THE OXFORD ENGLISH DICTIONARY

SECOND EDITION

THE OXFORD ENGLISH DICTIONARY

First Edited by

JAMES A. H. MURRAY, HENRY BRADLEY, W. A. CRAIGIE
and C. T. ONIONS

COMBINED WITH

A SUPPLEMENT TO THE OXFORD ENGLISH DICTIONARY

Edited by

R. W. BURCHFIELD

AND RESET WITH CORRECTIONS, REVISIONS
AND ADDITIONAL VOCABULARY

THE OXFORD ENGLISH DICTIONARY

SECOND EDITION

Prepared by

J. A. SIMPSON *and* E. S. C. WEINER

VOLUME VI

Follow–Haswed

CLARENDON PRESS · OXFORD

Oxford University Press, Great Clarendon Street, Oxford OX2 6DP
Oxford New York
Athens Auckland Bangkok Bogotá Buenos Aires Calcutta
Cape Town Chennai Dar es Salaam Delhi Florence Hong Kong Istanbul
Karachi Kuala Lumpur Madrid Melbourne Mexico City Mumbai
Nairobi Paris São Paulo Singapore Taipei Tokyo Toronto Warsaw
and associated companies in
Berlin Ibadan

Oxford is a registered trade mark of Oxford University Press

First published 1989
Reprinted 1991 (with corrections), 1998

British Library Cataloguing in Publication Data
Oxford English dictionary.—2nd ed.
1. English language—Dictionaries
I. Simpson, J. A. (John Andrew), 1953-
II. Weiner, Edmund S. C., 1950-
423
ISBN 0-19-861218-4 (vol. VI)
ISBN 0-19-861186-2 (set)

Library of Congress Cataloging-in-Publication Data
The Oxford English dictionary.—2nd ed.
prepared by J. A. Simpson and E. S. C. Weiner
Bibliography: p.
ISBN 0-19-861218-4 (vol. VI)
ISBN 0-19-861186-2 (set)
1. English language—Dictionaries. I. Simpson, J. A.
II. Weiner, E. S. C. III. Oxford University Press.
PE1625.087 1989
423—dc19 88-5330

Data capture by ICC, Fort Washington, Pa.
Text-processing by Oxford University Press
Typesetting by Pindar Graphics Origination, Scarborough, N. Yorks.
Manufactured in the United States of America by
World Color Book Services, Taunton, Mass.

KEY TO THE PRONUNCIATION

THE pronunciations given are those in use in the educated speech of southern England (the so-called 'Received Standard'), and the keywords given are to be understood as pronounced in such speech.

I. *Consonants*

b, d, f, k, l, m, n, p, t, v, z *have their usual English values*

g as in *go* (gəʊ)
h ... *ho!* (həʊ)
r ... *run* (rʌn), *terrier* ('tɛrɪə(r))
(r) ... *her* (hɜ:(r))
s ... *see* (si:), *success* (sək'sɛs)
w ... *wear* (wɛə(r))
hw ... *when* (hwɛn)
j ... *yes* (jɛs)

θ as in *thin* (θɪn), *bath* (bɑ:θ)
ð ... *then* (ðɛn), *bathe* (beɪð)
ʃ ... *shop* (ʃɒp), *dish* (dɪʃ)
tʃ ... *chop* (tʃɒp), *ditch* (dɪtʃ)
ʒ ... *vision* ('vɪʒən), *déjeuner* (deʒøne)
dʒ ... *judge* (dʒʌdʒ)
ŋ ... *singing* ('sɪŋɪŋ), *think* (θiŋk)
ŋg ... *finger* ('fɪŋgə(r))

(FOREIGN AND NON-SOUTHERN)

ʎ as in It. *serraglio* (ser'raʎo)
ɲ ... Fr. *cognac* (kɔɲak)
x ... Ger. *ach* (ax), Sc. *loch* (lɒx), Sp. *frijoles* (fri'xoles)
ç ... Ger. *ich* (ɪç), Sc. *nicht* (nɪçt)
ɣ ... North Ger. *sagen* ('za:ɣən)
c ... Afrikaans *baardmannetjie* ('ba:rtmanəci)
ɥ ... Fr. *cuisine* (kɥizin)

Symbols in parentheses are used to denote elements that may be omitted either by individual speakers or in particular phonetic contexts: e.g. *bottle* ('bɒt(ə)l), *Mercian* ('mɜ:ʃ(ɪ)ən), *suit* (s(j)u:t), *impromptu* (ɪm'prɒm(p)tju:), *father* ('fɑ:ðə(r)).

II. *Vowels and Diphthongs*

SHORT

ɪ as in *pit* (pɪt), *-ness*, (-nɪs)
ɛ ... *pet* (pɛt), Fr. *sept* (sɛt)
æ ... *pat* (pæt)
ʌ ... *putt* (pʌt)
ɒ ... *pot* (pɒt)
ʊ ... *put* (pʊt)
ə ... *another* (ə'nʌðə(r))
(ə) ... *beaten* ('bi:t(ə)n)
i ... Fr. *si* (si)
e ... Fr. *bébé* (bebe)
a ... Fr. *mari* (mari)
ɑ ... Fr. *bâtiment* (bɑtimɑ̃)
ɔ ... Fr. *homme* (ɔm)
o ... Fr. *eau* (o)
ø ... Fr. *peu* (pø)
œ ... Fr. *boeuf* (bœf) *coeur* (kœr)
u ... Fr. *douce* (dus)
ʏ ... Ger. *Müller* ('mʏlər)
y ... Fr. *du* (dy)

LONG

i: as in *bean* (bi:n)
ɑ: ... *barn* (bɑ:n)
ɔ: ... *born* (bɔ:n)
u: ... *boon* (bu:n)
ɜ: ... *burn* (bɜ:n)
e: ... Ger. *Schnee* (ʃne:)
ɛ: ... Ger. *Fähre* ('fɛ:rə)
a: ... Ger. *Tag* (ta:k)
o: ... Ger. *Sohn* (zo:n)
ø: ... Ger. *Goethe* ('gø:tə)
y: ... Ger. *grün* (gry:n)

NASAL

ɛ̃, æ̃ as in Fr. *fin* (fɛ̃, fæ̃)
ɑ̃ ... Fr. *franc* (frɑ̃)
ɔ̃ ... Fr. *bon* (bɔ̃)
œ̃ ... Fr. *un* (œ̃)

DIPHTHONGS, etc.

eɪ as in *bay* (beɪ)
aɪ ... *buy* (baɪ)
ɔɪ ... *boy* (bɔɪ)
əʊ ... *no* (nəʊ)
aʊ ... *now* (naʊ)
ɪə ... *peer* (pɪə(r))
ɛə ... *pair* (pɛə(r))
ʊə ... *tour* (tʊə(r))
ɔə ... *boar* (bɔə(r))

aɪə as in *fiery* ('faɪərɪ)
aʊə ... *sour* (saʊə(r))

The incidence of main stress is shown by a superior stress mark (') preceding the stressed syllable, and a secondary stress by an inferior stress mark (ˌ), e.g. *pronunciation* (prəˌnʌnsɪ'eɪʃ(ə)n).

For further explanation of the transcription used, see *General Explanations*, Volume I.

LIST OF ABBREVIATIONS, SIGNS, ETC.

Some abbreviations listed here in italics are also in certain cases printed in roman type, and vice versa.

a. (in Etym.)	adoption of, adopted from
a (as *a* 1850)	*ante*, 'before', 'not later than'
a.	adjective
abbrev.	abbreviation (of)
abl.	ablative
absol.	absolute, -ly
Abstr.	(in titles) *Abstract, -s*
acc.	accusative
Acct.	(in titles) *Account*
A.D.	*Anno Domini*
ad. (in Etym.)	adaptation of
Add.	Addenda
adj.	adjective
Adv.	(in titles) *Advance, -d, -s*
adv.	adverb
advb.	adverbial, -ly
Advt.	advertisement
Aeronaut.	(as label) in Aeronautics; (in titles) *Aeronautic, -al, -s*
AF., AFr.	Anglo-French
Afr.	Africa, -n
Agric.	(as label) in Agriculture; (in titles) *Agriculture, -al*
Alb.	Albanian
Amer.	American
Amer. Ind.	American Indian
Anat.	(as label) in Anatomy; (in titles) *Anatomy, -ical*
Anc.	(in titles) *Ancient*
Anglo-Ind.	Anglo-Indian
Anglo-Ir.	Anglo-Irish
Ann.	Annals
Anthrop., *Anthropol.*	(as label) in Anthropology; (in titles) *Anthropology, -ical*
Antiq.	(as label) in Antiquities; (in titles) *Antiquity*
aphet.	aphetic, aphetized
app.	apparently
Appl.	(in titles) *Applied*
Applic.	(in titles) *Application, -s*
appos.	appositive, -ly
Arab.	Arabic
Aram.	Aramaic
Arch.	in Architecture
arch.	archaic
Archæol.	in Archæology
Archit.	(as label) in Architecture; (in titles) *Architecture, -al*
Arm.	Armenian
assoc.	association
Astr.	in Astronomy
Astrol.	in Astrology
Astron.	(in titles) *Astronomy, -ical*
Astronaut.	(in titles) *Astronautic, -s*
attrib.	attributive, -ly
Austral.	Australian
Autobiogr.	(in titles) *Autobiography, -ical*
A.V.	Authorized Version
B.C.	Before Christ
B.C.	(in titles) British Columbia
bef.	before
Bibliogr.	(as label) in Bibliography; (in titles) *Bibliography, -ical*
Biochem.	(as label) in Biochemistry; (in titles) *Biochemistry, -ical*
Biol.	(as label) in Biology; (in titles) *Biology, -ical*
Bk.	*Book*
Bot.	(as label) in Botany; (in titles) *Botany, -ical*
Bp.	Bishop
Brit.	(in titles) *Britain, British*
Bulg.	Bulgarian
Bull.	(in titles) *Bulletin*
c (as *c* 1700)	*circa*, 'about'
c. (as 19th c.)	century
Cal.	(in titles) *Calendar*
Cambr.	(in titles) *Cambridge*
Canad.	Canadian
Cat.	Catalan
catachr.	catachrestically
Catal.	(in titles) *Catalogue*
Celt.	Celtic
Cent.	(in titles) *Century, Central*
Cent. Dict.	*Century Dictionary*
Cf., cf.	*confer*, 'compare'
Ch.	Church
Chem.	(as label) in Chemistry; (in titles) *Chemistry, -ical*
Chr.	(in titles) *Christian*
Chron.	(in titles) *Chronicle*
Chronol.	(in titles) *Chronology, -ical*
Cinemat., *Cinematogr.*	in Cinematography
Clin.	(in titles) *Clinical*
cl. L.	classical Latin
cogn. w.	cognate with
Col.	(in titles) *Colonel, Colony*
Coll.	(in titles) *Collection*
collect.	collective, -ly
colloq.	colloquial, -ly
comb.	combined, -ing
Comb.	Combinations
Comm.	in Commercial usage
Communic.	in Communications
comp.	compound, composition
Compan.	(in titles) *Companion*
compar.	comparative
compl.	complement
Compl.	(in titles) *Complete*
Conc.	(in titles) *Concise*
Conch.	in Conchology
concr.	concrete, -ly
Conf.	(in titles) *Conference*
Congr.	(in titles) *Congress*
conj.	conjunction
cons.	consonant
const.	construction, construed with
contr.	contrast (with)
Contrib.	(in titles) *Contribution*
Corr.	(in titles) *Correspondence*
corresp.	corresponding (to)
Cotgr.	R. Cotgrave, *Dictionarie of the French and English Tongues*
cpd.	compound
Crit.	(in titles) *Criticism, Critical*
Cryst.	in Crystallography
Cycl.	(in titles) *Cyclopædia, -ic*
Cytol.	(in titles) *Cytology, -ical*
Da.	Danish
D.A.	*Dictionary of Americanisms*
D.A.E.	*Dictionary of American English*
dat.	dative
D.C.	District of Columbia
Deb.	(in titles) *Debate, -s*
def.	definite, -ition
dem.	demonstrative
deriv.	derivative, -ation
derog.	derogatory
Descr.	(in titles) *Description, -tive*
Devel.	(in titles) *Development, -al*
Diagn.	(in titles) *Diagnosis, Diagnostic*
dial.	dialect, -al
Dict.	Dictionary; *spec.*, the *Oxford English Dictionary*
dim.	diminutive
Dis.	(in titles) *Disease*
Diss.	(in titles) *Dissertation*
D.O.S.T.	*Dictionary of the Older Scottish Tongue*
Du.	Dutch
E.	East
Eccl.	(as label) in Ecclesiastical usage; (in titles) *Ecclesiastical*
Ecol.	in Ecology
Econ.	(as label) in Economics; (in titles) *Economy, -ics*
ed.	edition
E.D.D.	*English Dialect Dictionary*
Edin.	(in titles) *Edinburgh*
Educ.	(as label) in Education; (in titles) *Education, -al*
EE.	Early English
e.g.	*exempli gratia*, 'for example'
Electr.	(as label) in Electricity; (in titles) *Electricity, -ical*
Electron.	(in titles) *Electronic, -s*
Elem.	(in titles) *Element, -ary*
ellipt.	elliptical, -ly
Embryol.	in Embryology
e.midl.	east midland (dialect)
Encycl.	(in titles) *Encyclopædia, -ic*
Eng.	England, English
Engin.	in Engineering
Ent.	in Entomology
Entomol.	(in titles) *Entomology, -logical*
erron.	erroneous, -ly
esp.	especially
Ess.	(in titles) *Essay, -s*
et al.	*et alii*, 'and others'
etc.	et cetera
Ethnol.	in Ethnology
etym.	etymology
euphem.	euphemistically
Exam.	(in titles) *Examination*
exc.	except
Exerc.	(in titles) *Exercise, -s*
Exper.	(in titles) *Experiment, -al*
Explor.	(in titles) *Exploration, -s*
f.	feminine
f. (in Etym.)	formed on
f. (in subordinate entries)	form of
F.	French
fem. (*rarely* f.)	feminine
fig.	figurative, -ly
Finn.	Finnish
fl.	*floruit*, 'flourished'
Found.	(in titles) *Foundation, -s*
Fr.	French
freq.	frequent, -ly
Fris.	Frisian
Fund.	(in titles) *Fundamental, -s*
Funk or *Funk's Stand. Dict.*	*Funk and Wagnalls Standard Dictionary*
G.	German
Gael.	Gaelic
Gaz.	(in titles) *Gazette*
gen.	genitive
gen.	general, -ly
Geogr.	(as label) in Geography; (in titles) *Geography, -ical*

Geol.	(as label) in Geology; (in titles) *Geology, -ical*
Geom.	in Geometry
Geomorphol.	in Geomorphology
Ger.	German
Gloss.	Glossary
Gmc.	Germanic
Godef.	F. Godefroy, *Dictionnaire de l'ancienne langue française*
Goth.	Gothic
Govt.	(in titles) *Government*
Gr.	Greek
Gram.	(as label) in Grammar; (in titles) *Grammar, -tical*
Gt.	Great
Heb.	Hebrew
Her.	in Heraldry
Herb.	among herbalists
Hind.	Hindustani
Hist.	(as label) in History; (in titles) *History, -ical*
hist.	historical
Histol.	(in titles) *Histology, -ical*
Hort.	in Horticulture
Househ.	(in titles) *Household*
Housek.	(in titles) *Housekeeping*
Ibid.	*Ibidem*, 'in the same book or passage'
Icel.	Icelandic
Ichthyol.	in Ichthyology
id.	*idem*, 'the same'
i.e.	*id est*, 'that is'
IE.	Indo-European
Illustr.	(in titles) *Illustration, -ted*
imit.	imitative
Immunol.	in Immunology
imp.	imperative
impers.	impersonal
impf.	imperfect
ind.	indicative
indef.	indefinite
Industr.	(in titles) *Industry, -ial*
inf.	infinitive
infl.	influenced
Inorg.	(in titles) *Inorganic*
Ins.	(in titles) *Insurance*
Inst.	(in titles) *Institute, -tion*
int.	interjection
intr.	intransitive
Introd.	(in titles) *Introduction*
Ir.	Irish
irreg.	irregular, -ly
It.	Italian
J., (J.)	(quoted from) Johnson's *Dictionary*
(Jam.)	Jamieson, *Scottish Dict.*
Jap.	Japanese
joc.	jocular, -ly
Jrnl.	(in titles) *Journal*
Jun.	(in titles) *Junior*
Knowl.	(in titles) *Knowledge*
l.	line
L.	Latin
lang.	language
Lect.	(in titles) *Lecture, -s*
Less.	(in titles) *Lesson, -s*
Let., Lett.	letter, letters
LG.	Low German
lit.	literal, -ly
Lit.	Literary
Lith.	Lithuanian
LXX	Septuagint
m.	masculine
Mag.	(in titles) *Magazine*
Magn.	(in titles) *Magnetic, -ism*
Mal.	Malay, Malayan
Man.	(in titles) *Manual*
Managem.	(in titles) *Management*
Manch.	(in titles) *Manchester*
Manuf.	in Manufacture, -ing
Mar.	(in titles) *Marine*
masc. (*rarely* m.)	masculine
Math.	(as label) in Mathematics; (in titles) *Mathematics, -al*
MDu.	Middle Dutch
ME.	Middle English
Mech.	(as label) in Mechanics; (in titles) *Mechanics, -al*
Med.	(as label) in Medicine; (in titles) *Medicine, -ical*
med.L.	medieval Latin
Mem.	(in titles) *Memoir, -s*
Metaph.	in Metaphysics
Meteorol.	(as label) in Meteorology; (in titles) *Meteorology, -ical*
MHG.	Middle High German
midl.	midland (dialect)
Mil.	in military usage
Min.	(as label) in Mineralogy; (in titles) *Ministry*
Mineral.	(in titles) *Mineralogy, -ical*
MLG.	Middle Low German
Misc.	(in titles) *Miscellany, -eous*
mod.	modern
mod.L	modern Latin
(Morris),	(quoted from) E. E. Morris's *Austral English*
Mus.	(as label) in Music; (in titles) *Music, -al; Museum*
Myst.	(in titles) *Mystery*
Mythol.	in Mythology
N.	North
n.	neuter
N. Amer.	North America, -n
N. & Q.	*Notes and Queries*
Narr.	(in titles) *Narrative*
Nat.	(in titles) *Natural*
Nat. Hist.	in Natural History
Naut.	in nautical language
N.E.	North East
N.E.D.	*New English Dictionary*, original title of the *Oxford English Dictionary* (first edition)
Neurol.	in Neurology
neut. (*rarely* n.)	neuter
NF., NFr.	Northern French
No.	Number
nom.	nominative
north.	northern (dialect)
Norw.	Norwegian
n.q.	no quotations
N.T.	New Testament
Nucl.	Nuclear
Numism.	in Numismatics
N.W.	North West
N.Z.	New Zealand
obj.	object
obl.	oblique
Obs., obs.	obsolete
Obstetr.	(in titles) *Obstetrics*
occas.	occasionally
OE.	Old English (= Anglo-Saxon)
OF., OFr.	Old French
OFris.	Old Frisian
OHG.	Old High German
OIr.	Old Irish
ON.	Old Norse
ONF.	Old Northern French
Ophthalm.	in Ophthalmology
opp.	opposed (to), the opposite (of)
Opt.	in Optics
Org.	(in titles) *Organic*
orig.	origin, -al, -ally
Ornith.	(as label) in Ornithology; (in titles) *Ornithology, -ical*
OS.	Old Saxon
OSl.	Old (Church) Slavonic
O.T.	Old Testament
Outl.	(in titles) *Outline*
Oxf.	(in titles) *Oxford*
p.	page
Palæogr.	in Palæography
Palæont.	(as label) in Palæontology; (in titles) *Palæontology, -ical*
pa. pple.	passive participle, past participle
(Partridge),	(quoted from) E. Partridge's *Dictionary of Slang and Unconventional English*
pass.	passive, -ly
pa.t.	past tense
Path.	(as label) in Pathology; (in titles) *Pathology, -ical*
perh.	perhaps
Pers.	Persian
pers.	person, -al
Petrogr.	in Petrography
Petrol.	(as label) in Petrology; (in titles) *Petrology, -ical*
(Pettman),	(quoted from) C. Pettman's *Africanderisms*
pf.	perfect
Pg.	Portuguese
Pharm.	in Pharmacology
Philol.	(as label) in Philology; (in titles) *Philology, -ical*
Philos.	(as label) in Philosophy; (in titles) *Philosophy, -ic*
phonet.	phonetic, -ally
Photogr.	(as label) in Photography; (in titles) *Photography, -ical*
phr.	phrase
Phys.	physical; (*rarely*) in Physiology
Physiol.	(as label) in Physiology; (in titles) *Physiology, -ical*
Pict.	(in titles) *Picture, Pictorial*
pl., plur.	plural
poet.	poetic, -al
Pol.	Polish
Pol.	(as label) in Politics; (in titles) *Politics, -al*
Pol. Econ.	in Political Economy
Polit.	(in titles) *Politics, -al*
pop.	popular, -ly
Porc.	(in titles) *Porcelain*
poss.	possessive
Pott.	(in titles) *Pottery*
ppl. a., pple. adj.	participial adjective
pple.	participle
Pr.	Provençal
pr.	present
Pract.	(in titles) *Practice, -al*
prec.	preceding (word or article)
pred.	predicative
pref.	prefix
pref., Pref.	preface
prep.	preposition
pres.	present
Princ.	(in titles) *Principle, -s*
priv.	privative
prob.	probably
Probl.	(in titles) *Problem*
Proc.	(in titles) *Proceedings*
pron.	pronoun
pronunc.	pronunciation
prop.	properly
Pros.	in Prosody
Prov.	Provençal
pr. pple.	present participle
Psych.	in Psychology
Psychol.	(as label) in Psychology; (in titles) *Psychology, -ical*
Publ.	(in titles) *Publications*
Q.	(in titles) *Quarterly*
quot(s).	quotation(s)
q.v.	*quod vide*, 'which see'
R.	(in titles) *Royal*
Radiol.	in Radiology
R.C.Ch.	Roman Catholic Church
Rec.	(in titles) *Record*
redupl.	reduplicating
Ref.	(in titles) *Reference*
refash.	refashioned, -ing
refl.	reflexive
Reg.	(in titles) *Register*

reg.	regular
rel.	related to
Reminisc.	(in titles) *Reminiscence, -s*
Rep.	(in titles) *Report, -s*
repr.	representative, representing
Res.	(in titles) *Research*
Rev.	(in titles) *Review*
rev.	revised
Rhet.	in Rhetoric
Rom.	Roman, -ce, -ic
Rum.	Rumanian
Russ.	Russian
S.	South
S.Afr.	South Africa, -n
sb.	substantive
sc.	*scilicet*, 'understand' or 'supply'
Sc., Scot.	Scottish
Scand.	(in titles) *Scandinavia, -n*
Sch.	(in titles) *School*
Sc. Nat. Dict.	*Scottish National Dictionary*
Scotl.	(in titles) *Scotland*
Sel.	(in titles) *Selection, -s*
Ser.	Series
sing.	singular
Sk.	(in titles) *Sketch*
Skr.	Sanskrit
Slav.	Slavonic
S.N.D.	*Scottish National Dictionary*
Soc.	(in titles) *Society*
Sociol.	(as label) in Sociology; (in titles) *Sociology, -ical*
Sp.	Spanish
Sp.	(in titles) *Speech, -es*
sp.	spelling
spec.	specifically
Spec.	(in titles) *Specimen*
St.	Saint
Stand.	(in titles) *Standard*
Stanf.	(quoted from) *Stanford Dictionary of Anglicised Words & Phrases*
str.	strong
Struct.	(in titles) *Structure, -al*
Stud.	(in titles) *Studies*
subj.	subject
subord. cl.	subordinate clause
subseq.	subsequent, -ly
subst.	substantively
suff.	suffix
superl.	superlative
Suppl.	Supplement
Surg.	(as label) in Surgery; (in titles) *Surgery, Surgical*
s.v.	*sub voce*, 'under the word'
Sw.	Swedish
s.w.	south-western (dialect)
Syd. Soc. Lex.	Sydenham Society, *Lexicon of Medicine & Allied Sciences*
syll.	syllable
Syr.	Syrian
Syst.	(in titles) *System, -atic*
Taxon.	(in titles) *Taxonomy, -ical*
techn.	technical, -ly
Technol.	(in titles) *Technology, -ical*
Telegr.	in Telegraphy
Teleph.	in Telephony
(Th.),	(quoted from) Thornton's *American Glossary*
Theatr.	in the Theatre, theatrical
Theol.	(as label) in Theology; (in titles) *Theology, -ical*
Theoret.	(in titles) *Theoretical*
Tokh.	Tokharian
tr., transl.	translated, translation
Trans.	(in titles) *Transactions*
trans.	transitive
transf.	transferred sense
Trav.	(in titles) *Travel(s)*
Treas.	(in titles) *Treasury*
Treat.	(in titles) *Treatise*
Treatm.	(in titles) *Treatment*
Trig.	in Trigonometry
Trop.	(in titles) *Tropical*
Turk.	Turkish
Typog., Typogr.	in Typography
ult.	ultimately
Univ.	(in titles) *University*
unkn.	unknown
U.S.	United States
U.S.S.R.	Union of Soviet Socialist Republics
usu.	usually
v., vb.	verb
var(r)., vars.	variant(s) of
vbl. sb.	verbal substantive
Vertebr.	(in titles) *Vertebrate, -s*
Vet.	(as label) in Veterinary Science; (in titles) *Veterinary*
Vet. Sci.	in Veterinary Science
viz.	*videlicet*, 'namely'
Voy.	(in titles) *Voyage, -s*
v.str.	strong verb
vulg.	vulgar
v.w.	weak verb
W.	Welsh; West
wd.	word
Webster	*Webster's (New International) Dictionary*
Westm.	(in titles) *Westminster*
WGmc.	West Germanic
Wks.	(in titles) *Works*
w.midl.	west midland (dialect)
WS.	West Saxon
(Y.),	(quoted from) Yule & Burnell's *Hobson-Jobson*
Yrs.	(in titles) *Years*
Zoogeogr.	in Zoogeography
Zool.	(as label) in Zoology; (in titles) *Zoology, -ical*

Signs and Other Conventions

Before a word or sense

† = obsolete
‖ = not naturalized, alien
¶ = catachrestic and erroneous uses

In the listing of Forms

1 = before 1100
2 = 12th c. (1100 to 1200)
3 = 13th c. (1200 to 1300), etc.
5-7 = 15th to 17th century
20 = 20th century

In the etymologies

* indicates a word or form not actually found, but of which the existence is inferred
:— = normal development of

The printing of a word in SMALL CAPITALS indicates that further information will be found under the word so referred to.

.. indicates an omitted part of a quotation.

- (in a quotation) indicates a hyphen doubtfully present in the original; (in other text) indicates a hyphen inserted only for the sake of a line-break.

PROPRIETARY NAMES

THIS Dictionary includes some words which are or are asserted to be proprietary names or trade marks. Their inclusion does not imply that they have acquired for legal purposes a non-proprietary or general significance nor any other judgement concerning their legal status. In cases where the editorial staff have established in the records of the Patent Offices of the United Kingdom and of the United States that a word is registered as a proprietary name or trade mark this is indicated, but no judgement concerning the legal status of such words is made or implied thereby.

follow ('fɒləʊ), *sb.* [f. next verb.]

1. a. The action of the verb FOLLOW.

1870 HARDY & WARE *Mod. Hoyle*, Dominoes 93 It is sometimes an advantage to hold heavy dominoes, as they not unfrequently enable you to obtain what is called a good 'follow'. **1889** *Spectator* 9 Nov. 635/1 And hark! the view-hollo! 'Tis Mack in full follow.

b. A supplementary portion (in a restaurant); also *pl.*, = AFTERS.

1910 A. A. MILNE *Day's Play* 213 At most restaurants you can get a second help of anything for half-price, and that is technically called a 'follow'. **1946** G. MILLAR *Horned Pigeon* ii. 31 Robeson..made us some kind of stew; and the 'follows'..were tinned 'yellow cling' peaches.

2. *Billiards.* A stroke which causes the player's ball to roll on after the object-ball which it has set in motion. Called also *follow-stroke*, and *following stroke.* Also, the impulse given to the ball by such a stroke.

1873 BENNETT & CAVENDISH *Billiards* 371 The reason for playing with side is, that, when the balls are so close, sufficient 'follow' cannot be got on. **1881** H. W. COLLENDER *Mod. Billiards* 38 The Follow-Stroke. *Ibid.* 39 The 'follow' can also be executed with the cue delivered as far as one-fourth below centre.

3. follow on. a. *Cricket.* The act of 'following on' (see FOLLOW *v.* 19 d); also applied to the innings itself. Also simply *follow.*

1876 *Baily's Mag.* Aug. 100 Against which [score] Yorkshire could only put 208..which, unfortunately, did not prevent a 'follow on'. **1881** *Standard* 14 June 3/8 A 'follow on' was necessary. **1884** *Lillywhite's Cricket Ann.* 60 With the follow saved there was no chance of completion of the game. **1892** *Sat. Rev.* 9 July 33/1 In the follow on things altered very much.

b. *attrib.* in Cricketing and general use.

1897 *Badminton Mag.* Apr. 441 The original 'follow-on' limit was 100. **1899** W. G. GRACE *Cricket. Remin.* 229 The compulsory follow-on innings. **1960** *Farmer & Stockbreeder* 15 Mar. 94/1 (Advt.), This new booklet contains advice about 'follow-on' feeding. **1964** *Financ. Times* 12 Mar. 19/1 A large follow-on order for..engines. **1964** *Economist* 28 Mar. 1280/2 The follow-on rate [for electricity]. **1971** *Nature* 19 Mar. 143/2 It recommended that follow-on Vikings should be held in abeyance until the results of the first missions are analysed.

4. follow-through. a. *Golf, Cricket*, etc. The action or an act of following through (see FOLLOW *v.* 21). Also *transf.*

1897 *Encycl. Sport* I. 465/1 Both force and direction are imparted by what is technically known as the 'follow through'. **1904** *Daily Chron.* 28 Apr. 3/2 It is..worthy of note that after the ball has departed, when the follow-through is nearly completed, Vardon's gaze is still fixed on the spot whence it has flown. **1920** D. J. KNIGHT in P. F. Warner *Cricket* 27 Another great factor of the batsman's art is what is known as the follow through. **1924** F. G. LOWE *Lawn Tennis* 46 The wrist brings the striking face square with the ball, and after impact gradually turns the striking face over until at the finish of the 'follow through' it almost faces the ground. **1931** *Times Lit. Suppl.* 17 Sept. 699/3 The upward swing of a bait-rod (that gentle easy follow-through). **1959** *Daily Mail* 20 Feb. 10/4 Bowlers cutting up the pitch with their follow-through. **1964** WODEHOUSE *Frozen Assets* i. 14 The Sergeant stamped some more papers. He had a wristy follow-through which at any other moment Jerry would have admired.

b. *fig.* or *gen.*

1926 *Socialist Rev.* Jan. 308 He should be familiar with what is meant by 'follow-through Departments', for the condition of a patient five years after he leaves is a good test of the Hospital's efficiency. **1955** *Times* 25 July 5/6 The follow-through from this beginning by our respective Governments will be decisive in the measure of this conference. **1959** *Times* 11 June 16/3 Kaffirs..eased later because of lack of 'follow through' buying. **1970** *Daily Tel.* 15 June 2/5 The test of the agreement will be on the success of the productivity follow-through.

5. follow-up. The action of following up; the pursuit or prosecution of something begun or attempted; see also quot. 1942. Also *attrib.*

1923 J. D. HACKETT in *Managem. Engin.* May, *Follow-up*, methods used by the personnel department to maintain friendly relations with employees. **1929** *Melody Maker* Jan. p. iii (Advt.), Sensational follow-up song in America, to *That's My Weakness Now.* **1929** *Sat. Even. Post* 14 Dec. 13/2 It's the follow-up of that injunction gag. **1931** *Brit. Jrnl. Psychol.* July 87 A 'follow up' investigation of one thousand particularly gifted children. **1938** W. S. CHURCHILL *Into Battle* (1941) 68 A follow-up department in the Ministry to see exactly what was the state of production in the different firms. **1942** *Ann. Internal Med.* XVI. 655 Many cases have repeated hospital admissions and form a long line of 'follow-ups' in the out-patient department. **1950** W. HAMMOND *Cricketers' School* xvi. 149 The umpire himself may be temporarily unsighted by the bowler's follow-up. **1956** C. WILLOCK *Death at Flight* xvii. 227 Mr. Goss had briefed this team with all the relevant facts necessary for the follow-up story. **1957** *Technology* Apr. 70/3 The manufacturer's attack on a market needs firepower..; but, as in war, there must also be consolidation, the 'follow-up'. **1959** B. WOOTTON *Social Sci. & Social Path.* ii. 60 Except for the occasional follow-ups of rehoused populations. **1968** *Brit. Med. Bull.* XXIV. 208/1 A nation-wide follow-up system for samples of patients classified in field surveys. **1968** *New Scientist* 21 Nov. 417/1 Follow-ups of persons who have attempted suicide are not carried through sufficiently.

follow ('fɒləʊ), *v.* Forms: α. 1-2 folȝian, 2-3 folȝie(n, (folȝhi), foleȝe(n, (foleȝi), 3 folien, folhen, 2-4 folȝe(n, (3 *Orm.* follȝhenn, 4 *south.* uolȝe(n, uolȝy), 3-5 folew(en, (3 *south.* uolewen, 4 follew(e), folwe(n, (4 follwe(n), folu(n, foluw(en, (3 *south.* uoluwen), 4-6 follow(e, foloe, (5 folaw(e, foloȝe, foloyn, 4-6 fowlow(e, 6 foolow(e), 6 *Sc.* fallow, 4-7 followe, 4- follow. β. 1-2 fylȝan, fylȝian, fylȝian, fylian, 2-3 fulien, (3 *south. pa. t.* vulede), 3-4 fulu(n, filȝe(n, filiȝ(en, filyh(en, filiyh(en, felu(n, 4-5 filow, fylow, felow, 5 filoe. [The two OE. types, *folȝian* (*o-* stem) and *fylȝan* (*-jo-* stem), are, as is usual in similar pairs of conjugational variants, representatives of an OTeut. vb. of the *-êjan* class; cf. OFris. *folgia, folia, fulia*, OS. *folgôn* (Du. *volgen*), OHG. *folgên* (MHG. *volgen*, mod.Ger. *folgen*), ON. *fylgja* (Da. *fölge*, Sw. *följa*); not recorded in Goth. Beside these forms, several of the Teut. langs. have synonymous and phonetically resembling words which are compounds of GANG and GO *vbs.*; OE. has *fulgangan*, pa. t. *ful-éode* (from *éode*, serving as pa. t. of *gân*) = OS. *fulgangan*, OHG. *folle gân.* The most natural explanation of these parallel forms is that the apparently simple vb. was originally a compound or a phrasal combination. The first element occurs in OE. *fylstan, fullǽstan*, OHG. *folleisten* to help, succour, minister to (cf. Goth. *laistjan* to follow), OHG. *follaziohan* to assist, support (= OE. **fultéon*, whence *fultéam*, *fultum* assistance), Goth. *fullafahjan* to worship, serve, minister to the needs of. In these cases the prefix seems to add to the sense of the simple vbs. the notion of doing something by way of service to another (so that sense 3 of the present vb. is probably nearest to the original meaning). It is on formal grounds probable that the prefix is identical with FULL; its function in the above-cited instances is perh. due to the circumstance that in some vbs. compounded with it the primary sense of 'satisfying' developed into the cognate sense of 'ministering to', 'serving'.]

I. *trans.* [In OE. and early ME. the object is usually in the dative case.]

1. a. To go or come after (a person or other object in motion); to move behind in the same direction. Also with advs., e.g. *about, out.*

c **1000** *Ags. Gosp.* John x. 27 Mine sceap ȝehyraþ mine stefne, and hiȝ folȝiaþ me. *c* **1200** ORMIN 12768 He fand ta Filippe & seȝȝde þuss till himm; follh me. *c* **1220** *Bestiary* 757 Ilk der ðe him hereð..foleȝeð him up one ðe wold. *a* **1300** *Cursor M.* 15193 (Cott.) Folus forth þat ilk man Right in to þe bi. *c* **1386** CHAUCER *Miller's T.* 74 As any kyde or calf folwynge his dame. *a* **1533** LD. BERNERS *Huon* xlvii. 159 They went all together and foolowed Huon as preuely as they coude. **1598** SHAKS. *Merry W.* III. ii. 6, I had rather (forsooth) go before you like a man, then follow him like a dwarfe. **1667** MILTON *P.L.* I. 238 Him followed his next Mate. **1750** GOADBY *Apol. Life Bampfylde Moore Carew* (ed. 2) v. 48 Parson Bryant followed him out. **1850** PRESCOTT *Peru* II. 200 The remainder of his forces when mustered were to follow him. **1860** W. COLLINS *Woman in White* xi, I opened the door for her in silence, and followed her out. **1863** GEO. ELIOT *Romola* III. xxi, It was plain that he had followed her, and had been waiting for her. **1865** M. C. HARRIS *Christine* xxx, Richard followed his brother slowly out into the path. **1877** A. SEWELL *Black Beauty* xlviii, I used to come to him in the field and follow him about. **1910** E. M. ALBANESI *For Love of Anne Lambart* 59 He follows me about like a dog.

b. To go forward along (a path), to keep in (a track) as one goes. *lit.* and *fig.*

a **1300** *Cursor M.* 4575 (Cott.), I folud siþen, me-thoght, a sti Vntil a feild. **13..** *E.E. Allit. P.* A. 127 þe fyrre I folȝed þose floty valez. *c* **1385** CHAUCER *L.G.W.* 2018 *Ariadne*, That..The same weye he may returne anon, Folwynge alwey the thred as he hath come. **1548** HALL *Chron., Rich. III* (an. 3) 50 Pleiyng the parte of a good blood hounde, [he] foloed the tract of yᵉ flier..by yᵉ sent. **1667** MILTON *P.L.* II. 1025 Sin and Death amain Following his track. **1711** STEELE *Spect.* No. 79 ¶3, I am Young, and very much inclined to follow the Paths of Innocence. **1826** in COBBETT *Rur. Rides* (1885) II. 25, I was resolved..not to follow the turnpike road one single inch further. **1874** E. D. SMITH tr. *Oehler's O.T. Theol.* I. §43. 151 Old Testament angelology follows the opposite path.

c. Phr. *to follow the drum*: to be a soldier. *to follow the hounds*: to keep up behind them in the chase; to hunt with hounds. *follow my leader*: a game in which each player must do what the leader does, or pay forfeit; also *fig. to follow one's nose*: to go straight on (without reflexion or preconceived plan). *to follow the plough*: said of the ploughman.

1650 B. *Discolliminium* 19 I'le follow Providence, or my Nose, as well as I can. **1674** N. COX *Gentl. Recreat.* v. (1686) 2 Without its Assistance in Dieting and Exercise, no Horse can follow the Hounds..without hazarding. **1692** BENTLEY *Boyle Lect.* ii. 34 The main Maxim of his Philosophy was, To trust to his Senses, and follow his Nose. **1732** BERKELEY *Alciphr.* I. §1 While he..follows the plough, or looks after his flocks. **1785** BURNS *Jolly Beggars*, '*I am a son of Mars*', As when I us'd in scarlet to follow the drum. **1832** WORDSW. *Resol. & Independence* vii, Following [ed. 1 (1807) behind] his plough, along the mountain-side. **1835** MARRYATT *Jac. Faithf.* xxxviii, One amusement..was a favourite one of the captain's as it made the men smart. It is called 'Follow my leader'. **1858** THACKERAY *Virgin.* xvi, It was time to follow the hounds. **1895** *Tablet* 14 Sept. 408 Englishmen are the last people in the world to play a blind game of follow-my-leader.

2. *fig.* **a.** To come after in sequence or series, in order of time, etc.; to succeed.

a **1300** *Cursor M.* 4599 (Gött.) Seuen ȝere hunger grett þat oþer neist sal be foluand þat neuer was suilk bifor in land. **1659** B. HARRIS *Parival's Iron Age* 241 One misfortune followes another. **1667** MILTON *P.L.* XII. 335 Such follow him, as shall be registerd, Part good, part bad, of bad the longer scrowle. **1728** POPE *Dunc.* III. 321 Signs following signs lead on the mighty year! **1802** LD. ELDON in Vesey's *Rep.* VII. 81 This case was followed by The Att.-Gen. *v.* Doyley. *c* **1817** HOGG *Tales & Sk.* V. 350 Punishment must follow conviction, not antecede it. **1860** TYNDALL *Glac.* I. vii. 51 Transverse ridges which follow each other in succession.

†**b.** To be second or inferior to. *Obs.*

1632 MASSINGER & FIELD *Fatal Dowry* II. ii, Her education Follows not any.

c. To come after or succeed as a consequence or effect; to result from. (Cf. sense 4.)

1593 SHAKS. *Lucr.* 357 Misty night Covers the shame that follows sweet delight. *a* **1616** BEAUM. & FL. *Thierry & Theod.* I. ii, A duty well discharg'd is never follow'd By sad repentance. **1842** TENNYSON *Morte d'Arth.* 92 What good should follow this, if this were done? What harm, undone?

d. To provide (a thing) *with* a sequel (cf. 22 c) or a successor.

1671 HEAD & KIRKMAN *Eng. Rogue* IV. viii. 125 At the first blow, I thought he had cut me in two, following that with three or four more. **1901** *Daily Chron.* 14 Dec. 8/2 He had arranged to follow 'Iris' with..'My Lady Virtue'. **1907** *Smart Set* Jan. 72 Her efforts to follow 'Anchored' with other stories.

†**e.** Of a side at *Cricket*: *to follow their innings*, to follow on (see sense 19 d). *Obs.*

1815 *Suffolk Chron.* 2 Sept. 4/4 The latter, immediately following their first innings, obtained 13. **1854** J. PYCROFT *Cricket Field* (ed. 2) xi. 251 The M.C.C...in playing Surrey followed their innings, being headed by 106. **1894** *Laws of Cricket* §53 The side which goes in second shall follow their innings if they have scored 120 runs less than the opposite side in a three days' match, or 80 runs in a two days' match.

3. a. To go after or along with (a person) as an attendant or companion; to accompany, serve, or attend upon.

O.E. Chron. an. 755 þa cuædon hie þæt..hie næfre his banan folȝian noldon. *c* **950** *Lindisf. Gosp.* Mark v. 37 Ne leort æniȝne monno to fylȝenne hine. *c* **1175** *Lamb. Hom.* 151 Monie kunnes men foleȝeden ure drihten ine þisse liue. *c* **1205** LAY. 95 Of kunne & of folke þe fulede þan duke. *a* **1300** *Cursor M.* 15339 (Cott.) Yee haf me folud hider-to. *c* **1385** CHAUCER *L.G.W.* 894 *Thisbe*, I wol the folwen ded and I wol be Felaw and cause eke of thy deth, quod she. *c* **1450** *St. Cuthbert* (Surtees) 6338 A seruand folowand his lorde. **1591** SHAKS. *Two Gentl.* I. i. 94 Thou for wages followest thy master. **1611** BIBLE *1 Sam.* xvii. 13 And the three eldest sonnes of Iesse went, and followed Saul to the battell. **1845** S. C. HALL *Whiteboy* vi. 51 The rheumatic.. creature who had 'followed' the family for more than forty years. **1875** JOWETT *Plato* (ed. 2) I. 37 You may depend on my following and not deserting him.

b. To go after as an admirer, auditor, or the like.

1602 SHAKS. *Ham.* II. ii. 349 Do they hold the same estimation they did when I was in the city? Are they so followed? **1756** MRS. F. BROOKE *Old Maid* No. 22 ¶3, I went ..with a friend, to hear one of the most followed and admired of them all [preachers]. *Ibid.* O! he is..a charming man!..thank God I have followed him these twenty years.

c. To attend (the body of a deceased person) to the grave; (*colloq.*) to attend a person's funeral. Also *absol.*

1814 *New Monthly Mag.* Feb. 103/1 Behind the waggon followed the chief mourner, who was his own riding horse, attached by the bridle. **1819** C. WOLFE in *Rem.* (1827) 155 Last night I helped to lay poor M—— in his coffin, and followed him this morning to his grave. **1820** *Kaleidoscope* New Ser. I. 142/3 His brothers..agreed to follow the body to the grave. **1831** J. BANIM *Smuggler* I. xi. 201 They renewed their cries for 'Hood! to follow in the funeral!' **1897** HALL CAINE *Christian* I. viii, Gimme a black cloth on the corfin, my dear, and mind yer tell 'im to foller. **1902** *Westm. Gaz.* 18 Dec. 12/2 In Norfolk it is customary to speak of attending a funeral as 'following' the remains. **1940** BRAHMS & SIMON *Don't, Mr. Disraeli* ii. 21 Defiantly Henrietta sent a wreath to the funeral. It did not follow her friend to the grave.

4. *fig.* To accompany, attend upon, 'go with'; to be a (necessary) concomitant or accompaniment to; to be consequent upon.

c **1000** *Ags. Ps.* lv[i]. 4 Ðæt minre spræce sped folȝie. *c* **1205** LAY. 1002 Wælde heom scal fulien. *a* **1300** *E.E. Psalter* xxii[i]. 6 And filigh me sal þi mercy. *c* **1450** tr. *De Imitatione* II. vi. 46 Sorwe foluiþ euer þe glory of þe worlde. **1526** TINDALE *1 Cor.* x. 13 There hath no temptacion taken you but soche as foloweth the nature of man. **1599** SHAKS. *Hen. V*, v. ii. 297 The liberty that follows our places. **1611** BIBLE *Ps.* xxiii. 6 Surely goodnes and mercie shall followe me all the daies of my life. **1667** MILTON *P.L.* II. 25 The happier state In Heav'n, which follows dignity. **1859** JEPHSON *Brittany* vi. 74 Under the feudal system, the title follows the land. **1868** MORRIS *Earthly Par.* I. 610 (*Pygmalion*) Seest thou how tears still follow earthly bliss? **1885** *Law Rep.* 29 Ch. Div. 283 The right to a grant of administration follows the right to the property.

5. a. To go in pursuit of, try to overtake or come up with; to pursue, chase.

Beowulf 2933 (Gr.) [He] folȝode feorhȝeniðlan. *a* **1300** *E.E. Psalter* xvi[i]. 38, I sal filghe mi faas, and um-lap þa. *a* **1340** HAMPOLE *Psalter* vii. 1 Make me safe of all folouand me. *c* **1400** MAUNDEV. (Roxb.) iv. 12 þe dragoun folowed and tuke þe knyght. **1548** HALL *Chron., Hen. VI* (an. 6) 105 The Englishemen folowed theim so faste, in killyng and takyng of their enemies. **1690** DRYDEN *Don Sebast.* I. i, 'Twas indeed the place To seek Sebastian: through a track of Death I follow'd him. **1783** COWPER *Epitaph on Hare* 2

Here lies, whom hound did ne'er pursue, Nor swifter greyhound follow.

b. *fig.* To pursue like an enemy. Also, †to visit (a person) *with* (affliction, etc.).

a **1310** in Wright's *Lyric P.* xv. 48 Evel ant elde, ant other wo, foleweth me so faste. *c* **1350** *Will. Palerne* 436 A fers feintise folwes me oft, & takes me so tenefully. **1606** SHAKS. *Ant. & Cl.* v. i. 36 O Antony! I haue followd thee to this. **1607** —— *Cor.* IV. v. 104 Since I haue euer followed thee with hate. **1671** LADY M. BERTIE in *12th Rep. Hist. MSS. Comm.* App. v. 22 Wee play sometimes at trante a courante where my old ill lucke follows mee to loose my money. **1688** BUNYAN *Jerus. Sinn. Saved* (1689) 155 Art thou followed with affliction.

c. *Sc.* 'To pursue at law' (Jam.), prosecute. Also *absol.*

1425 *Sc. Acts Jas. I* (1814) 9 The party scathit sall folowe, and the party trespassande sall defende, eftir the cours of the auld lawis of the realme. **1466** *Act. Audit.* (1839) 5/2 [He] comperit nouther be himself nor his procuraturis to folow thaim.

†**d.** To visit (an offence, an offender) with punishment. *Obs.*

1579–80 NORTH *Plutarch* 19 (*Theseus*) There was no man at that time that dyd followe or pursue his death. **1593** BILSON *Govt. Christ's Ch.* 295 Were you but once or twise well followed for other mens faultes, you woulde soone waxe weary of this generall and confused execution.

6. *fig.* **a.** To pursue (an object of desire); to endeavour to reach or attain to; to strive after, try to gain or compass, aim at.

a **1300** *Cursor M.* 23868 (Gött.) In eldrin men vr merrur [we] mai se quat forto fulv, quat forto fle. *c* **1400** *Apol. Loll.* 33 Dekunis to be chast, not..fowlowing fowle wynning. **1539** BIBLE (Great) *Heb.* xii. 14 Folowe peace wyth all men. **1549** LATIMER *3rd Serm. bef. Edw. VI* (Arb.) 97 He folowed gyftes, as fast as he that folowed the puddynge. **1754** CHATHAM *Lett. Nephew* iv. 24 To follow what they are pleased to call pleasure. **1842** TENNYSON *Ulysses* 31 Yearning in desire To follow knowledge like a sinking star. **1859** —— *Vivien* 474, I follow fame.

†**b.** To pursue (an affair) to its conclusion or accomplishment; to follow up, prosecute; to enforce (law). Also const. *on*, *upon*, *against* (a person). *Obs.*

a **1547** SURREY *Aeneid* II. 118 Ne could I fool refrein my tong from thretes..to folowe my reuenge. *c* **1585** R. BROWNE *Answ. Cartwright* 55 We shoulde first followe the Lawe on them, to thrust them out of the sheepefolde. **1595** DANIEL *Civ. Wars* IV. lxxxiii, Whereas the matter is so followed That he conuented is ere he could tell He was in danger. **1597** SHAKS. *2 Hen. IV*, I. i. 21 O, such a day, So fought, so followed and so fairly won. **1608** D. T. *Ess. Pol. & Mor.* 28 For that he did egerly follow the extreamitie of law against a certaine friende of his. **1653** HOLCROFT *Procopius, Vandal Wars* II. xi. 43 Belisarius followed no execution, thinking it enough with so small an Army to beat the enemy, and send him going. **1693** *Hum. Town* I. 30 Giving his Lawyer double Fees, that his Cause may be well followed.

7. *fig.* (Cf. sense 3). To treat or take (a person) as a guide, leader, or master; to accept the authority or example of, obey the dictates or guidance of; to adhere to, espouse the opinions, side, or cause of. Also, ***to follow a person's steps***.

c **1000** *Ags. Gosp.* Luke xvi. 13 He anum folȝaþ and oðerne forhoȝaþ. *c* **1200** *Vices & Virtues* (1888) 27 Ðat tu ne folȝih none dwelmenn, ðe muchel misleueð. *c* **1230** *Hali Meid.* 15 He seð þe folhen hire treoden. *c* **1374** CHAUCER *Anel. & Arc.* 21 First followe I Stace, and after him Corinne. *c* **1380** WYCLIF *Wks.* (1880) 381 Þat ȝe filow þe steppis of hym þat did no synne. *c* **1449** PECOCK *Repr.* 248 The sympler partie of hem folewiden the worthier and the more wijs partie. **1526** *Pilgr. Perf.* (W. de W. 1531) 1 b, Which doctours I folowe most communly in this poore treatyse. **1548** HALL *Chron., Hen. VI* (an. 34) 169 Favoryng and folowyng the part of kyng Henry. **1548–9** (Mar.) *Bk. Com. Prayer* Collect 18th Sund. after Trinity, With pure harte and mynde to folowe thee the onelye God. **1666** DRYDEN *Let. to Sir R. Howard* 10 Nov. Wks. (Globe) 41 Virgil..has been my master in this poem: I have followed him everywhere. **1706** ATTERBURY *Serm.* 1 Cor. xv. 19 (1723) II. 7 They [Beasts] follow Nature, in their Desires and Fruitions, carrying them no farther than she directs. **1732** BERKELEY *Alciphr.* IV. §16 We profess to follow reason wherever it leads. **1851** RUSKIN *Mod. Paint.* II. III. II. v. §15 The sacred painters must not be followed in their frankness of unshadowed colour, unless we can also follow them in its clearness.

8. a. To conform to, comply with, obey, act upon or in accordance with (advice, command, teaching, example, fashion, etc.); to take as a rule or model, act up to, 'walk after'.

a **1000** *Elene* 929 (Gr.) He forlæteð lare þine & manþeawum minum folȝaþ. *c* **1200** *Trin. Coll. Hom.* 185 Wule nu þanne foleȝ seinte andreues faire forbisne. *a* **1340** HAMPOLE *Psalter* xxi. 16 As hundes folus þer custom in berkyng & bitynge. *a* **1450** *Cov. Myst.* (1841) 268 Ȝyf ȝe wole folwe myn intent. **1548–9** (Mar.) *Bk. Com. Prayer* Collect Sunday bef. Easter, That all mankynde shoulde folowe the example of his greate humilitie. **1611** BIBLE *2 Sam.* xvii. 23 His counsell was not followed. **1671** MILTON *P.R.* I. 483 Most men admire Virtue, who follow not her lore. **1692** LOCKE *Educ.* § 89 (1699) 141 Ill Patterns are sure to be follow'd more than good Rules. **1719** DE FOE *Crusoe* (1840) II. xi. 239 Our men..followed their orders. **1771** *Junius Lett.* xlviii. 252, I..think that the precedent ought to be followed immediately. **1849** MACAULAY *Hist. Eng.* I. 446 Had his advice been followed, the laws would have been strictly observed. **1871** MORLEY *Voltaire* (1886) 5 Voltaire ..did not always refuse to follow an adversary's bad example.

¶ *intr.* const. *to*. *rare*$^{-1}$ (perh. an involuntary anacoluthon).

1523 LD. BERNERS *Froiss.* I. ccccxli. 777 To the whiche counsayle they were gladde to folowe.

†**b.** To conform to in likeness, resemble, take after; to imitate or copy. *Obs.*

c **1386** CHAUCER *Clerk's T.* 1133 Folweth Ekko, that holdeth no silence. *c* **1400** *Destr. Troy* 8723 The body of this bold, þat barely is ded, Most follow by fourme the freeltie of man: Hit may not long vpon loft ly vncoruppit. **1483** *Cath. Angl.* 137/1 To Folowe ye fader in maners, *patrissare*. **1597** HOOKER *Eccl. Pol.* v. xxviii. §1 We had rather follow the perfections of them whom we like not, than in defects resemble them whom we love. **1615** T. ADAMS *Spirit. Navig.* 41 Glasse among stones is as a foole amongst men: for it followes precious stones in colour, not in virtue. **1674** WOOD *Life* (Oxf. Hist. Soc.) II. 281 Mrs. Betty her daughter follows her.

9. To walk in, pursue, practise (a way of life, habit, method of acting); to engage in, occupy oneself with, addict or apply oneself to; *esp.* to practise (a calling or profession) for a livelihood. ***to follow the sea***: to practise the calling of a sailor.

971 *Blickl. Hom.* 25 Þa men þe þyssum uncystum fylȝaþ. *c* **1175** *Lamb. Hom.* 119 Monie þewas..ledað to deðe on ende þa þe heom duseliche folȝiað. *c* **1400** *Cato's Morals* 63 in *Cursor M.* 1670 Quat werk þou folow salle. **1601** SHAKS. *Twel. N.* I. iii. 99 O, had I but followed the arts! **1618** ROLFE in *Capt. Smith's Wks.* (1819) II. 37 Euery man followed his building and planting. **1651** LILLY *Chas. I* (1774) 177 While he was young, he followed his book seriously. **1709** STEELE & SWIFT *Tatler* No. 68 ¶4 When I was young enough to follow the Sports of the Field. **1800** COLQUHOUN *Comm. Thames* Pref., Those..who follow Nautical Pursuits. **1864** D. G. MITCHELL *Sev. Stor.* 269 He followed the profession of an artist. **1883** STEVENSON *Treas. Isl.* II. x, Mr. Trelawney had followed the seas. **1885** U. S. GRANT *Personal Mem.* I. xxi. 288 Whose occupation had been following the river in various capacities, from captain down to deck hand.

10. To watch the progress or course of (an object in motion).

1697 DRYDEN *Æneid* VI. 643 [He] follow'd with his Eyes the flitting Shade. **1819** BYRON *Juan* I. clx, With prying snub-nose and small eyes he stood Following Antonia's motions here and there.

11. To trace or attend to the course or sequence of; to keep up with (an argument, train of thought, etc.) so as to grasp its sequence and meaning; also, to keep up with and understand (a person) as he reasons or recounts.

1697 DRYDEN *Virg. Georg.* IV. 408 An ancient Legend I prepare to sing, And upward follow Fame's immortal Spring. **1866** L. CARROLL *Alice in Wonderld.* ix, I think I should understand that better..if I had it written down: but I can't quite follow it as you say it. **1875** JOWETT *Plato* (ed. 2) I. 64, I do not quite follow you, he said. *Ibid.* V. 12 The argument is too difficult for them to follow.

12. *Mech.* **a.** To go over the contour of (a piece of turned work with a tool). **b.** Of a piece of machinery: To receive its motion from, be a 'follower' to (another piece).

1703 MOXON *Mech. Exerc.* 213 They smoothen the work with the Edge..of a broken Knife..by following the Work with it: That is, holding the basil'd Edge of the Knife close against the Work while it comes about. **1851** L. D. B. GORDON in *Art Jrnl. Illust. Mag.* II. **/1 The act of giving motion to a piece is termed *driving* it, and that of receiving motion from a piece is termed *following* it.

13. ***to follow suit***: see SUIT *sb.*

II. Intransitive uses.

14. To go or come after a person or thing in motion; to move behind some object; also, to go as a person's attendant or companion. Const., *after*, †*on*, †*to*. Also *fig.* Cf. 1.

c **1250** *Gen. & Ex.* 3272 Egipcienes woren in twired wen queðer he sulden folȝen or flen. *c* **1340** *Cursor M.* 11435 (Trin.) Þei follewed on þe sterre beme Til þei coom to Ierusalem. *Ibid.* 19374 (Trin.) As bifore hem wrouȝt he þe wey So aftir him faste folewed þey. *c* **1400** *Rom. Rose* 6342 And with me folwith my loteby, To done me solas and company. *c* **1475** *Rauf Coilȝear* 421 He followit to him haistely..For to bring him to the king. **1513** MORE *Rich. III* (1641) 219 After whom folowed the King with his Crowne and Scepter. *c* **1600** SHAKS. *Sonn.* xli. 4 For still temptation follows where thou art. **1697** DRYDEN *Virg. Georg.* IV. 700 He first, and close behind him follow'd she. **1848** R. I. WILBERFORCE *Incarnat. Our Lord* xiv. (1852) 401 The Philosopher of Königsberg following in a measure in Plato's steps. **1874** GREEN *Short Hist.* ii. §6. 89 Gilbert was one of the Norman strangers who followed in the wake of the Conqueror.

15. a. To come (next) after something else in order or sequence. ***as follows***: a prefatory formula used to introduce a statement, enumeration, or the like. Cf. 2.

The const. in *as follows* is *impers.*, and the verb should always be used in the sing.; for the incorrect pl. see quots. 1776, 1797.

c **1300** *Cursor M.* 19135 (Edin.) Þe toþer dai þat folwid neste. *c* **1380** WYCLIF *Sel. Wks.* III. 107 Þe secunde part.. folweþ in þese wordes. **1426** in *Surtees Misc.* (1890) 9 Was done afterwarde als her fast folowys. **1486** *Bk. St. Albans* D iij, Now foloys the naamys of all maner of hawkys. **1548** HALL *Chron., Edw. IV* (an. 23) 247 He openly sayde as foloweth. **1607** TOPSELL *Four-f. Beasts* (1658) 229 Vegetius having commended the Persian Horses saith, that the Armenians and Sapharens do follow next. **1711** ADDISON *Spect.* No. 58 ¶6 The Subject of it (as in the rest of the Poems which follow). **1776** G. CAMPBELL *Rhetoric* I. II. iv. 495 Analogy as well as usage favour this mode of expression: 'The conditions of the agreement *as follows*,' and not *as follow*. A few late writers have inconsiderately adopted this last form through a mistake of the construction. **1797** GODWIN *Enquirer* II. xii. §1. 374 The reasons that dissuade us..are as follow. **1806–7** J. BERESFORD *Miseries Hum. Life* (1826) II. iv, Beat what follows if you can. **1843** MILL *Logic* I. iii. §7 There are philosophers who have argued as follows.

b. To happen or occur after something else; to come next as an event; to ensue. Const. *on*.

c **1400** *Lanfranc's Cirurg.* 120 If þe crampe folowe it is deedly. *a* **1533** LD. BERNERS *Huon* lxxxii. 254 It shall not folow after thy counsell. **1548** HALL *Chron., Hen. VI* (an. 5) 103 b, The Castle was almoste undermined, so that yeldyng must folowe. **1611** BIBLE *Exod.* xxi. 22 If men striue, and hurt a woman with child, so that her fruit depart from her, and yet no mischiefe follow. **1667** MILTON *P.L.* II. 206 When those who at the Spear are bold And vent'rous, if that fail them, shrink and fear What yet they know must follow. **1688** J. SMITH *Baroscope* 65 If Fair Weather follows immediately upon the Mercury's Rising. **1839** YEOWELL *Anc. Brit. Ch.* iii. (1847) 28 That the martyrdom of this blessed apostle followed very shortly after the writing of this Epistle. **1888** MRS. H. WARD *R. Elsmere* I. iii, That state which so often follows on the long confinement of illness. **1903** R. LANGBRIDGE *Flame & Flood* ii, A rich-souled organ poured out its absolution; following on the voice of the violin..

16. To result (as an effect from a cause, an inference from premisses); to be, or occur as, a consequent. Const. *from* (†*of*). Often *impers.* with a clause, ***it follows (that)***... Cf. 2 c.

a **1300** *Cursor M.* (Gött.) 2892 Fleis þat sine ouer al þis erde, Þe wreche þat foluis haue ȝe herd. *c* **1386** CHAUCER *Melib.* ¶110 And though that Salomon seith, That he ne fond never womman good, it folweth nat therfore that alle wommen ben wikke. *c* **1449** PECOCK *Repr.* II. i. 132 If this be trewe, thanne..it muste nedis folewe that [etc.]. **1624** W. SIMONS in *Capt. Smith's Wks.* (1819) I. 166 In a short time it followed, that could not be had for a pound of Copper, which before was sould vs for an ounce. **1678** DRYDEN *Limberham* I. Wks. 1883 VI. 27 But what followed of this dumb interview? **1698** KEILL *Exam. Th. Earth* (1734) 55 These are the effects which..would necessarily follow from the position of the Earths axis. **1751** JORTIN *Serm.* (1771) II. iii. 44 Though we have received a command to pray for our enemies, it follows not thence we may not wage war with them. **1843** MILL *Logic* II. i. §1 We say of a fact or statement, that it is proved, when we believe its truth by reason of some other fact or statement from which it is said to follow.

17. a. To go in chase or pursuit. Const. *after*, †*on*, †*upon*. Also *fig.* of things. Cf. 5.

c **1250** *Gen. & Ex.* 1751 He toc and wente and folwede on, And ðhoȝt in mod Iacob to slon. *c* **1400** *Destr. Troy* 10459 Theire fos on hom folowet. *c* **1420** *Anturs of Arth.* v, The king blue a rechase, Folut fast on the trase. **1535** COVERDALE *Prov.* xiii. 21 Myschefe foloweth vpon synners. **1611** BIBLE *Gen.* xliv. 4 Vp, follow after the men. **1623** BINGHAM *Xenophon* 115 They dare and will be readie to follow vpon vs, if we retire.

b. ***to follow after***: to strive to reach, gain, or compass. Cf. 6.

1362 LANGL. *P. Pl.* A. x. 189 Þauȝ þei don hem to donmowe..To folewen aftur þe Flucchen, fecche þei hit neuere. **1611** BIBLE *Ps.* cxix. 150 They draw nigh that follow after mischiefe. **1881** BIBLE (R.V.) *Heb.* xii. 14 Follow after peace with all men.

†**c.** ? To tend *to*. *Obs.*

c **1475** *Rauf Coilȝear* 508 Thow fand me fechand nathing that followit to feid.

†**18.** Of a person: To proceed with, or continue doing, something begun. Cf. 6 b. *Obs.*

a **1300** *Cursor M.* 12197 (Cott.) Ihesus þan folud on his speke. **1703** MOXON *Mech. Exerc.* 182 Having thus described the parts of a Common Lathe, I shall now follow with their other Tools also.

III. In combination with adverbs.

follow home. See HOME *adv.*

19. follow on. a. *intr.* To go on in the same direction as an object which is moving in front; to continue following.

c **1250** [see 17]. **1884** W. COOK *Billiards* 9 A following stroke is when you cause your ball to follow on after the ball it strikes.

†**b.** To go on or continue perseveringly (*to do* something). *Obs.*

1611 BIBLE *Hos.* vi. 3 Then shal we know, if we follow on to know the Lord.

c. *trans.* = *follow up* b.

1652 WADSWORTH tr. *Sandoval's Civ. Wars Spain* 363 If, after the taking of Torrelobaton, hee had followed on his victorie.

d. *intr.* Of a side at *Cricket*: To go in again at once after completing the first innings, in consequence of having made a prescribed number of runs less than their opponents in the first innings.

1865 F. LILLYWHITE *Guide to Cricketers* 86 Surrey 'followed on', but left only 23 runs for Oxford to get to win. **1882** *Standard* 9 Aug. 3/6 They consequently had to 'follow on'. **1891** *Leeds Mercury* 2 May 6/4 Being left in a minority of 93 they had to follow on.

20. follow out. *trans.* To pursue to a conclusion; to bring to a completion or final issue.

1762 LD. KAMES *Elem. Crit.* I. i. 36 Avarice having got possession of his mind, he follows out that theme to the end. **1884** CHURCH *Bacon* 22 While he was following out the great ideas which were to be the basis of his philosophy.

21. follow through. *intr.* *Golf*, etc. To continue the stroke, after the ball has been struck, to the full extent of the swing. (Cf. FOLLOW *sb.* 4.)

[**1895** H. G. HUTCHINSON *Golf* (ed. 5) iv. 87 The difficulty ..of getting the club to follow easily through after the ball.] **1897** *Encycl. Sport* I. 464/1 The player should have the habit, so important in this 'following through', of regarding the ball merely as a point *through* which the club head is to pass in the course of its circuit. **1909** P. A. VAILE *Mod. Golf*

xiv. 197 The timing of the stroke, so that the head of the driver..runs into the line of flight of the ball, hits it truly, and then follows through in a true vertical plane. **1967** *Know the Game: Tennis* 31 The racket is following through.

22. follow up. *trans.* **a.** To go after or pursue closely; to keep steadily in the track or pursuit of.

1847 Tennyson *Princ.* i. 203 We follow'd up the river as we rode. *Ibid.* iv. 446 It becomes no man to nurse despair, But..To follow up the worthiest till he die. **1888** *Times* 16 Oct. 10/5 The Forest bylaws..make no provision for wounded deer being followed up.

b. To prosecute with energy (an affair already in progress); to reinforce by further vigorous action or fresh support.

1794 Paley *Evid.* ii. ix. (1817) 216 It comes next to be considered how far these accounts are confirmed or followed up by other evidence. **1855** Macaulay *Hist. Eng.* IV. 354 The blow was speedily followed up. **1867** Smiles *Huguenots Eng.* ix. (1880) 143 Louis was not slow to follow up this intimation with measures of a more positive kind. **1878** Bosw. Smith *Carthage* 98 The Romans followed up their success by an attack on Olbia.

absol. **1854** Dickens *Hard T.* i. ii, He would go in and damage any subject whatever with his right, follow up with his left [etc.].

c. = sense 2 d.

1795 T. Paine *Age of Reason* ii. 66 Matthew..follows up this part of the story of the guard..with a second part. **1905** W. Bodie *Bodie Bk.* 173, I must explain these two statements, and then follow them up by a third.

23. *Comb.* **follow-me-lads** *sb. pl.* [cf. F. *suivez-moi-jeune-homme*], curls or ribbons hanging loosely over the shoulder; also *sing.*, *U.S. colloq.*, a furbelow in a woman's costume; **follow-spot**, a spotlight that follows a performer on the stage; also *fig.*

1862 *Times* 21 Jan. 10/1 Vagrant ringlets straying over the shoulder, better known by the name of 'follow me, lads'. **1872** *Spectator* (Farmer), 'Follow-me-lads' are not in themselves very pretty, though, like any other fashion, they become the Princess. **1874** Hotten *Slang Dict.*, *Follow-me-lads*, curls hanging over a lady's shoulder. **1901** Greenough & Kittredge *Words* (1902) 190 Kiss-me-quick, hug-me-tight, follow-me-lads,—names for articles of female attire. **1929** K. H. Brown *The Father* i, Miss Evelina Amberley, in all her frills and laces and follow-me-lads, as scalloped and frilled and fluted as her name. *Ibid.* ix, The knife sawed through Aunt Euphemia's follow-me-lad, slashed out a thick chunk of somber plush. **1957** J. Osborne *Entertainer* i. 12 The lighting is..bright and hard, or a simple follow-spot. **1960** Lawrence & Lee *Gang's All Here* 7 The follow spot is preparing to seek the man who will go to 1600 Pennsylvania Avenue.

follow, obs. form of fellow.

followable ('fɒləʊəb(ə)l), *a.* [f. prec. + -able.] That may or can be followed.

1548 Gest *Pr. Masse* 136 We ought to..embrace hys doyinges as followable and beleveable. **1611** Cotgr., *Imitable*, imitable, followable. **1830** N. S. Wheaton *Jrnl.* 199 A mistake which is followable by instant degradation. **1888** *Dublin Rev.* Jan. 219 The Church has..declared..his system of morals..to be void of error, and followable as a sure guide by any priest.

follower ('fɒləʊə(r)). [OE. *folȝere*, f. as prec. + -er[1].]

1. One who follows (in the literal sense).

1697 Dryden *Virg. Georg.* iii. 174 Clouds of Sand arise; Spurn'd, and cast backward on the Follower's Eyes. **1807** Hutton *Course Math.* II. 57 All the 10 arrows are taken by one of them, who goes foremost, and is called the leader; the other being called the follower, for distinction's sake.

b. Something that comes after or succeeds something else.

c **1450** Pecock (*title*) The Folewer to the Donet. **1581** Sidney *Apol. Poetrie* (Arb.) 50 One word so as it were begetting another, as..by the former a man shall haue a neere gesse to the follower. **1879** Furnivall *Rep. E.E.T.S.* 17 When the *Catholicon* is finisht, what its follower shall be can be discusst.

c. One who follows in order to catch or come up with another; a pursuer.

1593 Shaks. *3 Hen. VI* i. iv. 22 Ah, hark! the fatal followers do pursue. **1598** Grenewey *Tacitus' Ann.* iii. x. (1622) 105 Stealing by dangerous by-wayes [he] beguiled his followers.

2. a. One who follows another as his attendant, servant, retainer, or the like.

c **888** K. Ælfred *Boeth.* xxix. §1 Be ðam cyninge and be his folȝerum. *c* **1000** *Voc.* in Wr.-Wülcker 189/30 *Assecla*, folȝere. **1377** Langl. *P. Pl.* B. v. 549, I haue ben his folwar al þis fifty wyntre. *c* **1440** *Promp. Parv.* 169/2 Folware, or serwante folowynge hys mastyr or souereyne, *pedissequus*. **1548** Hall *Chron.*, *Edw. IV* (an. 2) 190 b, Certain of his henxmen or folowers wer taken. **1697** Dryden *Æneid* v. 1039 And forc'd Æneas..To leave his Foll'wers on a Foreign Coast. **1840** Dickens *Barn. Rudge* viii, The Captain eyed his follower over. **1844** *Regul. & Ord. Army* 275 All Followers and Retainers of the Camp.

b. One who follows another in regard to his teaching or opinions; an adherent or disciple; also one who follows an example, model, rule of conduct, etc.

c **1200** *Vices & Virtues* (1888) 41 Ȝe modi menn, ðes dieules folȝeres. *a* **1225** *Ancr. R.* 364 Sikerliche his feoleware mot mid pine of his flesche uoluwen his pinen. **1388** Wyclif *1 Cor.* xi. 1 Be ȝe my foleweris, as Y am of Crist. *c* **1440** *Promp. Parv.* 169/2 Folware, yn manerys, or condycions, *imitator*. *c* **1532** Dewes *Introd. Fr.* in Palsgr. 894 Arte is folower of nature. **1611** Bible *1 Pet.* iii. 13 If ye bee followers of that which is good. **1710** Berkeley *Princ. Hum. Knowl.* §11 Aristotle and his followers. **1781** Burke *Corr.* (1844) II. 437 We, who ought to have taken the lead in so noble a work, are but ill followers even of the examples which are set to us. **1849** Macaulay *Hist. Eng.* II. 13 It soon became clear that Halifax would have many followers. **1891** *Speaker* 2 May 526/2 To vindicate Horace Walpole from the aspersions of Macaulay and his followers.

c. *colloq.* A man who courts a maidservant; *esp.* one who calls at the house to see her.

1838 Dickens *Nich. Nick.* xvi, Five servants kept. No man. No followers. **1858** R. S. Surtees *Ask Mamma* xlv. 202 She granted [the servants]..every indulgence..in having their followers.

†**3.** *Sc.* A prosecutor (at law). Cf. follow *v.* 5 c.

a **1300** *Cursor M.* 28416 (Cott.) Wittnes foluar. **1449** *Sc. Acts Jas. II* (1814) II. 37 He salbe condampnit be the Juge in the expensis of the folowar.

4. *Sc.* and *north. dial.* The young of cattle.

1584 *Wills & Inv.* (Surtees 1860) II. 105 The beste cowe I haue..with her follower. *c* **1686** *Depredations on Clan Campbell* (1816) 61, 1 bull, 2 mares and followers. **1829** Scott *Doom of Devorgoil* i. i, Three cows, with each her follower. **1885** *Times* (weekly ed.) 16 Oct. 2/3 The crofter paying £10 should be able to keep four cows with their followers.

5. *Mech.* **a.** In various kinds of presses: The plate or block by which the pressure is applied.

1676 Worlidge *Cyder* (1691) 117 The lower end of the Toothed Bar must be fixed into a Follower of Wood. **1860** *All Year Round* No. 51. 19 A proper 'vat' and 'follower' made of solid mahogany [for making cheese]. **1882** Southward *Pract. Printing* 587 The piece [in a screw press] answering to the platen of a printing press is called the 'follower'.

b. In a pile-driving machine: A 'dolly' or block of timber placed between the ram and the head of the pile. Also, formerly, †the movable block and 'tongs' by which the ram is lifted and let fall.

1776 G. Semple *Building in Water* 36 Fig. 2 is the Follower playing in its Grooves..Fig. 3..the Follower and Ram, seemingly just ready to engage one another. **1868** *Min. Proc. Inst. Civ. Engineers* XXVII. 277 The piles..had to be driven with a follower, which was made of very tough oak, and well banded at both ends.

c. In wheel-work: (see quot. 1805).

1805 Brewster in *Ferguson's Lect.* I. 82 *note*, In a combination of wheels that which is acted upon by the power..is called a leader; and the other wheel on the same axis is called a follower. **1884** F. J. Britten *Watch & Clockm.* 291 Lantern pinions work very smoothly as followers though they are unsuitable as drivers.

d. (See quot.)

1874 Knight *Dict. Mech.*, *Follower* (Steam-engine), the cover or plug of a stuffing-box, which rests upon and compresses the packing; a gland.

6. *Stationery.* (See quots.)

1858 Simmonds *Dict. Trade*, *Follower*..a sheet of parchment, which is added to the first or indenture, etc. sheet. **1888** Jacobi *Printer's Voc.*, *Followers*, the following sheets after a heading—such as the ordinary plain-ruled paper used after the title-head of a long invoice.

'following, *pres. pple.* of follow *v.*, loosely used as quasi-prep.: as a sequel to, in succession to (an event), after.

1947 *Evening News* 11 Dec., The prologue was written by the company following an incident witnessed by them during anti-Jewish demonstrations following the hanging of two British soldiers in Palestine. **1948** E. Gowers *Plain Words* 56 Perhaps the fight against *following* as a preposition ought to be regarded as lost. **1968** *Observer* 24 Mar. 6/4 Used car prices are going up, following the Budget.

following ('fɒləʊɪŋ), *vbl. sb.* [f. as prec. + -ing[1].]

1. The action of the verb follow, in its various uses. Also with advs., as *following up*.

a **1300** *Cursor M.* 27832 (Cott.) O couaitise..cums..fals foluing, fals wittnesing. **1435** Misyn *Fire of Love* 66 In filoing of vertew. **1562** *39 Articles* No. 9 Originall sinne standeth not in the following of Adam. **1649** Drumm. of Hawth. *Hist. Jas. V.* Wks. (1711) 107 That the chace and following of hereticks is more necessary than that of infidels. **1801** Strutt *Sports & Past.* i. i. 13 Queen Elizabeth..frequently indulged herself in following of the hounds. **1875** Whitney *Life Lang.* viii. 143 The following-up of a series of acts.

2. *concr.* A body of followers, attendants, retainers or adherents; followers collectively.

c **1450** *Mirour Saluacioun* 1865 Abraham and his fylowing discomfit thaym be gods grace. **1695** Blair in *Blackmore's Hist. Conspir.* (1723) 117 He was a Man of great following and Interest in his Country. **1715** *Wodrow Corr.* (1843) II. 88 He reckons Mar's following must decrease. **1816** Scott *Old Mort.* xxvi. 191 The unfortunate Duke of Monmouth, who had..a numerous following, as it was called, in the southern parts of that kingdom. *a* **1859** Macaulay *Hist. Eng.* V. 110 Such a man, with a great name in the country and a strong following in Parliament. **1889** Jessopp *Coming of Friars* i. 39 [They] started lectures and secured a large following.

'following, *ppl. a.* [f. as prec. + -ing[2].]

1. That follows or moves after another.

1626 Bacon *Sylva* §844 By the more Equall spreading of the Tangible Parts, which thereby are more Sliding and Following. **1715–20** Pope *Iliad* xiv. 489 His following shield the fallen chief o'erspread. **1796–7** *Instr. & Reg. Cavalry* (1813) 125 The three's wheel from the pivot flank, which then becomes the following one.

2. That comes after or next in order or in time; succeeding, subsequent, ensuing.

In most collocations placed indifferently before or after the sb.; as, *in the following year*, *in the year following*.

a **1300** *Cursor M.* 11378 (Cott.) Þe nest yeire foluand. *c* **1330** R. Brunne *Chron.* (1810) 87 In þe ȝere folowand. *c* **1430** Maundev. (Roxb.) xxiv. 110 On þe nyght next folowand. **1535** Coverdale *2 Macc.* xii. 39 Vpon the daye folowinge. **1667** Milton *P.L.* x. 278 Living Carcasses design'd For death, the following day, in bloodie fight. **1742** Johnson *L.P.*, *Sydenham*, To continue the same office upon all following occasions. **1829** Marryat *F. Mildmay* xxii, They were *asked* in church the Sunday following. **1860** Tyndall *Glac.* i. viii. 57 Early on the following day. **1875** Whitney *Life Lang.* iv. 46 A sibilant with following palatal mute.

b. In introducing a statement, enumeration, etc.: That now follows; that is immediately to be set forth, mentioned, recounted, or the like. Also *absol.* (*the following*).

1340 *Ayenb.* 1 Þis byeþ þe capiteles of þe boc uolȝinde. **1545–8** *Yorksh. Chantry Surv.* 11 (Surtees) 461 In thandes of the personnes foloing. **1626** Bacon *Sylva* §846 They are all but the effects of some of these causes following. **1653** Walton *Angler* To Rdr., I think fit to tell thee these following truths. **1711** Steele *Spect.* No. 152 ¶2 My Friend answered what I said in the following manner. **1794** Sullivan *View Nat.* I. 225 The following..may not, as an example, be unworthy of notice. **1807** T. Thomson *Chem.* II. 148 The following bodies have the property of converting nitric oxide into nitrous oxide. **1841** Lane *Arab. Nts.* I. 123 Among the common dishes are the following.

c. Ensuing as an effect or consequence, resulting.

1593 Shaks. *Lucr.* 166 In his inward mind he doth debate, What following sorrow may on this arise. **1687** Shadwell *Juvenal* x. 46 The Conquerors used to put the following spoyls upon the stumps of Trees, which were call'd Trophies.

†**3.** Conformable, correspondent. answerable.

c **1340** *Gaw. & Gr. Knt.* 145 His wombe & his wast were worthily smale, & alle his fetures folȝande. *Ibid.* 859 Tapytez tyȝt to þe woȝe, of tuly & tars, & vnder fete, on þe flet, of folȝande sute.

4. Of wind or tide: ? Moving in the direction of the ship's course. (Cf. L. *ventus secundus.*)

1807 J. Boone in *Naval Chron.* XXIII. 406 She was assisted by a high following sea. **1839** Marryat *Phant. Ship* viii, You may sail for weeks with a cloudless sky and a following breeze, without starting tack or sheet. **1858** W. Cook in *Merc. Marine Mag.* V. 42 We had a following sea previous to falling in with this mist, but the sea then changed to a kind of boil, or topping sea.

5. *Billiards* and *Croquet.* ***following stroke*** = follow *sb.* 2.

1867 Dufton *Pract. Billiards* iii. 45. **1868** W. J. Whitmore *Croquet Tac.* 15 In making a following stroke, the player must follow with the mallet head, as a person follows with the cue at billiards. **1884** [See follow *v.* 19 a].

6. In various technical usages.

1839 Ure *Dict. Arts* 979 When a coal has a following or roof stone, which regularly separates with the coal. **1883** Gresley *Gloss. Coal-m.*, *Following dirt*, loose shale, etc., in a thin bed forming the roof of a coal seam. *Ibid.*, *Following-up bank*, a breadth of about 6 yards of coal taken off on either side of a leading bank. **1888** *Lockwood's Dict. Mech. Engin.*, *Following edge*, that edge of the blade of a screw propeller which leaves the water behind it, as distinguished from the leading edge. *Following joints*. The rings of which cylindrical boilers are built, being lap jointed, fit one within the other. Instead, therefore, of being parallel cylinders, they are necessarily frustra of cones, and as the joints all lap in one direction, they are termed following joints. *Following steady*, a steady which is attached to the back of the side rest of a lathe, and which embraces the work behind or after the tool and follows it along with the rest. **1967** *Gloss. Mining Terms (B.S.I.)* xi. 8 *Following roof*, a layer of roof which falls as coal is excavated, or soon after.

†**'followingly**, *adv. Obs.* [f. following *ppl. a.* + -ly[2].]

1. a. Afterwards in order or sequence, subsequently, ensuingly. **b.** As a result or consequence, consequently.

1382 Wyclif *2 Chron.* xxxii. 15 Ȝif forsothe no God of alle Gentilis..myȝte delyueren his puple..folowyngly ne ȝour God schal mowe delyuer ȝou. **1398** Trevisa *Barth. De P.R.* xiii. xxii. (1495) 454 Thenne folowingly is the coste that hyght Ligusticus. *c* **1449** Pecock *Repr.* ii. ix. 191 Into suche ..remembrauncis..and folewingli therbi into ful deuout preiers. **1502** *Ord. Crysten Men* (W. de W. 1506) iii. iii. 145 Unto hymself fyrste and folowyngly unto them [etc.]. **1559** *Homilies* i. (1859) 56 That consequently (or followingly) God should be the better honoured by them.

2. In what now follows; in the following words.

c **1450** *Mirour Saluacioun* 4085 Howe crist his woundes to his ffadere shewes is to here fylowingly. **1494** Fabyan *Chron.* vii. ccxix. 241 As folowyngly shalbe shewed. **1521** Fisher *Wks.* (1876) 307 In thende of this gospel folowingly is made by our sauyour a stronge argument.

†**'folly**, *a.* and *adv. Obs.* Also 3–4 foli(e, folliche, (folik), 4–5 foly(e, 5 fooly, 6 follie, folyche. [ME. *follich*, f. *fol*, fool *a.* and *sb.* + *-lich* -ly[1].]

A. *adj.* Foolish; also, lewd, unchaste.

a **1300** *Cursor M.* 4361 (Cott.) 'Bilete', he said, 'þi foli will'. **1387** Trevisa *Higden* (Rolls) VII. 233 A nyce folie couenant schulde nouȝt be i-holde. *c* **1400** *Lanfranc's Cirurg.* 267 Ther ben manie foli lechis. *a* **1450** *Knt. de la Tour* (1868) 52 No body shulde..make countenaunce nor lokes of foly loue there inne [the chirche], but yef it were of loue of mariage. **1577–87** Holinshed *Chron.* III. 305/1 Bankettings, dansings and other follie pastimes. **1604** Breton *Pass. Sheph.* (Grosart) 9/2 A Gowne of Veluet.. Shall now bewitche mine eyes with folly gazes.

B. *adv.* Foolishly; also, lewdly, unchastely.

c **1230** *Hali Meid.* 17 Ȝif ȝe þrafter þenne speken togedere folliche. *a* **1300** *Cursor M.* 27890 (Cott.) Drunkenhede dos ..man folik be traist and glad, quare he wit resun suld be radd. **1340** *Ayenb.* 43 þet uolk þet ne byeþ naȝt ine spoushod, louieþ ham togidere folliche. *c* **1369** CHAUCER *Bk. Duchesse* 874 Hyr lokynge nas not foly sprad.

Hence †'**folliness**, foolishness.

c **1340** *Cursor M.* 1278 (Trin.), I was dryuen fro paradis And lost hit bi my folynys. *c* **1449** PECOCK *Repr.* II. iv. 155 The dotage or..folynes..of the persoones. *c* **1450** BURGH *Secrees* 2579 The rede [heerys] also be signe of ffoolynesse.

folly ('fɒlɪ), *sb.*[1] Pl. follies. Forms: 3-5 foli(e, 3-6 foly(e, (4 fole, folle, fowlye), 5 fooly, 6-7 follie, 9 *south.* volly, 5- folly. [a. OF. and Fr. *folie*, f. *fol*, *fou* foolish, mad (see FOOL); corresponding to Pr. *folia*, *follia*, *folhia*, OSp. *folia*, It. *follia*.]

1. a. The quality or state of being foolish or deficient in understanding; want of good sense, weakness or derangement of mind; also, unwise conduct. †*to do folly*: to act foolishly. (*fond*, etc.) *to a folly*, to an absurd degree.

a **1225** *Ancr. R.* 52 Ant te wise ouh to uolewen wisdom, & nout folie. *c* **1330** *Amis & Amil.* 1982 'What foly', he seyd, 'can he sain? Is he madde of mode?' **1375** BARBOUR *Bruce* I. 344 To fenyhe foly quhile is wyt. *c* **1400** *Lanfranc's Cirurg.* 212 þan it is folie for to lete him blood. **1477** EARL RIVERS (Caxton) *Dictes* 127 To loue sapience, and to hate fooly. *a* **1533** LD. BERNERS *Huon* lxvi. 228 We haue done grete foly to departe. **1651** SIR E. NICHOLAS in *N. Papers (Camden)* 248 Sir Thomas Gardner will be ruined by his daughter's folly. **1742** GRAY *Ode Prospect Eton Coll.* 100 Where ignorance is bliss, 'Tis folly to be wise. **1766** GOLDSM. *Vic. W.* xxiv. When lovely woman stoops to folly. **1778** FRANKLIN *Lett.* Wks. 1889 VI. 206, I was fond to a folly of our British connections. **1784** *Laura & Augustus* I. 81 The people are hospitable to a folly. **1875** JOWETT *Plato* (ed. 2) V. 98 The folly of..nurses believes that the left hand is by nature different from the right.

b. *personified.*

1594 WILLOBIE in *Shaks. C. Praise* 9 And folly feedes where fury fretes. **1632** MILTON *Penseroso* 2 Deluding joys, The brood of folly without father bred. **1728** POPE *Dunc.* II. 418 All was hush'd, as Folly's self lay dead.

c. With *a* and *pl.* An example of foolishness; a foolish action, error, idea, practice, etc.; a ridiculous thing, an absurdity.

a **1300** *Cursor M.* 4124 (Cott.) To stint wald he, if he moght, þe foly þat his breþer thoght. **13..** *Coer de L.* 4761 We schole be wrothe, Swylke folyes yiff thou haunte. *c* **1489** CAXTON *Sonnes of Aymon* i. 21 Your father hath enterprised a great foly. *a* **1533** LD. BERNERS *Huon* xcv. 308 They knew well it was but a folye to folow me. **1648** EVELYN *Mem.* (1857) I. 255 The celebrated follies of Bartholomew Fair. **1725** WATTS *Logic* II. v. §4 The mistakes, imprudences, and follies, which ourselves or others have been guilty of. **1773** GOLDSM. *Stoops to Conq.* I. i. 49 In my time, the follies of the town crept slowly among us. **1832** HT. MARTINEAU *Life in Wilds* vi. 72 'Tis a folly to expect it.

†**2. a.** Wickedness, evil, mischief, harm. *Obs.*

c **1290** *S. Eng. Leg.* I. 30/36 He heold him faste in his folie. **1303** R. BRUNNE *Handl. Synne* 4119 He dede no man folye. **1340** HAMPOLE *Pr. Consc.* 357 Purgatory Whar saules er clensed of alle foly. *c* **1489** CAXTON *Sonnes of Aymon* iii. 80 Ye shall haue no leiser for to repente you of the folie that ye doo. **1535** COVERDALE *Josh.* vii. 15 Because he hath.. committed folye in Israel.

†**b.** With *a* and *pl.* A wrong-doing, sin, crime.

c **1250** *Meid. Maregrete* 1 Olde ant yonge i prei ou oure folies for to lete. **1393** LANGL. *P. Pl.* C. XVII. 135 Hit [Pouerte] defendeþ þe flessh fro folyes ful menye. **1535** COVERDALE *Judg.* xx. 6 They haue done an abhominacion and folye in Israel.

†**3. a.** Lewdness, wantonness. Cf. Fr. *folie*. *Obs.*

1303 R. BRUNNE *Handl. Synne* 2961 ȝyf þou to foly wuldest here wynne. *c* **1400** MAUNDEV. (1839) iv. 24 A comoun woman that dwelled there to resceyve men to folye. *a* **1450** *Knt. de la Tour* (1868) 76 The quene..beganne to desire to haue hym to foly with her. **1567** FENTON *Trag. Disc.* A a vij, Neyther had age so altered her complexion but there appered follie in all partes of her face. **1604** SHAKS. *Oth.* v. ii. 132 *Oth.* She turn'd to folly; and she was a whore. **1634** CANNE *Necess. Separ.* (1849) 291 One which calls a woman, 'Whore'..and commits folly with her.

b. With *a* and *pl.* A lewd action or desire.

c **1305** *Miracle St. James 3* in *E.E.P.* (1862) 57 He dude ane folie þat menie to helle bringeþ: þe sinne of lecherie. *c* **1320** *Sir Tristr.* 2181 Her folies vsen þai ay. **1603** SHAKS. *Meas. for M.* III. i. 91 Whose..deliberate word Nips youth i'th head, and follies doth emmew.

†**4.** Madness, insanity, mania (= F. *folie*); hence, rage, anger. *Obs.*

c **1400** *Destr. Troy* 1957 He frothet for folle, and his face chaunget. **1670** LASSELS *Voy. Italy* II. 212, I went to the Pazzorella, where they keep madmen and fooles, and saw there strange variety of humours in folly.

5. a. A popular name for any costly structure considered to have shown folly in the builder.

R. Wendover says that when (in 1228) a castle which Hubert de Burgh had begun to build, near the Welsh border, had to be razed to the ground on account of a treaty concluded with the Welsh, much amusement was excited by the recollection that Hubert had given to the building on its foundation the name of Hubert's Folly (*Stultitiam Huberti*). It was remarked that he had shown himself a true prophet. Probably the word used by Hubert was F. *folie*; the original meaning seems to have been not *stultitia*, but 'delight', 'favourite abode'. Many houses in France still bear the name *La Folie*, and there is some evidence that 'the Folly' was as late as the nineteenth century used in some parts of England for a public pleasure-garden or the like.

1654 WHITLOCK *Zootomia* 502 [He] buryeth it [his wealth] ..in Buildings needlesse, vain, or ill contrived, that stay but the finishing, and being called by his kind Gossip-neighbours his Folly. **1772** R. GRAVES *Spirit. Quixote* III. IX. vii, An object, amidst the woods, on the edge of the hill; which, upon enquiry, they were told was called Shenstone's folly. **1796** *Monthly Mag.* Feb. 20, I built a great many mounds in the form of sugar-loaves, very broad at bottom and pointed at top..Travellers call them my *folly*. **1801** COXE *Tour Monmouthsh.* I. 121 Hence it was called Kemeys Folly. **1885** W. H. RUSSELL in *Harper's Mag.* Apr. 752/1 'The Heights', on which the Folly is built.

b. *pl.* A revue notable for the glamour of its female performers; used esp. as a title, as ***Ziegfeld Follies***; also, the female members of such a revue.

[**1880** J. STIRLING tr. *Zola's Nana* v. 104 Maria Blond—a girl of fifteen—frightfully thin and frightfully vicious, who had just made her début at the Folies.] **1908** *Theatre Mag.* (U.S.) Aug. 201/1 In novelty of ideas, variety, talent of performers and general smartness of production, 'Follies of 1908' is fully up to the standard of the best this enterprising ..young manager [*sc.* Ziegfeld] has yet attempted. **1917** R. W. LARDNER *Gullible's Travels* (1926) iv. 202 They wouldn't nobody of ever mistook the women for *Follies* chorus girls. **1919** F. HURST *Humoresque* 300 The Moncrieff Follies—twenty-four of them, not counting two specialty acts and a pair of whistling Pierrots—burst forth into frolic. **1929** H. MILES tr. *Morand's Black Magic* I. 71 Head-dresses worthy of the Ziegfeld Follies. **1957** 'GYPSY ROSE LEE' *Gypsy* xxxiv. 309 Julie Bryan, my understudy in the *Follies* (less experienced than the maid), went to work as featured strip teaser for the Minskys. **1965** P. ZIEGFELD *Ziegfelds' Girl* ii. 43 The first *Ziegfeld Follies* opened at the Apollo Theater in Atlantic City and came to New York in July of 1907.

6. *Comb.*, as ***folly-blind***, ***-drenched***, †***-fallen***, ***-painting***, ***-stricken*** adjs.

1597 MIDDLETON *Paraphr. Wisd. Sol.* ix. 6 My raigne would be like fortunes, follie-blinde. **1601** SHAKS. *Twel. N.* III. i. 75 For folly that he wisely shewes is fit; But wisemens folly falne, quite taint their wit. **1638-48** G. DANIEL *Eclog.* III. 307 Thy follie-drenched Soule. **1726-46** THOMSON *Winter* 615 Lively wit..Or folly-painting humour. **1807** SYD. SMITH *Wks.* (1859) I. 80/2 The mournful and folly-stricken blockhead.

Hence '**folly** *v. intr.*, to commit folly, to act foolishly. '**follying** *vbl. sb.* also *attrib.*

1818 KEATS *Endymion* I. 612 Let me shun Such follying before thee. **1822** B. CORNWALL *Ludovico Sforza* i. 95 What! shall I in My age be follying? —— *A. Wentworth* ii. 27, In my follying days.

'**folly**, *sb.*[2] *dial.* A clump of fir-trees on the crest of a hill.

1880 R. JEFFERIES *Gr. Ferne F.* vi, 'Every hill seems to have a Folly'..'I mean a clump of trees on the top.' **1888** *Berks. Gloss.*, There are three such 'vollys' at Hampstead Norreys on the 'Volly Hill'.

folmard(e, obs. form of FOUMART.

Folsom ('fəʊlsəm). The name of a village in north-eastern New Mexico, U.S.A., applied *attrib.* to the remains of a prehistoric culture first found there, esp. to a type of projectile point (see quots.).

1928 H. J. COOK in *Sci. Amer.* July 39/3 The fact that these arrowheads were found under the conditions they were, makes it possible to designate it as evidence of a definite cultural stage, for which the name 'Folsom Culture' has been suggested. **1931** *Proc. Colorado Mus. Nat. Hist.* X. ii. 12 Fragments with long and broad lengthwise grooves.. with often long and sharp base points, are really the only ones that could be called 'Folsom points', strictu sensu, that is to say, points of same shape and technique as those actually found at Folsom and..made by the same ancient people. **1948** A. L. KROEBER *Anthropol.* xvi. 678 The typical fine 'Folsom points' are projectile heads made by pressure chipping. *Ibid.* 679 The true or specific Folsom culture.. seems more likely to have been glacial rather than postglacial; certainly terminal Pleistocene..rather than initial or middle. **1954** *Ann. Reg.* *1953* 387 In the New World, after 27 years of searching, the first bone (a rib) of Folsom Man was unearthed in New Mexico.

†**folt**, *sb.* *Obs.* Forms: 4 folet, folt, 4-6 folte, 5 folett, 6 foult. [a. OF. *folet*, f. *fol* mad, foolish: see FOOL *sb.*] A fool.

1303 R. BRUNNE *Handl. Synne* 8300 A kaynarde and an olde folte. *c* **1330** —— *Chron. Wace* (Rolls) 4527 A folet coupe he wel adaunte. *c* **1440** *Promp. Parv.* 168/2 Folett ..*stolidus*. *c* **1440** HYLTON *Scala Perf.* (W. de W. 1494) I. xxxiv, In þe day of pentecost..thei were made neyther foles ne foltis, but..wonder wyse. **1566** DRANT *Horace's Sat.* I. i. A iv, The foolishe frantycke foultes.

Hence †'**folthead**, †'**foltry** [see -RY], folly.

1399 LANGL. *Rich. Redeles* II. 7 Non..ȝoure name wolde nempne In ffersnesse ne in ffoltheed. *c* **1440** *Promp. Parv.* 169/1 Foltrye, *fatuitas, stoliditas.*

†**folt**, *v.* *Obs.* [f. FOLT *sb.*] *intr.* To act like a fool. Hence †'**folted** *ppl. a.*, foolish.

a **1300** *Cursor M.* 2239 (Gött.) þir folis foltid gadrid þaim þan. **1303** R. BRUNNE *Handl. Synne* 5839 Shrewes..helde hym foltede or wode For he was so mylde of mode. **13..** *Minor Poems fr. Vernon MS.* XXXVII. 605 þe wikked gost.. seide þat he was a folted mon. *c* **1440** *Promp. Parv.* 169/1 Foltyn, or doon as a foole.

†'**foltish**, *a.* *Obs.* Also 4 foltishe, foltisch, 5 foltysch, 6 foultish. [f. FOLT *sb.* + -ISH.] Foolish, besotted, silly.

c **1380** WYCLIF *Serm.* Sel. Wks. I. 309 Foltish chaffering. *c* **1430** LYDG. *Min. Poems* (Percy Soc.) 166 A foltissh face. **1566** DRANT *Horace's Sat.* II. iii. G iv b, No reason is this foultishe flocke from madnes to exile.

†**foltron.** *Obs. rare.*

1748 WESLEY *Wks.* (1872) XI. 509 Try foltron, a mixture of herbs to be had at many grocers', far healthier, as well as cheaper, than tea.

foly(e, obs. form of FOLLY.

‖**Fomalhaut** ('fəʊməl,hɔːt). *Astron.* Also 6, 8 **fomahant.** [Arab. *fum*[u] *'l-haut* mouth of the fish, Sp. *fomahant.*] A star of the first magnitude in the constellation Southern Fish (α *Piscis Australis*).

1594 BLUNDEVIL *Exerc.* III. I. xxvi. (ed. 7) 334 One..star of the first bignesse in his mouth called Fomahant. **1704** J. HARRIS *Lex. Techn.*, *Fomahant*, a Star of the first Magnitude in..Aquarius. **1884** BROWNING *Ferishtah* 137 Should I overlook Fomalhaut and declare some fen-fire King.

foman, obs. form of FOEMAN.

†'**fomblitude.** *nonce-wd.* [? f. FUMBLE, parodying *similitude.*] 'A weak comparison' (Halliw.).

1583 FULKE *Defence* iii. 112 As for your fomblitudes of Manlius and Iudas, two proper names, compared with image, and idoll..which be common names, I will not vouchsafe to answer them.

fome, obs. form of FOAM *sb.* and *v.*

'**foment**, *sb.* Now *rare.* In 7 foement. [ad. L. *fōmentum*, contraction for **fovimentum*, f. *fovēre* to cherish, warm.]

1. = FOMENTATION 1 b.

1540 HYRDE tr. *Vives' Instr. Chr. Wom.* I. ix. I iv, Those superfluous sauors & fomentes of the body. **1643** J. STEER tr. *Exp. Chyrurg.* xii. 47 Apply this following Foment. **1892** *Pall Mall G.* 21 Jan. 1/3 Ameliorating the symptoms by hot foments, mustard applications, and wet-sheet packings.

†**2.** *fig.* Fomentation, encouragement. *Obs.*

1642 QUARLES *Observ. Princes & St.* iv, Long-settled humors give foment to the distemper when it breakes forth.

†**b.** Some thing that foments or encourages; stimulus. *Obs.*

1604 T. WRIGHT *Passions* I. iv. 15 They rather serve them for instruments of vertue, than foments of vice. **1658** R. CRESHALD *Legacy* 10 Which by the distemper gave Foment and force to the approaching Maladie. **1660** MORE *Myst. Godl.* To Rdr. 14 The foments of strife and palliations of Hypocrisy. **1704** *Expedient for Innocence* in *Harl. Misc.* (1746) VIII. 13/1 What more seasonable Charity, than to abstract the Foment from these accursed Divisions, by prohibiting those Oaths, that..perpetuate our Janglings?

¶**3.** ? Confused with FERMENT 3.

1793 T. JEFFERSON *Writ.* (1859) III. 527 Should the present foment in Europe not produce republics everywhere.

foment (fəʊ'mɛnt), *v.* [ad. Fr. *foment-er*, ad. late L. *fōmentāre*, f. *fōmentum* FOMENT *sb.*]

1. *trans.* To bathe with warm or medicated lotions; to apply fomentations to. Also, †to lubricate.

1611 COTGR., *Bassiner*, to warme, foment. **1643** J. STEER tr. *Exp. Chyrurg.* xii. 47 Foment the place affected with the following foment. **1656** RIDGLEY *Pract. Physick* 131 Foment it with white wax. **1748** tr. *Vegetius' Distemp. Horses* 144 You shall foment it for the Space of four Days. **1802** *Med. Jrnl.* VIII. 516 The breasts were frequently fomented. **1894** FITZWYGRAM *Horses & Stables* §255 The leg..may be conveniently fomented by putting it in a deep bucket of warm water.

absol. **1612** WOODALL *Surg. Mate* Wks. (1653) 303 Foment not too long at any one time.

†**2.** 'To cherish with heat, to warm' (J.). Always in conjunction with another verb, as *chafe, heat, warm*. *Obs.*

1648 JOS. BEAUMONT *Psyche* I. clv, Creeps chillness on him? She foments and heats His flesh. **1667** MILTON *P.L.* IV. 669 All things..these soft fires..foment and warme.

†**3.** To rouse or stir up (a person or his energies); to excite, irritate. *Obs.*

1642 R. CARPENTER *Experience* v. xix. 326, I was active.. fomented with your envenomed suggestions. **1680** OTWAY *Orphan* IV. v. 1506 Still Chaft and fomented let my heart swell on. **1704** SWIFT *Batt. Bks.* (1711) 226 By its Bitterness and Venom..to foment the Genius of the Combatants. **1724** DE FOE *Mem. Cavalier* (1840) 127 The old general, not to foment him, with a great deal of mildness stood up.

†**b.** *intr.* for *refl.*: To become excited or heated.

1665 J. WEBB *Stone-Heng* 16 In like manner, this Doctor fomenteth, saying; The one stumbles upon an Alter-stone.. over which the other leaped clearly. **1680** OTWAY *Orphan* v. ii. 1851 To think Of Women were enough to taint my Brains, Till they foment to madness.

4. a. To promote the growth, development, effect, or spread of (something material or physical).

1644 QUARLES *Barnabas & B.* 150 That humour which foments thy malady. **1661** *Burning of Lond.* in *Select. Harl. Misc.* (1793) 463 A violent easterly wind fomented it, and kept it burning all that day. **1667** MILTON *P.L.* x. 1071 How we his gather'd beams Reflected, may with matter sere foment. **1707** *Curios. Husb. & Gard.* 180 Plants receive from their Roots this Nitre, which feeds, foments and preserves them. **1725** POPE *Odyss.* XIX. 77 While those with unctuous fir foment the flame.

b. To cherish, cultivate, foster; to stimulate, encourage, instigate (a sentiment, belief, pursuit, course of conduct, etc.). *Esp.* in a bad sense.

1622 BACON *Hen. VII*, 12 Which bruite was cunningly fomented by such as desired innouation. **1664** MARVELL *Corr.* Wks. 1872-5 II. 164 His Majesty..offers himself as a third to foment so amiable a controversy. **1725** POPE *Odyss.* XI. 226 Thy sire in solitude foments his care. **1726-7** SWIFT *Gulliver* I. iv, These civil commotions were constantly fomented by the monarchs of Blefuscu. **1774** FLETCHER *Equal Check* Wks. 1795 IV. p. v, Is not the Antinomianism of hearers fomented by that of preachers? **1868** M. PATTISON

Academ. Org. iv. 75 To encourage indolence or foment extravagance. **1873** H. ROGERS *Orig. Bible* ii. (1875) 59 Persecutions which the Jews always fomented.

Hence **fo'menting** *vbl. sb.* Also *attrib.*

1611 COTGR., *Bassinement*, warming, a fomentation or fomenting. **1894** FITZWYGRAM *Horses & Stables* §255 During the fomentation a thick rug should be thrown over the fomenting cloth.

†**fo'mentary.** *Obs. rare.* [as if ad. L. **fōmentāri-us*, f. *fōmentum*: see FOMENT *sb.* and -ARY.] One who or that which foments; a fomenter.

1657 HAWKE *Killing is M.* Pref. 1 The disparagement of Princes are the fomentaries .. of Sedition.

†**'fomentate,** *v. Obs. rare.* [f. L. *fōmentāt-* ppl. stem of *fōmentāre* to foment.] = FOMENT *v.* 1.

1569 R. ANDROSE tr. *Alexis' Secr.* IV. I. 23 Therwith washe the eyes, or else fomentate them with the water. *Ibid.* IV. I. 31 You must fomentate them with a peece of a milstone burned and quenched in vineger. **1613** SHERLEY *Trav. Persia* 85 The one a kingdome fomentated as a bar between you and the Portugals.

fomentation (fəumən'teɪʃən). [ad. late L. *fōmentātiōn-em*, n. of action f. *fōmentāre* to FOMENT. Cf. F. *fomentation.*]

1. *Med.* The application to the surface of the body either of flannels, etc. soaked in hot water, whether simple or medicated, or of any other warm, soft, medicinal substance. ***dry fomentation*** (see quot. 1882).

c **1400** *Lanfranc's Cirurg.* 252 þer upon þou schalt make a fomentacioun wiþ hoot water. **1541** R. COPLAND *Guydon's Formul.* Xj b. Fomentacyon with oyle and terebentyne medled & warmed. **1578** LYTE *Dodoens* I. xxxiv. 50 In manner of a fomentation or a warme bathe. **1661** LOVELL *Hist. Anim. & Min.* 289 Fomentation with sponges in vineger. **1702** J. PURCELL *Cholick* (1714) 133 Flannel, or a Thin Woollen Cloth worn next to the Skin .. is a lesser kind of perpetual Fomentation. **1704** J. HARRIS *Lex. Techn.* s.v., A Dry Fomentation. **1801** *Med. Jrnl.* V. 578 Fomentations with warm water. **1882** M. BECK in *Quain's Dict. Med.* s.v., The term 'dry fomentation' is sometimes applied to bags of salt, hot bran, or chamomile flowers; or pieces of flannel toasted before a fire and applied hot.

b. *concr.* The remedial means so applied.

1546 PHAER *Bk. Childr.* (1553) Rj a, Ye may make a fomentacion of hoate and moist herbes. **1643** J. STEER tr. *Exp. Chyrurg.* xv. 58 Boyle them in the Broth .. for a Fomentation. *c* **1720** W. GIBSON *Farrier's Dispens.* xi. (1734) 249 Fomentations are made only with aqueous Menstruums whereas Embrocations consist of [etc.]. **1789** W. BUCHAN *Dom. Med.* (1790) 311 Flannels wrung out of warm spirituous fomentations should likewise be applied. **1894** FITZWYGRAM *Horses & Stables* §314 Hot water makes the best fomentation.

fig. **1593** Q. ELIZ. *Boeth.* (E.E.T.S.) 30 Because the fomentations of my reason haue entred in the.

†**2.** The action or process of cherishing with heat or warming. *Obs.*

1669 GALE *Crt. Gentiles* I. III. iii. 42 In this discription .. we have the Spirit's Motion, Fomentation, and Formation of althings out of this Chaos. *Ibid.*, The Fomentation of an Hen, that sets abrood.

3. *fig.* The action or process of fomenting, fostering or stimulation; encouragement, instigation.

a **1612** DONNE *Βιαθανατος* (1644) 39 Denying to it lawfull refreshings, and fomentations. **1670-1** MARVELL *Corr.* Wks. 1872-5 II. 373, I am .. well pleased to find him and Mr. Whittington jealous of one another, which shall not want fomentation. **1742** YOUNG *Nt. Th.* v. 743 Dishonest fomentation of your pride. **1861** *Times* 29 Aug., The fomentation of Hungarian discontent by foreign intrigues.

b. A means of fomentation, an influence that foments, a stimulus.

a **1631** DONNE *Serm.* viii. 79 They [our works] cleave to us; whether as Fomentations to nourish us or as Corrosives to gnaw upon us. **1659** C. NOBLE *Inexpediency of Exped.* 5 Unless the .. slie Redarguings .. be a rise and fomentation to such a Dispute.

fomenter (fəʊ'mɛntə(r)). Also **fomentor.** [f. FOMENT *v.* + -ER[1].] One who or that which foments.

1633 PRYNNE *Histrio-M.* I. III. ii. 75 Fomentors of Crueltie, Quarrells [etc.]. **1660** WOOD *Life* (Oxf. Hist. Soc.) I. 360 Such lectures in the nation had been fomenters of the late rebellion. **1710** HEARNE *Collect.* 6 Mar., The Fomenters and Abettors of the Riot. **1780** COXE *Russ. Disc.* 139 The most inveterate fomenter of hostilities against the Russians. *c* **1817** HOGG *Tales & Sk.* VI. 116 The primal cause and fomentor of this cruel and bloody war. **1866** BRIGHT *Sp. Reform* 4 Dec., The fomenter of discord.

†**fo'mentress.** *Obs.*$^{-1}$ [f. prec. + -ESS[1].] A female fomenter.

1646 EARL MONMOUTH tr. *Biondi's Hist. Civ. Warres Eng.* II. IX. 208 The Dutchesse of Burgundy .. must be known to be fomentresse of the Forgery.

fomerel(l, -il, obs. forms of FEMERELL.

‖**fomes** ('fəumiːz). Pl. **fomites** ('fəumɪtiːz). [L. *fōmes, fōmitis* touchwood, tinder.] †**a.** The morbific matter (of a disease) (*obs.*). **b.** 'Any porous substance capable of absorbing and retaining contagious effluvia' (Mayne).

1773 *Gentl. Mag.* XLIII. 554 If this putrid ferment could be more immediately corrected, a stop would probably be put to the flux, and the *fomes* of the disease likewise removed. **1803** *Med. Jrnl.* X. 213, I cannot say that I have known it spread from fomites. **1851-9** A. BRYSON in *Man. Sc. Enq.* 248 Either simply through the medium of the atmosphere or by means of fomites. **1882** *Quain's Dict. Med.* s.v., The most important fomites are bed-clothes, bedding, woollen garments, carpets, curtains, letters, &c.

fig. **1658** J. OWEN *Temptation* vii. 126 Naturall tempers .. prove a great *Fomes* of sinne. *a* **1711** KEN *Hymnotheo* Poet. Wks. 1721 III. 327 Concupiscential Fomes, which possess'd The Parents thus, was on their Race impress'd.

fomie, fomy, obs. forms of FOAMY.

fomite ('fəumaɪt). *rare.* [incorrect back-formation from *fomites*, pl. of FOMES.] = FOMES.

1859 R. F. BURTON *Centr. Afr.* in *Jrnl. Geog. Soc.* XXIX. 134 This must be an efficacious fomite of cutaneous and pectoral disease.

fomon, obs. form of FOEMAN.

Fomorian (fəʊ'mɔːrɪən), *sb.* (and *a.*) *Celtic Mythol.* Pl. also **Fomori.** [f. Ir. *fomor* pirate, monster, f. *fo* under + *mor* sea (cogn. w. MARE *sb.*[2]) = Gael. *famhair* + -IAN.] In Irish legend, one of a race of pirates or giants, perhaps originally representing the gods of death and darkness. In Scottish legend, a giant. Also as *adj.*

1876 *Encycl. Brit.* V. 300/2 That the Fomorian and *Tuatha Dé Danaan* contests are mythological there can be no doubt. **1891** W. B. YEATS *John Sherman & Dhoya* 173 One evening Fomorian galleys had entered the Bay of the Red Cataract. **1898** J. HERON *Celtic Church* 5 Partholonians, Nemedians, and Fomorians, or sea-rovers, are .. the first .. to take possession [of Ireland]. **1901** J. RHŶS *Celtic Folklore* II. vii. 435 The Irish Morc .. and another called Conaing are represented in the legendary history of early Erin as the naval leaders of the Fomori. **1921** L. SPENCE *Introd. Mythol.* xi. 294 Among these warring elements the Fomorians are a race of Titans. **1926** *Contemp. Rev.* Mar. 352 Scottish folk lore knows the giants as Fomorians. Tale after tale tells of their great boulder-throwing contests on the Scottish hills. **1959** ALDINGTON & AMES tr. *Larousse Encycl. Mythol.* 236/1 After a battle with the Fomorians in which Conann and many Fomorian followers were killed, the remnants of the people of Nemed fled from the country. **1964** E. O. G. TURVILLE-PETRE *Myth & Religion of North* vii. 160 This second battle has been seen as one between the Tuatha Dé Danann, gods of light, life, day, and the Fomorians, gods of death and darkness.

†**fon,** *sb.* and *a. Obs.* Also 5 **fone,** 5-6 **fonn(e.** [Belongs to FON *v.*; but the mutual relation of the words is uncertain.

It is tempting to connect the sb. with Sw. *fån(e*, MDa. *fåne* fool, mod.Icel. *fáni* swaggerer, vain person; but the history of the Eng. words shows no trace of a long vowel, and the northern Eng. forms have *o*, and not the *a* which in that dialect normally represents ON. *á*. Besides, the primary sense of the Eng. vb. appears to be 'to lose savour, become insipid', and if so the sb. is prob. from the vb.]

A. *sb.* A fool.

a **1300** *Cursor M.* 9186 (Cott.) O þis manasses com amon, þat, als his fader, was a fon. *c* **1330** R. BRUNNE *Chron. Wace* (Rolls) 4051 After Eldolf, þys folted fon, Cam his sone hight Redyon. *c* **1450** *Cov. Myst.* 367 A! ȝe ffonnys and slought of herte ffor to beleve in holy Scrypture! *c* **1450** *St. Cuthbert* (Surtees) 5386 God some tyme chastys a fonn And he is made mare wyse. **1526** SKELTON *Magnyf.* 1200 Wenyst thou that I cannot make the play the fon? **1595** SPENSER *Col. Clout* 292 Ah! Cuddy, (then quoth Colin) thous a fon.

B. *adj.* Foolish, silly.

c **1440** *Gesta Rom.* lx. 248 (Harl. MS.) The lion stode besyde him, as he hadde be a ffonne shepe. **1538** STARKEY *England* I. i. 24 Yf wyse men .. wold have bent themselfe to that purpos, levyng such fon respecte of tyme and of place.

Hence **'fonly** *adv.*, foolishly, fondly; **'fonnish** *a.*, somewhat foolish.

c **1449** PECOCK *Repr.* II. iv. 156 Thilk fonnysch opinioun may sonne bi wise men be schewed .. to be vntrewe. **1481** TIPTOFT tr. *Cicero's De Amic.* (1530) B viij, What may be a more fonnysh thyng than whan [etc.]. **1526** SKELTON *Magnyf.* 659 Tusshe, fonnysshe Fansy, thou arte frantyke. **1579** SPENSER *Sheph. Cal.* May 58, I .. had rather be envied, All were it of my foe, than fonly pitied.

†**fon,** *v. Obs.* Also 5 **fonne,** 6 **fone.** [see prec. The later FUN *v.* (whence FUN *sb.*) is prob. etymologically identical.]

1. *intr.* To lose savour, become insipid or sickly in flavour. Only in pa. pple.: see FOND *a.*

2. To be foolish or infatuated; to act the fool; to become foolish.

c **1440** *York Myst.* ix. 89 Now Noye, in faythe þe fonnes full faste. *c* **1450** *Cov. Myst.* 36 Thou fonnyst as a best I gesse. **1508** DUNBAR *Tua Mariit Wemen* 274 With kissing, et with clapping, I gert the carill fon. **1570** BUCHANAN *Ane Admonitioun* Wks. (1892) 30 Yᵉ Dukis sone .. causit yᵉ rest of y hamiltonis to fon for faynnes.

3. *trans.* To befool, make a fool of.

c **1440** LYDG. *Secrees* 570 The fals Erryng hath fonnyd many Oon. *c* **1449** PECOCK *Repr.* II. ii. 145 Salomon .. fonned and bidotid with hise wifis, made ydolis. *c* **1460** *Towneley Myst.* (Surtees) 199 Soyn shalle we fon hym.

4. *Sc.* To toy with; to fondle.

1430 *Peblis to Play* vii. in Pinkerton *Scot. Ball.* (1783) I. 4 The fairest fallis me; Tak ye the laif and fone thame.

Hence **'fonning** *vbl. sb.*, foolishness, foolish behaviour.

c **1400** *Destr. Troy* 4880 Our werkes [shuld] all wisely [be] wroght by discrecioun, þat we fare with no foly ne fonnyng of pride. *c* **1450** *Cov. Myst.* 304 Be his meraclys and fals prechyng He bryngyth the pepyl in gret fonnyng.

fon, obs. form of FIND; Sc. pl. of FOE.

fond, *sb.* Also 7, 9 **fonds,** 8 **fonde.** Now only as an alien word, pronounced (fɔ̃). [a. F. *fond, fonds*:—OF. *fonz, fons* (see FOUNCE).

The word became fully naturalized in the 17th c. In the 18th c. it was superseded in ordinary use by FUND, which is a refashioned form after L. *fundus*. Subsequently, however, the F. word frequently appears (usually in italics) in Eng. writers. In F., the forms *fond* and *fonds*, formerly used indiscriminately, are now differentiated in sense; but Eng. writers often use the wrong form.]

1. Foundation, ground, groundwork (in various applications). (In Fr. now written *fond.*)

1664 EVELYN tr. *Freart's Archit.* 141 All sorts of precious Marbles .. cut and lay'd into a *fonds* or ground of black-Marble. **1665** SIR P. WARWICK in *Evelyn's Mem.* (1819) II. 162 The present Prizes .. being a better fond of credit. **1704** SWIFT *T. Tub* iv. 93 This Grandeur .. could not be maintained without a better Fonde than what he was born to. **1825** JEFFREY in *Edin. Rev.* Aug. 429 But the *fonds* of the character is the same. **1844** THACKERAY in *Fraser's Mag.* Feb. 155/2 The spirits are for the most part artificial, the *fond* is sadness. **1867** LOWELL *Lett.* (1894) I. 394 There is no early French literature of any value in which the Teutonic blood did not supply the *fond*.

b. *Lace-making.* (See quots.)

1882 CAULFIELD & SAWARD *Dict. Needlework*, *Fond*, Identical with Champ, Entoilage, and Treille, terms by which the groundwork of lace .. is distinguished from the Toilé, or pattern, which it surrounds and supports. These grounds are divided into Fonds Claire, Brides Claire, and Brides Ornées. The Fonds Claire include the Réseau or net patterned grounds and varieties of the same.

2. A source of supply, stock, store or stores. *Obs.* in material sense. (In Fr. now *fonds.*)

1685 DRYDEN *Albion & Albanus* Pref., Here, therefore, if they will Criticise, they shall do it out of their own *Fond*. **1704** SWIFT *T. Tub* vii. 142 Some new Fonde of Wit should, if possible, be provided. **1707** *Curios. in Husb. & Gard.* 92 The Juices of Plants are one of the richest Fonds of Physick. **1872** MRS. OLIPHANT *Ombra* I. ii, Kate herself was not indifferent to the *fond* of appreciation thus secured to her.

†**3.** A stock or sum of money, *esp.* one set apart for a particular purpose; pecuniary means, revenues. (In Fr. now *fonds.*) *Obs.*

1673 TEMPLE *Observ. United Prov.* Wks. 1731 I. 38 This *Fond* being not sufficient in Times of War, is supplied by the States with whatever more is necessary from other *Fonds*. **1690** WILL. III. *Sp. Parl.* 25 Nov. in *Lond. Gaz.* No. 2613/1 The Civil Government, which has no Fonds for its Support. **1691** T. H[ALE] *Acc. New Invent.* p. cxi, The want of any Fonds to support the Charge of such Office.

†**4.** A sum of money, a stock of goods, or amount of revenues, serving as a security for specified payments. (In Fr. now *fonds.*) *Obs.*

1677 CHAS. II. in Marvell *Growth Popery* 39 Without the sum Six hundred thousand pounds, or Credit for such a sum, upon new Fonds. *a* **1687** PETTY *Pol. Arith.* x. (1691) 114 Making a Fond of such value, to be security for all Commodities. **1693** *Mem. Ct. Teckely* I. 47 The Princess .. had seized the fonds whereupon the Pension of their Ministers was assigned. **1714** *Lond. Gaz.* No. 5260/4 Debts .. secur'd by Judgment, Statute, Recognizance, Fond, or Specialty.

†**5.** *Printing* = FOUNT. *Obs.*

1678 PHILLIPS, *Fond* or *Fund* .. Among Letter-founders, a parcel of Printing Letters, as many as are Printed at a time.

fond (fɒnd), *a.* and *sb.*[2] Forms: 4 **fonned, -yd,** 5 **fonnet,** 5- **fond,** 5-7 **fonde,** 9 *Sc.* and *dial.* **font.** [ME. *fonned*, f. FON *v.* + -ED[1].]

A. *adj.* (orig. *ppl. a.*).

†**1.** That has lost its savour; insipid; sickly-flavoured. *Obs.* exc. *dial.*

c **1380** WYCLIF *Wks.* (1880) 57 ȝif þe salt be fonnyd it is not worþi. **1388** —— *Prol.* x. 31 He is seid fonned salt, not prophitable to eny thing. **1784** CULLUM *Hist. Hawsted* 171 *Fond*, faint or fulsome; applied to smell or taste. *a* **1825** FORBY *Voc. E. Anglia*, *Fond*, luscious; fulsome; disagreeably sweet, in taste or in smell.

2. Infatuated, foolish, silly. Since 16th c. the sense in literary use has been chiefly: Foolishly credulous or sanguine. In dialects the wider sense is still current. Cf. FONNED *ppl. a.*

a **1340** HAMPOLE *Psalter* Cant. 523 Sho ioyed not .. in vanytes of þis lyfe as our fonnyd maydyns dos now. **1388** WYCLIF *Exod.* xviii. 18 Thou art wastid with a fonned trauel. *a* **1400-50** *Alexander* 5513 A fonned fantasy þan fell in his hert. *c* **1460** *Towneley Myst.* 199 This fond foylle. **1526** *Pilgr. Perf.* (W. de W. 1531) 63 b, And suche communly be as dotrelles, whiche is a fonde byrde. **1580** LYLY *Euphues* (Arb.) 241 He yat is young thinketh the olde man fond. **1650** FULLER *Pisgah* II. xii. 250 Never more to fright Children with fond tales of Bug-bears. **1681** GLANVILL *Sadducismus* Ded., I am not fond enough to phancy any Art .. to recommend it. *a* **1703** BURKITT *On N.T.* Heb. xi. 22 To dig mens' bones out of their graves, to enshrine them .. is fond and ridiculous. *a* **1748** WATTS *Improv. Mind* II. iii. §8, I am not so fond as to think I have [etc.]. **1798** W. HUTTON *Autobiog.* 36 Seized with a fond fit of farming, I took the place into my own hands. **1831** CARLYLE *Sart. Res.* II. ii. (1872) 65 Writing from the abundance of his own fond ineptitude. **1832** HARE in *Philol. Mus.* I. 247 An attempt to settle its age cannot with any justice be censured as a fond waste of time in mere literary trifling. **1847-8** H. MILLER *First Impr.* viii. (1857) 129 Evangelistic Dissent was fond enough to believe the cause a common one. **1855** ROBINSON *Whitby Gloss.*, *Fond*, foolish, weakminded.

quasi-*adv.* **1601** SHAKS. *All's Well* I. iii. 76 Fond done, done fond, was this King Priams ioy.

3. In stronger sense: Idiotic, imbecile, mad; also, dazed. †With *to*: Mad *for*. *Obs.* exc. *dial.*

c **1400** *Destr. Troy* 6182 The pepull of Poyem .. were fond to the fight. **1483** *Cath. Angl.* 137/1 Fonde, *arepticius, astrosus*. **1640** *Durh. Vestry Bks.* (Surtees) 303 For puttinge fond Allye's child to nursinge .. 1s. 4d. **1781** J. HUTTON *Tour* to Caves Gloss., *Fond*, silly, stupid like an ideot. **1876** *Mid-Yorksh. Gloss.*, *Fond*, silly. 'I'd a dizziness in my head that turned me fair fond.'

†**4.** Of things: Valued only by fools, trifling, trivial. *Obs.*

1603 SHAKS. *Meas. for M.* II. ii. 149 Ile bribe you.. Not with fond Sickles of the tested gold. **1645** USSHER *Body Div.* (1647) 239 When we sweare by.. bread, salt, fire, and many fond trashes.

5. a. Of persons, their actions and attributes: Foolishly tender; over-affectionate, doting. In later use without reproachful sense: Affectionate, loving, tender.

1579 LYLY *Euphues* (Arb.) 106 A cooling Carde for Philautus and all fond louers. **1641** HINDE *J. Bruen* x. 34 Fond affection without moderation. **1749** WESLEY *Wks.* (1872) XIII. 162 A loving husband is a very amiable character. A fond one I think is not so. **1759** ROBERTSON *Hist. Scot.* I. 10 A hero to whom the fond admiration of his country-men hath ascribed many fabulous acts of prowess. **1766** GOLDSM. *Vic. W.* xxii, I called up the many fond things I had to say. **1816** J. WILSON *City of Plague* I. iii. 60 She.. in the light Of her fond parents' love was fostered. **1854** MRS. OLIPHANT *Magd. Hepburn* III. 285 Ritchie is fond, and loves to see me fair arrayed.

b. Of opinions, sentiments, etc.: Cherished or entertained with strong or unreasoning affection.

1635 N. R. *Camden's Hist. Eliz.* (an. 21). II. 200 Don John .. resigned his fond ambition. **1683** SOAME & DRYDEN tr. *Boileau's Art of Poetry* IV. 63 In vain their fond Opinions you deride, With their lov'd Follies they are satisfy'd. **1750** CARTE *Hist. Eng.* II. 337 Edward's.. fond opinion of his own capacity. **1842** ABDY *Water Cure* (1843) 212 A practice which.. holds out a hope of giving an enduring reality to his fondest wishes. **1871** MACDUFF *Mem. Patmos* ix. 112 To defraud His servant of his fond expectation. **1872** RUSKIN *Eagle's N.* §121 Children.. Bred.. by their parents, in the fond poverty of learning.

6. Const. *of* (formerly †*on*): Having strong affection or liking for (a person or thing, a pursuit, etc.).

1590 SHAKS. *Mids. N.* II. i. 266 He may proue More fond on her, then she vpon her loue. **1601** HOLLAND *Pliny* I. 231 The she Apes.. are wonderous fond of their little ones. **1615** LATHAM *Falconry* (1633) 32 Many Hawks.. grow fond on them or him that doe.. bring them vp. **1665** BOYLE *Occas. Refl.* IV. ii. (1845) 175 So fond of the Sun. **1754** RICHARDSON *Grandison* I. xii. 68, I am fond of talking to this young Lady. **1774** GOLDSM. *Nat. Hist.* (1776) V. 294 They feed upon all sorts of grain, but are fondest of millet-seed. **1801** STRUTT *Sports & Past.* I. i. 4 Ædgar.. was extremely fond of the sports of the field. **1833** HT. MARTINEAU *Berkeley the Banker* I. ix. 169 Lewis has made his uncle and aunt very fond of him already.

†**b.** With *of*: Possessed with admiration for, proud of. *Obs.*

1702 ROWE *Tamerl.* Ded., There is no part in your Lordship's Character but what the World would be fond of. **1754** RICHARDSON *Grandison* I. i. 3 He is a vain creature you know, and seemed fond of what he had written.

†**7.** Eager for (some object), desirous of, or strongly inclined to (an action). Const. *of*. *Obs.*

1552 HULOET, Fonde or desierous. **1594** SHAKS. *Lucr.* 134 Those that much couet are with gaine so fond. **1666** MARVELL *Corr.* Wks. 1872–5 II. liv. 191 The redemption of the chimney money at eight years purchase we are very fond of. **1689** LUTTRELL *Brief Rel.* (1857) I. 604 Many persons have blamed duke Schonberg for not fighting the Irish army, which our men seem'd so fond of. **1719** DE FOE *Crusoe* (1840) I. xx, They would be fond of buying it. **1748** RICHARDSON *Clarissa* (1811) I. 16 The man was not fond of marrying at all. **1760** GOLDSM. *Cit. World* cxi, People are naturally fond of going to paradise at as small expense as possible. **1772** FOOTE *Nabob* III. (1778) 63, I fancy he will not be very fond of prolonging his visit. **1779** BURKE *Corr.* (1844) II. 256 Sentiments which no being in human form could.. be fond of owning.

b. With *to* and *inf.* (rarely with *that*): Having a liking, eager, glad to (do something). Now *rare*.

All the examples in 19th c. and nearly all those in late 18th c. are from Scottish writers.

1546 J. HEYWOOD *Prov.* (1867) 3 Both these, for loue to wed with me fond are. **1587** FLEMING *Contn. Holinshed* III. 1582/2, I find no great cause I should be fond to liue. **1695** BLACKMORE *Pr. Arth.* I. 738 They all seem fond to wear the Martyr's Crown. **1734** WATTS *Reliq. Juv.* (1789) 106 We are so fond to appear always in the right. **1748** RICHARDSON *Clarissa* (1811) V. 376 Nor could I be fond that they should see you. **1766** GOLDSM. *Double Transform.* 53 Fond to be seen, she kept a bevy Of powdered coxcombs at her levy. **1769** ROBERTSON *Chas. V*, VI. VI. 59 They are fond to interpret it as an omen of the bloody war that followed. **1826** *Literary Souvenir* 198 The bravest of the two is fond to whistle, that he may keep up the courage of his comrade. **1883** BLACKIE in *19th Cent.* Apr. 607 'The year of Charlie', as the Highlanders are fond to call it.

8. *Comb.*, as *fond-blind*, *-conceited*, *-hardy*, *-like*, *-sparkling* adjs.; **fond plough** = *fool-plough*: see FOOL *sb.* 6.

1594 BARNFIELD *Affect. Sheph.* II. xxiv. (Arb.) 16 Be thou *fond-blinde.. Thou are my Loue. **1590** GREENE *Orl. Fur.* Wks. (Rtldg.) 109/1 Follower of *fond-conceited Phaeton. **1659** TORRIANO, *Corrivo*.. *fond-hardie. **1632** BROME *Northern Lass* II. ii, Mine Vncle and he fell on other talke, of Lords and Ladies, and many *fond-like things. **1889** BARRIE *Window in Thrums* xix, But she was 'at he laid it on the fire fell fond-like. **1788** W. MARSHALL *Yorksh.* Gloss., *Fond-plufe.* **1831** HOWITT *Seasons* (1854) 43 The custom of the.. Fond Plough. **1786** BURNS *Yon wild mossy Mountains* vi, But kindness.. in the *fond-sparkling e'e, Has lustre outshining the diamond to me.

†**B.** *absol.* and *sb.* A foolish person, a fool.

1519 HORMAN *Vulg.* 19 It is vnlucky with fondis to do on the lyft sho first. **1575** CHURCHYARD *Chippes* (1817) 45 The fond will read awhile, but cares for nought.

†**fond**, *v.* *Obs.* Also 6 fonde. [f. FOND *a.*]

1. *intr.* To play the fool; to become foolish.

?**1530** *Exam. W. Thorpe* in Foxe *A. & M.* (1563) 164/2 And the clarke sayde. I fonded, and that I sayde not truthe. *Ibid.* Thou wouldest make vs to fonde with the. *a* **1541** WYATT *7 Penit. Ps.* Poet. Wks. (1861) 208 The sword shall pierce the heart of such that fonds.

2. Const. *on*, *over*, *upon*. To entertain a fond or foolish affection for; to dote upon. Also *simply*, to display fondness.

1530 PALSGR. 553/2, I fonde, or dote upon a thyng for inordynate love. **1567** TURBERV. *Ovid's Epist.* 154 Whilst thou.. did fonde on Phyllis. **1590** FENNE *Frutes* I. 53 Immoderately fonding over wife, sonne, daughter. **1601** SHAKS. *Twel. N.* II. ii. 35 My master loues her deerely, And I (poore monster) fond asmuch on him.

3. *trans.* To make a fool of; to befool.

1540 HYRDE tr. *Vives' Instr. Chr. Wom.* I. xvi. S ib, They dote and fonde [L. *dementant*] good yonge men. *a* **1547** SURREY *Æneid* IV. 489 Did I not him.. fonded [*demens*] eke invest Of halfe my realme? **1566** DRANT *Horace's Sat.* iv. B viij, Love of goods, or love of rule doth fonde him now and then. **1567** —— *Horace's Epist.* i. C iij, Such follye fondes a man and fondly makes him roue.

4. To show fondness for; to caress, fondle.

1676 DRYDEN *Aurengz.* IV. i, Howe'r unjust your jealousie appear.. I'll fond it, as the froward Child of Love. **1697** —— *Æneid* I. 962 The Tyrian hugs, and fonds thee on her breast.

b. To beguile; also to beguile *to* (disaster).

1627–77 FELTHAM *Resolves* I. xxvi. 45 The Meretricious world claps our cheeks, and fonds us to a cozening fail. **1682** SOUTHERNE *Loyal Brother* I I, My poor heart Would fain be fonded with the hopes of rest.

Hence **'fonded** *ppl. a.*, (*a*) deluded, foolish; (*b*) fondly loved. **'fonding** *vbl. sb.*, fondness.

1566 DRANT *Horace's Sat.* ii. B b, They, the sillye fonded fooles, Do feaste him. **1665** R. B. *Comment on 2 Tales* 99 Put on a smooth Brow, and feign a kind of Fonding. **1701** STEELE *Chr. Hero* III. 52 A brighter diadem than ever Fortune bestowed on the most fonded.. of her favourites.

fond: see FAND *v.* *Obs.*, to attempt, try, etc.

fond, obs. pa. t. FIND: obs. form of FOUND *v.*[1]

‖**fonda** (fɒnda). [Sp. *fonda* from Arab.: see FONDUK.] A hotel, an inn (in Spain or Sp. countries).

1826 CAPT. HEAD *Pampas* 127 They then came into the yard of the Fonda (inn). **1877** B. HARTE *Story of a Mine* iii, He plunged into the first Fonda at the wayside.

‖**fondaco** ('fondako). Also 6 fondego, 7 fundaco. [It., ad. Arab.; see FONDUK.] An inn; also, in North Africa, †a building containing a merchant's residence and sale rooms.

1599 HAKLUYT *Voy.* II. 183 At the death of one of their marchants in Alexandria.. the French Consul Vento sealing up his fondego and chamber tooke under his seal his goods. **1632** LITHGOW *Trav.* IX. 385 A Fundaco or Inne. **1833** J. H. NEWMAN *Lett.* (1891) I. 397 The landlady of the fondaco asked me if I was going to Paris.

fondak: see FONDUK.

fondant ('fɒndənt). [a. Fr. *fondant* sb. and pr. pple. of *fondre* to melt.] A sweetmeat made chiefly in France: (see quots.). Also *attrib.*

1877 *Encycl. Brit.* VI. 257 Fondants.. are made from solutions boiled to the point of crystallization, properly coloured and flavoured, and cast into moulds made of starch. **1892–4** *Encycl. Cookery* (Garrett) I. 602/1 *Fondants.* This term has become familiar to us for kinds of soft sweets that 'melt' in the mouth. *Ibid.* 602/2 Divide the Fondant-paste into two portions.

fondary: see FOUNDRY.

fondement, obs. form of FUNDAMENT.

fonding: see FANDING, FOUNDING *vbl. sbs.*

fondish ('fɒndɪʃ), *a.* [f. FOND *a.* + -ISH.]

a. Somewhat fond. **b.** *dial.* (See quot. 1876.)

1834 J. WILSON in *Blackw. Mag.* XXXV. 860 An old man .. fondish of literature. **1876** *Whitby Gloss.*, *Fondish*, shallow in point of intellect; whimsical.

fondle ('fɒnd(ə)l), *v.* [frequentative of FOND *v.* Cf. DANDLE, FADDLE.]

†**1.** *trans.* To treat with fond indulgence; to cocker, pamper. Also, to bring *to* (a state or condition) by indulgence. Also with *up*. *Obs.*

1694 DRYDEN *Love Triumphant* II. i, Ximena, you have fondled him to this. **1721** AMHURST *Terræ-Filius* No. 8 ¶ 11 Where one would stand it out.. twenty chose rather to be fondled up, and call'd mother's nown boys at any expence. **1732** BOLINGBROKE in *Swift's Lett.* (1766) II. 157 You shall be nursed, fondled, and humoured. **1757** JOHNSON *Rambler* No. 175 ¶ 5 Every day sends out, in quest of pleasure.. some heir fondled in ignorance. **1789** MAD. D'ARBLAY *Lett.* Apr., I knew you would.. fondle them [poultry] like your children.

2. To handle or treat with fondness; to caress. Also, to press fondly *to* (the heart).

1796 H. HUNTER tr. *St.-Pierre's Stud. Nat.* (1799) II. 52 The sheep, which he fondled when a lamb. **1832** W. IRVING *Alhambra* II. 36 The prince fondled it to his heart. 'Happy bird', said he. **1859** KINGSLEY *Misc.* (1860) I. 282 To fondle the reptile is to be bitten by it. **1874** GREEN *Short Hist.* vii. §3. (1876) 363 Elizabeth.. fondled her 'sweet Robin', Lord Leicester, in the face of the court.

fig. **1818** KEATS *Endym.* I. 311 Zephyr.. Fondles the flower amid the sobbing rain.

3. *intr.* To behave, play or speak fondly; to toy; also †to bestow caresses *on*.

1720 GAY *Work for a Cooper* 78 He.. fondled on her like his child. **1727** POPE, &c., *Art of Sinking* 102 He fondles like a mere stammerer. **1773** GOLDSM. *Stoops to Conq.* IV. (Globe) 667/2 Fondling together, as I'm alive. **1840** DICKENS *Old C. Shop* i, 'Foolish Nell', said the old man fondling with her hair. **1880** G. MEREDITH *Trag. Com.* 74 Unable to take such services without rewarding him, she fondled.

fig. **1836** LANDOR *Pericles & Aspasia* liii, Sighs full often fondle with reproofs. **1874** LOWELL *Agassiz* II. lvii, Persuasion fondled in his look and tone.

Hence **fondled** *ppl. a.* Also **'fondle** *sb.*, an act of fondling. **'fondler**, one who fondles.

1755 JOHNSON, *Fondler*. **1788** C. REEVE *Exiles* III. 169 Those fondled and spoiled children, who are disagreeable to all others. **1833** LAMB *Elia* (1860) 419 It was a stranger to the patient fondle, the hushing caress. **1876** MISS YONGE *Womankind* xviii. 135 Whether the elder brother starts as.. the champion and fondler.

fondlesome ('fɒnd(ə)lsəm), *a.* [f. FONDLE *v.* + -SOME.] Addicted to fondling.

1835 BECKFORD *Recoll.* 36 Turtle doves were never more fondlesome.

fondling ('fɒndlɪŋ), *vbl. sb.* [f. FONDLE *v.* + -ING[1].] The action of the vb. FONDLE; an affectionate handling; a fond gesture.

1714 MANDEVILLE *Fab. Bees* (1733) II. 211 The various expressions of their fondness for their infants, which fondling of them ever increases. **1781** MICKLE *Siege of Marseilles* II. iv, Cyrus made no.. amorous fondling To fan her pride. **1886** HALL CAINE *Son of Hagar* I. i, Embraced each other with the quiet fondling of lambs.

fondling ('fɒndlɪŋ). [f. FOND *a.* + -LING.]

†**1.** A 'fond' or foolish person. Also *transf.* of animals. *Obs.*

c **1440** *York Myst.* xix. 157 Þan schall þat fandelyng felle Be-lyue his bliss schall blynne. **1547–64** BAULDWIN *Mor. Philos.* (Palfr.) 56 The vicious & rich faulty fondling.. by whom common-weales are destroyed. **1589** NASHE *Anat. Absurd.* 29 How farre are these fondlings from imitating Crates the Philosopher. **1594** CHAPMAN *Shadow of Night* Eja, Thou and thy Nimphs shall.. mocke the fondling, for his mad aspire. **1613–16** W. BROWNE *Brit. Past.* II. i, See how yonder fondlings teare Their fleeces in the brakes. **1674** N. FAIRFAX *Bulk & Selv.* To Rdr., I should lacken it.. by making such a Fondling the Penman of it. **1781** J. HUTTON *Tour to Caves* Gloss., *Fondling*, an ideot.

2. One who is fondly loved; one who is much fondled or caressed; a pet. Also *fig.* Now *rare*.

1640 H. MILL *Nights Search* 128 When this Spark is from his Fondling gone. **1692** L'ESTRANGE *Fables* No. 248 Partiality in a Parent is commonly Unlucky.. for Fondlings are in danger to be made Fools. **1699** LOCKE *Hum. Und.* (ed. 4) IV. xix. §16 That may shew it [an opinion] to be a Fondling of our own. **1702** ROWE *Tamerl.* III. i. 1059 The Fondling once of her dear Father's Arms. **1788** MAD. D'ARBLAY *Diary* 5 Jan. Frogs.. kept in glasses for fondlings and favourites. **1834** SOUTHEY *Doctor* ix, He became his father's companion imperceptibly as he ceased to be his fondling.

fondling ('fɒndlɪŋ), *ppl. a.* [f. FONDLE *v.* + -ING[2].] That fondles; caressing, endearing.

1676 GLANVILL *Seasonable Refl.* 207 What can the fondling flesh and the world do for thee? *c* **1704** PRIOR *Henry & Emma* 65 He call'd her.. his Nut-brown Maid, The friends and tenants took the fondling word. **1768** GOLDSM. *Good-n. Man* IV. i, I will discard the fondling hope from my bosom. **1798** MAD. D'ARBLAY *Let.* Mar., He.. called out in a fondling manner. **1821** CLARE *Vill. Minstr.* II. 27 His chuff cheeks dimpling in a fondling smile. **1824** MISS MITFORD *Village* Ser. I. (1863) 211 By that fondling nursery name she best liked to be called. **1850** KINGSLEY *Alt. Locke* i. (1879) 13 And spoke to my mother in a fondling, patronizing way.

Hence **'fondlingly** *adv.*

1835 *New Monthly Mag.* XLV. 80 She clings fearingly and fondlingly to Lablache.

fondling, obs. form of FOUNDLING.

'fondly, *a. rare.* [f. FOND *a.* + -LY[1].] Fond; †foolish. Hence **'fondliness**, fondness.

1587 M. GROVE *Pelops & Hipp.* (1878) 77 Leaue such fondly toves. **1852** J. B. OWEN in Talbot *Meliora* Ser. I. 135 The fond old man.. squeezed [her hand] with a fondlier emotion than usual. **1821** *New Monthly Mag.* I. 646 Bright partners of the sky, each other's gloom Cheering with smile of mutual fondliness.

fondly ('fɒndlɪ), *adv.* [f. FOND *a.* + -LY[2].]

†**1.** Foolishly. *Obs.*

c **1340** *Cursor M.* 16461 (Laud) Iudas beheld & sie how fondly they with hym dalt. [Doubtful; MS. is 15th c.] **1401** *Pol. Poems* (Rolls) II. 97 Thou feynest fonnedli that oure Lord we sclaundre. **1483** *Cath. Angl.* 137 Fondely, *stulte*. **1551** UDALL, etc. *Erasm. Par. Matt.* ix. 23 Suche other thynges as menne be wont to doe verye fondly. **1634** FORD *P. Warbeck* IV. iv, He fondly angles who will hurl his bait Into the water, 'cause the fish.. dares not bite. **1648** JOS. BEAUMONT *Psyche* XIX. xxx, Still thy Adventure's management debases The fondly-founded credit of thy Bliss.

2. With self-pleasing or affectionate credulity.

1762 GOLDSM. *Cit. W.* xlvii. (1837) 189 You would fondly persuade me that my former lessons still influence your conduct. **1805** WORDSW. *Prelude* III. 482 That they needs Must keep to all, as fondly all believe, Their highest promise. **1824** W. IRVING *T. Trav.* II. 12, I will henceforth .. endeavour to be all that she fondly imagined me. **1851** GLADSTONE *Glean.* VI. lxix. 45, I.. am fondly perhaps but yet firmly assured [etc.]. **1862** LORD BROUGHAM *Brit. Const.* x. 131 [The English] have fondly traced the origin of our free institutions to the most remote ages. **1885** *Law Times*

LXXIX. 159/1 Legal learning is not, we fondly hope, a thing of the past.

3. Affectionately, lovingly, tenderly. Also, with show of affection, caressingly.

1593 SHAKS. *Rich. II*, III. ii. 9 As a long parted Mother with her Child, Playes fondly with her teares. **1737–8** SAVAGE *Volunteer Laureat* VI. 9 To be or fondly or severely kind..Parents shall learn from Her. **1757** FOOTE *Author* I. Wks. 1799 I. 131 You loved her, Sir..Fondly.—Nay, foolishly. **1797–1800** COLERIDGE *Christabel* Poems (1862) 287 Fondly in his arms he took Fair Geraldine. **1870** E. PEACOCK *Ralf Skirl.* III. 95 He never looked on her so fondly as now.

fondness ('fɒndnɪs). [f. FOND *a.* + -NESS.]

1. Foolishness, folly; 'weakness; want of sense or judgement' (J.); an instance of this. *Obs.* exc. *dial.*

c **1380** WYCLIF *Wks.* (1880) 266 þei seyn þat þe speche of holy writt is fals þat reuersiþ here owene fonnydnesse. **1434** MISYN *Mending of Life* 116 Slike lufe truly in þe begynnyng is labyr & fondnes. **1460** CAPGRAVE *Chron.*, *6 Hen. III* (Rolls) 151 In his fonnednesse he wold sey that he was so arayed for savacion of the world. **1533** FRITH *Answ. More* Gj, It were fondnes to fayne that the soule did other wise eate then do the Angellys in heauen. **1609** C. BUTLER *Fem. Mon.* iv. (1623) Hj, Others seeing the fondnesse of this opinion haue..taught that the Drone is a different species. *a* **1797** H. WALPOLE *Mem. Geo. II* (1847) I. iv. 85 Lord Lincoln..was the mimic of his fulsome fondnesses and follies. **1855** ROBINSON *Whitby Gloss.*, *Fondness*, foolishness.

2. Foolish affection; unreasoning tenderness.

1579–80 NORTH *Plutarch* (1676) 76 Persons..which suffer themselves to be overcome with such passions and fondness in their mourning. **1678** CUDWORTH *Intell. Syst.* 889 Neither his goodness being Fondness, nor his Justice Cruelty. **1702** *Eng. Theophrast.* 4 The players like their parts to a Fondness. **1727** GAY *Fables* I. iii. 31 By partial fondness shown, Like you, we doat upon our own. *a* **1859** MACAULAY *Hist. Eng.* V. 236 The object of her fondness was Spencer Cowper, who was already married.

3. Affectionateness, tenderness.

1603 SHAKS. *Meas. for M.* II. iv. 28 The generall subiect to a wel-wisht king..in obsequious fondnesse Crowd to his presence. **1703** *Rules of Civility* 25 It is not discreet for a man to express too much Fondness of his Wife before Company. **1727** SWIFT *To very yng. Lady* Wks. 1755 II. II. 41, I must likewise warn you..against the least degree of fondness to your husband before any witness whatsoever. **1782** HAN. MORE *Moses* I. 5 A mother's fondness reigns Without a rival. **1838** LYTTON *Alice* I. iii, The curate..was not insensible to the fondness of his beautiful pupil. **1868** HELPS *Realmah* xv. (1876) 400 The fondness of her words did not console him.

4. Instinctive or unreasoning liking or partiality; strong inclination, propensity or desire. Const. *for*, †*of*, †*to*, also †*to* with *inf.*

1654 HAMMOND *Fundamentals* xviii, Through indulgence to others, or fondness to any sinne in themselves. **1665** BOYLE *Occas. Refl.* x. (1845) 335 So conspicuous is this Creatures fondness of Light. **1713** STEELE *Guardian* No. 1 ¶1 They have a restless fondness for satisfying the world in the Mistakes [etc.]. **1735** MRS WHITEWAY *Swift's Lett.* (1768) IV. 141 Mr. ——'s great fondness to get his wife home, was to stop a prosecution she had begun against him. **1754** RICHARDSON *Grandison* I. viii. 40 Will he not attribute all I shall repeat of this sort..to that fondness of admiration. **1841** ELPHINSTONE *Hist. Ind.* II. 314 He showed no fondness for war. **1885** CLODD *Myths & Dr.* I. v. 94 The fondness of the negro races..for such fables is well known.

fondon. (See quot.)

1881 RAYMOND *Mining Gloss.*, *Fondon*, a large copper vessel, in which hot amalgamation is practiced.

fondre, obs. Sc. form of FOUNDER *v.*

†**'fondrel.** *Obs. rare*⁻¹. [f. FOND *a.*; ? after analogy of SCOUNDREL, etc.] A simpleton, ninny.

1614 *Sco. Venus* (1876) 27 No lisping tongue that fondrels count a grace.

fondu (fɔ̃dy). Also **fondus.** [a. F. *fondu* sing., *fondus* pl., pa. pple. of *fondre* to melt.] (See quots.)

1848 CRAIG, *Fondus* (*fondant*, melting, Fr.), that particular kind of painting on calico, paper-hangings, &c., in which the colours are blended in each other. **1875** *Ure's Dict. Arts* III. 479 The *fondu* or rainbow style of paper-hangings is produced [etc.].

‖**fondue** (fɔ̃dy). *Cookery.* Also *erron.* fondu. [ad. F. *fondue*, f. *fondre* to melt.] A dish composed of melted cheese with eggs, etc.

1878 *Cassell's Dict. Cookery* s.v., The fondu will rise very much. **1892–4** *Encycl. Cooking* (Garrett) I. 602/2 *Fondues*, these very favourite French savouries are made of melted cheese. **1895** *Daily News* 8 Jan. 6/4 Omelettes and fondues are equally dependent on this celerity of serving.

‖**fonduk** ('fɒndʊk). Also 8 **funduck**, 9 **fondak.** See also FONDACO. [Arab. *funduq* an inn, ad. Gr. πάνδοκος, πανδοκεύς innkeeper (whence πανδοκεῖον inn).] In North Africa; A hotel, an inn.

1704 J. PITTS *Acc. Mohammetans* 157 A Court, or Funduck, as they term it. **1883** *Academy* 20 Jan. 44/2 We drove from Tunis to Susa, spending a night on the way at the fonduk of Bîr-el-Bîtah. **1891** HALL CAINE *Scapegoat* xx, Between the village of Lemsa and the fondak which lies on the road to Tangier.

†**fone.** *Obs. rare*⁻¹. In 5 foine. [Of obscure origin and meaning; the *oi* stands for (oː).]

c **1460** *Towneley Myst.* (Surtees) 343 He was thi fode, thi faryst foine, Thi luf, thi lake, thi lufsom son.

fone, obs. form of FEW and obs. pl. of FOE.

fonel, fong(e, obs. ff. FUNNEL, FANG *v.*[1]

fonȝe, var. of FOIN *sb.*[1] *Obs.*

†**'fonkin.** *Obs.* [f. FON + -KIN.] A little fool.

1591 FRAUNCE *Yvychurch* I. i, If thou couldst, nay wouldst (and who would not, but a fonkin?)

fonly, fonnish: see FON *sb.* and *a.*

‖**fons et origo** (fɒnz ɛt ə'raɪgəʊ). [L.] The source and origin (*of*).

[**1809**, etc. examples of *fons et origo mali*: see Stanford's Dict. Anglicised Words.] **1873** BROWNING *Red Cott. Nt.-Cap* iii. 202 Never mind the cause, *Fons et origo* of the malady: Apply the drug with courage! **1890** W. JAMES *Princ. Psychol.* II. xx. 189 Many writers..hold that the consciousness of active muscular motion, aware of its own amount, is the *fons et origo* of all spatial measurement. **1897** *Westm. Gaz.* 12 Nov. 2/2 If we may reserve our opinion on the one point which was the *fons et origo* of Liberal Forwardism—the Eastern Question. **1927** A. H. MCNEILE *Introd. N.T.* 285 Papias, the *fons et origo* of many problems. **1930** *Times Lit. Suppl.* 20 Nov. 955/3 The *fons et origo* of the downfall of the West. **1966** *Listener* 12 May 701/1 That conjunction of..emotion and expression, that is the *fons et origo* of his music.

font (fɒnt), *sb.*[1] Forms: 1 font, fant, 2–6 funt(e, *Orm.* funnt (4 fant), 4–7 fount(e, (4 founȝt, fownte), 5–6 fonte, 2– font. [OE. *font*, *fant*, ad. Eccl. Lat. *font-em* or *fontes* (*baptismi*), lit. 'fountain' or 'fountains (of baptism)', a specific use of L. *font-em*, *fons*: see FOUNT. In ME. the compound FONT-STONE had the same sense. In sense 3 it may be regarded as a different word, a var. of FOUNT, refashioned after the Lat. etymon.

Cf. also F. *fonts* pl. (OF. *fonce*), Pr. *font*, Pg. and OSp. *fonte* (mod.Sp. *fuente*), It. *fonte*, of same meaning. Prob. by adoption from Eng., the word appears early in other Teut. langs.: OFris. *font*, *funt*, MDu. *vonte* (mod.Du. in comb. *doopvont*, from *doop* baptism), ON *funt-r* (Sw. *funt*, *dopfunt*, Da. *font*, *dobfont*).]

1. A receptacle, usually of stone, for the water used in the sacrament of baptism. Also, ***font of baptism, baptismal font. to stand at font for*** (a person): to be sponsor to.

c **1000** *Canons Ælfric* xxxvi, Ne do man nænne ele to þam fante. *a* **1175** *Cott. Hom.* 241 Ælc cristen man anon se stepð up of þe funte wer he ifulled is. *a* **1225** *St. Marher.* 1 Euch ifulhet in font oþe almihti federes nome. *c* **1380** *Sir Ferumb.* 548 Y-vollid on þe haly fant. **1447** BOKENHAM *Seyntys* (Roxb.) 111 Crystnyd I was in a funt of stoon. **1523** LD. BERNERS *Froiss.* I. ccccii. 698 They..brake downe the fownte wherin the erle was christned. **1611** CORYAT *Crudities* 35 A Font of baptisme, made of porphyrie stone. *a* **1658** CLEVELAND *To T. C.* 14 A gray Bark That stood at Font for Noah's Ark. **1756–7** *Keysler's Trav.* (1760) 490 The large marble font is divided by four partitions. **1865** KINGSLEY *Herew.* Prel. 6 The curse which Dunstan had pronounced against him at the baptismal font.

b. *pl.* (with singular sense). *rare.* (Cf. Fr. *fonts*, Eccl. Lat. *fontes* a font.)

The pl. has been explained as referring to the compound fonts of several basins found in some early baptisteries. But prob. *fontes baptismi*, originally meant only 'the fountains (i.e. the waters) of baptism', the application as the name of the vessel being secondary.

1877 J. D. CHAMBERS *Div. Worship* 186 The Fonts at the West end of the Nave.

2. *transf.* **a.** A receptacle for holy water. **b.** The reservoir for oil in a lamp.

1542–5 BRINKLOW *Lament.* (1874) 100 The wyne wyll waxe sower and stincke, as doth their holy water in the founte by longe kepinge. **1644** *Ord. Parlt.* in *Vestry Bks.* (Surtees) 322–3 Noe Copes, Surplices..or Holy water Fonts, to be any more used. **1872** O. SHIPLEY *Gloss. Eccl. Terms*, *Holy Water Font.* **1891** *Sale Catal. Glass Wks., Stourbridge*, Two hundred and fifty-five lamp fonts.

3. = FOUNT. Now only *poet.*

1611 CORYAT *Crudities* 26 Delicate fonts and springes. **1658** J. JONES *Ovid's Ibis* 2nd Ded., On Parnasse hill rose the Nectarian Font. **1735** SOMERVILLE *Chase* III. 342 Adown His tortur'd Sides the Crimson Torrents roll From many a gaping Font. *c* **1750** SHENSTONE *Elegies* i. 46 Near font or stream, in meditation, rove. **1878** B. TAYLOR *Deukalion* IV. ii, The font Bubbling and brightening with an inward life, Spins up in silver, tinkling as it falls.

4. *attrib.* and *Comb.*, as ***font-cloth, -cover, -taper, -vat***; also **font-name**, (one's) baptismal name; †**font-wife**, ? a woman appointed to collect donations at baptisms.

1553 *Inv.* in *Trans. Essex Archæol. Soc.* (1884) 10 Itm. a *ffownte clothe. **1885** R. W. DIXON *Hist. Ch. Eng.* III. 450 Font-cloths with altar-cloths. *a* **1661** FULLER *Worthies, Hartfordshire* II. (1662) 20 Seeing his own *font-name was a Papall one. **1679** BURNET *Hist. Ref.* (1865) I. 150 *note*, It seems unlikely that he [Bonner] alone in the grace should be written by his font name when all the others were by their surname. **1519** in W. L. Nash *Churchw. Acc. St. Giles, Reading* (Camden) 5, Ij standerds and the *ffont taper. *c* **1000** in Thorpe *Ags. Hom.* II. 268 Hæðen cild..bið ȝebroht synfull..to ðam *fant-fæte. *c* **1220** *Bestiary* 108 Naked [he] falleð in ðe funt-fat, and cumeð ut al newe. **1569** *Churchw. Acc. Stanford* in *Antiquary* Apr. (1888) 169 Eliza Yat..and Elenor Sauere were chossen *fount wyeffs this yer, but the gathered nothing this yer.

font (fɒnt), *sb.*[2] Also 7 **fonte.** [ad. Fr. *fonte*, f. *fondre* to melt, cast.]

1. a. The action or process of casting or founding. *lit.* and *fig. rare.* **b.** *concr.* Cast iron.

1578 *Inventories* (1815) 249 Ane moyane of fonte markit with the sallamandre having ane new stok without yron werk. **1676** MARVELL *Mr. Smirke* 34 A Sermon..that was preached before His Majesty, and by his special command to be Printed, is it seems making over again, there having been sure some error in the Fonte. **1883** C. C. PERKINS *Ital. Sculpt.* 273 When the figure was ready to be cast in bronze, Michelangelo seems suddenly to have remembered that, as he knew nothing of the processes of the font, he could not [etc.].

2. *Printing.* (In England usually FOUNT, q.v.)

†**font**, *v. Obs.* [f. prec. sb.] *trans.* To 'christen', name.

1652 *Persuasive to Compliance* 17 Flattery, rather then Truth, fonted them Fathers of their Country. *a* **1659** OSBORN *Queries* Wks. (1673) 593 It being likelier to have been the voice of Custom than Reason that fonted a bare Knowledge in Tongues with the title of Learning.

fontal ('fɒntəl), *a.* and *sb.* [ad. med.L. *fontālis*, f. *font-*, *fons* FOUNT, FONT.]

A. *adj.* **1.** Of or pertaining to a fountain or spring; coming as from a spring. *rare.*

1656–81 in BLOUNT *Glossogr.* *a* **1711** KEN *Hymn. Evang.* Poet. Wks. 1721 I. 69 O Jesu..Stream from thy fontal Fulness a small Rill, My soul to purify..and fill. **1753** CHAMBERS *Cycl. Suppl.* s.v. *Alga*, The alga's are some marine..others fontal, growing in springs. **1822** T. TAYLOR *Apuleius* III. 58 She made a libation..with fontal water. **1855** BAILEY *Mystic* 85 Within whose veins condensed the essential dew Flows fontal.

2. Pertaining to the source of anything; that is the source of other things; original, primary.

1677 GALE *Crt. Gentiles* I. IV. 272 The fontall Unitie and infinite Abyss of his own Essence. *a* **1711** KEN *Hymn. Evang.* Poet. Wks. 1721 I. 135 When Godhead Fontal and Deriv'd, co-breath. **1793** T. TAYLOR *Orat. Julian* 30 The fontal sun, then, subsists in Jupiter the perfect artificer of the world. **1817** COLERIDGE *Biog. Lit.* 95 The fontal truths of natural religion. **1858** E. CASWALL *Masque of Mary* 16 Hail, Mother of all ages! fontal source of humankind. **1883** A. ROBERTS *O.T. Revision* vii. 139 Whence was that fontal text derived?

3. Pertaining to the font, baptismal.

? **1797** COLERIDGE *Poems, Christen. Friend's Child* i, This day among the faithful placed, And fed with fontal manna. **1846** KEBLE *Lyra Innoc.* (ed. 3) 6 The fontal wave To each apart the glory gave, Washing us clean.

B. *sb.* †**1.** Source, 'well-spring' (*fig.*). *Obs.*

a **1711** KEN *Hymnotheo* Poet. Wks. 1721 III. 379 Love's the propensive Fontal of our Wills.

2. *Her.* (See quot. 1828–40).

1688 R. HOLME *Armoury* II. xvi. 365 A Sea Nymph..resting her Arm upon a Water-pot or Fontall, from whence issues water all proper. **1828–40** BERRY *Encycl. Her.* I. s.v., The gods of fountains and rivers and water nymphs are generally depicted with a water-pot from which flows the river they represent, which is termed a fontal.

Hence **'fontally** *adv.*

a **1617** BAYNE *Diocesans Tryall* (1621) 69 It presupposeth the power of jurisdiction to be given originally and fontally to one person of the Church.

fontanelle, fontanel (fɒntə'nɛl). Forms: 6–8 fontenel(l(e, 6 fontynelle, 7 funtanel, 7–9 fontanel(l(e, fontinel(l(e. [a. Fr. *fontanelle* (OF. *fontanele*, *fontenele* little fountain, also in the senses below), dim. of *fontaine* FOUNTAIN *sb.* Cf. It. *fontanella* little fountain, also hollow of the neck.]

1. *Anat.* †**a.** The hollow between two muscles.

Mentioned as the appropriate place for the application of a seton or a cautery: cf. sense 2.

1541 R. COPLAND *Guydon's Quest. Chirurg.* IV. Pj, For that cause be the cetons & canteres [*sic*] done behinde the necke, and in the fontenelles of the lacertes where as one is deuyded from the other. *Ibid.* Pij, On the homoplate vnder the font[en]elles of the armes. *Ibid.*, On the fontynelles vnder the knee.

b. One of several membranous spaces in the head of an infant which lie at the adjacent angles of the parietal bones. (*Syd. Soc. Lex.*) In some animals it is permanent.

1741 MONRO *Anat. Bones* (ed. 3) 71 That Part of the *parietal* and *frontal* Bones, where the *Fontanelle* is in Children. **1752** SMELLIE *Midwif.* I. 292 No perceiveable pulsation at the *Fontanelle*. *a* **1823** M. BAILLIE *Wks.* (1825) I. 187, I opened the head at the anterior fontinel. **1872** MIVART *Elem. Anat.* 127 The transitory fontanelle of man is permanent in some animals, as in Sharks. **1875** HUXLEY in *Encycl. Brit.* I. 755/1 A large space (fontanelle) covered in by membrane, which lies in the interorbital region [of the frog].

†**2.** *Med.* An artificial ulcer or a natural issue for the discharge of humours from the body. *Obs.*

1612 WOODALL *Surgeon's Mate* Wks. (1639) 7 The cauterizing Irons..are good to make a funtanell or Issue in the hinder part of the head. **1676** *Phil. Trans.* XI. 742 Fontinels or Issues naturally arising in the Arms and Feet. **1779** JOHNSON *Let. to Dr. Taylor* 3 Aug., He has a fontanel in his back.

b. In extended sense: An outlet for the discharge of secretions, etc. Often with mixture of the etymological sense 'fount'. Also *transf.* and *fig.*

1649 JER. TAYLOR *Gt. Exemp.* Disc. i. §9 Why hath nature given to Women two exuberant fontineles? **1650** —— *Holy Living* ii. §3 (1727) 75 The fontinel of whose desires hath been opened. **1660** WATERHOUSE *Arms & Arm.* 126 Whose fontenel sends forth matter with words. **1701** C. WOLLEY *Jrnl. in New York* (1860) 25 Nature..purgeth it by Fontanels and Issues of running waters in its irriguous Valleys. **1848** R. E. LANDOR *Fountain of Arethusa* III. ii. §1 Through this narrow fontanel of perforated rock.

‖**fontange** (fɔ̃tɑ̃ʒ). Also 7 **fountange**. [Fr. *fontange*, f. *Fontanges* the territorial title of a mistress of Louis XIV.] A tall head-dress worn in the seventeenth and eighteenth centuries.

1689 Shadwell *Bury F.* 11, What d'ye lack, Ladies? fine mazarine Hoods, Fontanges, Girdles. **1711** Addison *Spect.* No. 98 ¶1 These old-fashioned Fontanges rose an Ell above the Head. **1883** F. G. Stephens *Catal. Prints Brit. Mus.* IV. 282 An ugly old one-eyed woman in a fontange.

†**fontanier.** *Obs.* [ad. Fr. *fontainier*, f. *fontaine* fountain *sb.*] One in charge of a fountain or fountains.

1641 Evelyn *Diary* (1871) 36 The hedge of water..which the fontanier caused to ascend out of the earth. **1702** W. J. *Bruyn's Voy. Levant* xxxiv. 135 He lives at present at Loo.. in the Quality of chief Fontanier.

fontful (ˈfɒntfʊl). [f. font *sb.*[1] + -ful.] As much as a font will hold.

c **1386** Chaucer *Man of Law's T.* 259 Thogh she a fontful water with hir lede. **1866** Blackmore *Cradock Nowell* iii, Labourers moistened their semi-regenerate clay with many a fontful of good ale.

fontlet (ˈfɒntlɪt). [f. font *sb.*[1] + -let.] **a.** A little fountain. **b.** A little font (for baptism).

1831 Lamb *Elia* Ser. ii. *Newspapers 35 Y. Ago*, The tracing of some mighty waters up to their shallow fontlet. **1894** T. J. Ball *Dict. Elem. Ritual* vi. 52 In privately baptizing the officiant should pour water on the child..not sprinkle it out of a toy called a 'fontlet'.

†ˈ**font-stone,** *Obs.* [f. font *sb.*[1] + stone.] The stone font used in baptism.

c **1175** *Lamb. Hom.* 149 þet ȝe habbeð et þe fonstan underfonge. **1297** R. Glouc. (1724) 247 Of holy vantston. *c* **1380** *Sir Ferumb.* 548 Had he beo in crist be-lued, & fulled in holi fanston. **1426** Audelay *Poems* 11 This foreward furst we mad at the fonsston. **1594** ? Greene *Selimus* Wks. 1881–3 XIV. 267 They shal swear it vpon the font-stone. **1682** R. Burton *Admirable Curiosities* (1684) 121 As clean from my Sins as I was at the Font-stone. **1830** Scott *Demonol.* v. 147 If she would but deny..the faith she took at the font-stone.

†ˈ**font-water.** *Obs.* [f. font *sb.*[1] + water.] Water used in baptism.

c **1000** *Sax. Leechd.* II. 350 Wyrc þonne drenc font wæter rudan saluian [etc.]. **1610** Bp. Hall *Apol. Brownists* Ded., One of them hath washt off thy font-water as vncleane. **1656** J. Trapp *Comm. John* vi. 49 A man may go to hell with font-water on his face.

foo, obs. form of foe.

food (fuːd), *sb.* Forms: 1 fóda, 2–6 fode, 3 *south.* vode, (4 fod), 3–6 fud(e, (4 *Sc.* fute, 5 fotte, foyde, fudde, *Sc.* fwde, 6 fooade, *Sc.* fuid, fuode), 4–6 foode, 6– food. [OE. *fóda* wk. masc.; the exact equivalent (:—OTeut. type **fôdon-*) does not occur elsewhere; the synonymous ON. *fœðe* str. neut., *fœða* wk. fem. (Sw. *föda* fem., Da. *føde*), and Goth. *fôdeins* str. fem., are derivatives of the cognate vb. OTeut. **fôdjan* to feed. The Teut. root **fad, fôd* (whence also fodder and the cognates there mentioned) represents OAryan **pât-*, whence Gr. πατέεσθαι, to feed.]

1. a. What is taken into the system to maintain life and growth, and to supply the waste of tissue; aliment, nourishment, provisions, victuals.

c **1000** Ælfric *Sigew. Interr.* in *Anglia* VII. 34 On þære oðre fleringe wæs heora nytena foda ȝeloȝod. *a* **1225** *Ancr. R.* 260 He hefde uode ase ueol to him. *a* **1300** *Cursor M.* 23084 (Cott.), I was hungre, yee gaf me fode. **1375** Barbour *Bruce* x. 189 Syndri cornys that thai bair Woxe rype to wyn to mannys fude. *a* **1400–50** *Alexander* 1174 Him moneste..to send..fode for his oste. **1597** Hooker *Eccl. Pol.* v. xii. §5 Men at their owne home take common foode. *a* **1687** Waller *Upon Roscommon's Hor.* 57 They [Bees] give us food, which may with nectar vie. **1789** G. White *Selborne* Let. xv, Worms are their usual food. **1798** Malthus *Popul.* (1890) 288 Want of food..the most efficient cause of the three immediate checks to population. **1860–1** Flo. Nightingale *Nursing* 46 A tea-cupful of some article of food.

b. What is edible, as opposed to 'drink.'

1610 Shaks. *Temp.* i. ii. 160 Some food we had and some fresh water. **1697** Dryden *Virg. Georg.* iii. 790 Simple his Bev'rage, homely was his Food. **1855** Macaulay *Hist. Eng.* IV. 516 The crews had better food and drink than they had ever had before. **1859** Tennyson *Enid* 1138 And wine and food were brought.

†**c.** Sustenance, 'livelihood'. *Obs.*

a **1066** *Charter of Eadward* (*MS.* 14th c.) in *Cod. Dipl.* IV. 214 Ic wille ðat ðæt cotlif..ðe Leofcild..bequað Crist and sainte Peter into Westminstre ligge unðder into ðare munece fodan ellswa he hit geuðe. **1393** Langl. *P. Pl.* C. xviii. 19 Peter fysshed for hus fode and hus fere Andreu. **1548** Forrest *Pleas. Poesye* 287 Which such may compell to earn their Fooade. *a* **1605** Montgomerie *Sonn.* xlvii, He that.. to mak faggots for his fuid is fane.

d. Phrases: *to be food for* (*an animal, worms*): to be a prey to, to be devoured by. *to be food for fishes*: to be drowned. *food for powder*: fit only to be shot at or to die in battle.

a **1225** *Ancr. R.* 276 Ne schalt tu beon wurmes fode? **1596** Shaks. *1 Hen. IV*, iv. ii. 71 Good enough to tosse: foode for Powder, foode for Powder: they'le fill a Pit, as well as better. *Ibid.* v. iv. 86 *Hot.* No Percy, thou art dust And food for — *Prin.* For Wormes, braue Percy. **1601** —— *A.Y.L.* ii. vi. 7. **1894** Rider Haggard *Mr. Meeson's Will* xxii, He was food for fishes now, poor fellow.

e. An article of food; a kind of food.

1393 Gower *Conf.* III. 26, I you shall reherce, How that my fodes ben diverse. *c* **1449** Pecock *Repr.* iii. v. 303 Hauyng foodis..be we content. **1526** *Pilgr. Perf.* (W. de W. 1531) 5 b, God sent from heuen a swete fode for theyr brede called manna. **1617** Markham *Caval.* i. 56 In England..we have so many choyces of good foodes. **1674** N. Cox *Gentl. Recreat.* iv. (1677) 45 The larger the Pike the courser the food. **1754** *Dict. Arts & Sc.* II. 1288 Foods proper for preserving health. **1887** *Cassell's Fam. Physician* 911 What are the proper fuels, or foods, with which to supply it [the human machine].

2. a. With reference to plants: That which they absorb from the earth and air; nutriment.

1759 tr. *Duhamel's Husb.* i. i. (1762) 3 The proper food of the plant. **1765** A. Dickson *Treat. Agric.* iii. (ed. 2) 5 The vegetation of plants is promoted by communicating to the earth their food. **1869** Roscoe *Elem. Chem.* (1878) 372 Plants possess the peculiar power of selection, by the roots, of the mineral constituents of food.

b. *transf.*, as in ***skin food***.

1898 H. A. Browning *Beauty Culture* vii. 134 Let me, however, warn you to study your skin (and not to choose its 'food' hastily or casually). *Ibid.* x. 221 The face..is smeared with skin-food. **1907** *Yesterday's Shopping* (1969) 537/1 Skin food. Massage & complexion cream. *Ibid.* 538/3 Squaw hair food. **1908** *Queen* 30 May 932/1 The introducer of the Russian skin food Valaze is Dr. Lyruski. **1912** *Ibid.* 30 Nov. 1006/1 It is a skin food in the truest sense and really works wonders with the skin. **1942** N. Marsh *Death & Dancing Footman* ii. 43 A fat lot of good 'Hersey's Skin Food' is to your middle-aged charms.

3. *fig.* **a.** (In early use applied more widely than is now admissible.)

c **1000** in Thorpe *Ags. Hom.* II. 396 Gif he hi forlæt buton ðam godspellican fodan on heora andgite. *c* **1175** *Lamb. Hom.* 63 Swa bi-houeð þe saule fode, mid godes wordes mid gode mode. *a* **1300** *Cursor M.* 29058 (Cott.) Þat þi fast to saul fode mai falle. *a* **1340** Hampole *Psalter* cxxvii. 2 Trauels.. are now fode til soul. *c* **1430** *Hymns Virg.* (1867) 14 God, þou be my strengist fode. **1500–20** Dunbar *Poems* lxxii. 54 His face, the fude of angellis fre. **1538** Starkey *England* 55 Nuryschyd wyth the spiritual fode of hys celestyal word. **1595** Shaks. *John* iii. iv. 104 My faire sonne, My life, my ioy, my food, my all the world. **1600** —— *A.Y.L.* iv. iii. 102 Orlando..Chewing the food of sweet and bitter fancie. **1713** Steele *Englishm.* No. 10. 67 Praise is the Food of a great Soul. **1784** Cowper *Tiroc.* 620 Such is all the mental food purveyed By public hackneys in the schooling trade. **1801** Wordsw. *Sonn. To Liberty* i. iv, What food Fed his first hopes? **1891** *Edin. Rev.* July 132 Fiction is the only intellectual food of thousands.

b. In sense of: Matter to discuss or dwell upon.

1780 Burke *Corr.* (1844) II. 347 Our own manners afford food enough for poetry. **1825** Southey *Tale of Paraguay* iii. 19 A lively tale, and fraught With..food for thought. **1834** L. Ritchie *Wand. by Seine* 83 There the reflective will find food for their meditations.

4. *transf.* †**a.** Material for keeping up a fire.

a **1050** *Lib. Scintill.* x. (1889) 56 Foda fyres holt. *a* **1225** *Ancr. R.* 150 Bowes..to none þinge betere þen to fures fode.

b. = shoddy: (see quot.)

1857 C. B. Robinson in Best *Farm. Bks.* (Surtees) Gloss. s.v., The entire substance that falls on the floor being called 'shoddy' or 'food', and being sold at a high rate for top dressing grass land.

†**5.** The act of eating. *in food*: while eating or feeding. *Obs.*

c **1250** *Gen. & Ex.* 894 Wið bredes fode and wines drinc. *a* **1400–50** *Alexander* 2 Fayn wald þai here Sum farand þing efter fode to fayn þare her[t]. **1590** Shaks. *Com. Err.* v. i. 83 In food, in sport..To be disturb'd, would mad or man, or beast.

†**6.** That which is fed; a child, offspring. Also in wider sense: A creature, person, man. *Obs.*

In early use also *collect.*, a brood, race. Cf. OF. *norriture, nourriture*, med.Lat. *nutrimentum*, a young animal.

a **1250** *Owl & Night.* 94 Þu fedest on heom a wel ful fode. *a* **1300** *Cursor M.* 682 (Cott.) Fouxl o flight, and fiss on sand ..com and ȝode, Als he war fader o þair fode. *a* **1300** *K. Horn* 1384 Aþulf þe gode, Min oȝene child, mi leve fode. **1375** Barbour *Bruce* iii. 578 Men mycht se mony frely fute About the costis thar lukand. *c* **1400** *Ywaine & Gaw.* 1621 So fals a fode, Was never cumen of Kynges blode. ? *c* **1475** *Sqr. lowe Degre* 364 in Hazl. *E.P.P.* II. 37, I may not beleue ..My doughter dere he wyll betraye..That fode to long with no foly. *c* **1485** *Digby Myst.* iii. 942, I have a favorows fode, and fresse as the fakown.

7. *attrib.* and *Comb.* **a.** simple attrib., as ***food-crank, -faddist, habit, -pan, parcel, product, queue, -shortage, -supply, tax, -ticket, -truck***; in sense of 'fit or used for food', as ***food-bird, -fish, -grain, -plant, -stuff, -substance***.

1879 H. George *Progr. & Pov.* ii. iii. (1881) 116 If he but shoot hawks, *food-birds will increase. **1906** J. Condon *Let.* 17 Nov. (1966) 220 Don't think I am some sort of a *food-crank. **1951** R. Campbell *Light on Dark Horse* 150 Any Fabian food-crank. **1910** *Daily Chron.* 14 Apr. 4/2 The '*food faddists' or 'food reformers'. **1927** W. E. Collinson *Contemp. Eng.* 38 Some of the food-faddists went beyond the vegetarian stage and became fruitarians. **1953** A. Christie *Pocket Full of Rye* viii. 47 One of those food faddists who'll eat any mortal thing so long as it isn't cooked. **1970** *Guardian* 15 Aug. 6/6 Top pundits tend to make fun of food faddists. **1865** J. G. Bertram (*title*) The harvest of the sea. A contribution to the natural and economic history of the British *food fishes. **1884** S. E. Dawson *Handbk. Canada* 334 Herring, haddock and other food-fishes are abundant. **1880** C. R. Markham *Peruv. Bark* 486 This remarkable *food grain might doubtless be usefully cultivated in the Himalayas. **1927** *Maclean's Mag.* 1 June 32/1 *Food habits are important. **1871** Alabaster *Wheel of Law* 149 He..took his *food-pan, and went and sat under the shade of the great banyan tree. **1919** E. H. Jones *Road to En-dor* v. 52 He was comfortable enough himself (thanks to the contents of our *food parcels). **1946** J. B. Priestley *Bright Day* x. 310 He'd been sending some food parcels to his sister in England. **1967** *Guardian* 5 Sept. 7/5 The poorest depending on cash grants and food parcels from Turkey. **1872** Yeats *Techn. Hist. Comm.* 208 Novel and valuable *food-plants. **1897** *Daily News* 6 Mar. 6/4 The Select Committee on *food products adulteration. **1906** *Daily Chron.* 5 June 5/4 To enable Government inspectors to supervise, from hoof to can, the preparation of meat food-products. **1940** *Manch. Guardian Weekly* 5 Jan. 3 There is nothing more irksome and more damaging to a smooth-running war system than local shortages and *food queues. **1931** J. S. Huxley *What dare I think?* iv. 135 *Food-shortage..will..bring about an equilibrium. **1965** M. Hilton tr. Meuvret in *Pop. in Hist.* xxi. 511 Movements undertaken to escape regions experiencing food-shortage. **1872** Huxley *Phys.* vi. 138 *Food-stuffs have been divided into heat-producers and tissue-formers. **1881** W. D. Hay *300 Years Hence* i. 4 Inquiries about..*food supply and so on. **1957** P. Worsley *Trumpet shall Sound* vi. 120 The Japanese organized work-teams..to cultivate huge gardens for their own and the natives' food-supply. **1906** *Food-tax [see *food-taxer* below]. **1913** *Punch* 22 Jan. 67 Food taxes. **1907** *Westm. Gaz.* 12 Oct. 13/1 The *food-ticket is invaluable, when money might prove a danger. **1909** *Ibid.* 30 Jan. 2/2, I felt also bound to refuse the gift of a food-ticket until their cases had been investigated. **1937** Koestler *Spanish Testament* ii. 55 The revolutionary committees issued food tickets which the shopkeepers were obliged to honour. **1886** *Longm. Mag.* VII. 329 The *food-truck which has now for two years been supported by the readers of Longman's Magazine.

b. objective, as ***food-chopper, -gatherer, -grower, -mixer, -taxer***; ***food-collecting, -gathering*** (see also 8), ***-getting, -taxing***; ***food-producing*** ppl. adj.

1908 *Sears, Roebuck Catal.* 468/1 Enterprise *food chopper..will chop raw meat, cooked meat, vegetables. **1911** *Daily Colonist* (Victoria, B.C.) 6 Apr. 3/1 (Advt.), Meant to save and sure to please bargains we are offering Food Choppers, $1.75 kind..$1.25. **1911** J. A. Thompson *Biol. Seasons* iii. 294 The marked shortening of the daylight hours available for *food-collecting. **1932** E. Step *Bees, Wasps, Ants* 4 When she [*sc.* the bee] is not making food-collecting excursions, she sits upon the cell. **1865** Gosse *Land & Sea* 153 The pseudopodia are *food-gatherers as well as instruments of locomotion. **1927** Haldane & Huxley *Animal Biol.* xii. 288 The last task undertaken [by bees] before going out *food-gathering is that of sentry-duty. **1941** J. S. Huxley *Uniqueness of Man* xiv. 278 Practical activities of communal existence such as *food-getting and war. **1841** S. Smith in *Mem.* (1855) II. 457 Neither butcher, nor baker, nor *food-grower. **1959** *Observer* 19 Apr. 14/3 There are over a dozen brands of *food mixers on the market. **1961** *Times* 26 Apr. 25/4 Domestic appliances such as..food-mixers. **1870** Bryant *Iliad* II. xiv. 59 Lay one hand Upon the *food-producing earth. **1903** *Westm. Gaz.* 19 Aug. 5/1 Mr. Arnold-Forster a *food-taxer. **1906** *Daily Chron.* 13 Feb. 4/2 There was something for the Food-taxers also, for..the matter of food-taxes is 'not a question of principle'. **1905** *Ibid.* 25 Mar. 7/4 This *food-taxing policy.

8. Special comb.: **food additive**, a substance added to food so as to improve its colour, flavour, or preservation, or for any other non-nutritional purpose; **food-call**, the cry of a bird for food; also *transf.*; **food-card**, a card used in the rationing of food to indicate the amount of food allowed to a person for a specified period of time; **food-chain** *Ecology*, a series of organisms each dependent upon another for food, esp. by direct predation; **food-chemist**, one occupied in the analysis of foods; **food-controller**, an official having control of food supplies; **food-cycle** *Ecology*, an interdependent group of food-chains in a community; †**food-fit** *a.*, fit to be used as food; **food-gatherer**, *spec.* in *Anthropol.*, one who obtains food from natural sources rather than through agriculture, etc.; so **food-gathering** *sb.* and *attrib.*; **food-lift**, a lift for the conveyance of food; **food-poisoning**, any illness caused by the presence in food of harmful bacteria or toxic substances (as bacterial toxins or poisons from inedible plants); **food processor**, an electrical kitchen appliance for mixing, chopping, shredding, and otherwise preparing foods for cooking or for the table; **food-rent** (see quot.); †**food-sick** *a.*, sick for want of food; **food stamp** (see quot. 1967); **food-value**, value as food; *spec.* in dietetics, the relative nourishing power assigned to foods; also *fig.*; **food-vessel** *Archæol.*, a type of prehistoric pottery found in northern England (see quot. 1963); applied *attrib.* to the culture characterized by such pottery; also (*rare*) *food-vase*; **food-web** = *food-cycle*; **food-yolk**, the non-germinative part of the yolk of an egg, which nourishes the embryo.

1958 *U.S. Statutes at Large* (1959) LXXII. i. 2151 The petitioner shall furnish samples of the *food additive involved..and of the food in or on which the additive is proposed to be used. **1984** M. Hanssen *E for Additives* 8 Sugar and salt are perhaps the most common food additives and are very important in the preservation of foods. **1926** T. E. Lawrence *Seven Pillars* (1935) iii. xxxv. 207 Down the visible wind in the misted valley came the *food-call of Turkish bugles. **1949** *Brit. Birds* XLII. 236 She may utter food-calls as during incubation. **1956** Bannerman *Birds Brit. Isles* V. 196 The 'food calls' of the young..are uttered in excited chorus. **1918** *Times* 6 Feb. 8/2 *Food cards taken out for children educated at boarding schools. **1923** E. A. Ross *Russian Soviet Republ.* 113 Bread- and food-cards of four different colors were issued to four class divisions of the population. *Ibid.* 114 In the spring of 1920 there were only eight thousand adults in Petrograd who had not taken out food-cards, i.e. had not gone to work. **1927** C. Elton *Anim. Ecol.* v. 56 There are, in fact, chains of animals linked together by food, and all dependent in the long run upon plants. We refer to these as '*food-chains', and to all the food chains in a community as the 'food-cycle'. **1959** J. Clegg *Freshwater Life* (ed. 2) iv. 65 The algae provide the first link in the food-chain, utilising simple chemical substances in the water to build up their own structures; thereby making available abundant food for the lower animals. **1968** *Times* 17 Dec. 10/5 Birds of prey are particularly vulnerable.. because of their position at the end of a food chain. For example, worms eat contaminated vegetation, sparrows eat worms, and peregrines eat sparrows. **1916** *Act 6 & 7 Geo. V* c. 68 §3 For the purpose of economising and maintaining the food supply of the country during the present war, it shall be lawful for His Majesty to appoint a Minister of Food under the title of *Food Controller. **1927** *Food-cycle [see *food-chain*]. **1963** J. E. G. Raymont *Plankton & Productivity in Oceans* xviii. 542 Food cycles in the oceans commence with the synthesis of organic material by the phytoplankton. **1885** A. W. Blyth in *Leisure Hour* Jan. 24/2 A *food-chemist.. laying down the principles of diet. *c* **1611** Sylvester *Du Bartas* ii. iv. iv. *Decay* 423 As one same ground indifferently doth breed Both *food-fit Wheat and dizzie Darnell seed. **1928** C. Dawson *Age of Gods* iii. 49 Man was entirely at the mercy of nature—a mere scavenger who eked out a miserable existence as a *food-gatherer and an eater of shell-fish. **1949** W. F. Albright *Archaeol. of Palestine* iii. 61 The Natufians were still essentially food-gatherers, in spite of their discovery of the cultivation of grain. **1960** K. M. Kenyon *Archaeol. in Holy Land* i. 19 The men of the period were dependent for their existence on the food they could gather by hunting, fishing and other natural sources; they were food-gatherers. **1926** V. G. Childe *Aryans* v. 103 Men who had made the great advance from a *food-gathering to a food-producing economy. **1936** *Proc. Prehist. Soc.* II. 253 People dependent upon hunting, fishing and food-gathering tend everywhere to produce the same kind of art. **1958** *Listener* 30 Oct. 689/2 The food-gathering state when man was, economically at least, a savage like the early Eskimo. **1898** A. Bennett *Man fr. North* xvi. 139 The screen which hid the *food-lift. **1922** Joyce *Ulysses* 167 A diner.. stared towards the foodlift. **1887** *Practitioner* Apr. 302 (*heading*) Report on *food poisoning at a wedding breakfast. **1917** E. O. Jordan *Food Poisoning* i. 2 Most attacks of food poisoning are usually of a slight and apparently temporary nature. **1951** Whitby & Hynes *Med. Bacteriol.* (ed. 5) ii. 15 Potassium permanganate is much used in the tropics to kill food-poisoning bacteria on vegetables. **1951** E. W. H. Cruikshank *Food & Nutrition* (ed. 2) xiv. 285 Food poisoning may also occur.. by the ingestion of poisonous plants. **1970** *Daily Tel.* 6 May 19/8 A doctor is only compelled to notify the health authorities of certain infectious diseases and cases of food poisoning. **1974** *House Beautiful* July 40/2 The food machine that does nearly everything is the innovative *Food Processor made by Cuisinarts. **1979** *Sunset* Apr. 128/1 (Advt.), Here's a food processor you can't go wrong with—literally. Because *this* food processor has a mistake-proof computer built right in. **1875** Maine *Hist. Inst.* vi. 160 The rent in kind, or *food-rent. **1587** *Mirr. Mag., Sir N. Burdet* xxxii, When facing foysters fit for Tiburne frayes Are *food-sicke faynt. **1962** *Economist* 28 Apr. 363/2 The 146,000 certified [American] needy now receiving *food-stamps. **1967** *Ibid.* 15 July 214/3 The other 'anti-hunger' device, the Food Stamp Programme, allows families to purchase stamps at substantially less than their face value and use them to buy food at their local shops. **1970** *Guardian* 31 Mar. 11/1 The flower children fled to communes in New Mexico where pot is plentiful and Federal food stamps prevent starvation. **1899** E. G. White *Counsel to Editors* (1939) xxi. 104 Everything that the imaginative mind can think of is woven into the book, and presented to the world as mental food. But very often it has no *food value. **1907** *Chamber's Jrnl.* 29 June 495 The York Health and Housing Reform Association has published a table of food-values. **1909** *Ibid.* Jan. 6/2 The average Chinese and Japanese diet is rather richer in food-values than the average American. **1915** *Lit. Digest* (N.Y.) 4 Sept. 479/2 (Advt.), A nourishing and appetizing first course like.. Tomato Soup.. contributes rich food-value. **1960** C. Storr *Marianne & Mark* iii. 35 Aunt Pamela, though.. no expert on food values, was immensely keen on providing a good mixed diet. **1871** *Archaeologia* XLIII. 385 One of the four *food-vases.. is ornamented with fine punctures at the bottom. **1963** H. N. Savory in Foster & Alcock *Culture & Environment* iii. 34 The rim of a Corded Beaker, part of a jar with a rim deeply bevelled internally, which Piggott hailed as a possible ancestor of the southern 'Food-vase'. **1871** *Archaeologia* XLIII. 378 *Food vessels are rare in the barrows of Wiltshire and the South of England. **1930** F. Elgee *Early Man in N.E. Yorks.* viii. 68, I shall first describe the food-vessel skeleton burials. *Ibid.* 70 Burials in which no pottery was present, but which are nevertheless characteristic of the food-vessel period. **1963** E. S. Wood *Collins Field Guide Archæol.* i. iv. 62 In the North the 'Food Vessel' culture absorbed very obviously many of the traditions of the secondary neolithic and Beaker peoples, and produced a somewhat coarse pottery, with neck and shoulder, and much ornament in bands and panels, from which it takes its name. **1961** *Estuarine Bull.* VI. 12 (*title*) Sand shrimp: cross-link in an estuarine *food web. **1971** *Nature* 1 Jan. 14/1 Important links in the food web of the sea. **1851** Carpenter *Man. Phys.* (ed. 2) 474 Animals which are provided with a '*food-yolk'.

†**food**, *v. Obs.* [f. prec. sb.] *trans.* To supply food to; to feed, nourish, support.

1399 Langl. *Rich. Redeles* ii. 135 ȝe ffostrid and ffodid a ffewe of þe best. *Ibid.* iii. 52 And with hir corps keuereth him.. And ffostrith and ffodith till ffedris schewe.

¶ For the supposed fig. sense 'to beguile,' see fode *v.*

foodaholic (fu:də'hɒlɪk). *colloq.* (orig. *U.S.*). Also foodoholic. [f. food *sb.* + -aholic.] One who has an inordinate craving for or obsession with food.

1965 in *Amer. Speech 1974* (1983) LVIII. 176 Are you a foodoholic suffering from creeping overweight? **1975** *Sunday News* (N.Y.) 23 Mar. 11 Lynn [Redgrave] admits that she once had a weight problem. 'At 23, when I made 'Georgy Girl', I was a foodaholic,' she said. She dieted and trimmed her 5-foot-10 frame to a slim 135 pounds soon afterward. **1978** *Sunday Sun* (Brisbane) 26 Feb. 3/4 For 15 years foodaholic Judith Lincoln refused to look at herself in a mirror. **1985** *Woman's Own* 22 June 37/1 'I like thin women,' he says. 'I don't like foodaholics.'

fooder, obs. var. of fudder.

foodful ('fu:dfʊl). Chiefly *poet.* [f. food *sb.* + -ful.] Abounding with or supplying food. Also, rich in nutriment, nutritious.

1638 G. Sandys *Paraphr. Job.* 55 When I made The foodfull Earth. **1697** Dryden *Virg. Georg.* i. 204 From furrow'd Fields to reap the foodful Store. **1735** Somerville *Chase* iii. 248 The bleating Innocent, that claims in vain.. The foodful Teat. **1808** J. Barlow *Columb.* i. 796 The sturdy fig .. And foodful cocoa fan the sultry plain. **1868** Browning *Ring & Bk.* ix. 246 No more friskings o'er the foodful glebe. *fig.* **1791** Burke *App. Whigs* Wks. 1842 I. 522 The democratick commonwealth is the foodful nurse of ambition.

foodie ('fu:dɪ). *colloq.* Also foody. [f. food *sb.* + -ie.] One who is particular about food, a gourmet. Also *attrib.*

1982 V. Woods et al. in *Harpers & Queen* Aug. 66/4 Foodies are foodist. They dislike and despise all non-foodies. *Ibid.* 67/2 The [colour] supplements encouraged the foodie movement. **1982** *Observer* 10 Oct. 28/6 We foodies know her better as the author of the Penguin volume, 'An Invitation to Indian Cooking'. **1984** Barr & Levy (*title*) The official foodie handbook. **1984** *Listener* 27 Sept. 19/2 He told me about the foodie who sat next to him at a meal in a Chinese restaurant and went into transports of enthusiastic analysis about the way in which the chicken had been cooked. **1985** *Daily Tel.* 4 Jan. 12 'A la carte', IPC's newest and most lavish magazine.. is aimed at the nation's foodies. **1986** *Good Housekeeping* Sept. 11/1 Although I am by no means a fully paid-up foodie, I do pride myself on being something of a connoisseur of menus.

†'**fooding.** *Obs.* [f. food *v.* + -ing[1].] **a.** A feeding. **b.** Food.

c **1440** *Promp. Parv.* 168/2 Fodynge, or norschynge, *fomentum.* **1650** *Witt's Recreations* Epigr. No. 232 Thou might'st have thought.. (As Joan her fooding bought) som good, som bad.

foodless ('fu:dlɪs), *a.* [f. food *sb.* + -less.]

1. Without food. **a.** Of persons or animals: Having no food.

a **1400–50** *Alexander* 2155 Lo, oure folez bene in fere for fodeles to dye. *a* **1541** Wyatt *Poems, Ps.* xxxvii. 70 Nor yet [shall] his seed foodless seen for to be. **1725** Pope *Odyss.* xviii. 413 Both constrained to wield, Foodless, the scythe. **1821** Shelley *Prometh. Unb.* i. 170 Foodless toads Within voluptuous chambers panting crawled. **1880** Earl Dunraven in *19th Cent.* Sept. 454 Our entirely foodless stomachs.. indicated that it was past noon.

fig. **1887** Swinburne *Locrine* iv. i. 105 So shall fear, mistrust, and jealous hate Lie foodless.

b. Of a country, place, etc. Devoid of food; not yielding food; barren.

1636 G. Sandys *Paraphr. Ps* cvii. (1638) 131 He in foodless Deserts fed The Hungry. **1726–46** Thomson *Winter* 256 The foodless wilds Pour forth their brown inhabitants. **1842** R. Oastler *Fleet Papers* II. 359 Their home.. was foodless. **1861** Wynter *Soc. Bees* 199 Vast foodless tracts have to be traversed by her ships, the camels of the ocean.

2. Without the properties of food; innutritious.

1891 *Independent* (N.Y.) 13 Aug., Alcohol is shown to be foodless.

Hence '**foodlessness**.

1852 *Meanderings of Mem.* I. 10 Galls them no more their foodlessness or fag.

foody ('fu:dɪ), *a.* [f. as prec. + -y[1].]

1. Full of, or supplying, food. (Only in Chapman.)

c **1611** Chapman *Iliad* xi. 104 Who brought them to the sable fleet from Ida's foody leas. *Ibid.* xv. 638 Jove's great queen of birds.. Beholds where cranes, swans, cormorants, have made their foody fall. **1615** —— *Odyss.* ii. 558 She.. into well-sew'd sacks pour'd foody meal.

2. Of wool (expressing superior quality).

1805 Luccock *Nat. Wool* 123 Wool of this discription is distinguished by the epithets foody and flowery.

foodyr, obs. form of fodder.

foo-foo ('fu:fu:). Also foofoo, fou-fou. [Of West Afr. origin: recorded in Twi, Ewe, Wolof, etc. Cf. Cuban Sp. *fufú*.] A kind of dough made out of plantains: a traditional food of Negroes on both sides of the Atlantic.

These are variant spellings of fufu (q.v.).

1826 A. Barclay *Pract. View Slavery W.I.* 437 A negro.. would greatly prefer his own good substantial dish of *foofoo*, composed of eddoes, ochras, and mashed plantains. **1851** *Illustr. Catal. Gt. Exhib.* iv. i. 977/2 This mass [of plantain boiled whole], beaten in a mortar, constitutes the *foo-foo* of the negroes [of British Guiana]. **1858** Simmonds *Dict. Trade, Foo-foo*, a negro name for dough made from plantains; the fruit being boiled and then pounded in a mortar. **1899** J. Rodway *In Guiana Wilds* 54 There were fou-fou soup, pepper-pot, barbecued meat, and piles of oranges. **1924** *Glasgow Herald* 8 Nov. 5 The women pounded their 'fou-fou' in the courtyard of the [Ashanti] village. **1964** E. Huxley *Back Street New Worlds* xiv. 141 The Shepherd's Bush market has a shop devoted wholly to West African foods.. like.. garden eggs and fou-fou, edwene and dried snails.

†**fooker.** *Obs. rare*[−1]. [? var. of fogger *sb.*[1]; cf. Ger. *fucker.*] ? A capitalist, financier.

1607 Middleton *Five Gallants* ii. iii, Pist! a supply, cary't closely my little fooker,—how much.

fool (fu:l) *sb.*[1] and *a.* Forms: 3–4 fol, (3 folle), 3–6 fole, (4 foyl), 4–6 foule(e, (4 fowle), 4–7 foole, (6 foolle), 4–9 *Sc.* fule, 5–6 full(e, 5–7 *Sc.* fuil(l, -yll, (5 fwle), 4– fool. [ME. *fōl* sb. and adj., ad. OF. *fol* sb. and adj. (mod.F. *fou* sb., insane person, madman, *fou* adj. masc., before vowel *fol*, fem. *folle*), corresponding to Pr. *fol*, *folh*, It. *folle*:—L. *follem*, *follis*, lit. 'bellows,' but in late popular Lat. employed in the sense of 'windbag,' empty-headed person, fool.]

A. *sb.*

I. 1. a. One deficient in judgement or sense, one who acts or behaves stupidly, a silly person, a simpleton. (In Biblical use applied to vicious or impious persons.)

The word has in mod.Eng. a much stronger sense than it had at an earlier period; it has now an implication of insulting contempt which does not in the same degree belong to any of its synonyms, or to the derivative *foolish*. Cf. F. *sot*.

c **1275** Lay. 1442 Cniþt þou art mochel fol. **1340** Hampole *Pr. Consc.* 126 Elles es he a fole and noght wise. **1398** Trevisa *Barth. De P.R.* vi. xvii. (1495) 203 Telle a fole his defawte, and he shall hate the. **1481** Caxton *Godfrey* xxv. 57 There ben more fooles than wysemen. *a* **1550** *Christis Kirke Gr.* xxii, For faintness tha forfochtin fulis Fell doun lyk flauchtir fails. **1612** Dekker *If it be not good*, Prol., Fooles by lucky Throwing, oft win the Game. **1709** Pope *Ess. Crit.* 625 For Fools rush in where Angels fear to tread. **1773** Mrs. Chapone *Improv. Mind* (1774) II. 111 Unless you improve your mind.. you will be an insignificant fool in old age. **1816** Scott *Antiq.* xliii, 'Mony a wise man sits in a fule's seat, and mony a fule in a wise man's, especially in families o' distinction.' **1881** Besant & Rice *Chapl. Fleet* I. 144 No doubt, there have been fools before.

b. Phrase. *to be a fool to*: to be every way inferior to, to be as nothing compared to.

1596 Shaks. *Tam. Shr.* iii. ii. 159 Tut, she's a Lambe, a Doue, a foole to him. **1791** 'G. Gambado' *Ann. Horsem.* xvii. (1809) 137 Childers would have been a fool to him. **1885** Rider Haggard *K. Solomon's Mines* 79 The Black Hole of Calcutta must have been a fool to it.

†**c.** Used as a term of endearment or pity. *Obs.*

c **1530** *Beaut. Women* in Hazl. *Dodsley* I. 71 How say ye now by this, little young fool? *a* **1586** Sidney *Astrophel & Stella* lxxiii, O heau'nly foole, thy most kisse-worthy face [etc.]. **1611** Shaks. *Wint. T.* ii. i. 118 Doe not weepe (goode Fooles) There is no cause.

d. In various proverbial expressions.

c **1400** *Rom. Rose* 5266 A fooles belle is soone runge. **1539** Taverner *Erasm. Prov.* (1552) 4 A foles bolt is soone shotte. **1546** J. Heywood *Prov.* (1867) 46 There is no foole to the olde foole. **1563** B. Googe *Epit. N. Grimoald* Eglogs, etc. (Arb.) 74 But Fortune fa[u]ours Fooles as old men saye. **1606** Holland *Sueton.* Annot. 16 A foole or a physition. *c* **1645** Howell *Lett.* I. v. xxxix, A fool and his money is soon parted. **1670** Ray *Prov.* 91 Fools build houses, and wise men buy them. **1721** Kelly *Sc. Prov.* 101 Every Man at thirty is a Fool or a Physician.

2. a. One who professionally counterfeits folly for the entertainment of others, a jester, clown.

The 'fool' in great households was often actually a harmless lunatic or a person of weak intellect, so that this sense and sense 4 are often hard to distinguish.

? **1370** *Robert Cicyle* in *Nugæ Poet.* (1844) 54 Lyke a fole and a fole to bee, Thy babulle schalle be thy dygnyte! *c* **1440** *Ipomydon* 1643 He semyd a fole.. Bothe by hede and by atyre. **1532** *Privy Purse Exp. Hen. VIII*, 205 For making of gere for the kinges fole xxx *s.* **1609** Dekker *Gulls Horne-bk.* Proem, Wks. (Grosart) II. 205 He may be.. his crafty foole, or his bawdy Jester. **1651** Brome *Joviall Crew* v. Wks. 1873 I. 451 To beg the next Fool-Royal's place that falls. **1691** Luttrell *Brief Rel.* (1857) II. 311 Mr. Graham, the fool in King James time. **1847** L. Hunt *Jar Honey* vi. (1848) 75 He had all the humiliations.. of the cap and bells, and was the dullest fool ever heard of.

b. *to play the fool*: to act the part of a fool or jester; hence *gen.* to act like a fool (sense 1).

c **1532** Dewes *Introd. Fr.* in Palsgr. 939 To plee the fole, *baguenauder.* **1579** Fulke *Heskins' Parl.* 295 He playeth the foole with that bable. **1659–60** Pepys *Diary* 28 Feb., I staid up a little while, playing the fool with the lass of the house. **1722** De Foe *Relig. Courtsh.* i. i, I advise you not to play the fool with me any longer. **1847** James *J. Marston Hall* viii, The parliament was playing the fool in Paris.

c. *Feast of Fools* [=med.L. *festum stultorum*]: *properly* the burlesque festival which in the Middle Ages was sometimes celebrated in churches on New Year's Day; hence in various allusive uses.

c **1320** *Seuyn Sag.* (W.) 2748 Sire, hastou owt herde the geste, Whi men made folen feste? **1609** Dekker *Gulls Horne-bk.* Proem. Wks. (Grosart) II. 209 To the intent I may aptly furnish this feast of Fooles.

3. One who is made to appear a fool; one who is imposed on by others; a dupe. Now somewhat *arch.*, exc. in phrases *to make a fool of* (formerly also †*to put the fool on*), to dupe, befool; *to be a*

fool for one's pains, to have one's labour for nothing.

c **1440** *Jacob's Well* 81 A nunne, þat..made here as a fool, and obeyid here to alle here sustren as here fool. **1579** LYLY *Euphues* (Arb.) 89 Bicause I was content to be his Friend, thought he me meete to be made his Foole. **1592** SHAKS. *Rom. & Jul.* III. i. 141, I am Fortunes foole. **1625** COOKE *Pope Joan* in *Harl. Misc.* (Malh.) IV. 28 The dean made a fool of the alderman. *a* **1684** LEIGHTON *Comm. 1 Peter* i. 3 Worldly hopes..put the fool upon a man. **1715** DE FOE *Fam. Instruct.* I. iv, I won't be made a fool of. **1850** TENNYSON *In Mem.* iv, Thou shalt not be the fool of loss. *Mod.* He is the fool of circumstances.

†**4.** One who is deficient in, or destitute of reason or intellect; a weak-minded or idiotic person. *Obs.* exc. in ***natural*** or ***born fool***, a born idiot (now *rare* exc. as a mere term of abuse). ***to beg*** (a person) ***for a fool***: see BEG 5 a.

1540 *Act 32 Hen. VIII*, c. 46 Ideottes and fooles naturall. **1566** NASHE *Saffron Walden* C iv b, Fooles..(especiallie if they bee naturall fooles) are suted in long coates. **1601** SHAKS. *All's Well* IV. iii. 213 He was whipt for getting the Shrieues fool with childe, a dumbe innocent that could not say him nay. **1609** SKENE *Reg. Maj.* 37 The warde and custodie of lands and tenements perteining to naturall fuilis, be the law sould perteine to the King. **1670** LASSELS *Voy. Italy* II. 212 The Pazzorella, where they keep madmen and fooles. **1708** OCKLEY *Saracens* (Bohn 1848) 326 Towards the latter end of his days, he did really turn fool. **1824** R. CRABB *Tales* 142 He became well in his health; but he remained quite a fool for the rest of his life!

II. In combinations.

5. General combinations; **a.** simple attributive, as ***fool-cunningness***, ***-trap***, ***-work***.

a **1834** COLERIDGE *Lit. Rem.* III. 198 This conceit..was just suited to James's *fool-cunningness. **1691** DRYDEN *K. Arthur* Prol. 27 Bets at the first were *fool-traps. **1883** W. REIN *Life Luther* xxii. 178 Hoods and tonsure, eating and drinking, and similar *fool-work.

b. appositive, as ***fool-dancer***, ***-fury***, ***-gallant***.

1887 D. C. MURRAY & HERMAN *One Trav. Returns* vii. 100 A *fool-dancer, in his ochre-smeared kilt and head-dress..sprang and contorted for a reward. **1850** TENNYSON *In Mem.* cxxv, Ev'n tho' thrice again The red *fool-fury of the Seine Should pile her barricades with dead. **1714** POPE *Wife Bath* 95 Or else her wit some *fool-gallant procures.

c. objective, as ***fool-catcher***, ***-doctor***, ***-taker***; ***fool-frighting*** adj.

1594 NASHE *Vnfort. Trav.* Wks. (Grosart) V. 39 They..in fine left mee and my fellowes (their *foole-catchers) Lords of the field. *a* **1624** BRETON *Figure Foure* (Grosart) 5/2 A Foole-catcher, and a Cony-catcher. **1760** JORTIN *Erasm.* II. 170 None are greater Fools than they, who set up for *Fool-Doctors. *a* **1720** SHEFFIELD (Dk. Buckhm.) *Wks.* (1753) I. 177 Fiery meteors, and *fool-frighting ghosts. *c* **1600** NASHE (Grosart), *Foole-taker.

d. instrumental and originative, as ***fool-born***, ***-frequented***, ***-renowned*** adjs.

1597 SHAKS. *2 Hen. IV*, v. v. 59 Reply not to me, with a *Foole-borne Iest. **1780** COWPER *Table-t.* 756 The *fool-frequented fair of vanity. **1742** POPE *Dunc.* IV. 371 Mummius *Fool-renown'd.

e. similative, as ***fool-bold***, ***-fat***, ***-fine***, ***-heady***, ***-holy*** adjs.; ***fool-like***, ***fool-wisely*** advs. (Some of these imitate FOOLHARDY, and may perhaps better be referred to the adj.)

1549 LELAND *Itin.* F iij b, Some in corners hath bene *folebolde. **1613** CHAPMAN *Revenge Bussy D'Ambois* Plays 1873 II. 113 Men thither come to laugh and feede *fool-fat. **1593-4** SYLVESTER *Profit Imprisonm.* 638 Depending oft on his foole-fat-feeding word. **1603** H. CROSSE *Vertues Commw.* (1878) 64 To know the price of Sattin and Veluet, and toies to make him *fool-fine. **1611** SPEED *Hist. Gt. Brit.* VI. i. §5. 184 Begging pardon for his *foole-heady forwardnesse. **1592** GREENE *Groatsw. Wit* B iij, So *foole holy as to make scruple of conscience where profit presents itselfe. **1842** WHITEHEAD *R. Savage* (1845) II. viii. 286 *Foole-like, I forgot myself. **1605** CAMDEN *Rem.* (1637) 84 But *foole-wisely have some Peters, called themselves Pierius. **1611** W. SCLATER *Key* (1629) 111 Some of them resoluing, foole wisely, that images are to be worshipped.

6. Special comb, as **fool-bane**, poison for fools; **fool-begged** *a.*, ? foolish, idiotic (cf. BEG 5 a); **fool-duck** (*U.S.*), the ruddy duck, *Erismatura rubida*; †**fool-fangle**, a silly trifle; †**fool-finder**, *slang* (see quot.); **fool-fish** (*U.S.*) a poplar name for certain fishes (see quots.); †**fool-happy** *a.*, lucky without judgement or contrivance; **fool-hen** (*U.S.*), see quot.; **fool-plough** (see quot. 1777); †**fool-** or **fool's-rack**, 'a..pernicious spirit, in which..the stinging sea-blubber was mixed' (Yule); †**fool-taken** *a.*, 'taken in' like fools; †**fool-taking** *vbl. sb.*, a method of cozening.

1679 DRYDEN *Troilus & Cr.* Epil. 10 'Twere worth our cost to scatter *fool-bane here. **1590** SHAKS. *Com. Err.* II. i. 41 This *foole-beg'd patience in thee will be left. **1647** WARD *Simpl. Cobler* 30 Ape-headed pullets, which invent Antique *foole-fangles, meerly for fashion..sake. **1796** GROSE *Dict. Vulg. Tongue* (ed. 3), **Fool finder*, a bailiff. **1842** DE KAY *Nat. Hist. New York* IV. 335 Our fishermen apply to it [*Monocanthus broccus*] the whimsical name of *Fool-fish, in allusion to..its absurd mode of swimming. **1888** *Riverside Nat. Hist.* III. 279 The *Pleuronectes glaber*, which is called fool-fish at Salem, because they are easily decoyed. **1590** SPENSER *F.Q.* I. vi. 1 His *foolhappie over-sight. **1885** T. ROOSEVELT *Hunting Trips* iii. 90 In the early part of the season the young [grouse], and indeed their parents also, are tame and unsuspicious to the very verge of stupidity, and..are often known by the name of *'fool-hens'. **1777** BRAND *Pop. Antiq.* xiv. 175 The *Fool Plough goes about, a Pageant that consists of a Number of Sword Dancers, dragging a Plough with Music [etc.]. **1698** FRYER *Acc. E. Ind. & P.* i. 68 *Fool Rack, Brandy made of Blubber or Carvil, by the Portugals. **1608** DEKKER *Belman Lond.* H iv b, *Foole-taking..is done seuerall wayes [described at length]. *Ibid.*, *Foole-taken.

7. Comb. with genitive *fool's*: **a.** obvious combinations (sense 2), as ***fool's ba(u)ble***, ***-colours***, ***-staff***. Also in phr. †***to come home by Fool's acre***.

1603 H. CROSSE *Vertues Commw.* (1878) 63 They..come home by Need-ham crosse, and *fooles acre. **1578** LYTE *Dodoens* III. lxxix. 428 Fashioned like a *fooles bable. **1728** POPE *Dunc.* I. 84 And with her own *fools-colours gilds them all. **1692** WASHINGTON tr. *Milton's Def. Pop.* Pref. (1851) 17 You..deserve to have your Bones well-thrash'd with a *Fool's staff.

b. Special comb., as **fool's crochet** (see quot.); **fool's errand**: see ERRAND 2 c; †**fool's fire**, a will o'-the-wisp, *Ignis fatuus*; **fool's gold**, iron pyrites; **fool's haste**, foolish precipitation; **fool's-head**, a head void of sense or intelligence; also, a foolish person; (cf. *sheep's-head*); **fool's hood**, the hood worn by a fool or jester; also, a hood resembling this, worn in the seventeenth century; **fool's mate** (*Chess*): see MATE. Also FOOLSCAP, FOOL'S-COAT, FOOL'S PARADISE.

1882 CAULFEILD & SAWARD *Dict. Needlework*, **Fool's Crochet*, a name sometimes given to Tricot. **1631** WIDDOWES *Nat. Philos.* (ed. 2) 16 Fiery Dragons, darke streames, *fooles fire, and such like fiery Meteors. **1882** *Boston Jrnl. Chem.* Feb. 16/3 *'Fool's gold'. **1827** SCOTT *Jrnl.* 12 Jan., I wish it may not prove *fool's haste, yet I take as much pains too as is in my nature. **1577** BRETON *Floorish vpon Fancie, etc.* (Grosart) 24/2 In the ende..Shee makes him see a *Fooles head of his owne. **1598** SHAKS. *Merry W.* I. iii. 134. **1650** R. STAPYLTON *Strada's Low C. Warres* IV. 78 The Low-countrey Lords were not fools-heads. **1597** GERARDE *Herbal* I. xcix. 159 In shape like to a *fooles hood or cockscombe wide open. **1647** R. STAPYLTON *Juvenal* VIII. 191 When nightly, thy adulterous blood Conceales it's blushes in a French fooles-hood.

c. *esp.* in plant-names, as †**fool's ballocks**, an old name for *Orchis Morio*; **fool's cicely** = *fool's parsley*; **fool's (water) cress** (see quot. 1878); **fool's parsley**, a poisonous weed, the Lesser Hemlock (*Æthusa Cynapium*); hence, a book-name of the genus *Æthusa*; †**fool's stones**, an old name for *Orchis Morio* and *O. mascula*.

1578 LYTE *Dodoens* II. lvi. 222 This second kinde [of Orchis] is called..in English..*Fooles Balloxe. **1796** WITHERING *Brit. Plants* (ed. 3) II. 305 *Æthusa Cynapium*..*Fool's Cicely, Lesser Hemlock. **1861** MRS. LANKESTER *Wild Flowers* 31 The *Fool's-Cress, as it is called (*Sium nodiflorum*). **1878** BRITTEN & HOLLAND *Plant-n.*, Fool's Water Cress, *Helosciadium nodiflorum*..Because those who are ignorant or unobservant may mistake it for water cress. **1755** *Gentl. Mag.* XXV. 69 The lesser Hemlock, or *Fool's Parsley. **1816-20** GREEN *Univ. Herbal* I. 64 *Æthusa Fatua*, Fine-leaved Fool's Parsley. **1597** GERARDE *Herbal* I. xcix. §5. 159 The male *Foole stones hath fiue..long, broad and smooth leaues. *Ibid.* The female Fooles stones hath also smooth narrow leaues.

B. *adj.* Foolish, silly. Now *colloq.* (freq. in *U.S.*).

By the late 19th cent. this use was obs. in the U.K., exc. *Sc.* and *dial.* and *vulgar* (the vulgar use being prob. a new formation from the sb.).

a **1225** *Ancr. R.* 54 þe holi Gost lette writen one boc uor to warnie wummen of hore fol eien. *a* **1240** *Ureisun* in *Cott. Hom.* 200 Me nis he fol chepmon, ðet buð deore a woc þing? **1297** R. GLOUC. (1724) 568 þis lokinge was riȝt fol in such destresse iwis. *c* **1314** *Guy Warw.* (A.) 380. 10 Ich wene þou art a fole musard! *c* **1400** *Destr. Troy* 13841 Hit fell hym by fortune of a foole end. *c* **1450** *Mirour Saluacioun* 271 The wise virgines yᵗ oele vnto the fole maydens denyed. **1481** CAXTON *Tulle of Old Age*, Olde age is grevous..to the fole old man. **1541** R. COPLAND *Galyen's Terap.* 2 Dj, O foole and imprudent Thessalus. **1580** R. HARVEY *Pl. Perc.* (1590) 22 Let the wisest be the forwardest, and the most foole the frowardest. **1681** COLVIL *Whigs Supplic.* (1751) 130 Fighting is a fool thing. *a* **1776** *Song* in Herd's *Collect.* II. 192 The fool-thing is oblig'd to fast Or eat what they've refus'd. **1805** L. DOW *Jrnl.* (1806) II. 1. 76, I showed the contrast of a gentleman and a fool deist. **1815** SCOTT *Guy M.* xxxix, 'They couldna hae sell'd the auld inheritance for that fool-body's debts.' **1823** GALT *Entail* II. iii. 22 A fool posture..and no very commodious at this time. **1854** M. J. HOLMES *Tempest & Sunshine* ii. 25 Tempest..can hardly wait till I'm dead before she spends my money on fool fixins. **1862** S. HALE *Lett.* (1919) 13 Everybody talking such fool nonsense as sometimes almost to prevent digestion. **1896** M. CORELLI *Mighty Atom* xvi. 335 My fool tears a-flowin' on her coffin. **1902** W. N. HARBEN *Abner Daniel* 2 Oh, Alan, don't you see he's goin' to ruin us with his fool notions? **1912** R. A. WASON *Friar Tuck* xxiii. 165 It was the foolest lookin' group I was ever part of. **1924** W. M. RAINE *Troubled Waters* xxiii. 245 You've heard that fool story about Norma and Mac. **1932** E. WILSON *Devil take the Hindmost* ix. 104 The local banks have failed through the speculations of some fool gambler. **1951** 'J. WYNDHAM' *Day of Triffids* iv. 85 You never can tell what fool carelessness may go on.

fool (fu:l), *sb.*[2] [prob. a use of prec., suggested by the synonym *trifle*, mentioned in quot. 1598. (So Skeat in *Phil. Soc. Trans.* 1885-7).

Mahn's derivation from F. *fouler* to crush, is not only baseless, but inconsistent with the early use of the word.]

†**1.** (See quots.). *Obs.*

1598 FLORIO, *Mantiglia*, a kinde of clouted creame called a foole or a trifle in English. *c* **1600** DAY *Begg. Bednall Gr.* v. (Bullen) 114 My Mother..could have taught thee how to a made..fritters, pancakes, I and the rarest fools. **1637** B. JONSON *Sad Sheph.* I. vi, Your cheese-cakes, curdes, and clowted creame, Your fooles, your flaunes. **1688** R. HOLME *Armoury* III. iii. 82 Foole is a kind of Custard, but more crudelly; being made of Cream, Yolks of Eggs, Cinamon, Mace boiled: and served on Sippets with sliced Dates, Sugar, and white and red Comfits, strawed thereon.

2. A dish composed of fruit stewed, crushed, and mixed with milk, cream, or custard. Often ***gooseberry fool***.

1747 MRS. GLASSE *Art of Cookery* ix. 79 A Gooseberry-Fool. *a* **1845** HOOD *Hymen Retrospect.* I. ii, Just like gooseberries boil'd for a fool!

fool (fu:l), *v.* Forms: see the sb. [f. FOOL *a.* or *sb.*[1] Cf. OF. *folier*, *foleiier*: see FOLEYE.]

†**1.** *intr.* To be or become foolish or insane.

13.. *E.E. Allit. P.* B. 1422 So faste þay weȝed to hym wyne, wel neȝe he foles. **1489** *Barbour's Bruce* (Edin. MS.) IV. 222 Bot he fulyt [*the better text has* was fule], forowtyn weir That gaiff throuth till that creatur.

2. To act like a fool.

a. To act as a foolish or weak-minded person; to play the fool, trifle, idle. Also ***to fool about***, or ***on***, and ***to fool it***. †***to fool into***: to be brought *into* by one's folly. ***to fool along*** (*U.S.*): to proceed slowly or aimlessly; also *fig.* ***to fool (a)round*** (*U.S.*): to 'hang about' aimlessly. ***to fool with***: to play or meddle with foolishly; also in indirect passive.

1593 SHAKS. *Rich. II*, v. v. 60 While I stand fooling heere. **1608** —— *Cor.* II. iii. 128 Rather then foole it so, Let the high Office and the Honor go. *a* **1621** BEAUM. & FL. *Cust. Country* v. v, Must I needs fool into mine own destruction? **1676** WYCHERLEY *Pl. Dealer* IV. i, My heart is too much in earnest to be fooled with. **1685** J. SCOTT *Chr. Life* II. 134 [He] So fools and fleers on till he hath toyed and laughed himself out of all sense of Religion. **1754** RICHARDSON *Grandison* IV. xxxiii. 228 How you..fooled on with us, before you came to confession! **1810** *Sporting Mag.* XXXVI. 269, I do not think this man was taken to the watch-house because he was fooling. **1826** SCOTT *Woodst.* v, Zoons, Mark Everard, I can fool it no longer. **1837** A. GREENE *Glance at New York* (Farmer), He mustn't come foolin' round my gal, or I'll give him fits. **1861** HUGHES *Tom Brown at Oxf.* xii. (1889) 112 You and I, perhaps, go fooling about with him, and get rusticated. **1866** C. H. SMITH *Bill Arp* 44 You get a government contract for a few thousand pounds and you fool along with it, selling what you make to these drug men at a bigger price. **1870** *Galaxy* May 726/2 What did Abel come fooling around there for? **1884** *Manch. Exam.* 28 June 4/6 The accused..began fooling with a loaded gun. **1884** 'MARK TWAIN' *Huck. Finn* xxxiii. 338 You turn back and fool along slow, so as to get to the house about the time you ought to. **1885** *Century Mag.* XXIX. 545/1 They [the pursuers] seemed to stop and fool around awhile. **1934** H. VINES *This Green Thicket World* 20 They fooled along and did not much try to reach the ferry-man's house.

†**b.** To act as a fool or jester; to play the buffoon. Also with *up*. *Obs.*

1617 FLETCHER *Mad Lover* v. iv, Foole up, sirra, You may chance get a dinner. **1633** FLETCHER & SHIRLEY *Night Walker* v. iii, I'le foole vp and provoke ye [to be merry]. **1641** DENHAM *Sophy* IV. (1667) 50 If you have the luck to be Court-fools, those that have Either wit or honesty, you may fool withal, and spare not.

c. quasi-*trans.* with compl. phrase.

1601 SHAKS. *Twel. N.* v. i. 44 You can foole no more money out of mee at this throw.

3. a. *trans.* To make a fool of; to impose upon, dupe, trifle with. Also, to balk, frustrate.

1596 SHAKS. *1 Hen IV*, I. iii. 178 That you are fool'd, discarded, and shook off By him, for whom these shames ye underwent. **1606** —— *Ant. & Cl.* v. ii. 225 Why that's the way to foole their preparation. **1663** COWLEY *Occas. Verses, Ode on Ld. Broghill's Verses* 2 Be gon..Ingrateful Muse, and see What others thou can'st fool as well as me. **1706** ESTCOURT *Fair Examp.* IV. i, This Gentleman..that has fool'd your Faith, wou'd betray your Honour. **1784** BURNS *Epit. Henpeckd Sq.*, As father Adam first was fool'd. **1818** BYRON *Ch. Har.* IV. clviii, This Outshining and o'erwhelming edifice Fools our fond gaze. **1867** TROLLOPE *Chron. Barset* xxxviii, [He] ought not to have been fooled by such a woman.

b. To cheat *of* or delude *out of* (something); to entice, lure *into* or *to*; to put or fob *off* by trickery.

1650 TRAPP *Comm.* Gen. xxi. 1 He fools them not off with fair promises. **1663** J. SPENCER *Vulg. Prophecies* (1665) 28 An impatience of the ignorance of things to come, fooled the Jews..out of their Reason. **1664** H. MORE *Myst. Iniq.* 456 But so manifest Eviction..will not be fooled off for ever. **1678** MARVELL *Growth Popery* 28 The Additional Excise..which the Tripple League had fooled them into. *c* **1680** J. HAINES *Epil.* in *Collect. Poems* 34 They all fool Cit of his Wife. *a* **1716** SOUTH *Serm.* (1737) IV. iv. 140 Such as come to be thus happily frighted into their wits, are not so easily fooled out of them again. **1833** H. BLUNT *Lect. Hist. St. Paul* II. 200 It fools you into the belief that [etc.]. **1841-4** EMERSON *Ess.*, *Politics* Wks. (Bohn) I. 237 Nature..will not be fooled or abated of any jot of her authority. **1863** MRS. C. CLARKE *Shaks. Char.* vi. 144 The English have never yet been fooled to their ruin.

†**4.** To make foolish; to infatuate. *Obs.*

1605 SHAKS. *Lear* II. iv. 278 Foole me not so much To beare it tamely; touch me with noble anger. **1641** DENHAM *Sophy* III. (1667) 43 He's so fool'd with down-right honesty, He'l ne're believe it.

5. ***to fool away***, †***out*** (also simply): to throw away or part with foolishly; to spend (money, time) foolishly.

1548 *Detect. Unskilf. Physic.* in Recorde *Urin. Physick* (1651) 4, I scarce beleeve any wise man would fool out a groat on your judgment. **1628** WITHER *Brit. Rememb.* III. 406 Foole thy life away By tempting Heav'n. **1641** SIR E. DERING *Sp. on Relig.* 22 Nov. xv. (1642) 69 Let no Ammonite perswade the Gileadite to foole out his right eye. **1660** PEPYS *Diary* 1 June, Where I..fooled away all the afternoon. **1711** SWIFT *Jrnl. to Stella* 9 July, I have fooled away too much money that way already. **1728** YOUNG *Love*

Fame II. (1757) 91 What crime In such a paradise to fool their time? *a* **1761** LAW *Behmen's Myst. Magnum* lvi. (1765) 329 We see here how Adam has fooled away, and lost the Blessing. **1863** MRS. C. CLARKE *Shaks. Char.* xx. 507 He fools away his time, his money, and his health.

Hence **fooled** *ppl. a.*

1715 tr. *C'tess D'Aunoy's Wks.* 391 This impious Grognon, by the fool'd Support Of a fond Prince, made Cruelty her Sport. **1742** YOUNG *Nt. Th.* v. 35 The fool'd mind.

† **foolage,** *a.* and *sb. Obs.* Also 6 *Sc.* **fulage, -ege.** [a. OF. *folage* adj. and sb. (repr. popular L. types **follāticus, -um*), f. *fol* FOOL. The 17th c. sb. may be a new formation on FOOL + -AGE.]

A. *adj. Sc.* Foolish. Hence **foolageness.**

1560 ROLLAND *Crt. Venus* II. 70 ʒe haif preuit fulage For to offend that Souerane. **1563** WINȜET *Four Scoir Thre Quest.* To Rdr., Wks. 1888 I. 55 Sik proud fulege phantaseis. *Ibid.* 62 *Insipientia eorum*..that is, the fulegenes of thame.

B. *sb.* Foolish condition.

1676 *Cal. St. Papers, Amer. & W. Ind.* (1893) No. 937. 398 [Old Governor Berkeley altered, by marrying a young wife, from his wonted public good to a] covetous foolage.

† **foolane, foo'larum, foo'latum.** *humorous. Obs.* [arbitrarily f. FOOL.] = FOOL.

1684 J. LACY *Sir H. Buffoon* II. v. Dram. Wks. (1875) 248 [Said to a servant] Prethee, good Foolane, tell Alderman Buffoon that he may come in. **1741** RICHARDSON *Pamela* I. xix. 47 And what..have I said to her, Foolatum; but that she was pretty? **1799** S. J. PRATT *Tri. Benevolence* II. 267 What's the foolarum at now?

† **foo'lation.** *Obs.* [f. FOOL *v.* + -ATION.] The action of fooling; also *concr.* a foolish thing.

1628 SIR J. BINGLEY in Miss Hickson *Irel. 17th C.* (1884) I. Introd. 89 Altars adorned with images and other foolations. **1638** [see -ATION].

fooldom ('fuːldəm). [f. FOOL *sb.*[1] + -DOM.] The realm of fools; fools collectively.

1886 RUSKIN *Præterita* I. vi. 191 A sort of triumphant shriek..has gone up from the Fooldom of Europe.

fool(e, obs. form of FOAL.

fooler ('fuːlə(r)). [f. FOOL *v.* 3 + -ER[1].] A person or thing that 'fools' one.

1909 R. A. WASON *Happy Hawkins* 316 They finally located a mine that looked good-natured an' generous; but it was a fooler.

foolery ('fuːlərɪ). Also 7 **follery.** [f. FOOL *sb.*[1] + -ERY.]

1. The habit or practice of fooling or acting foolishly.

1579 SPENSER *Sheph. Cal.* Feb. 211 But sike fansies weren foolerie. **1604** PARSONS *3rd Pt. Three Convers. Eng.* 271 Whether Fox may not beare away the bell for follery. **1694** WOOD *Life* 23 June (Oxf. Hist. Soc.), An implacable enmity to immorality and foolery. **1725** WATTS *Logic* IV. ii. Rule 3 It is mere foolery to multiply distinct particulars in treating of things. **1813** *Sporting Mag.* XLI. 227 The oddities and simple foolery of this man. **1858** DORAN *Crt. Fools* 38 An immoderate amount of foolery.

2. A piece of fooling; a foolish or ridiculous action, performance, or thing.

1552 LATIMER *Serm.* Eph. vi. in *Fruitf. Serm.* (1584) 198 It is not that [ringing of belles] that will serue against y[e] deuill: yet we haue beleued such fooleries in tymes past. **1589** WARNER *Alb. Eng.* VI. xxxi. (1612) 156 With.. Fooleries more than few I courted her. **1657** *North's Plutarch* Add. Lives (1676) 80 When they have turmoil'd themselves about such fooleries [Horoscopes] a long time, they gain nothing thereby. **1662** EVELYN *Diary* 1 Jan., I went to London, invited to the solemn foolerie of the Prince de la Grange at Lincoln's Inn. **1772** *Town & C. Mag.* 125 The pleasing levities, and agreable fooleries of a girl. **1830** *Athenæum* 16 Oct., Sèvres china, buhl cabinets, Indian fans, and other fooleries. **1859** TENNYSON *Vivien* 263 Your pretty tricks and fooleries.

3. Fools as a class. *nonce-use.*

1843 SYDNEY SMITH *Let.* 19 Aug. in *Mem.* (1855) II. 494 He knows how to disguise liberal ideas, and to make them less terrible to the Foolery of a country.

'**fooless.** *jocular.* A female fool.

1852 SMEDLEY *L. Arundel* xxxvi, When the mind of a fool (or fool-*ess*, as the case may be) exalts it to an undue pre-eminence. **1884** G. P. HAWLEY *Wit, etc., Richter* 155 The fools and foolesses of the subsequent centuries.

† **foolhardice.** *Obs.* Forms: 5 **fool hardiesse,** 6 **fool(e)hardise, -ize,** 7 **foole-hardice.** [In 15th c. *folehardiesse*, f. FOOLHARDY, after HARDIESSE; subsequently assimilated in form to COWARDICE.] = FOOLHARDINESS.

1475 *Bk. Noblesse* (1860) 63 Whiche by theire fole-hardiesse..causid the patrimonie of Lelius and Scipion to be lost. **1591** SPENSER *Ruins Rome* xiv, With vaine fool-hardise Daring the foe. **1600** FAIRFAX *Tasso* V. xxiii. 79 Foole-hardice, rashnes, madnes.

†,**fool'hardiment.** *Obs.* [OF. *fol hardiement* foolish daring.] = FOOLHARDINESS.

[*Le Manuel des Pechiez* 1336 in R. Brunne *Handl. Synne* (1862) 23 Home qe par fol hardiement Iure par deu horriblement.] **1375** BARBOUR *Bruce* VI. 337 Vorschip Extremyteis has twa; Fule-hardyment the formast is, And the tothir is cowardiss. *c* **1430** *Pilgr. Lyf Manhode* I. xxvi. (1869) 17 Michel is he of foolhardiment. **1533** BELLENDEN *Livy* II. (1822) 204 The consul reprochit thaim..of thair ful hardiment.

'**fool,hardiness.** [f. FOOLHARDY + -NESS.] The quality of being foolhardy.

a **1340** HAMPOLE *Psalter* xxiv. 7 My iolifte & fole-hardynes. **1401** *Pol. Poems* (Rolls) II. 55 By woodnesse and foolhardinesse for heresie to dien. **1535** STEWART *Cron. Scot.* II. 440 Full hardines..Cumis alway of ill considderance. *a* **1677** BARROW *Wks.* (1686) III. xxxiv. 377 The fear of men..doth involve the wildest boldness, and most rash fool-hardiness in the world. **1874** MORLEY *Compromise* (1886) 229 To be willing to make such changes too frequently..is foolhardiness.

foolhardy ('fuːl,hɑːdɪ), *a.* [a. OF. *fol hardi*, comb. of *fol* foolish, FOOL *a.* with *hardi* bold, HARDY *a.*] Daring without judgement, foolishly adventurous or bold, rashly venturesome.

a **1225** *Ancr. R.* 62 Nis heo to muche cang, oðer to fol-herdi. **1303** R. BRUNNE *Handl. Synne* 667 Þou were euer so fole hardy. **1413** *Pilgr. Sowle* (Caxton 1483) IV. xxx. 78 How dar ther ony man ben so fole hardy for to dampnen hym seluen. **1508** FISHER *7 Penit. Ps.* Wks. 104 Theyr fole-hardy Iugement. **1596** DALRYMPLE tr. *Leslie's Hist. Scot.* II. 153 A rasche, ferce, and fulehardie ȝoung man. *a* **1680** BUTLER *Rem.* (1759) II. 302 He runs on boldly like a foolhardy Wit. **1796** NELSON in Nicolas *Disp.* (1845) II. 244 If they really are so fool-hardy as to go to war to please the French. **1860** HOLLAND *Miss Gilbert* xxiv. 418 Do not be guilty of this foolhardy business again.

Hence '**fool,hardily** *adv.* Also '**fool,hardihood,** † **foolhardiship** = FOOLHARDINESS.

a **1225** *Ancr. R.* 182 Vor moni makeð hire sec þuruh hire fol herdischipe. **1382** WYCLIF *2 Sam.* xviii. 13 If I hadde doon aȝens my soul foolhardili. **1609** HOLLAND *Amm. Marcell.* XIX. iv. 127 Who..used foole-hardily to sallie forth and fight most courageously. **1837** SOUTHEY in *Q. Rev.* LIX. 306 Two brothers had the foolhardihood to wait till midnight in the church-porch. **1879** G. MACDONALD *Sir Gibbie* xix. 102, I would not foolhardily add to my many risks of blundering.

† **fool-haste.** *Obs.* [a. OF. *fole haste*, f. *fole* fem. of *fol* FOOL *a.* + *haste* HASTE.] Foolish precipitation, unseemly or reckless haste.

1393 GOWER *Conf.* I. 316 Contek..Foolhast hath to his chamberlain. **1597** MONTGOMERIE *Cherrie & Slae* 417 Fuil-haist ay almaist ay Ouirsylis the sicht of sum.

† **fool-hasty,** *a. Obs.* Forms: 4 **foolhastif,** 7 **foolhastie** [a. OF. *fol hastif*, comb. of *fol* FOOL *a.* and *hastif* HASTY; cf. prec. and FOOLHARDY.] Foolishly hasty, precipitate.

1393 GOWER *Conf.* I. 334 The man whiche is malicious And foolhastif, full ofte he falleth. **1600** HOLLAND *Livy* XXII. xli. 458 The audaciousnesse of the foolhastie Consull.

Hence † **fool-hastiness.**

13.. *Minor Poems fr. Vernon MS.* xxxii. 617 Fool-hastines. **1393** GOWER *Conf.* III. 99 Fool hastifnesse.

† '**foolhead.** *Obs. rare.* In 4 **folehede, foulhed.** [f. FOOL *sb.*[1] + -HEAD.] Folly.

a **1340** HAMPOLE *Psalter* xlviii. 21 He rehercys þe foulhed [foly] of man. *c* **1340** *Cursor M.* 3116 (Fairf.) Fole hede ys giuen al men to pay.

† **fooli'aminy.** *Obs.* [burlesque formation on FOOL *sb.*[1]; cf. F. *brouillamini.*] A fool; fools collectively.

1607 MIDDLETON *Trick to Catch* I. iv. Wks. (Bullen) II. 266 My clients come about me, the fooliaminy and coxcombry of the country. *Ibid.* IV. v. 339 Now, good man fooliaminy, what say you to me now? **1622** MASSINGER *Virg. Mart.* III. iii, Worse; all tottering, all out of frame, thou fooliamini!

† '**foolify,** *v. Obs.* [f. FOOL *sb.*[1] + -(I)FY.] *trans.* To make a fool of, render foolish.

1581 M. HANMER *Jesuites Banner* A iij b, They are foolified in themselues. *a* **1641** BP. MOUNTAGU *Acts & Mon.* (1642) 80 God in Justice doth so foolifie their malice, that [etc.].

Hence '**foolified** *ppl. a.*; '**foolifying** *vbl. sb.*, the action of the vb.

1585 T. WASHINGTON tr. *Nicholay's Voy.* Ep. Ded. ¶ iij b, Talking fondly of a thing wherein I have no practise, as somtimes did foolified Phormio. **1618** BRETON *Court & Country* (Grosart) 8/2 Is not the Clownifying of wit the Foolifying of vnderstanding? **1632** VICARS tr. *Æneid* XI. 972 Circling, with policie, Her foolified foe.

fooling ('fuːlɪŋ), *vbl. sb.* [f. FOOL *v.* + -ING[1].] The action of the vb., in various senses.

1609 DEKKER *Gulls Horne-bk.* Proem, Wks. (Grosart) II. 205 The excellency of his fooling. **1681** COLVIL *Whigs Supplic.* (1695) 99 Knipper-dolings, Who troubled Munster with their foolings. **1746** WESLEY *Princ. Methodist* 46, I am glad you give this fooling up. **1891** BARING-GOULD *In Troubadour Land* ix. 125 It is quite possible that this was all solemn fooling.

b. Preceded by an adj. = Condition or humour for fooling.

1601 SHAKS. *Twel. N.* I. v. 36 Put me into good fooling. *Ibid.* II. iii. 23 and 86. **1827** SCOTT *Jrnl.* 3 Apr., I was in good fooling. **1830** *Ibid.* 21 June, Sir Adam was in high fooling, and we had an amazing deal of laughing.

foolish ('fuːlɪʃ), *a.* Forms: 4 **foles, foolis,** 4–7 **folisch, -is(s)he, -ys(s)h(e,** (5 **foolich, foulishe, -ysse),** 5–6 **fulich, -ische,** 6– **foolish.** [f. FOOL *sb.*[1] + -ISH.]

1. Fool-like, wanting in sense or judgement.

a **1300** *Cursor M.* 14802 (Cott.) Þe folk es foles, þat es wel sene. **1382** WYCLIF *Ecclus.* xv. 7 Men foolis shul not take it. *c* **1449** PECOCK *Repr.* II. iii. 151 Thou woldist seie y were.. vnwijs and folisch. **1561** T. NORTON *Calvin's Inst.* III. 201 The fooli-hest sorte amonge the lawyers. **1692** LOCKE *Educ.* §94 Wks. 1727 III. 38 Think no man..wiser or foolisher, than he really is. **1838** DICKENS *Nich. Nick.* iv, Women are so very foolish, Mr. Squeers. **1866** GEO. ELIOT *F. Holt* (1868) 19, I was foolish to expect anything else.

absol. *c* **1430** *Pilgr. Lyf Manhode* II. xc. (1869) 108 The maymed, the foolich, the founded, the froren. **1526** TINDALE *Luke* x. 21 Thou hast hyd these thynges from the wyse..and opened them to the folisshe. **1741** RICHARDSON *Pamela* I. 163 Well, well, Lambkin (which the Foolish often calls me).

2. Befitting a fool; proceeding from, or indicative of folly.

c **1374** CHAUCER *Troylus* I. 793 Thyn ire and folish wilfulnesse. *c* **1489** CAXTON *Blanchardyn* xliii. 170 The rewarde of his folyshe loue. **1526** *Pilgr. Perf.* (W. de W. 1531) 7 b, Here perauenture the carnall and beestly man wyll moue a folysshe questyon. **1628** EARLE *Microcosm., Plausible Man* (Arb.) 60 He can listen to a foolish discourse with an applausive attention. **1651** HOBBES *Leviath.* III. xxxii. 196 Selfe-conceit, and foolish arrogance. **1735** POPE *Prol. Sat.* 212 Where Wits..wonder with a foolish face of praise. **1784** COWPER *Tiroc.* 255 To follow foolish precedents..is easier than to think. **1828** SCOTT *F.M. Perth* v, Her foolish notions of a convent. **1859** TENNYSON *Enid* 433 Nor speak I now from foolish flattery.

3. Ridiculous, †amusing.

1514 BARCLAY *Cyt. & Uplondyshm.* (Percy Soc.) 21 Nought is more folysshe than suche wretches be. **1691** SOUTHERNE *Sir A. Love* IV. Wks. (1721) 222 'Twill be foolish enough to observe him, when he discovers me; pray stay and laugh with me. **1717** PRIOR *Alma* I. 115 A foolish figure He must make.

4. Humble, insignificant, paltry, poor, mean, trifling. *arch.* or *dial.*

1592 SHAKS. *Rom. & Jul.* I. v. 124 We haue a trifling foolish Banquet towards. **1596** —— *Merch. V.* I. ii. 130 Hee of all the men that euer my foolish eyes look'd vpon, was the best deseruing a faire Lady. **1597** GERARDE *Herbal* II. xxxii. §9. 235 Stalkes; whereupon do grow foolish idle flowers. **1625** JACKSON *Creed* V. iv. §5 Base Licinus hath a pompous Tombe..Wise Cato but a foolish one. **1833** CARLYLE *Misc.* (1857) III. 218 Owes favour..to the foolishest accident. **1862** MRS. BROWNING *Last Poems, Parting Lovers* ii. 5 Thou hast not seen a hand push through A foolish flower or two. **1890** BOLDREWOOD *Colonial Reformer* (1891) 420 A hundred miles is..no foolish ride.

5. *Comb.*, as ***foolish-bold, -compounded, -looking, -wise, -witty.*** Also, † **foolish fire,** *Ignis fatuus*; **foolish guillemot,** an aquatic bird, *Lomvia troile.*

1613 T. MILLES *Treas. Anc. & Mod. Times* VIII. xii. 769/2 Phlegyas became (in the end) so ouer-weening and *foolish-bold that [etc.] **1597** SHAKS. *2 Hen. IV.* I. ii. 8 The braine of this *foolish compounded Clay-man. **1605** VERSTEGAN *Rest. Dec. Intell.* 217 *Dwas-licht.* That which wee other-wise call the *Foolish-Fyre. **1867** SMYTH *Sailor's Word-bk.*, **Foolish Guillemot*, the web-footed diving-bird *Uria troile*, common on our coasts. **1851** MAYNE REID *Scalp Hunt.* vii, Gaudy and *foolish-looking uniforms. **1590** GREENE *Orl. Fur.* (1594) D i b, The heauen of loue is but a pleasant hell, Where none but *foolish wise imprisned dwell. **1592** SHAKS. *Ven. & Ad.* 838 How loue is wise in follie, *foolish wittie.

† **foolish-hardy,** *a. Obs.* = FOOLHARDY.

1533 FRITH *Answ. to More* L vij b, I can not be so folishe hardy as to condempne suche an infinite nombre for oure prelates pleasures. *a* **1632** T. TAYLOR *God's Judgem.* I. I. vii. (1642) 15 So..foolish hardy as to take up armour.

absol. **1561** DAUS tr. *Bullinger on Apoc.* (1573) 15 The Lord Christ..restreyneth the foolishhardy.

Hence † '**foolish-'hardiness,** foolhardiness.

1525 LD. BERNERS *Froiss.* II. ccxvii. (1812) 670 Their valyauntnesse turneth to folyssh hardynes. **1578** RICH *Allarme to Eng.* I i b (marg.), Not valiaunce, but foolish hardinesse.

foolishly ('fuːlɪʃlɪ), *adv.* [f. as prec. + -LY[2].] In a foolish manner.

c **1489** CAXTON *Sonnes of Aymon* ix. 243 'Alas', sayd Reynawde, 'ye speke folysly'. **1561** WINȜET *Exhortation Marie Q. Scottis* Wks. 1888 I. 21 Quha fuleschlie assentit to thair prydefull arrogance. **1609** SKENE *Reg. Maj.* 83 Gif ane Burges wife..answeres fulishlie in Court. **1711** ADDISON *Spect.* No. 98 ¶ 5 We..foolishly contrive to call off the Eye from great and real Beauties, to childish Gewgaws. **1795** BURKE *Corr.* IV. 327 The Catholics have foolishly.. disarmed themselves. **1874** MORLEY *Compromise* (1886) 148 Opinions..foolishly and unreasonably associated with pain.

foolishment ('fuːlɪʃmənt). [f. FOOLISH *a.* + -MENT] = FOOLISHNESS.

1918 *N.Y. Evening World* 4 Jan. 18/1 (*title of verse*) Foolishment. **1928** M. CHAPMAN *Happy Mountain* (1929) xxviii. 306 Don't you pay heed to Dena's foolishment. **1966** *Sunday Mail* (Brisbane) 18 Dec. 29/3 There's nothing nicer than a good foolishment.

foolishness ('fuːlɪʃnɪs). [f. as FOOLISHLY *adv.* + -NESS.]

1. The quality or condition of being foolish.

c **1470** HENRY *Wallace* V. 631 Quhat is this luff? no thing bot folychnes. **1611** BIBLE *Ps.* xxxviii. 5 My wounds stinke ..because of my foolishnesse. **1628** WITHER *Brit. Rememb.* VI. 442 Converts their wisedome into foolishnesse. **1718** PRIOR *Solomon* II. 900, I..shape my Foolishness to their Desire. **1858** DORAN *Crt. Fools* 95 Listening to the pretended foolishness of a jester.

2. A foolish practice, act, or thing; an absurdity.

1535 COVERDALE *Wisd.* xix. 3 They deuysed another folishnes. **1553** UDALL *Flowers Latine* (1560) 88 b, It is a foolishnesse to suffer that ill to bee dooen, that a man maye auoyde. **1843** J. B. ROBERTSON tr. *Moehler's Symbolism* I. 40 Those opinions, which make the doctrine of the fall a foolishness.

† **fool-large,** *a.* and *sb. Obs.* Forms: 3 **fol-large,** 4–5 **fole-, foollarge,** 6–7 **foole-large.** [a. OF.

follarge, f. *fol* FOOL *a.* + *large* liberal, munificent, prodigal: see LARGE *a.* Cf. FOOLHARDY.]

A. *adj.* Foolishly liberal, prodigal, wasteful.

1297 R. GLOUC. (1724) 389 In spenynge he was fol large. *c* **1386** CHAUCER *Pars. T.* ¶740 Certes he that is fool large, ne yeueth nat his catel but he leseth his catel. **1474** CAXTON *Chesse* III. viii, Fole large and waystours of theyr goodes. **1603** H. CROSSE *Vertues Commw.* (1878) 69 Foole-large in distributing his goods, to waste his patrimonie.

B. *sb.* **1.** A prodigal, spendthrift.

a **1420** HOCCLEVE *De Reg. Princ.* 4628 And syn fool large on gold settiþ his herte No more þan þe liberal.

2. = FOOL-LARGESSE.

1474 CAXTON *Chesse* III. viii. (1860) I iij, And ye shall vnderstonde that fole large is a ryght euyl vyce.

†ˌ**fool-ˈlargess.** *Obs.* Forms: 4 fool-largesse, 4–5 foly-larges(se, 5 folargesse. [f. prec. after LARGESSE.] Foolish lavishness, prodigality.

c **1386** CHAUCER *Pars. T.* ¶740. 813 Men oughten eschue fool-largesse, that men clepen wast. **1422** tr. *Secreta Secret., Priv. Priv.* (E.E.T.S.) 134 The exspensis of folargesse. **1525** LD. BERNERS *Froiss.* II. xxvi. 72 He neuer loued folly, outrage, nor foly-larges.

†ˈ**foolmonger.** *Obs.* [f. FOOL *sb.*[1] + -MONGER.] One who 'trades on' the credulity of fools.

1592 G. HARVEY *Pierce's Super.* Wks. (Grosart) II. 91 An ..arrant foolemunger. **1681** OTWAY *Soldier's Fort.* I. Wks. (1735) 12 Of all the rogues I would not be a foolmonger.

foolocracy (fuːˈlɒkrəsɪ). *humorous.* [f. FOOL *sb.*[1] + -(O)CRACY.] **a.** Government by fools. **b.** A governing class or clique consisting of fools.

1832 SYD. SMITH *Let.* 21 Nov. in *Mem.* (1855) II. 341 The foolocracy under which it has so long laboured. **1861** GEN. P. THOMPSON *Audi Alt.* III. cxliv. 127 The management of affairs has been..given up to, what may for conciseness be called a 'foolocracy'.

foolometer (fuːˈlɒmɪtə(r)). *humorous.* [f. as prec. + -(O)METER.] That which serves as a standard for the measurement of fools or of folly.

1837 SYD. SMITH *2nd. Let. Singleton* Wks. 1859 II. 285/1, I am astonished that these Ministers neglect the common precaution of a foolometer..I mean, the acquaintance and society of three or four regular British fools as a test of public opinion. **1851** *Fraser's Mag.* XLIII. 633 The weakest intellect was the foolometer by which all brains were to be tried at lessons.

foolosopher (fuːˈlɒsəfə(r)). *humorous.* Also 6 foolelosopher, 7 fooleosopher. [perversion of PHILOSOPHER, after FOOL *sb.*[1], imitating Gr. μωρόσοφος used by Erasmus.] A foolish pretender to philosophy.

1549 CHALONER *Erasm. Moriæ Enc.* A iij, Suche men.. that in deede are archdoltes, and woulde be taken yet for sages and philosophers, maie I not aptely calle theim foolelosophers. *c* **1600** *Timon* V. v. (1842) 94 What, stand yee idle, my fooleosophers [*printed* foolc-]? **1694** ECHARD *Plautus* 197 A fine foolosopher!

So fooˈlosophy, foolish pretence of philosophy.

1592 GREENE *Def. Conny Catch.* To Rdr. Wks. (Grosart) XI. 43 That quaint and mysticall forme of Foolosophie. **1617** S. COLLINS *Def. Bp. Ely* II. vi. §23. 241 Fine phoolosophyes.

fool-proof (ˈfuːlpruːf), *a.* orig. *U.S.* [f. FOOL *sb.*[1] + PROOF *a.* 1 b.] Proof against even the incompetence of a fool; simple and straightforward so as to respond even to the most inexperienced or careless handling; safeguarded against every sort of accident.

1902 A. C. HARMSWORTH et al. *Motors* 309 The car..is comparatively 'fool-proof'. **1904** *Westm. Gaz.* 24 Oct. 2/2 The car is so 'simple' that my daughters drive it—'fool-proof' the Americans call it. **1926** W. R. INGE *Lay Thoughts* 220 Everywhere we find the same demand to make life easy, safe, and fool-proof. **1928** GALSWORTHY *Swan Song* III. ii. 231 A base of operations with a fool-proof title was essential. **1960** *Farmer & Stockbreeder* 19 Jan. (Suppl.) 37/2 It should be as foolproof and as easy to manage as possible, even to the most amateur poultry keeper. **1968** *Times* 24 Oct. 7/7 The cost of making nuclear reactors absolutely foolproof would outweigh their economic advantages.

†**fool sage.** *Obs.* [a. OF. **fol sage* (= *saige fol*, Palsgr.), lit. 'wise fool'.] A fool or jester.

1377 LANGL. *P. Pl.* B. XIII. 423 ȝe lordes..þat fedeth foles sages [**1393** C. VIII. 83 fool sages], flatereres and lyeres. *c* **1400** *Ipomedon* (Kölbing) 351 He..made him a fole sage.

ˈfool's-cap, ˈfoolscap.

1. A cap of fantastic shape, usually garnished with bells, formerly worn by fools or jesters.

1632 MASSINGER *City Madam* IV. iv, A French hood too.. A fool's cap would show better. **1680** R. MANSEL *Narr. Popish Plot* Addr. C ij, Some or other will take the Fools-cap off from their heads, and put it upon ours. **1789** WOLCOTT (P. Pindar) *Ode* xiv. Wks. 1812 II. 247 The Muse shall place a Fool's-cap on their sculls. **1839** LONGF. *Beware* v, It is a fool's-cap for thee to wear.

b. A dunce's cap.

1831 *Blackw. Mag.* Feb. 409 Mr. Sadler crowns our prodigy on the spot..with a paper fool's cap. **1876** GRANT *Burgh. Sch. Scotl.* II. v. 207 Smart castigation is, in our opinion, much preferable to fool's cap, imprisonment [etc.].

Comb. **1831** *Blackw. Mag.* Feb. 410/1 Our fool's-cap-crowned Reviewer. **1823** BYRON *Juan* XI. lxxxii, A huge, dun cupola, like a foolscap crown On a fool's head.

2. The device of a 'fool's cap' used as a watermark for paper.

It has been asserted that the fool's cap mark was introduced by Sir John Spielmann or Spilman, a German who built a paper-mill at Dartford in 1580; but we have failed to find any trustworthy authority for this statement. The Brit. Mus. copy of Rushworth's *Hist. Coll.* (1659) is marked with this device. The watermark called by Sotheby (*Princ.* III.) a 'fool's cap', and said by him to occur in some copies of Caxton's *Golden Legend*, seems not to be correctly so called. The catalogue of the Caxton Exhibition (1877) states that examples of the fool's cap, dating from 1479, are found in a German collection there exhibited. There is no foundation for the often-repeated story that the Rump Parliament ordered a fool's cap to be substituted for the royal arms in the watermark of the paper used for the journals of the House.

1795 DENNE in *Archæologia* XII. 121 The Fool's cap is not in either the Paston Letters or Mr. Ord's Plates. The date of that device in Mr. Fisher's is as late as 1661.

3. A long folio writing- or printing-paper, varying in size (see quots. 1871, 1888).

A document of 1714, shown to us by Mr. R. B. Prosser, is written on paper bearing the fool's cap watermark, and measuring 16¼ × 13 in. In 1795 the mark was obsolete: see quot. in b.

a **1700** B. E. *Dict. Cant. Crew, Fool's-Cap*, a sort of Paper so called. **1711** *Act 10 Anne* c. 18 §37 For all Paper called.. Fine Fools Cap. **1843** LEFEVRE *Life Trav. Phys.* I. I. ii. 28 One side of a sheet of foolscap. **1871** *Amer. Encycl. Print., Foolscap*, a folded writing-paper, usually 12 by 15 inches, or 12½ by 16. **1888** JACOBI *Printer's Voc., Foolscap*, a size of printing paper 17 × 13½ inches; writing paper 16¾ × 13½ inches.

b. *attrib.* as *foolscap paper, sheet, etc.*; also, **foolscap folio, octavo, quarto**, said of a volume consisting of sheets of foolscap size folded in the manner specified.

1795 DENNE in *Archæologia* XII. 121 The Fool's cap paper has for its mark Britannia. **1818** BYRON *Beppo* lxxv, Fellows In foolscap uniforms turn'd up with ink. **1820** SOUTHEY *Lett.* (1856) III. 177 Verses which I used to send you by the foolscapsheetful. **1886** RUSKIN *Præterita* I. 409 An essay nine foolscap pages long. **1887** *Times* 27 Aug. 11/4 In a foolscap volume of 260 pages.

foolscapped (ˈfuːlzkæpt), *pa. pple.* and *ppl. a.* [f. FOOL'S-CAP + -ED[2].] Furnished with a fool's cap.

1909 A. NOYES in *Westm. Gaz.* 26 Aug. 1/3 Poor fool's-capped scholars. **1918** *Hist. Amer. Lit.* I. 265 He was never laurelled like Byron, never foolscapped like Keats by critics or public.

fool's coat.

1. The motley coat of a fool or buffoon.

1589 NASHE *Martins Months minde* To Rdr. Wks. (Grosart) I. 166 When they shall put off their fooles coat. **1599** B. JONSON *Ev. Man out of Hum.* III. i, Of as many colours, as ere you saw any fooles coat in your life.

transf. and *fig.* **1709** H. CHANDLER *Effort agst. Bigotry* 17 Non-Conformists, Church-men..or whatever Fool's Coat of Distinction their uncharitable envious Neighbours put upon them. **1718** WARDER *True Amazons* (ed. 2) 54 Their [the Wasps'] Fools Coat, and hoarse Voice, doth soon discover them. **1735** POPE *Donne Sat.* IV. 221 Our Court.. helps it [the stage] both to fools-coats and to fools.

2. (See quot.)

a **1700** B. E. *Dict. Cant. Crew, A Fool's-Coat*, a Tulip so called, striped with Red and Yellow.

3. A name for the goldfinch.

a **1682** SIR T. BROWNE *Birds Norfolk* Wks. 1852 III. 322.

4. A bivalve mollusc, *Isocardia cor*, better known as *heart-shell* (*Cent. Dict.*).

foolship (ˈfuːlʃɪp). [f. FOOL *sb.*[1] + -SHIP.]

1. The quality or state of being a fool or jester.

1630 J. TAYLOR (Water P.) *Laugh & be fat* Wks. II. 70/2 Rather then for fooleship we will brawle, You shall be foole at Court, on Thames, and all.

2. A mock title for a fool.

1643 OWEN *Puritan turned Jesuit* 29 Let thy great fooleship know that [etc.]. **1663** COWLEY *Cutter Coleman St.* IV. vi, The Law will allow her honourable Alimony out o' your Foolship's Fortune. **1746** W. HORSLEY *Fool* No. 24 ¶4 My Foolship cannot talk like other People's.

fool's paradise. Also 9 fool-paradise.

1. A state of illusory happiness or good fortune; enjoyment based on false hopes or anticipations.

1462 W. PASTON in *Paston Lett.* No. 457 II. 109, I wold not be in a folis paradyce. **1477** NORTON *Ord. Alch.* ii. in Ashm. (1652) 28 For lewde hope is fooles Paradice. **1528** ROY *Rede Me* (Arb.) 86 Thus my lady, not very wyse, Is brought in-to foles paradyse. **1687** BP. CARTWRIGHT in *Magd. Coll. & Jas. II* (Oxf. Hist. Soc.) 189 Populacy..is the Fool's Paradise. **1709** E. W. *Life of Donna Rosina* 148 Thus was an old experienc'd villain brought into a Fool's Paradice. **1806–7** J. BERESFORD *Miseries Hum. Life* (1826) XII. xxxii, You have been revelling in a fool's paradise of leisure. **1856** MRS. BROWNING *Aur. Leigh* IV. 341 Love's fool-paradise Is out of date, like Adam's.

†**2.** (See quot.) *Obs.*

1644 DIGBY *Nat. Bodies* I. xxix. 257 Those triangular glasses or prismes which some do call fooles Paradises.

foolyie, Sc. var. of FOIL *sb.*[1]

foomart, -murt, var. forms of FOUMART.

foome, obs. form of FOAM.

foon(e, obs. pl. of FOE.

foord, obs. form of FORD *sb.*[1]

foore, var. of FORE *sb. Obs.*, a track.

foorth, obs. and Sc. form of FORTH.

foose. *dial.* Also fews, fooz, fouse. The house-leek, *Sempervivum tectorum*.

17.. *H. Robertson's School of Arts* I. 57 (Jam.) Take a quantity of house-leek commonly called foose.

fooster (ˈfuːstə(r)). *Anglo-Irish.* Bustle.

Hence **ˈfooster** *v. intr.*, to bustle *off*.

1847 LE FANU *T. O'Brien* 25 Where is it you're going, my colleen Beg, in all this foosther? **1850** *N. & Q.* 1st Ser. II. 153 Full of fun and fooster, like Mooney's goose. **1892** JANE BARLOW *Irish Idylls* III. 56 The hen that had foosthered off with herself down the bog.

foot (fʊt), *sb. Pl.* feet (fiːt). Forms: *Sing.* 1–2 fót, 3–4 fot, *south.* vot, 3–6 fote, fut, (3 fhote, fott, 5 fowte, foyte), 5–6 fotte, 5–7 foote, (7 foott), 8–9 *dial.* fit, 3– foot. *Sc.* 4–7 fute, (4 fut, 6 fuit), 6– fit. *Pl.* 1–2 fét, fœ́t, fótas, 2 fiet, (*genit.* 1 fóta, 3 fote; *dat.* 1 fótum, 3 foten), 3–5 fet, (3 fett, fite, 4 fyte), 4–5 fete, (4 *Sc.* feyt, 5 feytt), 5–8 feete, (6 fette, fiete, 7 feeten), 5–6 fotes, (6 footes), 7 (9 in sense 22) foots, 4– feet. [Com. Teut.: OE. *fót* str. masc. (dat. sing. nom. and acc. pl. *fét*), corresponds to OFris. *fôt*, OS. *fôt*, *fuot*, (Du. *voet*), OHG. *fuoz*, (MHG. *vuoz*, mod.Ger. *fuss*), ON. *fótr*, (Sw. *fot*, Da. *fod*), Goth. *fôtus*. The OTeut. **fôt* (a consonant-stem) represents OAryan **pōd-*, which with the ablaut-variants **pĕd-*, *pŏd-*, is found with cognate senses in most of the Aryan langs.: cf. Skr. *pād* (gen. *padás*) foot, *pad* to go to, *padá* neut. footstep; Lith. *pėdà* footstep; Gr. πούς (Dor. Æol. πώς), gen. ποδός foot, πεζός (:—*pedyós*) on foot; Lat. *pēs*, accus. *pĕd-em* foot; ON. *fet* str. neut., step, foot as a measure, *feta* to make one's way, OE. *fæt* str. neut., step, OHG. *fezzan* to go; see also FETTER *sb.* Possibly FET *v.*, FETCH *v.*, FETLOCK may belong to the same root.]

I. 1. a. The lowest part of the leg beyond the ankle-joint.

Beowulf 745 (Gr.) Sona hæfde unlifiᵹendes eal ᵹefeormod fet and folma. *c* **950** *Lindisf. Gosp.* John xi. 2 Maria ..ᵹedryᵹde his foet mið herum fæx hire. *a* **1000** *Phœnix* 311 (Gr.) þæs fuᵹles..fealwe fotas. *c* **1200** *Trin. Coll. Hom.* 21 And nailed þarto his fet, and his honden. **1297** R. GLOUC. (1724) 490 He vel of is palefrey, & brec is fot. *c* **1350** *Will. Palerne* 1766 William & þe mayde þat were white beres, gon forþ..Fersly on here foure fet. **1375** BARBOUR *Bruce* II. 359 Knychtis..Wndyr horss feyt defoulyt. **1434** MISYN *Mending Life* x. 121 Sayntis feet ar to be waschyd for þai draw duste of þe erth. **1538** STARKEY *England* I. ii. 48 The fote to go, and hand to hold and rech. **1601** SHAKS. *Twel. N.* III. ii. 66 So much blood..as will clog the foote of a flea. **1674** N. COX *Gentl. Recreat.* II. (1677) 228 Having flown with a Goshawk..till March, give her some good Quarry in her Foot. **1845** FORD *Handbk. Spain* I. 52 No Spaniard.. ever took a regular walk on his own feet—a walk for the sake of mere health. **1851** RUSKIN *Stones Ven.* (1874) I. vii. 74 A foot has two offices, to bear up and to hold firm. **1881** R. M'LACHLAN in *Encycl. Brit.* XIII. 144/1 Plantulæ (much marked in the feet of *Diptera*, which climb polished surfaces, &c., by means of them).

fig. **1570–6** LAMBARDE *Peramb. Kent* (1826) 191 It wanteth not the feete of sound reason to stand upon.

†**b.** In the oath or exclamation, ***Christ's foot***, later ***'s foot*** or simply ***foot***. Cf. BLOOD 1 e. *Obs.*

c **1386** CHAUCER *Miller's T.* 596 Ey, Cristes fote! what wil ye do therwith? *c* **1600** *Distr. Emperor* III. i. in Bullen *O. Pl.* (1884) III. 212 Foote, man, let him be ten thousand preists and a will styll want somethynge. **1662** T. W. *Thorny Abbey* 13, 'S foot, doe you think we gave him warning.

†**c.** By some anatomists used for: The whole limb from the hip-joint to the toes. Also, ***great foot***. (Cf. *great hand* for the whole upper limb.) *Obs.*

1541 R. COPLAND *Guydon's Quest. Chirurg.* K iij b, The great fote lasteth fro the ioynt of the hukcle..vnto the ferdest parte of the toes. **1661** LOVELL *Hist. Anim. & Min.* 302 The foot is divided into fœmur..the tibia..and the foot extreme.

d. In the colloq. exclamation ***my foot!*** (also ***your foot!***), expressing a contemptuous contradiction.

1923 R. CROTHERS *Mary the Third* II. ii. 69 *Mother*: She was honest enough to tell me that... *Father*: Honest your foot! She's fooled you—deceived you. **1925** N. COWARD *Hay Fever* III, *Judith*: It's so silly to get cross at criticism —it indicates a small mind. *David*: Small mind my foot! **1928** D. L. SAYERS *Lord Peter views Body* xi. 262 'I thought he was doing a motor-tour.' 'Motor-tour your foot!' said the Inspector, with more energy than politeness. **1945** L. A. G. STRONG *Othello's Occupation* 72 Cooperation my foot. You're trying to trap me into admitting a motive for doing the old girl in. **1961** H. E. BATES *Day of Tortoise* 55 'But it's a serious matter for you.' 'Serious my foot. Why should I worry?'

2. a. Viewed with regard to its function, as the organ of locomotion. In rhetorical and poetical use often (in sing. or pl.) qualified by adjs. denoting the kind of movement (as *swift*, *slow*, *stealthy*, etc.), or employed as the subject of verbs of motion.

c **1000** *Ags. Ps.* xxxv[i]. 12 [11], (Spelm.) Ne cume me fot ofermodiᵹnysse. *a* **1340** HAMPOLE *Psalter* xviii. 4 þe fame of a good man gas ferrere þan his fote may. **1603** SHAKS. *Meas. for M.* v. i. 400 Death, Which I did thinke, with slower foot came on. **1667** MILTON *P.L.* XI. 848 Tripping ebbe, that stole With soft foot towards the deep. *a* **1774** FERGUSSON *Poems* (1789) II. 107 Eild wi' wyly fit, Is wearing nearer bit by bit. **1813** SCOTT *Trierm.* III. xxiv, Foot of man..hath ne'er Dared to cross the Hall of Fear. **1847** MARRYAT *Childr. N. Forest* xxi, I was not aware of your presence. Your foot is so light. **1875** JOWETT *Plato* (ed. 2) III. 28 Dogs..swift of foot. **1878** BROWNING *La Saisiaz* 18 Useful as is Nature, to attract the tourist's foot.

Proverb. *c* **1300** *Cursor M.* 28939 (Cott. Galba) Gangand fote ay getes fode. **1670** RAY *Prov.* 262 A walking foot is ay getting.

fig. **1607** SHAKS. *Cor.* IV. vii. 7 Unless by using means I lame the foot Of our design. **1633** BP. HALL *Hard Texts, N.T.* 103 No man can come to me by the foot of a true faith except my Father..inlighten his understanding.

b. Hence, a person as walking. *Obs.* exc. *dial.* in ***first foot*** (see FIRST C. 2); similarly † ***evil foot***, one whom it is unlucky to meet. †Also (*rarely*) used simply for 'person'.

c **1200** *Vices & Virtues* 29 Ðanne ðe cumþ eft sum euel.. ne ȝelief ðu naht al swa sume..seggeð þat hie imetten euel fot, priest oðer munec. *a* **1225** *Leg. Kath.* 2273 He het hetterliche, anan wiðuten þe burh, bihefden ham, euch fot. **1592** SHAKS. *Rom. & Jul.* V. iii. 19 What cursed foot wanders this wayes to night? **1609** SKENE *Reg. Maj., Burrow Lawes* cxxxiv, He..offers his awin fute for his pledge.

†**3.** Power of walking or running. *Obs.*

a **1300** *Cursor M.* 20885 (Cott.) Petre..to þe cripels he gaf þam fote. *a* **1400–50** *Alexander* 1236 Alle þe folke of his affinite..þat outhire fote had or fole to þe fliȝt foundid. *c* **1450** HENRYSON *Parl. Beistis* 32 Ay rinnis the Foxe, als lang as he fute has. [Similarly **1500–20** DUNBAR *Poems* xlix. 48]. **1737** BRACKEN *Farriery Impr.* (1757) II. 123 Horses may alter as to their Speed or Foot (as 'tis called).

4. *ellipt.* Foot-soldiers; in early use † ***men of foot***. Cf. FOOTMAN 1. Often immediately following an ordinal, 'regiment of' being omitted.

1568 GRAFTON *Chron.* II. 245 Men of armes, and ix thousand Archers, beside men of foote. **1597** SHAKS. *2 Hen. IV* II. i. 186 Fifteene hundred Foot, fiue hundred Horse. **1633** T. STAFFORD *Pac. Hib.* x. (1821) 120 The President was a Captaine of Foot. **1709** STEELE *Tatler* No. 17 ¶3 Their Foot repulsed the same Body of Horse in three successive Charges. **1849** MACAULAY *Hist. Eng.* I. 296 At the close of the reign of Charles the Second, most of his foot were musketeers. **1878** TRIMEN *Reg. Brit. Army* 89 Forty-Fourth Foot..captured the Eagle of the 62nd French Infantry at Salamanca.

5. a. The end of a bed, a grave, etc., towards which the feet are placed. Formerly often *pl.*, now *sing.* (cf. sense 19).

a **1300** *Cursor M.* 17288 + 218 (Cott.) þat one at þe fote of þe graf, þat other at the hede. *c* **1386** CHAUCER *Reeve's T.* 293 He..bare it soft unto his beddes fete. *c* **1442** HOCCLEVE *Min. Poems* (1892) 238 In a cofre at my beddes feet yee Shul fynde hem. *c* **1710** C. FIENNES *Diary* (1888) 239 There was such another screen or raile at yᵉ ffeete of the bed. **1821** KEATS *Isabel* xxxv, At her couch's foot Lorenzo stood. **1891** *Law Rep.* Weekly Notes 201/1 His trousers..were hanging over the foot of the bed.

b. The part of a stocking, etc. which covers the foot.

1577 HARRISON *England* II. ix. (1877) I. 206 He will carrie his hosen..to save their feet from wearing. **1726** SHELVOCKE *Voy.* (1757) 112 A sort of knit buskins without feet to them. **1882** CAULFEILD & SAWARD *Dict. Needlework* 463/1 Silk [hose] with cotton feet.

II. 6. *Prosody.* [transl. of L. *pēs*, Gr. πούς; the term is commonly taken to refer to the movement of the foot in beating time.] A division of a verse, consisting of a number of syllables one of which has the ictus or principal stress.

c **1050** *Byrhtferth's Handboc* in *Anglia* (1885) VIII. 313 þæt pentimemeris byð þe todælð þæt vers on þam oðrum fet & byð ȝemet healf fot to lafe. **1387** TREVISA *Higden* (Rolls) V. 147 Iuvencius þe preost wroot þe gospelles to þe chirche of Rome in vers of sixe feet. *c* **1560** B. GOOGE *Epit. T. Phayre* Poems (Arb.) 72 Virgils verse hath greater grace in forrayne foote obtaynde, Than in his own. **1600** SHAKS. *A.Y.L.* III. ii. 173 Some of them had in them more feete then the Verses would beare. **1700** DRYDEN *Pref. Fables* (Globe) 499 Some thousands of his verses..are lame for want of half a foot. **1803** COLERIDGE *Metrical Feet* 3 Spondee..strong foot! yea ill able Ever to come up with Dactyl trisyllable. **1830** S. FOX *Menologium* p. vi, In these compositions..trochaic feet predominate. **1846** WRIGHT *Ess. Mid. Ages* I. i. 14 The Saxons did not measure their verse by feet. **1888** A. S. COOK *Judith* p. l, A normal hemistich contains two metrical feet. **1942** J. C. POPE *Rhythm of Beowulf* 12 Sievers was only borrowing mistakes from contemporary metrical theory when he marked the 'feet' of his five types.

III. As a unit of measurement.

7. a. A lineal measure originally based on the length of a man's foot. (The English foot consists of 12 inches, and is ⅓ of a YARD.) Hence, a measure of surface and of solid space (explicitly ***square*** or ***superficial, cubic*** or ***solid foot***) equal to the content respectively of a square and a cube the side of which measures one foot.

Often in sing. when preceded by numerals.

a **1000** *Laws Æthelstan* iv. 5 in Thorpe I. 224, .ix. fota & .ix. scæfta munda & .ix. bere-corna. *c* **1205** LAY. 21996 He is imeten a bræde, fif & twenti foten; fif fote he is deop. **1325** *Chron. Eng.* 83 in Ritson *Metr. Rom.* II. 273 Fourti fet.. Into the see he made him lepe. **1459** *Contract* in Willis & Clark *Cambridge* (1886) I. 309 A doore in brede iiij foote standard. **1523** FITZHERB. *Surv.* 35 Howe many footes euery one of them be in length. **1624** MASSINGER *Parl. Love* v. i, I'll build A room of eight feet square. **1712** tr. *Pomet's Hist. Drugs* I. 89 The Indigo Plant grows about two Foot high. **1722** DE FOE *Col. Jack* (1840) 192 Our privateer..outsailed her, running two feet for her one. **1816** KEATINGE *Trav.* (1817) I. 87 Every foot of this tract is argillaceous wheat-land. **1833** HT. MARTINEAU *Loom & Lugger* I. vii. 115 Who stood about five feet in their shoes. **1862** ANSTED *Channel Isl.* iv. App. A (ed. 2) 565 The linear Jersey foot is equivalent to only eleven English inches.

b. Used to express 'the least distance or space,' with *a*, *one* or a negative. † ***each foot***: all the way.

a **1300** *Cursor M.* 7526 (Cott.) Forth a fote ne moght he ga. *Ibid.* 15391 (Cott.) Fra þan he ran him ilk fote, ne yode he noght þe pas. **13..** *Coer de L.* 2361 He shal not have a fote of lond. *c* **1435** *Torr. Portugal* 239 He durst go no fote Lest they wold hyme sle. **1596** SHAKS. *1 Hen. IV*, II. ii. 23 Ile starue ere I rob a foote further. *a* **1800** *Lizie Lindsay* in Child *Ballads* VIII. (1892) 265 Bonnie Lizie..a fit furder couldna win.

†**c.** Hence ***every foot*** (***and anon***): incessantly.

1561 P. MORWYNG tr. *Compend. Josephus' Hist. Jews* 56 b, Antipater made feastes euery foote [L. *singulis diebus*] for thy brother Pheroras and him selfe. **1601** HOLLAND *Pliny* II. 243 Such a worke they made sometime in chafing and frying their bodies against a good fire, but euery foot in bringing them abroad into the hot Sunne. **1639** GENTILIS *Servita's Inquis.* (1676) 855 The Inquisitors do every foot write to Rome. **1692** R. L'ESTRANGE *Fables* cccclviii. 434 This Man's Son would every foot and anon be taking some of his Companions into the Orchard. **1784** CULLUM *Hist. Hawsted* 171 *Every Foot anon* every now and then.

d. As a measure of coal gas: the amount of gas contained in one cubic foot of space.

1838 *Penny Cycl.* XI. 88/2 A sufficient quantity of gas was turned on to give a light equal to that of a mould candle; the consumption in this case was a foot and a half per hour. **1879** *Encycl. Brit.* X. 99/2 A burner passing 7 feet of gas per hour.

8. A measure in tin-mining: (see quot. 1778).

1602 CAREW *Cornwall* 13 b, They measure their black Tynne by..the Foote. **1778** PRYCE *Min. Cornub.*, *Foot*, an ancient measure for black Tin, two gallons; now a nominal measure, but in weight 60 lb.

9. A measure in sizing grindstones (see quot.).

1844 McCULLOCH *Dict. Commerce* 615 They [grindstones] are classed in eight different sizes, called foots, according to their dimensions..A grindstone foot is 8 inches: the size is found by adding the diameter and thickness together. Thus, a stone 56 inches diameter by 8 thick..is an 8-foot stone.

IV. Something resembling a foot in function or position.

10. a. The lower (usually projecting) part of an object, which serves to support it; the base.

1382 WYCLIF *Exod.* xxvii. 10 Twenti pilers, with so feele brasun feet. *c* **1400** MAUNDEV. (1839) ii. 10 Therfore made thei the Foot of the Cros of Cedre. **1509** FISHER *Fun. Serm. Hen. VII.* Wks. (1876) 274 He..kyssed..the lowest parte, the fote of the monstraunt. **1571** DIGGES *Pantom.* III. xv. S iij b, Admit *BCD* a piller..my desire is to knowe the waight of the fote. **1611** BIBLE *Exod.* xxx. 18 A Lauer of brasse, and his foote also of brasse. **1802** MAR. EDGEWORTH *Moral T.* (1816) I. 214 You have seen this vase..and..the lines inscribed on the foot of it. **1875** FORTNUM *Majolica* iii. 31 Dishes..with..a projecting circular 'giretto' behind, forming a foot or base.

b. (See quot. 1892).

1869 SIR E. REED *Shipbuild.* vii. 121 The frames behind armour in this part of the ship terminate in a foot at the lower deck. **1892** *Lockwood's Dict. Mech. Engin.*, *Foot*, a base or flange which sustains a casting or structure.

11. a. *Zool.* Applied to various organs of locomotion or attachment belonging to certain invertebrate animals; in more precise technical language distinguished by special names, as ***ambulacrum, podium, pseudopodium***, etc.

1835 KIRBY *Hab. & Inst. Anim.* I. v. 177 The foot, or base by which the common coral is attached to the rocks. **1835–6** TODD *Cycl. Anat.* I. 701/2 In..the Conchiferous mollusks ..the foot constitutes a principal part of the body. **1841–71** T. R. JONES *Anim. Kingd.* (ed. 4) 551 The little animal..is ..possessed of a 'foot,' often very long and moveable, by the aid of which it can crawl upon a solid surface. **1852** DANA *Crust.* I. 10 Feet ambulatory or prehensile.

b. *Bot.* In various uses. The part (of a petal) by which it is attached; the part (of a hair) below the epidermis; also, in ferns, mosses, etc. (see quot. 1882).

1671 GREW *Anat. Plants* I. v. (1682) 35 The Foot of each Leaf being very long and slender. **1882** VINES *Sachs' Bot.* 427 The foot is an organ by which the embryo attaches itself to the tissue of the prothallium, in order to draw nourishment from it. **1891** A. JOHNSTONE *Bot.* 144 The part within the epidermal surface developing into the foot, and the protruded portion into the body of the hair.

12. *Printing.* (See quots.)

1683 MOXON *Mech. Exerc.* II. 376 *Foot of the Letter*, the Break-end of the Shanck of a Letter. **1888** SOUTHWARD in *Encycl. Brit.* XXIII. 698 The groove *g* divides the bottom of the type into two parts called the feet.

13. The extremity of the leg (of a pair of compasses, a chair, etc.).

1551 RECORDE *Pathw. Knowl.* I. iii, Set one foote of the compasse in the verye point of the angle. **1703** MOXON *Mech. Exerc.* 206 Describe a Circle..by placing one Foot in the prick-mark, and turning about the other Foot. **1831** BREWSTER *Optics* iii. 25 Place one foot of the compasses in the quadrant *NF*.

14. Of a plough: (See quots. and PLOUGH-FOOT).

1523 FITZHERB. *Husb.* §4 A man maye temper for one thynge in two or thre places, as for depnes. The fote is one. **1688** R. HOLME *Armoury* III. viii. 333/2 The Foot, is the piece of Hooked or Bended Wood, at the end of the Plow, under the Suck. **1846** *Jrnl. R. Agric. Soc.* VII. 72 If the foot was not wide, it would cut into the soil.

15. Of an organ pipe (see quots.).

1852 SEIDEL *Organ* 78 The foot upon which the whole pipe rests. **1876** HILES *Catech. Organ* iv. (1878) 25 The foot [of a wooden organ pipe] is a tube introduced at the bottom of the pipe; it serves as a support, and also as a conductor of the wind.

16. In a sewing-machine: The small plate which is pressed on the cloth to hold it steady.

1877 KNIGHT *Dict. Mech.*, *Presser-foot.* **188.** *Direct. Singer's 'Medium' Sewing Mach.*, Adjust the corder-foot to the presser-bar..In placing each succeeding cord, guide the fabric with the last cord sewed in the second groove of the foot.

17. One of the marginal pieces forming a serrated edge round the carapace of the Hawkbill turtle; otherwise called 'hoofs' or 'claws'; in *pl.* the commercial name for the small plates of tortoise-shell which line the carapace.

V. The lowest part, bottom.

18. a. The lowest part or bottom of an eminence, or any object in an erect or sloping position, as a wall, ladder, staircase, etc. Chiefly governed by preps.

c **1200** *Trin. Coll. Hom.* 89 On þe fot of þe dune þe men clepen munt oliuete. *a* **1300** *Cursor M.* 2481 (Cott.) Vnder þe fote of mont mambre, þar he ches to seit his fee. **1387** TREVISA *Higden* (Rolls) III. 65 At þe foot of þe hille mount Olympus. **1497** BP. ALCOCK *Mons Perfect.* C iij, The fote [of the ladder] stode by hym. **1582** N. LICHEFIELD tr. *Castanheda's Conq. E. Ind.* ii. 6 b, A man..who was going to gather honny at the foote of a bush. **1667** MILTON *P.L.* III. 485 And now at foot Of Heav'ns ascent they lift thir Feet. **1678** *Trial of Coleman* 44 At the Foot of the Stair-case. **1717** BERKELEY *Let.* Wks. 1871 IV. 80 Torre del Greco, a town situate at the foot of Vesuvius. **1779** J. BURGOYNE *Lett. to Constit.* (ed. 3) 15 Even the feet of the gallows, were resorted to for other recruits. **1815** *Falconer's Dict. Marine*, The Foot of a Mast, is the lower end, or that which goes into the step. **1860** TYNDALL *Glac.* I. ii. 68 A forest of dark pines.. gathered like a cloud at the foot of the mountain.

b. The beginning or end of the slope (of a bridge).

c **1450** *Merlin* 227 Here be-fore the yates at the brigge foote. **1548** HALL *Chron., Hen. VI* (an. 28) 160 b, Yᵉ rebelles drave the citezens from the stoulpes at the bridge foote. **1739** LABELYE *Short Acc. Piers Westm. Bridge* p. vi, Westminster-Bridge Foot. *c* **1850** *Arab. Nts.* (Rtldg.) 597 They passed this bridge, at the foot of which they met with an old blind man.

c. Geom. ***foot of the perpendicular***: (see quot.).

1840 LARDNER *Geom.* xii. 147 The point..where the perpendicular meets the plane, is called the foot of the perpendicular.

d. *Naut.* (See quot. 1776.)

1697 DAMPIER *Voy.* I. xviii. 495 We rolled up the foot of our Sail on a pole fastned to it. **1776** FALCONER *Dict. Marine*, *Foot* of a sail, lower edge or bottom. **1882** NARES *Seamanship* (ed. 6) 127 Carry up the foot.

19. The lower end, bottom (of a page or document, a class or list, a table, etc.). ***at foot***: at the bottom (of a page).

1669 STURMY *Mariner's Mag.* IV. 142 Look in the Foot of the Table for the fifth Rhomb. **1683** MOXON *Mech. Exerc.* II. 377 He claps the Fingers of his Left Hand about the Foot of the Page. **1722** WOLLASTON *Relig. Nat.* ix. 218 At the foot of the page. **1855** THORPE *Pref. to Beowulf* (1875) 8 Placing the proposed correction at foot. **1884** G. MOORE *Mummer's Wife* (1887) 223 He was invited to take the foot of the table and help the cold salmon.

20. Law. ***foot of a fine*** (AF. *pee*, Anglo-Lat. *pes*): that one of the 'parts' of a tripartite indenture recording the particulars of a fine (see FINE *sb.*[1] 6 b), which remained with the court, the other two being retained by the parties.

When the undivided sheet was placed so that this counterfoil could be read, it was actually at the 'foot' of the parchment (the extant 'feet of fines' have therefore their indentation at the top); in the other two counterparts the direction of the writing was at right angles to that of the 'foot'. The expression *pes indenturae* 'foot of the indenture' also occurs. Horwood's suggestion, that the term (L. *pes*) arose from a misinterpretation of AF *pes, pais*, 'peace' is baseless.

[**1293** in *Year Bks. 21 & 22 Edw. I* (Rolls) 221 E ke cele fin se leva tel an coram &c. nus vochum le pee de la fin a garrantye.] **1581** *Act 23 Eliz.* c. 3. §1 The Concorde, Note and Fote of everye suche Fyne. **1876** DIGBY *Real Prop.* ii. §8. 93 A document was drawn up, called in later times the foot, chirograph, or indenture of the fine. **1895** POLLOCK & MAITLAND *Hist. Eng. Law* I. 198 This 'final concord' or 'fine', will be drawn up by the royal clerks and one copy of it, the so-called 'Foot of the Fine', will remain with the Court.

21. What is written at the foot.

†**a.** The sum or total (of an account). *Obs.*

1480 *Wardr. Acc. Edw. IV* (1830) 154 *note*, 'The foote of the deliveree of stuff'. **1520** *Churchw. Acc. St. Giles, Reading* 8 In the ffote of the same accompte xjˡⁱ xiiijˢ vijᵈ. **1623** BP. ANDREWES *Serm. Nativ.* xvi. (1629) 148 So, it signifies to make the foot of an account. We call it the foot, because we write it below at the foot. **1692** DRYDEN *Cleomen.* IV. i, A trifling sum of Misery, New added to the foot of thy Account. **1712** STEELE *Spect.* No. 346 ¶1 The generous man..will soon find upon the foot of his account that he has sacrificed to fools.

†**b.** The refrain or 'chorus' (of a song). ***to bear a foot***: to sing a refrain. *Obs.*

1552 HULOET, Dittye synger, or he that beareth yᵉ fote of the songs, *præsentor* [sic]. *c* **1568** in *Laneham's Let.* (1871) Pref. 127 Here entreth Moros..Synging the foote of many Songes, as fooles were wont. **1603** KNOLLES *Hist. Turkes* 777 A souldior..sung a dolefull dittie whereunto his fellows sighing bare a foot. **1621** MOLLE *Camerar. Liv. Libr.* v. ii. 322 In praise of him certaine jygges were made which the yong lads vsed to sing..the foot of them was this; A thousand, thousand, thousand, we..[etc.].

22. (Plural *foots*). That which sinks to and lies upon the bottom; bottoms, dregs; the refuse in refining oil, etc.; coarse sugar. Cf. *foot grease, sugar*.

1560 Let. in Hakluyt Voy. I. 306 Much of this Waxe had a great foote.. You must cause the foote to bee taken off before you doe weigh it. 1644 Nye Gunnery v. (1647) 11 Fill up the Barrel with earth.. afterwards pour.. clean water upon the earth.. then pull out the Taps or Spiggots.. and let the water drop out of that vessel into another.. this water when it hath dropped twice, is called water of Foot. 1687 B. Randolph Archipelago 91 They raise the foot of the oyl, so that thick and thin goes together. 1770-4 A. Hunter Georg. Ess. (1803) I. 318 The bottoms or foots of oil. 1871 Daily News 5 Jan., Lump sugar is 13d. a pound, foots moist 9d. 1886 Elworthy W. Somerset Word-bk, Foots, dregs, sediment. This here cyder 'ont suit me, there's to much voots in it.

VI. Footing, standing, basis.

†23. Foothold, standing-ground. *Obs.*

1579 Tomson Calvin's Serm. Tim. 148/1 Their getting foote may be to their owne destruction. 1652 F. Kirkman Cleris & Lozia 113 Hinder new love from getting foot in her heart. 1662 More Philos. Writ. Pref. Gen. (1712) 19 Considering also how far that Philosophy has already got foot in Christendom.

†24. a. The footing, basis, understanding, totality of conditions or arrangements, on which a matter is established; the agreed or understood position or status which a person or thing occupies in relation to another. = FOOTING *vbl. sb.* 8. *Obs.*

1559 Jewel Let. to Bulinger in Strype Ann. Ref. I. x. 131 Religion was restored on that foot on which it stood in King Edwards time. 1686 Lond. Gaz. No. 2116/1 The Salaries of all Officers.. are likewise retrenched. The Councils.. are to be reduced to the foot they were upon in the Year 1621. 1707 Freind Peterborow's Cond. Sp. 7 Matters were set upon a new Foot. 1735 Berkeley Def. Free-think. in Math. Wks. 1871 III. 325 If you defend Sir Isaac's notions.. it must be on the rigorous foot of rejecting nothing. 1745 P. Thomas Voy. S. Seas 305 The Viceroy.. found he expected to be received on the same Foot with himself. 1762-71 H. Walpole Vertue's Anecd. Paint. (1786) III. 278 Boit.. was upon so low a foot, that he went into the country, and taught children to draw. 1767 Franklin Lett. Wks. 1887 IV. 9, I wish all correspondence was on the foot of writing and answering when one can. 1827 Pollok Course T. ix. 727 When he should stand on equal foot beside The man he wronged.

†b. *on the foot of*: on the ground of. *Obs.*

1679 Penn Addr. Prot. II. 84 He laid the Sin of the Jews upon this Foot, viz., That they rejected him, after he had made proof of his Divine Mission. a1797 H. Walpole Mem. Geo II (1847) II. viii. 259 The Prince excused his own inapplication on the foot of idleness.

†25. Standard rate of calculation or valuation. *under foot*: below standard value. *Obs.*

1588 J. Mellis Briefe Instr. F viij b, Vse one Foote or Standerd of money in your accompt in your Leager. 1594 Death of Usurie 12 The man beeing driuen to distresse, sels his corne farre vnder foote. 1645 Quarles Sol. Recant. I. 44 Not deem'd a pen'worth under foot. 1691 Locke Lower. Interest Wks. 1727 II. 80 He must pay twenty per Cent. more for all the Commodities he buys with the Money of the new Foot. 1726 Berkeley in Fraser Life iv. (1871) 137, I know money is at present on a very high foot of exchange. 1734 tr. Rollin's Anc. Hist. (1827) I. I. iv. 195 The disparity between the ancient and modern measures which it is hard to estimate on a fixed and certain foot.

VII. Phrases.

26. a. †*to catch* or *have by the foot*: to catch as in a trap; to hold fast, keep from flying. †*to give* (a person) *a foot*: to trip (him) up. *to have one foot in the grave*: to be near death.

1550 Latimer Serm. Fruitf. Serm. (1571) 90b, In answering him to this they would haue caught him by the foote. 1632 Massinger & Field Fatal Dowry I. ii, When one foot's in the grave. 1643 Prynne Sov. Power Parl. I. (ed. 2) 52 The English Armies disband themselves, as dreaming they had now good fortune by the foote. 1767 H. Brooke Fool of Qual. V. 15 Harry, giving him a slight foot, laid him on the broad of his back. 1886 J. Payn Luck Darrells xv, He has twenty thousand a year.. And one foot in his grave.

b. In adv. phr.: †*feet against* (or *to*) *feet*, said with reference to the Antipodes. *foot to foot*: with one's foot against an opponent's; in close combat. †(*to come in*) *foot and hand*: stepping forward and dealing a blow at the same time. *feet first*: see FIRST *a.* 3 b. (*with one's*) *feet foremost*: lit., hence also 'as a corpse'.

c1400 Maundev. (1839) xvii 182 Thei that dwellyn under us, ben feet aȝenst feet. 1553 Eden Decades viii, The Antipodes (that is) such as go fiete to fiete ageynst us. 1596 Shaks. 1 Hen. IV, II. iv, 241 [These] Began to giue me ground: but I followed me close, came in foot and hand. 1603 Knolles Hist. Turks 879 They encountred one another, not with their missive weapons onely.. but with their drawne swords foot to foot. 1606 Shaks. Ant. & Cl. III. vii. 67 Fighting foot to foot. 1737 Ozell Rabelais II. 27 They never enter St. Denys but with their Feet foremost. 1856 Kane Arct. Expl. I. xxix. 384 Hans, Morton and myself crawled feet-foremost into our buffalo-bag. 1860 All Year Round No. 65. 350 It [the disease].. had carried him out with his feet foremost.

c. *to find* or *know the length of* (a person's) *foot*: to discover or know his weaknesses, so as to be able to manage him. *to measure another man's foot by one's own last*: to measure others by one's own standard, to judge others by oneself. *feet of clay*: see CLAY *sb.* 4 c.

1580 Lyly Euphues (Arb.) 290 You shal not know the length of my foote, vntill by your cunning you get commendation. 1598 R. Bernard tr. Terence 70 He measures an other mans foote by his owne last. a1617 Bayne On Eph. i. 15 (1643) 156 Persons who can humour them, and finde the length of their foote. 1861 Trollope Barchester T. xxxv, Farmer Greenacre's eldest son.. had from his earliest years taken the exact measure of Miss Thorne's foot.

27. With reference to standing. (*to be, jump up*) *upon* or (*to raise*) *to one's feet*: in, into or to a standing position. *to be on one's feet*: to be able to stand; hence, in health. *to set* (a person) *on his feet*, to make his position or means of living secure. *to carry* (a person) *off his feet*: (*fig.*) to 'carry away' with enthusiasm, or the like. *to drop* or *fall on one's feet*: see FALL *v.* 65 h. *to have one's feet on the ground*: to base oneself on realities; to be practical. *to keep one's feet*: to stand or walk upright or without falling. †*to stand upon one's own feet* or *its own foot*: to rely on one's own resources; (of a thing) to be judged on its merits.

c1440 Generydes 44 Vppe vppon his fete he was a non. c1500 Melusine xxiii. 156 Make here byfore me the feste as that I were now on my feet. 1657 Burton's Diary (1828) II. 67 I move.. that you would leave Serjeant Dendy's right to stand upon its own foot. 1801 Gabrielli Myst. Husb. iv. 146 A sixth [hundred pounds] would set her once more upon her feet. 1845 M. Pattison Ess. (1889) I. 26 The bishops.. hastened to raise the king to his feet. 1849 Macaulay Hist. Eng. I. 301 He could not keep his feet in a breeze. 1854 Mrs. Gaskell Let. 27 Oct. (1966) 316 I'll enclose you two pieces of Mr. S. Gaskell to show how *he's* carried off his feet. 1889 Repent. P. Wentworth III. 145 He positively carried me off my feet for a few minutes that evening. 1950 'P. Woodruff' Island of Chamba i. 21 El Hadramauti.. is a bit of a theorist and H.M. for all his oddity has his feet very firmly on the ground.

28. a. With reference to placing the feet. *to put one's foot down*: (*a*) to take up a firm position; (*b*) when driving a motor vehicle: to accelerate. *to put* (*set*) *one's foot* (*down*) *upon*: to have nothing to do with; to repress firmly. *to put a foot upon*: ? to get an unfair advantage of, to wrong. *to put one's foot in* or *into it*: to get into difficulties or trouble; to blunder (*colloq.*). *not* (or *never*) *to put a foot wrong*: to make no mistakes; hence *not to put a foot right*: to make many mistakes. †*to set one's foot by* or *to* (another or another's): to engage in combat with.

1536 St. Papers Hen. VIII, I. 506 No man can or dare set his fote by ours in proving of the contrary. c1609 Hieron Wks. (1624) I. 7 Saint Paul.. would not haue feared for profession of Religion, to set his foot to him that was holiest. 1663 Pepys Diary 23 May, I had a fray with Sir J. Minnes in defence of my Will in a business where the old Coxcomb would have put a foot upon him. 1798 Gent. Mag. in Spirit Pub. Jrnls. (1799) II. 57 The General had put his foot into it again. 1823 'Bee' Slang s.v. 'To put one's foot in it,' to make a blunder on the wrong side; to get into a scrape by speaking. 1833 Marryat P. Simple xii, I put my foot into it (as we say), for I was nearly killed. 1868 J. H. Blunt Ref. Ch. Eng. I. 65 Wolsey set his foot upon this plan. 1886 J. Payn Luck Darrells xxvi, She.. put her foot down.. upon the least symptoms of an unpleasantry. 1948 'N. Shute' No Highway iv. 108 His superiors could rest content that Mr. Symes would never put a foot wrong. 1959 I. Jeffries 13 Days viii. 98, I didn't feel I ought to put a foot wrong with Watson, the Ordnance Captain. 1959 Listener 22 Jan. 152/1 He never put a foot wrong. He was extraordinarily good in the House. 1961 H. Nicolson Let. 1 June (1968) III. 395 The Americans.. blame.. the 'diplomatists', meaning thereby their intelligence services. 'Why can't we put a foot right?' they wail. 1962 J. Braine Life at Top ii. 38, I put my foot down and the Zephyr gathered speed up the slope.

b. *to set* or *put* (*one's*) *foot at, in, into,* †*off, on,* †*out of* (a place).

c1489 Caxton Sonnes of Aymon ix. 222 I shall never sette foote there. 1542 Udall Erasm. Apoph. 46 It was a foule shame for a phylosophier to sette his foote into any hous where bawderie wer kepte. 1548 Hall Chron., Edw. IV. (an 15) 237 b, Whom if you permitte once to set but one foote, out of your power.. there is no mortall creature able.. to deliver hym from death. 1579 Tomson Calvin's Serm. Tim. 251/2 Sins which haue set in foote. 1596 Spenser State Irel. 81 In some places of the same they have put foote. 1596 Shaks. 1 Hen. IV, III. ii. 95 When I from France set foot at Rauenspurgh. 1719 De Foe Crusoe II. vi, I was never to set my foot off this island. 1838 Lytton Leila I. v, Since first thou didst set foot within the city. 1875 T. W. Higginson U.S. Hist. v. 38 Columbus was not the first to set foot on the mainland.

29. With reference to walking or running.

a. (*to go*) *on one's own feet* or †*foot*: walking. *to pull foot* (colloq.): to run away, be off. †*on the foot of*: ready to start upon. †*to set foot forward*: to advance; also to quicken one's pace. †*to set on one's foot*: to start on the way; depart. †*to show the feet*: to depart. †*give me your foot*: let me see you go. *to take one's foot in one's hand*: to depart; also, to make a journey. *to take to one's feet* (or †*foot*): to use the feet, go on foot, to walk as opposed to 'ride.' (*Mr.*) *Foot's horse* (jocularly): one's feet. *to catch* (a person) *on the wrong foot*: to catch unawares. *to get* (or *set,* etc.) *off on the right foot*: to start successfully; similarly *to get* (or *start,* etc.) *off on the wrong foot*: to start unsuccessfully; to fail to establish good relations.

a1400-50 Alexander 3246 Quen fortune foundis him fra and him þe fete schewis. 1500-20 Dunbar Poems xxi. 12 Oft falsett rydis with ane rowt, Quhen trewth gois on his fute abowt. 1508 Kennedy Flyting w. Dunbar 473 Throu Ingland thef, and tak the to thy fute. 1548 Hall Chron., Hen. IV. (an. 1) 18 He.. never set fote forward duryng the first .ij. monethes, for the reisyng of the siege. 1575 J. Still Gammer Gurton IV. ii, Go softly, make no noyse, giue me your foote sir John, Here will I waite vpon you, tyl you come out anone. 1600 Holland Livy III. xxvii. (1609) 106 Willing them to set foot forward, to mend their pace and make speed. 1601 Shaks. Jul. C. II. i. 332 Set on your foote, And.. I follow you. 1605 —— Macb. II. iii. 131 Donal. Let's away, Our Teares are not yet brew'd. Mal. Nor our strong Sorrow Vpon the foot of Motion. 1755 Smollett Don Quix. IV. iv. I. 232 Andrew.. made his bows, and as the saying is, took his foot in his hand. 1779 Mad. D'Arblay Diary 19 June, I took to my feet and ran away. 1818 M. G. Lewis Jrnl. W. Ind. (1834) 109 One of my ladies chose to pull foot, and did not return.. till this morning. 1864 Burton Cairngorm 5 The kind of scenes he may alight on if he 'take his feet in his hands'. 1883 Harper's Mag. 946/1 The privilege of taking this trip on 'foot's horse'. 1909 R. Beach Silver Horde xiii. 173, I want to see you get off on the right foot; I'd feel bad if you fell down. 1925 Country Gentleman (U.S.) Sept. 11/2, I know I got off on the wrong foot. It was manifest in the faces and general demeanor of the grave and reverend Senators. 1937 N. Coward Present Indicative VI. xi. 262 To me a round of applause.. even though it be conventional rather than spontaneous, almost always sets my performance off on the right foot. 1947 C. Witting Let X be Murderer iv. 43 They caught me on the wrong foot, Glad. What did the old fool want to go and ring up for? 1949 R. Chandler Little Sister xxxii. 232, I got off on the wrong foot. After that I just had to take my lumps. 1955 Times 12 May 11/2 Starting the Colonial Development Corporation off on the wrong foot. 1956 A. Wilson Anglo-Saxon Attitudes I. iii. 71 'Oh, he's brilliant all right,' said Robin.. 'But he obviously gets off on the wrong foot with his colleagues.' 1958 Listener 7 Aug. 195/2 There is that vast number of marriages.. where the marriage takes place to give the baby a name. The whole thing starts on the wrong foot. 1958 Times 18 Dec. 11/4 The least athletically inclined are frequently finding themselves.. bowled out, tackled or caught on the wrong foot. 1960 H. Innes Doomed Oasis II. iii. 120 The relationship hadn't been at all easy at first. 'They started off on the wrong foot, you see.' 1961 Times 9 May 13/3 The Commons-peerage question must be disposed of before these wider discussions can be got off on the right foot.

b. With reference to 'pace'. *to have leaden feet*: to move very slowly. *to have the foot of*: to be more speedy than. (*to move*) *at a foot's pace*: at walking pace. *to run a good,* etc. *foot* (of a horse): to run at a good pace, run at his best pace. *to put* (or *set*) *the* (or *one's*) *best foot first, foremost* or *forward*: see BEST *a.* 5. †*the better foot before*: at one's best pace. †*to put the wrong foot before*: to make a blunder.

1588 Shaks. Tit. A. II. iii. 192 Come on my Lords, the better foote before. 1589 R. Harvey Pl. Perc. 4 Thou putst the wrong foote before. 1601 Dent Pathw. Heaven 141 Though God haue leaden feet, and commeth slowly to execute wrath. a1613 Overbury A Wife (1638) 164 Hee is still setting the best foot forward. 1737 Bracken Farriery Impr. (1757) II. 123 A large, nimble, strong, well-moving Horse, that would run a pretty good Foot. 1785 Burns To Davie xi, And then he'll hilch, and stilt, an' jimp, And rin an unco fit. 1818 M. G. Lewis Jrnl. W. Ind. (1834) 362 Thus we proceeded crawling along at a foot's pace. 1849 E. E. Napier Excurs. S. Africa II. 373 We had to put our best foot foremost. 1856 Lever Martin's of Cro' M. 133 I threw out a 'tenpenny' in the midst. The 'blind' fellow saw it first, but the 'lame cripple' had the foot of him, and got the money!

c. With the sense of 'step'. *to miss one's foot*: to take a wrong step. †*foot by* (*for, with*) *foot*: step by step, gradually; keeping step together; also *fig.* *to change foot* or *feet*: see CHANGE *v.* 9. *to have a good foot on the floor* (Sc.): 'to dance well' (Jam.).

c1290 S. Eng. Leg. I. 143/1300 Send with us fot with fot ane legat. c1430 Pilgr. Lyf Manhode IV. lxi. (1869) 205 þe olde also, foot bi foot, comen þider. 1535 Stewart Cron. Scot. II. 378 Fit for fit to Forfar all tha fuir. 1579 Tomson Calvin's Serm. Tim. 347/2 Hee that walketh with a straight foote.. will not fetch many windlesses to drawne neere to God. 1626 A. Cook in Abp. Usher's Lett. (1686) 373 Your Lordship had need now to do something; for few go with a right foot, and the Enemies are many. 1631 Weever Anc. Fun. Mon. 216 Anselme.. followed his predecessors steps almost foot by foot. 1785 Burns Halloween xxvi, She jumpet, But mist a fit, an' in the pool Out-owre the lugs she plumpet.

30. Expressing position relatively to the feet.

a. *at* (a person's) *feet* or †*foot*: low on the ground close to him; also, *fig.*, in the attitude of supplicaton, homage, subjection or discipleship; similarly *to come,* etc. *to a person's feet; before, beside one's feet,* etc. See FALL *v.* 20.

c950 Lindisf. Gosp. Luke vii. 38 And stod bihianda æt fotum his mið tæherum. c1175 Lamb. Hom. 101 Ða ileaffullen brohton heore gersum and leiden heo et þere apostlan fotan. a1300 Cursor M. 9599 (Cott.) Be-for þe king fote sco stode. 1382 Wyclif Acts xxii. 3 A man Jew.. norischid forsoth in this citie bisydis the feet of Gamaliel. c1489 Caxton Sonnes of Aymon xxvi. 550 He cast hymself to the fete of hym. 1596 Shaks. Merch. V. III. i. 92, I would my daughter were dead at my foot. 1710 Berkeley Princ. Hum. Knowl. Ded. Wks. 1871 I. 133 To lay this treatise at your lordship's feet. 1715-20 Pope Iliad xxiii. 28 The bloody Hector stretch'd before thy feet. 1814 Scott Drama (1874) 203 The royal bear-ward.. lodged a formal complaint at the feet of her majesty. 1861 Trollope Barchester T. xxvii, It was all very well to have Mr. Slope at her feet. 1895 Bookman Oct. 23/1 The lessons that he had learnt at the feet of Mazarin.

b. †(*to follow*) *at* or *to foot*: closely. †*to foot and hand*: in close attendance, ready to render service (cf. 'to wait upon one hand and foot'). *with a foal at* (*her*) *foot*: said of a mare.

a **1300** *Cursor M.* 24031 (Cott.) We folud þam to fote. *Ibid.* 6394 (Gött.) þar had þai watir in wildernes land, Plente for men, to fhote and hand. *c* **1420** *Sir Amadace* (Camden) lviii, I ȝo cummawunde To serue him wele to fote and honde. **1602** Shaks. *Ham.* iv. iii. 56 Follow him at foote. **1612** Sir R. Boyle in *Lismore Papers* (1886) I. 10, 5 of them [mares] had horse colte at their feet. **1884** *West. Morn. News* 30 Aug. 1/6 Two excellent brood mares, with foals at foot.

c. *under* or *beneath a person's foot* or *feet*: *fig.* in subjection to him, at his mercy or at his absolute disposal. Cf. 33.

c **825** *Vesp. Ps.* viii. 8 [6] All ðu underdeodes under fotum his. *c* **1175** *Lamb. Hom.* 129 Al eorðlic þing ure drihten dude under his fotan. *a* **1225** *Juliana* 60 þu.. wurpe under hare fet hare fan alle. **1597** Shaks. *2 Hen. IV*, iii. i. 63 Who..layd his Loue and Life vnder my foot. **1867** Trollope *Chron. Barset* III. vii. Mr. Crawley was now but a broken reed, and was beneath his feet.

d. *to have* or *set one's foot on the neck of*: (fig.) to hold completely in subjection: see neck *sb.*[1] 3a.

31. (*to sell corn*) *on the foot*: 'to sell it along with the straw before it is thrashed off' (Jam.).

1780 A. Young *Tour Irel.* I. 330 The value sold on the foot is in general 8*l.* **1812** *Agric. Surv. Stirling* iv. 104 The tenant, shall not sell his victual upon the foot, as it is called, or with the straw.

32. on foot. (See also afoot.) **a.** On one's own feet, walking or running, in opposition to *on horseback*, etc. †Also, *of*, *upon foot*.

a **1300** *Cursor M.* 6267 (Cott.) He folud wit ost on hors and fote. *a* **1310** in Wright *Lyric P.* 90 The is bettere on fote gon, then wycked hors to ryde. *c* **1314** *Guy Warw.* (A.) 2397 When Gii seye þe douke of fot. *c* **1400** *Destr. Troy* 356 So faire freikes vppon fote was ferly to se. **1568** Grafton *Chron.* II. 238 The Englishmen..made three battayles on foote. **1667** Milton *P.L.* ii. 941 Treading the crude consistence, half on foot, Half flying. **1860** Dickens *Uncomm. Trav.* iv, I drove up..(fearful of being late, or I should have come on foot).

b. In motion, stirring, astir (in opposition to *sitting still*, or the like).

1592 Shaks. *Ven. & Ad.* 679 When thou hast on foot the purblind hare, Mark..How he outruns the wind. **1607** — *Cor.* iv. iii. 49 The Centurions, and their charges..to be on foot at an houres warning. **1674** N. Cox *Gentl. Recreat.* i. (1677) 99 When the Hare is started and on foot. **1818** M. G. Lewis *Jrnl. W. Ind.* (1834) 161 Every body in Jamaica is on foot by six in the morning. **1885** T. Roosevelt *Hunting Trips* 280 Though I got very close up to my game, they were on foot before I saw them.

c. In active existence, employment, or operation.

1588 Shaks. *L.L.L.* v. ii. 757 Since loues argument was first on foote, Let not the cloud of sorrow justle it. **1651** W. G. tr. *Cowel's Inst.* 190 Unlesse the lease which is on foot.. be within three yeares of expiring. **1711** Steele *Spect.* No. 262 ¶6 Those Gentlemen who set on Foot the Royal Society. **1779** Burke *Corr.* (1844) II. 283 Nothing seems to me more wild..than the subscriptions now on foot. **1818** Cruise *Digest* (ed. 2) V. 212 Terms for years, which are kept on foot by purchasers..are not barred by fine. **1862** Ld. Brougham *Brit. Const.* xvii. 264 If, then, a King were to retain the troops on foot without a Mutiny Bill. **1867** Trollope *Chron. Barset* xlvii, The bishop had decided to put on foot another investigation.

33. under foot. (Sometimes written as one word.) **a.** Beneath one's feet; often *to trample* or *tread under foot* (also †*feet*), in lit. sense, also *fig.* to oppress, outrage, contemn. †*to bring, have under foot*: to bring into, hold in subjection. †*to cast under foot*: to ruin.

c **1205** Lay. 11693 þis lond..he..hæfde al vnder fot. *c* **1305** *Pilate* 49 in *E.E.P.* (1862) 112 If he þat lond chasteþ wel: and bringeþ vnder fote. *c* **1420** Hoccleve *Compl.* 13 Deathe vnder fote shall hym thrist adowne. **1551** Robinson tr. *More's Utop.* (Arb.) 161 Dissention..hathe caste under foote..the..riches of many cities. **1593** Shaks. *2 Hen. VI*, v. i. 209 From thy Burgonet Ile rend thy Beare, And tread it vnder foot with all contempt. **1647** Clarendon *Hist. Reb.* ii. §12 He never deserted it till both it and he were over-run and trod under foot. **1652** Wright tr. *Camus' Nature's Paradox* 260 They trampled under feet all private considerations. **1700** S. L. tr. *Fryke's Two Voy.* 308 They [elephants] would have trampl'd us under foot. *Mod. colloq.* It is not raining, but it is very wet under foot.

b. *Naut.* 'Under the ship's bottom; said of an anchor which is dropped while she has headway' (Smyth *Sailor's Wd.-bk.*); also of the movement of the tide, etc. Also †*to have a good* etc. *ship under foot* (i.e. to be sailing in such a ship).

1633 T. James *Voy.* 79 This Cable had laine slacke vnder-foot. **1670** Wood in Hacke *Coll. Voy.* iii. (1699) 61 It must ..be a bad Port in Winter, when..a Storm blows at West.. and a Tide of Ebb under Foot. **1719** De Foe *Crusoe* x. (1840) 166 Running cheerfully before the wind, and with a strong tide or eddy under foot. **1726** Shelvocke *Voy.* (1757) 321, I had a pretty good ship under foot, though she made but a poor figure. **1804** Capt. Duff in *Naval Chron.* XV. 281 We have a good comfortable ship under foot. **1860** *Merc. Marine Mag.* VII. 180 The Pilot..dropped the port anchor under foot.

VIII. *attrib.* and *Comb.*

34. a. simple attrib., as *foot-clamper, -muscle, -part, -shackle, -wear, -wound*.

1856 Kane *Arct. Expl* I. xxii. 273 Pointed staves, *foot-clampers, and other apparatus for climbing ice. **1854** Woodward *Mollusca* (1856) 250 The *foot muscles. **1644** Evelyn *Diary* 19 Nov., The nave..is in form of a cross, whereof the *foot-part is the longest. **1848** Craig, *Foot-shackles, fetters, shackles for fixing the feet. **1881** *Chicago Times* 11 June, If values were based upon present quotations of leather, an advance would be necessary upon several descriptions of *foot-wear. **1922** *Daily Mail* 1 Nov. 8 Women and girls, with their short skirts, neat footwear, and other prevailing fashions. **1954** F. C. Avis *Boxing Ref. Dict.* 43 *Footwear*, regulation boots. *a* **1225** *Ancr. R.* 194 Vlesches fondunge mei beon iefned to *uot wunde.

b. In the sense of 'on foot', 'going on foot', as †*foot-chapman, -comer, -excursion, -farer,* †*-fight, -hawker,* †*-messenger, -party, -passenger, -people, -robber, -servant, -tour, -traveller, -walker, -wandering*; *foot-faring, -running* adjs.

1584 *Burgh Rec. Aberdeen* (Spald. Club) II. 54 That no extranear *fut chopmane copair resort to this toun fra this furtht. **1811** Coleridge in *Southey's Life Bell* (1844) II. 645 The entrance..is disagreeable even to *foot-comers. **1796** T. Twining *Trav. Amer.* (1894) 148 He was absent with some friends on a *foot excursion. **1861** G. Meredith *E. Harrington* I. vi. 95 Dividing his attention between the *footfarer and moon. **1868** G. Macdonald *R. Falconer* I. 190 Half a dozen *footfaring students from Aberdeen. **1580** Sidney *Arcadia* (1622) 171 So began our *foot-fight. **1884** S. Dowell *Taxes in Eng.* III. 38 The revenue from the *foot-hawkers' licences. **1688** R. Holme *Armoury* iii. 60/1 *Foot Messengers of Arms, are such *Foot Servants, as are imployed by the Heralds of Arms. **1856** Kane *Arct. Expl.* I. xx. 252 The ice had baffled three organized *foot-parties. **1832** Babbage *Econ. Manuf.* iv. (ed. 3) 34 When *foot-passengers are knocked down by carriages. **1807** Pike *Sources Mississ.* ii. (1810) 114 My Indians and *foot people were yet in the rear. **1754** *Scoundrel's Dict.* 29 The Low-Pad, or *Foot-robber. **1865** Kingsley *Herew.* I. i. 62 A *foot-running slave. **1883** F. M. Crawford *Dr. Claudius* iii, He was going away on his customary *foot tour. **1805** Wordsw. *Prelude* (1850) 152 *Foot-travellers side by side.. we pursued Our journey. **1751** Hume *Princ. Morals* iv. 71 *note*, Amongst *Foot-walkers, the Right-hand entitles a Man to the Wall. **1839** Bailey *Festus* v. (1852) 62 The fastings, the *footwanderings, and the preachings of Christ.

c. *esp.* in sense 'of or pertaining to infantry', as †*foot-arms,* †*-band, -barracks, -company, -drill,* †*-officer, -soldier,* †*-troop*. Also foot-folk, -guards.

1662 *Protests Lords* I. 26 For assessing all persons mentioned therein for horse, arms, and *foot-arms. **1598** Barret *Theor. Warres* ii. i. 26 A Captaine of Infanterie, or *foot-band. **1835** D. Booth *Analyt. Dict.* 157 Artillery-barracks, Horse-barracks, and *Foot-barracks. **1635** Barriffe *Mil. Discip.* lxvii. (1643) 178 The severall motions and grounds, for the disciplining of a *foot company. **1833** *Regul. Instr. Cavalry* i. 43 The position of the man as in *Foot-drill. *a* **1674** Clarendon *Hist. Reb.* xvi. §96 [Monk] had the reputation of a very good *Foot-Officer. **1622** Drayton *Poly-olb.* xxix. 155 Seauen Earles, nine hundred Horse, and of *Foot-souldiers more. **1874** Boutell *Arms & Arm.* viii. 133 The treatment..shown to the foot-soldier of England by the nobles. **1579** Fenton *Guicciard.* (1618) 271 The French..discouered the *foot-troopes of the Genoways.

d. In sense 'for the use of persons going on foot', 'serving for foot-traffic', as *foot-passage, -pavement, -road, -track, -walk*; also, *foot-boat, -bridge* in 35 below, and foot-path, -way.

1789 Brand *Newcastle* I. 15 Convenient *foot-passages have lately been opened out on each side of this gate. **1791** Boswell *Johnson* II. 528 When he had got down on the *foot-pavement, he called out 'fare you well'. **1863** Kinglake *Crimea* (1876) I. xiv. 276 Numbers of spectators ..crowded the foot-pavement. **1784** Bage *Barham D.* I. 220 [He] saw a well dressed young woman..take the *foot road down to the river side. **1891** C. T. C. James *Rom. Rigmarole* 125, I thought I would..quit the beaten *foot-track, and strike boldly across country. **1837** Hawthorne *Twice-Told T.* (1851) I. ix. 166 Leaving him to sidle along the *footwalk.

e. In the names of various appliances worked by the foot, as *foot-bellows, blower, -drill, -hammer, -lathe, -lever, -press, -vise*; esp. in names of speed and control appliances on vehicles, as *foot-accelerator, -brake, -braking, -clutch, -starter*; also *foot-acted, -operated* adjs.

1908 *Westm. Gaz.* 16 Jan. 4/2 A *foot accelerator is also fitted. **1908** *Daily Chron.* 21 Nov. 9/4 The three-speed gear in association with a *foot-acted brake. **1874** Knight *Dict. Mech.* I. 901/2 *Foot-bellows. **1884** W. A. Ross *Blowpipe* 1 A *foot-blower. **1888** *Lockwood's Dict. Mech. Engin.*, *Foot Brake. **1925** *Morris Owner's Man.* 11 Both foot and hand brakes operate on drums fitted to the back wheels. **1909** *Daily Chron.* 27 Feb. 7/7 *Foot braking is less fatiguing for prolonged spells of application. **1905** *Westm. Gaz.* 17 Oct. 4/2 Many motorists who find the working of a *foot-clutch trying. **1892** *Lockwood's Dict. Mech. Engin.* (ed. 2), **Foot-drill*, a light drilling machine driven by a treadle. **1812–6** J. Smith *Panorama Sc. & Art.* I. 58 *Foot lathes. **1892** *Lockwood's Dict. Mech. Engin.* (ed. 2), **Foot Lever*, a lever worked by the pressure of the foot alone. **1908** *Westm. Gaz.* 30 Jan. 4/1 A large *foot-operated contracting brake. **1959** *Times* 2 Oct. 11/3 The foot-operated dip switch. **1967** *Jane's Surface Skimmer Systems 1967–68* 9/1 The engine is controlled by a foot-operated accelerator. **1971** *Engineering* Apr. 69/2 A hydraulic master cylinder unit, coupled to a pivoted foot-operated lever.

f. objective, etc., as *foot-binder, -kisser, -swather, -washer, -wiper*; *foot-failing, -firm*, adjs.; instrumental, as †*foot-tempered* adj.; locative, etc., as *foot-feathered, -foundered, -gilt, -lame,* (also *-lameness*) adjs.; also, *footward* adv.

1886 *Wanderings in China* I. 168 *Foot-binders..women whose profession it is to produce this horrible distortion. **1609** J. Davies *Holy Roode* Wks. (Grosart) 9/1 To march vpon the Seas *foot-failing floore? **1818** Keats *Endym.* iv. 331 *Foot-feathered Mercury. **1813** 'Æditus' *Metrical Remarks* 29 The *foot-firm sand Stretches its lengthened course along the land. **1801** Bloomfield *Rural T.* 227 A poor old Man, *foot founder'd and alone. **1859** Tennyson *Vivien* 280 *Foot-gilt with all the blossom-dust of those Deep meadows. **1868** Browning *Ring & Bk.* ix. 1085 Born foot-washer and foot-wiper, nay *Foot-kisser to each comrade of you all. *c* **1305** *Pol. Songs* (Camden) 194 Sixti thousent on a day hue maden *fot lome. *c* **1325** *Poem Times Edw. II*, 264 Ibid. 335 Thus knihtshipe [is] acloied and waxen al fot lame. **1828** *Sporting Mag.* XXII. 347 He [a horse] was struck with *foot-lameness. **1762** Goldsm. *Cit. W.* iii. ¶6 Your nose-borers, *feet-swathers..would all want bread, should their neighbours want vanity. *c* **1420** *Pallad. on Husb.* vi. 182 Wel *foote-tempred morter theron trete. **1822** T. Mitchell *Aristoph.* II. 211 Cecrops..(what if thy dimensions end *Footward in a wily serpent?) **1871** R. Ellis tr. *Catull.* lxiv. 66 That footward-fallen apparel. **1868** *Foot-washer [see *foot-kisser* above]. **1870** Spurgeon *Treas. Dav.* Ps. li. 14 If we could be preacher, precentor, doorkeeper, pew-opener, footwasher..all in one. **1868** *Foot-wiper [see *foot-kisser* above].

35. a. Special comb.: **foot-ale** *dial.* (see quots.); †**foot-and-half-foot** *a.*, sesquipedalian; **foot-and-mouth disease**, 'a febrile affection of horned cattle and some other animals, communicable also to man' (*Syd. Soc. Lex.* 1884); **foot-bank** *Fortif.* = banquette (see also quot. 1626); **foot-base** *Arch.*, 'the moulding above the plinth of an apartment' (Ogilvie); †**foot-bass**, an instrument on which a bass is played by the feet (see quot.); **foot-bath**, †(*a*) a 'wash' for the feet; (*b*) the act of bathing the feet; (*c*) a vessel in which the feet are bathed; **foot-bearing** *Mech.*, a bearing for the foot of a vertical shaft: cf. foot-step; †**foot-bench** = banquette; †**foot-blast**, the blast produced by bellows worked with the foot; ?†**foot-boat**, a ferry-boat for foot-passengers only; **foot-bone**, the tarsus; **foot-bridge**, (*a*) a bridge for foot-passengers; (*b*) *Mech.* (see quot. 1872); **foot-candle**, a unit of illumination equivalent to the illumination of a surface all of which is at a distance of one foot from a point source of light having a luminous intensity of one candela (or formerly one international candle), corresponding to a luminous flux density of one lumen per square foot; †**foot-clapper**, a dancer; **foot-coal**, an underlying stratum of coal; **foot-cushion**, (*a*) a cushion for the feet; (*b*) *Entom.*, a pulvillus; **foot-dirt** = *foots* (see foot *sb.*); **foot-dragging**, a deliberate delay or slowness (cf. drag *v.* 1b); **foot-drain**, a shallow drain; cf. *foot-trench*; **foot-drop** *Path.*, a permanently extended position of the foot, due to paralysis of the flexor muscles; †**foot-fast**, a prisoner; †**foot-fastness**, captivity; †**foot-follower**, an attendant (transl. L. *pedisequus*, *-sequa*); **foot-free**, *a.* and *adv.*, with the foot or feet free; **foot-gang**, (*a*) 'a long, narrow chest, extending alongside a wooden bed; (*b*) as much ground as one can move on' (Jam.); †**foot-geld** (see quot. 1641); †**foot-gin**, a snare for the feet; †**foot-glove**, a kind of shoe; **foot-grease** (see quot.); †**foot-grene** = *foot-gin*; **foot-guard**, a guard or protection for the foot; **foot-halt**, a disease which attacks the feet of sheep; **foot-hedge** (see quots.); **foot-hole**, a hole in which to place the foot (in climbing); †**foot-husk** (see quot.); **foot-iron** (see quots.); **foot-jaw**, one of the anterior limbs of crustacea and other arthropoda which are modified so as to assist in mastication; **foot-key**, an organ pedal; **foot-knave** = footman; **foot-lambert**, a unit of luminance equal to the average luminance of a surface emitting or reflecting one lumen per square foot; †**foot-land-raker**, a foot-pad; **foot-length**, *Angling* (see quot.); **foot-level** (see quot.); **foot-ley**, *dial.* (see quot. 1881); **foot-licker**, 'a slave, an humble fawner, one who licks the foot' (J.); so **foot-licking** *ppl. a.*; **foot-line**, (*a*) *Printing* (see quots.); (*b*) *Fishing*, 'the lead-line or lower line of a net or seine' (*Cent. Dict.*); **foot-locker** *U.S.*, a small trunk or chest; **foot-log** *U.S.*, a log used as a foot-bridge; †**foot-maid**, †**-maiden**, a female attendant; **foot-maker** *Glass-making* (see quot. 1881); †**foot-match**, a running- or walking-match; **foot-muff**, a muff for keeping the feet warm; †**foot-nail**, some kind of nail; †**foot-organ** (cf. *foot-bass* above); **foot-ornament** *Arch.* (see quot.); †**foot-pack**, a pedlar's pack; **foot-pad**, a pad to protect the foot of a horse (Knight); also *Entom.* = *foot-cushion* (*Cent. Dict.*); also a device on a space vehicle; **foot-page**, a boy attendant or servant; **foot-pan**, (*a*) a foot-bath; (*b*) a foot-warmer; **foot-peat** (see quot. and cf. *breast-peat*); **foot-piece** *Mining* (see quot.); †**foot-pimp**, a pimp in attendance; **foot-plate** (see quots.); **foot-plough**, a plough without a wheel, a *swing-*

plough; †**foot-poet** (after *foot-man*, etc: see quot.); **foot-post**, a letter-carrier or messenger who travels on foot; postal delivery by means of such carriers; **foot-pound** *Mech.*, the quantity of energy required to raise a weight of one pound to the height of one foot; **foot-poundal**, a unit consisting of the energy of a pound weight moving at the rate of one foot per second; **foot-pound-second**, used to designate a system of units based upon the foot, the pound, and the second as units of length, force, and time respectively; **foot-race**, a race run by persons on foot, a running-match; so **foot-racing** *vbl. sb.*; **foot-rail**, (*a*) a rail (*esp.* a bar or cross-piece connecting the legs of a table or seat) upon which the feet are rested; (*b*) (see quot. 1874); (*c*) (see quot. 1867); (*d*) var. form of FOOTRILL; **foot-rest**, a bench, stool, or the like, used for supporting a person's feet; **foot-ring**, the circular rim on the base of a plate, vase, etc.; **foot-room**, space in which to move the feet; **foot-rope** *Naut.*, (*a*) the bolt-rope to which the lower edge of a sail is sewed; (*b*) a rope extended beneath a yard upon which the sailors stand when furling or reefing; **foot-rot**, (*a*) an inflammatory disease of the foot in cattle and sheep; whence *foot-rotting* (vbl. sb.), treating sheep that have the foot-rot; (*b*) a fungal disease of plants, affecting the base of the stem; **foot-rule**, a measuring rule one foot long; also *fig.*; **foot run** [RUN *sb.*[1] 13 a], a length of one foot measured lengthwise along a material or structure, esp. one conceived of as having a potentially variable length; **foot-rut** *Agric.* (see quot.); **foot-scent** *Hunting*, the scent of a trail; **foot-scraper** = SCRAPER 5; **foot-screw** (see quot.); †**foot-seam** (see quot.); **foot-seine** (see quot.); **foot-set** (see quot. 1854 and cf. *foot-hedge*); **foot-sheet**, a sheet formerly used to sit upon while dressing or undressing; also, 'a narrow sheet spread across the foot of a bed' (Jam. *Suppl.*); **foot-side**, *Sc.* (*a*) *adj.*, (of a garment), reaching to the feet; (*b*) *adv.*, step for step; phr. *to keep foot-side*, to keep pace (*with*); **foot-slope**, the slope at the foot of a hill; **foot-space-rail** *Naut.* (see quots.); †**foot-spore**, the mark or print of a foot; †**foot-stake**, a base or support; **foot-stay**, a stay or rest for the feet; **foot-stick**, *Printing* (see quot. 1888); †**foot-stock**, (*a*) a kind of fulling-stocks used by hatters; (*b*) a step or stool for the feet; (*c*) *Naut.* (see quot. 1598); **foot-stone**, †(*a*) a base, pedestal; (*b*) the foundation-stone of a building; (*c*) the stone at the foot of a grave; **foot-stove**, a stove to warm the feet; †**foot-strife**, strife or contention in running; **foot-stroke**, a stroke at the foot of a letter; **foot-stump**, = *foot-tubercle*; **foot-sugar** = *foots*: see FOOT *sb.* 22; †**foot-team**, '(apparently) the end of the drawing-gear which is fastened to a plough or harrow' (Skeat); **foot-ton**, the amount of energy capable of raising a ton weight to the height of one foot; **foot-tramp**, the tramp of the feet, also a tramp or expedition on foot; †**foot-trap**, (*a*) a trap or snare for the feet; (*b*) the stocks; **foot-trench**, a shallow trench (cf. *foot-drain*); **foot-tubercle** (see quot.); **foot-valve**, (in a steam-engine) the valve between the air-pump and condenser; **foot-waling** *Naut.* (see quots.); **foot-wall** *Mining*, the wall or side of rock which is under a vein or lode; **foot-warmer**, a contrivance for keeping the feet warm, *esp.* while travelling; **foot-washing**, the washing of another's feet, *esp.* as a religious observance; also, locally as a wedding-ceremony; **foot-weir**, some kind of weir; †**foot-wharf**, (see quot.); †**foot-wise** *adv.*, with the feet first, footling; †**foot-withy**, a shackle for the foot of an animal; **foot-wobbler** *slang*, a foot-soldier; **foot-work**, †(*a*) attrib. in *footwork silk* (? meaning); (*b*) a work to protect the foot of a structure; (*c*) *Football*, 'work' done with the feet, dribbling and kicking; (*d*) in other games, dancing, etc.: agility, sureness, and accurate placing of the feet; also *fig.*; **foot-worn** *a.*, (*a*) worn by the feet; (*b*) worn or wearied as to the feet, footsore.

1747 HOOSON *Miner's Dict.*, *Foot-ale, an old Custom amongst Miners, when a Man enters first into Work, to pay his first Days Wages for Ale. **1881** *Leicestersh. Gloss.*, s.v. *Footing*, A stranger..will generally be asked to 'stand his foot-ale'. **1598** B. JONSON *Ev. Man in Hum.* Prol., With.. helpe of some few *foot-and-halfe-foote words. **1862** *Edin. Vet. Rev.* IV. 506 Cows affected with the *foot and mouth disease. **1626** AINSWORTH *Annot. Pentat.* Lev. ii. 13 They laid on the salt..on the *foot-banke (of the altar,) and on the top of the Altar. **1706** PHILLIPS (ed. Kersey), *Foot-bank* or *Foot-step*..a Step..under a Parapet, or Breast-work; upon which the men get up to Fire over it. **1882** O'DONOVAN *Merv Oasis* I. xvi. 275 The footbank has crumbled away to such an extent that only a few inches in breadth remain. **1786** T. JEFFERSON *Writ.* (1853) II. 75, I have lately examined a *foot-bass newly invented... It is placed on the floor, and the harpsichord..is set over it, the foot acting in concert on that, while the fingers play on this. **1599** A. M. tr. *Gabelhouer's Bk. Physicke* 357/2 Take Oaken-leaues M.iij. Saulte M.j. make therof a *footebath. **1858** SIMMONDS *Dict. Trade*, *Foot-bath*, a pan in which to wash the feet. **1855** OGILVIE Suppl., *Foot*. In *Mech.*, the lower end of an upright or vertical shaft, and which works in a foot-step, or *foot-bearing. **1629** *S'hertogenbosh* 19 Trenches with double bankets or *feet benches. **1622** MALYNES *Anc. Law-Merch.* 273 Vent..for the Litargium..as it is cast vp by the *Foot-blast. **1778** PENNANT *Tour in Wales* I. 64 The Romans knew only the weak powers of the foot-blast. **1579** DEE *Diary* (Camden) 6 The *fote-bote for the ferry at Kew was drowned and six persons. **1841** HARTSHORNE *Salop. Antiq.* 430 *Foot-boat*. **1658** SIR T. BROWNE *Gard. Cyrus* iii. 58 The thigh-bone, legge, *foot-bone, and claws of Birds. **1833** R. MUDIE *Brit. Birds* (1841) I. 23 The tarsus, or foot-bone. **1506** GUYLFORDE *Pilgr.* (Camden) 31 There lay ouer the same a tree for a *fote brydge. **1807** CRABBE *Par. Reg.* I. 802 The foot-bridge fail'd—he plung'd beneath the deep. **1892** *Lockwood's Dict. Mech. Engin.* (ed. 2), *Foot Bridge*, an arched bridge which carries a footstep bearing. **1906** *Illum. Engin.* I. 66/1 Owing largely to the loose and ambiguous manner in which the various terms expressing light-measurements are used..the term '*foot-candle'.. expresses but a vague idea to the average architect and engineer. **1949** H. C. WESTON *Sight, Light, & Efficiency* v. 150 The term foot-candle..is still in common use..but lumen per sq. ft. is now the preferred expression. **1963** J. M. FRASER *Psychol.* (ed. 2) xvii. 224 For certain jobs..up to four hundred foot-candles (the equivalent of bright sunlight) have been tried. **1620** SHELTON *Quix.* II. xix. 120 For your *Foot-clappers, I say nothing, you would wonder to see vm bestirre themselues. **1712** F. BELLERS in *Phil. Trans.* XXVII. 542 A coarse sort of Coal, called the *Foot-Coal. **1840** *Knickerbocker* XV. 105 About a foot from the bottom of every vein, there is a layer of earth... This divides it into 'foot-coal' and 'upper coal'. **1879** G. F. JACKSON *Shropsh. Word Bk.* 91 Foot coal. *c* **1460** J. RUSSELL *Bk. Nurture* 884 þe said shete ouer sprad So þat it keuer þe *fote coschyn and chayere. **1816** KIRBY & SP. *Entomol.* (1843) II. 257 Foot cushions (*pulvilli*). **1811** *East Reports* XIII. 523 Before..oil is delivered, it is the constant custom..for a broker..to attend to make a minute of the *foot-dirt and water in each cask. **1966** *New Statesman* 16 Dec. 896/1 One likely result of all this *foot-dragging is that the Nato Council will fail this week to seize what might have been an excellent opportunity to simplify the arrangements for European defence. **1969** *Guardian* 31 Jan. 10/2 There is no university now which does not have some appeals machinery..though there has been some foot-dragging on other issues. **1807** VANCOUVER *Agric. Devon* (1813) 285 To receive the surface-water from *foot-drains laid out upon the surface of the morass. **1908** C. W. DANIELS in Hutchison & Collier *Index of Treatment* (ed. 4) 119 When the '*foot-drop' is extreme, a cradle should be used to prevent..increasing the deformity. **1920** *Glasgow Herald* 8 July 4 Conditions affecting the feet..e.g. foot-drop, corns and contracted toes, clawfoot. **1950** E. D. W. HAUSER *Dis. Foot* (ed. 2) v. 84 In most instances the paralysis that causes a valgoplanus is associated with paralysis of the dorsiflexors, which means that foot drop is present. *a* **1300** *E.E. Psalter* lxxviii[i] 11 Inga in þi sight to seene Sighynge of *fote-festes þat beene. *Ibid.* civ. [cv.] 18 þai meked of him fete þare, In *fote-festnes harde þat ware. **1382** WYCLIF *1 Sam.* xxv. 42 And fyue child-wymmen, hir *feet folewers, wenten with hir. —— *1 Kings* xx. 14 Bi the foot folowers of the pryncis of prouyncis. **1837** W. IRVING *Capt. Bonneville* I. 50 A horse that is '*foot free', is tied to one thus secured. **1871** BROWNING *Balaustion* 1438 Thou, who stood'st Foot-free o' the snare. **1663** *Inv. Ld. J. Gordon's Furniture*, Ane arm chair, two stooles and ane *foot gange conforme to the bed. **1814** *Saxon & Gael* I. 108 I'll warran' she'll keep her ain side of the house; an' a fit-gang on her half-marrow's. **1594** R. CROMPTON *Jurisd. des Courts* 197 *Footegeld. **1641** *Termes de la Ley* s.v., Foot-geld is an Amercement for not cutting out the balls of great Dogges feet in the Forest. **1382** WYCLIF *Jer.* v. 26 Grenes puttende, and *feet gynnes [Vulg. *pedicas*]. **1720** DE FOE *Capt. Singleton* 161 The Buskins and *Foot-Gloves we wore. **1892** SIMMONDS *Dict. Trade* Suppl., *Foot-grease, a name for refuse of cotton seed, after the oil is pressed out. **1382** WYCLIF *Job* xviii. 10 His *foot grene [Vulg. *pedica*] is hid in the erthe. **1874** KNIGHT *Dict. Mech.*, *Foot-guard, a boot or pad to prevent the cutting of the feet by interfering or overreaching. **1794** *Ann. Agric.* XXII. 364 Sheep are subject to a disease called the *Foot-halt, which is thought to be catching. **1750** ELLIS *Mod. Husbandm.* I. i. 93 A *foot-hedge is one that has no Ditch belonging to it. **1854** ANNE BAKER *Northampt. Gloss.*, *Foot-hedge*, a slight dry hedge of thorns, placed by the side of a newly-planted hedge, to protect the quick. **1860** TYNDALL *Glac.* I. xi. 77 To render my *foot-holes broad and sure, I stamped upon the frozen crust. **1869** R. B. SMYTH *Goldf. Victoria* 611 *Footholes*—Holes cut in the sides of shafts or winzes to enable miners to ascend or descend them. **1706** PHILLIPS (ed. Kersey), **Foot-husks*, are short Heads, out of which Flowers grow. **1842** FRANCIS *Dict. Arts*, *Foot Iron, an iron fastened to the foot, in order to preserve the shoe while digging. **1858** SIMMONDS *Dict. Trade*, *Foot-iron*, *Foot-plate*, a step for a carriage. **1828** STARK *Elem. Nat. Hist.* II. 183 *Feet-jaws membranous. **1845** BAIRD in *Proc. Berw. Nat. Club* II. No. 13. 153 Mouth possessed of foot-jaws. *c* **1400** *Ywaine & Gaw.* 2267 The laddes of his kychyn, And also..his werst *fote-knave. **1925** *Trans. Illum. Engin. Sci.* XX. 631 The *Foot-lambert is the average brightness of any surface emitting or reflecting one lumen per square foot, or the uniform brightness of a perfectly diffusing surface emitting or reflecting one lumen per square foot. **1942** *Jrnl. Aeronaut. Sci.* IX. 263/1 A brightness level of 0·01 foot-lambert is..comparable in order of magnitude with the brightnesses of roads and highways under moonlight. **1958** *Van Nostrand's Sci. Encycl.* (ed. 3) 686/2 A foot candle is a unit of incident light and a foot lambert is a unit of emitted or reflected light. **1591** SHAKS. *1 Hen. IV*, II. i. 81, I am ioyned to no *Foot-land-Rakers. **1875** 'STONEHENGE' *Brit. Sports* I. v. ii. §1. 235 The *Foot-Length, or the extreme portion of the line, is.. generally made of pieces of gut, knotted together.. comprising a length of from three to eight feet. **1727–41** CHAMBERS *Cycl.*, **Foot Level*, an instrument, which serves to do the office both of a level, a square, and a Foot rule. **1638** *Terrier of Claybrook Glebe* (Leicestersh. Gloss.), In the New Close a hadley and *footeleay butting North and South. **1881** *Leicestersh. Gloss.*, *Foot-ley*, the lowest 'land' in a grass field. **1610** SHAKS. *Temp.* IV. i. 219 Do that good mischeefe, which may make..thy Caliban For aye thy *foot-licker. **1866** CARLYLE *Remin.* (1881) I. 258 On visit to some foot-licker whose people lived there. **1821** T. MOORE *Mem.* (1853) III. 276 If they know no medium between brawling rebellion and *foot-licking idolatry. **1676** MOXON *Print Lett.* 6 The **Foot-line* is the lower line that bounds the Letter. **1888** JACOBI *Printer's Voc.*, *Footline*, the bottom line in a page. **1943** *Harper's* June 16 They sit obscurely on *foot lockers during the daytime, when they must keep off their bunks. **1943** *Infantry Jrnl.* Aug. 51 Others went to town and came in late stumbling against footlockers and cursing. **1969** *Eugene* (Oreg.) *Register-Guard* 3 Dec. 1A/3 Foot lockers, cabinets and standard doorways are painted in combinations of the bright yellow and orange. **1969** *Sears, Roebuck Catal.* 298 *Metal-covered Footlocker.* Features a removable full-length molded plastic tray. Sheet steel covers sturdy plywood frame, fiberboard..top and bottom. **1845** W. T. PORTER *Big Bear Arkansas* 130, I husseled off..Jem to the *foot log. **1945** B. A. BOTKIN *Lay my Burden Down* 252 Go to the mill and cross on a foot log. *c* **1450** *Cov. Myst.* (Shaks. Soc.) 72 Sche xal be here *foot-mayd to mynyster here most mylde. **1847** HALLIWELL, **Foot-maiden*, a waiting maid. **1869** LEICESTER in *Eng. Mech.* 3 Dec. 282/2 Another workman, called the '*footmaker', fastens on the piece of glass. **1881** *Spon's Encycl. Industr. Arts*, etc. III. 1069 Each chair is made up of a 'workman', a first assistant or 'servitor', a second assistant or 'footmaker', and one or more boys. **1707** *Lond. Gaz.* No. 4314/3 There will be..*Foot-Matches, and other Divertisements. **1856** KANE *Arct. Expl.* I. xvi. 183 He was coiled up, with his nose buried in his bushy tail, like a fancy *foot-muff. **1406** in Rogers *Agric. & Prices* (1866) III. 446 *Fotnail called spiking, 1 c../6. **1802** M. CUTLER in *Life, etc.* (1888) II. 60 The *foot organ is a prodigious addition to Forte-Pianos. **1848** RICKMAN *Styles Archit.* (ed. 5) 74 The pedestal on which the pier stands being always square, while the pier itself..is often round, an interval occurs at the angles which is frequently filled up with an ornament consisting most commonly of rude foliage, these are usually called *foot ornaments. **1526** *Tolls* in Dillon *Calais & Pale* (1892) 80 Everye Jeweller carriing any *footepacke inwardes. **1966** *New Scientist* 30 June 835/1 The mechanical properties seen in *Surveyor's*.. photographs..show that the spacecraft's *footpads penetrated the surface for one inch. **1969** *Times* 22 July (Moon Rep.) p. i/1 I'm at the foot of the ladder. The L.M. footpads are only depressed in the surface about one or two inches. **1585** *Nomenclator* 519/1 A *foot-page. **1814** SCOTT *Wav.* xxiv, Callum Beg, the sort of foot-page who used to attend his person. **1855** H. CLARKE *Dict.*, **Foot-pan*, footbath. **1884** KNIGHT *Dict. Mech.* IV. 353/2 The foot-pans which are used in the railway cars of Continental Europe. **1802** FINDLATER *Agric. Surv. Peeb.* 208 As the digger stands upon the surface and presses in the peat-spade with his foot, such peat is designed *foot-peat. **1869** R. B. SMYTH *Goldf. Victoria* 611 **Foot-Piece*—A wedge of wood or part of a slab placed against the footwall. **1690** DRYDEN *Amphitryon* II. i, I who am a god, am degraded to a *foot-pimp. **1849** WEALE *Dict. Terms*, **Foot-plate*, the platform on which the engine-man and fire-man of a locomotive engine attend to their duties. **1855** H. CLARKE *Dict.*, *Foot-plate*, carriage step. **1677** PLOT *Oxfordsh.* 247 There are two sorts used in Oxfordshire, the *Foot, and Wheel-plough; whereof the first is used in deep and Clay Lands, being accordingly fitted with a broad fin share. **1807** A. YOUNG *Agric. Essex* I. v. 127 Both swing, or foot, and wheel ploughs. **1697** DRYDEN *Æneid* Ded., Our Italian Translatour..is a *Foot-Poet, he Lacquies by the side of Virgil at the best, but never mounts behind him. **1602** CAREW *Cornwall* 85 a, For carrying of such aduertisements and letters euery thorow-fare weekly appoynteth a *foot-Poast. **1841** ELPHINSTONE *Hist. Ind.* II. VIII. iii. 243 Foot posts, to a certain extent, must be coeval with village establishments. **1850** JOULE in *Phil. Trans.* CXL. 70 Hence 773·64 *foot-pounds will be the force which..is equivalent to 1° Fahr. in a lb. of water. **1892** *Foot-pound-second [see F.P.S. s.v. F III. 3]. **1968** *Van Nostrand's Sci. Encycl.* (ed. 4) 1912/2 The length-force-time system to be discussed here is the foot-pound-second system. **1663** PEPYS *Diary* (1890) 172 The great *foot-race run this day on Banstead Downes. **1849** MACAULAY *Hist. Eng.* I. 252 He..won footraces in his boots against fleet runners in shoes. **1801** STRUTT *Sports & Past.* II. ii. 70 *Foot-racing was considered an essential part of a young man's education. **1867** SMYTH *Sailor's Word-bk.*, **Foot-rails*, narrow mouldings raised on a vessel's stern. **1874** KNIGHT *Dict. Mech.* I. 903/1 *Foot-rail*, a railroad rail having wide-spreading foot flanges, a vertical web, and a bulb-shaped head. **1861** BERESF. HOPE *Eng. Cathedr. 19th C.* 148 Only three of the ranges were really sittings, the remainder having served as steps and *footrests. **1937** *Proc. Prehist. Soc.* III. 52 A large vessel with slightly raised base and *foot-ring. **1952** G. SAVAGE *18th Cent. Eng. Porc.* xxiii. 309 Champion's plates are more numerous than those of Cookworthy... Mostly they have a double foot-ring to prevent the centre of the plate from sagging downward during firing. **1967** *Antiquaries Jrnl.* XLVII. 229 Large platter with thick wall and scarcely defined rim... The foot-ring is low but carefully moulded. **1776** MICKLE tr. *Camoens' Lusiad* 126 The mountain and the wide-spread lawn Afford no *foot-room for the crowded foe. *c* **1000** ÆLFRIC *Gloss.* in Wr.-Wülcker 167 *Propes*, *fotrap. **1772–84** COOK *Voy.* (1790) V. 1915 In lowering the main top-sail.. the violence of the wind tore it out of the foot-rope. **1840** R. H. DANA *Bef. Mast* v. 11 We got out upon the weather-side of the jib-boom, our feet on the foot-ropes. **1807** *Ess. Highl. Soc.* III. 430 **Foot-rot*—is frequently occasioned in the milking season. **1873** G. C. DAVIES *Mount. & Mere* xxii. 193 A sure preventative against footrot. **1899** G. MASSEE *Text-bk. Plant Dis.* 333 This disease is known as 'mal-di-gomma' in Italy, and 'foot-rot' in Florida. **1926** H. H. HUME *Cultiv. Citrus Fruits* xxix. 462 Its history in Europe extends back to about 1845, and foot-rot worked destruction in the groves of the Azores some years previous to that time. **1952** E. RAMSDEN tr. *Gram & Weber's Plant Dis.* 68/2 Foot rot is a similar condition in older plants. *Ibid.* 69/1 Sclerotia are rarely to be found on damping off or foot-rot lesions. **1884** MARCUS CLARKE *Mem.* 99 Young Hopeful..is set to work *foot-rotting. **1727–41** CHAMBERS *Cycl.*, *Foot rule [see *foot* *level*]. 1760 RAPER in *Phil. Trans.* LI. 774 The foot-rules found in old ruins at Rome, are of various lengths. 1856 EMERSON *Eng. Traits, Character* Wks. (Bohn) II. 59 They.. measure with an English footrule every cell of the Inquisition. 1903 *Westm. Gaz.* 16 June 2/2 The advantage of having a foot-rule, so to speak, by which to test agreements for purchase. 1904 *Daily Chron.* 12 May 3/2 Mr. Richard Bagot's work may not always satisfy the critical foot-rule. 1908 *Westm. Gaz.* 9 June 1/2 It was Mr. Chamberlain who had pointed to exports as a foot-rule with which he wanted us to measure up our trade as a whole. 1837 *Foot run [see RUN *sb.*[1] 13 a]. 1869 W. RICHARDSON *Timber Trades Price Bk.* 1 (*heading*) The price per foot run and its equivalent per 120·12 ft., irrespective of thickness or width. 1968 *Bodl. Libr. Rec.* VIII. 61 The installation..provides 12,500 foot-run of shelving for books up to 12 inches in height. 1846 *Jrnl. R. Agric. Soc.* VII. I. 72 At the head of the plough is a *foot rut, made of wood, and a wide piece of wood on the end, to prevent the plough going deep. 1875 'STONEHENGE' *Brit. Sports* I. I. iv. §4. 80 A good setter.. generally makes out a *foot-scent better than a pointer. 1872 *Harper's Mag.* XLIV. 547/2 *Foot-scrapers and mats were doubled at all the approaches. 1938 J. STEINBECK *Long Valley* 115 On the front and back porches foot-scrapers and cocoa-fibre mats kept dirt out of the house. 1874 KNIGHT *Dict. Mech.* I. 903/1 **Foot-screw*, a supporting foot, for giving a machine or table a level standing on an uneven floor. 1589 COGAN *Haven Health* cliv. (1636) 149 The fat which is left upon the water of the seething of Netes feet, called commonly *foot seame. 1874 E. W. H. HOLDSWORTH *Deep-Sea Fishing* iv. 157 Seans [sweep-nets] may be divided into three classes, namely, the sean proper..the 'tuck-sean', and the 'ground or *foot-sean'. 1601 HOLLAND *Pliny* I. 510 This was at first practised with *foot-sets for a prick-hedge. 1854 ANNE BAKER *Northampt. Gloss.*, *Foot-hedge*..called in some parts of the county a *foot-set*..a foot-set is described as two rows of quick, planted about a foot asunder on a slope. c1440 *Bk. Curtasye* 488 in *Babees Bk.* 193 Þo lorde schalle skyft hys gown at ny3t, Syttand on *foteshete tyl he be dy3t. 1494 *Househ. Ord.* 120 All this season the Kinge shall sit still in his footesheete. 1513 DOUGLAS *Æneis* VII. xi. 31 Gyrd in a garmont semely and *fut syd. 1780 M. SHIELDS *Faithf. Contendings* 38 The Lord is helping some to keep foot-side with the bretheren at home. 1873 GEIKIE *Gt. Ice Age* (1894) 437 The ice radiated outwards..to the *foot-slopes of the hills of Middle Germany. 1815 *Falconer's Dict. Marine*, **Footspace-rail*. c1850 *Rudim. Navig.* (Weale) 119 *Foot-space rail*, the rail that terminates the foot of the balcony, and in which balusters step. 1867 in SMYTH *Sailor's Word-bk.* c1000 *Sax. Leechd.* III. 286 Gif hit sy oðer feoh, sing on þæt *fotspor. 1481 CAXTON *Reynard* (Arb.) 38 Where his footspore stood there stryked he with his tayl. 1382 WYCLIF *Exod.* xxvii. 12 Ten pilers and as feele *footstakis [Vulg. *bases*]. 1658 SIR T. BROWNE *Gard. Cyrus* i. 37 The Crosse of our blessed Saviour..having in some descriptions an Empedon or crossing *foot stay. 1683 MOXON *Mech. Exerc.* II. 29 The *Foot-sticks [are placed] against the foot or bottom of the Page. 1888 JACOBI *Printer's Voc.*, *Footstick*, a bevelled stick put at the bottom of a page or pages to quoin up against. 1565 *Act 8 Eliz.* c. 11 §4 Untyll suche tyme as the same Cappe be..half thicked at the least in the *Footestocke. 1565 JEWEL *Def. Apol.* (1611) 384 Sapores.. when hee had conquered Valerianus the Roman Emperour ..used him afterward most villanously, as his foot-stocke. 1598 FLORIO, *Stamine*, the vpright ribs or peeces of timber of the inside of a ship, of some called footestocks, or footesteecks. 1610 HOLLAND *Camden's Brit.* I. 31 Ships they had, of which the keeles, the footstocks also, or upright standards were made of slight Timber. c1000 ÆLFRIC *Gloss.* Suppl. in Wr.-Wülcker 191 *Fultura* *fotstan. 1738 J. ANDERSON *Constit. Free Masons* 102 The King levell'd the Footstone of the New Royal-Exchange on 23 Oct. 1667. 1876 BROWNING *St. Martin's Summer* v, Headstone, footstone moss may drape,—Name, date, violets hide from spelling. 1885 C. A. HULBERT *Suppl. Ann. Almondbury* 167 When it was decided to restore the old Hall, and the work had been commenced, a footstone was discovered which clearly indicated the pitch of the front gables. 1818 *Art Preserv. Feet* 152 Our English travellers..should always be on their guard against the use of *feet-stoves. 1882 HOWELLS in *Longm. Mag.* I. 46 The foot-stove which one of his congregation..carried to meeting, and warmed his poor feet with. c1611 CHAPMAN *Iliad* xxiii. 689 For not our greatest flourisher can equal him in pow'r Of *foot-strife, but Æacides. 1676 MOXON *Print Lett.* 23 F..Is made like E, onely instead of the *Foot-stroke here is onely a Footing. 1872 BEAMES *Gram. Aryan Lang. Ind.* I. 60 The Panjabi *n* is that of Asoka's inscriptions, with the horizontal footstrokes sloped downwards and curved. 1882 *Standard* 9 Oct. 2/7 He had no faith in *'foot' sugar. 1523 FITZHERB. *Husb.* §4 Yf he wyll haue his plough to go a narowe forowe..than he setteth his *fote teame in the nycke nexte to the ploughe beame. 1558 *Wills & Inv. N.C.* (Surtees 1835) 162, Iiij fuyt teames xijs. 1868 *Morn. Star* 25 June, The total force hurled against the Plymouth shield was 117,666 *foot-tons. 1808 SCOTT *Marm.* III. xxxi, The *foot-tramp of a flying steed. 1856 KANE *Arct. Expl.* I. viii. 79 We are farther north..than any of our predecessors, except Parry on his Spitzbergen foot-tramp. 1388 WYCLIF *Job* xviii. 10 The *foot trappe [1382 foot grene, Vulg. *pedica*] of hym is hid in the erthe. 1585 *Nomenclator* 196 The stocks, or foote-trap. 1796 W. MARSHALL *Midl. Co.* (ed. 2) II. Gloss., **Foot-trenches*, superficial drains, about a foot wide. 1884 *Syd. Soc. Lex.*, **Foot tubercles*, the lateral processes on each segment of some of the Annelida; also called *Parapodia*. 1839 R. S. ROBINSON *Naut. Steam Eng.* 58 The *foot valve. 1650 BLANCKLEY *Naval Expos.*, **Foot waaling* is all the Inboard Planking, from the Keelson upwards to the Orlop Clamps. 1867 SMYTH *Sailor's Word-bk.*, *Foot-waling*, the inside planking or lining of a ship over the floor-timbers. 1860 *Mining Surveyors' Rep.* (*Victoria Dept. Mines*) XII. 213 Slabs ..being also placed longitudinally on the *foot-wall to save the wear of the oxhide buckets. 1869 R. B. SMYTH *Goldf. Victoria* 611 *Foot-wall*, the bounding rock beneath or on the lower side of a reef. 1812 SOUTHEY in *Q. Rev.* VII. 60 He would certainly chuse an eyder-duck for his *foot-warmer. 1858 HAWTHORNE *Fr. & It. Jrnls.* (1872) I. 1 A foot-warmer (a long, flat, tin utensil, full of hot water) was put into the carriage. 1883 *Harper's Mag.* Mar. 539/1 Charcoal to put in the little foot-warmers..used by all womenkind in Dutch churches. 1796 MORSE *Amer. Geog.* I. 281 They practise the *foot-washing, the kiss of love [etc.]. 1871 C. GIBBON *Lack of Gold* xxii, He would be ready to endure the ceremony of the 'Feet-washing' on the eve of his bridal. 1584 in *Descr. Thames* 1758 63 No Fishermen..or Trinkermen shall avaunce or set up any Wears, Engines, Rowte Wears, Pight Wears, *Foot Wears. 1721 PERRY *Daggenh. Breach* 52 A Buttress or *Foot Wharf on each side to keep in the Earth.. to prevent the Dam from spreading and settling out at Foot. 1545 RAYNOLD *Byrth Mankynde* (1564) 66 When the one [birth] commeth headlong, the other *footewise. 1569 *Richmond. Wills* (Surtees) 218, x ireon temes and *foite wedies. 1785 GROSE *Dict. Vulg. Tongue*, **Foot wabler*, a contemptuous appellation for a foot soldier, commonly used by the cavalry. 1814 SCOTT *Wav.* lxi, 'I was sure you could be none of the foot-wobblers, as my Nosebag calls them.' 1568 *Wills & Inv. N.C.* (Surtees 1835) 294 A Remnant of *footwork silke ijs. 1721 PERRY *Daggenh. Breach* 120 There may likewise be a small Foot-work made at the Low-water Mark..the better to preserve the Beach from being washed away. 1895 *Daily News* 16 Dec. 6/6 Their [the Northern team's] foot work. 1908 *Daily Chron.* 29 Jan. 9/2 (Wrestling) Vallotton..showed fine form, his footwork being wonderfully smart. *Ibid.* 25 June 3/3 (Tennis) It is foot-work that wins. 1921 A. W. MYERS *20 Yrs. Lawn Tennis* 167 So well controlled was her foot-work. 1929 WODEHOUSE *Mr. Mulliner Speaking* ii. 62 In face of the danger, his footwork, always impressive, took on a new agility. 1963 *Times* 8 May 5/5 Each offered brilliant foot-work [in dancing]. 1795–1814 WORDSW. *Excursion* v. 169 Sepulchral stones appeared with emblems graven, And *foot-worn epitaphs. 1820 KEATS *Eve St. Agnes* xli, The chains lie silent on the footworn stones. 1856 KANE *Arct. Expl.* I. xxxii. 440 Some of our foot-worn absentees.

b. With adv.: **foot-up** *Rugby football*, in scrummaging, the illegal lifting of either foot by any member of the front row of forwards on either side before the ball is put in the scrummage. Also *attrib.*

1921 E. H. D. SEWELL *Rugby Football* 361 Inadvertent offside, foot-up,..are..absolutely unavoidable at times. 1927 WAKEFIELD & MARSHALL *Rugger* 183 The forwards.. merely leant up against one another while the front row tried trick hooking and foot-up tactics. *Ibid.* 185 He must be careful..not to be penalised..for foot-up. 1963 *Times* 7 Mar. 3/5 For a foot-up offence, MacCormac..got three points for the Pay Corps.

†**foot**, *a. Obs. rare.* [the prec. sb. used attrib.] Of style or language (after L. *pedester*): Prosaic, 'low', without elevation.

1582 STANYHURST *Poems, Ps.* iii. *note* (Arb.) 131 Theese bace and foote verses (so I terme al, sauluing thee Heroical and Elegiacal). 1604 HIERON *Preachers Plea* Serm. (1614) 535 For a man (saith hee [Jerome]) that handleth holy matters, a lowe and (as it were) a foote oration [*pedestris oratio*] is necessary, and not such as is thickned with artificiall framing of words.

foot (fʊt), *v.* [f. prec. sb. Cf. G. *fuszen.*]

1. a. *intr.* To move the foot, step, or tread to measure or music; to dance. Esp. in phr. *to foot it.*

c1400 *Rom. Rose* 2323 If he can wel foote and daunce, It may hym greetly do avaunce. 1513 DOUGLAS *Æneis* XIII. ix. 110 Thai fut it so that lang war to devys Thair hasty fair. 1610 SHAKS. *Temp.* I. ii. 380 Foot it featly here and there. 1700 DRYDEN *Wife of Bath's T.* 216 He saw a Quire of Ladies in a round, That featly footing seem'd to skim the Ground. 1787 G. COLMAN *Inkle & Yarico* Finale, Hymen gay foots away, Happy at our wedding-day. 1863 MRS. C. CLARKE *Shaks. Char.* iv. 107 The dance of fairies..footing it to the cricket's song.

b. quasi-*trans.* with cogn. object (a dance, etc.); also (*nonce-use*) with obj. and *adv.* as compl.

c1450 *Crt. of Love* lxxxiv, Falsely now they footen loves daunce. 1589 R. HARVEY *Pl. Perc.* 8 All the picked youth.. footing the Morris about a May pole. 1633 T. ADAMS *Exp. 2 Peter* ii. 3 Herodias' daughter, that..footed away the head of John Baptist. 1636 FEATLY *Clavis Myst.* xxviii. 388 Teach their scholars how to foot the dance. 1842 S. C. HALL *Ireland* II. 338 *note*, Footing a hornpipe to the music of a pair of bagpipes.

2. *intr.* **a.** To move the feet as in walking; to step, pace, walk, go on foot. Also, to step or walk *on, over, upon* (with *indirect pass.*). Now *rare*. Of a ship: to move or sail with speed. Also with *it*. (In windward sailing, denoting speed as distinguished from pointing.)

1570 LEVINS *Manip.* 178 To Foote, *gressus ponere.* 1590 SPENSER *F.Q.* I. xi. 8 The dreadful Beast drew nigh..Halfe flying and halfe footing in his haste. 1598 SHAKS. *Merry W.* II. i. 126 Theeues doe foot by night. 1600 SURFLET *Countrie Farme* II. xxxi. 239 Saffron..groweth the better if it be a little footed vpon. 1634 FORD *P. Warbeck* III. iv, Since first you footed on our territories. 1637 MILTON *Lycidas* 103 Next Camus, reverend sire, went footing slow. 1642 ANNE BRADSTREET *Poems* (1678) 10 And Hemus, whose steep sides none foot upon. 1646 J. HALL *Poems* (1647) 98 All paths are footed over, but that one Which should be gone. 1824 MISS FERRIER *Inher.* lxix, He footed away as fast as his short legs ..permitted. 1865 G. MEREDITH *Rhoda Fleming* xliv, They footed together, speechless: taking the woman's quickest gliding step. 1899 *Daily News* 4 Oct. 3/1 Shamrock, under clever handling, and footing splendidly, again took the lead. 1901 *Daily Chron.* 27 Sept. 5/7 His boat seemed to be footing it better. 1905 *Ibid.* 19 May 5/5 The latter boat was closely pursued by Hamburg, which was footing splendidly.

b. *esp.* in phr. *to foot it.*

1576 FLEMING *Panopl. Epist.* Ded. ¶3 b, I..leasurly began to foote it forward. a1625 FLETCHER & MASS. *Elder Bro.* I. i, I am tyr'd, Sir, and nere shall foot it home. 1713 ADDISON *Guardian* No. 166 ¶6 My operator..used to foot it from the other end of the town every morning. 1893 EARL DUNMORE *Pamirs* I. 181 Riding for us was out of the question, so we all had to foot it.

3. *trans.* To set foot on; to tread with the feet; to walk or dance on, pass over or traverse on foot.

1557 NORTH tr. *Gueuara's Diall Pr.* 248 b, Lucil..vsed to fote the streates of Rome. 1603 KNOLLES *Hist. Turks* 23 The top of the wall: which was first footed by the Duke Godfrey. 1667 BP. S. PARKER *Free & Impart. Censure* 102 The famous Traveller of Odcomb..footed most parts of the known world. a1717 PARNELL *Fairy T.* xxiii, The fairies bragly foot the floor. 1812 J. HENRY *Camp agst. Quebec* 26 The ground we footed within the last three days is a very rugged isthmus. 1892 STEVENSON in *Illustr. Lond. News* 2 July 9/3 It was good to foot the grass.

4. a. To set or plant (a person) on his feet *in* a place; to settle, establish. Chiefly *refl.* and in *pass.* = to have or obtain a foothold *in*.

1599 SHAKS. *Hen. V*, II. iv. 143 For he is footed in this Land already. 1633 T. STAFFORD *Pac. Hib.* iii. (1821) 247 When they are footed in Mounster, the most part of the Countrey will joyne with them. 1658 R. NEWCOURT *Map of London* (heading), Hingest the Saxon..footing himselfe here. 1888 *Daily News* 27 Apr. 6/3 They will go through the Thanet sands with cylinders again until they foot themselves well into the chalk.

b. *intr. to foot well*: (of a horse) ? to get a good 'footing'.

1826 *Sporting Mag.* XVII. 385 If he have a hand on his horse, and will allow him to 'foot well' (as we call it) before he springs.

†**5.** *trans.* **a.** To strike or thrust with the foot; to kick; *fig.* to spurn. *Obs.*

1596 SHAKS. *Merch. V.* I. iii. 119 You that did..foote me as you spurne a stranger curre Ouer your threshold. a1616 BEAUM. & FL. *Wit at sev. Weapons* v. i, When you shall foot her from you, not she you. 1637 NABBES *Microcosm.* IV. E ij b, *Blood.* Carry your toes wider. *Tast.* Take heed that I foote not you. 1808 JAMIESON, *Foot*, to kick, to strike with the foot; a term used with respect to horses.

†**b.** To tread, press, or crush with the feet.

c1682 J. COLLINS *Making Salt* 16 It was footed or pressed into a Cask.

c. To push or shove with the foot or feet. Chiefly *Naut.* (see quots.).

1757 W. THOMPSON *R.N. Advoc.* 41 They sometimes produce the Standard Weight without Footing or Handing the Scale. 1769 FALCONER *Dict. Marine* (1776), *Jetter dehors le fond du hunier*, to foot the topsail out of the top. c1860 H. STUART *Seaman's Catech.* 49 The masthead men parrel the yard and foot it amidships.

d. *intr.* or *absol.* To use the feet in kicking; to do 'foot-work'. *colloq.* (*Football*).

1852 BRISTED *Upper Ten Thousand* ix. 223 Both teams were footing their very best.

6. *trans.* Of a bird of prey (*esp.* a hawk): To seize or clutch with the talons. Also *fig.*

1575 TURBERV. *Faulconrie* 130 Throwe hir out the leure and let hir foote a henne..and kill it. 1600 SURFLET *Countrie Farme* I. xvii. 111 A certaine kinde of swanne..[with] his right foote..catcheth and footeth his pray. 1611 SHAKS. *Cymb.* v. iv. 116 The holy eagle Stoop'd, as to foot us. 1642 MILTON *Apol. Smect.* (1851) 276 Now trust me not, Readers, if I be not already weary of pluming and footing this Seagull, so open he lies to strokes. 1891 HARTING *Bibl. Accipitr.* Gloss., *Foot*, to clutch.

absol. 1879 RADCLIFFE in *Encycl. Brit.* IX. 7/1 A hawk is said to 'foot' well or to be a 'good footer' when she is successful in killing.

7. To follow the tracks of; to trace. Also *absol.*

1772 T. SIMPSON *Vermin-Killer* 8 The rats will run it like a dog footing a hare. 1829 *Sporting Mag.* XXIV. 292 The quails squatted till the dogs footed up to their very tails. 1886 *S.W. Linc. Gloss.*, s.v., 'There was snow on the ground, and they footed him to the pond'.

8. To make, add, or attach a foot to.

1465 [see FOREFOOT *v.*]. 1570 LEVINS *Manip.* 178 To Foote a stoole, *pedem addere.* 1596 SHAKS. *1 Hen. IV*, II. iv. 130. 1609 C. BUTLER *Fem. Mon.* ii. E iij, The stone-stooles must bee footed as they may. 1663 COWLEY *Cutter Colman St.* IV. vi, She shall foot Stockings in a Stall for me. 1771 SMOLLETT *Humph. Cl.* I. Let. ii, The stockings which his wife footed for me. 1852 HAWTHORNE *Blithedale Rom.* v. (1883) 356 Absolutely footing a stocking out of the texture of a dream.

9. †**a.** To end (a letter) with a postscript. *Obs.*

1648 EVELYN *Let. to Sir R. Browne* 5 June, Postscript, I would foot this letter with what I have since learned.

b. To add up and set the sum at the foot of (an account, bill, etc.); to reckon or sum up. Now usually with *up*. Chiefly *dial.* and *colloq.*

1490 *Acta Dom. Conc.* (1839) 176/2 The tyme that his compt wes futit. 1828 WEBSTER s.v., To foot an account. 1852 MRS. STOWE *Uncle Tom's C.* xxxv, The wall-paper was ..garnished with chalk memorandums, and long sums footed up. 1873 J. RICHARDS *Wood-working Factories* 80 The breakages from accident, if footed up at the end of each year, would in most cases equal..the clear earnings.

fig. 1883 *Harper's Mag.* 893/2 [He] was doing a little sum in social arithmetic. He was footing me up, as it were.

c. *colloq.* To pay or settle (a bill).

1819 E. EVANS *Pedestrious Tour* in R. G. Thwaites *Early Western Travels* (1907) VIII. 183 My dogs..helped themselves to the first repast presented, leaving their master to foot the bills. 1848 DURIVAGE *Stray Subj.* 183 If our plan succeeded, the landlord was to foot the bill, and 'stand treat'. 1891 *Leeds Mercury* 18 July 6/7 The annual bill we foot is, after all, small compared with that of France.

d. *intr.* Of an account, number of items, etc.: To mount or total *up* to (a certain sum). Const. with or without *to*.

1867 *Times* 19 Sept. 10 The united debts of the colony foot up something like £250,000. 1893 PEEL *Spen Valley* 224 His total losses footed up to £5000.

†**10.** *trans.* ? to fewter (a spear). *Sc. Obs.*

a1557 *Diurnal Occurrents* (1833) 45 The Scottis..futtit thair speris, and slew..to the nomber of thre scoir.

11. To admit (a new hand) on payment of a FOOTING.

1825 *Examiner* 285/2 The workmen..had been partaking of some liquor..on account of footing a new comer.

†**12.** ? To sing the 'foot' or burden to (a song).

a **1553** UDALL *Royster D.* I. iv. (Arb.) 30, I will by myne owne selfe foote the song perchaunce.

footage ('fʊtɪdʒ). [f. FOOT *sb.* + -AGE.]

1. *Mining.* A piece-work system of paying miners by the running foot of work; the amount paid; also, the amount mined.

1892 *Rep. Mineral Industries* (11th Census U.S.) 220 Two systems are employed in extracting the ore, (1) the footage system, and (2) the tribute system. The footage system is usually employed in new labores. **1909** *Westm. Gaz.* 9 Dec. 10/4 The output was 15,800 tons, or 2·15 tons per head, and the development footage 3,700. **1923** *Glasgow Herald* 31 May 16 The fathoms broken in the stopes were 234,960 against 192,784, the development footage 104,447 against 87,159, the tons milled 3,786,666 as compared with 3,447,736. **1927** *Sunday Times* 23 Jan. 5 The Development Footage sampled totalled 5,530 feet.

2. The length in feet of cinematographic or television film used in photographing a scene, etc. Also *attrib.*

1916 'B. M. BOWER' *Phantom Herd* ii. 22 He visualized a stampede and the probable amount of footage it would require. **1918** H. CROY *How Motion Pictures are Made* v. 128 Directors..craftily working to keep the production expense as low as possible, do not altogether forget the footage possibilities of an exterior love-scene. *Ibid.* vi. 150 The amounts are added up and a footage rate determined. **1950** O. SKILBECK *ABC of Film & TV* 57 *Footage counter.* All ciné cameras are fitted with a meter showing the amount of film run off. **1967** *Spectator* 28 July 101/1 NBC decided to puff the footage up into a fifty minute documentary. **1970** *Which?* July 217/1 They all had a footage counter so that you could work out how much film you had left.

†'**footback.** *Obs.* A humorous formation after *horseback.* Chiefly in phr. *on* (or *a*) *footback* = (travelling) on foot.

1589 NASHE *Pref.* to *Greene's Menaphon* 17 Beggers [have forgot] that euer they caried their fardles on footback. *a* **1625** FLETCHER *Woman's Prize* I. iii, Like St. George at Kingston, Running a footback from the furious dragon. **1630** J. TAYLOR (Water P.) *Odcomb's Compl.* 79 Should foot-back trotting Trauellers intend To match his trauels.

football ('fʊtbɔːl). Also formerly **foot-ball.** [f. FOOT *sb.* + BALL *sb.*]

1. An inflated ball used in the game (see 2). It is now either spherical or (as in the Rugby game) elliptical, and consists of an inflated bag or bladder enclosed in a leather case.

1486 *Bk. St. Albans, Her.* E vj a, It is calde in latyn *pila pedalis* a fotebal. **1508** BARCLAY *Egloges* v, The sturdie plowmen..driuing the foote ball. **1650** BAXTER *Saints' R.* IV. (1653) 282 Like a Football in the midst of a crowd of Boys. **1708** MOTTEUX *Rabelais* IV. vii. (1737) 26 The Bladder, wherewith they make Footballs. **1795–1814** WORDSW. *Excursion* VII. 743 If touched by him, The inglorious foot-ball mounted to the pitch Of the Lark's flight.

2. a. An open-air game played with this ball by two sides, each of which endeavours to kick or convey the ball to the goal at the opposite end of the field.

There are various styles of playing the game, but the most widely recognized are the Association and the Rugby Union and League games, and American football (see sense b below).

1424 *Sc. Act Jas. I,* c. 18 The king forbiddes þt na man play at þe fut ball vnder þe payne of iiijd. **1531** ELYOT *Gov.* I. xxvii, Foote balle, wherin is nothinge but beastly furie and exstreme violence. **1663** *Flagellum* or *O. Cromwell* (ed. 2) 8 Players at Foot-ball, Cudgels, or any other boysterous sport or game. **1791** W. BARTRAM *Carolina* 509 The foot-ball is likewise a favorite, manly diversion with them [the Indians]. **1880** *Times* 12 Nov. 4/4 Not 15 years back, few men played football after they left school.

b. *spec.* = *American football* s.v. AMERICAN *a.* 3.

The term *soccer* is used in North America to distinguish what is in Britain called *(Association) football* or *soccer* from *American football.*

1881 *N.Y. Herald* 20 Nov. 8/5 A splendid game of football was played yesterday at the Polo Grounds between.. Harvard and Princeton. **1925** F. SCOTT FITZGERALD *Great Gatsby* i. 7 Her husband..had been one of the most powerful ends that ever played football at New Haven. **1954** W. STEVENS *Coll. Poems* 270 The negroes were playing football in the park. **1976** *Webster's Sports Dict.* 162/2 Even though the game is named football, kicking plays a relatively minor role other than in attempting a field goal or point after touchdown.

3. *fig.* (*esp.* a person or thing that is kicked or tossed about like a football).

1532 MORE *Confut. Tindale* Wks. 416/1 For so he maye translate the worlde in to a footeball yf he ioyne therewith certayn circumstaunces, and saye this rounde rollyng foote-ball that men walke vpon [etc.]. ? *c* **1600** *Distr. Emperor* II. i. in Bullen *O. Pl.* III. 186, I am the verye foote-ball of the starres. **1711** *Let. to Sacheverel* 14 England must always have a National Football, and you, at present, are That. **1879** FROUDE *Cæsar* xv. 231 The..institutions of the mistress of the world had become the football of ruffians.

4. *attrib.* and *Comb.*, as ***football-club, -day, -field, -ground, -match, -pitch, -play, -player, -playing,*** †***-sport,*** †***-swain, -union, -war;*** **football coupon,** a coupon used in an entry for a football pool; **football hooligan,** one who engages in violent behaviour, vandalism, etc., while attending (or travelling to or from) a football match; hence ***football hooliganism;*** **football pool,** an organized system of betting on the results of football matches; also, loosely, = *football coupon.*

1918 *Methodist Times* 5 Dec. 9/1 The amendment of the Gambling Laws, particularly in relation to *football coupons, [etc.]..is long overdue. **1940** S. O'CASEY *Star turns Red* I. 5 The concentration necessary to choose the right teams for entry in his football coupons. **1815** in Hone *Every-Day Bk.* I. 245 The coachman exclaimed..'It's *Foot-ball day'. **1887** SHEARMAN *Athletics & Football* 247 Shrove Tuesday..was..the great 'football day' in England for centuries. **1867** *Routledge's Handbk. Football* 59, I know of no prettier sight than a *Football field on a bright March afternoon. **1986** *Financial Times* 25 June 17/5 Post-World Cup Brazil is trying to get used to the idea of defeat on the football field. **1852** *Foot Ball Controversy* (New Haven) 2 We appoint the usual *football ground..as the..place. **1898** *Westm. Gaz.* 12 July 10/1 Would it [*sc.* St. Paul's] not make a good football ground on a wet day if all the chairs were moved from under the dome? **1985** *Guardian* 2 Feb. 6/3 The concentration of debris into an area scarcely larger than a football ground showed that the missile had crashed. **1967** *Observer* 3 Dec. 7/2 The problem, Dr Harrington believes, is to find out what is the typical *football hooligan. **1984** *Financial Times* 4 June I. 13 Mr. Abbot is never actually as funny as he is on the box as..that carrot-headed Scottish football hooligan. **1969** *New Society* 27 Nov. 859/2 The Home Secretary's latest measures to deal with *football hooliganism received little publicity. **1986** *Guardian Weekly* 11 May 2/4 How can the House express its indignant rejection of football hooliganism while setting such a persuasive example of undignified and daily indiscipline? **1711** BUDGELL *Spect.* No. 161 ¶3, I was diverted from a farther Observation of these combatants, by a *Foot-ball Match. [**1946** *Brentwoodian* Dec. 25 Football has been made compulsory on Thursdays and except when detention intervenes all six pitches are in use.] **1961** F. C. AVIS *Sportsman's Gloss.* 12 (*caption*) Association *Football pitch plan. **1986** *Financial Times* 26 Aug. 7/4 The development will have a dealing floor the size of Wembley football pitch. **1589** COGAN *Haven Health* i (1612) 2 Some are vehement, as dauncing, leaping, *foote ball play. **1805** SCOTT *Last Minstr.* v. vi, Some, with many a merry shout..Pursued the foot-ball play. **1605** SHAKS. *Lear* I. iv. 95 *Ste.* Ile not be strucken, my Lord. *Kent.* Nor tript neither, you base *Foot-ball plaier. **1583** STUBBES *Anat. Abus.* I. (1879) 137 Some spend the Sabaoth day..in..*foot-ball playing, and such other deuilish pastimes. **1929** *Times Index* Jan.–Mar. 59/2 *Football 'pool'. **1936** *Economist* 7 Mar. 517/2 We may.. put..the total 'rake off' of football pool promoters..at not less than 30 per cent. of the amounts staked. **1957** M. SPARK *Comforters* i. 6 Louisa Jepp sat at the table writing out her football pools. **1959** *Chambers Encycl.* VI. 159/2 In 1954 football pools were estimated to be worth about £10 million to the post office. **1971** R. ROBERTS *Classic Slum* x. 183 Football pools 'nationalised' a local form of gambling. Before their introduction bookmakers supplied men in factory and workshop with fixed odds football coupons weekly. **1589** GREENE *Menaphon* Wks. (Grosart) VI. 137 At *foote ball sport, thou shalt my champion be. **1653** WALTON *Angler* i. 35 Where, for some sturdy *foot-ball Swain, Jone strokes a Sillibub or twaine. **1714** GAY *Trivia* II. 226 Lo! from far, I spy the Furies of the *Foot-ball War.

football ('fʊtbɔːl), *v.* [f. prec. sb.] *trans.* To kick like a football; to kick about with the feet; also *fig.* Hence '**footballing** *ppl. a.*

1599 NASHE *Lenten Stuffe* Wks. (Grosart) V. 268 They footeballd their heades togither. **1627–47** FELTHAM *Resolves* II. lxxxiii. 427 To see how well meaning simplicity is foot-ball'd. **1860** *All Year Round* No. 42. 363, I knew he longed ..to football my unshorn head up and down the knubbly street. **1885** G. MEREDITH *Diana* I. v. 129 She became the Mrs. Warwick of our footballing world.

footballer ('fʊtbɔːlə(r)). [f. prec. sb. or vb. + -ER.[1]] One who plays football.

1880 *Melbourne Bulletin* 29 Oct. 5/1 The Champion Footballers race for a quarter mile.

'**footballist.** [f. as prec. + -IST.] = prec.

1882 *Society* 28 Oct. 18/1 When a Rugby Union footballist is running with a football..the practice is to collar..him.

footboard ('fʊtbɔəd). [f. FOOT *sb.* + BOARD.]

1. A board to support the foot or feet; a board to stand on; e.g. a small platform at the back of a carriage on which the footman stands; a board upon which to step when entering or alighting from a carriage; the foot-rest of a driving-box; in *U.S.* the foot-plate (see FOOT *sb.* 35) of a locomotive engine.

1766 SMOLLETT *Trav.* II. xxv. 5 [They] may be carried in a common chair, provided with a foot-board, on men's shoulders. *Ibid.* II. xxvii. 54 The ladies sit within, and the cicisbei stand on the foot-boards, on each side of the coach. **1815** *Sporting Mag.* XLV. 184 A foot-board behind for the accommodation of a servant. **1825** J. NEAL *Jonathan* II. xv. 58 His feet rested on a foot-board, which..was attached.. to the rough axle-tree. **1874** KNIGHT *Dict. Mech.* I. 902/1 *Foot-board,* the platform on which the driver and stoker of a locomotive stand. A foot-plate. **1885** MISS BRADDON *Wyllard's Weird* I. ii. 49 She was standing on the foot-board ..with her face to the [railway-] coach.

b. A treadle.

1874 in KNIGHT *Dict. Mech.* **1888** *Lockwood's Dict. Mech. Engin., Treadle* or *Foot Board,* a strip of wood actuated by the foot and connected to the crank of a lathe, grindstone.. or other small machine.

2. An upright board set across the foot of a bedstead.

1843 MRS. CARLYLE *Lett.* I. 232 Groping, with my hand, I felt the footboard at my head!

'**footboy.**

†**a.** A boy-attendant (*obs.*) **b.** A boy (in livery) employed in the place of or to assist a footman; a page-boy.

1590 GREENE *Mourn. Garm.* Wks. (Grosart) IX. 139 On he paceth with his men and his foot-boyes towardes Assyria. **1591** SHAKS. *1 Hen. VI,* III. ii. 69 Like Peasant foot-Boyes doe they keepe the Walls. **1644** PRYNNE & WALKER *Fiennes' Trial* 5 On Friday night late I received a Note from your Foot-boy. **1711** STEELE *Spect.* No. 96 ¶1 From my being first a Footboy at fourteen, to my present Station of a Nobleman's Porter. **1837** HAWTHORNE *Twice-Told T.* (1851) I. ix. 163 The smart maid-servant, and the dirty little footboy.

'**foot-breadth,** †**-brede.** [See BREADTH and BREDE *sb.*[2]] The breadth of a foot (as a measure).

1375 BARBOUR *Bruce* XI. 365 He gert men mony pottis ma Of a fut breid round. *c* **1384** CHAUCER *H. Fame* III. 952 That wel vnneth in that place Hadde I a fote brede of space. **1535** COVERDALE *Deut.* ii. 5, I wyl not geue you one fote bredth of their londe. [Also in **1611.**] **1768** ROSS *Helenore* III. 371 Charge them to halt, nor move on foot bred more. **1857** H. MILLER *Test. Rocks* iii. 125 Luxuriant herbage cumbered every foot breadth of the dank..soil.

'**foot-cloth.**

†**1.** A large richly-ornamented cloth laid over the back of a horse and hanging down to the ground on each side. It was considered as a mark of dignity and state. *Obs.*

1480 *Wardr. Acc. Edw. IV* (1830) 154 An herneys in russet velvet cloth of gold for an hakeney, and a footeclothe maade of russet velvet lyned with blac bokeram. **1589** *Mar Martine* 6 Plucke but the foote cloth from his backe, The Asse will soone be seene. **1612** W. PARKES *Curtaine-Dr.* (1876) 24 Sometimes he that robbes both Church and Common-wealth is seene to ride on his foot-cloth. **1702** *Lond. Gaz.* No. 3842/1 The Town-Clerk with a Gold Chain, and his Footman and Footcloth. **1805** SCOTT *Last Minstr.* v. xvii, Fair Margaret on her palfrey came, Whose footcloth swept the ground.

fig. **1594** NASHE *Vnfort. Trav.* Wks. (Grosart) V. 70 The scolasticall squitter bookes clout you vp cannopies & foot-clothes of verses.

2. A cloth to set the feet upon, a carpet.

1639 FULLER *Holy War* IV. i. (1640) 165 Milain, and many other cities in Italy..danced at this musick, made a foot-cloth of their Master's livery. **1726–7** SWIFT *Gulliver* I. ii. 38 A foot-cloth for your majesty's chief room of state. **1824** MACAULAY *Ivry* vi, Then on the ground..Fling the red shreds, a footcloth meet for Henry of Navarre. **1847** TENNYSON *Princ.* IV. 267 On the..footcloth, lay The.. child.

†**3.** *attrib.* and *Comb.* (sense 1), as ***foot-cloth horse, mule, nag, -page, -servant, -strider.***

1571 SADLER, SMITH & WILSON *Let.* 7 Sept. in Murdin *Coll. State Pap.* (1759) 149 So havyng prepared a Fotecloth Nag for him..he was..quietly brought into the tower. **1593** SHAKS. *2 Hen. VI,* IV. i. 54 Hast thou not..Bare-headed plodded by my foot-cloth Mule. **1594** —— *Rich. III,* III. iv. 86 Three times to day my Foot-Cloth-Horse did stumble. **1654** GAYTON *Pleas. Notes* I. vii. 26 The Mule, and glorious Foot-cloath-pages, and Harbingers, are all too little for these Patriarchs. *a* **1658** FORD, etc. *Witch Edmonton* v. i, I'll ..Serve some Briarean footcloth-strider.

footed ('fʊtɪd), *ppl. a.* [f. FOOT *sb.* and *v.* + -ED.] Furnished with or having feet (*rarely* a foot).

1. a. Of a man or animal: Furnished with feet; having feet *like* (a dog, goose, etc.).

a **1529** SKELTON *Elynour Rumming* 49 Foted lyke a plane. **1608** ARMIN *Nest Ninn.* A iv a, Footed broad and long, In Motly cotes, goes Jacke Oates. **1661** J. CHILDREY *Brit. Baconica* 18 The Seal-fish is..footed like a Moldwarp. **1727** *Philip Quarll* (1816) 18 An animal..faced and footed like a goat. **1854** H. H. WILSON *Rig-veda* II. 91 The footless dawn is the precursor of footed beings. **1860** RUSKIN *Mod. Paint.* V. IX. iii. §5. 220 Thighed and shouldered like the billows; —footed like their stealing foam.

b. in parasynthetic derivatives, q.v. under their first element (as *brazen-, cat-, claw-footed,* etc.), or as main words (e.g. BARE-, FOURFOOTED).

c. fig. ***footed as*** or ***with the wind:*** having feet as swift as the wind.

1612 DRAYTON *Poly-olb.* xiii. 216 Each followes as his horse were footed with the wind. **1865** SWINBURNE *Atalanta* 46 Fair as the snow and footed as the wind.

2. Of a shoe, stocking, piece of furniture, etc.: Having, or provided with, a foot or feet; also, mended with a (new) foot.

1453 *Test. Ebor.* (Surtees) II. 191, ij salers broken, of siluer gilted and footed. **1463** *Bury Wills* (Camden) 23 A chayer, iij. footyd stoolys. *c* **1530** in Gutch *Coll. Cur.* II. 301 Item oone pleyne Pece footid and with a Cover. **1613** PURCHAS *Pilgrimage* I. xvi. 85 Then..80. women were carried in chaires footed with gold. **1639** *Bury Wills* (Camden) 182, I giue and bequeath..my stone pott..footed and tipt. *a* **1652** BROME *City Wit* IV. ii. Wks. 1873 I. 348 A fellow that wore worsted stockings footed. **1844** ALB. SMITH *Adv. Mr. Ledbury* I. xiv. 181 Various new-footed boots and shoes..ranged in pairs. **1856** KANE *Arct. Expl.* II. x. 99 A large pair of footed trowsers.

†**3.** Having a length of (a specified number of) feet: in parasynthetic comb., as ***twelve-footed.*** *Obs.*

1616 SHELDON *Miracles Antichr.* 303 The twelue-footed man, as he is measured by Petrus de Natalibus!

†**4.** Composed in metrical feet. *Obs.*

1567 MAPLET *Gr. Forest* 103 In footed verse. *c* **1595** SOUTHWELL *St. Peter's Compl.* Ded., This measured and footed stile. **1601** CHESTER *Love's Mart.* (1878) 123 The.. swanne In footed verse sings out his deep annoy.

5. *Archery.* Of an arrow: (See quot.).

1856 H. A. Ford *Archery* v. 29 Arrows are either *selfs* or *footed*; the former are made of a single piece of wood; the latter..have a different and harder wood dovetailed on to them at the pile end.

footer ('fʊtə(r)), *sb.*[1] [f. FOOT *sb.* or *v.* + -ER[1].]
1. a. One who goes on foot, a pedestrian. *rare.*
1608 Topsell *Serpents* (1658) 780 Being none of the best footers she could hardly keep way with the Spider. **1890** Baring-Gould *Old Co. Life* 327 The tor is covered with horses, traps, carriages, footers.
b. One who walks in a place, a frequenter.
1890 *Univ. Rev.* 15 July 317 This shy footer of solitudes.
2. *Falconry.* Of the hawk: (see FOOT *v.* 6).
1879 [see FOOT *v.* 6]. **1879** Radcliffe in *Encycl. Brit.* IX. 10/2 They..are most deadly 'footers'. **1881** *Macm. Mag.* Nov. 40 A better 'footer'—more clever at seizing the quarry in his talons.
3. *Football.* **a.** A kick at a football. ? *Obs.* **b.** *slang.* The game itself.
1781 J. Hutton *Tour to Caves, etc.* (ed. 2) 89 *Footer*, a stroke at a foot-ball. **1863** *Boy's Own Vol.* July 36 A peculiar fashion of their own [at Harrow] which prompts them to call football 'footer'. **1896** *Westm. Gaz.* 12 Dec. 1/3 Who'd have thought of finding the old smug at a footer match? **1925** W. Deeping *Sorrell & Son* xvi, To perform on the footer field with a lot of young louts. **1945** E. Waugh *Brideshead Revisited* I. i. 30, I had to change for *F-f-footer*.
4. *Bowls.* (See quot. 1876.)
1863 *Feltham's Guide to Archery, etc.* 57 If a gentleman play a bowl without his foot being upon the footer. **1876** Wilkinson in *Encycl. Brit.* IV. 180/2 The 'footer' is the small piece of material—cocoa-nut matting is the best—whereon each player stands in delivering the ball.
5. With a numeral prefixed: A person or thing whose height or length is of that number of feet; as *six-footer*, *twenty-one-footer*, etc.
1844 J. T. Hewlett *Parsons & W.* xxxiii, I..inquired of a second six-footer. **1892** *Daily News* 21 July 3/6 The club also sailed a match for 21-footers on Tuesday.
6. (See quot.)
1927 T. Woodhouse *Artificial Silk* 95 In the manufacture of stockings..two machines are used... One of these machines, termed the 'legger', knits the upper and longer part of the stocking, whereas the other machine, termed the 'footer', knits the remainder of the stocking.

footer ('fuːtə(r)), *sb.*[2] *dial.* or *slang.* [? var. of FOUTRE.] (See quots.). ? Hence **'footer** *v.*, to trifle, 'potter about'. **'footering** *ppl. a.*
1753 A. Murphy *Gray's-Inn Jrnl.* No. 36 *True Intellig.*, A Thief, a low Fellow, a Footer. **1825** Jennings *Somerset Gloss.*, *Footer*..a scurvy fellow; a term of contempt. **1847** Halliwell, *Footer*, to idle. **1893** Stevenson *Vailima Lett.* (1895) xxx. 273 Fussy footering German barons.

'footfall, 'foot-fall.
The fall of the foot on the ground in walking; a footstep, tread.
1610 Shaks. *Temp.* II. ii. 12 Like Hedg-hogs, which.. mount Their pricks at my foot-fall. **1826** Scott *Jrnl.* 18 May, For weeks you could have heard a foot-fall. **1873** Black *Pr. Thule* xxvi, He did not hear her approach, her footfall was so light.

foot-fault ('fʊtfɒlt, -ɔː-). *Lawn Tennis.* [f. FOOT *sb.* + FAULT *sb.*] A fault or infringement of the rules made by overstepping the base-line while serving. Hence **'foot-fault** *v. intr.*, to make a foot-fault; *trans.*, to record a foot-fault against (a player). **'foot-faulter, 'foot-faulting** *vbl. sb.*
1886 J. Dwight *Lawn Tennis* I. i. 5 Frequent foot-faulting in a match spoils your service altogether. *Ibid.* II. v. 69 It is nearly impossible to call foot faults and to watch the service line too. **1889** W. M. Brownlee *Lawn-Tennis* III. v. 144 Be careful to put the toe of the left foot on the line, and you are not likely to be foot-faulted. **1902** *Westm. Gaz.* 6 Oct. 4/3 The ex-champion was annoyed at being several times pulled up for 'foot-faulting'. *Ibid.* 23 Oct. 6/2 The New Lawn Tennis Laws. The Foot-Fault Difficulty Abolished... The feet of more than one 'crack' had to be carefully watched by relentless linesmen to detect the slightest inclination to foot-fault. **1909** *Ibid.* 9 Feb. 12/2 The ruling..that players who ..lift the left foot before throwing up the ball, or while doing it, and then do the same with the right foot before the ball leaves the racket, are foot-faulters. **1921** A. W. Myers *20 Yrs. Lawn Tennis* 114 Larned..was the foot-fault judge in the Davis Cup doubles... When he foot-faulted,..he signalled to the umpire with his hand and the man in the chair called the foot-fault. **1922** W. T. Tilden *It's All in the Game* 35 In his anxiety he foot-faulted and his first serve was wasted. **1927** *Daily Express* 6 June 1 Tilden was foot-faulted by a special umpire in the fifth game of the third set.

foot-fell. *Sc.* Forms: 5 fut(e)fell, 6 futfaill, -vale, fytwale, 7, 9 fitfeal. [app. f. FOOT *sb.* + FELL.] The fell or skin of a lamb that has died soon after it was dropped (Jam.). Also *footfell skin.*
1452 Jas. II. *Let.* in *Chart. Aberd.* (1890) 25 Skorlings, skaldings, futefell [etc.]. **1495** in *Halyburton's Ledger* (1867) 90 Item out of the samyn sek 125 futfell. **1535** *Aberd. Reg.* V. 15 (Jam.) Ane dossund of futfaill sufficient stuf. *Ibid.*, Vij. dossund of futfaill skynnis. **1592** *Sc. Acts Jas. VI*, §80 Skynnis..callit in the vulgar toung Scorlingis, scaldingis, futefaillis. **1670** *Rates* (Jam.), Fitfeals and scadlings.

'foot-folk. [ME., f. FOOT *sb.* + FOLK. Cf. MHG. *vuozvolc*, Ger. *fuszvolk*, Du. *voetvolk*, etc.] Foot-soldiers, infantry.
In mod. use a new formation, prob. partly after G. *fussvolk*, as in quot. 1859.
1297 R. Glouc. (1724) 398 Fot volc wythoute nombre. **13** .. *Coer de L.* 4529 The foote folk and sympyl knaves, In hande they hente ful good staves. **1859** Thackeray *Virgin.* II. xv, Old George Frundsberg of Mindelheim, a colonel of foot-folk in the Imperial service. **1876** Morris *Æneids* VII. 793 A cloud of foot-folk follow him. **1903** *Daily Chron.* 11 Dec. 3/4 The British footfolk at close grips are the very devil. **1905** *Ibid.* 24 June 4/6 The Scottish army consisted almost exclusively of foot-folk.

footful ('fʊtfʊl). [f. FOOT *sb.* + -FUL.] As much as can be held with the foot. (Cf. *handful*.)
1850 *Fraser's Mag.* XLII. 35 When the bird had grasped a footful it threw the sand behind it.

'foot-gear. [FOOT *sb.* I.] Boots, shoes, or similar covering for the feet.
1837 Carlyle *Fr. Rev.* III. I. viii, Their foot-gear testified no higher than the ankle to the muddy pilgrimage. **1874** 'H. Churton' *Toinette* (1881) ix. 101 The heavy brogans and a part of the gray stockings which formed her foot-gear. **1891** *Scribner's Mag.* X. 279 The proper foot-gear is the canvas shoe with rubber sole. **1904** S. E. White *Silent Places* viii. 81 A man's standing..can be accurately gauged by the magnificence of his foot-gear.

'foot-guards, 'footguards. (Formerly also in *sing.*) A body of picked foot-soldiers for special service as a guard. The Footguards now comprise the Grenadier Guards, the Coldstream Guards, the Scots Guards, the Irish Guards, and the Welsh Guards.
1675 tr. *Machiavelli's Prince* (Rtldg. 1883) 289 His German foot-guards consisted formerly of 300 men. **1678** tr. *Gaya's Art of War* I. 75 When the Princes of blood..and the Generals of an Army pass through any Town, the Governours furnish them with a Foot-guard. **1703** Steele *Tend. Husb.* II. i, The joiner of the Foot-guards has made his Fortune by it. **1855** Macaulay *Hist. Eng.* IV. 588 A strong body of infantry, the English footguards leading the way, stormed..the outworks.

foot-hill ('fʊthɪl). orig. *U.S.* [FOOT *sb.* 18.] A hill forming a lower eminence at the foot of a mountain or mountain-range.
1850 *Western Star* (Milwaukie, Ore.) 21 Nov. 3/2 The most productive portions..have been in the foot-hills. **1870** W. Gladden in *Scribner's Monthly* I. 153 The road leading to it passes over and among a series of conical foot-hills that rest against the base of the mountains. **1873** J. H. Beadle *Undevel. West* xv. 253 In California, everything under two thousand feet high is called a hill; if it leads up to a mountain, a foothill. **1879** Miss Bird *Rocky Mount.* 232 The long ascent through sweeping foothills to the gates of rock at a height of 9000 feet. **1882** *Rep. Prec. Metals U.S.* 262 The mineral belt is in the western foot-hills of the Verde range of mountains. **1916** J. B. Thoburn *Hist. Oklahoma* II. 4 The Black Mesa is in reality one of the foot-hills of the Rocky mountains. **1971** *Nature* 4 June 330/2 This bandicoot is widespread in the forested foothills and lowlands of western New Guinea. **1971** *Daily Tel.* 19 July 7/1 Its primary object is the exploration of Hadley Rille, one of the Moon's mysterious 'ditches' in the foothills of the Apennine range.

foothold ('fʊthəʊld). [See HOLD *sb.*]
1. A hold or support for the feet: a surface (secure or otherwise) for standing or walking on; firm or stable position of the feet.
1625 F. Markham *Bk. Hon.* v. ii. 166 The onely readie and perfit scale (where is neither slipperie foot-holde, nor tottering ascent). **1692** R. L'Estrange *Fables* vi, He has nothing above him to Aspire to, nor any Foot-Hold left him to come down by. **1837** W. Irving *Capt. Bonneville* II. 222 The horses had no foothold, but kept plunging forward. **1871** L. Stephen *Playgr. Eur.* iv. (1894) 102 It was impossible to cut steps in it [ice] deep enough to afford secure foothold.
b. *transf.*
1692 R. L'Estrange *Fables* cccxxxiii. 291 All fell to Work at the Roots of the Tree, and left it so little Foot-hold, that the first Blast of Wind laid it Flat upon the Ground. **1880** *Contemp. Rev.* Mar. 418 The hyssop finds firm foot-hold in the wall. **1890** *Home & Ch. St. Gregory the Great* 10 The insertion of new foundations under the pillars, which were supported while workmen removed their footholds.
c. *fig.*
1660 H. More *Myst. Godl.* I. v. 15 Those parts of the World where their Philosophy had taken foot-hold. **1855** H. Reed *Lect. Eng. Lit.* IV. (1878) 150 The Saracen was driven slowly from his last foothold in the west of Europe. **1864** *Theolog. Rev.* Mar. 19 As one foothold of belief after another is taken away.
2. ? *U.S.* 'A kind of light india-rubber overshoe, leaving the heel unprotected; a sandal. Sometimes called a *tip*.' (*Cent. Dict.*)

foot-hook: see FUTTOCK.

ˌfoot-'hot, *adv.* ? *Obs.* [f. FOOT *sb.* + HOT *a.* or *adv.*; the sb. seems to be locative as in *footsore*; cf. the differently-formed synonym *hot-foot*.]
a. In hot haste, without pause or slackening of speed. **b.** In the phrase *to follow foot-hot*, the *adv.* was sometimes taken to mean 'closely'; hence it was used in other collocations to express mere proximity of situation.
c **1320** *Seuyn Sag.* (W.) 843 Als quik he dede his schon of drawe, And karf his vaumpes, fot-hot. *c* **1375** *Sc. Leg. Saints, Paulus* 1164 Paule..Is cumine till hyme now fut-hat. *c* **1420** *Pallad. on Husb.* II. 228 So that thair apples riped with foothoote The semynaire be sette in. *c* **1460** *Towneley Myst.* (Surtees) 150 Lett us ryn fote hote. **1470–85** Malory *Arthur* IX. xxviii, They chalengyd sire launcelot foote hote. **1513** Douglas *Æneis* I. Prol. 287, I knaw quhat payne is to follow him fute haite. *Ibid.* XI. xvi. 37 Vnder the montane law thar stude fute hoit A byng of erth. **1576** Turberv. *Venerie* 138 Those cruell curres..Which vowe foot hote to followe me. **1579–80** North *Plutarch* (1676) 415 Following him foot-hot, as we commonly say, before the barbarous People could take breath.

footie, var. FOOTY *sb.*

footing ('fʊtɪŋ), *vbl. sb.* [f. FOOT *v.* + -ING[1].]
1. a. The act of walking, pacing, or stepping; a step or tread. Now *rare.* †*to set footing*: to set foot (*in*, *on* a place), to enter. (Also *fig.*)
1583 Stanyhurst *Æneis* III. (Arb.) 89 He stutted, apaled And fixt his footing. **1593** Shaks. *2 Hen. VI*, III. ii. 87 Seeke not a Scorpions Nest Nor set a footing on this vnkinde Shore. **1606** —— *Tr. & Cr.* II. ii. 155 Can it be, That so degenerate a straine as this, Should once set footing in your generous bosomes? **1604** E. G. *Acosta's Hist. Indies* III. xv. 163 For that man hath not so long a sight, nor so nimble and swift footing as were needefull. *c* **1611** Chapman *Iliad* x. 294 This man makes footing towards thee, Out of the tents. **1637** G. Daniel *Genius of Isle* 431 Recall thy footings thence, Wander not in Darke waies. **1642** *Remonst. conc. Ch. & Kingd. Irel.* 7 They will, with the assistance of Spaine and France, set footing in England. **1820** Keats *Isabella* xxiii, Towards him they bent their footing through the dews.
†b. The action of setting foot upon land.
1604 Shaks. *Oth.* II. i. 76 The bold Iago, Whose footing heere anticipates our thoughts, A Senights speed.
c. Moving with measured tread, dancing; †also, a dance.
1561 Hoby tr. *Castiglione's Courtyer* (1577) Y v b, To daunce well without ouer nimble footings or to busy tricks. **1596** Davies *Orchestra* xiv, My feet..Did neuer yet the Art of footing know. **1652** Peyton *Catastr. Ho. Stuarts* (1731) 14 Queen Anne, who had trod so many stately Footings in Masks at Court. **1760** Goldsm. *Cit. World* lii. ¶6 A squire from the country..desirous of learning the new manner of footing.
2. A mark or impression left by the foot; a footprint, or footprints collectively; a trace, track, trail. Also *fig.* (cf. *footstep*). Now *rare.*
1572 tr. *Buchanan's Detect. Mary Q. Scots* M j, I will nat here precisely trace out all the footynges of the wickit doynges. **1576** Turberv. *Venerie* 64 Let him firste marke what manner of Slotte or footing it is. **1579** E. K. *Ep. Ded.* to *Spenser's Sheph. Cal.* §4 Poetes, whose foting this Author every where followeth. **1624** Sanderson *12 Serm.* (1637) 420 God hath imprinted..some steps and footings of his goodnesse in the Creatures. **1727** Bradley *Fam. Dict.*, s.v. *Hart*, The Tracts or Footing of divers sorts of Beasts. **1841** D'Israeli *Amen. Lit.* (1867) 69 In Normandy we trace the first footings of our national power. **1847** Marryat *Childr. N. Forest* v, See, here is her footing.
†3. Recovery (of a woman after confinement) ? *Obs.* exc. in *footing-time* (see 17). Cf. *on foot.*
1566 Painter *Pal. Pleas.* I. 46 a, He asked the wife how she did, and praied the Goddes to send her good footyng, and then inquired of her trauell, and painful panges.
4. a. The action of placing the feet so as not to slip or stumble; stable position of the feet, foothold.
1398 Trevisa *Barth. De P.R.* v. liv. (1495) 170 The sole of the fote is fleshly and playne forwarde and bakwarde to haue fotynge. *c* **1500** *Melusine* lv. 332 But footyng faylled hym, & [he] fell doun deed to the grounde. *a* **1529** Skelton *Col. Cloute* 1074 Stande sure and take good fotyng. **1670** Dryden *Conq. Granada* I. IV. ii, Fear makes men look aside, and then their footing miss. **1708** Prior *Turtle & Sparrow* 366 Her footing chanc'd to fail And down she fell. **1810** Scott *Lady of L.* I. xiv, Unless he climb with footing nice, A far projecting precipice. **1869** C. Gibbon *R. Gray* iv, 'Come awa, Dawnie, and mind your futting.'
b. The action or manner of placing the feet for standing in a given position.
1545 Ascham *Toxoph.* (Arb.) 147 The fyrste poynte is when a man shoulde shote, to take suche footyng and standyng as shal be both cumlye to the eye and profytable to his vse. **1856** H. A. Ford *Archery* ix. 62 The footing must be firm, yet at the same time easy and springy.
5. a. Support for the foot; surface (favourable or the contrary) for walking or standing upon.
1596 Shaks. *1 Hen. IV*, I. iii. 193 To o'erwalk a Current, roaring loud, On the vnstedfast footing of a Speare. **1627** May *Lucan* III. 602 The Roman ships slow keel'd would firmely stand, And lend sure footing like a fight by land. **1789** Mad. D'Arblay *Diary* 8 July, I am delighted with the soft air and soft footing upon the sands. **1810** Scott *Lady of L.* IV. xxi, Where scarce was footing for the goat. **1824** Heber *Jrnl.* (1828) II. 44 It was probable we should find safe footing.
†b. A notch or ledge for the foot, a 'step'. *Obs.*
1725 De Foe *Voy. round World* (1840) 266 We, by footings made in the rocks, descended, as we might say, down a pair of stairs.
6. *fig.* Firm or secure position; established place; foothold, establishment.
1586 Walsingham *Let.* 4 Mar. in Spottiswood *Hist. Ch. Scot.* (1655) 361 In former times, when England had a footing in France. **1642** Fuller *Holy & Prof. St.* v. xii. 407 A lie cursorily told takes little footing..in the tellers memory. **1710** Berkeley *Princ. Hum. Knowl.* §55 Those notions have gained but a very inconsiderable footing in the world. **1815** W. H. Ireland *Scribbleomania* 120 This clerical baronet has vainly endeavoured to gain a footing upon the theatrical boards. **1869** Trollope *He knew* xxii, She had made good her footing in her aunt's house.
†7. The foundation, ground, or basis on which anything rests or from which it springs. *Obs.*
1581 J. Bell *Haddon's Answ. Osor.* 407 All which do come altogether to utter ruine, if Purgatory decay once: but if Purgatory hold fast, then are they all of good footing. *a* **1617** Hieron *Wks.* 1619 II. 441 A thing for which we find no footing in the scripture. **1674** N. Fairfax *Bulk & Selv.* 46 This way of speaking has so good footing, that [etc.].
8. a. The conditions and arrangements, the understood state of things, on which an institution, etc. is established; the position or status due or assigned to a person, etc. in

estimation or treatment. ***on the same, on one*** or ***a footing*** (***with***): on an equality.

1657 CROMWELL *Sp.* 21 Apr., I think we are now to consider, not what we are in regard to our Footing and that of the Government which called this Parliament. **1657–8** *Burton's Diary* (1828) II. 440 It is not long since they got the title of Lords. Anciently, all were upon one footing of account. **1741** tr. *D'Argens Chinese Lett.* XX. 136 They resolved to put the Chinese on the same Footing as the Dutch. **1769** *Junius Lett.* No. 2 (1804) I. 24 *n.* 2 The army..was never upon a more respectable footing with regard to discipline. **1807–8** SYD. SMITH *Plymley's Lett.* Wks. 1859 II. 177/1 What the Catholics ask for is to be put on a footing with the Protestant Dissenters. **1818** JAS. MILL *Brit. India* II. v. iv. 424 Mahomed Ali was..placed upon the footing of an ally of the King of Great Britain. **1861** HUGHES *Tom Brown at Oxf.* i. (1889) 3 The eldest sons of baronets..were scarcely admitted on any other footing [than as gentlemen-commoners]. **1894** *Times* (weekly ed.) 9 Feb. 115/2 The Khedive..stands upon an altogether different footing from the Sultan.

b. The 'terms' on which a person stands in intercourse with another; degree of intimacy or favour; relative status (as an equal, superior, or inferior).

1742 FIELDING *J. Andrews* II. iv, Horatio and Lenora were what they call on a good footing together. **1766** GOLDSM. *Vic. W.* xx, I was admitted to his table upon the footing of half friend, half underling. **1796** JANE AUSTEN *Pride & Prej.* v. 188 You see on what a footing we are.

9. Entrance on a new position, etc. (in phr. ***to pay for one's footing***); hence, a fee demanded of a person on doing something for the first time or on being admitted to any trade, society, etc.

1710 *Brit. Apollo* III. No. 12. 2/2 Young..Sinners..not yet of Age to pay for their Footing in St. James's Park. **1777** [see CHUMMAGE 2]. **1833** MARRYAT *P. Simple* vii, 'Hand out my footing! What does he mean?' 'He means that you must fork out a seven-shilling bit.' **1862** TROLLOPE *Small Ho. at Allington* ii, Mr. Crosbie..had to pay half a crown for his footing to the haymakers.

10. The action of putting a foot to anything.

1805 W. TAYLOR in *Ann. Rev.* III. 65 Weaving, footing, and grafting silk stockings..are mostly performed by women. **1882** CAULFEILD & SAWARD *Dict. Needlework*, *Footing*, a term employed in the knitting of stockings.

11. *concr.* That with which something is 'footed'.

a. Material used to 'foot' boots, stockings, etc.

1591 PERCIVALL *Sp. Dict.*, *Cabeçado*, new footings of bootes. **1707** J. STEVENS *Quevedo's Com. Wks.* (1709) 222 It waits to be converted into Footing for Stockings.

†**b.** = FOOT *sb.* 10.

1659 TORRIANO, *Fústo*, the shank, the supporter, the stalk or footing of any thing.

c. *Lace.* (See quot. 1882.)

1692 *Lond. Gaz.* No. 2733/4 One..Petticoat, having 3 black Fringes, with Footings. **1697** *Ibid.* No. 3250/4, 3 yards of Silver Lace and Footing. **1869** MRS. PALLISER *Lace* xix. 215 Château-Renaud and Mézières were chiefly employed in the manufacture of footings. **1882** CAULFEILD & SAWARD *Dict. Needlework*, *Footing*..is used..to distinguish the edge of the Lace that is sewn to the dress from the scalloped and unattached edge. The Footing is sometimes worked with the rest of the design, and at others as a separate narrow lace, being then sewn on to the main part.

d. A piece of hard wood dovetailed on to the pile-end of an arrow.

1856 H. A. FORD *Archery* v. 30 For footing, any hard wood will do; and if this be solid for one inch below the pile, it will be amply sufficient. **1887** W. BUTT *Ford's Archery* iii. 37 Great care should be taken..that the footing exactly fits the pile, so as to fill entirely the inside of it.

e. *Printing*, etc. (See quots.)

1676 MOXON *Print. Lett.* 7 The Footing is the small Arches the Letter stands on, as the Arches upon the feet of Letter A is the Footing of that Letter. **1683** —— *Mech. Exerc.* II. 126 The Footing, is the straight fine Stroak or Stroaks that lie in the Foot-Line of Letters.

12. *Arch.* A projecting course or courses at the base or foundation of a wall or other erection to give it security.

1703 MOXON *Mech. Exerc.* 255 All Walls ought to have a Basis, or Footing, at least 4 Inches on a side broader than the thickness of the Wall. **1838** SIMMS *Pub. Wks. Gt. Brit.* 25 The footings of the abutments will be 18 inches below the level. **1881** YOUNG *Every man his own mechanic* §23 He should get a bricklayer to show him..how to put in the footings of his wall.

13. A place hollowed out or otherwise prepared for receiving the foot of a timber or the like.

1793 SMEATON *Edystone L.* §88 In the center of the house a slight footing was cut for the mast, suitable to a square of 18 inches.

14. The action of adding up a column of figures, etc.; the result thus obtained, sum total.

1855 H. CLARKE *Dict.*, *Footing*..reckoning..sum total. **1881** *Chicago Times* 4 June, The final footings of the debt of all cities..of the United States..were made last week. **1884** *Harper's Mag.* July 296/2 We could easily add twenty per cent. to the gross footings of the entire list.

15. The action of collecting turf; also, the heaps so formed. *Sc.* and *Irish dial.*

1802 FINDLATER *Agric. Peebles* 209 The peats..are placed on end three or four together, and leaning against each other; this is called footing the peats. **1825** JAMIESON, *Fittings*, turfs set on edge. **1841** S. C. HALL *Ireland* (1842) II. 263 *note*, 'Footing', which means collecting the turf into parcels of about six each. **1880** *Antrim & Down Gloss.*, *Footins*, small heaps of cut peat.

16. *Whale-fishing.* (See quot. 1858.)

1820 SCORESBY *Acc. Arct. Reg.* II. 402 The greasy animal matter called footje or footing. **1858** SIMMONDS *Dict. Trade*, *Footing*, the finer detached fragments of the fenks, or refuse whale blubber, not wholly deprived of oil.

17. *attrib.* and *Comb.*, as ***footing-place*** (also *fig.*); **footing-ale** (see quots.); **footing beam, f. dormant**, the tie-beam of a roof; **footing-time** (*dial.*), the time when a woman rises from childbed.

1824 *Craven Dialect* 75 **Footing-ale*, liquor or money given by a person on entering a new employment. **1825** JAMIESON, *Fittin-ale*, an entertainment given by parents when they have a child that taks the fit or foot, i.e., begins to walk. **1842** GWILT *Encycl. Archit.* Gloss., **Footing Beam*, the name given, in some of the provinces, to the tie-beam of a roof. **1846** BUCHANAN *Techn. Dict.*, **Footing Dormant* in carpentry, a name for the tie-beam of a roof. **1611** SPEED *Hist. Gt. Brit.* IX. xii. §74 The possession of the Citie of Vannes..the English-men still kept, that..they might haue some holde and certaine *footing-place. *a* **1828** D. WORDSWORTH *Tour Continent* in *Jrnls.* (1941) II. 288 A gulph..towards the edge of which our footing-place..sloped directly. **1891** O. WILDE *Intentions* 26 Facts are not merely finding a footing-place in history, but they are usurping the domain of Fancy. **1674** RAY *S. & E.C. Words* 66 **Footing time*, Norf. is the same with upsetting time in Yorksh. when the Puerpera gets up.

†**'footingly**, *adv. Obs. rare*$^{-1}$. [f. *footing* ppl. adj. (f. FOOT *v.*) + -LY^2.] With (proper) use of the feet in dancing, trippingly.

1566 DRANT *Horace's Sat.* I. ix. 24 Or who can daunce so footinglye, Obseruing tune and time?

footle ('fu:t(ə)l), *v. slang.* [Of obscure origin: Cf. FOOTER *sb.*^{2}] *intr.* To talk or act foolishly, to trifle or 'potter'. Hence **'footle** *sb.*, twaddle, 'rot'. **'footle** *a.*, paltry, trifling.

1892 F. ANSTEY *Voces Populi* Ser. II. 111 Now, really, Settee, do try not to footle like this! **1894** DU MAURIER *Trilby* I. 163 His palette in one hand, and his twiddling little footle pig's-hair brush in the other. **1895** F. ANSTEY *Lyre & Lancet* x. 106 I'm no good at poetry..It does seem to me such—well, such footle.

footler ('fu:tlə(r)). [f. FOOTLE *v.* + -ER^1.] One who footles.

1904 CHESTERTON *Nap. Notting Hill* IV. iii. 242 Drop your public-house flag, you footler! **1923** *Daily Mail* 22 June 7 Urbane persiflage directed against 'footlers', bores, and busybodies. **1923** U. L. SILBERRAD *Lett. J. Armiter* ix. 191 The rest are just footlers who'd piffle and gas. **1940** 'G. ORWELL' *Inside Whale* 133 A novelist who simply disregards the major public events of the moment is generally either a footler or a plain idiot.

footless ('fʊtlɪs), *a.* [f. FOOT *sb.* + -LESS. Cf. FEETLESS.] Having no foot or feet.

1398 TREVISA *Barth. De P.R.* XVIII. cxv. (1495) 856 Amonge wormes some ben fotelesse: as adders and serpentes. *c* **1400** *Destr. Troy* 6475 Mony foteles freike of his fell dinttes. **1591** SYLVESTER *Du Bartas* I. v. 89 Some [creatures] head-less are, Foot-less, and fin-less. **1675** HOBBES *Odyss.* (1677) 45 About him will his footless sea-calves lie. **1849** H. MILLER *Footpr. Creat.* ix. 157 The footless serpent, which 'goeth upon its belly'. **1886** W. J. TUCKER *E. Europe* 114 'What do you think of us?' asked the footless officer.

b. of things (e.g. a stocking).

1611 COTGR., *Breusse*, a dish, or footlesse cup. **1853** KANE *Grinnell Exp.* xx. (1856) 159 Some footless stockings, tied up at the lower end to serve as socks.

c. *transf.* and *fig.*

1795 COLERIDGE *Eolian Harp* 24 Melodies..Footless and wild, like birds of Paradise. **1855** TENNYSON *Maud* XVIII. viii, My love has..stol'n away To dreamful wastes where footless fancies dwell.

footlights ('fʊtlaɪts), *sb. pl.* **a.** A row of lights placed in front of the stage of a theatre, on a level with the feet of the actors, and furnished with reflectors so as to throw all their light upon the scene. ***across the footlights***: see ACROSS B. *prep.* 2b. Often *transf.* = the 'stage'; ***to smell of the footlights*** = to be redolent of the stage.

1836–9 DICKENS *Sk. Boz* (1850) 74/2 The foot-lights have just made their appearance. **1880** OUIDA *Moths* II. 322 My own art has a little too much smell of the footlights; I have..too many [hours] with the gaslit crowds before me. **1883** S. C. HALL *Retrospect* II. 270 His experience of the foot-lights had not chilled..his love of Nature.

b. *attrib.* (in *sing.*)

1870 LOWELL *Among my Bks.* Ser. I. (1873) 324 The foot-light style of phrase. **1894** G. EGERTON *Keynotes* 1 The mental picture of footlight flare and fantastic dance.

footling ('fʊtlɪŋ), *sb.* [f. FOOT *sb.* + -LING.]

†**1.** The footstalk or petiole of a flower. *Obs.*

1562 TURNER *Herbal* II. 41 b, A long small pediculo, that is a footlyng or footstalcke.

2. In a rowing boat: (see quot.).

1857 P. COLQUHOUN *Comp. Oarsman's Guide* 7 Footlings, or shifting battens..consist of long strips of board 2½ inches broad and an inch apart, secured by cross pieces underneath them.

footling ('fʊtlɪŋ), *adv. Obstetrics.* [f. FOOT *sb.* + -LING.] With the feet foremost.

1734 GIFFARD *Cases in Midwifery* lxxxix. 215 A delivery where the child came footling. **1801** *Med. Jrnl.* V. 312 The child was smaller than usual, and the presentation footling.

footling ('fu:tlɪŋ), *ppl. a.* [f. FOOTLE *v.* + -ING^2.] That footles or trifles; 'drivelling', 'blithering', trivial; hence of things.

1897 in *N.E.D.* s.v. *footle v.* **1905** G. B. SHAW in *Daily Chron.* 15 Mar. 6/3 They are paraphrases of great works, made by footling people. **1907** *Daily Chron.* 2 Apr. 4/4 That dreary room..with its footling little lace window curtains. **1923** A. BENNETT *Things that have interested Me* II. II. 20 A perfectly footling popular play which fails to be popular. **1930** T. THURSTON *Man in Black Hat* x. 181, I had heard it before from fatuous idealists and footling divines. **1930** W. S. MAUGHAM *Breadwinner* I. 46 You do talk the most footling rot. **1960** *Guardian* 14 Dec. 8/7 Wondering why he should do 'footling' experiments with ball bearings.

footlock: see FETLOCK.

†**'footlong**, *adv. Obs. rare*$^{-1}$. [See -LONG.] = FOOTLING *adv.*

1545 RAYNOLD *Byrth Mankynde* 74 a, Then must the mydwife helpe the byrth..that cometh fotelonge (yf she can) to returne it vpon the head.

'foot-loose, *a.* orig. *U.S.* [Cf. FOOT *sb.* 35.]

1. Free to move the feet, untrammelled.

a **1699** JOS. BEAUMONT *Psyche* (1702) XIII. cxlviii, Sedition was his Drift, and He could ne'r Persue that game unless he footloose were.

2. Free to act as one pleases; not hampered by any ties.

1873 J. H. BEADLE *Undevel. West* xxxi. 669 All my friends who were 'footloose' had the 'Arizona fever'. **1904** F. LYNDE *Grafters* xxvii. 347 If the mine should happen to explode..it'll be a comfort to have a foot-loose friend or two on the outside to pick up the pieces of us. **1910** W. M. RAINE *B. O'Connor* 52 We went in together for all the kinds of spreeing that young fellows who are footloose are likely to do. **1924** —— *Troubled Waters* x. 104 Oh, she's nice enough, when she isn't a little divvle. The trouble is she isn't foot-loose. **1943** FORSHAW & ABERCROMBIE *County of London Plan* §46 The London Docks..are not directly affected by the Plan: this is an industry that is not 'foot-loose'. **1959** T. S. ELIOT *Elder Statesman* I. 25 You see, I'm a widower, like you, Dick. So I'm pretty footloose. **1961** *Guardian* 6 Feb. 8/4 A migrant group is likely to include..some who are merely footloose, who will settle nowhere. **1971** 'E. CANDY' *Words for Murder Perhaps* xi. 125 I'm travelling around, you see. Footloose and fancy free, you might call me. I've no special ties anywhere.

footman ('fʊtmən). [f. FOOT *sb.* + MAN.]

1. One who goes on foot, a pedestrian. Also with adj., a (good, swift, etc.) walker or runner. Now somewhat *rare* exc. *dial.*

1382 WYCLIF *Numb.* xi. 21 Six hundryd thousandes of foot men ben of this puple. **1475** *Presentm. Juries* in *Surtees Misc.* (1890) 27 The fotmans cawse be for William Chawe dore is defectyffe. **1563** ABP. SANDYS in Strype *Ann. Ref.* I. xxxv. 396 His park, wherein is a path for footmen. **1623** COCKERAM II, A swift Foot-man, *celeripedian*. **1650** FULLER *Pisgah* I. xiii. 41 Fear makes good Footmen. *a* **1744** W. BYRD in Tyler *Amer. Lit.* (1879) II. 277 Practice will soon make a man of tolerable vigor an able footman. **1769** *De Foe's Tour Gt. Brit.* I. 153 The Ferry-keeper will demand Sixpence of every Horseman, and Twopence of every Foot-man. **1816** KEATINGE *Trav.* (1817) II. 28 A Foot-man is nearly lost in this forest of annuals. **1882** *Worcestersh. Gloss.*, *Footman*, a good walker is termed 'a good footman'. **1890** O. BELKNAP in Shields *Big Game N. Amer.* 298 A Buffalo appeared..at a point which we afterwards found taxed the climbing powers of a footman. **1890** BOLDREWOOD *Squatter's Dream* xxiii. 277 A 'footman' (as a person not in possession of a horse is termed in Australian provincial circles).

†**b.** One who competes in a foot-race. *Obs.*

1654 WEBSTER *Appius & Virg.* I. i, I have heard of cunning footmen that have worn Shoes made of lead, some ten days 'fore a race To give them nimble and more active feet. **1685** *Lond. Gaz.* No. 2062. 2/2 There will be a Plate Run for by Footmen at Wigan.

†**c.** A foot-pad. *Obs.*

1615 J. STEPHENS *Ess. & Charac.*, *Warrener* (1857) 201 If he doth not play the valiant Foot-man, and take tribute of passengers. **1666** PEPYS *Diary* (1879) VI. 84 Being wounded..last night, by footmen, in the highway.

2. A foot-soldier.

1297 R. GLOUC. (1724) 199 Wyþoute archers & vot men, wyþ tuo þousend hors y wrye. **13..** *Coer de L.* 5105 Off a footman a bowe he took. *c* **1450** *Merlin* 113 [Theí]..were well viij^{ml} knyhtes..and fotemen grete plente. **1598** BARRET *Theor. Warres* III. i. 40 Those battels..being verie aduantagious for footmen against footmen. **1630** tr. *Camden's Hist. Eliz.* I. 105 He put his footmen aboord the small vessels he had. **1798** CRAIG in Owen *Wellesley's Desp.* 601 A force of 10,000 horse, and as many footmen. **1864** KINGSLEY *Rom. & Teut.* iii. (1875) 72 The knights..left the foot-men to finish the work. **1896** *Times* 22 Apr. 7/3 They were suddenly attacked by a body of 200 horsemen, supported by a large body of footmen.

†**3.** An attendant or foot-servant. In early use, a runner in attendance upon a rider of rank; and, later, a servant who ran before his master's carriage, called more fully a ***running-footman***. *Obs.*

c **1450** *Bk. Curtasye* 621 in *Babees Bk.* (1868) 320 Fotemen þat rennen by þe brydels of ladys shene. **1552** HULOET, Fotemen for princes, or noble persons, *circumpedes*. **1612** W. PARKES *Curtaine-Dr.* (1876) 27 He needs must ride, That had my Foot-man lackying by his side. **1718** PRIOR *Alma* I. 58 Like Footmen running before Coaches, To tell the Inn what Lord approaches. **1791** *Bee* 13 July IV. 11 Coaches..were [*c.* 1760] generally accompanied by running footmen..whose assistance was often wanted to support the coach on each side, to prevent it from being overturned. **1818** SCOTT *Br. Lamm.* xxii, Two running footmen, dressed in white, with black jockey-caps, and long staffs in their hands, headed the train. **1856** *N. & Q.* Ser. II. I. 80/1 The sheriff and judges were preceded by two running footmen.

4. A man-servant in livery employed chiefly to attend the carriage and wait at table.

1706–7 FARQUHAR *Beaux' Strat.* I. i, There's neither Red-Coat in the Coach, nor Footman behind it. **1756–7** tr. *Keysler's Trav.* (1760) IV. 469 Some gentlemen of the bed-chamber were not able even to keep a footman. **1784**

COWPER *Tiroc.* 407 Means that would disgrace A.. footman out of place. **1848** DICKENS *Dombey* vii, The Princess's Arms.. much resorted to by splendid footmen. **1878** M. A. BROWN *Nadeschda* 23 A gilded coach.. bursts forth; Like gaudy birds are the footmen perched.

b. *fig.* (Cf. *lackey*.)

1834 MACAULAY *Pitt* (1851) 45 The Whigs, who ought, he said, to be ashamed to talk about liberty, while they submitted to the footmen of the Duke of Newcastle.

5. A stand to support a kettle, etc. before the fire.

1767 *Specif. Brodie & Williams Patent* No. 880. 3 A rest or footman to put the tea-kettle on. **1844** DICKENS *Mart. Chuz.* xx, From pot and kettle, face of brass footman, and black-leaded stove.

6. A moth of the family *Lithosiidæ*.

1819 G. SAMOUELLE *Entomol. Compend.* 249 *Lithosia quadra* (four-spotted footman). **1870** *Eng. Mech.* 21 Jan. 449/2 The scarce footman (*Lithosia caniola*) has not long been known as a British insect.

7. *appositively* and *Comb.*, as †*footman archer*; *footman-like* adj.; † **footman's inn**, gaol.

1598 GRENEWEY *Tacitus' Ann.* XIII. ix. (1622) 192 In the wings went the *footmen archers with the residue of the horsemen. **1604** *Penniles Parl. Threed-bare Poets* in *Harl. Misc.* (1744) I. 179 Those that depend on Destiny, and not on God, may chance look through a narrow Lattice at *Footmen's Inn. **1613** S. ROWLANDS *Knaue of Harts, A theeuing Knaue*, That he at last in foot-mans Inne must host. **1864** *Realm* 23 Mar. 4 The Globe, whose *footmanlike servility to the Ministry is notorious.

Hence **'footmanhood**, footmen collectively. **'footmanry**, the occupation of a footman.

1822 GALT *Sir A. Wylie* I. xxiii. 208 We were plagued by the sons of the patriarchal fixtures of Chastington-hall, coming here to learn the craft and mystery of footmanry. **1862** H. AÏDÉ *Carr of Carrl.* III. 136 The powdered footmanhood of London.

footmanship ('fʊtmənʃɪp). [f. prec. + -SHIP.]

1. The action of, or skill in, running or walking. *to lay on* or *make footmanship*: to run quickly. Now *rare* or *Obs.*

1562 J. SHUTE *Cambine's Turk. Wars* 18 Everye man by fotemanshyppe soughte to save one and to get into the citie. **1565** GOLDING *Ovid's Met.* I. (1593) 17 Twaine of them do straine themselves and lay on footemanship. **1580** BLUNDEVIL *Horsemanship* (1609) 4 b, Their sure footmanship.. their lofty pase. *a* **1603** T. CARTWRIGHT *Confut. Rhem. N.T.* (1618) 9 The Hart pursued of the dogges, maketh foote-manship to the soile. **1672** PETTY *Pol. Anat.* 328 The footman-ship for which the Irish 40 years ago were very famous, is now almost quite lost among them. **1769** *De Foe's Tour Gt. Brit.* II. 414 The People in this County [Stafford] have been more particularly famous than any other for good Footmanship. **1896** *Boston* (Mass.) *Jrnl.* 30 Jan. 10/6 The most important test is utterly ignored. This.. Footmanship, not erudition, is the thing.

fig. **1614** J. COOKE *City Wit* in Dodsley *O.P.* VII. 85 I'll try the nimble footmanship of your tongue.

2. The occupation or office of a footman (sense 4).

1833 *Fraser's Mag.* VIII. 632 The fundamental principles of footmanship.

† **'foot-mantle.** *Obs.* **a.** ? An over-garment worn by women when riding, to protect their dress. **b.** = FOOT-CLOTH 1.

c **1386** CHAUCER *Prol.* 472 A foot-mantel aboute hir hipes large. **1488** in *Ld. Treas. Acc. Scotl.* I. 147 Item, for thre elne of veluus til a fut mantil, price of the elne iij li. *c* **1610** SIR J. MELVIL *Mem.* (1735) 91 With them came a Servant of Lord Robert's with a Horse and Foot-mantle of velvet.. for me to ride upon. **1685** *Lond. Gaz.* No. 2031/1 Six Heralds in Coats with Foot-Mantles, bearheaded, two and two. **1818** SCOTT *Hrt. Midl.* iv, 'Horse graith and harnessing, forby broidered robes and foot-mantles, that wad hae stude by their lane wi' gold brocade.'

foot-mark, footmark ('fʊtmɑːk).

1. A mark on the foot; (in quot.) an ownership mark cut on the foot of a swan.

1641 BEST *Farm. Bks.* (Surtees) 123 Our footemarke is to cutte or slit them on both the in-webbes.

2. A mark made by the foot; a foot-print.

1826 SYD. SMITH *Counsel for Prisoners* Wks. 1859 II. 111/2 A foot-mark, a word, a sound.. all gave birth to the most ingenious inferences. **1855** DAWSON *Acadian Geol.* ix. 187 When examining the red sandstones.. I found in one of the beds a few footmarks of an unknown animal.

fig. **1858** R. A. VAUGHAN *Ess. & Rem.* I. 31 Possessed of data wherewith to discover the genuine footmark, we may now track the course of our author.

Hence **foot-mark** *v. trans.* †(*a*) To mark on the foot. †(*b*) To impress with the mark of a foot.

1641 BEST *Farm. Bks.* (Surtees) 123 The swanners gette up the younge swannes about Midsummer, and footemarke them for the owners. **1821** CLARE *Vill. Minstr.* I. 208 Where .. First foot-mark'd the ground by me, All is still.

† **'foot-meal,** *adv. Obs.* [OE. *fótmælum*: see -MEAL.] Step by step. (In quot. preceded by *by*.)

c **1050** *Gloss.* in Wr.-Wülcker 412 *Gradatim*, fægre, oððe fotmælum. **1579** FENTON *Guicciard.* xv. (1599) 728 The Spaniards not ceassing.. to win aduantage by footmeale.

'footnote ('fʊtnəʊt). A note or comment inserted at the foot of the text. *transf.* and *fig.* Hence **'footnote** *v.*, to furnish with a footnote or footnotes; to comment on in a footnote. Also **footnoted** *ppl. a.*, **footnoting** *vbl. sb.*

1841 SAVAGE *Dict. Printing* 88 *Bottom notes*.. are also termed *Foot Notes*. **1864** *Reader* 21 May 645, A supplemental little poem.. extensively footnoted. *Ibid.* The result of all this.. footnoting and appendix-noting, is that the volume has a most chaotic and bewildering look. **1875** E. WHITE *Life in Christ* IV. xxiv. (1878) 360 To refer in a footnote to the passages.. where these words occur. **1892** R. L. STEVENSON (*title*) A footnote to history. Eight years of trouble in Samoa. **1893** *N. & Q.* Ser. VIII. III. 190 Junius foot-notes a passing attack on Chatham thus. **1935** E. V. LUCAS in *Punch* 4 Sept. 269/3 What a glorious possession this Abbey is and what a footnote to history, science and art! **1942** *Sphere* 15 Aug. 220/2 A significant footnote to China's great struggle. **1965** *Listener* 3 June 834/1 Sir Colin Coote's breezy, affectionate life of his friend Walter Elliot provides a useful footnote.

foot-oak: see FUTTOCK.

foot-pace ('fʊtpeɪs). [See PACE *sb.*]

1. A walking pace. Chiefly in advb. phr. *a foot-pace, at* (or †*in*) *a foot-pace* = at a walking pace.

1538 ELIOT, *Pedepressim*, a foote pase, softly. **1562** J. HEYWOOD *Prov. & Epigr.* (1867) 149 The best lacketh feete, foote pace with vs to holde. **1607** TOPSELL *Four-f. Beasts* (1658) 315 Cause him every day to be led up and down a foot pace a quarter of an hour. **1637** BRETON *Poste w. packet* Wks. (Grosart) 41/1 For your foot-pace, I thinke you haue sore heeles, you walke so nicely, as vpon egge-shels. **1674** N. COX *Gentl. Recreat.* v. (1686) 5 Being oblig'd.. to toil their Horses all day, over deep Fallows, in a foot-pace only. **1810** *Sporting Mag.* XXXVI. 90 The child was riding only a foot pace. **1859** DICKENS *T. Two Cities* I. ii. 'Come on at a footpace, d'ye mind me?'

2. Something on which to tread or set the feet.

†**a.** A carpet or mat. *Obs.*

1585 *Nomenclator* 249/2 *Storea*.. a mat: a footepase of sedges. **1653** H. COGAN tr. *Pinto's Trav.* xl. 160 A Chair of State.. and at the foot of it a Cushion of the same, all upon an exceeding large foot-pace of tapestry. **1706** in PHILLIPS (ed. Kersey).

b. A raised portion of a floor; a dais or platform; e.g. the step or raised floor on which an altar stands.

1580 HOLLYBAND *Treas. Fr. Tong, Marche-pied*, a footepace, a threshold, a groundsill. **1598** in *Mem. Stepney Parish* (1890–1) 34 Item, that there be made about the communion table a raile wth a foote pace and mattes thereon to kneele vpon. **1612** BACON *Ess., Judicature* (Arb.) 456 The place of Justice is an hallowed place; and therefore not onely the bench, but the footepace and precincts and purprise thereof ought to bee preserued with-out scandall and corruption. *a* **1676** WHITELOCKE *Mem.* (1682) 609 At the upper end upon a Foot pace and Carpet, stood the Protector with a Chair of State behind him. *a* **1697** AUBREY *Nat. Hist. Surrey* (1719) V. 193 The Communion Table.. [is] placed on a fine black and white Footpace. **1845** *Ecclesiologist* IV. 102 The footpace, or altar-platform. **1872** SHIPLEY *Gloss. Eccl. Terms, Footpace*.. a raised flooring in a bay window.

c. A hearth-stone.

1652 GAULE *Magastrom.* 181 The crickets chirping behind the chimney stock; or creeping upon the foot-pace. **1703** T. N. *City & C. Purchaser* 220 Some Pavements, (as in Foot-paces before Chimneys). **1840** PARKER *Gloss. Archit., Foot-pace*. This term is also sometimes used for the hearth-stone.

d. A half landing on a staircase or flight of steps; also called *half-pace*.

1703 MOXON *Mech. Exerc.* 160 *Foot-pace*, is a part of a pair of Stairs.. where you make two or three paces before you ascend another step. **1842** GWILT *Encycl. Archit.* Gloss., Foot Pace or Half Pace.

footpad ('fʊtpæd). *Obs.* exc. *Hist.* [See PAD.] A highwayman who robs on foot.

1683 DRYDEN & LEE *Duke of Guise* Ded., Though they assault us like footpads in the dark. **1789** WOLCOTT (P. Pindar) *Subj. for Paint.* Wks. 1812 II. 179 I'm no Highwayman. No, there you are right. A Footpad only. **1840** DICKENS *Barn. Rudge* ii, Roads in the neighbourhood of the metropolis were infested by footpads or highwaymen.

Hence **'footpad** *v.*, to play the footpad; **'footpadding** *vbl. sb.* and *ppl. a.* Also **'footpaddery, -padry** (*nonce-wd.*), the occupation of a foot-pad.

1735 in W. C. Sydney *Eng. 18th C.* (1891) II. 282 Five condemned malefactors were executed at Tyburn, viz. Kiffe and Wilson for footpadding [etc.]. **1790** BURNS *Let. to Cunningham* 13 Feb., A glass of whisky-toddy with a ruby-nosed yoke-fellow of a foot-padding exciseman. **1860** GEN. P. THOMPSON *Audi Alt.* III. ciii. 7 From foot-padding upwards, it is always desirable to get at the principle. **1861** *Ibid.* III. clxxviii. 215 Highwaymanhood and foot-padry. **1874** W. C. SMITH *Borland Hall* 152 I'd sooner footpad it, and steal and rob. **1889** DOYLE *Micah Clarke* xxiii, They did not, as a rule, descend to footpaddery or robbery.

foot-path, footpath ('fʊtpɑːθ, -æ-).

1. a. A path for foot-passengers only.

1526 *Pilgr. Perf.* (W. de W. 1531) 141 Lyke as the fote path or waye ledeth to the cite. **1605** SHAKS. *Lear* IV. i. 58 *Glou.* Know'st thou the way to Douer? *Edg.* Both style, and gate; Horseway, and foot-path. **1786** BURNS *Brigs of Ayr* 100 Your poor, narrow foot-path of a street. **1842** MRS. CARLYLE *Lett.* I. 156 A foot-path about half-a-yard wide.. cuts across the bit of green field.

fig. **1535** COVERDALE *Ps.* cxviii. [cxix.] 15, I wil.. haue respecte vnto thy fotepathes.

b. A pavement.

1813 J. LAMBERT *Trav. N. Amer.* (ed. 2) II. 56 The street [*sc.* Broadway, New York] is well paved, and the foot-paths are chiefly bricked. **1908** *Westm. Gaz.* 21 Sept. 8/3 His car struck the footpath-face.. and the car staggered badly on the road. **1943** K. TENNANT *Ride on Stranger* vi. 50 The city swarm poured over the footpaths and across the taxi's front wheels.

†**2.** ? A pedestal. *Obs.*

1580 *Eccl. Proc. Bp. Barnes* (Surtees) 128 There remaneth in the quere certayne corbile stones which were some time fotte pathes for images.

3. *attrib.*

1611 SHAKS. *Wint. T.* IV. iii. 132 Jog-on, Jog-on, the foot-path way, And merrily hent the Stile-a. **1892** *Daily News* 15 Feb. 5/1 The National Footpath Preservation Society.

Hence **'footpath** *v. trans.*, to make a footpath or footpaths across.

1844 MRS. BROWNING *Drama of Exile* Poet. Wks. 1889 I. 81 This shall.. Turn back your rivers, footpath all your seas.

footprint ('fʊtprɪnt). The print or impression left by the foot; *spec.* in *Geol.* a fossilized one.

1552 HULOET, Fote prynte, or the printe of the fote, *peda*. **1623** COCKERAM I, *Traces*, the feet-print of rauening beasts. **1850** LYELL *2nd Visit U.S.* II. 304 Certain fossil foot-prints of a reptile said to have been found in strata of the ancient coal-formation. **1865** TYLOR *Early Hist. Man.* 115 The typical case is the sacred footprint of Ceylon. **1888** BURGON *Lives 12 Gd. Men* II. v. 25 Their footprints in yesterday's snow were all still there.

fig. **1674** PLAYFORD *Skill Mus.* I. xi. 38 Of which I do intend in this my Discourse to leave some foot-prints. **1839** LONGF. *Psalm of Life* vii, Leave behind us Foot-prints on the sands of time.

Hence **'foot-print** *v. trans.*, to mark with footprints.

1850 MRS. BROWNING *Poems* I. 201 Pavement fair, The antique wood-nymphs scarce would dare To footprint o'er.

† **foot rid.** *Obs.* [Of doubtful origin; perh. f. FOOT *sb.* + *rid* f. RID *v.* Cf. FOOTRILL.] (See quot.)

1665 DUDLEY *Metallum Martis* (1854) 27 Where the Coles is deep and but little Earth upon the measures of Coles, there the Colliers rid off the Earth, and dig the Coles under their feet; these Works are called Foot-rids. **1686** [see FOOTRILL].

footrill ('fʊtrɪl). *Coal-mining.* Also **footrail, futteril.** [Of unknown etymology: cf. prec.] (See quots.)

1686 PLOT *Staffordsh.* iii. 129 The open works.. where.. the Workmen rid off the earth, and dig the coal under their feet.. there being no need for these, of windless, roap or carf, whence these sort of Coale-works are commonly call'd Foot-ridds or Footrills. **1883** GRESLEY *Gloss. Coal Mining. Footrill, Futteril*, and *Footrail*, the entrance to a mine by means of a level driven into a hill-side, or a dip road, up which coal is brought. **1885** *Sheffield Daily Tel.* 30 June, Four Shafts and a Footrill have been sunk to the Coal.

† **foot-saunt.** *Obs.* [f. FOOT *sb.* + *saunt*, CENT[2].] App. = *cent-foot* (see CENT[2]).

The quots. for *cent-foot* seem to show that there was something about 'loving' in the language used in the game, whence prob. the allusion below.

1579 GOSSON *Sch. Abuse* (Arb.) 35 In our assemblies at playes in London, you shall see suche heauing, and shoouing .. suche playing at foote Saunt without Cardes.

footsie, var. FOOTY *sb.* 1.

foot-slog ('fʊtslɒg), *v.* [f. FOOT *sb.* + SLOG V. 2.] *intr.* To go on foot; to tramp, march. Also with *it*. Hence **'foot-slog** *sb.*, a tramp, march; **'foot-,slogger**, a foot-soldier, infantryman, pedestrian; **'foot-,slogging** *vbl. sb.* and *ppl. a.*

1894 C. H. DONOVAN *With Wilson in Matabeleland* ix. 198 Some of the Johannesburg 'Foot-Sloggers'.. were doing damage in the village. **1899** KIPLING *Five Nations* (1903) 185 We're foot—slog—slog—sloggin' over Africa! **1906** *Macm. Mag.* Apr. 472 Must get in and foot-slog it, that's all. **1916** 'PETER' *Trench Yarns* iv. 34 I'm not a Shop gunner, y'know. I'm only a miserable foot-slogger! **1921** E. R. G. R. EVANS *South with Scott* vi. 89 There were people who preferred foot-slogging to ski at any time. **1925** B. TRAVERS *Mischief* viii, Another long foot-slog.. in squelching shoes. **1927** *Chambers's Jrnl.* June 392/1, I.. had to foot-slog until I could find a British Consul to borrow from. **1928** *Observer* 26 Feb. 6/3 A world where people travel by preference footslogging. **1928** *Sunday Express* 28 Oct. 14/3 A long, long way to Berlin, especially for the poor bally foot-sloggers who did the fighting and the dying. **1929** *Daily Tel.* 1 Jan. 9/6 Do coroners think that footsloggers willingly ask for trouble? **1939** *War Illustr.* 7 Oct. 98/3 Their speed.. was not that of foot-slogging infantry but of motorized columns.

'foot-sole. The sole of the foot.

1612 AINSWORTH *Annot. Ps.* lxxxix. 52 The oracle, Gen. 3. 15, that the serpent should bruise the footsole of the womans seed. **1630** J. TAYLOR (Water P.) *Taylor's Goose* Wks. 105/2 The name of them [Soland geese] may well proceede From the Dams foot-sole, whence they all do breede. **1870** MORRIS *Earthly Par.* II. III. 16 A dreary road the weary foot-sole wears.

foot-sore ('fʊtsɔə(r)), *a.* and *sb.*

A. *adj.* Sore as to the feet, having sore feet.

1719 DE FOE *Crusoe* (L.), The heat of the ground made me footsore. **1814** *Sporting Mag.* XLIII. 83 He was extremely foot sore. **1856** KANE *Arct. Expl.* I. xix. 238 The dogs were .. no longer foot-sore, but well rested.

B. *sb.* A complaint of the foot. *nonce-use.*

1874 FREEMAN in Stephens *Life* (1895) II. 84 Some kind of foot-sore, rheumatic gout, I believe they call it.

Hence **'footsoreness.**

1849 SOUTHEY *Common-pl. Bk.* Ser. II. 646 Cure for Foot-soreness. **1884** BESANT *Childr. Gibeon* xvii, Weariness I complain not of, and footsoreness is my righteous punishment.

footstalk ('fʊtstɔːk). [f. FOOT *sb.* + STALK.] A slender stem or support fitted into a foot or base.

a. *Bot.* The stalk or petiole of a leaf; the peduncle of a flower.

1562 TURNER *Herbal* II. 41 A footlyng or footstalcke such as chyries grow on. **1597** GERARDE *Herbal* II. xl. §3 The flowers do growe betweene the footestalkes of those leaues. **1640** PARKINSON *Theat. Bot.* 1114 The flowers come forth at the joynts upon long footstalkes. **1775** ROMANS *Hist. Florida* 27 Laurel, with.. blue berries sitting on long foot-stalks. **1849** DANA *Geol.* App. i. 716 The footstalk into which the frond tapers is very long.

b. *Zoöl.* A process resembling the petiole of a plant; e.g. the muscular attachment of a barnacle, the stalk of a crinoid, etc.

1826 KIRBY & SP. *Entomol.* IV. xliv. 214 Each egg is furnished with a footstalk terminating in a bulb. **1849** H. MILLER *Footpr. Creat.* iii. 30 The scale-like shagreen of the dog-fish is elevated over it on an osseous pedicle or foot-stalk. **1859** DARWIN *Orig. Spec.* v. (1878) 110 In some of the crabs the footstalk for the eye remains, though the eye is gone.

c. *gen.*

1831 BREWSTER *Nat. Magic* viii. (1833) 194 A tumbler-glass with a footstalk. **1871** L. STEPHEN *Playgr. Eur.* v. 122 Huge blocks [of ice] balanced on narrow footstalks.

Hence **'foot-stalked** *a.*, attached by a footstalk.

1849–52 TODD *Cycl. Anat.* IV. 1185/1 [Tunicata] sessile or foot-stalked on the rock.

footstall ('fʊtstɔːl). [f. FOOT *sb.* + STALL *sb.*]

1. The base or pedestal of a pillar, statue, etc.

1585 HIGGINS *Nomenclator* 203 *Stylobata*.. The foote stal of a piller. **1626** AINSWORTH *Annot. Pentat.* Lev. i. 15 The Priest went up on the footstall (of the Altar). **1635** J. HAYWARD tr. *Biondi's Ban. Virgin* 19 His shield.. rested on the footestall of the statue. **1886** WILLIS & CLARK *Cambridge* II. 140 The bases and footstalls shewed that the whole of the piers stood on this lower level.

2. 'A woman's stirrup' (J.).

footstep ('fʊtstɛp). [See STEP.]

1. a. A step or tread of the foot; a foot-fall.

1535 COVERDALE *Ps.* xvi[i]. 5 Ordre thou my goynges in thy pathes, that my fote steppes slippe not. **1719** DE FOE *Crusoe* I. xi, What marks were there of any other footsteps? **1797** MRS. RADCLIFFE *Italian* ix, Wherever I go I hear only the echoes of my own footsteps. **1816** J. WILSON *City of Plague* I. iii, Methought I heard a footstep in the church.

b. The distance traversed by the foot in stepping, taken as a measure of length or area.

1796 STEDMAN *Surinam* I. vii. 142 Not a foot-step of land could we find, where we might cook our salt provisions in safety. **1855** F. LOCKER *Lond. Lyrics, Old Cradle* vi, At most 'tis a footstep from cradle to coffin.

2. a. The mark or print made by a foot.

c **1220** *Bestiary* 7 Alle hise fet steppes After him he filleð. *c* **1440** *Promp. Parv.* 174/2 Foote steppe, of a mann only, *peda*. **1611** BIBLE *Bel & Dr.* 20, I see the footsteps of men, women and children. **1735** SOMERVILLE *Chase* III. 229 Trembling he views His Footsteps in the sand. **1860** TYNDALL *Glac.* I. xvi, 111, I marched without hesitation or anxiety in the footsteps of my guide.

b. *fig.*, as *to follow* or ***walk in a person's footsteps*** = to follow his example or guidance.

1549 *Compl. Scot.* xvii. 148 ȝe ar obleist to follou the futsteppis of ȝour predecessours in vertu. **1668** DENHAM *Prudence* Poems 147 Clear-sighted Reason Wisdoms Judgment leads, And Sense, her Vassal, in her footsteps treads. **1878** J. P. HOPPS *Jesus* x. 37 To call upon his sorrowing disciples to be prepared to follow in his footsteps.

†**3.** *fig.* A vestige or trace; a mark, token, or indication left by anything whether material or immaterial. *Obs.*

1587 GOLDING *De Mornay* v. 59 All these are traces, foot-steps, and images.. of that high misterie. **1647** N. BACON *Disc. Govt. Eng.* i. 2 As touching their cruelty, I find no footsteps in story. **1650** BULWER *Anthropomet.* 141 In the part of the Tooth cut off, there appeared the footsteps of a Nerve. **1662** J. CHANDLER *Van Helmont's Oriat.* 80 There is no foot-step, for the most part, of mooved Air to be perceived. **1670** MILTON *Hist. Eng.* I. 3 Relations.. accounted fabulous have bin after found to contain in them many foot-steps and reliques of something true. **1699** BENTLEY *Phal.* 211 There are plain and visible footsteps, that he has stole it. **1756** J. WARTON *Ess. Pope* (1806) I. 21 Those who have examined the New Forest can discover no mark or footstep of any other place of habitation.. than what at present remains. **1785** PALEY *Mor. Philos.* (1818) II. 86 We find no footsteps of any distinction of days which [etc.].

†**4.** A foot-path, footway. *Obs.*

1620 J. WILKINSON *Court Leet* 119 High-waies or foot-steps stopped up.

5. a. A step or raised structure on which to set the foot in order to ascend or descend. †In *Fortif.* = *foot-bank* (see FOOT *sb.* 35).

1549 LATIMER *6th Serm. bef. Edw. VI* (Arb.) 166 It is the fotesteppes of the ladder of heauen. **1646** SIR T. BROWNE *Pseud. Ep.* IV. x. 205 At the footestep of the Altar. **1706** PHILLIPS (ed. Kersey), *Foot-bank* or *Foot-step* (in Fortif.). **1806** WORDSW. (1st line of Sonnet), Methought I saw the foot-steps of a throne. **1815** JANE AUSTEN *Emma* I. 184 She crossed the low hedge, and tottering footstep which ended the narrow slippery path.

†**b.** A treadle for working a machine (*obs.*). **c.** *Printing* (see quot. 1888). **d.** A bearing to sustain the foot of a vertical shaft or spindle.

1678 *Phil. Trans.* XII. 1007 The Footsteps or Treddles differ in nothing from those which are usually made use of. **1683** MOXON *Mech. Exerc.* II. 72 [Printing] The Foot Step is an Inch-Board about a Foot broad, and sixteen Inches long. **1855** OGILVIE Suppl., *Footstep*, In mech., the pillow in which the foot of an upright or vertical shaft works. **1888** JACOBI *Printer's Voc.*, *Footstep*, the inclined footstool the pressman puts his foot on when pulling the bar over.

6. *attrib.*: **footstep bearing** = sense 5 d.

1887 D. A. LOW *Introd. Machine Draw.* 110 Plan and sectional elevation of a footstep bearing for an upright shaft. **1888** *Lockwood's Dict. Mech. Engin.* 147 Footstep bearings are.. made adjustable by placing the bearing in the centre of a ring casting. **1959** *Chambers's Encycl.* II. 175/2 A 'footstep bearing' is a thrust bearing at the bottom of a vertical shaft to support the revolving parts.

Hence †**'footstepping** *vbl. sb.* = FOOTSTEP 3.

1622 COOKE *Pope Joan* in *Harl. Misc.* (Malh.) IV. 56 You must bring better proof than this, that you find no foot-stepping of it in the answers made unto them.

footstool ('fʊtstuːl).

1. a. A stool upon which to rest the foot or feet.

1530 PALSGR. 222/2 Fote stole, *marchepied*. *c* **1611** CHAPMAN *Iliad* XIV. 201 A footstool for the ease Of thy soft feet. **1725** POPE *Odyss.* XVII. 271 With many a footstool thund'ring at thy head. **1849** JAMES *Woodman* ii, There she sat with her feet on a footstool.

b. *fig.*

1535 COVERDALE *Ps.* cix. [cx.] 1 Syt thou on my right hande, vntill I make thine enemies thy fotestole. **1593** SHAKS. *3 Hen. VI*, v. vii. 14. **1668** H. MORE *Div. Dial.* IV. xxvi. (1713) 363 The Popes have as well made Foot-balls of the Crowns of Emperours as Foot-stools of their Necks. **1860** FARRAR *Orig. Lang.* iv. 86 A nobler destiny than to become the footstool of a few families.

c. *U.S. colloq.* The earth. (Cf. Isaiah lxvi. 1.)

1821 T. DWIGHT *Trav. New Eng.* (1823) III. 231 We felt a total superiority to all the humble beings who were creeping on the footstool beneath us. **1859** *Congress. Globe* 18 Feb. 1122/1, I would give that power [of declaring war] to no President—none that has ever stood upon this footstool. **1891** *Boston* (Mass.) *Jrnl.* 12 Sept. 5/1, I found Mauchline to be the most God-forsaken place on the footstool. **1906** *N.Y. Globe* 20 Feb. 8 This New York of ours, regarded by many the wickedest city on the footstool.

†**2. a.** A stool to step upon, in order to climb to a higher position. Also *fig.* **b.** (See quot. 1611.)

1599 MINSHEU, A Foot-stoole to lift a woman to horse, vide *Andilla*. **1611** COTGR., *Suppied d'orgues*, the foot-stoole, or pedalls to a paire of Organs. **1642** FULLER *Holy & Prof. St.* v. xv. 418 He.. by making a foot-stool of his friends head, climbs up the higher into the Princes favour. **1702** ROWE *Tamerl.* II. ii. 697, I would have taught thy neck to know my Weight And mounted from that Footstool to my Saddle.

Hence **'footstooled** *ppl. a.*, provided with a footstool.

1791 COWPER *Odyss.* I. 163 Leading her toward a foot-stool'd throne. **1856** DOBELL *Eng. in Time War, Grass fr. Battlefield*, My shoe, soft footstooled on this hearth.

footsy, var. FOOTY *sb.* 1.

footway ('fʊtweɪ). [f. FOOT *sb.* + WAY.]

1. A way or path for foot-passengers only.

1526 [see FOOT-PATH 1]. **1532–3** *Act 24 Hen. VIII*, c. 5 Any common high way, cartway, horseway, or foteway. **1712** HEARNE *Collect.* (Oxf. Hist. Soc.) III. 474 In the Foot Way from South Hinksey to Foxcomb. **1776** G. SEMPLE *Building in Water* 17 Each of the Foot-ways is.. raised about a Foot above the Carriage-way. **1879** C. GEIKIE *Christ* li. 600 A footway ran from Gethsemane over the top of Olivet.

2. *Mining.* (See quots.)

1778 PRYCE *Min. Cornub.*, *Footway*.. in deep Mines they have old Shafts with ladders in them.. by means of which they descend into the Mines; whence this is stiled the Foot-way; and those Shafts, when applicable to no other use, Footway Shafts. **1869** R. B. SMYTH *Goldf. Victoria* 611. **1881** RAYMOND *Mining Gloss.*, *Foot-way*, the series of ladders and sollars by which men enter or leave a mine.

footy ('fuːtɪ), *a.*[1] *dial.* and *colloq.* [var. of FOUGHTY.] Paltry, poor, mean, worthless; little and insignificant.

1752 W. DODD *Beauties Shaks.* I. Pref. 7 Many a critic.. has.. foisted in some footy emendation of his own. **1833** MARRYAT *P. Simple* xxxiii, It would be a very pretty bit of practice to the ship's company to take her out from under that footy battery. **1873** MISS BRADDON *Str. & Pilgr.* III. iv. 260 You could not possibly be married from that footy little house in the Boroughbridge-road. **1890** R. KIPLING *Phant. 'Rickshaw* 85 They fires a footy little arrow at us.

footy ('fʊtɪ), *a.*[2] [f. FOOT *sb.* + -Y[1].] Having foots or dregs (see FOOT *sb.* 22).

1864 in WEBSTER.

footy, -ie ('fʊtɪ), *sb. colloq.* **1.** [Jocular dim. of FOOT *sb.*: see -Y[6].] Amorous play with the feet; also *transf.* and *fig.* Also **footsy, footsie**, and redupl.

1935 S. LEWIS *It can't happen Here* xix. 215 Lindy and you, playing footie-footie these last couple years. **1944** G. FOWLER *Good Night, Sweet Prince* (1949) II. iv. 131, I played footsie with her during Don José's first seduction by Carmen. **1945** S. LEWIS *Cass Timberlane* (1946) xl. 291 You got to do something about Bradd and your wife. Town's beginning to talk. They're playing a little too much footie-footie. **1947** K. JAEDIKER *Tall, Dark, & Dead* ii. 36, I have neither the inclination nor the time to play footie with the police. **1948** A. KEITH *Three came Home* iii. 61 The eight guards.. lolling in the women's barrack playing footsy-footsy. **1955** D. W. MAURER in *Publ. Amer. Dialect Soc.* XXIV. 136 Sometimes the party out of power retains one or two fixers who play 'footsie' with the *fixer* for the party which is in power. **1959** J. THURBER *Years with Ross* iii. 49 In [a drawing].. showing a man and his wife and another woman at a table.. the designing minx was playing footy-footy with the husband. **1959** K. WATERHOUSE *Billy Liar* iii. 48 This was the sequence and rhythm of daylight love-play as she knew it, a kind of oral footy-footy that was the nearest she could get to intimate conversation. **1963** *Economist* 11 May 537/3 Pakistan is.. despite recent games of footsie with Peking, a staunchly anti-communist-ally. **1971** *Ink* 12 June 14/2 The real trouble started when he started playing footsie with the real capitalists.

2. Dim. of FOOTBALL. esp. *Austral.* and *N.Z.*

1940 *Bulletin* (Sydney) 31 Jan. 40/2 When school came out I played footy, and picked a row with a kid and had a fight. **1947** 'A. P. GASKELL' *Big Game* 14, I cleaned my footy boots. **1949** [see CLEAN *v.* 6 b]. **1949** *Hilltop* (N.Z.) I. 8, I got footie practice tonight. **1966** F. SHAW et al. *Lern Yerself Scouse* 44 A game a footee, a game of football. **1967** *Southerly* XXVII. 297 Evans.. strides off with her to ask race-goers, cinema queues and footy fans to sign peace petitions.

foozle ('fuːz(ə)l), *sb.* [Connected with next vb.; the exact relation of the two words is uncertain.]

1. One who is 'behind the times', a fogy. (See also quot. 1889.)

1860 THACKERAY *Round. Papers, Chalk-mark* 115 Have we not almost all learnt these expressions of old foozles? **1889** BARRÈRE & LELAND *Slang*, *Foozle* (American), a man who is easily humbugged, a fool.

2. *Golf.* [from the vb.] A 'foozling' stroke.

1890 HUTCHINSON *Golf* (Badm. Libr.) 124 On the very rare occasions on which he made a foozle. **1891** A. LANG in *Longm. Mag.* Apr. 688 A 'carry' of a quarter of a mile would be a mere 'foozle' to him.

foozle ('fuːz(ə)l), *v.* [Cf. Ger. dial. *fuseln*, variously meaning 'to work hurriedly and badly', 'to work slowly' (Grimm).]

1. *intr.* To waste one's time, to fool.

1857 [see FOOZLING *ppl. a.*]. **1893** in *Stand. Dict.*

2. *trans.* To do clumsily, 'make a mess of'; to bungle (a stroke, etc.). *Golf* and *slang*. Also *absol.*

1892 *Daily News* 14 Jan. 5/1 You 'will' your opponent to foozle his tee shot. **1894** *Ibid.* 18 Oct. 5/1 Had he taken to golf, he.. might be living and foozling yet. **1894** *Field* 9 June 816/1, I have seen a man, a practised shot, foozle all his overhead rocketers with 30 in. barrels.

Hence **'foozling** *ppl. a.*, in quot. foolish, 'fooling'. Also **'foozler**, one who foozles, a bungler.

1857 HUGHES *Tom Brown* II. iii. (1871) 264 Let's.. have no more of his foozling bird's nesting. **1896** *Clarion* 1 Feb. 40/5 A person who 'mulls' his stroke is said to be a 'foozler'.

foozled ('fuːz(ə)ld), *ppl. a.* [f. FOOZLE *v.* + -ED[1].] Bungled; esp. of a stroke in *Golf*.

1899 *Westm. Gaz.* 25 Aug. 3/1 Foozled drives or missed approaches. **1909** *Ibid.* 22 Jan. 5/2 A round freely interspersed with foozled tee shots.

So **'foozling** *vbl. sb.*, bungling.

1927 J. ADAMS *Errors in School* 187 In his playing the pupil finds no lack of errors, mistakes, foozlings, call them what you will. **1965** G. MCINNES *Road to Gundagai* xiv. 259 The rest of the eighteen holes were a miserable exhibition of foozling, duffing, [etc.].

fop (fɒp), *sb.* Also 5–7 fopp(e. [Connected with next. For the development of sense cf. F. *fat*, orig. 'fool' (L. *fatuus*), now 'fop, coxcomb'.]

†**1.** A foolish person, a fool. *Obs.*

c **1440** *Promp. Parv.* 170/1 Foppe, *supra*, *idem quod* folet. *c* **1450** *Cov. Myst.* 295 Spek man, spek! spek, thou fop! *c* **1590** GREENE *Fr. Bacon* vii. 110 To bring us such a fop for Henry's son. *a* **1716** SOUTH *Serm. Prov.* xxii. 6 (1737) V. 10 A blessed improvement doubtless, and such as the fops our ancestors (as some use to call them) were never acquainted with.

†**b.** Applied to a girl. *Obs.*

1714 C. JOHNSON *Country Lasses* I. i, Cousin, thou art a very wild fop.

†**2.** A conceited person, a pretender to wit, wisdom, or accomplishments; a coxcomb, 'prig'. *Obs.*

1755 YOUNG *Centaur* vi. Wks. 1757 IV. 253 These moral fops, ridiculously good. **1805** *Med. Jrnl.* XIV. 440 This serious charge, brought by the excellent physician of Pergamos against The medical fops of his age.

3. One who is foolishly attentive to and vain of his appearance, dress, or manners; a dandy, an exquisite.

1672–6 [see 4]. **1681** OTWAY *Soldier's Fort.* II. i. Wks. 1728 I. 353 Some taudry fluttering fop or another. **1710** PALMER *Proverbs* 193 A multitude of fops who love to have their persons admir'd. **1826** DISRAELI *Viv. Grey* v. vi, His tightened waist, his stiff stock [etc.].. denoted the military fop. **1876** MISS BRADDON *J. Haggard's Dau.* II. 71 The days of Charles II, when poets were fops and courtiers.

4. *attrib.* and *Comb.*, chiefly attributive, as ***fop-call, -gravity, -maker, -neighbour, -picture***; †**Fops' alley**, 'a passage up the centre of the pit in the old Opera House where dandies congregated' (Davies); †**fop-corner**, a resort of fops; †**fop-road**, the habits and practices of a fop.

1782 MISS BURNEY *Cecilia* II. iv, Sir Robert Floyer.. sauntering down *fop's alley, stationed himself by her side. **1820** BYRON *Let. to Murray* 12 Nov., He.. took his station in Fops' Alley. **1676** ETHEREDGE *Man of Mode* IV. i. Wks. (1888) 329 A fiddle in this town is a kind of *fop-call. **1673** DRYDEN *Marr. a la Mode* Prol. 3 *Fop-corner now is free from civil war. **1672** —— *Assignation* IV. iii, Now do I even long to abuse that *fop-gravity again. **1749** FIELDING *Tom Jones* I. xi, The captain owed nothing to any of these *fop-makers in his dress. **1795** WOLCOTT (P. Pindar) *Pindariana* Wks. 1812 IV. 183 Our *fop-neighbours see things with strange eyes. **1698** *Def. Dram. Poetry* 82 In all the Stage *Fop-pictures, the Play-house bids so fair for mending that Fool too, that [etc.]. **1677** MRS. BEHN *Town Fop* v. 66 And so put you quite out of *Fopp Road.

†**fop**, *v. Obs.* Also 7 phop. [Of uncertain origin; sense 2 agrees with Ger. *foppen* to hoax (see FOB

v.). The precise relation between the vb. and sb. is uncertain; the sb. appears earlier.]

†**1.** *intr.* To act like a fool; to play the fool.

a **1529** SKELTON *Replyc.* 120 Whan ye..in the pulpete hopped And folysshly there fopped.

2. *trans.* = FOB *v.*[1] **a.** To make a fool of, cheat, dupe. Also to cheat *into*, *out of*. **b.** *to fop off*: = 'to fob off'.

1602 HERING tr. *Oberndorff's Anat. True Physit.* 41 When he expected his present payment, he phopped him thus. **1604** SHAKS. *Oth.* IV. ii. 197, I..begin to finde my selfe fopt in it. **1605** *Lond. Prodigal* I. i, Doth hee thinke to fop of his posteritie with Paradoxes. **1690** CROWNE *Eng. Friar* V. Dram. Wks. 1874 IV. 107 I'll comfort myself by fopping Ranter into marriage. **1694** —— *Regulus* V. ibid. 211 We are all fopp'd here, fopp'd out of our lives.

†**fopdoodle.** *Obs.* [f. FOP *sb.* + DOODLE.] A fop, fool, or simpleton.

16.. in *Ashm. MS.* xxxviii. 145 b, Bee blith Fopdoudells. **1664** BUTLER *Hud.* II. ii. 998 Where sturdy Butchers broke your Noddle, And handl'd you like a Fop-doodle.

†**'fopical,** *a.* *Obs.*[—0] [f. FOP *sb.* + -IC + -AL[1].] Befitting a fop. Hence †**'fopicalness.**

1660 FISHER *Rusticks Alarm* Wks. (1679) 373 To see and feel the foppicalness thereof.

fopling ('fɒplɪŋ). Also 7–8 **foplin, foppling.** [dim. of FOP *sb.*: see -LING.] A petty fop.

1684 J. LACY *Sir H. Buffoon* II. ii, A fop is the fruit of a foplin, as a Wit is the kernel of a witlin. **1726** AMHERST *Terræ Fil.* xlvi. 247 Many of these transitory foplings..came to the university..in linsey-wolsey coats. **1807–8** W. IRVING *Salmag.* (1824) 215 When the foplings of fashion bedazzle my sight. **1885** MISS BRADDON *Wyllard's Weird* II. 204 The race of languid foplings.

attrib. **1714** PHILIPS in *Steele's Poet. Misc.* 36 Some Love-sick Foplin Rhyme.

†**foppasty.** *Obs. rare.* ? = FOPPOTEE.

1611 CHAPMAN *May Day* IV. 70 True, and how the foppasty his Lieftenant, stept in to perswade with her.

†**'fopper.** *Obs.* [? f. FOP *v.* + -ER[1]; cf. Ger. *fopper*, hoaxer, quizzer.]

1. = FOP *sb.* 1.

1598 FLORIO, *Tentennone*..a fopper, a fool.

2. ? A hoaxer, a buffoon.

1659 TORRIANO, *Fiappatore*, a flapper, a fopper. **1719** D'URFEY *Pills* V. 349 Kept Foppers..Pit-Plyers be still.

So **'fopperishness,** foolishness; †**'fopperly** *a.*, silly, foolish.

1599 NASHE *Lenten Stuffe* 41 Their fopperly god is not so good as a red herring. **1683** TRYON *Way to Health* Pref., The fopperishness of those things I speak against.

foppery ('fɒpərɪ). [f. FOP *sb.* and *v.* + -ERY; cf. Ger. *fopperei*, Du. *fopperij*, hoaxing.]

†**1.** Foolishness, imbecility, stupidity, folly. *Obs.*

1592 GREENE *Disput.* 25 He..was fauoured by the foolish sect for his foppery. **1681** R. KNOX *Hist. Ceylon* Pref., The Foppery of their Priests Religious Opinions and Practices. **1711** E. WARD *Vulg. Brit.* II. 136 They're fix'd Enemies to Pop'ry, As well as to Fanatick Fop'ry.

†**b.** A foolish action, practice, idea, statement, etc.; a folly, an absurdity; *concr.* something foolishly esteemed or venerated. *Obs.*

1546 BALE *Eng. Votaries* I. Pref. 7 With hys myters and mastryes, wyth his fannoms and fopperyes. **1563–87** FOXE *A. & M.* (1684) III. 375 He foresook his former studying of the School Doctors, and other such fopperies. **1611** SPEED *Hist. Gt. Brit.* VI. xxiii. (1632) 139 Holding it a foppery to write of those, of whose fauour or wrath the Inditers stood in hope or feare. **1718** ROWE tr. *Lucan* Notes 47 Thank God, the Foppery of Pilgrimages is out of Fashion in England. **1758** JORTIN *Erasm.* I. 170/1 Colet was out of patience to see those silly fopperies [reliques].

2. The behaviour or manner characteristic of a fop; silly affectation of elegance; coxcombry, dandyism; an instance of this.

1697 POTTER *Antiq. Greece* I. xxvi. (1715) 181 Soldiers shall not observe the punctilios of Spruceness and Foppery. **1752** HUME *Ess. & Treat.* (1777) I. 135 Modern politeness ..runs often into affectation and foppery. **1808** SYD. SMITH *Wks.* (1867) I. 106 The abominable military foppery of our own people. **1822** LAMB *Elia* Ser. II. *Detached Th. on Bks.*, A Shakespeare, or a Milton (unless the first editions), it were mere foppery to trick out in gay apparel. **1851** HELPS *Comp. Solit.* vi. (1874) 101 Too intent upon the fopperies of religion.

b. *concr.* in *pl.* or *collect. sing.* Foppish finery.

1711 ADDISON *Spect.* No. 45 ¶1 An act..for prohibiting the importation of French Fopperies. *a* **1763** SHENSTONE *Progr. Taste* I. 116 And, as my satire bursts amain, See, feather'd foppery strew the plain. **1840** DICKENS *Barn. Rudge* x, His riding-gear, though free from such fopperies as were then in vogue, was..well-chosen.

†**'foppet.** *Obs.*[—1] [dim. of FOP *sb.*: see -ET[1].] A petty fop; in quot. applied to a woman.

1605 *King Leir* in *Six old Plays* (1779) 402 These foppets ..know not whether to love a man or no.

foppish ('fɒpɪʃ), *a.* [f. FOP *sb.* + -ISH.]

†**1.** Resembling or befitting a 'fop' or fool; foolish, silly. *Obs.*

1605 SHAKS. *Lear* I. iv. 184 Wisemen are growne foppish, And know not how their wits to weare. **1657** G. STARKEY *Helmont's Vind.* Ep. to Rdr., I..oppose your Diaeticall prescriptions as foppish. *a* **1720** SHEFFIELD (Dk. Buckhm.) *Wks.* (1753) I. 25 Your tale..Of patient hopes, and dull delay, Love's foppish part.

2. Resembling or befitting a fop or dandy.

1699 EVELYN *Mem.* (1857) II. 366 He was a vain, foppish young man. **1734** FIELDING *Intrig. Chambermaid* I. iv, Dotingly fond of everything that is fine and foppish. **1752** HUME *Ess. & Treat.* (1777) I. 137 We must..condemn such instances..as foppish and affected. **1836** *Random Recoll. Ho. Lords* xv. 366 There is nothing foppish in his dress. **1872** BAKER *Nile Tribut.* xvii. 307 Bowing in a most foppish manner.

Comb. **1863** MISS BRADDON *Eleanor's Vict.* II. xix. 279 He was..foppish-looking even in his travelling costume.

Hence **'foppishly** *adv.*; **'foppishness.**

1611 COTGR., *Sotise*..absurditie, follie, foppishnesse. **1651** BIGGS *New Disp.* ¶252 Whatever the schools foppishly prattle. **1742** RICHARDSON *Pamela* IV. 338 That Foppishness of Dress and Appearance, which distinguishes the Petits-maitres. **1876** SAUNDERS *Lion in Path* xvi, A young man foppishly dressed. **1886** J. K. JEROME *Idle Thoughts* 153 A little foppishness in a young man is good.

†**'fopple,** *v.* *Obs. rare*[—1].

1756 J. Q. ADAMS *Diary* 15 Mar., Wks. 1850 II. 9 At one table sits Mr. Insipid, foppling and fluttering.

†**foppotee.** *Obs. rare*[—1]. [arbitrarily f. FOP *sb.* Cf. FOPPASTY.] A simpleton.

1663 COWLEY *Cutter Colman St.* II. v, Why does this little Foppotee laugh always?

'foppy, *a. rare.* [f. FOP *sb.* + -Y[1].] = FOPPISH.

1878 *Masque Poets* 188 And of all fops the foppiest was Saturn.

fopship ('fɒpʃɪp). [f. FOP *sb.* + -SHIP.] The personality of a fop or fool; in quots. a mock title.

1680 HICKERINGILL *Meroz* 13, I give your fop-ship to understand. **1708** MOTTEUX *Rabelais* V. xii. (1737) 50 We will *innocentise* your Fopship with a Wannion.

†**'fopster.** *Obs.* [? alteration of FOPPER: see -STER.] App. a fool, simpleton.

(Halliwell has '*fopster*, a cutpurse' with reference to Dekker; prob. a misreading of *foyster*, FOISTER.)

1607 W. S. *Puritan* I. iv, Why, do but try the fopster, and break it to him bluntly.

for (fɔː(r), fə(r)), *prep.* and *conj.* Also 2 fer, 3 *south.* vor, *Orm.* forr. [OE. *for* prep. = OFris., OS. *for*, Goth. *faur*; probably an apocopated form of OTeut. **fora* FORE *adv.* and *prep.*, arising independently in the various langs. (cf. the origin of MHG. and mod.Ger. *vor* from OHG. *fora*); it may however represent a parallel formation on the same stem with some other suffix. Another formation on this stem appears in OS. *fur*, *furi*, OHG. *furi* (MHG. *vur*, mod.Ger. *für*) prep., for, ON. *fyre(r* (Da. *for*, Sw. *för*) adv. and prep., before, for.

The use of *for* as a conj. has not been found earlier than the 12th c. The older lang. supplied the place of the conj. by locutions in which *for* prep. governed a neuter demonstrative pronoun followed by a relative particle: *for ðon ðe*, *for ðý ðe*, etc. (see FOR-THON, FOR-THY). The conjunctional use of *for* = *for ðon ðe* may be explained either as an extension of the functions of the prep. to govern a noun-sentence, or as an ellipsis.

In OE. *for* and *fore* seem to have been used indiscriminately as preps.; in ME. they were gradually differentiated.]

A. *prep.*

†**I.** = BEFORE in various uses. *Obs.* (see FORE.)

1. Of place. **a.** In front of; = BEFORE 2, 2 b.

Beowulf 358 (Gr.) He for eaxlum ʒestod Deniga frean. *a* **1000** *Cædmon's Gen.* 2108 (Gr.) For þæs eaʒum, þe þe æsca tir æt guþe forʒeaf! *a* **1300** *Cursor M.* 10497 (Cott.) Sco sagh þat angel for hir stand. **1601** SHAKS. *All's Well* IV. iv. 3 For whose throne 'tis needfull..to kneele.

b. In the presence or sight of; = BEFORE 3, 4.

Beowulf 1649 (Gr.) Þa wæs..on flet boren Grendles heafod..eʒeslic for eorlum. *c* **1175** *Lamb. Hom.* 113 Moni mon..is erm for worlde and uniseli for gode.

c. In asseveration; = BEFORE 5. (Cf. Gr. πρός.) In later use replaced by FORE.

c **1230** *Hali Meid.* 25 For gode hit is wlateful þing for te þenke þron. *c* **1380** *Sir Ferumb.* 2564 My prayer ys now ido. For gode..so ys myn al-so. *c* **1420** *Chron. Vilod.* 838 Ȝeysse for God, quod þe knyȝt, dede he was.

d. Into the presence of.

a **1000** *Cædmon's Gen.* 871 (Gr.) Ne dear nu forð gan for þe andweardne. *a* **1300** *Cursor M.* 23933 (Gött.) Leuedi..lede me wid þe for þi sun.

2. Of time; = BEFORE 7, 8, 9. *for lang*: long ago. (Cf. ON. *fyrer.*)

a **1000** *Leg. Fursæus* in *Rel. Ant.* I. 276 Ic wat þone man on Criste, þe wæs ʒe-gripen nu for feowertyne ʒearum. *c* **1200** ORMIN 3076 Itt wass forr maniȝ daȝȝ Ær cwidded þurrh prophetess. *Ibid.* 6996 Forrlange. *a* **1225** *Ancr. R.* 22 Bute ȝif hit beo holiniht vor þe feste. *a* **1300** *Cursor M.* 10716 (Cott.) Þe propheci Was said for lang of ysai.

3. In preference to, above; = BEFORE 11.

c **1000** *Rood* 93 (Gr.) He his modor..for ealle menn ʒeweorðode ofer eall wifa cynn. *c* **1205** LAY. 13919 Ah for alle ure goden deore..Woden hehde þa hæhste laȝe. *c* **1300** *Beket* 721 The statutz of Clarendone ech bischop holde scholde; And nameliche theo for alle other. **14..** *Sir Beues* 160 (MS. M.) Sir, blessud be ye for alle men! **1486–1504** *Let.* in Denton *Eng. in 15th Cent.* (1888) Note D. 318 It is mor meritory to support..yowre tenants rathere then a stronge man, the pore..for a gentylman or a gentylmans man.

II. Of representation, substitution or exchange.

4. a. Representing, as representative of.

'The member for —— shire' now belongs rather to 13 c.

a **1000** *Guthlac* 171 (Gr.) Se for ealle spræc feonda mengu. *a* **1225** *Leg. Kath.* 952 An, for ham alle, Onswerede ant seide. **1414** *Rolls of Parlt.* IV. 22/2 Youre humble and trewe lieges that ben come for the Co[mmun]e of youre lond. **1582** N. LICHEFIELD tr. *Castanheda's Conq. E. Ind.* v. 14 b, Their Xeque..which was there for the king. **1842** MACAULAY *Ess.* (1848) II. 187 The members for many counties and large towns. **1843** *Fraser's Mag.* XXVIII. 334 Walker returned thanks for his lady. **1891** *Law Times* XCII. 124/2 Lord Palmerston and the Earl of Mayo, both Irish Peers, sat for English constituencies.

b. In elliptical expressions, *once for all*, †*for all.* Cf. Ger. *ein für allemal.*

1611 SHAKS. *Cymb.* II. iii. 111 Learne now, for all, That I [etc.]. **1820** J. S. KNOWLES *Virginius* II. ii, Now, once for all, farewell! **1881** BIBLE (Revised) *Hebr.* vii. 27 For this he did once for all [**1611**: once], when he offered up himself.

5. In place of, instead of.

c **1000** *Ags. Gosp.* Matt. ii. 22 He ʒehyrde þæt archelaus rixode on iudea-þeode for ðæne herodem. *a* **1300** *Cursor M.* 9972 (Cott.) Maria..stondes vs for sceild and targe, Agains all ure wiþerwyns. *c* **1400** MAUNDEV. (Roxb.) vi. 19 He died ..and his broþer regned for him. **1553** T. WILSON *Rhet.* (1580) 223 Some..will saye..Blacke Vellet, for blacke Veluet. **1611** BIBLE *Luke* xi. 11 Will he for a fish giue him a serpent? **1697** DRYDEN *Virg. Georg.* I. 10 Bacchus and.. Ceres..gave us Corn for Mast, for Water Wine. **1742** YOUNG *Nt. Th.* I. 14 'Tis only change of pain..Severer for severe. **1802** MAR. EDGEWORTH *Moral T.* (1816) I. 248 She could not..write..the count had written all that was wanting for her. **1849** MACAULAY *Hist. Eng.* II. 208 For the old test..was substituted a new test. **1895** LAKE in *Law Times* XCIX. 468/2 They will employ somebody to do the business for them.

6. Of payment, purchase, sale, etc. = *in exchange for*: see EXCHANGE *sb.* 1 g.

a. Introducing the thing bought or sold, etc.: As the price of, or the penalty on account of. Also after verbs, e.g. PAY, q.v.

c **1000** *Ags. Gosp.* Matt. v. 38 Eaʒe for eaʒe and toð for toð. *c* **1175** *Lamb. Hom.* 9 Nouþer gold ne seoluer ne moste gan for þe. *c* **1200** ORMIN Ded. 143, I shall hafenn forr min swinnc God læn. *c* **1330** R. BRUNNE *Chron.* (1725) I. 174 Men gaf fiueten schillynges for a goos or a heen. **1542** *MS. Acc. St. John's Hosp., Canterb.*, To Nycholes for the byllet for the schyr and hys costis xv s. **1789** DURNFORD & EAST *Reports* III. 467 The right of a seller to his goods, where he cannot receive payment for them. **1895** *Bookman* Oct. 17/2 The Duc d'Aumale's great work..for which some of us would gladly give all the novels ever written.

b. In requital of.

c **1000** *Ags. Ps.* xxxiv. [xxxv]. 14 (Spelman) Aguldon me yfelu for godum. **1583** HOLIBAND *Campo di Fior* 107 That she giue vs something for our paines. **1677** PLOT *Oxfordsh.* 151 Being found to yield considerably better than most other wheat, viz. somtimes twenty for one. **1697** DRYDEN *Virg. Georg.* IV. 221 Describe we next the Nature of the Bees, Bestow'd by Jove for secret Services. **1818** M. G. LEWIS *Jrnl. W. Ind.* (1834) 209 A full punishment for all his misdeeds. **1885** BOWEN in *Law Rep.* 14 Q. Bench Div. 869 Counsel..who should take nothing for their services. **1895** A. I. SHAND *Life Sir E. B. Hamley* I. ii. 21 He was very soundly thrashed for his pains.

III. 7. a. In defence or support of; in favour of, on the side of. Opposed to *against*. Often *predicatively*: see BE *v.* 23 c.

c **1000** ÆLFRIC *Exod.* xiv. 14 And Drihten fiht for eow. *c* **1175** *Lamb. Hom.* 7 Heo sculen..bidden for heom. *c* **1380** WYCLIF *Sel. Wks.* III. 363 How shulde men fiȝte for a persone þat þei witen not [etc.]? **1550** CROWLEY *Epigr.* 204 Where euerye man is for him selfe, And no manne for all. **1599** SHAKS. *Much Ado* II. i. 386 My Lord, I am for you, though it cost mee ten nights watchings. **1676** HOBBES *Iliad* Pref. (1686) 9 Homer indeed maketh some Gods for the Greeks and some for the Trojans. **1690** LOCKE *Govt.* II. vi, Blinded contenders for monarchy. **1711** STEELE *Spect.* No. 118 ¶3 Take my Word for it she is no Fool. **1743** BULKELEY & CUMMINS *Voy. S. Seas* Ded. 8 The Right Honourable Persons who will one Day determine for or against us. **1795** *Hist.* in *Ann. Reg.* 82 Fortune declared at last for the convention. **1847–9** HELPS *Friends in C.* Ser. I. (1851) I. 177 You argue for it in vain. **1885** COTTON in *Law Rep.* 30 Ch. Div. 13, I do not think that the cases..carry out the proposition for which he has cited them.

b. In exclamations, indicating the person, etc. favoured.

1664 BUTLER *Hud.* II. ii. 604 Did ride..Crying, hey, for our town through the burrough. **1835** LYTTON *Rienzi* III. i, 'Hurrah for the knight of St. John' cried the mercenaries; 'and hurrah for fair France and bold Germany!'

c. In honour of. Also *to name a child for* (= after) a person (now *U.S.* and *Sc.*).

1800 H. WELLS *Const. Neville* I. 7 Louisa..had been named for the mother of Mr. Hayman. **1820** J. S. KNOWLES *Virginius* I. i, Cheer for him, if you are Romans. **1826** W. P. SCARGILL *Truth* I. ii. 7 'What is the name to be? I think your mother's was Matilda.'—'Yes, she was named for a great worthy, lady Matilda.' **1863** HAWTHORNE *Our Old Home* (1864) 20 He had named his two children, one for Her Majesty and the other for Prince Albert.

d. quasi-*sb.* *fors and againsts*: 'pros and cons'.

c **1815** JANE AUSTEN *Persuas.* II. 185, I was privy to all the fors and againsts, I was the friend to whom he confided his hopes. **1892** *Temple Bar Mag.* Nov. 424 The fors and againsts..so inextricably mixed.

IV. Of purpose or destination.

8. a. With a view to; with the object or purpose of: as preparatory to. *for company*: see

COMPANY 1 b. Also, in preparation for or anticipation of (the stated time of a dinner, etc.).

Beowulf 458 (Gr.) þu.. for arstafum usic sohtest. c1000 *Ags. Gosp.* John xi. 4 Nys þeos untrumnys na for deaðe ac for godes wuldre. 1340 Hampole *Pr. Consc.* 2889 For warnyng of frendes þat lyefes. c1489 Caxton *Sonnes of Aymon* xxiv. 505, I byleve that god hathe sente theym to vs for our savynge. 1523 Ld. Berners *Froiss.* I. cxxx. 159 The Englyshmen neuer departed fro their batayls for chasynge of any man. a1654 Selden *Table-T.* (Arb.) 82 The individual person set apart for the service of such a Church. 1719 De Foe *Crusoe* I. vi, I left the iron crow in the wreck for next day. 1838 Thirlwall *Greece* III. xix. 95 [He] set sail.. for the relief of Epidamnus. 1849 Macaulay *Hist. Eng.* I. 615 A considerable number of prisoners were immediately selected for execution. 1887 L. Carroll *Game of Logic* ii. §6. 50, I have been out for a walk. 1891 *Law Times* XC. 283/1 An order was made.. for the payment of the balance to the plaintiff. 1900 *Athenæum* 5 May 545/1 The Annual Dinner of the Society will take place on Wednesday, May 16 ..at 7, for 7.30 P.M. 1929 E. Wallace *Iron Grip* viii, You can please yourself about accepting.. No. 109 Grosvenor Place, and the hour is 7.30 for 8. 1970 J. Burke *Four Stars for Danger* iii. 49 'Seven-thirty,' he was saying, 'for eight. Right?'

b. For the purpose of being or becoming.

c1489 Caxton *Sonnes of Aymon* ix. 210 Berynge in theyr handes flowres and roses for a token. 1697 Dryden *Virg. Georg.* III. 253 Whom to reserve for Husband of the Herd. 1741 tr. *Fortunate Country Maid* I. 13 He shall hear Reason; or, Waunds, I'll go for a Soldier. 1852 Dickens *Bleak Ho.* vii, [He] went for a soldier, and never came back. 1885 G. Allen *Babylon* xiv, I'm going to leave my place.. and go for a pupil-teacher.

c. Conducive to.

a1553 Udall *Royster D.* I. i. (Arb.) 12 To keepe the Queenes peace is more for his behoofe. 1664 Tillotson *Wisd. being Relig.* 31 It is for the general good of humane society. c1710 C. Fiennes *Diary* (1888) 128 The Bishop does not care to stay long in this place not being for his health. 1791 Boswell *Johnson* Advt., Such remarks as were greatly for the advantage of the work. 1843 *Fraser's Mag.* XXVIII. 565 It is all for her good.

d. *for sale*: to be sold; also used *attrib.* or as adj. phr. Cf. also SALE *sb.*² 2 e. *for rent* (U.S.) = *to let*.

1884 *Boston* (Mass.) *Jrnl.* 6 Sept. Advt., Baltimore Warehouse for Rent. 1889 *Century Mag.* Aug. 590/2 The last time I saw it, it was for rent. 1938 R. Field *All this & Heaven Too* (1939) xxxviii. 488 The best houses in the neighbourhood suddenly stood empty with 'To Let' or 'For Sale' signs on their walls. 1965 K. Giles *Some Beasts no More* ii. 42 There was a For Sale notice which alluded to a fine residence and ninety acres of land.

9. a. In order to obtain. Also after verbs like *ask*, *search*, etc., or verbs implying motion, e.g. *to go*, *send*, etc. *for*: see the verbs.

So, with mixture of 21 or 6, in (*I would not*) *for anything*, *for a great deal*, *for all the world*, etc.

c1230 *Hali Meid.* 9 þat við þat tu eauer dides te into swuch þeowdom for worldliche wunne. c1300 *Havelok* 788 Hauelok was war þat Grim swank sore For his mete, and he lay at hom. c1450 *Chester Pl.* (Shaks. Soc.) 11 Naye, Lorde, that will we not indeede For nothinge treasspass unto thee. 1611 Bible *Prov.* xxviii. 21 For a piece of bread that man will transgresse. 1657 W. Rand tr. *Gassendi's Life Peiresc* I. 25 He would not for any thing but be present at the Solemnity to behold the same. 1697 Dryden *Virg. Georg.* IV. 620 Weary Proteus.. Retir'd for Shelter to his wonted Caves. 1728 Young *Love Fame* I. 50 What will not men attempt for sacred praise? 1806–7 J. Beresford *Miseries Hum. Life* (1826) v. xix, After having fee'd very high for places at Mrs. Siddons's benefit. 1849 Macaulay *Hist. Eng.* II. 84 To bring a suit for this sum in the Court of King's Bench. 1864 Holme Lee *In Silver Age* (1866) 403, I would not for the world hurt his feelings. 1883 *Manch. Exam.* 27 Nov. 5/5 The drawers.. struck work for an advance of wages. 1891 *Newcastle Even. Chron.* 29 Jan. 3/1 For two pins I'll throw the lamp at you.

b. Of an amount staked or an object risked, e.g. *to play for* (*a certain stake*): see PLAY *v.* Also in a wager, in asseverations, and in *a narrow escape for one's life*, *to try a man for his life*.

a1225 *Juliana* 16 For mi lif quoð hire feder þe schal laðin his luue for þu schalt beon ibeaten [etc.]. a1553 Udall *Royster D.* I. i. (Arb.) 12, I haue yond espied hym sadly comming, And in loue for twentie pounde, by hys glommyng. 1596 Shaks. *Tam. Shr.* III. i. 49 Now for my life the knaue doth court my loue. 1602 —— *Ham.* III. iv. 24 Dead for a Ducate, dead. 1836 Southey in *Q. Rev.* LVII. 10 Major Beltran.. had a narrow escape for his life. 1849 Macaulay *Hist. Eng.* II. 223 Rosewell.. had been tried for his life by Jeffreys.

c. *for* (*one's*) *life*: in order to save one's life; also in hyperbolical use, as if one's life depended on it, with one's utmost efforts. Also in phrases like *I cannot do it for the life of me*, *for my heart*, *soul*, etc., where the sense is sometimes 'if it were to save my life', etc., and sometimes 'if I were to give my life', etc.

a1250 *Owl & Night.* 1078 He ne mihte for his live Iseo þat man wiþ hire speke. 1576 Fleming *Panopl. Epist.* 52 He had never had the audacitie and boldnesse for his hart, to set one foote forward into Syria. 1596 Shaks. *Tam. Shr.* I. ii. 38, I .. could not get him for my heart to do it. 1603 —— *Meas. for M.* IV. iii. 160, I dare not for my head fill my belly. 1711 Addison *Spect.* No. 85 ¶1, I cannot for my Heart leave a Room, before I have studied [etc.]. 1786 Mackenzie *Lounger* No. 56. 197 A great many other things.. which I can't do for the heart of me. a1806 H. K. White in *Life & Rem.* (1825) 176 You can't for the soul of you, learn how to frown. 1809 [see LIFE *sb.* 3 c]. 1813 Byron *Giaour* 250 Away, away, for life he rides. 1831 L. E. Landon *Romance & Reality* (1848) 354 We must row for our lives. 1843 *Blackw. Mag.* LIV. 742, I could not resist a smile for the life of me. 1848 Dickens *Dombey* xix, Walter, for his life, would have hardly called her by her name. 1849 Macaulay *Hist. Eng.* I. 131 Charles fled for his life. 1887 *Times* 15 Apr. 9/6 Back! for your lives!

d. *to run*, etc. *for it*: see IT.

10. Indicating the object to which the activity of the faculties or feelings is directed: frequent after vbs., as *care*, *long*, *search*, etc., sbs., as *an eye*, *genius*, *talent*, *taste*, *desire*, *love*, etc., or adjs., as *eager*, *watchful*, etc. (see those words); also in exclamations expressing expectancy or desire, *now for*, *oh for*.

1592 Shaks. *Rom. & Jul.* II. ii. 159 O for a Falkners voice, To lure this Tassell gentle back againe. 1602 Marston *Antonio's Rev.* V. i. Wks. 1856 I. 133 O for a fat leg of ewe mutton! 1697 Dryden *Virg. Georg.* IV. 300 Such a Zeal they have for flow'ry Sweets. 1709 Steele *Tatler* No. 30. ¶5 Now for Colonel Constant's Epistle. 1834 Medwin *Angler in Wales* I. 37 Now for a cigar and Charters. 1842 Macaulay *Lays, Virginia* 102 Oh for the tents which in old time whitened the Sacred Hill!

11. a. Before an *inf.*, usually *for to*, (Sc. *till*), indicating the object of an action; = 'in order (to)'. Now *arch.* or *vulgar*. Cf. Fr. *pour*, Ger. *um zu*.

For *for to* in other connexions see FORTO *prep.* and *conj.*

a1175 *Cott. Hom.* 221 Forte don him understonden. a1200 *Moral Ode* 180 Ne brekeþ ne ure drihte hellegate for lesen hi of bende. c1200 Ormin 1006 All þeȝȝre lac wass swillc & swillc, Forr oþerr þing to tacnenn. c1205 Lay. 13307 Ich æm icumen þe þus næh for muchelere neode for suggen þe tiðende. 1297 R. Glouc. (1724) 25 He bi gan to schake ys axe, for to smyte anon. c1400 *Lanfranc's Cirurg.* 53 For to clense þe wounde use þe medicyn of mel roset. c1485 *Digby Myst.* IV. 528 What can þou saye, Thy-self for till excuse? 1535 Coverdale *Prov.* xxviii. 20 He.. maketh to moch haist for to be riche. 1578–1600 *Scot. Poems 16th C.* II. 162 For till obscure thy light. 1688 R. Holme *Armoury* II. 86/1 A Billet is a piece of Cleft Wood for to Burn. 1748 G. Washington *Jrnl.* 8 Apr., Writ. 1889 I. 6 You must ride round yᵉ back of yᵉ Mountain for to get below them. 1774 A. Adams in *J.Q. Adams' Fam. Lett.* (1876) 41 Having only put off its present glory for to rise finally to a more happy state.

b. Hence *for to* often occurs merely for *to* before an inf. *Obs.* in educated use.

a1225 *Ancr. R.* 54 þe eppel þæt ich loke on is forbode me to etene, & nout forto biholden. c1305 *St. Swithin* 14 in *E.E.P.* (1862) 43 Seint swythin.. swiþe ȝung bigan Forto seruie ihesu crist. c1340 *Cursor M.* 717 (Fairf.) Satanas .. þoȝt þat ioy for-til stynt. 1397 *Rolls of Parlt.* III. 379/2 It was my menyng and my wenyng for to haue do the best for his persone and for his estate. 1523 Ld. Berners *Froiss.* I. cxxvi. 152 The kyng of Englande.. wyst nat where for to passe the ryuer of Some, the which was large and depe. 1659 D. Pell *Impr. Sea* 328 *note*, Blustring winds.. make the Seas for to rage and roar. 1674 tr. *Scheffer's Lapland* 84 Birds, Beasts, Fishes, which it was unlawfull for to bring in at the foredoor.

12. Indicating destination. Cf. Fr. *pour*.

a. In order to arrive at; with the purpose of going to (a place). Formerly sometimes after *go*, *journey*, *travel*, etc. Now chiefly after verbs denoting the commencement of a journey, as *to depart*, *start*, *sail*, *leave*, or the act of directing movement, as *to steer*, *make*; also after the pple. *bound*. Also predicatively: see BE 23 b.

c1489 Caxton *Sonnes of Aymon* i. 36 She asked whi they were departed for the kynges courte. 1595 Shaks. *John* III. iii. 71 For England Cosen, goe. 1595 Drake *Will* in *Wills Doctor's Com.* (Camden) 77 Her Majesties fleete nowe in service for the west Indyes. 1646 Markham *Let.* in *12th Rep. Hist. MSS. Comm.* App. v. 2 [I am] most certainly informed that hee is at Newcastle and intends for France. 1660–1 Marvell *Corr.* Wks. 1872–5 II. 43 Mr. Mabbot is, shortly to goe for Ireland. 1704 Addison *Italy* Wks. 1804 V. 149 We sailed from hence directly for Genoa. 1706–7 Farquhar *Beaux Strat.* II. i. Wks. (1742) 17 Are you for church this morning? 1719 De Foe *Capt. Singleton* xviii, We steered directly for the gulf. 1724 —— *Mem. Cavalier* (1840) 285 We resolved for Newark. 1763 Wesley *Jrnl.* 20 Aug. (1827) III. 138 We concluded to try for Larn, though we knew not the way. 1791 'G. Gambado' *Ann. Horsem.* ix. (1809) 106 The curb broke, and he [a horse] ran straight on for the cliffs. 1820 Keats *St. Agnes* i, His frosted breath.. seem'd taking flight for heaven without a death. 1838 Thirlwall *Greece* II. 296 The Persian army was in full march for Athens. 1865 Kingsley *Herew.* (1884) 251 They rowed away for Crowland. 1879 Church *Spenser* i. 9 Spenser was sixteen or seventeen when he left school for the University. 1883 *Law Times Rep.* XLIX. 332/2 The Clan Sinclair.. headed for the Margaret. 1885 *Manch. Exam.* 12 Mar. 4/6 Lord Reay left London yesterday for India.

b. *transf.* of time.

1885 *Truth* 2 July 3/1 It was getting on for two before supper was served.

c. Introducing the intended recipient, or the thing to which something is intended to belong, or in connexion with which it is to be used.

1411 *Rolls of Parlt.* III. 650/1 Certein Commune of Pasture.. whiche the said Lord.. claymes for hymself and his tenantz. 1551 Turner *Herbal* I. F v b, Byrche.. is good to make.. twygges for baskettes. 1585 T. Washington tr. *Nicholay's Voy.* I. xxi. 27 Were set up 2 faire pavillions, the one for him.. the other for the Ambassador. 1591 Shaks. *Two Gent.* II. i. 131 *Val.* Madam, they are for you. 1636 Massinger *Bashf. Lover* V. i, Your bottles too, that I carry For your own tooth? 1660 *Act 12 Chas. II* c. 4 Sched. s.v. *Boxes*, French boxes for Marmelade or Gelly. 1759 Johnson *Idler* No. 42 ¶2 The Idler holds the shield for virtue, as well as the glass for folly. 1835–6 Todd *Cycl. Anat.* I. 518/1 For this group of animals M. D'Haan has proposed the name of Asiphonoidia. 1839 Cath. Sinclair *Holiday House* xii. 281 He bought gowns for all the maids. 1855 Macaulay *Hist. Eng.* III. 20 He had.. secured for himself a place in history. 1861 M. Pattison *Ess.* (1889) I. 45 A fireproof chamber for the muniments. *Ibid.* A stone-vaulted kitchen, where dinner could be dressed for an army of guests.

13. Of appointment, appropriation, or fitness. **a.** Following a vb., adj., or noun of quality, denoting appointment, appropriation, fitness, etc.

c1400 Maundev. (1839) Prol. 2 Dethe withouten ende, the whiche was ordeyned for us. *Ibid.* v. 56 A manere of Wode.. the whiche is goode for manye dyverse Medicynes. c1450 *Cov. Myst.* 318 We xal asay Yf the cros for the be mete. 1548 Hall *Chron., Hen. IV*, Introd. 9 Henry duke of Lancastre.. a prince apt for a kyndom. 1548–9 (Mar.) *Bk. Com. Prayer, Communion* Rubric, The vesture appoyncted for that ministracion. 1582 N. Lichefield tr. *Castanheda's Conq. E. Ind.* ii. 5 To put himselfe in a readinesse for that voiage. 1674 N. Cox *Gentl. Recreat.* III. (1677) 62 Fitter for a large Inne than a Lady's Chamber. 1722 De Foe *Plague* (1754) 9 Loaded with Baggage and fitted out for travelling. 1764 Foote *Patron* II. Wks. 1799 I. 349 Robinson Crusoe is advertis'd for this evening. 1789 Blake *Songs Innoc., Echoing Green* iii, Many sisters and brothers, Like birds in their nest, Are ready for rest. 1815 Jane Austen *Emma* (1849) 31 Very fit for a wife, but not at all for a governess. 1838 Thirlwall *Greece* III. xxii. 247 Quite sufficient for his purpose. 1840 *Ibid.* VII. 283 Seleucus, reflecting on Pithon's fate, augured that which was designed for himself. 1840 *P. Parley's Ann.* 54 What is a clock good for?

b. After adjs. or advs. qualified by *too*, *enough*, etc., the prep. is often equivalent to the infinitive combinations, 'to admit of', 'to require, call for', or the like.

1803–6 Wordsworth *Ode, Int. Immortality*, Thoughts that do often lie too deep for tears. 1832 *Westm. Rev.* XVII. 82 The passages.. are too frequent for quotation. *Mod.* The subject is quite important enough for separate treatment.

c. Following a sb., or predicatively: = Appointed or adapted for, proper or suitable for. (*there is*) *nothing for it but*: (there is) no way of meeting the case, no course open, but.

c1350 *Will. Palerne* 294 Clothed in comly cloþing for any kinges sone. 1486 *Bk. St. Albans* D iij b, That hauke is for a Baron. 1583 Holiband *Campo di Fior* 55, I will rather have him. He is for me. 1663 Pepys *Diary* 27 Apr., He is not for my family, he is grown so out of order and not to be ruled. 1669 Sturmy *Mariner's Mag.* v. 64 Sea-Carriages are made less, as the Block-maker that makes them hath Rules for. 1711 Addison *Spect.* No. 297 ¶6 By no means a match for his enemies. 1748 Richardson *Clarissa* (1811) III. 198, I have nothing for it.. but matrimony. 1818 M. G. Lewis *Jrnl. W. Ind.* (1834) 250 The sheets, a term for various ropes. 1840 *P. Parley's Ann.* 55 Do you know it is time for school? 1845 M. Pattison *Ess.* (1889) I. 4 The momentous questions which have interest only for noble minds. 1849 Macaulay *Hist. Eng.* I. 223 Lauderdale.. still continued to be minister for Scotch affairs. 1850 Carlyle *Latter-d. Pamph.* i. 37, I fear she is not long for this world! 1874 Dasent *Half a Life* I. 196 There was nothing for it but to grin and bear it. 1885 *Manch. Exam.* 22 Sept. 5/3 The old law making hanging the inevitable penalty for murder. 1886 *Ibid.* 3 Nov. 3/1 The Quarterly for October.

d. (*it is*) *for* (*a person*) *to do something*: becoming or permissible to, the duty or concern of.

1611 Bible *Prov.* xxxi. 4 It is not for kings to drinke wine. 1819 Corbett *Eng. Gram.* xvii. §193 It is for the guilty to live in fear. 1885 Bowen in *Law Rep.* 14 Q.B. Div. 872 It will be for the Rule Committee to alter the rule if [etc.].

e. *to be for it* (orig. *Mil. slang*): to have one's name on the crime sheet, i.e. to be marked down for punishment or trouble; hence, to be in for trouble.

1909 *Captain* Apr. 14/2 'He'll give the whole show away?' 'Then, I suppose, we'll all be for it.' 1915 'I. Hay' *First Hundred Thousand* xvi. 214 No more trial trips; no more chaperoning! This time, we decided, we were 'for it'. 1915 *War Illustr.* 21 Aug. 22/1 Then it is that he realises so acutely that if anything happens to his pilot he is 'for it', as the current flying phrase has it. 1917 P. MacGill *Brown Brethren* iv. 68 If Captain Thorley finds 'im missin' he'll be for it. 1919 *Athenæum* 25 July 664/1 'You're for it', *i.e.*, for the 'orderly room'. *Ibid.* 1 Aug. 695/1 'On the peg', to be charged with a 'crime'. 'You'll be for it', the sergeant's threat of 'the peg'. 1926 *Punch* 28 Apr. 466/1 Major Atlee.. declared that if the discipline of a unit broke down it was the officer in charge who should be 'for it'. 1928 [see BONZO]. 1940 *War Illustr.* 5 Jan. 567/1 If a bomb comes, one is 'for it'.

14. Of result or effect; used after words like *cause*, *ground*, *motive*, *reason*, etc. (See the sbs.)

15. Designating an amount to be received or paid; cf. 6. Also in Cricket scoring: With the result of (so many runs), at the cost of (so many wickets).

1776 *Trial of Nundocomar* 23/2 Bollakey Doss drew a draught on Benares.. for a lack of rupees. 1857 Hughes *Tom Brown* II. viii., The Lord's men were out by half-past twelve o'clock for ninety-eight runs. 1885 *L'pool Daily Post* 1 June 5/4 The University men were all out for 44. 1886 Stevenson *Dr. Jekyll* i. (ed. 2) 8 The signature was good for more than that. 1887 A. Birrell *Obiter Dicta* Ser. II. 159 [He] sent the author a bank-bill for £100. *Mod.* Put my name down for two guineas. (*Comm.*) We have this day drawn on you for £100. (*Cricket*) The score stood at 150 for 6 wickets.

V. Of advantage or disadvantage.

16. a. With the purpose or result of benefiting or gratifying; as a service to.

a1000 Cynew. *Crist* (Gollancz) 1423 Ic þæt for worulde ȝebolade. c1205 Lay. 62 þæt he þeos soðfeste word segge.. for his fader saule. a1225 *Ancr. R.* 22 þe uormest viue [Psalmes] uor ou sulf & for alle þet ou god doð. 1340 *Ayenb.* 1 þin holy blod þet þou sseddest ane þe rod uor me and uor mankende. 1605 Shaks. *Macb.* III. i. 65 If't be so For

Banquo's Issue haue I fil'd my Minde. c1630 MILTON *Passion* 12 Dangers..Which he for us did freely undergo. 1631 GOUGE *God's Arrows* v. Ded. 406 Leave me not to shift for my selfe. 1674 tr. *Scheffer's Lapland* 118 If he sees convenient he may set up for himself. 1816 BYRON *Parisina* iii, They only for each other breathe.

b. *ironically.*

1740 *Xmas Entertainm.* ii. (1883-4) 12, I will swinge his Jacket for him. 1855 SMEDLEY *H. Coverdale* liii, It would have been a mercy if I hadn't broken some of his bones for him.

17. As affecting the interests or condition of (a person or thing), whether for good or evil. Chiefly after adjs., sbs. of quality, or advbs.

In early Eng. the dative was used in this sense without prep. Cf. Gr. and Lat. uses.

1537 BIBLE (Matthew) *Ps.* cxviii. [cxix]. 71 It is good for me that I haue bene in trouble. 1632 J. LEE *Short Surv.* 7 Grain, butter, cheese, and such other commodities usefull for the life of man. 1883 *Daily News* 22 Sept. 4/6 This..bodes ill for the peace of Europe. 1891 SIR. A. WILLS in *Law Times* XCI. 233/2 Things had..begun to look badly for all concerned.

18. a. Governing a sb. or pers. pron. followed by an infinitive, forming a construction equivalent to '*that he*, etc. *may*, *might*, *should*', etc.

Originally, the prep. had the sense 13 or 16, the inf. being either the subject of the sentence or expressive of purpose; but the use was early extended to include cases to which this analysis is inapplicable. In the 15-16th c. the L. use of the accus. and inf. was often imitated in Eng.: e.g. 'Behold how good..it is, brethren to dwell together in unity' (*Ps.* cxxxiii. 1, Prayer-bk. version).

1508 FISHER 7 *Penit. Ps.* xxxii. Wks. (1876) 41 It is better for a synner to suffre trybulacyon..in this lyfe..than to be eternally tourmented in hell. 1548 HALL *Chron., Hen. V*, (an. 7) 65 b, A tent of purple velvet for the counsailers to mete in. 1582 N. LICHEFIELD tr. *Castanheda's Conq. E. Ind.* vi. 16 It was verye needefull and necessarye for him to take a Pilot. 1621 BRATHWAIT *Nat. Embass.* Ded. (1641) A ij, It is high time for the Satyrist to pen somthing which may [etc.]. 1697 DRYDEN *Virg. Georg.* IV. 219, I must forsake This Task; for others afterwards to take. 1777 WATSON *Philip II* (1839) 85 The [island] lay at so great a distance from Europe, as had made it almost impossible for the Christians to send assistance to the besieged. 1818 M. G. LEWIS *Jrnl. W. Ind.* (1834) 220 For a man who had such good blood to part with it so wantonly was a shame. 1843 *Frasers Mag.* XXVIII. 713 What a condition for me to come to! 1883 *Law Times* 20 Oct. 408/1 The new rules..render it more difficult for a defence to be kept up. 1896 M. FIELD *Attila* I. 19 When a girl becomes A woman, it is usual for her mother To speak to her of life.

b. in exclamatory use.

1757 FOOTE *Author* II. Wks. 1799 I. 156 For this low, lousy son of a shoemaker, to talk of families.

VI. Of attributed or assumed character; = as.

19. a. In the character of, in the light of, as equivalent to; *esp.* to introduce the complement after verbs of incomplete predication, e.g. *to have, hold*, etc. (see those verbs), where *as* or *as being* may generally be substituted. ***to beg (a person) for a fool***: see BEG *v.* 5 a.

Beowulf 1175 (Gr.) þæt þu for sunu wolde hererinc habban. c1000 ÆLFRIC *Deut.* xxxi. 20 And tellaþ min wedd for naht. c1200 ORMIN 387 Þatt mann hemm hallt forr gode menn. 1297 R. GLOUC. (1724) 142 Þis word was for dom yholde. 1377 LANGL. *P. Pl.* B xv. 578 ȝit knewe þei cryst..For a parfit prophete. c1400 *Lanfranc's Cirurg.* 110 Þer ben but .vj. boonys whanne þat þou rekenest os coronale for oon boon. a1533 LD. BERNERS *Huon* lxxxiv. 265 Know for trouth that..god loueth fayth. a1553 UDALL *Royster D.* III. iii. (Arb.) 44 He vaunteth him selfe for a man of prowesse greate. 1568 GRAFTON *Chron., Hen. V*, (an. 2) II. 446 The Englishe Ambassadours receyving this for aunswere, tooke their leave. 1644 EVELYN *Mem.* (1857) I. 78 Celebrated in France for the best in the kingdom. 1711 ADDISON *Spect.* No. 169 ¶11 Ill-nature among ordinary Observers passes for Wit. 1719 DE FOE *Crusoe* II. xi, You will be hanged for a pirate. 1725 WATTS *Logic* II. iii. §1 We mistake his Blunders for Beauties. 1760 FOOTE *Minor* I. Wks. 1799 I. 239, I wou'd engage to elude your penetration, when I am beau'd out for the baron. 1813 BYRON *Giaour* 37 A grotto..That holds the pirate for a guest. 1818 M. G. LEWIS *Jrnl. W. Ind.* (1834) 40 That distance went for nothing. 1843 *Fraser's Mag.* XXVIII. 702, I know for a fact that a courier was waiting. 1845 M. PATTISON *Ess.* (1889) I. 5 Mere chronology..is often mistaken for history. 1883 STEVENSON *Silverado Sq.* (1886) 34 The pines look down upon the rest for underwood.

b. So with an adjective, as in ***to take for granted, to leave for dead***, etc. ***for certain, sure***, †***wiss***, see those adjs.

Also, with mixture of sense 8, as in the formula of the Marriage Service (quot. 1549) where the sense is 'whether she prove better or worse', etc.

c1460 FORTESCUE *Abs. & Lim. Mon.* xi. (1885) 136, I holde it for vndouted, þat [etc.]. 1549 *Bk. Com. Prayer* Matrimony, I..take thee..to my wedded wife..for better for worse. 1651 BAXTER *Inf. Bapt.* 49 In the mean time I take it for granted. 1681 COTTON *Wond. Peak* 69 At the bottom he was left for dead. 1700 DRYDEN *Pal. & Arc.* III. 704 He quivered with his feet, and lay for dead. 1732 BERKELEY *Alciphr.* VI. §30 Admitted for morally certain. 1802 MAR. EDGEWORTH *Moral T.* (1816) I. 208 L's friends..gave the man up for lost. 1854 PATMORE *Angel in Ho.* I. ix, I..blamed the print for old.

c. ***what is he***, etc. ***for (a man***, etc.): what is (he) considered as (a man), i.e. what sort of a (man, etc.) is he? (Cf. Ger. *Was für ein?*) *Obs.* or *dial.*

1580 SPENSER *Shep. Cal.* iv. 17 What is he for a Ladde you so lament? 1623 BINGHAM *Xenophon* 136 When the Lacedemonians enquired, what Xenophon was for a man, he answered, that [etc.]. 1657 W. RAND tr. *Gassendi's Life Peiresc* II. 265 Consider..how many, and what for Epistles he sent to this very City. 1708 *Brit. Apollo* No. 63. 3/2 What are you for a Lover. a1757 CIBBER *Comical Lovers* 1, What is she for a Woman? 1827 SCOTT *Surg. Dau.* x, 'What is that for a Zenobia?' said Hartley.

d. (*I*, etc.) ***for one***: as one, as a unit in an aggregate. ***for one thing***: used parenthetically when one out of several reasons, instances, etc., is mentioned.

1719 DE FOE *Crusoe* II. ix, Will you go..? I will go for one. 18.. KEBLE *Lett. Spirit. Counsel* (1870) 176, I could say, for one thing, make your account beforehand with this trouble coming upon you. 1880 *Scribner's Mag.* XX. 356/1, I for one shall never do so.

e. ***for the first, second***, etc. ***time***: as a first, second, etc., instance. Cf. Fr. *pour la première fois.*

1730 A. GORDON *Maffei's Amphith.* 68 The Romans were for the first time forbid such Games. 1788 GIBBON *Decl. & F.* lxvi. VI. 431 *note*, He [Aldus] printed above sixty considerable works of Greek literature, almost all for the first time. 1818 M. G. LEWIS *Jrnl. W. Ind.* (1834) 177 There was a shower of rain for the first time since my arrival. 1863 TRAFFORD *World in Ch.* III. 253 Is he a man likely to fall in love for a second time? 1875 JOWETT *Plato* (ed. 2) I. 399 That they may converse with Socrates for the last time.

f. ***for good (and all)***: see GOOD.

g. With an adjective, in pleonastic use, as ***for free***, for no charge, without payment; ***for real***, real. Also in such phrases used *attrib.* Chiefly *U.S.*

1887 in *Amer. Speech* (1950) XXV. 39/2 When a for-true doctor come to see him. 1900, etc. [see FAIR *sb.*[2] 1 c]. 1942 in WENTWORTH *Amer. Dial. Dict.* (1944) 228/1 Railroads don't haul trash for free. 1943 *Amer. Speech* XVIII. 47 It might be reasonable to assume that 'for free' results from the confusion of 'free' and 'for nothing'. 1954 W. M. MILLER *Conditionally Human* (1963) 72 Don't worry, Richard. This time it's for real. 1957 *New Yorker* 21 Sept. 33/2 He said psychiatrists had been enthusiastic, patents have been applied for, and it's for real. 1957 G. SMITH *Friends* 147 Back home we pay if we're ill... You don't expect to be ill for free. 1958 K. AMIS *I like it Here* xi. 133 Bowen tried to buy some drinks, conscious of having been fed and made drunk for free. 1960 J. KIRKWOOD *There must be a Pony* (1961) xii. 95 A good guy; a movie cop..; a for-real cop.

VII. Of the cause or reason.

20. a. By reason of, under the influence of (a feeling or subjective condition).

Beowulf 338 (Gr.) Wen ic, þæt ȝe for wlenco, nalles for wræcsiðum ac for hiȝe-þrymmum Hroðȝar sohton. a1123 *O.E. Chron.* an. 1101 For heoran agenan mycelan unȝetrywþan. c1175 *Lamb. Hom.* 17 He..ȝef us seodðan ane muchele ȝef for his muchele eadmodnesse. 1297 R. GLOUC. (1724) 58 He by gan hym by þenche, And hys wraþþe toward þe kyng, for drede of þe erl, quenche. c1380 *Antecrist* in Todd 3 *Treat. Wyclif* 152 How may þei seie for shame þat þei folowen Crist truly? c1440 *Jacob's Well* 72 Boldere to synne for trust of þe mercy of god. 1580 SIDNEY *Arcadia* II. xvi. 172 Like the poore childe, whose father, while he beates him, will make him beleeue it is for loue. 1725 DE FOE *Voy. round World* (1840) 305 Our men raised a shout for joy. 1802 *Noble Wanderers* II. 32 Arsaces, panting for rage, had already grasped his poniard. 1827 SOUTHEY *Hist. Penins. War* II. 776 They had, for pure wantonness, set fire to some of the houses.

b. ***for fear of, that***, etc.: see FEAR *sb.*[1] 3 b.

1847 MARRYAT *Childr. N. Forest* v, Take your guns too, for fear of accident.

21. Because of, on account of:

a. a person or persons.

c1000 ÆLFRIC *Gen.* xx. 3 Þu scealt sweltan nu Abimeleh for þam wife þe þu name. c1205 LAY. 14458 Þin hired þe hateð for me & ich æm iuæid for þe. 13.. *K. Alis.* 2318 Al Pierce for him sorwith, y-wis. 1382 WYCLIF *Ps.* xxvi. 11 Dresse me in a riȝt path for myn enemys. 1549 *Chron. Gr. Friars* (Camden) 62 The cause was for them that rose in Essex. 1605 SHAKS. *Lear* II. iv. 55 Thou shalt haue as many dolours for thy daughters. 1819 COBBETT *Eng. Gram.* xvii. §196 When I see many *its* in a page, I always tremble for the writer.

b. a thing. Also in ***for cause*** (see CAUSE *sb.* 6) and after such sbs. as *charge, reputation*, etc., and adjs. as *sorry* (see those words). Some adjs. formerly construed with this prep. now take others; e.g. *glad of.*

c1000 ÆLFRIC *Exod.* xviii. 9 Þa wæs Iethro bliþe for eallum þam godum þe Drihten dyde Israhela folce. c1175 *Lamb. Hom.* 17 Þine frond þu luuest for þam goddede þe he þe deð. 1297 R. GLOUC. (1724) 113 Ac for ȝoure coming ich am glad. c1380 WYCLIF *Serm.* Sel. Wks. I. 25 Þei shulden not be aferd for perillis. 1483 CAXTON *G. de la Tour* D iij, The one is prowde for his scyence. 1631 GOUGE *God's Arrows* IV. xii. 390 Faith herein will make us thankfull for all manner of prosperity. 1704 ADDISON *Italy* Wks. 1804 V. 149 The gulf..is..remarkable for tempests. 1802 MAR. EDGEWORTH *Moral T.* (1816) I. 225 A mother respected..for her feminine virtues. 1849 MACAULAY *Hist. Eng.* I. 308 Notorious both for covetousness and for parsimony.

¶ In OE. *for* with the instrumental case of the neuter demonst. pron. formed advb. phrases = 'therefore', which, with the addition or ellipsis of the relative *ðe* became conjunctional phrases = 'because'. (For these phrases and their later representatives see FOR-THON, FOR-THY; cf. also FOR-WHY). Similarly, FOR THAT appears from 13th c. as a conjunction; and in the 16th c. there are a few examples of *for this* in the senses 'therefore' and 'because'.

a1553 PHILPOT *Exam. & Writ.* (1842) 352 If that he demand the reason why we do so, I will gladly satisfy his mind..For this [orig. *quia*] we know surely those things, as they have written, to have come unto us uncorrupt. *Ibid.* 396 For this [orig. *igitur*], Florebell, thou hast a high bishop and ruler of the church such a one peradventure as thou soughtest not after.

c. On account of one's regard for. So in ***for the sake of*** (see SAKE), used synonymously with *for* in this sense and in senses 7 and 8.

a1000 *Cædmon's Gen.* 2472 (Gr.) Þa ic for god wille ȝemund-byrdan. c1000 *Rood* 113 (Gr.) Se þe for dryhtnes naman deaðes wolde..onbyriȝan. a1200 *Moral Ode* 23 Þe him solue forȝet for wiue ne for childe. c1205 LAY. 13223 Ich bad hine for gode don þat child of hade. 1393 LANGL. *P. Pl.* C. III. 170 To be maried for monye mede hath a-sented. a1450 *St. Cuthbert* (Surtees) 981, I leeue þe prolog for shortnes. 1697 DRYDEN *Virg. Past.* x. 35 Lycoris..for thy Rival tempts the raging Sea. 1697 KEN *Evg. Hymn* ii, Forgive me, Lord, for Thy dear Son.

d. In adjurations = *for the sake of.* Also in exclamations, chiefly of pain or sorrow.

a1000 *Boeth. Metr.* i. 128 He..hi for Drihtne bæd..þæt hi [etc.]. c1205 LAY. 57 Nu bidded Laȝamon alcne æðele mon for þene almiten godd..þet he [etc.]. c1325 *Coer de L.* 1782 Mercy, Richard, for Mary maid! 1393 LANGL. *P. Pl.* C. II. 54 Ich fraynede hure faire þo, for hym þat hure made. c1460 *Towneley Myst.* (Surtees) 210 Alas! for my master..That yester even..Before Caiphas was broght. 1593 SHAKS. *Rich. II*, v. ii. 75 Heauen for his mercy: what treachery is heere? 1609 BIBLE (Douay) *Joel* i. 15 Crie ye to our Lord: A a a, for the day. 1741 RICHARDSON *Pamela* I. 81 But I have not found it so, Alas for me. 1820 BYRON *Blues* II. 64 *Lady Blueb.* Oh fie! *Miss Lil.* And for shame! 1820 KEATS *Lamia* 271 For pity do not melt! 1844 DICKENS *Christmas Carol* iii. 90 Alas for Tiny Tim.

†**e.** ***for because***: see BECAUSE A. 1, B. 1. *Obs.*

22. Of an efficient or operative cause: In consequence of, by reason of, as the effect of. (Now chiefly after comparatives; otherwise usu. replaced by *from, of, through.*) Also in ***for want of***: see WANT.

c1205 LAY. 27818 Þa eorðe gon beouien for þan vnimete blase. ?c1370 *Robt. K. Cicyle* 55 Bettur he were..So to do then for hunger dye. c1380 WYCLIF *Sel. Wks.* III. 349 Scarioth was þe worse for beyng in þis holi cumpanye. c1400 *Lanfranc's Cirurg.* 101 & þou fyndest a man havynge þe crampe for a wounde. 1491 CAXTON *Vitas Patr.* (W. de W. 1495) I. xl. A a, For the grete hete of the sonne She hadde the febres or axes. 1512 *Act 4 Hen. VIII*, c. 11 For defaute of such issue to remaigne to oure Soveraigne Lorde. 1548 HALL *Chron., Hen. IV*, (an. 1), To die for thirst standyng in the river. 1578 COOPER *Thesaurus* s.v. *Vetustas*, He lacketh teeth for age. 1641 J. JACKSON *True Evang. T.* II. 121 For the abundance of milk she [the cow] did give, the owner might eate butter. 1718 BP. HUTCHINSON *Witchcraft* Ded. (1720) 11 Her chin and her knees meeting for Age. 1766 GOLDSM. *Vic. W.* xxviii, In this very room a debtor of his..died for want. 1850 LYNCH *Theo. Trin.* v. 84 Shall we be the brighter spirits for being the duller men? 1887 A. BIRRELL *Obiter Dicta* Ser. II. 103 They breathed the easier for the news. *Mod.* He is worse for liquor. This coat is worse for wear.

23. Of a preventive cause or obstacle. **a.** In spite of, notwithstanding. Rare exc. in ***for all, any***, with a sb.; also absol. ***for all that***, etc.

O.E. Chron. an. 1006 Ac for eallum þissum se here ferde swa he sylf wolde. c1320 *Seuyn Sag.* (W.) 1135 For al that heuer he mighte do, His menesoun might nowt staunche tho. c1386 CHAUCER *Doctor's T.* 129 This mayde shal be myn, for any man. c1430 *Syr Gener.* 8058 Loue him she wold for ony drede. 1548 HALL *Chron., Hen. V*, (an. 4) 53 But for all that he could do, he lost almoste ccc of his fotemen. 1681 H. MORE *Exp. Dan.* iii. 68 This Alexander the Great for all his greatness died. 1794 BURNS *For a' that* i, The rank is but the guinea stamp; The man's the gowd for a' that. 1820 KEATS *St. Agnes* i, The owl, for all his feathers, was a-cold. 1871 ROSSETTI *Poems, Last Confess.*, I was a moody comrade to her then, For all the love I bore her. 1873 F. HALL *Mod. English* p. xv, For all that, I have contrived..to give some thought to my mother-tongue.

b. in conjunctional phrases: ***for all that, for all*** = notwithstanding (that), although. Now *rare* in literary use.

1523 LD. BERNERS *Froiss.* I. clvi. 189 For all that the frenche kynge sende to hym to delyuer the same castels, yet he refused so to do. 1588 *Marprel. Epist.* (Arb.) 21, I tell you D. Stannop (for all you are so proude). 1682 BUNYAN *Holy War* 24 [Conscience]..(for all he was now so debauched), did terrifie..them sore. 1786 MACKENZIE in *Lounger* No. 90 ¶7 For all her feelings are so fine. 1841 L. HUNT *Seer* (1864) 40, I am not a very bad play-fellow..for all I am so much bigger. a1866 KEBLE *Lett. Spirit. Counsel* (1870) 185 For all she seemed so calm, she had often to bear up against the same kind of feelings.

c. Indicating the presence or operation of an obstacle or hindrance. (Cf. ON. *fyrer*, Ger. *für, vor.*) In negative sentences; also after *if it were not, were it not*; occas. = for fear of. †***for to die for it*** = if I die for it. ***but for***: see BUT C. 29.

Beowulf 2549 (Gr.) Ne meahte horde neah unbyrnende æniȝe hwile deop ȝedyȝan for dracan leȝe. c1000 ÆLFRIC *Gen.* xvi. 10 Þæt man hit ȝeriman ne mæȝ for þære meniu. 1297 R. GLOUC. (1724) 177 Hii mowe noȝt wel fle Vor feblesse of her brode. 1377 LANGL. *P. Pl.* B. xv. 282 Þat no man miȝte hym se for mosse and for leues. a1430 *Octouian* 682 That wyf therst not say nay, For wordes ylle. c1489 CAXTON *Sonnes of Aymon* xii. 296, I shall never doo that, for to deye for it. a1592 GREENE *Alphonsus* (1861) 231 That you dare Not use your sword for staining of your hands. 1691 RAY *Creation* 213 Unhabitable for heat. 1744 BERKELEY *Let. to T. Prior* 19 June Wks. 1871 IV. 298 Last night being unable to sleep for the heat. 1751 *Affect. Narr. Wager* 92 This was like, not seeing the Wood for Trees. 1810 SCOTT *Lady of L.* v. 858 Spare not for spoiling of thy steed. 1876 GEO. ELIOT *Dan. Der.* VI. xliii, At times she could not stand for the beating of her heart.

†**d.** As a precaution against, or simply, against: (to beware) of; (to hinder, keep, prevent) from.

c1330 R. BRUNNE *Chron.* (1810) 122 Sone after mydnyght..In þe snowe for syght scho ȝede out in hir smok. 1377 LANGL. *P. Pl.* B. II. 230 Freres..for knowyng of comeres coped hym as a frere. a 1400-50 *Alexander* 285 þat wald for hurte or for harme any hathill kepe. 1523 FITZHERB. *Husb.* §51 Se that they..holde his heed hye ynoughe for drownynge. 1561 HOLLYBUSH *Hom. Apoth.* 40 b, He must also beware for taking cold. 1590 GREENE *Poems* Wks. (1861) 294 A hat of straw, like a swain, Shelter for the sun and rain. 1611 BARREY *Ram. Alley* I. ii, Ah, how light he treads, For dirting his silk stockings! 1703 MOXON *Mech. Exerc.* 205 That may hinder the Corner of the edge of the Chissel for coming at the Work. 1728 in Picton *L'pool Munic. Rec.* (1886) II. 88 To prevent..the constitution of it for being entirely subverted.

VIII. Of correspondence or correlation.

24. Prefixed to the designation of a number or quantity to which another is stated to correspond in some different relation. (Cf. similar use of *to*.)

1399 LANGL. *Rich. Redeles* II. 42 For on þat ȝe merkyd ȝe missed ten schore Of homeliche hertis. 1583 T. WATSON *Centurie of Loue* xcvii. (Arb.) 133 For eu'ry pleasure that in Loue is found, A thousand woes and more therein abound. 1674 N. COX *Gentl. Recreat.* v. (1686) 6, I will undertake to shew any man Twenty other Horses lame..for one Hunter. 1724 DE FOE *Mem. Cavalier* (1840) 255 They were..twice our number in the whole; and their foot three for one. 1806-7 J. BERESFORD *Miseries Hum. Life* (1826) VI. xxxvii, It contains..for one inch of lean four or five of stringy fat. 1887 L. CARROLL *Game of Logic* i. §3. 32 For one workable Pair of Premisses..you will probably find five that lead to no Conclusion at all.

25. Preceded and followed by the same sb. (without article or defining word), in idiomatic expressions indicating equality in number or quantity between objects compared or contrasted. ***bulk for bulk***: taking an equal bulk of each. ***word for word***: with exact identity of expression, verbatim; similarly ***point for point***. †***day for day***: on one day as on every other, hence = 'day by day'. †***to fight hand for hand***: = 'hand to hand'. ***to turn*** (something) ***end for end***: to reverse.

13.. *K. Alis.* 2922 Word for word thus they spake. c1386 CHAUCER *Clerk's T.* 521 Of Grisildis wordes..He tolde him point for point. c1450 *Chester Pl.* (E.E.T.S.) 256 Such marvayels..he ne dyd day for day. 1535 STEWART *Cron. Scot.* II. 118 Dongard..curage had for to fecht hand for hand With Constantyne. 1606 SHAKS. *Ant. & Cl.* IV. viii. 22 A Braine that..can Get gole for gole of youth. 1692 BENTLEY *Boyle Lect.* iv. 116 Bulk for bulk heavier than a Fluid. 1759 JOHNSON *Idler* No. 69 ¶6 May, Sandys and Holiday, confined themselves to the toil of rendering line for line. a1769 *Regul. Sea-Serv.* in Falconer *Dict. Marine* (1789) Kk iv b, If a foreign admiral..salutes them, he shall receive gun for gun. 1877 *Daily News* 10 Oct. 6/2 We turned the rope end for end. 1881 JOWETT *Thucyd.* I. 168 The prisoners..were exchanged man for man. 1885 *Manch. Exam.* 15 May 5/3 They will not be slow to return him like for like.

IX. Of reference.

26. a. As regards, with regard or respect to, concerning. Also in idiomatic expressions: †***for the general***, in general; †***for so far***, in so far; †***for my mind***, to my thinking; ***for my, his***, etc. ***part*** (see PART); ***for the rest*** (= F. *du reste*: see REST *sb.*). †***what for—***; = 'what with—' (see WHAT). ***as for***: see AS 33.

The parenthetic use, as in *for me* = as for me, for my part (= Fr. *pour moi*), is now obsolete.

1479 J. PASTON in *Paston Lett.* No. 849 III. 267, I have myche to pay her in London, what for the funerall costes, dettes, and legattes that [etc.]. 1551 T. WILSON *Logike* (1580) 75 He is delivered from the lawe, for so much as pertaineth to his condemnation, but he is not free, for so muche as belongeth to the due obedience, whiche he oweth unto God. 1590 MARLOWE *2nd Pt. Tamburl.* IV. i, For person like to prove a second Mars. 1628 HOBBES *Thucyd.* (1822) 99 This year..was of all other for other diseases most free. 1634 W. WOOD *New Eng. Prosp.* I. iv, The Soyle is for the generall a warme kinde of earth. 1658 W. BURTON *Comm. Itin. Antoninus* 176 For old Marinus, I know not how to excuse him. 1664-5 PEPYS *Diary* 7 Apr., Sir Philip did shew me nakedly the king's condition for money. 1710 BERKELEY *Princ. Hum. Knowl.* §111 For the rest, this celebrated author holds there is an absolute Space. 1740 *Xmas Entertainm.* iii. (1883-4) 21 All the Witches for my Mind are young Women. 1765 BLACKSTONE *Comm.* I. 466 Thus much..for the privileges and disabilities of infants. 1818 M. G. LEWIS *Jrnl. W. Ind.* (1834) 250 How he managed for water I could not learn. 1843 *Fraser's Mag.* XXVIII. 570 So much for our housemaid. 1852 R. S. SURTEES *Sponge's Sp. Tour* (1893) 361 Get married and trust to Providence for the rest.

b. So far as concerns (a person or thing). Used with a limiting or restrictive force (cf. 23). ***for all*** or ***aught I know***, I know nothing to the contrary. (***he may do it***) ***for me***, i.e. with no opposition from me.

a1300 *Cursor M.* 3206 (Cott.) 'Fader', he said, 'be þou ful bald, For me sal it neuer be tald'. 1578 TIMME *Calvin on Gen.* x. I. 238 Let them..for all me, inioy the fruite..of their labours. 1655 HARTLIB *Legacy* 160 This Art, for what I can perceive, is no way demonstrable à priori. 1731 POPE *Ep. to Burlington* 138 Some are Vellum, and the rest as good For all his Lordship knows. 1767 S. PATERSON *Another Trav.* I. 321 They shall have it untouched for me. 1809 J. MOSER *Don Quixote in Barcelona* II. v, [He] shall carry all the limbs he has got to heaven for me. 1837 LANDOR *Pentam.* Wks. 1846 II. 314/2 The banks of the Hebrus may be level or rocky, for what I know about them. 1890 BESANT *Demoniac* vi, After the first month you ought to have come home again, for all the good it has done. 1893 *Law Times* XCIV. 559/2 The consideration was left blank, and for all I know it is blank still.

c. with words signifying privation or want.

1653 tr. *Carmeni's Nissena* 75 He wanted for no care nor possible assistance. 1791 COWPER *Retired Cat* 73 With hunger pinched, and pinched for room. 1802 MAR. EDGEWORTH *Moral T.* (1816) I. ix. 71 In..distress for money. 1804 J. MARSHALL *Washington* II. i. 38 The people ..were in great distress for provisions, arms, and ammunition. 1855 THACKERAY *Rose & Ring* i, He need want for nothing.

d. ***for all the world***: used to emphasize assertions of likeness.

(The lit. sense and proper place of this phrase are uncertain.)

c1385 CHAUCER *L.G.W.* 218 For al the world ryght as a daysye Ycorouned ys with white leues lyte. 1602 MARSTON *Ant. & Mel.* I. Wks. 1856 I. 13 He..lookes For all the world like an ore-roasted pigge. 1753 FOOTE *Eng. in Paris* I. Wks. 1799 I. 38 Their water-gruel jaws, sunk in a thicket of curls, appear, for all the world, like a lark in a soup-dish!

27. In proportion to, considering; considering the nature or capacity of; considering what he, she, or it is, or that he, etc. is so and so.

[1594 MARLOWE & NASHE *Dido* IV. iv, Aeneas, for his parentage, deserves As large a kingdom as is Lybia.] 1631 WEEVER *Anc. Fun. Mon.* 536 This Lawier was a very honest man for those times. 1697 DRYDEN *Virg. Georg.* III. 782 His Bulk too Weighty for his Thighs is grown. 1754 RICHARDSON *Grandison* I. ii. 6 A man of an excellent character for a Lawyer. 1787 GAMBADO'S *Acad. Horsemen* (1809) 29 Should your horse prove, what is properly termed too many for you. 1861 MISS YONGE *Stokesley Secret* ii. (1862) 42 As poor a man for an esquire as her father was for a surgeon. 1886 *Manch. Exam.* 15 Mar. 5/4 The weather.. phenomenally severe for the season.

X. Of duration and extension.

28. a. Marking actual duration. During, throughout. Phr. ***for long, for a*** or ***the time***.

c1450 *Cov. Myst.* 129 Who seyth oure ladyes sawtere dayly for a ȝer thus. 1506 GUYLFORDE *Pilgr* (Camden) 39 We ..restyd vs for that nyght. 1564-78 BULLEYN *Dial. agst. Pest.* (1888) 10 His stewarde..applied the poore menne with the purse with muche deuotion for the tyme. 1602 SHAKS. *Ham.* III. i. 91 How does your Honor for this many a day? 1626 T. AILESBURY *Passion-sermon* 15 The Jewes for long were..the favourites of heaven. 1711 ADDISON *Spect.* No. 86 ¶2, I have seen an Eye curse for half an Hour together. a1792 BP. HORNE *Serm.* (1799) III. 68 Reflect for a moment, on these two pictures of virtue and vice. 1843 *Fraser's Mag.* XXVIII. 334 The *Brigand's Bride* ran for many nights. 1849 MACAULAY *Hist. Eng.* I. 166 The two great parties..had for a moment concurred. 1872 LIDDON *Elem. Relig.* i. 34 Would he even be interested for long in a philosophy which he believed to be only relatively true? 1885 *Law Rep.* 15 Q. Bench Div. 316 The catch..was worn away, and probably had been so for months.

b. Marking intended duration, e.g. *for life*; also in the phrases, ***for the*** or †***this present, for a while. for ay, ever***: see AY 3 a, EVER 5 b.

1548 HALL *Chron., Hen. V* (an. 4) 55 A peace was concluded..for a certain space. 1559 W. CUNNINGHAM *Cosmogr. Glasse* 8 Have you then for this present, your whole desire? 1632 J. LEE *Short Surv.* 53 For the present I let passe. 1636 *N. Riding Rec.* IV. 52 He shall enter bond for his good abeareing for a year. 1642 *Protests Lords* I. 11 Whether we shall adjourn for six months. 1692 E. WALKER tr. *Epictetus' Mor.* (1737) xv, What bounteous God did for awhile afford. 1706 *Acc. Soc. Propag. Gosp.* 33 The Society ..ordered fifty Pounds per annum to be ascertained to him for Three Years. 1719 DE FOE *Crusoe* I. viii, I resolved to sit down for all night. 1750 JOHNSON *Rambler* No. 59 ¶6 He is always provided with a curacy for life. 1764 STERNE in Traill *Life* 87 About Christmas I..fix my head-quarters at London for the winter. 1847-9 HELPS *Friends in C.* Ser. I. (1851) I. 101 If there were Peers for life..it would..meet most of your objections. 1849 MACAULAY *Hist. Eng.* II. 156 Four thousand pounds a year for two lives. 1870 MISS BRIDGMAN *R. Lynne* II. v. 117, I sha'n't get up for another hour. 1885 *Law Rep.* 14 Q. Bench Div. 892 The driver.. was practically placed at the disposal of the defendants for the day.

29. ***for once, for the nonce***: see ONCE, NONCE[1].

30. Marking an amount of extension, *esp.* in space, lineal or superficial: Over, over the space of, to the extent of, through.

1568 GRAFTON *Chron.* II. 36 The River of Trent in the moneth of June flowed not for the space of a mile. 1605 SHAKS. *Lear* II. iv. 304 For many Miles about There's scarce a Bush. 1818 M. G. LEWIS *Jrnl. W. Ind.* (1834) 159 After travelling for five and twenty miles. 1863 KINGSLEY *Water Bab.* 9 Not only did he own all the land about for miles. 1885 *Manch. Exam.* 28 Sept. 5/3 When a..man has walked briskly even for a mile.

†**XI. 31.** Misused for *fro*, FROM.

c1340 *Cursor M.* 13554 (Trin.) Anoon he had his siȝt For þenne was he no more led. c1440 *Partonope* 2260 Sornogoure swerde for the arson reft. c1440 *York Myst.* xxx. 222 He bese hurled for þe highnes he haunted. 1540 *Act 32 Hen. VIII*, c. 42 §1 All personnes of the said company..shalbe exempt for bearing of armure.

B. *conj.*

†**1.** Introducing the cause of a fact, the statement of which precedes or follows: Because. Cf. A. 21 b. *Obs.* exc. *arch.*

a1200 tr. *Alcuin's Virt. & V.* 115 in *Anglia* XI. 376 We sculen fleon þa unðeawes, na þa mænn sylfe..for heo synd godes gesceafte. c1205 LAY. 148 Eneam he..biheyte..al his drihliche lond for he nefde nenne sune. 1340 HAMPOLE *Pr. Consc.* 6807 þus for þai did ay ogayns Goddes lawe, Vermyn and wode bestes sal þam ay gnawe. c1435 *Torr. Portugal* 1333 For sir Torent the fend did fall, Gret lordys honoured hym all. 1450-1530 *Myrr. our Ladye* 11 And for god made all thinges in syx dayes..therfore, etc. 1600 FAIRFAX *Tasso* II. xix, Nor for he sweld with ire was she affraid. 1604 SHAKS. *Oth.* III. iv. 161 They are..iealious for they're iealious. 1691 DRYDEN *K. Arthur* I. ii. Wks. 1884 VIII. 148 Why comes not he?..For he's a puling sprite. 1799 ANNA SEWARD *Sonn.* xlix, In balance true Weigh it, but smile at the objections vain Of sickly Spirits, hating for they do. 1872 TENNYSON *Gareth & Lynette* 386 And, for himself was of the greater state..he trusted his liege-lord Would yield him this large honour all the more.

2. a. Introducing the ground or reason for something previously said: Seeing that, since. Cf. Gr. γάρ, L. *nam* or *enim*, Fr. *car*, Ger. *denn*.

c1150 *Serm.* in Kluge *Ags. Lesebuch* 71 Hwu sceal þiss ȝewurðen, for ic necann naht of weres ȝemane. 1154 *O.E. Chron.* an. 1135 On þis kinges time wes al unfrið..for ægenes him risen sone þa rice men. c1200 ORMIN 119 And teȝȝ wærenn..Rihhtwise menn..Forr eȝȝþerr here ȝede..Rihht affter Godess lare. ?a1400 *Morte Arth.* 219 Ffore he was demyde þe doughtyeste þat duellyde in erthe. 1480 CAXTON *Chron. Eng.* ccxliv. (1482) 298 Nowe is good tyme For al Englond praith for vs. 1559 W. CUNNINGHAM *Cosmogr. Glasse* 25 For xij. tymes 30. maketh 360. a1613 OVERBURY *A Wife* (1638) 202 A churchman she dare not venture upon; for she hath heard widowes complain of dilapidations. 1664 TILLOTSON *Wisd. being Relig.* 59 Just such is he who for fear of any thing in this world ventures to grieve God; for in so doing he runs away from men and falls into the hands of the living God. 1766 GOLDSM. *Vic. W.* iii, Near a fortnight had passed before [etc.]..for premature consolation is but the remembrancer of sorrow. 1838 T. THOMSON *Chem. Org. Bodies* 806 This oil or resinous-like body contains phosphorus; for..we find phosphoric acid in the residue. 1883 *Manch. Guard.* 22 Oct. 5/3 This is no party question, for it touches us not as Liberals or Conservatives, but as citizens.

b. Introducing a detailed proof.

1570 BILLINGSLEY *Euclid* I. xi, For forasmuch as DC is equal to CE, and [etc.] therefore [etc.]. 1812-16 J. SMITH *Panorama Sc. & Art* I. 588 For, let there be three bodies at H, O, and D; if [etc.]. 1840 LARDNER *Geom.* 106 For from the point B draw BD perpendicular to [etc.].

3. = WHETHER in an obj. sentence. *Obs. rare.*

c1250 *Gen. & Ex.* 2651 We sulen nu witen for it dede ðis witterlike, or in child-hede. c1394 *P. Pl. Crede* 350 Woldest þou me tellen For þei ben..syker on to trosten, y wolde quyten þe þi mede.

†**4.** In order that. Cf. A. 8. *Obs.*

c1305 *St. Katherine* 171 in *E.E.P.* (1862) 94 Noman ne ȝaf hire mete ne drinke: for heo scholde for hunger deye. c1380 *Sir Ferumb.* 907 þay..byndeþ þer-wiþ is eȝene about; for he ne schold noȝt sene. c1450 *St. Cuthbert* (Surtees) 4753 For þair trauail sulde noȝt be waste. 1593 SHAKS. *3 Hen. VI*, III. i. 9 And for the time shall not seeme tedious Ile tell thee what [etc.].

†**5.** ***for and***: = 'and moreover'. *Obs.*

a1529 SKELTON *Agst. Garnesche* 22 Syr Gawen, Syr Cayus, for and Syr Olyuere. 1605 SHAKS. *Ham.* V. i. 103 A Pickhaxe and a Spade, a Spade for and a shrowding-Sheete. 1617 MIDDLETON *Fair Quarrel* V. i. Wks. (Dyce) III. 544 *Chough* [sings] A hippocrene, a tweak, for and a fucus.

for-, *pref.*[1] Also 1 fær-, 3 *Orm.* forr-, 3-4 *south.* vor-, ver-, 4 fur-, 6-7 fore-. [OE. *for-*, *fær-* = OFris. *for-*, *far-*, OS. *for-*, *far-* (Du. *ver-*), OHG. *far-*, *fir-*, *fer-* (MHG. and mod.G. *ver-*), ON. *for-* (Sw. *för-*, Da. *for-*); the ON. *fyrer-* (see FORE- *pref.*) though formally distinct, often corresponds in use with this prefix. The OE. form (like the other forms quoted) seems to represent (with obscured vowel due to absence of stress) the three OTeut. prefixes **fer-*, *fra-*, *fur-* (Goth. *faír-*, *fra-*, *faúr-*), which correspond formally to Gr. περι-, προ-, παρα-, representing various ablaut-grades of the Aryan root **pr-*: see FOR and FORE. Functionally, the three prefixes do not seem to be clearly distinguished even in Gothic; but in most cases when a vb. with OE. *for-* or Ger. *ver-* has a Goth. equivalent, the prefix appears as *fra-*, which seems to have been orig. its *stressed* form: cf. the two OE. forms *'fracod* and *for'cúð* (see FORCOUTH), which are believed to be accentual variants of the representative of pre-Teut. **prognto-*, despicable.

From the predominant meaning of the root, it may be inferred that the primary notion expressed by the prefix is that of 'forward, forth'. The various uses in the Teut. langs. may be plausibly explained as originating from this, though the exact process of their development is in many points uncertain: see Grimm's *Deutsches Wb.* s.v. *ver-*. The vbs. formed with this prefix often correspond in signification to Gr. vbs. formed with one or other of the cognate prefixes περι-, προ-, παρα-, and to Lat. vbs. with *per-* or *pro-*.]

A prefix used to form verbs and adjs., primarily occurring in OE. words of Com. Teut. or WGer. origin, but employed in the formation of new words down to the beginning of the mod.Eng. period; it is now entirely obsolete. Its various functions are enumerated below. The words here explained and illustrated are all obsolete; the surviving words formed with the prefix, and those obsolete ones which require extended treatment, are given as main words in their alphabetical place.

I. Forming verbs.

1. Prefixed to verbs, giving the additional sense of 'away', 'off', as in FORCAST; **forshake**, to shake off; **forshoot**, to cast off, reject; **forthrow**, to throw off.

a1300 *E.E. Psalter* cviii. [cix.] 23 *For-schaken [Vulg. *excussus*] als gressop. a1300 *Cursor M.* 13663 (Cott.) Quen iesus wist him þus *for-scotten. 1340 *Ayenb.* 86 Zuo þet he ne may hit *uorþrawe to his wylle [mistranslation of *si que il ne sen peult pas jetter dehors a sa voulente*].

2. With the sense of prohibition, exclusion, or warding off, as in FORBID; **forrun**, to bar by running; **forsay**, to renounce, exclude by command. Also with the sense of concealing from view: **forcover**, FORWRAP.

In this use the sense closely approaches that of FOR-², FORE-; cf. FOR(E)FEND, FOR(E)SHIELD.

1382 WYCLIF *Gen.* xxvii. 16 She *forcoueride the nakid of the nak. *c* **1205** LAY. 12861 Costantin..bad þa wæi-witere *for-ærnen þa wateres. **1579** SPENSER *Sheph. Cal.* May 82 Sike worldly sovenance he..must *for-say. *Ibid.* July 79 Shepherds been foresayd From places of delight.

3. With the notion of passing by, abstaining from, or neglecting, as in FORBEAR, FORGO, FORHOW; **forheed**, to disregard. Also with the sense of missing or forfeiting something through what is expressed by the simple vb.: **forgreme**, to forfeit by displeasing (God); **forslip**, to let slip; **forslug**, to neglect through sluggishness.

c **1200** *Trin. Coll. Hom.* 35 He com..to giuende þe mihtes þe adam *for-gremede us alle. *c* **1275** LAY. 2579 Wimmen he *forhedde. *c* **1315** SHOREHAM 11 Hy..That cristneth twyes enne, Other..For-hedeth Wanne childe ariȝt cristnynge heth. **1610** HOLLAND *Camden's Brit.* II. 115 (127) He shifted off and dallied with them still, untill they had *forslipt the opportunitie of pursuing him. *c* **1315** SHOREHAM 114 Wanne man leteth adrylle That he god ȝelde schel, And *for-sluggyth [*printed* slaggyth] by wylle That scholde men to stel. *c* **1386** CHAUCER *Pars. T.* ⁋611 Accidie..forsluggeth, and destroyeth alle goodes temporeles by reccheleesnesse.

4. With the sense of 'wrongly', 'mis-', as **forraught**, perverted; **forworship**, to worship wrongly.

c **1200** ORMIN 14540 All mankinn..Wass..all *forrraht ȝæn Godd. *c* **1380** *Antecrist* in Todd 3 *Treat. Wyclif* 141 þei seyn we *forwirship.

5. Implying destructive, painful, or prejudicial effect, as in FORDEEM, FORDO; **forgab**, to defame, publish the misdeeds of; **forglut**, to waste in gluttony, devour; **forhang**, **-head**, to put to death by hanging, by beheading; **forpierce**, **forprick**; **forscald**, to scald, scorch; **forseethe**, to scald; **forsench**, to submerge, drown; **forsink**, to be submerged; **forswithe**, to torture or destroy by burning; **forwall**, to torture with boiling. Also in pa. pples.: **forfaded**; **forfrorn**, frozen up, stuck fast in the ice; **forroasted**, tortured by roasting; **forstived**, stifled, choked; **forswarted**, blackened; **fortossed**; **forwithered**, withered or dried up.

1413 *Pilgr. Sowle* (Caxton 1483) IV. xxviii. 73 Sone as the heye is drye the floure is *forfaded. **1481** CAXTON *Reynard* xxxiii. (Arb.) 95 She..wente in to the yse wherein she was *forfrorn. *c* **1394** *P. Pl. Crede* 631 Whoso *forgabbed a frere yfounden at þe stues..Hym were as god greuen a greit lorde of rentes. **1393** LANGL. *P. Pl. C.* XII. 66 These wrecches..in glotonye *For-glotten here goodes. *c* **1300** *Havelok* 2724 Ich shall slo þe, and hire *for-henge heye. **13..** *K. Alis.* 1366 He that the treson dude, Was *forhedid in that steode. **1413** *Pilgr. Sowle* (Caxton 1483) IV. xx. 68 Seeth how he is ..al *forpercid sore. **1297** R. GLOUC. (Rolls) 7490 þre stedes he slou vnder him..*Vorpriked and uor arnd aboute. **1413** *Pilgr. Sowle* (1483) III. viii. 55 So moche haue they woundyd and forprycked other folk about them, that [etc.]. *c* **1440** *Jacob's Well* 10 He was al *for-rostyd, fryed & scaldyd. *a* **1225** *Juliana* 70 [The pitch] leop wallinde hat up..ant *for scaldede of ham seoluen fifti and tene. *a* **1225** *Ancr. R.* 246 þu hauest forschalded þe drake heaued mid wallinde watere. *a* **1450** tr. *Higden* (Harl. MS.) VII. 528 Liȝtnyng forscalded [L. *ustulavit*] cornes. *a* **1225** *Ancr. R.* 312 Lete we teares, leste ure owune teares *uorseoðen us in helle! *c* **1315** SHOREHAM 165 For death scholde his meystryes kethe, and for-sopil and for-sethe In deathes bende. *a* **1225** *Juliana* 60 His [Adam's] team..sunegede swa swiðe þat tu hit *forsenchtest al in noes flode. *c* **1250** *Gen. & Ex.* 1114 So *for-sanc and brente ðat steden. **1563** SACKVILLE *Induct. Mirr. Mag.* xx, Here in sorrowe art for-sonke so depe. **13..** *Cast. Love* 1729 in *Minor Poems fr. Vernon MS.* (1892) App. xxxviii. 405, I am *for-styfyd among, Thi synne stynketh on me so strong! *c* **1305** *Pilate* 227 in *E.E.P.* (1862) 117 And iseȝ his bodie al *forswarted. *a* **1225** *Ancr. R.* 306 Ure inwit, uorkuliinde [*v.r.* *forswiðande] hire suluen mid þe fure of sunne. *c* **1250** *Gen. & Ex.* 1140 Ðo meidenes herden quilum seien, Ðat fier sulde al ðis werlde forsweðen. **1571** GOLDING *Calvin on Ps.* xxii. 2. 78 We shall be in deede *foretossed, howbeit our faith shall alwayes scape shipwrecke. *a* **1240** *Sawles Warde* in *Cott. Hom.* 251 þat pich ham *forwalleð aðet ha beon for mealte. **1563** SACKVILLE *Induct. Mirr. Mag.* xii, Her body small, *forwithered, and forespent.

b. With the sense of 'asunder, in pieces', as in FORBURST, FORGNAW; **forcleave**; **forhale**, *fig.* to distract; **forrend**. Also in pa. pples.: **forbrittened**, broken in pieces; **forcrazed**, fallen to pieces; **forfrushed**, shattered to pieces; **forpinched**, **forscattered**, **fortattered**, **fortorn**.

?*a* **1400** *Morte Arth.* 2273 Braynes..With brandez *forbrittenede one brede in þe laundez. *c* **1290** *S. Eng. Leg.* I. 231/418 He *for-clef is foule bouk in þre partyes at þe laste. *c* **1380** *Sir Ferumb.* 543 Atweyne i wol forcleue þyn hed. *c* **1320** *Seuyn Sag.* (W.) 724 Chaumbers, and..hegghe halle, Of old werk, *for-crased alle. *c* **1330** R. BRUNNE *Chron. Wace* (Rolls) 1180 Of grete roches þey fulle al doun, & al *fur-frusched bak & croun. *c* **1477** CAXTON *Jason* 58 b, Our ship is alle to broken and forfrusshid. **1568** C. WATSON *Polyb.* 63 The whole navie was in greate perill, and many of them sore forfrushed. **1579** SPENSER *Sheph. Cal.* Sept. 243 Nought easeth the care, that doth me *forhaile. **1614** DAVIES *Eclogue, Willie & Wernock* 26 Who [? = *whom*] whilom no encheson could fore-haile. *c* **1325** *Poem Times Edw. II* 303 in *Pol. Songs* (Camden) 337 Hit shal be so *for-pinched, to-toilled, and to-twiht. *c* **1440** *Jacob's Well* 118 þanne schal þat soule..ben all *for-rent wyth helle-ratchys. **1496** *Dives & Paup.* (W. de W.) v. viii. 206/1 Woo be to the shepherdes that..forrende the flocke of my lesue. **1430** LYDG. *Chron. Troy* I. ix, That like to shepe were *for-skatered wide. *c* **1460** *Towneley Myst.* (Surtees) 239, I am leverd a lap is lyke to no lede, *For-tatyrd and torne. **1496** *Dives & Paup.* (W. de W.) VI. xv. 258/2 That blyssful bodye..was for-rent and *for tourne.

c. Prefixed to sbs., forming vbs. used only in pa. pple. with the sense 'overpowered or troubled by' (what is expressed by the sb.), as **forstormed**, tempest-tossed; **forwintered**, reduced to straits by winter.

1393 GOWER *Conf.* I. 160 The schip which..is *forstormed and forblowe. **1481** CAXTON *Reynard* iii. (Arb.) 6 In the harde froste he had ben sore *forwynterd.

6. Expressing the notion of something done in excess or so as to overwhelm or overpower; in pa. pples.: **forbeft**, baffled; **forbolned**, puffed up; **forchafed**, overheated; **forfastened**; **forflitten**, scolded above measure; **forfried**, too much fried; **forfrighted**, greatly terrified; **forglopned**, overwhelmed with astonishment; **forladen**, **-lode**, overloaded, overpowered; **forpained**; **forpampered**, pampered to excess; **forswollen**; **forswong**, harassed; **fortaxed**, overburdened with taxation; **fortired**, excessively wearied.

1375 BARBOUR *Bruce* XVII. 793 Voundit, and wery, and *forbeft. **1413** *Pilgr. Sowle* III. ii. 50 A grete bely ful of wynd *forbolned and forblowen. **1523** LD. BERNERS *Froiss.* I. ccxxvi, Ther came to them Sir Olyuer of Clysson, *forchafed [*printed* forchased, F. *eschauffé*] and enflamed. **1488** CAXTON *Chast. Goddes Chyldern* 32 We ben *forfestned wyth a dart of his ferdnes. **1603** *Philotus* ci, I haue bene threatnit and *forflittin, Sa oft that I am with it bittin. *c* **1440** *Psalmi Penit.* 36 My bonus beth drie and forsoke, As scrachenis that beth *forfryed. *c* **1250** *Gen. & Ex.* 3519 Ðis *for-friȝted folc fiȝeren stod. *c* **1200** ORMIN 670 To beldenn and to frofrenn þe, ȝiff he þe seþ *forrgloppnedd. *c* **1300** *Cursor M.* 19634 (Edin.) Saul him quoke sua was he rad, forglopnid in his mode als mad. **1565** GOLDING *Ovid's Met.* II. (1593) 28 Winter..*Forladen with the isykles that dangled up and downe. *Ibid.* III. (1593) 75 As one forlode with wine. **13..** *E.E. Allit. P.* A. 246 Pensyf, payred, I am *for-payned. *c* **1440** *Jacob's Well* 10 Allas, þat euere J was baptysed..to be þus forpeyned! *c* **1374** CHAUCER *Boeth.* II. metr. v. 36 (Camb. MS.) They ne weere nat *for-pampred with owtrage. **1593** GOLDING *Ovid's Metam.* I. 15 The serpent Python so *forswolne. *a* **1400** *Leg. Rood* (1871) 194 When þow were so *for-swong, Among the iues þey did þe hong. *c* **1460** *Towneley Myst.* (Surtees) 98 We ar so hamyd, *For-taxed, and ramyd. *a* **1400–50** *Alexander* 1009 All þe ȝeres of owr youth bene ȝare syne passyd, And we fortraveld & *for-tyred. **1423** JAS. I *Kingis Q.* xxx, For-tirit of my thoȝt and wo begone. **1598** E. GILPIN *Skial.* (1878) 12 Perhaps fore-tyrde he gets him to a play.

b. Prefixed to intransitive verbs, forming compounds chiefly *intr.* with sense 'to weary or exhaust (oneself) by' doing what the vb. denotes, as in FORWALK, FORWANDER, FORWEEP. Also in pa. pples. and ppl. adjs.: **forcried**, **fordreamed**, **forfast(ed**, exhausted with fasting; **forlaboured**; **forlapped**, sated with lapping or drinking; **forplaint**, wearied with complaining; **forraked**, overdone with walking; **forrun** (*forarned*); **forsung** (**-songen**); **forswunk**, exhausted with labour; **fortoiled**; **forwake**, **-waked**, wearied with waking or watching; **forwallowed**, wearied with tossing about; **forwatched**.

a **1600** *Freirs of Berwyk* in *Maitland Poems* (1786) I. 73 For-knokit and *for-cryit, About he went, onto the tother syd. ?*a* **1400** *Morte Arth.* 3393 Than wakkenyde I i-wys, alle wery *for-dremyde. *a* **1300** *Cursor M.* 12940 (Cott.) þe warlau..sagh him hungri and *for-fast. *c* **1450** *Mirr. Saluacioun* 1535 (1888) 51 He hoped crist was for-fastid. **1483** CAXTON *Gold. Leg.* 395 b/2 A grete tempeste..in which they were..sore *for-laboured. *c* **1510** MORE *Picus* Wks. 11/2 Forlabored in the waie of sinne. *c* **1307** *Pol. Songs* (Camden) 238 When he is al *for-laped. **1423** JAS. I *Kingis Q.* lxxiii, For lak of myght and mynd, For-wepit and *forpleynit pitously. *c* **1440** *Towneley Myst.* (E.E.T.S.) 124, I am wery *for-rakyd and run in the myre. **1297** R. GLOUC. (Rolls) 7490 þre stedes..Vorpriked & *uor arnd aboute. *c* **1470** HENRY *Wallace* x. 704 Feill Scottis hors was..Forrown that day. ?*a* **1366** CHAUCER *Rom. Rose* 664 Chalaundres fele saw I there, That wery, nigh *forsongen were. *a* **1250** *Prov. Ælfred* in *O.E. Misc.*, If heo ofte a swote *for swunke [*a* **1275** for-swu[n]ken] were. **1589** *Mar Martine* 5 Sith swaines forswonke, and so forswat, moght, sayen what them list. **1567** DRANT *Horace's Epist.* II. ii. Hij, Snorting like a very hogge the *foretoylede did groyne. *a* **1310** in Wright's *Lyric P.* vi. 28 Ycham for wowyng al *for-wake. *c* **1386** CHAUCER *Man of Law's T.* 498 *For-waked in here orisoun, Slepeth Constaunce. *c* **1460** *Towneley Myst.* (Surtees) 104 So forwakyd is none in thy shyre. **1827** TENNANT *Papistry Storm'd* 163 Upo' the death-bed o' the floor, For-wakit and for-drunken. **1423** JAS. I *Kingis Q.* xi, For-wakit and *for-walowit..Wery, forlyin, I lestnyt sodaynlye. *a* **1483** *Liber Niger* in Tate *Househ. Ord. Edw II* (1876) 65 If any Squier for the body be..*forewatchid he shall haue sike liuerey with Knightes. **1557** *Tottell's Misc.* (Arb.) 139 His eyes were red and all forewatched.

7. With the sense 'all over', 'through and through'; prefixed to transitive vbs. as in FORBRUISE, or rendering intrans. vbs. transitive, as in FORGROW. So **forcratch**, to scratch all over; **fordin**, to fill with noise, resound through; **forseek**, to search thoroughly; **forspread**, to overspread; also **fordewed** *pa. pple.*, soaked with dew.

?*a* **1366** CHAUCER *Rom. Rose* 323 Nor she hadde no-thing slowe be For to *forcracchen al hir face. **1430** LYDG. *Chron. Troy* I. vi, All *fordewed were her wedes blake. **1501** DOUGLAS *Pal. Hon.* Prol. iii, Quhais schill noitis *fordinned all the skyis. **1563** SACKVILLE *Induct. Mirr. Mag.* lxxii, Foredinning the ayer with his horrible yel. *a* **1300** *E.E. Psalter* xxxv. 11 *For-sprede þi merci thorgh þe land.

8. Prefixed to transitive vbs. with intensive force, or, in many cases, without perceptibly modifying the sense, as in FORDREAD; **forrue**, to rue, regret. Also in pa. pples., **forbroiden**, wrought with embroidery; **forchanged**, **forcrooked**; **fordreved**, perturbed; **forpossed** (*posse* = push), pushed violently, tossed about; **forshend**, severely injured; **forwrithen**, wreathed in many coils; **forwrinked**, made tortuous.

a **1300** *Cursor M.* 28016 (Cott.) Biletts *for-broiden. *c* **1460** *Towneley Myst.* (Surtees) 224 Alas..Alle *for-changid is thy chere. *c* **1305** *Edmund Conf.* 336 in *E.E.P.* (1862) 80 þe hond was ek *forcroked. *c* **1200** ORMIN 2194 ȝiff ure laffdiȝ Marȝe wass Forrshamedd & *forrdrefedd. **1430** LYDG. *Chron. Troy* III. xxiv, Their tentes..*Forpossid were. *c* **1430** *Compleynt* 530 in Lydg. *Temple Glas* (1891) App. i. 66 Thus forpossid be-twene tweye..Now I cheuere, & now I swete. *c* **1425** WYNTOUN *Cron.* VII. 3295 The Kyng off Norway..And hys men *fer revyd sare That evyre thai arrywyd thare. *c* **1475** *Rauf Coilȝear* 540 Bot gif I fand the, forrow now to keip my cunnand. *c* **1475** *Partenay* 3306 The monkes all betrapped and *forshend, That neuer on soule scaped out-wardly. **1401** *Pol. Poems* (Rolls) II. 45 A! *forwrithen serpent, thi wyles ben aspied. **14..** LYDG. *Temple Glas.* 84 þe hous, That was *for-wrynkked bi craft of Dedalus.

9. Forming factitive vbs. from adjs. or sbs. of quality, or prefixed to factitive vbs. so derived: **forbliss**, to make happy; **fordeave**, to deafen; **forlength**, to prolong; **formeagre**, to make lean. Also in pa. pples. and ppl. adjs., **forderked**, darkened; **forfatted**, fattened; **forfeebled**, enfeebled; **forhoared**, become hoary; **foridled**, given up to idleness.

a **1300** *Cursor M.* 13108 (Cott.) þat man sal *for-blisced be þe quilk him sclanders noght for me. **1501** DOUGLAS *Pal. Hon.* I. iii, Thair ȝelpis wilde my heiring all *fordeifit. **1430** LYDG. *Chron. Troy* Prol. (1513), Of thinges passed *fordyrked of theyr hewe. **1586** FERNE *Blaz. Gentrie* 143 Through epicurisme and misdiet..*forefatted. **1513** DOUGLAS *Æneis* VII. Prol. 10 *Forfeblit wolx his [Phebus] lemand giltly lewyne. **1587** TURBERV. *Trag. T.* (1837) 37 Forfeebled as she was..she fell upon the grasse. **1591** HARINGTON *Orl. Fur.* XXIV. lxvii. (1634) 194 Inforcing his forefeebled voice. *c* **1450** *Guy Warw.* (C.) 11089 Thou olde and *forhoryd man. *a* **1225** *Ancr. R.* 116 Ase þeo þet beoð *foridled. *a* **1300** *E.E. Psalter* cxxviii[i]. 3 þair wickednesse *for-lenghþed þai. **1571** GOLDING *Calvin on Ps.* xxxix. 7 They *for-meygre themselves..bycause they imagin that all is too little for them.

II. In adjs. [Cf. the cognate L. *per-*, Gr. περι-.]

10. Giving to an adj. the sense of an absolute superlative, 'very', 'extremely'; as ***for-black***, ***-cold***, ***-dry***, ***-dull***, ***-faint***, ***-great***, ***-hoar***, ***-old***, ***-weary***; **fordead**, utterly speechless and still.

[OE. had *for-wel*, very well, very, *for-éaðe*, very easily, *for-oft*, very often; a stressed variant of the prefix is *fræ-*, as *fræmicel* 'eximius', *fræfætt* 'præpinguis', *fræofestlice* 'propere'. Cf. ON. *for-lítill*, very little, *for-mikill*, very great, etc.; also the use of Sw. *för*, Da. *for*, in the sense of 'too'. It is remarkable that nearly all Chaucer's examples of these compounds admit of being explained as instances of *for* prep. governing an adj.; thus in the quots. below, '*for-blak*' may be taken as = 'for black (that it was)', 'for blackness'; '*fordrye*, as whyt as chalk' may be read, omitting the comma, 'as white as chalk for dry (that it was)', 'on account of being so dry.' It is possible that Chaucer himself may have apprehended the combinations in this manner.]

c **1386** CHAUCER *Knt.'s T.* 1286 As any ravenes fether it shoon *for-blak. *c* **1320** *Seuyn Sag.* (W) 2623 He was *for-cold, and lokede aboute. **1592** G. HARVEY *Pierce's Super.* 66 Who would haue thought..to haue found..the elocution of the Divels oratour..so *fordead. *Ibid.* 133 There is..no such libbard for a lively ape as fordead silence. *a* **1386** CHAUCER *Sqr.'s T.* 401 Amidde a tree *fordrye, as whyt as chalk..Ther sat a faucon. *c* **1430** LYDG. *Min. Poems* (Percy Soc.) 191 To teche a rude *for-dull asse. *c* **1570** *Marr. Wit & Science* IV. iii. in Hazl. *Dodsley* II. 368 Ye sprites, for-dull with toil. *c* **1440** *Psalmi Penit.* (1894) 2 My soule hath ..*Forgret mester to make mouns. ?*a* **1366** CHAUCER *Rom. Rose* 356 Hir heed for-hoor was, whyt as flour. *c* **1340** *Gaw. & Gr. Knt.* 1440 On þe sellokest swyn swenged out þere Long sythen for þe sounder þat wiȝt *forolde [? or is this a vb.]. *c* **1386** CHAUCER *Knt.'s T.* 1284 He hadde a beres skin, col-blak, for-old. *c* **1350** *Will. Palerne* 2443 Wel out from alle weyes *for-wery þei hem rested. *c* **1400** *Rom. Rose* 3336 Forwery, for-wandred as a fool.

for-, *pref.*², OE. *for-*, is identical with FOR *prep.*, and in OE. and ME. it occurs frequently as a variant of FORE-, with the senses 'before', 'in front', 'on behalf of', etc.; cf. OE. *for-*, *forecuman* to come before, ME. *forganger* and FOREGANGER. Where a word occurs with both forms of the prefix, it is in this Dictionary placed under FORE-.

for-, *pref.*³, occurring only in words adopted from Fr., as FORCATCH, FORFEIT, FORPRISE, represents OF. *for-*, *fors-*, identical with *fors* adv. (mod.F. *hors*) outside, out:—L. *foris*, *forās*.

foracan, obs. f. HURRICANE.

forage ('fɒrɪdʒ), *sb.* Forms: 5–6 fourage (6 fourr-), 5–8 forrage, 6–7 forradge, 4– forage. [a. F. *fourrage*, f. OF. *feurre* fodder:—Com. Rom. **fodro*, of Teut. origin: see FODDER and -AGE.]

1. a. Food for horses and cattle; fodder, provender; in early use *esp.* dry winter food, as opposed to grass. Now chiefly provender for horses in an army.

c **1315** SHOREHAM 122 The oxe and asse..Tho that hy seȝen hare creature [= Creator] Lyggynde ine hare forage. *c* **1386** CHAUCER *Reeve's Prol.* 14 Gras-tyme is doon, my fodder is now forage. *c* **1430** LYDG. *Min. Poems* (Percy Soc.) 177 No comparisoun twen good greyn and forage. **1523** LD. BERNERS *Froiss.* I. xviii. 8 b/2 They had nother ootes nor forage for them [horses]. **1578** LYTE *Dodoens* I. xxxviii. 56 Spurry is good fourage or fodder for Oxen and kyen. **1610** MARKHAM *Masterp.* I. xciii. 182 Next vnto grasse is forrage, which is onely the blades of greene corne. **1683** *Lond. Gaz.* No. 1868/3 The Cavalry made hard shift to get Forage, many Horses dying for want thereof. **1720** DE FOE *Capt. Singleton* vi. 106 A herb like a broad flat thistle supplied the buffaloes for drink as well as forage. **1770** *Junius Lett.* xxxvi. 175 *note*, This gentleman..was contractor for forage. **1865** CARLYLE *Fredk. Gt.* VII. XVIII. viii. 254 Our Inns were now almost quite exhausted of forage in corn or hay.

b. *transf.* and *fig.*

1697 DRYDEN *Virg. Georg.* IV. 233 Some [Bees] o're the Publick Magazines preside, And some are sent new Forrage to provide. **1767** FAWKES *Horace's Sat.* II. vi, Those Heaps of Forage he [a mouse] had glean'd with Care. **1792** MAD. D'ARBLAY *Let.* 2 Oct., Sarah..seems perfectly satisfied with foreign forage. **1836** *Johnsoniana* I. 86 The minds of men who acquire no solid learning, and only exist on the daily forage they pick up by running about.

2. a. The action of foraging or providing forage; hence, a roving search for provisions of any kind; sometimes, a raid for ravaging the ground from which the enemy draws his supplies. † *in forage*: in search of forage.

1481 CAXTON *Godfrey* xxxviii. 76 The Captayns..were ordeyned for to lede the peple in fourage. *c* **1500** *Melusine* lix. 351 Sayeng that they were frendes and that they had be all that nyght in fourrage. **1613** PURCHAS *Pilgrimage* VI. vi. 492 And thence made forrages into the Countrey. **1777** W. DALRYMPLE *Trav. Sp. & Port.* iv, I went upon the forage to get something to eat. *a* **1873** LYTTON *Pausanias* 51 My own brother..headed a detachment for forage.

†**b.** *transf.* A raging or ravening. *Obs.*

1588 SHAKS. *L.L.L.* IV. i. 93 And he [the lion] from forrage will incline to play. **1667** WATERHOUSE *Fire Lond.* 91 The Inhabitants..fled before the Fire, leaving it to its forradge.

†**3.** In *pl.* Foragers. *Obs.*

1523 LD. BERNERS *Froiss.* I. xlix. 70 Their forages rode forthe, but they met nat, bycause the ryuer was euer bytwene them. **1603** KNOLLES *Hist. Turks* 18 Sallying out to haue cut off the forrages of the Christians.

4. *attrib.* and *Comb.*, attributive as *forage-crop*, *-plant*, *-store*; also **forage-boat**, a boat used for conveying forage; **forage-cap** (see quot. 1876); **forage-guard**, a guard detailed to cover a foraging party; **forage harvester**, an implement for harvesting forage grass (see quot. 1944); **forage-master**, an officer who attended to the forage, etc. of an army.

1848 *Blackw. Mag.* Aug. 210 By means of the *forage-boat. **1827** J. F. COOPER *Prairie* I. x, He wore a *forage-cap of fine blue cloth. **1844** *Regul. & Ord. Army* 157 The Forage Caps of the Non-commissioned Officers and Men. **1876** VOYLE *Milit. Dict.* (ed. 3), *Forage cap*, the undress cap worn by infantry soldiers and known as the Glengarry forage cap. **1875** in *Encycl. Brit.* I. 370/2 Herbage and *forage crops. **1819** REES *Cycl.*, **Forrage-guard.* **1944** C. CULPIN *Farm Machinery* (ed. 2) x. 226 The Allis Chalmers *forage harvester..is a machine which cuts the standing crop, conveys it..to a chopping cylinder, chops it into short lengths, and blows it into a trailer alongside. **1960** *Farmer & Stockbreeder* 12 Jan. 79/1 The forage-harvester..is the best thing that has hit grass farming; just as the binder revolutionized the cornfield. **1579** DIGGES *Stratiot.* 109 He ought also to assigne a sufficient number of Horse to attende on the *Forrage maister. **1823** CRABB *Technol. Dict.* s.v. *Forage*, *Forage-Master-General*, formerly an officer under the marshall, who saw to the forage for the army, which duty is now performed by the Quarter-Master-General. **1861** *U.S. Army Regul.* 149 No wagon-master or forage-master shall be interested..in any wagon or other means of transport employed by the United States. **1831** LOUDON *Encycl. Agric.* (ed. 2) Gloss. Index, *Herbage plants*, *forage plants, such as clover and other plants cultivated chiefly for the herb. **1868** *Regul. & Ord. Army* ¶ 584 Sentries over *forage stores.

forage ('fɒrɪdʒ), *v.* Forms: 5–8 forrage, 6 four(r)age, 6– forage. [ad. F. *fourrager*, f. *fourrage*: see prec.]

1. *trans.* To collect forage from; to overrun (a country) for the purpose of obtaining or destroying supplies; to lay under contribution for forage. Also in wider sense, to plunder, pillage, ravage.

1417 in Ellis *Orig. Lett.* Ser. II. I. 56 Burninge, forrageing, & destroyinge all his contry. **1569** STOCKER tr. *Diod. Sic.* I. xv. 24 They..spoyled and fouraged their territories. **1618** BOLTON *Florus* (1636) 319 They, having first foraged their next neighbours, retired themselves within their defences. **1650** FULLER *Pisgah* I. 357 Those fond entertainers..having forraged the elements of aire, earth and water for provision for their guests. **1700** ASTRY tr. *Saavedra Faxardo* II. 247 To raise a great number of Soldiers, suffering them to Forage whole Countries. **1852** MISS YONGE *Cameos* I. xxxiii. 280 After which he foraged the lands of the Earl of Chester. **1865** CARLYLE *Fredk. Gt.* IX. XXI. ii. 262 Noble and Peasant had been pillaged, ransomed, foraged, eaten-out by so many different Armies.

transf. and *fig.* **1641** SIR E. DERING in Rushw. *Hist. Coll.* III. (1692) I. 295 Who neglecting the best part of his office in God's Vineyard..forrageth the Vines. **1667** SOUTH *Serm.* Ps. lxxxvii. 2 The captivated ark, which foraged their country more than a conquering army.

2. *intr.* To rove in search of forage or provisions; *spec.* of soldiers in the field.

1530 in PALSGR. 553/2. **1531** ELYOT *Gov.* III. x, Oxen and bulls, whiche..his men had taken in foraginge. **1608** TOPSELL *Serpents* (1658) 610 When the Parents were gone abroad to forrage for them. **1697** DRYDEN *Virg. Georg.* IV. 283 Nor dare they [Bees] stray..Nor Forrage far, but short Excursions make. **1702** *Lond. Gaz.* No. 3828/2 The Left Wing of the Army foraged near the Villages. **1824** W. IRVING *T. Trav.* I. 286 A detachment..travelled slowly on, foraging among the villages.

b. To make an inroad *on*, *upon*; to raid. Also *transf.* and *fig.*

1642 CHAS. I *Message to Both Houses* 11 July, He permitteth his Souldiers to..forrage upon the Countrey. **1680** MORDEN *Geog. Rect.* (1685) 43 Under their King Cochliarius foraging upon the Seacoast of Gaul. **1857** H. REED *Lect. Eng. Poets* II. xv. 208 A boyish enterprise of foraging upon the hazel trees. **1886** LOWELL *Lett.* (1894) II. 323 The consciousness that I had it to do would be so constantly foraging on my equanimity.

3. To rove or hunt about as in search of supplies; to make a roving search *for*; to rummage.

1768–74 TUCKER *Lt. Nat.* (1852) II. 122 We may sally out boldly to forage for new discoveries in the field of contemplation. **1822** W. IRVING *Braceb. Hall* ii. 92 He passed many an hour foraging among the old manuscripts. **1845** FORD *Handbk. Spain* I. 24 He must forage abroad for anything he may want. **1876** GEO. ELIOT *Dan. Der.* IV. xxxiii, Sir Hugo..wanted Deronda to forage for him on the legal part of the question. **1893** Q. [COUCH] *Delect. Duchy* 217 He foraged in the pockets of his..coat.

†**4.** To glut oneself, as a wild beast; to raven. *lit.* and *fig.* Also, To batten or revel *in*.

1592 SHAKS. *Ven. & Ad.* 554 With blind fold furie she begins to forrage. **1599** —— *Hen. V*, I. ii. 110 Whiles his.. Father..Stood smiling, to behold his Lyons Whelpe Forrage in blood of French Nobilitie. **1670** STUCLEY *Gosp. Glass* xxxiv. 362 The Plague..forraged in London, and the parts adjacent. **1698** CROWNE *Calig.* v. 48 Go and prepare for this design to-night, And we'll to-morrow forrage in delight.

5. *trans.* To supply with forage or food.

1552 HULOET, Foraged to be..*pabulor.* **1698** J. FRYER *E. India & Persia* 125 They..are now out of distrust the Moguls should Forrage their Army here. **1715–20** POPE *Iliad* VIII. 627 Our steeds to forage and refresh our pow'r. **1810** in *Mem. Visc. Combermere* I. 139 We have been very well foraged since we have been here. **1880** DISRAELI *Endym.* xiii, He foraged their pony..and supplied them from his dairy.

6. To obtain by foraging or rummaging. Also with *out*.

1656 BP. HALL *Occas. Medit.* (1851) 74 This fowl..is ravenous: all is too little, that he can forage for himself. **1837** CARLYLE *Fr. Rev.* III. I. ii. (1872) 12 Two-thousand stand of arms..are foraged in this way. **1849** THACKERAY *Pendennis* xxxvi, His valet..went out and foraged knowledge for him. **1856** KANE *Arct. Expl.* II. i. 19 He has foraged out some raw cabbage.

Hence **'foraged** *ppl. a.*; **'foraging** *ppl. a.*

1624 CAPT. SMITH *Virginia* III. iv. 54 Two of our forraging disorderly souldiers. **1649** G. DANIEL *Trinarch., Hen. V*, cclxvi, Forraging Bees. *a* **1848** WHITTIER *Yorktown* v, With stolen beeves, and foraged corn. **1863** BATES *Nat. Amazon* II. v. 351 The Ecitons, or foraging ants. **1873** HOLLAND *A. Bonnic.* xix. 306 A foraging squirrel picked up his dinner almost at my feet.

†**'foragement.** *Obs.* [a. OF. *fourragement*: see FORAGE *v.* and -MENT.] The act of foraging.

1596 *Edw. III*, II. i. D j b, The Lyon doth become his bloody iawes, And grace his forragement by being milde, When vassell feare lies trembling at his feete.

forager ('fɒrɪdʒə(r)). Forms: α. 4–7 forager(e, 5–6 fourrager, (6 forageour, forragiour, foriger), 6–7 forrager, 6– forager. β. 6 foranger, -enger, -inger. [ad. OF. *forragier*, f. *forrage* FORAGE *sb.*; also a. OF. *fourrageour*, agent-n. f. *fourragier* FORAGE *v.* With the β. forms cf. *messenger*, *passenger*.]

†**1.** A harbinger, messenger. *Obs.* Cf. FORAYER 2.

1377 LANGL. *P. Pl.* B. xx. 84 Frenesyes & foule yueles forageres of kynde. **1616** J. LANE *Sqr.'s T.* (1888) 122 *note*, Much praisinge love (of peace the harbinger), mild truithes, sterne iustices kind foragere.

2. One of a party sent out to gather forage, etc. for an army. †Also a spoiler, ravager.

1489 CAXTON *Faytes of A.* I. xiv. 36 Not trust onely vpon that that his fourragers shall bringe. **1525** LD. BERNERS *Froiss.* II. xxxiii. 39 b/2 If the spanish forangers were stronger, than they wold take theyr forag fro them. **1552** HULOET, Forager or waster of a countrey, *populator.* **1581** STYWARD *Mart. Discipl.* I. 16 Horse..to gard and defend the foringers. **1624** HEYWOOD *Gunaik.* IV. 173 Certaine forragers and robbers that made sundry incursions into the countrie. **1799** WELLINGTON 7 Apr. in Gurw. *Desp.* I. 27 The foragers are coming in fast well loaded with forage. **1865** CARLYLE *Fredk. Gt.* X. XXI. vi. 119 The continual skirmishing with the Prussian foragers.

b. A foraging ant (*Eciton*).

[**1834** MEDWIN *Angler in Wales* II. 47 They [ants] keep a party of foragers constantly on the lookout.] **1863** BATES *Nat. Amazon* II. v. 352 One of the foragers, Eciton rapax.. hunts in single file through the forest.

3. One who goes foraging for himself. Also *fig.*

1621 G. SANDYS *Ovid's Met.* II. (1626) 34 The Wood's wild foragers espy'd. **1742** YOUNG *Nt. Th.* V. 253 This forager on others wisdom. **1777** MASON *Eng. Garden* II. 278 Down so smooth a slope, The fleecy foragers will gladly browse. **1890** *Century Mag.* May 48/1 A nervous restless disposition, which makes them [poultry]..excellent foragers.

4. = *forage-cap*.

1891 *Daily News* 14 Feb. 3/6 It is expected that the new folding cap..will be shortly condemned in favour of the all-round forager, which it was intended to supersede.

foraging ('fɒrɪdʒɪŋ), *vbl. sb.* [see -ING[1].]

1. The action of the vb. FORAGE in various senses.

1481 CAXTON *Godfrey* xxxv. 72 The noble men..sente out on fouragyng ouer alle the countrey. **1651–3** JER. TAYLOR *Serm. for Year* I. xvii. 216 A Libian Tiger drawn from his wilder forragings. **1832** W. IRVING *Alhambra* I. 20 They.. had been signally enriched by the foraging of the previous evening. **1861** HOLLAND *Less. Life* xxiii. 327 His Childe Harold is nothing but the record of his tireless foraging.

2. *Comb.*, as *foraging-expedition*, *-party*, *-ship*; **foraging-cap** = *forage-cap*.

1830 MOORE *Mem.* (1854) VI. 144 Dressed in a neat blue frock and a *foraging cap. **1863** BATES *Nat. Amazon* II. v. 363 This ant goes on *foraging-expeditions like the rest of its tribe. **1780** D. BRODHEAD in Sparks *Corr. Amer. Rev.* (1853) III. 10 Unless I send out *foraging parties, and impress cattle. **1809** *Naval Chron.* XXI. 394 *note*, The Conqueror.. was a *foraging ship.

forain(e(r, obs. form of FOREIGN, -ER.

foralite ('fɔərəlaɪt). *Geol.* [mod. f. L. *forā-re* to bore + -LITE.] (See quot.)

1859 PAGE *Handbk. Geol. Terms*, *Foralites*, applied to certain tube-like markings which occur in sandstones [etc.] and which seem to have been the burrows of *annelids*.

‖**foramen** (fɒ'reɪmɪn). Pl. **foramina** (fɒ'ræmɪnə). [L. *forāmen*, f. *forāre* to bore.] An opening or orifice, a hole or short passage, for the protrusion of an organ, or for the performance of organic functions. In various applications in *Anat.*, *Zool.*, etc. In *Bot. esp.* the ***foramen of an ovule*** (see quot. 1866). Also with defining name, as **foramen of Magendie** [described by François *Magendie* (1783–1855), French physiologist], the median aperture in the roof of the fourth ventricle of the brain; **foramen of Monro** [described by Alexander *Monro* (1733–1817), Scottish anatomist], a foramen in the brain connecting the third ventricle with each of the two lateral ventricles; the interventricular foramen; **foramen of Winslow** [described by Jakob Benignus *Winslow* (1669–1760), Danish anatomist], a narrow passage connecting the lesser sac and the greater sac of the peritoneal cavity of the abdomen; the epiploic foramen.

1671 GREW *Anat. Veg.* (1672) I. 3 At the thicker end of the Bean, in the outer Coat, a very small Foramen presents itself. **1682** T. GIBSON *Anat.* (1697) 20 Above, where it adheres to the Midriff, it has three foramina or holes. **1819** REES *Cycl.*, *Foramen*..a term applied to the apertures observable in some specimens of *echini*, distinct from the mouth and vent. **1826** J. & C. BELL *Anat. & Physiol. Human Body* (ed. 6) III. 274 My reader must now find his way into the marsupium, or purse of the omentum, viz. the porta omenti, the celebrated foramen of Winslow. **1826** KIRBY & SP. *Entomol.* (1828) III. xxx. 256 In many conical pupæ is the appearance of a vertical foramen. **1828** QUAIN *Elem. Anat.* (1837) 150 Round the optic foramen. **1831** R. KNOX *Cloquet's Anat.* 185 The intervertebral foramina. **1837** J. QUAIN *Elem. Anat.* (ed. 4) 901 (Index), Foramen of Monro. **1841–71** T. R. JONES *Anim. Kingd.* (ed. 4) 210 Innumerable foramina..give passage to as many tubular feet or protrusible suckers. **1866** *Treas. Bot.* s.v., The foramen of an ovule is an aperture through the integuments, allowing the passage of the pollen tubes to the nucleus. **1882** *Quain's Elem. Anat.* (ed. 9) II. 290 The roof or posterior wall [of the fourth ventricle]..is not quite complete, for there is a hole in it termed the foramen of Majendie [*sic*]. **1907** *Practitioner* Aug. 267 A hernia into the foramen of Winslow was discovered. **1910** *Ibid.* July 50 The orifice in the ependyma roofing the fourth ventricle, which is called the foramen of Magendie. **1951** J. T. & O. T. LEWIS tr. *Houssay's Human Physiol.* xxv. 226/2 Obstruction of Monro's foramen provokes dilatation in the ventricle occluded.

foraminate (fɒ'ræmɪnət), *a.* [ad. L. *forāminātus* bored, f. *forāmin-* FORAMEN.] = FORAMINATED.

foraminate (fɒ'ræmɪneɪt), *v.* [f. L. *forāmin-*, FORAMEN + -ATE[3].] *trans.* To bore, pierce, perforate.

1599 [see next]. **1668** WILKINS *Real Char.* II. ix. §4. 246 Perforate, foraminate, pierce. **1830** MAUNDER *Dict.*, *Foraminate*, to bore full of holes.

foraminated (fɒ'ræmɪneɪtɪd), *ppl. a.* [f. L. *forāmināt-us* (see FORAMINATE *a.*) + -ED[1].] Bored, pierced, perforated: see also quot. 1839.

1599 A. M. tr. *Gabelhouer's Bk. Physicke* 28/1 Fine totalle and not foraminated pearles. **1728** R. NORTH *Mem. Mus.* (1846) 37 Pipes..foraminated for changing the tone when there was occasion. **1839** ROBERTS *Dict. Geol.*, *Foraminated* ..Applied to a shell, the chambers of which are united by a small perforation or *foramen*. **1854** Woodward *Mollusca* II. 229 Orthidæ: Shell transversely oblong, depressed, rarely foraminated.

foraminifer (fɒrəˈmɪnɪfə(r)). [mod. f. L. *forāmin-*, foramen + *-fer* bearing; in F. *foraminifère*.] A rhizopod of the order *Foraminifera*.
1841–71 T. R. Jones *Anim. Kingd.* (ed. 4) 11 The young Foraminifers. **1842** Brande *Dict. Sc.* etc., *Foraminifers*..a tribe of minute shells.

‖**Foraminifera** (fɒˌræmɪˈnɪfərə), *sb. pl. Zool.* [mod.L. neut. pl. of prec.] An order of *Rhizopoda*, furnished with a shell or test, usually perforated by pores (*foramina*).
1835–6 Todd *Cycl. Anat.* I. 518/1 *note*, But M. D'Orbigny..has substituted the positive term *Foraminifera*. **1882** Geikie *Text-bk. Geol.* VI. iv. §1. 838 In some places it [nummulitic limestone] is composed mainly of foraminifera.

foraminiferal (fɒˌræmɪˈnɪfərəl), *a.* [f. as prec. + -al[1].] **a.** Pertaining to the *Foraminifera*. **b.** Consisting of or containing Foraminifera.
1865 Carpenter in *Intell. Observ.* No. 40. 278 Referable to the foraminiferal type. **1876** Page *Adv. Text-bk. Geol.* xix. 363 Foraminiferal strata. **1882** Geikie *Text-bk. Geol.* II. ii §6. 167 Calcareous (Foraminiferal) Ooze.

foraminiferous (fɒˌræmɪˈnɪfərəs), *a.* [f. as prec. + -ous.] *lit.* Furnished with foramina; said of the *Foraminifera* or their shells. Also (less correctly) = foraminiferal b.
1835–6 Todd *Cycl. Anat.* I. 114/2 The lowest foraminiferous cephalopods. **1859** J. R. Greene *Man. Anim. Kingd. Protozoa* 15 Many Foraminiferous shells. **1872** Nicholson *Palæont.* 65 Its Foraminiferous fauna. **1884** *Science* III. 591 Foraminiferous ooze.

†**foˌramiˈnose**, *a. Obs.* [ad. L. *forāminōs-us*, f. *forāmin-* foramen.] 'Full of holes'.
1727 in Bailey vol. II.

†**foˈraminous**, *a. Obs.* [f. L. *forāmin-* foramen + -ous.] Full of holes, perforated, porous.
1626 Bacon *Sylva* §215 Soft and Foraminous Bodies. **1658** Sir T. Browne *Gard. Cyrus* iii. 51 The..foraminous roundles upon the leaf. **1664** Power *Exp. Philos.* I. 8 Bespeck'd here and there with black spots..all foraminous. **1816** Faber *Orig. Pagan Idol.* III. 137 The rocky foraminous grotto.

foraminulate (fɒrəˈmɪnjʊlət), *a.* [f. next + -ate[2].] = foraminulous.
1884 in *Syd. Soc. Lex.*

foraminule (fɒˈræmɪnjuːl). [as if ad. L. **forāminul-um*, dim. of foramen.]
1866 in *Treas. Bot.* **1884** *Syd. Soc. Lex.*, *Foraminule*, the minute opening or ostiolum of the perithecium of some Fungi and Lichens, through which the spores escape.

foraminulose (fɒrəˌmɪnjuːˈləʊs), *a.* [f. as prec. + -ose.] = next.
1884 in *Syd. Soc. Lex.*

foraminulous (fɒrəˈmɪnjʊləs), *a.* [f. as prec. + -ous.] Pierced with fine holes or pores.
1664 Power *Exp. Philos.* I. 3 The eye of a Bee..black and all foraminulous. **1721** in Bailey. **1884** in *Syd. Soc. Lex.*

foran, foranent: see forne, fornent.

†**foˈraneous**, *a. Obs.*[−0] [f. med.L. *forāne-us* (Du Cange), f. *forum* market-place, court of justice + -ous.] Belonging to a market or court.
1656 in Blount *Glossogr.* **1721** in Bailey.

foranger, foringer: see forager.

foranize: see foreignize.

forarnen: see forrun in for *pref.*[1] 2 and 6 b.

forasmuch (fɒrəzˈmʌtʃ), *adv.* [The phrase *for as much*; now written as one word.] Only in the conjunctional phrase *forasmuch as*: **a.** In consideration that, seeing that, inasmuch as. Now somewhat *formal* or *arch.* In early use occasionally with ellipsis of the second *as*; rarely with substitution of *that*. †**b.** Occasionally used in the etymologically prior sense: So far as, with regard to so much as.
a. 1297 R. Glouc. (1724) 454 Vor as muche as we mowe fle in none manere. *c* **1400** Maundev. (Roxb.) Pref. 2 For as mykill as it es lang tyme passed. **1411** *Rolls of Parlt.* III. 650/2 For as myche I am a Justice. **1450–1530** *Myrr. our Ladye* 2 But for as moche as many of you..can not se what the meanynge therof ys: therefore, etc. **1606** G. W. tr. *Hist. Ivstine* 119 b, Forasmuch that this prouision made greatly for his furtherance. **1651** tr. *De las Coveras' Hist. Don Fenise* 89 Forasmuch an honest wife ought to have no other will but that of her husband. **1732** Lediard *Sethos* II. VII. 17 Forasmuch as of all the countries included under the torrid zone..those..are the most expos'd. **1818** Cruise *Digest* (ed. 2) IV. 489 Forasmuch as then the lease would never be at an end. **1879** Butcher & Lang *Odyss.* 227 My friend, forasmuch as thou utterly beliest me.
b. 1639 Ld. G. Digby *Lett. conc. Relig.* (1651) 37 For as much as belongs to that eating, we are neither defrauded of any good by not eating, nor enricht with any good by the eating of the sanctified bread, which, for as much as it hath of materials, goes into the belly. **1654** Ld. Orrery *Parthen.* (1676) 557 The latter, forasmuch as concerned his bringing off, was not difficult.

forastero (fɒræˈstɛərəʊ). [a. Sp. *forastero*, strange.] Any of a group of varieties of the cacao tree, *Theobroma cacao*.
1858 L. A. A. de Verteuil *Trinidad* vii. 262 The cacao forastero is hardier, more robust, and yields more abundantly. **1908**, **1929** [see criollo]. **1953** E. M. Chatt *Cocoa* ii. 16 Criollo means 'native' and Forastero 'foreign'. The contradistinction arose in Venezuela after the introduction of cacao trees from the West Indies, when the terms were used to denote the local and imported kinds of cacao.

†**ˈforastery.** *Obs. rare.* In 7 forastiery. [ad. It. *forestieria* of same meaning, f. *forestiere* stranger, = Med.L. *forasteri-us*, f. *foras* out of doors.] The guest-house (of a monastery).
1604 R. Parsons *3rd Pt. Three Convers. Eng.* 246 A more learned Doctor..that came sometymes as a ghest to the forastiery of the said Monastery of Bury.

†**ˈforate,** *v. Obs.* [f. L. *forāt-* ppl. stem of *forāre* to bore, pierce.] *trans.* To perforate.
1657 Tomlinson *Renou's Disp.* 105 Well covered with a paper not forated.

foray (ˈfɒreɪ), *sb.* Forms: α. 4–5 forray, (5 ferray), 5 forra, 5–7 forrey, (5 forey), 6–7 forreie, 9 foray. β. 6 forrow. [See next vb.]
1. A hostile or predatory incursion or inroad, a raid. †*in, of foray*: on a foray.
Revived in the 19th c. by Sir Walter Scott.
1375 Barbour *Bruce* II. 281 Sum sall wend to the forray. *c* **1400–20** *Judicium* (Roxb.) 7 Some at ayll howse I fande: and som of ferray. *c* **1470** Henry *Wallace* IX. 463 Thir four hundreth..A forray kest and sessit mekill gud. *c* **1540** tr. *Pol. Verg. Eng. Hist.* (Camd. No. 29) 16 The forrow was..mainteyned every waye, without resistance. **1633** T. Stafford *Pac. Hib.* I. xiii. 82 Had not our Horse been over-wearied with their long forrey. **1813** Scott *Trierm.* I. ii, The foray was long, and the skirmish hot. **1865** Livingstone *Zambesi* xxiii. 471 The continual forays of Mariano had spread ruin and desolation on our south-east.
transf. and *fig.* **1822** W. Irving *Braceb. Hall* xxv, They [the rooks] are apt now and then to issue forth from their castles on a foray. **1850** D. G. Mitchell *Rever. of Bachelor* (1852) 258 Forbid those earnest forays over the borders of Now, and on what spoils would the soul live?
†**2.** Booty taken in a foray; prey. Also *pl.*
c **1400** *Destr. Troy* 6426 Þat neuer of forray art full. *c* **1425** Wyntoun *Cron.* VIII. xl. 264 Þai na gret Forrais made. **1598** Grenewey *Tacitus' Ann.* II. vii. (1622) 148 Desirous to hunt after pillage and forreies.
†**3.** The advance-guard of an army.
c **1425** Wyntoun *Cron.* VIII. xl. 136 Willame of Dowglas, Þat Þan was Ordanyd in Forray for to pas. *c* **1470** Henry *Wallace* IX. 468 The forray tuk the pray, and past the playn, Towart the park. **1535** Stewart *Cron. Scot.* I. 339 Neirby in sicht the forrow to reskew. **1577–87** Holinshed *Chron.* III. 1216/2 The forreie was a little troubled with a fortie or fiftie Scots horssemen.

foray (ˈfɒreɪ), *v.* Forms: 4–7 forray, (4 forra, 5 forr(e)y, 6 fory, forrow, 7 furrow), 9 foray. *Pa. t.* 6–7 forrai(e)d. [ultimately from Rom. **fodro* (see forage *sb.*); the precise formation and the mutual relation of the vb. and sb. are somewhat obscure.
The supposition most free from difficulties is perh. that the sb. is f. the vb., and that the vb. is a back-formation from forayer (the forms *forrow*, *furrow*, may come from the form *furrour* of the sb.). The alternative is to regard foray *sb.* as a derivative of OF. *forrer* to forage (see forage *sb.*), and as having given rise to the Eng. vb.]
1. *trans.* To scour or ravage (a country) in search of forage or booty; to pillage; to seize and carry off (goods); to plunder the property of (a person).
Revived in the 19th c. by Sir Walter Scott.
13.. *E.E. Allit. P.* B. 1200 Stoken so strayt, Þat Þay ne stray myȝt A fote fro Þat forselet to forray no goudes. **1375** Barbour *Bruce* XV. 511 Than gert he forray all the land. **1513** Douglas *Æneis* XI. x. 62 Enee..A certane horsmen, lycht armyt for the nanis, Hes send befor for to forray the planis. **1590** Spenser *F.Q.* I. xii. 3 Dead now was their foe, which them forrayed late. **1644** D. Hume *Hist. Ho. Douglas* 167 Hee was scarce retired, when Creighton..furrowed the lands of Corstorphin. **1810** Scott *Lady of L.* IV. xxiii, When Roderick foray'd Devanside. **1852** Miss Yonge *Cameos* I. xxxix. 333 Bruce forayed Cumberland.
2. *intr.* To make a raid; to forage; to pillage.
1375 Barbour *Bruce* XIX. 643 Na we may forra for to get met. *c* **1450** *Merlin* 179 He herde telle that thei [the saisnes] come to forrey. *c* **1540** tr. *Pol. Verg. Eng. Hist.* (Camd. No. 29) 37 Certaine companies..hearing, as they forrowed abroad, spoyling the countrey, that [etc.]. **1593** *Sc. Acts Jas. VI* (1597) §174 Sum quha nightlie and dailie rieuis, forrayis, and committis open thieft. **1813** Hogg *Queen's Wake* 196 To drive the deer of Otterdale, Or foray on the Border side. **1838** Prescott *Ferd. & Is.* I. xv. II. 162 The people of Granada..foraying into the Christian territories.
Hence ˈ**foraying** *vbl. sb.*, the action of the vb.
c **1400** Maundev. (Roxb.) xxx. 135 Withouten certayne scales Þat er ordaynd for forraying. **1470–85** Malory *Arthur* V. ix. 175, I wyl that thou make the redy and goo thyder in foreyeng. **1591** Percivall *Sp. Dict.*, *Tala*, foraying, spoiling, *Depopulatio*.

forayer (ˈfɒreɪə(r)). Forms: 4 forrier, forreyer, ferrour, 4–5 forrayour, forrour, 4–6 -eour, 5 -ear, ferriour, -your, foreyour, 7 forreiar, 9 forayer. [from two different sources: ME. *forrier* is a. OF. *forrier*, (see also fourrier, furrier[1]):—med.L. type **fodrārius*, f. **fodro* fodder (see forage *sb.*); ME. *forrour*, *ferreour*, is a. OF. *forreor*, agent-n. f. *forrer* to forage. The two words coalesced, the trisyllabic forms alone surviving, and were regarded as the agent-n. belonging to foray *v.*]
1. One who forays; a forager, a raider.
c **1330** R. Brunne *Chron. Wace* (Rolls) 13228 He was cheftayn of fforreyers [*orig.* foriers]. *c* **1425** Wyntoun *Cron.* VIII. xl. 144 Ðe Forryowris Þare hard ware sete. **1600** Holland *Livy* II. xxxix. (1609) 69 Sending with forreiars certaine guides. **1805** Scott *Last Minstr.* IV. xvii, Light forayers, first, to view the ground, Spurr'd their fleet coursers loosely round.
†**2.** A fore-goer, harbinger, messenger, or courier.
1340 *Ayenb.* 195 Þe guode forriers Þet nimeÞ and agrayÞeÞ Þet hous of paradys to Þe riche manne. **1377** Langl. *P. Pl.* B. xx. 80 Kynd..sent forth his foreioures [*v.rr.* forreyours, forreouris, forreores] feures & fluxes [etc.]. **1549** *Compl. Scot.* xi. 99 Thai var re[n]contrit be the forreours and exploratours of the romanis.

forb (fɔːb). [f. Gr. φορβή fodder, forage (φέρβειν to feed).] A herbaceous plant of a kind other than grass: applied chiefly to any broad-leaved herbs growing naturally on grassland.
1924 Clements & Weaver *Exper. Vegetation* i. 21 The term 'forb' is here used for herbs other than grasses in order to afford a clear cut distinction and at the same time avoid an awkward phrase. **1952** A. W. Sampson *Range Managem.* x. 193 Forbs such as the clovers, filaree, dandelion, and cow parsnip contribute in no small way to the hay and pasture crops. **1960** N. Polunin *Introd. Plant Geogr.* xiii. 399 On well-drained banks there may be Grasses and some hardy but attractive forbs. **1970** *Nature* 25 July 340/2 High numbers of mixed-feeding or forb-feeding species may not produce economically significant damage.

†**forˈban**, *v. Obs.*[−1] In 3 forbonne. [a. OF. *forbannir*: see next.] *trans.* To banish.
a **1250** *Owl & Night.* 1093 He let forbonne Þene cniht Þat hadde idon so muchel unriht.

†**forˈbanish**, *v. Obs.* [ad. OF. *forbanniss-* lengthened stem of *forbannir*, f. *for-*, for- *pref.*[3] + *bannir* to banish.] *trans.* To banish; occas. with second obj. of place whence. Also, to dispossess, disinherit. Hence **forˈbanished** *ppl. a.*
c **1320** *Sir Beues* 4309 (MS. A) Þis for-banniiste man Is come to Þe land aȝan. *c* **1440** *Jacob's Well* 62 Þei ben outelawyd, or for-banysched Þe kynges lond. *c* **1489** Caxton *Sonnes of Aymon* iii. 79 Yf ye haue forbanysshed vs, well we know it.

†**forˈbar**, *sb. Coal-mining. Obs.* [f. for- (? *pref.*[2]) + bar *sb.*] = barrier **1 g.**
? **15..** in *N. & Q.* Ser. v. X. 307 [In Durham records (34th *Rep. Dep. Keeper P.R.* 207) is a reference to offences committed by miners in cutting through the 'forbarres' when working the mines of coal and iron ore.]

†**forˈbar, foreˈbar**, *v. Obs.* [ad. AF. *forbarrer*, f. *for-*, for- *pref.*[3] + *barrer* to bar.]
1. *trans.* To hinder, obstruct, prevent, prohibit (an action, event, etc.); to withhold (a thing).
a **1300** *Cursor M.* 8213 (Cott.) It es na thing Þat mai for-barr his will. **1303** R. Brunne *Handl. Synne* 106 Handyl Þy synnes..Elles forbarre Þey Þe blys of heune. **13..** *Coer de L.* 3514 Though he forbarre our vytayle..Off us non schal dye for hungyr. *c* **1380** Wyclif *Wks.* (1880) 66 Anticrist haÞ forbarrid Þe fredom of goddis lawe. *c* **1450** *St. Cuthbert* (Surtees) 4547 Alle on strenthe Þair thrist was sett, Oure batelle to forbarre.
b. To bar, barricade, confine (a person); to obstruct (a way).
c **1350** *Will. Palerne* 3333 Whi lete ȝe foulli ȝour fon for-barre ȝou her-inne. **1435** Misyn *Fire of Love* II. v. 78 Þe wast wildernes the way forbarris.
2. To shut out; to bar, deprive, or exclude (a person); *esp.* in *Law* (see quot. 1607). Const. *of*, *from*, and with double object.
[**1292** Britton IV. ii §11 Si homage ne le forbarre.] *c* **1330** R. Brunne *Chron.* (1810) 214 Tille ilk a lordyng suld ward & relefe falle, Bot tille Þe kyng no Þing, he was forbarred alle. **1340** Hampole *Pr. Consc.* 957 A man at Þe last forbard may be Of Þe blisful world. *c* **1430** Lydg. *Bochas* VI. i. (1554) 146 b, He was forbarred..of vittayle. **1574** tr. *Littleton's Tenures* 40 b, The Lords nor none other shalbee forbarred of theire villaines. **1586** Ferne *Blaz. Gentrie* 103 It was prouidentlye foreseene to forbarre euery person from the wearing of that coller except the Knight. **1671** F. Phillips *Reg. Necess.* 387 The Commons did Petition the King, That none of his Subjects be fore-barred of their due debts.
absol. *c* **1450** *St. Cuthbert* (Surtees) 8284 Aftir Cnud regned Edwarde, Edeldrede sonn, naman forbarde.
Hence **forˈbarring** *vbl. sb.*, the action of the vb.
c **1449** Pecock *Repr.* IV. iii. 432 Myche forbarring of synnes, which ellis wolde come forth. **1502** Arnolde *Chron.* (1811) 287 My Lorde of Winchester..in forbarring of the Kyngis hyghwaye lete drawe the chayne of the stulpis there.

†**forbate**, *a. Obs. rare*[−1]. [? f. OF. *forb-er* to counterfeit + -ate.] ? Counterfeit, imitation.
1558 *Treasurer's Acc.* in *Lauder's Tractate* (1864) Pref. 7, xxiiii ellis of forbate taffeteis of syndrie sortes of hewis.

†**forˈbathe**, *v. Obs.* [f. for- *pref.*[1] + bathe *v.*] *trans.* To bathe deeply, imbrue.
1430 Lydg. *Chron. Troy* III. xxvi, He on foote stode All forbathed in the grekes bloude. *a* **1547** Surrey *Æneid* II. 765

Troyè town.. Whose shore hath been so oft for-bath'd in blood. **1563** SACKVILLE *Induct. Mirr. Mag.* lxi., Conquerours hands forbathde in their owne blood.

forbear, forebear (fəˈbɛə(r), ˈfɔəbɛə(r)), *sb.* (Originally *Sc.*) Forms: 6 foirbear, 6–7 for(e)beer, (6 forebeerar), 5– forbear, 6– forebear. [f. FOR- *pref.*² or FORE- *pref.* + BEER *sb.*², lit. one who is or exists before.] An ancestor, forefather, progenitor (usually more remote than a grandfather).

c **1470** HENRY *Wallace* I. 21 His forbearis.. Of hale lynage, and trew lyne of Scotland. **1578–1600** *Scot. Poems 16th C.* II. 159 For in this seiknes I was borne And my forebeerars me beforne. **1623** LISLE *Ælfric on O. & N. Test.* Pref. ¶ 17 Looke back a little to this outworne dialect of our forebeers. **1782** BURNS *Death Malie* 39 So may they [sheep] like their great Forbears, For monie a year come thro the sheers. **1816** SCOTT *Antiq.* xl, This Roland Cheyne.. was my forbear. **1883** D. C. MURRAY *Hearts* I. 53 A yeoman whose forbears had once owned the land.

forbear (fəˈbɛə(r)), *v.* Pa. t. **-bore** (-ˈbɔə(r)), pa. pple. **-borne** (-ˈbɔən). Forms: see FOR *pref.*¹ and BEAR *v.*; in pa. t. also *rarely* 5 forbored, 6 -beared. [OE. *forberan* (= OHG. *far-*, *-fer-*, *forberan*, MHG. *verbern* to restrain, abstain, Goth. *frabairan* to endure, support); see FOR- *pref.*¹ and BEAR *v.*]

†**1.** *trans.* To bear, endure, submit to. *Obs.*

c **1000** ÆLFRIC *Hom.* in Grein-Wülcker *Prosa* III. 72 Se mildheorta hælend þe swa micel forbær for us synfullum. *c* **1386** CHAUCER *Merch. T.* 938, I may not.. Forbere to ben out of your compagnie. **1570** E. ELVIDEN *Newyeres Gift* 304 His bounden duetie is For to forbeare the payne. **1585** T. WASHINGTON tr. *Nicholay's Voy.* IV. i. 114 b, Hunting.. being an.. occasion to use men.. to forbeare heate and cold.

†**2.** To bear with, have patience with, put up with, tolerate. *Obs.* (but cf. sense 8).

c **897** K. ÆLFRED *Gregory's Past.* xxi. 150 Ðeah hit mon cuðlice wiete, hit is to forberanne. *c* **1000** *Ags. Gosp.* Matt. xvii. 17 Hu lange for-bere ic eow. *c* **1175** *Lamb. Hom.* 95 He.. forbere monna hufelnesse þurh his liðnesse. *a* **1225** *Ancr. R.* 218 Unðeawes, þet he er uorber ase he ham nout nuste. **1340** *Ayenb.* 148 Þanne þe guode man.. bereþ and uorbereþ alneway þe foles. **1413** *Pilgr. Sowle* (Caxton 1483) III. vi. 54 The plente of his grace that hath the forborne. **1526–34** TINDALE *Rev.* ii. 2 Thou cannest not forbeare them which are evyll. **1624** CAPT. SMITH *Virginia* III. ix. 79, I haue forborne your insolencies. **1742** YOUNG *Nt. Th.* II. 607, I then had wrote What friends might flatter: prudent foes forbear.

†**3.** To bear up against, control (emotion or desire). Also *refl.* to control one's feelings. *Obs.*

Beowulf 1877 (Gr.) Þæt he þone breostwylm forberan ne mehte. *a* **1000** *Guthlac* 775 (Gr.) [Hi] firenlustas forberað in breostum. *c* **1230** *Hali Meid.* 17 Onont ti fleschliche wil & ti licomes lust þat tu forberes her. *a* **1300** *Cursor M.* 24427 (Cott.) Quen i sagh þus all thinges skurn, vn-feland for þair lauerd murn, moght i me noght for-ber. *c* **1430** *Syr Gener.* (Roxb.) 5005 His sorow might not be forborn.

†**b.** *absol.* or *intr.* for *refl.*

c **888** K. ÆLFRED *Boeth.* xxxvi. § 1 Hwa mæȝ forbæran þæt he þæt ne siofiȝe. *c* **1175** *Lamb. Hom.* 15 Ne beo þu nefre ene wrað þer fore, ah forber for drihtenes luue. **1297** R. GLOUC. (1724) 526 The king ne miȝte tho uorbere, that he ne wep atte laste. *c* **1300** *Beket* 72 Hi ne miȝte forbere nomore; And wope also pitousliche.

†**4.** To endure the absence or privation of; to dispense with, do without, spare (a person or thing). *Obs.*

c **900** tr. *Bæda's Hist.* I. xvi. [xvii.] (1890) 70 Forþon seo æftere cneoris.. alle ȝemete is to forbeorenne & to forlætenne. *c* **1330** *Assump. Virg.* (BM. MS.) 60 Þeo þat in þe temple were Ne miȝte noȝt hire forbere. **1469** *Paston Lett.* No. 607 II. 348 Yᵗ lytyll [money] yᵗ I myght forbere.. I haue delyuᵘyd to Dawbeney. **1477** *Ibid.* No. 787 III. 175 If Syme myght be forborn it wer well done that he [etc.]. **1562** BULLEYN *Bk. Simples* 30 a, He is the beste bonde slave in the common wealthe, and least can be forborne. **1667** MILTON *P.L.* IX. 747 Fruits.. Whose taste, too long forborn, at first assay Gave elocution to the mute.

†**b.** To give up, part with or from, lose. *Obs.*

13.. *Coer de L.* 419 Hys styropes he forbare. *c* **1430** *Syr Gener.* (Roxb.) 146 Sith I haue this hert lorn, And my goode men forborn. **1430** LYDG. *Chron. Troy* I. vi, She hath forbore Her maydenhead. **1590** SPENSER *F.Q.* II. i. 53 Whenas my wombe her burdein would forbeare.

†**c.** To avoid, shun; to keep away from or keep from interfering with; to leave alone. *Obs.*

a **1300** *Cursor M.* 14560 (Cott.) Þe land o Iude he has forborn. *c* **1386** CHAUCER *Knt.'s T.* 27, I wolde yow haue toold.. But al that thyng I moot as now forbere. *c* **1470** HENRY *Wallace* I. 259 Scho.. Forbure the gate for wachis that war thar. **1581** SAVILE *Tacitus' Hist.* I. ii, Offices of honour likewise either to beare them, or forbeare them [was a capitall crime]. **1598** YONG *Diana* 220 Forbeare us a little.. for I will not have you beare witnes to the love that I have to impart. **1607** TOPSELL *Four-f. Beasts* 755 The beast it selfe liueth euermore in shadowy places, forbearing the sun. **1628** FORD *Lover's Mel.* III. ii, Forbear the room. **1673** TEMPLE *Observ. United Prov.* Wks. 1731 I. 17 The People in the Country forbear the Market.

5. To abstain or refrain from (some action or procedure); to cease, desist from.

c **1200** *Trin. Coll. Hom.* 39 Muneȝeð hem ofte unðewes to forberen and gode þeawes to folȝen. *a* **1300** *Cursor M.* 3454 (Cott.) Þat þai moght noght þair strif for-bere. *c* **1425** *Seven Sag.* (P.) 355 And I myghte forbere speche, Seven dayes and seven nyght. **1552** ABP. HAMILTON *Catech.* (1884) 30 Forbeare the eting of swynis flesche. **1655** SIR E. NICHOLAS in *N. Papers* (Camden) II. 223, I forebore pressing them further. **1722** DE FOE *Plague* (1756) 51 All public Assemblies at other Burials are to be forborn during the Continuance of this Visitation. **1810** SCOTT *Lady of L.* II. xxxiv, Madman, forbear your frantic jar! **1867** WHITTIER *Our Master* iv, The strife of tongues forbear.

6. *absol.* and *intr.* To abstain, refrain. Const. *to* (also †*but*) with *inf.*, also *from*, †*for*, †*of*.

c **1375** *XI Pains Hell* (Vernon) 110 in *O.E. Misc.* 226 To heere godus wordus þei han for-born. *c* **1400** *Rom. Rose* 4751 It is a slowe [*i.e.* a moth], may not forbere Ragges, ribaned with gold, to were. *c* **1449** PECOCK *Repr.* I. xiv. 78 Y must here therof abstene and forber. **1529** MORE *Dyaloge* IV. Wks. 286/1 On the morow forbare I to speake with hym. **1598** GRENEWEY *Tacitus' Ann.* III. v. (1622) 72 The Dictator.. forbare somtime for making any more [lawes]. **1658** W. BURTON *Comment. Itin. Antonin.* 8, I cannot forbear but transcribe all of it hither. **1676** HOBBES *Iliad* I. 402 From War forbear. *a* **1745** SWIFT *Hen. I.* Lett. 1768 IV. 278 He commanded his soldiers to forbear. **1751** JOHNSON *Rambler* No. 159 ¶ 6 Few have repented of having forborne to speak. **1787** A. HILDITCH *Rosa de Montmorien* I. 140 De Beaufort, whom Strickland could not forbear of accusing of unwarrantable caprice. **1841** ELPHINSTONE *Hist. Ind.* II. 315 He would have incurred more blame.. if he had forborne from attempting to recover them. **1878** B. TAYLOR *Deukalion* I. iv, Forbear! The knowledge must be mine alone. **1879** M. ARNOLD *Falkland* Mixed Ess. 234 The lovers of Hampden cannot forbear to extol him at Falkland's expense.

†**b.** *Naut.* (See quots.) *Obs.*

1627 CAPT. SMITH *Seaman's Gram.* vi. 27 Forbeare is to hold still any oare you are commanded. **1727–90** BAILEY, *Forbear* [Sea Term], a Word of Command in a Ship's Boat.

7. *trans.* To refrain from using, uttering, mentioning, etc.; to withhold, keep back. †Formerly const. *from*, *to*, or *dative*.

1297 R. GLOUC. (Rolls) 1355 As þe truage to rome þat non vorbore nere. *a* **1300** *Cursor M.* 693 (Gott.) Þe scorpion forbar his tunge Fra bestis þat he lay emonge. *c* **1430** LYDG. *Chichev. & Byc.* in Dodsley *O. Pl.* XII. 334 Meke wyfes.. That neither can at bedde ne boord Theyr husbondes nat forbere oon woord. **1580** TUSSER *Husb.* xiii. (1878) 29 The west [wind] to all flowers may not be forborne. **1590** MARLOWE *Edw. II*, v. v, Stay a while; forbear thy bloody hand. *a* **1619** FOTHERBY *Atheom.* I. ii. § 2 (1622) 11 Wee are forced to forbeare the strongest of our Authorities. **1676** HOBBES *Iliad* I. 206 Hold then. Your sword forbear. **1709** HEARNE *Collect.* 4 Apr., Charlet could not forbear his Venom. **1725** POPE *Odyss.* I. 437 Forbear that dear, disastrous name. **1808** SOUTHEY in *Lett.* (1856) II. 115 You may repent a sarcasm,—you never can repent having forborne one. **1884** RUSKIN *Pleasures Eng.* 16 *note*, Gibbon.. might have forborne, with grace, his own definition of orthodoxy.

b. *refl.* To restrain oneself, refrain. *rare.*

1535 COVERDALE *Esther* (Apocr.) xvi. 12 He coude not forbeare him self from his pryde. **1611** BIBLE *2 Chron.* xxxv. 21 Forbeare thee from medling with God. **1852** MISS YONGE *Cameos* I. vi. 42 If it be so, forbear thyself to fight. **1865** MERIVALE *Rom. Emp.* VIII. lxviii. 370, I forbear myself from entering the lists.

8. To abstain from injuring, punishing, or giving way to resentment against (a person or thing); to spare, show mercy or indulgence to. Now *rare*. Cf. sense 2, to which this closely approaches.

1154 *O.E. Chron.* an. 1137 Ouer sithon ne for-baren hi nouther circe ne cyrceiærd. *c* **1275** *Serm.* (Cott.) in *O.E. Misc.* 188 Þes persones ich wene, Ne beoþ heo noȝt for-bore. **1393** LANGL. *P. Pl.* C. IV. 430 He.. For-bar hym and hus beste bestes. *c* **1470** HENRY *Wallace* I. 169 No for the Pape thai wald no kyrkis forber. **1513** MORE in Grafton *Chron.* (1568) II. 765 His maister gave him in charge not to forbeare his rest. *a* **1533** LD. BERNERS *Gold. Bk. M. Aurel.* (1546) Q v b, The quycke fire doth not forbeare the wod be it wette or drye. **1606** BRYSKETT *Civ. Life* 27, I craue to be forborne in this your request. **1618** RALEIGH in *Four C. Eng. Lett.* 37, I forbare all partes of the Spanish Indies. **1665** *Sir T. Roe's Voy. E. Ind.* 438 That scruple they make in forbearing the lives of the Creatures made for men's use. **1745** *De Foe's Eng. Tradesm.* (1841) I. xiv. 125 He knows whom he may best push at, and whom best forbear. **1855** MILMAN *Lat. Chr.* (1864) V. IX. vii. 357 Those who had so long been forborne in mercy. **1887** BOWEN *Virg. Eclog.* x. 50 Ah, may the splinters icy thy delicate feet forbear!

†**b.** Const. *of* (a thing). *Obs.*

c **1275** *Passion Our Lord* 158 in *O.E. Misc.* 41 Vader.. if hit may so beo, Of þis liche calche nv forber þu me. **1529** MORE *Comf. agst. Trib.* II. Wks. 1194/1 He would pray God forbeare him of the remenaunt.

c. *intr.* (or *absol.*) To be patient or forbearing; to show forbearance. Const. *with*.

The proverbial phrase *to bear and forbear*, now taken in this sense, was orig. *trans.*: see quot. 1340 in sense 2.

1591 SHAKS. *Two Gent.* v. iv. 27 Loue, lend me patience to forbeare a while. **1683** *Apol. Prot. France* v. 66 He for-bore beyond all Patience. **1725** POPE *Odyss.* II. 247 With patience I forbear. **1782** COWPER *Mut. Forbearance*, The kindest and the happiest pair Will find occasion to forbear. **1826** E. IRVING *Babylon* II. 363 He forbore with Austria. **1842** TENNYSON *Two Voices* 218 Some.. Bore and forbore; and did not tire. **1852** MRS. STOWE *Uncle Tom's C.* xv, She.. forebore with his failings.

9. *trans.* To refrain from enforcing, pressing, or demanding; not to urge, press, insist on, or exact. Sometimes with double obj. Now *rare*. †Also *intr.* with *of*.

1570 ABP. PARKER *Corr.* (1852) 374, I am driven to forbear of my ancient rights. **1583** WHITGIFT *Let.* in Fuller *Ch. Hist.* IX. v. § 9 Desiring your Lordships.. to forbear my comming thither. **1633** FORD *'Tis Pity* III. ii, Let me advise you here to forbear your suit. **1643** PRYNNE *Sov. Power Parl.* II. 20 That all the Acts of Oxenford, should from thenceforth be utterly forborne and annulled. **1649** EVELYN *Mem.* (1857) III. 49, I desire you to forbear my reasons, till the next return. **1756** JOHNSON *Life K. of Prussia* Wks. IV. 542 The claim was forborn. **1858** CARLYLE *Fredk. Gt.* (1865) I. III. v. 170 And the Corpus-Christi idolatries were forborne the Margraf and his company this time.

b. *esp.* To abstain from enforcing the payment of (money) after it has become due. Now *rare*.

1570 *Act 13 Eliz.* c. 8 § 5 Any Money so to be lent or forborn. **1664** W. HAIG in J. Russell *Haigs* x. (1881) 273, I can have a friend here that will.. forbear it [money] a year and a half. **1674** JEAKE *Arith.* (1696) 577 If an Annuity be forborn, the Paiments increase as well as the Interest. **1827** HUTTON *Course Math.* I. 129 The money lent, or forborn, is called the Principal. **1845** STEPHEN *Comm. Laws Eng.* (1874) II. 161 Such [debts] as were incurred or forborne by means of fraud.

absol. **1856** BOUVIER *Law Dict.* s.v., When the creditor agrees to forbear with his debtor.

forˈbearable *a.* [f. FORBEAR *v.* + -ABLE.]

†**a.** Ready to forbear, patient, indulgent (*obs.*). **b.** That may be forborne or dispensed with.

1465 *Paston Lett.* No. 518 II. 216, I founde the juges ryght gentell and forberable to me. **1803** W. TAYLOR in *Ann. Rev.* I. 362 The commerce of inland towns consists in the manufacture of forbearable articles.

forbearance (fəˈbɛərəns). [f. as prec. + -ANCE.

Originally (like *abearance*) a legal term (sense 3), which accounts for the hybrid formation.]

1. The action or habit of forbearing, dispensing with, refraining or abstaining from (some action or thing). Const. *of*, *from*, *to* with *inf.*

1591 SHAKS. *1 Hen. VI*, II. iv. 19 Tut, tut, here is a mannerly forbearance. **1593** —— *Rich. II*, IV. i. 120 True Noblenesse would Learne him forbearance from so foule a Wrong. **1627–77** FELTHAM *Resolves* I. xxvi. 45 Bad, both in action, and forbearance! **1634** CANNE *Necess. Separ.* (1849) 95, I might here instance Daniel's forbearance of the king's meats. **1750** JOHNSON *Rambler* No. 19 ¶ 3 Without any.. remarkable forbearance of the common amusements of young men. **1765** H. WALPOLE *Otranto* iv. (1798) 65 His forbearance to obey would be more alarming. **1825** T. JEFFERSON *Autobiog.* Wks. 1859 I. 39 Laws which rendered criminal.. the forbearance of repairing to church. *a* **1871** GROTE *Eth. Fragm.* i. (1876) 12 The various acts and forbearances which a man supposes to constitute the sum of his duty.

2. Forbearing conduct or spirit; patient endurance under provocation; indulgence, lenity.

1599 PORTER *Angry Wom. Abingd.* (Percy Soc.) 41 Commending the vertue of patience or forbearance. **1645** BP. HALL *Remedy Discontents* 43 If their sufferings be just, my forbearances are mercifull. **1741** MIDDLETON *Cicero* II. x. 412, I have now put an end to my forbearance of him. **1831** BREWSTER *Newton* (1855) II. xxiv. 314 The man of the world treats the institutions of religion with more respect and forbearance.

3. Abstinence from enforcing what is due, *esp.* the payment of a debt.

1576 FLEMING *Panopl. Epist.* 385 You are forced (because of credit and forbearaunce) to give a greater price. **1590** RECORDE, etc. *Gr. Arts* (1640) 495 What is wonne or lost in the 100 pound forbearance for 12 moneths. **1691** LOCKE *Lower. Interest* Wks. 1727 II. 31 In Debts and Forbearances, where Contract has not settled it between the Parties. **1773** *Act 13 Geo. III*, c. 63 § 30 No Subject.. shall.. take.. above the Value of twelve Pounds for the Forbearance of one hundred Pounds for a Year. **1827** HUTTON *Course Math.* I. 129 Interest is the premium or sum allowed for the loan, or forbearance of money.

Prov. **1599** PORTER *Angry Wom. Abingd.* (Percy Soc.) 41 Forbearance is no quittance. **1667** MILTON *P.L.* x. 53 He.. soon shall find Forbearance no acquittance.

†**4.** *Comb.*: **forbearance money**, money paid to a creditor (in addition to the interest) for allowing the repayment of a loan to be deferred beyond the stipulated time.

1668 SEDLEY *Mulberry Gard.* II. ii, Thou and I might live comfortably on the forbearance money, and let the interest run on. **1751** E. HAYWOOD *Betsy Thoughtless* II. xiv. 155 It must be that she has kept it [the penalty of a bond] off by large interest and forbearance-money.

transf. (*allusively*). **1814** SCOTT *Drama* (1874) 220 Foote.. was only anxious to extort forbearance-money from the timid.

forbearant (fəˈbɛərənt), *a.* [f. as prec. + -ANT.] Forbearing, indulgent, patient.

1642 R. HARRIS *Serm. Ps.* x. 14, 17 p. 32 God is Wisdome it selfe; and therefore forbearant. **1830** *Examiner* 419/2 The temper of George IV may have been forbearant. **1859** SMILES *Self-Help* xii. (1860) 342 The world at large is not so forbearant.

Hence **forˈbearantly** *adv.*

1855 in OGILVIE Suppl., whence in mod. Dicts.

forbearer (fəˈbɛərə(r)). [f. FORBEAR *v.* + -ER¹.] One who or that which forbears.

1570 *Act 13 Eliz.* c. 8 § 5 Contracts.. whereupon is not reserved.. to the Lender, Contracter, Shifter, Forbearer or Deliverer, above the Sum of ten Pound. **1580** TUSSER *Husb.* xiii. (1878) 29 The West [wind] as a father all goodnesse doth bring, The East a forbearer, no manner of thing. **1642** J. BALL *Answ. Canne* Pref., Hee lived and dyed a strict forbearer.. of all such corruptions. **1755** JOHNSON, *Forbearer*, an intermitter; interceptor of any thing.

forbearing (fəˈbɛərɪŋ), *vbl. sb.* [f. as prec. + -ING¹.] The action of the vb. FORBEAR.

13.. *K. Alis.* 3826 There was yeve no forberyng; Bytweone favasour and kyng. **13..** *Minor Poems fr. Vernon MS.* XXXII. 780 Worschupe þou folly ffleschfadur.. And þat in two Maner of þinges: In boxumnesse and for-berynges. *c* **1440** HYLTON *Scala Perf.* (W. de W. 1494) I. lxxxi, What is synne but a wanting or a forberyng of good. **1529** *Supplic. to King* 41 Forbearinge of bodely workes & kepinge ydle holy dayes. **1533** MORE *Apol.* xii. 91 b, The leuyng out of felonye, sacrylege, & murder, is rather a token of wylynes then any forbering or fauour. **1570** *Act 13 Eliz.* c. 8 §5 The Loan or forbearing of a hundred Pound for one Year. **1641** HINDE *J. Bruen* v. 16 The for-bearing of meats and drinks. **1659** HAMMOND *On Ps.* x. 13 Paraphr. 55 Thy longanimity in forbearing of wicked men.

forbearing (fəˈbɛərɪŋ), *ppl. a.* [f. as prec. + -ING².] That forbears; patient under provocation, long-suffering; †abstinent.

c **1425** *Eng. Conquest Irel.* xxxvi. (1896) 88 He was..[of] mete, & of drynke ful meen & for-berynge. **1611** BIBLE *2 Tim.* ii. 24 The seruant of the Lord must not striue: but bee gentle vnto all men..patient [*marg.* Or, forbearing]. **1782** COWPER *Table T.* 401 There is a time..For long-forbearing clemency to wait. **1853** C. BRONTË *Villette* x. (1876) 85 Madame Beck was..forbearing with all the world.

Hence **for'bearingly** *adv.*, **for'bearingness**.

1831 *Examiner* 660/2 The fitness of whipping Mr. Muir was..forbearingly negatived. **1855** CLARKE *Dict.*, *Forbearingness.* **1874** HELPS *Soc. Press.* xxv. (1875) 406 Considerations of pity, tenderness, and forbearingness.

†**for'beat**, *v. Obs.* For forms see BEAT *v.* [f. FOR- *pref.*¹ + BEAT *v.*] **a.** *trans.* To beat severely; to cover with bruises or stripes. **b.** To beat down, overcome. **c.** *pa. pple.* only. Of a path: Well-beaten or trodden.

1393 LANGL. *P. Pl.* c. xxiii. 198 So elde and hue hit hadde a-feynted and forbete. *c* **1420** *Anturs of Arth.* li, Alle blake was thayre brees, forbetun with brandis. *c* **1430** *Hymns Virg.* (1867) 29 Al his fleisch bloodi for-bete. *c* **1430** *Pilgr. Lyf Manhode* ii. lxxii. (1869) 103 Thou art not the firste pilgrime ..the wey is al forbeten. *c* **1470** HARDING *Chron.* xxxiv. v, This king..Came home agayn..All for-beten.

forbecause: see BECAUSE A. 1 and B. 1.

†**'forbed**, *ppl. a.* [f. *forbe, a. OF. *forbir* (see FURBISH *v.*) + -ED¹.] = FURBISHED.

1413 *Pilgr. Sowle* (Caxton 1483) iv. xxxvi. 84 The honoure of suche persones is clene forbed harneys.

†**forbe'hest.** *Obs.*⁻¹ [f. FOR- *pref.*² + BEHEST.] A promise previously given.

a **1400** *Prymer* in Maskell *Mon. Rit.* (1875) II. 75 That we be maad worthi to the forbiheestis of crist.

forbesite (ˈfɔːbzaɪt). *Min.* [ad. G. *forbesit* (A. Kenngott *Uebersicht d. Resultate min. Forschungen 1862–1865* (1868) 47), f. the name of David *Forbes* (1828–76), English geologist and explorer, who first analysed it: see -ITE¹.] A hydrated arsenate of nickel and cobalt found in the Atacama desert, Chile, as greyish-white crusts.

1868 J. D. DANA *Syst. Min.* (ed. 5) 560 D. Forbes describes..a mineral occurring in the desert of Atacama in veins in a decomposed dioryte... Kenngott names it Forbesite. **1935** J. W. MELLOR *Inorg. & Theoret. Chem.* XIV. 424 The cobalt minerals include..Forbesite, $H_2(Ni,Co)_2(AsO_4)_2 \cdot 8H_2O$.

†**for'bid**, *sb. Obs. rare.* [f. next vb.] A forbidding. (Cf. FORBODE *sb.*)

1602 W. WATSON *Decacordon* 338 For what is more innouate preposterous, and beyond all gods forbid, then this new fanglenes in you to prefer [etc.]. **1740** CHEYNE *Regimen* ii. 72 With what an evident Forbid, the Jewish Law directs this permit of animal Food.

forbid (fəˈbɪd), *v.* Pa. t. **forbad**, **forbade** (-ˈbæd); pa. pple. **forbidden** (-ˈbɪd(ə)n). Forms: *Infin.* 1–2 forbéodan (*north.* forbéada), 2–4 forbeoden, 3–5 forbede(n, -yn, (4 -bedd, -beed, 5 -bidde, -bide, -byde), 4–6 *Sc.* forbeid, (7 forbidd), 4– forbid. *Pa. t.* 1 forbéad, 2–3 forbead, (3 -bæd, -bet(t), 3–5 forbed(e, forbode, (4 -baad, -badde, -bed, -beed), 5 -bat (6, 7 -bod(de), 6–8 forbid, 4– forbad, forbade. *Pa. pple.* 1 forboden, 3–6 forbode(n, (5 -bade, -bed(e), 5–8 forbod(de(n, 6–9 forbid, 6– forbidden. Also weak *pa. t.* 4 forbedde, -bedid, *pa. pple.* 5 forbedd. [OE. *forbéodan*, pa. t. *forbéad*, pl. *-budon*, pa. pple. *forboden*, f. FOR- *pref.*¹ + *béodan* to BID; = OFris. *forbiada*, Du. *verbieden*, OHG. *far-*, *forpiotan* (MHG. and Ger. *verbieten*), Goth. *faurbiudan*. Cf. ON. *fyrirbióða*.]

1. *trans.* To command (a person or persons) not to do, have, use, or indulge in (something), or not to enter (a place); to prohibit. In many diverse constructions.

a. with double object, of the person (orig. *dative*), and of the thing prohibited. Also in *pass.* with either the person or the thing as subject; in the latter case, the indirect obj., if a sb., is preceded by *to*.

O.E. Chron. an. 1048 And cwæð þet se papa hit him forboden hæfde. *a* **1175** *Cott. Hom.* 223 Hwi for-bead ȝeu god þes trowes westm. *c* **1250** *Gen. & Ex.* 2984 Anon ðis folc fore he for-bead. *a* **1300** *Cursor M.* 13029 (Cott.) He for-bedd him þat womman. *c* **1330** R. BRUNNE *Chron. Wace* (Rolls) 9158 He..þat þeym þe lond furst forbede. *c* **1386** CHAUCER *Wife's Prol.* 519 Forbeed us thing, and that desire we. *c* **1394** *P. Pl. Crede* 769 God wold..fals freres [wer] forboden þe fayre ladis chaumbres! **1450–1530** *Myrr. our Ladye* 21 That is forboden vs by holy chirche. **1529** RASTELL *Pastyme, Hist. Rom.* (1811) 29 It was ordeynyd that preestis Grekes myght haue wyfis, which to preestis Latens was forboden. **1597** SHAKS. *Lover's Compl.* 164 To be forbid the sweets that seemes so good. **1609** DOULAND *Ornith. Microl.* 20 There be some other Interuals, very rare, and forbidden to yong beginners. **1697** DRYDEN *Æneid* vi. 760 The chaste and holy Race Are all forbidden this polluted Place. **1710** LADY M. W. MONTAGU *Let. Burnet* 20 July, My sex is usually forbid studies of this nature. **1793** COWPER *On Spaniel Beau* ii, Against my orders, whom you heard Forbidding you the prey. **1838** LYTTON *Leila* i. ii, When strength and courage are forbid me. **1849** MACAULAY *Hist. Eng.* II. 351 The archbishop..had long been forbidden the court. **1853** J. H. NEWMAN *Hist. Sk.* (1873) II. i. iv. 187 Their [the Turks'] religion forbids them every sort of painting. **1865** DICKENS *Mut. Fr.* i. vi, Will you forbid him the house where I know he is safe?

b. with personal object (in OE. either *dat.* or *accus.*) and an infinitive (formerly with *for to*; rarely without *to*) as second object.

c **1000** *Ags. Gosp.* Matt. xix. 14 Nelle ȝe hiȝ for-beodan cuman to me. *c* **1200** ORMIN 6499 Till Herode king onnȝænn He þeȝȝm forrbæd to turrnenn. *a* **1225** *Ancr. R.* 54 Þe eppel þæt ich loke on is forbode me to etene, & nout forto biholden. **1382** WYCLIF *Acts* xvi. 6 Thei..weren forbodyn of the Hooly Gost for to speke the word of God in Asya. *c* **1450** tr. *De Imitatione* i. xxv, He lackiþ inwarde comfort, & he is forboden to seke eny outwarde. **1562** BULLEYN *Dial. Soarnes & Chir.* 42b, We be also forboden to use repercussiues. **1611** SHAKS. *Wint. T.* i. ii. 427 You may as well Forbid the Sea for to obey the Moone. *a* **1618** J. DAVIES *Wits Pilgr.* (Grosart) 19/1 But..I am forbod..to tell it you. **1817** LD. ELLENBOROUGH in Maule & Selwyn *Rep.* VI. 316 He distinctly forbids the defendants to accept any more of their drafts.

†**c.** with personal obj. and negative clause. *Obs.*

O.E. Chron. an. 675 Swa ic for beode þe and ealle þe biscopas þe æfter ðe cumon..þæt ȝe nan onsting ne hauen of þæt mynstre. *a* **1225** *Ancr. R.* 256 Ich forbeode ou þet non of ou ne ileue þes deofles sondesmon. *c* **1275** *Passion* 581 in *O.E. Misc.* 53 Iesus..hire þo for-bed, þat heo attryne ne scolde his honde ne his fet. **1387** TREVISA *Higden* (Rolls) I. 85 By þese trees þe grete kyng Alexander was forbode, þat he schulde neuere come in Babylon. **1599** SHAKS. *Pass. Pilgr.* 124 She silly Queene..Forbad the boy he should not passe those grounds.

d. with omission of personal object, and with the thing prohibited expressed (*a*) by sb. or pron. (†const. *from*); (*b*) by an infinitive; (*c*) by an obj.-sentence (in early use with a negative, which the later idiom omits); (*d*) by object and infinitive.

(*a*) *c* **1175** *Lamb. Hom.* 115 He scal..heordom for-beodan. *c* **1200** *Trin. Coll. Hom.* 13 Þe holie boc hit forbet. **1340** *Ayenb.* 8 Ine þis heste ys uorbede zenne of hate. **1477** NORTON *Ord. Alch.* i. in Ashm. (1652) 15 Almighty God From Great Doctours hath this Science forbod. **1533** ELYOT *Cast. Helthe* (1539) 78b, Wyne is not to be forboden. **1671** LADY M. BERTIE in *12th Rep. Hist. MSS. Comm.* App. v. 23 They say the King hath put out a Proclamation to for-bid maskerades. **1730** A. GORDON *Maffei's Amphith.* 67 In the Year 325, Gladiators were expressly forbid. **1875** JOWETT *Plato* (ed. 2) V. 34, I..think that the Lacedaemonian lawgiver was right in forbidding pleasure.

(*b*) **13..** *E.E. Allit. P.* B. 1147 To defowle hit euer vpon folde fast he forbedes. **1526–34** TINDALE *Luke* xxiii. 2 Forbiddynge to paye tribute to Cesar. **1723** *State of Russia* II. 282 For which reason he had forbidden to carry anybody of his Majesty's Retinue over the River.

(*c*) *c* **1000** *Ags. Gosp.* Luke xxiii. 2 For-beodende þæt man þam casere gafol ne sealde. **1297** R. GLOUC. (1724) 496 The king..vorbed that me ne ssolde non of is lond sowe. **1340** *Ayenb.* 8 Þis heste uorbyet þet non ne ssel slaȝe oþren. **1450–1530** *Myrr. our Ladye* 71 Yt is forboden vnder payne of cursynge, that no man shulde haue ne drawe eny texte of holy scrypture in to Englysshe. **1619** BRENT tr. *Sarpi's Counc. Trent* iv. (1629) 355 It was forbid..that the Patrone ..should not make the presentation to any but the Bishop. **1658** W. BURTON *Comment. Itin. Antonin.* 121 He forbad that not any body should..use a silver drinking cup.

(*d*) **1382** WYCLIF *Luke* xxiii. 2 Forbedinge tributis to be ȝouun to Cesar. **1651** HOBBES *Leviath.* ii. xxvi. 137 Another Law, that forbiddeth it to be put in execution. **1763** J. BROWN *Poetry & Mus.* v. 75 This [the Swiss] Song..is forbid to be sung among their Regiments hired in the Service of other Nations. **1865** KNIGHT *Sch. Hist. Eng.* iv. 115 The governor of the Castle forbad the Church Service to be performed.

e. with the personal object only. Const. *from*, †*of* (a thing). Now *rare*.

c **1175** *Lamb. Hom.* 27 He þe wule forbeode of his eȝane onsiht. **13..** *Coer de L.* 3795 In Godys name I thee for-bede ..Ryche ne pore lat non leve. *c* **1400** MAUNDEV. (1839) viii. 87 Therefore wolde he [David] make the Temple in that place: but oure Lord forbade him. **1526** *Pilgr. Perf.* (W. de W. 1531) 8b, I forbede all syngular persones from the studyenge of this treatyse. **1533** J. HEYWOOD *Pardoner & F.* B ij b, Of all temporall seruice are we forbode. **1596** SPENSER *F.Q.* vi. vi. 18 Whom though he oft forbad, Yet for no bidding..Would he restrayned be from his attendement. **1840** THIRLWALL *Greece* VII. 117 The soldiers wished to take part in it also; and, though forbidden, forced their way into the palace. **1841** LANE *Arab. Nts.* I. 122 He forbade both men and women from entering them. **1851** HUSSEY *Papal Power* ii. 61 He forbad Hilary Bishop of Narbonne from all metropolitan rights.

f. *absol.* or with ellipsis of both objects.

1591 SHAKS. *1 Hen. VI*, i. iii. 19 Haue patience Noble Duke, I may not open, The Cardinall of Winchester forbids! **1667** MILTON *P.L.* v. 62 Forbid who will, none shall from me withhold Longer thy offerd good.

2. In various modified uses.

a. *fig.* To exclude, keep back, hinder, restrain. Now chiefly of circumstances, conditions, etc.: To constitute a prohibition or imperative reason against; to render impossible or undesirable.

c **1000** *Ags. Ps.* cxix. 101 (Spelm.) Fram eallum weȝe yfelu ic forbead fet mine. *a* **1340** HAMPOLE *Psalter* xxxiii. 13 For bede þi tonge fra ill. **1388** WYCLIF *Jer.* v. 25 Ȝoure synnes forbediden good fro ȝou. **1573** BARET *Alv.* F 847 To forbidde, to lette, to stoppe, *inhibeo*. **1626** BACON *Sylva* §596 The way to hasten the Breeding of Salt-Petre, is to forbid the Sunne, and the Growth of Vegetables. **1697** DRYDEN *Virg. Georg.* iii. 740 Clouds of smouldring Smoke forbad the Sacrifice. **1715–20** POPE *Iliad* xii. 148 Whose spreading arms..Forbid the tempest and protect the ground. **1750** GRAY *Elegy* xvii, Th' Applause of list'ning Senates to command..Their Lot forbad. **1799** SHERIDAN *Pizarro* iv. i, The state I left her in forbids all hope. **1863** FR. A. KEMBLE *Resid. in Georgia* 19 A pool, that effectually forbids the foot of the explorer. **1869** J. MARTINEAU *Ess.* II. 138 His limits forbade him to draw copiously. **1870** HUXLEY *Crit. & Addr.* (1890) 51 The Bible..forbids the veriest hind..to be ignorant of the existence of other countries and other civilizations.

b. In deprecatory phr. ***God, Heaven, the Lord forbid***, usually with a clause or sentence as direct object, rarely with an indirect object; also *absol.* as an exclamation.

a **1225** *Ancr. R.* 8 Þet God forbeode ou. *a* **1300** *Cursor M.* 4372 (Cott.) Godd forbedd i suld him suike. **1375** BARBOUR *Bruce* xii. 255, I warne ȝow of a thing, To happyn thamme (as god forbeid!) *c* **1385** CHAUCER *L.G.W.* 910 *Thisbe*, God forbede but a woman can Ben as trewe and lovynge as a man. *a* **1400–50** *Alexander* 5590 Nay, driȝtin for-bede! *c* **1470** HENRY *Wallace* v. 624 Gret God forbede it suld be so with this. **1513** MORE in Grafton *Chron.* (1568) II. 760 Our Lorde forbid that ye love together the worsse for the selfe same cause that ye ought to love together the better. *c* **1592** MARLOWE *Massacre Paris* i. iii, The Heavens forbid your highness such mishap! **1601** SHAKS. *Twel. N.* ii. ii. 19 Fortune forbid my out-side haue not charm'd her. **1606** —— *Tr. & Cr.* ii. iii. 208 This L[ord] goe to him? Jupiter forbid. **1611** BIBLE *1 Chron.* xi. 19 My God forbid it mee that I should doe this thing. —— *Gal.* ii. 7 God forbid. **1712–4** POPE *Rape Lock* iv. 105 Gods! shall the ravisher display your hair, While the Fops envy..Honour fobid! **1738** —— *Epil. Sat.* i. 105 Good Heav'n forbid, that I should blast their glory. **1875** JOWETT *Plato* (ed. 2) I. 34 Do you mean a knowledge of shoemaking? God forbid.

†**c.** with weakened sense: To argue or give one's opinion against. *Obs.*

c **1205** LAY. 30244 Summe hit gonnen ræden summe to for-beoden.

†**d.** To deny, refuse. *Obs.*

c **1000** *Ags. Gosp.* Luke vi. 29 Ne for-beod him no þine tunecan. *c* **1205** LAY. 30226 Whaðer he hit wolde iunne oðer him for-beode. **1483** *Cath. Angl.* 137/2 To Forbed, *abdicare, abnuere*.

†**e.** To defy, challenge.

1588 BP. ANDREWES *Serm.* 1 Tim. vi. 17–19, I forbid them ..to shew mee in Rhemes or in Rome..such a shew as we have seene here these last two daies.

†**f.** To lay under a ban, curse, interdict.

1605 SHAKS. *Macb.* i. iii. 21 He shall liue a man forbid. **1819** B. CORNWALL *Dram. Scenes, Werner* ii, Oh, I shall pass ..my time in solitude..a man forbidden.

†**3.** To countermand. *Obs. rare.*

1665 SIR W. COVENTRY in *Pepys' Diary* VI. 106 Some [ships] were ordered and others forbid.

†**4.** To put off for a time, to postpone. *Obs.*

[Perh. another word (?**for-bide*), or an erroneous use: Caxton has *forborn*, which expresses the sense.]

1387 TREVISA *Higden* (Rolls) II. 339 Iosue..renewede þe circumsicioun þat was forbode fourty ȝere in wyldernesse. *Ibid.* III. 51 Olympiades..was i-holde ones in fyue ȝere, lesth he schulde be forȝete and it were lengere forbode.

†**for'bid**, *ppl. a. Obs.* = FORBIDDEN. **forbid tree** (see quot. 1662).

1592 DAVIES *Immort. Soul* Introd. vii, By tasting of that Fruit forbid. **1662** PEPYS *Diary* 14 Aug., Many trees there [Forest of Dean] left at a great fall in Edward the Third's time, by the name of forbid-trees, which at this day are called vorbid trees.

†**for'biddable**, *a. Obs.*⁻¹ [f. FORBID *v.* + -ABLE.] That may be forbidden.

c **1449** PECOCK *Repr.* 470 In which thei ben forbedable.

for'biddal. *nonce-wd.* [f. FORBID *v.* + -AL¹.] The act of forbidding.

1835 LYTTON *Rienzi* iii. ii, Nay, sweet lady mine, no forbiddal!

forbiddance (fəˈbɪdəns). [f. as prec. + -ANCE.] The action of forbidding, an instance of this; prohibition, interdiction; also, a command or edict against (something).

1608–11 BP. HALL *Epist.* v, Forbiddance doth but whet desire. **1739** CIBBER *Apol.* (1756) I. 180 This absolute forbiddance of what they had more mind to have been entertain'd with. **1855** R. BOYLE *B. v. Wiseman* 26 The act of forbiddance to say mass. **1873** OUIDA *Pascarèl* I. 98 My father's forbiddance had taken from me many of my old pleasures.

forbidden (fəˈbɪd(ə)n), *ppl. a.* [pa. pple. of FORBID *v.*] **a.** In senses of the vb.

c **1200** *Trin. Coll. Hom.* 35 Þe forbodene appel. *a* **1300** *Cursor M.* 19861 (Cott.) Forboden beistes war [*sc.* þai] in lede. *c* **1465** *Eng. Chron.* (Camden 1856) 57 That the said maister Thomas sholde say massis in forboden..placez. **1513** DOUGLAS *Æneis* i. ix. 128 Quhen scho to Troy forbodyn hymeneus socht. **1588** SHAKS. *L.L.L.* ii. i. 26 Before we enter his forbidden gates. **1619** BRENT tr. *Sarpi's Counc. Trent* iii. (1629) 293 To eate..forbidden meates, in Lent. **1782** COWPER *Retirem.* 216 His hours of leisure.. employs In drawing pictures of forbidden joys. *a* **1839** PRAED *Poems* (1864) II. 109, I entered that forbidden room.

b. *spec.* ***forbidden degrees***, certain degrees of relationship within which persons are forbidden to marry; ***forbidden fruit***, (*a*) that forbidden to Adam (Gen. ii. 17), also *fig.*; (*b*) hence, a name given to several varieties of *Citrus*, esp. *C. decumana*; ***forbidden line***, a spectral line produced by a forbidden transition; †*forbidden time* (*Sc. Law*), the close time for fish; *forbidden transition*, a transition between two states of a quantum-mechanical system (as a molecule, atom, or nucleus) that does not conform to some selection rules, esp. those for electric dipole radiation from an unperturbed system.

1609 SKENE *Quon. Attach.* lxxxvii. *heading*, Of forbiddin Tyme in Fishing. **1662** STILLINGFL. *Orig. Sacr.* III. iii. §5 He required from him the observance of that positive command of not eating of the forbidden fruit. **1663** *Flagellum or O. Cromwell* (ed. 2) 5 The stealing and tasting of the forbidden fruit of Soveraignty. **1818** M. G. LEWIS *Jrnl. W. Ind.* (1834) 212 Some sweet oranges, others bitter ones, others again forbidden fruit. **1858** SIMMONDS *Dict. Trade*, *Pomelloes*, a name under which forbidden fruit is sometimes sold in this country by fruiterers. **1866** *Treas. Bot.*, Forbidden Fruit *Citrus Paradisi*.—(of London) a variety of the shaddock *C. decumana*. **1872** *Gloss. Eccl. Terms* (ed. Shipley), *Forbidden Degrees*. **1923** H. L. BROSE tr. *Sommerfeld's Atomic Struct. & Spectral Lines* vi. 366 The forbidden lines.. belong to transitions in which n_i jumps by two or.. by three units. *Ibid.* 367 In the combinations (sp_i) in the H.S. or the II N.S. no forbidden transitions occur. **1939** J. W. T. SPINKS tr. *Herzberg's Molecular Spectra & Molecular Struct.* I. v. 305 Another forbidden transition, also involving magnetic dipole radiation, has been observed for oxygen. **1957** *Encycl. Brit.* II. 591/1 The two strong green lines in the spectra of the gaseous nebulae prove to be forbidden lines of doubly ionized oxygen.

Hence **for'biddenly** *adv.*; **for'biddenness**.

1611 SHAKS. *Wint. T.* I. ii. 417 He thinkes.. that you haue toucht his Queene Forbiddenly. **1647** BOYLE *Disc. agst. Swearing* vii. Wks. 1772 VI. 10 Since the sinfulness of swearing does consist, not in the diversity of our oaths, but in their forbiddenness. **1744** BIRCH *Life Boyle* 41 Nothing but the forbiddenness of self-dispatch hindered his acting it.

forbidder (fəˈbɪdə(r)). [f. FORBID *v.* + -ER[1].] One who forbids.

*c***1449** PECOCK *Repr.* v. ii. 92 Forbeders whiche wolden forbede wedding. **1526** *Pilgr. Perf.* (W. de W. 1531) 253 A forbydder of the trybute to be payed to Cesar. **1643** MILTON *Divorce* II. xx. (1851) 118 The Papists.. are the strictest forbidders of divorce. **1849** CURZON *Visits Monast.* i. 10 Another attendant upon public men, who.. is called a yassakji, or forbidder.

forbidding (fəˈbɪdɪŋ), *vbl. sb.* [see -ING[1].] The action of the vb. FORBID; a prohibition.

*a***1300** *Cursor M.* 20527 (Cott.) He ete ogain mi forbidding. *c***1380** WYCLIF *Wks.* (1880) 85 þis forbedyng is colourid by holynesse. **1601** DONNE *Progr. Soul* ix. Poems (1633) 5 Her whom the first man did wive, Whom, and her race, only forbiddings drive. **1667** MILTON *P.L.* IX. 753 But his forbidding Commends thee more. **1740** CHEYNE *Regimen* 142 It amounts almost to a total Forbidding.

forbidding (fəˈbɪdɪŋ), *ppl. a.* [see -ING[2].]

1. That forbids, in senses of the vb.

1573 BARET *Alv.* F 849 Forbidding, *vetans*. **1667** MILTON *P.L.* II. 475 But they Dreaded not more th' adventure then his voice Forbidding.

2. *esp.* That forbids, or disinclines to, a nearer approach; repellent, repulsive, uninviting:

a. chiefly of a person, his manner, looks, etc.

1712 BUDGELL *Spect.* No. 301 ¶2 That awful Cast of the Eye and forbidding Frown. **1717** BERKELEY *Tour in Italy* 3 June Wks. 1871 IV. 560 Doors and entrances of the houses dirty and forbidding. **1837** M. DONOVAN *Dom. Econ.* II. 199 A forbidding-looking creature. **1840** DICKENS *Old C. Shop* iii, An elderly man of remarkably hard features and forbidding aspect. **1863** FR. A. KEMBLE *Resid. in Georgia* 21, I do not know that I ever saw any winged creature of so forbidding an aspect.

b. of a country, sea-coast, the weather, etc.

1726 SHELVOCKE *Voy. round World* (1757) 280 Although the land is so desart and forbidding. **1856** KANE *Arct. Expl.* II. xxvi. 264 We saw the same forbidding wall of belt-ice. **1860** *Merc. Marine Mag.* VII. 262 The coast.. is exceedingly rocky and forbidding. **1887** T. HARDY *Woodlanders* II. i. 8 The morning looked forbidding enough.

Hence **for'biddingly** *adv.*; **for'biddingness**.

1848 CRAIG, *Forbiddingly*. **1880** KINGLAKE *Crimea* VI vi. 75 The.. Ravine.. [was] forbiddingly hard to crest. **1883** E. P. ROE in *Harper's Mag.* Dec. 45/1 The Beacon hills.. frown forbiddingly.

†**for'bind**, *v. Obs.* [OE. *forbindan*, f. FOR- *pref.*[1] + *bindan* to BIND.] *trans.* To bind up.

*c***897** K. ÆLFRED *Gregory's Past.* xvi. 104 Ne forbinde ȝe no ðæm ðerscendum oxum ðone muð. *a***1200** in *Fragm. Ælfric's Gloss.* (1838) 5 þæt wrecche wif.. forbindeþ þæs dædan muþ. *c***1200** ORMIN 4524 Itt forrbindeþþ all þweorrt ut & blendeþþ manness heorrte.

†'**forbirth**. *Obs. rare.* In 4 forbirth(e, -burth(e. [f. FOR- *pref.*[2] + BIRTH. Cf. Ger. *vorgeburt*.]

a. Birthright. **b.** The first-born.

*a***1300** *Cursor M.* 3518 (Cott.) Esau his forbirth sald. *Ibid.* 6091 (Gött.) All þe for-birthis sal i sla.

forbish, obs. form of FURBISH.

†**for'bite**, *v. Obs.* Pa. t. 3 forbat, -bot. [f. FOR- *pref.*[1] + BITE *v.*; = Du. *verbijten*, Ger. *verbeiszen*.] *trans.* To bite. Also *transf.* and *fig.*

*c***1205** LAY. 6497 þat deor.. ræsde o þene stede and forbat him þa breste. **1297** R. GLOUC. (Rolls) App. 76 þat luþer dur op sturte forbot his stedes breste. **1377** LANGL. *P. Pl.* B. XVI. 35 The Flesshe is a fel wynde.. forbiteth the blosmes. **1586** J. HOOKER *Girald. Irel.* in *Holinshed* II. 87/2 When his braines are forebitten with a bottle of nappie ale.

forblack: see FOR- *pref.*[1] 10.

†**for'bleed**, *v. Obs.* [f. FOR- *pref.*[1] + BLEED. Cf. Ger. *verbluten*.] In *pa. pple.* **for'bled**: exhausted with bleeding; covered with blood.

*a***1300** *Cursor M.* 24395 (Cott.) Quen þat mi sun was al for-bled. **1387** TREVISA *Higden* (Rolls) VII. 35 He was i-drawe al aboute þe feeldes.. al forbled. **1470–85** MALORY *Arthur* X. xxx, Sir Tristram waxte faynte and forbledde. **1496** *Dives & Paup.* (W. de W.) VI. xv. 257/2 He sente home his sharte full of woundes and of holes and all forbleded. **1535** STEWART *Cron. Scot.* (1858) I. 306 All the laif, rycht bludie and forbled, Tha left the feild.

†**for'blend**, *v.*[1] *Obs.*[−1] [f. FOR- *pref.*[1] + BLEND *v.*[1]; = Ger. *verblenden*.] *trans.* To blind.

*c***1200** ORMIN 2985 Sinne.. Forrblendeþþ all þin heorrte.

†**for'blend**, *v.*[2] *Obs.*[−1] [f. FOR- *pref.*[1] + BLEND *v.*[2]] *trans.* To confound.

*a***1300** *Cursor M.* 18056 (Cott.) Min wicked werkes eke For-blended wer thoru his aun speke.

forbliss: see FOR- *pref.*[1] 9.

†**for'blow**, *v. Obs.* [OE. *forblawan*, f. FOR- *pref.*[1] + *blawan* to BLOW.] *trans.* **a.** To blow about or away. **b.** To blow out, inflate.

*c***893** K. ÆLFRED *Oros.* v. iv. §5 Com an wind, ond forbleow hie ut on sæ. *c***1000** *Sax. Leechd.* II. 240 Gif mon sie forblawen. **1393** GOWER *Conf.* I. 160 The ship.. is forstormed and forblowe. **1413** *Pilgr. Sowle* (Caxton 1483) III. ii. 50 A grete bely ful of wynd forbolned and forblowen.

Hence **for'blown**, **for'blowing** *ppl. adjs.*

14.. LYDG. *Life V.M.* xviii. (1484) C vj, With your forblowe blowying vanyte. [*MS. Ashm.* 39 f. 28 b, has;—youre for-blowynge vanite.]

†**for'bode**, *sb. Obs.* exc. *arch.* Forms: 1–6 forbod (6 forbodd), 3–7, 9 forbode, 3, 5 forbot (5 -bote), 5–6 forbott. [OE. *forbod*. f. *forbéodan* to FORBID; = Du *verbod*, MHG., mod.Ger. *verbot*, ON. *forboð*.] A forbidding; a prohibition, interdiction, prohibitory ordinance. *to lay in forbode*: to put under prohibition, to prohibit.

*a***1000** *Pol. Laws Ælfred* xli, Gewitnes þæt hit þara manna forbod wære. *c***1200** *Trin. Coll. Hom.* 11 No prest ne mai him chastien, ne mid forbode, ne mid scrifte, ne mid cursinge. *a***1300** *Cursor M.* 765 (Cott.) Our lauerd in forbot has it laid. *c***1449** PECOCK *Repr.* III. iii. 291 If eny oon forbode, maad in Iewis lawe to preestis, schulde binde also Cristen preestis. **1548** UDALL, etc. *Erasm. Par. Luke* vi. 73 Why dooe ye this geare whiche it is against all gods forbod to dooe on the Sabboth daies. **1626** AINSWORTH *Annot. Pentat.* Exod. xx. 3 Gods forbode bindeth most strictly and alwayes.

b. *to pass, be above* or *beyond, God's forbode*: said of anything outrageous or extravagant.

1515 MORE *K. Rich. III*, in Grafton *Chron.* II. 826 King Richarde, whome he.. had holpen, susteyned and set forward above all Gods forbode. *a***1529** SKELTON *Image Hypocr.* Wks. II. 425 It passeth Godes forbod That ever it should be. **1596** NASHE *Saffron Walden* Wks. (Grosart) III. 99 He is beyond all reason, or Gods forbod, distractedly enamourd of his own beautie. **1602** W. WATSON *Decacordon* 247 Marry the course that was held by them passeth all Gods forbod: as our phrase is.

c. (*over*) *God's forbode* = God forbid.

1377 LANGL. *P. Pl.* B. VII. 176 Lordes forbode ellis! *c***1460** *Towneley Myst.* (Surtees) 12 Over Godes forbot be to the Thank or thew to kun me. **1598** FLORIO, *Diácene*, god forbid, gods forbode. **1820** SCOTT *Ivanhoe* x, 'Over God's forbode!' said Prince John.

d. A use of this phrase as an asseveration.

1575 *Durham Deposit.* (Surtees) 303 Who toke upon hir then, with mony oothe and forbotts, that ther was never man that was fawter with hir.

†**for'bode**, *v. Obs. rare.* [f. prec. sb.; cf. ON. *forboða*.] = FORBID.

*c***1400** *Destr. Troy* 6428 Forbode the firke þi fode for to wyn. *c***1475** *Rauf Coilȝear* 746 The curagious knichtis bad haue him to hing.. 'God forbot' he said, 'my thank war sic thing To him that succourit my lyfe!'

forbolned: see FOR- *pref.*[1] 6.

†**for'bow**, *v. Obs.* [OE. *forbúȝ-an*, f. FOR- *pref.*[1] + *búȝ-an* to BOW.] *trans.* To pass by or avoid by making a circuit; to shun.

*a***1000** *Byrhtnoth* 325 (Gr.) Næs þæt na se Godric, þe þa guðe forbeah. *c***1000** ÆLFRIC *Job* 164 Se wer wæs.. forbuȝende yfel. *c***1200** *Trin. Coll. Hom.* 63 Forbue iuel and do god. *c***1230** *Hali Meid.* 17 Fleh alle thinges & forbuh ȝeorne þat tus unboteliche lure of mahe arisen.

†**for'braid**, *v. Obs.* Forms: see BRAID *v.* [OE. *forbreȝdan*, *-brédan*, f. FOR- *pref.*[1] + *breȝdan*, *brédan*: see BRAID *v.*] **a.** *trans.* To transform, pervert, corrupt. **b.** *intr.* for *refl.* To become corrupt, decay.

*c***888** K. ÆLFRED *Boeth.* xxxviii. §1 þæt hio sceolde mid hire drycræft þa men forbredan. *c***1220** *Bestiary* 124 Đanne he is forbroken and forbroiden. *Ibid.* 174 If ðu hauest is broken Al ðu forbreðes [*sic*] forwurðes and forgelues. *a***1250** *Owl & Night.* 1384 The rihte i-kunde swo for-breideth.

Hence **for'broide(n** *ppl. a.*, distorted, monstrous.

*a***1250** *Owl & Night.* 1379 He is un-fele and for-brode. **1297** R. GLOUC. (Rolls) 490 Hii founde an vewe geans vorbroide [*v.rr.* forbreyden, forbredde] men as it were.

†**for'break**, *v. Obs.* [OE. *forbrecan* f. FOR- *pref.*[1] + *brecan* to BREAK.] *trans.* **a.** To break in pieces, crush. **b.** To interrupt.

*c***1000** *Ags. Gosp.* John xix. 31 þæt man forbræce hyra sceancan. *c***1250** *Gen. & Ex.* 3049 Trees it for-brac. **1297** R. GLOUC. (1724) 375 Rychard.. vor brec þere hys necke atuo. *a***1300** *E.E. Psalter* cxxiii. 7 þe snare for-broken es in ai. *c***1374** CHAUCER *Boeth.* IV. pr. i. 108, I.. for-brek þe entencioun of hir þat entended[e] ȝitte to seyne oþer þinges. **1387** TREVISA *Higden* (Rolls) VII. 101 Edmond had al forbroken þe Danes. **1413** *Pilgr. Sowle* (Caxton) I. xix. (1859) 19 Al my teethe ben wasted and forbroken.

forbrittened, -broiden: see FOR- *pref.*[1] 8.

†**for'bruise**, *v. Obs.* Forms: 4–5 forbrose, 5 forbrisse, forbruyse. [f. FOR- *pref.*[1] + BRUISE.] *trans.* Only in pa. pple. **a.** To bruise severely; to cover with bruises. **b.** To break to pieces.

*c***1386** CHAUCER *Monk's T.* 624 In a chare men aboute him bare Al for-brused, bothe bak and syde. **1413** *Pilgr. Sowle* (Caxton 1483) IV. xxxvi. 84 Helme and palet to beten and forbruysed. *c***1420** *Anturs of Arth.* li, Vnnethe myȝte these sturun men stond vppe ryȝte So for-brissutte, and for-bled. *c***1450** *Merlin* 239 Alle for brosed and full wery of trauayle.

†**for'burn**, *v. Obs.* For forms see BURN. [α. OE. *forbęrnan* (trans.) = OHG. *ferbrennan* (Ger. *verbrennen*). β. OE. *forbeornan*, *-byrnan* str. (intr.) = OHG. *farprinnan*.]

1. *trans.* To destroy, torture, or injure by burning.

O.E. Chron. an. 685 þone [Mul] mon eft on Cent forbærnde. *c***1000** ÆLFRIC *Exod.* iii. 3 Ic ga and ȝeseo.. hwi þeos þyrne ne si forbærned. *c***1175** *Lamb. Hom.* 27 He mahte iseon ane berninde glede þet hine al for-bernað þurut to cole. **1297** R. GLOUC. (1724) 378 Seyn Poules chyrche of Londone was ek verbarnd þo. *a***1400** *Octouian* 216 With ryght sche schall Be all for-brent. *c***1440** *Jacob's Well* 10 þus for-brent, he roryd as a deuyl for peyne.

2. *intr.* To burn, be burnt, or consumed. Also, To be on fire. *lit.* and *fig.*

Beowulf 1667 (Gr.) Forbarn broȝden mæl. *c***893** K. ÆLFRED *Oros.* VI. i, Com micel fyrbyrne on Romeburȝ, þæt þær-binnan forburnon xv tunas. *a***1250** *Owl & Night.* 419 Vor thu forbernest wel neȝ for onde. *a***1350** *Leg. Rood* (1871) 23 Euerich stude þat we on stepten for brende al wiþ vre fete. *c***1380** *Sir Ferumb.* 3286 Sone ous tyd her for-brenne wyþ sorȝe & deshonour.

†**for'burst**, *v. Obs.* [f. FOR- *pref.*[1] + BURST.] *intr.* To burst asunder; to break.

*a***1000** *Laws Ethelred* III. iv. in Thorpe *Anc. Laws* I. 294 Slea man hine þæt him forberste se sweora. *c***1205** LAY. 1912 [He] breid Geogmagog þat him þe rug for-berst.

forbush, obs. form of FURBISH.

†**for'buy**, *v. Obs.* For forms see BUY. [f. FOR- *pref.*[1] + BUY.] *trans.* To buy off. **a.** To ransom; *esp.* to redeem (from sin, hell, etc.). **b.** To atone for. **c.** To gain over; to bribe.

a. *c***1315** SHOREHAM 164 Ase man was thorȝ trowe bycouȝt, In trowe he scholde be for-bouȝt. *a***1330** *Otuel* 1710 Takeþ me on liue & sle me nouȝt, Leet mi lif be for-bouȝt. *c***1450** *Chester Pl.* (Shaks. Soc.) I. 192 Christe.. comen [is] man-kinde to forbye From God in mayistie.

b. **1340** *Ayenb.* 78 Hi couþen hire zennen uorbegge. *c***1450** *Chester Pl.* (Shaks. Soc.) II. 79 My Lorde uppon the roode tree Your synnes hath forboughte.

c. *a***1300** *Cursor M.* 17464 (Cott.) þai war for-boght þe soth to hele. **1393** GOWER *Conf.* I. 212 He which hindreth every kinde And for no gold may be forbought.

Hence **for'buyer**, a redeemer.

1382 WYCLIF *Isa.* liv. 8 The Lord, thi forbiere. *c***1450** *Chester Pl.* (E.E.T.S.) 400, I am he they call Messy, forebyar of Israell.

forby(e (fəˈbaɪ), *prep.* and *adv.* Also 3–5 forbi, (5 for be), 5–6 foreby, (7 forbay, 9 forebye). [f. FOR- *adv.* or *prep.* + BY. Cf. Du. *voorbij*, Ger. *vorbei*; also (from Ger.) Sw. *förbi*, Da. *forbi*.]

A. *prep.*

1. Of position: Hard by, near. *Obs.* exc. *Sc.*

1596 SPENSER *F.Q.* v. ii. 54 As when a Falcon hath with nimble flight Flowne at a flush of ducks, foreby the brooke. **1858** M. PORTEOUS *'Souter Johnny'* 11 The Smith.. Had.. his snug abode Forbye his smiddy.

2. Of motion: Past; close by. *Obs.* exc. *arch.* In early use following the *obj.*

*a***1300** *Cursor M.* 20884 (Cott.) A ded he quickend wit his schade Quils þat he him for-bi glad. **13..** *K. Alis.* 5487 Alisaunder cometh upon his mule.. And flyngeth gode skowr hem forby. *c***1386** CHAUCER *Doctor's T.* 125 Sche cam forby ther the juge stood. *c***1430** *Syr Gener.* (Roxb.) 5748 The spere.. forbi the visage glode. **1523** LD. BERNERS *Froiss.* I. clvii. 191 They passed foreby the frenchmens busshment. **1590** SPENSER *F.Q.* III. i. 15 A goodly Lady did foreby them rush. **1870** MORRIS *Earthly Par.* III. 316 She went on toward the sea, For by the port.

3. *fig.* †**a.** In preference to, before, beyond. *Obs.* †**b.** In transgression of. *Obs.*[−1]

a. *a***1300** *Cursor M.* 13314 (Cott.) To petre.. For-bi all his oþer feris, Mast priuelege he gaf. *c***1330** R. BRUNNE *Chron.* (1810) 26 A stone þat Hauelok kast wele forbi euer ilkone. *c***1400** MAUNDEV. (Roxb.) xxiii. 107 Sutell of witte.. forby any oþer folk of þe werld. *c***1450** *Mirour Saluacioun* 4930 To take ffleshe of thi wombe for be othere wymmen alle.

b. *c***1250** *Gen. & Ex.* 3988 For-bi min red, quað ðu non del.

†**4.** Beside, in comparison with. Also, by way of distinction from. *Obs.*

*a***1300** *Cursor M.* 27365 (Cott.) Hu soft [it es] her for to mend forbi þat pine wit-vten end. *c***1400** MAUNDEV. (Roxb.)

vii. 25 þat es þe cause þat þai er so gude chepe þare, forby in oþer places. *Ibid.* xxii. 101 Wymmen..þat er wedded beres crownes..þat þai may be knawen by forby þaim þat er vnweddid.

5. Besides; not to mention. Only *north.* or *arch.*

1536 BELLENDEN *Cron. Scot.* XIII. xvi, Forby thir thre erllis and lord foresaid. **1637–50** ROW *Hist. Kirk* (1842) 108 Twenty-four ministers..forby elders. **1676** W. ROW *Contn. Blair's Autobiog.* x. (1848) 272 The special causes were forby the confession of sins to beg a blessing to the King. **1817** LADY L. STUART in Scott *Fam. Lett.* (1894) I. 404 Forbye the young, I have met with an established Blue-stocking who had never heard of Sir William Temple. **1879** BROWNING *Ned Bratts* 18 The regular crowd forbye. **1894** CROCKETT *Raiders* 90 No doubt he had many a sin on his soul, forbye murder.

¶ 6. = BY 28.

1596 SPENSER *F.Q.* V. xi. 17 He tooke her forby the lilly hand, And her recomforted.

B. *adv.* **1.** Of motion: **a.** Aside.

c **1330** R. BRUNNE *Chron.* (1810) 286 He turned not forbi for leue ne for loth. *c* **1330** *Arth. & Merl.* 3361 A little forbi he smot. *a* **1800** *Brown Adam* viii in Scott *Minstr. Scot. Bord.* (1802) II. 18 When he cam to his ladye's bour door, He stude a little forebye.

b. Along, past. Now *rare*. Also, *fig.* † *to go forby*: to be passed over or slighted.

c **1330** R. BRUNNE *Chron.* (1810) 110 Right ȝede þer forby, þe barons did no skille. **1375** BARBOUR *Bruce* x. 345 But I will let fele of thame pas forby. **1423** JAS. I. *Kingis Q.* xxx, To se the warld and folk that went forby. *a* **1533** LD. BERNERS *Huon* cxvi. 413 He salutyd them in passynge forby. **1862** W. W. STORY *Roba di R.* (1864) 78 That time has been long forbye.

2. Besides, in addition.

1590 J. BUREL in Watson *Collect.* II. (1709) 14 The other Burgissis forby Wer cled in thair pontificall. **1724** RAMSAY *Tea-t. Misc.* (1733) I. 25 Forby, how sweet the numbers chime. *a* **1810** TANNAHILL *Poet. Wks.* (1846) 77 Forby he had a bashfu' spirit. **1886** STEVENSON *Kidnapped* xii, There are the bairns forby..that must be learned their letters.

†**forbyland.** *Yorksh. dial. Obs.* [f. prec. adv. + LAND.] ? Extra land.

1510 *MS. Grant of Land at Ryton, Yorks.*, One tenement with forbyland. **1621** *N. Riding Rec.* I. 27 A mesuage, a cotage, or forby lands (which I take to be demeisnes).

†**for'bysen,** *sb. Obs.* [f. FOR *prep.* + BYSEN.] **a.** An example, pattern, type. **b.** An illustration, parable. **c.** A proverb. **d.** A token.

a. *c* **1175** *Lamb. Hom.* 81 Her of me mei ane forbisne of twa brondes. *c* **1220** *Bestiary* 307 Ðe hert haueð kindes two and forbisnes oc al so. *c* **1320** *Cast. Love* 980 A forbysne of boxumnes. **1393** LANGL. *P. Pl.* C. XVIII. 277 He is a forbusne to alle busshopes.

b. *c* **1175** *Lamb. Hom.* 79 God almihti seið an forbisne to his folk in þe halie godspel and seið [etc.]. *c* **1308** *Song Times* in *Pol. Songs.* (Camden) 197 Of thos a vorbisen ic herd telle. **1362** LANGL. *P. Pl.* A. IX. 24 'Bi a forebisene' seide the frere, 'I schal the feire schewe.'

c. *a* **1250** *Owl & Night.* 99 Thar-bi men segget a vorbisne, Dahet habbe that ilke best, That fuleth his owe nest. **1340** *Ayenb.* 47 Vor ase zayþ þe uorbisne 'leuedi of uaire diȝtinge is arblast to þe tour.'

d. *a* **1300** *Cursor M.* 4593 (Gött.) For þoru þis for-bisin here, Witt þu þar sal be seuen ȝere of plente..in þi kingrike. **1485** CAXTON *Trevisa's Higden* II. i. (1527) 58 Soo some partes of a mannes bodye be forbyson & bodyng of wondres.

†**for'bysen,** *v. Obs.* Also 4 (erron.) **forbyse.** [f. prec. sb.]

1. *trans.* To furnish (a person) with examples.

a **1300** [see FORBYSENING *vbl. sb.*] *c* **1374** CHAUCER *Troylus* II. 1341 (1390) It nedeth me nought thee longe to forbyse.

2. To give (something) as an example.

Hence **for'bisned** *ppl. a.*

c **1220** *Bestiary* 589 Ðis forbisnede ði[n]g.

†**for'bysening,** *vbl. sb. Obs.* [see -ING[1].]

1. The action of the vb. FORBYSEN; *concr.* an example, symbol, type.

a **1300** *Cursor M.* 2682 (Cott.) þe werk of circumcising bers in it-self gret for-bise[n]yng. *Ibid.* 15327 (Gött.) For a for-biseneng nu ȝur fete [þus] haue I washen all. *c* **1425** WYNTOUN *Cron.* VIII. xli. 69 Syndry..cald it iwil forbysnyng.

2. A parable.

a **1300** *Cursor M.* 7916 (Cott.) þan come þe prophet to þe king And said him suilk a forbisening. *a* **1300** *E.E. Psalter* lxxvii[i]. 2, I sal open mi mouth in forbiseninges.

†**for'carve,** *v. Obs.* For forms see CARVE. [OE. *forceorfan*, f. FOR- *pref.*[1] + *ceorfan* to CARVE.] *trans.* To carve or cut asunder, down, in two, out, through; to cut to pieces.

O.E. Chron. an. 797 Her Romane Leone þæm papan his tungon forcurfon. *c* **1000** ÆLFRIC *Judith* 23 þæt heo healfne forcearf þone sweoran him. *c* **1230** *Hali Meid.* 11 Meidenhad is te blosme þat beo ha eanes fulliche forcoruen ne spruteð ha neauer eft. **13..** *Coer de L.* 1926 Seven chains, with his good swerde Our King for-carf amidward. *c* **1386** [see FORCUT]. **1460** *Lybeaus Disc.* 1325 He..smot a strok of mayne..And forkarf bon and lyre.

†**for'cast,** *v. Obs.* [f. FOR- *pref.*[1] + CAST; = Da. *forkaste*, Sw. *förkasta*.] *trans.* To cast away, reject; to fling away, do away with.

a **1225** *Ancr. R.* 278 Edmodnesse is forkesting of wurð-schipe. *a* **1300** *Cursor M.* 24550 (Cott.) þat hope for-kest mi care. *a* **1300** *E.E. Psalter* xxi[i]. 10 Of maghe for-kast I am in þe. **1340** *Ayenb.* 186 þe wolues draȝeþ uorþ þe children þet byeþ uorkest. **1393** GOWER *Conf.* II. 167 Where she lay A child for-cast.

†**'forcat.** *Sc. Obs.* Also **foirchet.** [ad. OF. **forcat* = *forchat* forked stick, f. *forche* FORK *sb.*] 'A rest for a musket' (Jam.).

1598 *Sc. Acts Jas. VI* (1814) IV. 169 Furnist with..ane muscat with forcat, bedrol, and heid pece. *Ibid.* 191 Or ellis with ane muscat foirchet bandroll and heidpeice.

†**for'catch,** *v. Obs.*[−1] [ad. ONF. *for-*, *forscachier* (= Central OF. *forchacier*), f. *for(s)-*, FOR- *pref.*[3] + *cachier* (*chacier*): see CATCH *v.* and CHASE *v.*] *trans.* To drive forth.

1393 GOWER *Conf.* Prol. 17 Fro the leese, whiche is pleine, Into the breres they forcacche Here orf.

force (fɔəs), *sb.*[1] Forms: 3–6 **fors, forse,** (4 **foors, forze**), 3– **force.** [a. F. *force* (= Pr. *forsa*, *forza*, Sp. *fuerza*, Pg. *força*, It. *forza*):—popular L. **fortia*, n. of quality f. L. *fortis* strong.]

I. Strength, power.

†**1. a.** Physical strength, might, or vigour, as an attribute of living beings (occas. of liquor). Rarely in *pl.* (= F. *forces*). *Obs.*

a **1300** *Cursor M.* 7244 (Cott.) Thoru his fax his force was tint. *c* **1350** *Will. Palerne* 3598 þouȝh he hade fors of foure swiche oþer. *a* **1400–50** *Alexander* 1006 And now vs failis all oure force & oure flesch waykis. **1508** DUNBAR *Tua mariit wemen* 189 He has a forme without force. **1576** FLEMING *Panopl. Epist.* 194 Chosen men, hugest in stature, and fullest of force. **1610** ROWLANDS *Martin Mark-all* 22 Their Beere is of that force, and so mightie, that it serueth them in steade of meate, drinke, fire, and apparrell. **1611** BIBLE *Deut.* xxxiv. 7 His eye was not dimme, nor his naturall force abated. **1697** DRYDEN *Virg. Georg.* I. 249 Young Elms with early force in Copses bow. **1715** POPE *Iliad* III. 89 Thy force, like steel, a temper'd hardness shows. **1816** KEATINGE *Trav.* (1817) I. 245 The great hero of antiquity, in the thieving line, was eminent by his physical forces.

†**b.** *of force*: full of strength, vigorous. *Obs.*

1577 B. GOOGE *Heresbach's Husb.* (1586) 75 The Willowes must be holpen with often waterings, that the nature of the tree may be of force [*ut natura ligni vigeat*].

c. †*with* (*one's*) *force*: with energy, with exertion of one's strength. *with all one's force*: putting forth all one's strength.

c **1380** *Sir Ferumb.* 3036 'Leggeþ on, Lordes,' said he, 'wiþ force & smyteþ strokes smerte.' *c* **1400** *Ywaine & Gaw.* 2897 With hir force sho hasted so fast That sho over-toke him at the last. *c* **1430** *Syr Tryam.* 829 He prekyd to the kyng with fors. **1582** N. LICHEFIELD tr. *Castanheda's Conq. E. Ind.* xxxiii. 80 b, And rowing with force tooke two of the Pledges. **1674** N. COX *Gentl. Recreat.* I. (1677) 95 The Hounds..running with all their force. **1841** LANE *Arab. Nts.* I. 86 Strike the ball..with all thy force.

†**d.** *to make great force*: to exert oneself. *to do one's force*: to do one's utmost. *Obs.*

c **1450** *St. Cuthbert* (Surtees) 6182 Forto witt he made grete force. *Ibid* 6904 To wirschip it he did his fors.

2. a. As an attribute of physical action or movement: Strength, impetus, violence, or intensity of effect. Also with reference to the force of wind described by numbers in the Beaufort scale.

c **1320** *Sir Beues* 3405 (MS. A.) With a dent of gret fors A-bar him doun of his hors. *c* **1400** *Ywaine & Gaw.* 2452 With grete force he lete it fall. **1582** N. LICHEFIELD tr. *Castanheda's Conq. E. Ind.* xxix. 73 b, The tackling..of the Shippes, with the great force of the winde, made such a terrible noyse. **1607** ROWLANDS *Famous Hist.* 35 And makes them curse that e're they felt the force of Christian blows. **1697** DAMPIER *Voy.* I. ix. 247 The Sea falls with such force on the shore. **1703** MOXON *Mech. Exerc.* 197 By the force and strength of the Wedge. **1774** GOLDSM. *Nat. Hist.* (1776) III. 67 They break the force of the fall. **1781** GIBBON *Decl. & F.* III. 80 The force of the strongest and sharpest tools had been tried without effect. **1787** BURNS *Fragm. Ode* iii, The snowy ruin smokes along, With doubling speed and gathering force. **1812–16** J. SMITH *Panorama Sc. & Art* I. 347 The force of a stream. **1867** SMYTH *Sailor's Word-bk.* s.v., *Force of wind*, now described by numbers, 0 being calm, 12 the heaviest gale. **1933, 1961** [see BEAUFORT SCALE]. **1963** *Listener* 21 Mar. 528/3 The wind is not only there, but assuming the proportions of a force-ten hurricane.

†**b.** said of the violent onset of combatants in battle. *Obs.*

a **1300** *Cursor M.* 7760 (Cott.) O þis batail þat was sa snell, þe force a-pon þe king it fell. **1375** BARBOUR *Bruce* II. 429 That war sa few that thai na mycht Endur the forss mar off the fycht. *a* **1533** LD. BERNERS *Huon* lix. 206 The forse of the paynyms was so gret that at length they coude not abyde it. **1582** N. LICHEFIELD tr. *Castanheda's Conq. E. Ind.* lxxix. 162 Heere..was all the force of the battaile.

†**c.** phr. *within one's force*: within the range of his attack or defence. (Cf. DINT *sb.* 2 d.)

1680 OTWAY *Orphan* I. ii, When on the brink the foaming Boar I met, And in his side thought to have lodg'd my spear, The desperate savage rusht within my Force, And bore me headlong with him down the Rock.

†**d.** Violence or 'stress' of weather. *in the force of weather*: exposed to the brunt of its attack. *Obs.*

1614 RALEIGH *Hist. World* III. viii. §4. 90 A creeke, which is a good harbour for ships, the force of weather being borne off by the head-Land and Isle. *c* **1630** RISDON *Surv. Devon* §215 (1810) 223 A high rock, called Crocken-Torr..where is a table and seats of moorstone..lying in the force of all weather, no house or refuge being near it.

3. a. Power or might (of a ruler, realm, or the like); *esp.* military strength or power.

1303 R. BRUNNE *Handl. Synne* 3685 ȝyf þou any man manasse þurghe force or power þat þou hasse. *c* **1330** —— *Chron.* (1810) 191 þe Sarazin force doun his, Jhesu we þank þe. *c* **1460** *Towneley Myst.* (Surtees) 55 If any were..That wold my fors down felle. **1500–20** DUNBAR *Poems* viii. 14 Quhois force all France in fame did magnifie. **1593** SHAKS. *3 Hen. VI*, v. i. 77 And lo, where George of Clarence sweeps along, Of force enough to bid his brother battle. **1756** BURKE *Vind. Nat. Soc.* Wks. I. 20 In the same place where his predecessors had..wasted the force of so extensive an empire. **1796** —— *Regic. Peace* ii. ibid. VIII. 245 From her aiming through commerce at naval force which she never could attain. **1888** *Fortn. Rev.* Nov. 564 A navy actually inferior in fighting force to that of France.

b. In early use, the strength (of a fortress, defensive work, etc.). Subsequently, the fighting strength (of a ship), as measured by number of guns or men. † *of (good) force*: (well) armed or fortified.

1577–87 HARRISON *England* I. xii, At this Poulruan is a tower of force. **1578** T. NICHOLAS *Conq. W. India* (1596) 102 The estate and force of the said Ships. **1585** T. WASHINGTON tr. *Nicholay's Voy.* I. vii. 7 The foundation, force, and situation of the citie of Alger. **1615** G. SANDYS *Trav.* 210 The wals neither faire nor of force. **1669** NARBOROUGH *Jrnl.* in *Acc. Sev. Late Voy.* I. (1711) 7 The Castle..hath but four Guns, and is of no force. **1697** DAMPIER *Voy.* I. iii. 46 Sending from Holland Ships of good force. **1779** in *L'pool Munic. Rec.* (1886) II. 183 Several ships of force..are now on the coast. **1867** SMYTH *Sailor's Word-bk.*, *Force*..Also, the force of each ship stated agreeably to the old usage in the navy, according to the number of guns actually carried.

†**c.** *with force*: with, or by the employment of, military strength or numbers. Cf. 5 b. Sometimes app. = *in force* (see 17). *Obs.*

1303 R. BRUNNE *Handl. Synne* 3366 Wyþ fors þey gun wyþ hym fyghte. *c* **1400** MAUNDEV. (1839) xxvii. 279 Thei assembled hem with force, and assayleden his Castelle. *c* **1435** *Torr. Portugal* 2209 [He] sent letters on every side, With fforce theder to hye. **1548** HALL *Chron.*, *Hen. VI* (an. 6) 106 The Englishemen, whiche with greate force, theim received and manfully defended. *Ibid. Edw. IV* (an. 2) 191 Suche Castles..as his enemies there held, and with force defended. [**1884** *Graphic* 21 June 595/2 The numerous private members..came down with such force that a count out was plainly impossible.]

4. *concr.* **a.** A body of armed men, an army. In *pl.* the troops or soldiers composing the fighting strength of a kingdom or of a commander in the field; also in *attrib.* use or in the possessive, esp. during the war of 1939–1945.

1375 BARBOUR *Bruce* XIX. 632 We may nocht with iuperdiss Our felloune fais forss assale. **1548** HALL *Chron.*, *Hen. IV* (an. 1) 13 b, The duke..seyng the force of the townes men more and more encreace. **1594** SHAKS. *Rich. III*, v. iii. 109 Looke on my Forces with a gracious eye. **1611** BIBLE *1 Macc.* xii. 42 When Tryphon saw that Ionathan came with so great a force. **1727** SWIFT *Gulliver* II. vi. 149 The valour and atchievements of our forces by sea and land. **1796** BURKE *Corr.* (1844) IV. 422 A naval force is a very unsure defence. **1849** MACAULAY *Hist. Eng.* I. 575 The only standing force should be the militia. **1851** DIXON *W. Penn* xiv. (1872) 119 One of the leaders of the Parliamentary forces. **1874** STUBBS *Const. Hist.* (1875) II. xiv. 14 A force of seven thousand men landed in Suffolk. **1942** *New Statesman* 3 Jan., I see that a new version of this feature is now to begin in the new year on the Forces Programme. **1943** E. OLIVIER *Night Thoughts of Country Landlady* iii. 25 The very inferior music often produced in the B.B.C. Forces' Programme. **1945** *News Review* 10 May, If you're a Forces bride you will be given a travelling warrant for the whole journey from your British home to your new home in America. **1945** *Manch. Guardian* 18 July, A statement in a 'forces' newspaper. **1952** GRANVILLE *Dict. Theatr. Terms* 80 *The Forces' sweetheart*. Vera Lynn, the British vaudeville and radio singer, was a great favourite with the troops in the second world war, hence the sobriquet. **1959** *Times Lit. Suppl.* 2 Oct. 556/4 The man and the girl,..whom we observe listening intently to Forces Favourites.

transf. **1841** MACAULAY in Trevelyan *Life* (1876) II. ix. 147 The force which will be arrayed against a Bill.

b. A body of police; the whole body of police on service in a town or district; often absol. *the force* = policemen collectively.

1851 MAYHEW *Lond. Labour* I. 16 One boy..vowed vengeance against a member of the force. **1861** MISS BRADDON *Trail Serpent* IV. vi. 226, I was nobody in the Gardenford force. **1875** HAMERTON *Intell. Life* VII. vi. 259 She will protect your tranquility better than a force of policemen.

†**c.** ? A fort. *Obs. rare*[−1].

1538 LELAND *Itin.* (1711) III. 15 About a Myle by West of Penare is a Force nere the shore.

d. *U.S.* (See quots.)

1807 C. W. JANSON *Stranger in Amer.* 309 Force, is here employed when speaking of the number of slaves employed in field labour on each plantation. **1834** W. G. SIMMS *Guy Rivers* II. 97 The force of the traveller—for such is the term by which the number of his slaves is understood—was small. **1837** H. MARTINEAU *Society in Amer.* I. II. 344 All the 'force' that could be collected on a hasty summons,—that is, almost every able-bodied man in the city and neighbourhood, was sent out with axes to build us a bridge. **1871** SCHELE DE VERE *Americanisms* (1872) 475 *Force* is a common name for a gang of laborers, whether they are Irishmen at work on a railway, or negroes employed on a plantation. **1899** *Monthly South Dakotan* (Mitchell) I. 138 A high wind..showered down hundreds of bushels of apples, [and] one is confronted by the alternative of sending for the 'force' to pick them up on Sunday or letting the sun scald and ruin them.

5. a. Physical strength or power exerted upon an object; *esp.* the use of physical strength to constrain the action of persons; violence or physical coercion. †*to make force*: to use violence *to*.

a **1340** HAMPOLE *Psalter* Comm. Cant. 497 Lord .i. suffire force [*vim patior*]. **1382** WYCLIF *Gen.* xix. 9 And foors thei maden [L. *vim faciebant*] to Loth moost hidowsly. **1413** *Pilgr. Sowle* (Caxton 1483) IV. xii. 63 Force is nouther ryght ne reson. **1582** N. LICHEFIELD tr. *Castanheda's Conq. E. Ind.*

ii. 7b, Deeming..that those blacke men meant him no harme, nor would offer anye force. **1667** MILTON *P.L.* I. 647 To work in close design, by fraud or guile, What force effected not. **1687** BOYLE *Martyrd. Theodora* i. (1703) 6 Such cruel methods being apt to make the world suspect that our best argument is force. **1789** BENTHAM *Princ. Legisl.* xiii. §2 Force can accomplish many things which would be beyond the reach of cunning. **1840** H. ROGERS *Introd. Burke's Wks.* 82 Nothing will justify force while any other means remain untried. **1889** A. LANG *Prince Prigio* ii. 10 The prince, after having his ears boxed, said that 'force was no argument'.

b. *esp.* in phr. ***by force*** = by employing violence, by violent means, also †under compulsion. †Formerly also ***through, with, of force***; also, ***par force, by perforce, force perforce*** (see PERFORCE). Also, †***by*** or ***with fine force, a-force fine***: see FINE *a.*[3] Often implying the use of armed force or strength of numbers: cf. 3 c.

c **1320** *Seuyn Sag.* (W.) 488 Par force he hadde me forht i nome. **1375** BARBOUR *Bruce* XII. 524 Mony worthy men and wicht Throu forss wes fellit in that ficht. *c* **1380** *Sir Ferumb.* 972 þanne þay asayllede Scot Gwylmer & toke him a-force fine. **1484** CAXTON *Fables of Æsop* II. xi, The thynge which is promysed by force & for drede is not to be hold. *c* **1500** *Lancelot* 2701 Sir gawan thar reskewit he of fors, Magre his fois. **1593** SHAKS. *2 Hen. VI*, I. i. 210 That Maine, which by maine force Warwick did winne. **1611** BIBLE *John* vi. 15 When Iesus therefore perceiued that they would come and take him by force, to make him a King. **1701** DE FOE *True-born Eng.* 36 The Bad with Force they eagerly subdue. **1754** HUME *Hist. Eng.* (1812) I. iii. 163 One of his train.. attempted to make his way by force. **1875** JOWETT *Plato* (ed. 2) V. 241 The common people..can only be made to sing and step in rhythm by sheer force.

c. *spec.* in *Law*: Unlawful violence offered to persons or things. ***by force and arms***: translation of Law L. *vi et armis*. ***a force***: a particular act or instance of unlawful violence.

c **1480** LITTLETON *Tenures* II. xi, Il defendera forsque tort & force [**1538** *transl.* he..shal defend but the wrong and the force]. *Ibid.* II. xii. (end), Le tenaunt..luy forstalla le voye ouesque force & armys. **1594** WEST *2nd Pt. Symbol.* §65 Force is either simple or mixt. **1619** DALTON *Country Just.* 196 Also, women, and children, may commit a force. **1628** COKE *On Litt.* §240. 161 b, Force, *vis*, in the Common Law is most commonly taken in ill part, and taken for unlawful violence. **1768** BLACKSTONE *Comm.* III. viii. 119 This distinction of private wrongs, into injuries with and without force. **1818** CRUISE *Digest* (ed. 2) I. 102 Where a person is prevented from barring an estate tail by force and management. **1826** *Act 7 Geo. IV*, c. 64 §20 That no Judgment..shall be stayed or reversed..for the Omission.. of the Words 'with Force and Arms'. **1842** TENNYSON *E. Morris* 131 It seems I broke a close with force and arms.

†**d.** In non-material sense: Constraint or compulsion exerted *upon* a person. Also, ***a force***, as ***to put a force upon***: to put compulsion or constraint upon, to constrain; to strain or wrest the meaning of. ***to be upon the force***: ? to act under self-constraint and against one's natural impulses. ***under a force***: under compulsion. *Obs.*

1387 TREVISA *Higden* (Rolls) VII. 141 Godwyne..swore þat he didde nevere suche þinges, bot constreyned by þe force of kyng Harold. **1576** FLEMING *Panopl. Epist.* 261 The monie which you sent us, uppon the force of our commaundement. **1662** SIR A. MERVYN *Sp. Irish Aff.* 4 We come not to criminate, or to force a ball into the Dedan, but if any brick-wall expressions happen, that cannot be designed otherwise, it is rather a force upon us. **1667** MILTON *P.L.* IX. 1173 Beyond this had bin force, And force upon free Will hath here no place. **1681** BURNET *Hist. Ref.* II. 252 In many places..Men were chosen by Force and Threats..upon which reasons he concludes that it was no Parliament, since it was under a Force. **1690** WOLSELY in *Lond. Gaz.* No. 2536/2 It was a very unfortunate Force, which the Soldiers..put upon me, to burn the Town. **1697** DRYDEN *Virg. Georg.* III. 411 Nor cou'd his Kindred, nor the Kindly Force Of weeping Parents, change his fatal Course. **1707** NORRIS *Treat. Humility* v. 203 A Man can't be always upon the force, the Actor will sometimes tire. **1729** BUTLER *Serm.* xiii. Wks. 1874 II. 173 They may all be understood to be implied in these words of our Saviour, without putting any force upon them. **1774** J. BRYANT *Mythol.* I. 136 The whole is effected with a great strain and force upon history. **1805** K. WHITE *Let.* 19 Dec., I have very little society and that is quite a force upon my friends.

6. Mental or moral strength. Now only (influenced by sense 2), power of vigorous and effective action, or of overcoming resistance. In early use also, power of endurance or resistance, fortitude.

c **1340** HAMPOLE *Prose Tr.* 10 þey erre with-owtten charyte and vertue and force of sawle to stand agayne all ill styrrynges. **1502** *Ord. Crysten Men* (W. de W. 1506) II. viii. 106 Force is an other vertue by the whiche a man under-taketh to do or suffre for the loue of god these thynges stronge and harde. **1534** WHITINTON *Tullyes Offices* I. (1540) 3 He can not be acompted a man of force that iudgeth payne and grefe to be moste mysery. **1576** FLEMING *Panopl. Epist.* 26 Bend the powers of your spirite, and the force of your minde, that, [etc.]. **1679** PENN *Addr. Prot.* II. iv. (1692) 124 What before we were Unable, this gives us Force to do. **1711** DENNIS *Refl. Ess. Crit.* 1 He..hath rashly undertaken a Task which is infinitely above his Force. **1871** R. H. HUTTON *Ess.* II. 322 Real men of any force have a free sphere of their own. **1876** TREVELYAN *Macaulay* I. i. 9 There was another Son who in force of character stood out among his brothers.

7. a. Of things (in non-material or moral relations): Power to influence, affect, or control (*esp.* men in their actions, sentiments, etc.). ***to have force*** (***to do***): to avail.

1582 LYLY in *T. Watson's Centurie of Loue* (Arb.) 29 Mine appetite of lesse force then mine affection. **1605** BACON *Adv. Learn.* I. ii. §4 (1873) 14 It [learning] teacheth men the force of circumstances. **1713** ADDISON *Cato* IV. ii, Let not her cries or tears have force to move you. **1751** JORTIN *Serm.* (1771) IV. vi. 117 Such prejudices arise from the prevailing force of education. **1816** KEATINGE *Trav.* (1817) I. 276 The force of habit is certainly very strong, and prejudices the mind throughout. **1821** LAMB *Elia* Ser. I. *Old Benchers I.T.*, S. was thought..a fit person to be consulted..from force of manner entirely. **1845** DISRAELI *Sybil* VI. iii, I never heard that moral force won the battle of Waterloo. **1890** F. W. ROBINSON *Very strange Fam.* 2 The force of circumstances had thrust me upon him.

b. Peculiar power resident in a thing to produce special effects; virtue, efficacy.

1590 SHAKS. *Mids. N.* II. ii. 69 On whose eyes I might approue This flowers force in stirring loue. **1671** MILTON *P.R.* I. 347 Think'st thou such force in bread? **1709** STEELE *Tatler* No. 34 ¶4 Beauty loses its force, if not accompanied with modesty.

c. *esp.* Power to convince or persuade the reason or judgement; convincing or appealing power. Often in phr. ***of*** (***great***, etc.) ***force***; †formerly also ***of force*** simply.

1551 T. WILSON *Logike* (1580) 36 This [argument] that followeth, is of as good force. **1591** SHAKS. *1 Hen. VI*, III. i. 157 Those occasions, Vnckle, were of force. **1685** BAXTER *Paraphr. N.T.* Matt. xvi. 28 Nor is Dr. H. his reason against it..of any force. **1729** BUTLER *Serm.* Pref. Wks. 1874 II. 13 The force of this conviction is felt by almost every one. **1748** J. MASON *Elocut.* 31 You can never convey the Force and Fulness of his Ideas to another till you feel them yourself. **1818** CRUISE *Digest* (ed. 2) II. 514 The argument of long enjoyment was of no force. **1847** GROTE *Greece* II. l. (1862) IV. 341 In both these two reasons there is force. **1849** MACAULAY *Hist. Eng.* II. 23 They harangued..with some force on the great superiority of a regular army to a militia.

d. Of discourse, style, artistic creations, etc.: Strength or vividness of effect.

1842 H. ROGERS *Introd. Burke's Wks.* 85 The passage already quoted..is full of force and splendour. **1863** MRS. C. CLARKE *Shaks. Char.* vi. 152 Slender comes out in this play with extraordinary force. **1879** *Cassell's Techn. Educ.* IV. 24/1 The introduction of a considerable amount of black ..gives great force to the pattern.

e. *Austral.* and *N.Z.* (See quots.)

1933 *Press* (Christchurch) 21 Oct. 15/7 *Force*, the power of dogs to move sheep... Huntaways are sometimes spoken of as *forcing dogs*; but the term *f[orce]* is also applied to the ability of a heading dog to pull sheep. **1960** BAKER *Drum* 110 *Force*, the ability of a sheepdog to control a mob of sheep, esp. without legging, i.e., leg-biting. A good dog is said to have a lot of force.

8. a. Of a law, etc.: Binding power, validity.

1594 HOOKER *Eccl. Pol.* I. x. §8 Hath not his edict the force of a law? **1613** SHAKS. *Hen. VIII*, I. ii. 101 Free pardon to each man that has denied The force of this commission. **1786** BURKE *W. Hastings* Wks. 1842 II. 177 A country..in which the native authority had no force whatever. **1863** H. COX *Instit.* I. v. 25 Proclamations which..should have the force of statutes.

†**b.** ***of force***: of binding power, valid. *Obs.*

1502 ARNOLDE *Chron.* (1811) 180 That alle lettres patentes or grauntis by you..be voyde and of noo fors. **1611** BIBLE *Heb.* ix. 17 For a Testament is of force after men are dead. **1679** PENN *Addr. Prot.* II. v. (1692) 163 Whatsoever they shall decree, ought to be of Force.

c. ***in force***: operative or binding at the time. Also, ***in full force***, † ***in his force***. So ***to put in force***, to enforce; ***to come into force*** (also †***to take force***), to come into operation, take effect.

1491 *Act 7 Hen. VII*, c. 10 The foreseid statute..shuld be in his force and virtue fro thens perpetuelly to endure. **1553** T. WILSON *Rhet.* (1580) 159 By an order realmes stande, and Lawes take force. **1603** KNOLLES *Hist. Turks* 100 Without respect vnto the league yet in force. **1611** BIBLE *2 Esdras* ix. 37 Notwithstanding the law perisheth not, but ramaineth in his force. **1724** *Act* in *Lond. Gaz.* No. 6270/7 The Officer.. is..to limit the Time..for such Permit..to continue in Force. **1847** L. HUNT *Jar Honey* (1848) 190 In the south this ancient custom still remains in full force. **1856** KNIGHT *Pop. Hist. Eng.* I. xvii. 234 He engaged to put in force the laws of Edward the Confessor. **1891** MATTHEWS in *Law Times* XCII. 96/1 The..Act..came into force immediately on its passing.

9. The real import or significance (of a document, statement, or the like); the precise meaning or 'value' (of a word, sentence, etc.) as affecting its context or interpretation; the power or value of a symbol or character.

1555 BONNER *Profit. Doctr.* M iij, Thyrde is to be considered, the vertue, force, and effecte of the sayd Sacrament. **1690** LOCKE *Govt.* I. v. §44 We will..consider the Force of the Text in hand. **1709** STEELE *Tatler* No. 58 ¶2 The Examination of the Force of the Particle *For*. **1732** BERKELEY *Alciphr.* VII. §5, I comprehend the force and meaning of this proposition. **1741** CHAMBERS *Cycl.* s.v., In our language the *s* between two vowels has the Force or power of a *z*..An unite before a cypher has the Force of ten. **1756** BURKE *Subl. & B.* III. §2 Several who make use of that word [proportion], do not always seem to understand very clearly the force of the term. **1767** BLACKSTONE *Comm.* II. 353 We are next to consider the force and effect of a fine.

10. †**a.** (Without article prefixed): A large quantity or number, plenty; const. *of*, which is omitted in quot. 13.. (cf. F. *force gens* and the like). ***most force***: the greater part (*obs.*). **b.** ***a force***: a large number or quantity, a great deal. ***the force***: ? the majority. *Obs.* exc. *dial.*

13.. *Coer de L.* 1383 Two hundred schyppys ben wel vytailid With force hawberks, swerdes and knyvys. **1375** BARBOUR *Bruce* VIII. 11 The men mast fors com till his pess. **1461** *Liber Pluscard.* XI. xi. (1877) 397 Of thi detturis maist force ar lukkin in clay. *c* **1570** *Satir. Poems Reform.* xlv. 969 The vther having force of freindis. **1722** DE FOE *Col. Jack* (1840) 255 Her maid, with a force of crying..said her master was dead. **1842** C. SUMNER *Let.* 16 Sept. in S. Longfellow *Life of H. W. Longfellow* (1886) I. 414 The force of my acquaintance was among lawyers, judges, and politicians. **1876** *Whitby Gloss.*, 'There was a foorce o' folks', great numbers were present.

11. *Physics*, etc. Used in various senses developed from the older popular uses, and corresponding to mod. scientific uses of L. *vis*.

a. (= Newton's *vis impressa*: cf. sense 5). An influence (measurable with regard to its intensity and determinable with regard to its direction) operating on a body so as to produce an alteration or tendency to alteration of its state of rest or of uniform motion in a straight line; the intensity of such an influence as a measurable quantity.

Recent physicists mostly retain the word merely as the name for a measure of change of motion, not as denoting anything objectively existing as a cause.

1665 SALUSBURY tr. *Galileus' Mech.* 294 It will..be better, the Force that moveth the Weight upwards perpendicularly ..being given, to seek the Force that moveth it along the Elevated Plane. **1686** NEWTON *Let.* 20 June in Brewster *Life* I. 440 In one of my papers..above fifteen years ago, the proportion of the forces of the planets from the sun, reciprocally duplicate of their distances from him, is expressed. **1803** J. WOOD *Princ. Mech.* i. 15 Whatever changes, or tends to change, the state of rest or uniform rectilinear motion of a body, is called force. **1866** ARGYLL *Reign Law* ii. (ed. 4) 72 All the particles of matter exert an attractive force upon each other. **1871** B. STEWART *Heat* §21 The force of gravity..is somewhat greater in London than at Paris. **1876** TAIT *Force* in *Rec. Adv. Phys. Sc.* (1885) 357 Unit force is..that force which, whatever be its source, produces unit momentum in unit of time.

b. (cf. sense 2). Formerly used for what Leibnitz called *vis viva*, now known as kinetic energy, and often extended to include potential energy: see ENERGY 6. ***conservation of force***: see CONSERVATION.

1841 *Penny Cycl.* XXI. 307/1 The high tide at Chepstow is accounted for on 'the principle of the conservation of force'. **1870** JEVONS *Elem. Logic* xxiv. 209 Force cannot be created or destroyed by any of the processes of nature.

c. The cause of any one of the classes of physical phenomena, e.g. of motion, heat, electricity, etc., conceived as consisting in principle or power inherent in, or coexisting with, matter; such principles or powers regarded generically.

According to the now prevailing view that all physical changes are modes of motion, *force* in its generic sense comes to denote the one principle of which the separate *forces* are specific forms. But sense 11 c is no longer recognized as belonging to the technical language of physics.

[**1732** BERKELEY *Alciphr.* VII. §9 Force is that in bodies which produces motion and other sensible effects.] **1842-3** GROVE *Corr. Phys. Forces* (1846) 8, I therefore use the term Force..as meaning that active principle inseparable from matter which induces its various changes. *Ibid.* 21 If Heat be a force capable of producing motion, and motion be capable of producing the other modes of force. **1851** CARPENTER *Man. Phys.* (ed. 2) 10 A large number of phenomena.. resulting from the agency of forces as distinct from those of Physics and Chemistry, as they are from each other..the forces from whose operation we assume them to result, are termed vital forces.

d. *transf.* and *fig.* An agency, influence, or source of power likened to a physical force.

1785 WILKINS *Bhagvat* iii. 49 He was impelled by some secret force. **1868** NETTLESHIP *Browning* i. 18 The passion.. whose existence as a force in the world..he recognises. **1891** *Law Times* XC. 443/1 The Nisi Prius advocate who has a fair knowledge of law is still a great force in the Profession.

II. Senses derived from FORCE *v.*[1]

†**12.** The plunger of a force-pump. *Obs.*

1596 HARINGTON *Metam. Ajax* (1814) 9 You may with a force of twenty shillings, and a pipe of eighteen pence the yard, force it from the lowest part of your house to the highest. **1659** LEAK *Waterwks.* 34 This manner of force-Pump..the forces do Rise and Fall Perpendicularly in their Barrels. **1747** HOOSON *Miner's Dict.*, *Force*, a kind of Pump often used in the Mines, that throws the Water a good height ..'tis now worn out of Vse.

13. The upper die in a metal-stamping machine.

1879 *Cassell's Techn. Educ.* IV. 263/2 The final strokes are given by a 'force' cast in brass. **1886** *Jrnl. Franklin Inst.* CXXII. 327 The upper die was the cameo, technically the male die, punch or 'force'.

14. *Card-playing*. An act of forcing.

1862 'CAVENDISH' *Whist* (1879) 111 You may assume that he is strong in trumps, and you should take the force willingly. **1886** *Academy* 10 Apr. 251/2 The young player will naturally be startled by the instruction to lead trumps to an adversary who has just refused a force.

15. a. *Billiards*. A kind of stroke (see quot.); a 'screw-back'. *U.S.*

1881 COLLENDER *Mod. Billiards* 23 *Draw*, or *Force*.— Striking the cue ball one-half or more below its centre, causing it, if played full at the object-ball, to recoil or return toward the player.

b. *Tennis*. (See quot. 1890[2].)

1662 [see 5 d above.] **1890** J. M. HEATHCOTE *Tennis* 50 The Force is the usual resource of a player who must try to win at very 'close chase', or who returns a ball which comes 'fair-off' from the end-wall. *Ibid.* 124 *Force*, a stroke played, either direct or boasted, for the dedans with some strength. **1927** *Daily Tel.* 26 Apr. 17/1 Some admirable tennis was seen, with good returns, short chases, and accurate forces. **1955** *Times* 2 May 4/1 Dear went all out for winning openings, making a severe attack on the *dedans*—he scored with 11 forces during the two sets.

III. Phrases (see also senses 1–10).

16. ***by force of***: by dint of, by virtue of; by means of (properly with the implication of strength inherent in the means). Also (later), ***by the force of***. [F. *à force de*.]

1411 *Rolls of Parlt.* III. 650/2 The forsaid Archebisshop, and Chamberleyn.. by force of the submission that the said Robert in hem hath maad, haven ordeyned. *c* **1450** *Merlin* 27 Thei can knowe many thinges be force of clergie that we can no skyll on. **1512** *Act 4 Hen. VIII*, c. 10 Fynes.. levyed.. by reason or force of the same Indentures. **1585** T. WASHINGTON tr. *Nicholay's Voy.* I. ii. 2 The ankers being weied, by force of oares [*à force de rames*] we went to the yle of If. **1611** BIBLE *2 Macc.* x. 24 Timotheus.. came as though hee would take Iewrie by force of armes. **1633** G. HERBERT *Temple, Priesthood* iii, By cunning hand And force of fire, what curious things are made. **1639** FULLER *Holy War* IV. xii. (1640) 188 Two hundred and fourty Gentlemen of note died by force of the infection. **1697** *C'tess D'Aunoy's Trav.* (1706) 32 Don Lewis was no sooner come to himself, by the force of Remidies. **1756** BURKE *Subl. & B.* III. §2 It is not by the force of long attention and inquiry that we find any object to be beautiful. **1879** *Daily Tel.* 17 June, Being by force of genius no less than by virtue of office at the head of the noble profession to which he belongs.

17. ***in force***: **a.** (see 8c).

b. *Mil.* Of a host, enemy, etc.: (Collected) in great military strength and large numbers (cf. sense 3). Also, ***in great force***. [Fr. *en force*.]

c **1315** SHOREHAM 156 Ryȝt develen for screawedhede Ever ine force scholle brede. **1793** BURKE *Rem. Pol. Allies* Wks. VII. 119 When the army of some sovereign enters into the enemy's country in great force. **1810** C. JAMES *Milit. Dict.* (ed. 3) s.v. *Force*, As the enemy were in force behind the mountains. **1836** ALISON *Europe* (1849) V. xxxi. §12. 306 The Republicans were unable to drive back their opponents from the.. heights, which they had occupied in force. **1885** *Times* (weekly ed.) 23 Jan. 3/2 The enemy is reported to be in force at Metamneh.

c. of persons (usu. ***in great force***): In full command of one's powers, energies, or abilities; *esp.* Displaying readiness and vivacity in conversation or oratory (*colloq.*).

1849 R. G. LEVINGE *Cromwell Doolan* II. vi. 130 The young ladies.. were in the greatest possible 'force', as Filagree termed it, and full of fun. **1851** CARLYLE *Sterling* II. vii. (1872) 142 Latterly Calvert was better.. He was in force again. **1857** A. H. ELTON *Below Surface* vi. (1860) 60 Sir Eliot Prichard, quite at his ease, and in high force. **1857** LD. HOUGHTON in *Life* (1891) II. xii. 18 M. Guizot is in great force, and full of political and literary gossip.

†**18.** ***of force***: with *inf.*, strong or powerful enough, able *to* do something. Cf. 1 b, 3 b, 7 c, 8 b.

1598 GERARDE *Herball* II. iv. 182 Lyons Turnep is of force to digest. **1613** SIR J. HAYWARD *Lives 3 Normans* 90 After his death, the inhabitants were of force to expell the strangers. **1632** LE GRYS tr. *Vell. Paterc.* Ep. Ded. A 3 b, I did not beleeve there had beene any power.. of force to make me [etc.]. **1677** N. COX *Gentlem. Recr.* (ed. 2) i. 95 Young Hares are neither of force nor capacity to use such subtleties.

†**19. a.** ***of*** (or ***on***) ***force***: of necessity, on compulsion, whether one will or no, unavoidably, necessarily, perforce. (Cf. PERFORCE, †AFFORCE.) Also, ***of fine force*** (see FINE *a.* 3), ***of very force***. *Obs.*

c **1400** *Rom. Rose* 1796 In wele and wo Of force togidre they must go. **1508** DUNBAR *Poems* iv. 95 On forse I man his nyxt pray be. **1587** TURBERV. *Trag. T.* Hist. iv, There laye he close in wayte within the cops whereas Full well he knew that Guardastan of very force must passe. **1605** BACON *Adv. Learn.* II. v. §2 (1873) 106 Their inquiries must of force have been of a far other kind than they are. *a* **1645** HEYWOOD & ROWLEY *Fort. by Land* II. Wks. 1874 VI. 381 Since you must hire one on force, as good him as another. **1703** ROWE *Ulysses* IV. i. 1477 You must of Force delay it.

†**b.** ***it is*** (***of***) ***force***: it is necessary or inevitable. Const. *that*.., or (*for a person*) *to do*. *Obs.*

1483 CAXTON *Cato* F iv, It was force that he shold retourne into the worlde. **1535** STEWART *Cron. Scot.* II. 566 For euirilk falt quhilk force is to fulfill. **1563** WINZET *Cert. Tractates* (1890) II. 60 Gif we sal begin to mixt noueltie with antiquitie.. force it is that this maner spring vp vniuersalie. *c* **1565** LINDESAY (Pitscottie) *Chron. Scot.* 104 It was force for the said Sir Patrick Hamilton to light on Foot. **1802** H. MARTIN *Helen of Glenross* III. 272 Is it of force you must render yourself contemptible?

†**20. a.** ***it is force***: it is of consequence or importance; usu. neg. ***it is no force*** (also, ***it maketh no force***), it does not matter. So (without verb) ***what force?***, ***no force*** = 'what matter?', 'no matter'. Const. *though*.., *if*.., *whether*.., or relative clause; also *absol.* and parenthetic. [So in OF.] *Obs.*

a **1300** *Cursor M.* 13044 (Cott.) Of hir nam es na force to tell. *c* **1340** *Ibid.* 20683 (Trin.), I shal ȝou telle for hit is fors where þenne bicome hir cors. *c* **1369** CHAUCER *Dethe Blaunche* 522 'A! goode sir, no fors' quod I. *c* **1386** —— *Merch. T.* 591 It is no fors how longe that we pleye. *a* **1400–50** *Alexander* 471 Þofe þou haue forfet, na force, so has fele othire. *a* **1450** *Knt. de la Tour* (1868) 33 He is but a tromper and a iaper, no fors, late us sende for hym. **1450–1530** *Myrr. our Ladye* 325 *Trino* or *terno*, no force whether. **1494** FABYAN *Chron.* vii. 575 What force, though sathan.. Do hym rewarde? **1540** SIR R. SADLER in *St. Papers* (1809) I. 25 'Well', quoth he, 'it is no force'. **1551** RECORDE *Pathw. Knowl.* I. xxvi, Parte that arche line into two partes, equall other vnequall, it maketh no force. **1581** T. HOWELL *Deuises* (1879) 210 Imbrace the good, as for the rest, no force how they thee take. **1612** J. DAVIES *Muses Sacrif.* etc. (Grosart) 82/2 She neuer yet so much as smiled on me; No force, sith I my selfe the better know. **1669** STURMY *Mariner's Mag.* I. 19 They are Dutch Colours: no force, the worst of Enemies.

†**b.** Const. *of* or *for* (a thing) = it does not matter about, no need to care for. *Obs.*

c **1330** R. BRUNNE *Chron.* (1810) 20 Of his body was no force, non for him wild murne. *c* **1374** CHAUCER *Compl. Mars* 197 But were she sauf, hit were no fors of me. **1486** *Bk. St. Albans* C j a, Bot therof it is no force iff she be hole. **1529** MORE *Dyaloge* I. Wks. 131/2 It was of lyklyhode the same night, or some other time sone after.. No force for the time quod he. **1578** WHETSTONE *Promos & Cass.* I. II. iv, No force for that, each shyft for one.

†**21.** ***to make*** (***do, give, take, have, let, kythe, set***) ***force***: to make account (of), attach importance (to), give heed (to), care (for). Const. *of* (rarely *for, at, by, in*); also with infin. or dependent clause, and *absol.* *Obs.*

1303 R. BRUNNE *Handl. Synne* 10286 Lytel fors of hym þou ȝyues. *c* **1325** *Metr. Hom.* 43 Elles forze wald he nan mak Quether his clething war quit or blac. **1350** *Will. Palerne* 3651 Of here fon no fors þei ne leten. *c* **1369** CHAUCER *Dethe Blaunche* 542 'I do no fors therof' quod he. *c* **1430** LYDGATE *Min. Poems* 160 Som yeve no fors for to be forsworn. *c* **1450** *St. Cuthbert* (Surtees) 5392 Monkes hors to gest he had na fors In a hyrne of his Innes. **1470–85** MALORY *Arthur* II. iii. 79, I take no force though I haue bothe their hedes. **1483** *Cron. Englande* (1510) R j a, Kynge Edwardes sone set by the Scottes no force. **1509** BARCLAY *Shyp Folys* (1874) I. 173 Thou ought to be asshamyd To set so great fors for sylver or for golde. **1523** LD. BERNERS *Froissart* (1812) I. 770 Sir Hugh Caurell made no force at his wordes. *Ibid.* I. 419 With the whiche the prince was sore displeased, and set lesse force in yᵉ men of the churche, in whom before he hadde great trust. **1581** J. BELL *Haddon's Answ. Osorius* 512 b, I make no force whether any medicine be applied. **1664** *Floddan Field* III. 26 And of their lives took little force.

†**22. a.** Hunting. ***to hunt*** (etc.) ***at force*** (also ***of*** or ***by force***): to run (the game) down with dogs; to hunt in the open with the hounds in full cry. *Obs.*

[Cf. OF. *courir les cerfs a force* (15th c. in Littré; F. *par force* remains in Ger. *parforcejagd*, the ordinary term for a formal 'hunt' in the English sense.]

1575 LANEHAM *Let.* (1871) 13 Too ryde foorth into the Chase too hunt the Hart of fors. **1576** TURBERV. *Venerie* i. 3 In hunting the Raynedeare at force. **1637** B. JONSON *Sad Sheph.* I. vi, *Rob.* And hunted yee at force? *Mar.* In a full cry. **1674** N. COX *Gentl. Recreat.* I. (1677) 45 If.. you should run him at force out of a Toil. *Ibid.* 55 The King of Poland makes use of them in his hunting of great Beasts by force.

†**b.** ***to make force at, to, upon***: to rush violently at, attack, assail. *Obs.*

1607 TOPSELL *Four-f. Beasts* 145 The dog.. made force vpon him, and the Lyon likewise at the Dogge. *Ibid.* 158 Vpon signs giuen them to which of the stragling beastes they ought to make force. **1674** N. COX *Gentl. Recreat.* I. (1677) 62 Their manner is.. to make force at him with their Horns.

IV. 23. *Comb.* (? of the sb. or the verb-stem): **force cup**, a rubber cup attached to a handle which by creating a vacuum in a blocked drain is used to clear it; **force(-)field**, a field of force (see FIELD *sb.* 17); esp. in *Science Fiction*, one that acts as an invisible barrier; **force-land** *v.* (see FORCED *ppl. a.* 2 d); **force-out**, in *Baseball*, the obligatory retirement of a base runner at the base he is forced to run to by a following base runner; **force-piece** (see quot.); **force-pipe**, the pipe of a force-pump in which the piston works. Also FORCE-PUMP.

1907 *Yesterday's Shopping* (1969) 118/3 Force Cup. For cleansing stopped pipes, drains, &c. **1951** *Good Housek. Home Encycl.* 257/1 Try using a rubber force cup with a vigorous up-and-down movement. **1960** D. V. DAVIS *Domestic Encycl.* i. 54 An emergency force cup can be made by cutting a piece out of an old rubber ball, placing the pole over the sink outlet and squeezing the ball several times. **1920** *Rep. Brit. Assoc. 1920* 236 Each atom must form the centre of an electromagnetic field of force. These force fields were first dealt with by Humphreys. **1926** *Bull. Nat. Res. Counc.* LIV. 294 A clear understanding of the form of the orbit and quantum conditions for central force fields is often essential in the theoretical interpretation of spectra. **1944** F. BROWN in B. Aldiss *Introd. SF* (1964) 74 'There is a barrier.' A force-field, of course. **1962** F. I. ORDWAY et al. *Basic Astronautics* iv. 120 There are four groups of phenomena: (1) interstellar and interplanetary particulate matter, (2) energetic particles, (3) electromagnetic radiations, and (4) force fields. **1964** *Observer* 13 Dec. 34/7 An electronic bird-repeller.. that will send out a science-fiction type 'force field' to keep birds away. **1896** H. CHADWICK *Spalding's Base Ball Guide* 76 The result being a force-out play to second, if not a double play. **1926** *N.Y. Times* 11 Oct. 24/1 His grounder to Bell was turned into a forceout of Ruth at second while Combs dashed on to third. **1968** *Washington Post* 4 July C 2/4 Wills.. took third on Gene Alley's single and scored on Roberto Clemente's force out. **1882** OGILVIE, *Force-piece in mining*, a piece of timber placed in a level shaft to keep the ground open. **1842** GWILT *Encycl. Archit.* §2222 When the height of the force pipe is greater or less than the length of the suction pipe.

force (fɔəs), *sb.*² *local.* Also foss. [a. ON. *fors* (Sw. *fors*, Da. *fos*).] A name in the north of England for a waterfall or cascade.

1600 CAMDEN *Brit.* 686 marg., (Westmorland) *Catadupæ*, The Forses. **1658** PHILLIPS, *Forses*, water-falls. **1769** GRAY *Let.* 18 Oct. in *Poems* (1775) 369 After dinner I went.. to see the falls, or force, of the river Kent. **1788** W. MARSHALL *Yorksh.* (1796) II. 320 *Foss*.. a waterfall. **1813** SCOTT *Trierm.* III. viii, Shingle and Scrae, and Fell and Force. **1839** BAILEY *Festus* xix. (1848) 221 Like to a foaming force.

†**force**, *sb.*³ *Obs.* [f. FORCE *v.*³] Only in ***gruel of force*** = 'gruel forced, afforced' (see FORCE *v.*³).

c **1420** *Liber Cocorum* (1862) 47.

force (fɔəs), *v.*¹ Forms: see the sb. [a. Fr. *forcer*, f. *force* FORCE *sb.*]

I. To apply force.

1. *trans.* To use violence to; to violate, ravish (a woman).

a **1300** *Cursor M.* 1577 (Cott.) Wimmen þai forced a-mang þaim. ? *a* **1400** *Morte Arth.* 978 He has forsede hir and fylede. **1483** CAXTON *G. de la Tour* lviii. E vij b, She saide to her lord that he wolde haue forced her. **1530** PALSGR. 349 The abbesse sawe that for her beaute she shulde be forced. *c* **1620** Z. BOYD *Zion's Flowers* (1855) 143 To force a maide, it sure will blot your name. **1701** SWIFT *Cont. Nobles & Com.* Wks. 1755 II. I. 10 One of them proceeding so far, as to endeavour to force a lady of great virtue. **1871** H. KING *Ovid's Met.* IV. 290 'Let Himself', she cried, 'Confess, he forced me!'

†**2.** To press hard upon (in battle). *Obs.*

c **1330** *Arth. & Merl.* 8951 Thai.. forced hem with mani dent hard, What thai come to king Riones standard. *c* **1400** *Destr. Troy* 7671 Þai.. fforsit hym with fight.. Vnhorset hym in hast.

3. a. To constrain by force (whether physical or moral); to compel; to overcome the resistance of. ***to force*** (***one's***) ***hand***: to compel one to act prematurely or to adopt a policy he dislikes. Cf. Fr. *forcer la main à quelqu'un*.

c **1400** *Destr. Troy* 1924 His fader vs forset with his fowle wille. **1551** T. WILSON *Logike* (1580) 16 Neither can any Lawe bee able, violently to force the inwarde thought of man. **1574** HELLOWES *Gueuara's Fam. Ep.* 64 To demand more tribute, to force thy people, to forget mee thy friend. **1593** SHAKS. *3 Hen. VI*, I. i. 230 Art thou King, and wilt be forc't? **1602** MARSTON *Antonio's Rev.* IV. v, Hee whose great heart Heaven can not force with force. **1697** DRYDEN *Æneid* VII. 808 To Force their Monarch, and insult the Court. **1764** GOLDSM. *Trav.* 168 Where the black Swiss.. force a churlish soil for scanty bread. **1827** WORDSW. *Persecut. Scot. Covenanters*, Who would force the Soul, tilts with a straw Against a Champion cased in adamant. **1860** MOTLEY *Netherl.* (1868) I. viii. 524 Sir Francis.. occasionally forced his adversaries' hands.

b. To put a strained sense upon (words). Also, ***to force*** (***words***) ***into a sense***.

1662 STILLINGFL. *Orig. Sacr.* III. ii. §2 Without forcing the words of Moses into such a sense. **1701** SWIFT *Cont. Nobles & Com.* Wks. 1755 II. I. 43, I am not conscious, that I have forced one example. **1875** E. WHITE *Life in Christ* IV. xxiv. (1878) 381 This is manifestly to force the Scripture.

c. *Card-playing*, esp. in *Whist.* (*a*) To compel (a player) to trump a trick, by leading a card of a suit of which he has none; (*b*) To make (a player) play so as to show the strength of his hand; (*c*) To cause a player to play (a certain card) by leading one which must have the effect of drawing it out.

1746 HOYLE *Whist* (ed. 6) 25 Your strong Suit forces their best Trumps. *Ibid.* 68 *Forcing*, Means the obliging your Partner or your Adversary to trump a suit of which he has none. **1862** CAVENDISH *Whist* (1870) 28 To force or to give a force is to lead a forcing card. *Ibid.* (1879) 111 If.. a good partner refrains from forcing you, you may be sure he is weak. **1878** H. H. GIBBS *Ombre* 16 Manille when led will necessarily force Basto if the latter be the other player's only trump.

d. *intr. Austral.* and *N.Z.* Of a sheep-dog: to move sheep. Cf. FORCE *sb.*¹ 7 e.

1920 PATON & REID in J. B. Cramsie *Managem. Sheep Austral.* v. 29 Close working [by a dog] in the open paddock is to be avoided because this means forcing, and forcing means over-heated sheep. **1934** J. LILICO *Sheep Dog Mem.* 27 [The dogs] would head, lead, hunt away, force and back though.. they were best at rouseabout work.

4. a. To compel, constrain, or oblige (a person, oneself, etc.) *to do* a thing (†sometimes with *to* omitted); to bring (things), to drive (a person, etc.) *to* or *into* (a course of action, a condition).

c **1400** *Destr. Troy* 6823 Þe grekes.. were forsit to þe fight. *Ibid.* 9965 Þai spake to þe kyng, For to force hym to fight, & his feris help. *c* **1425** WYNTOUN *Cron.* VIII. xxxvii. 164 Fortown forsyd hyr to be fa. **1530** PALSGR. 555/1, I force, I constrayne one to do a thyng. *c* **1592** MARLOWE *Jew of Malta* III. i, Which forc'd their hands divide united hearts. **1592** SHAKS. *Ven. & Ad.* 61 Forst to content, but neuer to obey, Panting he lies. **1652–62** HEYLIN *Cosmogr.* III. (1673) 82/1 Who.. being forced for to forsake their Country, came and settled here. **1673** R. HADDOCK *Jrnl.* in *Camden Misc.* (1881) 25 The wind.. forct us strick our yard. **1770** *Junius Lett.* xli. 218 Your fears have.. forced you to resign. **1803** *Med. Jrnl.* X. 510 Solid or fluid substances exciting vomiting.. act as powerful stimuli on the disordered state of the stomach, and force it to preternatural contraction. **1845** M. PATTISON *Ess.* (1889) I. 4 When men are forced into daily and hourly action in matters where they cannot be indifferent spectators. **1867** SMILES *Huguenots Eng.* vii. (1880) 121 Many of the fugitives.. appear to have been forced to attend Mass. **1874** GREEN *Short Hist.* ii. §8 Every knight was forced to arm himself with coat of mail.

b. *pass.* (of a thing) ***to be forced to be***, etc.: to be of necessity. Now *colloq.* or *vulgar*.

1691 T. H[ALE] *Acc. New Invent.* 47 The Rudder-Irons being eaten by the Rust, were forced to be shifted. *Ibid.* 49 The Lead was forced to be cut away in many places.

†**c.** *ellipt.* (= *force to believe*) To convince. *Obs.*

1581 SIDNEY *Astr. & Stella* viii, Forct, by a tedious proofe, that Turkish hardned hart Is not fit marke.

5. a. To urge, compel to violent effort; †to exert (one's strength) to the utmost. *spec.* in *Cricket*.

to force the pace or *the running* (in a race): to adopt, and thus force one's competitors to adopt, a rate of speed likely to harass them and improve one's own chance of winning. *to force the bidding*: at a sale by auction, to run the price up rapidly. *to force one's voice*: to attempt notes beyond the natural compass. *to force the game* in *Cricket*: Of a batsman: To run some risks in order to increase the rate of scoring, and so give one's side a better chance of winning a game. **1697** DRYDEN *Æneid* VI. 487 High on a Mounting Wave, my head I bore, Forcing my Strength, and gath'ring to the Shore. **1825** DANNELEY *Encycl. Mus.* s.v. *Force*, When..the instrument or voice is forced, sound becomes noise..To *Force* the voice, is to exceed its diapason and natural strength. **1897** *Encycl. Sport* I. 226/2 Under such conditions the batsmen should run a few risks to score runs quickly (in cricketers' parlance, 'to force the game') while they have the chance. **1904** P. F. WARNER *How We recovered Ashes* xiv. 276 Hopkins was evidently bent on forcing the hitting. **1908** W. E. W. COLLINS *County Cricketer's Diary* x. 168 An attempt..to force the game on a ground that does not lend itself to forcing tactics. **1963** A. ROSS *Australia 63* iii. 79 Dexter forced him through mid-wicket. **1970** *Times* 19 Aug. 6/3 They all pitched a little short, for fear of being driven, and because of this they were forced and hooked.

†**b.** *refl.* and *intr.* To do one's utmost endeavour, strive. *Obs.*

a **1300** *Cursor M.* 18089 (Cott.) And forces yow wit might and main Stalworthli to stand a-gain. *c* **1340** HAMPOLE *Prose Tr.* 6 Sothely fra þat tym furthe I forced me for to luf Jhesu. **1382** WYCLIF *Ecclus.* xxix. 19 He that forseth manye thingus to do, shall fallen in to dom. *a* **1400–50** *Alexander* 2659 Þof he hym forsyd hafe The charge of hys chiftane chefely to fylle. **1579** SPENSER *Sheph. Cal.* Apr. 24 Forcing with gyfts to winne his wanton heart. **1596** —— *F.Q.* V. vi. 11 Forcing in vaine the rest to her to tell.

6. To overpower by force. **a.** To make a forcible entry into; to take by force, to storm (a stronghold); to board (a ship). Also, To effect a passage through (mountains, a river, an enemy's lines) by force.

1581 SAVILE *Tacitus' Hist.* II. ix. (1591) 58 By whose per swasion his shippe was forced and taken. **1608** GOLDING *Epit. Frossard* I. 10 At length the Citie..was forced by assault. **1695** BLACKMORE *Pr. Arth.* IV. 517 The Invading Saxon forc'd our Lines. **1810** WELLINGTON in Gurw. *Desp.* VII. 56, I have no doubt, the enemy is not..able to force the position of the allies in this country. **1825** T. JEFFERSON *Autobiog.* Wks. 1859 I. 98 The people..forced the prison of Saint Lazare. **1839** KEIGHTLEY *Hist. Eng.* II. 43 The rebels once more prepared to force the ford. **1854** J. S. C. ABBOTT *Napoleon* (1855) I. iv. 86 Hannibal..forced the Alps: but we have turned them.

transf. **1627** MAY *Lucan* II. 463 Vntill The sea diuided him, and water forc'd The land. **1821** CLARE *Vill. Minstr.* I. 136 Stopping up the mimic rills, Till they forc'd their frothy bound.

b. To break open (a gate, etc.); to break (a lock); †to pierce (armour). Also *to force open.*

1623 BINGHAM *Xenophon, Lipsius' Compar.* 4 The Parthian Arrows forced all kinde of Armor. *a* **1639** SPOTTISWOOD *Hist. Ch. Scot.* IV. (1677) 188 The Citizens..being denied entry, forces the gates. **1781** GIBBON *Decl. & F.* III. 236 The..dwelling..was forced open by one of the powerful Goths. **1834** MEDWIN *Angler in Wales* II. 57 Having no means of forcing the gate. **1849** MACAULAY *Hist. Eng.* III. 302 No blacksmith..would force the lock of the President's lodgings. **1887** *Times* 31 Aug. 13/4 A window had been forced as well as a desk.

†**c.** To compel to give way or yield; to overpower (troops, a guard). *Obs.*

a **1641** BP. MOUNTAGU *Acts & Mon.* (1642) 246 He..dislodged, forced, apprehended many of them. **1718** *Col. Rec. Pennsylv.* III. 51 And fforced two of their men. **1781** GIBBON *Decl. & F.* II. 120 The emperor soon removed the only obstacle that could embarrass his motions, by forcing a body of troops which had taken post in an amphitheatre.

7. a. To drive by force, propel against resistance, impel. Chiefly const. with prep., or with advbs.

1582 N. LICHEFIELD tr. *Castanheda's Conq. E. Ind.* iii. 8 b, Their skinnes be so hard that no speare can pearce the same, albeit it be forced vpon it with great strength. **1634** BATE *Myst. Nat. & Art.* I. 17 Another manner of forcing water. *a* **1691** BOYLE *Hist. Air* (1692) 138 They set up some turfs on the lee side of the hole, to catch, and so force down the fresh air. **1700** S. L. tr. *Fryke's Voy. E. Ind.* 298 Those that delight in Hunting, may find great quantities of Beasts forced up into the Mountains at that time. **1704** ADDISON *Italy* 4 We were forc'd by contrary Winds into St. Remo. *a* **1732** T. BOSTON *Crook in Lot* (1805) 115 When ye work against him, to force up your condition. **1818** M. G. LEWIS *Jrnl. W. Ind.* (1834) 299 At least three inches of the blade were forced into his right side. **1849** JAMES *Woodman* i, Through which the stream seemed to have forced itself. **1878** BROWNING *La Saisiaz* 59 Idle hopes that lure man onward, forced back by as idle fears.

absol. **1588** GREENE *Pandosto* (1607) A iv b, Where fancy forced friendship was of no force.

b. *to force down*: to compel (an aircraft) to land.

1917 *War Illustr.* 15 Dec. 359 The German machine..was 'forced down' on the French front in an intact state, and its airmen were made prisoners. **1958** *Times* 30 June 10/5 U.S. aircraft forced down by Soviet fighters.

8. a. *intr.* To make one's way by force. Also with *in, out, up.* Now *rare.*

1653 HOLCROFT *Procopius* II. 46 The Marriners rowed, and with much toyle forced up. **1697** DRYDEN *Virg. Georg.* III. 426 For Love they force thro' Thickets. **1707** *Lond. Gaz.* No. 4380/3 The Firebrand..drove off, and forc'd in under a Fore-Course for the Light of St. Agnes. **1713** WARDER *True Amazons* 150 When you feel them..ready to force out of your Hand. **1791** MRS. INCHBALD *Simp. Story* III. xii. 178 You have dared to visit her—to force into her presence and shock her. **1853** KANE *Grinnell. Exp.* xliv. (1856) 406 We gradually force ahead, breasting aside the floes.

b. *Tennis.* To use the force stroke (see prec. 15 b).

1890 J. M. HEATHCOTE *Tennis* 52 It is impossible to force as severely, difficult to force as accurately, with a back-hand as with a fore-hand stroke.

9. *trans.* **a.** To press, put, or impose (something) forcibly *on, upon* (a person), and *simply.* Also, *to force* (a person) *on, upon* (something): to oblige to resort to.

1601 SHAKS. *Twel. N.* III. i. 127 To force that on you..Which you knew none of yours. **1683** A. D. *Art Converse* 30 This barbarous custom of forcing drink upon men. **1709** SWIFT *Adv. Relig.* Wks. 1755 II. I. 106 New men, whose narrow fortunes have forced them upon industry and application. **1751** JORTIN *Serm.* (1771) II. iii. 43 An observation which will force itself upon you. *a* **1848** R. W. HAMILTON *Rew. & Punishm.* viii. (1853) 383 The warfare is forced upon us. **1856** DE QUINCEY *Confess.* 238 Nervous irritation forced me..upon frightful excesses; but terror from anomalous symptoms sooner or later forced me back. *Ibid.* 269 The..riotous prodigality of life naturally forces the mind more powerfully upon the antagonist thought of death. **1872** J. L. SANFORD *Estim. Eng. Kings, Chas. I*, 334 However plainly the facts of the case were forced on his attention. **1903** R. LANGBRIDGE *Flame & Flood* xxiv, Her lack of money had forced her back upon the most respectable costume which she had.

†**b.** To lay stress upon, press home, urge. *Obs.* Also, To enforce (a law, etc.).

1580 H. GIFFORD *Gilloflowers* (1875) 87 But will that stately Dame, Still bad me write, not forcing any blame? **1603** SHAKS. *Meas. for M.* III. i. 110 Has he affections in him That thus can make him bite the Law by th' nose, When he would force it? **1607** DRAYTON *Cromwell* ii. in *Mirr. Mag.* (1610) 520 Forcing my good, excusing of my ill.

c. In *Conjuring with cards* (see quot. 1888).

1880 BROWNING *Dram. Idyls* Ser. II. *Clive* 116 You forced a card and cheated! **1888** KUNARD *Card Tricks* 13 *To force a card*..consists in making a person select from a pack any particular card you desire him to take, while he imagines he is taking one quite at haphazard. *Ibid.* 14 To force, you must never be in a hurry..Four cards from the same pack were forced upon him.

10. To bring about, effect, or produce by force or effort; to bring about of necessity, or as a necessary result. Also, *to force a passage, one's way. lit.* and *fig.*

1551 T. WILSON *Logike* (1580) 42 b, Yet are thei not any cause to force the effect. **1593** SHAKS. *Lucr.* 689 This forced league doth force a further strife. **1640** HABINGTON *Edw. IV*, 35 The Nobility in generall lookt discontented, or else but forc'd a smile. **1651** HOBBES *Leviath.* xxix. 173 A..strong endeavour of the Heart, to force a passage for the Bloud. **1680** OTWAY *Orphan* II. i. 413 What man of sense would..force a grave starch't face When he's a very Libertine in 's heart? **1693** CONGREVE *Old Bach.* I. iv, I don't force appetite, but wait the natural call of my lust. **1697** DAMPIER *Voy.* I. i. 6 We should..force our way through their Country. **1711** SHAFTESBURY *Charac. Misc.* II. i. (1737) III. 46 If these Dealers are numerous, they will force a Trade. **1790** CATH. GRAHAM *Lett. Educ.* 30 Hearers, who could hardly force such a seeming attention as is consistent with common politeness. *c* **1802** C. JAMES *Milit. Dict.*, *To force a passage*, to oblige your enemy to retire..and thus open a way into the country which he had occupied. **1809** ROLAND *Fencing* 81 You may..force a favourable opportunity to deliver the thrust you had thus premeditated. **1875** JOWETT *Plato* (ed. 2) III. 416 These studies force their way by their natural charm.

11. To obtain or take by force; to win by violence; to draw forth (*lit.* and *fig.*) as a necessary consequence; to extort, elicit. Also, *to force away, out.*

1602 MARSTON *Antonio's Rev.* I. ii, A modest eye forceth affection. *Ibid.* IV. iii, What I here speake is forced from my lips By the pulsive straine of conscience. **1655** STANLEY *Hist. Philos.* I. (1701) 46/2 Cleobulus..and Periander..forced a reputation. **1676** HOBBES *Iliad* I. 375 His Officers from me have forc't my prey. **1697** DRYDEN *Æneid* x. 538 It stuck so fast..That scarce the Victor forc'd the Steel away. **1703** POPE *Thebais* 301 How long shall man..force unwilling vengeance from the sky! **1715** LADY M. W. MONTAGU *Town Eclogues* II. 46 A lady..with gentle strugglings let me force this ring. **1719** DE FOE *Crusoe* I. iv, This forced tears from my eyes. **1723** ATTERBURY *Answ. Consid. Spirit M. Luther* 65 The Heat of the Dispute had forc'd out from him Expressions that seem'd to make his Doctrine run higher than really it did. **1818** JAS. MILL *Brit. India* II. v. ix. 715 Means..were employed to force out the real state of the facts. **1818** M. G. LEWIS *Jrnl. W. Ind.* (1834) 56 Somebody..had endeavoured to force it [a medal] away. **1845** M. PATTISON *Ess.* (1889) I. 14 A moral power..forcing from them a sort of recognition of its claims.

12. To hasten by artificial means the maturity of (plants, fruit, etc.). Also *intr.* for *refl.*

1719 LONDON & WISE *Compl. Gard.* 304 We force Sorrel and wild Endive. **1823** *New Monthly Mag.* IX. 453/2 The Scarlets will force in a peach-house, or vinery. **1832** *Examiner* 801/1 Nomination burghs have been forced like mush-rooms. **1842** BRANDE *Dict. Sc.* etc. s.v. *Forcing*, Cherries having been forced..from the time of Charles II. *Mod.* A premature scholar forced in a so-called 'preparatory' school.

II. To give, add, have force.

†**13. a.** To give force or strength to; to strengthen, reinforce; also, to fortify, garrison (a place), to man (fortifications). *Obs.*

c **1430** LYDG. *Bochas* I. ix. (1544) 20 a, Polinices to forcen his partie Ywedded had the kinges doughter dere. **1535** STEWART *Cron. Scot.* (1858) I. 13 Syne forcit it [the stronghold] with fowseis..And dowbill dykes. **1560** ROLLAND *Crt. Venus* II. 847 With stark draw brig, weil forcit with fortalice. **1605** SHAKS. *Macb.* v. v. 5 Were they not forc'd with those that should be ours, We might haue..beate them backward home. *a* **1618** RALEIGH *Apol.* (1650) 28 If you shall find that any great number of Souldiers be newly sent into Orrenoque..and that the Passages be already Forc'd. **1794** W. HUTCHINSON *Hist. Durham* III. 175 The ground..appears to have been forced, and is trenched round. **1810** C. JAMES *Milit. Dict.* (ed. 3), *To force*, to man the works of a garrison.

†**b.** To fine (wine) by a short process. *Obs.*

1731–3 P. SHAW *Chem. Lect.* (1755) 208 These are the common Methods of Forcing at present used in the Wine-Business. **1802** WILLICH *Dom. Encycl.* II, Forcing of Wine: *see* Clarification. **1839** HARTLEY *Wine & Spirit Merchants' Comp.* 44 Fine or force this wine with the whites and shells of ten eggs.

†**14.** Chiefly in negative sentences: **a.** (*a*) *trans.* To attach force or importance to; to care for, regard; often with a strengthening phrase, as *a bean, a pin, a straw. Obs.*

c **1400** *Destr. Troy* 1929 We fors not his frendship, ne fere of his hate. **1509** BARCLAY *Shyp of Folys* 71 a, They forse no thynge so they may money wyn. **1587** TURBERV. *Epit. & Sonn.* (1837) 394 Force nat the face, regard nat feature so. **1593** SHAKS. *Lucr.* 1021, I force not argument a straw. **1606** J. RAYNOLDS *Dolarney's Prim.* (1880) 92 They feare not death, they force him not a pin. **1614** CHR. BROOKE *Poems* (Grosart) *Rich. III*, 50, I forst no public wrack..So I might rule.

†(*b*) with a sentence as obj. *Obs.*

1500–20 DUNBAR *Poems* lviii. 22 Thay fors bot litill how it fure. **1568** *Jacob & Esau* II. ii, I force not what it were, so that I had to eate. **1580** H. GIFFORD *Gilloflowers* (Grosart) 98 Let them speak and spare not, I force not a beane. **1611** SPEED *Hist. Gt. Brit.* IX. xx. (1632) 985 They forced not what part they tooke so that they might bee reuenged.

†(*c*) with *inf.* as *obj.* To care *to*, think it of consequence, or worth while *to.* Also, to hesitate, scruple. *Obs.*

1509 BARCLAY *Shyp of Folys* 170 b, To theyr company none forsyth to resort. **1546** BALE *Eng. Votaries* I. (1550) 60 b, He forced not to be perjured. **1563** *Homilies* II. *Right Use of Church* II. (1859) 163 Another..forceth not to hear the common prayer of the minister. **1588** SHAKS. *L.L.L.* v. ii. 440 Your oath once broke, you force not to forsweare. **1591** HARINGTON *Orl. Fur.* I. lxix, His name I will not force To tell, sith you desire to know the same.

†**b.** *intr.* To trouble oneself, be concerned, care. Const. *for, of*, rarely *on. Obs.*

?*a* **1471** RIPLEY *Comp. Alch.* v. xxxv. in Ashm. (1652) 156 He forsyth lyttyll of other menys losse. **1513** MORE in Grafton *Chron.* (1568) II. 785 The Fryer forced for no shame. **1547** RECORDE *Judic. Ur.* 2, I force nott though he doubt also of my truth in the same. **1548** HALL *Chron. Hen. VIII* an. 22 (1809) 774 He [Wolsey] forced litle on Simony. **1573** *New Custom* II. iii, I force not I, so the vyllaine were dead. **1605** CAMDEN *Rem.* Wise Sp. 190 The Duke answered: I force not of such fooleries.

†**15.** *impers.* or quasi-*impers.* To be of force, importance, or weight; to matter, signify. *Obs.*

a **1400–50** *Alexander* 2001 Þen how fele be att þe flote, it forcez bot lityll. **1553** T. WILSON *Rhet.* (1580) 75 What forceth when we die. **1603** OWEN *Pembrokesh.* (1891) 150 Whose soever they be yt forceth not.

†**force**, *v.*[2] *Obs.* [ad. AF. *forcer*, f. *forces* fem. pl.:—L. *forfices, forfex* clipping-shears.] *trans.* To clip or shear (wool, the beard); *esp.* to clip off the upper and more hairy part of (wool).

[**1429** *Act 8 Hen. VI*, c. 22 Ceux qi clakkent & forcent les bones lains du roialme.] *c* **1440** *Promp. Parv.* 170/2 Foorcyn, or clyppyn, *tondeo.* **1543** tr. *Act 8 Hen. VI*, c. 22 That do clackke and force the good wolles of the realme. **1607** COWELL *Interpr.* s.v. *Clack*, To force wooll is to clip of the vpper and more heary part of it. **1641** BEST *Farm. Bks.* (Surtees) 9 This the shepheardes call forcinge of them. **1706** in PHILLIPS. **1721–90** in BAILEY.

Hence **'forced** *ppl. a.*; **'forcing** *vbl. sb.* Also **force** *sb. Shetl. dial.* (see quot. 1819).

c **1440** *Promp. Parv.* 170/2 Foorcyd, as mennys beerdys ..*capitonsus. Ibid.*, Foorcyd, as wulle, *tonsus. Ibid.*, Foorcynge, *tonsura.* **1819** REES *Cycl.* XXXII. s.v. *Sheep*, When the new fleece has acquired about two months' growth, the rough hairs termed *fors* spring up..[The 'fors'] is separated from it [the wool] in dressing the fleece, by an operation called *forsing.* **1866** EDMONDSTON *Shetl. Gloss.*, *Forsens*, the refuse of wool.

†**force**, *v.*[3] *Obs.* [Alteration of FARCE *v.*[1], by confusion with FORCE *v.*[1]]

1. = FARCE *v.*[1] I.

In the 15th c. Cookery-bks. *aforce* is often used in the same contexts as this vb.; in some passages the sense may be 'to strengthen' (as by adding gravy), 'to season, spice.'

?*a* **1400** *Tourn. Tott.* Feast x, Dongesteks in doralle Was forsed wele with charcoll. *c* **1420** *Liber Cocorum* (1862) 27 Fors hit with spicys. *c* **1450** *Two Cookery-bks.* II. (1888) 117 Yiffe þou wilt haue it forced, hete milke [etc.]. **1747** MRS. GLASSE *Cookery* 18 To Force a Leg of Lamb.

fig. **1606** SHAKS. *Tr. & Cr.* II. iii. 232 Force him with praises, poure in, poure in, his ambition is dry. *Ibid.* v. i. 64 Wit..larded with malice and malice forced with wit.

2. = FARCE *v.*[1] 3. Also, to fatten (animals).

a **1571** JEWEL *Serm.* (1603) 227 Here wil I speak nothing of forcing and quaffinge, God keepe it farre from Christian tables. **1793** *Residence in France* (1797) I. 355 Forcing him with bons morceaux till he has an indigestion. **1847** HALLIWELL, *Force*..to fatten animals. *East.*

Hence **'forced** *ppl. a.*; **'forcing** *vbl. sb.*

[*c* **1390** in S. Pegge *Forme of Cury* (1780) 12 Grewel forced.] **14..** *Noble Bk. Cookery* (Napier 1882) 88 Gruelle enforced.] **1538** ELIOT, *Pulmentarium*, potage made with fleshe or fyshe, as forced gruell. **1688** R. HOLME *Armoury* III. iii. 82/2 A Forced Leg of Mutton. **1709** ADDISON *Tatler* No. 148 ¶3 High Soups, seasoned Sauces, and forced Meats. **1790** GROSE *Provinc. Gloss.* (ed. 2) Suppl., *Forcing*, fattening. *Norf.*

†'**forceable**, *a.* *Obs.*$^{-1}$ [ad. OF. *forçable*, f. *forcer* to force.] That may be forced.
1574 HELLOWES *Gueuara's Fam. Ep.* 201 In humane lawes there be more things arbitrable than forceable.

forceable, obs. form of FORCIBLE.

†'**forceage**. *Obs. rare.* [f. FORCE *sb.*^{1} + -AGE.] The action of forcing, compulsion.
c **1470** HARDING *Chron.* Ded. vii. 4 Y^e sharpe spurre of marciall forceage.

forced (fɔəst), *ppl. a.* [f. FORCE *v.*^{1} + -ED^1.]
1. Subjected to violence.
1621 G. SANDYS *Ovid's Met.* I. 705 She..implores the liquid Sisters Aid To change her Shape and pity a forc'd Maid. *Ibid.* III. 694 Let his forc'd breath Expire in groans.
2. a. Compelled, imposed, or exacted by force; enforced, compulsory; not spontaneous, voluntary, or optional. spec. ***forced labour*** (also as attrib. phr.); †*forced man*: a pressed man.
1576 FLEMING *Panopl. Epist.* 261 Wherein is declared the merite of free obedience and forced duetie. **1621** G. SANDYS *Ovid's Met.* II. 107 To this alone I give a forc'd Consent. **1661** *Papers on Alter. Prayer-bk.* 77 They had many Lyturgies in one Princes Dominion, and those alterable, and not forced. **1702** DENNIS *Comic. Gallant* 49 A forced Marriage is but a lawful Rape. **1734** tr. *Rollin's Anc. Hist.* (1827) VI. xv. xiii. 205 A forced peace is soon followed by war. **1748** *Anson's Voy.* I iii. 28 Spaniards being no strangers to the dissatisfaction of their forced men. **1781** GIBBON *Decl. & F.* III. 110 Forced or fictitious testaments. **1798** NELSON 27 Jan. in Nicolas *Disp.* (1845) III. 4 There ought to be the greatest difference made between a forced man and the man who voluntarily offers his life to preserve his country. **1812** BYRON *Ch. Har.* II. vii, There no forced banquet claims the sated guest. **18..** R. C. BROWNE *Milton's Poems* Introd. p. li, From March 1626 to July 1627, when the system of forced loans was in full operation. **1866** CRUMP *Banking* vii. 145 The forced paper currency. **1872** YEATS *Growth Comm.* 35 The forced labour of slaves. **1931** *Economist* 17 Jan. 105/2 Some of the worst features of the report..are those relating to what is euphemistically described as the official recruitment of labour, for export, mainly to Fernando Po, and to forced labour conditions. **1941** KOESTLER *Scum of Earth* 276 They..were kept in the Moroccan forced-labour battalions to work in mines and quarries. **1942** *Ann. Reg. 1941* 175 Trials of people for kindness towards prisoners of war and foreigners doing forced labour. **1960** *Guardian* 15 Nov. 8/5 Lord Altrincham's call for conscription seems to be for both military service and civil jobs such as road making. The latter is ordinarily termed forced labour.
b. ***forced move***: in a game, one rendered inevitable by the action of the adversary or the position of the piece. Cf. *forced put*, FORCE-PUT.
1847 H. STAUNTON *Chess-Player's Handbk.* I. ii. 22 When a player has only one legal move at command, it is said to be a *forced move.* **1890** R. F. GREEN *Chess* 31 The capture of a Pawn *en passant* is a forced move, if none other be possible.
c. ***forced feeding*** = *force-feeding* (see FORCE-FEED *v.*).
1901 G. C. WATSON *Farm Poultry* ix. 161 It is quite possible to injure the digestion of laying hens by a system of forced feeding. **1923** H. A. ROBERTS *Commercial Poultry Raising* xv. 207 Forced feeding must not be carried to the point where it affects and impairs stamina and health.
d. ***forced landing***: the unpremeditated landing of an aircraft in an emergency; hence ***force-land*** v. intr., to make a forced landing.
1917 'CONTACT' *Airman's Outings* 8 That aerial highwayman the forced landing. **1921** *Flight* XIII. 440/2 They left Croydon..in a Goliath, which had, unfortunately, to force-land at Amiens. **1928** [see CRASH *v.* 6 b]. **1936** *Jrnl. R. Aeronaut. Soc.* XL. 28 An engine failure is defined as engine trouble (apart from fuel system) causing a forced landing. **1958** *Oxf. Mail* 21 Jan. 1/1 A United States Navy plane..force-landed about 450 miles from its destination. **1961** L. VAN DER POST *Heart of Hunter* viii. 120 Some R.A.F. men..had made a forced landing in the desert.
e. ***forced-choice***: used *attrib.* of a question, technique, etc., in which the participant must choose between a number of pre-arranged alternatives.
1944 SHIPLEY & GRAHAM *Summary Res. on Personal Inventory* 1 Its items..are cast in forced-choice form to promote valid answering. **1957** E. BOTT *Family & Social Network* vi. 170 Answers to forced-choice questions need not represent the subject's attitudes. **1964** D. B. FRY in D. Abercrombie et al. *Daniel Jones* 62 The listener is placed in a 'forced choice' situation. **1967** J. F. CORSO in H. Helson et al. *Contemp. Approaches Psychol.* vii. 304 To predict performance in a forced-choice test, an extension of the decision model is required. **1970** *Jrnl. Gen. Psychol.* Jan. 96 These statements were mimeographed and presented in the form of a forced-choice true and false test. **1970** *Language* XLVI. 304 Despite their close agreement in the 'forced-choice' selections, the preceptive reaction of UK and US subjects shows them sharply polarized in the judgment test.
3. a. Produced or maintained with effort; strained. ***forced march***: 'one in which the marching power of the troops is forced or exerted beyond the ordinary limit' (Adm. Smyth).
1596 SHAKS. *1 Hen. IV*, III. i. 135 'Tis like the forc't gate of a shuffling Nagge. **1677** YARRANTON *Eng. Improv.* 132 No forc't hast; but Thrashing and carrying the corn to the Granary in times wherein his servants have leisure. **1769** ROBERTSON *Chas. V*, III. VII. 39 He..by a forced march got into Fertè. **1825** BENTHAM *Ration. Rew.* 271 This being sold at a forced price, the merchant will take care not to replace it. **1840** THIRLWALL *Greece* VII. liv. 38 Alexander..by a forced night-march, reached the Hydrastes at day-break. **1889** MILFORD *Pocket Dict. Mining, Forced production*, to work a mine so as to make it produce a greater output than can be maintained.
b. In literary usage: Strained, distorted. Cf. FORCE *v.*^{1} 3 b.
1583 FULKE *Defence* i. §52. 67 Neither doth Caluine..thinke it..a forced translation. **1678** CUDWORTH *Intell. Syst.* 309 The Greek Etymologies of this word, seem to be all..Violent and Forced. **1724** A. COLLINS *Gr. Chr. Relig.* 173 Forc'd interpretations. **1782** PRIESTLEY *Corrupt. Chr.* I. II. 163 Without any forced Construction it may be turned against this favourite opinion. **1812** WOODHOUSE *Astron.* xxxvi. 360 Without any forced analogies.
c. Of actions, demeanour, gestures, etc.: Affected, artificial, constrained, unnatural.
1621 WITHER *Motto* B j a, For much I hate the forced Apish tricks, Of those our home-disdaining Politicks. **1687** DRYDEN *Hind & P.* III. 78 Her forc'd civilities, her faint embrace. **1891** C. T. C. JAMES *Rom. Rigmarole* 80 In spite of her forced calmness.
†**4.** Artificially made or prepared; as opposed to *natural*. Chiefly of soils. *Obs.*
1622 FLETCHER *Beggar's Bush* II. i, Call in your crutches, ..Forc'd eyes and teeth, with your dead arms. **1650** FULLER *Pisgah* III. x. 433 The very bottome or floor thereof (being forced ground). **1664** EVELYN *Kal. Hort.* (1729) 200 Pot them [Tuberoses] in natural not forc'd earth. **1688** *Lond. Gaz.* No. 2363/4 Lost..a light bay Gelding..6 years old, with a forced mark on the Forehead.
5. Of plants, a crop, etc.: Made to bear, or produced, out of the proper season. Cf. FORCE *v.*^{1} 12.
1695 CONGREVE *Love for L.* v. ii, I'm..none of your forced trees, that pretend to blossom in the fall, and bud when they should bring forth fruit. **1866** MRS. GASKELL *Wives and Dau.* xxviii, Our forced strawberries are just ready.
†**6.** Fortified, made strong against attack. *Obs.*
1548 HALL *Chron., Hen. V* (an. 6) 59 b, And beside that chayne he sette vp a new forced bridge. **1602** WARNER *Alb. Eng.* Epit. (1612) 356 Seuerus his forced vallie, with other strong..fabrications.
7. Of a draught: produced artificially; so ***forced-air***, ***ventilation***; ***forced (feed) lubrication***, force-feed lubrication (see FORCE-FEED *sb.*).
1865 WEBSTER s.v. *Draught*, *Forced draught*, the draft produced by a blower, as by compressing the air beneath a fire. **1885** *Marine Engineer* VII. 39/1 (*heading*) On the Application of moderate forced draught to the furnaces of small steam vessels. **1887** *Encycl. Brit.* XXII. 496/2 Where forced draught has been substituted for chimney draught. **1898** *Westm. Gaz.* 18 May 2/3 In our service we are satisfied with a forced draught trial of four hours as a rule. **1901** *Feilden's Mag.* IV. 441/2 The forced-air draught fans... Forced-air draught is preferable to steam blast. **1907** J. G. HORNER *Encycl. Pract. Engin.* V. 40/2 It is hardly possible to overrate the importance of forced lubrication in modern practice. **1907** *Westm. Gaz.* 19 Nov. 4/2 Forced feed lubrication. **1909** *Ibid.* 12 Aug. 4/2 Designing an engine on the forced-induction principle. **1930** *Engineering* 28 Feb. 280/3 Forced lubrication is employed for the main engine and for the turbo-blower. **1960** *Farmer & Stockbreeder* 19 Jan. 108/1 The forced-draught cabinet incubators. **1971** *Sci. Amer.* May 73/3 In a forced-draft [cooling] tower the fan is at the bottom and pushes the air up through the tower.

‖**force de frappe** (fɔrs də frap). [Fr., lit. 'striking force'.] A striking force; *spec.* the French independent nuclear striking force. Also *attrib.*
1962 *Observer* 6 May 10/2 Britain has had her 'independent deterrent' for several years, and General de Gaulle is now trying to give France her own 'force de frappe'. **1962** *Spectator* 31 Aug. 294 Useless objects of conspicuous consumption like steel mills in underdeveloped countries or *forces de frappe* elsewhere. **1965** A. WERTH *De Gaulle* x. 344 De Gaulle continued to look upon his *force de frappe* as absolutely essential to France's independence and her status as a great power. **1968** S. SERFATY *France, de Gaulle & Europe* vi. 119 While the left is staunchly against the force de frappe, judged 'inefficient, ruinous and dangerous', it remains nonetheless true that the French atomic forces originated during leftist governments. **1968** *Listener* 4 July 2/1 Their leaders were evidently trained and equipped as a *force de frappe*, and acted in accordance with the precepts of Debray's guerrilla manual.

forcedly ('fɔəsɪdlɪ), *adv.* [f. FORCED *ppl. a.* + -LY^2.] In a forced manner.
1548 THOMAS *Ital. Dict.*, (1567), *Sforzatamente*, forcedly, or by constrainte. **1571** GOLDING *Calvin on Ps.* xxvii. 9 That which followeth some Hebrew interpreters expound a little more forcedly. **1646** P. BULKELEY *Gospel Covt.* I. 153 They follow him not forcedly, but..they submit willingly to his regiment. **1872** BLACK *Adv. Phaeton* xxv. 343 In a forcedly merry way. **1885** *Manch. Exam.* 10 Sept. 2/1 The passage may be not forcedly construed as meaning [etc.].

forcedness ('fɔəsɪdnɪs). [f. as prec. + -NESS.] The quality of being forced.
1660 H. MORE *Myst. Godl.* v. xvi. 193 So much of forcedness and incoherency is there in the making out this false Hypothesis. **1725** BRADLEY *Fam. Dict.* s.v. *Plover*, The Forcedness of the Motion. **1704** WORTHINGTON *Millennium* in *Miscell.* 2 Against the forcedness and incongruity of this sense much might be said.

forced put: see FORCE-PUT.

force-'feed, *v.* [f. FORCE *sb.*^{1} 23 + FEED *v.*] To feed by force; also *fig.* So **force-'feeding** *vbl. sb.*
1909 WEBSTER, *Force feeding*, feeding (poultry, etc.) by pushing food forcibly down the throat, as by a cramming machine. **1912** D. F. LAURIE *Poultry Foods & Feeding* v. 83 Machine or force feeding is the most..satisfactory method of feeding large numbers of fattening chickens. **1938** S. BECKETT *Murphy* 182 Otherwise he had to be force-fed. **1962** *Times* 15 Feb. 15/5 We had..put her [*sc.* a dolphin] in a small side tank in order to force-feed her. **1964** *Economist* 8 Feb. 504/2 The feeders who buy the animals and force-feed them nearly two tons of grain. **1964** D. VARADAY *Gara-Yaka* vi. 52 He brought a jug of lukewarm beef tea, and the task of force-feeding began. **1971** *Guardian* 26 Aug. 10/5 Being force-fed information is a habit one can break.

force-'feed, *sb.* [f. FORCE *sb.*^{1} 23 + FEED *sb.*, or f. prec.] A supply, esp. of lubricant, that is maintained under applied force or pressure. Usu. *attrib.*
1918 V. W. PAGÉ *Aviation Engines* vii. 19 When a force-feed lubricating system is used, the oil..is thrown off at a tangent to the crank-pin circle in all directions. **1921** W. H. BERRY *Mod. Motor Car Pract.* i. 44 This system of partial force-feed has been developed into a true forced-feed system. **1938** C. CULPIN *Farm Machinery* viii. 116 It has the advantage of all force-feed drills, and gives a more continuous flow of seed than the external-feed type. **1966** *McGraw-Hill Encycl. Sci. & Technol.* VII. 607/1 In the force-feed system the pump pressure insures a steady replacement of the oil which has been heated by friction work with fresh cool oil.

†**force-fish**. *Obs. rare.* [f. FORCE *v.*^{3}, after FORCEMEAT.] ? Stuffing for fish.
1741 *Compl. Fam.-Piece* I. ii. 132 You may put some Oysters and Marrow in your Force-fish, if you please.

forceful ('fɔəsfʊl), *a.* [f. FORCE *sb.*^{1} + -FUL.]
1. Full of force, powerful, strong, vigorous.
1616 CHAPMAN *Homer's Hymn to Venus* I. 204 From all the Fayre Of this so forcefull concourse. **1697** DRYDEN *Virg. Georg.* III. 374 The Waters..Black Sands, as from a forceful Engine throw. **1725** POPE *Odyss.* VI. 150 With forceful strength a branch the Heroe rends. **1784** COWPER *Task* IV. 315 The lands..Upturn'd so lately by the forceful share. **1824** SCOTT *Let. to Ld. Montagu* 15 June in *Lockhart*, The Turf is no doubt a very forceful temptation. **1888** BRYCE *Amer. Commw.* III. lxxvii. 18 In the hands of a forceful minister.
b. Of speech, style, etc.: Cogent, impressive, efficacious, effective.
1571 GOLDING *Calvin on Ps.* lxxiv. 18 A forcefull manner of speaking. **1591** SYLVESTER *Du Bartas* I. ii. 480 A Word so force-full and significant. **1746** COLLINS *Manners* 72 Each forceful thought. **1828** *Blackw. Mag.* XXIV. 8 His clear classical, forceful style. **1870** PROCTOR *Other Worlds* vi. 147 A forceful argument. **1886** RUSKIN *Præterita* I. ii. 54 Melodious and forceful verse.
2. Acting with force or violence; boisterous, impetuous, violent.
1592 WYRLEY *Armorie* 145 The forcefull floud his vessell doth not spaire. **1606** SYLVESTER *Du Bartas* II. iv. *Trophies* 1038 Whose forceful stream runs smoothly serpenting. **1812** *Examiner* 28 Sept. 620/1 The forceful ejection of a man and his family from their home. **1846** KEBLE *Lyra Innoc.* (1873) 149 Her forceful knocking must Heaven's door assail. **1871** BLACKIE *Four Phases* i. 49 As trees by forceful artifice are made to grow downwards..instead of upwards.
b. Driven with force or violence.
1697 DRYDEN *Æneid* II. 65 Against the Steed he threw His forceful Spear. **1776** MICKLE tr. *Camoens' Lusiad* 164 Deep through the ranks the forceful weapon past.
3. quasi-*adv.* = FORCEFULLY.
1718 ROWE *Lucan* IV. 1023 While his broad Knee bears forceful on his Groin. **1774** GOLDSM. *Nat. Hist.* (1862) I. xiii. 71 The water would burst out as forceful from the one as the other.
Hence '**forcefully** *adv.*; '**forcefulness**.
a **1774** GOLDSM. *Surv. Exper. Philos.* (1776) I. 415 The external fluid..presses against it as forcefully as its contents press out. **1822** *Examiner* 616/2 He sang very pleasingly, if not forcefully. **1825** HONE *Every-day Bk.* I. 1076 By.. forcefulness of wealth. **1832** *Blackw. Mag.* XXXI. 117 It will butt forcefully against the ramparts. **1866** *Contemp. Rev.* II. 156 The idiomatic forcefulness of Calvin.

†**forcehead**, corrupted form of FAUCET.
1598 FLORIO, *Spina*, a spigot, a gimblet, a forcehead, or tap to drawe drinke with.

†'**forcel**. *Obs.* [a. OF. *forcelle* (in 16th c. *fourcelle*), dim. of *forche* FORK.] = CANNEL-BONE 2.
(R. Holme mistakenly identifies it with CANNEL-BONE 3.)
1610 MARKHAM *Masterp.* II. iv. 219 Then is there the two spade-bones, and from thence to the forcels or canel bones other 2 bons called the marrow-bones. **1688** R. HOLME *Armoury* II. 153/2 The Forcels or canal bones [of a Horse].. are the Bones about the Knee.

forceless ('fɔəslɪs), *a.* [f. FORCE *sb.*^{1} + -LESS.] Without force; devoid of force.
1532 MORE *Confut. Tindale* Wks. 572/2 He waxeth forcelesse and carelesse. **1561** T. NORTON *Calvin's Inst.* IV. xix. (1634) 723 *marg.*, Extreme annointing is a forcelesse and unwarranted ceremonie. **1604** EDMONDS *Observ. Cæsar's Comm.* 58 The practise of the Romaines in taking in any towne, was to leaue them forcelesse. **1742** COLLINS *Simplicity* 39 Love, only love, her forceless numbers mean. **1813** SCOTT *Rokeby* I. xxiv, Feeble heart and forceless hand. **1883** MOMERIE *Personality* iv. 106 A mass of forceless atoms.
Hence †'**forcelessly** *adv.*
1611 COTGR., *Imbecillement*, weakly..forcelessly.

†'**forcelet**^{1}. *Obs.* Forms: 4–7 force (l)let(t, 4–5 fors(e)let. [a. AF. *forcelet* (whence Anglo-Lat. *forcelletum*), f. *force*: see FORCE *sb.*^{1}] A little fort or fortress.
13.. *E.E. Allit. P.* B. 1200 þay ne stray myȝt A fote fro þat forselet to forray no goudes. *a* **1400–50** *Alexander* 4358 A full faynt forcelett. **1548** HALL *Chron., Hen. VI* (an. 19) 141 Or thei could attain to any toune, or forcelet. **1616** SURFL. & MARKH. *Country Farme* VII. xix. 670 This house must bee made like vnto a little forcellet or fort strong.

†'**forcelet**[2]. *Obs.* Also forslet. [Corruptly a. OF. *forceret*, dim. of *forcer*: see FORCER[1].] A small 'forcer' or coffer.

c **1475** *Partenay* 1081 A forcelet wrought fresh of yuor bon. **1532** in Weaver *Wells Wills* (1890) 167 Elyn Samplyn my serv a copull of benches and a forslet. **1565** JEWEL *Def. Apol.* (1611) 281 To carrie home the Sacrament in their Napkins, and to keepe it in forcelets.

†'**forcely,** *a.* and *adv. Obs.* [f. FORCE *sb.*[1] + -LY[1] and [2].]

A. *adj.* Of strong build, vigorous. **B.** *adv.* By or with force or power, vigorously, violently.

a **1488** HENRYSON *Poems* (1865) 169 The foullis fair sa forcelie thay fle. **1508** DUNBAR *Tua Mariit Wemen* 430 Full oft I blenk by my buke.. To se quhat berne.. forgeit is maist forcely. **1535** STEWART *Cron. Scot.* III. 150 In thair defence thair war tha slane ilk man, Syne forcelie on thame the toun tha wan.

‖**force majeure** (fɔrs maʒœr). [Fr., lit. 'superior strength'.] Irrestible force or overwhelming power.

[**1858** SIMMONDS *Dict. Trade, Force-majeure*, a French commercial term for unavoidable accidents in the transport of goods, from superior force, the act of God, &c.] **1883** *Academy* 8 Sept. 158/1 Tyranny, upheld by law, will generally be 'tempered' by outrage, so long as a *force majeure* prevents its being met in any other way. **1886** *Macm. Mag.* Sept. 342/1 They [*sc.* politicians] will not combine except under *force majeure.* **1902** *Encycl. Brit.* XXV. 112/1 The expression 'act of God'.. is not synonymous with *force majeure*; but it includes every loss by *force majeure* in which human agency, by act or negligence, has had no part. **1907** W. DE MORGAN *Alice-for-Short* i, Hindered from.. determined effort by a *force-majeure* trying to the temper but heroically endured. **1916** 'PETER' *Trench Yarns* v. 51 *Force majeure* being on George's side, the transaction was accomplished to the accompaniment of awful threats as to George's lurid future. **1930** W. DE LA MARE *Poems for Children* p. xxix, Whose right is often founded solely on *force majeure.* **1941** A. L. ROWSE *Tudor Cornwall* xi. 265 It was thought.. that the mayor had yielded the town by treachery, but later they learned that it was rather by *force majeure.* **1959** G. MITCHELL *Man who grew Tomatoes* iii. 39 One cannot be a respected and highly respectable Civil Servant for twenty years without learning to bow to the *force majeure* of public opinion.

force-meat ('fɔəsmiːt). [f. FORCE *v.*[3] + MEAT.] Meat chopped fine, spiced, and highly seasoned, chiefly used for stuffing or as a garnish. Also *attrib.*, as ***force-meat ball.***

1688 R. HOLME *Armoury* III. iii. 82/2 *Force Meat*, is Meat with a stuffing of Herbs, or other things made to that purpose. **1747** MRS. GLASSE *Cookery* 13 To make Force-Meat Balls. *Ibid.* 44 Stuff the Bellies of the Pigeons with Force Meat made thus. **1853** SOYER *Pantroph.* 147 Preserve the intestines entire, and.. fill them with force meat. **1892** *Encycl. Cookery* (Garrett) I. 605 Forcemeat Cutlets.

forcement ('fɔəsmənt). [a. F. *forcement* f. *force-r*: see FORCE *v.*[1] and -MENT.]

†**1. a.** Strengthening; in quot. *fig.* encouragement. **b.** *concr.* Something which strengthens; a fortification. *Obs.*

1382 WYCLIF *Isa.* xxv. 12 And the forsemens, or strengthis [Vulg. *munimenta*] of thin heȝe walles shul togidere falle, and be lowid. **1533** BELLENDEN *Livy* v. (1822) 314 Thir wourdis gif.. grete audacite and forcement to the Volschis.

†**2.** An act of deforcement: see DEFORCEMENT 2.

1479 *Act. Dom. Conc.* (1839) 33 Vnlawis of grenewod, mureburne, forsmentis.

†**3.** Compulsion; also, a compelling motive.

1524 PACE *Let. Hen. VIII.* in Strype *Eccl. Mem.* I. App. xi. 20 Without great forcement to go bolt upright, wee could not avoide to fal down headlyng. **1541** CRANMER in *St. Papers* (1836) I. 691 Al that Derame did unto her was of his importune forcement. **1565** GOLDING *Ovid's Met.* XI. (1593) 266 Thine owne renowme, thy grandsire Jove are forcements thereunto. **1607** DEKKER *Hist. Sir T. Wyatt* Wks. 1873 III. 122 It was impos'd vpon vs by constraint.. And will you count such forcement treacherie? **1634** W. WOOD *New Eng. Prosp.* (1865) 24 They have seene a Deare leape three score feet at little or no forcement.

4. *Gunnery.* (See quot.)

1892 *Field* 10 Dec. 915/2 Neither the diameter of the chamber nor the 'forcement' of the projectiles has any primary influence on the recoil. *note*, This is a French word, for which we have no English equivalent.. it has, however, been Anglicised, and is now generally used in gunnery treatises. Its signification is the excess of diameter of the projectile over that of the bore.

†**forcene,** *v. Obs.* Also forsene. [a. F. *forcener, forsener*, f. *fors* (see FOR- *pref.*[3]) + OF. *sen* sense.] *intr.* To be or become mad or frantic.

1490 CAXTON *Eneydos* xviii. 68 O man of all other the moost forcened oute of thy wyt. *Ibid.* xxviii. 108 She all atones forsened as a persone that ys madde.

‖**forcené** ('fɔːs(ə)neɪ). *Her.* [a. F. *forcené*, pa. pple. of *forcener*: see prec.] (See quot.)

1725 COATS *Dict. Herald., Forcené*, as Cheval Forcené, is a Horse rearing or standing on his hinder Legs. **1889** in ELVIN *Dict. Her.*

†**forcenery.** *Obs.* [a. OF. *forcenerie*, f. *forcener*: see FORCENE *v.*] Madness.

1480 CAXTON *Ovid's Met.* x. vii, Yf it be of rage or forcenerye. **1484** —— *Ryall Bk.* C vj, Suche folye is callyd forsenerye or woodnesse.

†'**forceness.** *Obs.* [? f. FORCE *v.*[1] + -NESS.] Force, strength, violence.

13.. *Gaw. & Gr. Knt.* 646 Þat alle his forsnes he fong at þe fyue ioyez [of the Virgin Mary]. **1519** HORMAN *Vulg.* 268 We may dispoynt and alaye the forcenes of our ennemies by ofte remouynge of the hoste.

forcepped ('fɔːsɛpt), *a. nonce-wd.* [f. FORCEP(S + -ED[2].] Having or provided with forceps.

1845 HOOD *Winter Nosegay* ii, Sour leaf To garden thief, Forcepp'd or winged, was never a temptation.

forceps ('fɔːsɛps). *sing.* and *pl.* Also 8 *sing.* forcep, *pl.* 7–8 forcipes, 9 forcepses. [a. L. *forceps*, pl. *forcipes* in same sense.]

1. An instrument of the pincers kind, used for seizing and holding objects, *esp.* in surgical and obstetric operations.

sing. **1670** BOYLE *Wks.* (1772) III. 369 Motions.. excited by our rousing her with a forceps. **1759** STERNE *Tr. Shandy* II. xi. 70 Thou hast left thy *tire tête*,—thy new-invented forceps.. behind thee. **1822** IMISON *Sc. & Art* I. 279 A forceps, or pair of pliers, for taking up insects or other objects. **1832** BABBAGE *Econ. Manuf.* xix. (ed. 3) 187 The forceps draws the wire on to a distance equal in length to one pin. **1855** RAMSBOTHAM *Obstetr. Med.* 292 One of the most valuable instruments employed in Obstetric Surgery.. is the Long Forceps.

pl. 1634 T. JOHNSON *Parey's Chirurg.* XVII. xiii. (1678) 389 Then must the tooth be taken hold of with some of these toothed forcipes. **1685** *Lond. Gaz.* No. 2054/4 A pair of Steel Forceps. **1823** H. H. WILSON in *Oriental Mag.* I. 352 They were, therefore, pincers, nippers, or forcipes. **1875** BUCKLAND *Log-bk.* 140 By using a long pair of forceps.

2. *Anat.*, *Ent.*, and *Zoöl.* Some organ or part of the body that has the shape of, or may be used as, a forceps. †Also, one of the two branches of this.

sing. **1661** LOVELL *Hist. Anim. & Min.* Introd., The Squillæ have a taile, but no forceps. **1759** GOLDSM. *Bee* No. 4 (Globe) 378/2 Furnished with a forceps above the mouth. **1765** *Univ. Mag.* XXXVII. 9/1 The eggs at the origin of each forceps.. would contain but one forcep. **1828** STARK *Elem. Nat. Hist.* II. 153 P. *corrugatus*, Bosc.. forceps serrated. **1871** DARWIN *Desc. Man* I. ix. 329 One of the two posterior legs.. is converted into a forceps.

pl. **1667** E. KING in *Phil. Trans.* II. 425 Never leaving to pinch them on the head with their Forceps or Claws. **1713** DERHAM *Phys. Theol.* IV. xi. 190 Which is done by piercing their Prey with their Forcipes. **1859** DARWIN *Orig. Spec.* vii. (1873) 191 These forceps can seize firmly hold of any object. *Ibid.*, Tridactyle forcepses.. certainly exist on some star-fishes.

3. *attrib.* and *Comb.* (with reference to obstetric practice), as ***forceps-case, -delivery, -practice.***

1879 J. M. DUNCAN *Lect. Dis. Women* ii. (1889) 6 The result of injury, as by forceps-delivery. *Ibid.* vi. 26 Simply spoken of as forceps cases. *Ibid.* 27, I shall here make one remark in judging of the forceps-practice referred to.

'**force-pump.** [f. FORCE *sb.* or *v.* + PUMP *sb.*]

1. A pump employed to force water, etc. beyond the range of atmospheric pressure.

1659 LEAK *Waterwks.* 34 This manner of force-Pump, which is one of the best Inventions. **1754** W. EMERSON *Princ. Mech.* (1758) 276 Force pump, a pump that discharges water by pressing it upwards. **1825** J. NICHOLSON *Operat. Mechanic* 281 The fire-engine by Rowntree is a double force-pump.

2. (See quot.)

1858 SIMMONDS *Dict. Trade, Force-pump*.. the plunger pump for supplying the boiler of a locomotive engine.

'**force-put.** *Now dial.* Also 7–8 forced put. [perh. *forced put* was a term of some game, = 'forced move'; see FORCED *ppl. a.* 2 b and PUT.] An action rendered unavoidable by circumstances; a 'Hobson's choice'.

1657 G. STARKEY *Helmont's Vind.* 328 To give poysons to purge, in expectation that Nature being forced to play a desperate game, and reduced to a forc't put, may [etc.]. **1662** SIR A. MERVYN *Speech on Irish Affairs* 3 It must be therefore a forc'd Put, that presseth us on to this address. *c* **1680** HICKERINGILL *Hist. Whiggism* Wks. 1716 I. 118 Sometimes the Laws being put in Execution at a force-put, and then again slackning the Reins and following natural inclination. **1748–61** S. RICHARDSON *Clarissa H.* (1811) VII. 63 It is, truly, to be ingenuous, a forced put: for my passions are so wound up, that I am obliged either to laugh or cry. **1772** NUGENT *Hist. Friar Gerund* I. 526 He thought that it might pass for a case of necessity, or forced-put. **1876** in *N. & Q.* Ser. v. V. 266 A tradesman [of Torquay] told me.. that he had left his house very early.. 'but not from choice, 'twas a force-put'. **1892** *Northumb. Gloss.*, Force-put.

†'**forcer**[1]. *Obs.* Forms: 4 fosser, 4–5 forcere, (5 foorcere, forcyer), forser, (6 fo(r)sar), 5–6 focer, (6 fostler), 4–7, 9 *Hist.* forcer. [a. OF. *forcer*, *forcier*. Cf. It. *forziere.*]

A chest, coffer, or casket.

13.. *E.E. Allit. P.* A. 263 Her were a forser for þe in faye, If þou were a gentyl Iueler. *c* **1400** *Sowdone Bab.* 2303, I have a girdil in my Forcer. *c* **1460** *La Belle Dame sanz Mercy* 65 in *Pol. Rel. & L. Poems* (1866) 54 Fortune with strengthe the forcere hath vnshete where-ynne was spradde al my worldly richesse. **1530** PALSGR. 203/1 Casket or fosar, *escrain.* **1531** in Weaver *Wells Wills* (1890) 148 My wif shall have her coffer and her fostler to her own use. **1577** HANMER *Anc. Eccl. Hist.* (1619) 244 A basket or forsar full of Gold. **1669** STURMY *Mariner's Mag.* Suppl. Summ. 2 Any Painted Wares, Forsers, Caskets.. are forfeited if any such be Imported.. *Vide* Stat. 4 Edw. 4. **1863** SIR G. SCOTT *Glean. Westm. Abb.* (ed. 2) 96 A forcer, a receptacle for documents, not unlike a kettledrum in shape.

Comb. **1411** *Close Roll, 12 Hen. IV*, b, Johannes Whiteberd, forcermaker.

forcer[2] ('fɔəsə(r)). [f. FORCE *v.*[1] + -ER[1].]

1. a. One who or that which forces.

1556 *Aurelio & Isab.* (1608) K iij, They will that she dey the which hathe beane forcede, and the forcer liffe. **1581** MULCASTER *Positions* xiv. (1887) 67 Where feare is the forcer, and not free will. **1601** HOLLAND *Pliny* I. 175 The conqueror and great forcer of cities. **1616** CHAPMAN *Homer's Hymn Hermes* 669, I, in no similitude apper'd Of powre to be the forcer of a Herde. **1659** MILTON *Civ. Power* Wks. 1738 I. 551 How much bloodshed have the forcers of Conscience to answer for. *a* **1749** CHALKLEY *Wks.* (1766) 381 Those Forcers know not of what Spirit they are of. **1832** *Examiner* 258/2 Necessity is a great forcer.

b. One who produces forced crops.

1789 J. ABERCROMBIE (*title*) The complete kitchen gardener and hot-bed forcer. **1902** *Westm. Gaz.* 4 Apr. 8/2 There are forcers who have a dozen large hothouses devoted solely to Easter lilies. **1905** *Ibid.* 21 Feb. 12/1 A 'forcer' in Kent gets a living from strawberry-forcing on less than half an acre of land.

2. An instrument or means for forcing.

†**a.** Something with which to force (window bars); ? a crowbar. *Obs.*

1649 CHAS. I. *Let.* in Kingston *Hertfdsh. in Civ. War* (1894) 126 If I had a forcer, I would make no question of it, but having nothing but fyles.. my time will be too scant.

b. The plunger or piston of a force-pump.

1634 J. B[ATE] *Myst. Nat.* 8 A Forcer is a plug of wood exactly turned and leathered about. **1725** *Specif. R. Newsham's Patent* No. 479 The forcers being guided by the arch of a double wheel. **1825** J. NICHOLSON *Operat. Mechanic* 267 On the descent of the forcer, the lower valve shuts. **1867** in SMYTH *Sailor's Word-bk.*

c. A force-pump.

1731 BEIGHTON in *Phil. Trans.* XXXVII. 8 Besides these four Forcers, there are four more placed at the other Ends of the Libræ, or Levers. **1778** PRYCE *Min. Cornub.* 321 *Forcer* a small pump worked by hand, used in sinking of small.. Pits. **1883** in GRESLEY *Gloss. Coal Mining.*

†**d.** A contrivance for propelling water. *Obs.*

1598 STOW *Surv.* iii. (1603) 18 Thames water conueyed into mens houses by pipes of leade, from a most artificial forcier. **1610** HOLLAND *Camden's Brit.* I. 435 Maurice.. by meanes of a forser or wheele.. brought water.. into a great part of the city. **1730–6** BAILEY (folio), *Forcier*, a water-mill; an engine to convey water from one place to another.

†**e.** An agent for quickening the growth of plants, etc. *Obs.*

a **1722** LISLE *Husb.* (1752) 136 Nitre, blood, soot &c. all have been found great forcers.

†'**forcer**[3]. *Obs. rare.* [f. FORCE *v.*[2] + -ER[1].] One who forces wool.

1553 *Act 1 Mary* Sess. III. c. 7 §1 Sheer-men and Dyers, Forcers of Wools, Casters of Wools and Sorters of Wools.

†'**forcet.** *Obs.* Forms: 5–8 forset, (6 forçet, forsset), 6–8 fosset, 6–7 forcet. [? shortened form of FORCELET[2].] A little 'forcer' or chest.

1426 *E.E. Wills* (1882) 70 þe forset that Thomas Essexie wot where is. **1548** THOMAS *Ital. Gram.* (1567) N ij b, *Forciere*, a forset or a little coafer. **1577–87** HOLINSHED *Chron.* II. 590 A number of chests, coffers, and forssets. **1656** in BLOUNT *Glossogr.* **1721–92** in BAILEY.

†'**forcets,** *sb. pl. Obs. rare.* [a. AF. *forcettes* scissors, dim. of *forces*: see FORCE *v.*[2]] Scissors.

1474 CAXTON *Chesse* 77 In his right hand a payr of sheris or forcettis.

forchafed, forchanged: see FOR- *pref.*[1] 6, 8.

†**for'chase,** *v. Obs.* [ad. OF. *forschacier*, f. *fors-*, FOR- *pref.*[3] + *chacier* to chase. Cf. FORCATCH.] *trans.* **a.** To chase or drive away; to put to flight. **b.** To tire with chasing or running.

a **1300** *Cursor M.* 6977 (Cott.) An hundreth moght for-chace, Quils þai wit þam had godds grace. *a* **1510** DOUGLAS *King Hart* I. xxxiii, Radour ran hame full fleyit and for-chaist. **1549** CHALONER *Erasm. Moriæ Enc.* P ij a, Manfully forchasyng of hir enemies.

†**forche,** *sb. Obs.* [a. OF. *forche*: see FORK *sb.*]

1. In *pl.* Gallows.

c **1380** *Sir Ferumb.* 2881 þan scholtou don þe forchys there.. And to-morwe let þes be þar an honge. *Ibid.* 2970 þar þat þe fourchys was. **1584** J. HOOKER *Descr. Excester* (1765) 82 He commanded Forches and Gallows to be set up in sundry Places.

2. *Hunting.* (See FOUCH.)

forche ('fɔːʃeɪ), *a. Her.* [ad. F. *fourchée*, fem. of *fourché*, f. *fourche* fork.] (See quot.)

1889 ELVIN *Dict. Her., Forche* or *Fourchée*, divided into two parts towards the extremity.

forche: var. of FOURCHE. *v. Obs.*

†'**forcher.** *Obs. rare.* [prob. a derivative of OF. *forche, fourch* (see FOUCH).] The hindermost part of a deer's nombles or entrails.

1486 *Bk. St. Albans* E vij b, The hyndermost parte of the nomblis thene That is to say the Forchers. **1595** MARKHAM *Gentl. Acad.* 35 b, The hindermost part of the vmbles be called the Forchers.

forchet, obs. form of FORGETT.

†'**forchure.** *Obs. rare.* [ad. F. *fourchure* (f. *fourche* fork) in same sense.] The fork of the body.

c **1380** *Sir Ferumb.* 551 A man of gret stature . . & long man in forchure.

forcibility (ˌfɔəsɪ'bɪlɪtɪ). [f. next: see *-bility*, -ITY.] The quality of being forcible.

1770 *Char.* in *Ann. Reg.* 52/2 The repeated justice of his opinions, and forcibility of his pleadings. **1886** *Academy* 16 Oct. 253/3 Two people who . . cannot be denied a certain originality of opinion and forcibility in expressing it.

forcible ('fɔəsɪb(ə)l), *a.* Also 6–8 **forceable**, 8 **forciable.** [a. OF. *forcible*, f. *force* FORCE *sb.* The form *forceable* is as if f. FORCE + -ABLE.]

1. Done by force; involving the use of force or violence: *esp.* in Law, ***forcible detainer***, ***entry*** (see quot. 1769).

a. [**1391** *Act 15 Rich. II*, c. 2 A toutz les foitz que tielx forcibles entrees soient faitz.] *c* **1422** HOCCLEVE *Learn to die*, *Joys Heaven*, For the kyngdam of heuene souffrith forcible and mighty assautes of vertu. **1527** RASTELL *Abridgm. Stat.* 96 Them that make forcyble entre in beneficis. **1555** EDEN *Decades* 273 They prouided for th[e] indempnitie of theyr owne estate by forcible extenuatinge the goddes . . of them whom they desired to kepe in subiection. **1651** HOBBES *Leviath.* II. xxi. 113 That Liberty of Forcible Entry, was taken away by a Statute made in Parliament. **1667** MILTON *P.L.* II. 793 In embraces forcible and foule. **1767** BLACKSTONE *Comm.* II. 390 The stealing, or forcible abduction, of such property as this, is also felony. **1769** *Ibid.* IV. xi. 147 A forcible entry or detainer; which is committed by violently taking or keeping possession, with menaces, force, and arms, of lands and tenements, without the authority of law. **1816** J. SCOTT *Vis. Paris* (ed. 5) p. xlvi, A forcible dissolution of it [the Chamber] was intended. **1837** ADOLPHUS & ELLIS in *Rep. K. Bench Div.* III. 817 A conviction of forcible detainer dated September 3d, 1834. **1844** H. H. WILSON *Brit. India* II. 316 To compel, by forcible means . . submission to the authority which was to be substituted. **1868** FREEMAN *Norm. Conq.* (1876) II. vii. 152 He determined . . on a forcible return to his country.

β. **1548** UDALL, etc. *Erasm. Par. Luke* v. 19 The shame of forceable breakyng into this or that mannes house. **1683** SALMON *Doron Med.* I. 50 Which is a forceable drawing away. **1688** *Col. Rec. Pennsylv.* I. 236 Praying relief against a forceable Entry and Deteiner.

2. Possessing force. †**a.** Of persons, material things, natural agencies, etc.: Strong, powerful.

a. **1555** EDEN *Decades* 311 Dryuen by forcyble wynde to an vnknowen lande. **1555** ABP. PARKER *Ps.* cx. 5 Most forcible, He shall great kyngs and Cesars wound, In day of wrath. **1578** BANISTER *Hist. Man* III. 42 In the inside of the wrest, is a forcible Ligament. **1614** RALEIGH *Hist. World* v. vi. §11 He prepared a forcible armie to attend him. **1677** HALE *Prim. Orig. Man.* I. i. 29 Those subtil, invisible and forcible Engins which we call the Animal Spirits. **1700** PRIOR *Carmen Sec.* 419 Like mingled Streams, more forcible when join'd. **1802** BINGLEY *Anim. Biog.* (1813) III. 70 Indeed, so thick and so forcible was the shoal, as to carry before it every other kind of fish.

β. **1561** T. NORTON *Calvin's Inst.* II. 158 Strong forceable defences, whereby it may be safe against outward violence. *a* **1618** RALEIGH *Prerog. Parl.* (1628) 19 The forceable Lords his enemies. **1634–5** BRERETON *Trav.* (Chetham Soc.) 54 The wind . . was so forceable as it repelled the waters.

†**b.** followed by *to* with *inf. Obs.*

a. **1594** HOOKER *Eccl. Pol.* III. x. §3 That punishment, which hath bene sometimes forcible to bridle sinne. **1601** R. JOHNSON *Kingd. & Commw.* (1603) 167 Cosmus, a kind of charmed-sower-mares milke verie forcible to turne the braine. **1658** *Whole Duty Man* x. §8. 80 There being generally nothing more forcible to bring men into any sinful practice, than the seeing it used by others.

β. **1576** FLEMING *Panopl. Epist.* 34 Which reasons of his, are verie forceable to make him yeald to the foresaide matter in question. *a* **1641** BP. MOUNTAGU *Acts. & Mon.* iii. 222 Nothing is more forceable to convince all forrainers. **1710** T. FULLER *Pharm. Extemp.* 349 These [pills] are forceable to bring the necessary Pains in Child-Birth.

c. Of actions, words, representations: Producing a powerful effect, telling. Of reasoning: Having logical force, strong, convincing.

a. **1573** G. HARVEY *Letter-bk.* (Camden) 47 So forcible an antecedent it was most likeli there would follow as effectual a consequent. **1594** T. B. *La Primaud. Fr. Acad.* II. 527 But that argument of all others is most forcible. **1729** BUTLER *Serm.* Wks. 1874 II. 39 We may observe somewhat very forcible and expressive in these words. **1790** BURKE *Fr. Rev.* 105 Reasons, at least as forcible as those which [etc.]. **1865** DICKENS *Mut. Fr.* I. vi, With the natural need of a strong rough man in anger, to do something forcible. **1874** L. STEPHEN *Hours in Library* (1892) I. i. 13 One man sees everything in the forcible light and shade of Rembrandt. **1884** CHURCH *Bacon* ix. 223 His Latin . . is singularly forcible and expressive.

β. **1570–6** LAMBARDE *Peramb. Kent* (1826) 483 Against which assertion, that which is saide 10. H. 3. . . is not greatly forceable. **1612** T. TAYLOR *Comm. Titus* ii. 14 Another forceable argument. **1738** WARBURTON *Div. Legat.* I. 54 In Beasts the Instinct is invincibly forceable.

d. Hence of an author, painter, etc.

1787 G. GREGORY tr. *Lowth's Sacred Poetry Hebrews* II. xxi, He is at once elegant and sublime, forcible and ornamented. **1791** BURKE *Let. Langrishe* Wks. 1842 I. 560, I might have been more forcible and more clear, if I had not been interrupted as I have been. **1828** D'ISRAELI *Chas I*, II. xi. 286 The most forcible of portrait-painters.

†**3.** Necessary, unavoidable, indispensable. *Obs.*

1622 R. HAWKINS *Voy. S. Sea* (1847) 116 Our forcible businesse being ended. **1574** HELLOWES *Gueuara's Fam. Ep.* (1577) 70 Their forceable and necessarie perils.

†**4.** 'Valid, binding, obligatory' (J.). *Obs.*

1584 FENNER *Def. Ministers* (1587) 149 The Lawe was enacted, and stoode forceable.

5. quasi-*adv.* = FORCIBLY.

a. **1582** N. LICHEFIELD tr. *Castanheda's Conq. E. Ind.* iii. 8 b, Sea Woulfes . . so wilde and fierce, that they do forcible set vpon men. **1601** HOLLAND *Pliny* II. 621 Neither doth it strike or pierce the sight so forcible as the Rubies do. **1719** DE FOE *Crusoe* I. xi, The wind blew more forcible.

β. **1598** MANWOOD *Lawes Forest* i. §3 (1615) 23/2 Y^{e} more forceable to shew ye same, there is used this word.

Hence '**forcibleness.**

1563 FULKE *Meteors* 24 Either for the smal quantitie & lesse forcibles [? a misprint; or perh. for **forciblesse*]. **1581** SIDNEY *Apol. Poetrie* (Arb.) 67 Bewrayed, by that same forciblenes . . of the writer. *a* **1652** J. SMITH *Sel. Disc.* vi. 229 The forcibleness of its operation upon the heart of the prophet. **1890** TALMAGE *From Manger to Throne* 244 Mark's greater forcibleness of statement.

'**forcible** '**feeble.** [after Shakspere: see quot. 1597.] A feeble person who makes great pretence of vigour; also used *attrib.* or as *adj.*

[**1597** SHAKS. *2 Hen. IV*, III. ii. 179, *Shal.* Francis Feeble! *Fee.* Here, Sir . . *Fal.* I cannot put him to a priuate souldier, that is the Leader of so many thousands. Let that suffice, most Forcible Feeble.] **1844** DISRAELI *Coningsby* I. v, Italics, that last resource of the Forcible Feebles. **1850** *N. Brit. Rev.* XIII. 2 Epithets . . in the bad taste of the forcible-feeble school. **1896** *Daily News* 15 June 6/6 The forcible Feebles who control the destinies . . of the Party.

forcibly ('fɔəsɪblɪ), *adv.* [f. FORCIBLE + -LY^{2}.] In a forcible manner.

1. By or with force; also, against one's will.

1543 tr. *Act 15 Rich. II*, c. 2 Any that holdeth suche place forcybly after suche entrye made. *a* **1641** BP. MOUNTAGU *Acts & Mon.* iv. (1642) 283 His father . . intended to take her from him forceably. **1796** MORSE *Amer. Geog.* I. 173 Points and islands, which forcibly shift the bed of the river. **1867** SMILES *Huguenots Eng.* ix. (1880) 147 A Roman Catholic relative . . had the girl forcibly conveyed to the convent.

2. With powerful effect, energetically, strongly, vigorously; also, convincingly.

1578 T. WILCOCKS *Serm. Pawles* 20 The Spirit of God dothe moste forceably expresse this matter by this word. **1585** T. WASHINGTON tr. *Nicholay's Voy.* II. xii. 46 b, Working so forcibly with ores, that wee entred into the port. **1642** H. MORE *Song of Soul* II. iii. II. xiii, It shall thy reason forceably convince. **1782** PAINE *Let. Abbé Raynal* (1791) 47 Perhaps no two events ever united so forceably to expel prejudice. **1843** MRS. CARLYLE *Lett.* I. 214 He reminded me forcibly of the Princess Huncamunca. **1874** L. STEPHEN *Hours in Library* (1892) II. i. 5 It would be impertinent to say again in feebler language what Carlyle has expressed so forcibly.

forcing ('fɔəsɪŋ), *vbl. sb.* [see -ING^{1}.]

1. The action of the vb. FORCE.

1382 WYCLIF *2 Kings* v. 16 And whanne forsynge he made, vtturly he assentyde not. **1398** TREVISA *Barth. De P.R.* VII. xv. (1495) 234 Leest there be grete dyssolucion of the brayne by a forsynge of voyce. **14..** *Tretyce* in *Walter of Henley's Husb.* (1890) 50 Se welle þ^{t} yor mowere hold not his ryght honde afore to hyghe be hynde hym so þat he kyt asonder þe grasse in þe mydis and þis defaute is callid forsyng. **1514** BARCLAY *Cyt. & Uplondyshm.* (Percy Soc.) 27 Forsynge of women, murdre and rapyne. **1634** J. B[ATE] *Myst. Nat.* I. 15 The forcing of water by pressure. **1704** *Lond. Gaz.* No. 4047/4 A black Mare, with some white Hairs in her forehead by forcing. **1849** MACAULAY *Hist. Eng.* II. 306 The forcing of his [Hough's] door was everywhere mentioned with abhorrence.

†**2.** *concr.* A material used in 'forcing' wine.

1731–3 P. SHAW *Chem. Lect.* (1755) 209 Skimmed Milk likewise is a proper Forcing for all white Wines. **1743** *Lond. & Country Brew.* IV. (ed. 2) 331 The Victualler puts . . with it the usual Forcing or Fining.

3. *attrib.* and *Comb.* **a.** attributive, as ***forcing-apparatus***, ***-furnace***, ***-pipe***. Also **forcing-engine**, a fire-engine; **forcing-hazard** (*Billiards*), a stroke requiring more than the usual amount of force; **forcing-pen** (*Austral.* and *N.Z.*), a pen into which sheep are forced or driven in order to guide them to a certain point, as in a drafting yard; a crush-pen; **forcing-yard** (*Austral.*), a yard into which cattle are forced or driven, in order to keep each sort by itself.

1875 J. H. COLLINS *Metal Mining* 123 The *forcing apparatus is a kind of clockwork, which is wound up each morning. **1855** OGILVIE, Suppl., **Forcing-engine*, a fire-engine. **1652** FRENCH *Yorksh. Spa* vi. 62 A *forceing furnace. **1923** W. PERRY et al. *Sheepfarming in N.Z.* iii. 16 [The sheep yards] should consist of receiving yards at each end, *forcing pen, and drafting race. **1950** *N.Z. Jrnl. Agric.* July 5/2 If the forcing pens and . . check pens run up a slight incline, it is quite satisfactory to have the rest of the yards on level ground. **1965** J. S. GUNN *Terminol. Shearing Indust.* I. 28 *Forcing pen*, a narrow area through which sheep are forced on their way to the sheep shower. **1731** BEIGHTON in *Phil. Trans.* XXXVII. 8 *Forcing Pipes. **1890** BOLDREWOOD *Colonial Ref.* (1891) 217 They did not find it difficult to urge the . . animals into the smaller *forcing-yards.

b. *esp.* in combs. relating to the forcing of flowers, etc., as ***forcing-bed***, ***-field***, ***-frame***, ***-glass***, ***-ground***, ***-house***, ***-pit***, ***-wall***; and quasi-*adj.* with the sense 'suitable for forcing', as in ***forcing rose***, ***variety***.

1877 M. M. GRANT *Sun-Maid* iii, Large *forcing beds of lilies of the valley and of violets. **1865** *Spectator* 14 Jan. 44 The turnips in his *forcing field. **1741** *Compl. Fam. Piece* II. iii. 352 If you would have forward Fruits in *forcing Frames. **1819** REES *Cycl.*, **Forcing-ground*, the space . . that is destined to the purpose of forcing or raising vegetable productions by means of artificial heat. **1806–7** J. BERESFORD *Miseries Hum. Life* (1826) XXI. xi, Attending an Amateur-gardener, in the Dog-days, through all his *Forcing-houses. **1870** LOWELL *Study Wind.* 210 The fruits of the literary forcing-house. **1819** REES *Cycl.*, **Forcing-wall*, a wall constructed with flues for the purpose of conveying fire-heat, in order to ripen . . various kinds of tree-fruits.

forcing ('fɔəsɪŋ), *ppl. a.* [f. FORCE *v.*^{1} + -ING^{2}.]

a. That forces, in senses of the vb. *spec.* in *Cricket* (cf. FORCE *v.*^{1} 5) and in *Bridge.*

1551 T. WILSON *Logike* (1580) 42 b, Any forcyng cause. **1659** MILTON *Civ. Power* Wks. (1851) 317 The forcing protestant . . yet takes it to himself and his teachers, of far less autoritie then to be called the church. **1686** HORNECK *Crucif. Jesus* xiv. 302 The confederates drank of it, to make . . the execration more dreadful, and consequently more forcing. **1791** NEWTE *Tour Eng. & Scot.* 153 The thin, early, forcing, and sandy soil of Murray. **1809** W. NICOL (*title*), The Forcing, Fruit, and Kitchen Gardener. **1862** 'CAVENDISH' *Whist* (1870) 28 A forcing card is a card which compels one of the players to trump in order to win the trick. **1886** *Pall Mall G.* 28 July 6/1 A changeable and far from forcing summer. **1888** STEEL & LYTTELTON *Cricket* ii. 57 The ball most to be dreaded for the forcing stroke is the hanging ball, which stops and does not come on evenly and fast to the bat. **1891** W. G. GRACE *Cricket* viii. 236 There are many other points to be considered, such as knowing when to play a slow, patient game, or a forcing game. **1930** E. CULBERTSON *Contract Bridge Blue Bk.* vii. 95 The Forcing principle is a logical and necessary extension of the Approach principle with the added proviso that . . both partners are required to keep the bidding *unconditionally* open until the game bid is selected. The reason for the *Forcing* bids is: a majority of strong hands contain a choice between . . suit bids and no-trump; a game . . is assured provided *neither partner passes* before the best fitting bid is selected. **1933** C. VANDYCK *Contract Contracted* iii. 28 The Forcing Take-Out is a jump bid in a new suit. *Ibid.* iv. 32 The Forcing Call for the Opening Hand is variously known as the Forcing Two, Demand Two and Big Two. **1935** *Times* 4 Nov. 4/7 With no flourish or eccentricity, he was a forcing batsman who scored at an immense rate. **1939** N. DE V. HART *Bridge Players' Bedside Bk.* 137 Clearly he has made a forcing pass, leaving it to North to double or to go on in Hearts or Spades. **1947** S. HARRIS *Fund. Princ. Contract Bridge* iii. 27 The only way in which East can make a forcing bid over North is to double informatively, or overbid North in his own suit. **1959** REESE & DORMER *Bridge Player's Dict.* 95 Traditional Acol players do not regard a change of suit by responder as forcing unless it is combined with a jump. **1970** *Globe & Mail* (Toronto) 26 Sept. 51/4 Partner must have at least two aces for his jump raise (forcing).

b. *spec.* **forcing dog** *Austral.* and *N.Z.*, a dog with the power to move sheep in the direction it wishes.

1933 [see FORCE *sb.*^{1} 7 e].

Hence †'**forcingly** *adv.*, in a forcing manner.

1593 NASHE *Christ's T.* (1613) 176 [He] commanded all the Clergie . . to assemble in praier . . and deale forcingly beseeching with God, to intermit his fury. **1616–61** HOLYDAY *Persius* 305 Yet doth he cry . . and forcingly will make The gods to hear.

'**forcing-pump.** = FORCE-PUMP I, 2.

1727–41 CHAMBERS *Cycl.* s.v. *Pump*, The forcing Pump which . . raises water to any height at pleasure. **1800** VINCE *Hydrostat.* viii. (1806) 90 Some kinds of forcing pumps act by condensed air. **1838** *Civil Engin. & Arch. Jrnl.* I. 322/1 A substitute for the Forcing-pump in supplying Steam Boilers. **1842** H. ROGERS *Ess.* I. i. 26 His mind was a fountain, not a forcing-pump.

†'**forcipal,** *a. Obs.*$^{-1}$ [f. L. *forcip-* FORCEPS + -AL^{1}.] Of the nature of a forceps.

1658 SIR T. BROWNE *Gard. Cyrus* ii. 43 Mechanicks make use hereof in forcipal Organs.

forcipate ('fɔːsɪpeɪt), *a. Bot.* and *Zool.* [f. as prec. + -ATE^{2}.] Formed like a forceps.

1668 WILKINS *Real Char.* 124 Two forcipate claws. **1826** KIRBY & SP. *Entomol.* (1828) III. xxix. 121 These organs of forcipate construction. **1849** JOHNSTON in *Proc. Berw. Nat. Club* II. No. 7. 367 A mandibular shaft forcipate at the apex. **1862** COOKE *Bot. Terms*, *Forcipate*, forked like pincers.

'**forcipated,** *a.* [f. as prec. + -ED^{1}.] = prec.

1646 SIR T. BROWNE *Pseud. Ep.* v. iii. 236 Locusts have . . a forcipated tayle behinde. **1713** DERHAM *Phys. Theol.* 190 *note*, Their forcipated Mouth. **1836–9** TODD *Cycl. Anat.* II. 864/1 Distinguished from the Brachelytra by the forcipated anus.

forci'pation. [f. as prec. + -ATION.]

†**1.** Torture by nipping with forceps or pincers.

1592 BACON *Observ. on Libel* Wks. 1826 V. 464 A punishment . . of less torment far than . . forcipation.

2. *Zoöl.* The state of being forcipated; forfication, bifurcation (*Cent. Dict.*).

forcipressure (ˌfɔːsɪ'prɛʃ(j)ʊə(r)). [f. L. *forci(p)-*, *forceps* + PRESSURE *sb.*] (See quot. 1890.)

1879 S. WELLS in *Brit. Med. Jrnl.* 21 June 928/2 Useful in forcipressure and in torsion. **1890** GOULD *Med. Dict.*, *Forcipressure*, the arrest of a minor hæmorrhage by pressing the end of the divided vessel with a pair of spring forceps.

forcite ('fɔəsaɪt). Also **forsite.** [f. FORCE + -ITE.] A variety of dynamite (see quot. 1889).

1883 *Pall Mall G.* 28 Mar. 7/2 A dangerous explosive known as forsite. [So in other journals of the same day.] **1884** GEN. ABBOT in Eissler *Mod. Explosives* (1890) 41 Forcite presents the appearance of a plastic mass having power of nitro-glycerine. **1889** CUNDILL *Dict. Explos.* 51 *Forcite* has been described as a mixture of nitro-glycerine with cellulose, the latter being gelatinised.

† **ˈforcive**, *a. Obs.* [f. FORCE *sb.*[1] + -IVE.] = FORCIBLE.

c **1600** DAY *Begg. Bednall Gr.* IV. iii. (1881) 100 By forcive means. **1634** W. WOOD *New Eng. Prosp.* I. xii, I will use no forcive arguments to perswade any. **1651** DAVENANT *Gondibert* Pref., Great men fence often with her [i.e. Justice], and with a forcive sleight put by her sword.

forcleave: see FOR- *pref.*[1] 5 b.

† **forˈclem**, *v. Obs. rare*$^{-1}$. [f. FOR- *pref.*[1] + CLEM *v.*[1] Cf. Ger. *verklemmen.*] *trans.* To pinch with hunger.

13.. *E.E. Allit. P.* C. 395 Al schal crye for-clemmed, with alle oure clere strenþe.

† **forˈcling**, *v. Obs.* [OE. *forclingan*, f. FOR-[1] + *clingan* to CLING.] *intr.* To shrink up, wither.

a **800** *Corpus Gloss.* 1744 *Rigentia*, forclingendu. *c* **1000** *Veronica* (Gr.-Wülk.) 163 Wæron sume on forclungenum treowe ahangene. *c* **1200** ORMIN 13851 þatt herrte, þatt wiþþinnenn uss Iss hefiȝliȝ forrclungenn þurrh fakenn trowwþe towarrd Godd. *c* **1305** *Pilate* 216 in *E.E.P.* (1862) 117 His lymes so forclonge to noȝte So hi dude alle tofore here deþ. *c* **1430** *Hymns Virg.* (1867) 13 As a clot of clay þou were forclonge.

forclose: see FORECLOSE.

† **forˈclutch**, *v. Obs. Pa. pple.* vorcluȝt. [f. FOR- *pref.*[1] + CLUTCH.] *trans.* ? To cramp.

a **1300** *Leg. S. Patrick* 376 in Horstm. *Altengl. Leg.* (1875) 165 Vp hor ton hi sete al uorcluȝt, & quaked al uor fere.

forcold: see FOR- *pref.*[1] 10.

forcome: see FORECOME.

† **forˈcouth**, *a. Obs.* Forms: 1 forcúþ, 3 forcud. [OE. *forcúþ*, an accentual variant of *fracoð, fracod*, corresp. to Goth. *frakunþs* despised; see FOR- *pref.*[1] and COUTH.

Kluge suggests that the form with stressless prefix may have arisen from the compound '*unforcúþ*.']

Perverse, infamous, worthless, vile.

c **888** K. ÆLFRED *Boeth.* xxxvii. §3 Hi habbaþ þæs mennisces þone forcuþestan [*v.r.* forcuþeran] [dæl] ȝehealden. *c* **1000** ÆLFRIC *Hom.* I. 268 Swa he oftor on ðære fandunge abryð, swa he forcuðra bið. *a* **1175** *Cott. Hom.* 219 þa warð he and halle his iferen forcuðran þanne ænig oðer ȝesceafte. *c* **1205** LAY. 28240 Som forcouþ cniht. *c* **1230** *Hali Meid.* 33 þea þat fondeð ham meast; ifindeð ham forcudest.

forcover, forcratch, forcrazed: see FOR- *pref.*[1] 2, 5 b, 7.

† **forˈcremp**, *v. Obs. rare*$^{-1}$. [f. FOR- *pref.*[1] + CREMP = MHG. *verkrempfen.*] ? *intr.* for *refl.* To cramp oneself up.

a **1250** *Owl & Night.* 510 A sumere cheorles awedeth And forcrempeþ and forbredeþ.

forcried: see FOR- *pref.*[1] 6 b.

† **forˈcrier**. [f. FOR- *pref.*[2] + CRIER; cf. L. *proclamator.*] A crier.

a **1440** *Found. St. Bartholomew's* (1895) 37 This gylfull manne, namyd Alureid the bedyl or forcryer.

forcrooked: see FOR- *pref.*[1] 8.

† **forˈcurse**, *v. Obs. rare.* [OE. *forcursian*, f. FOR- *pref.*[1] + *cursian* to CURSE.] *trans.* To curse utterly, lay under a heavy curse.

1154 *O.E. Chron.* an. 1137 Hi ueron al for cursæd and for suoren. *a* **1300** *Cursor M.* 10262 (Cott.) Qua has in israel na side [*read* sede], He es forcursd als we rede.

† **forˈcut**, *v. Obs.* Forms: 4 forkutte, *pa. pple.* 4–5 forkute, -kytte: see CUT *v.* [f. FOR- *pref.*[1] + CUT *v.*] *trans.* To cut into, cut in pieces; to injure by cutting.

c **1386** CHAUCER *Manciple's T.* 236 As a swerd for-kutteth and for-kerueth An Arm atwo. **1387** TREVISA *Higden* (Rolls) VIII. 153 þe burgeys sone þat he had i-slawe for-kutte his wombe wiþ a knyf. **1398** —— *Barth. De P.R.* (1495) XVII. xcii. 660 Letuse.. heelyth synewes that are for-kytte. **1440** J. SHIRLEY *Dethe K. James* (1818) 19 The Kyng strogild with hem, for to have berevyd thame thare knyvys; by the which labur his handis wer all forkute.

† **ˈforcy**, *a. Obs.* Chiefly *north.* [f. FORCE *sb.*[1] + -Y[1].] Full of force, powerful, strong.

1375 BARBOUR *Bruce* II. 242 Othir fele folk, forsye in fycht. *c* **1470** HENRY *Wallace* v. 291 The forseast ay rudely rabutyt he. **1508** DUNBAR *Tua mariit Wemen* 85 A forky fure, ay furthwart, and forsy in draucht. **1586** WARNER *Alb. Eng.* III. xiv. 66 An Armie greate Of forcie Gawles.

ford (fɔəd), *sb.*[1] Forms: 1 ford, 3 *south.* vord, 4–6 fo(o)rde, 4–5 furd, forth(e, (4 fourde, foorth, 5 furthe, 6 furde), 6–7 foord, 7 foard, 3– ford. [OE. *ford* str. masc. = OS. *-ford* (in place-names), OHG. *furt* (MHG. *vurt*, mod.Ger. *furt*):—WGer. **furdu-z*:—pre-Teut. **pr̥tú-s*, found in OWelsh *rit*, now *rhyd* ford, L. *portus* PORT, harbour, f. Aryan root **per-*, Teut. **fer-, far-, fur-* to go, pass: see FARE *v.* The ON. *fiǫrðr* FIORD (:—**ferþu-z*:—**pértus*) differs in ablaut grade.]

1. A shallow place in a river or other water, where a man or beast may cross by wading.

c **893** K. ÆLFRED *Oros.* v. xii. §2 Neh þæm forda þe mon hæt Welengaford. *c* **1000** ÆLFRIC *Gen.* xxxii. 22 He.. oferfor þone ford. *c* **1205** LAY. 20159 Arður.. for-stod heom þene uord. *c* **1330** R. BRUNNE *Chron.* (1810) 187 Passage non he nam, þe forthes wer withsette. **1382** WYCLIF *Josh.* ii. 7 Thei ..folweden hem bi the weye that ledith to the foordis of Jordan. *c* **1425** WYNTOUN *Cron.* VIII. xxvi. 115 Ane met þame in þe Forde, Ðat prewaly.. Led þame wp by þe Wattyr syne. **1535** COVERDALE *Isa.* x. 28 At Machmas shal he muster his hooste, and go ouer yᵉ foorde. **1792** BURKE *Corr.* (1844) IV. 27 The fords must have been impassable in those floods. **1850** TENNYSON *In Mem.* vi, Her future Lord Was drown'd in passing thro' the ford. **1875** F. HALL in *Lippincott's Mag.* XVI. 749/1 The guide had strayed off the ford, and I was foundering in a quicksand.

Proverb. **1575** GASCOIGNE *Cert. Notes of Instr.* (Arb.) 34 Let vs take the forde as we finde it. **1637** RUTHERFORD *Lett.* (1862) I. ciii. 262, I praise and commend the ford (as we use to speak) as I find it.

† **2. a.** A tract of shallow water. **b.** Used (like L. *vadum*) for: The sea (*rare*$^{-1}$). **c.** *poet.* A stream, current (primarily with reference to passage). *Obs.*

1563 FULKE *Meteors* 56 b, Brookes, boornes or fordes, bee small streames of water, that ronne in a channell. *Ibid.*, Ryuers are caused by the meatynge.. of many brookes and fordes. **1565** GOLDING *Ovid's Met.* VI. (1593) 143 Their ship from land with ores was haled on the foord. *a* **1599** SPENSER (Webster 1864), With water of the ford Or of the clouds, to moisten their roots dry. **1610** W. FOLKINGHAM *Art of Survey* I. x. 24 Boggie.. grounds are.. fastened and firmed by frequent ouer-flowing them with Fords or Land-floods. *c* **1645** HOWELL *Lett.* (1688) IV. 495 A deep Foard wherein an Elephant might swim. **1661** LOVELL *Hist. Anim. & Min.* Introd., They live in the deep sea, and when they bring forth, they goe to foords and shores. *a* **1780** *Ball. Johnie Cock* iii. in Child *Ballads* v. cxiv. (1888) 3/1 And for a drop of thy heart's bluid, They wad ride the fords of hell.

3. *attrib.*, as ***ford-way***.

1721 in Temple & Sheldon *Hist. Northfield, Mass.* (1875) 223 Between Deerfield and Northfield.. 20 rods west of the fordway. **1858** J. F. REDFIELD *Law Railways* (1869) I. 231 Where a ford-way was destroyed, by the erection of a dam across a river.

Ford (fɔəd), *sb.*[2] The name of Henry *Ford* (1863–1947), American manufacturer of motor vehicles, used to designate the products of the company he founded. Also *fig.* (see quots. 1964, 1968).

1914 *Scotsman* 14 Oct. 12/1 Ford Chassis £105. **1918** *Automobile Engineer* Mar. 85/2 The minimum-priced car, represented by the Ford. **1920** *Blackw. Mag.* Jan. 105/2 It is the sort of road that even a Ford would hesitate to tackle. **1925** A. P. HERBERT *Laughing Ann* 48 Like the starting of a Ford. **1927** A. HUXLEY *Let.* 8 Oct. (1969) 292, I don't know whether one's interests are better looked after by an individual or a Ford factory. **1937** [see ANTI-FREEZE *a.* and *sb.*]. **1958** B. NICHOLS *Sweet & Twenties* vi. 83 She saw a Ford van in the window. **1964** W. L. GOODMAN *Hist. Woodworking Tools* 100 The Stanley-type plane may be described.. as the Ford of woodworking tools. **1968** J. IRONSIDE *Fashion Alphabet* 87 *Ford*, a best-seller, a winner. A line which continues from season to season.

ford (fɔəd), *v.* [f. FORD *sb.*[1]]

1. *trans.* To cross (water) by means of a ford; to wade through.

1614 RALEIGH *Hist. World* I. iii. §6 Adam's shin-bones must haue contayned a thousand fadome.. if he had foorded the Ocean. *a* **1674** CLARENDON *Hist. Reb.* IX. §88 His Horse ..should at the same time Ford the Severn.. and so joyn with his Foot. **1725** DE FOE *Voy. round World* (1840) 340 They found the river so shallow, that they easily forded it. **1849** GROTE *Greece* II. lxx. (1862) VI. 260 As no mention is made of a bridge, we are to presume that they forded the river. **1884** *Sat. Rev.* 14 June 780/1 An old woman in a cart is fording the brook.

fig. *a* **1641** BP. MOUNTAGU *Acts & Mon.* (1642) 299 The truth at last he foorded. **1642** MILTON *Apol. Smect.* (1851) 318 His last Section which is no deepe one, remains only to be foarded. **1701** ROWE *Amb. Step-Moth.* I. i, This Advantage may at least be made To ford his Shallow Soul.

b. *causatively.*

1726 DE FOE *Hist. Devil* I. xi, God intended to ford the Israelites over the Sea. **1903** A. ADAMS *Log of Cowboy* vii. 88 You can hardly imagine what a difference there is in fording this herd, between a cool cloudy day and a clear hot one.

2. *intr.* To cross (*over*) by means of a ford.

1675 OGILBY *Brit.* 90 You ford over the Owse. **1727** *Philip Quarll* (1816) 5 In some places too shallow for boats, and in others too deep to ford over. **1796** H. HUNTER tr. *St. Pierre's Stud. Nat.* III. 93 She durst not venture to put her feet into it for the purpose of fording over. **1823** SOUTHEY *Hist. Penins. War* I. 727 Some of their detachments forded both on the right and left of the Spaniards' position.

b. To wade. *rare.*

1748 *Voy. Disc.* I. 93 Goslings in the londs, amongst which our People had the greatest Success, as they could ford into the Water, and reach them with Cutlashes.

fig. **1817** COLERIDGE *Lay Serm.* 408 In the New Testament there are shallows where the lamb may ford, and depths where the elephant must swim.

ford, ford-: see FORTH, FORTH-.

fordable (ˈfɔədəb(ə)l), *a.* [f. FORD *v.* + -ABLE.] That may be forded.

1611 FLORIO, *Vadásile*, foardable, wadable. **1614** RALEIGH *Hist. World* I. iii § 9 Plinie placeth the Schenite vpon Euphrates, where the same beginneth to be foordable. **1724** DE FOE *Mem. Cavalier* (1840) 142 It was a little brook, fordable with ease. **1807** G. CHALMERS *Caledonia* I. i. ii. 108 The river Clyde, from Douglas upwards, was, in those days, fordable. **1886** STEVENSON *Kidnapped* xiv, It occurred to me that perhaps the creek was fordable.

fig. **1614** RALEIGH *Hist. World* Pref. B a, Hee found by Catesby, who sounded him, that he was not fordable. **1646** H. LAWRENCE *Comm. Angells* 176 The scriptures, though deepe, are foordable by those who are holy. **1710** *Fanatick Feast* 16 Thou art the shallowest, most fordable Monster in the Universe.

Hence **ˈfordableness**.

1727 in BAILEY vol. II.

fordage (ˈfɔədɪdʒ). *rare.* [f. as prec. + -AGE.] A fording-place, a ford.

1728 MORGAN *Algiers* II. v. 303 The Spaniards.. found a Fordage, not much above knee-deep.

fordead: see FOR- *pref.*[1] 10.

† **ˈfordeal**. *Obs.* Forms: 5 fordele, -deel, 6 fordaill, 6–9 fordel(l, (7 fortell). [f. FOR- *pref.*[2] + DEAL *sb.*, part; = Du. *voordeel*, Ger. *vorteil.*]

1. Advantage.

1470–85 MALORY *Arthur* v. viii, The bataille was grete, and oftsydes that one party was at a fordele and anone at an afterdele. **1481** CAXTON *Reynard* xxx. (Arb.) 78 Preferre the honour, worship, fordul and proffyte of theyr Lord. **1523** *St. Papers Hen. VIII*, I. 143 Which newes beyng true, shalbe a mervailory fordell to your intended purposes. **1637** R. MONRO *Exped.* I. 74 The enemy also, had another fortell, or advantage by reason of a new worke, which was uncomplete.

2. The first place, precedence, preference. *Sc.*

1513 DOUGLAS *Æneis* v. iii. 99 And now hes Pristis the fordaill. **1535** STEWART *Cron. Scot.* III. 276 Thair wes.. Ane flatterar and fenȝear for ane fordell, Semdill in the kirk and rich oft in the bordell. *a* **1651** CALDERWOOD *Hist. Kirk* (1843) II, So long as men of vertue and honour.. sall stand a fordell, to controll their.. wicked proceidings.

fordeave: see FOR- *pref.*[1] 9.

† **ˈfordeed**. *Obs.* In 3–5 fordede. [f. FOR *prep.* + DEED.] A deed done on behalf of some one; a benefit, favour.

a **1225** *Ancr. R.* 394 Neuer uere swuch fordede ne dude uor his owne uere. *c* **1350** *Will. Palerne* 5182 King william þe king of spayne þonkes Of al þe faire fordede þat he hade for hem wrouȝt. *c* **1460** *Towneley Myst.* 317 When had thou nede of oure fordede? When did we alle this dede for the?

† **forˈdeem**, *v. Obs.* [OE. *fordéman*, f. FOR- *pref.*[1] + DEEM *v.* Cf. ON. *fordœ́ma*, OHG. *fur-, fortuomen.*] *trans.* To condemn.

c **1000** *Ags. Gosp.* Matt. xxvii. 3 Ða ȝeseah iudas.. þæt he fordemed wæs, þa ongann he hreowsian. *c* **1175** *Lamb. Hom.* 95 Ac he nalde mid his to-cume þa sunfullen fordemen. *a* **1250** *Owl & Night.* 1098 And him fordeme lif and lime. *c* **1320** *Cast. Love* 447 Nout.. þat nis destrued and to-dreued, And dreynt, for-loren, and for-demed.

forder-: see FURTHER-.

forderked, -dewed: see FOR- *pref.*[1] 7, 9.

† **forˈdight**, *v. Obs.* In 3 pa. pple. **fordight**. [f. FOR- *pref.*[2] + DIGHT *v.*] *trans.* To prepare, predestine.

a **1300** *Cursor M.* 23583 (Cott.) To wirscip þat godd þam had fordight, þai graid þam bath mode and might.

† **forˈdilghe**, *v. Obs.* [OE. *fordileȝian*, f. FOR- *pref.*[1] + *dilȝian* = OS. *diligôn*, OHG. *tiligôn* (mod.Ger. *tilgen*) to destroy; cf. Ger. *vertilgen.*] *trans.* To exterminate, destroy.

c **900** tr. *Bæda's Hist.* I. xii. [xvi.] (1891) 54 þæt heo oð forwyrd æghwær fordilȝode ne wæron. *c* **1200** ORMIN 14541 All mannkinn.. Wass.. forrrahht ȝæn Godd, & wurrþ To wurrþenn all forrdillȝhedd.

† **forˈdill**, *v. Obs. rare.* [f. FOR- *pref.*[1] + DILL *v.*[2]] *trans.* To soothe.

a **1300** *Cursor M.* 23975 (Cott.) Hir dule ne ma i noght for-dill [*c* **1340** for-dille] Bot wit hir wepeing wepe i will.

† **forˈdim**, *v. Obs.* [OE *fordimmian*, f. FOR- *pref.*[1] + *dimmian* to DIM.] *trans.* To dim, obscure.

a **1050** *Liber Scintill.* xxv. (1889) 99 Se þe gaderaþ þæt biþ fordimmod. **1430** LYDG. *Chron. Troy* Prol., Fordimmed eke the letters aureat.

fordin: see FOR- *pref.*[1] 7.

fording (ˈfɔədɪŋ), *vbl. sb.* [f. FORD *v.* + -ING[1].]

a. The action of crossing a ford; also *attrib.* **b.** A fording-place or ford.

1833 M. SCOTT *Tom Cringle* xiv. (1859) 327 The hollo.. guided us to the fording which we had crossed on our first arrival. **1854** J. L. STEPHENS *Centr. Amer.* (1854) 278 We reached the bank; but here there was no fording-place. **1881** *Gentl. Mag.* Jan. 68 In two fordings we had narrowly escaped plumping into holes.

† **forˈdit**, *v. Obs.* [OE. *fordyttan* (*-duttan*), f. FOR- *pref.*[1] + *dyttan* to stop.] *trans.* To shut or stop up.

a **800** *Corpus Gloss.* 1414 *Obstruit*, fordytte. *c* **825** *Vesp. Psalter* lvii[i]. 5 Swe nedran deafe & forduttænde earan hire. *c* **1200** *Trin. Coll. Hom.* 197 þe neddre secheð a ston and leið hire on eare þer to and hire oðer eare pilteð hire tail þer inne and swo for-ditteð eiðer. *c* **1205** LAY. 17139 Mi gast hine iwarðeð.. & mine wise word for-dut. *a* **1240** *Lofsong* in *Cott. Hom.* 211 þine fif wunden iopened o rode wið neiles uordriuene and seoruhfulliche fordutte. **13..** *Coer de L.* 4170 The pytte.. was feld and fordytte, Up to the bank maad al playn.

fordless ('fɔədlɪs), *a.* [f. FORD *sb.*[1] or *v.* + -LESS.] Without a ford; that cannot be forded.

a **1649** DRUMM. OF HAWTH. *Hist. Jas. IV*, Wks. (1711) 63 The water of Till running deep and fordless upon the right hand. **1808** J. BARLOW *Columb.* IV. 294 Pierce the known thicket, breast the fordless tide. **1879** MALLOCK *Life Worth Liv.* 133 A deep and fordless river.

fordo, foredo (fə-, fɔə'duː), *v.* Pa. t. -did (-'dɪd). Pa. pple. -done (-'dʌn). Forms: see DO. [OE. *fordón*, f. FOR- *pref.*[1] + *dón* to DO. Cf. OS. *fardôn* (Du. *verdoen*), OHG. *fartuon* (MHG. *vertuon*. Ger. *verthun*).]

1. *trans.* To put (a living being) out of existence, to kill; to put an end to (life). *Obs.* exc. *arch.*

a **1000** *Pœnit. Ecgberti* II. §2 in Thorpe *Anc. Laws* II. 180 Be þam wifmen þe..hire bearn fordeð. *c* **1250** *Gen. & Ex.* 426 Caym ðat abel for-dede. *a* **1300** *Cursor M.* 2867 (Cott.) For if ani fische þar-in bigane..þe lijf it es for-don wit stink. *c* **1385** CHAUCER *L.G.W.* 2557 *Phyllis*, She for dispayr fordede hyre self. *c* **1460** *How Goode Wif Taught Doughter* 140 in Hazl. *E.P.P.* I. 189 Many for folye hem self fordoothe. *a* **1547** SURREY *Æneid* IV. 843 Offspring of each race With mortal warr eche other may fordoe. **1602** SHAKS. *Ham.* v. i. 244 This doth betoken The Coarse they follow, did with disperate hand, Fore do it owne life. *a* **1659** BP. BROWNRIG *Serm.* (1674) I. xxi. 274 He trembles, despairs, is ready to foredo himself. **1870** MORRIS *Earthly Par.* II. III. 348 By the sword's edge his life shall be foredone.

†**b.** *to fordo into* or *to*: see DESTROY *v.* 7. *Obs.*

c **950** *Lindisf. Gosp.* Matt. x. 28 Ah is rehtræ ðone ondredes seðe mæȝe & ða s[a]uel & lic-homa fordoa in tintergo. *c* **1175** *Lamb. Hom.* 17 Betere hit is þet heo beon ispilled of heore licome þenne mid alle fordon to þes deofles hond. *a* **1200** *Moral Ode* 274 And al þo þe ani wise deuel iquemde þo beð mid hem in helle fordon and demde.

2. To destroy, ruin, spoil, wreck (a place or thing); to lay waste (land). *arch.*

c **900** tr. *Bæda's Hist.* II. x. [xiv.] (1890) 138 Se biscop..towearp & fordyde þa wigbed. **1154** *O.E. Chron.* an. 1137 Þe land was al fordon mid suilce dædes. **1303** R. BRUNNE *Handl. Synne* 884 A tempest þat tyme began to falle And fordede here vynys alle. **1357** *Lay Folks Catech.* 489 Sklaundir for to fordo a mannes gode fame. **1375** BARBOUR *Bruce* v. 410 Syne tuk he salt..And ded horss, and fordid the well. **1399** LANGL. *Rich. Redeles* III. 141 They..ffor doth the coyne..And maketh the peple ffor pens-lac in pointe ffor to wepe. *c* **1460** *How Wise Man Taught Son* 76 in Ritson *Anc. Pop. P.* (1791) 86 Were thy complexion neuyr so strong, Wyth surfet thou mayst fordo that. **1581** J. BELL *Haddon's Answ. Osor.* 375 He raysed upp..consciences that were utterly foredone. **1845** BAILEY *Festus* 388 Throne wrecked on throne, All ruined and foredone.

†**3.** To ruin or undo (a person). Also (in late use), To deprive *of*. *Obs.*

c **1380** *Sir Ferumb.* 2269 Now helpeþ ȝow silue on þes cas: or ellis ȝe buþ for-done. **1571** GOLDING *Calvin on Ps.* ix. 13 He [God]..keepeth in his bosome, those which (as touching the fleshe) seeme vtterly fordoone. **1647** H. MORE *Poems* 264 Those bad arts that have fore-done Many a bold wit. **1764** CHURCHILL *Poems, Independence* II. 12 Lioness of royal whelps foredone.

4. †**a.** To abolish (an institution, etc.); to annul (a law, etc.). *Obs.*

O.E. Chron. an. 986 Se cyning fordyde þæt b'rice æt Hrofe ceastre. *c* **1320** R. BRUNNE *Medit.* 186 A newe testament he gan sone, þe olde sacryfyce to fordone. **1494** FABYAN *Chron.* VII. 320 The enterdyccion was adnullyd & fordoon, in the moneth of Julii. **1508** FISHER 7 *Penit. Ps.* li. Wks. (1876) 136 Oblacyons and sacrefyces whiche be now vtterly fordone. **1528** MORE *Dyaloge* II. Wks. 198/2 Ye would not I truste that lent were fordone. **1532** in Strype *Eccl. Mem.* I. App. xli. 109 To cause the said injust exactions..to cease & to be foredoen for ever. **1568** GRAFTON *Chron.* II. 149 All statutes and ordynaunces made before made..were utterly fordone and set at naught. **1833** WHITTIER *Ex. New Eng. Leg.* 3 How has New England's romance fled..Its rites foredone, its guardians dead.

b. To do away with, put away, remove. Chiefly with immaterial obj., *esp.* sin. *Obs.* or *arch.*

a **1300** *Cursor M.* 10052 (Gött.) Gastly gladnes was hir emydd, þat al ille heuynes it for-didd. **1340** HAMPOLE *Pr. Consc.* 3391 Syns þat er veniele..may be here Fordon on light manere. **1398** TREVISA *Barth. De P.R.* XVII. cxliv. (1495) 701 The barke and fruyte of the Ellern soden wyth salt water fordooth swellynge of fete. *c* **1430** *Syr Gener.* (Roxb.) 2432 The lauender That neuer might for noo washing For-doo the spottes of the weping. **1600** HOLLAND *Livy* XLI. iii. (1609) 1098 To..wipe away and foredoe the shamefull blot. **1894** F. S. ELLIS *Reynard* 146 Now Reynard, to foredo the brand Of sin, will to the Holy Land.

†**5.** To undo, bring to nought; to render powerless, counteract, neutralize (poison, temptation, etc.). *Obs.*

c **1175** *Lamb. Hom.* 105 þenne maȝe we fordon swa þa deofliche ȝitsunge. *a* **1225** *Leg. Kath.* 484 Ichulle fordon þe wisdom of þeos wise worldmen. *a* **1250** *Owl & Night.* 822 þonne is þes hundes smel fordo. *a* **1300** *Cursor M.* 11947 (Cott.) þat i do þou it for-dos. *c* **1330** R. BRUNNE *Chron.* (1810) 87 For soth it was grete skathe, his passage was fordone. **1377** LANGL. *P. Pl.* B. XVIII. 152 Venym for-doth venym. **1601** HOLLAND *Pliny* I. 26 They will fordoe and frusrate the dangers pronounced.

†**6.** To change, transform. *Obs.*

1624 HEYWOOD *Gunaik.* I. 53 Nisus and Scilla are in shape foredoone, He to a hawke, she to a larke is shifted.

7. Pa. pple. only: Exhausted, overdone, wearied out, 'done up'. *arch.*

a **1547** SURREY *Æneid* II. 785 Go see where thow hast left Anchises thy father fordone with age. **1591** *Troub. Raigne K. John* II. (1611) 79 My heart is maz'd, my sences all foredone. **1718** ROWE tr. *Lucan* VI. 744 Universal Nature stands foredone. **1796** COLERIDGE *Ode Depart. Year* Epode ii, All foredone with toil and wounds Death-like he..dozes among heaps of dead. **1867** M. ARNOLD *Southern Night* vii, With Indian heats at last fordone.

Hence **for'doing** *vbl. sb.* Also **for'doer**.

c **1440** *Jacob's Well* (E.E.T.S.) 84 Þe secunde fote brede of wose, in dede of enuye, is a fordoyng; þat is, whanne, for enuye in þi dede, þou dystroyest him, þat wolde do ryȝt. **1631** J. DONE *Polydoron* 129 Desperate Foredoers of themselves denote that they turn'd their backs upon God.

fordone (fə'dʌn), *ppl. a.* [pa. pple. of FORDO *v.*] Exhausted, overcome, tired out. (See FORDO 7.)

1590 SPENSER *F.Q.* I. v. 41 If either salves, or oyles, or herbes, or charmes, A fordonne wight from dore of death mote raise. **1866** CARLYLE *Remin.* II. 241, I reached home after my evening ride, the most foredone of men.

†**for'dote,** *v. Obs. rare*[−1]. [f. FOR- *pref.*[1] + DOTE *v.*] *trans.* To make quite foolish or doting.

c **1533** *Articles imputed to Latimer* in Foxe *A. & M.* (1563) 1313 Here, for lacke of helpe, we may..dishonor god, fordote oure-selues.

†**for'dovered,** *pple.* and *ppl. a. Obs. Sc.* [f. FOR- *pref.*[1] + DOVER *v.* + -ED[1].] Overcome with slumber.

1513 DOUGLAS *Æneis* II. vi. 35 That tyme quhen the fyrst quiet Of naturale sleip..Stelis on fordoverit mortale creaturis. *Ibid.* IX. vi. 20 Apon the gyrs..Fordoveryt, fallyn down als drunk as swyne.

†**for'draw,** *v. Obs. Pa. t.* 4 fordroȝ. *Pa. pple.* fordraun, -draw(e)n. [f. FOR- *pref.*[1] + DRAW *v.*]

1. *trans.* ? To stretch on the rack, torture.

a **1300** *Cursor M.* 21235 (Cott.) Barnabas..sufferd paines strang..Bath for-draun and brint wit feir. *c* **1380** *Sir Ferumb.* 1796 þe deuel þe for-drawe.

2. a. To defer, put off. **b.** To draw on (as a tempter.)

a **1300** *Cursor M.* 26135 (Cott.) Him..for-think his lang delaiance þat he for-draun has his penance. **1382** WYCLIF *Prov.* vii. 21 With flatering of lippis she fordroȝ him.

†**for'dread,** *v. Obs.* [f. FOR- *pref.*[1] + DREAD *v.*] *intr.* To be in dread *of*.

c **1200** ORMIN 147 [Zacariȝe] warrþ drefedd & forrdredd Off þatt he sahh þatt enngell. *c* **1250** *Gen. & Ex.* 1557 Quan ysaac it under-nam..Wel selkuðlike he wurð for-dred. **1297** R. GLOUC. (Rolls) 2088 Gracian þe emperour..of him uor dradde ynou. *a* **1310** in Wright's *Lyric P.* 88 Myn herte of dedes wes for-dred.

fordreamed: see FOR- *pref.*[1] 6 b.

†**for'drench,** *v. Obs.* [OE. *fordrencan*, f. FOR- *pref.*[1] + *drẹncan* to DRENCH; = MLG. *vordrenken*.]

trans. **a.** To make drunk, intoxicate. *lit.* and *fig.* **b.** To drown. Also *intr.*

a. *c* **1000** ÆLFRIC *Gen.* xix. 32 Uton fordrencan urne fæder færlice mid wine. *c* **1175** *Lamb. Hom.* 91 þas men beoð mid miste fordrencte. *a* **1225** *Leg. Kath.* 2343 þe þæt wes fordrenct wið þes deoules puisun.

b. *a* **1225** *Juliana* 61 þe reade sea..þear as al pharaones forde fordrencte. **1430** LYDG. *Chron. Troy* II. xvii, Alterat with Bachus myghty Jous And affered of tournynge of the hous And fordreynt on the drye land.

fordreved: see FOR- *pref.*[1] 8.

†**fordrift.** *Obs. rare*[−1]. [f. FOR-[2], FORE- *pref.* + DRIFT.] ? Purpose, preconceived design.

1549 CHALONER tr. *Erasm. Moriæ Enc.* Sj b, Thynges smallie sensed..as which liue by no arte nor fordrifte [orig. *sollicitudine*].

†**for'drive,** *v. Obs.* [OE. *fordrífan*, f. FOR- *pref.*[1] + *drífan* to DRIVE; = OHG. *far-*, *fertrîban*.] *trans.* To drive forth, drive about.

O.E. Chron. an. 774 Norðhymbra fordrifon heora cining Alhred of Eoferwic. *c* **1220** *Bestiary* 527 Ðe sipes ðat arn on se fordriuen. *a* **1300** *Cursor M.* 22635 (Cott.) þe deuels vte sal be fordriuen. *c* **1430** LYDG. *Bochas* VI. (1494) V iij a, With wynde and tempest fordryuen also was he. **1513** DOUGLAS *Æneis* I. i. 56 Scho thame fordrivis, and causis oft ga will Frawart Latium.

†**for'drunken,** *ppl. a. Obs.* [OE. *fordruncen*, f. FOR- *pref.*[1] + DRUNKEN; = MLG. *vordrunken*.] Drunk, overcome with drink.

c **897** K. ÆLFRED *Gregory's Past.* xl. 295 Ab[i]gall..forsuigode ðæt dysiȝ hiere fordruncnan hlafordes. *c* **1175** *Lamb. Hom.* 143 þe prude, þe for-drunken, þe chidinde. *c* **1386** CHAUCER *Miller's Prol.* 12 The Myller that fordrunken was al pale. **1513** DOUGLAS *Æneis* III. ix. 81 Sow-pit in sleip, his nek fourth of the cave He straucht, for-drunkin.

†**for'dry,** *v. Obs.* [OE. *fordrúȝian* (intr.), f. FOR-[1] + *drúȝian* to DRY. The trans. use is f. FOR-[1] + DRY *a.*] *intr.* To dry up.

a **1000** *Boeth. Metr.* xx. 207 Hio wære fordrugod to duste. *a* **1225** *Ancr. R.* 148 Ant te grene bowes beoð al uordruwede. *a* **1350** *Leben Jesu* 596 Ase a luþur braunche, and fur druyt. **1398** TREVISA *Barth. De P.R.* IX. vi. (Tollem. MS.) þe sonne ..ripeþ frutes and flouris..and fordrieþ and wasteþ superfluiteis. *Ibid.* XVII. xiii. (1495), Pouder therof layed therto fordrieth the bleding. **1413** *Pilgr. Sowle* (Caxton 1483) III. iii. 51 Some of them were all fordryed and lene. **1494** FABYAN *Chron.* VII. ccxxvii. 256 The ryuer of Trent was so fordryd..y[t] men went ouer drye.

fordry, -dull: see FOR- *pref.*[1] 10.

†**for'dull,** *v. Obs.* Also 4 fordoll. [f. FOR- *pref.*[1] + DULL *v.*; cf. MLG. *vordullen* and FORDILL *v.*] *trans.* To make dull; to stupefy. Only in pa. pple. Hence **for'dulled** *ppl. a*

13.. *Leg. Rood* (1871) 141 Alle þei seiden þei weore sori, For-dolled in a dronknyng dred. **13..** *E.E. Allit. P.* A 11, I dewyne for-dolled [*printed* dolked] of luf daungere. **1430** LYDG. *Chron. Troy* I. vi, Fordulled is myne imagynatyfe. **1513** DOUGLAS *Æneis* IV. Prol. 158 To droup like a fordullit as. **1578** T. PROCTOR *Gorg. Gallery* in *Heliconia* I. 163 O feeble wit! forduld with woe, awake thy wandering thought. **1592** R. WILMOT *Tancred & Gism.* II, What well of teares may serue To feed the streames of my fore-dulled eies. **1605** MONTGOMERIE *Sonnets* xi, Quhat mervell than, thoght our fordullit hedes..be mare amaisd.

†**for'dwine,** *v. Obs.* [f. FOR- *pref.*[1] + DWINE; = MDu. *verdwijnen*.] *intr.* To fade away, decay, wither; to vanish.

c **1000** ÆLFRIC *Saints' Lives* (E.E.T.S.) II. 268 Se deofol þær-rihte for-dwan swa swa smic of þæs halȝan ȝesihðe. *a* **1300** *Old Age* vi. in *E.E.P.* (1862) 149 When i bi-hold on mi schennen m'in dimmiþ al for-dwynnen. *c* **1305** *Pilate* 215 *ibid.* 117 His bodi gan al fordwyne. ? *a* **1366** CHAUCER *Rom. Rose* 366 Bothe hir hondes lorn, fordwyned.

†**'fordy,** *a. Obs. rare.* In 6 fourdie, -ye. [f. FORD *sb.*[1] + -Y[1].] Full of fords.

1570 in LEVINS *Manip.* 97. **1580** in BARET *Alv.* F 1050.

†**fore,** *sb. Obs.* Forms: 1 fór, 3-5 fore, vore, 4 foore, 5 fowre. [OE. *fór* str. fem. = OHG. *fuora* (MHG. *vuore*, mod.Ger. *fuhre*):—OTeut. **fôrâ-*, f. **fôr-*, ablaut-var. of **far-* to go: see FARE *v.*]

1. A going, journey, expedition. Also, an expeditionary force.

c **900** tr. *Bæda's Hist.* v. ix. (1891) 412 He his fore ȝeȝearwede. *c* **1205** LAY. 5568 Brennes..mid starkere fore ferde toward Rome. *Ibid.* 5858 þe cnihtes weoren on fore fer ut of Rome. **1297** R. GLOUC. (1724) 386 Wyllam ysey..bote he adde help of hys men, hys fore nas ryȝt noȝt. *c* **1400** in *Rel. Ant.* I. 160 Sori is the fore Fram bedde to the flore.

b. A rush, onset, charge.

c **1205** LAY. 1676 In þera ilke uore heo fælden of his iueren. **13..** *K. Alis.* 2355 Theose braken, at one fore, Heore launces on Nycanore.

2. A track, trace.

c **1250** *Owl & Night.* 817 And so forleost þe hund his fore. *c* **1386** CHAUCER *Sompn. T.* 227 Who folweth Cristes gospel and his fore. **1387** TREVISA *Higden* (Rolls) IV. 153 þere were afterward i sene foores and steppes of men and of hors. **1398** —— *Barth. De P.R.* IX. viii. (1495) 353 The foores and the sygnes of Somer that is goon is all dystroyed.

3. The course of an affair; a proceeding, adventure.

c **1205** LAY. 15578 For swa wes al þa uore. *Ibid.* 15810 Iwhiten þu wult þa uore nu þu hit scalt ihere. *c* **1320** *Cast. Love* 1156 No tonge may tellen of þat fore.

fore, obs. var. of FURROW.

fore (fɔə(r)), *a.* Also 6 *Sc.* foir. [The use of *fore* as adj. arises out of an analysis of sbs. which are combinations of FORE- *pref.*, e.g. *forepart*. These being occasionally written as two words, the first member came to be treated as an adj.]

I. As adj. *in concord.*

1. Situated or appearing in front, or in front of something else; usually with an opposition expressed or implied to *back*, *hind-*.

1500-20 DUNBAR *Poems* xlii. 68 Than Bissines..Straik doun the top of the foir tour. *c* **1540** *Order in Battayll* A vij b, When thou hast invaded thyne enemyes with the fore and hinder warde. *a* **1639** SPOTTISWOOD *Hist. Ch. Scot.* v. (1655) 271 The Cannon having made great breaches in the fore and back walls. **1655** GURNALL *Chr. in Arm.* Introd. v. (1669) 171 It comes in at the Back-door, while we are expecting it at the Fore. **1703** MOXON *Mech. Exerc.* 107 In the fore side of this wooden Piece is a square hole. **1715** CHEYNE *Philos. Princ. Relig.* I. i. (ed. 2) 13 Resistance in Fluids arises from their greater Pressing on the Fore, than Hind part of the Bodies moving in them. **1762** STERNE *Tr. Shandy* V. xxvi, Susannah had but just time to make her escape down the back-stairs, as my mother came up the fore. **1805** FORSYTH *Beauties Scotl.* II. 192 In the fore wall of the church..there has plainly been an aperture. **1880** HUXLEY *Crayfish* ii. 61 The alimentary canal may therefore be distinguished into a fore and a hind gut.

†**2.** Anterior, previous, former. *Obs.*

1490 CAXTON *Eneydos* xxiv. 90 The fore loue reneweth hym selfe. **1526** R. WHYTFORD *Martiloge* (1893) 84 The duke dyd the moost..commun seruyce notwithstandyng his fore estate. **1535** COVERDALE *2 Esdras* vii. 12 The intraunces of the fore worlde were wyde and sure. **1597** MORLEY *Introd. Mus.* 12 The great musicke maisters who excelled in fore time. *a* **1634** CHAPMAN *Alphonsus* Plays 1873 III. 239 Alexander and Meritz have the fore dance. **1718** *Entertainer* xxvi. 175 That Place which in a fore Time was Stil'd the Temple of Dagon.

II. quasi-*sb.* or *elliptically*.

3. The fore part of anything, e.g. the bow of a ship, the fore-quarter of beef, etc.

1888 *Pall Mall G.* 16 Jan. 14/1 The sensation was stronger in the fore of sailing vessels. **1890** *Daily News* 11 July 2/8 American refrigerated hind-quarters..thirds..fores.

b. *Naut.* *(at) the fore*: (see quot. 1883).

1860 MOTLEY *Netherl.* II. xix. 475 Medina Sidonia hoisted the royal standard at the fore. **1883** W. C. RUSSELL *Sailor's Lang.* s.v. *Fore*, At the fore, means at the fore-royal mast-head.

4. to the fore. (Sc. and Anglo-Irish phrase, introduced into English literary use in the 19th c.) **a.** Of a person: Present, on the spot, within call.

1637 RUTHERFORD *Lett.* (1862) I. 363 If Christ had not been to the fore in our sad days, the waters had gone over our soul. **1656** EARL MONM. *Advt. fr. Parnass.* 416 Some Italian Princes who were yet to the fore, could not be weighed. **1726** R. ERSKINE *Sonnets* II. i. §6 Yield not..The Lion strong of Judah's tribe, Thy Husband, 's to the fore. **1815** SCOTT *Guy M.* xlv, 'I wuss auld Sherra Pleydell was to the fore here!' **1829** MRS. S. C. HALL *Sk. Irish Char.* (1842) 60 Why didn't you give it me, and I to the fore? **1852** LEVER *Daltons* II. xxxv, If he hasn't me to the fore to prove what I said, he can do nothing.

b. Still surviving, alive.

1695 EARL CROMARTY *Vindic. Robt. III*, 14 The said Lord John..being to the fore, and on Life. **1724** RAMSAY *Tea-t. Misc.* (1733) I. 22 As lang's Sandy's to the fore Ye never shall get Nansy. **1787** BURNS *Let. W. Nicol* 1 June, Gif the beast be to the fore. **1818** SCOTT *Hrt. Midl.* xliii, 'While this grey head is to the fore, not a clute o' them but sall be as weel cared for as if they were the fatted kine of Pharaoh.' **1888** J. PAYN *Myst. Mirbridge* vi, The steward..though stricken in years—was still to the fore.

†**c.** *to the fore with*: in advance of. *Obs.*

1646 R. BAILLIE *Lett.* (1775) II. 221, I am now two to the fore with you, albeit I wrote none the last post.

d. Of money, etc.: Ready at or to hand, forthcoming; available. † *to go to the fore*: to be put to one's credit.

1636 RUTHERFORD *Lett.* (1862) I. 181 Therefore my wages are going to the fore up in heaven. **1640** *Dumbarton Burgh Rec.* in Irving *Hist. Dumbartonsh.* (1860) 525 Gif thay had common guid to the foir. **1660** SHARP *Let.* 11 May in Wodrow *Hist.* I. Introd. 25 Is his broad Sword to the fore? **1639** R. BAILLIE *Lett.* (1775) I. 126 He had a good estate, and well to the fore. **1828** SCOTT *F.M. Perth* viii, If these are not to the fore, it is the Provost's fault, and not the town's. **1848** THACKERAY *Van. Fair* xxv, How many captains in the regiment have two thousand pounds to the fore.

e. In recent use sometimes taken to mean 'in full view, conspicuous'. So *to come to the fore* occurs for: 'to come to the front', 'to come into view'.

1842 BARHAM *Ingol. Leg., Auto-da-Fe*, Magnificent structures..As our Irish friends have it, are there 'to the fore'. **1876** *World* V. No. 106. 5 These vermin seldom venture to come to the fore themselves. **1880** *Manch. Guard.* 23 Nov., The vexed question of local taxation reform must come to the fore next session.

fore (fɔə(r)), *adv.* and *prep.* [Com. Teut.: OE. *fore* = OFris. *fara*, OS. *fora* (Du. *voor*), OHG. *fora* (MHG. *vor(e*, mod.Ger. *vor*), Goth. *faura*. The root is the same as in L. *prō*, *præ*, *per*, Gr. πρό, παρά, παραί, περί, Skr. *purā*. The precise form in OTeut. is disputed: one opinion is that it was **forai* = Gr. παραί, with a dative case-ending.

From 16th c. the word has often been regarded as an abbreviation of *before*, and hence written *'fore*.]

†**A.** *adv. Obs.*

1. Before, at some earlier time, previously.

c **1000** *Ags. Ps.* (Th.) lxxvii[i]. 14 [12] He on Egypta ӡenum lande, worhte fore wundur mære. *a* **1300** *Cursor M.* 10938 (Cott.) Elizabeth..was anna sister, als i for tald. *c* **1350** *Will. Palerne* 2076 þe welþe & welfare i haue him wrouӡt fore. *a* **1375** *Joseph Arim.* 208 Wiþouten faute oþer faus as þei fore seiden. *c* **1600** SHAKS. *Sonn.* vii, The eyes (fore dutious) now..looke an other way.

b. Forward or onward, forth.

a **1300** *Cursor M.* 18267 (Cott.) Fra nu for, vnderstand þou wele Hu fele pines ai sal þou fele.

2. Beforehand, in advance.

a **1225** *Juliana* 47 Ah wel ich warni þe uore, hit nis nawt þin biheue. *c* **1500** *Melusine* xxiv. 184 To see a remedy be had to it rather to fore than to late.

B. *prep.* = FOR *prep.* in various uses.

†**1. a.** Before, in front of, in the presence of; = FOR 1 a, b. *Obs.*

Beowulf 1064 (Gr.) þær wæs sang and sweg..fore Healfdenes hildewisan. *c* **1300** *Beket* 31 The manere of Engelonde this Gilbert hire tolde fore. *c* **1320** *Cast. Love* 1030 So stille and derne he [Jesus] was þe fend fore. *c* **1550** *Northren Mothers Blessing* vi. (1597) E v, What man that shall wed the fore God with a ring. **1608** J. DAY *Law-Trickes* I. ii. (1881) 18 Y'are..much to rude, To shew this kindnesse fore a multitude. **1611** SHAKS. *Wint. T.* IV. iv. 401 Contract vs fore these Witnesses.

b. In asseveration or adjuration; = FOR 1 c.

c **1435** *Torr. Portugal* 745 Fore Sen Jame! What ys the gyantes name. **1601** SHAKS. *All's Well* II. iii. 51 Fore God I thinke so. **1687** CONGREVE *Old Bach.* III. ii, No, foregad! I'm caught. **1756** FOOTE *Eng. fr. Paris* II. Wks. 1799 I. 111 Foregad I believe the Papistes ha' bewitch'd him. **1840** BARHAM *Ingol. Leg., Ghost*, 'Fore George, I'm vastly puzzled what to do.

†**2.** Of time: Before; = FOR 2. *Obs.*

a **1000** *Crist* 1031 (Gr.) Fore Cristes cyme. *a* **1300** *Cursor M.* 22429 (Cott.) Fore domes-dai þat sal be sene. **1601** SHAKS. *Meas. for M.* II. ii. 160 At any time 'fore-noone.

†**3.** Before, in preference to; = FOR 3. *Obs.*

1591 SHAKS. *1 Hen. VI*, I. iii. 22 Prizest him 'fore me? **1594** MARLOWE & NASHE *Dido* III. iv, I follow one that loveth fame fore me. **1634** MASSINGER *Very Woman* II. i, You prefer My safety 'fore your own.

†**4.** = FOR 6. *Obs.*

1463 *Bury Wills* (Camd.) 17 And alle here costez payd fore.

†**5.** In support of, in favour of; = FOR 7. *Obs.*

c **900** tr. *Bæda's Hist.* v. v. (1891) 396 þæt he..him fore ӡebæde. *a* **1000** *Crist* 1202 (Gr.) Eal þa earfeðu, þe he fore ældum adreaӡ. *a* **1300** *Cursor M.* 11291 (Cott.) For to do fore him þat dai, þe settenes of þe ald lai. *c* **1340** *Ibid.* 9610 (Trin.) If my sister saue miӡt al þat she wolde fore [*other texts* for] crie & cal.

†**6.** On account of, because of; = FOR 21 b. *Obs.*

c **1175** *Lamb. Hom.* 27 þu ne derst cumen bi-foren him fore þine gulte. *c* **1340** *Cursor M.* 13756 (Trin.), I dampne þe nat þi synne fore. *c* **1440** *Jacob's Well* (E.E.T.S.) 45 þe fals tythere rehersyth aӡen in his fals tythyng þe synne, þat crist was do fore to deth.

†**7.** As a precaution against; = FOR 23 d. *Obs.*

c **1450** *Two Cookery-bks.* II. 106 And holde a dissh vnderneth, fore spilling of the licour.

8. *Comb.* †**fore-belly**, padded clothing in front of the belly; **fore-dawn**, the time preceding the dawn (also *attrib.* or *adj.*); †**fore-eternal** *a.*, †**fore-everlasting** *a.*, that is or was before the eternal or everlasting; in quots. *absol.* or quasi-*sb.*; **fore-sabbath**, the day that precedes the sabbath; †**fore-south** *a.*, facing the south.

1638 JASPER MAYNE tr. *Lucian's Dial.* (1664) 363, I forbear to speake of his stuft Brests, and *fore-Bellyes, which make an adventitious and artificiall corpulency. **1884** J. PAYNE *Tales fr. Arabic* II. 33 It was the *fore-dawn hour. **1894** HALL CAINE *Manxman* v. ii. 283 Sometimes he was up in the vague fore-dawn. **1587** GOLDING *De Mornay* vi. 80 Porphyrius..saying, that there is an euerlasting or eternall Mynd, and yet..afore the same a *Foreëternall, or former euerlasting. *Ibid.* And that betweene the *Foreeuerlasting and the Euerlasting, Eternitie resteth in the middest. **1656** TRAPP *Comm.* (1868) 415 The Jews..before their sabbath [had] their *fore-sabbath. **1686** PLOT *Staffordsh.* 386 The *fore-South windows..being cover'd with Matt to preserve the hony.

fore (fɔə(r)), *int. Golf.* [Probably a contraction of BEFORE.] (See quot. 1878.)

1878 PARDON *Football, etc.*, 82 Fore! a warning cry to people in front of the stroke.

fore, obs. pa. t. of FARE.

fore-, *prefix.* In OE. the adv. FORE (like its equivalent in various other Teut. langs.) was used as a prefix (1) to verbs, giving the additional sense of 'before' (either in time, position, order, or rank), and (2) to sbs. either forming designations of objects or parts of objects occupying a front position, or expressing anteriority in time. (Cf. OE. *forecweðan*, Goth. *fauraqiþan*, OHG. *foraquedan* to predict; OE. *foregangan*, Goth. *fauragaggan* to precede; OE. *foretóð*, Ger. *vorzahn* front tooth, etc.). The prefix has through all stages of the language continued to be a living formative in all its uses. The principal combinations are in this work treated as Main words in their alphabetical place; those which are of merely occasional use, or self-explanatory, are enumerated in this article.

I. In verbs, ppl. adjs., agent-nouns and nouns of action. (Stress on the verb.)

1. With the sense 'in front', as in *foregird*, *-lie*, *-lift* (all *Obs.* or *arch.*). Also in agent-nouns, as †*forespurrer*, FORERUNNER, FOREWALKER.

1610 HOLLAND *Camden's Brit.* I. 791 Severus *foregirded and fensed Britain with a ditch from sea to sea. **1590** SPENSER *F.Q.* II. iii. 29 A golden bauldricke, which *forelay Athwart her snowy brest. *Ibid.* I. xi. 15 *Fore-lifting up aloft his speckled brest. **1769** FALCONER *Shipwr.* III. 582 The ship, fore-lifted by the sea. **1596** SHAKS. *Merch. V*, II. ix. 95 This *fore-spurrer.

2. = 'Beforehand', 'previously', 'in advance'.

Formerly, esp. in 16–17th c., the prefix was used with any vb. to which it was desired to give this additional meaning. The number of recorded combinations of this kind is therefore enormous, and only a selection of them can here be given. Now, however, the use of the prefix, except in established combinations such as *foresee*, *foretell*, or in new combinations closely analogous to these, is felt to be somewhat archaistic or affected; in ordinary prose usage the meaning is expressed by the addition of an adverb, or (in verbs of obvious Lat. or Rom. derivation) by the prefix *pre-*.

a. in verbs, as ***fore-accustom***, ***-acquaint***, ***-adapt***, ***-admonish***, ***-advertise***, ***-advise***, ***-allot***, ***-answer***, ***-assign***, ***-balance***, ***-bespeak***, ***-bless***, ***-calculate***, ***-compose***, ***-comprehend***, ***-conclude***, ***-condemn***, ***-consider***, ***-contrive***, ***-count***, ***-date***, ***-declare***, ***-decree***, ***-design***, ***-dispose***, ***-divine***, ***-engage***, ***-exist***, ***-expect***, ***-express***, ***-fear***, ***-figure***, ***-fit***, ***-fix***, ***-grasp***, ***-haste***, ***-instruct***, ***-learn***, ***-lend***, ***-mean***, ***-order***, ***-paint***, ***-picture***, ***-plan***, ***-poison***, ***-promise***, ***-reckon***, ***-repent***, ***-report***, ***-request***, ***-resemble***, ***-scent***, ***-season***, ***-seize***, ***-send***, ***-shape***, ***-shoe***, ***-sing***, ***-smell***, ***-sound***, ***-steep***, ***-study***, ***-suffer***, ***-summon***, ***-suspect***, ***-threaten***, ***-trace***, ***-use***, ***-utter***, ***-vow***, ***-ween***, ***-weep***, ***-weigh***.

1640 BP. REYNOLDS *Passions* xxii, *Fore-accustoming the mind to evil. **1624** GATAKER *Transubst.* To Rdr., This is all that..I was desirous by way of Preface to *fore-acquaint thee withall. **1696** WHISTON *Th. Earth* IV. (1722) 294 He foresaw and *foreadapted the entire Frame. **1633** BP. HALL *Hard Texts, N.T.* 396 Who *fore-admonished me that [etc.]. **1598** BARRET *Theor. Warres* IV. ii. 105 To *fore aduertise the souldiers by the drumme maior. **1664** H. MORE *Myst. Iniq.* 206 Fore-advertising them..of all their affairs of Importance by the mouths of his Prophets. **1604** HIERON *Wks.* I. Advt. to Rdr. 671 This short catechisme..*foreaduiseth thee of the certainty of diuers afflictions. **1587** GOLDING *De Mornay* ix. 121 Whatsoeuer he had *foreallotted them of his goodnesse. **1620** BP. HALL *Hon. Mar. Clergy* I. §1 If all my proofes be..*fore-answered by his Bellarmine. **1713** BENTLEY *Free-thinking* I. xxix. 147 Notwithstanding he had foreanswered..all that he can say about Different Interpretations. **1675** BROOKS *Gold. Key* Wks. 1867 V. 333 God the Father, who from eternity hath *fore-assigned Christ to this office of a mediator. **1612** J. COTTA *Dangers Practisers Phys.* I. v. 43 Where..the strength of nature hath..bene carefully *foreballanced betweene hope and hazard. **1682** BUNYAN *Holy War* 67 Thy evil fruit *fore-bespeaks thee not to be a good tree. **1630** DRAYTON *Moses* I. 63 By th' eternal prouidence *fore-blest. **1864** *Spectator* 20 Aug. 963/1 Some great crisis not to be definitely *fore-calculated. **1684** BAXTER *Twelve Argts.* §1. 5 No man knoweth before-hand, whether a Minister hath studied and *fore comp[o]sed his..Sermon. **1652** GAULE *Magastrom.* vii. 78 Whether it be not quite contradictory to the nature of future contingents to be *fore-comprehended by any created intellect. **1618** DANIEL *Hist. Eng.* 12 They held the same confederation *fore-concluded by Alfred. **1642** MILTON *Apol. Smect.* (1851) 258 To prejudice and *forecondemne his adversary in the title for slanderous and scurrilous. **1677** OTWAY *Cheats of Scapin* II. i. Wks. 1728 I. 208 These things premis'd, and *fore-consider'd. **1652** BP. HALL *Invis. World* I. §6 Abraham saw an angel *fore-contriving the work. **1642** FULLER *Holy & Prof. St.* III. ix. 173 They *forecount their wives fair, fruitfull, and rich. **1859** LD. LYTTON *Wanderer* (ed. 2) 97 But why should I forecount as yet The ravage of that vulture brood? **1858** H. BONAR *Hymns Faith & Hope* 10 Faith *foredates the joyful day. **1625** K. LONG tr. *Barclay's Argenis* III. iii. 155 His death..had bin *fore-declared. **1696** WILLARD *Body of Divinity* (1726) 359/2 The same which was foredeclared by the angel. **1618** DANIEL *Hist. Eng.* 162 God had *foredecreed to make it his owne worke by a cleaner way. **1645** WITHER *Vox Pacif.* 141 Of that, which God himselfe, did *fore-designe. **1715** CHEYNE *Philos. Princ. Relig.* (J.), All the steps of the growth and vegetation..have been..foredesigned by the wise Author of nature. *a* **1661** FULLER (Webster), King James had by promise *foredisposed the place on the Bishop of Meath. **1607** WALKINGTON *Opt. Glass* 142 Which doe *fore-divine, and are, as it were, prophets. **1649** BP. HALL *Cases Consc.* II. vii. (1654) 132 Your former vow or oath hath *fore-ingaged you to a just discovery. **1662** J. CHANDLER *Van Helmont's Oriat.* 33 If the disposed matter do *fore-exist. **1864** PUSEY *Lect. Daniel* vi. 298 They, then, fore-existing; this, derived from them. **1633** BP. HALL *Hard Texts, N.T.* 47 So as no man can *fore-expect the day. **1628** WITHER *Brit. Rememb.* 276 The fourth true token which doth *fore-expresse The ruine of a land for wickednesse. **1586** WHETSTONE *Engl. Mirror* 121 Little *forefeared he that God would make him the capitall offender of the Romish superstition. **1534** MORE *Treat. Passion* Wks. 1323/2 The old sacrifices..*fore fygured the ..sacrifice of Christes blessed bodye. **1622** S. WARD *Life Faith in Death* (1627) 57 Such as..fore-know their death, yet..*fore-fit themselues neuer the more carefully. **1571** GOLDING *Calvin on Ps.* xxi. 9 The time which the heavenly father hath *fore fixed. **1878** B. TAYLOR *Deukalion* I. iii. 28 They who made us and forefixed our fate, The Titans. **1880** G. MACDONALD *Diary of an Old Soul* 5 May, A greater thing Than purest imagination can *foregrasp. **1820** MILMAN *Fall Jerusalem* 154 Am I in heaven, and thou *forehasted thither To welcome me? **1617** BP. HALL *Quo Vadis?* §24 Let them carefully *fore-instruct..themselues with the sound knowledge of the principles of religion. **1855** SINGLETON *Virg. Georg.* I. 344 Hence can we *forelearn The weather in th' uncertain sky. **1596** SPENSER *F.Q.* IV. iii. 6 Carelesse of perill..As if that life to losse they had *forelent. **1608** B. JONSON *Masque Beauty* Wks. (Rtldg.) 548/2 As being the place, by Destiny *forement. *a* **1743** SAVAGE *Wks.* (1775) II. 221 (Jod.) Has he foremeant some distant age to bless? **1870** LOWELL *Among Bks.* Ser. I. (1873) 224 Without foremeaning it, he had [etc.]. **1873** *Ibid.* Ser. II. 87 Providence therefore *foreordered two ends to be pursued by man. **1627** S. WARD *Christ All in All* 11 As if the Scriptures..had not *forepainted out such an Antichrist. **1634** JACKSON *Creed* VII. *Christ's Answ.* §54 By the fall of Lebanon..he *forepictures the extirpation of David's royal race. **1796** JANE AUSTEN *Sense & Sens.* iii. 46 What had been already..*foreplanned in her own mind. **1584** *Discov. Throckmorton's Treas.* 2 Such as are not forestalled, or rather *forepoysoned..with the lies alreadie spred. **1565** T. STAPLETON *Fort. Faith* 65 The calling of the gentils *fore-promised. *a* **1656** BP. HALL *Specialties in his life* (1660) 27 It was fore-promised to one of my fellow Chaplains. **1856** MRS. BROWNING *Aur. Leigh* IV. 469, I, who should have known, *Forereckoned mischief! **1590** GREENE *Neuer too late* (1600) 62 He that *forerepents, forsees many perils. **1642** FULLER *Holy & Prof. St.* III. xxiii. 218 But Fame falls most short..chiefly in *fore-reporting the Happinesse in heaven. **1655** —— *Ch. Hist.* II. iii. §38 Offa had *fore-requested the granting of these Priviledges from the Pope. **1641** MILTON *Ch. Govt.* v. (1851) 113 He..argues that Christ..was as well *fore-resembled by the Kings then, as by the high Priest. **1652** GAULE *Magastrom.* xxvi, Metoposcopy, boasts herself to *foresent all the beginnings, the progresses, and the ends of men. **1598** E. GILPIN *Skial.* (1878) 45 Hauing so well *fore-season'd thy minds caske. **1682** TATE *Abs. & Achit.* II. 976 Proceed, illustrious, happy chief..*Foreseize the garlands for thy brow decreed. **1818** MILMAN *Samor* 87 To foreseize from Fate Thy slow existence. *c* **1000** ÆLFRIC *Gram.* xxviii. (Z.) 172 *Praemitto*, ic *foresende. *c* **1586** C'TESS PEMBROKE *Ps.* CV. v, He for them to Ægipt had foresent The slave-sold Joseph. **1842** SIR H. TAYLOR *Edwin* III. iii, We shall so *foreshape the minds of men That..It shall be hailed acceptable. *a* **1691** BOYLE *Hist. Air* (1692) 174 They begin to travel again in a white sand, being *fore-shod with shoes, whose single soles are made [etc.]. **1563** *Mirr. Mag., Hastings* liv, Swannelyke I *foresong my death. **1634** HABINGTON *Castara* (Arb.) 35 He was a Prophet, and fore-sang my love. *a* **1651** CALDERWOOD *Hist. Kirk.* (1843) II. 343 Manie of his servants *forsmelling danger, left him. **1648** HERRICK *Hesper.* 146 Which *fore-sounds A plentious harvest to your grounds. **1565** GOLDING *Ovid's Met.* VII. (1593) 155 The ground then soking makes The seed *foresteept in poison strong. **1553** GRIMALDE *Cicero's Offices* II. 81 Lucius Crassus did showe himself in open courte to do that verie-well having *forestudied. **1647** FULLER *Good Th. in Worse T.* (1841) 134 The party praying ..fore-studieth not every expression. **1839** BAILEY *Festus* xxviii. (1848) 335 But I foresee, *fore-suffer. **1923** T. S. ELIOT *Waste Land* iii. 17 And I Tiresias have foresuffered all. **1597** DANIEL *Civ. Wars* VII. lxii, The Parlement.. Which his Associates had *fore-summoned. *a* **1612** DONNE *Βιαθανατος* (1644) 68 *Fore-suspecting that hee should not easily remove that desire of dying. **1598** J. DICKENSON

Greene in Conc. (1878) 103 Which these so many, and so manyfest likelihoodes did *forethreaten. **1656** Trapp *Comm. Matt.* iii. 10 Edom is forethreatened for not harbouring them when scattered by the Chaldeans. **1833** Wordsw. *Warning* 133 Paths no human wisdom can *foretrace! *a* **1612** Donne *Βιαθανατος* (1648) 216 Except where a competent diligence being *fore-used, a mistaking in our conscience may provide an excuse. **1583** Stanyhurst *Æneis* iii. (Arb.) 88 Theese stoans king Helenus, theese ragd rocks rustye *forevttred. **1839** Bailey *Festus* xxxii. (1848) 352 The prophecies Of God fore-uttered through the tongues of Time. **1615** Daniel *Hymen's Tri.* Poems (1717) 124 A Heart *forevow'd unto a better Choice. **1587** T. Hughes *Misfort. Arthur* iii. i. (1828) 46 *Foreweening nought what perils might insue. **1763** Churchill *Poems, Duellist* i, The sky in sullen drops of rain *Forewept the morn. **1819** Crabbe *T. of Hall, Patron* 75 When each indulgence was *foreweigh'd with care.

b. in ppl. adjs., as ***fore-bemoaned, -biased, -boasted, -commended, -created, -dated, -defined, -denounced, -described, -deserved, -devised, -devote, -done, -fated, -formed, -hinting, -impressed, -inclined, -intimated, -led, -made, -misgiving, -noted, -obtained, -opinioned, -penned, -pretended, -provided, -recited, -rehearsed, -remembered, -settled, -specified, -typified, -vouched, -wished, -wonted.*** Also **fore-littering**, littering prematurely; **fore-riped**, ripened too early; premature. **fore-wrought**, ? tampered with beforehand.

c **1600** Shaks. *Sonn.* xxx, The sad account of *fore-bemoned mone. **1720** Welton *Suffer. Son of God* II. xxix. 751 The Malicious Prejudices..of His accusers and *fore-byass'd Judges. **1602** Warner *Alb. Eng.* ix. xlix. 228 Gods sole Prouidence Did cleare *fore-bosted Conquest..hence. **1642** Cudworth *Lord's Supper* vi. (1676) 34 Which I will confirm from that *forecommended place. **1587** Golding *De Mornay* ix. 118 Whether the Worlde was created after the pattern of a thing *forecreated, or of a thing without a beginning. **1641** Milton *Ch. Govt.* ii. (1851) 148 An abortive and *foredated discovery. **1640** Bp. Hall *Episc.* ii. iv. 103 The proper and *fore-defined sence. **1604** Hieron *Wks.* I. To Rdr. 553 Romes long-deserued and *fore-denounced ouerthrow. **1581** Sidney *Apol. Poetrie* (Arb.) 28 The *foredescribed name of Poets. **1580** —— *Arcadia* iv. (1598) 416 Their *fore-deserued punishment. **1579** Fenton *Guicciard.* (1618) 38 It was a deliberation voluntary and *foredeuised. **1889** *Sat. Rev.* 7 Sept. 262/1 There is a sort of tourists *foredevote to mischance. **1862** F. Hall *Hindu Philos. Syst.* 125 The fruit of *foredone sacrifices. **1839** Bailey *Festus* (1848) 38 The statesman makes new laws for growing worlds, Through their *fore-fated ages. **1767** H. Brooke *Fool of Qual.* II. viii. 31 No *foreformed evasions or contrivances for escape. **1868** Bushnell *Serm. Living Subj.* 420 A strange, enigmatic, yet apparently *forehinting utterance. **1642** H. More *Song of Soul* ii. iii. ii. lx, Swayd By sense, and *fore-imprest Astronomie. **1640** Bp. Hall *Episc.* iii. ii. 227 A *fore-inclined minde. **1631** Gouge *God's Arrows* Ded. 5 The *fore-intimated arrowes. **1662** J. Chandler *Van Helmont's Oriat.* 101 Their *fore-led life. **1583** Stanyhurst *Æneis* Ded. (Arb.) 8 Like as *forelittring bitches whelp blynde puppies. **1642** Fuller *Holy & Prof. St.* iii. xxiii. 217 If such *foremade reports prove true. **1565** Golding *Ovid's Met.* x. (1593) 248 Her *foremisgiving mind did also make her sad. **1583** Stanhurst *Æneis* iv. (Arb.) 118 Thee *forenoted offrings. **1568** T. Howell *Arb. Amitie* (1879) 43 Perpend the grace, the trust and trade, of *foreobteyned wyfe. **1627–77** Feltham *Resolves* i. xxviii. 48 Men are *fore-opinion'd of him for a politic man. **1549** Chaloner tr. *Erasm. Moriæ Enc.* A j, Their longe and *fore-penned oracions. **1709** Strype *Ann. Ref.* I. liv. 587 All.. were but *fore-pretended falsehoods. **1850** Lynch *Theo. Trin.* i. 15 *Fore-provided signals. **1613** Shaks. *Hen. VIII*, i. ii. 127 The *fore-recited practises. **1661** J. Stephens *Procurations* 142 According to the fore-recited Act. **1526** Tindale *N.T.* Prol., This *forerehearced newe testament. **1577–87** Holinshed *Chron.* III. 1230/2 The *fore-remembred Coniers vicar of saint Martins in Norwich. **1631** Weever *Anc. Fun. Mon.* 170 My fore remembred Author. **1534** Ld. Berners *Gold. Bk. M. Aurel.* (1546) O viij, The *fore ryped prymetyme prouoked them therto. **1587** Golding *De Mornay* Pref. 10 For..*fore-setled opinions doo bring in bondage. **1647** Sprigge *Anglia Rediv.* i. ii. 12 The *fore-specified commands. **1693** Chauncy *Enq. Gosp. New Law* 34 The great Sacrifice so long *fore-typified. **1605** Shaks. *Lear* i. i. 223 Your *fore-voucht affection [must] Fall into taint. **1592** Wyrley *Armorie, Chandos* 98 Had I taken the oportunitie..The towne had I surprised speedilie And well atchiued *fore-wished pretence. **1647** H. More *Song of Soul* App. iii. xviii, Even so the ghosts..Walk in their *forewonted coast. **1611** Speed *Hist. Gt. Brit.* ix. viii. §16. 489 To reduce those partes to his Allegiance..was no hard matter to effect; the greater part of Commaunders there (being *fore-wrought) expecting nothing more..then these perfidious assaults.

c. in vbl. sbs., as ***fore-aboding, -accounting, -being, -building, -catching, -damning, -enjoying, -fearing, -glooming, -living, -misgiving, -placing, -planting, -poling, -schooling, -shaping, -understanding, -whipping, -whispering.***

a **1711** Ken *Edmund* Poet. Wks. 1721 II. 199 Yet from some *Fore-abodings I divine, I David like, the Temple may design. **1580** Sidney *Arcadia* i. 85 But *fore-accounting oft makes builders misse. **1561** Daus tr. *Bullinger on Apoc.* (1573) 10 For this is it, that he meaneth by ioyning the *forebeyng to the present beyng. **1662** Glanvill *Lux Orient.* xii. (1682) 92 In the state of our Fore-Beings. **1581** Mulcaster *Positions* v. (1887) 26 That, which must follow their *forebuilding. **1625** Gill *Sacr. Philos.* i. 86 Some *fore-catchings of the shadowes of things to come. **1615** Byfield *Expos. Coloss.* iii. 6 That can but seriously consider..God's reprobating or *fore-damning of millions of men. **1640** Bp. Reynolds *Passions* (1658) 985 Under pretence of devoting themselves to contemplation and a *fore-enjoying of the light of God. **1674** N. Fairfax *Bulk & Selv.* 65 The *forefearing that if emptiness far and wide were not granted, the world would not be bounded. **1880** W. Watson *Prince's Quest. Vanishings* (1892) 147 Vague *foreglooomings of the Dark to be. **1430** Lydg. *Chron. Troy* v. xxxvi, The Kynge was to her in all his *fore liuinge Louyng and true in all maner thinge. **1565** Golding *Ovid's Met.* vi. (1593) 143 The *foremisgiving of his mind did make them sore afraid. **1611** Cotgr., *Premise*, a *fore-placing, a setting before. *Ibid.*, *Preplantement*, a *fore-planting or former setting. **1881** R. W. Raymond *Gloss. Mining Terms, Fore-poling*, a method of securing drifts in progress through quicksand by driving ahead poles, lath, boards, slabs, etc., to prevent the inflow of the quicksand on the sides and top, the face being protected by breastboards. **1967** *Gloss. Mining Terms (B.S.I.)* xi. 8 *Forepoling*, the use of girders or bars projecting forward in cantilever as temporary supports beneath newly exposed roof. **1886** Lowell *Pr. Wks.* (1890) VI. 163 Is it so good a *fore-schooling for Life? **1892** *Athenæum* 16 Apr. 496/2 Some clear *foreshapings of that new order. **1550** Bale *Sel. Wks.* (1849) 498 And I (saith St. John) perceived it evidently in my *fore-understanding, that this woman..was all drunken in the bloody slaughter of saints. **1613** T. Godwin *Rom. Antiq.* (1625) 194 This *forewhipping I take to be a matter vnquestionable. **1880** W. Watson *Prince's Quest.* (1892) 20 Perchance To hear *forewhisperings of their destiny.

d. in nouns of action, as ***fore-advice, -choice, -consent, -designment, -determination, -guidance, -payment, -proffer, -provision, -revelation, -spousals, -sufferance, -trial.***

1598 Florio, *Premonitione*, a premonition..a *foreaduise. **1614** Raleigh *Hist. World* ii. (1634) 260 God's ..promise. and *fore-choice of his people. **1615** Chapman *Odyss.* xiii. 194 The *fore-consent Thou hadst vouchsafed it. *a* **1641** Bp. Mountagu *Acts & Mon.* (1642) 21 A *fore-designement of better things to come. **1565** Jewel *Def. Apol.* (1611) 38 His owne blinde preiudices, and *fore-determinations. **1610** Guillim *Heraldry* iv. xv. (1611) 230 Without the *fore-guidance of a valiant leader. **1807** Southey *Lett.* (1856) II. 9, I had 100*l.* of him in *forepayment for the first edition. **1548** Udall, etc. *Erasm. Par. Luke* i. 77 A *foreprofer to the abolishing of synne. **1611** Cotgr., *Preparation*, a preparation or *fore-prouision. *a* **1680** Charnock *Attrib. God* (1834) I. 552 The event did answer his *fore-revelation. *a* **1639** Webster *App. & Virg.* iv. ii, Divorc'd from her *fore-spousals with Icilius. **1629** Jackson *Creed* vi. ii. xxxii. §7 His experience on *foresufferance of the like evils. **1868** Hanna *Ministry in Galilee* iii. 50 A short *fore-trial might be made of the work.

II. Prefixed to sbs. (Stress chiefly on the prefix, exc. where this is liable to be apprehended as an adj.; in many words the stress is variable).

3. With reference to place. **a.** With sense, 'that is in the front', or 'in front of something', 'directed to the front'; = front- (by which it is now often replaced), as ***fore-axle, -chamber, -corner, -courtyard, -covert, -desk, -face, -flap, -gallery, -glass, -hall, -hill, -log, -nook, -parlour, -pillow, -place, -plate, -porch, -post, -quarter, -rank, -rib, -shop, -skirt, -tail, -way, -wedge, -wheel.***

1822 Imison *Sc. & Art* I. 103 The *fore-axle must sustain as much more friction. **1622** H. Sydenham *Serm. Sol. Occ.* (1637) 106 Gluttony is the *fore-chamber of lust. **1852** Grote *Greece* ii. lxxxii. X. 665 The fore-chambers and back-chambers of the various temples. **1805** Mrs. Wakefield *Dom. Recreat.* x. 137 The *fore-corner of the same eye-lid. **1623** *Crt. & Times Jas. I.* (1849) II. 430 The *forecourt-yard of the French ambassador's house. **1609** Holland *Amm. Marcell.* xxiv. vi. 249 Of undermining and the fabrickes *fore-covert and defence, Nevita and Dagalaiphus had the charge. *c* **1515** in Willis & Clark *Cambridge* (1886) I. 483 Lvj Stalles in the lower degrees with the *foredeskes for the same. **1545** Raynold *Byrth Mankynde* i. ix. (1634) 32 From the right side..and *foreface of the great arterie. **1607** Beaum. & Fl. *Woman-hater* v. i, My *foreflap hangs in the right place. **1775** S. J. Pratt *Liberal Opin.* (1783) IV. 3 The fore-flap of his coat. **1715** Leoni *Palladio's Archit.* (1742) II. 19, I have made the *Fore-galleries..as I fancy they ought to have been. **1741** Richardson *Pamela* (1824) I. 125, I was afraid of Robin's looking back, through the *fore-glass [of the coach]. **1882–3** Schaff *Encycl. Relig. Knowl.* I. 210 To the one side a *fore-hall, the schoolroom. **1776** *Phil. Trans.* LXVI. 527 Its *forehills are almost every where composed of rocks and strata, rising very steep to the horizon. **1883** Mrs. Rollins *New Eng. Bygones* 68 They [the backlogs] were buried in embers and then supplemented with *forelogs. **1641** Best *Farm. Bks.* (Surtees) 36 They beginne with the farr *fore-nooke, and after that with the neare fore-nooke, then with the farr hinder nooke. **1747** *Scheme Equip. Men of War* 59 Their *Fore-Parlours, or Dining Rooms. **1617** Markham *Caval.* vi. 51 The *fore-pillowes must stand so directly that they may defend the Ryders knees from the neather point of the bare tree. **1878** Morley *Carlyle* 194 Laughter has a *fore-place in life. **1715** Desaguliers *Fires Impr.* 108 The first Piece or *fore-Plate. **1535** *Goodly Primer* Ps. c. 3 Into his *foreporches with praise. **1870** *Daily News* 24 Sept., A Jager regiment formed the infantry *foreposts in a line of villages. *c* **1430** *Two Cookery-bks.* i. 6 Take fayre beef of þe rybbys of þe *fore quarterys. **1883** *Harper's Mag.* Feb. 367/2 A fore-quarter of lamb. **1599** Shaks. *Hen. V*, v. ii. 97 Compris'd Within the *fore-ranke of our Articles. **1863** J. G. Murphy *Comm. Gen.* xlix. 10 Judah had the forerank among the tribes in the wilderness. **1861** Mrs. Beeton *Bk. Househ. Managem.* xii. 276 *Fore quarter.* Five ribs, called the *fore-rib.—This is considered the primest roasting piece [of beef]. **1895** *Daily News* 9 Jan. 6/2, 17 foreribs of beef. **1633** Ford *Love's Sacr.* iii. i, Shut up your *fore-shop, I'll be your journeyman no longer. **1613** Shaks. *Hen. VIII*, ii. iii. 98 Honours traine Is longer than his *fore-skirt. **1665** J. Wilson *Projectors* ii. i. Dram. Wks. (1874) 218 One doublet with a new pair of foreskirts. **1732** E. Forrest *Hogarth's Tour* 8 The *fore-tail of his shirt. **1631** *Househ. Ord.* 349 The *foreway for the chappell. **1523** Fitzherb. *Husb.* §4 *Forewedge and helewedge. **1728** Vanbr. & Cib. *Prov. Husb.* i. Wks. (1730) 222 The two *fore-wheels came crash down at once. **1822** Imison *Sc. & Art* I. 103 In all four-wheeled carriages, the fore-wheels are made of a less size than the hind ones.

b. Indicating the front part of something; as ***fore-brain, -palate, -shaft, -shoulder.***

1879 tr. *Haeckel's Evol. Man* II. xx. 225 The highest activities of the animal body..have their seat in the *fore-brain. **1872** Beames *Comp. Gram. Aryan Lang. India* I. ix. 326 A larger portion of the tongue's surface being brought into contact with the *fore-palate. **1883** Im Thurn *Indians Guiana* xi. 245 The *foreshaft [of arrow] and the blunt head. **1857** Holland *Bay Path* xvii. 196 Then he'll let me have it just back o' the *fore-shoulder.

c. Indicating one of the front limbs of an animal; as ***fore-claw, -fin, -flipper, -hoof, -knee, -limb, -pad, -paw,*** † ***-talon.*** (Stress often on the sb.)

1769 *Phil. Trans.* LX. 37 On its *fore-claws are five strong long nails. **1779–80** Cook *Voy.* (1785) II. 457 The dam.. holds the young one between her *fore-fins. **1853** Kane *Grinnell Exp.* xlv. (1856) 417 Behind the *fore-flippers. **1770** G. White *Selborne* xxviii. 79 The *fore-hoofs were upright and shapely. **1607** Topsell *Four-f. Beasts* 121 And then stayeth his body vpon the *fore-knees. **1794–6** E. Darwin *Zoon.* (1802) I. 199 Quadrupeds that have collar-bones use their *fore-limbs in some measure as we use our hands. **1879** Jefferies *Wild Life in S.C.* 8 These animals, [rabbits], strike with the *fore-pads as if boxing. **1825** J. Neal *Bro. Jonathan* I. 110 Throwing one of the bear's great *fore-paws at him. *a* **1682** Sir T. Browne *Tracts* 113 They opened the vein of the *fore talon.

d. *Naut.* Chiefly in words denoting some 'part of a ship's frame and machinery which lies near the stem, or in that direction, in opposition to *aft* or *after*' (Adm. Smyth); also of parts connected with the foremast (opposed to *main-*, *mizen-*); as ***fore-bitts, -bonnet, -bowline, -brace, -bridge, -cap, -cat-harpings, -chains, -cluegarnet, -course, -downhaul, -hatch, -hatchway, -hood, -keel, -lee, -rake, -rigging, -royal, -scuttle, -shrouds, -spoke, -spritsail, -tackle, -truck, -trysail.***

1833 Marryat *P. Simple* (1863) 411 Their first shot went right through the hull of the brig, just abaft the *fore-bits. **1669** Sturmy *Mariner's Mag.* i. 17 Unbind all things clear of it, and bring too the *Fore-bonnet. *Ibid.* 18 Hawl bout *fore Bowline. *Ibid.* 17 Hawl aft the Sheets, get aft on the Quarter Deck, the *fore Braces. **1833** Marryat *P. Simple* (1863) 213 The jaws of the fore-brace block. **1893** Adm. Markham in *Daily News* 3 July 5/7 The Admiral came forward to the *fore-bridge. **1748** *Anson's Voy.* iii. i. 297 The Gloucester's *forecap split. **1867** Smyth *Sailor's Word-bk.*, **Fore Cat-harpings*. **1720** *Fore-chains [see chain 14 b]. **1820** Scoresby *Acc. Arctic Reg.* II. 193 From the stem to the fore-chains. **1825** H. B. Gascoigne *Nav. Fame* 51 The *Forecluegarnets are Let-run of all. **1626** Capt. Smith *Accid. Yng. Seamen* 96 The fore sayle called sometimes the *fore course. **1707** *Lond. Gaz.* No. 4380/3 The Firebrand..forc'd in under a Fore-course for the Light of St. Agnes. **1669** Sturmy *Mariner's Mag.* i. 17 Belay the *fore doon hall. **1840** R. H. Dana *Bef. Mast* xxxi. 112 A large sheep-pen which had been built upon the *forehatch. **1790** Beatson *Nav. & Mil. Mem.* II. 162 The *fore-hatch-way. **1819** J. H. Vaux *Mem.* I. 226 Certain parts of the stem, called the *fore-hoods, were loose. **1653** H. Cogan tr. *Pinto's Trav.* lxvi. 267 The *Fore-keel of our Poup. *a* **1802** *Young Man* v. in Child *Ballads* viii. ccxlv. (1892) 377/1 She'll..gae out your *fore-lee. **1627** Capt. Smith *Seaman's Gram.* ii. 4 The *fore Rake is that which giues the ship good way. **1805** in Nicolas *Disp. Nelson* (1846) VII. 167 *note*, Employed knotting and splicing our *fore-rigging. **1882** *Daily Tel.* 12 Sept. 2/1 He was ordered on to the *foreroyal yard along with another youngster. **1800** Colquhoun *Comm. Thames* ii. 55 He placed the two trunks close to the *fore-scuttle. **1699** Dampier *Voy.* II. iii. 64 Let us go a little way up the *Fore-shrouds. **1833** Marryat *P. Simple* (1863) 107 The captain and first lieutenant went aft, and took the *fore-spokes of the wheel. *a* **1661** Holyday *Juvenal* 229 A *fore-sprit-saile. **1823** Crabb *Technol. Dict.* s.v. *Fore*, **Fore-tackle*, a tackle on the fore-mast. **1669** Sturmy *Mariner's Mag.* v. 64 They nail down Quoyners to the *Fore-Trucks of heavy Guns. **1895** *Century Mag.* Aug. 594/2 The admiral's flag at the fore-truck. **1857** C. Gribble in *Merc. Mar. Mag.* (1858) V. 3 *Fore-try-sail.

4. With reference to time. **a.** Giving the additional sense of precedence or anticipation; as ***fore-age, -ancestor, -assurance, -care, -consciousness, -counsel, -day, -gleam, -glimpse, -handsel, -hope, -impression, -king, -light, -luck, -martyr, -messenger, -notice, -notion, -order, -parent, -precedent, -resolution, -restraint, -scene, -scent, -sense, -sentence, -shift, -sign, -sin, -splendour, -tenant, -thrift, -year.***

1581 J. Bell *Haddon's Answ. Osor.* 453 b, Where be these Records..of auncient Antiquitye, and of all *foreages? **1563–87** Foxe *A. & M.* (1596) 120 Our *fore-ancestors. **1631** Donne *Biathanatos* (1644) 74 A *fore-assurance that else they would escape death by death. **1615** P. Smalle *Mans May* B iij a, Prudence, *Fore-care, and Diligence.. are the flow'rs of May. **1843** Lowell *Glance behind Curtain* Poet. Wks. (1879) 49 A *fore-consciousness of their high doom. **1839** Bailey *Festus* (1848) 32/1 *Forecounsel, wisdom, and experience. *a* **1300** *Cursor M.* 19049 (Cott.) A man was criplid in þe parlesi, And had ben mast all his *fordais. **1857–8** Sears *Athan.* xi. 98 We get even now intimations and *fore-gleams of what it is. **1894** *Advance* (Chicago) 5 Apr., A *fore-glimpse of the Day of Judgment. **1574** tr. *Marlorat's Apocalips* 9 A *forehansell of the newe lyfe. **1603** Sir C. Heydon *Jud. Astrol.* x. 233 If therefore through this *fore-hope..the excesse of immoderate ioy be abated. **1597** Daniel *Civ. Wars* vi. xxii, A *fore-impression of the right he has. **1876** Tennyson *Harold* iv. iii, Thy fierce *fore-kings had clench'd their pirate hides To the bleak church doors. **1853** J. Cumming *Lect. Miracles* (1854) 126

One of the *forelights of the restoration of all things. **1659** TORRIANO, *Buona-mano*..good hanzell or good *fore-luck. **1577** HANMER *Anc. Eccl. Hist.* (1636) 75 The other *foremartyrs..hasten themselves unto Martyrdome. **1548** UDALL, etc. *Erasm. Par. Luke* i. 17 The *foremessagier of the former cumming. **1574** NEWTON *Health Mag.* Tjb, A fore-messanger or waymaker to Feuers, Apostumations and Abscesses. **1678** T. RYMER *Trag. Last Age* 38 Some *fore-notice of it. **1604** DANIEL *Vision 12 Goddesses* Wks. (1717) 239 To the end thou may'st have *Fore-Notion what Powers ..take here this Prospective. **1594** CAREW *Tasso* (1881) 29 And for all wants *foreorder layd. **1526** *Pilgr. Perf.* (W. de W. 1531) 41 Our *fore parentes Adam and Eue. **1577–87** HOLINSHED *Chron.* III. 1114/1 The said alleaged *fore-presidents against me. **1629** T. ADAMS *Soules Refuge*, Wks. 910 Men that want this *fore-resolution. **1594** CAREW *Tasso* (1881) 106 How he scornde his rule and *fore-restraint. **1857–8** SEARS *Athan.* 12 If the light of the after-scene were turned full on the *fore-scene. **1834** I. TAYLOR *Sat. Even.* 231 Not free from an appalling *forescent of his own near discomfiture. **1621** CADE *Serm.* 3 With too little..*fore-sence of vengeance, or pricke of conscience. **1840** CLOUGH *Amours de Voy.* III. 123 The steady fore-sense of a freer and larger existence. **1598** SYLVESTER *Du Bartas* II. ii. Ark 599 This..old-man..toucht with true repentance, W^th Prophet-mouth 'gan thus his Son's *fore-sentence. **1891** *Labour Commission* Gloss. s.v. *Shift*, One set or shift go underground early in the morning..these are called '*foreshift men'. The second set go underground about 9 a.m., and are called 'backshift men'. **1548** UDALL, etc. *Erasm. Par. Mark* i. 13 Undoubtedlye he maketh a *foresigne. **1659** MACALLO *Can. Physick* 43 Foresigns of life or death. **1530** TINDALE *Answ. More* II. iii. (1573) 293/2 To make satisfaction for his *fore-sinnes. **1831** CARLYLE *Sart. Res.* (1858) 115 Fore-shadows, call them rather *fore-splendours, of that Truth. **1814** SOUTHEY *Roderick* II, The *fore-tenant of that holy place. **1869** R. LYTTON *Orval* 217 The force of *fore-thrift in the fear of want. **1615** CHAPMAN *Odyss.* VIII. 603 The sauing trade, The Reuerend for her wisedome (Circe) had In *foreyeares taught him.

b. Indicating the early part of; as ***fore-night, -summer, -year; foreday*** = morning. Chiefly *Sc.*

1818 HOGG *Brownie Bodsbeck* I. 13 He saw them as weel as it had been *fore-day. **1808–79** JAMIESON, **Forenicht*, the interval between twilight and bed-time. **1887** *American* XIV. 234 The terrible winter and *foresummer of 1854–55. **1545** BRUNSTON in Tytler *Hist. Scot.* (1864) III. 372 The said cardinal [Beaton] entendis..to bring us gret support in the *foir yere.

5. Special combinations. **a.** With reference to place: **fore-action**, the movement of a horse's front legs; † **fore-alley**, (in a meeting-house) the alley or passage in front of the desk; † **fore-beak**, the prow of a vessel; **fore-bitter**, a sea song (see quots.); † **fore-board**, the deck or fore-deck; **fore-boot**: see BOOT *sb.*[1] 4 c; † **fore-bowels**, the part of a horse's belly in front of the girths; † **fore-bush** (of hair) = FORELOCK; † **fore-buttock** (jocular), the breast (of a woman); **fore-caddie** *Golf*, a caddie who goes in advance of the players to watch where the balls fall; **fore-car**, an obsolete form of motor-cycle having the passenger's seat in front; † **fore-cloth**, the covering of a horse's shoulders; † **fore-cock** (of a hat), see quot. and COCK *sb.*[6] 3; † **fore-crag** (see quot.); † **fore-crop** (see quot.); **foredeep** *Geol.*, a trench or elongated depression along the edge of an orogenic belt, often beneath the sea; **fore-dune**, the part of a dune system nearest to the sea; † **fore-entry** (*a*) = FORE-COURT, (*b*) the porch or gate-house; † **fore-fellows**, fellow-soldiers in the preceding rank; † **fore-flank**, (*a*) the front part of the flank, (*b*) (see quot. 1796); † **fore-gallant**, the chief performer (in a morrice-dance); † **fore-gear**, (*a*) armour for the front of the body, (*b*) harness for the front horses of a team; **fore-hanging, fore-hearth** (see quots.); **fore-heater**, *Salt-making* (see quot.); † **fore-hip**, a trick in wrestling; **fore-hock**, the hock of the fore-leg of pork or bacon; **fore-hooks**, *Naut.* = *breast-hooks*; **fore-kidney** = PRONEPHRON; † **fore-knight** *Naut.* (see quot.); **fore-lighter**, the first in a 'gang' of lighters; † **fore-lines**, lines drawn directly forward; **fore-march**, a march forward, in quot. *fig*; **fore-mark**, ? a conspicuous model for imitation; **fore-milk**, (*a*) the colostrum (Dorland, 1901); (*b*) the first milk drawn from a cow at each milking; **fore-page**, the first page (in a printed work); **fore-piece** (see quot.); **fore-pipe**, a brass pipe near the muzzle of a musket, etc., to receive the ramrod; **fore-pitch**, ? projection; also *fig.* (G. M. Hopkins); **foreplay**, stimulation or love-play preceding sexual intercourse; **fore-pleasure** [tr. G. *vorlust* (S. Freud *Drei Abhandlungen zur Sexualtheorie* (1905) iii. 56)], pleasure induced by sexual stimulation; † **fore-smock**, ? an article of dress worn in front of the smock, an apron; † **fore-spar** *Sc.*, a swingle-tree for attaching the front horses of a team; **fore-starling** (see quot.); **fore-step**, (*a*) a step forward, (*b*) *pl.* steps in front, tracks; **fore-stone**, a mass of rock that interrupts a vein of ore; also, the front cross-piece of a blast furnace; **fore-thwart, fore-train** (see quots.); † **fore-tow** *Sc.*, a rope for attaching the front horses of a team; **fore-winning** (see quot.).

1816 KEATINGE *Trav.* (1817) I. 159 The Spanish horse carries his head high, and his *fore-action is regulated hereby. **1716** S. SEWALL *Diary* 9 Sept., They stood in the *Fore-Ally and were admitted, Confessing their Sin of Fornication. *a* **1656** USSHER *Ann.* VI. (1658) 551 After they had ran violently upon one another with their *forebeaks. **1906** C. BRIDGE in C. Stone *Sea Songs* p. iv, In the Royal Navy the term sea song was unknown. What landsmen would have so designated, blue-jackets called '*Fore-bitters'. **1962** A. G. COURSE *Dict. Naut. Terms* 79 *Fore bitters*, sea songs sung round the fore bitts... Sea shanties were never sung on these occasions. **1591** HARINGTON *Orl. Fur.* XIII. xv, In vaine it was to pull down all our sailes, And on the *foreboord close to couch the mast. **1580** BLUNDEVIL *Horses Diseases* cxi. 51 b, All the shoulder [of the horse] from the maine downward, and betwixt the *forebowels. **1674** N. COX *Gentl. Recreat.* v. (1688) 65 You shall observe your Horse's Sweat, under his Saddle, and Forebowels, if it appear White. **1591** PERCIVALL *Sp. Dict.*, *Copete*, the *forebush of the haire. **1727** SWIFT, etc. *Sylv.*, *Misc.* IV. 137 Her *Fore Buttocks to the navel bare. **1792** *Scots Mag.* LIV. 223/2 Dickson was then performing the duty of what is now commonly called a *fore-cadie. **1926** *Glasgow Herald* 27 Dec. 6 An intelligent forecaddy..can materially enhance his prospects. **1904** *Motor Cycle* 11 Apr. 348/1 One of the most highly developed *forecars we have yet seen. **1908** *Westm. Gaz.* 21 May 4/3 My machine was a three-wheeler, known in those days as a forecar. **1963** BIRD & HUTTON-STOTT *Veteran Motor Car* 90 Tricar, fore-car and light car proper. **1526** *Househ. Ord.* (1790) 205 The King's sadles, bridles, bytts, *forecloathes, and other necessaries. **1627** *Crt. & Times Chas. I* (1848) I. 256 He..lay in the field all night with two horses' forecloths under and two cloaks over him. **1668** ETHEREDGE *She wou'd if she cou'd* III. iii, Never hat took the *fore-cock and the hind-cock at one motion so naturally. **1591** *News fr. Scotl.* in Brand *Pop. Antiq.* (1849) III. 8 Found the enemy's mark to be in her [the witch's] *forecrag, or fore part of her throat. **1523** FITZHERB. *Husb.* §57 Se that they [fatte-oxen] be soft on the *fore-croppe, behynde the shulder. **1909** H. B. C. SOLLAS tr. *Suess's Face of Earth* IV. v. ix. 295 These depressions mark the subsidence of the foreland beneath the recent folds. They have received the name of 'fore-troughs'. But..their two sides are of different structure, and it therefore seems advisable to call them '*fore-deeps'. **1968** R. W. FAIRBRIDGE *Encycl. Geomorphol.* 35 'Pacific' tectonics are those associated with contemporary orthogeosynclines, island arcs, oceanic trenches and active foredeeps. **1921** L. COCKAYNE *Veget. N.Z.* II. iv. 73 A typical, highly developed dune-area in New Zealand consists of a fairly even-topped low wall of sand the *foredune which rises from the upper strand beyond reach of an ordinary tide. **1964** V. J. CHAPMAN *Coastal Veget.* vi. 140 In the absence of sand couch grass, the fore-dunes are generally colonized by the Lyme grass. **1598** BARRET *Theor. Warres* III. i. 43 Each one hauing a care to his *forefellowes ..discharge altogether at one vollie. **1796** W. MARSHALL *Midl. Co.* I. 355 (E.D.S.) **Fore-flank*..a projection of fat, upon the ribs, immediately behind the shoulder. **1856** *Farmer's Mag.* Jan. 10 He was especially good in his back and fore-flank. **1589** NASHE *Pasquill & Marforius* 12 The *fore-gallant of the Morrice, with the treble belles. *a* **1658** FORD, etc. *Witch Edmonton* II. i, If you..know me..for a.. fore-gallant in a morris, my father's stable is not unfurnish'd. **1496** in *Ld. Treas. Acc. Scotl.* (1877) I. 300 Fore towis, harnys, and quhelis, and all *foregere. **1560** ROLLAND *Crt. Venus* IV. 613 The peirt persing of foirgeir into deid. **1528** TINDALE *Obed. Chr. Man* 91 b, Christe hath brought us all into the inner temple, within the vayle or *forehanginge. **1881** RAYMOND *Mining Gloss.*, **Fore-hearth*, a projecting bay in the front of a blast-furnace hearth, under the tymp. **1880** *Lib. Univ. Knowl.* XIII. 76 The brine..is placed in large shallow iron pans called the '*foreheaters', when it is boiled until the impurities have been deposited. **1602** CAREW *Cornwall* 76 a, Many sleights and tricks appertaine hereunto..Such are the Trip, *forehip [etc.]. **1923** R. E. DAVIES *Pigs & Bacon Curing* 29 The side may be made into smaller cuts by either of the following divisions:—First: *fore hock, thick streaky, thin streaky, flank, gammon, corner, long loin, back and ribs, and collar. **1867** SMYTH *Sailor's Word-bk.*, **Fore-hook*. **1892** J. A. THOMSON *Outl. Zool.* 404 The pronephros or *fore-kidney persists. **1678** PHILLIPS, **Fore-knight* and *Main-knight*, in Navigation are two short thick pieces of Wood carved with the head of a Man, fast bolted to the Beams upon the second Deck. **1891** A. J. FOSTER *Ouse* 170 First comes the *fore-lighter with the name of the owner painted on the bows. **1626** BACON *Sylva* §204 Sounds though they spread round ..yet they..go furthest in the *Fore-lines from the first local impulsion of the air. **1822** GOOD *Study Med.* (1834) IV. 89 This *fore-march of nature should be timely checked. **1863** MRS. C. CLARKE *Shaks. Char.* xvi. 405 The *foremark and exemplar of a commercial nobleman. **1904** *Daily Chron.* 15 July 3/7 Thousands of bacteria have been found in the '*fore' milk, whereas the 'middle' milk was..germ-free. **1908** *Stratford-upon-Avon Herald* 24 July 7/1 The rejection of foremilk and the discontinuance of wet milking. **1949** *New Biol.* VII. 21 During any one milking time the fat-content of the milk increases very rapidly from the thin 'fore-milk' to the rich 'strippings'. **1623** LISLE *Ælfric on O. & N. Test.* Pref. ¶5 The *fore page of this Worke. **1874** KNIGHT *Dict. Mech.* I. 905 **Fore-piece* (Saddlery) the flap attached to the fore-part of a side-saddle, to guard the rider's dress. **1837** *Regul. & Ord. Army 93 Repairs to Rifles*, For long *Fore-pipe, brass 1*s.* 0*d.* **1870** G. M. HOPKINS *Jrnl.* 19 Dec. (1959) 201 Each [icicle] like a *forepitch of the shape of the piece of potsherd it grew on, like a tooth to its root for instance. **1871** *Ibid.* Mar. 204 Possibly each tuft [of cloud] in forepitch or in origin is quained and a crystal. **1881** —— *Sermons* (1959) II. viii. 196 There is..in the works of creation..the order of intention,..not only intention in understanding and intention in will but also intention or forepitch of execution, of power or activity. **1929** J. B. EGGEN in Calverton & Schmalhausen *Sex in Civilization* 594 The difference between perversion and *fore-play. **1950** M. MEAD *Male and Female* II. iii. 73 Love-affairs are matters of the eyes, foreplay is almost completely concentrated in a glance-exchanging courtship. **1953** A. C. KINSEY et al. *Sex. Behav. Hum. Female* II. ix. 364 Many persons..feel that the intensity of the ultimate orgasm is heightened by extended foreplay. **1961** R. LISWOOD *Doc. Speaks* (1963) iv. 64 When there is adequate foreplay..intercourse is more satisfying. **1910** A. A. BRILL tr. *Freud's Three Contributions to Theory of Sex* iii. 62 In contradistinction to the end-pleasure, or pleasure of gratification of sexual activity, we can properly designate the first as *fore-pleasure. The fore-pleasure is then the same as that furnished by the infantile sexual impulse, though on a reduced scale. **1925** J. RIVIERE et al. tr. *Freud's Coll. Papers* IV. 183 The increment of pleasure which is offered us in order to release yet greater pleasure arising from deeper sources in the mind is called an 'incitement premium' or technically, 'fore-pleasure'. **1951** C. BERG *Unconscious Significance of Hair* vii. 58 Lingering at the stage of 'fore pleasure' relations to the sexual object. **1536** LADY BRIAN *Let.* in Strype *Eccl. Mem.* I. App. lxxi. 172 She hath neither gowne nor kirtell..nor *foresmocks. **1496** in *Ld. Treas. Acc. Scotl.* (1877) I. 298 Item for iiij *fore sparris to turs to the oost. **1874** KNIGHT *Dict. Mech.* I. 905 **Fore-starling*, an ice-breaker in advance of the starling of a bridge. **1562** J. HEYWOOD *Prov. & Epigr.* (1867) 203 If one backstep be as much as *foresteps three. **1611** SPEED *Hist. Gt. Brit.* IX. v. §27 Following the fore-steps of your famous Ancestors. **1668** GLANVILL in *Phil. Trans.* II. 770 A Rock called a *Fore-stone. **1839** URE *Dict. Arts* 756 The front of the furnace is open for about 12 inches from the lower part of the front cross-piece called fore-stone. **1884** Fore-stone [see *work-stone* s.v. WORK *sb.* 34]. **1867** SMYTH *Sailor's Word-bk.*, **Fore-thwart*. The seat of the bowman in a boat. **1496** [see *foregear*] *Fore-towis. **1797** *Sporting Mag.* X. 296 The *fore-train consists of the neck, the shoulders, the breast, and the fore-legs. **1881** RAYMOND *Mining Gloss.*, **Fore-winning*, advanced workings.

b. With reference to time: † **fore-eatage**, the opportunity of pasturing one's cattle before others; † **fore-fetch**, a reaching forward in thought, forethought (see FETCH *sb.*[1] 1); † **fore-goodsire** = FORE-GRANDSIRE; † **fore-great-grandfather** = *great-great-grandfather*; **fore-rent**, 'a year's rent of a farm payable six months after entry' (Jam.); † **forestore**, a store laid up beforehand; † **fore-title**, prescriptive title; † **fore-wages** (*Sc.*), wages paid in advance.

1641 BEST *Farm. Bks.* (Surtees) 117 They may have the *fore-eatage of the towne-side. **1554** BALE *Decl. Bonner's Art.* xi. (1561) 35 He is a man of a great *fore fatche. **1535** STEWART *Cron. Scot.* III. 19 His *foirgudschir king Malcome Canmoir. *a* **1693** URQUHART *Rabelais* III. xxxvii. 310 Caillets *fore-great Grandfather. **1813** R. KERR *Agric. Surv. Berw.* 141 The..mode of payment..termed *fore-rent or forehand rent. **1556** J. HEYWOOD *Spider & F.* x. 110 To begerie from richesse *Forestore lasht out, in excreable excesse. **1611** SPEED *Hist. Gt. Brit.* IX. viii. §5 No man hath Right or any other *fore-Title to succeede another..vnlesse [etc.]. **1606** *Sc. Acts Jas. VI* (1816) IV. 287 Samony of thame as sall ressaue *foirwageis.

fore-aboding, etc.; see FORE- *pref.*

foreacre (ˈfɔərеɪkə(r)). Now *dial.* [f. FORE- *pref.* + ACRE. Cf. Ger. *voracker.*] (See quots.)

1736 PEGGE *Kenticisms* (E.D.S.) 28 *Fore-acre*, an head-land. **1887** *Kent Gloss.*, *Fore-acre*, a headland: the land at the ends of the field where the furrows cross.

foreˈact *v.* [f. FORE- *pref.* + ACT *v.*] *trans.* and *intr.* To act beforehand (see senses of ACT *v.*).

1757 DYER *Fleece* I. 261 Sagacious care foreacts. **1840** R. I. WILBERFORCE *5 Empires* 33 The great deeds of the Son of God foreacted in dumb show in the ordinances of God's worship.

Hence **fore-acted** *ppl. a.*; **fore-acting** *vbl. sb.*

a **1618** SYLVESTER *Job Triumph.* Proem 865 To finde some hole in my fore-acted Life. **1652** CARYL *Exp. Job* xi.–xiv. 507 These dispensations being (*præludia gloriæ*) the fore-actings of a glorified estate. **1682** *2nd Plea for Nonconf.* 26 Their fore-acted Conspiracies.

fore-adapt, -advise, etc.: see FORE- *pref.*

† **ˌfore-aˈgain, -aˈgainst**, *prep. Obs.* Also 5 foragayne, 6 foraganis, forayenst. [f. FORE *prep.* or *adv.* + AGAIN, AGAINST. Cf. FOREGAIN(ST, FORNENT.] Directly opposite, facing.

1494 FABYAN *Chron.* VI. clxxx. 178 For agayne the olde towne of Notyngham. **1506** *Will of Wyttylbury* (Somerset Ho.), Forayenst the place where my fader lieth. **1577–87** HOLINSHED *Chron.* I. 178/1 That part that lieth fore against France, was assigned to Edmund. **1596** DALRYMPLE tr. *Leslie's Hist. Scot.* I. 87 Nathir to thay best partes in Albion in the Easte foraganes Irland. **1631** HEYLIN *St. George* II. viii. 312 They..set, by two and two: every one with his fellow, which is foreagainst him in his stall.

fore-age: see FORE- *pref.* 4.

† **ˌfore-aˈlleged**, *ppl. a. Obs.* [f. FORE- *pref.* + ALLEGED.] Previously alleged or quoted.

1587 GOLDING *De Mornay* iv. 47 The forealledged Oracles. **1610** HEALEY *St. Aug. Citie of God* I. xxvi. (1620) 30 It must needs be that which is fore-alledged. **1701** NORRIS *Ideal World* II. iii. (1704) 154 The fore-alledged instance.

fore-alley, -allot: see FORE- *pref.* 2 a, 5.

fore and aft, *adv.*, *a.*, and *sb. Naut.*

A. *adv.*

1. Of position: In or at both bow and stern; hence, along the length of or all over the ship.

1627 CAPT. SMITH *Seaman's Gram.* xiii. 61 A health to you all fore and aft. **1743** BULKELEY & CUMMINS *Voy. S. Seas* 9 My Rigging is all gone, and broke fore and aft. **1793** SMEATON *Edystone L.* §123 Her deck raised, and laid flush fore and aft. **1822** G. W. MANBY *Voy. Greenland* (1823) 63 And the bulwark, fore and aft, was washed away. **1835**

MARRYAT *Pirate* vii, Awnings were spread fore and aft to protect the crew from the rays of the sun.

2. Of motion or direction: Alternately towards the bow and stern, backwards and forwards.

1726 SHELVOCKE *Voy. round World* (1757) 406 So incommoded by them, that we could hardly move, fore and aft, through the throng of them [Indians]. **1840** R. H. DANA *Bef. Mast* xxiii. 73 To walk fore and aft in the waist. **1865** LIVINGSTONE *Zambesi* vi. 151 Every night they [rats] went fore and aft rousing with impartial feet every sleeper.

3. From stem to stern, lengthwise.

a **1618** [see AFT 2 c]. **1709** *Lond. Gaz.* No. 4543/2 He.. raked her fore and aft with his Cannon. **1823** J. BADCOCK *Dom. Amusem.* 208 The pontons should be..sharpish fore and aft. **1867** SMYTH *Sailor's Word-bk., Fore and aft*..also implies in a line with the keel.

B. *adj.* **a.** (usu. with hyphens). Placed or directed in the line of the vessel's length. Of sails (see quot. 1867); hence, of a vessel rigged with such sails. Also Comb. *fore-and-aft rigged* ppl. adj.

1820 SCORESBY *Acc. Arctic Reg.* II. 197 *note*, I have confined the term..gaff sails to the fore and aft sails. **1834** M. SCOTT *Cruise Midge* (1859) 329 A large fore-and-aft rigged vessel. **1856** *Farmer's Mag.* Nov. 426 The Dean Richmond is a fore-and-aft schooner of 380 tons register. **1867** SMYTH *Sailor's Word-bk., Fore-and-aft sails*, jibs, staysails, and gaffsails; in fact, all sails which are not set to yards. **1878** [see AFT 2 c]. **1879** THOMSON & TAIT *Nat. Phil.* I. I. §325 'Fore-and-aft' rig is any rig in which..the chief sails come into the plane of mast or masts and keel, by the action of the wind upon the sails when the vessel's head is to wind.

b. *spec.* Applied to a field service cap.

1940 *War Illustr.* 5 Jan. 571/2 Boys in the same battle-kit that the British Army wears, but with a maple-leaf badge in their fore-and-aft caps. **1950** A. BARON *There's no Home* viii. 87 He wore a British soldier's fore-and-aft cap with the flaps buttoned under his chin.

C. *sb.* ? A cap with peaks both before and behind.

1888 *Harper's Mag.* Sept. 494 Women in jockey caps and fore-and-afts.

ˌfore-and-ˈafter. [f. FORE AND AFT *adv.*, + -ER[1].] **a.** A 'fore and aft' schooner. **b.** (see quot. 1867.)

1823 J. F. COOPER *Pioneer* xv. (1869) 66, I went a few trips in a fore-and-after. **1867** SMYTH *Sailor's Word-bk., Fore-and-after*, a cocked hat worn with the peak in front instead of athwart.

fore-anent: see FORNENT.

ˌfore-aˈnnounce, *v.* [f. FORE- *pref.* + ANNOUNCE.] *trans.* To announce beforehand.

1846 TRENCH *Mirac.* (1889) 453 [God] might have used Caiaphas to fore-announce other truths of his Kingdom. **1860** PUSEY *Min. Proph.* 5 After foreannouncing the miseries at the destruction of Samaria.

Hence **fore-aˈnnounced** *ppl. a.*; **fore-aˈnnouncing** *vbl. sb.* Also **fore-aˈnnouncement,** a notification or declaration beforehand.

1864 PUSEY *Lect. Daniel* vi. 355 His foreannounced justice. *Ibid.* v. 236 The fore-announcing of our Lord's coming. **1864** —— *David* 626 A foreannouncement of events.

fore-answer: see FORE- *pref.* 2 a.

ˌfore-aˈppoint, *v. arch.* [f. FORE- *pref.* + APPOINT.] *trans.* To appoint beforehand.

1561 T. NORTON *Calvin's Inst.* II. 148 Whosoeuer..hope to knowe more of Christ than god hath foreapointed them by his secret decree. **1637–50** ROW *Hist. Kirk* (1842) 485 To dissolve the meeting of the Councill that day, albeit it was fore-appoynted for answering the subjects petitions. **1726–31** TINDAL *Rapin's Hist. Eng.* (1743) II. XVII. 126 Days and Places which you..shall thereunto fore-appoint. **1836** J. GILBERT *Chr. Atonem.* iii. (1852) 62 So steadily had this purpose been entertained, and so clearly this event foreappointed that, [etc.]. **1886** J. PAYNE *Decameron* I. 33 The place fore-appointed of them.

Hence **fore-aˈppointed** *ppl. a.*; **fore-aˈppointing** *vbl. sb.* and *ppl. a.* Also **fore-aˈppointment,** previous appointment, preordination.

1577 tr. *Bullinger's Decades* (1592) 643 The ende of predestination or foreappointment is Christ. **1580** SIDNEY *Arcadia* (1622) 413 Her fore-appointed end. **1589** GREENE *Tullie's Loue* Wks. (Grosart) VII. 189 The aspectes of the fore-appointing stars. **1654** TRAPP *Comm. Job* xvi. 11 The foreappointed affliction. **1656** —— *Comm. Gal.* iv. 9 [God's] gracious fore-knowing and fore-appointing of us to eternal life. **1677** HALE *Contempl.* II. Lord's Prayer 105 By the determinate Counsel and Fore appointment of God. **1833** KEBLE *Serm.* vii. (1848) 166 The fore-appointed safeguard of the integrity of our Lord's holy sacraments.

forearm (ˈfɔərɑːm), *sb.* [f. FORE- *pref.* + ARM *sb.*] The part of the arm between the elbow and the wrist; sometimes the whole arm below the elbow. Also, the corresponding part in the forelegs of quadrupeds, or in the wings of birds.

1741 MONRO *Anat. Bones* (ed. 3) 251 The fore-arm consists of two long Bones, the *Ulna* and *Radius*. **1758** J. S. *Le Dran's Observ. Surg.* (1771) 156 The Swelling upon the ..Fore-Arm increased. **1835–6** TODD *Cycl. Anat.* I. 294/2 Birds in general possess two flexors..of the fore-arm. **1843** BETHUNE *Sc. Fireside Stor.* 128 In such a manner as to leave the whole of the fore-arm bare. **1856** KANE *Arct. Expl.* I. xxix. 388 She tore down by single efforts of her forearms the barrels of frozen beef. **1880** HAUGHTON *Phys. Geog.* vi. 283 The bones of the forearm and leg.

forearm (fɔərˈɑːm), *v.* [f. FORE- *pref.* + ARM *v.*] *trans.* To arm beforehand; *lit.* and *fig.*

1592 GREENE *Disc. Coosnage* II. 1 Forewarned, forearmed. **1682** DRYDEN *Medal* 68 Who helps a pow'rful Friend, forearms a Foe. **1768–74** TUCKER *Lt. Nat.* (1852) II. 429 Knowing that forewarned is forearmed. **1862** GOULBURN *Pers. Relig.* III. iv. (1873) 190 We are forearmed against surprises.

fore-axle: see FORE- *pref.* 3.

†**ˌfore-ˈbackwardly,** *adv. Obs. rare*[−1]. [f. FORE *adv.* + BACKWARD + -LY[2].] Beginning at the wrong end, preposterously.

1581 SIDNEY *Apol. Poetrie* (Arb.) 62 Exercise indeede wee doe, but that, very fore-backwardly: for where we should exercise to know, wee exercise as hauing knowne.

fore-balance, -bald: see FORE- *pref.* 2 a.

†**ˈfore-ball.** *dial. Obs.* (See quot.)

1602 CAREW *Cornwall* 74 a, The Hurlers are bound to the obseruation of many lawes, as..that he must deale no Foreball, viz. he may not throw it to any of his mates standing neerer the goale, then himselfe.

fore-bay (ˈfɔəbeɪ). [f. FORE- *pref.* + BAY *sb.*[3]] **a.** *Naut.* **b.** *Hydraulics.* (see quots.)

1867 SMYTH *Sailor's Word-bk., Fore-bay*..the galley or sick-bay. **1874** KNIGHT *Dict. Mech., Forebay*, a reservoir or conductor between a mill-race and a waterwheel. The discharging end of a head or mill-race.

fore-beak, -beam, -being: see FORE- *pref.*

†**ˈfore-bell.** *Obs.* [f. FORE- *pref.* + BELL.] The first of a peal of bells.

1484 *Churchw. Acc. Wigtoft, nr. Boston* (Nichols 1797) 79 For shotyng of an irren bolte to the forbell whele. **1529** *Churchw. Acc. St. Giles Reading* 37 Iron werk for the fore bell. **1546** *Ludlow Churchw. Acc.* (Camden) 26 Pesynge of the for belle rope. **1801** STRUTT *Sports & Past.* III. v. §18. 171 These [morris-dancers'] bells were of unequal sizes and differently denominated, as the fore bell, the second bell, the treble, the tenor or great bell.

fore-bemoan, -bespeak, -bias: see FORE- *pref.*

†**ˈfore-bit.** *Obs.* [f. FORE *adv.* + *bit*, BITTEN.] = DEVIL'S-BIT 1.

1597 GERARDE *Herbal* II. ccxxxvii. 587 It is commonly called *Morsus Diaboli* or Diuels bit, of the root (as it seemeth) that is bitten off..in French *Mors du Diable*..in English Diuels bit, and Fore-bit. **1611** COTGR., *Mors du diable*, the hearbe Forebit, or Diuels bit.

foreˈbitten, *ppl. a. Obs.* [f. FORE- *pref.* + BITTEN.] Bitten in front; only in *forebitten more* = FOREBIT.

1597 GERARDE *Herbal* App., Forebitten More is Diuels bit.

fore-bless, -blind, -board, etc.: see FORE- *pref.*

forebode (fɔəˈbəʊd), *v.* [f. FORE- *pref.* + BODE *v.*]

1. *trans.* To announce beforehand, predict, prognosticate.

1664 BUTLER *Hud.* II. iii. 172 Do not our great Reformers use This Sidrophel to fore-boad News. **1709** STEELE *Tatler* No. 30 ¶5 To Morrow will be a Day of Battle, and something forebodes in my Breast that I shall fall in it. **1816** J. WILSON *City of Plague* III. i, Then many heard..a voice foreboding woe. **1879** DIXON *Windsor* I. xxvi. 265 Old men foreboded evil days to come.

b. Of things: To betoken, portend.

1656 COWLEY *Pindaric Odes, Isa.* XXXIV. v, Though no new Ills can be foreboded there. **1718** *Freethinker* No. 62 ¶7 Palpitations of the Heart..foreboded the Infidelity of a Friend. **1780** COWPER *Progr. Err.* 604 Long flights forebode a fall. **1868** E. EDWARDS *Raleigh* I. xiii. 254 The Earl's administration of Irish affairs foreboded at its outset the issue.

2. To feel a secret premonition of, have a presentiment of (*usually* evil); to anticipate, to apprehend beforehand. Const. *simple obj.* or *subord. cl.*

1603 KNOLLES *Hist. Turks* (1621) 235 You see the dangers and injuries I indure in this my journy, and my minde forbodeth greater to ensue. **1677** HORNECK *Gt. Law Consid.* v. (1704) 271 An evil conscience, which foreboded an all-revenging arm. **1725** POPE *Odyss.* IX. 248 My soul foreboded I should find the bower Of some fell monster. **1793** LD. SHEFFIELD in *Ld. Auckland's Corr.* (1862) III. 118, I foreboded mischief the moment I heard of its division. **1848** DICKENS *Dombey* 341 Stragglers..foreboding that their misery there would be but as a drop of water in the sea. **1895** M. CORELLI *Sorrows Satan* 321 Neither to regret the past nor forbode the future.

b. *intr.* or *absol.* To conjecture, forecast.

1711 ADDISON *Spect.* No. 7 ¶4 One of these Antiquated Sibyls, that forebodes and prophesies from one end of the Year to the other. **1782** COWPER *Gilpin* 166 And if I well forebode, My hat and wig will soon be here. **1850** HAWTHORNE *Scarlet L.* x. (1892) 161 There can be, if I forebode aright, no power short of the Divine mercy, to disclose [etc.].

Hence **foreˈboded** *ppl. a.* Also †**forebode** *sb.*, **foreˈbodement,** a foreboding.

a **1679** T. GOODWIN *Wks.* II. IV. 72 There is upon many forebodes..one great Fate to come upon the Churches of Christ. **1755** JOHNSON, *Presagement*, forebodement, presension. **1853** M. ARNOLD *Poems, World's Triumphs*, Thy foreboded homage. **1860** ADLER *Fauriel's Prov. Poetry* xi. 234 He was wont to tremble at every forebodement.

†**foreˈboden,** *ppl. a. Obs. rare.* [FORE- *pref.* + *boden* pa. pple. of *bede* BID *v.*] Presented beforehand.

1602 CAREW *Cornwall* 25 b, It was taken at first for a forboden token.

foreboder (fɔəˈbəʊdə(r)). [f. FOREBODE *v.* + -ER[1].] One who or that which forebodes; †a prognosticator.

1687 R. L'ESTRANGE *Answ. Diss.* 43 These Fore-boders, are..the most Pernicious of Wizzards. **1782** BURNS *Song*, O why the deuce should I repine, And be an ill foreboder. **1805** WORDSW. *Waggoner* III. 130 This explanation..Cured the foreboder like a charm. **1876** BANCROFT *Hist. U.S.* IV. xxxiv. 568 Merchants..who feared a war as the fore-boder of their own bankruptcy.

foreboding (fɔəˈbəʊdɪŋ), *vbl. sb.* [f. FOREBODE *v.* + -ING[1].]

1. The action of the vb. FOREBODE; hence, a prediction, presage. (Now only of evil.)

1387 TREVISA *Higden* (Rolls) IV. 401 As so as it was by a forbledynge [*v.rr.* for bedynge, forbodyng] he hadde þat name Seneca. **1618** BOLTON *Florus* IV. xii. 320 Marcus Crassus..tooke the word as a faire foreboding. **1838** THIRLWALL *Greece* IV. xxxiv. 357 By which the forebodings of Socrates were realised. **1860** TYNDALL *Glac.* I. ii. 12 Heedless of the forebodings of many prophets of evil weather.

b. A portent, omen.

1387 TREVISA *Higden* (Rolls) VII. 351 Þis Remigius semede ny3 a wonder forbeddynge [*v.rr.* forbodyng, vorbodyng]. **1692** R. L'ESTRANGE *Fables* clxxviii. moral 149 The Fancy of Omens, Forebodings, Old Wives Tales and Visions. **1871** PALGRAVE *Lyr. Poems* 28 Great Ossa..lay Like the foreboding of a coming woe.

2. A presentiment of something to happen, *esp.* of approaching or overhanging evil.

1603 KNOLLES *Hist. Turks* (1621) 186, I say no more for griefe, and foreboding of euill fortune. **1799** SHERIDAN *Pizarro* II. iii, I..cannot fly from the foreboding which oppresses me. **1883** S. C. HALL *Retrospect* II. 149 She had a foreboding of early death.

foreboding (fɔəˈbəʊdɪŋ), *ppl. a.* [f. as prec. + -ING[2].] That forebodes, in senses of the vb.

1679 EVERARD *Popish Plot* 7 By a fore-boding guilt they knew perfectly..I had grounds enough wherewith to accuse them. **1795** BURKE *Th. Scarcity* Wks. 1842 II. 257, I can never quote France without a foreboding sigh. **1860** PUSEY *Min. Proph.* 486 That he by a foreboding name should be called Haggai, i.e. 'festive'.

Hence **foreˈbodingly** *adv.*; **foreˈbodingness.**

1801 COLERIDGE *Let.* in Mrs. Sandford *T. Poole & Friends* (1888) II. 48 My gloom and forebodingness respecting pecuniary affairs. **1823** *New Monthly Mag.* VIII. 284 He gave me a squeeze of the hand, which was forebodingly forcible. **1857** W. COLLINS *Dead Secret* III. ii. (1861) 79 Her head shaking forebodingly from time to time.

fore-body (ˈfɔəˌbɒdɪ). [f. FORE- *pref.*]

†**1.** The front part of a dress. *Obs.*

1611 COTGR. s.v. *Robert*, A Doublet whose forebodie is fine stuffe, and the backe parts course. **1691** *Islington Wells* 10 The Lady by her Manteaus Forebody, Sure takes a Pride to Dress like no Body.

2. *Naut.* (See quots.)

1830 HEDDERWICK *Marine Archit.* 113 *Fore-body*, every part of the hull before..the dead-flat frame. **1867** SMYTH *Sailor's Word-bk., Fore-body*, an imaginary figure of that part of the ship afore the midships or dead-flat, as seen from ahead. **1883** *Fortn. Rev.* 1 Sept. 324 Thus making the afterbody longer and finer than the forebody.

†**ˈforebow**[1]. *Obs.* exc. *dial.* Also 6 **fore-bough,** 7 **-boothe.** [f. FORE- *pref.* + BOUGH *sb.* (sense 1), BOW *sb.*[3]] **a.** In *pl.* The shoulders of a quadruped, as seen from the front; the breast. **b.** The beak or prow of a ship.

1569 STOCKER tr. *Diod. Sic.* III. viii. 115 It is difficile and harde to laye abord about the beake or forebough of a Gallie. **1610** MARKHAM *Masterp.* I. lii. 110 Bathe all his breast and foreboothes with the oyle of Peter. **1614** —— *Cheap Husb.* (1623) 86 His dew-lap extending from his neather lip downe to his fore-boothes. **1714** *Lond. Gaz.* No. 5253/4 Strayed.. a Black Mare..a small White Spot between her Forebows. **1828** *Craven Dial., Forbows*, the breast of an animal.

†**ˈforebow**[2]. *Obs.* [f. FORE- *pref.* + BOW *sb.*[1]] The arched frame in the front of a saddle. (Cf. Fr. *arçon.*)

1725 BRADLEY *Fam. Dict.* s.v. *Saddle*, The Toes or Points of the Saddle's Fore-bow press too much the Horse's Side. **1835** BOOTH *Analyt. Dict.* 296 The Saddle has a round knob on the fore-part or Fore-bow, called the Pommel.

fore-bowels, -bowline, etc.: see FORE- *pref.*

ˈforebreast. [OE. *forbréost* (rendering L. *præcordia*), f. FOR-[2], FORE- *pref.* + *bréost*, BREAST *sb.*]

1. *Sc.* The fore part of anything.

c **1470** HENRY *Wallace* VII. 1189 At the forbreist thai prewit hardely. **1825–80** JAMIESON, *Fore-breast*, as the fore-breast o' the laft, the front-seat of the gallery in a church. **1871** W. ALEXANDER *Johnny Gibb* i. (1873) 13 And then, mounting the 'forebreist' [of a cart] himself, started again. *attrib.* **1513** DOUGLAS *Æneis* XI. xv. 19 The forbreist lappis.

2. *Mining.* (See quot.) = FOREFIELD.

1747 HOOSON *Miner's Dict., Forebrest, Forfield* or *Forehead*. Those are all the same but the most Antient Name amongst the Old Miners is Forfield; and it is always that Quantity of Wholes which he takes in his compass before him, as he cuts his way be it more or less. **1880** C. C.

ADLEY in *Rep. Pioneer Mining Co.* 2 Oct. 1 The rock in the forebreast of the level has become very hard.

forebroads (ˈfɔəbrɔːdz). *Sc.* [f. FORE- *pref.*; cf. Icel. *broddr* 'milk of cows immediately after calving' (Vigf.).] = BEESTINGS.

1811 W. AITON *Agric. Surv. Ayrsh.* 443 (Jam.) The young calves are fed on the milk, first drawn, locally termed fore-broads. **1842** J. AITON *Clerical Economics* iv. 173 The milk first drawn from the cow, locally termed the forebroads.

†**forebudding.** ? = FOREBODY 2.

1811 *Chron.* in *Ann. Reg.* 96/1 She [a fishing smack] drifted down on a boat a-head of her and took the point of her boom into her forebuddings.

foreburden, corrupt var. of FABURDEN.

1603 HOLLAND *Plutarch's Mor.* 476 The foreburthen of their canticle was this.

fore-bush, -buttock: see FORE- *pref.* 5.

†**fore'buyer.** *Obs.* [f. FORE- *pref.* + BUYER.] One who buys at first hand to sell again, a wholesale buyer.

1558 *Merch. Adv. Newcastle* (Surtees) 88 Woll and skynnes, bought of any glovers or forebyers. **1559** *Ibid.* 48 An acte concernyng the byeng of wooll..of for-byers..Men that byes it of other men that growes it, callyde forbyers. **1597** SKENE *De Verb. Sign.* s.v. *Regrateris,* That they are fore-byars of quheate, beare, aites [etc.].

'fore-cabin. [f. FORE- *pref.* + CABIN *sb.*] A cabin in the forepart of the vessel; *spec.* one for second-class passengers in which the accommodation is inferior to that in the saloon.

1816 *Gentl. Mag.* LXXXVI. I. 102 The fore-cabin made close, and a hatchway so as to keep out the water. **1833** MARRYAT *P. Simple* (1863) 61 The cashier, with his chest of money..was shown into the fore-cabin. **1877** W. THOMSON *Voy. Challenger* I. i. 11 The fore-cabin, a handsome room 30 ft. long by 12 wide.

fore'call, *v.* [f. FORE- *pref.* + CALL *v.*] *trans.* To call or ordain beforehand. (In first quot. perh. for **forcall* = FORSPEAK, to bewitch.)

c **1650** *Suppl. to Vicary's Anat.* 113 If a man be fore-called, doe this nine dayes, and hee shall be whole. **1667** WATERHOUSE *Fire Lond.* 61 He predisposes and forecalls severalties to their Randezvous. **1880** L. A. TOLLEMACHE in *Jrnl. Educ.* Oct. 225 Cats were his Cardinals made..Each forecalled by the name of an unborn Cynic apostle.

'fore-carriage. [f. FORE- *pref.* + CARRIAGE.] †**a.** Carriage forward or out from home; opp. to *back-carriage.* **b.** The front part of the framework of a carriage, *esp.* the front axle and fore-wheels.

1549 *Privy Council Acts* (1890) II. 349 Shod wheles for fore cariages. **1677** YARRANTON *Eng. Improv.* 118 All things would be fitted for fore and back carriage. **1892** *Melbourne Age* 31 Dec. 10/2 Waggonette for Sale, English forecarriage.

forecast (ˈfɔəkɑːst, -æ-), *sb.* [f. next vb.]

1. a. The action, habit, or faculty of forecasting; foresight of consequences and provision against them, forethought, prudence. Now *rare.*

a **1541** WYATT *Poet. Wks.* (1861) 183 The wisdom and forecast, Which woe to realms, when that the King doth lack! **1644** QUARLES *Barnabas & B.* 243 Give me a wise forecast, that the subtlety of the devil may not entrap me. **1754** RICHARDSON *Grandison* (1781) I. vii. 109 He has invention, forecast, and contrivance. **1831** CARLYLE *Sart. Res.* (1858) 177 The doctrine, which Swift, with the keen forecast of genius, dimly anticipated. **1838** PRESCOTT *Ferd. & Is.* (1846) III. xvi. 168 Evils which no forecast could avert.

b. A forecasting or anticipation; a conjectural estimate or account, based on present indications, of the course of events or state of things in the future, *esp.* with regard to the weather.

a **1673** CARYL in Spurgeon *Treas. Dav.* Ps. cvi. 7 What were these fearful forecasts..but the overflowings of unbelief. **1822** LAMB *Elia* Ser. II. *Confess. Drunkard,* A forecast of the wearisome day that lies before me. **1862** *Times* 12 Apr., Too little critical attention has been given to the 'wet or dry' part of our forecasts. **1873** SYMONDS *Grk. Poets* i. 10 Is not the shield of Achilles..a forecast of the future? **1930** *Observer* 14 Sept. 17 The previous forecast of no serious gale. **1955** *Ann. Reg. 1954* 2 It proved to be one of those occasions when the forecast says 'widespread rain' and all that follows is a display of cloud. **1957** *Times* 11 May 7/1 Forecasts for period 6 a.m. to midnight.

†**2. a.** Design, purpose, aim. **b.** A plan, scheme, or device made beforehand. *Obs.*

a. 1549 COVERDALE, etc. *Erasm. Par. Jas.* iv. 1-6 To set theyr forcastes vpon muckryng vp of riches. *c* **1686-8** *Invinc. Pride Wom.* in *Roxb. Ball.* (1890) VII. 21 It is her forecast to contrive to rise about the hour of Noon.

b. 1535 COVERDALE *Wisd.* ix. 14 Oure forecastes are but vncertayne. **1674** N. FAIRFAX *Bulk & Selv.* 162 That forecast or decree by the power of which the world was. **1754** RICHARDSON *Grandison* (ed. 7) VIII. 172 What an admirable forecast in my dearest life! A repast so elegant [etc.].

†**3.** A projection. *Obs.*

1580 HOLLYBAND *Treas. Fr. Tong, Projects de maisons,* when houses haue a little forecast or wall before the gate.

forecast (fɔəˈkɑːst, -æ-, ˈfɔə-), *v.* Pa. t. and pa. pple. forecast, forecasted. [f. FORE- *pref.* + CAST *v.*]

1. *trans.* To contrive or scheme beforehand; to arrange or plan before execution; to foreordain, predestine.

1388 [see FORECASTING *vbl. sb.*]. **1413** *Pilgr. Sowle* (Caxton 1483) III. iii. 52 For sothly his deth was fore cast but if he the better sawe to hym self. **1587** GOLDING *De Mornay* xiii. (1617) 203 At the first sight the thing which was forecast by good order, seemeth to happen by adventure. **1678** tr. *Gaya's Art of War* I. 6 [He] to whom a Soveraign hath intrusted the command of an Army, should well forecast his measures, before he go into the Field. **1751** G. WEST *Educ.* I. xlviii, He..warily forecasting to evade The giant's furious arm, about him wheel'd. **1835** *Tait's Mag.* II. 257 The advantageous part her ambition had forecasted. **1871** ROSSETTI *Poems, Ave* 45 On some day forecast in Heaven.

absol. **1578** BANISTER *Hist. Man* I. 3 Since Nature..needfully forecasted, let vs see to what end and purpose, were these Processes ordeined. **1593** NASHE *Christ's T.* 79 b, They fore-cast for backe doores, to come in and out by vndiscouerd. **1674** N. FAIRFAX *Bulk & Selv.* 151 Fore-casting also for the young ones a coming.

b. To consider or think of beforehand.

1534 WHITINTON *Tullyes Offices* III. (1540) 145 Who so euer wyll not forecast this, no fraude fro hym wyll be absent. **1577** HANMER *Anc. Eccl. Hist.* (1619) 213 He forecast also what God he were best to call upon for aide. **1671** MILTON *Samson* 254 Fore-casting in what place To set upon them.

2. To estimate, conjecture, or imagine beforehand (the course of events or future condition of things). Sometimes with *clause* as *obj.*

1494 FABYAN *Chron.* VII. 561 The whiche forecastyng yͤ great shedyng of Cristen mannys bloode..made such affectuouse labour, yͭ [etc.]. **1548** HALL *Chron., Edw. IV* (an. 8) 211 Quene Margaret..ever forcastyng and doubtyng, the chaunce that might happen. *a* **1602** W. PERKINS *Cases Consc.* (1619) 220 Ionah..fore-casted dangers in his calling. **1731** SWIFT *Strephon & Chloe* Misc. 1735 V. 42 A prudent Builder should forecast How long the Stuff is like to last. **1762** FALCONER *Shipwr.* II. 613 No skill ..could forecast The..approach of this destructive blast. **1845-6** TRENCH *Huls. Lect.* Ser. I. vii. 113 How little..could friend or foe..have forecast that out of it..should unfold itself a poetry..greater..than any which the old world had seen. **1868** G. DUFF *Pol. Surv.* 134, I am..quite unable to forecast the future with regard to this matter.

absol. *a* **1533** LD. BERNERS *Gold. Bk. M. Aurel.* (1546) P, A shypmayster..forcasteth, and is in gret thought and feare of tempestes and stormes to come. **1627** MILTON *Vac. Exerc.* 13 If it happen as I did forecast. **1633** G. HERBERT *Temple, Discharge* xi, Either grief will not come: or if it must, Do not forecast. *a* **1853** ROBERTSON *Serm.* Ser. III. (1872) ii. 24 The merchant, who forecasts, saves, denies himself systematically through years to amass a fortune.

3. (? from the *sb.*) To take a forecast of (the sky, weather); to exhibit a forecast of; to foreshadow.

1883 MRS. ROLLINS *New Eng. Bygones* 94 They forecasted the sky, and planned the toils of the morrow. **1889** J. M. ROBERTSON *Ess. towards Crit. Meth.* 33 His..explication of æsthetic impressions forecasts Diderot.

Hence **fore'casted** *ppl. a.*

1882 *Nature* XXVI. 552 A single communication of forecasted weather.

forecastable (fɔəˈkɑːstəb(ə)l, -æ-, ˈfɔə-), *a.* [f. FORECAST *v.* + -ABLE.] That may be forecast.

1897 'MARK TWAIN' *Following Equator* 546 In India, the annual man-killings by snakes are..as forecastable as the tiger-average and suicide-average. **1965** *Philos.* XL. 340 This must not be..forecastable within the calendar.

forecaster (fɔəˈkɑːstə(r), -æ-, ˈfɔə-). [f. FORECAST *v.* + -ER[1].] One who forecasts.

1639 J. CLARKE *Parœmiologia* 252 A good forecaster is better than a bad worker. **1862** *Times* 12 Apr., The forecasters of probable weather. **1870** *Standard* 13 Dec., The end of which the boldest forecaster of political events dare not venture to determine.

†**forecastful,** *a. Obs.* [f. FORECAST *sb.* + -FUL.] Full of forecast, foresight, or forethought.

1576 NEWTON *Lemnie's Complex.* (1633) 183 Neither by use, forecastfull, sharpe witted, nor crafty. **1594** CAREW *Huarte's Exam. Wits* (1616) 204 It is necessarie that he hold a difference of imagination, fore-castfull, warie.

forecasting (fɔəˈkɑːstɪŋ, -æ-, ˈfɔə-), *vbl. sb.* [f. FORECAST *v.* + -ING[1].] The action of the vb. FORECAST.

1388 WYCLIF *Job* xxxiv. 27 Whiche ȝeden awei fro hym bi castyng afore [*v.r.* fore castynge: Vulg. *de industria*]. *a* **1529** SKELTON *Sp. Parrot* 457 So myche forcastyng. **1548** HALL *Chron., Edw. IV* (an. 11) 224 His besy divises, and pollitique forcastynges. **1829** CARLYLE *Misc.* (1857) II 86 The forecasting of the most indubitable Seer. **1842** MANNING *Serm.* (1848) I. xxiv. 350 All feelings, all cares, all forecastings.

forecasting (fɔəˈkɑːstɪŋ, -æ-, ˈfɔə-), *ppl. a.* [f. as prec. + -ING[2].] That forecasts, in senses of the vb.

1548 HALL *Chron., Hen. IV* (an. 1) 13 By his prudent and forecastyng councell. **1622** BACON *Hen. VII,* 5 Being..not very apprehensiue or forecasting of future Euents. **1688** BOYLE *Final Causes Nat. Things* iv. 166 A forecasting, as well as a designing, agent. **1807** SCOTT *Lett.* 15 May, Your Ladyship will..commend my early and fore-casting prudence in this matter. **1856** LEVER *Martins of Cro' M.* 296 Dreamy, projective and forecasting existence.

Hence **fore'castingly** *adv.*

1548 THOMAS *Ital. Gram.* (1567), *Prouidamente,* wisely or forecastyngly. **1677** MIEGE *Eng.-Fr. Dict.,* Forecastingly, *avec prevoiance.* **1860** *All Year Round* No. 39. 299 Enmities had to be forecastingly provided against.

'forecastle. Also written fo'c'sle, after sailors' pronunc. (ˈfəʊks(ə)l). [f. FORE- + CASTLE.]

1. *Naut.* A short raised deck at the fore end of a vessel. In early use raised like a castle to command the enemy's decks. *Obs.* exc. *arch.* or *Hist.*

c **1400** *Destr. Troy* 5657 The forcastels full of fuerse men of armys. *a* **1533** LD. BERNERS *Huon* xxiii. 440 The fore castell of whyght crystal. **1624** CAPT. SMITH *Virginia* III. vi. 62 Targets..about the forepart of our Boat like a fore-castle. **1748** *Anson's Voy.* I. iii. 29 The forecastle was manned with its customary watch. **1805** in Nicolas *Disp. Nelson* (1846) VII. 203 *note,* Her people still firing from her tops, forecastle and lower-deck. **1863** LONGF. *Wayside Inn, Saga of Olaf* XIX. vi, On the forecastle Ulf the Red watched the lashing of the Ships.

2. The fore part of a ship (see quots. 1704, 1867). ***to ride forecastle in,*** i.e. with bows under.

1490 CAXTON *Eneydos* xxxi. 116 Theyr chyeff maryner.. was halfe a slepe vpon the forcastell. *a* **1529** SKELTON *Col. Cloute* 1253 The forecastell of my shyp Shall glyde, and smothely slyp Out of the waves wod Of the stormy flod. *a* **1661** HOLYDAY *Juvenal* 232 Sometimes the one end, as the fore-castle, sometimes the other, as the sterne. **1704** J. HARRIS *Lex. Techn., Fore-castle of a Ship* is that part where the Fore-Mast stands, and 'tis divided from the rest of the Floor by a Bulk-head; that part of the *Fore-castle* which is aloft, and not in the Hold, is called the Prow. **1719** DE FOE *Crusoe* I. 9 Our Ship rid Forecastle in. **1794** NELSON 26 Oct. in Nicolas *Disp.* (1845) I. 499 We are riding forecastle in. **1867** SMYTH *Sailor's Word-bk., Forecastle*..is now applied in men-of-war to that part of the upper deck forward of the after-shroud.

3. In merchant vessels, the forward part of the vessel, under the deck, where the sailors live.

1840 R. H. DANA *Bef. Mast* ix. 19 No man can..know what sailors are, unless he has lived in the forecastle with them. **1888** W. C. RUSSELL *Death Ship* I. xviii. 251 A ship of which there were a thousand stories afloat in every forecastle throughout the world.

4. *attrib.* and *Comb.* Chiefly attributive (of or pertaining to the forecastle), as ***forecastle-deck, -hatch, -joke, -netting, -rail, -song, -yarn;*** also **forecastle-man,** a sailor stationed on the forecastle.

1726 SHELVOCKE *Voy. round World* (1757) 229 The *forecastle conversation. **1851** H. MELVILLE *Whale* i. 5 The ..pure air of the *forecastle deck. **1869** C. GIBBON *R. Gray* vi, He laid down near the *forecastle hatch. **1867** SMYTH *Sailor's Word-bk.,* **Forecastle-jokes,* practical tricks played upon greenhorns. **1804** *Naval Chron.* XII. 246 Except the *Forecastlemen. **1823** J. F. COOPER *Pioneer* xx, He handles an axe much the same as a forecastleman his marlin-spike. **1867** SMYTH *Sailor's Word-bk.,* **Forecastle-nettings. Ibid.,* **Forecastle-rail,* the rail extended on stanchions across the after-part of the forecastle-deck in some ships. **1856** KANE *Arct. Expl.* II. xxiv. 243 Their old *forecastle songs. **1873** [T. E. BROWN] (*title*), Betsy Lee: a *fo'c's'le yarn.

fore-catching, -chains, -chamber: see FORE- 2 c, 3 a, d.

†**'fore-chase.** *Obs.* [f. FORE- *pref.* + CHASE *sb.*]

1. A chase, hunt, or rush forwards.

c **1611** CHAPMAN *Iliad* XVII. 637 Not a man sustain'd The forechace, nor the after-fight.

2. The bow chase-guns of a ship.

1726 SHELVOCKE *Voy. round World* (1757) 202 Plying us with his forechase. **1745** P. THOMAS *Jrnl. Anson's Voy.* 281 We..began the Engagement with our Fore-chace.

†**fore'choose,** *v. Obs.* [f. FORE- *pref.* + CHOOSE *v.*] *trans.* To choose beforehand, pre-elect.

a **1400** *Prymer* (1891) 27 God ches hyre and forches hire, And he maketh hire dwelle in his tabernacle. *c* **1400** MAUNDEV. (1839) xii. 132 Sche was forchosen from the begynnynge of the World. **1553** *Short Catech.* 38 a, We are forechosen..to euerlasting lyfe.

Hence **fore'chosen** *ppl. a.;* **fore'choosing** *vbl. sb.,* the action of the vb.

1577-87 HOLINSHED *Chron.* III. 1054/1 Not vnderstanding God..and how through all dangers he saueth his forechosen. **1580** SIDNEY *Arcadia* (1622) 109 Without framing out of her owne will the fore-chosing of any thing.

ˌfore-'cited, *ppl. a.* [f. FORE- *pref.* + CITED.] Previously cited.

1576 FLEMING *Panopl. Epist.* 194 The forecited young men. **1674** ALLEN *Dang. Enthus.* 49 The Prophesie fore-cited. **1736** POPE *Dunc.* I. *note,* The forecited critic. **1875** E. WHITE *Life in Christ* II. xv. (1878) 174 The fore-cited passages.

fore-claw: see FORE- *pref.*[1] 3 c.

foreclosable (fɔəˈkləʊzəb(ə)l), *a.* [f. FORECLOSE *v.*[2] + -ABLE.] That may be foreclosed.

1890 *Harper's Mag.* June 154/2 A highly foreclosable mortgage in stock. **1892** *Nation* (N.Y.) 1 Dec. 407/2 We continue to regard railroad bonds as foreclosable.

foreclose (fɔəˈkləʊz), *v.* Forms: 3-6 forclose, 6 *Sc.* foirclois, 6- foreclose. [f. *forclos-,* stem of *forclore,* f. *for-,* FOR- *pref.*[3] + *clore* to CLOSE. Some of the senses may have originated from or have been influenced by the identification of the prefix with FOR-[1] (cf. OE. *forclýsan* to close, stop up), or with FOR-[2], FORE- (cf. *preclude*).]

1. *trans.* To bar, exclude, shut out completely.

[**1292** BRITTON VI. ii. §8 Les plus proscheins heirs, qi par les feffours en sount forclos.] **1413** *Pilgr. Sowle* (Caxton) I. xxi. (1859) 21 Thenne am I nought forclosyd oute of this court [orig. *forclos donques ne suis ie pas*]. *c* **1489** CAXTON *Sonnes of Aymon* xii. 289 He forclosed me fro all my kynsmen. **1563** *Mirr. Mag., Ld. Hastings* xvii, Greenish waues and heauie lowring skies All comfort else forclosed our exiled eies. **1581** J. BELL *Haddon's Answ. Osor.* 314 b, [They] ought not deteigne, and foreclose other men from the knowledge of Holy Scripture. **1732** NEAL *Hist. Purit.* I. 229 The Puritans being thus foreclosed and shut out of the Church. **1850** BLACKIE *Æschylus* II. 125 My flight to foreclose from the chase of my foes! **1883** L. O. PIKE *Yearbks. 11 & 12 Edw. III*, Pref. 24 The certificate of the bishop.. would be a sufficient answer to foreclose her should she bring a writ of dower.

†**b.** To bar or stop up (one's) passage. *Obs.*

c **1290** *S. Eng. Leg.* I. 303/143 þe se for-closede hire sone.

†**2.** To close fast, close or stop up, block up (an opening, way, etc.) *Obs.*

1547 HALL *Chron., Hen. VII*, 43 a, All by waies beyng stopped and forclosed. **1561** T. NORTON *Calvin's Inst* II. 106 The entrie vnto it is forclosed and impossible to be come to. **1600** HOLLAND *Livy* VIII. xxiv. (1609) 298 The continuall raines..had foreclosed and stopped the passages. **1655** CALTHROP *Reports* (1670) 158 If any common way or common course of water be foreclosed or letted. **1751** J. BROWN *Shaftesb. Charac.* 178 Every avenue is foreclosed, by which virtue should enter.

3. To preclude, hinder, or prohibit (a person) *from* (an action) or *to do* something; to hinder the action, working, or activity of.

1536 *Act 28 Hen. VIII*, c. 7 §6 Children borne.. vnder the same mariage..shall be..vtterly forclosed, excluded and barred to claime..as laufull heyre. **1602** CAREW *Cornwall* 19 b, The Imbargo with Spaine..foreclosed this trade. *Ibid.* 112 b, Foreclosing all others, saue themselves, from dredging of Oysters. **1648** PRYNNE *Plea for Lords* 36 This Protestation did not foreclose the Lords..to give Judgement against Commoners. **1681** LUTTRELL *Brief. Rel.* (1857) I. 145 He had obtained his liberty on bail..but..the court had since..found there was an impeachment against him..and therefore their hands being foreclosed, they discharged his bail. **1705** STANHOPE *Paraphr.* I. 187 [He] had thereby..foreclosed himself from remitting the Guilt and Punishment. **1720** WATERLAND *Answ. Whitby's Reply* §14 You resolve..to make a show of saying something, though you find yourself already foreclosed. **1732** BERKELEY *Serm. Soc. Prop. Gosp.* Wks. III. 245 A mind not hardened by impenitency, nor foreclosed by pride. **1796** COLERIDGE *Ode Departing Year* i, Ere yet the enter'd cloud foreclosed my sight.

b. To debar from the enjoyment *of.*

1865 NICHOLS *Britton* II. 31 We will that the lords be foreclosed of such homage. **1876** LOWELL *Poet. Wks.* (1879) 470 Are we..Foreclosed of Beauty by our modern date?

c. To preclude or prevent (an action or event).

1546 in *St. Papers Hen. VIII* (1852) XI. v. 121 Consydre ..wheder forclosing of victailling shalbe expedyent. **1813** SCOTT *Rokeby* VI. 17 Nor hope discovery to foreclose By giving me to feed the crows.

4. *Law of Mortgage.* To bar or exclude (the person entitled to redeem) upon non-payment of money due; to deprive of the equity of redemption. Const. *from*; also with double *obj.*

1728 VERNON *Rep.* II. 235 The first Mortgagee brought a Bill against the second, to compel him to redeem or to be foreclosed, and foreclosed him accordingly. **1734** *Act Geo. II*, c. 20 §1 Mortgagees frequently..commence Suits in his Majesty's Courts of Equity, to foreclose their Mortgagors from redeeming their Estates. **1844** WILLIAMS *Real Prop.* (1877) 428 He may be foreclosed his equity of redemption.

b. To bar (a right of redemption); to take away the power of redeeming (a mortgage).

1704 *Lond. Gaz.* No. 4057/4 The Equity of Redemption is foreclosed on certain Mortgages. **1824** W. IRVING *T. Trav.* (1849) 390 Tom Walker never returned to foreclose the mortgage.

5. To close beforehand; to answer or settle by anticipation.

1722 DE FOE *Moll Flanders* (1840) 80 He had foreclosed all manner of objection. **1849** *Tait's Mag.* XVI. 399/2 Warburton has confessed that Charles was a despot, and has thereby foreclosed his case. **1865** GROTE *Plato* I. vi. 254 Points already settled and foreclosed.

6. To establish an exclusive claim to.

1599 DANIEL *Musophilus* cxxxi, That immense and boundless ocean Of Nature's riches, never yet found out, Nor foreclosed with the wit of any man. **1817** COLERIDGE *Biog. Lit.* I. xi. 228 Instead of being foreclosed and immovable, it [church property] is in fact the only species of landed property that is essentially moving and circulative. **1838** EMERSON *Addr., Cambridge (Mass.)* Wks. (Bohn) II. 195 And finding not names and places..but even virtue and truth foreclosed and monopolized.

Hence **fore'closed** *ppl. a.*; **fore'closing** *vbl. sb.*

1594 CAREW *Tasso* (1881) 23 Passages forclosde wide ope to make. **1598** SIR T. NORREYS in *Lismore Papers* Ser. II. (1887) I. 15 The Tenants to haue the forclosinge of there owen Tythes. **1883** *Gd. Words* 240 A foreclosed mortgage. **1895** *Daily News* 6 June 5/4 There are 149 of such foreclosed estates to come under the hammer.

foreclosure (fɔə'kləʊʒ(j)ʊə(r)). [f. FORECLOSE *v.* + -URE.] The action of foreclosing (a mortgage) or depriving (a mortgagor) of the power of redeeming a mortgaged estate; a proceeding to bar the right of redeeming mortgaged property. attrib., *foreclosure action.*

1728 VERNON *Rep.* II. 235 The Defendant pleaded the former suit and decree of foreclosure. **1818** CRUISE *Digest* (ed. 2) II. 103 The decree of foreclosure was obtained by.. fraud. **1875** LE FANU *Willing to Die* xxxiv. 202 Foreclosures, bills of exchange hovering threateningly in the air.

transf. **1865** *Daily Tel.* 6 Nov. 5/4 The Arab..has been driven by foreclosure from the plains into the mountains.

attrib. **1862** *Macm. Mag.* July 185 The advertisements.. are chiefly of patent medicines..and foreclosure sales. **1905** *Westm. Gaz.* 15 May 2/1 [The] suggestion of a foreclosure without a foreclosure action. **1929** *Encycl. Brit.* IX. 494/2 A foreclosure action is brought by the mortgagee against the mortgagor in the chancery division of the High Court in England. **1959** JOWITT *Dict. Eng. Law* I. 818/1 Foreclosure actions are now comparatively rare in practice.

fore'come, *v. rare.* [OE. *for-, forecuman*, f. FOR-², FORE- *pref.* + *cuman* COME *v.* Chiefly used in imitation of L. *prævenire.*] †**a.** *intr.* To come before the usual time; to come early (*obs.*⁻¹). **b.** *trans.* To come before, anticipate (*rare*). †**c.** To gain the advantage of, overcome (*obs.*).

c **900** tr. *Bæda's Hist.* IV. xxvi. [xxv]. (1891) 350 þætte þu seo forecumende Drihtnes onsyne [orig. *præoccupando Dei faciem*] in andetnisse. *c* **1000** *Ags. Ps.* xvi[i]. 14[13] (Spelman), Aris, Drihten, forcum hi. *a* **1300** *E.E. Psalter* ibid., Ris up, Laverd, for-come him swa. *Ibid.* cxviii. [cxix.] 147, I for-come in ripenes, and made crie. *c* **1300** *Cursor M.* 10068 (Cott.) Quar-thoru þe warlaw, wirid wight, For-cummen es and has tint his might. **1860** PUSEY *Min. Proph.* 513 We are forecome by the grace of God.

Hence **fore'coming** *ppl. a.*; **fore'comingness.**

1839 BAILEY *Festus* (1848) 29/2 The..forecomingness of things. **1860** PUSEY *Min. Proph.* 502 God's forecoming love.

fore-commend, etc.: see FORE- *pref.*

†**fore-conceit.** *Obs.* [f. FORE- *pref.*] A conception previously formed; a preconception.

1581 SIDNEY *Apol. Poetrie* (Arb.) 26 That Idea or fore-conceite of the work. *a* **1600** HOOKER *Eccl. Pol.* VII. (1617) 472 A fore-conceit thus qualified. **1640** BP. REYNOLDES *Passions* xl. 522 The Fore-conceipt of eternall blisse.

†ˌ**fore-con'ceited,** *ppl. a.* [f. FORE- *pref.*] Conceived beforehand. (But the orig. has *pour-pensée.*)

1591 SYLVESTER *Du Bartas* I. i. 213 Some fantastick fore-conceited Plot.

†ˌ**forecon'ceive,** *v. Obs.* [f. FORE- *pref.*] *trans.* To conceive beforehand, to preconceive.

1553 GRIMALDE tr. *Cicero's Offices* (1556) 31 b, The other proceedes of a greate witt, to fore conceiue in minde thinges to comme. **1597** BACON *Coulers Good & Evill* (Arb.) 149 By expecting, or foreconceyuing, that [etc.]. **1628** BP. HALL tr. *Rotomagensis Anon.* Wks. 815 Which He..hath foreconceiued in His certaine and vnchangeable decree. **1659** TORRIANO, *Premeditáre*, to forethink, to fore-conceive in mind.

Hence ˌ**forecon'ceived** *ppl. a.*

1561 T. NORTON *Calvin's Inst.* III. 175 The foundation hereof is a fore conceiued perswasion of the truthe of God. **1600** FAIRFAX *Tasso* VIII. lxxiii, But fore-conceiued griefes.. The ire still nourished. **1662** GLANVILL *Lux Orient.* xi. (1682) 88 Their own fore-conceived notions.

fore-conclude, -course, etc.: see FORE- *pref.*

foreconscious (ˌfɔə'kɒnʃəs), *a.* (*sb.*). *Psychol.* [tr. G. *vorbewusst* (see PRECONSCIOUS *a.*), f. FORE- + CONSCIOUS *a.*] Pertaining to that part of the mind, below the threshold of immediate conscious attention, whose memories and perceptions can re-enter the conscious field; = PRECONSCIOUS *a.* Also as *sb.*

1915 C. R. PAYNE tr. *Pfister's Psychoanalytic Method* 47 Freud distinguishes foreconscious ideas which lack only the conscious investment of energy, from the real unconscious, but attributes to this distinction more practical than theoretical value. **1915** STEDMAN *Med. Dict.* (ed. 3) 348/1 *Fore-conscious*, noting an unconscious mental process which becomes conscious only on the fulfillment of certain conditions. **1920** T. P. NUNN *Education* (1923) 49 The complex may be on the 'fore-conscious' level—that is the ideas belonging to its activity, though forgotten, may be capable of being recalled. **1921** *Sat. Westm. Gaz.* 1 Oct. 16/2 The fore-conscious or marginal region of the mind. **1924** E. E. CUMMINGS *Let.* 27 Feb. (1969) 105 Many voices answer ..but not mine because *gas-bill* flashed thru our hero's foreconscious. **1942** J. G. MILLER *Unconsciousness* i. 20 Preconscious and foreconscious. These are psychoanalytic terms used synonymously. **1957** R. L. MUNROE *Schools of Psychoanalytic Thought* II. iii. 82 The perceptual conscious is what we are actually aware of at any given moment. This rather narrow field extends into the preconscious or foreconscious (the terms are interchangeable), which includes the host of immediate perceptions and memories available to us if our attention requires them.

fore-court ('fɔəkɔət). [f. FORE- *pref.* + COURT *sb.*]

The court or enclosed space in front of a building, the first or outer court. *spec.* the petrol-dispensing part of a filling-station.

1535 COVERDALE *Ezek.* x. 5 The sounde of the Cherubins wynges was herde in to the forecourte. **1668** EVELYN *Diary* 14 Aug., A slip of ground..to enlarge my fore-court. **1814** SCOTT *Wav.* xv, Waverley repaired to the fore-court as it was called. **1865** ELIZA METEYARD *Life Wedgwood* I. 252 The ivy-clad cottage, with its forecourt or garden standing to the front, the kilns and sheds behind. **1884** C. MARVIN *Centr. Asia* 28 Through the crowded forecourt and bazaar. **1958** *Motor* 24 Sept. 239 Most motorists patronize a particular garage when they are on their home ground, having found that the forecourt service is efficient and.. reflects good workmanship in the premises behind. **1961** *Oxford Mail* 4 Oct. 2/5 Girl or boy to train as forecourt attendant. **1969** *Guardian* 11 Aug. 5/6 Stamps are 'paid' for on the forecourt by artificially high prices.

fig. **1867** J. H. STIRLING in *Fortn. Rev.* Oct. 377 These to him (with Ontology, but only as fore-court) constituted Metaphysic.

fore-covert, -crop, etc.: see FORE- *pref.* 3, 5.

†**fore-currour.** *Obs. rare*⁻¹. [f. FORE- *pref.* + *currour*, COURIER *sb.*] = AVANT-COURIER.

1548 UDALL, etc., *Erasmus Par. Mark* i. 9 John..played the forecurrour.

fore-dated, -day: see FORE- *pref.* 2 b, 4 a.

fore-dawn: see FORE *adv.* and *prep.* 8.

†'**fore-deck.** *Obs.* [f. FORE- *pref.*¹ + DECK *sb.*] The deck at the fore-part of a ship; the fore-part of the deck.

1565 GOLDING *Ovid's Met.* III. (1593) 76 The god..out of the foredecke cast His eie upon the sea. **1653** H. COGAN tr. *Pinto's Trav.* xx. 73 The remainder..retired in disorder towards the foredeck. **1747** CARTE *Hist. Eng.* I. 306 At the stern and on the foredeck.

fig. **1637** GILLESPIE *Eng. Pop. Cerem.* Ep. B iij, Because the foredecke and hindecke of all our Opposites probations, doe resolve and rest finally into the Auctority of a Law.

fore-declare, -decree, -define: see FORE-.

†ˌ**fore'deem,** *v. Obs.* [f. FORE- + DEEM.]

1. *trans.* To form a judgement of beforehand; to forecast, presage. Also *intr.* with *of.*

1542 UDALL *Erasm. Apoph.* 288 b, To foredeme the wurste. **1557** N. T. (Genev.) *Acts* xvi. 16 *marg. note*, Which [maid] could gesse and foredeeme of things past, present and to come. *a* **1639** SPOTTISWOOD *Hist. Ch. Scot.* v. (1677) 272 Many did foredeem that he should not escape some misfortune. **1660** *Plea Minist. Sequestration* 6 Too truly foredeeming their own turbulent subsequent actions if they regain their power.

2. To deem or account in advance.

1612 WEBSTER *White Devil* I. i, Laugh at your misery, as foredeeming you An idle meteor.

Hence **fore'deemed** *ppl. a.*; **fore'deeming** *vbl. sb.*

1587 T. HUGHES *Misfort. Arthur* IV. iii. (1828) 67 You frame a cause of long foredeemed doome. **1587** GOLDING *De Mornay* Pref. 10 Foredeemings and fore-setled opinions. **1610** HOLLAND *Camden's Brit.* I. 8 The deceitfull conjectures and foredeemings of one Merline.

†'**foreden.** *Obs.* Also 3 fareden. [repr. OE. *fáræden, f. *fá*, FOE + *ræden* condition: see -RED. The modern form would have been *foered.*] Foeship, enmity.

c **1205** LAY. 4067 Cloten heo o-scuneden & his færedene for-howede. **1297** R. GLOUC. (Rolls) App. G. 59 And Cloten hi for leten & his foredene for howede. *a* **1300** *Cursor M.* 895 (Cott.) Fra þis dai fareden [*Gött.* foredin] sal be, Forsoth, bituix womman and þe.

fore-denounced, -desk, etc.: see FORE- *pref.*

fore'destine, *v.* [f. FORE- *pref.* + DESTINE *v.*] *trans.* To destine beforehand, predestine.

a **1300** *Cursor M.* 417 (Cott.) He fordestend tuin creature to serue him in þat hali ture. *Ibid.* 25270 (Cott.) All þat þou has fordestind ar, to þe kingrike of heuen blis. **1880** W. WATSON *Prince's Quest* (1892) 105 Our king foredestined from his mother's womb.

fore'destiny. [f. FORE- *pref.* + DESTINY.] †**a.** A declaration of what is destined to happen, prediction (*obs.*). **b.** = DESTINY 4.

1548 HOOPER *Declar. 10 Commandm.* iv. F j, These blind coniectures and foredestenis. **1871** MORLEY *Voltaire* (1886) 2 Invincible forces of grace, election and foredestiny.

foredoom ('fɔədu:m), *sb.* [f. FORE- *pref.* + DOOM *sb.*] A doom or judgement pronounced beforehand; destiny.

1563 SACKVILLE *Induct. Mirr. Mag.* lxiii, Ioves vnmooved sentence and foredoome On Priam kyng. **1625** K. LONG tr. *Barclay's Argenis* II. xvii. 125 Kings Councels, and the gods fore-doome..She knows. **1839** BAILEY *Festus* (1854) 346 An opening scene in Heaven, wherein The fore-doom of all things..Is shewn.

foredoom (fɔə'du:m), *v.* [f. FORE- *pref.* + DOOM *v.*]

1. *trans.* To doom beforehand: **a.** to condemn beforehand (*to* a destiny, or *to do* something); **b.** to foreordain, predestine (a thing).

a. 1608 SHAKS. *Lear* V. iii. 291 (Qo. 2) Your eldest daughters haue fore-doom'd [*Qo.* 1 foredoome; *Fol.* foredone] themselues. **1647** MAY *Hist. Parl.* I. ii. 23 Men.. fore-doomed by an Oracle to a bad fortune. **1715–20** POPE *Iliad* XVI. 545 Sons of gods, foredoom'd to death, Before proud Ilion. **1808** J. BARLOW *Columb.* IV. 20 O hapless prelate!..Foredoom'd with crimes a fruitless war to wage. **1855** H. REED *Lect. Eng. Hist.* viii. 270 The ruthless judges, who had foredoomed her. **1878** BOSW. SMITH *Carthage* 150 His efforts were, for the present foredoomed to failure.

b. 1674 N. FAIRFAX *Bulk & Selv.* 162 Foredooming that which is to be, and is not, till so foredoom'd. **1712–4** POPE *Rape Lock* III. 5 Here Britain's statesmen oft the fall fore-doom Of foreign tyrants. **1814** SOUTHEY *Roderick* XI, A field ..For bloody theatre of famous deeds Foredoom'd. **1844** MRS. BROWNING *Drama of Exile* Poems 1850 I. 62 Had God foredoomed despair, He had not spoken hope.

2. To determine beforehand as a doom; to forecast, foreshadow, presage.

a **1592** GREENE *George a Greene* Wks. (Rtldg.) 261/2 A wizer wizard never met you yet, Nor one that better could foredoom your fall. **1818** KEATS *Endym.* I. 252 Broad leaved fig trees even now foredoom Their ripen'd fruitage.

Hence **fore'doomed** *ppl. a.* Also **fore'doomer.**

1591 *Troub. Raigne K. John* II. (1611) 75 Disturbed thoughts, foredoomers of mine ill. **1700** DRYDEN *Pal. & Arcite* III. 636 As Fate foredoom'd, and all things tend..to their appointed End. **1868** E. EDWARDS *Raleigh* I. xxv. 603 To face..the perils of a foredoomed enterprise.

'fore-door. [f. FORE- *pref.* + DOOR.] A door in the front of a building, a front-door. Now *rare.*

1581 LAMBARDE *Eiren.* II. vii. (1588) 295 His brother.. shut the foredoore against them that pursued. **1674** tr. *Scheffer's Lapland* 84 Two doors, one, a foredoor, and the other, a backward. **1696** EDWARDS *Exist. & Provid. of God* II. 20 With the mouth (that so visible and useful fore-door of this our humane habitation) we take in food. **1761** *Brit. Mag.* II. 558 The rogues..fastened the fore-door before they left the house. **1811** W. AITON *Agric. Surv. Ayrsh.* 115 (Jam.) The principal door—was named the fore-door.

†**'foredrove.** *Obs.* [f. FORE- *pref.* + DROVE.] An animal or animals driven before the corpse at a funeral, a corse-present or mortuary.

1504 *Will of J. Osburne* in *Trans. Essex Archæol. Soc.* Ser. II. I. 167, I bequeth ij shepe of a yere age for my fore Drove. **1536** *Will of W. Perte* ibid. 168 A shepe price ijs. which I will shall be dreven before me in the day of my buryall for a foredrove.

fore-eatage: see FORE- *pref.* 5 b.

fore-edge ('fɔərɛdʒ). [f. FORE- *pref.* + EDGE.] The front or outer edge; *esp.* of a leaf in a book, or of the book itself. ***fore-edge painting*** (see quot. 1960).

1665 HOOKE *Microgr.* 174 The fore-edge..is arm'd with a multitude of little bristles. **1880** *Print. Trades Jrnl.* No. 32. 1 To cut heads, tails, and fore-edges at one time. **1886** WILLIS & CLARK *Cambridge* III. 420 The book is placed on the shelf with the fore-edge turned outwards. **1892** ZAEHNSDORF *Binding of Bks.* 14 Catch each succeeding leaf up by the forefinger on the top corner as near the for-edge as possible. **1912** A. J. PHILIP *Business of Bookbinding* 199 *Foredge painting*, pictures found, usually in old books, on the fore-edge of books. **1938** *Times Lit. Suppl.* 17 Dec. 808/2 A seventeenth-century English Bible..with a signed fore-edge painting. **1960** G. A. GLAISTER *Gloss. Bk.* 143/2 *Fore-edge painting*, a water colour painted on the fanned out fore-edge of a book. **1969** *Canad. Antiques Coll.* Apr. 23/1 Fore-edge paintings in rare books provide not only delight to collectors but mysteries in more ways than one.

fore-elders ('fɔərɛldəz), *pl.* Chiefly northern. For forms see ELDER. [f. FORE- *pref.* + ELDER(S. Cf. ON. *foreldrar* in same sense (Da. *forældre*, Sw. *föräldrar* parents).] Ancestors, progenitors.

a **1300** *Cursor M.* 18362 (Cott.) þou has þam drund and don forfare, Als þou til ur for-eildres suare. *c* **1425** WYNTOUN *Cron.* IX. xvii. 6 As þare For-elderis ware slane to Dede. **1525** Q. MARG. in M. A. E. Wood *Lett. R. & Illustr. Ladies* (1852) I. 372 They may..live under him as his subjects, as their foreelders has done in time past. **1627** SANDERSON *Serm.* I. 265 Our Romish catholicks often twit us with our fore-elders. What, say they, were they not all down-right papists? **1710** BP. NICOLSON in Ellis *Orig. Lett.* Ser. I. III. 359 Principles on which their fore-elders built the gude wark of reformation. **1843** *For. & Colon. Q. Rev.* II. 349 The former must have been visited by the fore-elders of mankind earlier than Egypt. **1876** *Mr. Gray & his Neighbours* I. 26 John Dannay lived upon his own lands as his fore-elders had done from time immemorial.

fore-end ('fɔərɛnd). [f. FORE- *pref.*[1] + END.]

1. a. Of place: The fore part, front. Now chiefly *Naut.*

c **1425** *Found. St. Bartholomew's* (E.E.T.S.) 39 Seynt Barthilmewe..with his holy hande drewe forth the shippe by the for ende. *c* **1489** CAXTON *Blanchardyn* vii. 29 He dyde cut of the hed, & henged hit atte forende of his sadel. *a* **1626** BACON *New Atl.* Wks. 1778 I. 352 In the fore-end of it which was towards him, grew a..branch of palm. **1833** MARRYAT *P. Simple* xiv, Mr. Chucks then sat down upon the fore-end of the booms. **1878** W. C. RUSSELL *Wreck of Grosvenor* xxi, I crawled to the fore-end of the poop.

b. The fore part of the stock of a gun, which supports the barrel. Also *attrib.*

1881 GREENER *Gun* 250 The finisher..has to file up and shape the stock and fore-end. *Ibid.* 256 All that is required being a sufficient grip to keep the fore-end to the barrels. *Ibid.* 487 Grasp the gun..close to the fore-end tip.

c. = *fore-hock.*

1906 MRS. BEETON *Househ. Managem.* 628 Fore end.. weight about 17 lb. **1951** *Good Housek. Home Encycl.* 343/1 For boiling, choose a piece of fore-end or gammon. **1960** *Farmer & Stockbreeder* 16 Feb. (Suppl.) 11/2 Good length, well-shaped hams..fine fore-end and head.

d. *pl.* The forward space in a submarine, used for the storage of torpedoes and as living-quarters for members of the crew; also, the submarine ratings quartered there. *colloq.*

1940 G. HACKFORTH-JONES *Submarine Flotilla* i. 24 A torpedo..had slipped through its carrying-band and plunged into the 'fore-ends'. **1942** —— *One-One-One* i. 7 Petty Officer John Rodgers, the Torpedo Gunner's Mate, was browsing over his torpedo tubes in the 'Fore-ends' of the *Plunger*. *Ibid.*, Those [torpedoes] ready for firing lying concealed in the tubes..were the pride of the 'Fore-ends' crew. **1958** J. D. DRUMMOND *H.M. U-Boat* vii. 105 Naval Intelligence..indicated that the 'Salmon and Gluckstein'—as the fore-ends lightly nicknamed the enemy heavy units—were ready to make a dash for it. *Ibid.* viii. 118 The long-suffering Scots in the fore-ends.

2. Of time: The beginning, early part. Now *dial.*; chiefly = *spring.*

1611 SHAKS. *Cymb.* III. iii. 73 Where I haue..payed More pious debts to Heauen, then in all The fore-end of my time. **1768** WALES in *Phil. Trans.* LX. 123 In the fore end of December, I went to one of the hunters tents. **1816** SCOTT *Antiq.* xxvii, 'I will be back about the fore end o' har'st.' **1855** ROBINSON *Whitby Gloss.*, 'The fore end of the year', spring. **1890** W. A. WALLACE *Only a Sister* xiv, 'Yow've read about her i' the papers maybe last fore-end?'

3. *Comb.* **fore-end loader** *Agric.*, a loader attached to the front of a tractor or other vehicle; a FORE-LOADER.

1958 *Times* 15 Dec. 2/5 The indiscriminate use of fore-end loaders can add materially to the dirt tare. **1964** J. C. TURNER *Farm Machinery* ix. 82 When using a fore-end loader the following..should be remembered... The load should not be lifted higher than necessary.

fore-engage, -estate, etc.: see FORE- *pref.*

†**fore-entry, -entresse.** Chiefly *Sc. Obs.* [f. FORE- *pref.* + ENTRY, ENTRESSE.] A front entrance, vestibule.

1535 COVERDALE *Jer.* xxxvii. 21 In the fore entrie off the preson. *a* **1557** *Diurn. Occurrents* (1833) 44 With tuelf cannonis on the foirentres. *a* **1572** KNOX *Hist. Ref.* Wks. 1846 I. 121 The Englismen..hasarded a schoote at the for-entree of the Castell. **1673** WEDDERBURN *Voc.* 11 (Jam.) *Propylaeum*, a fore-entresse.

forefather ('fɔəfɑːðə(r)). For forms see FATHER. [f. FORE- *pref.* + FATHER. ON. had *forfaðir*. Cf. FORM-, FORN-, FORTH-FATHER.] An ancestor, a progenitor. Chiefly *pl.* ***forefathers' day*** (U.S.): the anniversary of the day on which the first settlers landed at Plymouth, Mass.

a **1300** *Cursor M.* 5464 (Cott.) Jacob..went out of þis wreched werld, And til his forfaders fard. **1377** LANGL. *P. Pl.* B. v. 501 Feddest with thi fresche blode owre forfadres in derknesse. *c* **1450** *Chester Pl.* xii. 163 Our forfather ouercomen was..to doe evill. **1526** *Pilgr. Perf.* (W. de W. 1531) 14 b, Theyr forefathers were baptysed in the reed see. *a* **1682** SIR T. BROWNE *Tracts* (1684) 17 Our Forefathers before the Floud. **1750** GRAY *Elegy* 16 The rude Fore-fathers of the Hamlet. **1821** J. Q. ADAMS in C. Davies *Metr. Syst.* III. (1871) 120 Measures which they and their fore-fathers, time out of mind had employed. **1848** LOWELL *Lett.* (1894) I. 147 It is Fore-fathers' Day, you remember.

transf. and *fig.* **1593** SHAKS. *Rich. II*, II. ii. 35 Conceit is still deriu'd From some fore-father greefe. **1834** HT. MARTINEAU *Moral* I. 6 It is a great thing to possess improved breeds of animals in the place of their forefathers.

Hence **'fore,fatherly** *a.*, of or pertaining to one's forefathers, ancestral.

1855 in CLARKE *Dict.* **1873** *Contemp. Rev.* XXI. 213 Abstruse Englisc, forefatherly and foremotherly as we are assured it is. **1880** G. MEREDITH *Trag. Com.* vi, The clever assortment of our forefatherly heaps of bones.

forefaultry, see FORFAULTRY.

forefeel (fɔə'fiːl), *v.* [f. FORE- + FEEL *v.*] *trans.* To feel beforehand, have a presentiment of.

1580 SIDNEY *Arcadia* II. xviii. 181 b, Erona..forefeeling the harmes which after fell to her. *c* **1611** CHAPMAN *Iliad* XIV. 13 With unwieldy waves the great sea forefeels winds That both ways murmur. *a* **1632** T. TAYLOR *God's Judgem.* I. I. iii. (1642) 410 Sinners..fore-feeling the approach of hell. **1810** W. TAYLOR in *Monthly Mag.* XXIX. 320 To forefeel Her coming joy, redoubles my delight. **1851** MAURICE *Patriarchs & Lawg.* vi. (1867) 122 Those objects were in very deed foreshown and forefelt in his childish aspirations.

Hence **'forefeel** *sb.*; **fore'feeling** (whence **fore'feelingly** *adv.*), **fore'felt** *ppl. adjs.*

1580 SIDNEY *Arcadia* (1622) 380 Fore-felt Desire, begin to sauour part Of comming gladnesse. **1607** TOPSELL *Serpents* (1658) 782 A divine prudence and forefeeling knowledge originally inbred by Nature. **1805** SOUTHEY *Madoc* I. xi, His spirit..beheld with no forefeeling joy The rising sons of song. **1808** —— *Lett.* (1856) II. 117 Well might W. fore-feelingly call our rulers 'A venal band'. **1839** BAILEY *Festus* xxii, Like a fore-feel of madness about the brain.

forefeeling ('fɔəfiːlɪŋ), *vbl. sb.* [f. prec. + -ING[1].] The action of the vb. FOREFEEL; a feeling beforehand, presentiment.

1551 ROBINSON tr. *More's Utop.* (Arb.) 147 Some priuie and secret fore-feiling of the punishement now at hande. **1605** CAMDEN *Rem.*, *Epitaphs* 28 The inuention of them proceeded from the presage or forfeeling of immortality. **1715** tr. *C'tess Daunoy's Wks.* 425 An ominous fore-feeling of their approaching Misfortune. **1803** SOUTHEY *Lett.* (1856) I. 241 His father has..the same forefeeling that..he will not live to be a man. **1878** DOWDEN *Stud. Lit.* 147 Within him lay a forefeeling of the great destiny.

fore-fellow: see FORE- *pref.* 5.

†**'forefence**, *sb. Obs.* [f. FORE- *pref.* + FENCE *sb.*] A first or front defence; a bulwark.

1609 HOLLAND *Amm. Marcell.* XIV. ii. 4 Within their thicke growne Fastnesses and Fore-fences..they maintained and enriched themselves. **1610** —— *Camden's Brit.* I. 755 The Iland Walney as a fore fence or countremure lying along by it. **1677** PLOT *Oxfordsh.* 320 A praetentura, or fore-fence of the Romans raised against the Britans.

Hence **'forefence** *v. trans.*, to serve as an outer defence or bulwark to.

1610 HOLLAND *Camden's Brit.* I. 627 The mountaines of Talgar and Ewias doe as it were forefense it.

forefend: see FORFEND.

forefield ('fɔəfiːld). *Mining.* Also 7–8 forfield. [f. FORE- *pref.* + FIELD *sb.*] (See quots.)

1681 HOUGHTON *Compl. Miner* (E.D.S.), *Forfield*, the furthest place that a man has wrought in his ground, or the end of a meer above-ground. **1755** *Phil. Trans.* XLIX. 401 There was a miner working at the forfield, or east end of the vein. **1881** RAYMOND *Mining Gloss.*, *Forefield*, the face of the workings. The *forefield-end* is the end of the workings farthest advanced.

†**'forefight.** *Obs.* [f. FORE- *pref.* + FIGHT *sb.*] **a.** The foremost defence or bulwark (see FIGHT, *sb.* 5 b). **b.** The front rank (of an army).

c **1611** CHAPMAN *Iliad* XII. 274 The Greeks..repair'd the fore-fights of their wall With hides of oxen. *Ibid.* XV. 277 These were they, that bravely furnish'd then The fierce forefight.

fore-'fighter. *rare*[−1]. [f. FORE- *pref.* + FIGHTER.] One who fights in the front rank.

1883 LEAF *Iliad* IV. 79 Then the forefighters and glorious Hector yielded.

fore-figure, -fin: see FORE- *pref.* 2 a, 3 c.

forefinger ('fɔəfɪŋgə(r)). [f. FORE- *pref.* + FINGER.] The finger next the thumb: also called the *first* or *index finger*.

c **1450** *Voc.* in Wr.-Wülcker 626 Forefyngure, *index.* **1579–80** NORTH *Plutarch* (1676) 43 *note*, When they were conquer'd they held up their fore-finger in sign of yeelding. **1612** PEACHAM *Drawing* II. v, Polymnia shall bee drawne as it were acting her speech with her forefinger. **1713** BERKELEY *Guardian* No. 39 ¶3 Her fore-fingers stuck in her ears. **1847** TENNYSON *Princ.* II. 356 Jewels five-words-long That on the stretch'd forefinger of all Time Sparkle for ever.

fore-fit, -flank, -flipper, etc.: see FORE- *pref.*

[**foreflow** *v.*, 'to flow before', *Dryden*, in Webster (1832) and later Dicts., is a mistake for *foreslow*: see FORSLOW 2. quot. 1682.]

fore-foot ('fɔəfʊt), *sb.* [f. FORE- *pref.* + FOOT.] The stress is variable, the prefix being often felt as an adj.

1. One of the front feet of a quadruped.

1481 CAXTON *Reynard* (Arb.) 18 He had loste his eeris and the skynne wyth the clawes of his forefeet. **1525** LD. BERNERS *Froiss.* II. 312 a, The grayhounde..wolde..leape with his fore fete vpon the Kynges shulders. **1604** BRETON *Pass. Sheph.* Past. iii. 26 To see..the little black-haird Cony ..With her fore-feete wash her face. **1697** *Lond. Gaz.* No. 3330/4 Throws his fore Foot out like a Turky Horse. **1770** G. WHITE *Selborne* xxviii. 79 From the fore-feet to the belly behind the shoulder, it [the moose-deer] measured three feet and eight inches. **1834** MCMURTRIE *Cuvier's Anim. Kingd.* 60 The long claws of their fore-feet enable them to dig with great effect. **1869** DUNKIN *Midn. Sky* 16 The Great Bear's right fore-foot.

†**b.** *jocularly.* The hand.

1599 SHAKS. *Hen. V*, II. i. 71 Giue me thy fist, thy fore-foote to me giue.

2. *Naut.* 'The foremost piece of the keel, or a timber which terminates the keel at the forward extremity, and forms a rest for the stem's lower end' (Adm. Smyth).

[**1644** MANWAYRING *Sea-mans Dict.* sv., There is no such place of a ship which is termed her fore-foote; but..when two ships saile, so that one doth lie with her stem so much a-weather the other, that keeping their courses, that ship which doth so lie, will goe-out a head with the other, then we say, that she doth lie with the fore-foote of the other, as she stands or comes with her fore-foote..so that this word fore-foote, implies no more, but one ships lying, or sayling a-crosse an other ships way.] **1770** *Chron.* in *Ann. Reg.* 153/1 She hung upon this rock by the fore-foot, her stern being amazingly depressed. **1840** R. H. DANA *Bef. Mast* xviii. 51 We saw a..whale, slowly crossing our fore-foot.

†**forefoot**, *v. Obs. rare*[−1]. [f. FORE- *pref.* + FOOT *v.*] *trans.* ? To repair (a boot) with new upper leather, to vamp.

1465 *Manners & Househ. Exp.* 302 To pay for fforfotenge of his botuys. *Ibid.*, For forfotynge [*Norf. MS.* fotynge] of a payre of botes.

†**fore-footman.** *Obs.* [FORE- *pref.* + FOOTMAN.] A footman who ran before his master.

(A rendering of *vautrarius* FEWTERER, misread as *vantrarius* and supposed to be connected with F. *avant.*)

1610 HOLLAND *Camden's Brit.* I. 331 He should be, the Kings fore-foot-man, until he had worne out a paire of shooes.

forefront ('fɔəfrʌnt). [f. FORE- *pref.* + FRONT.]

1. The principal face or foremost part of anything (*esp.* of a building). Now *rare.* (In early use opposed to †*back front.*)

c **1470** HENRY *Wallace* IX. 831 He gert thaim tak Syllys off ayk, and a stark barres mak, At a foyr frount, fast in the forest syd. **1548** HALL *Chron.* (1809) 639 The fore-frontes of euery gallery were hanged with..Sarcenet. **1551** ROBINSON tr. *More's Utop.* II. G v b, The forefrontes or frontiers of the ij corners [of the Ilande], what wythe fordys & shelues, & what with rockes be very..daungerous. **1659** EVELYN *To R. Boyle* 3 Sept., To the entry fore front of this a court, and at the other back front a plot walled in of a competent square. **1664** POWER *Micros. Observ.* in Sir T. Blount *Nat. Hist.* (1693) 314 These Eyes are plac'd all in the forefront of their [Spiders'] Head. **1671** CHARENTE *Let. Customs* 53 The.. forefronts of the Houses are very little handsomer than those of our Country Villages. **1698** VANBURGH *Prov. Wife* III. iii, I love to sit in the fore-front of a box; for, if one sits behind, there's two Acts gone before one's found out. **1726** LEONI *Alberti's Archit.* I. 39/2 From the..Fore-front of the Work

I draw a Line quite thro' to the Back-front. **1866** G. MACDONALD *Ann. Q. Neighb.* ii. (1878) 19 This little gallery was..larger than was just necessary for the organ..and a few of the parishioners had chosen to sit in its fore-front. **1876** *Whitby Gloss.*, *Foore-front*, the face of the building.

b. The 'front' of an army, the front rank.

1513 DOUGLAS *Æneis* XI. ix. 14 The Troiane barnage.. With ordinance of Tuscan, that did spreid In forfront al the large feyldis on breid. **1631** QUARLES *Samson* Div. Poems (1717) 302 They brought him bound To the forefront of the Philistian Band. **1737** WHISTON *Josephus' Hist.* I. iv. §7 He was in the fore-front, in the utmost danger. **1864** KINGSLEY *Rom. & Teut.* v. (1875) 130 He thrust himself into the fore-front of the battle.

c. *fig.* (Now the most frequent use.)

1589 NASHE in *Greene's Menaphon* (Arb.) 10 In the fore-front of whom [i.e. men of import], I cannot but place that aged Father Erasmus. **1607** DAY *Trav. Eng. Bro.* G iv b, True constancie's my fore-front and my back. **1846** TRENCH *Mirac.* Introd. (1862) 49 The position which it has won in the very forefront of the world. **1874** GREEN *Short Hist.* iv. §3. 176 The great statutes which stand in the forefront of our laws.

2. The beginning, commencement (of a book, document, or literary work). *Obs.* or *arch.*

1577-87 HOLINSHED *Chron.* II. 40/1 Iohannes Duns Scotus an Irishman borne, as in the forefront of this treatise I haue declared. **1612** T. TAYLOR *Comm. Titus* iii. 8 The author of it is set in the forefront or face of it. **1870** SPURGEON *Treas. Dav.* Ps. l. 1 In royal decrees the names and dignities of monarchs are placed in the forefront.

3. The front of the body as opposed to the 'back'.

1880 BROWNING *Dram. Idylls* Ser. II. *Mule'ykeh* 34 Her forefront whitens indeed Like a yellowish wave's cream-crest..Her fetlock is foam-splashed too. **1894** CROCKETT *Raiders* 74, I was to do nothing except lie thus prone on my forefront.

Hence **'forefront** *v. trans.*, to build a (*new*) forefront to.

1761 STERNE *Tr. Shandy* IV. xxxi, He would new fore-front his house, and add a new wing to make it even.

†**foregad**: affected pronunc. of *Fore God*: see FORE *prep.* 1 b.

†**fore'gain, fore'gains(t.** Chiefly *Sc. Obs.* [f. FORE- *prep.* or *adv.* + GAIN, GAINST. Cf. FORE-AGAIN(ST.] Directly opposite to; also, in the opposite scale to.

1375 BARBOUR *Bruce* XVI. 555 Ay forgane the schippis. **1535** STEWART *Cron. Scot.* (1856) I. 133 Ane messinger wes cuming him forgane. *a* **1547** SURREY *Æneid* II. 889 My spouse clasping my feet Foregainst his father young Iulus set. **1563** *Aberdeen Council Reg.* (1844) 254 In the Gallowgett of the said burght..forgains the gray freiris place. **1588** A. KING tr. *Canisius' Catech.* H vj, Foregainst ye quhilk is placed ye golden nombre of yat ȝere. **1639** RUTHERFORD *Lett.* cclxxxix. (1836) II. 188 If ye go to weigh Jesus his sweetness..and lay foregainst him your ounces or drachms of suffering for him. **1709** PHILP *Let.* 24 Sept. in Dunbar *Social Life* (1865) 50 Two ships ryding at ankor forgainst this place. **1725** RAMSAY *Gentl. Sheph.* III. ii, On Skelfs foregainst the Door.

fore-gallant, -gallery; see FORE- *pref.* 3, 5.

'fore-game. [FORE- *pref.*] A preliminary game; *lit.* and *fig.* Cf. AFTER-GAME.

1594 KYD *Cornelia* IV. G ij b, The Gaules were but a fore-game fecht about For ciuill discord. *a* **1635** NAUNTON *Fragm. Reg.* (Arb.) 28 His play was chiefly at the fore-game. **1643** TREVOR in Carte *Collect.* (1735) 260 Neither side can yet brag of the foregame. **1741** *Compl. Fam. Piece* II. i. 288 The Huntsman should therefore be..good at both Fore and After-Game.

foreganger ('fɔəgæŋə(r)). [f. FORE- *pref.* + GANGER; = Ger. *vorgänger*, Du. *voorganger*.]

†**1.** One who or that which goes before: **a.** a fore-runner, a harbinger; **b.** a predecessor. *Obs.*

1340 HAMPOLE *Pr. Consc.* 4152, I hald þir gret mysdoers Als anticrist lyms and his forgangers. *c* **1460** *Towneley Myst.* (Surtees) 165, I go before bodword to bere, And as forgangere am I send.

2. *Naut.* **a.** 'A short piece of rope immediately connecting the line with the shank of the harpoon, when spanned for killing' (Adm. Smyth). Cf. FOREGOER, -RUNNER. **b.** (See quot. 1867.) [So Du. *voorganger*.]

1794 *Rigging & Seamanship* I. 64 Yarn for foregangers is made of the best dressed long hemp. **1823** SCORESBY *Jrnl. Whale Fishery* 288 The 'fore-ganger', or that part of the line immediately connected with the harpoon. **1867** SMYTH *Sailor's Word-bk.*, *Fore-ganger* of the Chain Bower Cables, is a length of 15 fathoms of stouter chain, in consequence of greater wear and tear near the anchor.

foregarth ('fɔəgɑːθ). *dial.* [a. ON. *forgarð-r*, f. *for-*, FORE- + *garð-r* GARTH (= OE. *ȝeard* YARD).] = FORE-YARD[1].

1641 BEST *Farm. Bks.* (Surtees) 137 The helme in the foregarth will doe somethinge more then shelter three waines. **1684** *MS. Indenture* (Yorksh.), All that cottage, foregarth and little close.

foregate ('fɔəgeɪt). [f. FORE- *pref.* + GATE.]

1. The front gate or principal entrance.

1503 in *Lib. Cart. S. Crucis* (1840) lvii, Item, for vij punschionis of plaister to the turatis of the foryet..iiij lib. xviij s. **1610** HOLLAND *Camden's Brit.* II. 81 A castle also.. and a foregate at the entrance unto it. **1726** LEONI *Alberti's Archit.* I. 101/1 Chambers near the vestibule or fore-gate. **1856** FROUDE *Hist. Eng.* II. 430 There was..to be but one entrance only, by the great foregate.

transf. and *fig.* **1613** J. DAVIES *Muse's Teares* E ij b, Beare vp the Crosse; and euer looke vpon't As on the only Key of Heau'n's fore-gate. **1692** G. STRADLING *Serm. & Disc.* 381 They [the Jesuits] were..turned out of the Foregates of those States.

Prov. c **1645** HOWELL *Lett.* I. v. xxi, When distrust enters in at the foregate, love goes out at the Postern. **1686** W. DE BRITAINE *Hum. Prud.* vii. 31 When passion enters in at the fore-gate, Wisdom goes out at the postern.

2. *Sc.* 'The high or open street' (Jam.).

1560 in *Burgh Rec. Aberdeen* (1844) 327 Diuerse personis hes biggit and dalie biggis choppis vnder stairis vpoune the forgettis. **1567** *Sc. Acts Jas. VI* (1814) 43 The samyn to be saulde and toppit be honest personis in þe foir-gait in oppin and publict tavernis. *a* **1583** *Chalm. Air* in *Balfour's Practicks* (1754) 588 Gif thair be ony swine cruivis biggit on the fore-gait, stoppand the samin.

foregather: see FORGATHER.

fore-gear: see FORE- *pref.* 5.

†**foregengl.** *Obs.*[−1] [f. FORE- *pref.* + *gengl = OHG. *gengil* goer, f. root of GANG *v.*] A foregoer, predecessor.

c **1205** LAY. 25082 Þeos weoren mine ælderen, mine aðǝele uore-genglen.

foregift ('fɔəgɪft). [f. FORE- *pref.* + GIFT.] *Law.* 'A premium for a lease' (Wharton 1867).

1744 in *N. Riding Rec.* VIII. 109 A fine or foregift was paid to the late Lady Stapleton. **1845** STEPHEN *Comm. Laws Eng.* (1874) II 737 That no fine or foregift be taken for the lease. **1881** *Law Rep.* Chancery Div. XVI. 598 There was reserved on every demise..the best yearly rent without taking any fine, premium or foregift.

fore-gird: see FORE- *pref.* 1.

†**fore-'give,** *v. Obs.* [f. FORE- *pref.* + GIVE *v.* Cf. *misgive.*] *intr.* To have a foreboding, anticipate.

1600 HOLLAND *Livy* XXV. xxxv. (1609) 575 As commonly mens minds use to fore-give and tell aforehand [L. *præsagientibus*] when there is some mischiefe and ill toward them.

foreglance ('fɔəglɑːns, -æ-). [f. FORE- *pref.* + GLANCE *sb.*] The action of glancing forward; also, a view or glance beforehand.

1825 COLERIDGE *Rem.* (1836) II. 126 A misprint..arising from an anticipation by foreglance of the compositor's eye. **1860** ELLICOTT *Life Our Lord* ii. 49 With the rapid fore-glance of thought she must have seen in the clouded future, scorn, dereliction..death. **1889** HISSEY *Tour in Phaeton* 131 How intensely interesting it would be to have a fore-glance into a science text-book of a century hence.

fore-glass, -gleam, -glimpse: see FORE-.

forego ('fɔəgəʊ), *sb. rare*[−1]. [f. next.] Something that goes or happens before.

1880 GORDON *Bk. Chron. Keith* 63 The..'Death-Watch' ..was conjectured to be a forego of a Death or a Flitting.

forego (fɔə'gəʊ), *v.* Pa. t. forewent; pa. pple. foregone. Forms: see GO. [OE. *fore-gán*, f. FORE- *pref.* + *gán* to GO.]

1. *trans.* To go before or in advance of; to precede: either in position or time.

c **900** tr. *Bæda's Hist.* v. xxi. [xxiii.] (1891) 476 Oðer [steorra] hiora foreeode þa sunnan on morȝen. **1515** T. MORE *Chron. K. Edw. V*, in Grafton II. 757 And the yere fore goyng his death he had obtayned the towne of Barwike. **1548** GEST *Pr. Masse* 116 That part of the masse that forgoeth consecration. **1577-87** HOLINSHED *Chron.* I. Pref., Summarie contents foregoing euerie chapter. **1587** GOLDING *De Mornay* xxx. 491 A Christ..whom being forgone by an Elias, it behoued to preach the Kingdome of God. *a* **1619** FOTHERBY *Atheom.* II. iii. §2 (1622) 214 The cause doth alwayes his effect fore-goe. **1668** CULPEPPER & COLE *Barthol. Anat.* II. vii. 109 The constriction of the Earlets does always forego the Diastole of the Ventricles. **1879** E. ARNOLD *Lt. Asia* 3 Over half the earth a lovely light Forewent the morn. **1884** J. PAYNE *Tales fr. Arabic* I. 15 His head forewent his feet and he fell to the ground. *Ibid.* 185 So Abdulmelik went away to his house, whither he found that the money had foregone him.

2. *intr.* To go before, precede in place or time. Also quasi-*trans.* with cognate obj.

c **825** *Vesp. Ps.* lxxxviii. 15 Mildheortnis & soðfestnis foregað biforan onsiene ðinre. *a* **1300** *E.E. Psalter* xcvi[i]. 3 Fire bi-fore him sal for-gane. *c* **1555** HARPSFIELD *Divorce Hen. VIII*, 45 The wife and the man with their mutual consent adhibited and fore-going enter into religion. **1563** *Mirr. Mag.*, *Hastings* i. 5 Cleaving my tombe the waye my fame forewent. **1579** SPENSER *Sheph. Cal.* July 117 And now they bene to heauen forewent. **1622** T. SCOTT *Belg. Pismire* 30 To purchase honour without some worthy action fore-going..is not truely to be Noble. **1865** MRS. WHITNEY *Gayworthys* I. 116 A gait, sublimely unaffected by all that had foregone.

forego: see FORGO.

foregoer (fɔə'gəʊə(r)). Forms: 4-6 forgoer, (4 forgoere, 5 goar, 6 foregoere), 5- foregoer. [f. FORE- *pref.* + GOER.]

†**1.** A messenger sent before, a forerunner, a harbinger; *spec.* a purveyor. *Obs.*

c **1340** *Cursor M.* 13208 (Trin.) To helle bifore crist [Ion] ferd..þerfore is he called forgoer. **1393** LANGL. *P. Pl.* C. III. 198 Ac gile was forgoere to gyen al the puple, For to wisse hem the weye and with Mede a-byde. **1502** *Caxton's Chron. Eng.* kvj b/1 He was..The forgooer of Antecryst, the fulfyller of heresye. **1580** *Ord. of Prayer* in *Liturg. Serv. Q. Eliz.* (1847) 568 He sent Hornets and wild Beasts, as foregoers of his host. **1580** SIDNEY *Arcadia* (1622) 216 O Mercurie, foregoer to the euening. **1601** F. TATE *Househ. Ord. Edw. II* §90 (1876) 53 Their shalbe a fore-goer in the kinges household. **1662** PHILLIPS, *Foregoers*, Purveyours going before the King or Queen in progresse. **1745** BLOMEFIELD *Norf.* II. 605 There was one always at each (Leper) House called the Foregoer, who used to beg daily for them.

2. One who or that which goes in front or 'leads the way'; a leader; hence, an example, pattern.

1382 WYCLIF *Josh.* iii. 3 Whanne ȝe seen the ark..folwe ȝe the forgoers. **1485** CAXTON *St. Wenefr.* 10 They made her in alle thynges a forgoar and ensample to them. **1549** COVERDALE, etc. *Erasm. Par. 1 Tim.* ii. 11 It is conuenient for them [women]..to be folowers, and not foregoers. **1596** DAVIES *Orchestra* 73 All the followers [flying cranes] their heads doe lay On their forgoers backs. **1658** BAXTER *Saving Faith* xii. 85 The promised Glory, and the future blessings that are its necessary Foregoers. **1869** BLACKMORE *Lorna D.* II. i. Each [reaper] casting leftwards his rich clearance on his foregoer's double track.

3. One that has gone before; a predecessor.

1553 GRIMALDE *Cicero's Offices* II. (1558) 102 He..in knowledge clerely exceded all his foregoers. **1602** CAREW *Cornwall* (1769) 68 Two young men of the parish are yerely chosen by their last fore-goers, to be wardens. **1868** DIXON *Spiritual Wives* II. xi. 90 His foregoers had been settled in Massachusetts since the days of the Mayflower. **1877** MORLEY *Crit. Misc.* Ser. II. 348 The order in which each state of society has followed its foregoer.

4. *Naut.* = FOREGANGER 2 a.

1694 *Acc. Sev. Late Voy.* II. (1711) 161 Before this hollow part, the Fore-goer is fasten'd or ty'd. **1867** in SMYTH *Sailor's Word-bk.* **1892** *Daily News* 8 June 5/3 We quickly bent on the line to the foregoer, clapped the harpoon into the gun.

foregoing (fɔə'gəʊɪŋ), *vbl. sb.* [f. FOREGO *v.* + -ING[1].]

1. The action of the vb. FOREGO; a going before, preceding, or leading the way.

1581 SIDNEY *Apol. Poetrie* (Arb.) 21 After whom, encouraged..with theyr excellent fore-going, others haue followed. **1656** tr. *Hobbes' Elem. Philos.* (1839) 130 Their verity depends not upon our knowledge, but upon the fore-going of their causes.

†**2.** That which goes before. *Obs.*[−1]

1598 FLORIO, *Preambulo*, a preamble, a foregoing.

foregoing (fɔə'gəʊɪŋ), *ppl. a.* [f. as prec. + -ING[2].] That goes or has gone before, preceding (in position or time).

1450-1530 *Myrr. our Ladye* 306 Heyle starre forgoynge. **1532** MORE *Confut. Tindale* II. IV. 119 They doo not merite with anye forgoyng good dedes. **1605** VERSTEGAN *Dec. Intell.* Pref. Ep., The ensuing matter will be answerable to the foregoing title. **1737** WHISTON *Josephus' Hist.* I. xix. §2 The multitude..were emboldened by their foregoing victory. **1828** J. H. MOORE *Pract. Navig.* (ed. 20) 229 From the foregoing examples it is plain, that the operation is the same. **1841** EMERSON *Addr.*, *Method Nat.* Wks. (Bohn) II. 226 A fruit which it cost all the foregoing ages to form and ripen.

b. *absol.* (quasi-*sb.*) and *ellipt.*

1662 STILLINGFL. *Orig. Sacr.* II. ii. §7 The Political and civil part of it, which may better be called wisdom then most of the fore-going. **1762-71** H. WALPOLE *Vertue's Anecd. Paint.* (1786) II. 185 Besides the foregoing, Lord Breadalbane has..eleven portraits. **1874** HELPS *Soc. Press.* iii. 54 The foregoing must not be confounded with purely communistic theories.

foregone (fɔə'gɒn, -ɔː-), *ppl. a.* [f. FORE- *pref.* + GONE, pa. pple. of GO.] That has gone before or gone by; (of time) past.

c **1600** SHAKS. *Sonn.* xxx, Then can I grieve at grievances foregone. **1656** COWLEY *Pindar. Odes* I. iii, With Oblivion's silent Stroke deface Of foregone Ills the very Trace. **1794** BURKE *Rep. Lord's Jrnls.* Wks. 1842 II. 610 With no light from any principle, precedent, or foregone authority of law. **1824** LAMB *Elia* Ser. II. *Capt. Jackson*, A bare scrag—cold savings from the foregone meal. **1870** LOWELL *Cathedral* Poet. Wks. (1879) 441/2 This has made poets dream of lives foregone In worlds fantastical.

b. *foregone conclusion*: a Shaksperian phrase, variously interpreted by commentators (see CONCLUSION 15). Now used for: A decision or opinion already formed before the case is argued or the full evidence known (hence *foregone intention*, *opinion*, etc.); also, a result or upshot that might have been foreseen as inevitable.

1604 SHAKS. *Oth.* III. iii. 428. **1821** LAMB *Elia* Ser. I. *New Year's Eve*, I plunge into foregone visions and conclusions. **1856** FROUDE *Hist. Eng.* (1858) I. iii. 286 Starting always with a foregone conclusion, he arrived of course where he wished to arrive. **1868** J. H. BLUNT *Ref. Ch. Eng.* I. 186 The Archbishop was simply carrying out..the foregone intention of the King. **1878** BOSW. SMITH *Carthage* 387 That struggle was heroic..but the conclusion was foregone.

Hence **fore'goneness.** (*nonce-wd.*)

1892 *Athenæum* 6 Aug. 191/2 [The book is] affected..by the 'foregoneness' of its conclusion.

†**,fore-'grandsire.** *Sc. Obs.* Forms: see FORE- *pref.* and GRANDSIRE. [f. FORE- *pref.* + GRANDSIRE.] **a.** A grandfather; = L. *avus.* **b.** A great-grandfather; = L. *proavus.* **c.** A great-great-grandfather. **d.** An ancestor.

a. 1513 DOUGLAS *Æneis* XII. vi. 95 The name he bair of his fore grandschir wycht.

b. 1474 *Acta Audit.* (1839) 34/2 Þai fand þe said Robertis forgrantsire deit last vest & sesit of þe said landes. **1500-20** in *Dunbar's Poems* (1893) 315 My foir grandschir, hecht Fyn Mackcowll.

c. **1541** *Books Counc. & Sess.* B 18. 44 (Jam.) Be his fader, gudschir, grandshir, and forgrandshir, lardis of Fingiltoun. **1633** *Acts Chas. I* (1814) V. 64/2 To the forsaids persones.. thair fathers guidschirs grandschirs foirgrandschirs [etc.]. d. **1549** *Compl. Scot.* (1873) 3 Your foir grandscheir gode-froid of billon kyng of iherusalem.. deffendit his pepil. *fig.* **1581** N. BURNE *Disp. Relig.* xviii. 62/2 Frere Martine Lauter your foirgrandschir passed mair cannelie to vorke.

foreground ('fɔəgraʊnd), *sb.* [f. FORE- *pref.* + GROUND.]

1. a. That part of a view which is in front and nearest the observer; *esp.* as represented in a picture.

1695 DRYDEN *Art of Paint.* 167 White can subsist on the fore-ground of the Picture. **1799** G. SMITH *Laboratory* I. 353 Such as lie nearer the fore-ground you are to imitate according to nature. **1834** MEDWIN *Angler in Wales* II. 19 The desolate crag—a fit foreground to the still more desolate prospect that the land presented. **1841** W. SPALDING *Italy & It. Isl.* II. 401 A mother in the foreground, seated beside her two dead infants.

b. *fig.* The most conspicuous or prominent position.

1816 BENTHAM *Chrestom.* 247 The desirable property,—which on this occasion stands as the principal object, and occupies the fore-ground. **1833** MACAULAY *Ess., Walpole's Lett. to Mann* (1854) 264/2 He was content.. to keep in the background and to leave the foreground to the author. **1873** SYMONDS *Grk. Poets* v. 127 The Aeolians occupied the very foreground of Greek literature.

2. The ground in front of an object. *rare*$^{-1}$.

1858 J. MARTINEAU *Stud. Chr.* 134 The high priest.. touched with finger dipped in blood, the sacred lid and foreground of the Ark.

3. *attrib.* ***foreground music*** (opp. *background music*: see BACKGROUND *sb.* 1 e).

1827 STEUART *Planter's G.* (1828) 362 Several groups of fine foreground Trees with extensive tops were already formed. **1887** RUSKIN *Præterita* II. 165, I made two fore-ground studies in colour. **1961** *Time* 21 July 36/1 When his wife asks where the cash came from, he mumbles something about the stock market and adds, as cellos groan ominously in what ought to be called the film's foreground music, 'I made a killing.' **1967** L. DEIGHTON *London Dossier* 30 Deafening foreground music is provided by a giant jukebox.

'foreground, *v.* [f. the sb.] *trans.* To place in the foreground. Hence **'foregrounding** *vbl. sb.*; *spec.* in *Linguistics* [rendering Czech *aktualisace* modernization (Havránek and Weingart *Spisovná čeština a jazyková kultura* (1932))], the use of unorthodox or unexpected devices in language.

1892 'MARK TWAIN' *Amer. Claimant* xvi. 153 We could do a prodigious trade [in portrait-painting] with the women if we could foreground the things they like, but they don't give a damn for artillery. **1959** R. QUIRK in Quirk & Smith *Teaching of English* i. 45 The Prague School notion of what has been translated as 'foregrounding'.. is defined by Mukařovský as 'the aesthetically intentional distortion of the linguistic components' in relation to the normal standard language on the one hand and to 'the traditional aesthetic canon' on the other. **1962** S. R. LEVIN *Ling. Struct. Poetry* ii. 17 Foregrounded linguistic elements.. call attention to themselves. **1964** P. L. GARVIN *Prague School Reader* p. viii, *Automatization* refers to the stimulus normally expected in a social situation; *foregrounding*—in Czech *aktualisace*—on the other hand refers to a stimulus not culturally expected in a social situation and hence capable of provoking special attention.

†fore'guard, *v. Obs.*$^{-1}$ [f. FORE- *pref.* + GUARD *v.*] *trans.* To guard beforehand or in front.

1588 GREENE *Metam.* Wks. (Grosart) IX. 23 In that we foregarded all our actions with vertue. *Ibid.* 89.

foreguess (fɔə'gɛs), *v.* [f. FORE- *pref.* + GUESS.] *trans.* To guess beforehand; to forecast, anticipate, conjecture. Const. with simple obj. or with obj. clause. Also *absol.*

Hence **fore'guessing** *vbl. sb.* and *ppl. a.*

1388 WYCLIF *Wisd.* xvii. 10 *marg. note* Bi forgessing grete yuels to comynge on it silf. **1548** UDALL, etc. *Erasm. Par. Luke* xii. 54 Obseruing and markyng al lykelyhodes and foregeassynges of tempestes. **1598** FLORIO *Presago*, a.. fore-guessing man. **1640** BP. HALL *Chr. Moder.* 28/1 Melancthon could foreguess that the time should come wherein [etc.]. **1895** W. H. TURTON *Truth of Chr.* 88 He may also have foreknown, what we can only foreguess.

fore-guidance, -hall: see FORE- *pref.* 2 d, 3.

†fore'halsen, *v. Obs. rare.* [f. FORE- *pref.* + HALSEN *v.*] *trans.* (*absol.*) To presage.

1594 CAREW *Tasso* I. iv, One day perhaps, my pen fore-halsening Will dare, what now of thee tis purposing. **1602** —— *Cornwall* 124 b, A fore-halsening of this rebellion.

'fore-,hammer. *Sc.* and *north. dial.* [f. FORE- *pref.* + HAMMER. Cf. Du. *voorhamer* (in Kilian 1598 *veurhamer*), Da. *forhammer*.] The large hammer which strikes first; a sledge-hammer.

1543 *Richmond. Wills* (Surtees) 43 Item iiij fore hamers. **1592** *Sc. Act Jas. VI* (1814) III. 538 Breking vp his chalmer durris with foirhammeris. **1785** BURNS *Scotch Drink* xi, The strong forehammer. **1818** SCOTT *Hrt. Midl.* v, The unceasing clang of the heavy fore-hammers. **1894** CROCKETT *Raiders* 315 From the other side.. came the sound of a forehammer thundering on a gate.

forehand ('fɔəhænd), *a.* and *sb.* and *adv.* [f. FORE- *pref.* + HAND.] **A.** *adj.*

†1. *Archery.* ***forehand*** (***shaft***): an arrow for shooting straight before one. Opposed to *underhand*. *Obs.*

1545 ASCHAM *Toxoph.* (Arb.) 126 The forehande must haue a bigge breste to bere the great myghte of the bowe. **1597** SHAKS. *2 Hen. IV*, III. ii. 52 Hee would haue.. carryed you a fore-hand Shaft at foureteene and foureteene and a halfe.

2. Done or given at some earlier time. Of payments, etc.: Made in advance. ? *Obs.* exc. *dial.*

1599 SHAKS. *Much Ado* IV. i. 51 She did embrace me as a husband, And so extenuate the forehand sinne. **1678** *St. Trials, Popish Plot* Introd. VI. 1490, I wonder I had no fore-hand notice of it [my trial]. *a* **1679** T. GOODWIN *Wks.* I. III. 25 This forehand Union hath.. such virtue in it. **1790** W. MARSHALL *Midland Co.* I. 20 Covenanting to pay what is called a 'forehand rent'. **1825–80** JAMIESON s.v., Fore-han'-payment is payment in advance, as is generally the rule with school fees.

3. Foremost, leading. Also, *fore-a-hand.* ***forehand stone*** (*Curling*): see quot. Also *ellipt.* or quasi-*sb.*: The first or foremost player.

1664 BUTLER *Hud.* II. ii 618 A Nag That might pass for a forehand Stag. **1816** SCOTT *Old Mort.* vii, Our auld fore-hand ox. **1825** JAMIESON s.v., The forehand stane is the stone first played in *curling*. Clydes. **1831** *Blackw. Mag.* Dec. 983 A canny forehan'. **1892** KERR *Curling* Gloss. in *Skating, etc.* (Badm. Libr.) 380 *Fore-han'*, the first player or lead.

4. ? = FOREHANDED *a.* 2 b.

1784 BAGE *Barham Downs* I. 172 Would any man in his senses that was not a very forehand man indeed, live in the elegant way you do?

5. *Lawn Tennis.* **a.** Said of a stroke made by holding the racket with the palm of the hand turned forwards. **b.** Applied to the area of a court in which a player uses the forehand stroke.

1889 H. W. W. WILBERFORCE *Lawn Tennis* 21 When about to make a forehand stroke, the feet should be apart. *Ibid.* 36 Supposing it [*sc.* the return] comes to the player's forehand, he may.. return it in the direction it came but at an acuter angle. *Ibid.* 37 From the forehand court the return will be either—(*a*) Down the line... (*b*) Across the court. **1890** C. G. HEATHCOTE *Tennis* 212 The moment it is seen that the ball will come to the fore-hand, the left foot should be brought across and in front of the right. **1921** A. W. MYERS *20 Yrs. Lawn Tennis* 9 He attacked the Australian's backhand corner (the forehand corner of a right-handed player) very adroitly. **1929** *Morn. Post* 13 July 16/2 The Forehand Grip. **1958** *Everyman's Encycl.* VII. 663/1 In the forehand drive the hitting arm is extended fully.

B. *sb.*

1. a. The position in front or above. **†*to have the forehand of, to be to the forehand with*** (Sc.): to have the upper hand or advantage of.

1557 PHAER *Æneid* v. M iij b, And yet not formost al, nor al her keele hath forhand wonne. **1588** PARKE tr. *Mendoza's Hist. China* 143 a, Hee determined.. to depart and procure .. to get the forehande of them.. and to ayde and helpe them [etc.]. **1599** SHAKS. *Hen. V*, IV. i. 297 But for Ceremonie, such a Wretch.. Had the fore-hand and vantage of a King. **1646** JENKYN *Remora* 28 God keeps on the fore-hand with you, let us follow hard after him. **1825–80** JAMIESON, s.v., 'I'm to the forehand wi' you', I have got the start of you.

b. That which holds the front position; the vanguard, hence the mainstay.

1606 SHAKS. *Tr. & Cr.* I. iii. 143 The great Achilles.. The sinew and the fore-hand of our Hoste.

2. That part of a horse which is before the rider.

1617 MARKHAM *Caval.* I. 12 They haue most excellent forehandes. **1683** *Lond. Gaz.* No. 1890/4 A light Grey Mare .. handsome forehand but thin behind. **1816** SCOTT *Antiq.* xxxvi, What fine fore-hands!—what capital chargers they would make! **1884** E. L. ANDERSON *Mod. Horsemansh.* I. i. 2 For our purposes, we shall consider as the Forehand of the horse all that part which is in front of the saddle.

3. *Lawn Tennis.* A forehand stroke. ***on the forehand***: forehanded.

1908 H. S. MAHONY in A. W. Myers *Compl. Lawn Tennis Player* 246 Of their ground-play, especially on the fore-hand, there is nothing to be said but praise. **1924** G. W. HILLYARD *40 Yrs. Lawn Tennis* 69 He.. never did acquire the right method of hitting the ball on the forehand. **1934** *Times* 26 July 5/4 His forehand became utterly wild... It was on the forehand that he made the losing stroke.

C. *adv. Lawn Tennis.* (See quot.)

1925 S. LENGLEN *Lawn Tennis* 24 The ball is cut fore-hand when it is struck below the centre of its circumference and across from right to left.

'fore,handed, *a.* [f. as prec. + -ED[2].]

†1. Having a forehand (see FOREHAND B. 2); 'formed in the foreparts' (J.). Usually with a defining *adj.* or *adv.* Said of horses, and *transf.* *Obs.*

1591 GREENE *Farew. Folly* Wks. (Grosart) IX. 327 The Gentleman is well forehanded and well foreheaded. **1614** MARKHAM *Cheap Husb.* I. i. (1668) 4 Observe.. to have them fore-handed, that is good neck, breast and shoulders. **1680** *Lond. Gaz.* No. 1489/4 A dark brown Gelding.. lofty Forehanded.

2. Looking to the forehand (see prec. B. 1); careful as to the future, prudent, thrifty. Now only *U.S.*

1650 JER. TAYLOR *Holy Living* (1727) 12 An early and forehanded care. **1777** J. Q. ADAMS *Wks.* (1854) IX. 454 Here and there a farmer and a tradesman, who is forehanded and frugal enough to make more money than he has occasion to spend. **1870** LOWELL *Study Wind.* 76 They were.. a thrifty forehanded race.

b. That has made provision for the future; in easy circumstances, 'well-to-do'. Now only *U.S.*

1658 GURNALL *Chr. in Arm.* II. 576 They that are fore-handed, are willing to give time and able to forbear long. **1828** WEBSTER, *Forehanded*.. 2 In America, in good circumstances as to property. **1837–40** HALIBURTON *Clockm.* (1862) 132 A big man, and one that's considerable fore-handed, and pretty well to do in the world. **1851** S. JUDD *Margaret* ix. (1871) 47 In popular phrase a forehanded man, his house and barns were large, and his grounds indicated thrift. **1883** MRS. ROLLINS *New Eng. Bygones* 156 The wives of forehanded farmers and professional men were apt to be somewhat exalted.

3. *Lawn Tennis.* With a forehand stroke. Also *adv.*

1889, 1890 [see BACK-HANDED *a.* 2]. **1908** A. W. MYERS *Compl. Lawn Tennis Player* 129 Lawford attempted to take them forehanded. **1922** [see BACK-HANDED *a.* 2].

fore'handedness. *U.S.* [f. FOREHANDED *a.* 2.] The quality of being 'forehanded'.

1840 R. H. DANA *Bef. Mast* (1854) 262 Regular habits, forehandedness (if I may use the word) in worldly affairs. **1897** A. T. MAHAN *Life Nelson* II. 277 The incident shows at once the forehandedness of Nelson. **1905** *Springfield (Mass.) Weekly Republ.* 8 Dec. 1 The attempt.. to persuade people to do their Christmas shopping early appears to be making headway. Such forehandedness is in the interest of the buyers. **1937** *Times Lit. Suppl.* 13 Feb. 99/3 His [*sc.* Ezra Pound's] forehandedness makes this new volume particularly exciting.

forehander ('fɔə,hændə(r)). *Lawn Tennis.* [f. FOREHAND + -ER[1].] A forehand stroke.

1922 A. E. CRAWLEY *Lawn Tennis Do's & Don'ts* 25 If you hold [the racket] across your chest, you may be too late for a forehander.

fore-handsel, -hanging: see FORE- *pref.* 4 a, 5.

forehard ('fɔəhɑːd). [f. FORE- *pref.* + HARD.] (See quot.)

1853 URE *Dict. Arts* II. 563 The forehard, or proper twist in the strands for all sizes of ropes, is.. attained.

fore-haste, -hatch, etc.: see FORE- *pref.*

forehead ('fɒrɪd, 'fɔəhɛd). Forms: see HEAD. [OE. *forhéafod*, f. FOR-[2], FORE- *pref.* + *héafod* HEAD.]

1. That part of the face which reaches upward from the eyebrows to the natural line of the hair. Also, the corresponding part in beasts, etc.

c **1000** ÆLFRIC *Gloss.* in Wr.-Wülcker 156 *Caluarium*, for-heafod. *c* **1175** *Lamb. Hom.* 127 Ure forhefod. *a* **1225** *Ancr. R.* 18 Makieð.. a large creoiz mit þe þreo vingres vrom abuue þe vorheaued dun to þe breoste. *c* **1305** *Edmund Conf.* 65–6 in *E.E.P.* (1862) 72 In mie foreheuede iwrite mi name þu schalt iseo. Signe þerwiþ þi forheued. *c* **1380** *Sir Ferumb.* 3927 Hys hors.. bar a sterre on his for-hed. *c* **1489** CAXTON *Sonnes of Aymon* i. 48 He frompeled his forhede. **1513** DOUGLAS *Æneis* XIII. iii. 128 Thy plesand forret schapely and ene cleir. **1582** T. WATSON *Centurie of Love* Ep. Ded. (Arb.) 26 Malicious high foreheads. **1612** WOODALL *Surg. Mate* Wks. (1653) 363 Applyed cold to the forr-head, or place grieved. **1662** STILLINGFL. *Orig. Sacr.* II. vi. §8 The placing of the motto.. upon the High Priests fore-head. **1726** LEONI *Alberti's Archit.* III. 34/2 From the Forhead to the Hinder-part of the head. **1842** TENNYSON *Locksley Hall* 25 On her pallid cheek and forehead came a colour and a light. **1886** A. WINCHELL *Walks & Talks Geol. Field* 256 The dinoceras.. had.. perhaps three pairs of horns, one on the snout, one on the cheeks, and one on the forehead.

b. *transf.* and *fig.*

1602 SHAKS. *Ham.* III. iii. 63 Euen to the teeth and fore-head of our faults. **1607** —— *Cor.* II. i. 57 The forhead of the morning. *c* **1611** CHAPMAN *Iliad* XVI. 692 Two fierce kings of beasts, oppos'd in strife about a hind Slain on the forehead of a hill. **1642** MILTON *Apol. Smect.* (1851) 258 Tis manifest his purpose was only to rub the forehead of his title with this word modest. **1766** FORDYCE *Serm. Yng. Wom.* (1767) I. iv. 149 Those writings carry on their very forehead the mark of the beast. **1795–1814** WORDSW. *Excursion* VII. 593 And oak ..on whose forehead inaccessible The raven lodged in safety. **1839** LONGF. *Hyperion* I. vi. (1865) 30 High and hoar on the forehead of the Jettenbuhl stands the castle of Heidelberg.

c. Phrase. **†*to take time* (*or occasion*) *by the forehead***: now usually *by the forelock* (see FORELOCK *sb.*[2] 2).

1592 GREENE *Farew. Folly* Wks. (Grosart) IX. 311 Take time now by the forehead, she is bald behind. **1599** BEN. JONSON *Cynthia's Rev.* IV. i, Let us then take our time by the forehead. **1633** HEYWOOD *Eng. Trav.* III. Wks. 1874 IV. 47 Take Occasion by the forehead.

†2. Used (like L. *frons*) for the countenance as capable of expressing shame, etc. In two opposite applications: **a.** Capacity of blushing; sense of shame or decency; modesty. **b.** Command of countenance, unblushing front; assurance, impudence, audacity. *Obs.*

1560 BECON *New Catech.* IV. Wks. 1564 I. 384 b, With what forhead.. dare we say in the Lord's prayer 'Forgeue vs our trespasses'. **1631** J. BURGES *Answ. Rejoined* 236 No man can deny it, who hath any forehead left. **1675** *Mistaken Husband* II. i. in *Dryden's Wks.* (1884) VIII. 599 With what forehead Darest thou call me so? **1775** T. SHERIDAN *Art Reading* 371 No body but a modern freethinker could have the forehead or folly to turn it into ridicule.

3. The front part, forefront. **†a.** *gen.* (*Obs.* exc. with conscious metaphor: see 1 b.)

1525 LD. BERNERS *Froiss.* II. clvii. [cliii.] 429 She rode on the one syde by the quenes lytter, and it was assysted with the duke of Thourayne, and the duke of Burbone, at the fore heed on bothe sydes.

b. *Mining*, etc. The end, for the time being, of a level.

1747 HOOSON *Miner's Dict.* Ij b, Forebrest, Forfield, or Forehead. **1862** SMILES *Engineers* III. 130 When I arrived at the forehead of the dip. **1885** *Trans. Cumbld. & Westmld. Antiq. Soc.* VIII. 9 From the forehead of the level it was conveyed to the day by means of a wooden railroad.

c. *Naut.* (See quot.)

a **1642** SIR W. MONSON *Naval Tracts* III. (1704) 332/2 In the Forehead or Mizon-yard.

d. *dial.* (See quots.)

1798 *Ann. Agric. Som.* XXX. 354 Foreheads or head-lands. **1810** *Devon & Cornw. Voc.* in *Monthly Mag.* June 436 *Forehead* about six feet space wide of earth round the hedges of a field, which is ploughed up, mixed with lime and carted or wheeled upon the field for manure.

†**4.** One holding the place of honour; a leader.

[Not derived from sense 1; strictly a new formation.]

c **1640** J. SMYTH *Lives Berkeleys* (1883) II. 380 To have rated the forehead of his hounds, then in chase after a wrong bucke. **1641** SIR E. DERING *Sp. on Relig.* 20 Nov. xiv. (1642) 45 Pretending to be a fore-head of Divinity.

5. *attrib.* and *Comb.*, as ***forehead-band, -bone, -wrinkle***; **forehead-bald** *a.*, bald as to the forehead; **forehead-cloth**, a cloth or bandage formerly worn on the forehead by ladies; †**forehead-piece** (see quot.).

1530 TINDALE *Lev.* xiii. 41 Then he is *foreheadbalde. **1809** A. HENRY *Trav.* 24 A fillet, or *forehead-band. **1646** SIR T. BROWNE *Pseud. Ep.* III. xiii. 137 It was rather the *forehead bone petrified, then a stone within the crany. **1793** HOLCROFT tr. *Lavater's Physiog.* vii. 44 The forehead bones remain unaltered. **1561** *Gifts to Queen* in Nichols *Progr. Q. Eliz.* (1823) I. 116 Three *forehed-clothes of cameryk netted with gold. **1677** *Lond. Gaz.* No 1245/4 Four laced Forehead Cloaths. **1767** *Connoisseur* (ed. 5) III. No. 80. 71 A store of clouts, caps, forehead-cloths. **1673** WYCHERLEY *Gentl. Dancing-Master* IV. i, Every night since he came, I have worn the *forehead-piece of bees' wax and hogs' grease. **1572** HULOET (ed. Higins), *Forehead wrinkles ..*rugæ frontis.*

'foreheaded, *ppl. a.* [f. prec. + -ED².] Having (a) forehead.

1. With adj. or adv. prefixed, as ***high, low, well foreheaded.*** †***tender-foreheaded***: modest, meek.

1591 [see FOREHANDED *a.* 1]. **1659** GAUDEN *Tears of Church* 47 The Gnosticks..were tender-foreheaded..people compared to those high-crested and Seraphick Sophisters. **1670** NARBOROUGH *Jrnl.* in *Acc. Sev. Late Voy.* I. (1711) 64 These People are..low Fore-headed. **1892** *Pall Mall G.* 30 Jan. 3/1 High-foreheaded, colourless Madonnas.

†**2.** Hardened with effrontery, brazen. *Obs.*

16.. PAIN *Let. to Feild* in Heylin *Hist. Presbyt.* (1670) 278 This For-headed Age.

'foreheadless, *a.* [f. as prec. + -LESS.] Having no FOREHEAD (sense 2): †**a.** having no sense of shame (*obs.*); **b.** destitute of confidence.

a **1603** T. CARTWRIGHT *Confut. Rhem. N.T.* (1618) 713 They are thus foreheadlesse in forging Scriptures. **1621** S. WARD *Serm. Jethro's J.P.* 25 What doe our audacious and fore-headlesse Swaggerers require? **1844** BROWNING *Colombe's Birthday* v. Poems 1849 I. 369 *Mel.*..How Behaved our spokesman with the forehead? *Berth.* Oh, Turned out no better than the foreheadless.

fore'hear, *v.* [f. FORE- *pref.* + HEAR *v.*] *trans.* and *intr.* To hear beforehand.

1599 *Soliman & Perseda* G ij, Hauing forehard of Basiliscoe's worth. **1623** WEBSTER *D'chess Malfy* III. iv, How that the Pope, forehearing of her looseness Hath seiz'd.. The dukedom which she held as dowager. **1800–24** CAMPBELL *Death-boat of Heligoland* 4 Brains..that maddening forehear the last trumpet of doom. **1813** BYRON *Giaour* 1076 *note*, His troublesome faculty of forehearing.

†**'forehearse.** *Obs. rare*⁻¹. [f. FORE- *pref.* + HEARSE, app. in the sense of F. *herse* portcullis.] ? That which guards the front.

1589 GREENE *Menaphon* (Arb.) 87, I feele him wound the forehearse of my heart.

fore-hearth, -heater: see FORE- *pref.* 5.

†**fore'heed,** *v. Obs.* [f. FORE- *pref.* + HEED.] *trans.* To take care against beforehand; to provide against. With simple obj., or *that* introducing subord. sentence.

1526 *Ord. Hen. VIII* in *Househ. Ord.* (1790) 212 Foreheeding alwayes that none of them depart the court before the expences of their offices be brought to the Masters of the household. **1631** R. BYFIELD *Doctr. Sabb.* 68 A..casualty that could not be foreseene or foreheeded.

forehele, var. of FORHELE *v.*, to conceal.

†**fore'hent,** *v. Obs.* [f. FORE- *pref.* + HENT.] *trans.* To seize beforehand; **a.** to cut off (in flight), overtake. **b.** To take in advance.

1590 SPENSER *F.Q.* III. iv. 49 A fearefull Dove..Having farre off espyde a Tassell gent..Doubleth her hast for feare to bee for-hent. **1593** GOLDING *Ovid's Met.* XI. 267 [He] toake the pleasure which the sonne of Maia had forehent.

forehew, erron. form (in Dicts.) for FORHEW.

fore-hill, -hinting, -hip: see FORE- *pref.*

forehold ('fɔəhəʊld). [f. FORE- *pref.* + HOLD *sb.*]

†**1.** The action of holding on in front; advance.

1641 BEST *Farm. Bks.* (Surtees) 12 Aboute the middle of Aprill, when the fields have gotten some foreholde.

2. *Naut.* (See quot. 1867).

1790 BEATSON tr. *Nav. & Mil. Mem.* 322 Started 30 tons of water in the fore-hold to lighten her forward. **1835** SIR J. Ross *Narr. 2nd Voy.* vii. 94 The forehold was restowed. **1867** SMYTH *Sailor's Word-bk.*, *Fore-hold*, the part of the hold before the fore hatchway. **1884** SIR R. COUCH in *Law Rep.* 9 App. Cases 422 The master improperly loaded the forehold of the steamer.

[**foreholding**: a spurious word in Johnson; in his quot. from L'Estrange (*Fables* clxxviii) the word should be *Forebodings*.]

fore-hood, -hoof, etc.: see FORE- *pref.*

'fore-horse. [f. FORE- *pref.* + HORSE.] The foremost horse in a team, 'leader'.

1483 *Fun. Edw. IV*, in *Lett. & Pap. Rich. III* (Rolls) I. 7 Upon the fore horse, and the thil horse sat ij chariot men. **1592** GREENE *Upst. Courtier* in *Harl. Misc.* (Malh.) II. 218 They wore beesoms of thrift in their hats like fore-horses. *a* **1670** HACKET *Abp. Williams* I. (1692) 28 None of his fellows had cause to repent that he rode upon the fore-horse. **1718** *Freethinker* No. 144 ¶8 The Nobleman is but the Fore-Horse in the Team. **1824** MISS MITFORD *Village* Ser. I. (1863) 199 The fore-horse decked with ribbons.

transf. and *fig.* **1601** SHAKS. *All's Well* II. i. 30, I shal stay here the for-horse to a smocke. **1645** PAGITT *Heresiogr.* (1661) 177 [He useth this passage] as the fore-horse or leading Authority, to bring in whatsoever Calumnies he pleaseth afterward. **1816** T. JEFFERSON *Writ.* (1830) IV. 290 The fore-horse of this frightful team is public debt.

attrib. **1480** *Wardr. Acc. Edw. IV* (1830) 123 A forehors bridelle. **1636** SAMPSON *Vow-breaker* v. i. I iij, Have I not borrow'd the fore Horse-bells his Plumes, and braveries?

foreign ('fɒrɪn), *a.* and *sb.* Forms: 3, 5–6 foren(e, 3–4, 6–7, 9 forein(e, -eyn(e, 4, 6–8 for(r)ain(e, 5–6 -ayn(e, 4–6 forreyn(e, 5–7 -ayne, 6–8 forr-en, -ei(g)ne, -aign(e, (7 foran, furraine), 6– foreign. [a. OF. *forain*:—popular L. type **forānus*, f. *forās, for-is*: see FOR- *pref.*³

Med.L. had *forāneus* (Sp. *foraneo*) on the analogy of *extrāneus*; also *forinsecus* adj. (f. class. L. *forinsecus* adv.), which in Eng. Law Latin is the usual equivalent of *foreign*.]

A. *adj.*

†**1. a.** Out of doors; outside. ***a chamber foreign***: a privy (cf. FOREIGN *sb.*). ***foreign darkness*** = 'outer darkness'. *Obs.*

1297 R. GLOUC. (1724) 310 In to a chambre forene þe gadelyng gan wende. *c* **1374** CHAUCER *Boeth.* I. metr. ii. 3 (Camb. MS.) Mintinge to goon in to foreine derknesses. *c* **1430** LYDG. *Min. Poems* 234 This is the name that chaceth away the clips Of foreyn dirkenesse.

†**b.** Concerned with matters at a distance from home; outside; opposed to *domestic*. *Obs.*

1605 in *Archæologia* (1800) XIII. 316 [The steward] is to see into all offices, soe well forraine, as at home. *a* **1619** FOTHERBY *Atheom.* II. xiii. §1 (1622) 348 By writing, we may giue direction for our foraine Businesses, though we stay at home; and for our domestical, though we be abroad.

†**c.** *nonce-use.* ? Excluded, kept away (from court, or from employment in affairs).

The sense is doubtful: it may be 'resident abroad' (cf. 7), or 'outside the circle of one's intimate friends' (cf. 2 b).

1613 SHAKS. *Hen. VIII*, II. ii. 129 You enuide him; And fearing he would rise..Kept him a forraigne man still.

2. a. Belonging to other persons or things; not one's own; = L. *alienus*. Now *rare*.

c **1374** CHAUCER *Boeth.* I. pr. iv. 9 (Camb. MS.) For nede of foreyne moneye [mistranslation of *æris alieni necessitate*, 'through pressure of debt'] *Ibid.* II. pr. v. 32 (Camb. MS.) Fortune ne shal neuer makyn þat swyche thynges ben thyne, þat nature of thinges hath maked foreyne fro the. **1633** G. HERBERT *Temple, Church Porch* lxi, Keep all thy native good, and naturalize All forrain of that name; but scorn their ill. **1733** POPE *Ess. Man* III. 21 Nothing is foreign; parts relate to whole. **1851** HUSSEY *Papal Power* i. 35 The interference of Bishops in foreign Sees.

†**b.** Not of one's household or family. *Obs.*

1604 SHAKS. *Oth.* IV. iii 89 They..powre our Treasures into forraigne laps. **1608** —— *Per.* IV. i. 34, I loue the king your father..with more then forraine heart.

†**c.** Of possessions, expenses: Other than personal. *Obs.*

1589 PUTTENHAM *Eng. Poesie* I. xviii. (Arb.) 53 Quick cattel being the first property of any forreine possession. I say forreine, because alway men claimed property in their apparell and armour, and other like things made by their owne..industry. **1721** STRYPE *Eccl. Mem.* II. II. ii. 260 To have their foreign expences after the rate of 100*l.* a year.

3. Proceeding from other persons or things.

c **1374** CHAUCER *Boeth.* III. pr. iii. 55 (Camb. MS.) Than ..hath a man nede to seken hym foreyne helpe by whyche he may deffende hys moneye? **1561** T. NORTON *Calvin's Inst.* I. 16 The truthe is then set free from all douting, when not vpholden by forayne aides it self alone sufficeth to susteine it self. **1659** HAMMOND *On Ps.* Pref. §3. 2 For this ..we must appeal to forreign testimonies. **1712** BLACKMORE *Creation* I. 395 Machines..Move by a foreign impulse, not their own. **1834** MRS. SOMERVILLE *Connect. Phys. Sc.* x. (1849) 81 If the system be not deranged by a foreign cause.

4. Alien in character; not related to or concerned with the matter under consideration; irrelevant, dissimilar, inappropriate. Now only const. *from, to.*

1393 GOWER *Conf.* I. 279 A vice foreine fro the lawe. **1622** CALLIS *Stat. Sewers* (1647) 103 The Lord of the Copyhold is not to be taxed for the Soil of the Copyhold: for although he might come to it by forfeiture committed, yet that is a forain possibility. **1665** GLANVILL *Scepsis Sci.* 64 Our Author's sense and interpretation seems to me..forraign, arbitrary, and unnatural. **1672** MARVELL *Reh. Transp.* I. 118 This is a matter forreign to my Judicature. **1701** SWIFT *Sacramental Test* Wks. 1755 II. I. 128 This design is not so foreign from some people's thoughts. **1724** A. COLLINS *Gr. Chr. Relig.* 193 To tell the woman Ye worship ye know not what relates..to a matter wholly foreign. **1735** BERKELEY *Def. Free-think. in Math.* §42 All you have been saying..is quite foreign to the argument. **1756** BURKE *Subl. & B.* III. vi, To leave these foreign examples; if beauty in our own species was annexed to use, men would be much more lovely than women. **1821** LAMB *Elia* Ser. I. *Grace bef. Meat*, [The diet] least stimulative to appetite, leaves the mind most free for foreign considerations. **1828** SCOTT *F.M. Perth* xix, However foreign to his nature and disposition. **1873** HELPS *Anim. & Mast.* i. (1875) 16 A purpose foreign from his pursuits.

5. Introduced from outside; not belonging to the place in which it is found; *esp.* in Surgical use, of substances embedded in tissues of the body. *spec.* in phr. ***foreign body***.

1621 BURTON *Anat. Mel.* II. ii. III. (1651) 262 Excluding forrain aire and winds. **1626** BACON *Sylva* §334 A Foreign Spirit, stronger and more eager than the Spirit of the Body. **1664** POWER *Exp. Philos.* II. 133 Yet in its dilation will admit of no aether or forrain Substance to enter the pores thereof. **1767** GOOCH *Treat. Wounds* I. 123, I discovered, by the probe, this foreign body. **1770** PRIESTLEY in *Phil. Trans.* LX. 204 Part of the electric matter natural to the body must be repelled, to make room for the foreign electricity. **1875** *Lyell's Princ. Geol.* I. II. xv. 331 A hard chlorite rock equally foreign to the immediate neighbourhood. **1898** *Daily News* 30 Nov. 8/1 The presence of the 'foreign body'—a disguising euphemism for half an ounce..of lead entering a man at great velocity. **1961** *Brit. Med. Dict.* 577/1 *Foreign body*, a substance present in any part of the body in which normally it is not found, and usually of external origin. **1964** S. DUKE-ELDER *Parsons' Dis. Eye* (ed. 14) xxvi. 375 Foreign bodies,..particles of coal dust, emery, steel, etc.—may pitch upon the conjunctiva or..cornea.

6. a. Situated outside an estate, manor, district, parish, province, etc.

[**1292** BRITTON III. viii. §5 Vivers foreyns.] **1495** *Act 11 Hen. VII*, c. 7 Dwelling in a foren Shire. **1512** *Act 4 Hen. VIII*, c. 4 Preamb., Outlawries had ageynst theym in forreyn Counties. **1523** FITZHERB. *Surv.* 3 b, It is to be inquered of forren pastures that is comyn..what the lorde may haue in the same. **1676** DEGGE *Parson's Counsellor* II. v. 166 To be imployed in a Forrain Parish. **1885** E. B. IVATTS *Railw. Managem.* 547 To the employees of railway 'A' all other railways in respect to traffic are 'foreign'.

b. Belonging to or coming from another district, county, society, etc.

c **1460** in *Eng. Gilds* (1870) 317 Ye schall couer no foren stranger yn no wys under yoʳ franches. **1568** GRAFTON *Chron.* II. 437 The markethouse..was buylded for the free-sale of the foreyn Boocher, and of the foreyn Fishmonger. *c* **1638** *Order Priv. Counc.* in Penkethman *Artach.* H ij b, The forreigne Bakers which bring their Bread to be sold in the market of any Citie. **1891** *Daily News* 18 Sept. 3/3 There has been a great demand for foreign labour in Kent. **1895** *Guardian* 6 Mar. 363/3 The foreign examiners [at Durham] are the Regius Professor of Hebrew, Oxford, and the Dixie Professor of Ecclesiastical History, Cambridge.

†**c.** ? Dealing with matters outside (the manor).

1708 *Lond. Gaz.* No. 4465/6 In the Hands of the foreign Bailiff of Dudley.

7. Situated outside the country; not in one's own land.

In this and the following senses, the word is in British use not applied to parts of the United Kingdom, nor, ordinarily, to (former) colonies chiefly inhabited by English-speaking people. In the U.S. the designations of ***foreign corporation, foreign port***, are sometimes applied to those belonging to other States of the Union.

1393 GOWER *Conf.* II. 160 [Isles] that fro the lond forein Leie open to the wynd al plein. *Ibid.* III. 185 A place, Which is forein out in an ile. *c* **1400** MAUNDEV. (1839) xvii. 183 Whan men gon beȝonde tho iourneyes, toward Ynde and to the foreyn Yles. *c* **1450** *Merlin* 577 Kynge Alein of the forayn londes. **1524** *Act 14 & 15 Hen. VIII*, c. 1 Preamb., The said outwarde and foren regions. **1611** HEYWOOD *Gold. Age* I. Wks. 1874 III. 9 Whil'st I in forreigne Kingdomes search my Fate. **1700** WALLIS in *Collect.* (Oxf. Hist. Soc.) I. 313 In some forain universities. **1875** JOWETT *Plato* (ed. 2) III. 385 In some foreign clime which is..beyond our ken. **1888** BRYCE *Amer. Commw.* II. xxxviii. 63 They usually talk of corporations belonging to other States as 'foreign'.

8. a. Pertaining to, characteristic of, or derived from another country or nation; not domestic or native. ***foreign legion***: see LEGION 1 b.

1447 BOKENHAM *Seyntys* (Roxb.) 29, I am but foreyn in this cuntre. **1535** in Ellis *Orig. Lett.* Ser. III. II. 325 No more jurisdiction wᵗʰ in this realme than anie oodre foreyne bisshoppe. **1579** FENTON *Guicciard.* (1618) 7 To build his suretie vpon forreine strength, seeing he had no confidence in his owne forces. **1611** HEYWOOD *Gold. Age* I. Wks. 1874 III. 8 If my owne land proue thus vnnaturall I'le purchase forraine aid. **1655** H. VAUGHAN *Silex Scint.* I. Pref. (1858) 5 Plentifully furnished with various Foraign Vanities. **1676** HOBBES *Iliad* Pref. (1686) 2 Forein words. **1709** STEELE *Tatler* No. 49 ¶9 The Foreign Ministers residing at the Hague. **1771** *Junius Lett.* lix. 308 A foreign force..actually landed upon our coast. **1832** LEWIS *Use & Ab. Pol. Terms* iii. 32 The foreign and native commodity. **1849** HARE *Serm.* II. 435 The plan sprang up in the heart of a forein king. **1875** H. JAMES *R. Hudson* iv. 140 She spoke with a vague foreign accent.

b. *transf.* Unfamiliar, strange.

1881 ILLINGWORTH *Serm. in Coll. Chapel* 74 Such language may be a little foreign, but the experience is universal.

c. ***foreign devil*** [tr. Chin. *yang kuei-tzu* (also, formerly, *fan kuei(-tzu)*, and other regional forms)]: a term of contempt for a foreigner (esp. a European) in China; also *transf.*

[**1842** *China as it Was* viii. 51 Be it remarked, that the term Fan-Qui, signifying literally 'barbarian wanderer', or 'outlandish demon' is applied invariably by the subjects of the 'Celestial Empire' to all foreigners.] **1860** *Englishman in China* 237 All rush to their doors, and press to see the '*Fan Qui*', or foreign devils; though I must here add that but once was that name applied to us, and really they were all of them most civil. **1889** G. B. SHAW *Fabian Ess. Socialism* 174 A Frenchman or Scotchman was a natural enemy: a Muscovite was a foreign devil. **1926** A. HUXLEY *Jesting Pilate* III. 248 The trees might just be saying, 'Foreign Devil, Foreign Devil', and repeating it monotonously, mile after mile. **1937** E. SNOW *Red Star over China* I. iv. 43 It was the perfect setting for the blotting-out of a too inquisitive foreign devil. **1965** P. ORDWAY *Night of Reckoning* (1967) ii. 39 Most of us foreign devils [in Spain] found seasonal rentals a very necessary source of additional income. **1969** V. G. KIERNAN *Lords of Human Kind* v. 167 Against these new barbarians China was building a new Great Wall, of hatred. Wherever they went they were saluted with cries of 'foreign devil'.

9. Carried on or taking place abroad, into or with other countries. *spec.* opp. *inland*, as ***foreign bill, exchange*** (see EXCHANGE *sb.* 4 and quots.).

1548 HALL *Chron., Hen. VI* (an. 32) 167 When foren warre and outward battailes, were brought to an ende. **1576** FLEMING *Panopl. Epist.* 176 To take on mee a forreigne voyage. **1632** SANDERSON *Serm.* 475 A forraigne Invasion abroad. **1653** WALTON *Angler* i. 32 A man whose forraign imployments in the service of this Nation, and [etc.]. **1691** [see EXCHANGE *sb.* 4]. **1810** C. JAMES *Milit. Dict.* (ed. 3), *Foreign Service*.. any service done out of the limits of Great Britain, Ireland..etc. **1840** MALCOM *Trav.* 34/1 The foreign trade is extinct. **1849** [see INLAND *a.* 2]. **1940** *Manch. Guardian Weekly* 5 Jan. 3 Behind all these questions of supply lie the inexorable limitations of foreign exchange and shipping space. **1948** G. CROWTHER *Outl. Money* (ed. 2) vii. 202 (*heading*) The Foreign Exchanges. *Ibid.* 210 The foreign exchange market was originally the 'foreign-bills-of-exchange market'. It was the place where bills payable in New York, Shanghai, Buenos Aires and half a hundred other places could be bought. **1951** J. R. WINTON *Dict. Econ. Terms* (ed. 3) 38 *Foreign exchange*, strictly, this term denotes the transaction of exchanging one currency for another but, in practice, it is often used to refer to actual currency, e.g. foreign currency notes or the means of obtaining such through travellers' cheques or letters of credit. **1971** *Daily Tel.* 10 May 14/2 The currency of any other country is 'foreign exchange'.

10. Dealing with matters concerning other countries. ***Foreign Office***: the department of the 'Secretary of State for Foreign Affairs'; the building in which the business of this department is carried on. Also, intended for use in transactions or correspondence with other countries, as in ***foreign bill*** (see quot. 1767), ***foreign letter-paper***. Also in *Journalism*.

1611 CORYAT *Crudities* Epist. Dedic., The Observations of my trauels..I hope..will be very delectable to every Reader that loueth to heare of forraine affaires. **1623** J. CHAMBERLAIN *Let.* 21 Nov. (1939) II. 527 The selected commissioners for forain affaires sit much. **1655** SIR E. NICHOLAS in *N. Papers* (Camden) II. 241 Other furraine newes I heare not. **1659** MARVELL *Corr.* Wks. 1872–5 II. 12 John Milton, Esqire, Secretarye for the Forrain affaires. **1682** SCARLETT *Exchanges* 15 So are usually all Foreign Bills. **1745** *De Foe's Eng. Tradesman* Introd. (1841) I. 2 Such as carry on foreign correspondences. **1767** BLACKSTONE *Comm.* II. xxx. 467 These bills [of exchange] are either foreign, or inland foreign, when drawn by a merchant residing abroad upon his correspondent in England or *vice versa*. **1848** THACKERAY *Pendennis* I. xxx, Look! here comes the Foreign Express galloping in. *Ibid.*, Mr. Doolan..is foreign sub-editor, and sees the mail on the newspaper sheet before he goes to his own. **1856** EMERSON *Eng. Traits, Result* Wks. (Bohn) II. 133 The foreign policy of England. **1859** *Sat. Rev.* VIII. 62/2 The army and the Foreign Office have, to a certain extent, escaped the constitutionalizing process. **1870** *Nation* (N.Y.) 27 Jan. 54/2 There is..a column of telegrams from Europe in every issue of the daily papers, which editors are accustomed to refer to as furnishing the latest 'foreign intelligence'. **1877** *Harper's Mag.* Dec. 53/2 Foreign correspondence in the hands of a foreign editor. **1892** E. REEVES *Homeward Bound* 113 No contribution to exceed six pages of foreign note paper. **1959** C. OGBURN *Marauders* (1960) ii. 47 A reporter and a writer on the foreign desk of *The Chicago Daily News*. **1967** [see *city page* s.v. CITY 9]. **1971** *Guardian* 22 July 11/8 Foreign correspondents during the previous days used, perforce, comments from the angry hippies.

11. Law. ***foreign apposer, attachment*** (see the sbs.); ***foreign answer, matter, plea, service*** (see quots. 1607). †***foreign intent***: a constructive sense not implied in the wording of the instrument to be interpreted; opposed to *common intent*.

1512 *Act 4 Hen. VIII*, c. 2 Of feyned and untrew Foreyn pleyes triable in foreyn Countes. **1607** COWELL *Interpr.* s.v., *Forein aunswer*..such an answer, as is not triable in the countie where it is made. [With a reference to *Act 15 Hen. VI*, c. 5, which reads: Jesques au temps que chescun des ditz foreins severalx responses soit trie.] **1607** COWELL *Interpr.*, *Forein Apposer* (forinsecarum oppositor). *Ibid.*, *Forein attachment* (attachiamentum forinsecum). *Ibid.*, Forein mater..mater triable in another countie. *Ibid.*, *Forein-plea* ..a refusal of the Iudge as incompetent, because the mater in hand was not within his precincts. *Ibid.*, *Forein seruice*.. such service, whereby a meane Lord holdeth ouer of another, without the compasse of his owne fee..or else that which a tenant performeth..out of the fee. *a* **1626** BACON *Max. & Uses Com. Law* x. (1636) 43 The graunts of a common person..shall be extended as well to a forrein intent as to a common intent. **1685** KEBLE *King's Bench Rep.* II. 132 The Defendant pleads a forein attachment in London of 50 li. **1800** DURNFORD & EAST *Cases King's Bench* VIII. 417 A foreign attachment in the Mayor's court at the suit of the plaintiff.

†¶ **12.** Used to translate L. *forensis*: Made in open court, public.

c **1374** CHAUCER *Boeth.* III. pr. iii. 55 (Camb. MS.) For whennes comyn elles alle thyse foreyne compleyntes.

13. quasi-*adv.* (***to fit, go, sail***, etc.) ***foreign***, i.e. for foreign parts. (*Naut. colloq.*)

1829 MARRYAT *F. Mildmay* v, We were ordered to fit foreign. **1840** —— *Poor Jack* xiii, In consequence of our being about to sail foreign. **1844** J. T. HEWLETT *Parsons & W.* xix, But the captain is going foreign, is he not?

14. *Comb.* Chiefly locative and parasynthetic, as ***foreign-built, -foliaged, -going, -looking, -made, -manned***, †***-nationed, -owned*** (= owned by a foreigner, of foreign ownership), ***-wrought***, etc. adjs.. Also ***foreign aid*** [AID *sb.* 3 c], ***-born*** (= born abroad), ***-language*** attrib.

1958 *Foreign-aid [see AID *sb.* 3 c]. **1968** B. TURNER *Circle of Squares* viii. 51 The foreign aid we have lashed out so lavishly. **1969** *New Yorker* 31 May 68/3 Because foreign-aid resources have been so limited, Indonesia's economic-development efforts..have been confined largely to food production. **1856** J. P. HAMBLETON *H. A. Wise* 57 Both the Alien and Sedition laws were intended for the oppression of *foreign born citizens. **1940** J. H. JAGGER *English in Future* 124 Native-born with one parent foreign-born. **1964** P. F. ANSON *Bishops at Large* ix. 440 A foreign-born Mexican citizen. **1678** in Marvell *Growth Popery* 64 The Agatha, *Foreign built, 250 Tuns. **1898** *Westm. Gaz.* 16 June 1/3 A *foreign-controlled department of public works. **1898** *Daily News* 5 Nov. 6/3 The commander of the *foreign drilled troops. **1890** BOLDREWOOD *Col. Reform.* (1891) 54 The vast *foreign-foliaged, primeval forests. **1863** H. COX *Instit.* III. v. 658 Masters and mates of *foreign-going vessels. **1905** *Daily Chron.* 22 Nov. 6/3 Our corn is part home-grown and part *foreign-grown. **1933** BLOOMFIELD *Lang.* iii. 54 The factor of *foreign-language speaking does not lend itself to measurement. **1938** *Times Lit. Suppl.* 20 Aug. 514/3 The kind of Americans of foreign-language origin who are members of the population of the United States. **1959** *Encounter* Dec. 56/2 The BBC set new standards for foreign-language broadcasts. **1971** *Incorporated Linguist* X. 39/1 No one would claim that British foreign-language policy towards Europe is or should be principally determined by the extent to which English is known and used in Europe. **1830** MISS MITFORD *Village* Ser. IV. (1863) 213 A dark, sallow, *foreign-looking personage. **1895** *Daily News* 15 June 5/4 *Foreign-made machinery. **1599** R. LINCHE *Fount. Anc. Fict.* Hj b, The vncertaine steps of *forren-nationed pilgrimes. **1878** A. L. PERRY *Elem. Pol. Econ.* 556 American-built but *foreign-owned ships. **1906** *Daily Chron.* 13 Aug. 4/7 The *foreign-trained fitters and machinists. **1513** MORE in Grafton *Chron.* (1568) II. 808 Lawes..agaynst..*foreign wrought wares.

B. quasi-*sb.* and *sb.*

†**1. a.** = FOREIGNER 1. Also, a foreign vessel. *Obs.*

1330 R. BRUNNE *Chron.* (1810) 322 þe tounes, þe countes, þe foreyns alle aboute, To þe kyng felle on knes. **1429** *Pol. Poems* (Rolls) II. 143 Outrayeng foreyns that cam from Babilon. **1509** BARCLAY *Shyp of Folys* (1570) 197 Of these false forrains renneth so great a bande Vnto our shippes, that [etc.]. **1612** BREREWOOD *Lang. & Relig.* iii. 19 Ambassages ..or whatsoever other business of the provincials, or forraigns. **1643** *Decl. Lords & Com., Reb. Ireland* 50 They took yesterday a Forrain laden with deales.

†**b.** One not a citizen, or more particularly not a member of the guild, a stranger, an outsider.

c **1350** in *Eng. Gilds* (1870) 361 ȝef a foreyne empledy þe teþynge. **1487** in *Ann. Barber-Surg. Lond.* (1890) 581 Ye shall not admytt eny foren to be of this misterie. **1540** HYRDE tr. *Vives' Instr. Chr. Wom.* (1592) N vj, For citicens favour more one another, than they do forrains.

†**2.** Short for *chambre foreine* (see A. 1). *Obs.*

1303 R. BRUNNE *Handl. Synne* 7436 Ful foule ys þat forreyne þat ys comoun for al certeyne. *c* **1385** CHAUCER *L.G.W. 1962 Ariadne*, The tour..Was ioyning in the walle to a foreyne. **1505** in Gage *Thingoe Hundred* 140 To be wrought with calion and breke, with foreyns and other necessaries. **1570** LEVINS *Manip.* 201/8 A Forayne, *forica*.

3. a. That part of a town which lies outside the borough or the parish proper. Now *local*.

1668 PLOT *Staffordsh.* viii. §82. 314 All the Villages and Hamlets belonging thereunto [Walsall]..which they call the forraigne. **1782** NASH *Worcestersh.* II. 39 The inhabitants of the foreign of Kidderminster, so called to distinguish them from the inhabitants of the borough. **1856** GLEW *Walsall* 3 The parish is in two townships, called the Borough and Foreign. **1875** *Sussex Gloss.* s.v. *Foreigner*, At Rye..that part of the parish which lies out of the boundary of the corporation, is called the Foreign of Rye.

b. *pl.* The outer court of a monastery; also, the space immediately outside the monastic precincts. *Obs.*, but surviving as proper name in various places where monasteries existed.

1668 WILKES *Plan Canterbury* cited in Willis *Monast. Canterb.* (1869) 152 Ye forrins. **1799** HASTED *Kent* IV. 575 The space of ground *without* or foreign to it [the jurisdiction of the church] called *the Foreigns*, now vulgarly the *Follings*. **1872** *Gloss. Eccl. Terms* (ed. Shipley), *Foreign Court*..Also called Foreigns.

4. a. ***in foreign***: abroad.

c **1618** FLETCHER *Q. Corinth* III. i, One that hath As people say in forraigne pleasur'd him.

b. ellipt. for *foreign language, foreign parts, foreign service*, etc.

1906 R. BROOKE *Let.* 3 Feb. (1968) 39 The Calendar has appeared. There are about eight foreigns [*sc.* matches against teams from other schools]. **1907** A. QUILLER-COUCH *Major Vigoureux* ix. 90, I was thinking that—she being from foreign and the Islands the first place she've touched at—I might pick up a bravish order in the way of fresh milk and eggs. **1955** G. FREEMAN *Liberty Man* I. iii. 49 'On leave, Jack?' 'Yeah... Just back from foreign.' **1962** *Times* 13 Feb. 12/6, I had tried to explain I'd just arrived from 'foreign' [*sc.* foreign service]. **1971** P. O'DONNELL *Impossible Virgin* v. 103 He was a foreigner, and he babbled in foreign.

Hence **'foreignly** *adv.*; **'foreignness**.

1611 COTGR., *Peregrinité*..forrainenesse. **1661** BOYLE *Style of Script.* (1675) 249 The forreignness and obscurity of some texts. **1876** GEO. ELIOT *Dan. Der.* I. v. 32 His English had little foreignness except its fluency. **1880** J. CAIRD *Philos. Relig.* vi. 169 When a being or object reveals itself to feeling, it, so to speak, loses any vestige of foreignness or estrangement. **1880** G. MEREDITH *Trag. Com.* ix. 169 He rose out of his amazement..foreignly beholding himself.

†**fo'reign**, *v. Obs.*$^{-0}$ [f. prec.] (See quot.)

1598 FLORIO, *Esternare*, to alienate, estrange, forraine.

foreig'neer, *v. vulgar.* [f. FOREIGN + -EER[1] (marking contempt). Cf. *electioneer* vb.] Only in **foreig'neering** *vbl. sb. attrib.*, concerned with foreign matters; also *ppl. a.* foreign, like a foreigner.

1827 *Sporting Mag.* XIX. 194 Since I sent you a despatch on foreigneering business. **1841** *Blackw. Mag.* Apr. 501 There is no teaching these foreigneering fellows the proper usage of their parts of speech. **1890** HALL CAINE *Bondman* I. iv. 65 The sailor was like..a foreigneering sort of man in a skin cap and long stockings.

foreigner ('fɒrɪnə(r)). [f. FOREIGN *a.* + -ER[1].]

1. a. A person born in a foreign country; one from abroad or of another nation; an alien.

In ordinary use chiefly applied to those who speak a foreign language as their native tongue; thus in England the term is not commonly understood to include Americans.

1413 *Pilgr. Sowle* (Caxton) IV. xxxviii. (1859) 64 They were straunge foreyners, nought of his propre peple. **1526** *Pilgr. Perf.* (W. de W. 1531) 302 Whome that foreyner & straunger Pylate wolde oftentymes..haue delyuered. **1561** T. NORTON *Calvin's Inst.* IV. 138, I am here a foriner and stranger, as all my fathers were. **1637** *Decree Star Chamb.* §12 in *Milton's Areop.* (Arb.) 15 That no..forreigner..be suffered to bring in..any booke or bookes printed beyond the seas. **1703** *Lond. Gaz.* No. 3916/3 Having reviewed all the Horse and Foot under his Command, as well English as Foreigners. **1835** THIRLWALL *Greece* I. vii. 268 Besides the Dorians, there were foreigners of other nations.

b. *transf.* Some thing produced or brought from abroad; *esp.* a foreign vessel.

1677 PLOT *Oxfordsh.* 148 Beside what I have seen amongst forreigners [plants] in Gardens. **1716** ADDISON *Freeholder* No. 22 ¶3 The lemons, the brandy, the sugar, and the nutmeg, were all foreigners. **1823** SCORESBY *Jrnl. Whale Fishery* 68 Nine or ten ships were assembled..none of them followed us, excepting a foreigner. *Ibid.* 419 The black rat and the common mouse are enumerated..but both these are foreigners imported by the shipping. **1891** *Daily News* 21 Nov. 5/3 The failure of the English walnut crop has enhanced the price of 'foreigners'.

c. *pl.* Foreign stocks and shares.

1898 *Westm. Gaz.* 14 Feb. 9/1 Foreigners are quiet. **1904** *Ibid.* 10 May 11/1 The Account Changes in Foreigners. **1964** *Financ. Times* 3 Mar. 19/2 Among Foreigners, Baltic bonds attracted buying interest.

2. One of another county, parish, etc.; a stranger, outsider. In early use *esp.* one not a member of any particular guild, a non-freeman. Now *dial.*

14.. *Customs of Malton* in *Surtees Misc.* (1890) 59 Yffe any man..als wele a foraner as Burges, be sommonyd to any cowrte. *c* **1460** in *Eng. Gilds* (1870) 317 Ye shall not.. counsell any forynar to dwell wᵗʸn þe franschys of this craft. **1565** in Picton *L'pool Munic. Rec.* (1883) I. 75 No foreigner, as men of Bolton, Blackburne or any other places. **1676** DEGGE *Parson's Counsellor* II. v. 166 There is no difference between the Case of a Parishioner and a Forrainer, where [etc.]. **1700** *Grassmens' Acc.* (Surtees) 96 If any Forraner or Freeborn come. **1855** MRS. GASKELL *North & S.* xvii, 'You're just a foreigner, and nothing more', said he, contemptuously. 'Much yo know about it.' **1875** *Sussex Gloss.*, *Foreigner*, a stranger, a person who comes from any other county but Sussex. **1966** O. NORTON *School of Liars* viii. 129, I know very little about him. He's a foreigner in the village. **1968** M. ALLINGHAM *Cargo of Eagles* xiv. 157 He was a poor silly foreigner from Kent. **1968** J. DRUMMOND *Gantry Episode* ii. 23, I want the lot of you foreigners out of Gantry... I don't like interference.

†**3.** *fig.* A stranger, outsider; a little-known person; *rarely*, a person other than oneself (cf. FOREIGN *a.* 2). *Obs.*

1586 T. B. *La Primaud. Fr. Acad.* I. (1594) 75 He, that would not be a stranger to the universe, an alien to felicity, and a foreiner to himself. **1597** HOOKER *Eccl. Pol.* v. lxviii. §1 Forreiners and strangers from the Church of God. **1621** BURTON *Anat. Mel.* III. iii. I. i. (1651) 591 Jealousie is..a fear or doubt, lest any forrainer should participate or share with him in his love. **1641** DENHAM *Sophy* v. 52 Joy is such a forrainer, So meere a stranger to my thoughts, I know Not how to entertaine him.

foreignism ('fɒrɪnɪz(ə)m). [f. as prec. + -ISM.]

1. The imitation of what is foreign.

1879 SIR G. SCOTT *Recollect.* v. 202, In my essays..I do not recollect any tendency to foreignism. **1892** *Review of Rev.* Aug. 165 Journalists in the German language encourage foreignism.

2. An idiom, phrase, or term of foreign origin.

1877 *Congregationalist* (U.S.) 15 Aug. (Cent.), That he [Miles Coverdale] left in his Bible some few foreignisms.. is not surprising. **1887** L. SWINBURNE in *Scribner's Mag.* II. 508 It is astonishing, indeed, how many of these foreignisms have crept into the common speech.

foreignize ('fɒrɪnaɪz), *v.* [f. as prec. + -IZE.]

1. *intr.* To grow or become foreign; to take after, or display a resemblance to, foreign types.

a **1661** FULLER *Worthies, Warwick* (1662) 129 *marg.*, Our Countryman Pits did foranize with long living beyond the Seas. **1860** *Ecclesiologist* XXI. 179 The style of course foreignizes.

2. *trans.* To render foreign; to refashion after foreign models; to give a foreign air to.

1832 *Fraser's Mag.* V. 372 Instructors.. have sought.. to foreignise our people. **1861** G. MEREDITH *E. Harrington* I. iii. 37 Her sisters said she was 'foreignised' over-much. **1894** *Nation* (N.Y.) LVIII. 360/3 We needlessly foreignize our tongue by multiplying the single *f*, *l*, and *v* endings.

†**ˌfore-iˈmagine**, *v.* *Obs.* [f. FORE- *pref.* + IMAGINE *v.*] *trans.* To imagine beforehand.

1602 [see the *ppl. a.*]. **1603** FLORIO *Montaigne* I. xxiii. (1632) 55, I am fully perswaded you fore-imagine what I will charge you with. **1624** BP. HALL *Heaven vpon Earth* §3 To ..fore-imagine the worst in all casuall matters.

Hence **fore-imagined** *ppl. a.* So **fore-imagination**, something imagined beforehand.

1602 CAREW *Eng. Tongue* (1723) 11 A fore-imagined possibilitie. **1625** DONNE *Serm.* lxvi. 667 All that is well done..is..done according to Preconceptions, Fore-imaginations.

fore-inclined, -instruct, etc.: see FORE-.

ˌfore-inˈtend, *v.* [f. FORE- *pref.*] *trans.* To intend beforehand. Hence **ˈfore-intended** *ppl. a.*

1580 SIDNEY *Arcadia* (1622) 249 Shee was put from the bias of her fore-intended lesson. **1622** WITHER *Mistr., Philar.* Wks. (1633) 635 What the Fates doe fore-intend, They never change agaíne. **1641** BEST *Farm. Bks.* (Surtees) 90 That hee give him notice what is to bee done or foreintended. **1866** G. MACDONALD *Ann. Q. Neighb.* xv. (1878) 325 Whether she foreintended her following conduct.

†**ˈfore-intent.** *Obs.* [f. FORE- *pref.* + INTENT.] A pre-arranged purpose.

1627–77 FELTHAM *Resolves* I. lxxxiii. 127 One may fail me by accident, but the other will do it out of fore-intent.

forejudge (fɔəˈdʒʌdʒ), *v.* Also 7 forjudge. [f. FORE- *pref.* + JUDGE *v.*]

1. *trans.* To judge or determine beforehand or without a fair trial; to prejudge. Also *absol.*

1561–80 [see the *ppl. a.* and *vbl. sb.*]. **1647** CLARENDON *Hist. Reb.* III. §195 If his Majesty might take notice what Bills were passing in either House, and declare His Own opinion, it was to forejudge Their Counsels. **1656** in *Burton's Diary* (1828) I. 215 We ought not to forejudge the petition. **1860** ELLICOTT *Life Our Lord* iv. 174 Pharisees whom Judæa and Jerusalem..had sent forth to forejudge and to condemn.

†**2.** To form a judgement or opinion of beforehand. Also *intr.* with *of*. *Obs.*

1603 SIR C. HEYDON *Jud. Astrol.* To Rdr. 7 They rashely foreiudge what I thinke. *a* **1716** SOUTH *Serm.* (1717) V. 300 Those false Rates and Grounds, by which Men generally fore-judge of the Issue or Event of Actions. **1734** W. GIFFARD *Case Midwif.* lvii. 129, I..prepared to attempt the delivery, forejudging the inconveniencies I might meet with. **1792** G. WASHINGTON *Lett.* Writ. 1891 XII. 177 Some infallible rule by which we could fore-judge events.

3. (See quot.)

1611 COTGR., *Prejuger*, to..foreiudge; to rule, or direct the opinion of Iudges by a former iudgement.

Hence **foreˈjudged** *ppl. a.*; **foreˈjudging** *vbl. sb.* and *ppl. a.*

1561 T. NORTON *Calvin's Inst.* IV. 54 The determination of the Councell may haue his force, and be as a foreiudged sentence, and yet not hinder the aforesaid examination. **1571** GOLDING *Calvin on Ps.* xlii. 8 This proud vaunting rose of..malicious forejudging. **1580** SIDNEY *Arcadia* v. (1598) 433 If you will suffer attentiue iudgement and not fore-iudging passion, to bee the waigher of my wordes. **1633** FORD *Broken H.* IV. iii, Cleave not my heart..With your fore-judging fears.

forejudge: see FORJUDGE.

forejudgement (fɔəˈdʒʌdʒmənt). Also 6 for-. [f. FORE *pref.* + JUDGEMENT: cf. prec.]

1. Judgement determined or formed beforehand.

1548 UDALL, etc. *Erasm. Par. Mark* Pref. 3 a, It is not my part to make any ones title either better or worse with my fore-iudgment. **1591** SPENSER *Muiopotmos* 320 All the Gods ..Did surely deeme the victorie his due: But seldome seene, forejudgement proveth true. **1862** SEWARD in *Sat. Rev.* (1863) 404 The only foreign nation steadily contributing in every indirect way possible to verify its forejudgment.

†**2.** A judgement previously pronounced; a judicial precedent. *Obs.*

1599 BLUNDEVILE *Art Logic* IV. iii. 104 What call you Foreiudgementes or Ruled Cases? They bee iudgementes or sentences heretofore pronounced, whereby Iudges take example to giue like iudgement in like cases.

fore-keel, -king, -knee, -knight: see FORE-.

foreknow (fɔəˈnəʊ), *v.* Also 6 forknow. [f. FORE- *pref.* + KNOW *v.*] **a.** *trans.* To know beforehand, have previous knowledge of.

1450–1530 *Myrr. our Ladye* 141 Before all tymes, I was forknowen and ordeyned of god to be made. **1680** ALLEN *Peace & Unity* 16 St. Paul..fore-knew there would be Heresies among them. **1732** BERKELEY *Serm. to Soc. Prop. Gosp.* Wks. III. 239 Are not the times and seasons fore-known only to God? **1817** SHELLEY *To Ollier* 11 Dec., You ..foreknew all that these people would say. **1855** KINGSLEY *Westw. Ho!* (1889) 5/1 He foreknew it would give her pain. *absol.* **1754** EDWARDS *Freed. Will* II. xi. (ed. 4) 138 If God does not fore-know, he cannot foretell.

b. *intr.* To have previous knowledge *of*.

1703 ROWE *Ulyss.* II. i. 858 Thetis..Wept for her Son, fore-knowing of his Fate.

Hence **foreˈknown** *ppl. a.*; **foreˈknowing** *vbl. sb.* and *ppl. a.* (whence **foreˈknowingly** *adv.*). Also †**foreˈknowable** *a.*, that may be foreknown; †**foreˈknower**, one who foreknows.

c **1374** CHAUCER *Troylus* I. 79 This Calkas..for to departen softely Took purpos ful this forknowinge wyse. **1423** JAS. I. *Kingis Q.* cxlix, Fortune is..strangest evermore Quhare leste foreknawing..Is in the man. **1450–1530** *Myrr. our Ladye* 4 Hauynge her endelesly as presente in the syghte of hys Godly forknowynge. **1548** UDALL, etc. *Erasm. Par. Matt.* xxv. 34 God the foreknower of al thinges. **1562** J. HEYWOOD *Prov. & Epigr.* (1867) 115 The fore knowne ill to man, would call Fore felt greefe, of fore knowne vnrest. **1647** JER. TAYLOR *Lib. Proph.* xiii. 198 He does very imprudently serve his ends who seeingly and fore-knowingly loses his life in the prosecution of them. *a* **1660** HAMMOND *Third let. Prescience* §75 Wks. 1674. I. 598 The foreknower is not cause of all that are foreknown. **1667** MILTON *P.L.* XI. 773 Evil..Which neither his foreknowing can prevent. **1678** CUDWORTH *Intell. Syst.* 712 We cannot but grant such things therefore to be foreknowable. **1849** GROTE *Greece* II. lxviii. (1862) VI. 143 Foreknowing and consistent agents. **1860** PUSEY *Min. Proph.* 259 That regularity itself of God's creation sets forth those other foreknown operations of God.

foreknowledge (fɔəˈnɒlɪdʒ). [f. FORE- *pref.* + KNOWLEDGE.] Knowledge of an event, etc. before it exists or happens; prescience.

1535 COVERDALE *Judith* ix. 6 Thy iudgmentes are done in thy euerlastinge fore knowlege. **1555** EDEN *Decades* Contents (Arb.) 45 The foreknowleage that the poet Seneca had of the fyndynge of the newe worlde. **1667** MILTON *P.L.* III. 118 If I foreknew, Foreknowledge had no influence on their fault. **1729** BUTLER *Serm.* Wks. 1874 II. Pref. 19 It is not foreknowledge of the punishment which renders us obnoxious to it. **1847** GROTE *Greece* II. xi. III. 139 Money lent with the foreknowledge that the borrower will be unable to repay it. **1863** DICEY *Federal St.* II. 210 [An astrologer promises to] give to the public a fore-knowledge of all the general affairs through life.

Hence **foreˈknowledged** *ppl. a.*, known beforehand as liable *to*, destined *to*. *Obs.*[−1]

1577 tr. *Bullinger's Decades* (1592) 643 Thou art..fore-knowledged, as they saye, to damnation.

forel, forrel (ˈfɒrəl). Forms: 3–6 forel, (5 furel), 5–7 forell(e, 7 forrell, foroll, 9 for(r)el, forrill. [a. OF. *forrel*, *fourrel* (Fr. *fourreau*), dim. f. *forre*, *fuerre* case, sheath, etc. (see FUR *sb.*).]

1. †**a.** A sheath (*obs.*). †**b.** A case or box (*obs.*).

a **1300** *Cursor M.* 15791 (Cott.) O þe forel a suerd he drogh. ? *a* **1430** *Wyclif's Job* xx. 25 Out of his shethe, or out of the furel. **1578** LYTE *Dodoens* VI lxi. 737 The fruit [of Date tree] ..lapped in a certayne long and brode forrell or covering.

c. A case or covering in which a book or manuscript is kept, or into which it is sewn. Now *dial.*

1393 LANGL. *P. Pl.* C. XVI. 103 And take his felawe to wittnesse, What he fond in a forel of a freres lyuynge. *c* **1440** *Promp. Parv.* 171/2 Forelle, to kepe yn a boke, *forulus*. **1519** HORMAN *Vulg.* 84 b, I hadde leuer haue my boke sowed in a forel: than bounde in bourdis. **1523** *St. Papers Hen. VIII*, VI. 134 His letters shalbe enclosed in a forel directed to the Treasorer. **1825** J. JENNINGS *Observ. Dial. West Eng.* 38 *Forrel*, the cover of a book. **1893** *Wiltsh. Gloss.*, *Forel*, the.. cover of a book.

2. A kind of parchment dressed to look like vellum, used for covering books (now only for account-books).

1549 (Mar.) *Bk. Com. Prayer* Colophon, No manner of persone shall sell this present book, unbounde, above the price of two shillynges and two-pence; and bounde in forell for iis. *xd.* **1824** J. JOHNSON *Typogr.* II. 529 The tympans are covered with vellum, forrels, or parchment.

attrib. **1883** *Kerry's St. Lawr. Reading* 203 Good paper —forel binding.

3. A selvedge or border.

1691 *Lond. Gaz.* No. 2653/4 A Crimson Piece of Spanish Cloth 23 yards long..with a yellow Foroll and a White List. **1697** *Ibid.* No. 3316/4 Three pieces of Super-fine Black Cloath for Men's ware, marked with..D. Chance in length in the Forell. **1774** *Act 14 Geo. III*, c. 25 Frauds are frequently committed..by taking off..the..Forrel or other Marks, of..Cloth. **1847** HALLIWELL, *Forrel*, the border of a handkerchief. *West.* **1886** ELWORTHY *W. Somerset Word-bk.*, *Forrel*, the stripe which is woven across the ends of a piece of cloth to show that it is a whole piece.

†**ˈforel, ˈforrel**, *v.* *Obs.* [f. prec. sb.] *trans.* To cover with a 'forel'. Hence **ˈforelled** *ppl. a.*

1642 FULLER *Holy & Prof. St.* III. xxiv. 227 The second edition of the Temple..as it was new forrelled and filleted with gold by Herod. **1696** *E. Budleigh Churchw. Acc.* in *Trans. Devonsh. Assoc.* (1892) XXIV. 264 Pd for a great foreld booke 00. 05. 0.

ˈforelady. *U.S.* = FOREWOMAN b.

1889 FARMER *Americanisms*, *Forelady*, a forewoman. **1904** *N.Y. Even. Post* 6 Oct. 3 (Advt.), Help Wanted. Designer and Forelady for long-established waist factory near Chicago. **1906** U. SINCLAIR *Jungle* x. 125 Miss Henderson, the fore-lady in her department. **1909** *Public Ledger* (Philadelphia) 24 June 14/1 Umbrella forelady, to take charge of finishers in large umbrella factory. *a* **1910** 'O. HENRY' *Trimmed Lamp* (1916) 15 Two of the most 'refined' women in the store—a fore-lady and a cashier—had a few 'swell gentlemen friends'. **1923** M. WATTS *L. Nichols* 191 She had advanced..to..the position of forewoman—again, pardon!—of forelady at Stein and Merkel's.

foreland (ˈfɔələnd). Forms: 4 forlonde, (farlande), 5–7 forland(e, (7 furland), 6 forelonde, -lande, 5– foreland. [f. FORE- *pref.* + LAND. Cf. Du. *voorland*; also Icel. *forlendi* land between hills and the sea.]

1. A cape, headland or promontory.

13.. *Gaw. & Gr. Knt.* 699 Alle þe iles of Anglesay on lyft half he haldez, & farez ouer þe fordez by þe for-londez. ? *a* **1400** *Morte Arth.* 880 See ȝe ȝone farlande with ȝone two fyrez. *a* **1490** BOTONER *Itin.* (Nasmith 1778) 153 Unum forland vocat. le Holyhede. **1535** STEWART *Cron. Scot.* I. 374 The schippis draif on forland and on craigis. **1551** RECORDE *Cast. Knowl.* (1556) 83 The great forelonde of Affrike, commonly called the cape of Good hope. **1671** NARBOROUGH *Jrnl.* in *Acc. Sev. Late Voy.* I. (1711) 24 At the face of this Foreland lie six rocky Islands. **1796** MORSE *Amer. Geog.* I. 117 A cape, which..he [Frobisher in 1576] called Queen Elizabeth's Foreland. **1876** L. MORRIS *Epic Hades* (1878) 35 To where the wave-worn foreland ends the bay.

2. A strip of land in front of something.

a. (See quots.) Esp. in *Physical Geogr.*, land deposited by the action of the sea in front of a coast, usu. with no intervening water; also, such land forming a cape (cf. sense 1).

1580–1 *Act 23 Eliz.* c. 13. §2 Certeyne Shelves and Fore-landes..lyeng betwene the Walles and Boundes of the said Marshes..and the River of Thames. **1795** J. PHILLIPS *Hist. Inland Navig.* Add. 178 The forelands on the north side also are not to be less than thirty feet wide. **1807** *Trans. Soc. Arts* XXVI. 35 By the erection of a new bank or sea wall they get a foreland to their former estate. **1867** SMYTH *Sailor's Word-bk.*, *Foreland*..a space left between the base of a canal bank, and an adjacent drainage cut or river, so as to favour the stability of the bank. **1896** *Bull. Geol. Soc. Amer.* VII. 400 At a later stage transportation of material alongshore begins and the waste from the edge and bottom of the land, together with the river sediment, is built out at certain points in front of the older mainland in deposits of various shapes, which are appropriately grouped together under the general term forelands. **1959** C. A. M. KING *Beaches & Coasts* viii. 261 The Paekakariki coast north of Wellington, where a wide sandy foreland fills in a broad bay in the wide northern part of Cook Strait.

b. *Fortif.* (See quot. 1853.)

1704 J. HARRIS *Lex. Techn.*, *Foreland*..the same with *Berme*. **1717** tr. *Frezier's Voy. S. Sea* 93 A Berm, or Fore-land, being a small space of Ground between the Wall and the Moat. **1853** STOCQUELER *Milit. Dict.*, *Foreland*..a confined space of ground between the rampart of a town or fortified place and the moat..Now usually called a berm.

3. Land or territory lying in front.

1851 KITTO *Bible Illustr.*, *Life & Death Our Lord* 29, I looked towards the west, and beheld the forelands of Carmel. **1870** *Daily Tel.* 22 Sept., Alsace and Lorraine.. will form a German foreland.

†**4.** *Sc.* 'A house facing the street, as distinguished from one in a close or alley' (Jam.). *Obs.*

1489 *Acta Audit.* 149/2 A foreland of ane tennenment liand in þe said Cannoungate.

5. *Geol.* A firm unyielding block of the earth's crust which is opposed to or partially surrounds an orogenic belt and towards which the folding is inclined.

1907 W. B. SCOTT *Introd. Geol.* (ed. 2) xxiii. 506 In folded mountain ranges three zones may be distinguished: (1) A rigid, unyielding mass which is not folded, (2) the zone of folding, (3) the zone of diminishing action, where the folding gradually dies away or ends in a fault... The side of the range toward which the overturned folds incline is called the foreland, and may be either the unfolded mass or the zone of diminishing action. **1909** [see BACK-LAND 3]. **1937** WOOLDRIDGE & MORGAN *Physical Basis Geogr.* vi. 76 The African 'hinterland' is believed to have moved northward towards the European 'foreland'. **1968** R. W. FAIRBRIDGE *Encycl. Geomorphol.* 734/1 The Mediterranean-Alpine-Himalayan belt is double sided, the folds tending to be overthrust against forelands..both to the north and to the south, while in between lie block-faulted collapsed regions. **1970** *Nature* 28 Nov. 838/2 All of these 'orogenies' have resulted in thrusts and overturned folds directed towards the foreland.

6. *attrib.*, in †*Foreland-men* (see quot.).

1666 *Lond. Gaz.* No. 19/4 The Foreland Men, viz. The Colliers of Sandwich, and the several Ports of Thanet, stay in expectation of Convoy.

forelay (fɔəˈleɪ), *v.* [f. FORE- *pref.* + LAY *v.*]

1. *trans.* To lie in wait for, waylay. *Obs.* exc. *dial.*

1548 HALL *Chron.*, *Hen. IV*, Introd. 9 He was forelayed and taken. **1603** HOLLAND *Plutarch's Mor.* 667 For feare (quoth he) that I be forlaied by the way, and rifled by him. **1700** DRYDEN *Palamon & A.* I. 493 An ambush'd thief fore-lays a traveller. **1887** *Kentish Gloss.*, *Fore-lay*, to waylay.

†**b.** To lie in ambush about or near (a place).

1563 GOLDING *Cæsar* (1565) 80 b, Hys enemys might.. for-lay the wayes. **1611** SPEED *Hist. Gt. Brit.* VI. lii. (1632) 180 His opposites had forelaid the country, and hemmed him about. **1683** *Brit. Spec.* 106 They had forelaid the Passages by land.

c. *fig.* To lay obstacles in the way of; to plot or take action against; to embarrass, frustrate, hinder, interfere with. Now *rare.*

1571 GOLDING *Calvin on Ps.* v. 11 The Lord..forlayeth their craftynesse. **1612** DRAYTON *Poly-olb.* iv. 58 Then Ebwith, and with her slides Srowy; which forelay Her progresse. **1612–15** BP. HALL *Contempl.*, *O.T.* XX. ix, How cunningly doth he forelay their confidence. **1697** DRYDEN *Virgil* XI. 781 With chosen Foot his Passage to forelay, And place an Ambush in the winding way. **1832** JOHN BREE *Saint Herbert's Isle* II. v, She would her own sweet peace forelay.

2. To lay down or plan beforehand; to pre-arrange; with both material and immaterial *objs.* *Obs.* exc. *dial.*

1605 DANIEL *Philotas* Wks. (1717) 350 Envy will most cunningly forelay The Ambush of their Ruin. *a* **1619** F. DAVISON *Poet. Rhapsody* (1826) II. 361 Privy snares my foes fore-lay. **1643** [ANGIER] *Lanc. Vall. Achor* 1 The wise God ..forelaid a double-foundation, of sin in the enemy, and humiliation in his people. *a* **1716** SOUTH *Serm.* (1744) XI. 252 An excellent artificer, who in all his works of art, has forelaid in his mind a perfect model of his intended fabric. **1815** *Mr. John Decastro* I. 52 Thus the ground was forelaid for great rejoicing. **1876** in *Whitby Gloss.*

Hence **ˈforelaid** *ppl. a.*; **foreˈlaying** *vbl. sb.*

1600 HOLLAND *Livy* v. xxviii. (1609) 199 There was no feare of ambushments and forelayings. **1640** LD. J. DIGBY *Sp.* in *Ho. Com.* 9 Nov. 8, I levell at no man with a forelayd designe. **1643** SIR T. BROWNE *Relig. Med.* I. §16 The constituted and fore-laid principles of his Art. **1815** *Mr. John Decastro* I. 259 Thus far by way of..forelaying of the ground.

†**foreleader.** *Obs.* Also 4, 6 for-. [f. FORE- *pref.* + LEADER.] One who leads the advance; a chief or principal leader.

a **1300** *Cursor M.* 14410 (Cott.) Moyses was þair for-leder. **1535** JOYE *Apol. Tindale* 18 Christe is the firste frutis and fore leader of them that sleap. **1576** GASCOIGNE *Diet for Drunkards* (1789) 17 Would God that we learned not, by the foreleaders before named, to charge and coniure each other vnto the pledge. **1611** SPEED *Hist. Gt. Brit.* VII. v. §1 Hengist for valour, policie, and strength, was the fore-leader. **1648** HERRICK *Hesper.* (1869) 326 Know, for truth, I meant You a fore-leader in this testament. **1876** *Whitby Gloss.*, *Fooreleader*, chief captain.

foreleg (ˈfɔəlɛg; but the stress is variable.) [f. FORE- *pref.* + LEG *sb.*] One of the front legs of a quadruped; also, rarely one of the anterior limbs of a biped.

1483 CAXTON *Gold. Leg.* (1692) 1079 A grete wulfe syttyng and embracyng the heed betwene his forleggys. **1509** HAWES *Past. Pleas.* XXXVII. iii, His forelegges latyn, and of fethers full. **1616** SURFL. & MARKH. *Country Farme* 133 When a Horses neere fore-legge, and his neere hinder-legge..are so fastened together. **1658** OSBORN *Adv. Son* (1673) 83 A Carver at Court..being laughed at by him [King James] for saying the wing of a Rabbit, maintained it as congruous as the fore-leg of a Capon, a Phrase used in Scotland. **1749** FIELDING *Tom Jones* XI. ii, The beast now unluckily making a false step, fell upon his fore legs. **1862** HUXLEY *Lect. Wrkg. Men* 23 The foreleg of the Horse. **1875** W. S. HAYWARD *Love agst. World* 13 Though he got his fore legs well on the bank he was short with his hind ones.

fore-lend, -lie: see FORE- *pref.* 2 a, 1.

fore-lift, -lighter, -line, etc.: see FORE- *pref.*

forelive (fɔəˈlɪv), *v.* [f. FORE- *pref.* + LIVE *v.*] *trans.* To live before another.

1599 DANIEL *Musophilus* lxii, All those great worthies of antiquity Which long forelived thee, and shall long survive. *c* **1645** HOWELL *Lett.* (1812) II. 530 They who fore-liv'd and preceded us may be called our Ancestors. **1805** SOUTHEY *Madoc* II. iii, Then do I forelive the race of men, So that the things that will be, are to me Past.

b. *intr.* (or *absol.*)

1839 BAILEY *Festus* xix. (1848) 208 Some believed..that the soul..had forelived in Heaven.

foˈrelle [a. Ger. *forelle.*] A kind of trout.

1881 BLACKMORE *Christowell*, I. xvii. 268, I dare say, he doesn't know a trout from a Forelle. [**1891** G. MEREDITH *One of our Conq.* II. iv. 88 Fresh *forellen* for lunch.]

ˈfore-loader. [LOADER[1] 1 c (*a*).] A loader mounted on the front of a tractor or other vehicle. Cf. *fore-end loader.*

1954 *Farmers Weekly* 4 June 65/2, I bought a fore-loader for use with the hydraulic lift of a modern tractor. **1958** *Times* 27 Oct. 15/4 The obvious loading tool is the tractor-mounted foreloader, to be found on most farms today. **1960** *Farmer & Stockbreeder* 8 Mar. 112/2 This makes it possible for a tractor and foreloader to go in for cleaning out the manure. **1963** *Times* 14 Jan. 13/2 Silage is machine-chopped and blown into the feed truck, meal and potatoes being added by foreloader.

forelock (ˈfɔəlɒk), *sb.*[1] Also 5–7 forlock. [f. FORE- *pref.* + LOCK *sb.*[1]]

†**1. a.** ? Some piece of horse-harness. **b.** (See quot. 1889.) *Obs.*

1467 *Mann. & Househ. Exp.* (1841) 408 My mastyr paid for mendynge of a forlokke, j.d. **1889** *Cent. Dict.*, *Forelock*, in medieval armor, a clasp or catch serving to hold the helm, or in some cases the beaver or the mentonnière, to the gorgerin or breast-plate in front.

2. A wedge (usually of iron) thrust through a hole in the end of a bolt in order to keep it in its place. Now chiefly *Naut.*

1514 *Wigtoft Churchw. Acc.* (1797) 209 For yᵉ forlock to yᵉ grete bell, 4*d.* **1534** *Yatton Churchw. Acc.* (Som. Rec. Soc.) 149 For forks, forlocks, pynnes to yᵉ bales [bells]. **1613–39** I. JONES in Leoni tr. *Palladio's Archit.* (1742) I. 103 The Bolts and Forelocks of Fir, that fasten the Timber. **1762** FALCONER *Shipwr.* II. 273 The forelocks drawn, the frappings they unlace. **1869** SIR E. J. REED *Shipbuild.* xvii. 340 The various parts of the work are..temporarily secured ..by means of pins and cotters, or forelocks.

3. *Comb.*: **forelock-bolt, -hook** (see quots.).

1627 CAPT. SMITH *Seaman's Gram.* ii. 5 Fore locke bolts hath an eye at the end, whereinto a fore locke of iron is driuen to keepe it from starting backe. **1769** FALCONER *Dict. Marine* (1789), *Cheville à goupilles*, a forelock-bolt, or bolt fitted to receive a forelock. **1794** *Rigging & Seamansh.* 54 *Fore-lock-hooks* are made of iron, with a long neck and handle. **1874** KNIGHT *Dict. Mech.* I. 905 *Forelock Hook* (Rope-making), a winch or whirl in the tackle-block by which a bunch of three yarns is twisted into a strand.

forelock (ˈfɔəlɒk), *sb.*[2] [f. FORE- *pref.* + LOCK *sb.*[2]]

1. A lock of hair growing from the fore part of the head, just above the forehead.

c **1000** *New Aldhelm Gloss.* in *Anglia* (1891) XIII. 37 Foreloccas, *antie frontis.* **1650** BULWER *Anthropomet.* 87 A square forehead, upon which those forelocks of the Hair abide moderately elevated. **1667** MILTON *P.L.* IV. 302 Hyacinthin Locks Round from his parted forelock manly hung Clustring. **1832** HT. MARTINEAU *Each & All* v. 62 There was plenty of bobbing from the girls and pulling of forelocks from the boys. **1878** BESANT & RICE *Celia's Arb.* xxii, All had a word to say to the Captain, touching their forelocks by way of preface.

transf. **1619** BAINBRIDGE *Descr. Late Comet* (1629) 9 This Comets forelock was a better Ephemeris for the Sunnes place then many in great request.

b. Of a horse, etc.: A detached lock above the forehead.

1711 ADDISON *Spect.* No. 59 ¶4 The Forelock of the Horse. **1781** COWPER *Charity* 176 Loose fly his forelock and his ample mane. **1791** —— *Iliad* XIX. 306 The bristly forelock of the boar. **1870** BRYANT *Iliad* I. III. 94 Clipped away the forelocks of the lambs.

2. *fig.*; *esp.* in phrase ***to take time, opportunity,*** etc. ***by the forelock.***

(Suggested by the representation described in Phædrus *Fab.* v. viii, 'Calvus, comosa fronte, nudo occipitio,.. Occasionem rerum significat brevem.')

1589 GREENE *Menaphon* (Arb.) 65 Thinking to..take opportunitie by her forelockes. **1594** SPENSER *Amoretti* lxx, The ioyous time wil not be staid, Unlesse she doe him by the forelock take. **1639** MASSINGER *Unnat. Combat* v. i, I'll take occasion by the forelock. **1775** ADAIR *Amer. Ind.* 301, I took time by the fore-lock. **1871** B. TAYLOR *Faust* (1875) I. 231, I became a philosopher, to catch..Wisdom by the forelock. **1874** MOTLEY *Barneveld* I. vii. 213 The occasion..was bald behind, and must be grasped by the forelock.

forelock (ˈfɔəlɒk), *v.* [f. FORELOCK *sb.*[1]] *trans.* To fasten with a forelock; also with *in.*

1769 FALCONER *Dict. Marine* (1789) Y iij b, Bolts, which.. are fore-locked or clinched upon rings. **1839** R. S. ROBINSON *Naut. Steam Eng.* 89 The paddle arms..keyed or forelocked there. **1882** NARES *Seamanship* (ed. 6) 86 A bolt is put through the mast..and forelocked in.

Hence **ˈforelocked** *ppl. a*, **ˈforelocking** *vbl. sb.*

1839 R. S. ROBINSON *Naut. Steam Eng.* 85 A crank pin.. secured by a forelocking pin. **1874** THEARLE *Naval Arch.* §231. 244 The channel rail is secured to the channel by iron straps, fastened by forelocked bolts.

fore-log: see FORE- *pref.* 3.

forelong, obs. form of FURLONG.

fore-loofe, obs. Sc. form of FURLOUGH.

forelook (ˈfɔəlʊk), *sb.* [f. FORE- *pref.* + LOOK *sb.*; cf. next.] **a.** A look forward (*obs.* exc. *U.S.*) †**b.** The habit or power of looking forward; Foresight, providence.

1357 *Lay Folks Catech.* 143 The saule..went untill hell and toke oute thas..Whilke he in his forloke wold that wer saued. *c* **1420** *Sir Amadas* (Weber) 373 Ther Y had an hondorthe marke of rent; Y spentte hit all in lyghtte atent, Of suche forlok was Y. **1583** GOLDING *Calvin on Deut.* cxc. 1181 It is to be concluded then, that Moses had a further forelook. **1882** E. P. GOODWIN *Serm. bef. Amer. Bd. Comm. For. Missions* 7 The gospel was to be preached..with equal ..forelook of triumph to all who would receive it. **1883** HALE *Christm. in Palace* viii. 192 She had a week's provant in the house; and that was a very long forelook for her.

forelook (fɔəˈlʊk), *v.* Also for-. [f. FORE- *pref.* + LOOK *v.* (In sense 3 perh. f. FOR- *pref.*[1])]

1. *trans.* To look at or see ahead or beforehand, foresee; to watch over. Also *refl.*

a **1300** *Cursor M.* 8211 (Cott.) Godd..þat all for-lokes in his sight. *c* **1300** *Ibid.* 28056 (Cott. Galba) Ilk man suld him forloke..þat his conciens be clene. **1340** HAMPOLE *Pr. Consc.* 1946 Na man..can þe tyme of þe dede forluke.

2. *intr.* To look ahead or forward.

1494 FABYAN *Chron.* VII. 551 He shall dylygentlye foreloke and see that Goddys wylle be done. **1603** B. JONSON *King's Entertainm.* 19 Wks. (Rtldg.) 529/2 Then did I forelook, And saw this day mark'd white in Clotho's book. **1847** EMERSON *Poems* (1857) 146 The World-soul knows his own affair, Forelooking, when he would prepare For the next ages.

†**3.** To bewitch by a look. Cf. *overlook. Obs.*

1596 THOMAS *Ital. Dict.* (1606), *Fascino*, to bewitch..to forelooke. **1611** COTGR., *Ensorceler*..To charme..fore-looke, eye-bite.

Hence **foreˈlooking** *ppl. a.* Also **foreˈlooker,** one who forelooks.

1382 WYCLIF *Ecclus.* iii. 34 God is the forlookere [Vulg. *prospector*] of hym that ȝeldeth grace. *Ibid.* xi. 32 As the forlookere seende the falling of his neȝhebore. **1870** EMERSON *Soc. & Solit.* vi. 118 A forelooking tenderness.

forelooper, foreloper (fɔəˈluːpə(r), -ˈləʊpə(r)). *South Africa.* [ad. Du. *voorlooper*, f. *voor-* FORE- + *looper* runner, f. *loopen* to run.]

A boy who walks with the foremost pair of a team of oxen, in order to guide them. Hence **foreˈloop** *v. intr.*, to do the work of a forelooper.

1863 W. C. BALDWIN *Afr. Hunting* iv, I managed to start on March 31, with only a driver and foreloper. **1881** FENN *Off to Wilds* iii. 21 The foreloper, whose duty it is to walk with the foremost oxen. **1889** *Catholic Household* 30 Nov. 7 Fr. Le Bihan in like manner 'fore-louping' because one of their boys had cut his foot.

forelorn, obs. form of FORLORN.

†**ˈfore-maid.** *Obs. rare*⁻¹. [f. FORE- *pref.* + MAID.] A forewoman.

1555 *Will of T. Sidney* (Somerset Ho.), Mary Hilles once the formayde of my shop.

foreman (ˈfɔəmən). Pl. foremen. Also for-. [f. FORE- *pref.* + MAN; cf. ON. *formaðr*, gen. *-manns* (perh. the source), also Du. *voorman*, Ger. *vormann.*]

†**1.** One who goes in front; a leader. *Obs.*

c **1425** *Eng. Conq. Irel.* lvii. 134 Steuenessone was forman, & opened the wey to þe Erl. **1580** BARET *Alv.*, A foreman, a guide, *auspex.* **1592** G. HARVEY *Pierce's Super.* 8 They cannot..bellow lustely like the foreman of the Heard. **1612** T. TAYLOR *Comm. Titus* i. 8 In the practice of this duty, the Apostle requireth that the Minister be the foreman. **1674** tr. *Scheffer's Lapland* 117 The men are led up by a Laplander, whom they call Automwatze, or foreman, then follows the Bridegroom.

†**b.** *pl.* The front rank. *Obs.*

1577 HANMER *Anc. Eccl. Hist.* (1619) 387 When..they had foiled the foremen, they turned themselves back. **1598** GRENEWEY *Tacitus' Ann.* I. ii. (1622) 21 The enemy..lightly skirmishing with the flanks and the foremen; set amaine on the hindmost.

†**c.** The man in front (of another). *Obs.*

1598 BARRET *Theor. Warres* III. i. 36 Keeping the lower end of his pike on the one side of his foremans legge. **1607** DEKKER & WEBSTER *Sir T. Wyat* D.'s Wks. 1873 III. 113 Euerie face Is lifted vp aboue his foremans head.

2. The principal juror, who presides at the deliberations of the jury, and communicates their verdict to the court.

1538 FITZHERB. *Just. Peas* 89 The counterpane of the offyce..to remayne with the forman of the enquest. **1607** DEKKER *Northw. Hoe* II. i. Wks. 1873 III. 20, I will looke grauely..like the fore-man of a Jury. **1711** ADDISON *Spect.* No. 122 ¶3 He..has been several times Foreman of the Petty-Jury. **1818** SCOTT *Hrt. Midl.* xxiv, The foreman, called in Scotland the chancellor of the jury. **1840** HOOD *Kilmansegg, Her Death* xvi, At the Golden Lion the Inquest met, Its foreman a carver and gilder.

transf. **1697** C. LESLIE *Snake in Grass* (ed. 2) 221 It is Subscrib'd by a Bakers Dozen of them; and George Fox the Fore-Man, in the Name of themselves.

3. One who takes the most prominent part; the chief or leader (of a party); the president (of a deliberative body). *Obs.* exc. *locally* in municipal use.

1603 FLORIO *Montaigne* II. xii. 294 Socrates, the foreman of his Dialogues doth ever aske and propose his disputation. **1643** PRYNNE *Sov. Power Parl.* I. (ed. 2) 17 The Kings principall wicked Counsellers; of whom Winchester being the foreman, appealed. **1702** S. PARKER tr. *Cicero's De Finibus* 280 The Old Peripateticks too, and among them Aristotle, their Foreman. **1790** PORSON *Lett. Travis* 379 The foreman of the Apostles, Peter. **1805** SOUTHEY *Lett.* (1856) I. 307 At length all the inhabitants of the grave arose, St. John at their head for foreman. **1835** *Rep. Commiss. Municip. Corp.* XXVI. 2287 The Foreman of the commons [of Huntingdon] is appointed by a committee of burgesses.

4. The principal workman; *spec.*, one who has charge of a department of work. ***foreman of the yard***: one who superintends the gangers. ***working foreman***: one who divides his time between labour and supervision.

1574 *Life Abp. Canterb.* Pref. to Rdr. E v, It was but rough hewen by one of the prentises, and wanted sum polishing by the forman. **1631** T. POWELL *Tom All Trades* 174 Thomas the fore-man of the shop. **1641** BEST *Farm. Bks.* (Surtees) 46 The foreman, whose office is to mowe and place the sheaues aright. **1691** DRYDEN *K. Arthur* Epil. Wks. 1884 VIII. 200 This precious fop Is foreman of a haberdasher's shop. **1703** MOXON *Mech. Exerc.* 257 The Master-Bricklayer, or his Foreman, must take care to see all the Foundations set truly out. **1793** SMEATON *Edystone L.* §164 One of the masons..offered himself as foreman over the stone-cutters. **1863** P. BARRY *Dockyard Econ.* 79 Mr. Brown is the foreman of all the framework. **1878** JEVONS *Prim. Pol. Econ.* 38 Foremen plan out the work, and allot it to the artisans. **1893** *Labour Commission* Gloss., *Foremen of the Yards*, a class of officers next above the 'leading men'..and to whom the leading men are directly responsible.

b. ? An overseer or bailiff.

1774 J. Q. ADAMS *Fam. Lett.* (1876) 7, I sometimes think I must come to this—to be the foreman upon my own farm. **1856** KANE *Arct. Expl.* II. xxix. 294 Petersen had been foreman of the settlement. **1894–5** *Kelly's Oxford Direct.* 342 J. Belcher, foreman to John Birt esq. Wood End farm.

†**5.** ? *slang.* ? A goose. *Obs.*

1622 BEAUM. & FL. *Philaster* v. iii, Ile soile you euer[y] long vacation a brace of foremen, that at Michaelmas shall come vp fat and kicking. [Differently in 1st ed.]

¶**6.** ? Used as ad. Du. *voerman*, carrier.

1641 EVELYN *Diary* (1871) 25, I tooke wagon to Rotterdam, where we were hurried in less than an hour.. so furiously do these Foremen drive. **1699** R. L'ESTRANGE *Colloq. Erasm.* (ed. 3) 260 We wait for the Antwerp Waggon ..You must rise betimes to find a Fore-man [L. *aurigam*] Sober.

Hence **ˈforeman** *v. trans. rare*, to direct or oversee as a foreman. **ˈforemanship**, the office, post, or position of a foreman.

1853 'MARK TWAIN' *Let.* (1917) I. 24 If he cannot get a foremanship. **1859** SMILES *Self-Help* 17 The foremanship of a large workshop. **1886** T. WRIGHT in *19th Cent.* XX. 534 The all-round workman requires as a rule very little foremaning. **1941** H. J. MASSINGHAM *Remembrance* viii. 74 The craftsman..drilled the thin slabs with the slat-pick..in tune with the foremanship of the seasons.

foremarch, -mark, -martyr: see FORE- *pref.*

foremast ('fɔəmɑːst, -æ-). [f. FORE- *pref.* (and FORE *prep.*) + MAST.]

1. The forward lower-mast in all vessels.

1582 N. LICHEFIELD tr. *Castanheda's E. Ind.* ix. 25 b, The tacklings of their formast. **1591** PERCIVALL *Sp. Dict., Ostay*, a cord that goeth from the boltsprit to the saile of the foremast. **1697** DAMPIER *Voy.* I. xvi. 452 The fury of the Wind..snapt off the Boltsprit and Fore-mast both at once. **1719** DE FOE *Crusoe* I. i, The Mate and Boat-swain begg'd the Master of our Ship to let them cut away the Fore-mast. **1848** W. IRVING *Columbus* I. 240 The latter..from the weakness of her foremast, could not hold the wind.

2. ? The station of being 'before the mast'; only *attrib.*, as **foremast man, seaman,** a sailor below the rank of a petty officer; hence quasi-*adj.*, characteristic of a foremast man.

1626 CAPT. SMITH *Accid. Yng. Seamen* 6 The Younkers are the yong men called Foremast men. **1707** *Lond. Gaz.* No. 4366/3 Eighty of the Foremast-Men belonging to the Jersey were..order'd to be discharg'd. **1793** SMEATON *Edystone L.* §163 In the light of a foremast seaman, he appeared to be quite a Genius. **1823** BYRON *Island* II. xx, His foremast air, and somewhat rolling gait..spoke his former state. **1849** MACAULAY *Hist. Eng.* I. 303 He was inferior in seamanship to every foremast man on board.

fore-mean: see FORE- *pref.* 2 a.

ˌfore'mention *v.* [f. FORE- *pref.* + MENTION.] To mention beforehand.

1660 N. INGELO *Bent. & Urania* (1682) II. 12 They found themselves sick of the Diseases which he had forementioned. *Ibid.* II. 143 For the Reason which I forementioned.

Hence **ˌfore'mentioned** *ppl. a.* previously mentioned. Also *ellipt.*

1587 GOLDING *De Mornay* ix. 133 The forementioned Chaos. **1631** GOUGE *God's Arrows* I. xiv. 19 Yet hath God his wayes and means to deliver the righteous in the forementioned cases. **1697** LOCKE in Fox Bourne *Life* II. xiii. 383 In the forementioned new law to be enacted. **1750** tr. *Leonardus' Mirr. Stones* 145 There are other species.. which with the fore-mentioned, make up the number twelve.

fore-messenger, -misgiving: see FORE-.

†**fore'mind,** *v. Obs.* [f. FORE- + MIND *v.*] *trans.* To contemplate or intend beforehand.

1513 MORE *Rich. III*, Wks. 38/1 Were it that the duke.. hadde of olde foreminded this conclusion. **1583** STANYHURST *Æneis* IV. (Arb.) 103 Neauer I foreminded.. For toe slip in secret by flight.

†**foremore,** *a. rare.* [Perversion of FORMER (cf. FOREMOST).]

1801 W. TAYLOR in *Monthly Mag.* XII. 219 Some of the foremore poems celebrate the return from captivity. **1815** *Ibid.* XXXVIII. 43 Of Simon's works, only the two foremore can now merit an importation into English literature.

foremost ('fɔəməʊst, -məst), *a.* and *adv.* (*superl.*) Forms: 1 **formest, fyrmest, (firmest),** 2–7 **formest,** 3 *south.* **vormest,** (4 **furmest,** 5 **for-, foremest(e,** 6 **formes),** 3–4 **firmest,** 3–7 **formast,** (4 **formaste),** 6–7 **formost(e,** 6– **foremost.** See also FORTHMOST. [OE. *formest, fyrmest*: = OFris. *formest*, Goth. *frumist-s*, f. OTeut. **formo-* (FORME *a.*) with additional superlative suffix (see -EST). Afterwards written so as to suggest a derivation from FORE *a.* + MOST *adv.*]

A. *adj.*

†**1.** In regard to time: Prior to all others in occurrence, existence, etc.; = FIRST A. 1. *Obs.*

a **1300** *Cursor M.* 1525 (Cott.) Noema was þe formest webster þat man findes o þat mister. *Ibid.* 1051 Þe formast barn þat sco him bare was caim. **1485** CAXTON *Chas. Gt.* 195 To repayre thoffence of our formest fader adam. **1587** GOLDING *De Mornay* v. 56 If they could haue had any beginning, the Sonne had bin formost in that case.

†**b.** *absol.* or *ellipt.* Also in advb. phrase *at the foremost. Obs.*

c **1200** *Trin. Coll. Hom.* 219 Þe laste man isib þe formeste, þe was biforn us. **1389** in *Eng. Gilds* (1870) 4 Atte firmast to-fore þe day of þe a compte of þe maistres. *a* **1400** *Hymn Virg.* 8 in *Min. Poems Vern. MS.* (E.E.T.S.) 134 Heil logge that vr lord in lay, The formast that neuer was founden in fable.

†**c.** After the name of a day of the week: Next following; = FIRST 1 h. *Obs.*

c **1330** R. BRUNNE *Chron.* (1810) 308 Þe Wednesday formest þe Kyng had fulle grete hy.

†**2.** First in serial order; = FIRST A. 2. *Obs.*

c **1000** *Sax. Leechd.* III. 274 Feower heafod windas synd, se fyrmesta is easterne wind. *c* **1200** *Trin. Coll. Hom.* 17 Þe formeste word of þe salme. *a* **1225** *Ancr. R.* 18 Sigge ðe vormeste vers, 'Adoramus te, Christe,' fif siðen kneolinde. *a* **1300** *Cursor M.* 26877 (Cott.) Þe quilk I talde þe of resun in þe neist formast questiun. **13..** *E.E. Allit. P.* B. 494 Monyth þe fyrst þat fallez formast in þe 3er. *c* **1475** *Rauf Coilȝear* 288 Is not the morne ȝule day, formest of the ȝeir? **1542** RECORDE *Gr. Artes* 135 b, The bowynge of the foremost fynger, and settynge the ende of the thombe between the 2 foremost or hyghest ioyntes of it.

†**b.** *absol.* or *ellipt.* Also in advb. phrases, *a formest, an alre formest. Obs.*

a **1225** *Ancr. R.* 116 As we seiden þer uppe a vormest. *Ibid.* 180 Understondeð þeonne an alre uormest. **1398** TREVISA *Barth. De P.R.* III. xx. (1495) 55 The formest hyghte Ymaginatiua, the mydle Logica, the thyrde memoratiua. **1588** A. KING tr. *Canisius' Catech.* 126 Gif he fallis, the latter pairt is warst nor yᵉ formest. **1709** ADDISON *Tatler* No. 24 ¶13 The Foremost of the whole Rank of Toasts..are Mrs. Gatty and Mrs. Frontlet.

3. Most forward or advanced in position; front: = FIRST A. 3. †Also in agreement with sb. to indicate the front part or front of. (Cf. L. *summus mons*, etc.)

c **1205** LAY. 23801 A þen feoremeste flocke feouwerti hundred. *c* **1350** *Will. Palerne* 2324 Þe prouost wiþ al þe puple presed forþ formast. *a* **1400** *Octouian* 1106 An ax.. That heng on hys formest arsoun. *c* **1450** *Merlin* 46 He wolde come..formeste of his company. **1585** T. WASHINGTON tr. *Nicholay's Voy.* IV. xiii. 126 b, The whole skinne of a great Lion, fastened with the two formost feet before upon the brest. **1658** A. FOX *Wurtz' Surg.* II. xxv. 152 The foremost part of the Arms bones are broken. **1667** MILTON *P.L.* II. 28 Who here Will envy whom the highest place exposes Formost to stand against the Thunderers aime Your bulwark? **1766** GOLDSM. *Vic. W.* xiii, The giant..was foremost now; but the Dwarf was not far behind. **1781** GIBBON *Decl. & F.* II. xxvi. 41 The king himself fought and fell in the foremost ranks of the battle. **1875** W. S. HAYWARD *Love agst. World* 14 The foremost hounds are close on him.

b. *absol.* or *ellipt.* Also in advb. phrase, †*a formest*.

c **1205** LAY. 24611 Bedeuer a uormest eode mid guldene bolle. *a* **1310** in Wright *Lyric P.* xii. 41 So the furmest hevede y-don, ase the erst undertoc. *c* **1400** *Song Roland* 807 We haue the formest feld to the ground. *c* **1489** CAXTON *Sonnes of Aymon* vi. 137 Reynawde wente out of Bordews, the formest of all his folke. **1553** T. WILSON *Rhet.* (1580) 67 Good will settyng me forthe with the foremost: I can not chuse but write. **1774** GOLDSM. *Nat. Hist.* (1776) III. 175 Those [dogs] which are young, fierce, and unaccustomed to the chace, are generally the foremost. **1828** SCOTT *F.M. Perth* xxxiv, The Smith of the Wynd..had been the foremost in the crowd that thronged to see the gallant champions of Clan Quhele. **1872** BLACK *Adv. Phaeton* xxiii, She was determined to march with the foremost.

c. in *proverb* denoting continuous action.

1606 *Sir G. Goosecappe* III. i. in Bullen *O. Pl.* III. 44 Never stir if he fought not with great Seckerson four hours to one, foremost take up hindmost.

d. In adverbial phrases *head, end, stern,* etc. *foremost*, i.e. with the head, etc. first or in front.

1697 DAMPIER *Voy.* I. iii. 49 It flys down head foremost. **1842** C. WHITEHEAD *R. Savage* (1845) III. ix. 420 Wigs.. wrong-side foremost. **1856** FERRIER *Inst. Metaph.* Introd. 46 This is a science which naturally comes to us end foremost. **1865** DICKENS *Mut. Fr.* I. i, The boat drove stern foremost before it [the tide].

4. Most notable or prominent, best, chief. Also more emphatically *first and foremost*: = FIRST A. 4.

c **1000** *Ags. Gosp.* Matt. xx. 27 Seþe wyle betweox eow beon fyrmest sy he eower þeow. **1483** CAXTON *G. de la Tour* E j, And suche one is that weneth to be first and formest that often fyndeth her the last of all. **1546** BP. GARDINER *Declar. Art. Joye* 72 b, Christ in his speach trulye affirmed his choise, which was chief, principall, and formest. **1644** MILTON *Areop.* (Arb.) 40 Men ever famous, and formost in the achievements of liberty. **1791** COWPER *Iliad* I. 83 Calchas, an augur foremost in his art. **1851** DIXON *W. Penn* xvi. (1872) 137 Foremost of these sufferers were the Quakers.

absol. or *ellipt. c* **1000** *Ags. Gosp.* Matt. xix. 20 Soðlice manega fyrmeste beoð ytemeste; & ytemeste fyrmesta. *c* **1400** *Destr. Troy* 278 Hit was þe formast on flete þat on flode past. *a* **1610** HEALEY *Cebes* (1636) 136 The fore-most of them, Right knowledge, the rest are her sisters.

B. *adv.* First, before any other or anything else, in position or rank; †formerly also, in time, serial order, etc.; = FIRST B. 1. Also in strengthened phrase, *first and foremost.*

a **1000** *Elene* 68 (Gr.) þæs þe hie feonda ȝefær fyrmest ȝesæȝon. *a* **1175** *Cott. Hom.* 235 Si forme lage þat is si ȝecende lage, þe god sett formest an þes mannes heorte. *c* **1250** *Gen. & Ex.* 1472 Esau was firmest boren And iacob sone after. *c* **1350** *Will. Palerne* 268 He swor formest þat ȝe schuld have no harm. **1551** T. WILSON *Logike* (1580) 4 The Logician first and formoste, professeth to knowe wordes, before he..knitte sentences. **1599** T. M[OUFET] *Silkwormes* 66 He formost dies, and yeelds to fatal dart: Ne liues she long. **1650** TRAPP *Comm. Numb.* ii. 3 Judah encamped foremost. It was fit the Lion should leade the way.

b. In the first place, firstly. See FIRST B. 1 c.

1393, 1583 [see FIRST B. 1 c.]. **1603** HOLLAND *Plutarch's Mor.* 3 First and formest requisite it is, that the ground be good.

Hence †**'foremostly** *adv. Obs.*, in the foremost place, in front.

1607 DEKKER & WEBSTER *Sir T. Wyat* D.'s Wks. 1873 III. 113 Norfolke rides formostly, his crest well knowne. ? *a* **1700** *Ballad of Jephthah* in *Percy's Reliq.* (1876) I. 184 When he saw his daughter dear Coming on most foremostly, He wrung his hands.

foremother ('fɔəmʌðə(r)). [f. FORE- *pref.* + MOTHER, after *forefather*.] A female ancestor.

1582 BENTLEY *Mon. Matrones* Pref. B. iij b, Looking in this glasse of the holie liues of their foremothers. **1655** *Songs Costume* (Percy Soc.) 145 Where is the decency become Which your fore-mother had? **1806–7** J. BERESFORD *Miseries Hum. Life* XX. xxv. (1826) 254 Unheard-of fore-fathers and fore-mothers of your host's family. **1878** H. H. GIBBS *Ombre* 1 Ombre, the delight of our forefathers and foremothers.

foren: see FORNE.

forename ('fɔəneɪm), *sb.* [f. FORE- *pref.* + NAME.] A person's first or 'Christian' name; in *Rom. Ant.* = PRÆNOMEN.

1533 CATH. PARR tr. *Erasm. Comm. Crede* 74 The name and the forename of Pylate. **1610** HOLLAND *Camden's Brit.* 320 His sonne, carrying the same fore-name [Bartholomew]. *a* **1656** USSHER *Ann.* VI. (1658) 753 It was provided by an Edict, that none of that family should have the forename of Marcus. **1716** M. DAVIES *Athen. Brit.* III. *Crit. Hist.* 99 The Ancient Roman Women had a Fore-name, or a Christen-Name besides their Sir Name. **1870** SWINBURNE *Ess. & Stud.* (1875) 34 The counsellor whose name is Reason, whose forename is Interest. **1883** *Academy* 15 Dec. 394 Mary Martha Brooke, whose twofold fore-name is intended to symbolise her character.

transf. **1610** HOLLAND *Camden's Brit.* I. 519 This place [Cole Ouerton] hath a Cole prefixed for the fore name.

†**'forename,** *v. Obs.* [f. FORE- *pref.* + NAME *v.*] *trans.* **a.** To name or mention beforehand. **b.** To give a name to beforehand.

1610 HEALEY *St. Aug. Citie of God* V. xvi. (1620) 209 The vertues of such worthies as we forenamed. *a* **1633** AUSTIN *Medit.* (1635) 53 Behold a Virgin shall conceave A Sonne, fore nam'd Emmanuel.

Hence **'forenamed** *ppl. a.*, named or mentioned before; fore-cited.

1490 CAXTON *Eneydos* xiii. 47 The two sustres fore named. **1535** STEWART *Cron. Scot.* II. 317 This foirnamit king. **1628** T. SPENCER *Logick* 224 The forenamed Axiomes are compounded of simple axiomes. **1737** WHISTON *Josephus' Antiq.* VIII. xi. §1 The woman..grieved at the death of the fore-named child. **1823** J. BADCOCK *Dom. Amusem.* 30 Flour which is mixed with the fore-named adulterations.

absol. or *ellipt.* **1578** LYTE *Dodoens* I. i. 2 Besides the two forenamed there is found a thirde kinde. **1655** FULLER *Ch. Hist.* II. i. §7 Besides the fore-named, they had Neptune.

†**'foreness.** *nonce-wd.* [f. FORE *a.* + -NESS.] Priority.

1587 GOLDING tr. *De Mornay* 136 Euen according to Aristotles owne doctrine, forenesse, afternesse, and continuance of tyme do followe forenesse, afternesse, and continuance of mouing.

'forenext, *a. Obs. rare*⁻¹. In 3 fore-neist. [f. FORE *adv.* + NEXT.] ? Next preceding.

a **1300** *Cursor M.* 8146 (Cott.) Þe night fore-neist o paradis Him thoght in sueuen he was þar-bi.

forenight ('fɔənaɪt). [f. FORE- *adv.* and *prep.*]

†**1.** The previous night. *Obs.*

1583 STANYHURST *Æneis* II. (Arb.) 66, I that in forenight was with no weapon agasted, Now shiuer at shaddows.

2. *Sc.* The evening, the interval between twilight and bed-time.

1513 DOUGLAS *Æneis* IX. vi. 63 Serranus That all the fornycht in ryot..had spendit. **1810** *Cromek's Rem. Nithsdale Song* 299 We kent nae but it was drunken fowk riding to the fair, i' the fore night. **1865** G. MACDONALD *A. Forbes* xvi. 67 There were long forenights to favour the plot.

fore-nook: see FORE- *pref.* 3.

forenoon ('fɔənuːn). [f. FORE *prep.* + NOON.]

1. The portion of the day before noon.

1506 GUYLFORDE *Pilgr.* (Camden) 35 We..spent that fore noone there in prayers and deuocion. **1582** N. LICHEFIELD tr. *Castanheda's Conq. E. Ind.* iii. 10 At tenne of the Clocke in the fore noone. **1669** WORLIDGE *Syst. Agric.* (1681) 168 When..the Nights [are] yet cold, water in the Fore-noons. **1727** A. HAMILTON *New Acc. E. Ind.* II. xxxiii. 12 The Fore-noons being dedicated to Business. **1838** MRS. CARLYLE *Lett.* I. 107 He sat with me one forenoon, last week. **1872** BLACK *Adv. Phaeton* xxvi. 352 He begged us to start for our forenoon's walk.

2. *attrib.*

a **1602** W. PERKINS *Cases Consc.* (1619) 325 Some persons ..are good forenoone-men, but bad afternoone-men. **1658** GURNALL *Chr. in Arm.* II. xii. §3. 138 Physicians that they call fore-noon men..because commonly they are drunk in the after-noon. *a* **1806** *Yng. Beichan & Susie Pye* xxxviii. in Child *Ballads* II. liii. (1884) 471/1 Then out and spak the forenoon bride. **1833** M. SCOTT *Tom Cringle* xix. (1859) 542 My stormy forenoon watch is at length over. **1878** HUXLEY *Physiogr.* 8 The forenoon shadow.

fore-noted, -notice, -notion: see FORE- *pref.* 2 b, 4.

†**fo'rensal,** *a. Obs.* [f. L. *forens-is* (see FORENSIC) + -AL¹.] = FORENSIC.

1660 H. MORE *Myst. Godl.* V. xii. 164 All which, as Grotius interprets the place in a Forensal sense, is of a very large extension. **1670** in BLOUNT *Glossogr.* **1676–1732** in COLES.

forensic (fə'rɛnsɪk), *a.* and *sb.* Also 7 forinseck. [f. L. *forens-is* (f. *forum* FORUM) + -IC.]

A. *adj.* Pertaining to, connected with, or used in courts of law; suitable or analogous to pleadings in court. *forensic medicine*: medicine in its relations to law; medical jurisprudence.

1659 HAMMOND *On Ps.* cvi. 31 It signifies much more than justification, as in the forinseck sense that is opposite to condemning. **1690** LOCKE *Hum. Und.* II. xxvi. (1695) 189 Person..is a Forensick Term. **1768** BLACKSTONE *Comm.* III. 84 That the students might not be distracted from their studies by legal process from distant courts, and other forensic avocations. *a* **1779** WARBURTON *Div. Legat.* III. iv. Wks. 1788 II. 89 Lactantius, from a forensic Lawyer now become an advocate for Christianity. **1837** CARLYLE *Fr. Rev.* I. IV. iv. (1872) 122 Such admired forensic eloquence. **1845** STEPHEN *Comm. Laws Eng.* (1874) I. 8 A sort of mixed science known by the name of Forensic Medicine or Medical Jurisprudence. **1865** DICKENS *Mut. Fr.* II. viii, In an imposing and forensic manner.

B. *sb. U.S.* A college exercise, consisting of a speech or (at Harvard) written thesis maintaining one side or the other of a given question.

1830 *Collegian* 241 in B. H. Hall *College Words*, Themes, forensics [etc.]. **1837** *Ord. & Regul. Harvard Univ.* 12 Every omission of a theme or forensic.

† **fo'rensical**, *a. Obs.* Also 6-8 forinsecal, -sicall, (7 forensecal). [f. as prec. + -AL[1].] = prec. *adj.*
1581 J. BELL *Haddon's Answ. Osor.* 357 In forinsicall, and temporall causes. 1654 WARREN *Unbelievers* 231 Justification is a forensical, judicial act. 1740 NORTH *Examen* II. v. §37. 336 Acts of the supreme Power, or (in forinsecal style) legislative Acts or Acts of Parliament.

Hence **fo'rensically** *adv.*, in a forensic manner.
1845 MOZLEY *Ess., Laud* (1878) I. 218 Laud was put into the humiliating position of having to stand up and forensically guard every little thing he had done. 1876 —— *Univ. Serm.* v. 102 The Church..contemplates war forensically, as a mode of settling national questions.

† **fo'rensive**, *a. Obs.* [See -IVE.] = FORENSIC.
a 1670 HACKET *Abp. Williams* I. (1693) 97 His Forensive or Political Transactions.

† **fore-oath**. *Obs.* exc. *Hist.* [OE. *foreáþ*, *foráþ*, f. FORE- *pref.* + *áþ* OATH.] In OE. Law: An oath required of the party commencing a suit unless the fact complained of was manifest.
a 1000 *Laws Ath.* i. §23 Ofga ælc man his tihtlan mid foreaðe. 1641 *Ancient Cust. Eng.* in *Harl. Misc.* (1808) I. 240 He might, afterward, with his fore-oath his lord's part play at any need. 1895 POLLOCK & MAITLAND *Hist. Eng. Law* I. 16 A fore-oath was needless if a man sued for wounding and showed the wound to the Court.

fore-obtained, -opinioned: see FORE- *pref.* 2 b.

foreordain (ˌfɔərɔː'deɪn), *v.* [f. FORE- *pref.* + ORDAIN.] *trans.* To ordain or appoint beforehand; to predestinate.
c 1440 *Partonope* 3155 The fayrest shapen creature That euer was foordened thorow nature. [But is this a mistake for *foddened*?] 1561 T. NORTON *Calvin's Inst.* III. 302 Some to be foreordeined to saluation, other some to destruction. 1611 BIBLE *1 Pet.* i. 20 Who verily was foreordeined before the foundation of the world. 1647 *Westm. Conf. Faith* iii. §3 Others foreordained to everlasting death. 1736-1879 [see below].

Hence ˌ**foreor'dained** *ppl. a.*; ˌ**foreor'daining** *vbl. sb.* and *ppl. a.* Also ˌ**foreor'dainment**, predestination.
c 1420 *Wyclif's Mark* Prol., The for-ordenede John Zakaries sone. 1667 BP. S. PARKER *Free & Impart. Cens.* 236 His foreordaining him to that employment. 1736 BUTLER *Anal.* II. iv. Wks. 1874 I. 200 According to general foreordained laws. 1864 PUSEY *Lect. Daniel* v. 250 God's foreordaining love. 1879 MACLEAR *Mark* i. 15 *note*, The great fore-ordained and predicted time of the Messiah. 1879 FARRAR *St. Paul* II. 492 The foreordainment, and the result of this Gospel in uniting the Jew and Gentile.

fore-order: see FORE- *pref.* 4.

† **fore'ordinance**. *Obs.* [f. FORE- *pref.* + ORDINANCE.] = FORE-ORDINATION.
1450-1530 *Myrr. our Ladye* 181 The endelesse fore ordenaunce of god. 1587 GOLDING *De Mornay* xi. 151 Which nature, that is to say the foreordinance of the Creator doeth for them.

ˌ**fore'ordinate**, *v.* [f. FORE- *pref.* + ORDINATE.] *trans.* To foreordain. Hence **fore'ordinated** *ppl. a.*
1858 BUSHNELL *Nat. & Supernat.* xv. (1864) 525 The grand, fore-ordinated circle of existence.

ˌ**foreordi'nation**. [f. prec.: see -ATION.] Previous ordination or appointment, predestination; an instance of this.
1628 BP. HALL tr. *Rotomagensis Anon.* Wks. 815 Neither can His will be frustrated..nor His fore-ordinations altered. *a* 1680 CHARNOCK *Attrib. Gosp.* (1834) I. 346 A fore-ordination of him [Christ] was before the foundation of the world. 1855 *Ess. Intuit. Morals* 108 If Fore-ordination be reduced to Ordination. 1879 FARRAR *St. Paul* I. 427 In accordance with..Divine fore-ordination.

fore-pad, -parlour, etc.: see FORE- *pref.* 3.

fore'pale, fore'pole, *v. Mining* and *Engineering.* [f. FORE- *pref.* PALE, POLE.] *trans.* To protect (a work in progress) from falling débris, quicksand, etc. by timbers driven in front.
1871 *Trans. Amer. Inst. Mining Engineers* I. 352 After driving fifty yards through heavy rock tumbles, where every foot had to be forepaled. 1881 RAYMOND *Mining Gloss.*, *Fore-poling*, a method of securing drifts in progress through quicksand by driving ahead poles..slabs, etc. *Ibid. Forpale* or *Forepale*.

fore-part, forepart ('fɔəpɑːt). [f. FORE- *pref.* + PART.]

1. The foremost, first, or most advanced part; the front.
c 1400 *Burgh Lawis* c. 105 Þai sall leilly lyne..baith foir part and back part of þe land. 1435 MISYN *Fire of Love* I. xvii. 38 All þe inar forpartis of my saule with swetnes of heuenly myrth ar fulfild. 1483 *Cath. Angl.* 138/2 Þe For-parte of yᵉ hede, *cinciput*. 1548 HALL *Chron., Rich. III* (an. 3) 49 b, They of the Castell vexed their enemies on the foreparte. *c* 1611 CHAPMAN *Iliad* XVI. 324 Betwixt his neck, and foreparts. 1714 S. SEWALL *Diary* 12 Nov. (1882) III 26 The Snow and Rain..beat on the fore-part of the Calash. 1836 *Random Recoll. Ho. Lords* xvi. 383 His dark hair..stands on end on the fore part of his head.

b. *esp.* The bow or prow of a vessel. ? *Obs.*
1526 TINDALE *Acts* xxvii 41 And the foore parte stucke fast. 1555 EDEN *Decades* 160 Turnynge the stemmes or forpartes of their shyppes ageynst the streame. 1699 DAMPIER *Voy.* II. I. 74 The head or fore-part is not altogether so high as the Stern.

†2. An ornamental covering for the breast worn by women; a stomacher. *Obs.*
1600 *Q. Eliz. Wardr.* in Nichols' *Progresses* (1823) III. 507 Item, one foreparte of clothe of sylver. 1607 WEBSTER *Northw. Hoe* I. iii. Wks. (Rtldg.) 256/1, I confess I took up a petticoat and a raised forepart for her. 1640 SHIRLEY *Constant Maid* IV. iii, They were a midwife's Fore part.

3. The earlier part.
1614 RALEIGH *Hist. World* iii. §7 All the fore-part of the day. 1633 EARL MANCH. *Al Mondo* (1636) 131 He lives twice that bestowes the fore-part of his life well. 1722 SEWEL *Hist. Quakers* (1795) I. v. 369 In the fore part of the year 1659. 1727 A. HAMILTON *New Acc. E. Ind.* II. l. 217 In the Fore-part of the seventeenth Century. 1852 MRS. STOWE *Uncle Tom's C.* xv, In some long-forgotten fore part of the day.

† '**foreparty**. *Obs.* [f. FORE- *pref.* + PARTY.] = FOREPART.
1398 TREVISA *Barth. De P.R.* v. ii. (1495) 102 In the fore party the heed is somdele comyng narough and hygh. *c* 1400 *Lanfranc's Cirurg.* 67 In þe fore partye of þe þrote.

forepass: see FORPASS *v. Obs.*

'**fore-ˌpassage**. *Naut.* [f. FORE- *pref.* + PASSAGE.] **a.** A passage leading to the forepeak. **b.** A passage leading from the hatchway to the forward magazine. (*Cent. Dict.*)

forepassed, -past (fɔə'pɑːst, -æ-), *ppl. a.* [f. FORE- *pref.* + PASSED, PAST.] That has previously passed, or been passed. Now only of time.
1557 *Tottell's Misc.* (Arb.) 143 O Lord..for my helpe make haste To pardon the forepassed race that carelesse I haue past. 1596 RALEIGH *Discov. Gviana* 21 Neither could any of the forepassed vndertakers..discouer the country. 1622 DRAYTON *Poly-olb.* xxii. (1748) 353 Those forepassed hours. *a* 1713 ELLWOOD *Autobiog.* (1714) 12 The Actions of my fore-past Life. 1830 SOUTHEY *Yng. Dragon* I. 36 Forepast times..With no portent could match it.

†**b.** quasi-*adv.* On a past occasion. *Obs.*
1664 *Floddan F.* III. 24 What he had said fore-past was nought.

fore-paw, -payment: see FORE- *pref.* 2 d, 3 c.

'**forepeak**. *Naut.* Also 7 forepike. [f. FORE- *pref.* + PEAK *sb.*[2]] The extreme end of the forehold in the angle of the bows.
1693 R. LYDE *Retaking a Ship* 11, I will command three of them down into the Fore-pike. *Ibid.* 17 A Scuttle..that went down into the Forepeak. 1835 MARRYAT *Three Cutt.* i, Luxury..is not wholly lost, even at the fore-peak. 1890 *Times* 6 Feb. 5/6 The collision-bulkhead, separating the forepeak from the watertight compartments.

fore-piece ('fɔəpiːs). [f. FORE- *pref.* + PIECE.] The foremost, first, or front piece: **a.** *gen.* **b.** *Theatr.* A 'curtain-raiser'. **c.** *Saddlery* (see quot. 1874).
1788 M. CUTLER in *Life Jrnls. & Corr.* (1888) I. 401 Broke the forepiece of my sulky, which detained us. 1814 *Monthly Mag.* XXXVII. 333 Tragedies of the last age..could be shortened into permanent fore-pieces. 1874 KNIGHT *Dict. Mech.* I. 905 *Fore-piece* (Saddlery), the flap attached to the fore-part of a side saddle, to guard the rider's dress.

fore-pillow: see FORE- *pref.* 3.

forepine: see FORPINE.

fore-place, -placing, -plan: see FORE- *pref.*

'**fore-plane**. [f. FORE- *pref.* + PLANE *sb.*] (See quot. 1842.)
1703 MOXON *Mech. Exerc.* 65 It is called the Fore Plane because it is used before you come to work either with the Smooth Plane, or with the Joynter. 1842 GWILT *Encycl. Archit.* Gloss., *Fore Plane* in carpentry and joinery the first plane used after the saw or axe. 1847 EMERSON *Repr. Men, Uses Gt. Men* Wks. (Bohn) I. 278 Every carpenter who shaves with a fore-plane borrows the genius of a forgotten inventor.

fore-planting, -plate: see FORE- *pref.* 2 c, 3.

† **fore'plead**, *v. Obs.*—[0] [perh. for **forplead*, f. FOR- *pref.*[1] (sense as in *forswear*) + PLEAD.] ? *trans.* To overreach in pleading. Hence **fore'pleading** *vbl. sb.*, unfair argument.
1624 BEDELL *Lett.* iii. 54 The forepleadings and aduantages to bee vsed against Heretikes.

† '**fore-plot**. *Obs.* [f. FORE- *pref.* + PLOT.] Premeditation. Similarly **fore'plot** *v.*, to contrive beforehand; **fore'plotted** *ppl. a.*
1641 PRYNNE *Antip.* 10 Which fore-plotted treason was the occasion of this Vision. 1647 N. BACON *Disc. Govt. Eng.* I. xl. (1739) 62 Which last they called Abere Murther, or Murther by foreplot or treachery. 1655 FULLER *Ch. Hist.* VI. iii. 315 His Wife..might..be presumed honest, if such a fore-plotted occasion had not debauched her.

† **fore-'point**, *v. Obs.* Also 6 forepoint. [f. FORE- *pref.* + POINT *v.*]

1. *trans.* **a.** To appoint or determine beforehand; to predestine *to* or *unto*. **b.** To forebode. **c.** To mark by points beforehand.
a. *c* 1550 CHEKE *Matt.* xvi. 17 *note*, Everlastingnes, and happines wheerunto his chosen be forpointed. 1589 GREENE *Menaphon* (Arb.) 84 Unfortunate Samela born to mishaps, and forepointed to sinister fortunes. 1593 LODGE *Longbeard*, etc. (1880) 56 He is the man forpointed to be my husband.
b. 1590 GREENE *Never too late* (1600) 69 As the Marble drops against raine, so their teares fore-poynt mischiefe.
c. 1570 DEE *Math. Pref.*, Which point we shall atteyne, by Notyng and forepointyng the angles and lines, by a sure and certain direction and connexion.

2. *intr.* To point beforehand.
1601 WEEVER *Mirr. Mart.* A iv b, He might haue seene how Fate that day fore-pointed. 1613-18 DANIEL *Coll. Hist. Eng.* (1626) 20 Thus (as fore pointing to a storme that was gathering on that coast) began the first difference with the French nation.

Hence **forepointing** *ppl. a.* Also **forepointer**, one who or that which points out beforehand.
1587 GREENE *Eupheus Cens.* Wks. (Grosart) VI. 171 The fathers and forepointers of wysedom. 1589 —— *Menaphon* (Arb.) 27 Some further forepoynting fate. 1590 —— *Mourn. Garm.* (1616) 23 Desires aboue Fortunes, are the forepointers of deep falls.

† ˌ**fore-po'ssess**, *v. Obs.* [f. FORE- *pref.* + POSSESS.] *trans.* To possess beforehand *with*.
1579 TOMSON *Calvin's Serm. Tim.* 625/2 Wee are fore-possessed and seised with so many vanities that [etc.]. 1635 SANDERSON *12 Serm., ad Cler.* (1681) 63 Any rational man not extremely fore-possessed with prejudice.

fore-post, -precedent: see FORE- *pref.* 3, 4 a.

† **fore-prepa'ration**. *Obs.* [f. FORE- *pref.* and FORE *prep.*] Preparation beforehand; also, *nonce-use*, the day before the (Jewish) 'preparation'.
1580 SIDNEY *Arcadia* (1622) 207 Hauing much aduantage both in number, valure, and fore-preparation. 1656 TRAPP *Comm. John* xix. 31 The Jews, before their preparation, had their fore-preparation.

† ˌ**fore-pre'pare**, *v. Obs.* [f. FORE- *pref.* + PREPARE.] *trans.* To prepare beforehand. Hence ˌ**forepre'pared** *ppl. a.*
1642 FULLER *Holy & Prof. St.* III xiv. 187 His fore-prepared Sepulchre. 1648 BP. HALL *Select Th.* §24 The evils, which we look for, fall so much the less heavily, by how much we are foreprepared for their entertainment. 1650 FULLER *Pisgah* I. III. vi. 372 They were rivetted into holes fore-prepared of purpose.

fore-pretended: see FORE- *pref.* 2 b.

† **fore'prise**, *v. Obs.* Also 6 forprise, 7 foreprize, -prizz. [f. FORE- *pref.* + *-prise*, after the analogy of *apprise*, *comprise*, etc.]

trans. To take beforehand: **a.** To assume, take for granted. **b.** To deal with, allow for, or mention beforehand; to provide for or determine beforehand; to forestall, anticipate. **c.** To take *into* or include by anticipation.
a. 1577 STANYHURST *Descr. Irel.* in Holinshed *Chron.* VI. Ep. Ded., The truth of the matter being forprised.
b. 1594 HOOKER *Eccl. Pol.* v. lxxi. §4 God hath fore-prised things of the greatest weight and hath therein precisely defined..that which every man must perform. 1607 BODLEIGH *Let.* 19 Feb. in *Abp. Ussher's Lett.* (1686) App. 21 As if the thing that they sought had been by prevention fore-priz'd by others. *a* 1641 BP. R. MOUNTAGU *Acts & Mon.* (1642) 499 Daniel forepriseth him, as a spirituall and eternall Prince. 1659 T. WHITE *Middle State of Souls* 28 Those holy Fathers..by their testimonies foreprize our exceptions. 1693 BEVERLEY *True St. Gospel Truth* 1 To be resolved in some Cases of Doubt, in others Foreprized, or Guarded against.
c. 1692 BEVERLEY *Disc. Dr. Crisp* 5 The Sins to come were Forepriz'd into it.

Hence ˌ**fore'prised**, ˌ**fore'prising** *ppl. adjs.*
1605 *Play Stucley* 1961 in Simpson *Sch. Shaks.* (1878) I. 236 If in the Basilisks fore-prizzing eye Be safely for the object it beholds Then [etc.]. *a* 1641 BP. R. MOUNTAGU *Acts & Mon.* (1642) 552 These fore-prised passages.

foreprise, -prize: see FORPRISE *sb.* and *v.* (*Law*).

† **fore-'prophesy**, *v. Obs.* [f. FORE- *pref.* + PROPHESY *v.*] *trans.* and *intr.* To prophesy beforehand. (Frequent in 16-17th c.)
1581 J. BELL *Haddon's Answ. Osor.* 379 When as we promise or foreprophecy in the name and person of God, things to come to passe. 1654 S. CLARKE *Eccl. Hist.* I. (ed. 2) 16 Who spake by the Spirit of God: Fore-seeing and fore-prophesying of those things which we now see are come to pass. 1676 W. ROW *Contn. Blair's Autobiog.* xii. (1848) 486 Foreprophesying that they would be employed against themselves.

fore-provided: see FORE- *pref.* 2 b.

'**fore-purpose**, *sb.* [f. FORE- *pref.* + PURPOSE.] A purpose settled beforehand, previous design. Similarly **fore'purpose** *v. trans.*, to purpose beforehand; **fore'purposed** *ppl. a.*
1551 T. WILSON *Logike* (1580) 43 A fore purposed choice. 1581 MARBECK *Bk. of Notes* 128 It is nothing els but his eternall determination fore purposed in his brest. 1587 GOLDING *De Mornay* ix. 121 Vpon new deuise, or vpon euerlasting forepurpose. *Ibid.* 135 To haue brought to passe and perfected all that euer he had forepurposed, betokeneth an incomparable might and power. *c* 1611 CHAPMAN *Iliad* xx. 17 The rest of these fore-purposes. 1829 SOUTHEY *Sir T. More* I. 105 The mystery whereby the free will of the subject is preserved, while it is directed by the fore purpose of the state.

† **fore-'quote**, *v. Obs.* [f. FORE- *pref.* + QUOTE.] *trans.* To quote or cite beforehand.

Hence **fore-quoted** *ppl. a.*
1598 SYLVESTER *Du Bartas* II. ii. IV. *Columnes* 454 Fore-quoting Confusedly th' Events most worthy noting. **1637** GILLESPIE *Eng. Pop. Cerem.* III. i. 4 In the forequotted place. **1670** W. CLARKE *Nat. Hist. Nitre* 14 According to the fore-quoted author.

fore-rake, -rank: see FORE- *pref.* 3, 3 d.

† **'foreranger.** corruption of *foranger*, FORAGER.
1612 PAULE *Life Whitgift* 40 The fore-rangers and harbingers of their further designes.

† **'forereach,** *sb. Naut. Obs.* [f. next vb.] ? The projection of the forepart of a vessel, beyond the end of the keel; = *fore-rake.*
1626 CAPT. SMITH *Accid. Yng. Seamen* 10 Her rake, the fore reach, plankes.

,fore-'reach, *v.* Chiefly *Naut.* [f. FORE- *pref.* + REACH *v.*]
1. *intr.* To shoot ahead. Also, *to fore-reach on, upon* (see quot. 1644).
1644 MANWAYRING *Sea-mans Dict.* 42 When two ships saile together, or after one another, she which sailes best (that is fastest) doth Fore-reach upon the other. **1748** *Anson's Voy.* II. iv. 163 We found that we had both weathered and fore-reached upon her considerably. **1800** C. STURT in *Naval Chron.* IV. 394 Mr. Weld's cutter fore-reached, but I gained to windward. **1834** M. SCOTT *Cruise Midge* (1859) 252 She..had forereached on us so far as to be well before our beam by this time. **1842** R. H. DANA *Seaman's Man.* 106 *Fore-reach*, to shoot ahead, especially when going in stays.
2. *trans.* To reach beyond, gain ground upon, pass. Also *fig.* To get the better of.
1803 *Naval Chron.* XXIII. 398 To endeavour to fore-reach her. **1845** NAPIER *Conq. Scinde* II. ii. 253 The general, coming back by a different route, had fore-reached them in such a scheme. **1870** *Daily News* 12 May, At 8.30 the Sappho was rapidly forereaching her opponent.
3. *trans.* To seize beforehand, anticipate. *rare.*
1874 WHITTIER *My Triumph* xvii, I..Fore-reach the good to be And share the victory.
Hence **,fore-'reaching** *ppl. a.*, pushing, eager.
1864 SKEAT *Uhland's Poems* 102 Every hand and every spirit works Fore-reaching, active, for the general weal.

† **fore-'read,** *v. Obs.* [f. FORE- *pref.* + READ.] *trans.* **a.** To read beforehand. **b.** To betoken or signify beforehand. **c.** To predestine.
a. 1620 BP. SAUNDERSON *Twelve Sermons* (1637) 303 Not onely to foreknow the extraordinary plagues..but also to fore-read in them Gods fierce wrath and heavie displeasure.
b. 1591 SPENSER *Muiopotmos* 29 His young..yeares..to him forered, That he..would..proue such an one. **1612** DRAYTON *Poly-olb.* xiii. 219 The first part of whose name, Godiua, doth foreread Th' first syllable of hers.
c. *a* **1636** FITZGEOFFREY *Eleg.* III. E vij b, Had Fate fore-read me in a Croude to dye.
Hence **fore-'reading** *vbl. sb.* and *ppl. a.*
1557 GRIMALDE in *Tottell's Misc.* (Arb.) 116 Good luck, certayn forereadyng moothers haue. *a* **1656** HALES *Gold. Rem.* (1688) 347 Your fore-reading of Suetonius.

fore-recited, -report, etc.: see FORE- *pref.*

fore-resemble, -rib, etc.: see FORE- *pref.*

† **fore-'ride,** *v. Obs.* [OE. *for-rídan*, f. FOR-[2], = FORE- *pref.* + *rídan* to RIDE.] *trans.* To ride before or in advance of.
O.E. Chron. an. 894 þa for rad sio fierd hie foran. *c* **1205** LAY. 26931 þat þa Rom-leoden heom for riden hafueden. **1570** LEVINS *Manip.* 117 To Foreryde, *præcurrere.*

fore-rider ('fɔəraɪdə(r)). [f. FORE- *pref.* + RIDER *sb.*; = Ger. *vorreiter.* Cf. FORRIDEL.] One who rides in front; *esp* † **a.** one of the vanguard; † **b.** a scout; **c.** an outrider or postillion; † **d.** a harbinger.
c **1470** HENRY *Wallace* III. 76 Thair for rydar was past till Ayr agane. **1494** FABYAN *Chron.* VI. clxiii. 156 Y^e^ fore rydars y^t^ put themselfe in prese with theyr sharpe launcys to wynne the firste brunte of the feelde. **1513** DOUGLAS *Æneis* XIII. *Prol.* 20 And Esperus..Vpspringis, as forridar of the nycht. **1548** HALL *Chron., Rich. III* (an. 3) 55 Therle of Richmond knewe by his forriders that the kyng was so nere embattayled. **1601** F. TATE *Househ. Ord. Edw. II* (1876) §56. 43 Each [charetter] shal have a fore rider which charetters and fore riders shal drive the charettes and keepe the horses. **1888** *Pall Mall G.* 8 Oct. 5/2 Then the mounted foreriders; and then the Emperor's carriage.

fore-rigging: see FORE- *pref.* 3 d.

foreright (,fɔə'raɪt), rarely with advbl. gen. *-s* **forerights,** *adv., prep., a.* and *sb.* [f. FORE *adv.* + RIGHT *adv.* and *adj.*]
† **A.** *adv.* Directly forward, in or towards the front, straight ahead. *fore-right against*, directly opposite. *Obs.*
1398 TREVISA *Barth. De P.R.* XVIII. lxiv. (1495) 819 A yonge Cowe is..compellyd to folowe euen and foreryght the steppes and fores of oxen. **1548** ELYOT, *Aduersus*..fore ryght againste. **1548** UDALL, etc. *Erasm. Par. Luke* xix. 30 The litell toune y^t^ ye see yonder foreright ayenst you. **1608** ARMIN *Nest Ninn.* (1842) 1 To looke fore-right I can not, because judgment out-lookes mee. **1659** LEAK *Water-wks.* 30 The difference is that, this here is seen fore-right, and that other upon one side. **1663** STAPYLTON *Slighted Maid* 3 *Fil.* Hey boy! how sits the wind? *Gios.* Fore-right, and a brisk Gale. **1715–20** POPE *Iliad* XXII. 189 No less fore-right the rapid chace they held. **1761** STERNE *Tr. Shandy* III. xl, Surveying it transversely..then foreright,—then this way, and then that. **1796** C. MARSHALL *Garden.* xii. (1813) 166 Let them [shoots] not advance far foreright.
B. *prep.*
† **1.** Straight along. *Obs.*[—1]
1650 FULLER *Pisgah* II. v. vii. 156 Sailing (not athwart the breadth..but) almost foreright the length of the lake.
2. Opposite, over against. *dial.*
1858 in Hughes *Scouring White Horse* 140 Vp, vorights the Castle round They did zet I on the ground.
C. *adj.*
† **1. a.** Of a path, road, etc.: Directly in front of one, straight forward. *Obs.*
1624 MASSINGER *Parl. Love* III. iii. Plays (1868) 179/2 You did but point me out a fore-right way To lead to certain happiness. *a* **1669** SOMNER *Roman Ports & Forts* 50 A direct and foreright continued current and passage. **1703** MOXON *Mech. Exerc.* 145 A straight or Foreright Ascent. **1748** RICHARDSON *Clarissa* Wks. (1883) VII. 315 You have only had the foreright path you were in overwhelmed.
† **b.** Of a wind: Straight on the line of one's course, favourable. *Obs.*
1605 CHAPMAN, etc. *Eastw. Hoe* III. ii, Ther's a foreright winde continuall wafts vs till we come at Virginia. **1615** —— *Odyss.* III. 244 Nor ever left the wind his foreright force. **1632** QUARLES *Div. Fancies* II. xciv. (1660) 95 His sayle Being fill'd and prosper'd with a fore-right Gale.
2. Of a branch, etc.: Shooting straight out.
1741 *Compl. Fam. Piece* II. iii. 388 Take off all fore-right or trailing Branches. **1802** W. FORSYTH *Fruit Trees* ii. (1824) 34 They will frequently throw out small dugs, or foreright shoots. **1882** *Gard. Chron.* XVII. 675 Removing..all foreright shoots.
3. *dial.* Of persons: **a.** Going straight ahead without regard of consequences, headstrong. **b.** Honest, straightforward; also, plain-spoken, blunt.
a. *a.* **1736** PEGGE *Kenticisms* (E.D.S.) s.v. (given as a 'Hants' word). **1853** COOPER *Sussex Gloss.* (ed. 2).
b. 1810 *Devon & Cornw. Voc.* in *Monthly Mag.* June 436 'A foreright man', that is, a plain honest man. **1880** MRS. PARR *Adam & Eve* II. 213 Be foreright in all you do.
D. *sb.* [The *adj.* used *absol.*]
† **a.** Something straightforward (*obs.*). **b.** A foreright shoot; cf. C. 2. **c.** *dial.* (see quot.).
a. *a.* **1754** RICHARDSON *Grandison* VII. xiii. 75 We women sometimes choose to come at a point by the round-abouts, rather than by the fore-rights.
b. 1882 *Jrnl. Horticulture* 6 Apr. 288 The forerights unless strong being treated similarly.
c. 1797 R. POLWHELE *Old Eng. Gentl.* 54 Then..Cut from the buttock a convenient slice, And..Salute the fore-right with as keen a knife. *Note*, 'Foreright' is the coarsest sort of wheaten bread, made of the meal, with all the bran.

fore-riped: see FORE- *pref.* 2 b.

'fore-room. [f. FORE- *pref.* + ROOM.]
† **1.** ? The forecastle of a ship. *Obs.*
c **1565** LINDESAY (Pitscottie) *Chron. Scot.* (1728) 101 With ..two-handed swords in your fore-rooms. **1589** GREENE *Sp. Masquerado* Wks. (Grosart) V. 272 That woorthy Gentleman..valiantly standing in the fore roome deliuered with Cannon his Ambassage to the Enemie.
2. The front room or parlour. Now only *US.*
1728 VANBR. & CIB. *Prov. Husb.* I. i. 32 She has a Couple of clever Girls there a stitching i' th' Fore-room. **1774** FOOTE *Cozeners* II. Wks. 1799 II. 174 In the fore-room, up one pair of stairs. **1880** E. H. ARR *New Eng. Bygones* 46 This was the 'best-room' or as my grandfather called it, the 'fore' room. **1893** *Boston* (Mass.) *Youth's Comp.* 16 Mar. 140/4 So we went into the fore-room.

fore-royal: see FORE- *pref.* 2 d.

fore-run (fɔə'rʌn), *v.* [f FORE- + RUN.]
1. *intr.* To run on in front. OE. only.
c **1000** *Ags. Gosp.* John xx. 4 Se oðer leorning-cniht for-arn [*c* **950** *Lindisf.* forearn] petrus forne.
2. *trans.* To outrun, outstrip. *Obs.* exc. *fig.*
1513 DOUGLAS *Æneis* XII. vi. 61 That thai forryn and gois befor alway Zephirus and Nothus. **1536** BELLENDEN *Cron. Scot.* (1821) I. 186 Gif the haris had forrun the hundis. **1842** TENNYSON *2 Voices* 88 Forerun thy peers. **1879** CHURCH *Spenser* v. 119 Even genius..cannot forerun the limitations of its day.
† **3.** To run in front of; hence, to act as harbinger of (a person). Also *transf.* to precede. *Obs.*
1570 LEVINS *Manip.* 188 To forerunne, *præcurrere.* **1615** G. SANDYS *Trav.* 173 They often compassing the sepulcher in a ioynt procession, are fore-run and followed by the people. **1621** QUARLES *Argalus & P.* (1678) 6 Chris-cross foreruns the Alphabet of love. **1708** STANHOPE *Paraphr.* (1709) IV. 335 And thou, my Child John, shalt fore-tell and immediately fore-run this Saviour. **1750** COVENTRY *Pompey Litt.* (1752) 36 Thus our hero, with three footmen fore-running his equipage, set out in triumph.
absol. *a* **1643** W. CARTWRIGHT *Siege* v. iii, To forerun And lead the way t' Elysium [is] but a duty She would not thank me for.
4. To be the precursor of (a future event, etc.).
1590 GREENE *Never too late* (1600) 71 Lightning, that beautifies the heauen for a blaze, but foreruns stormes and thunder. **1593** SHAKS. *Rich. II*, II. iv. 15 These signes fore-run the death of Kings. **1652** COTTERELL *Cassandra* v. II. (1676) 487 This felicity was to fore-run the last I now can hope for. *a* **1711** KEN *Hymns Evang.* Poet. Wks. 1721 I. 219 A Star..which Eastern Gentiles guess'd was to forerun The wish'd-for Dawn of the Eternal Sun. **1834** GOOD *Study Med.* (ed. 4) II. 359 The symptoms that forerun the chicken-pox. **1859** TENNYSON *Idylls, Guinevere* 131 The cold wind that foreruns the morn.
5. To anticipate, forestall.
1591 RALEIGH *Last Fight Rev.* 15 By anticipating and forerunning false reports. **1655** H. VAUGHAN *Silex Scint.*, *Rules & Lessons* (1858) 73 Our Bodies but forerun The Spirit's duty. **1849** LONGF. *Mrs. Kemble's Readings Shaks.*, The great poet who foreruns the ages, Anticipating all that shall be said!
Hence **'fore,running** *vbl. sb.* and *ppl. a.*
1565 HARDING *Let. to Jewel* in Strype *Ann. Ref* I. App. xxx. 72 Your forerunning sermon. **1580** HOLLYBAND *Treas. Fr. Tong, Advantcourement*, forerunning. **1660** MILTON *Free Commw.* Wks. (1847) 449/2 The diabolical forerunning Libels. **1690** PENN *Rise & Progr. Quakers* (1834) 50 The consummation of the legal, and fore running of the Gospel times. **1818** S. E. PIERCE *Bk. Psalms* II. 460 Sorrows and griefs, forerunning figures of what would befall Messiah. **1872** LONGF. *Div. Trag.* Introitus 53 The sublime fore running of their time.

forerunner (fɔə'rʌnə(r)). [f. prec. + -ER[1].]
1. a. One who runs before, *esp.* one sent to prepare the way and herald a great man's approach, a harbinger; also, a guide. Chiefly *transf.* and *fig.*
First used *fig.* as rendering of L. *præcursor*, *esp.* of John the Baptist as 'the Forerunner of Christ'.
a **1300** *Cursor M.* 13208 (Cott.) For-þi es he cald his foriner [*MS. app. reads* former; *Gött.* forinnier], And cristes aun messenger. *c* **1440** *York Myst.* xxi. 16 Þus am I comen in message right, And be fore-reyner in certayne. **1541** COVERDALE *Old Faith* ix. (1547) F viij, John the baptist, whych was the fore runner of..Christ. **1576** FLEMING *Panopl. Epist.* 292 Followyng ye infallible foot-steps of thy forerunner Nature. **1634** HEYWOOD *Witches Lanc.* I. i. Wks. 1874 IV. 175 Farewell Gentlemen, Ile be your fore-runner, To give him notice of your visite. *a* **1711** KEN *Preparatives* Poet. Wks. 1721 IV. 144 Death our Fore-runner is, and guides To Sion. **1725** POPE *Odyss.* I. 520 Did he some loan ..require, Or came fore-runner of your scepter'd Sire? **1860** PUSEY *Min. Proph.* 594 The Forerunner of our Lord. **1878** BOSW. SMITH *Carthage* 75 When Claudius the..forerunner of the Roman army, appeared at Rhegium.
b. Applied *transf.* to things.
1579 E. K. *Gloss. Spenser's Sheph. Cal.* Mar. 11 The swallow..useth to be counted..the forerunner of springe. **1622** SPARROW *Bk. Com. Prayer* (1661) 115 Advent Sundaies..are to Christmas Day..forerunners to prepare for it. **1674** N. FAIRFAX *Bulk & Selv.* Contents, Chap. I The Introduction or forerunner. **1751** CHESTERF. *Lett.* (1792) III. ccxlii. 109 A sort of panegyric of you..which will be a very useful fore-runner for you.
c. *pl.* The advance-guard of an army. Chiefly *transf.* and *fig.*
1535 COVERDALE *Wisd.* xii. 8 Thou..sendest ye forerunners of thyne hoost, euen hornettes. **1645** PAGITT *Heresiogr.* (1661) 276 They..cryed out, that they were the fore-runners of Popery. **1878** BOSW. SMITH *Carthage* 233 Four thousand cavalry..had been sent forward by Servilius as his forerunners.
d. *Skiing.* [tr. G. *vorläufer.*] A skier who runs over the course as a preliminary to a skiing race.
1949 P. CUMMINGS *Dict. Sports, Forerunner* (Skiing), one who breaks a trail first before a competition starts. **1964** *Times* 31 Jan. 4/1 Three forerunners then came down to open the course.
2. One whom another follows or comes after, a predecessor; also, an ancestor.
1595 SHAKS. *John* II. i. 2 Arthur, that great fore-runner of thy bloud. **1683** D. A. *Art Converse* 7 Long descriptions of their own Pedigree, and grandure of their fore-runners. **1768** STERNE *Sent. Journ.* (1775) I. 13 My..observations will be altogether of a different cast from any of my fore-runners. **1866** J. MARTINEAU *Ess.* I. 15 Comte claims Hume as his chief forerunner in philosophy.
transf. **1663** GERBIER *Counsel* A iv a, The fore-runner of this Discourse was printed and dedicated to the King.
3. That which foreruns or foreshadows something else; a prognostic or sign of something to follow.
1589 GREENE *Menaphon* (Arb.) 39 The wrongs of my youth are the fore-runners of my woes in age. **1612** WOODALL *Surg. Mate* Wks. (1653) 88 A convulsion oftentimes is a fore-runner or a messenger of death. **1764** HARMER *Observ.* xvii. 42 A squall of wind and clouds of dust are the usual forerunners of these first rains. **1878** BOSW. SMITH *Carthage* 112 The famine and the pestilence which are usually the last outcome and not the forerunners of a siege.
4. *Naut.* **a.** A rope fastened to a harpoon. Cf. FORE-GANGER. **b.** A rope rove through a single block on the foremast. **c.** (See quots.)
a. *a.* **1694** *Acc. Sev. Late Voy.* II. (1711) 158 The first of them is ty'd to the Fore-runner, or small Line.
b. 1805 in Nicolas *Disp. Nelson* (1846) VII. 189 *note*, Got forerunners and tackles forward to secure foremast.
c. 1815 *Falconer's Dict. Marine* (ed. Burney), *Fore-Runner of the Log-line*, a small piece of red buntin, laid into that line at a certain distance from the log. **1841** R. H. DANA *Seaman's Man.* 106 *Fore-runner*, a piece of rag, terminating the stray-line of the log line.
Hence **'fore,runnership,** the condition or dignity of a forerunner.
1881 A. B. BRUCE *Chief End Revelat.* vi. 300 This fore-runnership of Christ.

foresaid ('fɔəsɛd), *a.* [f. FORE- *pref.* + SAID.] = AFORESAID. (In Sc. writings of 16th c., and in legal formulæ until 18th c., it occurs with plural ending *forsaidis.*) Now *rare.*
c **1000** ÆLFRIC *Josh.* vi. 22 Iosue cwæþ þa siððan to þam foresædan ærendracum. *a* **1300** *Cursor M.* 6392 (Cott.) Moyses..smat it wit þis forsaid wand. **1340** *Ayenb.* 190 þe uorzede manne. **1413** *Pilgr. Sowle* (Caxton 1483) v. xiv. 105, I sawe a semely persone standyng nyhe the forsaid tree. **1563** SHUTE *Archit.* B j b, The measures of the forsayde Pillours. **1585** JAS. I. *Essayes in Poesie* (1869) 55 Many of thir foirsaides precepts. **1679** DRYDEN *Tr. & Cr.* III. i. Wks. 1883 VI. 325 All of these foresaid men are fools. **1775** ADAIR *Amer. Ind.* 321 When the fore-said warriors returned home. **1787** COWPER *Let.* 17 Nov., 'Foresaid little Bishop and I had

much talk about many things, but most about Homer. **1821** SCOTT *Kenilw.* xii, An archway surmounted by the foresaid tower.

ellipt. **1556** LAUDER *Tractate* 140 Off thir forsaids ȝe sall be sure. **1688** R. HOLME *Armoury* III. 336/2 The foresaid are kind of Bottles which Reapers..use to carry their Drink or Milk in. **1752** J. LOUTHIAN *Form of Process* (ed. 2) 120 All Cost, Skaith, Damage and Expences, he or his foresaids [*i.e.* his 'executors, assigns, etc.'] may happen to sustain therethrough.

fore-sail (ˈfɔəseɪl). [f. FORE- *pref.* + SAIL; = Ger. *vorsegel.*] The principal sail set on the foremast; in square-rigged vessels, the lowest square sail on the foremast; in fore-and-aft rigged, the triangular sail before the mast.

1481–90 *Howard Househ. Bks.* (Roxb.) 50 A bolte roppe for the foreseile. **1582** N. LICHEFIELD tr. *Castanheda's Conq. E. Ind.* xxix. 72 b, They brought themselves vnder their foresailes againe. **1630** J. TAYLOR (Water P.) *Urania* Wks. I His Sprit-saile, Fore-saile, Main-saile, and his Mizzen. **1745** P. THOMAS *Jrnl. Anson's Voy.* 27 The next Day we split the Fore-sail. **1855** O. W. HOLMES *Poems* 165 Many a foresail..Shall break from yard and stay.

attrib. **1549** *Compl. Scot.* vi. 40 Hail..the foir sail scheit, hail out the bollene.

†**ˈforesaw.** *Obs. rare.* [f. FORE- *pref.* + SAW *sb.* saying.] **a.** A previous saying. **b.** A fore-saying, prediction.

1387 TREVISA *Higden* II. 177 And now the more world is discreued in oure four sawes in þe firste book [L. *in præcedentibus*]. **1555** WATREMAN *Fardle Facions* II. viii. L iv a, In the beginning of yᵉ yere, assemblying together, thei [the Sages] foreshewe of raine..For aswell the kynge as the people, ones vndrestandyng their foresawes..shone the euilles.

fore-say (fɔəˈseɪ), *v.* [OE. *foresęcgan*, f. FORE- *pref.* + *sęcgan* to SAY.] *trans.* To say beforehand, foretell, predict. Now *rare.*

c **900** tr. *Bæda's Hist.* Contents III. xiii. (1890) 14 Ðæt se biscop Aidan þam scypfarendum þone storm towardne foresæȝde. *a* **1300** *Cursor M.* 1606 (Cott.) A propheci, þat forsaid was bi his merci. **1543** GRAFTON *Contn. Harding* 549 Kyng Henry yᵉ Sixte did foresaye the same, and in like maner prophecy of hym. **1561** T. NORTON *Calvin's Inst.* IV. 9 He foresayth yᵗ the people shalbe gathered together agayne. *a* **1641** BP. R. MOUNTAGU *Acts & Mon.* (1642) 176 Homer took much out of her verses, which she foresaw and foresaid he should doe. **1886** J. PAYNE *Decameron* I. 12 The pleasance and delight..which belike, were it not foresaid, might not be looked for from such a beginning.

Hence **foreˈsaying** *vbl. sb.*

1548 UDALL, etc. *Erasm. Par. Mark* i. 2 The prophecies and foresayinges of the Prophetes. **1608–11** BP. HALL *Epist.* III. iii. Wks. (1627) 319 Whose foresayings verified in all particular issues are more than demonstratiue.

fore-scene, -scent, etc.: see FORE- *pref.*

†**ˈfore-seat.** *Obs.* [see FORE- *pref.* 3.] A seat or position in front.

1615 CROOKE *Body of Man* 133 The fore-seate of the Hollow veine, where it groweth to the Liuer. **1715** S. SEWALL *Diary* 20 Mar. (1882) III. 42 Mr. Pemberton spake to me as he went by the foreseat in the morning.

foresee (fɔəˈsiː). Also 4–6 forsee, (6 force, *Sc.* foirsee). [OE. *foresēon*, f. FORE- *pref.* + *sēon* to SEE; cf. Ger. *vorsehen.*]

1. *trans.* To see beforehand, have prescience of. Often with obj. and *inf.* or with *clause* as obj.

c **1000** *Ags. Ps.* cxxxviii. [cxxxix.] 2 (Th.) Þu ealle mine weȝas wel fore-sawe. *c* **1400** *Destr. Troy* 2247 Þat hedis to þe first, And for-sees not the fer end, what may falle after. **1513** MORE in Grafton *Chron.* (1568) II. 781 He that of good heart and courage foresawe no perilles. **1581** MARBECK *Bk. Notes* 331 God did fore-see and fore-knowe, that they should be dampned. **1611** BIBLE *Prov.* xxvii. 12 A prudent man foreseeth the euil, and hideth himselfe. **1630** PRYNNE *Anti-Armin.* 116 God from all eternity foresaw them in themselues to be such. **1725** DE FOE *Voy. round World* (1840) 41, I presently foresaw, that, if I went to the extremity, I should spoil the voyage. **1815** JANE AUSTEN *Emma* iv, Emma had very early foreseen how useful she might find her. **1883** FROUDE *Short Stud.* IV. I. x. 112 The empire might be laid under interdict, with the consequences which everyone foresaw.

absol. **1667** MILTON *P.L.* I. 627 What power of mind Foreseeing or presaging, from the Depth Of knowledge past or present. *a* **1881** ROSSETTI *House of Life* x, The shadowed eyes remember and foresee.

†**b.** *Sc.* To see previously; to have an interview with (a person) beforehand; to inspect or consider beforehand. *Obs.*

1592 *Sc. Acts Jas. VI* (1814) III. 627 For dyuerss vtheris wechtie caussis and guid consideratiounis foirsene be his hienes. **1625** *Burgh Rec. Glasgow* (1876) 348 That na maner of persoun..pas heirefter to..England without thai first foirsie the prouest and bailleis. **1663** SPALDING *Troub. Chas. I* (1829) 66 Thir articles were foreseen by the tables at Edinburgh, and order given to refuse the samen.

†**2.** To prepare beforehand or provide; in early use with *dat.* of person, later with *to.* Also, to provide *of* or *with* (something). *Obs.*

c **900** tr. *Bæda's Hist.* IV. i. (1891) 256 Þæt he him on his biscopscire ȝerisne stowe foreseȝe and salde. **1513** DOUGLAS *Æneis* X. xii. 134 Thou sall de fyrst, quhat evyr to me forseyne Or providyt has mychty Jove. **1637** R. MONRO *Exped.* II. 133 This Leaguer..at all sorting Ports, being well foreseene with slaught-bomes and triangles.

†**b.** To see to or take care about beforehand; to provide for or against. With simple *obj.*, or *obj.* clause introduced by *that. Obs.*

c **900** tr. *Bæda's Hist.* I. xxvii. (1891) 66 Swylce eac be heora ondlifne is to þencenne and to foreseonne þæt [etc.]. **1526** *Househ. Ord.* 139 The sewers..to have semblably charge to forsee that no part of the fruict..be in any wise purloyned. **1565** *Act 8 Eliz.* c. 13 §1 The Master, Wardens and Assistants of the Trinity-house..are bound to foresee the good Increase and Maintenance of Ships. **1577** HANMER *Anc. Eccl. Hist.* 251 He supposed it was his bounden duety to foresee lest the..decrees of that councell should..be impayred. **1590** GREENE *Never too late* (1600) 62 He that forerepents forsees many perils. **1604** *Nottingham Rec.* (1889) IV. 267 The 7 Aldermen,..be ouerseers for the towne to forsee the daunger of the visitacion. **1622** CALLIS *Stat. Sewers* (1647) 5 The King..was bound to see and foresee the safety of this Realm. **1626** BACON *Sylva* §699 In Horse-Races Men are curious to fore-see, that there be not the least Weight upon the one Horse, more than vpon the other.

†**3.** *intr.* To exercise foresight, take care or precaution, make provision. Also, to look *to* or *into* beforehand. *Obs.*

1551 T. WILSON *Logike* (1580) 84 Fire, nor yet water doe harme of them selves, but..the negligence of man, whiche forseeth not to them. *a* **1590** *Marr. Wit & Wisd.* (1846) 8 Well, as for that I shall for-se. **1594** *First Pt. Contention* (1843) 33 Well hath your grace foreseen into that Duke. **1624** QUARLES *Div. Poems, Job* (1717) 228 He plots, complots, forsees, prevents, directs. *a* **1626** BACON (J.), A king against a storm must foresee to a convenient stock of treasure.

†**4.** (*alway*) *foreseen* or *foreseeing that*: provided that.

1434 *E.E. Wills* (1882) 99 Forseen alwey, that yf..my doughtres dye [etc.]. **1533** ELYOT *Cast. Helthe* II. i. (1541) 16 b, Forseene alwaye that they eate withoute gourmandyse. **1550** *Privy Council Acts* (1891) III. 79 Forseing that of their waiges they content their hostes for their victailes. **1600** W. VAUGHAN *Direct. Health* (1633) 32 Foreseene also that they that shall drinke it thus, be not subject to the Chollicke.

Hence **foreˈseeing** *vbl. sb.*; **foreˈseeing** *ppl. a.*, characterized by foresight. **fore-ˈseeingly** *adv.*

c **1374** CHAUCER *Troylus* IV. 961 (989) It were rather an opinyon Uncertein, and no stedfast forseynge. **1536** LATIMER *2nd Serm. bef. Convocation* Wks. I. 43 Ought we to attribute it to..the forseeing of the kings grace? **1567** *Triall Treas.* (1850) 18 Be circumspect, therefore, forseing and sapient. **1594** MARLOWE & NASHE *Dido* IV. iii, Follow your fore-seeing stars in all. *a* **1653** GOUGE *Comm. Heb.* xi. 39 Gods..fore-seeing of this and that is justly stiled a providing it. **1728** VANBR. & CIB. *Prov. Husb.* I, What prudent care does this deep foreseeing nation take for the support of its worshipful families! **1802** H. MARTIN *Helen of Glenross* I. 105 Your gloomy croaking ominous fore-seeings. **1848** W. H. KELLY tr. *L. Blanc's Hist. Ten Y.* II. 567 A wise and foreseeing policy. **1857** RUSKIN *Elem. Drawing* iii. 205 You must go straight through them, knowingly and foreseeingly, all the way.

foreseeable (fɔəˈsiːəb(ə)l), *a.* [f. prec. + -ABLE.] That may be foreseen. Freq. in phr. ***foreseeable future.***

1804 W. TAYLOR in *Ann. Rev.* II. 367 A rise and a fall foreseeable. **1840** MILL *Diss. & Disc., Bentham* (1859) I. 387 The morality of an action depends on its foreseeable consequences. **1932** *Nation* June 613 The population problem..does not seem likely to be solved in the foreseeable future. **1958** *Spectator* 22 Aug. 241/3 Nobody is going, within the fore-seeable future, to lay a finger on the trade unions. **1959** *Cambr. Rev.* 2 May 469/1, I cannot picture fewer motorists in the city during the foreseeable future. **1965** *New Statesman* 30 Apr. 672/3 The sad fact is that, in the readily foreseeable future, governments have to persuade us to ration ourselves to one child each on the average.

foreseen (fɔəˈsiːn), *pple.* and *ppl. a.* [*pa. pple.* of FORESEE.]

†**1.** *pple.* That has seen beforehand; previously acquainted or instructed *in*; aware *of. to make foreseen*: to acquaint or inform previously. *Obs.*

1569 MURRAY *To L.B.* (Harl. Lib. 37. B. 9 fo. 43) Her highness had been foreseen in the dukes design. **1577** LOCHLEVIN *Let. to Morton* in Robertson *Hist. Scot.* App. 72, I tho't good to make your grace forseen of the same. **1597** LOWE *Chirurg.* IV. vii. (1634) 89 For the which the parents and friends would be foreseene of the danger which may happen. *a* **1651** CALDERWOOD *Hist. Kirk* (1678) II. 490 Kerseweil was rebooked for accepting the Bishoprick of the Isles, without making the Assembly foreseen.

2. *ppl. a.* That is seen beforehand; also, †known beforehand by sight *to.*

1532 MORE *Confut. Tindale* Wks. 573/1 An elect foresene to god from the beginning. *a* **1600** HOOKER *Answ. Travers' Supplic.* §22 They are not reiected..without a fore-seene worthinesse of reiection going..in order before. **1697** DRYDEN *Æneid* VI. 1088 At his fore-seen Approach, already quake The Caspian Kingdoms. **1790** BURKE *Fr. Rev.* Wks. V. 145 A burst of enthusiasm on the foreseen consequences of this happy day. **1837–8** SIR W. HAMILTON *Logic* xxiii. (1866) I. 454 To move in a foreseen, and, consequently, a determinate direction. **1856** EMERSON *Eng. Traits, Lit.* Wks. (Bohn) II. 113 No sublime augury cheers the student, no secure striding from experiment onward to a foreseen law.

foreseer (fɔəˈsiːə(r)). Also 6 foresear. [f. FORESEE *v.* + -ER¹.] One who foresees.

1548 HALL *Chron., Rich. III* (an. 2) 33 b, That you be..a vigilante foresear. **1621** AINSWORTH *Annot. Deut.* xviii. 10 A fore-seer or presager. **1799** *Spirit Publ. Jrnls.* (1800) III. 364 There are many sagacious foreseers who can calculate the loss of a reputation.

foreset (fɔəˈsɛt), *v.* [OE. *fore-sęttan*, f. FORE- *pref.* + *sęttan* to SET.]

†**1.** To set in front, put to the front. *Obs.*

c **825** *Vesp. Psalter* lxxxv[i]. 14 Ða unrehtwisan..na [*MS.* non] foresetton þec beforan ȝesihþe his. *a* **1300** *E.E. Psalter* cxxxvi[i]. 6 If I for-set þe noght Ierusalem, ai, In biginning of mi fainenes al dai.

2. To set, arrange, or settle beforehand; to prearrange, predetermine. Now *rare.*

1561 DAUS tr. *Bullinger on Apoc.* (1573) 143 b, Hereby is the tyme betokened and foreset. **1587** *Misfort. Arth.* II. iii, No Fate But is foreset. **1633** BP. HALL *Hard Texts* 150 To foresee and foreset the daies and times for his judgments. **1839** BAILEY *Festus* iv. (1848) 35 No man can foreset thy coming.

Hence **foreˈsetting** *vbl. sb.*, the action of setting or arranging beforehand; also quasi-*concr.* a purpose. †**ˈforeset** *sb.*, set purpose.

a **1300** *E.E. Psalter* xlviii. 5 [xlix. 4], I sal open in sauter mi forsettinge. **1561** NORTON & SACKV. *Gorboduc* II. ii, Whan kinges of foreset wyll neglecte the rede Of best aduise. **1571** GOLDING *Calvin on Ps.* lxxv. 3 The foresettinge of ende and measure untoo mischaunces.

foreset, *ppl. a.* [f. the vb.] **1.** (fɔəˈsɛt) Set or determined beforehand.

1550 BALE *Image Both Ch.* II. xiv. §11 H viij b, To committe theym by faythfull prayer to his purposed decrees or for set ordinaunces. **1669** WOODHEAD *St. Teresa* I. Pref. 2 Rigidly exacting of herself the foreset portion of time for it.

2. (ˈfɔəsɛt). *Geol.* [directly f. FORE- *prefix* + SET *ppl. a.*] In a delta or similar deposit, designating a series of inclined layers of sediment formed by successive deposition on the advancing forward slope and usu. situated between bottom-set beds and top-set beds. Also *ellipt.*

1905, 1942 [see *bottom-set bed* s.v. BOTTOM *sb.* 20]. **1939** W. H. TWENHOFEL *Princ. Sedimentation* xiv. 507 Foreset lengths are largely directly controlled by quantity of sands and inversely by velocity of currents. Foresets may range in length to 30 meters or more but about 3 meters is an average high maximum. **1957** G. E. HUTCHINSON *Treat. Limnol.* I. ii. 183 As more and more foreset beds are laid down, the mouth of the river is carried out into the lake. **1971** *Nature* 13 Aug. 448/1 The foreset slopes of major deltas.

foreset: see FORSET, to obstruct, waylay.

foreset, var. f. of FORCET, *Obs.*

fore-settled: see FORE- *pref.* 2 b.

foreshadow (ˈfɔəʃædəʊ), *sb.* [f. FORE- *pref.* + SHADOW *sb*; suggested by next vb.] *fig.* A shadow cast before an object; an indication or imperfect representation of something to come.

1831 CARLYLE *Sart. Res.* (1858) 115 Fore-shadows..of that Truth and Beginning of Truths, fell mysteriously over my soul. **1852** J. M. LUDLOW *Master Engineers* 132 A truce is often the foreshadow of a peace. **1887** KINGLAKE *Crimea* VIII. 280 The foreshadow of death was then falling on the mind of the Chief.

foreshadow (fɔəˈʃædəʊ), *v.* [f. FORE- *pref.* + SHADOW *v.*] *trans.* To serve as the shadow thrown before (an object); hence, to represent imperfectly beforehand, prefigure. Also rarely (of a person), to have a foreboding of.

1577 VAUTROUILLIER *Luther on Ep. Gal.* 146 The ceremonies commanded in the law did foreshadow Christ. *a* **1677** BARROW *Serm.* Wks. 1761. II. xxvii. 288 Our Saviour's death..was by manifold types fore-shadowed. **1855** H. SPENCER *Princ. Psychol.* (1872) II. VI. xxvii. 297 These intuitions are fore-shadowed in the very first stages of an incipient consciousness. **1860** MOTLEY *Nether l.* (1868) I. i. 23 The surrender of Ghent foreshadowed the fate of Flanders. **1864** DICKENS *Our Mut. Fr.* II. xiv, Another consequence that he had never foreshadowed was [etc.].

Hence **foreˈshadowed** *ppl. a.*; **foreˈshadowing** *vbl. sb.* Also **foreˈshadower,** one who or that which foreshadows.

1848 DICKENS *Dombey* xx, The feeling..of which he had had some old foreshadowing in older times..was full-formed now. **1866** GEO. ELIOT *F. Holt* xvii, Phrases that class our foreshadowed endurance among those common and ignominious troubles. **1870** MORRIS *Earthly Par.* I. I. 306 Dim foreshadowings of what yet might come. **18..** *Chamb. Jrnl.* (Cent. Dict.) The foreshadowers of evil.

fore-shaft, -shape: see FORE- *pref.* 2 a, 3 b.

fore-sheet (ˈfɔəʃiːt). *Naut.* [f. FORE- *pref.* + SHEET.]

1. The rope by which the lee corner of the foresail is kept in place.

1667 DAVENANT & DRYDEN *Tempest* I. i, Flat-in the fore-sheet there. **1669** STURMY *Mariner's Mag.* I. 16 Round aft the Main sheets, and Fore-sheets. **1745** P. THOMAS *Jrnl. Anson's Voy.* 28 We broke our Larboard Fore-sheet and fixed a new one.

2. *pl.* The inner part of the bows of a boat, fitted with gratings upon which the bow-man stands (Adm. Smyth).

1719 DE FOE *Crusoe* II. xii, Two of the enemy's men entered the boat just where this fellow stood, being in the fore-sheets. **1833** MARRYAT *P. Simple* (1863) 99, I stowed myself away under the fore-sheets. **1883** STEVENSON *Treas. Isl.* III. xiii, In a jiffy I had slipped over the side, and curled up in the fore-sheets of the nearest boat.

3. *Comb.*, as *fore-sheet horse, traveller* (see quots.).

1846 YOUNG *Naut. Dict., Fore-Sheet Horse*, an iron rod or piece of wood fastened at its ends athwart the deck of a single masted vessel, before the mast, for the foresail sheet to travel upon. *Ibid.* s.v. *Traveller*, The Fore-sheet Traveller is a ring ..which traverses on the fore-sheet horse.

† **fore'shield**, *v. Obs.* Also for-. [f. FOR- *pref.* or FORE- *pref.*[1] + SHIELD *v.*] *trans.* To ward off, avert; only in asseverations, as *God forshield (that..)*: = FORFEND 2.

a **1549** *Murning Maidin* xv, That I you sla, that God forscheild! **1562-83** FOXE *A. & M.* (1583) 1583 God foreshield that I should so do. **1663** COWLEY *Cutter Coleman St.* v. x, Marry, Heav'n foreshield!

foreshift: see FORE- *pref.* 4.

foreshine ('fɔəʃaɪn), *sb. rare.* [f. FORE- *pref.* + SHINE *sb.*; suggested by Ger. *vorschein.*] A shining seen in advance.

1864 CARLYLE *Fredk. Gt.* IV. II. v. 72 The appearance, or indubitable foreshine, or Friedrich Wilhelm's bayonets.

† **fore'shine**, *v. Obs.* [f. FORE- *pref.* + SHINE *v.*] *intr.* To shine forth; also, to shine in front, throw light forward. Hence **fore'shining** *vbl. sb.*

1571 GOLDING *Calvin on Ps.* xviii. 7 When fayth foreshyneth untoo us..then truly is the gate set open for us. *Ibid.* xxv. 12 By the foreshining of the light of the Spirit they may understand what is needful to be done. **1611** CORYAT *Crudities* App. 15 The Lyon old, whose princely heart foreshineth in his breast.

foreship ('fɔəʃɪp). [OE. *forscip*, f. FOR- *pref.*[2]; FORE- *pref.* + *scip*, SHIP.] The fore part of a ship or vessel; the prow.

c **1000** ÆLFRIC *Voc.* in Wr.-Wülcker 166 *Prora*..forscip. **13..** *Coer de L.* 2618 Kynge Rychard..With hys axe in foreschyp stood. **1432-50** tr. *Higden* (Rolls) V. 159 The erle ..inquirede of hym syttinge in the foreschippe, wheþer he see of Athanasius. **1526** TINDALE *Acts* xxvii. 30 As though they wolde have caste ancres out off the forshippe. **1895** *Daily News* 1 Feb. 7/2 The stem..is gone above water to the third frame, but there is no water in the foreship.

'fore-shock. *Seismology.* [FORE- *pref.* 5.] A lesser shock preceding the principal shock of an earthquake.

1902 *Q. Jrnl. Geol. Soc.* LVIII. 393 (*heading*) Fore-shocks of 1901. **1959** *Times* 3 Jan. 4/1 It is not uncommon to have a preliminary or 'foreshock' followed by the main shock. **1970** *Nature* 18 July 317/2 Small local foreshocks and aftershocks which often precede and follow larger earthquakes.

fore-shoe, -shop: see FORE- *pref.* 2 a and 3.

foreshore ('fɔəʃɔə(r)). [f. FORE- *pref.* + SHORE] **1.** The fore part of the shore; that part which lies between the high- and low-water marks; occas. the ground lying between the edge of the water and the land which is cultivated or built upon.

1764 *Skeffling Inclos. Act* 13 Land or ground, as a new fore shore to the said river. **1839** STONEHOUSE *Axholme* 56 Stone heaps which are put out for the defence of the foreshores. **1864** J. G. BERTRAM *Notes Trav.* 1862-3. 67 The moment the tide runs back the foreshore is at once overrun with a legion of hungry people. **1894** SALA *Lond. up to date* xxiv. 360 Many grand patrician houses existed on this foreshore [of the Thames] from Essex Street down to Hungerford. *transf.* **1874** T. HARDY *Madding Crowd* II. i. 15 The foreshores and promontories of coppery cloud which bounded a green and pellucid expanse in the western sky.

2. *Hydraul. Engin.* (See quot. 1874.)

1841 BREES *Gloss. Civ. Engin.* 34, D, the foreshore. **1873** F. ROBERTSON *Engineering Notes* 61 A slope..terminating in a long nearly level berm called a foreshore. **1874** KNIGHT *Dict. Mech.* I. 905/1 *Fore-shore* (Hydraulic Engineering) (*a*), a bank a little distance from a sea-wall to break the force of the surf; (*b*), the seaward projecting, slightly inclined portion of a breakwater.

foreshorten (fɔə'ʃɔːt(ə)n), *v.* [f. FORE- *pref.* + SHORTEN *v.*]

1. *trans.* Of the effect of visual perspective: To cause (an object) to be apparently shortened in the directions not lying in a plane perpendicular to the line of sight. Of a draughtsman: To delineate (an object) so as to represent this apparent shortening.

1606 PEACHAM *Art Drawing* 28 If I should paint..an horse with his brest and head looking full in my face, I must of necessity foreshorten him behinde. **1650** BULWER *Anthropomet.* 261 Much Art being used to make the Foot shew as foreshortned. *a* **1680** BUTLER *Rem.* (1759) I. 263 'Tis a greater Mystery in the Art Of painting to foreshorten any Part, Than draw it out. **1784** SIR J. REYNOLDS *Disc.* xii. (1876) 51 The best of the painters could not even foreshorten the foot. **1838** DICKENS *Nich. Nick.* iii, His legs fore-shortened to the size of salt-spoons. **1853** HERSCHEL *Pop. Lect. Sc.* v. §9 (1873) 184 To fore-shorten its whole length into one joint.

transf. and *fig.* **1768** SPENCE *Parallel* 22 After he had taken to this way of fore-shortening his reading, if I may be allowed so odd an expression. **1850** TENNYSON *In Mem.* lxxvii, Lives, that lie Fore-shorten'd in the tract of time. *absol.* **1841** W. SPALDING *Italy & It. Isl.* II. 356 The master's mechanical skill, especially in foreshortening on the ceiling.

2. *nonce-use.* In literal sense: To shorten or curtail in advance.

1839 BAILEY *Festus* xiii. (1848) 122 Youth forestalling and foreshortening age.

Hence **fore'shortened** *ppl. a.*

1654 MARVEL *First Anniversary*, Foreshortned time its useless course would stay. **1831** BREWSTER *Nat. Magic* v. (1833) 122 The fore-shortened figure of a dead body lying horizontally. **1859** GULLICK & TIMBS *Paint.* 147 It was by such means that Correggio painted his wonderful fore-shortened figures. **1874** LADY HERBERT tr. *Hübner's Ramble* I. vii. (1878) 88 Placed close together these mountains all look to us foreshortened.

fore'shortening, *vbl. sb.* [f. prec. + -ING[1].] The action of the vb. FORESHORTEN.

1606 PEACHAM *Art Drawing* 27 Of fore-shortning. **1686** AGLIONBY *Painting Illustr.* Explan. Terms, Shortning is, when a Figure seems of greater quantity than really it is.. Some call it Fore-Shortning. **1784** BLAGDEN in *Phil. Trans.* LXXIV. 205 The fore-shortening..of the tail. **1859** GULLICK & TIMBS *Paint.* 39 Correct foreshortening is one of the greatest difficulties in art. **1860** PUSEY *Min. Proph.* 494 Prophecy, in its long perspective, uses a continual foreshortening.

foreshot ('fɔəʃɒt). [f. FORE- *pref.* + SHOT.]

1. A projecting part of a building.

1839 BLACK *Hist. Brechin* viii. 189 The Timber Market, formerly so obstructed with foreshots covered with thatch.

2. In distilling: The spirits which first come over.

1893 *Brit. Med. Jrnl.* 1 Apr. 708/1 The alcohol which had not passed over in the 'fore-shots' and the 'clean spirits'.

fore-shoulder: see FORE- *pref.* 3 b.

† **'foreshow**, *sb. Obs.* [f. FORE- *pref.* + SHOW *sb.*] A manifestation beforehand; a previous indication or token; a prefiguration.

1548 UDALL, etc. *Erasm. Par. Mark* iii. 35 Here was made a foreshewe of the churche, that should be gathered together. **1584** R. SCOT *Discov. Witcher.* XI. vi. 157 Pretending that everie bird and beast, &c., should be sent from the gods as foreshewes of somewhat. **1600** FAIRFAX *Tasso* XIII. liv. 245 With vermile drops at eau'n his tresses bleed, Foreshowes of future heat. **1603** FLORIO *Montaigne* I. xxv. (1632) 69 The foreshew of their inclination whilest they are young is so uncertaine.

foreshow (fɔə'ʃəʊ), *v.* [OE. *foresceáwian*, f. FORE- *pref.* + *sceáwian* to SHOW.]

†**1.** *trans.* To look out for; to provide; to contemplate in the future. Only OE. and early ME.

c **1000** ÆLFRIC *Judg.* vi. 8 He him foresceawode sumne heretoȝan. *a* **1175** *Cott. Hom.* 227 Se time com þe god forescewede. *c* **1200** *Vices & Virtues* (1888) 17 Ðare hierte ðe ne wile forsceawin h(w)ider he scal ðanne he henen farð.

2. To show or make known beforehand; chiefly, to foretell, prognosticate.

1561 T. NORTON *Calvin's Inst.* II. 82 God there fore-sheweth some peculiar thing concerning his electes. **1642-46** in Quincy *Hist. Harvard Univ.* (1840) I. 517 No scholar shall..unless foreshowed and allowed by the President..be absent from his studies..above an hour. **1651** C. CARTWRIGHT *Cert. Relig.* I. 110 He foreshews that many should come in his name. **1711** POPE *Temp. Fame* 462 Astrologers, that future fates foreshew. **1826** E. IRVING *Babylon* II. 316 He gave Enoch a commission to foreshow the deluge. **1879** BUTCHER & LANG *Odyss.* 196 If thou hurtest them, I foreshow ruin for thy ship.

b. Of things: To indicate beforehand, give promise or warning of; to foreshadow, prefigure.

1601 CHESTER *Love's Mart.* cix. (1878) 71 The Sunne did frowne, Fore-shewing to his men a blacke-fac't day. **1776** G. HORNE *Psalms* xlvii. 3 That great conquest, foreshewed by the victories of Joshua. *c* **1790** IMISON *Sch. Art* I. 132 The falling of the mercury foreshews thunder. **1834** GOOD *Study Med.* (ed. 4) II. 245 Aphthæ frequently..foreshow imminent death. **1860** PUSEY *Min. Proph.* 40 God had.. enjoined sacrifice, to foreshow and plead to Himself the one meritorious Sacrifice of Christ.

†**3.** To show forth, betoken, display. *Obs.*

1590 [TARLTON] *News Purgat.* (1844) 91 Glances that fore-shewed good will. **1607** H. ARTHINGTON *Princ. Points* I. v, To view God's Creatures..How do they all his loue fore-shew. **1608** SHAKS. *Per.* IV. i. 86 Your lookes fore-shew You haue a gentle heart.

Hence **fore'shown** *ppl. a.* Also **fore'shower**, one who or that which foreshows.

1555 WATREMAN *Fardle Facions* Pref. 13 Deuilles, fore-shewers of thinges. **1585** ABP. SANDYS *Serm.* (1841) 388 The signs..which should be the foreshewers of this terrible day. **1658** BROMHALL *Treat. Specters* IV. 258 [They] were fore-shewers of a happy voyage. **1755** JOHNSON, *Foreteller*, predicter, foreshower. **1844** MRS. BROWNING *Drama of Exile* Poems 1850 I. 68 The voices of foreshown Humanity. **1852** PEACOCK *Wks.* (1875) III. 380 To all mankind death is the foreshown doom.

foreshowing (fɔə'ʃəʊɪŋ), *vbl. sb.* [f. prec. vb. + -ING[1].] The action of the vb. FORESHOW.

a **1050** *Liber Scintil.* vi. (1889) 28 Atihtincge his mid eallum ȝeþances bigenge on godes foresceawunge [*contemplatione*] ȝefæstnað. *a* **1300** *Cursor M.* 5745 (Cott.) Þis was fore-sceuing scene O moder bath and maiden clene. **1561** T. NORTON *Calvin's Inst.* I. 56 b, The vnbeleuers..do faine that their felicitie or misery doth hang on the decrees and foreshewinges of the starres. **1609** BIBLE (Douay) *Proph. Bks.* Comm., Al the old Testament is a general prophecie, and forshewing of the New. **1846** TRENCH *Mirac.* xv. (1862) 261 Many..found in these healing influences of the pool of Bethesda a foreshowing of future benefits.

fore-shrouds: see FORE- *pref.* 3 d.

foreside ('fɔəsaɪd). Also 5-7 for-. [f. FORE- *pref.* + SIDE. Cf. Du. *voorzijde*, Ger. *vorseite.*]

1. The fore part; the front; also, the upper side (of anything). Now *rare* exc. *techn.*

c **1400** *Lanfranc's Cirurg.* 161 Þese .vij. ribbis..in þe for-side of a man..have no fastnynge to no boon. **1489** CAXTON *Faytes of A.* I. xxvii. 82 Sharp yrons were dressed to the foresyde of the same engyn. **1548** UDALL, etc. *Erasm. Par. Luke* vii. 85 b, The tables..letted hir to..cast hir self down prostrate on the foresyde, at the fete of Jesus. **1569** *Wills & Inv. N.C.* (Surtees 1835) 311 On lytlye pattlett sett wth pearll on the forsyd. **1642** *Relat. Action bef. Cyrencester* 8 The Colonell perceiving the garden wall..too high to be entred on the foreside. **1670-98** LASSELS *Voy. Italy* II. 103 The picture..turns upon a frame, and shews you both the fore-side of those combatants, and their backsides too. **1738** [G. SMITH] *Curious Relat.* I. iv. 470 They have another Skin ..which covers their Back, and a square one to cover their Foreside. **1762** STERNE *Tr. Shandy* V. xxix, Over-turning it upside-down, and fore-side back. **1884** F. J. BRITTEN *Watch & Clockm.* 9 Making the backs of the escape wheel teeth radial and the foresides curved.

fig. **1596** SPENSER *F.Q.* v. iii. 39 When these counterfeits were thus uncased Out of the foreside of their forgerie..All gan to jest and gibe full merilie. *a* **1655** VINES *Lord's Supp.* (1677) 343 There [at the bottom] lies abundance of self-love, and self-interest, even when there is a good countenance and fore-side. **1685** RENWICK *Serm.*, etc. xiii. (1776) 159 Hills and Vallies..are all written over, backside and fore-side with legible characters of the knowledge of God.

2. The front side or edge.

1703 MOXON *Mech. Exerc.* 164 *Raiser*, is a Board set on edge under the Fore-side of a step.

3. *attrib.*

a **1643** W. CARTWRIGHT *Lady-Errant* v. i, This foreside blow Cuts off thrice three, this back-blow thrice three more.

foresight ('fɔəsaɪt). [f. FORE- *pref.* + SIGHT. Cf. OHG. *forasiht*, Ger. *vorsicht.*]

1. The action or faculty of foreseeing what must happen; prevision.

14.. LYDG. *Secrees* 173 Haue ther with Consyderacyon Be a forsyght and cleer inspeccyon. **1553** T. WILSON *Rhet.* 17 b, Foresight is a gatheryng by conjectures what shall happen. **1656** BP. HALL *Occas. Medit.* (1851) 19 Want of foresight makes thee more merry. **1791** BURKE *Th. on Fr. Affairs* Wks. VII. 83 The effects rather of blind terrour than of enlightened foresight. **1815** JANE AUSTEN *Emma* III. iii, On fire with speculation and foresight. **1856** SMYTH *Roman Family Coins* 245 Nor had he foresight enough to see the true interests of his country.

2. a. The action of looking forward (*lit.* and *fig.*); also, a look forward (at some distant object).

1591 SPENSER *Muiopot.* 389 The foolish flie without fore-sight. **1656** BP. HALL *Occas. Medit.* (1851) 22 My very eye is weary with the foresight of so great a distance. **1667** MILTON *P.L.* XI. 368 Let Eve..Here sleep below, while thou to foresight wak'st. **1778** PENNANT *Tour Wales* (1883) I. 20 From the Summit of Garreg..the traveller may have an august foresight of the lofty tract of Snowdon. **1885** WHYTE MELVILLE *In Lena Delta* iv. 50 Aftersight informed us of much that our foresight had overlooked.

b. Perception gained by looking forward; prospect; a sight or view into the future.

1422 *E.E. Wills* (1882) 49 Hauyng gode in forsyght, I haue maad and ordened this my..last wylle. *c* **1422** HOCCLEVE *Learn to Die* 527 Forsighte at al ne haan tho wrecches noon Of the harm which ther-of moot folwe neede. **1594** CAREW *Huarte's Exam. Wits* xi. (1596) 169 The thoughts of mortal men are timorous, and their foresights vncertaine. **1649** BP. HALL *Cases Consc.* v. (1654) 30 Joseph, out of the fore-sight of a following dearth, bought up the seven yeares graine for Pharaoh. *a* **1674** CLARENDON *Surv. Leviath.* (1676) 176 Upon a fore-sight that the fire may come thither. **1736** BUTLER *Anal.* I. ii. 49 Our foresight of those consequences, is a warning given us. **1876** MOZLEY *Univ. Serm.* iii. 62 We are guarded against the naked effect of the perpetual foresight of death.

3. a. Care or provision for the future.

1375 BARBOUR *Bruce* xx. 314 With sa gude forsicht and sa viss, Or his furth-passyng ordanit he, That [etc.]. **1430** LYDG. *Chron. Troy* I. v, If by prudent forsyght, Thou haddest had grace for to record aryht. **1513** DOUGLAS *Æneis* VIII. ix. 74 Gyf it be sa ȝour godhed..Be prescience provyd hes, and forsichtis. **1603** KNOLLES *Hist. Turks* (1638) 111 Counsell grounded vpon no wise foresight or approued experience, was more dangerous to him. **1732** LEDIARD *Sethos* II. VIII. 257 He had had the foresight to order [it]. **1833** HT. MARTINEAU *Manch. Strike* viii. 85 Those least disposed to foresight could not help asking..what was to be done next time. *a* **1862** BUCKLE *Misc. Wks.* (1872) I. 155 In hot climates, nature being bountiful, man is not obliged to use foresight.

†**b.** (*God's, divine*) *foresight*: = PROVIDENCE. Also, an instance or effect of Divine Providence.

a **1300** *Cursor M.* 284 (Cott.) Þis lauerd þat is so mikil of miȝt puruaid al in his for-sight. **1375** BARBOUR *Bruce* I. 460 God..Preserwyt thaim in hys forsycht. **1559** *Mirr. Mag., Dk. Clarence* lvi, Wo wurth the wretch y[t] strives with gods forsighte. **1635-56** COWLEY *Davideis* II. 827 Shapd in the glass of the divine Foresight. **1664** MARVELL *Corr.* Wks. 1872-5 II. 167, I find now..that my want of language hath been but a foresight of the King my Master, and a fit complement upon His part.

4. *Surveying.* (See quot.). ? U.S. only.

1855 DAVIES & PECK *Math. Dict.* (1857), *Foresight*, any reading of the leveling-rod, after the first, taken at a given station. The first reading is called a *back-sight*.

5. The foremost of the two sights on a gun; the muzzle-sight.

1806 M. LEWIS in *Orig. Jrnls. Lewis & Clark Exped.* (1905) IV. 169 Labuish,..having by some accedent lost the fore sight of his gun shot a great number of times but killed only the number mentioned. **1847** [see SIGHT *sb.*[1] 14 b]. **1859** *Musketry Instruct.* 25 Raise the folding sight and the eye.. until the fore-sight is in a line with the bull's-eye. **1880** *Times* 18 Oct. 4/3 In using the rifle a native rarely avails himself of the foresight.

foresighted ('fɔəsaɪtɪd), *ppl. a.* [f. prec. + -ED[2].] Gifted with or having foresight;

characterized or controlled by foresight. Hence **ˈforesightedness.**

1660 tr. *Amyraldus' Treat. conc. Relig.* I. iv. 54 A fore-sighted and rational conduct of things to their end. **1700** ASTRY tr. *Saavedra-Faxardo* II. 37 The Thebans did not desire Princes so foresighted. **1775** ADAIR *Amer. Ind.* 286 The fore-sighted French knew their fickle and treacherous disposition. **1891** ATKINSON *Last of Giant Killers* 121 The most foresighted and farsighted of mortals. **1909** 'MARK TWAIN' *Speeches* (1910) 179 You complimented Mr. Rogers on his foresightedness. **1924** *Glasgow Herald* 10 Apr. 9 Knowing the foresightedness of the Prime Minister the consensus of opinion is that he has taken an opportune moment to test the feeling of the country. **1926** *Proc. U.S. Naval Inst.* Jan. 116 No limit should be placed on the foresightedness of a commander.

foresightful (ˈfɔəsaɪtfʊl), *a.* [f. as prec. + -FUL.] Full of or possessed of foresight.

1580 SIDNEY *Arcadia* (1622) 104 The foresightfull care he had of his silly successour. *Ibid.* 205 Giue vs foresightfull mindes. **1668** G. C. in H. More *Div. Dial.* 2nd Pref. (1713) 27 Foresightful Solicitude in the behalf of the Kingdom of God. **1855** SINGLETON *Virgil* II. 75 Thou also, O most holy prophetess Foresightful of futurity. **1889** F. HALL in *Nation* (N.Y.) XLVIII. 389/1 A.. well informed, and, for the most part, foresightful writer.

foresightless (ˈfɔəsaɪtlɪs), *a.* [f. as prec. + -LESS.] Without foresight. Implied in **ˈforesightlessness**, the condition of being without foresight.

1880 G. MACDONALD *Diary Old Soul* 28 Mar., Lost in oblivion and foresightlessness.

fore-sign: see FORE- *pref* 4.

foresignifiˈcation. *rare*⁻¹. [f. FORE- *pref.* + SIGNIFICATION.] A signification in advance of some future event; a premonition.

1592 tr. *Junius on Rev.* viii. 1 The seventh seale is the next foresignification.

foresignify (fɔəˈsɪgnɪfaɪ), *v.* [f. FORE- *pref.* + SIGNIFY *v.*] *trans.* To signify beforehand.

a. To betoken beforehand, prefigure, typify.

1565 JEWEL *Repl. Harding* (1611) 348 In the Sacrament it selfe there is a thing foresignified. **1613–18** DANIEL *Coll. Hist. Eng.* (1626) 57 An exceeding great Ecclipse of the Sun .. was taken to fore-signifie his death. **1697** DRYDEN *Virgil* Life (1721) I. 63 He hardly ever describes the rising of the Sun, but with some Circumstance, which fore-signifies the Fortune of the Day. **1860** PUSEY *Min. Proph.* 559 That symbolic Blood, by which, foresignifying the new Covenant, He made them His own people.

†**b.** To intimate beforehand, foretell. With simple *obj.* or with object sentence. *Obs.*

1597 HOOKER *Eccl. Pol.* v. lxii. §8 Christ had foresignified, that.. his absence would soone make them apt to fast. **1614** RALEIGH *Hist. World* v. vi. §3 His death.. was foresignified vnto Perseus, by Calligenes. **1678** CUDWORTH *Intell. Syst.* 701 [Spectres] sometimes do fore-signifie unto men future events. **1695** BP. PATRICK *Comm. Gen.* 271 God hereby fore-signified their Sins should be expiated by Sacrifices.

Hence **foreˈsignifying** *vbl. sb.* and *ppl. a.*

1592 tr. *Junius on Rev.* vi. 1 The foresignifying.. of all the evils which God powreth out upon this world. **1860** PUSEY *Min. Proph.* 285 Jonah.. wore a foresignifying character.

fore-sin, -sing: see FORE- *pref.* 2 a and 4.

foreskin (ˈfɔəskɪn). [f. FORE- *pref.* + SKIN *sb.*] The prepuce.

1535 COVERDALE *Exod.* iv. 25 Then toke Zipora a stone, and circumcyded the foreskynne of hir sonne. **1643** MILTON *Divorce* II. vi. (1851) 77 Not sparing the tender fore-skin of any male infant. **1712** SWIFT *Wonderful Proph.* Wks. 1755 III. I. 174 The Free-thinkers.. shall be converted to Judaism: and the Sultan shall receive the foreskins of Toland and Collins. **1804** ABERNETHY *Surg. Obs.* 167 Sometimes.. the disease shifts its ground and attacks the foreskin. **1868** *Chambers' Encycl.* III. 50 The cutting off the foreskin.. [is] a rite widely diffused among ancient and modern nations.

fig. **1535** COVERDALE *Jer.* iv. 4 Be circumcided in the Lorde, and cut awaye the foreskynne of youre hertes.

fore-skirt: see FORE- *pref.* 3.

foreslack: see FORSLACK.

foresleeve (ˈfɔəsliːv). [f. FORE- *pref.* + SLEEVE.] **a.** The fore part of a sleeve. †**b.** (See quot. 1538.) (*obs.*). †**c.** A loose ornamental sleeve formerly worn over the ordinary sleeve (*obs.*). **d.** That part of a dress-sleeve which covers the fore-arm.

1377 LANGL. *P. Pl.* B. v. 81 Of a freres frokke were the forsleues. *c* **1523** *Inv. Goods Dame Hungerford* in *Archæologia* (1860) XXXVIII. 372 Item, a doblet of blake satten, the forsleves and the plagarde of tyncell. **1538** ELYOT *Dict.*, *Cubitale*, a forsleue of a garmente, whiche keuereth the arme from the elbowe downwarde. **1548** HALL *Chron.*, *Hen. VIII* (an. 12) 83 Ruffed sleves with foresleves pendant. **1649** *Bury Wills* (1850) 221, I give to my sister Fuller my.. pair of foresleeues. **1892** *Daily News* 29 July 3/3 A collar, sash, and foresleeves to match carried out the scheme of colour.

foreslow: see FORSLOW.

fore-smell, -smock, etc.: see FORE- *pref.*

foresold (fɔəˈsəʊld), *pple. Comm.* [f. FORE- *pref.* + *sold* pa. pple. of SELL *v.*] Of a manufacturer, etc.: That has sold goods not yet produced.

1883 *Scotsman* 9 May 8 Makers are heavily foresold, and prices are very firm.

forespar: see FORE- *pref.* 5.

forespeak (fɔəˈspiːk), *v.* Also for-. [f. FORE- *pref.* + SPEAK *v.*]

1. *trans.* To speak beforehand; to speak of beforehand, *esp.* to fortell, predict. Now *rare.* †Occasionally of a thing: To betoken.

1375 BARBOUR *Bruce* I. 630 Let hym with the lettir passe, Till entyr It, as for-spokin was. **1548** GEST *Pr. Masse* 110 Hys antecedent.. was not to sacryfyce his body wherof he forspoke never word. **1654** H. L'ESTRANGE *Chas. I* (1655) 91 Every man would now be wise and fore-speak fair weather .. how truly a few moneths will discover. **1667** *Disc. Religion of England* 27 Though a peoples discomposure doth not forespeak Warrs and Tumults, yet it may denounce Woe and Misery. **1850** BLACKIE *Æschylus* I. 165, I must flee.. and hie me where the god Forespoke me refuge. **1877** J. B. TAYLOR in *Internat. Rev.* IV. 417 He [Tennyson] has not.. forespoken the deeper problems which shall engage the generation to come.

†**b.** To speak to (a person) beforehand. *Obs.*

1635 J. HAYWARD tr. *Biondi's Ban. Virgin* 143 My Physitian had, in fore-speaking the women.. made every of them beleeve, that [etc.]. **1692** WAGSTAFFE *Vind. Carol.* Pref., Our Author has forespoken his Reader with a long Preface.

†**2.** *intr.* To speak beforehand; *chiefly*, to utter predictions, prophesy.

a **1300** *Cursor M.* 2947 (Cott.) Als sco for spak, right sua þai wrought. **1557** *N.T.* (Genev.) *Epist.* *iv, First Isaie forespake vnto, how that he sholde be borne of a Virgine. **1586** J. HOOKER *Girald. Irel.* in *Holinshed* II. 43/1 The Irish prophet.. forespeaking of this battell said [etc.]. **1646** P. BULKELEY *Gospel Covt.* I. 110 These are the days fore-spoken of. **1656** CROMWELL *Sp.* 17 Sept. in *Burton's Diary* (1828) Introd. I. 155 The head of the anti-Christian interest, that is.. so fore-spoken of.

†**3.** *trans.* To speak forth or out; to proclaim.

1546 J. HEYWOOD *Prov.* (1867) 31 Forspeake not your fortune, nor hide not your neede. *a* **1547** SURREY *Ps.* lxxiii. 66 My unworthy lips.. Shall thus forespeak thy secret works, in sight of Adams race.

4. To speak for or bespeak in advance.

1659 H. L'ESTRANGE *Alliance Div. Off.* 36 That they might the better forespeak impunity for so strange boldness. **1882** OGILV., *Forespeak*.. to buy a thing before it is fit or in the market; to bespeak; as, that calf is forespoken. (*Scotch*).

Hence **foreˈspeaking** *ppl. a.*

1650 W. SCLATER *Malachy* Ep. Ded. II. Forespeaking and .. conjecturing natures.

forespeak: see FORSPEAK, to bewitch, etc.

†**foreˈspeaker.** *Obs.* [f. FORESPEAK *v.* + -ER¹.]

1. One who speaks for another; an advocate. (The later examples are Sc.)

c **1175** *Lamb. Hom.* 83 Þes Mon bi-com uorspeker. **13..** in *Rel. Ant.* II. 229 Come, shuppere, Holy Gost.. Thou that art cleped vorspekere. **1427** *Sc. Acts Jas. I* (1814) II. 16 Consalers & forspekars nedful til his caus. **1533** BELLENDEN *Livy* II. (1822) 183 The hous of Fabis.. made Ceso Fabius, consul, to be forespekare for thaim. **1609** SKENE *Reg. Maj.* 12 The defender, nor his forespeaker sould nocht be challenged be anie petition of the persewer. **1768** ROSS *Helenore* (1789) 104 She.. nae forspeakers has her cause to ca'.

2. One who speaks first; the leader of a meeting.

1552 HULOET, Forespeaker, or whych speaketh firste, *antiloquus*. **1745** WESLEY *Wks.* (1830) I. 491 A congregation so.. noisy, encouraged thereto by their forespeaker, a drunken alehouse keeper.

3. *Sc.* The foreman of a jury.

a **1600** *Aberd. Reg.* (Jam.).

forespeaking, *vbl. sb.* [f. as prec. + -ING¹.] The action of the vb. FORESPEAK; †a preliminary speech, preface; †a prediction.

1480 CAXTON *Descr. Brit.* 31 This place is but a forspekyng and not a full tretis ther of. **1548** UDALL, etc. *Erasm. Par. John* xii. 33 Sum.. which did conjecte (bicause of the forespeakyng of death) that he had spoken of the torment of the crosse. **1563–87** FOXE *A. & M.* (1596) 107/2 The fore-speaking of Austin was heere verified upon the Britains. **1614** RALEIGH *Hist. World* II. (1634) 237 The.. mysticall fore-speakings of Christ. **1645** R. NORWOOD in Prynne *Disc. Prodigious New Blazing-Stars* App. 26 Horrible fore-speakings, threatnings.. and censures have been publikely denounced against me. **1694** PEPYS in *Academy* 9 Aug. (1890) 110/3 Your Fount for Musick, which I am pleas'd with yoʳ fore-speaking soe well of.

forespecified: see FORE- *pref.* 2 b.

†**ˈforespeech.** *Obs.* [f. FORE- *pref.* + SPEECH; in OE. *foresprǣc, -spǣc.*]

1. An introductory speech, a preface.

c **1000** ÆLFRIC *Gloss.* Supp. in Wr.-Wülcker 172 *Praefatio*, forespæc. **1340** *Ayenb.* 105 Nou hest þou yherd þe uore-speche of þe holy pater noster. **1578** J. STOCKWOOD *Serm.* 24 Aug. 4, I will vse no fore-speech.. set out with some Rhetoricall florishe. **1599** THYNNE *Animadv.* (1875) 5 In your forespeche to the reader, yoᵘ saye [etc.]. **1688** R. HOLME *Armoury* III. 200/1 A Prologue, Preface or fore-speech.. opens the state of a Comedy or Fable.

2. ? A speaking for or on behalf of.

c **1300** *Cursor M.* 28762 Or elles in word or werk helpand, oþer in for-specе or in consail, þat mai þe nede oght auail. *c* **1585** PILKINGTON *Expos. Nehem.* ii. 9 Where God delivered his people by the forespeech of their enemies.

forespeed (fɔəˈspiːd), *v. rare*⁻¹. [See FORE- *pref.*] *trans.* To speed in front of, outrun.

1872 BLACKIE *Death Columba, Lays Highl. & Isl.* 22 Eager at the sound, Columba In the way forespeд the rest.

†**foreˈspell,** *v. Obs.* [f. FORE- *pref.* + SPELL.] *trans.* To spell beforehand. **a.** To predict. **b.** To decipher beforehand.

1611 *Panegyr. Verses* in *Coryat's Crudities* Some barde.. had forespeld That it should stand.. Till Whiting over it did ferrie. **1652** GAULE *Magastr.* 10 So written in legible characters, that a man may forespell and fore-read them.

foreˈspent, *ppl. a.* [f. FORE- *pref.* + SPENT, pple. of SPEND.] Spent previously.

1578 *Chr. Prayers* in *Priv. Prayers* (1851) 541 Such as that part of our life hath been, such will the residue be. **1590** SPENSER *F.Q.* I. ix. 43 Is not enough thy euill life forespent? **1611** SHAKS. *Cymb.* II. iii. 64 Towards himselfe, his goodnesse fore-spent on vs, We must extend our notice. **1624** HEYWOOD *Gunaik.* II. 88 My happier dayes Are all forespent. **1641** BROME *Joviall Crew* II. Wks. 1873 III. 380 A confession of my forespent life. **1884** G. B. SHAW *Let.* 15 Apr. (1965) 83 The additional ten hours depend for their table producing power on the forespent other ten hours.

forespoke: see FORE- *pref.*

†**ˈforespoken,** *ppl. a. Obs.* [f. FORE- *pref.* + SPOKEN; in OE. *foresp(r)ecen.*] That has been spoken of before, aforesaid, before-mentioned.

c **888** K. ÆLFRED *Boeth.* xxxviii. §3 Do þæs lean to þam forespecenan godum. **1625** F. MARKHAM *Bk. Hon.* II. iv. §5 Without these fore-spoken disabilities.

fore-spritsail: see FORE- *pref.*

forest (ˈfɒrɪst), *sb.* Also 4–5 foreste, (5 foreist, -eyst, *Sc.* forast), 6–7 forrest. [a. OF. *forest* (Fr. *forêt*), ad. med.L. *forest-em* (*silvam*) the 'outside' wood (i.e. that lying outside the walls of the park, not fenced in), f. *foris* out of doors.]

1. a. An extensive tract of land covered with trees and undergrowth, sometimes intermingled with pasture. Also, the trees collectively of a 'forest'.

a **1300** *Cursor M.* 3608 (Cott.) Bath in feild and in forest. *c* **1350** *Will. Palerne* 3 In þat forest.. þat woned a wel old cherl. *c* **1440** *Ipomydon* 370 With youre houndis more and lesse, In the forest to take my grese. *a* **1631** DONNE *Paradoxes* (1652) 75 Tylting, Turnying, and riding in Forrests. **1639** S. DU VERGER tr. *Camus' Admir. Events* 23 To have acknowledged their victories with Crowns, a Forrest of Laurell would scarce have sufficed. **1730–46** THOMSON *Autumn* 320 The stooping forest pours A rustling shower of yet untimely leaves. **1799** COLEBROOKE in *Life* (1873) 410 The prevalence of forest renders Bejeygerh a very unwholesome spot. **1835** W. IRVING *Tour Prairies* 149 He was whisked away over prairies, and forests. **1860** TYNDALL *Glac.* I. xxvii. 196 The black pine forests on the slopes of the mountains.

transf. and *fig.* **1602** SHAKS. *Ham.* III. ii. 286 A Forrest of Feathers. **1627** DRAYTON *Agincourt* clxxvii, Vpon these French our Fathers wan renowne, And with their swords we'll hewe yan Forrest down. **1645** FULLER *Good Th. in Bad T.* (1841) 43 London (that forest of people). **1669** DRYDEN *Tyrannic Love* I. i. Wks. 1883 III. 394 With a forest of their darts he strove. **1784** COWPER *Task* IV. 74 Forests of no meaning spread the page In which all comprehension wanders lost. **1867** A. BARRY *Sir C. Barry* iii. 70 A forest of spires sprang up. **1875** E. WHITE *Life in Christ* IV. xxvii. (1876) 475 A whole forest of verbal arguments.

b. In Great Britain, the name of several districts formerly covered with trees, but now brought more or less under cultivation, always with some proper name attached, as *Ashdown, Ettrick, Sherwood, Wychwood Forest.*

2. *Law.* A woodland district, usually belonging to the king, set apart for hunting wild beasts and game, etc. (cf. quots. 1598 and 1628); having special laws and officers of its own.

1297 R. GLOUC. (1724) 375 Þe nywe forest, þat ys in Souþhamtessyre. *c* **1425** WYNTOUN *Cron.* VII. iv. 28 In huntyng.. On a day in þe Neu Forast. **1494** FABYAN *Chron.* (1811) 356 Confirmacon of yᵉ statutes of yᵉ forest. **1598** MANWOOD *Lawes Forest* i. §1. 1 a, A Forrest is certen Territorie of wooddy grounds & fruitfull pastures, priuiledged for wild beasts and foules of Forrest, Chase and Warren, to rest and abide in, in the safe protection of the King, for his princely delight and pleasure. **1628** COKE *On Litt.* §378 A Forest and Chase are not but a Parke must bee inclosed. **1674** N. COX *Gentl. Recreat.* I. (1677) 22 A Chase .. may be in the hands of a Subject, which a Forest in its proper nature cannot be. **1767** BLACKSTONE *Comm.* II. 414 The forests.. having never been disposed of in the first distribution of lands, were therefore held to belong to the crown. **1883** F. POLLOCK *Land Laws* ii. 40 The presence of trees.. is not required to make a forest in this sense. The great mark of it is the absence of enclosures.

†**3.** A wild uncultivated waste, a wilderness.

c **1320** *Seuyn Sag.* (W.) 846 He wente into a forest wild Into desert fram alle men. *c* **1511** *1st Eng. Bk. Amer.* (Arb.) Introd. 33/1 In our lande is also a grete deserte or forest. **1578** LYTE *Dodoens* II. xxix. 182 Therefore we haue named them Camomill of the Forest, or wildernesse. **1659** D. PELL *Impr. Sea* Proem B iij b, Away she betakes her self into the great and wide Forrest of the Sea.

4. *attrib.* and *Comb.* **a.** simple attrib., as *forest-administration, -alley, -bough, -brother, -craft, -deep, fire* (also *fig.*), *-floor, -folk, -fruit, -glade, -hearse, -house, -land, -lawn, -leaf, -life, -lodge, -lord, -matter, -nymph, -path, pathology,* *reserve, -ridge, -rights, -road, -shade, -sheriff, -side, -skirt, -sport, -steading, stream, -top, -walk, -wood.* Also *forest-like* adj.

1838 *Penny Cycl.* X. 359/2 The laws and regulations of *forest administration. **1844** CLOUGH *Wirkung in der Ferne* Remains (1869) II. 35 In perspective, brief, uncertain, Are the *forest-alleys closed. **1727–46** THOMSON *Summer* 299 The *Forest-Boughs..dance..to the playful Breeze. *a* **1835** MRS. HEMANS *Last Constantine* xc. Poems (1849) 232 Mountain storms, whose fury hath o'erthrown It's *forest-bretheren. **1894** *Academy* 8 Sept. 175/3 The influence of German *forest-craft is seen in every page. **1842** TENNYSON *Sir Lancelot* 7 In *forest-deeps unseen. **1878** F. B. HOUGH *Rep. Forestry* I. 158 The frequent occurrence of *forest-fires along railroad-lines. **1958** *Spectator* 8 Aug. 183/2 He was forced to intervene in the island to protect Turkish nationals, to prevent indirect aggression, and to put out a neighbouring forest fire. **1849** THOREAU *Week Concord Riv.* 233 Ere the black bear haunted Thy red *forest-floor. **1864** LOWELL *Fireside Trav.* 10 Green..decay on forest-floors. **1847** MARY HOWITT *Ballads* 125 The *forest-folk they sing their songs. **1697** DRYDEN *Virg. Georg.* I. 222 Trees their *Forrest-fruit deny'd. **1727–46** THOMSON *Summer* 58 Along the *Forest-Glade The wild Deer trip. **1820** KEATS *Isabella* xliii, She..went into that dismal *forest-hearse. **1646** BUCK *Rich. III*, 118 In a Lodge, or *Forest-house. **1649** MILTON *Eikon.* Wks. (1847) 296/2 Their possessions..taken from them, one while as *forest land, another while as crown land. **1805** KING in *Hist. Rec. Austral.* 1st Ser. V. 586 Forest land: [land which] abounds with Grass and is the only Ground which is fit to Graze; according to the local distinction, the Grass is the discriminating Character and not the Trees, for by making use of the Former it is clearly understood as different from a Brush or Scrub. **1936** *Discovery* Apr. 107 A typical Finnish scene of water and forest-land. **1968** G. JONES *Hist. Vikings* IV. ii. 383 He headed into the forestlands of Dalarna. **1809** WORDSW. *Sonn.*, '*Advance—come forth*', The hunter train..Have roused her [Echo] from her ..*forest-lawn. **1727–46** THOMSON *Summer* 1120 And stirs the *Forest-Leaf without a Breath. **1880** C. R. MARKHAM *Peruv. Bark* 165 This, the first day of our *forest-life. **1611** COTGR., *Forestier*, woodie, *forrest-like. **1824** MISS MITFORD *Village* Ser. I. (1863) 46 The more beautiful for being shut in with a forest-like closeness. **1847** MARY HOWITT *Ballads* 147 My mother she loves that *forest-lodge. *a* **1847** ELIZA COOK *There Would I be* iv, Where the dark *forest-lords tangle their boughs. **1659** RUSHW. *Hist. Coll.* III. (1692) I. 129 Illegal Actions in *Forest-matters. **1612** DRAYTON *Poly-olb.* ii. 25 A *Forest-Nymph, and one of chaste Diana's charge. **1821** MRS. HEMANS *Vespers of Palermo* II. ii, Oh! the *forest-paths are dim and wild. **1944** *Forestry Terminol.* (Soc. Amer. Foresters) 3/2 *Forest pathology borders on a number of related fields, such as forestry, plant pathology, mycology. **1882** *North Amer. Rev.* Oct. 400 Preserving certain portions..as Government *forest reserves. **1945** *Craig* (Colo.) *Empire-Courier* 25 July 2/4 There's forest reserve country up there that's just waiting for you. **1822** MANTELL *Fossils S. Downs* 17 The *Forest-ridge constitutes the north-eastern extremity of the county. **1863** J. R. WISE *New Forest* iv. 46 Cattle may..be turned out, by those who have *Forest rights. **1847** MARY HOWITT *Ballads* 140 That every soul from Elverslie The *forest-roads might take. **1704** POPE *Summer* 62 Chaste Diana haunts the *forest-shade. **1808** SCOTT *Marm.* II. Introd. 85 The *Forest-Sheriff's lonely chace. *c* **1386** CHAUCER *Wife's T.* 990 In his wey it happed him to ryde.. under a *forest syde. **14..** *Sir Beues* 3360 (MS. M.) Tyl they cam to a forest syde. **1845** G. MURRAY *Islaford* 44 Breezy jauntings..On *forest-skirt. **1852** JAMES *Agnes Sorel* (1860) I. 131 Well accustomed to *forest-sports. **1879** *Encycl. Brit.* X. 18 The '*forest-steading of Galashiels' is first mentioned in history shortly after the beginning of the 15th century. **1847** MARY HOWITT *Ballads* 127 The *forest-streams..with a talking sound went by. **1819** BYRON *Juan* II. ciii, Its growing green..waved in *forest tops. **1588** SHAKS. *Tit. A.* II. i. 114 The *Forrest walkes are wide and spacious. **1593** —— *Rich. II*, III. i. 23 You haue..fell'd my *Forrest Woods.

b. *esp.* with names of living beings, with sense 'haunting or inhabiting a forest': as, *forest-bear, -bee, -boar, -boy, -dove, -pony.*

1593 SHAKS. *3 Hen. VI*, II. ii. 13 Whose hand is that the *Forrest Beare doth licke? **1738** WESLEY *Psalms* civ. III, Darkness He makes the Earth to shroud, When *Forest-Beasts securely stray. **1885** J. S. STALLYBRASS tr. *Hehn's Wand. Plants & Anim.* 463 This keeping of *forest-bees was the business of the bee-master. **1870** BRYANT *Iliad* II. XVII. 195 Like hounds That spring upon a wounded *forest-boar. **1847** MARY HOWITT *Ballads* 123 He did not run about with the *forest-boys at play. *a* **1835** MRS. HEMANS *Sicilian Captive* Poet. Wks. (1849) 413 Bowers wherein the *forest-dove her nest untroubled weaves. **1823** in Cobbett *Rur. Rides* (1885) I. 393 As ragged as *forest-ponies in the month of March.

c. objective, as *forest-feller, -felling.*

1618 CHAPMAN *Hesiod. Bk. Days* 68 Let thy *forest-feller cut thee all Thy chamber fuel. **1841** CARLYLE *Heroes* 53 Among the Northland Sovereigns..I find some..*Forest-felling Kings.

d. instrumental, locative, and originative; as *forest-belted, -born, -bosomed, -bound, -bred, -clad, -crowned, -dweller, -dwelling, -frowning, -rustling.*

1875 LONGF. *Pandora* VI, Have the mountains..the *forest-belted, Scattered their arms abroad. **1600** SHAKS. *A.Y.L.* v. iv. 30 This boy is *forestborn. **1837** *Southern Lit. Messenger* III. 238 The walls..once resounded with the accents of the forest-born Demosthenes. **1841** H. S. FOOTE *Texas & Texans* I. 120 It was in fact perfectly natural..that 'forest-born' orators [should have come forward] to rouse.. the spirit of resistance. **1817** SHELLEY *Athanase* II. ii. 50 Like wind upon some *forest-bosomed lake. **1835** J. P. KENNEDY *Horse Shoe R.* xiii, The sequestered and *forest-bound region in which Adair resided. **1882** J. HAWTHORNE *Fort. Fool* I. xiii, A specimen of art such as the *forest-bred lad had never happened to see before. **1880** A. R. WALLACE *Isl. Life* 208 Its [the Mississippi's] sources are..in *forest-clad plateaux. **1727–46** THOMSON *Summer* 459 On the Sunless side Of a romantic Mountain *Forest-crown'd. **1866** PEACOCK *Eng. Ch. Furniture* 14 The shepherd, the hunter, the *forest-dweller, and the sea-rover. **1891** ATKINSON *Last of Giant Killers* 202 Wild or *forest-dwelling creatures. **1794** COLERIDGE *Monody Death Chatterton* 72 Some hill, whose *forest-frowning side Waves o'er the murmurs of his calmer tide. **1726–46** THOMSON *Winter* 151 From the shore ..And *forest-rustling mountain, comes a voice.

5. Special combinations: **forest-bed**, *Geol.*, a stratum originating from a primæval forest; †**forest-bill**, a woodman's bill-hook; **forest-brown** *a.*, the trade designation of a colour used for ladies' dresses; †**forest-cloth**, ? some woollen fabric; **forest-court** (see quot.); †**forest-fever**, jungle-fever; **forest-fly**, a fly of the genus *Hippobosca*, esp. *H. equina*; **forest-green** *a.* and *sb.*, applied by Scot to the 'Lincoln green', said in the ballads to be the special costume of Robin Hood and his men; hence (?), used as the commercial name of a shade of green in dress-material; **forest-kangaroo**: see FORESTER 3 b; **forest-laws**, laws relating to royal forests, enacted by William I and other Norman kings; **forest mahogany**, a name used for several species of the genus *Eucalyptus*, especially *E. resinifera*; **forest marble** (see quot.); **forest-oak** (see quot.); **forest-peat**, wood-peat (*Cent. Dict.*); **forest red gum**, *Eucalyptus tereticornis*; **forest-school**, a school for giving instruction and training in the management of forests; **forest shrew**, a name used for several African shrews of the genus *Myosorex*; **forest-stone** (see quot.); **forest-tree**, any tree of large growth, fitted to be a constituent part of a forest; **forest-wards** *adv.*, towards the forest; †**forest-white**, a kind of cloth; †**forest-work**, a decorative representation of sylvan scenery.

1840 *Forest bed [see CROMER]. **1861** *Geologist* IV. 70 The dark sandy clay, known as the Forest bed, from the abundance..of stems and trunks of trees found in and on it. **1865** PAGE *Geol. Terms* (ed. 2), *Forest-bed*, the name given by English geologists to a stratum which underlies the Glacial Drift at Cromer in Norfolk. **1488** *Mem. Rip.* (Surtees) I. 311 Cum quodam le *Forest byll..in capite percussit. **1828–40** BERRY *Encycl. Herald.* I. *Forest-bill* or *Wood-bill* an instrument for lopping trees, &c. **1892** *Daily News* 29 Sept. 6/2 A tea-gown of *forest brown velvet. **1769** *Dublin Mercury* 16–19 Sept. 2/2 All kinds of broad cloths, *forest cloths, beaver druggets. **1768** BLACKSTONE *Comm.* III. vi. 71 The *forest courts, instituted for the government of the king's forests..and for the punishment of all injuries done to the king's deer [etc.]. **1799** COLEBROOKE in *Life* (1873) 427 This disorder did not assume the worst shape of what is denominated the *forest fever. **1658** ROWLAND tr. *Moufet's Theat. Ins.* 934 The greater..is the *Forrest-fly. **1773** G. WHITE *Selborne* liii. (1875) 143 A species of them [*Hippoboscæ*] is familiar to horsemen in the south of England under the name of forest-fly. **1836–39** TODD *Cycl. Anat.* II. 867/2 The forest-fly is..troublesome to horses in the summer. **1810** SCOTT *Lady of L.* IV. xii, As gay [is] the *forest-green. **1820** —— *Ivanhoe* iii, His dress was a tunic of forest green. **1892** *Daily News* 16 Sept. 3/3 A dark forest-green gown is lined with tartan silk in brown and green. **1852** MRS. MEREDITH *My home in Tasmania* I. 244 The Great or *Forest Kangaroo (*Macropus giganteus*). **1598** MANWOOD *Lawes Forest* vi. 34 Those that were vnlearned in the *Forrest lawes. **1839** KEIGHTLEY *Hist. Eng.* I. 103 No part of the royal despotism was so galling..as these forest-laws. **1884** A. NILSON *Timber Trees N.S.W.* 10 The most valuable and best-known species of *Eucalyptus* are those called..'Red or *Forest Mahogany'. **1889** F. VON MUELLER *Eucalyptographia* I, s.v. *Eucalyptus resinifera*, It bears the colonial name of Red or Forest-Mahogany, which appellations are very inaptly given, inasmuch as the wood bears no real similarity to that of the true West Indian Mahogany. **1858** *Forest Marble [see BATHONIAN *a.* 2]. **1865** PAGE *Handbk. Geol. Terms, Forest Marble*, an argillaceous laminated shelly limestone..forming one of the upper portions of the Lower Oolite. It derives its name from Whichwood Forest in Oxfordshire. **1882** J. SMITH *Dict. Pop. Names Plants* 294 *Casuarina equisetifolia* and *C. torulosa*..In Australia they are known by the names of.. She Oak, *Forest Oak [etc.]. **1904** J. H. MAIDEN *Forest Flora N.S.W.* II. 1 '*Forest Red Gum'... This species is.. usually found in open forest country, hence I recommend the adoption of the prefix 'Forest' to Red Gum, the name by which it is very commonly known, with the view to save confusion. **1931** E. MAXWELL *Afforestation in Southern Lands* lxiv. 273 This other Red Gum, the Forest Red Gum, will grow under conditions that the River Red Gum will not. **1957** *Forest Trees Austral.* (Commonw. Forestry & Timber Bur.) 86 Forest red gum..extends beyond the shores of Australia to the drier parts of Papua. **1888** *Pall Mall G.* 4 Apr. 5/1 The difference between skilled and unskilled management would more than repay the cost of a *forest school. **1958** G. DURRELL *Encounters with Animals* I. 25 If anything lives to eat, this *forest shrew does. **1787** G. WHITE *Selborne* iv. (1789) 10 [A] sort of stone, called by the workmen sand, or *forest-stone..composed of a small roundish crystalline grit, cemented together by a brown, terrene, ferruginous matter. **1712** J. JAMES tr. *Le Blond's Gardening* 145 The Trees hitherto mention'd, are..called *Forest-Trees. **1814** SCOTT *Ld. of Isles* v. xxvii, The rest move slowly forth with me, In shelter of the forest-tree. **1833** HT. MARTINEAU *Briery Creek* vi. 139 She looked out, *forest-wards, for long before she tried to rest. **1551–2** *Act 5 & 6 Edw. VI*, c. 6. §1 All Clothes commonly called Pennystones or *Forest Whites. **1647** H. MORE *Song of Soul* I. I. xli, All *forrest-work is in this tapestry. **1745** *De Foe's Eng. Tradesman* xxii. (1841) I. 207 Finely painted in forest-work and figures.

forest ('fɒrɪst), *v.* [f. prec.] *trans.* **a.** *nonce-use.* To place in a forest. **b.** To plant with trees, convert into a forest.

1818 KEATS *Endymion* II. 305 O Haunter chaste Of river sides, and woods..Where..Art thou now forested? **1865** *Q. Rev.* July 18 A comparatively small surface of this vast range of wild country has been forested. **1885** *Pall Mall G.* 11 Mar. 4/2 Ground that has not been forested.

†**'fore-staff.** *Naut. Obs.* [f. FORE- *pref.* + STAFF.] = CROSS-STAFF 2 (see quot. 1867).

1669 STURMY *Mariner's Mag.* II. 82 Thus I have shewed you how to take an Observation by the Fore-Staff. **1719** HALLEY in *Phil. Trans.* XXX. 993 The Moon was not too high to be well observed with a Forestaff. **1769** FALCONER *Dict. Marine* (1789), *Arbalette*, a cross-staff or fore-staff. **1867** SMYTH *Sailor's Word-bk.*, *Fore-staff*, an instrument formerly used at sea for taking the altitudes of heavenly bodies..takes its name hence, that the observer in using it turns his face towards the object, in contradistinction to the back-staff.

'fore-stage. *Naut.* In 5 forstage. [f. FORE- *pref.* + STAGE.] †**1.** = FORECASTLE 1; hence a ship with a forecastle. Also, *ship of forestage, forestage ship. Obs.*

?**1345** [MS. (? of this date) is cited by J. Bree *Cursory Sketch* (1791) 110 for 'ships of forstage'.] **1462** *Paston Lett.* No. 443 II. 94 Thei sey, there shulde come in to Seyne CC. gret forstages out of Spayne. *c* **1465** *Eng. Chron.* (Camden 1856) 85 That the seyde Lord Ryvers shulde kepe certeyne grete forstage shyppys that were the erles of Warrewyk. **1481** CAXTON *Orat. G. Flamineus* F iij b, Gayus Flammineus Publius..had delyuerd to my gouernaunce ten shippis of forstage. **1867** SMYTH *Sailor's Word-bk.*, *Fore-stage*, the old name for forecastle.

2. *Theatre.* That part of the stage which lies nearest to the audience, freq. extending in front of the curtain.

1923 G. B. SHAW *Shaw on Theatre* (1958) 163 Mr. Granville-Barker..had reconstructed the London and American stages on which he worked by building a forestage out into the auditorium. **1934** T. S. ELIOT *Rock* i. 31 On the fore-stage, an agitator is addressing a tattered crowd. **1958** *Times* 22 Oct. 6/3 A stepped forestage that gives access to a semi-circular apron, placed, in the manner of a Greek orchestra, immediately before it.

forestage ('fɒrɪstɪdʒ). [f. FOREST + -AGE. In sense 1 ad. med.L. *forestāgium*, ad. OF. *forestage.*]

†**1.** *Law.* Given in various Dicts. as the rendering of Anglo-Lat. *forestagium*, explained to mean 'duty paid by foresters to the king', 'duty paid to the king's foresters', 'right to take reasonable estovers from the forest' (see Du Cange). *Obs.*$^{-0}$

2. *collect.* Tree-growth, forest.

1855 BAILEY *Mystic* 83 Siberian forestage of spiry pine.

†**'fore-stair.** *Sc. Obs.* exc. *Hist.* [f. FORE- *pref.* + STAIR.] (See quot. 1797.)

1500–20 DUNBAR *Poems* lxxxii. 17 ȝour foirstairis makis ȝour housis mirk, Lyk na cuntray bot heir at hame. **1775** in Cramond *Annals of Banff* (1891) I. 323 James Alexander has erected a forestair adjoining the South front of his new house. **1797** *G. M. Berkeley's Poems* Pref. 61 The houses at St. Andrews are disfigured by..a fore-stair, that is an open staircase on the outside in a zigzag manner across the front of the house.

forestal ('fɒrɪstəl), *a.* [f. FOREST *sb.* + -AL[1].] Of or pertaining to a forest.

1827 HALLAM *Const. Hist.* (1876) II. viii. 10 The king's forestal rights. **1859–62** LEWIN *Invas. Brit.* 51 Any strong military fastness, of a forestal character, such as the Britons are said to have occupied. **1878** *Fraser's Mag.* XVIII. 276 These Asiatic provinces teem with forestal riches.

forestall ('fɔəstɔːl), *sb.* Forms: 1 for(e)steal(l, 2–9 forstal(l, 7 foristell, 8 forestal, 6– forestall. In sense 2 also 7–9 fostal. [In sense 1, OE. *for-, foresteall*, f. FORE- *pref.* + *steall*, STALL, app. used in the sense of 'position taken up'; for sense cf. the vbs. FORELAY, FORSET. In sense 2 f. FORE- *pref.* + STALL.]

†**1.** In OE.; an ambush, plot; an intercepting, waylaying, rescue. Hence in *Law*, the offence of waylaying or 'intercepting in the highway'; also, the jurisdiction in respect of this offence, often enumerated amongst feudal rights. *Obs.*

Cf. *Laws Hen. I*, §4, Forestel est, si quis ex transverso incurrat, vel in via expectet et assaliat inimicum suum. Also *Concilium Culintonense, Laws of Edmund* (Schmid) 181, Et dictum est de investigetione et quæstione pecoris furati, ut ad villam investigetur, et non sit foristeallum aliquod illi vel aliqua prohibitio itineris vel quæstionis.

c **1000** ÆLFRIC *Hom.* II. 242 Ða Iudeiscan ealdras.. smeadon hu hi Hælend Crist acwellan mihton; ondredon him swa-ðeah þæs folces foresteall. *c* **1000** *Laws of Æthelred* v. §31 (Schmid), Gif hwa forsteal oððon openne wiðer-cwyde onȝean lah-riht Cristes oððe cyninges ahwar ȝewyrce. *c* **1155** *Charter Hen. II* in *Anglia* VII. 220 Grithbriches & hamsocne & forstalles, & infangenes thiafes. *c* **1250** *Gloss. Law Terms* in *Rel. Ant.* I. 33 *Forstal*, ki autri force desturbe. **1610** HOLLAND *Camden's Brit.* II. 75 Who granted unto them all Regall liberties except foure Pleas, namely of Burning, Rape, Forstall and Treasure Trove. *Ibid.* I. 350 Quite and quiet from all custome, beside for Robbery, peace-breach, and Foristell.

2. Something situated or placed in front.

†**a.** ? *gen. Obs.*$^{-1}$

1556 J. HEYWOOD *Spider & Fl.* lxv. 83 Without trenching or such defensife forstalles, Ordnance they ley, to batter that castell walles.

†**b.** The front part (of a cart). *Obs.*

1598 HAKLUYT *Voy.* I. 95 The house was vpon the carte.. A fellow stood in the doore of the house, vpon the forestall of the carte driuing forth the oxen.

c. The space in front of a farm-house, or the approach to it from the road. *dial.* only.

1661 *Aylesford Par. Reg.* in *N. & Q.* Ser. VIII. V. 244 Henry Gorham and John Allen.. going into yᵉ River at Jerman's fforstall to wash themselves.. were both drowned. **1674** RAY *S.C. Words*, A *Fostal* forte *Forestal*: A way leading from the high way to a great House. **1736** PEGGE *Kenticisms* (E.D.S.), *Forstal*.. a green place before an house; but otherwise I have known that part of a farmer's yard lying just before the door call'd the *forstal*. **1836** COOPER *Sussex Gloss.*, *Fostal* [corruption of *Forestall*], a paddock near a farm-house or a way leading thereto.

3. A (horse's) frontlet. Cf. *headstall.*

1519 HORMAN *Vulg.* 170 b, The forstall [*frontalia*] is full of gylte bollyons. **1880** L. WALLACE *Ben-Hur* 117 A bridle with a forestall of gold.

4. In the writings of Gerard Manley Hopkins (see quots.).

c **1883** G. M. HOPKINS *Sermons* (1959) II. iii. 150 The.. act (of consenting to grace) is really necessary... But if after this we are left to ourselves for a leisurely and deliberate avowal or disavowal of this 'forestall' (as I shall call it), [etc.]. *Ibid.* 155 Remark that prayer understood in this sense, this sigh or aspiration or stirring of the spirit towards God, is a *forestall* of the thing to be done, as on the other side grace prevenient is God's forestall of the same.

forestall (fɔə'stɔːl), *v.* Also 4-6 **forstal(l(e**, 6-9 **forestal**. [ME. f. OE. *foresteall*: see prec. sb. First recorded in the specific sense 2; cf. AF. *forstaller*, whence the agent-n. *forstallour* (13th c.).]

†**1.** To lie in wait for, intercept, cut off (a person or animal). *Obs.*

1413 *Pilgr. Sowle* (Caxton) I. xvii. (1859) 18 He hath.. greuously pursued in al that he couthe or myght ley for me in a wayte, and forstallyd in weyes. **1570** LEVINS *Manip.* 13/18 To Forestall, *intercipere*. **1674** N. COX *Gentl. Recreat.* I. (1677) 52 Which is seldom hunted at force or with Hounds, but onely drawn after with a Bloodhound, and forestall'd with Nets and Engines. **1741** CHAMBERS *Cycl.*, *Forestalling* is particularly used in Crompton, for stopping a deer broken out of the forest, and preventing its return home again.

†**b.** To intercept and appropriate (a living, a revenue). Also with *away*. *Obs.*

1581 MULCASTER *Positions* xxxvii. (1887) 163 To supplant the learned, and forstaull away their liuinges. **1618** BOLTON *Florus* III. xvii. (1636) 225 The Gentrie.. forestalled the publick revenewes [L. *interceptis vectigalibus*].

2. To intercept (goods, etc.) before they reach the public markets; to buy (them) up privately with a view to enhance the price: in former days an indictable offence. *Obs.* exc. *Hist.*

[**1353** *Act 27 Edw. III*, I. c. 5 Que nul Marchant Engleis nengrosse ne forstalle vins en Gascoigne.] **1467** in *Eng. Gilds* (1870) 374 That they forstalle no fysshe by the wey. **1567** DRANT *Horace's Ep. Numitius* D j b, Take ship betyme, leste sum forestal, and bye vp all this good. **1592** GREENE *Upst. Courtier* Wks. (Grosart) XI. 283 First I alledge against the Grasier that he forestalleth pasturs and medow grounds, for the feeding of his cattell.

absol. **14..** *Chalmerlain Ayr* i. (*Sc. Stat.* I.), All þe names of þe furth duelland forstallaris of þe forsaid burgh byand and selland forstalland. **1551** ROBINSON tr. *More's Utop.* (Arb.) 44 Suffer not these riche men to bie up al, to ingrosse and forstalle. [See also FORESTALLING *vbl. sb.*]

transf. and *fig.* **1727** SWIFT *Petition of Colliers* Wks. 1755 III. I. 129 To confine, forestall, and monopolize the beams of the sun. **1775** SHERIDAN *Rivals* II. i, I am not my own property; my dear Lydia has forestalled me.

b. To anticipate or prevent sales at (a fair, market) by buying up or selling goods beforehand or by dissuading persons from bringing in their goods. † ***to forestall the burgh***: to make a profit out of the inhabitants by such practices (*Sc. obs.*).

1362 LANGL. *P. Pl.* A. IV. 43 He.. Forstalleþ my Feire. Fihteþ in my chepynges. **1550** LEVER *Serm.* (Arb.) 84 As couitous carles do here in Englande forstall the markettes. **1609** SKENE *Reg. Maj.* 148 Quha forestalles the said burgh, be buying and selling. **1769** BLACKSTONE *Comm.* IV. 158 The offence of forestalling the market is also an offence against public trade. **1849** JAMES *Woodman* v, 'Tis thus he always forestalls the market.

fig. **1639** FULLER *Holy War* III. vii. (1647) 121 Philip, thinking to forestall the market of honour, and take up all for himself, hasted presently to Ptolemais.

†**3.** To beset, obstruct by armed force (a way or passage); to bar the entrance to (a house) by a force stationed before it. *Obs.*

1535 in W. H. Turner *Select. Rec. Oxford* 131 Gwent and others.. stode at yᵉ dore and forestalled yᵉ houses wᵗʰ swordes drawen, and thretned me. **1544** tr. *Littleton's Tenures* 54 b, The tenant.. encountreth him & forestalleth him the way with force & armes. **1581** LAMBARDE *Eiren.* II. iv. (1588) 155 If a disseisor of a house, or Land, shall forestall the way of the disseisee (with force and armes). **1611** SPEED *Hist. Gt. Brit.* VII. xxxvi. §22 The.. Inhabitants.. begirt them about with their hoast, and forestalled the passages of all supply of victuals.

4. Hence *gen.* To hinder, obstruct, or prevent by anticipation. Now *rare*; cf. 5.

1579 SPENSER *Sheph. Cal.* May 273, I you pray, With your ayd to forstall my neere decay. **1615** LATHAM *Falconry* (1633) 109 Garlicke and wormewood shall forstall and correct them. **1667** MILTON *P.L.* x. 1024 God Hath wiselier arm'd his vengeful ire then so To be forestall'd. **1675** BAXTER *Cath. Theol.* II. VIII. 146 You must not forestall the Truth by any of these false suppositions. **1768** BLACKSTONE *Comm.* III. 160 This has frequently occasioned offenders.. to begin a suit, in order to forestall and prevent other actions. **1818** JAS. MILL *Brit. India* II. v. iv. 443 That he should not forestall the wishes of his allies, by the precipitate conclusion of a peace. **1863** H. COX *Instit.* I. viii. 98 Endeavours to forestal a free election by papers, in the nature of warrants.

†**b.** To bar or deprive (a person) by previous action *from*, *of*, *out of* (a thing). *Obs.*

1577-87 HOLINSHED *Chron.* I. 26/1 Purposing.. to forestall the Romans from vittels. **1579** SPENSER *Sheph. Cal.* Sept. 231 With heede and watchfullnesse, Forstallen hem of their wilinesse. **1611** SHAKS. *Cymb.* III. v. 69 May This night fore-stall him of the comming day. **1643** PRYNNE *Sov. Power Parl.* I. (ed. 2) 3 Who would have murthered him in his.. Cradle to forestall him of the Crowne of England? **1660** BAKER *Chron.* (1674) 260 King James.. thought it stood not with his honour to be fore-stalled out of his own Realm.

†**5.** To pre-occupy, secure beforehand; also, to influence beforehand, prejudice. *Obs.*

1572 BUCHANAN *Detect. Mary* K ij, The mindis of the maist pairt of men weir.. forestallit wyth rewardis. **1600** HAKLUYT *Voy.* (1810) III. 240 Suffered the fit places.. to be forestalled and taken up by the Britons of Saint Malo. **1618** BOLTON *Florus* Ep. Ded. (1636) A ij, Seeing the glory of a great Historian forestall'd by Livie. **1635** SIBBES *Soules Confl.* xiii. §3. 193 The Jewes.. were fore-stalled with vaine imaginations against sound repentance. **1685** BOYLE *Enq. Notion Nat.* 3 Most men will be forestall'd with no mean prejudices against so venturous an Attempt.

b. To pre-occupy the place of.

1877 C. GEIKIE *Christ* liv. (1879) 653 An unworthy attempt to forestall them in their Master's favor.

6. To be beforehand with in action; to anticipate the action of, or simply, to anticipate; often with the additional sense of rendering ineffective, nugatory, or useless. (The chief current sense.)

c **1585** *Faire Em* I. 305 Then hie thee, Manvile, to forestall such foes. **1589** GREENE *Menaphon* (Arb.) 59 Well did you forestall my exception. **1682** BUNYAN *Holy War* 43 And this he did to forestal any tidings. *a* **1683** OLDHAM *Poet. Wks.* (1686) 18 Let your deeds forestal intent, Forestal ev'n wishes. **1712** ADDISON *Spect.* No. 363 In Milton the former part of the description does not forestall the latter. **1732** WATERLAND *Wks.* X. 464, I shall not forestall your own thoughts. **1751** LABELYE *Westm. Br.* 97, I will not forestall the Readers in the Pleasure of pronouncing the Result. **1828** SCOTT *F.M. Perth* viii, I will teach him to forestall my sport! **1860** PUSEY *Min. Proph.* 293 Micah forestalls our Lord's words, I am the good Shepherd, in his description of the Messiah. **1865** KINGSLEY *Herew.* ii, Whatever they were going to say the ladies forestalled. **1867** FREEMAN *Norm. Conq.* (1876) I. ii. 50 He forestalled our age in exploring the Northern Ocean.

7. To think of, deal with, or introduce before the appropriate or due time; 'to meet' (misfortune, etc.) 'halfway'.

1634 MILTON *Comus* 362 What need a man forestall his date of grief. **1725** POPE *Odyss.* XVIII. 183 His boding mind the future woe forestalls. **1786-1805** H. TOOKE *Purley* 52 In order to explain it, I must forestall something of what I had to say concerning conjunctions. **1828** SCOTT *F.M. Perth* xxxiii, Dorothy, whose talents for forestalling evil.. are known to the reader. **1862** GOULBURN *Pers. Relig.* III. vi. (1873) 213, I cannot help so far forestalling this part of the subject. *a* **1871** GROTE *Eth. Fragm.* iv. (1876) 109 There is no inclination to forestall his wants.

†**b.** To place in the fore-front, bring forward.

1657 *North's Plutarch, Add. Lives* 42 To prove his [Charlemain's] said Ambition, the said Writers do usually forestall two of his Actions.

forestalled (fɔə'stɔːld), *ppl. a.* [f. FORESTALL *v.* + -ED¹.] In senses of the vb.; bespoken, or taken beforehand; anticipated; prejudiced.

1543 *Act 25 Edw. III*, III. c. 3 The thinges forstalled shalbe forfeyt to the kynge. **1590** SPENSER *F.Q.* II. iv. 39 Abandon this forestalled place at erst. **1642** ROGERS *Naaman* 99 His prejudicate and forestalled heart. **1872** W. R. GREG *Enigmas* (1873) 104 By long indulgence and forestalled desires.

forestaller (fɔə'stɔːlə(r)). [f. FORESTALL *v.* + -ER¹.] One who forestalls.

1. One who buys up goods before they reach the public market. Also ***forestaller of the market***.

[**1292** BRITTON I. xxi. §11 Et ausi de forstallours.] **14..** *Chalmerlain Ayr* i. (*Sc. Stat.* I.), þe furth duelland forstallaris of þe forsaid burgh. **1472** *Presentm. Juries* in *Surtees Misc.* (1890) 25 Forstallers of samen comyng toward the marketť in Selby. **1527** RASTELL *Abridgem. Stat.* s.v., Forstallers of wynes. *a* **1626** BACON *Max. & Uses Com. Law* (1635) 11 They are.. to punish Forestallers, regrators, and engrossers. **1712** HEARNE *Collect.* (Oxf. Hist. Soc.) III. 471 Goods forfeited by the Forestallers of the Market. **1837** CARLYLE *Fr. Rev.* (1872) III. III. i. 101 A forestaller or two hung up at the doorlintels. **1881** W. R. SMITH *Old Test. in Jewish Ch.* xii. 347 The landowners became merchants and forestallers of grain.

†**2.** One who bars or obstructs the way. *Obs.*

1623 BINGHAM *Xenophon* 62 They should.. giue a signe with the trumpet, and descend and charge the forestallers of the knowne way.

†**3.** A taster. *Obs.* (? *nonce-use.*)

1611 COTGR., *Preguste*, a Taster, or Forestaller; one that takes th' essay of meats.

4. One who or that which acts in anticipation of another person or thing.

1870 *Daily News* 15 Nov., That sweeping forestaller of letters, the telegraph. **1895** *Westm. Gaz.* 9 Oct. 7/2 The.. withdrawal of Red Heart.. is the most severe blow which 'forestallers' have received.

forestalling (fɔə'stɔːlɪŋ), *vbl. sb.* [f. FORESTALL *v.* + -ING¹.] The action of the vb. FORESTALL.

†**1.** The action of obstructing a person in the highway or a deer on its way back to the forest.

1387 TREVISA *Higden* (Rolls) II. 95 Forstallynge, wrong oþer let i-doo in þe kynges hiȝe weie. **1544** tr. *Littleton's Tenures* 54 b, Yf by suche forstallynge and manassynge he that hath Rent charge.. is forstalled. **1570-6** LAMBARDE *Peramb. Kent* (1826) 178 Acquitted of all actions and customes of charge, except fellonie, breach of the peace, and forstalling. **1594** CROMPTON *Auth. & Jurisd. Crts.* 153 b, Mes si le cheine per chaunce obuie vn Dame et luy tue, ceo nest forestalling.

2. The buying up of goods beforehand, etc.

1548 CRANMER *Catech.* 77 By forstalling, regratyng, agreements in haules to raise the price of thinges. **1609** SKENE *Reg. Maj.* Burrow Lawes 141 That na man of quhat estate he be may repledge his man, for foristallinge fra the Court of the burgh. **1735** KIRBY *Suffolk Trav.* (1764) 53 The Practice of Forestalling is carried to such a height, as [etc.]. **1800** ADDISON *Amer. Law Rep.* 27 Usury is.. a forestalling of money. **1872** YEATS *Growth Comm.* 379 Edicts were directed against forestalling, that is, transacting any business before the opening of the fair.

3. The action of being before or beforehand with some one or something else; anticipation.

1642 R. CARPENTER *Experience* I. xvi. 112 With her forestalling of death, and singing her owne obsequies. **1782** PAINE *Let. Abbé Raynal* Introd. (1791) 4 The forestalling the Abbe's publication by London editions. **1833** I. TAYLOR *Fanat.* v. 95 A proud forestalling of misery. **1867** FREEMAN *Norm. Conq.* (1876) I. v. 315 This sounds very much like a forestalling of the Gunpowder Plot.

†**4.** The action of appropriating beforehand. *Obs.*

1655 FULLER *Ch. Hist.* III. ix. §26. 115 Such forestalling of Livings to Forrainers was forbidden.

forestalling (fɔə'stɔːlɪŋ), *ppl. a.* [f. as prec. + -ING².] That forestalls, in senses of vb.

1592 GREENE *Upst. Courtier* Wks. (Grosart) XI. 262 To bridle the extorting and forestalling coosenage. **1634** MILTON *Comus* 284 Perhaps forestalling night prevented them. **1799** *Spirit Publ. Jrnls.* I. 148 The monopolizing and fore-stalling butchers cannot take in the public. **1839** HOOD *Open Question* xii, No children, with forestalling smiles, Throng, happy, to the gates of Eden Minor.

forestalment (fɔə'stɔːlmənt). [f. FORESTALL *v.* + -MENT.]

The action of forestalling in various senses; an instance of this. **a.** *Law.* Hindering from entry on land, etc. **b.** Buying up goods beforehand. **c.** Anticipation in general; †prejudice.

a. 1628 COKE *On Litt.* 162 a, A forestallment with such a menace [of death or mutilation] is a disseisin.

b. 1861 RILEY *Liber Albus* 172 A fine exacted for the Forestalment of cloths.

c. 1611 COTGR., *Anticipation*.. forestallment. **1612-15** BP. HALL *Contempl. N.T.* IV. xxx, One dram of prejudice or forestalment turns the scales. **1664** POWER *Exp. Philos.* III. 187 Which.. rash censure and forestallment of their endevours, does not [etc.]. **1876** MOZLEY *Univ. Serm.* iv. 87 The canonisation of men.. professes to be a forestalment.. of the final judgment. **1882** T. HARDY *Two on Tower* II. v. 85 He had learnt the fatal forestallment of his stellar discovery.

†'**forestam.** *Obs.* Also 4 **forestayne**, 5 **forstanyg** (? read *forstavyng*), 5 **forestaven.** [f. FORE- *pref.* + ME. *stam*, *staven*, OE. *stæfn* prow (see STEM).]

1. The prow of a ship.

? *a* **1400** *Morte Arth.* 742 Frekes one þe forestayne, fakene þeire coblez. *c* **1470** HENRY *Wallace* IX. 55 Frekis in forstame [*v.r.* foirstam, forstarne] rewllit weill thar ger. *c* **1475** *Voc.* in Wr.-Wülcker 804 *Hec prora*, a forstanyg. ? *c* **1475** *Sqr. lowe Degre* 822 in Ritson *Met. Rom.* III. 179 With eighty ores at the fore staven. **1513** DOUGLAS *Æneis* v. iii. 78 Fra thair foirstammys the buller brayis and raris.

2. *Sc.* The front, forehead.

1790 SHIRREFS *Poems* Gloss. 15 *Forestum* [sic], the forehead. *a* **1809** in *Skinner's Misc. Poet.* 132 His enemy.. Raught him a rap on the forestam.

fore-starling: see FORE- *pref.* 5.

forestated, *ppl. a.* [f. FORE- *pref.* + *stated*, pa. pple. of STATE *v.*] Stated or mentioned previously.

1691 NORRIS *Ideal World* I. iv. (1701) 223 According to the forestated measures.

fore-stay ('fɔəsteɪ). [f. FORE- *pref.*]

1. *Naut.* A stay or strong rope reaching from the foremast-head towards the bowsprit end.

1373 *Indenture* in Riley *Lond. Mem.* (1868) 369 Forstiez.. backstiez. **1626** CAPT. SMITH *Accid. Yng. Seamen* 14 The fore stay, the maine stay. **1630** J. TAYLOR (Water-P.) *Navy Landships* Wks. I. 81/1 She had neither Forestay or Backstay. **1748** *Anson's Voy.* I. viii. 82 We learnt that they had broke their fore-stay.

b. A sail hoisted on the fore-stay; in full ***fore-stay-sail.***

1742 WOODROOFE in Hanway *Trav.* (1762) I. II. xxiii. 100 With great difficulty we wore the ship with the foresail and forestaysail. **1762** FALCONER *Shipwr.* II. 190 While the fore stay-sail balances before. **1875** BEDFORD *Sailor's Pocket-bk.* vi. (ed. 2) 214 The jib is the forestay.

2. (See quot. 1888).

1833 J. HOLLAND *Manuf. Metal* II. 208 Supported by the standard or forestay, are two grooved rods. **1888** JACOBI

Printer's Voc., *Forestay of press*, the leg which supports the frame or ribs of a hand-press.

forested (ˈfɒrɪstɪd), *ppl. a.* [f. FOREST *sb.* or *v.* + -ED.] **a.** Converted into forest. *rare.* **b.** Furnished or abounding with forest, covered with large trees, thickly wooded.

a. 1612 DRAYTON *Poly-olb.* ii. 27 Whereby shee..became first forrested. **1885** *Pall Mall G.* 11 Mar. 4/2 On forested ground the gillies usually put their feet in a grouse nest, when found.
b. 1796 A. AVERELL *Diary* in *Mem.* vii. (1848) 149 The finely forested park of Lord Kenmare. **1859** CORNWALLIS *New World* I. 104 The dark forested ridges. **1884** *Harper's Mag.* May 882/2 The..district is heavily forested.
transf. **1863** J. A. SYMONDS in *Biog.* (1895) I. 278 The whole descent, forested with spires, was seen naked beneath us.

fore-steep, -step: see FORE- *pref.* 2 a and 5.

forester (ˈfɒrɪstə(r)). Forms: 4–7 forster(e, (5 *Sc.* forestar, 6 forstar), 7–8 forrester, 3– forester. Also FOSTER. [ad. OF. and Fr. *forestier*, f. OF. *forest* FOREST.]

1. An officer having charge of a forest (see quot. 1598); also, one who looks after the growing timber on an estate. †*forester in* or *of fee*: one who holds his office in fee: see FEE *sb.*[2] 4 a. In poetical and romantic use sometimes a huntsman.

1297 R. GLOUC. (1724) 499 Ne that bailif, ne forester. *c* **1320** *Sir Tristr.* 496 Þe forster for his riȝtes þe left schulder ȝaf he. **1458** *Tomb in Newland Ch.* (co. Glouc.), Here lythe Jun Wyrall forester of fee. *c* **1460** FORTESCUE *Abs. & Lim. Mon.* (1714) 124 Sum Forester of the Kyngs. **1523** SKELTON *Garl. Laurel* 27 Faire fall that forster that so well can bate his hownde. **1598** MANWOOD *Lawes Forest* xxi. §4 (1615) 200–1 A Forester is an officier of a forest of the King (or of an other man) that is sworne to preserue the Vert and Venison of the same forest, and to attend vpon the wild beasts within his Bailiwick, and to attach offendors there..and the same to present at the courts of the same forest. **1607** COWEL *Interpr.* s.v. *Forester*, Some haue this graunt to them and their heires and thereby are called Foristers or Fosters in fee. **1646** G. DANIEL *Poems* Wks. 1878 I. 67 This wounded Heart..Who whilome was the fairest Beast impal'd, The fforsters cheife delight. **1735** SOMERVILLE *Chase* III. 224 The painful Forrester Climbs the high Hills. **1809** CAMPBELL *O'Connor's Child* viii, Come with thy belted forestere. **1843** JAMES *Forest Days* iv, He rode straight towards the foresters.

b. *Forester of the King of France*: an early title of the governor of Flanders.

1387 TREVISA *Higden* (Rolls) VI. 379 Flaundres..was i-ruled by þe kynges forsters. **1494** FABYAN *Chron.* VI. clxvi. 161 The ruler there of [Flanders] was callyd the forester of the kynge of Fraunce.

†**2.** One versed in forest-craft. *Obs.*

c **1645** HOWELL *Lett.* (1688) IV. 455 You are cryed up, my Lord, to be an excellent Horseman, Huntsman, Forester.

3. One who lives in a forest.

1513 DOUGLAS *Æneis* VII. ix. 15 Quhilk thyng..first steryt the wild forstaris fell To move debait, or mak thame for battell. **1664** EVELYN *Sylva* xxxii. Paraenesis §3. 112 Foresters and Borduerers, are not generally so civil, and reasonable, as might be wished. **1807** WORDSW. *White Doe Rylstone* v, Above the loftiest ridge..Where foresters and shepherds dwell. **1821** DWIGHT *Trav.* II. 459 A considerable part of those, who begin the cultivation of the wilderness, may be denominated foresters, or Pioneers.

b. A bird or beast of the forest; *spec.* one of the rough ponies bred in the New Forest. In Australian use, the great kangaroo (*Macropus giganteus*).

1630 DAVENANT *Just Italian* v. Dram. Wks. 1872 I. 274 Each feather'd forester roosts in my beard. **1713** J. WARDER *True Amazons* 58 The Queen doth so far surpass her Subjects in Shape and Beauty, as the finest Horse that ever ran on Banstead Downs, doth the most common Forrester. **1782** COWPER *Prog. Err.* 362 Without discipline the favourite child, Like a neglected forester, runs wild. **1795** SOUTHEY *Joan of Arc* VIII. 281 He loved to see the dappled foresters Browze fearless on their lair. **1826** DISRAELI *Viv. Grey* VI. ii. 294 Vivian took his horse, an old forester, across it with ease. **1832** BISCHOFF *Van Diemen's Land* ii. 27 There are three or four varieties of kangaroos; those most common are denominated the forester and brush kangaroo. **1890** BOLDREWOOD *Miner's Right* xix. 181 A brace of stray 'foresters' from the adjacent ranges.

c. A popular name of several moths of the family *Zygænidæ*.

1819 G. SAMOUELLE *Entomol. Compend.* 245 *Ino Statices* (forester). **1867** STAINTON *Brit. Butterflies & Moths* 33 The Foresters and Burnets frequent dry grassy slopes.

d. = *forest-tree*.

1664 EVELYN *Kal. Hort.* (1729) 224 You may transplant not only any Fruit Trees, but remove also any of the Foresters. **1664** —— *Sylva* (1776) 38 Foresters, which only require diligent weeding and frequent cleansing till they are able to shift for themselves. **1840** POE *Gold Bug* Wks. 1864 I. 63 The tulip-tree..the most magnificent of American foresters. **1893** *Illustr. Sport. & Dram. News* 22 July 751/3 A few fruit trees, and a few more arborescent foresters.

4. A member of the 'friendly society' known as the 'Ancient Order of Foresters'.

1851 MAYHEW *Lond. Lab.* II. 178 There are numerous benefit-clubs made up of working men of every description, such as Old Friends, Odd Fellows, Foresters [etc.]. **1875** BRABROOK in *Jrnl. Statist. Soc.* June 187 The Ancient Order of Foresters which has now..276 districts [etc.]

5. *Comb.* **forester oats** (see quot.); **forester sphinx** (see quot. 1867).

1794 HUTCHINSON *Hist. Cumberland* I. 166 *note*, The tenants..pay forester oats..these oats were a duty paid to the forester [of Inglewood]. **1867** STAINTON *Brit. Butterflies & Moths* 123 *Procris statices*, the Forester Sphinx.

Hence **ˈforestership**, the office of forester.

a **1634** COKE *On Litt.* IV. lxxiii. (1648) 310 The Forestership is become void. **1886** *Athenæum* 20 Nov. 672/3 It is now announced that he [Chaucer] held the forestership of North Petherton.

forestful (ˈfɒrɪstfʊl). [f. FOREST *sb.* + -FUL.] As much or as many as a forest will hold.

1832 *Fraser's Mag.* IV. 745 The roaring of a forest-full of shaggy monarchs. **1886** in *Advance* (Chicago) 30 Sept., The ladies wear whole forestfuls of birds on their bonnets.

forestial (fəˈrɛstɪəl), *a.* [f. as prec. + -IAL.] Of or pertaining to the forest.

1696 BROOKHOUSE *Temple Opened* 55 The Temporal Power is the Forrest, w^h^ encloses the Fruitful Field of the Church..Christ presides over the Forrestial Kingdoms. **1840** *Blackw. Mag.* XLVIII. 320 One of the royal forestial demesnes of merry England.

†**foˈrestic**, *a.* *Obs.*$^{-1}$ [f. as prec. + -IC.] = prec.

1650 R. GENTILIS tr. *Malvezzi's Consid.* 181 The people of Rome..feared he would lose the beauty of his forestick horridnesse, by meanes of manuring.

†**foˈrestical**, *a.* *Obs.*$^{-1}$ [f. prec. + -AL[1].] = prec.

1659 M. JAMES *Best Fee-simple* 21 A Country, in respect of the Sandy and Forestical part, affording such variety of pleasures.

fore-stick (ˈfɔəstɪk). *U.S.* [f. FORE- *pref.*] The front stick lying on the andirons in a wood fire.

1793 *Massachusetts Spy* 7 Mar. (Th.), He found his companion lying in a large body of live coals, her head on the backlog and knees on the forestick. **1821** [see CHUNK *sb.*[1] 1 b]. **1872** O. W. HOLMES *Poet Breakf.-t.* i. (1885) 26 The fore-stick and back-log of ancient days. **1878** MRS. STOWE *Poganuc P.* ix. 71 Backlog and forestick were soon piled.

forestine (ˈfɒrɪstɪn, -aɪn), *a.* [f. FOREST *sb.* + -INE.] Of or pertaining to forests.

1881 G. ALLEN *Evolutionist at Large* 166 Much more formidable forestine rodents. **1883** —— in *Longm. Mag.* III. 288 We have only to suppose such a reptile to acquire forestine habits.

forestish (ˈfɒrɪstɪʃ), *a.* [f. FOREST *sb.* + -ISH.] Somewhat resembling a forest.

1815 SIMOND *Jrnl. Tour Gt. Brit.* II. 223 The country..begins to look forestish.

forestless (ˈfɒrɪstlɪs), *a.* [f. FOREST *sb.* + -LESS.] Devoid of forests, unwooded.

1884 *American* IX. 183 A forestless area of grass. **1885** tr. *Hehn's Wand. Plants & Anim.* 228 A substitute for firewood in the forestless south.

fore-stone, -store: see FORE- *pref.* 5, 5 b.

†**foreˈstop**, *v.* *Obs.* [f. FORE- *pref.* + STOP *v.*] **a.** *trans.* To stop up in front. **b.** *intr.* or *absol.* To put in a stay or support for earth in advance of the work. Hence **fore-stopping** *vbl. sb.*; in quot. *concr.*

1566 DRANT *Wail. Hierem.* K v b, He [God] hath fore-stopde my pathes with stone. **1747** HOOSON *Miner's Dict.* I ij, To Forestop with Polings driven down with care. *Ibid.*, It may be put in without disturbing the fore-stoping.

†**ˈforestress**. *Obs.* [f. FORESTER + -ESS.] A female forester; a lady fond of hunting.

1513 DOUGLAS *Æneis* IX. xi. 23 Alcanor..Quham Hybera, the wild foresteres knaw. **1647** R. STAPYLTON *Juvenal* 272 Diana the fair forrestresse. **1650** —— *Strada's Low C. Warres* I. 21 The Governess was much delighted in..Hunting, whereupon they..called her the Forestress.

†**ˈfore-stroke**. *Obs.* [f. FORE- *pref.*] A forward stroke (in bell-ringing and in sword-play).

1674 N. FAIRFAX *Bulk & Selv.* 96 If the forestroke give us but a little tick, the backstroke will be sure to give him a knocker. **1684** R. H. *School Recreat.* 86 So must they successively strike one after another, both Forestroke and Backstroke, in a due Musical Time. **1688** BUNYAN *Jerus. Sinner Saved* (1886) 64 God's word hath two edges; it can cut back-stroke and fore-stroke. **1779** FORREST *Voy. N. Guinea* 237 He..draws his sword, with which, fore stroke and back stroke, he cleaves the air.
attrib. **1726** AMHERST *Terræ Fil.* xiv. 72 'Tis such fore-stroke and back-stroke play.

forestry (ˈfɒrɪstrɪ). [ad. OF. *foresterie*, f. *forest* FOREST; or f. FOREST *sb.* + -RY. In sense 4 f. FOREST(E)R + -Y.]

1. *Sc. Law.* The privileges of a royal forest. **b.** An estate to which this privilege is attached.

1693 VISCT. STAIR *Instit. Law Scot.* II. iii. §67. 235 The King having..granted a Forrestry to the Laird of Fascally. **1751** LD. BANKTON *Instit. Laws Scot.* I. II. iii. 573 The lands must be erected into a free forrestry. *a* **1763** ERSKINE *Inst. Law Scot.* II. vi. §14 Lands erected by the crown with the right of forestry had all the privileges of a King's forest. **1872** *Bell's Princ. Law Scot.* (ed. Guthrie) §753 The right of forestry is not conferred by erection into a barony.

2. Wooded country; a vast extent of trees.

1823 BYRON *Juan* x. lxxxii, Lost amidst the forestry Of masts. **1865** *Morning Star* 20 May, Let this amphitheatre be filled with a forestry of genealogical trees. **1879** BROWNING *Ivan Ivanovitch* 19 Through forestry right and left.

3. The science and art of forming and cultivating forests, management of growing timber.

1859 TENNENT *Ceylon* II. VII. v. 211 A knowledge of..forestry, pharmacy, and toxicology have each been demanded. **1881** HORNE *Fiji* 137 A person with a fair knowledge of forestry.
attrib. **1881** *Atlantic Monthly* XLVII. 166 Forestry, fishery, and farm products. **1885** *Manch. Exam.* 28 Jan. 5/5 Mr. Gladstone..has been engaged in forestry operations.

4. The principles and organization of the 'Ancient Order of Foresters'.

1861 *Morning Star* 21 Aug. 3 It is..about 30 years since forestry, in its present development, took its rise.

fore-study, etc.: see FORE- *pref.* 2 a.

†**ˈforesty**, *a.* *Obs.* [f. FOREST + -Y[1].] Forest-like, covered with forests or woods.

1622 DRAYTON *Poly-olb.* xxii. (1748) 341 When this whole country's face was foresty. *a* **1661** FULLER *Worthies* II. (1662) 17 This Forrestie-Ground.

foret, obs. form of FERRET *sb.*[1] and [2].

fore-tack (ˈfɔətæk). *Naut.* [f. FORE- *pref.* + TACK *sb.*] The rope by which the weather corner of the fore-sail is kept in place.

1669 STURMY *Mariner's Mag.* I. 16 Aboard Main-Tack, aboard Fore-tack, a Lee the Helmne. **1790** BEATSON *Nav. & Mil. Mem.* II. 62 His foretack and all his braces being cut at the same time. **1859** M. SCOTT *Tom Cringle's Log* xv. 368 He ..got the fore tack on board again.

fore-tackle, -tail: see FORE- *pref.* 3, 3 d.

†**foreˈtake**, *v.* *Obs.* [f. FORE- *pref.* + TAKE *v.*] *trans.* To take beforehand: **a.** to anticipate; **b.** to assume beforehand, presuppose.

1588 FRAUNCE *Lawiers Log.* II. xvi. 113 Mans wit..now and then preventeth and foretaketh the conclusion. **1674** N. FAIRFAX *Bulk & Selv.* 144 The places and bodies mov'd in them, are fore-taken to be altogether without parts.

Hence **foreˈtaken** *ppl. a.*, previously taken or adopted; **foreˈtaking** *vbl. sb.*, the action of the vb.; also, previous capture.

1563–87 FOXE *A. & M.* (1596) 1090/2, I..declared what was happened..of maister Garrets escape. He was glad, for he knewe of his foretaking. **1580** SIDNEY *Arcadia* (1622) 407 Yet remained there such footsteps of the foretaken opinion. **1590** SWINBURNE *Testaments* 15 There were foure seuerall kindes of legacies..by challenge, by condemnation, by suffering, by foretaking [*per præceptionem*]. **1618** LATHAM *2nd Bk. Falconry* (1633) 8 Present cold, and foretaken or former heat. *a* **1627** HAYWARD *Four Y. Eliz.* (Camden) 9 Desiring them..that they would lay aside all foretaken conceits.

ˈforetalk, *sb.* *rare.* [f. FORE- + TALK *sb.*] A preliminary talk or speech, introduction, preface.

1565 JEWEL *Repl. Harding* Pref. (1611) 7 Your foretalke, which is before the shewing of your Booke. **1879** FURNIVALL *Rep. E.E.T.S.* 9 Prof. Skeat has written an interesting foretalk to it.

So **foreˈtalking** *vbl. sb.*

1872 FURNIVALL *3rd Rep. Chaucer Soc.* 12, I propose to keep this name of Chaucer's own [Preamble] for these fore-talkings of his fellows.

fore-talon: see FORE- *pref.* 3 c.

foretaste (ˈfɔəteɪst), *sb.* [f. FORE- *pref.* + TASTE *sb.*] A taste beforehand; an anticipation, partial enjoyment in advance.

1435 MISYN *Fire of Love* II. vii. 86 It is trowde of euerlastynge swetnes a fortaste. *c* **1450** tr. *De Imitatione* III. vii, It is..a maner of fortaste of þe heuenly cuntre. **1604** BILSON *Survey* Table s.v. *Hell*, The foretast of iudgement in Hell. *a* **1716** SOUTH *Serm.* Wks. 1737 I. 37 It is the fore-taste of heaven, and the earnest of eternity. **1838** THIRLWALL *Greece* III. xix. 123 This foretaste of the evils of war did not damp the general ardour. **1880** DIXON *Windsor* III. xxv. 248 The monster..trembled with a foretaste of the stake.

foretaste (fɔəˈteɪst), *v.* Also 5 **fortaste**. [f. FORE- *pref.* + TASTE *v.*]

1. *trans.* To taste beforehand, have a foretaste of.

c **1450** tr. *De Imitatione* III. xviii, Felicite..suche as gode true cristen men abidin, & spiritual men fortastiþ. **1526** [see the *vbl. sb.*]. *a* **1711** KEN *Preparatives* Poet. Wks. 1721 IV. 92 Saints thus Celestial Joys fore-taste. **1834** GOOD *Study Med.* (ed. 4) I. 395 The Epicureans..fore-tasting the spirit of the Lavoisierian system..contended that it [heat] was a substance sui generis.

2. 'To taste before another' (J.).

1667 [see FORETASTED *ppl. a.*].

Hence **foreˈtasted** *ppl. a.*; **foreˈtasting** *vbl. sb.* and *ppl. a.* Also **foreˈtaster**.

1526 *Pilgr. Perf.* (W. de W. 1531) 280 b, The foretastynges of ye glory of heuen. **1632** SHERWOOD, A foretaster, *preguste*. **1667** MILTON *P.L.* IX. 929 Foretasted Fruit Profan'd first by the Serpent. *a* **1711** KEN *Hymns Evang.* Poet. Wks. 1721 I. 74 Give me..Of heav'nly Joys a sweet foretasting view.

foreˈteach, *v.* *rare.* [f. FORE- *pref.* + TEACH *v.*] *trans.* To teach beforehand.

1591 GREENE *Farewell to Folly* Wks. (Grosart) IX. 245 Eua..following nothing but what hir husbande foreshewed and foretaught hir. **1661** BOYLE *Style of Script.* (1675) 126 Those few duties which nature herself hath foretaught us. **1876** MORRIS *Æneids* x. 843 The father's soul foretaught of ill, afar their wail he knew. **1909** tr. *Sermons of St. Bernard on Advent & Christmas* 152 They are foretaught by the Holy Spirit.

Hence **foretaught** *ppl. a.*, previously taught.

1534 MORE *On the Passion* Wks. 1346/2 Theyr foretaught and fro tyme to tyme kept and continued faith. **1563** *Mirr. Mag., Blacksmith* xxxvi, Whose foretaught wyt of treason knoweth the payne. **1590** SPENSER *F.Q.* I. vii. 18 The sacred thinges, and holy heastes foretaught.

† **'foreteam.** *Obs.*—¹ [f. FORE- *pref.* + TEAM *sb.*, misused in the sense of L. *temo.*] The front part of the pole of a chariot.

a **1611** CHAPMAN *Iliad* XVI. 350 Their chariots in their foreteams [ἐν πρώτῳ ῥυμῷ] broke.

fore-teeth: see FORE-TOOTH.

foretell (fɔə'tɛl), *v.* Also 3 **fortell,** 7–9 **foretel.** [f. FORE- *pref.* + TELL *v.*]

1. *trans.* To tell of (an event, etc.) beforehand; to predict, prophesy.

a **1300** *Cursor M.* 9265 (Cott.) Crist was for-tald wit propheci. **1639** A. WHEELOCKE in *Lett. Lit. Men* (Camden) 158 Augustine fore-tould and threatned theire death. **1727** DE FOE *Syst. Magic* I. ii. (1840) 42 These Magi..foretold things to come, or, at least, made the people believe so. **1732** BERKELEY *Alciphr.* iv. §15 He foretells to them, that..in half an Hour they shall meet Men or Cattle. **1837** WHEWELL *Hist. Induct. Sc.* (1857) I. 225 To whom the astrologers had foretold glorious old age. **1869** LECKY *Europ. Mor.* II. i. 2 The object of the Pagan systems was to foretell the future.

b. Of things: To give notice of beforehand, indicate the approach of, foreshow.

1593 SHAKS. *3 Hen. VI,* II. i. 43 Thou, whose heauie Lookes fore-tell Some dreadfull story hanging on thy Tongue. **1672** SIR W. PETTY *Pol. Anat.* (1691) 50 There is the Instrument to measure and foretel Frost and Snow. **1753** J. WARTON *Virgil* (T.), These ills prophetic signs have oft foretold. **1862** ANSTED *Channel Isl.* I. vii. (ed. 2) 144 A signal station, to foretel storms.

†**2.** To tell (i.e. either inform or enjoin) beforehand. With sb. or clause as second obj. (See TELL). *Obs.*

a **1300** *Cursor M.* 14552 (Cott.) Þis was bi him he þaim fortald Thoru quam he wist he suld be sald. **1581** LAMBARDE *Eiren.* II. v. (1602) 168 If the maister..take his vsuall seruants with him, not foretelling them what hee intendeth to doe. **1590** GREENE *Mourn. Garm.* (1616) 58 Had I beleeued what I was foretold. **1610** SHAKS. *Temp.* IV. i. 149 These our actors, (As I foretold you) were all Spirits. **1631** WEEVER *Anc. Fun. Mon.* 209 Hauing beene prophetically foretold that hee should die in Ierusalem. **1641** BEST *Farm. Bks.* (Surtees) 36 Forkers are to be foretolde that they give upp goode forkefulls. *a* **1679** HOBBES *Rhet.* III. xiii. 120 A Man is free to fore-tell, or not, what points he will insist upon.

†**3.** *intr.* To utter prediction *of*, prophesy *of*.

a **1300** *Cursor M.* 9858 (Cott.) Þis barn þat ysai of fortald. **1557** N. T. (Genev.) *Acts* iii. 24 Al the Prophetes haue fore tolde of these dayes. **1667** MILTON *P.L.* XII. 242 To introduce One greater, of whose day he shall foretell.

Hence **fore'telling** *vbl. sb.*, prediction, prophecy. **fore'telling** *ppl. a.*, that foretells. Also **fore'teller,** one who or that which foretells.

1548 UDALL, etc. *Erasm. Par. Luke* xxii 176 a, Of whome the foretellynges of the prophetes doe make mencion. **1580** HOLLYBAND *Treas. Fr. Tong, Pronostiqueur,* a foreteller, a deuine which telleth thing to come. *a* **1640** W. FENNER *Sacr. Faithfull* (1648) 201 If a man lie sicke, and they see death in his face, they call it the foretelling signe. *a* **1716** SOUTH *Serm.* (1737) VI. x. 357 Buds and blossoms are the foretellers of fruit. **1826** MISS MITFORD *Village* Ser. II. (1863) 439 The genuine gipsy tact with which she adapted her foretellings to the age [etc.]..of her clients. **1879** FARRAR *St. Paul* (1883) 252 There was scarcely a Roman family that did not keep or consult its own foreteller of the future.

fore'tellable, *a.* [f. FORETELL *v.* + -ABLE.] Capable of being foretold.

1912 F. VON HÜGEL *Eternal Life* 212 The very range and slowness of such an immense, assumedly necessary, foretellable evolution. **1927** H. G. WELLS in *Sunday Express* 20 Feb. 12/3 A foretellable disaster.

fore-tenant: see FORE- *pref.* 4.

forethink (fɔə'θɪŋk). Also **for-.** [OE. *foreþenc(e)an*, f. FORE- *pref.* + *þenc(e)an* to THINK.]

†**1.** *trans.* To consider or think out beforehand, contrive, plan. *Obs.*

c **897** K. ÆLFRED *Gregory's Past.* xv. §5. 95 Se lareow sceal ..foreðencean..ðæt he nane ðinga ðæt ryht to suiðe..ne bodiʒe. *a* **1300** *Cursor M.* 845 (Cott.) Our lauerd had ranscond [man] On suilk a wis, als he for-thoght. *c* **1430** *Pilgr. Lyf Manhode* II. civ. (1869) 141 Ther is no time no thing wel doon..but it be forthouht bi my wit. **1513** MORE in Grafton *Chron.* (1568) II. 759 He long time in king Edwardes life, forethought to be king. **1587** FLEMING *Contn. Holinshed* III. 1394/1 If he..did now forethink the treason. **1715** ROWE *Lady Jane Gray* III, My brain fore-thought And fashion'd every action of my life.

absol. **1634** FORD *P. Warbeck* IV. iv, You're men know how to do, not to forethink.

2. To think of or contemplate beforehand; to anticipate in the mind, to presage (evil). Now *rare.*

1547–64 BAULDWIN *Mor. Philos.* (Palfr.) 106 Humility & gentlenes will rather of a friend hope the best, then forethinke the worst. **1627** P. FLETCHER *Locusts* IV. xxxvi, Oh how my daunting heart leapes in my breast But to forethinke that noble tragedie. **1724** R. WELTON *28 Disc.* 20 It [is] very unaccountable for a man so little to fore-think what will shortly befall him. **1890** *Illustr. Lond. News* 4 Oct. 426/2 Each forethinks, as the full cups circle, how well he may take his next meal in Paradise.

†**3.** *intr.* To think beforehand *of*. *Obs.*

1587 GREENE *Euphues his Censure* Wks. (Grosart) VI. 248 Age and time..men may forethink of, but not preuent. **1657** J. SMITH *Myst. Rhet.* 62 Thou dost not forethink of the difficulty. **1701** J. NORRIS *Ideal World* I. ii. 27 He could not make it without forethinking of it.

Hence **fore'thinking** *vbl. sb.*, forethought; also, †a contrivance, plot. **fore'thinking** *ppl. a.* Also **fore'thinker,** one who forethinks.

1632 [I. L.] *Womens Rights* 352 Felonies..forethinkings, and all that is against the Kings peace. **1709** STRYPE *Ann. Ref.* I. xxxi. 360 Concerning which, conscientious and forethinking Men had very Melancholy Thoughts. **1846** GROTE *Greece* I. iii. I. 102 Prometheus and Epimetheus the forethinker and the after-thinker. **1874** M. COLLINS *Frances* I. 182 Hope is the fire that the Forethinker stole.

forethought ('fɔəθɔːt), *sb.* [f. FORE- *pref.* + THOUGHT *sb.*]

1. a. A thinking out or contriving beforehand. (*crime, evil,* etc.) *of forethought*, premeditated.

a **1300** *Cursor M.* 27661 (Cott.) O nith cums bitternes o thoght..wit wicked for-thoght And conspiraciun. **1692** R. L'ESTRANGE *Fables* ccccxcix, He..is equally Undone, whether it be by a Spitefulness of Forethought, or by the Folly of Oversight. **1788** BURKE *Sp. agst. W. Hastings* Wks. XIII. 12 We urge no crimes, that were not crimes of forethought. **1853** WHITTIER *My Namesake* xix, His good was mainly an intent, His evil not of forethought done.

b. Previous thought or consideration; anticipation; also, a thought beforehand.

a **1300** *Cursor M.* 26727 (Cott.) Scrift agh be made wit god for-thoght. *c* **1440** *Jacob's Well* (E.E.T.S.) 172 ȝif þe contricyoun for þi synne haue a forthowȝt, & be pryue to god alone. **1539** TAVERNER *Erasm. Prov.* (1552) 3 Better is one forethought than two after. **1626** DK. BUCKHM. in Rushw. *Hist. Coll.* (1659) I. 378 The Earl..nominated the Duke to be his Successor, without the Dukes privity or fore-thought of it. **1650–3** tr. *Hales' Dissert. de Pace* in *Phenix* (1708) II. 366 These shall..be discarded from the Forethought..of eternal Joy. **1863** GEO. ELIOT *Romola* II. viii, The title which she had never given him before came to her lips without forethought.

†**2.** A pre-conceived idea or design, an anticipation or forecast. *Obs.*

a **1400** in *Leg. Rood* 145 Alle þe werkes þat I haue wrouht Weore founden in þe ffaderes fore-þouht. *c* **1440** *York Myst.* ii. 74 Þis materis more ȝitt will I mende, so for to fulfill my for-thoght. **1729** SHELVOCKE *Artillery* IV. 217 All these things were only so many Forethoughts of our Hand-Grenado's.

3. Thought for the future, provident care.

1719 DE FOE *Crusoe* I. 300 True Seamen are, perhaps, the least of all Mankind given to Fore-thought. **1766** BLACKSTONE *Comm.* II. II. xi. 172 Formal deeds..are presumed to be made with great caution, fore-thought, and advice. **1875** JOWETT *Plato* (ed. 2) IV. 283 Just so much forethought as is necessary to provide for the morrow.

Hence **forethoughted** *a.*, marked by forethought.

1816 L. HUNT *Rimini* III. 60 Fore-thoughted chess, and riddle rarely missed.

forethought ('fɔəθɔːt), *ppl. a.* [pa. pple. of FORETHINK *v.*]

1. Thought out or contrived beforehand; premeditated; *esp.* in Law, *forethought felony*, (*of, with, upon*) *malice forethought.* Cf. AFORETHOUGHT.

c **1425** WYNTOUN *Cron.* VII. ix. 502 Quheþir it wes of reklesnes Or it of forthoucht Felny wes. *c* **1540** in *Fisher's Wks., Life* p. liv, He began..to speake of his forethought divorse with Queene Catherin. **1628** COKE *On Litt.* 287 b, Murder is when one is slaine..with malice prepensed or forethought. **1662** HICKERINGILL *Wks.* (1716) I. 307 What Rebels shall be hereafter, must needs be so upon malice fore-thought. **1752** J. LOUTHIAN *Form of Process* (ed. 2) 103 The Pannel..by Premeditation and forethought Felony.. wounded the deceas'd. **1828** SCOTT *F.M. Perth* xx, A deed of foul and fore-thought murder.

†**2.** Anticipated. *Obs.*

1666 SPURSTOWE *Spir. Chym.* (1668) 108 The stroke of a forethought evil is more gentle and soft than if it were wholly unexpected.

forethoughtful (fɔə'θɔːtfʊl), *a.* [f. FORETHOUGHT *sb.* + -FUL.] Full of or having forethought; thoughtful for the future, provident.

1809–10 COLERIDGE *Friend* (1818) III. 205 The '*prudens quæstio*' (the forethoughtful query). **1853** LYTTON *Harold* x. vi. (ed. 3) 240 That it is which, free and fore-thoughtful [ed. 1 (1848) prethoughtful] of every chance, ye should now decide. **1876** G. MEREDITH *Beauch. Career* II. iii. 48 Neither of them had a forethoughtful head for the land at large.

Hence **fore'thoughtfully** *adv.*; **fore'thoughtfulness.**

1647 J. TRAPP *Comm. Matt.* vi. 34 Let us..not, by too much fore-thoughtfulnesse,..suffer fained or future evils before they seize upon us. **1874** DYKES *Relat. Kingdom* 71 That moral forethoughtfulness by which existence is both sustained and adorned. **1891** G. MEREDITH *One of our Conq.* III. v. 84 He made his way forethoughtfully to the glass-sheltered seats.

forethreaten, -thrift, etc.: see FORE- *pref.*

foretime ('fɔətaɪm), *sb.* and *adv.* [f. FORE- *pref.* + TIME *sb.*] Former time; a former time. †**a.** In advb. phrase, *in foretime*(*s* = AFORETIME(S.

c **1540** tr. *Pol. Verg. Eng. Hist.* (Camden) I. 98 If there were in foretimes enie hatred on their partes towards the Romaines. **1610** HOLLAND *Camden's Brit.* I. 507 It was called in foretime Norton Dany.

b. The time gone by, the past; also, the early days (of a city or state).

1853 GROTE *Greece* II. lxxxvii. XI. 380 That conception of Athens in her foretime which he [Thucydides] is perpetually impressing on his countrymen. **1868** GLADSTONE *Juv. Mundi* v. (1869) 124 The single great Achaian voyage of the traditionary fore-time, that of the ship Argo to the Euxine.

c. *attrib.* (quasi-*adj.*)

1894 F. S. ELLIS *Reynard* 116 He who thought the world to win, His foretime poverty was in. **1896** C. HARRISON in *Daily News* 8 Jan. 6/3 For though You now have passed away from us The foretime Dedication still holds good.

†**B.** *adv.* = AFORETIME. *Obs.*—¹

c **1590** GREENE *Fr. Bacon* ix. 128 Lest thou dost lose what foretime thou didst gain.

foretimed (fɔə'taɪmd), *ppl. a.* [f. FORE- *pref.* + TIMED.] Assigned to a too early time or date; antedated.

1832 SOUTHEY in *Q. Rev.* XLVII. 507 As Hampden had not reached that stage of the reformer's progress, it [this language] appears to have been fore-timed.

foretitle: see FORE- *pref.* 5 b.

foretoken ('fɔətəʊk(ə)n), *sb.* Also 6 *Sc.* corruptly **foreta(i)king.** [OE. *foretácn* (= OHG. *forazeichan*), f. FORE- *pref.* + *tácn*, TOKEN.] A premonitory token; a prognostic.

c **888** K. ÆLFRED *Boeth.* xl. §2 Hit sie foretacn ecra goda. *c* **1175** *Lamb. Hom.* 87 And wes iseȝen godes fortacne uppon ane dune. *c* **1250** *Gen. & Ex.* 2994 Ðis fortoken godes gastes is. *a* **1300** *E.E. Psalter* lxxvii. 43 He set..his for-taknes in felde of Than. **1393** GOWER *Conf.* I. 137 To him a foretokne [MS. aforetokne] he sende. **1562** WINȜET *Cert. Tract.* Wks. 1888. I. 24 Ane gret portent and foretaiking of ignorance. **1580** *Ord. of Prayer* in *Liturg. Serv. Q. Eliz.* (1847) 571 We find not that any such foretoken happened against the coming of this earthquake. **1607** TOPSELL *Four-f. Beasts* (1658) 523 There are in Swine many presages and foretokens of foul weather. **1713** R. NELSON *Life Bp. Bull* lv. (1714) 304 A foretoken of his future Incarnation. **1834** GOOD *Study Med.* (ed. 4) III. 340 The foretoken has always been found to be true. **1858** TORREY *Neander's Ch. Hist.* IX. II. 568 The foretokens of a thoroughly antichristian tendency.

foretoken (fɔə'təʊk(ə)n), *v.* [f. prec. sb. OE. had *foretácnian* in same sense.] *trans.* To be a foretoken of; to indicate or betoken beforehand.

1598 GRENEWEY *Tacitus' Ann.* XV. viii. (1622) 232 There hapned..a dolefull chance, but yet..foretokening good luck. *a* **1661** FULLER *Worthies* (1840) III. 312 The northern [waterfall] sounding clear and loud, fore-tokeneth fair weather. **1817** COLERIDGE *Biog. Lit.* 300 The evidence.. foretokening that..the graces propounded to us in Christ are what he needs. **1867** R. PALMER *Life Philip Howard* 150 Mutterings..which..foretokened the greatest evils.

Hence **fore'tokening** *vbl. sb.*

a **1300** *E.E. Psalter* lxx[i]. 7 Made am I als for-takeninge [Vulg. *tanquam prodigium*] Unto mani. **1600** HOLLAND *Livy* VI. 245 The Dictatour..hath given a good foretokening and presage of a consull Commoner. **1853** J. H. NEWMAN *Hist. Sk.* (1876) II. I. vii. 128 Such general foretokenings are borne out..in the Vandalic conquest of Africa.

foretold (fɔə'təʊld), *ppl. a.* [pa. pple. of FORETELL *v.*] †**a.** Before mentioned (*obs.*). **b.** Predicted.

a **1300** *Cursor M.* 21169 (Cott.) Efter þe riht-wis fortald iacob O iurselem he was biscop. **1589** NASHE *Anat. Absurd.* B iv, He thinketh this is the foretold Earthquake. **1661** BOYLE *Style of Script.* (1675) 37 That those..should know the foretold events, before they do come to pass.

fore-tooth ('fɔətuːθ). [f. FORE- *pref.* + TOOTH.]

1. One of the front teeth. *rare* in *sing.*

c **1000** ÆLFRIC *Gloss.* in Wr.-Wülcker 157 *Praecisores*, foreteð. ? *a* **1400** *Morte Arth.* 1089 With..þe flesche in his fortethe fowly as a bere. *c* **1440** *Bone Flor.* 1609 Hys for tethe owte he spytt. **1581** LAMBARDE *Eiren.* IV. iv. (1588) 425 By ..beating out his foreteeth. **1661** PEPYS *Diary* 8 May, My wife..had a foretooth drawn out to-day. **1754** RICHARDSON *Grandison* (1781) V. xxi. 121 Our Aunt Nell has lost two more of her upper fore-teeth. **1834** LANDOR *Imag. Conv.* Wks. 1846 II. 240 One..had lost..many fore-teeth by a cudgel.

†**2.** Only in *pl.* The first or milk-teeth. *Obs.*

1601 HOLLAND *Pliny* VII. xvi. 164 Children breed their fore-teeth in the seventh moneth after they are borne. **1651** WITTIE tr. *Primrose's Pop Err.* III. 187 Nature doth then give unto children their foreteeth, when they have need of solid meat.

foretop ('fɔətɒp). Also **for-.** [f. FORE- *pref.* + TOP.]

†**1.** The fore part of the crown of the head; sometimes, loosely, the top of the head. *Obs.*

1382 WYCLIF *Deut.* xxxiii. 20 As a lioun he restide, & he took arme and fortop [L. *verticem*]. **1387** TREVISA *Higden* (Rolls) IV. 217 Heer faillede on his moolde and on his fortop. *c* **1430** LYDG. *Min. Poems* (Percy Soc.) 115 He felle and brake hys fore tope Apon the bare growend. *a* **1529** SKELTON *Col. Cloute* 533 When the good ale sop Dothe daunce in theyr fore top. **1675** J. SMITH *Chr. Relig. Appeal* Pref. 1 The Abantes..were wont to shave their foretops and chins. *c* **1774** T. ERSKINE in *Spirit Pub. Jrnls.* (1800) III. 321 Puppies of France, with unrelenting paws That scrape the foretops of our aching heads. **1779–81** JOHNSON *L.P., Milton* Wks. II. 139 His hair..parted at the foretop.

fig. **1654** GATAKER *Disc. Apol.* 12 This charge..appeering with an apparent lie in the foretop.

†**2. a.** The lock of hair which grows upon the fore part of the crown, or is arranged

ornamentally on the forehead; the similar part of a wig. *Obs.*

c **1290** *S. Eng. Leg.* I. 317/625 Þe Rym-forst..cleouez on hegges..I-chot wel, on mi fore-top it hauez wel ofte i-do. ?*a* **1400** *Morte Arth.* 1078 His fax and his foretoppe was filterede to-geders. **1599** MARSTON *Sco. Villanie* III. xi. 228 Hauing knit the brow, Stroke vp his fore-top. **1603** H. CROSSE *Vertues Commw.* (1878) 76 Poking stickes, perriwigs, embroided fore-tops. **1667** EVELYN *Mem.* (1857) I. 385 Her Majesty in the same habit, her fore-top long and turned aside very strangely. **1703** MRS. CENTLIVRE *Beau's Duel* IV. i, I believe you have got the fore-top of some Beau's Wig. **1712** HEARNE *Collect.* (Oxf. Hist. Soc.) III. 331 Henry Prince of Wales in his own short Hair, with his foretop standing up. **1772** NUGENT *Hist. Friar Gerund* II. 3 He was as keen a pair of scissars at trimming a sermon as adjusting a foretop. **1814** SCOTT *Wav.* xi, The foretop of his riding periwig.

fig. **1607** TOURNEUR *Rev. Trag.* II. i. Wks. 1878 II. 51 Faire trees, those comely fore-tops of the Field.

†**b.** *fig.*; *esp.* in phrase ***to take occasion, opportunity*** or ***time by the foretop*** (= FORELOCK). *Obs.*

a **1577** GASCOIGNE *Flowers, Hearbes, etc.* Wks. (1587) 255 You hauing occasion fast by the foretop, did dally with him so long. **1602** MARSTON *Antonio's Rev.* v. iii, Opportunity shakes us his foretop. **1624** HEYWOOD *Captives* III. iii. in Bullen *O. Pl.* IV, Loose not this advantadge But take tyme by the fore-topp. **1694** DRYDEN *Love Triumph.* III. i, Now take the blest occasion by the foretop.

†**c.** One who wears a foretop; hence, a fop.

1597 *1st Pt. Return fr. Parnass.* IV. i. 1237 This cringer, this foretopp. *Ibid.* v. i. 1435.

3. The tuft of hair hanging between the ears of an animal, *esp.* of a horse or (*U.S.*) a sheep; = FORELOCK.

1607 TOPSELL *Four-f. Beasts* (1658) 222 A fore-top, which is granted to Horses not only for ornament sake, but also for necessity to defend their eyes. **1689** *Lond. Gaz.* No. 2467 4 A Nag..with a thin Mane, without a Foretop. **1725** BRADLEY *Fam. Dict.* s.v. *Travelling Horse*, His Foretop, Mane and Tail should be wetted with a wet Mane-Comb. **1798** BLOOMFIELD *Farmer's Boy, Summer* 236 He..Seizes the shaggy fore-top of the bull. **1816** KEATINGE *Trav.* (1817) II. 264 *note*, Wool..the tail..and the fore-top. **1866** *Ret. Agric. Soc. Maine* 149 They all had the large foretop on the forehead. **1874** *Rep. Vermont Board Agric.* II. 416 When young they should have good foretop, and the skin a light pink.

4. a. The TOP of a foremast. ***military foretop***: an armed foretop of a war vessel.

1509 BARCLAY *Shyp of Folys* (1570) 48 His place is best Hye in the foretoppe of our foolishe barge. **1610** *Englands Eliza* Induct. 84 in *Mirr. Mag.* 777 Each..nimblie capring on the purple waue, With loftie foretops did the welkin brave. **1697** DAMPIER *Voy.* I. xvi. 453 Three men were in the Fore-top when the Fore-mast broke. **1795** NELSON 8 July in Nicolas *Disp.* (1845) II. 51 The Alcide..took fire, by a box of combustibles in her fore-top. **1833** MARRYAT *P. Simple* (1863) 29 'Captain of the foretop', said he, 'up on your horses'. **1895** *Century Mag.* Aug. 595/1 The sub-lieutenant in the military foretop was taking sextant angles.

fig. **1641** MILTON *Reform.* II. (1851) 47 Spanioliz'd Bishops swaggering in the fore-top of the State.

b. Short for *fore-topgallant-masthead*.

1800 *Naval Chron.* III. 113 Commodore J. W. Payne's Broad Pendant is flying at the Foretop.

5. *U.S.* The front seat on the top of a vehicle.

1850 B. TAYLOR *Eldorado* xliii. (1862) 430 When one has to face the cold from the foretop of a diligence. **1872** 'MARK TWAIN' *Innoc. Abr.* xii. 77 It was worth a lifetime of city toiling..to perch in the foretop with the driver.

6. *Comb.* (sense 4), as **foretop-head, -shroud** = *fore-topmast-head, -shroud*; **foretopman**, one of the men stationed in the foretop.

1710 *Lond. Gaz.* No. 4752/3 Sir Edward Whitaker hoisted the White Flag on the Foretop-head of her Majesty's Ship the Monmouth. **1816** 'QUIZ' *Grand Master* I. 7 Those fore-top-men I shall flog. **1860** GEN. P. THOMPSON *Audi Alt.* III. ci. 3 There is a young man, a fore-topman, sitting now with his Esquimaux wife.

Hence **'fore-,topping** = sense 3.

1683 *Lond. Gaz.* No. 1807/4 A black Gelding..a sore place under the Fore-topping.

fore-topgallant (fɔətɒp'gælənt). *a. Naut.* [f. FORE- *pref.* + TOPGALLANT.] Used in *Comb.* **fore-topgallant-mast**, the mast above the fore-topmast; hence with sense of 'of or belonging to the fore-topgallant-mast', as ***fore-topgallant-sail (-yard), -stay, -yard (-arm)***.

1627 CAPT. SMITH *Seaman's Gram.* iv. 17 The fore top gallant Mast, the fore top gallant saile yard. **1669** STURMY *Mariner's Mag.* I. 16 Take in your Main and Fore-top-gallant-sails. **1745** P. THOMAS *Jrnl. Anson's Voy.* 138 And the next Day got up the Fore-top-gallant-mast and Yard. **1805** NELSON 10 Oct. in Nicolas *Disp.* (1846) VII. 104 A Union Jack is to be suspended from the fore top-gallant stay. **1825** H. B. GASCOIGNE *Nav. Fame* 119 The fore-top gallant yard Is torn away. **1844** *Regul. & Ord. Army* 35 The flag of the Lord High Admiral [shall be hoisted] at the fore-top-gallant-mast-head.

fore-topmast (fɔə'tɒpmɑːst, -æ-). *Naut.* [f. FORE- *pref.* + TOPMAST.] The mast above the fore-mast; also *attrib.*, as ***fore-topmast crosstrees, -head***, etc.

1626 CAPT. SMITH *Accid. Yng. Seamen* 12 The fore top mast. **1692** *Lond. Gaz.* No. 2763/1 He spread his Flag at the Fore-top-mast-head. **1858** *Merc. Marine Mag.* V. 199 Hauled down fore topmast-staysail. **1869** *Daily News* 10 Dec., The Monarch will display..the American ensign abreast of the foretopmast crosstrees.

fore-topsail (fɔə'tɒpseɪl, -s(ə)l). *Naut.* [f. FORE- *pref.* + TOPSAIL.] The sail above the fore-sail; also *attrib.*, as ***fore-topsail yard***.

1582 N. LICHEFIELD tr. *Castanheda's Conq. E. Ind.* xxviii. 71 a, In trimming the sayles..and foretop sayles. **1627** CAPT. SMITH *Seaman's Gram.* iv. 17 The fore top-saile yard. **1790** BEATSON *Nav. & Mil. Mem.* II. 62 As that hung on her fore-top-sail and backed it, he had no command of his ship. **1833** M. SCOTT *Tom Cringle* ii. (1859) 64 We..handed the foretopsail and presently she was alongside.

†**fore'touch**, *v. Obs.* [FORE- *pref.*] *trans.* To touch, or touch upon, beforehand; to blame or censure beforehand. Hence **fore'touched** *ppl. a.*

c **1450** *Mirour Saluacioun* 3453 This Resurexionne of crist was be a stone fortouchid [L. *prætaxata*] Whilk was reprovid some tyme of thaym yᵗ the temple beldid. **1710** NORRIS *Chr. Prud.* i. 44 All the fortouch'd considerations.

fore-tow, -trace, etc.: see FORE- *pref.*

foretype ('fɔətaɪp), *sb.* [f. FORE- *pref.* + TYPE *sb.*] = ANTETYPE.

1848 LYTTON *Harold* XI. vi, Rough foretype of the coming crusader. **1864** A. LEIGHTON in *Reader* 23 July 97/2, I have seen their foretypes in the head of J. N. a hundred times.

foretype (fɔə'taɪp), *v. rare.* [f. prec. sb.] *trans.* To be a foretype of; to prefigure.

a **1618** SYLVESTER *Maidens Blush* 409 A Day full oft to be fore-typ't..by Prophets manifold. **1839** BAILEY *Festus* (1848) 32/2 O Thou..Whom all the faiths, and creeds, and rites of old..Foreshadowed and foretyped.

fore-typified, -use, -utter: see FORE- *pref.*

forever (fə'rɛvə(r)), *adv.*

1. The phrase *for ever* (see EVER 5 b), written as one word. Chiefly *U.S.* exc. in sense 'incessantly'.

1670 EACHARD *Cont. Clergy* Pref., An honest..wisher, that the best of our clergy might forever continue as they are. **1696** TATE & BRADY *Ps.* cxxviii. 1 Forever blest be God the Lord. **1768–74** TUCKER *Lt. Nat.* (1852) II. 250 The only true estate forever we can purchase by our care and diligence, lies in the sentiments of the heart. **1825** J. NEAL *Bro. Jonathan* III. 322, I will speak of them forever, to my last breath. **1839** CARLYLE *Chartism* iii. (1858) 14 The whole result is forever unattainable. **1875** T. HILL *True Order Studies* 91 The children..are forever questioning concerning the great lumps of pudding stone.

2. quasi-*sb.* Eternity, perpetuity.

1858 KINGSLEY *Farewell* 7 Make life, death, and that vast for-ever One grand sweet song. **1881** E. COXON *Basil Pl.* II. 232 This short for-ever of earth.

So **fo'revermore** *adv.*: see EVERMORE 1 b.

1837 CARLYLE *Fr. Rev.* III. IV. viii. (1871) 170 Farewell forevermore, ye Girondins. **1872** LONGF. *Christus* Introitus 46 Forevermore, it shall be as it hath been heretofore.

fore-view ('fɔəvjuː), *sb.* [f. FORE- *pref.*] A view beforehand, prospect, anticipation.

1831 E. IRVING *Let.* 17 Jan. in Mrs. Oliphant *Life* (1862) II. 170 In the foreview of it I ask your prayers. **1865** C. J. VAUGHAN *Plain Words on Chr. Living* 9 It was not the mere foreview of death which thus convulsed and agonized a brave and constant spirit.

†**fore-'view**, *v. Obs.*$^{-1}$ [f. FORE- *pref.* + VIEW *v.*] *trans.* To view or see beforehand.

a **1711** KEN *Edmund* Poet. Wks. 1721 II. 260 To die, for both their parting Hour fore-view'd.

fore-vouched, -vow, etc.: see FORE- *pref.*

†**fore'walker.** *Obs.* [f. FORE- *pref.* + WALKER] = FORERUNNER.

1529 SIR T. MORE *Dyaloge* 126 a/1 Antichrist (of whome these folke be yᵉ for walkers). **1548** UDALL, etc. *Erasm. Par. Mark* i. 9 John the forewalker of Christe.

†**'forewall.** *Obs.* [FORE *prep.* or *pref.*] A wall of defence; a wall or outwork raised to defend another.

a **1000** *Cædmon's Exod.* 297 Syndon þa foreweallas fægre ȝestepte..oð wolcna hrof. **1388** WYCLIF *Isa.* xxvi. 1 The wal and the fore wal [Vulg. *antemurale*]. **1609** BIBLE (Douay) *Lam.* ii. 8 The forewal [Vulg. *antemurale*] hath mourned, and the wal is destroyed together.

†**'foreward**, *sb.*[1] *Obs.* Forms: 2 foreweard, 3–4 **foreward(e**, (3 voreward, 4 vorewerde), 3–6 **forward(e**, (5 forwart). [OE. *foreweard* str. fem., *forewarde* wk. fem., f. FORE- *pref.* + *weard* str. fem. security, precaution: see WARD *sb.* Cf. Du. *voorwaarde*, ON. *forvǫrðr*.] An agreement, compact, covenant, promise.

O.E. Chron. an. 1109 Dær wurdon þa fore-wearda full worhte. *c* **1205** LAY. 1091 Al þat forward was ileft. **1340** *Ayenb.* 215 Þet me maki uorewerdes. *c* **1450** *Chester Pl., Deluge* 345 A forwarde noe with thie I make.

†**'foreward**, *sb.*[2] *Obs.* Also 4–6 forward(e, 5 fowarde. [f. FORE- *pref.* + WARD *sb.*]

1. The first line of an army, vanguard, front. ***in foreward***: in the van.

c **1400** *Destr. Troy* IV. 1148 Nestor..Fare shall before the forward to lead. *c* **1489** CAXTON *Sonnes of Aymon* i. 41 Fyrste of alle came the forewarde wyth the Oryflame. **1548** PATTEN *Exped. Scotl.* in Arb. *Garner* III. 62 Upon the side whereof our Foreward stood. **1631** WEEVER *Anc. Fun. Mon.* 617 After a short resistance hee discomfited the Foreward of King Richard. **1664** *Flodden F.* vi. 52 And that in foreward with his Grace He should him find fit for to fight.

fig. **1566** T. STAPLETON *Ret. Untr. Jewel* III. 90 M. Iuell hath made but a simple brauerye in this forewarde of his doctours. **1589** PUTTENHAM *Eng. Poesie* III. xii. (Arb.) 176 This one word..placed in the foreward.

2. The command of the van; a position in the van.

c **1400** *Sowdone Bab.* 502 King Lukafer..shalle have the Fowarde. *Ibid.* 732. *c* **1460** *Otterbourne* 102 in *Percy's Reliq.*, Thou arte my eme, The forwarde I gyve to the. **1570–6** LAMBARDE *Peramb. Kent* (1826) 7 The forward in all battels belongeth to them.

fig. **1555** HOOPER in Coverdale *Lett. Mart.* (1564) 122 Doubtles it is a singuler fauour of God..to geue you this foreward and preeminence.

Hence **fore-'warder**, one of the foreward or vanguard.

1611 SPEED *Hist. Gt. Brit.* VI. v. §5. 192 Caligula..lost the defense of his fore-warders, and the straitnesse of the place permitted not his gard to follow.

†**fore'ward**, *v. Obs.*$^{-1}$ [f. FORE- *pref.* + WARD *v.*] *trans.* To guard, or fortify in front.

1610 HOLLAND *Camden's Brit.* I. 817 Which she hath so forewarded againe with a counter-scarfe.

forewarn (fɔə'wɔːn), *v.* [f. FORE- *pref.* + WARN *v.*]

1. *trans.* To warn, caution, or admonish beforehand; also, to give previous notice to. Const. *of*, *to* with *inf.*, or *that* with obj. sentence.

c **1330** R. BRUNNE *Chron.* (1810) 96 Þe bisshop þouht treson, for warned was Henry. **1548** UDALL, etc. *Erasm. Par. John* xvi. 4, I thought mete to fore-warne you hereof. **1593** SHAKS. *3 Hen. VI*, IV. vii. 17 We were fore-warned of your comming, And shut the Gates. **1667** MILTON *P.L.* VII. 41 The..Arch-angel had forewarn'd Adam..to beware Apostasie. **1692** WASHINGTON tr. *Milton's Def. Pop.* ii. (1851) 60 As Samuel forewarns the People that theirs would degenerate into..Tyranny. **1741** MIDDLETON *Cicero* II. VII. 101 That which I have told, and forewarned you of. **1836** H. COLERIDGE *North. Worthies* (1852) I. 27 Their..member forewarns them of the difficulties likely to stand in their way.

absol. **1651** C. CARTWRIGHT *Cert. Relig.* I. 110 He fore-shews that many should come in his name..and forewarnes to beware of them. **1667** MILTON *P.L.* XII. 507 But in thir room, as they forewarne, Wolves shall succeed for teachers. **1860** *Merc. Marine Mag.* VII. 360 The progress of a cyclone may be telegraphed, and might secure many a ship from danger by forewarning.

Prov. [**1592**, **1768–74**; see FOREARM *v.*] *a* **1688** BUNYAN *Heart's Ease* 148 Forewarned, forearmed. **1855** KINGSLEY *Glaucus* (1878) 31 To be forewarned is to be forearmed.

†**2.** To announce beforehand, prophesy. *Obs.*

1583 STANYHURST *Æneis* III. (Arb.) 82 The Harpye Celaeno Forwarns much mischiefe too coom.

forewarn: see FORWARN *Obs.*, to prohibit.

forewarner (fɔə'wɔːnə(r)). [f. FOREWARN *v.* + -ER[1].] One who or that which forewarns.

c **1425** *Found. St. Bartholomew's* (E.E.T.S.) 43 The forwarners of variaunte tempeste to come. **1626** (*title*) *Sir Walter Rawleigh's Ghost*, or England's Forewarner. **1684** T. BURNET *Th. Earth* II. 87 It may indeed be made a question, whether this fiery vengeance..will not precede the general conflagration..as a fore-runner and forewarner to the world. **1842** LYTTON *Zanoni* VI. v, There both Mother and Forewarner stood.

forewarning (fɔə'wɔːnɪŋ), *vbl. sb.* [f. as prec. + -ING[1].] A warning beforehand.

1548 UDALL, etc. *Erasm. Par. Mark* i. 15 To geue them forewarning yᵗ Messias & the kyngdome of God were at hand. **1570** DEE *Math. Pref.* 1 They had no forwarnyng and information..whereto his doctrine tended. **1659** MILTON *Civ. Power* Wks. (1851) 323 That wise forewarning of Gamaliel. **1848** LYTTON *Harold* VIII. iv, Edward's sinister forewarnings.

fore'warning, *ppl. a.* [f. as prec. + -ING[2].] That forewarns, in senses of the vb.

1576 FLEMING *Panopl. Epist.* 193 My presignificant speach, and forewarning watchwordes, were counted unworthy credite. **1591** LAMBARDE *Archeion* (1635) 181 These offences might be made exemplary, and forewarning to other men. **1852** MRS. STOWE *Uncle Tom's C.* xl. 348 Tom heard the message with a forewarning heart.

Hence **fore'warningly** *adv.*

1839 BAILEY *Festus* (1848) 43/1 As sings the swan with parting breath, So I to thee..Forewarningly.

fore-way, -wedge, etc.: see FORE- *pref.*

†**'fore-while.** *Obs. rare.* [f. FORE- *pref.* + WHILE *sb.*] The space of time or interval before a future event happens.

1615 CHAPMAN *Odyss.* II. 256 Let us consult yet, in this long forewhile, How to ourselves we may prevent this ill.

†**'fore-wind.** *Obs.* Also for-. [f. FORE- *pref.* + WIND *sb.* Cf. Du. *voorwind.*] A wind that blows a ship forward on her course, a favourable wind.

1561 EDEN *Arte Nauig.* A iij b, They founde it to serue with a forewynde. **1603** DRAYTON *Barons' Wars* IV. xix, A for-wind now for Harwich fitly blowes. **1676** HOBBES *Iliad* I. 461 A good forewind Apollo with them sent.

fig. **1682** S. PORDAGE *Medal Rev.* 104 All with the fore-wind of Religion Saile.

fore-winning: see FORE- *pref.* 5.

†**fore-wise.** *Obs.* [f. FORE- *pref.* + WISE.] Wise beforehand, prescient, far-seeing.

c **1400** *Destr. Troy* 3950 Wise of his dedis, In fele thinges forwise, & a fer caster.

So **fore-'wisdom**, prescience, forethought.

1576 FLEMING *Panopl. Epist.* 20 What providence and forewisedome did he use. **1882** BERESF. HOPE *Brandreth* I.

xvi. 252 The husband who devises this ingenious proof of confidence is well advised in his forewisdom.

†**'fore-wit**, *sb. Obs.* Also 4-6 forwit. [f. FORE- *pref.* + WIT.]

1. Fore-knowledge, foresight, prudence.

1377 LANGL. *P. Pl.* B. v. 166 Seynt Gregorie..had a gode forwit. **1503** HAWES *Examp. Virt.* v. (Arb.) 16 Thinges.. with a forwytte kepte in store. **1546** J. HEYWOOD *Prov.* (1867) 15 Yet is one good forewit woorth two after wits. **1631** GOUGE *God's Arrows* III. lix. 292 Had the fore-wit of the Aramites beene as good as their after-wit.

2. A leading 'wit', a leader in matters of taste or literature.

1637 B. JONSON *Sad Sheph.* Prol. 41 Nor that the Fore-wits that would draw the rest Vnto their liking, alwayes like the best.

†**fore-'wit**, *v. Obs.* Pres. 1st, 3rd sing. **-wot**. Also for- [OE. *fore-*, *forwitan*, f. FORE- *pref.*, FOR- *pref.*² + *witan*, WIT *v.*] *trans.* To know beforehand.

*c***888** K. ÆLFRED *Boeth.* xxxix. §5 On þam hean sceoþperde þe eall forewat hu hit ȝeweorþan sceal. *c***1374** CHAUCER *Troylus* IV. 1043 (1071) Thilke sovereyn purveyaunce, That forwoot alle, withouten ignoraunce. *c***1384** —— *H. Fame* (Sk.) 45 If the soule..Be so parfit.. That hit forwot that is to come. *c***1400** *Test. Love* III. (1532) 352 God by necessitee forwote al thynges comyng.

Hence **fore-'witting** *vbl. sb.*, fore-knowledge. Also **fore-'witter**, one who knows beforehand.

*c***1374** CHAUCER *Boeth.* v. pr. vi. 178 God byholder and forwiter of alle þinges dwelliþ aboue. *c***1386** —— *Nun's Pr. T.* 423 Goddis worthy forwetyng Streigneth me needely for to do a thing.

forewoman ('fɔəwʊmən), pl. **-women** (-wɪmɪn). [f. FORE- *pref.* + WOMAN.] A woman who acts as chief of other women: **a.** in a jury of matrons; **b.** in a shop or department.

1709 STEELE *Tatler* No. 84 ¶1 The learned Androgyne, that would make a good Fore-woman of the Pannel. **1752** J. LOUTHIAN *Form of Process* (ed. 2) 216 If the Forewoman shall say, She is with quick Child..then [etc.]. **1838** DICKENS *Nich. Nick.* x, Miss Knag, the forewoman, shall have directions to try you with some easy work at first. **1869** MRS. PALLISER *Lace* vii. 109 There were only three forewomen and sixty-three lace-makers.

fore-wonted: see FORE- *pref.* 2 b.

foreword ('fɔəwɜːd, 'fɔːwəd). [f. FORE- *pref.* + WORD. Cf. Ger. *vorwort.*] A word said before something else; hence, an introduction, a preface.

1842 DASENT tr. *Prose or Younger Edda* Pref. 6 The Translator..has felt no hesitation in placing the 'Foreword to the Edda'..at the end of the volume. **1868** FURNIVALL (*title*), The Babees Book, etc...with some Forewords on Education in early England. **1879** *19th Cent.* June 1092 After these few forewords I will quote the letter. **1888** BESANT *Inner House* v, All the dancing, courting, pretty speeches, and tender looks, meant only the fore-words of Love in earnest.

†**forework.** *Obs.* [f. FORE- *pref.* + WORK *sb.*] A 'work' or defensive structure in the front of a building or fortified place.

1497 in *Ld. Treas. Acc. Scotl.* (1877) I. 334 The bigging of the fore werk of Dunbar. **1502** *Acc.* in *Lib. Cart. S. Crucis* (1840) lvi, To Walter Merlioun, mason, in part payment of his task of the foirwerk and the new hall in Halyrudhous.

fore-world ('fɔəwɜːld). [f. FORE- *pref.* + WORLD. Cf. Ger. *vorwelt.*] The primeval world.

1796 W. TAYLOR in *Monthly Rev.* XX. 517 Monuments of the Fore-world. **1801** SOUTHEY *Thalaba* IX. 324 It were as wise to bring from Ararat The fore-world's wood to build the magic pile. **1849** *Reverberations* II. 95 From the Fore-world's chaotic night, Gleaming and streaming into light.

fore-write (fɔə'raɪt), *v.* [f. FORE- *pref.* + WRITE.] *trans.* To write before or beforehand.

1634 FORD *P. Warbeck* II. iii, Time alone debates Quarrels forewritten in the book of fates. **1872** LONGF. *Div. Trag.* I. *Marriage in Cana*, What is to be Hath been fore-written in the thought divine From the beginning.

Hence ˌ**fore-'written** (*-of*) *ppl. a.* Also **'fore-writ**, something written before, a title; †**fore-'writer**, one who writes, or has written, beforehand.

*c***1460** J. RUSSELL *Bk. Nurture* 1243 As for ryme or reson, þe forewryter was not to blame, For as he founde hit aforne hym, so wrote he þe same. **1560-78** *Bk. Discipl. Ch. Scot.* (1621) 37 The fore-written Provinces. **1570** LEVINS *Manip.* 149/28 Ye Forewrit, *titulus, prescriptum.* **1578** BANISTER *Hist. Man* I. 13 By the probable assertions of the best forewriters. **1599** NASHE *Lenten Stuffe* Wks. (Grosart) V. 214 The forewritten-of Bishop of Norwich. **1649** BP. HALL *Cases Consc.* III. (1654) 207 Such, as must have their grounds from fore-written truths. **1839** BAILEY *Festus* (1848) 47/1 The forewritten hour.

fore-wrought: see FORE- *pref.* 2 b.

fore-yard¹ ('fɔəjɑːd). [f. FORE- *pref.* + YARD¹.] The yard or court in front of a building.

1388 WYCLIF *Ezek.* x. 4 The halle [*v.r.* forȝerde; L. *atrium*]. **1420-30** *Lay-Folks' Prayer Bk.* (E.E.T.S.) 46 In the forȝerdis of the hous of oure God. **1699** S. SEWALL *Diary* 21 June (1878) I. 498 A Pack of Cards are found strawed over my fore-yard. **1741** RICHARDSON *Pamela* II. 288 She would not come in, but sat fretting on a Seat in the Fore-yard. **1860** J. WHITE *Hist. France* (ed. 2) 90 Where gentle lawns sloping downward from the door must be converted into a foreyard.

fore-yard² ('fɔəjɑːd). [f. FORE- *pref.* + YARD².]

1. *Naut.* 'The lowest yard on the fore-mast' (W. C. Russell).

1627 CAPT. SMITH *Seaman's Gram.* iii. 16 The fore Yard [must be] 19 yards long, and 15 inches diameter or thick. **1745** P. THOMAS *Jrnl. Anson's Voy.* 145 Her Fore-top-mast broke short, and in its Fall, meeting with the Fore-yard broke it in the Slings. **1844** W. H. MAXWELL *Sports & Adv. Scot.* ix. (1855) 91 At sea, when the bell is struck at noon, the sun is said to be 'over the fore-yard'. **1854** H. MILLER *Sch. & Schm.* (1858) 6 After toiling on the foreyard in a violent night-squall.

†**2.** *pl.* = ANTENNÆ. *Obs.*

1658 ROWLAND *Moufet's Theat. Ins.* 937 The fore-yards are thin, black and short.

fore-year: see FORE- *pref.* 4, 4 b.

†**for'faint**, *a. Obs.* [f. FOR- *pref.*¹ + FAINT *a.*] Very faint. So †**for'fainted** *ppl. a.*

14.. *Why I can't be a Nun* 112 in *E.E.P.* (1862) 141 At that worde for-feynte I fylle. **1563** SACKVILLE *Induct. Mirr. Mag.* xv, With that worde of sorrowe all forfaynt She looked vp. **1566** DRANT *Wail. Hierem.* 3 For foode to theyr forefainted soules.

forfalt, -fault, -faute: see FORFEIT.

†**for'famel**, *v. Obs. rare*⁻¹. [f. FOR- *pref.*¹ + **famel*, ad. OF. *fameil-er* to be hungry.] Only in *pa. pple.*: Starved to death.

*c***1400** *Sowdone Bab.* 2282 He charged hem to wacche wel all abowte That thay for-famelid might dye.

†**forfang, -feng.** *Obs.* [OE. *for(e)fang, -feng*, f. FORE- *pref.* + FANG, FENG *sbs.*]

1. *OE. Law.* A rescuing of stolen property; the reward for this.

*a***1000** *Laws Ine* liii, Be forstolenes monnes forefenge. *a***1000** *Laws Æthelst.* vi, Forfang..æt men fiftene peningas.

2. By post-Conquest lawyers explained (perh. by conjecture based on the etymology) to mean: The fine for taking provisions from a market before the royal purveyors were served.

*c***1250** *Gloss. Law Terms* in *Rel. Ant.* I. 33 *Forfeng*, quite de avant prise (avent le rei).

†**for'fare**, *v.*¹ *Obs.* For forms see FARE *v.*¹ Cf. FORFERE. [OE. *forfaran* (f. FOR- *pref.*¹ + *faran*, FARE *v.*) = OFris. *forfara*, OHG. *fer-, for-, furfaran*, Ger. *verfahren.*]

1. *intr.* To pass away, perish, decay.

O.E. Chron. an. 910 Hi þær mæst ealle siððan forforon. *Ibid.* an. 1091 Seo scip fyrde..æl mæst earmlice forfor. *c***1175** *Lamb. Hom.* 141 Þet fole wes welnech for-faren drinkeles. *c***1250** *Gen. & Ex.* 3018 To-morȝen, but he muȝen vt-pharen, Egyptes erf sal al for-faren. **1375** BARBOUR *Bruce* I. 478 Thys lord the brwyss..Saw all the kynryk swa forfayr. *c***1420** *Pallad. on Husb.* IV. 951 They seynge her dwellyng so forfare, So fle away. **1494** FABYAN *Chron.* v. lxxxiii. 61 *marg.*, Thonge Castell..is now Forfaryn. **1578** *Scot. Poems 16th C.* II. 178 This warld sall all forfair.

b. *pa. pple.* Worn out with travel, age, etc.

1393 GOWER *Conf.* I. 45 As it were a man forfare Unto the wode I gan to fare. **1460** *Lybeaus Disc.* (1890) 1574 No kniȝt ..Thauȝ he schold be forfard, Ne geteth her non ostell. **15..** *Merchant & his Son* in Hazl. *E.P.P.* I. 142 For-faren wyth the fyre stynk. **1787** BURNS *Brigs of Ayr* 109 Wi' crazy eild I'm sair forfairn. *a***1810** TANNAHILL *Kebbuckston Wedding* Poems (1846) 139 Though sair forfairn, He vows that he'll wallop twa sets with the howdie.

2. *trans.* To cause to perish, destroy.

*a***1000** *Laws Edw. & Guth.* §11 On earde forfare [man] hy mid ealle. *c***1205** LAY. 11454 Wulleð Romleode..foruaren vs mid fehte. *c***1330** R. BRUNNE *Chron.* (1810) 158 Two busses wer forfaren. **1413** *Pilgr. Sowle* (Caxton 1483) IV. ii. 58 A worme had forfaren these pepyns and corrumped them withynne. *c***1450** *Bk. Curtasye* 220 in *Babees Bk.* (1868) 305 Thre enmys..þer are, þat coueyten alle men to for-fare,— The deuel, þe flesshe, þe worlde also. *a***1605** POLWART *Flyting w. Montgomerie* 48 Make obedience In time, for feare leist I forfaire thee.

¶**3.** By Skene associated with F. *forfaire*, med.L. *forisfacĕre.* (See quot.)

1597 SKENE *De Verb. Sign.* s.v. *Forisfactum*, It is taken for fornication committed be ane woman..to fore-fair, or abuse her bodie. **1609** —— *Reg. Maj.* 39 Wemen..gif they forfair or abuse their bodies in fornication..sall be disherrissed.

†**for'fare**, *v.*² *Obs.* [f. FOR- *pref.*² + FARE *v.*] *trans.* To pass along (a way, etc.) before others.

O.E. Chron. an. 897 For foron him þone muðan foran on uter mere. *c***1205** LAY. 27373 What beoð þeos ut-laȝen þa þisne wei us habbeoð for-uaren [*c***1275** forfare].

Forfars ('fɔːfəz). [f. *Forfar* the name of the Scotch county in which it is chiefly made.]

1882 CAULFEILD & SAWARD *Dict. Needlework*, *Forfars* a coarse, heavy description of linen cloth, made of unbleached flax.

forfast(ed, -fastened, -fatted: see FOR- *pref.*¹

†**'forfaultry, forefaultry.** *Sc. Obs.* [f. *forfault*, FORFEIT *sb.* + -RY.] = FORFEITURE.

*c***1565** LINDESAY (Pitscottie) *Chron. Scot.* (1728) 41 A sufficient cause to tyne his life..and deserving forfaultry. **1676** W. ROW *Contn. Blair's Autobiog.* xi. (1848) 367 The Lord Warriston being summoned under pain of forfaultry.

†**for'fear**, *v. Obs.* [f. FOR- *pref.*¹ + FEAR *v.*] *trans.* To terrify. Only in pa. pple., which often coincides in sense with the phrase *for ferd*: see FERD *sb.*² Const. with *of* or *subord. cl.*

*c***1200** ORMIN 674 ȝiff he seþ þatt mann iss ohht Forrfæredd off hiss sihhþe. *c***1320** *Seuyn Sag.* (W.) 3078 He slogh him sone that ilk day, Forfered that he sold oght say. *c***1386** CHAUCER *Sqr.'s T.* 519 Myn herte..For-fered of his deeth..Graunted him loue. *c***1400** *Ywaine & Gaw.* 1679 He sperd his yate, and in he ran, For fered of that wode man.

for-feebled: see FOR- *pref.*¹ 9.

forfeit ('fɔːfɪt), *sb.* Forms: α. 4-5 forfet(t(e, (4-5 furfatt, -fet, 6 forfect, forefaicte), 4-6 forfaite, -ayt(te, -eite, -ete, -eyte, 6- forfeit. β. *Sc.* 6 foir-, forfalt, -fault, 7 forfaute. [a. OF. *forfet*, *forfait*:—med.L. *foris factum* trespass, fine, neut. pa. pple. of *foris facĕre* to transgress, f. *foris* outside (see FOR- *pref.*³) + *facĕre* to do. The Sc. forms β. are corrupted by assimilation to *fault* or *default.*]

†**1.** A misdeed, crime, offence, transgression; hence, wilful injury. Also with *of*: Transgression against or in respect of, breach or violation *of*. *Obs.*

in forfault (Sc. Law): under charge of wrong doing, guilty of breaking the law. (Jam.)

α. *a***1300** *Cursor M.* 15814 (Cott.) Petre was in hand nummen for forfait he had don. **1393** GOWER *Conf.* III. 245 That he the forfete of luxure Shall tempre and reule. **1423** JAS. I. *Kingis Q.* xcii, Thus were thai wrangit that did no forfet. **1481** CAXTON *Reynard* (Arb.) 53 Ye may frely..ete them wythoute ony forfayte. **1483** —— *G. de la Tour* E v, Men ought wel to kepe hem self fro the forfait of maryage. *a***1533** LD. BERNERS *Gold. Bk. M. Aurel.* (1546) C iij, The Censure..dayly toke hede to the forfaytes done. **1668** TEMPLE *Let. to Ld. Arlington* Wks. 1731 II. 90 No.. Corruption of Ministers, can preserve them long from paying what they owe to any Forfeits of their Duty.

β. **14..** tr. *Burgh Lawis* c. 19 in *Sc. Acts* (1814) I. 336 Gif ony man or ony woman in the burgh be in forfaute of brede or ale [*sit in forisfacto de pane vel cervisia*]..gif he faltis twyis he sall be chastyte twyis for his forfaute. **1572** *Lament Lady Scot.* 373 in *Scot. Poems 16th C.* (1801) II. 253 Thir foirfalts that I haue done reheirs, That lords, lairds, ladys and lawers dois exerce.

2. Something to which the right is lost by the commission of a crime or fault; hence, a penal fine, a penalty for breach of contract or neglect of duty. Phr. *to take (the) forfeit of*, *to pay (the) forfeit* (*lit.* and *fig.*).

*c***1450** *Bk. Curtasye* 577 in *Babees Bk.* (1868) 318 Of þe lordes courtes and forfetis. **1480** CAXTON *Chron. Eng.* ccxix. 179 They taken the goodes..and lete hem calle his forfaytz. **1538** FITZHERB. *Just. Peas* 38 b, The forfayt therof is al the pewter and brasse so cast and wrought. **1555** WATREMAN *Fardle Facions* I. v. 70 The forfect for non paiment of the lone. **1596** SHAKS. *Merch. V.* IV. i. 207, I craue the Law, The penaltie and forfeite of my bond. **1625** FLETCHER & SHIRLEY *Nt. Walker* iv, Thou hast undone a faithful Gentleman, By taking forfeit of his Land. **1713** YOUNG *Force Relig.* II. (1757) 62 Life is a forfeit we must shortly pay. **1843** LEVER *J. Hinton* xviii, To be free of the transaction, I this morning offered to pay half forfeit. **1857** BUCKLE *Civiliz.* I. viii. 543 The forfeit incurred by many of those illustrious thinkers who [etc.].

b. *transf.* of a person.

1603 SHAKS. *Meas. for M.* IV. ii. 167 Claudio..is no greater forfeit to the law than Angelo.

3. A trivial mulct or fine imposed, e.g., for breach of some rule or by-law in a tavern parlour, a club, etc. Also, in certain games, an article (usually something carried on the person) which a player gives up by way of penalty for making some mistake, and which he afterwards redeems by performing some ludicrous task.

1603 SHAKS. *Meas. for M.* v. 323 The strong Statutes Stand like the forfeites in a Barbers shop, As much in mocke, as marke. **1642** FULLER *Holy & Prof. St.* v. x. 395 No more than the forfeits in a barbers shop, where a Gentle-mans pleasure is all the obligation to pay. **1660-1** PEPYS *Diary* 4 Feb., And here I took pleasure to take forfeits of the ladies. **1714** GAY *Trivia* II. 175 The..Wits shall frequent Forfeits pay. **1766** GOLDSM. *Vic. W.* ii, Walking out, drinking tea, country dances, and forfeits, shortened the rest of the day. **1814** SCOTT *Wav.* lxix, We played the game boldly, and the forfeit shall be paid. **1837** DICKENS *Pickw.* xxviii, We.. beguile the time with forfeits and old stories. **1865** J. HATTON *Bitter Sweets* xxxii, In the games of forfeit, he played his part.

4. [from the vb.] The losing of something by way of penalty: = FORFEITURE.

to set to forfalt (Sc. Law): to attaint, outlaw.

α. **1393** GOWER *Conf.* III. 177 To give..and to withdrawe The forfet of a mannes life. **1423** JAS. I. *Kingis Q.* cxxix, Vertu sall be the cause of thy forfet. **1596** SHAKS. *Merch. V.* IV. i. 212, I will be bound to pay it..On forfeit of my hands, my head, my heart. **1629** MILTON *Nativity* i, That he our deadly forfeit should release. **1644** —— *Educ.* Wks. (1847) 98/1 You would to the forfeit of your own discerning ability, impose on me [etc.]. **1716** LADY M. W. MONTAGU *Let. to C'tess Bristol* 22 Aug., Debts..they could clear no other way but by the forfeit of their honour.

β. **1536** BELLENDEN *Cron. Scot.* XIII. xv, Eftir his forfalt, the constabillary wes geuyn to the Hayis of Arroll. **1570** BUCHANAN *Chamæleon* Wks. (1892) 46 Ye parliament set to forfalt sic lordis as had fled in Ingland.

forfeit ('fɔːfɪt), *a.* Forms: see prec. [ad. OF. *forfait*, pa. pple. of *forfaire*:—late L. *forisfacĕre*:

see prec. In early use serving as pa. pple. of next.]

That has been lost or has to be given up as the penalty of a crime or fault or breach of engagement. Const. †*till*, *to*, *unto*.

α. **1393** GOWER *Conf.* I. 194 That ye this thing no lenger let, So that your life be nought forfete. **1425** WYNTOUN *Cron.* VII. viii. 716 Hale he tuk in-til Ethchet As þai had fallyne til hym forfet. **1538** FITZHERB. *Just. Peas* (1514) 38 b, The value of them is forfayt, halfe to the fyndours or serchers therof. **1594** PLAT *Jewell-ho.* I. 5 Forfeit and confiscate vnto the crowne. **1601** SHAKS. *All's Well* IV. iii. 216 His braines are forfeite to the next tile that fals. **1608** MARKHAM & MACHIN *Dumb Knight* V. i, This monster.. Whose forfait life is witnesse to his shame. **1697** DRYDEN *Virg. Georg.* IV. 711 And his long Toils were forfeit for a Look. **1735** SOMERVILLE *Chase* III. 63 Behold the just Avenger, swift to seize His forfeit Head. **1827** HALLAM *Const. Hist.* (1876) II. ix. 110 These have half redeemed his forfeit fame. **1847** EMERSON *Poems* (1857) 43 The wish To tread the forfeit Paradise. **1859** GLADSTONE *Horace's Odes* III. ix, My forfeit life I'll freely give, So she, my better life, may live.

β. **1423** JAS. I. *Kingis Q.* cxli, All though my lyf suld forfaut be therefore.

forfeit ('fɔːfɪt), *v.* Forms: α. *Infin.* 4–6 forfet(e(n, -yn, 5–6 -fett(e, (5 foffet), 5–7 forfait(e, 5–6 -fayt(te, -feyt, (5 -fite, 6 -fyt, -fect, -feict), 6 *Sc.* forfat, -fit, 6– forfeit. *Pa. t.* and *pa. pple.* -ed. Also *pa. t.* 5 forfett(e; *pa. pple.* 4–5 forfet(e, 6 -feyte (see FORFEIT *a.*). β. *Sc.* 4–7 forfalt, 6–9 forfault, 7–9 forefault; *pa. pple.* 4 forfalt, 5 forfaut. [f. prec. sb.]

†**1.** *intr.* To do amiss, sin, transgress. *Obs.*

a **1325** *Prose Psalter* cxviii[i]. 119 Ich told alle the sinȝers of erthe for-fetand [L. *prævaricantes*.] *c* **1386** CHAUCER *Pars. T.* ¶ 199 And al this suffred Ihesu crist þat neuere forfeted. **1496** *Dives & Paup.* (W. de W.) I. li. 91 They forfete hyghely ayenst the fyrst commaundement. *c* **1530** LD. BERNERS *Arth. Lyt. Bryt.* (1814) 348 Ye saye yt she hath forfeyte with this knight; for he can not forfeyte with her, but yt she must be accorded with him.

b. *trans.* To transgress against, violate (one's faith or oath). *rare.*

[So OF. *forfaire*: but there is an admixture of sense 2.] **1654** tr. *Scudery's Curia Pol.* 28 Having known you so notoriously to forfeit your Faith. **1800** tr. *Invisible Man* II. 208 You have received my oath; I am incapable of forfeiting it.

2. *trans.* To lose, lose the right to; to render oneself liable to be deprived of (something); also, to have to pay (a sum of money) in consequence of a crime, offence, breach of duty, or engagement. Const. *to* (the receiver). **a.** in a strictly legal sense.

α. **1466** *Mann. & Househ. Exp.* 176 They schal kontente me fore my parte of skenes that were foffetede, iiij. li. **1581** MULCASTER *Positions* xxxvii. (1887) 152 Neither he, ne yet his parentes, can forsake their prince, vpon any colour without forfaiting more than a quarters scholehire. **1663** MARVELL *Corr.* xl. Wks. 1872–5 II. 88 The House adjourned till Wednesday fortnight.. every one absent to forfeit five pounds. **1723** DE FOE *Col. Jack* (1840) 242 My life and effects were all forfeited to the English government. **1827** JARMAN *Powell's Devises* II. 261 The Court held the estate not to be forfeited by non-performance. **1833** HT. MARTINEAU *Tale of Tyne* i. 15 You forget what you forfeit, if you have your indentures broke.

β. **1535** STEWART *Cron. Scot.* III. 75 That ather.. suld.. forfalt all in the kingis hand. **1609** SKENE *Reg. Maj.* 13 They sall tine and forfalt all their cattell. **1688** *Ess. Magistracy* in *Harl. Misc.* I. 5 Whoever goes about to subvert it.. forefaults his own title. **1717** *Wodrow Corr.* (1843) II. 339 Such.. should for that time forfault their part in the settlement of a parish.

b. *gen.* To lose by misconduct.

13.. *E.E. Allit. P.* A. 638 Oure forme-fader hit con forfete þurȝ an apple. *c* **1400** *Destr. Troy* 4450 To forfet þat faire place & offense make. **1611** SPEED *Hist. Gt. Brit.* IX. xxiv. (1632) 1147 Wee had.. forfaited it [Calais] so that wee could enter into no other Article of peace. **1770** BURKE *Pres. Discont.* Wks. 1808 II. 303 The first franchise of an Englishman.. is to be forfeited for some offence which no man knows. **1847** HAMILTON *Rew. & Pun.* vi. (1853) 263 The angels forefeited all happiness.. when they sinned. **1865** TROLLOPE *Belton Est.* xxv. 298 He had done nothing to forfeit her love.

c. In wider sense: To lose or give up, as a necessary consequence.

? *a* **1400** *Morte Arth.* 437 Are I be fechyde wyth force, or forfette my landes. **1591** SHAKS. *1 Hen. VI*, IV. iii. 27 So should we save a valiant gentleman, By forfeiting a traitor and a coward. **1615** CROOKE *Body of Man* 197 But shall we therefore forfet our knowledge because some men cannot conteine their lewd and inordinate affections? **1802** *Med. Jrnl.* 389 Nor can any one regulate his professional conduct by it, without forfeiting all claim to consistency. **1847** EMERSON *Repr. Men, Montaigne* Wks. (Bohn) I. 350 The moral sentiment.. never forfeits its supremacy. **1871** NAPHEYS *Prev. & Cure Dis.* I. viii. 231 The liquid forfeits part of its strength on exposure to the air.

d. *absol.* or *intr.* To incur the penalty of forfeiture or (*obs.*) confiscation.

1727 POPE, etc. *Art of Sinking* 124 It shall be reckoned a neglect of her business, and she shall forfeit accordingly. **1755** *Mem. Capt. P. Drake* i. 2 The Family remained in peaceable possession of this Estate.. until the War.. when .. they forfeited, and were driven to shift for themselves.

3. Of the executive power: **a.** To subject (land, etc.) to forfeiture; to confiscate. *Obs.* exc. *Hist.*

α. **1382** WYCLIF *Dan.* ii. 5 Your housis shuln be maad commoun, or forfetid [Vulg. *publicabuntur*]. **1611** BIBLE *Ezra* x. 8 All his substance should be forfeited. **1700** DRYDEN *Pref. Fables* (Globe) 495 Let them be staved or forfeited, like counterbanded goods.

β. **1375** BARBOUR *Bruce* XIII. 499 All his land was sesit, and forfalt to the kyng. *a* **1834** SURTEES *Poem* in Taylor *Life* (Surtees) 246 If thou wilt not ride with us, Yet shall thy lands forfaulted be. **1895** CROCKETT *Mosshaggs* 163 As for Earlstoun, we heard it was to be forfaulted very soon.

b. Chiefly *Sc.* To subject (a person) to forfeiture or confiscation (*of* estates, etc.); to confiscate the estates of. *Obs.* exc. *Hist.*

α. ? *a* **1400** *Morte Arth.* 1155 We mone be forfetede in faith, and flemyde for ever! **1565** EARL OF BEDFORD in Ellis *Orig. Lett.* Ser. I. II. 209 That the Earles.. sholde have byne forfited yf the kinge coulde not be perswaded. **1639** DRUMM. OF HAWTH. *Queries of State* Wks. (1711) 177 Whether it be lawful to proscribe and forfeit country-men. **1707** DK. ATHOL in *Vulpone* 20 It is the height of Injustice.. to forfeit any Person without a Hainous Crime. **1816** SCOTT *Old Mort.* xxix, With the purpose of forfeiting and fining such men of property whom [etc.]. **1862** LD. BROUGHAM *Brit. Const.* xv. 236 Seventy individuals.. were forfeited for their adherence to the King.

β. **1535** STEWART *Cron. Scot.* II. 637 The Thane of Calder for tressoun and cryme Forfaltit wes. **1567** *Satir. Poems Reform.* iii. 201 Quha did forfault him of his land and rent. **1582–8** *Hist. James VI* (1804) 71 The regent.. causit forfalt my Lord Fleyming. **1676** W. ROW *Contn. Blair's Autobiog.* xi. (1848) 350 The Parliament did for-fault all those that were upon that jury. **1755** CARTE *Hist. Eng.* IV. 284 The Scotch parliament.. forefaulted general Ruthven for refusing to surrender the castle of Edinburgh.

†**4.** To exact a forfeit or fine from. Also *absol.*

c **1592** MARLOWE *Jew of Malta* II. ii, With extorting, cozening, forfeiting, I fill'd the jails with bankrouts. **1736** FIELDING *Pasquin* I, I dare not go into the Green-room; I shall be forfeited if I go in there.

†**5.** To cause the forfeiture, loss, or ruin of. *Obs.*

α. *a* **1611** BEAUM. & FL. *Maid's Trag.* IV. i, Such another forgetfulness Forfeits your life. **1670** DRYDEN *Conq. Granada* I. i, Outrage unpunish'd when a Prince is by, Forfeits to Scorn the Rights of Majesty. **1673** *Essex Papers* (Camden) I. 62 Any Practice of this kind would immediately forfeit their commands. **1679** L. ADDISON *Mahumedism* 29 This had utterly forfeited him the reputation of a Prophet. **1704–5** WYCHERLEY *Let. to Pope* 25 Jan. in *Pope's Wks.* (1737) V. 4 Your good wit never forfeited your good judgment but in your partiality to me and mine.

β. **1639** CHAS. I. *Declar. Tumults Scot.* Wks. 361 Albeit.. yet that doth not.. forefault the Kirk's right.

forfeitable ('fɔːfɪtəb(ə)l), *a.* [f. prec. + -ABLE.] Liable to be forfeited; subject to forfeiture.

1467 in *Eng. Gilds* (1870) 383 Them [goods] that be forfetable by the lawe. **1495** *Act 11 Hen. VII*, c. 64. §6 All Castels.. be not.. forfeitable in eny wise to the Kyng. **1683** LUTTRELL *Brief Rel.* (1857) I. 247 Neither the charter of the citty of London or of any other corporation is forfeitable by law. **1767** BLACKSTONE *Comm.* II. 133 A moiety of the husband's lands.. forfeitable by incontinency. **1841** *Fraser's Mag.* XXIII. 385 The lives of these official Shylocks were forfeitable. **1884** *Weekly Notes* 9 Feb. 31/2 The interest of the tenant.. becomes forfeitable.

Hence **'forfeitable,ness.**

1727–36 in BAILEY.

forfeited ('fɔːfɪtɪd), *ppl. a.* [f. as prec. + -ED[1].] In senses of the verb.

α. **1530** *Act 22 Hen. VIII*, c. 15 Al issues forfaited fines and amerciaments affiered. **1752** *Scots Mag.* Nov. (1753) 554/2 His family, as.. being.. connected with the *forfeited person*, would be.. suspected. *a* **1859** MACAULAY *Hist. Eng.* V. 272 They determined to vest in the trustees of the forfeited lands an estate. **1893** STEVENSON *Catriona* 15 He's a forfeited rebel.

β. **1687** *Crim. Lett. agst. Burnet* in Burnet *Six Papers* 54 Forfaulted Traitors. **1708** J. CHAMBERLAYNE *St. Gt. Brit.* II. II. v. (1743) 381 His deputy holding in his hand one escutcheon of the arms of the forefaulted person.

forfeiter ('fɔːfɪtə(r)). [f. as prec. + -ER[1].] One who forfeits: †**a.** An evil-doer. **b.** One who forfeits (property, etc.) or incurs forfeiture.

α. **1413** *Pilgr. Sowle* (Caxton 1483) IV. xxxiv. 83 Offycers .. to done execucion of lawe vpon forfetours. *c* **1490** *Paston Lett.* III. 365 Mysdoers and forfaytours, as wesellis [etc.]. **1611** SHAKS. *Cymb.* III. ii. 38 Though forfeytours you cast in prison. **1642** ROGERS *Naaman* 607 Their forfeit is a double mulct and losse to the forfeiter. **1848** CRAIG, *Forfeiter*, one who incurs punishment by forfeiting his bond.

β. **1535** STEWART *Cron. Scot.* II. 54 Thair freindis als that tyme forȝet he nocht, Into the tyme that tha forfaltouris inbrocht. **1560** ROLLAND *Crt. Venus* IV. 262 Desperance was found ane Forfaltour.

forfeiting ('fɔːfɪtɪŋ), *vbl. sb.* [f. as prec. + -ING[1].] The action of the vb. FORFEIT.

α. *c* **1440** *Promp. Parv.* 172/1 Forfetynge. **1545** BRINKLOW *Compl.* 2 The forfetting of the londes.. of traytours.

β. **1570** *Satir. Poems Reform.* xvi. 56 Als he gat Setoun out of hands, From forfalting he sauit his lands. **1584** LD. HUNSDANE to *Sir F. Walsingham* in Calderwood *Hist. Kirk* (1843) IV. 173 That there may be nothing done.. for the forfaulting of their livings and goods. **1884** *Gd. Words* Nov. 750/2 The forefaulting of Patrick, Earl of Orkney.

forfeiting ('fɔːfɪtɪŋ), *ppl. a.* [f. as prec. + -ING[2].] That forfeits, or incurs forfeiture.

1791 NEWTE *Tour Eng. & Scot.* 277 The heirs of the forfeiting families. *a* **1859** MACAULAY *Hist. Eng.* V. 272 An estate greater than had ever belonged to the forfeiting landholders.

†**'forfeitment.** *Obs. rare*⁻¹. In 6 forfaitment. [f. FORFEIT *v.* + -MENT.] Something paid by way of forfeit: a penalty.

1597–8 BP. HALL *Sat.* II. i. 17 Manie a Lollerd would in forfaitment Beare paper-fagots ore the pavement.

forfeiture ('fɔːfɪtjʊ(r)). Forms: see FORFEIT. [a. OF. *forfeture, forfaiture*, f. *forfait* FORFEIT *sb.*]

†**1.** Transgression or violation of a law; crime, sin; *spec.* in *Law*. *Obs.*

c **1380** WYCLIF *Wks.* (1880) 348 Hereof schulden men not fayle wiþouten greet forfeture. **1414** BRAMPTON *Penit. Ps.* lxxiii. (Percy Soc.) 28 Whan I do ony forfeture, A contrite heart I offere to the. **1628** COKE *On Litt.* 59 To do a thing against or without Law or Custome, and that legally is called a forfeiture.

†**b.** In weaker sense: A breach of rules. *Obs.*

1576 TURBERV. *Venerie* 134 If.. he touch the shoulder.. with any other thing than his knyfe.. it is a forfayture.

†**c.** *forfeiture of marriage*: (see quot.). *Obs.*

1607 COWELL *Interpr.*, *Forfeiture of mariage*, is a writ lying against him, who houlding by knights seruice, and being vnder age and vnmaried, refuseth her, whome the Lord offereth him.. and marieth another.

2. The fact of losing or becoming liable to deprivation of (an estate, goods, life, an office, right, etc.) in consequence of a crime, offence, or breach of engagement. Const. *of*, †*on*.

α. **13..** *Coer de L.* 257 Forfeyture on lyff and londe. **1389** in *Eng. Gilds* (1870) 76 No brother.. shalle discuse þe counseil of þis fraternite to no straungere, vp þe payne of forfeture of þe fraternite. **1467** *Ibid.* 384 Vppon peyne of forfetor of xl[s]. **1495** *Act 11 Hen. VII*, c. 58 §1 Actes of atteyndre and forfeiture made in the seid parliament. **1523** FITZHERB. *Surv.* 13 b, That there may be made due proues without fauoure.. on payne of forfeyture of his offyce. **1614** SELDEN *Titles Hon.* 31 Henrie iv., possessing it by the forfeiture of the Lord Scrop. **1741** CHAMBERS *Cycl.* s.v., *Full Forfeiture*.. is a forfeiture of life and member, and all else that a man has. **1767** BLACKSTONE *Comm.* II. 267 Forfeiture is a punishment annexed by law to some illegal act, or negligence, in the owner of lands, tenements, or hereditaments; whereby he loses all his interest therein. **1864** BP. OF LINCOLN *Charge* 6 The minimum which will satisfy the inspector, and save the forfeiture of the grant. **1868** E. EDWARDS *Raleigh* I. vi. 94 The large forfeitures which followed the suppression of the rebellion of the Desmonds.

β. **1542** *Sc. Acts Mary* (1814) II. 416/2 The said sentence of forfaltoure was gevine vpoune þe fift day of þe samin moneth. **1609** SKENE *Reg. Maj.*, *Treatise* 132 The paine of treason is tynsell, and forefaltour of life, lands, gudes, and geir. **1755** R. KEITH *Catal. Scot. Bps.* (1824) 178 The same year he is witness to the forefaulture of the Earl of Ross.

transf. and *fig.* **1637–50** ROW *Hist. Kirk* (1842) 539 The undoing of my peace, and foirfalture of my Saluation. **1655** STANLEY *Hist. Philos.* I. (1701) 27/1 What forfeiture you impose on others, undergo your self. **1713** SWIFT *Cadenus & Vanessa* Wks. 1755 III. II. 28 He has a forfeiture incurr'd. *a* **1853** ROBERTSON *Serm.* Ser. III. viii. (1863) VI. 110 A proud remorse does not forgive itself the forfeiture of its own dignity.

†**b.** The penalty of the transgression; punishment for an offence. *Obs.*

1390 GOWER *Conf.* II. 268 This shall be thy forfeiture; With that she both his sones slough Before his eye. **1667** MILTON *P.L.* III. 221 Much less that durst upon his own head draw The deadly forfeiture, and ransom set.

3. *concr.* That which is forfeited; a pecuniary penalty, a fine. ? *Obs.*

α. **1399** *Pol. Poems* (Rolls) I. 412 Alle his ffynys.. ne fforffeyturis ffele.. myȝte not areche to paie the pore peple. **1483** in *Eng. Gilds* (1870) 336 The same forfetoures to be enployed halfe to the said cite, and the oder halfe to the said ffraternite. **1588** LD. BURGHLEY in Ellis *Orig. Lett.* Ser. I. III. 27 The forfeycture for every publique offence committed without the College to be collected by the bedells. **1607** *Nottingham Rec.* IV. 287 The order for v. li. forfeyture for refusinge to be Chamberlaynes. **1709** ADDISON *Tatler* No. 116 ¶ 7, I pronounced the Petticoat a Forfeiture. **1781** GIBBON *Decl. & F.* II. 57 One of the finest breeds [of horses].. was the forfeiture of a rebel. **1818** COBBETT *Pol. Reg.* XXXIII. 712 A forfeiture, part of which went to the informer.

β. *c* **1610** SIR J. MELVIL *Mem.* (1735) 226 Promising each of his Party a Share of the Forfaulters of the Queen's Lords. **1661** LAUDERDALE in *L. Papers* (1884) I. 93 Fines and forfaultures are wholly at my disposall.

transf. and *fig.* **1602** *Narcissus* (1893) 611 Helpe mee foorth, els I am the rude woods forfeiture. **1754** RICHARDSON *Grandison* II. vii. 105 Extraordinary merit has some forfeitures to pay. **1786** HENLEY tr. *Beckford's Vathek* (1868) 10 The exaction of these forfeitures [their beards].

forfend, forefend (fə'fɛnd, fɔə'fɛnd), *v.* [f. FOR-*pref.*[1] (see sense 2) + FEND *v.*]

†**1.** *trans.* To forbid, prohibit. With the thing forbidden as object, or with personal object and an *infinitive* with *to* as second object. *Obs.*

1382 WYCLIF *2 Kings* xii. 8 And the prestis ben forfendid to eny more takyn monee of the puple. *c* **1400** *Apol. Loll.* 70 þe wedding of prestis, or of cosynis in þe þrid or ferd degre, is not forfendid bi þe autorite of þe oolde lawe. **1493** *Dives & Paup.* (Pynson) I. i. Bj b, Gregory.. prised him for.. he forfendyd them to worshyp ymages. **1530** PALSGR. 555/2 Naye, I forfende that, for that is no playe. **1548** UDALL, etc. *Erasm. Par. Mark* i. 10 That law forfended to were any clothing of linsaye wolsaye. **1635** PAGITT *Christianogr.*, *Relig. Britans* 29 Anselme.. forefended Priests to have Wives. **1660** STILLINGFL. *Iren.* II. viii. (1662) 390 Whether it be forefended by Goddes Law. **1823** J. BADCOCK *Dom. Amusem.* 86 This ingenious veterinarian forefends the practice of mixing clay in the stuffing.

2. To avert, keep away or off, prevent; *esp.* in deprecatory phr. *God* (etc.) *forfend*; often with sentence as object; also *absol.* as an exclamation. *arch.*

1382 WYCLIF *2 Sam.* xxiv. 25 The veniaunce is forfendyd fro Yrael. **1530** SIR T. MORE *Ordin.* in *Ann. Barber-Surgeons Lond.* (1890) 583 As God forfende. **1582** N. LICHEFIELD tr. *Castanheda's Conq. E. Ind.* lvii. 120 There stood in the water.. a great number, alwaies forfending our landing. **1591** SHAKS. *1 Hen. VI*, v. iv. 65 Now heauen forfend, the holy Maid with child? **1639** HORN & ROB. *Gate Lang. Unl.* xcix. §984 They joyn themselves in company with the godly..as guardians to forefend mischiefes. **1732** FIELDING *Covent Gard.* I. iii, Behold thee carted—oh! forefend the sight. **1848** LYTTON *Harold* II. iii, 'The fiend forfend' said the grim Earl. **1859** I. TAYLOR *Logic in Theol.* 226 May we not forfend the successes of our rivals by adopting their principles. **1887** BOWEN *Virg. Æneid* III. 265 Gods forefend this menace.

†**b.** To check, refrain, withhold. *Obs.*

1382 WYCLIF *Gen.* viii. 2 And the watris ben lessid..and reynes fro hevene ben forfendid. —— *Prov.* i. 15 Forfende thi foot fro the sties of hem.

3. To secure or protect by precautionary measures. Now chiefly *U.S.*

1592 WILMOT *Tancred & Gismunda* Pref. iii, Gismond..doth humbly pray, Heauens to forefend your loues from like decay. **1875** HOLYOAKE *Co-op. Eng.* I. 250 Some men by..energy, and enterprise are able to forfend themselves against suffering. **1887** in *Amer. Missionary* Oct. 283 This is forefended by the fact that [etc.]. **1892** *Nation* (N.Y.) 28 Apr. 327/2 'The sacrifice of the Mississippi'..was forefended against even the treason of Wilkinson.

Hence **for'fended** *ppl. a.*; **fore'fending** *vbl. sb.*

c **1380** WYCLIF *Serm.* Sel. Wks. II. 223 Adam and Eve syneden..by etyng of þe forfendid appul. *c* **1440** *Promp. Parv.* 170/1 Forbedynge..or forefendynge..*prohibicio.* **1605** SHAKS. *Lear* v. i. 11 Haue you neuer found my Brothers way, To the fore-fended place?

†**for'fere**, *v. Obs.* [OE. *forféran*, f. FOR- *pref.*[1] + *féran*, FERE, *v.* Cf. FORFARE *v.*] **a.** *intr.* To perish. **b.** *trans.* To destroy.

a. *O.E. Chron.* an. 1098 For neah ælc tilð on mersc lande for ferde. *a* **1225** *Ancr. R.* 334 Forði heo uoruerden wið [uten] hope. **13..** *E.E. Allit. P.* B. 560 Quen four-ferde alle þe flesch þat he formed hade.

b. *c* **1205** LAY. 7280 Heo for-ferde Rome. *c* **1340** *Gaw. & Gr. Knt.* 1617 þe bores hed watz borne bifore þe burnes seluen þat him for-ferde in þe forþe.

†**for'ferly**, *v. Obs.* Also 4 forfarly. [f. FOR- *pref.*[1] + FERLY *v.*] *trans.* To astonish greatly. (Only in pa. pple.)

a **1300** *Cursor M.* 17361 (Cott.) Ful for-farled þan war þai. *c* **1375** *Sc. Leg. Saints* iii. 950 He wes forferlyt grettumly.

forfex ('fɔːfɛks). [a. L. *forfex* pair of scissors.]

1. *Humorously pedantic.* A pair of scissors.

1712–4 POPE *Rape Lock* III. 147 The peer now spreads the glittering forfex wide, To inclose the lock. **1837** E. HOWARD *Old Commod.* II. iv. 95 With the glittering forfex in his hand the Doctor gave chase.

2. *Ent.* (See quot.)

1826 KIRBY & SP. *Entomol.* III. 391 *Forfex* (the *Forfex*). A pair of anal organs, which open or shut transversely, and cross each other.

forficate ('fɔːfɪkət), *a. Ent.* [f. L. *forfic-*, *forfex*, + -ATE[2].] Shaped like a pair of scissors.

1816 KIRBY & SP. *Entomol.* (1843) II. 106 *note*, The mandibles are forficate. **1889** *Cent. Dict.* s.v. *Frigate-bird*, It has..a long forficate tail.

forficated ('fɔːfɪkeɪtɪd), *a. Ent.* = prec.

1752 SIR J. HILL *Hist. Anim.* 505 The Loxia with a forficated beak. **1860** in WORCESTER.

forfication (fɔːfɪ'keɪʃən). [f. L. *forfic-*, *forfex* + -ATION.] The condition of being forficate; forficate portion.

1889 *Cent. Dict.* s.v., The forfication of the tail is three inches deep.

forficulate (fɔː'fɪkjʊlət), *a. Ent.* [f. L. *forficula*, dim. of *forfex* + -ATE[2].] Shaped like a pair of small scissors.

1889 *Cent. Dict.* s.v., The forficulate palpi of certain scorpions.

forficulate (fɔː'fɪkəleɪt), *v. nonce-wd.* [f. mod.L. *forficul-a* (see prec.) + -ATE[3].] *intr.* To have a 'creeping' sensation, as if a *forficula* or earwig were crawling over one's skin.

1849 LYTTON *Caxtons* VII. iii, There is not a part of me that has not..crept, crawled, and forficulated ever since.

†**for'fight**, *v. Sc. Obs.*[−1] In 7 forefight. [back-formation from FORFOUGHTEN.] *trans.* To exhaust or over-fatigue (oneself) with fighting.

1661 *Mercur. Caled.* (Jam.), These noble gentlemen..may..forefight themselves in our excellent fields.

†**for'fighter.** *Obs.*[−1] [f. FOR *prep.* + FIGHTER.] A defender.

1382 WYCLIF *Isa.* xix. 20 He shal sende to them a saueour, and a forfiȝtere [Vulg. *propugnatorem*], that delyuere them.

†**for'flit**, *v. Obs.*[−1] In 5 forflytte. [f. FOR- *pref.*[1] + FLIT *v.*] *trans.* To remove.

c **1420** *Sir Amadas* (Weber) 381 As a fole Y am for-flytte.

forflitten: see FOR- *pref.*[1] 6.

for'foughten, *pple.* and *ppl. a. Obs.* exc. *Sc.* and *north. dial.* For forms see FIGHT *v.* and FOUGHTEN; also 8–9 forfoughen. [f. FOR- *pref.*[1] + FOUGHTEN.] Wearied and worn-out with fighting.

c **1275** LAY. 26189 On wis cniht com ride to þis kinges ferde þat was al for-fohte. *c* **1350** *Will. Palerne* 3686 ȝour mene..þat feynt ar for-fouten in feld. *c* **1450** LONELICH *Grail* xlv. 765, I was so forfowhte That non lengere stonden I mowhte. **1470–85** MALORY *Arthur* III. vi, We are forfoughten, & moche blood haue we loste. *a* **1550** [see FLAUGHTER *sb.*] *a* **1775** *Hobie Noble* xxviii. in Child *Ballads* VII. (1890) 3/2 I'm but like a forfoughen hound, Has been fighting in a dirty syke. **1787** BURNS *Let. to W. Nicol* 1 June, As forjesket and forniaw'd as a forfoughten cock. **1818** SCOTT *Rob Roy* xxviii, This good little gentleman, that seems sair for-foughen, as I may say, in this tuilzie.

b. *transf.* Wearied, over-fatigued.

1786 *Harvest Rig* in Chambers *Pop. Poems Scotl.* (1862) 50 They're a' right glad the kemp is done, For they're forfoughten ilka ane. *c* **1817** HOGG *Tales & Sk.* IV. 253 Both he and his master were alike sore forefoughten. **1832–53** *Whistle-Binkie* (Sc. Songs) Ser. I. 39 In case some drift-driven strangers come forfoughten to our bield.

†**for'fret**, *v. Obs.* [f. FOR- *pref.*[1] + FRET *v.*] *trans.* To devour, gnaw; to eat up or into, corrode.

a **1225** *Ancr. R.* 138 Also wiðuten wisdom, fleshs, ase wurm, uoruret hire, & westeð hire suluen. **1297** R. GLOUC. (Rolls) 186 þe gret evel..þat vorfreteþ menne limes. *c* **1350** *Will. Palerne* 2376 þe werwolf..ran forþ..as he wold þat barn bliue haue for-frete. **1377** LANGL. *P. Pl.* B. XVI. 29 Coueityse..forfret neigh þe frute þorw many faire siȝtes.

Hence †**for'fretten** *ppl. a.*

c **1420** *Pallad. on Husb.* III. 331 The long endurid, old, forfreton vine Is not to helpe.

forfrorn, -frush, -fry, -gab: see FOR- *pref.*[1]

†**for'gall**, *v. Obs.* Also *pa. pple.* forgalded. [f. FOR- *pref.*[1] + GALL *v.*] To gall thoroughly.

1563 *Mirr. Mag., Hen. Dk. Buckhm.* lxxxiv, The Bull chased with Dartes, And with dyepe woundes forgald and gored. **1576** GASCOIGNE *Philomene* (Arb.) 117 That horse which..lothes the griefe of his forgalded sides.

†**for'gar**, *v. Obs.* [f. FOR- *pref.*[1] + OE. *ȝearwian* to make ready. Cf. ON. *fyrirgøra* (Da. *forgiöre*, Sw. *förgöra*) to forfeit.] *trans.* **a.** To lose. **b.** To destroy, corrupt.

c **1200** ORMIN 14584 Mannkinn þatt all wass full off sinne & all forrgarrt ȝæn Godd. *Ibid.* 17531 þurrh whatt wass heffness whel forrgarrt To dreȝhenn helle pine? **13..** *E.E. Allit. P.* A. 321 Hit watz for-garte, at paradys greue. *Ibid.* B. 240 To lyue þer..& thenne enherite þat home þat aungelez for-gart. *a* **1400** *Pol. Poems* (1859) I. 344 This fellowship han forgard her grace.

forgather, foregather (fə'gæðə(r), fɔə-), *v.* Chiefly *Sc.* Also 6 -gadder, *Sc.* -gader. [f. FOR- *pref.*[1] + GATHER. Cf. Du. *vergaderen*, Flem. 16th c. *vergaederen* to assemble.]

1. *intr.* To gather together, assemble.

1513 DOUGLAS *Æneis* VII. xiv. 30 Ane ost of futmen..Thik forgadderis the large feyldis about. **1535** STEWART *Cron. Scot.* II. 62 The Scottis all forgadderit in Argyle. *a* **1774** FERGUSSON *King's Birthday* Poems (1845) 1 In London town Whare fouk..Forgather aft..To drink and tipple. **1895** H. P. ROBINSON *Men born equal* 329 Three or four other men forgathered with them in the wine-room over the coffee and cigars.

2. To encounter, meet; *esp.* to meet *with*. 'Now commonly used to denote an accidental meeting' (Jam.).

1600 R. LOGAN in Pitcairn *Crim. Trials* (1833) II. 282 Incase ye and M.A.R. forgader,..be very var vith his raklese toyis of Padoa. **1676** W. ROW *Contn. Blair's Autobiog.* ix. (1848) 142 They forgathered with a mighty hurricane out of the north-west. **1737** RAMSAY *Scot. Prov.* Ded., Ye fergather wi' your friends at kirk. **1786** BURNS *Twa Dogs* 6 'Twas in that place..Twa dogs..Forgather'd ance upon a time. **1873** G. C. DAVIES *Mount. & Mere* xix. 178, I foregathered with an ancient fisherman.

b. To associate *with*. *to forgather up*: to take *up* with, become attached to.

1782 BURNS *Death Poor Mailie* x, O, may thou ne'er forgather up Wi' ony blastit, moorland toop. **1858** *Times* 30 Nov. 6/6 For this..purpose he forgathered with the privates of the regiment, and treated them.

3. ? To come together in marriage.

1768 ROSS *Helenore* II. 100 Fouk ay had best begin wi' dealing fair, Altho' they sud forgather ne'er so bare.

Hence **for'gathered** *ppl. a.*, assembled. **for'gathering** *vbl. sb.*, the action of gathering together; also, an assembly, gathering, or meeting.

1823 TENNANT *Cardinal Beaton* II. i. 33 'You're awing me a pint o' gin for this forgatherin.' **1839** BAILEY *Festus* xix. (1848) 206 There rose a shout From the foregathered multitudes. **1868** DICKENS *Let.* 21 Mar., We hold all sorts of hearty foregatherings. **1884** *St. James's Gaz.* 8 Aug. 3/1 The fears and doubts of nations are laid to rest by the foregathering of the imperial cousins.

forge (fɔədʒ), *sb.* Also 5 foorge, 6 fordg. [a. OF. *forge* (= Pr., Catal. *farga*, Sp. *forja*, also *fragua*, Pg. *forja*):—Com. Rom. **faurga*:—L. *fabrica*: see FABRIC.]

†**1.** Manufacture, construction; style of construction, make, workmanship; = FABRIC 5, 6. In late use a new formation on the vb. *Obs.*

1390 GOWER *Conf.* I. 78 An horse of brass..Of suche entaile, of such a forge. **1569** J. SANFORD tr. *Agrippa's Van. Artes* 124 b, If it [Husbandrie] did not teache so many monstruouse forges of plantes. **1690** DRYDEN *Don Sebast.* v. Wks. 1883 VII. 464 His soft metal..runs in the mould, And needs not further forge. **1691** RAY *Creation* II. (1692) 93 In the greater Bodies the Forge was easie, the Matter being ductile and sequacious.

2. A smithy.

c **1386** CHAUCER *Miller's T.* 576 A smith..That in his forge smithed plough-harneys. **1484** CAXTON *Fables of Æsop* III. xii, A serpent entyrd som tyme within the forge of a smythe. *a* **1547** SURREY *Descr. Fickle Affect.* 24 The hammer of the restlesse forge. **1689** *Lond. Gaz.* No. 2482/1 In the meantime the Enemies Vanguard attack'd the Village Forge. **1712** POPE *Statius* 309 The o'er-labour'd Cyclop from his task retires, The Aeolian Forge exhausted of its Fires. **1861** DICKENS *Gt. Expect.* v, Joe had got..his leather apron on, and passed into the forge.

transf. and *fig.* *a* **1536** *Beauty & Prop. Women* C j, Rather than to be made in natures forge An angell thou wouldist iudge him, I make auow. **1658** T. WALL *Charact. Enemies Ch.* 45 The Forge of their own fancies. **1697** COLLIER *Ess. Mor. Subj.* II. (1703) 78 The brain..is the forge in which all the speculations of the understanding..are hammered-out. **1880** *Victorian Rev.* I. 545 England..became..the great forge and factory of the world.

3. An apparatus consisting of an open hearth or fireplace with a bellows attached, used by blacksmiths for heating iron to render it malleable; a similar apparatus on wheels for military use.

1481–90 *Howard Househ. Bks.* (Roxb.) 381 For makenge of the belowes to the forge. **1549** *Privy Council Acts* II. 349/2 Smithes forges complet, ij. **1667** MILTON *P.L.* XI. 564 At the forge Labouring. **1753** DODSLEY *Pub. Virtue, Agric.* I. iii. 164 A ponderous lump..to the hammer tam'd, Takes from the forge, in bars, its final form. **1810** C. JAMES *Milit. Dict.* (ed. 3) s.v., The cavalry have portable forges as well as the artillery. **1839** LONGF. *Village Blacksmith*, They love to see the flaming forge.

transf. and *fig.* **1577** FENTON *Gold. Epist.* (1582) 106 The hearte being the forge whereon our wicked plottes are wrought. **1598** SHAKS. *Merry W.* IV. ii. 239 Come to the Forge with it, then shape it: I would not haue things coole. **1654** GAYTON *Pleas. Notes* IV. v. 198 They..out of their own sparkling forges have found delight and pleasance for the whole time of their stay. **1791** BURKE *Let. Member Nat. Assembly* Wks. VI. 14 All black with the smoke and soot of the forge of confiscation and robbery. *a* **1839** PRAED *Poems* (1864) II. 130 In laboured phrase and polished lie Wrought by the forge of flattery.

4. A hearth or furnace for melting or refining metals. Also, the workshop, etc., where this work is carried on.

1601 HOLLAND *Pliny* VII. lvi. 188 The forges and furnaces of brasse. **1674** MARTINIERE tr. *Voy. N. Countries* 9 The Forges which are..much of the same nature with the Copper Forges..some separating, some washing, some melting, others refining, and others coining, for..his Majesty. **1796** MORSE *Amer. Geog.* I. 591 Forges to refine pig-iron into bars. **1839** URE *Dict. Arts, Forge*..the great workshop where iron is made malleable..a shingling mill. **1874** KNIGHT *Dict. Mech., Forge*..3 a place where iron is puddled and shingled.

5. In market reports, short for *forge iron*.

1890 *Daily News* 10 Jan. 3/7 Staffordshire forge ranged from 65*s.* to 70*s.*

6. *attrib.* and *Comb.* **a.** simple attributive, (of or pertaining to the forge), as ***forge-bellows***, ***-coal***, ***-furnace***, ***-hammer***, ***-hearth***, ***-house***, ***-iron***, ***-master***, ***-smith***, ***-tongs***.

1855 LARDNER *Hand-bk. Nat. Phil., Hydrost.*, etc. 211 The *forge-bellows. **1892** *Daily News* 5 Sept. 7/1 For good *forge coal from 9*s.* to 10*s.* is asked. **1858** SIMMONDS *Dict. Trade*, **Forge Furnace*, a blacksmith's open furnace. **1815** J. SMITH *Panorama Sc. & Art* I. 13 The *forge hammer, invented by George Walby of London. **1583** STANYHURST *Æneis* VIII. (Arb.) 137 His hoate *fordgharth. **1633** W. STRUTHER in Spurgeon *Treas. Dav.* Ps. cxix. 168 A furnace and *forge-house for evil. **1884** *Imp. & Mach. Rev.* 1 Dec. 6733/1 *Forge iron of North of England brands. *a* **1628** F. GREVILLE *Of Warres* xii. Wks. (Grosart) II. 107 These *forge-masters of our woes. **1886** J. GILLOW *Lit. & Biog. Hist. Eng. Catholics* II. 402 A labouring *forge-smith. **1851** D. WILSON *Preh. Ann.* (1863) II. 84 The rude pair of iron *forge-tongs.

b. Special comb., as **forge-cart** (*Mil.*), a travelling forge for service in the field; **forge-cinder** (see quot.); **forge-fire**, (*a*) a smith's fire; (*b*) a puddling furnace; **forge-man**, a forger or smith; *spec.* (see quot. 1858); **forge-master**, one having charge or ownership of a forge; also *fig.*; **forge-mill** (see quot.); **forge-pig**, a pig of forge-iron, also *collect.*; **forge-roll** (see quot.); **forge-roller**, a workman in a rolling mill (?); **forge-scale** = *hammer-scale* (HAMMER *sb.*[1] 7); **forge-wagon** = *forge-cart*; **forge-water**, water in which heated irons have been dipped, formerly in popular use as a medicine.

1810 WELLINGTON 25 July in Gurw. *Desp.* VI. 292 The *forge carts of the Royal Dragoons. **1881** RAYMOND *Mining Gloss.*, **Forge-cinder*, the slag from a forge or bloomary. **1855** KINGSLEY *Heroes, Argon.* IV. 126 The *forge-fires shone like sparks through the darkness. **1888** *Lockwood's Dict. Mech. Engin., Forge Fire*..a puddling furnace. **1621** BURTON *Anat. Mel.* Democr. to Rdr. (1657) 63 Smiths, *Forge-men, Brewers, Bakers, Metal-men. **1858** SIMMONDS *Dict. Trade, Forge-man*, a superior class of coach-smith, having a hammer-man under him. *a* **1628** *Forge-master [see FORGE *sb.* 6 a]. **1814** M. BIRKBECK *Journey through France* 71 The sale of the ore to the forge-masters. **1959** *Times Rev. Industry* July 75/2 Wire-drawers, forgemasters and other consumers of semi-finished steel products. **1969** *Daily Tel.* 24 Jan. 4/6 Crankshaft makers and forgemasters. **1738** CHAMBERS *Cycl.* s.v. *Mill*, 6 *Forge-Mills turned by water serve to raise and let fall one or more huge hammers. **1839** URE *Dict. Arts* 719 The average quantity of fine metal obtainable from the *forge-pigs. **1892** *Daily News* 29 July 2/4 Northampton forge pig is 43*s.* 6*d.* **1874** KNIGHT *Dict. Mech.*, **Forge-rolls*, the train of rolls by which the slab or bloom in converted into puddled bars. **1885** *Instr. to Census Clerks* 92 [Workmen engaged in] Wrought Iron Manufacture..*Forge Roller. **1883** *Specif. Alnwick & Cornhill Rlwy.* 9 To substitute a portion of *forge scales or cinders. **1940** *Chamber's Techn. Dict.* 349/1 *Forge scale*, the iron oxide coating which forms on iron and steel during forging. **1810** C. JAMES *Milit. Dict.* (ed. 3) s.v. *Cart*, *Forge-Wagons are travelling machines fitted up for the purpose of assisting the artillery in the field, and in repairing or replacing any iron work. **1725** BRADLEY *Fam. Dict.* s.v. *Turkey*, Let em Drink *Forge Water. **1798** W. BLAIR *Soldier's Friend* 23 Half a pint of strong forge-water.

forge (fɔədʒ), *v.*[1] Also 5 forgyn, 5, 7 fourge, 6 fordge, furge. [ad. OF. *forgier* (Fr. *forger*):—L. *fabricāre*: see FABRICATE.]

1. *trans.* To make, fashion, frame, or construct (any material thing); = FABRICATE *v.* 1. *Obs.* exc. as coincident with *transf.* use of 2. ***to forge together***: to frame together, weld.

a **1300** *Cursor M.* 28395 (Cott.) A-mang myn oþer wark vn-lele haf i oft forged fals sele. **1382** WYCLIF *Exod.* iv. 11 Who forgide the dowmbe and the deef, the seer and the blynde? **1390** GOWER *Conf.* III. 67 Of wexe he forged an ymage. *a* **1450** *Le Morte Arth.* 967 There myght none feyrer sayle on flode, Ne better forgid as of tree. *c* **1475** *Partenay* 6103 So by hym was made and furged again Off Maillers the church. **1578** BANISTER *Hist. Man* I. 9 This same bone.. seemeth to be forged with fiue sides. **1624** HEYWOOD *Gunaik.* I. 17 The image of Victorie most curiouslie forged. **1812** H. & J. SMITH *Rej. Addr.* 3 Forging for this isle a yoke.

2. To shape by heating in a forge and hammering; to beat into shape; †to coin (money). Also with *out*.

13.. *E.E. Allit. P.* B. 343 Hit watz fettled & forged & to þe fulle grayþed. *c* **1477** CAXTON *Jason* 72 b, After thys was ordeyned that ther sholde be forgid moneye in the cite. *a* **1533** LD. BERNERS *Huon* xliv. 148 Cursyd be he of Mahunde that forgyd thy sword. **1568** GRAFTON *Chron.* II. 364 They forge in Fraunce newe Floreyns wherewith ye shall be payde. **1703** MOXON *Mech. Exerc.* 28 The Key-hole being finished, forge your Key. **1782** COWPER *Charity* 237 Sin forged, and ignorance made fast, the chain. **1845** JAMES *A. Neil* ii, Did you ever see a blacksmith forge a horse-shoe? *fig.* **1601** BP. W. BARLOW *Serm. Paules Crosse* 39 An opinion forged at the fire of hell. **1682** SIR T. BROWNE *Chr. Mor.* II. §2 If the substantial subject be well forged out, we need not examine the sparks which irregularly fly from it. **1853** C. BRONTË *Villette* xxxvi, Out of men's afflictions and affections were forged the rivets of their servitude.

b. *absol.* or *intr.* To work at the forge; to do smith's work.

1382 WYCLIF *Ps.* cxxviii[ix]. 3 Vpon my bac forgeden [*fabricaverunt*] synneres. *c* **1386** CHAUCER *Pars. T.* ¶480 In this forseyde develes fourneys ther forgen three shrewes. **14..** LYDG. & BURGH *Secrees* 2135 Hym to Enfoorme.. Why his sone.. Sauf oonly to forge wolde take noon informacion. **1605** VERSTEGAN *Dec. Intell.* ix. 310 The Smith, that forgeth at the fire. **1770** J. CLUBBE *Physiogn.* 43 They can saw, but not plane; they can forge, but not polish.

†**c.** ***to forge and file***: to bring into shape, fashion completely, make ready. *Obs.*

c **1381** CHAUCER *Parl. Foules* 212 Besyde a welle I say Cupyde our lord his arwes forge and fyle. **1447** BOKENHAM *Seyntys* (Roxb.) 13 If the crafth of descrypcyoun I cowde.. bothe forge and fyle. **1626** T. H. *Caussin's Holy Crt.* 424 It was in her shop, where all these Councells plotted for his ruine, were forged, and fyled.

†**3.** To frame or fashion (something immaterial); to contrive, devise, invent. *Obs.* exc. as in 4.

c **1400** *Destr. Troy* 12551, I will tell how.. fortune, full fell, forget þere end. *c* **1430** LYDG. *Bochas* VI. i. (1554) 145 b, Like your conceites ye forge me and peint. **1562** WINȜET *Bk.* 83 *Quest.* To Chr. Rdr., Wks. (1887–8) I. 52 Forgeing thair sermonis for the plesuir of euery auditour.

†**b.** To invent, 'coin' (a word, etc.). *Obs.*

1549 COVERDALE, etc. *Erasm. Par. 1 Cor.* i. 13 Why then forge ye to your selfes any other name. **1571** DIGGES *Pantom.* III. Introd. Q, To forge newe English wordes. **1605** CAMDEN *Rem.* (1637) 78 Some thinke it to be no ancient name, but forged by the writer of King Arthurs historie. **1690** LOCKE *Hum. Underst.* III. viii. 230 Those few [names] that the Schools forged, and put into the mouths of their Scholars, could never yet get admittance into common use.

4. *esp.* To fabricate, frame, invent (a false or imaginary story, lie, etc.); to devise (evil). Also, to pretend (something) to have happened, to fable.

c **1386** CHAUCER *Pars. T.* ¶536 In which delit they wol forge a long tale. *c* **1440** *Partonope* 4459 Anon she forged a fayre lesyng. **1545** BRINKLOW *Compl.* 24 b, Then the matter was forged that he hangyd hymselfe. **1547** *Homilies* I. *Falling fr. God* I. (1859) 82 Let no man forge evil in his heart against his brother. **1648** JOS. BEAUMONT *Psyche* XV. cxli, How fine a story they can forge and fashion Of no Materials but Imagination! **1752** FIELDING *Amelia* II. ii, I.. forged a meeting to have been between me and my imaginary mistress. **1794** GODWIN *Cal. Williams* 289 Who had forged the basest and most atrocious falsehoods. **1859** KINGSLEY *Misc.* (1860) I. 77 A charge.. forged by that villain. **1876** E. MELLOR *Priesth.* vii. 334 Ever listening for words which they could forge into accusations. **1887** STEVENSON *Mem. & Portraits* vii. 110 The hope was one of those that childhood forges for a pastime.

absol. **1580** LYLY *Euphues* (Arb.) 298 A gentleman.. whose name I will not conceale, least thou shouldest.. thinke me to forge. **1610** A. COOKE *Pope Joan* in *Harl. Misc.* IV. 10 They are driven to feign, to forge, to cog.

5. To make (something) in fraudulent imitation of something else; to make or devise (something spurious) in order to pass it off as genuine.

c **1330** R. BRUNNE *Chron.* (1810) 155 Þat was a fals brefe, & forged wele. **1494** FABYAN *Chron.* v. cxxiii. 100 He then vsyd gyle.. and deuysed or forged certeyn letters in the name of Brunechieldys. **1552** HULOET, Forge or falsifie a writinge as chartre, dede, or testament. **1605** *Lond. Prodigal* III. iii, You forg'd a will. **1635** PAGITT *Christianogr.* III. (1636) 94 Many of these their Reliques were forged. **1712** STEELE *Spect.* No. 264 ¶3 He has carried his Skill in Imitation so far, as to have forged a Letter from my Friend Sir Roger. **1741** MIDDLETON *Cicero* (1742) III. xi. 241 Nothing was more common, than to have sayings forged for his. **1845** S. AUSTIN *Ranke's Hist. Ref.* III. ii. 47 Elector Joachim demanded.. that the name of the liar who had forged this treaty should be published. **1891** E. PEACOCK *N. Brendon* I. 81 Forge a pedigree if you haven't one.

b. To imitate fraudulently; to counterfeit.

1535 *Act 27 Hen. VIII*, c. 2 If anie person.. falsely forge and counterfaite the kinges signe manuel. **1677** WOOD *Life* (Oxf. Hist. Soc.) II. 392 Frankland.. had forged the University seal. **1887** R. BUCHANAN *Heir of Linne* v, As if I had.. forged the laird's name.

6. *intr.* To commit forgery.

1591 SHAKS. *1 Hen. VI*, III. i. 12 Thinke not.. that I haue forg'd or am not able *Verbatim* to rehearse the Methode of my Penne. **1738** POPE *Epil. Sat.* II. 190 But Pens can forge, my Friend, that cannot write. **1855** MACAULAY *Hist. Eng.* IV. 245 He wandered.. about Ireland.. begging, stealing, cheating, personating, forging. **1885** TENNYSON *Despair* xii, One son had forged on his father and fled.

forge (fɔədʒ), *v.*[2] [Of unknown origin; it has been conjectured to be a mispronunc. of FORCE (cf. *dispoge* for dispose), or a transferred use of FORGE *v.*[1], with allusion to the effect of repeated blows of a sledge hammer.]

1. *intr.* Of a vessel: To make way, 'shoot ahead' (Adm. Smyth), *esp.* by mere momentum, or the pressure of tide. Often with *ahead*; also with *along*, *off*, *on*; and with cognate obj.

The first quot. seems, from the elaborate nautical imagery of the context, to be a fig. example of this sense, though so much earlier than any other known instance.

[**1611** SPEED *Hist. Gt. Brit.* IX. xix. 715 For albeit the Barke of his begunne adventures had without perill well passed the straightes.. he feared the gust of every wind.. His inward study therefore still forged.. to cleave his passage by taking those dangerous lets away.] **1769** FALCONER *Dict. Marine* (1789), *Franchir une roche*, to pass over, or forge off from a rock. **1779** FORREST *Voy. N. Guinea* 23 As she forged on without any sail. **1830** MARRYAT *King's Own* xvi, The latter [frigate].. continued to forge in-shore. **1833** —— *P. Simple* xxxv, The four-decker forged ahead. **1849** DE QUINCEY *Eng. Mail-coach, Dream-fugue* Wks. IV. 344 Off she forged without a shock. **1886** J. H. MCCARTHY *Doom* 20 As the Atlantis slowly forged her way out to sea.

transf. and *fig.* **1861** *Sat. Rev.* 14 Sept. 280 Presently he drops behind, and I take advantage of the lull in the tempest to forge ahead. **1887** *Pall Mall G.* 2 Feb. 11/1 Canada is 'forging ahead', as they say in the North. **1887** JESSOPP *Arcady* viii. 223 The artizan who forges ahead.. is.. in ninety-nine cases out of a hundred a born townsman. **1893** F. HALL in *Academy* 25 March 266/3 No good reason is obvious why our little Tellus, though ever so crank, should not forge along till the year 2000.

2. *trans.* (See quot.)

1815 *Falconer's Dict. Marine* (ed. Burney), *To Forge over* is to force a ship violently over a shoal by the effort of a great quantity of sail.

forge (fɔədʒ), *v.*[3] [? From FORGE *v.*[1] 2, with ref. to the sound.] *intr.* Of a horse: = CLICK *v.*

1831 [see CLICKING *vbl. sb.* b].

forgeable (ˈfɔədʒəb(ə)l), *a.* [f. FORGE *v.*[1] + -ABLE.] That may be forged, admitting of forging.

1382 WYCLIF *Bible* Pref. Ep vi. 67 Forgers treten forgeable thingis. **1869** G. DODD *Dict. Manuf., etc.* s.v. *Iron*, Ductile, moderately forgeable and weldable. **1878** *Ure's Dict. Arts* IV. 551 At a red heat it was easily forgeable.

Hence **forgeaˈbility**.

1878 *Ure's Dict. Arts* IV. 552 Carbon affects the forgeability of steel more than silicon.

forged (fɔədʒd), *ppl. a.* Also 4 i-forged. [f. FORGE *v.* + -ED[1].] In senses of the vb.

†**1. a.** Fashioned, framed. In quot. 1382 *alle forgid trees* = all kinds of wooden instruments. *Obs.*

1382 WYCLIF *2 Sam.* vi. 5 Dauid and al Yrael pleiden before the Lord, in alle forgid trees, and harpis.

2. Fashioned at the forge. †Of money: Coined.

c **1386** CHAUCER *Miller's T.* 70 Full brighter was the shynyng of hir hewe, Than in the tour the noble yforged newe. **1621** G. SANDYS *Ovid's Met.* v. 13 Nor shall thy wings, nor Jove in forged gold, Work thy escape. **1679** *Essex Papers* (Camden) I. 235 Soe that it may be.. wrought as forged Iron is. *a* **1839** PRAED *Poems* (1864) I. 259 Whose broken chain Than new forged bonds is far more dear. **1881** *Daily News* 11 Aug. 1/6 The 'Standard' Forged Horse Nails.

†**3.** Fabricated, 'got up', 'made up', invented.

14.. LYDG. *Secrees* 75 That double of tonge hatyd adulacyon, ffals Repoort.. fforgyd talys with oute sekirnesse. **1583** GREENE *Mamillia* Wks. (Grosart) II. 183 His fained faith and forged flatterie. **1615** G. SANDYS *Trav.* 135 The Priests.. by diuulging forged miracles, increased the number of her Votaries. *a* **1639** SPOTTISWOOD *Hist. Ch. Scot.* (1655) 37 Upon a forged quarrell. **1671** J. WEBSTER *Metallogr.* i. 11 The learning attributed to Hermes Trismegist, is but of late years standing, and both the Author and it but forged and feigned.

4. Made in fraudulent imitation of something genuine; counterfeit, false, spurious.

1484 *Certificate* in *Surtees Misc.* (1890) 42 A forget testimonyall. **1509** *Act 1 Hen. VIII*, c. 7 Many.. forged informacions. **1561** T. NORTON *Calvin's Inst.* I. 38 This monstrous forged deuise. **1592** WARNER *Alb. Eng.* VII. xxxv. (1612) 168 Lambert the forged Yorkest. **1621** G. SANDYS *Ovid's Met.* IX. 75 What hope has thou, a forged Snake, to scape? **1628** COKE *On Litt.* lxxv. 172 This forged release. *a* **1641** BP. R. MOUNTAGU *Acts & Mon.* (1642) 169 Many forged and counterfait writings. **1817** *Parl. Debates* 716 A forged Bank of England note. **1858** GREENER *Gunnery* 246 Any such forged or counterfeit stamp. **1876** HUMPHREYS *Coin-Coll. Man.* xxvi. 404 Acquainted with the aspect of forged coins.

Hence †**ˈforgedly** *adv.*

1579 LYLY *Euphues* (Arb.) 91 If thou wast minded both falsely, and forgedly to deceive me. **1675** tr. *Camden's Hist. Eliz.* III. 355 That her Adversaries might easily.. write many things forgedly and falsly.

†**ˈforgeful**, *a. Obs.* [f. FORGE *v.* + -FUL.] Apt to forge, creative.

1751 STORMONT *Elegy Frederick Pr. Wales* 14 Th' illusive scenes That forgeful Fancy plan'd. **1814** CARY *Dante, Purg.* xxv. 63 For each limb Is in the heart by forgeful nature plann'd.

forgeless (ˈfɔədʒlɪs), *a.* [f. FORGE *sb.* + -LESS.] Without a forge.

1888 R. DOWLING *Miracle Gold* I. x. 196 This house of bankrupt and forgeless Vulcan.

†**forˈgender**, *v. Obs.* (Frequent in Trevisa.) *trans.* To disregard, neglect, slight.

1387 TREVISA *Higden* (Rolls) V. 221 Þe holy places of Godes were forgendred. *Ibid.* VI. 407 Þe Kentisshe men forgendrede þe kynges heste. *Ibid.* VI. 239 To forgendre what is detty and riȝtfull.

forger[1] (ˈfɔədʒə(r)). [f. FORGE *v.* + -ER[1].] One who forges, in senses of the vb.

1. A maker or framer (of something material or immaterial); an author or creator. Now only in bad sense, a fabricator, inventor (of false stories, etc.).

c **1380** WYCLIF *Serm.* Sel. Wks. II. 19 Joseph was a forgere of trees, þat is to seie a wriȝte. **1382** —— *Job* xiii. 4 Rathere shewende ȝou forgeris of lesingus. —— *Eccl.* xi. 5 God, that is forgere of alle thingus. *a* **1541** WYATT *Poet. Wks.* (1861) 81 Your fault is forger of this note. **1563** WINȜET *Vinc. Lirin.* Ded. Wks. (1887–8) II. 5 Al forgearis and manteaneris of schisme and errour. **1609** BIBLE (Douay) *Deut.* xiii. 5 That prophete or forger of dreames. **1747** WEST *Resurrection* 347 No Forger of Lies. **1805** WORDSW. *Prelude* v. 523 Forgers of daring tales.

2. One who forges (metal) or works at a forge; a smith; †a coiner (of money); also, an owner of forges or rolling mills.

1382 WYCLIF *Bible* Pref. Ep. vi. 67 Forgers treten forgeable thingis. **1424** *Paston Lett.* No. 4 I. 13 The forgeers and makers of the seyd billes. **1474** CAXTON *Chesse* III. ii. E vj b, Forgers and makers of money. **1491** —— *Vitas Patr.* (W. de W. 1495) 19 Saynt Appellen was a forgeur of yren. *a* **1605** MONTGOMERIE *Misc. Poems* xlii. 13 The forger when he feeds his fyre With sparks of water. *a* **1679** T. GOODWIN *Justif. Faith* I. vi. Wks. (1697) IV. 29 Thus God is the immediate Forger of every Linke of that golden Chain. **1827** HONE *Every-day Bk.* II. 879 The brawny forger. **1858** GREENER *Gunnery* 91 The inventors, forgers, and finishers of this great gun. **1884** *Manch. Exam.* 13 Sept. 4/7 A file forger. **1891** *Daily News* 26 Oct. 2/6 Forgers say that they could do much more work if it was forthcoming.

3. One who makes fraudulent imitations (of documents, coins, etc.); a counterfeiter.

1552 HULOET, Forger of dedes or wrytynges, *falsarius subiector.* **1565–73** COOPER *Thesaurus, Adulterator monetæ*.. a forgier or false coynar of mony. *a* **1680** BUTLER *Sat. Plagiaries* 12 Rem. 1749 I. 168 Mark them with characters and brands Like other forgers of men's hands. **1790** PALEY *Horæ Paul.* Rom. i. 11 The forger of the epistle.. inserted in it the passage upon which our observations are founded. **1791** BURKE *Let. Member Nat. Assembly* Wks. VI. 18 Forgers of paper currency. **1859** DICKENS *T. Two Cities* II. i, The forger was put to Death. **1875** JOWETT *Plato* (ed. 2) V. 22 Whether we can attribute the worst parts of a work to a forger and the best to a great writer.. depends.

†**ˈforger**[2]. *Law. Obs. rare*[−1]. [a. AF. *forger* = FORGE *v.*[1]; see -ER[4].] The action of forging. (Cowel 1607, and some later writers who quote the statute, have mistaken the word for prec. sb.)

1562 *Act 5 Eliz.* c. 14 §4 The Party.. grieved.. shall.. sue his Action of Forger of false Deeds upon this Statute. **1641** *Termes de la Ley* 164 b, Forger of false Deeds.. is used in our Law for the fraudulent making and publishing of false writings to the prejudice of another mans right.

†**ˈforgerer.** *Obs.* [f. FORGER[1] or FORGERY: see -ER[1] 3.] One who commits forgery, a forger.

1607 TOPSELL *Four-f. Beasts* 628 Forgerers and periured persons. **1696** PRIDEAUX *Lett.* (Camd.) 183 The forgerer was acquitted. **1765** *Chron.* in *Ann. Reg.* 58/2 The forgerer.. suffered.. the February following. **1826** BENTHAM in *Westm. Rev.* VI. 462 A forgerer is comparatively at his ease.

So †**ˈforgering** *ppl. a.*, practising forgery.

1618 BARNEVELT'S *Apol.* G iv, If these forgering fellows would manifest and discover themselues.

†**ˈforgeress.** *Obs.*[−1] [f. FORGER[1] + -ESS.] A female forger, fashioner, or maker.

c **1430** *Pilgr. Lyf Manhode* II. cxlviii. (1869) 134 Dame justice, the smythiere of vertues, and the forgeresse.

forgery (ˈfɔədʒərɪ). [f. FORGE *v.* + -ERY.]

†**1.** The action or craft of forging metal. *Obs.*

1609 BIBLE (Douay) *Hab.* ii. 18 Because the forger therof hath hoped in his forgerie, to make dumme idols. **1671** MILTON *Samson* 131 Useless the forgery Of brazen shield and spear.

b. *concr.* A piece of forged work. *rare.*

1850 BLACKIE *Æschylus* II. 184 On his shield, stout forgery of brass.. He shows.. The terrible Sphynx.

2. Invention, excogitation; fictitious invention, fiction. Now only *poet.* Formerly also with more reproachful sense: †Deception, lying; a fraudulent artifice, a deceit.

1583 STANYHURST Æneis II. (Arb.) 46 Hee fabled sundrye reportes, Mee to trap in matters of state, with forgerye knauish. 1593 SHAKS. 3 Hen. VI, III. iii. 175 To sooth your Forgery and his. 1599 —— Pass. Pilgr. 4 Vnskilful in the worlds false forgeries. 1602 —— Ham. IV. vii. 90 So farre he past my thought, That I in forgery of shapes and trickes, Come short of what he did. 1633 P. FLETCHER Poet. Misc. 61 My never-slak't desire Will cast to prove by welcome forgerie, That for my absence I am much the nigher. 1782 COWPER Retirement 323 [Speaking of insanity] 'Tis not, as heads that never ache suppose, Forgery of fancy, and a dream of woes.

3. The making of a thing in fraudulent imitation of something; also, *esp.* the forging, counterfeiting, or falsifying of a document. For the use in *Law* see quot. 1769.

1593 SHAKS. Lucr. 920 Guilty of treason, forgerie, and shift. 1605 ROWLANDS Hell's Broke Loose 5 Manes.. published a fift Gospell of his owne forgerie. 1696 PRIDEAUX Lett. (Camden) 169 Severall very notorious acts of forgery haveing been proved against Dean. 1741 MIDDLETON Cicero I. i. 40 The..art..of raising a kind of enthusiasm..in his army, by the forgery of auspices and divine admonitions. 1769 BLACKSTONE Comm. IV. 245 Forgery, or the crimen falsi..'the fraudulent making or alteration of a writing to the prejudice of another man's right.' 1853 C. BRONTE Villette xxxv, In their eyes..I write essays; and with deliberate forgery, sign to them my pupils' names. 1883 Contemp. Rev. Dec. 842 It was natural that literary forgery should thrive.

b. The fact of being forged. *rare.*

1665 J. SPENCER Disc. Vulg. Proph. 83 A sign of the forgery of the whole Prophecy. 1845 GRAVES Rom. Law in Encycl. Metrop. 756/1 The forgery of the Tabula Marliana is now generally admitted.

c. *concr.* Something forged, counterfeited, or fabricated; a spurious production.

1574 tr. Marlorat's Apocalips 25 Their wicked forgeries. 1641 MILTON Ch. Govt. II. iii. (1851) 157 A pure tyrannical forgery of the Prelats. 1781 GIBBON Decl. & F. II. 99 A manifest forgery was attested by a person of the most sacred character. 1833 HT. MARTINEAU Berkeley the Banker I. iv. 92 He told several people in confidence that forgeries of their notes were abroad. 1875 JOWETT Plato (ed. 2) V. 4 That.. one of the most excellent writings bearing the name of Plato should be a forgery..would be a singular phenomenon in ancient literature.

forget (fəˈgɛt), *sb.* Chiefly *colloq.* [f. next vb.] An act of forgetting; a lapse of memory.

1861 IVATTS Handbk. Railw. Station Managem. 27 Errors of Judgment and Casual Mistakes, including 'Forgets'. 1880 J. PAYN Confid. Agent I. 111, I thought you might have made a forget of it. 1885 T. MOZLEY Remin. Towns, etc. I. ix. 44, I was very liable to momentary forgets, transpositions and misplacings of words.

forget (fəˈgɛt), *v.* Pa. t. forgot (-ˈgɒt), *arch.* forgat (-ˈgæt). Pa. pple. forgotten, *arch.* and *poet.*, forgot (-ˈgɒt(ə)n, -ˈgɒt). For forms see GET. [OE. *forȝietan* str. vb. (*forȝeat, -ȝéatun, -ȝiten*) corresponding to OS. *far-getan* (Du. *vergeten*), OHG. *fargezan* (MHG. *vergezzen*, Ger. *vergessen*); f. OTeut. **getan* (see GET *v.*) in the sense 'to hold, grasp', the force of the prefix being that illustrated under FOR- *pref.*[1] 3. The etymological sense is thus 'to miss or lose one's hold'; but the physical application is not recorded in any Teut. lang.]

1. *trans.* To lose remembrance of; to cease to retain in one's memory. †Formerly sometimes with *out*. Often with clause as obj. Also *colloq.* in admonitory phrases. Phr. *forget it*: take no more notice of it, don't mention it.

c888 K. ÆLFRED Boeth. xlii, Næfre nauht he ne forgeat. c1050 Byrhtferth's Handboc in Anglia (1885) VIII. 326 Þæt þu neforgyte þæt ic þe nu secge. a1200 Moral Ode 98 Nabbeð hie no þing forȝieten of þat hie her iseien. c1300 Beket 1956 Here names for here schrewede ne beoth noȝt forȝute ut [MS. Laud 108 nout forȝite ȝuyt]. 1375 BARBOUR Bruce I. 16 Swa that na lenth of tyme it let Na ger it haly be forȝet. 1525 LD. BERNERS Froiss. II. lxii. [lxv.] 210 That I sholde forgete out ony thynge that I have knowen to be done. c1540 Howers of Blessed Virgin E. & L. 104 They shall Be registred so, they shall not be forgetten. c1676 LADY CHAWORTH in 12th Rep Hist. MSS. Com. App. v. 34 The D. of Monmouth Mr. Griffin and Mr. Godolphin and a fourth whose name I have forgot. 1757 WESLEY Wks. (1872) IX. 279 Have you forgot that every man is now born in as good a state as Adam was made at first? 1845 S. AUSTIN Ranke's Hist. Ref. I. 387 Frederic..did not forget his numerous wrongs and affronts. 1874 GREEN Short Hist. i. §1. 5 Men forgot how to fight for their Country when they forgot how to govern it. 1888 Detroit Free Press 6 Oct. (Farmer Amer.), You don't want to fool with those Quakers any, and don't you forget it. 1890 R. K. FOX Slang Dict. N.Y. 48 'And don't you forget it' [and other slang expressions] are all, or nearly all, Californianisms. 1903 R. L. MCCARDELL Conversat. Chorus Girl 91, I gave him the laugh, and said, 'Forget it!' 1909 E. C. HALL Aunt Jane of Kentucky ii. 32 He was the Rev. Lemuel Page, and don't you forgit it. 1915 Let. in C. Mackenzie My Life & Times (1966) V. 13 The next bloody army I join is the Salvation bloody army and don't you forget it. 1930 R. MACAULAY Staying with Relations xx. 302 Well, then, forget it... I sure don't want to wait any more. 1932 [see AW int.]. 1951 'A. GARVE' Murder in Moscow xxii. 181 'By the way, Jeff—thanks!' 'Forget it.' 1960 'W. HAGGARD' Closed Circuit ix. 111 'I hope I'm not interrupting you...' 'Forget it.' 1970 W. SMITH Gold Mine xxxi. 78 She was genuinely puzzled by the question... 'What's he got to do with it?' 'All right, forget it.'

Prov. c1530 R. HILLES Common-pl. Bk. (1858) 140 Seld sene sone forgotyn.

b. To fail to recall to mind; not to recollect.

1787 'GAMBADO' Acad. Horsemen (1809) 28 He says much the same of rabbits and onions, but I forgot [? *read* forget] how he brings that to bear. 1847 MARRYAT Childr. N. Forest xv, I forget the sign [of the inn].

c. const. *to* a person = as a matter of reproach against him. *rare.*

1822 T. MOORE Diary 31 Jan., The thing has never been forgotten to Etienne since.

d. *absol.* (or *intr.*) Also, *to forget about*: not to recall the facts concerning; not to remember to take action in the matter of (*colloq.*).

1382 WYCLIF Isa. xliv. 18 Thei forȝeeten, lest ther eȝen seeȝen, and lest thei vnderstoden in ther herte. c1435 Torr. Portugal 824 The kyng wold not foreget. 1592 SHAKS. Rom. & Jul. I. i. 243 Farewell thou can'st not teach me to forget. 1611 BIBLE Ps. x. 11 Hee hath said in his heart, God hath forgotten. a1839 PRAED Poems (1864) I. 363 He'll learn..To feign and to forget. 18.. TENNYSON Flight i, Are you sleeping? have you forgotten? 1897 N. GOULD Seeing him Through xix, He had forgotten about that, it was such a long time ago. a1915 R. BROOKE Mem. in Coll. Poems (1918) p. xxv, I often wonder whether I haven't written several of them myself under a pseudonym, and forgotten about it.

2. To omit or neglect through inadvertence. Chiefly with *infinitive* as obj. In poetry sometimes *fig.* of natural agents, etc.

c950 Lindisf. Gosp. Mark x. 21 An ðe is forgeten. c1000 Ags. Gosp. Matt. xvi. 5 Hiȝ forgeton þæt hiȝ hlafas namon. a1300 Cursor M. 1730 (Cott.) Þe folk to preche for-gate he noght. c1386 CHAUCER Prioress' T. 59 This widwe hir litel sone y-taught Our blisful lady..To worshipe ay, and he forgat it naught. c1420 Sir Amadace (Camden) xxviii, To sadulle his horse was noȝte forȝetun. 1548 HALL Chron., Edw. IV (an. 10) 216 God dyd neither forgeve nor forget to punishe the duke. 1697 DAMPIER Voy. I. xvi. 444, I quite forgot to put it into my Journal. 1710 POPE Windsor For. 353 The winds forgot to roar. 1718 ROWE tr. Lucan IX. 1389 Straight His Blood forgot to flow, his Heart to beat. 1842 TENNYSON Gardener's Dau. 85 The steer forgot to graze.

b. To omit to take, leave behind inadvertently.

a1300 Cursor M. 1690 (Cott.) Fouxul ne worme forget þou noght. Ibid. 3163 (Cott) Suerd and fire forgat he noght. 1535 COVERDALE Deut. xxiv. 19 Whan thou hast reaped downe thine haruest in the felde, and hast forgotten a shefe in the felde. 1596 SHAKS 1 Hen. IV, III. i. 6 Hotsp. A plague vpon it, I haue forgot the Mappe. Glend. No, here it is. 1768 GOLDSM. Good-n. Man IV. i, I had almost forgot the wedding ring! 1860 TYNDALL Glac. I. xi. 72 We had no candles, they had been forgotten.

†c. with complementary adj. or adv. *Obs.*

a1340 HAMPOLE Psalter vi. 6 Þat nane be forgetyn vnpunyst. c1400 Three Kings Cologne (1886) 127 Þes þinges oure lady forgat bihynde hir whan sche ȝede oute of þat plaas in to Egypte. 1513 DOUGLAS Æneis XI. xvi. 69 Hys feris all hes hym forȝet allane.

d. To omit to mention, leave unnoticed, pass over inadvertently.

1538 ELYOT, Prætermitto, to leue vntouched, to forgete, to leue oute. 1548 HALL Chron., Hen. V (an. 3) 49 b, I may not forget how the Frenche men..sent a herault. 1625 BACON Ess., Cunning (Arb.) 439 He would pass ouer that, that he intended most, and goe forth, and come backe againe, and speake of it, as of a Thing, that he had almost forgot. 1674 tr. Scheffer's Lapland 93, I had almost forgot Tobacco, of which they are very great admirers. 1775 S. J. PRATT Liberal Opin. (1783) III. 187 Pray don't forget me to your uncle. 1881 FREEMAN Subj. Venice 166 Not forgetting a gate which has been made out in the long walls.

3. To cease or omit to think of, let slip out of the mind, leave out of sight, take no note of.

c1000 Ags. Ps. (Th.) xii. 1 Hu lange wilt þu, Drihten, min forgitan. c1200 Vices & Virtues (1888) 7 Hie forȝiteð to swiðe hem seluen wið-innen. a1300 Floriz & Bl. 497 (Camb. MS.) Ne schal ihc neure forȝete þe. a1300 Cursor M. 20208 (Cott.) O þat bode forgat scho noght. 1382 WYCLIF Ps. cxviii[i]. 176 Thin hestis I haue not forȝeten. c1450 Bk. Curtasye 196 in Babees Bk. 305 Þou schalle neuer lose for to be kynde; That on forȝetis anoþer hase in mynde. 1593 SHAKS. 3 Hen. VI, IV. vii. 45. 1651 ISAACKSON in Fuller's Abel Rediv., Andrewes (1867) II. 168 He forgat not his patron, Dr. Watts, at his end. 1717 POPE Eloisa 208 The world forgetting, by the world forgot. 1797 NELSON Aug. in Nicolas Disp. (1845) II. 437, I shall not be surprised to be neglected and forgot, as probably I shall no longer be considered as useful. 1888 MISS BRADDON Fatal Three I. v. Are you forgetting luncheon?

b. used in connexion with *forgive*; also *absol.* passing into proverb.

a1225 Ancr. R. 124 Al þet hurt & al þet sore were uorȝiten & forȝiuen uor glednesse. 1421–2 HOCCLEVE Dialogus 672 Mochil thyng haast thow write, That they nat foryeue haue, ne foryite. 1576 FLEMING Panopl. Epist. 380 Hee did both forgive and forgett offences committed against his majestie. 1621 ELSING Debates Ho. Lords (Camden) 74, I am sorry for it: I praye forgive and forgett. 1775 SHERIDAN Rivals IV. ii, Come, come, Mrs. Malaprop, we must forget and forgive. 1841 TRENCH Parables xxiv. (1877) 411 Though God may forgive, man is not therefore to forget.

†c. To drop the practice of (a duty, virtue, etc.); to lose the use of (one's senses). ***to forget to do*** = to forget how to do (something). *Obs.*

13.. E.E. Allit. P. B. 203 He forȝet alle his fre þewes, And wex wod to þe wrache. c1385 CHAUCER L.G.W. 1752 Lucrece, Desire That in his herte brent as any fire So wodely that hys witte was foryeten. 1390 GOWER Conf. II. 20 So clene his wittes he foryete. 1590 SHAKS. Com. Err. III. ii. 1 And may it be that you haue quite forgot A husbands office? 1592 —— Ven. & Ad. 1061 Her joints forget to bow. 1670 MILTON Hist. Eng. II. 36 The terrour of such new and resolute opposition made them forget thir wonted valour.

4. In stronger sense: To neglect wilfully, take no thought of, disregard, overlook, slight.

1297 R. GLOUC. (1724) 445 He verȝet al þe strong oþ, þat he adde byuore To emperesse. 1340 HAMPOLE Pr. Consc. 2051 Whiles þai lyf þai have na mynde Of God, bot forgettes hym. c1380 WYCLIF Serm. Sel. Wks. I. 201 Þis lore is forȝete and þe fendis lore take. a1400–50 Alexander 3276 The gome þat hys god forgatt. 1571 BUCHANAN Ane Admonition Wks. (1892) 21 It may seame..that I..forȝettis my devoir. a1703 BURKITT On N.T. Jas. ii. 5 Men wallow in wealth, and forget God. 1797 MRS. RADCLIFFE Italian ii, Why should I be in danger of forgetting what is due to my father?

5. ***to forget oneself.*** **a.** To omit care for oneself. **b.** To lose remembrance of one's own station, position, or character; to lose sight of the requirements of dignity, propriety, or decorum; to behave unbecomingly. **†c.** To lose one's way. **d.** To lose consciousness.

a. a1200 Moral Ode 25 Þe þe him selfe forȝeit for wiue oðer for childe He sal cumen on euel stede. a1225 Leg. Kath. 1377 Feire is us ifallen: ah ȝet we forȝeoteð us.

b. 1593 SHAKS. Rich. II, III. ii. 83 Aum. Comfort, my liege; remember who you are. K. Rich. I had forgot myself: am I not king? a1627 MIDDLETON & ROWLEY Changeling III. iv, Push! you forget yourself; A woman dipp'd in blood, and talk of modesty! 1697 COLLIER Immor. Stage i. 4 Jacinta, Elvira, Dalinda..forget themselves extreamly: And almost all the Characters..are foul and nauseous. 1794 NELSON 29 July in Nicolas Disp. (1845) I. 462 These Agents forget themselves very much. 1856 READE Never too late xi, How is he to answer my question if he holds his tongue? you forget yourself. 1891 19th Cent. Dec. 856 When any speaker so far forgot himself as [etc.].

c. 1582 N. LICHEFIELD tr. Castanheda's Conq. E. Ind. xl. 93 b, The Captaine Generall..founde..missing one of his greate Shippes, in the which went Sancho..vnto whome it did well appeare, by reason it was night, that he had forgotten himselfe.

d. 1390 GOWER Conf. II. 21, I myself foryete, That I wot never, what I am, Ne whider I shall, ne whenne I cam. c1430 Syr. Gener. (Roxb.) 7561 Hir self she forgute, With-out spech stil she sute. 1717 POPE Eloisa 24 Though cold like you, unmov'd and silent grown, I have not yet forgot myself to stone. Mod. I was nearly asleep, I had just forgotten myself.

Hence **forˈgetter**, one who forgets.

1398 TREVISA Barth. De P.R. XII. vii. (1495) 417 The colouore is..foryeter of wronges. c1440 Promp. Parv. 174/1 Forȝetare [v.r. forgeter], immemor. 1613 BEAUM. & FL. Captain IV. iii, I think her A strange forgetter of herself. 1755 JOHNSON, Forgetter, a careless person. 1826 LAMB Elia Ser. II. Pop. Fallacies, We are not..so careless as that Imperial forgetter of his dreams. 1869 SPURGEON Treas. Dav. Ps. ix. 17 Forgetters of God.

forget, var. FORGETT.

†forˈgetel, *a.* *Obs.* Forms: 1 forȝyttol, 4 forgetel, -il, 4–5 foryetel(l, 5 forȝetylle, forgetyll. [OE. *forgytol, forȝeotul, forȝitel*, f. *forȝietan*: see FORGET *v.*; corresp. to Fris. *forgittel*, Du. *vergetel*, LG. *forgetel*.] Forgetful, forgetting.

c1000 ÆLFRIC Hom. II. 118 He..wæs forgyttol, ac ȝefæstnode his lare on fæsthafelum ȝemynde. a1340 HAMPOLE Psalter cxviii. 10 He þat sekis noght god in all his hert he is forgetil. 1390 GOWER Conf. III. 98 Foryetel, slow and wery sone Of every thing. 1430 LYDG. Chron. Troy IV. xxxv, As I were foryetell reckles To remember. c1440 Promp. Parv. 174/1 Forȝetylle..obliviosus.

Hence **†forˈgetelness, -ship**, forgetfulness. *Obs.*

a1000 Lamb. Ps. lxxxvii[i]. 12 (Bosw.) On lande forgytelnysse. c1200 Trin. Coll. Hom. 71 Ten þing ben þe letten men of here scrifte..forgetelnesse, nutelnesse [etc.]. a1300 E.E. Psalter cxxxvi[i]. 5 If I for-gete þe, Jerusalem land, To for-getelnesse given be mi right hand. c1330 R. BRUNNE Chron. (1810) 176 So did Kyng Philip with sautes on þam gan pres, Bot for a forgetilschip R. & he boþe les. c1386 CHAUCER Pars. T. ¶753 The fifthe is foryetelnesse by to muchel drynkynge. c1450 St. Cuthbert (Surtees) 2441 Þai knew þair forgetilnes.

forgetful (fəˈgɛtfʊl), *a.* [f. FORGET *v.* + -FUL.]

1. Apt, inclined, or liable to forget; having a bad memory. Also, that forgets: const. *of*.

1382 WYCLIF Jas. i. 25 Not maad a forȝetful herer, but a doer of werk. c1449 PECOCK Repr. II. v. 165 We ben ful freel and forȝeteful. 1509 FISHER Fun. Serm. C'tess Richmond Wks. (1876) 291 She wolde not be..forgetfull of ony kyndnes or seruyce done to her before. 1601 SHAKS. Jul. C. IV. iii. 255 Beare with me good Boy, I am much forgetfull. 1794 COLERIDGE Death of Chatterton 115 Wisely forgetful. 1860 TYNDALL Glac. I. xiv. 97 Forgetful of the glory of the past.

2. Heedless, neglectful. Const. *of* or inf.

1526–34 TINDALE Heb. xiii. 2 Be not forgetfull to lodge straungers. 1697 DRYDEN Virg. Georg. IV. 709 Th' unwary Lover cast his Eyes behind, Forgetful of the Law. 1720 PRIOR Horace I. ix. 16, I..intend To serve myself, forgetful of my Friend. 1859 TENNYSON Enid 53 Forgetful of his glory and his name.

3. That causes to forget, inducing oblivion. Chiefly *poet.* (Cf. *oblivious*.)

1557 Tottell's Misc. (Arb.) 271 Reason runnes about, To seke forgetfull water. 1667 MILTON P.L. II. 74 If the sleepy drench Of that forgetful Lake benumme not still. 1697 DRYDEN Æneid VI. 1017 Compell'd to drink the deep Lethean Flood, In large forgetful draughts. 1787 Generous Attachm. I. 157 The self same bed..once received an honoured parent..to its soft forgetful down. 1850 TENNYSON In Mem. xxxv, The sound of that forgetful shore.

Hence **forˈgetfully** *adv.*, in a forgetful manner.

a1716 SOUTH Serm. (1744) VIII. xiv. 416 It is our duty.. forgetfully, to accept the oppression. 1731 BOYSE From C. Dryden's Horti Arlingtoniani Poems 36 Through the Maze forgetfully they stray. 1859 CORNWALLIS New World I. 70 One of them having forgetfully left his umbrella behind him.

forgetfulness (fəˈgɛtfʊlnɪs). [f. prec. + -NESS.] The quality or state of being forgetful.

1. The quality of being apt to forget, the state of forgetting.

1477 EARL RIVERS (Caxton) *Dictes* 19 Establisshe & ease.. thy foryetfulnesse with thyn remembraunce. **1553** T. WILSON *Rhet.* III. 112 a, Where ouer much cold is..there is euer muche forgetfulnesse. **1699** BENTLEY *Phal.* 282 This.. he did not do out of design, but pure forgetfullness. **1725** POPE *Odyss.* XII. 366 Each in slumber shares A sweet forgetfulness of human cares. **1783** HAILES *Antiq. Chr. Ch.* iv. 81 *note*, Such was..the constitutional forgetfulness of Claudius. **1838** DICKENS *Nich. Nick.* xxx, He smiled upon all present in happy forgetfulness of having exhibited symptoms of pugnacity.

2. The condition of forgetting or losing recollection of everything.

1398 TREVISA *Barth. De P.R.* XIII. i. (1495) 440 In Boecia ben two welles, that one makith good mynde, and that other makyth foryetfulnesse. **14..** *Epiph.* in *Tundale's Vis.* 116 Euer with deth cometh forgetfulnes. **1597** SHAKS. *2 Hen. IV*, III. i. 8 O gentle Sleepe..thou no more wilt weigh my eye-lids downe And steepe my Sences in Forgetfulnesse.

3. The state of being forgotten, oblivion. ? *Obs.*

1561 T. NORTON *Calvin's Inst.* IV. xviii. (1634) 704 This Masse..shamefully..putteth his death in forgetfulnesse. **1663** CHARLETON *Chor. Gigant.* 5 Monuments themselves are subject to Forgetfulness even while they remain. **1779–81** JOHNSON *L.P.*, *Mallet*, [His] Amyntor and Theodora..is now lost in forgetfulness. **1829** LYTTON *Devereux* I. xiv, The forgetfulness of one buried is nothing to the forgetfulness of one disgraced.

4. Disregard, inattention, neglect.

1576 FLEMING *Panopl. Epist.* 272 It doeth kindle in his mynde, forgetfulnesse of himselfe. **1757** JOHNSON *Rambler* No. 180 ¶5 He..naturally sinks from omission to forgetfulness of social duties. **1875** JOWETT *Plato* (ed. 2) V. 211 Victory sometimes produces forgetfulness of education.

forgetive (ˈfɔədʒɪtɪv), *a.* [? f. FORGE *v.*[1] + -TIVE.] A Shaksperian word, of uncertain formation and meaning. Commonly taken as a derivative of FORGE *v.*[1], and hence used by writers of the 19th c. for: Apt at 'forging', inventive, creative.

1597 SHAKS. *2 Hen. IV*, IV. iii. 107 A good Sherris-Sack.. makes it [the braine] apprehensiue, quicke, forgetiue, full of nimble, fierie, and delectable shapes. **1800** MALONE *Life Dryden* Pr. Wks. I. I. 382 Corinna's forgetive imagination. **1814** CARY *Dante, Purg.* XVII. 14 O quick and forgetive power! that sometimes dost So rob us of ourselves. **1871** M. COLLINS *Mrq. & Merch.* I. iv. 127 Her temperament.. strangely quick, sensitive, apprehensive, forgetive.

forˈget-me-ˌnot. [In sense 1, a translation of the OF. name *ne m'oubliez mye*, whence late MHG. *vergiz mîn niht* (mod.Ger. *vergisz mein nicht*), Sw. *förgäta mig ej*. In the 15th c. the flower was supposed to have the virtue of ensuring that those wearing it should never be forgotten by their lovers. (See quots. in Grimm *Wb.* s.v.) The application of the name to the ground-pine (sense 3) is app. exclusively Eng.; whether this plant was credited with the same magical properties as its namesake, or whether it was named 'on account of the nauseous taste that it leaves in the mouth' (Prior) is not ascertained.]

1. a. The name of various kinds of *Myosotis*, esp. *M. palustris*, a plant which flourishes in damp or wet soil, having bright blue flowers with a yellow eye. Also applied to the closely resembling species, *M. azorica*, *M. arvensis*, and others.

c **1532** DEWES *Introd. Fr.* in *Palsgr.* 1024 A flour of forget me nat, *une fleur de ne moubliez mye.* **1817** COLERIDGE *Sibyll Leaves, Keep-sake* 13 Hope's gentle gem, the sweet Forget-me-not. **1833** TENNYSON *Poems* 46 Eyes..Blue as the blue forget-me-not. **1840** AGNES STRICKLAND *Queens Eng.* III. 84 This royal adventurer..Lancaster, appears to have been the person who gave to the *myosotis arvensis*, or, 'forget-me-not', its emblematic and poetic meaning. **1880** OUIDA *Moths* III. 216 He laid on her knee some forget-me-nots.

b. Applied with qualifying words to other varieties of *Myosotis* (see quots.).

1865 GOSSE *Land & Sea* (1874) 235 The early scorpiongrass or hill forget-me-not. **1867** SOWERBY *Eng. Bot.* VII. 102 Alpine Forget-me-not, *M. alpestris. Ibid.*, Creeping water Forget-me-not, *M. repens. Ibid.* 106 Dwarf Forget-me-not, *M. collina. Ibid.* 104 Wood Forget-me-not, *M. sylvatica. Ibid.* 108 Yellow and blue Forget-me-not, *M. versicolor.*

2. The Germander Speedwell (*Veronica Chamædrys*). [So also in German writers of 15–16th c.]

1853 G. JOHNSTON *Nat. Hist. E. Bord.* I. 151 *Veronica chamædrys*..often miscalled the Forget-me-not.

†**3.** The Ground Pine (*Ajuga Chamæpitys*).

1578 LYTE *Dodoens* I. xviii. 28 Of Ground Pyne..There be three sortes..called..in English also Chamæpitys, Ground Pyne, Herbe Iue, Forget me not. **1597** GERARDE *Herbal* II. cxlii. §3. 422 Ground Pine is called in English herbe Iuie, Forget me not.

4. *attrib.* and *Comb.*, as ***forget-me-not blue***, ***brooch***, ***eyes***, ***ring***; ***forget-me-not-hued*** adj.; also *ellipt.* for *forget-me-not brooch* or *ring*.

1836 DICKENS *Sk. Boz* II. 154 A small gold chain and a 'Forget me not' ring, the girl's property. **1844** C. M. YONGE *Abbeychurch* vi. 118 Jane gave me the pretty forget-me-not brooch I wore yesterday. **1854** —— *Heartsease* I. I. v. 85 There—that forget-me-not—the first ring I ever had. **1863** A. D. WHITNEY *Faith Gartney* xx. 131 There was the forget-me-not ring lying in her box of ornaments. *Ibid.* xxiv. 170 You must wear this, now, and keep the forget-me-not for a guard. *a* **1877** OUIDA *Tricotrin* I. 522 The treacherous.. glitter in her forget-me-not-hued eyes. **1887** J. A. STERRY *Lazy Minstr.* (1892) 148 A smart little crew..In ivory-white and forget-me-not blue. *Ibid.* 174 This sweet little lass, Raises two Forget-me-not eyes. **1894** *Daily News* 22 June 6/6 Dressed in forget-me-not blue chené silk.

forgetness (fəˈgɛtnɪs). *rare.* [f. FORGET *v.* + -NESS.] Forgetfulness.

1474 CAXTON *Chesse* III. vi. H iij b, The vice of glotonye prouoketh lecherye; wherof cometh forgetenes of his mynde. **1892** *Daily News* 11 Oct. 4/7 It is easier to imagine the disappearance of Westminster Abbey from the face of the earth, the forgetness that such a place ever existed among men, than, etc.

forget(t) (ˈfɔːdʒɪt). *Glove-making.* Also 7 forchet, (forge), 9 forchette, forget(te, forgit. [originally *forchet*, a. F. *fourchette* of same meaning, lit. 'fork'.]

(See quots.)

1681 *Min. Glover Incorp. Perth* in Beck *Gloves* (1883) 153 That no Gloves be made with tard forchets but allenerly with Cliven forchets. **1688** R. HOLME *Armoury* III. 18/1 The Forges, the peeces between the Fingers. **1862** MRS. H. WOOD *Mrs. Hallib.* I. xxiii. (1864) 125 The long strips, running up inside the fingers, are the forgits. **1886** [see FOURCHETTE 1 d]. **1891** *19th Cent.* No. 178. 939 The pieces for the thumbs, and the forgets—*i.e.* the little side pieces for the fingers. **1921** *Dict. Occup. Terms* (1927) §429 Side pieces for fingers of glove (called fourchettes or forgets).

forgettable (fəˈgɛtəb(ə)l), *a.* [f. FORGET *v.* + -ABLE.] That may be forgotten.

1845 CARLYLE *Cromwell* (1871) I. 55 Indistinct and instantly forgettable particulars. **1868** M. PATTISON *Academ. Org.* v. 184 Wasting six months in cramming up a minimum of forgetable matter.

forgetting (fəˈgɛtɪŋ), *vbl. sb.* [f. FORGET *v.* + -ING[1].]

1. The action of the vb. FORGET; also, †the state of being unconscious, oblivion.

1340 *Ayenb.* 18 Ingratitude, þet is, uoryeti[n]ge of god and of his guodes. **1398** TREVISA *Barth. De P.R.* XVII. clxxxiv. (1495) 724 Wyne bredyth in the soule foryetynge of anguyssh. *c* **1440** *Jacob's Well* (E.E.T.S.) 109 Fforgetyng makyth a man in his schryfte to forȝete boþe smale synnes & grete. **1538** ELYOT *Dict.*, *Prætermissio*, forgetynge, or leuinge out of a thynge. **1614** W. BARCLAY *Nepenthes* in Jas. I *Counterbl.* (Arb.) 116 It maketh and induceth..the forgetting of all sorrowes and miseries. **1643** MILTON *Divorce* II. xxii. (1851) 128, I am not willing to discover the forgettings of reverend men. **1803–6** WORDSW. *Intim. Immort.* v, Our birth is but a sleep and a forgetting.

†**2.** The state of being forgotten, oblivion. *Obs.*

a **1050** *Liber Scintill.* lvi. (1889) 174 Heo na byð on forgytincge [*oblivione*]. *a* **1340** HAMPOLE *Psalter* Cant. 498 þou gaf til forgetynge all my synnys. *c* **1449** PECOCK *Repr.* II. xv. 236 That thilk mynde die not and falle not into forȝeting. **1583** GOLDING *Calvin on Deut.* i. 4 God had..prouided to preserue it from forgetting.

forgetting (fəˈgɛtɪŋ), *ppl. a. rare.* [see + -ING[2].] That forgets, forgetful.

1847 EMERSON *Poems, Uriel*, A forgetting wind Stole over the celestial kind. **1855** in CLARKE *Dict.*

Hence **forˈgettingly** *adv.*, in a forgetful manner; forgetfully; through forgetfulness.

1605 B. JONSON *Volpone* IV. vi, I fear I haue (forgettingly) transgrest Against the dignity of the Court. **1650** HALL *Grounds Monarchy* in Harrington *Oceana* (1700) 14 Which ..partly in this penury of Books, forgettingly I pass.

†**forˈgettingness.** *Obs. rare.* [f. as prec. + -NESS.] Forgetfulness.

1387 TREVISA *Higden* (Rolls) I. 5 Forȝetingnes all wey kypinge þe craft of a stepdamme, he is enmy of mynde. *Ibid.* II. 323 Moyses..made tweie rynges, oon of mynde and anoþer of forȝetyngnesse.

†**forˈgift.** *Obs.* Forms: 4 forȝefthe, -ȝyft, 4–5 -gyft, (5 -yifte). [f. FORGIVE *v.* after GIFT.] Forgiveness.

c **1315** SHOREHAM 40 Two thynges her wythynne beth Forȝefthe and repentynge. *c* **1380** *Sir Ferumb.* 5736 þou most byleue on holychurche..And on for-ȝyft of synne. **1532** *Wedn. Faste* (W. de W.), Kynge Davyd fasted for mercy! Nineve dyd ye same And had forgyft of synne.

forging (ˈfɔədʒɪŋ), *vbl. sb.*[1] [f. FORGE *v.*[1] + -ING[1].]

1. The action of the vb. FORGE in various senses; an instance of the same. Also, used gerundially with the omission of *in*.

1382 WYCLIF *Ecclus.* xxxii. 8 In forging [**1388** the making] of gold signe is of a smaragd. *c* **1400** tr. *Secreta Secret., Gov. Lordsh.* (E.E.T.S.) 100 þe craft of fforgynge. **1523** LD. BERNERS *Froiss.* I. clxx. 208 Forgyng of moneys. *a* **1568** ASCHAM *Scholem.* (Arb.) 120 Which tooles..be not of myne owne forging. **1594** WEST *2nd Pt. Symbol.* II. Indict. §66 Forging of false and fraudulent writings. **1667** OLDENBURG in *Phil. Trans.* II. 415 The melting, forging, and tempering of it [iron]. **1774** GOLDSM. *Nat. Hist.* (1862) I. viii. 36 In this great elaboratory of nature, a thousand benefits and calamities are forging. **1839** URE *Dict. Arts*, etc. 703 The forging and drawing out of the iron.

b. *concr.* A product of forging; a forged mass (of iron, etc.).

1858 GREENER *Gunnery* 95 The skill..displayed in welding large forgings of wrought iron into shafts. **1882** *Worc. Exhib. Catal.* iii. 15 Tyres and forging of Whitworth steel.

2. *attrib.*, as ***forging-hammer***, ***-mill***.

1874 KNIGHT *Dict. Mech.* I. 906 *Forging-hammer*, a hammer used by gold-beaters. **1887** HISSEY *Holiday on Road* 73 The requisite water-power for forging or other mills.

forging, *vbl. sb.*[2] [f. FORGE *v.*[3] + -ING[1].] = CLICKING *vbl. sb.* b.

1831 [see CLICKING *vbl. sb.* b]. **1892** in *Funk's Stand. Dict.*, In *forging*, a horse merely hits one of his forward shoes with his hind shoes, making a disagreeable noise. **1963** BLOODGOOD & SANTINI *Horseman's Dict.* 9 *Forging* or *clicking*: when the foreshoe strikes the hind shoe on the same side.

forging (ˈfɔədʒɪŋ), *ppl. a.* [f. as FORGING *vbl. sb.*[1] + -ING[2].] That forges, in senses of the vb.

1592 SHAKS. *Ven. & Ad.* 729 Till forging nature be condemn'd of treason. **1679** DRYDEN & LEE *Œdipus* IV. Wks. 1883 VI. 204 Let..not a greybeard forging priest come near. **1739** G. OGLE *Gualth. & Gris.* 66 A forging Hand he found, and scheming Head.

forgivable (fəˈgɪvəb(ə)l), *a.* Also **forgiveable**. [f. FORGIVE *v.* + -ABLE.] That may be forgiven, pardonable, excusable.

1550 LATIMER *Last Serm. bef. Edw. VI* (1562) 123 b, An vnexcusable sin; yet to him that will truly repent, it is forgeueable. **1611** COTGR., *Pardonnable*..forgiueable. **1821** COLERIDGE *Lett. Convers., etc.* II. xxiii. 39 A neglect of this kind may be forgiveable, but it is utterly inexcusable. **1872** M. COLLINS *Pr. Clarice* I. ix. 139 To know one's own dulness ought to make it forgiveable.

Hence **forˈgivableness**, the quality of being forgivable; **forˈgivably** *adv.*, in a manner that is excusable or deserves forgiveness.

1898 *Expositor* Aug. 105 When general unbelief prevails in the forgivableness of transgression, it is a truth worth proclaiming. **1926** *Spectator* 29 May 917/2 The quality which distinguishes his great prototype Pepys, we mean the quality of forgivableness. **1926** H. W. PHILLIPS *Mod. Foreign Exch.* 31 Then came the reaction from the strain and privation of the war, expressing itself quite forgivably in an orgy of spending. **1927** *Sunday Times* 13 Mar. 6/4 [The part] was quite ludicrously, if forgivably, presented by a substitute. **1968** *Times Lit. Suppl.* 2 May 460/3 'Voices'.. forgivably crowd the earlier note-books.

†**forˈgivance.** *Sc. Obs.* Forms: 5 forgivance, 6 foirgiffance, forgev(e)ance. [f. FORGIVE *v.* + -ANCE.] Forgiveness, pardon.

1490 *Acta Dom. Conc.* (1839) 153 And ask..forgeuance of þe deth of þe said Johne. *a* **1575** *Diurn. Occurr.* (Bannatyne Club) 339 The said laird..askit the haill peopill foirgiffance in his name.

forgive (fəˈgɪv), *v.* Pa. t. forgave (fəˈgeɪv). Pa. pple. forgiven (fəˈgɪv(ə)n). Forms: see GIVE. [OE. *forȝiefan* (f. FOR- *pref.*[1] + *ȝiefan*: see GIVE *v.*), corresponding to Du. *vergeven*, OHG. *far-*, *fer-*, *for-*, *furgeban* (Ger. *vergeben*), ON. *fyrirgefa* (Sw. *förgifva*, MDa. *forgive*) to forgive, Goth. *fragiban* to grant.]

†**1.** *trans.* To give, grant. *Obs.*

c **900** tr. *Bæda's Hist.* I. xvi. [xxvii.] (1890) 84 Forþon ne bið þæt forȝifen þætte alefed bið, ac þæt bið riht. **971** *Blickl. Hom.* 31 Ealra þara gifa þe he middanȝearde forgeaf þurh his tocyme. *a* **1175** *Cott. Hom.* 229 He forȝiaf blinde manne ȝesechðe. **1377** LANGL. *P. Pl.* B. XVIII. 76 For he was knyȝte & kynges sone kynde forȝaf þat tyme, þat non harlot were so hardy to leyne hands vppon hym. **1483** *Vulgaria abs Terentio* 2 b, The grettist tresoure that j hadd j forgafe the.

†**2.** To give up, cease to harbour (resentment, wrath). Also, to give up one's resolve (*to* do something). *Obs.*

c **1200** ORMIN 1466 A33 whannse þu forrȝifesst tuss þin wraþþe. *c* **1305** *Pilate* 167 in *E.E.P.* (1862) 115 He wende ..þat he hadde forȝeue him his wraþþe. *c* **1380** WYCLIF *Paternoster* Wks. (1880) 200 Here men moten forȝeue þe rancour..of here herte to here neiȝeboris. *a* **1533** LD. BERNERS *Huon* lxxxiii. 257 Oberon..forgaue all the yll wyll that he had to Huon. **1564** *Carsewell's Lett.* in *Wodr. Soc. Misc.* 285, I can nocht forgif to do my sobir diligens in furderance of the kirk.

3. To remit (a debt); to give up resentment or claim to requital for, pardon (an offence). Const. **a.** with simple object.

a **1000** *Cædmon's Gen.* 662 (Gr.) He forgirð hit. *c* **1175** *Lamb. Hom.* 67 Ower hating forȝefe ȝe. *c* **1200** *Trin. Coll. Hom.* 29 þanne beð þe synne forgiuen. **13..** *Cursor M.* 25109 (Cott. Galba) Lord forgiff þou dettes ours. *c* **1400** *Destr. Troy* 11581 All hir gilt to forgiff. **1503** *Kalender of Sheph.* Pater Noster, Forghewe the fawlys doyeng ageyns them. **1596** SHAKS. *Merch. V.* IV. i. 26 Forgiue a moytie of the principall. **1651** HOBBES *Leviath.* III. xlii. 274 An Authority to Forgive, or Retain Sins. **1781** BURNS *Why am I loth* ii, Fain would I say, 'Forgive my foul offence!' **1855** TENNYSON *Maud* xii, Should I fear..to say 'Forgive the wrong'. **1882** *19th Cent.* No. 61. 348 The amount of rent that has been forgiven in the past two years has been very large.

b. with the thing in the acc., and the person in the dat., or preceded by †*til*, *to*, *unto* (or as subj. of vb. in pass).

c **1000** *Ags. Gosp.* Matt. vi. 12 And forgyf us ure gyltas. *c* **1175** *Lamb. Hom.* 37 Ne mei þe preost forȝefen nane men his sunne. *a* **1300** *Cursor M.* 19019 (Edin.) Giu sal forgiuin be giur sak. *Ibid.* 25109 (Cott.) Forgiue þou til us dettes vrs. *c* **1320** *Sir Tristr.* 2568 Forȝeuen hem was her wo, No were þai neuer so dere. **1382** WYCLIF *Matt.* xviii. 27 Sothely the lord of that seruant.. forȝaue to hym the dette. *c* **1430** *Hymns Virg.* (1867) 128 Lord your deth forgyffe it me. **1503–4** *Act 19 Hen. VII*, c. 37 Preamb., It pleased your Highnesse..to forgyve unto your seid Subgiect all the seid Mesprisions. **1611** BIBLE *Isa.* xxxiii. 24 The people that dwel therein shalbe forgiuen their iniquitie. **1665** WALTON *Life Hooker* H.'s Wks. 1888 I. 39 Forgiving him his first-fruits. **1726–31** TINDAL *Rapin's Hist. Eng.* (1743) II. XVII.

153 She forgave him what she had lent his father. 1782 COWPER *Charity* 634 Let Charity forgive me a mistake That zeal, not vanity, has chanced to make. 1826 T. MOORE *Mem.* (1854) V. 46 Clonmell never forgave this to Grattan.

c. with indirect (personal) obj. only, either in *dative* (a construction now merged in 4), or †preceded by *to*, *till*, *unto*.

c 1000 *Ags. Gosp.* Matt. xviii. 21 Mot ic him forgyfan oð seofon siþas. *c* 1175 *Lamb. Hom.* 39 þu scalt forȝeuen þon monne þe wið þe agultet. *a* 1340 HAMPOLE *Psalter* vi. 1 Forgifynge til him þat synnes in vs. 1382 WYCLIF *Matt.* vi. 12 As we forȝeue to oure dettours. 1484 CAXTON *Fables of Æsop* I. xviii, The myghte and puyssant must pardonne and forgyue to the lytyll and feble.

4. To give up resentment against, pardon (an offender). Const. *for*, †*of*, or dependent clause, rarely †*to* with *inf.* Also (now *rarely*) to abandon one's claim against (a debtor).

[*c* 1000, *c* 1175: see 3 c.] *c* 1200 ORMIN 4960 To forrȝifenn oþre menn Wiþþ word & ec wiþþ herrte. *c* 1340 *Cursor M.* 8396 (Fairf.) ȝe ar for-giuen of þat vn-riȝt. *c* 1450 *Mirour Saluacioun* 91 How y[t] crist forgaf mavdelen marie. 1591 SHAKS. *Two Gent.* II. iv. 172 Forgiue me that I doe not dreame on thee. 1607 WILKINS *Miseries Inforced Marriage* II. Dj, I do forgiue thee with my hart. 1715 DE FOE *Fam. Instruct.* I. i, He forgives them for the sake of Jesus Christ. 1742 RICHARDSON *Pamela* III. 387 An Example so much better—forgive me to say—before her. 1785 BURNS *1st Epist. Lapraik* xvii, I like the lasses—Gude forgie me! 1828 SCOTT *F.M. Perth* xxi, Forgive me if I remind you, that [etc.]. 1866 G. MACDONALD *Ann. Q. Neighb.* xxii. (1878) 403 He asks you to forgive the man who wronged you.

5. *absol.* (of 3 and 4, which in this use coincide).

c 1000 *Ags. Gosp.* Luke vi. 37 Forgyfaþ & eow byð forgyfen. 1398 TREVISA *Barth. De P.R.* VI. v. (1495) 192 Chyldren ben sone playsyd and lyghtly they forgyue. 1611 BIBLE *1 Kings* viii. 30 And when thou hearest, forgiue. 1709 POPE *Ess. Crit.* 525 To err is human, to forgive, divine. 1841 TRENCH *Parables* xxiv. (1877) 411 Though God may forgive, man is not therefore to forget.

6. To make excuse or apology for, regard indulgently. Now only in *imper.* as an entreaty.

1667 MILTON *P.L.* x. 956 Thy frailtie and infirmer Sex forgiv'n. 1738 POPE *Epil. Sat.* I. 63 Dear Sir, forgive the Prejudice of Youth. 1782 COWPER *Truth* 582 Forgive their evil, and accept their good. 1850 TENNYSON *In Mem.* Prol. xi, Forgive these wild and wandering cries.. Forgive them where they fail in truth.

†**7.** = MISGIVE. (So also GIVE). *Obs. rare.*

1600 HOLLAND *Livy* 754 Anniball, whose mind forgave him that such a thing would fall out, had prepared shipping.

8. *dial.* (See quots.)

1790 GROSE *Prov. Gloss* (ed. 2) s.v., *Forgive*, to thaw. *a* 1825 FORBY *Voc. E. Anglia*, *Forgive*, to begin to thaw.

forgive-, stem of prec. used in derivatives; as †**for'giveful** *a.* [see -FUL], full of forgiveness; ready to forgive. **for'giveless** *a.* [see -LESS], disinclined to forgive; unforgiving. †**for-'ȝivelich** *a.* ME. (OE. *forȝifenlic*) [see -LY[1]], likely to be forgiven; pardonable, venial.

c 1000 *Ags. Gosp.* Matt. xi. 24 Ic secȝe eow, Ðæt Sodumwara lande byð forȝyfenlicre on domes dæȝ, þonne ȝe. *a* 1225 *Ancr. R.* 346 O sunne uorȝiuelich mei beon ful deadlich. 1563 MAN *Musculus' Commonpl.* 126 a, He is also forgeuefull and mercyfull. 1861 *Temple Bar Mag.* I. 356 They live their lives, forgotten and dead, Forgiveless and unforgiven.

forgiven (fə'gɪv(ə)n), *ppl. a.* [pa. pple. of FORGIVE *v.*] In senses of the vb.

1548 ELYOT *Dict.*, *Condonatus*.. geuen, forgeuen, pardoned. 1607 SHAKS. *Timon* v. iv. 79 Faults forgiuen. 1717 POPE *Eloisa* 255 Soft as the slumbers of a saint forgiv'n. 1859 TENNYSON *Elaine* 1096 A face, bright as for sin forgiven.

forgiveness (fə'gɪvnɪs). Forms: 1 **forȝife(n)nys, -ȝyfe(n)nys, forȝif(e)nes**; for later forms cf. FORGIVE and -NESS. [OE. *forȝifennys*, f. *forȝifen*, FORGIVEN *ppl. a.* + -NESS. Cf. Du. *vergiffenis*.]

1. The action of forgiving; pardon of a fault, remission of a debt, etc. †In OE. also: Indulgent permission.

The etymological sense, 'condition or fact of being forgiven', is not clearly evidenced even in OE., though in expressions like 'the forgiveness of sins' the word may admit of being thus interpreted.

c 900 tr. *Bæda's Hist.* I. xvi. [xxvii]. (1890) 82 Ðis ic cweðo æfter forgifnesse [*secundum indulgentiam*] nales æfter bebodo. 971 *Blickl. Hom.* 19 þonne we.. us forgifnessa biddaþ. *a* 1200 *Moral Ode* 298 Nis noþer inne helle ore no forȝiuenesse. 1297 R. GLOUC. (1724) 58 þat bid me for ȝefnesse, & to amende hys trespas. 1340 *Ayenb.* 32 Vor non ne may habbe uoryeuenesse: wyþ-oute zoþe ssrifte. *c* 1400 MAUNDEV. (Roxb.) xiii. 59 A man schuld all anely ask him forgifnes wham he trespast to. 1480 CAXTON *Chron. Eng.* ccxxviii. 238 The pope yafe hem.. foryeuenes of al hir sinnes that [etc.]. 1584 POWEL *Lloyd's Cambria* 235 All the brethren desired the father forgiuenes. 1729 BUTLER *Serm.* Pref. Wks. 1874 II. 21 Forgiveness of injuries is one of the very few moral obligations which has been disputed. 1863 GEO. ELIOT *Romola* II. xxxi, He would have to encounter much that was unpleasant before he could win her forgiveness.

2. Disposition or willingness to forgive.

c 1200 ORMIN 1477, & are & millce & mildherrtleȝȝc & rihht forrȝifenesse. 1535 COVERDALE *Dan.* ix. 9 Vnto the.. pertayneth mercy and forgeuenesse. 1678 SPRAT *Serm.* (1710) 99 Meekness, Forgiveness, Bounty and Magnanimity.

b. in *plural. rare.* (A Hebraism.)

1611 BIBLE *Dan.* ix. 9 To the Lord our God belong mercies and forgiuenesses.

forgiver (fə'gɪvə(r)). [f. FORGIVE *v.* + -ER[1].] One who forgives.

a 1225 *Ancr. R.* 256 *note* (MS. Titus), Hire forȝeouere. 1388 WYCLIF *Rom.* iii. 25 Whom God ordeynyde forȝyuer [1382 an helpere; Vulg. *propitiationem*]. *c* 1449 PECOCK *Repr.* III. v. 306 Ful grete forȝeuers of dettis. 1557 *Primer, Godly Prayers* O ij, Not onlye a forgever but also a revenger. 1625 USSHER *Answ. Jesuit* 102 [He] is the forgiver of sinnes. 1742 RICHARDSON *Pamela* III. 69, I was thus lifted up to the State of a sovereign Forgiver, and my lordly Master became a Petitioner. 1872 J. G. MURPHY *Comm. Lev.* xvi. *ad fin.*, The great Forgiver.

forgiving (fə'gɪvɪŋ), *vbl. sb.* Also 5–6 *Sc.* **forgiffine, -yne.** [f. FORGIVE *v.* + -ING[1].] The action of the verb FORGIVE.

c 1385 CHAUCER *L.G.W.* 1852 *Lucrece*, Be as be may, quod she, of forgyfynge. *a* 1460 *Let. Jas. II*, Chart. Aberd. 62 (Jam.) Not agaynstanding ony relessing, gyft, forgiffyne, or accordyng. *c* 1526 FRITH *Disput. Purgat.* Wks. (1573) 29 Albeit man repente his forgeuyng and after-wards sue for his debt. 1533 GAU *Richt Vay* (1888) 8 Quhair thay sal get grace marcie and forgiffine of thair sinnis.

forgiving (fə'gɪvɪŋ), *ppl. a.* [f. as prec. + -ING[2].] That forgives; inclined to forgive; indicating forgiveness.

1690 NORRIS *Beatitudes* (1694) I. 188 A mild, meek and forgiving Spirit. 1703 ROWE *Fair Penit.* IV. i. 1574 One forgiving Glance. 1820 KEATS *Isabella* xix, Of thee we now should ask forgiving boon. 1855 MACAULAY *Hist. Eng.* III. 458 He was of no gentle or forgiving temper.

Hence **for'givingly** *adv.*; **for'givingness**.

1667 FLAVEL *Saint Indeed* (1754) 84 Never did any carry it more peaceably and forgivingly. 1742 RICHARDSON *Pamela* III. 82 So much Sweetness, and so much Forgivingness. 1857 W. COLLINS *Dead Secret* 249 Remember me forgivingly, Arthur. 1865 J. GROTE *Moral Ideas* viii. (1876) 114 Active forgivingness, the returning of good for evil.

forglopned, -glut: see FOR- *pref.*[1] 5 and 6.

†**for'gnaw**, *v. Obs.* [OE. *forgnaȝan*, f. FOR- *pref.*[1] + *gnaȝan* to GNAW.] *trans.* To gnaw in pieces, eat up; *lit.* and *fig.*

c 1000 ÆLFRIC *Hom.* (Th.) II. 194 Gærstapan forgnoȝon swa hwæt swa se haȝol belæfde. *a* 1225 *Ancr. R.* 338 Godis god, hwon ich hit do.. min vuel hit forgnaweð. *c* 1290 *Altenglische Legenden* (Horstmann) I. 161 Somme.. hor wreche flesch uor gnowe. *c* 1325 *Body & Soul* 269 in *Map's Poems* 343 Wormes for-gnowen heor alre throte. 1413 *Pilgr. Sowle* (Caxton 1483) II. xlv. 24 Somme had feete al forgnawen.

†**for'gnide**, *v. Obs.* Pa. t. **forgnode.** [OE. *forgnídan*, f. FOR- *pref.*[1] + *gnídan* to crush.] *trans.* To break, break to pieces; to destroy.

a 1000 *Lamb. Ps.* civ. [cv.] 16 He forgnad.. treow ȝemæru heora. *a* 1300 *E.E. Psalter* ibid., He.. alle festnes of bred forgnode. *Ibid.* cvi[i]. 16 He forgnod yhates brased ware.

forgo, forego (fə-, fɔə'gəʊ), *v.* Pa. t. **for-, forewent.** Pa. pple. **for-, foregone.** Forms: see GO. [OE. *forgán*, *-gangan*, f. FOR- *pref.*[1] + *gán*, *gangan*: see GO.]

†**1.** *intr.* To go away, go past, pass away. *Obs.*

c 950 *Lindisf. Gosp.* Matt. v. 18 Enne pricle.. ne forgæs from ae wið ða huile alle sie. *a* 1300 *Cursor M.* 6264 (Cott.) þe see on aiþer side þam stod Als walles tua, quils þai for yod. 1563 SACKVILLE *Induct. Mirr. Mag.* xlix, And fast by him pale Malady was plac'd: Sore sick in bed, her colour all foregone.

†**2.** *trans.* To go by, pass over. *lit.* and *fig.* Hence, to leave alone or undone, neglect, overlook, slight. *Obs.* exc. *arch.*

c 1000 ÆLFRIC *Hom.* (Th.) I. 92 Seðe þis forgæið his sawul losað. *c* 1000 —— *Exod.* xii. 23 He [Drihten] forȝæþ þæs huses duru. *a* 1300 *Cursor M.* 25344 (Cott.) Grant vs þi maght.. to luue vr euen cristen sua þat we þair lastes ma forga. ? *a* 1500 *Trevisa's Barth. de P.R.* (1535) VI. xvi, He [the euyll seruant] forgeth [1398 forgendreþ] all his lordes nedes, and leaueth them vndone. 1858 BUCKLE *Civiliz.* (1869) II. i. 29 He.. never.. allowed the claims of his profession to make him forego the superior claims of his country.

†**3.** To avoid, elude. *Obs. rare*[−1].

c 1305 *Edmund Conf.* 301 in *E.E.P.* (1862) 79 þer lurnede þis holi man.. þe deueles poer forgon.

†**b.** To overreach, deceive. *Obs. rare*[−1].

1382 WYCLIF *Col.* Prol. 429 Thei weren forgon of false apostlis.

4. To go from, forsake, leave. *Obs.* exc. *arch.*

a 1300 *Cursor M.* 17012 (Gött.) Mannes saul.. wold neuer if it might þe bodi self forga. *c* 1340 *Ibid.* 13280 (Trin.) Petur and andrew.. wiþ o word haue þei ship forgone. 1530 PALSGR. 556/1 Shall I forgo your company nowe. 1622 CALLIS *Stat. Sewers* (1647) 191 When D. was Banished, he then forewent his local Habitation. 1697 DRYDEN *Virg. Past.* IV. 46 When to ripen'd Manhood he shall grow, The greedy Sailer shall the Seas forego. 1725 POPE *Odyss.* XII. 450 Vengeance, ye Gods! or I the skies forego. 1821 WORDSW. *Sonn.*, *Clerical Integrity*, Their altars they forego, their homes they quit. 1844 MRS. BROWNING *Catarina to Camoens* iv, And if they looked up to you, All the light which has forgone them Would be gathered back anew.

5. To abstain or refrain from (some action or procedure). Rarely with *to* and *inf.* as object.

a 1000 *Laws Cnut* §85 in Thorpe *Anc. Laws* I. 424 þæt he .. smeaȝe.. hwæt him sy to donne & to forganne. 1297 R. GLOUC. (1724) 290 þys god man Seyn Dunston Hatede muche to crouny hym, ȝyf he yt myȝte ver gon. *c* 1420 *Sir Amadace* (Camden) xviii, Vnnethe he myȝte forgoe to wepe. 1587 TURBERV. *Trag. T.* (1837) 9 The Authour here declareth the cause why hee.. forewent the translation of the learned Poet Lucan. 1768 BEATTIE *Minstr.* II. xlvi, Then jarring appetites forego their strife. 1842 PUSEY *Crisis Eng. Ch.* 72 We forewent much which any of us might have desired to do. 1860 HAWTHORNE *Transform.* xv, He had foregone to be a Christian reality. 1871 FREEMAN *Hist. Ess.* Ser. I. x. 313 We forego any comparison between the two men.

absol. 1810 SCOTT *Lady of L.* II. xxxiv, Chieftains, forego! I hold the first who strikes my foe.

6. To abstain from, go without, deny to oneself; to let go or pass, omit to take or use; to give up, part with, relinquish, renounce, resign.

a 1175 *Cott. Hom.* 221 Forgang þu ones treowes westm. *a* 1225 *Ancr. R.* 8 Fleschs forgon oþer visch. *c* 1400 *Melayne* 307 Bid hym hawkes & houndes forgoo, And to dedis of armes hym doo. 1561 T. NORTON *Calvin's Inst.* IV. 3 No greate pleasure shoulde be foregone thereby. 1606 SHAKS. *Tr. & Cr.* v. viii. 9, I am vnarm'd, forgoe this vantage, Greeke. 1653 MILTON *Hirelings* Wks. (1847) 435/1 Though Paul were pleas'd to forgo his due, and not to use his Power .. yet he had a Power. 1714 GAY *Trivia* III. 300 Ah hapless Swain.. Canst thou forgo Roast-Beef for nauseous Pills? 1748 HARTLEY *Observ. Man* II. iii. 343 The Pleasures are to be foregone, and the Pains accepted. 1828 E. IRVING *Serm.* I. p. liv, Whatever He.. forewent of infinite glory.. is to be placed to the account of mankind. 1848 KINGSLEY *Saint's Trag.* II. iv, Wear but one robe the less—forego one meal. 1849 M. ARNOLD *New Sirens*, Those slackened arms forgo The delight of death-embraces.

†**7.** To go without (compulsorily), to be without; to miss, lack. *Obs. rare.*

a 1300 *Cursor M.* 3443 (Cott.) His wijf þat lang had child for-gane Now sco bredes tua for ane. *c* 1340 *Ibid.* 23292 (Trin.) Mercy shul þei euer forgoon. *c* 1400 MAUNDEV. (Roxb.) xxxii. 147 Alssone as þai forga þe smell of þam þai dye. *a* 1400–50 *Alexander* 188 And gett agayn his awyn gronde at he forgais nowe.

†**b.** To let go (involuntarily), lose, forfeit. *Obs.*

c 1205 LAY. 22130 Alc mon þe his lond hafde for-gan. *c* 1491 *Chast. Goddes Chyld.* 9 Hem thynken oftymes that they maye neuer forgoo the likyng that they haue. 1587 GOLDING *De Mornay* xxvi. 395 He had sodainly forgone his sight, which was afterward restored againe.

absol. *c* 1450 tr. *De Imitatione* III. liv. þere shal be plente of all good wiþoute drede of lesyng or forgoyng.

†**8.** Only in pa. pple.: Exhausted with going, wearied, faint. Also, faint with emotion. *Obs.*

a 1300 *Cursor M.* 3527 (Cott.) Quen he al weri was forgan Ham he tok his wai o-nan. 13.. *Coer de L.* 5472 Myn [horses] ar wery and forgon. *c* 1330 *Amis & Amil.* 1054 Than seighe he a weri knight forgon, Vnder a tre slepeand alon. *c* 1384 CHAUCER *H. Fame* I. 115 He that wery was for-go On pilgrimage myles two. 1597 T. BEARD *Theat. Gods Judgem.* (1612) 350 The poor slave, all forgone at this.. ouglie sight, looked everie minute to be devoured.

Hence **for'going** *vbl. sb.*; **for'gone** *ppl. a.* Also **for'goer**, one who forgoes (something).

1549 COVERDALE, etc. *Erasm. Par. Col.* ii. 12 After suche forgoyng of your bodyes, which were thral to sinne. 1611 COTGR., *Abandonneur*.. forgoer. 1627 SANDERSON *Serm.* I. 268 They chuse to be still ignorant, rather than hazard the forgoing of any part of that freedom. 1736 BUTLER *Anal.* I. v. Wks. 1874 I. 93 The voluntary foregoing many things which we desire. 1828 WEBSTER, *Foregoer*, one who forbears to enjoy. *Ibid.*, *Foregone*, forborne to be possessed or enjoyed.

forgotten (fə'gɒt(ə)n), *ppl. a.* [pa. pple. of FORGET *v.*] **a.** Not remembered, that has passed from the mind or out of remembrance. **b.** Omitted or neglected through inadvertence.

1429 *Wills & Inv. N.C.* (Surtees 1835) 78, I gyf to the vicar of Seint Nicholas kyrk for forgetyn tendes c[s]. 1527 *Will* in *Southwell Visit.* (1891) 128 For forgoten tithes vjs. viijd. 1597 SHAKS. *2 Hen. IV*, IV. v. 116 Onely compound me with forgotten dust. 1870 L'ESTRANGE *Miss Mitford* I. v. 113 A good deal of forgotten poetry. 1887 BOWEN *Virg. Æneid* I. 358 A forgotten treasure that lay Long from the daylight buried.

forgottenness (fə'gɒt(ə)nnɪs). [f. FORGOTTEN *ppl. a.* + -NESS.] The state of being forgotten; oblivion.

1924 *Brit. Weekly* 4 Sept. 483/4 Archbishop Leighton's writings are apt to be relegated to forgottenness to-day. 1924 L. M. WATT *Prayers Public Worship* 159 Awake them from the lethargy of forgottenness. 1947 *Sat. Rev. Lit.* 22 Nov. 17 No one has fewer illusions about that forgottenness.

†**for'graith**, *v. Obs.* [f. FOR- *pref.*[2] + GRAITH *v.*] *trans.* To get ready beforehand, prepare. Hence †**for'graithing** *vbl. sb.*, preparation.

a 1300 *E.E. Psalter* ix. 38 [x. 17] For-gra[i]þynge of þair hert herd ere þine. *Ibid.* xx[i]. 12 In þaire leuynges forgraiþe lickam of þa.

forgreat, -greme: see FOR- *pref.*[1] 3, 10.

†**for'grow**, *v. Obs. rare* exc. in *pa. pple.* **forgrown.** Forms: see GROW. [OE. *forgrówan*, f. FOR- *pref.*[1] + *grówan*: see GROW *v.*]

1. *intr.* To grow to excess or out of shape. Only in pa. pple. *forgrown*, overgrown, misshapen.

a 1000 *Riming Poem* (Gr.) 46 Brondhord ȝeblowen breostum in forgrowen. 1399 *Sarcastic Verses* in *Archæol.* XXI. 89 þis is a busch þat is forgrowe. 1543 GRAFTON *Contn. Harding* 599 A pylgremes hat.. with a long and for-growen bearde. 1565 GOLDING *Ovid's Met.* I. (1593) 14 So foule a Dragon.. so monstrously for-growne. 1576 NEWTON *Lemnie's Complex.* (1633) 133 Although the party be fat and forgrowne. 1601 BP. ANDREWES *Serm.* Matt. xxii. 21 (1641) II. 96 The fat and foregrown rammes within our own fold.

fig. 1583 GOLDING *Calvin on Deut.* clxxxii. 1129 An euill custome is nothing else than an errour forgrowen.

2. *trans.* To overgrow, cover with a growth (usually one that is excessive or unsightly).

c **1200** *Trin. Coll. Hom.* 129 Forþi is þis westren forgrouwen mid brimbles. **1399** *Pol. Poems* (Rolls) I. 363 The long gras that is so grene..forgrowen hit hath the fellde. **1494** FABYAN *Chron.* v. cxx. 97 The towne of Westmynster ..that tyme was forgrowen with busshes. *a* **1535** MORE *Wks.* 74 The ground that is al foregrowen with nettels. **1575** LANEHAM *Let.* (1871) 14 Hombre Saluagio..forgrone all in moss and Iuy.

b. In pa. pple. (of aged persons): Overgrown or covered (with hair). Hence (? or from sense 1), Extremely old.

c **1430** LYDG. *Bochas* IX. x. (1554) 201 b, With heere forgrowen body and visage. *c* **1440** *Generydes* 3667 A man that was right ferr in age..And all for growe. **1494** FABYAN *Chron.* VII. 605 In the bordour of this dilicious place..Stode ii. forgrowen faders, reasemblyng Ennok and Hely. **1527** *Prose Life St. Brandan* (Percy) 52 He was olde and forgrowen so that no man myght se his body.

†**for'guilt**, *v. Obs.* Forms: 3 *Orm.* forrgilltenn. *Pa. t.* 3 forgilt, -gult. *Pa. pple.* 2–3 forgilt, -gult, *Orm.* -gilltedd. [OE. *forgyltan, f. FOR- *pref.*[1] + *gyltan* to sin.]

1. *trans.* To bring into a state of guilt. Only *refl.* or in *pass.* Const. *wið*, *ȝæn*.

c **1175** *Lamb. Hom.* 27 ȝif þu ert swiðe for-gult wið þine eorðliche lauerd he [etc.]. *c* **1200** ORMIN 2619 þe deofell.. stannddeþþ..To don uss to forrgilltenn uss ȝæn Godd. *a* **1225** *Ancr. R.* 388 Al þet is iðe worlde he werp under ure uet bestes ant fueles, ear we weren uorgulte.

2. To forfeit by guilty conduct. Also, to bring *into* by guilt.

c **1175** *Lamb. Hom.* 19 Er we weren al forgult in to helle. *c* **1200** *Trin. Coll. Hom.* 211 He forgilt heuene wele, and haueð helle wowe. **1297** R. GLOUC. (1724) 1 Plente me may in Engelond of alle gode y se, Bute folc yt for gulte oþer ȝeres þe worse be. *c* **1300** *Harrow. Hell* 166 þou laddest ous to parays, We hit forgulten ase vnwys. ? *a* **1350** *Arth. & Merl.* (Linc. Inn MS.) 593 Til Lucifer hit forgult wiþ pryde.

forhale, -hang: see FOR- *pref.*[1] 5.

†**for'hard**, *v. Obs.*$^{-1}$ [ME. *forhardien* (trans.), OE. *forheardian* (intr.), f. FOR- *pref.*[1] + *heardian* to become or make hard.] *trans.* To harden.

c **1250** *Gen. & Ex.* 3338 For it [*sc.* the manna] malt at ðe sunne-sine, Oc oðer fir for-hardede [*printed* forhadede] hine.

†**for'harden**, *v. Obs.*$^{-1}$ [f. FOR- *pref.*[1] + HARDEN *v.*] *trans.* = prec.

1571 GOLDING *Calvin on Ps.* lxxiii. 15 They become forhardened, and shaking of the feare of God, do therwithal cast away the hope of salvation.

†**for'hare**, *v. Obs. rare*$^{-1}$. [f. FOR- *pref.*[1] + HARE *v.*[1]] *trans.* To affright or harry exceedingly.

1659 BP. GAUDEN *Serm. at Fun. Bp. Brounrig* (1660) 55 Elisha's cry is not..a bare clamor insignificant, as one scared and forehared.

forhead, -heed: see FOR- *pref.*[1] 3, 5.

†**for'hecche**, *v. Obs.* Pa. pple. forhaht. [f. FOR- *pref.*[1]: the verbal element is obscure.] *trans.* To despise.

c **1230** *Hali Meid.* 41 He forhoheð [*v.r.* forhecched] þe anan. *a* **1310** in Wright's *Lyric P.* x. 37 Thenne mihti..ben hated ant for-haht.

†**for'hele**, *v. Obs.* Pa. pple. forholen. [OE. *forhelan*, f. FOR- *pref.*[1] + *helan* to hide = OFris., OS. *farhelan* (Du. *verhelen*), OHG. *far-*, *ferhelan* (MHG. *verheln*, Ger. *verhehlen*).]

trans. To hide, conceal; with personal obj. in dat. or preceded by *wiþ*.

c **888** K. ÆLFRED *Boeth.* xvii, Ðæt mine cræftas and anweald ne wurden forgitene and forholene. *c* **1000** ÆLFRIC *Gen.* xviii. 17 Hu mæȝ ic forhelan Abrahame, ðe ic don wille. **1154** *O.E. Chron.* an. 1137 [Hi] wenden ðæt it sculde ben forholen. *c* **1200** ORMIN 2468 Itt shollde wurrþenn wel Forrholenn wiþþ þe defell. **13..** *K. Alis.* 6967 Thy traitour schal beo forhole. *c* **1430** *How Good Wijf tauȝte Douȝtir* in *Babees Bk.* (1868) 39 Schewe it to þi freendis, & for-hile þou it noȝt.

†**for'hevedness**. *Obs.* [OF. *forhæfedness*, f. *forhæfed* (pa. pple. of *forhabban* to restrain, f. FOR- *pref.*[1] + *habban* to HAVE, hold) + -NESS.] Restraint, continence, abstinence.

c **900** tr. *Bæda's Hist.* IV. xxvi. [xxv]. (1890) 352 He..in micelre forhæfdnesse Drihtne þeowade. *c* **1175** *Lamb. Hom.* 101 To michel forheuednesse on hete and on wete macað þene mon unhalne.

†**for'hew**, *v. Obs.* Forms: *Pa. t.* 3 forheow. *Pa. pple.* 4–5 forhewen. [OE. *forhéawan* (f. FOR- *pref.*[1] + *héawan* to HEW) = OS. *forhawan*, OHG. *furhouwan* (MHG. *verhouwen*, Ger. *verhauen*).] *trans.* To hew or cut to pieces.

a **1000** *Byrhtnoth* 115 (Gr.) He mid billum wearð..swiðe forheawen. *a* **1205** LAY. 4593 He for-heow þænne mæst a-two riht amidden. *c* **1380** *Sir Ferumb.* 899 And eke ys noble aketoun was [al] for-hewe & schente. *c* **1450** *Merlin* 234 Er thei were alle ynne ther were many slayn and for hewen. **1470–85** MALORY *Arthur* VII. xii, Their sheldes and theyr hauberkes were al forhewen. **1563** SACKVILLE *Induct. Mirr. Mag.* lvii, His face forhewed with woundes.

†**for'hide**, *v. Obs.* [OE. *forhýdan* f. FOR-[1] + *hýdan* to HIDE); = LG. *ferhüden*.] *trans.* To hide.

c **1000** *Ags. Ps.* cxxxix. [cxl.] 5 (Gr.) Forhyddan oferhydge me inwit-gyrene. *c* **1250** *Gen. & Ex.* 1875 Longe it weren ðor forhid. *c* **1340** *Cursor M.* 5263 (Fairf.) Sone quy squa forhidde þou þe.

†**for'hight**, *v. Obs.* Forms: 1 forhátan, 2–3 forhote. *Pa. t.* 3–4 forhet, 4 *Sc.* forhicht. [OE. *forhátan* str. vb., f. FOR- *pref.*[1] + *hátan* to promise, command: see HIGHT *v.*]

1. *trans.* To promise not to do, enjoy or practise (something); to renounce.

c **1000** ÆLFRIC *Past. Ep.* §47 Buton he hit forhaten hæbbe. *c* **1200** *Trin. Coll. Hom.* 199 Ðanne forsake we ure sinnes mid heorte and for-hoteð mid muðe. *a* **1225** *Ancr. R.* 192 ȝe ..ine blostme of ower ȝuweðe uorheten alle worldes blissen. *c* **1305** *Edmund Conf.* 86 in *E.E.P.* (1862) 73 He..forhet bifore hire truliche wommanes mone. *c* **1375** *Sc. Leg. Saints, Nicolaus* 965 þai forhicht mare to steile.

2. To forbid.

c **1315** SHOREHAM 162 Thou dedest by thine wyves stevene Thet was for-hote.

3. To promise. [Cf. Ger. *verheiszen*.]

a **1300** *Cursor M.* 11334 (Cott.) Godd has..sent þam þat he lang for-hight.

†**for'hill**, *v. Obs.* [f. FOR- *pref.*[1] + HILL *v.*] *trans.* To cover; to protect.

a **1300** *E.E. Psalter* xc[i]. 14 For-hile him I sal, for mi name knewe he. *a* **1400–50** *Alexander* 1063 Ane hert with a hoge heued..Was to behald as a harrow foreheld [forhelid] with tyndez.

Hence **for'hilling** *vbl. sb.*, in quot. quasi-*concr.* protection. Also **for'hiller**, a protector.

a **1300** *E.E. Psalter* xvii[i]. 18 Made is Laverd mi forhilinge. *Ibid.* 30 For-hiler es he Of al þat in him hopand be.

forhoar(ed: see FOR- *pref.*[1] 9, 10.

†**for'hold**, *v. Obs.* [OE. *forhealdan* (in sense forsake, lose), f. FOR- *pref.*[1] + *healdan* to HOLD; = MLG. *vorholden*.]

trans. To detain, withhold. Hence **for'holde(n** *ppl. a.*, held over, kept too long.

Beowulf 2381 (Gr.) Hæfdon hy forhealden helm Scylfinga. *c* **888** K. ÆLFRED *Boeth.* xxix. §1 Oððe hi beoþ beȝen forhealden. *c* **1250** *Gen. & Ex.* 2026 An time he was at hire tȝeld..she him his mentel for-held. *c* **1275** *xi Pains of Hell* 78 in *O.E. Misc.* 149 A water..þat..stynkeþ so forholde lych.

for'how, *v. Obs.* exc. *Sc.* Forms: 1 forhoȝian, 2 -huȝian, 3 -howien, -hoȝien, -huȝien, 4–8 forhue, 9 forhoo, forhooy, 8– forhow. [OE. *forhoȝian*, f. FOR- *pref.*[1] + *hoȝian* to think, care.]

†**1.** *trans.* To despise, scorn. *Obs.*

c **900** tr. *Bæda's Hist.* II. ii. (1890) 102 Gif he þonne eow eac forhoȝie..sy he þonne from eow forhoȝad. *c* **1160** *Hatton Gosp.* Matt. xviii. 10 þæt ȝe ne for-huȝien ænne of þissen lytlingen. *a* **1225** *Ancr. R.* 166 Worldliche þinges to.. forhowien. *c* **1230** *Hali Meid.* 25 Forhohe for to don hit þat he þuncheð uuel of. *a* **1300** *Cursor M.* 15107 (Cott.) We wend he had for-huud vs all.

2. To forsake, quit.

a **1300** *Cursor M.* 23047 (Edin.) þe formast raw..þat sinne and sak for him forhuid. *c* **1450** *St. Cuthbert* (Surtees) 8258 þar fore saint dunstan he pursued Whils he englande forhued. **1753** A. MURPHY *Gray's-Inn Jrnl.* No. 39 ¶1 It gives me muckle Trouble to see the English forehuing their Neest, and giving it up to the Cheeld of Israel. **1768** ROSS *Helenore* 99 Ye did her so treach'rously forhow. *a* **1835** HOGG *Kilmeny* xxiv, And the merl and the mavis forhooyed their young. **1871** W. ALEXANDER *Johnny Gibb* ii. (1873) 15 The laird wud hae to forhoo's bit bonny nest.

Hence †**forhower**, a forsaker. †**forhoght**, contempt.

a **1300** *E.E. Psalter* cxviii. [cxix.] 22 Bere fra me vpbraidinge and for-hoghte. **1513** DOUGLAS *Æneis* XII. i. 36 ȝon ilk Troiane forhowar of Asya [*desertorem Asiæ*].

†**for'hunger**, *v. Obs.* [f. FOR- *pref.*[1] + HUNGER *v.*; = Ger. *verhungern*.] *trans.* To make very hungry; to cause to die of hunger; to starve. Only in *pa. pple.* and *ppl. adj.* **for'hungered**.

c **1200** ORMIN 11567 Iesu Crist forrhunnggredd wass. *c* **1275** LAY. 23562 Mid þan wrecche folke þat lai þar forhongered. *c* **1350** *Will. Palerne* 2515 þei..eten at here ese, for þei were for-hungred. *c* **1425** *Seven Sag.* (P.) 964 The knave..was for-ungrid sore. **1481** CAXTON *Reynard* (Arb.) 114 They..eten them lyke as they were forhongred hounds. **1894** F. S. ELLIS *Reynard* 324 They..rob them like forhungered hounds.

†**for'hush**, *v. Obs.* Only in pa. t. forhuste. [f. FOR- *pref.*[1] + ? OE. *hyscan* to mock.] *trans.* To deride.

c **1205** LAY. 29021 þe king heo for-husten.

†**'foricate**, *v. nonce-wd.* [f. L. *forica* a privy + -ATE[3].]

1615 SIR E. HOBY *Curry-combe* title-p., In answer to a lewd Libell lately foricated by Jabal Rachil.

foridled: see FOR- *pref.*[1] 9.

forinsec (fə'rɪnsɪk), *a. Obs.* exc. *Hist.* Also 8 *erron.* forensic. [ad. L. (*servitium*) *forinsecum*, med.L. (adj.) f. L. *forinsecus* (adv.) out of doors, f. *foris* + *secus*, after the analogy of *extrinsecus*.]

Only in *forinsec service* = 'foreign service': see FOREIGN *a.* 11.

1741 CHAMBERS *Cycl.* s.v. *Service*, Forensic or extrinsic Service..was a service which did not belong to the chief lord, but to the king. **1855** BRICHAN *Orig. Paroch. Scot.* II. 406 Every other service except the forinsec service of the king when required.

†**fo'rinsecal**, *a. Obs.* Also 6 forincy-, forynsicall, 6–7 forinsecall. [f. as FORINSEC *a.* + -AL[1].] = FOREIGN *a.* in various senses; alien, extrinsic; in, pertaining to, or coming from another country.

1539 T. CHAPMAN in *Chron. Gr. Friars* (Camden Soc.) p. xvi, Not to follow the supersticious tradicions of ony foryncicall potentate or peere. *c* **1540** tr. *Pol. Verg. Eng. Hist.* (Camd. No. 29) I. 110 While they mayntained forinsecall battayles. **1658** J. ROBINSON *Eudoxa* II. 126 All salts, whether vitriol or allum, whose encrease is by apposition of forinsecall matter. **1659** D. PELL *Impr. Sea* Proem. Bb, Who will say that this Act (under God) is not Englands safety from Forinsical Invasions? **1732** BERKELEY *Alciphr.* III. vi, They disdain all forinsecal motives to it; and love Virtue only for Virtue's sake.

forint ('fɒrɪnt). [Hungarian, f. It. *fiorino*: see FLORIN.] The principal monetary unit of Hungary; a coin of this denomination.

1946 *Times* 31 Aug. 7/4 The National Bank of Hungary's buying rate for sterling remittances from the United Kingdom is at present 46.96 forint = £1. **1947** [see FILLER[3]]. **1962** R. A. G. CARSON *Coins* 383 Hungary, declared a republic in 1946, began a new coinage with a new unit, the forint consisting of 100 filler.

†**for'irk**, *v. Obs.* [f. FOR- *pref.*[1] + IRK.] *intr.* To grow weary or disgusted. Const. *of* or *to* with *inf.*

c **1250** *Gen. & Ex.* 3658 Of manna he ben for-hirked to eten. **1563** *Mirr. Mag., Hen. Dk. Buckhm.* xlvi, His wife foreyrked [*ed.* **1587** foreyrking] of his raygne, Sleping in bed this cruel wretche hath slayne.

forisfamiliate (ˌfɔərɪsfə'mɪlɪeɪt), *v. Civil* and *Sc. Law.* Pa. pple. *Sc.* 7 -at, 9 -ate. [f. ppl. stem of med.L. *forisfamiliāre*, f. *foris* outside + *familia* family.] (See quots.)

1609 SKENE *Reg. Maj.* Table 80 Forisfamiliat the sonne is be the father, quhen the father giues to him ane certaine part of his heretage, and he is content therewith. **1754** ERSKINE *Princ. Sc. Law* I. (1809) 110 A child who gets a separate stock ..even though he should continue in the father's house, may be said to be emancipated or forisfamiliated. **1879** W. E. HEARN *Aryan Househ.* 132 A son was said to be foris-familiated if his father assigned to him part of his land and gave him seisin thereof. **1880** J. SKELTON *Crookit Meg* xiii. 157 The lasses are a' forisfamiliate.

ˌforisfaˌmili'ation. The action of forisfamiliating (a son); also *transf.*

1767 A. CAMPBELL *Lexiph.* (1774) 25 A forisfamiliation out of the universe. **1818** SCOTT *Rob Roy* iii, My father could not be serious in the sentence of forisfamiliation. **1837** HALLAM *Hist. Lit.* III. iv. §99. 399 That [period] of emancipation or foris-familiation.

for'jeskit, *pple. Sc.* [Cf. FOR- *pref.*[1] and DISJASKET.] Jaded, tired out.

1785 BURNS *2nd Ep. to J. Lapraik* ii, Forjesket sair, with weary legs. **1826** G. BEATTIE *John o' Arnha'* in *Life* 228 The fiend, forjeskit, tried to 'scape.

†**for'joust**, *v. Obs.* [f. FOR- *pref.*[1] + JOUST *v.*] *trans.* To overcome or overthrow in jousting.

? *a* **1400** *Morte Arth.* 1398 Syr Marschalle de Mowne es.. fforc-justyde at that journee. *a* **1440** *Sir Degrev.* 1897 At Portgaff was he slone, ffor-justyd with a Soudone. *c* **1470** HARDING *Chron.* CXLVII. xiii, He foriust the duke full manly. **1470–85** MALORY *Arthur* VIII. xxxix, He foriusted alle that were there.

forjudge, forejudge (fə'dʒʌdʒ), *v.* Also 4–5 forjuge, (5 forjugge), 5–7 forjudge, 6–9 forejudge. [In sense 1, ad. OF. *for-*, *fors-*, *fourjugier*, f. *for(s-*, FOR- *pref.*[3] + *jugier* JUDGE *v.* In sense 2 the prefix seems to have been taken as FOR-[1].]

1. To exclude, oust, or dispossess by a judgement. Const. *from*, *of*, or with *double obj.* *Obs.* exc. in *Law.*

[**1292** BRITTON I. xiv. §4 Si soint il forjugez de chescune ley et hors de nostre pes.] *c* **1470** HARDING *Chron.* CXIV. xix, He was depriued of his estate..Foriuged hole from [all] his magestee. **1491** *Act 7 Hen. VII*, c. 16 It was enacted..that John Duke of Norfolk..shuld..be..forjuged of all honour. *a* **1577** SIR T. SMITH *Commw. Eng.* (1609) 90 His lands..in all cases of felony are commonly lost from him and his heires, if he be foreiudged, that is, condemned for a felon by the law. **1641** *Termes de la Ley* 164 If an Attorneyy or other officer in any Court bee put out and forbidden to use the same, he is said to be forjudged the Court. **1642** tr. *Perkin's Prof. Bk.* v. §432. 186 If..the tenant bringeth a Writ of Mesne against the Mesne, and forejudgeth him. **1643** PRYNNE *Sov. Power Parl.* I. 12 The same Justices were forejudged of their lives. **1765** BLACKSTONE *Comm.* I. 134 It is enacted by the statute 5 Edw. III. c. 9. that no man shall be forejudged of life or limb, contrary to the great charter. **1883** F. POLLOCK *Land Laws* (1887) 25 When a man is forejudged of life and lands for cowardice in battle.

†**b.** To prohibit (*from*). *Obs.*

1675 *Camden's Hist. Eliz.* IV. 589 The Navigation of the English into those Parts would for the future be forejudged and wholly barred. **1697** *View Penal Laws* 151 For the fourth shall be forejudged from ever keeping an Inn again.

†**2.** To condemn judicially (*to* a penalty). *Obs.*

1390 GOWER *Conf.* III. 192 Alisaundre..a worthy knight Of sodein wrath and nat of right Forjuged hath. **1423** JAS. I *Kingis Q.* iii, From estate, by fortune a quhile Foriugit was to pouert in exile. **1494** FABYAN *Chron.* VII. 568 [They] were takyn as prysoners in the Towre of London, and soone after foriugyd, hanged, and hedyd. **1571** GOLDING *Calvin on Ps.* xli. 1 The greater part of men forjudge miserable folk to destruction. **1752** CARTE *Hist. Eng.* III. 606 She..being already condemned and forejudged to die.

Hence **for'judging** *vbl. sb.*

1651 N. BACON *Disc. Govt. Eng.* II. iii. (1739) 20 No.. forejudging of Life..against the form of the Grand Charter.

†**forjudgement.** *Obs.* [a. OF. *forjugement*, f. *forjugier* to FORJUDGE.] = next.

1531 *Dial. Laws of Eng.* II. xliii. 89 a, It is comonly holden that if an enfant had nat ben excepted in the statute of foriugement, that the foriugement sholde haue bounde him. **1628** COKE *On Litt.* II. vi. §142. 100 The iudgement in case of foriudgement is [etc.].

forjudger (fəˈdʒʌdʒə(r)). *Law.* Also 5 forjugger, 8–9 forejudger. [a. Anglo-Fr. *forjuger* = OF. *forjugier* pres. inf. (see FORJUDGE *v.*) used as sb.; cf. DEMURRER.] A judgement or sentence of deprivation, expulsion, or banishment. Applied *spec.* to the ousting of a mesne lord by a writ of mesne.

1496–7 *Act 12 Hen. VII*, c. 11 §1 The seid Acte..of.. forjugger and forfeiture. **1628** COKE *On Litt.* II. vi. §142. 100 Foriudger in that case is not given against his heire. **1641** in *Termes de la Ley* 164. **1850** in BURRILL *Law Dict.*

transf. **1716** M. DAVIES *Athen. Brit.* II. To Rdr. 23 The Insatiable Rich..become Drum- and Trumpet-Proof to the sacred Forejudgers, *Mat.* 25. 41, 42, *Luke* 14. 13, 21 [etc.].

†**for'jure, forejure,** *v. Obs.* [a. OF. *forjure-r* = med.L. *forisjurāre*, really two distinct words: (1) f. *for-*, FOR- *pref.*[3] + *jurer*:—L. *jurāre* to swear; (2) f. med.L. *foris* prep. outside + *jūra* laws, rights.]

1. *trans.* To forswear; to abandon, abjure, quit.

1601 F. TATE *Househ. Ord. Edw. II*, §90 (1876) 53 No man shalbe avantalour who hath forjured the Court.

2. To exclude from civil rights.

1647 N. BACON *Disc. Govt. Eng.* I. lxix. (1739) 182 Bail shall not be allowed to Outlaws fore-jured.

fork (fɔːk), *sb.* Also 1 forca, (*myx-*)force, 3 *pl.* furken, 4–6 forcke, 4–7 forke. [OE. *forca* wk. masc., *force* wk. fem., ad. L. *furca* fem., fork (for hay, etc.), forked stake, gallows, yoke.

The use of the word in Eng. was doubtless extended by the influence of the ONF. form *forque, fourque* (Central OF. *forche, fourche*), from which some of the Eng. senses are derived. The L. word is found in nearly all the Rom. and Teut. langs.: cf. Pr. *forca*, Sp. *horca*, Pg. *forca*, It. *furca*, OHG. *furcha* (mod. Ger. *furke*), Du. *vork*, all chiefly in sense 'pitchfork'; also ON. *forkr*, forked stake.]

I. A pronged instrument.

1. a. An implement, chiefly agricultural, consisting of a long straight handle, furnished at the end with two or more prongs or tines, and used for carrying, digging, lifting, or throwing; also with word prefixed indicating its use, as ***digging-, dung-, hay-***, etc. ***fork***: see those words; also FIRE-FORK, PITCH-FORK, etc.

c **1000** ÆLFRIC *Hom.* (Th.) I. 430 Ða cwelleras..wið-ufan mid heora forcum hine ðydon. *c* **1000** —— *Gloss.* in Wr.-Wülcker 154 *Furcilla*, litel forca. *a* **1310** in Wright's *Lyric P.* 110 Mon in the mone..on is bot forke is burthen he bereth. **1382** WYCLIF *1 Sam.* xiii. 21 Eggys..of diggynge yrens, and of forkis..weren blunt. **1413** *Pilgr. Sowle* (Caxton 1483) III. viii. 55 Suche folke..to bynde in fagottes and cast them with forkes into the fyre. **1523** FITZHERB. *Husb.* §24 A good husbande hath his forkes and rakes made redye in the wynter before. **1573** BARET *Alv.* F 892 A Forke, or trout speare with three points, *fuscina*. **1573** TUSSER *Husb.* liii. (1878) 120 At Midsommer, downe with the brembles and brakes, and after, abrode with thy forks and thy rakes. **1700** DRYDEN *Cock & Fox* 727 The crew, With forks and staves the felon to pursue. **1719** LONDON & WISE *Compl. Gard.* VIII. 196 We must use an Iron Fork to draw them out of the Nursery-Beds. **1784** COWPER *Task* III. 479 Lightly, shaking it with agile hand From the full fork. **1860** DELAMER *Kitch. Gard.* (1861) 16 A fork for taking up potatoes, &c., and spreading dung.

fig. in *Proverb.* *a* **1700** B. E. *Dict. Cant. Crew*, *Fork is often Rakes Heir*, or after a scraping Father comes a scattering Son. **1725** *New Cant. Dict.*, *Fork* is also used for a Spendthrift, etc.

†**b.** A similar implement used as a weapon.

13.. *K. Alis.* 1191 Fiftene thousand of fot laddes, That.. hadde, Axes, speres, forkis, and slynges. **1598** GRENEWEY *Tacitus' Ann.* 78 Some with poles or forks ouerthrew this sluggish lump: leauing them for halfe dead lying on the ground. **1678** tr. *Gaya's Arms of War* 29 The Forks are the same with the common Forks, but they have little Hooks.

†**c.** The forked tongue (popularly supposed to be the sting) of a snake. *Obs.*

1603 SHAKS. *Meas. for M.* III. i. 16 Thou dost feare the soft and tender forke Of a poore worme. **1605** —— *Macb.* IV. i. 16.

2. a. An instrument with two, three, or four prongs, used for holding the food while it is being cut, for conveying it to the mouth, and for other purposes at table or in cooking. For ***carving-, dessert-, fish-, pickle-, table-fork***, etc. see those words.

1463 *Bury Wills* (Camden) 40, I beqwethe to Davn John Kertelynge my silvir forke for grene gyngour. **1554** *Ibid.* 147, I geve and bequeath my neighbor..my spone with a forke in the end. **1589** *Pasquil's Ret.* D iij, At the signe of the siluer forke and the tosted cheese. **1605** B. JONSON *Volpone* IV. i, Then must you learn the use And handling of your silver fork at meals. **1724** R. FALCONER *Voy.* (1769) 65, I had in my Pocket a Knife and Fork. **1766** SMOLLETT *Trav.* 35 The poorest tradesman in Boulogne has..silver forks with four prongs. **1838** DICKENS *Nich. Nick.* vii, He laid down his knife and fork.

b. ***forks and knives***: the name of the club-moss *Lycopodium clavatum*.

1853 G. JOHNSTON *Nat. Hist. E. Bord.* I. 257.

3. a. Used in *pl.* for the prongs of a fork. Also *transf.* Cf. 12.

1674 N. COX *Gentl. Recreat.* IV. (1677) 40 An Eel-spear.. is made for the most part with three Forks or Teeth. **1702** ADDISON *Dial. Medals* Wks. 1721 I. 447 A thunderbolt with three forks. **1767** H. KELLY, etc. *Babler* I. 280 A couple of tushes that project a surprising way from the mouth, like the forks of an elephant.

b. *pl.* (*slang*). The fingers. Hence, a pick-pocket (B. E. *Dict. Cant. Crew* ?*a* 1700).

1812 J. H. VAUX *Flash Dict.*, *Forks*, the two fore-fingers; to *put your forks down*, is to pick a pocket. **1834** AINSWORTH *Rookwood* III. v, No dummy hunter had forks so fly.

4. A steel instrument with two prongs which, when set in vibration, gives a musical note; called more fully a *tuning-fork*.

1799 YOUNG in *Phil. Trans.* XC. 134 The fork was a comma and a half above the pitch..of an imaginary C. *c* **1865** J. WYLDE in *Circ. Sc.* I. 275/1 If the fork be struck against any hard body..its prong..vibrates.

II. Applied to various objects having two (or more) branches.

†**5. a.** A gallows. Also *pl.* Cf. FORCHE 1.

[So OF. *fourche(s*, L. *furca*; the Roman gallows was originally of the shape ʌ.]

c **1205** LAY. 5720 þe furken [*1275* forkes] weoren aræred, heo teuwen up þa ȝisles, and heom þer hengen. **1399** *Pol. Poems* (Rolls) I. 379 He shulde have hadde hongynge on hie on the fforckis. **1596** DALRYMPLE tr. *Leslie's Hist. Scot.* I. 121 Lat him end his lyf vpon ane fork. *a* **1680** BUTLER *Rem.* II. 195 They had run through all punishments, and just 'scaped the fork.

b. *Rom. Ant.* Used to render L. *furca*, (*a*) the 'yoke' under which defeated enemies were made to pass as a token of their submission; (*b*) the forked stake used as a whipping-post.

a **1616** BEAUM. & FL. *Bonduca* II. iv, The forks Where you shall have two lictors with two whips Hammer your hide. **1618** BOLTON *Florus* I. xvi. 48 Passing them naked under Forkes, or Gallowses. **1683** DRYDEN & LEE *Duke of Guise* IV. v, We passed Like beaten Romans underneath the fork.

6. A stake, staff, or stick with a forked end; **a.** as a prop for a vine or tree; **b.** a rest for a musket; cf. FORCAT. **c.** (See quot.). **d.** *Mining* (Derbysh.): see quot. 1881. **e.** A divining-rod.

a. 1389 *Helmingham MS.* 21. 17 b, Forkis..to bere up þe vyne. **1626** BACON *Sylva* §423 Some have put two little Forks about the bottom of their Trees, to keep them upright. **1816** KEATINGE *Trav.* (1817) I. 43 The boughs.. propped up by forks.

b. 1591 GARRARD *Art Warre* 7 To traine hys Forke or Staffe after hym whilest he..doth charge hys Musket.

c. 1726 *Gentlem. Angler* 149 A Fork. Vide Rest [for a fishing rod].

d. 1747 HOOSON *Miner's Dict.* G iij b, If..we think it will let the Forks settle when they come to be weighted, we put a Sill under them. **1881** RAYMOND *Mining Gloss.*, *Fork*..a piece of wood supporting the side of an excavation in soft ground.

e. 1886 A. WINCHELL *Walks & Talks Geol. Field* 137 Some..even resorted to the witch-hazel fork [in 'prospecting' for petroleum].

7. *Building.* See quots. 1868, 1883.

c **1420** *Pallad. on Husb.* I. 522 Let make an hous for bestis ..Of forkis, & of boord. **1792** MASTIN *Hist. Antiq. Naseby* 9 The most antique architecture, called forked building, which forks are all of oak. **1841** *Anc. Laws Wales* 351 Thirty pence is the value of every fork that shall support the roof tree. **1868** ATKINSON *Cleveland Gloss.*, *Forks*, the centres, in the timber-work of the roof of a shed, house or other building; commonly, 'a pair of forks'. **1883** SEEBOHM *Village Community* 239 Their [the trees'] extremities bending over make a Gothic arch, and crossing one another at the top, each pair makes a fork, upon which the roof-tree is fixed. These trees supporting the roof-tree are called gavaels, forks, or columns.

†**8.** *Anat.* ***fork of the throat*** or ***breast***: app. the sternal bone together with the clavicles. *Obs.*

[= med.L. *furcula*, OF. *fourcelle*; the words seem to have been used very vaguely, and it is often impossible to determine the exact sense.]

c **1400** *Lanfranc's Cirurg.* 316 For brekyng of þe forke of þe þrote and of þe brest. *c* **1535** DEWES *Introd. Fr.* in Palsgr. 900 The forke of the brest..*fourcelle*. **1639** DE GRAY *Compl. Horsem.* 39 The Forke or Throat hath five [bones].

†**9.** The barbed head of an arrow. *Obs.*

1605 SHAKS. *Lear* I. i. 146 Make from the shaft. *Kent.* Let it fall rather, though the forke inuade The region of my heart.

10. In various technical uses. **a.** A piece of steel fitting into the socket or chuck of a lathe, used for carrying round the piece to be turned.

1858 in SIMMONDS *Dict. Trade.*

b. (also *forks*): see quot.

1888 *Lockwood's Dict. Mech. Engin.*, *Belt Fork*, or *Strap Fork*, a pair of prongs standing out from a strap bar and enclosing a space within which the belt or strap of a machine fitted with fast and loose pulleys runs. **1893** *Labour Commission* Gloss., *Forks*. In mill sawing machinery the forks are two upright pieces of iron one on each side of the band moved by a lever to throw the band on or off the driving wheels.

c. The front or back projection of a saddle.

1833 *Reg. Instr. Calvalry* I. 46 The pummel or fore fork. *Ibid.* 42 The Blanket..to be raised well into the fork.

d. The part of a bicycle frame in which the (front or back) wheel revolves; also *attrib.*, as ***fork-blade, -crown, -end, -head***. Also *pl.*

1871 *English Mechanic* XIII. 144 Can any reader give me a description of socket and fork of 'Ariel' bicycle? **1880** *Scott. Football Ann.* (Advt.), The Howe Bicycle, all the latest improvements, hollow oval fork, &c. **1892** *Work* 27 Aug. 379/2 Front mud-guard should be fixed to fork crown with a bolt and nut. **1898** *Cycling* 48 The fork ends. **1902** *Captain* VII. 83/1 The fork head of the Raleigh. **1908** *Daily Chron.* 7 Nov. 7/1 In a fog it is better to carry one's lamp on the fork-blade than high up. **1957** *Encycl. Brit.* III. 544/2 The fork crown (at the top of the forks) is fixed to the steering column. **1952** *Cycling* ('Know the Game') (1964) 17 The wheel revolves on a spindle contained in the hub and this is usually secured in the forks of the cycle by means of two ordinary nuts. **1968** [see FRAME *sb.* 11 f].

11. *Mining.* (See quots.)

1778 PRYCE *Min. Cornub.*, *Forcque, Fork*, the bottom of the Sumph. Forking the water, is drawing it all out; and when it is done, they say..'the Engine is in Fork'. **1869** R. B. SMYTH *Goldf. Victoria* 611 When a mine is in fork the bottom of the engine-shaft is clear of water.

12. [From the verb.] A forking, bifurcation, or division into branches; the point at which anything forks. Hence, each of the branches into which anything forks. **a.** *gen.*

1398 TREVISA *Barth. De P.R.* V. xviii. (1495) 123 The endes of thyse bones ben departed and haue two forkes. **1615** CROOKE *Body of Man* 375 The forked values making certain gaping fissures betweene their forkes. **1674** N. COX *Gentl. Recreat.* IV. (1677) 10 Those sixty Carps were from Eye to Fork from fifteen Inches to eighteen Inches. **1830** HERSCHEL *Stud. Nat. Phil.* 84 We cross the two first fingers of one hand, and place a pea in the fork between them.

b. In the human body, the part at which the lower limbs proceed from the trunk. Also (*sing.* and *pl.*), the lower limbs themselves; the lower half of the body. Cf. FORCHURE.

1605 SHAKS. *Lear* IV. vi. 121. **1631** [see CHINING *vbl. sb.*]. **1812** *Examiner* 12 Oct. 652/a, You are not long enough in the fork for the—dragoons. **1872** BAKER *Nile Tribut.* xiv. 234 The thigh, and entire leg from the fork to the ankle.

c. The point at which a river divides into two, or the point of junction of two rivers; a branch or tributary. Chiefly *U.S.*

1753 C. GIST *Jrnls.* (1893) 80 We..got to the big fork of said river. **1837** W. IRVING *Capt. Bonneville* (1849) 41 The fork of the Nebraska, where it divides itself into two equal and beautiful streams. **1839** MURCHISON *Silur. Syst.* I. xxix. 372 N. and S. forks of the great estuary of Milford Haven. **18..** *Scenes Rocky Mts.* 50 (Bartlett) Their village, at the Forks of the Platte. **1877** J. A. ALLEN *Amer. Bison* 515 Great herds on the east fork of the Salmon River.

d. of a road.

1839–40 W. IRVING *Wolfert's R.* (1855) 281 A fork in the road. **1860** PUSEY *Min. Proph.* 241 Taking the fork where the ways parted, in order to intercept the fugitives. **1883** HOWARD *Roads* (ed. 3) 47 Here take the right hand fork.

e. of a plant or tree.

1776 WITHERING *Brit. Plants* (1796) II. 200 Fruit-stalk.. rising from the fork of the stem. **1843** *Zoologist* I. 228 The raven's nest was placed in a fork..of one of these trees. **1871** G. MEREDITH *H. Richmond* xv, Torches were struck in clefts of the trees, or in the fork of the branches.

f. A flash (of forked lightning); a tongue of flame.

1859 TENNYSON *Vivien* 939 Dazzled by the livid-flickering fork. **1871** PALGRAVE *Lyr. Poems* 58 A fork of flame from Vesuvius Through his black cone went on high.

g. *Chess.* A simultaneous attack on two pieces, esp. by a knight.

1656 BEALE *Royall Game of Chesse Play* vii, Forke is, that when you see two of the enemies Noble-men standing in the same ranke, and but one house betwixt them, advance a pawne, guarded with an other, unto the middle house before them both, and you may commonly take one of them. **1688** R. HOLME *Armoury* (1905) 66/2 A Fork or dilemma, is a way of takeing a chesse man, by runing vp a pawn to the rank next two great men of the aduerse part standing in one rank with a house betweene them, where if one be saued, the other wilbe taken. **1761** E. HOYLE *Ess. Chess* A4, Take care of a Fork or a Check by Discovery, or a Stale mat. **1764** R. LAMBE *Hist. Chess* 98 A Fork is, when an adverse Pawn must take one of your Pieces, by standing upon a Square of the next Line, between two of them. **1890** R. F. GREEN *Chess* v. 17 A frequent and fatal fork. The White Knight..attacks both the Black King and Queen. **1969** A. GLYN *Dragon Variation* ix. 293 Carl was threatening a Knight fork against Boghossian's Queen and other Rook.

†**13.** *fig.* **a.** *nonce-use.* The union of two lines of descent. **b.** A dilemma, choice of alternatives; also, a dichotomy, distinction. *Obs.*

1559 *Mirr. Mag., Dk. Clarence* vi, Of which two houses ioyned in a forke, My father..was lawful heire beget. *a* **1616** BEAUM. & FL. *Bloody Brother* III. ii, There is a fork, sir, In death..Man may be two ways killed. **1670** HOBBES *Behemoth* (1840) 214 Declining the force of true reason by verbal forks..distinctions that signify nothing.

14. ***Caudine Forks*** = L. *Furcæ* or *Furculæ Caudinæ*: proper name of a defile near Caudium, in Samnium, where the Romans were intercepted in the second Samnite war. Hence proverbially used for: A crushing defeat.

1618 BOLTON *Florus* I. xvi. 48 The most notable and famous foyle..was received at the Forkes of Caudium. **1781** J. Q. ADAMS in *Fam. Lett.* (1876) 403 The Romans never saw but one Caudine Forks in their whole history. Americans have shown the Britons two in one war.

III. *attrib.* and *Comb.* (see also sense 10 d).

15. a. objective, as ***fork-grinder***, etc.; **b.** parasynthetic and similative, as ***fork-like, -shaped, -tongued*** adjs.; ***fork-wise*** adv.

1844–5 DODD *Dict. Manuf.*, s.v. *Fork-making*, The *fork-grinders are too often a reckless body of men. **1889** *Daily News* 11 Nov. 2/6 With the exception of the fork grinders there is no actual agitation. **1611** COTGR., *Fourcheure*, A forkinesse..a *fork-like diuision. **1889** *Daily News* 9 Oct. 5/5 They frequently fix the faces of the prisoners with fork-like irons towards the burning sun. **1835-6** TODD *Cycl. Anat.* I. 334/2 The vessel then passes between the clavicle and the *fork-shaped bone. **1636** MASSINGER *Gt. Dk. Florence* III. i, They..Had trod on *fork-tongued adders. **1541** R. COPLAND *Guydon's Quest. Chirurg.* D ij, The veynes ..renne *forkewyse in to two partyes. **1668** CULPEPPER & COLE *Barthol. Anat.* I. xvi. 40 Divided forkwise into two twigs.

16. a. Special comb.: **fork-beam** *Naut.* (see quot.); **fork-beard**, a name given to various fishes of the genus *Phycis*; **fork-breakfast** (see quot.); **fork-carving** *a.*, that uses a fork in carving; **fork-chuck** (*Wood-turning*), a chuck with two or more teeth: see quot. 1874; **fork-fish**, ? a kind of thornback; **fork-lift truck**, etc. a vehicle fitted with a pronged device in front for lifting and carrying heavy goods; also *fork-lift* ellipt.; **fork-moss**, a kind of moss (*Dicranum bryoïdes*); **fork-ribbed** *a.*, having ribs branching off like the prongs of a fork; **fork-shaft**, the handle of a fork; **fork-staff-plane**, a kind of joiner's plane used for working convex cylindrical surfaces; **fork-way**, a point where two roads meet or diverge, a fork; **fork-wrench** (see quot.). Also FORK-HEAD, FORK-TAIL.

c **1850** *Rudim. Navig.* (Weale) 95 **Fork-Beam*, a forked piece of timber nearly of the depth of the beam, scarphed, tabled, and bolted, for additional security to the sides of beams athwart large openings in the decks. **1864** COUCH *Brit. Fishes* III. 122 Lesser *Forkbeard. **1812** *Sporting Mag.* XXXIX. 163 *Le dejeuner à la fourchette*, or *fork-breakfast, is so called, because in eating meat you have occasion for a fork. **1882** H. C. MERIVALE *Faucit of B.* II. xv, In this country..the French midday fork-breakfast, is unknown. *c* **1618** FLETCHER *Q. Corinth* IV. i, Your T beard..doth express the enamour'd courtier, As full as your *fork-carving traveller. **1842** FRANCIS *Dict. Arts*, **Fork Chuck.* **1874** KNIGHT *Dict. Mech.*, *Fork-chuck* (Turning), a piece of steel projecting from the live spindle and carrying the front center and a pair of joints which enter the wood and rotate it. **1601** HOLLAND *Pliny* I. 261 The Puffen or *Fork-fish.. lieth in await..ready to strike the fishes that passe by with a sharpe rod or pricke that he hath. **1706** PHILLIPS, *Fork-fish*, a kind of Thorn-back, so call'd from its forked Tail. **1946** *Engin. Index 1945* 557/2 Use of carrier *fork lift trucks capable of handling filled cable reels. **1950** *Jrnl. R. Aeronaut. Soc.* LIV. 521/1 Fork lifts, and in exceptional cases loading ramps, were used for the bulky awkward items. **1955** *Radio Times* 30 Sept., Modern package-handling machines—fork-lifts they are called. **1958** *Times* 1 July p. iv/7 The tractor is fitted with a fork lift loader to lift 35 cwt. capacity pallets. **1968** *Times* 11 Mar. p. ii. (*caption*), A heavy load..handled by a forklift truck. **1860** GOSSE *Rom. Nat. Hist.* 192 The sight of the *fork-moss would ever afterwards call up a vivid recollection of that desolate scene. **1858** CARPENTER *Veg. Phys.* § 196 As regards their leaves, the Cryptogamia may be characterized as *fork-ribbed. **1641** BEST *Farm. Bks.* (Surtees) 34 Shorte *forke-shaftes made of seasoned ashe. **1848** A. B. EVANS *Leicester Words*, *Fork-shaft*, handle of a fork, whether pitchfork or any other. **1816** J. SMITH *Panorama Sc. & Art* I. 111 A plane..with a concave sole, is also distinguished by the name of a *fork-staff-plane. **1819** W. TAYLOR in *Monthly Mag.* XLVII. 308 Hecate, Luna, Diana, who meet in a *fork-way. **1874** KNIGHT *Dict. Mech.*, **Fork-wrench*, a spanner with two jaws which embrace a nut or square on a coupling.

b. fork supper (also *-buffet*, *-dinner*, *-lunch(eon*, etc.), a meal served at a buffet, etc., consisting of food suitable for eating with fork alone, making the provision of set places at table unnecessary.

1940 N. MITFORD *Pigeon Pie* i. 12 He came to all the week-end parties, tea parties, fork luncheons. **1949** *Antiquity* XXIII. 121 After a sumptuous fork-luncheon they all set off for Amiens. **1952** A. COLBY *Beauty Bk.* 230 The buffet supper..is a 'fork supper'. **1957** H. CROOME *Forgotten Place* vii. 89 We'll have a party. Just a fork supper, and a bit of dancing. **1958** *TV Times* 18 July 18/3 The party is always on a Sunday or Monday—fork buffets, of course. **1965** *Courier-Mail* (Brisbane) 9 Oct. 17/11 A fork dinner for 40 young friends. **1971** *Times* 22 Jan. 14/3 Aspirants..would be well-advised to practise the art of conversing while wielding wine glass and loaded plate, because the plan is to hold a two-hour fork luncheon before the selection meeting.

fork (fɔːk), *v.* [f. prec.]

1. a. *intr.* To form a fork; to divide into branches, divaricate. Of lightning: To play forkedly. Also with *away*, *off*, or *out*.

1598 SYLVESTER *Du Bartas* II. ii. I. *Noah* 243 Adam's Trunk (of both-our Worlds the Tree) In two faire branches forking fruitfully. **1796** H. HUNTER tr. *St. Pierre's Stud. Nat.* (1799) I. 239 Others [trees] ascend vertically, and.. fork off in various tiers. **1808** J. BARLOW *Columb.* v. 276 The flames fork round the semivault of heaven. **1840** *Jrnl. R. Agric. Soc.* I. IV. 419 The parsnip..forks away into fingers. **1847** ANSTED *Anc. World* viii. 170 Rays..forking off towards the end. **1851** MAYNE REID *Scalp Hunt.* xli, The lightning forked and flashed. **1853** PHILLIPS *Rivers Yorksh.* ix. 240 Here the road forked.

b. Of corn: To sprout.

1707 MORTIMER *Husb.* 265 Throw the frozen outsides into the middle till the Corn begin to fork and warm in the Couch. **1725** BRADLEY *Fam. Dict.* s.v. *Malt.*

c. *Chess. trans.* To attack (two pieces) simultaneously with the same piece.

1745 E. HOYLE *Piquet & Chess* 61 Take care that no guarded Pawn of your Adversary's fork two of your Pieces. **1891** E. FREEBOROUGH *Chess Endings* 116 The Queen may be forked by a diverging check, with the Kt, preceded by B-Kt 7 ch. **1891** R. B. SWINTON *Chess for Beginners* 73 Sometimes a Pawn can play a shrewd trick by 'forking' two pieces. **1899** E. E. CUNNINGTON *Mod. Chess Primer* 20 There is nothing, in chess, more dangerous than to allow one of your opponent's men to..'fork' two of your men by one move. **1922** A. EMERY *Elem. Chess* 68 When a knight checks, and at the same time attacks a man which can be captured with advantage on the next move the latter is said to be 'forked'.

†**2.** *fig.* **a.** Of witnesses: To disagree in their testimony. **b.** Of the tongue [after F. *fourcher*]: To stumble, trip. *Obs.*

a **1300** *Cursor M.* 16074 (Cott.) In þair aun sagh þai said, oft-sith for-kid þai. *Ibid.* 17754 (Gött.) þai did þaa thre men þan to sunder, And askid seluen ilkan sere, Oo þair forking fain wald þai here. **1652** URQUHART *Jewel* Wks. (1834) 265 Philoplutaries, my tongue forks it, I have mistaken..one word for another, I should have said Philosophers.

3. *trans.* To make or put into the form of a fork; to make fork-shaped. † *to fork the fingers*: to extend them towards a person as a mark of contempt.

1640 *Witts Recreat.* C ij, His wife..Behind him forks her fingers. **1668** CULPEPPER & COLE *Barthol. Anat.* I. viii. 315 The *Ramus Iliacus* is forked out on each side. **1774** GOLDSM. *Nat. Hist.* (1776) VII. 348 The tail..is forked into two horns. **1816** J. SMITH *Panorama Sc. & Art* I. 376 A lever.. which is forked at the lower part to receive the pendulum. **1816** BYRON *Ch. Har.* III. xcv, The mightiest of the storms ..through these parted hills hath fork'd His lightnings. **1817** COLERIDGE *Biog. Lit.* 289 Bertram..stands..with his lower limbs forked.

fig. **1683** DRYDEN & LEE *Dk. of Guise* IV. iii, Angel-traitors ..Forked into ills, and split into deceits.

4. To raise or move with or as with a fork; to dig, take, or throw *in*, *out*, *up*, etc., with a fork.

1802 A. KIRKWOOD *Jrnl.* in *Mem.* (1856) 24, I..forked some hay for Mr. Black. **1829** *Rep. Doncaster Commission, Bone Manure* 30 Fold manure..should be forked up to a considerable height. **1833** M. SCOTT *Tom Cringle* xv, Bang ..was gobbling his last plantain, and forking up along with it..slices of cheese. **1846** J. BAXTER *Libr. Pract. Agric.* II. 191 The ancient practice of forking out each parsnip from the ground. **1850** KINGSLEY *Alt. Locke* xi, He..set to work forking up some weeds on a fallow. **1851** GLENNY *Handbk. Fl. Gard.* 24 The border should be prepared..by forking in some peat. **1858** —— *Gard. Every-day Bk.* 75/1 The beds should now be forked over. **1882** TENNYSON *Promise of May* II, And you an' your Sally was forkin' the haäy.

fig. **1647** TRAPP *Mellif. Theolog.* in *Comm. Epist.* 643 He leaves it [his wealth] to a prodigall, that..forks it abroad, as fast as the miser his father raked it together. [Cf. FORK *sb.* 1 *fig.*] **1828** LANDOR *Imag. Conv.* III. 101 Society is not yet trodden down and forked together by you, into one and the same rotten mass.

absol. **1683** J. ERSKINE *Jrnl.* 11 Sept. (1893) 16, I was seeing the corn cut in the barnyard and whiles forking.

5. *transf.* (*colloq.* or *slang.*) **a.** *to fork out, over,* or *up*: to give up, hand over, pay.

1831 TRELAWNY *Adv. Younger Son.* xxxvi, Fork out something better than this. **1839** *Observer & Reporter* May 18 The gambler should fork over his illgotten gains. **1843** *Punch* V. 86/2 'Oblige me with that hod', and 'Have the kindness to hand me that gimlet', are phrases which might be well substituted for a request to 'chuck' or 'fork up' 'this here' and 'that 'ere'. **1849** D. NASON *Jrnl.* 113 As he was the biggest man I had to fork over $1·25. **1865** DICKENS *Mut. Fr.* III. i, Fork out your balance in hand. **1866** J. C. GREGG *Life in Army* xv. 132 Every person..forks over his picayune. **1871** *Scribner's Monthly* I. 601 So the governor forked this up, though it's my selection entirely. **1883** *Harper's Mag.* Aug. 486/1 He forked over the money. **1918** E. POUND in *Lett. J. Joyce* (1966) II. 424, I will fork up the remaining £20 of the fifty promised. **1932** H. CRANE *Let.* Jan. (1965) 395 The family will just have to fork up a loan or something for me.

absol. **1836** *Franklin Repos.* (Chambersburg, Pa.) 29 Mar. 1/2 'Fork up, and that instantly, or take the contents of this,' he added fiercely, as he thrust the cold barrel of the pistol against the supplicant's cheek. **1839** *Observer & Reporter* Nov. 23 Well then, fork up, and be quick. **1856** READE *Never too Late* lv, See it for twenty-four hours or I won't fork out. **1857** *Quinland* II. III. iii. 167 The plethoric dog of a New Jersey Jew has got the 'tin', and will fork up as soon as the matter is fixed. **1875** A. R. HOPE *My Schoolboy Fr.* 154 I'll tell Vialls if you do not fork out.

b. (*U.S.*) See quots.

1839 MARRYAT *Diary Amer.* Ser. I. II. 231, I heard a young man..in Vermont, say,..'Well, how he contrived to fork into her young affections, I can't tell'. **1851** B. H. HALL *College Wds.*, *Fork on.* At Hamilton College, *to fork on*, to appropriate to one's self.

6. *intr.* (*colloq.*) To protrude awkwardly.

1882 *Fraser's Mag.* XXV. 532, I noted a number of heads forking over the side of the ship. **1890** W. C. RUSSELL *Ocean Trag.* II. xiv. 20 He came slowly forking up through the hatch. *Ibid.* xix. 133 Leathery noses forking up out of a hedge of whisker.

7. *slang.* (*trans.*) *to fork a person*: to pick his pocket. Cf. FORK *sb.* 3.

a **1700** B. E. *Dict. Cant. Crew*, *Let's fork him*, let us Pick that Man's Pocket. **1785** in GROSE *Dict. Vulg. Tongue.*

8. *intr.* (*Sc.*) To look out, strive *for* (something).

1681 COLVIL *Whigs Supplic.* (1710) 73 That Pauls Iniquities, mystery working, Was men, then for precedency forking. **1825-80** JAMIESON s.v. *Forking*, 'Forkin' for siller'; 'Forkin' for a job.

9. *Mining.* (*trans.*) To pump (a mine) dry; to remove (water) by pumping. Cf. FORK *sb.* 11.

1702 SAVERY *Miner's Fr.* 56 What signifies your Engine.. if it be not capable of Sinking or Forking an Old Mine. **1859** *Times* 27 Apr., He had forked the heaviest waters in the whole country. **1869** *West. Daily Mercury* 20 Mar., They have resolved on forking the water. **1893** *Pall Mall G.* 14 Jan. 2/1 The mine has been 'forked'.

10. To bestride or mount (a horse). *U.S.*

1903 A. ADAMS *Log of Cowboy* xix. 295 So fork that swimming horse of yours and wet your big toe again in the North Platte. **1920** J. M. HUNTER *Trail Drivers of Texas* 245 Throw your rope and whatever it falls on, fork him.

forkals, *pl. jocular.* [f. FORK *sb.* + -AL[1].] Legs.

1828 *Sporting Mag.* XXIII. 33 The piece of mahogany under which my old forkals had so merrily rested.

forked (fɔːkt), *ppl. a.* [f. FORK *sb.* + -ED[2].]

1. Having a fork or fork-like end; shaped like a fork, bifurcate, branching.

a **1300** *Cursor M.* 18843 (Cott.) Forked fair þe chin he bare. *c* **1386** CHAUCER *Prol.* 270 A Marchant..with a forked berd. **1398** TREVISA *Barth. De P.R.* XII. xxii. 428 The swalowes..tayles ben forkyd as a payr of sherys. *c* **1400** *Lanfranc's Cirurg.* 158 þat oþere partie of þe veyne passiþ to þe arm hoolis & þere he is forkid. **1534** FITZHERB. *Husb.* §21 He hath a forked stycke a yarde longe. **1597** SHAKS. *2 Hen. IV*, III. ii. 334 Hee was, for all the world, like a forked Radish, with a Head fantastically caru'd vpon it. **1667** MILTON *P.L.* x. 518 Hiss for hiss returnd with forked tongue To forked tongue. **1692** *Lond. Gaz.* No. 2830/4 Stolen..2 silver Spoons, a Fork, 2 small Spoons forkt. **1729** T. COOKE *Tales*, etc. 40 Forked Light'nings fright the World below. **1821** CLARE *Vill. Minstr.* I. 53 On two forked sticks with cordage tied, Their pot o'er pilfer'd fuel boils away. **1861** MISS PRATT *Flower. Pl.* I. 3 A stem is termed forked when it divides into two branches of equal, or nearly equal size. **1870** HOOKER *Stud. Flora* 24 Arabis..with forked or stellate hairs. **1887** BOWEN *Virg. Æneid* II. 211 Forked tongues are flickering seen.

fig. **1649** G. DANIEL *Trinarch.*, *Hen. IV*, xvii, Thus forked Novelty Spreads.

b. Of a road: Making a fork; having two or more diverging branches.

1525 LD. BERNERS *Froiss.* II. xci. [lxxxvii.] 271 When we had rydden a ii. leages, we came to a forked waye. **1600** HOLLAND *Livy* XXXVIII. xlv. (1609) 1011 At every forked high way leading on both hands. **1633** *Gate of Tongues Unl.* 114 A forked way or carfax is deceitfull. **1888** J. PAYN *Myst. Mirbridge* iii, They came to the forked road.

c. Of a mountain: Divided at the summit, cleft.

1606 SHAKS. *Ant. & Cl.* IV. xiv. 5 Sometime we see..A forked Mountaine, or blew Promontorie. *a* **1628** SIR J. BEAUMONT *To Muses 2* in *Bosworth F.* (1629) 9 Sweet Sounds are raised upon the forked Hill Of high Parnassus. **1821** SHELLEY *Prometh. Unb.* I. i, Yon forked and snowy hill.

†**d.** of a mitre.

1509 BARCLAY *Ship of Folys* (1874) II. 279 No wyse man is desyrous to obtayne The forked cap without he worthy be. **1545** BRINKLOW *Compl.* 4 Banyysshed my natyue contry..by the cruelty of the forkyd cappes of Ingland. **1641** MILTON *Ch. Govt.* vi. (1851) 128 She..sends her haughty Prelates from all parts with their forked Miters.

e. *Her.* = FORCHE. (Robson *Brit. Her.* 1830).

1486 *Bk. St. Albans, Her.* c vj a, A certan forkyd cros..hit is called forkyd: for as moch as that all thendys of hit ar clouyn and forkyd.

f. Having (a specified number of) forks or prongs, as *three-forked*.

1535 COVERDALE *1 Sam.* ii. 13 A three forked fleshoke. **1583** STANYHURST *Æneis* II. (Arb.) 59 With toonge three forcked furth spirts fyre. *a* **1628** F. GREVILLE *Monarchy* dclii, To stirre, or calm the ocean's race, As royalties of his [Neptune's] three-forked mace. **1887** BOWEN *Virg. Æneid* II. 475 Some viper..darting a three-forked flickering tongue.

†**g.** Of an arrow: Barbed. *Obs.*

1549 STOURTON *Let.* in *Wilts. Arch. Mag.* (1864) VIII. 296 His crosse bow bent, and forked arrow in the same. **1611** COTGR., *Fer de flesche à oreilles*, a forked or barbed arrowe head. **1673** DRYDEN *Assignation* III. i, I am wounded with a forked Arrow, which will not easily be got out.

2. Having the lower half of the body divided; two-legged.

1605 SHAKS. *Lear* III. iv. 113 A poore, bare, forked Animall as thou art. **1771** *Exmoor Scold.* 48 Thee wut come oll a gerred, and oll horry zo vurs tha art a vorked [= i-forked].

3. Of building: Characterized by the use of 'forks' (see FORK *sb.* 7).

1792 J. MASTIN *Hist. Naseby* 9 Some [houses]..of the most antique architecture, called forked building.

4. Horned; also *spec.* of deer: see quot. 1674.

1591 SYLVESTER *Du Bartas* I. iv. 476 The more she [the Moon] Fills her Forkéd Round. **1598** *Ibid.* II. i. III. *Furies* 600 With fisking train, with forked head, and foot Himselfe, th' Ayre, th' Earth, he beateth. **1674** N. COX *Gentl. Recreat.* (1677) I. 13 Heads having doubling Croches, are called Forked Heads, because the Croches are planted on the top of the Beam like Forks.

b. 'Horned', 'cornuted', cuckolded. *a knight of the forked order*: a cuckold.

1586 T. B. *La Primaud. Fr. Acad.* I. 455 Thou puttest thy selfe in great danger, least thy rounde heade become forked. **1592** GREENE *Disput.* Wks. (Grosart) X. 257 Let him dub her husband knight of the forked order. **1639** MAYNE *City Match* in Dodsley *O. Pl.* (1780) IX. 373 And I am fork'd? hum! **1673** F. KIRKMAN *Unlucky Citizen* 95, I should be sure to be dubb'd a knight of the forked order.

†**5.** Of an argument, etc.: That points more than one way; containing a dilemma; ambiguous, equivocal. *Obs.*

1551 BP. GARDINER *Explication* 80b, What hath this auctor wonne nowe by his forked question? **1604-13** R. CAWDRY *Table Alph.* (ed. 3), *Dilemma*, a forked kinde of argument. **1605** B. JONSON *Volpone* I. i, Giue forked counsel; take prouoking gold On eyther hand, and put it vp. **1663** J. SPENCER *Prodigies* (1665) 324 To this forked Objection I return these five considerations. **1681** CROWNE *Hen. VI*, IV. 46 Must Justice starve because we want a Lawyer's forked distinctions to feed her neatly with?

†**b.** Of a fee: Taken from both parties in a suit.

1648 HERRICK *Hesper.* (1869) 216 Ere thy palm shall know A postern-bribe took, or a forked-fee To fetter Justice.

6. Done with a fork. *nonce-use.*

1611 CORYAT *Crudities* 91 To imitate the Italian fashion by this forked cutting of meate.

7. *ellipt.* for *forked-headed* or *-tailed.*

1674 N. COX *Gentl. Recreat.* II. (1677) 161 The Forked Kite and bold Buzzard. 1769 PENNANT *Zool.* (1776) III. 170 Forked Hake..is known on the coast of Cornwall by the name of the great forked beard, where it was first discovered by Mr. Jago. 1864 COUCH *Brit. Fishes* III. 125 Forked Hake.

8. *Comb.*: parasynthetic and similative, as ***forked-wise*** adv.; also †**forked-beard** = *fork-beard*; **forked-head**, a forked or barbed arrow, a fork-head; **forked-tailed** *a.*, having a forked tail; *esp.* in the names of birds (cf. *fork-tailed*).

1713 RAY *Syn. Pisc.* 163 The great *Forked-beard. *Ibid.* 164 The lesser Forked-beard. 1574 J. FORTESCUE in *Hist. Fam. of F.* (1869) II. 228 Arrows..as well *forked-heads as others. 1600 SHAKS. *A.Y.L.* II. i. 24 It irkes me the poore dapled fooles..Should..with forked heads Haue their round hanches goard. 1556 J. HEYWOOD *Spider & F.* xxxi. 95 A sorte of *forkte tailde flise. 1691 RAY *Creation* (1701) 167 The fork'd-tail'd Kite. 1843 YARRELL *Brit. Birds* III. 520 The Forked-tailed Petrel. 1586 LUPTON *Thous. Notable Th.* (1675) 23 Children with a cloven upper lip, and *forked-wise, called an Hare-lip.

Hence **'forkedly** *adv.*, in a forked manner; **'forkedness**, the condition of being forked.

1603 DEKKER *Wonderf. Yeare* E iv, Tongues forkedly cut. 1611 COTGR., *Fourcheure*..forkednesse. a 1665 GOODWIN *Wks.* (1692) III. 601 The forkedness of the Arrows. 1748 RICHARDSON *Clarissa* (1811) VI. 50 Sally..snapt her fingers at me, and pointing two of each hand forkedly at me, bid me [etc.]. 1789 G. WHITE *Selborne* xviii. (1843) 230 Distinguished..by the length and forkedness of their tails. 1881 DUFFIELD *Don Quix.* II. 555 [She] flung her body..across the saddle, and remained forkedly, as if she had been a man.

forken ('fɔːk(ə)n), *a. Obs.* exc. *dial.* In 8–9 *dial.* **forkin.** [f. FORK *sb.* + -EN[5], or after str. pa. pples.] Forked. ***forken-robin***, the earwig.

1603 KNOLLES *Hist. Turks* (1638) 52 He had a forken beard and bald head. 1691 RAY *N.C. Words, Forkin-robbin*, an earwig; called from its forked tail. So in BAILEY (1721) and ATKINSON *Cleveland Gloss.* (1868).

forker ('fɔːkə(r)). [f. FORK *v.* + -ER[1].]

†**1.** = FORK *sb.* 2; perh. mispr. for FORKET. *Obs.*

a 1603 T. CARTWRIGHT *Confut. Rhem. N.T.* (1618) 416 The Italians now take their meate with a forker.

2. One who forks: **a.** One who throws up (hay, etc.) with a fork. **b.** *slang.* (See quot. 1867).

1641 BEST *Farm. Bks.* (Surtees) 35 One of the men is a loader, the other a forker. 1867 SMYTH *Sailor's Word-bk., Forkers*, those who reside in seaports for the sake of stealing dockyard stores, or buying them, knowing them to be stolen.

†**3.** Something forked: **a.** A forked tongue, a 'sting'. **b.** A forked arrow, a fork-head. *Obs.*

1589 NASHE *Martins Months Minde* Wks. (Grosart) I. 155 His arrowes all are forkers. 1616 J. LANE *Contn. Sqr.'s T.* ix. 388 A..snake..crawld vp her to stinge, with forker blewe. c 1640 J. SMYTH *Lives Berkeleys* (1883) I. 205 An vnderkeeper..with a forker out of his Crosbowe slewe one Oliffe.

†**4.** *slang. to wear a forker*: to be 'cornuted'.

1606 MARSTON *Parisitaster* II. i, Why? my lord, tis nothing to weare a forker.

5. ('In Suffolk, an unpaired partridge.' F. Hall.)

1657 R. LIGON *Barbadoes* (1673) 4 They [? flying fish]..flye as far as young Partridges, that are forkers.

†**'forket.** *Obs.* Also 5 **forkette.** [? f. FORK *sb.* + -ET[1]; cf. F. *fourchette* table-fork.]

1. A small fork. Also, a prong of a fork.

1583 HOLLYBAND *Campo di Fior* 209 Picke not thy teeth with a forkette. 1611 COTGR., *Fourcheon*, a forket; the tooth, or graine of a forke.

2. (See quot.)

1708 *Phil. Trans.* XXVI. 78 Fossils..Bidentula. The Forket.

forkful ('fɔːkfʊl). [f. FORK *sb.* + -FUL.] As much as may be lifted on a fork.

1641 BEST *Farm. Bks.* (Surtees) 36 Forkers are to bee foretolde that they give upp goode forkefulls. 1768 *Case of J. Ruffle* 3 He would rather they should cheat him of a forkful..of corn. 1882 *Garden* 14 Jan. 31/2 Putting a forkful of long manure on the corners.

'fork-head.

†**1.** An arrow with barbed head. *Obs.*

1590 SPENSER *F.Q.* III. v. 19 Through his haberjeon the forkehead flew.

2. *Mech.* **a.** (see quot. 1874); **b.** = CROSS-TAIL.

1839 [see CROSS-TAIL]. 1874 KNIGHT *Dict. Mech., Fork-head*, the double head of a rod which divides in order to form a connection by means of a pin.

†**'forkin.** *Obs. rare*⁻¹. [a. OF. *fourquon* of same meaning.] ? A baker's shovel.

c 1475 *Pict. Voc.* in Wr.-Wülcker 808 *Hec pala*, a forkyn.

forking ('fɔːkɪŋ), *vbl. sb.* [f. FORK *v.* + -ING[1].] The action of the vb. FORK.

a 1300 [see FORK *v.* 2 a]. 1866 GEO. ELIOT *F. Holt* xxxiii, At this forking of the street there was a large space. 1884 BOWER & SCOTT *De Bary's Phaner.* 314 Where the branching appears and remains as a forking of the main axis.

forking ('fɔːkɪŋ), *ppl. a.* [f. FORK *v.* + -ING[2].] That forks; characterized by forking.

1851 GLENNY *Handbk. Fl. Gard.* 221 A forking..habit of growth. 1877–84 F. E. HULME *Wild Fl.* p. vi, Stems forking. 1892 *Blackw. Mag.* Apr. 549 A forking creek.

forkless ('fɔːklɪs), *a.* [f. FORK *sb.* + -LESS.] Without a fork.

(WORCESTER (1846) cites *Phil. Mag.*).

fork-tail, *a.* and *sb.*

†**A.** *adj.* = *forked-tail(ed. Obs.*

1611 FLORIO, *Follo*, an eare-wig..or fork-taile vermine.

B. *sb.*

1. (See quot. 1753.)

1753 CHAMBERS *Supp., Forktail*..a name given to the salmon, while in the fourth years growth. 1818 in TODD. 1861 *Act 24 & 25 Vict.* c. 109. §4 Salmon..known by the names..blue pole, fork tail..or by any other local name.

2. (See quot. 1893.)

1893 NEWTON *Dict. Birds, Forktail*, of old time used in England for the Kite, but now applied in India to the birds of the genus *Henicurus*.

Hence **fork-tailed** *a.*, having a forked tail; used in the names of birds, etc. (cf. *forked-tailed*).

1694 J. RAY in *Lett. Lit. Men* (Camden) 200 A kind of fork-tail'd..sea-swallow. 1828 SIR J. S. SEBRIGHT *Hawking* 44 The fork-tailed kites were much flown, some years ago. 1868 WOOD *Homes without H.* v. 103 The Fork-tailed Date Shell (*Lithodomus caudigera*).

†**forkulie**, *v. Obs.* [Of unknown formation.] *trans.* To blacken by heat.

a 1225 *Ancr. R.* 50 Þe blake cloð bitockneð þet te soðe sunne, þet is Iesu Crist, haueð wiðuten vorkuled ou. *Ibid.* 306 Ure inwit, uorkuliinde hire suluen mid þe fure of sunne.

forky ('fɔːkɪ), *a.* [f. FORK *sb.* + -Y[1].]

1. Shaped like a fork, forked.

[1508 (see FORCY: the sense is not clear).] 1697 DRYDEN *Virg. Georg.* III. 666 A Snake..brandishing his forky Tongue. a 1700 —— *Ovid's Met.* I. 425 Parnassus whose forky rise Mounts thro' the clouds. 1727 SWIFT *Circumcision E. Curll* Wks. 1755 III. I. 166 A meagre man with a..black forky beard. 1762 FALCONER *Shipwr.* I. 256 A skilful marksman o'er his head suspends The forky prongs. 1808 SCOTT *Marm.* I. viii, The last..On high his forky pennon bore. a 1851 D. MOIR *Sir Eliduc* Poet. Wks. 1852 II. 192 The tree by the forky lightnings scathed.

b. *fig.* and *allusively.*

1702 WATTS *Epit. Will. III*, x, Slander gnaw her forky tongue. 1821 BYRON *Cain* I. i. 227 Those he spake to with his forky tongue.

2. *Comb.*, as ***forky-tongued*** adj.

1727 WATTS *Poems* (1743) 235 Cares never come With..Malice forky-tongued.

Hence **'forkiness**, the condition of being forky.

1611 COTGR., *Fourcheure*, a forkinesse. 1766 PENNANT *Zool.* (1768) II. 242 The house swallow is distinguished from all others by the superior forkiness of its tail.

forlaboured, -laden: see FOR- *pref.*[1] 6, 6 b.

†**for'lain**, *ppl. a.* Also 6 *Sc.* **forlane.** [pa. pple. of FORLIE *v.*]

I. 1. Of a woman: That has lost her chastity. Also, as a term of abuse for either sex.

c 1290 *S. Eng. Leg.* I. 462/6 A womman..that was sunful and for-lein. c 1450 HENRYSON *Test. Cres.* 140 Now allace! that seid with froist is slane, And I fra luifferis left and all forlane. [But this may belong to sense 2.] 1508 DUNBAR *Tua Mariit Wemen* 137 That carybald forlane.

II. 2. App. used for: (? Laid aside), forgotten.

c 1320 *Sir Tristr.* 1586 Tristrem, þis þef is he, þat may be nouȝt for lain. [c 1450: see under sense 1] 1560 ROLLAND *Crt. Venus* IV. 496 All faltis bygane..He did or said..Be quite forȝet, ouirsene, and all forlane.

†**for'lance**, *v. Obs.* [? a. OF. **forlancer* to throw out (in mod.F. *spec.* to drive out an animal from his lair), f. *for-*, FOR- *pref.*[3] + *lancer* to throw, LAUNCH.] *intr.* or *absol.* To throw out.

13.. *Gaw. & Gr. Knt.* 1334 Þen brek þay þe bale, þe balez out token, Lystily forlancyng.

forlapped: see FOR- *pref.*[1] 6 b.

†**for'lay**, *v. Obs.* [f. FOR- *pref.*[1] + LAY *v.*] *trans.* To lay aside.

a 1300 *Cursor M.* 24328 (Cott.) We stemmed still als stan, Þof lijf was vs for-laid.

forlay: see FORELAY.

†**for'lead**, *v.*[1] *Obs.* [OE. *forlǽdan*, f. FOR- *pref.*[1] + *lǽdan*: see LEAD *v.*; cf. OS. *farlêdean* (Du. *verleiden*), OHG. *far-*, *fir-*, *forleitan* (Ger. *verleiten*).] *trans.* To mislead, seduce.

Beowulf 4084 (Gr.) Hie forlæddan to þam lindpleȝan swæse ȝesiðas. c 1000 ÆLFRIC *Gram.* xlvii (Z.) 277 *Seduco*, ic bepæce oððe forlæde. c 1275 LAY. 1333 For hire workes beoþ so swete þat fale men [heo] for-ledeþ. c 1315 SHOREHAM 164 The fendes privé gyle The man for-ledde.

†**for'lead**, *v.*[2] *Obs.* [f. FOR- *pref.*[2] + LEAD *v.*] *trans.* To lead forward, lead before. Hence **for'leading** *vbl. sb.*

a 1300 *E.E. Psalter* cxxxi[i]. 17 Þethen sal I for-lede [Vulg. *producam*] David horn. 1387 TREVISA *Higden* (Rolls) I. 29 By such forledynge [L. *his præviis*].

†**for'leave**, *v. Obs.* [f. FOR- *pref.*[1] + LEAVE *v.*; = OHG. *firleiben.*] *trans.* To leave behind, give up, abandon, forsake, depart from.

c 1225 *Juliana* 33 Ich am wilcweme ne forleaf þu me nawt luuiende lauerd. c 1325 *Poem Times Edw. II* 374 in *Pol. Songs* (Camden) 340, I drede me that God us hath for-laft out of his hond. c 1374 CHAUCER *Boeth.* I. metr. iii. 5 (Camb. MS.) Dirknesses for-leften me. c 1440 HYLTON *Scala Perf.* (W. de W. 1494) I. xxxviii, In a lityll I forlefte the.

forlength: see FOR- *pref.*[1] 9.

†**for'lere**, *v. Obs.* [OE. *forlǽran*, f. FOR- *pref.*[1] + *lǽran* LERE *v.* to teach.] *trans.* To teach wrongly, pervert, seduce.

a 1000 *Andreas* 1364 (Gr.) Ðu leoda feala forleolce and forlærdest. c 1200 *Trin. Coll. Hom.* 29 Þat is þe flesliche lust þe mankinne forlereð, and al hit is bi þe deuel þat men þus forlerede. a 1250 *Owl & Night.* 924 That thi dweole song heo ne for-lere.

†**for'lese**, *v. Obs.* Forms: *Infin.* 1 forléosan, 2–3 -leosen, 3 -losen, -lesen, 4–5 -lese, (6 *Sc.* -leir). *Pa. t.* 1 forléas, *Northumb.* -léos, *pl.* -luron, 3 forleas, (2nd pers. sing. forlure), 3–4 forles, 6–7 forlore, *Sc.* forloir. *Pa. pple.* 1–4 forloren, 4 *north.* forlose(n, -in, 4–8 forlorne, 6–7 forelorn(e, 3–9 forlore, (5 forlo(o)r, 6 *Sc.* forloir, 8 forelore), 3- forlorn. [OE. *forléosan*, pa. t. *forléas*, pl. *forluron*, pa. pple. *forloren*; = OFris. *forliasa*, *-liesa*, OS. *far-*, *forleosan*, *-liosan*, OHG. *far-*, *fer-*, *for-*, *furleosan*, *-liosan* (MHG. *verliesen*, Ger. *verlieren*), Goth. *fraliusan*; f. FOR- *pref.*[1] + *-léosan*, ME. *lesen*: see LESE *v.*

After 15th c. only in pa. pple., and (rarely) in the new forms, inf. (Sc.) *forleir*, pa. t. *forlore* (Sc. *forloir*).]

1. *trans.* To LOSE, in various senses.

Beowulf 2861 (Gr.) Æt þam ȝeongum..þam þe ær his elne forleas. c 1175 *Lamb. Hom.* 83 Mon hefde uorloren efre stephne bi-uore gode. c 1205 LAY. 213 Creusa..þe Eneas his fader in Troie for-leas. a 1225 *Ancr. R.* 246 Þe weorreur of helle mei longe asailen ou, & forleosen al his hwule. a 1250 *Owl & Night.* 815 An so for-lost the hund his fore. a 1300 *Cursor M.* 714 (Cott.) To win þe blis he had forlosin. c 1374 CHAUCER *Boeth.* IV. pr. iv. 100 (Camb. MS.) Yif þat a man hadde al for-lorn hys syhte. c 1430 *Hymns Virg.* 124 Thy honde warke þat þou hast wrowyth, My dere son, forlese hem nowhte! c 1460 *Towneley Myst.* (Surtees) 188 My right ere I have forlorne. 1581 J. BELL *Haddon's Answ. Osor.* 322 b, It may seeme we have..forlorne all mercy and compassion. 1600 FAIRFAX *Tasso* VII. i, Her feeble hand the bridle raines forlore. 1663 *Robin Hood & Curtal Friar* xiii. in Child *Ballads* v. cxxiii. (1888) 124/1 Carry me over the water..Or else thy life's forlorn.

2. To destroy, cause to perish, cut off.

a 1000 *Cædmon's Gen.* 1281 (Gr.) He wolde..forleosan lica ȝehwilc. c 1200 *Vices & Virtues* (E.E.T.S.) 73 Gif he [a pot] ðar inne bersteð and brekð, he is forloren and sone ut-ȝeworpen. c 1250 *Gen. & Ex.* 1143 Ðo meidenes..wenden..ðat man-kinde were al for-loren. 1390 GOWER *Conf.* I. 314 Thus they that comen first to-fore Upon the rockes ben forlore. 1560 ROLLAND *Crt. Venus* III. 274 Becaus Diomeid wald forleir The fers Troians. 1614 SYLVESTER *Bethulia's Rescue* VI. 175 For the God of Power Th' Assyrian Forces hath this Night forlorn. 1664 *Flodden F.* I. 2 Worthy Lords by him forlorne.

b. *intr.* for *refl.* To perish, come to nought.

a 1225 *St. Marher.* 3 Ne ne let tu neauer mi sawle forleosen wið þe forlorne. a 1225 *Leg. Kath.* 2254 Nalde nawt godd leoten his martirs licomes liggen to forleosen.

c. *trans.* To bring to ruin, put to shame, confound; also, to lead astray to one's ruin. (Usually in passive.)

c 1200 *Trin. Coll. Hom.* 5 Forleteð yure synne. þat ȝe ne ben ifunden on sunne and swo forlorene. a 1300 *E.E. Psalter* cxlii[i]. 12 And for-lese my faas in merci þine. c 1400 *Melayne* 77 Late never my sawle be forlorne. a 1471 *Pol. Poems* (Rolls) II. 241 Unavysyd clerk soone may be forlore Unto that theef [Simony] to donne obeysaunce. 1578 *Gude & Godlie Ballates* 193 Lowse me or I be forloir And heir my mone. 1591 SPENSER *Vis. Worlds Vanitie* vi, O! how great vainnesse is it then to scorne The weake, that hath the strong so oft forlorne!

3. To leave, abandon, desert, forsake.

c 1460 *Pol. Rel. & L. Poems* (1866) 97 The order of preesthode he has forlorne. 1590 SPENSER *F.Q.* III. ix. 52 Her frail witt, that now her quite forlore. 1600 FAIRFAX *Tasso* III. lxxvi, The birds their nests forlore.

Hence **for'lesing** *vbl. sb.*, loss, perdition.

1340 *Ayenb.* 156 Uor þet me be-ulyȝt hire folye and hire uorlyezinge. *Ibid.* 243.

†**for'let**, *v.*[1] *Obs.* Forms: see LET *v.*[1] Also pa. pple. 7 erron. **forlitt.** [OE. *forlǽtan*, f. FOR- *pref.*[1] + *lǽtan* LET *v.*[1]; = OS. *forlátan* (Du. *verlaten*), OHG. *firlâzzan* (MHG. *verlâzen*, Ger. *verlassen*), ON. *fyrirláta* (Sw. *förlåta*, Da. *forlade*).]

1. *trans.* To allow, permit.

c 900 tr. *Bæda's Hist.* I. xxvii, Sum eorþlic æ forlæteþ, þætte [etc.]. a 1300 *E.E. Psalter* cxxv. 3 For noght forelete sal he Yherde of sinful for to be Over lote of rightwis.

2. To leave, go away from (a person or place), forsake; to abandon (possessions).

971 *Blickl. Hom.* 27 Hine þa forlet se costiȝend. a 1175 *Cott. Hom.* 219 To chiesen ȝief[h]y wolden hare sceppinde lufie oðer hine ferleten. c 1205 LAY. 30599 Þat ufel hine gon for-leten. a 1300 *Cursor M.* 13295 (Cott.) He for iesu al for-lete. c 1350 *Will. Palerne* 2311 Alle þe breme bestes þat a-boute vs were, for-lete vs & folwed him forþ. 1508 DUNBAR *Tua Mariit Wemen* 381, I him forleit as a lad.

b. To leave (a person) helpless or destitute.

a 1000 *Andreas* 459 (Gr.) Næfre forlæteð lifȝende god eorl on eorðan, ȝif his ellen deah! a 1225 *St. Marher.* 8 Ne forlet tu me nawt luuende lauerd. 1340–70 *Alisaunder* 679 Whan Philip in his foule will hathe þee forlete..Him tides to take þee aȝain. 1413 *Pilgr. Sowle* (Caxton 1483) IV. xx, He is forlete and al forpercid sore and pytously. a 1553 PHILPOT *Exam. & Writ.* (1842) 345 Who may say that God forletteth his church right, so that he may permit those things to.. decay, without the which it may not consist?

c. To leave (land) desolate or uncultivated; to leave (a building, etc.) to decay.

a **1300** *Leg. Rood* (1871) 34 So þat þulke stude was vor-lete mony aday. **1390** GOWER *Conf.* III. 104 But yet there ben of londes fele..Which of the people be forlete As londe deserte. **1480** CAXTON *Chron. Eng.* b 7 b, He yaf hem a contre that was forleten where in they myght duelle. **1528** *Will* in W. Molyneux *Burton-on-Trent* (1869) 58 The seyd brygge ys lyke to be decayed and forlett. **1610** HOLLAND *Camden's Brit.* I. 513 The three Channels or draines have a long time beene forlet and neglected.

d. To leave off, renounce (a custom, habit, sin).

c **1175** *Lamb. Hom.* 19 Nu sculle we forlete þes licome lust. *c* **1200** *Trin. Coll. Hom.* 103 Hwi luuest þu þine fule sunnes . forlet hem. **1303** R. BRUNNE *Handl. Synne* 3779 Wraþþe and oþer synne forlate [*printed* foolate]. *c* **1386** CHAUCER *Pars. T.* ¶ 45 In þe drede of god man forleteth his synne. **1535** STEWART *Cron. Scot.* II. 64 He thoucht he wald mak peice agane With Scot and Pecht, and all weiris forleit. **1601** HOLLAND *Pliny* I. 84 Soone after this custome was for-let and cleane giuen ouer.

e. To forsake, cease to regard (a law, etc.).

c **1250** *Gen. & Ex.* 4068 For luue of ðis hore-plaȝe Manie for-leten godes laȝe. *a* **1300** *Cursor M.* 9448 (Cott.) Sua sun als he þat apel ete, þe laghes bath he þan for-lete. **1340** *Ayenb.* 184 Roboam..uorlet þane red of þe yealden guode men uor þane red of yonge. **1535** STEWART *Cron. Scot.* (1858) I. 60 Lautie wes lost, forleit wes all the lawes.

¶**f.** Used as a term of Sc. constitutional law.

1689 EARL OF BALCARRAS *Let. Jas. II on St. Scot.* 61 (MS.) The Committee..found great difficulty how to declare the Crown vacant. Some were for abdications..Others were for using an old obsolete word (fforleiting) used for a Birds forsaking her nest. **1689** LUTTRELL *Brief Rel.* (1857) I. 518 The throne of Scotland is vacant, the late King James the 7th haveing forlitt or forfeited the crown.

3. To leave out, omit; to let alone, abandon.

c **1200** *Trin. Coll. Hom.* 71 We shule no þing seien þere þat les beo, and no þing of þe soðe forlete. *c* **1220** *Bestiary* 230 Finde ȝe ðe wete corn ðat hire qwemeð. Al ȝe forleteð ðis oðer seð. *a* **1300** *Cursor M.* 21777 (Gött.) Eline..wald noght for-lett þe nailes in his hend and fete..ful gern scho soght Till scho þaim fand ne fined noght. *c* **1300** *Beket* 1998 All that he i handled hadde the houndes hit forlete. **13..** *E.E. Allit. P.* B. 101 Be þay fers, be þay feble for-lotez none.

b. To cease from; to cease *to* do something.

c **1175** *Lamb. Hom.* 35 Ne forlete ȝe for nane scame þat ȝe ne seggen þam preoste alle eower sunne. *c* **1200** ORMIN 18875 All follc well neh forrlet To þenkenn ohht off heffne. *a* **1250** *Owl & Night.* 36, I-wis for þine fule lete Wel oft ich mine song forlete. *c* **1374** CHAUCER *Boeth.* III. pr. xi. 75 (Camb. MS.) Whan it forletiþ to ben oone it mot nedis dien.

4. To let go, release or lose from one's hold or keeping.

c **1150** *Departing Soul's Addr. Body* 19 Thine godfæderes ihaten ær heo the forleten that [etc.]. *c* **1200** ORMIN 3768 He wollde hiss aȝhenn lif Forr hise shep forrlætenn. *a* **1225** *Juliana* 47 Forlet me mi leafdi & ich chulle al bileaue þe. *a* **1225** *St. Marher.* 6 Weila wummon hwuch wlite þu leosest ant forletest for þin misbeleaue. *a* **1300** *Cursor M.* 4006 (Cott.) Formast his lijf he suld for-lete. *c* **1374** CHAUCER *Boeth.* I. metr. ii. 3 (Camb. MS.) Allas how the thowt of man dulleth and forletith his propre cleernesse.

b. To remit (a debt); to forgive.

1340 *Ayenb.* 262 And uorlet ous oure yeldinges: ase and we uorleteþ oure yelderes.

c. To dismiss from attention. *Sc.*

1813 PICKEN *Poems* I. 121 Sae let's forleet it—gie's a sang; To brood on ill unken'd is wrang.

Hence **for'let(en** *ppl. a.*; **for'leting** *vbl. sb.* Also **for'letness**, the state of being let alone.

a **1300** *E.E. Psalter* cxxii[i]. 3 For of for-letenesse mikel filled we are. *Ibid.* 4 Up-braiding To mightand, and to proude for-leting. **13..** *K. Alis.* 2889 As a stude for-let, Is now Thebes. *c* **1374** CHAUCER *Boeth.* I. pr. i. 2 (Camb. MS.) A forletyn and a despised elde. *c* **1440** *Jacob's Well* (E.E.T.S.) x. 11 An old for-latyn cote. **1506** GUYLFORDE *Pilgr.* (Camden) 33 An olde for leten ruynous churche. **1610** HOLLAND *Camden's Brit.* (1637) 188 The language of our ancestours..lay forlet and buried in oblivion.

†**for'let**, *v.*[2] *Obs.* [f. FOR- *pref.*[1] + LET *v.*[2]] *trans.* To hinder, prevent, stop. Const. *inf* or *that* with *not.* Also in deprecatory phr. *God forlet it!*

a **1555** PHILPOT *Exam. & Writ.* (1842) 351 But God forelet it that I should not believe the gospel! **1568** C. WATSON *Polyb.* 95 a, The Romans..being in league with the Carthaginenses..forlet him not to aide them. **1575** R. B. *Appius & Virg.* E ij, It is naught in dry sommer, for letting my drinke.

†**for'lie**, *v. Obs.* Forms: see LIE *v.*[1] [OE. *forlicȝan* (f. FOR- *pref.*[1] + *licȝan* LIE *v.*[1]) = OHG. *farligan* (MHG. *verligen*).

Cf. Gr. aorist παρελέξατο lay with (a woman) secretly, which is etymologically equivalent.]

I. 1. *refl.* Of a woman: To prostitute herself.

c **893** K. ÆLFRED *Oros.* III. vi. §2. *a* **1000** *Laws Cnut* liv.

2. *intr.* for *refl.* (Often conjugated with *be*). To commit fornication. Const. *by* or *with.*

c **1200** ORMIN 3118 Forr þa mann munnde trowwenn wel þatt ȝho forrleȝenn wære. *c* **1450** *St. Cuthbert* (Surtees) 519 And with him to be forlayne. **1513** DOUGLAS *Æneis* VI. i. 54 Prevalie with the bull forlane wes sche. *Ibid.* x. vii. 72 The quhilk Anchemolus..had forlayn his awin stepmoder by.

3. *trans.* Of the man: To lie with, violate.

c **1205** LAY. 15375 Heo for-læiȝen þa wif. **13..** *Coer de L.* 924 Forleyn was his doughter yyng. *a* **1420** HOCCLEVE *De Reg. Princ.* (Roxb.) 191 How many a wyfe & maide hathe be forlayne. **1480** CAXTON *Chron. Eng.* e iij b, He wolde haue forlayne that maide.

II. 4. To smother by lying upon, to overlie.

a **1300** *Cursor M.* 8623 (Cott.) þat was for-lain Moght neuer couer þe lijf again. *c* **1340** *Ibid.* 8602 (Fairf.) An womman had hir childe for-layne.

III. 5. To be fatigued with lying (in bed).

1423 JAS. I. *Kingis Q.* xi, For-wakit and for-walowit, thus musing Wery forlyin..I herd the bell to matyns ryng, And vp I rase, no langer wald I lye.

†**forline**, *v. Obs.* [a. OF. *forlignier.*] *intr.* To degenerate.

c **1374** CHAUCER *Boeth.* III. pr. vi. (1886) 61 þat they ne sholden nat owtrayen or forlynen fro the vertuus of hyr noble kynrede. *Ibid.* metr. vi, Thanne nis ther no forlyned wyht but yif he norysse hys corage vn to vyces.

†**forlive**, *v. Obs.* [f. FOR- *pref.*[1] + LIVE *v.*] *intr.* To outlive one's strength, become decrepit; in pa. pples. *-lived*, *-liven*, decrepit.

a **1300** *Cursor M.* 5315 (Cott.) Als man of eild, and lang forliuen [**1340** *Fairf.* for liued]. **1398** TREVISA *Barth. De P.R.* XII. xvi. (Tollem. MS.) A forlyued..cok leyeþ egges in his laste elde.

forlode: see FOR- *pref.*[1] 6.

forloff, obs. Sc. form of FURLOUGH.

†**forloin**, *sb. Obs. Hunting.* [f. next vb.]

1. The action of forloining.

14.. *Le Venery de Twety* in *Rel. Ant.* I. 152 Why blowe ye so? For cause that the hert is seen, an ye wot nevere whedir that myn hundys be become fro myn meyne. And what maner of chase clepe ye that? We clepe it the chace of the forloyne [orig. *la chace de Forloyng*]. **1486** *Bk. St. Albans* F j, What is a forloyng, for that is goode to here.

2. A note of recall.

c **1369** CHAUCER *Dethe Blaunche* 386 Therwith the hunte wonder faste Blew a forloyn at the laste. **1735** in BAILEY, *Forloyn*, a Retreat when the Dogs are called off from a wrong Scent. *O*[*ld Word*].

†**for'loin**, *v. Obs.* Forms: 4-6 forloyne, 6-7 foreloin, -loyne, 6- forloin. [ad. OF. *for-*, *forsloignier*, f. *fors* (see FOR- *pref.*[3]) + *loin*:—L. *longē* far.]

1. *trans.* To leave behind at a distance, forsake.

13.. *E.E. Allit. P.* A. 368 þaȝ I forloyne my dere endorde. *Ibid.* B. 1165 þay forloyne her fayth & folȝed oþer goddes.

b. *intr.* To stray, err.

13.. *E.E. Allit. P.* B. 282 He knew och freke forloyned fro þe ryȝt wayez. *Ibid.* B. 750 ȝif I for-loyne as a fol.

2. *Hunting. trans.* To leave (the pack) far behind. Said of the stag, or of individual hounds. Also *absol.*

1486 *Bk. St. Albans* F j, When..the beest is stoll away owt of the fryth Or the houndes that thow hast meten therwith And any other houndes before than may with hem mete Thees oder houndes arn then forloyned..For the beste and the houndes arn so fer before And the houndes behynde be weere and soore So that they may not at the best cum at ther will The houndes before forloyne hem. **1576** TURBERV. *Venerie* 118 A harte doth foreloyne and breake out before the houndes for divers reasons. **1686** BLOME *Gentl. Recreat.* II. 79 When a Hound meeteth a Chase, and goeth away with it far before the rest, then say, he Foreloyneth.

†**for'long**, *v.*[1] *Obs.* In 3 *Orm.* forrlangenn. [f. FOR- *pref.*[1] + *langen* to LONG; = MHG. *verlangen.*] To be possessed with longing.

c **1200** ORMIN 1280 ȝiff þatt tu forrlangedd arrt To cumenn upp till Criste.

Hence **for'longing** *vbl. sb.*

a **1225** *Ancr. R.* 274 Heorte-sor uor worldliche þinge, deori uorlonginge, & ȝiscunge of eihte.

†**for'long**, *v.*[2] *Obs.*[−1] [f. FOR- *pref.*[1] + LONG *a.*; after L. *prolongāre.*] *trans.* To keep or continue longer; to prolong.

1496 *Dives & Paup.* (W. de W.) VII. xxii. 310/1 They haue leuer to gyue .xx. shellynges to forlonge the soules in payne all a yere.

†**for'loppin**, *a. Sc. Obs.* [f. FOR- *pref.*[1] + *loppin*, pa. pple. of *loup*, LEAP *v.*] Fugitive, runaway, vagabond.

1500–20 DUNBAR *Poems* xxxiii. 7 Me thocht a Turk of Tartary Come throw the boundis of Barbary And lay forloppin in Lumbardy. **157.** *Satir. Poems Reform.* xlv. 8 Ane fals, forloppen, fenyeit freir.

forlore: see FORLESE and next.

forlorn (fəˈlɔːn), *a.* and *sb.* Forms: see FORLESE. [pa. pple. of FORLESE.] **A.** *adj.*

†**1.** Lost, not to be found. *Obs.*: see the vb.

1577 HARRISON *England* II. ix. (1877) I. 190 To the end they should lie no more in corners as forlorne books and vnknowne.

†**2.** Morally lost; abandoned, depraved. *Obs.*

1154 *O.E. Chron.* an. 1137 Hi [the lawless barons in Stephen's time] weron al forcursæd, & forsworen & forloren. *c* **1250** *Gen. & Ex.* 546 Miȝti men, and fiȝti, [and] for-loren. *a* **1300** *Cursor M.* 25074 (Cott.) þe quick þe godmen er and chosen, þe ded þe wick þat ar for-losen. **1578** *Gude & Godlie Ballates* 30 The Forlorne Sone, as it is writtin in the xv. Chapter of Luk. **1598** DRAYTON *Heroic. Ep.* xvi. 53 He that's in all the Worlds blacke sinnes forlorne. **1683** *Apol. Prot. France* ii. 20 They hire forlorn Wretches to go to the Sermons of the Protestant Ministers.

†**3.** 'Lost', ruined, doomed to destruction. *Obs.*

c **1386** CHAUCER *Frankl. T.* 309 Lord Phebus, cast thy merciable eye On wrecche Aurilie, which that am for-lorne. *c* **1440** HYLTON *Scala Perf.* (W. de W. 1494) I. xxxviii, As thou were a forloor man. **1554** TRAVES in Strype *Eccl. Mem.* III. App. xxxiii. 88 As though ye were a man forlore. **1696** TATE & BRADY *Ps.* vi. 1 And spare a Wretch forlorn. **1719** YOUNG *Busiris* V. i, What urge these forlorn rebels in excuse For choosing ruin?

†**b.** *forlorn boys* (= Fr. *enfants perdus*), *fellows*, etc.: men who perform their duty at the imminent risk of their life. *forlorn fort*: one held at extreme risk. See also FORLORN HOPE.

1577–87 HOLINSHED *Chron.* III. 1137/2 Fortie or fiftie forlorne boies. **1598** BARRET *Theor. Warres* II. i. 17 He shall set abroad certaine forlorne Sentinels without the Word. **1618** BOLTON *Florus* (1636) 137 Some new band of forlorne fellowes appeared. **1700** S. L. tr. *Fryke's Voy. E. Ind.* 298 To march to a Forlorn Fort..six Leagues from [etc.].

c. Desperate, hopeless.

1603 KNOLLES *Hist. Turks* 591 Everything..seemed as altogither lost and forlorne. **1710** BERKELEY *Princ. Hum. Knowl.* Introd. Wks. 1871 I. 137 [We] sit down in a forlorn Scepticism. **1791** BOSWELL *Johnson* an. 1732, In the forlorn state of his circumstances. **1836** W. IRVING *Astoria* II. 183 Having seen these three adventurous bands depart upon their forlorn expeditions. **1874** MORLEY *Compromise* (1886) 8 The home of great and forlorn causes.

4. Of persons or places: Abandoned, forsaken, deserted; left alone, desolate.

1535 *Goodly Primer* (1834) 120 An old forlorn house. **1559** *Mirr. Mag.*, *Dk. Clarence* xvii, To help King Henry vtterly forlorne. **1621** G. SANDYS *Ovid s Met.* VIII. (1626) 152 Whither fly'st thou? leauing me for-lore. **1667** MILTON *P.L.* I. 180 Yon dreary Plain, forlorn and wilde. **1704** POPE *Autumn* 22 To the winds I mourn; Alike unheard, unpity'd, and forlorn. **1726** SHELVOCKE *Voy. round World* (1757) 79 Dreading an accident in so forlorn a place, I..stood out to sea again. **1814** CARY *Dante, Inf.* xxx. 16 A wretch forlorn and captive. **1829** HOOD *Eugene Aram* x, Horrid stabs in groves forlorn And murders done in caves. **1850** TENNYSON *In Mem.* lx, The little village looks forlorn. **1863** F. LOCKER *Lond. Lyrics, Reply to Invit. Rome* ii, Perhaps you think your *Love forlore* Should pine unless her slave be with her.

b. Const. *of*, †*from*: Forsaken by (a person); bereft, destitute, or stripped of (a thing).

c **1150** *Departing Soul's Addr. Body* v, Eart thu forloren from al that thu lufedest. **1579** SPENSER *Sheph. Cal.* Apr. 4 Or art thou of thy loved lasse forlorne? **1667** MILTON *P.L.* x. 921 Forlorn of thee Whither shall I betake me. **1697** DRYDEN *Iliad* I. Fables (1700) 208 The good old Man, forlorn of human Aid, For Vengeance..pray'd. **1798** COLERIDGE *Anc. Mar.* VII. xxv, He went like one that..is of sense forlorn. **1832** TENNYSON *Œnone* 15 Mournful Œnone wandering forlorn Of Paris once her playmate. **1871** ROSSETTI *Love's Nocturn* ii, Dreamland lies forlorn of light.

5. In pitiful condition, wretched.

1582 T. WATSON *Centurie of Loue* xiii, Such as lay with pestilence forlorne. *a* **1628** F. GREVILLE *Alaham* IV. iii, Nothing can come amisse to thoughts forlorne. **1724** R. WELTON *18 Disc.* 454 They saw so great a man in so forlorne a plight. **1781** GIBBON *Decl. & F.* II. xli. 549 His forlorn appearance. **1866** MISS MULOCK *Noble Life* xii, Ay, be it the forlornest bodily tabernacle in which immortal soul ever dwelt.

b. Of a wretched appearance, meagre.

1588 SHAKS. *Tit. A.* II. iii. 94 The Trees, though Sommer, yet forlorne and leane. **1597** —— *2 Hen. IV*, III. ii. 335 Hee was so forlorne, that his Dimensions (to any thicke sight) were inuincible. **1875** F. HALL in *Lippincott's Mag.* XV. 338/2 Forlorn pullets, certainly from the same farmyard with the lean kine of Egypt.

†**B.** *sb. Obs.*

1. A forlorn person.

c **1506** DUNBAR *Littill Interlud* 165 The Gret Forlore Of Babylon. **1593** SHAKS. *3 Hen. VI*, III. iii. 26 Henry..Is..forc'd to liue in Scotland a Forlorne. **1710** STEELE *Tatler* No. 210 ¶6 [An old maid writes] I am surrounded with both, though at present a Forlorn. **1814** *Forgery* II. ii, There, poor forlorns, divide the little there.

2. Short for FORLORN HOPE; a body of troops detached to the front, a front line, vanguard. Also *pl.*, the men forming a forlorn hope.

1645 CROMWELL *Let. to Lenthall* 14 Sept., Captain Ireton with a forlorn of Colonel Rich's regiment. **1677** W. HUBBARD *Narrative* II. (1865) 181 The Forlorne of our Forces. **1688** J. S. *Art of War* 54 The General must send his Forlorns to post themselves on the highest places. **1702** C. MATHER *Magn. Chr.* II. App. (1852) 187 Four companies of these were drawn out as forlorns. **1724** DE FOE *Mem. Cavalier* (1840) 287, I..rode up to the forlorn.

transf. and *fig.* **1648** JOS. BEAUMONT *Psyche* IV. cxliii, Next these, a large Brigade was marshallèd, For whose forlorn first march'd the hardy Boar. **1655** GURNALL *Chr. in Arm.* Introd. i. (1656) 10 The fearful are in the forlorne of those that march for hell. **1666** *Lond. Gaz.* No. 68/4, 12 or 14 as the Vauntguard or Forlorn of their Fleet. **1680** R. L'ESTRANGE *Season. Mem. Liberties Press & Pulpit* 4 There started out a Party upon the Forelorn, to make Discoveries, and try the Temper of the Government. **1681** CROWNE *Thyestes* v. Dram. Wks. 1873 II. 70 Sometimes they'll..stand A flight of beams from the forlorn of day. **1674** DRYDEN *Epil. Open. New Ho.* 10 Criticks..Who..still charge first, the true forlorn of wit.

for'lorn ˌhope. [ad. Du. *verloren hoop* (in Kilian 1598), lit. 'lost troop' (*hoop* = HEAP, Ger. *haufen*). Cf. Fr *enfants perdus.* (Among sailors mispronounced *flowing hope.*)]

1. In early use, a picked body of men, detached to the front to begin the attack; a body of skirmishers. Now usually, a storming party.

In the 17th c. sometimes applied to the rear-guard.

1579 DIGGES *Stratiot.* 102 He must also so order the Forlorn hope in yᵉ front of hys Battayle with new supplies. **1581** STYWARD *Mart. Discipl.* II. 136 The which the Germaine calls, their Forlorne hoope. **1600** DYMMOK *Ireland* (1841) 32 Before the vantguarde marched the forlorn hope. **1642** *True State Ireland* 5 Likewise for the forlorn hope of the Rear, Captain Pate commanded 40 Dragooners. **1678** tr. *Gaya's Art of War* II. 74 Called the Forlorn Hope, because they..fall on first, and make a Passage for the rest. **1799** WELLINGTON in Gurw. *Desp.* I. 31 The forlorn hope of each attack consisted of a sergeant and twelve Europeans. **1874** L. STEPHEN *Hours Libr.* (1892) I. vii. 245 Compelled to lead a forlorn hope up the scaling ladders.

b. *transf.* and *fig.*, chiefly of persons in a desperate condition.

c **1572** GASCOIGNE *Fruits Warre* (1831) 211 The forlorne hope which haue set vp their rest By rash expense, and knowe not howe to liue. **1572** J. JONES *Bathes of Bath* Pref. 3 A booteless matter to perswade the forlorn hope, suche as have decreed to caste awaye them selves. *a* **1661** FULLER *Worthies* (1840) II. 11 [Object of Christ's descent into hell] To preach, useless where his auditory was all the forlorn hope. **1698** FRYER *Acc. E. India & P.* 128 The busy apes, the Forlorn hope of these declining Woods, deeming no place safe where they beheld us.

c. *pl.* The men composing such a body; hence, reckless bravos.

1539 TONSTALL *Serm. Palm Sund.* (1823) 67 To make this realme a praye to al..spoylers, all snaphanses, all forlornehopes, all cormerauntes. *c* **1645** T. TULLY *Siege of Carlisle* (1840) 31 Toppam had yᵉ honour of yᵉ forlorn hopes, and gave them a gallant charge. **1867** SMYTH *Sailor's Word-bk.*, Forlorn-hopes was a term formerly applied to the videttes of the army.

d. A perilous or desperate enterprise.

1768 J. BYRON *Narr. Wager* (1778) 89 We saw them a little after, setting out upon their forlorn hope, and helping one another over..rocks. **1771** *Junius Lett.* lix. 311 The wary.. never went upon a forlorn hope.

2. *slang.* **a.** The losers at a gaming-table. **b.** (See quot. 1785.)

1608 DEKKER *Lanthorne & Candle-light* D ij, They that sit downe to play, are at first called Leaders. They that loose, are the Forlorne Hope. *a* **1700** B. E. *Dict. Cant. Crew, Forlorn Hope*, losing Gamesters. **1785** GROSE *Dict. Vulg. Tongue, Forlorn hope*, a gamester's last stake.

3. With word-play or misapprehension of the etymology: A faint hope, a 'hope against hope'; an enterprise which has little chance of success.

1641 J. SHUTE *Sarah & Hagar* (1649) 108 If we sin, upon a presumption that we shall conceal either our actions or persons from God, it is a forlorn hope; our iniquities will finde us out. **1806–7** J. BERESFORD *Miseries Hum. Life* (1826) II. xxi, In hopes of making your hearer think that you had been only singing all the while. A forlorn hope indeed. **1885** *Harper's Mag.* Mar. 594/1 She had had a forlorn hope of a letter, but it had died away.

forlornity (fəˈlɔːnɪtɪ). orig. *U.S.* [f. FORLORN *a.* + -ITY.] **a.** Forlornness. **b.** A forlorn person.

a **1870** In *D.A.E.* s.v., *Forlornity*, forlorn condition. **1878** 'MARK TWAIN' *Let.* (1917) I. 341 Livy and Clara sat down forlorn, and cried... Last night the forlornities had all disappeared. **1904** B. VON HUTTEN *Pam* III. ii, 'Oh!' she added, breaking into rueful laughter at the sight of his fat forlornity. **1917** H. T. COMSTOCK *Man thou Gavest* 320 Thomas explained and apologized for the admittance of the two 'forlornities', as he called them. **1922** *Contemp. Rev.* Oct. 489 In their rusty forlornity.

forlornly (fəˈlɔːnlɪ), *adv.* [f. FORLORN *a.* + -LY².] In a forlorn manner or degree.

1630 GAULE *Defiance to Death* 30 Why are you so desperately and forlornely afraid of death? **1633** BP. HALL *Hard Texts* 566, I will..goe up and downe heavily and forelornely. **1879** E. GARRETT *House by Wks.* I. 170 She found the girl sitting forlornly on her low bed.

forlornness (fəˈlɔːnnɪs). [f. as prec. + -NESS.] The state of being forlorn (see the adj.).

c **825** *Vesp. Psalter* lxxxvii. 12 In forlorenisse [Vulg. *in perditione*]. *a* **1225** *Ancr. R.* 110 Vor hore uorlorennesse þet drowen him to deaðe. **1579** TOMSON *Calvin's Serm. Tim.* 160/2 Albeit there be at this day an horrible forlornenesse, so that it may well seeme that we are verie miserable creatures. **1668** H. MORE *Div. Dial.* II. xv. (1713) 135 The forlornness and desolateness of that forsaken Habitacle, the Body of a natural Fool. **1791** MRS. RADCLIFFE *Rom. Forest* ii, Adeline felt the forlornness of her condition with energy. **1850** L. HUNT *Autobiog.* II. xvii. 265 The beautiful vegetation immediately about it..completes this look of forlornness.

†**forˈlose**, *v. Obs.* [f. FOR- *pref.*¹ + LOSE.] *trans.* To lose. Hence **forˈlost** *ppl. a.*

c **1374** CHAUCER *Troylus* III. 231 (280) She for-lost, and thou right nought y-wonne. *Ibid.* IV. 728 (756) She held hire self a forlost creature. *c* **1440** *Partonope* 6904 He hath forlost his steede.

†**forˈlot**, *v. Obs. rare.* [f. FOR- *pref.*² + LOT *v.*] *trans.* ? To allot beforehand.

1566 DRANT *Horace's Sat.* V. C iv, To sterte up in astrologie the casuals of men, To limit and forlote by arte.

†**forˈlyten**, *v. Obs.* In 4 fore-. [f. FOR- *pref.*¹ + LYTE *a.* + -EN⁵.] *trans.* To diminish.

? *a* **1400** *Morte Arth.* 254 We hafe..forelytenede the loos þat we are layttede.

form (fɔːm), *sb.* Forms: 3–7 forme, 4– form; also 3–4 furme, 3–7 fourme, 5 foorme; fourm. [a. OF. *fo(u)rme, furme*, ad. L. *forma*, primarily shape, configuration; the derived senses below were for the most part developed in class. or post-class. Lat.

Some philologists refer the word to the root of *ferīre* to strike; others compare it with Skr. *dharman* neut., holding, position, order, f. *dhar, dhṛ*, to hold. The word has been adopted, and is in familiar use, in all the Rom. and mod. Teut. langs.: Pr., Sp., Pg., It. *forma* (Sp. *Mech.* also *horma*), Ger., Sw., Da. *form*, Du. *vorm*.

Todd 1818 assigns to the word in senses 6 b, 17, 21 the pronunciation (fɔəm), in other senses (fɔːm). The distinction, if it was ever recognized, is now obsolete.]

I. Shape, arrangement of parts.

1. a. The visible aspect of a thing; now usually in narrower sense, shape, configuration, as distinguished from colour; occasionally, the shape or figure of the body as distinguished from the face.

1297 R. GLOUC. (Rolls) 3326 þat ychanged hii were Hii þre in þe oþeres fourme. *a* **1300** *Fragm. Pop. Sc.* (Wright) 311 After the eiȝte and twenti dayes, forme hit [the seed] gynneth to nyme. *c* **1325** *Metr. Hom.* 92 An angel bi wai he mette, In mannes fourm. *c* **1400** *Rom. Rose* 2810 Hir shappe, hir fourme, hir goodly chere. *c* **1400** *Lanfranc's Cirurg.* 127 þis schal be þe fourme of a trepane. **1562** TURNER *Herbal* II. 99 The whyte asp differeth..from the blak..in the form of the lefe. **1585** T. WASHINGTON tr. *Nicholay's Voy.* I. viii. 7 b, A great building made in forme of a Citadelle. **1697** DRYDEN *Virg. Georg.* IV. 587 The slipp'ry God will..various Forms assume, to cheat thy sight. **1750** JOHNSON *Rambler* No. 82 ¶2 Stones of remarkable forms. **1849** MACAULAY *Hist. Eng.* II. 257 Her face was expressive: her form wanted no feminine charm. **1875** JOWETT *Plato* (ed. 2) III. 571 The world was made in the form of a globe.

b. *pl.* The shape of the different parts of a body. [So Fr. *les formes du corps*.]

1837 LANE *Mod. Egypt.* I. 50 In the Egyptian females the forms of womanhood begin to develop themselves about the ninth or tenth year. **1871** FREEMAN *Norm. Conq.* (1876) IV. xviii. 211 The buildings of the city..presenting forms dear to the antiquary.

c. *spec.* in *Crystallogr.* (See quots.)

1878 GURNEY *Crystallogr.* 38 This group of faces, which are required to co-exist with a given face by the law of symmetry of the system is called a crystallographic form. **1878** HUXLEY *Physiogr.* 60 A set of faces symmetrically related, such as the six faces of the prism of rock-crystal, is called technically a form.

d. Abstractly considered as one of the elements of the plastic arts.

1851 RUSKIN *Mod. Paint.* II. III. II. iv. §9 Form we find abstractedly considered by the sculptor. **1879** ROOD *Chromatics* xviii. 314 In painting..colour is subordinate to form.

†**e.** Beauty, comeliness. [so L. *forma*.] *Obs.*

1382 WYCLIF *Wisd.* viii. 2 And loouere I am mad of the foorme of it [wisdom]. **1568** T. HOWELL *Arb. Amitie* (1879) 19 Forme is most frayle, a fading flattering showe. **1611** BIBLE *Isa.* liii. 2 Hee hath no forme nor comelinesse. **1632** RANDOLPH *Jealous Lovers* II. vii, You punish'd The queen of beauty with a mole; but certainly Her perjury hath added to her form.

†**f.** Style of dress, costume. *Obs. rare*⁻¹.

1664 PEPYS *Diary* 15 July, There comes out of the chayre-roome Mrs. Stewart, in a most lovely form..A lovely creature she in this dress seemed to be.

†**2.** An image, representation, or likeness (of a body). Also *fig. Obs.*

a **1225** *Ancr. R.* 138 Ure deorewurðe goste, Godes owune furme. *c* **1290** *S. Eng. Leg.* I. 25/43 Ane Croyz of seluer with þe fourme of god huy leten a-rere. **1340** *Ayenb.* 87 Oure riȝte uader..þet..ssop þe zaule to his anlycnisse an to his fourme. *c* **1400** MAUNDEV. (Roxb.) viii. 32 In þe whilk roche es þe prynte and þe fourme of his body. *c* **1600** SHAKS. *Sonn.* ix, That thou no forme of thee hast left behind. **1610** GUILLIM *Heraldry* I. vii. (1611) 29 An escocheon is the forme or representation of a shield.

3. A body considered in respect to its outward shape and appearance; *esp.* that of a living being, a person.

1297 R. GLOUC. (Rolls) 4218 King Arthure..Toward þis grisliche fourme mid god herte him drou. *c* **1385** CHAUCER *L.G.W.* 1768 *Lucretia*, Right so, thogh that her forme wer absent, The plesaunce of hir forme was present. *c* **1400** *Lanfranc's Cirurg.* 27 þat þei moun bynde manye þingis in oon foorme, as þe panicle of þe heed byndiþ sevene boones. **1639** MASSINGER *Unnat. Combat* V. ii, Are your aerial forms deprived of language? **1697** DRYDEN *Æneid* VI. 389 Here Toils, and Death, and Death's half-brother, Sleep, Forms terrible to view, their Centry keep. **1817** COLERIDGE *Lewti* 2 To forget the form I loved. **1841** LANE *Arab. Nts.* I. 77 To his surprise, this very form stood before him.

4. *Philos.* **a.** In the Scholastic philosophy: The essential determinant principle of a thing; that which makes anything (*matter*) a determinate species or kind of being; the essential creative quality.

This use of *form* (Aristotle's μορφή or εἶδος) and *matter* (ὕλη) is a metaphorical extension of their popular use. In ordinary speech, a portion of matter, stuff, or material, becomes a 'thing' by virtue of having a particular 'form' or shape; by altering the form, the matter remaining unchanged, we make a new 'thing'. This language, primarily applied only to objects of sense, was in philosophical use extended to objects of thought: every 'thing' or entity was viewed as consisting of two elements, its form by virtue of which it was different from, and its matter which it had in common with, others.

c **1385** CHAUCER *L.G.W.* 2228 *Philomene*, Thou yiver of the formes that hast wrought The faire world. **1413** *Pilgr. Sowle* (Caxton 1483) IV. xxv. 71 The body was only mater, to whiche thou [the soul] were the fourme, of whome now is he naked another fourme accidentale..maye he wel haue, but forme substancial is hit nought that he hath. **1570** DEE *Math. Pref.* *j, To behold in the Glas of Creation, the Forme of Formes. **1594** HOOKER *Eccl. Pol.* I. iii. §4 *note*, Form in other creatures is a thing proportionable unto the soul in living creatures..According to the diversity of inward forms, things of the world are distinguished into their kinds. **1605** P. WOODHOUSE *Flea* (1877) 10 Reason's the forme of man, he who wants this, May well be like a man, but no man is. **1643** SIR T. BROWNE *Relig. Med.* I. §33, I beleeve..that they [spirits] know things by their formes, and define by specificall difference what we describe by accidents and properties. **1645** MILTON *Tetrach.* (1851) 169 The Form by which the thing is what it is. **1665** GLANVILL *Scepsis Sci.* xxii. 137 That the Soul cannot be separated from the Body, because 'tis it's Form. **1676** BATES *Exist. God* iv. 66 Supposing the self subsistence of Matter..could the World, full of innumerable Forms, spring by an Impetus from a dead, formless Principle? **1690** LOCKE *Hum. Und.* III. vi. §10 That the several Species of Substances had their distinct internal substantial Forms.

b. So in *Theol.*, a sacrament is said to consist of *matter* (as the water in baptism, the bread and wine in the Eucharist) and *form*, which is furnished by certain essential formulary words.

1597 HOOKER *Eccl. Pol.* V. lviii. §2 To make complete the outward substance of a sacrament, there is required an outward form, which form sacramental elements receive from sacramental words. *a* **1600** *Ibid.* VI. iv. §3 Forasmuch as a sacrament is complete, having the matter and form which it ought. **1727–41** in CHAMBERS *Cycl.*

c. In Bacon's modification of the Scholastic use: The real or objective conditions on which a sensible quality or body depends for its existence, and the knowledge of which enables it to be freely produced.

1605 BACON *Adv. Learn.* II. vii. §5 To inquire the form of a lion, of an oak, of gold, nay, of water, of air, is a vain pursuit: but to inquire the forms of sense..of colours..of density, of tenuity, of heat, of cold, and all other natures and qualities..to inquire, I say, the true forms of these, is that part of metaphysic which we now define of.

d. In the usage of Kant and Kantians: That factor of knowledge which gives reality and objectivity to the thing known, and which Kant regards as due to mind, or as (in his sense) subjective; the formative principle which holds together the several elements of a thing.

1803 *Edin. Rev.* I. 258 The subjective elements are by Kant denominated forms. **1862** H. SPENCER *First Princ.* I. iii §5 (1875) 49 If Space and Time are forms of thought, they can never be thought of. **1874** SIDGWICK *Meth. Ethics* I. ix. 93 This notion of 'ought'..is a necessary form of our moral apprehension. **1889** CAIRD *Philos. Kant* I. 279 The forms of unity by which it [the mind] determines sensible objects. *Ibid.* I. 349 The categories or forms of synthesis which belong to the pure understanding.

5. a. The particular character, nature, structure, or constitution of a thing; the particular mode in which a thing exists or manifests itself. Phr. ***in the form of, to take the form of.***

a **1300** *Cursor M.* 1591 (Gött.) For-þi in form of iugement A neu vengans on þaim he sent. *c* **1310** *Poems Harl. MS.* 2253 (Böddeker) 193 Iesu..graunte ous..þe vnderfonge in fourme of bred. *c* **1400** *Lanfranc's Cirurg.* 81 Alwey stiryng til it..come into þe foorme of an oynement. **1559** W. CUNNINGHAM *Cosmogr. Glasse* Pref. A vj b, I have reduced it into the forme of a Dialoge. **1605** CAMDEN *Rem.* 8 When they had..brought them into forme of a province. **1756** C. LUCAS *Ess. Waters* III. 117 Iron is not, in the metallic form, produced by nature. **1850** MCCOSH *Div. Govt.* I. (1874) 53 Pantheism is the form in which infidelity prevails on the Continent of Europe in the present day. **1860–1** FLO. NIGHTINGALE *Nursing* 50 An egg, whipped up with wine, is often the only form in which they can take this kind of nourishment. **1875** JOWETT *Plato* (ed. 2) I. 399 The Dialogue necessarily takes the form of a narrative.

b. One of the different modes in which a thing exists or manifests itself; a species, kind, or variety.

1542 RECORDE *Gr. Artes* 116 b, This sorte is in two fourmes commenly. The one by lynes, and the other without lynes. **1597** MORLEY *Introd. Mus.* 76 To make your descant carrie some forme of relation to the plaine song. **1651** HOBBES *Leviath.* II. xviii. 94 The Power in all formes [of Commonwealth], if they be perfect enough to protect them, is the same. **1733** POPE *Ess. Man* III. 303 For Forms of Government let fools contest. **1821** J. MARSHALL *Const. Opin.* (1839) 256 To this argument, in all its forms, the same answer may be given. **1843** C. H. SMITH *Naturalist's Library* I. 291 The group is intermediate between the bisontine form and the bovine. **1849** MACAULAY *Hist. Eng.* I. 157 They had refused to declare that any form of ecclesiastical polity was of divine origin. **1855** BAIN *Senses & Int.* II. ii. §8 The sensation of wetness seems to be nothing else than a form of cold.

c. *Gram.* (*a*) One of the various modes of pronunciation, spelling, or inflexion under which a word may appear. (*b*) In generalized sense: the external characteristics of words (*esp.* with reference to their inflexions), as distinguished from their signification. Also in extended uses in *Linguistics*. Cf. *linguistic form*.

1861 M. MÜLLER *Lect. Sci. Lang.* vii. 255 The Chinese sound *ta* means without any change of form, great, greatness, and to be great. **1889** F. HALL in *Nation* (N.Y.) XLVIII. 267/3 In 1530, Palsgrave recorded the form *topsy tyrvy*. **1921** E. SAPIR *Lang.* iv. 63 The evolution of forms like *teeth* and *geese*. **1926** BLOOMFIELD in *Language* II. 155 The vocal features common to same or partly same utterances are forms. *Ibid.*, Thus a form is a recurrent vocal feature which has meaning. **1933** —— *Lang.* 168 A form like *John* or *run*, ..without, for instance, any specification as to final-pitch, is, properly speaking, not a real linguistic form, but only a lexical form; a linguistic form, as actually uttered, always contains a grammatical form. **1953** J. B. CARROLL *Study of Lang.* ii. 49 The comparative linguist can attempt to trace back the forms of a given language to the forms of another, older language. *Ibid.*, Historical linguists have prepared lists of 'reconstructed' forms. **1962** E. F. HADEN et al. *Resonance-Theory Linguistics* ii. 15 Two language entities, between which there is a state of Resonance, may be found to be 'sames' as to their Form. **1966** J. M. SINCLAIR in C. E. Bazell *In Memory of J. R. Firth* 430 A form, in this article, is a stretch of language which has not yet been assigned a lexical status.

d. *Math.* A homogeneous polynomial in two or more variables; a quantic.

1859 G. Salmon *Less. Mod. Higher Alg.* xii. 88 A quadratic form can be reduced in an infinity of ways to a sum of squares, yet the number of positive and negative squares in this sum is fixed. **1903** Grace & Young *Alg. Invariants* i. 4 The transformation of the binary form $a_0x^2_1 + 2a_1x_1x_2 + a_2x^2_2$. **1928** H. W. Turnbull *Theory of Determinants* iii. 31 It is a linear homogeneous form in *n* arguments. *Ibid.* viii. 133 A homogeneous polynomial is a form or quantic. **1953** F. Blum tr. *van der Waerden's Mod. Algebra* (ed. 2) I. iii. 48 A polynomial is said to be homogeneous or to be a form if all of its terms are of the same degree.

e. *Librarianship.* Used *attrib.* in ***form-catalogue, -class***, etc., to denote a catalogue or catalogue entry in which books of a certain kind (poetry, almanacs, fiction, etc.) are listed together.

1876 C. A. Cutter *Rules Dict. Catal.*, Contents, Form-catalogue. *Ibid.* 14 *Form-entry*, registry under the name of the kind of literature to which the book belongs. *Ibid.* 49 In the catalogues of libraries consisting chiefly of English books, if it is thought most convenient to make form-entries under the headings Poetry, Drama, Fiction, it may be done. *Ibid.*, There is no reason but want of room why only collections should be entered under form-headings. *Ibid.*, In the case of English fiction a form-list is of such constant use that nearly all libraries have separate fiction catalogues. **1913** J. H. Quinn *Library Catal.* 30 Form-Catalogue is one in which the entries are arranged according to the forms of literature and the languages in which the books are written, either alphabetically or according to the relations of the forms to one another. **1966** T. Landau *Encycl. Librarianship* (ed. 3) 105/2 Form Classes or divisions are used to contain those works which are required more for the way in which they are written or presented than their subject content.

6. †**a.** *gen.* A grade or degree of rank, quality, excellence, or eminence; one of the classes forming a series arranged in order of merit, official dignity, proficiency in learning, etc. *Obs.*

[So late L. *forma prima, secunda*, etc., used of the various orders in the clergy, etc.]

c **1430** Lydg. *Bochas* i. viii. (1544) 12 b, Minos..Made statutes..Of righteousnes they toke the fyrst fourme. **1579** E. K. *Gen. Argt. Spenser's Sheph. Cal.* §3 These..Æclogues ..may be..deuided into three formes or ranckes. *c* **1609** *Beaumont Papers* (1884) 21, I looke for no ordinarie cocke, hauyng of myne owne of that fourme more then I know what to doe withall. **1662** Stillingfl. *Orig. Sacr.* ii. ii. §6 Certainly this kind of Learning deserves the highest form among the *difficiles Nugæ*. **1687** Burnet *Reply to Varillas* 123 He cannot bear my saying that such matters were above men of his form. **1700** Pepys *Let. in Diary* VI. 225 Thinking is working, though many forms beneath what my Lady and you are doing. **1702** Steele *Funeral* ii. (1704) 40 The Tongue is the Instrument of Speech to us of a lower Form. **1710** *Acc. Last Distemp. Tom Whigg* i. 22 The Doctor was a Physician of the first form.

b. *spec.* One of the numbered classes into which the pupils of a school are divided according to their degree of proficiency.

In English Schools the sixth form is usually the highest; when a larger number of classes is required, the numbered 'forms' are divided into 'upper' and 'lower', etc. The word is usually explained as meaning originally 'a number of scholars sitting on the same *form*' (sense 17); but there appears to be no ground for this.

1560 Daus tr. *Sleidane's Comm.* 160 b, The maner of teaching the youth, and diuiding them into fourmes. **1655** Heywood *Fort. by Land* iii. Wks. 1874 VI. 399 We two were bred together, Schoole fellows, Both of one form and like degree in School. **1740** J. Clarke *Educ. Youth* (ed. 3) 110 The Master is obliged to divide his Time amongst Boys of different Forms. **1871** M. Collins *Mrq. & Merch.* I. i. 13 He was in the fifth form at Eton.

fig. **1774** Fletcher *Ess. Truth* Wks. 1795 IV. 124 If there are various forms in the School of Truth.

†**7.** A model, type, pattern, or example. *Obs.*

1382 Wyclif *1 Thess.* i. 7 So that 3e ben maad fourme, or ensaumple, to alle men bileuynge. *c* **1425** Wyntoun *Cron.* vii. vi. 19 Hys Lyf wes fowrme of all meknes, Merowr he wes of Rychtwysnes. **1690** Locke *Hum. Und.* iii. iii. (1695) 230 To make abstract general Ideas, and set them up in the Mind, with Names annexed to them, as Patterns, or Forms, (for in that sence the word Form has a very proper signification).

8. Due shape, proper figure; orderly arrangement of parts, regularity, good order; also, military formation.

1595 Shaks. *John* iii. iv. 101, I will not keepe this forme vpon my head, When there is such disorder in my witte! **1597** —— *2 Hen. IV*, iv. i. 20 In goodly form comes on the enemy. **1652** Evelyn *Diary* 22 Mar., His garden, which he was now desirous to put into some forme. **1681** Dryden *Abs. & Achit.* i. 531 'Gainst form and order they their power employ, Nothing to build, and all things to destroy. **1697** —— *Virg. Georg.* iv. 606 Where heaps of Billows..In Form of War, their wat'ry Ranks divide. **1719** De Foe *Crusoe* ii. x, They came dropping in..not..in form, but all in heaps. **1775** R. King in *Life & Corr.* (1894) I. 9 As soon as one Man was shot down in the front, another from the Rear immediately filled his place, and by that means [they] kept their Body in form.

9. Style of expressing the thoughts and ideas in literary or musical composition, including the arrangement and order of the different parts of the whole. Also, method of arranging the ideas in logical reasoning; good or just order (of ideas, etc.), †logical sequence.

1551 T. Wilson *Logike* (1580) 84 b, The faulte that is in the forme, or maner of makyng [of a syllogism]. **1576** Fleming *Panopl. Epist.* 81 It reasoneth with itselfe in this forme and order. *c* **1600** Shaks. *Sonn.* lxxxv. 8 In polish'd form of well-refined pen. **1602** —— *Ham.* iii. i. 171 Nor what he spake, though it lack'd form a little, Was not like madness. **1667** Temple *Let. Gourville* Wks. 1731 II. 32, I am very little satisfied with the Queen of Spain's Letter..I think the Form is faulty, as well as the Substance. **1864** Bowen *Logic* vi. 149 Every correct step of Reasoning, considered simply as such, or in reference to its Form. **1871** Morley *Voltaire* (1886) 6 Hardly a page of all these countless leaves is common form. **1876** Stainer & Barrett *Dict. Mus. Terms, Form*, the shape and order in which musical ideas are presented. **1879** Green *Read. Eng. Hist.* xxvii. 139 He read the Sonnets of Petrarca, and he learnt what is meant by 'form' in poetry. **1889** Lowell *Latest Lit. Ess.* (1892) 144 Form..is the artistic sense of decorum controlling the coordination of parts and ensuring their harmonious subservience to a common end.

†**10.** Manner, method, way, fashion (of doing anything). ***in like form***: in like manner. *Obs.*

1297 R. Glouc. (1724) 447 3yf byssop..ded were, He grantede, þat þoru kyng non destourbance nere, þat me ne chose in ry3te fourme anoþer anon. *c* **1380** Wyclif *Serm.* Sel. Wks. I. 177 Crist 3yveþ his prechours foorme how þei shal lyue in þis work. **1475** *Bk. Noblesse* (1860) 24 It is in like fourme knowen of high recorde. **1509** Barclay *Shyp of Folys* (1874) I. 195 In lyke fourme who comyth unto confessyon [etc.]. **1585** T. Washington tr. *Nicholay's Voy.* iv. viii. 119 Over their shoulders, in the fourme and maner as the picture following doth shew. **1641** J. Jackson *True Evang. T.* ii. 115 He..was crucified..as his master was, but after a diverse forme, with his head downward.

11. a. A set, customary, or prescribed way of doing anything; a set method of procedure according to rule (*e.g.* at law); formal procedure. ***a matter of form***: a point of formal procedure; orig. a legal phrase; hence *colloq.* = a merely formal affair; a point of ordinary routine.

1297 R. Glouc. (1724) 491 & in gode fourme acorded hii were. *a* **1300** *Cursor M.* 19981 (Cott.) þe form þat him bitaght was ar O baptis3ing, he held it þar. **1596** Spenser *State Irel.* (Globe) 622/2 The wrongfull distrayning of any mans goodes. agaynst the forme of the Common Lawe. **1599** Shaks. *Much Ado* iv. i. 2 The plaine forme of marriage. **1647** Clarendon *Hist. Reb.* viii. §284 Their general; who used, in all dispatches made by himself, to observe all decency in the forms. **1711** [see form *sb.* 15]. **1713** Steele *Englishm.* No. 55. 355 The Lords..only laid hold of some Forms of Law to have prevented Judgment. **1727** Swift *Gulliver* iii. iv. 205 He was content to go on in the old forms. **1787** T. Jefferson *Writ.* (1859) II. 272 A paper from the admiralty..sent to me as a matter of form. **1805** T. Lindley *Voy. Brasil* (1808) 77 To make his report..from whence he came, &c. (a form to which the Portuguese merchantmen are all subject). **1818** Jas. Mill *Brit. India* II. v. ix. 706 The other commissioners being seldom called to deliberate, or so much as assemble for form sake. **1824** H. J. Stephen *Treat. Princ. Pleading* ii. §1. 254 As the party has no option in accepting the issue, when well tendered, and as the similiter may in that case be added for him, the acceptance of the issue when well tendered, may be considered as a mere matter of *form*. **1870** Lubbock *Orig. Civiliz.* i. (1875) 2 The form of capture in weddings.

b. ***in form*** (now usually ***in due or proper form***): according to the rules or prescribed methods; also, as a matter of merely formal procedure, formally; ***the form*** (somewhat *colloq.*): the state of affairs, what is happening or going on, the position; the correct procedure.

[**1556** *Aurelio & Isab.* (1608) D vj, It sholde be putte in writinge, and reduitede in fourme of lawe.] **1703** Luttrell *Brief Rel.* (1857) V. 350 Count de Frize, governor of Landau, writes, that [he] expects to be attackt in form. **1711** Addison *Spect.* No. 164 ¶5 He recovered himself enough to give her the Absolution in Form. **1736** Lediard *Life Marlborough* I. 24 The Art..of besieging a strong Town in Form. **1749** Fielding *Tom Jones* i. xi, The citadel was defended in form, and at length, in proper form surrendered at discretion. **1756–82** J. Warton *Ess. Pope* II. x. 128 The publisher..makes a grave apology..in form. **1805** T. Lindley *Voy. Brasil* xix, The laws, which heretofore existed only in form, have been thoroughly enforced. **1934** E. Waugh *Handful of Dust* 21 'I'm going to Hetton tomorrow.'..'What's the form?' 'Very quiet and enjoyable.' **1936** P. Fleming *News from Tartary* ii. ii. 76, I sent a wire to..Reuter's Correspondent at the capital..who..would be sure to know the form. **1940** N. Mitford *Pigeon Pie* xii. 192 She read somewhere that this was the form in Imperial Russia. **1951** 'N. Shute' *Round Bend* 87 He came along to the hotel each morning and evening to find out the form and when I wanted him. **1958** J. Cannan *And be a Villain* i. 36 Eve, you know the form—telephone for a doctor.

†**c.** In University language: The regular course of exercises, attendance on lectures, etc., prescribed for a particular degree. Only in phrase ***for his form*** = L. *pro forma*. *Obs.*

c **1470** Harding *Chron.* cx. *heading*, At Oxenford, where the clerkes be sworne they shall not rede for theyr fourme at Stamforde. **1523–9** *Act 14–15 Hen. VIII*, §3 in *Oxf. & Camb. Enactm.* 10 A Graduat of Oxforde or Cantebrygge which hath accomplisshed all thyng for his fourme. **1574** M. Stokys in Peacock *Stat. Univ. Camb.* (1841) App. A. 19 Iff a Bachelar off Dyvynyte preche for his Frurme.

12. a. A set or fixed order of words (*e.g.* as used in religious ritual); the customary or legal method of drawing up a writing or document.

1399 *Rolls of Parlt.* III. 424/1 3e renounsed and cessed of the State of Kyng..uppe the fourme that is contened in the same Renunciation and Cession. **1526** *Pilgr. Perf.* (W. de W. 1531) 9 Our lorde and sauyour Jesu Chryst hath gyuen vs a forme how to praye. **1597** Hooker *Eccl. Pol.* v. xxvi. §1 A strange conceit, that to serve God with any set form of common prayer is superstitious. **1648** [see flat *v.*[2] 6 b]. **1660** Pepys *Diary* 17 Nov., I inquired..for a form for a nobleman to make one his Chaplain. But I understanding that there is not any, I did draw up one. **1711** Addison *Spect.* No. 121 ¶1 Monsieur Bayle..delivers the same Opinion, tho' in a bolder Form of Words. **1732** Law *Serious C.* xiv. (ed. 2) 241, I think a form of prayer very necessary. **1818** Cruise *Digest* (ed. 2) V. 106 The form of this fine is—' And the agreement is such, to wit, that [etc.].' **1855** Dickens *Dorrit* i. x. You'll memorialise that Department (according to regular forms which you'll find out) for leave to memorialise this Department.

b. A formulary document with blanks for the insertion of particulars.

1855 Dickens *Dorrit* i. x, I can give you plenty of forms to fill up. **1885** *Act 48 Vict.* c. 15 Sched. ii. Forms ii. Form A, You are hereby required to fill up accurately the underwritten form. **1895** *Times* 5 Feb. 12/3 A message written on a telegraph form.

†**c.** A formula, recipe, prescription. *Obs.*

1484 Caxton *Fables of Poge* (1634) 213 A young man, that made pilles, after a certaine forme that he [a Physition] had shewed vnto him. **1607** Topsell *Four-f. Beasts* (1658) 147 Armetia..prescribeth this form for the cure of this evill: let the Dog be put into the water..and then..let his hair be shaved off [etc.]. **1610** Barrough *Meth. Physick* vii. xxiii. (1639) 410 The form and making wherof [ointments] is to be sought out of the Antidotaries.

†**13.** A formal agreement, settlement, or arrangement between parties; also, a formal commission or authority. *Obs.*

1297 R. Glouc. (Rolls) 8766 An fourme hii made þat eiþer helde is owe lond in is hond. *c* **1305** *St. Kenelm* 314 in *E.E.P.* (1862) 56 Hi makede a forme þat [etc.]. **1411** *Rolls of Parlt.* III. 650/1 Hym to harme and dishonure, agayn the fourme of a Loveday taken bytwen the same parties.

14. a. A set method of outward behaviour or procedure in accordance with prescribed usage, etiquette, ritual, etc.; a ceremony or formality. (Often *slightingly*, as implying the absence of intrinsic meaning or reality.)

1612 Davies *Discov. Causes why Ireland etc.* 234 That the Parliamentes of Ireland, might want no desent or honorable forme that was vsed in England. **1643** Burroughes *Exp. Hosea* iv. (1652) 212 Many who have no religion but a forme, yet neglect Gods forme. **1676** Etheredge *Man of Mode* i. i, The Forms and Civilities of the last Age. **1732** Berkeley *Alciphr.* i. §1 After the usual forms at first meeting, Euphranor and I sat down by them. **1805** T. Lindley *Voy. Brasil* (1808) 29 The sacrament, which was administered with all its forms. **1818** Jas. Mill *Brit. India* ii. v. vii. 620 They put on the forms of distance; and stood upon elevated terms [with the envoys]. **1850** Tennyson *In Mem.* cv, For who would keep an ancient form Thro' which the spirit breathes no more?

†**b.** A way of behaving oneself, an instance of behaviour of a given kind; in *pl.* = manners. *Obs.*

1591 Shaks. *Two Gent.* v. iv. 56 If the gentle spirit of mouing words Can no way change you to a milder forme. **1616** J. Haig in J. Russell *Haigs* vi. (1881) 140 My brother ..breaks up the letter, whilk was no gentlemanly form. **1625** Bacon *Ess., Ceremonies* (Arb.) 25 It doth much adde to a Mans Reputation..to have good Formes. *a* **1639** Spottiswood *Hist. Ch. Scot.* vi. (1655) 395 When he perceived the Kings countenance not to be towards him..he changed his forms.

15. a. Behaviour according to prescribed or customary rules; observance of etiquette, ceremony, or decorum. ***in (full, great) form***: with due ceremony. Often *depreciatively*: Mere outward ceremony or formality, conventional observance of etiquette, etc.

c **1386** Chaucer *Prol.* 305 Not o word spak he more than was nede, And that was said in forme & reverence. **1602** Shaks. *Ham.* iii. i. 161 The glass of fashion and the mould of form. *a* **1672** Wood *Life* (1848) 118 A fellow of little or no religion, only for forme-sake. **1703** Steele *Tend. Husb.* v. i, We'll eat the Dinner, and have a Dance together, or we shall transgress all form. **1711** —— *Spect.* No. 147 ¶2 When I reflected on my former Performance of that Duty, I found I had run it over as a matter of Form. **1722** De Foe *Plague* (1884) 116 They cou'd no more bury in Form, Rich or Poor. **1776** Foote *Bankrupt* i. Wks. 1799 II. 100 There is so much confinement, and form, even in the most fashionable families. **1788** Ld. Auckland *Diary* Lett. 1861 II. 74 We went in the evening in a carriage in full form. **1804** J. Grahame *Sabbath* 37 Of giving thanks to God—not thanks of form, A word and a grimace, but rev'rently. **1805** T. Lindley *Voy. Brasil* (1808) 126 These officers accordingly attended in great form. **18..** Arnold in Stanley *Life & Corr.* (1844) II. App. A. 344 Whether while we worshipped Thee in form, we worshipped Thee in spirit and in truth. **1871** Farrar *Witn. Hist.* iii. 97 To plant the standard of Christian freedom upon the ruins of Levitical form.

b. ***good*** (or ***bad***) ***form***: said of behaviour, manners, etc. which satisfy (or offend) the current ideals of 'Society'; (good or bad) manners. *colloq.*

1868 *Daily News* 24 Dec., Happily it is not good form even to purchase the Bacchanalian handkerchiefs of the Burlington-arcade. **1883** E. B. England Notes Eurip. *Iphig. in Tauris* 122 This excellent sentiment makes us wonder if οἱ νέοι in Euripides's day thought energy 'such awf'ly bad form, you know'. **1890** *Spectator* 7 June 791 It is not good intellectual form to grow angry in discussion.

16. a. *Sporting.* Of a horse: Condition in regard to health and training; fitness for running or racing; style and speed in running (as compared with competitors). (See quot. 1861.) ***in form***: fit to run, 'in condition'; so ***out of form***. Said also of athletes (*e.g.* oarsmen, cricketers) and players generally.

1760 R. Heber *Horse Matches* ix. 148 A horse in a very high form. **1787** 'G. Gambado' *Acad. Horsemen* (1809) 47 Bringing horses of different forms together over Newmarket. **1834** Medwin *Angler in Wales* II. 115 To enable him to run in his best form. **1861** Walsh & Lupton *Horse* vi. 84 When we say that a horse is 'in form' we intend to convey to our hearers that he is in high condition and fit to run. **1869** Lady Barker *Station Life N. Zealand* xvii. (1874) 126 One of the new chums, who was not supposed to be in good form for a long walk. **1880** W. Day *Racehorse in Training* xvi. 157 The mare had simply lost her form—she was not so good as a three- as she was as a two-year-old. **1882** *Standard* 20 Nov. 2/8 Mitchell was in good form, whilst Peall did not play so well as on previous days [at billiards]. **1883** *Times* 22 Oct. 10/2 Glocke..has not run in this country, but has shown fair form abroad. **1884** *Camb. Rev.* 10 Dec. 131 In the winning crew: M...kept his form well.

b. *transf.* Liveliness, high spirits, conversational powers, or the like. *colloq.*

1877 Mrs. Church *Father's Name* (Tauchn.) II. i. 17 The Misses Lillietrip were in great form. **1884** *Nonconformist & Indep.* 7 Feb. 130/2 The Irish members..did not appear to have recovered their usual form. **1895** *Pall Mall Mag.* Sept. 114 Macturk was in great form after his breakfast, apologising to my wife with the grandest air.

c. *slang.* (Without preceding article.) A 'police record'; a criminal conviction.

1958 F. Norman *Bang to Rights* III. 151 You can get at least a five..for getting captured with a shooter especially if you've got a bit of form behind you. **1960** 'M. Underwood' *Death by Misadventure* vi. 91 He has form for false pretences, mostly small stuff. **1964** J. Prescot *Case for Court* vi. 107 There's loads of form written down on my conviction card... Juvenile court, police court, quarter sessions and assizes—I've seen 'em all.

II. Denoting various material objects.

17. A long seat without a back, a bench.

[So OF. *forme*, med.L. *forma*, applied also to the stalls in a choir, with back, and book-rest. For the origin of this use of the word, cf. OF. *s'asseoir en forme*, to sit in a row or in fixed order.]

1387 Trevisa *Higden* (Rolls) IV. 99 Benches, stoles, formes. *c* **1440** *Promp. Parv.* 172/1 Foorme, longe stole, *sponda*. **1494** Fabyan *Chron.* vii. ccxxii. 246 The munkes, with fourmes and candelstyckes, defended theym. **1539** *Act 31 Hen. VIII*, c. 10 The same fourme that the arche-bishop of Canterburie sitteth on. **1607** Hieron *Wks.* I. 282 To sitte in the schoole of Christ vpon the learners forme. **1641** *Vestry Bks.* (Surtees) 191 Item for 2 short fourmes to sett a coffin uppon. **1694** Evelyn *Diary* 5 Oct., I went to St. Paul's to see the choir..The pulling out the formes, like drawers, from under the stalls is ingenious. **1745** P. Thomas *Jrnl. Anson's Voy.* 320 They have no Seats, as in our Churches, only Forms. **1833** L. Ritchie *Wand. by Loire* 33 A large cold room, garnished with deal tables and forms. **1875** A. R. Hope *My Schoolboy Fr.* 35 Abbing was made to stand upon a form. **1877** J. D. Chambers *Divine Worship* 139 The First Three Lessons..were read by Boys from each side alternately from the first Form.

18. a. *Mech.*, etc. A mould or 'shape'; an implement on which anything is shaped or fashioned.

a **1653** Gouge *Comm. Heb.* iii. 1 If the form be square or round, so will the metall be. **1669** Sturmy *Mariner's Mag.* v. 63 To have a form of Wood turned to the height of the Cartredge. **1727-41** Chambers *Cycl.*, *Form*..a kind of mould, whereon a thing is fashioned or wrought. Such are the hatters Form, the papermakers Form, &c. **1858** in Simmonds *Dict. Trade.* **1867** Smyth *Sailor's Word-bk.*, *Forms*, the moulds for making wads by.

b. A temporary structure for containing fresh concrete and giving it the required shape while it sets.

1908 T. Potter *Concrete* (ed. 3) xvi. 281 There are no set methods for making forms; a common-sense joiner will soon develop ideas of his own..especially if he sees castings turned out a few times. **1964** *Economist* 6 June 1151/1 A 'slip form paver'..pulls along behind it its own shuttering or 'forms' which keep the concrete from spreading sideways as it sets.

†**19. a.** A window-frame. [So F. *forme*.] *Obs.*

1463 *Bury Wills* (Camden) 39 The glas and the foorme of stoon that longith vnto the same wyndowe.

b. A case or box. *Obs.*

1594 Plat *Jewell-ho.* iii. 1 Cause new fourmes of Lead to be made..in euerie of which fourmes place one flower..let these fourmes be well fitted with their apt couers, and sodered verie close.

20. *Printing.* A body of type, secured in a chase, for printing at one impression. (Often spelt *forme.*)

1481 Caxton *Godfrey* ccxii. 312 Whiche book I.. sette in forme & enprynted the xx day of nouembre. *c* **1483** —— *Bk. for Trav.* 24b, At Westmestre by london In fourmes enprinted [Fr. *En formes impressee*]. **1594** T. B. *La Primaud. Fr. Acad.* ii. 337 The Printer that putteth ynke vpon the fourmes. **1691** Wood *Ath. Oxon.* II. 315 He flew to the Printing-house and commanded the Compositors to distribute the form. **1771** Franklin *Autobiog.* Wks. 1887 I. 93 On occasion, I carried up and down stairs a large form of types in each hand. **1882** Pebody *Eng. Journalism* xv. 107 The printers, even with three sets of formes, often found themselves working off papers half through the night. **1888** J. Southward in *Encycl. Brit.* XXIII. 700 The pages of types..are then ready to be made into a forme.

21. a. The nest or lair in which a hare crouches. Also *rarely*, of a deer.

c **1290**, etc. in M.E.D. *a* **1300** *Fragm. Pop. Sc.* (Wright) 318 I-buyd as an hare Whan he in forme lyth. *c* **1386** Chaucer *Shipman's T.* 104 As in a fourme sitteth a wery hare. *c* **1440** *Promp. Parv.* 172/1 Foorme of an hare, or oþer lyke, *lustrum*. **1576** Turberv. *Venerie* 161 When a hare ryseth out of the fourme. **1616** Surfl. & Markh. *Country Farme* 695 The first point..for the killing of the Hare, consisteth in finding out her forme. **1735** Somerville *Chase* ii. 38 In the dry crumbling Bank Their Forms they delve. **1799** J. Robertson *Agric. Perth* 329 The young [deer] keep close to their form, until the dam return to raise them. **1845** Darwin *Voy. Nat.* iii. (1852) 46 The Indians catch the Varying Hare by walking spirally round and round it when on its form. **1916** Blunden *Harbingers* 63 Strange streams Flow flagging in the undescribed deep fourms Of creatures born the first of all. **1952** R. Campbell tr. *Poems of Baudelaire* 77 Whereon as in a fourm you would fill out And mould your hair.

b. *transf.*

1589 *Pappe w. Hatchet* (1844) 19 The knaue was started from his Fourme. **1642** Fuller *Holy & Prof. St.* iii. xxiii. 215 Some Fames are most difficult to trace home to their form. **1655** Gurnall *Chr. in Arm.* i (1656) 141 After he had hunted Pharoah out of all his formes and burrowes.

III. 22. *Comb.*, as ***form-establishing, -fitting, -shifting*** adjs.; (sense 6 b) ***form-fellow, -master, -room***; (sense 12 b) ***form-filling*** vbl. sb.; **form-board**, (*a*) a device used in intelligence tests; (*b*) = form *sb.* 18 b; **form book** [form *sb.* 16], a record of the performances of a racehorse; also *transf.*; **form-class**, (*a*) *Forestry* (see quot. 1905), (*b*) *Linguistics*, a class of linguistic forms having some feature in common, such as being usable in the same position within a given construction, or being spoken with exclamatory final pitch; **form-criticism** *Theol.* [tr. G. *formgeschichte*], a method of literary criticism mainly applied to the Bible, and carried out by first classifying passages as belonging to certain forms (e.g. sayings, myths), and then tracing the early history of these forms with the aim of discovering the original form and relating this to its historical setting; so **form-critic**, one who engages in form-criticism; ***form-critical*** adj.; **form drag** *Aeronaut.*, the drag on a moving body that depends directly on its shape and is due to the unequal pressure over its surface that results from the disturbance of the fluid; **form factor** *Forestry* (see quots.); **form-genus** *Biol.*, a collective group of **form-species**, showing morphological similarities but not necessarily a genetic relationship; **form-historical** *a.* = *form-critical* adj.; also ***form-historian, -history***; **form letter**, a standardized letter, esp. one that can be sent to correspondents who inquire about routine matters or topics of frequent occurrence; **form-line** *Cartography*, (usu. *pl.*) lines drawn on a map to indicate the estimated configuration or elevation between the contour lines; †**form-pieces** *Arch.*, *pl.* the pieces of stone which constitute the tracery of a window: cf. form *sb.* 19 a; **form quality** [tr. G. *gestaltqualität* (C. von Ehrenfels 1890, in *Vierteljahrsschrift f. wissensch. Philos.* XIV. 256] (see quot. 1901); **form-species**: see *form-genus*; **form-symbol**, a symbol designating the form of a crystal (see form *sb.* 1 c); **form-word** *Gram.*, a word serving the function of an inflexion; also *gen.*, a word expressing a formal or grammatical feature; a function word; = functor 2; **formwork**, timber, steel, etc. made up into a form or set of forms for concrete (see form *sb.* 18 b).

1917 L. M. Terman et al. *Stanford Rev. Binet-Simon Scale* vii. 142 In the *form-board test, the younger subjects were a little superior to the older. **1947** P. L. Harriman *Dict. Psychol.* 141 *Form-board*, a measure of intelligence which consists of blocks to be fitted into a recess. **1952** *Brit. Jrnl. Psychol.* Feb. 79 Two versions of the test, of which the first is a 'formboard' requiring the actual placing of a piece to complete the pattern. **1958** *Archit. Rev.* CXIII. 222/1 Formboards are laid between their flanges, mesh reinforcement is laid over tees and formboard, and gypsum concrete is pumped on to make a roof of about 3 in. thick. **1923** Wodehouse *Inimitable Jeeves* xiv. 180 The race went by the *form-book all right. **1934** —— *Right Ho, Jeeves* i. 14 Gussie Fink-Nottle, against all the ruling of the form book, might have fallen in love. **1955** T. Rattigan *Separate Tables* i, According to this form book, Marston Lad is worth a bob or two each way. **1962** *John o' London's* 1 Feb. 115/1 Her acting range, when you go through the form-book, though deep, is also somewhat narrow. **1905** *Terms Forestry & Logging* 12 **Form class*, all trees in a stand so similar in form that the same form factor is applicable in determining their actual volume. **1921** E. Sapir *Lang.* Index 252 Form-classes. **1932** *Forestry* VI. 143 Each tree was placed in its form-class according to the value of the girth quotient. **1933** Bloomfield *Lang.* ix. 146 All English substantives belong to a form-class. *Ibid.* xii. 202 The form-class of limiting adjectives is much smaller than that of descriptive adjectives. **1958** C. F. Hockett *Course in Mod. Ling.* xviii. 162 A class of forms which have similar privileges of occurrence in building larger forms is a form-class. **1962** Householder & Saporta *Probl. Lexicogr.* 280 The principle of form-class equivalence, that glosses should be perfect and complete translations in respect to grammatical class. **1970** A. Cameron et al. *Computers & O.E. Concordances* 48 Through the form classes, the user has an index to various class correlations—agreement, concord, [etc.]. **1933** V. Taylor *Format. Gospel Trad.* i. 19 The *Form-Critics..appear to proceed as if they had lighted upon a method which supersedes all others. **1951** H. Gardner *Business of Criticism* ii. ii. 105 The fundamental question which the form-critic asks is 'Why was the story told?' or 'What is the point of the story?' **1933** V. Taylor *Format. Gospel Trad.* i. 19 The historical sketch will have served the purpose..of introducing the leading members of the *Form-critical School. **1957** D. E. Nineham *Stud. Gospels* p. x, He seemed largely to accept Bultmann's very negative assessment of the historical value of the Gospels as seen through form-critical eyes. **1928** B. S. Easton *Gospel before Gospels* ii. 32 With Dibelius form-history is raised to the rank of a distinct discipline..in his hands 'form-history' becomes '*form-criticism'. **1935** C. H. Dodd *Parables of Kingdom* iv. 111 The most recent school of Gospel criticism, that of *Formgeschichte*, or 'Form-criticism' , has taught us that in order to understand rightly any passage in the gospels we must enquire into the 'setting in life'..in which the tradition underlying that passage took form. **1951** N. Annan *L. Stephen* vi. 183 Some critics declare that form-criticism, which discloses the tradition of the early Church, rather than source-criticism, is the most fruitful method of interpreting the evidence. **1963** C. H. Dodd *Hist. Trad. in Fourth Gosp.* 6 The application of form-criticism opened up new lines of approach. **1931** T. G. Whitlock *Appl. Aerodynam.* iii. 38 *Form drag..is not a frictional or rubbing force acting tangentially to the surface, like skin friction. **1937** *Jrnl. R. Aeronaut. Soc.* XLI. 1120 Air resistance consists of the skin friction and of the drag due to the inertia of the medium ('form drag' according to modern terminology). **1951** D. O. Dommasch et al. *Airplane Aerodynam.* vi. 146 The various types of drag..are as follows: (1) form or pressure drag; (2) skin-friction drag; (3) induced drag; and (4) wave drag. **1970** A. C. Kermode *Flight without Formulae* 63 That part of the drag which is due to the shape or 'form' of a body, and which can be reduced by streamlining, is called form drag. **1599** Daniel *Musophilus* Wks. (1717) 388 *Form-establishing Devotion. **1895** W. Schlich *Man. Forestry* III. i. 36 Under '*form factor' is understood the proportion which exists between the volume of a tree and that of a regularly shaped body which has the same base and height as the tree. **1953** *Brit. Commonw. For. Term.* I. 63 *Form factor*, the ratio of the volume of a tree or its part to the product of its basal area and height. **1659** Fuller *App. Inj. Innoc.* i. 55 The Brittaines, *form-fellowes with the Grecians, were wholly given to Idolatry. **1820** Byron *Let. to Murray* 6 Oct., I met..my old school and form fellow. **1857** Dickens *Dorrit* ii. viii. 387 The work of *form-filling,..memorandum-making. **1960** *Guardian* 3 Feb. 6/4 A minimum of fuss but plenty of form-filling. **1897** *Sears, Roebuck Catal.* 237/2 Balbriggan Drawers... Elastic and *form fitting. **1970** J. Sangster *Touchfeather* iv. 87 A girl like me, with a trim little form-fitting uniform to wear, has absolutely no place where she can conceal a gun. **1873** *Q. Jrnl. Microsc. Sci.* XIII. 411 He is careful to retain a complete and concise enumeration of the various 'artificial species', '*form-genera', or 'phases', in which the natural species may manifest themselves. **1886** *Encycl. Brit.* XXI. 399/2 Billroth came forward in 1874 with the startling view that the various 'form-species' and 'form-genera' are only different states of one and the same organism. **1935** E. A. Bessey *Text-bk. Mycol.* xiv. 375 Since the genera based on asexual structures do not necessarily indicate true relationships of the included species the term 'form genus' was suggested for such groups by Schroeter. **1960** H. H. Swinnerton *Fossils* x. 58 These genera are therefore not based upon genetic affinity but upon outstanding similarities of form. They are in fact morphological or form genera marking grades of evolution. **1928** B. S. Easton *Gospel before Gospels* ii. 31 The Synoptic material, obviously, offers a tempting field to the *form-historian. *Ibid.* iii. 59 In 1924 such an examination appeared, *The Form-Historical Method*, by Licentiate Emil Fascher. **1934** F. C. Grant in *Bultmann's Form Criticism* i. 7 To grasp the main outlines of the form-historical method. **1954** *Scott. Jrnl. Theol.* VII. 339 There is considerable evidence on form-historical principles themselves. **1909** *Sat. Even. Post* 13 Feb. 8/1 The credit man..had a perfect passion for *form letters. **1921** *Daily Colonist* (Victoria, B.C.) 11 Mar. 16/7 The original bill and the polite note are as nothing compared with the 'form' letter sent out by firms which make a business of debt collecting. **1922** S. Lewis *Babbitt* iii. §3 The fortnightly form-letter, to be mimeographed and sent out to a thousand 'prospects'. **1932** Crooks & Dawson *Etheridge's Dict. Typewriting* (ed. 3) 147 *Form letters*..are printed forms or skeleton letters which are allotted numbers for identification by the typists when they are instructed..to send stock letters in reply to inquiries which do not warrant separate letters. **1968** *Globe & Mail* (Toronto) *Mag.* 17 Feb. 5 A form letter to boys who send in asking for hockey photos. **1935** *Geogr. Jrnl.* LXXXVI. 253 The topography sketched in by the use of *formlines at intervals of approximately 200 feet. **1951** F. Stark *Beyond Euphrates* 231, I am still in hectic work over my map, which has to have all the heights and form-lines fixed by Tuesday. **1961** L. D. Stamp *Gloss. Geogr. Terms* 125/1 Many cartographers are careful to draw a distinction between 'contours' which are based on instrumental survey and 'form-lines' which are sketched in from general observations. **1888** *Daily News* 10 Sept. 5/3 The active rivalry of *form masters. **1360** *Ely Sacrist. Roll* (Parker *Gloss. Arch.*) In 2 lapidibus vocat *fourme peces empt. 5*s*. **1450** in *Hist. Dunelm. Script. tres* (Surtees) 325 Pro factura ij formpeys. **1901** Baldwin *Dict. Philos.* I. 391/2 **Form quality*, that which characterizes a mental whole as being of a particular form, as being formed, or as having relations of parts. **1938** R. S. Woodworth *Exper. Psychol.* xxv. 623 The form quality of the tune does not reside in the constituent notes but in their pattern and mutual relations. **1948** *Mind* LVII. 23 We can..apprehend directly such form-qualities as sketchiness and schematicity. **1955** F. H. Allport *Theories of Perception* xviii. 498 Form-qualities are one type of such universals, for..they transcend the particular receptor pattern made by the stimulus-object of the moment. **1875** *Cliftonian* Apr. 40 Let the admirer of antiquity confine his excitement to the *form-room. **1897** H. W. Bleackley *Short Innings* xv, The bell..signified that all the boys should be in their form rooms. **1907** C. L. Thomson *Teaching English* 11 The form-room library, under the control of the form mistress. **1593** Nashe *Christ's T.* Wks. (Grosart) IV. 225 A *forme-shyfting deuill disguised in mans lykenesse. **1959** *Dana's Man. Mineral.* (ed. 17) ii. 27 Miller indices also may be used as *form symbols and are then enclosed in braces. **1875** Whitney *Life Lang.* ii. 21 The auxiliary apparatus of inflections and *form-words. **1889** *Cent. Dict.*, *Formword*,..a word showing relation only or chiefly; an independent word performing an office such as in other languages..is performed by the formative parts of words. **1892** H. Sweet *New Eng. Gram.* I. 22 We call such words as *the* and *is* form-words, because they are words in form only. When a form-word is entirely devoid of meaning, we may call it an empty word, as opposed to full words such as *earth* and *round*. **1937-8** *Proc. Arist. Soc.* XXXVIII. 196 Such form-words as *all, some, this, not,* and *and implies*. **1964** *English Studies* XLV. 241 Such formwords as *thou, yon(der,* and *there*. **1967** [see functor 2]. **1918** Hool & Johnson *Concrete Engineers' Handbk.* ii. 94 *Formwork, of course, should in every case leave the finished concrete true to line and surface. **1943** J. S. Huxley *TVA* 83 (*caption*) The arrangement of rough timber formwork into which the concrete is poured. **1962** *Engineering* 31 Aug. 267/1 A method of using precision-made steel formwork for the placing *in situ* of structural concrete in room width tunnel sections.

form (fɔːm), *v.*¹ Also 4-6 fourme(n, (4-5 foorme, fowrme, fowrym). [a. OF. *fourme-r* (Fr. *former*) = Pr. and Sp. *formar*, ad. L. *formāre*, f. *forma* FORM *sb.*]

1. a. *trans.* To give form or shape to; to put into or reduce to shape; to fashion, mould.

1340-70 *Alex. & Dind.* 600 We..No figure of fin gold fourme þer-inne. **1667** MILTON *P.L.* VIII. 470 The Rib he formd and fashond with his hands. **1738** WESLEY *Hymn, 'All Glory to the dying Lamb'* v, Send down the Spirit of thy Son To form my Heart divine. **1809** ROLAND *Fencing* 64 Return to nearly the same position..but forming the parade with a firm, supple, and precise motion.

absol. **1869** WARD tr. *Curtius' Hist. Greece* II. II. iv. 74 Here artists had formed in clay from a very early date.

†**b.** To express in formal shape; to formulate; to state formally. Also with *up*. *Obs.*

c **1330** R. BRUNNE *Chron.* (1810) 99 þe bisshop of Parys þe pes þan formed he. **1614** B. JONSON *Barth. Fair* IV. vi, Hee'll go neare to forme to her what a debauch'd Rascall I am. **1675** BROOKS *Gold. Key* Wks. 1867 V. 286, Seven several pleas, that all sincere Christians may form up.

c. To give a specified form to; to mould or fashion *into* a certain shape, or *after*, *by*, *from*, *upon* a certain pattern or model; to conform *to*.

1297 R. GLOUC. (Rolls) 3179 Yfourmed as a dragon ase red ase fur. **1303** R. BRUNNE *Handl. Synne* 3781 God louyþ euery creature þat he formed to hys fygure. *c* **1330** *King of Tars* 578 Yif Mahoun and Jovin con Make hit iformed aftur mon, With lyf and lymes ariht. *c* **1400** MAUNDEV. (Roxb.) vii. 25 þat worme es turned till a fewle perfitely fourmed. *c* **1440** *Gesta Rom.* xviii. 332 (Add. MS.) The soule, sette aboute with vertues, whan god fourmed it to his liknesse. *a* **1533** LD. BERNERS *Huon* lxxxiii. 263 By yᵉ lorde that fourmyd me to his semblaunce. **1674** tr. *Scheffer's Lapland* 64 Charles..divided the Countrey into several parts, and formed it into better order. **1683** SALMON *Doron Med.* I. 107 Forme it into Lozenges of what Fashion you please. **1875** JOWETT *Plato* (ed. 2) V. 172 A state formed after the model of Crete should..have a character for virtue.

d. *intr.* To shape itself *into*. Also, †to agree in form, fit *with*.

1703 MOXON *Mech. Exerc.* 183 In short time wears the outside of that Corner to comply and form with the hollow of the Gouge. **1871** L. STEPHEN *Playgr. Eur.* iii. (1894) 72 A ridge of rocky peaks, forming into two ridges about its centre.

†**e.** *trans.* To express by form, to 'body forth'.

1590 SPENSER *F.Q.* III. i. 1 Sith it [Chastity] is shrined in my Soveraines brest, And form'd so lively in each perfect part, That [etc.].

†**f.** To agree formally *to do* something. *Obs.*

c **1400** *Destr. Troy* 10946 There þai fourmyt a fest.. Serten dayes by-dene duly to hold.

g. *Electr.* (i) [after F. *former* (G. Planté 1872, in *Compt. Rend.* LXXIV. 593).] To convert electrolytically the surface of (a positive or †negative plate of a lead-acid accumulator) into its active form by passing a direct current through it in both directions alternately.

1881 S. P. THOMPSON *Storage Electr.* 11/2 M. Planté.. minutely describes the process of 'forming' the cell. *Ibid.*, The charges may last several hours, and by the end of several months, the cell will be well 'formed'. **1932** ALTHOUSE & TURNQUIST *Mod. Storage Battery Pract.* iii. 73 After the active materials have been pasted into the plates, the plates are formed by a series of charges and discharges. **1964** G. SMITH *Storage Batteries* ii. 23 Planté negatives have been obsolete for many years, and it is modern practice to form Planté positives against plain lead sheets, or 'dummies'.

(ii) To subject (a semiconductor device or some kinds of rectifier) to a relatively large current or voltage in order to produce or modify permanently certain electrical characteristics.

1926 [implied by FORMING *vbl. sb.* b]. **1949** BARDEEN & BRATTAIN in *Physical Rev.* 2nd Ser. LXXV. 1210/1 When the two points were connected as emitter and collector, and the collector was electrically formed, transistor action was obtained. **1953** R. A. HARVEY *Battery Chargers* iv. 92 Once the [selenium] rectifier is formed it remains reasonably stable. **1962** L. P. HUNTER *Handbk. Semiconductor Electronics* (ed. 2) viii. 15 A procedure similar to that of forming a point contact can be used to create small-area PN junctions under a metal contact.

2. a. To mould by discipline or education; to train, instruct. Now *rare*, exc. with the mind, a faculty, etc. as object. Also *refl.* to shape one's conduct, style, etc. *on* or *upon* (a model).

a **1340** HAMPOLE *Psalter* xvii. 29 þaire maners ere fourmed of samen lifynge. **1697** DRYDEN *Virg. Georg.* III. 305 Thus form'd, for speed he [a horse] challenges the Wind. **1724** A. COLLINS *Gr. Chr. Relig.* 140 It seems..natural for a body of slaves..to be form'd by their masters. **1746** *Col. Records Pennsylv.* V. 51 One of Your Royal Blood, form'd upon your Majestie's Example. **1749** SMOLLETT *Gil Bl.* v. i, On this hint I formed myself. **1770** LANGHORNE *Plutarch* (1879) II. 715/2 The reward he gave him for forming his son was.. honourable. **1778** EARL PEMBROKE *Equitation* 87 There is a great deal of good sense in Xenophon's method of forming horses for war. **1781** GIBBON *Decl. & F.* III. 2 The most skilful masters..had laboured to form the mind and body of the young prince. **1812** SIR H. DAVY *Chem. Philos.* 18 Van Helmont..was formed in the school of Alchemy. **1847** L. HUNT *Men, Women & B.* II. vii. 96 Formed under their auspices, our parrot soon equalled his instructors. **1889** JESSOPP *Coming of Friars* iv. 197 Rudely scrawled by some one whose hand is not yet formed.

absol. **1377** LANGL. *P. Pl.* B. xv. 371 But if gyle be mayster And flaterere his felawe vnder hym to fourmen.

b. To inform *of*; also, to instruct. *Obs.*

1399 LANGL. *R. Redeles* IV. 58 Somme..to þe kyng wente, And fformed him of foos, þat good ffrendis weren. *c* **1400** *Apol. Loll.* 71 What may þey do, but..abid til þei be formid wiþ holy writ, how hem is best to do?

†**c.** To instigate, persuade. *Obs.*

1399 LANGL. *R. Redeles* I. 107 þe ffrist þat 3ou fformed to þat ffals dede, He shulde have hadde hongynge on hie on þe fforckis. *c* **1400** *Destr. Troy* 8027 How þat faire, by his fader, was fourmet to wende To the grekes.

3. a. To place in order, arrange. Also, to embody, organize (persons or things) *into* (a society, system, etc.). Cf. 8 a.

1362 LANGL. *P. Pl.* A. VIII. 39 þat I ne schal sende 3or soules saaf in-to heuene, And bi-foren þe Face of my Fader fourmen or seetes. *c* **1420** *Pallad. on Husb.* I. 1101 But setis make yfourmed as thee list. **1667** *Decay Chr. Piety* xv. 360 Our divisions with the Romanists..are thus form'd into an interest. **1700** S. L. tr. *Fryke's Voy. E. Ind.* 309 We were commanded..to form ourselves into a Ring. **1772** SIMES *Mil. Guide* (1781) 12 The routes must be so formed, that no column cross another on the march. **1874** GREEN *Short Hist.* ii. §6. 93 The Clerks of the Royal Chapel were formed into a body of secretaries.

b. *intr.* for *refl.* (Cf. 8 b.)

1821 CLARE *Vill. Minstr.* I. 44 The noisy rout..Form round the ring superior strength to show.

4. a. To construct, frame; to make, bring into existence, produce. Const. *from*, *of*, *out of* (the material or elements). Also, to articulate, pronounce (a word, etc.).

c **1300** *Havelok* 36 God..Formede hire wimman to be born. **1382** WYCLIF *Gen.* ii. 7 God thanne fourmede man of the slyme of the erthe. *c* **1400** *Lanfranc's Cirurg.* 139 He answerde me bablynge as a childe þat begynneþ to speke but he my3te formen non worde. *c* **1440** *Gesta Rom.* xlvii. 204 (Harl. MS.) Adam, the whiche was shapin and formide in the felde of Damaske. **1514** BARCLAY *Cyt. & Uplondyshm.* (Percy Soc.) 10 When the worlde was fourmed & create. **1551** BP. GARDINER *Explic. Transubst.* 107 Whenne God formed Adam of claye. **1577** HELLOWES *Gueuara's Chron.* 75 He made the Goddesse Venus in Alabaster..and of waxe did fourme the whole Island Creta. **1611** BIBLE *2 Esdras* vi. 39 The sound of mans voice was not yet formed. **1667** MILTON *P.L.* XI. 570 The liquid Ore he draend Into fit moulds prepar'd; from which he form'd First his own Tooles. **1800** tr. *Lagrange's Chem.* II. 151 The oxygen of the oxide of the gold seizes on the hydrogen and forms water. **1849** MACAULAY *Hist. Eng.* I. 294 It had recently been formed out of the cavalry who had returned from Tangier. **1860** TYNDALL *Glac.* I. xxvii. 202 The snow had given way, forming a zigzag fissure across the slope. **1885** *Antiquary* Sept. 89/1 Henry VIII...was the first English king to form a gallery of pictures.

b. To frame in the mind, conceive (an idea, judgement, opinion, etc.). †Formerly also, to imagine; occas. *to form to oneself* (= Fr. *se figurer*), and with complement.

1595 SHAKS. *John* IV. iii. 45 Could thought, without this obiect, Forme such another? **1667** *Decay Chr. Piety* xv. 357 The defeat of the secular Design, is commonly the routing those Opinions which were formed for the promoting it. **1678** DRYDEN *All for Love* II. Wks. 1883 V. 369, I formed the danger greater than it was, And now 'tis near, 'tis lessened. **1703** ROWE *Fair Penit.* II. i. 424 My sad Soul Has form'd a dismal melancholy Scene. **1712** STEELE *Spect.* No. 533 ¶2 Form to yourself what a persecution this must needs be to a virtuous and chaste mind. **1779** BURKE *Corr.* (1844) II. 270, I do not form an estimate of the ideas of the churches of Italy and France from the pulpits of Edinburgh. **1861** M. PATTISON *Ess.* (1889) I. 44 The reader..may form to himself some notion of what [etc.]. **1866** J. MARTINEAU *Ess.* I. 277 We form no judgments till we have got language.

c. *Parliamentary.* = CONSTITUTE 6 b.

1825 T. JEFFERSON *Autobiog.* Wks. 1859 I. 11 Many members being assembled, but the House not yet formed.

d. *refl.* and *intr.* for *refl.*

1801 SOUTHEY *Thalaba* I. xxiv. Three years no cloud had form'd. **1830** TENNYSON *Sea-Fairies* 25 The rainbow forms and flies on the land Over the islands free. **1864** BRYCE *Holy Rom. Emp.* vii. (1875) 113 Very early..had the belief formed itself that [etc.]. **1880** J. A. SPALDING *Eliz. Demonol.* 128 Stop the butter from forming in the churn. **1893** *Law Times* XCV. 40/1 A sheet of ice had formed in front of Proctor's house.

5. To develop in oneself, acquire (habits); to enter into (a junction); to contract (an alliance, friendship, etc.).

1736 BUTLER *Anal.* I. v. Wks. 1874 I. 90 Active habits are to be formed by exercise. **1781** *Hist. Eur.* in *Ann. Reg.* 2/1 The French..formed a junction with the Spaniards. **1784** COWPER *Task* II. 634 We..form connexions, but acquire no friend. **1828** D'ISRAELI *Chas. I*, II. xii. 309 With the Flemings..our country had from the earliest times formed an uninterrupted intercourse. **1842** LYTTON *Zanoni* 22 He formed no friends. **1891** *Speaker* 2 May 531/1 Those methodical readers, who have formed the useful habit of keeping commonplace books.

6. a. To be the components or material of; to go to make up, to compose. **b.** To serve for, constitute; to make *one* or *part of*.

1377 LANGL. *P. Pl.* B. XVII. 169 The fyngres fourmen a ful hande to purtreye or peynten. **1717** tr. *Frezier's Voy. S. Sea* 48 The Continent, with which it [the island] forms two Passages. **1781** COWPER *Friendship* 14 The requisites that form a friend. **1817** COLERIDGE *Sibyll. Leaves, Fire, Famine & Slaughter*, Letters four do form his name. **1849** MACAULAY *Hist. Eng.* I. 294 The Life Guards..now form two regiments. **1873** *Act 36 & 37 Vict.* c. 77. §39 The soil forming such butt or target. **1874** GREEN *Short Hist.* vi. §2. 275 Yeomen and tradesmen formed the bulk of the insurgents. **1885** *Manch. Exam.* 15 July 5/2 A common mould fungus..forming a kind of black velvety mass.

b. 1821 CLARE *Vill. Minstr.* II. 35 Every molehill forms a seat. **1841** BREWSTER *Mart. Sc.* vi. (1856) 91 His eminent pupil Viviani formed one of his family. **1845** M. PATTISON *Ess.* (1889) I. 27 The volume of the canons which had formed the object of his study. **1869** FREEMAN *Norm. Conq.* (1876) III. xi. 59 A realm of which Northumberland constitutionally formed a part.

c. With mixture of sense 2: To render fit *for*.

1711 STEELE *Spect.* No. 49 ¶3 These are the Men formed for Society. **1777** ROBERTSON *Hist. Amer.* (1778) I. II. 84 All these qualities formed him for command.

7. *Gram.* **a.** To construct (a new word) by derivation, composition, etc. **b.** Of a word or word-stem: To have (a case, tense, etc.) expressed by a specified inflexion.

1824 L. MURRAY *Gram.* I. 348 Dissyllables, formed by prefixing a syllable to the radical word. **1872** MORRIS *Eng. Accid.* xiii. 168 The verbs of the strong conjugation form the past tense by a change of the root-vowel.

8. *Milit.* and *Naval.* **a.** To draw up (troops, etc.) in order. Also with *up*.

[*c* **1330** R. BRUNNE *Chron.* (1725) 115 Walter Spek ros on hand, þe folk to forme & taile. *c* **1400** *Destr. Troy* 6334 The fourthe batell in feld, he fourmet to leng With Archelaus]. **1816** KEATINGE *Trav.* (1817) II. 5 The troops mount, and, the whole being formed, move off the ground. **1833** *Regul. Instr. Cavalry* I. 56 The left files to be formed up, and sit at ease. **1838-42** ARNOLD *Hist. Rome* III. xliii. 78 Hannibal.. forming his men as fast as they landed, led them instantly to the charge. **1870** BRYANT *Iliad* I. II. 69 For there was none to form their ranks for fight. **1893** FORBES-MITCHELL *Remin. Gt. Mutiny* 41 We were then formed up and served with some rations.

b. *refl.* and *intr.* Of troops, ships, etc.: To arrange themselves in or assume some particular disposition or formation, according to prescribed rules. Also with *up*. *to form on* (some other body): see quot. 1802.

1722 DE FOE *Col. Jack* (1840) 236 Our army formed immediately. **1736** LEDIARD *Life Marlborough* II. 494 The first Squadrons..had much ado to form themselves. **1795** NELSON 10 Mar. in Nicolas *Disp.* II. 11 The Admiral made the signal to form in the Order of Battle. **1796** *Instr. & Reg. Cavalry* (1813) 77 They will at once form up. **1799** HARRIS in Owen *Wellesley's Desp.* 119 The right wing of the army under my command formed on the picquets of the right. **1802** C. JAMES *Milit. Dict.*, To *Form on*, is to advance forward, so as to connect yourself with any given object of formation, and to lengthen the line. **1803** LAKE in Owen *Wellesley's Desp.* 405 The infantry formed in two columns. **1832** HT. MARTINEAU *Hill & Valley* viii. 126 The soldiers formed themselves round the waggon. **1859** TENNYSON *Riflemen Form!* ii, Form, Form, Riflemen Form! Ready, be ready to meet the storm! **1883** *Army Corps Orders* in *Standard* 22 Mar. 3/3 When the 'assemble' sounds both Forces will form up by Brigades.

c. *trans.* To arrange themselves in the form of (battalions, a line, etc.). Esp. in the orders *form fours!* and *form two deep!*

1772 SIMES *Mil. Guide* (1781) 12 The companies will.. form battalions as they advance to the head of the line, and then halt. **1796** *Instr. & Reg. Cavalry* (1813) 152 The whole are ordered to halt, with an intention of forming line in the new direction. *Ibid.* 225 Form open column of divisions behind the right. **1889** *Infantry Drill* 152 The companies that will form the side faces will form fours in the required direction. *Ibid.* 154 On the words Form Two-Deep, the original rear-rank men will take one pace to the rear. **1915** 'I. HAY' *First Hundred Thousand* i, 'Squoad—'Shun! Move to the right in fours. Forrm—*fourrrs*!'..'On the command "form fours", odd numbers will stand fast.'..'Forrm—two *deep*!'

d. *to form the siege* (of a place) [Fr. *former un siège*]: to commence active siege-operations (against it).

1766 GIBBON *Decl. & F.* I. xi. 218 The siege of that great city was immediately formed. **1802** C. JAMES *Milit. Dict.* s.v. *Siege, To form the Siege, or lay Siege to a place*..there must be an army sufficient to furnish five or six reliefs for the trenches, pioneers, guards, convoys, escorts, &c. and artillery, with all the apparatus thereto belonging; magazines, etc. **1871** FREEMAN *Norm. Conq.* (1876) IV. xviii. 155 The whole army now drew near; the siege was formed.

form (fɔːm), *v.*² [f. the sb.: see FORM *sb.* 21.] *intr.* Of a hare: To take to her form; to seat.

1575 TURBERVILE *Art Ven.* lviii. 162 To looke about hir, and to choose out a place to forme in. **1612** DRAYTON *Poly-olb.* ij, The melancholy hare is formed in brakes and briers. **1637** B. JONSON *Sad Sheph.* II. vii, First think which way shee fourmeth, on what wind: Or North, or South. **1725** COATES *Dict. Herald.*, *Seateth* or *Formeth* are the Terms that note where the Hare has its resting Place. **1801** STRUTT *Sports & Past.* I. i. 17 A hare [was said to be] formed, a rabbit set.

form- (fɔːm), in *Chem.*, combining form of FORMIC or FORMYL, as in **formal** ('fɔːmæl) *sb.*², any of the acetals derived from formaldehyde, having the general formula $CH_2(OR)_2$; *spec.* METHYLAL, $CH_2(OCH_3)_2$; **'formamide**, the amide of formic acid; **for'mamidine**, the postulated compound $NH_2{\cdot}CH{:}NH$, which is known only as its salts; **for'manilide**, a white crystalline compound, $C_6H_5{\cdot}NH{\cdot}COH$, used as an antipyretic, analgesic, and local anæsthetic. (Cf. the termination of *chloro-form*.)

1900 DORLAND *Med. Dict.*, *Formal*, methylol or methylene dimethylate..: a clear, fragrant liquid. It is anesthetic and hypnotic. **1952** E. H. RODD *Chem. Carbon Compounds* I. xvi. 1031 A mixture of the isomeric formals is obtained from glycerol, trioxymethylene and conc. HCl at 100°. **1852** Formamide [see *formanilide*]. **1863** A. W. HOFMANN in *Jrnl. Chem. Soc.* XVI. 72 Half-way between formate of ammonium and hydrocyanic acid, theory justifies us in searching for formamide. *Ibid.* 73 This substance, which is equally soluble in water, alcohol and ether is formamide. **1869** ROSCOE *Chem.* 349 *Formamide*, obtained by acting on ethyl formate with ammonia. **1890** *Lancet* 11 Oct. 783/2 Injections..of a 1 per cent. solution of formamide of mercury. **1882** *Jrnl. Chem. Soc.* XLI. 266 The solid therefore obtained by the action of the substance, 2HCN + 3HCl, upon alcohol is the hydrochloride of the base.. formamidine. **1952** *Jrnl. Appl. Chem.* II. 203 It is now possible to report a simple method for the synthesis of formamidine hydrochloride. **1852** W. GREGORY *Handbk. Org. Chem.* 337 Formanilide, the analogous compound to which, formamide, is not known. **1966** MILLAR & SPRINGALL *Sidgwick's Org. Chem. Nitrogen* (ed. 3) vii. 224 The formylation of aromatic amines proceeds very readily; formanilide, H·CONHPh, is rapidly formed on boiling dilute formic acid with aniline.

-form (fɔːm), repr. F. *-forme*, L. *-formis*, f. *forma* FORM *sb.*, a termination used to form adjs. (1) with the sense 'having the form of' (what is denoted by the Lat. sb.), as in *cruciform*, *cuneiform*, *filiform*; (2) referring to number of forms, as *diversiform*, *multiform*, *uniform*. The former class includes many words of recent origin used in natural science, *esp.* in Botany, as *acinaciform*, *calathiform*, *corolliform*, *fusiform*, *vermiform*; new words of this type are still frequently formed.

The termination is always preceded by *-i-*, either representing the Lat. stem-vowel or its weakened form in combination, or inserted after consonant stems. By some this *i* has been ignorantly supposed to be the genitive ending; hence such misspellings as *fabæform*, *tabulæform*.

formable ('fɔːməb(ə)l), *a.* [f. FORM *v.*[1] + -ABLE.]

1. That may be formed. In early use: Workable, plastic.

1398 TREVISA *Barth. De P. R.* XVII. xxiv. (1495) 617 The cypresse tree is fourmable. **1572** BOSSEWELL *Armorie* II. 95 b, The Cypres next vnto yᵉ Cedar tree is most formable. **1600** DEKKER *Old Fortunatus* in Dodsley *O. Pl.* (1816) III. 166 God bless me from suffering you to love me, if you be not so formable. **1629** T. ADAMS *Wks.* 696 The Papists..not shaming to call that sacred Writ a nose of waxe, formable to any construction. **1674** GREW *Anat. Plants* IV. I. iii. (1682) 225 Not generable, formable, or transformable. **1884** J. FISKE *Evolutionist* xii. 312 A good many of his nervous connections are not yet formed, they are only formable.

†**2.** Exhibiting agreement with prescribed forms; formal, proper, shapely. *Obs.*

1479 J. PASTON in *Paston Lett.* No. 841 III. 256 Lomnore and I..drew ought a formable bylle ought of your, and send it ayen to th' Exchetore. **1483** *Cath. Angl.* 138/1 Formabylle; *ubi* ordinate. **1586** W. WEBBE *Eng. Poetrie* (Arb.) 90 That whatsoeuer he wryteth he may so expresse and order it, that hys narration may be formable. **1622** F. MARKHAM *Bk. War* II. v. 58 One of the first which gaue light to our late Postures, and formable motions.

Hence **forma'bility**, capability of formation.

1825 COLERIDGE *Aids Refl.* App. C. (1858) I. 394 Of infinite capacity and formability.

†**'formably**, *adv. Obs.* [f. prec. + -LY[2].] According to customary or prescribed form; formally; in good form; speciously.

c **1400** *Apol. Loll.* 79 Þis cosynage..may not be known formably bi proue after þe court of plete. *c* **1450** *Chester Pl.* (Shaks. Soc.) I. 6 See that you, telers..The storye of the Assention formablye doe frame. **1479** in *Eng. Gilds* (1870) 416 Such thinges as I..haue not duely ne formably executed. **1481** CAXTON *Reynard* (Arb.) 31 The foxe made his excuse so wel and formably..that [etc.]. **1509** HAWES *Past. Pleas.* 123 As I shall shew anone more formably.

†**for'mad**, *ppl. a. Obs.* In 4 formadd. [pa. pple. of OE. **formǣdan*, f. FOR- *pref.*[1] + (*ȝe*)*mǣdan*: see AMAD.] Driven mad, frantic.

a **1300** *Cursor M.* 24539 (Cott.), I murnand moder þus formadd In sterin stanging was i stadd.

†**for'make**, *v. Obs.* [f. FOR- *pref.*[1] + MAKE *v.*] *trans.* To make over again, ? repair.

c **1483** CAXTON *Vocab.* 21 *Poul le couvelier faict et refaict les cuves*, Poule the couper Maketh and formaketh the keupis.

formal ('fɔːməl), *a.* and *sb.*[1] [a. L. *formālis*, f. *forma* FORM *sb.*: see -AL[1]. Cf. F. *formel.*]

A. *adj.*

1. Of or pertaining to FORM, in various senses.

a. *Metaph.* Pertaining to the form or constitutive essence of a thing; essential. Opposed to *material*. So *formal cause* (see CAUSE *sb.* 5).

c **1386** CHAUCER *Melib.* ¶433 The cause material been the fyve woundes of thy doghter. The cause formal is the manere of hir werkinge. *c* **1430** *Art of Nombrynge* (E.E.T.S.) 1 Sothely .2. manere of nombres ben notifiede; Materialle, as nombre is vnitees gadrede to gedres; Formalle, as nombre is a collеccione of vnitees. **1447** BOKENHAM *Seyntys* Introd. (Roxb.) 1 The more clere That it may be the formal cause [He] Settyth in dew ordre clause be clause. **1587** GOLDING *De Mornay* ii. (1617) 25 They be good, as in respect of their bare being: and euill, as in respect that they forgoe their formal being that is to say their goodnesse. **1628** T. SPENCER *Logick* 55 Man is..fit to loue the knowne good..this fitnes floweth from his reasonable soule or formall being. **1669** HOLDER *Elem. Speech* 22 Of Letters the Material part is Breath and Voice; the Formal is constituted by the Motions and Figure of the Organs of Speech affecting Breath with a peculiar sound, by which each Letter is discriminated. *a* **1703** BURKITT *On N.T.* Luke xii. 32 The goodwill..of God is the original spring and formal cause, from whence all divine favours do proceed. *a* **1716** SOUTH *Serm.* (1744) X. 37 For deceit is the formal, constituent reason of hypocrisy. **1814** CARY *Dante, Par.* II. 71 Different virtues needs must be the fruits Of formal principles. **1827** WHATELY *Logic* II. v. §3 Whatever Term can be affirmed of several things, must express either their whole essence..or a part of their essence, (viz. either the material part, which is called the Genus, or the formal and distinguishing part, which is called Differentia).

†**b.** Pertaining to the specific form of an animal or plant. Of a seed or germ: Endowed with a principle of form. *Obs.*

c **1400** *Lanfranc's Cirurg.* 21 Þe foormal vertu which almyȝty god haþ ȝeue to þe maris ordeyneþ and diuidid euery partie of þese spermes..til þat þe child be born. **1605** BACON *Adv. Learn.* II. iv. §5. 19 Being as a plant that cometh of the lust of the earth without a formal seed. **1677** HALE *Prim. Orig. Man.* III. vi. 277 Although it be admitted that Insects and *spontaneè orta* do or may arise from a *Semen* or Principle that is not univocal or formal.

c. Pertaining to the outward form, shape, or appearance (of a material object); also, in immaterial sense, pertaining to the form, arrangement, external qualities (*e.g.* of a work of art, a composition, etc.). †Also, occas. of knowledge: Theoretical as opposed to practical.

1639 EVELYN *Diary* (1827) I. 15 Musick, in which I afterwards arriv'd to some formal knowledge, though to small perfection of hand. **1655** G. S. in Hartlib *Ref. Commw. Bees* 27 Honey..out of which they [the Bees] doe separate a more fat substance, which they also transmute into Wax, with a formal transmutation. **1837** WHEWELL *Hist. Induct. Sc.* (1857) I. 273 The distinction of formal and physical Astronomy. *a* **1853** ROBERTSON *Serm.* Ser. III. iii. (1872) 39 All living unity is spiritual, not formal. **1860** RUSKIN *Mod. Paint.* V. VIII. i. 158 Invention Formal, otherwise and most commonly called technical composition.

d. *Logic.* Concerned with the form, as distinguished from the matter, of reasoning. ***formal concept*** [tr. G. *formaler begriff*]: a concept of logic, free from the descriptive content that would restrict it to any particular subject-matter (see quots.); ***formal implication*** (see quots.).

c **1856** SIR W. HAMILTON *Lect. Logic* xxvii. (1860) II. 64 The harmony of thought with the form of thought, is.. Formal Truth. *Ibid.* 231 App. I. The doctrine which expounds the laws by which our scientific procedure should be governed, in so far as these lie in the forms of thought, or in the conditions of the mind itself..may be called Formal, or Subjective, or Abstract, or Pure, Logic. **1864** BOWEN *Logic* ii. 42 All this, however, is but the elimination of Formal error. **1870** JEVONS *Elem. Logic* vii. 69 It is no part of formal Logic to teach us how to interpret the meanings of sentences. **1903** B. RUSSELL *Princ. Math.* §15 The relation of formal implication..holds between propositional functions when the one implies the other for all values of the variable. **1922** tr. *Wittgenstein's Tractatus* 4. 126 In the sense in which we speak of formal properties we can now speak also of formal concepts. (I introduce this expression in order to make clear the confusion of formal concepts with proper concepts which runs through the whole of the old logic.) **1932** LEWIS & LANGFORD *Symbolic Logic* 101 The relation of formal implication is transitive, like material implication. **1939** G. RYLE in *Mind* XLVIII. 149 To use the language of Kant and Wittgenstein, we were trying to treat formal concepts as if they were 'proper' or material concepts. *Ibid.* 151 A formal concept is one which may have a place in a proposition about any subject-matter you please, and some ..will be present in any proposition... 'Not', 'exists', 'some', 'other',..and many others are not peculiar to any special topics. **1955** A. N. PRIOR *Formal Logic* 197 The Russellian 'formal' implication is simply universal material implication. **1965** E. J. LEMMON *Beginning Logic* iv. 154 The term 'formal implication' was coined by Russell to describe the universal quantification over a material implication: i.e. a proposition of the form '$(x)\ (Fx \rightarrow Gx)$'.

e. Of or pertaining to customary form or conventionality.

1712 POPE *1st. Ep. Miss Blount* 42 Still in constraint your suff'ring Sex remains, Or bound in formal, or in real chains.

2. Characterized by, or regarded according to, its form; that is (so and so) in respect of form.

a. *Theol.* ***formal sin***: one which is such in the full sense, as including not merely the outward act which is forbidden, but the circumstances which constitute it as sinful, *e.g.* evil intention. So ***formal schism***, ***schismatic***, etc. Opposed to ***material sin***, etc.

1641 J. JACKSON *True Evang. T.* II. 92 Therefore was there a positive Law..not to seeth the Kid in the mothers milke. Not that there was any direct, or formal sin, in that manner of Cookery. ? **1656** BRAMHALL *Replic.* i. 66 Cannot God pardon formall, much more materiall Schism. *Ibid.* ix. 341 They are not formall, but only materiall Schismaticks.

†**b.** That is such in essence; strictly so called, essential. *Obs.*

1691 RAY *Creation* II. (1704) 289 The bottom of the Eye where the formal Organ of Vision is situate.

†**c.** That is such merely in outward form or appearance. *Obs.*

1581 SIDNEY *Apol. Poetrie* (Arb.) 35 Pretty Allegories, stealing vnder the formall tales of Beastes. **1633** EARL MANCH. *Al Mondo* (1636) 155 Formall penitents will easily part with so much of their sinne as may abate nothing of their profit. **1634** CANNE *Necess. Separ.* (1849) 231 The formal Protestants in England. **1737** BRACKEN *Farriery Impr.* (1756) I. 286 It is a Kind of formal Leprosy which often begins in the Neck, Mane or Tail.

†**d.** Of quoted statements: Exact with regard to form. *Obs.*

1563 FOXE *A. & M.* 708/1 What were the formall wordes, or at the least-wise in substance that I the sayde Bishop then vttered.

3. a. That is according to recognized forms, or to the rules of art or law. Formerly occas. const. †*to*.

1390 GOWER *Conf.* III. 89 The wise man accompteth After the formal proprete Of algorismes a, be, ce. *c* **1425** WYNTOUN *Cron.* IX. Prol. 56 Now Modyr of þe Makare..To fair formale Fyne my labouris þow lede. **1526** *Pilgr. Perf.* (W. de W. 1531) 168 The fourth condicyon of yᵉ prayer of yᵉ clene hert is, that it must be formall: that is to saye, it must be formed and ordred after the order of charite. **1529** MORE *Dial. Touchyng Pest. Sect Luther* C ij b, A sylogysme & resonynge, almoste as formall as is the argumente. **1597** MORLEY *Introd. Mus.* 74 It followeth to speake of a formall closing without a dis-cord or Cadence. **1602** DANIEL *Trag. Philotas* IV. ii, And haue his Tryal formal to our Laws. **1622** MALYNES *Anc. Law-Merch.* 394 You may not say in the Bill, It may please you to pay..and most men will not vse the words (Make him good Payment) but the fewer words the more formall. **1722** DE FOE *Col. Jack* (1840) 235 No one place..could have held out a formal siege. **1749** FIELDING *Tom Jones* VI. vii. (*heading*) A picture of formal courtship in miniature, as it always ought to be drawn.

†**b.** Made in proper form, regular, complete. Also in familiar use, 'regular', unmistakable. *Obs.*

1635 EARL STRAFFORDE *Lett.* (1739) I. 410 An Indisposition which hath hindred me from writing..a formal Fit of the Gout. **1673** EVELYN *Mem.* (1857) I. 89 We went..to see the formal and formidable camp on Blackheath, raised to invade Holland. **1684** *Lond. Gaz.* No. 1953/1 Though the Lower Town has no other defence than a single Wall, yet his Highness found it convenient to make formal approaches to it. **1719** DE FOE *Crusoe* I. 247 As there was a Door or Entrance there into my Cave, I made a formal fram'd Door-case, and a Door to it of Boards.

†**c.** Of a story, etc.: Elaborately constructed, circumstantial. *Obs.*

1592 WARNER *Alb. Eng.* VII. xxxv. (1612) 168 At full he could his lessons, and a formale lie would tell. **1662** MORE *Philos. Writ.* Pref. Gen. (1712) 23 Such was that formal story of his casting incense on the Altar of an Idol. **1663** BUTLER *Hud.* I. ii. 41 And never coyn a formal Lye on't, To make the Knight o'ercome the Giant. **1708** SWIFT *Sacr. Test* Wks. 1755 II. I. 121 When the earl of Pembroke was in Ireland..a formal story was very gravely carried to his excellency.

†**4. a.** Regular, having a definite principle, methodical. **b.** Of feature, stature, etc.: Regular, shapely. **c.** Normal in intellect, sane. *Obs.*

a. 1413 *Pilgr. Sowle* (Caxton) I. iii. (1859) 4 The ouer-most of the erthe was moost clere, and alwey the clerenesse amenussing dounward by verray formal processe. **1701** ROWE *Amb. Step-moth.* V. ii. 2874 Formal Justice that severely strikes, And in an instant is serene and calm.

b. 1525 LD. BERNERS *Froiss.* II. clxiv. [clx.] 455 Therle of Foiz..was a goodly prince and of a formall stature. **1548** HALL *Chron., Edw. IV* (an. 3) 194 b, She was a woman more of formal countenaunce, then of excellent beautie, but yet of such beautie and favor that [etc.]. **1576** FLEMING *Panopl. Epist.* 377 Every joynte and limme..verie formall, and passing hansome.

c. 1590 SHAKS. *Com. Err.* V. i. 105 With wholsome sirrups, drugges, and holy prayers To make of him a formall man againe.

5. Done or made with the forms recognized as ensuring validity; explicit and definite, as opposed to what is matter of tacit understanding.

1547 BOORDE *Brev. Health* Preamble, Let him loke to it, and make a formal wyl or testament. **1560–78** *Bk. Discipl. Ch. Scot.* (1621) 21 It hath power to excommunicate the obstinate, formall processe being led. **1622** BACON *Holy War* Misc. Wks. (1629) 127 As there are Formall and written Leagues, Respective to certaine Enemies; So is there a Naturall and Tacite Confederation, amongst all Men against the common Enemy of Humane Society. **1626** CHAS. I in Ellis *Orig. Lett.* Ser. I. III. 249 For Blennill he has yet but made his formale demands concerning the Ships. **1771** *Junius Lett.* lxii. 321 Nor has there ever been a formal decision against them in any of the superior Courts. **1838** THIRLWALL *Greece* II. xiv. 228 Cleomenes, without waiting for a formal commission, immediately repaired to Ægina. **1856** FROUDE *Hist. Eng.* (1858) II. vii. 129 Both the king and the archbishop had disobeyed a formal inhibition.

¶ Predicatively of a law: Of unmistakable import, decisive. [A Gallicism.]

1701 tr. *Le Clerc's Prim. Fathers* 260 He could not be transferred to Constantinople without breaking the Fifteenth Canon of the Council of Nice which is formal thereupon.

6. a. Connected with or accompanied by form or ceremony; ceremonial, 'state'.

1602 WARNER *Alb. Eng.* XI. lxvi. 283 Scarce Cleopatras Anthony was feasted with more cheere..than Jenkinson was heere: In formall Hawking, Hunting, Chace not them came Tristram neere. **1841** ELPHINSTONE *Hist. Ind.* I. xi. 355 The most general practice on formal occasions is [etc.]. **1875** W. S. HAYWARD *Love agst. World* 3 It will save the squire a formal call.

†**b.** Of apparel: Ceremonial, proper to a dignity or office. Cf. FORMALITY 10. *Obs.*

1593 *Rites & Mon. Ch. Durh.* (Surtees) 43 [Pictures of bps. etc.] most largly and sumptuously sett fourth in there formall apparell. **1656** STANLEY *Hist. Philos.* IV. (1701) 136/1, I will not with a formal robe disgrace Myself.

7. That is merely matter of form: **a.** Done or adopted for the sake of form or convention; perfunctory; having the form without the spirit or substance. **b.** That is matter of routine only, not of substantial import.

a. 1648 MILTON *Tenure Kings* (1650) 45 A formal preachment huddl'd up at the odd hours of a lazy week. **1676** DRYDEN *Aurengz.* II. i, Of formal duty, make no more thy boast. **1720** WATTS *Hymn, Come Holy Spirit*, In vain we tune our formal songs, In vain we strive to rise.

b. **1818** CRUISE *Digest* (ed. 2) IV. 256 This doctrine..does not extend to mere formal acts.

8. Of persons, their manners and actions: Rigorously observant of forms; precise; prim in attire; ceremonious. Chiefly in reproachful use: Unduly precise or ceremonious, stiff.

1514 BARCLAY *Cyt. & Uplondyshm.* (Percy Soc.) 1 Amyntas was formalle & propre in his gere. **1594** SHAKS. *Rich. III*, III. i. 82 Thus like the formall Vice, Iniquitie, I morallize two meanings in one word. **1596** —— *Tam. Shr.* III. i. 61 Are you so formall, sir? **1607–12** BACON *Ess.*, *Ceremonies* (Arb.) 26 Especially they [Ceremonies] be not to be omitted to Straungers and formall Natures. **1679** PENN *Addr. Prot.* I. vii. (1692) 27 He is reported Formal, that will not be Rude to Sacred Things. *c* **1689** PRIOR *Ode*, '*While Blooming Youth*' 25 Forc'd compliments and formal bows. **1693** *Hum. & Conv. Town* 125 The distant Justice of Peace, his formal Spouse, and Daughters. **1711** ADDISON *Spect.* No. 119 ¶5 To make Conversation too stiff, formal and precise. **1749** CHESTERF. *Lett.* (1792) II. cxciii. 220 All the evening in formal fine company. **1853** LYTTON *My Novel* II. vii, More familiar with his master than we formal English permit our domestics to be.

9. a. Marked by extreme or excessive regularity or symmetry; stiff or rigid in design; wanting in ease or freedom of outline or arrangement.

1597 SHAKS. *Lover's Compl.* 29 Her hair, nor loose, nor tied in formal plat. **1753** HOGARTH *Anal. Beauty* vi. 34 When any part of dress has not the excuse of fitness or propriety for its uniformity of parts, the ladies always call it formal. **1807–8** W. IRVING *Salmag.* (1824) 116 Your plaited shirts, Your formal bag-wigs. **1873** BLACK *Pr. Thule* xxi. 353 Small windows with formal red curtains. **1874** L. STEPHEN *Hours in Library* (1892) I. iii. 120 Pope..was one of the first ..to break through the old formal school of gardening.

b. In immaterial sense: Having a 'set' or rigorously methodical aspect or character.

1726 SHELVOCKE *Voy. round World* (1757) 423 It would perhaps be too formal to enter upon a discourse concerning their government. **1846** MCCULLOCH *Acc. Brit. Empire* (1854) II. 367 Formal harangues of this sort are about the least efficient of all the modes in which information can be conveyed to the student. **1865** GROTE *Plato* (1875) Pref. 5 The dramatic—as contrasted with the formal and systematising.

B. *sb.* A thing that is formal; *esp.* (orig. and chiefly *U.S.*) (an) evening dress; an engagement at which such dress is worn.

1605 TIMME *Quersit.* II. iv. 14 Simples may be distinguished into those things which are simple formes, and into those which are simple matters; or into those things which are simply formals, and into those which are simply materials. Those things which are simply formall are astrall and spirituall. **1875** WHITNEY *Life Lang.* v. 95 They are etherealized formals. **1941** *Amer. Speech* XVI. 96 They are all right for casuals or spectator wear, but I'd get that formal in either Waltz Blue or Coronado Coral. **1946** *New Yorker* 28 Sept. 27/2 The neighboring children were strange, with ..their queer talk of dates, and formals, and going steady. **1948** *Ibid.* 27 Mar. 29/1 The initiates wore evening dresses (formals, formals, Emily reminded herself to say). **1961** M. BEADLE *These Ruins are Inhabited* (1963) v. 71 If a dinner invitation does not specify 'informal', guests assume that black ties will be worn. Young ladies then wear short formals, and old ladies wear floor-length evening dresses. **1968** 'A. YORK' *Predator* vi. 86 She looked sufficiently virginal to be attending her first formal.

formal, var. form of FORMEL.

formaldehyde (fɔːˈmældɪhaɪd). *Chem.* [f. FORM- + ALDEHYDE.] A choking gas, CH_2O, usually prepared as an aqueous solution, and used as a preservative, an antiseptic, and in large quantities as a raw material in the chemical and plastics industries.

1872 *Jrnl. Chem. Soc.* XXV. 234 (*heading*) Reduction of formic acid to formaldehyde and methyl alcohol. **1894** *Athenæum* 11 Aug. 199/1 Last year a patent was granted for a solution of formaldehyde as a new antiseptic material, under the name of 'formalin'. **1947** R. L. WAKEMAN *Chem. Commercial Plastics* iii. 28 Formaldehyde, made by oxidation of methanol, is an essential component of all of the large volume thermosetting resins now produced. **1957** *New Scientist* 9 May 11/2 Salk and his colleagues..had shown that poliomyelitis viruses could be grown in tissue culture in bulk and treated with formaldehyde to make a vaccine. **1958** *Times Rev. Industry* Feb. 77/1 Monsanto Chemicals (Australia) has announced that its latest formaldehyde unit will double the capacity of the plant laid down some years ago.

formalin (ˈfɔːməlɪn). Formerly also **-ine**. [f. FORMAL(DEHYDE + -IN[1].] An aqueous formaldehyde solution, stabilized with methanol, containing 37 per cent by weight of formaldehyde. Hence ˌ**formaliniˈzation**, treatment with formalin; ˈ**formalinize** *v. trans.*, to treat with formalin; ˈ**formalinized** *ppl. a.*

1893 *Brit. Pat. 7038*, The new antiseptic material, herein called formalin,..contains 40% of pure formaldehyde combined with 60% of water. **1894** [see FORMOL]. **1901** *Westm. Gaz.* 25 July 5/3 The formalin treatment of consumption. **1907** *Practitioner* Apr. 570 The use of formalinised gut is advised. **1958** *Listener* 23 Jan. 153/2 The vaccine used in Britain and America is 'dead'—that is to say the virus is killed with formalin before it is made up for use. **1960** *Proc. Soc. Exper. Biol. & Med.* CIII. 158/2 After formalinization, these cells were not subject to hemolysis. **1964** M. HYNES *Med. Bacteriol.* (ed. 8) xi. 145 Toxoid, which can be prepared by formalinizing the purified toxin, may be used for active immunization of the human subject.

formalism (ˈfɔːməlɪz(ə)m). [f. FORMAL *a.* + -ISM. Not in Johnson, Todd, or Richardson.]

1. Strict or excessive adherence to prescribed forms; an instance or variety of this.

1840 in SMART. **1850** KINGSLEY *Alt. Locke* xiii. (1879) 151 Useless formalism! which lets through the reckless..and only excludes the honest and the conscientious. **1852** MRS. JAMESON *Leg. Madonna* Introd. (1857) 25 The rigid formalism of the degenerate Greek school. **1862** MERIVALE *Rom. Emp.* (1865) III. xxii. 12 Completely enchained by their dogmatic formalisms. **1875** STUBBS *Const. Hist.* III. xviii. 273 The constitutional formalism of three reigns.

2. a. The disposition to exalt what is formal or outward at the expense of what is spiritual; the practice of using forms of worship and of religious profession without real devotion or conviction.

1856 R. A. VAUGHAN *Mystics* (1860) II. 219 Formalism does not lie in these outward things themselves—it consists in the spirit in which they are used. **1878** MORLEY *Carlyle*, *Crit. Misc.* Ser. I. 201 The cant and formalism of any other degenerate form of active faith. **1883** FROUDE *Short Stud.* IV. II. iv. 208 The family devotions were long, but there was no formalism.

b. *Theology.* (See quot. 1957.)

1931 K. E. KIRK *Vision of God* i. 8 Formalism, as we have defined it hitherto,—the demand for a definite rule of life —has rigorism as one of its branches. **1937** O. WYON tr. *Brunner's Divine Imperative* vii. 65 The fact that the knowledge of God has become obscure also leads to the fatal dilemma—either the formalism of the legalistic ethic..or eudaemonistic materialism. **1957** *Oxf. Dict. Chr. Ch.* 513 *Formalism*... Of theories of ethics which look for the ground of moral action in the form of the moral law alone..without reference to any specific purposes or values which it is desired through the action to achieve or realize.

3. *Math.* **a.** The conception of pure mathematics as the manipulation according to certain formal rules of symbols that are intrinsically meaningless.

1913 tr. L. E. J. Brouwer in *Bull. Amer. Math. Soc.* XX. 82 On what grounds the conviction of the unassailable exactness of mathematical laws is based has for centuries been an object of philosophical research, and two points of view may here be distinguished, intuitionism (largely French) and formalism (largely German). **1933** M. BLACK *Nature of Math.* 148 'Formalism' has always been the working attitude of a group of practising mathematicians rather than a fully explicit philosophy. **1940** E. T. BELL *Devel. Math.* xxiii. 527 Formalism denies logicalism and seeks to controvert the conclusions of intuitionism. **1970** H. WEYL *Appreciation* in C. Reid *Hilbert* 270 Hilbert's formalism restores the principle of the excluded middle which was the main target of Brouwer's criticism.

b. (See quot. 1940.)

1940 E. T. BELL *Devel. Math.* xiii. 262 'Formalism' in analysis means manipulation of formulas involving infinite processes without sufficient attention to convergence and mathematical existence. **1947** COURANT & ROBBINS *What is Math.?* (ed. 4) p. vii, There exists the danger of frustration and disillusionment unless students and teachers try to look beyond mathematical formalism and manipulation and to grasp the real essence of mathematics. **1964** H. EVES *Introd. Hist. Math.* (rev. ed.) xii. 360 Euler's work represents the outstanding example of eighteenth-century formalism.

4. *Theatre.* A movement originating *c* 1890 in Russia which, at first a reaction against excessive naturalism in stage production, after the Revolution led to excessive emphasis on symbolism and stylization.

1927 J. DOLMAN *Art Play Prod.* xviii. 396 Most of the attempts at formalism today are really compromises—accidental compromises with stylization..or intentional compromises with realism or symbolism. **1931** SELDEN & SELLMAN *Stage Scenery* I. i. 28 Among the more popular styles..are: Realism,..Stylization,..Formalism, the mode of using forms which mark a place for action but do not attempt to represent or suggest any given locality. **1966** A. NICOLL *Devel. Theatre* (ed. 5) i. 3 We are here [*sc.* in the Nō plays] confronted by a theatre in which formalism is dominant. **1967** A. S. GILLETTE *Introd. Scenic Design* xii. 165 Theatres with conventional proscenium arches have been adapted to formalism by the substitution of drapery backgrounds for scenery.

5. a. The theory held by a Russian literary group in existence between 1916 and 1930 that technique and form are both the means to and the goal of artistic creation. **b.** Subsequently, a term often used pejoratively in Communist criticism to denote an artist's concentration on form at the expense of social reality and content.

1943 V. UGHET tr. *Miliukov's Outl. Russ. Culture* II. 118 It [*sc.* Socialist Realism] was directed against 'formalism' with its tendency to degenerate into mere aesthetic preoccupation with literary forms. **1955** V. ERLICH *Russ. Formalism* I. i. 4 Formalism was..the first critical movement in Russia which attacked in systematic fashion the problems of rhythm and meter, of style and composition. **1957** C. HUNT *Guide to Communist Jargon* xxi. 73 The *Political Dictionary* defines formalism as 'putting to the forefront the outer side of a question, the detachment of form from content'. *Ibid.* 75 The charge of formalism will commonly mean that a novelist has devoted too much attention to plot, characterization and description, and that his work lacks the requisite inspirational quality. **1962** *Listener* 19 July 115/1 The best circles in the West are now almost exclusively preoccupied with technical means for their own sake, with what their colleagues on the wrong side of the Iron Curtain would describe as 'formalism'.

6. [cf. G. *formalismus* in same sense (Hilbert et al. 1928, in *Math. Ann.* XCVIII. 1–30).] A particular mathematical theory or mode of description of a physical situation or effect.

1934 *Ann. Math.* XXXV. 29 (*heading*) On an algebraic generalization of the quantum mechanical formalism. **1955** J. A. WHEELER in W. Pauli *Niels Bohr* 177 These circumstances make it appropriate to discuss the spontaneous fission rates of even very heavy nuclei in terms of the liquid drop formalism. **1968** C. G. KUPER *Introd. Theory Superconductivity* xii. 193 In the field-theoretical approach to the theory of solids, quasiparticles enter the formalism in precisely the same way as 'physical' particles enter the formalism of elementary particle physics. **1970** *Nature* 12 Sept. 1087/2 A fresh attempt to impose a simple formalism on the kinetics and equilibrium of the oxygenation reaction.

formalist (ˈfɔːməlɪst), *sb.* and *a.* [f. as prec. + -IST.]

A. *sb.* †**1.** A formal person, a solemn pretender to wisdom. *Obs.*

1607–12 BACON *Ess.*, *Of Seeming Wise* (Arb.) 214 There are in pointe of wisedome..that doe nothing or litle verie solemlye..It is a ridiculous thing..to see what shiftes theis Formalists have..to make superficies to seeme body, that hath depth and bulk.

†**2.** One who formally adheres to the prevailing system; a time-server in religion. *Obs.*

1609 DOWNAM *Chr. Liberty* 75 Do not many..thinke themselues the more religious, for refusing obedience..to the lawes, and censure others as formalists and time-seruers? **1621** BURTON *Anat. Mel.* IV. iv. I. v, New Gods.. will have new ceremonies..to which every wise man as a good formalist should accommodate himself. **1632** D. LUPTON *Lond. & Co. Carbonadoed, Exchange* (1857) 276 A great Formalist. and an hazardable temporizer.

3. a. One who is excessively attached to forms; a stickler for fixed rule, etiquette, routine, or ceremonial. **b.** One who has the form of religion without the power.

1637 GILLESPIE *Eng. Pop. Cerem.* III. iv. 47 The Ceremonies are Idols to Formalists. **1642** MILTON *Apol. Smect.* (1851) 316 Though the formalist will say, what no decency in Gods worship? **1706–7** *Reflex. upon Ridicule* 183 Those Formalists who demand Explications of the least ambiguous Word. **1742** YOUNG *Nt. Th.* IV. 638 Oh ye cold-hearted, frozen, formalists! On such a theme, 'tis impious to be calm. **1814** SCOTT *Drama* (1874) 221 The former may be called the formalist of dramatic criticism. **1855** MACAULAY *Hist. Eng.* III. 19 Nobody..except the solemn formalists at the Spanish embassy, thought his youth an objection to his promotion. **1870** SPURGEON *Treas. Dav.* Ps. xxviii. 1 Mere formalists may be content without answers to their prayers, but genuine suppliants cannot.

†**4.** *Sc.* ? An authority on legal forms. *Obs.*

1612 SPOTTISWOOD *Let.* in Scot *Apol. Narr.* (1846) 236 To make choice of my Lord Secretary to be our formalist and adviser of our acts.

5. A follower or advocate of FORMALISM (3, 4, 5).

1913 tr. L. E. J. Brouwer in *Bull. Amer. Math. Soc.* XX. 83 For the formalist..mathematical exactness consists merely in the method of developing the series of relations, and is independent of the significance one might want to give to the relations or the entities which they relate. **1926** *Encycl. Brit.* III. 635/2 The 'Formalists' held that the naturalistic theatre was not art, but a soulless attempt to photograph life. **1934** P. A. MARKOV *Soviet Theatre* vii. 119 The 'formalists'..stressed the need for freeing the actor from the bonds of realism or æstheticism. **1941** COURANT & ROBBINS *What is Math.?* iv. 216 The clash between the intuitionists and the formalists has been much publicized by passionate partisans of these schools. **1954** A. J. AYER *Philos. Essays* ix. 221 The formalist aims to get rid of numbers by construing statements about numbers as statements about signs. **1955** V. ERLICH *Russ. Formalism* I. vi. 95 By focussing sharply on the specific aims and methods of literary scholarship, the Formalists had induced their Marxian opponents to get off the high horse of dialectical generalizations. **1967** A. S. GILLETTE *Introd. Scenic Design* xii. 165 The goal of the formalists originally was to return to a completely functional theatre. **1971** *Sci. Amer.* Aug. 92/2 A Formalist is likely to say that the real-number line is whatever we define it to be.

B. *adj.* Of or pertaining to formalism, in various senses; formalistic.

1900 B. RUSSELL *Philos. Leibniz* xiv. 170 But as a method of pursuing philosophy, it had the formalist defect which results from a belief in analytic propositions, and which led Spinoza to employ a geometrical method. **1926** *Proc. Lond. Math. Soc.* 2nd Ser. XXV. 339, I hold that mathematics is part of logic, and so belong to..the logical school as opposed to the formalist and intuitionist schools. **1931** K. E. KIRK *Vision of God* III. iii. 132 The characteristic dangers of Judaism..were exactly the dangers that formalist codification tends to foster. **1955** V. ERLICH *Russ. Formalism* I. iii. 47 In Petersburg..the first steps of the Formalist movement were marked by a close alliance with the poetic avant-garde. **1967** G. H. HAMILTON *Painting & Sculpt. in Europe* 5 The scope of strictly formalist criticism has undoubtedly been enlarged by surrealism and by the doctrines of social realism. **1970** *Times Lit. Suppl.* 23 July 787/2 The Formalist philosophy was an exemplary one in several respects.

formalistic (fɔːməˈlɪstɪk), *a.* [f. prec. + -IC.] Characterized by formalism.

1856 MISS WINKWORTH *Life Tauler* (1857) 107 Partakers of a spiritual in opposition to a formalistic piety. **1875** POSTE *Gaius* IV. Comm. (ed. 2) 516 Its shortcoming was not so much its formalism (the following system was equally formalistic). **1941** COURANT & ROBBINS *What is Math.?* ii. 88 In some way or other,..even under the most uncompromising formalistic, logical, or postulational aspect, constructive intuition always remains the vital element in mathematics. **1957** C. HUNT *Guide to Communist Jargon* xxi. 77 The resolution [of 10 Feb. 1948] went on to censure for their 'formalistic perversions and anti-democratic tendencies' all the more prominent Soviet composers. **1962** *Listener* 19 July 115/2 The Sixth

[Symphony of Shostakovich] was denounced as empty and 'formalistic'.

formality (fɔːˈmælɪtɪ). [ad. L. *formālitās*, f. *formālis* FORMAL *a.* Cf. F. *formalité* (1497 in Hatz.-Darm.).]

†**1.** Formal or essential nature; the characteristic or distinctive property by which a thing is defined. Also, the condition of possessing formal existence.

1570 DEE *Math. Pref.* 3 Creatures..brought, from Nothing, to the Formalitie of their being and state. **1596** BELL *Surv. Popery* III. ix. 378 The formalitie of original sin is of two sorts. **1649** JER. TAYLOR *Gt. Exemp.* III. xvii. 66 This calamity in its own formality..is a punishment. **1672** GREW *Anat. Plants, Idea Philos. Hist.* §7 Those Formalities, wherein their [plants'] Essence doth consist. **1686** GOAD *Celest. Bodies* III. iii. 449 Motion is the Formality of Wind. **1737** WATERLAND *Eucharist* 19 Mr. Scandret, distinguishing a Sacrament, according to its precise Formality, from a Sacrifice, observes [etc.].

†**b.** Formal aspect or category. *Obs.*

1620 J. HEALEY *Augustine's City of God* I. xiv. 23 The City being nothing but a multitude of men vnited in one formality of religion and estate. **1660** JER. TAYLOR *Duct. Dubit.* I. iii, If it be propounded as evil, the will that chooses it under that formality is criminal. **1668** CULPEPPER & COLE *Barthol. Anat.* I. xxviii. 70 The womb is sensible of Odours, not under the formality of Odours, but is only affected by the..subtile vaporous matter conjoyned.

†**2.** That which pertains to outward form; also, an outward appearance or semblance (*of* something). *Obs.*

1615 J. STEPHENS *Ess. & Char., Impudent Censurer* (1857) 134 The walking Apes; which on the Mountaines seeme carefull Inhabitants, but at your approach, the formality of man only. **1640** BP. HALL *Episc.* II. xxii. 215 There may be some appendances and formalities of government alterable by the wisdome of the Church; yet for the main substance, it is now utterly indispensable. **1645** MILTON *Tetrach.* (1851) 191 Sacred things not perform'd sincerely..are no way acceptable to God in their outward formality. **1649** —— *Eikon.* xxvii, To root up all true virtue and honour, or to be contented only with some leaves and withering formalities of them, without any real fruits.

†**3.** Method, regularity. Also, uniform procedure. *Obs.*

1603 HOLLAND *Plutarch's Mor.* 423 Who greatly commended the Eliens for observing such good order and formality at the Olympick games. **1628** LE GRYS tr. *Barclay's Argenis* 101 Meleander..had..escaped [poison] by the carefulnesse of his seruants, who did looke to his meate and his clothes with a curious formality. **1647** CLARENDON *Hist. Reb.* III. §182 Such Judges (whose formality was first to Imprison, and after, at their leisure, to Examine). *a***1650** MAY *Satir. Puppy* (1657) 15 A strange dejected humour possest him three months, his actions were quite void of formality, his domestick affaires by himselfe neglected. **1655** FULLER *Ch. Hist.* IV. ii. §5 The Archbishop ..was very punctual and ceremonious in his proceedings.. the formality of his exemplary justice [etc.].

4. Accordance with legal form.

1660 *Trial Regic.* 51 When a man would plead any thing, because he would Plead it in Formality, Councel is allowed. **1693** CREECH *Juvenal* xiii. 179 If Men forswear the Deeds and Bonds they draw, Tho' Sign'd with all formality of Law.

†**5.** Literary or artistic form; agreement with the laws of form. *Obs.*

1531 ELYOT *Gov.* I. xiv. (1883) 149 Than appoynte they howe many plees maye be made for euery parte, and in what formalitie they shulde be sette, whiche is the seconde parte of Rhetorike, called disposition. **1597** MORLEY *Introd. Mus.* 76 In descanting you must not onelie seeke true cordes, but formalitie also: that is, to make your descant carrie some forme of relation to the plaine song. **1674** PLAYFORD *Skill Mus.* III. 14 If in the first Rule the Notes follow not in expected formality. **1677** *Phil. Trans.* XII. 838 Formality [in music] requires, that the succeeding Notes be agreable to the former.

6. Conformity to established rule; customary propriety. Often in depreciative sense, rigid or merely conventional observance of forms.

1597 HOOKER *Eccl. Pol.* v. xxix. §1 The attyre..being a matter of meere formalitie. *a***1625** CHAS. I *Let.* in *Athenæum* 24 Feb. (1872) 241/3 Which I wryt not for formalities sake, but doe indede fynd myselfe ingaged both in honnor and affection. **1706** ATTERBURY *Serm. Funeral Mr. Bennet* 13 Nor was his Attendance on Divine Offices a matter of Formality and Custom, but of Conscience. **1874** MORLEY *Compromise* (1886) 179 If the religious spirit is only a fine name for..mere social formality. **1881** TYLOR in *Nature* No. 623. 529 To give an idea of the state of formality into which life has come among these supposed free-and-easy savages.

7. Ceremony, elaborate procedure.

1666 PEPYS *Diary* 11 Apr., To Gresham College; where a great deal of do and formality in choosing of the Council and officers. **1705** STANHOPE *Paraphr.* II. 329 Our Enemy makes his Approaches toward us with less Formality..than He.. could do against the Holy Jesus. **1725** DE FOE *Voy. round World* (1840) 96 Prodigious state and formality. **1865** MAFFEI *Brigand Life* I. 240 Without a moment's delay, and with scarcely any formality, the sentence was carried into effect.

8. A ceremony; a formal act or observance; a legal, authorized, or customary procedure.

1674 MARTINIERE tr. *Voy. N. Countries* 52 The pleasant Funeral formalities among the Muscovian Laplanders. **1741** MIDDLETON *Cicero* I. vi. 530 After the election, he was installed, with all the usual formalities, by Hortensius. **1749** FIELDING *Tom Jones* XVI. iv, I insist on the formality of its being delivered me, with a full ratification of all the concessions stipulated. **1862** TROLLOPE *Orley F.* i, A codicil to his will, executed with due legal formalities.

9. Something required to be done for form's sake; a requirement of etiquette, custom, etc. (Often *depreciatively*, implying mere attention to externals.)

1647 CLARENDON *Hist. Reb.* I. §20 It would put an end.. to all those Formalities, which..might yet retard the Infanta's voyage into England. **1664** H. MORE *Myst. Iniq.* 453 Antichrist and his adherents..boasting of works and dead formalities. **1685** *Gracian's Courtiers Orac.* 169 He shall never gain the esteem of an able man, who sticks too much upon Formalities. **1840** CARLYLE *Heroes* (1858) 282 How, by fasts, vigils, formalities and mass-work, a man's soul could be saved. **1856** KANE *Arct. Expl.* I. viii. 90 Many a warm shake of the hand showed me that our good-bye was not a mere formality. **1874** GREEN *Short Hist.* iv. §2 174 Their presence..became so pure a formality that [etc.].

†**b.** Ceremonious attention (paid to a person).

1603 KNOLLES *Hist. Turks* (1638) 96 The Emperour.. became his host, entertaining him with all the formalities that feigned friendship could deuise. **1692** LUTTRELL *Brief Rel.* (1857) II. 564 The mayor and aldermen attended on the prince and princesse daily; but had received notice..to desist paying those formalities. **1726** SHELVOCKE *Voy. round World* (1757) 407 Those..they guessed..to be above the common sort. These they always received with such formality as could not be expected in such a place.

10. *pl.* or *collect. sing.* Robes or insignia of office or dignity. *Obs.* exc. *Hist.* †Also (*rarely*) in *sing.*, an armorial bearing.

1575 R. LANEHAM *Letter* (1871) 41 Appeerez then a fresh, in hiz ful formalitee with a louely loock. **1614** SELDEN *Titles Hon.* 196 Neither haue they now the Crown as a part of their habit, but a formalitie only on their Armorie. **1614** T. LORKIN *Let.* in Willis & Clark *Cambridge* (1886) III. 35 Doctors in their formalityes and vpon their foots-cloths. **1696** *Lond. Gaz.* No. 3176/1 In the morning the Magistrates went to Church in a Body, and in their Formality. **1751** JOHNSON *Rambler* No. 173 ¶8 Divest themselves with too much haste of their academical formality. **1753** in *Lond. Even. Post* 9 Aug., The corporation of Scarborough waited upon the Rt. Hon. Henry Pelham, Esq., in their formalities. **1894** BOASE *Exeter Coll.* (Oxf. Hist. Soc.) p. xlvii, The picture of a man kneeling, with his gown and formalities upon him.

†**b.** In wider sense: Ceremonial or significant garments of any kind. *Obs.*

1672 CAVE *Prim. Chr.* III. v. (1673) 367 They appeared in all the Formalities of Sorrow and Mourning. **1717** MRS. CENTLIVRE *Bold Str. for Wife* v, I hoped to have been quiet, when once I had put on your odious formality here [i.e. a Quaker dress].

11. The attribute of being formal; precision, rigid decorum of manners; excessive regularity or stiffness (of style, outline, etc.).

1599 NASHE *Lenten Stuffe* (1871) 33 A universal merchantly formality, in habit, speech, and gestures. *a***1674** CLARENDON *Hist. Reb.* VI. §396 That which look'd like Formality, was a Punctuality in preserving his dignity. **1789** BELSHAM *Ess.* I. iii. 66 The frozen formality..of Charles occasioned extreme disgust. **1830** HOOD *Haunted H.* I. xxv, The very yew Formality had train'd To such a rigid pyramidal stature. **1834** MACAULAY *Pitt, Ess.* (1889) 301 His heart was a little cold..his manners decorous even to formality. **1849** *Florist* 285 On our left the lake, the formality of its smooth banks elegantly broken by those willows.

formalization (ˌfɔːməlaɪˈzeɪʃən). [f. FORMALIZE: see -ATION.] The action of the vb. FORMALIZE; also, †an expression of offended dignity.

1656 FINETT *For. Ambass.* 68 His Majesty..stormed much at it, till (Sir Thomas Edmonds..being sent..from his Majestie with some formalization to that purpose) The Ambassador was said the next day to have made his excuse. **1682** BURTHOGGE *Argument* (1684) 114 The Holy Scripture no where intimates..any such Formalization, Incorporation, or Distinguishing Association of Righteous good men. **1875** McCOSH *Scot. Philos.* lvii. 417 He attempts too much by logical differentiation and formalisation.

formalize (ˈfɔːməlaɪz), *v.* [f. FORMAL *a.* + -IZE. Cf. F. *formaliser.*]

†**1.** *trans.* To give formal being to; to impart or constitute the form, essence, or characteristic attribute of; to 'inform', as the soul the body.

1597 HOOKER *Eccl. Pol.* v. lvi. §11 The same Spirit..doth ..formalize, vnite, and actuate his whole race. **1627** HAKEWILL *Apol.* I. iv. §1. 39 Quickned and formaliz'd, as the body of man is by its reasonable Soule. **1678** GALE *Crt. Gentiles* IV. III. 68 The malice and vitiositie which formalised the action as theirs, is no way imputable to Gods act.

†**2.** To adorn, give a specious appearance to.

1597 DANIEL *Civ. Wars* II. lviii, To formalize his deed, He kneeles him downe. **1604** EDMONDS *Observ. Cæsar's Comm.* 4, I graunt that it is not altogether wealth that doth grace and formalize the actions of men: for in some cases penurie.. makes men more valorous.

3. To give formal or definite shape to.

1646 BP. MAXWELL *Burd. Issach.* in *Phenix* (1708) II. 298 They establish'd and formaliz'd the Judicatory, by constituting a Moderator, a Clerk, and other essential Members of the Court. **1647** *Answ. to Let. to Dr. Turner* 19 The Apostles..did in their latter dayes formalize and bound out that power which still we do call Episcopacy. **1844** LD. HOUGHTON *Palm Leaves* 89 You can fix and formalize The Power on which you raise your eyes. **1877** MRS. OLIPHANT *Makers Flor.* ii. 50 The gates..shut against him, did no more than formalize that sentence of banishment.

†**4.** To cause to take sides definitely; *refl.* to range oneself, or pronounce, for or against. [So formerly Fr. *se formaliser.*] *Obs.*

1599 SANDYS *Europæ Spec.* (1632) 206 Whereby both parts are formalized and settled in their oppositions. **1656** FINETT *For. Ambass.* 219 For his Majesty to establish an order, and after to break it..could not but be to him of so hard a digistion..yet he must (if offered)..formalize himself against it.

5. To render formal: **a.** To give legal formality to (a document). **b.** To render ceremonious, precise, or rigid. **c.** To imbue with formalism.

1855 *Fraser's Mag.* LI. 628 Its seal..frequently formalizes legal documents. **1856** RUSKIN *Mod. Paint.* III. IV. xiii. §28 It sought eminently for orderliness..formalized whatever decoration it put into its minor architectural mouldings. **1866** J. H. NEWMAN *Let. Pusey* 85 When it is formalized into meditations or exercises, it is as repulsive as love-letters in a police report. **1870** GOULBURN *Cathedr. Syst.* iii. 42 Having a tendency to familiarise them with holy things, and to lower their standard of reverence, or, at best to formalize them.

6. *intr.* To act with formality; to be formal or ceremonious; to show the spirit of a formalist.

*a***1656** HALES *Ser. Duels* Rem. (1673) 84 Many times indeed our Gallants can formalize in other words, but evermore the substance, and usually the very words are no other but these of Cain, Let us go out into the Feild. **1697** [see FORMALIZING *vbl. sb.*]. **1721** BAILEY, *Formalize*, to play the Formalist. **1830** [see FORMALIZING *ppl. a.*].

†**7. a.** *trans.* To cavil at, raise scrupulous objections to. **b.** *intr.* To cavil, raise scruples; to take umbrage; also, to affect scruples. ***to formalize upon***: to scruple at, demur to, haggle over.

[Cf. F. *se formaliser*, to take umbrage.]

a. 1599 SANDYS *Europæ Spec.* (1632) 95 By culling out the errours..by formalizing the contrarieties; mis-interpreting the ambiguitie, intangling more the obscurities..in the most renowmed authors. **1603** KNOLLES *Hist. Turks* (1621) 1195 His resolution was to take part with the Christian emperour, if the great Bassaes..should seeke..to formalize his actions..in this maner of the obtaining of his government. **1668** R. L'ESTRANGE *Vis. Quev.* (1708) 236 That is to say, whether in Reason of State, it ought to be done; and we are formalizing the Matter, whether in point of Equity and Justice it may be done.

b. 1597 LOWE *Chirurg.* (1634) 57 But, because such as delight in this pastime, will formalize..I will not altogether condemne it. **1641** *Nicholas Papers* (Camden) I. 41 Ye kings answer to ye parlement..is now to noe purpose. Ye house haveing formalized uppon it, ye king hath recalled it. **1655** *Ibid.* II. 216 Some of the townes suspecting the intention began to formalise. *a***1674** CLARENDON *Life* (1761) I. III. 148 Particulars..which the Officers on the King's Side, (who had no Mind to a Cessation) formalized much upon. **1692** R. L'ESTRANGE *Josephus' Antiq.* XVII. xi. (1733) 471 It seems a strange thing..that Archelaus should be now formalizing about his Title to a Kingdom after so absolute an Exercise of sovereign Power over it already. *a***1734** NORTH *Lives* II. 301 He went not only willingly, but ambitiously, and formalized upon nothing that led towards the end he most earnestly desired. *a***1797** H. WALPOLE *Mem. Geo. II*, (1847) I. xii. 418 He..told him that they had formalized at his professions.

Hence **ˈformalized** *ppl. a.*; **ˈformalizing** *vbl. sb.* and *ppl. a.* Also **ˈformalizable** *a.*, capable of being formalized; **ˈformalizer**, one who formalizes.

*a***1656** HALES *St. Peter's Fall* Rem. (1673) 111 They turned..their true Fasting into Formalizing and partial abstinence. **1697** COLLIER *Immor. Stage* iv. §3 (1730) 145 Vanity and Formalizing is Lord Foplington's Part. *a***1734** NORTH *Lives* II. 65 The ministers turned formalisers; and the court mysterious. —— *Exam.* III. viii. §26 He found no formalising Scruples on the Lord Keeper's Part. **1830** CROLY *Geo. IV*, 364 The spirit of the juntas was timid, frivolous, and formalizing. **1849** RUSKIN *Sev. Lamps* vi. §3. 165 Those gloomy rows of formalised minuteness. **1875** WHITNEY *Life Lang.* v. 90 A complete formalizing of what was before solid, positive, substantial. **1944** H. REICHENBACH in P. A. Schilpp *Philos. B. Russell* 27 This formulation given at a later stage was anticipated by Russell's original distinction of formalizable and non-formalizable parts of logic. **1965** N. CHOMSKY *Aspects of Theory of Syntax* i. 19 No adequate formalizable techniques are known for obtaining reliable information concerning the facts of linguistic structure.

†**ˈformall.** *Obs. rare.* [? f. FOR-², FORE- *pref.* + MALL. Cf. FOREHAMMER.] (See quot.)

1572 BOSSEWELL *Armorie* II. 123/b, A Sledge or an Hammer, of some called a formall.

formally (ˈfɔːməlɪ), *adv.* [f. FORMAL *a.* + -LY². (Cf. FORMLY.)]

1. In formal respects; as regards form.

a. *Metaph.* (see FORM *sb.* 4 a, FORMAL A. 1 a): With regard to, or by virtue of, the form or distinctive essence. Also in *Logic*: With regard to the form, as opposed to the matter of reasoning.

1570 DEE *Math. Pref.* 13 But formally, Number, is the Vnion, and Vnitie of Vnits. **1581** E. CAMPION in *Confer.* IV. (1584) Bbj, When..the Iewes were commanded to steale from the Egyptians, it was in the act theft, but not formally theft. **1678** GALE *Crt. Gentiles* III. 32 Neither..that God doth properly move to sin simply and formally taken, or sin as sin. **1685** BAXTER *Paraphr. N.T.* 1 Cor. xi. 23-4 The same thing which is materially Gold and Silver, may formally be the King's Coyn..or a badge of Honour..[etc.]. **1697** tr. *Burgersdicius' Logic* I. xxvi. 106 Words..are said to be taken materially when for themselves; formally, when for the things by them signified. **1713** SMALLRIDGE *Serm.* (1724) 331 The heathen and the Christian may agree in the material acts of charity; but that which formally makes this a Christian grace, is the spring from which it flows. **1864** BOWEN *Logic* ii. 24 Hence what is formally correct may be materially false. **1877** E. CAIRD *Philos. Kant* II. vi. 295 A judgment is formally right when its predicate is contained in the conception of the subject; formally wrong when it is not

b. With regard to form or outline.

1868 SWINBURNE *Ess. & Stud.* (1875) 360 His..painting is..the faultless..expression of an exclusive worship of things formally beautiful.

†**c.** In outward appearance, seemingly. *Obs.*
1602 WARNER *Alb. Eng.* XII. lxxiv. (1612) 305 The gentle-woman (formally then modest) blushing, said. **1608** MIDDLETON *Mad World* IV. iv, The very devil assum'd thee formally; That face, that voice. **1649** BALL *Power of Kings* 7 Even so there is..an Act, or Being Really just, and seemingly or formally just..which may be in itself unjust.

†**2.** In good form: **a.** In good order, style, or method. **b.** Handsomely. *Obs.*
c **1400** *Beryn* 3457 He reportid the tale riȝt formally. **1548** HALL *Chron., Hen. IV* (an. 14) 32 b, This kyng was of a mean stature wel proporcioned and formally compact.

†**3.** According to the principles of art or science.
1509 HAWES *Past. Pleas.* V. xi, All the eyght partes..Are Laten wordes, annexed properly To every speche, for to speke formally. **1597** MORLEY *Introd. Mus.* Pref., Any of but meane capacitie..may..perfectly learn to sing, make discant, and set partes well and formally togither.

b. According to logical form; hence, †logically, convincingly.
c **1526** FRITH *Disput. Purgat.* (1829) 112 Therefore this argument holdeth not formally. **1548** GEST *Pr. Masse* 89 If thys be formallye argued..then it argueth etc.

†**4.** Regularly: **a.** In the ordinary or proper way. **b.** 'As a rule'; under normal circumstances. **c.** With exact correspondence. *Obs.*
1607 TOPSELL *Four-f. Beasts* (1658) 237 When they [horses] came to hand to lay upon their backs a little boy flat on his belly; and afterward to make him sit upon him formally, holding him by the head. **1627** CAPT. SMITH *Seaman's Gram.* ii. 9 The entering Ladder is in the Waist, made formally of wood. **1674** PLAYFORD *Skill Mus.* III. 13 What Cords have held good in this ascending and descending of the Bass, answer in the contrary by the very same rule, though not so formally as the other.

5. Explicitly, expressly.
1526 *Pilgr. Perf.* (W. de W. 1531) 19 b, Though the gyftes of the holy goost spekeths not formally all these wordes before sayd. *a* **1600** HOOKER (J.), You and your followers do stand formally divided against the authorised guides of the church, and the rest of the people. **1682** NORRIS *Hierocles* Pref. 28 Though this be not formally intended by the Agent. **1765** BLACKSTONE *Comm.* (1793) 48 Though perhaps in no instance it has ever been formally expressed at the first institution of a state. **1841** MYERS *Cath. Th.* III. xx. 3 A book of Maxims and of Precepts everywhere formally didactic. **1853** C. BRONTE *Villette* xxxvii, I cannot say that Paulina.. formally proposed to herself the task of winning him to reflection.

†**b.** In identical form. *Obs.*
1682 *Case Prot. Eng.* 8 All the Profits..are to be refunded if they be extant and found among their Goods, formally, or but so much as equivalently.

6. In prescribed or customary form; with the formalities required to give validity or definiteness to the action; in set form, statedly.
1564 *Child Marriages* (E.E.T.S.) 135 This deponent made a certen note of her Will..and after she was dede, this examinant made it formallie. **1597** WARNER *Alb. Eng.* VIII. xli. 200 At length at full and formally he courted her for grace. **1634–5** BRERETON *Trav.* (Chetham Soc.) 9 They.. the wife and husband..conclude formally in writing..that the longest liver take all. **1688** *Lond. Gaz.* No. 2319/3 The place was not to be formally besieged, but by a numerous Army. **1741–2** H. WALPOLE *Lett. H. Mann* (1834) I. xxi. 86 Waller was to have been the other but has formally refused. **1838** THIRLWALL *Greece* V. xxxviii. 63 He was now formally accused by Iphicrates. **1860** TYNDALL *Glac.* I. v. 40, I formally took up my position there.

7. With formality of manner, ceremoniously.
c **1611** CHAPMAN *Iliad* III. 239 He stood a little still..His sceptre moving neither way, but held it formally, Like one that vainly doth affect. **1697** COLLIER *Ess. Mor. Subj., Pride* (1703) 26 To be stiff and formally reserved, as if the Company did not deserve our Familiarity. **1800** MRS. HERVEY *Mourtray Fam.* IV. 66 Courtesying formally, she abruptly left her.

8. As a matter of form.
1870 ROGERS *Hist. Gleanings* Ser. II. 235 Convocation.. never met, except formally, for near a century.

formalness ('fɔːməlnɪs). [f. as prec. + -NESS.] The quality of being formal.
1684 H. MORE *Answer* 24 To awaken them out of their remissness and litherly formalness. **1727** BAILEY vol. II, *Formalness*, ceremony, affectation. **1890** *Pall Mall G.* 4 Oct. 2/3 An altogether unnecessary formalness of design in his studies for scratched plaster work.

†**'formament.** *Obs.*$^{-0}$ [f. L. *formāment-um*, f. *formāre* to form. Cf. OF. *formement*.]
1727 BAILEY vol. II, *Formament*, a Mould, Form or Shape.

†**for'manging**, *vbl. sb. Obs. rare.* [f. ME. **formang-en* to barter (f. FOR- *pref.*[1] + *mangen*, whence MONGER + -ING[1]).] Barter, exchange.
a **1300** *E. E. Psalter* liv. 20 [lv. 19] Noght es to þam for-manging [mistransl. Lat. *commutatio*].

formant ('fɔːmənt). [a. G. *formant* (Hermann and Matthias 1894, in *Arch. f. d. ges. Physiol.* LVIII. 262), f. L. *formant-*, *-ans* pres. pple. of *formāre* to FORM: see -ANT[1].] **1.** *Phonetics.* The characteristic pitch of a vowel-sound; *spec.* one of several characteristic bands of resonance, a combination of which determines the distinctive sound-quality of a vowel (or *transf.*, of a musical instrument).
1901 *Nature* 26 Dec. 187/2 A vowel, according to him [*sc.* Hermann], is a special acoustic phenomenon, depending on the intermittent production of a special partial, or 'formant' or 'characteristique'. The pitch of the 'formant' may vary a little without altering the character of the vowel. **1930** *Times Lit. Suppl.* 3 July 545/1 Later investigators have developed a theory of the vowel as a *formant*, which, though occupying a definite region of pitch, nevertheless manages somehow to affect the whole sound-complex. **1952** *Electronic Engin.* XXIV. 368 The peaks of the transmission curve are the resonant frequencies, and generate formants, which have been defined as the frequencies of energy concentration of the speech signal. **1956** JAKOBSON & HALLE in Saporta & Bastian *Psycholinguistics* (1961) 349/1 The clear-cut formant structure of a vowel. **1957** A. C. BAINES *Woodwind Instrum.* 34 Harmonics that fall within certain zones of pitch ('formants') tend to dominate. **1964** J. B. CARROLL *Lang. & Thought* ii. 12 Vowel quality is directly correlated with the relative positions, on the frequency scale, of two or three formants, or bands of strong resonance overtones, present in the frequency spectrum of a sound. **1968** J. LYONS *Introd. Theoret. Ling.* iii. 110 The acoustic analysis of vowels in terms of their constituent formants..correlates quite well with their description in terms of the articulatory dimensions.

2. *Philol.* An affix to a root or stem, forming a longer root or stem. (Sometimes used more loosely.)
1935 G. K. ZIPF *Psycho-Biol. Lang.* (1965) iv. 144 The stem (root plus formant) to which endings are added. **1956** J. WHATMOUGH *Language* viii. 136 Some morphemes occur only as parts of words, e.g. English *-ing* in *loving*, or *-nt-* in Latin *amantis*.., and these are known as 'formants'.

‖**forma pauperis** ('fɔːmə 'pɔːpərɪs). [L.] = *in forma pauperis* (s.v. ‖IN 10). Also †*under forma pauperis*.
1627 MIDDLETON et al. *Widow* II. i, I scorn to get thee under *forma pauperis*. **1633** T. ADAMS *Exp. 2 Peter* ii. 6. 621 Doe they not sue for their inheritance in heaven, *Formâ pauperis*; refusing to give the least scrap of their superfluitie for eternall life? **1907** *Daily Chron.* 4 Mar. 3/5 In the Divorce Court..fees to the lawyers are supposed to be paid even in formâ pauperis causes. **1959** JOWITT *Dict. Eng. Law* II. 947/2 Appeals may still be taken *in forma pauperis* to the House of Lords. The Appeal (Forma Pauperis) Act, 1893, enables the House to refuse leave to appeal.

format ('fɔːmæt, ‖fɔrma), *sb.* [F. *format*, (according to Littré ad. L. (*liber*) *formātus*, (a book) *formed* in such or such a way).] **1. a.** Shape and size of a book, e.g. octavo, quarto, etc.
1840 MOORE *Mem.* (1856) VII. 272 To bring out the 'History'..in a better shape than that vile Lardnerian *format*. **1883** *Sat. Rev.* 5 May LV. 580 The book..is not undeserving of the pretty square format in which it appears. *Mod. Prospectus*, Format and paper of present Prospectus.

b. *transf.*
1936 O. S. PUCKLE tr. *von Ardenne's Telev. Reception* ii. 42 The photograph shows the evenness of the illumination and the almost perfect rectangularity of the picture format. **1962** *Listener* 1 Feb. 224/1 The low relief and the often square format of the canvas also establish the pictures as firmly constructed panels. **1971** *Daily Tel.* 13 Oct. 6/7 The Brick Development Association proposed a single metric brick format which was adopted by the industry. It was slightly smaller than the imperial format: 225 mm × 112·5 mm × 75. **1971** D. POTTER *Brit. Eliz. Stamps* iii. 32 The first vertical format double-size stamp was issued.

2. a. A style or manner of arrangement or presentation; a mode of procedure.
1955 *Times* 3 June 9/2 It is a tribute to the attractive format..that one does not realize that the report runs to 83 pages. **1957** *N.Y. Times* 29 Dec. IV. 3/2 It is so fundamental that the President must never appear before the American people in a minor role that the choice of this format is inexplicable. **1958** *Spectator* 1 Aug. 167/1 The principal performer..had to write the scripts herself, and when..she attempted to heed criticism and alter the format, she was told that the show, however bad, must go on. **1958** *Listener* 23 Oct. 648/2 Goldberg has developed from the sectional, chopped-up forms of de Kooning to a large centralized format. **1963** *Amer. Speech* XXXVIII. 165 The slang items in this study are subdivided into two major groupings... The format followed supplies first the denotative word or phrase which was used to elicit the slang responses. Next, [etc.]. **1967** *Times* 6 Jan. 15/1 The usefulness of the I[ndustrial] R[eorganization] C[orporation] will be in its ability to help the two sides agree upon a new supply format. **1970** *Daily Tel.* 19 Nov. 14/4 This programme format, consisting of a report followed by a public meeting arranged for television, never seems to me satisfactory. **1971** *Homes & Gardens* Oct. 175/2 The noise generated by tape play-back systems..is the most serious drawback of the small cassette format.

b. *Computers.* A particular arrangement of data or characters in a record, instruction, word, etc., in a form that can be processed or stored by a computer.
1955 *Computers & Automation* Jan. 16/2 Logical operations of verifying format, insuring proper placement of significant characters,.. are all performed in less than ½ second. **1959** *Jrnl. Assoc. Comput. Mach.* VI. 325 One such typical program..might involve the conversion and rearrangement of data from the format in which it is stored on external units to a format compatible with internal use, e.g. the conversion of characters from decimal to binary form. **1963** B. F. GREEN *Digital Computers in Research* v. 84 An associated format statement..specifies the precise manner in which the quantities appear in the input or output medium. **1968** *Amer. Documentation* Jan. 74/2 A format routine converts scanner output to element form for entry in the central data file. **1970** *Nature* 4 July 7/2 A scheme for coding rock and mineral names into a format suitable for computers.

format ('fɔːmæt), *v.* Pa. t. and pa. pple. **formatted**; pres. pple. **formatting**. [f. the sb.] *trans.* To arrange or put into a format: used chiefly in connection with *Computers* (see FORMAT *sb.* 2 b). Also **'formatted** *ppl. a.*, **'formatting** *vbl. sb.*
1964 *CIS Gloss. Automated Typesetting* (Composition Information Services, Calif.) 14 Book formatting. **1965** *Adv. Computers* VI. 7 These systems have come to be known as formatted file systems, since the input data are arranged into various formats for ease of storage and retrieval. **1968** *Guardian* 23 Sept. 9/2 We formatted this Top 100 Sounds, covering the top sounds both east and west of the Atlantic. **1969** *Computers & Humanities* IV. 98 Little or no composition control data or formatting punctuation is encoded with the input data. *Ibid.* 99 We format pages internally and then pass them to an output module tailored to a specific output device. **1970** A. CAMERON et al. *Computers & O.E. Concordances* 48 A concordance, however, if formatted along appropriate lines..can shorten this mind-wearying labour tremendously. **1970** *McGraw-Hill Yearbk. Sci. & Technol.* 160/1 The principal formatting function in the graphic arts is justification, which is frequently coupled with hyphenation.

formate ('fɔːmət), *sb. Chem.* Also less analogically **formiate**. [f. FORM(IC) + -ATE.] A salt of formic acid.
1807 T. THOMSON *Chem.* (ed. 3) II. 316 Formic acid may be obtained from formate of lead. *Ibid.* 521 Salts.. Formiates. **1825** HAMILTON *Handbk. Terms, Formates.* **1853** W. GREGORY *Inorg. Chem.* (ed. 3) 153 A formiate. **1876** HARLEY *Mat. Med.* 105 Formiate of potash.

†**'formate**, *v.*[1] *Obs.* [f. L. *formāt-* ppl. stem of *formāre* to FORM.]
1. *trans.* To form, mould.
1599 A. M. tr. *Gabelhouer's Bk. Physicke* 50/1 Intermixe it with whyte waxe, and formate therof little Candles.

2. ? To state in a precise form; to formulate.
1656–7 *Burton's Diary* (1828) I. 361 Unless you will have me to say nothing, but what you shall formate to me.

formate (fɔː'meɪt), *v.*[2] *Aeronaut.* [Back-formation from FORMATION 4 b.] *intr.* Of an aircraft or its pilot: to take up formation *with*, to fly in formation. Also const. *on*. Also (*rare*) of a boat: to proceed in formation.
1929 *Times* 6 Mar. 5/6 He saw Mr. Sealy-Allin 15 minutes before the collision and attempted to formate with him. **1933** *Aeroplane* 19 Apr. 690/1 The Avros formated by themselves. **1934** T. E. LAWRENCE *Lett.* (1938) 805 We are all up to the teeth in 5 more target boats. Three or four are [to] formate from here to Bridlington. **1934** V. M. YEATES *Winged Victory* xiii. 106 He kept getting in everybody's way. If there was one thing a pilot ought to do properly, it was to formate. **1935** *Flight* 23 May 549/1 It is possible to recollect a number of occasions when, as passenger in a big machine, one has been 'formated' on by odd and sometimes gay pilots. **1942** *We speak from Air* xvi. 51 The other Beauforts formated on me until we separated near the target.

formation (fɔː'meɪʃən). [ad. L. *formātiōn-em*, n. of action f. *form-āre* to FORM: see -ATION.]
1. a. The action or process of forming; a putting or coming into form; creation, production.
c **1450** *Chester Pl.* (Shaks. Soc.) I. 10 The worlde..I forme in the formacion With a dongion of darcknes. **1480** CAXTON *Chron. Eng.* cclvii, Aboute this tyme there was a great formation of monasteries. **1530** PALSGR. 12 The rules that I shall gyve for the formation of tenses. **1656** COWLEY *Davideis* IV. note xxvi, The Formation of the Body in the Womb. **1707** *Curios. in Husb. & Gard.* 315 The Formation of Barnacles is exactly the same. **1830** D'ISRAELI *Chas. I*, III. iv. 43 The complete formation of this administration was interrupted by the death of the Earl. **1853** W. GREGORY *Inorg. Chem.* (ed. 3) 52 The escape of hydrogen and the formation of a neutral salt. **1863** GEO. ELIOT *Romola* I. xi, His mind had really reached a new stage in its formation of a purpose.

b. *Electr.* The action or process of forming an accumulator plate, a semiconductor device, etc. (see FORM *v.* 1 g).
1881 S. P. THOMPSON *Storage Electr.* 12/1 The amount of charge will..depend on the size of the plates and on the degree to which the process of 'formation' has been carried out. **1926** L. B. W. JOLLEY *A.C. Rectification* (ed. 2) xv. 372 During the process of formation the oxide film is being deposited on the anode. **1964** G. SMITH *Storage Batteries* ii. 22 A forming agent is added to the sulphuric acid, which.. accelerates the production of the lead dioxide coating when current is passed through the plate during formation.

2. *concr.* The thing formed.
1646 SIR T. BROWNE *Pseud. Ep.* III. vi. 117 The Chorion, a thick..membrane obscuring the formation, and which the Dam doth teare asunder. **1800** *Med. Jrnl.* III. 501 Productive of some disgusting formation in their children. **1872** MORRIS *Eng. Accid.* xviii. 234 Modern formations are numerous, as *acquittal* [etc.].

3. a. The manner in which a thing is formed with respect to the disposition of its parts; formal structure, conformation.
1774 GOLDSM. *Nat. Hist.* (1776) II. 324 These holes are dug with so much art, that there seems the design of an architect in the formation. **1808** *Med. Jrnl.* XIX. 325 Remarks..as to the formation of clouds. **1845** BUDD *Dis. Liver* 253 The liver..varies much in size, in different persons..from mere peculiarities of formation. **1867** SMYTH *Sailor's Word-bk., Formation*..the particulars of a ship's build.

b. The disposition of fibres in a sheet of paper.
1937 E. J. LABARRE *Dict. Paper* 110/1 *Formation*, the disposition or texture of the fibres in a sheet of paper. **1952** J. P. CASEY *Pulp & Paper* I. viii. 417 Formation..is a highly important property and influences many of the properties of the final paper, such as strength and appearance. **1953** J. N. STEPHENSON *Pulp & Paper Manuf.* III. 119 Formation is that quality which describes the structure of a sheet of paper, the manner in which the fibers are interlaced.

4. a. *Mil.* An arrangement or disposition of troops.

1796–7 *Instr. & Reg. Cavalry* (1813) 98 The formation becomes the same as to the front. **1802** in C. James *Milit. Dict.* **1832** *Regul. Instr. Cavalry* II. 20 The..Formations must be executed as often by the left as by the right. **1879** Froude *Caesar* xxii. 388 The usual Roman formation in battle was in triple line.

b. *Aeronaut.* The orderly disposition of a number of aircraft in flight.

1914 *Engineering* 4 Dec. 680/3 Formation Flying... In the handling of a single squadron, the formation adopted may evidently be fairly elastic. **1917** 'Contact' *Airman's Outings* p. xiv, Dotted everywhere, singly or in formations of two, three, four, or six, were..the single-seater fighting scouts. **1931** H. A. Jones *War in Air* III. iv. 296 They were made to..practise..flying in formation. **1941** E. C. Shepherd *Military Aeroplane* 4 Anti-aircraft fire can..break up the formations. **1963** *Amer. Speech* XXXVIII. 117 The bomber then comes slowly up behind the tanker and flies a close formation with it. **1971** D. N. James *Gloster Aircraft* 211 Three Gladiators of No. 87 Squadron flew tied-together formation aerobatic sequences with cord connecting their interplane struts.

5. a. *Geol.* (See quots.)

1815 W. Phillips *Outl. Min. & Geol.* (1818) 88 The term formation is not always used to express a deposite consisting only of a single stratum..it is also commonly used to designate a series of..strata, which being intimately associated, and containing the same description of organic remains, are thence..considered to be of contemporaneous formation. **1833** Lyell *Elem. Geol.* i. (1874) 4 The term 'formation'..expresses..any assemblage of rocks which have some character in common, whether of origin, age, or composition. **1881** *Nature* XXIV. 14 The formation, by which, adopting a terminology now in much favour on the Continent, we mean the lithological character and origin of the rock.

b. *Ecol.* [a. G. *formation* (A. Grisebach 1838, in *Linnaea* XII. 160).] A community formed by groups of plants which have adapted themselves to similar climatic conditions.

1898 *Bot. Gaz.* XXV. 394 The grass formations are more or less intermediate between the sand hill and the foothill formations. **1909** Groom & Balfour tr. *Warming's Oecology of Plants* xxxv. 140 A formation may then be defined as a community of species,..which have become associated together by definite external..characters of the habitat. **1929** Weaver & Clements *Plant Ecol.* i. 6 No formation is uniform throughout its entire extent. **1960** N. Polunin *Introd. Plant Geogr.* xi. 333 Each formation usually covers a wide area involving various conditions.

6. *attrib.*, as ***formation-stage***; **formation dancing**, a variety of (competitive) ballroom dancing in which members of a team dance in formation through a sequence of routines; **formation-level** (see quot.); **formation-rule** *Logic*, one of a set of rules together specifying which combinations of symbols are to count as well-formed formulas in a given system (opp. *transformation rule*).

1936 *Dancing Times* Aug. 515/2 There was also a very fine demonstration of Mrs. Ripman's 'Formation Dancing' in Valse and Fox-trot. **1967** Silvester & Whitman *Compl. Old Time Dancer* 137 Some competitors have found that experience of formation dancing has helped them in various ways. **1985** *Financial Times* (Weekend Suppl.) 10 Aug. p. i/3 Walking back along the promenade I looked through a window—to watch a group of elderly ladies doing formation dancing in the front room of a private hotel. **1888** *Lockwood's Dict. Mech. Engin.*, *Formation Level*, the level of the tops of the embankments and bottoms of the cuttings of a railway upon which the ballast is laid. **1937** A. Smeaton tr. *Carnap's Logical Syntax Lang.* § 1. 2 The difference between syntactical rules in the narrower sense and the logical rules of deduction is only the difference between formation rules and transformation rules. **1948** H. Reichenbach *Elem. Symb. Logic* i. 16 Formation rules..tell us under what conditions a set of signs is meaningful. **1965** P. Caws *Philos. of Sci.* xvi. 119 Formation-rules..specify how primitive or other terms may be put together to form acceptable expressions. **1966** *Amer. Philos. Q.* III. 7/1 Speech activities ..proceed in accordance with formation rules. **1892** Gladstone in *Daily News* 8 Sept. 3/1 In the formation stage of its existence.

¶ = information.

c **1470** Henry *Wallace* v. 977 Pardown he ast off the repreiff befor; and said, he suld no mor Formacioune [*ed.* **1570** Information] mak off him that was so gud.

Hence **for'mational** *a.* [see -al[1]], of or pertaining to formation or formations; **for'mationally** *adv.*, in respect of formation, as regards formation.

1886 *Amer. Jrnl. Sc.* Ser. III. XXXII. 244 Formational and historical geology. **1898** *Bot. Gaz.* XXV. 382 The forests of Mexico..are both floristically and formationally distinct from the northern forests. **1953** C. E. Bazell *Linguistic Form* 51 Phonemically the form [*wished*] is on a par with the formationally underivable *fist*, etc.

formative ('fɔːmətɪv), *a.* (*sb.*) [a. OF. *formatif*, *-ive* (12th c.), as if ad. L. **formātīv-us*, f. *formāre* to form: see -ive.] **A.** *adj.*

1. Having the faculty of forming or fashioning.

1490 Caxton *Eneydos* xvi. 64 The arteres formatyue of speche were stopped wythin hym. **1614** Selden *Titles Hon.* Pref. B iv, The formatiue power of the Parents. **1653** Gauden *Hierasp.* 74 All other creatures rising up, as bubbles ..so soon as the formative Word of God..fell..on the face of the great deep. **1824** *Examiner* 451/2 Associations formative of lasting mind and character. **1859** Darwin *Orig. Spec.* ix. (1873) 235 The formative organs themselves are perfect in structure.

2. Of or pertaining to formation or moulding.

1850 Leitch *Müller's Anc. Art* §346. 417 The formative art. **1867** J. Hogg *Microsc.* II. i. 256 The formative processes of plant-life. **1875** Whitney *Life Lang.* iv. 46 The early formative period of the Christian church.

3. *Biol.* and *Path.* (See quots.)

1877 Bennett tr. *Thomé's Bot.* 41 A special tissue to which the names of formative or generating tissue and meristem have been given. **1894** Duane *Dict. Med.*, *Formative*, producing, or attended with the production of, new tissue.

4. *Gram.* Serving to form words: said chiefly of flexional and derivative suffixes or prefixes.

1711 J. Greenwood *Eng. Gram.* 186 The formative Terminations. **1797** W. Taylor in *Monthly Mag.* III. 338 The use of formative syllables. **1872** Morris *Eng. Accid.* xviii. 211 To get at the root of a word we must remove all the formative elements.

B. *sb.* *Gram.* A formative element (see A. 4); also 'a word formed in accordance with some rule or usage, as from a root' (W.); (cf. *derivative*). Also *gen.*, a formative agent.

1816 *Q. Rev.* XV. 363 The element or formative, he seems to think, is employed to express the thing which modifies or connects itself with the idea suggested by the primitive. **1865** J. Davies *Temporal Augment* 31 In this language prefixed particles or augments are used as verbal formatives. **1907** Galsworthy *Country House* I. iv, That essential formative of character, east wind. **1953** C. E. Bazell *Linguistic Form* i. 8 A unit of formation, commonly called (*allo-*) *morph* in America and *morpheme* in Europe (outside Copenhagen), and for which the present writer has proposed the term *formative*. **1965** N. Chomsky *Aspects of Theory of Syntax* i. 3 The rules that specify the well-formed strings of minimal syntactically functioning units (*formatives*). **1965** B. M. H. Strang *Metaphors & Models* 18 In the first stage a terminal *string* is generated by applying an ordered set of rules, the formula *F*, to some of a finite repertoire or set, *Σ*, of formatives.

Hence **'formatively** *adv.*; **'formativeness.**

1654 tr. *Behmen's Myst. Magnum* xxxvii. 254 That which he introduced out of the deity into the humanity, that is, neither nature, nor creature, yet in our humanity formatively. **1849** *Fraser's Mag.* XXXIX. 664 These are the pure links of nature, wholly innocent of human formativeness. **1874** Pusey *Lent. Serm.* 318 'Having or holding', S. Paul says, a 'formativeness of godliness' [2 Tim. iii. 5 μόρφωσιν].

† **formator.** *Obs. rare.* [a. L. *formātor*, agent-n. f. *formāre* to form.] A person or thing that forms; a creator, maker.

1656–81 Blount *Glossogr.*, *Formator* (Lat.) he that instructeth, maketh or formeth. **1794** Sullivan *View Nat.* IV. 247 If fire was its spring or formator.

‖ **formatore** (fɔːma'tɔəreɪ). [It., agent-n. f. *formare* to form.] A modeller in wax or plaster; a technical assistant who repairs or restores pottery, metalwork, etc.

1862 *Catal. Internat. Exhib., Brit.* II. No. 5451 Formatore to the Science and Art Department, the Trustees of the British Museum, and the Royal Academy of Arts. **1899** *Proc. Zool. Soc.* 776 Assistant formatore in the Museum.

'formatory, *a.* *nonce-wd.* [f. form *v.* after the analogy of reformatory *a.*] Tending to form.

1868 Ruskin *Arrows of Chace* (1881) II. 199 The real and noblest function of labour is..not to be Reformatory but Formatory.

† **for'matrix.** *Obs.* Also 8 formatrice. [a. late L. *formātrix*, fem. agent-n. f. *formāre* to form.] Formative faculty. Also ***vertue formatrix***.

a **1648** Ld. Herbert *Life* (1886) 35 Since in my mother's womb this *plastica*, or formatrix, which formed my eyes, ears, and other senses, did not intend them for that noisome place. **1650** Bulwer *Anthropomet.* 82 The natural heat which is the instrument of the vertue formatrix. **1678** Cudworth *Intell. Syst.* I. iii. 180 The soul endued with a plastick power [is] the chief Formatrix of its own body.

formature ('fɔːmətjʊə(r)). [ad. L. *formātūr-am*, f. *formāre* to form.] The action of forming.

1659 Hammond *On Ps.* cxxxiii. 3 Annot. 659 That first formature of rain. **18..** *Churchman* LIV. 498 (Cent.) These infant communities were easily susceptible of formature by leading men.

† **for'may,** *v.* *Obs. rare.* [f. for- (? *pref.*[3]) + *-may* in amay, dismay, etc.] *trans.* = dismay.

c **1470** Harding *Chron.* ccix. xi, He went into Burgoyne all formayed.

† **'forme,** *a.* *Obs.* Forms: 1 forma, -e, 2–6 forme, 3 *Orm.* forrme, 3 firme, furme, vorme, 3–5 form, 5 ferme. [OE. *forma* = OFris. *forma*, OS. *formo*:—OTeut. **formon-*, a superlative (with *-m-* suffix as in L. *prīmus*) from the root of fore *adv.* A variant is OE. *fruma* (early ME. frume, beginning) = Goth. *fruma*.]

1. Earliest in time or serial order, first; also, the first of two, former.

Beowulf 2286 (Gr.) Frea sceawode fyra fyrnȝeweorc forman siðe. *c* **888** K. Ælfred *Boeth.* xv, Hu ȝesæliȝ seo forme eld was þises middanȝeardes. *a* **1250** *Owl & Night.* 818 The vox kan..turne ut from his forme weie. *a* **1330** *Otuel* 1572 King karnifees..slouȝ him ate forme dunt. *c* **1425** *Seven Sages* (P.) 373 Yf I speke loude or stille, With the forme word I sal deye. *c* **1450** *Mirour Saluacioun* 4006 Oure forme fadere and modere.

absol. and *ellipt.* *c* **1000** *Ags. Gosp.* Matt. x. 2 Se forma ys Simon. *a* **1175** *Cott. Hom.* 243 Of the formen seieð sanctus paulus. Non est [etc.]. *c* **1205** Lay. 25151 Þe uorme wes Belin. **13..** *E.E. Allit. P.* C. 38 Hit arn fettled in on forme, þe forme & þe laste. *c* **1420** *Pallad. on Husb.* II. 447 As iij is nyne, as ij is ten, the forme Thelleuth is with.

b. Previous to the present; former, early.

a **1300** *Cursor M.* 22229 (Cott.) In form tide. *c* **1340** *Ibid.* 8583 (Trin.) Þe forme dawes.

c. quasi-*sb.* The beginning.

13.. *Gaw. & Gr. Knt.* 499 Þe forme to þe fynisment foldez ful selden.

2. Foremost in position, rank, etc.

14.. *Rom. Alexander* in *Roland & V.* (1836) p. xx. Antiogus hadde the form gard, Tholomeu the rereward. **1523** Skelton *Garl. Laurel* 595 And with his forme foot he shoke forth this wrytyng.

3. quasi-*Comb.*, in **forme-fader** (*a*) (our) first father, Adam; (*b*) = forefather; **forme-moder,** (our) first mother, Eve; **forme-mete,** early meat, breakfast; **forme-ward,** vanguard.

a **1175** *Cott. Hom.* 231 Me..sceolde..ȝiefe him his forme-mete þat him to lang ne þuhte to abiden oð se laford to þe none inn come. *a* **1200** *Moral Ode* 195 Ure forme fader gult, we abuȝeð alle. **13..** *K. Alis.* 5733 Of the forme-ward he herd grete cry For hy weren assailed of olifauntz. *a* **1340** Hampole *Psalter* cxviii. 21 Oure form-fadirs þat god blamyd. *c* **1394** *P. Pl. Crede* 808 He..descended a-doune to þe derke helle, And fet oute our formfaderes. *c* **1440** *York Myst.* xxiii. 81 Oure fforme-ffadyrs full fayne Wold see this solempne sight. *c* **1450** Lonelich *Grail* xxx. 404 The grete wronge That oure form Modir dyde.

forme (*Printing*): see form *sb.* 20.

formé, -ée ('fɔːmeɪ), *a.* *Her.* Also anglicized formy. [a. F. *formé*, *formée*, pa. pple. of *former* to form.] Of a cross: Narrow in the centre and broad at the extremities: = pattée.

1610 Guillim *Heraldry* II. vii. (1660) 80 Gules, a Cheuvron between ten Crosses, Formee, Argent. **1661** Morgan *Sph. Gentry* II. 9 Crosse Forme or Patee. **1828–40** Berry *Encycl. Her.* I, *Formé* or *Formy*, the same as pattée. **1864** Boutell *Heraldry Hist. & Pop.* xxi. §1 (ed. 3) 356 Four crosses formées fitchées.

formeagre: see for- *pref.*[1] 9.

formed (fɔːmd), *ppl. a.* [f. form *v.* + -ed[1].]

1. In senses of the vb.

c **1440** *Promp. Parv.* 172/1 Foormyd, *formatus.* **1611** Bible *Wisd.* x. 1 The first formed father of the world. **1669** Woodhead *St. Teresa* I. Pref. 24 Without any formed words, Exterior or Interior. **1692** Ray *Dissol. World* II. iii. (1732) 123 Petrified shells now passing under the name of formed stones. **1717** tr. *Frezier's Voy. S. Sea* 119 Form'd Apples, half green, and quite ripe, all together. **1796–7** *Instr. & Reg. Cavalry* (1813) 187 The formed part of the regiments. **1871** Freeman *Hist. Ess.* Ser. I. vii. 173 A tongue which is as..a formed and polished speech.

2. *esp.* † **a.** Drawn up according to rule; formal, set. **b.** That has obtained distinct development or formulation; decided, definite, settled. **c.** Perfected by training or discipline; matured.

a. 1647 Clarendon *Hist. Reb.* III. §3 A long, form'd discourse. **1725** tr. *Dupin's Eccl. Hist. 17th C.* I. v. 68 In the First he treats of the canonical or form'd Epistles. *Ibid.* 69 Gerard Rodolphus..whose Book of Canonical, Form'd.. and Dimissory Letters were printed at Cologne in 1582.

b. 1605 Bacon *Adv. Learn.* I. iv. §12. 23 Besides the which there are some other rather peccant humours, then fourmed diseases. **1676–7** Marvell *Corr.* cclxxvii. Wks. 1872–5 II. 506 It tooke not so much place as to come to a formed question. **1681–6** J. Scott *Chr. Life* (1747) III. 386 Government is essential to formed and regular Societies. **1771** Mackenzie *Man of Feeling* xl. (1803) 90 Though he had no formed complaint, his health was manifestly on the decline. **1818** Jas. Mill *Brit. India* II. v. viii. 659 Without any formed intention of mendacity.

c. 1833 *Regul. Instr. Cavalry* I. 83 A formed horse must be rode on the bit entirely. **1834** J. H. Newman *Par. Serm.* (1837) I. xv. 276 The spontaneous acts of the formed Christian temper. **1865** M. Arnold *Ess. Crit.* viii. (1875) 326 An effect not only upon the young and enthusiastic.. but upon formed and important personages.

† **d.** ***formed bachelor*** (= med.L. *baccalaureus formatus*), a bachelor who has performed the whole of his 'forma': see form *sb.* 11 c.

This was the highest stage in the degree of B.D. in mediæval universities, the earlier stages being those of *cursor* or *biblicus*, and *sententiarius*.

1727–41 Chambers *Cycl.* s.v. *Bachelor*, At present, *formed bachelor* denotes a person who has taken the degree regularly, after the due course of study..by way of opposition to a *currant bachelor* who is admitted in the way of grace, or by diploma.

3. *Her.* = formé, -ée, pattée.

1592 Wyrley *Armorie* 111 Ten formed croslets.

† **formedon** ('fɔːmɪdɒn). *Law.* Also 5 fourme doon, 5–6 form(e)downe, 6–7 formdon(e. [AF., f. Law Lat. phr. *forma dōnī* form of gift.] A writ of right formerly used for claiming entailed property (see quot. 1628).

[**1485, 1523, 1598, 1768**: see descender[1].] **1495** *Act 11 Hen. VII*, c. 60 §1 The seid Hugh..[may] pursue for the recovere of the same londes by fourme doon or otherwise. **1523** Fitzherb. *Surv.* xi. (1539) 17 The Kynges writte of Formdone. **1628** Coke *On Litt.* 326 b, There be three kinde of Writs of Formedon, viz. The first in the Discender to be brought by the issue in taile, which claime by discent Per formam doni. The second is in the Reuerter, which lieth for him in the reuersion or his heires or Assignes after the state taile be spent. The third is [in] the Remainder, which the Law giueth to him in the remainder, his Heires or Assignes after the determination of the estate taile. **1680** Filmer *Patriarcha* iii. §17 (1884) 71 Who brought a formedon against a poor man. **1741** T. Robinson *Gavelkind* vi. 106 The Writ of Formedon brought by Daughters. **1876** Digby

Real Prop. iv. §3. 193 This was called the writ of 'formedon in the descender'.

† **'formel, formal,** *sb. Obs.* Also 4-5 **formaylle,** 7 **formale, fore-male.** [a. F. *formel* adj. (see FORMAL), which occurs in *faucon formel*, and latinized as *formelus* in a letter of Magnus of Norway to Edw. I, as an epithet applied to hawks. As the female hawk was greatly superior for purposes of sport, the sense of *formel* in this application may be 'regular', 'proper' (see FORMAL *a.*).

Cf. F. *forme*, 'a term of Hawking, the female of a bird of prey that gives its name to the species' (Littré).]

The female of the eagle or the hawk. Also *attrib.*

c **1381** CHAUCER *Parl. Foules* 371 To chese or for to take, By hir acord, his formel or his make. *Ibid.* 373 Nature held on hir honde A formel egle. ? *a* **1400** *Morte Arth.* 4003, I salle neuer..ffawkone ne formaylle appone fiste handille. *a* **1605** MONTGOMERIE *Misc. Poems* xviii. 38 Quhilks vhen they sau they wroght in vane, The formels fair auay they fure. **1616** SURFL. MARKH. *Country Farme* 712 Of Merlins there are both males and females..the female is called the formale. **1674** N. COX *Gentl. Recreat.* II. (1677) 215 If you will fly with a Merlin at a Partridge, chuse the Formal, which is the Female. The Jack is not worth the training. **1688** R. HOLME *Armoury* II. 239/1 Fore-Male, the term given to all Females of Hawks.

for'mel, *v. dial.* [a. ON. *formæla* to appoint, f. *for-*, FOR- *pref.*², FORE-¹ + *mæla* to speak.

The pa. t. and pa. pple. *formelt* in *Cursor Mundi* may belong to **formeld*, f. FOR- *pref.*² + MELD.]

trans. †**a.** To mention beforehand; also *intr.* to speak beforehand *of*. **b.** *dial.* To bespeak.

a **1300** *Cursor M.* 10181 þe toþer part, als was for-melt, It was bi-tuix þe prestes delt. *Ibid.* 10387 (Gött.) þe hundrid schepe þat i for-melt To all þe comune war þai delt. **1674** RAY *N.C. Words* 18 To Format [*sic: read* Formal] or Formel: to bespeak anything. **1869** in *Lonsdale Gloss.* **1878** *Cumbld. Gloss.* s.v., 'He formelt a par o' shun wi' stee cokers and girt heedit nails at t' boddam'.

†**formell.** *Obs.* [ad. Anglo-Lat. *formella* (substituted, perh. by mistake, for FOTMAL in one version of the *Assisa de Ponderibus*), a dim. of *forma* FORM, in the sense of 'mould'; cf. *formella* a cheese (Du Cange).] = FOTMAL.

1674 JEAKE *Arith.* (1696) 80 Lead..By the Ordinance abovesaid, 1 Load 30 Formells..So was the Formel 70 Pounds, a Weight now grown obsolete.

† **for'melt,** *v. Obs.* [f. FOR- *pref.*¹ + MELT *v.* (str. and weak).] *intr.* (strong) and *trans.* (weak). To melt, melt away.

c **893** K. ÆLFRED *Oros.* v. iv, Ealle þa scipu formulton. *c* **1200** *Trin. Coll. Hom.* 151 þe sunne hete þe snow, þat he hit for-melteð to watere. *c* **1230** *Hali Meid.* 13 þat ha ne merren ne formealten þurh licomliche lustes. *a* **1240** *Sawles Warde* in *Cott. Hom.* 251 þat pich ham forwalleð aðet ha beon for mealte.

Hence **for'melting** *ppl. a.*

1606 CHAPMAN *Gentl. Usher* IV, I vow..By the.. imaginarie ioyes Of vntride nuptialls; by loues vshering fire Fore-melting beautie and loues flame itselfe.

formene ('fɔːmiːn). [f. FORM(IC) + -ENE.] Methane or marsh-gas (CH_4). Hence **for'menophone** [Gr. φωνή sound]: see quot.

1884 *Athenæum* 19 July 86/3 Formene..cooled in boiling ethylene..is resolved into an extremely volatile colourless fluid. **1894** *Pop. Sci. Monthly* XLIV. 576 An instrument which he calls a formenophone has been invented by..M. E. Hardy, for..estimating the proportions of gaseous impurities of an atmosphere by the sound they give in a pipe.

†**for'menge,** *v. Obs.* [OE. *formęngan*, f. FOR- *pref.*¹ + *męngan*, MENG *v.* to mix; = Du., Ger. *vermengen.*] *trans.* To confound, trouble.

a **1300** *Cursor M.* 17292 Alle for-menged in þar mode.

former ('fɔːmə(r)), *sb.*¹ [f. FORM *v.* + -ER¹.]

1. One who forms or gives form to something; a maker, creator, fashioner, framer.

c **1340** *Cursor M.* 24411 (Fairf.) þe elementis þen mirkenid alle quen þai sagh þaire fourmer falle. *c* **1386** CHAUCER *Doctor's T.* 19 He that is the former principal Hath maked me his vicaire general, To forme and peynten erthely creaturis Right as me list. *c* **1400** MAUNDEV. (1839) Prol. 2 He that was formyour of alle the World. **1552** HULOET, Brycke former or maker. **1610** HEALEY *St. Aug. Citie of God* XII. xxvi. (1620) 443 Porphyry..affirmeth directly that these gods..are but the forgers of our prisons, and not our formers but only our iaylors. **1678** CUDWORTH *Intell. Syst.* 440 The Framer and Former of the Vniverse. *a* **1711** KEN *Christophil* Poet. Wks. 1721 I. 456 Thou in the New Creation art The Former of the Heart. **1841** D'ISRAELI *Amen. Lit.* (1867) 102 The first former of the vernacular literature of Italy. **1891** *Bookseller* July 647/2 The writer does not concern himself with education as a former of character.

†**2.** An instructor, instigator. *Obs.* (Cf. FORM *v.*¹ 2.)

1401 *Pol. Poems* (Rolls) II. 42 Iak Uplond..thourȝ formyng of his formere thus freyneth a frere. *Ibid.* 43 Jak, thi formur is a fole, that thus thee hath yfourmed, to make so lewid an argument.

3. a. Applied to various instruments or tools used in forming articles (see quots.).

1847 HALLIWELL, *Former*..also an instrument for holding different pieces of a table together. **1874** KNIGHT *Dict. Mech.*, *Former*, a templet, pattern, or gage by which an article is shaped, as pottery or an object in the lathe. A cutter by which patterns, blanks, wads or pieces are cut from sheets for various purposes. **1884** F. J. BRITTEN *Watch & Clockm.* 129 For polishing, formers of brass to begin..For soft stones the formers are of lead. **1888** *Lockwood's Dict. Mech. Engin.*, *Former* or *Copy*, the templet used for the cutting of wheel teeth, and other works in copying machines.

b. *Gunnery*, etc. (See quot. 1867.)

1644 MANWAYRING *Sea-mans Dict.*, *A Former* is a peece of wood, turned round, somewhat lesse then the bore of the Peece for which it is made..The use whereof, is to make upon it Paper Carthrages or Linnen Carthrages. **1669** STURMY *Mariner's Mag.* v. 86 Dip an Inch of the Case in Water, the Formor in him. **1794** NELSON 9 July in Nicolas *Disp.* (1845) I. 430 The Victory has a Former for twenty-six pounders. **1867** SMYTH *Sailor's Word-bk.*, *Former*, a small cylindrical piece of wood on which musket or pistol cartridge-cases are rolled and formed. The name is also applied to the flat piece of wood with a hole in the centre used for making wads, but which is properly *form*. **1873** E. SPON *Workshop Receipts* Ser. I. 124 To roll up the cases [of rockets] you must have a smooth round ruler, or, as it is called, a former.

c. (See quot.)

1802 C. JAMES *Milit. Dict.*, *Formers* were likewise used among officers and soldiers to reduce their clubs [CLUB *sb.* 6] to a uniform shape, before the general introduction of tails.

d. *Electr.* A frame or core about which a coil is wound.

1891 J. W. URQUHART *Dynamo Constr.* v. 76 The first matter to attend to in winding the bobbins is to ensure that there shall be no possibility of metallic contact between the wire and..the metal of the reel or former. **1910** *Encycl. Brit.* VIII. 772/1 The coils are either wound by hand directly on to the armature core, or are shaped on formers prior to being inserted in the armature slots. **1943** *Electronic Engin.* XVI. 80/2 A high quality ceramic coil former..for aerial coupling coils.

e. *Aeronaut.* A transverse member that strengthens and gives shape to a wing or fuselage.

1919 H. SHAW *Text-bk. Aeronaut.* ix. 110 In order to maintain the front portion of the upper surface [of the wing] it is customary to place false ribs or formers from the leading edge to the main spar. **1930** *Flight* 28 Nov. 1384/2 The fuselage formers or frames..are attached to the longerons by angle-section brackets. **1951** 'N. SHUTE' *Round Bend* 261 The great empty cabin, floored with duralumin, with bare stringers and formers supporting the outer skin of the walls. **1966** D. STINTON *Anat. of Aeroplane* 203 The skin is usually formed of metal sheets riveted, or spot-welded, to metal frames, formers and bulkheads.

4. *attrib.* and *Comb.*, as **former-wound** *a.*, of an armature coil, wound on a former before being mounted.

1902 *Encycl. Brit.* XXVII. 583/2 The former-wound coils have the advantage that they are perfectly symmetrical and interchangeable. **1906** A. RUSSELL *Treat. Altern. Curr.* II. 328 The winding of the stator of a polyphase motor is simple. It may be made up of rectangular former-wound coils, that is, coils which are wound into shape on a rectangular wooden block before being fixed on the stator. **1940** [see *bar-wound* adj.].

† **'former,** *sb.*² *Obs.* Also 6 **formour.** [ad. OF. *formoir* chisel, f. *form-er* to FORM; subsequently altered into *fermoir*: see FIRMER.] A kind of chisel or gouge, used by carpenters and masons (see quot. 1688; the description may have been influenced by false etymology).

1530 PALSGR. 222/1 Formour or grublyng yron. **1553** T. WILSON *Rhet.* 83 The mason [hath] his former, and his plaine. **1688** R. HOLME *Armoury* III. viii. §135 The second is termed a Former, it is a Chissel used before the Paring Chissel in all works. *Ibid.* ix. §142 The Clenser, or Former, is a broad ended Iron Plate, or Old [? Cold] Chessel, with a broad bottom, set in an Handle; with which Tool they smooth and make even the Stone after it is cut into that form and Order, as the Work-man will have it. **1727-51** CHAMBERS *Cycl.* s.v. *Chissel*, The chissels used in carpentry and joinery are, 1. The former, which is used first of all before the paring-chissel, and just after the work is scribed.

former ('fɔːmə(r)), *a.* Also 2-4 **formere,** 6 **formar(e,** (*Sc.* **formair),** 7 **formore.** [First recorded in the 12th century; a comparative formed on the analogy of *formest*, FOREMOST. In 16-17th c. the ending was sometimes assimilated to MORE.]

1. a. Earlier in time. Now chiefly in the more specific sense: Pertaining to the past, or to a period or occasion anterior to that in question.

The sense 'the earlier of two' (in strictly temporal application) is *obs.* or *arch.* exc. with reference to the halves of a period of time.

c **1160** *Hatton Gosp.* Matt. xxi. 36 Ða sende he eft oðre þeowas selre þanne þa formere [*earlier text* þa ærran] wæron. *c* **1380** WYCLIF *Sel. Wks.* III. 363 þe pope may..revoke his former errour. **1545** JOYE *Exp. Dan.* viii. 126 As the later waues thruste forthe the former sourges. **1576** FLEMING *Panopl. Epist.* 104 In my former letters. **1611** BIBLE *Hos.* vi. 3 He shall come vnto vs..as the latter and former raine. **1632** J. LEE *Short Surv.* 73 Having..the next yeare gathered together a farre greater army then the former. **1642** PERKINS *Prof. Bk.* vii. §479. 210 The testament..shall stand, notwithstanding that it hath the former date and was written before the other testament. **1676** DRYDEN *Aurengz.* IV. i. 1589 Trust on, and think to Morrow will repay: To Morrow's falser than the former Day. **1699** DAMPIER *Voy.* II. I. 177 The former part of the night we had much Rain. **1711** ADDISON *Spect.* No. 94 ¶8 With many melancholy Reflexions upon his former and his present State of Life. **1852** MRS. STOWE *Uncle Tom's C.* xxvi, Eva appeared more like her former self than ever she had done since her sickness. **1875** JOWETT *Plato* (ed. 2) I. 176 The admission of that, he replied, would belie our former admissions.

†**b.** followed by *than. Obs. rare.*

1382 WYCLIF *John* i. 30 He was the formere than I. **1611** SPEED *Theat. Gt. Brit.* (1614) 138/1 All which shew a former interest for Ireland then that which by conquest under Henry the second was made.

†**c.** In ME. it sometimes took the place of the earlier FORME, first, primeval, as in ***former father, days***; with similar sense ***the former age*** (Chaucer).

a **1300** *Cursor M.* 5464 (Gött.) Jacob..to his former fadris ferd. *Ibid.* 9156 (Gött.) He was þe first..þat ded men raysed in former dais [*Cott.* in form dais]. *c* **1374** CHAUCER *Former Age* 2 A Blysful lyf..Ledden the peoples in the former age. *c* **1400** MAUNDEV. (1839) Prol. 2 The Synne of oure formere Fader Adam. **1529** SIR T. MORE *Dyaloge* 126 a/2 From oure formar father Adam to yᵉ laste day.

d. Formerly possessed, occupied, frequented, etc.

1388 WYCLIF *Judg.* xvi. 28 ȝelde thou now to me the formere strengthe, that Y venge me of myn enemyes. **1607** SHAKS. *Cor.* v. iii. 202 Out of that Ile worke My selfe a former Fortune. **1697** DRYDEN *Virg. Georg.* III. 153 In Peace t' enjoy his former Palms and Pains. *Ibid.* IV. 790 This finish'd, to the former Woods repair.

e. Used to designate a former holder of an office; = British *ex-*. *U.S.*

1905 *N.Y. Herald* 5 Feb. 47 Former President Cleveland is among the arrivals of the week at the Lakewood Hotel. **1919** MENCKEN *Amer. Lang.* iv. 118 Such clumsy quasi-titles as ex-United States Senator,..and former Chief of the Fire Department. **1948** *Minneapolis Morn. Tribune* 28 Sept. 1/6 Sen. George Wilson, threatened by Democratic former Sen. Guy M. Gillette, was frankly warned by Dewey's advisers to intensify his campaign. **1970** *Encycl. Brit.* XXII. 650/1 President Hayes..appointed former Senator David M. Key..to his cabinet.

2. With reference to order. ***the former*** (often *absol.*, with ellipsis of sb.): **a.** The first of two. †Also, the (immediately) preceding; and *occas.* in connexion with a cardinal numeral = FIRST *a.* 2 e.

1588 A. KING tr. *Canisius' Catech.* H iij, In yᵉ ȝere besydes yᵉ 52 owkes yair is ane day ode, quhilk makis yᵉ dominical lettre to be changeit euerie ȝere in the formair. **1609** BIBLE (Douay) *2 Kings* Comm., In the seventene former chapters, are recorded [etc.]..The other eight chapters conteine other thinges donne in Juda. *a* **1703** BURKITT *On N.T.* Mark iii. 4 The former part of this chapter reports to us a miraculous cure. **1824** L. MURRAY *Eng. Gram.* (ed. 5) I. 348 Of dissyllables, formed by affixing a termination, the former syllable is commonly accented.

b. The first mentioned of two; opposed to *latter*.

A use app. of late introduction, but now so prominent that the other uses have become restricted to contexts in which the word could not be misinterpreted in this sense.

1597 HOOKER *Eccl. Pol.* v. iv. §3 Of the former kinde are all manner vertuous duties. **1606** SHAKS. *Ant. & Cl.* III. xiii. 80 Wisedome and Fortune combatting together, If that the former dare but what it can, No chance may shake it. **1674** tr. *Scheffer's Lapland* 84 Two doors, one, a foredoor, and the other, a backward; the former bigger and more ordinarily used, the latter less. **1717** POPE *Wks.* Pref., A bad Author deserves better usage than a bad Critic; a man may be the former merely thro' the misfortune of an ill judgment, but [etc.]. **1789** BENTHAM *Princ. Legisl.* xvii. §6 The latter mode is not less certain than the former. **1841** LANE *Arab. Nts.* I. 76 Therefore, in this work, I call the former 'a piece of gold', and the latter 'a piece of silver'. **1886** A. WINCHELL *Walks & Talks Geol. Field* 180 The former locality..has for many years been a favourite collecting-ground of geologists.

†**c.** Spoken of before, aforesaid. *Obs.*

1607 TOPSELL *Four-f. Beasts* (1658) 14 She presently threw herself from the former rock, and so she ended.

†**3.** Situated more forward; front, fore. *Obs.*

1382 WYCLIF *2 Macc.* iii. 25 He with fersnesse..rushide the former feet to Heliodore. *a* **1400** *Octouian* 1040 Two bole-axys..In hys former arsun were y-honge. **1544** PHAER *Regim. Life* (1560) S v b, Apply it to the former part of yᵉ heade. **1558** *Will of R. Fetlawe* (Somerset Ho.), Rynge that I weare upon my former fynger. **1593** *Rites of Durham* (Surtees) 17 In the former part of the Quire. **1601** SHAKS. *Jul. C.* v. i. 80 Comming from Sardis, on our former Ensigne Two mighty Eagles fell, and there they pearch'd. **1668** CULPEPPER & COLE *Barthol. Anat.* I. iv. 7 In the former part of a Mans Neck. **1678** tr. *Gaya's Art of War* II. 66 To fire in gaining of ground, the Battalion is commanded to advance as fast as the former Ranks discharge.

4. In the absol. or elliptical use, sometimes inflected as a *sb.* †**a.** With plural suffix (*obs. rare*). **b.** With genitive suffix.

a. **1548** W. PATTEN *Exped. Scot.* Pref. A iij a, We must be content in commune speche to vse the termes of our formers deuised. **1606** WARNER *Alb. Eng.* XV. xciii. 374 Pictish Britons did Brittish Reuolts inuaid, Because those Lattres (basely thought those Formers) Rome obaid.

b. **1613** T. JACKSON *Comm. Apost. Creede* I. 380 The manner..of the formers dissolution. **1824** L. MURRAY *Eng. Gram.* (ed. 5) I. 102 The former's phlegm was a check upon the latter's vivacity.

-former. [f. FORM *sb.* 6 b + -ER¹.] In schools, a member of a specified class or form, as ***sixth-former***.

1869 Third-former [see THIRD *a.* 5]. **1927** J. ELDER *Thomasina Toddy* xi, Sixth and Fifth formers who were in the Elevens. *Ibid.* xii, They gained on the Sixth-formers' boat. **1928** *Daily Express* 31 Aug. 15/2 One of them inquired of a small fourth-former whether he had seen any suspicious characters about. **1960** D. POTTER *Glittering Coffin* vi. 82 The choice of grammar school sixth-formers would be Oxford or Cambridge first. **1969** *Listener* 20 Feb. 252/1 A more likable, fourth-former-to-fourth-former note.

formeret (ˈfɔːmərɪt). *Arch.* [a. F. *formeret*; according to Hatzf.-Darm. f. *forme* FORM *sb.*]
1872 *Gloss. Eccl. Terms* (Shipley), *Formaret*, rib moulding placed at the junction of a vault with the vertical wall.

formerly (ˈfɔːməlɪ), *adv.* [f. FORMER *a.* + -LY².]
†**1.** Before another or something else; first, beforehand. *Obs.*
1596 SPENSER *F.Q.* VI. i. 38 Calidore..Nimbler handed Preuented him before his stroke could light And on the helmet smote him formerlye. *c* **1645** HOWELL *Lett.* (1655) IV. xi. 29 If I had not formerly read the Barons Wars in England, I had more admir'd that of the Liguers in France.
2. In former days, at some past time.
1599 HAKLUYT *Voy.* II. 181 Requiring for the visiting no more then formerly they were accustomed to pay at their first comming. **1607** SHAKS. *Cor.* IV. i. 53 You shall Heare from me still, and neuer of me ought But what is like me formerly. **1674** MARTINIERE *Voy. N. Countries* 58 After supper we went to our lodging, which as formerly was upon Bear-skin spread upon the floor. **1709** STEELE & ADDISON *Tatler* No. 114 ¶1, I had formerly conversed with him at this House. **1856** SIR B. BRODIE *Psychol. Inq.* I. i. 5 We were sensible that we were not what we had been formerly. **1857** BUCKLE *Civiliz.* I. xi. 626 The superstitious reverence with which kings were formerly regarded is extinct.
†**3.** A little time before, just now. *Obs.*
1590 SPENSER *F.Q.* II. xii. 67 Her faire locks, which formerly were bownd Up in one knott, she low adowne did lose. **1596** SHAKS. *Merch. V.* IV. i. 362. **1665** MANLEY *Grotius' Low C. Warres* 681 They who had formerly gone out of the Battel, to be refreshed and comforted, came in again. **1697** POTTER *Antiq. Greece* IV. iv. (1715) 194 As has been formerly observed. **1766** GOLDSM. *Vic. W.* xxxii, Those..whom I formerly rebuked with such sharpness.

†ˈ**formerness.** *Obs.* [f. FORMER *a.* + -NESS.] The quality of being former; anteriority.
1587 GOLDING *De Mornay* vii. 98 Where order is, there is a formernesse and an afternesse. **1674** N. FAIRFAX *Bulk & Selv.* 14 To shut out formerness and afterness.

†ˈ**formerward.** *Obs. rare*⁻¹. [f. FORMER *a.* + WARD: cf. FOREWARD².] The vanguard.
13.. *K. Alis.* 7786 Antioche hadde the former-warde, And Tolomê the reirwarde. [Cf. quot. **14..** in FORME *a.* 2.]

formest: see FOREMOST.

formet, obs. form of FOUMART.

formful (ˈfɔːmfʊl), *a.* [f. FORM *sb.* + -FUL.] Full of form or forms: **a.** Apt to create forms (of the imagination). **b.** Shapely.
1727–46 THOMSON *Summer* 1632 As fleets the vision o'er the formful brain. **1798** BLOOMFIELD *Farmer's Boy, Winter* 289 Fancy's formful Visions. **1832** *Blackw. Mag.* XXXI. 999 He is familiar with Chantrey's form-full statues.

‖**Formgeschichte** (ˈfɔːmgəˌʃɪçtə). [G., f. *form* form + *geschichte* history.] = *form-criticism.*
1923 *Harvard Theol. Rev.* XVI. 92 Two monographs on special phases of gospel 'Formgeschichte'. **1932** *Expos. Times* XLIII. 396/1 The 'investigations'..of the German school of *Formgeschichte*. **1935** [see *form-criticism*]. **1954** *Scott. Jrnl. Theol.* VII. 334 The work of R. Bultmann and M. Dibelius in the field of Formgeschichte in the Gospels. **1970** *Computers & Humanities* IV. 199 It offers a scientific method of crossing..the quagmire of *Formgeschichte* which has seemed to be the limit of Synoptic studies.

formiate: see FORMATE *sb.*

formic (ˈfɔːmɪk), *a.* [for **formicic*, f. L. *formic-a* ant + -IC. Cf. F. *formique*.]
1. *Chem. formic acid*: a colourless irritant volatile acid contained in a fluid emitted by ants.
formic ethers, ethers obtained by substituting alcoholic radicals for the basic hydrogen of formic acid.
1791 HAMILTON *Berthollet's Dyeing* II. II. i. 52 Formic acid acts on indigo like the muriatic. **1807** T. THOMSON *Chem.* (ed. 3) II. 313 Of formic acid. **1871** TYNDALL *Fragm. Sc.* (1879) I. xvii. 449 For barely visible redness formic aether is more opaque than sulphuric. **1884** BOWER & SCOTT *De Bary's Phaner.* 68 By distilling the nettle plant with sulphuric acid formic acid is obtained.
2. Occas. in *gen.* sense: Of or pertaining to ants.
1816 KIRBY & SP. *Entomol.* (1843) II. 88 A nest of ants. enjoying the full sun, which seems the acmé of formic felicity. **1857** *Chamb. Jrnl.* VII. 300 Republicanism is made to find its antitype in the formic community.

‖**formica**¹ (fɔːˈmaɪkə). [L. *formīca* ant.]
1. *Ent.* The typical genus of the family *Formicidæ*; the ant.
1865 LIVINGSTONE *Zambesi* ix. 190 We could not [sleep] because of the attacks by the fighting battalions of a small species of *formica*. **1878** BELL *Gegenbaur's Comp. Anat.* 272 Many Hymenoptera, Formica, Cynips, also possess it.
2. A kind of abscess, ulcer, or excrescence, occurring *esp.* in a hawk's bill or a dog's ears.
c **1400** *Lanfranc's Cirurg.* 213 Pustule þat comeþ of humours corrupt as ignis persicus & miliaris & fformica schall be purged. **1543** TRAHERON tr. *Vigo's Chirurg.* II. vi. 20b, Formica is a lytle pustle, or many pustles that come upon the skynne..The thyrde [sygne] is pryckynge, and it is a sodayn bytyng as it were of an ante wherof it hath hys name. **1614** MARKHAM *Cheap Husb.* (1623) 161 The Formicas in Hawkes is a hard horne growing vpon the beake of a Hawke. **1674** N. COX *Gentl. Recreat.* II. (1677) 248 Of the Formica. This is a Distemper which commonly seizeth on the Horn of Hawks Beaks, which will eat the Beak away. **1846** J. BAXTER *Libr. Pract. Agric.* (ed. 4) I. 225 Formica or Scab in the Ears [of a dog].

Formica² (fɔːˈmaɪkə). Also formica. The proprietary name of a hard, durable plastic laminate used esp. as a decorative surfacing material. Also *attrib.* and *Comb.*
1922 *Official Gaz.* (U.S. Pat. Off.) 10 Jan. 409/2 The Formica Insulation Company, Cincinnati, Ohio..*Formica*. Electric Insulating Compound. **1946** *Ibid.* 12 Mar. 179/2 The Formica Insulation Company, Cincinnati, Ohio... *Formica*. For laminated sheets of wood, fabric, or paper impregnated with synthetic resin and consolidated under heat and pressure, for use on table tops, furniture and wall panelling. **1957** *Oxf. Mail* Suppl. 16 Oct. 6/5 Red upholstered chairs with chromium legs and tables in formica. **1958** *House & Garden* Feb. 91 (Advt.), Furniture surfaced for ever with Formica decorative laminates. **1958** *Woman's Own* 5 Mar. 11/4 Formica-topped units link the automatic electric cooker (with eye-level grill) and sink unit into an ideal one-level working surface. **1959** H. HOBSON *Mission House Murder* i. 9 One tinselly formica-and-chrome establishment. **1960** *Guardian* 25 Apr. 2/4 A Formica-covered table top.

formican (fɔːˈmaɪkən), *a. rare.* [f. FORMICA¹ + -AN.] Of or pertaining to ants.
1880 *Daily Tel.* 16 Nov., If the Queen-ant is removed from a nest, the formican politicians settle down soon into a steady-going Republic. **1884** G. ALLEN in *Longm. Mag.* V. 42 These singular results of formican selection.

formicant (ˈfɔːmɪkənt), *a.* [ad. L. *formīcant-em*, pr. pple. of *formīcāre* to crawl like ants (said of the pulse or skin), f. *formīca* ant.] Crawling like an ant; in *Path.* of the pulse (see quot. 1893).
1707 FLOYER *Physic. Pulse-Watch* 51 A formicant Pulse is like the motion of an Ant, who moves her feet oft without going much forward. **1842** DUNGLISON *Dict. Med.* (ed. 3), *Formicant*, an epithet given to the pulse when extremely small, scarcely perceptible, unequal, and communicating a sensation like that of the motion of an ant through a thin texture.

formiˈcarian, *a.* [f. L. **formīcāri-us* (see FORMICARY) + -AN.] Relating to or resembling ants.
1607 TOPSELL *Four-f. Beasts* (1658) 29 It is called a Formicarian Bear; for..whereas that Countrey is..annoyed with..Ants, that beast doth..prey and feed upon them. —— *Serpents* (1658) 769 This formicarian or Pismire-like Phalanx.

formicarioid (fɔːmɪˈkɛərɪɔɪd), *a.* [f. as prec. + -OID.] Of or belonging to the *Formicarioideæ* or ant-thrushes. Also *sb*, a member of this family.
1874 A. R. WALLACE in *Ibis* Ser. III. IV. 413 Formicaroid [*sic*] Passeres.

formicarium (fɔːmɪˈkɛərɪəm). [a. med.L: see FORMICARY.] = FORMICARY.
1834 MEDWIN *Angler in Wales* I. 161 For I found that our bungalow..was a 'formicaria' [*sic*]. **1863** BATES *Nat. Amazon* I. 32 A Formicarium or ant-colony. **1892** *Edin. Rev.* July 46 The formicarium or burrow of the ants.

formicary (ˈfɔːmɪkərɪ). [ad. med.L. *formīcārium* neut. sing. of **formīcārius* pertaining to ants, f. L. *formīca* ant.] An ants' nest, ant-hill.
1816 KIRBY & SP. *Entomol.* (1843) II. 47 They are conducted into the interior of the Formicary. **1880** LUBBOCK in *Jrnl. Linn. Soc.* XV. No. 83. 176 The queen was alone within an artificial glass formicary.

formicate (ˈfɔːmɪkət), *a. rare*⁻⁰. [f. L. *formīca* ant + -ATE.] Resembling an ant.
1840 in SMART.

formicate (ˈfɔːmɪkeɪt), *v.* [f. ppl. stem of L. *formīcāre*: see FORMICANT.] *intr.* To crawl like ants; *transf.* to swarm *with* moving beings. Hence ˈ**formicating** *ppl. a.* = FORMICANT.
1684 tr. *Bonet's Merc. Compit.* VI. 180 A languid, unequal, or formicating Pulse. **1854** LOWELL *Jrnl. Italy* Prose Wks. 1890 I. 165 An open space, which formicated with peasantry.

formication (fɔːmɪˈkeɪʃən). *Path.* [ad. L. *formīcātiōn-em*, n. of action f. *formīcāre* (see FORMICANT).] An abnormal sensation as of ants creeping over the skin.
1707 FLOYER *Physic. Pulse-Watch* 313 Pains in the Limbs, Formications, Lassitudes. **1844** HECKER *Epid. Middle Ages* 279 Many patients experienced..a disagreeable creeping sensation or formication on their hands and feet. **1861** WYNTER *Soc. Bees* 457 Figs produced formication of the palate and fauces.

formicative (ˈfɔːmɪkeɪtɪv), *a.* [f. L. *formīcāt-* ppl. stem of *formīcāre* (see prec.) + -IVE.] Of, or of the nature of, formication.
1834 GOOD *Study Med.* (ed. 4) III. 356 To remove the.. pricking or formicative pain from the limbs.

†**formice.** *Obs. rare.* [ad. L. *formīca* ant. Cf. OF. *formiz, formis.*] The ant.
1484 CAXTON *Fables of Æsop* II. xvii, A fable Of the ante or formyce and of the flye. **1491** —— *Vitas Patr.* (W. de W. 1495) I. xxxviii. 52 a/2 Salamon the whyche sente the slowthfull to the formices or Auntes.

formicic (fɔːˈmɪsɪk), *a.* = FORMIC.
[**1874** KEY *Lang.* 137 In our language a chemist speaks of *formic* acid rather than *formicic*.] In some mod. Dicts.

formicid (ˈfɔːmɪsɪd), *sb.* and *a.* Also formicide. [ad. mod.L. *Formīcid-æ*: see -ID.]
A. *sb.* A member of the family *Formicidæ* or ants. **B.** *adj.* Of or belonging to this family.
1878 *Pop. Sci. Monthly* XII. 197 The Formicide family.

ˈ**formicine**, *a. rare.* [ad. L. *formīcīnus*, f. *formīca* ant: see -INE.] Of, or of the nature of, ants.
1885 H. O. FORBES *E. Archip.* 31 Every trading vessel in the tropics has its formicine fauna.

ˌ**formidaˈbility.** [f. FORMIDABLE *a.*: see *-bility*, -ITY.] The quality of being formidable.
1745 H. WALPOLE *Lett. H. Mann* (1834) II. cxliii. 91 A Mackintosh has been taken, who reduces their formidability by being sent to raise two clans. **1754** H. P. *Hiberniad* iii. 24 There would be an Air of Formidability in..his.. Assertions. **1860** in WORCESTER (citing *Q. Rev.*).

formidable (ˈfɔːmɪdəb(ə)l), *a.* [a. F. *formidable* (15th c.), ad. L. *formīdābil-em*, f. *formīdāre* to fear, dread: see -ABLE.] That gives cause for fear or alarm; fit to inspire dread or apprehension. Now usually (with some obscuration of the etymological sense): Likely to be difficult to overcome, resist, or deal with; giving cause for serious apprehension of defeat or failure.
1508 FISHER *7 Penit. Ps.* xxxviii. e e v b, The countenaunce of god shall be so formydable and fereful that [etc.]. **1548** HALL *Chron., Hen. VII*, 5 Of whiche name..foreyne prynces trymbled and quaked, so muche was that name to all nacions terrible and formidable. **1658** T. WALL *Gods Revenge Enemies Ch.* 30 The Leopard..being..of a formidable aspect. **1678** WANLEY *Wond. Lit. World* v. i. §97. 468/1 Charles..defeated Barbarossa, that formidable Pirat. *a* **1687** PETTY *Pol. Arith.* (1690) 80 The decay of Timber in England is no very formidable thing. **1759** ROBERTSON *Hist. Scot.* I. III. 178 A party formidable by their number. **1834** L. RITCHIE *Wand. by Seine* 74 Swords of formidable dimensions. **1844** THIRLWALL *Greece* VIII. lx. 7 He set sail with a formidable armament. **1860** TYNDALL *Glac.* I. xiv. 97 Along the edge of a formidable precipice of rock.
b. Const. *to.*
1665 BOYLE *Occas. Refl.* II. viii. (1808) 38 These commotions of the Appetite which would not else be formidable to me. **1855** MACAULAY *Hist. Eng.* III. 495 The Episcopal schismatics, thus reinforced, would probably have been as formidable to the new King..as [etc.].
c. Often applied playfully or sarcastically.
1697 DRYDEN *Æneid* Ded., Unless I wou'd swell my Preface into a Volume, and make it formidable to your Lordship, when you see so many Pages yet behind. **1777** SHERIDAN *Sch. Scand.* IV. i, Here, now, is a maiden sister of his..done by Kneller, in his best manner, and esteemed a very formidable likeness. **1816** KEATINGE *Trav.* (1817) I. 275 His majesty has..a *corps de musique* of most formidable establishment equally in point of execution as of numbers. **1879** *Cassell's Techn. Educ.* VII. 23/2 The Thames..is not a very formidable river at that point.

formidableness (ˈfɔːmɪdəb(ə)lnɪs). [f. prec. + -NESS.] The quality of being formidable.
1659 *Gentl. Calling* viii. §17. 447 That by which we use to discriminate base fear from just caution, is the formidableness of the object feared. **1709** J. JOHNSON *Clergm. Vade-m.* II. p. lxxviij, A talk of the formidableness of Church-power. **1832** *Examiner* 260/1 Our author straightway forgets the formidableness of our antagonist. **1891** H. S. CONSTABLE *Horses, Sport & War* 218 The formidableness of Russia comes, also, from her increasing population.

formidably (ˈfɔːmɪdəblɪ), *adv.* [f. as prec. + -LY².] In a formidable manner.
1685 DRYDEN *Thren. August.* 512 The British cannon formidably roars. **1715–20** POPE *Iliad* XI. 54 His fourfold helm..With nodding horse-hair formidably graced. **1855** MACAULAY *Hist. Eng.* IV. 237 She was so formidably manned that all attempts to board her failed. **1858** FROUDE *Hist. Eng.* III. xiv. 254 England lay formidably open to attack.

†ˌ**formidoˈlose**, *a. Obs.*⁻⁰ [ad. L. *formīdolōs-us*: see next and -OSE.] (See quot.) Hence **formidoˈlosity.**
1727 BAILEY vol. II, *Formidolose*, fearful; also to be feared, dreadful. [Hence in mod. Dicts.] *Ibid.*, *Formidolosity*, fearfulness, very great dread.

†**forˈmidolous**, *a. Obs.* [ad. L. *formīdolōs-us* (better *-dulōsus*) causing or feeling dread, f. *formīdo* dread.] Fearful, terrible; also, feeling fear, timorous.
1656 BLOUNT *Glossogr.*, *Formidolous*, fearful, that feareth, dreadful, dangerous. **1773** J. ROSS *Fratricide* II. 618 (MS.) Why this so sudden, this formidolous change?

forming (ˈfɔːmɪŋ), *vbl. sb.* [f. FORM *v.*¹ + -ING¹.]
a. The action of the vb. FORM; the fact or process of being formed.
1401 [see FORMER *sb.*¹ 2]. *c* **1440** HYLTON *Scala Perf.* (W. de W. 1494) II. iv, Syth that man in hys fyrste fourmynge of God was sette in his free wyll. **1530** PALSGR. Introd. 17 At theyr fyrst formyng [they] open theyr mowth. **1651** HOBBES *Leviath.* II. xxviii. 165 The forming of mens wils to the observation of the Law. *a* **1856** H. MILLER *Notes on Fossils* in *Footpr. Creat.* (1861) 326 Our knowledge is but in the forming, and still very incomplete.
b. *spec.* in *Electr.* = FORMATION 1 b.
1902 *Encycl. Brit.* XXV. 26/2 Faure..greatly shortened the time required for 'forming' by giving the plates a preliminary coating of red lead. **1926** *Physical Rev.* 2nd Ser. XXVII. 813 No forming is necessary so the rectifier is immediately operative when the alternating voltage is

applied. **1956** L. P. HUNTER *Handbk. Semiconductor Electronics* iv. 17 The transistor before forming shows a collector resistance of the order of 10^5 ohms... After forming, the collector resistance is usually about 2×10^4 ohms. **1962** SIMPSON & RICHARDS *Junction Transistors* viii. 181 The other is reverse-biased and forms the collector. It is given a special heat treatment called 'forming' which consists of passing a large current through it in the reverse direction for a short time.

forming ('fɔːmɪŋ), *ppl. a.* [f. as prec. + -ING².] **a.** That forms; formative, creative.

1644 DIGBY *Nat. Bodies* (1645) I. 289 A forming virtue or *Vis formatrix*. **1701** ROWE *Amb. Step. Moth.* I. i, The thought that labours in my forming Brain. **1711** STEELE *Spect.* No. 167 ⁋3 What august Palaces..have grown under my forming Imagination. **1739** G. OGLE *Gualth. & Gris.* 37 She still improv'd beneath their forming hands.

b. That is in process of being formed.

1805 *Rec. Greenhead United Presbyt. Ch. Glasgow*, To be taken under their consideration as a forming congregation. **1875** WHITNEY *Life Lang.* v. 96 The construction was in a forming and doubtful state.

c. That forms or brings about formation (see FORM *v.* 1 g).

1914 H. PENDER *Amer. Handbk. Electr. Engineers* 105 After the forming charge the plates are dried and are ready for the market. **1962** L. P. HUNTER *Handbk. Semiconductor Electronics* (ed. 2) iv. 42 The forming pulse..heats the germanium in the neighborhood of the collector point to a relatively high temperature. **1964** [see FORMATION 1 b].

†**for'mirken**, *v. Obs.* In 5 formerken. [f. FOR-*pref.*¹ + MURKEN *v.*] *intr.* To darken.

c **1430** *Chev. Assigne* 362 Alle his feyre federes fomede vpon blode, And alle formerknes þe watur, þer þe swanne swymmethe.

†**'formity.** *Obs.* [formed after INFORMITY.] The quality of possessing form or shape.

1623 COCKERAM II. A v, *Beauty*, Pulchritude, Formity. **1635** SWAN *Spec. M.* vi. §2 (1643) 184 The informity was expressed before, when Moses said that the Earth was void and invisible..but the formitie is then..declared when the waters are gathered, and the dry-land made apparent.

formity, obs. form of FRUMENTY.

†**formize**, *v. Obs.*⁻¹ [f. FORM *sb.* + -IZE.] *trans.* To put into definite form.

1649 J. E. tr. *Behmen's Ep.* vi. 65 All Beings are but one onely Being, which hath..severized and formized it selfe.

formless ('fɔːmlɪs), *a.* [f. FORM *sb.* + -LESS.] Devoid of, or wanting in, form; shapeless; having no determinate or regular form. Said both of material and immaterial things.

1591 SPENSER *Tears Muses* 502 Things she formed of a formelesse mas. **1595** SHAKS. *John* III. i. 253. *a* **1631** DONNE *Poems, Elegie* xv. *Julia* 25 Countlesse multitudes Of formlesse curses, projects unmade up. **1667** MILTON *P.L.* III. 12 The rising world of waters..Won from the void and formless infinite. **1680** G. HICKES *Spirit of Popery* 27 That unprescribed Formless way of Worship, which they now use. **1819** SHELLEY *Cenci* III. i, Like a ghost shrouded and folded up In its own formless horror. **1869** TYNDALL *Chem. Rays* in *Fortn. Rev.* 1 Feb. 244 This formless aggregate of infinitesimal particles. **1870** MORRIS *Earthly Par.* I. I. 169 Brown birds..Twittered their sweet and formless tune.

Hence **'formlessly** *adv.*; **'formlessness.**

1727 BAILEY vol. II, *Formlesness.* **1825** COLERIDGE *Aids Refl.* App. C. (1858) 394 We leave space dimensionless.. and therefore the representative of absolute weakness and formlessness. **1845** CARLYLE *Cromwell* (1873) I. i. 9 They had form, but they are changing into sheer formlessness. **1884** SEELEY in *Contemp. Rev.* Oct. 500 Goethe [was].. impatient of the formlessness which had begun to reign in literature. **1888** HOWELLS *Annie Kilburn* vi, His long coat hung formlessly from his shoulders.

†**'formly**, *a. Obs. rare*⁻¹. [f. FORM *sb.* + -LY¹.] Having (proper) form, shapely.

1548 VICARY *Eng. Treas.* (1626) 12 Through him every member is made the formelier, and taketh the better shape.

†**'formly**, *adv. Obs.* Forms: 4 forma-, formelich(e, -ly, 5 fourmely. [f. FORM *sb.* + *-liche*, -LY².] In proper form; also, with regard to the 'form' or essential nature; = FORMALLY.

c **1374** CHAUCER *Boeth.* v. pr. iv. 128 (Camb. MS.) It biholdeth alle thingis so as I shal seye bi a strok of thogth formely [L. *formaliter*] with owte discours or collation. —— *Troylus* IV. 469 (497) O where hastow ben hid so longe in muwe That canst so wel and formely [*v.r.* formaly] arguwe? **1377** LANGL. *P. Pl.* B. xv. 366 For is none of þis newe clerkes ..þat can versifye faire ne formalich [C. XVIII. 109 formeliche] enditen. **1470** FORTESCUE in *Gov. England* (1885) 350 How the lawe may be fourmely kepte.

formo- ('fɔːməʊ). *Chem.* Combining form of FORMIC, as in ˌ**formoben'zoic** (*acid*), an obs. name for MANDELIC *acid*; hence ˌ**formo'benzoate**, a salt of this acid.

1834 MRS. SOMERVILLE *Connect. Phys. Sc.* xxiv. (1849) 229 Formobenzoate of silver. **1873** *Fownes' Chem.* (ed. 11) 823 Formobenzoic or Mandelic Acid $C_8H_8O_3$.

formol ('fɔːmɒl). [Former trade name, app. arbitrarily f. FORMALDEHYDE.] = FORMALIN. Also *attrib.*, as **formol titration** *Biochem.*, a method of estimating amino acids involving the use of formalin. Hence **'formolize** *v. trans.*, = FORMALINIZE *v.*; **'formolized** *ppl. a.*

1894 *Brit. Med. Jrnl.* 22 Dec. 1429/2 Formol was introduced by Professor Leber; it was supplied under two names—formol or formaline. **1910** *Chem. Abstr.* IV. 606 The conclusion of Soerensen, that amino acid N can be determined by means of the formol titration..is confirmed. **1932** *Proc. Soc. Exper. Biol. & Med.* XXIX. 456 We.. succeeded in immunizing guinea pigs with formolized Rickettsia suspensions. **1949** MILES & PIRIE *Nature Bacterial Surface* i. 7 The partly lysed bacteria were formolized and washed repeatedly on the centrifuge. **1961** GREENSTEIN & WINITZ *Chem. Amino Acids* I. iv. 516 (*heading*) Formol titration constants of amino acids and peptides at 30°. **1964** *Bull. World Health Org.* XXX. 46/1 The cells were formolized by a modification of Csizmas' (1960) method.

Formosa (fɔː'məʊsə). [See next.] Used *attrib.* in names of products of Formosa, esp. *Formosa tea* (also *ellipt.*).

1889 *Jrnl. Soc. Chem. Ind.* 30 Nov. 931/1 Formosa camphor in the Hong Kong market rose to 30 dols. per picul. **1892** [see PEKOE *v.*]. **1896** J. D. CLARK *Formosa* 58 The fear lest Formosa Tea, being converted into Congou by the Indian methods of preparation..should thereby lose the distinguished position it occupies as Oolong. **1951** W. G. COPSEY *Law's Grocer's Man.* 157/1 *Formosa tea.* This is a distinctive leaf tea known as Formosa Oolong. It is semi-fermented in character and variegated in colour.

Formosan (fɔː'məʊsən), *a.* and *sb.* [f. *Formosa*, orig. fem. (sc. *insula* island) of L. *formōsus* beautiful; a name (orig. Portuguese) of the island Taiwan, off the south-east coast of China: see -AN.] **A.** *adj.* Of or pertaining to the island of Formosa, its inhabitants, or their language. **B.** *sb.* **a.** A native or inhabitant of Formosa. **b.** The language of the indigenous Formosans.

1650 H. JESSEI tr. *Sibellius's Conv.* 5,900 *E. Indians* 4 M. Junius being carryed by the good hand of God to the Formosan Island, in the East-Indies, preached in Dutch. *Ibid.* 8 M. Junius..translated certaine Psalmes into the Formosan Islanders Language. **1704** G. PSALMANAZAR *Descr. Formosa* 122 The Formosan Alphabet. *Ibid.* 335 The Lord's Prayer, Apostle's Creed, and the Ten Commandments, translated by the Author into Formosan. **1707** —— (*title*) A dialogue between a Japonese and a Formosan, about some points of the religion of the time. *Ibid.* (Pref.), You'll see a Formosan, like a willing Prisoner, endeavouring to bring his friend unto the same Condition as he is himself. **1731** R. MILLAR *Hist. Propag. Christ.* II. viii. 318 Mr. Robert Junius..translated certain psalms into the Formosan language. **1879** *Encycl. Brit.* IX. 416/2 The Formosan fauna has been but partially ascertained. **1915** W. CAMPBELL *Sks. fr. Formosa* xvi. 122 Some of the Formosan tribes boil down every head brought in to a thick jelly, from which thin oblong cakes are made, for being nibbled to inspire fresh courage. **1933** BLOOMFIELD *Lang.* iv. 71 The languages of the great islands of the East, such as Formosan, Javanese (20 millions), Sundanese (6½ millions) [etc.]. **1955** H. KURNITZ *Let.* 29 Dec. in G. Marx *Groucho Lett.* (1967) 250 The Krasnas had a Xmas party with Chinese food, which..was cooked by some Formosan tribesmen. **1962** *Times* 20 Aug. 9/4 The Kuomintang has no appeal to the younger generation in Formosa whether they are children of those who came from the mainland or native Formosans.

†**formose, formous**, *a. Obs.* Also 6 *Sc.* formois. [ad. L. *formōs-us* beautiful, f. *forma* FORM: see -OSE.] Beautiful, comely.

14.. *Nine Ladies Worthie* 27 in *Chaucer's Wks.* (1561) 342 Of all femine moste formous flour. *c* **1450** *Mirour Saluacioun* 4003 Moises faire and formouse. **1530** LYNDESAY *Test. Papyngo* 104 Amang the flowris fresche, fragrant, & formose. **1567** *Satir. Poems Reform.* iii. 59 Of face formois and vult heroycall. *a* **1658** CLEVELAND *Vit. Uxoris* iii. Wks. (1687) 267 If he chuse one most Formose, Ripe for't, shee'll prove libidinous. **1684** I. MATHER *Remark. Provid.* (1856) 175 The nymphs..were dæmons, presenting themselves in shapes very formose.

formose ('fɔːməʊz, -s), *sb. Chem.* [a. G. *formose* (O. Loew 1886, in *Jrnl. f. prakt. Chemie* XXXIII. 328), f. FORM(ALDEHYDE + -OSE².] A mixture of hexose sugars, originally thought to be a single compound, produced by the condensation of formaldehyde in the presence of weak alkalis.

1886 *Jrnl. Chem. Soc.* L. 610 Formose, $C_6H_{12}O_6$, is obtained by shaking a 3·5 to 4 per cent. solution of formaldehyde with an excess of milk of lime. **1957** J. C. SOWDEN in W. Pigman *Carbohydrates* ii. 103 Formaldehyde condenses in the presence of weak bases to form a complex mixture of sugars called formose or methose. **1969** *New Scientist* 13 Nov. 342/3 NASA scientists are studying the formose sugar synthesis.

formosity (fɔː'mɒsɪtɪ). *Obs.* exc. *arch.* [a. OF. *formosité*, ad. L. *formōsitāt-em*, f. *formōsus*: see FORMOSE, FORMOUS *a.* and -ITY.] Beauty; also, a beauty.

1489–99 *Inscription* in Wood *Life* (Oxf. Hist. Soc.) II. 409 Thys chapill floryschyd with formosyte spectabyll. *a* **1521** *Helyas* in Thoms *Prose Rom.* (1858) III. 27 The beaute and formosite of hir noble persone. **1647** R. BARON *Cyprian Acad.* 8 A Damsell of exquisite formosity. **1652** F. KIRKMAN *Clerio & Lozia* 122 It is idolatrous for him to bend before so many graces and formosities. **1893** T. F. HENDERSON *Old World Scot.* xv. 172 Squalor and dirt were thoroughly antagonistic to adornment and 'formosity'.

†**form-speckle.** *Obs. rare*⁻¹. [? Perversion of FERNTICLE or the synonymous dialectal *fan freckle.*] A freckle.

1702 *Lond. Gaz.* No. 3815/8 John Hewitt, a Bricklayer.. straight Hair, and Form-Speckles on his hands and Face.

formula ('fɔːmjʊlə). Pl. formulæ, -as. [a. L. *formula*, dim. of *forma* FORM *sb.* Cf. F. *formule.*]

1. a. A set form of words in which something is defined, stated, or declared, or which is prescribed by authority or custom to be used on some ceremonial occasion.

[**1581** E. CAMPION in *Confer.* IV. (1584) Ee ij b, The *Formula* of the second covenant, is Christ. *Charke.* You vnderstand not..what *Formula* is.] *a* **1638** MEDE *Wks.* (1672) I. xxii. 83 What is the meaning of this Formula [of the Jews—'Let his memory be blessed']? **1685** *Lond. Gaz.* No. 2031/2 The Lord Register reading the Formula, the Lyon King at Arms..Fenced the High Court of Parliament. **1723** *Act 9 Geo. I*, c. 24 §8 All Papists..shall..make and subscribe the Declaration called the Formula, as the same is recited in an Act of Parliament of Scotland [of 1700]. **1752** J. LOUTHIAN *Form of Process* (ed. 2) 51 Before inclosing of the Assize, the Clerk, by Order of the Court, leaves a Formula with them for their Direction. **1792** BURKE *Let. to Sir H. Langrishe* Wks. 1842 I. 555 You have sent me several papers..I think I had seen all of them, except the formula of association. **1798** EDGEWORTH *Pract. Educ.* (1811) II. 23 The grammatical formulæ may then by gentle degrees be committed to memory. **1844** H. H. WILSON *Brit. India* III. 318 Forcing the Brahmins..to repeat the Mohammedan formula of faith. **1892** *Speaker* 3 Sept. 293/2 The excellent scholastic formula *Transeat*, meaning either 'Not proven', or 'Nothing to the purpose'.

b. In recent use, after Carlyle, often applied more or less disparagingly, e.g. to rules unintelligently or slavishly followed, to fettering conventionalities of usage, to beliefs held or professed out of mere acquiescence in tradition, etc.

Carlyle's use of the word was clearly suggested by the words used of Mirabeau by his father, 'Il a humé toutes les formules'. This really meant that M. had unreflectingly 'swallowed' the watchwords, or cant phrases of his revolutionary friends; but Carlyle mistranslated *humé* by 'swallowed up, made away with', and frequently alludes to the passage as thus misinterpreted. Carlyle's use of *formula*, however, though suggested by a mistake, is in itself a very natural development from the ordinary sense.

1837 CARLYLE *Fr. Rev.* III. II. i. (1872) 58 Man lives not except with formulas; with customs, ways of doing and living. **1861** KINGSLEY *Lett.* (1878) II. 132 Men who try to speak what they believe, are naked men fighting men quilted sevenfold in formulae. **1871** EARLE *Philol. Eng. Tongue* §649 The man of formulas often directs, and sometimes practically determines the action of his superior. **1874** H. R. REYNOLDS *John Bapt.* IV. iv. 252 They bound the religious life of their disciples with ever stiffening formulæ which left no room for the free play of the conscience.

c. A form of words serving to reconcile different aims, opinions, or points of view.

1905 ASQUITH in *Westm. Gaz.* 9 Oct. 2/3 The recovery of freedom of negotiation, the reloading of the big revolver, the summoning of an open conference, and all the other temporising formulæ of the Balfourian school. **1928** GALSWORTHY *Swan Song* I. i. 5 We shall sit and glower at each other, and use the word 'formula' at stated intervals. **1940** WODEHOUSE *Quick Service* i. 18 It was plain that this girl and he were poles apart and could never hope to find a formula. **1971** A. BULLOCK *20th Cent.* 51/1 At the Yalta Conference (February 1945) verbal formulae were found to disguise growing differences between the Russians and the Anglo-Americans.

d. *Literary Criticism.* In various technical and semi-technical uses (see quots.).

1888 A. S. COOK *Judith* p. lii, Rime and various forms of assonance are occasionally employed by Old English poets, sometimes for the purpose of uniting more closely the two halves of the same line,..rarely in formulas or compounds within the same hemistich. **1903** L. F. ANDERSON *Anglo-Saxon Scop* 39 Grein gives four examples of the occurrence of the formula ['*singan and secgan*'] in Anglo-Saxon. **1921** B. TARKINGTON *Let.* 26 Mar. (1959) 49 The formulas that have prevailed are now all familiar to the audience. **1932** M. PARRY in *Harvard Stud. Class. Philol.* XLIII. 8 Each idea to be expressed in the poetry has its formula for each metrical need. **1934** H. J. ROSE *Handbk. Gk. Lit.* ii. 31 There are embedded in it [*sc.* the style of Homer] many formulae, epithets and turns of expression which strongly indicate.. the existence of an age of balladry before the date of the epics. **1935** A. C. BARTLETT *Larger Rhet. Patterns Anglo-Saxon Poetry* 91 Although not every Anglo-Saxon poem has a formal introductory passage, there is a type of opening sentence which occurs so often as to allow its being called a formula. **1953** *Speculum* XXVIII. 446 The unlettered singer ordinarily composing rapidly and extempore before a live audience, must and does call upon ready-made language, upon a vast reservoir of formulas filling just measures of verse. **1958** T. B. L. WEBSTER *From Mycenae to Homer* iii. 89 Homer preserves much of this manner [*sc.* of second-millennium poetry] in his noun-epithet formulae, typical scenes, formulae for opening and closing of speeches, refrain lines, etc. **1965** M. HODGART *Faber Bk. Ballads* 14 A formula is a theme expressed in identical or almost identical words and metre. **1967** C. L. WRENN *Study of O.E. Lit.* iii. 47 *Andreas*, a heroic hagiographical poem of the early ninth century, begins with exactly the same exordial formula..as does *Beowulf*. **1971** *English Studies* LII. 350, I..fail to see why syntactic, idiomatic and even single semantic units must be called 'formulas' because they occur in OE poetry.

2. A prescription or detailed statement of ingredients; a recipe.

1706 PHILLIPS (ed. Kersey), *Formula*..a Physician's Prescription or Bill appointing Medicines to be prepared by an Apothecary. **1792** W. YONGE in Beddoes *Calculus* (1793) 34, I am very glad to hear of your intention to publish your formula. **1801** *Med. Jrnl.* V. 546 My formula has been, the tincture joined with the dec. lin. so as to administer from fifteen to twenty or thirty drops to children..twice or thrice within the twenty-four hours. **1830** M. DONOVAN *Dom. Econ.* I. 293 White Currant Wine May be made according to the same formula.

3. a. *Math.* A rule or principle expressed in algebraic symbols.

1796 KIRWAN *Elem. Min.* (ed. 2) I. Pref. 6 An algebraic formula. **1836** EMERSON *Nature, Idealism* Wks. (Bohn) II. 163 In physics..the memory..carries centuries of observation in a single formula. **1850** DAUBENY *Atomic Theory* v. (ed. 2) 156 A general formula for calculating the specific heat of each class of compounds. **1864** BOWEN *Logic* i. 25 The algebraist easily recalls to mind a few brief formulas.

b. *Chem.* An expression of the constituents of a compound by means of symbols and figures.

1846 G. E. DAY tr. *Simon's Anim. Chem.* II. 480 If..the formulæ for the morbid deposits are calculated in relation to C_{48}, their connexion with the formula for protein will be more obvious to the eye. **1853** W. GREGORY *Inorg. Chem.* (ed. 3) 266 So that MR is the general formula for a mono-basic salt. **1881** WILLIAMSON in *Nature* No. 618. 414 Thus chloro-carbonic acid was represented as a compound of carbonic acid with carbonic chloride, and..the formula was made to contain the formulæ of those bodies.

c. In general scientific use, a group of symbols and figures containing a condensed tabulation of certain facts. ***dental formula***: see DENTAL. Hence sometimes used for the set of facts that might be expressed by a formula.

1855 BAIN *Senses & Int.* II. iv. §9 Each species of animal has its particular formula of ordering the legs in walking.

4. *Motor Racing.* The class or specification of a racing car, usu. expressed in terms of engine capacity. Also *attrib.*

1927 *Autocar* 20 May 850/2 Half an hour later we knew for certain that we had won the race on formula. **1939** *Motor Sport* June 181/1 Last year..Indianapolis was run under the Grand Prix formula laid down by the A.I.A.C.R., specifying engine limits of 3-litres supercharged and 4½-litres unsupercharged. **1958** *Times* 31 Oct. 15/4 There is little doubt that the new Grand Prix formula recommended by the C.S.I. will be accepted by the F.I.A. at their next meeting. **1965** *Listener* 3 June 841/1 This was the weekend of the Monaco Grand Prix, when the faded Edwardian *pensions* seemed stunned and shaken by the noise of Formula One racing engines.

formulable (ˈfɔːmjʊlab(ə)l), *a.* [f. FORMUL(ATE + -ABLE.] That may or can be formulated; capable of formulation.

1891 W. JAMES *Let.* 21 Sept. in R. B. Perry *Tht. & Char. of W. J.* (1935) II. 174 The way in which you squeeze the last drops of formulable truth out of the facts is admirable. **1902** M. H. LIDDELL *Introd. Sci. Study Eng. Poetry* p. vii, Certain fundamental laws as definitive and formulable in the one case as in the others. **1934** T. S. ELIOT *Eliz. Ess.* 151 If we may use the word 'purpose' for something more profound than any formulable purpose can be. **1939** *Mind* XLVIII. 202 The class *k* of non-analytic declarative sentences formulable in a given language.

formulaic (fɔːmjʊˈleɪɪk), *a.* [f. FORMULA + -IC.] Of the nature of a formula.

formulaic equation, an identical equation.

1882 CASSELL, *Formulaic equations.* **1892** AGNES M. CLERKE *Fam. Stud. Homer* i. 28 Formulaic and other expressions common to both. **1933** M. PARRY in *Trans. Amer. Philol. Assoc.* LXIV. 179 (*title*) Whole formulaic verses in Greek and South-slavic heroic song. **1952** C. M. BOWRA *Heroic Poetry* vi. 222 Not all heroic poetry shows these two kinds of formulaic elements on the same scale. **1953** *Speculum* XXVIII. 446 Parry, aided by Lord, demonstrated that the characteristic feature of all orally composed poetry is its totally formulaic character. **1963** R. QUIRK in Brown & Foote *Early Eng. & Norse Studies* 171 While formulaic utterances and habitual collocations are the necessary starting point in the study of the early alliterative poetry, they are *only* a starting point. **1967** C. L. WRENN *Study of O.E. Lit.* iii. 51 *Word-hord onlēac* is a formulaic phrase from oral tradition. **1971** *New Statesman* 16 Apr. 529/2 There is something in the Homeric poems that carries them far beyond the standards of the oral, formulaic poetry of the Southern Slavs.

Hence **ˌformuˈlaically** *adv.*

1957 *Archivum Linguisticum* IX. II. 96 *Cena* (with which *yantar* was paired off formulaically). **1963** J. LYONS *Structural Semantics* vi. 111 This convention..makes for easier reading of syntactic equivalences, formulaically expressed. **1966** S. B. GREENFIELD in E. G. Stanley *Continuations & Beginnings* 153 The first-person speaker recounts graphically (however formulaically) his tribulations as an exile upon the sea.

formular (ˈfɔːmjʊlə(r)), *a.* and *sb.* [ad. L. type **formulār-is*, f. FORMULA. As sb., a. F. *formulaire.* See -AR[1], [2].] **A.** *adj.*

1. Formal, correct or regular in form.

1773 JOHNSON in *Boswell* 29 Apr., A speech on the stage, let it flatter ever so extravagantly, is formular. It has always been formular to flatter Kings and Queens.

2. Pertaining to formulæ; formulary.

1880 MUIRHEAD *Gaius* III. §180 *note*, Under the formular system in use in the classical period.

B. *sb.* A prescribed or set form, formulary; hence, a model, type. ? *Obs.*

1563 ABP. PARKER *Corresp.* (1853) 183, I had of mine own head moved my lord of London to bethink himself of some formular of common prayer. **1578** SIR H. SYDNEY in *Lett. & Mem. State* (1746) I. 246 He ys a rare Ornament to thys Age, the very Formular, that all well dysposed young Gentylmen of ouer Court, do form allsoe thear Maners and Lyfe by. **1603** FLORIO *Montaigne* III. ix. (1632) 564 Before I had ever seene any, I would have beene glad to have had but a paterne or formular of one. *a* **1734** NORTH *Exam.* III. vi. §20 (1740) 437 The Liturgy must be deprived of all the primitive Formulars.

formularism (ˈfɔːmjʊləˌrɪz(ə)m). [f. FORMULAR(Y + -ISM.] Rigid adherence to or dependence on formularies. So **ˈformularist**.

1896 HARDY *Jude* II. i. 95 The well-known three, the enthusiast, the poet, and the formularist. **1927** *Observer* 30 Oct. 7 The cut-and-dried formularism of the Socialist theory.

ˌformulaˈristic, *a.* [f. FORMULAR *a.* and *sb.* + -IST + -IC.] Pertaining to or exhibiting formularization.

1864 WEBSTER (citing EMERSON).

formularization (ˌfɔːmjʊləraɪˈzeɪʃən). [f. next + -ATION.] The action of formularizing; also, a formularized statement.

1881 B. W. RICHARDSON in *Gentl. Mag.* CCL. 159 The formularisation of rules. **1886** MUIRHEAD in *Encycl. Brit.* XX. 677/2 The great majority of these so-called enactments were probably nothing more than formularizations as of customary law.

formularize (ˈfɔːmjʊləraɪz), *v.* [f. FORMULAR *a.* + -IZE.] *trans.* To express in a formula or formal statement; to formulate.

1852 *Fraser's Mag.* XLV. 90 Every process is formularized in the most scientific language. **1862** GOULBURN *Educ. World* in *Replies to Ess. & Rev.* 37 Her doctrines were evolved..by formularizing the thoughts embodied in the record of the Church of the Apostles. **1876** BARTHOLOW *Mat. Med.* (1879) 247 The comparative merits of tannic and gallic acids may be formularized as follows: for local effects tannic acid, for systemic effects gallic acid is to be preferred.

Hence **ˈformularizing** *vbl. sb.*

1891 *Athenæum* 15 Aug. 222/3 A clumsy formularizing in general of Talleyrand's sharpest and most famous *mot.*

formulary (ˈfɔːmjʊlərɪ), *sb.* and *a.* [ad. F. *formulaire* sb. = collection of formulæ, ad. L. **formulārium*, neut. sing. of *formulārius* (recorded in sense 'lawyer skilled in formulæ'): see FORMULA, FORMULAR, and -ARY.]

A. *sb.* A collection or system of formulas; a statement drawn up in formulas; a document containing the set form or forms according to which something is to be done (*esp.* one that contains prescribed forms of religious belief or ritual).

1541 R. COPLAND (*title*) Questyonary of Cyrurgyens, with the formulary of lytell Guydo in Cyrurgie. *a* **1626** BACON *On Libel* in 1592 Wks. 1861 VIII. 204 In the practice of all law, the formularies have been few, and certain, and not varied according to every particular case. *c* **1645** HOWELL *Lett.* I. xxxii. (1655) 274, I beleeve evry one hath som mode and modell or formulary of his own, specially for his private cubicular devotions. **1723** WATERLAND *Ath. Creed* iv. Wks. IV. 223 They received this Creed..as an orthodox formulary, and an approved rule of faith. *a* **1734** NORTH *Life Guildford* (1742) 260 A committee of council to settle the formulary of the coronation. **1782** BURNEY *Hist. Mus.* (1789) II. ii. 121 It contains..a Formulary of the Ecclesiastical tones. **1827** BENTHAM *Ration. Evid.* Wks. 1843 VI. 441 Take up a history of an old French lawsuit..it is the same dull formulary in every case. **1877** J. D. CHAMBERS *Div. Worship* 110 The Anglican Formularies, however, do not recognize Hymns at all.

b. ? A formula.

1782 WARTON *Enq. Poems Rowley* 23 These poems abound with modern words, and modern formularies of expression. **1874** J. SULLY *Sensation & Intuition* 112 A boundless faith in the primitive formulary 'I can'.

B. *adj.* Of the nature of a formula or prescribed form; of or relating to formulas.

1728 MORGAN *Algiers* II. iv. 293 Visiting his Tomb, they say a Fedha, or formulary sort of Prayer for Success. **1766** JOHNSON in *Boswell* Feb., The formulary and statutory part of law. **1775** —— *Let. to Mrs. Thrale* 11 June, Part of it [an epitaph], which tells the birth and marriage, is formulary, and can be expressed only one way. **1862** HELPS *Organiz. Daily Life* 120 All that is merely formulary, and that depends solely upon rules. **1875** POSTE *Gaius* III. Comm. (ed. 2) 445 Under the formulary system the term was still employed.

b. Of a person: Closely adhering to formulas.

1837 CARLYLE *Fr. Rev.* III. III. ii. 155 There is..in the incorruptible Seagreen himself, though otherwise so lean and formulary, a heartfelt knowledge of this latter fact.

formulatable (ˌfɔːmjʊˈleɪtəb(ə)l), *a.* [f. FORMULAT(E *v.* + -ABLE.] = FORMULABLE *a.*

1895 H. JAMES *Notebk.* 22 Dec. (1947) 239 Everything is formulated and formulatable to the child. **1923** *Spectator* 29 Sept. 426/1 Reduction to a small number of formulatable principles. **1946** C. I. LEWIS *Analysis of Knowledge* II. viii. 204 Only by confining statements to an intent thus formulatable in expressive terms can anything be proved conclusively by single experiences.

formulate (ˈfɔːmjʊleɪt), *v.* [f. FORMULA + -ATE[3]. Cf. F. *formuler.*] *trans.* To reduce to a formula; to express in (or as in) a formula; to set forth in a definite and systematic statement.

1860 EARL CARNARVON *Recoll. Druses Lebanon* v. 49 The Druse doctrines were..rapidly formulated into a system. **1862** H. SPENCER *First Princ.* I. iv. §26 (1875) 88 Besides that definite consciousness of which Logic formulates the laws, there is also an indefinite consciousness which cannot be formulated. **1880** KINGLAKE *Crimea* VI. ix. 225 Lord Raglan did not unconsciously formulate for himself any settled design. **1883** *Q. Rev.* CLVI. 326 The Heads of Houses..entrusted the Provost..with the responsibility of formulating the document. **1893** A. CONAN DOYLE *Mem. S. Holmes* 12, I listened..to the dialogue of the two detectives. Gregory was formulating his theory. **1906** E. PHILLPOTTS *Portreeve* I. x, She..stood for the moment powerless to formulate a clear pathway through this thicket of ideas. **1907** *Smart Set* Mar. 134 He resolved to send her some volumes of Ruskin and to formulate a graduated course of reading. **1910** E. M. ALBANESI *For Love of Anne Lambart* 91 Anne began to put into movement the scheme that had formulated itself in her mind. **1924** A. D. SEDGWICK *Little French Girl* I. vii. 69 It was strange to her, as she spoke, to feel how deeply she knew all this about Giles, though she had never before formulated it to herself.

Hence **ˈformulator**; **ˈformulated**, **ˈformulating** *ppl. adjs.*

1860 MARSH *Eng. Lang.* 235 Formulated doctrine. **1876** C. M. DAVIES *Unorth. Lond.* 99 An established, formulated, orthodox spiritism. **1895** *Athenæum* 24 Aug. 253/1 The formulating effects of his [Laud's] churchmanship. **1919** K. PEARSON in C. Goring *Eng. Convict* 12 The use by the formulator of a thoroughly unscientific method does not justify us in rejecting his hypothesis. **1966** *New Statesman* 13 May 682/1 The three officials..should not be regarded..simply as civil servants. Stan Morris..is more a formulator of policy.

formulation (fɔːmjʊˈleɪʃən). [f. prec.: see -ATION.] **a.** The action of the vb. FORMULATE.

1876 DOUSE *Grimm's L.* §1. 1 The concise formulation of which it [Grimm's Law] is susceptible. **1885** CLODD *Myths & Dr.* I. iv. 67 Facts which led..to the formulation of the solar theory.

b. A material or mixture prepared according to a particular formula.

1958 *New Scientist* 19 June 208/1 Different formulations of rubber vary..in their performance as cushioning materials. **1959** *Ibid.* 2 Apr. 744/2 The preparation of the liquid mix from which plastic tools are moulded is said to be simplified by a new series of pre-measured formulations. **1964** *Times Rev. Industry* Feb. 7/1 Between 40 and 50 new drugs and formulations are marketed every year and each one will involve the consideration of masses of data.

formulatory (ˈfɔːmjʊləˌtərɪ), *a. rare.* [f. as prec. + -ORY.] Relating to formulation.

1887 *Westm. Rev.* CXXVIII. 841 Put in this bald formulatory fashion, the difference between the two may seem unimportant.

† **ˈformule**, *sb. Obs.* [a. F. *formule*, ad. L. *formula*: see FORMULA.]

1. = FORMULA.

1677 GALE *Crt. Gentiles* IV. 164 A wel-governed Republic is bounded by the formule of certain Laws. **1773** *Gentl. Mag.* XLIII. 170 The first trial of this formule was on the observations from whence he had deduced it, of which he gives a table for each station.

2. ? A little form or shape.

1829 *Young Lady's Bk.* 469 A series of frames, or formules, is obtained..The principal formule is to be placed on a piece of London drawing-board.

formule (ˈfɔːmjuːl), *v. rare.* [ad. F. *formuler*, f. *formule* FORMULA.] = FORMULATE.

1852 R. KNOX *Gt. Artists & Anat.* 13 Could we formule the doctrine as simply as [etc.]. *Ibid.* 103 The doctrine..cannot be formuled in so clear a manner.

formulism (ˈfɔːmjʊlɪz(ə)m). [f. FORMUL-A + -ISM. Cf. next.] Adherence to or dependence upon formulas; also, a system of formulas.

1840 CARLYLE *Heroes* (1858) 312 Triviality, Formulism and Commonplace were come for ever. **1851** RUSKIN *Stones Ven.* II. viii. §51 The..love of systematizing, which gradually degenerated into every species of contemptible formulism. **1881** *Encycl. Brit.* XII. 603/1 The whole of this complex theory is ruled by a mathematical formulism of triad, hebdomad, etc.

formulist (ˈfɔːmjʊlɪst). [ad. F. *formuliste*: see -IST.] One fond of formulas.

1852 R. KNOX *Gt. Artists & Anat.* 15 The mere formulist (Cuvier also was a formulist in a sense).

formulistic (fɔːmjʊˈlɪstɪk), *a.* [f. prec. + -IC.] Displaying fondness for formulas.

1873 MORLEY *Rousseau* II. xvi. 310 Its prudential didactics, its formulistic Sociality. [Cf. **1837** CARLYLE *Fr. Rev.* III. IV. vi. (1871) 162 The uncalculating Spirit of Jacobinism, and Sansculottic sansformulistic Frenzy!]

formulization (ˌfɔːmjʊlaɪˈzeɪʃən). [f. next + -ATION.] The action of the vb. FORMULIZE.

1851 RUSKIN *Stones Ven.* III. ii. §86 The curious tendency to formulization and system which, under the name of philosophy, encumbered the minds of the Renaissance schoolmen. **1873** *Contemp. Rev.* XXI. 774 Every formulization of truth is not absolute but relative.

formulize (ˈfɔːmjʊlaɪz), *v.* [f. FORMULA + -IZE.] *trans.* To reduce to or express in a formula; to construct a formula for.

1851 WESTCOTT *Introd. Study Gosp.* i. (1875) 49 The labours of Priests and Scribes in after time formulized what the Prophets had taught. **1859** MASSON *Brit. Novelists* iv. 255 The ideas of Liberty, Equality, and Fraternity which that Revolution had promulgated and formulized. **1882** T. MOZLEY *Remin. Oriel* II. cv. 228 They have formulized their religion into these two monosyllables.

Hence **ˈformulized** *ppl. a.* Also **ˈformulizer**, one who formulizes.

1864 KINGSLEY *Rom. & Teut.* x. 293 The formulizers of that law were none other than the celibate Roman clergy. **1865** PUSEY *Truth Eng. Ch.* 94 That vast formulized theory.

formy (ˈfɔːmɪ), *a.* [ad. F. *formé*: see FORMÉ.]

1. *Her.* Of a cross: = PATTÉE.

1562 LEIGH *Armorie* 56 b, He beareth Azure, a crosse formye vecked Argent. *Ibid.* 57 b, A Crosse formie Sable. **1889** ELVIN *Dict. Her.*, *Formy*, a cross pattée.

†**2.** Of the fæces: = FIGURATE A. 2 a. *Obs.*

1576 TURBERV. *Venerie* 65 From midde July untill the ende of August they make theyr fewmishing altogether formie.

formyl (ˈfɔːmɪl). *Chem.* [f. FORM- + -YL.] The hypothetical radical (CHO) of formic acid.

1879 *Cassell's Techn. Educ.* IV. 118/2 Formyle is the hypothetical radical of formic acid, first discovered in the red ant.

formylate (ˈfɔːmɪleɪt), *v. Chem.* [f. FORMYL + -ATE[3].] To introduce one or more formyl groups into (a compound or molecule). So **ˈformylated, -ing** *ppl. adjs.*; also **ˈformylatable** *a.*

1931 *Jrnl. Amer. Chem. Soc.* LIII. 3491 The scheme of formylating by distilling a mixture of toluene, formic acid and methionine. **1964** *Jrnl. Molec. Biol.* VIII. 836 Artificially formylated [^{35}S]methionyl-RNA was prepared. **1965** *Ibid.* XIV. 64 The methionyl-sRNA synthetase and the formylating enzyme were separated by precipitation. *Ibid.* 65 Methionine was formylated after esterification to sRNA. **1970** *Nature* 29 Aug. 918 Reticulocyte initiation factors bind a formylatable methionine tRNA but not a non-formylatable tRNA.

formylation (fɔːmɪˈleɪʃən). *Chem.* [f. as prec. + -ATION.] The introduction of one or more formyl groups into a compound or molecule by means of a chemical reaction.

1930 *Jrnl. Biol. Chem.* LXXXVI. 695 (*heading*) The formylation of amino acids. **1962** *Lancet* 29 Dec. 1381/1 The introduction of the no. 2 carbon to form the purine ring proceeds via formylation of A.I.C.A.R. to the 4-formamido compound. **1964** *Jrnl. Molec. Biol.* VIII. 835 The formylation of the free α-amino group of methionine..takes place.

fornace, obs. form of FURNACE.

fornacic (fɔːˈnæsɪk), *a. rare*[−1]. [f. L. *fornāc-, fornax* furnace + -IC.] Pertaining to a furnace.

1807 HEADRICK *View Min. Arran* 216 The smelting of iron, and other fornacic uses.

fornage: see FURNAGE.

fornale, *v. Sc.* Also 9 forenail. [Of obscure origin; Jam. suggests the sense 'to NAIL or fasten up beforehand'.] *trans.* To alienate the income of (an estate) in advance; in mod. use 'to spend (money) before it is gained' (Jam.).

1478 *Acta Dom. Conc.* (1839) 13 He sall nouther sell..na fornale, langar na sevin ȝeris, nane of his landis.

†**forne**, *adv.*, *a.*, and *prep. Obs.* Forms: 1 foran, forn(e, 3 foren, 3–5 forn, *Orm.* forrn, 4–7 forne. [OE. *foran* (Northumb. *fora*), *forne* adv. = OS. *foran, forana*, OHG. *forna* (MHG., mod.Ger. *vorne, vorn*); f. root of FOR, FORE *adv.*

The adj. appears to be an English development from the adv., and not an adoption of the ON. *forn* ancient.]

A. *adv.*

1. With respect to place. **a.** Of position: In front, before the eyes; in or on the front, opp. to *behind*. **b.** Of motion: Forwards, to the front.

a. *a* **1000** *Riddles* liv. 8 (Gr.) Wonnum hyrstum Foran ȝefrætwed. *c* **1380** *Sir Ferumb.* 4361 Þat host abod behynde & forn. *a* **1400–50** *Alexander* 3925 Þis breme best bare.. Before forne in þe fronte thre fell tyndis.

b. *c* **1000** *Daniel* 557 (Gr.) Þæt þæt treow sceolde telgum besnæded foran afeallan. *c* **1205** LAY. 26899 And ten þusend hehte aneouste foren wenden. **1430** LYDG. *Chron. Troy* III. xxii, He rode forne Brenning full hote.

2. With respect to time: **a.** Formerly; in former time. **b.** Thenceforward, in future.

13.. *Gaw. & Gr. Knt.* 2422 Þes wer forne þe freest þat folȝeð alle þe sele. **14..** *Trentalle S. Gregorii* in *Tundale's Vis.* (1843) 80 For pynes thar hym dred non forne Of purgatory no of helle.

3. Prefixed to prepositions, and occas. to another adverb: **a.** Prefixed to *again, against*, adv. and prep.: Right in front. **b.** *forne an, at*: before, in front of. **c.** *forne in*: straight before. **d.** *forne to*: before, both of place and time. **e.** *forne on*: right forward, seriatim.

c **1000** *Ags. Gosp.* Matt. xxi. 2 Farað on þæt castel þæt foran [*c* **1160** *Hatton* foren] onȝen eow ys. *c* **1200** ORMIN 553 Þeȝȝ tokenn eft fornnon To serrfenn wukemalumm. *c* **1205** LAY. 20120 Up bræid Arður his sceld foren to his breosten. *Ibid.* 23968 His hereburne gon to falsie, foren an his hafde. *Ibid.* 24032 Arður beh to þan ȝæte, forn at þere burȝe. *Ibid.* 29269 And foren to þære nihte fur þer on brohte. **1388** WYCLIF *Mark* xv. 39 The centurien that stood forn aȝens siȝ, that [etc.]. *c* **1400** *Destr. Troy* 7759 There met hym þis Mawhown.. Euyn forne in his face.

B. *adj.* **a.** Of place: Anterior, front. **b.** Of time: Former.

c **1440** *Promp. Parv.* 172/2 Forne parte of a schyppe, or forschyppe. **1485** CAXTON *Trevisa's Higden* II. i. 71 a, From the begynnyng of his forne dedes. **1565** JEWEL *Def. Apol.* (1611) 340 It was true in Old forne yeeres, about twelue hundred yeeres agoe.

C. *prep.*

a. Of motion: Before, in front of, in advance of.

O.E. Chron. an. 894, Þa for rad sio fierd hie foran. *c* **1000** [see FORE-RUN]. *c* **1175** *Lamb. Hom.* 51 Leofe moder swim þu foren me. *c* **1250** *Gen. & Ex.* 3541 Mac us godes foren us to gon. *c* **1380** *Sir Ferumb.* 3649 Þe kyng hem passede withinne a wyle, Forn hem þe mountance of two myle.

b. Of position: Before, before the face of, in sight of. Hence of fighting: In behalf of.

c **1250** *Gen. & Ex.* 3866 God [bad]..foren hem smiten on ðe ston. **13..** *Guy Warw.* (A.) 200 Gij stode forn him in þat flett. *c* **1440** *Partonope* 2172 To see hym dye me forn. *a* **1450** *Le Morte Arth.* 3211 Agaynste her fone I faught hem forne. **1602** *2nd Pt. Return fr. Parnass.* Prol. 70 Stories of love, where forne the wondring bench, The lisping gallant might inioy his wench.

c. Of time: Before.

a **1300** *Cursor M.* 22429 (Gött.) Forn domes-dai.

d. Of cause: On account of.

c **1440** *Bone Flor.* 67 To mykyll bale was sche borne, And many a man slayn hur forne.

D. *Comb.*, as **forn-cast** *v.* = FORECAST *v.*, to premeditate; **forn-father** = FOREFATHER; **forn-goer**, a predecessor; **forn-had** *ppl. a.*, formerly possessed; **forn-said** *ppl. a.* = FORESAID *ppl. a.*

c **1374** CHAUCER *Troylus* III. 472 (521) He..Hadde every thing that her-to might avayle *Forn-cast. *c* **1386** —— *Pars. T.* ¶ 374 Malice ymagined, avysed, and forncast. *c* **1400** *Test. Love* I. Chaucer's Wks. (1561) 290 b, Enuie, forne-caste and ymagined. *c* **1340** *Cursor M.* 9768 (Fairf.) Þe gilt Adam our *forn-fadir spylt. **1450–1530** *Myrr. our Ladye* 26 The worshyp of god ys songe..after the maner of oure forne-fathers. **1483** CAXTON *Gold. Leg.* 258/1 He hath lerned of his *forn goers whiche dyd that ought not to be forgoten. **1382** WYCLIF *Judges* xvi. 28 Lord..ȝeeld to me nowe the *fornhad [*pristinam*] strength. **1509** *Bury Wills* (Camden) 109 My lord ye abbot off ye monastery in Bury *ffornseyd.

†**fornean**, *adv. Obs.* [f. FOR *prep.* + *néan* wk. dat. neut. of *néah* NIGH.] Nearly, almost.

c **1000** *Ags. Ps.* lxxii[i]. 1 Me for nean syndon losode nu þa ealle on foldan fota gangas. *a* **1175** *Cott. Hom.* 227 For nean en ende þissere wurold.

‖**forˈnello.** *Mil. Obs.*[−1] [a. It. *fornello*, dim. of *forno* (lit. 'oven'):—L. *furnus* oven.] A cavity in which powder is placed for blasting.

1687 B. RANDOLPH *Archipelago* 70 How many mines, and fornellos were blown up.

fornent (fɔːˈnɛnt), **fornenst** (fɔːˈnɛnst), *adv.* and *prep. Sc.* and *north.* Forms: 6 foir-, for-, fore-anempst, -ane(i)nst, -(a)nent(s, -nence, -nens(t, -nentis, 9 foore-, for(e)-(a)nen(s)t, 6– fornent. [f. FORE *adv.* + ANENT.]

1. Right opposite to, over against; facing.

1524 *St. Papers Hen. VIII*, VI. 236 For defence of his Borders foranempst Scotland. **1582–8** *Hist. James VI*, (1804) 204 In the straitt passage foirnent the goldsmyths shopp. **1649** BP. GUTHRIE *Mem.* (1702) 64 The Earl of Athol ..Encamp'd fornent him. **1807** J. STAGG *Poems* 61 Reeght for nenst them up they gat. **1864** *Glasgow Herald* 11 June, My house is right fornent the tank.

†**2. a.** (Ready) against. **b.** With regard to.

1533 BELLENDEN *Livy* (1822) 15 Reddy fornence all aventuris that micht occur. **1709** *Rob. III's Answ.* in *Watson's Collect.* II. p. iv, But we will do you understand What we declare fornent Scotland.

†**3.** quasi-*adv.* Opposite. *Obs.*

1548 THOMAS *Ital. Gram. & Dict.* (1567), *Dirimpetto*, foranenst. **1596** DALRYMPLE tr. *Leslie's Hist. Scot.* (1888) I. 35 The bray foranent vpon Laudian syde.

forneys, obs. form of FURNACE.

fornical (ˈfɔːnɪkəl), *a.* [f. L. *fornic-em* arch + -AL[1].] 'Pertaining to the fornix' (*Cent. Dict.*).

†**fornicarer.** *Obs. rare*[−1]. [? f. L. *fornicār-ius* + -ER[1].] A fornicator.

c **1400** *Apol. Loll.* 37 Seynt Poule..forbediþ us to tak meit or comyn wiþ þeis..fornicarers.

†**forniˈcarious**, *a. Obs. rare*[−1]. [f. as next + -OUS.] Of or pertaining to fornication.

1688 J. NORRIS *Theory Love* II. ii. 105 Fornicarious mixture..must of necessity be a sin.

†**ˈfornicary**, *sb.* and *a. Obs.* Also 3 fornic-, fornycarie, 5 fornycary. [ad. L. *fornicāri-us* masc., *fornicāria* fem., f. *fornic-*: see next and -ARY. Cf. OF. *fornicaire.*] **A.** *sb.* A fornicator.

1382 WYCLIF *Isa.* lvii. 3 Sonus..of a fornycarie [Vulg. *fornicariæ*]. **1496** *Dives & Paup.* (W. de W.) VI. viii. 243/1 God shall deme fornycaryes, & them that do auoutrye.

B. *adj.* Addicted to fornication, lecherous.

1382 WYCLIF *Ecclus.* xli. 25 Shame ȝee..fro biholdyng of a fornycarie womman. **1387** TREVISA *Higden* (Rolls) VII. 469 He schulde doo riȝt of preostes fornicaries [*de sacerdotibus fornicariis*] and of hire concubynes.

fornicate (ˈfɔːnɪkeɪt), *v.* [f. L. *fornicāt-*, ppl. stem of *fornicārī* of same meaning, f. *fornic-, fornix* brothel, originally arch, vault (see FORNIX).] *intr.* To commit fornication.

1552 HULOET, Fornicaten, or commit fornication or lechery, *fornicor*. **1649** MILTON *Eikon.* xxviii. Wks. (1847) 336/2 These shall hate the great Whore..and yet shall lament the fall of Babylon, where they fornicated with her. **1668** ETHEREDGE *She wou'd if she cou'd* II. ii, We..are resolved to fornicate in private. **1824** LANDOR *Imag. Conv.* I. 155 He hunted and drank and fornicated.

Hence **ˈfornicating** *vbl. sb.* and *ppl. a.*

1620 BP. HALL *Hon. Mar. Clergy* I. viii. 42 The heroicall spirit of Luther..chose rather..to be an honest Husband, than a fornicating Frier. **1625** BP. SAUNDERSON *Twelve Serm.* (1637) 207 Their fornicating both bodily with the daughters, and spiritually with the Idols of Moab.

fornicate (ˈfɔːnɪkət), *a.* [ad. L. *fornicāt-us*, f. *fornix* arch, vault: see -ATE[2].] = FORNICATED; *spec.* in *Bot.*, *Conchol.*, and *Entom.*

1828 WEBSTER, *Fornicate*, arched, vaulted like an oven or furnace. **1829** LOUDON *Encycl. Pl.* 1099 *Fornicate*, arched. **1839** SOWERBY *Man. Conchol.* Gloss., *Fornicate*, arched. **1856–8** W. CLARK *Van der Hoeven's Zool.* I. 326 Four setæ of haustellum, and an upper fornicate.

fornicated (ˈfɔːnɪkeɪtɪd), *ppl. a.* [f. L. *fornicāt-us* (see FORNICATE *a.*) + -ED[1].] Arched, bending over; *esp.* in *Bot.* of a leaf, etc.

1750 G. HUGHES *Barbadoes* 218 The Stylus..is divided at the top into three fornicated branches.

¶ With word-play on FORNICATE *v.*

1641 MILTON *Ch. Govt.* II. iii. (1851) 173 [She] gives up her body to a mercenary whordome under those fornicated arches which she cals Gods house.

fornication[1] (fɔːnɪˈkeɪʃən). [a. OF. *fornication, -acion*, f. late L. *fornicātiōn-em*, n. of action f. *fornicārī*: see FORNICATE and -ATION.] Voluntary sexual intercourse between a man (in restricted use, an unmarried man) and an unmarried woman. In Scripture extended to adultery.

a **1300** *Cursor M.* 27938 Þis sin [lechery] has branches fele ..fornicacion es an. **1303** R. BRUNNE *Handl. Synne* 7352 'Fornycacyoun' [ys], whan two vnweddyde haue mysdoun. *a* **1450** *Knt. de la Tour* (1868) 57 King David..felle into avowtry and fornicacion with her. **1494** FABYAN *Chron.* VII. ccxxiv. 251 Takynge of fynes of preestis for cryme of fornycacion. **1535** COVERDALE *Matt.* v. 32 Whosoeuer putteth awaye his wyfe (except it be for fornicacion). **1603** SHAKS. *Meas. for M.* V. i. 195 Shee..accuses him of Fornication. **1779** JOHNSON 10 Oct. in *Boswell*, Fornication is a crime in a single man. **1874** VAN BUREN *Dis. Genit. Org.* 41 Fornication is always irregular.

b. *fig.*; esp. in Scripture: The forsaking of God for idols; idolatry; also, ***spiritual fornication***.

a **1340** HAMPOLE *Psalter* lxxii. 26 Þou lost all þat dos fornycacioun fra þe. **1691–8** NORRIS *Pract. Disc.* (1711) III. 47 'Tis a kind of Spiritual Fornication..to admit any Creature into a Partnership with him in our Love. **1860** PUSEY *Min. Proph.* 298 All forsaking of God being spiritual fornication.

fornication[2] (fɔːnɪˈkeɪʃən). *Arch.* [ad. L. *fornicātiōn-em*, f. *fornicātus* vaulted, f. *fornix* arch, vault: see -ATION.] An arching or vaulting.

1703 T. N. *City & C. Purchaser* 138 Fornication, In Architecture, is an Arching, or Vaulting. **1810** C. JAMES *Mil. Dict.* (ed. 3) App., *Fornication* is an arching, or vaulting.

fornicator (ˈfɔːnɪkeɪtə(r)). [a. L. *fornicātor*, agent-n. f. *fornicārī*: see FORNICATE.]

1. One who commits fornication.

1377 LANGL. *P. Pl.* B. II. 180 Oure cart shal he drawe, And fecche forth oure vitailes of fornicatores. **1477** EARL RIVERS (Caxton) *Dictes* 11 Kepe you oute of the companyes of.. fornicatours. **1552** ABP. HAMILTON *Catech.* (1884) 10 Fornicatouris and provokaris to the synne of lechorie. *a* **1710** BP. BULL *Serm.* Wks. I. ix. 237 What will become of ..the adulterer, the fornicator..and such like? **1869** SPURGEON *Treas. Dav.* Ps. x. 3 If a man is a fornicator, or a drunkard.

†**2.** *Billiards.* (See quot.) *Obs.*

1674 *Cotton's Compl. Gamester* i. 29 Make your Adversary a Fornicator, that is, having past your self a little way, and the other's Ball being hardly through the Port, you put him back again, and it may be quite out of Pass.

†**ˈfornicaˌtory**, *a. Obs.* [f. prec.: see -ORY.] Of the nature of fornication.

1651 BAXTER *Inf. Bapt.* 88 It was not the unlawfulness as Fornicatory, but as impious directly which they suspected.

fornicatress (ˈfɔːnɪkeɪtrɪs). [f. FORNICATOR + -ESS[1]. Cf. OF. *fornicateresse.*] A woman addicted to or guilty of fornication.

1593 NASHE *Christ's T.* (1613) 160 Those that haue been dayly fornicatresses. **1603** SHAKS. *Meas. for M.* II. ii. 23. **1621** AINSWORTH *Annot. Pentat.* Deut. xxiii. 17 Common whore, fornicatresse.

†**fornicatrice.** *Obs.* [ad. L. *fornicātrīce-m, fornicātrix*: see next. Cf. F. *fornicatrice.*] = prec.

c **1450** *Mirour Saluacion* 912 Inpossible is y[t] this woman be ffornicatrice.

fornicatrix (ˈfɔːnɪˌkeɪtrɪks). Pl. -trixes. [a. L. *fornicātrix*, fem. of *fornicātor.*] = prec.

1586 *Perth Session Rec.* in C. Rogers *Soc. Life Scot.* (1884) II. xii. 244 To shave the heads of fornicators and fornicatrixes. **1655** in Kirkton *Hist. Ch. Scot.* (1817) 171 *note*, One quadrilapse fornicatrix. **1768** *Life & Adv. Sir B. Sapskull* II. 130 What, sir (exclaimed the old fornicatrix).

forniciform (fɔːˈnɪsɪfɔːm), *a. Bot.* [f. L. *fornic-em, fornix* arch, vault + -(I)FORM.]

1860 MAYNE *Expos. Lex.*, *Forniciform*, *Bot.*, resembling an arch or vault; vaulted.

†**forˈnim**, *v. Obs.* Also 4 forneme; *pa. pple.* 3 fornumen, fornomen. [OE. *forniman*, pa. t. *fornam, fornóm*, pa. pple. *fornumen*, f. FOR- *pref.* + *niman* to take.] *trans.* To take away, do away with, destroy; also, to take up, appropriate by encroachment.

Beowulf 1205 (Gr.) Hine Wyrd fornam. *c* **1000** *Saxon Leechd.* I. 118 Wið weartan, ȝenim þas ylcan wyrte..hy beoð sona fornumene. *c* **1250** *Gen. & Ex.* 2228 Min two childre aren me for-numen. *a* **1300** *E.E. Psalter* cviii. [cix.] 23 Als schadw, when heldes, for-nomen I am. *c* **1350** in *Eng. Gilds*

(1870) 359 Euerych tannere..shal, for þe stret þt he fornemeþ, twey shullynges by þe ȝere. *c* **1430** *Compleynt* 56 in Lydg. *Temple Glas* (1891) App. 60 Ȝee..Han me for-nome tunge & speche.

fornix (ˈfɔːnɪks). [a. L. *fornix* arch, vaulted chamber.] Something resembling an arch.

a. *Anat.* esp. an arched formation of the brain.

1681 tr. *Willis' Rem. Med. Wks.* Vocab., *Fornix*, a hollow place in the brain, bending like an arch. **1799** *Med. Jrnl.* II. 329 The fornix..raised at its anterior extremity. **1881** MIVART *Cat* 268 This fornix is made up of two white cords closely approximated anteriorly.

b. *Bot.* (See quots.)

1823 CRABB *Technol. Dict.* s.v. *Arch*, Fornix, a small elongation of the corolla, which commonly covers the stamina. **1862** M. C. COOKE *Man. Bot. Terms*, *Fornix*, arched scales in the orifice of some flowers.

c. *Conchol.* 'The excavated part of a shell, situated under the umbo. It also signifies the upper or convex shell in the Ostrea' (Craig 1848).

†**forˈnumb,** *v. Obs. rare*$^{-1}$. [f. FOR- *pref.*[1] + NUMB *v.*] *intr.* To become numbed.

1571 GOLDING *Calvin on Ps.* li. 9 How much so euer they fornommed, whosoever is touched earnestly wt the feare of God, hee will wishe none other remedy.

for-old. *a.*: see FOR- *pref.*[1] 10.

†**foˈrold,** *v. Obs.* [OE. *forealdian*, f. FOR- *pref.*[1] + *ealdian* to grow old, f. *eald*, OLD *a.* Cf. OHG. *faralten* (mod.Ger. *veralten*).] *intr.* To grow old, wear out with age.

c **900** tr. *Bæda's Hist.* III. iv. [vi.] (1890) 166 Ne forealdiȝe þeos hond æfre. *a* **1300** *Holy Rood* 74 (Ashm.) in *Leg. Rood* (1871) 24 It ne bar noþer lef ne rynde as it uorolded [*MS. Vernon* for-oldet] were. *c* **1305** *Edmund Conf.* 175 in *E.E.P.* (1862) 75 He hem forbrende stilleliche: for hi forolþed [*S. Eng. Legendary, S. Edmund* 175: for-olde] were.

foroughe, obs. form of FURROW.

†**foˈrout, foˈrouten,** *prep. Obs.* Forms: 1 foruton, 4 foroutyn. -owtyn, -outen, forout(e, 4–5 forowt, (4 foreowt), 5–6 foroutin, 6 forowtin, 7 foroutten. [OE. *forúton*, *-útan*, f. FOR *prep.* + *úton*, *-an*, f. *út* OUT.]

1. a. Except. OE. only. **b.** Besides.

O.E. Chron. an. 1122, Se fir..for bearnde ealle þe minstre for uton feawe bec. **1375** BARBOUR *Bruce* XI. 110 Fifty thousand of archerys He had, forouten the hoblerys. *c* **1425** WYNTOUN *Cron.* VIII. xlii. 126 He had..Foure scor off hardy armyd men, For-owte archeris.

2. Without.

c **1350** *Will. Palerne* 2681 To late hire lengþe fulle a fourteniȝt for-oute alle greues of sauȝtes to þe cite. *c* **1425** WYNTOUN *Cron.* VIII. xxxvii. 66 He for-owt gruchyng Delyveryt hym of coursis thre. **1513** DOUGLAS *Æneis* III. x. 59 Forowtin faill. **1609** SKENE *Reg. Maj.* 111 Quhere dome is given foroutten Judge sitand, that is na dome of law.

†**foˈrouth,** *adv.* and *prep. Sc. Obs.* Also 4 forrouth, 4–5 forow(e)th. [app. a var. of FORWITH; cf. Sc. (Barbour) *owtouth* = *out with*. Perhaps FORROW is a shortened form of this.]

A. *adv.* **a.** Of position: In front. **b.** Of direction: Forward. **c.** Of time: Before, beforehand.

1375 BARBOUR *Bruce* VI. 202 Ta Fifty weill Armyt, and forouth ga. *Ibid.* XIV. 242 The Erll thomas wes forrouth ay. *Ibid.* XVI. 504 As ȝe forrouth herd me tell.

B. *prep.* Of time or place: Before.

1375 BARBOUR *Bruce* I. 163, I sall Hald It..as myn eldris forouch [*sic MS.*: ? *read* forouth] me. *Ibid.* XI. 341 Evyn forrouth hym suld ga The vaward. *c* **1375** *Sc. Troy-bk.* II. 722 The Gregeois swyth Aryvede..A litill foroweth þe evennynge. **1425** WYNTOUN *Cron.* VIII. xxxviii. 134 Ðai gaddryd þame all..And schupe þame forowth þame to be.

forow, obs. f. FURROW; var. FORROW, *Obs. Sc.*

forpained, -pampered: see FOR- *pref.*[1] 6.

†**forˈpass,** *v. Obs.* Also **forepass.** [ad. OF. *for-*, *fourpasser*, f. *fors*, FOR- *pref.*[3] + *passer* to PASS; in Spenser's quasi-archaic use the prefix seems to be taken as FORE-.]

1. *trans.* To go beyond, surpass, excel. [So in OF.; in quot. 1374 Skeat takes *for* as a conj.]

c **1374** CHAUCER *Troylus* I. 101 In al Troyes citee Nas noon so fair, for passing every wight, So aungellyk was hir natyf beautee. **153.** STARKEY *Let. to Cromwell* in *England* p. lxxii, So my wytt and capacyte hit for-passyth. **1550** COVERDALE *Spir. Perle* xxx. 83 b, Lyke as the spyryte forepasseth and ouercommyth the fleshe in Christe. **1579** TOMSON *Calvin's Serm. Tim.* 303/2 They..know that it forepasseth all our wits.

b. To exceed (a time-limit).

1622 BACON *Hen. VII*, 72 The Subiect should haue his time of Watch for fiue yeares..which if hee fore-passed his Right should be bound for euer after.

2. *intr.* To pass beyond. In Spenser: To go past, pass.

1496 *Bk. St. Albans, Fishing* D iv, Whether over the water he woll forpas. **1590** SPENSER *F.Q.* III. x. 20 One day as hee forpassed by the plaine With weary pace. **1591** —— *M. Hubberd* 519 Scarse can a Bishoprick forpas them by.

forpierce, -pinch: see FOR- *pref.*[1] 5 and 5 b.

forˈpine, *v. Obs.* exc. *arch.* Also 6–7 **forepine.** [f. FOR- *pref.*[1] + PINE *v.*] *trans.* To cause to pine or waste away; to torture, famish, waste. (Often in *pa. pple.*; perh. *intr.*)

c **1205** LAY. 29130 Munekes he for-pinede on mani are wise. **1297** R. GLOUC. (Rolls) 1159 He lai uorpined in þe wounde. ? *a* **1366** CHAUCER *Rom. Rose* 365 Hir face frounced and forpyned. **1571** GOLDING *Calvin on Ps.* li. 9 He was forpyned with extreme sorow. **1577** *St. Aug. Manual* (Longm.) 30 Whom meates puff up, whom fastynges forepine. *a* **1618** J. DAVIES *Commend. Poems* (Grosart) 20/1 Its wood to be fore-pinde with wastefull carke. **1626** *Sir F. Drake revived* in Arb. *Garner* V. 545 Our long fasting..might somewhat forepine and waste us. **1865** *Reader* No. 117. 338/3 Forpined my cheek you see.

Hence **forˈpined, forˈpining** *ppl. adjs.*

1377 LANGL. *P. Pl.* B. VI. 157 For-pyned schrewe! *c* **1386** CHAUCER *Prol.* 205 Pale as a for-pyned goost. **1597–8** BP. HALL *Sat.* v. ii. 91 Grim Famine sits in their forepined face. **1818** MILMAN *Samor* 92 Forepining day, and vigilant sleepless night.

forpit, forpet (ˈfɔːpɪt). *Sc.* and *north. dial.* [corruption of *fourth part.*] The fourth part of some other measure, now of a peck.

1793 *Statist. Acc. Scot., Lanarks.* VI. 77 As much land as is requisite for sowing a cap-full, or forpet of seed. *a* **1794** in Ritson's *Sc. Songs* I. 184, I ha'e brew'd a forpet o' ma't. **1799** J. ROBERTSON *Agric. Perth* p. vi, 4 lippies or forpits = 1 peck or ¼ of a bushel or firlot respectively. **1824** SCOTT *Redgauntlet* ch. vii, 'A forpit or twa of sault.' **1862** HUNTER *Biggar & House of Fleming* v. 60 Two pecks and two forpits of bear at the cost of 2/2*d.* **1892** in *Northumb. Gloss.*

for-plaint, -possed, -prick: see FOR- *pref.*[1]

forprise (ˈfɔːpraɪz), *sb.* Also 7 **foreprise.** [a. AF. *forprise*, f. *forpris*: see next.] An exception or reservation.

[**1292** BRITTON II. xv. §6 Sauntz fere nule forprise.] **1530** *Act 22 Hen. VIII*, c. 15 The excepcions, forprises, and prouisions in this present pardon hereafter mencioned. **1602** FULBECKE *1st Pt. Parall.* 10 Hee woulde haue leuied the Fine with a foreprise or exception of certaine acres. **1613** SIR H. FINCH *Law* (1636) 18 He shall make no foreprise in his Writ. **1676** in COLES. **1848** in WHARTON *Law Lex.*

forprise (fəˈpraɪz), *v.* Forms: 5–8 **forprise,** (6 **-yse**), 6–8 **foreprise,** (6 **-ice,** 7 **-yse, forseprise**), 7– **foreprize.** [f. AF. *forpris*, *-se*, pa. pple. of *forprendre*, *forsprendre* to except, f. *for*(*s-*, FOR- *pref.*[3] + *prendre* to take.]

trans. To take out, except, or reserve; *esp.* in Law phr. ***except(ed and forprised.*** Now *rare.*

[**1303** *Lib. Custum.* in *Munim. Gildhallæ* II. I. 168 Le Duc de Brabaunt..qe est forspris par nostre Seignour le Rei dEngleterre.] **1488** *Act 3 Hen. VII*, c. 3 §111 The Townes of Berwyk and Carlile oonly except and forprised. **1535** *Act 26 Hen. VIII*, c. 6 §4 Any games..the game of shotinge onely exceptyd and forprised. **1565** JEWEL *Def. Apol.* (1611) 384 Dame Ioane, I trow, ye will haue foreprised out of this number. **1620** BP. HALL *Hon. Mar. Clergy* III. iii, Foreprizing none but such as haue the gift of continencie. **1686** *Royal Proclam.* 10 Mar. in *Lond. Gaz.* No. 2120/2 Excepted and always foreprized out of this Our Pardon, all Treasons [etc.]. **1797** TOMLINS *Law Dict.* s.v. *Forprise*, Leases and conveyances, wherein excepted and forprised is an usual expression. **1864** SIR F. PALGRAVE *Norm. & Eng.* III. 115 One individual alone foreprized.

forquhy, Sc. form of FORWHY.

†**forˈquiche,** *v. Obs.*$^{-1}$ [f. FOR- *pref.*[1] + OE. *cwician*, f. *cwic*, QUICK *a.*] *intr.* To come to life.

c **1200** *Trin. Coll. Hom.* 77 We don, alse þing doð, þe haueð lein on swete, forquichieð þan here time cumeð.

forˈquidder. *Obs.*$^{-1}$ In 3 **forcwiddare.** [f. FOR-[2], FORE- *pref.* + **cwiddere*, agent-n. f. *cwiddian* to tell.] A foreteller.

a **1225** *Ancr. R.* 212 Þeos beoð hore owune prophetes forcwiddares.

forraine, obs. form of FOREIGN.

for-raked, -raught: see FOR- *pref.*[1] 6 b, 4.

forra(r)der: see FORWARDER *a.* and *adv.*

forra(y), obs. form of FORAY.

†**foˈrrede,** *v. Obs.* [OE. *forrǽdan* = OHG. *for-*, *ferrâten* (Ger. *verrathen*).] *trans.* To deceive, betray, seduce.

a **1000** WULFSTAN *Hom.* (Napier) 160 Eadwerd man forrædde and syððan acwealde. *c* **1205** LAY. 14867 Þurh his dohter Rouwenne mine uader he uor-radde. *a* **1225** *Juliana* 18 Ne nullich leauen ower read þat forreadeð ou seoluen. *c* **1250** *Gen. & Ex.* 2192 Ðo was Iosep sore for-dred Ðat he wore oc ðhurȝ hem for-red. *a* **1300** *Body & Soul* in *Map's Poems* 337 The world..that mani a soule haved for-rad.

forrede, obs. form of FURRED.

forrel(l, forrester: see FOREL, FORESTER.

for-rend: see FOR- *pref.*[1] 5 b.

forrey, -eie, obs. ff. of FORAY.

†**foˈrridden,** *pple.* and *ppl. a. Obs.* [f. FOR- *pref.*[1] + *ridden* pa. pple. of RIDE *v.*] **a.** Of a person: Wearied with riding. **b.** Of a horse: That has been ridden to excess (in quot. *transf.*).

1500–20 DUNBAR *Poems* lxi. 62 The court hes done my curage cuill, And maid me [ane] forriddin muill. **1635** CRANLEY *Amanda* 23 Young bold-faced Queanes, and old fore-ridden Iades. **1820** *Scots Mag.* May 422 Sare forridden, my merry menyie Left me my livan' lane.

†**forridel.** *Obs.* [OE. *forridel*, f. FOR- *pref.*[2] + root of *rídan* to RIDE.] One who rides in advance. Also *fig.* a precursor, a preliminary.

c **1000** ÆLFRIC *Hom.* II. 168 Cyning..Totilla..sende his forridel..cyðan his to-cyme ðam halgan were. *a* **1225** *Ancr. R.* 206 Oðer swuche uor-rideles. *Ibid.* 300 Al þe uorrideles þet brouhten in þe sunne þet is þe deofles heaued þet me schal totreden anon.

forrill, var. of FOREL.

forrit (ˈfɒrɪt), *adv. Sc.* [repr. FORWARD, or a coalescence of this with FORERIGHT.] Forward.

1786 BURNS *Pastoral Poetry* vi, Come forrit, honest Allan! **1816** SCOTT *Old Mort.* xxxviii, 'What for are ye no getting forrit wi' the sowens?' **1826** J. WILSON *Noct. Ambr.* Wks. 1855 I. 145 Things wunna retire and come forrit as I wish.

Hence ˈ**forritsome** *a.*, forward, 'pushing'.

1894 CROCKETT *Raiders* 200 'I'm not..a forritsome man.'

forroast: see FOR- *pref.*[1] 5.

†**foˈrroot,** *v. Obs.* [ME. *forroten*, f. FOR- *pref.*[1] + *roten*, ROOT *v.*] *intr.* To 'root' as a swine.

c **1230** *Hali Meid.* 13 Ha in hare wurðunge as eaueres forroteden.

†**foˈrrot,** *v. Obs.* [OE. *forrotian*, f. FOR- *pref.*[1] + *rotian* to ROT; = MLG. *vorroten* (Ger. *verrotten*).] *intr.* To rot away, putrefy.

a **900** *Kentish Gloss.* in Wr.-Wülcker 64 *Et..putrescet*, and forrotað. *c* **1175** *Lamb. Hom.* 111 Þine welan forrotiað biforan þine eȝan. *a* **1225** *Ancr. R.* 138 Wiðuten salt fleshs..forroteð sone. *a* **1300** *Seven Sins* iv. in *E.E.P.* (1862) 17 Þou salt..for-roti to axin and erþe.

fig. **1340** *Ayenb.* 205 Chastete..þet uorrotede ine þe watere of uoule lostes.

Hence **foˈrrotted** *ppl. a.*, putrefied, rotten.

c **897** K. ÆLFRED *Gregory's Past.* xvii. (1871) 124 Ðæt sio reðnes ðæs wines ða forrotedan wunde..clænsiȝe. **1340** *Ayenb.* 148 Þe leme uorroted ssolde ssende þe hole.

†ˈ**forrow,** *adv.* and *prep. Sc. Obs.* [prob. short. f. FOROUTH, FORWITH; cf. *otow* = *outouth*, *outwith*. See AFORROW, TOFORROW.] **A.** *adv.* Beforehand, in advance. **B.** *prep.* Before (in time or place).

1375 BARBOUR *Bruce* I. 120 Walys ensample mycht have bene To ȝow, had ȝe it forow sene. *Ibid.* VII. 145, I will that he ga forrow vs. **1474** *Acta Audit.* (1839) 35 On friday forou witsonday. **1535** STEWART *Cron. Scot.* (1858) I. 73 On that nycht ane lytill forrow da.

forrow, obs. form of FORAY.

for-rue, -run: see FOR- *pref.*[1] 2, 6 b and 8.

†**forˈsado.** *Obs. rare.* [a. Sp. *forçado*, now written *forzado*.] A galley-slave.

1625–6 PURCHAS *Pilgrims* II. 1367 There were many other Christian Slaues, but more then two hundred Forsados. **1722** D. COXE *Carolina* 28 The Majority of the Inhabitants, are Forc'adoes or forc'd People, having been Malefactors in some Parts of Mexico.

forsaid: see FORESAID.

forsake (fəˈseɪk), *v.* Pa. t. forsook (fəˈsʊk). Pa. pple. forsaken (fəˈseɪk(ə)n). Forms: *Pres. t.* 1 **forsace,** (*Northumb.* **foresacco**), 2–3 *south.* **vorsake,** (**fursake,** 4 *south.* **vorsake, forsak,** 6 **forsayke**), 2– **forsake.** *Pa. t.* 1 **forsóc,** 3–4 **forso(c)k,** *south.* **vorsoc, -k,** 3–6 **forsoke,** (4 **forsuk(e,** 6 **foresoke**), 6–7 **forsooke,** 4– **forsook;** also 7 *weak form* **forsaked.** *Pa. pple.* 1 **forsacen,** 3–4 **fursake(n, forsakin, -yn,** 3 **forsoc,** 4–6 **forsake,** 6–9 **forsook(e,** (7 **forsoken**), 3– **forsaken;** *weak forms* 3–4 **forsaked, -id.** [OE. *forsacan*, f. FOR- *pref.*[1] + *sacan* to contend, dispute, deny; cf. OS. *forsakan* (Du. *verzaken*), OHG. *firsahhan* to deny, repudiate, renounce.]

†**1.** *trans.* To deny (an accusation, an alleged fact, etc.). *Obs.*

c **1250** *Gen. & Ex.* 1767 Stalðe ic for-sake. **1297** R. GLOUC. (1724) 473 Ȝuf eni clerc as felon were itake, & vor felon iproued, & ne miȝte it noȝt uorsake. *c* **1374** CHAUCER *Boeth.* II. pr. iv. 27 (Camb. MS.), I ne may nat for-sake the ryht swyfte cours of my prosperite. **1389** *Serm.* (MS. Helm.), Þei [Ananie and Safira] forsoken to Petir here monei þat þei hadden. *c* **1440** *Promp. Parv.* 172/2 Forsakyn, and denyyn, *abnego*. *c* **1511** *1st Eng. Bk. Amer.* (Arb.) Introd. 31/1 They forsake that maria is the moder of god.

†**b.** To deny knowledge of (a person). *Obs.*

c **1340** *Cursor M.* 15997 (Trin.) Petur..had forsake his lord þries on a rowe. *c* **1400** MAUNDEV. (1839) viii. 91 Seynt Peter forsoke our Lord thries.

†**c.** To deny, renounce, or repudiate allegiance to (God, a lord, etc.). Also rarely, ***forsake to.***

a **1225** *Juliana* 33 Mi feader & mi moder for þi þat ich nule þe forsaken; habbe forsake me. *a* **1300** *Cursor M.* 22205 Þan sal all þaa..Es funden lele in cristen lai, Oither to iesu crist for-sake, Or underli sa wraful wrake. *Ibid.* 25149 Wicked man, þat godd forsakes. **1483** CAXTON *Gold. Leg.* 81 b/2 For we haue not folowed the synne of our fadres that forsoken theyr God. **1537** *Bury Wills* (Camden) 131, I forsake the Bysshoppe of Romes vsurpyt pouer.

†**d.** To 'deny' (oneself); = DENY *v.* 7. *Obs.*

c **1175** *Lamb. Hom.* 145 Forsake him seolf, and bere his rode. *c* **1440** HYLTON *Scala Perf.* (W. de W. 1494) I. xlii,

Who soo wyll come after me, forsake hymself. **1576** FLEMING *Panopl. Epist.* 80 As renouncing and forsaking mee selfe.

†**2.** To decline or refuse (something offered). With simple *obj.* or *to* and *inf.* *Obs.*

a **800** *Corpus Gloss.* 650 *Detractauit*, forsooc. *c* **893** K. ÆLFRED *Oros.* II. iv. §2 An consul.. forsoc þone triumphan. *a* **1000** *Laws Edgar* ii. §8 þone [mynet] nan man ne forsace. *a* **1225** *Juliana* 11 Sei me hwi þu forsakest þi sy & ti selhðe. **1297** R. GLOUC. (1724) 411 Roberd hym byþo3te.. þat yt was wel gret trauayl, to be kyng of þulke lond.. War þoru he ..vorsoc yt al out. *c* **1375** *Lay Folks Mass Bk.* (MS. B) 250 þai offerd gold ensense & myrre, and þou forsoke none of þirre. **1395** *E.E. Wills* (1882) 9 My sone and.. his wif haue forsake to be myne executours. **1470–85** MALORY *Arthur* VI. xviii, The thre knyghtes.. yelded hem vnto syr kay and sir kay forsoke hem and said he foughte neuer with hem. **1593** GREENE *News fr. Heaven & Hell* D iij b, This Brick-layer who forsooke to goe into Heauen because his wife was there. **1605** CAMDEN *Rem.* (1637) 275 He.. forsooke a right worshipful roome when it was offered to him. [**1697** DRYDEN *Virg. Georg.* III. 335 He.. forsakes his Food.]

absol. **1382** WYCLIF *Prov.* I. 24, I clepede, and 3ee forsoken.

†**b.** To decline or refuse to bear, encounter, have to do with, undertake; to avoid, shun. *Obs.*

a **1225** *Ancr. R.* 182 Nolde me tellen him alre monne dusi3est, þet forsoke enne buffet, uor one speres wunde. **1375** BARBOUR *Bruce* XIV. 315 Na multitud he forsuk of men, Quhill he hade ane aganis ten. **1389** in *Eng. Gilds* (1870) 54 Qwo-so be chosen.. & he forsake his offyce he xal paye.. iijs. **1398** TREVISA *Barth. De P.R.* XVI. lxiii. (Tollem. MS.), A noþer kynde of magnas, þat forsakeþ yren and dryueþ it awey. *c* **1400** *Lanfranc's Cirurg.* 173 If a leche be in straunge cuntre.. he schal forsake alle maner of curis þat ben harde to do. **1573** TUSSER *Husb.* (1580) 81 Hanging on the Crosse, no shame he did forsake. **1576** FLEMING *Panopl. Epist.* 33 We followe libertie, and forsake servitude.

†**c.** To refuse respect or obedience to (a command, duty, etc.); to disregard. Also, to neglect (*to do* something). *Obs.*

c **1175** *Lamb. Hom.* 111 Swa saul þe king dude þe forsech godes heste. *a* **1300** *Cursor M.* 6523 Sum of þaim þis fast forsoke. *Ibid.* 28246 Ic for-soke oft to kyrk at ga. **1340** HAMPOLE *Pr. Consc.* 4406 Al þas men.. þat sal forsake to wirk Cristes werk. **1387** TREVISA *Higden* (Rolls) VI. 273 þe kynges kny3es.. forsook Clito his faire byhestes.

3. To give up, renounce. **a.** To give up, part with, surrender (*esp.* something dear or valued). Passing into sense 4.

c **893** K. ÆLFRED *Oros.* I. xii. §3 He þæt wæs eall forsacende. *c* **1200** *Trin. Coll. Hom.* 147 Hie forsoken þe wereld and eorðliche wele. *a* **1240** *Ureisun* in *Cott. Hom.* 195 Vor þine luue ich uorsoc al þet me leof was. *a* **1300** *Cursor M.* 23045 þaa þat.. al þis werld welth forsok. *c* **1400** MAUNDEV. (Roxb.) xix. 88 He hase forsaken wyf and childer and all þe ricches.. of þe werld. **1582** BENTLEY *Mon. Matrones* ii. 12, I rather did forsake my right than to behold such cruelnesse. **1585** T. WASHINGTON tr. *Nicholay's Voy.* I. ix. 12 b, Forsaking the name of a Captayne any longer, caused himselfe to be called king. **1593** SHAKS. *Lucr.* 157 For himself himself he must forsake. **1781** COWPER *Hope* 585 Forsaking country, kindred, friends.

b. To break off from, renounce (an employment, design, *esp.* an evil practice or sin; also, a belief, doctrine). †Till 17th c. occas. with *inf.* as object.

c **1175** *Lamb. Hom.* 81 He scal his sunne uor-saken. *c* **1200** *Vices & Virtues* (1888) 23 Nu ðurh godes grace þu hes hafst forsaken. *c* **1305** *St. Andrew* 6 in *E.E.P.* (1862) 98 þis oþere here nettes gonne forsake. **1382** WYCLIF *Heb.* x. 25 Not forsakynge oure gederinge to gidere, as it is of custom to sum men. *c* **1400** MAUNDEV. (Roxb.) xi. 42 þe emperour.. forsuke Cristen fayth. **1401** *Pol. Poems* (Rolls) II. 49 Who wil allege the temple for glorie of our chirche, fforsake he to be cristen. *c* **1460** *Pol. Rel. & L. Poems* (1866) 236 Vertu, godede, & almisdede, arn al for-sake. **1548–9** (Mar.) *Bk. Com. Prayer* (Baptism), Doest thou forsake the deuill and all his workes? **1558** BP. WATSON *Sev. Sacram.* xxix. 186 He must forsake to dwel with hys father and mother. **1601** CHESTER *Love's Mart., Dialogue* ccxvii, Haue I forsooke to bathe me in the fluods. **1697** DRYDEN *Virg. Georg.* IV. 218 Streighten'd by my Space, I must forsake This Task. **1703** MAUNDRELL *Journ. Jerus.* (1732) 140 We were forc'd to forsake our intended visit. **1844** STANLEY *Arnold* (1858) II. viii. 14 Nor that the doctrine of Christ crucified has been so forsaken. **1894** J. T. FOWLER *Adamnan* Introd. 56 The southern Picts.. had forsaken idolatry.

4. To abandon, leave entirely, withdraw from; *esp.* to withdraw one's presence and help or companionship from; to desert. †*to forsake patch*: ? to quit the spot.

a **1300** *Cursor M.* 1228 He þaim for-soke in al þer nedis. *a* **1340** HAMPOLE *Psalter* vi. 7 Til whaim now he spekis forsakand þaire felaghschip. *c* **1386** CHAUCER *Friar's T.* 224, I wol holde company with the, Til it be so that thou forsake me. *c* **1422** HOCCLEVE *Learn to Die* 506 Forsake y am, frendshipe y can noon fynde. *c* **1489** CAXTON *Sonnes of Aymon* xxi. 461 Whan mawgys sawe that they forsoke the place, he followed theym not. *a* **1533** LD. BERNERS *Huon* cxxxviii. 516 They.. forsoke theyr horses on the see syde. **1548–9** (Mar.) *Bk. Com. Prayer* Matrimony, And forsaking all other kepe thee only to her. **1602** CAREW *Cornwall* 135 a, The Foy men gave them so rough entertaynment at their welcome, that they were glad to forsake patch, without bidding farewell. **1674** MARTINIERE *Voy. N. Countries* 64 The night forsook us quite, the Sun continuing always in our sight. **1713** ADDISON *Cato* II. vi, Thou hast forsook Thy Juba's cause. **1774** GOLDSM. *Nat. Hist.* (1776) V. 318 Larks ..forsake that climate in winter. **1816** J. WILSON *City of Plague* II. iv, I implored her to forsake the city. **1833** L. RITCHIE *Wand. by Loire* 115 The road forsakes the river. **1841–4** EMERSON *Ess., Love* Wks. (Bohn) I. 71 This passion ..though it begin with the young, yet forsakes not the old. **1860** TYNDALL *Glac.* I. xxvii. 197 It [a hut] was forsaken, and half buried in the snow. **1881** JOWETT *Thucyd.* I. 45 Those who forsake allies whom they have sworn to defend.

absol. *a* **1839** PRAED *Poems* (1864) I. 363 He'll learn to flatter and forsake. **1841** LANE *Arab. Nts.* I. 100 If thou forsake, we verily do the same.

†**b.** Of things: To fail, disappoint the hopes of. *Obs.*

1526 *Pilgr. Perf.* (W. de W. 1531) 6 The corruptyble rychesse of this worlde.. forsaketh and deceyueth him whan he weneth best. **1610** BP. CARLETON *Jurisd.* v. 73 It is not to be marueiled, if the truth of Religion afterward forsaked them. **1774** GOLDSM. *Nat. Hist.* (1776) V. 361 Their food.. never forsakes them in those warm latitudes.

forsaken (fəˈseɪk(ə)n), †**forsake**, *ppl. a.* [pa. pple of FORSAKE *v.*] In senses of the verb.

1. Deserted, left solitary or desolate.

c **1305** *Pilate* 238 in *E.E.P.* (1862) 117 He.. caste hit wiþoute þe toun among olde walles forsake. **1388** WYCLIF *Ps.* lxii[i]. 3 In a lond forsakun. *c* **1430** LYDG. *Venus-Mass* in *Lay Folks Mass Bk.* (1879) Notes 395 Me semeth amonges all I am on of the most for-sake. **1590** SPENSER *F.Q.* I. iii. 3 Forsaken, wofull, solitarie mayd. **1614** RALEIGH *Hist. World* II. (1634) 532 This banished Nation retained their.. love of their forsaken Country. **1791** MRS. RADCLIFFE *Rom. Forest* ii, This apparently forsaken edifice might be a place of refuge to banditti. **1871** FREEMAN *Norm. Conq.* (1876) IV. xviii. 218 Their forsaken state was not owing to any oppression.

†**b.** Of words: Disused, obsolete. *Obs.*

1612 BREREWOOD *Lang. & Relig.* vi. 53 The articles of league.. could very hardly in his time be understood, by reason of the old forsaken words.

†**2.** Morally abandoned. Also *absol.* *Obs.*

1572 *Satir. Poems Reform.* xxx. 206 Bot, quhair the iust dois ioyne thame with forsakin, Be war thay get not wickit Acabs takin. **1597** HOOKER *Eccl. Pol.* v. xlii. §13 Those impious forsaken miscreants.

Hence **forˈsakenly** *adv.*; **forˈsakenness.**

1591 HARINGTON *Orl. Fur.* XXXII. xlvii, Leaves.. Forsakenly about the tree doth lye. **1621** LADY M. WROTH *Urania* 93 To make me the more miserably end with neglectiue forsakennesse. **1840** CARLYLE *Heroes* (1858) 252 So could the Hero [Dante], in his forsakenness.. still say to himself. **1876** GEO. ELIOT *Dan. Der.* I. xvii Tragedies of the copse.. where the helpless drag wounded wings forsakenly.

forsaker (fəˈseɪkə(r)). Now *rare.* [f. FORSAKE *v.* + -ER[1].] One who forsakes.

1382 WYCLIF *Isa.* xxx. 1 Wo! 3ee sonus forsakeres seith the Lord. ? **1507** *Communyc.* (W. de W.) B ij, Of synne a forsaker. **1689** *Def. Liberty agst. Tyrants* 139 They may justly be called forsakers and traytors. **1821** *Examiner* 803/2 The faithless forsakers of Parga. **1879** GEO. ELIOT *Theo. Such* 159 In this sort of love it is the forsaker who has the melancholy lot.

forsaking (fəˈseɪkɪŋ), *vbl. sb.* [f. FORSAKE *v.* + -ING[1].] The action of the vb. FORSAKE.

c **1320** *Cast. Love* 1637 Then helpeth ther no pledyng there, Ne forsakyng. *c* **1440** HYLTON *Scala Perf.* (W. de W. 1494) I. xxxviii, Traueyle.. whiche to an uncunnyng man semyth a forsakyng of god. **1526** *Pilgr. Perf.* (W. de W. 1531) 23 b, For yᵉ forsakyng of one worlde, we shall haue more.. than there is.. in an.. hondred thousande worldes. **1611** BIBLE *Isa.* vi. 12 Vntill.. there be a great forsaking in the midst of the land. *a* **1612** DONNE *Βιαθανατος* (1644) 16 Ever in his forsakings there are degrees of Mercy. **1842** MANNING *Serm.* (1848) I. xviii. 268 The forsaking of the light of God's countenance is our portion in the lot of sinners.

†ˈ**forsar(y.** *Obs.* [ad. Fr. †*forsaire, -çaire*, now superseded by *forçat.*] A galley-slave.

1546 *St. Papers Hen. VIII*, XI. 284 As toching the forsares, He could not of his honour rendre them, having before gyven them libertye. *a* **1572** KNOX *Hist. Ref.* I. (1586) 182 The Masse was said in the Gallies.. in Presence of the Forsaris. **1721** STRYPE *Eccl. Mem.* II. I. xviii. 149 A proclamation.. that.. every such author.. be committed into the galleys, there to row in chains, as a slave or forsary.

‖ˈ**forsat.** *Obs. rare*[−1]. [Fr.; now written *forçat.*] In phrase *to play at forsat* (= F. *jouer au forçat*): to adhere strictly to certain rules the observance of which is not generally obligatory.

1674 COTTON *Compl. Gamester* in Singer *Hist. Cards* 340 If you play at forsat (that is the rigour of the play) he that deals wrong loseth one and his deal.

forsay, -scald, -scattered: see FOR- *pref.*[1]

forse: see FORCE.

†**forsee**, *v.* *Obs.* [OE. *forséon*, f. FOR- *pref.*[1] + *séon* to see; = OS. *forsehan* (Du. *verzien*), OHG. *far-*, *fersehan* (mod.Ger. *versehen*).] *trans.* To disregard, despise, overlook.

971 *Blickl. Hom.* 37 Ne forseoh þu næfre þine 3ecynd. *c* **1175** *Lamb. Hom.* 113 Ne bið his mehte nohwer for-se3en. *a* **1225** *St. Marher.* 15 Ha blindlunge gað and forseoð godd. *a* **1300** *E.E. Psalter* xci. 12 [xcii. 11] For-segh min egh, lokande, þas þat ere mine ille-willande.

forsee: see FORESEE.

†**forˈseek**, *v.* *Obs.* [f. FOR- *pref.*[1] + SEEK.] *trans.* To seek thoroughly, seek out.

a **1300** *Sarmun* 50 in *E.E.P.* (1862) 2 þe wormis þat hit habbiþ al for-so3t. **1584** GREENE *Carde of Fancie* Wks. (Grosart) IV. 161 To deuise his destruction which simply foresought thy preferment. **1614** J. DAVIES *Eclog.* 98 Wks. (Grosart) II. 20/1 Vartue it's sed (and is an old said saw) Is for hur selfe, to be forsought alone.

b. To weary (oneself) with seeking.

a **1300** *Cursor M.* 17597 þair sandes come again vn-spedd þai war for-soght þam vp and dun.

forseethe: see FOR- *pref.*[1] 5.

forsemens: see FORCEMENT.

for-sench: see FORE- *pref.*[1] 5.

forsene: see FORCENE.

forset (fəˈsɛt), *v.* Now *dial.* Also 6, 9 fore-. [OE. *forsettan*, f. FOR- *pref.*[1] + *settan* to SET; = MHG. *versetzen*. OE. had *forsittan* in same sense.]

1. *trans.* To beset (*lit.* and *fig.*); to bar (a way; with *dat.* of person); to surround, invest (a city, etc.); to waylay, entrap (a person or animal).

c **900** tr. *Bæda's Hist.* III. xiv. [xix.] (1891) 212 þæt heo him þone heofonlican we3 forsette & fortynde. **13..** *E.E. Allit. P.* B. 78 My gomez.. for-settez on vche a syde þe cete aboute. *c* **1330** R. BRUNNE *Chron. Wace* (Rolls) 1815 Forsetten byfore, & eke byhynde Wyþ crokes ilkon oþer gan bynde. ? *a* **1400** *Morte Arth.* 1896 Thay hade at 3one foreste forsette vs the wayes. *c* **1430** *Chev. Assigne* 251 Thow haste forsette þe 3onge qwene. *c* **1470** HARDING *Chron.* CLXXI. iv, Knightes, A litell fro Duresme their waye forsett. **1577** HOLINSHED *Chron.* I. Scotl. 437/1 The Earle of Angus caused the Castell to be forsette. **1598** MANWOOD *Lawes Forest* xx. §4 (1615) 171/1 They might hunt and chase the wild beasts.. towards the forest, so that they do not forestal nor foreset them in their return. **1872** *Daily News* 13 Aug., The watcher and policeman then 'foreset' the defendants, whom they captured. **1882** *Lanc. Gloss.*, *For-set* (Furness), to waylay.

2. *Sc.* To overburden or overpower with work.

1500–20 DUNBAR *Poems* xxii. 11 Forsett is ay the falconis kynd, Bot euir the mittane is hard in mynd.

Hence †ˈ**forset** *sb.* *Obs.* ? A stratagem.

c **1330** R. BRUNNE *Chron. Wace* (Rolls) 2912 Ne schal nought Brenne bede me trypet þat y ne schal turne hym wiþ a forset.

forset, obs. form of FAUCET.

forshake: see FOR- *pref.*[1] 1.

†**forshakel.** *Obs.* [f. FOR- *pref.*[2] + *shakel*, SHACKLE *sb.*] (See quot.)

1304 in Rogers *Agric. & Prices* I. xxi. 538 [The forshakel of Cheddington (1304) and the lustlegg of Trillek and Troy (1308, 1328) are local equivalents of the plough-shoe].

†**forˈshame**, *v.* *Obs.* [OE. *forsceamian*, f. FOR- *pref.*[1] + *sceamian*: see SHAME *v.*] *intr.* To be greatly ashamed. In OE. also *impersonal.*

c **897** K. ÆLFRED *Gregory's Past.* xxi. 150 Ðæt hie on3ieten ðæt hie mon tæle.. & hie forscami3e. *a* **1050** *Liber Scintill.* viii. (1889) 40 On him sylfum be his synnum a3enum forsceami3ean. *c* **1200** ORMIN 12528 þe deofell wennde awe33 anan Forrshamedd off himm sellfenn.

†**forˈshape**, *v.* *Obs.* For forms see SHAPE *v.* [OE. *forsceppan* str. vb., f. FOR- *pref.*[1] + *sceppan*: see SHAPE *v.*] *trans.* To metamorphose, transform; to misshape, disfigure.

c **1000** ÆLFRIC *Gen.* 308 (Gr.) Heo ealle forsceop drihten to deoflum. *a* **1225** *Ancr. R.* 120 Hwat 3if eni ancre.. is forschupped to wuluene. *c* **1350** *Will. Palerne* 4394 Ich forschop þe þanne In þis wise to a werwolf. **1398** TREVISA *Barth. De P.R.* XVII. cxlii. (1495) 698 Ydo made a mawmet: and forshaped it in the stede of god. **1480** *Descr. Brit.* 54 A man and a woman most nedes ben.. forshapen in to likenes of wolues. *c* **1532** DEWES *Introd. Fr.* in *Palsgr.* 956 To forshape, *transmuer.* **1884** CHILD *Ballads* II. xxxi. 291/2 Her stepmother had forshapen her.

Hence **forˈshaped, forˈshapen** *ppl. adjs.*, transformed, misshapen. **forˈshaping**, a deformity. Also **forschuppild** (-y-) [see -ILD], a transformer.

a **1225** *Ancr. R.* 120 Wreððe is a uorschuppild. *c* **1320** *Cast. Love* 640 He were al soþfast mon, þat no forschippyng weore him on. *c* **1440** HYLTON *Scala Perf.* (W. de W. 1494) II. vi, Remedyes.. by the which a forshapen soule maye be restored agayne. **1530** PALSGR. 157 A monstre, a wonderfull thyng or forshapen.

forshend, -shoot: see FOR- *pref.*[1] 1 and 8.

forshield: see FORESHIELD.

†**forˈshrink**, *v.* *Obs.* [OE. *forscrincan*, f. FOR- *pref.*[1] + *scrincan*, SHRINK *v.*] *intr.* To shrink up, dry up.

c **1000** ÆLFRIC *Job* vii. 5 Min hyd.. is forscruncen. *c* **1000** *Ags. Gosp.* Matt. xxi. 19 Ða sona forscranc þæt fic-treow. *a* **1500** *Flower & Leaf* lii, The beauty of hir fresh coloures, Forshronke with heat.

†**forˈshut**, *v.* *Obs.* [OE. *forscyttan*, f. FOR- *pref.*[1] + *scyttan* to SHUT.] *trans.* To shut off or out; hence, to preclude, prohibit.

c **1000** ÆLFRIC *Hom.* I. 540 Hi heofodon folces synna, and heora wrace on him sylfum forscytton. *c* **1150** *Departing Soul's Addr. Body* 13 Nu is thin muth forscutted. *c* **1430** *Pilgr. Lyf Manhode* I. xlv. (1869) 27 It forshetteth yow from passinge ouer. **1530** PALSGR. 109 *Forclorre*, to schutte out or forschut.

forsight: see FORESIGHT.

forsin, *sb.*: see FORE- *pref.*[1] 4 a.

†**forˈsin**, *v.* *Obs.* [OE. *forsyn3ian* weak vb., f. FOR- *pref.*[1] + *syn3ian*: see SIN *v.*] In *pa. pple.*, Ruined by sin, burdened with sin.

a **1000** *Laws of Edgar, Of Penitents* §12 Ne wurð æni3 man on worlde swa swiðe forsyn3ad, þe he. *c* **1175** *Lamb. Hom.* 95 He demað stiðne dom þam forsune3ede. *c* **1200** *Trin. Coll. Hom.* 187 To freurende þo forsine3ede.

forsink: see FOR- *pref.*[1] 5.

†**for'sit**, *v. Obs.* [OE. *forsittan*, f. FOR- *pref.*[1] + *sittan* to SIT.]

1. *trans.* To defer, delay; to neglect, omit.

a **940** *Laws of Æthelstan* II. §20 (Schmid) Gif hwa ȝemot forsitte þriwa. *c* **1205** LAY. 28518 Wah swa hit for-sete [*c* **1275** for-seate] þat þe king hete.

2. = FORFEIT. (? Miswritten for *forfette*.)

?*a* **1400** *Ipomadon* (Kölbing) 1854 When he ys in þis contre, At his will well ye maryede be, Ellyes forsytte youre londe.

forsite: see FORCITE.

†**for'slack, foreslack**, *v. Obs.* [f. FOR- *pref.*[1] + SLACK *v.*]

1. *intr.* To be or grow slack; to pall. *rare.*

a **1300** *Cursor M.* 23794 We wreches wit vr will for-sakes, þat selenes þat neuer for-slakes. **1579** TOMSON *Calvin's Serm. Tim.* 223/2 The tentations whiche sinne hath wrought, may in no wise make vs worse or forslake in our calling.

2. *trans.* To be slack in, neglect; to lose or spoil by slackness or delay. Also with *inf.* as *obj.*

1563-87 FOXE *A. & M.* (1596) 62/1 Bicause..we foreslacke our praieng, or be not so vigilant therein as we should. *Ibid.* 77/2 The Officiall thinking to foreslacke no time..laide handes upon this Peter. **1594** CAREW *Tasso* (1881) 27 He spitefull warie is, ne ought foreslackes Hierusalem with new force to supply. **1596** SPENSER *F.Q.* VII. vii. 45 They..love eschewed That might forslack the charge to them foreshewed. **1636** FEATLY *Clavis Myst.* xxi. 266 Be not negligent, nor fore slacke thy opportunity. **1660** H. MORE *Myst. Godl.* v. xvii. 210 This Prophecie of the Churches change into so excellent a state may be foreslacked by the ill management and faithlesness of them.

Hence **for'slacking** *vbl. sb.*, delay, hesitation.

1600 HOLLAND *Livy* XLII. lvii. (1609) 1148 All forslacking ..now would greatly prejudice their reputation.

†**forsleep**, *v. Obs.* [f. FOR- *pref.*[1] + SLEEP *v.*]

a. *intr.* Only in pa. pple.: Overcome with sleep. **b.** *trans.* To neglect through sleep.

1382 WYCLIF *Prov.* xxiii. 34 The steris man al forslept, the steer staf lost. **1571** CAMPION *Hist. Irel.* vii. (1633) 21 Before the generall flood..when every man foreslept the monition.

†**for'sling**, *v. Obs.*[−1] In 5 *pa. pple.* verslongen. [ad. Du. *verslinden*: cf. Ger. *verschlingen*.] *trans.* To swallow down, gobble up.

1481 CAXTON *Reynard* (Arb.) 10 Of xv. [chyldren] I haue but foure in suche wyse hath this theef forslongen them.

†**for'slinger**, *v. Obs.*[−1] In 5 forslynger. [a. Du. *verslingeren*, f. *ver-* = FOR- *pref.*[1] + *slingeren*, to twist, throw.] *trans.* To beat, belabour.

1481 CAXTON *Reynard* (Arb.) 16 That one had an leden malle, and that other a grete leden wapper, therwyth they wappred and al for slyngred hym.

forslip: see FOR- *pref.*[1] 3.

†**for'slocken**, *v. Obs.*[−1] [f. FOR- *pref.*[1] + SLOCKEN.] *Pa. pple.* only: Drowned.

1401 *Pol. Poems* (Rolls) II. 40 The moone is al blodi and dymme..that signefieth lordship forslokend in synne.

†**for'sloth**, *v.* [f. FOR- *pref.*[1] + SLOTH *v.*] *trans.* To lose, miss, neglect, spoil, or waste through sloth. Also with *inf.* as *obj.*

1297 R. GLOUC. (1724) 197 Wanne hii [France & oþer londes] for soke ys, & for slewþed [*v.r.* uorslewede] & to non defence ne come. *c* **1386** CHAUCER *Nun's Pr. T.* 276 Thou wolt..for-sleuthen wilfully thy tyde. **1390** GOWER *Conf.* II. 190 The prelats now..Forslouthen that they sholden tille. **1393** LANGL. *P. Pl.* C. VIII. 52 Ich..botere, melke, and chese For-sleuþe[d] in my seruice. *c* **1440** *Ps. Penit.* (1894) 33 Y haue forsleuthid thi service. *c* **1470** in *Myrc's Par. Priest* (1868) 64 Alle graces that thowe hast forslowthed. **1555** ABP. PARKER *Ps.* xxxiii, Forslouth not thys. *a* **1557** MRS. BASSET tr. *More's Treat. the Passion* Wks. 1362/2 Hee forslouthed to praye and call for gods help.

for'slow, fore'slow, *v. Obs.* exc. *arch.* Forms: 1 forsláwian, 3-4 for-, *south.* vorslewe, 6-7 for(e)slow(e, (6 foresloe). *Pa. t.* 6-7 for(e)slowed, (6 -slowe). *Pa. pple.* 3 vorslewede, 6 for(e)slowed, -slowne, 9 foreslowen. [OE. *forsláwian*, f. FOR- *pref.*[1] + *sláwian* to be slow, f. *sláw*, SLOW *a.*]

†**1.** *trans.* To be slow or dilatory about; to lose or spoil by sloth; to delay, neglect, omit, put off. Also with *inf. obj. Obs.* exc. *arch.*

c **888** K. ÆLFRED *Boeth.* x, þu naht ne forslawodest þæt þu þin aȝen feorh for hine ne sealdest. **1297** R. GLOUC. (Rolls) 4055 Wanne hii vorsoke is & uorslewede [*v.r.* for slewþed] & to none defense ne come. *c* **1315** SHOREHAM 114 Hyt hys thorwe besynesse That men for-slewyth hyt. *c* **1386** CHAUCER *Pars. T.* ¶611 This foule sinne Accidie.. forsleweth and forsluggeth, and destroyeth alle goodes temporeles. **1507** *Will of Duke* (Somerset Ho.), My tithes forgoten or forslewyd. **1585** ABP. SANDYS *Serm.* (1841) 172 By procrastination..& forslowing our turning to the Lord. **1591** HARINGTON *Orl. Fur.* XLI. xlvii, He foresloed when he was on ground To be baptized. **1633** HANMER *Chron. Irel.* 171 Do good then here, fore slow no time. **1677** W. HUBBARD *Narrative* 71 They were resolved to foreslow no opportunity. **1862** SIR H. TAYLOR *St. Clement's Eve* III. vi, Rash attempts shall fitly be foreslowen.

†**2.** To make slow, delay, hinder, impede, obstruct; to slacken. *Obs.* exc. *arch.*

1563-87 FOXE *A. & M.* (1596) 274/2 He foreslowed not his iourneie. **1579** SPENSER *Sheph. Cal.* June 119 Least night with stealing steppes doe you forsloe. **1603** SIR C. HEYDON *Jud. Astrol.* xxi. 474 Saturne doth onely foreslow the operation of the Moone; the rest of the Planets doe all further her working. *a* **1660** HAMMOND *Wks.* (1684) IV. 565 If they be any time foreslowed and trashed by either outward or inward restraints. **1682** DRYDEN *To Duchess on her return* 15 The wond'ring Nereids..Foreslow'd [*Bell printed* foreflowed] her passage to behold her form. **1855** SINGLETON *Virgil* I. 140 What delay foreslows the laggard nights.

absol. **1615** CROOKE *Body of Man* 261 Nature..doth not either preuent or foreslow vnlesse shee be prouoked.

†**3.** *intr.* To be slow or dilatory. *Obs.*

1571 GOLDING *Calvin on Ps.* xi. 8 Although God forslow and delay for a while, yit..the time of vengeance will surely come. **1593** SHAKS. *3 Hen. VI*, II. iii. 56 Foreslow no longer, make we hence amaine.

Hence **for'slowed** *ppl. a.*, **for'slowing** *vbl. sb.* Also **for'slower**, one who 'forslows'.

c **1590** CARTWRIGHT in *Presbyt. Rev.* Jan. (1888) 116 Much les cast you into forfiture for a foresloed [*printed* fooresto ed] letter. **1593** NASHE *Christs T.* 81 b, Of these foreslowers it is sayde..I will spue them out of my mouth. **1611** COTGR., *Accrochement*..a staying, delaying, or foreslowing, of a Suit.

forslug: see FOR- *pref.*[1] 3.

forsment, obs. form of FORCEMENT.

†**for'smerl**, *v. Obs.*[−1] [f. FOR- *pref.*[1] + SMERLES ointment.] *trans.* To anoint.

a **1300** *Cursor M.* 19985 (Edin.) In quilc [cristis] nam forsmerlid tald es he.

†**for'smite**, *v. Obs.* [f. FOR- *pref.*[1] + SMITE.] *trans.* To smite in pieces; to strike down.

c **1205** LAY. 1598 He hine for-smat a-midden. *c* **1314** *Guy Warw.* (A.) 3621 For-smiten þai be þat neuer after schullen y-the. *c* **1420** *Pallad. on Husb.* III. 272 As thyng with leyt forsmyton, wol they die. *c* **1475** *Partenay* 2104 Fighting ful manly, On all for-smete.

†**forso'much**, *adv. Obs.* = FORASMUCH.

1454 in Burton & Raine *Hemingbrough* 393 Forsomykill as I have certeyn knawledge. **1561** WINȜET *Cert. Tract.* ii. (1888) 16 Forsamekle as [etc.]. **1611** BIBLE *Luke* xix. 9 Forsomuch as he also is the sonne of Abraham. **1648** Z. BOYD in *Zion's Flowers* (1855) App. 30/1 Forsameikle as [etc.].

forsongen: see FOR- *pref.*[1] 6 b.

forsooth (fəˈsuːθ), *adv.* Forms: 1 forsóð, 3-4 forsoþ(e, 4 *south.* vorzoþe, 3-6 forsoth(e, (3 forsotht(h, 4 for-suth, 4 forsoothe), 4-5 *Sc.* for-suth, (4 *Sc.* fursuth, 5 for-sute, *Sc.* -suith), 6 forsouth, (*Sc.* -soith), 6- forsooth. [OE. *forsóð*, f. FOR *prep.* + *sóð*, SOOTH *sb.*, written as one word.]

1. †**a.** In truth, truly. Also in phrase, *forsooth to say, forsooth and forsooth* (cf. *verily, verily*), *forsooth and God. Obs.* **b.** Now only used parenthetically with an ironical or derisive statement.

c **888** K. ÆLFRED *Boeth.* xiv. §3 Wite þu forsoþ þæt nan ȝod ne deraþ þam þe hit ah. *a* **1225** *Ancr. R.* 88 Auh forsoðe so hit is. *c* **1300** *Harrow. Hell* 40 He nam him..Vnto helle for soþe to sei. **1393** LANGL. *P. Pl.* C. XVII. 303 And when a man swereþ for soþ, for soþ he hit troweþ. *c* **1481** *Plumpton Corr.* 42 For sute, madam, I lost all that I payd for him. **1523** LD. BERNERS *Froiss.* Pref. 2 Forsothe and God, this hath moued me at the highe comaundement of my..lorde kynge Henry the VIII. **1547** *Homilies* I. *Of Faith* (1859) 43 He confirmeth with a double oath, saying, Forsoothe and forsooth I say unto you [etc.]. **1642** R. CARPENTER *Experience* I. xiv. 107 After every word even when they speake to young greene Boyes, they come with yes forsooth, and no forsooth. **1667** PEPYS *Diary* 25 Mar., By and by comes Mr. Lowther and his wife and mine, and into a box, forsooth, neither of them being dressed. **1711** STEELE *Spect.* No. 79 ¶9 She has no Secrets, forsooth, which should make her afraid to speak her Mind. **1789** MRS. PIOZZI *Journ. France* I. 109 That they might be at liberty forsooth to clap and hiss. **1809-10** COLERIDGE *Friend* (1865) 202 He reproaches me with treachery, because forsooth I had not sent him a challenge! **1842** BROWNING *Waring* I. ii, How, forsooth, was I to know it? **1863** P. BARRY *Dockyard Econ.* 165 Reserve forsooth! **1880** MRS. FORRESTER *Roy & Viola* I. 21 A very happy couple we should have made, for-sooth.

2. quasi-*sb.* An act of saying *forsooth*.

1712 STEELE *Spect.* No. 266 ¶4 Her innocent *forsooths, yes's, and't please you's.*

Hence **for'sooth** *sb.*, one who uses the word frequently, an affected speaker. **for'sooth** *v. trans.* to say 'forsooth' to, treat ceremoniously.

1604 B. JONSON *Penates* Wks. (Rtldg.) 541 You sip so like a forsooth of the city. **1660-1** PEPYS *Diary* 16 Jan., The sport was how she had intended to have kept herself unknown, and how the Captaine..of the Charles had forsoothed her, though he knew her well and she him.

†**for'sopil**, *v. Obs.* [f. FOR- *pref.*[1] + ? *sopil*, SUPPLE. But the reading and sense are doubtful.]

c **1315** SHOREHAM 165 For death scholde his meystryes kethe and for-sopil and for-sethe In deathes bende.

†**for'span**, *v. Obs.* [OE. *forspanan*, f. FOR- *pref.*[1] + *spanan* to entice; = OS. *forspanan*, OHG. *farspanan*.] *trans.* To entice, seduce.

c **1000** ÆLFRIC *Hom.* II. 226 Gehwa seðe oðerne to leahtrum forspenð..is manslaȝa. *a* **1175** *Cott. Hom.* 223 Warþ þa þat wif for-spannen þurh þe deofles lare.

forspeak (fəˈspiːk), *v.* Also fore-. [f. FOR- *pref.*[1] + SPEAK. OE. had *forspecan* to deny.]

1. *trans.* To bewitch, charm. *Obs.* exc. *Sc.*

c **1440** *Promp. Parv.* 173/1 For-spekyn, or charmyn, *fascino.* *c* **1460** *Towneley Myst.* (Surtees) 115 Sythen told me a clerk, that he was forspokyn. **1584** R. SCOT *Discov. Witchcr.* III. ii. 45 They [the witches] saie they have.. forespoken hir neighbour. **1601** HOLLAND *Pliny* II. 296 Whosoeuer shall enchant or fore-speake any corne or fruits of the earth. *a* **1658** FORD, etc. *Witch Edmonton* II. i, Urging, That my bad tongue..Forespeaks their cattle. **1895** [see below].

†**2.** To forbid, renounce. *Obs.*

1565-73 COOPER *Thesaurus, Abdicere*..to forspeake: to cast of or renounce. **1579** J. STUBBES *Gaping Gulf* E viij b, If he should speede (which God forspeake).

†**3.** To speak against, speak evil of. *Obs.*

a **1300** [see below]. **1606** SHAKS. *Ant. & Cl.* III. vii. 3 Thou hast forspoke my being in these warres, And say'st it is not fit. **1611** W. SCLATER *Key* (1629) 84 The fashion of most men, in such iudgements, is to cry out of ill tongues that have fore-spoken them.

Hence **for'speaking** *vbl. sb.* and *ppl. a.*; **for'spoken** *ppl. a.* Also **for'speaker**, a witch.

a **1300** *E.E. Psalter* xliii. 17 Fra steven of up-braidand and for-spekand. **14..** *Voc.* in Wr.-Wülcker 582 *Facimia*, a forspeker or a tylyystere. **1483** *Cath. Angl.* 138/2 A Forspekynge, *fascinacio.* **1570** T. NORTON tr. *Nowel's Catech.* (1853) 127 They..which abuse the name of God in ..enchantments, in forespeakings, or in any other manner of superstition. **1895** *Longm. Mag.* Nov. 39 She told him he had been 'forespoken'..and made him drink water mixed with earth from the 'fore-speaker's' grave.

forspend, forespend (fəˈspɛnd), *v.* [OE. *forspendan*, f. FOR- *pref.*[1] + *spendan* to SPEND. Cf. OHG. *vorspentôn*.] *trans.* To spend completely: †**a.** To exhaust (money or property).

c **893** K. ÆLFRED *Oros.* I. i. §23 Swiðost ealle hys speda hy forspendað. *c* **1175** *Lamb. Hom.* 31 Swa þet ic mine oðre god al ne fors-spende.

b. To wear out with toil, etc.; *rare* exc. in pa. pple.

1571 GOLDING *Calvin on Ps.* li. 9 His livelynes was almoste forspent. **1652-62** HEYLIN *Cosmogr.* III. (1682) 146 Fore-spent with age, and with the travel of the Wars. **1799** SOUTHEY *Eng. Eclog., etc.* Poet. Wks. III. 142 A painful march..Forespent the British troops. **1814** CARY *Dante, Inf.* I. 21 A man..Forespent with toiling. **1884** *Punch* 23 Feb. 88 Camel and leader onward fare forespent.

Hence **for'spent, fore'spent** *ppl. a.*

1563 SACKVILLE *Induct. Mirr. Mag.* xii, Her body small soe withered and forespent. **1576** NEWTON *Lemnie's Complex.* (1633) 108 Their languishing and forespent body forsaketh their soule. **1821** LAMB *Elia* Ser. II. *Valentine's Day*, The weary and all forspent twopenny postman.

†**for'spill**, *v. Obs.* [OE. *forspillan*, *-spildan*, f. FOR- *pref.*[1] + *spillan* to destroy, SPILL. Cf. OHG. *farspildan*.] *trans.* To destroy, lose.

c **893** K. ÆLFRED *Oros.* III. ix. §4 þa wolde he hiene selfne ..forspillan. *a* **1300** *E.E. Psalter* lxxxviii. 11 [lxxxix. 10] þou ..In mighte of þine arme forspilt þi faas. *c* **1340** *Cursor M.* 4332 (Fairf.) Almast made ho him forspilt.

forspread: see FOR- *pref.*[1] 7.

forstage, forstall: see FORE-STAGE, -STALL.

†**for'stand, fore'stand**, *v.*[1] *Obs.* [OE. *forstandan*, f. FOR- *pref.*[1] + *standan* to STAND.]

1. *trans.* To oppose, withstand; to bar.

In quot. 1599 perh. = 'neglect' (cf. FORSIT, or read *foreslow'd*).

a **1000** *Boeth. Metr.* i. 44 Ne meahte þa seo wea laf wiȝe forstandan. *c* **1205** LAY. 20159 Arður wende his speres ord, and for-stod heom þene ford. **1599** *Life Sir T. More* in Wordsw. *Eccl. Biog.* (1853) II. 58 He fore-stood nothing for the happie expedition of the same. [**1892** STOPF. BROOKE *E.E. Lit.* II. xxv. 264 A mighty angel there forstood them.]

2. = UNDERSTAND. [Cf. Ger. *verstehen*.]

c **888** K. ÆLFRED *Boeth.* v. §3 Uneaþe ic mæȝ forstandan þine acsunga. **1682** *New News from Bedlam* 47 How the.. Papists will approve of it, we cannot forestand. **1768** ROSS *Helenore* 145 A cripple I'm not, ye forsta me.

†**for'stand**, *v.*[2] *Obs.* [f. FOR- *pref.*[2] + STAND *v.*] *trans.* To stand up for, defend, represent.

[*a* **1000** *Laws Ine* lxii. in Thorpe *Anc. Laws* I. 142 Gif hine ..nelle forstandan.] **1642** *Vindic. Parlt.* in *Harl. Misc.* (Malh.) V. 277 The members of the parliament are chosen by us, and forstand us.

†**for'steal**, *v. Obs.* [OE. *forstelan*, f. FOR- *pref.*[1] + *stelan* to STEAL.] *trans.* To steal away.

a **940** *Laws of Æthelstan* v. vi. §3 Gif hine man forstæle. *c* **975** *Rushw. Gosp.* Matt. vi. 19 In eorþe..þær ðiofes adelfaþ and forstelaþ. *c* **1175** *Lamb. Hom.* 109 Heouene..þer nan þeof ne mei [his] maðmas forsteolan. *c* **1200** *Prayer to our Lady* 9 in *O.E. Misc.* 192 Slep me hað mi lif forstole richt half oðer more.

forsteal(l, obs. form of FORESTALL.

forsterite (ˈfɔːstəraɪt). *Min.* [f. the surname *Forster* + -ITE.] A silicate of magnesium found in yellowish crystals.

1824 LEVY in *Ann. Phil.* Ser. II. VII. 62, I have chosen for it the name of forsterite.

forstid ('fɔːstɪd). *Mining.* Also 7–9 **forestid**, 8–9 **fausted.** [Of unknown origin.] Rarely *pl.* Chiefly *attrib.*, as ***forstid ore*** (see quot. 1874).

1653 MANLOVE *Lead-Mines* 266 Forstid-oar and Tees. **1681** HOUGHTON *Compl. Miner* (E.D.S.), *Fore-stid ore.* **1747** HOOSON *Miner's Dict.* D iv b, With this [Bucker] they knock Ore, or anything that is mixed with Ore, Fausteds, &c. *Ibid.* M ij, All the Fausted Ore was to be Free. **1802** MAWE *Min. Derbysh.* 204 *Fausted,* refuse lead ore to be dressed finer. **1874** *Gloss.* to *Manlove's Lead-Mines* (E.D.S.), *Forstid-ore* or *Forestid ore,* ore that is gotten out of earth and dirt that has been previously washed and deprived of part of its ore.

forstived: see FOR- *pref.*[1] 5.

Forstner bit ('fɔəstnə(r)). [The name of Benjamin *Forstner,* who patented the invention in 1874 and 1883 (U.S. patents 155,148 and 280,026).] A type of wood-drilling bit.

1902 G. L. SUTCLIFFE *Mod. Carpenter* II. 131 (*caption*) Forstner Auger bit. **1931** REID & HIGGINS *Fund. Woodworking Trades* viii. 90 Forstner bits..are guided by their circular rim instead of a spur in the centre... They are especially adapted for delicate work. **1966** A. W. LEWIS *Gloss. Woodworking Terms* 8 *Forstner bit,* bit with a very short centre point and sharp cylindrical rim.

†for'stop, *v. Obs.* [f. FOR- *pref.*[1] + STOP *v.*; = MDu. *verstoppen.*] *trans.* To stop; to stifle (breath); also, to dam up, in quot. *fig.*

a **1225** *Ancr. R.* 72 3e al þisses weis pundeð ower wordes, & forstoppeð ouwer þouhtes. **13..** *Coer de L.* 4843 The wynde..forstoppyd the Crystene onde.

forstormed: see FOR- *pref.*[1] 5 c.

†for'straught, *pa. pple.* [f. FOR- *pref.*[1] + *straught* in DISTRAUGHT.] Distracted.

c **1386** CHAUCER *Shipman's T.* 105 A very hare..al forstraught with houndes grete and smale. *c* **1440** *Ps. Penit.* (1894) 58 For-straught to the yfled am y.

†for'strive, *v. Obs. rare*⁻¹. [f. FOR *prep.* + STRIVE.] *trans.* To strive for.

c **1315** SHOREHAM 93 Coveyte none mannes wyf, Ne nauȝt of hys for-stryve.

†for'sume, *v. Obs. rare*⁻¹. [f. FOR- *pref.*[1] + ?*-sume* in CONSUME. But cf. OHG. *firsûmen*, mod.G. *versäumen* to procrastinate.] *trans.* To waste, consume.

a **1510** DOUGLAS *K. Hart* II. xxv, And gif 3e be ane counsalour sle, Quhy suld 3e sleuthfullie your tyme forsume?

forsung: see FOR- *pref.*[1] 6 b.

†for'swallow, *v. Obs.* [OE. *forswelȝan, -sweolȝan,* f. FOR- *pref.*[1] + *swelȝan* to SWALLOW.] *trans.* To swallow up, devour utterly.

Beowulf 2089 (Gr.) Grendel..leofes mannes lic eall forswealȝ. *c* **1175** *Lamb. Hom.* 123 þenne bið he gredi..and forswoleȝeð þene hoc forð mid þan ese. *a* **1225** *Ancr. R.* 66 þe luðere coue deouel..uorswoluweð al þæt god þæt heo istreoned habbeð. **1340** *Ayenb.* 67 Onleak þe erþe and uorzualȝ datan and abyron. *c* **1400** *Solomon's Bk. Wisdom* 259 Sone hadden þe Lyouns forswelewed hem vchone.

forswarted: see FOR- *pref.*[1] 5.

†for'swat, *ppl. a.* [pa. pple. of *forsweat, f. FOR- *pref.*[1] + SWEAT *v.*] Covered with sweat.

c **1325** *Pol. Songs* (Camden) 158 Of thralles y am ther thral, That sitteth swart ant forswat. **1375** BARBOUR *Bruce* VII. 2 The kyng toward the rod is gane, Wery for-swat. *c* **1450** *Merlin* 296 Com a knyght right well armed vpon a grete steede all for swette. **1580** SIDNEY *Arcadia* (1622) 138 A couple of foreswat melters.

†for'sweal, *v. Obs.* [OE. *forswǣlan,* f. FOR- *pref.*[1] + *swǣlan*: see SWEAL.] *trans.* To burn up.

c **1000** ÆLFRIC *Hom.* II. 494 We sind mid liȝum forswælede. *c* **1205** LAY. 16228 Al hit for-swælde þat þer inne wunede. *c* **1425** *Eng. Conq. Irel.* xxiv. 58 A fyr..shal Irlond al about for-swely.

forswear (fɔə'swɛə(r)), *v.* Pa. t. **forswore** (-'swɔə(r)). Pa. pple. **forsworn** (-'swɔːn). Forms: see FOR- *pref.* and SWEAR. [OE. *forswerian* str. vb., f. FOR- *pref.*[1] + *swerian* to SWEAR.]

1. *trans.* To abandon or renounce on oath or in a manner deemed irrevocable; = ABJURE. ***to forswear the land,*** etc.: to swear to abandon it for ever. Also with *inf.* as obj.

Beowulf 804 He sigewæpnum forsworen hæfde. **1297** R. GLOUC. (1724) 387 He made hym, vor hys treson, vorsueryе Engelond. *c* **1330** R. BRUNNE *Chron.* (1810) 97 þe lond boþe forsuore. *c* **1470** HENRY *Wallace* x. 214, I wald forswer Scotland for euirmair. **1561** T. NORTON *Calvin's Inst.* IV. 109 By suche contempt the grace offred is refused and as it were forsworne. **1599** SHAKS. *Pass. Pilgr.* 33 A woman I forswore; but I will prove, Thou being a goddess, I forswore not thee. **1622** DRAYTON *Poly-olb.* xii. 84 They the Land at last did vtterly forsweare. **1660** MILTON *Free Commw.* Wks. 1738 I. 588 The solemn Ingagement, wherin we all forswore Kingship. **1775** SHERIDAN *Rivals* II. i, I shall forswear your company. **1826** DISRAELI *Viv. Grey* V. xiii, I foreswore, with the most solemn oaths, the gaming table. **1845** S. AUSTIN *Ranke's Hist. Ref.* III. 369 The whole system of pensions should be for ever forsworn.

b. with *inf.* as *obj.*

1592 SHAKS. *Rom. & Jul.* I. i. 229 She hath forsworne to loue. **1607** —— *Cor.* v. iii. 80 The thing I haue forsworne to graunt.

2. To deny or repudiate on oath or with strong asseveration. †Also with *inf.* or sentence as *obj.*

c **1400** *Apol. Loll.* 109 Appily I be not..constreyin be nede to..forsuer þe name of my Lord God. **1532** MORE *Confut. Tindale* Wks. 603/2 Peter..sinned not deadly at the time when he forswore Chryst. **1565–73** COOPER *Thesaurus, Abiurauit creditum,* he hath forsworne his debt. **1590** SHAKS. *Com. Err.* v. i. 11 That selfe chaine about his necke, Which he forswore most monstrously to haue. **1596** —— *1 Hen. IV,* v. ii. 39 His Oath-breaking: which he mended thus, By now forswearing that he is forsworne. *a* **1625** BOYS *Wks.* (1629) 491 Who did euer offend in word more than Peter? forswearing his owne master. **1712** ARBUTHNOT *John Bull* III. ix, If thou durst, [thou] would'st forswear thy own hand and seal. **1738** POPE *Epil. Sat.* I. 112 A Peer or Peeress..Who..forswears a Debt.

3. *intr.* To swear falsely, commit perjury.

a **1000** *Laws of Edw. & Guth.* §3 Gyf ȝehadod man..forsweriȝe oþþe forlicȝe. **1382** WYCLIF *Matt.* v. 33 Thou shalt not forswere. *a* **1592** GREENE *Jas. IV,* v. iv, You swear, forswear, and all to compass wealth. **1681** COTTON *Wond. Peake,* To swear, curse, slaunder, and forswear More natural is to your Peak Highlander. *a* **1763** SHENSTONE *Charms of Precedence* 22 Do ye not flatter, lye, forswear,.. And all for this. **1876** FARRAR *Marlb. Serm.* xxvii. 265 The relative heinousness of forswearing by the temple and forswearing by its gold.

b. *refl.* To swear falsely, perjure oneself. Also *pass.* to be guilty of perjury.

a **1000** *Laws Ecgb. P.* II. §24 3if hwylc læwede man hine forsweriȝe..fæste iiii. ȝear. *c* **1000** ÆLFRIC *Josh.* ii. 20 We ne beoþ forsworene. *c* **1175** *Lamb. Hom.* 13 Ne for-swerie þu þe. *c* **1205** LAY 4124 Nu heo beð for-sworne mid heore swike-dome. **1340** *Ayenb.* 6 Yef he zuereþ uals be his wytinde; he him uorzuerrþ. *c* **1400** *Rom. Rose* 5973–4 If I forswere me, than am I lorn, But I wol never be forsworn. **1523** LD. BERNERS *Froiss.* I. cclxxx. 419 He sware by his fathers soule, wherby he was neuer forsworne. **1526–34** TINDALE *Matt.* v. 33 Thou shalt not forswere thy selfe, but shalt performe thyne othe to God. **1666** WOOD *Life* (Oxf. Hist. Soc.) II. 89 Dr. Pelham forswore himself, having 800 *li.* lying by him. **1709** STEELE *Tatler* No. 105 ¶3, I hope you won't be such a perjured Wretch as to forswear your self. **1838** LYTTON *Leila* v. iii, Hear one who never was forsworn. **1871** BLACKIE *Four Phases* I. 17, I have sworn to obey the laws, and I cannot forswear myself.

†c. *trans.* To defraud of by perjury. *Obs.*

1668 ROLLE *Abridgem., Tit. Action sur Case* (F.) pl. 12. 40 Si home dit dun auter, He did forswear me..40*s.* worth of Tithes in Canterbury Court. Nul Action gist pur ceux Parols.

†4. a. To swear by (a thing) falsely or profanely.

c **1325** *Song Mercy* 151 *E.E. Poems* (1862) 123 We stunt noþer for schame, ne drede To..For-swere his [God's] soule, his hert al-so.

b. To swear (something) falsely; to break (an oath); to forsake (sworn allegiance).

1580 [see FORSWORN 2]. *a* **1631** DONNE *Woman's Constancy* 7 Wilt thou then..say..that oathes, made in reverentiall feare Of Love and his wrath, any may forsweare? **1871** R. ELLIS tr. *Catullus* lxvii. 8 Duty of years forsworn, honour in injury lost.

†5. To swear or vow to bring about. *Obs. rare*⁻¹.

a **1300** *Cursor M.* 14561 (Cott.) þe land o Iude he has forborn, For þar þai hafe his ded forsuorn.

Hence **for'swearing** *vbl. sb.* and *ppl. a.* **for'swearer,** one who forswears (himself), a perjurer.

1340 *Ayenb.* 57 þise ten boȝes we moȝe alsuo nemni ydelnesse..lyesynges, vorzueriinges [etc.]. **1413** *Pilgr. Sowle* (Caxton 1483) III. v. 53 Ye lyers, forswerers and witnessers of falshede. **1490** CAXTON *Eneydos* xxvi. 93 Dydo whan she dyde remembre the forsweryng of laomedon.. made grete doubte to folowe theym. **1561** T. NORTON *Calvin's Inst.* IV. xviii. (1634) 711 With forswearings..to enter forceably into any mans possession. **1583** GOLDING *Calvin on Deut.* xxxix. 230 God will in the end vtter his wrath both against forswearers and against theeues. **16..** *Let. to Friend* in *Select. Harl. Misc.* (1793) 484 The nonswearing, or forswearing clergy and laity, who will help forwards another revolution. **1720** DE FOE *Capt. Singleton* i. (1840) 7 Forswearing..was the stated practice of the ship's crew.

†for'swelt, *v. Obs.* [OE. *forsweltan,* str. vb., f. FOR- *pref.*[1] + *sweltan,* SWELT *v.* to die.]

1. *intr.* To die, perish.

c **888** K. ÆLFRED *Boeth.* xxxi. §1 Maniȝ wif forswilt for hire bearne. *a* **1225** *Juliana* 19 He schal þe forreaden & makie to forswelten.

2. *trans.* To cause to perish, to kill.

a **1225** *St. Marher.* 5 Mi sweord schal uorswelten and forswolhen þi flesch. **13..** *K. Alis.* 7559 Her was the gult, To ben forbarnd, to ben forswelte.

†for'swift, *v. Obs.*⁻¹ In 6 *pa. pple.* **forswiftet.** [f. FOR- *pref.*[1]; cf. SWIFT *a.* and ON. *svipta* to sweep off.] *trans.* To sweep away.

1513 DOUGLAS *Æneis* III. iii. 97 Forswiftet fro our richt cours, gane we ar.

forswithe, -swong, -swonk: see FOR- *pref.*[1]

for-swollen, *pa. pple.*: see FOR- *pref.*[1] 6.

fig. *c* **1450** *Merlin* xxvii. 538 'Ha boyes' quod the kynge, 'thow art fell, and for-swollen'.

forsworn (fɔə'swɔːn), **†forswore,** *ppl. a.* [pa. pple. of FORSWEAR.]

1. That has forsworn himself, perjured.

O.E. Chron. an. 1094 [He] hine forsworenne & trywleasne clypode. *a* **1100** *Ags. Voc.* in Wr.-Wülcker 337 *Periurus,* forsworen. *c* **1290** *S. Eng. Leg.* I. 135/1011 Puyrliche forsuore we schullen him preoui. *c* **1400** *Apol. Loll.* 37 For sworn men, cursars, drunksum men. **1571** GOLDING *Calvin on Ps.* iii. 84 God will mainteyne the faithfulnesse of his promises against such forsworne naughty packs. **1680** FALKLAND *Life Edw. II* in *Select. Harl. Misc.* (1793) 49 His forsworn traiterous murderers enter his chamber. **1718** *Freethinker* No. 20. 135 The Forsworn Enemies of the Protestant Succession. **1849–53** ROCK *Ch. of Fathers* III. x. 501 Our pastors, from the sainted Austin down to the forsworn Cranmer. **1887** BOWEN *Virg. Æneid* II. 195 By lips forsworn of a cunning liar, the tale Credence finds.

Proverbs. *c* **1330** *Amis & Amil.* 1102 Forsworn man shal neuer spede! **1591** *Troubl. Raigne K. John* II. (1611) 92 Once forsworne, and neuer after sound. **1619** DALTON *Countr. Just.* (1630) 297 Once forsworne ever forlorne.

absol. *c* **1000** ÆLFRIC *Hom.* I. 132 Ða forsworenan mid forsworenum..forwurðað. *a* **1200** *Moral Ode* 103 Hwet sculen ordlinghes don þa swicen and ta forsworene? **1597** DANIEL *Civ. Wars* III. xxx, One says he never should endure the sight Of that Forsworn.

2. Falsely sworn.

1580 SIDNEY *Arcadia* (1622) 184 Plexirtus, mingling forsworne excuses with false-meant promises.

Hence **for'swornness,** false swearing, perjury.

c **1000** ÆLFRIC *Hom.* II. 328 Cypmannum ȝedafenað þæt hi..lofian heora ðing buton laðre forsworennysse. *c* **1175** *Lamb. Hom.* 103 Stale and lesunge, and forsworenesse. **1828** WEBSTER, *Forswornness,* the state of being forsworn.

†for'swounden, *pa. pple. Obs.* [pple. of *forswinden vb. = OHG. *farswindan* (mod.Ger. *verschwinden*) to swoon.] Implied in **for'swundenleȝc, for'swundenness,** indolence, remissness.

c **1200** ORMIN 2623 Unnlusst & forrswundennleȝȝc Iss Drihhtin swiþe unncweme. *Ibid.* 4736 Himm iss idellnesse laþ & all forrswundennesse.

forswunk: see FOR- *pref.*[1] 6 b.

forsythia (fɔː'saɪθɪə). [mod.L. (M. Vahl *Enumeratio Plantarum* (1805) I. 39), f. the name of William *Forsyth* (1737–1804), English botanist: see -IA[1].] A plant of the genus of spring-flowering shrubs so named, native to Albania and eastern Asia and belonging to the family Oleaceæ; cultivated for their bright yellow, bell-shaped flowers.

1846 *Jrnl. R. Hort. Soc.* I. 227 The species obtained by Mr. Fortune is very distinct from the original Forsythia. **1851** *Curtis's Bot. Mag.* LXXVII. 4587 The original *Forsythia,* established on a Chinese plant cultivated in Japan ..appears to have been introduced into Holland in 1833. **1893** [see *golden bell*]. **1905** *Daily Chron.* 2 Aug. 3/1 Daffodils in the grass under drooping Forsythia. **1927** E. H. M. COX *Evol. Garden* xiii. 250 The Forsythias with bright yellow flowers. **1965** S. C. EMBERTON *Shrub Gardening* ix. 52 The gardens along the line bubble over with sugar-pink almond blossom and irrepressible yellow forsythias.

fort (fɔət), *sb.*[1] Also 6 **forthe.** [a. F. *fort,* absol. use of *fort* adj.: see next.]

1. *Mil.* A fortified place; a position fortified for defensive or protective purposes, usually surrounded with a ditch, rampart, and parapet, and garrisoned with troops; a fortress.

1557–75 *Diurn. Occurr.* (1833) 52 The forthe of Aymouth [was] decernit to be cassin down. **1568** GRAFTON *Chron.* II. 15 He..builded a forte, where as at thys day standeth newe Castell upon Tyne. **1592** BABINGTON *Comf. Notes Gen.* vii. §12 When..forts, trees, nor any tall towers can saue a man. **1725** DE FOE *Voy. round World* (1840) 280 Strong forts erected..and strong garrisons maintained in them. **1844** H. H. WILSON *Brit. India* III. 178 A detachment from the British force..drove the insurgents out of the fort. **1873** MISS BRADDON *L. Davoren* Prol. i, To make his way back to a far distant fort in quest of provisions.

b. *fig.* A strong position, stronghold. Phr. ***to hold the fort***: to act as a temporary substitute; also, to remain at one's post, to maintain one's position, to 'cope'.

1568 FULWELL *Like Will to Like* (1587) D iv, The forte of Vertue, oh man assaile. **1592** DANIEL *Compl. Rosamond* Wks. (1717) 40 Having but..weak feeble Hands To hold their Honours Fort unvanquished. **1605** BACON *Adv. Learn.* I. v. §11 If there were sought in knowledge..a fort or commanding ground for strife. **1640** BP. HALL *Chr. Moder.* 29/2 Such [parts of the body] as wherein the main fort of life doth not consist. **1708** *Brit. Apollo* No. 39. 1/2 They look upon this Passage in the Revelations as their strongest Fort. *c* **1870** P. P. BLISS *Sacred Songs & Solos sung by Ira D. Sankey* (1874) 3 'Hold the fort, for I am coming,' Jesus signals still; Wave the answer back to heaven, 'By Thy grace we will.' **1928** D. H. LAWRENCE *Phoenix II* (1968) 601 Thirty-six years ago men.. still believed in the fight for life and the fun of it. 'Hold the fort, for I am coming.' **1936** E. S. GARDNER *Case Sleepwalker's Niece* x. 73 In the meantime I want to put in a telephone call. You hold the fort. **1941** A. L. ROWSE *Tudor Cornwall* 341 Elizabeth and her archbishops..had held the fort until their church had come ..to have an ethos of its own. **1960** J. STROUD *Shorn Lamb* viii. 107 I'm going out for an hour or so, can you hold the fort? **1962** J. WAIN *Strike Father Dead* v. 243, I shan't need more than ten minutes, if you can hold the fort that long. **1966** *Times* 22 Sept. 11/5 Mr. George Brown's determination to hold the Foreign Office fort and to sally forth as little as possible.

c. In British North America and parts of the U.S.: A trading station (originally fortified).

1776 ADAM SMITH *W.N.* v. i. (1869) II. 328 Their.. settlements and habitations, which they [the Hudson's Bay Company] have honoured with the name of forts.

2. The place of security (of a wild animal).

1653 URQUHART *Rabelais* II. xxvi, A..roe-buck which was come out of his Fort. **1674** N. COX *Gentl. Recreat.* I. (1677) 130 If a Boar intends to abide in his Den, Couch, or Fort.

†3. *Astrol. Obs.*
1686 GOAD *Celest. Bodies* I. xii. 48 Unless the Semisextile on each side..be reduced to the ☌, and the Quincunx likewise to the Opposition, as their Matrices, their Forts and Principals; the Conjunction..will be found the most insignificant Aspect in the pack.

4. Strong part or point. Now written FORTE, q.v.

5. *attrib.* and *Comb.*, as ***fort-breach***; ***fort-crowned*** adj.; **fort-adjutant**, 'an officer in a garrison who is responsible for its internal discipline, and the appropriation of the men to the several corps'; **fort-major**, in a fort or fortress, the officer next to the governor or commandant. Also FORT-ROYAL.
1876 VOYLE *Milit. Dict.*, *Fort-adjutant. **1649** G. DANIEL *Trinarch., Hen. V*, cxciii, As they..had found Some *fort-breach. **1894** *Daily News* 26 Nov. 4/6 The *fort-crowned heights. **1715** *Lond. Gaz.* No. 5300/5 *Fort-Major of the said Town. **1844** *Regul. & Ord. Army* 3 Officers employed as Town or Fort Majors.

fort, *sb.*[2] (See quot.)
1867 FRY *Playing-Card Terms* in *Philol. Soc. Trans.* 56 *Fort*, an oiled sheet, (usually large enough for twenty cards) formerly used in making the stencilling-plate for stencilling the colors of the court-cards or the pips of the other cards.

†**fort**, *a. Obs.* Also 5 forte. [a. F. *fort*:—L. *fortem* strong.] Strong, powerful.
13.. *K. Alis.* 7710 Sampson theo fort, also, Daliada dude him wrong and wo. **14..** *Pol. Rel. & L. Poems* 238 þou most fort wit wele or wo. *a* **1450** *Knt. de la Tour* (1868) 92 Dalide, that was wiff to Sampson forte. *c* **1450** LONELICH *Grail* xlii. 471 Which dwk was bothe Riche & fort. **1494** FABYAN *Chron.* VII. 371 John..after many fort assautes wanne the sayd castell. *c* **1611** CHAPMAN *Iliad* XVII. 112 Why should Fame make thee fort 'gainst our harmes.

fort (fɔət), *v.* ? *Obs.* Also 6 forte. [f. FORT *sb.*[1]] *trans.* To defend or protect with a fortification; to fortify; to enclose in a fort; also with *in*.
1559 in *Sir R. Sadler's Papers* (1809) II. 185 The Frenches are to take summe other part of the countrey, and forte it. *a* **1572** KNOX *Hist. Ref.* Wks. 1846 I. 406 To fortifie our tounis..and to lay sa strang garnisouns of straingearis thairin. **1747** in *Westfield (Mass.) Jubilee* (1870) 132 To Consider what measures to take about forting the Town. **1756** G. WASHINGTON *Lett.* Writ. 1889 I. 360 While you remain..forted in, as if to defend yourselves were the sole end of your coming. **1757** *Ibid.* 508 The few families that are forted on the Branch. **1834** D. CROCKETT *Narr. Life* vii. 52 The fort was built right in the middle of a large old field, and in it the people had been forted so long and so quietly, that they didn't apprehend any danger at all. **1838** *Southern Lit. Messenger* IV. 295 The settlers were sometimes forted. **1851** W. DE HASS *Hist. W. Virginia* 315 Of those forted at Grave creek, was a William McIntosh, wife and child. **1853** B. YOUNG in *Jrnl. Discourses* I. 165 Suppose we should say to all the wards in this city, the time has come to fort up. **1878** J. H. BEADLE *Western Wilds* xii. 186 They lit on the Yorker and his friends and druv 'em back into Miller's Store, when they forted and held their own. **1905** G. E. COLE *Early Oregon* iv. 53 We started on and arriving at Grave creek, found the people 'forted up'. **1948** E. N. DICK *Dixie Frontier* 267 Castleman warned the pioneers to 'fort'.
absol. **1723** in G. Sheldon *Hist. Deerfield, Mass.* (1895) I. 396 These towns can't stand the strain upon them to watch and ward, scout and fort without pay.
Hence **'forted** *ppl. a.* **'forting** *vbl. sb.*
1566 NUCE *Seneca's Octavia* I. iv, sig. C ij, Through top of fortred [? *read* forted] towre. **1603** SHAKS. *Meas. for M.* v. i. 12 It deserues..A forted residence, 'gainst the tooth of time. **1808** J. BARLOW *Columb.* v. 760 They dare oppose Their fielded cohorts to the forted foes. **1756** in G. Sheldon *Hist. Deerfield, Mass.* (1895) I. 647 Voted..to Consider..in what ..manner to carry on ye forting.

†**for'take**, *v. Obs.* exc. *arch.* [f. FOR- *pref.*[1] + TAKE *v.*] *trans.* To take away.
c **1460** *Towneley Myst.* (Surtees) 263 It was my gylt he was fortayn, And nothing his. [**1892** STOPF. BROOKE *E.E. Lit.* I. vii. 153 Famine-death fortook fortitude from men.]

fortalice ('fɔːtəlɪs). Forms: 5 fortalys, -alyce, fortilitie, 6 fortilesse, fortilage, fortelleze, fortelace, 7, 9 fortiless, 9 -alise, 6- fortalice. [The surviving form, which is also the earliest recorded, is ad. med.L. *fortalitia*, *fortalitium*, a derivative of *fortis* strong; cf Pr., Sp., Pg. *fortaleza*, It. *fortalizio*, *fortilizio*, OF. *fortelesce* (cf. the parallel formation *forteresce* FORTRESS). Some of the obsolete forms are from Fr. or other Romanic langs.]
In early use = FORTRESS; by mod. writers chiefly used for: 'A small outwork of a fortification' (W.); a small fort.
c **1425** WYNTOUN *Cron.* VIII. xxix. 31 Ðare-in þai made a Fortalyce. **1494** *Act 11 Hen. VII*, c. 18 Any Person..being in his Service within his Towns and Fortilities of Berwick and Carlyle. **1560** ROLLAND *Crt. Venus* II. 847 With stark draw brig, weil forcit with fortalice. **1590** SPENSER *F.Q.* II. xii. 43 Nought feard their force, that fortilage to win. **1642** PRYNNE *Sov. Antidote* 24 Castles, Fortresses, Fortilesses. **1754** ERSKINE *Princ. Sc. Law* (1809) 181 Fortalices, or small places of strength. **1816** SCOTT *Old Mort.* xi, The fortalice thus commanding both bridge and pass. **1870** *Echo* 9 Nov., We canter off to the as yet unfinished fortalice of Des Bordes.
transf. and *fig.*
1826 SCOTT *Woodst.* xxii, This makes Understanding bar himself up within his fortalise. **1830** MARRYAT *King's Own* xxxiii, Seymour and Jerry descended from their little fortalice aloft. **1884** *Mag. of Art* Jan. 102 In the circular fortalice on its [an elephant's] back are troopers with buff coats. **1887** RUSKIN *Præterita* II. 393 A majestic, but unterrific fortalice of cliff, forest, and meadow.

for-tattered, -taxed: see FOR- *pref.*[1] 5 b, 6.

†**forte, fort**, variant of FORTO *prep.* and *conj.* *Obs.* Also sometimes standing for *for to* before an infinitive: see FOR *prep.* 11, 11 b.
a **1175** *Cott. Hom.* 235 Nas tid..þat god ne send gode mænn his folc forte ȝelaðie to his rice. *a* **1225** *Ancr. R.* 96 ȝif eni mon bit fort iseon ou. *c* **1300** *Beket* 86 He ȝeode forte awaite what that wonder were. **1307** *Elegy Edw. I*, ii, Al Englond ahte forte knowe, Of wham that song is. **1362** LANGL. *P. Pl.* A. II. 4 Teche me the kuynde craft forte knowe the False. *c* **1425** *Seven Sag.* (P.) 44 Into his hert fort reche Al the clergy undir sonne That we seven clerkes cunne.

forte ('fɔːti, 'fɔːteɪ, formerly fɔːt), *sb.* Also 7-8 fort. [a. F. *fort*, absolute use of *fort* strong: see FORT *a.* As in many other adoptions of Fr. adjs. used as sbs., the fem. form has been ignorantly substituted for the masc.; cf. *locale*, *morale* (of an army), etc.]
1. The strong point (of a person), that in which he excels.
1682 SHADWELL *Medal* Epil. A b, His Fort is, that he is an indifferent good Versificator. **1768** GOLDSM. *Good-n. Man* Epil., Those things are not our forte at Covent Garden. **1805** W. IRVING in *Life & Lett.* (1864) I. 158 The artful designing hypocrite is his forte, and in Iago he is admirable. **1870** MISS BRIDGMAN *R. Lynne* II. xii. 244 Mr. Selwyn had a forte for horse-racing.
2. *Fencing.* The strongest part of a sword-blade.
a **1648**, **1755**, **1837**, **1879** [see FOIBLE B. 2]. **1692** SIR W. HOPE *Fencing Master* 3 The Strong, Fort, or Prime of the Blade is Measured from the Shell..to the middle of the Blade. **1809** ROLAND *Fencing* 3 The sword being supported by the fort of it in your left hand.
b. *fig.*
1772 in Simes *Milit. Guide* 6 They would more easily discover the fort or foible of their respective commands. **1823** DE QUINCEY *Lett. Yng. Man* Wks. XIV. 27 A student of mature age must be presumed to be best acquainted.. with his 'forte' and his 'foible'.
3. *Pugilism.*
1815 *Sporting Mag.* XLVI. 109 He covered his head with his left hand, went in, and got to his forte.

‖**forte** ('forte, 'fɔːteɪ), *a.* (*adv.*) and *sb.* *Mus.* [It. = strong, loud:—L. *fortis*.] **A.** *adj.* (*adv.*) A musical direction indicating a strong, loud tone in performance. Also ***forte forte*** very loud. (Abbreviated *f.*, *ff.*) Also *attrib.*
1724 *Short Explic. For. Words in Mus. Bks.* 32 *Forte*..is to play or sing loud and strong, and *Forte Forte*, or *FF*, is very loud. **1818** in TODD. **1852** SPENCER *Use & Beauty* Ess. 1891 II. 373 Forte passages in music must have piano passages to relieve them. **1884** *Pall Mall G.* 8 Sept. 4/2 The usual jubilant and unsuitable forte chorus.
B. *sb.* 'Forte' tone; a 'forte' passage. Also, in the Harmonium, an apparatus used for producing a forte effect.
1759 STERNE *Tr. Shandy* I. xxiii, The forte or piano of a certain wind instrument they use. *a* **1774** FERGUSSON *Poems* (1845) 5 Banish vile Italian tricks Frae out your quorum Nor fortes wi' pianos mix. **1883** *Athenæum* 28 Apr. 549/3 His tone in the fortes is rather coarse.

†**for'tee**, *v. Obs.* [OE. *fortéon* (= OHG. *farziuhan*, Ger. *verziehen*), f. FOR- *pref.*[1] + *téon* to draw.] *trans.* To draw away (to evil): to seduce.
a **1000** *Crist* 270 (Gr.) To þam..æðelan rice þonan us..se swearta gæst forteah. *c* **1200** *Trin. Coll. Hom.* 87 þe fule gost ..forteð þat child..to here wille. *a* **1250** *Prov. Ælfred* 334 in *O.E. Misc.* 122 For hit seyþ in the l[e]oþ as scumes forteoþ ..þat cold rede is quene red.

forten, obs. form of FORTUNE *v.*

forte-piano ('fɔːteɪpɪ'ɑːnəʊ), *a.* (*adv.*) and *sb.* [It.; see FORTE and PIANO.]
A. *adj.* (*adv.*) A musical direction indicating sudden but transient emphasis; loud, then immediately soft. (Abbreviated *fp.*) Also as *sb.*, such a succession of notes or chords.
1897 in *N.E.D.* **1917** G. B. SHAW *How to become Mus. Critic* (1960) 294 Sir Thomas Beecham..seems to have no conception of the dynamic range of Mozart's effects, of the fierceness of his *fortepianos*.
B. *sb.* **a.** An early name of the PIANOFORTE.
1769 *Publ. Advertiser* 24 May 4/3 A very large Forte ex [*read* e *or* et] Piano in a Harpsichord Carcase. **1771** T. JEFFERSON *Let.* Writ. 1892 I. 395, I have since seen a Forte-piano and am charmed with it. **1824** *Dict. Musicians* s.v. *Bach*, The King..invited Bach to try his forte-pianos made by Silvermann. **1879–80** GROVE *Dict. Mus.* I. 556 Fortepiano—afterwards changed to pianoforte..was the natural Italian name for the new instrument which could give both loud and soft sounds, instead of loud only, as was the case with the harpsichord. **1948** *Penguin Music Mag.* Oct. 25 How many domestic pianists would relish having to revert to the thin-toned *forte-piano* of Beethoven's day? **1961** *Proc. R. Mus. Assoc.* LXXXVII. 43 It is well known that J. C. Bach preferred the forte piano to the harpsichord. It is, indeed, the ideal instrument for accompanying.
b. *attrib.*, as ***forte-piano maker***, ***teacher***.
1840 MARRYAT *Poor Jack* xiii, He must have been a forty piany teacher. **1844** J. W. CROKER *Guillotine* (1853) 47 One Schmidt, a forte-piano maker.

Fortescue, fortescue ('fɔːtɪskjuː). *Austral.* [perh. alteration of the pop. name *forty skewer* after the proper name *Fortescue*.] A scorpænid fish, *Centropogon australis*.
1874 E. S. HILL in J. E. Tenison-Woods *Fish N.S.W.* (1882) 49 The scorpion or Fortescue..bear that name no doubt in memory of the pain they have hitherto inflicted; and for its number and array of prickles it enjoys in this country the *alias* 'Forty skewer' or 'Fortescure'. **1882** J. E. TENISON-WOODS *Ibid.*, The 'Fortescue'..is a common fish in Port Jackson, with a very long dagger-shaped preorbital spine. **1896** F. G. AFLALO *Nat. Hist. Austral.* 228 Fortescue (*Pentaroge*)..is a terrible pest, lurking among the *débris* in the nets and all but invisible. **1951** T. C. ROUGHLEY *Fish Austral.* 129 Most fishermen on the eastern Australian coast are familiar with..the fortesque (*Centropogon australis*). **1968** G. P. WHITLEY et al. *Animals of World: Austral.* 21/2 Several related fishes such as the..Fortescue (*Centropogon australis*) are less severe in their toxic effects.

forteyn(e, obs. form of FORTUNE *v.*

forth (fɔəθ), *adv.*, *prep.*, and *sb.* Forms: 1 **forð**, **forþ**, (fordh, forht), 3-4 *south.* vorth, 3-6 forthe, (3 ford, 4 ferth, forgh), 4-6 furth(e, (5 firth), 5-6 fourthe, 6-7 forrth. [OE. *forð* = OFris., OS. *forth* (Du. *voort*), MHG. *vort* (mod.Ger. *fort*):—OTeut. **furþo-* (represented also in Goth. *faurþis* FURTHER):—pre-Teut. **prto-*, a derivative with suffix *-to-* of the root which appears in FORE *adv.*
Criticized as obsolete by Gray in letter to Dr. Beattie 8 Mar. 1771.]
A. *adv.*
1. Of movement or direction: Forwards; opposed to backwards. *Obs.* exc. in ***back and forth***, now only *U.S.* (? or *dial.*) = 'backwards and forwards'. †Also, with ellipsis of *go*. Cf. 6 b.
c **1000** ÆLFRIC *Josh.* viii. 20 [Hi] ne mihton ðanon fleon, ne forþ ne underbæc. *c* **1380** WYCLIF *Wks.* (1880) 155 þat riȝtwisnesse may not forþ in her vertuouse lyuynge. *c* **1430** *Hymns Virg.* 97 While riȝt schal forþ, & no mercie. **1535** COVERDALE *Ezra* v. 8 Ye worke goeth fast forth. **1543** T. BASIL in Strype *Eccl. Mem.* I. l. 383 If his grace go forth as he hath begun, he shall [etc.]. **1548** HALL *Chron.*, *Hen. V* (an. 3) 49 Eche armye..beyng in open sight..every man cried furth, furth. **1599** SHAKS. *Hen. V*, II. ii. 189 Then forth, deare Countreymen. **1607** DEKKER & WEBSTER *Northw. Hoe* I. i, Forth, Son. **1613** T. JACKSON *Apost. Creede* I. 196 Lengthning the time by..vnnecessarie turnings, backe and forth. **1839** [see BACK *adv.* 14]. **1882** *Macm. Mag.* XLVI. 203 Back and forth her needle goes.
†**b.** Expressing promptitude or eagerness for action. *to set* (a person) *forth*: to urge forward. ***to make oneself forth***: to bestir oneself, prepare.
c **1470** HENRY *Wallace* IV. 482 To tak him in thai maid thaim redy ford. *Ibid.* VIII. 752 The knycht Cambell..At the north ȝett, and Ramsay maid thaim ford. **1553** T. WILSON *Rhet.* (1580) 67 Good will settyng me forthe with the foremost: I can not chuse but write. **1560** ROLLAND *Crt. Venus* II. 209 In euerie Camp the proudest man armait His pray was ay, and maid him euer ford.
†2. Onwards from a specified point; continuously in one direction; without deviation or interruption. So ***right forth*** (see RIGHT *a.*); FORTH ON.
847 *Charter Æthelwulf* in *O.E. Texts* 434 From ðæm stane forð on ðone herepað on ðone dic. **1297** R. GLOUC. (Rolls) 171 Fram þe on ende of engelond vorþ to þe other end. **1424** *E.E. Wills* (1882) 61 And þanne forth as hit is a-fore declared. **1450–1530** *Myrr. our Ladye* 292 The seconde parte, that ys from Laudamus te furthe to the ende. **1535** COVERDALE *Ezek.* vi. 14 From the wildernesse off Deblat forth.
†**b.** Appended to another adv., giving the additional notion of 'for some distance in the specified direction, everywhere in the specified locality', as ***beneath-***, ***within-***, ***without-forth*** (for quots. see those words); also ***about-forth***, for some distance round; ***otherwise forth***, in all other respects. *Obs.*
c **1400** *Lanfranc's Cirurg.* 223 Whanne þou wolt kutte þis enpostym, þou schalt but kutte aboutefor þ in þe skyn. **1587** FLEMING *Contn. Holinshed* III. 1955/2 He would..not onelie restore him to his former libertie, but otherwise forth be readie to pleasure him.
†**c.** In early ME. *forth mid*, later *forth with* = 'along with'. Also *absol.*, along with him, them, etc.: at the same time with something else.
c **1175** *Lamb. Hom.* 117 þenne losiað fele saulen and he seolf forð mid for his ȝemeleste. *Ibid.* 123 þenne bið he gredi þes eses and forswoleȝeð þene hoc forð mid þan ese. *a* **1200** *Moral Ode* 90 in *E.E.P.* (1862) 28 To heuenriche he scullen, ford mid vre drihte. *c* **1325** *Know Thyself* 95 ibid. 132 Amende þe mon euene forþ mydde. *c* **1386** CHAUCER *Pars. T.* ¶345 There is also costlewe furringe in hir gounes..forth with the superfluitee in lengthe of the forseide gownes. **1460** *Lybeaus Disc.* 1474 (Kaluza) Forþ wiþ þe scholder bon His riȝt arm fell anoon Into þe feld.
†**d.** *forth with that*: at the same moment that. Cf. FORTHWITHAL and FORTHWITH. *Obs.*
1541 R. COPLAND *Galyen's Terap.* 2 A iv, The ende of the bathynge..shalbe forth with that the partycle becometh ruddy and ryse in a lumpe.
3. Of extent in time: Onwards, immediately afterwards and continuously. Now only in phrases ***from this time*** (*day*, etc.) ***forth*** (somewhat *arch.*), and in combs. HENCEFORTH, THENCEFORTH, etc. †*always forth*: continually,

ever more and more, so *ever forth, aye forth* (OE. *á forð*), for which see EVER, AYE.

a **700** *Epinal Gloss.* 529 *In dies crudesceret*: a fordh. *c* **1230** *Hali Meid.* 25 þat laðliche beast leaueð & last forð. *a* **1300** *Cursor M.* 3758 In dew and gress sere o þorth Sal be þi blissing fra no forth. *a* **1450** *Le Morte Arth.* 1668 In the castelle thay gan forthe lende. **1535** COVERDALE *Haggai* ii. 10 Considre then from this daye forth. **1559** FECKNAM in Strype *Ann. Ref.* I. App. ix. 24 Which of them bothe is.. allwayes forth one and agreeable with it self. **1577** HOLINSHED *Scot. Chron.* I. 394/2 The King..assigned hir foorth sufficient reuenewes. **1601** SHAKS. *Jul. C.* IV. iii. 48 From this day forth, Ile vse you for my Mirth. **1611** BIBLE *Ps.* cxiii. 2 Blessed be the name of the Lord: from this time forth. **1850** DICKENS *Child's Dream Star, Househ. Wds.* I. 25 From that hour forth, the child looked out upon the star as on the Home he was to go to.

†**b.** Expressing continuity or progressiveness of action; joined to a verb, and giving the sense 'to go on doing' what the verb denotes. Cf. *on. Obs.*

Beowulf (Z.) 948 Heald forð tela niwe sibbe! *O.E. Chron.* an. 534 (Laud MS.) Cynric..rixade forþ xxvi wintra. **1297** R. GLOUC. (Rolls) 6576 þat water dude uorþ is kunde & wax euere uaste. *c* **1330** R. BRUNNE *Chron.* (1725) 174 If he forth has grace, as he now bigynnes. *c* **1380** WYCLIF *Wks.* (1880) 135 Possessioners may holden forþe here seculer lordischipis. **1399** *Pol. Poems* (Rolls) I. 371 Beholde the book onys..and if ȝe savere sum delle, se it fforth overe. **1428** *E.E. Wills* (1882) 81, I woll that myne Executours.. parfourme forth my deuouacions forth as I was wonte. **1477** EARL RIVERS (Caxton) *Dictes* 7 b, Pray him of his merci he wol kepe you forthe. **1542** RECORDE *Gr. Artes* C iv b, Whiche, after you haue well practysed, then maie you learne forth. **1563** *Homilies* II. *Agst. Idolatry* III. (1859) 216 If you read on forth, it expoundeth itself. *a* **1615** *Brieue Cron. Erlis of Ross* (1850) 17 He bigged furth the Dortour. **1808** SCOTT *Marm.* II. xxx, Now, men of death, work forth your will.

†**c.** *to make forth* (*long, longer*): to protract.

1565–73 COOPER *Thesaurus, Contexere longius*..I might make forth this verse longer. **1611** SHAKS. *Cymb.* IV. ii. 149 The Boy Fideles sickenesse Did make my way long forth.

†**d.** Further, moreover, also. *Obs.*

c **1315** SHOREHAM 9 Ne mede ne forthe no other licour That chaungeth wateres kende, Ne longeth nauȝt to cristendom. **1481** CAXTON *Reynard* (Arb.) 34 My lorde the kynge, and dere quene, and forth alle ye that here stande.

†**4.** At or to an advanced point: **a.** of position or progress. *Obs.*

a **1225** *Ancr. R.* 374 Monie þet beoð ful uorð iðe weie touward heouene. *a* **1300** *Cursor M.* 11027 (Gött.) Elizabeth, þat wele forth stadd. *Ibid.* 11203 (Cott.) þan was sco gan sua forth, þat mild, þat sco was at hir time o child. *c* **1400** MAUNDEV. (1839) xvii. 180 More forthe toward the parties septemtrioneles: it [the North Pole] is 62 Degrees.

†**b.** of time. *forth days, nighte*; *forth in with even*: late in the day, night, or evening. *Obs.*

a **1300** *Birth of Jesus* 576 in *Altengl. Leg.* (Horstm.) 91 Vorþ niȝte hit was. **1388** WYCLIF *Mark* vi. 35 Whanne it was forth daies [*cum hora multa fieret*], his disciplis camen. *a* **1400** *Sir Perc.* 825 Tille one the morne at forthe dayes, He mett a wyche. *a* **1400–50** *Alexander* 3055 þen quen þai fange to ȝe fliȝt was furth in with euyn. **1470–85** MALORY *Arthur* XX. v. 804 Or it be forth dayes.

5. Forward, into view. Only with such verbs as *bring, come, show, put*, etc.: see the verbs.

c **900** tr. *Bæda's Hist.* v. xiv. [xiii.] (1890) 438 þa teah heora oðer forð fægre boc. *c* **1050** *Byrhtferth's Handboc* in *Anglia* VIII. 298, & forð stæpð wel orglice binnan feower wintrum. *c* **1200** ORMIN 3078, & ec he droh þatt wittness forþ Off Ysayȝess lare. *c* **1340** *Cursor M.* 11988 (Fairf.) He..oþer childer forþ hit kid. **1388** WYCLIF *2 Sam.* vi. 6 Oza helde forth the hond to the arke of God. **1551** T. WILSON *Logike* (1580) 3 b, A question is either a worde or sentence put foorthe, as when I aske what suche thyng is. **1692** E. WALKER *Epictetus' Mor.* xx, If tis nigh, Stretch forth your Hand, take share with Modesty. **1719** YOUNG *Busiris* I. i, This day the court shines forth in all its lustre. **1872** JENKINSON *Guide Eng. Lakes* (1879) 159 Skiddaw, which stands forth in all its majesty.

†**b.** with ellipsis of *come* or *go*. *forth with* = come forth with, (come) out with, utter. *Obs.*

c **1400** *Lanfranc's Cirurg.* 139 He myȝte forþ wiþ no word. **1551** ROBINSON tr. *More's Utop.* To Rdr. (Arb.) 19 To Imprintinge it came..against my wyll. Howebeit.. perceauing therfore none other remedy, but that furth it shoulde.

6. Away or out from a place of origin, residence, or sojourn.

c **1000** ÆLFRIC *Exod.* xiii. 19 Alædaþ mine ban forþ mid eow. *c* **1175** *Lamb. Hom.* 5 þat folc eode þar ford to processiun to munte olueti. *c* **1250** *Gen. & Ex.* 113 Forð glod ðis oðer dais niȝt. *a* **1300** *Fall & Passion* 47 in *E.E.P.* (1862) 14 God is angle anon forþ send. *c* **1400** *Destr. Troy* 2984 Sho..Hade hom radly arayed for þe rode furth. **1596** SHAKS. *Tam. Shr.* v. ii. 104 Swinge me them soundly forth vnto their husbands. **1697** DRYDEN *Virg. Georg.* IV. 104 In form of Battel drawn, they issue forth. **1771** BEATTIE *Minstrel* I. iii, Nor need I here describe..How forth the Minstrel far'd in days of yore. **1852** MISS YONGE *Cameos* I. i. 5 The Vikings..sailed fearlessly forth.

b. with ellipsis of *go.* Now *arch.*

c **1175** *Lamb. Hom.* 81 Nu is þes deakne forþe. *c* **1330** R. BRUNNE *Chron.* (1810) 309 No lenger suld þei bide, bot forth & stand to chance. **1481** CAXTON *Godfrey* clix. 234 The goyng forth of therle of tholouse..caused them moche to haue the wyll forth. **1607** SHAKS. *Cor.* I. iii. 99 Indeed, I will not foorth. **1837** CARLYLE *Fr. Rev.* I. VII. iv, Maternity must forth to the streets. **1860** W. COLLINS *Antonina* xii, The slaves..are forth to pursue me.

†**7.** Of position: Abroad; not at home; in the field; at sea. Cf. ABROAD 3 and 4. *Obs.*

14.. *Chalmerlain Ayr* (*Sc. Stat.* I), Alswele induellande as furth duelland. **1590** SHAKS. *Com. Err.* II. ii. 212 Say he dines forth. **1596** —— *Merch. V.* I. i. 15 Had I such venture forth. **1598** —— *Merry W.* II. ii. 276 At that time..her husband will be forth. **1607** —— *Cor.* I. iii. 108 The Volcies haue an Army forth.

†**8.** In senses 5 and 6, the adv. was formerly used in many idiomatic combinations with verbs, where for the most part *out* is now substituted. *Obs.*

c **1430** *Two Cookery-bks.* I. 23 Coloure it with Safroun, an sethe an serue forth. **1513** DOUGLAS *Æneis* XIII. Prol. 164 Furth quynching gan the starris, one be one. **1513** MORE in Grafton *Chron.* (1568) II. 770 The fetching forth of this noble man..out of that place. **1584** *Vestry Bks.* (Surtees) 16 Laid forthe by the foresaid churchwardens..vij s. vj d. **1593** *Tell-Troth's N.Y. Gift* 34 New conceites are easly remoued but engrauen thoughtes will not be rubbed forth. **1590** SHAKS. *Com. Err.* IV. iv. 98 Say, wherefore didst thou locke me forth to-day. **1593** —— *3 Hen. VI*, II. i. 12, I..watcht him how he singled Clifford forth. **1596** —— *Merch. V.* I. i. 143 To finde the other forth. **1611** BIBLE *Transl. Pref.* 1 He gaue foorth, that hee had not seene any profit. **1659** D. PELL *Impr. Sea* 280 If they finde them so doing, they will blow them [candles] forth. **1688** R. HOLME *Armoury* III. 182/1 The Library Keeper is..to keep the Books clean, to lend none forth.

9. Phraseological combinations.

a. forth of = *out of* in various senses. Now only *poet.* or *rhetorical*, and only in lit. sense expressive of motion from within a place. In 16–17th c. occas. †*from forth of.* †*forth of door(s, forth adoors*: out of doors; see ADOORS. †*forth of hand* = out of hand, at once.

c **1500** *Doctry. Gd. Servaunts* (Percy Soc.) 8 Whan your mayster is forth of towne. **1513** DOUGLAS *Æneis* III. viii. 26 Furth of his eft schip a bekyn gart he stent. **1537** POLE *Let. to King* in Strype *Eccl. Mem.* I. App. lxxxii. 203 There was never man..that by offence was forth of the grace & favor of God. **1552–3** *Inv. Ch. Goods, Staffs.* in *Ann. Lichfield* IV. 51 Thes parcells followynge were stolne furthe of the sayd churche at Cristmas. **1564** HAWARD *Eutropius* v. 51 They shuld be all slaine forthe of hande. *c* **1592** MARLOWE *Massacre Paris* III. iii, I'll..root Valois his line from forth of France. **1594** SHAKS. *Rich. III*, IV. iv. 176 Humfrey Hower ..call'd your Grace To Breakefast once, forth of my company. **1607** WILKINS *Miseries Enforct Marr.* v, Off with your coate then, get you forth a dores. **1614** *North Riding Rec.* (1884) II. 54 A woman presented for that she will not sell anie of her ale forth of doores except it [etc.]. **1622** in Picton *L'pool Munic. Rec.* (1883) I. 212 Forth of his wayges ..soe much money shall be abated. **1632** ROWLEY *Woman never vext* IV. 59 My..Vncle [being] poore, I him relieving was thrust forth of dores. **1633** T. JAMES *Voy.* 61 Forth adores we could not go. **1671** J. WEBSTER *Metallogr.* i. 14 A Roman Hermit, whose Writings were translated forth of the Arabick Language into Latine. **1751** *Affect. Narr. Wager* 63 He threw his Pistol aside, and came forth of the Tent. **1816** KEATINGE *Trav.* (1817) I. 49 He who is exiled forth of the land, endures his punishment at home. **1867** SWINBURNE in *Fortn. Rev.* Nov. 541 Flee from the foot of the lion..forth of his den.

b. and so forth. †(*a*) And then onwards; and then in regular sequence. †(*b*) And similarly (in the remaining cases); usually followed by *of* (OE. *be*). (*c*) Now used only (like *and so on*) in breaking off an enumeration, quotation, etc.: And the like, etcetera. Formerly also, †*or so forth.*

(*a*) *c* **1000** ÆLFRIC *Gram.* xxv. (Z.) 144 And swa forþ. *c* **1290** *S. Eng. Leg.* I. 473/400 To his schyp he wende: and so forz [*read* forþ] in þe se. *c* **1340** *Cursor M.* 6122 (Fairf.) At the kyng he first by gan And so forth slow beste & man. **1377** LANGL. *P. Pl.* B. XIV. 159 Moche murthe in Maye is amonges wilde bestes, And so forth whil somer lasteth her solace dureth. **1551** RECORDE *Pathw. Knowl.* II. lvi, If a line bee drawen by bothe their centres, and so forthe in lengthe. **1574** WHITGIFT *Def. Answ.* III. i. 9 Looke at the 2. Admonition especially, and so foorth, where [etc.].

(*b*) *c* **1000** *Starcraft fr. Bæda* 4 in *Sax. Leechd.* III. 250 And swa forð be ðam oðrum. *c* **1400** MAUNDEV. (Roxb.) xxx. 137 A Kyng es porter..anoþer sewer, anoþer marschall, and so furth of all oþer officez þat langes till his courte. **1450–1530** *Myrr. our Ladye* 3 Why an hympne ys callyd an hympne..why an Antempne is callyd an Antempne and so fourth of other. ? *a* **1500** *Wycket* (1828) 4 They spared not the sonne of God..and so forth of the apostels and martirs.

(*c*) *c* **1574–5** ABP. PARKER *Corresp.* (1853) 474, I toy out my time, partly with copying of books..partly in genealogies, and so forth. **1602** SHAKS. *Ham.* II. i. 61 *Videlicet*, a Brothell, or so forth. **1670** G. H. *Hist. Cardinals* III. I. 239 These were such as declar'd him a Heretick..a Profaner, and so forth. **1745** P. THOMAS *Jrnl. Anson's Voy.* 44 Some Jewels, abundance of Gold and Silver Twist, and so forth. **1816** KEATINGE *Trav.* (1817) II. 155 Coal beds..piscatory exuviæ, and so forth. **1841** MACAULAY *Let. Napier* in Trevelyan *Life* (1876) II. ix. 127 This lady..called the Marquis of Hertford 'Earl of Hertford', and so forth.

†**c. as** or **so forth**: as or so far, to such an extent or degree (*as, that*). Cf. FAR-FORTH.

a **1000** *Ags. Laws, Oaths* xi, Swa forð swa uncre wordȝecwydu fyrmest wæron. *a* **1225** *Leg. Kath.* 2304 ȝef þu.. wult greten ure godes ase forð as þu ham hauest igremet. *a* **1225** *Juliana* 15 þat tu hauest wið ute me se forð þi luue ileuet þat [etc.]. *Ibid.* 47 And wurche his wil ouer al ase forð as imei. *c* **1386** CHAUCER *Man of Law's Prol.* 19 (Harl. MS.) Leseþ no tyme, as forþe as ȝe may.

B. *prep.*

†**1.** Forward to, up to, to the extent or limit of. Chiefly with *even*: see EMFORTH, EVEN-FORTH. Also in conjunctional phrase, *forth that*: until.

c **888** K. ÆLFRED *Boeth.* xxxviii. § 5 On cnihthade and swa forþ eallne ðonne ȝioȝoþhad. *c* **1175** *Lamb. Hom.* 91 Forð þet ic alegge þine feond under þine fot-sceomele. *c* **1200** *Trin. Coll. Hom.* 87 Forð þat hie understonden wurldes wit. *c* **1449** PECOCK *Repr.* 52 The processis forth and afore the textis ligging. *Ibid.* I. xvii. 100 The processis forth and aftir, bifore and behinde, where thilke textis ben writun.

2. Forward, out or away from; out of, from out of. Now *rare.*

1566–75 PAINTER *Pal. Pleas.* (1813) II. 114 In saying so, the teares gushed forth hir eyes. **1594** DANIEL *Cleopatra* II. i, And forth her trembling Hand the Blade did wrest. **1595** HUNNIS *Joseph* 5 They stript him forth his party cote. **1670** P. HENRY *Diaries & Lett.* (1882) 231 [He] went forth his Desk. **1678** OTWAY *Friendship in Fash.* v. (1736) 107 Discharge them of their punishment, and see 'em forth the gates. **1814** CARY *Dante* (Chandos) 210 Never fire, With so swift motion, forth a stormy cloud, Leap'd downward. **1864** BLACKMORE *Clara Vaughan* xxxiv, The brambled quarry standing forth the trees.

b. Preceded by *from.*

a **1592** MARLOWE & NASHE *Dido* II. i, Poor Troy..From forth her ashes shall advance her head. **1598** SHAKS. *Merry W.* IV. iv. 53 Let them from forth a saw-pit rush at once. **1671** MILTON *Samson* 922 That I may fetch thee From forth this loathsome prison-house. **1820** KEATS *St. Agnes* xxx, He from forth the closet brought a heap Of candied apple.

†**C.** *sb.* In phrase, *to have one's forth*: to have outlet; *fig.* to have free course, to have one's 'fling'. Hence (*rarely*) as independent sb.: Free course, wide publicity. *Obs.*

1362 LANGL. *P. Pl.* A. III. 153 Letteþ so faste, þat Feiþ may not han hus forþ. **1496** *Dives & Paup.* (W. de W.) VIII. vii. 329/1 These men of lawe..for mede withdrawe them to ..lette falsebede haue his forth. **1567** JEWELL *Apol.* 327 Wee ..geeue God thankes, that..hath published..the name of his Sonne in euery place..The foorth, and force thereof greeueth you nowe..as it did..your Fathers..that cried.. All the worlde renneth after him. **1597** J. KING *On Jonah* (1599) 362 Thorough Propontis, where the sea is patent againe, and hath his forth. **1597** HOOKER *Eccl. Pol.* v. lxii. § 8 The Church..was contented to let Donatists haue their foorth by the space of threescore yeares. **1611** SPEED *Hist. Gt. Brit.* IX. viii. § 32 Obstacles..which all must be done and voided before the Pope can haue his full forth.

D. forth- in composition. In OE. and ME. the combinations of *forth* adv. with vbs. are hardly to be considered compound words; whether the adv. precedes or follows the vb. depends on euphonic or other conditions which do not affect the sense. The agent-nouns, nouns of action, and ppl. adjs. corresponding to these verbal locutions were formed by prefixing *forth* to the verbal noun or adj. corresponding to the verb. In mod.Eng. compound vbs. formed with *forth-* are rare; but *forth-* is often used as a prefix in the formation of nouns of agent and action, and ppl. adjs. corresponding to the verbal phrases (compound verbs in sense but not in form) in which the adv. follows the verb. More frequently, however, the agent-noun, etc. is followed by the adv.; thus we have *a setter forth*, but *forthsetter is app. not recorded. For the formation of ppl. adjs. the prefix is the only means available; and in poetry from Pope onwards it is very common in pres. pples.

In some OE. and ME. words, *forth-* appears as a substitute for FORE-: see FORTHFATHER, FORTHWARD, FORTHWITH 2.

The more important compounds of *forth-* will be treated in their alphabetical place as Main words; those enumerated in this article are nonce-words or of rare occurrence.

1. Verbs; as *forth-leap, -throw*, and renderings of Lat. vbs. with *pro-*, as *forth-cut, -follow, -look.*

1382 WYCLIF *Isa.* xxviii. 24 Whether al day shal ere the erere, that he sowe and *forth kutten [Vulg. *proscindet*], and purge his erthe. *a* **1300** *E.E. Psalter* lxviii. 27 [lxix. 26] For wham þou smate, *forth-filiyhed [Vulg. *persecuti sunt*] þa. **13..** *E.E. Allit. P.* C. 154 Mony ladde þer *forth-lep to laue & to kest. *a* **1300** *E.E. Psalter* lxxxiv. 12 [lxxxv. 11] Fra heven *forth-loked [Vulg. *prospexit*] rightwisenes. **1557** *Tottell's Misc.* (Arb.) 195 To stay my life pray her *furththrowe swete lokes whan I complaine.

2. Nouns: **a.** vbl. sbs.; as *forth-carrying, -flowing, -giving*, †*-living, -shedding, -shining, -stretching.* Also, †**forth-getting**, a shoot, sprout; †**forth-growing**, an outgrowth. **b.** nouns of action; as, *forth-flow, -look*, †*-progress, -roll*, †*-speed.* **c.** agent-nouns, as *forth-speaker.*

1716 in *Wodrow Corr.* (1843) II. 137 The old..woman.. died in the *forth-carrying. **1870** J. DUNCAN *Colloq. Peripat.* 138 The *forthflow of the one life of the Universe. **1886** A. B. BRUCE *Miraculous Elem. Gosp.* vii. 258 The *forth-flowing of that love. **1382** WYCLIF *Jer.* v. 10 Doth awei his *forthgetingus [Vulg. *propagines*], for thei ben not the Lordis. **1887** L. PARKS *His Star in East* ii. 52 The creation of a father is the *forthgiving of a father's life. **1562** TURNER *Herbal* II. 40 b, In the top of (the braunches of Lithospermon) is ther a double *furthgrowyng or a double thyng growing out. ? *c* **1450** *MS. St. John's Coll. Oxon* (No. 117 fo. 123 b) in Maskell *Mon. Rit.* III. 356 Loke thi beginning of thi lif, care and sorwe: thi *fo[r]thliuing, trauail ..and disese. **1865** A. B. GROSART *Mem. H. Palmer* 45 A worn, wistful, sad *forth-look that is unspeakably touching. *c* **1475** *Partenay* 3199 To thys *forth-progresse Geffray made redy. **1891** G. MEREDITH *One of our Conq.* I. viii. 144 The noble *forthroll of the notes. **1526** *Pilgr. Perf.* (W. de W. 1531) 254 His great effusyon or *forthshedynge of his blode. **1875** E. WHITE *Life in Christ* II. xi. (1878) 121 The full *forthshining of the light came only with the Christ. **1873** D. FRASER *Synopt. Lect.* III. 2 The prophet, or *forth-speaker. **1494** FABYAN *Chron.* VI. clxix. 162 Which tydynges lettyd hym of his *forth spede in that iourney. *c* **1400** tr. *Secreta Secret., Gov. Lordsh.* (E.E.T.S.) 69 *Forth-strechynge of þe membres makys stalworth þe body.

3. Adjectives and participles: a. Pres. pples. and ppl. adjs., as *forth-beaming*, *-flowing*, *-giving*, *-gleaming*, *-issuing*, *-standing*; also †*forth-werþand*, casting out. b. Pass. pples., as †*forth-fet*, †*-sent*; also, †**forth-grown**, brought up; †**forth-straȝt**, stretched out (= Lat. *directæ*).

1725 POPE *Odyss.* XIII. 501 Nor longer in the heavy eyeball shined The glance divine, *forth-beaming from the mind. *c* **1425** *Seven Sag.* (P.) 2440 Anon hys sone was *forthe fete And ladde ther he schulde dee. **1866** R. S. CANDLISH *1st Ep. John* xxvii. 306 Is all clear and open free and *forthflowing between thee and him. **1883** *Life Mrs. Prentiss* ix. 290 She was peculiarly free and..*forthgiving. *a* **1835** MRS. HEMANS *Eng. Mart.* i, Rolls like a furling banner, from the brows Of the *forth-gleaming hills. *c* **1400** *Test. Love* I. Chaucer's Wks. (1532) 331 b, The cytie of London..in whiche I was *forthe growen. **1725** POPE *Odyss.* xx. 181 To the sage Greeks convened in Themis' court, *Forth-issuing from the dome, the prince repaired. **1611** W. SCLATER *Key* (1628) To Reader, My desire was to haue *forth-sent them with greater company and better furniture. **1715–20** POPE *Iliad* XIII. 93 As a Falcon..*Forth-springing instant, darts her self from high. **1866** BLACKMORE *Cradock Nowell* xlvii, The pupils *forthstanding haggardly. **1382** WYCLIF *Ecclus.* xxxix. 29 The weies of it to the weies of them ben *forth straȝt. *a* **1300** *E.E. Psalter* xvi[i]. 11 Me um gaf nou me *forth werpand [Vulg. *projicientes*].

†**forth**, *v.* *Obs.* Forms: 1 **forðian** (also **ȝeforðian**: see AFFORD), 2–4 **forthen**, 3 *Orm.* **forthenn**, 5 **forthe**. [OE. *forðian*, f. FORTH *adv.*; formally, it corresponds to L. *portāre* to carry.]

1. *trans.* To accomplish, carry out; also, to manage *to* (do something). See AFFORD 1, 2, and 3.

O.E. Chron. an. 675 (Laud MS.) Hwilc man swa haueð behaten to faren to Rome, and he ne muȝe hit forðian. *c* **1200** ORMIN 212 Þu shallt ben dumb Till þatt itt shall ben forþedd. *a* **1225** *Juliana* 67 Forðe al þi feaders wil þes feondes of helle. **1340–70** *Alex. & Dind.* 570 Of more make ȝe avaunt, þan ȝe mowe forþen. *a* **1400–50** *Alexander* 1774 Vnneth may þou forthe þine awen caitefe cors to clethe, & to fede. *c* **1460** *Towneley Myst.* (Surtees) 45 Alle that I say I shalle forthe.

2. To put forward, offer.

c **1200** *Trin. Coll. Hom.* 43 Vnderstonde we..his holie wordes, and forþe [*proferamus*] we him ure rihte bileue.

forth(e, obs. f. FORD *sb.*[1]

fortham, -than: see FORTHON.

for that, *conj.* Also 7 **for that that**. [See FOR *prep.* 21 b.]

1. For the reason that, because. *arch.*

c **1200** ORMIN 3826 Þa wakenenn to frofrenn Forr þatt hi wisste wel þatt teȝȝ Off himm fordrædde wærenn. *a* **1250** *Owl & Night.* 365 And seist for þat ich fleo bi nihte þat ich ne mai iseo bi lihte. *c* **1400** *Lanfranc's Cirurg.* 14 In moiste bodies for þat þe smale lymes ben feble. **1598** SHAKS. *Merry W.* III. iv. 82 For that I love your daughter..I must advance the colours of my love. **1620** J. WILKINSON *Coroners & Sherifes* 1 The Statute of Westminster..rehearseth, For that that people of small condition..be..chosen [etc.]. **1641** J. SHUTE *Sarah & Hagar* (1649) 116 For that her mistress had corrected her, her stomack riseth against it. **1782** COWPER *Gilpin* 26 For that wine is dear, We will be furnish'd with our own. **1894** *Yellow Bk.* I. 67 It is hard to trace folly, for that it is inconsequent, to its start.

¶ The mod. use of *for that* in reported speech (when both words are conjs.) is to be distinguished from the above.

1774 GOLDSM. *Grecian Hist.* II. 8 The courier conjured him..that he should read them forthwith, for that they contained matter of great importance. **1821** KEATS *Lamia* 306 Bidding him raise His drooping head..For that she was a woman. **1855** MACAULAY *Hist. Eng.* (1889) II. xvii. 282 He had told them to go to their supper..for that nothing more would be done that day. **1873** TRISTRAM *Moab* i. 6 That we were needlessly encumbering ourselves, for that..rice might be procured..in the villages.

†2. For the purpose that; in order that. *Obs.*

c **1200** ORMIN 1019 Þatt waȝherifft wass hengedd tær, Forr that itt hidenn shollde All [etc.]. **13..** *Guy Warw.* (A.) 146 Al folk he dede him loue, For þat noman schuld him schoue. **1428** in *Surtees Misc.* (1890) 7 For þ^t pair praiers suld stand John Lyllyng to availl. **1572** R. H. tr. *Lauaterus' Ghostes* (1596) 104, I thought good to repeate these things..the rather for that the reader might see, that [etc.].

†**forth'bear**, *v.* *Obs.* [OE. *forðberan*, f. FORTH *adv.* + *beran* to BEAR.] *trans.* a. In OE.: To bring forth, produce. b. To bear forth, bring out. c. To promote, uphold.

c **900** tr. *Bæda's Hist.* I. vii. (1890) 34 Þone æðelan Albanum seo wæstmberende Bryton forðbereð. *c* **1305** *St. Edmund King* 85 in *E.E.P.* (1862) 89 Þe wolf makede þo deol ynouȝ, þo hi þat heued forþþere. *c* **1400** tr. *Secreta Secret., Gov. Lordsh.* (E.E.T.S.) 55 Ouer alle þinges it fallys to a kynge..to forthbere religious men.

†**'forthbirth.** *Obs. rare*$^{-1}$. = FORBIRTH b.

a **1300** *Cursor M.* 6122 (Gött.) He..þe forth-birth [*Cott.* forbirth] slow bath [best] and man.

†**forth'bring**, *v.* *Obs.* [OE. *forðbringan*, f. FORTH *adv.* + *bringan* to BRING.] *trans.* = *bring forth* in various senses: a. To bear (offspring, fruit); to bring to pass. b. To bring forward; to bring out, utter. c. To bring up, rear.

a. *c* **971** *Blickl. Hom.* 37 Ealle þa wæstmas þe eorþe forþbringeþ. *a* **1300** *Cursor M.* 384 Þe dri [he] cald erth þat lauerd kyng, and bad it gress and frut forthbring. *Ibid.* 10722 Of rote of iesse þar suld spring A wand þat suld a flur forth bring. **1340** HAMPOLE *Pr. Consc.* 5866 Sons and doghtirs þat þai forthebroght. *c* **1460** *Towneley Myst.* (Surtees) 1 After my wille this is furth broght.

b. *c* **1000** *Ags. Gosp.* Luke vi. 45 Yfel man of yfelum goldhorde yfel forþbringþ. *c* **1305** *St. Edmund Conf.* 570 in *E.E.P.* (1862) 86 He sat longe in þoȝte, & al laȝinge an englisch þuse wordes forþ broȝte. *c* **1325** *Songe of Deo Gracias* 5 ibid. 124, I seiȝ a clerk a boke forthe brynge. *c* **1425** *Seven Sag.* (P.) 3116 The childe was forthe broght.

c. *c* **1430** *Syr Gener.* 879 From a childe she him forth broght.

Hence **forth'bringing** *vbl. sb.*, the action of the vb.; †*esp.* the carrying forth of a body for burial. Also **forth'bringer**, one who, or that which, brings forth or produces.

1398 TREVISA *Barth. De P.R.* VIII. i. (1495) 296 Though the worlde seme fader and forthbrynger and feder of bodyes. **1429** *Wills & Inv. N.C.* (Surtees 1835) 78, I wylle yat eu'y prest seculer..haue..to be at my dirges and forthbryngyng j noble. **1546** BALE *Eng. Votaries* I. (1548) 17 b, Saynt Kentigerne..had..a fayre mayde to his forthebrynger. **1584** *Lanc. & Chesh. Wills* (1884) 98 After my forth bringinge, the rest of my goodes to be devided equaly to my wif and Children. **1874** PUSEY *Lent. Serm.* 12 The forerunner and forthbringer of the next week's or next month's deadly sin. **1889** *Athenæum* 7 Sept. 321/1 The success of the book depending so largely upon its artistic forthbringing.

†**forthby**, *adv.* *Obs.* = FORBY *adv.* 1 b.

c **1386** CHAUCER *Pardoner's T.* 340 (Harl. MS.) What corps is [this] þat passeth her forþ by? **14..** LYDG. *Temple Glas* 230 Forth-bi as he doþ pace. **1483** CAXTON *Gold. Leg.* 84 b/1 Seuen deuylles..which slew all them that passed forthby. *c* **1489** —— *Sonnes of Aymon* xxviii. 586 Thenne cam a pylgrym forthby.

†**forth'call**, *v.* *Obs. rare.* [f. FORTH *adv.* + CALL *v.*] *trans.* a. To provoke; = L. *provocare*. b. To call or summon forth.

a **1300** *E.E. Psalter* lxxvii[i]. 58 In þar graves at nithe þai forth-kalled him als. **1748** THOMSON *Cast. Indol.* II. xii, Forth-calling all with which boon earth is fraught.

†**forth'cast**, *v.* *Obs.* [f. FORTH *adv.* + CAST *v.*] *trans.* To cast forth.

a **1300** *E.E. Psalter* xlix. [l.] 17 Þou..forth-keste mi saghes hind-ward þare. *a* **1340** HAMPOLE *Psalter* xvi. 12 Forth-kastand me now þai haf vmgifen me. **1674** N. FAIRFAX *Bulk & Selv.* 120 When motion is shifted or begotten in the thing mov'd or forthcast.

Hence †**forth'cast** *ppl. a.* Also †**'forthcast** *sb.*, a thing cast forth, a projectile.

1674 N. FAIRFAX *Bulk & Selv.* 122 This comes not home to the business of forthcast things. *Ibid.* 129 Only herein the motion that nature gives, is unlike to that which we bequeath to forthcasts.

†**forth'clepe**, *v.* *Obs.* [OE. *forþclipian*, f. FORTH *adv.* + *clipian*, CLEPE *v.*] *trans.* To call forth, invite forward. Also, to incite, provoke.

?*c* **1000** *Gal.* v. 26 (Lye) Forþclypiend us betwynan, *provocantes invicem*. *a* **1175** *Cott. Hom.* 231 Ȝef he frend were me hine sceolde derewrlice forð clepien. **1382** WYCLIF *Deut.* xxxii. 11 As an egle forthclepynge his bryddis to flee.

†**'forthcome**, *sb.* *Obs. rare.* [f. FORTH *adv.* + OE. *cyme*, COME *sb.*[1]] A coming forth.

c **1000** ÆLFRIC *Gen.* xxxviii. 28 On ðæra cilda forþcyme. *a* **1300** *E.E. Psalter* civ. [cv.] 38 Fained es Egipt in forth-come of am.

forthcome (fɔəθ'kʌm), *v.* [f. FORTH *adv.* + COME *v.*] *intr.* To come forth. Now only as an occasional back-formation from the *ppl. a.*: To be forthcoming.

a **1000** *Cædmon's Gen.* 122 (Gr.) Metod..heht..leoht forð-cuman. **1340** HAMPOLE *Pr. Consc.* 713 Man..als a flour bright, First forth comes here til þis light, And es sone broken and passes away. **1848** KINGSLEY *Saint's Trag.* II. vii, This food forthcomes not. **1886** *Spectator* 2 Jan. 12/1 If funds be forthcoming (and..funds will forthcome).

Hence **forth'come** *ppl. a.*, that has come forth or been issued. Also **forth'comer**.

1812–14 SIR R. WILSON in *Sat. Rev.* XII. 384/1 Their quantity and quality astonish the Prussians, and gain the English many a gaze as forthcomers from a country where [etc]. **1827** LAMB *Let. to B. Barton* in *Life & Lett.* xvi. Wks. (1865) 50 A forthcome or coming review of foreign books. **1840** *New Monthly Mag.* LVIII. 497 The last forthcomer from Paternoster-row, or Albemarle-street. **1863** MASSON in *Reader* 7 Nov. 527/3 [Books] no longer forthcoming, but actually forthcome within the last few days.

forthcoming (fɔəθ'kʌmɪŋ), *vbl. sb.* [f. FORTH *adv.* + COMING *vbl. sb.*[1]]

1. A coming forth; *esp.* †appearance in court.

1533 MORE *Apol.* xxxvii. Wks. 903/1 He woulde..rather ..suffer them [his harmes] paciently, then to..proue them with his forth comming agaÿne. **1591** *Child Marriages* (1897) 149 Richard Wilson vndertaketh for the furth-coming of Robert Kirks. **1640** *Order of Lords* in Rushw. *Hist. Coll.* III. (1692) I. 127 The Lords ordered him to give 10000*l.* Bail for his forth-coming. **1703** J. LOGAN in *Pa. Hist. Soc. Mem.* IX. 224 Take security of them for their..forth-coming when called for. **1822–34** GOOD *Study Med.* (ed. 4) IV. 353 He had notice of their [i.e. the worms'] forth-coming by a sense of heat in the urinary canal. **1856** C. J. ANDERSSON *Lake Ngami* 362 My other waggons..had not yet arrived..Whilst abiding their forthcoming, I busied myself in mapping.

2. *Sc. Law.* See quot. 1861 and cf. FORTHCOMING *ppl. a.* 1 b.

1754 ERSKINE *Princ. Sc. Law* (1809) 36 In forthcomings, in poindings of the ground, in mails and duties. **1861** W. BELL *Dict. Law Scotl.*, *Forthcoming*, is the action by which an arrestment is made available to the arrester. **1886** *Act* 49 *Vict.* c. 23 §3 Such winding up shall..be equivalent to an arrestment in execution and decree of forthcoming.

forthcoming (fɔəθ'kʌmɪŋ), *ppl. a.* [f. FORTH *adv.* + COMING *ppl. a.*]

1. a. About to or likely to come forth; also *simply*, coming or approaching (in time); *esp.* ready to appear or be produced when required, at one's disposal or within one's reach, 'get-at-able'. Said both of persons and things. † *to keep* (a person) *forthcoming*: to keep in safe custody. † *to see* (a person) *forthcoming*: ? to make amenable to control.

1521–32 BP. LONGLAND in Ellis *Orig. Lett.* Ser. III. xcv. 248 That he be forth comyng to his answere when your Grace shall commaund. **1565–73** *Durham Deposit.* (Surtees) 219 To arreste the said Isabell..and to kepe her furthcomyng unto the morning. **1621** BURTON *Anat. Mel.* I. i. II. vii, Memory layes up all the species which the senses have brought in and records them as a good register that they may be forth coming when they are called for. *a* **1635** NAUNTON *Fragm. Reg.* (Arb.) 17 If you think to rule here, I will take a course to see you forth-coming. **1640–1** *Kirkcudbr. War-Comm. Min. Bk.* (1855) 80 To..find sufficient suretie that the samen shall be furth-cumand to the publict. **1647** CLARENDON *Hist. Reb.* IV. §151 The Members should be forth coming assoon as a Legal Charge should be preferred against them. **1674** N. FAIRFAX *Bulk & Selv.* 170 His everlasting Essence..must be forth-coming. **1795** LD. AUCKLAND *Corr.* (1862) III. 354, I am forthcoming any day except Monday next. **1829** LYTTON *Disowned* 3 When neither Canary, Palermo, nor Sherry are forthcoming. **1859** LANG *Wand. India* 270 He had forgotten all about the forthcoming execution. **1893** *Law Times* XCIV. 601/1 Possible but never forthcoming claimants.

b. *Sc. Law* in phrase *to make forthcoming*.

1609 SKENE *Reg. Maj.* 24 The ordinator..is bound..to finde and make forthcumand to him ane bondman. **1693** V'CT STAIR *Instit.* III. i. §36. 374 This action for making Sums or Goods arrested forthcoming is ordinary.

2. Ready to make or meet advances. Also, informative, responsive.

1835 T. MOORE *Mem.* (1856) VII. 81 Nothing could be more frank or forthcoming than his manner. **1885** L. MALET *Col. Enderby's Wife* III. vi, She was extremely gracious and forthcoming; but one might detect a certain watchfulness and hardness behind her genial manner. **1942** *Punch* 8 July 12/1 The War Minister..got into a brisk row with most of the House when he was not very forthcoming on the question of dive-bombers. **1971** J. AIKEN *Nightly Deadshade* v. 54 'Some of your colleagues,' I say, 'are not so forthcoming as you seem to wish to be.'

Hence **forth'comingness**.

1808 BENTHAM *Sc. Ref.* 21 Means of securing forthcomingness, on the part of persons and things, for legal purposes. **1818** T. MOORE *Mem.* (1853) II. 133, I see no chance for my escape but in the forthcomingness of his uncle Sheddon. **1969** *Daily Tel.* (Colour Suppl.) 7 Feb. 30/1 The people have that unsophisticated forthcomingness tempered by a subtle irony.

†**'forthdeal.** *Obs.* = FORDEAL.

1542 UDALL *Erasm. Apoph.* 38 That is to saye: as good a forthdeale and auantage towardes the ende of the werke, as if a good porcion of the same wer already finyshed.

†**forth'do**, *v.* *Obs.* [OE. *forþdón*, f. FORTH *adv.* + *dón* to DO.] *trans.* To put forth; to utter (words).

c **900** tr. *Bæda's Hist.* v. ii. (1891) 388 Heht he his tungan forðdoon of his muðe. *c* **1250** *Gen. & Ex.* 3993 Sal ic non wurd muȝen forð-don, Vten ðat god me leið on.

†**forth'draw**, *v.* *Obs.* [f. FORTH *adv.* + DRAW *v.*] *trans.* To draw forth.

?*a* **1300** *Leg. Gregory* (Schulz) 347 Þe fischer þan þe child forþ drouȝ. **1340** *Ayenb.* 98 Þet he ous delyuri of þe zeue dyadliche zennes..and uorþdraȝe þe zeue uirtues.

†**'forthe(n**, *adv.* *Obs.* Forms: 1 **furþum, -on, -an, forþum**, 2 **forþon, -an**, 3 **forþe(n**, *Orm.* **forþenn**. [OE. *furþum*, f. OTeut. **furþ-, forþ-* (see FORTH *adv.*) with suffix of dat. pl.] Even.

971 *Blickl. Hom.* 179 Nære næfre næniȝ toþæs haliȝ mon on þissum middanȝearde ne furþum næniȝ on heofenum. *c* **1000** *Ags. Gosp.* Matt. vi. 29 Furðon salomon on eallum hys wuldre næs [etc.]. *c* **1175** *Lamb. Hom.* 5 He mihte ridan..on riche stede..nalde he no, na forþon uppon þa muchele assa, aȝe uppon þa lutthle fole. *c* **1200** ORMIN 825 He nolde giltenn Ne forþenn þurrh an idell word. *c* **1200** *Trin. Coll. Hom.* 13 Ne forðe gef man haueð to done mid his rihte spuse [etc.]. *c* **1205** LAY. 3012 Al þat is on liue nis nig swa dure swa me is þin an lime forðe min ahȝene lif.

forther, forther-: see FURTHER.

†**'forthfare**, *sb.* *Obs.* [OE. **forðfaru* (Lye), f. FORTH *adv.* + *faru* FARE *sb.*[1]] A going forth.

1. Decease, death.

c **1205** LAY. 6009 Vmbe feole ȝere æfter Belinnes forð-fare.

b. The passing-bell rung at a person's death.

1551 HOOPER *Injunct.* xxxiii. Wks. (Parker Soc.) II. 137 Item, that from henceforth there be no knells or forth-fares rung for the death of any man.

2. The going forth of a corpse; funeral.

1473 *Churchw. Acc. St. Edmund's, Salisbury* 17 (MS.) Item for the grete belle at his furthfare xij*d.* **1538–9** *Will of A. Hamon* (Somerset Ho.), Thexpenses and charges of my forthfare thirtye Day & Anniversary.

†**forth'fare**, *v.* *Obs.* [OE. *forðfaran*, f. FORTH *adv.* + *faran* to go: see FARE *v.*[1]]

1. *intr.* To go forth, go away, depart, journey.

c **888** K. ÆLFRED *Boeth.* xxxiii. §4 Swa ðætte hi æȝþer ȝe forþ faraþ ȝe eftcumaþ. *a* **1200** *Moral Ode* 340 Go we..þene wei grene þer forð-fareð lutel folc. *a* **1300** *E.E. Psalter* x[i]. 1, I sal forth fare, ife I wil, Als a sparwe in to þe hil. **13..** *K. Alis.* 6936 Sorwe and care That day thei letten forth fare.

2. To decease, die.

O.E. Chron. an. 571, On þam ilcan ȝeare he forþfor. *a* **1175** *Cott. Hom.* 225 Noe lefede..niȝon hund ȝeare and fifti, and he þa forðferde. *c* **1205** LAY. 11458 þenne þu beost forð faren. *c* **1320** *Cast. Love* 218 Atte laste he moste dyen and forþ-fare. *c* **1350** *Will. Palerne* 5266 þemperour was forþ-fare faire to crist.

Hence **forth'faring** *ppl. a.* (also *absol.*). *arch.*

a **1225** *Ancr. R.* 210 þeos seoue bestes..iðe wildernesse ..þet alle þe uorðfarinde uondeð to uordonne. **1876** SWINBURNE *Erechth.* 1323 A terror to forthfaring ships by night.

† **'forthfather.** *Obs.* [OE. *forþfæderas*, f. FORTH *adv.* + FATHER.] *pl.* = FOREFATHERS.

c **1000** ÆLFRIC *De vet. Test.* in Grein *Ags. Prosa* I. 4 Abrahames forðfæderas. *a* **1225** *St. Marher.* 4 þine forðfederes beoð forfarene reowliche. *a* **1225** *Leg. Kath.* 94 ȝef þeo weren todreauet..þæt hire forð-fadres hefden ifostret.

† **forth'fill,** *v. Obs.* [f. FORTH *adv.* + FILL *v.*] *trans.* To fulfil; also to discharge (a legacy).

c **1400** *Apol. Loll.* 3 As feiþ is forþfillid of þe werkis, so is also desir. *c* **1420** *Chron. Vilod.* 425 þus was forthfulde þe prophecy of þe sweuene. **1550** *Richmond. Wills* (Surtees) 69, I geue my executrix..the resydew of my gouds, my debts payd, and legocyes furthfilled, to dispose forther as [etc.].

† **'forthfore.** *Obs.* [OE. *forðfór*, f. FORTH *adv.* + *fór* a going: see FORE *sb.*] A going forth: **a.** OE. only: Decease, death; = FORTHFARE *sb.* 1. **b.** Used as rendering of Lat. *transitus*, given by Jerome as the literal meaning of *pascha* (passover).

c **900** tr. *Bæda's Hist.* III. xix. (1891) 210 Forðon him cuð fordfor toweard wære & unȝewiis seo tid þære ilcan forðfore. *c* **1250** *Gen. & Ex.* 3158 Ðat niȝt sal ben fest pasche, forð for, on engle tunge, it be.

† **'forthgang,** *sb. Obs.* [OE. *forðgang*, f. FORTH *adv.* + *gang* a going.] A going forth or out; progress, advance.

c **900** tr. *Bæda's Hist.* v. xxii. (1891) 476 þæs cyninges rice ȝe foreweard ȝe forðgong..moneȝum..styrenessum wiþerweardra ðinga..ȝemengde syndon. *a* **1225** *Ancr. R.* 318 Ich was þe beginnunge hwi swuch þing hefde uorðȝong. *Ibid.* 374, I uorðȝong of gode liue; and iðe last ende. *a* **1300** *E.E. Psalter* cxliii[i]. 14 Noght es falling of stane walle swa, Ne forth-gang, ne crie, in waies of þa.

† **forth'gang,** *v. Obs.* [OE. *forþgangan*, f. FORTH *adv.* + *gangan* to go.] *intr.* To go forth.

a **1000** *Byrhtnoth* 3 (Gr.) Het þa hyssa hwæne.. forðgangan. *a* **1300** *Cursor M.* 5998 (Gött.) Pharao..þe folk ne wild he late forthgang.

† **forth'go,** *v. Obs.* [OE. *forþgán*, f. FORTH *adv.* + *gán* to GO.]

1. *intr.* To go forth: see FORTH *adv.* 5 and 6. Occas. with cognate object. Of day, night, etc.: To pass, pass away.

O.E. Chron. an. 1075, Raulf..wolde forðgan mid his folce. *c* **1175** *Lamb. Hom.* 91 Swa þet ileiden þa untrummen men bi þere stret þere petrus forð-eoðe. *c* **1200** *Trin. Coll. Hom.* 9 Ðe niht is forð-gon and dai neihleched. *c* **1250** *Gen. & Ex.* 2819 Nu is forð gon ðe ðridde dai. *a* **1300** *E.E. Psalter* lxxxviii[i]. 42 Bi-reved him alle forth-gaand þe wai. **1382** WYCLIF *Gen.* xliv. 4 And now the cyte thei ȝeden oute and forth ȝeden a litill. —— *Judith* xvi. 27 Forsothe she was in feste daȝes forth goende [Vulg. *procedens*] with gret glorie. *c* **1425** *Seven Sag.* (P) 761 Thay..dyde ham bothe forth goo. *c* **1440** *Promp. Parv.* 173/2 Forthegone, *profectus.* **1600** FAIRFAX *Tasso* XVIII. xix. 6 Whereat amazd he staid, and well prepard For his defence, heedfull..foorthwent.

b. *fig.* esp. To advance in age (also, in power or dignity). Of a treaty: To be carried into effect.

c **1250** *Gen. & Ex.* 834 Sum was wið miȝte so forð gon, ðat hadden he under hem mani on. *a* **1300** *Cursor M.* 10757 He was sumdel forthgan in lijf. *c* **1330** R. BRUNNE *Chron.* (1810) 185 Philip vnderstode, R. wild not consent, þat ilk conant forth ȝode, þat þe Soudan sent.

2. To come forth as from a source, proceed.

c **1000** *Ags. Gosp.* Mark vii. 15 þa ðing þe of ðam men forðgað, þa hine besmitað. *a* **1325** *Prose Psalter* Athanasian Creed 22 Nouȝt fourmed, noȝt biȝeten, bot forþgoand. *c* **1340** *Cursor M.* 10240 (Fairf.) Ioachym here shalle none Offryng of thy hond forþ-gone. *c* **1400** *Apol. Loll.* 10 þe maker of mankynd takyng a soulid body of þe virgyn..& forþgoing man wiþ out seed may gif vs His Godhed.

forthgoing (fɔəθ'gəʊɪŋ), *vbl. sb.* [f. FORTH *adv.* + GOING *vbl. sb.*] A going forth.

1382 WYCLIF *Ps.* Prol. 737 The forth going of profitende men. *c* **1440** HYLTON *Scala Perf.* (W. de W. 1494) II. xxxi, A lityll of the forthgoyng fro that refourmyng to the hygher refourmyng. **1587** GOLDING *De Mornay* v. 56 A certeine couert forewardnesse or foorthgoing of the will towards the thing that is loued. **1833** CHALMERS *Const. Man* (1835) I. i. 72 To the fiat and forthgoing of whose will it owes its existence. **1852** ROCK *Ch. of Fathers* III. I. 210 His hopes that God's angels would come for his soul at its forth-going. **1870** W. ARNOT *Life J. Hamilton* iv. 180 With a great forthgoing towards the common people.

forthgoing (fɔəθ'gəʊɪŋ), *ppl. a. rare.* [f. FORTH *adv.* + GOING *ppl. a.*] That goes forth; *esp.* disposed to make advances; enthusiastic; gracious. Cf. FORTHCOMING *ppl. a.* 2.

1851 J. HAMILTON *Royal Preacher* xx. (1854) 258 The great desires of his forthgoing patriotism and piety. **1876** MRS. WHITNEY *Sights & Ins.* xxxii. 307 But to him she may have been forthgoing.

forthingdole: see FARTHINGDEAL.

† **for'think,** *v. Obs.* Forms: see THINK. Also 4-6 forethink. [repr. two distinct words: *a.* OE. *forðencan* (f. FOR- *pref.*[1] + *ðencan* to THINK) = OHG. *fordenchen* (Ger. *verdenken*). *β.* f. FOR- *pref.*[1] + OE. *þyncan* to seem. Cf. MHG. *verdunken* and ON. *forþykkja* to displease.]

I. Senses from OE. *ðyncan.*

1. *trans.* To displease, cause regret to.

a **1225** *Juliana* 16 Ne ich ne seh him neuer þat me sare forþuncheð. *c* **1325** *Metr. Hom.* (Small) xvi, To king William bodword was broht Of this tithing, that him for thoht. *c* **1374** CHAUCER *Troylus* II. 1365 (1414), I nas, ne nevere to be I thenke, Ayens a thing that myght the forthenke. *c* **1430** *Syr Gener.* (Roxb.) 6446 If..it had you forthoght, Ye might [etc.]. *c* **1530** *Adam Bel* 548 in Hazl. *E.P.P.* II. 161, I hav y-graunted them graces, And that forthynketh me. **1535** STEWART *Cron. Scot.* (1858) I. 200 Full sair for-thinkis me, The greit injuris..Done to my sister.

2. *impers.* and quasi-*impers.* (*it*) *forthinks* (*me, him,* etc.): I, etc., feel regret, repent, or am sorry. Const. *of, for,* or *that,* with dependent clause.

a **1300** *Cursor M.* 2732 If sco did it hir for-thoght. **13..** *E.E. Allit. P.* B. 285 Me forthynkez ful much þat euer I mon made. **1393** LANGL. *P. Pl.* C. XXI. 92 Sore hit me for-þynkeþ Of þe dede þat ich haue don. *c* **1420** *Sir Amadace* (Camd.) xviii, For his dedus him sore for-thoȝte. **1548** UDALL *Erasm. Par. Luke* xxiv. 46 The Lorde hath sworne and it shall not forthynke hym. **1578–1600** *Scot. Poems 16th C.* (1801) II. 166 Baneist is faith now euery quhair And sair forthinkes me. **1588** A. KING tr *Canisius' Catech., Confession* 12 It forthinkes me sore that I haue sinned.

II. Senses from OE. *ðencan.*

3. a. *trans.* To despise or neglect. OE. only. **b.** *intr.* To be reluctant.

c **1000** *Ags. Ps.* (Th.) xlviii. Argt., He lærde þæt þa ðearfan hy ne forðohton. *a* **1300** *Cursor M.* 16427 Pilate forthoght þam..to wrath.

4. *trans.* To think upon with pain; to regret, repent of, be sorry for; *rarely* passive.

? *a* **1250** *Ags. Poem* clxxvi. in Hickes *Thes.* (1705) I. 224 Se þæt mai and nele ðeder come, Sore hit sel uorðenche. **13..** *E.E. Allit. P.* B. 557 þe souerayn in sete so sore for-þoȝt þat euer he man vpon molde merked to lyuy. *c* **1375** *Sc. Leg. Saints, Johannes* 445 He..þane sa fore-thocht his mysded þat he gret sare. *c* **1425** WYNTOUN *Cron.* v. xii. 1310 Wyth Rewth of Hart for-thynk youre syn. *c* **1430** *How Wise Man taught Son* 32 in *Babees Bk.* (1868) 49 þou myȝte seie a word to-day þat .vij. ȝeer after may be for-þouȝt. **1470–85** MALORY *Arthur* XVII. xv, Yf thou entre thou shalt forthynke hit. **1548** W. PATTEN *Exp. Scotl.* Pref. in Arb. *Garner* III. 58 They forthink that inroad. *a* **1639** SPOTTISWOOD *Hist. Ch. Scotl.* II. (1677) 37 Suddenly forethinking what he had done, he [etc.]. **1704** *Min. of Torryburn Sess.* in *Ess. on Witchcraft* (1820) 131 She would make Jean Riȝet forethink what she had done.

5. *refl.* To change the direction of one's thoughts; to experience a change of mind or purpose; to repent, be sorry. Const. *of, that,* or *to* with *inf.*

a **1300** *Cursor M.* 24786 O þis tiþand he him for-thoght. *c* **1550** CHEKE *Matt.* xxvii. 3 Joudas..seing y[t] he was condemned, did forthink himself. **1553** T. WILSON *Rhet.* (1580) 40 Nor yet you shall forthinke your self, that you haue obeyed..myne aduise. **1589** WARNER *Alb. Eng., Æneidos* 156 Wel may I fore think mee so to haue done. **1599** *Life Sir T. More* in Wordsw. *Eccl. Biog.* (1853) II. 98 The whole counsell began to forethink them of their forwardness.

b. *intr.* for *refl.* Const. *of.*

c **1380** WYCLIF *Serm.* Sel. Wks. I. 279 þe fende shal..ever forþinke. *c* **1410** LOVE *Bonavent. Mirr.* xxii. 48 (Gibbs MS.), I..come to ȝowe..forthynkynge inwardly of þat I haue offendet. **1509** BARCLAY *Shyp of Folys* (1570) 132 He..then forthinketh, but late is his complaint. **1535** STEWART *Cron. Scot.* II. 468 He forthocht full soir Of the grit wrang. **1562** J. HEYWOOD *Prov. & Epigr.* (1867) 118 Better foresee, than forthinke. **1578** WHETSTONE *Promos & Cass.* II. v, Forethinke of thy forepassed faultes.

6. Occasional uses: **a.** *trans.* To change one's mind about; to renounce. **b.** *intr.* To think or plan something wrong; to conspire.

1483 *Festivall* (W. de W. 1515) 73 b, By tentacyon of the fende they forthought all theyr purpose. **1494** *Coll. Hist. Staff.* XII. (1891) 334 Sir Humfrey Stanley, with xx persons, forthought ayens your pease and lawis.

forthink: see FORETHINK.

† **for'thinking,** *vbl. sb. Obs.* The action of the vb. FORTHINK; also, repentance.

a **1225** *Ancr. R.* 110 þet of-þunchung [*v.r.* forðinchinge] þet he hefde wiðinnen him. **1340** *Ayenb.* 20 þet þou nere naȝt digneliche y-diȝt be ssrifþe and by vorþenchinge. *a* **1400** *Relig. Pieces fr. Thornton MS.* (1867) 8 Sothefaste forthynkynge þat we hafe of oure syne. **1555** W. WATREMAN *Fardle Facions* II. xii. 289 Let him sorowe, not with a lighte forthinckinge. **1587** GOLDING *De Mornay* xvii. 269 The.. Cerimonies of al Nations, doe witnesse vnto vs a certeyne forethinking and remorce of sinne against God.

† **for'thirst,** *pa. pple.* In 3 *Orm.* forrþrisst. [f. FOR- *pref.*[1] + *thirst*, pa. pple. of THIRST *v.*] Overpowered with thirst.

c **1200** ORMIN 8635 He..seȝȝde þatt he wass forrþrisst. *c* **1440** *Promp. Parv.* 173/2 Forthyrst, *sitibundus, siciens.*

† **forth'lead,** *v. Obs.* [OE. *forðlǽdan*, f. FORTH *adv.* + *lǽdan* to LEAD.] *trans.* **a.** To lead forth. **b.** To put forth (horns, etc.); = Lat. *producere.*

a **1000** *Satan* (Gr.) 566 Freodrihten hine forðlædde to ðam halȝan ham. *a* **1300** *E.E. Psalter* lxviii. 32 [lxix. 31] Kalf.. Forthledand [Vulg. *producentem*] hornes and klees his. *c* **1425** *Seven Sag.* (P.) 2443 There was many a wepyng heye As the childe was forth ladde.

† **'forthly,** *a. Obs.* Forms: 3 forthlich, 4 forthely. [f. FORTH *adv.* + -LY[1].] Healthy, likely to live; also, full of energy.

c **1230** *Hali Meid.* 35 ȝif hit wel iborn is & þuncheð wel forðlich, fearlac of his lure is anan wið him iboren. *c* **1330** R. BRUNNE *Chron.* (1810) 160 Felawes were þei alle, als forthely as he.

† **'forthmost,** *a.* and *adv. Obs.* [f. FORTH *adv.* + MOST.] = FOREMOST.

c **950** *Lindisf. Gosp.* Matt. xx. 27 Seðe wælle betuih iuh forðmest wossa sie iuer ðea. *c* **1425** *Engl. Conq. Irel.* (1896) 16 Robert was..euer with the forthmost in euery fight. *c* **1450** *Mirour Saluacioun* 22 The certein guyse es this That of the new law forthemast a sothe reherced is.

† **forth'nim,** *v. Obs.* [f. FORTH *adv.* + NIM *v.*]

1. *trans.* To consume. Cf. FORNIM.

c **1175** *Lamb. Hom.* 95 þes fares [? fures] icunde is þet hit forðnimeð swa hwet him neh bið.

2. *intr.* To go forth, go away, proceed.

c **1250** *Gen. & Ex.* 3351 Forð nam ðis folc, so god taȝte him, to ðe desert of rafadim. *Ibid.* 3640 Twelf moneð forð ben alle cumen, Or he fro synay ben forð numen.

† **forth on, forthon,** *adv. Obs.* For forms see FORTH. [f. FORTH *adv.* + ON *adv.*]

1. Of space: Forwards; = FORTH 1. In quot. with ellipsis of *go.* Also, onwards, straight on, without deviation; = FORTH 2.

1529 MORE *Dyaloge* II. Wks. 183/1 Let us forth on a litle further. **1607** SHAKS. *Timon* I. i. 49 My free drift..Flies an Eagle flight, bold, and forth on.

2. Of time: Onwards; = FORTH 3.

1474 CAXTON *Chesse* 11 He..shold be his frend fro than forthon. *c* **1500** *Melusine* lix. (1895) 361 Thy fortres fro this day fourthon shalbe quyte of ony trybute. **1587** GOLDING *De Mornay* xxxi. 505 From the beginning foorthon, Moyses and the Prophets gaue it you.

b. Straightway, at once, forthwith.

a **1000** *Martyrol.* (E.E.T.S.) 154 þa het Valerianus se refa hi forðon acwellan. *c* **1250** *Gen. & Ex.* 3162 Ilc firme bigeten ..was storuen on morwen and dead forðan.

† **for-'thon,** *conj. Obs.* Also 1 forþám, -þan, 2-4 forthan, 7 forthen. [In OE. two words: FOR *prep.* + *þon* instr., *þám* dat., of THE. The dat. and instr. forms coalesced in ME.]

1. For this reason, therefore. In ME. sometimes repeated, *forþon..forþon* 'for this reason..that'.

c **900** tr. *Bæda's Hist.* III. xiii. [xv.] (1890) 198 He forðon eallum ȝe þisse worulde aldormonnum wæs leof. *c* **1000** *Ags. Gosp.* Matt. vi. 25 Forþam [*c* **1160** *Hatton* Forþan] ic secȝe eow þæt [etc.]. *c* **1175** *Lamb. Hom.* 95 Forðon wes þe halia gast on culfren onlicnesse bufan criste, forðon he wes [etc.]. *c* **1205** LAY. 989 For þon [*c* **1275** for þan] ȝif hit eow bi-loueð ..fare we from þisse londe. *c* **1320** *Cast. Love* 1072 He scholde neuer die for þon. *c* **1394** *P. Pl. Crede* 27 By a fraynyng for-þan faileþ þer manye. **1447** BOKENHAM *Seyntys* (Roxb.) 43 Not forthan I wyl not blynne. **1674** RAY *N.C. Words* 19 Forthen and Forthy, therefore.

2. For the reason that, because.

Beowulf (Gr.) 150 Forþam wearð [sorȝcearu] ylda bearnum undyrne cuð. *c* **1175** *Lamb. Hom.* 17 Hit is riht þet me hem spille, forþan betere hit is [etc.]. *c* **1250** *Gen. & Ex.* 1996 Putifar..boȝte ioseph al forðan He wulde don is lechurhed wið ioseph.

So **for-thon the,** later **forthon that** = 2.

c **893** K. ÆLFRED *Oros.* I. i. (1883) 24 For ðon þe sio sunne þær gæð near on sett þonne on oðrum lande, þær [etc.]. *c* **1000** *Ags. Gosp.* Matt. xiv. 24 For-þam [*c* **1160** *Hatton* for-þan] þe hyt wæs strang wind. *c* **1175** *Lamb. Hom.* 53 For þon þet he scolde swote smelle. *c* **1200** *Trin. Coll. Hom.* 107 Leomene fader we clepeð ure drihten for þan þe he sunne atend. *c* **1250** *Owl & Night.* 780 And for þan þat hit no wit not Ne mai his strenghe hit ischilde. **1340** *Ayenb.* 184 Vor þan þet roboam..uorlet þane red of þe yealden guode men ..he uor-leas þet gratteste del of his kingdome.

forthought: see FORETHOUGHT.

† **forth'pass,** *v. Obs.* [f. FORTH *adv.* + PASS *v.*] *intr.* To pass forth, go, proceed.

1382 WYCLIF *Gen.* xxviii. 2 But go, and forthpasse into Mesopotany..to the hows of Batuel. **1435** MISYN *Fire of Love* I. viii. (1896) 16 þe holy goste of þe fadyr & þe sone forthpassynge. *c* **1440** HYLTON *Scala Perf.* (W. de W. 1494) I. lxxxvi, By cause of synne he forthpassith [**1533** passeth farre] liuyng in this worlde in this ymage of synne.

† **forthputter.** *Obs. rare*[−1]. [f. FORTH *adv.* + PUTTER.] One who puts forth; a braggart.

a **1610** HEALEY *Theophrastus* xxiii. (1636) 79 A vanter or forth-putter is he, that boastes upon the Exchange that he hath store of banke-mony.

forthputting (fɔəθ'pʊtɪŋ), *vbl. sb.* [f. FORTH *adv.* + PUTTING *vbl. sb.*]

1. The action of putting forth.

1640 BP. REYNOLDS *Passions* (1658) 1009 The effects of Hope..arising out of want, contention, and forth-putting of the mind. **1833** CHALMERS *Const. Man* (1835) II. II. i. 163 An obvious..forth-putting of skill. **1875** M[c]LAREN *Serm.* Ser. II. ii. 24 A continuous forth-putting of power.

2. *U.S.* Obtrusive behaviour.

1861 LOWELL *Biglow P.* Poems 1890 II. 216 To secure myself against any imputation of unseemly forthputting.

forthputting (fɔəθ'pʊtɪŋ), *ppl. a.* [f. FORTH *adv.* + PUTTING, pr. pple. of PUT *v.*] That puts forth;

esp. that puts oneself forward; forward, obtrusive, presumptuous. (Now chiefly *U.S.*)

c **1570** *Pride & Lowl.* (1841) 33 For soft, and no whit forth-putting was he. **1647** Trapp *Comm. Matt.* xviii. 21 Peter is still the same, ever too forwardly and forth-putting. **1854** Hawthorne *Eng. Note-bks.* (1879) II. 312, I should wrong her if I left the impression of her being forth-putting and obtrusive. **1883** Howells *Register* i, Do you think it was forth-putting at all, to ask him?

† **for'thrast**, *v. Obs.* [OE. *forðræstan*, f. for- *pref.*[1] + *ðræstan* to crush.] *trans.* To crush, shatter.

c **825** *Vesp. Ps.* ix. 36 [x. 15] Forðræst earm ðes synfullan. *a* **1300** *E.E. Psalter* xlvii[i]. 7 In strange gaste schippes of Thars for-thrist saltou. **13..** *Visions St. Paul* 34 in *O.E. Misc.* (1872) 224 Synful soules, and al for-þrast. **13..** *E.E. Allit. P.* B. 249 Bot in þe þryd [act of God's vengeance] watz for-þrast al þat þryue schuld.

forthren, obs. f. further *v.*

forthright (fɔəθ'raɪt, 'fɔəθraɪt), rarely with advb. gen. *-s* **forthrights**, *adv.*, *a.*, and *sb. arch.* [f. forth *adv.* + right *a.* and *adv.*, in OE. *riht, rihte*: cf. downright.] **A.** *adv.*

1. Directly forward, in or towards the front, straight before one.

a **1000** *Ags. Gloss.* in Haupt's *Zeitschr.* IX. 406 *Indeclinabiliter*, forðrihte. *c* **1205** Lay. 1523 Brutus..iwende forð-rihtes to þon ilke weie þer him iwised wes. ? *a* **1366** Chaucer *Rom. Rose* 295 She mighte loke in no visage Of man or womman forth-right pleyn. **1398** Trevisa *Barth. De P.R.* v. ii. (1495) 104 That heryth not only fourth ryght but all abowte. **1580** Sidney *Arcadia* ii. 115 He ever going so just with the horse, either forth-right or turning. **1697** Dryden *Æneid* xii. 1076 Now forthright and now in Orbits wheel'd. **1818** Keats *Endym.* ii. 331 Until impatient in embarrassment He forthright pass'd. **1879** G. Meredith *Egoist* III. viii. 153 Reach the good man your hand, my girl: forth-right from the shoulder, like a brave boxer.

† **b.** Straight out, horizontally. *Obs.*

1640 Parkinson *Theat. Bot.* 356 The fruite..standing some forthright, and some upright.

2. Straightway, immediately, at once.

c **1200** Ormin 2481 He..wollde forrþrihht hire himm fra All stillelike shædenn. *a* **1225** *St. Marher.* 15 Ant tenne some agulteð eawiht [*sc.* ha moten] gan anan forðriht þæt ha [etc.]. **1590** Spenser *F.Q.* ii. vii. 35 Whose dore forthright To him did open as it had beene taught. **1609** C. Butler *Fem. Mon.* (1634) 131 You may see some slain forthright with the thrust of the Spear. **1659** Torriano, *A ribibo*, forthright, as it were carelesly. **1882** Swinburne *Tristram of Lyonesse* 49 Forthright upon his steed [he] Leapt.

B. *adj.*

1. Proceeding in a straight course, directly in front of one, straight forward.

c **1000** Ælfric *Gloss.* in Wr.-Wülcker 222/30 *Directanei*, forðrihte. **1398** Trevisa tr. *Barth. De P.R.* ix. i. (1495) 345 Streyghte and forthryghte meuynge. **1657** S. Purchas *Pol. Flying-Ins.* 190 Having two points forth-right, not barbed like a Bees. **1824** Scott *St. Ronan's* xxxvi, Now in making feints, now in making forthright passes. **1865** C. J. Vaughan *Words fr. Gosp.* 71 Must thine eye be thus roving thy forthright vision thus distracted? **1878** Stevenson *Inland Voy.* 145 A headlong, forth-right tide.

2. *fig.* Going straight to the point, straightforward, unswerving, outspoken; also, unhesitating, dexterous.

1855 Browning *Men & Wom.* II. *Andrea del Sarto* 5 This low-pulsed forthright craftsman's hand of mine. **1867** Swinburne in *Fortn. Rev.* July 22 In clear forthright manner of procedure..it resembles the work of Chaucer. **1870** Lowell *Study Wind.* 261 The home-thrust of a forth-right word. **1879** Farrar *St. Paul* I. 422 The practical, forthright, non-argumentative turn of his mind.

C. *sb.* A straight course or path; *lit.* and *fig.* (Chiefly after Shakspere.)

1606 Shaks. *Tr. & Cr.* iii. iii. 158 If you giue way Or hedge aside from the direct forth right. **1610** —— *Temp.* iii. iii. 3 Here's a maze trod indeede Through fourth rights, and Meanders. **1880** Browning *Dram. Idylls* Ser. ii. *Clive* 12 Thought..Notes this forthright, that meander. **1884** Bp. Barry in *Contemp. Rev.* Sept. 409 Materialism with its maze of 'forthrights and meanders' is utterly at fault. **1887** Lowell *Pr. Wks.* (1890) VI. 186 He has not allowed himself to be lured from the direct forthright by any [etc.].

Hence **'forthrightly** *adv.*; **'forthrightness**, the quality of being forthright; straightforwardness.

1873 Lowell *Among my Bks.* Ser. ii. 123 Dante's concise forthrightness of phrase. **1879** Farrar *St. Paul* I. 225 He..carried into his arguments that intensity and forthrightness which awaken dormant opposition. **1934** Webster. Forthrightly. **1957** G. Ashe *King Arthur's Avalon* i. 32 The druids fortified their flocks with the doctrine of immortality. They taught it more forthrightly and dogmatically than any other priesthood in Europe. **1965** S. Gibbons in J. Gibb *Light on C. S. Lewis* 98 These qualities come out forthrightly—as if, with a sigh of pleasure, all the brakes had been taken off—in his seven books for children, the Narnia stories. **1979** *Daily Tel.* 28 July 10/5 We might take the initiative..in forthrightly defending our principles in the international fora. **1985** *New Yorker* 11 Mar. 68/1 He bought a rubber plantation..and forthrightly christened it Fordlandia.

† **for'thring**, *v. Obs. rare.* [f. for- *pref.*[1] + thring *v.* to press. The OE. *forðringan* (for- *pref.*[2] ?) occurs once, app. in the sense 'to urge forward'.] *trans.* To press heavily upon, oppress.

Beowulf (Gr.) 1084 þæt he ne mehte..þa wea-lafe wiȝe for-þringan þeodnes þeȝne. *c* **1200** Ormin 6169 Himm þatt i cwarrterrne liþ Forrbundenn & forrþrungenn.

forthrow: see for- *pref.*[1] 1.

† **forth'set**, *v. Obs.* [f. forth *adv.* + set *v.*[1]] *trans.* To set forth; to present to view, display.

c **1565** Lindesay (Pitscottie) *Chron. Scot.* (1728) I. 1 They, that are most forthy in the ingyring and forthsetting them-selves. **1585** Jas. I *Ess. Poesie* (Arb.) 37, I had farr rather Babell tower forthsett, Then [etc.].

Hence **forth'setting** *vbl. sb.*

1528 J. Hacket *to Wolsey* (*MS. Cott. Galba* B. ix. 181) Yt myght be a forthesettyng of Frenchemen to make ther bragges. *a* **1572** Knox *Hist. Ref.* Wks. 1846 I. 344 Being conveaned..in the name of Jesus Christ, for furth-setting of his glorie. *a* **1847** Chalmers *Posth. Wks.* I. 76 Let me not enter on the vain attempt to enhance the impression of this celebrated story by any forthsetting of mine. **1863** A. B. Grosart *Small Sins* Pref. (ed. 2) 10 It has seemed therefore to me advisable to..select less obvious forth-setting of the same great Truths.

† **forth'show**, *v. Obs.* [f. forth *adv.* + show *v.*] *trans.* To show forth, declare, exhibit.

a **1300** *E.E. Psalter* cxliv. [cxlv.] 4 Strende and strende..sal..þi might forth-schewe. *c* **1330** R. Brunne *Chron.* (1810) 54 þei durst it not forth schewe. **1553** Q. Kennedy *Compend. Tract.* in *Wodr. Soc. Misc.* 127 Quhat and he be blynd quhilk suld furthschaw the way to utheris. **1556** Lauder *Tractate* 503 Now haue I breuelie heir furthschawin ..How that ȝe suld [etc.].

† **'forthsithe.** *Obs.* [f. forth *adv.* + *síð* journey.] Departure, decease; hence, death-bed.

O.E. Chron. an. 992, Æfter Oswaldes..forðsiðe. *a* **1240** *Ureisun* in *Cott. Hom.* 197 Ich þe bidde þet tu kume to mine uorð-siðe.

† **forth'tee**, *v. Obs.* [OE *forðtéon*, f. forth *adv.* + *téon*: see tee *v.*] *trans.* **a.** To manifest outwardly. **b.** To bring forward, adduce, quote. **c.** To draw (a person) on, seduce, beguile.

c **1200** *Trin. Coll. Hom.* 35 þe deuel teð forð geres hwile after fox..hwile after oðre, and on ech of hise deden is iefned to þe deore wuas geres he forðteoð. *Ibid.* 145 þe fewe word þe ich nu forð-tegh he specð of [etc.]. *Ibid.* 199 Man mid is gele, eggeð us and fondeð and forþ-teþ to idele þonke.

forthtell (fɔərθ'tɛl), *v. rare.* [f. forth *adv.* + tell *v.*] *trans.* To tell forth, publish abroad. So **forth'teller**.

1549–62 Sternhold & H. *Ps.* cxlviii. 14 His Saints shall all forthtell His praise and worthinesse. **1561** Kethe *Ps.* c. 1 Hym serue with feare, his praise forth tell. **1889** T. Wright *Chalice of Carden* xv. 108 'Imprinted', as its title page forthtold, in the last year of Elizabeth. **1920** *Glasgow Herald* 17 July 4 Mr Wells takes himself much more seriously as historian than as humorous novelist, or 'forthteller' of scientific development. **1964** G. A. Williamson *World of Josephus* iii. 63 A prophet was not primarily a foreteller, but a forthteller.

† **'forthward**, *sb. Obs.* Also 5 *Sc.* **forðward, forthwart.** [See forth *adv.*] = foreward *sb.*[1]

c **1340** *Cursor M.* 13959 (Fairf.) þe Iewes wiþ þaire fals forþward..þai soȝt ihesu to þe dede. *c* **1470** Henry *Wallace* xi. 487 For thi manheid this forthwart to me fest. **1535** Stewart *Cron. Scot.* iii. 254 As plesit him his fordward to fulfill.

'forthward, with adv. gen. *-s* **forthwards**, *adv.* and *a. Obs.* exc. *arch.* Forms: see forth and -ward. [OE. *forðweard* (= OS. *forðwerd*, *forðwardes*), f. forth *adv.* + -ward.] **A.** *adv.*

1. Of place: Towards a place or part in front or before, onward(s, forward. ***to be forthward***: to be on one's way. ***to set forthward***: to help on.

c **1175** *Lamb. Hom.* 51 And tech me hu ic scal swimmen forðward. *c* **1205** Lay. 5370 Feouwer daies fulle forð ward [*c* **1275** forþwardes] heo wenden. **1297** R. Glouc. (1724) 245 þo þys ost al ȝare was, vorþward vaste hii drowe. *c* **1400** *Lanfranc's Cirurg.* 315 Drawe þe boon forþward. *c* **1430** *Pilgr. Lyf Manhode* i. xciii. (1869) 51 Me thinketh riht longe þat I ne were forthward and set in þe wey. *c* **1450** *St. Cuthbert* (Surtees) 6097 He went forthward with þe wayne. **1530** *Test. Ebor.* (Surtees) V. 301 Also to the peir, if it go furthwardes, xls. **1560** Rolland *Crt. Venus* iv. 659 Fordward I fuir. **1588** A. King tr. *Canisius' Catech.* 39 Besyddis y[at] we set furthwart, be all meanis possible ye proffeit of our nyghbour. *Ibid.* 205 b, Gif thou preiss forduart. **1655** Fuller *Ch. Hist.* v. iv. §35 That unity and concord in opinions..may encrease and goe forthward. **1768** Ross *Helenore* 8 'Tweish twa hillocks the poor lambie lies, An' ay fell forthert, as it shoope to rise.

b. Prominently, in public.

1504 Atkynson tr. *De Imitatione* iii. lix, He wyll also apere forthwarde, and haue the syghte and experyens of many thynges by his outwarde senses.

2. Of time: **a.** (OE. only.) Continually, prospectively. **b.** For the future onwards. Also, ***ay, (from) hence, now, then forthward***; ***from that*** or ***this day*** or ***time forthward***.

c **1000** *Ags. Ps.* l[i]. 79 (Gr.) þæt min ȝehernes hehtful weorðe..forðweard to þe! *c* **1000** Ælfric *Gram.* xxi. (Z.) 125 Ðis ȝemet [the imperative mood] sprecð forþwerd. *c* **1200** Ormin 5226 þatt itt [þatt twifalde gast] beo nu forrþwarrd inn me. *c* **1340** *Cursor M.* 14905 (Fairf.) Of his passion þat is sa harde þat ȝe sal here now forþwarde. *c* **1380** *Sir Ferumb.* 2605 If y þys day forþward spare Sarasyn ouþer torke, for euere mot y þan for-fare. *c* **1440** *Gesta Rom.* l. 225 (Harl. MS.) & þere for, fadir, dothe to me fro hennys forþeward as þe likithe. *c* **1450** *St. Cuthbert* (Surtees) 6930 þare he ordayned þe bischop se Ay forthward forto be. *c* **1460** Fortescue *Abs. & Lim. Mon.* (1885) 147 Wich wages shall than forthwarde cesse. **1541** *Act 33 Hen. VIII*, c. 13 From that time furthward.

B. *adj.* = forward *a.*

c **1470** Henry *Wallace* iii. 46 Growand in curage; Forthward, rycht fayr. *Ibid.* x. 78 So weill beseyn, so forthwart, stern, and stult. **1881** Duffield *Don Quix.* II. 560 Don Quixote went..on his forthward way.

Hence **'forthwardly** *adv.*

c **1470** Henry *Wallace* x. 653 So forthwartlye thai pressyt in the thrang. **1494** Fabyan *Chron.* vi. clxxxvii. 189 Richarde..toke vpon hym the rule of his owne signory, and grewe & encreased forthwardly.

† **for'thwax**, *v. Obs.* [OE. *forðweaxan*, f. forth *adv.* + *weaxan* to wax.] *intr.* To grow forth, grow to excess, increase.

a **900** ? Werfrith *Greg. Dial.* ii. xxvii. (Bosw.-T.) Forþweox his feondscipe. *c* **1250** *Gen. & Ex.* 1211 Wintres forð wexen on ysaac.

† **'forthwise**, *v. Obs.* [OE. *forþwísian*, f. forth *adv.* + *wísian* to show, guide.] *trans.* To guide forth, direct; hence, to bring up (a child).

Beowulf (Gr.) 1795 Him seleþeȝn..forð wisade. *c* **1315** Shoreham 68 The fader and moder That hyne fleschlyche forthwyseth.

forthwith (ˌfɔəθ'wɪθ, -'wɪð), *adv.* [For *forth with* (prep.), = earlier *forth mid*, along with, see forth *adv.* 2 c. The adv. *forthwith* originates from this phrase, the prep. being used *absol.* or with ellipsis of its regimen.]

Immediately, at once, without delay or interval.

1450–1530 *Myrr. our Ladye* 3 Other before the letter or after or else fourthe wyth togyther. **1461** J. Paston in *P. Lett.* No. 384 II. 4 Ther was a certeyn person forth wyth after the jurney at Wakefield. **1463** *Bury Wills* (Camden) 17 Y[t] y[e] messe of requiem may begynne forthwith whan y[t] is doo. **1637** *Decree Star Chamb.* §17 in *Milton's Areop.* (Arb.) 17 That the Master and Wardens of the Company of Stationers, doe foorthwith certifie [etc.]. **1712** Hearne *Collect.* (Oxf. Hist. Soc.) III. 424 It shall be done forthwith. **1814** Cary *Dante, Par.* viii. 50 Forthwith it grew In size and splendour. **1848** Wharton *Law Lex.* s.v., When a defendant is ordered to plead forthwith, he must plead within twenty-four hours. **1867** Smiles *Huguenots Eng.* iv. (1880) 53 The King determined that they should forthwith be reconverted to Roman Catholicism.

¶ Used for forwith *adv.* and *prep.* (which is a variant reading in all the passages).

a **1300** *Cursor M.* 10752 Amang þir men es forthwit tald, He come al forto ber his wand. *Ibid.* 11423 þe stern went forth-wit þat þam ledd. *c* **1340** *Ibid.* 11001 (Trin.) In septembre moneth þe foure & twenty nyȝt was..Forþwiþ þe annunciacioun.

† **'forthwithal**, *adv. Obs.* [f. forth *adv.* + with *prep.* + all. See forth *adv.* 2 d.] = prec.

c **1200** Ormin 1336 Let itt eornenn forþwiþþ all Vt inntill wilde wesste. **1390** Gower *Conf.* III. 262 And forthwithall ..A naked swerd..She toke, and through hir hert it throng. *a* **1500** *Assembl. Ladies* cv. in *Chaucer's Wks.* (1561) 261 Than eche of vs toke other by the sleue And forth withal, as we shulde take our leue. **1548** in Strype *Eccl. Mem.* II. App. D. 27 Yf thou take hym that is not trew unto hys prynce, punysh him forthwithall.

forthy ('fɔəθɪ), *a. Sc.* and *dial.* [f. forth *adv.* + -y[1].] Disposed to put oneself forth or forward; forward, outspoken, unrestrained.

c **1565** [see forthset *v.*]. **1846** *Spec. Cornish Prov. Dial.* 55 A yungster comed out very forthy, 'Here come I, St. George'. **1880** *E. Cornwall Gloss.*, *Forthy*, officious; forward. **1892** *Northumb. Gloss.*, *Forthy*, industrious, well doing, free, kindly spoken.

† **for-'thy**, *conj. Obs.* Also 1 **forðí**, 2–5 **forthi**, 3 *south.* **forðui**, 3–4 **forthe.** [OE. *forðí, forðý*, f. for *prep.* + *ðý*, instr. of the. Cf. forthon.] For this reason, therefore.

c **1000** *Ags. Gosp.* John vii. 22 Forðy Moyses eow sealde ymbsnydenysse. *c* **1175** *Lamb. Hom.* 21 Forðon a þis world winð onȝein us..for-þi we suneȝiet on-ȝein drihtenes welle. *c* **1230** *Hali Meid.* 9 For þi seli meiden forȝet ti folc. *a* **1250** *Owl & Night.* 69 Forthe the sulve mose Hire thonkes wolde the to-tose. **13..** *E.E. Allit. P.* A. 234 My joy for-þy watz much þe more. **1377** Langl. *P. Pl.* B. Prol. 187 For-þi I conseille alle þe comune to lat þe catte worthe. *c* **1450** Henryson *Mor. Fab.* 45 The morning myld, my mirth was maire forthy. **1501** Douglas *Pal. Hon.* i. xxii, For thy I knew the signe Was Acteon. **1590** Lodge *Euphues Gold. Leg.* in Halliw. *Shaks.* VI. 22 Forthy, Montanus, follow mine arreede. **1647** H. More *Song of Soul* ii. i. ii. xxviii, Forthy let first an inward centre hid Be put.

b. ***not-for-thy***: nevertheless. ***what for-thy***: what of that?

1375 Barbour *Bruce* v. 319 Vndir the mantill nocht-forthi He suld be armyt preualy. **1413** *Pilgr. Sowle* (Caxton) i. xv. (1859) 13 Nought for thy, this I byhote expresse. *c* **1430** *Syr Tryam.* 736 The fyrste that rode noght for thy, Was the kyng of Lumbardy. *c* **1450** *Cov. Myst.* (1841) 120 Nevyr the les, what for-thy..Withowith mannys company She myght not be with childe.

Hence **forthy that**, earlier **forthy the**, because.

c **1000** *Ags. Gosp.* John vii. 22 Na forði ðe heo of Moyses sy. *c* **1175** *Lamb. Hom.* 41 On þon deie þa engles of heofene ham iblissieð: forði þe þa erming saulen habbeð rest of heore pine. *a* **1225** *Ancr. R.* 56 Al þæt vuel of Dina..ne com nout forðui þæt te wummen lokede cangliche o weopmen. **1340** Hampole *Pr. Consc.* 2698 Forthy þat sum has na knawyng Of purgatory..þarfor [etc.]. *c* **1400** Maundev. (Roxb.) vi. 18 þare also gert kyng Nabugodonosor putte þe three childer in þe fyre, forþi þat þai held þe riȝt beleue.

†**forth'yete**, *v. Obs.* [OE. *forðʒéotan*, f. FORTH *adv.* + *ʒéotan* to pour.] *trans.* To pour out.

c **900** tr. *Bæda's Hist.* IV. xxix. [xxviii.] (1890) 370 He.. forðʒotenum tearum..Dryhtne his willan bebead. **1513** DOUGLAS *Æneis* I. iii. 55 The deip furtht ȝet in schaldis heir and thair. —— IV. viii. 88 All for nocht the teris war furth ȝet.

fortieth ('fɔːtɪɪθ), *a.* (*sb.*) Forms: α. **féowertiʒoða**, *erron.* **-teoða** (fem., neut. **-ðe**), 2 **furteohte**, 3 **fowertiðe**, **-tuðe**, **-tiȝthe**, **fuwertiðe**, **fourtiand**, 4 *south.* **vourtaȝte**, **fourtithe**, **-tied**, 5 **fowrtyde**, **fortith**, 6 **fourteth**, 7 **fourtieth**, 6– **fortieth**; β. 6 **fourtyest**. [OE. *féowertiʒoða* :—prehistoric **fiwortigunþon-*, corresponding to ON. *fertugonde*, *-ande* (Sw. *fyrationde*, Da. *fyrretyvende*), f. FORTY on the analogy of TENTH.

The rare 13th c. *fourtiand* is of Scandinavian origin. The 16th c. *fourtyest* is noteworthy as being formed with the same suffix as in the Low and High Ger. equivalents (Du. *veertigste*, OHG. *fiorzugôsto*); cf. also late Icel. *fertugasti*.]

The ordinal numeral belonging to the cardinal forty. ***the fortieth man***: one man in forty. ***fortieth part***: one of forty equal parts into which a quantity may be divided. Also *absol.* and quasi-*sb.*

c **1000** ÆLFRIC *Deut.* i. 3 On þam feowerteoðan ʒeare. *c* **1175** *Cott. Hom.* 229 Drihten þa an þa furteohte deʒe his æristes astah to heofene. **1258** *Charter of Hen. III*, in Tyrrell *Hist. Eng.* (1700) II. App. 25 In the two and fowertiȝthe geare of ure crunninge. **1357** *Lay Folks Catech.* 152 The fourtied day after that he ras..he stegh in-till heuen. *c* **1425** WYNTOUN *Cron.* VI. iv. 89 Of hys kynryk þe fowrtyde yhere. **1502** *Ord. Crysten Men* (W. de W. 1506) I. vi. 52 The fourtyest daye after his resurreccyon. **1590** SIR J. SMYTH *Disc. Weapons* in *Lett. Lit. Men* (Camden) 51 Of which, scarce the fortieth man escaped with life. **1611** BIBLE *Chron.* xxvi. 31 In the fourtieth yeere of the reigne of Dauid. *a* **1631** DONNE *Love's Diet* 23 Ah! what doth it availe To be the fourtieth name in an entail? **1724** SWIFT *Drapier's Lett.* Wks. 1755 V. II. 138 It is not above the fortieth part in value to the rest of Britain. **1758** S. HAYWARD *Serm.* v. 145 In that fortieth of Isaiah how is that Jehovah set forth? **1800** YOUNG in *Phil. Trans.* XCI. 55 A large card, divided..into fortieths of an inch. **1855** MILMAN *Lat. Chr.* (1864) V. IX. vii. 324 All prelates [etc.]..were summoned to contribute at least a fortieth to this end.

fortifiable ('fɔːtɪfaɪəb(ə)l), *a.* [f. FORTIFY *v.* + -ABLE; cf. F. *fortifiable*.] That may be fortified.

1609 OVERBURY *Observ. 17 Prov.* Wks. (1856) 223 The countrey every where fortifiable with water. **1755** in JOHNSON. **1886** RUSKIN *Præterita* I. vii. 207 The quadrilateral plan of my fortifiable dispositions.

†**for'tificate**, *v. Sc. Obs.* [f. ppl. stem of L. *fortificāre*.] = FORTIFY.

1560 ROLLAND *Crt. Venus* III. 188 The vther part gif thay fortificat In ȝour contrair.

fortification (ˌfɔːtɪfɪ'keɪʃən). [a. F. *fortification*, ad. L. *fortificātiōn-em*, n. of action f. *fortificā-re* to FORTIFY.]

I. The action of fortifying; in senses of the vb.

†**1.** Strengthening, corroboration, ratification.

1530–1 *Act 22 Hen. VIII*, c. 14 [They] haue..procured many men..to the..practise of archerie..to the greate encrease and fortificacions of the same outwarde realmes. **1557–75** *Diurn. Occurr.* (Bannatyne) 122 To come to Edinburgh to subscriue the fortificatioun of the kingis coronatioun. **1563–87** FOXE *A. & M.* (1684) III. 454 For the more fortification of that which hath been said. **1609** SKENE *Reg. Maj.*, *Forme of Proces* 116 The defender quha propones the exception, for fortification therof, may propone ane duply, against the libell and reply. **1614** RALEIGH *Hist. World* II. (1634) 442 Much common good therby likely to arise with mutual fortification of both those kingdoms. **1623** CONWAY in Ellis *Orig. Lett.* Ser. I. III. 155 His actes had not need of theire fortification.

2. a. The strengthening of wine with alcohol.

1885 *Pall Mall G.* 7 Sept. 5/2 Spirits exported to Spain for the fortification of native wines. **1893** *Manch. Guard.* 19 May 5/4 The duty was raised..to discourage the fortification of Spanish wines with coarse spirits.

b. The addition of nutrients, usually vitamins, to food.

1939 *Milbank Mem. Fund Q.* XVII. 241 (*heading*) The public health aspects of the fortification of foods with vitamins and minerals. **1941** *Lancet* 20 Dec. 773/1 Fortification must be considered solely in relation to the proven need..for a given nutrient. **1967** *New Scientist* 9 Nov. 328/3 Fortification of cereals and cereal flours with proteins offers the best immediate prospect for alleviating the world's shortage of protein foods.

3. *Mil.* **a.** The action of fortifying or providing with defensive works.

1562 WHITEHORNE tr. *Machiavel* (*title*) Certain waies of the orderyng of Souldiers in battelray, & settyng of battailes ..also plattes for fortificacion of Townes. **1882** STEVENSON *New Arab. Nts.* (1884) 129 He had no means of fortification, and lay open to attack.

b. The art or science of fortifying or constructing works of defence.

1642 HOWELL *For. Trav.* (Arb.) 80 The art of Navigation and Fortification. **1688** CAPT. J. S. *Fortification* 23 *Fortification*, or Military Architecture, is a Science [etc.]. **1751** JOHNSON *Rambler* No. 103 ¶2 We range from city to city, though we profess neither architecture nor fortification. **1828** J. M. SPEARMAN *Brit. Gunner* (ed. 2) 201 *Fortification*..is divided into two parts, which are called Permanent or Field Fortification. **1879** *Cassell's Techn. Educ.* I. 21/2 The science..is termed Fortification.

fig. **1649** JER. TAYLOR *Gt. Exemp.* II. ix. 124 Observe what object is aptest to inflame thee, and by speciall arts of fortification, stop up the avenues to that part.

II. *concr.*

4. a. *Mil.* A defensive work; a wall, earthwork, tower, etc. Chiefly *collect. plural.*

1489 CAXTON *Faytes of A.* II. xxiv. 137 Upon euery yate muste be made dyuerse deffences and fortyfycacions. **1512** *Act 4 Hen. VIII*, c. 1 §1 To make Bulwerkes, Brayes..and al other fortificacions. **1604** SHAKS. *Oth.* III. v. 5 This Fortification (Gentlemen) shall we see't? **1683** *Brit. Spec.* 18 Strong fortifications do secure thy Ports. **1719** DE FOE *Crusoe* I. iv, I..made me a Door to come out, on the Outside of my Pale or Fortification. **1794** SULLIVAN *View Nat.* II. 362 In the neighbourhood of Lexington..are the remains of two ancient fortifications. **1841** W. SPALDING *Italy & It. Isl.* I. 223 We find all the Seven Hills embraced within a fortification which the legendary history ascribes to Servius Tullius. **1863** LYELL *Antiq. Man* 40 Extensive fortifications to protect them from their enemies.

b. *Comb.*: **fortification-agate** (see quot.).

1882 in CASSELL. **1892** *Dana's Syst. Min.* (ed. 6) 189 *Ruin-agate* or *Fortification-agate* is a variety with light to dark brown shades, showing, when polished, curious markings well described by the name.

c. *transf.* and *fig.* A means of defence.

a **1586** SIDNEY *Arcad.* I. x. 40b, The Stagge thought it better to trust to the nimblenes of his feete then to the slender fortification of his lodging. **1653** WALTON *Angler* ii. 41 The gloves of an Otter are the best fortification for your hands against wet weather. **1656–7** *Burton's Diary* (1828) I. 363 That..is the best fortification for all honest men. **1742** *Lond. & Country Brew.* I. (ed. 4) 80 Horse-dung should be laid to the Windows as a Fortification against them [winds]. **1751** JOHNSON *Rambler* No. 26 ¶7 He was happy in this fortification [an arrangement of bolts and bars].

5. †**a.** *gen.* A means of strengthening. *Obs.*

1655 *Advt.* in *Culpepper's Pract. Physic*, It [*aurum potabile*] is an Universal Fortification for all Complexions and ages. **1678** DRYDEN *Kind Keeper* IV. i, Go, provide..the Westphalia ham, and other fortifications of nature.

b. *spec.* The strengthening timbers, etc. of a whaling vessel: see FORTIFY *v.* 1 b.

1820 SCORESBY *Acc. Arctic Reg.* II. 191 The next important part of the fortification is the pointers.

†**c.** *Gunnery.* The additional thickness of metal serving to strengthen certain portions of a cannon.

1626 CAPT. SMITH *Accid. Yng. Seamen* 32 To..know her leuell poynt blanke..her fortification, the differences of powder [etc.]. **1669** STURMY *Mariner's Mag.* v. 65 Canon-Powder is best..for in taking up much room it hath the greater length or fortification of metal about it in the Piece.

fortified ('fɔːtɪfaɪd), *ppl. a.* [f. FORTIFY *v.* + -ED[1].] **1.** Strengthened; provided with means of defence; protected with fortifications.

1538 ELYOT, *Firmus*, stable, constant, well fortified. **1611** BIBLE *Micah* vii. 12 He shal come..from the fortified cities. *a* **1657** LOVELACE *Poems* (1864) 234 Your days fare, a fortified toast. **1692** in *Capt. Smith's Seaman's Gram.* II. xviii. 128 A Well Fortified Gun, hath her Metal at the Vent or Touch-hole as thick as her Diameter at the Bore. **1757** *York Courant* 18 Oct., A well-fortified vessel for the coasting trade..has been long wanted. **1790** BURKE *Fr. Rev.* Wks. V. 247 The Orsini and Vitelli in Italy, who used to sally from their fortified dens to rob the trader and traveller. **1861** M. PATTISON *Ess.* (1889) I. 45 Three fortified and portcullised gateways.

2. a. Of food: supplied with added nutrients.

1910 C. WATSON *Food & Feeding* iv. 36 Milk fortified with starch. *Ibid.* viii. 139 A 'fortified cocoa' can be prepared as follows:—..cocoa..milk..sugar..water..cream. **1940** *Nature* 27 July 117/1 The white loaf would be fortified with a supplement of vitamin B_1 (aneurin) and a calcium salt. **1970** *Guardian* 7 Aug. 3/8 Modern bakeries..have pushed out fortified bread to tickle the palate.

b. Of wines: strengthened with alcohol. Cf. FORTIFY *v.* 4.

c **1906** *Harmsworth Encycl.* VIII. 6320/2 Madeira is a sherry type of fortified wine. **1954** R. W. SCHERY *Plants for Man* xx. 525/2 Fortified wines are 'cocktail' or 'dessert' wines such as port, sherry, and vermouth, in which the alcoholic content is supplemented by the additon of brandy ..to a strength unobtainable by simple fermentation. **1968** *Daily Tel.* (Colour Suppl.) 13 Dec. 41/1 So often in statistics no distinction is made between table wine, fortified wine, and aperitif wine.

fortifier ('fɔːtɪfaɪə(r)). [f. next + -ER[1].] One who or that which fortifies: **a.** One who constructs fortifications. **b.** One who or that which strengthens; a supporter, an upholder.

a. 1552 HULOET, Fortifier, *munitor.* **1589** IVE *Fortif.* 33 Admonishing the Fortifier..to vse..the considerations before in them alleaged. **1599** HAKLUYT *Voy.* II. I. 123 A fortifier, had deuised a certaine kinde of ioyned boords, the which being caried of the souldiers, defended them from the shot of the Harquebuzers. **1602** CAREW *Cornwall* 149 The fortifier made his aduantage of the commoditie, affoorded by the ground. **1873** *Daily News* 7 Nov. 5/3 General Chabeau Latour, the fortifier of Paris.

b. *c* **1565** LINDESAY (Pitscottie) *Chron. Scot.* (1728) 45 But also reproached the fortifiers and allowers of him in such wickedness. **1569** MURRAY 15 Oct. in H. Campbell *Love Lett. Mary Q. Scots* App. 58 We wer constranit to nominate the said Quene..as maintenar and fortifiar of the executouris thairof. **1878** *Daily News* 11 Sept. 4/7 The opinion is at least a fortifier against adverse criticism. **1894** *Ibid.* 15 Feb. 5/3 An egg beaten in a very little whisky and water will be found an excellent fortifier.

fortify ('fɔːtɪfaɪ), *v.* [ad. F. *fortifier*, ad. L. *fortificāre*, f. *fortis* strong + *-ficāre*: see -FY.]

I. To make strong.

1. a. *trans.* To strengthen structurally. Now somewhat *rare.*

c **1450** *Merlin* 187 He made to a-mende and fortyfie the wallis of the town ther, as thei were most feble. **1697** DRYDEN *Virg. Georg.* IV. 262 The grave experienc'd Bee.. Employ'd at home..To fortify the Combs, to build the Wall. **1726** LEONI tr. *Alberti's Archit.* II. 113/2 They shou'd also be fortifyed all round with strong brick work. **1886** WILLIS & CLARK *Cambridge* III. 545 Fortifying the woodwork of the Dome and Lantern.

b. *spec.* To strengthen (a gun) by additional thickness of metal. Cf. FORTIFICATION 5 c. Also, to strengthen (a ship) for especial emergency, by means of additional timbers, etc.

1627 CAPT. SMITH *Seaman's Gram.* xiv. 71 Those small Peeces are better fortified than the greater. **1669** STURMY *Mariner's Mag.* v. 62 You must work as if the Piece were fortified no more than only so much as the thinnest part of the Metal is. **1820** SCORESBY *Acc. Arctic Reg.* II. 508 The new ship..is fortified within the bow. **1853** KANE *Grinnell Exp.* xv. (1856) 112 She was..fortified with three additional strips of boiler iron.

c. To cover or bind with some protective material or appliance. (Now coloured by senses 7–8.)

1607 TOPSELL *Four-f. Beasts* (1658) 372 Men armed with shields, and fortified all over with thongs of leather. **1669** BOYLE *Contn. New Exp.* II. (1682) 21 A little [air] brake into the Reciever..because I had neglected to fortifie the cover with Turpentine. **1697** POTTER *Antiq. Greece* III. xv. (1715) 130 The whole Fabrick..was fortified with Pitch to secure the Wood from the Waters. **1706** HEARNE *Collect.* 7 Feb., Being us'd to fortifie himself against weather by..a thick Robe. **1798** W. BLAIR *Soldier's Friend* 31 Ingenious modes of fortifying shoes, and rendering them water-proof. **1803** WELLINGTON 20 Jan. in Gurw. *Desp.* I. 397 Kegs of six gallons each, well fortified with iron hoops. **1850** MERIVALE *Rom. Emp.* (1865) I. v. 193 Camillus..fortified the shield with a rim of metal.

2. To impart strength or vigour to (the body, its organs, or powers, †a plant); to give (a person, oneself) strength or endurance for some effort.

14.. LYDG. & BURGH *Secrees* 1959 Wyn..ffortefieth the heete in the body natural. **1578** LYTE *Dodoens* II. lxxi. 241 It doth fortefie and strengthen the harte. **1686** W. HARRIS tr. *Lemery's Course Chem.* II. xxii. (ed. 3) 624 The Turks will take of it [opium] to the bigness of a hazle Nut to fortifie themselves when they are going to fight. **1691** RAY *Creation* Ded. (1704) 3 To fortifie you in your Athletic Conflicts. **1719** LONDON & WISE *Compl. Gard.* 212 We endeavour to fortifie it, and make it grow big all Summer, by watering and cropping it. **1849** CLARIDGE *Cold Water-cure* 42 Cold water, as a beverage, fortifies the stomach and intestines. **1865** DICKENS *Mut. Fr.* I. xiii, Mr. Inspector hastily fortifying himself with another glass.

†**3. a.** To render more powerful or effective; to strengthen, reinforce with additional resources or co-operation; to garrison (a fortress); to provide (an army, etc.) with necessaries. *Obs.*

1470–85 MALORY *Arthur* I. xviii, They had..moo than eyght thousand for to fortyfye alle the fortresses in the marches of Cornewaylle. **1480** *Robt. Devyll* in Thoms *Prose Rom.* 6 He ever prayed to God to send hym a chyld..to multyply and fortyfy his lynage. **1523** LD. BERNERS *Froiss.* I. lxxii. 94 The countesse..fortifyed all her garisons of euery thyng yᵗ they wanted. **1548** HALL *Chron.*, *Hen. VI* an. 31) 165 He fortified Burdeaux with Englishmen and victayle. **1612** WOODALL *Surg. Mate* Wks. (1653) 190 It fortifieth the other medicines, and doubleth their forces. **1670** COTTON *Espernon* I. II. 69 The Inhabitants of the Suburbs of St. Germains were order'd to slip in to fortifie the attempt. **1701** SWIFT *Contests Nobles & Com.* Wks. 1755 II. I. 11 They admitted three thousand into a share of the government; and thus fortified, became the cruellest tyranny upon record. **1725** DE FOE *Voy. round World* (1840) 28, I fortified myself with the French captain, and the supercargo.

b. To arm, strengthen with weapons. Cf. 7. *rare.*

1711 ADDISON *Spect.* No. 121 ¶3 That great Variety of Arms with which Nature has differently fortified the Bodies of several kind of Animals, such as Claws, Hoofs, and Horns.

4. a. To strengthen (liquors) with alcohol.

1880 *Act 43 & 44 Vict.* c. 24 §70 Any spirits warehoused ..may be used in the warehouse for fortifying wines. **1894** C. N. ROBINSON *Brit. Fleet* 142 In 1869 the present practice of fortifying the [lime] juice with rum was resorted to.

b. To add nutrients, usually vitamins, to (food).

1940 *Nature* 27 July 118/2 There will now be two outstanding examples of fortified foodstuffs, bread and margarine. **1941** *Ann. Reg. 1940* 345 Recognition..of the need to fortify various products such as bread, margarine etc., with vitamins. **1942** *Endeavour* I. I. 30/2, 1 gram of calciferol is sufficient to fortify 40 tons of margarine. **1967** *New Scientist* 9 Nov. 328/3 By 1969..all emergency shipments of grain will be fortified to the optimal extent either with amino acids or with protein concentrates.

5. a. To strengthen mentally or morally; to endow with immaterial resources; to impart fortitude to; to cheer, encourage.

1477 EARL RIVERS (Caxton) *Dictes* 19 It apparteigneth to euery man..to seke science and ther with to fortiffie hym hauyng a good eye vpon his enemyes. **1573** BARET *Alv.* F 948 To haue a hart fortified with wisedome. *a* **1586** SIDNEY *Arcadia* II. (1629) 111 Which..so greatly fortified her desires, to see that her mother had the like desires. **1699** LOCKE *Educ.* §70. 100 A young Man, before he leaves the shelter of his Father's House, should be fortified with Resolution to secure his Vertue. **1751** JOHNSON *Rambler* No. 155 ¶8 Every delay gives vice another opportunity of fortifying itself by habit. **1761** HUME *Hist. Eng.* II. xxiii. 69 The king..fortified by this unsuccessful attempt to dethrone him. *a* **1794** GIBBON *Life* viii. (1839) 238 Timidity was fortified by pride. **1865** M. ARNOLD *Ess. Crit.* vii. (1875) 269 Their courage was fortified by a fervent prayer.

b. To confirm, corroborate, add support to (a statement, etc.). *to fortify oneself*: to confirm one's statement, etc. †Also (*rarely*) *intr.* for *refl.*

c **1449** PECOCK *Repr.* 285 To fortofie and strength the same badde answere. **1529** MORE *Dyaloge* I. Wks. 164/1 That glose he would haue fortified..with another worde of Christ. *c* **1532** DEWES *Introd. Fr.* in *Palsgr.* 1063 My lorde the President fortifyeng sayd that we be nat bounde by the lawe to say. **1678** *Trans. Crt. Spain* 5 To fortifie his Reasons, he sent us a Manifesto. **1833** HT. MARTINEAU *Loom & Lugger* II. v. 96 A distinct charge is brought against you, fortified by particulars. **1847** EMERSON *Repr. Men, Plato* Wks. (Bohn) I. 295 If he made transcendental distinctions, he fortified himself by drawing all his illustrations from sources disdained by orators.

†**6.** *intr.* To gain strength, grow strong. *Obs.*

1605 BACON *Adv. Learn.* II. xxii. §6 How they [the affections] gather and fortify. **1658** EVELYN *Fr. Gard.* (1675) 165 Leaving the least to bear seed, and that the plant may fortifie. **1660** SHARROCK *Vegetables* 126 Bind up..the strongest and forwardest first, letting the other fortifie.

II. To strengthen against attack.

7. *trans.* To provide (a town or its walls) with defensive works; to protect with fortifications.

1436 *Pol. Poems* (Rolls) II. 166 To fortefye anone he dyd devyse Of englysshe townes iij. **1485** CAXTON *Chas. Gt.* (1880) 165 The walles of that cyte ben fortefyed with towres. **1582** N. LICHEFIELD tr. *Castanheda's Conq. E. Ind.* lvii. 120 All their houses well fortified with sundry trenches round about. **1611** BIBLE *Isa.* xxii. 10 The houses haue yee broken downe to fortifie the wall. **1759** ROBERTSON *Hist. Scot.* I. II. 152 These were immediately commanded to fortify Leith. **1816** KEATINGE *Trav.* (1817) I. 86 It is environed with walls, but not regularly fortified. **1893** *Academy* 13 May 411/2 The opposite bank..was admirably fortified.

transf. **1601** HOLLAND *Pliny* I. 111 This isle is fortified with the mount Prion. **1705** ADDISON *Italy* 8 A Rock that runs out into the Sea, and is well fortify'd by Nature. **1726** LEONI tr. *Alberti's Archit.* II. 121/1 A Pier..to fortifie a Port.

fig. **1548** HALL *Chron., Rich. III* (an. 3) 42 b, Realmes and countries are fortified and munited with a double power. **1644** MILTON *Areop.* (Arb.) 50 Shut and fortifie one gate against corruption. **1775** JOHNSON *Tax. no Tyr.* 31 His house is fortified by the law. **1850** MERIVALE *Rom. Emp.* (1865) I. ix. 355 He..fortified his position against the malevolence of a future consul.

8. To surround (an army, oneself) with defences; to put in a position of defence.

1548 HALL *Chron., Hen. V* (an. 3) 48 b, The fotemen were hedged about with the stakes..This device of fortifiyng an army was at this tyme fyrst invented. **1590** MARLOWE *2nd Pt. Tamburl.* III. ii, I'll have you learn..the way to fortify your men. **1837** W. IRVING *Capt. Bonneville* III. 47 Here they proceeded to fortify themselves.

9. *intr.* To erect fortifications; to establish a position of defence.

1570–6 LAMBARDE *Peramb. Kent.* (1826) 185 Sailing up the River of Thamise, he fortifieth at Middleton. *c* **1600** SIR R. CECIL *Let.* in Naunton *Fragm. Reg.* (Arb.) 61 They will first fortifie and learn the strength of the Rebels. **1774** PENNANT *Tour Scotl. in 1772.* 293 No people will give themselves the trouble of fortifying amidst the security of friends. *a* **1885** U. S. GRANT *Personal Mem.* I. 331 The enemy was fortifying at Corinth.

transf. and *fig.* **1591** LYLY *Endym.* I. iii, I will withdraw myselfe to the river, and there fortifie for fish. *c* **1600** SHAKS. *Sonn.* lxiii, For such a time do I now fortifie Against confounding Ages cruell knife.

Hence **'fortifying** *ppl. a.*

1863 W. B. JERROLD *Sign. Distress* 22 Soup, made of sound and fortifying materials. **1872** BAGEHOT *Physics & Pol.* (1876) 217 The fortifying religions..those which lay the plainest stress on the manly parts of morality.

fortifying ('fɔːtɪfaɪɪŋ), *vbl. sb.* [f. prec. + -ING[1].] The action of the vb. FORTIFY. Also gerundially with omission of *in*.

1580 HOLLYBAND *Treas. Fr. Tong, Fortifiement*, a fortifying. **1719** DE FOE *Crusoe* I. iv, I laid aside..my building, and fortifying. **1774** S. COOPER in *Franklin's Wks.* (1887) V. 364 The entrance into this town is now fortifying by the soldiery. **1820** SCORESBY *Acc. Arctic Reg.* II. 191 Fortifying, is the operation of strengthening a ship's stern and bows. **1832** J. H. NEWMAN *Lett.* (1891) I. 287 Lying down is an instant specific for it [sea-sickness], and eating, a certain alleviation and fortifying against it. **1866** GEO. ELIOT *F. Holt* (1868) 40 Sir Maximus Debarry who had been at the fortifying of the old castle.

†**b.** *concr.* A fortification, defence. *Obs.*

1523 LD. BERNERS *Froiss.* I. cclxxxiii. 422 The fote men.. beate downe the fortifyeng and barryers. **1553** BRENDE *Q. Curtius* VII. 138 b, The King of Scythia..iudging y[t] the fortifieng vpon the ryuers side, shuld be as a yoke to his neck. **1573** BARET *Alv.* F 950 A proppe, a fortifying..*fulcimentum.*

†**for'tiht**, *v. Obs.* (early ME.) [OE. *fortyhtan*, f. FOR- *pref.*[1] + *tyhtan* to draw.] *trans.* To draw aside (to evil); to seduce.

a **1000** *Elene* 208 (Gr.) Swa se ealda feond..leode fortyhte. *c* **1200** *Trin. Coll. Hom.* 87 Seuene oðre gostes..fortehten hit [þat child]. *Ibid.* 107 Þe deuel mid his fortihtinge bringeð unnut þonc on mannes hearte.

fortilage, fortiless, obs. ff. of FORTALICE.

†**'fortin**, *sb.*[1] *Obs.* [a. F. *fortin*, dim. of *fort*: see FORT *sb.*] A small fort; a field-fort.

1706 PHILLIPS (ed. Kersey), *Fortin*, or *Field-fort*. **1721–36** in BAILEY. **1744** HANMER *conjecture* in *Shaks. 1 Hen. IV*, II. iii. 55 Of palisadoes, fortins [**1623** frontiers], parapets.

Fortin ('fɔːtɪn), *sb.*[2] The name of J. *Fortin* (1750–1831), French physicist, used attrib. or in the possessive to designate a type of mercury barometer invented by him.

1875 *Encycl. Brit.* III. 382/2 (*caption*) Fortin's Barometer. **1930** *Meteorol. Gloss.* (*Met. Office*) (ed. 2) 80 *Fortin barometer*, a portable form of mercurial barometer in which the zero of the scale is fixed by a pointer, inside the cistern. By making the cistern partly of leather and providing an adjusting screw, the level of mercury in the cistern can be brought up to the scale zero before each reading is taken. **1970** *Encycl. Brit.* III. 181/1 Since the Fortin barometer is not a primary instrument, its instrumental errors must be determined by comparison with a standard barometer.

†**'fortin**, *a. Obs. rare*[−1]. [a. OF. *fortin* (used only of Samson), f. *fort* strong.] Strong.

1340 *Ayenb.* 204 Samson fortin.

fortingle, var. f. of FARTHINGDEAL, *Obs.*

1721–36 in BAILEY.

for-tired: see FOR- *pref.*[1] 6.

fortis ('fɔːtɪs), *sb.* and *a.* [f. L. *fortis* adj., strong.] **A.** *sb.* A variety of dynamite: see quot.

1889 MAJOR CUNDILL *Dict. Explosives, Glycero-Nitre*.. This explosive has been submitted for authorisation in this country under the name of 'Fortis'.

B. *adj.* Of one of two or more homorganic consonants: strongly articulated. Opp. *lenis.* So also as *sb.* (pl., -es), such a consonant.

1909 WEBSTER, Fortis *a.* **1932** G. K. ZIPF *Sel. Stud. Rel. Freq. Lang.* I. 4 The fortis tenuis aspirata is decidedly more conspicuous than the faint lenis media. **1933** BLOOMFIELD *Lang.* vi. 99 In English the unvoiced stops are aspirated fortes. **1962** A. C. GIMSON *Introd. Pronunc. Eng.* iv. 32 A voiceless/voiced pair such as [s, z] are distinguished not only by the presence or absence of voice but also by the degree of breath and muscular effort involved in the articulation... Those English consonants which are usually voiced tend to be articulated with relatively weak energy, whereas those which are always voiceless are relatively strong. Thus, it may be important to define [s]..as strong or *fortis* and [z] as weak or *lenis.* **1964** JAKOBSON & HALLE in D. Abercrombie et al. *Daniel Jones* 100 The distinctive mark in a fortis-lenis pair. **1965** *Language* XLI. 480 The stop is of greater duration and fortis articulation. **1969** *Jrnl. Lancs. Dial. Soc.* 14 The weakening of the fortis consonants in Jestetten was a phonetic change which threatened the stability of the whole consonant system.

‖**for'tissimo**, *adv.* and *sb. Music.* [It. *fortissimo*, superl. of *forte*: see FORTE.] **A.** *adv.* Very loud. (Abbreviated *ff.*, *ffor.*, or *fortiss.*) Also quasi-*adj.*

1724 *Short Explic. For. Words in Music* 32 *Fortissimo*, is Extream loud. **1767** STERNE *Tr. Shandy* IX. xi, Amen, cried my father, *fortissimo*. **1883** MISS BRADDON *Golden Calf* I. ii. 50 If their pianissimo passages failed in delicacy, there was no mistake about their fortissimo. **1889** *Athenæum* 6 Apr. 448/3 A splendid effect being gained by the sudden entry of the combined chorus *fortissimo* to the words 'Hosannah! Lord of Lords!'

B. *sb.* A very loud passage or point; *fig.* a high pitch of excitement.

1856 GEO. ELIOT *Jrnl.* in *Lett.* (1954) II. 243 It was a crescendo of delight when we found a 'Strawberry', and a *fortissimo* when I..saw..an Anthea Cereus. **1885** G. B. SHAW *How to become Mus. Critic* (1960) 69 He [*sc.* Massenet] pours forth all his energy in a screeching, grinding, rasping *fortissimo* of extraordinary exuberance and vigor. **1928** *Observer* 5 Feb. 12/5 The hard and sudden fortissimos. **1928** *Daily Express* 17 Mar. 9/7 As this jazz harmony reached its fortissimo. **1931** E. SACKVILLE-WEST *Simpson* III. xiii, Flinging a fortissimo of emotion—whether of anger or of delight—with sudden and deafening violence on to everything which twitched the robe of his soul. *a* **1963** C. S. LEWIS *Poems* (1964) 59 Those who have seen no lions must revere A bull for Pan's *fortissimo.*

[fortition, spurious word: see SORTITION.]

fortitude ('fɔːtɪtjuːd). [a. F. *fortitude*, ad. L. *fortitūdo*, f. *fortis* strong: see FORT *a.*]

†**1.** Physical or structural strength. *Obs.*

1553 EDEN *Treat. Newe Ind.* (Arb.) 15 A beast..excellinge all other beastes in fortitude and strength. **1591** SHAKS. *1 Hen. VI*, II. i. 17 Dispairing of his owne armes fortitude. **1604** —— *Oth.* I. iii. 222 The Fortitude of the place is best knowne to you. **1703** T. N. *City & C. Purchaser* 50 Bonding of Brick-work..conduces very much to its Fortitude.

2. Moral strength or courage. Now only in passive sense: Unyielding courage in the endurance of pain or adversity. (One of the cardinal virtues.)

[*c* **1386** CHAUCER *Pars. T.* ¶654 Agayns..Accidie..ther is a vertu that is called Fortitudo.] **1500–20** DUNBAR *Poems* lxviii. 77 Fortitude, prowdence, and temperance. **1609** BIBLE (Douay) *Zech.* xiii. Comm., The Apostles fleing God recalled them, and streingthened them with fortitude. **1713** STEELE *Englishm.* No. 22. 144 Fortitude is the peculiar Excellence of Man. **1754** MRS. DELANY *Let.* 10 Nov., The Duchess of Queensbury bears her calamity with great fortitude. **1818** HAZLITT *Eng. Poets* ii. (1870) 27 Fortitude does not appear at any time to have been the distinguishing virtue of poets. **1848** DICKENS *Dombey* vi. (C. D. ed.) 40 She could bear the disappointments of other people with tolerable fortitude.

3. *Astrol.* A position or circumstance which heightens the influence of a planet; a dignity.

1547 BOORDE *Astronamye* Contents in *Introd. Knowl.* (1870) Forewords 23 The iii[i]. capytle doth shew of the fortitudes of the planetes. **1695** CONGREVE *Love for L.* II. i, Sure the Moon is in all her Fortitudes.

fortitudinous (fɔːtɪ'tjuːdɪnəs), *a.* [f. L. *fortitūdin-em* (see FORTITUDE) + -OUS.] Endowed with or characterized by fortitude.

1752 FIELDING *Amelia* Wks. 1775 X. 224 As fortitudinous a man as any in the King's dominions. **1781** GIBBON *Decl. & F.* III. lii. 262 These fortitudinous heroes are awed by the superior fierceness of the lions and tigers. **1878** MORLEY *Carlyle* 175 Right service performed in fortitudinous temper.

fortlet ('fɔːtlɪt). Also 4, 6 fortelet. [f. FORT *sb.* + -LET. (In quot. 1330 it may be an error for *forcelete* or *fortelece*: see FORCELET, FORTALICE.)] A small fort.

c **1330** R. BRUNNE *Chron. Wace* (Rolls) 4822 Hys pleyn londes he let hym haue, Bot his forteletes he dide saue. **1538** LELAND *Itin.* VII. 55 A lytle poore Steple as a Fortelet for a Brunt. **1613** SIR H. FINCH *Law* (1636) 354 As if he that took them driue them to a Fortlet or Castle. **1781** JUSTAMOND *Priv. Life Lewis XV*, III. 372 The troops were employed in burning a fortlet. **1817** G. CHALMERS *Pref. to Churchyard's Chips, Murton's Trag.* 159 The master defended the donjon of the fortlet against the regent. **1859** *Times* 26 Dec. 7/2 The new fortlets have been completed.

fortnight ('fɔːtnaɪt). Forms: 3 furten-, 3–5 fourte-, (5 fourtee-, fowerte-), 4–5 fourten-, fowrt(e-, 5–7 fo(u)rth-, 6 fourt-, (fortk-), 6– fort-: see NIGHT. [Contracted form of OE. *féowertýne niht* fourteen nights. Cf. SENNIGHT. For the ancient Germanic method of reckoning by nights see Tacitus *Germania* xi.]

1. A period of fourteen nights; two weeks.

a **1000** *Laws of Ina* §55 Oþ ðæt feowertyne niht ofer Eastron. *c* **1275** LAY. 25675 Nou his folle fourteniht [*c* **1205** feowertene niht] þat he hire haueþ i-holde forþ riht. **13..** *Guy Warw.* (A.) 4236 Al a fourten niȝt sike he lay. *c* **1440** *Generydes* 5342 It passith not a fourthnyght sithe it was. **1530** PALSGR. Introd. 20 It is but a senyghtes labour, or, at the moste, a fourtnyghtes. **1639** *Hamilton Papers* (Camden) 81, I shall make ane end of uhuat I can do in on fortnighte. *c* **1720** PRIOR *Case Stated* 8 It wanted a fortnight to Bartlemew-fair. **1879** FROUDE *Cæsar* viii. 69 During the brief fortnight of his seventh consulship.

b. *this day, Monday,* †*Monday was* (*a*), etc. *fortnight*: a fortnight from (this day, etc.).

1389 in *Eng. Gilds* (1870) 71 Y[e] tridde shal been ye sunday fowrtenytz aftere hestern. **1470–85** MALORY *Arthur* x. ii, I.. haue remembraunce of your promyse that ye haue made with me to doo bataille with me this day fourtenyght. **1605** *Nottingham Rec.* IV. 278 To be payd..10 li. this day fortnight. **1712** STEELE *Spect.* No. 533 ¶2 On Monday was fortnight it was my misfortune to come to London.

†**2.** *attrib.*; occas. quasi-*adj.* = FORTNIGHTLY.

1549 LATIMER *4th Serm. bef. Edw. VI* (Arb.) 120 There was thre wekes sessions at newgate, and fourthnyghte Sessions at the Marshialshy. **1563** *Child Marriages* (E.E.T.S.) 59 At the fortnight end, he maried her not, but [etc.].

fortnightly ('fɔːtnaɪtlɪ), *a.*, *adv.*, and *sb.* [f. prec. + -LY.] **A.** *adj.* Happening or appearing once in a fortnight. **B.** *adv.* Once in a fortnight.

1800 *Dundee Mag.* Dec. Pref., He then published a Fortnightly Magazine which was carried on for two years. **1820** LAMB *Elia*, Ser. I. *South-Sea Ho.*, His fine suite of official rooms..resounded fortnightly to the notes of a concert. **1854** H. MILLER *Sch. & Schm.* (1858) 325 The masons.. were paid fortnightly. **1881** *Macm. Mag.* XLIII. 436/1 Fort-nightly Sunday concerts are to be given next season.

C. *sb.* A newspaper or magazine published fortnightly. Cf. *biweekly* s.v. BI-[2] 4 a.

Quots. 1865 and 1929 refer specifically to the *Fortnightly Review* (1865–), re-titled *The Fortnightly* from July 1934.

1865 G. H. LEWES *Jrnl.* 13 May in G. Eliot *Lett.* (1955) IV. 192 The *First Number of the Fortnightly* appeared. **1929** *Fortnightly Rev.* Aug. p. ii (Advt.), The Fortnightly announces for September *The Car Mind* By G. R. Stirling-Taylor... Also other notable articles, stories and poems. **1966** in *Random House Dict.* **1984** G. SMITH *Eng. Compan.* (1985) 96 *Private Eye*, an offset-litho fortnightly begun in 1961.

†**'forto, 'fort(e,** *prep.* and *conj. Obs.* [f. FOR *prep.* + TO *prep.*]

A. *prep.* Till, until; up to, as far as.

c **1200** *Trin. Coll. Hom.* 33 Al mankin was wunende on muchele wowe..forte þat ilke time þat [etc.]. *a* **1225** *Ancr. R.* 38 'Aue Maria', uort 'Dominus tecum'. **1297** R. GLOUC. (1724) 463 þe kyng..vorto Mydewynter ney byseged þe emperesse. *c* **1330** *Arth. & Merl.* 4796 That strengthe him last Fort arnemorwe. **1387** TREVISA *Higden* (Rolls) II. 25 Alle þe woke longe, forto Saturday at none.

b. In conjunctional phrase, *fort(e that*: until.

c **1200** *Trin. Coll. Hom.* 51 þe king of babilonie bilai þe burh ierusalem, forte þat hit [= he it] wan. *c* **1275** LAY. 11518 Mauric verde vorþ riht..forte that he come to Maximian. *c* **1330** *King of Tars* 396 The mayden..al niht lay and wepe Forte that day gon dawe. **1362** LANGL. *P. Pl.* A. VII. 2 A gyde, That mihte folwen us vch a fote forte that we come there. *c* **1450** *Two Cookery-bks.* 114 Wash hem [peson] clene in cold water, fort that ye holys go of.

B. *conj.* Till, until.

c **1200** *Trin. Coll. Hom.* 23 For to þe time cam þat he heregede helle. *c* **1275** LAY. 7563 Alle dai was þat fiht forte hit were dorcke niþt. **13..** *Guy Warw.* (A.) 668 No grome louen y no may Fort he be kniȝt. *c* **1440** *Marriage Serv.* in *Bk. Offices* (MS. Hereford Cath. No. 45), Ich —— take the —— to my wedded wife..forte deth us departe. *c* **1450** *Two Cookery-bks.* II. 114 Nym a pond of ris, seth hem fort hit berste.

†**fortoggle**, *v. Obs. rare*[−1]. [f. FOR- *pref.*[1] + *toglen*, TOGGLE *v.*] *trans.* To distract.

a **1300** *Cursor M.* 24606 Fortoglid [*Gött.* fortugild] þus wit trei and tene.

fortoiled: see FOR- *pref.*[1] 6 b.

fortoken, -told, -top, -touch: see FORETOKEN, etc.

fortorn, -tossed: see FOR- *pref.*[1] 5 b and 5.

Fortran (ˈfɔːtræn). *Computers.* Also **FORTRAN, fortran.** [f. *for(mula tran(slation.*] A high-level programming language used chiefly for scientific and mathematical calculations. Freq. *attrib.*

1956 *Computers & Automation* Nov. 9/2 More recently, John Backus' group at IBM has prepared FORTRAN (FORmula TRANslation) for the IBM-704 computer. FORTRAN will translate into computer language a program written very close [*sic*] the language of the mathematician or scientist. **1957** J. W. BACKUS et al. in *Proc. Western Joint Computer Conf.* Feb. 188 (*heading*) The FORTRAN automatic coding system. *Ibid.*, The programmer attended a one-day course on FORTRAN and ..then programmed the job in four hours using 47 FORTRAN statements. **1966** *Listener* 15 Dec. 895/2 The technologist can always write his fortran and the literato compose his iambics. **1967** *Electronics* 6 Mar. 140/1 The Norden program features... Fortran language, which permits it to be used on any computer having a Fortran compiler. **1969** P. B. JORDAIN *Condensed Computer Encycl.* 223 The principal dialects today are FORTRAN II (now obsolescent) and FORTRAN IV.

†fortravail, -vel, *v. Obs.* [f. FOR- *pref.*[1] + TRAVAIL *v.*] *trans.* To exhaust with labour.

c **1305** *St. Kenelm* 314 in *E.E.P.* (1862) 56 Fortrauailled hy were sore: þat hi moste slepe echon. **1375** BARBOUR *Bruce* III. 326 The king saw that he..wes for-trawaillyt. **1496** *Dives & Paup.* (W. de W.) IX. ii. 349/1 The fende..thre houres togydre..fortrauayled hym. **1523** LD. BERNERS *Froiss.* I. xviii. 20 His men of warre..were meruailously fortrauailed. **1819** W. TENNANT *Papistry Storm'd* (1827) 129 The sutor-folk..Wi' flings fortravail'd and forfairn.

†forˈtread, *v. Obs.* [OE. *fortredan*, f. FOR- *pref.*[1] + *tredan* to TREAD.] *trans.* To tread down, tread under foot; to destroy by trampling.

c **1000** ÆLFRIC *Hom.* II. 90 Weȝferende hit [ðæt sæd] fortrædon. *c* **1200** *Trin. Coll. Hom.* 155 Sum of þe sed..fel bi þe wei, and was fortreden. *c* **1386** CHAUCER *Pars. T.* ¶116 In helle schulle þay be al fortrode of deueles. *c* **1450** *Chester Pl.* (Shaks. Soc.) II. 143 Eatinge over all that he coulde fonge The remnant he fore-treade.

fig. *c* **1374** CHAUCER *Boeth.* IV. pr. i. 85 It [vertue] is cast vndyr and fortroden vndyr the feet of felonos foolk.

fortress (ˈfɔːtrɪs), *sb.* Forms: 4-5 **forteresse**, *Sc.* **fortrace, fortrass**, 4 **forceress** (? read *fort-*), 5-7 **fortresse**, 6 **fortres**, 4- **fortress.** [a. OF. *forteresse* strength, a strong place, f. *fort* strong; a variant of, or parallel formation with, *fortelesce* FORTALICE.]

1. A military stronghold, fortified place; in mod. use chiefly one capable of receiving a large force; often applied to a strongly fortified town regarded from a military point of view.

13.. *K. Alis.* 2668 Wel they warden gatis alle, The fortresses and the walle. *c* **1330** R. BRUNNE *Chron. Wace* (Rolls) 7143 When he had alle þys forceresses..3yt he þoughte [etc.]. *c* **1450** *Merlin* 192 Kynge Arthur hadde wele garnysshed alle the forteresses of hys londe. **1553** T. WILSON *Rhet.* Ep. A j, Divers stronge Castels and Fortresses were peaceably geven up. **1665** MANLEY *Grotius' Low C. Warres* 759 There was a strong Fortress raised close by the City. **1769** ROBERTSON *Chas. V*, II. II. 90 Those in garrison at Goletta threatened to give up that important fortress. **1861** M. PATTISON *Ess.* (1889) I. 45 Thick walls and turrets at the angles gave the whole the aspect and the reality of a fortress.

transf. and *fig.* **1477** EARL RIVERS (Caxton) *Dictes* 104 The hertis of good peple ben the castell & forterescis of secretes. **1513** MORE in Grafton *Chron.* (1568) II. 757 Affection towardes hym, had bene to his noble children..a merveilous fortresse and sure armor. **1603** R. NICCOLS *Fun. Orat. Q. Eliz.*, Her countrie was the fortresse of banisht men. **1738** WESLEY *Psalms* xviii. 1 My Rock and Fortress is the Lord.

2. *attrib.* and *Comb.*: **a.** simple attrib., as *fortress-company, -engineer*. **b.** appositive, as *fortress-castle, -chapel, -church, -city, -palace, -prison, -rock, -tomb, -town*. Also in phrases of the type *Fortress America, Europe* [after G. *Festung Europa*]. **c.** instrumental, as *fortress-guarded* adj.

1951 *N.Y. Herald Tribune* 25 Feb. 24 The central thesis.. is the idea that *fortress America could survive alone. **1960** *Times* 13 Jan. 13/7 American interest in civil defence shelters might be interpreted as implying American belief in a Fortress America. **1966** *Guardian* 21 Apr. 18/3 A retreat to a 'fortress America' concept. **1906** *Westm. Gaz.* 16 Aug. 2/3 No Imperial *fortress-castle is strong enough to Germanise the vast plains where peer and peasant alike are still passionately Polish. **1838** MISS PARDOE *River & Desert* II. 52 The *fortress-chapel of Nôtre-Dame-de-la-Garde. **1963** *Times* 9 Feb. 11/2 Characteristic is its *fortress-church. **1909** *Westm. Gaz.* 22 Feb. 1/3 The buried *fortress-city of Jericho. **1893** *Daily News* 24 Jan. 5/7 A garrison company of artillery, a *fortress company of engineers. **1894** *Westm. Gaz.* 4 Oct. 4/3 A company of *fortress engineers. **1942** *Nation* 19 Dec. 682 It was the Italian press which first launched the idea of *Fortress Europe. **1944** *Sat. Even. Post* 27 May 12/1 We shall still face the real problem of Fortress Europe, the penetration of the German mind. **1971** *Guardian* 22 July 4/1 The Prime Minister..said..'I have never seen a European policy as a policy of withdrawal into a fortress Europe.' **1887** *Pall Mall G.* 24 Jan. 1/2 Across the *fortress-guarded frontier. **1905** *Westm. Gaz.* 11 Sept. 3/1 The gloomy *fortress-palaces. **1955** J. THOMAS *No Banners* viii. 70 A fire-gutted convent which had been transformed under the Franco *régime* into a *fortress prison. **1838** MISS PARDOE *River & Desert* I. 218 Our *fortress-rock of Gibraltar. **1835** WILLIS *Pencillings* I. xii. 90, I crossed the Tiber at the *fortress-tomb of Adrian. **1937** *Discovery* Aug. 250/2 The *fortress-town..enclosed an area of about 270 by 200 metres.

fortress (ˈfɔːtrɪs), *v.* [f. prec. sb.] *trans.* To furnish with a fortress or fortifications; to protect with or as with a fortress. Chiefly *transf.* and *fig.*

1542 BECON *Pathw. Prayer* Wks. (1564) 68 a, Hitherto I haue fortressed this my treatise with the sayinges of yᵉ godly learned Doctors. **1545** JOYE *Exp. Dan.* xii. 232 That holy hyghe mount of Sion, well fortreced and turretted. **1546** in Strype *Eccl. Mem.* I. lii. 390 Our most puissant..King fortressed his most flourishing monarchy..with all things that a man can invent. **1602** MARSTON *Ant. & Mel.* Induct., So impregnably fortrest with his own content. **1652** WHARTON tr. *Rothmann's Chiromancy* Ded. Wks. (1683) 2 Learning is best Fortress'd of those by whom she is most understood. **1848** LOWELL *Biglow P.* Poems 1890 II. 34 Want was the prime foe these hardy exodists had to fortress themselves against. **1857** *Fraser's Mag.* LVI. 499 Those grassy banks that fortressed him and his household from the rage of waters.

Hence **ˈfortressed** *ppl. a.*, **ˈfortressing** *vbl. sb.*

1542 BECON *David's Harp* Wks. (1564) 159 b, There was no kyngdom so inuincible, strong, and fortressed, but that he..was able easly to ouercome. **1624** CHAPMAN *Homer's Hymn Venus* Wks. (1858) 95 Venus, that owes in fate the fortressing Of all maritimal Cyprus. **18..** LOWELL *To Garrison* Poet. Wks. 1890 I. 284 The lesson taught of old.. In our single manhood to be bold, Fortressed in conscience. **1895** *Reliquary* Oct. 194 The stern, severe, massive fortressed work of their sister city, Florence.

†ˈfort-ˌroyal. *Obs.* [f. FORT + ROYAL *a.* Cf. Fr. *bastion royal* a great bastion.] Some kind of fort of great size and strength: see quot. 1706.

1645 N. STONE *Enchir. Fortif.* 39 To convert a Square Fortresse..into a Fort-Royall. **1672** *Essex Papers* (Camden) I. 4 Kinsale might haue a Forte Royall erected on it [the Harbour]. **1706** PHILLIPS (ed. Kersey), *Fort Royal*, a Fort that has 26 Fathoms for the Line of Defence.

fig. **1650** HUBBERT *Pill Formality* 12 Hypocrisie is the devils Fort-Royal. **1681** *Whole Duty Nations* 36 To acknowledge this Union the Fort-Royal against the hostile Invasions of Popery.

†fortuit, *a. Obs.* Also 7 **-ite.** [a. F. *fortuit*, ad. L. *fortuitus*: see FORTUITOUS.] Fortuitous.

c **1374** CHAUCER *Boeth.* V. pr. I. 117 (Camb. MS.) Fortuit hap. **1530** PALSGR. *Introd.* 16 Utterly fortuyt and done by chaunce. **1621** BURTON *Anat. Mel.* II. iii. v, False feares and all other fortuit inconueniences. **1668** M. CASAUBON *Credulity* (1670) 15 That the world was made by a fortuit concourse of Atomes.

Hence **†fortuitness.**

1642 SIR K. DIGBY *Observ. Religio Medici* (1659) 18 Fortuitnesse or Contingency of things.

†fortuˈition. *Obs. rare*⁻¹.

a **1641** BP. MOUNTAGU *Acts & Mon.* (1642) 417 They inferred fate, fortuition..and co-incidency of all things.

fortuitism (fɔːˈtjuːɪtɪz(ə)m). [f. FORTUIT-OUS + -ISM.] The belief that adaptations in nature are produced by natural causes operating 'fortuitously'. So **forˈtuitist**, one who believes in fortuitism.

1881 *St. James's Gaz.* 14 Apr. 13/1 There will always be teleologists, no doubt, and there will always be fortuitists (if we may coin a needful correlative term); but..Professor Mivart's teleology now so nearly approaches Mr. Darwin's fortuitism that [etc.]. **1890** *Univ. Rev.* 15 June 239 In assigning the lion's share of development to the accumulation of fortunate accidents, he tempted fortuitists to try and cut the ground from under Lamarck's feet.

fortuitous (fɔːˈtjuːɪtəs), *a.* [f. L. *fortuit-us*, f. *forte* by chance, f. *fors* chance + -OUS.] That happens or is produced by fortune or chance; accidental, casual. ***fortuitous concourse of atoms***: see CONCOURSE 3. ***fortuitous event*** (Law): see quot. 1856.

1653 H. MORE *Antid. Ath.* III. xv. (1712) 135 This Argument against the fortuitous concourse of Atoms. **1712** ADDISON *Spect.* No. 293 ¶4 The highest Degree of it [Wisdom] which Man can possess, is by no means equal to fortuitous Events. **1806** FELLOWES tr. *Milton's 2nd Def.* Wks. (Bohn) I. 240 This extraordinary kindness..cannot be any fortuitous combination. **1823** SCOTT *Peveril* Pref. Let., A fortuitous rencontre. **1856** BOUVIER *Amer. Law Dict.*, *Fortuitous event*, a term in the civil law to denote that which happens by a cause which cannot be resisted..Or it is that which neither of the parties has occasioned or could prevent. **1865** *Pall Mall G.* 27 Oct. 6 The epithet he [Lord Palmerston] applied to the coalition of parties against him on the China question in 1857—'a fortuitous concourse of atoms'. **1877** SPARROW *Serm.* xviii. 241 Neither fortuitous nor necessitated, but entirely under the governmental control of the great and good God.

absol. **1855** H. SPENCER *Princ. Psychol.* IV. ii. (1872) I. 408 All grades, from the necessary to the fortuitous.

fortuitously (fɔːˈtjuːɪtəslɪ), *adv.* [f. prec. + -LY[2].] In a fortuitous manner, by chance.

a **1652** J. SMITH *Sel. Disc.* VI. viii. (1821) 258 This gift was not so fortuitously dispensed as to be communicated without any discrimination of persons. *a* **1711** KEN *Hymnotheo* Poet. Wks. 1721 III. 97 Wiles, Trech'ry, Lies, Guilt, Flattery, Deceit, Like Atoms here fortuitously meet. **1871** TYNDALL *Fragm. Sc.* (1879) II. v. 64 Atom is added to atom..not boisterously or fortuitously.

fortuitousness (fɔːˈtjuːɪtəsnɪs). [f. as prec. + -NESS.] The quality of being fortuitous; accident, chance, fortuity.

1652 GAULE *Magastrom.* 132 How have men been crucified betwixt inevitable fatation and undeterminate fortuitousness! **1798** W. TAYLOR in *Monthly Rev.* XXVII. 580 Whether the personages were brought together..by the pretended fortuitousness of a nicely contrived probability. **1844** *N. Brit. Rev.* I. 116 They allow them to be guided by no accident or fortuitousness.

fortuity (fɔːˈtjuːɪtɪ). [irreg. f. L. *fortuitus*: see FORTUITOUS and -ITY.] Fortuitous character, fortuitousness; accident, chance; an accidental occurrence. Occasionally used for: Appearance of fortuitousness or unstudiedness.

a **1747** D. FORBES *Incredulity* 80 How they can be sure, that those deserved judgments were the effect of mere fortuity. **1790** PALEY *Horæ Paul.* Wks. 1825 III. 194 Forgeries confirming and falling in with one another by a species of fortuity. **1829** I. TAYLOR *Enthus.* vi. (1867) 110 It is by the fortuities of life that the religious enthusiast is deluded. **1860** READE *Cloister & H.* II. 245 One of the company, by some immense fortuity, could read. **1860** GEO. ELIOT *Mill on Fl.* I. vii, She looks..at her bracelets, and adjusts their clasps with that pretty studied fortuity which [etc.]. **1885** J. MARTINEAU *Types Eth. Th.* (1886) II. II. i. 372 Nothing that might not happen in a universe of fortuity.

†ˈfortunable, *a. Obs.* [a. OF. *fortunable* ('unfortunate', Godef.): see FORTUNE and -ABLE.]

1. Favoured by fortune, fortunate.

c **1470** HARDING *Chron.* CCXXV. ii, The lord Wiloughby, full fortunable. **1486** *Bk. St. Albans, Her.* A iij, He the wich berith in his Cote armur that stone, fortunable of victori in his kinges battayl shall be. **1556** *Aurelio & Isab.* (1608) B, It behoveth that suche persons be well fortunable.

2. Bringing good fortune, lucky.

c **1465** *Pol. Rel. & L. Poems* (1866) 3 There was neuer birde brede vnder þe stone More fortunable in a felde þan þat birde hath be. **1513** DOUGLAS *Æneis* I. xi. 75 We the beseik, this day be fortunable To ws Tirianis.

3. Pertaining to fortune or chance, fortuitous.

1509 BARCLAY *Shyp of Folys* (1570) 46 Thus is that man voyde of all intelligence Whom fortune fedeth with chaunce fortunable. **1606** BRYSKETT *Civ. Life* 253 Such things as are subiect to change; and may be and not be; may be done or not done; and (when al is said) are fortunable.

Hence **† ˈfortunably** *adv.*, by fortune.

1555 ABP. PARKER *Ps.* (1556) C iv, If by chaunce thou fallest amonges thyne enemies, and yet hast fortunably escaped them.

†ˈfortunacy. *Obs.* [f. FORTUNATE *a.*: see -ACY.] Fortunateness, good fortune.

1580 LODGE *Forb. & Prisc.* (Shaks. Soc.) 94 The fortunacie of Forbonius is..unfortunate for thy selfe. **1624** [T. SCOTT] *Vox Cœli* 29 Ending these warres with more fortunacie.

†ˈfortunary. *Obs.*⁻¹ [f. FORTUNE *sb.* + -ARY.] One who deals in fortunes, a fortune-teller.

1652 GAULE *Magastrom.* 147 And why doe our Fataries and Fortunaries so confound them: especially in their prognostications or predictions?

fortunate (ˈfɔːtjʊnət), *a.* (and *sb.*) Also 4-5 **fortunat**, 5 **fortenat.** [ad. L. *fortūnāt-us*, f. *fortūnāre* (see FORTUNE *v.*).]

1. Favoured by fortune; possessed of or receiving good fortune; lucky, prosperous. Said of persons; also, of an enterprise, event, etc. Const. *to* and *inf.*

c **1386** CHAUCER *Nun's Priest's Prol.* 10 Whan a man.. clymbeth vp and wexeth fortunat. **1390** GOWER *Conf.* III. 115 He shall be..fortunate to marchandy. *c* **1430** LYDG. *Min. Poems* 37 Wold God of myhte, I had be borne, by influence hevenly, So fortunate, that [etc.]. **1514** BAINBRIDGE in Ellis *Orig. Lett.* Ser. II. I. 232 Which [enterprise] I shall besiche the blisside Trynitie to make fortunate. **1603** KNOLLES *Hist. Turks* (1621) 13 Their attempts more desperate..and their success fortunater. **1607** SHAKS. *Cor.* IV. iii. 39, I am most fortunate, thus accidentally to encounter you. **1647** CLARENDON *Hist. Reb.* I. §70 Nor was he very fortunate in the election of those Dependants. **1705** J. PHILIPS *Blenheim* 48 Burleigh (fortunate..to serve The best of Queens). **1830** D'ISRAELI *Chas. I*, III. vii. 150 [He] was fortunate enough to save himself by flight. **1849** MACAULAY *Hist. Eng.* I. 171 He.. might think himself fortunate when [etc.].

transf. **1870** LOWELL *Study Wind.* 335 Authors who.. have written one or two pieces so facile in thought and fortunate in phrase as to be carried lightly in the memory.

b. ***Fortunate Islands*** (= L. *Fortunatæ Insulæ*), fabulous isles of the Western Ocean, the abode of the blessed dead. Also *fig.*

1432-50 tr. *Higden* (Rolls) I. 321 The Yles Fortunate. **1553** EDEN *Treat. Newe Ind.* Contents, The fortunate Ilandes, otherwyse called the Ilandes of Canaria. **1639** T. BRUGIS tr. *Camus' Mor. Relat.* 273 Keepe his course towards the fortunate Ilands of Parmenes favour.

2. Bringing or presaging good fortune; auspicious, favourable, lucky.

c **1391** CHAUCER *Astrol.* II. §4 They wol caste that thei have a fortunat planete in hir assendent. **1582** BENTLEY *Mon. Matrones* II. 5 Thou..also hast giuen vnto mee the right fortunate gift of grace. **1676** LILLY *Guide Astrol.* 75 To consider in Nativities..if a Fortune fortunate and no way afflicted be in the seventh. **1741** MIDDLETON *Cicero* I. i. 20 Postumius..proclaming it to be a fortunate omen. **1841** LANE *Arab. Nts.* I. 68 Thursday and Friday are considered fortunate. **1849** MACAULAY *Hist. Eng.* I. 154 It ought to be considered as a most fortunate circumstance that [etc.].

1880 MRS. FORRESTER *Roy & V.* I. 11 'This is fortunate', she cries gaily.

3. a. *absol.* passing into a *sb.* (See next sense.)

1655 STANLEY *Hist. Philos.* I. (1701) 29/1 The rich is more able to satisfie his desires..yet the fortunate excels him. **1710** STEELE *Tatler* No. 202 ¶5 Each coming upon the same Errand, to know whether they were of the Fortunate in the Lottery. **1776** GIBBON *Decl. & F.* I. xv. 379 The fortunate are satisfied with the possession of this world.

b. *sb.* (with *pl.*) A fortunate person or thing; *esp.* in *Astrol.* a fortunate planet, sign, etc.

1614 TOMKIS *Albumazar* v. i, Search your Natiuitie: see if the Fortunates And Luminaries bee in a good Aspect. **1655** H. VAUGHAN *Silex Scint.* (1858) 37 Marriage of all states Makes most unhappy, or most fortunates. **1894** W. B. HARTE in *Arena* (Boston) June 3 The colony of fortunates whom Almighty God sent ready booted and spurred to ride over the millions.

†**'fortunate,** *v. Obs.* Also 6 *pa. pple.* fortunate. [f. L. *fortūnāt-*, ppl. stem of *fortūnāre*: see FORTUNE *v.* and -ATE[3].] *trans.* To make fortunate, give good fortune to, prosper. Also *absol.*

c **1420** *Pallad. on Husb.* I. 180 Let sowe hit on, and God hit fortunate. **1535** SHAXTON *Let. Cromwell* in Strype *Eccl. Mem.* I. App. lxi. 152 [I] shall rejoyce that God hath fortunate my writing. **1611** SPEED *Hist. Gt. Brit.* IX. xiii. (1632) 730 These petty braues thus giuen to the King, were farther fortunated with a little victory. **1647** LILLY *Chr. Astrol.* xxvii. 169 If the Lord of the third fortunate the Lord of the second..he will be assisted in procuring an Estate. **1792** SIBLY *Astrology* I. 18 Some heavenly influence..that ..fortunateth or infortunateth by mistake of words, signals, or acts.

†**'fortunateling.** *Obs.* [f. FORTUNATE *a.* + -LING.] A favourite of fortune.

1605 A. WARREN *Poor Man's Pass.* cxvii, Succour and meanes of maintenance to mee, The..ayre, the woods, and waters giue, Though Fortunatelings hate it so to bee.

fortunately ('fɔːtjʊnətlɪ), *adv.* [f. FORTUNATE *a.* + -LY[2].] In a fortunate manner; by or with good fortune, happily, luckily, successfully. In mod. use often qualifying the whole sentence, intimating that the fact stated is fortunate.

1548 HALL *Chron., Hen. V* (an. 4) 54 After this victorye fortunately obteined. **1600** HOLLAND *Livy* II. xvi. (1609) 54 In that yeare the Romanes fought with the Sabines fortunatelie [*bene pugnatum*]. **1681** DRYDEN *Abs. & Achit.* 51 These Adam-wits, too fortunately free, Began to dream they wanted Liberty. **1706** MAULE *Hist. Picts* in *Misc. Scot.* I. 16 The Roman Emperors who warred fortunatly against them. **1794** PALEY *Evid.* I. I. I. iv. 82 When, fortunately for their preservation, they were not found at home. **1796** MORSE *Amer. Geog.* I. 122 Fortunately, Lord De la War.. met them the day after they had sailed. **1855** MOTLEY *Dutch Rep.* (1864) I. 171 As vacillating and incompetent a statesman as he was prompt and fortunately audacious in the field. **1860** TYNDALL *Glac.* I. xi. 72, I fortunately possessed a box of wax matches.

fortunateness ('fɔːtjʊnətnɪs). [f. as prec. + -NESS.] The quality or state of being fortunate.

1530 PALSGR. 222/2 Fortunatnesse, *bienheureté.* **1580** SIDNEY *Arcadia* (1622) 117 Whose greatest fortunatenesse is more vnfortunate, then my sisters greatest vnfortunatenesse. **1664** MARVELL *Corr.* Wks. 1872–5 II. 122 The fortunateness of his Armes. **1825** COLERIDGE *Aids Refl.* (1848) I. 30 Felicity, in its proper sense, is but another word for fortunateness, or happiness. **1860** RUSKIN *Mod. Paint.* V. IX. x. §9. 308 A sign of fortunateness.

†**fortu'nation.** *Obs.* [f. FORTUNATE *a.* or *v.*: see -ATION.] The action of making fortunate, the being favoured by fortune.

c **1470** HARDING *Chron.* XI. ii, He..Reioysed highly of his fortunacion. **1727** BAILEY vol. II, *Fortunation*, luckiness, etc.

fortune ('fɔːtjʊn), *sb.* Also 4–6 fortoun, 6 fortun. [a. F. *fortune* (12th c. in Hatz.-Darm.), ad. L. *fortūna*, related to *forti-*, *fors* chance, and *ferre* to BEAR.]

1. a. Chance, hap, or luck, regarded as a cause of events and changes in men's affairs. Often (after Latin) personified as a goddess, 'the power supposed to distribute the lots of life according to her own humour' (J.); her emblem is a wheel, betokening vicissitude.

a **1300** *Cursor M.* 32719 Dame fortune turnes þan hir quele And castes vs dun vntil a wele. *c* **1374** CHAUCER *Troylus* I. 781 (837) Wele fynde I that Fortune is my fo. **1390** GOWER *Conf.* III. 106 The chaunces of the worlde also, That we fortune clepen so. **1489** CAXTON *Faytes of A.* III. xxi. 218 As longe as fortune was for them. **1500–20** DUNBAR *Poems* xv. 44 To fecht with fortoun is no wit. **1593** SHAKS. *3 Hen. VI*, IV. iii. 47 Though fortune's malice overthrow my state, My mind exceeds the compass of her wheel. **1683** HACKE *Collect. Voy.* (1699) I. 41 Yet fortune did not favour them. **1770** *Junius Lett.* xli. 212 Here..you have fortune on your side. **1849** MACAULAY *Hist. Eng.* I. 497 When fortune changed..his real propensities began to show themselves.

b. ***in the name of fortune***: see NAME.

†**c.** phr. ***by fortune***: by chance. ***upon fortune***: as it fell out. *Obs.*

1390 GOWER *Conf.* III. 152 The worldes good was first comune, But afterward upon fortune Was thilke comun profit cessed. *c* **1400** MAUNDEV. (1839) xxvi. 267 Thoghe it happene, sum of hem, be Fortune, to gon out. *a* **1533** LD. BERNERS *Gold. Bk. M. Aurel.* (1546) C vj, Yf by fortune he falle. **1604** SHAKS. *Oth.* v. ii. 226 That Handkerchiefe..I found by Fortune, and did giue my Husband.

d. with a defining phrase added, as ***the fortune of war***, etc.

1390 GOWER *Conf.* III. 12 The fortune of every chaunce ..To man it groweth from above. **1484** CAXTON *Fables of Æsop* IV. xiv, When the toune is taken..by fortune of warre. *c* **1489** —— *Sonnes of Aymon* xxiv. 524 By fortune of wedryng they were well eyght moneths vpon the See. *a* **1533** LD. BERNERS *Huon* lvii. 191 Fortune of yᵉ se hath brought vs hyder. **1709** STEELE *Tatler* No. 58 ¶1 One who was his by the Fortune of War. **1827** HALLAM *Const. Hist.* (1876) II. x. 177 It remained only..to try once more the fortune of war.

e. ***a soldier of fortune*** (see quots. 1802, 1810). (F. *soldat de fortune* is explained by Littré in the sense given in quot. 1810, but this meaning is rare in English.)

1661 BOYLE *Style of Script.* (1675) 186 Like war which is wont as well to raise soldiers of fortune as to ruine men of fortune. **1685** SOUTH *Serm.* (1823) I. 212 Every warrior may in some sense be said to be a soldier of fortune. **1775** R. H. LEE in Sparks *Corr. Amer. Rev.* (1853) I. 13, I refer you to Mr. Frazer..who goes to the camp a soldier of fortune. **1802** C. JAMES *Milit. Dict., Soldier of Fortune.* During the frequent wars which occurred in Italy, before the military profession became so generally prevalent in Europe, it was usual for men of enterprise and reputation to offer their services to the different states that were engaged..They afterwards extended their services, and under the title of *soldiers of fortune* fought for employment in every country or state that would pay them. **1810** *Ibid.* (ed. 3) s.v. *Fortune*, A soldier of Fortune, a military man who has risen from the ranks by his own merit. **1850** MRS. JAMESON *Leg. Monast. Ord.* (1863) 338 A brave, reckless, profligate soldier of fortune. **1889** J. CORBETT *Monk* xi. 156 He [Monk] patiently resumed his unassailable position of the obedient and disinterested soldier of fortune.

†**2. a.** A chance, hap, accident; an event or incident befalling any one, an adventure. *Obs.*

c **1350** *Will. Palerne* 157 As þis fortune bi-fel þat i told of bi-fore. *c* **1500** *Melusine* xiii. 49 The Erle thought euer on Raymondyn..that som ffortune he had fonde at the fontayne of Soyf. **1579** FENTON *Guicciard.* I. 26 That in all accidents and fortunes, that citie should not faile to minister to him. **1596** SHAKS. *Tam. Shr.* III. ii. 23 What euer fortune stayes him from his word. **1655** STANLEY *Hist. Philos.* III. (1701) 75/1 Many other good Fortunes happening to the Athenians upon this day are Recorded by Ælian. **1726** *Adv. Capt. R. Boyle* Pref. A iv, A Detail of Fortunes I have run through for many Years.

b. A mishap, disaster. ***to run a fortune*** (= F. *courir fortune de*): to run a risk. *Obs.*

c **1489** CAXTON *Blanchardyn* xxxii. 121 Wher they arryued in fewe dayes wythout eny fortune. *c* **1500** *Three Kings' Sons* (E.E.T.S.) 67 It was tyme nowe to leue of alle sorowe & lamentacion for any fortune that was befalle. **1627** *Lisander & Cal.* II. 29, I had rather run a fortune in giving way unto your desire, than refuse you so small a matter.

3. a. The chance or luck (good or bad) which falls to any one as his lot in life or in a particular affair. Also in *pl.* †***extreme fortune*** (= L. *res extremæ*): the last extremity.

c **1374** CHAUCER *Boeth.* II. metr. iii. 27 (Camb. MS.) Wolthow thanne trusten in the tomblynge fortunes of men? ? *a* **1400** *Morte Arth.* 1177 Ne had my fortune bene faire, fey had I leuede! **1484** CAXTON *Fables of Æsop* 2 First begynneth the lyf of Esope with alle his fortune. **1523** LD. BERNERS *Froiss.* I. ccccii. 698 He that hath any yuell fortune, men wyll speke the worst therof. **1531** ELYOT *Governour* II. ii. (1534) 100 b, It is no lyttell thyng to meruayle at, the maiestie showed in extreme fortune and mysery. **1582** N. LICHEFIELD tr. *Castanheda's Conq. E. Ind.* 5 b, Thanking God for their..good fortune in this their first brunt of daunger. **1598** SHAKS. *Merry W.* IV. v. 48 To know if it were my Masters fortune to haue her, or no. **1607–12** BACON *Ess., Of Fortune*, Chieflie the mould of a Mans fortune is in himself. **1699** DAMPIER *Voy.* II. II. 22 It was my fortune to be at the Helm from 6 a Clock in the Evening till 8. **1726** *Adv. Capt. R. Boyle* 125 The Women of Morocco, I mean all that I had the Fortune to see, were very handsome. **1752** HUME *Ess. & Treat.* (1777) I. 3 Good or ill fortune is very little at our disposal. **1827** HALLAM *Const. Hist.* (1876) III. xvi. 232 Scotland was now doomed to wait on the fortunes of her more powerful ally. **1852** THACKERAY *Esmond* II. iii, Some good fortune at last occurred to a family which stood in great need of it. **1874** GREEN *Short Hist.* iii. §2. 121 On the fortunes of Philip hung the fortunes of English freedom.

b. attributed to things, purposes, undertakings.

1665 BOYLE *Occas. Refl.* Pref. (1845) 34 They that would compleat the Good Fortune of these Papers. **1697** DRYDEN *Virg. Georg.* IV. 132 And undecided leave the Fortune of the Day. **1769** ROBERTSON *Chas. V*, V. IV. 367 The fortune of the day was quickly changed. **1880** MᶜCARTHY *Own Times* IV. lx. 324 The fortunes of the war were virtually decided in a day.

c. phr. ***to try one's fortune***: to make trial how it will turn out (with the hope of its proving favourable). Similarly (with mixture of senses 5, 6) ***to seek one's fortune***.

1573 BARET *Alv.* F 955, I will aduenture, or trie and seeke my fortune. **1700** S. L. tr. *Fryke's Voy. E. Ind.* 13 Any one that hath a mind to see the Indies, and to try his Fortune. *a* **1745** SWIFT (J.), His father dying, he was driven to London to seek his fortune. **1749** FIELDING *Tom Jones* VII. x, To seek his fortune at sea, or rather, indeed, to fly away from his fortune on shore. *c* **1790** WILLOCK *Voy.* 94 They thought proper to sail towards the western isles, and try their fortune a little longer.

d. That which is to befall a person in the future: chiefly in phr. ***to tell a person his fortune*** and ***to tell fortunes*** (said of would-be seers).

1375 BARBOUR *Bruce* IV. 640 For, or ȝe pass, I sall ȝow schaw Of ȝour fortoun a gret party. **1413** *Pilgr. Sowle* (Caxton 1483) IV. v. 60 Alisandre..fond two trees, whiche trees told hym his fortunes. **1647** COWLEY *Mistress*, My fate 19 You, who men's fortunes in their faces read. **1668** PEPYS *Diary* 11 Aug., This afternoon my wife and Mercer..to see the gypsies at Lambeth, and have their fortunes told. **1688** *Lond. Gaz.* No. 2375/2 The Visier then demanded, if he could tell his own Fortune? **1847** MARRYAT *Childr. N. Forest* xi, They were great thieves, and told fortunes, and played all manner of tricks.

4. *absol.* (= good fortune): Good luck; success, prosperity.

1390 GOWER *Conf.* III. 166 Though thou victoire have on honde, Fortune may nought stonde alwey. *c* **1490** *Adam Bel & Clym of Clough* 429 in Ritson *Anc. Pop. P.* 21 Then went they to supper, Wyth such meat as they had, And thanked god of ther fortune. **1523** LD. BERNERS *Froiss.* I. xxix. 43 He was entred into such fortune and grace of the people. **1546** J. HEYWOOD *Prov.* (1867) 62 God sendeth fortune to fooles. **1596** HARINGTON *Metam. Ajax* (1814) 9 A herald by great fortune found out his pedigree in an old church book. **1625** BACON *Ess.* Ep. Ded. (Arb.) 498 Your Fortune, and Merit both, haue been Eminent. *a* **1698** TEMPLE *Misc.* II. Wks. 1720 I. 163 This Terrestrial Globe..has since been surrounded by the Fortune and Boldness of several navigators. **1855** MOTLEY *Dutch Rep.* I. ii. (1866) 98 Saint Quentin being thus reduced, Philip was not more disposed to push his fortune.

5. One's condition or standing in life; often *absol.* a prosperous condition, as in ***to make one's fortune*** = to win a good position in the world. Also *pl.*

1600 SHAKS. *A.Y.L.* I. ii. 263 My pride fell with my fortunes. **1649** MILTON *Eikon.* 14 A private conscience sorts not with a public Calling: but declares that Person rather meant by nature for a private fortune. **1677** DRYDEN *State Innoc.* v. 1 No, he shall eat, and dye with me, or live: Our equal crimes shall equal fortune give. **1680** OTWAY *Orphan* I. i, Unable to advance her Fortune He left his Daughter to our Master's care. **1683** HACKE *Collect. Voy.* (1699) I. 23 Had reason but ruled them, we might all have made our Fortunes. **1807–8** W. IRVING *Salmag.* xv. (1860) 355 If you only make a great man laugh now and then, your fortune is made. **1886** RUSKIN *Præterita* I. v. 142 John..went soon to push his fortune in Australia.

6. Position as determined by wealth; amount of wealth; *concr.* a person's possessions collectively, wealth, 'substance'; †formerly also *pl.* in the same senses. ***a man,*** etc. ***of fortune***: one possessing great (usually inherited) wealth. Also (with *a* and *pl.*) a stock of wealth, accumulated by an individual or received by inheritance, as a marriage portion, etc.; ordinarily implying a somewhat ample amount. Phr. ***to make a, one's fortune***.

a small fortune (colloq.): used hyperbolically to designate the extravagantly large amount paid for some object of expenditure, or any large sum of money.

1596 SPENSER *F.Q.* VI. ix. 30 For wisedome is most riches; fooles therefore They are which fortunes doe by vowes devize. **1601** SHAKS. *All's Well* III. vii. 14 You haue shew'd me that which well approues Y' are great in fortune. **1604** —— *Oth.* v. ii. 366 Seize vpon the Fortunes of the Moore. **1606** —— *Ant. & Cl.* II. v. 49 Make thee a Fortune from me. **1647** CLARENDON *Hist. Reb.* I. §123 He paid much too dear for his Wife's Fortune, by taking her Person into the bargain. **1653** H. MORE *Antid. Ath.* Ep. Ded. (1712) 4 Those ample Fortunes that Divine Providence has bestowed upon you. **1725** BERKELEY *Proposal* Wks. III. 222 There is no prospect of making a fortune by this small trade. **1732** —— *Alciphr.* I. §12 Men of rank and fortune. **1791** MRS. RADCLIFFE *Rom. Forest* iii, A chevalier of family, but of small fortune. ? *a* **1800** *Song*, 'My face is my fortune, Sir', she said. **1836** MARRYAT *Midsh. Easy* xxii, Imagining them ..to be young Englishmen of fortune on their travels. **1874** HARDY *Far fr. Madding Crowd* I. vi. 65 He played on with spirit, and in half an hour had earned in pence what was a small fortune to a destitute man. **1875** JOWETT *Plato* (ed. 2) III. 39 They might have made large fortunes out of them. **1886** SIR J. PEARSON in *Law Rep.* 32 Ch. Div. 46 Every one of the partners is liable to the full extent of his fortune for all the debts incurred by the partnership. **1912** T. DREISER *Financier* iv. 37 If he had been able to buy them all and dispose of them all as readily as he had his soap, he would have made a small fortune. **1951** E. PAUL *Springtime in Paris* iii. 53 Gobelin tapestries on the walls and old French rugs on the floors, each one worth a small fortune. **1962** D. MAYO *Island of Sin* ii. 16 It's one of the least known islands in the group, and Doreen pays a small fortune to keep it that way.

†**7.** Short for: A woman of fortune; an heiress.

1655 A. JOHNSON in *Nicholas Papers* (Camden) II. 251 The Lady Bath (one of the greatest fortunes here). **1676** D'URFEY *Mad. Fickle* III. ii, She's his Neece, a Widow, an approv'd fortune. **1711** STEELE *Spect.* No. 19 ¶2 He is secretly married to a great Fortune. **1752** FIELDING *Amelia* II. ii, She certainly was handsome..and a very considerable fortune. **1823** BYRON *Juan* XII. xxxii.

8. *Astrol.* A name for the planets Jupiter and Venus (see also quot. 1819).

1671 SALMON *Syn. Med.* I. viii. 22 A Planet is said to be a Fortune when he is conjoyned to the Fortunes or beseiged of them or their beams. **1679** MOXON *Math. Dict., Fortunes*, the two benevolent Planets ♃ and ♀, by reason of their kind and friendly Nature. **1819** J. WILSON *Dict. Astrol.* s.v., The Sun..The Moon and Mercury are likewise esteemed as fortunes when well aspected by ♃ and ♀, and free from affliction. **1855** SMEDLEY *Occult. Sc.* 309 Jupiter, 'the greater fortune'.

9. *Comb.*, as ***fortune-maker, -seeker***; †***fortune-bit, -curst, -favoured, -proof, -trodden*** adjs.; also **fortune-book**, 'a book consulted to know fortune or future events' (J.); **fortune cookie** *N. Amer.*, a dessert, freq. served in Chinese restaurants, made from a thin dough folded and cooked around a slip of paper bearing a prediction or maxim; **Fortune 500** *U.S.*, (an annual list of) the five hundred most profitable U.S. industrial corporations; also *attrib.*; †**fortune-flinger**, *humorous* for FORTUNE-TELLER; †**fortune-speller** = FORTUNE-TELLER;

†**fortune-stealer**, one who runs off with an heiress; so †**fortune-stealing**.

1682 MRS. BEHN *City Heiress* 56 Was ever man thus *Fortune bit, that he shou'd cross my hopes just in the nick? **1646** CRASHAW *Love's Horosc.* 12 A Face, in whose each looke, Beauty layes ope loves *Fortune-booke. **1962** K. ORVIS *Damned & Destroyed* xx. 149, I didn't need to break a *fortune-cookie to know about her. Your voice told me she is a very special girl. **1970** *Toronto Daily Star* 24 Sept. 6/3 Chinese fortune cookies. **1649** G. DANIEL *Trinarch., Rich. II*, cxcvii, And 'tis but only Fooles are *Fortune-curst. **1898** *Daily News* 6 Oct. 6/7 The more *fortune-favoured individuals. **1915** W. J. LOCKE *Jaffery* i, He had put poor old Jaffery and fortune-favoured me in the shade. [**1955** *Fortune* July (Suppl.) (*title*) The Fortune directory of the 500 largest U.S. industrial corporations.] **1972** *N.Y. Times* 26 May 44/5 Speaking at the *Fortune 500 dinner at the St. Regis Hotel, Mr. Regan said, 'the growing and blind prejudice against bigness may cripple our ability to compete internationally.' **1983** *Forbes* (N.Y.) Fall 223/3 Most of it is in the form of ownership of productive capital, potentially enough dough to buy up the Fortune 500 and still get change back. **1642** SHIRLEY *Sisters* III. i, More antics yet? What nation have we here? *Fortune-flingers! *a* **1616** BEAUM. & FL. *Bonduca* I. i, Are these the men that conquer by inheritance, The *fortune-makers. **1656** DUCHESS OF NEWCASTLE *True Relat. Nature's Pict.* 383 And Misery hath tried us, and finds us *Fortune-proof. **1906** *Daily Chron.* 5 May 4/7 A vast throng of *fortune-seekers. **1652** GAULE *Magastrom.* 23 Away, then, with all..Planet Prognosticators, and *fortune spellers! **1712** ADDISON *Spect.* No. 311 ¶1 Those audacious young Fellows among us who commonly go by the name of *Fortune-Stealers. **1680** OTWAY *Orphan* Epil. 19 The next Sparks that go a *Fortune-stealing. **1622** H. SYDENHAM *Serm. Sol. Occ.* II. (1637) 137 Hee that's *fortune-trodden.

fortune ('fɔːtjʊn), *v.* Also 5 forteyn(e, 6 forten, fortone. [a. OF. *fortune-r* to assign fortune to, make fortunate, ad. L. *fortūnāre* to make fortunate, f. *fortūna*: see FORTUNE *sb.*]

†**1.** *trans.* To assign a (certain) fortune to (a person, affair, etc.); to allot, regulate, or control the fortunes of. *Obs.*

c **1386** CHAUCER *Knt.'s T.* 1519 O stronge god..that..hast in euery regne and euery lond Of armes al the brydel in thyn hond, And hem fortunest as thee list deuise. **1390** GOWER *Conf.* III. 361 With many an other mo, Which hadden be fortuned sore In loves cause. *c* **1440** *Generydes* 1431 Atte last, as god wold fortune it. **1606** SHAKS. *Ant. & Cl.* I. ii. 77 Deere Isis, keep decorum, and Fortune him accordingly!

†**b.** To ordain (a person), as his fortune or luck, *to do* something; to ordain (something) *to* happen, or *that* it shall happen. *Obs.*

c **1430** *Syr Gener.* 1187 If god you fortune oones come to elde. **1463** *Bury Wills* (Camden) 18 What day God fortune yᵗ I desesse. **1536** BELLENDEN *Cron. Scot.* (1821) II. 371 Gif God fortunit him to be on live. **1600** FAIRFAX *Tasso* V. xci, That Lord..Shall Fortune all your Actions well to speed.

†**c.** in *Astrol.*: To ascribe a (certain) fortune to.

c **1386** CHAUCER *Prol.* 419 Wel cowde he fortune the ascendent Of his ymages for his pacient. **1477** NORTON *Ord. Alch.* v. in Ashm. (1652) 60 With Astrologie joyne Elements also, To fortune their Workings as theie goe.

†**d.** To give good fortune to, make fortunate.

14.. LYDG. *Temple Glas* 903, I myself also Shal þe fortune er þi tale be do.

2. To endow with wealth or a fortune; to dower. (*rare*: cf. FORTUNED.) Also, *to fortune off* or *out*: to get (a daughter) off one's hands by dowering her.

1748 RICHARDSON *Clarissa* (1811) II. xxv. 166 He is to fortune her out to a young lover. **1835** *Tait's Mag.* II. 31 In order that they may save a few hundreds for fortuning off their girls. **1838** *Ibid.* V. 253 They have dowered their wives, and fortuned their daughters. **1881** MISS LAFFAN in *Macm. Mag.* XLIV. 389 She grumbled..over the expensive schooling of her two grand-daughters. The money, in her opinion, would have been far better kept to 'fortune them off'.

†**3.** *intr.* Of events, etc.: To happen, chance, occur. Const. *to*, *unto*, or dative obj. *Obs.*

c **1369** CHAUCER *Dethe Blaunche* 288 Swiche meruayles fortuned than. **1424** *Paston Lett.* No. 4 I. 14 What so ever fortunyd in the seyd pleynt. *c* **1450** *Cokwolds Daunce* 168 in Hazl. *E.P.P.* I. 45 Hym selfe, noble kyng Arthour, Hath forteynd syche a chans. **1532** HERVET *Xenophon's Househ.* (1768) 42 If any thynge fortuned well to vs, we gaue her parte of it. **1547** BOORDE *Brev. Health* ccl. 84b, The impedimentes whiche doth fortune to the synewes. **1620** *Frier Rush* 23 This night hath fortuned to me a great aduenture. **1739** G. OGLE *Gualth. & Gris.* 104 All that fortunes, fortunes for the Best.

b. impers. *it fortunes* = it happens or befalls. Const. with clause; also *to*, *with* (a person) or with dative obj. Also with omission of *it*. *arch.*

1462 J. PASTON in *P. Lett.* No. 461 II. 115 It so fortuned your seid besecher cowd not performe the seid apoyntement. **1470–85** MALORY *Arthur* IX. xvii, Hit fortuned me that I was a slepe in the wyndowe. *c* **1500** *Melusine* xxiii. 156 Sith it hath fortuned thus with me. *c* **1510** *Gesta Rom.* Add. Stories (W. de W.) ii. 431 It fortuned after..yᵗ he gaue batayll. **1590** MARLOWE *Edw. II*, II. iii. ii, How fortunes that he came not? **1622** BACON *Hen. VII* (ed. Lumby) 172 It so fortuned, that he was taken by pirates at sea. **18..** LOWELL *Dara* Poet. Wks. (1879) 378 When it fortuned that a king more wise Endued the realm with brain and hands and eyes. **1886** BURTON *Arab. Nts.* I. 14 So it fortuneth that I am toiling..while thou takest thine ease.

†**c.** followed by *object* and *inf.* (Sometimes a dative obj.; sometimes the phrase is equivalent to L. acc. and inf., or to the subj.-clause in 3 b.) *Obs.*

c **1420** *Pol. Rel. & L. Poems* (1866) 204 A solom cite me fortunyd to fynde. **1487** *Will* in *Surrey Archæol. Collect.* III. 163 At that auter before which it shall fortune me to be buried. **1508** FISHER 7 *Penit. Ps.* i. Wks. (1876) 32 It may also fortune a man to be sory for his synne. **1577–87** HOLINSHED *Chron.* III. 1119/1 If it fortune no issue male to be borne of this matrimonie. **1591** SPENSER *M. Hubberd* 631 Therefore if fortune thee in Court to liue. **1603** KNOLLES *Hist. Turks* (1621) 1279 If hereafter it should fortune any detriment..to be by any man..done unto the Hungarians. **1628** DIGBY *Voy. Medit.* (1868) 3 If it should fortune each to loose other.

†**4.** With person or thing as subject: To happen or chance *to be* or *to do* (something). *Obs.*

1454 *E.E. Wills* (1882) 134 All myne other goodes whatsoeuer they fortune to be, in valour. **1521** FISHER *Serm. agst. Luther* Wks. (1876) 313 These daungerous tempestes of heresyes, whan so euer they fortune to aryse. **1570** THORNE *Song, This world is but a vanety* vi. (1848), Yf thow fortune to be poore. **1658** BROMHALL *Treat. Specters* II. 182 The Birth-day of the Emperor Augustus fortuned to be on that very time. **1728** POPE *Dunc.* II. 73 Here fortun'd Curll to slide. **1798** YOUNG *Let.* in *Mem. Dalzel* (1862) 163 The Dean himself fortuning to be absent.

b. To come by chance *upon* (something). *rare*$^{-1}$.

1662 EVELYN *Sculpt.* iv. 38 Albert Durer..had performed wonders both in Copper and Wood, had he once fortun'd upon the least notion of that excellent manner, which came afterwards to be in vogue.

†**c.** *ellipt.* To chance to come *to* (a place).

a **1520** *Joseph of Armathia* 133 They fortuned to a countre of a tyraunt kene Called wales.

†**d.** To have a certain fortune, to fare. *Obs.*

1513 BRADSHAW *St. Werburge* II. 1830 Whan ye in trauelyng vpon her do call..Ye fortune and spede well.

†**'fortune,** *adv.* *Obs.* [Cf. FORTUNE *v.* 3 b and CHANCE *sb.* C.] Mayhap, haply, perchance.

1513 MORE in Grafton *Chron.* (1568) II. 797 If..one of hys tormentours might fortune breake his heade for marring of the play. *a* **1605** MONTGOMERIE *Misc. Poems* v. 56 3our feet are not so sicker sett Bot fortun 3e may fall.

fortuned ('fɔːtjʊnd), *ppl. a.* Now *rare.* [f. FORTUNE *sb.* and *v.* + -ED.] Having fortune (of a specified kind); †also, = fortunate (*obs.*). Of an event: Characterized by a (specified) fortune.

c **1374** CHAUCER *Compl. Mars* 180 My lady is..so wel fortuned and thewed. *c* **1470** HENRY *Wallace* VIII. 685 A fortonyt man. **1484** CAXTON *Fables of Æsop* III. iii, He that is wel fortuned and happy. —— *Curial* 15 O fortuned men. **1606** SHAKS. *Ant. & Cl.* IV. xv. 24 The full-Fortun'd Cæsar. **1887** SAINTSBURY *Hist. Elizab. Lit.* (1894) 202 The poisoning being like Juliet's a mere trick though differently fortuned.

b. Possessed of a 'fortune' or portion.

1631 SHIRLEY *Love in Maze* I. i, This Gerard is a gentle-man Of handsome parts, And, they say, fortuned. **1748** RICHARDSON *Clarissa* (1811) I. xl. 299, I must go to him, and to his, as an obliged and half-fortuned person.

'fortune-,hunter. One who seeks to win a fortune; *esp.* one who tries to capture an heiress.

1689 J. CARLISLE (*title*), The Fortune Hunters, or two Fools well met, a Comedy. **1755** *Gentl. Mag.* XXV. 111 Several Irish brigades..may be formed out of those able bodied men which are called Fortune-hunters. **1838** LYTTON *Alice* I. I. x. 36 If she were of our sex, [she] would make a capital fortune-hunter.

So **'fortune-,hunting** *vbl. sb.* and *ppl. a.*

1766 GOLDSM. *Vic. W.* v, There is no character more contemptible than a man that is a fortune-hunter; and I can see no reason why fortune-hunting women should not be contemptible too. **1793** MRS. ELIZA PARSONS *Woman as she should be* II. 122 Poor Harry..is gone a fortune hunting to India. **1870** LOWELL *Among my Bks.* Ser. I. (1873) 125 [A] fortune-hunting count.

†**'fortunel,** *a.* *Obs.* [a. OF. *fortunal*, *-el*: see FORTUNE *sb.* and -AL¹.] Fortuitous, accidental.

c **1374** CHAUCER *Boeth.* v. metr. i. 117 (Camb. MS.) The wateres I medlyd wrappith or implieth many fortunel [L. *fortuitos*] happis or maneres.

'fortuneless, *a.* [f. FORTUNE *sb.* + -LESS.] Without (good) fortune, luckless, unfortunate. Also, destitute of a 'fortune' or portion.

1596 SPENSER *F.Q.* IV. viii. 27 Against all hard mishaps and fortunelesse misfare. **1669** *Raleigh's Troub.* in *Select. Harl. Misc.* (1793) 227 Being a person not full twenty years old, left friendless and fortuneless. **1836** *Fraser's Mag.* XIII. 314 Flaunting, fortuneless, over-educated girls. **1864** HAWTHORNE *Grimshawe* iv. (1891) 41 The utilitarian line of education..especially desirable for a fortuneless boy.

'fortune-,teller. [See FORTUNE *sb.* 3 d.] One who 'tells fortunes'.

1590 SHAKS. *Com. Err.* v. i. 239 One Pinch..A thred-bare Iuggler, and a Fortune-teller. **1612** J. MASON *Anat. Sorc.* 46 They travelled about the country, as fortune-tellers..and such like do with us. **1716** SWIFT *Phillis* 51 Long ago a Fortune-teller Exactly said what now befel her. **1874** BURNAND *My Time* xii. 101 The fortune-teller, who, from the lines engraved on the open palm, predicts a destiny.

'fortune-,telling, *vbl. sb.* [Cf. prec.] The practice of 'telling fortunes'.

1577 NORTHBROOKE *Dicing* (1843) 56 Forbidding..euill and vnprofitable arts..or fortune tellings. **1598** SHAKS. *Merry W.* IV. ii. 184 We are simple men; wee doe not know what's brought to passe vnder the profession of Fortune-telling. **1655** WALTON *Angler* v. (ed. 2) 161 The Gypsies were then to divide all the money..got..by Fortune telling. **1732** BERKELEY *Alciphr.* VI. §21 They are..addicted to..astrology, fortune-telling, and presages of all kinds.

So **'fortune-telling** *ppl. a.* Also (*nonce-wd.*) **'fortune-tell** *v.*, a back-formation from prec.

1598 SHAKS. *Merry W.* IV. ii. 196 Out of my doore, you Witch!..Ile coniure you, Ile fortune-tell you. *a* **1659** CLEVELAND *Fuscara* 26 Wks. (1687) 2 He tipples Palmestry, and dines On all her Fortune-telling Lines. **1681** COLVIL *Whigs Supplic.* (1751) 49 He finds both comets and eclipses, But pretty fortune telling gipsies. **1795–1814** WORDSW. *Excursion* VII. 88 Belong they to the fortune-telling Tribe?

†**for'tunity.** *Obs.* [a. OF. *fortunité* (ill) hap: see FORTUNE and -ITY.] ? Fortune, hap. (Cf. INFORTUNITY.)

c **1470** HARDING *Chron.* X. v, Seyng Iuly this fals fortunite The soroes greate in hym so multiplied, That there for shame of his fortunite, In no wyse would [he no] lenger dwell ne byde. **1614** SELDEN *Titles Hon.* 365 By aduenture of his fortunitie. **1652** GAULE *Magastrom.* 187 That they here..vaticinate or ominate of..fortunity, infortunity.

†**'fortunize,** *v.* *Obs. rare.* [f. FORTUNE *sb.* + -IZE.] *trans.* To regulate the fortunes of; to make fortunate. Hence **'fortunizing** *ppl. a.*, fortune-telling.

1596 SPENSER *F.Q.* VI. ix. 30 Fooles therefore They are which fortunes doe by vowes devize, Sith each unto himselfe his life may fortunize. **1652** GAULE *Magastrom.* 98 Else, how can the fortunizing Genethliack foretell that the child new born shall be a Traveller?

†**fortunous,** *a.* *Obs.* [a. OF. *fortuneus*: see FORTUNE *sb.* and -OUS.]

1. Pertaining to fortune or chance, fortuitous.

c **1374** CHAUCER *Boeth.* I. pr. vi. 17 (Camb. MS.), I ne trowe nat in no manere, that so certeyn thinges sholden be moeued by fortunows fortune. *Ibid.* II. pr. iv. 29 (Camb. MS.) Thinges that ben fortunous and temporel.

2. Fortunate, successful.

c **1470** HARDING *Chron.* IX. iv, He wanne the felde in batell fortunous.

†**fortuny.** *Obs.*$^{-0}$ (See quot.)

1676 COLES, *Fortuny*, a kind of Tournement or running a tilt with launces on horseback. [So in some later Dicts.]

forty ('fɔːtɪ), *a.* and *sb.* Forms: 1 **féowertiᵹ, féowurtiᵹ,** *Northumb.* **feuortiᵹ,** 2 *Orm.* **fowwerrtiᵹ, feortiᵹ,** 2–3 **f(e)owerti,** 3 **feouwerti, f(e)uwerti, fuerti, feowrti, fourte,** 3–4 **fourti,** *south.* **vourti, -y,** (3 **forti**), 3–8 **fourty,** 4 **faurty,** 5 **fourthi, -y,** 6 **fourtie, -ye, fortie,** 6– **forty.** [OE. *féowertiᵹ* = OFris. *fiuwertich*, OS. *fiwartig*, *fiartig*, *fiortig* (MDu. *viertich*, Du. *veertig*), OHG. *fiorzug* (MHG. *vierzic*, mod.Ger. *vierzig*), ON. *fiórer tiger*, *fiǫrutigi*, *fiǫrutíu* (Sw. *fyratio*, *fyrtio*, Da. *fyrretyve*, *firti*), Goth. *fidwôr tigjus*: see FOUR and -TY.]

A. *adj.* **a.** The cardinal number equal to four tens, represented by the figures 40, xl, or XL. Also in comb. with numbers below ten (cardinal and ordinal), as *forty-one*, *forty-first*, etc.

c **950** *Lindisf. Gosp.* Matt. iv. 2 & mið ðy ᵹefæste feuortiᵹ daᵹa & feowertiᵹ næhta. *a* **1175** *Cott. Hom.* 227 He hi afedde feorti3 wintre. *c* **1200** *Trin. Coll. Hom.* 61 Adam was in helle in pine fuwerti hundred wintre for his sinne. **1297** R. GLOUC. (1724) 419 More þan a uourty 3er hyt was þat he was ybore. *c* **1386** CHAUCER *Can. Yeom. Prol. & T.* 808 If that thee list it haue, Ye shul paye fourty pound. *c* **1489** CAXTON *Sonnes of Aymon* i. 55 He hadde noo moo wyth hym but fourthi. *c* **1585** R. BROWNE *Answ. Cartwright* 43 In the fourtie and eyght Psalme. **1698** FRYER *Acc. E. India & P.* 94 At the end of their Quarentine, which is Forty days. **1707** HEARNE *Collect.* (Oxf. Hist. Soc.) I. 323 He died in the fourty fifth year of his Age. **1803** HATCHETT in *Phil. Trans.* XCIII. 89 It..was found to contain one forty-eighth of antimony. **1825** J. NEAL *Bro. Jonathan* II. 188 The day..according to his calculation, was about forty-eight hours. **1860** READE *Cloister & H.* xxv, Dietrich's forty years weighed him down like forty bullets.

b. Used indefinitely to express a large number. *like forty* (*U.S. colloq.*): with immense force or vigour, 'like anything'.

1607 SHAKS. *Cor.* III. i. 243 On faire ground I could beat fortie of them. **1619** G. HERBERT *Let.* 19 Jan. Wks. 1859 I. 381, I have forty businesses in my hands: your Courtesy will pardon the haste of your humblest Servant. **1692** R. L'ESTRANGE *Fables* cccv, He that's Well, already, and upon a Levity of Mind, Quits his Station, in hopes to be Better, 'tis Forty to One, he loses by the Change. **1852** MRS. STOWE *Uncle Tom's C.* viii, 'I has principles and I sticks to them like forty'.

c. †*forty pence*: a customary amount for a wager. *forty winks* (colloq.): a short nap, *esp.* after dinner.

1567 HARMAN *Caveat* viii. 46 Forty pence gaged vpon a matche of wrastling. **1613** SHAKS. *Hen. VIII*, II. iii. 89 How tastes it? is it bitter? forty pence, no. **1872** *Punch* 16 Nov. 208/2 If a..man, after reading steadily through the Thirty-nine Articles, were to take forty winks. **1887** SIMS *Mary Jane's Mem.* 228 I'm tired, and I want my forty winks.

†**d.** = FORTIETH. *Obs.*

1559 *Homilies* I. *Good Wks.* III. (1859) 58 Sectes..were neither the forty part so many among the Jewes, nor [etc.].

e. *the forty hours* (also qualifying *devotion*, etc.; It. *le quarant' ore*): in the R.C. Church, the continuous exposition of the Host for forty hours, used as an occasion of special devotion or intercession.

1759 A. BUTLER *Lives Saints* IV. 560 The saint..ordered the forty hours prayer for his recovery. **1839** K. H. DIGBY

Mores Cath. IX. iii. 79 The devotion of the forty hours prayer instituted by a poor Capuchin friar, Joseph of Milan. **1869** A. T. DRANE *Life Mother Margaret Hallahan* vii. 189 During the Octave of Corpus Christi this year the Devotion of the Forty Hours was for the first time celebrated in St. Catherine's Convent. **1922** *Cath. Encycl.* Suppl. 29/1 The Forty Hours' Adoration. **1967** *New Cath. Encycl.* V. 1036/1 Forty hours devotion. A continuous period of prayer before the Blessed Sacrament, begun and terminated with a solemn high Mass, procession where possible, Litany of the Saints, and special prayers. *Ibid.* 1036/2 Forty Hours has come to be a devotion simply honoring the Blessed Sacrament rather than a means of making reparation or of petitioning for peace.

B. *sb.*

1. a. The age of 40 years. **b.** ***the forties***: the years between 40 and 50 of a century or of one's life.

1732 BERKELEY *Alciphr.* I. §1 Alciphron is above forty. **1885** *Athenæum* 18 July 83/1 His *magnum opus* was published in Edinburgh some time in the forties. **1893** GEO. HILL *Hist. Eng. Dress* II. 243 What were called half-caps were worn in the early forties.

2. ***the forty***: a designation applied to certain public bodies in various countries and at various periods, from the number of their members; e.g. to several courts of justice in the Venetian republic; to a body of itinerant justices in ancient Attica, empowered to try petty actions; to the French Academy, and (occasionally) to the Royal Academy of Arts in London.

1820 BYRON *Mar. Fal.* I. i. 24 'Tis not for us To anticipate the sentence of the Forty.

3. A yacht of forty tons burden.

1894 *Field* 9 June 836/1 The two big cutters had left.. the two forties many miles astern.

4. ***the roaring forties***: see ROARING FORTIES as main entry.

5. One fourth of a quarter section of land, comprising forty acres. *U.S.*

1845 C. M. KIRKLAND *Western Clearings* 2 Eighties and forties.. are plain enough when one is habituated to them. **1873** E. EGGLESTON *Myst. Metrop.* i. 19 It was just so many quarter sections, 'eighties', and 'forties' to be bought low. **1902** S. E. WHITE *Blazed Trail* i. 13 The men who were to fell the trees, Radway distributed along one boundary of a 'forty'. **1913** G. STRATTON-PORTER *Laddie* (1917) xiv. 276, I had thought we would commence on the east forty when planning the work [of ploughing]. **1947** *Pacific Discovery* Jan.–Feb. 5/1 This was wilderness, as distinct from the back forty.

6. A period of forty minutes' play.

1913 *Field* 25 Oct. 904/2 Light forwards are bound to be worn down in two 'forties' by heavier.

7. A 'crook', thief, sharper (in quot. 1879, a convict). *Austral. slang.*

1879 MRS. C. COOK *Comic Hist. N.S.W.*, Fifteen of the 'Forties' became free of the colony this June. **1882** *Sydney Slang Dict.* 8/2 *The Forties*, the worst types of 'the talent' who get up rows in a mob, .. and sometimes assault and rob, either in barrooms or the streets. **1885** *Australasian Printers' Keepsake* 116 Ah, them were jolly days indeed, Long ere the Vandemonian swarm had come, .. Or ere the 'Forty' had capsized our trade. **1927** M. M. BENNETT *Christison* xxii. 194 Their numbers swelled with rowdies and 'forties'—gambling sharpers who travelled from shed to shed making five pounds by cheating for every five shillings they earned.

C. in Combination.

1. Combination of the simple numeral with a sb. (used *attrib.* or *ellipt.* as sbs.), and parasynthetic derivatives of these: **forty-acre** *U.S.* and *N.Z.*, a section of land comprising forty acres (cf. B. 5); **forty-foot**, †(*a*) = *forty legs*; (*b*) see quot. 1889; **forty-footer**, a forty-foot yacht; **forty-knot**, 'the *Alternanthera Achyrantha*, a prostrate amarantaceous weed of warm countries' (*Cent. Dict.*); **forty legs**, a popular or dialectal name of the centipede; †**forty pence**, ? a jocular designation for a servant who runs errands; **forty-penny nail**, a nail of such size that one thousand of them weigh forty pounds (see PENNY); †**forty penny piece**, a coin worth 40 pence Scots, i.e. 3⅓*d.* sterling; **forty rod lightning**, *U.S. slang*: see quot.; **forty-rod whisky** = prec.; also *ellipt.*; **forty skewer**: see FORTESCUE; **forty-spot**, the Tasmanian name for a bird, *Pardalotus quadragintus* (Gould, *Birds Austr.*, 1848); **forty-tonner** = B. 3.

1742 *New Hampshire Probate Records* III. 94, I give to my Grand Son.. one *Forty Acre Lot. **1860** in A. F. Ridgway *Voices from Auckland* 48 The Forty-acre men will ruin the country. **1869** J. MAY *Guide to Farming in N.Z.* 42 We were lately on the sections of two 'forty-acre men'. **1877** C. B. GEORGE *40 Yrs. on Rail* xi. 227, 'I live just over there', pointing to his house across a forty-acre lot. **1943** C. CROW *Gt. Amer. Customer* 185 There was no reason why a farmer could not plant a whole forty-acre field in wheat. **1673** E. BROWN *Trav. Europe* (1677) 17 An Indian Scolopendria, or *Forty-foot. **1889** *N. W. Linc. Gloss.*, *Forty-foot*, a right of forty-foot which the tenants of certain manors had over the soil of an adjoining manor. **1902** *Essex Inst. Hist. Coll.* XXXVIII. 256 The schooner-yacht 'Excelsior' was one of the earliest of the '*forty-footers'. **1697** DAMPIER *Voy.* I. xi. 320 Centapees, call'd by the English *40 Legs. **1750** G. HUGHES *Barbadoes* 89 The Forty-legs in Surinam are a great deal larger than what are bred in Barbados. **1866** BROGDEN *Provinc. Words Lincolnsh.*, *Forty-legs*, a centipede. **1616** *Englishm. for my Money* F iiij a, Farewell *fortipence, goe seeke your Signor. **1769** in Hawkesworth *Voy.* (1773) II. 182 No nails less than *fortypenny were current. *c* **1850** *Rudim. Navig.* (Weale) 135 *Nails of sorts* are, 4, 6, 8.. and 40-penny nails. **1681** COLVIL *Whigs Supplic.* (1751) 58 Butter and cheese, and wool fleeces, For groats and *Fourty penny pieces. **1889** FARMER *Americanisms*, **Forty Rod Lightning*, whisky of the most villainous description, so called because humorously warranted to kill at forty rods. **1892** STEVENSON *Wrecker* 124 *Forty-rod whisky was administered by a proprietor as dirty as his beasts. **1863** W. H. RUSSELL *My Diary North & South* II. 11 Their cries for water were incessant to allay the internal fires caused by '40 rod' and '60 rod'. **1869** 'MARK TWAIN' *Sks. New & Old* (1875) 70 Trading for forty-rod whiskey.. has played the everlasting mischief. **1873** J. H. BEADLE *Undevel. West* xiii, The standard drink is whisky—'stone fence', 'forty-rod', and 'tarantula-juice'. **1916** 'ANZAC' *On Anzac Trail* v. 77 Shebangs [in Cairo] where they sell you whisky that takes the lining of your throat down with it.. a soothing liquid that licks 'forty-rod', 'chained lightning', or 'Cape smoke' to the back of creation. **1919** Forty-rod [see BOOT-LEGGING]. **1948** *Daily Oklahoman* (Okla. City) 7 June 8/1 The mere possession of a few gills of forty rod is not counted as an ample offset to planned assassination. **1895** *Daily News* 11 June 2/4 For the second match, *forty-tonners, three entered.

2. a. Substantival uses of the compound numerals (see A. 1): **forty-eight**, (*a*) a flowerpot of the third smallest size, of which there are 48 in a 'cast'; (*b*) *pl.* a sheet of a book folded into forty-eight leaves; (*c*) the forty-eight preludes and fugues of J. S. Bach; **forty-eightmo**, the size of a book in forty-eights; **forty-four**, (*a*) a forty-four gun ship; (*b*) a bicycle with a wheel 44 inches in diameter; †**forty-nine**, a 17th c. name for some kind of liquor; **forty-one** *Hist.*, the Venetian council by whom the Doge was elected; **forty-two** *attrib.* in ***forty-two man***, a man of the 42nd regiment.

1851 GLENNY *Handbk. Fl. Gard.* 227 They must be potted off into moderately small pots, say *forty-eights. **1808** C. STOWER *Printers' Gram.* 192 A Half Sheet of Forty-eights, with Two Signatures. **1839** T. C. HANSARD *Print. & Type-Founding* 168 Forty-eights to be paid 2s. per sheet extra. **1873** H. C. BANISTER *Music* (1889) III. xxvi. 206 Bach's Fugue in C♯ Minor, No. 4 of the 48. **1902** *Westm. Gaz.* 29 Dec. 1/3 Those famous fugues and preludes known to all musicians as the 'Forty-Eight'. **1965** G. HUGHES *Handbk. Gt. Composers* vii. 45 At times the.. counterpoint seems to spring from the interweaving of rhythmic figures rather than of melodic phrases—as in the prelude in F sharp major from the second book of the 'forty-eight'. **1888** C. T. JACOBI *Printers' Vocab.*, **Forty-eightmo*, a sheet of paper folded into forty-eight leaves. **1821** BYRON *To Murray* 7 Feb., The giant element.. made our stout *forty-four's.. timbers creak again. **1884** *Century Mag.* Nov. 55/2 His hand resting .. on the handle of his forty-four. **1692** A. P[ITCAIRNE] *Babell* 2 (Maitl. 1830) 5 Assist me all, ye Muses nyne! With a beer glass of *fourtie nyne. **1723** MESTON *Knight* (1767) 21 A glass or two of forty-nine He can pull off before he dine. **1612** W. SHUTE tr. *Fougasses' Venice* II. 481 The *forty one being assembled.. they.. chose him Prince. **1816** SCOTT *Antiq.* xliii, Here comes an old *forty-two man, who is a fitter match for you than I am.

b. In abbreviated dates, as *forty-one*, *-two*, *-three*, etc., colloquially used to designate a year of the current or preceding century. Hence **forty-niner** *U.S.*, one of those who settled in California during the 'gold fever' about 1849.

1710 H. BEDFORD *Vind. Ch. Eng.* 1 The Spirit of Forty-one is reviving. **1853** *Mt. Echo* (Downieville, Calif.) 12 Feb. 1/1 Speeches were made by some of the worthy old forty-nin-ers. **1887** *Council Bluffs Herald* (Iowa U.S.) 17 Jan., Running the 'pony express' in the exciting days of the '49-ers'. **1890** BOLDREWOOD *Miner's Right* xliv. 384 All old prospectors and 'forty-niners'.

forty-five. **a.** ***the Forty-five***: the year 1745, and the Jacobite rebellion of that year. **b.** *Card-playing.* A game in which each trick counts five and the game is forty-five. Also ***forty-fives***. **c.** A revolver of ·45 calibre. *U.S.* **d.** A 45 r.p.m. 7-inch microgroove gramophone record; also written **45**.

a. 1832 SCOTT *Redgauntlet* ch. xi, Ye have heard of a year they call the *forty-five*. **1895** D. MARSHALL in *Scot. Antiq.* X. 77 In the 'Forty-five, Burleigh Castle.. was garrisoned for King George.

b. 1875 WOOD & LAPHAM *Wait. Mail* 32 The others.. gathered round the table to enjoy the Irish game of 'forty-fives'.

c. 1881 G. W. ROMSPERT *Western Echo* 285 We now used the six-shooters,—known as forty-fives,—and which were also deadly weapons. **1926** J. BLACK *You can't Win* iii. 21 He owned the latest pattern of repeating rifle and a couple of 'forty-fives'.

d. [**1949** *Gramophone* Nov. 108/2 Single, double and treble speed motors fitted with heavy non-magnetic turntables, suitable for high fidelity reproduction of 78, 45 and 33⅓ r.p.m. records.] **1950** *Ibid.* Dec. 162/2, I have had an opportunity of hearing the Rachmaninov No. 2 and the Tchaikovsky No. 1 Pianoforte Concerto on these 45 discs. **1968** R. CLAPPERTON *No News on Monday* vii. 82, I did a forty-five for Sunny Coast Records once that had as much impact as a handful of sand.

fortyish, *a.* Looking forty years old.

1821 *New Monthly Mag.* II. 324 A sort of Tom Shuffleton grown flat, staid, and fortyish.

foruh, obs. form of FURROW.

forum ('fɔərəm). [a. L. *forum.*]

1. *Rom. Ant.* The public place or market-place of a city. In ancient Rome the place of assembly for judicial and other public business.

1460 CAPGRAVE *Chron.* 29 Thoo places in which juges herd causes he [Foroneus] cleped hem aftir his name, 'forum', that is to say, 'a hopen place', or 'a market'. **1601** HOLLAND *Pliny* II. 117 The said Scipioes statue erected in the Forum or publick hall. **1647** R. STAPYLTON *Juvenal* 61 The city of Rome had four great forums or piazzas. **1781** GIBBON *Decl. & F.* II. 15 The principal Forum; which appears to have been of a circular, or rather elliptical form. **1838** ARNOLD *Hist. Rome* I. 38 He [Tarquinius] made a forum or market place and divided out the ground around it for shops and stalls, and made a covered walk around it.

b. as the place of public discussion; hence *fig.*

1735 THOMSON *Liberty* I. 160 Foes in the forum in the field were friends. **1818** BYRON *Ch. Har.* IV. cxiv. 1025 Rienzi.. The forum's champion, and the people's chief. **1831** CARLYLE *Sart. Res.* (1858) 8 To descend.. into the angry noisy Forum, with an Argument that cannot but exasperate and divide.

2. A court, tribunal. ***law of the forum***: the legal rules of a particular court or jurisdiction.

1848 WHARTON *Law Lex.*, *Forum*, the court to the jurisdiction of which a party is liable. **1857** PARSONS *Contracts* II. II. ii. §6 (ed. 2) 103 Limitation and prescription are applied only according to the law of the forum. **1858** LD. ST. LEONARDS *Handy-bk. Prop. Law* II. 4 As the law of property is now administered in the different forums.. it exhibits a splendid.. code of jurisprudence.

b. *transf.* and *fig.* (Cf. med.L. *in foro interno*, *in foro conscientiæ*).

1690 *Case Univ. Oxford* 48 A right to be impleaded in their own Forum only. **1756** BURKE *Subl. & B.* v. v, Of this, at first view, every man, in his own forum, ought to judge without appeal. **1852** GLADSTONE *Glean.* (1879) IV. xiv. 151 In every country of Europe, except one, when excusable collision arises between the civil and the religious power it must be in the external forum. **1874** MORLEY *Compromise* (1886) 147 It is truth that in the forum of conscience claims an undivided allegiance.

3. *attrib.*, as ***forum-area***, ***-orator***.

1812 SOUTHEY in *Q. Rev.* VIII. 347 A forum orator some years ago published a tour. **1893** *Archæologia* LIII. 544 The forum area was trenched but not excavated.

forur(e, var. FURRURE *Obs.*, fur trimming.

†**for'vay**, *v. Obs.* Also 4 (Gower) forsveie, 5 forvoyen, -wey(e, -way(e, 5–6 for-, fourvey(e. [ad. OF. *forvoier*, *forsvoier*, f. *for(s)-*, FOR- *pref.*[3] + *voie* way.] *intr.* To go out of the way, go astray; *fig.* to err, make a mistake. Hence **for'vaying** *vbl. sb.*

1390 GOWER *Conf.* I. 76 [MS. Fairfax] That þei be Duistres of þe weie Forþi if eny man forsueie [*Pauli prints* forswey] Thurgh hem þei be noght excusable (Also III. 224, 272, 275). **1413** *Pilgr. Sowle* (Caxton) I. i. (1859) 2 Ther nys no pylgrym that goth so redyly but that oftymes he mote foruoyen. *c* **1430** *Pilgr. Lyf Manhode* IV. lxv. (1869) 207 Þe forueyinge of ooþere shulde ben warnynge. **1483** CAXTON *G. de la Tour* K vj, This yonge man forweyeth. *c* **1500** *Melusine* xix. 101, I was forwayed of my way to comme to lusygnen. **1508** DUNBAR *Gold. Targe* 204 As drunkyn man he all forvayit. **1513** DOUGLAS *Æneis* III. Prol. 18 Tharfore wald God I had thair eris to pull Misknawis the creid and threpis othir forwayis. *c* **1560** A. SCOTT *Poems* (S.T.S.) iii. 15 Forvey no tyme, be reddy day and nicht.

forwake(d: see FOR- *pref.*[1] 6 b.

†**forwal.** *Obs. rare*[−1]. [perh. mis-written for **forfal*, a. ON. *forfall* (law term) hindrance.] A legitimate excuse.

c **1205** LAY. 31590 Þa andswarede Cadwalan þe kene.. Oswy haueð for-wal [Wace: *essoine le tient*].

†**for'walk**, *v. Obs.* Also 6 fore-. [f. FOR- *pref.*[1] + WALK.] *trans.* To weary with walking; to over-tire. Hence **for'walked** *ppl. a.*

In the Sc. examples prob. confused with *forwaked*: see FOR- *pref.*[1] 6 b.

c **1350** *Will. Palerne* 2236 Þei þeder come al wery for walked. **1377** LANGL. *P. Pl.* B. XIII. 204 Whan thow art wery for-walked. **1513** DOUGLAS *Æneis* II. vi. [v.] 35 Quhen the first quyet Of natural slepe.. Stelis on forwalkit [*so Ruthven MS.*; *ed. Small* fordoverit] mortall creaturis. **1533** BELLENDEN *Livy* II. (1822) 204 The Romanis.. sett on the Volschis, wery and forwalkit. **1612** [see FORWELK.]

for-wall, -wallowed: see FOR- *pref.*[1] 5, 6 b.

for'wander, *v. Obs.* exc. *arch.* or *Sc.* [f. FOR- *pref.*[1] + WANDER.] *intr.* To weary oneself with wandering; to wander far and wide. Hence **for'wandered** *ppl. a.*

c **1350** *Will. Palerne* 739 He.. forwandreþ in wo & wakeþ .. on niȝtes. **1377** LANGL. *P. Pl.* B. Prol. 7, I was wery forwandred and went me to reste. **1563** SACKVILLE *Mirr. Mag.*, *Buckingham* lxxiv, All forsake.. forwandred in despayer. **1590** SPENSER *F.Q.* I. vi. 34 A wearie wight forwandring by the way. **1890** G. A. SMITH *Isaiah* II. xvi. 254 Among the bruised, the prisoners, the forwandered of Israel. **1894** CROCKETT *Raiders* 158 A poor lost forwandered lad.

forward ('fɔːwəd), *a.*, *adv.* and *sb.* Forms: 1 fore-, forweard, -werd, 4–7 foreward(e, 4–6 forwarde, 6 foret, 9 *dial.* forat, forrad, -at, 4– forward. See also FORRIT. [OE. *for(e)weard*, adj. and adv.; see FORE *adv.* and -WARD. The adj. seems to have been obsolete after the OE. period, and to have been redeveloped from the adv. in the 16th c. The adv. (OE. *foreweard*) was app. in origin the neut. acc. of the adj.]

A. *adj.*

†1. In OE. used in partitive concord: The front part of (any thing material); the first or earliest part of (a period of time, etc.). *Obs.*
c900 tr. *Bæda's Hist.* v. xiii. [xii]. (1891) 422 In forewearde neaht. **c1000** ÆLFRIC *Hom.* II. 266 Ure Forewearde heafod.

2. a. Situated in the fore part. *Obs.* exc. *techn.*
1601 SHAKS. *All's Well* v. iii. 39 Let's take the instant by the forward top. **1692** LUTTRELL *Brief Rel.* (1857) II. 503 The guides conducted the forwardest of the party..a wrong way. **1876** HOLLAND *Sevenoaks* x. 131 He fixed a knob of tallow upon the forward sight of Mr. Balfour's gun.

b. *Naut.* Belonging to the fore part (of a vessel).
1881 *Daily Tel.* 24 Feb., The nine forward men are divided into three watches. **1893** *Westm. Gaz.* 21 Mar. 5/3 The forward-house and forecastle bulkhead were stove in.

†**c.** Principal, foremost, chief. *Obs.*
1581 SAVILE *Tacitus' Agric.* (1622) 184 Many haue beene wasted by casuall chances, the most sufficient and forward by the cruelty of the Prince.

d. That lies in front; now only, that lies in the direction towards which one is moving.
1643 LIGHTFOOT *Glean. Ex.* (1648) 17 In the five preceding Plagues, the obduration of Pharaohs heart is attributed to himselfe, in these five forward, it is attributed to God. **1800–24** CAMPBELL *Dream* ii, Shadow'd in the forward distance Lay the land of Death. **1844** KINGLAKE *Eothen* xvii. (1878) 233 Out of the forward horizon.

3. a. Directed towards a point in advance, onward; also 'outward' as opposed to 'return'.
1603 DRAYTON *Bar. Wars* I. xlvi, She [fortune], dispos'd his forward course to let. **1814** CARY *Dante, Par.* XXIX. 136 Let us seek The forward path again. **1840** BURY *Select Comm. on Railw.* Q. 2398 You spoke of sending an engine to meet the train; on what line would that go?—It must go on the forward line. **1844** H. H. WILSON *Brit. India* II. 46 General Wood was compelled..to undertake a forward movement. **1884** *G.W.R. Time Tables* July 87 *Return Tickets* are available..for completion of the forward and backward journeys.

b. Of the face: (Looking) straight in front.
1700 DRYDEN *Cymon & Iph.* 594 The lovers close the rear, With forward faces not confessing fear. **1850** TENNYSON *In Mem.* cxiv, She [knowledge] sets her forward countenance And leaps into the future chance.

c. Of a ship's beak: Moving onwards.
1871 R. ELLIS tr. *Catullus* lxiv. 12 Scarcely the forward snout tore up that wintery water.

d. ***forward play*** in *Cricket*: the method of playing forward: see the *adv.* 3 b. So ***forward batsman, block, cut, drive, glance, lunge, player, point, stroke.*** Cf. BACKWARD *a.* 1.
1876 *Haygarth's Cricket Scores & Biogr.* 1855–75 v. 38 A steady, forward batsman. **1849** *Boy's Own Bk.* 85 Smother it by the forward block. **1851** J. PYCROFT *Cricket Field* vii. 145 The Forward Cut..sends the ball between point and middle wicket. **1836** E. JESSE *Angler's Rambles* 301 He would draw diagrams of the angles of incidence and reflexion: shew ..the exact length which he could cover in a forward drive. **1903** P. F. WARNER in H. G. Hutchinson *Cricket* iii. 64 The back glance and the forward glance have practically taken the place of the leg hit. **1861** 'OLD CRICKETER' *Cricket-Bat* 66 The forward cut, also called the forward lounge, is an off hit. **1828** G. T. KNIGHT in W. Denison *Cricket: Sk. Players* (1846) 41 The method then [c 1804] introduced was running in at the ball, hard hitting, and a bold forward play. **1891** W. G. GRACE *Cricket* §4 in *Outdoor Games & Recr.* 19 Practise both backward and forward play. **1851** J. PYCROFT *Cricket Field* vii. 126 The best forward players may err. **1870** Forward player [see BACKWARD *a.* 1]. **1851** J. PYCROFT *Cricket Field* xi. 222 With a fine forward player, a near Middle-wicket or forward point often snaps up a catch. **1897** RANJITSINHJI in *Daily News* 10 Aug. 6/1 In order to make a forward-stroke effectively aggressive, the batsman must throw himself into the correct attitude. **1906** A. E. KNIGHT *Compl. Cricketer* ii. 66 A forward stroke..generally known in our time as the 'Push stroke'.

e. ***forward movement***: recently often used to denote a special effort made by a political party, a religious or benevolent organization, etc., in order to make more rapid progress. Cf. 9.
1896 *Indep. & Nonconf.* 31 Dec. 494 The Colonial Missionary Society Forward Movement. **1897** *Westm. Gaz.* 9 Jan., The Liberal Forward Movement.

4. *Comm.* Of a business transaction, contract, delivery, exchange, material etc.: Prospective, relating to future produce.
1883 *Manch. Exam.* 6 Nov. 4/4 In the old days, when it took three or four months to send out goods to India..there was a real ground for forward buying. **1891** *Daily News* 23 Nov. 2/7 The rate for good furnace coke is 14s...but consumers will not pay this price for forward contracts. **1930** M. CLARK *Home Trade* 107 'Forward delivery' [means] that the goods will be delivered..at a future date. **1930** [see FORWARD *adv.* 1 c]. **1957** *Economist* 21 Dec. 1076/2 If they could offset that reduction cheaply by larger purchases of forward rubber they might do so, but rubber three months forward commands a premium of about ½d. per lb. **1962** *Ibid.* 28 Apr. 367/2 A forward exchange operation is a contract to exchange one currency for another at a future date at a rate of exchange fixed now.

5. a. That is in an advanced state or condition; progressing towards maturity or completion. Chiefly *predicative* and barely distinguishable from the *adv.*
1526 *Pilgr. Perf.* (W. de W. 1531) 72 b, How moche we profyte & be forewarde in euery day by our labour. **1561** T. HOBY tr. *Castiglione's Courtyer* I. C b, It is nowe well forwarde in nyghte. **1743** BULKELEY & CUMMINS *Voy. S. Seas* 86 To acquaint him how forward the Boat was [in making]. **1805** *Med. Jrnl.* XVII. 515 The [vaccinated] arms of Sarah..were in a more forward state than the rest. **1848** *Jrnl. R. Agric. Soc.* IX. I. 7 The sheep..get exceedingly forward in condition. **1866** MRS. H. WOOD *St. Martin's Eve* iv, A sturdy little fellow..sufficiently forward in walking to get about the room.

b. Of a plant, a crop, or the season: Well advanced, early.
1591 SHAKS. *Two Gent.* I. i. 45 As the most forward Bud Is eaten by the Canker ere it blow. **1601** R. JOHNSON *Kingd. & Commw.* (1603) 13 The inhabitants of Turon..enjoy as forward a summer, as those of Provence. **1707** *Curios. in Husb. & Gard.* 254 Fruit, the soundest and forwardest of any on the Tree. **1796** C. MARSHALL *Garden.* xix. (1813) 344 Sow three or four seeds..in a small pot, which being placed on a gentle heat, will be much forwarder and finer. **1821** CLARE *Vill. Minstr.* I. 18 He 'gins again 'Bout signs in weather, late or forward spring. **1832** HT. MARTINEAU *Homes Abroad* ii. 23 Place our hungry brethren where nature's work is forwardest.

c. Of a pregnant animal: *in* or *with foal*, etc.
1684 *Lond. Gaz.* No. 1910/4 A Red Cow..forward with Calf. **1707** *Ibid.* No. 4312/3 Lost..a bay Saddle Mare.. forward in Fole. **1839** *Lincoln, etc. Gaz.* 12 Feb. 2/3 Eleven ewes forward in lamb. **1857** *Jrnl. R. Agric. Soc.* XVIII. I. 19 The mares are indulged a little as they get forward with foal.

6. a. Ready, prompt, eager (in an action or a cause); *esp.* with const. *to* (do something).
1523 LD. BERNERS *Froiss.* I. xxxi. 45 At the first assaute he was so forwarde, that he was stryken to the erth. **a1568** ASCHAM *Scholem.* I. (Arb.) 56 God grafte in vs the trewe knowledge of his woorde, with a forward will to folowe it. **1631** GOUGE *God's Arrows* v. Ded. 406 Be not backward to patronize what you have been forward to produce. **a1633** AUSTIN *Medit.* (1635) 231 Neither can it be collected..that hee [St. Bartholomew] was ever forward of his Tongue, as some of the Rest were. **1644** LAUD *Wks.* (1854) IV. 181 His Majesty's piety was so forward, that nothing needed to be extorted from him. **1702** C. MATHER *Magn. Chr.* II. App. (1852) 203 He was much forwarder to give his assent than they were to ask it. **1818** JAS. MILL *Brit. India* III. VI. i. 52 Their followers were to be ranked as the most forward and loud, who denounced parliament as so corrupt. **1875** M. PATTISON *Casaubon* 40 Authors were always forward to send him copies of their learned publications.

†**b.** Inclined *to* or *for* (something). *Obs.*
1581 J. BELL *Haddon's Answ. Osor.* 256 b, If I had bene.. so foreward to sedition..there wanted not..fautoures of the cause. **1681** BAXTER *Apol. Nonconf. Min.* 4 The forwardest to Peace. **1727** SWIFT *Art Polite Lying* Wks. 1755 III. I. 118 A hot-headed crack-brained coxcomb forward for a scheme of moderation.

c. Ardent, eager, spirited, zealous. ? *Obs.*
1587 FLEMING *Contn. Holinshed* III. 1551/2 Three sonnes, all forward, martiall, and valorous gentlemen. **1593** SHAKS. *Rich. II,* IV. i. 72 How fondly do'st thou spurre a forward Horse? **1611** TOURNEUR *Ath. Trag.* II. i. Wks. 1878 I. 41 His forward spirit press'd into the front. **1680** OTWAY *Orphan* I. i, They both have forward, gen'rous active Spirits. **1804** WELLINGTON in Gurw. *Desp.* III. 468 He is a gallant, forward officer.

d. *transf.* and *fig.* of things. ? *Obs.*
1605 CAMDEN *Rem.* Ded. 1 This..Treatise was once vnaduisedly forward to haue bin dedicated to your good worship. But..It recalled it selfe in good time. **1695** BLACKMORE *Pr. Arth.* I. 654 Their forward genius without teaching grows. **1719** DE FOE *Crusoe* II. iii, These stakes also, being of a wood very forward to grow. **1736** BUTLER *Anal.* I. i. Wks. 1874 I. 18 We are accustomed, from our youth up, to indulge that forward delusive faculty [imagination].

7. Well-advanced for one's years, precocious.
1591 LYLY *Endym.* II. ii, It will be a forward cock that croweth in the shell. **1593** SHAKS. *3 Hen. VI,* I. i. 203 Long liue thou, and these thy forward Sonnes. **1600** —— *A.Y.L.* III. iii. 14 When..a mans good wit [cannot be] seconded with the forward childe vnderstanding. **1714** *Restoration* in *Villiers' Wks.* (1775) 8 He's a pretty forward boy about four and twenty. **1869** PRINCESS ALICE *Mem.* 25 Apr. (1884) 215 My children..are so forward, clever, and spirited.

8. In bad sense: Presumptuous, pert; bold, immodest.
1561 T. NORTON *Calvin's Inst.* III. xxii. (1634) 454 Some ..doe raile at this doctrine with greater maliciousnesse, than that their forward pride ought to be suffered. **1602** WARNER *Alb. Eng.* IX. xlvii. (1612) 221 They tould how forward Maidens weare, how proude if in request. **a1704** T. BROWN *Praise Poverty* Wks. 1730 I. 94 A forward prating cox-comb. **1711** STEELE *Spect.* No. 51 ¶1, I have..a great Aversion to the forward Air and Fashion which is practised in all publick Places. **1775** SHERIDAN *Duenna* I. iv, Clara..would think this step of mine highly forward. **1806–7** J. BERESFORD *Miseries Hum. Life* (1826) VII. lxix, Hearing your favourite poem..mammocked by the mouth of a forward Puppy. **1844** DICKENS *Mart. Chuz.* xl, 'The favouritest young for'ard huzzy of a servant gal as ever come into a house.' **1888** J. PAYN *Myst. Mirbridge* v, 'Do you call him forward?' ..'He was certainly free in his manners'.

9. Of persons, opinions: Advanced, extreme; in mod. use, favouring vigorous aggressive action.
1608 F. JOHNSON *Cert. Reasons & Argts.* To Rdr., The Books of the forward Preachers now abroad. **1885** *Pall Mall G.* 7 May 1/2 You of all people in the world, the Forwardest of the Forward school, cannot complain of the advance of Empire. **1887** *Ibid.* 10 June 7/1 Denouncing outrage and dynamite, and what are generally known as 'forward' measures.

B. *adv.*

1. a. Of extent in time: Towards the future, immediately afterwards and continuously onwards. Chiefly (and now only) in phrases ***from this day*** (***time***, etc.) ***forward.*** †Also, ***from this, from hence, (from) now, and so forward.*** Cf. FORTH *adv.* 3.
a1000 *Cædmon's Gen.* 788 (Gr.) Gif hie wolden lare godes forweard fremman. **a1300** *Cursor M.* 5480 (Gött.) In egipt held he þaim ful hard, As i sal tell you sone forward. *Ibid.* 13958 (Gött.) Ai fra þat dai for-warde..þe Iuus..soght iesu to do to dede. **1303** R. BRUNNE *Handl. Synne* 744 Alle my ꝥys grete Fro ꝥys forwarde wyl y lete. **c1391** CHAUCER *Astrol.* II. §12, & fro that time forward..shal the verrey degree of the sonne shewe the howr of the planete. **c1440** *Gesta Rom.* lxi. 261 (Harl. MS.), I Resseyve [yow] fro hens forwarde to my Ioye. **1552** LATIMER *Serm. 2nd Sund. in Advent* (1562) 132 If we..intend to amend our life now forward. **1600** HOLLAND *Livy* II. xli. 71 This is the first time that the law Agraria was published: and so forward unto this present hower, it was never debated of. **c1680** BEVERIDGE *Serm.* (1729) I. 547 From that time forward whatsoever he did..was in order to that end. **1853** MAURICE *Proph. & Kings* iii. 42 From that day forward..the Spirit of God came upon David. **1871** SMILES *Charac.* iii. (1876) 68 The elder student from that time forward acted as the Mentor of the younger one.

b. With vbs., as *look, think*: esp. ***to look forward***: to look ahead, to look expectantly towards the future or *to* a coming event.
1741 WATTS *Improv. Mind* I. i. Wks. (1813) 9 To think forward a little. **1742** RICHARDSON *Pamela* III. 343 One who can look forwarder than the Nine Days of Wonder. **1768** FOOTE *Devil on 2 Sticks* I. Wks. 1799 II. 249 Banish your fears, and let us look forward, my love. **1816** KEATINGE *Trav.* (1817) II. 23 Like chess-players, they seem always to look three moves forward. **1837** DISRAELI *Venetia* III. i, His visit to the hall was looked forward to with interest. **1875** JOWETT *Plato* (ed. 2) IV. 45 He looks forward to all future systems sharing the fate of the past.

c. *Comm.* For future delivery or payment. ***to date forward***: to postdate.
1882 *Daily News* 4 Mar., The orders being neither numerous nor large, and not a few dated forward. **1884** *Manch. Exam.* 12 May 4/4 Dating forward..is a thing unknown among shippers, for payment is usually made a week or so after the goods have been delivered. **1894** *Daily News* 28 Mar. 7/3 Maize still..dear, but cheaper forward. **1930** *Economist* 23 Aug. 350/1 It by no means follows that the policy of buying forward will always operate to the buyer's advantage, for unless a foreign buyer simultaneously covers himself by a corresponding forward exchange operation, he may find that an adverse movement of the exchange has destroyed his profit on the shipment.

†**2. a.** Onward or further on in a series; onwards from a specified point. ***and so forward***: = and so forth, et cetera. Cf. FORTH *adv.* 2. *Obs.*
c1440 *Promp. Parv.* 173/2 Forwarde, or more vtyr, *ultra, ulterius.* **1582** N. LICHEFIELD tr. *Castanheda's Conq. E. Ind.* i. 2 a, Whether that from the Cape of Buena Esperansa forwarde there were anye Nauigation to the East India. **1583** STUBBES *Anat. Abus.* II. (1882) 34 If sixtie would serue, they must have an hundred, and so forward. **1659** HAMMOND *On Ps.* Annot. 3 From that tenth Psalm forward. **1663** MARVELL *Corr.* xlvii. Wks. 1872–5 II. 96, I am this day beginning my long voyage to Archangel, and so forward.

b. In the first place, foremost: in phr. ***first and forward.*** *Obs.*
1362 LANGL. *P. Pl.* A. x. 127 Furst and foreward to folk that ben i-weddet. **c1386** CHAUCER *Melib.* ¶275 First and forward, ye han erred in [etc.].

3. a. Towards the front, in the direction which a person or thing faces. ***forward of*** (U.S.): in front of. ***to put*** or ***set foot forward***: see FOOT *sb.* 29.
1513 MORE in Grafton *Chron.* (1568) II. 758 He came into the world with the feete forward. **1548** etc. [see FOOT *sb.* 29]. **1669** STURMY *Mariner's Mag.* II. 82, I..bow the Head forward or backward, or over the one side or the other. **1674** PLAYFORD *Skill Mus.* II. 103 You must begin with your Bow forward, though the Bow be drawn forward the Note before. **1703** MOXON *Mech. Exerc.* 226 Its middle part..stands about an Inch forwarder than the Foreside of the Puppet. **1762** FOOTE *Lyar* III. Wks. 1799 I. 308 Your hood a little forwarder, Miss. **1811** *Lett. fr. Eng.* II. xlix. 270 The skirts of the coat..brought forward to meet over the thigh. **1852** J. H. NEWMAN *Scope Univ. Educ.* 242 He may have no power at all of advancing one step forward of himself. **1856** C. J. ANDERSSON *Lake Ngami* 256 The ostrich..always strikes forward [with its foot]. **1891** M. S. WILKINS *Humble Rom.* 165 Two little thin dancing curls..just forward of her cap!

b. ***to play forward,*** in *Cricket*: to reach forward in order to play a rather short-pitched ball.
1851 J. PYCROFT *Cricket Field* x. 191 A good ball..is pushed forward to middle wicket. *Ibid.*, Shortleg is standing sharp in forward. **1884** *Lillywhite's Cricket Ann.* 101 Rather too fond of playing forward. **1891** W. G. GRACE *Cricket* §5 in *Outdoor Games & Recr.* 23 If he [the batsman]..plays forward, pitch shorter and shorter..until he makes a mistake.

4. a. Of continuous motion: Towards what is in front; (moving) onwards, on.
a1400–50 *Alexander* 847 Þe faster forward him he faris þe faster he snaipirs. **1526** *Pilgr. Perf.* (W. de W. 1531) 8 b, Suche..be not mete to..go forwarde in this pilgrymage. **1639** FULLER *Holy War* IV. viii. (1840) 190 His ships were manned, victualled, and sailing forward. **1697** DAMPIER *Voy.* I. xiii. 346 Meeting very strong Westerly Winds, we got nothing forward in many days. **1732** BERKELEY *Alciphr.* IV. §15 In case they walk straight forward, in half a hour they shall meet men. **1791** MRS. RADCLIFFE *Rom. Forest* i, He was desirous to hasten forward. **1855** MRS. GATTY *Parables fr. Nat.* Ser. I. (1869) 50 The river is rushing forward; the clouds are hurrying onward.

b. with ellipsis of some part of the vb. *go.* Also *Mil.*, as a word of command ***forward! for'ard on!*** in *Fox-hunting*: of the fox: Gone on in front.
a1533 LD. BERNERS *Huon* lv. 186 His horse wolde nother forwarde nor backe warde. **1583** GOLDING *Calvin on Deut.* xv. 86 Therefore let us on forewarde as he commandeth. **1833** *Regul. Instr. Cavalry* I. 25 The word *Forward*..is given by the commander. **1848** W. H. KELLY tr. *L. Blanc's Hist. Ten Y.* II. 207 Ibrahim..had but to cry 'Forward', and Constantinople was his.

c. In advance, in front, ahead.

1838 THIRLWALL *Greece* V. 369 Dercylus seems to have been sent forward. **1860** TYNDALL *Glac.* I. xxv. 182 One of our porters..was sent forward to test the [snow] bridge.

d. ***back*** or ***backward and forward***: to and fro; see BACK *adv.* 14 and BACKWARD *adv.* 5 b.

5. To the front or to a prominent position (from being behind or in the background), into view; *esp.* in phrases, as ***to bring forward*** (see also BRING *v.* 17). ***to come forward***: see COME *v.* 62; also, to come into existence. ***to put*** or ***set forward***: to put forth, advance, allege, offer; also *refl.* to give oneself (undue) prominence.

1611 BIBLE *2 Esdras* iii. 6 Before euer the earth came forward. **1651** HOBBES *Leviath.* III. xl. 252 To set forward.. such doctrine as was agreeable to Moses. **1783** BURKE *Rep. Affairs Ind.* Wks. XI. 304 He certainly has it in his power.. to keep it back, and bring it forward at his own times. **1794** MRS. RADCLIFFE *Myst. Udolpho* xliv, Dorothee, who had lingered far behind, was called forward. **1836** NEWMAN *Parochial Sermons* (ed. 2) II. xxiv. 325 Now, it is plain that there are two sorts of men in the world;—those who put themselves forward, and speak much; and those who retire. **1849** JAMES *Woodman* xviii, Who are you, my good friend, who put yourself so forward? **1895** COULSON KERNAHAN *God & Ant* Apol. (ed. 4) 9 The worst of all reasons which inexperienced writers put forward for setting pen to paper.

†**6. a.** In front, on the front or front side. *Obs.*

1618 BOLTON *Florus* I. xviii. 57 All their wounds were forward. **1663** GERBIER *Counsel* 101 Caused..the windowes which were forward to be made up.

b. *fig.* In a prominent position.

1796 BURKE *Let. to C. J. Fox* Wks. 1842 II. 391 A young man..who stands very forward in parliament.

7. a. At an advanced point; at a point or position which is beyond or further than another. Cf. FORTH *adv.* 4.

1523 LD. BERNERS *Froiss.* I. xvii. 18 All his barones went out of the cite, and ye first nyght they lodged vi. myle forwarde. **1611** BIBLE *Num.* xxxii. 19 Wee will not inherite with them on yonder side Iordane, or forward. **1647** SPRIGGE *Anglia Rediv.* IV. ii. 189 To secure the landing of Irish or Welch supplies so much the forwarder towards the east. **1656** H. PHILLIPS *Purch. Patt.* (1676) 162 Adding a cipher, and setting the (·) a figure forwarder. **1712** J. JAMES tr. *Le Blond's Gardening* 52 A little forwarder you find small Cross-ways with four Alleys.

b. Of time: In advance.

1571 HANMER *Chron. Irel.* (1633) 38, I thinke they are too forward in their computation. **1810** VINCE *Elem. Astron.* xxiv. 289 The time at the place of observation is forwarder than that at Greenwich.

8. *Naut.* **a.** Of motion: Towards the fore part of a vessel.

1669 STURMY *Mariner's Mag.* I. 17 Hawl forward the main Bowline. **1743** BULKELEY & CUMMINS *Voy. S. Seas* 15 The Carpenter going forward to inspect the Chain-Plates.

b. Of position: At or in the fore part of a vessel. ***forward of*** (U.S.): in front of. †***forward on***: at the fore end, forward.

1630 J. TAYLOR (Water P.) *Wks.* I. 88/1 The Sayler imagined that his horse was too much laden ahead, or foreward on (as the sea phrase is). **1688** *Lond. Gaz.* No. 2317/1 Captain Killegrew..being at the same time forward by the Gang-Way. **1691** T. H[ALE] *Acc. New Invent.* 124 The butt-ends..have been as it were abolished forward on for the easie passage of the Vessel through the water. **1743** BULKELEY & CUMMINS *Voy. S. Seas* 110 Being oblig'd to lie forward with the Men. **1794** NELSON 5 Nov. in Nicolas *Disp.* I. 504 Transports laying..with their Truce Flag hoisted forward. **1840** R. H. DANA *Bef. Mast* xxii. 67 Her only fault being..that she was wet forward. *a* **1864** HAWTHORNE *Amer. Note-bks.* (1879) I. 112 Forward of the ward-room.. is the midshipmen's room.

9. *fig.* Onward, so as to progress or advance. Chiefly in phr. ***to go forward*** (rarely with ellipsis of *go*): to be in progress or 'on foot', to be going on. ***to build forward***: to continue building.

1513 MORE in Grafton *Chron.* (1568) II. 760 There must it needes be long ere any good conclusion go forwarde. **1535** COVERDALE *Ezra* iii. 8 To se that the worke of the house of the Lorde wente forwarde. *a* **1600** HOOKER in *Eccl. Pol.* v. (1888) App. i. §3 It is the nature of Gods most bountiful disposition to build forward where his foundation is once laid. **1610** SHAKS. *Temp.* III. ii. 91 Now forward with your Tale. **1665** MANLEY *Grotius' Low C. Warres* 177 He would not forget to help forward the Belgick Affairs. **1717** tr. *Frezier's Voy. S. Sea* 119 The Climate is so fertile..that the Fruit is coming forward all the Year. **1766** GOLDSM. *Vic. W.* xi, Mr. Burchell..was always fond of seeing some innocent amusement going forward. **1788** FRANKLIN *Autobiog.* Wks. 1840 I. 181, I am got forward too fast with my story. **1793** SMEATON *Edystone L.* §124 My models and preparatory matters were now so far brought forward. **1832** HT. MARTINEAU *Life in Wilds* i. 18 Dinner was going forward. **1865** *Sat. Rev.* 5 Aug. 165 Unless..extreme partisans.. make concessions, there is no getting any forwarder. **1891** R. KIPLING *City Dreadf. Nt.* 43 Let's go in here—there may be something forward.

10. Phrases. ***to put*** or ***set forward*** (a person): to start onward, give a start to. *lit.* and *fig.* ***to set forward*** (intr.): to start on a journey, set out.

1546 J. HEYWOOD *Prov.* (1867) 17 Set forward, ye shall neuer labour yonger. **1582** N. LICHEFIELD tr. *Castanheda's Conq. E. Ind.* vii. 18 Such gale as would serue to put him forward on his iourney. **1650** HUBBERT *Pill Formality* 202 The trips and slidings shall but set thee forwarder on thy journey. **1766** GOLDSM. *Vic. W.* iii, The next morning we all set forward together. **1832** HT. MARTINEAU *Hill & Valley* ii. 19 To set his young people forward in the same way of life with himself. **1859** JEPHSON *Brittany* xvi. 258 Her godfather ..straightway sets forward to avenge her death.

11. *Comb.* **a.** with *pres. pple.*, as ***forward-bearing***, ***-creeping***, ***-flowing***, ***-looking*** adjs. **b.** with *pa. pple.*, as ***forward-turned*** adj. **c.** ***forward-looker***.

1647 H. MORE *Song of Soul* III. II. xxiii, Strong *forward-bearing will or appetite. **1850** TENNYSON *In Mem.* ciii. 37 The *forward-creeping tides. **1830** —— *Recoll. Arab. Nts.* i, The *forward-flowing tide of time. **1919** MENCKEN *Amer. Lang.* ix. 302 The *forward-looker, whose belief in the continuity..of the evolutionary process takes on the virulence of a religious faith. **1923** [see BABBITT]. **1933** P. GODFREY *Back-Stage* xiii. 164 It is this vanguard which makes the studio or art theatre possible. These serious people are prompted by feelings of responsibility towards the rest of humanity. They are the forward-lookers. **1800** WORDSW. *Michael* 158 A child..Brings hope with it, and *forward-looking thoughts. **1843** H. D. THOREAU *Let.* 8 June in R. B. Perry *Tht. & Char. W. James* (1935) I. 48 He [*sc.* H. James, sen.] is a refreshing, forward-looking and forward-moving man. **1922** S. LEWIS *Babbitt* xvi. 209 Weeklies and monthlies..as practical and forward-looking, as the real-estate columns. **1928** F. HURST *President is Born* xxii. 235 A man born into his time as snugly as a bug into his rug. Forward-looking. Backward-heeding. Un-neurotic. Normal. **1962** *BSI News* June 25/1 A forward-looking attitude prevails. *c* **1611** CHAPMAN *Iliad* v. 46 It took his *forward-turned backe, and lookt out of his breast.

C. *sb.* [The *adj.* used absolutely.]

†**1.** The fore or front part, the first part. ***on forward***: in the beginning (see AFOREWARD). *Obs.*

c **1000** ÆLFRIC *Deut.* xxviii. 13 Drihten þe ʒesett simle on foreweard & na on æfterweard. *c* **1175** *Lamb. Hom.* 73 On forward þos cristendomes ech man leorned his bileue er he fulht underfenge.

†**2.** A trick in wrestling; a throw which causes one's opponent to fall forward on his face. *Obs.*

1602 CAREW *Cornwall* 76 Many sleights and tricks appertaine hereunto..Such are the..forward and backward. **1612** DRAYTON *Poly-olb.* i. 6 They practise..The forward, backward, falx.

3. *Naut.* (See quot.)

1892 *Labour Commission* Gloss., *Foreward*..the fore end of a barge or other craft.

4. *Football.* One who plays in the front line; one of the body of players termed 'forwards', as opposed to 'backs' (see BACK *sb.* 21), whose duty is to be foremost in the attack. Also in various other games.

1879 *Encycl. Brit.* IX. 367/2 Under the Rugby code.. fifteen a side [is] the usual number of players—ten 'forwards', two 'half backs', one 'three-quarters back', and two 'backs'. **1889** *Pauline* VIII. 33 There is much to be learnt by the forwards. **1895** *Daily Chron.* 17 Jan. 6/4 The side whose forwards were beaten won the match. **1895** J. M. BROWN *Polo* 78 The two 'forwards', No. 1 and No. 2, should work together, and, if possible, be exactly the same class of player. **1897** *Encycl. Sport* I. 517/2 All the forwards should make a point of taking passes with their sticks. **1929** *Encycl. Brit.* III. 182/2 The duty of the forwards [in basket-ball] is primarily to make goals. **1956** *Men's Hockey* (Know the Game Series) (rev. ed.) 17/2 At long corners the defence come out in two waves, the forwards in the first wave each making for his attacking number. **1968** EAGLESON & MCKIE *Terminol. Austral. Nat. Football* II. 7 *Forward*, a player occupying a forward position.

forward ('fɔːwəd), *v.* [f. FORWARD *adv.*]

1. *trans.* To help or push forward; to advance, assist, hasten, promote, urge on. Also, †to put forward, set on foot (*obs. rare*).

1596 SHAKS. *1 Hen. IV*, I. i. 33 Then let me heare..What yesternight our Councell did decree In forwarding this deere expedience. **1605** VERSTEGAN *Dec. Intell.* vi. (1628) 172 Hee was greatly encouraged and forwarded in the matter by diuers of his most inward friendes. **1728** MORGAN *Algiers* II. i. 219 The Moriscoes of Africa..were often forwarded and assisted by them in their nocturnal Expeditions. **1780** BURKE *Let. to Burgh* Wks. IX. 243 He [Lord North]..forwarded two bills, that for encouraging the growth of tobacco, and that for giving a bounty on exportation of hemp from Ireland. **1786** MAD. D'ARBLAY *Diary* 24 July, After doing whatever I can to forward my dress for the next morning, I go to bed. **1806** WELLINGTON in Owen *Desp.* lxxvi, This prince..showed every disposition to impede rather than to forward the operations of the British army. **1871** FREEMAN *Norm. Conq.* (1876) IV. xvi. 33 To protect its rights and to forward its interests.

2. To accelerate the growth of (plants, etc.).

1626 BACON *Sylva* §412 So wee may House our owne Countrey Plants to forward them, and make them come in the Cold Seasons. **1707** *Curios. in Husb. & Gard.* 266 A Dunghill..is of wondrous Efficacy to forward the Flowers. **1720** SWIFT *Apollo to Dean* Wks. 1755 IV. I. 16 Whenever I shine, I forward the grass, and I ripen the vine. **1845** *Florist's Jrnl.* 55 They [plants] will be forwarded, or retarded, according to the state of the season.

3. To send forward, send to an ulterior destination (a thing, *rarely* a person). In commercial language often loosely, to dispatch, send by some regular mode of conveyance.

1757 FRANKLIN *Let. to Wife* in Bigelow *Life* (1881) I. 378 The black silk was sent to Mr. Neates, who undertook to forward it in some package of his. **1757** *Affect. Narr. Wager* 33 Where they might meet with..an Opportunity also of being forwarded to their own Home. **1790** BURKE *Fr. Rev.* Pref. 3 That letter..has been since forwarded to the person to whom it was addressed. **1844** LINGARD *Anglo-Sax. Ch.* (1858) I. iii. 122 Who..forwarded him in safety to Rome. **1883** F. M. PEARD *Contrad.* xii, There is a letter which should be forwarded to my brother. *Mod.* (*Comm.*) We have this day forwarded to your address per S.W.R. three boxes marked [etc.].

†**b.** To pass on, publish abroad. *Obs.*

1713 *Guardian* No. 1 ⁋ 1 His countenance is communicated to the publick..and forwarded by engravers, artists by way of mezzo-tinto, etc.

4. *Bookbinding.* To get (a sewed book) ready for the 'finisher' by putting a plain cover on (see FORWARDING *vbl. sb.* 2).

Hence **'forwarded** *ppl. a.* (in 17th c. occas. †forwardly disposed, eager); **'forwarding** *ppl. a.*

a **1674** CLARENDON *Surv. Leviath.* (1676) 208 None are more glad to see those punishments inflicted, or more forwarded to promote it, then [etc.]. **1691** NORRIS *Pract. Disc.* 315 Enough to ingage us to seek out for the best and most forwarding Assistances. **1776** BARKER in *Phil. Trans.* LXVI. 371 The latter part of that month was warm and forwarding. **1796** C. MARSHALL *Garden.* xv. (1813) 238 When these forwarded beans are planted in rows singly. **1894** MRS. H. WARD *Marcella* III. 96 She had received a forwarded letter from that old friend.

forward: see FOREWARD.

forwardal (fɔːˈwɔːdəl). [f. FORWARD *v.* + -AL.] = FORWARDING *vbl. sb.*

1911 *Supt. Govt. Printing India* Form No. 283 Books, The book..is available, price Rs.— inclusive of forwardal charges.

forwarder ('fɔːwədə(r)), *sb.* [f. FORWARD *v.* + -ER[1].]

1. One who or that which forwards.

1549 COVERDALE, etc. *Erasm. Par. Eph.* Prol., A fyne forewarder of the ghospels lybertie. **1611** COTGR., *Poulseavant*..an overseer, and forwarder of a worke that requires hast. **1611** BARREY *Ram Alley* v. i, Nor am I.. seconder, perswader, forwarder, Principall, or maintainer of this late theft. **1681** CHETHAM *Angler's Vade-m.* xli. §2 (1689) 308 Fresh Water being a great Forwarder of Fishes feeding. **1797** BURKE *Regic. Peace* iii. Wks. 1808 VIII. 274 Contempt of the suppliant is not the best forwarder of a suit. **1840** CARLYLE *Heroes* ii. (1858) 222 Mecca..had at one time a population of 100,000; buyers, forwarders of those Eastern and Western products.

2. *Bookbinding.* (See quot. 1890.)

1870 *Echo* 20 Dec., The men..are divided into two classes, forwarders and finishers. **1875** *Ure's Dict. Arts* I. 424 The ends of the cords are then drawn by the 'forwarder' through holes pierced in the boards. **1890** ZAEHNSDORF *Binding Bk.* 18 *Forwarder*, the workman who takes the books after they are sewn, and advances them to the covering department.

forwarder ('fɔːwədə(r)), *a.* and *adv.* [compar. of FORWARD *a.* and *adv.*] Further forward. Often in jocular colloq. use in the (orig. dial. or vulgar) form **forra(r)der** ('fɒrədə(r)), in the phr. (***to get***) ***no*** or ***any forra(r)der***.

1796 F. BURNEY *Camilla* x. vii, She ventured to bend forwarder, to take a view of the side wings. **1813** JANE AUSTEN *Pride & Prej.* III. xiii, Kitty is forwarder than either of us. **1814** —— *Mansf. Park* I. xviii, Without his being much the forwarder. **1860** H. SPENCER *First Princ.* (1863) ii. 33 And so on in an infinite series, leaving us at last no forwarder than at first. **1888** 'R. BOLDREWOOD' *Robbery under Arms* II. vii. 143 Every week..we found ourselves a lot forrader. **1898** *Daily Tel.* 15 Dec. (Ware), Whether the Liberal Forwards will get any 'forrader' over the light claret [etc.]. **1918** W. OWEN *Let.* 6 Mar. (1967) 537 Am no forrader with my Chest of Drawers. The man won't sell as it is, & says he has no time yet to work on it. **1966** *Times* 10 Oct. 1/2 The case of Gerald Brooke, the British lecturer sentenced in Russia, was discussed but, in the words of a British source, 'We got no forrader.'

'forwarding, *vbl. sb.* [f. FORWARD *v.* + -ING[1].]

1. The action of the vb. FORWARD in various senses. Also gerundially, with omission of *in*.

1635 J. GORE *Well-doing* 17 Like that which Bias calls ἐγκοπὴν προκοπῆν the Backeward forwarding of a cause. **1707** *Curios. in Husb. & Gard.* 268 Horse-dung, and Kennel-Water, contribute..to the forwarding of Plants. **1711** SWIFT *Jrnl. to Stella* 28 Sept., The people in general know that a peace is forwarding. **1817** *Evans' Parl. Debates* 1381 Sir J. Newport urged the immediate forwarding of the measure.

2. *spec.* in *Bookbinding.* The operation of putting a plain cover on a book previously sewn, and otherwise making it fit for the 'finisher's' hands.

1893 E. G. DUFF *Early printed Bks.* 193 Even a study of the forwarding of a binding is of great help. **1895** ZAEHNSDORF *Hist. Book binding* 13 His backs were firm, and his forwarding excellent.

3. *attrib.* as ***forwarding agency***, ***department***, ***establishment***, ***house***, ***mechanism***, ***-room***, ***yard***; **forwarding agent**, **merchant**, one whose business is the receiving and shipment or transmission of goods; **forwarding-note** (see quot.).

1837 W. JENKINS *Ohio Gaz.* 126 It has..ten heavy forwarding houses, connected with lake and canal transportation. **1839** STORY *Bailments* Index, Forwarding merchant. **1847** H. HOWE *Hist. Coll. Ohio* 43 The harbor of Ashtabula..has several forwarding establishments. *Ibid.* 331 Toledo..has..9 forwarding and commission houses. **1869** *Pall Mall G.* 10 Aug. 10 The same building also includes..a telegraph office, and a forwarding department, where remittances are sent from friends of emigrants, and all other miscellaneous letters received and forwarded. **1879** *Cassell's Techn. Educ.* IV. 40 The book now passes from the women to the forwarding room, where several processes occur. **1882** CASSELL, *Forwarding note* (*Comm.*), a note in which is entered a description of goods or parcels, with the names and addresses of the consignor and consignee, to be sent along with goods, &c., conveyed by a carrier (*American*). **1892** E. REEVES *Homewd. Bound* 327 He employed a forwarding agent. **1897** *Outing* (U.S.) XXX. 197/2 The tourist should look after his own mount..and he should not send it by an independent forwarding agency. **1950** *N.Z. Jrnl. Agric.* July 7/3 The receiving yards [for sheep] usually communicate with the forwarding yards or pens. **1968** *Gloss. Terms Offset Lithogr. Printing* (*B.S.I.*) 34 *Forwarding mechanism*, a device on a machine or feeder by which the top sheet is advanced in its normal direction of travel.

forwardly ('fɔːwədlɪ), *adv.* (and *a.*) [f. FORWARD *a.* + -LY.]

A. *adv.*

1. In a forward manner; readily, promptly, eagerly; presumptuously, pertly.

1552 HULOET, Forwardly or towardly, *recte.* **1587** FLEMING *Contn. Holinshed* III. 1579/2 He was not so suddenlie come, as forwardlie welcome. **1651** JER. TAYLOR *Serm. for Year* I. Ep. Ded., You must not admire too forwardly for your own sake. **1690** LOCKE *Hum. Und.* IV. viii. §3, I grant, as forwardly as any one, that they are all true. **1712** STEELE *Spect.* No. 504 ¶5 The fellow..very forwardly, and like a man who was willing to deal, told him [etc.]. **1812** W. GODWIN *Let.* in Hogg *Life Shelley* (1858) II. iii. 86, I shall still acknowledge as forwardly as ever the lovely qualities. **1813** *Examiner* 15 Feb. 103/2 Men being forwardly obedient to all the impulses they receive from themselves.

†**2.** In a forward position, in the fore part. *Obs.*

1578 BANISTER *Hist. Man* I. 24 The Cartilages, which the ribbes forwardly produce, are diuerse. **1646** SIR T. BROWNE *Pseud. Ep.* V. xix. 261 If the horne have this situation, and be so forwardly affixed. **1654** tr. *Scudery's Curia Pol.* 189 When his valour marched so forwardly in the Van.

3. In a forward direction, towards the front. *U.S.*

1876 MRS. WHITNEY *Sights & Ins.* vi. 82 We did not come upon it forwardly..we moved alongside it. **1884** *Harper's Mag.* Jan. 263/1 The..hands were stretched out forwardly, as though feeling the way.

†**4.** Early, prematurely. *Obs.*

a **1641** BP. R. MOUNTAGU *Acts & Mon.* (1642) 546 Mary, Cleophas his daughter, was forwardly married, and a mother before she was 5 yeers old.

†**B.** *adj.* **a.** Eager, ready. **b.** Advanced (in growth or progress). Also, of a season: Early.

1581 MULCASTER *Positions* xxxvii. (1887) 151 Til the childe be either in the grammar schole, by orderly ascent, and not by two forewardly hast. **1598** BARCKLEY *Felic. Man* Ded. (1603) *iv b, It was so forwardly that I could not well hinder the impression. **1647** TRAPP *Comm. Matt.* xviii. 21 Peter is still the same; ever too forwardly and forth-putting. **1670** W. HUGHES *Compl. Vineyard* (1683) 39 Neither ought it to be done, unless it be a forwardly Spring..If your Vines be forwardly, you ought..[to] break off some of the Leaves.

Hence †'**forwardliness**, forward condition.

1647 TRAPP *Comm. Luke* xxi. 38 Let our people look upon their forwardliness. **1667** *Lond. Gaz.* No. 220/2 The two Men of War that were building..are in a good forwardliness.

forwardmost ('fɔːwədməst), *a.*, *superl. rare*$^{-1}$. [f. FORWARD *a.* + -MOST.] Most to the front, foremost; nearest.

1834 M. SCOTT *Cruise Midge* (1863) 24 Making the sweeps ..appear as black as ebony, between us and the flash of the forwardmost gun.

forwardness ('fɔːwədnɪs). [see -NESS.]

1. The state or condition of being forward; advancement towards completion or perfection.

1523 LD. BERNERS *Froiss.* I. xxviii. 41 Whan this croisy was in gret forwardnesse, for there was no spekyng but therof. **1596** DRAYTON *Leg.* I. 677 Whilst in so faire forwardnesse it was. **1661** MARVELL *Corr.* xxiv. Wks. 1872–5 II. 59 That Bill, which is in good forwardnesse to be presented to the House. **1711** *Lond. Gaz.* No. 4836/1 Funds ..which are hitherto in no forwardness of being compleat. **1779** FORREST *Voy. N. Guinea* 298 The arts are in no kind of forwardness here. **1793** SMEATON *Edystone L.* §129 Mr. Jessop had..got other things in forwardness that had been committed to his charge. **1851** HELPS *Comp. Solit.* xii. 242 Till it [a work] is in some state of forwardness.

†**b.** Furtherance, advancement. *Obs.*

1591 *Troub. Raigne K. John* II. (1611) 89 Thus fortune (Lords) acts to your forwardnesse. **1742** RICHARDSON *Pamela* IV. 209 If you should [chuse to be divorced from me], I will give your Wishes all the Forwardness that I honourably can.

2. (Unusual) advancement towards maturity: **a.** of a child; **b.** of a crop, the season, etc.

1693 *Humours & Conv. Town* 21 Parents..bring them to a bold Confidence..and this they miscall Wit, and hopeful forwardness. **1709** STEELE *Tatler* No. 95 ¶4 The Satisfaction the Father took in the Forwardness of his Son. **1789** MRS. PIOZZI *Journ. France* II. 376 The forwardness of the season. *c* **1790** WILLOCK *Voy.* 99 Gardens..all in great forwardness. *a* **1864** HAWTHORNE *Amer. Note-bks.* (1879) II. 139 Our peas are in such forwardness.

3. The quality of being forward; readiness, promptness, eagerness, zeal. †Also, proneness or inclination *to*.

1526 *Pilgr. Perf.* (W. de W. 1531) 69 In my body and flesshe I fynde no good, ne forwardnes to perfeccyon. **1555** EDEN *Decades* 58 A man of..apt forwardenes to attempte thynges. **1611** BIBLE *2 Cor.* ix. 2, I know the forwardnesse of your mind. **1631** GOUGE *God's Arrows* I. xlii. 68 Not by reason of any forwardnesse in him to anger. **1696** SOUTHERNE *Oroonoko* IV. ii, I speak..in my desire And forwardness to serve so great a man. **1817–18** COBBETT *Resid. U.S.* (1822) 84, I have observed in the American farmers..not the least backwardness, but great forwardness, to applaud and admire my mode of cultivating these crops. **1852** GROTE *Greece* II. lxxx. X. 480 The extreme forwardness with which these leaders exposed themselves. **1875** JOWETT *Plato* (ed. 2) III. 217 Forwardness to take office.

4. Over-readiness, presumptuous self-confidence; hence, lack of becoming modesty, boldness.

1600 SHAKS. *A.Y.L.* I. ii. 159 Since the youth will not be intreated His owne perill on his forwardnesse. **1612** WOODALL *Surg. Mate* Wks. (1653) 162 There is a fault in young Surgeons of forwardnesse in taking too much blood at Sea. **1677** *Govt. Venice* 145 It is indecency and too much forwardness in young Men to enquire into the Institution of their Laws, and demand Reasons for them. **1705** ADDISON *Italy* 45 In France it is usual to bring their Children into Company, and to cherish in 'em, from their Infancy, a kind of Forwardness and Assurance. **1827** LYTTON *Pelham* xii, Nobody will call your civility forwardness and pushing. **1875** MRS. RANDOLPH *W. Hyacinth* I. 129 She snubs him in the..most remorseless manner..His forwardness is quite amazing.

forwards ('fɔːwədz), *adv.* (and *a.*) [f. FORWARD with advb. genitive *-s*: see -WARDS.]

A. *adv.* = FORWARD *adv.* in its various senses.

The present distinction in usage between *forward* and *forwards* is that the latter expresses a definite direction viewed in contrast with other directions. In some contexts either form may be used without perceptible difference of meaning; the following are examples in which only one of them can now be used: 'The ratchet-wheel can move only *forwards*'; 'the right side of the paper has the maker's name reading *forwards*'; 'if you move at all it must be *forwards*'; 'my companion has gone *forward*'; 'to bring a matter *forward*'; 'from this time *forward*'. The usage of earlier periods, and of modern dialects, varies greatly from that of mod. standard English. In U.S. *forward* is now generally used, to the exclusion of *forwards*, which was stigmatized by Webster (1832) as 'a corruption'.

c **1400** MAUNDEV. (1839) v. 61 Fro this forewardes nevere entred such Filthe. **1470–85** MALORY *Arthur* I. vii, And sire Brastias was maade wardeyn to wayte vpon the northe fro Trent forwardes. **1489** CAXTON *Faytes of A.* I. ix. 24 To marche forwardis a quantite of paaces. **1551** T. WILSON *Logike* (1580) 10 Thei will..with good endevour fillip Nature forewardes. **1560–78** *Bk. Discipl. Ch. Scot.* (1621) 47 We leave it..to be weighed by your honours wisdome, and set forwards by your authority. **1691** T. H[ALE] *Acc. New Invent.* 122 An..unlevel keel drooping forwards. **1703** MOXON *Mech. Exerc.* 17 The Teeth of the File are made to cut forwards..for it cuts not coming back. **1785** PALEY *Mor. Philos.* (1818) II. 283 When..we carry forwards our views. **1809** PINKNEY *Trav. France* 57 If he can come forwards, and prove..that he has merely been absent. **1844** DICKENS *Mart. Chuz.* xxxiii, He was backwards and forwards constantly. **1885** *Manch. Exam.* 16 May 5/1 Police-men.. have to carry him backwards and forwards between the police station and the workhouse.

†**B.** *adj.* = FORWARD *a.* *Obs. rare.*

1598 GRENEWEY *Tacitus' Ann.* III. x. (1622) 78 A valiant warriour, and forwards in all his charges. **1625** BACON *Ess.*, *Travaile* (Arb.) 524 Let him be rather aduised in his Answers, then forwards to tell Stories. **1626** —— *Sylva* §422 Quere, if laying of Straw some height about the Body of a Tree, will not make the Tree forwards.

forward scattering. **a.** *Physics.* Scattering in which the direction of the scattered radiation or particles makes an angle of less than ninety degrees with the original direction. **b.** *Telecommunications.* Scattering or reflection of high-frequency radio waves by irregularities in the troposphere or ionosphere so that some of their energy returns to earth beyond the horizon of the point of transmission. Hence (as a back-formation) **forward-scatter** *v. trans.*; also **forward-scattered** *ppl. a.*

1950 *Proc. IRE* XXXVIII. 406/1 This formula for forward scattering applies no matter what may be the relation of the scale of turbulence to the wavelength. **1952** *Physical Rev.* LXXXVI. 1 (*heading*) Forward scattering of light by a Coulomb field. **1953** *Jrnl. Geophysical Res.* LVIII. 90 The amplitude of the forward-scattered signal exceeds that of an equivalent back-scattered signal. **1954** *Proc. IRE* XLII. 530/1 Echoes forward-scattered from individual meteor ionization trails. **1967** RODBERG & THALER *Introd. Quantum Theory of Scattering* xii. 370 For a large target of uniform particle density..only forward scattering will occur. **1968** W. G. BURROWS *V.H.F. Radio Wave Propag.* 6 The propagation of a VHF wave beyond the radio horizon by forward scattering.

So **forward(-)scatter** *sb.*, (*a*) forward scattering (sense b); (*b*) radio waves that have returned to earth after being scattered in this way. Also *attrib.*

1954 *Canad. Jrnl. Physics* XXXII. 450 Reflections from meteoric trails can support, intermittently, high frequency radio transmissions well beyond the line-of-sight... The Stamford workers have developed a theory of this forward-scatter transmission. **1956** *Ann. Reg. 1955* 409 Waves reflected from the E-layer..and sent on by 'forward scatter'. **1958** *Times* 30 Apr. 6/6 Experiments are to be carried out in Britain to ascertain whether television pictures can be transmitted by the 'forward scatter' technique over distances of 200 miles or more. **1960** *Gloss. Terms Telecomm.* (*B.S.I.*) 168 A signal received by forward scattering is often referred to as forward scatter.

†**for'warn, fore'warn,** *v. Obs.* [OE. *forwiernan*, f. FOR- *pref.*^{1} + *wiernan* to forbid: see WARN *v.*^{2}] *trans.* To prohibit, forbid. With double *obj.*, or *obj.* of the person and *to* with *inf.* or *from*.

Beowulf (Gr.) 429 þæt þu me ne forwyrne..þæt ic mote [etc.]. *c* **893** K. ÆLFRED *Oros.* II. iv. (Sweet) 76 Him þær se ȝiunga cyning þæs oferfæreldes forwiernan mehte. *a* **1175** *Cott. Hom.* 221 Hwi wolde god swa litles þinges him forwerne. *c* **1205** LAY. 3497 Nule heo me do na wurse þanne hire lond forwurnen. *c* **1380** *Sir Ferumb.* 2809 þus damesels for-werneþ al, þat me greueþ werst. **1583** GOLDING *Calvin on Deut.* xxvii. 163 He forewarneth vs here to make any vndergods or meane gods. **1606** HOLLAND *Sueton.* 67 He prohibited and forewarned them the companie of strangers. **1690** SHADWELL *Am. Bigot* III, This wicked Duenna..has forwarn'd her the house. **1708** S. SEWALL *Diary* 8 Sept. (1879) II. 236, I meet the Workman by Mr. Pemberton's Gate, and forewarn him from making of it. **1820** LAMB *Elia* Ser. I. *Christ's Hosp. 35 years ago*, He did not know that the thing had been forewarned.

†**for-'wary,** *v. Obs.* [f. FOR- *pref.*^{1} + OE. *werȝan*, WARY *v.* to curse; cf. OHG. *furwergen*.] *trans.* To curse. Hence **for'waried** *ppl. a.*

c **1200** ORMIN 8048 þatt tatt man iss forrwarrȝedd þatt [etc.]. *c* **1340** *Cursor M.* 1350 (Trin.) Abelle þat kaym slouȝe for-waryed wiȝt.

†**for'waste,** *v. Obs.* Also 6–7 forewaste. Pa. pple. 6 forwaste. [f. FOR- *pref.*^{1} + WASTE *v.*] *trans.* = WASTE *v.* in various senses; to lay waste; to use up, exhaust; to render emaciated or feeble; to spend wastefully.

1563 SACKVILLE *Induct. Mirr. Mag.* xi, A piteous wight, whom love had al forwaste. *a* **1577** GASCOIGNE *Flowers, Jocasta* Wks. (1587) 91 Then set aside these vaine forewasted words. **1580** SIDNEY *Arcadia* (1622) 365 The rest both in face and apparell so forewasted, that they seemed to beare a great conformitie with the sauages. **1590** SPENSER *F.Q.* I. xi. 1 And their forwasted kingdom to repayre. **1630** LORD *Banians & Persees* 31 To make their forewasted powers..to renew their vigour.

forwatched: see FOR- *pref.*^{1} 6 b.

†**for'wax,** *v. Obs.* [OE. *forweaxan*, f. FOR- *pref.*^{1} + *weaxan*, WAX *v.* Cf. Ger. *verwachsen*.] *intr.* To grow to excess, overgrow, swell. Hence **for'waxen** *ppl. a.*

c **897** K. ÆLFRED *Gregory's Past.* xl. (1872) 292 Sumu [treowu] he cearf..ðylæs hie to ðæm forweoxen ðæt hie forsearoden. *c* **1000** *Sax. Leechd.* I. 80 Wið þon þe man on wambe forweaxen sy. *c* **1475** *Partenay* 2990 Horrible gret was, a forwoxen grome, Such another neuer had he sain.

forwe, obs. form of FURROW.

†**for'wean,** *v. Obs.* [OE. **forwęnian*; only in pa. pple. *forwęned*, 'insolens' Corpus Gloss.; cf. Ger. *verwöhnen*.] *trans.* To accustom to bad habits, spoil by over-indulgence, pamper.

1362 LANGL. *P. Pl.* A. v. 33 *v.rr.* Let no wynnyng forwanye hem, let no welthe for-wany hem. **1399** —— *Rich. Redeles* I. 27 [They] walwed in her willis fforweyned in here youthe.

†**for'wear,** *v. Obs.* [f. FOR- *pref.*^{1} + WEAR *v.*] *trans.* To wear out, wear away, exhaust.

c **1205** LAY. 14479 þenne mihte þu mid winne þi lif al uorwerien mid haueken & mid hunden hired-plæie luuien. *a* **1240** *Sawles Warde* in *Cott. Hom.* 251 þah ich hefde a þusent tungen of stele and talde aðet ha weren alle forwerede. *c* **1394** *P. Pl. Crede* 736 Wiþ cloutede schon & cloþes ful feble Wel neiȝ for-werd. **1398** TREVISA *Barth. De P.R.* XIV. ii. (Tollem. MS.), Meuynge of watres, þat diggeþ and forwereþ [**1535** wereth] þe nesche parties of þe erþe. **1413** *Pilgr. Sowle* (Caxton) I. xix. (1859) 19 Teethe had he none, but they were al forbroke, forweryd, and forfaren. *a* **1577** GASCOIGNE *Flowers, Jocasta* Wks. (1587) 104 You a weake old woman forworne with yeares.

Hence **for'wearing** *vbl. sb.*

1609 R. BARNERD *Faithf. Sheph.* 85 Some in meditating doe vse to speake and gesture; but this a forewearing of the spirits, and too Histrionian like.

forweary *a. Obs.*: see FOR- *pref.*^{1} 10.

forweary (fə'wɪərɪ), *v. Obs.* or *arch.* Also 6–9 fore-. [f. FOR- *pref.*^{1} + WEARY *v.*] *trans.* To weary, tire out.

¶ An intr. sense, 'to become wearied' is given in the *Cent. Dict.* with reference to Palsgr., but he has only the trans. sense. Many of the examples of the pa. pple. might admit of being referred to the intrans. use.

c **1250** *Gen. & Ex.* 3894 Forð ðeðen he comen to salmona, for-weried grucheden he ðoa. **1494** FABYAN *Chron.* VII. 239 Nowe shaketh my hande, my pen waxeth dulle, For weryd and tyred. **1587** FLEMING *Contn. Holinshed* III. 1320/2 The foure foster children of desire entered in a braue chariot..as men forewearied and halfe ouercome. **1603** KNOLLES *Hist. Turks* (1621) 8 The Christians forewearied with long travel, were not able farre to follow the Chace. **1819** W. TENNANT *Papistry Storm'd* (1827) 112 Hawkey..Within the byre forwearyt stood. **1832** MOTHERWELL *Tim the Tacket* 10 A spectre-ship, Forwearied of the storm and ocean. **1867** MORRIS *Jason* I. 389 A pleasant bed For tired limbs..Of sandalled nymph, forewearied with the chase.

Hence **forwearied** *ppl. a.*; **forwearying** *vbl. sb.*

1562 LEIGH *Armorie* (1597) 126 b, As forwearied souldiers. **1571** GOLDING *Calvin on Ps.* xvii. 15 After long forweryïng, he lay as it were in a slomber. **1592** NASHE *P. Penilesse* Wks. (Grosart) II. 134 The verie thought..woulde haue inspired thy forewearied Muse with new furie. **1855** SINGLETON *Virgil* I. 210 His forwearied limbs.

†**for'weep,** *v. Obs.* Pa. pple. forwepe, -weped, -wept(e. [f. FOR- *pref.*^{1} + WEEP.] *intr.* **a.** To exhaust oneself with weeping. **b.** Of a vine: To bleed excessively.

c **1350** *Will. Palerne* 2868 þe quen was wery for-wept & went to bedde. *c* **1420** *Pallad. on Husb.* III. 1149 Vines that forwepe & turne away ffrom fruit. **1423** JAS. I. *Kingis Q.* lxxiii, For-wepit and for-pleynit pitously. *a* **1500** *Chaucer's Dreme* Wks. (1687) 606/2 With visage and ein all forwept, And pale, as man longe vnslept.

†**for'wel(e)we**, *v. Obs.* [ME., f. FOR- *pref.*¹ + *welewe*, ? related to WELK *v.*] *intr.* To wither, decay, dry up. Only in *pa. pple.*

a **1300** *Leg. Rood* (1871) 22 Þe stapes he [Seth] vond uorwelwed. *c* **1300** *Life Jesus* (Horstm.) 846 Þe figer felde a non is lef.. And fur weolewede as a stok. *c* **1340** *Cursor M.* 1255 (Trin.) In þat weye shal þou.. se þe steppes of þi moder & me For welewed in þat gres grene.

†**for'welk**, *v. Obs.* [f. FOR- *pref.*¹ + WELK *v.*] *trans.* To wither. Hence **for'welked** *ppl. a.*

?*a* **1366** CHAUCER *Rom. Rose* 361 A foul forwelked thing was she. **1593** NASHE *Christ's T.* 73 b, They weare away with continuance, euen as Time doth weare and fore-welke [**1612** fore-walke] vs. **1616** BULLOKAR, *Forewelked*, dried vp.

†**for'wend**, *v. Obs.* [f. FOR- *pref.*¹ + WEND. Cf. MLG. *vorwenden*, MHG. *verwenden.*] *trans.* To turn *into* (something); to turn, incline, dispose.

c **1250** *Gen. & Ex.* 1121 So ist nu forwent mirie dale In to dririhed. *c* **1340** *Cursor M.* 24728 (Fairf.) We prai þat lauedi be for-wende þat we mai finde hir sone our frende.

†**for'werpe, forworpe**, *v. Obs.* [OE. *forweorpan*, f. FOR- *pref.*¹ + *weorpan*, WARP *v.*, to throw.] *trans.* To cast away, cast off, reject.

Beowulf (Gr.) 2872 Mæg secȝan, se þe wyle soð sprecan .. þæt he.. ȝuðȝewædu.. forwurpe. *c* **1175** *Lamb. Hom.* 105 God nele þet we beon gredie ȝitseras, ne ec for weorld ȝelpe forworpan ure ehtan. *c* **1220** *Bestiary* 345 Forwerpen pride euril[c] del, so hert doð his hornes. *a* **1225** *Ancr. R.* 150 Al so god dede þet wule adeaden forworpeð hire rinde, þet is, unheleð hire. *a* **1300** *E.E. Psalter* l. 12 [li. 11] Ne for-werpe me fra face of þe.

†**for'while.** *Obs. rare*⁻¹. Something that lasts only 'for a while'.

c **1550** CHEKE *Matt.* xiii. 21 He.. hath noo root in himself, and y^eerfoor is but a forwhile.

†**for'whore**, *v. Obs.* [f. FOR- *pref.*¹ + WHORE *sb.*] *trans.* To lead into unchastity; to debauch, defile. Also *refl.* and *fig.*

c **1200** ORMIN 2043 Ȝho forrhoredd wass þurrh ful forrleȝerrnesse. *a* **1225** *Ancr. R.* 394 Heo muhte uorhoren hire mid oðer men. *Ibid.* Ne beo neuer his leofmon uorhored mid so monie deðliche sunnen. *c* **1315** SHOREHAM 59 The gode for-horede the fend Wyth hys blaundynge stevene.

Hence **for'whored** *ppl. a.*

c **1200** *Trin. Coll. Hom.* 81 Iuelmennish and forhored mannish [*generacio mala et adultera*] acseð after fortocne.

†**for'why**, *adv.* and *conj. Obs.* Forms: 1 for-hwí, -hwý, 2–4 -hwi (3 -we, -wi), 3–5 -qui, -quy, 3–6 -whi, 4– -why. [OE. *for-hwí*, f. FOR *prep.* + *hwí*, WHY *adv.* I ¶, instr. of *hwæt*, neut. of *hwá* who?]

A. *adv.*

1. As *direct interrog.* For what reason? Why?

c **1000** *Ags. Ps.* cxiii. 5 Þu, Iordanen, for hwi ȝengdest on bæcling? *c* **1175** *Lamb. Hom.* 153 Ach for-hwi nemneð ure drihten þis fa to neddre. *c* **1200** ORMIN 12690 Forrwhi wass þatt tatt Sannt Iohan amang þe leode seȝȝde off Crist, tatt [etc.]. *a* **1300** *Cursor M.* 11157 Ioseph, dauid sun, for-qui [*c* **1340** (Fairf.) for-why] Wil þou leue þi spuse mari? *c* **1475** *Partenay* 3464 Alas! this for-whi hast thou me in hate?

b. *ellipt.* and quasi-*int.* Cf. the use of WHY?

In many early examples the interpretation 'because' (see B.) would be equally suitable, the punctuation being merely due to the editors.

c **1200** *Trin. Coll. Hom.* 7 Ure helendes on tocume þincð .. grisliche alle manne. Forwi! for þat [etc.]. **1513** BRADSHAW *St. Werburge* II. 1019 The horses had no power any part to take: For why? by myracle theyr heedes all.. Were vp holden in the ayre. **1561** KETHE *Ps.* c. 4 '*All people that on earth do dwell*', For why? The Lord our God is good. **1601** in Farr *S.P. Eliz.* (1845) II. 425 For why? temptations doe approach vs fast.

2. As indirect *interrog.* For what reason, why.

c **1175** *Lamb. Hom.* 81 Her me ah to understonden for-whi hit seið alf quic. *a* **1225** *Leg. Kath.* 507 Schaw sumwhet of ham, for hwi ha beon wurðe for to beon iwurðȝet. *c* **1320** *Cast. Love* 115 The reson is good and feir for-whi. *c* **1384** CHAUCER *H. Fame* I. 20 To knowe.. the causis Ffor-why this is more then that cause is. *a* **1400–50** *Alexander* 4325 And I sall quethe þe forqui & quat is þe cause.

ellipt. **1710** SWIFT *Jrnl. to Stella* 23 Dec., I will tell you no more at present, guess for why.

3. With connective force: On account of which, for which cause; wherefore.

c **1275** *Death* 31 in *O.E. Misc.* 170 Ah seoððen moni mon biȝet bores and halle For-hwi þam þe wrecche sawle schal in-to pine ualle. **1340** HAMPOLE *Pr. Consc.* 2478 Alle our syns þat may be knawen, Commes of our-selven.. For-why, withouten God we syn sone. *a* **1400–50** *Alexander* 4584 Ȝe say ȝe sawe neuire soile, ne na citis biggis.. For-quy as bestis on þe bent ȝe growe on þe greuys. *c* **1430** *Pilgr. Lyf Manhode* I. xli. (1869) 59 The doublet is maad with poynynges, For whi it is cleped a pourpoynt. **1502** ARNOLDE *Chron.* (1811) 18 For why we wyl and stedfastly commaunde that [etc.].

B. *conj.* **1.** Because; = FOR *conj.* I.

a **1300** *Cursor M.* 6975 (Gött.) For-qui þai held þair lay lastand, Was na folk þaim miht wid-stand. *c* **1384** CHAUCER *H. Fame* II. 45 And al my felynge gan to dede For whi hit was to grete affray. **14..** *Lanfranc's Chirurg.* 214 For-micam þou schalt brenne, fforwhi a cauterie drawiþ out al þe matere þat is corrupt. *c* **1489** CAXTON *Sonnes of Aymon* ix. 202 But no man that hath ony rayson in his hede ought not to counseyll you the same for whi the daunger is there grete. **1584** R. SCOT *Discov. Witchcr.* x. ii. 144 Regard no dreames, for why the mind Of that in Sleepe a view doth take, Which [etc.]. **1674** N. FAIRFAX *Bulk & Selv.* 188 The Argument.. will ever fall short upon this score: For why, there is not a full reckoning up of those attributes of his [God's] that have to do in the work. **1883** E. A. FREEMAN *MS. letter*, It will be pleasant if you go to the Old Borough.. Forwhy in that case you will certainly come on hither.

b. *for why that*: (*a*) = sense 1; (*b*) on the consideration that; provided that.

a **1300** *Cursor M.* 3500 Þe fader luued esau for fode, For-qui þat he was archer gode. *a* **1450** *Le Morte Arth.* 389 (Roxb.) Thou shalt haue yiftis good, For why þat thou wilte dwelle wyth me.

2. = FOR *conj.* 2 (= L. *nam, enim*).

a **1300** *Cursor M.* 15242 Drinckes all o þis he said For-qui it es mi blod. **1388** WYCLIF *Gen.* iii. 5 For whi [Vulg. *enim*] God woot that, in what euere dai ȝe schulen ete therof [etc.]. *c* **1449** PECOCK *Repr.* IV. iv. 445 Forwhi whi schulde he thanne more correcte.. than be correctid. **1460–70** *Bk. Quintessence* (1866) 18 Saturne þe planete.. is enemye to al kynde. For why, euery snow [etc.] comeþ of him. **1513** BRADSHAW *St. Werburge* I. 2607 Her merytes were.. manyfest and playne For why by her merytes.. Sygnes and myracles were shewed full playne. **1603** KNOLLES *Hist. Turks* 618 A camell might well carrie one of them [fieldpieces].. for why, Solyman.. had.. brought no greater pieces of batterie with him.

forwintered: see FOR- *pref.*¹ 5 c.

†**forwith**, *adv.* and *prep. Obs.* See also FOROUTH, FORROW. [f. FOR *adv.* or FOR- *pref.*² + WITH.] = BEFORE *adv.* and *prep.* (used of place, time, order, etc.).

a **1300** *Cursor M.* 215 Drery days fiuten.. sal cum for-wit domesday. *Ibid.* 1068 (Gött.), Þis caym þat i forwid melte vnto his broþer ire he bare. *Ibid.* 11006 He þat suld cum help vr hele Sent him forwit his bedele. *Ibid.* 11007 For-þi sent iesus iohn forwith, Ar he himself til vs wald kyth. *Ibid.* 11499 Melchior.. Wit recles forwit him he fell. *a* **1400–50** *Alexander* 15, I forwith ȝow alle ettillis to schewe Of ane Emperoure. *Ibid.* 1675 As our fadirs has folowid forwith þis time. *Ibid.* 2242 Quare-to feynys þou þis fare for-with myne eȝen?

b. With *ere, than.*

a **1300** *Cursor M.* 10904 Als neuer did womman forwit ar. *Ibid.* 10953 He praid in þe kyrk allan, Als he forwit þan was wont. *Ibid.* 14423 Als i haf teld you forwit are.

¶ = FORTHWITH. ? = Immediately, at once.

c **1430** *Two Cookery-bks.* I. 41, & put raw ȝolkys of Eyroun ij or iij þer-to, & choppe for-with. **1609** BIBLE (Douay) *Josh.* ii. 7 They being gone out the gate forwith was shutte.

forwithered: see FOR- *pref.*¹ 5.

†**for'witting**, *sb. Obs.* [f. FOR- *pref.*¹ + WITE *v.* + -ING¹; after Du. *verwijten.*] Reproach.

1481 CAXTON *Reynard* (Arb.) 91 Parauenture ye remembred not that I shal now saye, not to ony forwyttyng of yow, for ye be worthy alle worship.

†**for'wlench**, *v. Obs.* [OE. *forwlęncean*, f. FOR- *pref.*¹ + *wlęncean* to make proud, f. *wlanc* proud.] *trans.* To render proud.

c **897** K. ÆLFRED *Gregory's Past.* xxvi. (1871) 182 Ðonne hiene ne maȝon ða welan forwlencean. *a* **1310** *Lyric P.* (Böddeker) 183 When we beþ wiþ þis world forwleynt.

†**for'wonder**, *v. Obs.* [f. FOR- *pref.*¹ + WONDER; cf. Ger. *verwundern* to be astonished at.] Only in pa. pple.: Astonished.

c **1200** ORMIN 3417 Iwhillc mann þatt herrde itt ohht Forwunndred wass þæroffe. *a* **1300** *Cursor M.* 18163 Þai war for-wondred o þat light. **1375** BARBOUR *Bruce* VI. 10 Till him tald all haill the cass, That tharof all forvounderit wass.

for'worden, *ppl. a. Obs.* exc. *dial.* Also *irreg.* 3 *Orm.* **forwurrþenn(-like), forworthyn**, 9 *dial.* **forwoden.** [OE. *forworden*, pa. pple. of *forweorðan*: see FORWORTH *v.*] Perished, gone to ruin. Hence (*Orm.*) **forwurþenlike** *adv.*, corruptly, perversely.

c **1200** ORMIN 6245 Þeȝȝ wirrkenn ȝunnkerr weorrc Forrwurrþennlike & ille. *c* **1440** *Jacob's Well* (E.E.T.S.) 106 Þou faryst as a forworthyn man, þat had leuere to lyen & rottyn in prisoun, þan to do penaunce. **1508** DUNBAR *Flyting w. Kennedie* 105 Forworthin fule, of all the warld reffuse. **1513** DOUGLAS *Æneis* VIII. iv. 21 A grysly den and ane forworthyne gap of Cacus. **1691** RAY *N.C. Words* 27 Forewordén with Lice, Dirt etc., i.e. over-run with. **1847** HALLIW. *Fore-warden*, destroyed, undone. *North.* **1855** ROBINSON *Whitby Gloss.*, They are lost and forwoden i' muck.

†**for'work**, *v. Obs.* [OE. *forwyrcan*, f. FOR- *pref.*¹ + *wyrcan* to WORK; cf. OS. *farwirkian*, OHG. *firwirken* (MHG., mod.Ger. *verwirken*), Goth. *frawaurkjan.*]

1. *trans.* To forfeit (a possession, privilege, etc.), ruin (oneself) by one's own conduct.

a **1000** *Crist* 921 (Gr.) He bið.. eȝeslic.. to ȝeseonne .. þam þær mid firenum cumað forð forworhte. *a* **1175** *Cott. Hom.* 221 Þæt wuniunge on hefen rice, þe se deofel forwo[r]hte mid modinesse. *c* **1200** ORMIN 13734 Forr affterr þat ta forrme menn Adam & Eve.. Forrwrohhte wærenn ȝæness Godd. *Ibid.* 17534 Hu wærenn þeȝȝ forrwrohhte To dreȝhenn wa wiþþ mikell rihht Inn helle wiþþ þe defell? **1481** CAXTON *Reynard* (Arb.) 52 Have I forwrought, and angred my frendes.

2. To do wrong to, injure.

c **1205** LAY. 16694 Þat þu hauest þas hæȝe burh swa swiðe for-worht.

3. To overwork, exhaust with toil. Only in pa. pple. **for'wrought.**

13.. *E.E. Allit. P.* C. 163 Þen þo wery for-wroȝt wyst no bote. *c* **1400** *Destr. Troy* 5861 He was very [= wery] forwroght, & woundet full sore. *c* **1500** *Lancelot* 888 So forwrocht hys lymmys ver ilkon. **1535** STEWART *Cron. Scot.* III. 44 Werie forwrocht, and richt weilsum of wane.

forworn (fəˈwɔːn), *ppl. a. arch.* [mod.Eng. (strong) pa. pple. of FORWEAR *v.*] Worn out, exhausted, decayed, grown old, the worse for wear.

1508 FISHER 7 *Penit. Ps.* li. Wks. (1876) 117 To botche or mende an olde forworen thynge. **1570** DEE *Math. Pref.* A iij b, They, who haue.. requested me, (an old forworne Mathematicien) to take pen in hand. **1590** SPENSER *F.Q.* I. vi. 35 A silly man, in simple weedes forworne, And soild with dust. **1625** *Gonsalvio's Sp. Inquis.* 64 He was an old forworne soldiour. **1631** WEEVER *Anc. Fun. Mon.* 545 Old, wearied, and for-worne Hackneyes. **1849** J. A. CARLYLE tr. *Dante's Inferno* 32 Those spirits who were foreworn and naked, changed colour. **1870** MORRIS *Earthly Par.* III. IV. 410 Slowly he went, for afternoon it was, And with the long way was he much foreworn.

forworship: see FOR- *pref.*¹ 4.

†**for'worth**, *v. Obs.* [OE. *forweorðan* str. vb., f. FOR- *pref.*¹ + *weorðan* to become (see WORTH *v.*); cf. OHG. *farwerdan.*

In early northern ME. occasionally conjugated weak.]

1. *intr.* To perish, come to nought, go wrong.

c **1000** *Ags. Gosp.* Matt. xxvi. 52 Mid swurde hiȝ forwurþað. *c* **1175** *Lamb. Hom.* 109 Þurh his ahȝene ehte forwurð a on echnesse. *c* **1200** *Trin. Coll. Hom.* 155 Sum [sed] ful among þornes, and forwarð. *c* **1220** *Bestiary* 175 If ðu hauest is broken Al ðu forbreðes, forwurðes and forȝelues. *a* **1300** *E.E. Psalter* lxxxii. 9 [lxxxiii. 10] Þai forworthed in Endor. **1340** HAMPOLE *Pr. Consc.* 780 His werkes for-worthes þat he bygynnes.

2. To degenerate into, become (something inferior).

a **1225** *Ancr. R.* 370 Þeo þet schulden one lecnen hore soule.. uorwurðeð fisiciens & licomes leche. *Ibid.* 422 Ancre ne schal nout forwurðen scolmeistre.

†**for'wound**, *v. Obs.* [OE. *forwundian*, f. FOR- *pref.*¹ + *wundian*, WOUND *v.*] *trans.* To wound sorely. Hence **for'wounded** *ppl. a.*

O.E. Chron. an. 882, & þa wæron miclum forslæȝene & for wundode ær hie on hond eodon. *c* **1175** *Lamb. Hom.* 81 He com bi þis forwundede mon. *c* **1205** LAY. 14713 Hors forð riht þer for-wundede Catiger. **1297** R. GLOUC. (Rolls) 1287 Þat folc vel doun vorwounded & aslawe in eiþer side. *c* **1350** *Will. Palerne* 3686 Ȝour mene.. þat feynt ar for-fouten in feld & for-wounded. *c* **1400** *Rom. Rose* 1830 Upon my feet I roos up than Feble, as a forwoundid man. **1496** *Dives & Paup.* (W. de W.) VI. xv. 258/2 He was so forwounded that by waye of manhode.. nedely he muste dye.

†**for'wrap**, *v. Obs.* Also 6 fore-. [f. FOR- *pref.*¹ + WRAP *v.*] *trans.* To wrap up. Also *fig.*

c **1386** CHAUCER *Pard. T.* 390 Why artow al for-wrapped save thi face? —— *Pars. T.* ¶ 246 Al moot be seyd, and no thyng excused, ne forwrapped. **1571** FORTESCUE tr. *Mexia's Forest* 43 a, Whereunto he [Tamburlayne] answeared forewrapped in coller, Supposest thou [etc.].

†**for'wray**, *v. Obs.* [OE. *forwréȝan*, f. FOR- *pref.*¹ + *wréȝan* to accuse: see BEWRAY.] *trans.* To accuse, betray, charge with a crime.

O.E. Chron. an. 1009, Brihtric.. forwreȝde Wulfnoð.. to þam cyning. *a* **1200** *Moral Ode* 97 Þer sculle ben deofles swo fele þe wulleð us forwreien. *a* **1225** *Juliana* 46 Oðer ichulle forwreien to mi meinfule feder. **1303** R. BRUNNE *Handl. Synne* 11448 Þe synne hymself shal forwreye.

†**for'wrecche**, *v. Obs.*⁻¹ [f. FOR- *pref.*¹ + OE. *węccan* to rouse.] *trans.* To rouse to wrath.

c **1440** *Jacob's Well* (E.E.T.S.) 36, I.. sorwe more, þat I haue forwrecchyd my god, þan I drede.. to gon to helle.

forwrinked, -writhen: see FOR- *pref.*¹ 8.

†**for'wrought**, *ppl. a. Obs.* [See FORWORK *v.*] Destroyed, ruined, accursed. In quot. *absol.*

c **1250** *Gen. & Ex.* 266 Quan al man-kinde.. Sal ben fro dede to liue broȝt, And seli sad fro ðe forwroȝt.

†**fo'ryellow**, *v. Obs. rare.* [f. FOR- *pref.*¹ + YELLOW.] *intr.* To turn yellow, fade.

c **1220** [see FORWORTH *v.*].

†**for'yeme**, *v. Obs.* [OE. *forȝéman, forȝýman*, f. FOR- *pref.*¹ + *ȝieman, ȝýman*, YEME *v.*, to take care.] *trans.* To disregard, neglect.

Beowulf (Gr.) 1751 He þa forðȝesceaft forȝyteð and forȝymeð. *c* **1175** *Lamb. Hom.* 13 Gif ȝe.. mine heste forȝemeð. *c* **1200** ORMIN 7502 Þurrh þatt teȝȝ Godess bodeword Forr-letenn & forrȝemmdenn. *a* **1250** *Prov. Ælfred* 207 in *O.E. Misc.* 114 Monymon.. for his seoluer hym seolue for-ȝemeþ. *c* **1320** *Cast. Love* 947, I seo þe mislyken and al for-ȝemed, And out of þin owne lond i-flemed. *c* **1440** *Ps. Penit.* (1894) 26 For me that hath thi feyth foryemed.

†**for'yield**, *v. Obs.* [f. FOR- *pref.*¹ + YIELD *v.*; = OHG. *fargeltan* (mod.Ger. *vergelten*).]

1. *trans.* To repay, recompense, requite. With personal obj. in *dative*, and direct obj. of the thing. Also *intr.* (const. *of*). Phr. ***God**, etc. **foryield*** (it).

971 *Blickl. Hom.* 45 Þa wæs him forȝolden æfter his aȝenum ȝewyrhtum. *c* **1175** *Lamb. Hom.* 65 For godes luue forȝeue we al, for he hit wel forȝelden scal. *c* **1205** LAY. 2298 An þu mi muchele swinc mid sare forȝeldest. *a* **1300** *Cursor M.* 4883 Sir, godd þe for-yeild.. Of al þi god, and haue god day. **1362** LANGL. *P. Pl.* A. VII. 263 Þis is a loueli lesson vr lord hit þe for-ȝelde! *c* **1460** *Towneley Myst.* (Surtees) 102 And men say lyght chepe Letherly for-yeldys. **1560** ROLLAND *Crt. Venus* II. 560 God ȝow forȝeild.

2. To afford, permit.

c **1420** *Pallad. on Husb.* I. 311 Thyn hous.. to repare as may thi londe foryelde.

Hence **for'yielding** *vbl. sb.*, the action of the vb., an instance of this; retribution, a reward.
a **1300** *E.E. Psalter* cii[i]. 2 And nil forgete alle his for-yheldinges.

forytt, obs. f. FERRET *sb.*[1]

‖**forzando** (fɔr'tsando), *adv. Mus.* [It. gerund of *forzare* to force.] With force: an indication that a note or passage is to be rendered with force or emphasis; = SFORZANDO.
1828 in BUSBY *Mus. Man.* **1876** in STAINER & BARRETT.

Fosbury ('fɒzbərɪ). The name of Richard ('Dick') *Fosbury* (b. 1947), U.S. athlete and 1968 Olympic gold-medallist, used *attrib.*, esp. as ***Fosbury flop***, to designate a method of high jumping popularized by him, in which the athlete leaps head-first and facing outwards, attempting to clear the bar under his (or her) back; hence ***Fosbury-flop*** vb. intr.
1968 *Listener* 24 Oct. 560/2 It is very seldom that a new technique makes such an impact as did the high-jumping of Dick Fosbury in winning the Olympic title. With his incredible 'Fosbury Flop' he has invented a technique for clearing the bar which seems to be more efficient than all others. **1972** *Sunday Tel.* 30 Apr. 35/5 In the junior..high jump Alan Dainton Fosbury-flopped over 6 ft. 2 in. **1973** *Times* 2 Feb. 11/7 It was at Cosford just over a year ago that Miss Peters first experimented with the Fosbury style of high jumping in which the athlete crosses the bar on her back. **1984** *Washington Post* 1 Aug. D5/2 Hu Hongfei..did not know of the Fosbury Flop jumping style..until three years after Dick Fosbury used it to win a gold medal in Mexico City in 1968.

foschip, foshipe, obs. forms of FOESHIP.

fosile, obs. form of FOCILE.

fosper, var. f. of *footspore* (see FOOT *sb.* 35).
1570 LEVINS *Manip.* 73/44.

foss, var. form of FORCE *sb.*[2], FOSSE.

‖**fossa**[1] ('fɒsə). *Anat.* Pl. **fossæ**. [L. *fossa* ditch, fem. pa. pple. (understand *terra*, earth) of *fodĕre* to dig.] A shallow depression, pit, or cavity.
1830 R. KNOX *Béclard's Anat.* 68 The inflation of the abdomen..causes the contents of the stomach to flow..into ..the nasal fossæ or the mouth. **1856–8** W. CLARK *Van der Hoeven's Zool.* II. 505 *Sphenostoma*..Nostrils basal, placed in a fossa. **1870** ROLLESTON *Anim. Life* 6 Between the temporal and the antorbital fossae.

fossa[2], **foussa** ('fɒsə, 'fuːsə). Also **fosa**. [Malagasy: see FOSSANE.] **a.** A mammal (*Cryptoprocta ferox*), related to both cats and civets, which is the largest carnivore found in Madagascar. **b.** *Fossa fossa* (popular names FOSSANE, *foussa*, and *fanaloka*), a monotypic genus of civets also found in Madagascar.
1838 W. ELLIS *Hist. Madagascar* I. ii. 47 An animal of the badger kind, found chiefly, if not exclusively, in the Sakalava country; it is called fosa. **1883** *Encycl. Brit.* XV. 435/2 *C. ferox*, the 'foussa' of the Malagasy. **1887** CHISHOLM tr. *Vogt & Specht's Nat. Hist. Anim.* I. 184 The Fossa of the Malagasies or in scientific nomenclature Cryptoprocta ferox. **1916** *Ann. & Mag. Nat. Hist.* 8th Ser. XVII. 413 The Fossa (*Cryptoprocta*) has probably received more anatomical attention than any single genus of Carnivora. **1945** F. HARPER *Extinct & Vanishing Mammals of Old World* 249 Fossane..is presumably a diminutive of fossa and lesser fossa is an English translation of it. **1964** E. P. WALKER et al. *Mammals of World* II. 1262/1 Fossas walk in a flat-footed manner on the soles of their feet. *Ibid.* 1238/2 Fanalokas, Fossanes, Malagasy Civets... The fact that the generic name of this animal [*Fossa*] is the same as the vernacular name of another Madagascar mammal, the fossa (*Cryptoprocta*) should not lead to confusion, as they are distinctly different animals.

†'**fossage**. *Obs.*[−0] [ad. med.L. *fossāg-ium*, f. L. *fossa* ditch.] (See quot.)
1721–92 BAILEY, *Fossage*, a Composition paid, to be excused from the..maintaining the Ditches round a Town.

fossak ('fɒsæk). (See quot.)
1888 *Athenæum* 21 Apr. 503/2 The tidal trout, or so-called 'fossak' of the Inver and other rivers.

fossane ('fɒseɪn). [a. F. *fossane*; French travellers give *foussa* as the native name.] A species of weasel or genet, found in Madagascar, etc.
1781 PENNANT *Quadrup.* II. 349 Weesel..Fossane. W. with a slender body [etc.]. **1855–82** in OGILVIE.

fosse (fɒs). Also 7–9 foss. [a. F. *fosse*, ad. L. *fossa* (see FOSSA[1]).]
1. An excavation narrow in proportion to its length; a canal, ditch, or trench; †a cart-rut.
a **1440** *Sir Degrev.* 1640 The stede stert over a fosse and strykys astray. **1477** NORTON *Ord. Alch.* i. in Ashm. (1652) 19 As water in fosses of the Carte-wheele. **1555** EDEN *Decades* 137 Fosses or trenches made of oulde tyme. **1606** HOLLAND *Sueton.* 185 Hee had an intention..from thence by a Fosse to let the Sea into old Rome. **1664** EVELYN *Sylva* (1776) 44 You may plant them in double Fosses. **1806** SURR *Winter in Lond.* (ed. 3) III. 41, I stripped off several of his garments, which I threw into a fosse. **1853** G. JOHNSTON *Nat. Hist. E. Bord.* I. 254 With mounds and parallel fosses that have evidently an artificial origin.
fig. **1549** *Compl. Scot.* i. 19 The diuyne sapiens..garris them fal in the depe fosse of seruitude.

2. *esp.* in *Fortif.* and *Archæol.* A ditch or dike formed to serve as a barrier against an advancing foe, a moat surrounding a fortified place.
c **1400** MAUNDEV. (1839) iv. 32 There nyghe is the Fosse of Mennon, that is alle round. **1549** *Compl. Scot.* xiv. 113 Thai maid tua lang depe fosses about al the toune. **1678** tr. *Gaya's Art of War* II. 113 A Trench, a casting up of Earth by way of Parapet, with a Ditch or Foss on the side of the Enemy. **1774** PENNANT *Tour Scotl. in 1772*, 95 A round British camp surrounded with two fosses. **1807** G. CHALMERS *Caledonia* I. I. iv. 157 It..was defended by three strong ramparts, and two large fosses. **1872** BAKER *Nile Tribut.* iv. 51 A deep fosse is a safeguard against a sudden surprise. **1882** SWINBURNE *Tristram of Lyonesse* 122 What fosse may fence thee round as deep as hate?
transf. **1860** MOTLEY *Netherl.* II. ix. 22 [The Meuse] was now..in the power of the Spaniards, The Province of Brabant became thoroughly guarded again by its foss.
b. In full ***fosse-road***. = FOSSE-WAY.
1130–35—*a* **1450** [in M.E.D.]. **1882** *Encycl. Brit.* XIV. 424/2 The Fosse road from Lincolnshire..passes by Leicester to Watling Street; the *Via Devana*..joins the Fosse at Leicester on its way to Chester. **1937** COLLINGWOOD & MYRES *Roman Brit.* (ed. 2) vi. 91 The Fosse begins at Seaton..on the Devonshire coast. **1969** C. COCHRANE *Lost Roads of Wessex* i. 14 No Roman way has been listed as located between Salisbury and the southern part of the Fosse. *Ibid.* vi. 119 For a short distance the Roman quarrystone paving of the Foss was intact.
†**3. a.** A deep hole dug in the ground; a pit. Also, a burying-ground, grave. *Obs.*
1474 CAXTON *Chesse* IV. vii, Than he herde a voyce that yssued out of the fosse or pitte of the sacrefises. **1669** WORLIDGE *Syst. Agric.* (1681) 137 Its usual to apply good Mould..to fill up the Foss after the placing the Tree. **1727** BRADLEY *Fam. Dict.* s.v., The Foss or Pit for the Bait should be under it as at *A.B.C.D.* *a* **1777** FAWKES *Apollonius Rhodius* III. 1277 A deep round foss he made, And on the kindling wood the victim laid. **1855** SMEDLEY *Occult Sc.* 129 Most of the spirits..hover over the foss and its bloody libation.
b. *Hist.* A pit [= med.Lat. *fossa*] in which women condemned for felony were drowned.
1825–80 JAMIESON s.v. *Pit & Gallows*, In some old deeds ..these terms [*furca et fossa*] are rendered *furc* and *fos*.
†**4.** A waterway or navigable channel. *Obs.*
1601 HOLLAND *Pliny* I. 117 In the fosse and mouth of this riuer Phasis.
5. An abyss, chasm, or gulf. [transl. It. *bolgia*.]
1814 CARY *Dante, Inf.* VIII. 74 We came within the fosses deep, that moat This region comfortless.
6. *Anat.* = FOSSA[1].
1730–36 BAILEY (folio), *Foss* [with Anatomists] a kind of cavity in a bone, with a large aperture, but no exit or perforation. **1847** JOHNSTON in *Proc. Berw. Nat. Club* II. No. 5. 215 Its origin was marked by a deep incissure or fosse in the back. **1883** *Knowledge* 13 July 22/2 Between the margin and the feelers..there may be a groove or foss.
7. *attrib.* and *Comb.*, as ***foss-ditch***; **foss-work**, *Hist.* (*Feudal*), work done on the town foss.
1772 BURKE *Corr.* (1844) I. 402 The nature of the Turkish frontier provinces, an immense foss-ditch (if I may so call it) of desert, is a defence made..at the expense of mankind. **1775** ASH, *Foss-work*.

‖**fossé** (fose). Also anglicized forms 8 faussee, fossée, -ee; and Sc. FOWSIE. [F. *fossé*:—late L. *fossātum*, neut. pa. pple. of *fossāre*, freq. of *fodĕre* to dig.]
A fosse, ditch, or sunk fence.
1708 *Lond. Gaz.* No. 4470/3 In the Night we made the Descent of the Fossés of the Counterguard on the Right. **1727** S. SWITZER *Pract. Gard.* IX. lxxvii. 366 The digging of the fossee round will go a great way in raising the ground. **1761** HUME *Hist. Eng.* II. xxxvii. 312 Having ordered Andelot..to drain the fossée, he commanded an assault. **1769** *De Foe's Tour Gt. Brit.* II. 175 The Orangery..is separated from the Lawn by a Faussee. **1802** C. JAMES *Milit. Dict.*, *Fossé* in fortification. See *Ditch*.

fossed (fɒst), *a.* [f. FOSSE + -ED[2].] Encircled with or as with a fosse.
1682 WHELER *Journ. Greece* I. 60 A square Toure, or Castle, Fossed without but not very deep. **1831** LANDOR *Siege Ancona* Wks. 1846 II. 584 Burnt-offerings raised In your high places, and fossed round with blood!

fosser, obs. form of FORCER[1].
1601 HOLLAND *Pliny* XVI. xl, These trees be good for caskets and fossers.

fosset, obs. form of FACET, FAUCET, FORCET.

fossette (fɒ'sɛt). [a. F. *fossette* dimple, dim. of *fosse* ditch: see FOSSE.] A little hollow, depression, or dimple; *esp.* **a.** *Zool.* (see quot. 1856). **b.** *Path.* 'A small ulcer of the transparent cornea, the centre of which is deep' (Ogilv.).
1848 CRAIG, *Fossette* (French) a little hollow; a dimple. **1852** DANA *Crust.* I. 49 Inner antennæ without fossettes, and elongated. **1856–8** W. CLARK *Van der Hoeven's Zool.* I. 178 *Cestoïdea.*—Head usually furnished with fossettes or suctorial oscules. **1862** DANA *Man. Geol.* 273 Showing..the depression or fossette in the star on one side.

Fosse-way, Fosse Way ('fɒsweɪ). *Hist.* Also Foss Way, Foss-way. [f. FOSSE 2 + WAY *sb.*[1]]
One of the four great Roman roads in Britain, so called from the ditch or fosse on each side; it probably ran from Axminster to Lincoln, via Bath and Leicester.
1610 HOLLAND *Camden's Brit.* I. 562 Thus much of the Feldon, or champion part, which, that ancient Fosse-way (a thing that would not bee overpassed) cutteth over-thwart. *c* **1703** C. FIENNES *Journeys* (1949) IV. vi. 333, I came..to High Crosse which is esteemed the middle off England, where the two great Roads meete that divides the kingdom in the Saxons tyme in 4 parts, the Whatling Streete.., and the Fosse Way. **1797** *Encycl. Brit.* V. 26/1 The fosse-way, which comes from Scotland, passes through this county and town to Totness in Devonshire. **1838** *Penny Cycl.* X. 381/1 From Aquæ Solis the Foss-way continued its course in a pretty direct line to Ischalis (Ilchester), of which town it forms the principal street. **1876** *Encycl. Brit.* V. 792/2 The junction of the Fosse-way with the Ermin and Icknield streets. **1937** COLLINGWOOD & MYRES *Roman Brit.* (ed. 2) xxi. 353 Even if we assume that..the south-east of Britain as far as the Fosse Way had passed by 442 under Saxon dominion, there is other fifth-century evidence which is hard to reconcile with such an idea. **1965** TIMPERLEY & BRILL *Anc. Trackways of Wessex* xxii. 131 As the trackway came near to the Avon it may have been superseded by the Foss Way for the rest of its journey to join up with the Cotswold Ridgeway.

fossick ('fɒsɪk), *v. Austral.* [app. of Eng. dial. origin; cf. '*Fossick*, a troublesome person, *fossiking*, troublesome. *Warw.*' (Halliwell).]
1. *intr.* in *Mining.* To search for gold by digging out crevices with knife or pick, or by working in washing-places and abandoned workings in the hope of finding particles or small nuggets overlooked by others. Also, ***to fossick about***.
1852 W. H. HALL *Diggings Victoria* 16 (Morris) Fossicking (picking out the nuggets from the interstices of the slate formation) with knives and trowels. **1855** CLARKE *Dict.*, *Fossick*, to undermine a man's gold-digging. **1864** ROGERS *New Rush* I. 18 We'll fossick wherever we think there is gold. **1874** A. BATHGATE *Colonial Experiences* xi. 138 [These unsocial miners], so long as they can make a living by 'fossicking' about, are happy. **1886** M. KERSHAW in *Spectator* 4 Dec. 1630 When a Chinaman fossicks about for gold or tin.
2. *gen.* To rummage or hunt about; to search.
1887 *Illustr. Lond. News* 12 Mar. 282/3 'Fossicking' among books and memoranda I came upon an..example. **1889** BOLDREWOOD *Robbery under Arms* (1890) 165 We fossicked about for a while to see if the man..had left anything behind him. **1890** *Melbourne Argus* 2 Aug. 4/3 Half the time was spent in fossicking for sticks. **1938** F. S. ANTHONY in D. M. Davin *N.Z. Short Stories* (1953) 213 Why not bung about ten cows each up there and let them fossick for tucker in the bush. **1956** E. HISCOCK *Around World in Wanderer III* xiii. 180 A place where people go to fossick, i.e. to gather shells and coral at low water on the reef. **1968** *Times* 11 Sept. 11/5 Unpaved backstreets..where old crones fossicked.
3. *trans.* To dig *out*, to hunt *up* (something).
1857 C. R. THATCHER *Goldrush Songster* (1958) 77 Next morning I well fossicked it. *a* **1870** LEMAITRE *Songs of Gold Fields* 14 He ran from the flat..Without waiting to fossick the coffin lid out. **1893** J. A. BARRY *Steve Brown's Bunyip* 8 I'll have to fossick up them mokes, Mariar.
Hence '**fossicking** *vbl. sb.* and *ppl. a.* Also '**fossicker**, one who fossicks, *esp.* a pocket-miner or a prospector for gold.
1853 E. CLACY *Lady's Visit Gold Diggings Austral.* vii. 123 William was the one whose fossicking-knife first brought its hidden beauties to light. **1859** CORNWALLIS *New World* I. 130 A plain leather belt, in which he..carries his fossicking knife. **1864** ROGERS *New Rush* II. 32 Steady old fossickers often get more Than the first who opens ground. **1880** SUTHERLAND *Tales Goldf.* 22 He commenced working..at surface digging and fossicking. **1891** *Melbourne Argus* 25 July 13/2 One could wish that all irrigationists would take the view that most of the native birds, and above all the swamp fossickers, are not merely friends but allies. **1916** J. B. COOPER *Coo-oo-ee* xiv. 213 All the same, I don't think Hawley got much colour for all his 'fossickin'. **1936** F. CLUNE *Roaming round Darling* xxv. 273 Gorrie..had given up cooking and taken to fossicking, as a mate of his found a gold nugget on Christmas Eve worth £130. **1970** K. GILES *Death in Church* iv. 77 No suspicion of illegal fossicking or buying.

fossiform ('fɒsɪfɔːm), *a.* [f. L. *fossa* (see FOSSA[1]) + -(I)FORM.] Taking the form of a FOSSA[1].
1846 DANA *Zooph.* (1848) 188 Cells fossiform.

fossil ('fɒsɪl), *a.* and *sb.* Also 6 focille, 7–8 fossile, (7 -ill, 8 fosile, fossel). [a. F. *fossile*, ad. L. *fossil-is* dug up, f. *fodĕre* to dig.]
A. *adj.*
1. a. Obtained by digging; found buried in the earth.
[**1563** W. FULKE *Meteors* (1640) 1 Those bodies, that are generated in the earth called *Fossilia*.] **1654** VILVAIN *Epit. Ess.* III. lxx, Seven unmixt fossil Metals are forecited. **1669** WORLIDGE *Syst. Agric.* (1681) 25 Lime, Chalk, Marle, or any cold fossile Soils, are an extraordinary Improvement to dry, sandy, hot Lands. **1673** RAY *Journ. Low C.* 101 Fossile Dice, which they say they dig out of the Earth. **1732** ARBUTHNOT *Rules of Diet* 269 All fossil Salts, as Sea-Salt, Rock-Salt, etc. **1816** J. SMITH *Panorama Sc. & Art* II. 354 Fossil coal, and..bitumen, contain a large quantity of carbon.
†**b.** ***fossil fishes***: fishes anciently supposed to live in water underground. *Obs.*
1661 LOVELL *Hist. Anim. & Min.* Introd. [*a* **1661** FULLER *Worthies Lancashire* II. (1662) 107 These Pisces Fossiles or Subterranean Fishes must needs be unwholesome.]
c. ***fossil fuel***: combustible material obtained from below ground and formed during the geological past; now esp. contrasted with sources of nuclear energy. Also *attrib.*
1835 [J. HOLLAND] (*title*) The history and description of fossil fuel, the collieries and coal trade of Great Britain. **1854** RONALDS & RICHARDSON *Chem. Technol.* (ed. 2) I. 54 The oldest of all kinds of fossil fuel, the anthracite. **1921** *Sci.*

Amer. 14 May 292/3 The early exhaustion of our fossil fuels will require the use of such other sources of power as water, wind, and sun. **1949** *Science* 4 Feb. 107/2 In view of the eventual exhaustion of fossil fuels, it is of interest to know to what extent water power can be depended upon to replace them. **1952** AYRES & SCARLOTT *Energy Sources* i. 4 The combustion of fossil fuels or the accelerated nuclear fission of elements. **1955** *Times* 9 Aug. 8/2 This would exhaust the known reserves of coal, oil and natural gas (the so-called fossil fuels) within less than a century. **1969** R. B. FULLER *Operating Man. Spaceship Earth* viii. 122 Physical energy.. is ever increasingly deposited as a fossil-fuel savings account aboard our Spaceship Earth through photosynthesis and.. topsoil fossilization.

2. a. Now applied in narrower sense to the remains of animals and plants, belonging to past (usually prehistoric) ages, and found embedded in the strata of the earth. (Commonly apprehended as an attrib. use of the sb.)

fossil ivory, ivory furnished by the tusks of mammoths preserved in Siberian ice; *fossil screws* (see quot. 1882).

1665 *Phil. Trans.* I. 111 Of Fossile wood and Coals. *c* **1680** *Enquiries* 2/1 Is there any.. Amianthus, Fossile teeth, or any kind of Ore unknown to you? **1695** WOODWARD *Nat. Hist. Earth* VI. (1702) 251 The fossil Shells are many of them of the same kinds with those that now appear upon the neighbouring Shores. **1753** CHAMBERS *Cycl.* Suppl. s.v. *Ivory*, Fossile Ivory. **1754** *Phil. Trans.* XLVIII. 801 It is.. considerably lighter than any fossile petrifaction. **1758** FOTHERGILL *ibid.* L. 688 The fossill Bones of an Alligator found.. near Whitby. **1802** PLAYFAIR *Illustr. Hutton. Th.* 196 This is true likewise of the fossil-pitch of Coal-Brookdale. **1850** LYELL *2nd Visit U.S.* II. xxx. 177 A fossil forest. **1875** MASKELL *Ivories* 2 Another kind of real ivory —the fossil ivory. **1880** HAUGHTON *Phys. Geog.* vi. 264 Its fossil eggs are estimated at twenty-four pounds weight each. **1882** CASSELL, *Fossil-screws*, a popular name for the casts in the rock left by spiral shells, or for those of encrinites when their impressions are horizontally furrowed.

fig. **1841–4** EMERSON *Ess.*, *Poet* Wks. (Bohn) I. 162 Language is fossil poetry. **1849** ROBERTSON *Serm.* Ser. I. xii. (1866) 206 Words are fossil thoughts. **1877** CONDER *Basis Faith* i. 34 The fossil impression of a dead faith.

b. Used in names of certain mineral substances fancifully considered to resemble organic products, as *fossil copal*, *cork*, *farina*: see the sbs.; *fossil flax*, *paper*, *wood*, *wool*, varieties of asbestos; *fossil flour*, *meal*, ? = *fossil farina*.

1859 PAGE *Handbk. Geol. Terms*, *Fossil-Paper*, *Fossil-Wool*. **1882** CASSELL, *Fossil-flour*. *Ibid.*, *Fossil-wood*. **1882** OGILVIE, *Fossil-flax*. **1883** *Cassell's Fam. Mag.* Dec. 62/2 'Fossil meal' is the name given to a composition.. used for coating steam pipes and boilers.

3. Applied contemptuously to persons, ideas, etc.: Belonging to the past, out of date; 'petrified', incapable of growth or progress.

1859 T. PARKER in Weiss *Life* (1863) II. 103 The Pope is a fossil ruler, pre-mediæval. **1894** LD. ROSEBERY in *Westm. Gaz.* 22 Mar. 5/2 Those fossil politicians—for there is a fossil Radicalism as well as a fossil Toryism.

B. *sb.* † **1. a.** In early use: Any rock, mineral, or mineral substance dug out of the earth. *Obs.*

1619 H. HUTTON *Follie's Anat.* (Percy Soc.) 23 So that he seemes as if black Vulcan's art Of diverse fossiles had compil'd each part. **1665–6** *Phil. Trans.* I. 111 Of some Fossils as Sand, Gravel, Earths. **1744** BERKELEY *Siris* §23 Its being dug out of the earth shews it to be a fossil. **1799** *Scott. Descr.* (ed. 2) 15 An infinite diversity of minerals and other fossils. **1807** HEADRICK *View Min. etc. Arran* 58, I could not find any solid rock of that fossil [pitchstone]. **1814** tr. *Klaproth's Trav.* 382 The chief mass of this porphyry seems .. to be a distinct fossil from basalt.

† **b.** A fossil fish: see A. 1 b. *Obs.*

1569 E. FENTON *Secr. Nat.* 50 b, The auncient Philosophers affirme, that there haue bene founde fishes vnder the earth, who (for that cause) they called Focilles.

c. *humorously*. Something dug out of the earth.

1855 LADY HOLLAND *Mem. Syd. Smith* I. 376 You always detect a little of the Irish fossil, the potato, peeping out in an Irishman.

2. Now only in restricted sense: Anything found in the strata of the earth, which is recognizable as the remains of a plant or animal of a former geological period, or as showing vestiges of the animal or vegetable life of such a period.

[**1707** *Curios. in Husb. & Gard.* 296 When a Plant petrifies, it degenerates by degrading it self to the Rank of Fossiles.] **1736** P. COLLINSON in *Darlington's Mem.* (1849) 73 What are called fossils—being stones.. that have either the impressions, or else the regular form of shells, leaves, fishes, fungi [etc.]. **1774** GOLDSM. *Nat. Hist.* (1776) I. 26 These shells and extraneous fossils are not productions of the earth. **1831** BREWSTER *Newton* (1855) II. xvi. 100 He regarded fossils as the real remains of plants and animals which had been buried in the strata.

3. *fig.* Something 'petrified', that has lost its vitality or capacity for growth or progress. Also, contemptuously applied to a person of antiquated notions or habits.

1844 EMERSON *Lect.*, *Yng. Amer.* Wks. (Bohn) II. 300 Government has been a fossil; it should be a plant. **1857** C. BRONTE *Professor* iv, When a man endures what ought to be unendurable he is a fossil.

4. *attrib.* and *Comb.*, attributive or similative, as *fossil-like* adj.; objective, as *fossil-bearing* adj.; parasynthetic, as *fossil-fuelled* adj.; **fossil-botanist**, one skilled in **fossil-botany**, the study of fossil plants; **fossil-ore** (see quot.).

1886 A. WINCHELL *Walks & Talks Geol. Field* 195 These lowest *fossil-bearing strata. **1850** H. MILLER *Footpr. Creat.* x. (1874) 183 The *fossil botanist who devoted himself chiefly to the study of microscopic structure. **1882** CASSELL, **Fossil-botany*. **1964** J. B. MCCLURE in *Trans. World Power Conf.* (Lausanne) IA. 326 The early application of higher efficiency in *fossil fueled processes is limited by declining fuel costs.. and high capital costs. **1967** *Technology Week* 23 Jan. 34/2 The nuclear power plants currently being constructed will be competitive with fossil-fueled plants. **1970** *Times* 10 Apr. 31/5 The bugbear of short range with existing battery electric systems could be overcome in the short term.. by offering a small fossil-fuelled engine alternator. **1874** SAYCE *Compar. Philol.* i. 61 Long-forgotten strata of society which our *fossil-like records reveal to us. **1881** RAYMOND *Mining Gloss.*, **Fossil ore*, fossiliferous red hematite.

Hence † **'fossilry**, ? a collection of fossils.

1755 *Gentl. Mag.* XXV. 567 Verses occasion'd by seeing the Fossilry at Tenderves in Cornwall.

fossil(l(e, var. form of FOCILE.

1612 WOODALL *Surg. Mate* Wks. (1653) 151. **1656** RIDGLEY *Pract. Physic* 242.

fossilate ('fɒsɪleɪt), *v.* [f. FOSSIL *sb.* + -ATE[3].] *trans.* or *intr.* To make or become fossil. Hence **'fossilated** *ppl. a.* Also **fossi'lation**, the action of the vb.; = FOSSILIZATION.

1819 G. S. FABER *Dispensations* (1823) I. 143 The fossilated ruins of the productions of the third, and fifth, and sixth demiurgic periods. **1832** *Fraser's Mag.* V. 553 The fossilated remains of their skeletons. **1886** A. WINCHELL *Walks & Talks Geol. Field* 128 There are two suggestions in reference to the way in which iron-ore particles have been accumulated:—first, fossilation of ancient iron-bogs; second, segregation.

fossildom ('fɒsɪldəm). [f. FOSSIL *sb.* + -DOM.] The condition or character of being a fossil or a lifeless piece of antiquity.

1898 *Daily News* 3 Dec. 5/7 Spurious vulgar fossildom secretly urges members to oppose this non-party measure. **1905** J. RICKABY *Development* 48 Protestantism, even Anglican Protestantism, is essentially fossildom.

fossiled ('fɒsɪld), *ppl. a. rare.* [f. FOSSIL *sb.* + -ED[1].] Made fossil, fossilized.

1868 G. STEPHENS *Runic Mon.* I. 28 Everywhere both living and fossiled word-foliage, everywhere transition.

fossiliferous (fɒsɪ'lɪfərəs), *a.* [f. FOSSIL *sb.* + -(I)FEROUS. Cf. F. *fossilifère.*] Bearing or containing fossils or organic remains.

18.. LYELL *Princ. Geol.* (1875) II. II. xxi. 194 The fossiliferous deposits of modern date. **1858** GEIKIE *Hist. Boulder* vi. 97 Richly fossiliferous beds of the mountain limestone.

fossilification (fɒ,sɪlɪfɪ'keɪʃən). [f. FOSSILIFY: see -FICATION.] The action of the vb. FOSSILIFY; petrifaction.

1846 WORCESTER (cites WAILES). **1855** in OGILVIE Suppl.

fo'ssilify, *v. rare*$^{-0}$. [f. FOSSIL *sb.* + (I)FY.] *trans.* and *intr.* = FOSSILIZE.

In recent Dicts.

fossilism ('fɒsɪlɪz(ə)m). [f. FOSSIL *sb.* + -ISM.]

1. The scientific study of fossils. *rare*$^{-1}$.

1796 COLERIDGE in J. Cottle *Early Recollect.* (1837) I. 192, I would thoroughly understand Mechanics; Hydrostatics.. Fossilism; Chemistry [etc.].

2. The state of being a fossil, the character or nature of a fossil.

1861 *Med. Times* 18 May 526/1 Precocity may talk of superfluous laggards and obstructive fossilism.

fossilist ('fɒsɪlɪst). Now somewhat *rare.* [f. as prec. + -IST.] One who studies fossils, an authority on fossils, a palæontologist.

1746 [see ARGUMENT *v.* 4]. **1766** PENNANT *Zool.* (1768) I. 41 Those remains which fossilists distinguish by the title of diluvian. **1806** *Guide to Watering Places* 115 The fossilist and botanist may here find ample amusement. **1876** PAGE *Adv. Text-bk. Geol.* vi. 113 Battles of opinion were fought between Cosmogonists, Diluvialists, and Fossilists.

fossility (fɒ'sɪlɪtɪ). [f. as prec. + -ITY. Cf. F. *fossilité.*] The quality or state of a fossil.

1860 in WORCESTER (citing *Penny Cycl.*).

fossilization (,fɒsɪlaɪ'zeɪʃən). [f. FOSSILIZE *v.* + -ATION. Cf. F. *fossilisation.*]

1. The action or process of fossilizing; the conversion of vegetable and animal remains into fossils.

1819 G. S. FABER *Dispensations* (1823) I. 124 The human species alone.. entirely escaped fossilization. **1827** G. HIGGINS *Celtic Druids* 142 Draw up one of the piles driven into the Danube by Trajan, and see how far in it the process of fossilization has proceeded. **1872** NICHOLSON *Palæont.* 3 Fossilisation may be applied in a general sense to all the processes through which an organic body passes in order to become a fossil.

2. The process of becoming, or state of having become, antiquated.

1886 [see FLUIDITY 1 b.]

fossilize ('fɒsɪlaɪz), *v.* [f. FOSSIL *sb.* + -IZE. Cf. F. *fossiliser.*]

1. a. *trans.* To turn or change into a fossil.

1794 HUNTER in *Phil. Trans.* LXXXIV. 407 Bones that are fossilized become so in the medium in which they were deposited at the animal's death. **1854** F. C. BAKEWELL *Geol.* 32 'Petrifying wells' do not, however, fossilize the things put into them. **1878** HUXLEY *Physiogr.* 229 There is much more likelihood that the remains of animals.. should be fossilized.

b. *intr.* To become, or be changed into, a fossil.

1828 in WEBSTER; and in later Dicts.

2. *fig.* **a.** *trans.* 'To cause to become antiquated, rigid, or fixed'; 'to place beyond the influence of change or progress' (Webster 1864); *rarely*, to preserve as if in fossil form. **b.** *intr.* for *refl.*

a. 1856 MRS. BROWNING *Aur. Leigh* VIII. 532 Ten layers of birthdays on a woman's head Are apt to fossilise her girlish mirth. **1862** R. H. PATTERSON *Ess. Hist. & Art* 98 Poetry, — which last century became temporarily fossilised from a slavish worship.. of antiquated models. **1877** A. B. EDWARDS *Up Nile* iv. 100 Sakkarah fossilises the name of Sokari, one of the special denominations of.. Osiris.

b. 1864 WEBSTER, *Fossilize*, to become antiquated, rigid, or fixed, beyond the influence of change or progress. **1888** *Co-op. News* 2 June 550 If it is to flourish, and not fossilize.

3. *intr.* To search for fossils. *colloq.*

1845 LYELL *Trav. N. Amer.* I. 158, I fossilized for three days very diligently.

Hence **'fossilized** *ppl. a.*; **'fossilizing** *vbl. sb.* and *ppl. a.*

1819 G. S. FABER *Dispensations* (1823) I. 124 No proper fossilized portion of the human subject has ever yet been detected. **18..** LYELL *Princ. Geol.* (1875) I. I. xiv. 314 The Fossilizing process. **1861** STANLEY *Lect. Eccl. Hist.* p. xxxviii, The fossilised relics of the old Imperial Church. **1887** FRITH *Autobiog.* I. xviii. 228 The Academy 'has changed all that', as well as other fossilized rules. **1891** *Athenæum* 28 Nov. 715/1 The fossilizing influence of the patristic theologians.

† **fo'ssilogy.** *Obs.* [Incorrectly f. FOSSIL *sb.* + -LOGY.] That branch of science which deals with fossils; palæontology; also, a treatise on this. So † **fo'ssilogist**, one who studies this science.

1776 G. EDWARDS (*title*) Elements of Fossilogy. **1776** DE COSTA *Conchology* 250 The Gryphytæ of fossilogists. **1806** *Guide to Watering Places* 176 In fossilogy we shall notice the echini, shark's teeth, and ammoniæ. **1812** *Gentl. Mag.* LXXXII. I. 206 An accurate and learned fossilogist. **1866** PHILLIPS in *Athenæum* 2 May (1874), Natural History and 'Fossilogy', as we then termed the magnificent branch of study now known as Palæontology.

fossi'lology. *rare*$^{-0}$. A less incorrect form (in Dicts.) of FOSSILOGY. So **fossilo'logical** *a.*, pertaining to 'fossilology'. **fossi'lologist**, one who studies this science.

1837 WHEWELL *Hist. Induct. Sc.* III. XVIII. iii. §2. 525 When.. earlier writers.. spoke of mineralogical and fossilological maps. **1864** WORCESTER (cites Buchanan), *Fossilology*. **1882** CASSELL, *Fossilologist*.

† **'fossion.** *Obs. rare*$^{-0}$. [ad. L. *fossiōn-em*, n. of action f. *fodĕre* to dig.] A digging.

1656–81 BLOUNT *Glossogr.*, *Fossion*, a digging or delving.

‖ **fossor** ('fɒsə(r)). [L. *fossor* in late L. sense of 'grave-digger'.] **1.** *Eccl.* An officer of the early Church charged with the burial of the dead.

1854 CDL. WISEMAN *Fabiola* (1855) 205, I saw it all, answered the old fossor. **1877** WITHROW *Catacombs of Rome* (ed. 3) 519 A very numerous class in the economy of the primitive church was that of the fossors, or grave-diggers.

2. [ad. mod.L. *Fossores* (P. A. Latreille 1817, in *Nouveau Dictionnaire d'Histoire Naturelle* X. 287), name of a group of Hymenoptera.] One of the burrowing Hymenoptera, the digger-wasps, formerly described as Fossores.

1899 *Cambr. Nat. Hist.* VI. 95 The apterous condition of females of the Multillides and Thynnides is very anomalous in the Fossors. **1919** *Jrnl. E. Afr. Nat. Hist. Soc.* XV. 440 The Fossors are not true wasps. *Ibid.* 441 Each Fossor lives entirely an independent life.

fossorial (fɒ'sɔərɪəl), *a.* and *sb.* Chiefly *Zool.* [f. L. *fossōri-us*, f. *fossor*, agent-n. of *fodĕre* to dig + -AL[1].] **A.** *adj.*

1. Having a faculty of digging, able to burrow, burrowing, fodient. Cf. prec.

fossorial Hymenoptera, a family of insects called *Fossores*.

1836–9 TODD *Cycl. Anat.* II. 46/2 The recently discovered American fossorial animal, the *Chlamyphorus*. **1837** W. E. SHUCKARD (*title*) Essay on the indigenous fossorial Hymenoptera. **1845** *Zoologist* III. 847 Some species of Fossorial Hymenoptera. **1877** COUES *Fur Anim.* ix. 280 Other animals are as decidedly fossorial as the Badger. **1880** *Notes from Leyden Museum* II. 225 (*title*) On two new exotic species of fossorial Hymenoptera. **1935** *Bull. Soc. Sci. Nat. Maroc* XV. 1 (*title*) On some fossorial Hymenoptera from the Soudan.

2. Of or pertaining to fodient animals, adapted for or used in burrowing.

1845 TODD & BOWMAN *Phys. Anat.* I. 148 Among the Edentata those tribes possess a clavicle whose habits are fossorial. **1854** OWEN in *Circ. Sc.* (*c* 1865) II. 107/1 The fossorial (digging and scratching) character of the.. mechanism of the limbs. **1865** WOOD *Homes without H.* 22 The fossorial limbs of the badger.

B. *sb.* A fossorial animal.

1855 in OGILVIE Suppl., *Fossorials*.

fossorious (fɒ'sɔərɪəs), *a.* [f. as prec. + -OUS.] = FOSSORIAL.

1826 KIRBY & SP. *Entomol.* (1828) III. xxxv. 545 The first pair of legs are fossorious.

‖ **fossula** ('fɒsjʊlə). [L. *fossula*, dim. of *fossa*: see FOSSA[1].] A small fossa; *spec.* **a.** *Anat.* 'One of the numerous slight depressions on the surface of the cerebrum' (1894 Gould *Dict. Med.*). **b.** *Zool.* A vacant space representing one of the primitive septa of certain corals; more fully *septal fossula*.

1843 J. G. WILKINSON *Swedenborg's Anim. Kingd.* I. i. 21 They lie on the base of the tongue in superficial crypts or fossulæ. **1879** NICHOLSON in *Encycl. Brit.* VI. 382/1 The septal fossula.

fossulate ('fɒsjʊlət), *a. Anat.* and *Zool.* [f. L. *fossula* (see FOSSULA) + -ATE².] Having one or more long narrow grooves or depressions.

1839–47 TODD *Cycl. Anat.* III. 297/1 In the kangaroo.. there is a large fossulate papilla near the base of the tongue.

fossule ('fɒsjʊl). [anglicized form of FOSSULA.] = FOSSULA.

1889 in *Cent. Dict.*

fossulet ('fɒsjʊlɪt). *Entom.* [dim. of FOSSULE: see -ET¹.] An elongated shallow groove.

1889 in *Cent. Dict.*

† **'fossure.** *Obs. rare*⁻⁰. [ad. L. *fossūr-a*, f. *fodĕre* to dig.] 'A digging' (1727 Bailey vol. II.).

† **'fostal,** *sb. Obs. rare*⁻¹. In 5 *pl.* fostalx. [? a contraction of FOOTSTALL (not recorded in this sense).] The track of a hare.

1486 *Bk. St. Albans* E viij b, When he [a hare] rennyth in the way drye or weete Then men may finde fostalx of clees or of feete.

fostal, var. form of FORESTALL *sb.* 2.

† **'fostell.** *Obs. rare*⁻¹. [? a. OF. *fustaille* (mod.F. *futaille*) cask.] ? A cask.

a **1510** DOUGLAS *K. Hart* II. lxi, Grein Lust, I leif to the at my last ende, Of fantisie ane fostell fillit fow.

fosten, obs. form of FUSTIAN.

foster ('fɒstə(r)), *sb.*¹ *Obs.* exc. in *Comb.* [OE. *fóstor*, str. neut. = ON. *fóstr*:—OTeut. **fôstrom*, f. root **fôð-* (see FOOD) + instrumental suffix *-tro-*.]

1. Food, nourishment.

c **1000** *Saxon Leechd.* II. 198 Sio is blodes timber, & blodes hus, & fostor. *c* **1230** *Hali Meid.* 15 Ure licomes lust is he feondes foster.

Proverb. a **1420** HOCCLEVE *De Reg. Princ.* 60 Styntyng the cause, th' effect styntethe eke, No lenger forster, no longer lemman. **1670** RAY *Proverbs* 94 No longer foster no longer friend.

2. Guardianship, keeping, fostering. *at foster*, at nurse (with a foster-parent).

c **1460** *Towneley Myst.* (Surtees) 320 Now shalle thai have rom in pyk and tar ever dwelland, Of thare sorow no some, bot ay to be yelland In oure fostre. **1861** G. W. DASENT *Burnt Njal* II. 166 They had children out at foster there.

3. a. Offspring, progeny. **b.** One nourished or brought up; a foster-child, nursling. **c.** An animal of one's own breeding.

a. *a* **1175** *Cott. Hom.* 225 Ic ȝegaderi in-to ðe of diercynne and of fuȝel cynne simle ȝemacan, þat hi eft to fostre bien. *a* **1225** *Leg. Kath.* 451 Ant ti semliche schape schaweð wel þæt tu art freo monne foster. **13..** *E.E. Allit. P.* B. 257 For hit was þe forme-foster þat þe folde bred. **1513** DOUGLAS *Æneis* VI. xv. 86 Ne neuer, certis, the ground of the Romanis Of ony foster sall hym so avance.

b. *c* **1205** LAY. 25921 Eleine min aȝen uoster. **1585** M. W. *Commendat. Verses to Jas. I's Ess. Poesie* (Arb.) 10 Lo heir the fructis, Nymphe, of thy foster faire.

c. 1609 SKENE *Reg. Maj.* 108 This.. beast.. is my leill, lawfull, and hamehalde cattell, or my inborne foister, the quhilk was thifteouslie stollen fra me.

4. *attrib.* and *Comb.*, as *foster-home, -milk*, FOSTER-BROTHER, -SISTER; FOSTER-CHILD, -SON and synonymously *foster-babe, -daughter*. Also FOSTER-FATHER, -MOTHER and in the synonyms *foster-dam*, † *-mame* (Sc.), *-parent, -sire*; hence in sense of 'acting as a foster-mother or nurse', *foster-city, -earth*.

1818 BYRON *Ch. Har.* IV. lxxxix, All thy *foster-babes are dead. **1618** BOLTON *Florus* III. xviii. (1636) 228 All Etruria and Campania, finally Italy, rose joyntly in armes against the mother and *foster city. **1697** DRYDEN *Æneid* VIII. 843 There, by the Wolf, were laid the Martial Twins.. The *foster-Dam loll'd out her fawning Tongue. *c* **1616** WEBSTER *Duch. Malfy* II. ii, Go, go, give your *foster-daughters good counsel. **1708** J. PHILIPS *Cyder* I. 9 The nursling Grove Seems fair awhile, cherish'd with *foster Earth. **1886** *Longm. Mag.* VII. 647 *Foster-homes under the boarding-out system. **1606** BIRNIE *Kirk-Buriall* (1833) 17 Superstition, the *foster mame of all error. **1582** BENTLEY *Mon. Matrones* iii. 272 Like a louing mother, and tender nursse, giving my *foster-milke, the foode of thy word and Gospell, aboundantlie to all. **1649** JER. TAYLOR *Gt. Exemp.* 37 That little love which is abated from the *Foster-parents upon publick report that they are not natural. **1816** *Gentl. Mag.* LXXXVI. I. 11 The Gentleman's Magazine being very justly considered as the foster-parent of English Topography. **1878** M. A. BROWN *Nadeschda* 16 Scarce had the beauteous maiden ceased When Miljutin, her kind *foster sire.. approached.

Hence **'fostership** = FOSTERAGE.

1861 CLINGTON *Frank O'Donnell* 110 The tie of fostership is, or at least was, held as sacred as that of natural brothers.

'foster, *sb.*² *Obs.* exc. *arch.* Also 1–3 fostre. [OE. (*cild-*) *fóstre* wk. fem., nurse, = MDu. *voester* (also *voetster*, mod.Du. *voedster*), ON. *fóstra*:—OTeut. **fôstrôn-*, f. **fôstr-om*: see prec. ON. had *fóstre* wk. masc., foster-father, of similar formation.

In the sole recorded OE. instance, a variant reading is *cild fēstre*, which is prob. a genuine form:—prehistoric **fôdistra*, f. root of FOOD + fem. agent-suffix *-istrôn*, -STER.]

A foster-parent, nurse.

a **1000** *Laws of Ine* lxiii[i], Mot he habben.. mid him.. his cildfostran [*v.r.* -festran]. *a* **1225** *St. Marher.* 8 þu art foster ant feder to helplese children. *c* **1250** *Gen. & Ex.* 2620 Sche forð-ran, And brogt hire a fostre wimman. *Ibid.* 2624–5 Iakabeð wente bliðe agen, ðat ȝhe ðe gildes [cildes?] fostre muste ben. *a* **1563** BECON *Humble Supplic.* Wks. 1563 III. 21 b, Heretofore we had suche shepeheardes, as were tender fosters of thy flocke. **1601** HOLLAND *Pliny* xv. iv, The Greekes, whom wee may count the very fathers and fosters of all vices. **1640** R. BAILLIE *Canterb. Self-Convict.* Pref. 10 Your sweete Fosters the Bishops have brought the Pope upon you and your Children. **1737** WATERLAND *Eucharist* 157 The Word is all Things to the Infant, a Father, a Mother, a Preceptor, a Foster. **1851** LONGF. *Gold. Leg.* II. *Village Church*, This is the Black Pater-noster, God was my foster, He fostered me Under the book of the Palm-tree!

† **'foster,** *sb.*³ *Obs.* Also 5 fostere. [contracted f. FORESTER; used in AF.] = FORESTER.

c **1386** CHAUCER *Prol.* 117 A forster [*v.r.* foster] was he, soothly, as I gesse. *c* **1430** *Syr Tryam.* 1063 Then swere the fosters alle twelve, They wolde no wedd but hymselfe. **1460** CAPGRAVE *Chron.* 111 Flaundres.. had no othir governouris but the Fosteres of the Kyng of Frauns. **15..** *Adam Bel* 561 in Hazl. *E.P.P.* II. 162 Forty fosters of the fe, These outlawes had y-slaw. **1590** SPENSER *F.Q.* III. i. 17 A griesly Foster forth did rush. **1594** [see FORESTER 1]. **1597** DOWLAND *1st Bk. Songs* (1844) 90 And love as well the foster can, As can the mighty nobleman. **1607** [see FORESTER 1].

Hence **'fostership**, the office of forester.

1628 COKE *On Litt.* 20 a, The Office of a Fostership [was] intailed.

foster ('fɒstə(r)), *v.* Forms: 1 ? fóstrian, 3 fostren, -in, (*Orm.* fosstrenn), 3–6 fostre, (3 *south.* vostre, 4 fostire), 5 foustre, (5 fostare, 7 fauster), 3– foster. [OE. **fóstrian* (Lye), = ON. *fóstra* (Sw. *fostra*, Du. *fostre*), f. *fóstor*, FOSTER *sb.*¹ The recorded OE. *fēstr(i)an* may be either f. the same stem or f. *fēstre* nurse: see FOSTER *sb.*²]

† **1.** *trans.* To supply with food or nourishment; to nourish, feed, support. In early quots. *to feed and foster*. *Obs.* in lit. sense.

[*a* **1050** *Liber Scintill.* lxxxi. (1889) 222 Mann byþ festrud [*nutritur*] and byð ȝefedd.] *c* **1200** ORMIN 1558 Annd Jesu Crist himm sellf shall ben Uppo þatt bodiȝ hæfedd, To fedenn & to fosstrenn hemm. *c* **1300** *Havelok* 1434 Vnto this day, Haue ich ben fed and fostred ay. *c* **1386** CHAUCER *Manciple's T.* 71 Lat take a cat, and fostre him wel with milk, And tendre flesh. **1483** CAXTON *Gold. Leg.* 434 b/1 Wold to god I had mylke to foustre the wythal. **1611** SHAKS. *Cymb.* II. iii. 119 One, bred but of Almes, and foster'd with cold dishes. [**1719** YOUNG *Busiris* v. i, The infant of my bosom! Whom I would foster with my vital blood.]

fig. a **1340** HAMPOLE *Psalter* xxx. 4 For þi name þou sall lede me & fostire me. *a* **1400–50** *Alexander* 3495 His flesche is fostard & fedd be fiȝt & by sternes. **1526** *Pilgr. Perf.* (W. de W. 1531) 108 b, They sholde be.. with swete consolacyons fostred & nourysshed. **1647** H. MORE *Song of Soul* II. ii. III. iv, Fauster'd and fed with hid hypocrisie.

† **2.** To bring up (a child) with parental care; often, to bring up as a foster-child, be a foster-parent to. Also with *forth, up*. *Obs.*

c **1205** LAY. 25900 Ich wes hire uoster-moder, and feire heo uostrede. *c* **1340** *Cursor M.* 3070 (Trin.) Here shal þou wiþ him wone & foster forþ here þi sone. **1357** *Lay Folks Catech.*, Fleshli fadir and modir That getes and fosters us forthe in this world. *c* **1386** CHAUCER *Man of Law's T.* 177 Thy yonge doughter fostred up so softe. **1470–85** MALORY *Arthur* I. vi, Your wyf that as wel as her owne hath fostred me and kepte. **1529** MORE *Supplic. Soulys* Wks. 337/2 Oure fathers also, whiche while we liued fostred vs vp so tenderly. **1588** SHAKS. *Tit. A.* II. iii. 153 Some say, that Rauens foster forlorne children. **1606** BRYSKETT *Civ. Life* 34 Such children as were borne vnperfect.. should not.. be fostered vp. **1697** DRYDEN *Æneid* VII. 941 The son of Mulciber, Found in the Fire, and foster'd in the Plains.

† **b.** To bring up, educate, nurture *in* (beliefs, habits, etc.). *Obs.*

c **1386** CHAUCER *Sec. Nun's T.* 122 This mayden.. Was.. from hir cradel fostred in the faith Of Crist. **1483** CAXTON *Gold. Leg.* 378/1. **1588** A. KING tr. *Canisius' Catech.* 50 Fosterit, teachit, and brocht vp in continuall exercise. **1580** SIDNEY *Arcadia* II. (1590) 138 b, A Prince.. fostred [ed. **1598** fostered vp] in blood by his naughty Father.

c. with reference to FOSTERAGE 2. Also *absol.*

1515 in *St. Papers Hen. VIII* (1834) II. 13 Some sayeth, that the Englyshe noble folke useith to delyver therre children to the Kynges Irysshe enymyes to foster. **1596** SPENSER *State Irel.* Wks. (Globe) 638/2 These evill customes of fostring and marrying with the Irish most carefully to be restrayned. **1775** JOHNSON *West. Isl.* 313 A Laird, a man of wealth and eminence, sends his child, either male or female, to a tacksman or tenant, to be fostered. **1887** STOKES tr. *Tripartite Life Patrick* 141 He gave him to bishop Bron to be fostered.

d. *to foster on* (a lamb): to put it to a ewe, which is not its mother, to be nourished.

1816 KEATINGE *Trav.* (1817) II. 264 Sometimes it is necessary to.. compel the ewes to admit the lambs, either their own or fostered on, to suck them. *Note*, To foster on a lamb, they tie the ewe, and at night compel her to give suck to the lamb two or three times.

e. *transf.* and *fig.* of a country, etc.

a **1300** *Cursor M.* 22102 Bethsaida and corozaim, þir tua cites sal foster him. **1577** tr. *Bullinger's Decades* (1592) 145 Euery mans countrie.. which fed, fostered, adorned, and defended him. **1583** STANYHURST *Æneis* I. (Arb.) 35 Such barbarus vsadge What soyle wyld fosters?

3. To 'nurse', tend with affectionate care; to 'nurse', cherish, keep warm (in the bosom).

c **1386** CHAUCER *Clerk's T.* 166 And in greet reverence and charitee Hir olde poore fader fostred she. —— *Merch. T.* 143 No man hateth his flesh, but in his lyf He fostreth it. **1388** WYCLIF *Prov.* v. 20 Mi sone, whi art thou disseyued of an alien womman; and art fostrid [*foveris*] in the bosum of an othere? **1483** CAXTON *G. de la Tour* I iv b, She hadde grete pyte of wymmen whiche were at theyre childbedde and vysyted and foustred them. **1603** KNOLLES *Hist. Turks* (1638) 330, I was so foolish and inconsiderate to foster vp as it were in my bosom this my domesticall and neglected enemy. **1766** GOLDSM. *Vic. W.* xxxi, What a viper have I been fostering in my bosom! **1821** KEATS *Lamia* 140 But the god fostering her chilled hand, She felt the warmth.

4. To encourage or help to grow; to promote the growth of (a fire, plant, etc.). Also, with †*forth, up*. Now only with mixture of sense 3.

a **1225** *Ancr. R.* 296 þe sparke lið & keccheð more fur, & fostreð hit forð, & waxeð from lesse to more. **1377** LANGL. *P. Pl.* B. XVII. 206 Wex and weyke and hote fyre togyderes Fostren forth a flaumbe. **1555** W. WATREMAN *Fardle Facions* I. i. 24 The moste pleasaunt plot of the earth, fostered to flourishe with the moisture of floudes on euery parte. **1576** GASCOIGNE *Philomene* 4 Westerne windes do foster forth our floures. **1615** G. SANDYS *Trav.* (1652) 133 They [the priests] shave their heads and foster their beards, contrary to the laity. **1850** TENNYSON *In Mem.* viii, A flower.. Which once she foster'd up with care. **1856** KANE *Arct. Expl.* I. ix. 98 Fostered by the reverberation of solar heat from the rocks, we met a flower growth.

5. To encourage, cherish, harbour fondly, nurse (a feeling, etc.); to encourage, promote the development of; (of things, circumstances) to be favourable or conducive to. Also with *up*.

1570 BUCHANAN *Ane Admonit.* Wks. (1892) 31 The hamiltonis fosterit yair vane hoip. **1585** ABP. SANDYS *Serm.* x. 166 The Arrians, the Anabaptists, the Family of loue, with all others of the like sort, fostered vp their errors in secret and darke corners. **1755** *Monitor* (1756) I. ii. 17 They always foster up a jealousy in the minds of the people. **1783** JOHNSON *Let. to Mrs. Thrale* 8 July, Of Miss H — whom you charge me with forgetting, I know not why I should much foster the remembrance. **1785** BURKE *Sp. Nabob of Arcot's Debts* Wks. IV. 207 The system of concealment is fostered by a system of falsehood. **1809–10** COLERIDGE *Friend* (1865) 192 Rivalry between two nations.. fosters all the virtues by which national security is maintained. **1844** H. H. WILSON *Brit. India* II. 216 Thus fostered, the insurrection was rapidly gaining head. **1844** DISRAELI *Coningsby* VII. viii, The enmities that are fostered between you and my grand-father. **1868** ROGERS *Pol. Econ.* viii. (1876) 76 The genius of financiers was directed towards fostering exportation, checking importation. **1885** CLODD *Myths & Dr.* I. iii. 40 The superstitions which mountainous countries especially foster.

† **b.** To encourage, indulge *in* a habit, etc. *Obs.*

1568 GRAFTON *Chron.* II. 64 Rather to be brideled for his presumption, then to bee fostered and encouraged therin. **1633** PRYNNE *1st Pt. Histrio-mastix* VI. vi. 505 Stage-playes serve.. to drawe men on by degrees to idlenesse, or to foster, to foment them in it.

Hence **'fostered** *ppl. a.*

1583 STANYHURST *Æneis* I. (Arb.) 17 Junoes long fostred deadlye reuengment. **1608** ARMIN *Nest Ninn.* (1842) 50 The Citty.. placed him as a fostred fatherless child. **1639** G. DANIEL *Ecclus.* xxix. 95 Thou shalt be revil'd.. even by the ffoster'd Child Of thy owne Charity. **1790–1811** W. COMBE *Devil upon Two Stick's in Eng.* (1817) IV. 201 The fostered habits of his mind.

fosterable ('fɒstərəb(ə)l), *a.* [f. FOSTER *v.* + -ABLE.] That may be fostered.

1869 *Anc. Laws Irel.* II. 165 To return a fosterable child without necessity.

fosterage ('fɒstərɪdʒ). Also 7 fosteridge. [f. as prec. + -AGE.]

1. The action, also the office or charge, of fostering or bringing up (another's child).

1614 RALEIGH *Hist. World* I. (1634) 182 Some one or other adjoyning to this Lake, had the charge and fosteridge of this childe. **1828** SCOTT *F.M. Perth* xxvii, Thou art already envied of many of our tribe, for having had the fosterage of the young Chief. **1882** J. PAYNE *1001 Nts.* I. 161 For the sake of my fosterage of thee.. spare this young lady.

b. The condition of being a foster-child.

1867 PEARSON *Hist. Eng.* I. 114 It was rather a sort of clientship or fosterage. **1872** E. W. ROBERTSON *Hist. Ess.* 157 Placed upon a footing with the foster-child during his fosterage.

2. The custom of putting (a child) under the care of a foster-mother; *esp.* the now obsolete custom amongst the Irish and Scottish nobility of giving over their children to a tenant to be nursed and brought up.

1775 JOHNSON *West. Isl.* Wks. X. 484 There still remains in the islands, though it is passing fast away, the custom of fosterage. **1875** MAINE *Hist. Inst.* viii. 241 This was Fosterage, the giving and taking of children for nurture. **1893** JOYCE *Short Hist. Irel.* 85 One of the leading features of Irish social life was fosterage.

attrib. **1881** *Leisure Hour* Apr. 226 Where the fosterage ties had most strength.. were the north-west of Ulster.. and Munster. **1893** JOYCE *Short Hist. Irel.* 86 A fine of two-thirds of the fosterage fee.

3. The action of encouraging or helping forward.

1816 KEATINGE *Trav.* (1817) I. 125 A branch of human morals so important; one which calls for the statesman's fosterage, the patriot's countenance. **1824** MISS MITFORD *Village* Ser. II. (1863) 262 [Under her] fosterage our evil habits throve apace. **1834** *Tait's Mag.* I. 848 Its [a conspiracy's] fosterage and management Richmond described very graphically. **1867** *Q. Rev.* Apr. 430 The scope afforded by one and all to the fosterage of the imaginative quality.

ˈfoster-brother. [OE. *fóster-bróðor*, f. FOSTER *sb.*[1] So ON. *fóstbróðir*.] A male child nursed at the same breast as, or reared together with, another of different parentage.

a **1000** *Ags. Voc.* in Wr.-Wülcker 268 *Alumnus*, foster-broþor. **1470–85** MALORY *Arthur* I. vi, My sone your foster broder Syre Kay. **1653** H. COGAN tr. *Pinto's Trav.* liv. (1663) 212 The Chaumigrem his Foster-brother was Commander in Chief. **1752** FIELDING *Amelia* Wks. 1775 X. 78 He had been her foster-brother. **1828** SCOTT *F.M. Perth* xxxiv, Eachin MacIan placed himself in the second line betwixt two of his foster-brothers.

transf. and *fig.* **1587** FLEMING *Contn. Holinshed* III. 1320/1 Foure of fansies fellowes, fosterbrothers to desire, and drie nurst by despaire. **1610** BEAUM. & FL. *Maid's Trag.* IV. i, My wrongs, Which are my foster-brothers. *a* **1735** ARBUTHNOT *Wks.* (1751) I. 195 The Bear with her Cubs and their Foster-Brother. **1860** *All Year Round* No. 63. 295 The nestling cuckoo ungratefully ejects his legitimate foster-brethren out of the family nest.

Hence **foster-ˈbrotherhood.**

1886 *Athenæum* 6 Feb. 194/1 A more picturesque story of foster-brotherhood was never imagined.

ˈfoster-child. [OE. *fóstercild*, f. FOSTER *sb.*[1]] A child as related to persons who have reared it as their own, or (*esp.* in Ireland and the Highlands) to its wet-nurse and her husband; a nursling.

a **1200** *Voc.* in Wr.-Wülcker 538 *Alumnus*, fostercild. **1590** SPENSER *F.Q.* III. ii. 33, I avow, by this most sacred head Of my deare foster childe, to ease thy griefe. **1612** DAVIES *Why Ireland, etc.* (1787) 135 The foster-children do love, and are beloved of their foster-fathers. **1717** ADDISON *Ovid's Met.* III. 346 The Goddess thus beguil'd, With pleasing Stories, her false Foster-child. **1828** SCOTT *F.M. Perth* xxxiv, Torquil, who entertained for his foster-child even a double portion of that passionate fondness.

fig. **1820** KEATS *Ode on Grecian Urn* 2 Thou foster-child of Silence and slow Time. **1846** H. ROGERS *Ess.* (1874) I. iv. 153 Leibnitz..[was] a foster-child of literature.

fosterer (ˈfɒstərə(r)). [f. FOSTER *v.* + -ER[1].]

1. One who nurses and brings up (a child); a nurse, foster-parent; *esp.* with reference to the custom of FOSTERAGE.

1589 GREENE *Menaphon* (Arb.) 48 What sparkes they haue of inconstancie, they drawe from their female fosterers. **1612** DAVIES *Why Ireland, etc.* (1787) 135 In Ireland..they put away all their children to fosterers. **1747** W. HARRIS in Southey *Comm.-Pl. Bk.* Ser. II. 362 If any love or faith is to be found among the Irish, you must look for it among the fosterers and their foster-children. *a* **1873** LYTTON *Pausanias* 81 My fosterer, my saviour, my more than father.

fig. *a* **1571** JEWEL *On 1 Thess.* (1611) 153 Peace..is the Nurse and fosterer of the Church of God. **1836** LYTTON *Athens* (1837) II. 577 Fountains and Rivers and ye Trojan Plains, I loved ye as my fosterers.

2. One who cherishes or cultivates (a plant, etc.).

1628 PRYNNE *Love-lockes* 27 All our Impudent, Ruffianly, and Shamelesse Love-locke fosterers. **1871** M. COLLINS *Mrq. & Merch.* II. vi. 167, I don't pretend to guess whether she prefers the fosterer of flowers or the smiter of steel.

3. A patron, protector, favourer (of persons or things); one who, or something which, promotes or encourages the growth of (a feeling, an institution, etc.).

1581 SIDNEY *Apol. Poetrie* (Arb.) 54 Dooth not knowledge of Law..being abused grow the crooked fosterer of horrible iniuries? **1586** J. HOOKER *Girald. Irel.* in *Holinshed* II. 132/1 The most notable offenders and their fosterers. **1659** RUSHW. *Hist. Coll.* I. 616 His Mother was a Recusant, and a fosterer of Recusants. **1691** WOOD *Ath. Oxon.* I. 819 Being found unfit..because he was a fosterer of faction, he resign'd. **1837** WHEWELL *Hist. Induct. Sc.* (1857) I. 210 The Arabians became the fosterers and patrons of philosophy. **1848** LYTTON *Harold* IV. vii, His character, as the foe of all injustice and the fosterer of all that were desolate.

4. *Anglo-Irish.* A foster-brother.

1735 SWIFT *Lett.* (1766) II. 217 When I had credit..at court, I provided for above fifty people..of which, not one was a relation. I have neither followers, nor fosterers, nor dependers. **1828** C. CROKER *Fairy Leg.* II. 238 He has an eye on the farm this long time for a fosterer of his own.

ˈfoster-father. [OE. *fósterfæder*, f. FOSTER *sb.*[1] (also *fēster-*: cf. related forms under FOSTER *sb.*[2] and *v.*). Cf. ON. *fóstrfaðir*.] **a.** One who performs the duty of a father to another's child. **b.** The husband of a nurse (*esp.* in Ireland and the Highlands).

a **800** *Corpus Gloss.* 140 *Altor*, fostorfaeder. ? *a* **1000** *Martyrol.* (Cockayne) 62 He is ure festerfæder on Criste. *c* **1200** ORMIN 8855 Annd till hiss fossterrfaderr ec He wass buhsumm & milde. **13..** *Guy Warw.* (A.) 169 Gij a forster fader hadde That him lerd and him radde. **1548** UDALL, etc. *Erasm. Par. Luke* ii. 37 a, The chylde..beeyng vnder the guydyng of his mother, and his foster-father. **1622** BACON *Hen. VII* Mor. & Hist. Wks. (Bohn) 342 The duke of Britain having been..a kind of parent or foster-father to the king. **1711** ADDISON *Spect.* No. 123 ¶5 Florio lived at the House of his Foster-father. **1848** DICKENS *Dombey* ii, He motioned his child's foster-father to the door.

fig. **1561** T. NORTON *Calvin's Inst.* IV. 161 Esay.. promiseth that kinges shalbe fosterfathers of ye Chirch. *a* **1652** J. SMITH *Sel. Disc.* iii. 51 Epicureans (who are not the true, but foster-fathers of that natural philosophy they brag of).

†**ˈfoster-ˌfeeling.** ? *nonce-wd.* One who 'fosters feeling', a sentimental person.

1784 *Unfortunate Sensibility* II. 119 The luke-warm rhetoric of foster-feelings.

ˈfosterhood. *rare.* [f. FOSTER *sb.*[1] + -HOOD.] The condition of being fostered or nursed tenderly.

1834 *Tait's Mag.* I. 242 Margaret would..bid her not spoil the boy by over-fosterhood.

ˈfostering, *vbl. sb.* [f. FOSTER *v.* + -ING[1].]

1. The action of the vb. FOSTER in various senses.

c **1230** *Hali Meid.* 33 Jn his fostrenge forð. *c* **1400** *Rom. Rose* 6113 In Gile & in Ipocrisie, That me engendred & yaf fostryng. **1447** BOKENHAM *Seyntys* Introd. (Roxb.), Of Seynt Margrete..The byrthe, the fostryng and how she cam Fyrst to the feyth. **1548** HALL *Chron., Edw. IV* (an. 13) 225 b, For the long mainteinyng, and fosteryng of Quene Margarete, and her soonne Prince Edwarde. **1885** *Athenæum* 3 Oct. 441/2 The withdrawal of such official and quasi-official fostering as architecture already has.

b. = FOSTERAGE 2. *Obs.* exc. *Hist.*

1596 SPENSER *State Irel.* Wks. (Globe) 638/1 The chiefest cause of the bringing in of the Irish language, amongest them, was specially theyr fostring, and marrying with the Irish. **1612** DAVIES *Why Ireland, etc.* (1787) 135 In the opinion of this [the Irish] people fostering hath always been a stronger alliance than blood. **1827** HALLAM *Const. Hist.* (1876) III. xviii. 354 The English settlers..connected themselves with them [Irish] by the national custom of fostering.

2. *concr.* Food, nourishment, sustenance.

c **1386** CHAUCER *Sompn. T.* 137, I am a man of litel sustenaunce. My spirit hath his fostring in the Bible.

fostering (ˈfɒstərɪŋ), *ppl. a.* [f. as prec. + -ING[2].] That fosters, in senses of the verb.

1568 T. HOWELL *Arb. Amitie* (1879) 35 The fethred foule ..his fostring foode, with chirping bill he peckes. **1697** DRYDEN *Virg. Georg.* I. 9 Bacchus and fost'ring Ceres, Pow'rs Divine. **1764** GOLDSM. *Trav.* 368 Thou transitory flower, alike undone By proud contempt, or favour's fostering sun. **1795** BURNS *To Cunningham* 4 The furrow'd, waving corn is seen Rejoice in fostering showers. **1840** MACAULAY *Ranke's Hist.* Ess. 1851 II. 145 Edinburgh has owed less to..the fostering care of rulers.

Hence **ˈfosteringly** *adv.*

1838 CARLYLE *Misc.* (1857) IV. 205 Sheltered and fosteringly embowered.

ˈfoster-land. *rare*[−0]. [after FOSTER-MOTHER, etc. OE. had *fósterland* 'land allotted for the support of monks' (= *ad cibum monachorum*, Domesday).] 'One's adopted country' (Cassell, 1882).

fosterling (ˈfɒstəlɪŋ). [OE. *fóstorling*: see FOSTER *sb.*[1] and -LING.] A foster-child, nursling.

c **1000** ÆLFRIC *Gloss.* Supp. in Wr.-Wülcker 170 *Uerna*, *uel uernaculus*, imberdling, *uel* fostorling. *c* **1205** LAY. 28574 Þer weoren of-slaȝe..þa Bruttes alle of Arðures borde, and alle his fosterlinges. **1630** B. JONSON *New Inn* V. i. I'll none of your Light Heart fosterlings, no inmates, Supposititious fruits of an host's brain..to be put upon me. **1872** MORRIS *Love is enough* (1873) 70 Bid farewell to thy fosterling while the life yet is in me. **1886** *Sat. Rev.* 20 Feb. 272 He has no special fosterling of his own, no pet theory for which he is bent on securing..recognition.

†**ˈfosterment.** *Obs. rare.* [f. FOSTER *v.* + -MENT.] Food, nourishment, subsistence.

1593 NASHE *Christ's T.* 33 b, She had no other refuge of fosterment, she was constrained..hauing but one onely sonne, to kill him and rost him. **1623** in COCKERAM.

ˈfoster-mother. [OE. *fóster-*, *fóstormódor*, f. FOSTER *sb.*[1] Cf. ON. *fóstrmóðir*. (OE. had also *féstermódor*; cf. *féstre* = FOSTER *sb.*[2]).] **1.** A woman who nurses and brings up another's child: **a.** as an adoptive mother; **b.** in the capacity of a nurse.

? *a* **1000** *Martyrol.* (1894) 154 Þa cwæð þæs cnihtes fostor-modor to þam fæder: ȝif [etc.]. *c* **1205** LAY. 25899 Ich wes hire uoster-moder. *a* **1300** *Cursor M.* 3347 Hir foster moder wit hir sco ledd. *c* **1470** HENRY *Wallace* II. 270. **1634** SANDYS *Prudence* x. 127 That Childe that receiveth nutriment from his Foster Mother. *a* **1735** ARBUTHNOT *Wks.* (1751) I. 196 The young Gentleman told his Foster-Mother..that [etc.]. **1855** MACAULAY *Hist. Eng.* IV. 582 Maine.. was loved by Lewis with the love of a father, by Madame de Maintenon with the not less tender love of a foster mother. **1894** *Daily News* 12 Mar. 6/5 Each home..will be in charge of a foster-father and foster-mother.

fig. **1526** *Pilgr. Perf.* (W. de W. 1531) 80 Obedience..is the nouryce or fostermother of all vertues. **1637** LD. CAREY *Romulus & Tarq.* 201 Liberty belongs to equals, flattery to inferiours, the one is the Common-wealths Nurse, the other the Tyrants foster-mother. **1876** BANCROFT *Hist. U.S.* VI. xxxiii. 129 France became the foster-mother of republicanism.

2. An apparatus for rearing chickens hatched in an incubator.

1907 *Yesterday's Shopping* (1969) p. xxxv/4 Foster mothers. **1911** J. W. HURST *Successful Incubation* 78 A cheap form of ordinary lamp should never be used, as is sometimes attempted..by makers of home-made brooders and foster-mothers. **1914** *Poultry* 2 Jan. 1042 When my Chicks are in your Foster-Mothers I can rest comfortably at night, and so can the Chicks. **1960** *Farmer & Stockbreeder* 19 Jan. Suppl. 37/3 There is still much to be said for the old foster-mother as this not only provides a brooder but a house as well.

ˈfoster-nurse. [f. FOSTER *sb.*[1]] A nurse who brings up another's child as her own.

1607 WILKINS *Miseries Inforst Marr.* I. Biij, Your hands haue bin to me like bounties purse, Neuer shut vp, your selfe my foster-Nurse. **1856** FROUDE *Hist. Eng.* II. 245 The foster nurse first chanted the spell over the cradle.

fig. **1600** SHAKS. *A.Y.L.* II. ii. 40 Fiue hundred Crownes ..Which I did store to be my foster Nurse. **1873** SYMONDS *Grk. Poets* x. 311 In the North nature is rather an awful mother than a kind foster-nurse and friend of man.

ˈfoster-sister. [f. FOSTER *sb.*[1] In OE. **fóstersweoster* (Lye). Cf. ON. *fóstrsystir*.]

A female child nursed at the same breast as, or reared together with, another of different parentage.

1649 JER. TAYLOR *Gt. Exemp.* 37 Scipio Asiaticus.. pardoned them at the request of his Foster-sister. **1840** DICKENS *Barn. Rudge* xx, [Dolly] had ever since been the humble friend of Miss Haredale, whose foster-sister she was.

ˈfoster-son. [f. FOSTER *sb.*[1] Cf. ON. *fóstrsonr*.] One who is brought up as a son though not one by birth.

a **1450** *Le Morte Arth.* 2955 That fals traytor, sr Mordreid, The Kynges foster sone [*Furniv.* soster son] he was. **1697** DRYDEN *Virg. Past.* IV. 66 O of Cœlestial Seed! O foster Son of Jove. **1894** J. T. FOWLER *Adamnan* Introd. 82 He was called the foster-son or *alumnus* of Adamnan.

†**ˈfostler.** *Obs. rare*[−1]. [? metathetic corruption of FORCELET.] = FORCELET[2].

1531 PH. STRONGE in Weaver *Wells Wills* (1890) 148 My wif shall have her coffer and her fostler to her own use.

fostress[1] (ˈfɒstrɪs). Also 7 fost(e)resse. [fem. of FOSTERER: see -ESS.] A female who fosters, in the senses of the vb.

1603 HOLLAND *Plutarch's Mor.* 161 That hope..the nurse and fostresse of old age. **1611** HEYWOOD *Gold. Age* IV. i. Wks. 1874 III. 54 Great Athens The nurse and fostresse of my infancy. *a* **1637** B. JONSON *Sp. at Pr. Henry's Barriers* Wks. (Rtldg.) 578/1 Glory of knights..Come forth; your fostresse bids! who from your birth Hath bred you to this hour. **1648** HEXHAM, *Een Mamme*..a Nurse, a Fosteresse, or a Foster-Mother. **1883** SWINBURNE *Century of Roundels*, *In Guernsey*, My mother sea, my fostress. **1891** —— *Eton: an Ode* in *Athenæum* 30 May 700/1 With England Eton her child kept pace as a fostress of men to be.

appositively. **1882** SWINBURNE *Tristram of Lyonesse*, *Athens* 176 Woven about the fragrant forehead of the fostress maiden's town.

†**ˈfostress**[2]. *Obs.* In 6 *Sc.* fostaress. [f. FOSTER *sb.*[3] + -ESS.] = FORESTRESS.

1501 DOUGLAS *Pal. Hon.* I. xxiii, Sine ladyis come with lustie giltin tressis, In habit wilde maist like till fostaressis.

†**ˈfostrild.** *Obs. rare*[−1]. [f. FOSTER *v.* + fem. suffix -ILD.] A nurse. In quot. *fig.*

a **1225** *Ancr. R.* 72 So hit is ine monie, ase seint Gregorie seið; Silence is wordes fostrild.

fot(e, fotch(e, obs. ff. of FOOT, FETCH.

fother (ˈfɒðə(r)), *sb.* Forms: 1 fóðer, 3–4 *south.* voðer, 4–6 fother, -yr, futher, -ir, (6 fouther, fowther), 5–7 fuder, -yr, fudder, *Sc.* -ir, 5–9 fodder, (5–6 foder, -yr, 6 fodar, 7 fooder), 6–7 *Sc.* fidder, 4– fother. [OE. *fóðer* str. neut. = OS. *fôthar* (MDu. *voeder*, Du. *voer*), OHG. *fuodar* (MHG. *vuoder*, Ger. *fuder*):—WGer. **fôþr(o)*; the continental words mean 'cartload', 'a certain weight supposed to represent a cartload', 'a certain measure of wine' (see FOODER, FUDDER). The root is usually believed to be an ablaut variant of *fap-* to stretch out: see FATHOM *sb.*]

1. A load; a cart-load (of hay, turf, wood, etc.). *Obs.* exc. *dial.*

O.E. Chron. an. 852 (Laud MS.) He scolde gife ilca ȝear in to þe minstre sixtiȝa foðra wuda and twælf foður græfan and sex foður ȝearda. *c* **1205** LAY. 25762 Ban unimete, bi atlinge heom þuhte þritti uoðere. **1375** BARBOUR *Bruce* x. 198 Ane fudyr..greter..Than eny he broucht..befor. *c* **1386** CHAUCER *Prol.* 530 With him ther was a Plowman, was his brother That hadde y-lad of dong ful many a fother. *c* **1450** *St. Cuthbert* (Surtees) 6007 Þe sledd it bare so grete fothir. **1469** *Plumpton Corr.* 21 Your tenant..hath not gotten but xii foder of hay. **1490** *Acta Dom. Conc.* 181 Withhaldin.. fourtj fuder of pettis [= peats] of ane yere bipast. **1568** *Wowing Jok & Jynny* vii, Fyve fidder of raggis to stuff ane jak. **1569** in *Wills & Inv. N.C.* (Surtees 1835) 307 Lxxx fudders of barke xx *l.* **1774–5** *Act 14 Geo. III* in Brand *Newcastle* (1789) I. 652 Four fother of clod lime, and fifteen fothers of good manure, on each acre. **1813** *Misc.* in *Ann. Reg.* 507/2, 20 fothers of additional thickness in clay were thrown in. **1892** *Northumbld. Gloss.* s.v., A fother of muck, or of lime, &c.

fig. *a* **1225** *Ancr. R.* 140 Þu hauest imaked uoðer to heui uorte ueðren mide þe soule.

b. *transf.* A mass; a quantity, 'lot'.

13.. *K. Alis.* 1809 Darie..makith thretyng ful a fothir. *Ibid.* 6467 Heore nether lippe is a foul fother. *c* **1450** LONELICH *Grail* xiii. 490 Vnder hem bothe was there fair fothir. **1513** DOUGLAS *Æneis* x. Prol. 159, I compt not of thir pagane Goddis ane futhir. **1515** *Scot. Field* 44 There they fell, at the first shotte Many a fell fothir. **1567** *Satir. Poems Reform.* vi. 52 King, Quene and Lord, they pass into ane fidder.

c. Used for an enormous quantity, a 'cart-load' of gold or money.

c **1386** CHAUCER *Knt.'s T.* 1050 Another, That coste largely of gold a fother. **14..** *Partonope* App. 3147 Ffor though a man wolde gyfe a fother Of golde he myght not sell to another. **1500–20** DUNBAR *Poems* xxvi. 62 Out of thair throttis thay schot on vdder Hett moltin gold, me thocht a fudder. **1863** ROBSON *Bards Tyne* 287 Where the brass hez a' cum frae nebody can tell..But..they mun have at least had a fother.

2. *spec.* A definite weight of some specified substance. **a.** Of lead: Now usually $19\frac{1}{2}$ cwt.

1375–6 [see FOTMAL]. **1463** *Mann. & Househ. Exp.* 154 My mastyre sent to my lorde a fodyr and di. off leede. **1541** *Ld. Treas. Acc. Scotl.* in Pitcairn *Crim. Trials* I. 310 For þe fraucht of thre fidder of leid. **1622** MALYNES *Anc. Law-Merch.* 269 Foure of these Loads will make a Fother of Lead of twentie hundreth. **1747** HOOSON *Miner's Dict.* J iv, In both the Peaks the Merchants deal and sell the Lead by Fodders. **1866** ROGERS *Agric. & Prices* I. x. 168 The charrus contains nearly $19\frac{1}{2}$ hundreds, that is, it corresponds to the fodder, or fother, of modern times.

b. *ellipt.* in phr. ***to fall as a fother (of lead)***; hence, a crushing blow.

13.. *Coer de L.* 1732 On his head falleth the fother. *c* **1380** *Sir Ferumb.* 641 Euery strok þat þou me rauȝt falleþ doun as a foþer.

c. Of coals: (see quot. 1851).

1607 COWELL *Interpr.*, *Fother* is a weight of twenty hundred which is a waine or cartload. **1765** *Lond. Chron.* 17 Dec. 582 Several fothers of coals this week have been found short of the standard measure. **1851** GREENWELL *Coal-trade Terms Northumb. & Durh.* 26 *Fother*, a measure of coals, being one-third of a chaldron, of $17\frac{2}{3}$ cwt.; a good single horse cart load.

fother ('fɒðə(r)), *v. Naut.* Also 9 fodder. [prob. ad. Du. *voederen* (now *voeren*), or LG. *fodern* = Ger. *füttern* to line (used also *Naut.* as below); cf. further ON. *fóðra* to line, f. OTeut. **fôðro-* sheath, etc. (mentioned under FODDER *sb.*: see also FUR, FOREL).]

1. *trans.* To cover (a sail) thickly with oakum, rope yarn, or other loose material fastened on it, with the view of getting some of it sucked into a leak, over which the sail is to be drawn.

1789 A. DUNCAN *Mariner's Chron.* (1805) IV. 36 The leak began..to gain upon them, a second sail was fothered and got under the bottom. **1790** *Ann. Reg.* 263 Fothering it round with oakum, to fill up. **1811** *Naval Chron.* XXV. 4 The..sail had been fothered, and drawn under the ship. **1833** M. SCOTT *Tom Cringle* iii. (1859) 93 Get the boatswain to fother a sail then.

2. To stop a leak by this method.

1800 *Naval Chron.* III. 473 By foddering, and those excellent pumps, we kept her above water. **1820** SCORESBY *Acc. Arctic Reg.* II. 449 The different plans which..had been adopted to stop a leak..were..1. To fother.

Hence **'fother (fodder)** *sb.*, the material used for fothering. **'fothering** *vbl. sb.*, the action of the vb. Also *attrib.*, as ***fothering-mat, -sail.***

1800 *Naval Chron.* III. 473 We could get a sail with fodder over. **1815** *Falconer's Dict. Marine* (ed. Burney) s.v., A superior method of fothering is now practised. **1819** J. H. VAUX *Mem.* I. 226 Applying what is termed a fothering mat to her bows. **1820** SCORESBY *Acc. Arctic Reg.* II. 451 A bunch of rope-yarns..might enter some of the larger leaks ..through the medium of a fothering sail.

fother, obs. form of FODDER.

† **'fotion.** *Obs.*$^{-1}$ [as if ad. L. **fōtiōn-em*, n. of action f. *fovēre* to cherish.] A cherishing.

1656 in BLOUNT *Glossogr.* **1668** WILKINS *Real Char.* II. ix. §2. 233 Action Vegetative 4. Fotion, cherishing, foster, foment, brood. **1721–92** in BAILEY.

† **'fotive,** *a. Obs.*$^{-1}$ [f. L. *fōt-* ppl. stem of *fovēre* to cherish + -IVE.] Cherishing, warming.

a **1639** T. CAREW *Cœlum Brit.* iv. Wks. (1824) 168 If I not cherish them With..fotive heat, They know no vegetation.

† **'fotmal.** *Obs.* See also FORMELL. [app. a use of OE. *fótmæl*, foot measure (see FOOT *sb.* and MEAL); the L. *pes* seems to have been used in the same sense. The reason for the name is obscure.] A weight used for lead, app. about 70 lbs., the thirtieth part of a FOTHER or load.

? *a* **1300** *Assisa de Ponderibus* in *Stat. of the Realm* I. 205 Item charrus plumbi constat ex xxx fotmals; Et quodlibet fotmal constat ex vj petris, ij libris minus; Et quelibet petra constat ex xij. libris. [The transl. printed with this passage (taken from ed. 1751) has *formel* instead of *fotmal*; for the Lat. text which this version seems to represent, see FORMELL.] **1375–6** *Abingdon Acc.* (1892) 30 Et ad iactandum xvj vothres vj votmels [*printed* votinels] plumbi in pondere, Cs. **13..** *Meas. of Weight* in *Rel. Ant.* I. 70 Sex waxpunde makiet .j. ledpound .xij. ledpunde .j. fotmel..xxiij fotmel .j. fothir of Bristouwe. **1866** ROGERS *Agric. & Prices* I. x. 168 This [charrus] contained thirty fontinelli [*misread for* fotmelli], fotmael, pedes, or pigs.

fott(e, obs. f. FET, FOOD, FOOT.

‖**fotus.** *Obs.* [L. *fōtus* (-u stem) noun of action from *fovēre* to warm, cherish.] A fomentation.

1586 W. BAILEY *Preserv. Eye-sight* (1633) 21 If the eyes be over-dry, we humect them..with a fotus of Mallows..and Violets. **1714** *Spect.* No. 572 ¶5 The Anodine Fotus.

† **fou** (fuː), *sb. Sc. Obs.* [? subst. use of *fou* FULL *a.*] A bushel.

a **1700** *Sir Patrick Spens* viii. in Child *Ballads* III. (1885) 25/2, I brought half a fou o good red goud Out oer the sea with me. **1786** BURNS *Auld Mare, Maggie* 99 For my last fou, A heapit stimpart, I'll reserve ane Laid by for you.

fou (fuː), *a. Sc.* Also 6–8 fow, 8 fu'. [var. of FULL *a.*, q.v. for other senses, in which this spelling is no longer commonly used.] Drunk.

1535 LYNDESAY *Satyre* 139 Na he is wod drunkin I trow; Se ȝe not that he is wod fow? **1602** *Shetland Law Rep.* in *Scotsman* (1886) 29 Jan. 7/1 Magnus Crasmusson for being fow and drunken, etc. **1768** ROSS *Helenore* III. 113 Awa', she says, fool man, ye're growing fu'. **1785** BURNS *Death & Dr. Hornbk.* 14, I wasna fou, but just had plenty. **1820** SCOTT *Monast.* Introd. Epist., He is as fou as a piper by this time. **1858** PORTEOUS *Souter Johnny* 13 The rogue gied monie a hearty smack When he was fou.

fou, var. of FAW, *Obs.*, dial. f. FOUL.

† **'fouat.** *Sc.* = FOOSE.

1822 SCOTT *Nigel* ii, There is hay made at the Cross, and a dainty crop of fouats in the Grassmarket.

Foucault (fuko, 'fuːkəʊ). The name of J. B. L. *Foucault* (1819–1868), French physicist, used *attrib.* and in the possessive to designate experiments or discoveries made, or apparatus designed, by him; as ***Foucault current***, an eddy current; ***Foucault (knife-edge) method, test***, a method of testing lenses and mirrors for surface irregularities; ***Foucault('s) pendulum***, a pendulum designed to demonstrate the rotation of the earth by the rotation of its plane of oscillation; ***Foucault prism***, a polarizing prism resembling a Nicol prism but having the two halves separated by a film of air.

1852 *Phil. Mag.* 4th Ser. III. 331 (*heading*) A mathematical theory of M. Foucault's pendulum experiment. **1882** L. WRIGHT *Light* xi. 251 A large Foucault prism is only about one-fourth the cost of a Nicol of the same aperture. **1883** ATKINSON tr. *Ganot's Physics* (ed. 11) 869 The currents..produced in solid conductors and which are converted into heat, are often spoken of as Foucault currents. **1923** GLAZEBROOK *Dict. Appl. Physics* IV. 329/1 For the investigation of spherical aberration errors Foucault's original knife-edge method is still frequently employed. **1930** L. C. MARTIN *Introd. Appl. Optics* I. 204 In case a prism is wanted for purposes of ultra-violet polarimetry, the Foucault type..is employed. *Ibid.* 257 (*caption*) The Foucault knife-edge test. **1931** *Discovery* May 164/1 A knowledge of the rotation of our world might be gained by such means as the Foucault pendulum or the gyro-compass. **1952** F. TWYMAN *Prism & Lens Making* (ed. 2) xi. 373 Correcting mirrors by local polishing with the help of the Foucault test. **1953** P. KEMP *A.C. Electr. Engin.* (ed. 8) x. 96 These e.m.f.s..set up local circulating currents known as Foucault or Eddy Currents and give rise to a loss of power. **1966** *McGraw-Hill Encycl. Sci. & Technol.* IX. 618 A Foucault pendulum is a spherical pendulum suspended so that its plane of oscillation is free to rotate.

† **fouch.** *Obs.* Forms: 4 fourche, 5 forche, 6 fowche, 7 fouch(e. Also FURCH. [ME. *fourche*, a. OF. *fourche, forche*, lit. 'fork': cf. FORCHE.]

1. ? The fork of the legs.

c **1330** R. BRUNNE *Chron. Wace* (Rolls) 1824 Wiþ fet in fourche [*v.r.* fouche] ilk oþer tok [said of wrestlers].

2. The hind quarters of a deer; also *pl.*

13.. *Gaw. & Gr. Knt.* 1357 Þay..henged þenne a[y]þer bi hoȝes of þe fourchez. **1486** *Bk. St. Albans* F iij b, And after the Ragge boon cuttis euen also The forchis. **1491** [see FURCH]. *c* **1550** *Wyl Bucke His Test.* B 3 b, For to cut out kindely the fowche. Take of the buttockes..let both the loynes sitte together..and leue therin the kidneys. **1631** BRATHWAIT *Whimzies, Forrester* 36 To present some.. gentleman in his masters name, with a side or a fouch. **1671** in *12th Rep. Hist. MSS. Comm.* App. VII. (1890) 382 Given to Mr. Bellingham's man that brought a fouch of venison, 2s.

Hence **fouch** *v. trans.*, to divide a buck into four quarters (Halliwell).

fouch, obs. form of VOUCH *v.*

foud (faʊd). *dial.* Also 6, 9 fowd(e, 7 fold, 8 feud. [Adoption of the local Scand. form:—ON. *fógeti* (Da. *foged*, Sw. *fogde*) = Ger. *vogt*, ad. med.L. *vocātus*, pa. pple. of *vocāre* to call.]

In Orkney, Shetland, and the Faroe Isles, a bailiff, magistrate, or governor; formerly the President of the Supreme Court in Orkney and Shetland.

1581 *Sc. Acts Jas. VI* (1814) III. 255 Gevand—to the said lord robert stewart and his..schireffis and fowdis foirsaidis, full power [etc.]. **1602** *Min. District Crt. Dunrossnan* in *J. Mill's Diary* (1889) 178 Provin in the foldis buikis to have disobeyit to gang to my lordis wark in Scallowy. **1703** BRAND *Descr. Orkney, etc.* 121 In this parish..the Principal Feud or Judge of the Country used to sit and give Judgment. **1889** GOUDIE *J. Mill's Diary* Introd. 38 Originally in Shetland..every..parish had its court, presided over by the parish Foud. **1894** *Scotsman* 10 Nov. 10/6 The Foude [in Faroe] is collector, or rather treasurer of all kinds of skat.

Hence **'foudrie** [see -RY], the office of a foud; also, the district over which his jurisdiction extended.

1581 *Sc. Acts Jas. VI.* (1814) III. 254 Our souerane lord ..grantis to the said lord robert stewart..the offices..of schirefschip and fowdrie. **1592** *Ibid.* 619 Landis lyand wᵗʰin the diocie of orknay wᵗʰin the fauderie of orknay and Zetland. **1693** J. WALLACE *Descr. Orkney* 91 Foudrie, the Government of the Foud.

foude, var. form of FOOD *v.*

foudre, var. of FOULDRE, *Obs.*

foudroyant (fuː'drɔɪənt, Fr. fudrwajɑ̃), *a.* [a. Fr. *foudroyant*, pr. pple. of *foudroyer* to strike with or as with lightning, f. *foudre*: see FOULDRE.]

1. a. Thundering, stunning, noisy. **b.** Flashing, dazzling.

1840 DE QUINCEY *Style* Wks. 1859 XI. 210 When..the 'foudroyant' style of the organist commenced the hailstone chorus. **1860** O. W. HOLMES *Elsie V.* xxi. 292 With Helen Darley as a foil..she must be foudroyant.

2. *spec.* in *Pathol.* of a disease: Beginning in a very sudden and severe form.

fouel, obs. form of FOWL.

‖ † **'fouet.** *Obs.* [Fr. *fouet* whip.] A whip.

1491 CAXTON *Vitas Patr.* (W. de W. 1495) II. 296 a/2 Thenne he delyuered to hym a fouet & his hogges to kepe.

‖**fouetté** (fwete), *sb. Ballet.* [Fr., pa. pple. of *fouetter* to whip.] A step in which the dancer stands on one point and executes a rapid sideways 'whipping' movement with the free leg, freq. turning on the point at the same time.

1830 R. BARTON tr. *Blasis's Code of Terpsichore* II. 102 Afterwards come the..attitudes..the *grands fouettés*, facing and revolving. **1922** BEAUMONT & IDZIKOWSKI *Man. Class. Theatr. Dancing* II. iv. 80 Execute a *Fouetté à terre en dedans*. **1932** A. HASKELL *Ballet in Eng.* iii. 20 It is straightforward, strong, helpful music, a powerful aid in the famous (notorious?) 32 fouettés. **1947** *Ballet Ann.* I. 96 In the early classical ballets where we have the repetitive execution of steps (the *fouetté* is a good example), the pace will vary with the dancer. **1959** *Times* 2 Mar. 12/5 Technically, apart from a miscalculation in the *fouettés* of the third act, her dancing was smooth.

fougade (fuː'gaːd). [a. Fr. *fougade*, ad. It. *fugata*.] = FOUGASSE; also *fig.*

1643 SIR T. BROWNE *Relig. Med.* 37 'Twas not dumbe chance; that to discover the Fougade or Powder Plot, contrived a miscarriage in the letter. **1686** *Lond. Gaz.* No. 2163/1 The Enemy sprang five Mines or Fougades at the foot of the Breach. **1827** SOUTHEY *Penins. War* II. 126 The explosion of two fougades..scarcely appeared to impede their progress. **1904** *Daily Chron.* 4 June 5/5 The explosion of a number of mines and fougades.

fougasse (fuː'gɑːs). [a. Fr. *fougasse*, according to Hatz.-Darm. an alteration of FOUGADE.] 'A small mine from 6 to 12 feet under ground, charged either with powder or loaded shells' (Voyle).

1832 SOUTHEY *Penins. War* III. 414 Under the three angles of the glacis they placed fougasses. **1851** J. S. MACAULAY *Field Fort.* 224 The point at which it is intended to fire the fougasse.

fouge: see FOG *sb.*[1]

fough, var. of FAUGH *int.*

fought (fɔːt), *ppl. a.* [pa. pple. of FIGHT *v.*] In senses of the vb.; also with *out*. *rare* in attrib. use exc. with advs., as ***well-fought***. † ***close-fought*** (nonce-use): used in hand-to-hand fighting.

1550 J. COKE *Eng. & Fr. Heralds* § 125 He had in his dayes ben in .xxvi. fought battayles. **1615** CHAPMAN *Odyss.* II. 727 No touch away with him bore..of close-fought sword. **1827** SOUTHEY *Penins. War* II. 562 The circumstances of that well-fought field. **1865** SWINBURNE *Atalanta* 2059 The lord of fought fields Breaketh spearshaft from spear. **1895** *Daily News* 17 Apr. 7/2 A keenly fought out match.

foughten ('fɔːt(ə)n), *ppl. a.* [Archaic form of pa. pple. of FIGHT *v.*: see prec.]

1. ***foughten field***: one in which there is or has been fighting; a battle-field. *Obs.* exc. *poet.*

1568 GRAFTON *Chron.* II. 424 Was taken prisoner..in a pitched and foughten fielde. **1676** HOBBES *Iliad* 78 With all the horrour of a foughten field. **1819** KEATS *Otho* I. iii, A thousand foughten fields. **1870** EDGAR *Runnymede* 53 You will doubtless live to see..many foughten fields.

2. Of persons: † **a.** That has fought (*obs.*). **b.** *Sc.* FORFOUGHTEN.

1631 CHAPMAN *Cæsar & Pompey* Plays 1873 III. 166 So many staid and dreadfull soldiers?..long foughten? **1786** BURNS *Twa Dogs* 173 Are we sae foughten an' harrass'd.

'foughty, *a. dial.* Also 7 faughty, foughtie, 9 fouty. See also FOOTY. [app. repr. OE. **fúhtiȝ* (corresp. to Du. *vochtig*, Sw. *fuktig*, Da. *fugtig*, damp), f. *fúht* damp. The form *faughty* may be due to confusion with *fauty*, FAULTY. At Sheffield the pronunciation is (fʌʊtɪ) or (foʊtɪ).] Musty.

1600 SURFLET *Countrie Farme* VI. ii. 731 A mustie and foughtie taste in the wine. **1625** MARKHAM *Farew. Husb.* (1625) 115 Neither will the Corne corrupt or grow faughty, as long as the wormewood remaines amongst it. **1888** *Sheffield Gloss.*, Meat or broth which has lost its freshness.. or a pudding made of old suet, is fouty.

‖**fougue** (fuːg). *Obs.* Also 7 fogue. [a. Fr. *fougue*, ad. It. *foga*.] Fury, passion; ardour, impetuosity.

1660 DRYDEN *Astræa Redux* 203 Henceforth their fogue must spend at lesser rate. *c* **1665** MRS. HUTCHINSON *Mem. Col. Hutchinson* (1885) II. 55 The governor only laughed at his fogue. **1683** TEMPLE *Mem.* Wks. 1731 I. 452 After some Fougue spent for about a Fortnight..those Ambassadors began to grow soft and calm again.

‖**foujdar** (ˈfaʊdʒdar). Also 7 **fous-**, 8 **phous-**, 9 **fouge-**, **faoja-**. [Pers. *faujdār* f. Arab. *fauj* troop.] 'In India, an officer of the Moghul Government, who was invested with the charge of the police, and jurisdiction in criminal matters. Also, used in Bengal last century for a criminal judge' (Yule).

1683 SIR W. HEDGES *Diary* 8 Nov. (Hakluyt Soc.) I. 136 The Fousdar received another Perwanna. **1702** in Wheeler *Madras* (1861) I. 405 Perwannas directed to all Foujdars. **1763** ORME *Hist. Milit. Trans. Indostan* I. v. 374 The Phousdar of Velore..made overtures, offering to acknowledge Mahomed ally. **1809** LD. VALENTIA *Voy. & Trav. India* I. viii. 409 The Faojadar, being now in his capital, sent me an excellent dinner of fowls. **1828** HEBER *Journ. India* I. xvi. 419 The 'Foujdar' (Chatellain) of Suromunuggur. **1862** BEVERIDGE *Hist. India* II. v. v. 369 The majority..dismissed the fougedar.

Hence ‖ˈ**foujdary** *a.* [Pers.], pertaining to a foujdar.

1862 BEVERIDGE *Hist. India* II. v. vi. 413 Each zemindar.. was 'to exercise a fougedary jurisdiction'. **1892** *Wharton's Law Lex., Foujdarry-court*, a tribunal for administering criminal law. *Indian.*

foul (faʊl), *a.*, *adv.* and *sb.* Forms: 1 fúl, 2–3 ful, (3 ? fuȝel), 2–5 fule, (5 fulle), 4 fole, (feule), 4–7 foule, fowl(e, 4 *south.* voule, (5–6 foull, fow(e)ll), 9 *dial.* feaw, fou, 3– foul. [OE. *fúl* = OFris. *fûl(nisse)* (Du. *vuil*), OHG. *fûl* (MHG. *vûl*, Ger. *faul*), ON. *fúll* (Sw. *ful*, Da. *fuul*), Goth. *fûls*:—OTeut. **fûlo-*, f. root **fu-* (also in ON. *fúenn* rotten, *feyja*:—**faujan* to cause to rot):—Aryan **pu-* (in Skr. *pū* to stink, Gr. *πύον*, L. *pūs* purulent matter, L. *pūtēre* to stink, *puter* rotten).] A. *adj.*

I. 1. a. Grossly offensive to the senses, physically loathsome; primarily with reference to the odour or appearance indicative of putridity or corruption.

a **800** *Corpus Gloss.* 1031 *Holido*, fule. **971** *Blickl. Hom.* 59 Se lichoma þonne on þone heardestan stenc..þone fulostan bið ȝecyrred. *c* **1175** *Lamb. Hom.* 43 Ful stunch. *c* **1250** *Gen. & Ex.* 2556 Summe he deden in vn-ðewed swinc, for it was fuȝel and ful o stinc. *c* **1325** *Metr. Hom.* 77 Wykked folk sall fall doun Into hell that foule dongoun. *a* **1535** MORE *Wks.* (1557) 477 Lest he finally fall into the fowle smoke of helle, where he shall neuer see after. **1667** MILTON *P.L.* IV. 841 Thou resembl'st..Thy..place of doom obscure and foule. *Mod.* The foul smells of the place soon drove us away. The foul dens to be found in our great cities.

b. Of a disease or a person affected with disease: Loathsome. †*the foul disease* or *evil*: (*a*) epilepsy, (*b*) syphilis, etc. *foul brood*: a disease of larval bees (see quot. 1896); hence *foul-broody* adj., infected with foul brood.

c **900** *Bede Gloss.* 50 in Sweet *O.E. Texts* 181 *Feda peste*, fulre adle. **1393** LANGL. *P. Pl.* C. IV. 96 Feueres oþer fouler yueles. **1486** *Bk. St. Albans* C v b, That is tokyn of the foule glet. **1529** S. FISH *Supplic. Beggers* (E.E.T.S.) 1 The foule, vnhappy sorte of lepres. **1542** BOORDE *Introd. Knowl.* ii. 127 As 'the foule euyll', whyche is the fallyng syckenes, is at the ende of euery skottysh mans tale. **1607** TOPSELL *Four-f. Beasts* (1658) 567 The disease called the Foul evill. **1697** DRYDEN *Virg. Georg.* III. 711 On Winter Seas we fewer Storms behold, Than foul diseases that infect the Fold. **1744** BERKELEY *Siris* §63 Useful in gouts, dropsies, and rheums, as well as in the foul disease. **1863** *Jrnl. Hort.* 28 July 78/1 It..occurred to me that all the mischief might possibly arise from that fatal scourge of continental and American apiaries denominated 'foul brood'. **1875** J. HUNTER *Man. Bee-keeping* 193 Twenty stocks..were foul-broody, and I lost them all. **1888** *Gd. Words* 353 The terrible disease [of bees] known as 'foul-brood'. **1896** *Board of Agriculture Leaflet* No. 32 Foul brood or Bee pest is the most terrible scourge of apiculture. It..is caused by a rod-shaped micro-organism, called *Bacillus alvei*..Hives in which foul brood exists give forth a sickly and unpleasant smell.

c. Charged with offensive matter; 'full of gross humours' (J.). Of a carcase: Tainted with disease.

c **1400** *Lanfranc's Cirurg.* 93 Þis is þe difference bitwene a cankre & a foul ulcus. **1606** SHAKS. *A.Y.L.* II. vii. 60, I will through and through Cleanse the foul bodie of th' infected world. **1609** SKENE *Reg. Maj., Stat. Robt. III*, c. 40. 59 b, Fvle Swine, or Corrvpted Salmon, sould be not sauld. **1799** *Med. Jrnl.* II. 350 A comparative view of a foul ulcer, with one in a healing state. **1837** CARLYLE *Fr. Rev.* I. II. iii. (1872) 32 Foul Product of still fouler corruption.

II. Opposed to CLEAN *a.* II.

(The implication of disgust etymologically belonging to the word was formerly often absent in these senses; in present use association with sense 1 has commonly restored it, exc. in certain technical or idiomatic expressons.)

2. Dirty, soiled; covered with or full of dirt. Of ground, a road: Miry, muddy. Now *arch.* or *dial.*, exc. with mixture of sense 1: Disgustingly dirty, filthy.

c **1000** ÆLFRIC *Gloss.* in Wr.-Wülcker 125 *Stigmentum*, ful maal on ræȝel. *c* **1175** *Lamb. Hom.* 81 Þes oðer..luueð his sunnen alse deð þet fette swin þet fule fen to liȝȝen in. *c* **1230** *Hali Meid.* 13 Þa ilke sari wrecches þat i þat ilke fule wurðunge unweddede walewið. *c* **1300** *Havelok* 555 In a poke, ful and blac, Sone he caste him on his bac. **1387** TREVISA *Higden* (Rolls) I. 287 Torfes..smelleþ wors þan wode, and makeþ fouler askes. *c* **1450** *St. Cuthbert* (Surtees) 7214 Þe way was foule, and wendyng hard. *c* **1483** CAXTON *Vocab.* 16 Yf it [the vrinall] be foull. So rubbe it within. **1516** *Will of R. Peke of Wakefield* 4 June, To ament a fowll holle abowt the brige. **1535** COVERDALE *Zech.* iii. 4 Take awaye ye foule clothes from him. **1655** H. VAUGHAN *Silex Scint.* I. *Stars* (1858) 56 The night Is dark, and long; The Rode foul. **1700** S. L. tr. *Fryke's Voy. E. Ind.* 341 One of the Washers, came..to fetch People's foul Linnen. **1807** *Med. Jrnl.* XVII. 107 The sick..dressed in their foulest clothes. **1889** *Whitby Gaz.* 25 Oct. 3/3 If the way be foul so as not to be passable.

fig. **1588** SHAKS. *L.L.L.* IV. i. 139 Come, come, you talke greasily, your lips grow foule. **1715** DE FOE *Fam. Instruct.* I. iv. (1841) 86 If you hold of this Mind, we are like to have a foul house with you quickly.

3. a. †Of handwriting: Blotted, illegible (*obs.*). ***foul case*** (see quots. 1872, 1963); ***foul copy***: a first copy, defaced by corrections (now *rare*); so †***foul books***, etc.; ***foul papers***, a draft or working manuscript, as opposed to a fair copy; ***foul proof***: see quots. (Cf. CLEAN *a.* 3 c, FAIR *a.* 8 c.)

1467 *Paston Lett.* No. 575 II. 307 By cause of the foule wrytyng and interlynyeng. *c* **1625** in *Library* (1925) 4th Ser. VI. 152 The Booke where by it was first Acted from is lost: and this hath beene transcribed from the fowle papers of the Authors wch were found. **1628** EARLE *Microcosm.* (Arb.) 85 Acquaintance is the first draught of a friend, whom we must lay downe oft thus, as the foule coppy. **1659** *Burton's Diary* (1828) IV. 470 The particulars in his hands were foul books and papers, out of which those he had returned were extracted. **1683** MOXON *Mech. Exerc.* II. 377 *Foul Proof*, when a Proof has many Faults markt in it. **1729** J. GAY *Polly* Pref. p. iii, I take this occasion in the most solemn manner to affirm, that the very copy I delivered to Mr. Rich was written in my own hand some months before at the Bath from my own first foul blotted papers. **1758** JORTIN *Erasm.* I. 46 He sent a foul Copy..to Ammonius, begging him to get it transcribed. **1872** W. BLADES *Shaks. & Typogr.* 74 The compositor works with two of these cases slanting up in front of him, and, when from a shake, a slip, or any other accident, the letters become misplaced, the result is technically known as a 'foul case'. **1888** JACOBI *Printer's Voc., Foul proof*—a proof distinct from a clean proof. **1955** *Essays & Studies* VIII. 3 Investigators have worked out theories about how we can recognize 'foul papers' ('author's manuscript in its last stage before the making of a fair copy', to quote a recent definition). **1959** F. BOWERS *Textual & Lit. Crit.* iii. 75 Formerly, both quartos were thought to be printed from Shakespeare's foul papers. **1963** KENNEISON & SPILMAN *Dict. Printing* 73 *Foul case*, a case of type in which the separate pieces of type have been distributed into the wrong compartments.

b. ***foul bill of health***: see BILL *sb.*[3] 10.

1867 SMYTH *Sailor's Word-bk.* s.v. *Bill of Health.*

4. a. Charged with defiling or noxious matter; *esp.* said of air, water, etc. †Of a ship: ***to make foul water*** (see quot. 1769). Cf. CLEAN *a.* 2.

foul air, *water*, exc. in technical uses as *Naut.* or *Mining*, are now used with a mixture of sense 1.

1535 COVERDALE *Jer.* ii. 18 To drinke foule water. **1627** CAPT. SMITH *Seaman's Gram.* ix. 44 Fowle water is when she comes into shallow water where shee raise the sand or ose with her way. **1653–4** WHITELOCKE *Jrnl. Swed. Emb.* (1772) I. 132 [The ship].. made fowle water by striking as she passed over the Riffe. **1756** C. LUCAS *Ess. Waters* I. 35 The Seine..is foul and turbid as the Avon. **1769** FALCONER *Dict. Marine* (1789), *Eau changée*, foul water; or water whose colour is changed by approaching the shore, or otherwise. **1805** T. LINDLEY *Voy. Brasil* (1808) 48 Oppressed with breathing the foul air. **1817** COLERIDGE *Sibyl. Leaves* (1862) 271 The unwholesome plain Sent up its foulest fogs. **1851** GREENWELL *Coal-trade Terms Northumb. & Durh.* 26 *Foul*, in an inflammable state, from fire-damp having accumulated. **1885** *Manch. Exam.* 5 June 5/2 Old workings charged with foul gas. **1891** E. PEACOCK *N. Brendon* I. 2 Coal pits..make the atmosphere foul with smoke.

b. Dirty-coloured, discoloured. Also *fig. rare.*

1601 SHAKS. *All's Well* I. iii. 6 We..make foule the clearnesse of our deseruings. **1657** R. LIGON *Barbadoes* (1673) 12 Those teeth, which at a distance appear'd rarely white, are yellow and foul. **1717** tr. *Frezier's Voy. S. Sea* 183 Glass made with Saltpeter..is green, foul, and ill wrought. **1799** G. SMITH *Laboratory* I. 136 Put into this your yellow-coloured or foul pearls.

5. a. Of food: Coarse, gross, rank. Hence, applied to the eating of such food, or the eaters of it (in present use, with the stronger notion of feeding on unclean or putrid food).

1713 FELTON *On Classicks* 67 They are all for rank and foul Feeding. **1726** SHELVOCKE *Voy. round World* (1757) 256 Not one of us had an hour's sickness, notwithstanding we fed on such foul diet as we did, without bread or salt. **1727** ARBUTHNOT *John Bull* Postscript ch. x, How the Esq: from a foul-feeder grew dainty. *Mod.* The vulture is a foul feeder.

b. Of a horse: Sluggish from want of exercise. †Hence, torpid. [Cf. Ger. *faul* lazy.]

1580 FRAMPTON *Dial. Yron & Steele* 133 For if they cast the juyce uppon him, it maketh him fowle [Sp. *lo entorpece*]. **1737** BRACKEN *Farriery Impr.* (1757) II. 92 Any Horse that has too little Exercise, and is what we call foul, may puff and blow when moved quick up a Hill.

6. Clogged, choked, or encumbered with something foreign. Cf. CLEAN *a.* 3 b. **a.** *gen.* ? *Obs.*

c **1470** HENRY *Wallace* II. 377 Thoct it [the blaid] was foule, nobill it was of steyll. **1572** HULOET, *Fowle corn*, being full of weedis. **1759** B. MARTIN *Nat. Hist. Eng.* I. Devon 31 The Head of it lies in a fowl, barren ground. **1793** *Trans. Soc. Arts* (ed. 2) V. 77 Ground that is either foul of weeds or grass. **1809** *Med. Jrnl.* XXI. 75 Swamps, muddy banks, and foul shores.

b. of a gun-barrel, or a chimney.

1674 S. VINCENT *Gallant's Acad.* 17 The Body of it [a gun] is fowl..by being too much heated. **1805** W. SAUNDERS *Min. Waters* 32 The scourings of a foul gun barrel. **1846** GREENER *Sc. Gunnery* 137 If the gun be allowed to get very foul. **1860–1** FLO. NIGHTINGALE *Nursing* 24 If your chimney is foul, sweep it.

c. Naut. ***foul bottom, coast, ground*** (see quot. 1867). Also, of a ship: Having the bottom overgrown with seaweed, shell-fish, etc.

1622 R. HAWKINS *Voy. S. Sea* (1847) 117 The norther part of the bay hath foule ground and rockes under water. **1683** HACKE *Collect. Voy.* I. (1699) 23 Yet she out-sailed us, she being clean and we as foul as we could be. **1717** tr. *Frezier's Voy. S. Sea* 293 The Sea running high..made us fear, because the Coast is foul. **1790** BEATSON *Nav. & Mil. Mem.* 405 The Monmouth now became very foul and leaky. **1808** FORSYTH *Beauties Scotl.* V. 515 The navigation of the Sound of Ilay is dangerous..from foul ground. **1867** SMYTH *Sailor's Word-bk., Foul Bottom*..the bottom of the sea if rocky, or unsafe from wrecks. *Foul Coast*, one beset with reefs and breakers. *Foul Ground*, synonymous with foul bottom. **1875** BEDFORD *Sailor's Pocket-bk.* v. (ed. 2) 157 The launch should be sent in the direction of the foulground.

†**d.** Of plants: Infested with insect parasites. Cf. FILTH 2 c. ? *Obs.*

1811 *Sporting Mag.* XXXVII. 33 The peas fine, but foul [with plant-lice].

e. *Path.* Of the tongue: Coated with fur, furred.

1800 *Med. Jrnl.* IV. 422 We misunderstand one of the most common appearances..I mean a foul tongue. **1849** CLARIDGE *Cold Water-cure* 166 Foul tongue and pain at the pit of the stomach.

7. a. Morally or spiritually polluted; abominable, detestable, wicked. For ***foul fiend***, see FIEND. ***foul thief***: the devil. ***foul spirit*** = unclean spirit. Cf. CLEAN *a.* 4.

a **1000** *Crist* 1482 (Gr.) Þu þæt sele-ȝescot..þurh firenlustas fule synne unsyfre besmite. *a* **1175** *Cott. Hom.* 243 Euel ȝeþanc and fule lustes. *c* **1205** LAY. 27634 His fule saule sæh in to helle. *c* **1275** *Death* 206 in *O.E. Misc.* 181 Þer ich schal imete mony o ful wiht. **1297** R. GLOUC. (1724) 380 Kyng Wyllam..bygan sone..to febly..Vor trauayl of þe foul asaȝt. *a* **1300** *Cursor M.* 7444 (Gött.) Goli, þat etin, In foul hordam was he getin. *c* **1320** *Sir Tristr.* 1007 Þou lexst a foule lesing. *c* **1386** CHAUCER *Pars. T.* ¶72 Ne a fouler thral may no man..maken of his body than for to yeuen his body to synne. *c* **1420** *Metr. St. Kath.* (Halliw.) 10 Helle hounde, thou fowle wyght. *c* **1425** *Seven Sag.* (P.) 681 The fule thefe ..He was aboute my wyf to spyle. **1526** *Pilgr. Perf.* (W. de W. 1531) 129 b, Theyr suggestions & thoughtes be foule & unprofytable. **1526–34** TINDALE *Rev.* xviii. 2 Babilon..ys become..the holde of all fowle sprettes. **1610** SHAKS. *Temp.* IV. i. 139, I had forgot that foule conspiracy Of the beast Calliban. **1679** PENN *Addr. Prot.* II. v. (1692) 186 To be Led ..in ways we see to be foul or wrong. **1719** WATTS *Ps.* cxxi. (L.M.) 25 On thee foul spirits have no power. **1781** COWPER *Expostulation* 213 Grace abused brings forth the foulest deeds, As richest soil the most luxuriant weeds. **1817** COLERIDGE *Sibyl. Leaves* (1862) 216 Beneath the foulest mother's curse No child could ever thrive. **1838** THIRLWALL *Greece* IV. 267 Aristophanes must stand convicted..of the foulest motives. **1855** MACAULAY *Hist. Eng.* III. 60 A court foul with all the vices of the Restoration.

ellipt. **1788** PICKEN *Poems* 81 O' a' the Nine, the foul a ane [= devil a one] Inspiris like thee.

†**b.** Guilty of a charge or accusation; criminally implicated. *Obs.* Cf. CLEAN *a.* 4 b.

a **1300** [see CLEAN *a.* 4 b]. **1575** CHURCHYARD *Chippes* (1817) 194, I must..Prooue foule, or cleane, and by my peeres be tried. *c* **1575** BALFOUR *Practicks* (1754) 611 Efter the offendar be anis fund foul of the first offence. **1621** ELSING *Debates Ho. Lords* (Camden) 36 Twedy is very fowle in this buissines.

8. Of speech, etc.: Filthy, obscene; also, disgustingly abusive.

a **1000** *Voc.* in Wr.-Wülcker 458 *Obscæne*, þære fulan. *c* **1450** *Grosseteste's Househ. Stat.* in *Babees Bk.* 330 That they be-haue them selfe honestly, with-out stryffe, fowle-spekyng, and noyse. **1477** EARL RIVERS (Caxton) *Dictes* 15 Beware that..ther escape out of your mouth noo foule wordes. *c* **1530** H. RHODES *Bk. Nurture* 107 in *Babees Bk.* 74 Foule speech deserues a double hate. **1590** SPENSER *F.Q.* I. v. 50 The bold Semiramis..her fowle reproches spoke. **1603** SHAKS. *Meas. for M.* v. i. 309 In foule mouth..To call him villaine. **1757** *Affect. Narr. Wager* 32 He poured out a deal of foul Language. **1833** HT. MARTINEAU *3 Ages* ii. 47 The..gentlemen present had..set the fiddlers..to sing all the foul songs. **1834** MEDWIN *Angler in Wales* I. 145 If you don't stop that foul mouth of yours, I'll [etc.]. **1852** MISS YONGE *Cameos* I. xii. 80 Keep..your foul tongue to yourself.

9. †**a.** Of persons: Ceremonially unclean. Of food: Defiling, not fit for use. *Obs.*

c **1000** ÆLFRIC *Judg.* xiii. 4 Ne naht fules ne þicȝe! *c* **1400** MAUNDEV. (Roxb.) xi. 41 So foule men schuld noȝt comme in to so haly place.

b. In mod. use applied to fish at or immediately after spawning. Cf. CLEAN *a.* 5 b.

†**c.** See quot., and cf. CLEAN *a.* 5 d; also *foul-cut* in C. 6.

1811 *Sporting Mag.* XXXVIII. 212 A foul horse—not a complete gelding.

†**10.** Of language, diction: Incorrect, inelegant. *Obs.*$^{-1}$ Cf. FAIR *a.* 4, CLEAN *a.* 7 a.

1303 R. BRUNNE *Handl. Synne* 8627 To my sawe blame may be leyde For foule englysshe.

III. Opposed to FAIR *a.*

11. a. Of persons and material objects: Ugly. Now *rare* in literary use, but in many (midl. and north.) dialects the current sense. Cf. FAIR *a.* 1 a.

c **1386** CHAUCER *Wife's Prol.* 265 And if that she be foul thou seist, that she Coveiteth every man that she may se. **1393** LANGL. *P. Pl.* C. XIX. 54 Thenne tok ich hede, Whether the frut were faire other foul to loken on. **1413** *Pilgr. Sowle* (Caxton 1483) IV. ii. 58 These pepyns myght nought kyndely sprynge to a fayre appeltree but to fowle buskes and wylde. **1483** CAXTON *G. de la Tour* G vij, Soone after another [sone] they hadde whiche was fowle and lame. **1509** *York Manual* (Surtees) 27 For fayrer for fouler. **1533** FRITH *Another Bk. agst. Rastell* (1829) 225 He hath made a foul hole in his kinsmans best coat. **1568** TILNEY *Disc. Mariage* E vij, Daylie we maye see a foule deformed woman, that [etc.]. **1583** HOLLYBAND *Campo di Fior* 15 Thou callest me fowle [Fr. *laide*, It. *brutta*] wenche. **1603** KNOLLES *Hist.*

Turks (1621) 53 Hee was set upon a foule lean cammell. 1604 SHAKS. *Oth.* II. i. 141. 1607 —— *Timon* IV. iii. 28. 1616 W. BROWNE *Brit. Past.* II. i. 10 None could be foule esteem'd compar'd with her. 1836 EMERSON *Nature, Beauty* Wks. (Bohn) II. 145 There is no object so foul that intense light will not make beautiful. 1841 TRENCH *Parables* xii. (1877) 232 He loved her foul, that He might make her fair.

b. Of a part of an animal: ? Ill-shaped. ? *Obs.*

1688 *Lond. Gaz.* No. 2336/8 Lost.. a middle-siz'd Fleet-Hound Bitch, very strong made.. a foul stern. 1703 *Ibid.* 3881/4 Stolen.. a thick punching Horse.. a little white on one of his Heels, and a foul Head. [1765: cf. 20 a.]

†**c.** Unattractive, poor in quality. *Obs.*

1535 COVERDALE *1 Sam.* xv. 9 What was foule and nothinge worth, that they damned. 1606 SHAKS. *Tr. & Cr.* I. iii. 359 Let vs (like Merchants) show our fowlist Wares, And thinke, perchance, they'l sell.

†**d.** Of the face: Disfigured by distress or tears.

*c*1400 *Destr. Troy* 8507 Thies fellyn hym to fete with a foule chere. 1611 BIBLE *Job* xvi. 16 My face is fowle with weeping.

12. Of sounds: Ugly, disagreeable. Now *dial.* (Common in north midlands). Cf. FAIR *a.* 2.

*c*1440 *York Myst.* xxxi. 320 O! ȝe make a foule noyse for þe nonys. 1568 GRAFTON *Chron.* II. 274 The Genowayes.. made another leape and a foule crie. 1606 HOLLAND *Sueton.* 81 The Frogges.. chaunced to make a foule noyse.

13. a. Disgraceful, ignominious, shameful. Cf. 7.

*a*1300 *Cursor M.* 7829 (Gött.) A fouler dede þan ani may driue. *c*1400 *Apol. Loll.* 55 þe Son of God wold be condempnid to fowlist deþ. *c*1420 *Sir Amadace* (Camd.) ii, Thenne made I a fulle fowle ende! 1529 MORE *Comf. agst. Trib.* III. Wks. 1213/2 Thys vngracious secte of Mahomette, shall haue a fowle fall. 1559 *Mirr. Mag., Northumberland* xi, This fowle despite did cause vs to conspire. 1590 SHAKS. *Mids. N.* III. ii. 197 Haue you conspir'd.. To baite me with this foule derision? 1659 D. PELL *Impr. Sea* 605 This is a foul blot in the Sailors Scutchion. 1756 C. LUCAS *Ess. Waters* II. 144, I should be glad.. to acquit the college.. of this foul charge. 1808 SCOTT *Marm.* VI. xv, A letter forged! .. Did ever knight so foul a deed!

b. Revolting, disgusting. *slang.*

1911 D. COKE *Wilson's* vi. 59, I was stopping somebody making a foul row. 1930 A. P. HERBERT *Water Gipsies* xxi, 'Hullo, Gordon! My dear, it's a *foul* night. Arctic!' She shivered charmingly. 1930 *Punch* 20 Aug. 200/1 'How foul!' I said... 'How dare the creature long to meet me!' 1963 'J. LE CARRÉ' *Spy who came in fr. Cold* xxv. 212 Mundt won. London won—that's the point. It was a foul, foul operation. But it's paid off, and that's the only rule.

14. *Sporting* and *Games.* Contrary to rule or established custom, irregular, unfair; said also of the player. ***foul ball*** (Baseball): a ball struck so that it falls outside the lines drawn from the home base through the first and third bases. Cf. FAIR *a.* 10.

1797 *Sporting Mag.* IX. 283 His antagonist having struck him two foul blows. *a*1861 MRS. BROWNING *Last Poems, Garibaldi* i, Perhaps that was not a foul trick. 1882 *Field* 28 Jan. (Cassell), Thus, at billiards, if a player makes a foul stroke and scores, his adversary has the option of not enforcing the penalty. 1882 *Sydney Slang Dict.* 4/1 *Foul-riding,* boring a competitor against the rails. 1892 J. KENT *Ld. G. Bentinck* ii. 48 Colonel Leigh.. accused Sam Chifney of foul riding.

b. *esp.* in ***foul play***: unfair conduct in a game; *transf.* unfair or treacherous dealing, often with the additional notion of roughness or violence: see 17. So also †***foul player.*** Cf. *fair-play,* FAIR *a.* 10 c.

[Cf. *c*1440 in 17.] 1580 LYLY *Euphues* (Arb.) 289 Foule gamesters, who hauing lost the maine.. thinke to face it out with a false oath. 1610 SHAKS. *Temp.* I. ii. 58 What fowle play had we, that we came from thence? *c*1672 WOOD *Life* (Oxf. Hist. Soc.) I. 383 Supposing.. that Dr. Thomas Jones .. would act foul play in the election. 1674 tr. *Scheffer's Lapland* 109 To strike the ball with their bandies over the others line (for it is foul play to fling it with their hands). *Ibid.,* Any one that is found delinquent in this kind, is branded for a fowl plaier. 1737 M. GREEN *Spleen* (1738) 21 And when he can't prevent foul-play, Enjoys the folly of the fray. 1814 *Sporting Mag.* XLIV. 241 After the fifteenth round 'Foul play!' was loudly called. 1825 LYTTON *Zicci* 5 There can be no foul play at the public tables. 1887 RIDER HAGGARD *Jess* xxii, At any rate that does not look like foul play.

c. †Of a return: Fraudulent (*obs.*). Also, in ***foul loss***: see quot. 1848.

1685 LUTTRELL *Brief Rel.* (1857) I. 341 Foul returns [of elections] made in many places. 1848 ARNOULD *Mar. Insur.* (1866) II. III. ix. 1004 If after a loss has been paid, the underwriter discovers that there was fraud, misrepresentation or concealment.. such payment is familiarly termed in insurance law a foul loss.

†**d.** ***foul honesty***: (? an oxymoron) false pretence of honesty. *Obs.*

1550 HOOPER *Serm. on Jonas* iii. 40 b, Then washeth he hys handes with as much foule honestie as he can.

15. Of the weather, etc.: Unfavourable; wet and stormy. Cf. FAIR *a.* 12.

*c*1380 WYCLIF *Serm.* Sel. Wks. I. 101 Foule wedir and coold. *a*1541 WYATT in Warton *Hist. Eng. Poetry* (1840) III. xxxviii. 47 In foule wether at my booke to sit. 1595 SHAKS. *John* IV. ii. 108 So foule a skie cleres not without a storme. 1628 DIGBY *Voy. Medit.* (1868) 9 And att night wee had foule weather. 1661 PEPYS *Diary* 19 Apr., It being so foule that I could not go to Whitehall. 1719 DE FOE *Crusoe* I. xiii, A very foul Night it was after it. 1776 ADAM SMITH *W.N.* I. x. (1869) I. 107 A mason.. can work neither in hard frost nor in foul weather. 1865 PARKMAN *Champlain* iii. (1875) 228 For labor or amusement in foul weather.

16. Of the wind: Contrary, unfavourable.

1726 G. ROBERTS *4 Years' Voy.* 3 Untoward Weather, as well as a foul Wind. 1795 NELSON 22 May in Nicolas *Disp.* II. 39 Continued foul winds.. from the day of our sailing. 1883 S. C. HALL *Retrospect* II. 300 The packet could not sail in the teeth of a foul wind.

17. Of a means or procedure, and of language: Harsh, rough, violent. Cf. FAIR *a.* 15.

*c*1440 *Gesta Rom.* lx. 248 (Harl. MS.), Tristing in himselfe that the lion wolde have I-made a foule pleye withe þe lorde & withe þe lady. 1592 SHAKS. *Ven. & Ad.* 573 Foul words and frowns must not repel a lover. 1608 *Yorksh. Trag.* I. vii, A fouler strength than his O'erthrew me with his arms. 1639 T. BRUGIS tr. *Camus' Moral Relat.* 171 He would not have gathered by faire meanes or foule, that which he so impatiently desired. 1659 D. PELL *Impr. Sea* 79 Some of you get foul checks. 1704 [see FAIR *a.* 15]. 1856 EMERSON *Eng. Traits, Aristocracy* Wks. II. 85 War is a foul game.

18. *Naut.,* opposed to *clear*: 'Entangled, embarrassed, or contrary to' (Adm. Smyth). Const. *of,* †*on.* ***to fall, run foul of***: see the vbs. ***foul berth, hawse***: see quot. 1867.

1627 CAPT. SMITH *Seaman's Gram.* xiii. 61 We are fowle on each other, and the ship is on fire. 1697 DAMPIER *Voy.* I. x. 303 She.. coming foul of the same shole.. was in great danger of being lost. 1743 BULKELEY & CUMMINS *Voy. S. Seas* 115 In weighing the Grapenel.. we found it foul among some Rocks. 1748 *Anson's Voy.* I. i. 10 And we were in no small danger of driving foul of the Prince Frederick. 1769 FALCONER *Dict. Marine* (1789), *Tour de cable,* a foul hawse; a turn or elbow in the hawse. 1822 G. W. MANBY *Voy. Greenland* (1823) 13 A small axe to cut away the line, in case of its getting foul when running out. 1829 MARRYAT *F. Mildmay* xxiii, Topsail-tie is foul. 1840 R. H. DANA *Bef. Mast* vii. 16 We [the ship] were continually swinging round, and had thus got a very foul hawse. 1867 SMYTH *Sailor's Word-bk., Foul Berth,* when a ship anchors in the hawse of another she gives the latter a foul berth. *Foul Hawse,* when a vessel is riding with two anchors out, and the cables are crossed round each other outside the stem, by the swinging of the ship when moored in a tide-way.

b. ***foul anchor***: see quot. 1769. Also, the badge of the British Admiralty.

1769 FALCONER *Dict. Marine* (1789), Foul *Anchor*: it is so called when it.. hooks some other anchor, wreck, or cable.. or when.. the ship.. straying round the bed of her anchor entangles her slack cable about the upper fluke of it. 1840 R. H. DANA *Bef. Mast* xiii. 31 On one of his broad arms he had the crucifixion, and on the other the sign of the 'foul anchor'. 1882 NARES *Seamanship* (ed. 6) 203 Put a foul-anchor strop round the crown.

19. Of a charge of powder.

1799 G. SMITH *Laboratory* I. 9 If the rocket rises a little, and falls back, the charge is foul.

IV. 20. *Comb.* **a.** parasynthetic, as ***foul-aired, -browed, -faced, -minded*** (hence ***foul-mindedness***), ***-thighed, -tongued, -vizored.*** Also FOUL-MOUTHED.

1883 *Century Mag.* XXVI. 213 The whole place unclean and *foul-aired. 1610 HEALEY *St. Aug. Citie of God* 765 The holy.. servants of the true God live in this *foule-browed world. 1602 *2nd Pt. Return fr. Parnass.* I. i. (Arb.) 7 Then *foule faced Vice was in his swadling bands. 1849 KINGSLEY *Poetry Sacr. & Leg. Art* Misc. I. 244 Every form of prudish and prurient *foulmindedness. 1765 *Treat. Dom. Pigeons* 95 Let it [another colour] fall here, or on any other part of the thigh, it is called *foul-thigh'd. 1549 COVERDALE, etc. *Erasm. Par. Rom.* iii. 8 *Foule tounged people. 1608 MACHIN *Dumb Knight* I. i, *Foule vizard coynes.

b. in *attrib.* (quasi-*adj.*) uses of ***foul weather*** (sense 15); also ***foul-weather-like*** adj.

1768 WALES in *Phil. Trans.* LX. 108 Over these they have a kind of foul-weather jacket. *c*1793 *Spirit Pub. Jrnls.* (1799) I. 75, I don't care a stale chaw of tobacco for the foul-weather looks of any fair-weather Jack in the three kingdoms. 1837 MARRYAT *Dog-fiend* xii, He remained in his .. foul-weather hat. 1793 SMEATON *Edystone L.* §275 The sky began to look foul-weather-like.

B. *sb.* [The adj. used *absol.* or *elliptically.*]

1. That which is foul (in senses of the adj.): something foul. ***for foul nor fair***: on no account, by no means. For ***foul befall*** see note on FAIR *sb.*[2] 1.

*a*900 *Halsuncge* in Sweet *O.E. Texts* 176 Ðis mon.. scal reda ofer ða feta ðe ful infalleð. *a*1000 *Elene* 769 þæs he in ermðum sceal earla fula ful fah þrowian. *c*1386 CHAUCER *Man of Law's T.* 525 But what she was, she wold no man seye For foul ne fair. *c*1400 *Sowdone Bab.* 199 And foule shal hem this day bifalle. 1430 LYDG. *Chron. Troy* I. v, All the foule shall couertly be wryed. *c*1470 HENRY *Wallace* I. 430 Foule mot yow fall. 1477 NORTON *Ord. Alch.* iv. in Ashm. (1652) 47 Foule and cleane by naturall lawe Hath greate discord. 1594 J. DICKENSON *Arisbas* (1878) 54 Foule fall the wagge that lost so rare a iewell. 1768 STERNE *Sent. Journ.* (1778) II. 7 Foul befal the man who ever lays a snare in its way!

*Prov. a*1661 FULLER *Worthies, Cheshire* I. (1662) 177 Frost and Fraud both end in Foul.

2. A disease in the feet of cattle and sheep. Also, a disease in dogs (see quot. 1854). Cf. FILE *sb.*[2] 6 b.

1523 FITZHERB. *Husb.* §63 There be bestes, that wyll haue the foule and that is betwene the cleese, sometyme before, and some tyme behynde, and it wyll swell, and cause hym to halt. 1614 MARKHAM *Cheap Husb.* II. xxiii. (1668) 79 Troubled with that disease which is called the Foule. 1737 BRACKEN *Farriery Impr.* (1756) I. 315 What the Cow-Leeches term the Foul in a Cow's Foot. 1810 *Ann. Reg.* 629, I have had them disordered in the feet with the fouls, but not the foot-rot. 1854 E. MAYHEW *Dogs* (1861) 114 Foul is not one disease, but an accumulation of disorders, brought on by the absence of exercise, with a stimulating diet.

3. a. (In sense partly derived from FOUL *v.*) A collision or entanglement, *esp.* in riding, rowing, running, etc.; an irregular stroke, piece of play, etc. ***to claim a foul***: to claim a favourable award because of unfair action on the part of an opponent. In *Baseball*: A foul hit: see A. 14.

1754 *Dict. Arts & Sc.* II. 1311 Foul imports, also, the running of one ship against another. 1864 *Home News* 19 Dec. 21/2 Coombes.. boring his opponent too closely to the shore, a foul occurred. 1867 F. FRANCIS *Angling* v. (1880) 150 The drop will fall over the stretcher, and a foul will be the consequence. 1873 BENNETT *Billiards* 480 The player who made the foul must follow suit. 189. *Billiard Rules* xix, A player may claim a foul if he sees his opponent touch a ball .. (except with his cue, when making a stroke).

b. ***foul-up***: a state of muddle or confusion. orig. *U.S.*

1953 'S. RANSOME' *Drag Dark* (1954) vii. 69, I couldn't judge how far I could rely on you to find the way out of this foul-up. 1958 'P. BRYANT' *Two Hours to Doom* 30 Second weapon to be used if there's any foul up with the first. 1967 *Observer* 14 May 2/8 He traces the foul-up back to 1953.

C. *adv.* [In early ME. *fule, foule,* f. the adj. with advb. ending *-e*; after 14th c. not distinguished in form from the adj.]

†**1.** In a manner offensive to the sense of smell.

*c*1200 ORMIN 1201 Gat iss.. Gal deor, and stinnkeþþ fule. *c*1275 *XI Pains of Hell* 123 in *O.E. Misc.* 150 þe stude.. stinkeþ fulre þane þe hund. *a*1300 *Cursor M.* 18147 þou hell, sua fule stinkand thing. *c*1340 *Ibid.* 6353 (Trin.) þe wattres þat so foule stank. 1563 W. FULKE *Meteors* (1640) 67 b, Lead also, which maketh it to bee in colour so black and so fowle to corrupt.

†**2.** In an ugly manner. ***to fare foul***: To behave in an unseemly way, 'go on' outrageously.

?*a*1366 CHAUCER *Rom. Rose* 155 Y frounced foule was hir visage. *a*1400-50 *Alexander* 4082 Women.. þat frely faire ware of face bot foule ware clethid. *c*1425 *Seven Sag.* (P.) 484 Scho.. To-rente hyre clothes and foule ferde. *c*1450 *Merlin* 116 Foule were thei skorched with the fier.

†**3.** Disgracefully, shamefully. *Obs.* ***to call (a person) foul***: to call by a bad name. *Obs.*

*c*1275 *Doomsday* 48 in *O.E. Misc.* 164 So fule he [þe cwed] vs blende. *c*1325 *Poem temp. Edw. II* (Percy) lxi, He shal be foul afrounted. 1362 LANGL. *P. Pl.* A. III. 179 And þou hast famed me foule bifore the kyng heer. 1385 CHAUCER *L.G.W.* 1307 *Dido,* Ye wil nat fro your wyf thus foule fleen? *c*1386 —— *Pars. T.* ¶741 He leseth foule his good þat ne seketh with the yifte of his good no thyng but synne. *c*1430 *How Wise Man taught his Son* 100 in *Babees Bk.* 51 To calle hir foule it is þi schame. *a*1450 *Knt. de la Tour* 13 [In confession] ye shulde telle the synne as foule as ye do it, and in the same manere. *c*1450 *Merlin* 12 Hir bewte was foule spente, seth it was loste in soche manere. 1594 SHAKS. *Rich. III,* III. ii. 44 Ile haue this Crown of mine cut from my shoulders, Before Ile see the Crowne so foule mis-plac'd.

4. †**a.** Badly, ill, grievously. *Obs.*

*a*1225 *Ancr. R.* 108 Heo is a grucchild, & ful itowen. *c*1340 *Cursor M.* 1639 (Trin.) þe erþe wiþ synne is foul shent. ?1366 CHAUCER *Rom. Rose* 1061 They.. foule abate the folkes prys. 1377 LANGL. *P. Pl.* B. x. 472 Selden falle thei so foule.. As clerkes of holikirke. *c*1400 *Rom. Rose* 2655 Than shalt thou goon, ful foule aferd. 1426 W. PASTON in *P. Lett.* No. 7 I. 26, I am foule and noysyngly vexed with hem. *c*1460 *Towneley Myst.* (Surtees) 114 Ille spon weft, I wys, ay commys foulle owte. 1590 SPENSER *F.Q.* I. v. 23 Two of three her nephews are so fowle forlorne.

b. Not in the correct or regular manner.

1683 *Lond. Gaz.* No. 1840/4 [He] trots and gallops foul. 1686 *Ibid.* No. 2136/4 Stolen or stray'd.. a red roan Gelding .. trots foul.. cuts behind. 1715 *Ibid.* No. 5331/4 Carries his Tail foul. 1884 *Western Daily Press* 16 Apr. 7/2 A well-known.. amateur.. in spurring his first bird fastened the spur on 'foul', the result being that the first blow it made cut its own throat.

5. Unfairly; contrary to the rules of the game. Also *fig.* in ***to play (a person) foul***: to deal treacherously with.

1707 *Reflex. upon Ridicule* 261 You are fond of Gaming and you Play foul. 1755 YOUNG *Centaur* 105 He that plays foul the most dexterously is sure to be undone. 1799 NELSON 17 Oct. in Nicolas *Disp.* IV. 60 Our Allies have.. played us foul.

6. *Comb.,* as ***foul-feeding, -reeking, -smelling, -spoken*** adjs.; also **foul-biting** *sb.* (see quot.); **foul-cut** *a.,* imperfectly gelded (cf. FOUL *a.* 9 c); **foul-hooked** *a.,* of a fish, hooked anywhere on the body except in the mouth.

1822 IMISON *Sc. & Art* II. 429 Otherwise you will have parts bit that were not intended, which is called *foul-biting. 1811 *Sporting Mag.* XXXVIII. 213 It was a *foul-cut horse. 1634 BP. HALL *Serm. Rom.* xii. 2. Wks. II. 301 There is an *appetitus caninus,* that.. falls upon unmeet and *foule-feeding morsels. 1684 OTWAY *Atheist* I. i, The dirty Dugs of a foul-feeding Witch. 1898 *Westm. Gaz.* 6 Oct. 4/2 Without doubt this fish was *foul-hooked, though it was surely a heavy one. 1959 *Cape Times* 9 Mar. 3/6 Galjoen, haarders, and white steenbras, most of which were foul hooked, were landed. 1971 *Country Life* 11 Mar. 533/3 If there is a fish in the run, casts subsequent to the first will tend to fall across it and disturb it, if indeed it is not pricked or foul-hooked. 1593 SHAKS. *Lucr.* 799 O night, thou furnace of *foul-reeking smoke. 1869 E. A. PARKES *Pract. Hygiene* (ed. 3) 55 In the case of any *foul-smelling or suspected water. 1588 SHAKS. *Tit. A.* II. i. 58 *Foule spoken Coward That thundrest with thy tongue. 1848 HARE *Guesses* Ser. II. (1873) 527 They who are too fairspoken before you, are likely to be foulspoken behind you.

foul (faʊl), *v.*[1] [In form repr. OE. *fúlian* intr. = OHG. *fûlôn* (MHG. *vûlen,* mod.G. *faulen*). In the trans. use, which begins in the 14th c, it may be regarded as a new formation; cf. FILE *v.*[2], to which the early ME. *fulen* trans. belongs.]

1. a. *intr.* To be foul, become foul.

*c*893 K. ÆLFRED *Oros.* I. i. (Sweet 21) Ðær licȝað þa deadan men swa lange and ne fuliað. *c*1000 *Ags. Ps.* (Th.) xxxvii[i]. 5 Mine wunda rotedan and fuledon. *c*1200 *Trin. Coll. Hom.* 37 Sume men ladeð here lif on etinge and on drinkinge alse swin, þe uulieð. 13.. *E.E. Allit. P.* B. 269 So ferly fowled her flesch þat þe fende loked, How [etc.]. 1691 T. H[ALE] *Acc. New Invent.* 41 So apt to foul, or difficult to clean as Wood. 1858 GREENER *Gunnery* 400 Prince's breech-loader.. fouls in the proportion of at least 3 to 1 more.

b. Also with *up*.

1922 D. H. LAWRENCE *England, my England* 238 He could smell the cold, rotten clay that fouled up into the water. 1960 E. L. DELMAR-MORGAN *Cruising Yacht Equip. & Navig.* xii. 146 Tendency of a two-stroke to 'oil up' or to 'foul up'.

2. a. *trans.* To render (materially) foul, filthy, or dirty; to destroy the cleanness or purity of; = DEFILE *v.*[1] 2, FILE *v.*[2] 1.

c1420 *Chron. Vilod.* 937 Lest þ[t] holy plase w[t] þat blod y folud shuld be. c1440 CAPGRAVE *Life St. Kath.* v. 1594 It is neyther wurshipful ne honest On-to mankeende to foule soo his nest. c1450 *Bk. Curtasye* 110 in *Babees Bk.* 302 To foule þe borde clothe with þi knyfe. 1526 *Pilgr. Perf.* (W. de W. 1531) 177 He y[t] hath a precyous.. garment, wyll be loth to ..foule it. 1611 BIBLE *Ezek.* xxxiv. 19 They drinke that which yee haue fouled with your feete. 1683 TRYON *Way to Health* 303 A close heavy substance.. that fouls and makes the blood thick and gross. 1705 OLIVER in *Phil. Trans.* XXV. 2181 'Tis farther observable, he never foul'd his Bed. a1745 SWIFT *Wks.* (1841) II. 355 The waiting maid.. fouls a smock more in one hour, than the kitchen maid does in a week. 1756 C. LUCAS *Ess. Waters* II. 141 It fouls itself with a pale ochrous sediment. 1865 KINGSLEY *Herew.* II. xxii. 368 Any more than the wolf would forgive the lamb for fouling the water below him. 1883 *Manch. Exam.* 20 Nov. 5/5 Manchester gas is fouled by sulphur compounds.

b. *absol.* To cause filth or dirt, to drop ordure.

1483 CAXTON *G. de la Tour* G v, It fortuned that the swalowe dyd fowle within the eyen of Thobye. 1814 J. GILCHRIST *Reason* 56 Thus they croaked, and crawled, and spawned, and fouled.

3. *fig.* and in immaterial sense. To defile or pollute (with guilt); to dishonour, disgrace.

a1300 *Cursor M.* 10637 (Gött.) To saule þat fowlid was in sinne. 1362 LANGL. *P. Pl.* A. VII. 137 Leste þe Fend and heore flesch fouleden heore soules. c1380 WYCLIF *Serm.* Sel. Wks. II. 264 Many þenken þei [þe freres] ben heretikes and foulen men þat maynteynen hem. c1440 *Jacob's Well* (E.E.T.S.) 297 For venyall synnes þat foulyth vs yche day. 1581 SAVILE *Tacitus' Hist.* I. xlii. 41 Fouling his infamous life with a slow and dishonest departing. 1612 T. TAYLOR *Comm. Titus* ii. 14 He careth not to be filthy still.. and to fowle.. all that come in his companie. 1748 CHESTERF. *Lett.* (1792) II. cxxxix. 372 Your *Commensaux*, who.. foul themselves with.. scoundrel gamesters. 1791 BURKE *App. Whigs* Wks. VI. 15 With hands not fouled with confiscation. 1862 GOULBURN *Pers. Relig.* III. x. (1873) 241 Whose imaginations have been fouled of evil. 1870 MORRIS *Earthly Par.* I. II. 621 No weariness of good shall foul thy name.

†**b.** To throw discredit on. *Obs.*

c1440 *Gesta Rom.* xvii. 62 (Add. MS.) The new lawe that he made, and fowled [*v.r.* fylid] not the other.

†**c.** To violate the chastity of, debauch. *Obs.*[−1]

1607 TOURNEUR *Rev. Trag.* I. iii. Wks. 1878 II. 33 Sweare me to foule my sister!

d. Also with *up*: to spoil, (cause) to bungle or muddle (something or someone). Chiefly *U.S.*

1947 *Harper's Mag.* May 425/1 'Wing Ding' has a tricky opening where the sax and trumpet play against each other, accenting different beats... Sparrow came in a beat late, fouling it up. 1950 'S. RANSOME' *Deadly Miss Ashley* xii. 143 It would foul us up for fair this time. 1951 J. D. SALINGER *Catcher in Rye* ix. 80 Boy, I *really* fouled that up. 1954 J. & W. HAWKINS *Death Watch* (1959) ii. 55, I got all fouled up in the chain of command. 1958 S. ELLIN *Eighth Circle* (1959) II. ix. 100 You've got fine bone structure, but look at the way you're fouling it up. 1971 N. FREELING *Over High Side* III. 201 Everybody still has their mouth far too close to the utterly fouled-up microphone.

4. To make ugly (see FOUL *a.* 11); to deface, disfigure, spoil the look of.

a1340 HAMPOLE *Psalter* iv. 7 Swa to foule þis ymage [of God] þ[t] it kan noght knaw til whas lycnynge it is made. 1377 LANGL. *P. Pl.* B. XIX. 309 Kammokes and wedes Fouleth þe fruite in þe felde þere þei growe togyderes. a1450 *Knt. de la Tour* (1868) 23 So was the wiff fouled and maymed alle her lyff. 1557 *Tottel's Misc.* (Arb.) 158 He.. fowlth with haile the winters face. 1884 BROWNING *Ferishtah* (1885) 25 The cloud, which fouled so late Thy face.

5. Chiefly *Naut.* Cf. FOUL *a.* 18. **a.** To cause (an anchor, a cable) to become entangled. Also, To jam or block, render immovable or incapable of working; to make (a sea bottom) 'foul' or obstructed.

1726 G. ROBERTS *Four Years Voy.* 401 'Tis generally said, That the West-of-England-men fouled this Bay, by heaving their Stone Ballast over-board in it. 1827 HOOD *Sailor's Apol.* ii, 'Twas all along of Poll, as I may say, That fouled my cable, when I ought to slip. 1835 MARRYAT *Pirate* viii, See that she does not foul her anchor. 1885 *Manch. Exam.* 17 Jan. 5/4 The Manchester express.. ran into a mineral train by which the line was fouled. 1892 *Law Times Rep.* LXV. 590/1 A ship.. fouled her propellor. 1895 *Daily News* 9 Sept. 3/3 Station him at the east.. section of the Circus to prevent the traffic from east to west 'fouling' the crossing. *fig.* 1865 DICKENS *Mut. Fr.* I. xiv, His luck's got fouled under the keels of the barges.

b. *intr.* To get foul; to become entangled. Also (chiefly *U.S.*) *fig.* with *up*.

1857 P. COLQUHOUN *Comp. Oarsman's Guide* 32 To foul, or get foul, is to get entangled. 1860 C. HARROLD in *Merc. Marine Mag.* VII. 173 The chain fouled on the windlass. 1867 F. FRANCIS *Angling* v. (1880) 166 He will be perpetually fouling in the branches. 1957 P. FRANK *Seven Days to Never* (1959) VIII. iv. 184 Somewhere in his career he had fouled up. 1958 'P. BRYANT' *Two Hours to Doom* 16 A man marked for high rank.. if he did not foul up on the way.

c. *trans.* To run foul of, collide with.

1859 *Guardian* 2 Mar. 195 In attempting to make the harbour [she].. fouled the pier. 1861 HUGHES *Tom Brown at Oxf.* ii. (1889) 16 He managed.. to get into Iffley lock on the way up without fouling the gates. 1868 KINGLAKE *Crimea* (1877) IV. xiii. 389 Her jib-boom fouled the jib-boom of the Agamemnon. 1875 W. S. HAYWARD *Love agst. World* 125 Keep to the left, or you'll foul me.

6. *Sporting* and *Games.* Cf. FOUL *a.* 14. To handle or strike an opponent in a 'foul' manner. **b.** *Baseball.* To hit a foul ball. ***to foul out***: to be caught 'out' from a foul ball.

Hence '**fouling** *ppl. a.* Also '**fouler**, one that fouls or makes dirty.

a1050 *Liber Scintill.* ix. (1889) 45 Fuligendum limum. 1630 J. TAYLOR (Water P.) *Praise cleane Linen* 13 Wks. II. 166 Prayers for the cleane amendment of all foulers of Linnen. 1896 *Daily Chron.* 23 Mar. 3/2 Ridding our soot-charged passages of the fouling stuff.

†**foul, fowle,** *v.*[2] *Obs.* [a. F. *fouler* to tread, trample, press. Cf. FULL *v.*, FOIL *v.*[1]] *trans.* To trample, tread, tread down.

a1400–50 *Alexander* 4681 And be þar gold in oure gate.. We do bot foulis it with oure fete. 1483 CAXTON *Gold. Leg.* 24 b/2 The presse I have torned and fowled all allone. a1533 LD. BERNERS *Huon* cxl. 524 The countre is sore fowllyd and opressyd. 1643 PRYNNE *Popish R. Fav.* 46 He caused the Image of the Crosse to be redressed, and that men should not foule it under their feete.

†'**foulage.** *Obs. rare*[−1]. [f. FOUL *v.*[1] + -AGE.] Defilement, dirt. In quot. *fig.*

a1603 T. CARTWRIGHT *Confut. Rhem. N.T.* (1618) 457 Made fruitfull by the sweet shower of the grace and mercy of God, and not by the filthy foulage and dung of mans merit. *Ibid.* Pref. p. xxx, Fowlage [*printed* fowtage].

foulard (fular, fuːˈlɑːd). [a. Fr. *foulard.*]

1. A thin flexible material of silk, or of silk mixed with cotton.

1864 E. SARGENT *Peculiar* II. 137 Laura was attired in a light checked foulard silk. 1885 *Yng. Ladies' Jrnl.* 1 July 42/1 The new cambrics.. very much resemble foulards.

2. A handkerchief of this material.

1879 BODDAM-WHETHAM *Roraima* 60 Stores filled with gay-coloured foulards. 1888 *19th Cent.* Apr. 514 A foulard has become a common attire with the St. Petersburg house-maids.

fould, obs. form of FOLD.

fouldage, obs. form of FOLDAGE.

†'**fouldenhead.** *Obs.* Also 8 foudenhed. [f. *foulden*, var. of FOLDEN *ppl. a.* + HEAD.]

1747 HOOSON *Miner's Dict.*, *Foudenhed*, a small Pick, and the least of all the Tools that belong to a Miner.. so thin and slender, that it will not abide to have an Eye struck in it.. but is made by laping over in form of a Noose, with-out any Head at all. *Ibid.* O iv b, Foulden-Head.

†'**foulder,** *v.*[1] *Obs.* [ad. OF. *fouldrer*, f. *fouldre*: see FOULDRE.] *trans.* To flash or thunder forth; to send forth as a thundercloud or a gun. Also *absol.*

1559 *Mirr. Mag.*, *Mortimers* iv, Which forced enuy foulder out the rust That in mens hearts before did lie and smother. 1594 W. PERCY *Cœlia* x, From the leads of that proud Citadell Do foulder forth two fierie Culuerines.

Hence '**fouldering** *ppl. a.*

1590 SPENSER *F.Q.* II. ii. 20 Loud thunder.. Did rend the rattling skyes with flames of fouldring heat.

†'**foulder,** *v.*[2] *Obs.*[−1] [? f. FOUL *a.*, after the analogy of MOULDER.] *intr.* To crumble.

1610 HOLLAND *Camden's Brit.* 251 When the leaues were touched they fouldred to dust.

†**fouldre.** *Obs.* Also 4–5 foudre. [a. OF. *fouldre* (Fr. *foudre*):—vulg. Lat. **fulgĕr-em* (L. *fulgur* neut.).] Lightning; a thunderbolt.

c1384 CHAUCER *H. Fame* II. 27 That thing that men calle foudre That smoot somtyme a tour to powdre. c1450 *Mirour Saluacioun* 3413 His face like foudre shynyng. 1483 CAXTON *G. de la Tour* F iij, Sodome and Gomorre.. were.. brente.. by fyre of sulphur and of fouldre.

foule, obs. form of FOAL.

‖**foulé** (fule). [Fr. *foulé* pressed (cloth), pa. pple. of *fouler* FULL *v.*, FOUL *v.*[2]] A light woollen dress material with a glossy surface.

1894 *Daily News* 18 Sept. 6/4 A.. dainty little dress.. in biscuit-coloured foulé.

fouled (faʊld), *ppl. a.* [f. FOUL *v.*[1] + -ED[1].] In various senses of the vb. ***fouled anchor***: = 'foul anchor' (see FOUL *a.* 18 b).

1388 WYCLIF *Lev.* vii. 20 A pollutid [*v.r.* foulid] soule. 1552 HULOET, Fowled, *maculatus.* 1704 DERHAM in *Phil. Trans.* XXV. 1786 Some of the fouled Oyl of the Pump spirtled on the Wheels. 1885 *Pall Mall G.* 6 May 11/1 The fouled water from inside the house. 1889 *Daily News* 6 Aug. 6/1 The red flag, with a fouled anchor emblazoned thereon.

†'**foulhead.** *Obs.* [f. FOUL *a.* + -HEAD.] Foulness.

a1300 *Cursor M.* 1160 (Gött.) Felauschip and broþerhede Ne miht þe drau fra foulhede. c1330 *Amis & Amil.* 2395 All his foulehed away was go. 1340 *Ayenb.* 257 And zuo þenche his uoulhede and his ziknesse.

fouling (ˈfaʊlɪŋ), *vbl. sb.* [f. FOUL *v.*[1] + -ING[1].]

1. The action of the vb. FOUL in various senses.

c1380 WYCLIF *Sel. Wks.* III. 514 Þe gospel oweþ to be kept, wiþouten ony foulinge, of alle Cristene men. 1552 HULOET, Foulinge or defilynge, *vitiatio.* 1580 HOLLYBAND *Treas. Fr. Tong*, *Salissure*, fouling. 1691 T. H[ALE] *Acc. New Invent.* 80 As to its fouling, it fouls nothing near so soon as a Wood-sheathing. 1865 *Sat. Rev.* 11 Mar. 293 The fouling of two boats in a solemn funeral procession.

attrib. 1893 R. KIPLING *Many Invent.* 248 The rifle.. uncleaned, with the fouling marks about breech and muzzle.

2. *concr.* A foul deposit, filth. Also, †a foul person, a wretch.

1382 WYCLIF *Ezek.* xxiv. 11 That.. the foulinge therof be wellid togidre in the mydil therof. c1450 *Cov. Myst.* (Shaks. Soc.) 306 Spek, I say, thou foulyng. 1882 J. H. WALSH *Modern Sportsm.* I. 382 The chamber where the fouling collects. 1891 *Daily News* 23 Oct. 5/8 A rousing flood.. will effectually cleanse out this fouling.

'**foulish,** *a.* [See -ISH.] Somewhat foul.

1753 N. TORRIANO *Gangr. Sore Throat* 76 Her Tongue was foulish.

foully (ˈfaʊllɪ), *adv.* [f. FOUL *a.* + -LY[2]; in OE. *fúllíce.*] In a foul manner.

1. Fetidly, noisomely, filthily, disgustingly.

a1300 *Cursor M.* 6353 Þe water was al suete alson, þe water þat sua fuli stanc. c1400 MAUNDEV. (Roxb.) xxi. 96 It es better þai be eten with fewles.. þan foully to be eten in þe erthe with wormes. 1568 GRAFTON *Chron.* II. 77 Though she were sweete, nowe fowly doth she stinke. 1642 QUARLES *Feast for W.* IX. ix. 36 Their service is unsweet and foully taint.

fig. 1697 POTTER *Antiq. Greece* III. iv. (1715) 48 There is scarce any Passage.. which does not.. foully disgust their curious.. Palates.

2. Hideously; with gross disfigurement.

c1425 WYNTOUN *Cron.* VI. iii. 8 Fowlyly hym demenbryd þai. c1450 *St. Cuthbert* (Surtees) 7809 It was sa fouly sa defuyled. 1566 DRANT *Horace's Sat.* I. iii, We calle him goose, and disarde doulte, and fowlye fatted nowle. 1577–87 HOLINSHED *Chron.* III. 1035/1 Houses.. burned, and fowlie defaced with fire. 1592 WYRLEY *Armorie, Ld. Chandos* 65 Fairest truth I fouliest masked. 1632 SANDERSON *12 Serm.* 466 Foulely defaced with Sinne. 1728 SWIFT *Answer* 261 Your numerous virtues foully stain'd.

3. Abominably, disgracefully, shamefully; with revolting wickedness, cruelty, or treachery.

c1230 *Hali Meid.* 11 Meidenhad is te blosme þat beo ha eanes fulliche forcoruen, ne spruteð ha neauer eft. c1340 *Cursor M.* 16461 (Trin.) Iudas.. bihelde & seȝe how foulely þei wiþ him dalt. c1430 *Hymns Virg.* (1867) 127 So betyn, so woundyd, Entretyd so fuly. 1577–87 HOLINSHED *Chron.* III. 1233/2 His goods by the commons fowlie despoiled. 1583 STANYHURST *Æneis* III. (Arb.) 72 Al trust fowlye breaking. 1605 CAMDEN *Rem.* 212 Forsooth, yee doe fowly to smite a King annoynted. 1666 BUNYAN *Grace Abound.* ¶159, I had not.. transgressed so foully as he. 1714 GAY *What d'ye call it?* II. iii, Filbert still is true; I foully wrong'd him. 1859 TENNYSON *Enid* 459 From mine own earldom foully ousted me. 1880 MISS BRADDON *Just as I am* iii, He was foully murdered one October evening.

b. Impurely, obscenely.

a1050 *Liber Scintill.* xxviii. (1889) 106 Wel oft soðlice ȝyfernyss & ȝenihtsumnyss wines fullice [*turpiter*] on galnysse tolæt. 1603 SHAKS. *Meas. for M.* II. ii. 174 Dost thou desire her fowly, for those things That make her good? 1864 NEALE *Seaton. Poems* 265 Still Madlier the revel, foullier went the jest.

4. With gross contumely, insultingly. Now only with strong mixture of sense 3, with reference to slander or coarse language.

a1340 HAMPOLE *Psalter* xxi. 13, I am slane of thaim as fouly as watere is helt. c1340 *Cursor M.* 24085 (Fairf.) Fouli þai on him spitte. 1393 LANGL. *P. Pl.* C. XXI. 96 Thenne gan faith foully þe false Iewes to despisen. 1577 tr. *Bullinger's Decades* (1592) 129 The things wherein Gods name is fowly abused. 1596 SHAKS. *1 Hen. IV*, I. iii. 154 For whose death we.. Liue scandaliz'd, and fouly spoken of. a1627 HAYWARD *Edw. VI* (1630) 96 The other two [letters] did fully and fowly set forth his obstinacie. 1639 FULLER *Holy War* III. xxx. (1647) 163 The Pope hearing thereof, belibelled him more fouly than ever before. 1855 MACAULAY *Hist. Eng.* IV. 234 The gentlemen who had been so foully slandered.

†**5.** Badly, grievously. *Obs.*

c1330 R. BRUNNE *Chron.* (1810) 42 Bot ever was Eilred fouly begiled. 1375 BARBOUR *Bruce* VI. 156 Quha vist euir men sa fouly fall As vs, gif that we thusgat leif? 1539 TONSTALL *Serm. Palm Sund.* (1823) 81 Surely they be fowelye deceyued. 1577 HANMER *Anc. Eccl. Hist.* (1619) 360 He erred fowly in the.. vnderstanding thereof. 1603 KNOLLES *Hist. Turkes* (1621) 1217 Hee fell sicke of the small poxe, wherewith hee.. was.. foulely tormented. 1655 FULLER *Ch. Hist.* II. v. §1 Pope Formosus was foully offended. [1881 R. BUCHANAN *God and Man* II. vi, An innocent man foully taxed and troubled.]

foulmouth (ˈfaʊlmaʊθ), *a.* and *sb.* [f. FOUL *a.* + MOUTH.]

†**A.** *adj.* = FOUL-MOUTHED. *Obs.* **B.** *sb.* A foul-mouthed person.

a1640 W. FENNER *Christ's Alarm* II. (1657) 10 Hearing what this fowl-mouth [Goliath] said. 1692 WASHINGTON tr. *Milton's Def. Pop.* 390 Infamous foulmouth wretch. 1966 AUDEN *About House* 39 A foul-mouth gets the cold Shoulder.

foul-mouthed (ˈfaʊlˌmaʊðd), *a.* [f. FOUL *a.* + MOUTH + -ED[2].] Of persons and their utterances: Using obscene, profane, or scurrilous language.

1596 SHAKS. *1 Hen. IV*, III. iii. 122 Like a foule-mouth'd man as hee is. 1655 FULLER *Ch. Hist.* IX. vii. §17 Those foule mouth'd papers like Blackmoors did all look alike. 1730 A. GORDON *Maffei's Amphith.* 95 One of those foul-mouth'd Poets. 1838 MACAULAY *Ess.*, *Temple*, Temple.. complained, very unjustly, of Bentley's foul-mouthed raillery. 1873

SYMONDS *Grk. Poets* iv. 101 This runaway soldier and foul-mouthed Ionian satirist [Archilochus].

Hence **'foul,mouthedness.**

1834 LANDOR *Exam. Shaks.* Wks. 1846 II. 275 Thou hast aggravated thy offence.. by thy foul-mouthedness. **1884** *Sat. Rev.* 22 Nov. 645/2 The country.. has had a taste of Radical foulmouthedness.

foulness ('faʊlnɪs). [f. FOUL *a.* + -NESS.]

1. A foul or dirty condition; dirtiness, impurity, pollution, uncleanness. Rarely *pl.*

1552 HULOET, Fowlenes or fylthines, *sorditudo.* **1582** *N.T.* (Rhem.) *John* xiii. Annot., The fovlnes of the fute.. signifieth the earthie affections. **1667** PEPYS *Diary* (1877) V. 429 My wife and I fell out a little about the foulness of the linen of the table. **1725** BRADLEY *Fam. Dict.* s.v. *Fish*, It is the Foulness of the Ponds.. that stenches the Water. **1744** BERKELEY *Siris* §4 A medicine.. useful in.. foulnesses of the blood. **1809–10** COLERIDGE *Friend* (1865) 214 With such.. eagerness as to neglect the foulness of the road. **1853** KANE *Grinnell Exp.* xxxi. (1856) 271 The.. foulness of air in the between-deck.. cannot be amended.

fig. **1755** YOUNG *Centaur* iv. Wks. 1757 IV. 194 Few know the foulness of their own hearts.

b. Of the weather: Storminess. Of a sea-bottom: Rockiness, roughness.

1603 KNOLLES *Hist. Turks* (1621) 1028 Such was the foulenesse of the winter weather. *a* **1718** PENN *Wks.* (1726) I. Life 64 Being.. wearied with the Foulness of the Ways and Weather. **1748** *Anson's Voy.* II. i. 115 To secure them [the cables] from being rubbed by the foulness of the ground.

c. *concr.* Foul matter; something that is or makes foul; a foul crust or deposit; filth; †a purulent affection (of the skin). Also *pl.*

1398 TREVISA *Barth. De P.R.* XVI. lii. (1495) 570 It.. clensyth the eyen of fowlenes and fylthe. **1583** HOLLYBAND *Campo di Fior* 25 Washe well the fowlenesse which is about the jointes of the fingers. **1648** WILKINS *Math. Magick* II. xii. (1680) 246 The spots or foulness of other cloaths are washed out. **1740** STACK in *Phil. Trans.* XLI. 424 If a glass Globe filled with Water be rapidly turned on its Axis, one sees little Foulnesses. **1768–74** TUCKER *Lt. Nat.* (1852) II. 396 The dust and smoke of earth will continually throw a foulness upon our glass. **1782** W. HEBERDEN *Comm.* xxiii. (1806) 122 Efficacious in cleansing the skin from many foulnesses. **1889** R. B. ANDERSON tr. *Rydberg's Teut. Myth.* 214 The floors were made of serpents encased in foulness.

fig. *a* **1654** SELDEN *Table-T.* (Arb.) 18 They had a Foulness about them, viz. Original Sin, that could not be washed away but by Baptism. *a* **1716** SOUTH *Serm.* (1737) II. 199 The wickedness of a whole life, discharging all its filth and foulness into this one quality. **1790** G. WALKER *Serm.* II. xxx. 331 What debasing shame must sink the wretched soul, when foulnesses without number shall be revealed.

2. Moral impurity; disgusting wickedness.

c **1532** DEWES *Introd. Fr.* in *Palsgr.* 905 The foulenesse, *la turpitude.* **1578** T. N. tr. *Conq. W. India* 135 Grievous sinnes.. for the foulnesse whereof I name them not. **1599** SHAKS. *Much Ado* IV. i. 155 Claudio.. lou'd her so, that speaking of her foulnesse, Wash'd it with teares. **1624** BACON *New Atlantis* Wks. 1857 III. 152 There is not.. a nation.. so free from all pollution or foulness. **1719** YOUNG *Busiris* v. i, The foulness of thy guilt secures thee From my reproach. **1879** FARRAR *St. Paul* (1883) 208 Those umbrageous groves were the dark haunts of every foulness.

†3. Ugliness, hideousness, repulsiveness. *Obs.*

1382 WYCLIF *Bible, Pref. Ep. St. Jerome* vii. (1850) I. 73, I wole not, that thou be offendid in holi scripturis.. thurȝ foulness of words. **1398** TREVISA *Barth. De P.R.* XII. xxxii. (1495) 432 The pecok arereth his fethers.. and thenne he.. seeth the fowlenesse of his fete. **1600** SHAKS. *A.Y.L.* III. v. 66 Hees falne in loue with your foulnesse. **1697** DRYDEN *Æneid* VII. 582 The Fury.. with new methods try'd The foulness of th' infernal Form to hide.

†4. Unfairness, dishonesty. Also, roughness, violence. Cf. FOUL *a.* 14, 17. *Obs.*

1523 LD. BERNERS *Froiss.* I. cccxxi. 202 a, Outher with fayrnesse or foulnesse. **1596** DALRYMPLE tr. *Leslie's Hist. Scot.* II. 150 Be fairnes ather be foulnes. **1654** HAMMOND *Fundamentals* 99 Piety is opposed to.. all falsness or foulness of intentions.

foulsome, foulter, obs. of FULSOME, FALTER.

foulzie, var. of FULYIE, *Sc.*

foumart ('fuːmət). Forms: 4 folmarde, 5 ful(e)merd(e, -mert, 5–6 -mard(e, 5–7 -mer(e, (5 -mare), 5 fullimart, 6 fullymart, 7 ful-, 7–8 fuli-, 7–9 foul(e)mart, 5–7 fow-, 7, 9 fu-, 8, 9 foomart, (6 foumerd, 7 fummer, 8 formet), 8– foumart. [ME. *fulmard*:—OE. **fúl mearð* (*fúl*, FOUL *a.* + *mearð* marten).]

1. The polecat (*Putorius fœtidus*).

13.. *E.E. Allit. P.* B. 534 Þe fox & þe folmarde to þe fryth wyndez. *c* **1450** *Chester Pl., Noah's Flood* 170 (Pollard), Atter and foxe, fullimartes alsoe. **1486** *Bk. St. Albans* B vij b, That no fulmertis nor fecheus ne other vermyn com nott in to hir. **1523** FITZHERB. *Husb.* §146 To se that they be well kepte from.. fully martes & other vermin. *a* **1592** H. SMITH *Serm.* (1622) 102 Vsurers.. lurke about the City like Rats, and Wesels, and Fulmers. **1772** T. SIMPSON *Vermin Killer* 23 The Polecat, Fitchat, Fitchew, Formet. The same animal called by different names in different countries. **1815** SCOTT *Guy M.* xxii, 'Sicken a day as we had wi' the foumarts and the tods.' **1863** N. MACLEOD *Remin. Highland Par.* iii, Rats, fumarts, wild cats [etc.].

b. Used as a term of contempt or opprobrium.

1508 KENNEDIE *Flyting w. Dunbar* 517 Fowmart, fasert, fostirit in filth and fen. *a* **1605** MONTGOMERIE *Flyting w. Polwart* 69 False fecklesse foulmart, loe heere a defyance! **1633** B. JONSON *Tale of Tub* I. iv, You stote! Was ever such a fulmart for an huisher, To a great worshipful lady, as myself! **1892** J. PAYN *Mod. Dick Whittington* I. 112 He and that foulmart, the parson, have just gone.

2. *attrib.*, as ***foumart-hunt***, ***-skin***; **foumart-dog**, a dog used for hunting the foumart.

1612 *Sc. Bk. Customs* in Halyburton *Ledger* (1867) 329 Skins called.. Fowmart skins. *c* **1746** J. COLLIER (Tim Bobbin) *Lanc. Dial.* Wks. (1862) 52 Mezzil fease.. gran like a Foomurt-Dog. **1855** WAUGH *Lanc. Sketches, Heywood*, etc. (1869) 182 Now and then a foomart-hunt takes place.

foun, obs. form of FAWN, FEW.

†founce, *sb. Obs.* Also founs. [AF. *founz* = OF. *fonz*, *funz* (mod.Fr. *fonds*):—popular L. **fundus* neut. = class. L. *fundus* masc.] The bottom of anything.

13.. *E.E. Allit. P.* A. 113 In þe founce þer stonden stonez stepe. *a* **1400–50** *Alexander* 4130 Þai flee as fast in-to flode & to þe founce plangid. *c* **1500** *Melusine* xxiv. 172 The founs of the valey.

†founce, *v. Obs.* [app. a. F. *foncer*, f. OF. *fonz*: see prec.] **a.** In *passive*: ? To have one's attention fixed *upon*. **b.** *intr.* To come down with force *upon*.

1430 LYDG. *Chron. Troy* v. xxxvi, By the power of this sorceresse I was so founced upon her fayrenesse; That [etc.]. **1530** PALSGR. 557/2, I fownce (Lyd[gate]), I dent a thing. *Je fonce.* This terme is nat yet in comen use. **1565** JEWEL *Def. Apol.* (1611) 645 Yet is his soule.. crushed with the beetle of the whole earth, that founceth downe vpon it.

found (faʊnd), *sb.*[1] *Sc.* [f. FOUND *v.*[2]] = FOUNDATION; see also quot. 1846.

1818 *Edin. Mag.* Dec. 503 Our milkhouse.. micht hae stude to the last day; but its found had been onner-minit by the last Lammas-spait. **1846** BUCHANAN *Technol. Dict.*, *Found*, in architecture, the trench or excavation made to receive the foundation stones of a wall.

found (faʊnd), *sb.*[2] [f. FOUND *v.*[3]] The process of founding (metal, materials for glass). †*of found* (Sc.) = made of cast metal (cf. FONT *sb.*[2] 1).

1540 *Sc. Act Jas. V* (1597) §94 Ane Hagbutte of Founde, called Hagbute of Crochert. **1566** in T. Thompson *Inv. R. Wardrobe* (1815) 166 Foure new cannonis of found. **1818** SCOTT *Hrt. Midl.* xii, Guns, cross-bows, hagbuts of found. **18..** *Glass-making* 120 (*Cent. Dict.*) The success of the subsequent melting or found.

found, *sb.*[3] A comb-maker's tool (see quot.).

1874 KNIGHT *Dict. Mech.* I. 909 *Found*, a three-square, single-cut file or float, with one very acute angle.

found, obs. var. of FOUNT[2].

found (faʊnd), *ppl. a.* Forms: see FIND *v.* [pa. pple. of FIND *v.*]

1. a. Discovered, met with, ascertained, etc. (see the verb). Also, with adv. prefixed, as ***new found***, †***rare found***.

c **1380** WYCLIF *Sel. Wks.* III. 347 But ȝif he took more charge upon him bi his newe foundun ordenaunce. *c* **1450** *Mirour Saluacioun* 231 Also the founden shepe broght home yt arst was lorne. **1553** EDEN (*title*) A treatyse of the newe India, with other new founde landes and Ilandes. **1571** DIGGES *Pantom.* IV. prob. xxiv. Ee iij b, The square of the Dodecaedrons founde side. **1594** BLUNDEVIL *Exerc.* I. (ed. 7) 96 Double the foresaid found Root 13. **1603–8** KNOLLES *Hist. Turks* (1638) 214 His great vertues, and rare found courtesie. **1720** DE FOE *Capt. Singleton* xiii. (1840) 225 Our lost, but now found comrade. *a* **1823** *May Collin* in Child *Ballads* I. (1882) 58/1 Who owns this dapple grey? 'It is a found one', she replied, 'That I got on the way.'

†b. Said of children exposed or abandoned; ***found child*** (***brat***, etc.) = FOUNDLING. *Obs.*

1655 *Valentine & Orson* 53 This Found-fellow I perceive growes in great favour with the King. *Ibid.* xii. 56 They call me Found-brat. **1662** PETTY *Taxes* 4 The maintenance of orphans, found and exposed children.

c. ***found stones***: stones obtained from the surface of the ground without quarrying.

1885 *Blacklaws Quarry Price List, Ruble & Founds* Found Stones, not above 7 in. thick per sup. foot 4½*d.*

2. Furnished with stores, supplies, or the like; of a ship, equipped; only with defining word prefixed, as ***well found***, ***single found*** (see quot. 1799).

1793 SMEATON *Edystone L.* §94 A strong and very well found sloop. **1799** *Naval Chron.* I. 216 Her materials were what is called *single found*, i.e. she had only one anchor, one cable, etc. **1857** R. TOMES *Amer. in Japan* ii. 35 The strongest-moored and best found vessels. **1864** BURTON *Scot Abr.* II. ii. 144 The garrison is large, and well found.

3. *absol.* in *pl.* Advertisements of found articles, usually in phr. ***losts and founds***.

1913 G. B. DIBBLEE *Newspaper* 126 The most important groups of classified advertising are as follows: financial, theatrical, public notices, losts and founds, educational.

†found, *v.*[1] *Obs.* Forms: 1 fundian, 2–3 fundie(n, 3–5 fund(e, 4–6 found(e, 5 fownd(e; also 3–5 fond(e. [OE. *fundian* = OS. *fundôn*:—OTeut. type **fundôjan*, f. **fund-*:—OAryan **pn̥t-* (whence Gr. πάτος way), ablaut var. of **pent-*: see FIND *v.* Cf. OHG. *funden* (:—**fundjan*) of the same meaning; also the cognate FAND *v.*]

1. *intr.* To set out, start, hasten; to go, depart, betake oneself; to travel, journey. (In its later use chiefly *north.*) Cf. FAND *v.* 8.

a **1000** *Seafarer* 47 Ac a hafað longunge se þe on lagu fundað. *c* **1000** ÆLFRIC *Saints' Lives* xxvi. 224 And lædde forð mid him þær he fundode to. *c* **1200** *Trin. Coll. Hom.* 117 Ðo þe ure louerd ihesu crist fundede lichamliche fro eorðe to heuene. *c* **1250** *Gen. & Ex.* 2958 Ðis folc of londe funden ne mot. *a* **1300** *Cursor M.* 6034 (Gött.) Þe folk to fond [*Cott.* fund, *Fairf.* founde] i sal giue leue. **1375** BARBOUR *Bruce* x. 256 [Bruce] syne our all the land can found. *c* **1440** *York Myst.* ix. 80, I am nouȝt bowne to fonde nowe ouer þere ffellis. *c* **1470** HENRY *Wallace* x. 32 Nane off that place had power for to found. **1535** STEWART *Cron. Scot.* III. 435 With clarions cleir.. Quhomeof the sound did found attouir the fell. **1596** DALRYMPLE tr. *Leslie's Hist. Scot.* III. 182 Spangs vp on a swofte horse, and founde away at speid.

b. followed by *inf.* expressing the purpose.

Beowulf (Gr.) 1819 We fundiað Higelac secan. *a* **1000** *Cædmon's Gen.* (Gr.) 2269 Hwider fundast þu.. siðas dreoȝan? *a* **1300** *Cursor M.* 5091 To fotte mi fader sal yee fund.

c. To rush or dash forcibly *into*; to strike out *at* (with a weapon).

c **1420** *Anturs of Arth.* xli, He foundes into the freke with a fresche fare. *Ibid.* xlvii, Fast he foundes atte his face With a squrd kene. *c* **1435** *Torr. Portugal* 2469 But lordys of other lond, Every one to other ffond.

2. *to found to* (an object): to strive or yearn towards, try to arrive at or reach; also, to take or betake oneself *to* (flight, war, etc.).

a **1000** *Crist* 1671 (Gr.) Nu þu most feran þider þu fundadest longe and ȝelome. *a* **1000** *Guthlac* (Gr.) 1062 Sawul fundað of lic-fate to þam longan ȝefean. *a* **1250** *Owl & Night.* 848 And techest hom that hi fundieth honne Up to the songe that evre i-lest. **1352** MINOT *Poems* (Hall) i. 12 When Edward founded first to were. *c* **1400** *Destr. Troy* 10276 Þai foundyt to flight.

3. Const. with *inf.* (a development from 1 b): To set about, set oneself, try, begin or prepare (*to do* something); to proceed or go on (*to do*).

c **1205** LAY. 17858 Vther.. fundede to uarene wið Passent to fehten. **12..** *Prayer to our Lady* 7 in *O.E. Misc.* 192 Dai and nicht ich fundie to wendende heonne. *c* **1250** *Gen. & Ex.* 2831 Moyses, friȝti, ðo funden gan to speken wið ietro ðat riche man. **1387** TREVISA *Higden* (Rolls) V. 53 He foundede [*v. rr.* fonded, vondede] biseliche.. to fulfille [orig. *implere satagebat*] þe counsail of the gospel. *c* **1460** *Towneley Myst.* (Surtees) 135 If thou Wyll saue thy self vnshent ffownde the fast to fare. *c* **1470** HENRY *Wallace* III. 203 On horsis some.. can found To socour thaim. **1674–91** RAY *N.C. Words* 141 *Found*, idem quod *fettle* [*Fettle*, to set or go about any thing].

b. with clause: To try to find *how* (one may, etc.).

1390 GOWER *Conf.* III. 139 [He] foundeth howe he might excite The juges through his eloquence Fro deth to torne the sentence.

4. *trans.* **a.** To try, test, tempt (a person).

c **1175–1400** [see FOUNDING *vbl. sb.*].

b. To make experiment of, prove, try (something); also, to follow after, practise.

1340–70 *Alex. & Dind.* 392 Alle leccheries lust vs loþeth to founde. *Ibid.* 913 And oþur wordliche werk wisly to founde. *c* **1374** CHAUCER *Anel. & Arc.* 241 Ferther wol I neuer founde Non other help, my sores for to sounde. *c* **1420** [see FAND *v.* 3].

Hence **'founding** *vbl. sb.*: (*a*) setting forth, faring, etc.; (*b*) trial, temptation.

O.E. Chron. an. 1106, Forþam þe he nolde on his fundunge ofer sæ hired healdan. *c* **1175** *Lamb. Hom.* 67 Ne led us noht in to costnunga, þet is an cun [*printed* cum] of fun-dunga. *c* **1400** *Apol. Loll.* 87 Þe createris of God are maad in to hate, & foundingis [*Vulg. Sap.* xiv. 11 *in tentationem*] to þe soul of men. *a* **1400–50** *Alexander* 4154 Þe writhe of þe wale god I wate on vs liȝtis For oure foundyng ouire his forbod so ferre to þe est. *c* **1450** *Guy Warw.* (C) 4486 He was tryste in all fowndynge.

found (faʊnd), *v.*[2] Forms: 4–5 fund(e, fond(e, fownd(e, 4– found. Pa. t. and pa. pple. founded: also 4–5 founde, fund(e, fond, and in pa. pple. (by confusion with that of FIND), fonden, -yn, founden, -un. [a. F. *fonder*:—L. *fundāre*, f. *fundus* bottom, foundation.]

1. *trans.* To lay the base or substructure of (a building, etc.); to set, fix, or build *on* a firm ground or base. (Sometimes used simply = build, erect.)

c **1330** *Arth. & Merl.* 1443 Tel me now.. Whi noman no may founde Castel here opon þis grounde. *c* **1340** *Cursor M.* 7876 Dauid.. an hous bigon to founde. **1382** WYCLIF *Matt.* vii. 25 It felle nat doun, for it was foundid [**1388** foundun] on a stoon. *c* **1384** CHAUCER *H. Fame* III. 891 Yet hit [the house] is founded to endure. *c* **1400** *Rom. Rose* 4156 A sturdy wal, Which on a cragge was founded al. **1611** BIBLE *Matt.* vii. 25. **1752** HUME *Ess. & Treat.* (1777) II. 97 The House.. is.. solidly built and founded.

b. To serve as the base or foundation of.

1728 POPE *Dunc.* I. 160 A folio Common-place Founds the whole pile, of all his works the base.

2. To build (an edifice, town, etc.) for the first time; to begin the building of, be the first builder of.

c **1290** *Becket* 374 in *S. Eng. Leg.* I. 117 Þe churche of Redinge þat i-founded was and a-rerd þoruȝ henri þe oþur kingue. **1362** LANGL. *P. Pl.* A. I. 62 That is the castel of care.. Ther-inne woneth a wiht.. he foundede it him-seluen. *c* **1400** *Destr. Troy* 11662 Here foundit he first the faire place Ylion. **1609** HOLLAND *Amm. Marcell.* XIV. vii. 17 Seleucia, founded and built by King Seleucus. **1718** PRIOR *Solomon* II. 16, I founded palaces, and planted bowers. **1835** THIRLWALL *Greece* I. ii. 58 His son Lycaon founds the first city, Lycosura.

3. *fig.* To set up or establish for the first time (an institution, etc.), *esp.* with provision for its perpetual maintenance; to originate, create, initiate (something which continues to exist thenceforward).

a **1300** *Cursor M.* 20901 Quen he of antioche had fund þe kirk. *c* **1330** R. BRUNNE *Chron.* (1810) 127 He lis.. In an abbey of pris he founded with lond & rent. **1368** in *Eng. Gilds* 54 In septembre þis fraternite is funded and stabeled. **1377** LANGL. *P. Pl.* B. x. 215 Alle thise sciences I my-self sotiled and ordeyned And founded hem formest folke to deceyue. *c* **1460** FORTESCUE *Abs. & Lim. Mon.* xix, For þeras oþer kynges haue ffounded byshopriches.. þe kyng shall þan haue ffounded an holl reaume, and endowed it with gretter possescions [etc.]. **1611** BIBLE *2 Macc.* ii. 13 He founding a librarie. **1671** MILTON *P.R.* III. 295 By great Arsaces led, who founded first That empire. **1712** ADDISON *Spect.* No. 413 ¶5 The Breed is incapable of propagating its Likeness, and of founding a new Order of Creatures. **1790** PALEY *Horæ Paul.* Rom. ii. 18 That city where he had founded a church. **1845** M. PATTISON *Ess.* (1889) I. 12 The abbey of Marmoutier, founded by St. Martin himself. **1861** MAINE *Anc. Law* 113 The glossators who founded modern jurisprudence. **1874** L. STEPHEN *Hours in Library* (1892) I. v. 169 De Foe founded the modern school of English novelists. **1874** GREEN *Short Hist.* v. §1. 218 Flemish weavers had come over with the Conqueror to found the prosperity of Norwich. **1885** *Manch. Exam.* 8 June 5/2 Bismarck is eager to found colonies in all parts of the world.

†**b.** To endow, make provision for the maintenance of (persons who are to perform certain functions). *Obs.*

1377 LANGL. *P. Pl.* B. xv. 319 And ȝiueth to bidde for ȝow to such that ben riche, And ben founded and feffed eke to bidde for other. *c* **1450** LONELICH *Grail* liii. 309 Kyng Galaaz.. fowndid an hows of the Trenite, And there-inne syxty monkes serteinle, And therto fownded hem with good inowhe. *c* **1500** *Melusine* lix. 361 Yf thou wylt edyfye an hospital, and founde therin a preste to syng dayly for thy faders sowle. **1535** COVERDALE *2 Kings* xxiii. 5 The Kemurims, whom the kynges of Iuda had founded, to burne incense vpon the hye places. **1612** DRAYTON *Poly-olb.* xxiv. 873 Gilbert.. who founded those Diuines, Monasticks all that were, of him nam'd Gilbertines.

4. To set or establish (something immaterial) on a firm basis; to give a basis or firm support to; to construct as on a ground or underlying reason or principle; to base, ground. Const. *on, upon.*

a **1300** *Cursor M.* 127 þar-for þis werc sal I fund Apon a selcuth stedfast grund. **1390** GOWER *Conf.* III. 342 Lo, what it is to be well grounded, For he hath ferst his love founded Honestelich as for to wedde. *a* **1400-50** *Alexander* 4641 Pure is ȝoure tecches, Mare fonden opon foly þan ficchid on reson. **1526** *Pilgr. Perf.* (W. de W. 1531) 1 b, Therfore on it I founde this poore treatyse. **1604** SHAKS. *Oth.* III. iv. 94 A man that all his time Hath founded his good fortunes on your love. **1662** STILLINGFL. *Orig. Sacr.* II. v. §5 The question which Moses supposeth, is founded upon clear and evident reason. **1711** ADDISON *Spect.* No. 162 ¶6 The most humourous Character in Horace is founded upon this Unevenness of Temper. **1850** L. HUNT *Autobiog.* I ii. 77 A play founded on a Barbadian story. **1865** M. ARNOLD *Ess. Crit.* iii. 85 Greatness can never be founded upon frivolity and corruption. **1879** LUBBOCK *Sci. Lect.* ii. 42 A classification of insects founded on larvæ would be quite different from that founded on the perfect insects. **1886** *Law Rep.* 31 Ch. Div. 626 The order appealed from was founded on the Chief Clerk's certificate. *Mod.* This novel is believed to be founded on fact.

b. const. *in.*

1667 *Decay Chr. Piety* xvii. 383 The opinion of some schoolmen, that dominion is founded in Grace. **1690** LOCKE *Of Govmt.* I. ix. §97 A right to the use of the creatures being founded originally in the right a man has to subsist. **1733** POPE *Ess. Man* III. 109 God, in the nature of each being, founds Its proper Bliss. **1832** LEWIS *Use & Ab. Pol. Terms* iii. 21 A claim founded in justice and expediency. **1837-9** HALLAM *Hist. Lit.* I. viii. i. §23. 432 Remarks so delicate in taste and so founded in knowledge.

†**c.** with *obj.* a person: To establish in a firm position (in controversy, etc.); to ground *in* (a subject of instruction, etc.); also *refl.* to take one's stand *upon* (a ground for argument, etc.). *Obs.*

c **1394** *P. Pl. Crede* 47 It is but a faynt folk i-founded vp-on iapes. **1481** CAXTON *Myrr.* II. viii. 81 This knewe they by their grete.. vnderstandyng of astronomye in whiche they were endowed and founded. **1483** —— *Gold. Leg.* 162/2 He was ryght sore founded in humylyte. **1643** SIR T. BROWNE *Relig. Med.* I. §43 They that found themselves on the radical balsome, or vital sulphur of the parts, determine not why Abel lived not so long as Adam. **1644** MILTON *Educ.* Wks. (1847) 98/2 Because our understanding cannot in this body found itself but on sensible things. **1676-7** MARVELL *Corr.* cclxxxiv. Wks. 1872-5 II. 516 If you find yourselves so firmly founded as we imagine you.

d. Of a thing: To serve as, or furnish, a basis or ground for.

1690 LOCKE *Hum. Und.* II. xxviii. §19 The comparing them then in their Descent.. is enough to found my Notion of their having.. the Relation of Brothers. **1885** B. COLERIDGE in *Law Times Rep.* LII. 585/1 The relationship between the parties was.. one of bailment, and therefore could not found criminal proceedings. **1894** *Solicitors' Jrnl.* XXXIX. 2/2 The further report, if it is to found jurisdiction for an order for public examination, must state that [etc.].

e. *intr.* (for *refl.*: cf. 4 c). To base oneself or one's opinion, to base itself, to be based (*on, upon*). Chiefly *Sc.*

1836-7 SIR W. HAMILTON *Metaph.* vi. (1870) I. 99 The legitimacy of every synthesis is.. dependent on the legitimacy of the analysis which it presupposes, and on which it founds. **1837** CARLYLE *Fr. Rev.* III. I. v, All Delineation.. must either found on Belief and provable Fact, or have no foundation at all. **1856** DOVE *Logic Chr. Faith* v. ii. 311 All that course of argumentation which founds on the occurrences of the outward World. **1882** OGILVIE s.v., 'I found upon the evidence of my senses'.

†**5.** To fasten or attach *to.* Also *fig. Obs.*

1541 R. COPLAND *Guydon's Quest. Chirurg.*, The bone.. wherto the tongue is founded. **1641** MARMION *Antiquary* III. Dram. Wks. (1875) 240, I see you are growing obdurate in your crimes, Founded to vice, lost to all piety.

Hence ˈ**founding** *vbl. sb.*

c **1400** *Destr. Troy* v. *heading*, Of the Foundyng of New Troye. **1571** HANMER *Chron. Irel.* (1633) 41 Some twenty five yeeres before the founding of Armagh. **1682** WOOD *Life* 20 Mar., The vice-chancellor asked 'whether they denied the founding of the lecture itself, or the conditions?' **1697** *Conf. at Lambeth* in W. S. Perry *Hist. Coll. Amer. Col. Ch.* I. 40 Particularly, the word founding, which is always the Law Word for a perpetual fund of maintenance, is always put into these Revenues. **1859** TENNYSON *Vivien* 409 When first the question rose About the founding of a Table Round. **1889** *Athenæum* 9 Feb. 178/2 [He dies] a 'Poor Brother' in the hospital of his own founding.

found (faʊnd), *v.*[3] Also 4, 8 fond. [ad. F. *fondre*:—L. *fundĕre* to pour, melt, FUSE.]

†**1.** *trans.* To dissolve or mix *together*. *Obs.*$^{-1}$

?*c* **1390** *Form of Cury* in Warner *Antiq. Culin.* 18 Take wyne and hony and fond it togyder.

2. To melt (metal) and run it into a mould; to form (an article) by running molten metal into a mould; to cast.

1562 WHITEHORNE tr. *Macchiavelli's Arte of Warre* (1573) II. 44 a, The Pottes.. may also serue to found metalles in. **1601** HOLLAND *Pliny* XXXIV. ii. 487 Famous for metall-founding, and casting of images. **1667** MILTON *P.L.* I. 703 A second multitude With wondrous Art founded the massie Ore. *Ibid.* VI. 518 Veins.. of mineral.. Whereof to found.. their balls Of missive ruin. **1672** MARVELL *Reh. Transp.* I. 6 Lead, when moulded into Bullets, is not so mortal as when founded into Letters! **1796** MORSE *Amer. Geog.* II. 93 A bell at Moscow, founded in Czar Boris's time.

b. To melt or fuse (the materials for making glass); to make (glass) by melting the materials in a furnace.

1782 [see *vbl. sb.* below]. **1853** URE *Dict. Arts* I. 907 A Bohemian furnace in which.. window glass is founded. *Ibid.* 914 The fourth is called the *arch of the materials*, because it serves for drying them before they are founded.

c. *fig.* (? A pun: cf. FOUND *v.*[2] 3 b.)

1624 FLETCHER *Rule a Wife* IV. ii, A fellow founded out of charity, And moulded to the height, contemn his maker, Curb the free hand that fram'd him?

Hence ˈ**founding** *vbl. sb.* Also *attrib.*

1658 W. BURTON *Comm. Antoninus' Itin.* 156 The magnificent Acts [*read* Arts] of Statuarie, Founding, Mowlding. **1779** HERVEY *Naval Hist.* III. II. 50 Ship-building, and the founding of iron cannon, were the sole [arts] in which the English excelled. **1782** WEDGWOOD in *Phil. Trans.* LXXII. 320 The fonding heat of the glass furnaces.. was.. 114° for flint-glass. **1853** URE *Dict. Arts* I. 908 The founding-pots are filled up with these blocks of frit. *Ibid.* 917 These three stages are called the first, second, and third fusion or founding.

†**found**, *v.*[4] *Obs.* Aphetic form of CONFOUND.

1382 WYCLIF *Isa.* xlvi. 8 Remembreth this, and beth foundid [Vulg. *confundamini*]. *a* **1592** GREENE *George a Greene* Wks. (Rtldg.) 267/2 A plague found you!

†**found**, *v.*[5] Also 6 pa. pple. **fundied**. [aphetic f. *affound*, ad. OF. *enfondre*: see first quot.] To be chilled or numbed with cold.

[**13..** CHAUCER *To Rosemounde* 21 My love may not refreyd be nor affound.] *c* **1430** *Pilgr. Lyf Manhode* II. xc. (1869) 108 The maymed, the foollich, the founded [*morfondue*], the froren. **1560** ROLLAND *Crt. Venus* IV. 736 Becaus I was baith fundeit, faint, and cald. **1562** TURNER *Herbal* II. 108 [Pyrethio] is excellently good for any parte of the body yᵗ is fundied or foundered or made allmost num, with to much colde.

†ˈ**foundable**, *a. Obs. rare*$^{-1}$. [f. FOUND *v.*[2] + -ABLE.] That can be founded.

1413 *Pilgr. Sowle* (Caxton) v. xiv. (1859) 82 Ouer fantastyk, nought grounded, nor foundable in holy Scripture.

foundation (faʊnˈdeɪʃən). Forms: 4-6 f(o)undacio(u)n, -yon, 5-6 f(o)undatio(u)n, -yo(u)n, (6 foundasyon), 7 fund-, fondation, 5- foundation. [ad. L. *fundātiōn-em*, n. of action f. *fundāre*: see FOUND *v.*[2] Cf. OF. *fondacion* (1322).]

1. The action of founding or building upon a firm substructure; the state or fact of being founded.

c **1385** CHAUCER *L.G.W.* 739 *Thisbe*, This wal.. Was cloven a-two, right fro the toppe adoun, Of old tyme of his fundacioun. *c* **1400** MAUNDEV. (1839) xxi. 223 The foundacion of the Tour of Babylon. **1535** COVERDALE *Ezra* iii. 12 Many of the olde prestes.. which had sene the house afore in his foundacion. **1611** BIBLE *John* xvii. 24 Thou louedst mee before the foundation of the world. **1719** TICKELL *Death Addison* 44 Ne'er to these chambers where the mighty rest, Since their foundation, came a nobler guest.

2. *fig.* The action of establishing, instituting, or constituting on a permanent basis.

c **1400** MAUNDEV. (Roxb.) xi. 44 þat was þe fundacion of þe Templeres and of þaire ordre. **1548** HALL *Chron., Edw. IV* (an. 9) 206 b, For the more sure foundacion of the newe amitie, Edward Prince of Wales, wedded Anne. **1619** SEMPIL *Sacrilege Handled* 84 Heere then was but a Nuncupation, a Fundation of Priesthood. **1841** LANE *Arab. Nts.* I. 73 Extending to the foundation of the Empire of Baghdad. **1874** GREEN *Short Hist.* viii. §5. 506 The foundation of the linen manufacture which was to bring wealth to Ulster.

3. a. *esp.* The establishing of an institution, together with an endowment or provision for its perpetual maintenance.

1389 in *Eng. Gilds* (1870) 67 Theyse arne the ordinaunces of the Gylde of Seynt Katerine.. ordeynyd.. in the fyrste fundacion. *c* **1460** FORTESCUE *Abs. & Lim. Mon.* xix. (1885) 185 To establysh and.. amortyse þe same lyuelod to is crowne.. wych than wold be as a newe ffundacion of is crowne. **1513** BRADSHAW *St. Werburge* I. 2449 What landes he gaue towarde the fundacyon Of the sayd monastery. **1587** FLEMING *Contn. Holinshed* III. 1349/2 In ech vniuersities by the foundation of the ordinarie and publike lessons. **1859** C. BARKER *Assoc. Princ.* i. 7 The piety.. evidenced by bequests of broad acres, the foundation of religious houses.

†**b.** The charter of establishment or incorporation of a society, institution, etc., with rules and ordinances for its government. *Obs.*

1389 in *Eng. Gilds* (1870) 110 [heading] *Certificacio fundacionis et regiminis gilde*.. [ending with] Other fundacioun es ther non. **1530-1** *Act 22 Hen. VIII*, c. 12 Euery person.. bounden by reason of any foundacion or ordynaunce to gyue or distribute any money in almes. **1546** *Mem. Ripon* (Surtees) III. 20 As in the First Chauntrie at large is declared as apperyth by Foundacion dated [etc.].

4. a. That which is founded or established by endowment; an institution (e.g. a monastery, college, or hospital) established with an endowment and regulations for its maintenance.

1513 MORE in Grafton *Chron.* (1568) II. 808 He begun to founde a College of a hundred priestes, which foundation with the founder shortly tooke an ende. **1669** WOODHEAD *St. Teresa* II. xxviii. 175 It was our Lord's pleasure, that no Foundation should be erected without great troubles to me. **1843** COLERIDGE in Stanley *Arnold's Life & Corr.* (1844) I. i. 9 Corpus is a very small establishment,—twenty fellows and twenty scholars, with four exhibitioners, form the foundation. **1867** FREEMAN *Norm. Conq.* (1876) I. iv. 190 He was with difficulty hindered from becoming a monk in his own foundation of Jumièges.

b. *on* (or †*of*) *the foundation*: said of the members of an endowed college or similar society.

1491 *Act 7 Hen. VII*, c. 19 William Priour of Cristchurche of Caunterbury of your noble fundacion. **1588** LD. BURGHLEY in Ellis *Orig. Lett.* Ser. I. III. 26 No Scholer nor Fellowes of the foundation of any Howse of Learninge. **1761** GRAY *Lett.* Wks. 1884 III. 86 If the boy was to be on the foundation [at Eton]. **1839** DE QUINCEY *Recoll. Lakes* Wks. 1862 II. 71 He.. was removed to.. London, and placed on the great foundation of Christ's Hospital. **1881** *Oxford Univ. Calend.* 163 There are now fourteen Fellowships and fifteen Scholarships on the old Foundation at this College.

c. The fund or revenues appropriated to endow such an institution. Also *U.S.* (see quot. 1851).

c **1430** LYDG. *Min. Poems* 136 To sette of tithes a fundacioun. **1593** NASHE *Christ's T.* 83 b, They peruert foundations, and will not bestow the Bequeathers free almes. **1655** FULLER *Ch. Hist.* VI. iii. 312 None [of the Convents] was left standing in the whole Diocesse of Bangor, where no Foundation was valued at full seventy pounds per annum. **1851** B. H. HALL *College Words* 134 *Foundation*.. In America applied to a donation or legacy appropriated especially to maintain poor and deserving.. students at a college.

5. a. The solid ground or base (natural or built up) on which an edifice or other structure is erected; also, the lowest part of a building, usually constructed below the ground-level.

1494 FABYAN *Chron.* v. cxxxiv. 119 Albeit yᵗ many [buildings] stande vpon theyr first foundacion, as this yet doth. **1585** T. WASHINGTON tr. *Nicholay's Voy.* I. viii. 8 b, Where as yet are seene the foundations of the auncient citie. **1697** DRYDEN *Æneid* III. 27, I lay the deep Foundations of a Wall. **1802** C. JAMES *Milit. Dict.* s.v., If the earth to be built upon is.. such that the natural foundation cannot be trusted. **1850** MRS. JAMESON *Leg. Monast. Ord.* (1863) 22 In digging the foundations of the monastery of Monte Cassino.

transf. and *fig.* **1398** TREVISA *Barth. De P.R.* v. lvii. (1495) 172 The bones ben the foundacion of al the body and the byldynge of all the body is sette thervpon. **1535** COVERDALE *Ps.* cii. 25 Thou Lorde in the begynnynge has layed yᵉ foundacion of the earth. **1597** DANIEL *Civ. Wars* VI. 54 Which engines of protests, and proffers kind.. So shook the whole foundation of his mind, As they did all his resolution move. **1648** HERRICK *Hesper., Hock-cart* 29 The large and cheefe Foundation of your Feast, Fat Beefe. **1697** DRYDEN *Virg. Georg.* I. 455 The Rocks are from their old Foundations rent. **1705** S. SEWALL *Diary* 19 Jan. (1879) II. 122 The Horses went away with the foundation and left the Superstructure of the Slay and the Riders behind.

†**b.** The 'seat' of the body, the 'fundament'.

1681 COLVIL *Whigs Supplic.* (1751) 131 Who quarrels pick with neighbour nations Get halberts thrust thro' their fundations.

6. *fig.* **a.** A basis or groundwork on which something (immaterial) is raised or by which it is supported or confirmed; an underlying ground or principle; the basis on which a story, fiction, or the like is founded.

c **1400** *Hist. & Art. Masonry* 28 Hit was cause and fundacion of all craftys and sciens. **1529** MORE *Dyaloge* I. Wks. 161/1 This one poynt is the very fond foundacion and ground of all his great heresyes. **1611** BIBLE *Transl. Pref.* 4 The Edition of the Seuentie was vsed by the Greeke fathers for the ground and foundation of their Commentaries. **1628** T. SPENCER *Logick* 182 The principles, and foundation of a demonstration, are necessary axiomes. **1674** PLAYFORD *Skill Mus.* III. 1 The Bass, which is the lowest part and foundation of the whole Song. **1695** WOODWARD *Nat. Hist. Earth* III. ii. (1723) 179 There being no reasonable Foundation to believe that the Deluge did come to pass this Way. **1711** STEELE *Spect.* No. 91 ¶1 The Subject I am now going upon would be much more properly the Foundation of a Comedy. **1716**

LADY M. W. MONTAGU *Let. to Lady Rich* 1 Dec., The report ..I can assure you..has no real foundation. **1765** BLACKSTONE *Comm.* I. 47 The only true and natural foundations of society are the wants and the fears of individuals. **1843** MILL *Logic* I. iii. §9, I shall term the sensation of white the foundation of the quality whiteness. **1875** JOWETT *Plato* (ed. 2) I. 313 Thus far Socrates has proceeded in placing religion on a moral foundation.

†**b.** A ground or reason upon which men act; an understanding, basis of agreement. *Obs.*

1642 R. CARPENTER *Experience* IV. ii. 132 He may kill his adversary, upon this foundation, because he must either kill or be killed. **1727** A. HAMILTON *New Acc. E. Ind.* II. xli. 107 That the English might again repair to their respective Houses, and trade on the old Foundation. **1793** SMEATON *Edystone L.* §30 Upon this foundation Captain Lovet engaged Mr. John Rudyerd to be his engineer.

c. *pl.* [tr. G. *grundlagen*, etc.] The underlying principles or logical basis (of a subject), esp. as a separate matter for study.

1817 COLERIDGE *Biog. Lit.* x. 194, I retired to a cottage in Somersetshire..and devoted my thoughts and studies to the foundations of religions and morals. **1897** B. RUSSELL (*title*) An essay on the foundations of geometry. **1931** F. P. RAMSEY (*title*) The foundations of mathematics. **1941** COURANT & ROBBINS *What is Math.?* ii. 87 Paradoxes like this have led Russell and others to a systematic study of the foundations of mathematics and logic. **1944** H. REICHENBACH (*title*) Philosophic foundations of quantum mechanics. **1965** A. S. & E. H. LUCHINS *Logical Found. Math.* xviii. 377 Despite the popularity of the term *foundations*, there are wide differences of opinion as to the importance of foundations for psychology.

7. *transf.* **a.** That upon which any structure is built up; a body or ground upon which other parts are overlaid; in various technical uses: e.g. in *Dressmaking*, an underskirt over which the outer skirt is hung or draped; also, a material used for stiffening a garment, etc.; in crochet-work and knitting, the first set of stitches, to which the rest are secured. **b.** *attrib.* **c.** = *foundation garment*.

1845 [see BODY *sb.* 7 b]. **1865** M. EYRE *Lady's Walks* xvii. 195 The materials to be used are..neatly tacked on the silk —any foundation could..be used; merino, cloth, or whatever material was thought best suited for curtains. **1874** KNIGHT *Dict. Mech.* I. 909 *Foundation*..the body of a hat, of wool or inferior fur, upon which the napping of superior fur is laid and united at the battery. **1882** CAULFEILD & SAWARD *Dict. Needlework, Foundation net*, a coarse quality of Net..employed for stiff foundations in Millinery and Dressmaking. **1893** G. HILL *Hist. Eng. Dress* II. 270 Six skirts of tulle over a foundation of satin. **1907** *Westm. Gaz.* 9 Mar. 13/2 Such a coat is..mounted on a foundation silk. **1939** P. J. MARQUAND *Wickford Point* 370 She said that she had heard that I worked in a department store and she wanted to know about foundations. **1960** [see BACKLESS *a.* b].

d. A base for cosmetics. Used esp. *attrib.*, as ***foundation cream, lotion, make-up.***

[**1911** G. STRATTON-PORTER *Harvester* xiii. 279 She found a box of cream and rubbed it on for a foundation. Then she opened some pink powder, and carefully dusted her cheeks.] **1929** D. L. MOORE *Pandora's Let. Box* x. 179 A thick layer of powder..may be spread on a foundation cream having almost the consistency of paste. **1935** 'E. ANN' *Beauty Adorned* x. 86 A greaseless foundation-cream as a base. **1939–40** *Army & Navy Stores Catal.* 434/3 Foundation Cream—3/6. Foundation Lotion—4/6. **1942** D. POWELL *Time to be Born* (1943) x. 227 Miss Finkelstein..checked on her Chinese yellow foundation make-up. **1952** C. W. CUNNINGTON *Eng. Women's Clothing* viii. 265 Starting with foundation lotion over cherry-coloured cream rouge..this is followed by cameo powder and cherry lipstick. **1959** *News Chron.* 12 Aug. 5/5, I don't use foundation now. It dries my skin. **1965** [see CLEANSING *ppl. a.*]. **1966** *Guardian* 25 Apr. 6/2 Lipsticks (and foundations) in rich as well as pale colours for the darker woman.

8. *attrib.* and *Comb.* **a.** simple attrib. (= belonging to or serving as a foundation, fundamental).

1665 GLANVILL *Scepsis Sci.* xi. (1680) 98 If any ask, how the Soul came by those foundation-Propositions. **1670** *Devout Commun.* (1688) 160 Christ, that foundation-mercy, that hath all mercies folded up in him. **1726** VANBRUGH *Journ. to Lond.* I. i, It is a settled foundation-point that every child that is born shall be a beggar, except one; and that he —shall be a fool. **1875** E. WHITE *Life in Christ* III. xx. (1878) 262 He builds everywhere on the foundation-thought that a Christian is [etc.].

b. = belonging to a foundation (sense 4), as ***foundation-charter, child,*** †***master, scholar,*** †***undergraduate.*** Also applied to persons, etc. belonging to or associated with the founding of a society or institution, as ***foundation member.*** Cf. FOUNDER *sb.*[2] 5.

1900 *Westm. Gaz.* 28 June 1/1 The Royal herd and flock at Sandringham were established in 1863, when the *foundation animals were selected from some of the best stocks in England. *c* **1670** WOOD *Life* (1848) 129 A copie of the *foundation-charter of Canterbury college in Oxon. **1845** STOCQUELER *Handbk. Brit. India* (1854) 156 The *foundation children, fifty in number, are elected from the Christian population of Calcutta. **1706** HEARNE *Collect.* 17 Feb., He was a *Foundation Master (as they call them). **1928** *Daily Mail* 31 July 8/5 The subscription will be 5s. a year for *foundation members. **1965** DOUGHTY & WAHL in *Rossetti Lett.* I. 41 James Collinson,..a foundation member of the P.R.B. **1970** *Morning Star* 26 Aug. 5 A foundation member of the Communist Party, Tommy Strudwick,..has died in New Zealand. **1883** *Cassell's Fam. Mag.* Aug. 525/1 The number of free or *Foundation scholars has been increased. **1687** W. SHERWIN in *Magd. Coll. & Jas. II* (Oxf. Hist. Soc.) 216 Any *foundation-undergraduate.

c. Special comb.: **foundation-chain**, the first stitches in a piece of crochet-work; **foundation deposit**, an object placed in the foundation of a building; **foundation garment**, a woman's corset, or corset-substitute; **foundation-muslin, -net**, gummed fabrics used for stiffening dresses and bonnets; **foundation-school**, an endowed school; **foundation-stone**, one of the stones forming the foundation of a building; *spec.* a stone laid with public ceremony to celebrate the founding of the edifice; also *fig.*; **foundation-stop**, in an organ (see quot. 1881); **foundation-trench** (see quot. 1954).

1882 CAULFEILD & SAWARD *Dict. Needlework*, **Foundation Chain.* **1955** L. WOOLLEY *Alalakh* ii. 84 It is tempting to regard these concealed 'cupboards' as intended to receive *foundation-deposits. **1962** D. HARDEN *Phoenicians* 225 As a foundation-deposit under one wall there was a late geometric amphora with twisted handles. **1927** *Daily Express* 12 Sept. 5/5 These are best described as cami-bockers, plus a skirt, and are quite the most sensible *foundation garment. **1952** M. MCCARTHY *Groves of Academe* (1953) iv. 54 Courses tailored to the individual need, like their own foundation-garments. **1957** *Times* 25 Nov. 11/1 It is wise first of all to give thought to the question of the right foundation garments. Unconditioned muscles tire less with the support of a well-fitted brassière and pantie-belt. **1858** SIMMONDS *Dict. Trade*, **Foundation-muslin.* **1882** CAULFEILD & SAWARD *Dict. Needlework*, **Foundation net.* **1833** MARRYAT *P. Simple* (1863) 92, I had been..educated at a *foundation school. **1651** HOBBES *Leviath.* III. xlii. 302 The *Foundation-Stone of the Church. **1856** J. A. SYMONDS *Let.* 28 June (1967) I. 74 The laying of the Foundation Stone of the New Aisle. **1874** MORLEY *Compromise* (1886) 250 The first foundation-stone for the doctrine of liberty is to be sought in the conception of society as a growing and developing organism. **1887** *Spectator* 9 July 924/1 The foundation-stone of the Imperial Institute was laid by the Queen. **1846** RIMBAULT in *North Mem. Musicke* 121 Smith seems to have excelled in the diapason or *foundation stops. **1881** C. A. EDWARDS *Organs* 148 Foundation stops are those that give a note corresponding to the key pressed. **1942** *Oxoniensia* VII. 28 The purpose of this enclosure is obscure. The rectangular sides suggest a *foundation-trench for a masonry building, but no trace of masonry or even rubble was found in the section. **1954** M. WHEELER *Archaeol. fr. Earth* (1955) vi. 72 A trench, known as the 'foundation-trench', is cut along the line of the proposed wall in order that the foundations of the latter may rest upon the solid sub-soil rather than upon the relatively unstable soil that is commonly found on the surface.

Hence †**foun'dation** *v.*, to ground.

1627–77 FELTHAM *Resolves* II. xxvii. 215 He that foundations not himself with the Arts, will hardly be fit to go out Doctor, either to himself or others.

foundational (faʊn'deɪʃənəl), *a.* [f. as prec. + -AL[1].] Of, pertaining to, or of the nature of a foundation; fundamental.

1683 E. HOOKER *Pref. Ep. Pordage's Mystic Div.* 44 Foundational Doctrines. **1728** R. MORRIS *Ess. Anc. Archit.* 100 The foundational Laws of Beauty and Proportion. **1865** RUSKIN *Sesame* 161 His command of it should be foundational and progressive, hers, general and accomplished for daily and helpful use.

Hence **foun'dationally** *adv.*

1878 T. SINCLAIR *Mount* 133 Never till then can they construct foundationally.

foundationary (faʊn'deɪʃənərɪ), *a.* [f. as prec. + -ARY.] Of or belonging to a foundation.

1762 tr. *Busching's Syst. Geog.* V. 440 [It] was converted into a foundation of canons..It has its own foundationary amt-office. **1864** *Daily Tel.* 2 Aug., The foundationary funds attached to them [schools].

foundationer (faʊn'deɪʃənə(r)). [f. as prec. + -ER[1].] One who is 'on the foundation' of an endowed school or college.

1839 ARNOLD *Let.* in Stanley *Life & Corr.* (1844) II. ix. 155 The difference which I had always made between Non-foundationers and Foundationers. **1876** FOX BOURNE *Locke* I. i. 17 A new charter, which in addition to the forty foundationers..provided for the education of eighty other boys.

foundationless (faʊn'deɪʃənlɪs), *a.* [f. as prec. + -LESS.] Without foundation, baseless.

1648 HAMMOND *Serm. 2 Cor.* vii. 1 Wks. 1684 IV. 506 A flattering, fallacious, foundationless..hope. **1821** *Examiner* 2/1 The rumour..was not altogether foundationless. **1849** RUSKIN *Sev. Lamps* vi. 165 Tottering, foundationless shells of splintered wood and imitated stone.

Hence **foun'dationlessness.**

1895 *Blackw. Mag.* July 33 Its one foundation is the foundationlessness of other systems.

†**foundator.** *Obs.* Also -atour, *Sc.* fundatour. [ad. L. *fundātor*, agent-n. f. *fundāre*, refashioned after FOUND *v.*[2]] = FOUNDER *sb.*[2]

c **1425** *Found. St. Bartholomew's* (E.E.T.S.) 19 And with ofte visitacions solempne laude yeldid to God, with the foundatoure. **1549** *Compl. Scot.* xv. 128 Lauberaris of the grond..var foundatouris of al there triumphand prosperite. **1585** T. WASHINGTON tr. *Nicholay's Voy.* IV. xxiv. 140 Penetropolis..afterwards of his foundator Philippopoli. **1596** DALRYMPLE tr. *Leslie's Hist. Scotl.* I. 324 The Abbay.. quhairof he is namet fundatour.

†**founday.** *Obs.* [? f. FOUND *v.*[3]] (See quot.)

1674 RAY *Collect. Words* 126 Every six days they call a Founday, in which space they make 8 Tun of Iron, if you divide the whole summ of Iron made by the Foundays: for at first they make less in a Founday, at last more. *Suss*[*ex*].

founded ('faʊndɪd), *ppl. a.* [f. FOUND *v.*[2]]

1. Based, having a (specified) base or ground (with qualifying adverb). †Also without adv. = 'well founded', well grounded, etc. (*obs.*).

1605 SHAKS. *Macb.* III. iv. 22 Then comes my Fit againe. I had else beene perfect, Whole as the Marble, founded as the Rocke. **1671** MILTON *Samson* 1504 Thy hopes are not ill founded. **1771** *Junius Lett.* lv. 291, I mean..of such charges..to show that they are not founded. **1774** tr. *Helvetius' Child of Nature* I. 132 A young woman of your prudence must be founded in her behaviour. **1780** BURKE *Sp. at Bristol* Wks. III. 398 Supply them with just and founded motives to disaffection. **1792** *Anecd. W. Pitt* III. xliii. 152 If Ministers are founded in saying there is no sort of treaty with France. **1855** MACAULAY *Hist. Eng.* III. 248 These complaints were in many cases well founded.

2. Endowed, 'on the foundation'. *rare.*

1895 J. M. BULLOCH *Hist. Aberdeen Univ.* 99 The greater part of the founded members had been 'quyte abolisched'.

foundement: see FUNDAMENT.

†**'founder,** *sb.*[1] *Obs.* [f. FOUND *v.*[1] + -ER[1].] One who tests: only in ***ale-founder*** = ALE-CONNER.

c **1500** *Bk. of Brome* (1886) 164 Enquere..of yower alle-founders, ȝef they hawe do yer office well and trwly.

founder ('faʊndə(r)), *sb.*[2] [f. FOUND *v.*[2] + -ER[1]: cf. OF. *fondeor, -eur.*]

1. a. 'One who raises an edifice; one who presides at the erection of a city' (J.).

1387 TREVISA *Higden* (Rolls) II. 79 Þe foundour of þis citee is vnknowe. *c* **1440** *Bone Flor.* 11 Antenowre..fownder of Jerusalem. **1611** CORYAT *Crudities* 8 Julius Cæsar was the first founder of this tower. **1728** NEWTON *Chronol. Amended* i. 161 Every City set up the worship of its own Founder. **1838** *Murray's Handbk. N. Germ.* 477 The building displays ..the taste of different founders.

†**b.** A maker or creator. *Obs.*

a **1375** *Joseph Arim.* 68 He þat is mi foundeor may hit folfulle, þat was ded on þe cros & bouȝte us so deore.

2. One who sets up or institutes for the first time; one who gives its first beginning to (an institution, sect, etc.). Formerly in wider use, an originator (of a practice or custom).

1340–70 *Alex. & Dind.* 664 He [Mars] was fihtere fel & foundur of werre. **1389** in *Eng. Gilds* (1870) 101 Y[e] first foundurs of y[is] gilde. **1548** HALL *Chron., Hen. VII*, 32 b, No man could tell who was the authoure and founder of that rumoure. **1563** *Homilies* II. *Wilful Rebel.* IV. (1859) 583 Sathan, the first founder of Rebellion. **1678** CUDWORTH *Intell. Syst.* I. i. Contents §17 Leucippus and Democritus.. were..the Founders of that Philosophy which is Atheistically Atomical. **1697** DRYDEN *Virg. Georg.* I. 24 Pallas..Thou Founder of the Plough and Plough-man's Toyl. **1776** GIBBON *Decl. & F.* I. 357 Like Augustus, Diocletian may be considered as the founder of a new empire. **1855** MACAULAY *Hist. Eng.* IV. 24 George Fox, the founder of the sect of Quakers. **1874** HELPS *Soc. Press.* iii. 52 The founders of great fortunes and great families.

3. One who founds or establishes (an institution) with an endowment for its perpetual maintenance.

1303 R. BRUNNE *Handl. Synne* 2584 He was fyrst founder and syre Of þe cherche of Knares myre. **1535–6** *Act 27 Hen. VIII*, c. 28 Suche as pretende to be foundours, patrons or donours of suche relygyous houses. **1682** PRIDEAUX *Lett.* (Camden) 122 Our founders monument being defaced in the late wars, I am again restoreing it. **1693** BENTLEY *Boyle Lect.* II. 8 The Honourable Founder of this Lecture. **1856** EMERSON *Eng. Traits, Universities* Wks. (Bohn) II. 89 The pictures of the founders hang from the walls.

†**4.** One who supports or maintains another. *Obs.*

1548 HALL *Chron.* (1809) 491 He [Perkyn Warbeck].. with all hys complices and confederates, and Jhon Awater.. one of hys founders and hys sonne, were..arreyned and condempned at Westmynster. **1613** BEAUM. & FL. *Captain* I. iii, What a vengeance ails you, To be so childish to imagine me A founder of old fellows?

5. founder member, a person belonging to or associated with the founding of a society or institution; **founder's-shares, (-parts)** *pl.*, shares issued to the founders of a public company, as part of the consideration for the business or concession which is taken over, and not forming a part of the ordinary capital. Cf. FOUNDATION 8 b.

1889 *Daily News* 24 Oct. 7/2 The value of..founders' shares has grown unwieldy. **1896** *Athenæum* 1 Feb. 143/2 The invention of 'founders' shares'..dates only from 1889. **1909** *Westm. Gaz.* 23 Apr. 9/3 The committee of the Aero Club of the United Kingdom have decided that after the first thousand members have been elected, such thousand members being founder members, the subscription will be raised and an entrance fee charged. **1960** *Farmer & Stockbreeder* 8 Mar. 63/2 A founder-member of the British Charollais Committee..said many farmers would like to see Charollais imported.

founder ('faʊndə(r)), *sb.*[3] [f. FOUND *v.*[3] + -ER[1]. Cf. OF. (and mod.F.) *fondeur.*]

1. One who founds or casts metal, or makes articles of cast metal. Often in comb., with the metal or article specified, as ***bell-, iron-, type-founder.***

1402 in *Rot. Parl.* III. 520 Bartilmew Dekene, Founder. **1560** BIBLE (Genev.) *Jer.* vi. 29 The lead is consumed in the fyre: the founder melteth in vaine. **1637** *Decree Star Chamber* xxvii. in Arb. *Milton's Areop.* 21 That there shall be foure Founders of letters for printing allowed. **1681** GREW *Musæum* III. iii. 334 Founders add a little [antimony] to their Bell-Metal, to make it more sonorous. **1705**

LUTTRELL *Brief Rel.* (1857) V. 581 Her majesties founder has orders to cast 60 heavy cannon. **1724** SWIFT *Drapier's Lett.* Wks. 1755 V. II. 28 Let Mr. Wood and his crew of founders and tinkers coin on. **1892** *Labour Commission* Gloss. s.v., Master founders are the owners or managers of a foundry for making iron or brass castings.

b. One who founds glass.

1853 URE *Dict. Arts* I. 905 The glass-founder. **1885** *Instr. Census Clerks* 89 Glass Manufacture [Workmen employed in] Metal Making: Founder.

2. *Comb.*, as ***founder's dust, sand*** (see quots.).

1858 SIMMONDS *Dict. Trade, Founders' Dust*, charcoal powder, and coal and coke dust ground fine and sifted for casting purposes in foundries. *Ibid., Founders' sand*, a species of sand obtained from Lewisham, Kent, and other districts, for making foundry moulds.

founder (ˈfaʊndə(r)), *sb.*[4] [f. FOUNDER *v.*]

†**1.** *pl.* Grounds, lees, sediment. Cf. F. *fondrilles. Obs.*

c **1450** *M.E. Med. Bk.* (Heinrich) 176 Do awey þe foundres [*v.r.* groundes] vndernepe.

2. The action of the verb FOUNDER; a landslip.

1882 *Cornh. Mag.* Dec. 738 A series of founders or landslips, caused by the undermining of the solid strata.

founder (ˈfaʊndə(r)), *sb.*[5] [app. f. *found*, pa. pple. of FIND *v.* + -ER[1].]

†**1.** = FINDER. *Obs.*

1577 FRAMPTON *Joyful News* in *App. Jas. I's Counterbl.* (Arb.) 84 Lorde Nicot..first founder out of this hearbe.

2. *spec.* in *Derbysh. Lead-mining* (see quot. 1851).

1601 *High Peak Art.* l. in Mander *Derbysh. Min. Gloss.* (1824) 130 Who..were or pretended to be possessed of the same ground as taker of a Fore-field for an old founder. **1851** TAPPING *Lead-mining Terms* (E.D.S.), *Founder* is the mining term expressive of the finder of a vein, or rake, or in ordinary language, a miner.

3. That portion of a lead-mine which is given to the first finder of the vein; hence, the part first worked. Called also ***founder-meer, -shaft.***

1653 MANLOVE *Lead-Mines* 59 (E.D.S.) If two Founders in one Rake be set. **1747** HOOSON *Miner's Dict.* I ijb, Sometimes it happens that there is two Founders in the same Vein, for a Vein may be found at a distance from my Founder. **1802** MAWE *Min. Derbysh.* 204 *Foundermere*, the first 32 yards of ground worked. *Ibid., Foundershaft*, the first shaft that is sunk. **1851** *Act 14 & 15 Vict.* c. 94 §2 The Word 'Founder' shall mean the Point at which a Vein of Ore shall be first found..the Words 'Founder-Meers' shall mean the Two first Meers to be set out to the Finder.

founder (ˈfaʊndə(r)), *sb.*[6] Also 6 fownder. [f. FOUNDER *v.* (senses 4–5).]

1. Inflammation of the laminar structures of a horse's foot, resulting usually from overwork; a similar disease in dogs.

1547 SALESBURY *Welsh Dict., Fraeo val march*, fownder. **1708** J. C. *Compl. Collier* (1845) 34 They are subject to Beat or Founder to their Feet or Leggs. **1825** LOUDON *Agric.* §6517 (1831) 987 Founder of the feet. **1884** SPEEDY *Sport* iii. 31 Kennel lameness, founder, and rheumatism [in dogs] are often caused by [etc.]

2. A rheumatic affection of the muscles of the chest in horses. Called also ***body-, chest-founder.***

1737 BRACKEN *Farriery Impr.* (1756) I. 275 They were often mistaken even in what they call the Chest or Body-founder. **1818** *Sporting Mag.* II. 171, I agree with the French writers that the founder is a fluxion.

founder (ˈfaʊndə(r)), *v.* [a. OF. *fondrer* to plunge to the bottom, submerge; also *intr.* to collapse, fall in ruins:—f. L. *fundus* bottom.

The simple vb. *fondrer* appears to be rare in OF.; the compounds *esfondrer, enfondrer*, are common, and occur in most of the senses below; cf. AFOUNDER, ENFOUNDER, of which *founder* in some uses may be an aphetic form. The *r* in the OF. vb. is variously accounted for: see Hatz.-Darm. s.v. *effondrer*, Körting *Lat.-Rom.-Wb.* s. vv. *exfundulare, infundulare*; a popular Lat. type **fundorāre* may have existed, f. *fundora* (see Du Cange) pl. of *fundus* neut., whence Fr. *fonds*, FOUNCE.]

†**1.** *trans.* To burst or smash (something) in; to force a passage through. *Obs.*

13.. *Coer de L.* 5266 He gaff Richard a sory flatt, That foundryd bacynet and hatt. *c* **1330** R. BRUNNE *Chron.* (1725) 183 And whan he was withinne, & fauht as a wilde leon, He fondred þe Sarazins otuynne & fauht as a dragon.

†**2.** To send to the bottom, cause to be swallowed up or engulfed. *Obs.*

13.. *E.E. Allit. P.* B. 1014 Þis watz a uengeaunce violent þat voyded þise places, þat foundered hatz so fayr a folk & þe folde sonkken. **1490** CAXTON *Eneydos* xxvii. 97 Haue no mercy..of ony man that lyueth, foundre & droune altogider [F. *effondres tout*] in-to the botome of the sea.

3. *intr.* Of the earth, a building, etc.: To fall down, give way.

1489 CAXTON *Faytes of A.* II. xxxv. 153 The toure foundred and sanke doune in to the grounde. *a* **1697** AUBREY *Wilts.* (Royal Soc. MS.) 106 (Halliw.) A quantity of earth foundred and fell downe a vast depth. **1830** LYELL *Princ. Geol.* I. 274 We find that the cliffs of Bawdsey and Felixtow are foundering slowly.

†**b.** *trans.* To undermine. Also *fig. Obs.*

1655 FULLER *Ch. Hist.* III. iv. §13 King John having his soul battered without, with forrain fears, and foundred with-in by the falsenesse of his Subjects, sunk on a sudden beneath himself. *a* **1656** USSHER *Ann.* v. (1658) 60 The river ..foundering the wall thereof 20 furlongs in length, bare it down.

4. *intr.* (Chiefly of a horse or its rider.) To stumble violently, fall helplessly to the ground, collapse; to fall lame; *occas.* to sink or stick fast (in mire or bog).

c **1386** CHAUCER *Knt's. T.* 1829 For which his hors for feere gan to turne, And leep asyde, and foundred as he leep. *c* **1450** *Golagros & Gaw.* 1022 As he loutit our ane bra, His feit founderit hym fra. **1513** DOUGLAS *Æneis* x. xiv. 157 Down swakkis the knycht sone with a fellon fayr, Foundris fordwart flatlingis on hys spald. *c* **1560** A. SCOTT *Poems* (S.T.S.) ii. 163 To grund, for fersness, he did funder. **1563** *Homilies* II. *Rogation Week* IV. (1859) 498 Where-by thy poor nyghbour, sitting on his seelly weak beast, foundereth not in the deep thereof. **1713** STEELE *Guard.* No. 132 ¶6 The man is a thick-skull'd puppy, and founders like a horse. **1875** F. HALL in *Lippincott's Mag.* XVI. 749/1 The guide had strayed off the ford, and I was foundering in a quicksand. **1880** MUIRHEAD *Gaius* III. §219 When a man has ..driven another's horse so hard as to cause it to founder.

5. *trans.* To cause to break down or go lame; *esp.* to cause (a horse) to have the founder, thus disabling him.

1593 NASHE 4 *Lett. Confut.* 51 A broken-winded..Iade, that..now is quite foundred and tired. **1608** *Yorksh. Trag.* I. viii, O stumbling jade..Plague founder thee. **1674** N. COX *Gentl. Recreat.* I. (1677) 97 You will surbate or founder your Hounds. **1680** HACKE *Collect. Voy.* II. (1699) 3 A very bad Path, which with our being necessitated to wade the River.. almost foundred our Men. **1732** GAY *Achilles* I, He will quite founder himself with galloping from place to place to look after me. **1884** W. C. SMITH *Kildrostan* 74 She..rode my pony till she foundered him.

b. *fig.*

1589 R. HARVEY *Pl. Perc.* 18 Such firie Agues fall soonest into a surfeit, and founder themselues with their intemperate behauiour. **1645** MILTON *Colast.* (1851) 365 Founder himself to and fro in his own objections. **1658** BRAMHALL *Consecr. Bps.* vi. 148 And so your Consequence ..is foundered of all four, and can neither passe nor repasse.

¶**c.** Confused with FOUND *v.*[5]: To benumb.

1562 [see FOUND *v.*[5]]. **1578** LYTE *Dodoens* III. xix. 342 The Oyle..is good..for members that are benummed or foundered.

6. *intr.* Of a vessel: To fill with water and sink, go to the bottom. [= OF. *s'enfondrer*: cf. sense 2.]

1600 HAKLUYT *Voy.* III. 398 Already she had receiued in much water, insomuch that she beganne to founder. **1719** DE FOE *Crusoe* I. i, The seamen every now and then cried out she would founder. **1882** WHITE *Naval Archit.* 13 Ships founder when the entry of water into the interior causes a serious and fatal loss of floating power.

b. *fig.* To 'come to grief', be wrecked.

1613 SHAKS. *Hen. VIII*, III. ii. 40 But in this point All his tricks founder. **1816** KEATINGE *Trav.* (1817) I. 56 *note*, Spain began to founder from the loss of the Low Countries: but a first-rate ship does not go down like a wherry.

7. *trans.* To cause (a ship) to fill with water and sink; to send to the bottom.

1659 D. PELL *Impr. Sea* 305 When a vessel is, or comes once to bee foundered, there is no possibility of her being helped up. [But this may be sense 6.] **1748** F. SMITH *Voy. Disc.* I. 52 Capable of pierceing a Ship under her Bends, so foundering her. **1893** G. ALLEN *Scallywag* III. 110 A great ship was being foundered and ground to pieces by some invisible force within a few yards of them.

8. *Golf.* To hit (a ball) into the ground.

1880 'CAPT. CRAWLEY' *Football, etc.* 96 The young Golfer ..is likely to founder the ball, or drive it only a comparatively short distance.

¶**9.** *erron.* = Fr. *fondre*: To burst (into tears).

c **1477** CAXTON *Jason* 5 The damoiseau Jason..began thenne to foundre in teeris right habondantly. [Often in Caxton.] *c* **1530** LD. BERNERS *Arth. Lyt. Bryt.* (1814) 51 The king foundred all in teeres.

Hence **ˈfoundering** *vbl. sb.* and *ppl. a.*

1548 HALL *Chron., Hen. VI* (an. 13) 127 Matthew Gouth, by founderyng of his horsse, was taken. **1602** WARNER *Alb. Eng.* IX. liii. (1612) 238 No one thing quailes Religion more than foundring Presbytrie. **1614** MARKHAM *Cheap Husb.* I. li. (1668) 62 Of Foundring in the Feet there be two sorts, a dry and a wet. **1802** C. JAMES *Milit. Dict.* s.v., Foundering in the feet..Foundering in the chest. **1813** SCOTT *Rokeby* I. xvii, Rescued from our foundering skiff.

foundered (ˈfaʊndəd), *ppl. a.* [f. FOUNDER *v.* + -ED[1].]

†**1.** Undermined, made to give way. *Obs.*

a **1661** FULLER *Worthies* (1840) I. 119 A foundered and failing foundation.

2. Of a horse: Affected with founder; lamed.

1543 tr. *Act 20 Rich. II*, c. 5 The sayde horses become al lost and foundred [original AF. *foundez*]. **1599** B. JONSON *Cynthia's Rev.* I. i, As tender as the foot of a foundred nagge. **1640** FULLER *Joseph's Coat* 1 Cor. xi. (1867) 81 So our judgment will be partial and favourable to us, as foundered feet will never tread hard. **1726** SWIFT *Corr.* Wks. 1841 II. 596 Shall gallop a foundered horse ten miles upon a causeway and get home safe. **1869** BLACKMORE *Lorna D.* xxiii, Your horse was greatly foundered.

fig. **1642** FULLER *Holy & Prof. St.* II. i. 51 He not only hears but examines his Client, and pincheth the cause, where he fears it is foundred. **1822** BYRON *Vis. Judg.* xci, Ere he could get a word Of all his founder'd verses under way.

3. Of a vessel: Sunk, wrecked.

a **1700** B. E. *Dict. Cant. Crew, Founder'd, Ship at Sea*, that sprung a Leak and Sunk downright. **1762–9** FALCONER *Shipwr.* III. 634 They..Across the founder'd deck o'erwhelming roar.

founderous (ˈfaʊndərəs), *a.* Also foundrous. [f. FOUNDER *v.* + -OUS.] Causing or likely to cause to founder; miry, full of ruts and holes.

1767 *Hull & Anlaby Road Act* 2 The other roads..are become very founderous for travellers. **1796** BURKE *Regic. Peace* iii. Wks. VIII. 267, I have travelled through the negotiation, and a sad founderous road it is. **1805** WORDSW. *Waggoner* 111, Poor pilot I, by snows confounded, And many a foundrous pit surrounded! **1844** WILLIAMS *Real Prop.* (1873) 314 Where a public way is foundrous, as such ways frequently were in former times.

foundership (ˈfaʊndəʃɪp). [f. FOUNDER *sb.*[2] + -SHIP.] The position of a founder.

1565 ABP. PARKER *Corr.* (1853) 252, I would wish a better in his place to govern the house, and he to hold him in his foundership if he will. **1622** CALLIS *Stat. Sewers* (1647) 213 Many Inheritances I found in reason freed from these Taxes and Lays, as Tythes in Spiritual hands..Presentations, Founderships. **1841** *Fraser's Mag.* XXIII. 92 There seems to be a patriotic schism..as to the foundership of the Temperance societies. **1869** *Contemp. Rev.* XII. 67 It.. harmonizes with his foundership of the Olympic games.

ˈfounding, *ppl. a.* [f. FOUND *v.*[2]] Associated with or marking the establishment of (something specified); that originated or created. Spec. ***founding father*** (freq. with capital initials), an American statesman of the Revolutionary period, esp. a member of the American Constitutional Convention of 1787; also *transf.*; ***founding member*** = *founder member.*

1903 *Westm. Gaz.* 17 Nov. 10/1 Founding members are now being elected for the Ladies' Military and Naval Club. **1914** K. B. UMBRIET (*title*) Founding fathers: men who shaped our tradition. **1953** *Manch. Guardian Weekly* 8 Oct. 5/1 The Hyde Park-Kenwood Community Conference was formed. Many of the 'founding-fathers' of the conference were Quakers. **1957** C. HUNT *Guide to Communist Jargon* viii. 21 The invitation to the founding Congress of the Comintern. **1958** C. BAKER *Friend in Power* i. 14 The Founding Fathers, eternized in dark oils, looked benignly down from the white and gold walls. **1959** *Ann. Reg. 1958* 180 Article 4 provided that the control commission should consist of seven members, one representative each from the three founding nuclear Powers [etc.]. **1959** *Listener* 5 Mar. 419/2 It is possible, too, that some of the founding families [in Tarentum] may have enjoyed political privileges. **1961** *Ibid.* 7 Sept. 336/1 Sociologists tend to accept the distinction stressed by their Founding Father, Max Weber, between fact and value. **1966** *Times* 28 Feb. (Canada Suppl.) p. v/1 One third of Canadians are not of the founding races. **1967** *Observer* (Colour Suppl.) 15 Oct. 44/2 It was with abuses of this sort..in mind that Lord Keynes and the founding fathers of the new regime at Covent Garden set to work in 1945. **1969** P. A. ROBINSON *Sexual Radicals* (1970) II. 84 Roheim..rejected the naïve attempts of the founding fathers to explain culture in terms of a simple-minded rationalistic psychology.

foundling (ˈfaʊndlɪŋ). Forms: 4 **fynd(e)ling,** 4–8 **fondling,** 4–6 **-elyng,** 4–6 **found(e)lyng,** (4 **-eling**), 4–5 **fund(e)ling, -lyng,** 4, 6 **foundling.** [ME. *fundeling* (= Du. *vondeling*, MHG. *vundelinc*), f. *funden*, pa. pple. of FIND *v.* + -LING; ME. had also *findling* (= Ger. *findling*), f. the pres. stem of the vb. Cf. also ME. *funding*.]

1. A deserted infant whose parents are unknown, a child whom there is no one to claim. Also *transf.*

a **1300** *E.E. Psalter* lxvii[i]. 5 (Horstm.) Of fadre of foundlinges ma. *c* **1305** *Judas* 56 in *E.E.P.* (1862) 108 So þat þe quene vpbreid adai: þat he fyndling was. *c* **1440** *Promp. Parv.* 182/2 Fundelynge, as he þat ys fowndyn, and noman wote ho ys hys fadur, ne hys modyr. **1549** COVERDALE, etc. *Erasm. Par. Phil.* iii. 5, I am an Israelite, not by engraffynge, but by kyndred: not a straunge foundlyng, but a Jewe, beynge borne of the Jewes. **1602** WITHALS *Dict.* 271/1 A childe which is laid and found in the streete..or else-where, which they call commonly a foundling. **1735** BERKELEY *Querist* §372 Whether there should not be erected..an hospital for orphans and foundlings, at the expense of old bachelors? **1789** G. WHITE *Selborne* xliv. 113, I myself have seen these foundlings in their nest displaying a strange ferocity of nature. **1840** DICKENS *Barn. Rudge* xxxix, He roared again until the very foundlings near at hand were startled in their beds.

appositively. *a* **1712** KING *Ulysses & Tiresias* 25 Tho' he a foundling bastard be. *a* **1853** ROBERTSON *Serm.* Ser. IV. xxiii. (1876) 250 The discovery of a foundling orphan.

b. *fig.*

1587 GOLDING *De Mornay* Pref. 8 As for lying or vntruth, it is a foundling, and not a thing bred. **1827–38** HARE *Guesses* (1867) 210 Employ such words as have the largest families, keeping clear of foundlings and of those of which nobody can tell whence they come unless he happens to be a scholar. **1853** TRENCH *Proverbs* 39 The great majority of proverbs are foundlings, the happier foundlings of a nation's wit, which [etc.].

2. ***the Foundling***: the Foundling Hospital, London.

1829 GEN. P. THOMPSON *Exerc.* (1842) I. 123 It would be as wise to recommend wolves for nurses at the Foundling, on the credit of Romulus and Remus.

3. *attrib.* and *Comb.*, as **foundling-hospital,** †**-house,** an institution for the reception of foundlings; **foundling-stone,** an erratic boulder.

1756 NUGENT *Gr. Tour, France* IV. 39 The *enfants trouvés*, or *foundling-hospital. **1875** JOWETT *Plato* (ed. 2) III. 166 The Crêches of Paris, or the foundling hospital of Dublin. **1750** JOHNSON *Rambler* No. 12 ¶6 What, you never heard of the *Foundling House? **1892** *Edin. Rev.* Apr. 305 *'Foundling-stones' innumerable have become objects of popular superstition and scientific curiosity.

foundment: see FUNDAMENT.

foundress[1] (ˈfaʊndrɪs). Forms: 5 fowndowr-, 5–6 founderesse, (7 -ess), 5–7 foundresse, 7–8 -res, 7– foundress. [f. FOUNDER *sb.*[2] + -ESS.] A female founder; *esp.* a woman who founds or endows an institution, etc.

c**1430** LYDG. *Min. Poems* 11 Gramer..Cheeff ffounderesse and roote of alle connyng. **1490** CAXTON *Eneydos* vi. 23 Dydo..foundresse of the noble cyte of cartage. **1568** GRAFTON *Chron.* II. 898 [Perkin] retourned againe to the Lady Margaret his first foolish foundresse. **1631** WEEVER *Anc. Fun. Mon.* 387 The chiefe Foundresse of this religious house. **1778** LOWTH *Transl. Isaiah* Notes (ed. 12) 328 Semiramis was the foundress of this part also of the Babylonian greatness. **1875** JOWETT *Plato* (ed. 2) III. 530 The goddess who is the common foundress of both our cities.

†**ˈfoundress**[2]. *Obs.* [f. FOUNDER *sb.*[3] + -ESS.] A woman who founds or casts metals.

1638 FORD *Fancies* III. ii, The great bell of my heart is crack'd and never Can ring in tune again, till't be new cast By one only skilful foundress.

foundry (ˈfaʊndrɪ). Forms: 7 fondary, -ery, founderie, 8 -ary, 8–9 -ery, 9 foundry. [a. F. *fond(e)rie*, f. *fondre*: see FOUND *v.*[3]]

1. The art or business of founding or casting metal; *concr.* founders' work, castings.

1601 HOLLAND *Pliny* II. 565 This art of grauing images in stone is of greater antiquitie by farre, than..founderie and casting statues. **1793** SMEATON *Edystone L.* §279 *note*, The ingenious Mr. Prickett, to whom the Iron Foundery of this kingdom owes much. **1890** *Daily News* 6 Jan. 2/3 Cut nails are advanced..and a similar run is declared in heavy iron foundry, mill-rolls, wheels, etc.

2. An establishment or building in which founding of metal or glass is carried on.

1645 EVELYN *Mem.* (1819) I. 194 The founderie where they cast ordinance. c**1730** BURT *Lett. N. Scotl.* (1818) I. 258 This man..dwelt near an English foundery in Glengary. **1853** URE *Dict. Arts* I. 915 (art. *Glass-making*). **1880** MISS BRADDON *Just as I am* xliii, Fellow-workmen together in the same foundry.

fig. **1711** SHAFTESB. *Charac.* (1737) I. 320 Thus I contend with fancy and opinion; and search the mint and foundery of imagination. **1794** SULLIVAN *View Nat.* IV. 249 The nursery of irresistible legions, the foundary of the human race.

†**b.** (See quots.) *Obs.*

1670–98 LASSELS *Voy. Italy* I. 3 The Fondaries or Stilling-Houses of the Great Duke of Florence. **1674** BLOUNT *Glossogr.*, *Fondery* (Fr.) a Stilling-house.

3. *attrib.* and *Comb.*, as ***foundry-coke***, ***-furnace***, ***-goods***, ***-man***; **foundry-iron**, iron containing sufficient carbon to make it suitable for castings; **foundry-proof**, the final proof before stereotyping or electrotyping (Jacobi).

1892 *Daily News* 6 Aug. 8/6 Wanted by Colliery Proprietors, an Agent, to sell *foundry coke. **1884** KNIGHT *Dict. Mech.* IV. 355 **Foundry Furnace*..Reverberating and blast furnaces. **1831** J. HOLLAND *Manuf. Metal* I. 71 That endless variety of smaller and generally useful articles, denominated *foundery goods. **1863** ROBSON *Bards of Tyne* 357 He..keeps 'a the *foundrymen starvin' till neet.

fount[1] (faʊnt). Chiefly *poet.* [Appears late in 16th c.; ad. F. *font* or L. *font-em* on the analogy of *mount*, *mountain*, etc.] A spring, source, FOUNTAIN *sb.*

1593 SHAKS. *Lucr.* 850 Why should..toads infect fair founts with venom mud? **1613** —— *Hen. VIII*, I. i. 154 Proofes as cleere as Founts in Iuly, when Wee see each graine of grauell. **1641** J. JACKSON *True Evang. Temper* I. 8 As naturall a fluxe and emanation forth of it..as the water in the rivelet hath from the fount. **1667** MILTON *P.L.* III. 357 And flours aloft shading the Fount of Life. **1725** POPE *Odyss.* XIX 562 Thy milky founts my infant lips have drained. **1728–46** THOMSON *Spring* 398 High to their fount ..trace up the brooks. a**1839** PRAED *Poems* (1864) II. 308 By Kedron's brook, or Siloa's holy fount.

b. *transf.* and *fig.*

1593 DRAYTON *Eclog.* iv. 107 From this Fount did all those Mischiefs flow. **1833** MRS. BROWNING *Prometh. Bound* Poems 1850 I. 144 Because I stole The secret fount of fire. **1842** TENNYSON *Locksley Hall* 188 Ancient founts of inspiration well thro' all my fancy yet. **1874** GREEN *Short Hist.* v. §3. 235 The Archbishop turned fiercely upon Oxford as the fount and centre of the new heresies.

fount[2] (faʊnt), **font** (fɒnt). *Printing.* Also 8 found; cf. FUND. [See FONT *sb.*[2]] A complete set or assortment of type of a particular face and size. Also fully, ***fount of letter*** or ***type***.

1683 MOXON *Printing* No. II. ¶2. 13 A Fount (properly a Fund) of Letter of all Bodies. *Ibid.* No. XXIII. 377 *Fount* is the whole number of Letters that are Cast of the same Body and Face at one time. **1687–8** BOYLE *Let.* 5 Mar. in Birch *Life* 417, I caused a font of Irish letters to be cast. **1714** MANDEVILLE *Fab. Bees* (1725) I. 258 Break down the printing-presses, melt the founds. **1771** P. LUCKOMBE *Hist. Print.* 248 A Complete Fount of Letter. **1834** SOUTHEY *Doctor* I. ii. 27 We discussed the merits of a new font. **1862** BURTON *Bk. Hunter* 76 The largest font of Italics possessed by the establishment. **1878** F. S. WILLIAMS *Midl. Railw.* 630 He set up a complete fount of type.

fountain (ˈfaʊntɪn), *sb.* Forms: 5–6 fontayn(e, -eyn(e, 5–7 -taine, fountayn(e, 6 fontane, 6–7 fountaine, 7– fountain. [late ME. *fontayne*, a. OF. *fontaine*:—late L. *fontāna* (whence Pr., Sp., Pg., It. *fontana*, Welsh *ffynnawn*, *-on*), fem. of L. *fontānus* pertaining to a fount, f. *font-*, *fons* FOUNT *sb.*[1]]

1. a. A spring or source of water issuing from the earth and collecting in a basin, natural or artificial; also, the head-spring or source *of* a stream or river. Now *arch.* or *poet.* exc. *fig.*

c**1450** *Merlin* 308 To this fountayn ofte tyme com nimiane for to disporte. c**1489** CAXTON *Sonnes of Aymon* xviii. 400 A fore the gate sprange a quycke fontaine. **1535** COVERDALE *Gen.* viii. 2 The fountaynes of the depe and the wyndowes of heauen were stopte. **1588** SHAKS. *Tit. A.* II. v. 23 Like to a bubling fountaine stir'd with winde. **1635** N. CARPENTER *Geog. Del.* II. ix. 163 Some would haue the great riuer Tanais not to haue his head or fountaine in the Riphæan mountains. **1671** MILTON *Samson* 581 God, who caused a fountain at thy prayer From the dry ground to spring, etc. **1692** RAY *Dissol. World* II. ii (1732) 83 Making Rivers to ascend to their Fountains. **1727** DYER *Grongar Hill* 20 So oft I have, At the fountain of a rill Sate upon a flow'ry bed. **1812** BRACKENRIDGE *Views Louisiana* (1814) 105 The greatest objection to this country is the want of fountains and running streams. **1842** TENNYSON *Amphion* 96 The vilest herb that runs to seed Beside its native fountain.

b. Used with reference to baptism (cf. FONT).

[**1526** TINDALE *Eph.* v. 26 Clensed it in the fountayne of water thorowe the worde.] **1548–9** (Mar.) *Bk. Com. Prayer* Offices 8 Them which at this fountayne forsake the deuill and all his workes.

c. *transf.*

1526–34 TINDALE *Mark* v. 29 And streyght waye her fountayne of bloude was dryed vp. **1592** SHAKS. *Rom. & Jul.* I. i. 92 With purple fountains issuing from your veins.

d. *fig.* A spring, source, 'well'. (Often in *pl.*)

1398 TREVISA *Barth. De P.R.* I. (1495) 6 God is the fountayne of all godenesse and of all vertue. **14..** *Balade to our Ladie* (Chaucer's Wks. 1561) Fountain al filthlesse, as birell current clere. **1481** CAXTON *Myrr.* I. vi. 30 Parys Oxenford & Cambryge ben the fontayns where men may drawe out most science. **1548–9** (Mar.) *Bk. Com. Prayer*, Post-Communion, Almightie God, the fountayn of all wisdome. **1589** *Pasquil's Ret.* C iij, This mischiefe hath many fountaines. **1660** BARROW *Euclid* Pref. (1714) 3 Some principal Rules of practical Geometry, reducing them to their original Fountains. **1766** BLACKSTONE *Comm.* II. 223 The French law, which is derived from the same feodal fountain. **1844** LD. BROUGHAM *Brit. Const.* xvii. (1862) 268 The Crown is the fountain of honour. **1861** TULLOCH *Eng. Purit.* i. 116 Long-practised craft had poisoned the very fountains of trust in him.

2. a. A jet or stream of water made to rise or spout up artificially; the structure built for such a jet or stream to rise and fall in; also, an erection in a public place for a constant supply of fresh water for drinking (more fully, ***drinking fountain***). Applied also to a natural jet of water, as that of a geyser.

1509 HAWES *Past. Pleas.* XVIII. ix, A dulcet spring and marvaylous fountaine Of golde and asure made all certaine. **1590** SPENSER *F.Q.* II. xii. 60 In the midst of all a fountaine stood, Of richest substance that on earth might bee. **1601** SHAKS *Jul. C.* II. ii. 77 My Statue, Which like a Fountaine, with an hundred spouts Did run pure blood. **1625** BACON *Ess.*, *Gardens* (Arb.) 561 Fountaines I intend to be of two Natures: the One that sprinckleth or Spouteth Water; the Other a Faire Receipt of Water,..without Fish, or Slime, or Mud. a**1631** DONNE *Poems* (1650) 23 A stone fountaine weeping out the yeare. **1717** LADY M. W. MONTAGU *Let. to Lady Rich* 1 Apr., There were four fountains of cold water in this room. **1726** *Adv. Capt. R. Boyle* 28 It had been formerly a Fountain, but was only choak'd up..I ask'd..if he had ever known it to play. **1841–4** EMERSON *Ess.*, *Art* Wks. (Bohn) I. 145 Let spouting fountains cool the air, Singing in the sun-baked square. **1882** CASSELL s.v. *Drinking-fountain*, Modern drinking fountains began to be erected in Liverpool in 1857. The first one in London was opened to the public on April 12, 1859. **1886** A. WINCHELL *Walks & Talks in Geol. Field* 84 Instantly the fountain [of the Great Geyser of Iceland] began to play with the utmost violence.

b. A metal vessel containing aerated water for drinking; a box containing ice and a coil through which aerated water is drawn (= *soda-fountain*). *U.S.*

1843 'R. CARLTON' *New Purchase* I. 52, I shall make no attempt to record their..puns—good things of the sort, like soda-water, had better be taken at the fountain. **1873** J. H. BEADLE *Undevel. West* xxxi. 675 A drink equal to the best soda from fountains. **1936** *Amer. Speech* XI. 38 The craze for this sort of fountain entertainment seems to be on the wane. **1955** H. ROTH *Sleeper* xvi. 131 He had neglected to tip the fountain man.

3. *Her.* A roundel, barry wavy of six, argent and azure.

1610 GUILLIM *Heraldry* III. iv. 96 He beareth..a Bend.. betweene six Fountaines Proper. **1864** BOUTELL *Her. Hist. & Pop.* v. 25 In representation, the Bezant, Plate, and Fountain, are flat. **1868** CUSSANS *Her.* iv. 70 A Bend between six Fountains forms the Coat of the Stourton Family.

4. A reservoir or compartment for holding oil, ink, etc., in an Argand lamp, a printing-press, etc.

5. *Conchol.* (See quot.)

1895 *Edin. Rev.* Oct. 355 Fountains and watering-pots.. and helmet-shells..names which have been locally.. applied to a few of the multitudinous species of Mollusca.

6. *attrib.* and *Comb.* **a.** simple attrib. (chiefly appositive and *fig.* = belonging to or of the nature of a spring or source, original).

1645 RUTHERFORD *Tryal & Tri. Faith* (1845) 5 The fountain-love, the fountain-delight, the fountain-joy of men and angels. **1648** BOYLE *Seraph. Love* xviii. (1700) 111 His Love is the first Original and Fountain-blessing. a**1652** J. SMITH *Sel. Disc.* IX. 446 The universal fountain-fulness of one supreme almighty goodness. **1662** J. CHANDLER *Van Helmont's Oriat.* 286 The Fountain-light of the soul. **1678** MARVELL *Def. Howe* Wks. 1875 IV. 192 The original and fountain-Being. **1803–6** WORDSW. *Intimat. Immort.* ix, Those shadowy recollections, Which be they what they may, Are yet the fountain light of all our day. **1846** TRENCH *Mirac.* vi. (1862) 191 In contact with Him who is the fountain-flame of all life.

b. *Comb.*, as ***fountain-brim***, ***-side***; ***fountain-fruitful*** adj.; also **fountain-fish**, a ctenophoran; **fountain-pen**, a pen furnished with an ink-reservoir; **fountain-pipe**, a pipe which supplies a fountain with water; **fountain-tree**, a name for the deodar (*Treas. Bot.* 1866); also, 'a tree in the Canary Isles which distills water from its leaves' (W.); †**fountain-water**, fresh water from a spring, spring-water.

1634 MILTON *Comus* 119 By dimpled brook and *fountain-brim. **1641** G. SANDYS *Paraphr. Song Sol.* IV. ii, The *Fountain-fruitfull Lebanon. **1710** M. HENRY *Expos. Bible*, *Zechariah* iv. 2 Without any further Care they [*sc.* lamps] received Oil as fast as they wasted it, (as in those which we call Fountain Inkhorns, or *Fountain Pens). **1789** F. BURNEY *Diary* 18 Aug. (1842) 51, I took my fountain pen, and wrote my rough journal. **1823** *Dict. Math. & Phys. Sc.*, Fountain-pen. **1833** *Mechanics' Mag.* XIX. 319/1 The introduction of this paper will go far to supersede the use of fountain-pens of all kinds. **1892** E. REEVES *Homewd. Bound* 164 One silver pocket-knife and fountain-pen. **1664** EVELYN *Kal. Hort.* (1729) 226 Look to your *Fountain-Pipes. **1667** MILTON *P.L.* IV. 326 By a fresh *fountain-side. **1725** POPE *Odyss.* XV. 480 Descry'd By road frequented, or by fountain-side. **1572** MASCALL *Plant. & Graff.* (1592) 78 Mingled with a little *Fountaine or running water. **1612** *Enchir. Med.* II. 7 Let it be boyled in foure pints of fountaine water. **1678** R. RUSSELL *Geber* IV. iv. 245 Common Salt is dissolved in clear Fountain Water.

ˈfountain, *v.* [f. the sb.] **a.** *intr.* To rise like the waters of a fountain. **b.** *trans.* To cause to well up in the manner of a fountain.

1903 HARDY *Dynasts* I. I. iii. 27 Soon stars will shut..And sunbeams fountain forth. **1948** G. H. JOHNSTON *Death takes Small Bites* vii. 174 And then a high log broke and dropped into the ashes of the fire and the sparks fountained. **1967** D. KNIGHT *Turning On* 94 Fire fountained from the church spire, red sparks floating on the wind. **1969** *Daily Tel.* (Colour Suppl.) 16 May 45/3 Seven tons of water fountained up at 125 m.p.h. to a height of over 400 feet. *Ibid.* 28 Nov. 8/1 A water main..suddenly fountained 20,000 gallons of water down the Haymarket.

fountained (ˈfaʊntɪnd), *ppl. a.* [f. FOUNTAIN *sb.* + -ED[2].] Provided with a fountain or fountains; also with attributive prefixed, as ***many-fountained***.

1818 KEATS *Endym.* II. 717 O fountain'd hill! Old Homer's Helicon! **1832** TENNYSON *Œnone* 22 O mother Ida, many-fountain'd Ida. **1852** MISS MITFORD *Recollect.* II. 3 Fountained garden and pillared court.

†**fountaiˈneer**. *Obs.* In 7 -e(e)r(e, -iere; also FONTANIER. [ad. F. *fontainier*, *fontenier*: see -EER[1].] One who has charge of a fountain.

1603 HOLLAND *Plutarch's Mor.* 220 No gardener nor fountainer. **1644** EVELYN *Diary* 27 Feb., A basilisc of copper, wh[ch] managed by the fountainere, casts water neere 60 feet high..The fountainiere represented a showre of raine from the topp. **1652** WRIGHT tr. *Camus' Nature's Paradox* 28 Like those Fountaineers, who shewing curious Water-works and Grotta's..set themselves in some known place where they remain dry, whilst every one else is wetted to the skin.

ˈfountain-head. 1. A fountain or spring from which a stream flows; the head-spring or source of a stream.

1585 T. WASHINGTON tr. *Nicholay's Voy.* I. viii. 9 This tower was made..for the garding and keeping of the fountayne heads which from thence are brought..into the citie. **1635** SWAN *Spec. M.* vi. §2 (1643) 200 The sea..is the fountain-head from whence all fountains have their heads. **1708** J. C. *Compl. Collier* (1845) 26 Any Water coming from the Fountain, will rise to the height of that Fountain Head. **1774** J. BRYANT *Mythol.* II. 60, I passed through the regions of the north to the fountain-head of the Ister. **1872** RAYMOND *Statist. Mines & Mining* 57 Taking the waters of the streams from their fountain-heads.

2. *fig.* The chief or prime source of anything; the quarter whence anything originates; *esp.* an original source of information, news, etc.

1606 BRYSKETT *Civ. Life* 114 These two vnruly..powers, which are the spring and fountaine head of all disordinate affections. **1655** *Nicholas Papers* (Camden) II. 326 As I am ..assured from some heere very neare the fountayne head at Bruxells. **1754** FOOTE *Knights* I. Wks. 1799 I. 64 You are about the court; and so, being at the fountain-head, know what is in the papers before they are printed. **1787** BENTHAM *Def. Usury* x. 94 To trace an error to its fountain-head is to refute it. **1855** MACAULAY *Hist. Eng.* III. 28 The Convention was the fountain-head from which the authority of all future Parliaments must be derived.

fountaining (ˈfaʊntɪnɪŋ), *ppl. a.* [f. FOUNTAIN + -ING[2].] = FOUNTING *ppl. a.*

1883 G. MEREDITH *Poet. Wks.* (1912) 218 A chariot, cleaving the storm, Clove the fountaining lake with a plough. **1923** *Glasgow Herald* 5 Sept. 8 When the sun plays on the foam the impression of innumerable fountaining pearls is conveyed. *Ibid.* 11 Dec. 6 The pale fountaining gold of the clumps of tall windlestraws. **1955** S. SPENDER *Coll. Poems 1928–1953* 131 This early summer prepares its feasts In the garden..Fountaining bird-song, criss-crossed with bees.

fountainless (ˈfaʊntɪnlɪs), *a.* [f. FOUNTAIN *sb.* + -LESS.] Without fountains.

1671 MILTON *P.R.* III. 264 Barren desert, fountainless and dry. **1816** SCOTT *Old Mort.* (1830–2) II. xviii. 164 Like Hagar watching the waning life of her infant amid the fountainless desert. **1842** DE QUINCEY *Philos. Herodotus* Wks. IX. 207 A..wilderness..everywhere fountainless.

'fountainlet. *nonce-wd.* [See -LET.] A little fountain.

a **1661** FULLER *Worthies, Huntingdon* II. (1662) 48 In the afore-said Village there be two Fountaine-lets.

fountainous ('faʊntɪnəs), *a. rare.* [f. FOUNTAIN *sb.* + -OUS.] **a.** Of the nature of a fountain or source. *lit.* and *fig.* **b.** Containing fountains or springs of water.

1655 STANLEY *Hist. Philos.* I. (1701) 18/1 From the Fountainous Idea's there proceeded others. **1664** BEALE in *Evelyn's Pomona* 29 If the Land be neither dry..nor fountainous. **1747** E. POSTON *Pratler* I. 42 From this vast fountainous Cause we may plainly trace all the Sins and Follies of Mankind. **1855** BAILEY *Mystic* 72 The angels.. unsealed The secret wealth of many a fountainous hill.

Hence **'fountainously** *adv.* (= as from a source).

1662 J. CHANDLER *Van Helmont's Oriat.* 195 The light of the same proceeding immediately and fountainously from the Father of Lights.

fountful ('faʊntfʊl), *a. poet.* [f. FOUNT[1] + -FUL.] Full of founts or springs.

c **1611** CHAPMAN *Iliad* xx. 204 The foot of Ida's fountful hill. **1621** G. SANDYS *Ovid's Met.* xv. (1626) 315 Where yellow Tybris runs From fountfull Appenines. **1715–20** POPE *Iliad* XII. 114 Fountful Ide. **1809** MRS. WEST *Mother* (1810) 144 On the top of fountful Pisgah.

founting ('faʊntɪŋ), *ppl. a. rare.* [f. FOUNT[1] + -ING[2].] Welling up like a spring; *transf.* drooping in the form of a falling fountain.

1827 HOOD *Mids. Fairies* iii, And there were founting springs to overflow Their marble basins. *Ibid.* xlviii, We bend each tree in proper attitude, And founting willows train in silvery falls.

[**foupe,** *v.* Error for *soupe* (see SWOOP *v.* 2 b), through misprint of f for ſ.

1605 CAMDEN *Rem., Languages* 23 To soupe [edd. 1614–37 foupe; 1657, etc. soupe] their words out of the throat with fat and full spirits. Hence **1755** in JOHNSON [quoting the above with the reading 'foupe']. **1775** in ASH. Corrected by TODD, 1818.]

four (fɔə(r)), *a.* and *sb.* Forms: 1–3 **féower, féwer,** (2 **fure**), 2–3 **f(o)uwer,** 3 **feouwer, fowuer, fower,** *Orm.* **fowwerr, foo(u)r, fuȝer, fur,** *south.* **vor,** 3–4 *south.* **vour,** 3–7 **fowre, foure,** (3 **fawre, fowr,** *Orm.* **fowwre**), 4 **faur(e,** 3– **four.** [Com. Teut. and Aryan: OE. *féower* = OFris. *fiuwer, fior,* OS. *fiwar, fiuwar, fiori* (Du. *vier*), OHG. *fior, fier* (MHG., mod.Ger. *vier*), ON. *fiórer* masc., *-ar* fem., *fiogor* neut. (Sw. *fyra,* Da. *fire*), Goth. *fidwôr.* In comb. OE. had a form *fyðer-, fiðer-,* Anglian *feoðor-, -ur;* cf. OSw. *fiæþer-,* Frankish *fitter-* (Lex Salica), Goth. *fidur-.* The phonological relation of the Teut. forms to those in other Aryan langs. presents anomalies of which the explanation is still disputed; the OAryan type is **qetwer-, -wŏr-, qetur-* (with other ablaut-variants of somewhat uncertain form), regularly represented by Skr. *catvār-, catur-,* Gr. *τέσσαρες* (Dor. *τέτορες*), L. *quattuor,* OIrish *cethir,* OWelsh *petguar* (mod. Welsh *pedwar*).] The cardinal number next after *three,* represented by the symbols 4 or IV.

A. as *adj.*

1. a. In concord with the sb. expressed.

the four corners, quarters, etc. (*of the earth, heavens* or *world*): the remotest parts; see CORNER *sb.*[1] 8. ***the four corners*** (of a document): the limits or scope of its contents; see CORNER *sb.*[1] 1 e. ***within the four seas:*** within the boundaries of Great Britain. †***of all four sides:*** entirely, thoroughly.

a **1000** *Crist* 879 (Gr.) From feowerum foldan sceatum þam ytemestum eorðan rices englas..blawað byman. *c* **1175** *Lamb. Hom.* 159 þas fure kunnes teres boð þe fuwer wateres þa þe beoð ihaten us on to weschen. *c* **1205** LAY. 5154 Com þa tiðinde to þan feouwer kinggen þat Belin king wes icumen. *a* **1225** *Juliana* 9 þa leaden him i cure up o fowr hweoles. *a* **1300** *Cursor M.* 14241 Mari and martha..þai had ben wepand þar four dais. *c* **1400** *Destr. Troy* 8808 þen þos maisters gert make..Fovre lampis full light..all of gold fyne. *c* **1489** CAXTON *Sonnes of Aymon* vi. 151 Reynawde is well a noble gentylman of all foure sides. **1533** WRIOTHESLEY *Chron.* (1875) I. 19 A rich canapie of cloath of silver borne over her heade by the fower Lordes of the Portes. **1642** FULLER *Holy & Prof. St.* v. i. 359 So be it he goeth not out beyond the Foure seas. **1745** P. THOMAS *Jrnl. Anson's Voy.* 156 They fired four Guns as Signals of Distress. **1886** MRS. LYNN LINTON *Paston Carew* iii, He..was the safest confidant to be found within the four seas. **1893** *Law Times* XCV. 29/2 It may be necessary to look beyond the four corners of the agreement.

b. ***four corners,*** a game: see quots. Also, in *Horsemanship* (see quot. 1753).

1730–36 BAILEY (folio), *Four-corners* [with Horsemen]. **1753** CHAMBERS *Cycl. Supp., Four-corners,* in the manege, or to work upon the four corners, is to divide in imagination the volt or round into four quarters, so that upon each of these quarters, the horse makes a round or two at trot or gallop; and when he has done so upon each quarter, he has made the four corners. **1801** STRUTT *Sports & Past.* III. vii. 241 Four-corners is so called from four large pins which are placed singly at each angle of a square frame. **1881** in *Isle of Wight Gloss.* 64 The game of Skittles is also altered from nine pins to four, and is called 'Four Corners'.

c. ***the history of the Four Kings*** (see quot.).

1760 FOOTE *Minor* I. Wks. 1799 I. 241 Come, shall we have a dip in the history of the Four Kings this morning? **1894** BREWER *Dict. Phrase & Fable* s.v., The History of the Four Kings (*Livre des Quatre Rois*), a pack of cards.

2. a. With ellipsis of sb., which may usually be supplied from context. †***four for four:*** in fours.

c **1205** LAY. 4046 Feowere here weren riche þe haueden ferden muchele. **13..** *E.E. Allit. P.* B. 938 þe aungelez.. enforsed alle fawre forth at þe ȝatez. **1535** STEWART *Cron. Scot.* II. 201 Syne four for four togidder than tha fuir, And sone all aucht. **1611** BIBLE *2 Sam.* xxi. 22 These foure..fell by the hand of Dauid. *a* **1699** LADY HALKETT *Autobiog.* (1875) 53 All Fowre were in the place apointed.

b. with omission of *hours,* as ***four o'clock.***

1575 LANEHAM *Let.* (1871) 32 (Az vnhappy it waz for the bride) that cam thither too soon, (and yet waz it a four a clok). **1727** SWIFT *To Earl of Oxford* Wks. 1755 III. II. 44, I shall think of that no more, If you'll be sure to come at four. **1875** JEVONS *Money* (1878) 266 The bustle and turmoil of the work grow to a climax at four o'clock.

c. with omission of *horses.*

1815 L. SIMOND *Tour Gt. Brit.* I. 3 An elegant post-chaise and four stopped at the door. **1858** MRS. CARLYLE *Lett.* II. 363 As pleasant as a barouche and four.

†**d.** In phrases ***on (upon, of) all four*** (sc. feet or limbs); also ***on*** or ***upon four.*** *Obs.*; now *on* ALL-FOURS.

13.. *E.E. Allit. P.* B. 1683 He fares forth on alle faure. **1430–40** LYDG. *Bochas* I. ix. 37 What thyng..Goth fyrst on foure, or els gothe he nought? **1470–85** MALORY *Arthur* II. xviii, Thenne balan yede on al four feet and handes and put of the helme of his broder. **1611** BIBLE *Lev.* xi. 20 All foules that creepe, going vpon all foure, shalbe an abomination vnto you. **1641** MARMION *Antiquary* I. in Hazl. *Dodsley* XIII. 431 You'll hardly find..beast that trots sound of all four: There will be some defect. **1662** J. DAVIES tr. *Olearius' Voy. Ambass.* (1669) 157 [Babies] will crawl stark naked of all four about the House and into the fields. **1699** BENTLEY *Phal.* 128 What a sorry cripled Argument's here, even lame upon all four? **1712** ARBUTHNOT *John Bull* II. iv, I would crawl upon all four to serve you. [**1719** DE FOE *Crusoe* 211, I was oblig'd to creep upon all Fours.] **1722** *Lett. from Mist's Jrnl.* I. 294 An old black Horse, that can scarce crawl upon Four. **1877, 1883** [see ALL FOURS *phr.* 2]. **1909** H. G. WELLS *Tono-Bungay* II. iii. §2. 191 'It's just on all fours with the rest of things,' he remarked; 'only more so. You needn't think you're anything out of the way.' **1931** *Economist* 8 Aug. 277/1 The railways maintain that conditions in Great Britain and America are not on all fours. **1940** W. S. CHURCHILL *Into Battle* (1941) 186 It was only natural that the Admiralty, since this war began, should have brought this precedent—although it is not exactly on all fours, and there are some differences—..to the notice of His Majesty's Government. **1961** *Ann. Reg. 1960* 49 It was impossible to make an agreement exactly on all fours with the Anglo-American bomber base agreement.

3. Coupled with a higher cardinal or ordinal numeral following, so as to form a compound (cardinal or ordinal) numeral.

c **1205** LAY. 2092 [Brutus] hæfde þis lond fower and twenti winter on his hond. **1398** TREVISA *Barth. De P.R.* XII. xi. (1495) 421 Amonge foules oonly the rauen hath fowre and syxty chaungynges of voyce. **1579** FULKE *Heskins' Parl.* 416 The foure and thirtieth Chapter sheweth the vse of the Masse. **1818** SCOTT *Heart Midl.* viii, My breath is growing as scant as a broken-winded piper's when he has played for four-and-twenty hours at a penny wedding.

B. as *sb.*

1. a. The abstract number four.

a **1300** *Cursor M.* 21748 O four and thre qua tels euen, He sal þe numbre mak o seuen. **1398** TREVISA *Barth. De P.R.* XIX. cxviii. (1495) 921 One doo to thre makyth foure. **1837** WHEWELL *Hist. Induct. Sc.* (1857) I. 47 Four..was held to be the most perfect number.

b. The figure (4) denoting this number.

2. A set of four persons or things: *esp.* **a.** A card, domino, or the side of a die marked with four pips or spots; a throw of the die by which the 'four' comes uppermost. **b.** *Card-playing* (*Poker*). A set of four cards of the same value. **c.** A four-oared boat or a crew of four oarsmen. ***fours,*** races for four-oared boats. **d.** *Cricket,* etc. A hit for which four runs are scored. **e.** *pl.* (See quot. 1888.) Also ***in fours*** (formerly †***in fours and fours***), arranged in groups of four; *spec.* in *Bibliography* used to indicate the number of leaves in a sheet or gathering. **f.** The four players of a game, esp. of Bridge. Also *fig.*

a. 1599 MINSHEU *Sp. Dict., Dial.* iii. 26 *R.* I did lift an Ace. —*L.* I a foure. **1674** COTTON *Gamester* vi. 80 The Deuces, Treys, Fours, and Fives. **1728** SWIFT *Jrnl. Mod. Lady* Wks. 1755 III. II. 196 When lady Tricksey play'd a four You took it with a mattadore. **1870** HARDY & WARE *Mod. Hoyle* 81 Suppose your hand consists of a four, five, and six of spades.

b. 1883 *Longm. Mag.* Sept. 499 Fours, or four [cards] of a kind. **1894** MASKELYNE *Sharps & Flats* 84 If he had been so fortunate as to possess another ace among the cards..he would have a 'four'.

c. 1861 DICKENS *Gt. Expect.* liv, A Four and two sitters.. up with one tide and down with another. **1891** *Outdoor Games & Recreat.* 137 He must graduate through his college fours, and Torpid races. *Ibid.* 144 The 'Coxswainless Fours', These 'Fours'..are inter-collegiate races.

d. 1836 in 'Bat' *Cricketer's Man.* (1850) 100 Threes, fours, and fives appear as easy for him to get. **1894** A. LANG *Ban & Arrière Ban* 67 When Oxford's bowling always goes For 'fours', for ever to the Cords.

e. 1488 in *Ld. Treas. Acc. Scotl.* I. 84 Item, a frete or the Quenis oure set with grete perle sett in fouris and fouris. **1888** JACOBI *Printers' Voc., Fours,* a familiar term used by compositors for 'quarto'. **1890** H. O. SOMMER *Malory's Arthur* II. Introd. 9 The first part has signatures A to Z.. in fours.

f. 1895 KIPLING *Day's Work* (1898) 348 Can't I get him to make up a four at tennis with the Hammon girls? **1905** H. A. VACHELL *Hill* vii. 144 Bridge.... We could get up a four in this house. **1924** C. MACKENZIE *Old Men of Sea* vii. 113 Cosway was called away to make up a four at bridge. **1971** *Times* 9 Aug. 4 A four in the East-West bridge game.

3. Short for: **a.** four-shilling beer (see quot.); **b.** four-pennyworth (of spirits); **c.** (*pl.*) four-percents; **d.** *pl.* (in form *fourses*). A light meal taken in the fields at four o'clock in the afternoon. *local.* Cf. BEVER *sb.* 3.

a. 1633 W. R. *Match at Midn.* II. in Hazl. *Dodsley* XIII. 43 *Tim.* What is 't, brother? Four or six? *Capt.* Four or six! 'tis rich Canary... *Tim...* Now I think on 't, a cup of this is better than our four-shilling beer at home.

b. 1869 E. YATES *Wrecked in Port* xxii. 241 'Fours' of rum, and 'sixes' of brandy. **1876** BESANT & RICE *Gold. Butterfly* i. 20 The girl..set before him a 'four' of brandy and the cold water.

c. 1887 *Daily News* 15 Nov. 5/6 Fully-paid-up stock..in exchange for the converted Fours and Four-and-a-Halfs.

d. 1823 E. MOOR *Suffolk Words* 132 Foorzes. **1849** [see ELEVENS]. **1887** E. S. SUFFLING *Land of Broads* (ed. 2) 266 At 4 p.m., when they have their 'fourses'. **1895, 1923** [see ELEVENS]. **1953** A. JOBSON *Household & Country Crafts* ii. 28 Another speciality..was the harvest-cake or biscuit, also known as a bever cake... This was a most welcome addition to the 'fourses' provided by the farmer's wife for the harvest field. **1966** G. E. EVANS *Pattern under Plough* xv. 154 A substitute harvest horn..did service to summon up the women and children to bring their *elevenses* and *fourses* into the harvest field.

C. *attrib.* and *Comb.*

Comb. **1. a.** Combined with sbs. forming adjs., as ***four-acre, -button, -cylinder, -day, -door, -gallon, -gun, -line, -mile, -story, -year-old.***

1868 GLADSTONE *Juv. Mundi* xi. (1870) 420 A *four-acre field. **1896** *Daily News* 2 July 8/7 White kids sewn with black ..as well as lavender, chiefly in *four-button length. **1902** *Westm. Gaz.* 8 Sept. 7/3 Quadruple expansion *four-cylinder engines of 4,000 horse-power. **1936** *Discovery* Feb. 37 Improved four-cylinder compound locomotive with poppet-valves and double blast-pipe. **1902** *Daily Chron.* 1 Sept. 5/2 The half-yearly *four-day closing of the British Museum reading room. **1909** *Westm. Gaz.* 3 Sept. 12/1 Thus making the first four-day westward voyage. **1935** *Discovery* Aug. 221/1 The five-day week has already arrived, the four-day week will come and there will be increasing leisure to be employed. **1960** *News Chron.* 9 Apr. 1/3 Thousands of men stayed away from work..trying..to enforce a four-day week. **1957** P. FRANK *Seven Days to Never* i. 13 A *four-door sedan. **1879** MISS BIRD *Rocky Mount.* I. 264, I told him to fill up the *four-gallon kettle. **1862** LATHAM *Channel Isl.* III. xvii. (ed. 2) 400 A *four-gun cutter. **1827** *Gentl. Mag.* XCVII. II. 501 Underneath this a stave or *four-line verse. **1897** S. L. HINDE *Fall of Congo Arabs* 115 The whole crowd jumped into the river, here about a hundred yards wide, with a *four-mile current. **1903** KIPLING *Five Nations* 90 From the Four-mile Radius roughly to the plains of Hindustan. **1835** C. F. HOFFMAN *Winter in West* I. 95 [In Detroit] there are..many *four-story stores erecting. **1888** A. K. GREEN *Behind Closed Doors* vi, A four-story brick building. **1832** LYTTON *Eugene A.* I. v, The *four-year-old mutton..affecting the shape and assuming the adjuncts of venison. **1855** TENNYSON *Brook* 137 'That [colt] was the four-year old I sold the Squire.'

b. In parasynthetic adjs. with suffix -ED[2], as ***four-barrelled, -chambered, -columned, -decked, -faced, -fingered, -headed, -legged, -lettered, -lined, -roomed, -sided, -snouted, -spined, -stranded, -stringed, -tined, -toed.***

1881 *Times* 15 Jan. 5/6 A high power of firing for a *four-barrelled gun. **1870** GILLMORE *Reptiles & Birds* Introd. 2 The heart is *four-chambered, transmitting venous blood to the lungs. **1768–74** TUCKER *Lt. Nat.* (1852) I. 386 We are now poring over all the nothings in a *four-columned newspaper. **1833** MARRYAT *P. Simple* xxxv, Nothing would suit Nelson but this *four-decked ship. **1878** GURNEY *Crystallogr.* 86 A cube with a low four-sided pyramid on each face..is sometimes called a *four-faced cube. **1802** BINGLEY *Anim. Biog.* (1813) I. 89 The *four-fingered monkey. **1864** PUSEY *Lect. Daniel* ii. 75 The *four-headed creatures in Ezekiel's vision. **1663** BUTLER *Hud.* I. i. 402 To guard the magazine i' th' hose From two-legg'd and from *four-legg'd foes. **1778** HUTTON in *Phil. Trans.* LXVIII. 57 The whole being supported by a four-legged stand. **1828** SCOTT *F.M. Perth* xi, Louise..calling her little four-legged companion, had eagerly followed in the path. **1652** H. C. *Looking-Glasse for Ladies* 4 That *four-letter'd name, rare and Divine. **1831** SOUTHEY *Lett.* (1856) IV. 214 The poem ..is in *four-lined stanzas. **1890** BOLDREWOOD *Col. Reformer* (1891) 234 A new *four-roomed cottage. **1669** STURMY *Mariner's Mag.* I. 26 Of *four-sided Figures. **1647** R. STAPYLTON *Juvenal* v. 55 Thou drain'st a foule *four-snouted glasse, that's call'd The Beneventine Cobler. **1836** YARRELL *Brit. Fishes* I. 83 The *four-spined Stickleback. **1769** FALCONER *Dict. Marine* (1789) Uuiij, The middle strand of a *four-stranded rope. **1742** BERKELEY *Let. to Gervais* in Fraser *Life* viii. (1871) 284 The instrument she desired to be provided was a large *four-stringed bass violin. **1765** *Univ. Mag.* XXXVII. 33/1 A *four-tined fork. **1872** BAKER *Nile Tribut.* ii. 27 The first time I saw the peculiar *four-toed print of the hippopotamus's foot.

c. In parasynthetic sbs. with suffix -ER[1], as ***four-boater, -decker, -master, -year-older.***

1889 *Century Dict.,* **Four-boater,* a whaling-ship carrying four boats on the cranes. **1833** MARRYAT *P. Simple* xxxv, She was a *four-decker. **1826** DISRAELI *Viv. Grey* I. vii, Any stray *four-year-older not yet sent to bed.

d. In advb. sense (= in four parts) with pa. pples., as ***four-cleft, -parted*** adjs.

1793 MARTYN *Lang. Bot.,* *Four-cleft leaf. *Folium quadrifidum.* **1846** DANA *Zooph.* (1848) 139 Mouth prominent, four-cleft within. *a* **1619** FOTHERBY *Atheom.* II. vii. §3 (1622) 264 The *foure-parted Image. **1793** MARTYN *Lang. Bot.,* Four-parted leaf. *Folium quadripartitum.*

2. Special comb.: **four-ale,** (*a*) ale sold at fourpence a quart; also *attrib.*; (*b*) a four-ale bar; **four-ball** *a.,* defining a foursome at golf in which four balls are used, the best ball on each side counting at each hole; also *absol.*; **four-baller**, a golfer playing in a four-ball match; **four-by-two**, (*a*) *Mil. colloq.*, the cloth attached to a pull-through; (*b*) also, rhyming slang for a Jew; **four-cant** (see quot.; cf. *four-strand*); **four-centred arch** (*Arch.*), one described from four centres; **four-chromatic** *a.* = *four-colour* adj.; **four-colour** *a.*, having, or pertaining to the use of, four colours; ***four-colour problem***, the as yet unsolved problem of proving as a mathematical theorem that on any plane map only four colours are needed to give different colours to any regions that have a common boundary; hence **four-coloration, four-colour** *v. trans.*, **four-colouring** *vbl. sb.*; †**four-corner** *a.* = next; **four-cornered** *a.*, having four corners, square; ***four-cornered cap***, a college cap or 'square'; hence **four-cornerwise** *adv.*, so as to form four corners; **four-coupled** *a.*, having four coupled wheels; **four-course** (*Agric.*), a four years' course or series of crops in rotation (in quots. *attrib.*; see COURSE *sb.* 24); **four-crossway(s**, the place where two roads cross or four roads meet; **four-cycle** *a.* = FOUR-STROKE *a.*; **four-dimensional** *a.* (*Math.*), of or belonging to a fourth dimension; **four-dimensioned** *a.*, having four dimensions; †**four-double** = FOURFOLD *a.* 1; †**four-eared** *a. fig.*, twofold; **four-eyes**, (*a*) see quot. 1755; (*b*) the name of a fish (see quot. 1879); (*c*) *slang* (see quot. 1874); †**four-fallow** *v.*, to fallow fourfold; **four-field course** (*Agric.*), a series of crops grown in four fields in rotation; **four-figure** *a.*, (*a*) consisting of four figures, i.e. a thousand or over (but less than ten thousand), a thousand pounds or over, etc.; (*b*) evaluated to or containing four significant figures or four decimal places; **four figures**, i.e. an amount of one thousand pounds or over (whence ***four figured*** adj., that sells for four figures); **four-foil** (*Arch.*), a quatrefoil; **four-foot (way)**, the space (really 4 ft. 8½ in.) between the rails on which the train runs; **four-four time** *Mus.*, time or rhythm consisting of four crotchets in a bar (also *ellipt.*); **four freedoms**: see FREEDOM 4; **four-half** (*slang*), half ale, half porter, at four-pence a quart; **four-high** *a.*, having four rolls one over another, as a rolling-mill (cf. *two-high* s.v. TWO B. IV. 2); **four-horse, four-horsed** *adjs.*, that is drawn by four horses; **four-hours** *Sc.*, a light refreshment taken about four o'clock; also †***four hours penny*** (see quot. 1651); **four hundred** *U.S.*, the highest society of a locality; **four-inch** *a.*, that measures four inches, also *ellipt.* = four inch rope; †**four-inched** *a.*, four inches wide; **four-lane-end(s** *dial.*, = *four-crossways*; **four-leaf clover**, a rare form of clover leaf having four leaflets, regarded as a lucky charm or sign of good fortune; cf. FOUR-LEAVED *a.*; **four-letter** *a.*, consisting of four letters; applied esp. to any of several monosyllabic English words, referring to the sexual or excretory functions or organs of the human body, that are conventionally excluded from polite use; ***four-letter man***, an obnoxious person; †**four-millioneer**, one who is worth four millions of money; **four-minute mile**, a mile run by an athlete in four minutes or less (first achieved by R. Bannister in 1954); hence **four-minute miler**, an athlete who performs this feat; freq. used hyperbolically; **four-nooked** *a.*, four-cornered (*obs.* exc. *dial.*); **four-oar**, a boat rowed with four oars; **four-oared** *a.*, propelled by four oars or oarsmen; also *absol.* (= four-oared boat); **four-part** *a.* (*Music*), composed for four parts or voices; **four paws** *U.S. logging* (see quot. 1905); **four-place** *a.* = *four-figure* adj. (*b*); **four-point assay** *Chem.* (see quot.); **four-point bearing** *Naut.* (see quot. 1948); **four-post, -posted** *adjs.*, (of a bedstead) having four posts (to support a canopy and curtains); **four-poster**, a four-posted bedstead; **four-pounder**, (*a*) a gun to carry a four-pound shot; (*b*) a loaf four pounds in weight; **four-rowed**, (of barley) having four rows of awns; **four-seater**, a car with seating accommodation for four people, also *attrib.*; **four-shilling** *a.*, that costs four shillings (in quot., †of beer, 4*s.* the barrel); **four-spot**, a four of a suit in cards; **four-star** *a.*, designating a (high) rank in a grading system for hotels, etc., usu. with four or five grades; also *transf.*, of a high degree of excellence; also ***four-starred*** adj.; **four-strand**, (of a rope) having four strands; **four-tailed bandage** (see quot.); **four thieves' vinegar** (see quot.); **four-tooth** (see quot.); **four-vector** *Math.* [ad. G. *vierervektor* (A. Sommerfeld 1910, in *Ann. d. Physik* 4th Ser. XXXII. 750)], a vector defined by four scalar components, esp. a space-time vector in the theory of relativity; **four-walled** *a.*, having or enclosed within four walls; **four walls**, the walls of a room or a house; hence, *allusively*, in reference to confinement within the limits of a (small) building; **four-way(s** = *four-crossways*; **four-way** *a.* (in ***four-way cock*** or ***valve***), having communication with four pipes; **four-winged** *a.*, having four wings or wing-like appendages; **four-wings** (see quot.).

1883 *Daily News* 8 Sept. 3/1 Nearly every man seemed to order nothing more mischievous than 'half-a-pint of *four ale'. **1902** *Daily Chron.* 23 Sept. 6/7 He had been to a 'four-ale club'. **1930** *Ibid.* 6 Nov. 5/7 The man had been in his [public-]house—in the four-ale bar. **1953** DYLAN THOMAS *Under Milk Wood* (1954) 2 Night in the four-ale, quiet as a domino. **1966** 'H. CARMICHAEL' *Suicide Clause* vi. 73 A kindred spirit beside me in the four-ale bar. **1904** *Westm. Gaz.* 25 Mar. 4/1 The players in a *four-ball match. **1909** *Ibid.* 8 Mar. 12/2 Four-ball foursomes. **1969** *Times* 25 Sept. 15/1 In the wake of that extraordinary feature of American golf, the four-ball, gang mowers at last got to work on the fairways. **1927** *Observer* 31 July 15/5 A selfish '*four-baller', intent solely on his own pleasure, has blocked the way. **1925** FRASER & GIBBONS *Soldier & Sailor Words* 97 **Four by two*, the term for the piece of flannel issued as a 'pull through' for cleaning a rifle. From its size, four inches by two. **1930** P. MACDONALD *Link* 88 Cross maintains that the oil-bottle and four-by-two must have been to clean the rifle. **1936** J. CURTIS *Gilt Kid* vii. 69 That's all right so long as it's not ham... I'm a four-be two, you see. **1968** L. BERG *Risinghill* 106 It was like the rhyming slang 'four-by-twos' for 'Jews', used..perhaps with an under-tone of lurking contempt. **1970** E. MCGIRR *Death pays Wages* iii. 60 'This Marx, was he a four by two?' demanded Quimple. 'Pardon?' 'A Jew, sir, a Jew.' **1867** SMYTH *Sailor's Word-bk.*, **Four-cant*, a rope composed of four strands. **1812–16** J. SMITH *Panorama Sc. & Art* I. 154 Its arch is very often *four-centred, which at once decides its date. **1952** G. A. DIRAC in *Jrnl. London Math. Soc.* XXVII. 85 (*title*) A property of *4-chromatic graphs and some remarks on critical graphs. **1962** A. DOIG tr. *Berge's Theory of Graphs* xxi. 214 The following theorem which has never yet been proved is known as the four-colour problem: every planar graph is 4-chromatic. **1967** O. ORE *Four-Color Probl.* xii. 210 This..can be extended..to give a 4-coloration of G. [**1879** CAYLEY in *Proc. R. Geogr. Soc.* I. 260 The theorem then is, that if an area be partitioned in any manner into areas, these can be, with four colours only, coloured in such wise that in every case two attached areas have distinct colours.] **1879** A. B. KEMPE in *Amer. Jrnl. Math.* II. 200, I will conclude with a theorem... It is one of which I long endeavoured to obtain an independent proof, as a means of solving the *four-colour problem. **1897** P. J. HEAWOOD in *Q. Jrnl. Math.* XXIX. 270 (*title*) On the four-colour map theorem. **1931** *Everyman's Encycl.* IV. 209/1 The early years of the twentieth century have seen many improvements in working the three-colour block process, while in America especially the four-colour process has been developed. **1941** COURANT & ROBBINS *What is Math.?* v. 247 The four color theorem has indeed been proved for all maps containing less than thirty-eight regions. *Ibid.*, In the four color problem the maps may be drawn either in the plane or on the surface of a sphere. **1963** E. L. JOHNSON in *Calif. Univ. Operations Res. Center Rep.* No. 28 (*title*) A proof of four-coloring the edges of a regular three-degree graph. *Ibid.* 8 The edges of the reduced graph G^1 can be 4-colored. **1967** E. CHAMBERS *Photolitho-Offset* xv. 236 The demand for colour, especially four-colour half-tone work, either for catalogue or carton use, has brought about the development of four and six-colour machines. **1971** *Daily Tel.* (Colour Suppl.) 8 Jan. 21/4 The best four-colour lithographic printers in the country. **1963** G. A. DIRAC in *Proc. London Math. Soc.* XIII. 195 Theorem 2 establishes the truth of the four-colour conjecture for a new class of planar graphs..and ..furnishes a procedure for verifying that a given suitable planar graph is 4-colourable without having to find a *4-colouring for the whole of it. **1967** O. ORE *Four-Color Probl.* viii. 107 To define a four coloring of the faces in G. **1640–1** LD. J. DIGBY *Sp. in Ho. Com.* 9 Feb. 9 The Lawne sleeves, the *foure corner Cap, the Cope. *c* **1440** *Promp. Parv.* 175/2 *Fowre corneryd, *quadrangulus*. **15..** in Strype *Parker* App. (1711) No. 40 Every Hedde of College..to weare when they goo abrode, longe Gownes..and square or four cornered Capps. **1719** DE FOE *Crusoe* II. xv, It [the idol] had..a mouth extended four-cornered, like that of a lion. **1823** SCOTT *Let. to Ld. Montagu* 18 June in *Lockhart*, Think of a vile four cornered house with plantations laid out in scollops. **1607** TOPSELL *Four-f. Beasts* 509 The common kind of this moustrap is made of wood, long, and *foure cornerwise. **1889** *Daily News* 21 June 6/3 A *four coupled engine drew an excursion train of 13 vehicles. **1846** J. BAXTER *Libr. Pract. Agric.* (ed. 4) II. 245 By what is termed the *four-course shift, having equal proportions of fallow, barley, clover, peas or beans, and wheat in each year. **1894** SCRIVENER *Fields & Cities* 28 This 'Four-Course' system, as it is called, produces five entirely different plants, namely, turnips, barley, beans, clover, and wheat. [*a* **1490** BOTONER *Itin.* (1778) 176 At the crosse yn Baldwyne strete been *IIII crosse wayes metyng.] **1647** W. BROWNE *Polexander* I. 48 He came to a foure crosse way. **1842** *P. Parley's Ann.* III. 288 Do you mean..that your husband was buried in a four-crossways? He must then have killed himself. **1909** *Westm. Gaz.* 25 Mar. 4/1 It is open to question if a two-cycle engine will ever be produced which will show the same economy of fuel as the *four-cycle. **1924** *Times* 29 Nov. (Trade & Engin. Suppl.) 250/4 Four-cycle double-acting engines. **1950** *Engineering* 19 May 577/3 Fuel within this range..can be burnt successfully in four-cycle [diesel] engines. **1880** *Four-dimensional [see DIMENSIONAL *a.* 2]. **1886** MYERS *Phantasms of Living* II. 314 Four-dimensional space (if that exists). **1880** *Daily News* 20 Oct. 5/1 The unfamiliarity of a début in this world to a spirit more at home in *four-dimensioned space. **1527** ANDREW *Brunswyke's Distyll. Waters* Aij, With a *foure dowble clowte, or with hempen towe steped in the same..do as ye dyde before twyse or thryse a daye. **1599** A. M. tr. *Gabelhouer's Bk. Physicke* 249/2 Wet therin a fourdubble cloth, and applye him theron. **1704** *Lond. Gaz.* No. 3990/4 A small Gold Chain 4 double fastened to the Watch. **1600** E. BLOUNT *Hosp. Incurable Fooles* 62 A ridiculous and *foure-eared foole. **1614** BRETON *I would & I would not* lxxxii. Wks. (Grosart) I. 10, I would I were the gallanst Courtizan, That euer put a four-Ear'de Asse to schoole. **1755** AMORY *Mem.* (1769) I. 199 Some people have named this bird [the golden eye] the *four-eyes. **1874** *Slang Dict.*, *Four eyes*, a man or woman who habitually wears spectacles. **1879** BODDAM-WHETHAM *Roraima* 130 The little fish known as 'Four Eyes', *Anableps Tetraophthalmus*. **1577** B. GOOGE *Heresbach's Husb.* (1586) 22 b, You must not only twyfallow and threefallow your ground, but also *fourfallow it. **1842** TENNYSON *Audley Court* 33 We..discuss'd the farm, The *four-field system, and the price of grain. **1844** *Jrnl. R. Agric. Soc.* V. I. 162 It is usually cropped on the four-field or Norfolk course. **1842** *Penny Cycl.* XXIII. 499/2 *Four-figure logarithms on a card. **1877** *Porcupine* 17 Feb. 741/1 The same modest four-figure price. **1968** FOX & MAYERS *Computing Methods for Scientists & Engineers* iii. 51 The fifth digit in our four-figure computation. **1970** *Daily Tel.* 8 June 4/3 The newcomers should help to send Dame Patricia back to Westminster with a good four-figure majority. **1893** *Pall Mall G.* 12 Jan. 3/2 The two best yearlings sold for *four figures. **1895** *Daily News* 7 Jan. 3/4 The total amount of capital invested in these '*four-figured'..animals. **1860** RUSKIN *Mod. Paint.* V. VI. iv. 29 The normal of *four-foils is therefore [etc.]. **1896** *Daily News* 9 Mar. 5/5 The body of the lady, who was lying in the *four-foot. **1826** J. F. DANNELEY *Mus. Gram.* (Index) 100 *Four-four time. **1853** C. ENGEL *Pianist's Handbk.* 49 The *Allemande*, in the style of an old German dance, in $^4_4$ time, in moderate movement. **1880** [see COMPOUND *a.* 2f]. **1959** *Listener* 5 Feb. 264/2 Alternating bars of five-four and four-four. **1966** *Crescendo* Dec. 26/1 The time signature 4/4 seems to be at its most productive rhythmically when 12/8 is imposed on it. *Ibid.*, To superimpose 18/8 on to 4/4. **1884** *Punch* 29 Nov. 257/1 Drinks anything stronger or dearer than '*four-half'. **1878** *Iron Age* 5 Dec. 3/5 The use of Bleckly's *four-high wire mill..has been attended with very satisfactory results. **1928** *Jrnl. Iron & Steel Inst.* CXVII. 840 The chief object of the four-high mill is to provide an exceedingly rigid working roll of relatively small working diameter. **1958** *Times* 7 Jan. 14/2 Heavy, medium and light plates all rolled in two 4-high mills. *Ibid.*, The new slabbing mill and the 4-high plate mills. **1765** A. DICKSON *Treat. Agric.* II. (ed. 2) 254 In a *four-horse plough yoked in pairs. **1842** DICKENS *Amer. Notes* (1850) 91/1 The mail takes the lead in a four-horse wagon. **1382** WYCLIF *Isa.* lxvi. 15 The Lord in fyr shal come, and as a whirlewynd his *foure horsid carres. **1887** BOWEN *Virg. Æneid* VI. 587 Borne on his four-horsed chariot ..Over the Danaan land. **1637** RUTHERFORD *Lett.* (1862) I. 243 We think all is but a little earnest, a *four-hours, a small tasting, that we have..in this life. *a* **1651** CALDERWOOD *Hist. Kirk* (1843) II. 125 When the craftsmen were required to assemble..they went to their foure houres pennie. *Note*, The name of the after-noon refreshment of ale [etc.]..taken at four o'clock. **1870** RAMSAY *Remin* v. (ed. 18) 118 When I get my four hours, that will refresh me. **1888** *N.Y. Tribune* 8 Apr. 5/1 Not all of 'the *400' have yet returned from the South. **1948** *Coronet* Aug. 36/1 To social strivers she is Queen of the 400. **1858** GLENNY *Gard. Every-day Bk.* 254/1 Seedlings..must be pricked off into *four-inch pots. **1840** MARRYAT *Poor Jack* xii, Here's a good long piece of *four-inch. **1605** SHAKS. *Lear* III. iv. 57 To ride..ouer *foure incht Bridges. **1787** PEGGE in *Archæol.* VIII. 203 He being also anathematized, was interred at a *four-lane-end without the city. **1927** *Melody Maker* June 573/2 Nick Lucas is as good as ever in '*I'm Looking Over a *Four-Leaf Clover*'. **1959** I. & P. OPIE *Lore & Lang. Schoolch.* xi. 222 It is not usually considered enough merely to find a lucky object... The only exception seems to be the four-leaf clover, the discovery of which appears to be felt singular enough to be lucky in itself. **1985** *N.Y. Times* 31 Dec. A11/2 Parcells is superstitious and proud of it, and..he told of a four-leaf clover a dry-cleaner's delivery man had left intentionally in the coach's jacket pocket. **1923** J. MANCHON *Le Slang* 265 *Shit*,..un type embêtant... L'euph. est **four-letter-man*. **1924** J. SUTHERLAND *Circle of Stars* xxiii. 236 Carter isn't that kind of a four letter man if he does soak. **1927** C. S. LEWIS *Let.* 12 Dec. (1966) 122 Louis the Pious was 'a man of blameless and virtuous habits'—tho' every other sentence in the chapter makes it clear that he was a four letter man. **1934** *Amer. Speech* IX. 264/1 The obscene 'four-letter words' of the English language are not cant or slang or dialect, but belong to the oldest and best established element in the English vocabulary. *Ibid.* 267/1 For most people, the bare word forms of these four-letter words have become sexual fetishes. **1935** E. HEMINGWAY *Green Hills Africa* (1936) II. iii. 97 Ashamed at having been a four-letter man about books. **1947** A. HUXLEY *Let.* 9 Mar. (1969) 568 She would bring him to amorous life again by re-assuming her cockney accent..going very nearly to the point of murmuring four-letter words into his ear. **1960** *Times* 7 Nov. 17/4 Having regard to the state of current writing, it seems that the prosecution against *Lady Chatterley* can only have been launched on the ground that the book contained so-called four-letter words. **1962** I. MURDOCH *Unofficial Rose* xvii. 164 Felix regarded Randall as a four-letter man of the first order. **1969** N. COHN *AWopBopaLooBop* (1970) xx. 191 He was heckled. Immediately, he exploded in a rash of four-letter words and the curtain came down. **1666–7** DENHAM *Direct. Paint.* II. ix. 14 Find out the Cheats of the *four Millioneer. **1955** T. STERLING *Evil of Day* iv. 40 These people would believe I was going to die if they saw me running the *four minute mile. **1958** *Sunday Times* 30 Nov. 38/6 His phenomenal series of four-minute miles. **1963** *Listener* 31 Jan. 209/2 A 4-minute miler could take 3.6 seconds off his time under the influence of amphetamine. **1969** J. WAINWRIGHT *Take-Over Men* i. 16 He broke the four-minute mile to position her chair. *c* **1205** LAY. 21999 *Feower noked he is and þer inne is feower kunnes fisc. **1536** BELLENDEN *Cron. Scot.* (1821) I. 286 The mone beand in opposition, quhen it is maist round, apperit suddanly as it war foure nukit. **1876** *Whitby Gloss.*, *Four-neuk'd*, square or four-cornered. **1844** LD. MALMESBURY *Mem.* (1884) I. 154 We then returned home in the *four-oar. **1685** *Lond. Gaz.* No. 2023/4 A six Oared Barge..and a *four Oared Boat. **1861** DICKENS *Gt. Expect.* liv, If we had seen a four-oared galley going up with the tide. **1870** DASENT *Eventful Life* I. 141 Leaving the boat-hook of a four-oared, which I steered. **1664** PEPYS *Diary* (1879) III. 79 We sung..Ravenscroft's *4-part psalms. **1890** E. PROUT *Counterpoint* 143 Four-part counterpoint. **1905** *Terms Forestry & Logging* 35 *Double couplers*, two coupling grabs joined by a short cable, used for fastening logs together. Syn.: *four paws. **1957** *Brit. Commonw. Forest Terminol.* II. 76 *Four paws*,..used for fastening a skidding chain or cable to large logs. **1888** *Encycl. Brit.* XXIII. 13/1 A *four-place table. **1927** CAREY & GRACE (*title*) Four-place mathematical tables with forced decimals. **1940** A. L. BACHARACH et al. in *Biochem. Jrnl.* XXXIV. 1464 The comparison of activity with that of a stable standard preparation..can be done by means of the '*four-point assay'; two doses of the standard and two doses of test material are used. **1926** G. BRADFORD *Gloss. Sea Terms* 19/1 Bow and beam bearing..is also called a *four point bearing. **1948** R. DE KERCHOVE *Internat. Maritime Dict.* 278/2 *Four-point bearing*, the simplest and most commonly used method of determining the distance off a terrestrial object when coasting. The object is observed when it is four points (45°) on the bow and again when it is abeam. **1818** M. G. LEWIS *Jrnl. W. Ind.* (1834) 110, I saw none without a *four-post bedstead and plenty of bedclothes. **1823** BYRON *Juan* VI. xxv, Beds, *Four-posted and silk curtain'd. **1856** MRS. CARLYLE *Lett.* II. 285, I expect to sleep in my great comfortable four-posted bed. **1836–9** DICKENS *Sk. Boz* (1850) 265/2 His small French bedstead was converted into a regular matrimonial *four-poster. **1684** J. PETER *Siege Vienna* 109 *Four Pounders. **1854** MRS. GASKELL *North & S.* xvii, I ha' gone and bought a four-pounder out o' another baker's shop to common on such days. **1876** BANCROFT *Hist. U.S.* IV. xxv. 573 It was boarded by the provincials, who carried off four four-pounders and twelve swivels. **1882** J. HARDY in *Proc. Berw. Nat. Club* IX. No. 3. 444 It might have been once used for husking big, or *four-rowed barley. **1909** *Westm. Gaz.* 16 Nov. 4/2 The famous 15-h.p. *four-seater touring-car. **1922** *Times* 20 June 8/5 The increased convenience and comfort of a four-seater. **1633** [see B. 3 a] *Four-shilling beer. **1878** B. F. TAYLOR *Between Gates* 193 We are a *four-spot of dirty spades. **1920** C. E. MULFORD *J. Nelson* x. 100 I'm layin' down as fine a pair of four-spots as I've ever held. **1921** *Automobile Assoc. Ann. Rep.* 4 Upwards of 2,000 firms carry the official appointment of the Association. During the past year the work of inspecting and appointing, on a '*four-star' classification basis, has continued. **1952** E. GRIERSON *Reputation for Song* xvii. 138 The 'Golden Fleece'..was a four-star hotel. **1958** K. AMIS *I like it Here* xiii. 155 A four-star monastery with chanting and flagellation. **1959** *Sunday Express* 21 June 6/6 Oscar Heinrich's life is four-star reading for anyone who [etc.]. **1968** *Listener* 1 Aug. 159/1 No one has ever shown that a car which will run happily, without pinking, on, say, four-star petrol will run any better—faster, or more economically—on five-star. **1970** *Daily Tel.* 30 June 3/1 Ladbroke's, the bookmakers, announced yesterday that they are going to build a four-star hotel in the centre of Leeds. **1950** A. CHRISTIE *Murder is Announced* viii. 85 George, it's my own particular, one and only, *four starred Pussy. The super Pussy of all old Pussies. **1867** SMYTH *Sailor's Word-bk.* s.v. *Ropes*, **Four-strand* is..laid with four strands, and a core scarcely twisted. **1844** HOBLYN *Med. Dict.* (ed. 2), **Four-tailed bandage*, a bandage for the forehead, face and jaws. **1868** *Paxton's Bot. Dict.*, **Four thieves' vinegar*, a preparation from *Rosmarinus officinalis*. **1793–1813** *Agric. Surv. Dorset* 8 (E.D.S.), **Four-tooth*, a two-year-old sheep. **1914** L. SILBERSTEIN *Theory of Relativity* v. 148 The length, thus defined, of a *four-vector may be either real, or purely imaginary, or nil, according as we have..a space-like, a time-like, or a singular vector. **1952** E. G. RAMBERG tr. *Sommerfeld's Electrodynam.* III. 213 The four-vector attains a meaning in the four-dimensional world which is independent of the choice of the coordinate system. **1968** *Physics Bull.* Nov. 370/2 The four-vector potential of the electromagnetic field. **1905** *Daily Chron.* 18 Aug. 3/7 A *four-walled prison life. **1908** C. W. WALLACE *Children Chapel Blackfriars* 7 The four-walled coach-court of the public inn. [**1834** tr. *Jacquemont's Journ. India* I. 156, I was much more comfortable under it..than within *four naked walls.] **1849** N. P. WILLIS *Rural Lett.* 17 Between five in the morning and 'flower-shut' I feel as if four walls and a ceiling would stop my breath. **1922** 'E. PERCY' (*title*) If four walls told. **1930** HARRISON & CARTWRIGHT (*title*) Within four walls. **1598** FLORIO, *Quadriuio*, a *fower-way, a way that hath fower turnings, a place where fower waies meete. **1891** H. HALIBURTON *Ochil Idylls* 72 Peasants flock in from the fields to the four-ways. **1824** R. STUART *Hist. Steam Engine* 161 A considerable improvement on the *fourway-cock. **1841** BREES *Gloss. Civ. Engin.*, *Four-way Cock*..a description of valve..for passing the steam to the cylinder; it was invented by Leopold in about the year 1720. *a* **1711** KEN *Urania* Poet. Wks. 1721 IV. 457 She'll strive to soar as high, As *four-wing'd Seraphs fly. *c* **1755** GARDEN in *Phil. Trans.* LI. 931 They are followed by pretty large four-winged fruit. **1878** BELL *Gegenbaur's Comp. Anat.* 248 In the other four-winged orders. **1889** *Century Dict.*, **Four-wings*, a name of the goatsuckers or night-jars of the genera *Macrodipteryx* and *Cosmetornis*, in which some of the flight-feathers are so much elongated that the birds seem to have four wings.

†**fourb(e**, *sb. Obs.* Also 7 fowrb. [a. F. *fourbe* masc. and fem. (two distinct words), f. *fourbir* to FURBISH, taken in fig. sense. Cf. FOB *sb.*[1]]

1. A cheat, an impostor.

1668 DENHAM *Passion of Dido* 107 Thou art a false Impostor and a Fourbe. **1680** C. BLOUNT *Philostratus* 43, I have never met with greater Fourbs than those Quaking Saints. **1736** CARTE *Ormonde* II. 273 He was a fourbe in his politicks..and thought to be a secret convert to the Roman Catholick Religion. **1761** W. SANDBY *Port. Inquis.* 17 (Stanf.) The various tricks put in practice by this notable Fourbe, to introduce the Inquisition.

2. A trick, an imposture.

1654 tr. *Scudery's Curia Pol.* 133 Many Polititians yeeld and perswade, that..fraud and fowrbs are commendable and innocent instruments. **1691** BAXTER *Cert. of Worlds of Spirits* 89, I began to suspect a Fourbe.

†**fourb(e**, *v. Obs.* [a. F. *fourber*, f. *fourbe*: see prec.] *trans.* To cheat, impose upon, trick.

1654 *Nicholas Papers* (Camden) II. 122 Lord Jermyn hath lustily fourbed the Queene of all her jewells. **1713** *Gentl. Instr.* (ed. 5) 244, I ask then, how those who fourb'd others become Dupes to their own contrivance?

†'**fourbery**. *Obs.* Also 7 furbery. [ad. F. *fourberie*, f. *fourber*: see prec.] A piece of deception; a fraud, trick, imposture.

1642 HOWELL *For. Trav.* (Arb.) 43 Young Travellers must be cautious..to avoyd one kind of Furbery or cheat, whereunto many are subiect. **1690** *Secr. Hist. Chas. II & Jas. II*, Pref. A ij b, Let all the world judg of the Furberies and Tyranny of those times. **1737** FIELDING *Hist. Reg.* III. Wks. 1882 X. 232 This, sir, I think is a very pretty Pantomime trick, and an ingenious burlesque on all the fourberies which the great Lun has exhibited in all his entertainments. [**1856** SMYTH *Catal. Roman Family Coins* 165 Alessandro had a strong vein of fourberie in ancient matters.]

fourbour, var. of FURBER *Obs.*

fourbusher: see FURBISHER.

Fourcault ('fʊəkəʊ). The name of Émile *Fourcault*, Belgian inventor (1862–1919), used *attrib.* to designate a continuous process for making sheet glass in which the glass is drawn vertically upwards through a slot in a debiteuse. Also ***Fourcault machine***, etc.

1908 W. ROSENHAIN *Glass Manuf.* 359 (Index), Fourcault process. **1948** L. M. ANGUS-BUTTERWORTH *Manuf. Glass* xvii. 158 The great disadvantage of the Fourcault process was that it was necessary to continue drawing the sheet up vertically after it left the furnace. **1949** P. DAVIS *Devel. Amer. Glass Industry* viii. 192, 44 per cent of total window-glass production in 1929 was made by the Fourcault machine. **1965** *Glass Technol.* VI. 27A The one-compartment Fourcault tanks..must necessarily have a certain length to permit the glass to cool down sufficiently on its way towards the drawing compartment.

†**fourch(e**, *v. Obs.* [a. F. *fourcher* to fork, f. *fourche* fork.]

1. *intr.* = FORK *v.*; *spec.* of a hart: see quot. Hence **fourched** *ppl. a.*, forked.

c **1320** *Sir Tristr.* 503 Þe rauen he ȝaue his ȝiftes Sat on þe fourched tre, On rowe. **1413–22** *Venery de Twety* in *Rel. Ant.* I. 151 Alleway we calle [a hart one] of the fyrst hed tyl that he be of x. of the lasse. And fyrst whan an hert hath fourched, and then auntlere ryall, and surryall, and forched on the one syde, and troched on that other syde, than is he an hert of x. and of the more. **1486** *Bk. St. Albans* E j b, And that in the toppe so when ye may hym keen Then shall ye call hym forchyd an hert of tenne.

2. *Law*: see FOURCHER.

1613 SIR H. FINCH *Law* (1636) 429 The Pl' and Def. if they list, may fourch infinitely by the common Law.

fourche, earlier form of FOUCH, *Obs.*

fourche, var. f. of FORCHE, *Obs.*, gallows.

fourché(e ('fʊəʃeɪ), *a. Her.* [a. F. *fourchée*: see FORCHE *a.*] = FORCHE *a.*

1706 PHILLIPS (ed. Kersey), s.v., A Cross fourché, is a Cross forked at each end. **1864** BOUTELL *Her. Hist. & Pop.* xviii. § 1 (ed. 3) 288 A lion rampt. arg., the tail fourchée.

‖'**fourcher**. *Law. Obs.* [Law F. *fourcher*: see FOURCH(E *v.*] A mode of delay practised by two defendants in a suit, and consisting in their appearing (or being essoined) alternately instead of together.

1602 *Les Termes de la Ley* 166 Fourcher is a deuice vsed to delay the plaintife or demaundant in a suite against two.

fourchette (fuːr'ʃɛt). [a. F. *fourchette*, dim. of *fourche*: see FORK *sb.*] **1.** A fork; something forked or resembling a fork. **a.** *Anat.* (See quot.)

1754–64 SMELLIE *Midwif.* I. 93 The Fraenum or Fourchette, which bounds the inferior part of the Fossa magna and os externum. **1844** HOBLYN *Dict. Med.* (ed. 2), *Fourchette*..the thin commissure, by which the labia majora of the pudendum unite together.

b. *Surg.* A forked instrument formerly used to divide the frænum of the tongue when short (*Syd. Soc. Lex.* 1885.)

1854 in MAYNE *Expos. Lex.*

c. *Ornith.* The furcula of a bird.

1854 in MAYNE *Expos. Lex.* **1862** J. SMITH *Newer Plioc. Geol.* 14 A marine deposit, containing the bones of..sea-fowl. *Foot-n.* The fourchette of a diver.

d. *Glove-making.* The forked piece between two adjacent fingers of a glove; a forgett. Also *Comb.*, as ***fourchette-cutter***, **-*puncher***.

1862 *Catal. Internat. Exhib., Brit.* II. No. 4942 The Children's [gloves] have an improved fourchette. **1881** *Instr. Census Clerks* (1885) 76 Thumb and Fourchette Cutter and Puncher. **1886** *Chambers's Jrnl.* 226/2 He cut pieces for the thumbs and fourchettes or sides of the fingers—usually pronounced 'forgets'. **1957** M. B. PICKEN *Fashion Dict.* 136/1 *Fourchette*, small forked piece of leather or other material set in between fingers of well-fitted gloves.

2. *Card games.* (See quots.)

1885 R. A. PROCTOR *Whist* 241 King and Knave make the *fourchette* to the Queen led; Queen and ten make the *fourchette* to the Knave; and so on. **1898** 'CAVENDISH' *Princ. Whist* 102 When you have the *fourchette* it is almost always right to cover. **1906** 'CUT-CAVENDISH' *Compl. Bridge Player* 131 A fourchette is the combination of cards in one hand immediately above and below the card led, such as knave, nine, sitting over the ten. It applies to the cards of the second player over the leader, and to the cards of the third player over the second. **1907** *Westm. Gaz.* 18 May 14/1 In the unusual case of holding a hand that is full of fourchettes, the middle heart is the correct opening.

fourcrœa: see FURCRÆA.

†**fourd**, *v. Obs. rare*[−1]. [Aphetic var. of AFFORD.] *trans.* To supply, AFFORD.

1581 *Disc. Comm. Weal Eng.* (1893) 66 He could not fourde his paper as good cheape as that came from beyonde the seaze.

Fourdrinier (fuːə'drɪnɪeɪ, fuːdrɪ'nɪə(r)). The name of Henry (1766–1854) and Sealy (d. 1847) *Fourdrinier*, British printers, used attrib. (†or in the possessive) to denote esp. the paper-making machine invented by them, and also the wire cloth used for draining the pulp in the machine.

[**1825** J. NICHOLSON *Oper. Mech.* 369 The machines which are now almost universally employed..the invention of Messrs. Fourdrinier.] **1837** *Rep. Sel. Comm. Fourdrinier's Pat.* 9 in *Parl. Papers* XX. 35 Do you understand the working of the machine which is called Fourdrinier's Patent Machine for making paper? **1839** URE *Dict. Arts* II. 930 One of the Fourdrinier machines made at London by Mr. Donkin. **1845** *Encycl. Metrop.* VIII. 766 Fourdrinier's machine.—This was the first successful attempt at supplying machinery to perform the duties of the deckle or mould. **1874** *Art of Paper-Making* 164 They certainly well deserve to be immortalised in the name of the present Fourdrinier. *Ibid.* 182 It is this shaking movement, though it is very trifling (about ¼ inch), which makes the Fourdrinier paper superior to that made on a cylinder-machine. *a* **1877** KNIGHT *Dict. Mech.* I. 912/1 *Fourdrinier-machine*, a paper-making machine, the first to make a continuous web. **1964** *Gloss. Paper Terms (B.S.I.)* 16 *Fourdrinier machine*, a machine for the production of a continuous sheet of paper or board which is formed by drainage on an endless wire cloth unit known as the 'Fourdrinier wire part'. **1966** H. WILLIAMSON *Methods Bk. Design* (ed. 2) xviii. 295 Almost any Fourdrinier is huge; the biggest is colossal. *Ibid.* 298 It is the drying cylinders which extend the Fourdrinier machine to its enormous size.

†**fourdrye**, *v. Obs. rare*[−1]. [? Corruptly ad. OF. *fouldrié*, *foudroyé*, struck by lightning.]

1483 CAXTON *G. de la Tour* E iiij b, So were the seuen cytees brenned and fourdryed in stynkyng sulphure.

fourer ('fɔərə(r)). *Cricket.* [f. FOUR + -ER[1].] A hit from which four runs are scored. (No longer current.)

1875 *Field* 8 May 458/1 Boys made a 'fourer'. **1901** R. H. LYTTELTON *Out-door Games* 14 The public only applaud him [*sc.* the batsman] when he hits a fourer. **1927** *Observer* 29 May 28/5 At the other end I'll make old Brown bowl full half-volleys wide of the off-stump and have an outer ring of three to save the fourers.

four flush, *sb. U.S.* [FLUSH *sb.*[3] 1.] In poker, a flush containing only four (instead of five) cards, and hence almost worthless; a bob-tail flush. Hence *attrib.* or as *adj.*, lacking in genuineness. So **four-flush** *v. intr.*, to act in a 'bluffing' or fraudulent manner; chiefly as **four-flushing** *vbl. sb.* and *ppl. a.*

1887 J. W. KELLER *Draw Poker* 35 If in opening a pot a player finds in his hand a pair and a four flush, or four straight, he may break his pair. **1896** ADE *Artie* iv. 37 'I thought he was going to fight.' 'Not that boy. He was four-flushin'.' **1899** —— *Fables in Slang* (1911) 12 She always saw the same old line of Four-Flush Drummers from Chicago and St. Louis. **1901** 'J. FLYNT' *World of Graft* 46 That's what I call four-flushin'. **1901** [see *call-down* s.v. CALL *sb.* 15]. **1904** *N.Y. Even. Post* 20 Feb. 10 Mayor Harrison's assertion that the Sunday closing law is a 'four-flush' law..one that was meant to deceive and not meant for actual enforcement. **1942** W. STEGNER *Mormon Country* 286 A four-flushing holdup man named Gunplay Maxwell.

Hence '**four-flusher**, a pretender, braggart, humbug.

1904 'No. 1500' *Life in Sing Sing* xiii. 255 *Four-flusher*, one who poses for effect. **1910** *Outlook* 25 June 376 Many doubted his intention, and one newspaper called him a 'four-flusher'. **1916** 'B. M. BOWER' *Phantom Herd* ii. 30 Some of the four-flushers..kept eyeing that bluff. **1920** A. B. BAXTER *Parts Men Play* xxi. § 1, Vot you mean, you great big fourflusher? **1923** R. D. PAINE *Comrades of Rolling Ocean* vi. 106, I could have sized up this Maddigan four-flusher if he had merely walked across the campus in my freshman year. **1924** W. M. RAINE *Troubled Waters* ii. 22 You're a fine bunch of four-flushers. **1944** L. A. G. STRONG *Director* xiii. 112 You shouldn't let these four-flushers come it over you.

fourfold ('fɔəfəʊld), *a.*, *adv.*, and *sb.* [f. FOUR + -FOLD.]

A. *adj.*

1. Consisting of four things; made up of four parts.

c **1275** LAY. 1356 To þan lond hii verden þare hii leof folk funden fouruald ferde. *a* **1300** *Cursor M.* 28974 Chastiyng o flexs foure fald to tak, In praier, fasting, wand, and wak. **1660** BOYLE *New Exp. Phys. Mech.* ix. 70 A four-fold Advantage. **1823** H. J. BROOKE *Introd. Crystallogr.* 58 A four-fold cleavage, or one in four directions, will produce a tetrahedron. **1838** THIRLWALL *Greece* II. xi. 4 The four-fold distribution of the country is the foundation of another tradition. **1877** A. B. EDWARDS *Up Nile* xii. 341 The four-fold surroundings of Philæ—the cataract, the river, the desert, the environing mountains.

2. Four times as great or numerous: quadruple.

c **1000** *Ags. Gosp.* Luke xix. 8 Gif ic ænigne bereafode ic hit be feowerfealdum agyfe. **1557** RECORDE *Whetst.* B ij, Quadrupla. 4 to 1: 8 to 2..Fowerfolde. *a* **1650** MAY *Old Couple* IV. i, *2nd Neigh.* All happiness betide you. *3rd Neigh.* And a reward four-fold in th' other world.

3. *Comb.*, as ***fourfold-visaged*** adj.

1667 MILTON *P.L.* VI. 845 Nor less on either side tempestuous fell, His arrows, from the fourfold-visag'd foure.

B. *adv.* In fourfold proportion.

1535 COVERDALE *2 Sam.* xii. 6 The shepe also shal he make good foure folde. **1873** B. STEWART *Conserv. Energy* i. 14 Its penetrating power is increased nearly fourfold. **1875** SCRIVENER *Lect. Text N. Test.* 7 [They] amount to at least fourfold that quantity.

C. *sb.* A fourfold amount. †Also *spec.* in *U.S.*, 'A quadruple assessment for neglect to make return of taxable estate'; hence **'fourfold** *v.*, 'to assess in a fourfold ratio' (Webster *Compend. Dict.* 1806).

c **1380** WYCLIF *Serm.* Sel. Wks. II. 209 ȝif y have ought bigiled ony Y ȝelde aȝen þe forefold. **1611** BIBLE *Luke* xix. 8, I restore him foure fold. **1779** *Vermont St. Papers* (1823) 296 The listers shall add the sum total of such additions and four-folds, to the sum total before mentioned.

four-foot, *a.* *Obs.* exc. *poet.* [f. FOUR *a.* + FOOT *sb.*] = FOUR-FOOTED.

[*c* **893** K. ÆLFRED *Oros.* II. iv. §3 Ælces cynnes feowerfetes feos an. *c* **900** tr. *Bæda's Hist.* IV. xxx. [xxix.] (1891) 374 He..nales ðæt aan feðerfotra neata..ðone teoðan dæl..sealde.] *c* **1300** *Cursor M.* 19848 (Edin.) Alle fourfote bestis saȝ he bune. **1732** SWIFT *Beasts' Confess.* 201 For libelling the four-foot race. **1864** SWINBURNE *Atalanta* 149 Yea, lest they smite us with some four-foot plague.

'four-ˌfooted, *a.* [f. FOUR *a.* + FOOT *sb.* + -ED[2].] Having four feet, quadruped.

c **1175** *Lamb. Hom.* 43 Innan þan ilke sea weren unaneomned deor summe feðer fotetd. *a* **1300** *Cursor M.* 19848 All four foted bestes sagh he bun. **1553** EDEN *Treat. Newe Ind.* (Arb.) 19 Foure footed beastes. **1714** BERKELEY *Serm.* Wks. 1871 IV. 606 Birds and fourfooted beasts. **1887** SIR R. H. ROBERTS *In the Shires* ix. 150 Many a four-footed friend ..would eat from no hand but mine.

b. Of or pertaining to four-footed animals.

a **1682** SIR T. BROWNE *Chr. Mor.* iii. §14 Expose not thyself by four-footed manners unto monstrous draughts, and caricatura representations. **1698** DRYDEN *Ovid's Metam.* Fables (1700) 435 Whose Art in vain From Fight dissuaded the four-footed Train. **1840** HOOD *Kilmansegg, Her Accident* vi, The Maid rides first in the fourfooted strife.

c. quasi-*adv.* On four feet.

1718 PRIOR *Knowledge* 631 All the living that four-footed move Along the shore, the meadow, or the grove.

'four-ˌfooter. [f. FOUR *a.* + FOOT *sb.* + -ER[1].] A creature having four feet; a quadruped.

1906 R. WHITEING *Ring in New* xxxviii. 281 They [*sc.* tigers] are four-footers, we are two—perhaps that's all the difference. **1920** GALSWORTHY *In Chancery* II. x, 'Strange life a dog's,' said Jolyon suddenly; 'the only four-footer with rudiments of altruism, and a sense of God!'

‖**fourgon** (furgɔ̃). [a. F. *fourgon.*] A baggage-wagon, a luggage-van.

1848 THACKERAY *Van. Fair* lxii, Lord Bareacres' chariot, Britska, and fourgon, that any body might pay for who liked. **1866** MRS. H. WOOD *St. Martin's Eve* xxv. (1874) 309 Your wedding-dress is come, with lots more things, nearly a fourgon full, Louise says. **1884** *Health Exhib. Catal.* p. xxxix, Fourgons containing the equipment of Hospital Corps.

four-handed, *a.*

1. Having four feet which resemble the hands of a man; quadrumanous.

1774 GOLDSM. *Nat. Hist.* (1776) IV. 249 Animals of the monkey kind..From this general description of four-handed animals, we perceive what [etc.]. **1833** TENNYSON *Poems* 3 When, in the darkness over me, The fourhanded mole shall scrape. **1846** OWEN *Brit. Fossil Mammals & Birds* 3 Arboreal Mammalia of the four-handed order.

2. Suitable for four persons. Also, *rarely*, of a piece of pianoforte music: Adapted for four hands (Fr. *à quatre mains*), i.e. two players; a duet.

1824 MISS MITFORD *Village* Ser. I. (1863) 217 If we could both have won—if it had been four-handed cribbage, and she my partner. **1840** DICKENS *Old C. Shop* xxix, We'll make a four-handed game of it, and take in Groves. **1885** *Pall Mall G.* 20 Mar. 5/2 Among those who are wedded to their first love of normal chess, the four-handed game does not gain much favour.

†**four-herned**, *a.* *Obs.* *rare*[−1]. In 3 -huyrned. [f. FOUR + HERN corner + -ED[2].] Four-cornered.

c **1290** *S. Eng. Leg.* I. 416/462 Þo hiet he is desciples þat huy ane put four-huyrned him made.

†**'fourhood.** *Obs. rare.* In 5 -hede. [f. FOUR + -HEAD, -HOOD.]

c **1400** tr. *Secreta Secret., Gov. Lordsh.* (E.E.T.S.) 109 Yn ffourhede er oon, two, thre, and ffoure, and if þou geder hem to-gedre þey make tene; þe nombre of ten ys þe perfeccion of hem þat enbracen ffourhede.

Fourier ('fʊərɪeɪ). The name of J. B. J. *Fourier* (1768–1830), French mathematician, used *attrib.* or in the possessive to designate certain principles enunciated by him and many mathematical expressions and techniques arising out of his work, as ***Fourier analysis***, the analysis of a periodic function into a number of simple harmonic functions or, more generally, into a series of functions from any orthonormal set; ***Fourier's law***, that any non-sinusoidal periodic vibration can be regarded as the sum of a number of sinusoidal vibrations each having a frequency that is an integral multiple of some fundamental frequency; ***Fourier('s) series***, a series of the form $\frac{1}{2}a_0 + (a_1 \cos x + b_1 \sin x) + (a_2 \cos 2x + b_2 \sin 2x) + \ldots$, where the constants a_0, a_1, b_1, etc. are defined in terms of a function $f(x)$ to which the series may converge; ***Fourier's theorem***, (*a*) that if a function $f(x)$ satisfies certain conditions within the interval $-\pi \leqslant x \leqslant \pi$, it can be represented within that interval by a Fourier series; (*b*) (see quot. 1880); ***Fourier transform***, a function $f(x)$ related to a given function $g(t)$ by the equation

$$(2\pi)^{\frac{1}{2}} f(x) = \int_{-\infty}^{\infty} g(t)e^{\pm itx}dt,$$ used to represent a non-periodic function by a spectrum of sinusoidal functions. Also ***Fourier coefficient, expansion, integral, transformation***, etc.

1834 *Rep. Brit. Assoc. 1833* 343 If the interval of the roots be determined, by the application of Fourier's theorem of the succession of signs of the original function X and its derivatives. **1842** A. DE MORGAN *Differential & Integral Calculus* xx. 641 In applying Fourier's theorem..to discontinuous functions, we find that at the point where the discontinuity takes place, and a function which generally can have but one value might be expected to have two, it takes neither, and gives only the mean between them. **1877** RAYLEIGH *Theory of Sound* I. ii. 24 The pre-eminent importance of Fourier's series in Acoustics. **1880** G. S. CARR *Synopsis Pure & Appl. Math.* I. I. 134 Fourier's Theorem.—Fourier's functions are..$f(x)$, $f'(x)$, $f''(x)$ ...$f^n(x)$...As x increases, Fourier's functions lose *one* change of sign for each root of the equation $f(x) = 0$, through which x passes, and r changes of sign for r repeated roots. **1884** A. DANIELL *Text Bk. Princ. Physics* v. 127 Longitudinal vibrations of a string or rod..whose ends are held fixed obey the same principles as transverse vibrations. Fourier's law holds good. **1902** E. T. WHITTAKER *Course Mod. Anal.* vii. 152 The question arises..whether the Fourier expansion is *unique*. **1911** *Proc. R. Soc.* A. LXXXV. 14 We can also sum the series of the products of the Fourier coefficients of two such functions. **1912** *Phil. Mag.* 6th Ser. XXIV. 866 Fourier's integral. **1923** *Proc. Cambr. Philos. Soc.* XXI. 463 The notion of Fourier transforms arises from Fourier's integral formula,..which gives..reciprocal relations..connecting the two functions $f(x)$ and $F(x)$. **1929** V. BUSH *Operational Circuit Analysis* x. 186 Direct operational methods may be regarded as shorthand processes of evaluating and tabulating the results of Fourier analysis. **1936** *Discovery* Apr. 114/2 All sound-waves (except those from a flute, closed organ-pipe, etc.) are composed of many combined vibrations whose composition follows Fourier's law. **1957** R. S. LONGHURST *Geom. & Physical Optics* xi. 226 The Fraunhofer pattern is the Fourier transform of the amplitude across the diffracting aperture and vice versa. **1963** R. W. DITCHBURN *Light* (ed. 2) iv. 89 The 'top-hat curve' shown in fig. 4.6 can be represented by an appropriate Fourier series..for all values of x_0 because the curve to be represented is periodic. **1964** *Oceanogr. & Marine Biol.* II. 14 The correlation coefficient $f_u(\tau)$ is related by a Fourier transformation to the spectrum function $F_u(n)$. **1965** PEARSON & MALER *Introd. Circuit Anal.* ix. 439 The Fourier transform..is useful in analyzing pulses from a frequency standpoint. **1967** CONDON & ODISHAW *Handbk. Physics* (ed. 2) II. iii. 26/2 The part of $F(t)$ effective in exciting the oscillator is the component in its Fourier integral representation associated with the natural frequency of the oscillator.

Hence vbl. uses, as ***Fourier-analyse, -transform*** vbs.; ***Fourier-transformed*** ppl. adj.

1962 W. B. THOMPSON *Introd. Plasma Physics* vi. 108 To get a numerical value, the curve may be Fourier analysed, and the effect of each harmonic component discovered. **1967** *Oceanogr. & Marine Biol.* V. 24 For several North Sea ports..continuous sea-level records were Fourier-analysed to determine if any non-tidal periods were present. **1968** C. G. KUPER *Introd. Theory Superconductivity* iv. 57 These Fourier-transformed quantities. **1970** *Nature* 5 Sept. 1032/1 The Fourier co-efficients..could then be inversely Fourier transformed to reconstruct the specimen in three dimensions.

Fourierism ('fʊərɪərɪz(ə)m). [in F. *Fouriérisme*, f. the name *Fourier*: see -ISM.] A system invented by the French socialist Charles Fourier for the re-organization of society; phalansterianism.

1841–4 EMERSON *Ess., Nom. & Real* Wks. (Bohn) I. 251 Mesmerism..Fourierism, and the Millennial Church..are poor pretensions enough, but good criticism on the science, philosophy, and preaching of the day. **1864** R. CHAMBERS *Bk. Days* 7 Apr. 486/1 Fourierism found many adherents in France and the United States.

Fourierist ('fʊərɪərɪst). [f. as prec. + -IST.] An adherent of the system of Fourierism.

1843 EMERSON *Let.* in *Atlantic Monthly* (1892) May 581 He thinks himself sure of W. H. Channing as a good Fourierist. **1856** LEVER *Martins of Cro' M.* 386, I was pitched out into the gutter..and I got up a Radical, a Democrat, a Fourierist.

2. *attrib.* or *adj.* Of the Fourierists; Fourieristic.

1870 *Athenæum* 5 Feb. 187 The Fourierist communities were, with one or two exceptions, equally short-lived.

Hence **Fourieristic** *a.*, of or pertaining to the Fourierists or to Fourierism.

1883 R. T. ELY *Fr. & Ger. Socialism* 102 All the strictly Fourieristic experiments tried in France thus far have failed.

'Fourierite [See -ITE.] = FOURIERIST.

1844 MARY HENNELL *Soc. Syst.* 209 The Fourierites have spread themselves..widely through France.

attrib. or *adj.* **1850** LONGF. in *Life* (1891) II. 175 L—— at me again to edit his book on Fourierite Analogies!

four-in-hand.

1. a. A vehicle with four horses driven by one person.

1793 *European Mag.* XXIII. 46 Swift thro' Hyde Park I drive my four-in-hand. **1825** DISRAELI in Smiles *Life J. Murray* (1891) II. xxvi. 188 The four-in-hands of the Yorkshire squires. **1842** TENNYSON *Walking to Mail* 103 As quaint a four-in-hand As you shall see—three pyebalds and a roan.

fig. **1837** LONGF. in *Life* (1891) I. 277 This four-in-hand of outlandish animals [the foreign instructors at Harvard College], all pulling the wrong way, except one.

b. A kind of necktie of the variety designed to be tied in a loose knot with hanging ends. Also ***four-in-hand tie***. Chiefly *U.S.*

1892 *Pall Mall G.* 11 Oct. 7/2 You do not need..slippers, nor *four-in-hand ties. **1902** S. HALE *Let.* (1919) 374 The young men in Tuxedos, four-in-hands, panamas. **1909** 'O. HENRY' *Roads of Destiny* x. 166 While trying to figure out Jimmy's method of tying his four-in-hand he cordially gave information. **1909** *Public Ledger* (Philadelphia) 24 June 5/1 Knitted and French Four-in-hands, made of fiber and short lengths of silk. **1919** T. K. HOLMES *Man fr. Tall Timber* xix. 224 She had fashioned..a crimson four-in-hand to be tied at the low, rolling collar of her blouse. **1942** E. PAUL *Narrow St.* ii. 12 His twinkling blue eyes..noted my American felt hat and four-in-hand tie. **1967** *Boston* (Mass.) *Herald* 1 Apr. 21/2 The traditional four-in-hand or ascot.

2. quasi-*adv.* With a four-in-hand.

1812 COMBE (Dr. Syntax) *Picturesque* xx. 145 Thus off they went, and, four-in-hand, Dash'd briskly tow'rds the promis'd land. **1871** M. COLLINS *Mrq. & Merch.* II. ix. 276 He drives them down four-in-hand.

3. a. *attrib.* and *Comb.*, as ***four-in-hand club, -driver, -driving***; **four-in-hand tie**: see sense 1 b.

1849 E. E. NAPIER *Excurs. S. Africa* I. 169 A style that completely outdoes the..most renowned members of the *'Four in hand' Club at home. **1877** M. M. GRANT *Sun-Maid* ii, He considered himself equal to the best whip in the Four-in-Hand Club. **1812** *Sporting Mag.* XXXIX. 153 Flash *Four-in-Hand and Donkey drivers. **1848** THACKERAY *Van. Fair* x, Boxing, rat-hunting..and *four in hand driving were then the fashion of our British aristocracy.

b. quasi-*adj.*

1799 HAN. MORE *Fem. Educ.* (ed. 4) I. 75 The intrepid female, the hoyden..the swinging arms, the confident address, the regimental, and the four-in-hand. **1807–8** W. IRVING *Salmag.* iii. (1811) 41 It is excessively pleasant to hear a couple of these four-in-hand gentlemen retail their exploits over a bottle. **1856** WHYTE MELVILLE *Kate Cov.* xx, The tobacco-smoking, four-in-hand Miss Coventry.

‖**fou rire** (fu rir). [Fr., lit. 'mad laughter'.] (A fit of) wild or uncontrollable laughter.

[**1897** P. G. HAMERTON *Autobiogr.* vii. 51 The eldest boy in our class was liable to fits of perfectly uncontrollable laughter (what the French call *le fou rire*).] **1914** R. BROOKE *Let.* 3 Sept. (1968) 613 Murmurs of subdued applause from me. Eddie [Marsh] had a *fou rire*. **1919** G. SAINTSBURY *Hist. Fr. Novel* II. iv. 137 But I own that an access of *fou rire* once came upon me when I was told in a printed page that *La Chartreuse de Parme* was a 'very lively and very amusing book'. **1924** M. MACCARTHY *Nineteenth-Cent. Childhood* vii. 75 Adela and I exchange glances... We recover quickly from our hidden *fou-rire*. **1963** P. H. JOHNSON *Night & Silence* xxvi. 194 Halfway up the stairs she..fell into a *fou rire*.

'four-leaved, *a.* [f. FOUR + LEAF + -ED[2].] Having four leaves.

1793 MARTYN *Lang. Bot.*, Four-leaved tendril. **1839** LOVER *Four-leaved Shamrock* 1 I'll seek a four-leaved shamrock in all the fairy dells. **1847** LONGF. *Ev.* I. iii. 19 The marvellous powers of four-leaved clover.

b. ***four-leaved grass***: †(*a*) a four-leaved variety of *Trifolium repens*; (*b*) the plant *Paris quadrifolia*.

c **1450** *Alphita* (Anecd. Oxon.) 152/1 *Quadrafolium*, fowrleuedgras. **1597** GERARDE *Herbal* 1029 The other is called *Lotus quadrifolia*, or fower leafed Grasse, or purple Woort. **1640** PARKINSON *Theat. Bot.* 1112 *Quadrifolium fuscum.* Fower leafed or purple grass. **1863** PRIOR *Plant-n.* 86 Four leaved grass..the Herb Trulove, *Paris quadrifolia*.

fourling ('fɔəlɪŋ). [f. FOUR *sb.* + -LING.]

1. 'One of four children born at the same time' (Ogilvie 1855 and mod. Dicts.).

2. *Min.* A twin crystal made up of four independent individuals (*Cent. Dict.*).

fourm(e, var. FORM *sb.*

†**'fourment.** *Obs. rare* [a. F. *fourment*, 16th c. var. of *froment*, ad. L. *frumentum.*] Corn; rendering L. *frumentum*.

1601 HOLLAND *Pliny* I. 557 Of all graine, there are two principall kinds..first Fourment, containing vnder it wheat and Barley, and such like: secondly, Pulse.

†**fourneau.** *Mil. Obs.* [a. F. *fourneau*, lit. oven, OF. *fornel*:—late L. type *furnellus*, dim. of *furnus* (F. *four*) oven.] = FORNELLO.

1678 tr. *Gaya's Arms of War* 56 Blowing up the Bastions of a Place besieged, by means of Mines and Fourneaus.

†**fourneil.** *Obs. rare*[−1]. [a. OF. *fornel* furnace, kiln: see FOURNEAU.] A kiln.

1483 CAXTON *Gold. Leg.* 195 b/2 As I wente..after one of my sowes I fonde a fourneil of lyme meruelously grete.

†**fournie.** *Obs.*

1548 *Privy Council Acts* (1890) II. 174 Fournies for cartouches, v...canvas for cartouches, l elles.

Fournier (ˈfʊənɪeɪ). The name of P. S. *Fournier* (1712–68), French engraver and type-founder, used to designate a style of type designed by him and revived in modern use. ***Fournier('s) point***, a unit of measurement of type.

1902 T. L. De Vinne *Pract. Typogr.* 146 Attempts have been made to return to the Fournier point by making it in accord with the new measures. *Ibid.* 155 In the Fournier system 1000 points made 35 centimetres. **1927** in O. Simon *Introd. Typogr.* (ed. 2, 1963) v. 92 Fournier, a specimen of a classic old face designed by Pierre Simon Fournier (*Fournier-le-jeune*) Paris ca. 1750 & now first revived by the Lanston Monotype Corporation Ld...1927. **1930** H. Carter *Fournier on Typefounding* p. xxxv, The traditional 'Fournier point', long used in Belgium, was ·013728 English inch. **1935**, **1945** [see Bembo]. **1962** D. B. Updike *Printing Types* (ed. 3) I. ii. 32 Fournier's point is scarcely used nowadays, except in Belgium. **1963** O. Simon *Introd. Typogr.* (ed. 2) iii. 13 Fournier, Plantin and Imprint are.. more successful in their smaller sizes.

fournymente, var. of furniment. *Obs.*

four o'clock.

1. (More fully ***four o'clock flower***.) A name for the plant *Mirabilis Jalapa* or Marvel of Peru.

1756 P. Browne *Jamaica* 166 Jalap or Four-o-clock-flower. **1794** Martyn *Rousseau's Bot.* xvi. 211 In the west Indian Islands, where it [Marvel of Peru] is very common, they call it four o'clock flower. **1852** Mrs. Stowe *Uncle Tom's C.* iv, Here also..various brilliant annuals, such as marigolds, petunias, four-o'clocks, found an indulgent corner. **1882** J. Smith *Dict. Plants* 269 Marvel of Peru (*Mirabilis Jalapa*)..This and *M. longiflora* are handsome garden plants, opening their pretty tube-like flowers..in the after-noon, hence called Four o'clock-flower.

2. The Australian friar-bird, *Philemon corniculatus*, so called from its cry.

1848 J. Gould *Birds Austral.* IV. Descr. pl. 58, *Tropidorhynchus Corniculatus.* Friar Bird. From the fancied resemblance of its notes to those words, it has obtained from the Colonists the various names of..'Four o'clock', etc.

3. A seed-head of the dandelion. Cf. *one o'clock*.

1883 Talmage in *Chr. Globe* 13 Sept. 819/1 The hand that had plucked four o'clocks in the meadow.

4. A light meal taken by workmen about four o'clock in the afternoon.

1825 Jamieson Supp. s.v. *Four-hours*, A slight refreshment taken by workmen in Birmingham is called a four o'clock. **1841** Hartshorne *Salop. Antiq.* 432 *Four o'clock*, a lunch or bait taken by labourers at this hour in the harvest. **1881** *Oxf. Gloss.* Supp., *Four o'clock*, a tea in the hayfield.

fourpence (ˈfɔəpəns). [f. four *a.* + pence.] A sum of money or coin equal to four pennies. ***fourpence-halfpenny***: see quots. 1722, 1860.

The Irish shilling of Elizabeth circulated in England under the name and at the value of 'ninepence'; it is inferred that the 'fourpence-halfpenny' was the Irish sixpence of the same period.

1722 De Foe *Col. Jack* (1840) 46 Ninepences, and fourpence-halfpennies..Scotch and Irish coin. **1852** R. S. Surtees *Sponge's Sp. Tour* (1893) 319 'Well, there's sixpence for you, my good woman', said he..'It's nabbut fourpence', observed the woman. **1860** Bartlett *Dict. Amer.* s.v. *Federal Currency*, The [Spanish] half real..is called..in New England, fourpence ha'penny, or simply fourpence. **1872** O. W. Holmes *Poet Breakf.-t* iii. (1885) 75 Give me two fo'pencehappenies for a ninepence.

fourpenny (ˈfɔəpənɪ), *a.* [f. four *a.* + penny.]

1. a. That costs or is valued at four pence. ***fourpenny ale***, ale sold at four pence a quart; ***fourpenny bit*** or ***piece***, a silver coin of the value of four pence; so ***fourpenny-halfpenny piece***.

1597 *1st Pt. Return fr. Parnass.* II. i. 517 Simple plaine felowes..that weare foure-pennie garters. **1678** *Lond. Gaz.* No. 1348/4 Three pieces of Four-peny broad black taffaty Ribon. **1691** Locke *Lower. Interest* Wks. 1727 II. 97 A sufficient Quantity of Four-penny, Four-penny half-penny, and Five penny Pieces should be coined. **1756** *Monitor* I. No. 25. 220 How often do we see these fourpenny boarders, in red coats, turning the family out of their beds. **1868** Yates *Rock Ahead* III. i, He looked as if he'd lost a four-penny-piece. **1871** M. Collins *Mrq. & Merch.* I. ii. 61 He set..to work to intoxicate himself with fourpenny ale. **1890** *Pall Mall G.* 27 Nov. 2/3 The once familiar fourpenny bits have ceased from circulation.

b. quasi-*sb.* A fourpenny piece.

1883 Stevenson *Treasure Isl.* I. i, He promised me a silver four-penny on the first of every month.

c. ***fourpenny one***: a blow, hit; also, a scolding. *colloq.*

1936 *Evening News* 29 Feb. 11/6 The chairman rang the lift bell... Great was our mirth..when the little messenger ..said: 'Blimey, guv'nor,..George won't 'alf give you a fourpenny one when he comes down.' **1953** N. Balchin *Sundry Creditors* 89 On the last bend someone went hard into the retaining fence and took what looked like a fourpenny one. **1964** N. Freeling *Double-Barrel* II. xi. 73, I think he got mad because he gave her a real four-penny one. I bet she has a black eye.

2. ***fourpenny nail*** [see penny *a.*]: a nail $1\frac{1}{2}$ in. long, of which 4 lbs. go to the 'thousand' (i.e. 10 nominal hundreds or 1120).

1481 *Nottingham Rec.* II. 320 Et de dimidio centum de forpeny nayl. **1703** Moxon *Mech. Exerc.* 244 Another sort are four Penny, and six Penny Nails. *c* **1850** *Rudim. Navig.* (Weale) 135 *Nails of sorts* are 4, 6, 8..and 40-penny nails.

fourreau (ˈfuːrəʊ). [F. *fourreau*, lit. sheath, scabbard.] A tight-fitting dress; an underslip as part of a dress. (Cf. slip *sb.*³ 4 c.)

1872 *Young Englishwoman* Dec. 645/1 The fourreau dress, reminding one of modes of the First Empire. **1908** [see *sheath gown* s.v. sheath¹]. **1913** in C. W. Cunnington *Eng. Women's Clothing* (1952) iii. 118 Evening gown..mounted on flesh pink marquisette with a fourreau of sea-green charmeuse. **1921** *Glasgow Herald* 22 Jan. 4 A fourreau of black charmeuse, with which..is worn a simple over-dress of crepe de chine. **1927** *Observer* 10 Apr. 22 The whole dress is also slit from throat to hem, permitting a glimpse of a contrasting fourreau. **1964** O. Coburn tr. *Braun-Ronsdorf's Wheel of Fashion* 112/1 In such a sheath dress (called *fourreau*), which fitted the hips tightly..a lady could scarcely move.

ˈ**fourrier.** *Obs.* exc. *Hist.* or as an alien word. Also 7–8 fourier. [a. F. *fourrier*, var. of OF. *forrier*: see forayer.]

1. = forayer.

1481 Caxton *Godeffroy* lxxxiii. 131 They made semblaunt for to take fourriers and the horses nyghe them. **1604** E. Grimstone *Hist. Siege Ostend* 30 The Arch-duke had caused a Fourrier or Harbinger..to be put in prison. **1646** Buck *Rich. III*, I. 34 This was the preparative and fourrier of the rest. **1823** Scott *Quentin D.* xxviii, He that decoyed us into this snare shall go our fourrier to the next world, to take up lodgings for us.

2. A quartermaster. Also ***brigadier-fourrier*** (see quot. 1895).

1678 tr. *Gaya's Art of War* II. 47 The Fourier ought to have a List of all the Soldiers of a Company. **1781** in Simes *Mil. Guide* (ed. 3) 7 He makes the Fourier mark the head-quarters, and the quarters of the General Officers. **1895** *Daily News* 22 Oct. 6/4 He had worked his way up to the enviable position of brigadier-fourrier, a sub-officer charged with accounts, lodging of men, etc.

fourscore (ˈfɔəskɔə(r)), *a.* [f. four *a.* + score *sb.*] Four times twenty, eighty. Formerly current as an ordinary numeral; now *arch.* or *rhetorical.*

c **1250** *Gen. & Ex.* 2911 Fowre score ȝer he was hold. **1297** R. Glouc. (1724) 382 Þo deyde he in þe ȝer of grace of þousend..And four score and seuene. **1340** Hampole *Pr. Consc.* 754 If in myghtfulnes four score yhere falle, Mare es thair swynk and sorow with-alle. *c* **1585** R. Browne *Answ. Cartwright* 58 The fourescore and nynthe Psalme. **1598** Shaks. *Merry W.* III. i. 56, I haue liued foure-score yeeres, and vpward. **1600** —— *A.Y.L.* II. iii. 74 At seauenteene yeeres, many their fortunes seeke But at fourescore, it is too late a weeke. *c* **1720** Prior *Daphne & Apollo* 70 We mortals seldom live above fourscore. **1750** Chesterf. *Lett.* (1792) II. ccxix. 345 An Italian book..written by one Alberti about fourscore or a hundred years ago. **1870** Bryant *Iliad* I. II. 64 Nestor who came To war on Troy with four-score ships and ten. **1871** Morley *Voltaire* (1886) 5 The fourscore volumes which he wrote are the monument..of a new renascence. **1878** O. W. Holmes *School-boy* (1879) 73 Fourscore, like twenty, has its tasks and toys.

†ˈ**fourscorth**, *a.* *Obs.* [f. fourscore *a.*: see -th¹.] Eightieth.

1571 Golding *Calvin on Ps.* xlv. 1 In the fowerscorthe Psalme, there is put yᵉ plurall nomber (Lillyes). **1587** —— *De Mornay* viii. 100 What euidentnesse or certeintie is there in the Greeke histories afore the fourescorth Olympiade. **1657** *North's Plutarch* Add. Lives (1676) 2 (*Constantine*) Great Britain, of which he was the fourscorth King. **1713** Addison *Guardian* No. 137 ¶7 An Aunt..who..is supposed to have died a Maid in the fourscorth Year of her Age.

foursenery, var. f. of forcenery. *Obs.*

1483 Caxton *Gold. Leg.* 428 b/1 Madde folke..were delyuerd fro theyr foursenerye or madnesse.

foursenyd, var. of *forcened*: see forcene.

c **1500** *Melusine* xlii. 315 They that are foursenyd with yre.

foursome (ˈfɔəsəm), *a.* and *sb.* orig. *Sc.* [f. four *a.* + -some.] **A.** *adj.*

1. a. Four (together). Also *absol.*

15.. Douglas *K. Hart* I. 198 The fouresum baid and huvit on the grene. *c* **1560** A. Scott *Poems* (S.T.S.) ii. 145 For, wer ȝe foursum in a flok, I compt ȝow noᵗ a leik.

b. Used for the nonce as *adv.*

1875 Morris *Æneid* VII. 509 Come from the cleaving of an oak with foursome driven wedge.

2. Performed by four persons together.

1814 Scott *Wav.* xxviii, Dancing full merrily in the doubles and full career of a Scotch foursome reel. **1884** J. Payne *1001 Nts.* IX. 388 The Murebbes or foursome song occurs once only in the Nights.

B. *sb.* **1.** *Golf.* A match in which four persons take part, two playing on each side.

1867 *Cornh. Mag.* Apr. 493 Perhaps you find three men who, with yourself, will make a good foursome.

2. A company, party, or dance of four persons.

1926 [see eightsome *a.*]. **1926** *Amer. Speech* I. 630/2 The expressions *onesome, twosome, threesome, foursome, fivesome,* are coming to be used in other fields than golf, as a 'threesome at tennis', a 'foursome for bridge', a 'fivesome for dinner'. **1971** *Petticoat* 17 July 15/1 Your friend wants you to make up a foursome with her boyfriend's unknown friend. **1971** G. Mitchell *Lament for Leto* i. 26 Do you play bridge?.. I want to make up a foursome.

four-square, *a.* (*adv.*), and *sb.* [f. four *a.* + square.]

A. *adj.* Having four equal sides; square.

a **1300** *Cursor M.* 19843 A mikel linnen clath four squar Laten dun, him thoght was þar. **1470–85** Malory *Arthur* I. iii, There was sene in the chircheyard ayenst the hyghe aulter a grete stone four square. **1523** Fitzherb. *Husb.* §34 Whyte wheate is lyke polerde wheate in the busshell..and the eare is foure-square. **1634** Sir T. Herbert *Trav.* 59 Adjoyning is another foure-square room. **1745** Eliza Heywood *Female Spect.* (1748) II. 279 A four-square looking-glass. **1849** Ruskin *Sev. Lamps* vi. 164 The four-square keep of Granson.

transf. and *fig.* **1603** Holland *Plutarch's Mor.* 1304 Sixteene is a number quadrangular or foure-square. **1877** Dowden *Shaks. Prim.* vi. 135 Goneril is..the more incapable of any hatred which is not solid and four-square. **1886** Lowell *Wks.* (1890) VI. 176 One of Aristotle's four-square men, capable of holding his own in whatever field he may be cast.

b. quasi-*adv.* In a square form or position.

c **1430** *Two Cookery-bks.* I. 46 Caste by þe cake round abowte, & close hym four-square. **1522–3** Fitzherb. *Husb.* §13 Bere barleye..hathe an eare thre ynches of lengthe or more, sette foure square. **1852** Tennyson *Death Dk. Wellington* 39 That tower of strength Which stood four-square to all the winds that blew!

fig. **1845–6** Trench *Huls. Lect.* Ser. I. iii. 47 We have a Gospel which stands four-square, with a side facing each side of the spiritual world. **1877** L. Morris *Epic Hades* III. 260 It is strength To live four-square. **1884** Warfield in *Chr. Treas.* Feb. 90/1 A masterly argument..set four-square against all possible opposition.

B. *sb.* A figure having four equal sides.

1587 Golding *De Mornay* xv. 241 A fiuesquare conteineth both a Fowersquare and a Triangle. **1613** M. Ridley *Magn. Bodies* 32 You may forme the stone..into a foure-square. **1696** Temple *Ess.* iii. §2 (ed. 4) 175 Peking.. is a regular Four-square; the Wall of each side is six Miles in length. **1787** M. Cutler in *Life, Jrnl. & Corr.* (1888) I. 224 The whole roof forms the base of the steeple in a four-square. **1844** Upton *Physioglyphics* 174 It is then of a shape between a circle and four-square.

Hence †ˈ**four-squared** *ppl. a.* = four-square *a.* Also **foursquarewise** *adv.*, forming a square.

1513 Douglas *Æneis* VII. ix. 78 He Stude schydand ane four-squayr akyne tre. **1535** Coverdale *Lam.* iii. 9 He hath stopped vp my wayes with foure squared stones. **1551** Turner *Herbal* I. O ij, Walwurt..hath a forsquared stalk and full of ioyntes. **1610** Holland *Camden's Brit.* I. 701 The West part, is compassed in with a uerie faire wall and the river together, fouresquarewise. **1694** Molyneux in *Phil. Trans.* XVIII. 181 Our Irish Basaltes is composed of Columns, whereof none are four-squared. **1708** Motteux *Rabelais* IV. xl. 160 It threw..four squar'd Steel Boults.

four-stroke, *a.* [four *a.* + stroke *sb.*¹] In internal combustion engines, designating a cycle of operations which consists of four strokes (intake, compression, combustion, and exhaust); also ***four-stroke engine, working***.

1900 W. W. Beaumont *Motor Vehicles* xi. 190 The two cylinders give an impulse for each revolution with a four-stroke cycle. **1902** P. N. Hasluck *Automobile* vi. 113 Petrol motors employed on automobiles belong..to the compression and explosion type, and the Beau de Rochas four-stroke cycle of operations, known in Great Britain as the Otto cycle, is employed almost exclusively. **1906** *Motor Boat* 12 July 14/1 A four-stroke engine. **1951** *Engineering* 6 July 2/1 Valve..drives are more heavily stressed in two-stroke working than in four-stroke working.

fourteen (fɔəˈtiːn, ˈfɔətiːn), *a.* and *sb.* Forms: 1 **féowerténe, -týne,** *Northumb.* **-téno,** 2 **fowertene,** 3 **feo(u)wertene,** 3 **furten, fourtine,** *south.* **vourtene,** (6 **fowertene**), 4–6 **four(e)ten,** (4 **faurten**), 6–7 **fourteene,** 6– **fourteen.** [OE. *féowerténe* = OFris *fiuwertîne*, OS. *fiertein* (Du. *veertein*), OHG. *fiorzehan* (MHG. *vierzehen*, mod.Ger. *vierzehn*), ON. *fjórtan* (Sw. *fjorton*, Da. *fjorten*), Goth. *fidwōrtaihun*: see four and -teen.] The cardinal number composed of ten and four, represented by the symbols 14, xiv, or XIV.

A. as *adj.*

1. In concord with the sb. expressed.

c **950** *Lindisf. Gosp.* Matt. i. 17 From oferfaer babilones wið to crist cneuresua feower-teno. **1297** R. Glouc. (Rolls) 5491 Aboute vourtene ȝer king þer after he nas. **1340** Hampole *Pr. Consc.* 6552 Omang alle þat þar has bene sene, I fynde wryten paynes fourtene. **1490** Caxton *Eneydos* xxxi. 119 Whan this foureten persones were come to Crete the kyng made theym to be putte wythin the forsayd house. **1538** Wriothesley *Chron.* (1875) I. 79 Fowertene yeares past. **1611** Bible *1 Chron.* xxv. 5 Fourteene sonnes. **1751** *Affect. Narr. Wager* 24 Our ill-fated Vessel struck abaft on a sunken Rock, in fourteen Fathom Water. **1894** C. W. Boase *Reg. Coll. Exon.* p. xxxii, The fellowships were.. tenable for rather less than fourteen years.

†**b.** (*a*) ***fourteen night*** (rarely ***fourteen day***): a fortnight. *Obs.*

a **1000** *Laws of Ine* §55 Oþ-ðæt feowertyne niht ofer Eastron. *c* **1175** *Lamb. Hom.* 123 Easter dei þe nu bið to dei on fowertene niht. *c* **1205** Lay. 28236 Ah feowertene niht fulle þere læi þa uerde. *c* **1290** *S. Eng. Leg.* I. 65/406 And fourtene niȝt þare-aftur-ward. **1477** *Surtees Misc.* (1888) 27 The purpressures come in this day xiiij day. **1561** Hollybush *Hom. Apoth.* 39 Do this a fourten night and it shall auoyde. **1726** Lady M. W. Montagu *Let. to C'tess Mar* 15 Apr., I have been confined this fourteen-night to one floor.

2. With ellipsis of sb.

1480 Caxton *Chron. Eng.* ccxliv. 303 With other tounes fortresses and vyllages in to the nombre of fourtene. **1592** Shaks. *Rom. & Jul.* I. iii. 13–14 Ile lay fourteene of my teeth ..shee's not fourteene. **1685** Baxter *Paraphr. N.T.* Matt. i. 14, I reduce them to fourteen in the recitation, for memory-sake. **1818** Scott *Heart Midl.* viii, A tall gawky silly-looking boy of fourteen or fifteen.

†**3.** = fourteenth *a.* *Obs.*

c **1300** R. Glouc. (Rolls) App. xx. 261 In þe kinges fourteþe ȝere [*v.r.* fourtene ȝeer of þe kyng] hure sone henri com Of king dauid of scotlond. *c* **1430** *Freemasonry* 245 The fourtene artycul.. Scheweth the mayster how he schal don. **1553** Wilson *Rhetorike* (1567) 35 a, The fowertene of Julie.

4. *Comb.*, as **fourteen-foot** *a.*, fourteen feet in length; **fourteen-gun** *a.*, (a vessel) carrying fourteen guns; †**fourteen-shilling piece**, the Scottish 'merk' (see quot. 1695).

1695 *Act Priv. Counc. Scot.* in Cochran-Patrick *Rec. Coinage Scot.* II. 252 The value of thretteen shilling four pennies was never put upon the merk peice after they were raised to fourteen shilling, neither were they tearmed therafter merk peices but fourteen shilling peices. **1862** Latham *Channel Isl.* III. xvii. (ed. 2) 400 A fourteen-gun schooner.. some boats, and forty men constituted the authority. **1890** Boldrewood *Col. Reformer* (1891) 120 A fourteen-foot whip in your hand.

B. as *sb.*

1. The abstract number fourteen.

c **1050** *Byrhtferth's Handboc* in *Anglia* (1885) VIII. 302 Twia seofon beoð feowertyne.

†**2.** A fourteen shilling piece: see A. 4. *Obs.*

1693 *Sc. Presbyt. Eloq.* (1738) 129 The Preacher seeing him in Church, took a Fourteen out of his Pocket.

3. *pl.* Candles fourteen to the pound.

1883 *Goole Weekly Times* 14 Sept. 4/5 Dip Candles (Fourteens).

fourteener (fɔə'tiːnə(r)). [f. prec. + -ER[1].]

a. A poem of fourteen lines. *rare*$^{-1}$. **b.** A line of fourteen syllables. Also *attrib.*

1829 Lamb *Let. to Procter* xvii. 157 Study that sonnet.. and was this a fourteener to be rejected by a trumpery annual? **1884** Saintsbury *Ess. Eng. Lit.* (1891) 350 Few men manage the long 'fourteener' with middle rhyme better than Lockhart. **1887** —— *Hist. Elizab. Lit.* i. 9 The attempt to arrange the old and apparently almost indigenous 'eights and sixes' into fourteener lines and into alternate fourteeners and Alexandrines.

fourteenth (fɔə'tiːnθ, 'fɔətiːnθ), *a.* and *sb.* Forms: 1 **féowertéoða, -teoȝða,** 3 **fourteothe, fowrtuðe,** 3-4 **four-,** *south.* **vourteþe, fourtend,** (3 **four-, fortend**), 4 **faurtend, fourtenþe, -teneth,** 6- **fourteenth.** [OE. *féowertéoða*, f. *féowertýne* FOURTEEN on the analogy of *téoða* tenth. (For the subsequent history of the forms cf. FIFTEENTH.)] The ordinal numeral belonging to the cardinal fourteen.

A. *adj.* in concord with sb. expressed; also *ellipt.* ***fourteenth part***: one of 14 equal parts into which a whole is divided.

c **900** tr. *Bæda's Hist.* I. iv. (1890) 32 Se wæs feowerteoþa fram Agusto þam casere. ? *a* **1000** *Martyrologium* 82 On þone feowerteoȝðan dæȝ þæs monðes bið þara haliȝra þrowung sancte Victores ond sancte Coronan. *a* **1225** *Juliana* 79 þe fowrtuðe Kalende of mearch þat is seoððen. **1297** R. Glouc. (1724) 408 þe vourteþe day of Jenyuer vor honger þanne hii wende. *c* **1300** *St. Brandan* 331 The thretteoth [brother] fram the to the ylle of ankres schal wende, And the fourteothe to helle al quic. **1340** Hampole *Pr. Consc.* 6581 þe fourtend payne despayre es cald. **1579** Fulke *Heskins' Parl.* 181 The fourteenth Chapter expoundeth the same text. **1662** Stillingfl. *Orig. Sacr.* II. vii. §3 The fourteenth of Nisan was passed before the sanctification of the Temple was finished. **1805** W. Saunders *Min. Waters* 18 Aquatic trees.. contain only about a fourteenth part of their weight of solid matter. **1861** M. Pattison *Ess.* (1889) I. 44 The massive and imposing style of the fourteenth century.

B. *sb.* **a.** A fourteenth part. **b.** *Mus.* The octave or replicate of the seventh.

1597 Morley *Introd. Mus.* 71 *Phi.* Which distances make discord? *Ma.* A ninth, aleuenth, a fourteenth, etc. **1800** Young in *Phil. Trans.* XCI. 59 Its transverse diameter must be diminished one-fourteenth.. of an inch.

Hence **fourteenthly** *adv.*, in the fourteenth place.

a **1642** Sir W. Monson *Naval Tracts* III. (1704) 322/1 Fourteenthly, They ought to Sign Estimates. **1691-8** Norris *Pract. Disc.* (1711) III. 170 And Fourteenthly, That our Blessed Lord himself was thus treated.

fourth (fɔəθ), *a.* and *sb.* Forms: 1 **féorða, féowerða,** *Northumb.* **féarða,** (2 **forðe**), 2-3 **feorðe,** (3 **feorthe, foerth,** *south.* **veorðe**), 3-4 **ferþe,** *south.* **verþ(e, fierþ(e,** (4 **firþe,** 5 **firthe**), 3-5 **fe(e)rthe,** 3-6 **ferth,** (3-4 **feirth, ferith, feurth, furth, firth**), 4-5 **furthe,** (**furþe, forthe, fourþe, -the**), 3-6 **ferd(e,** (3-4 **feird,** *south.* **veorde,** 4 **feyrd, fyrde, furde,** 6 *Sc.* **faird**), 4-6 **ford(e,** 4-7 **fourt(e,** (4 **fowrte, forte**), 5-6 **fowerth,** (5 **faw-, fowrith, fowrth(e**), 3- **fourth.** [OE. *féorða*, corresp. to OS. *fiorðo* (Du. *vierde*), OHG. *fiordo* (MHG. *vierde*, mod.G. *vierte*), ON. *fióröe* (Sw., Da. *fjerde*):—OTeut. **fi(đ)(w)orþo-n-* repr. Com. Aryan **qeturto-* or **qetwrto-*, whence Skr. *caturtha*, OSl. *cetvrĭtŭ*, Gr. τέταρτος, L. *quartus*.] The ordinal numeral belonging to the cardinal four.

A. *adj.*

1. In concord with the sb. expressed.

fourth estate: see ESTATE *sb.* 7 b.

c **950** *Lindisf. Gosp.* Matt. xiv. 25 Ðiu feorða waccen næhtes. *c* **1175** *Lamb. Hom.* 13 Honora patrem tuum et matrem tuam þet wes þe feowerþe heste þet godalmihti het. *c* **1250** *Gen. & Ex.* 157 Forþ glod ðis ferðe dais niȝt, ðo cam ðe fifte dais liȝt. *c* **1330** R. Brunne *Chron.* (1810) 82 In his ferþe ȝere he went tille Aluerton. *c* **1400** *Destr. Troy* v. 2007 The furthe day fell all þe fuerse wyndes. **1486** *Bk. St. Albans* E j b, The fowrith yere a Stagge call hym by any way. **1588** A. King tr. *Canisius' Catech.* 109 Euerie fourt ferie (callid wenesday). **1637-50** Row *Hist. Kirk* (1842) 127 The ferd Acte condemned the Presbiterie as ane judgement not allowed by the King's law. **1674** Playford *Skill Mus.* II. 112 For the Tuning of your Violin.. the Bass or Fourth String is called G sol re ut.

2. a. With ellipsis of the sb.

c **1175** *Lamb. Hom.* 39 þat forðe is þat þu scalt wakien for þines drihtenes luue. *a* **1300** *Ten Commandm.* 33 in *E.E.P.* (1862) 16 þe verþ, loue þi neiȝbore as þine owe bodi. **1377** Langl. *P. Pl.* B. XIV. 294 þe fierthe is a fortune þat florissheth þe soule Wyth sobrete fram all synne. **1435** *Nottingham Rec.* II. 360 And ilk of thre payis, iiijs. viijd., and ye forte, iijs. **1562** Bulleyn *Bk. Simples* 52 b, It is hotte and drie, in the thirde degree, and in the beginnyng of the fowerth. **1669** Sturmy *Mariner's Mag.* I. 33 Three Right Lines being given, To find a fourth in proportion to them.

b. *esp.* with ellipsis of 'day'. ***the Fourth*** (*of July*) U.S., the anniversary of the Declaration of Independence; also *attrib.* Also quasi-*sb.* in *pl.* Hence ***Fourth-of-Julyism***.

[**1777** *Jrnls. Cont. Congr.* VIII. 625 There is due.. a bill for material, workmanship, &c. furnished for the fire works on the 4 July, the sum of 102 69/90 dollars.] **1779** *New Haven Colony Hist. Soc. Coll.* VI. 317 Toasts were drank, to wit:.. the Fourth of July, '76: The memorable era of American Independence. **1807** M. L. Weems *Lett.* (1929) II. 369 From these reflections.. we may collect some good fourth-of-July ideas. **1827** Longf. in *Life* (1891) I. viii. 121 We did not celebrate the 'glorious Fourth' here. **1830** S. Breck *Recoll.* (1877) 91 On the Fourth, being a national holiday, there was a great parade on the Common. **1834** *Southern Lit. Messenger* I. 156, I do not know that the celebration of a Fourth of July in a country village has ever been thought worthy of appearing in print. **1853** *Ibid.* XIX. 473/1 Fourth-of-Julyisms fled to the stump or the national anniversary barbecues. **1854** W. G. Simms *Southward Ho!* xiii. 253 Ordinarily admirable, our dinner on the glorious Fourth was worthy of the occasion. **1872** E. Eggleston *End of World* xi. 76 No more electin' presidents.., no more Fourths,.. no more nothin. **1874** B. F. Taylor *World on Wheels* II. i. 183 A Fourth-of-Julyism has somehow become an object of contempt. **1888** Lowell *Pr. Wks.* (1890) VI. 202 This is what may be called the Fourth of July period of our history. **1891** C. James *Rom. Rigmarole* 74 As I write I picture, here in my lonely study, bright Fourths of June. **1894** *Westm. Gaz.* 2 Jan. 6/1 The amounts passing through on the 4ths of the months for 1893. **1909** 'O. Henry' *Roads of Destiny* xiii. 206 It reminds me of a Fourth I helped to celebrate down in Salvador. **1967** D. Francis *Blood Sport* viii. 94 I'm glad you could take me at such short notice, with the Fourth coming up this weekend.

3. ***fourth part***, †***deal***: one of four equal parts into which a thing may be divided. See also FARTHINGDEAL.

c **1000** *Ags. Gosp.* Luke iii. 1 Feorþan dæles rica. *c* **1350** [see DEAL *sb.*[1] 1 b]. **1375** Barbour *Bruce* IX. 593 For gif thai fled, thai vist that thai Suld nocht weill ferd part get away. ? *a* **1400** *Morte Arth.* 946 The fourtedele a furlange be-twene þis he walkes. **1480** Caxton *Chron. Eng.* ccxxiii. 221 Yet saw I neuer the ferth part of the wynge fyght. **1585** T. Washington tr. *Nicholay's Voy.* II. v. 35 Two buts of wine of Chio, two fourth parts of muscadell. **1893** Stevenson in *Daily News* 11 Apr. 6/3 Of the remaining three-fourth parts of my said father's estate, one-fourth part of the three-fourth parts I give and bequeath [etc.].

B. *sb.*

1. The fraction indicated by a unit in the fourth place in the sexagesimal, decimal, or any other system of fractional notation having a constant modulus. Hence, in Scotland, a weight of account, $= \frac{1}{712}$ (i.e. $1 \div 24^4$) of a grain Scots.

1594 Blundevil *Exerc.* I. xxvii. (ed. 7) 65 They divide every whole thing that had no usuall parts into 60 minutes, and every minute into 60 seconds, and every second into 60 thirds, and so forth into 60 fourths, fifths, sixths [etc.]. **1604** *Proclam. James I.* in Ruding *Coinage Gt. Brit.* (1840) I. 363 Pieces of Gold.. v.s. 1 denier 23 grains 7 primes, 18 seconds, 8 thirds, $10\frac{3}{4}$ fourths. **1608** R. Norton tr. *Stevin's Disme* C ij, $3^{(1)} 7^{(2)} 5^{(3)} 9^{(4)}$, that is to say, 3 Primes, 7 Seconds, 5 Thirds, 9 Fourths.. of.. valew. **1674** Jeake *Arith.* (1696) 209 As to set down 3 Fourths, and 4 Fifths, thus, 0,00034.

2. = *fourth part.*

1741 tr. *D'Argens Chinese Lett.* xxxi. 229 The idle Fables and gross Lyes, with which Three-fourths of the European Authors stuff their Works. **1892** E. K. Blyth in *Law Times* XCIII. 489/1 The cases requiring pleadings are not more at the outside than a fourth of the contested cases.

3. *Mus.* A tone four diatonic degrees above or below any given tone; the interval between any tone and a tone four degrees distant from it; the harmonic combination of two such tones.

1597 Morley *Introd. Mus.* 71 *Phi.* Which distances make discord or dissonant sounds? *Ma.* All such as doe not make concords: as a second, a fourth. **1674** Playford *Skill Mus.* I. v. 20 This Rule serves for the rising of Fourths or Fifths, etc. **1788** Cavallo in *Phil. Trans.* LXXVIII. 238 When those sounds are considered with respect to the first, they are called.. the prime or key-note.. fourth, fourth major, [etc.]. **1869** Ouseley *Counterp.* ii. 6 The fourth, which in strict counterpoint is always treated as a discord. **1879** Grove *Dict. Mus.* I. s.v., Fourth is an interval comprising two whole tones and a semitone. It is called a fourth because four notes are passed through in going from one extreme of the interval to the other.

4. *pl.* Articles of the fourth degree in quality.

1832 G. R. Porter *Porcelain & Gl.* 186 Crown glass is sold, according to its quality, under four different denominations—firsts, seconds, thirds, and fourths. **1890** *Daily News* 7 Jan. 2/7 Butter.. classified as follows:—Firsts, 0; seconds, 9; thirds, 36; fourths, 9.

†**5.** ***by fourths***: by fours. *Obs.*

c **1430** *Art of Nombrynge* (E.E.T.S.) 17 First thow most compt the figures by fourthes, that is to sey in the place of thousandes.

6. A player who comes in to complete a party of four in a game or at a social event.

1803 *Lett. Miss Riversdale* I. 155 He.. insisted upon Marlow's leaving with him to come and make up a rubber for his sister, knowing he could depend upon me for a fourth. **1841** Dickens *Let.* 10 Feb. (1969) II. 209 Browne.. dines with me... The gay and festive Thompson also joins us. Will you make a fourth? **1865** —— *Mut. Friend* I. II. iv. 196 [He] implores to be asked to.. make a fourth at the play. **1902** E. Glyn *Refl. Ambrosine* 159 The men played Bridge. Augustus made one of the fourths. **1959** T. S. Eliot *Elder Statesman* II. 43 I'll feel more confidence after a fortnight.. of people not staring.. or wanting a fourth at bridge.

7. The fourth forward gear of a motor vehicle.

1900 J. S. V. Bickford *Faults & how to find Them* §1173 Changing down. By this we mean changing from a high speed to a lower (fourth to third, third to second etc.). **1968** *Autocar* 12 Sept. 30/1 By 4,500 rpm (73 mph in fourth, almost 80 mph in fifth) this resonance has practically died away.

8. A place in the fourth class in an examination list.

[**1911** *Encycl. Brit.* X. 42/1 In the 15th century the candidates for the mastership of arts were divided into three classes.. while a fourth, which was not published, contained the names of those who failed.] **1914** C. Mackenzie *Sinister St.* II. III. xi. 714, I shall never get my Blue. I shall get a fourth in Greats. *Ibid.* xii. 746 If he stays up ten years he'll never get a Fourth. **1945** E. Waugh *Brideshead Revisited* I. i. 24 You want either a first or a fourth. There is no value in anything between. **1946** C. L. Wrenn *Word & Symbol* (1967) 163 The consciousness in the minds of the Oxford authorities that Sweet had obtained a 'fourth' in Greats.

C. *Comb.*: **a. fourth arm** (see ARM *sb.*[2] 9); **fourth-born** *a.*, that is born fourth; **Fourth-day**, the name given by members of the Society of Friends to Wednesday; **fourth dimension**, a supposed or assumed dimension, additional to length, breadth, and thickness (see DIMENSION 3 *note*); hence **fourth-dimensional** *a.*, of or relating to the fourth dimension, *fig.* superhuman, extraordinary; hence ***fourth-dimensionalism***; **fourth estate** (see ESTATE *sb.* 7 b); **fourth-hand** *a.*, that has passed through the hands of four persons; **fourth leader**, from 1922 to 1966, the fourth leading article in *The Times*, usually of a light or humorous nature; **fourth (cranial) nerve** *Anat.*, either of the trochlear nerves (see TROCHLEAR *a.* 1), together also called the ***fourth pair of nerves***; **fourth party** *Eng. Hist.*, a group of politicians (1880-85) led by Lord Randolph Churchill, forming a party independent of the three existing political parties; **fourth position** *Dancing* (see quot. 1957); **fourth ventricle** *Anat.*, a rhomboidal cavity situated between the medulla oblongata and the pons Varolii in front and the cerebellum behind; **fourth wall** *Theatr.*, the proscenium opening through which the audience sees the performance; **fourth wheel** (see quot.).

1559 *Mirr. Mag.*, *Dk. Clarence* viii, The *fowerth borne. **1592** Warner *Alb. Eng.* VIII. xi. 196 Gylford Dudly fourth-borne Sonne vnto Northumberland Had married her. **1697** S. Sewall *Diary* 14 Sept. (1878) I. 459 *Fourth-day was a storm, else might have husbanded it so as to have come to Rehoboth that night. **1820** J. H. Wiffen in A. A. Watts *Life A. Watts* (1884) I. 102 She.. must necessarily lay the matter before the monthly meeting next fourth day. **1875** G. H. Lewes *Problems* II. 279 We have no experiences out of which a *fourth dimension could be constructed. **1895** W. D. Howells *My Lit. Passions* 202 The fourth dimension of the poem which is not yet made palpable or visible. **1904** B. Russell in *Mind* XIII. 574 The merit of speculations on the fourth dimension.. is chiefly that they stimulate the imagination, and free the intellect from the shackles of the actual. **1934** *Discovery* Aug. 239/1 The Fourth and higher Dimensions. **1964** C. Chaplin *Autobiogr.* xvii. 303 Wells said that as a struggling young writer he had written one of the first scientific articles touching on the fourth dimension. **1902** E. Carpenter *Civilisation* ii. 70 An immaterial mediation or a *fourth-dimensional mediation.. would simply remove the problem out of the regions of scientific analysis. **1908** *Westm. Gaz.* 28 July 2/1 A forcible proof of superhuman or fourth-dimensional power. **1921** *Quest* Oct. 55 These few crude remarks on fourth-dimensionalism and the time-enigma are ventured solely as the tentative opinions of a layman. **1599** Marston *Sco. Villanie* I. ii. 176 Tail'd, and retail'd, till to the pedlers packe, The *fourth-hand ward-ware comes. [**1946** *Times* 28 June 5/6 Those of your readers who are under a perpetual obligation to the charm of the fourth leading article may like to be reminded of Dr. Johnson's praise of the Scottish breakfast.] **1949** 'M. Innes' *Journeying Boy* vi. 64 He picked up *The Times*... He was mildly diverted by the *fourth leader. **1964** E. S. Turner *How to measure a Woman* 165 *The Times*.. has allowed its Fourth Leader writer, more than once, to drool over the temptation the alarm provides. **1966** *Times* 6 Oct. 9/6 'If it was not so tragic it would make a fine fourth leader for *The Times*,' said a seasoned observer of the Commonwealth Parliamentary Association conferences that meet round the world annually. **1681** S. Pordage tr. *Remaining Med. Works of T. Willis* 140 The *fourth conjugation of nerves (which we call rightly the fourth by order and succession, although it is accounted the eighth and last by Fallopius) hath a diverse origine from all the rest. **1685** S. Collins *Syst. Anat.* II. Tab. xlviii, The Pathetic, or Fourth pair of Nerves. **1858** Gray *Anat.* 478 The Fourth, or trochlear nerve, is the smallest of the cranial nerves. **1963** Brock & Krieger *Basis Clin. Neurol.* (ed. 4) xii. 189 The superior oblique muscle [of the eye] is innervated by the fourth nerve. **1880** H. Wolff *Let.* 29 Sept. in W. S. Churchill *Ld. R. Churchill* (1906) I. 166 My dear Randolph,—After you left yesterday I received two very handsome tributes to the *Fourth Party. **1897** J. McCarthy *Hist. Own*

Times from 1880 to Jubilee 27 Now came Lord Randolph with his new group, having its distinct individual purpose, and it claimed to be recognised as the Fourth party. **1966** R. S. CHURCHILL *Winston Churchill* I. iii. 44 This led to the formation of the Fourth Party—Lord Randolph Churchill, Sir Henry Drummond Wolff, Mr John Gorst, with Mr Arthur Balfour, Lord Salisbury's nephew, in loose attendance. **1884** D. ANDERSON *Compl. Ball-Room Guide* 10 **Fourth position*, put out right foot in a straight line with left toe, right heel about four inches from left toe. **1957** G. B. L. WILSON *Dict. Ballet* 124 In the fourth position..one foot is placed before the other in an extension of the first position with the weight evenly distributed, both feet being fully turned out and separated by a distance of about one foot. **1578** J. BANISTER *Hist. Man* f. 100ᵛ The *fourth ventricle is not much capable, and is comprehended of the thinne membran. **1685** S. COLLINS *Syst. Anat.* II. Tab. l, The Scobs which makes the fourth ventricle. **1848** *Quain's Elem. Anat.* (ed. 5) II. 723 The fourth ventricle, or ventricle of the cerebellum. **1962** *Gray's Ant.* (ed. 33) 956 The cavity of the rhombencephalon is expanded to form the fourth ventricle. **1807** L. HUNT *Crit. Ess.* 60 The stage appears to be his room, of which the audience compose the *fourth wall. **1910** E. F. SPENCE *Our Stage* v. 111 That fourth wall, the existence of which Mr. Jerome K. Jerome rather quaintly..suggested by the fender and fireirons laid in front of the foot-lights. **1959** *Listener* 4 June 997/2 His music-hall experience made him aware of the artificiality of the 'fourth wall' which in the legitimate theatre separates the stage from the auditorium: the music-hall comedian speaks directly to the audience. **1967** *Times* 19 Apr. 6/4 In the last act, Andrey..breaks the fourth wall and delivers his assault..straight out to the audience. **1884** BRITTEN *Watch and Clockm.*, **Fourth Wheel*, the wheel in a watch that drives the escape pinion, and to the arbor of which the seconds hand is attached.

b. Prefixed to certain sbs., as *class*, *form*, *rate*, etc. forming a comb. which is used attrib. and passes occas. into an *adj.*, and through the absolute use into a *sb.* ***fourth-class matter*** (*U.S. Postal system*), matter containing merchandise.

1689 *Lond. Gaz.* No. 2453/2 Their Majesties Ship the Nonsuch, a small fourth Rate of 36 Guns. **1694** *Ibid.* No. 3021/3 This day were Launched..two new fourth Rate Ships. **1857** HUGHES *Tom Brown* I. vi. The fourth form are uncertain in their belief. *Ibid.* I. vii. [A] fourth-form boy. **1889** *Advance* (Chicago) 7 Mar. 190 More sham than school, taught by fourth-rate teachers, because they are cheap.

Hence **'fourthly** *adv.*, in the fourth place, †for the fourth time.

1526 *Pilgr. Perf.* (W. de W. 1531) 8 b, Fourthly they must trust onely in the grace & mercy of god. **1613** SYLVESTER (*title*), Du Bartas his Deuine Weekes and Workes..Now fourthly corr: and augm. **1772** *Ann. Reg.* 247/2 Fourthly, Because [etc.].

fourvey(e, var. of FORVAY *v. Obs.*

four-went, *a. dial.* [f. FOUR + *went*, pa. pple. of WEND to turn.] Only in ***four-went way***(*s*, a point where four roads meet.

1777 T. FISHER *Kent. Trav. Comp.* (1787) 50 This lane will bring the traveller to a four-went way. **1865** *Monthly Packet* June 609 A 'four-want-way', where suicides were buried in times past.

'four-wheel, *sb.* A four-wheeled carriage.

1848 CLOUGH *Bothie* I. 45 In the four wheel they drove to the place of the clansmen's meeting. **1859** HUGHES *Scouring W. Horse* vi. 119, I would go behind in the four-wheel.

'four-wheel, *a.* **1.** Of a horse-drawn or motor vehicle: = FOUR-WHEELED *a.*

1740 W. ELLIS *Mod. Husb.* I. 131 Four-wheel Carriages.. go easier, when the Weight..is laid on the hinder Wheels. **1777** P. THICKNESSE *Year's Journey* I. iii. 16, I have sold my four-wheel post-chaise. **1820** J. S. FRY *Ess. Constr. Wheel-Carriages* vi. 75 A four-wheel Coach, as at present constructed. **1902** P. N. HASLUCK *Automobile* xviii. 441 The Decauville voiturette is the first of the four-wheel voiturettes to be described.

2. Of the braking or driving system of a motor vehicle: operating on all the four wheels.

1924 *Nation* 29 Oct. 461 Vast multitudes are entirely content, entirely occupied with their four-wheel brakes and their radios. **1926** *Encycl. Brit.* I. 229 Another vehicle, of a different type, is the '4-wheel drive' lorry, in which the wheels are driven independently. **1956** 'N. SHUTE' *Beyond Black Stump* ii. 60 A big four-wheel-drive truck. **1969** *Times* 12 May 16/2 A four-wheel drive forward control tractor.

'four-wheeled, *a.* [f. FOUR *a.* + WHEEL *sb.* + -ED².] Having or running upon four wheels.

1622 in *Crt. & Times Jas. I* (1849) II. 327 One [proclamation] against four-wheeled carts or waggons, that with their weight mar and tear the highways. **1725** POPE *Odyss.* IX. 286 Scarce twenty four-wheel'd cars, compact and strong, The massy load could bear. **1865** TROLLOPE *Belton Est.* i. 14 The four-wheeled carriage..came to the door.

transf. **1876** T. HARDY *Ethelberta* (1890) 230 She might pull up some distance short of the castle, and leave the ass at a cottage before joining her four-wheeled friends.

four-'wheeler. [f. FOUR + WHEEL *sb.* + -ER¹.] A vehicle with four wheels; *esp.* a four-wheeled hackney carriage.

1846 JAS. TAYLOR *Upper Canada* 26 Farmers' wives.. enter the market with their neat four-wheeler and pair. **1860** *All Year Round* No. 44. 415 A four-wheeler is let to a driver for about twelve shillings a day. **1874** W. BLACK *Princ. Thule* x, He, having sent on all their luggage by a respectable old four-wheeler, got into the hansom beside her.

†**fous**, *a. Obs.* Forms: 1 fús, 2–3 fus, (3 fuus, fuss), 3–5 fous, (*south* vous(e). [OE. *fús* = OS. *fús*, OHG. *funs*, ON. *fúss*:—OTeut. **funso-*:—pre-Teut. **pn̥t-to-*, f. root **pent-*, *pont-*, *pn̥t-* to go, set out; cf. FIND, FAND, FOUND *vbs.*] Eager, ready. Const. with *of*, *to*, and *inf.*

Beowulf (Z.) 1805 Wæron æðelingas eft to leodum fuse to farenne. *c* **1200** ORMIN 16997 He wass fus to lernenn. *a* **1300** *Cursor M.* 21881 He sends us þis all in warning..Of vr saul to be ai fus. *Ibid.* 23749 þe flexs es ai to filthes fus. **1460** *Lybeaus Disc.* 288 To dele ech man rappes Ever he was fous.

Hence **'fouse** *v.*, *intr.* and *trans.*, to hasten.

Substituted in the later text of Layamon II. 19546 and 29780 for FUSE (*ü*).

fousie, -y: see FOWSIE.

foussa, var. FOSSA².

fous(s)on, fousty, obs. ff. FOISON, FUSTY.

†**foutch.** *Obs.* [Cf. *fouchon*, FALCHION.] ? = FALCHION.

1580 HOLLYBAND *Treas. Fr. Tong*, *Malcus*, a foutch, a kinde of sword.

fouth (fu:θ). *Sc.* Also 6 fouht, fowith, 6–8 fowth. [Sc. form of FULTH.] Fullness, plenty. †*at fouth*: in plenty.

1501 DOUGLAS *Pal. Hon.* III. xiii, Thow sall haue fouth of sentence and not scant. **1535** STEWART *Cron. Scot.* III. 509 Of neidfull thing weill furneist all at fouth. **1725** RAMSAY *Gentle Sheph.* I. i, I..took a fouth O' sweetest kisses frae her glowing mouth. **1837** R. NICOLL *Poems* (1842) 84 The earth has fouth o' trusty hearts.

foutre, fouter ('fu:tə(r)). Forms: 6–7 footra, footre, fowtre, 7 foutra, foutree, foutir, 9 fouter. [a. OF. *foutre*:—L. *futuĕre* (the inf. used subst.).]

1. In phrases, ***a foutre for***, (***to care***) ***not a fouter.***

[*a* **1592** GREENE *James IV*, v. ii, *Jaques*..faites bonne chere: foutre de ce monde!] **1597** SHAKS. *2 Hen. IV*, v. iii. 103 A footra [*Q.* footre] for the World, and Worldlings base. **1622** FLETCHER *Sea Voy.* v. i, Therefore footra, When I am full, let 'em hang me, I care not. **1638** SUCKLING *Goblins* III. (1646) 26 Shall I so?—why then foutree for the Guise. **1871** R. ELLIS *Catullus* xvii. 17 He leaves her alone to romp idly, cares not a fouter.

2. Applied contemptuously to persons.

1780–1808 J. MAYNE *Siller Gun* III. xxv, The astonish'd tailor..swearing he was better stuff Than sick a fouter. **1786** *Harvest Rig* in *R. Chambers' Pop. Poems Scotl.* (1862) 50 A sutor, Most manfully about does lay—A tough auld fouter. **1833** MARRYAT *P. Simple* (1863) 145 O'Brien declared that he was a liar, and a cowardly *foutre*.

†**'fouty**, *a. Obs.* Also futie. [Sc. f. of FOOTY *a.*¹] = FOOTY *a.*¹

1722 HAMILTON *Wallace* XII. vi. 353 He..beat out another fouty Rascal's Brains. **1785** R. FORBES *Poems in Buchan Dial.* 31 Then to blame me Is futie an' mislear'd.

fovea ('fəʊvɪə). *Anat.*, *Zool.*, *Bot.* [a. L. *fovea* small pit.] A small depression or pit; *esp.* a depression of the retina of the eye; ***fovea centralis***, the fovea of the retina.

1849 JOHNSTON in *Proc. Berw. Nat. Club* II. No. 7. 364 A ..furrow..beginning behind the eye..terminating in a deeper fovea, and with a foveola near the centre. **1858** GRAY *Anat.* 560 In the centre of the posterior part of the globe, the retina presents a yellow spot..having a central depression, *fovea centralis*. **1882** VINES *Sachs' Bot.* 480 In consequence of cell-division..the sporangium soon appears as a swelling in the fovea. **1924** R. M. OGDEN tr. *Koffka's Growth of Mind* iii. 71 The eye is turned until the fixated object falls upon the place of clearest vision lying at the centre of the retina (the *fovea centralis*). **1970** T. S. & C. R. LEESON *Histol.* (ed. 2) xx. 488 The fovea centralis is a shallow, rounded pit lying 4 mm. to the temporal side of the optic disk.

†**'foveable**, *a. Obs. rare*⁻¹. [f. prec. + -ABLE.]

1541 COPLAND *Guydon's Quest. Chirurg.*, Other [bones] be foueable or holow.

foveal ('fəʊvɪəl), *a.* [f. FOVEA + -AL¹.] Of or pertaining to or situated in a fovea.

1889 in *Cent. Dict.* **1904** *Westm. Gaz.* 15 June 1/3 In the *fovea centralis* there are cones only, so that in direct or foveal vision the rods are out of play. **1931** *Brit. Jrnl. Psychol.* Jan. 286 Some persons possess a quite appreciable proportion of foveal rods. **1962** H. C. WESTON *Sight, Light & Work* (ed. 2) i. 4 Each of these foveal cones has its own separate nerve path to the brain. **1966** M. KABRISKY *Proposed Model Visual Information Processing Human Brain* ii. 19 The 100,000 foveal receptors are allocated about 100,000 channels in the optic nerve, leaving the rest of the 125 million receptors only about 900,000 channels.

foveate ('fəʊvi:eɪt), *a.* [f. FOVEA + -ATE².] = next.

1854 in MAYNE *Expos. Lex.* **1866** in *Treas. Bot.*

foveated ('fəʊvi:eɪtɪd), *a. Anat.*, *Zool.*, *Bot.* [f. as prec. + -ED¹.] Marked with foveæ, pitted.

1846 HARDY in *Proc. Berw. Nat. Club* II. No. 14. 196 Thorax..less deeply foveated at the base. **1883** *Quain's Med. Dict.* s.v. *Vaccination*, There is then left a cicatrix, which is circular, somewhat depressed, foveated, etc.

†**'fovent**, *a. Obs. rare*⁻¹. [ad. L. *fovent-em*, pr. pple. of *fovēre* to keep warm.] Producing pleasant or salutary warmth.

1614 RALEIGH *Hist. World* II. (1634) 272 All Starres haue a certain fovent heate.

‖**foveola** (fəʊ'vi:ələ). [L. dim. of FOVEA.] A small fovea.

1849 [see FOVEA].

foveolate ('fəʊvi:ələt), *a.* [f. prec. + -ATE.] Marked with little depressions or pits; pitted.

1848 JOHNSTON in *Proc. Berw. Nat. Club* II. No. 6. 289 The back flattened, foveolate.

foveolated ('fəʊvi:əleɪtɪd), *ppl. a.* [f. prec. + -ED.] = FOVEOLATE.

1819 G. SAMOUELLE *Entomol. Compend.* 168 Foveolated thorax. **1847** HARDY in *Proc. Berw. Nat. Club* II. 249 Head oblong-ovate..obsoletely foveolated on the forehead.

foveole ('fəʊvi:əʊl). [ad. L. *foveola*: see FOVEOLA.] A foveola; in *Bot.* 'the perithecium of certain fungals' (*Treas. Bot.* 1866).

fovilla (fəʊ'vɪlə). *Bot.* [mod.Lat., used by Linnæus in 1766 (*Syst. Nat.* II. 6).] The substance contained in the pollen-cells.

In ed. 1735 Linnæus calls it *farina*, in 1744 *pulvis*, in 1758 *elater*; it is stated (Bischoff *Bot. Term.*) that he somewhere uses the word *favilla* in the same sense. Perh. *fovilla* is an alteration of *favilla*, suggested by the word *fovere* to cherish, which actually occurs in the context in ed. 1766.

1793 MARTYN *Lang. Bot.*, *Fovilla*, a fine substance, imperceptible to the naked eye, exploded by the pollen in the anthers of flowers. **1816** KEITH *Phys. Bot.* 114 Emitting a subtile and elastic vapour, or sort of fovilla which swims on the surface. **1870** BENTLEY *Bot.* 255 The matter contained within the coat or coats of the pollen-cell is called the fovilla.

†**fow**, *v. Obs.* Also 7 foe. [a. ON. *fága*: see FAY *v.*²] *trans.* To clean, cleanse (*out*). Also *fig.*

13.. *Sir Beues* 1120 (MS. A.) Beter be-come þe iliche, For to fowen an olde diche þanne for to be dobbed kniȝt. *c* **1350** *Med. MS.* in *Archæologia* XXX. 351 Chyldys vryne þin ere fowe, And helpe þin ere on a throwe. *c* **1440** *Jacob's Well* (E.E.T.S.) 266 Take mekenes in herte, & þat schal fowyn out all trouble and vnreste. **1530** PALSGR. 557/2 Thou shalte eate no buttered fysshe with me, tyll thou wasshe thy handes, for thou hast fowed a gonge late. **1633** T. ADAMS *Exp. 2 Peter* i. 10 They are only good, when on the sabbath day they are fowing tap-houses.

Hence †**'fowing** *vbl. sb.* Also †**'fower**, one who cleanses.

c **1440** *Promp. Parv.* 174/2 Foware, or clensare of donge, as gongys, and oper lyke, *fimarius*, *oblitor*. *Ibid.* 175/1 Fowynge, or clensynge, *emundacio*. **1636** JAMES *Iter Lanc.* (Chetham Soc.) 9 *note*, He had found six thousand infants' heads in the foing of his fish ponds.

fow, var. of FOU *a. Sc.*, full, drunk.

†**fow(e.** *Obs.* A kind of fur. See FAW *a.* 2.

fowage, var. of FEUAGE, *Obs.*

1523 LD. BERNERS *Froiss.* V. ccxli. 351/2 This fowage.. shulde have been well worthe every yere a xii thousand from euery fyer to have payed yerely a franke. **1529** RASTELL *Pastyme, Hist. Brit.* (1811) 225 He levyed a fowage in Guyan agaynst the myndes of the lordes. **1592** WYRLEY *Armorie* 84 Wanting which a fowage was desierd To pay the soldiers for this iourney hierd. **1611** SPEED *Hist. Gt. Brit.* IX. xii. §136 The Prince of Wales had..propounded a demaund for fowage, or of money to be leuied by the Chimney. **1834** SIR H. TAYLOR *1st Pt. Artevelde* II. vi, What were the fowage and the subsidies When bread was but four mites that's now a groat?

fowayle, -el, obs. ff. of FUEL.

fowe, var. of FAW *a. Obs.*; obs. f. of FEW *a.*

fowie, *a. Sc.* [f. *fow*, FULL.] Jolly-looking.

1590 A. HUME *Hymns, &c.* (1832) 9 Why monethly the Moone renewes hir hew and hornes so paill, Why monethlie hir fowie face is round and lightned haill.

†**'fowker.** *Obs.* [a. Ger. *fucker*: see FOGGER, FOOKER.] A capitalist, financier.

1630 *R. Johnson's Kingd. & Commw.* 72 Some great Fowker or Agent for a whole kingdome.

†**'fowkin.** *Obs. rare*⁻¹. = FART *sb.*

?*a* **1600** *Turnament of Totenham* 89 He gurde so fast his gray mare, That she lete a fowkyn fare At the rewarde.

fowl (faʊl), *sb.* Forms: 1 fuȝel, -ol, -ul, 2–3 fuȝel, -hel, -wel, *south.* vuhel, 3–4 foȝel, *south.* voȝel, (3 feoȝel, fohȝel), 4–5 foghel, -il(l, -ul, (4 fughil, foxl, -ul, foxul, -ul, fuxl, fuxol, -ul, 5 foghle), 3–7 foul(e, 3–4 fou-, fowel, (*south.* vowel), fuel, 4 fule, (fouul), 5 f(e)wle, -ylle, 4–7 fowle, 6– fowl. [Com. Teutonic; OE. *fuȝel*, *fuȝol*, *fuȝul* str. masc. = OFris. *fugel*, OS. *fugol* (Du. *vogel*), OHG. *fogal* (MHG. and Ger. *vogel*), ON. *fugl* (Sw. *fogel*, Da. *fugl*), Goth. *fugls*:—OTeut. **foglo-z*, *fuglo-z*; usually believed to be a dissimilated form of **floglo-*, *fluglo-*, f. *flug-* to FLY; cf. the OE. adj. *fluȝol* 'fugax', and the form *fluȝlas heofun* in the Rushworth Gloss. Matt. xiii. 32, rendering *volucres cæli*; the Lindisf. gloss has *fleȝende*, the Wessex gospel *fuhlas*.]

The forms containing *x* are from the Cotton MS. of the *Cursor Mundi*; perh. miscopied from an original which had ȝ (or possibly þ).

1. a. Any feathered vertebrate animal; = BIRD *sb.* 2 (q.v. with note attached). Now *rare* exc. *collect.*

Beowulf 218 (Gr.) Gewat þa ofer wæȝholm winde ȝefysed flota famiȝheals fuȝle ȝelicost. *c* **1000** *Ags. Gosp.* Matt. viii. 20 Foxas habbað holu and heofenan fuȝlas [*c* **1160** *Hatton* fuȝeles] nest. *c* **1175** *Lamb. Hom.* 81 A vuhel com flon from houene into orðe. *a* **1225** *Ancr. R.* 298 We speken of fuwelene cunde, þet beoð iefned to ancre. *a* **1300** *Cursor M.*

621 Fiss on sund, and fouxl on flight. **1340** *Ayenb.* 254 þe herte is ase þe uoȝel þet wolde vly to his wylle. **1375** BARBOUR *Bruce* VII. 188 Tharfor he slepit as foul on twist. *c* **1450** *Mirour Saluacioun* 1002 Thi son wham we..seke als foghil the day. **1526** *Pilgr. Perf.* (W. de W. 1531) 2 b, Fowles, & all other creatures..hath place deputed..to them. **1597** MONTGOMERIE *Cherrie & Slae* 460, I leuir haue euer Ane foule in hand, or tway, Nor seand ten fleand About me. **1599** SHAKS. *Much Ado* II. iii. 95 Stalke on, stalke on, the foule sits. **1607** TOPSELL *Four-f. Beasts* (1658) 213 To defend them from Eagles and other ravening Fowls. **1640** FULLER *Joseph's Coat, David's Punishm.* xxii. (1867) 235, I for your fowls of Phasis do not care. **1719** DE FOE *Crusoe* I. xxv, I saw a great fowl, like a hawk, sit upon a tree. **1791** COWPER *Iliad* XVII. 293 And the fowls sate with his flesh.

collect. **1603** DRAYTON *Bar. Wars* VI. lxv, The fearefull Fowle all prostrate to her power. **1605** CAMDEN *Rem.* (1637) 1 Stored with infinite delicate fowle. **1769** GOLDSM. *Rom. Hist.* (1786) II. 273 In this was served up..seven thousand fowl of the most valuable kinds. **1865** KINGSLEY *Herew.* xvi, All the fowl of heaven were flocking to the feast.

†**b.** In narrower sense: Winged game. *Obs.*

1646 EVELYN *Mem.* (1857) I. 252 Sometimes we shot at fowls and other birds: nothing came amiss. **1763** H. WALPOLE *Vertue's Anecd. Paint.* III. 85 In the great anti-chamber [at Chatsworth] are several dead fowl over the chimney finely executed.

†**c.** With some modifying addition; as, ***fowl of chase, flight, game, prey, ravin.*** *Obs.*

c **1381** CHAUCER *Parl. Foules* 323 The foules of ravyne Were hyest set. **1398** TREVISA *Barth. De P.R.* XII. vi. (1495) 416 The owle semyth lyke to foules of pray. *c* **1420** *Chron. Vilod.* 280 Wyld bestes and folys of flyȝt. **1485** CAXTON *Paris & V.* 26 Faulcens and many other fowles of chace. **1671** MILTON *P.R.* II. 342 Beasts of chase, or fowl of game In pastry built.

fig. *a* **1300** *Cursor M.* 21276 (Gött.) þe firth Iohn, fowel of [*Cotton MS.* on] flight.

d. A troublesome sailor, one unamenable to discipline. *slang.*

1937 in PARTRIDGE *Slang Dict.* **1938** 'GIRALDUS' *Merry Matloe Again* 145, I was a 'fowl' of the first water. I was always getting 'run-in', always in trouble and had no zeal for the Navy whatsoever.

†**2.** In wider sense: Winged creatures. Also *collect.* in plural sense. *Obs.*

1382 WYCLIF *Ecclus.* xi. 3 Short in foules [Vulg. *in volatilibus*] is a bee. **1398** TREVISA *Barth. De P.R.* XII. Introd. (Tollem. MS.), To þe ornament of þe eyer parteyneþ briddes and foules [*volatilia*]. **1613** PURCHAS *Pilgrimage* VIII. x. 789 They offered to him [the Sunne] Fowles, from the Butter-flie to the Eagle. **1648** GAGE *West Ind.* xii. (1655) 45 Battes, or Rear-mice and other fowle.

3. The prevailing sense: A 'barn-door fowl', a domestic cock or hen; a bird of the genus *Gallus*. In the U.S. applied also to 'a domestic duck or turkey' (*Cent. Dict.*). Often with some modifying word prefixed: as, ***barn-door-, game-, guinea-fowl***, for which see those words.

1580 SIDNEY *Arcadia* III. (1590) 311 As folkes keep foul when they are not fat enough for their eating. **1697** DAMPIER *Voy.* I. iv. 76 The Inhabitants plant Corn..and breed a few Fowls. **1841** LANE *Arab. Nts.* I. 123 Fowls simply roasted or boiled. **1879** FARRAR *St. Paul* (1883) 43 The Talmud.. devotes one whole treatise..to the method of killing a fowl.

4. a. The flesh of birds used for food. Now only in the phrases ***fish, flesh, and fowl***, etc. **b.** In narrower sense: The flesh of the 'barn-door' or domestic fowl.

1673 O. WALKER *Educ.* (1677) 169 A feast suggests..Fish, Foul, Flesh. **1861** BEETON *Bk. Househ. Man.* §978 Fricasseed Fowl. Ingredients—The remains of cold roast fowl [etc.].

5. *attrib.* and *Comb.* **a.** simple attrib., as ***fowl-flight, -house, -net, -yard.*** **b.** objective, as ***fowl-keeping, -rearing, -stealer, -stealing.*** **c.** Special comb., as **fowl-cholera** = *chicken-cholera*: see CHOLERA 4; **fowl-foot**, the plant *Ornithopus perpusillus*; **fowl-grass, fowl-meadow-grass**, *Poa trivialis*; **fowl paralysis**, Marek's disease, a type of cancer affecting poultry; **fowl pest**, (*a*) = *fowl plague*; (*b*) = *Newcastle disease*; **fowl plague**, an acute, highly contagious virus disease of the domestic fowl and other birds that is usually fatal; **fowl pox**, a virus disease of the domestic fowl and other birds, in which lesions appear on feather-free parts of the body or on the mucous membranes of the mouth, nose, or throat; **fowl-run**, a place where fowls may run, an establishment for breeding fowls.

1883 *Gd. Words* 179 The epidemic among fowls, called *fowl-cholera. *c* **1250** *Gen. & Ex.* 3321 At euen cam a *fuȝel-fliȝt, fro-ward arabie. **1578** LYTE *Dodoens* IV. xxix. 487 *Ornithopodium*..This wild herbe is called in Brabant Uoghelvoet, that is to say in English, Birdes foote, or *Fowle foote, bycause his huskes or cods are lyke to a birdes foote. **1839** *Lincoln, etc. Gaz.* 12 Feb. 3/4 They went to Mr. F.'s; whose *fowl-house they broke open. **1894** *Jrnl. R. Agric. Soc.* June 303 It is *fowl-keeping on this modest scale that pays. **1774** J. Q. ADAMS *Diary* 28 Feb., Shall I try to introduce *fowl-meadow, and herds-grass into the meadows? **1786** M. CUTLER in *Life, Jrnls. & Corr.* (1888) II. 264 Fowl meadow-grass is cultivated in wet meadows. **1856** KANE *Arct. Expl.* II. xiii. 134 Tinkering over..*fowl-nets or other household-gear. **1932** *Ann. Reg. Scientific Poultry Breeders' Assoc.* 75 There seems little doubt that there is a special condition affecting poultry which, for want of a better name, is termed *fowl paralysis. **1960** *Farmer & Stockbreeder* Suppl. 22 Mar. 1/2 An outstanding feature is the resistance to leucosis and fowl paralysis. **1909** WEBSTER, *Fowl pest. **1912** J. R. MOHLER et al. tr. *Hutyra & Marek's Spec. Path. Dis. Dom. Animals* I. I. xiii. 290 Fowl pest is an acute, contagious, infectious disease of fowls. **1953** 'M. INNES' *Christmas at Candleshoe* x. 110 The other gentlemen had fallen into a grave discourse of fowl-pest, hard-pad and foot-and-mouth disease. **1970** *Times* 21 Oct. 10/1 The current upsurge of fowl pest is at its most destructive in the factory farming units. **1937** *Poultry World Ann.* 82 *Fowl plague or pest is a very highly infectious disease caused by a virus... The so-called Newcastle Disease closely resembles Fowl plague in many respects, but is caused by a different virus. **1970** *Q. Poultry Bull.* (Brit. Oil & Cake Mills) Dec. 13 The Fowl Pest Order of 1936 with amendments lays down the legislation governing both Newcastle Disease and Fowl Plague. **1908** M. H. HAYES tr. *Friedberger & Fröhner's Vet. Path.* (ed. 6) II. 425 The causative agents in *fowl-pox belong to the group of so-called filtrable agents of infection. **1932** GAIGER & DAVIES *Vet. Path. & Bact.* xxvii. 388 Fowl-pox occurs naturally in fowls, turkeys and other birds. **1953** L. ROBINSON *Mod. Poultry Husbandry* xx. 551 Fowl pox is extremely contagious. **1894** *Jrnl. R. Agric. Soc.* June 302 A point of cardinal importance..in..*fowl-rearing. **1886** H. F. LESTER *Under Two Fig Trees* 179 In one corner of the little estate is a *fowl-run. **1825** *Sporting Mag.* XVI. 336 Have we ..no *fowl stealers. **1892** *Pall Mall G.* 24 Mar. 2/1 Poaching is closely allied to *fowl-stealing. **1889** *Ibid.* 27 May 2/3 The lack of interest displayed in their *fowl-yards by..British farmers.

fowl (faʊl), *v.* [OE. *fuȝ(e)lian*, f. *fuȝel* FOWL.] *intr.* To catch, hunt, shoot, or snare wildfowl.

c **1000** ÆLFRIC *Gram.* xxv. (Z.) 146 *Aucupor*, ic fuȝlie. **1399** LANGL. *Rich. Redeles* II. 157 Thus ffoulyd this ffaukyn on ffyldis abouȝte. **1519** *Presentm. Juries* in *Surtees Misc.* (1888) 32 þ[t] no man fyshe nor fewle in the dam. **1530** PALSGR. 557/2, I fowle after byrdes, *Je vas a la pipée.* **1697** DAMPIER *Voy.* I. vii. 192 The Tenour of them [Commissions] is, to give a Liberty to fish, fowl, and hunt. **1766** BLACKSTONE *Comm.* II. xxvii. 419 Such persons as may thus lawfully hunt, fish, or fowl. **1850** MRS. JAMESON *Leg. Monast. Ord.* (1863) 86 He went out fowling in a small skiff.

†**b.** *fig.* with *after, for.*

a **1420** HOCCLEVE *De Reg. Princ.* 2442 But tonge of man.. Nat may be tamed..And after repreef fissheth, clappeth, fouleth. **1596** DALRYMPLE tr. *Leslie's Hist. Scot.* VI. 314 Heir hes thou a commodious and meit place for the slauchtir, that thou foules for.

†**c.** quasi-*trans.* To hunt over, beat (a bush).

1611 B. JONSON *Catiline* I. i, They..Fowl every brook and bush to please Their wanton taste.

fowl(e, obs. forms of FOAL, FOUL.

fowler ('faʊlə(r)). [OE. *fuȝelere*, agent-n. f. *fuȝelian* to FOWL.]

1. One who hunts wild birds, whether for sport or food, *esp.* with nets; a bird-catcher. Now *rare.*

c **893** K. ÆLFRED *Oros.* I. i. §14 Ðær huntan ȝewico don oþþe fisceras oþþe fuȝeleras. *a* **1225** *St. Marher.* 3 As þe fuhel þe is fon i þe fuheleres grune. **1382** WYCLIF *Amos* iii. 5 Wher a brid shal falle into grane of erthe, withouten a fouler. *c* **1385** CHAUCER *L.G.W.* Prol. 138 The foweler we deffye, And al his crafte. *c* **1430** LYDG. *Min. Poems* 186 A bleryeed fowler trust not though he wepe. **1657** W. COLES *Adam in Eden* 305 Boyes and Fowlers use the Berries [of the Ash] as Baites to catch Blackbirds, etc. **1723** *Lond. Gaz.* No. 6222/9 Simon Teatford..Fisher and Fowler. **1815** ELPHINSTONE *Acc. Caubul* (1842) I. 77 Fowlers catching quails among the wheat. **1879** JEFFERIES *Wild Life in S.C.* 296 A fowler..had a cock chaffinch in a cage covered with a black cloth.

fig. **1340** *Ayenb.* 254 þe herte ualþ ofte into þe grines of the uoȝelere of helle.

Comb. **1685** CROWNE *Sir C. Nice* Epil., There fowler-like the watching gallant pores Behind his glove.

†**2.** A species of catapult. *Obs.*

1420 *Siege Rouen* in *Archæol.* XXI. 52 A stronge fowlere there was leyde lowe..that he miȝt throwe.

†**3.** A kind of light cannon, *esp.* for use on board ship. *Obs.* Cf. Du. *vogheler*, whence Fr. *veuglaire*.

1548 *Privy Council Acts* (1890) II. 197 The municions folowing..fowlers of iron xij. **1622** R. HAWKINS *Voy. S. Sea* (1847) 206 Fowlers and great bases in the cage workes. **1642** SIR W. MONSON *Naval Tracts* III. (1704) 357/1 Fowlers.. are Pieces of greatest Importance, after a Ship is Boarded.

fowlerite ('faʊləraɪt). *Min.* [named after Dr. S. Fowler: see -ITE.] A flesh-red variety of rhodonite containing zinc.

1832 C. U. SHEPARD *Min.* 186 Fowlerite. Ferro-Silicate of Manganese. **1884** in *Dana's Min.*

fowlery. A place where fowls are kept.

1845 *Bachel. Albany* (1848) 185 A fowlery and a piggery.

fowling ('faʊlɪŋ), *vbl. sb.* [f. FOWL *v.* + -ING[1].]

1. The action of the vb. FOWL; the art or practice of hunting, shooting, or snaring wild fowl.

1413 *Pilgr. Sowle* (Caxton 1483) IV. xxxvii. §84 Alle suche labourers that trauaylen..in fysshyng and fowlynge. **1555** EDEN *Decades* 83 Owre Spanyardes..are ignorant in foulynge. **1663** PEPYS *Diary* (1875) II. 210 His birding-piece going off, as he was a-fowling. **1743** BULKELEY & CUMMINS *Voy. S. Seas* 62 Launch'd the Yawl to go a fowling; shot several Geese, Ducks..and Sea-pies. **1879** DIXON *Windsor* I. iv. 38 Exercise in riding and fowling had kept him spare.

2. *attrib.* and *Comb.*, as ***fowling-cutter, -gun, -net, -pole.***

1882 SIR R. PAYNE-GALLWEY *Fowler in Ireland* v, A *fowling-cutter on the bleak coast of a wide estuary. **1647** *Archives of Maryland* IV. 323 Tho. Greene..demandeth of Richard Span a *fowling Gunne. **1847** *Knickerbocker* XXX. 239 Reader, in your younger days you have, no doubt, left your fowling gun slyly hid in a fence corner. **1530** J. HALL in Weaver *Wells Wills* (1890) 114 Xij hangyng and *fowlyng netts. **1810** G. LANDT *Descr. Feroe Islands* 241 They are caught with the *fowling-pole and net.

'fowling-piece. [f. prec. + PIECE *sb.*]

1. A light gun for shooting wild fowl.

1596 *Lanc. Wills* III. 4 A foulinge piece. **1643** [ANGIER] *Lanc. Vall. Achor* 31 God sent a deadly messenger out of a Fowling-Piece to one of them. **1727–41** CHAMBERS *Cycl.* s.v., Of Fowling pieces, those are reputed the best, which have the longest barrel. **1839** G. BIRD *Nat. Phil.* 130 The well-known double report of a fowling-piece, fired at a distance. *a* **1864** HAWTHORNE *S. Felton* (1883) 244 The old fowling-piece of seven-foot barrel.

2. A picture of game.

1888 *Athenæum* 7 Jan. 21/2 The fowling-piece, which is something like the fine picture at the Prado.

†**'fowl-kin.** [OE. *fuȝel-cynn*, see FOWL and KIN.] **a.** The race of birds. **b.** A species of bird.

c **1000** ÆLFRIC *Gen.* i. 30 Eallum nytenum and eallum fuȝelcynne. *c* **1175** *Lamb. Hom.* 95 Forðon þe þet fuȝel-cun is swiðe bilehwit. *c* **1205** LAY. 8109 Of an fohȝel [*c* **1275** foȝel] cunne ne mai hit na mon kennen. *a* **1250** *Owl & Night.* 65 Thu art loth al fuel-kunne.

fowness, Sc. var. of FULLNESS.

†**'fowsie.** *Obs.* Also 6 fous(s)ie, -y, fowse(a. Sc. form of FOSSÉ, ditch.

1501 DOUGLAS *Pal. Hon.* III. lxxxviii, That gudlie garth.. Quhilk with a large fousie..Inueronit was. *a* **1572** KNOX *Hist. Ref.* Wks. 1846 I. 175 His head was brokin..and he castin in the fowsea. **1637** ADAMSON in R. Ford *Harp of Perthsh.* (1893) 5 Turning home we spared nor dyke nor fowsie. [**1861** W. BELL *Dict. Law Scot.*, *Fossa*, a pit or fowsie.]

fowsome, fowte, Sc. var. of FULSOME, FOOT.

fox (fɒks), *sb.* Also 3–7 foxe, 3, 4, 6 vox, (6 wox). [Com. Teut.: OE. *fox* str. masc. corresponds to Du. *vos*, OHG. *fuhs* (MHG. *vuhs*, mod. Ger. *fuchs*); the ON. *fox* neut., fraud, may be a different word. The OTeut. type is **fuhs-*, from the same root as the feminine formation OHG. *foha* (MHG. *vohe*, vixen, fox, ON. *fóa*, Goth. *fauhô* fox, f. OTeut. **fuh-*:—pre-Teut. **puk-*, which some scholars plausibly connect with Skr. *puccha* tail.

With regard to the Eng. and Du. *o* for OTeut. and HG. *u* before *hs*, cf. OE. *lox* = Du. *los* = OHG. *luhs*, lynx; also Du. *drossaerd* = OHG. *truhsâzzo* steward.]

I. 1. a. An animal of the genus *Vulpes*, having an elongated pointed muzzle and long bushy tail. Usually *V. vulgaris*, preserved in England and elsewhere as a beast of the chase.

c **825** *Vesp. Psalter* lxii[i]. 11 [10] Sien sald in hond sweordes daelas foxa bioð. *a* **1225** *Ancr. R.* 294 Nimeð & keccheð us..anon þe ȝunge uoxes. *a* **1300** *Vox & Wolf* 208 in Hazl. *E.P.P.* I. 65 Ȝe, quad the vox, al thou most sugge. *a* **1300** *Cursor M.* 7151 Thre hundreth fox he samun knitt. **1375** BARBOUR *Bruce* XIX. 663 In-till the luge a fox he saw, That fast can on a salmond gnaw. **1486** *Bk. St. Albans* F vj b, A skulke of Foxis. **1597** HOOKER *Eccl. Pol.* v. lxxix. §16 As if the world did..thinke the Foxe a goodly creature. **1674** N. COX *Gentl. Recreat.* I. (1677) 8 Fox..is called the first year, a Cub. The second year, a Fox, and afterwards an old Fox. **1718** PRIOR *Knowledge* 210 The lonely fox roams far abroad, On secret rapine bent. **1835** FONBLANQUE *Eng. under 7 Administ.* (1837) III. 245 If the esteem of the people were made as much a pursuit as a stinking fox's brush. **1870** YEATS *Nat. Hist. Comm.* 266 The red fox of America.

b. with allusion to its artfulness and cunning.

c **1200** *Trin. Coll. Hom.* 195 þe fox mid his wrenches walt oðer deor and haueð his wille þerof. *a* **1634** RANDOLPH *Ode* 64 Nor will we spare To hunt the crafty fox. **1735** SOMERVILLE *Chase* III. 23 The wily Fox remain'd A subtle pilf'ring Foe, prowling around In Midnight Shades. **1791** BURNS *3rd Ep. R. Graham* 17 Foxes and statesmen, subtile wiles ensure.

c. in various proverbial expressions.

c **1450** HENRYSON *Mor. Fab.* 29 Aye runnes the Foxe as long as hee feete hes. *c* **1460** *Towneley Myst.* (Surtees) 10 Let furth youre geyse, the fox wille preche. **1539** TAVERNER *Erasm. Prov.* (1552) 27 An olde foxe is not taken in a snare. **1545** BRINKLOW *Compl.* xxiv. Hv, As y[u] mayest knowe a foxe by his furred taile. **1562** J. HEYWOOD *Prov. & Epigr.* (1867) 153 When the foxe preacheth, then beware our geese. **1607** WALKINGTON *Opt. Glass* 38 A Fox is known by his bush. **1662** PEPYS *Diary* 26 Dec., We shall endeavour to joyne the lion's skin to the fox's tail.

d. Phrases: †***to catch, hunt the fox***: to get drunk. ***to flay the fox***: see FLAY *v.* 6. ***to play (the) fox***: (*a*) to act cunningly, (*b*) to sham. †***to smell a fox***: to be suspicious.

1599 MINSHEU *Span. Dial.* 19 Whosoeuer loues good wine, hunts the foxe once a yeere. **1611** MIDDLETON & DEKKER *Roaring Girle* I. D.'s Wks. 1873 II. 145 Now I do smell a fox strongly. **1647** WARD *Simp. Cobler* 6 Tiberius play'd the Fox with the Senate of Rome. *a* **1700** B. E. *Dict. Cant. Crew* s.v. *Fox*, He has caught a Fox, he is very Drunk. **1894** CROCKETT *Raiders* 329, I played fox several times, pretending to be in pain.

2. *fig.* **a.** A man likened for craftiness to a fox.

c **1000** *Ags. Gosp.* Luke xiii. 32 Gað & secȝað þam foxe, deofol-seocnessa ic utadrife. **1548** HALL *Chron.*, *Hen. VI* (an. 31) 164 b, This auncient Fox, and pollitique Capitayne lost not one houre..till [etc.]. **1712** ARBUTHNOT *John Bull* I. iv, Don't you see how that old fox steals away your customers? **1851** MAYNE REID *Scalp Hunt.* l. 383, I could not help reflecting on the strange stratagem by which the old fox [Rube] had saved himself.

b. ? Used as *adj.*: Fox-like, cunning.

c **1200** ORMIN 6646 þatt mann iss fox & hinnderrȝæp . . þatt . . follȝheþþ deofless wille. *a* **1300** *Long Life* in *O.E. Misc.* 156 Fox and ferlich is his wren[c]h.

c. An attractive woman. *U.S. slang.*

1963 R. I. MCDAVID in Mencken *Amer. Lang.* xi. 745 A cat in hot pursuit of a chick or fox is said to have his nose wide open. **1964** L. HAIRSTON in J. H. Clarke *Harlem* 290 Daddy, she was a real fox! **1967** WENTWORTH & FLEXNER *Dict. Amer. Slang* (Suppl.) 684 *Fox*, an energetic, attractive, desirable girl, esp. one having a happy and alert personality. Orig. Negro use. Pop. into white use during 1963 by heavyweight boxer Cassius Clay. **1970** R. H. GREENAN *Nightmare in Colour* (1971) lviii. 181 A fox is a girl. A fox is a chick, you see?

3. The fur of the fox.

1501 *Bury Wills* (Camden) 88 My tawney gown furryd w[t] ffoxe. **1603** SHAKS. *Meas. for M.* III. ii. 9 A fur'd gowne to keepe him warme; and furd with Foxe and Lamb-skins too. **1882** BECK *Draper's Dict.*, *Fox*. . Of this fur there are several varieties.

4. One of the northern constellations (*Vulpecula*).

1868 LOCKYER *Guillemin's Heavens* (ed. 3) 398 Situated between the constellations of the Swan and the Fox.

5. a. Some beast or fish likened to a fox, *esp.* the gemmeous dragonet (*Callionymus lyra*), called also *fox-fish*. ***flying fox, sea fox***: see those words.

1611 COTGR., *Spase*. . the sea-fox, or fox dog-fish. **1646** SIR T. BROWNE *Pseud. Ep.* III. xxiv. 169 Some are called the Fox, the Dog, the Sparrow, or Frog-fish. **1769** PENNANT *Zool.* III. 302 These fish [carp] are extremely cunning, and on that account are by some styled the river fox. **1836** YARRELL *Brit. Fishes* I. 302 Fox. . The common Skulpin.

b. Short for *fox-moth* (see 16 b).

II. Senses of obscure development.

†**6.** A kind of sword. *Obs.*

It has been conjectured that this use arose from the figure of a wolf, on certain sword-blades, being mistaken for a fox.

1599 PORTER *Angry Wom. Abingd.* (Percy) 60, I had a sword . . a right fox, i faith. **1633** FORD *Love's Sacr.* v. ii, 'Tis a tough fox, will not fail his master. **1821** SCOTT *Kenilw.* iv, Put up your fox, and let us be jogging.

7. *Brewing.* (See quot.) Cf. FOX *v.* 5.

1750 W. ELLIS *Country Housewife* 377 (E.D.S.) That poisonous damage called in great brewhouses the fox, which gives the drink a sickish nasty taste.

8. *Naut.* (See quots. 1769, 1815.)

1769 FALCONER *Dict. Marine* (1789), *Fox* a sort of strand, formed by twisting several rope-yarns together, and used as a seizing, or to weave a mat or paunch, etc. **1815** *Falconer's Dict. Marine* (ed. Burney), Spanish *Fox*, a single rope-yarn untwisted, and then twisted up the contrary way and rubbed smooth. It is used for small seizings. **1833** MARRYAT *P. Simple* (1863) 38 Mr. Jenkins desired the other men to get half-a-dozen foxes and make a spread eagle of me. *c* **1860** H. STUART *Seaman's Catech.* 27.

9. A drain carried under another water-course by means of a tunnel. Cf. FOX *v.* 3.

1784 *M. Weighton Drainage Award* 13 The Fox made under the canal.

10. See quot. Also FOX-TAIL.

1874 KNIGHT *Dict. Mech.* I. 912 *Fox-bolt*, a description of bolt which is made tight by a fox or wedge driven into a split in the end.

11. *pl.* A variety of ironstone. *dial.*

1793–1813 A. YOUNG *Agric. Surv. Sussex* 13 (E.D.S.).

12. *slang.* An artificial sore.

1862 MAYHEW & BINNY *Criminal Prisons Lond.* 305 Daring youths . . were constantly in the habit of making 'foxes' (artificial sores).

13. *In U.S. Colleges*: A freshman. Cf. Ger. *fuchs.*

1839 LONGF. *Hyperion* (1865) 77 A procession of new-comers or Nasty Foxes, as they are called in the college dialect. **1847** *Yale Lit. Mag.* Jan. XII. 116 'Halloo there, Herdman, fox!' yelled another lusty tippler.

†**14.** ? = FOXGLOVE 1. *Obs.*

1684 tr. *Bonet's Merc. Compit.* XIV. 473 Bathes wherein proper Herbs, especially Foxes, have been boiled.

III. *attrib.* and *Comb.*

15. a. simple attrib., as ***fox bitch, -burrow, -cover, -craft, -cub, -earth, -head*** (used attributively); (used for taking the fox), as ***fox-gin, -trap***; (sense 6), as ***fox-blade, -broadsword.***

a **1611** BEAUM. & FL. *Philaster* IV. i, When my *fox-bitch Beauty grows proud, I'll borrow him. *c* **1640** [SHIRLEY] *Capt. Underwit* I. in Bullen *O. Pl.* II. 321 And old *fox blade made at Hounsloe heath. **1826** SCOTT *Woodst.* i, A good *fox broad-sword. **1550** WILSON *Logike* (1567) 37a, The huntesman . . will sone espie when he seeth a hole, whether it be a *Foxe borough, or not. **1831** GEN. P. THOMPSON *Exerc.* (1842) I. 371 Who . . turns his farm into a *fox-cover. **1654** VILVAIN *Epit. Ess.* IV. xcii. 87 Two fals Scotsh Earls of *Fox-craft fraud composed. **1857** HUGHES *Tom Brown* I. iii, To watch the *fox cubs playing in the green rides. **1530** PALSGR. 222/2 *Foxe erthe, *taisniere.* **1824** MISS MITFORD *Village* Ser. I. (1863) 141 Amongst broken ridges and fox-earths. **1669** WORLIDGE *Syst. Agric.* (1681) 216 Small Iron-gins like *Fox-gins. **1852** R. S. SURTEES *Sponge's Sp. Tour* xviii. (1893) 88 A large gold *fox-head pin. **1605** B. JONSON *Volpone* v. iii, Let his sport pay for 't. This is call'd the *Fox-trap. **1856** KANE *Arct. Expl.* I. v. 53 Places of deposit for meat, and rocks arranged as foxtraps.

b. objective, as ***fox-follower, -stealer, -worship; fox poisoning*** vbl. sb.

1781 COWPER *Conversat.* 410 Though the fox he follows may be tamed, A mere *fox-follower never is reclaimed. **1890** *Daily News* 7 July 3/8 Attempts at *fox-poisoning. **1852** R. S. SURTEES *Sponge's Sp. Tour* liii. (1893) 284 The poachers and *fox-stealers of the village. **1880** MISS BIRD *Japan* I. 71 *Fox-worship being one of the most universal superstitions in Japan.

c. parasynthetic, as ***fox-nosed, -visaged*** adjs.

1889 *Century Dict.* s.v., The lemurs called *fox-nosed monkeys. **1892** A. M. *Yoshiwara Episode* 41 The wares the *fox-visaged, bullet-headed gyn kept on crying.

d. similative, as ***fox-red*** adj.

1910 GALSWORTHY *Inn Tranq.* (1912) 53 The wet *fox-red drifts under the beech-trees. **1926** D. H. LAWRENCE *David* x. 70 Thou hast spied out every hair in his beard. Is he not fox-red? **1956** G. DURRELL *My Family* vii. 87 A tall, square Venetian mansion, with . . green shutters and a fox-red roof.

16. a. Special comb., as **fox-beagle**, a beagle used for fox-hunting; **fox-bench**, 'indurated sand' (*Chesh. Gloss.*); **fox-bolt** (see quot.); **fox-brush**, the tail of a fox used *similatively*; †**fox-case**, the skin of a fox; **fox-chase**, (*a*) = FOX-HUNT: (*b*) a game in imitation of this, also *attrib.*; **fox-colour**, a reddish-yellow colour, whence ***fox-coloured*** adj.; †**fox-court**, a place or yard in which foxes may be kept; **fox-dog**, a fox-hound; †**fox-drunk** *a.* (see quot.); **fox-evil**, 'a disease in which the hair falls off' (1842 Johnson *Farmer's Encycl.*), alopecia (see also 16 e); †**fox-hen**, ? a payment of a hen for the maintenance of fox-hunting; **fox-hound**, a superior variety of hound trained and used for fox-hunting; **fox-key** (see quot.); †**fox-lungs**, some medicinal preparation; **fox-mould**, a name given to green sand when coloured by an oxide of iron; **fox-skin**, the skin of a fox, also *attrib.*; **fox-sleep**, a pretended sleep; †**fox-stones** *pl.*, (*a*) the testicles of a fox; (*b*) an old name for *Orchis mascula*; **fox-terrier**, one of a breed of short-haired terriers, used for unearthing foxes, but kept chiefly as pets; **fox-wedge** (see quot.); †**fox-whelp**, (*a*) a cub of the fox (used also as a term of contempt); (*b*) app. a kind of cider (cf. quot. 1664; **fox-wood** (see quot.; cf. FOX-FIRE).

1676 *Lond. Gaz.* No. 1108/4 A black *Fox Beagle Bitch. **1816** KEATINGE *Trav.* (1817) II. 155 Geology brings to mind here all the connexion of ideas of *fox-bench, with the denudation of forests, coal-beds, iron. **1874** *Fox-bolt [see sense 10]. **1891** *Daily News* 1 June 2/5 Some large tails of *fox brush orchids. **1610** GUILLIM *Heraldry* III. xxiii. (1611) 170 Where the Lion's skin is too scant it must bee peeced out with a *fox case. *a* **1625** FLETCHER *Woman's Prize* II. ii, You old fox-case. *a* **1704** T. BROWN *Praise Poverty* Wks. 1730 I. 98 A kind of *Fox-chace pleasure. **1732** POPE *Ep. Cobham* 74 Mad at a Fox-chase, wise at a Debate. **1856** KANE *Arct. Expl.* I. xiii. 145 A 'fox-chase' round the decks. **1796** WITHERING *Brit. Plants* IV. 193 Gills white, in pairs: pileus *fox colour, convex. **1641** BEST *Farm. Bks.* (Surtees) 84 *Foxe coloured lambes. **1879** ROOD *Chromatics* iv. 45 A fox-coloured yellow. **1781** P. BECKFORD *Hunting* (1802) 328 If you breed up cubs, you will find a *fox-court necessary. **1708** MOTTEUX *Rabelais* IV. xliv. (1737) 178 Some of your Badger's or *Fox-Dogs. **1592** NASHE *P. Pennilesse* Wks. (Grosart) II. 82 The eighth [kind of drunkenness] is *Fox drunke, when he is craftie drunke. **1659** TORRIANO, *Alopecia*, the falling or shedding of a mans hair through foul diseases, called the *Fox-evil. **1528** SIR R. WESTON in Dillon *Calais & Pale* (1892) 93 He hath of every householde . . a henne by name of the *'fox henne', for the which he ys lykewyse bounde to hunt the foxe. *a* **1763** SHENSTONE *Œcon.* I. 94 Who lavishes his wealth On racer, *fox-hound, hawk or spaniel. **1874** KNIGHT *Dict. Mech.* I. 912 **Fox-key* (Machinery), a splitcotter with a thin wedge of steel driven into the end to prevent its working back. **1660** *Act 12 Chas. II*, c. 4, Rates Inwards, [In List of Drugs] *Fox lungs the pound iiis. **1807** VANCOUVER *Agric. Devon* (1813) 42 A moist peaty earth on a reddish brown clay, highly retentive of water, and commonly called *fox mould. **1598** HAKLUYT *Voy.* I. 71 Who gaue vnto eche of vs a gowne made of *Foxe-skinnes. **1856** KANE *Arct. Expl.* II. App. xi. 311 Dressing in fox-skin clothing. **1596** LODGE *Margarite Amer.* (1876) 30 Entering Arsadachus chamber [they] found him in his *foxe sleepe. **1623** HEXHAM *Tongue-Combat* Ep. Ded. 3 That stupide Lethargie or reserued Foxe-sleepe of Policie, wherein they lye bed-rid. **1597** GERARDE *Herbal* I. cxiii. (1633) 212 There be divers sorts of *Fox-stones. **1604** MARSTON & WEBSTER *Malcontent* II. ii, Jelly of cock-sparrows, he-monkey's marrow, or powder of fox-stones. **1823** BYRON *Juan* VII. xxiv, Unless they are game as bull-dogs and *fox-terriers. **1888** GREENWELL *Coal-trade Terms Northumb. & Durh.* (ed. 3), **Fox-wedge*, a long wedge driven between two other wedges with their thick ends placed in the opposite direction. *c* **1320** *Sir Beues* 1733 Aȝilt þe, a seide, þow *fox welp. *c* **1374** CHAUCER *Boeth.* IV. pr. iii. 78 Yif he . . reioyseth him to rauisshe by wyles, thou shalt seyn him lyke to the fox whelpes. [**1664** EVELYN *Pomona* iv. 14 For the kinds then of Cider-Apples in being . . Some commend the Fox-Whelp.] **1837** SOUTHEY *Doctor* Interch. xvi, Fox-whelp, a beverage as much better than Champagne, as it is honester, wholesomer and cheaper. **1889** *Century Dict.*, **Fox-wood*. . decayed wood, especially such as emits a phosphorescent light [U.S.].

b. *esp.* in names of animals, etc. having a real or fancied resemblance to the fox, as †**fox-ape**, ? the opossum; **fox-bat** = FLYING FOX; **fox-fish**, see FOX *sb.* 5; **fox-lynx**, a variety of lynx; **fox-moth**, a greyish-brown European bombycid moth (*Lasiocampa rubi*); **fox-shark**, the sea-fox (*Alopias vulpes*); **fox-snake**, a large harmless snake of the United States (*Elaphe vulpina*); **fox-sparrow**, a North American sparrow (*Passerella iliaca*); **fox-squirrel**, a North American squirrel (*Sciurus cinereus*, *S. niger*, etc.).

1594 BLUNDEVIL *Exerc.* v. (ed. 7) 570 Gesner calleth this Beast an Ape-Foxe, or a *Fox-Ape. **1834** CAUNTER *Orient. Ann.* xiv. 187 The *fox-bat bustled from his covert among the tombs. **1862** H. MARRYAT *Year in Sweden* II. 439 The Räflo, or *fox-lynx, of a soft reddish-white fur. **1828** STARK *Elem. Nat. Hist.* I. 385 The *Fox Shark. **1857** *Trans. Ill. Agric. Soc.* II. 658 They are also found in the stomachs of the milk-snake, . . and of the large *fox-snake (Scotophis vulpinus). **1958** R. CONANT *Field Guide Reptiles U.S.* 157 *Fox snake*. . . Ground color varies from yellowish to light brown, and the dark spots and blotches from chocolate to black. **1869** J. BURROUGHS in *Galaxy Mag.* (N.Y.) Aug., The *fox-sparrow . . comes to us in the fall. **1791** W. BARTRAM *Carolina* 283 The great black *fox squirrel. **1844** GOSSE in *Zoologist* II. 707 Some towering oaks, on which several fox squirrels (*Sciurus capistratus*) were frisking.

c. in plant-names, as **fox-bane**, a species of monkshood (*Aconitum Vulparia*); **fox-berry** = BEARBERRY; **fox-chop** (see quot.); **fox-finger(s** = FOXGLOVE; **fox-geranium, -grass**, herb Robert (*Geranium Robertianum*); **fox-grape**, a name for several North American species of wild grapes. Also FOXGLOVE, FOXTAIL.

1840 PAXTON *Bot. Dict.*, **Foxbane*. **1866** *Treas. Bot.*, *Fox-chop, *Mesembryanthemum vulpinum*. **1657** W. COLES *Adam in Eden* lxvii. 126 Some call it *Fox-finger. **1657** AUSTEN *Fruit Trees* I. 59 The *Fox Grape is a faire large fruit. **1683** PENN *Wks.* (1782) IV. 302 The great red grape (now ripe) called by ignorance, 'The fox-grape', (because of the relish it hath with unskilful palates). **1849** LOWELL *Biglow P.* Poet. Wks. (1879) 176 Growing so fairly . . as a fox-grape over a scrub-oak in a swamp.

d. in the names of various games in which one of the players acts as a fox, as **fox and geese**, a game played on a board with pegs, draughtsmen, or the like; **fox and hounds**, a boys' game, in which the 'hounds' chase the 'fox'; †**fox in** *or* **to the** *or* **thy hole** (see quots.).

1633 MARMION *Fine Companion* II. v, Let him sit in the shop . . and play at *fox and geese with the foreman. **1856** MRS. BROWNING *Aur. Leigh* IX. Poems 1890 VI. 351 Though you played At 'fox and goose' about him with your soul. **1821** CLARE *Vill. Minstr.* II. 37 Noise of blind-man's buff, and *fox-and-hounds. **1585** J. HIGINS *Junius' Nomenclator* 298 A kinde of playe wherein boyes lift up one leg and hop on the other; it is called *fox in thy hole. **1648** HERRICK *Hesper.*, *New Yeares Gift* (1869) 134 The wassel-boule, That tost up after Fox-i-th' hole. **1783** AINSWORTH *Lat. Dict.* (Morell) VI. *Discoliasmus*, Children's play, called Fox to thy hole.

e. with genitive *fox's*, as **fox's cough** (see quot.); †**foxes evil** = *fox-evil*; **fox's foot**, a kind of grass (*Dactylis glomerata* L.); in early use, perh. *Sparganium simplex*; **fox's tail** (see FOXTAIL).

1611 COTGR., *Toux de regnard*, the *Foxes cough; a rooted, or old-growne cough, which waits on a man to his graue. **1607** TOPSELL *Four-f. Beasts* (1658) 379 Troubled with the *foxes evill. **1671** H. M. tr. *Colloq. Erasm.* 134 The foxes evil (falling off of the hair) had made him almost quite bald. *c* **1000** *Sax. Leechd.* I. 150 Genim þysse wyrte wyrttruman þe man . . *foxesfot nemneð. **1853** JOHNSTON *Nat. Hist. E. Bord.* I. 216 *Dactylis glomerata*, Fox's-foot, which the clustered panicle somewhat resembles.

fox (fɒks), *v.* [f. prec. sb.]

1. †**a.** *trans.* To play the fox for; to compass by crafty means (*obs.*). **b.** *intr.* To play the fox, dissemble, sham. Now *dial.* and *slang.*

1602 WARNER *Alb. Eng.* IX. liii. (1612) 239 Insociable, Maleparte, foxing their priuate good. **1646** R. BAILLIE *Lett. & Jrnls.* (1841) II. 351 The other pettie princes are foxeing alreadie for fear. **1884** *Chester Gloss.*, *Fox*, to sham. **1886** D. C. MURRAY *1st Pers. Singular* xxix, He had played the fox for so many years, that now to his mind everybody was dodging and foxing.

2. a. *trans.* To intoxicate, befuddle. Also (? *nonce-use*), to redden (one's nose) with drinking.

1611 [TARLTON] *Jests* (1844) 21 Before they parted they foxt Tarlton at the Castle in Pater Noster Row. **1649** BLITHE *Eng. Improv. Impr.* (1652) 258 It [Cider] serves as well . . for men to fox their noses. **1660** PEPYS *Diary* 26 Oct., The last of whom I did almost fox with Margate ale. *a* **1734** NORTH *Exam.* II. iv. §41 (1740) 251 Mr. Atkins was . . at Greenwich, and there, at an Entertainment of some Ladies, soundly foxed, the Attorney General threw up.

†**b.** *transf.* To stupefy (fish). *Obs.*

1650 H. MORE *Enthus. Triumph.* (1656) 86 For ought you know, it may be onely a charm to fox fishes. **1787** BEST *Angling* (ed. 2) 67 Take heart-wort, and lime, mingle them together, and throw them into a standing water, and it will fox them [fishes]. **1805** *Sporting Mag.* XXVI. 178 Two gentlemen . . were foxing fish in the river Calder.

c. *fig.* To delude.

a **1660** H. PETERS in South *Serm.* (Bohn) I. 540 Fox them a little more with religion. *a* **1734** NORTH *Exam.* I. ii. §115 (1740) 93 When the Faction had . . once foxed the People with an ill Opinion of the Government. **1835** A. B. LONGSTREET *Georgia Scenes* 63 Has he foxed you? **1906** E. PHILLPOTTS *Portreeve* I. xv, Don't fox yourself to think that. That's mad. *Ibid.* II. xviii, Love makes a man cunning. . . I foxed you fifty times. **1942** *Times* 1 June 4/3 'We had the guns absolutely foxed,' a pilot said. **1963** *Times* 25 Feb. 13/5, I like to imagine some house-holder in the next century trying to piece together our lives and interests. Will she be foxed by literature addressed to Mr. H.-T. (my husband)?

†**d.** *intr.* To get drunk. *Obs.*

1649 LOVELACE *Lucasta* (1864) 8 The humble tenant, that does bring A chicke or egges . . Is tane into the buttry, and does fox Equall with him that gave a stalled oxe.

†**3.** *trans.* To pierce with a 'fox' (see FOX *sb.* 6).

1567 EDWARDS *Damon & Pithias* in Hazl. *Dodsley* IV. 68 *Jack.* By the mass, I will box you. *Will.* By Cock, I will fox you. **1589** *Pasquil's Ret.* Nashe's Wks. (Grosart) I. 123 Diuinitie . . holding of her hart as if she were sicke, because Martin would have foxed her.

4. *trans.* To discolour (the leaves of a book). See FOXED *ppl. a.*

5. *intr.* Of beer: To turn sour in fermenting; also *trans.* (causatively).

1744-50 W. ELLIS *Mod. Husb.* II. i. 130 (E.D.S.) She.. took out the wort.. laying it thin enough to be out of danger of foxing. **1830** M. DONOVAN *Dom. Econ.* I. 213 In this way the fermentation may fearlessly be conducted during the warmest weather without risk of foxing.

6. *trans.* To repair (boots or shoes) by renewing the upper leather; also to ornament (the upper of a shoe) with a strip of leather.

1796 GROSE *Dict. Vulg. Tongue* (ed. 3), *Foxing a Boot*, mending the foot by capping it. **1889** FARMER *Americanisms*, *Fox*, a shoemaker's term, to repair boots.

7. *intr.* To hunt the fox. *U.S.*

1877 [see FOXING 1].

†**8.** *trans.* ? To trim (a horse's ears) in some manner. *Obs.*

1806 *Spirit Pub. Jrnls.* (1807) X. 109 He.. appears.. What the jockies call a roarer. His owners are anxious to have his ears foxed; but we think he is more in need of cropping and docking.

9. *Comb.* † **fox-mine-host** (see quot. and sense 2).

1622 MARBE tr. *Aleman's Guzman d'Alf.* I. III. ii. 194 They may afterwards play at Foxe mine Host, or some other Drinking Game at Cards or Dice for their recreation.

foxaline ('fɒksəli:n). [Fanciful formation on FOX *sb.*] Imitation fox-fur.

1907 *Ladies' Field* 12 Jan. (Advt.), White Foxaline long Stole. **1923** *Daily Mail* 16 Apr. 4 White Foxaline Tie. **1927** *Daily Express* 13 Sept. 5/2 Grey Chinese cat (sometimes called foxaline). **1930** R. MACAULAY *Staying with Relations* ii. 18 One of those mythical animals imagined by the fur trade, like the foxaline, the pony-seal, and the rabbit-skunk. **1963** *Retail Trading-Standards Assoc. Bull.* Aug.-Sept. 3/1 *Animal*, hare flank... *Accepted trade name*, foxaline.

foxed (fɒkst), *ppl. a.* [f. FOX *v.* + -ED[1].] In senses of the vb.

1. Intoxicated, drunk, stupefied.

1611 [see COLUMBERED]. **1673** SHADWELL *Epsom Wells* IV. Wks. 1720 II. 248 Udsooks, I begin to be fox'd. **1896** *Q. Rev.* Jan. 16 Will Symons had often seen him 'foxed' amid the most undignified surroundings.

2. Trimmed with fox-fur. In quot. *punningly*.

1609 W. M. *Man in Moone* (1849) 26 His gowne is throughly foxt, yet he is sober.

3. Of the leaves of books, also of timber; Discoloured by decay; stained with brownish-yellow spots.

1847 HALLIWELL *s.v.*, Timber is said to be foxed, when it becomes discoloured in consequence of incipient decay. *Warw.* **1848** HARE *Guesses* Ser. II. 335 A torn or foxt and dog's-eared volume. **1885** A. DOBSON *At Sign Lyre* 83 The Burton I bought for a florin, And the Rabelais foxed and flea'd.

4. Of beer: Turned sour.

1743 *Lond. & Country Brew.* 106 The evil stinking Scent that arises therefrom, which has brought it under the Denomination of being foxed.

5. Of a boot: (see FOX *v.* 6, FOXING 2).

1880 *Antrim & Down Gloss.* s.v., Women's cloth boots are foxed when they have a binding of leather on the cloth all round next the sole.

foxery ('fɒksərı). [f. FOX *sb.* + -ERY.] The character, manners, or behaviour of a fox; wiliness, cunning.

c **1400** *Rom. Rose* 6795, I.. have wel lever.. Bifore the puple patre and prey, And wrye me in my foxerye Under a cope of papelardye. *c* **1540** *Pilgr. T.* 278 in *Thynne's Animadv.* (1865) App. i. 85, I had rehersid nothing but papry, sprong owt of Antichrist, full of foxry. **1893** R. F. BURTON tr. *Il Pentamerone* I. 178 The fox, never dreaming that the other was a quintessence of foxery, found a woman more a fox than herself.

fox-fire. Now only *U.S.* The phosphorescent light emitted by decaying timber.

1483 *Cath. Angl.* 140 Fox Fire, *glos, glossis.* **1824** J. DODDRIDGE *Notes Virginia & Pennsylv.* 290 If they had seen any thing like fire, between that and the fort, it must have been fox fire. **1832** J. P. KENNEDY *Swallow Barn* I. xxviii. 311 The fox-fire—as the country people call it—glowed hideously from the cold and matted bosom of the marsh. **1853** KANE *Grinnell Exp.* xxiv. (1856) 193 The fox-fire of the Virginia meadows. **1872** E. EGGLESTON *End of World* xxxii. 210 The 'fox-fire', rotting logs glowing with a faint luminosity, startled her several times. **1920** J. M. HUNTER *Trail Drivers of Texas* 149 There is where you could see phosphorescence (fox fire) on our horses' ears.

'fox-fur. The fur of the fox, used to face gowns; hence, a gown trimmed with fox-fur.

1599 MARSTON *Sco. Villanie* II. vii. 204 Let him but in iudgements sight vncase, He's naught but budge, old gards, browne fox-fur face. **1649** G. DANIEL *Trinarch., Hen. IV* lxxxvii, The Alderman has won his Fox-furre here. **1876** OUIDA *Winter City* vii. 183 The dying daylight on the silver fox-furs.

'fox-furred. [f. prec. + -ED.]

1. Trimmed with fox-fur.

1579 GOSSON *Sch. Abuse* (Arb.) 49 Take heed of the foxe-furd nightcap. **1606** DEKKER *Devils Answ.* Wks. (Grosart) II. 139 Shall my Fox-furde gownes be lockt vp from me?

2. Wearing fox-fur, wearing a fox-furred gown.

1591 GREENE *Disc. Coosnage* (1859) 12 Those Fox-furd Gentlemen that hyde under their gownes faced with foynes, more falshood then all the Conny-catchers in England. **1597** *Pilgr. Parnass.* v. (1886) 21, I thinke not worser of faire Parnassus' hill For that it wants that sommer's golden clay, The idol of the foxfur'd usurer. **1648** *Hunting of Fox* 38 Some few of the Fox-furred Aldermen.

foxglove ('fɒksglʌv). [OE. *foxes glófa* (? pl.) see FOX *sb.* and GLOVE.

The reason for the second part of the name is obvious, as the flower resembles a finger-stall in shape; cf. the Lat. name. Why the plant was associated with the fox is not so clear; but cf. Norw. *revbjelde* = 'fox bell'.]

1. The popular name of *Digitalis purpurea*, a common ornamental flowering plant.

c **1000** *Sax. Leechd.* I. 54 Herba tricnos manicos þæt is foxes clofe [*v.r.* glofa]. *c* **1265** *Names Plants* in Wr.-Wülcker 556/6 *Saluinca*.. foxesgloue. *a* **1387** *Sinon. Barthol.* (Anecd. Oxon.) 15 *Ceroterica, Ceroteca vulpis*, foxglove. **1578** LYTE *Dodoens* II. xxiv. 175 Foxe gloue floureth chiefly in July and August. **1664** EVELYN *Kal. Hort.* (1729) 214 Columbines, Iron-colour'd Fox-gloves, Holly-hocks. **1810** SCOTT *Lady of L.* I. xii, Fox-glove and nightshade, side by side, Emblems of punishment and pride.

b. Used in medicine: see DIGITALIS.

1801 *Med. Jrnl.* V. 209 The Fox-glove of which the tincture is made, is commonly procured from the Hall. **1861** GEO. ELIOT *Silas M.* 13 Recalling the relief his mother had found from a simple preparation of foxglove.

2. Applied to various plants of other genera; *e.g.* formerly to the Mullein (*Verbascum Thapsus*).

1587 MASCALL *Govt. Cattle* (1600) 242 The iuyce of heg-taper, called Foxegloue.

3. *attrib.* and *Comb.*, as *foxglove-bell, -leaf, -spire*; **foxglove-shaped** *a.* (see quot.).

a **1821** KEATS *Sonn.* iii, Where the deer's swift leap Startles the wild bee from the *foxglove bell. **1811** A. T. THOMSON *Lond. Disp.* (1818) 610 Take of *foxglove leaves dried, a drachm. **1856** HENSLOW *Dict. Bot. Terms*, **Foxglove-shaped*, a nearly cylindrical but somewhat irregular and inflated tube, formed like the corolla of a Digitalis. **1850** TENNYSON *In Mem.* lxxxiii, The *foxglove-spire.

'fox-hole. [See HOLE *sb.* 1 b; the compound *fox(e)hole* (OE. *fox-hol*) appears in early local designations, e.g. in Domesday Book, and persists in place-names.] A hole in the ground used by a soldier for protection; a slit trench. Also *transf.* and *fig.*; also used *attrib.*, as **foxhole circuit** (see quot. 1946[2]).

1919 *Red Cross Mag.* Apr. 29/1 The bitter weeks of the Argonne when the same Yank lay hungry, cold, wet, and exhausted in some insufficient fox-hole. **1928** BLUNDEN *Undertones of War* xii. 143 Those dead men in field grey overcoats at the entrances, and others flung down by their last 'foxholes' near by. **1942** *Hutchinson's Pict. Hist. of War* 18 Mar.-9 June 130 Slit trenches used for protection by troops were called 'fox-holes' by American soldiers fighting against the Japanese on Bataan peninsula. **1944** *Newsweek* 31 July 60 The performers who were selected to make up the first entertainment.. wave, as part of USO-Camp Show's 'Foxhole Circuit'. **1946** W. V. THOMAS in Hawkins & Boyd *War Report* xviii. 351 Fox-holes with the Germans manning bazookas. **1946** *Amer. Speech* XXI. 223/1 *Foxhole circuit*, a theater circuit at the fighting fronts played by American troupes. **1955** *Sci. News Let.* 19 Feb. 116/1 Simple foxhole shelters provide 'surprising protection' from this invisible radioactivity. **1957** *Economist* 28 Sept. 1003/2 The arrangement.. might get trade flowing without abandoning the principle of reunion through elections, and yet it might conceivably inveigle the communists out of their foxholes. **1964** D. F. DOWD in I. L. Horowitz *New Sociol.* 59 The academic profession in America is the social critic's refuge; even, in extreme cases, his foxhole. **1968** *Times* 4 Apr. 8/6 The pound is in the same foxhole as the dollar.

'fox-hunt. The chase of a fox with hounds.

1816 *Sporting Mag.* XLVII. 288 Next after a fox-hunt, the finest sight in England is a stage-coach just ready to start. **1875** W. S. HAYWARD *Love agst. World* 11 This is my first fox-hunt.

So **'fox-hunting** *vbl. sb.*, the sport of hunting the fox; **'fox-hunting** *ppl. a.*; and (back-formation) **'fox-hunt** *v. intr.*, also † *to fox-hunt it*. Also **'fox-hunter, 'fox-huntress, 'fox-huntsman**, one who hunts the fox.

1674 N. COX *Gentl. Recreat.* I. (1677) 106 Fox-hunting is very pleasant. **1692** R. L'ESTRANGE *Fables* civ, The fox-hunters went their way. **1768** G. WASHINGTON *Writ.* (1889) II. 232 Rid up to Toulston in order to fox hunt it. **1772** DK. RICHMOND in *Burke's Corr.* (1844) I. 393, I have engaged a large party.. to come here.. and stay a month to fox-hunt. **1827** *Sporting Mag.* XX. 93 No bad stem to graft a fox-huntsman on. **1829** *Ibid.* XXIV. 32 A female fox-huntress. **1830** N. S. WHEATON *Jrnl.* 59 A fox-hunting, horse-racing.. people. **1837** HOWITT *Rur. Life* I. iv. (1862) 31 Fox-hunting is now the chief amusement of the true British sportsman. **1852** R. S. SURTEES *Sponge's Sp. Tour* lvi. 318 Breaking their necks being, as she conceived, the inevitable end of fox-hunters.

Foxian ('fɒksıən), *a.* [f. the surname *Fox* or *Foxe* (see below) + -IAN.] Pertaining to: **a.** John Foxe, author of the *Book of Martyrs*; **b.** George Fox, founder of the Society of Friends or 'Quakers'.

1641 MILTON *Animadv.* (1851) 197 They which one of your Bishops scornfully termes the Foxian Confessors. **1642** —— *Apol. Smect.* (1851) 289. **1823** LAMB *Elia, Quaker's Meeting*, Once only.. I witnessed a sample of the old Foxian orgasm.

foxie, foxy ('fɒksı). *Austral.* and *N.Z. colloq.* [Abbrev. of *fox-terrier* + -Y[6].] A fox-terrier.

1906 E. DYSON *Fact'ry 'Ands* xviii. 246 Like er bally foxie after er rat. **1933** *Bulletin* (Sydney) 13 Sept. 21/1 The first dog I loved lived long—a fat old foxie older than I. **1948** D. W. BALLANTYNE *Cunninghams* (1963) II. xv. 192 The dog—a dirty-coated foxie—whimpered across the kitchen. **1966** *Weekly News* (N.Z.) 27 Apr. 40 (*caption*) The smooth-haired 'foxie' probably developed later than the wire-haired type.

foxing ('fɒksıŋ), *vbl. sb.* [f. FOX *v.* + -ING[1].]

1. The action of the vb., in various senses.

c **1220** *Bestiary* 435 And in ure skemting he doð raðe a foxing. **1742** *Lond. & Country Brew.* I. (ed. 4) 43 Foxing is a Misfortune, or rather a Disease in Malt Drinks, occasioned by divers Means. **1868** *Chambers' Encycl.* I. 809 The sugar in the worts will become partially converted into acetic acid, or, as it is termed, foxing occurs. **1873** *N. & Q.* Ser. IV. XI. 216 Is there any known means to prevent foxing in books? **1877** HALLOCK *Sportsman's Gaz.* 17 With us of the North, foxing is by some followed during.. winter.

2. *concr.* (See quots. and FOX *v.* 6.)

1865 MRS. WHITNEY *Gayworthys* II. 75 Say wore cloth boots, with patent foxings. **1874** KNIGHT *Dict. Mech.* I. 912 *Foxing*.. an outer covering or upper leather over the usual upper. 2. Ornamental strips of a different material on the uppers of shoes.

† **'foxish,** *a. Obs.* [f. FOX *sb.* + -ISH.]

1. Of or pertaining to a fox, fox-like.

c **1400** *Lanfranc's Cirurg.* 196 Four different kinds of Leprosy are distinguished.. 3. *alopicia* and *vulpina* foxissch. **1571** GOLDING *Calvin on Ps.* xxviii. 3 This foxish wylynesse. **1583** —— *Calvin on Deut.* xxxvi. 215 If the fathers bee woolues they would haue their Children wooluish: if they bee olde foxes they would haue them to bee foxish.

2. *fig.* Like a fox in nature, crafty, cunning.

14.. LYDG. in *Pol. Rel. & L. Poems* (1866) 25 Among foxys be foxische of nature. **1535** JOYE *Apol. Tindale* 44 By his foxisshe example he pretendeth [etc.]. **1699** T. C[OCKMAN] *Tully's Offices* (1706) 273 Your.. crafty, foxish, juggling kind of Fellows.

Foxite ('fɒksaıt). [see -ITE.] A political follower of Charles James Fox. Also *attrib.*

1782 DR. WOLCOT (Peter Pindar) *Lyric Odes* iii. 41 His muzzle, form'd of opposition stuff Firm as a Foxite, would not lose its ruff. **1808** SCOTT *Fam. Lett.* 8 Feb., During the Foxites' interval of power. *a* **1845** HOOD *To Mrs. Fry* v, The Pittite hues will sadden there, Whereas the Foxite shades will all show fair! [Used punningly: cf. FOXIAN b.]

'foxless, *a.* [f. FOX *sb.* + -LESS.] Void of foxes.

1891 *Field* 7 Mar. 331/2 To show that the fine country they ranged over is not foxless, it may be stated that in the course of the day they moved eight or nine.

fox-like ('fɒkslaık), *a.* [f. as prec. + LIKE *a.*] Like a fox; *esp.* crafty, cunning.

1577-87 HOLINSHED *Scot. Chron.* (1808) V. 577 This Mudiard and his companions imbued with more than fox-like conditions, did (deceiuing their keepers) returne to their owne caues. **1654** TRAPP *Comm. Job* xxxiii. 26 Reconciliations are for the most part Fox-like friendships. **1868** DARWIN *Anim. & Pl.* I. i. 25 The domestic dogs on the coast of Guinea are fox-like animals.

† **'foxly,** *a.* and *adv. Obs.* In 2 adv. -liche. [f. as prec. + -LY[1] and [2].] Like a fox.

A. *adj.* Crafty, cunning. **B.** *adv.* Craftily.

c **1175** *Lamb. Hom.* 31 He wile seggen and foxliche smeþien mid worde, Nabbe ic nawiht þer-of. **1528** in Furnivall *Ballads fr. MSS.* I. 354 By foxly polecy þou dyd them in toll. **1594** WILLOBIE *Avisa* 18 Your painted box, and goodly preach, I see doth hold a foxly reach.

fox-mark ('fɒksmɑ:k). [f. FOX *v.* 4 + MARK *sb.*[1]] A brown spot or stain on a print, book, etc., caused by damp affecting impurities in the paper. Hence *fox-marking*; also *fox(e)y* adj., *foxiness*.

1880 W. BLADES *Enemies of Books* ii. 23 It grieves the heart to see 'foxey' stains common in his most superb works. **1931** *Book-Collectors' Q.* June-Aug. 13 A recent attempt was made to get at the cause of fox-marks. *Ibid.*, One portion of a leaf separated into two parts was sent to one chemist, and the other portion to another chemist, to report on the fox-marking. **1935** C. A. MITCHELL *Docum. & Sci. Exam.* 24 The so-called 'foxy' appearance of paper caused by the oxidising action of mould fungi or chemical processes of oxidation. **1937** E. J. LABARRE *Dict. Paper* 149/2 *Foxed, foxing* or *foxy*, stains, specks or spots in paper, e.g. prints, books, mostly due to mould or paper-mildew. **1956** *Bookman's Conc. Dict.* 117/2 *Foxiness*, decay or spottiness of book pages. **1958** *Oxf. Mail* 19 Mar. Suppl. 21/4 First a word on 'fox-marks'. These brown stains.. are caused by damp. **1960** G. A. GLAISTER *Gloss. Bk.* 28/2 Fox marks and certain apparently indelible stains on printed paper can be removed by bleaching.

foxship ('fɒksʃıp). [f. FOX *sb.* + -SHIP.]

1. The character or qualities of a fox.

1607 SHAKS. *Cor.* IV. ii. 18 Had'st thou Foxship To banish him that strooke more blowes for Rome Then thou hast spoken words?

2. As a mock title.

1863 W. LANCASTER *Praeterita* 41 If I meet thy foxship afterdays.. I'll mar that serpent face.. And leave thy surgy rock without a king. **1870** *Standard* 13 Dec., His fox-ship was 'run into' between Culgaith and Longwathby.

'foxtail. [f. as prec. + TAIL *sb.*]

1. The tail of a fox, a fox's brush. Formerly one of the badges of the fool or jester. † *flap with a foxtail*: see FLAP *sb.* 1 b.

? *a* **1370** *Robt. Cicyle* 57 The fole Roberd with hym went, Clad in a fulle sympulle garment, With foxe tayles to renne abowte. **1553**, **1717** [see FLAP *sb.* 1 b]. [*a* **1605** MONTGOMERY *Misc. P.* iv. 48 Then tak me with the foxis taill a flap, Since that the Hevins are hinderers of my hap.] **1613** PURCHAS *Pilgrimage* ii. §2 (R.) Such a one is carried about the town with a boord fastned to his necke, all be-hanged with foxe-tayles. **1852** SEIDEL *Organ* 24 When they pulled out this stop, suddenly a large fox-tail flew into their faces. **1893** T. B. FOREMAN *Trip to Spain* 31 Their bells and ornaments of fox-tail.

2. As the name of a plant: **a.** One of various species of grass with soft brush-like spikes of flowers, *esp. Alopecurus pratensis.*

1552 HULOET, Foxe taile, herbe, *Alopecurus.* **1597** GERARDE *Herbal* I. lviii. §1. 81 Foxetaile hath many grassie leaues or blades. **1799** J. ROBERTSON *Agric. Perth* 208 The meadow fox tail (alopecurus pratensis). **1846** J. BAXTER *Libr. Pract. Agric.* (ed. 4) I. 359 The foxtail flowers in April, May, and..June.

b. A club-moss (*Lycopodium clavatum*).

[**1800** WORDSW. *Idle Shepherd-boys,* That plant which in our dale We call stag-horn or fox's tail.] **1866** in *Treas. Bot.*

3. In various technical uses (see quots.).

1712 J. JAMES tr. *Le Blond's Gardening* 195 These Pipes are..subject to Fox-Tails, which are the Roots of very small Trees, which passing by the Pores of the Earthen Pipe.. grow to such Length and Bigness, as to stop up the Pipe entirely [so Fr. *queue de renard* (Littré)]. **1854** BADHAM *Halieut* 313 Willughby tells us that salars caught in the Ribble, those of the first year are called smolts..those of the fourth, fox-tails. **1873** *Weale's Dict. Terms* (ed. 4), *Fox-tail* in metallurgy, the cinder obtained in the last stage of the charcoal-finery process; it is a cylindrical piece hollow in the centre. [So Fr. *renard,* quoted by Littré from Buffon.]

4. *attrib.* and *Comb.,* as **foxtail-grass** = FOXTAIL 2 a; **foxtail-saw, -wedging** (see quots.).

1597 GERARDE *Herbal* I. vii. §1. 8 The great *Foxe-taile grasse. **1711** J. PETIVER in *Phil. Trans.* XXVII. 377 Rough ear'd Fox-tail Grass. **1813** SIR H. DAVY *Agric. Chem.* (1814) 362 Meadow fox-tail grass. **1874** KNIGHT *Dict. Mech.* I. 912 **Fox-tail saw,* a dovetail saw. **1825** HAMILTON *Dict. Terms,* **Foxtail wedging.* **1842–76** GWILT *Archit. Gloss., Fox-tail Wedging,* a method of fixing a tenon in a mortise by splitting the end of the tenon and inserting a projecting wedge, then entering the tenon into the mortise and driving it home.

'foxtailed, *a.* [f. prec. + -ED².] Having a tail like a fox. ***foxtailed asparagus,*** the horsetail (*Equisetum maximum*) (Britten and Holland).

1774 GOLDSM. *Nat. Hist.* (1790) IV. 237 The saki, or cagui ..has been often termed the foxtailed monkey.

'foxter. *Sc.* Also 7 fochsterrie, fox trie. The foxglove (*Digitalis purpurea*).

1623 in Pitcairn *Crim. Trials Scot.* II. 538 Issobell confessit that scho send furth hir sone to gether fochsterrie leaueis. **1636** in *Dalyell's Darker Superst. Scotl.* (1831) 113 Ane drink of fox trie leaves. **1818** HOGG *Wool-gatherer, Brownie of Bodsbeck,* etc. II. 183 They [the fairies] 'll hae to ..gang away an' sleep in their dew-cups an' foxterleaves till the gloaming come again.

'fox-trot, *sb.* **1.** A pace with short steps, as in changing from trotting to walking.

1872 F. M. A. ROE *Army Lett.* (1909) 70 He has a fox trot, which is wonderfully easy. **1888** *Century Mag.* Oct. XXXVI. 897 She heard a horse approaching at a *fox-trot. **1894** R. KIPLING *Day's Work* (1898) 58 Would you consider a fox-trot, an' single-foot, an' rack, an' pace, *an'* amble, distinctions not worth distinguishin'? **1946** M. C. SELF *Horseman's Encycl.* 134 *Fox trot,* a slow, shuffling trot, the fox-trot is one of the gaits permitted in a five-gaited saddler as a 'slow-gait'.

2. A modern dance, of American origin, consisting chiefly of alternating measures of long and short steps; also, a piece of music suitable as an accompaniment for the fox-trot.

1915 *Truth* 17 Mar. 1/5 A new dance, the 'Fox-trot', a relation of..'Ragtime'. **1915** *Victor Record Catal.* May, Dance records... Fox trots. **1917** S. B. LEACOCK *Frenzied Fiction* (1919) v. 70 The others were dancing the fox-trot to the victrola on the piazza. **1919** G. D'EGVILLE *How & what to Dance* (1922) 55 The Fox-Trot is a dance of many steps, and to the casual observer everybody seems to have different ones. **1919** E. SCOTT *All about Latest Dances* 68 The true basis of the American Fox-Trot is an alternation of four slow and four or eight quick movements, depending on the step chosen. **1923** —— *A.B.C. of Dancing* 84 The foxtrot is not a dance in the sense that the waltz and polka are dances because it has no distinctive rhythm and no characteristic step or figure. **1928** *Melody Maker* Feb. 127/1 You have just heard a fox-trot, 'I call her honey because she sticks to me'. **1946** R. CAPELL *Simiomata* II. 48 Kirou remembers Macaskie singing foxtrots.

Hence **'fox-trot** *v. intr.,* to dance a fox-trot; **'fox-trotter,** one who fox-trots; **'fox-trotting** *vbl. sb.*

1916 *Daily Colonist* (Victoria, B.C.) 11 July 3/7 Such [folk] dances should not be classed with fox-trotting, bunny-hugging, Wilson gliding, [etc.]. **1919** *Punch* 26 Feb. 166/2 I've fox-trotted in Stranraer, Irish-jigged in Mullingar. **1919** E. SCOTT *All about Latest Dances* 72 Some fox-trotters spin round at intervals on the soles of their feet. **1923** R. D. PAINE *Comrades of Rolling Ocean* v. 75 A dozen couples..fox-trotted in a clear space of the forward deck. **1928** F. N. HART *Bellamy Trial* i. 18 He seems to have spent most of his time perfecting his golf game and his fox-trotting abilities. **1967** V. NABOKOV *Speak, Memory* (ed. 2) xiii. 254 On the Cunard liner *Pannonia* which left Greece on May 18, 1919..I learned to foxtrot.

foxy ('fɒksɪ), *a.* [f. FOX *sb.* + -Y¹.]

1. a. Fox-like: *esp.* crafty, cunning.

1528 ROY *Rede me* Ded. (Arb.) 23 An hole or denne of falce foxy hipocrites. *a* **1536** TINDALE *Wks.* (1573) 148 Oh foxy Pharisay. **1601** W. PARRY *Trav. Sir A. Sherley* 30 Having merrily passed the time with this foxy fryer. **1859** TENNYSON *Guinevere* 62 Modred's narrow foxy face. **1895** W. C. GORE in *Inlander* Dec. 110 *Foxy,* cunning, wary, clever, tricky, politic. 'That's a foxy trick.' 'The French ambassador is a foxy old bird.' **1946** G. MILLAR *Horned Pigeon* xx. 335 And he is much too foxy to let a poor girl even smell at his antecedents. He is so clever that he speaks even his native language without accent. **1957** MEZZROW & WOLFE *Really Blues* (Gloss.) 373 *Foxy,* sly, clever.

b. Of weather: misleadingly bright.

1876 in *Eng. Dial. Dict.* **1909** *Westm. Gaz.* 10 July 3/1 Fine 'foxy' days, when hot sunshine burns the breeze up, don't last. **1933** 'L. LUARD' *All Hands* 240 'Tis foxy old weather.

2. a. Fox-coloured, reddish brown or yellow.

1850 *Jrnl. R. Agric. Soc.* XI. I. 132 There are many patches of a deep, loose, foxy soil. **1879** G. MACDONALD *Sir Gibbie* I. xiv. 198 Its forehead was high, with a mass of foxy hair over it.

b. *Painting.* Marked by excessive predominance of reddish tints; over-hot in colouring.

1783 SIR J. REYNOLDS *Notes on Du Fresnoy* 105 That [style] of Titian, which may be called the Golden Manner, when unskilfully managed becomes what the Painters call Foxy. **1821** CRAIG *Lect. Drawing* ii. 128 They allowed such an excessive brownness in their shadows, as to make them sometimes perfectly foxy. **1861** THORNBURY *Turner* II. 342 In some of the England series there is a violent foxy tone, very hot and oppressive.

3. Used to denote various defects of colour and quality resulting from atmospheric conditions, improper treatment, etc. Cf. also FOX-MARK.

1805 R. W. DICKSON *Pract. Agric.* (1807) II. 260 The substance will be what is termed foxy. **1817** W. TUCKER *Family Dyer & Scourer* iii. 28 Should the silks appear rusty, or what is known to the dyers by the name of copper burst, or foxy, it is customary to [etc.]. **1830** M. DONOVAN *Dom. Econ.* I. 351 Salt..stiffens the clammy soft dough made from new flour, and gives it a fair colour, when otherwise it would be foxy. **1846** YOUNG *Naut. Dict., Foxey* implies 'a defect in timber of a reddish cast or hue, arising from over age or other causes'. **1877** *N.W. Linc. Gloss.* (ed. 2), Turnips when they turn leathery are said to be foxy. **1883** in *Standard* 18 May 6/5 Foxy to fine ordinary Guatemala [Coffee], at 48s. **1888** ELWORTHY *W. Somerset Word-bk., Foxy,* specked, spotted—as with spots of mould or mildew. Also, clouded or uneven in shade of colour..Said of some bad dyeing. **1888** *Lockwood's Dict. Mech. Engin., Foxey,* timber is said to be foxey when there is an excessive proportion of green sapwood present in it.

4. Of beer, wine, etc.: Turned sour in the course of fermentation, not properly fermented.

1847 in HALLIW. **1864** in WEBSTER.

5. Of grapes: Having the coarse flavour of the fox-grape.

1864 in WEBSTER.

6. *U.S. slang.* Of a woman: attractive, desirable, pretty; sexy.

1913 *Dialect Notes* IV. 21 *Foxy,* stylish looking, attractive. Usage widespread in Nebraska. 'She's a *foxy* looking little lady.' **1959** *Esquire* Nov. 70 *Foxy,* beautiful. Example: Man, but she's foxy. **1961** R. RUSSELL *Sound* xii. 218, I mean all the studs in fancy duds and foxy chicks togged to the bricks is gonna be there. **1964** L. HAIRSTON in J. H. Clarke *Harlem* 292 Me and Oleta was hittin' it off fine. And she was lookin' foxier by the minute. **1978** J. HYAMS *Pool* xi. 172 The word around town is that she's a foxy lady. **1983** *Easyriders* Feb. 81/1 W/f [white female]..21 years old and foxy, would like to hear from a gorgeous man with a terrific body.

7. *Comb.,* as ***foxy-eyed, -featured, -looking, -red*** adjs.

1878 HUXLEY *Physiogr.* 26 Its inky taste, and the foxy-red sediment which it deposits..attest the presence of iron. **1880** W. J. FLORENCE in *Theatre* (U.S.) Oct. 215 The foxy-eyed party near us. **1899** S. R. CROCKETT *Black Douglas* x. 67 A red, foxy-featured man, with mean and shifty eyes. **1924** J. MASEFIELD *Sard Harker* 56 A middle-aged, foxy-looking man.

Hence **'foxiness.**

1875 LASLETT *Timber* viii. 47 Oak timber..in its worst stage of 'foxiness'. **1889** J. JACOBS *Æsop's Fables* I. 209 To him [early man] cunning was foxiness.

foxy, var. FOXIE.

†**foy,** *sb.*¹ *Obs.* [a. F. *foi,* later form of *fei* FAY *sb.*¹, faith.] **a.** Faith, allegiance, homage. **b.** As an asseverative exclamation.

1590 SPENSER *F.Q.* II. x. 41 Did foy and tribute raise. **1694** CONGREVE *Double Dealer* I. iv, O foy! Sir Paul! what do you mean?

foy (fɔɪ), *sb.*² Now *dial.* [a. Du. *fooi* (in Kilian *foye, voye*), prob., as Kilian suggests, a. Fr. *voie* way, journey.] A parting entertainment, present, cup of liquor, etc., given by or to one setting out on a journey. In different parts of Scotland applied variously to a party given in honour of a woman on the eve of her marriage; to a feast at the end of the harvest or fishing season; and the like.

1496–7 *Recs. Burgh Prestwick* 6 Feb. (Maitl.) 34 He said the said balȝeis was foy takaris, and held na courtis. *c* **1645** HOWELL *Lett.* II. xii, Hoping to enjoy you before you go, and to give you a frendly foy. **1668** J. GIBSON *Let. to F. Wright* 24 Aug., My due deserved thanks..for yᵉ friendly foy you pleased to giue me at our parting. **1700** FARQUHAR *Const. Couple* I. i, I'll pay my foy, drink a health to my King ..and away for Hungary to-morrow morning. **1741** RICHARDSON *Pamela* (1824) I. xxxvii. 343 Under the notion of my foy, I slid a couple of guineas into the good woman's hand. **1854** *Phemie Millar* 175 Mr. Millar could not reconcile himself to Isabella's foy being passed over without notice. **1856** ELIZA EDMONSTON *Sk. & T. Shetland Isl.* iv. 46 At the Foys, the time-honoured toast is, The Lord open the mouths of the gray fish. **1896** MACKAY *Hist. Fife & Kinross* x. 196 The Foy or farewell supper before Martinmas was specially a ploughman's feast.

foy (fɔɪ), *v. local.* ['Mr. G. H. Haswell informs us that on the north-east coast (esp. at Shields), a *foy-boat* was a small boat used (before the introduction of steam-tugs) to tow vessels in and out of harbour. The boat carried a small anchor or "kedge", and was rowed a certain distance ahead of the vessel being towed; the kedge was then dropped, and the men on the ship "hove upon" the kedge with a windlass until the vessel came over it, when the kedge was taken up and the process repeated. The operation was called *foying,* and the men employed *foy-men.* (See *The Maister: a Century of Tyneside Life,* p. 39.)' (*N.E.D. Addenda*).] *intr.* To go off to ships with provisions and assist them when in distress (Simson *Historic Thanet* 110). Hence **'foyer,** one who does this; **foy-boat,** a boat used by 'foyers'.

1813 R. EDINGTON *Coal Trade* 225 Not less than 500 pilot and foy-boats. **1830** *Beauties Thanet* I. 71 The Foyers of this town form a numerous and hardy class.

foyaite ('fəʊjəaɪt). *Min.* [f. *Foya* a place in Portugal, where it is found.] A kind of syenite.

1878 LAWRENCE tr. *Cotta's Rocks Class.* 169 In the syenite group we also include..foyaite. **1879** RUTLEY *Study Rocks* x. 108 Elæolite is a constituent of the rocks zircon-syenite, foyaite, miascite, and ditroite.

‖**foyer** ('fɔɪjeɪ, fwaje). [Fr.: see note s.v. FOCUS *sb.*]

1. a. = FOCUS 4.

1878 A. M. HAMILTON *Nerv. Dis.* 157 But that when the softening follows typhus fever, puerperal, and other general diseases, the foyers will be multiple.

b. Hearth, home.

1908 *Daily Chron.* 28 Jan. 4/6 The love of parents for their children..makes the every-day life of the foyer lovely. **1959** R. POSTGATE *Every Man is God* xxiii. 210 Happy families are centripetal; they have a heart, a centre to which all the rest are attracted..there is a warm *foyer* of love to hold that group together.

2. Originally, the green-room in French theatres; now usually, a large room in a theatre, concert-hall, etc., to which the audience may retire during the intervals of the performances; the entrance hall of a hotel, restaurant, theatre, etc.

1859 SALA *Tw. round Clock* (1861) 263 This model *foyer* is to have something of the Haymarket and something of the Adelphi. **1882** *Harper's Mag.* Feb. 327 Twice a year it is held in the foyer of the Academy of Music. **1901** *Dialect Notes* II. 140. **1910** *Bradshaw's Railway Guide* Apr. 1116 The Restaurant with Foyer is one of the prettiest Dining Rooms in London. **1915** 'BARTIMEUS' *Tall Ship* iv. 77 There were at least half a dozen mothers in the *foyer* of the big.. hotel. **1938** E. BOWEN *Death of Heart* III. iv. 380 She had proposed to meet him in the entrance foyer of Quayne and Merrett's.

3. = FOCUS *sb.* 5 b.

1799 MALTHUS *Jrnl.* 29 May (1966) 36 The Emperor of Russia had..been..misinformed in supposing that Hamburgh was the foyer of Democrats. **1939** A. J. TOYNBEE *Study Hist.* VI. 36 A political *foyer* for acts of religious creation.

foygne, obs. form of FOIN *v.*

foyle, foyl(l, obs. ff. of FOAL, FOOL, FOIL.

foyn(e, foynȝe(e, obs. forms of FOIN *v.* and *sb.*

foyne, obs. form of FEW.

foysen, -so(u)n, -zon, etc., obs. ff. FOISON.

foyst(e, foyster, var. of FOIST, FUSTER.

foyte, obs. form of FOOT.

fozy ('fəʊzɪ), *a. Sc.* and *dial.* [cf. Du. *voos* in Kilian also *voosch, vooghs,* 'spongiosus, rarus et levis instar fungi'); also Norw. *fos* spongy, LG. *fussig* porous, spongy.] Spongy, loose-textured; also of flesh = FOGGY 3. Also *fig.,* 'fat-witted'. Hence **'foziness.**

1821 *Blackw. Mag.* X. 753 The weak and young Whigs have become middle aged, and their foziness can no longer be concealed. **1823** J. WILSON *Ibid.* XIII. 593 A certain ingenious person..met with a turnip of more than common foziness in his field. **1826** —— *Noct. Ambr.* Wks. 1855 I. 15 The language is out of condition—fat and fozy, thickwinded,..and plethoric. **1894** IAN MACLAREN *Beside Bonnie Brier Bush* 206 He's fair fozzy wi' trokin' in his gairden an' feeding pigs.

fra, obs. form of FRO.

frab (fræb), *v. dial.* [Onomatopœic; cf. *crab* and *fret, fratch,* etc.] *trans.* To harass, worry.

1848 MRS. GASKELL *M. Barton* iv. (1882) 7/2, I was very frabbit with him. **1853** —— *Ruth* III. xii. 298, I was not kind to you. I frabbed you, and plagued you from the first. **1865** B. BRIERLEY *Irkdale* I. 34 What toylin an' frabbin ther needs Through this woald to get decently poo'd.

†**'frabble,** *sb. Obs. rare*⁻¹. [Cf. next.] Confused wrangling.

1685 H. MORE *Paralip. Prophet.* 370 Rather a frabble of words than a distinct disagreement of senses.

'frabble, *v. rare.* [dim. or freq. of FRAB. Cf. BRABBLE.] *intr.* To bicker, wrangle.

1885 *Manch. Even. News* 6 July 2/2 It is distinctly undesirable that the matter should be made a peg on which to hang further misunderstandings and frabblings.

frabjous ('fræbdʒəs), *a.* A nonsense-word invented by 'Lewis Carroll' (C. L. Dodgson), app. intended to suggest 'fair' and 'joyous'; used vaguely by others in various contextual senses. Hence **'frabjously** *adv.*

1872 'L. CARROLL' *Through Looking-Glass* i. 24 O frabjous day! Callooh! Callay! **1899** KIPLING *Stalky & Co.* 144 Oh, you frabjous asses! *Ibid.* 244 You're a dirty little schoolboy. Besides bein' frabjously immoral. **1935** 'D. SMITH' in *Famous Plays 1935–36* 171 I'm frabjously late. **1937** D. L. SAYERS *Busman's Honeymoon* iv. 96 Oh, frabjous day!.. All my life I have waited to hear those exquisite words, *Peter darling, The sweep's come.* **1970** *New Yorker* 10 Jan. 6/1 A frabjous sort of place in a somewhat vorpal neighborhood.

fracas ('frækɑː, fraka; in U.S. 'freɪkəs). Also *Sc.* fraca (Jam.). [a. Fr. *fracas*, ad. It. *fracasso*, vbl. sb. f. *fracassare* to make an uproar.] A disturbance, noisy quarrel, 'row', uproar.

1727 LADY M. W. MONTAGU *Let. to C'tess Mar* Apr., He ..occasions such fracas among the ladies of gallantry that it passes description. **1785** BURNS *Scotch Drink* 1 Let other Poets raise a fracas 'Bout vines, an' wines, an' drunken Bacchus. **1848** THACKERAY *Van. Fair* xxxvi, A violent fracas took place between the infantry-colonel and his lady.

‖**fra'cedo.** *Obs.* [mod.L. *fracēdo*, f. *frac-idus* FRACID, after the analogy of *dulcēdo* sweetness.] Putrefying heat. Hence **fra'cedinous** *a.*, erroneously *fra'cedonous*, productive of heat through putrefaction; pertaining to putrid fermentation.

1669 W. SIMPSON *Hydrol. Chym.* 253 The several sorts of Earth, are various coagulations of water, according to the difference of the Fracedinous seeds dispersed and implanted therein. *Ibid.* 329 The Fracedinous Odor. **1677** HALE *Prim. Orig. Man.* IV. ii. 306 Some Insects.. have an Origination.. by very strength and *fracedo* of the Earth and Waters quickened by the vigorous Heat of the Sun. *a* **1691** BOYLE *Hist. Air* xiii. (1692) 75 Their several malignant, congelative and fracedonous Natures and Qualities.

frache. ? *Obs.* Also 9 **fraiche.** A metal tray for holding glass-ware in the annealing process.

1662 MERRETT tr. *Neri's Art of Glass* 244 After some time these Glasses are put into Iron Pans.. call'd Fraches, which by degrees are drawn.. all along the Leer.. that the Glasses may cool Gradatim. **1799** G. SMITH *Laboratory* I. 167 Fraches. **1832** G. R. PORTER *Porcelain & Gl.* 158 The annealing oven.. is.. furnished with numerous shallow iron trays, which can be passed easily along the level bottom of the chamber. These trays are called lier-pans or fraiches.

†**'fracid,** *a. Obs.* [ad. L. *fracid-us*, f. *frac-*, *frax* lees of oil.] Rotten from over-ripeness.

1655 G. S. *Let. to Hartlib* in *Ref. Commw. Bees* 23 Insects ..is.. Natures recreation, which she out of the fracid ferment of putrifying Bodies doth form. **1656** BLOUNT *Glossogr.*, *Fracid*, more then ripe, rotten-ripe, putrified. **1721** in BAILEY. **1866** *Treas. Bot.*, *Fracid*, Of a pasty texture; between fleshy and pulpy.

fracin, frackne, var. of FRECKEN *sb. Obs.*

frack, Sc. var. of FRECK, *Obs.*

fracle, obs. form of FRECKLE.

†**fract,** *ppl. a. Obs.* [ad. L. *fract-us*, pa. pple. of *frangĕre* to break.] **a.** Broken, cracked. **b.** Of a number: Fractional.

1547 BOORDE *Brev. Health* lxx. 29 b, A mans skull.. may be fract or broken. **1715** *Phil. Trans.* XXIX. 211 Mr. Newton introduced into his Analytical Computations, the Fract, Surd, Negative and Indefinitive Indices of Dignities.

†**fractable,** *sb. Arch. Obs.* [f. prec. + TABLE.] (See quot. 1862.) Also **fractabling.**

1688 R. HOLME *Armoury* III. 451/2 Of the outsides of an House.. are.. the Fractables and Corbells. **1862** *Dict. Arch.* (Arch. Publ. Soc.), *Fractable*, or *Fract Table*; *Fractabling* at Liverpool. A term used, in the middle ages, for the *crest table* or coping running up and down the gables of a building.

fractal ('fræktəl), *sb.* (and *a.*) *Math.* [a. F. *fractal* (B. B. Mandelbrot 1975, in *Les Objets Fractals*), f. L. *fract-us*, pa. pple. of *frangĕre* to break: see -AL[1].] A mathematically conceived curve such that any small part of it, enlarged, has the same statistical character as the original. Freq. *attrib.* or as *adj.*

1975 *Sci. Amer.* Nov. 144/3 It seems that mountain relief, islands, lakes, the holes in Appenzeller and Ementhaler cheeses, the craters of the moon, the distribution of stars close to us in the galaxy and a good deal more can be described by the use of generalized Brownian motions and the idea of the fractal dimension. **1977** B. B. MANDELBROT *Fractals* i. 1/2 Many important spatial patterns of Nature are either irregular or fragmented to such an extreme degree that..classical geometry..is hardly of any help in describing their form... I hope to show that it is possible in many cases to remedy this absence of geometric representation by using a family of shapes I propose to call fractals—or fractal sets. **1977** *Sci. News* 20 Aug. 123 Sets and curves with the discordant dimensional behavior of fractals were introduced at the end of the 19th century by Georg Cantor and Karl Weierstrass. **1978** [see *snowflake curve* s.v. SNOWFLAKE 7]. **1984** *Nature* 4 Oct. 419/2 Parts of such patterns, when magnified, are indistinguishable from the whole. The patterns are characterized by a fractal dimension; the value $\log_2 3 \simeq 1{\cdot}59$ is the most common. **1985** *Ibid.* 21 Feb. 671 Mandelbrot has argued that a wide range of natural objects and phenomena are fractals; examples of fractal trees include actual trees, plants such as a cauliflower, river systems and the cardiovascular system.

'fracted, *ppl. a.* [f. L. *fract-* (see FRACTABLE *sb.*) + -ED[1].]

†**1.** Broken, in various senses. Of a number: Fractional. *Obs.*

1547 BOORDE *Brev. Health* §321 If..the memory [be] fracted with the pregnance of it [some matter above his capacity]. **1599** SHAKS. *Hen. V*, II. i. 130 His heart is fracted and corroborate. **1607** —— *Timon* II. i. 22 My reliances on his fracted dates Have smit my credit. **1674** JEAKE *Arith.* (1696) 161 If the Addends be Fracted Geodaeticals.. Then proceed in the Addition with the Fractions. **1706** W. JONES *Syn. Palmar. Matheseos* 163 This Proportion will hold, whether *n* be.. Whole, Fracted, or Surd Quantity.

2. *Her.* Having a part displaced as if broken.

1828–40 BERRY *Encycl. Her.* I. *Fracted*, broken or parted asunder..[e.g.] a fesse debruised, fracted or removed.

fractile ('fræktɪl), *a.* [f. as prec. + -ILE[1].] Pertaining to fraction or breakage; indicating liability to breakage or cleavage.

1727 BAILEY vol. II, *Fractile*, Frail or Brittle. **1893** *Scribner's Mag.* Apr. 470/2 The fractile lines of the sandstone.

fraction ('frækʃən), *sb.* Also 4–6 **fraccion, -yon.** [a. OF. *fraccion* (Fr. *fraction*), ad. eccl.L. *fractiōn-em*, n. of action f. *frangĕre* to break.]

1. The action of breaking: **a.** in the Eucharist: the breaking or dividing of the bread.

1504 ATKYNSON tr. *De Imitatione* II. xi. 190 Many foloweth hym to beparteners of the fraccyon of his brede. **1602** T. FITZHERBERT *Apol.* 50 Though it may be said.. that he suffreth fraction or breaking in the Sacrament when it is broken.. yet [etc.]. **1737** WATERLAND *Eucharist* 67 The distributing the Bread to the Company, after the Benediction and Fraction, was customary among the Jews. **1877** J. D. CHAMBERS *Div. Worship* 377 The Fraction is the most solemn, ancient, and significant Action of the whole of the Formulary of Consecration.

†**b.** with reference to material things in general, and to lines, etc.; also, refraction (of light). *Obs.*

1571 DIGGES *Pantom.* I. xxi. G j b, Glasses transparent, whiche by fraction should vnite or dissipate the images. **1612** WOODALL *Surg. Mate* Wks. (1653) 271 Fraction is the breaking of some matter with ones hand, or with an instrument. **1656** tr. *Hobbes' Elem. Philos.* (1839) 195 The bending or curvation of a strait line into the circumference of a circle.. is fraction continually increasing. **1684** BURNET *Th. Earth* I. iii. 30 Several parcels of Nature that retain still the evident marks of fraction and ruine. **1813** T. BUSBY *Lucretius* I. Comment. xxi, Had compound bodies been subject to unlimited fraction.

c. with reference to immaterial things; chiefly in obsolete uses, e.g. a disturbance (of the mind), an infraction or rupture (of the peace).

1547 BOORDE *Brev. Health* 27 This impediment [dreames] ..may come.. specially of fraction of the mynde. **1627–77** FELTHAM *Resolves* II. v. 170 When the Affections are glewed to the world, Death makes not a Dissolution, but a Fraction. **1721** STRYPE *Eccl. Mem.* I. iv. 51 The French king having lost his friendship by divers fractions of the peace with England. **1842** SIR H. TAYLOR *Edwin the Fair* I. v, The blackbird sang us forth.. loud and full at first.. then with pause And fraction fitfully.

†**2.** The result of breaking; the state of being broken; a broken place, breach, fissure, rupture; *spec.* in *Surg.* a fracture. *Obs.*

1587 FLEMING *Contn. Holinshed* III. 1349/1 Healing of bones broken, termed commonlie fractions. **1658** A. FOX *Wurtz' Surg.* II. vii. 67 Carefully feel with your finger, whether there be any fraction. **1685** TRAVESTIN *Siege Newheusel* 20 We.. made large Fractions in the Bastion. **1690** T. BURNET *Th. Earth* III. 36 If we had seen the mountains.. when the earth was fresh broken.. the fractions ..of them would have appear'd very gastly. **1705** CHERRY in Hearne *Collect.* (Oxf. Hist. Soc.) I. 22 A fall.. caus'd a great fraction in my nose. **1798** W. BLAIR *Soldier's Friend* 74 Wounds, fractions, and dislocations.

†**3.** An interruption of good feeling or harmony; discord, dissension; a rupture. In early use also: A breach of the peace, brawling. *Obs.*

1502 *Ord. Crysten Men* (W. de W. 1506) IV. ix. 193 Whiche taketh wylfully ony persone.. in the chyrcheyarde ..or yᵉ whiche there maketh ony fraccion. **1591** HORSEY *Trav.* (Hakl. Soc.) 262 Betwen the Poll and them fractions, and factions among themselves. **1606** SHAKS. *Tr. & Cr.* II. iii. 107. **1670** COTTON *Espernon* II. VI. 262 By which means ..a fraction betwixt them must of necessity ensue. *a* **1713** SHAFTESBURY *Char.* (1749) III. 143 Fractions at Court.—Ship-wreck of Ministrys. **1721** [see 1 c].

4. a. Something broken off; a disconnected portion; a fragment, scrap, small piece. Said with reference both to material and immaterial things. ***by fractions***: piecemeal, by halves. Now *rare.*

1606 SHAKS. *Tr. & Cr.* V. ii. 158 The fractions of her faith, orts of her loue. **1607** —— *Timon* II. ii. 220. **1641** PRYNNE *Antip.* To Rdr., My primitive intention was, to have presented thee with this.. Antipathy intirely at the same instant without fractions. **1656** DAVENANT *Siege Rhodes* I. To Rdr., Why my numbers are so often diversify'd and fall into short fractions. **1657** SANDERSON *Pref. to Serm.* (1681) §23 Whilest they are still crumbling into Fractions and Factions. **1796** H. HUNTER tr. *St. Pierre's Stud. Nat.* (1799) II. 19 No one is disposed to be a friend by fractions. **1840** CARLYLE *Heroes* (1858) 233 Mahomet's followers found the Koran lying all in fractions.

†**b.** ? A paragraph or section (of a book). *Obs.*

1625 BURGES *Pers. Tithes* 44 In the next Fraction after that branch of the Statute.. it is said; Prouided alwaies [etc.].

5. *Math.* **a.** *Arith.* A numerical quantity that is not an integer; one or more aliquot parts of a unit or whole number; an expression for a definite portion of a unit or magnitude.

common or ***vulgar fractions*** are those in which the numerator and denominator are represented by numbers placed the one above, the other below, a horizontal line. Sometimes *fraction* is used for 'vulgar fraction', or for a quantity expressed by means of a numerator and denominator; e.g. 'the fraction $\frac{4}{2} = 2$'. For *complex, compound, continued, decimal, proper* and *improper fractions*, see those words.

c **1391** CHAUCER *Astrol.* Prol. §3 Smallest fraccions ne wol nat ben shewed in so smal an instrument. **1542** RECORDE *Gr. Artes* 130 b, Thenne maye I boldly enstructe you in yᵉ arte of fractions or broken nomber. **1614** RALEIGH *Hist. World* II. (1634) 214 But the very minutes and lesser fractions were to be observed by him. **1668** WILKINS *Real Char.* 393 A Fraction may be exprest.. by the Adjective Neuter. **1705** ARBUTHNOT *Coins* (J.), Pliny put a round number near the truth, rather than a fraction. **1811** W. IRVING in *Life & Lett.* (1864) I. 269 This place would suit you to a fraction. **1812–16** PLAYFAIR *Nat. Phil.* II. 243 The deflection.. if reduced to feet, comes out 16 and a small fraction. **1827** HUTTON *Course Math.* I. 86 The vulgar fraction may be reduced to a decimal, then joined to the integer, and the root of the whole extracted. **1838** DE MORGAN *Ess. Probab.* 30 The probability of an event is measured by the fraction which the number of favourable cases is of all that can happen. **1846** GREENER *Sc. Gunnery* 392 The Belgians too find the same result to a fraction. **1847** GROTE *Greece* I. xxviii. (1862) III. 43 The village is a fraction, but the city is an unit. **1878** HUXLEY *Physiogr.* 11 The fraction which denotes the ratio of the two distances is sometimes termed the representative fraction.

b. *Alg.* An expression analogous to an arithmetical vulgar fraction, in which the numerator and denominator are algebraical terms or expressions.

1812–16 PLAYFAIR *Nat. Phil.* (1819) I. 39 This fraction is a maximum, when the denominator $A + B +$ [etc.] is a minimum.

6. A portion of a section (sense 2 e (b)) of land. *U.S.*

1789 in C. Cist *Cincinnati* (1841) 209 The whole of the township and fraction to be surveyed. **1815** D. DRAKE *Cincinnati* vi. 202 The principal wall or embankment, encloses an entire block of lots and some fractions. **1837** J. M. PECK *Gaz. Illinois* I. 77 Fractions are parts of quarter sections intersected by streams or confined claims. **1847** in H. Howe *Hist. Coll. Ohio* 206 Matthias Denman.. had purchased the fraction of land on the bank of the Ohio, and the entire section adjoining it on the north. **1901** S. E. WHITE *Westerners* xviii. 156 Thar is a lode.. over on the J. G. fraction that's shore th' purtiest bit of quartz lead you ever see.

7. Any one of the portions, differing in physical or chemical properties, into which a mixture may be separated, esp. by physical methods.

1857 *Phil. Mag.* 4th Ser. XIII. 134, I selected the fraction boiling in the fifteenth rectification at 240°F. to make a preliminary experiment upon. **1873** *Ibid.* XLV. 129 In such a case each fraction of the distillate will have the same composition as every other fraction and as the original mixture. **1904** [see FRACTIONALLY *adv.*]. **1913** A. R. WARNES *Coal Tar Distill.* 52 When it is not desired to recover the anthracene, the heavy creosote and anthracene oil fractions are sometimes not separated, but worked as one fraction. **1955** *Sci. Amer.* Aug. 92/3 Electrophoresis is the special name given to the technique of separating molecular mixtures into fractions. **1958** *New Scientist* 9 Jan. 12/1 The purification of these liquids gives rise to aromatic fractions suitable for use as gasoline components. **1960** L. PICKEN *Organization of Cells* v. 188 Five different particle fractions were.. separated from the homogenate at five different speeds and times of centrifugation. **1971** *Nature* 13 Aug. 455/2 Textural variation depends on changes in the proportions of sand and clay with the silt fraction remaining fairly constant.

8. In Communist use: see quots. 1922 and 1927. Also, a deviant or schismatic group. Hence **'fractionism,** the views or policies of such a group; **'fractionist,** a member or adherent of such a group. Also (all forms) *transf.* Cf. FRACTIONAL *a.* c.

1922 *Communist Party Gt. Brit.: Rep. Organisation* ii. 25 Besides his area group, every member will have some special task. He may be on the Speakers' Group, or working in the Local Labour Party Fraction. *Ibid.* 26 A Fraction is a Party organisation inside a representative or delegate body. (It is also used for a grouping of all the Communists and their followers inside a trade union or similar organisation.) **1927** *Communist Party Training* (*Communist Party Gt. Brit.*) 117 A fraction is composed of all Party members inside any unit or representative committee of a non-party organisation, united for the purpose of conducting Party work in same. **1949** *Times* 10 Jan. 6/1 Other new words recently collected from this paper include *fractionist* (akin to deviationist). **1952** *New Yorker* 25 Oct. 106/2 Among Marty's other criminal fractionisms were that he thought American imperialism in France was of only secondary importance. **1952** M. MCCARTHY *Groves of Academe* (1953) xiii. 262 In the fraction, I was given the assignment of recruiting Mulcahy to the Party. **1954** *Encounter* Feb. 48/2 Last came the rank and file, whose work consisted of making speeches, distributing leaflets, attending party and fraction meetings. **1954** KOESTLER *Invis. Writing* xxiii. 255 It is essential to.. discredit a person or fraction 'in the eyes of the masses' before he or they are liquidated. **1958** *New Statesman* 1 Feb. 136/2 The fact is that Conservatives, Liberals, Socialists and Roman Catholics all hold 'fraction meetings' and decide what their policy is to be in the trade unions. **1959** B. & R. NORTH tr. *Duverger's Pol. Parties* (ed. 2) I. iii. 174 The development of fractions is not a sign of the liberty of members..: rather does it point to differences of opinion between members of the ruling class.

Hence ˈ**fraction** *v.*, to break into fractions or pieces. ˈ**fractionlet**, a small fragment.

1830 CARLYLE in Froude *Life in Lond.* (1882) II. 88 Wrote a fractionlet of verse, entitled 'The Beetle'. **1840** —— *Heroes* ii. 47 The Nation fractioned and cut asunder by deserts.

fractional (ˈfrækʃənəl), *a.* [f. FRACTION + -AL[1].]

a. Of, pertaining to, or dealing with a fraction or fractions; comprising or constituting a fraction; of the nature of a fraction. Hence, incomplete, partial, insignificant. ***fractional currency*** (see quot.). ***fractional distillation***: see DISTILLATION 3. ***fractional note*** (*N. Amer.*), a note in fractional currency. ***fractional section*** = FRACTION *sb.* 6.

1675 OGILBY *Brit.* Pref., Not regarding the Fractional Parts of a Mile. *a* **1806** Fox *Speech, Proc. Ld. Melville* Sp. 1815 VI. 584 The right honourable gentleman.. has amused the House with an account of fractional sums of 8*s.* 6*d.*, 14*s.*, and 2*s.* **1815** D. DRAKE *Cincinnati* 129 Cincinnati is built upon one entire and two fractional sections. **1828** D'ISRAELI *Chas. I*, II. ii. 32 At length we are surprised that these fractional disputes close into one mighty..enmity. **1858** MILL *Liberty* iv. (1865) 45/1 The interest which society has in him individually..is fractional. **1861** GOSCHEN *For. Exch.* 102 Realizing a fractional profit for the convenience which they afford. **1863** *Stat. at Large U.S.A.* (1864) XII. 711 In lieu of postage and revenue stamps for fractional currency, and of fractional notes, commonly called postage currency, ..the Secretary of the Treasury may issue fractional notes of like amounts in such form as he may deem expedient. **1878** *Congress. Rec.* 29 Jan. 638/2 [Silver] is not like our fractional notes, a promise to pay. It is payment. *Ibid.* 4 Feb. 727/2 The fractional currency had become so ragged and so dirty that people were willing to surrender it for almost anything. **1879** WEBSTER, Supp., *Fractional currency*, small coin, or paper notes, in circulation, of less value than the monetary unit. **1892** *Daily News* 20 Dec. 7/3 Messrs. B. decline to accept Messrs. M.'s fractional certificates in exchange for bonds. **1903** R. STILES *4 Yrs. under Marse Robert* 63 In the South during the war banks, municipalities, companies, and .. individuals issued fractional notes or shin plasters which passed as currency supplementary to the Treasury notes issued by the Confederate Government. **1946** J. T. ADAMS *Album Amer. Hist.* III. 135 Later (July, 1862) Congress legalized small change notes by providing for the issuance of fractional currency in denominations of 3, 5, 10, 15, 25 and 50 cents.

b. *Chem.* Designating a process in which different fractions of a mixture are separated in consequence of their differing physical properties. So ***fractional crystallization***, ***distillation*** (see DISTILLATION 3), ***precipitation***, etc.

1857 W. A. MILLER *Elem. Chem.* III. i. 9 This process of *fractional* distillation is well adapted to the separation of liquids. **1886** *Chem. News* 10 Sept. 131/1 Fractional crystallisation has yielded new results with didymium. *Ibid.*, Working with the samarskite earths, fractional precipitation with oxalic acid separates first erbia, holmia, and thulia, then terbia, and lastly yttria. **1897** G. F. BECKER in *Amer. Jrnl. Sci.* CLIV. 257 (*heading*) Fractional crystallization of rocks. *Ibid.* 258 The process..usually known as fractional crystallization..has been employed in the purification of compounds ever since chemistry was pursued. **1949** ALEXANDER & JOHNSON *Colloid Sci.* II. xxvii. 797 Fractional solution may also be employed, a series of solvents of increasing solvent power being used to extract the unfractionated polymer. **1950** N. V. SIDGWICK *Chem. Elements* I. 456 Fractional precipitation of the hydroxides is useful in isolating the very weakly basic $Sc(OH)_3$ or the strongly basic $La(OH)_3$. **1960** TURNER & VERHOOGEN *Ign. & Metamorph. Petrol.* (ed. 2) iv. 85 The nature of the liquid fraction of a crystallizing magma at a given moment depends on..the degree to which fractional crystallization has already been effective. **1966** *McGraw-Hill Encycl. Sci. & Technol.* XI. 118 Fractional distillation to remove iron, lead, and cadmium from crude zinc. **1968** COULSON & RICHARDSON *Chem. Engin.* (ed. 2) II. xiv. 577 It is often possible to separate a mixture of two soluble salts by fractional crystallization.

c. In Communist use: of, or pertaining to, a fraction (sense 8). Hence ˈ**fractionalism**, the doctrine or policy of a fraction; an instance of deviating from the official line of the Communist Party; ˈ**fractionalist**, an adherent or supporter of fractionalism; also *attrib.* or as *adj.* Also (all forms) *transf.* Cf. FRACTIONISM, -IST (s.v. FRACTION *sb.* 8).

1929 *Communist Party Gt. Brit.: New Line* 77 Greater attention must be given to..the strengthening of all fractional activities within the trade unions. **1941** KOESTLER *Scum* 157 The *abstentionisme* of the Chamber was intended to be a subtle fractional device; in fact it was a declaration of irresponsibility. **1945** —— *Yogi & Commissar* 203 Behind the façade of Popular-Front Committees..the air was thick with Comintern-intrigue and fractional conspiracy. **1950** E. H. CARR *Bolshevik Rev.* I. viii. 202 The criticism of individuals or even of groups would be tolerated within the party, but the opposition must not organize: that would be to commit the sin of 'fractionalism'. **1953** *Newsweek* 2 Mar. 38/3 Two months ago he was finally ousted from the French Communist Party as a 'fractionalist'. **1959** *Oxf. Mail* 28 Jan. 1/7 Mr. Podgorny..said the 'fractional activity of the group had been exposed. **1959** *Times* 29 Jan. 8/3 The anti-party group members were accused of 'fractionalism'. **1960** *Spectator* 19 Feb. 241 These last he dismissed as 'fractionalist' because, he claimed, they subordinated the national interest to that of fractions of the nation in coalition.

Hence ˈ**fractionally** *adv.*, in a fractional manner or degree; by a fraction or fractions; in *Chem.*, so as to separate into fractions.

1871 *Jrnl. Chem. Soc.* XXIV. 405 Bromotetracodeine is conveniently obtained as hydrobromide by..dissolving the residue in the smallest possible quantity of weak hydrobromic acid, and fractionally precipitating by cautious addition of stronger acid. **1883** *Daily News* 7 Nov. 4/7 American prices were firm, but foreign Government stocks receded fractionally. **1888** *Ibid.* 4 Dec. 7/2 A surplus, applied to augment that dividend fractionally. **1904** F. SODDY *Radio-Activity* 17 If the active barium chloride was fractionally crystallised, the activity tended to concentrate in the least soluble fraction. **1954** REILLY & RAE *Physico-Chem. Methods* (ed. 5) II. 253 Intimate mixtures are fractionally disintegrated.

fractionalize (ˈfrækʃənəlaɪz), *v.* [f. FRACTIONAL *a.* + -IZE.] *trans.* To break up or separate into distinct parts or fractions. Hence ˈ**fractionalizing** *vbl. sb.* Also ˌ**fractionaliˈzation**, an act of, or the process of, fractionalizing.

1931 *Economist* 5 Sept. 420/2 Their report underlines even more categorically..the disadvantages which result from the fractionalising of the economic life of Europe. **1945** *Annals Amer. Acad. Pol. & Soc. Sci.* Jan. 55/1 Hampered by political fractionalization..the countries of eastern Europe have nevertheless made rapid progress. **1947** *Amer. Friend* 24 July 286/1 It is so easy to sectionalize and fractionalize humanity. **1955** *N.Y. Times* 17 June 14/7 John B. Hollister ..said he thought it would be a mistake to begin an 'early fractionalization' of foreign aid activities. **1957** L. F. R. WILLIAMS *State of Israel* 158 The Israel system has the disadvantage of so fractionalizing the representation in the legislature that no party has yet succeeded in gaining an absolute majority. *Ibid.* 159 The fractionalization of representation in the Knesset between some fourteen groups. **1967** *Times Rev. Industry* July 89/1 It [*sc.* information] is fractionalised; in other words, it is scattered about between different departments and different people.

fractionary (ˈfrækʃənərɪ), *a.* [f. FRACTION + -ARY[2]. Cf. Fr. *fractionnaire.*] **a.** = FRACTIONAL. **b.** Dealing with or carried on by fractions or fragments. **c.** Tending to divide into fractions.

a. **1674** JEAKE *Arith.* (1696) 32 But the further practise therewith must be referred to Fractionary or Contract Operations. **1847** GILFILLAN in *Tait's Mag.* XIV. 523 To discharge even a fractionary part of what would never in whole be defrayed.

b. **1840** MRS. CARLYLE *Lett.* I. 128 Fritters away my time in fractionary writing. **1847** DE QUINCEY in *Tait's Mag.* XIV. 666 Beyond what can be supplied by the fractionary life of petty brokerage or commerce.

c. **1867** *Contemp. Rev.* V. 154 The 'fractionary' ecclesiastical spirit of the African Christians has been traced in the enormous numbers of the African bishops.

fractionate (ˈfrækʃəneɪt), *v.* [f. FRACTION + -ATE[3].] **1. a.** *trans.* To separate (a mixture) by distillation or otherwise into portions of differing properties. Hence ˈ**fractionated** *ppl. a.*

1867 W. R. BOWDITCH *Coal Gas* 5 These heavy oils were obtained by passing the gas over carefully fractionated pure light coal oils. **1894** *Nature* 23 Aug. 410/2 By fractionating Russian petroleum the author had obtained hydrocarbons [etc.].

b. *gen.* = FRACTIONALIZE *v.*

1961 in WEBSTER. **1963** C. D. SIMAK *They walked like Men* xxvi. 155 Might there not be no more than a single one of them, with that one fractionated into units the size of bowling balls? **1965** *Listener* 12 Aug. 233/2 We spend much of our time fractionating living matter. We break it up with sonic oscillations..or by chilling it in solid carbon dioxide and hitting it with a hammer. **1970** *Sci. Jrnl.* Apr. 5/1 Pollution matters beat even space activities for the extent to which they are fractionated between different departments —no less than 12 are involved.

2. *intr.* To break up into fractions.

1957 G. E. HUTCHINSON *Treat. Limnol.* I. viii. 543 If the drop fractionates, small daughter drops may be carried to the top of the cloud in an updraft.

Hence ˈ**fractionating** *ppl. a.* and *vbl. sb.*; ***fractionating column***, a long vertical chamber for fractionating liquids in which vapour from a still passes upwards to a condenser and mixes intimately with falling condensate on the way, so becoming enriched in the lower-boiling fractions.

1908 *Jrnl. Chem. Soc.* XCIV. II. 17 (*heading*) A Fractionating Column... A condenser is provided inside the top of the..apparatus, and the distilled liquid is collected at the lower part, being returned to the distillation flask or run off as desired. **1922** C. S. ROBINSON *Elem. Fract. Distill.* iii. 17 The second general method by which fractionating can be obtained, is fractional condensation. **1952** SMITH & STINSON *Fuels & Combustion* i. 22 The vapors are passed into the fractionating column where the oil is separated into several fractions. **1970** R. M. E. DIAMANT *Appl. Chem. Engineers* (ed. 2) xiv. 248 The degree of separation of the liquid into upper and lower fractions depends upon the number of plates or the length of the fractionating column.

fractionation (frækʃəˈneɪʃən). [f. FRACTIONATE: see -ATION.] The action or an act of fractionating.

1878 KINGZETT *Anim. Chem.* 210 It may..be separated from that substance by a process of fractionation. **1926** *Encycl. Brit.* II. 164/1 The production of an innumerable series of colour-forms, as in the sweet pea, is almost certainly due to the fractionation of the colour-complex. **1934** H. C. WARREN *Dict. Psychol.* 109/2 *Fractionation*, a piecemeal method of describing a conscious experience, in which the situation is repeated exactly..a number of times with varied instructions. **1951** G. HUMPHREY *Thinking* 68 The subject might be required to notice..what happened in consciousness before the stimulus word appeared. This was the method of fractionation. **1963** *Language* XXXIX. 11 'Position' in a sentence is defined by successive fractionations, i.e. when a sentence has just two positions, each of which may be occupied by a word or a phrase, and when each constituent phrase in turn may be divided into two positions. **1966** *Rep. Comm. Inquiry Univ. Oxf.* I. 135 The growth and present size of most departments now means that these duties are far beyond the grasp of a single head, and fractionation has become essential to well-being and progress.

fractionize (ˈfrækʃənaɪz), *v.* [f. FRACTION + -IZE.] *trans.* (and *absol.*) To break up into fractions.

1675 COLLINS in Rigaud *Corr. Sci. Men* (1841) I. 216 If the second term of an equation be wanting, the penultimate may be removed into the room of it..and that without fractionizing. **1831** SOUTHEY in *Q. Rev.* XLV. 443 They fractionize, they divide. **1841** *Fraser's Mag.* XXIV. 207 To ..fractionise..the Conservative party, would be an act of treachery. **1872** *Contemp. Rev.* XX. 583 All of these fragmentary ideas..fractionize, but do not resolve the problem.

fractious (ˈfrækʃəs), *a.* [f. FRACTION (sense 3), after *captious*, etc.

The original sense seems to have been 'disposed to make breaches, factious'; the more trivial use now current may be due to association with FRATCH.]

Refractory, unruly; now chiefly, cross, fretful, peevish; *esp.* of children.

1725 DE FOE *Voy. round World* (1840) 353 Having had an account how mutinous and fractious they had been. **1776** FOOTE *Capuchin* III. Wks. 1799 II. 399 The young slut is so headstrong and fractious. **1824** W. IRVING *T. Trav.* II. 30 A terrible peevish fractious fellow. **1847** ALB. SMITH *Chr. Tadpole* lxi. (1879) 510 Baby would be getting so very fractious. **1857** BUCKLE *Civilisation* vii. 402 The fractious and disloyal conduct of many of the hierarchy. **1880** L. WALLACE *Ben-Hur* ix. 46 Men struggling doubtfully with fractious cows and frightened sheep.

transf. **1821** COLERIDGE in *Blackw. Mag.* X. 261 The fractious noise of the dashing of a lake on its border.

Hence ˈ**fractiously** *adv.*; ˈ**fractiousness**.

1727 BAILEY vol. II, *Fractiousness.* **1736** —— (folio), *Fractiously.* **1753** MISS COLLIER *Art Torment.* 159 She will ..ask your pardon..for having indulged your own fractiousness. **1855** MACAULAY *Hist. Eng.* IV. 54 The treason of Russell is to be attributed partly to fractiousness. **1858** POLSON *Law & L.* 99 His fractiousness, and his want of patience. **1878** MRS. H. WOOD *Pomeroy Abb.* (ed. 3) 122 'How stupid you are, Bridget!' she fractiously said.

fracto- (ˈfræktəʊ), used as comb. form of L. *fractus* broken, in *Meteorology* (see quots.).

1896 *Internat. Cloud-Atlas* (*Internat. Meteorol. Committee*) 18 (*heading*) International designations of cloud-forms... Fr. Cu... Fracto-cumulus. Fr. N... Fracto-nimbus. Fr. S... Fracto-stratus. **1917** A. G. MCADIE *Princ. Aërography* 115 The true cumulus..is often torn by strong winds,..('fracto-cumulus'). *Ibid.*, If the mass of nimbus is torn up into small patches..they may be called 'fracto-nimbus', the 'scud' of the sailors. **1926** —— *Man & Weather* 68 The word *fracto*..is now in general use to designate a cloud form in which the mass is broken into small divisions. **1956** J. C. SWAYNE *Conc. Gloss. Geogr. Terms* 62 *Fracto-nimbus cloud* (*scud*), ragged fragments of cloud drifting rapidly in a strong wind often under rain clouds.

fracturable (ˈfræktjʊərəb(ə)l, -tʃərəb(ə)l), *a.* [f. FRACTURE *v.* + -ABLE.] That can be fractured.

1897 *Kodak News* May 6 Nor should there be anything easily fracturable. **1911** H. S. HARRISON *Queed* xxxi, He might fracture all of the decalogue that was refinedly fracturable.

fracture (ˈfræktjʊər), *sb.* Also 6 fractour. [a. Fr. *fracture*, ad. L. *fractūra*, f. *fract-* ppl. stem of *frangĕre* to break.]

1. The action of breaking or fact of being broken; breakage; *spec.* in *Surg.* (the earliest use), the breaking of a bone, cartilage, etc.

1541 R. COPLAND *Galyen's Terap.* 2 Bj, Ye must begyn the lygature at the vlcerate party, in ledynge it towarde the hole partye, as Hyppocrates wylleth in the fractour of bones. **1677** HALE *Prim. Orig. Man.* I. i. 38 Without any great fracture of the more stable and fixed parts of Nature. **1720** DE FOE *Capt. Singleton* xiv. (1840) 241 The shock of the air, which the fracture in the clouds made. **1832** BABBAGE *Econ. Manuf.* iv. (ed. 3) 33 Time is requisite for producing the fracture of the ice. **1878** T. BRYANT *Pract. Surg.* (1879) II. 39 Fracture of the sterno-costal cartilages is a rare accident.

fig. **1842** LD. COCKBURN *Jrnl.* I. 315 Preparations have begun to be made for..fracture of the Church.

2. a. The result of breaking; a crack, division, split; †a broken part, a splinter.

1641 'SMECTYMNUUS' *Answ.* §18 (1653) 71 Their Fractures were so many, they knew not which Religion to chuse if they should turne Christians. **1651** JER. TAYLOR *Holy Dying* iv. §8 (1727) 177 Reconcile the fractures of his family. **1654** GAYTON *Pleas. Notes* I. v. 16 Besides, the losse of his Launce, though it stuck emblematically on his sides, yet the fractures went to his heart. **1798** W. CLUBBE *Omnium* 33 He got off his box, and went to splicing the fractures [of the harness]. **1814** SCOTT *Ld. of Isles* v. vi, O'er chasms he pass'd, where fractures wide Craved wary eye and ample stride. **1832** DE LA BECHE *Geol. Man.* (ed. 2) 29 No appearances of fracture are visible in the hills. **1876** J. S. BREWER *Eng. Stud.* ii. (1881) 78 They admitted no such fracture in the chain of our political existence.

b. *Surg.* For *comminuted*, *compound*, *simple fracture*, see those words.

1525 tr. *Brunswick's Surg.* G iiij, If the fracture be lytell it shall be cured like yᵉ contusyon aforesayd. **1599** A. M. tr. *Gabelhouer's Bk. Physicke* 306/2 Whether it be a wounde or a Fracture. **1633** G. HERBERT *Temple, Repentance* vi, Fractures well cur'd make us more strong. **1656** RIDGLEY *Pract. Physick* 161 Fractures of the Nose, Cheek-bones.. fasten again in twenty or twenty-four days. **1789** W.

BUCHAN *Dom. Med.* (1790) 593 The art of reducing fractures. **1835–6** TODD *Cycl. Anat.* I. 443/1 In one [bone] the fracture had not united. **1843** BETHUNE *Sc. Fireside Stor.* 11 The fracture was a simple one.

fig. **1859** HOLLAND *Gold F.* vi. 98 Old fractures of character that refuse to unite.

3. The characteristic appearance of the fresh surface in a mineral, when broken irregularly by the blow of a hammer. More fully, ***surface of fracture***.

1794 SULLIVAN *View Nat.* I, Sparkling in its fracture like sugar. **1812–16** J. SMITH *Panorama Sc. & Art* I. 2 The fracture of which is of a dark colour. **1830** HERSCHEL *Stud. Nat. Phil,* I. iii. 47 The rock at once splits with a clean fracture. **1831** BREWSTER *Optics* xii. 101 The two surfaces of fracture were absolutely black. **1869** PHILLIPS *Vesuv.* iii. 65 It breaks with a resinous fracture.

†**4.** = FRACTION 5. *Obs.*$^{-1}$

1674 JEAKE *Arith.* (1696) 230 Forasmuch as alwayes an whole Year..is not the subject of the Question..but sometimes Parts or Fractures of the whole are useful.

5. *Phonology.* The euphonic substitution of a diphthong for a simple vowel, owing to the influence of a following consonant (in OE. *h, l, r*); the diphthong so produced.

1891 A. L. MAYHEW *O.E. Phonol.* §81 Short *eo* corresponds to Germ. *e*, as the result of fracture before final *h*. *Ibid.* §84 *eo* = *io* the fracture of Germ. *i* before *h* + cons.

6. *attrib.* and *Comb.*, as ***fracture-bed, -bedstead***; (of fracture in the earth's crust): ***fracture-line, -system, -zone***; **fracture-surface** (= sense 3).

1884 *Health Exhib. Catal.* 102/1 *Fracture Beds. *Ibid.* 102/2 *Fracture Bedstead. **1925** J. JOLY *Surface-Hist. Earth* viii. 140 The long rift valley of South Australia, mainly meridional in direction, as well as meridionally-directed *fracture-lines along the eastern side of that continent. **1805–17** R. JAMESON *Char. Min.* (ed. 3) 135 The *fracture-surfaces or planes thus exposed. **1922** *Encycl. Brit.* XXXI. 214/2 Rectilinear and regularly intersecting *fracture-systems. **1965** A. HOLMES *Princ. Physical Geol.* (ed. 2) xxvi. 939 By far the most astonishing structures of the East Pacific Rise are the E–W fracture zones which have sliced the Rise into long crustal slabs.

fracture (ˈfræktjʊə(r)), *v.* [f. prec. sb.]

1. a. *trans.* To cause a fracture in, *esp.* a bone, etc.; to break the continuity of; to crack.

[**1612–1794** see the ppl. adj.] **1803** M. CUTLER in *Life, Jrnls. & Corr.* (1888) II. 134, I fell upon a large round timber and fractured two ribs. **1830** LYELL *Princ. Geol.* I. 132 Before our secondary strata were formed, those of older date..were fractured and contorted. **1858** LARDNER *Hand-bk. Nat. Phil., Hydrost.* 7 A liability of bursting or fracturing some parts of the machine might arise. **1859** W. COLLINS *Q. of Hearts* I. ii. 42 She would..fracture her skull with the pony.

b. To impress, excite, amuse greatly. *U.S. slang.*

1946 H. BROWN *Sound of Hunting* II. 116 This guy Muller fractures me. **1951** M. SHULMAN *Many Loves of Dobie Gillis* (1953) 41 We're a riot, hey. We play all kinds of funny stuff. We fracture the people. **1955** L. FEATHER *Encycl. Jazz* (1956) x. 346 *Fracture*, impress, excite, amuse. **1966** *Crescendo* Aug. 20/2, I know he fractured you the same as he did me. **1970** H. E. ROBERTS *Third Ear* 7/1 *Fracture v.*, to make one laugh.

2. *intr.* for *refl.* To suffer fracture; to break.

18.. *Science* IV. No. 16. 5 (Cent.) The implements..are of sandstone [or] quartzite, neither of which fractures properly when subjected to heat.

3. *Phonology.* (*trans.*) To subject to fracture.

1889 ELLIS *E.E. Pronunc.* v. 496 The peculiar manner of fracturing the vowels in the A-, A', Æ, E-, EA', O' words by prefixing an accented (ee) or (*ii*) and reducing the vowel itself to indistinct (ɐ).

Hence **ˈfractured** *ppl. a.*; **ˈfracturing** *vbl. sb.* and *ppl. a.*

1612 WOODALL *Surg. Mate* Wks. (1653) 149 Nothing cureth a fractured bone so much as rest. *a* **1763** SHENSTONE *Economy* III. 38 Behold his chair, whose fractur'd seat infirm An aged cushion hides. **1794** SULLIVAN *View Nat.* I. 104 That mass of fractured and sinking country. **1830** HERSCHEL *Stud. Nat. Phil.* 285 The sudden application of convulsive and fracturing efforts. **1834** MRS. SOMERVILLE *Connex. Phys. Sc.* xxx. (1849) 350 The part which originally had a north pole acquires a south pole at the fractured end. **1886** A. WINCHELL *Walks & Talks Geol. Field* 221 Much fracturing of the crust must have resulted.

frae, Sc. form of FRO.

‖**frænulum** (ˈfriːnjʊləm). *Anat.* Also **frenulum** (ˈfrɛnjʊləm). [dim. of FRÆNUM.] **1.** A small frænum; a frænum.

1706 in PHILLIPS (ed. Kersey). **1840** YOUATT *Horse* viii. (1847) 204 A portion of the tongue of a mare, extending as far as the frænulum beneath. **1843** J. G. WILKINSON tr. *Swedenborg's Anim. Kingd.* I. ii. 59 Each of the lips has its peculiar frænulum.

2. *Ent.* A bristle or group of bristles attached to the base of the hind wing in many Lepidoptera, and interlocking with a process on the front wing, thus uniting the two wings of a side in flight. Hence **ˈfrenate, ˈfrenular** *adjs.*

1892 G. F. HAMPSON *Fauna Brit. India, Moths* I. 6 The fore and hind wings of the majority of families of moths are united by a 'frenulum' arising from the base of the costa of the hind wing and fitting into a 'retinaculum' on the fore wing. **1898** A. S. PACKARD *Text-bk. Entomol.* 122 In many Lepidoptera they [*sc.* the wings] are loosely connected by the loop and frenulum. **1925** A. D. IMMS *Gen. Textbk. Entomol.* III. 418 Among Hetero-neura two main types of wing-coupling apparatus are also evident, viz: the frenate and the amplexiform. In the frenate type a sexual difference is very noticeable. **1969** R. F. CHAPMAN *Insects* viii. 175 Many other Lepidoptera have the frenulum well developed. *Ibid.*, In Micropterygidæ the jugum is folded under the fore wings and holds the frenular bristles.

‖**frænum, frenum** (ˈfriːnəm). Pl. **fræna, frena**. [L. *frēnum, frænum*, bridle.]

1. *Anat.* A small ligament or membranous fold which bridles or restrains the motion of the organ to which it is attached; *e.g.* that of the tongue.

1741 MONRO *Anat.* (ed. 3) 147 The Frænum of the Tongue. **1754–64** [see FOURCHETTE 1 a.]. **1807–26** S. COOPER *First Lines Surg.* (ed. 5) 382 In persons born dumb, the state of the frænum should always be examined. **1872** COHEN *Dis. Throat* 51 The glosso-epiglottic fold..or frænum of the epiglottis.

2. (See quot. 1859.)

1859 DARWIN *Orig. Spec.* vi. 192 Pedunculated cirripedes have two minute folds of skin, called by me the ovigerous frena, which serve, through the means of a sticky secretion, to retain the eggs until they are hatched. **1877** HUXLEY *Anat. Inv. Anim.* vi. 295 The ovigerous fræna of Lepas.

frag (fræg), *v.* *U.S. Mil. slang.* [Abbrev. of *fragmentation (grenade).*] To throw a fragmentation grenade at one's superior officer, esp. one who is considered over-zealous in his desire for combat. So **ˈfragging** *vbl. sb.*

1970 *Daily Colonist* (Victoria, B.C.) 9 Dec. 5/4 Another spectacular technique is 'fragging'. 'To frag' is a term meaning to use a fragmentation grenade 'to cool the ardor of any officer or NCO too eager to make contact with the enemy'. **1971** *Courier-Mail* (Brisbane) 19 May 1/3 There were 209 fragging incidents last year, according to the Army and 34 deaths were listed as probably due to these. **1972** *Sat. Rev.* 8 Jan. 12/1 Fragging is a macabre ritual of Vietnam in which American enlisted men attempt to murder their superiors. The word comes from the nickname for hand grenades, a weapon popular with enlisted men because the evidence is destroyed with the consummation of the crime.

fraght, obs. form of FRAUGHT.

fragile (ˈfrædʒaɪl, ˈfrædʒɪl), *a.* Also 6 **fragyll**, 8 **fragil**. [a. F. *fragile* (14th c.), ad. L. *fragil-is*, f. *frag-* root of *frangĕre* to break. See FRAIL *a.*]

1. a. Liable to break or be broken; easily snapped or shattered; in looser sense, weak, perishable, easily destroyed. Also *fig.*

1607 SHAKS. *Timon* v. i. 204 Throwes That Natures fragile Vessell doth sustaine In lifes vncertaine voyage. **1626** BACON *Sylva* §841 Of Bodies, some are Fragile; and some are Tough, and not Fragile. *a* **1668** DENHAM *Progr. Learn.* 188 When subtile Wits have spun their thred too fine, 'Tis weak and fragile, like Arachne's line. **1671** MILTON *P.R.* III. 388 Much ostentation vain of fleshly arm And fragile arms. **1756** BLACKLOCK *Soliloquy* 281 Secure, thy steps the fragile board could press. **1832** G. R. PORTER *Porcelain & Gl.* 248 Threads..render the material [glass] extremely fragile. **1856** KANE *Arct. Expl.* I. xxvii. 356 We found the spot..hemmed in by loose and fragile ice.

b. Of persons, etc.: Of weak or tender frame or constitution, delicate (= FRAIL, but used with an allusion to the primary sense).

1858 FROUDE *Hist. Eng.* III. xvii. 435 The..people saw as yet but a single fragile life between the country and a disputed succession. **1883** OUIDA *Wanda* I. 43 An old lady, so delicate..so pretty and so fragile.

†**2.** Liable to err or fall into sin; frail. *Obs.*

1513 BRADSHAW *St. Werburge* I. 1875 More lyke an angell ..Than a fragyll mayde of sensuall appetyte. *Ibid.* I. 2776 A wanton prynce folowynge sensualyte And his fragyll appetyte. **1548** HALL *Chron., Edw. IV* (an. 23) 248 b, Suche is the blyndnes of our fraile and fragile nature, euer giuen to carnal concupiscence.

3. quasi-*sb* in *pl.* = fragile articles or goods.

1882 *Pall Mall G.* 19 June 10/1 Cases..marked ..'Fragiles'.

Hence **ˈfragilely** *adv.*, **ˈfragileness**.

1727 BAILEY II, *Fragileness.* **1864** WEBSTER, *Fragilely.*

fragility (frəˈdʒɪlɪtɪ). [a. F. *fragilité* (12th c.), ad. L. *fragilitātem*: see FRAILTY.]

1. The quality of being fragile or easily broken; hence, liability to be damaged or destroyed, weakness, delicacy.

1474 CAXTON *Chesse* 147 Hit is not fittyng for a woman to goo to bataylle for the fragylite and feblenes of her. **1604** R. CAWDREY *Table Alph., Fragilitie*, brittlenes, or weakenesse. *c* **1620** BACON *Wks.* (1857) III. 807 Three things are chiefly to be observed: the colour: the fragility or pliantness: the volatility or fixation. **1707** *Curios. in Husb. & Gard.* 25 Man ought not to regard.. Flowers without reflecting..on their Fragility and small Duration. **1756** BURKE *Subl. & B.* III. xvi, An air of robustness and strength is very prejudicial to beauty. An appearance of delicacy, and even of fragility, is almost essential to it. **1866** TATE *Brit. Mollusks* iv. 131 The shell of this species is..characterized by its extreme thinness and fragility.

b. *fig.*

1603 KNOLLES *Hist. Turks* (1638) 54 That which was left of his body..lay, as..the miserable spectacle of mans fragilitie. **1750** JOHNSON *Rambler* No. 71 ¶9 General forgetfulness of the fragility of life. **1751** *Ibid.* No. 143 ¶3 They would..lament..the fragility of beauty. **1886** SIR H. MAINE *Pop. Govt.* in *Fortn. Rev.* N.S. XXXIX. 171 The controversy as to the relative fragility, or the relative difficulty, of popular government and other forms of government.

†**2.** Moral weakness, frailty. *Obs.*

1398 TREVISA *Barth. De P.R.* I. (1495) 8 In case that bi humayne fragilyte or freyltee thou trespas ayenst the commaundement of almyghty god. *a* **1533** LD. BERNERS *Huon* I. 167 Adam & Eue..the whiche by theyr fragylyte brake goddes commaundement. **1579** FULKE *Heskins' Parl.* 273 God condescending to our fragilities. **1600** HOLLAND *Livy* VIII. 307 Beseeching the Dictatour to forgive this humane fragilitie and youthfull folly of Qu. Fabius. *a* **1624** SWINBURNE *Spousals* (1686) 156 The fragility and mutability of the fæminine Sex considered.

fragment (ˈfrægmənt), *sb.* [a. F. *fragment* (16th c.) or ad. L. *fragment-um* (f. *frangĕre* to break).]

1. A part broken off or otherwise detached from a whole; a broken piece; a (comparatively) small detached portion of anything.

1583 HOLLYBAND *Campo di Fior* 75 They promised me to bring me..some of the leavinges, or fragmentes [of a feast]. **1611** BIBLE *John* vi. 13. **1632** LITHGOW *Trav.* vi. 280 The valley..now filled up with fragments of old walles. **1704** NEWTON *Optics* II. III. v. 55 If a thin'd or plated Body.. should be..broken into fragments of the same thickness with the plate. **1716** POPE *Iliad* VIII. 493 Their Car in Fragments scatter'd o'er the Sky. **1807–26** S. COOPER *First Lines Surg.* (ed. 5) 155 Extracting..the fragments of bone. **1814** SCOTT *Wav.* xvi, A mere precipice, with here and there a projecting fragment of granite. **1848** W. H. BARTLETT *Egypt to Pal.* x. (1879) 221 Fragments of old pottery.

2. *transf.* and *fig.* A detached, isolated, or incomplete part; a (comparatively) small portion of anything; a part remaining or still preserved when the whole is lost or destroyed.

1531 ELYOT *Gov.* I. xix, At that tyme Idolatry was nat clerely extincte, but diuers fragmentes therof remained in euery region. **1571** DIGGES *Pantom.* III. vi. Q iij b, Howe fragmentes or partes of a Globe are measured. **1607** SHAKS. *Timon* IV. iii. 399 Where should he haue this Gold? It is some poore Fragment, some slender Ort of his remainder. **1809–10** COLERIDGE *Friend* (ed. 3) III. 109 However irregular and desultory his talk, there is method in the fragments. **1852** ROBERTSON *Serm.* Ser. I. xix. (1866) 318 Fragments of truth torn out of connection. **1870** E. PEACOCK *Ralf Skirl.* II. 100 This fragment of the County of Lincoln [the isle of Axholme]. **1871** FREEMAN *Norm. Conq.* (1876) IV. xviii. 189 Thegns of the shire who retained some small fragments of their property.

b. An extant portion of a writing or composition which as a whole is lost; also, a portion of a work left uncompleted by its author; hence, a part of any unfinished whole or uncompleted design.

1595–6 CAREW in *Shaks. C. Praise* 20 Shakespeare and Marlows fragment. **1628** EARLE *Microcosm., Critic* (Arb.) 56 He conuerses much in fragments and *Desunt multa's*. **1662** STILLINGFL. *Orig. Sacr.* I. ii. §11 The fragments of Manetho in Eusebius. **1712** ADDISON *Spect.* No. 333 ¶8 Claudian in his Fragment upon the Gyants War. *a* **1748** WATTS *Improv. Mind* I. xx. (1801) 183 Cowley, in his unfinished fragment of the Davideis. **1875** JOWETT *Plato* (ed. 2) III. 191 The 'New Atlantis' is only a fragment.

†**c.** applied to a person as a term of contempt.

1606 SHAKS. *Tr. & Cr.* v. i. 9 From whence, Fragment? **1607** —— *Cor.* I. i. 226 Go get you home, you Fragments.

†**3.** = FRACTION 5. *Obs. rare.*

1674 JEAKE *Arith.* (1696) 41 The next sort..are Fractions, sometime called Fragments. *Ibid.* 60 If $\frac{1}{84}$ be divided by any of the three Fragments.

fragment (ˈfrægmənt, frægˈmɛnt), *v.* [f. the sb.] *trans.* and *intr.* To break or separate into fragments.

1818 KEATS *Endymion* iii. 845 For what poor mortals fragment up, as mere As marble was there lavish. **1901** H. MCINTOSH *Is Christ Infallible?* I. iii. 76 They vainly dream that they can fragment and vivisect the Spirit's embodiment and environment of Christ's teaching. **1919** *Proc. Class. Assoc.* 27 Specialism..has fragmented the specialities themselves in a way that makes the outlook hazardous. **1961** *Time* 7 July 30 The Revolutionary Council..was fragmenting in despair.

fragmental (ˈfrægməntəl, frægˈmɛntəl), *a.* [f. FRAGMENT *sb.* + -AL[1].] = FRAGMENTARY; *spec.* in *Geol.* (see quot. 1882).

1798 JANE AUSTEN *Northang. Abb.* (1833) II. ix. 159 Some fragmental journal, continued probably to the last gasp. **1837** WHEWELL *Hist. Induct. Sc.* (1857) I. 218 Collected from his lips, or from fragmental notes. **1845** MOIR in *Blackw. Mag.* LVIII. 410 The treasuries Of half-forgotten and fragmental things. **1882** GEIKIE *Text-bk. Geol.* (1885) 116 Fragmental rocks are formed either of the débris of older rocks, or of the aggregated remains of plants or animals.

Hence **fragmentally** *adv.*

1814 LAMB *Let. to Coleridge* 26 Aug., Inquire in seven years' time for the 'Rokebys' and the 'Laras', and where shall they be found? fluttering fragmentally in some thread-paper. **1848** *Blackw. Mag.* LXIV. 540.

fragmentary (ˈfrægməntərɪ), *a.* [f. FRAGMENT *sb.* + -ARY. Cf. mod.F. *fragmentaire*.

Johnson 1755 cites Donne, and says 'a word not elegant, nor in use'. It has been common since 1835.]

Of the nature of, or composed of, fragments; not complete or entire; disconnected or disjointed.

1611 DONNE *Lett.* (1651) 158 With those fragmentary recreations I must make shift. *a* **1631** —— *Progr. Soul*, 2nd Anniv. 82 What fragmentary rubbidge this world is Thou know'st. **1835** BROWNING *Paracelsus* II. 32 A few Discoveries, as appended here and there, The fragmentary produce of much toil. **1844** THIRLWALL *Greece* VIII. lxiv. 275 We have but scanty and fragmentary notices of his operations. **1856** KANE *Arct. Expl.* I. xx. 248 Becoming embarrassed in fragmentary ice. **1875** JOWETT *Plato* (ed. 2) III. 527 His knowledge is fragmentary and unconnected.

b. *spec.* in *Geol.* Composed of fragments of previously-existing rocks, etc.

1836 MACGILLIVRAY tr. *Humboldt's Trav.* xxi. 305 The rocks were found to be fragmentary, consisting of pieces of coral, cemented by carbonate of lime, and interspersed with quartzy sand.

Hence **'fragmentarily** *adv.*; also **'fragmentariness.**

1836 J. STERLING *Ess. & Tales* (1848) I. p. lxxxvii, I have always had..a sense of fragmentariness from not having been there. **1856** EMERSON *Eng. Traits, Universities* Wks. (Bohn) II. 94 Pamphleteer or journalist..must read meanly and fragmentarily. **1860** WESTCOTT *Introd. Study Gosp.* vi. (ed. 5) 329 The various narratives of the Resurrection place the fragmentariness of the Gospel [of St. Luke] in the clearest light. **1871** *Daily News* 18 Sept., Where an enterprising enemy might have cut them off fragmentarily.

fragmentation (frægmən'teɪʃən). [f. FRAGMENT *sb.* + -ATION. Cf. F. *fragmentation.*]

1. A breaking or separation into fragments; *spec.* in *Biol.* separation into parts which form new individuals.

1881 *Times* 24 Dec., Fragmentation of work, not attacking too many points at once. **1882** E. R. LANKESTER in *Nature* XXVIII. 88 The 'fragmentation', or division of the chlorophyll corpuscles of both Hydra and Spongilla. **1882** VINES *Sachs' Bot.* 946 This process of nuclear division has been termed fragmentation. **1920** H. G. WELLS *Outl. Hist.* I. VI. xxx. 380/1 The state of Europe beneath its political fragmentation was a social disorder. **1943** *Roof over Britain* ii. 10 The fragmentation of metals under certain conditions. **1958** *Spectator* 15 Aug. 213/1 The fragmentation of French political parties. **1959** *Listener* 23 July 152/2 The music is a study in fragmentation.

2. Comb.: **fragmentation bomb, grenade,** one designed to disintegrate into small fragments on explosion.

1918 *Aviation* 15 Nov. 502/2 Deliveries of the 'demolition' and 'fragmentation' bombs..were made in April. **1944** *Times* 10 Feb. 4/6 An airfield was hit with fragmentation bombs. **1957** F. KROLLMANN *Langenscheidts Fachwörterbuch Wehrwesen* 647/1 Fragmentation shell.. fragmentation grenade. **1970** *Peace News* 3 Apr. 5 (*caption*) This Vietnamese woman was the victim of a fragmentation bomb (made in the USA). **1970** Fragmentation grenade [see FRAG *v.*]. **1971** *Daily Tel.* 22 Apr. 4/5 Incidents of American soldiers in Vietnam tossing fragmentation grenades at officers more than doubled, to 209, last year.

fragmented ('frægməntɪd, -'mɛntɪd), *pa. pple.* and *ppl. a.* [f. FRAGMENT *sb.* + -ED[2]. Cf. F. *fragmenté.*] Broken into fragments, made fragmentary.

*a***1817** JANE AUSTEN *Northanger Abbey* (1818) II. ix. 172 In the shape of some fragmented journal, continued to the last gasp. **1830** *Fraser's Mag.* II. 128 What follows is a song from the same fragmented masque. **1852** WILLIS *Summer Cruise in Medit.* xxiii. 143 Heaps of fragmented columns. **1864** *Reader* 2 July 20 Examples of bones fragmented by man of animals extinct in that part of Europe. **1893** *19th Cent.* Nov. 839 The tumbled crags..Lie fragmented in horror. **1955** *Times* 24 June 10/7 The necessity of avoiding such isolation..was felt more profoundly than elsewhere in a Europe fragmented by history. **1964** G. L. COHEN *What's Wrong with Hospitals?* v. 99 With responsibility for the expectant mother fragmented or frantically shuffled between three authorities (hospital, local health, general practice).

fragmentist ('frægməntɪst). [f. FRAGMENT *sb.* + -IST. Cf. F. *fragmentiste.*] A writer of fragments or of works which survive only in fragments.

1874 H. R. REYNOLDS *John Bapt.* v. §2. 314 The Wolfenbüttel fragmentist. **1882-3** SCHAFF *Encycl. Relig. Knowl.* I. 390 The [Muratorian] fragmentist.

fragmen'titious, *a. rare.* [f. FRAGMENT *sb.*, after *commentitious* or the like.] = FRAGMENTARY.

1827 J. S. MILL in Bentham *Rationale Jud. Evid.* III. 573 The papers..were..left by him in a very incomplete and fragmentitious state. **1837** HARRIS *Great Teacher* 404 Instead of resting in any fragmentitious excellence, it only sends him in thought to the great Archetype.

fragmentize ('frægməntaɪz), *v.* [f. as prec. + -IZE.] *trans.* To break into fragments. So ˌ**fragmenti'zation.**

1815 MURRAY *Let. Byron* in Smiles *Life* (1891) I. xv. 354 You should fragmentize the first hundred [lines], and condense the last thirty. **1885** W. C. RUSSELL *Strange Voy.* I. xiii. 182 You can..fragmentize her into a medley of spars, ropes, and planks. **1951** *Yale Rev.* Spring 514 The majority of the population, up in arms against a fragmentization of their native land. **1968** *New Scientist* 21 Mar. 617/1 The French Minister for Science, M. Maurice Schumann objected, we have been told, to the use of the phrase 'fragmentization of Europe' in the draft report of last week's OECD meeting.

†**'fragor**[1]. *Obs.* Also -our. [a. L. *fragor*, f. *frag-* stem of *frangĕre* to break.] A loud harsh noise, a crash, din.

1605 DANIEL *Philotas* Wks. (1717) 339 Those thund'ring Fragors that affright the Earth. **1660** F. BROOKE tr. *Le Blanc's Trav.* 392 This Streight is vexed with forcible tides ..which..encounter with a most obstreperous fragour. **1702** WATTS *Horæ Lyr., Vict. Poles over Osman*, Scarce sounds so far The direful fragor, when some southern blast Tears from the Alps a ridge of knotty oaks.

†**fragor**[2]. *Obs. rare.* Also -our. [a. It. *fragore* = *frägrore* f. L. *frāgr-*: see FRAGRANT.] Fragrance.

1638 SIR T. HERBERT *Trav.* 185 The gardens challenge our attention; than which for grandeur and fragor no Citie in Asia out-vies her. *Ibid.* 322 [The musk] by its fragor is oft found by the carelesse passenger.

fragrance ('freɪgrəns). [a. OF. *fragrance*, ad. late L. *frāgrantia*, f. *frāgrans*: see FRAGRANT.] Sweetness of smell; sweet or pleasing scent.

1667 MILTON *P.L.* IX. 425 Eve separate he spies, Veiled in a cloud of fragrance. **1725** POPE *Odyss.* VI. 92 A cruise of fragrance, formed of burnish'd gold. **1751** GRAY *Spring* 10 Cool Zephyrs through the clear blue sky Their gather'd fragrance fling. **1817** MOORE *Lalla R.* (1824) 131 As they sat in the cool fragrance of this delicious spot. **1853** C. BRONTE *Villette* xxx, Inhaling the fragrance of baked apples from the refectory.

fig. **1821** KEATS *Isabella* x, To meet again..and share The inward fragrance of each other's heart. **1838** J. H. NEWMAN *Par. Serm.* (1839) IV. xvii. 297 Years that are past bear in retrospect so much of fragrance with them.

Hence **'fragrance** *v. nonce-wd.* (*trans.*), to fill with fragrance.

1854 *Tait's Mag.* XXI. 449 The rose-bush fragrances all the vale.

fragrancy ('freɪgrənsɪ). Now *rare.* [see prec. and -ANCY.] The quality of being fragrant; sweetness of smell. Occas. with *pl.*

1578 BANISTER *Hist. Man* v. 79 b, He hath lost the sauour of the roses and frangrantie [*sic*] of their nature. **1607** TOPSELL *Four-f. Beasts* (1658) 120 The fragrancy of every green herb yeeldeth such a savour as [etc.]. **1693** SALMON *Pharm. Bat.* I. (1713) 78/2 Thus have you..one of the most abominable Scents upon Earth, made one of the greatest Fragrancies in the whole World. **1725** POPE *Odyss.* IX. 245 The goblet crown'd Breath'd aromatic fragrancies around. **1764** HARMER *Observ.* iv. 201 The fragrancy of the fruit is admirable. **1876** J. P. NORRIS *Rudim. Theol.* i. 10 The pleasant fragrancy of the fine pollen that floats into the air.

fig. *a***1631** DONNE in *Select.* (1840) 124 When others give allowance of our works, and are edified by them, there is their savour, their odour, their perfume, their fragrancy. **1689** *Trial Pritchard v. Papillon* 6 Nov. 1684 11 Pray let us have none of your Fragrancies, and Fine Rhetorical Flowers, to take the People with. **1817** COLERIDGE *Biog. Lit.* 100 The High German is indeed a *lingua communis*..the choice and fragrancy of all the dialects.

fragrant ('freɪgrənt), *a.* Also 6 **fragraunt**; see also FLAGRANT 6. [a. F. *fragrant* (16th c. in Godefroy) or ad. L. *frāgrant-em*, pr. pple. of *frāgrāre* to smell sweetly.] Emitting a sweet or pleasant odour, sweet-smelling.

1500-20 DUNBAR *'Now fayre, fayrest'* 7 Freshe fragrant floure. **1514** BARCLAY *Cyt. & Uplondyshm.* (Percy Soc.) xxxii, The fragraunt odour & oyntment of swete floure. **1596** SPENSER *F.Q.* IV. i. 31 As fresh and fragrant as the floure-deluce She was become. **1667** MILTON *P.L.* IV. 645 Fragrant the fertil earth After soft showers. *a***1721** PRIOR *Garland* ii, The flowers less blooming than her face, The scent less fragrant than her breath. **1871** B. TAYLOR *Faust* (1875) I. xxi. 178 The springtime stirs within the fragrant birches.

fig. **1651** *Fuller's Abel Rediv., Erasmus* 84 In Basil He did end his dayes, As full of yeeres as fragrant fame. **1782** COWPER *Conversation* 631 Their fragrant memory will outlast their tomb. **1827** KEBLE *Chr. Y., Churching* i. This hallow'd air Is fragrant with a mother's first and fondest prayer.

Hence **'fragrantly** *adv.*; †**'fragrantness.**

1515 BARCLAY *Egloges* iv. (1570) C vj/2 As medoes paynted with floures redolent The sight reioyce of suche as them beholde: So man indued with vertue excellent Fragrantly shineth with beames manyfolde. **1555** ABP. PARKER *Ps.* xxxiv. 85 Gods goodnes smelleth most fragrantly. **1616** SURFL. & MARKH. *Country Farme* 449 To keepe the aromaticall fragrantnesse in those which smell sweet. **1707** J. MORTIMER *Husb.* 137 As the Hops begin to change colour ..and smell fragrantly, you may conclude them ripe.

fraiche: see FRACHE; also obs. f. FRESH.

†**fraid,** *a. Obs.* [app. the pa. pple. of **fraid* v. ad. OF. *freidir*: see FRETISH *v.*[1]] (See quot.)

1577 B. GOOGE *Heresbach's Husb.* (1586) III. 123 b, If a horse have..taken cold, which the Germanes call *Verfangen*, in English foundred, or in some places fraide.

fraid: see FRAYED *ppl. a.*[1]

'fraid (freɪd), *a. colloq.* [aphet. f. AFRAID *ppl. a.*] (I'm) afraid. So (chiefly *Children's*) phr. *fraid cat* (also *fraidy cat*), a coward. Cf. FRAYED *ppl. a.*[1]

1888 KIPLING *Story of Gadsbys* (1889) 85 'Fraid you won't be entered in the Stud Book correctly unless you go Home? **1895** —— *Day's Work* (1898) 195 Wish I could, Lizzie. 'Fraid I can't. **1908** G. JEKYLL *Children & Gardens* (*caption*, facing p. 64), 'Fraid I've dropped a stitch! *c***1910-23** in WENTWORTH *Amer. Dial. Dict.* (1944) 'Fraidy cat. **1912** *Dialect Notes* III. 576 *Fraid-cat*, a coward. **1942** C. MORLEY *Thorofare* xlix. 286 You're an old fraid-cat. **1945** N. L. MCCLUNG *Stream runs Fast* iv. 26 He might not have been so composed, if he had known he had two fraidy-cats to take care of him. **1968** C. AIRD *Henrietta Who?* i. 4 'Accident?' shouted the man at the wheel... ''Fraid so,' shouted back Ford. **1968** D. GRAY *Died in Red* xiii. 65 'So you won't go on working here?' 'No. 'Fraid not.'

fraik. *Sc.* Some kind of sea-bird.

1830 *Edin. Encycl.* V. 220 Scarfs, marrots, fraiks and other seafowl hatch in the rocks.

frail (freɪl), *sb.*[1] Forms: 4-5 frayel, fraell(e, fraiel, 4-6 frayle, 5-6 frale, 6 fraile, 7 freal, 6- frail. [a. OF. *frayel*, of unknown origin.]

1. A kind of basket made of rushes, used for packing figs, raisins, etc.; the quantity of raisins, etc. (30 to 75 lbs.) contained in this.

13.. *Coer de L.* 1549 Fyggys, raysyns, in frayel. **1382** WYCLIF *Jer.* xxiv. 2 One fraiel hadde good figus. *c***1420** *Pallad. on Husb.* XI. 494 A multitude of reysouns..take, And into russhy frayels rare hem gete. **1483** *Cath. Angl.* 141/1 A frale [*v.r.* fraelle] of fygis, *palata.* **1562** TURNER *Herbal* II. 144 b, A kind of..sea rishe (whereof the frayles are made that fyges and rasines are carried hether in out of Spayne). *c***1618** FLETCHER *Q. Corinth* II. iv, Three frailes of spratts.. Ore as much meat as these. **1791** COWPER *Iliad* XVIII. 719 In frails of wicker bore the luscious fruit. **1836** *Fraser's Mag.* XIV. 286 Sixteen frails of Zante currants. **1880** W. WHITELEY *Diary & Alman.* 82 Frail of figs = 32 to 56 lbs.

2. 'A rush for weaving baskets' (Johnson 1755).

3. *Comb.*, as *frail basket, -bent, -rush.*

1548 TURNER *Names Herbs* (E.D.S.) 76 Spartum herba.. may be called in english Frailbente. **1578** LYTE *Dodoens* IV. lii. 511 The frayle Rushe or panier Rushe, bycause they use to make figge frayles and paniers therwithall. **1815** A. CONSTABLE *Let.* 27 Jan. in *J. Constable's Correspondence* (1962) I. 112 The frail basket in which the turkey is, is your own. **1900** A. MORRISON *Cunning Murrell* i. 9 Over his shoulder he carried a large gingham umbrella..and from its handle hung a frail basket.

frail, *sb.*[2] ? *Obs.*

1691 T. H[ALE] *Acc. New Invent.* 119 Observations upon loading of a Ship with Lead..Salt, Frail, and Timber.

frail, *sb.*[3] *slang* (chiefly *U.S.*). [Subst. use of FRAIL *a.*] A woman.

1908 H. GREEN *Maison de Shine* 50 Aw, the frails is all the same... A guy comes along and shoots that old con about how he's the grandest thing on earth, an' the wisest of 'em fall. **1926** *Amer. Speech* I. 462/1 The Apollo Theater in London prints the following glossary of slang in its program as a guide to 'Is Zat So?' *Dame, Frail,*..Girl. **1931** E. LINKLATER *Juan in Amer.* II. xvi. 177 Bullets whistling through the air to..threaten widowhood for the ravished frail. **1945** P. CHEYNEY *I'll Say she Does* v. 141 She's a swell dish—a lovely piece of frail. **1970** K. PLATT *Pushbutton Butterfly* (1971) iv. 36 A smaller soggy shape was huddled behind him... An Angel and his frail challenging another night.

frail (freɪl), *a.* Forms: 4-5 fre(e)(l)l(e, (4 freile, 5 fraiel, frale, freall, freyle), 5-7 fraile, -yle, 6- frail. [ad. OF. *fraile, frele* (Fr. *frêle*) = It. *fraile*:—L. *fragilis* FRAGILE.]

1. Liable to break or be broken; easily crushed or destroyed.

1382 WYCLIF *Wisd.* xiv. 1 An other thinkende to seilen.. the tree berende hym, inwardli clepeth a more frele tree. *c***1440** *Promp. Parv.* 177/2 Freyl, and brokulle, or brytylle, *fragilis.* **1535** COVERDALE *Wisd.* xv. 13 He yᵗ of earth maketh frayle vessell and ymages, knoweth himself to offende aboue all other. *c***1586** C'TESS PEMBROKE *Ps.* xcii. 7 The wicked grow Like fraile, though flowry grasse. **1600** FAIRFAX *Tasso* VI. xlviii, Their armours forged were of mettall fraile. **1713** YOUNG *Last Day* II. 63 Thus a frail model of the work design'd First takes a copy of the builder's mind. **1812** J. WILSON *Isle of Palms* II. 496 In that frail bark the lovers sit. **1879** STAINER *Music of Bible* 82 Their great age renders the wood from which they were made extremely frail.

b. Of immaterial things, sometimes with conscious metaphor: Subject to casualties, liable to be suddenly shattered, transient.

*c***1450** *St. Cuthbert* (Surtees) 2482 How freele is werldly welefare. *a***1533** LD. BERNERS *Gold. Bk. M. Aurel.* (1546) C ij b, It is no new thyng that men gape for hygh and frayle thynges. **1656** COWLEY *Pindar. Odes 2nd Olympique* vi, With a frail good they wisely buy The solid Purchase of Eternity. **1703** ROWE *Ulyss.* IV. i. 1523 Grasp thy frail Life, and break it like a Bubble. **1770** GOLDSM. *Des. Vill.* 291 But when those charms are past, for charms are frail. **1843** J. MARTINEAU *Chr. Life* (1867) 295 A profounder but a frailer bliss.

2. Weak, subject to infirmities; wanting in power, easily overcome.

1382 WYCLIF *Rom.* viii. 3 That was vnpossible to the lawe, in what thing it was syk, or freel, by fleisch. **1398** TREVISA *Barth. De P.R.* v. lxii. (1495) 178 The flesshe..was freell and brotyll of mankynd. *c***1450** tr. *De Imitatione* I. xxii. 29 Al þe while þat we bere þis fraiel body, we can not be wiþoute synne. **1545** JOYE *Exp. Dan.* ii. 28 b, Because the toes were parte yerne and parte baked erthe, this empyre shalbe partely stronge and partely frayle and weak. **1593** SHAKS. *Lucr.* 227 Wil not my tongue be mute, my fraile ioints shake? **1611** BIBLE *Ps.* xxxix. 4 That I may know how fraile I am. **1790** BEATSON *Nav. & Mil. Mem.* I. 291 The Governor and Council..knowing the frail condition of the place, were greatly alarmed. **1853** MRS. CARLYLE *Lett.* II. 222 Too weak and frail to be out of bed. **1871** R. ELLIS *Catullus* lxv. 18 Lest ..these words..Seem too soon from a frail memory fallen away.

b. *dial.* (See quot.)

[Cf. **1387** in 5.] **1886** *S.W. Linc. Gloss.*, *Frail*, weak-minded, timid, frightened: as 'She was born frail, poor lass.'

3. Morally weak; unable to resist temptation; habitually falling into transgression.

Now sometimes applied as a half-jocular euphemism, to a woman who lives unchastely or has fallen from virtue.

*a***1340** HAMPOLE *Psalter* xxiv. 8 See how frele I am of kynd. **1362** LANGL. *P. Pl.* A. III. 117 Heo is frele of hire Flesch, Fikel of hire tongue. **1597** HOOKER *Eccl. Pol.* v. xxii. §10 In our speech of most holy things, our most fraile affections many times are bewrayed. **1667** MILTON *P.L.* III. 404 Purposed not to doom frail Man So strictly. **1713** YOUNG *Force Relig.* I. (1757) 54 Though with ill frail nature will be mov'd, I'll bear it well. **1824** W. IRVING *T. Trav.* I. 250 The leniency of one who felt himself to be but frail. **1868** FREEMAN *Norm. Conq.* (1876) II. vii. 90 Most likely a child of the frail Abbess of Leominster.

†**4.** Tender. *Obs.*

1590 SPENSER *F.Q.* III. viii. 31 That sight..smote Deepe indignation and compassion frayle Into his hart.

5. *Comb.*, as *frail-bodied*, *-floreted*, *-lived*, *-strung*, *-witted*.

1850 LYNCH *Theo. Trin.* xi. 211 Trinal was a *frail-bodied man. **1860** RUSKIN *Mod. Paint.* V. VI. i. §1 Infinite orchards wreathing the hills with *frail-floretted snow. **1859** LD. LYTTON *Wanderer* (ed. 2) 204 *Frail-lived April's newliest nurtured blossoms. **1820** KEATS *Lamia* I. 309 The self-same pains Inhabited her *frail-strung heart. **1387** T. USK *Test. Love* III. vii (Skeat) 57 *Freelwitted people supposen in such poesies to be begyled.

Hence †**'frailful** *a.* [+ -FUL], extremely frail. **'frailish** *a.* [+ -ISH], somewhat frail, feeble. **'frailly** *adv.*, in a frail manner.

a **1300** *Cursor M.* 25689 Man..þat frelli fra þi [God's] frenscep fell. *a* **1541** WYATT *Domine ne in furore tuo* Poet. Wks. 216, I know my frailful wickedness. **1630** J. TAYLOR (Water P.) *Whore* 33 Wks. II. 108/2 King Dauid frailely fell. **1854** LOWELL *Lett.* (1894) I. 209 A rather frailish kind of stuff. **1860** *Chamb. Jrnl.* XIV. 50 The two garments linked frailly by a half-yard of string.

frail, *v. U.S. dial.* [prob. f. Eng. dial. *frail* flail.] *trans.* To beat, thrash. Hence **'frailing** *vbl. sb.*

1851 M. L. BYRN *Arkansaw Doctor* 82 (Th.), The old man plainly told her..he would frail her worse than a dog would a pole-cat. *Ibid.* 123 (Th.), He..did not like the thought of getting a frailing for it. **1890** J. C. HARRIS in *Century Mag.* Dec. 287/1 He uped an' frailed me out, an' got the gal to boot. **1896** *Peterson Mag.* Jan. 89/2 A frailing with a dead branch left him [*sc.* a mule] unmoved. **1901** W. CHURCHILL *Crisis* I. xii. 97 Reckon I'd frail 'em good ef he catched hold of me with his black hands. **1932** W. FAULKNER *Light in August* (1933) xi. 229 I'll frail the tar out of you.

frailness ('freɪlnɪs). Now *rare.* [f. FRAIL *a.* + -NESS.] The quality of being frail; liability to be broken or destroyed, fragility; lack of permanence; weakness, physical or mental; moral weakness, inability to resist temptation.

a **1300** *Cursor M.* 25337 Thurgh frelnes of oure fless. *c* **1374** CHAUCER *Boeth.* IV. pr. ii. 87 (Camb. MS.) Yif thou knowe clerly the frelenesse of yuel, the stidefastnesse of good is knowen. *c* **1380** WYCLIF *Sel. Wks.* III. 405 Freelnesse and towghnesse [of bread]. **1447** BOKENHAM *Seyntys* (Roxb.) 195 In a uergyn pure The freelnesse took of oure nature. *c* **1450** *Cov. Myst.* (Shaks. Soc.) 108 ȝe must consyder the frelnes of mankende. **1509** BARCLAY *Shyp of Folys* (1570) 236 Let hir [fortune] passe and hir fraylenes defye. **1535** COVERDALE *Rom.* xv. 1 We that are stronge ought to beare yᵉ fraylenesse of them which are weake. **1545** *Richmond. Wills* (Surtees) 55 After mannes fraylnes of condycons deyth to every creatour is certan. **1687** J. NORRIS *Misc., Of Courage* 166 There is nothing among all the frailnesses and uncertaintys of this sublunary world so tottering and unstable as the virtue of a Coward. **1871** BROWNING *Balaust.* 160 Pity for the frailness found in flesh. **1882** C. A. DAVIS in Spurgeon *Treas. Dav.* Ps. cxix. 81–8 The depression arising from mortal frailness.

frailty ('freɪltɪ). [ad. OF. *fraileté*:—L. *fragilitātem*, f. *fragilis* FRAGILE.]

1. Liability to be crushed or to decay, either in a material or immaterial sense; perishableness, weakness; an instance of this; †also, a frail feature or spot, a flaw. Now *rare.*

1382 WYCLIF *Heb.* vii. 28 The lawe ordeynede men prestis hauynge sykenesse or freelte. *c* **1400** MAUNDEV. (1839) Prol. 5 Mynde of Man ne may not ben comprehended ne witheholden, for the Freeltee of Mankynde. **1593** NASHE *Four Lett. Confut.* 29 No frailtie hath thy fame, but the imputation of this Idiots friendship. **1615** G. SANDYS *Trav.* 216 Tyrus is now no other then an heape of ruines; yet.. they..instruct the..beholder with their exemplary frailty. **1635** QUARLES *Embl., Hierogl.* vi, Behold the frailty of this slender snuff. **1665** HOOKE *Microgr.* Pref. a b, The like frailties are to be found in the Memory; we often let many things slip away from us. **1781** COWPER *Convers.* 554 The works of man inherit..Their author's frailty, and return to dust. **1818** CRUISE *Digest* (ed. 2) IV. 230 A person may feel conscious of such weakness, and frailty of mind. **1883** *Manch. Exam.* 26 Nov. 5/3 The frailty of the vessels which are employed in the lake traffic.

2. Moral weakness; instability of mind; liability to err or yield to temptation.

a **1340** HAMPOLE *Psalter* xxi. 2 To shew þe frelte of mannys fleysse. *a* **1400** *Prymer* (1891) 105 Alle the synnes þat they han doon by freelte of worldli lifynge. *c* **1440** *Gesta Rom.* xi. 37 (Harl. MS.) If we synne by..frailte..late vs with shrifte..do it away. **1538** STARKEY *England* I. i. 18 They consydur not the fraylty of man, wych seyng the best folowyth the worst. **1604** SHAKS. *Oth.* IV. iii. 100 Is't Frailty that thus erres? **1661** COWLEY *Disc. Govt. O. Cromwell* Verses & Ess. (1669) 57 Sir, it may be you have spoken all this rather to try than to tempt my frailty. **1725** WATTS *Logic* Introd., Something of this Frailty is owing to our very Constitution. **1876** C. M. DAVIES *Unorth. Lond.* 78 All frailty is taken clean away.

b. A fault arising from infirmity; a 'weakness'.

1606 SHAKS. *Ant. & Cl.* x. ii. 123, I..do confesse I haue Bene laden with like frailties, which before Haue often sham'd our Sex. **1635** QUARLES *Embl.* III. vi. (1718) 150 See not my frailties, Lord, but through my fear. **1718** LADY M. W. MONTAGU *Let. to Abbe Conti* 19 May, My vanity (the darling frailty of mankind) [is] not a little flattered. **1750** GRAY *Elegy* 126 No farther seek..to..draw his frailties from their dread abode. **1877** MOZLEY *Univ. Serm.* vii. 159 There is some characteristic frailty at the bottom of every human heart.

frain(e, var. of FRAYNE, *v. Obs.*

†**frais,** *v. Sc. Obs.* Also frase. [Of obscure origin; cf. Sw. *frasa* to rustle.] *intr.* To creak, make a grating noise.

1513 DOUGLAS *Æneis* I. ii. 60 Cabillis can freit and frais. *Ibid.* VI. ix. 52 Feill crewell strakis smytting hard thai sound, Frasing of irn fetteris and chenȝeis.

‖**fraischeur.** *Obs. rare.* In 6 frechure. [F. *fraischeur* (now *fraîcheur*), f. *frais, fraiche* fresh.] Freshness.

1599 A. HUME in *Chron. S.P.* III. 388 The breathless flocks drawes to the shade And frechure of their fald. **1647** W. BROWNE tr. *Polexander* I. 12 That fair and delightfull country..conserves a perpetuall spring and continuall fraischeur. **1661** DRYDEN *On Coronation* 102 Hither in summer-evenings you repair, To taste the fraischeur of the purer air. [**1862** THACKERAY *Adv. Philip* II. vii. 163 What innocence! What *fraîcheur*! What a merry good-humour!]

fraise (freɪz), *sb.*¹ [a. F. *fraise* fem.

The F. word is app. a transferred use of the earlier *fraise* mesentery of a calf; for a similar development of meaning see CHITTERLING; cf. also FRILL *sb.*¹]

1. A ruff such as was worn in the 16th century.

1801 C. SMITH *Solit. Wanderer* II. 136 The stranger had already caught a glimpse, between the trees, of the white fraise she wore. **1830** JAMES *Darnley* xv, A beautiful standing ruff, or fraise, as the French termed it. **1876** OUIDA *Winter City* ii. 22 She had..a high fraise; sleeves, etc.

2. *Fortif.* A palisade, made horizontal or slightly inclining to the horizon, placed for defence round a work near the berm.

1775 R. MONTGOMERY in Sparks *Corr. Amer. Rev.* (1853) I. 470 By the time we arrived there, the fraise around the berme would be destroyed. **1851** J. S. MACAULAY *Field Fortif.* 91 The stakes of the fraise should be 11 feet long. **1876** BANCROFT *Hist. U.S.* VI. liv. 427 The storming party ..broke through the fraises and mounted the parapet.

fraise (freɪz), *sb.*² [a. F. *fraise* fem., f. *fraiser, fraser*, to enlarge a circular hole, f. *fraise* (see prec.).] A tool used for enlarging a circular hole; also, in Watchmaking, for cutting teeth in a wheel.

1874 KNIGHT *Dict. Mech.* I. 912 *Fraise*..2 a tool used by marble-workers to enlarge a hole made by a drill. **1884** F. J. BRITTEN *Watch & Clockm.* 125 If the fraise chosen is too large, it will cut a jagged and uneven tooth.

fraise (freɪz), *sb.*³ *dial.* [cf. FRAIS *v.*] A 'fuss', commotion.

1725 RAMSAY *Gentl. Sheph.* I. ii, He may, indeed, for ten or fifteen days, Mak meikle o' ye, wi' an unco fraise. **1801** R. ANDERSON *Cumberld. Ball.* (1808) 18 Atween the twee there's sec a frase. **1809** F. DONALDSON *Poems* 77 (Northumbld. Gloss.) The auld wives aften mak' a fraise. **1871** C. GIBBON *Lack of Gold* xxvi, Let him have his own way, instead of standing here making a fraise about nothing.

b. *Comb.*

1683 T. HUNT *Def. Charter Lond.* 10 This Frace-maker and Scaramuchi to the vain youth of the nation, is ever enterchanging the characters of men.

fraise (freɪz), *v.* [ad. F. *fraiser*, f. *fraise*: see FRAISE *sb.*¹] *trans.* To fence or defend with or as with a fraise.

1706 PHILLIPS (ed. Kersey), To *Fraise* a Battalion. **1802** C. JAMES *Milit. Dict.* s.v. *Fraiser, Fraiser un battaillon* is to fraise or fence all the musquetry-men belonging to a battalion with pikes, to oppose the irruption of cavalry. **1876** BANCROFT *Hist. U.S.* V. iv. 371 The counterscarp and parapet were fraised with sharpened stakes.

fraise, var. of FROISE, a pancake.

†**fraist,** *v. Obs.* Forms: 3–4 frest, fraist(e, 4 frayst(e, 5 frast. [a. ON. *freista* (Sw. *fresta*, Da. *friste*) = Goth. **fraistan* (whence *fraistubni* temptation).]

1. *trans.* To try, put to the proof, test.

a **1300** *Cursor M.* 18672 (Cott.) Iesus him kidd til þaim all neu, To frest if þai in trouth war tru. *Ibid.* 25670 (Gött.) Leuedi mari! wele þu wast, þe feindes fraistes me ful fast. *a* **1300** *E.E. Psalter* xi. 7 Silver fraisted with þe fire. *c* **1330** R. BRUNNE *Chron.* (Rolls) 8391 In bataille now þey wil vs frayst. *c* **1400** *Destr. Troy* 6947 Therfore, feris, bes fell, fraistes your strenght! *c* **1460** *Towneley Myst.* (Surtees) 36 My servand I wille found and frast, Abraham, if he be trast.

2. To try, attempt.

c **1400** *Ywaine & Gaw.* 3253 His felow fraisted with al his mayn, To raise him smertly up ogayn. *c* **1440** *York Myst.* ii. 71 With fedrys fayre to frast þer flight fro stede to stede whe þai will stand. *Ibid.* xl. 158 Fraste þer-on faithfully, my frendis you to feede.

3. To learn or know by trial; to experience.

c **1330** R. BRUNNE *Chron.* (1810) 175 ȝour douhtynesse of blode þe Saraȝins salle freist. **1340** HAMPOLE *Pr. Consc.* 1090 Many men þe world here fraistes, Bot he is noght wise þat þar-in traystes.

4. *trans.* and *intr.* To ask. Also *at* (a person).

13.. *Gaw. & Gr. Knt.* 1395 'Þat watz not forward', quod he, 'frayst me no more'. ? *a* **1400** *Morte Arth.* 435, I salle be foundyne in Fraunce, fraiste when hym lykes, The fyrste daye of Feuerȝere. *a* **1400** *Isumbras* 669 The lady..fraystes at hym there 'Was thou euer gentylle mane?' **1400** *Destr. Troy* 97 Ffrayne will I fer and fraist of þere werkes. *c* **1460** *Towneley Myst.* (Surtees) 25 My [wife] wille I frast what she wille say.

5. *trans.* To seek, search for, desire.

13.. *E.E. Allit. P.* A. 169 þe more I frayste hyr fayre face. **13..** *Gaw. & Gr. Knt.* 279 Nay, frayst, I no fyȝt, in fayth I þe telle. ? *a* **1400** *Morte Arth.* 1227 The kyng fraystez a furth ouer the fresche strandez. *c* **1420** *Awntyrs Arthur* 412 (Thornton MS.) For fyghtynge to frayste I fowndede fra hame.

Hence †**'fraisting** *vbl. sb.*, the action of the vb. Also †**fraist** *sb.*, trial, assault.

a **1300** *Cursor M.* 9884 Þis castel..a-pon þe marche it standes traist, O fede ne dredes it na fraist. *c* **1440** *York Myst.* xl. 49 In frasting we fonde hym full faithfull and free.

fraiter, -our: see FRATER, refectory.

frak, obs. var. FRECK *a.*

†**'fraked,** *a. Obs.* [OE. *fracoð, fracod*: see FORCOUTH.] Wicked, vile.

a **900** tr. *Bæda's Hist.* III. xv. [xxi.] (1891) 222 Ond cwæð, þæt heo fracuðe & earme wære, þæt heo ne woldon heora Gode hyran. *c* **1200** *Trin. Coll. Hom.* 83 Þis frakede folc. *Ibid.* 189 Nis non werse fo þene frakede fere.

†**'frakel,** *a. Obs.* Also 2 frekel. [? repr. OE. **fræcel*, **frécel*, implied in *frécelnes* dangerousness, *frécelsian* to endanger.] Dangerous, deceitful.

c **1175** *Lamb. Hom.* 21 Ne beo heo [the sin] swa frekel, ne swa heh. *Ibid.* 25 He bið wið-uten feire and frakel wið-innen. *a* **1225** *Ancr. R.* 204 Þet euerich..boruwe et tisse urakele worlde so lutel so heo euer mei. *a* **1250** *Prov. Ælfred* 257 in *O.E. Misc.* (1872) 118 And oft mon of fayre frakele icheoseþ. *c* **1275** *Luue Ron* 12 ibid. 93 Vikel and frakel.

fraken(e, -yn(e, var. ff. FRECKEN. *Obs.*

Fraktur ('fræktuː(r)). *Typogr.* [G.] A German style of black-letter.

[**1886** T. L. DE VINNE *Historic Printing Types* ii. 18 Considering its angularity, the name, Fractur, which Germans give to their modern German character is well chosen.] **1904** —— *Mod. Meth. Bk. Composition* 253 Though black and forbidding, fraktur is a thin character. **1926** S. MORISON *Type Designs* 11 [Gutenberg's] informal type is..interesting..mainly as the ancestor of the *fraktur* and *schwabacher* later employed for vernacular and less important uses. **1965** *Amer. Speech* XL. 106 In handwriting and printing, the German *Fraktur* script was used exclusively [amongst German-Americans]. **1969** H. CARTER *View Early Typogr.* iii. 57 The Schwabacher was the normal vehicle for German from 1490 until, about 1540, it was outdone in favour by Fraktur. *Ibid.* iv. 69 The Fraktur..is a revolution within the gothic, expressing, as it does, a courtly taste of the highest secular majesty. **1970** *Times Lit. Suppl.* 7 Aug. 884/5 Among the vernaculars, the German *Fraktur* still survives.

fram: see FROM.

framable, frameable ('freɪməb(ə)l), *a.* [f. FRAME *v.* + -ABLE.] Capable of being framed; †comformable.

1577 STANYHURST *Descr. Irel.* 10 in *Holinshed* (1587) II, Ech of these fiue, where they are framable to ciuilitie..be sundred into shires or counties. *a* **1600** HOOKER *Serm. Jude* 17–21 §30 Wks. 1888 III. 696 Framable to the truth, not like rough stone..refusing to be..squared for the building. **1607** HIERON *Wks.* I. 417 An obiection..frameable out of these words. **1658** tr. *Porta's Nat. Magick* I. iii. 4 The Air.. doth make mens bodies framable to her temperature. **1879** G. MACDONALD *P. Faber* I. xvii. 221 The absolute lie, if such be frameable by lips of men.

Hence **'framableness.**

1617 HIERON *Wks.* II. 65 To bring them to a more frameablenesse to His own will. **1654** S. ASHE *Funeral Serm. R. Strange* 2 Their natural, inbred ingenuity or acquired frameablenesse to that which is good.

frambœsia (fræm'biːzɪə). *Path.* [mod.L., f. F. *framboise* raspberry: see FRAMBOISE.] A chronic contagious disease peculiar to the negro, and characterized by raspberry-like excrescences; the yaws.

[**1768** F. B. DE SAUVAGES *Nosol. Method.* II. 554 Frambæsia; Yaw Guineesium; Epian vel Pian Americanorum Est morbus contagiosus apud Guineenses.] **1803** T. WINTERBOTTOM *Sierra Leone* II. viii. 145 The pians ..has been improperly included with the former [yaws] under the term framboesia. **1814** BATEMAN *Cutaneous Dis.* (ed. 3) 316 For, like the febrile eruptions, the Frambœsia affects the same person only once during life. **1876** DUHRING *Dis. Skin* 443 Frambœsia..is an endemic disease.

Hence **fram'bœsioid** *a.* [see -OID], like or indicating frambœsia.

1885–9 BUCK *Handbk. Med. Sc.* V. 77 (Cent.) Growths.. at first wart-like, later profusely hypertrophic— frambœsioid.

framboise, *sb.* and *a.* Also 6 **framboye,** 6–7 **frambois, -boys.** [a. F. *framboise* (from 12th c.), usually regarded as a corruption of Du. *braambezie* = Ger. *brombeere* blackberry, lit. bramble-berry: see BRAMBLE, BROOM, BERRY. But some French scholars doubt this.]

†**A.** *sb.* The raspberry (*Rubus Idæus*). *Obs.*

[**1551–62** Turner cites the word as French only.] **1578** LYTE *Dodoens* VI. v. 662 Of Framboys, Raspis, or Hyndberie. The Framboye is a kinde of bremble. **1620** VENNER *Via Recta* vii. 125 Strawberries are..to be preferred before the Framboise. **1651** tr. *Bacon's Life & Death* 31 Of this sort the chief are Borage..Frambois or Raspis, &c.

B. *adj.* Of raspberry colour. Also *absol.*

1904 *Daily Chron.* 24 Sept. 8/3 The soft..framboise tones. **1959** *Times* 28 Sept. 13/2 It [*sc.* a suit] can also be obtained in size 18..in framboise.

frambousier [F. *framboisier*], a raspberry bush.

a **1648** LD. HERBERT *Life Hen. VIII* (1683) 89 A Frambousier or Raspis-Bush.

frame (freɪm), *sb.* [In sense 1, perh. a. ON. *frame* furtherance, advancement, or repr. the neut. of OE. *fram* adj., forward (see FROM *prep.*); cf. FREME *sb.* In the remaining senses, f. the vb.]

†**I. 1.** Advantage, benefit, profit. *Obs.*

c **1200** ORMIN Ded. 17 Þu þohhtesst tatt itt mihhte wel Till mikell frame turrnenn. *c* **1250** *Gen. & Ex.* 2540 Pharao..

dede ðe ebris frame. **1303** R. BRUNNE *Handl. Synne* 9604 Sey..'Y crysten þe [etc.]'..And ȝive what thou wylt hyt a name, And kast on water; than ys hyt frame. *c* **1330** —— *Chron.* 162 We trowe it is our frame, his resurrectioun.

II. Action or manner of framing.

2. †**a.** The action of framing, fashioning, or constructing; a contrivance. *Obs.*

1558 BP. WATSON *Sev. Sacram.* i. 3 He openeth our eyes to see the frames of our enemyes. **1599** SHAKS. *Much Ado* IV. i. 191 The practise of it liues in John the bastard, Whose spirits toile in frame of villanies. **1642** ROGERS *Naaman* 28 The first happy moover in this frame of miraculous cure. **1645** USSHER *Body Div.* (1647) 96 A man which will teach a child in the frame of a letter, will first teach him one line of the letter.

†**b.** ? *nonce use.* Upbringing. Cf. FRAME *v.* 5 d.

1632 LITHGOW *Trav.* v. 182 Thou Tharsus, brookes a glorious name, For that great Saint, who in Thee had his frame.

c. = FRAME-UP. *U.S. slang.*

1914 JACKSON & HELLYER *Vocab. Criminal Slang* 35 *Frame*,..a prearranged plan of action; a secret implying sinister intention; a 'frame-up'. **1924** G. BRONSON-HOWARD *Devil's Chaplain* ii. 36 This louse woulda beat us to the frame if I hadn't plugged him. **1948** 'J. EVANS' *Halo for Satan* (1949) xiii. 175 He..wasn't a killer but just the victim of a frame.

3. The manner or method of framing; construction, structure; constitution, nature.

1590 SPENSER *F.Q.* III. i. 31 The goodly frame, And stately port of Castle Joyeous. **1607** TOPSELL *Four-f. Beasts* 3 Apes do..resemble men..in the inward frame of the hand. **1705** *Col. Rec. Pennsylv.* II. 204 Upon Account of the whole frame of the act. **1736** BUTLER *Anal.* I. v. 126 We have in our inward frame various affections. **1829** LYTTON *Devereux* I. iii, My youngest brother..was of a very different disposition of mind and frame of body. **1884** SIR J. PEARSON in *Law Times Rep.* LIII. 6/1 There was a trust created..which might be enforced even though the deed in its form and frame were inoperative.

4. a. An established order, plan, scheme, system, *esp.* of government.

1599 SHAKS. *Much Ado* IV. i. 130 Grieu'd I, I had but one? Chid I, for that at frugal Natures frame? **1605** —— *Macb.* III. ii. 16 But let the frame of things dis-ioynt, Both the Worlds suffer. **1630** PRYNNE *Anti-Armin.* 118 Which ouerthrowes the whole foundation, frame, and method of the Scriptures. **1694** ATTERBURY *Serm.* (1723) I. iv. 150 The Law of Moses..had nothing in the Frame and Design of it apt..to recommend it to its Professors. **1759** FRANKLIN *Ess.* Wks. 1840 III. 180 Mr. Penn left his frame at least in a very imperfect state. **1825** MACAULAY *Ess., Milton* (1854) 22 His death dissolved the whole frame of society. **1844** LD. BROUGHAM *Brit. Const.* xvii. (1862) 253 The democratic principle enters largely into the frame of our mixed monarchy.

†**b.** A form or arrangement of words; a formula; a form of reasoning, type of syllogism. *Obs.*

1603 DANIEL *Def. Rhime* Wks. (1717) 7 All verse is but a Frame of Words. **1628** T. SPENCER *Logick* 273 This frame containes a proposition negatiue vniversall, an assumption affirmatiue speciall, and a conclusion negatiue speciall. **1646** BP. MAXWELL *Burd. Issach.* in *Phenix* (1708) II. 261 To make this frame good, they maintain, that [etc.]. **1739** G. OGLE *Gualth. & Gris.* 66 Take, for your Plan, some old Pontific Frame.

†**c.** ? Warlike array; a host. *Obs.*

c **1430** *Hymns Virg.* 44 Þe deuelis gadriden þer greet frame, And heelden þer perlament in þe myst.

d. In full *frame of reference*: (i) A system of co-ordinate axes in relation to which position may be defined and motion conceived of as taking place.

1897 A. E. H. LOVE *Theoret. Mech.* i. 5 A set of lines of reference such as *OA, OB, OC* with respect to which the position of a point *P* can be determined will be called a frame of reference. *Ibid.* xiii. 360 'Acceleration', and by consequence 'force', have no meaning except as dependent on a frame; 'acceleration' means 'acceleration relative to a frame', and similarly with force. **1928** A. S. EDDINGTON *Nature Physical World* iii. 61 The particular frame in which we are relatively at rest has a symmetry with respect to us which other frames do not possess. **1942** SYNGE & GRIFFITH *Princ. Mech.* i. 12 Latitude and longitude define position on the earth's surface; we are here using the earth as a frame of reference. **1965** J. D. NORTH *Measure of Universe* xvi. 362 The triply-infinite set of inertial frames connected by the Lorentz transformations is often referred to as a new 'Absolute'. **1967** RODBERG & THALER *Introd. Quantum Theory of Scattering* x. 260 The *S* matrix we have been using ..describes collisions in an arbitrary reference frame.

(ii) *fig.* and *transf.* (Always as *frame of reference.*) A set of standards, beliefs, or assumptions governing perceptual or logical evaluation or social behaviour.

1924 *Sci. Amer.* Dec. 401/1 This is the mind's 'frame of reference' for the facts of the outer world. **1933** G. B. SHAW *Polit. Madhouse Amer.* 16 If I may borrow an expression from my friend Professor Archibald Henderson, who is a mathematician, he had no frame of reference. He had no scientific postulates of any kind. He was in the air. **1936** M. SHERIF *Psychol. Soc. Norms* ii. 9 We shall give concrete examples to illustrate the existence of norms or frames of reference which are different from those that are taken by western civilization to be as 'natural' as air or water. **1949** KOESTLER *Insight & Outlook* xxvii. 366 In each pair two universes clash, two self-contained frames of reference, two hierarchies of values intersect. **1957** V. G. CHILDE *Dawn Europ. Civilization* (ed. 6) x. 176 But his [*sc.* Montelius's] disciples and imitators have clumsily extended his system beyond the regions for which it was devised and have used it as a frame of reference into which cultural phenomena in Central Europe, South Russia, and even Turkestan must be fitted! **1958** *Listener* 6 Nov. 724/1 There is as yet no assured frame of reference for comparisons between the scrolls and the New Testament. **1967** A. ARENT *Gravedigger's Funeral* xii. 192 That was the thing about Jenny. Her frame of reference. She was solid.

†**5.** Adapted or adjusted condition; definite form, regular procedure; order, regularity, 'shape'. Frequent in phrases (*to bring, set,* etc.) *in, into, out of, to* (*a good,* etc.) *frame. Obs.*

1494 FABYAN *Chron.* v. cvi. 80 Arthur by his marcyal knyghthode, brought theym in such frame..that [etc.]. **1535** COVERDALE *Bible* Ded., It causeth all prosperite, and setteth euery thyng in frame. **1581** MULCASTER *Positions* xx. (1887) 84 It [walking] is good for..the throte, the chest, when they be out of frame. **1602** SHAKS. *Ham.* III. ii. 321 Good my Lord put your discowrse into some frame. **1641** *Vind. Smectymnuus* xiii. 125 To plant and erect Churches to their due frame. **1695** WOODWARD *Nat. Hist. Earth* IV. (1723) 199 The Strata..owe their present Frame and Order to the Deluge. **1718** SWIFT *Horace's Odes* IV. ix. 9 Your steady soul preserves her frame. **1737** BRACKEN *Farriery Impr.* (1757) II. 41 When Nature finds any Member.. weakened or out of Frame. **1801** W. SEWARD *Yordes Cave* 2 Box-trees are cut into a curious frame. **1810** SCOTT *Lady of L.* I. xxxii, To her lips in measured frame The minstrel verse spontaneous came.

6. Mental or emotional disposition or state (more explicitly, *frame of mind, soul,* etc.).

a. Natural or habitual disposition, temper, turn of thought, etc. (now *rare*). **b.** Temporary posture of mind, state of feeling, mood, condition of temper. *frames and feelings*: often used in religious literature of the 18th and 19th c. as a disparaging term for emotional states as a criterion of the reality of spiritual life.

a. *c* **1665** MRS. HUTCHINSON *Mem. Col. Hutchinson* (1846) 31 So had he the most merciful, gentle, and compassionate frame of spirit. **1711** STEELE *Spect.* No. 167 ¶3, I am a Fellow of a very odd Frame of Mind. *a* **1754** FIELDING *Char. Man* Wks. 1784 IX. 409 That heavenly frame of soul, of which Jesus Christ himself was the most perfect pattern. **1878** BOSW. SMITH *Carthage* 110 It did not occur to a body of so conservative a frame of mind, that [etc.].

b. **1665** BOYLE *Occas. Refl.* (1845) 28 The way of thinking we would recommend, does very much dispose men to an attentive frame of mind. **1702** C. MATHER *Magn. Chr.* III. xvi. 117 He would compose himself unto a most heavenly Frame in all things. **1719** DE FOE *Crusoe* I. xv, In this thankful frame I continued. *c* **1741** BRAINERD in Edwards *Life* i. (1851) 3 All my good frames were but self-righteousness. **1774** FLETCHER *Ess. on Truth* Wks. 1795 IV. 114 The modish doctrine of a faith without frame and feeling. **1806** A. KNOX *Rem.* I. 10 The concluding stanza shews..in what frame he wrote. **1828** E. IRVING *Last Days* 45 Hence arose that substitution of frames and feelings for the sacraments..of the church. **1838** J. H. NEWMAN *Par. Serm.* (1839) IV. viii. 144 Consider the different frames of mind we are in hour by hour. **1874** STUBBS *Const. Hist.* I. xiv. 131 He was in no patient frame.

III. A framed work, structure.

* *generally.*

7. a. A structure, fabric, or engine constructed of parts fitted together. Now *obs.* or *arch.*, exc. in the particular applications under 8, 9. †In early *Sc.* applied *spec.* to a rack; in 16–18th c. to a gallows, an easel, a scaffolding, etc.

c **1375** *Sc. Leg. Saints, Laurentius* 338 Þar-eftyre gert hyme straucht In til framis with al þare macht. *Ibid. Agatha* 168 He gert strek hire in a frame, & torment hir in syndry vyse. **15..** *Hickscorner* in Hazl. *Dodsley* I. 158 Yea, at Tyburn there standeth the great frame, And some take a fall that maketh their neck lame. **1526** *Pilgr. Perf.* (W. de W. 1531) 147 The way of perfeccyon is as a frame, in the whiche one thynge dependeth of an other. **1558** PHAER *Æneid* IV. 653 Make out with ores, in ships, in boates, in frames. **1577** B. GOOGE *Heresbach's Husb.* I. (1586) 41 b, They use a greater Sythe..fenced with a crooked frame of stickes. **1632** LITHGOW *Trav.* v. 171 At Ierusalem I lodg'd..in a Cloystred frame. *a* **1641** SUCKLING *Lett.* Wks. (1646) 87 If I should see Van Dike with..his Frame and right Light. **1645** EVELYN *Diary* (1889) I. 189 At Naples they use a frame [a 'maiden', sort of guillotine], like ours at Halifax. **1697** DRYDEN *Alexander's Feast* 162 Divine Cecilia came, Inventress of the vocal frame. **1700** —— *Palamon & A.* II. 554 The gate was adamant; eternal frame. **1726** LEONI *Alberti's Archit.* II. 121/2 He made use of Frames to shut out the River.

†**b.** ? A snare; = ENGINE. *Obs.*

1509 BARCLAY *Shyp of Folys* (1874) I. 164 The deuyll.. labours to get vs in his frame. [Cf. **1558** in 2.]

8. Applied to the heaven, earth, etc. regarded as a structure.

1561 T. NORTON *Calvin's Inst.* I. 21 Y^e knowledge of God ..in the frame of the world and all the creatures is..plainly set forth. **1594** MARLOWE & NASHE *Dido* v. ii, Ye gods, that guide the Starry frame..Grant [etc.]. **1602** SHAKS. *Ham.* II. ii. 310 This goodly frame the Earth. **1667** MILTON *P.L.* v. 154 These are thy glorious works, Parent of good, Almightie, thine this universal Frame. **1774** J. BRYANT *Mythol.* II. 371 Power supreme..to thee I sue, to thee, coeval with the mundane frame. **1856** STANLEY *Sinai & Pal.* xii. (1858) 403 The thunderstorm..begins by making the solid frame of Lebanon and Sirion to leap for fear.

9. a. Applied to the animal, *esp.* the human body, with reference to its make, build, or constitution.

1599 B. JONSON *Cynthia's Rev.* III. i, As you enter at the door, there is opposed to you the frame of a wolf in the hangings. *c* **1600** SHAKS. *Sonn.* lix. 10 This composed wonder of your frame. **1617** J. TAYLOR (Water P.) in *Shaks. C. Praise* 126 His post-like legs were answerable to the rest of the great frame which they supported. **1658** SIR T. BROWNE *Hydriot.* Ep. Ded., How long in this corruptible Frame some Parts may be uncorrupted. **1749** SMOLLETT *Regicide* I. vi, Simple woman Is weak in intellect, as well as frame. **1775** JOHNSON *Tax. no Tyr.* 65 Amidst the terror which shakes my frame. **1812–16** J. SMITH *Panorama Sc. & Art* I. 298 A lever of the third sort became most admirably adapted to the animal frame. **1867** FREEMAN *Norm. Conq.* (1876) I. v. 398 One whose vigorous frame had won him his distinctive surname [Ironside].

b. *Austral.* and *U.S.* An emaciated animal; *spec.* in *pl.* in *Austral.*, draught cattle. (Cf. sense 11.)

1880 *Bradstreet's* 29 Sept. 3/4 The north British farmers are finding it profitable to import what the American dealers graphically call 'frames' to feed for market. **1903** 'T. COLLINS' *Such is Life* 249 By-the-way, there's four of your frames left—out near those coolibahs. **1934** *Bulletin* (Sydney) 10 Oct. 21/4 No poorer or weaker old frames ever travelled the Birdsville stock route.

** A supporting or enclosing structure.

10. a. A structure of timbers, joists, etc. fitted together to form the skeleton of a building.

c **1440** *Promp. Parv.* 176/1 Frame of a worke, *fabrica.* **1533** UDALL *Flowers Latine Speaking* 84 b, *Fabrica*, proprely is a forge or frame of a carpenter. **1545** *Act 37 Hen. VIII*, c. 6 The secret burnynge of frames of tymber..redy to be sett up, and edified for houses. **1579** *Nottingham Rec.* (1889) IV. 182 For the frame of the house at Fre Scole. **1626** BACON *Sylva* §505 Great Castles made of Trees vpon Frames of Timber..were anciently matters of Magnificence. **1703** MOXON *Mech. Exerc.* 132 Taking away the wooden Blocks.. from under the corners of the Frame, they let it fall into its place. **1741** P. TAILFER, etc. *Narr. Georgia* 107 The Frame of the Orphan-house is up. **1835** W. IRVING *Tour Prairies* 251 The bare frames of the lodges, and the brands of extinguished fires, alone marked the place. **1904** W. N. HARBEN *Georgians* 299 Half a dozen expert workmen were putting up the frame of a two-storied building on massive pine sills.

b. A building; in later use, one composed chiefly or entirely of wood. Also = FRAME-HOUSE 2. *Obs.* exc. *U.S.*

c **1425** *Found. St. Bartholomew's* (E.E.T.S.) 13 He reysid vppe a grete frame. **1509** in C. Welch *Tower Bridge* (1894) 85 A Trinite and ij aungellis set in the new Frame upon the bridge. *c* **1639** in Quincy *Hist. Harvard Univ.* (1840) I. 452 The frame in the College yard. **1667** *Boston Rec.* (1881) VII. 37 The Complaint of seuerall Inhabitants of a frame sett vp. **1732** *Rec. Early Hist. Boston* (1885) XII. 40 Henry Gibbs has very lately Incroched on the Towns Land on Dock Square by Erecting Frames thereon. **1766** ENTICK *London* IV. 334 A large..frame of timber and brick was set thereon. **1841** C. CIST *Cincinnati* 41 Of these last [buildings] 200 were brick and 121 frames. **1884** *N.Y. Herald* 27 Oct. 4/6 The house is a three story frame, and was full of guests at the time. **1892** 'MARK TWAIN' *Amer. Claimant* 28 The 'mansion'..was a ricketty old two-story frame.

c. *ellipt.* as adj. (= FRAMED *ppl. a.*) or sb. (= FRAMEWORK 1). *U.S.*

1790 *Pennsylvania Packet* 3 Apr. 3/3 A good frame loaf bread bake house with one oven. **1816** U. BROWN *Jrnl.* in *Maryland Hist. Mag.* (1915) X. 268 The 3rd House is Log and frame with Double Porches. **1836** J. HALL *Statistics of West* iv. 66 The dwelling houses are usually large edifices of brick or frame. **1872** 'MARK TWAIN' *Roughing It* (1882) xiii. 74 Block after block of trim dwellings, built of 'frame' and sunburnt brick. **1897** J. L. ALLEN *Choir Invisible* ii. 12 Rude dwellings of logs now giving way to others of frame and of brick. **1924** C. E. MULFORD *Rustlers' Valley* iv. 38 The street was a busy one in front of a line of lighted buildings, frame, one-story shacks all.

11. a. A structure which serves as an underlying support or skeleton, or of which the parts form an outline or skeleton not filled in.

In mod. dialects used for the skeleton of a person or animal (see Cheshire and Wilts. Glossaries, E.D.S.).

1536 in W. H. Turner *Select. Rec. Oxford* 183 To Wesburne, carpenter, settyng upon the frame and bells in St. Fryswides steple, xiiijs. **1579** E. K. *Gloss. Spenser's Sheph. Cal.* Nov. 161 *Beare*, a frame, whereon they vse to lay the dead corse. **1657** R. LIGON *Barbadoes* (1673) Index 84 The Frame where the Coppers stand..is made of Dutch Bricks. **1665** BOYLE *Occas. Refl.* v. x. (1845) 335 For placing broken Looking-glasses upon a moveable Frame betwixt their Nets. **1697** DAMPIER *Voy.* I. ii. 20 Lay there all night, upon our Barbecu's, or frames of Sticks. **1816** J. SMITH *Panorama Sc. & Art* II. 26 The tube and basin are fixed to a frame of wood. **1833** J. HOLLAND *Manuf. Metal* II. 143 The whole of the machine is made of iron, the length and breadth of the frame being regulated according to the size of the article to be turned. **1846** YOUNG *Naut. Dict.* 330 The paddle-shafts and intermediate shaft rest on the top of a strong frame. **1853** URE *Dict. Arts* I. 1086 The powerful uprights or standards called housing frames, of cast iron, in which the gudgeons of the rolls are set to revolve. **1858** SIMMONDS *Dict. Trade, Frame*..the ribs or stretchers for an umbrella or parasol. **1866** ROGERS *Agric. & Prices* I. xxi. 542 The frame or body of the cart. **1884** *Longm. Mag.* Mar. 486 The terrible jars which its rubberless wheels and springless frame communicated to the system of the rider.

fig. **1642** ROGERS *Naaman* Ep. Ded. 1 These two Graces.. are the chiefe frame of these my ensuing lectures.

b. *Horology.* (See quots.)

1704 J. HARRIS *Lex. Techn.*, *Frame* is the Out-work of a Clock or Watch, consisting of the Plates and Pillars. **1884** F. J. BRITTEN *Watch & Clockm.* 106 [The] Frame ..[comprises] the plates of a watch or clock that support the pivots of the train.

c. *Printing.* (See quot. 1874.)

1683 MOXON *Mech. Exerc.* II. 22. **1874** KNIGHT *Dict. Mech.* I. 912/2 *Frame*..7 (*Printing*) a desk containing two pairs of cases, containing roman and italic letters for the use of a compositor (see *Case*), or the stand supporting them.

d. *Naut.* (See quots.)

1769 FALCONER *Dict. Marine* (1789) D b, A frame of timbers..is composed of one floor-timber..whose arms branch outward to both sides of the ship: two or three futtocks..and a top timber. **1867** SMYTH *Sailor's Word-bk.*, *Frames*, the bends of timbers constituting the shape of the ship's body—when completed a ship is said to be *in frame.* **1883** NARES *Const. Ironclad* 4 The frames, which correspond to the ribs or timbers of a wooden ship are of iron about ½ inch thick.

e. That part of a pair of spectacles which encloses the lenses and holds them in their proper position. Also *attrib.*

1847 *Penny Cycl.* XXII. 328/2 Where side-pieces are added to the frame..the instrument is denominated simply a pair of spectacles. **1895** *Montgomery Ward Catal.* 203/2 Steel frame spectacles. **1939–40** *Army & Navy Stores Catal.* 921/2 Lenses fitted to any of the above frames or customers' own frames. **1969** *Which?* Feb. 45 Two-thirds of those buying spectacles pay several pounds extra on private frames.

f. The fixed part of a bicycle. Hence ***frame-bag*** (a bag for carrying articles, fixed within the frame).

1871 *English Mechanic* 10 Feb. 491/3 The great ease in riding..the makers attribute to the form of the frame. **1897** *Westm. Gaz.* 14 Aug. 7/2 In the frame bag was a package containing blocks of writing paper. **1898** *Cycling* 8 Lacking the elaborate plant of the great firms—especially that for frame building—they are apt to fit their frames together untruly. **1968** *Which?* Aug. 233 We measured the strength of front forks (the parts of the frame which are likely to bend or crack first), pedal cranks and carriers. **1971** *Oxford Mail* 6 Oct. 16/1 (Advt.), Boys bicycles, 16 in. frame, relatively little used.

g. In Pool, the triangular form used in setting up the balls; also, the balls as set up, or the round of play required to pocket them all; similarly in Skittles and Tenpin Bowling; also, one of the several innings forming a game.

1890 C. C. Moore *Games of Pool* 79 These balls are placed in the form of a triangle upon the table, as in Pyramids, a wooden frame or 'triangle' being employed to save trouble and insure correctness. **1897** R. F. Foster *Compl. Hoyle* 608 (Tenpins) Each player rolls ten frames or innings. **1910** *Hints on Skittles, Offic. Rules* 23 The Frame shall be 4-ft. 6-in. square, the Plate circular, 3-in. in diameter, and 22½-in. from centre to centre. *Ibid.* 24 The ball is not dead until it is motionless on, or off the frame. **1929** *Encycl. Brit.* III. 978/1 The teams roll one frame (2 balls) on one alley, and for the next frame alternate and use the other alley. **1930** A. P. Herbert *Water-Gipsies* xxi, There were thirty competitors for the Cup, and each of them played seven frames. **1958** *Economist* 20 Dec. 1085/1 If he succeeds in spilling all ten pins with one ball, this is called a 'strike', and the bowler is credited with ten points in that particular section of the game (each such section is called a 'frame'). **1968** Mrs. L. B. Johnson *White House Diary* 8 Oct. (1970) 718, I..rolled two balls that went in the gutter for my second frame. **1971** J. Wainwright *Last Buccaneer* I. 10 He could play snooker. It was a three-frame match and he had already won the first frame.

h. The horizontal skeleton of a motor vehicle that supports the body, the engine, and the various mechanisms; also, the structural framework of an aircraft (now usu. *air frame* (air *sb.*[1] B. III. 6)).

1900 W. W. Beaumont *Motor Vehicles* I. 232 The frame is built up of tubes, and is carried on double-leaf springs on the front axle, which carries stud axles at its ends with forwardly projecting steering arms. **1902** A. C. Harmsworth et al. *Motors* II. x, A frame which has some diagonal stays or parts which act as diagonals is very desirable, though few car frames are so made. **1909** *Flight* 20 Feb. 103 *Frame*, in French, the term 'chassis' is sometimes used, but more often the word 'fuselage' on account of the bodies of most monoplanes being spindle-shaped. *Ibid.*, *Half-Elliptic Frames*, a frame of the fusiform type which has been curtailed at the middle. **1921** *Chambers's Jrnl.* 341/1 The rattle and jolt of the little frame-car and the noise of the motor made conversation..inaudible. **1922** *Encycl. Brit.* XXX. 24/1 The body [of an aeroplane] is most often a frame of wood compression members and wire bracing. *Ibid.*, To these spars are attached transverse ribs which give the shape of the wing and a light wood edge completes the frame. **1929** *Encycl. Brit.* XV. 893/2 The type of frame which has become practically standard consists of two longitudinal beams..with cross members spanning between them at intervals... The frame with the mechanical parts of the car assembled upon it is called the chassis. **1959** *'Motor' Man.* (ed. 36) i. 13 The cruciform bracing could be applied to a frame only to the rear of the engine and gearbox. **1968** G. N. Georgano *Compl. Encycl. Motorcars* 574 Based on light and simple tubular frames, the cars were easily adaptable for various racing classes.

i. *Aeronaut.* A transverse structural member in a fuselage, wing, etc., which follows the outline of the part and supports the longitudinal members and the skin.

1925 E. H. Lewitt *Rigid Airship* i. 13 All the loads carried by the ship are supported by this corridor, which transmits their weight to the transverse frames. **1930**, **1966** [see former *sb.*[1] 3 e]. **1933** W. Munro *Marine Aircraft Design* v. 74 The scantlings of a wing float frame are given in Fig. 55. The frames are spaced about 8 in. apart. **1966** *McGraw-Hill Encycl. Sci. & Technol.* V. 587/2 Most..stiffened-shell fuselages use both frames and stringers to support the skin.

12. a. That in which something, *esp.* a picture, pane of glass, etc. is set or let in, as in a border or case.

c **1600** Shaks. *Sonn.* xxiv, My body is the frame wherin 'tis held. **1666** Pepys *Diary* (1890) 280 Paid him £14 for the picture, and £1 5*s.* for the frame. **1762** H. Walpole *Vertue's Anecd. Paint.* I. iv. 89 It had a glass over it, and a frame curiously carved. **1811** A. T. Thomson *Lond. Disp.* (1818) p. lxxxviii, These [filters] are generally made..with the mouth stretched on a hoop or frame. **1849** C. Bronte *Shirley* xix, The mill yawned all ruinous with unglazed frames. **1892** *Photogr. Rev. of Rev.* I. 452 Pictures in unusual frames.

fig. **1848** C. Bronte *J. Eyre* xxxvii, A grass-plat..set in the heavy frame of the forest.

b. *Cinematography.* One of the series of separate pictures on a film.

1916 E. W. Sargent *Technique Photoplay* (ed. 3) 362 *Frame*. A single photograph in the roll of film. A picture one inch wide by three-fourths of an inch high. There are sixteen of these frames to the foot. **1918** H. Croy *How Motion Pictures are Made* 32 The light revealed the postures of the dancer as she appeared on the 'frames' in front of the viewing aperture. **1936** *Discovery* June 192/2 Red figures underneath the black shutter speeds show the standard ciné speeds from 8 to 96 frames per second. **1966** *Listener* 24 Feb. 286/2 The very last (and most horrifying) frame. **1971** *Sci. Amer.* Oct. 35/2 Frame-by-frame analysis of motion pictures of the head movements and eye movements.

c. *Television.* A single complete image or picture built up from a series of lines; formerly also = field *sb.* 16 d. Also *attrib.*, as ***frame frequency***.

[**1928** *Television* I. II. 10/3 All that is required is simply an adjustment to bring the picture properly into its 'frame'.] **1935** E. H. Robinson *Televiewing* iii. 49 This number of complete 'frames' or pictures is barely sufficient to prevent flicker in the receiver. **1936** O. S. Puckle tr. *von Ardenne's Telev. Reception* i. 5 The Marconi-E.M.I. television system transmits 25 complete pictures per second each of 405 total lines. These lines are interlaced so that the frame and flicker frequency is 50 per second. **1943** [see field *sb.* 16 d]. **1943** *Gloss. Terms Telecomm. (B.S.I.)* 77 In interlaced scanning the frame-frequency is an integral multiple of the picture-frequency. **1955** J. W. Wentworth *Color Telev. Engin.* ix. 249 It takes two fields to produce a complete television image or frame. In a field-sequential color system, it takes 6 fields or 3 frames to produce a complete color picture, since each line must eventually be scanned in all three colors. **1971** *Sci. Amer.* Sept. 183/2 Television stations broadcast 30 frames per second, each frame containing 525 scan lines.

13. a. Hence applied to various utensils of which the 'frame' or border is an important part.

1727–41 Chambers *Cycl.* s.v. *Frame*, The founder's Frame is a kind of ledge inclosing a board; which being filled with sand, serves as a mould to cast their work in. **1874** Knight *Dict. Mech.* I. 912 *Frame*..3 the head of the batten in a loom. *Ibid.*, *Frame*..10 (Soap-making) a box whose sides are removable when required, and locked together when the soap is to be poured in.

b. *Embroidery* and *Weaving.* In early use: A loom (*obs.*). Now short for *lace-frame*, *stocking-frame*, etc.: see also quot. 1727.

The early uses should perh. be referred to sense 7 or 11.

1523 Skelton *Garl. Laurel* 792 The frame was brought forth with his wevyng pin. **1530** Palsgr. 222/2 Frame to worke in, *metier*. **1592** Davies *Immort. Soul* IV. x. (1714) 36 Narrow Webs on narrow Frames are weav'd. **1727–41** Chambers *Cycl.*, *Frame* is more particularly used for a sort of loom, whereon artizans stretch their linens, silks stuffs &c. to be embroidered, quilted or the like. **1797** *Monthly Mag.* III. 243 Many frames are entirely stopped, and others but partially employed. **1812** *Examiner* 11 May 291/2 Frames..indisputably lessen the number of workmen. **1849** James *Woodman* ii, Two young girls..sat near with tall frames before them, running the industrious needle in and out. **1849** C. Bronte *Shirley* i, He expects two waggon loads of frames and shears.

c. *Horticulture.* A glazed structure, portable or fixed, for protecting seeds and young plants from frost, etc.

1664 Evelyn *Kal. Hort.* (1729) 207 Covering..the Tree ..with a glaz'd Frame. **1782** Cowper *Pineapples & Bee* 9 The frame was tight, And only pervious to the light. **1858** Glenny *Gard. Every-day Bk.* 276/1 Stocks..are mostly sown in frames. **1882** *Garden* 4 Feb. 73/3 The whole of these were placed in..a propagating frame.

d. An open box of slats in which bees build and which can be removed from the hive. Also *attrib.*

1673 *Phil. Trans. R. Soc.* VIII. 6097 The Frame for the Bees to fasten their Work upon. **1875** J. Hunter *Man. Bee-keeping* 137 Select a frame of comb. **1881** *Gardening Illustr.* III. 123 Remove the top, and four or five of the frames, so as to let the bees drop in the hive. *Ibid.*, The bees will run up into the frame hive. **1908** Kipling *Actions & Reactions* (1909) 98 Melissa found a far-off frame so messed and mishandled by abandoned cell-building experiments that, for very shame, the bees never went there. **1955** A. C. Waine *Background to Bee-keeping* v. 46 Part of this problem was solved by the blind Swiss naturalist Huber (1789) who induced his bees to build their combs within wooden frames each of which could be conveniently handled. **1971** D. Galton *Bee-keeping in Russia* ii. 10 The movable frames.. now in standard use in Russia as elsewhere.

14. *Mining.* (See quots.)

1747 Hooson *Miner's Dict.*, *Frame*, This is for Sinking in Sand and Water..it is made of four good Planks..placed in the Top of a Sand, [it] may be let down with ease enough as one Sinks. **1869** R. B. Smyth *Goldf. Victoria* 612 Frame of Timber—Differs (as some say) from a 'set' in width, and the legs are placed perpendicularly. **1875** J. H. Collins *Metal Mining* Gloss., *Frame*, an inclined board over which a gentle stream of water is made to flow, for the purpose of washing away the waste from small portions of ore which are placed upon it from time to time.

15. *attrib.* and *Comb.* General relations: **a.** simple attrib., as (sense 10) ***frame barn***, ***-building***, ***construction***, ***-cottage***, ***-dwelling***, ***shop***; (sense 11) ***frame-boat***, ***tent***; (sense 11 d) ***frame-bend***, ***-timbers***; (sense 12) ***frame-door***; (sense 13 b) ***frame-smith***; (sense 13 c) ***frame-cucumber***, ***yard***. See also senses 11 f, 12 c.

1753 in *New Jersey Archives* (1897) 1st Ser. XIX. 284 To be Sold... Plantation..there is on it..a large *frame barn, and stables. **1825** *Colonial Advocate* (Toronto) 5 Jan. 1/4 For Sale... A Frame Barn with Stabling, Forty by Forty-two. **1831** J. M. Peck *Guide Emigrants* 182 He may put up a frame barn. **1847** Carlyle *Lett.* 2 Oct. (1904) II. 50 You will be very wise to get that frame barn you speak of. *c* **1850** *Rudim. Navig.* (Weale) 120 *Frame-timbers*, Various timbers that compose a *frame bend. **1888** T. T. Wildridge *Northumbria* 124 *Frame-boats covered with skins. **1858** *Merc. Marine Mag.* V. 93 The machinery is in a *frame building. **1935** *Archit. Rev.* LXXVII. 64/3 All Wright houses look like *frame-construction houses. **1956** J. M. Richards in A. Pryce-Jones *New Outl. Mod. Knowledge* 381 Rhythmic façade patterns that frame-construction naturally promotes. **1881** G. W. Cable *Mme. Delphine Carancro* iv. 12 A little *frame cottage, standing on high pillars. **1890** *Daily News* 26 June 2/6 *Frame cucumbers, 1*s.* 6*d.* to 2*s.* per dozen. **1851** Greenwell *Coal-trade Terms Northumb. & Durh.* 23 A *frame door is set in a proper frame, made for the purpose. **1760** in *New Jersey Archives* (1898) 1st Ser. XX. 425 To be sold, a certain Tract of Land,..with three good *frame Dwelling-houses. **1832** J. P. Kennedy *Swallow Barn* I. xix. 192 Half a dozen frame dwellings..were scattered over the landscape. **1913** J. London *Valley of Moon* III. xiv, He had just begun work on a small frame dwelling. **1894** 'Mark Twain' *Pudd'nhead Wilson* i, Two or three brick stores..towered above interjected bunches of little *frame shops. **1725** *Lond. Gaz.* No. 6385/4 John Smith..*Frame-Smith. **1861** *Stamford Mercury* 1 Feb. 6/2 Apprenticed..to a frame-smith. **1874** A. Bathgate *Colonial Experiences* x. 134 We reached the township of Maori Point..consisting of ..a few '*frame tents', as fixed tents usually lined with green baize or druggeting are called. **1961** *Spectator* 23 June 933 Frame tents are what liken the camping fields of Europe to Agincourt. **1963** *Guardian* 21 Jan. 5/2 The frame tent..is built on a folding tubular frame, with four or five uprights. **1970** *Which?* May 132/1 A frame tent usually consists of two tents. *Ibid.* 136/1 The number of people a frame tent can sleep is determined by the width of the inner tent. **1846** Young *Naut. Dict.*, *Frames*, or *Frame-timbers, in shipbuilding, the floor timbers, which..compose what is termed the frame. **1899** *Daily News* 28 Oct. 7/6 The early chrysanthemums..are well worth a visit. Ask for the '*frame-yard'. **1933** *Jrnl. R. Hort. Soc.* LVIII. I. 13 The plants..should be..left on the beds for two or three days before removing to the frame yard.

b. objective, as ***frame-bender***, ***-maker***. **c.** instrumental, as ***frame-knit***, ***-knitted***, ***-knitter***, ***-knitting***, ***-tape***, ***-worker***.

1882 *Standard* 13 Oct. 2/3 The dispute originated with the *frame benders and steel platers. **1696** *Lond. Gaz.* No. 3226/4, 5 dozen of superfine Rolling *Frame Knit Hose. **1892** *Scott. Leader* 30 Mar. 5 He presented a petition from the *frame-knitters to Parliament. **1882** Caulfeild & Saward *Dict. Needlework*, *Frame Knitting*, a description of Frame Work, which when finished has the appearance of Knitting. **1762** Walpole *Vertue's Anecd. Paint.* (1765) II. 57 *note*, Norrice, *frame-maker to the Court. **1822** Mrs. Hofland *Son of a Genius* iv, His frame-maker agreeing to take his pictures off his hands. **1882** Caulfeild & Saward *Dict. Needlework*, *Frame Tape*, this is a stout half bleached linen tape..The prefix 'Frame' refers to the loom on which it is woven. **1812** Byron *Let. to Ld. Holland* 25 Feb., Practices which have deprived the *frame-workers of employment.

16. Special comb.: **frame aerial** *Radio*, an aerial composed of a rectangle or loop of wire, adapted for directional reception; **frame-breaker**, one of those who resisted with violence the introduction of frames for weaving stockings, etc.; so **frame-breaking**; **frame-bridge** (see quot.); **frame-dam** (see quot.); **frame-level** (see quot.); **frame story**, a story which serves as a framework within which a number of other stories are told; **frame-stud**, one of the uprights of the frame of a building; **frame-tubbing** (see quot.). Also frame-house, frame-saw.

1921 *Wireless World* 10 Dec. 562/2, I can receive the Dutch Concert..on a..*frame aerial. **1924** *Wireless Weekly* 8 Oct. 745/1 A good range of receivers, including reflex sets using small frame aerials. **1960** *Gloss. Terms Telecomm. (B.S.I.)* 122 *Loop aerial* (frame aerial), a closed circuit designed to be used as an aerial. **1812** in *Spirit Pub. Jrnls.* (1813) XVI. 160, I have had an application from Nottingham to chalk for the *frame-breakers. **1849** C. Bronte *Shirley* ii, I only wish..the frames..were safe here ..Once put up, I defy the frame-breakers. **1816** *Parl. Debates* 10 July, Lord Sidmouth moved the third reading of the *Frame Breaking Bill. **1863** Kingsley *Water Bab.* i, The frame-breaking riots, which Tom could just remember. **1882** Ogilvie, **Frame-bridge*, a bridge constructed of pieces of timber framed together on the principle of combining the greatest degree of strength with the smallest expenditure of material. **1851** Greenwell *Coal-trade Terms Northumb. & Durh.* 26 A *frame-dam is formed of balks of fir wood, placed endwise against the pressure. **1874** Knight *Dict. Mech.* I. 913 **Frame-level*, a mason's level. **1924** F. Edgerton *Panchatantra Reconstructed* II. i. 4 Each of the five books contains not only a primary story, which we call the '*frame-story', but also at least one, and usually several, 'emboxt' stories. **1960** J. V. Cunningham *Trad. & Poetic Struct.* 60 For the second feature—the general idea of a frame story—it is agreed that no particular model need be sought. **1770–4** A. Hunter *Georg. Ess.* (1804) II. 195 In wooden cottages, the *frame-studs are to be six inches by five. **1883** Gresley *Gloss. Coal Mining*, **Frame Tubbing*, solid wood tubbing.

frame (freɪm), *v.* [OE. *framian* to be helpful or profitable, to make progress, f. *fram* forward *adj.* and *adv.* (see from); cf. the equivalent ON. *frama* to further, advance, get on with. The cognate ON. *fremja* (= OE. *fręmman*, *fręmian*: see freme *v.*) to further, execute, perform, may have influenced the development, as it has no umlaut in pa. t. and pa. pple. (*framðe*, *framdr*).]

† **1.** *intr.* To profit, be of service. Const. with *dat.*; also quasi-*impers.* Also, to supply the needs of. *Obs.*

c **961** Æthelwold *Rule St. Benet* lvii. (Schröer) 95 Forðy, þe he bydæle þære stowe mid his cræfte framað. *c* **1230** *Hali Meid.* 31 Þat tu understonde hu lutel hit frameð ham. *c* **1250** *Gen. & Ex.* 1642 At set time he sulden samen ðor [i.e. at the well] hem-self & here orf framèn. *c*1330 R. BRUNNE *Chron. Wace* (Rolls) 11112 To nemne hem here, litel hit frames.

†**2.** To gain ground, make progress; to 'get on' (*with*); to prosper, succeed. Also, in neutral, sense with adv., to get on *well, ill*, etc. *Obs.*

*a*1050 *Liber Scintill.* iv. (1889) 20 Eadmodness swa micelum swa heo is ahyld to neowlum swa micelum heo framað [*proficit*] on heahnysse. 1509 BARCLAY *Shyp of Folys* (1874) II. 253 But oft full yll they frame That wyll be besy with to hye thynges to mell. 1526 SKELTON *Magnyf.* 1863 The feldfare wolde have fydled, and it wold not frame. 1550 LATIMER *Last Serm. bef. Edw. VI*, Wks. I. 228 Now I could not frame with it, nor it liked me not in no sauce. 1559 *Mirr. Mag., Dk. York* xxiii, God that causeth thinges to fro or frame. 1577–87 HOLINSHED *Chron.* I. 186/2 When the world framed contrarie..to his purpose. 1582 T. WATSON *Centurie of Loue* lxxxi. (Arb.) 117 So frames it with mee now, that I [etc.]. *c*1611 CHAPMAN *Iliad* IV. 13 The two..are pleas'd to see how well the..fight did frame. 1634 RUTHERFORD *Lett.* (1862) I. 126 Even howbeit the business frame not, the Lord shall feed your soul. 1669 WORLIDGE *Syst. Agric.* (1681) 184 It framed not according to expectation.

†**3.** *trans.* To prepare, make ready for use; also, to furnish or adorn *with*. *Obs.*

*c*1250 *Gen. & Ex.* 3146 So mikil hird so it noten mai, Ben at euen folc sum to samen, And ilc folc is to fode framen, And eten it bred. 13.. *Coer de L.* 1859 The knights framed the tree-castel Before the city upon a hill. *c*1400 *Destr. Troy* 6206 A cloth all of clene gold, Dubbit full of diamondis.. Framet ouer freshly with frettes of perle.

†**4.** To prepare (timber) for use in building; to hew out; to prepare the timbers, perform the carpenter's work for (a building). Phrase, *to frame and rear, frame and set up*. *Obs.*

*c*1374 CHAUCER *Troylus* III. 481 (530) This timber is al redy up to frame. *c*1440 *Promp. Parv.* 176/2 Framyn tymbyr for howsys, *dolo*. 1520 WHITTINTON *Vulg.* (1527) 1 To square tymbre, frame and rere ony buyldynge. *c*1520 *Mem. Ripon* (Surtees) III. 205 Will'mo Caruer framyng the sayd fertter per ij dies & alias, 2*s.* 2*d.* 1542–3 *Act 34 & 35 Hen. VIII*, c. 25 It shalbe lawfull..to erecte, make, frame and set vp..one good..windemill. 1557 *Trin. Coll. Acc.* in Willis & Clark *Cambridge* II. 472 Carpenter 4 dayes in framing tymber for yᵉ upper floor. 1603 *Ibid.* II. 491 A bargayne to frame finish and set vp yᵉ roofe. 1707 MORTIMER *Husb.* 302 The Carpenters Work to Hew the timber, saw it out, frame it, and set it together. 1724 in Temple & Sheldon *Hist. Northfield, Mass.* (1875) 199, I hope the fort and houses will be framed and set up this month.

5. To shape, give shape to; to fashion, form. **a.** with material obj. *Obs.* exc. with additional notion as in 6 and 7.

1553 EDEN *Treat. Newe Ind.* (Arb.) 30 They frame the roofes of these cotages with sharpe toppes. 1576 FLEMING *Panopl. Epist.* 190 This brittle bottle framed out of clay. 1615 G. SANDYS *Trav.* 181 The effigies of Saint Ierome, miraculous framed by the naturall veines of the stone. 1678 R. BARCLAY *Apol. Quakers* v. xxiii. 171 The Iron..is softned and framed. 1703 MOXON *Mech. Exerc.* 9 Batter it out.. pretty near its shape; and so by several Heats..frame it into Form and Size. *Ibid.* 183 The Gouge..may..also frame pretty near the hollow Moldings required in the Work.

b. To shape, compose, give (specified) expression to (the countenance).

1565–73 COOPER *Thesaurus, Frons castigata*, a Countenance so well framed that it cannot be reprehended. 1593 SHAKS. *3 Hen. VI*, III. ii. 186 Why I can..frame my Face to all occasions. 1632 J. HAYWARD tr. *Biondi's Eromena* 21 The Admirall (framing the best countenance he could) departed thence.

c. To shape, direct (one's thoughts, actions, powers, etc.) to a certain purpose. Also with a person, etc. as obj., to shape the action, faculties, or inclinations of; to dispose. †In early use, to train, discipline; = FORM *v.* 2. †Also in *passive*, to be in a certain frame or mood. Const. *for, to, to do*.

1547 J. HARRISON *Exhort. Scottes* 210 You shall..frame his youthe with verteous preceptes. 1552 *Bk. Com. Prayer, Ordering of Deacons*, To frame..youre owne lyues.. according to the doctrine of Christ. 1556 HOBY tr. *Castiglione's Courtyer* (1577) Q ii. v, The good man of the house..firste with faire woordes, afterward with threatninges, attempted to frame hir to do his pleasure. 1569 J. PARKHURST *Injunctions*, You must endeuour so to order and frame your selues in the setting foorth of Gods true Religion. 1579 LYLY *Euphues* (Arb.) 127 Two whelpes..the one he framed to hunt, and the other [etc.]. 1599 B. JONSON *Every Man out Hum.* II. i. (Rtldg.) 38/1, I cannot frame me to your harsh vulgar phrase, 'tis against my genius. 1637 RUTHERFORD *Lett.* clxxxvii. (1891) 367 Frame yourself for Christ, and gloom not upon His cross. 1640 MARCOMBES in *Lismore Papers* Ser. II. (1888) IV. 117 It will be a harder matter for me to frame them to their bookes. 1660 PEPYS *Diary* 26 Jan., We were as merry as I could frame myself to be. 1662 NEWCOMBE *Diary* (Chetham Soc.) 44, I got up about 8, and was but ordinarily framed. 1675 tr. *Camden's Hist. Eliz.* (ed. 3) Introd. 6 b, She..framed her Tongue to a pure and elegant way of Speaking. 1742 RICHARDSON *Pamela* III. 177 She cannot quite..frame her Mouth to the Sound of the Word Sister. 1775 MAD. D'ARBLAY *Let. to Mr. Crisp* 8 May in *Early Diary*, I cannot frame myself to anything else. 1814 CARY *Dante, Par.* III. 110 God knows how, after that, my life was framed. 1846 KEBLE *Lyra Innoc.* (1873) 150 Such is Thy silent grace, framing aright our lowly orisons.

d. To direct (one's steps); to set out upon (a journey). Also *refl.* and *absol.* To shape one's course; to betake oneself, resort. *Obs.* exc. *dial.* = 'go'.

1576 FLEMING *Panopl. Epist.* 169 Many..men..have framed themselves to my conversation. 1590 SPENSER *F.Q.* III. i. 20 A stately Castle far away she spyde, To which her steps directly she did frame. 1598 YONG *Diana* 61, I frame my selfe to the seruice of some Lord or Gentleman. 1608 SHAKS. *Per.* Prol. 32 The beauty of this sinful dame Made many princes thither frame. 1637 HEYWOOD *Dial.* i. Wks. 1874 VI. 100 Pilgrimage I'l frame Vnto the blessed Maid of Walsinghame. 1847 E. BRONTE *Wuthering Heights* v, 'Frame upstairs, and make little din.' *Ibid.* xiii, A threat to set Throttler on me if I did not 'frame off', rewarded my perseverance. 1865 B. BRIERLEY *Irkdale* I. 120, I fraimt up to her and sed.

e. *intr.* for *refl.*, in various applications, now chiefly *dial.*: (*a*) To put oneself in a posture of doing something; to set about, make an attempt or pretence *to* do; (*b*) to go about a work in a promising manner; to give promise of becoming skilful; (*c*) to manage, contrive, *to* do something.

Cf. *shape* intr., used dialectally in all these meanings.

1602 *2nd Pt. Return fr. Parnass.* IV. v. (Arb.) 62 Schollers must frame to liue at a low sayle. 1611 BIBLE *Judg.* xii. 6 He could not frame to pronounce it right. 1634–5 BRERETON *Trav.* (Chetham Soc.) 119 The masters..not..knowing how to frame to till, and order their land, the ground hath been untilled. 1664 *Flodden F.* ix. 83 For defence they fiercely frame. 1674 N. FAIRFAX *Bulk & Selv.* 130 Before he could frame to get loose of her. 1863 MRS. TOOGOOD *Yorksh. Dial.*, She frames with the butter, does Mary Ann. 1867 MISS PARR *Mr. Wynyard's Ward* II. 79, 'I frames to get about, but I'se racked wi' rheumatiz terrible—terrible.' 1876 *Whitby Gloss.* s.v., 'She frames at eating a bit'..'He frames badly at wark.' *Ibid.*, 'It's framing for wet.' 1887 H. SMART *Cleverly Won* iv. 31 If..the mare framed well for jumping..he would [etc.]. 1888–9 *Longm. Mag.* XIII. 442 'And when the other maids was back, she was framin' to be asleep, with her cap of rushes on.' 1894 *Westm. Gaz.* 15 June 5/3 He was just framing to play when a ball..came right through the next net. 1894 MRS. H. WARD *Marcella* II. 265 He frames well in speaking.

6. a. *trans.* To adapt, adjust, fit (chiefly an immaterial object) *to* or *into* (something).

*c*1550 *Lusty Juventus* in Hazl. *Dodsley* II. 93 Unto his teaching your life ye will not frame. 1639 S. DU VERGER tr. *Camus' Admir. Events* 10 Rosana..framed her selfe unto all the humours of the Prince. *a*1656 USSHER *Power Princes* II. (1683) 131 To frame our wills to the chearful performance of that duty. 1663 GERBIER *Counsel* 15 Carpenters do frame their Railes to Ballesters. *Ibid.* 94 Carpenters do frame them so exact to the width..of the window. 1703 MOXON *Mech. Exerc.* 131 They are to be framed into one another. *a*1716 SOUTH *Serm.* (1744) II. 305 The desires of the righteous are ..framed to an agreeableness with the ways of God. 1806 WORDSW. *Intimations* vii, Unto this he frames his song.

†**b.** *intr.* for *refl.* To adapt oneself, conform. Of things: To suit, fit. *Obs.*

1533 MORE *Confut. Barnes* VIII. Wks. 783/1 How would then those wordes frame. 1586 W. WEBBE *Eng. Poetrie* (Arb.) 80 It will not frame altogether so currantlye in our English as the other, because the shortnesse of the seconde Penthimimer will hardly be framed to fall together in good sence. 1606 HOLLAND *Sueton.* 76 Having in..ardent heat begun a Tragædie, when he saw his stile would not frame thereto..he..wiped it quite out. 1642 ROGERS *Naaman* 436 Bids us try the Unicorne whether he..will..draw our cart ..meaning that his wildnesse will not frame to it.

7. *trans.* To make, construct. Now always implying the combination and fitting together of parts, and adaptation to a design; in 16–17th c. often used more widely.

1555 EDEN *Decades* 58 They framed a new carauel shortly after. 1571 DIGGES *Pantom.* I. vi. C ij b, Couple yᵉ endes of those two right lines togither with a thirde, and so haue you framed a Triangle equall to the former. 1577 B. GOOGE *Heresbach's Husb.* I. (1586) 39 b, [Hemp] serveth both for makyng of Canvesse, and framing of Ropes. *Ibid.* IV. 185 They be greater, as though their bodies were purposely framed for generation. 1598 BARRET *Theor. Warres* IV. i. 116 To frame bridges ouer rivers. 1607 TOPSELL *Four-f. Beasts* (1658) 264 Alexander the Great caused Lysippus..to frame the pictures of all those knights which..were slain at the river Granicus. 1612 *Enchir. Med.* 94 A cataplasme framed of crumbs..and milke with oile of Roses. 1667 MILTON *P.L.* IV. 691 It was a place Chos'n by the sovran Planter, when he fram'd All things to mans delightful use. 1691 T. H[ALE] *Acc. New Invent.* 120 The principal things..to be considered in framing and fitting of a Ship. 1725 DE FOE *Voy. round World* (1840) 321 Their rafts..were lifted off from the place where they were framed. 1726 LEONI tr. *Alberti's Archit.* I. 72/2 You may frame wooden dams. 1810 SCOTT *Lady of L.* III. v, The fieldfare framed her lowly nest. 1847 EMERSON *Repr. Men, Plato* Wks. (Bohn) I. 291 If the tongue had not been framed for articulation man would still be a beast in the forest. 1875 JOWETT *Plato* (ed. 2) III. 418 The things in heaven are framed by the Creator in the most perfect manner. 1879 *Cassell's Techn. Educ.* IV. 189/2 This is really the first stage in the operation of 'framing' a wood ship.

8. In various immaterial applications. **a.** To contrive (a plot, etc.); to devise, invent, fabricate (a rule, story, theory, etc.); to put together, fashion, compose; to put into words, express.

1514 BARCLAY *Cyt. & Uplondyshm.* (Percy Soc.) 23 Than frame they fraudes man slyly to begyle. 1570–6 LAMBARDE *Peramb. Kent* (1826) 187 Leland calleth it Noviodunum, which word is framed out of the Saxon Niwanðune. 1576 FLEMING *Panopl. Epist.* 150, I will frame an aunsweare, to your two severall letters. 1577 B. GOOGE *Herebach's Husb.* I. 16 He can not so easely frame a false accompt. 1587 TURBERV. *Trag. T.* (1837) 127 Shee ever lookt when he Would frame his humble sute. 1608 BP. HALL *Char. Virtues & V.* 122 (*Slothfull*) He is wittie in nothing but framing excuses to sit still. 1658 BRAMHALL *Consecr. Bps.* vii. 153 He who had so great a hand in framing the Oath. 1674 PLAYFORD *Skill Mus.* I. xi. 40 Who hath framed to himself a manner of Singing. 1682 BURNET *Rights Princes* ii. 27 This was a Story framed long after. 1767 BLACKSTONE *Comm.* II. 128 We may observe, with how much nicety and consideration the old rules of law were framed. 1791 COWPER *Odyss.* II. 226 But let us frame Effectual means. 1808 SCOTT *Marm.* I. vii. Frame love-ditties passing rare. 1856 FROUDE *Hist. Eng.* (1858) I. iv. 359 The convocation.. had framed their answer in the same spirit. 1859 KINGSLEY *Misc.* (1860) I. 67 Statutes..Which must needs have been framed for some purpose or other.

b. To form, articulate, utter (words, sounds).

1609 BIBLE (Douay) *Num.* ix. comm., God answered by a voice framed by an Angel. 1702 POPE *Dryope* 80 When first his infant voice shall frame Imperfect words. 1782 HAN. MORE *Belshazzar* I. 62 Then may my tongue refuse to frame the strains Of sweetest harmony. 1880 G. MEREDITH *Trag. Com.* (1881) 153 She framed the words half aloud.

c. To form or construct in the mind; to conceive, imagine. More fully ***to frame to oneself***. †Also with *out*.

1597 HOOKER *Eccl. Pol.* V. ii. §2 Frame to themselues a way more pleasant. *a*1618 RALEIGH *Sceptick* in *Rem.* (1651) 21 As several humours are predominant, so are the..conceits severally framed and effected. 1653 H. MORE *Antid. Ath.* I. iii. (ed. 1712) 13 An Idea of a Being absolutely..Perfect, which we frame out by attributing all conceivable Perfection to it. 1710 BERKELEY *Princ. Hum. Knowl.* §98 Whenever I attempt to frame a simple idea of time. 1782 HAN. MORE *Moses* III. 14 A mother's fondness frames a thousand fears. 1814 CARY *Dante, Par.* II. 48 With thoughts devout, Such as I best can frame. 1863 GEO. ELIOT *Romola* I. ix, He could frame to himself no probable image of love-scenes between them.

†**d.** To cause, produce, bring to pass. *Obs.*

1576 FLEMING *Panopl. Epist.* Epit. A iv b, Can you name A better place then countrie blest? Where..Summers frame Joyes. *a*1592 GREENE *Alphonsus* V. Wks. (Rtldg) 243/1 His daughter..by her marrying did his pardon frame. 1593 SHAKS. *2 Hen. VI*, V. ii. 32 Feare frames disorder. 1597 —— *2 Hen. IV*, IV. i. 180 Which Heauen so frame.

e. ***to frame up***: to pre-arrange (an event) surreptitiously and with sinister intent; to plan in secret; to fake the result of (a contest, etc.). *U.S. slang*.

1906 A. H. LEWIS *Confess. Detective* ii. 26 One of the gang ..cried out to his fellows: 'Hold off! He's pulled his cannister; an' if you crowd him he's framed it up to do Red.' 1910 E. A. WALCOTT *Open Door* vii. 86 'An' then he frames up dis job on me,' said Jimmy bitterly. 1913 C. E. MULFORD *Coming of Cassidy* vii. 119 As long as this deal was framed up, we'll say it was this mornin'. 1919 *Detective Story Mag.* 25 Nov. XXVIII. 5 If you give me the signal I'll frame up something. 1923 R. D. PAINE *Comrades of Rolling Ocean* vii. 121 All I need is a little work with your catcher, to frame up signals and so on.

9. [from the sb.] To set in a frame; to enclose in or as in a frame; to serve as a frame for. Also with *in*.

1705 ADDISON *Italy* 7 The winding Rocks a spacious Harbour frame. 1842 MRS. CARLYLE *Lett.* I. 138, I have your..Villa framed and hung up. 1876 W. H. POLLOCK in *Contemp. Rev.* June 63 Scenery and machinery were employed to frame the play. 1878 BROWNING *Poets Croisic* 56 Somebody saw a portrait framed and glazed. 1883 LD. R. GOWER *My Remin.* I. xiii. 237 The lovely lake, framed in by a background of soft-swelling hills.

10. To concoct a false charge or accusation against; to devise a scheme or plot with regard to; to make the victim of a 'frame-up'. *slang* (orig. *U.S.*).

1922 E. TITUS *Timber* xxvi. 234 So they were after Bryant were they? They were framing him? 1926 C. E. MULFORD *Cassidy's Protégé* iv. 40 He had seen honest men framed, and guilty men let off for political reasons. 1926 J. BLACK *You can't Win* xxii. 347 The police..knew I was trying to frame myself out; they began framing me in. 1927 *Observer* 6 Nov. 21 Her heart has been given to Tom Mix, who, in consequence, is 'framed'. 1931 *Daily Tel.* 19 Jan. 11/6 They're for ever after me all the time, trying to frame me. 1956 R. BRADDON *Nancy Wake* vii. 70 If they were prepared to lie about Marseille then obviously they intended to frame her.

Hence **'framing** *ppl. a.*, that serves as a frame.

1876 GEO. ELIOT *Dan. Der.* II. xxxiv. 382 Her yellow face with its framing rouleau of grey hair.

‖**'framea.** *Ant.* [L.; presumably a Teut. word.] A kind of javelin used by the ancient Germans (see quot.). By modern archaeologists the word has been applied to a particular type of lance found in ancient German tombs, etc., and also to a form of socketed stone celt.

1598 GRENEWEY *Tacitus' Germany* i. (1622) 259 [They] carry Iauelines, or as they term them Frameas, with a narrow and short iron, but so sharpe..that..with the same weapon they can fight both at hand, and a farre off.

framed (freɪmd), *ppl. a.* [f. FRAME *v.* + -ED[1].] In senses of the vb; *spec.* in U.S. of houses (cf. FRAME *sb.* 10, 15).

*c*1440 *Promp. Parv.* 176/1 Framyd, *dolatus*. 1496 in C. Welch *Tower Bridge* (1894) 83 [The carriage of loads of 'framed timber' figures in the accounts of 1496.] 1566 in Peacock *Eng. Ch. Furniture* 65 A Rood loft whearof is made a framde table. 1578 TIMME *Caluine on Gen.* 91 The principal point of wisdom is, framed sobriety to the obedience of God. 1598 BARRET *Theor. Warres* II. i. 21 In Ordinances, or framed battels..the Ensignes do march in one large or long ranke iointly. 1605 BACON *Adv. Learn.* I. 3, I cannot..propound unto you framed particulers. 1639 in *Virginia Mag. of Hist. & Biog.* (1895) III. 30 Others have undertaken to build framed howses to beautifye the place. 1719 DE FOE *Crusoe* II. i, To carry a framed sloop on board the ship. 1751 in *New Jersey Archives* (1897) 1st Ser. XIX. 68 To be sold, a plantation containing..a good fram'd Barn. 1784 *Maryland Jrnl.* 11 May, Advt. (Th.), A large framed House almost as good as new. 1816 JAMESON *Charac. Min.* 207 Framed or squared fluor-spar (*chaux fluatée encadrée*). 1823 E. JAMES *Long's Exped. Rocky Mts.* I. 82 This town.. contained..several framed dwellings of two stories. 1837 J. M. PECK *Gaz. Illinois* II. 133 The rough..cabin is giving place to comfortable framed or brick tenements. **1874** MICKLETHWAITE *Mod. Par. Churches* 319 Framed pictures require to be placed where they may be seen.

framed, Sc. var. of FREMD.

'frame-house. [f. FRAME *sb.* and *v.* + HOUSE.] †**1.** A house in which things are framed or fashioned. *Obs.*

a **1555** BRADFORD in *Certain Lett.* (1564) 276 The crosse.. is the framehouse in the which god frameth his children like to his sonne Christe.

2. A house constructed with a wooden framework or skeleton covered with boards.

1817 J. BRADBURY *Trav. Amer.* 331 Every planter.. is able to erect a handsome frame-house. **1856** OLMSTED *Slave States* 394 In a little white frame-house we found a company of engineers. **1887** *Spectator* 26 Mar. 412/2 A master-carpenter.. lived in a comfortable two-story frame-house.

frameless ('freɪmlɪs), *a.* [f. FRAME *sb.* + -LESS.] Without frame, having no frame.

1862 T. A. TROLLOPE *Marietta* II. vii. 110 Smaller frameless canvasses. **1882** J. PAYN *Thicker than Water* iii, He had a frameless, stringless glass, which stuck in his eye with the tenacity of a limpet.

†**'framely**, *adv.* *Obs.* [f. FRAME *sb.* + -LY[2].]

1561 NORTON & SACKV. *Gorboduc* I. i. That.. my purpose may more framelie [*later edd.* firmelie] stande.

framer ('freɪmə(r)). [f. FRAME *v.* + -ER[1].] One who frames; a maker, contriver, inventor. Also, one who frames a picture, etc.

1561 T. NORTON *Calvin's Inst.* I. 41, I maruel what these framers of new Gods do meane. **1613** PURCHAS *Pilgrimage* IV. vi. (1614) 367 It is the Minde of the minde which is framer of the fierie world. **1690** LOCKE *Govt.* II. xiii. (Rtldg.) 156 The first framers of the government. **1741** MONRO *Anat. Nerves* (ed. 3) 16 The Framers of this Objection. **1796** KIRWAN *Elem. Min.* (ed. 2) I. Pref. 12 Leske, the framer of the present collection. **1827** KEBLE *Chr. Y.*, *Evening* ix, Thou Framer of the light and dark. **1864** A. J. HORWOOD *Yearbks. 32 & 33 Edw. I* Pref. 34 The framer of the Latin version translated from the French form. **1870** SWINBURNE *Ess. & Stud.* (1875) 315 Without more form of order than has been given by the framers and hangers.

'frame-saw. [f. FRAME *sb.* + SAW.] A thin saw stretched in a frame which gives it sufficient rigidity in its work (Knight).

1678 MOXON *Mech. Exerc.* I. 99 The office of the Cheeks made to the Frame-Saw is, by the twisted Cord and Tongue ..to..strain the Blade of the Saw the straighter. **1761** *Brit. Mag.* II. 299 An oak fructed, proper, having a frame-saw, transversely fixed. **1832** BABBAGE *Econ. Manuf.* xxii. (ed. 3) 217 The horny exterior is then cut into three portions with a frame-saw.

'frame-up. *colloq.* (orig. *U.S.*). [See FRAME *v.* 8 e, 10.] Anything that has been pre-arranged or concocted, esp. with a sinister intent; a conspiracy or plot, e.g. for the purpose of incriminating a person on false evidence.

1900 'FLYNT' & WALTON *Powers that Prey* 141 He could arrange a 'frame-up', and relieve 'Soapy' of the stolen pocketbook, after 'Soapy' had lifted it from his victim's pocket. **1913** C. E. MULFORD *Coming of Cassidy* vii. 116 The crookedness would not come more than once in a deal if the frame-up was 'single-odd'. **1919** *New Appeal* (Girard, Kans.) 11 Jan. 1/5 They were the victims of a frameup inspired by class hatred. **1924** *Westm. Gaz.* 12 Feb., The Government, he said, were guilty of manufacturing a plot which never existed. He claimed that the plot was from beginning to end a 'frame-up'. **1956** A. L. ROWSE *Early Churchills* xi. 214 Their signatures were very cleverly forged. Coming at such a moment it looks like a frame-up. **1971** *It* 2–16 June 5/2 While serving a six month sentence.. Ian learned a lot about frame ups, about prison conditions.

'framework. [f. FRAME *sb.* + WORK *sb.*]

1. a. A structure composed of parts framed together, *esp.* one designed for inclosing or supporting anything; a frame or skeleton.

1644 MILTON *Areop.* (Arb.) 64 What a fine conformity would it starch us all into? doubtless a stanch and solid peece of frame-work, as any January could freeze together. **1703** MOXON *Mech. Exerc.* 132 Laying a Block.. under the corner of the Frame-work to bear it hollow off the Foundation. **1822** T. MITCHELL *Aristoph.* I. 192 Let ribs of beef this frame-work line. **1874** BURNAND *My Time* iii. 28 The old arm-chair, whose framework had been made any number of years ago. **1885** F. TEMPLE *Relat. Relig. & Sc.* vi. 164 The framework [of vertebrate animals] as a whole always exhibiting the same fundamental type.

b. *transf.* and *fig.* ***framework of reference***, †*axes* = *frame of reference* (now chiefly in sense (ii)).

1816 J. SCOTT *Vis. Paris* (ed. 5) 10 That the frame-work of a nation may be strong, each of its divisions must be let closely into others. **1856** STANLEY *Sinai & Pal.* i. (1858) 67 Those grand frameworks, such as at Marathon and elsewhere correspond to the event they have encompassed. **1876** FREEMAN *Norm. Conq.* V. xxii. 7 The outward framework of law and government still keeps its ancient shape. **1910** E. T. WHITTAKER *Hist. Theories Aether & Electr.* xii. 446 The physicist.. finds it convenient to construct a framework of axes in space and time for the purposes of fitting his experiences into an orderly arrangement. **1914** L. SILBERSTEIN *Theory of Relativity* i. 4 We are compelled to give up our earth as a system of reference and replace it.. by a framework of axes pointing from an initial point fixed in the sun. *Ibid.* 3 The earth loses its privilege as a framework of reference. **1931** *Amer. Jrnl. Orthopsychiatry* Oct. 493 Clearly the framework of reference within which a department of life is thought partly determines the basic attitude. **1959** *Listener* 14 May 857/1 The idea of a Luddite phase is clearly important in his framework of reference.

2. (Written as two words or with a hyphen.) Work done in or with a frame. **a.** Knitting or weaving done on a 'stocking-frame'; cf. FRAME *sb.* 13 b, and see 3 below. **b.** (See quot.)

1882 CAULFEILD & SAWARD *Dict. Needlework*, *Frame Work*, this work, also called *Travail au Métier*, is formed with wools and silk upon a flat solid wooden Frame cut to the size required.

c. *Gardening.* (See quot.)

1819 REES *Cycl.*, *Frame-work*, that sort of forcing and raising vegetable productions at an early period, which is performed by means of frames and artificial heart applied by them.

3. *Comb.*, as ***framework-knitted***, ***-knitter***.

1716 *Lond. Gaz.* No. 5484/4 John Hathoway.. Frame-work knitter. **1788** *Act 28 Geo. III*, c. 55 An Act for the.. Punishment of Persons destroying.. Framework knitted Pieces, Stockings, and other Articles. **1858** SIMMONDS *Dict. Trade*, *Frame-work Knitter*, an operative in the hosiery trade, who weaves the worsted or cotton thread up into a knitted fabric.

framing ('freɪmɪŋ), *vbl. sb.* [f. FRAME *v.* + -ING[1].] The action of FRAME *v.* in various senses.

†**1.** The action of making profit. *Obs.*

c **1440** *Promp. Parv.* 176/2 Framynge or afframynge or wynnynge, *lucrum, emolumentum*.

2. The action, method, or process of constructing, making, or shaping anything whether material or immaterial; †also, hewing of timber (*obs.*). Also gerundial with omission of *in*.

c **1440** *Promp. Parv.* 176/2 Framynge of tymbyr, *dolatura*. *a* **1569** KINGESMYLL *Man's Est.* ix. (1580) 45 There is a stone framyng, it shall be laied in Sion. **1633** P. FLETCHER *Purple Isl.* III. iii, This curious Isle, whose framing yet Was never ..known to any humane wit. **1697** DAMPIER *Voy.* I. vii. 189 Captain Bond had the framing.. of it [a Fire ship]. **1703** MOXON *Mech. Exerc.* 123 To pin the Frame.. of a Roof together, whilst it is framing. **1867** SMYTH *Sailor's Word-bk.*, *Framing*, the placing, scarphing, and bolting of the frame-timbers of a ship. **1883** *Manch. Exam.* 16 June 4/7 The clause in dispute was of Lord Salisbury's own framing.

3. *Mining.* See quot. and cf. *framing-table*.

1874 KNIGHT *Dict. Mech.* I. 913 *Framing*.. 2 (Mining) an operation upon pounded or stamped ores by which they are sorted into grades of comparative weight and consequent richness.

4. *concr.* Framed work; a framework; a frame or set or system of frames.

1703 T.N. *City & C. Purchaser* 142 The Timber.. to make 3 Square of Framing. **1823** SCORESBY *Jrnl. Whale Fishery* 455 The pannels of the captain's state-room door were forced out of the framing. **1828** TREDGOLD *Elem. Princ. Carpentery* title-p., Pressure and Equilibrium of Timber Framing. **1886** *Pall Mall G.* 22 July 4/2 Walls of bamboo framing filled in with mud.

5. *attrib.*, as ***framing-house***, ***-timber***; also **framing-chisel**, a heavy chisel for making mortises; **framing-table** *Mining* (see quot. and sense 3).

1874 KNIGHT *Dict. Mech.* I. 914 **Framing-chisel*. **1583** HOLLYBAND *Campo di Fior* 57 The colledge.. is the *framing house, and as it were, The shoppe of men. **1874** KNIGHT *Dict. Mech.* I. 913/2 The *framing-table is.. suspended in an inclined position, on pivots, so that it may be tipped into a vertical position when full, discharging its contents into separate cisterns beneath. **1522** *Mem. Ripon* (Surtees) III. 188 Le *framyng tymbre. **1940** *Chambers's Techn. Dict.* 353/1 *Framing timber*, the Australian equivalent of carcassing timber. **1957** *N.Z. Timber Jrnl.* Mar. 52/2 *Framing timber*, wood used in the carcassing of buildings. **1968** *Gloss. Formwork Terms* (*B.S.I.*) 9 *Carcassing timber* (framing timber), timber used for any structural purpose in the support of the forms, but not normally in contact with the concrete.

†**framp**, *v.* *Obs.* *rare*$^{-1}$. *intr.* ? To revel, indulge greedily.

1532 MORE *Confut. Tindale* Wks. 716/1 Which not content with.. manna.. murmured y[t] they might not frampe in fleshe.

†**'frample**, *v.* *Sc.* *Obs.* [? freq. of FRAMP *v.*] To swallow or gobble *up*.

a **1598** ROLLOCK *2 Thess.* iii, xii. (1606) 146 When thou hast beene an idle vagabound.. and yet stops to thy dinner, and framples vp other mens trauels, that is vnlawfull eating.

'frampler. pseudo-*arch.* *rare*$^{-1}$. [Cf. FRAPLER, FRAMPOLD.] A brawler; = FRAPLER.

1820 SCOTT *Monast.* xxvii, A rude low-born frampler and wrangler.

'frampold, *a.* *Obs.* exc. *dial.* Forms: 6–7 **frampold**, **frompall**, 7 **frampald**, **-pard**, **frompered**, **frampel(l**, **-ple**, **-pole**, **-poll**, **-pull**, **(phrampell)**, 7, 9 *hist.* **frampal(l**, 7, 9 *dial.* **frampled**. [Of obscure origin; it is uncertain which of the many divergent forms is the earliest; formation on *fram*, FROM + POLL head, would suit sense 2. Cf. *frommard* = FROMWARD, FROWARD; also FRUMP, and Sc. *frample* 'to put in disorder'.]

1. Sour-tempered, cross, disagreeable, peevish.

1598 SHAKS. *Merry W.* II. ii. 94 She leads a very frampold life with him. *c* **1600** DAY *Begg. Bednall Gr.* II. ii. (1881) 37, I think the fellow's frompall:—I ask thee where my Cloak is. **1617** COLLINS *Def. Bp. Ely* II. x. 539 If a Priest were so frampoll.. as to refuse to baptize a poore infant in that case. **1633** B. JONSON *Tale Tub* II. iv, I pray thee, grow not fram pull now. **1674** N. FAIRFAX *Bulk & Selv.* To Rdr., An ill will'd and frampled waspishness. **1688** BUNYAN *Solomon's Temple Spiritualized* xlix. 9 Babes.. have.. babyish tricks.. their childish talk and frompered carriage must be borne withal. *a* **1825** FORBY *Voc. E. Anglia*, *Frampled*, cross, ill-humoured.

2. Of a horse: Fiery, mettlesome, spirited.

1603 HOLLAND *Plutarch's Mor.* 14 Like a skittish and frampold horse. **1611** MIDDLETON & DEKKER *Roaring Girle* D.'s Wks. 1873 III. 170 Coachman.. are we fitted with good phrampell iades. **1823** SCOTT *Peveril* xxxii, The two 'frampal jades' (to use the term of the period). [**1876** *Whitby Gloss.*, *Frample* v., to paw on the ground, as a horse when kept standing in one place.]

framward: see FROMWARD. *Obs.*

franc (fræŋk). Forms: 4–8 **frank**, 9 **franc**. [a. F. *franc*, said to be derived from the legend *Francorum rex*, 'king of the Franks', on the first coins which were so called.

The F. word appears as the name of a gold coin in an official document of 1360 (Hatz.-Darm.); the legend *Francorum rex* occurs on a gold coin struck in the same year.]

The name of a French coin or money of account, of different values at different periods. **a.** A gold coin, in the 14th c. weighing about 60 grs., and intrinsically worth about 10*s.* 6*d.* (1897), but afterwards depreciated. **b.** (Sometimes ***pound franc***.) A silver coin, first struck in 1575, identical with the livre tournois of 20 sols; in the 18th c. English money-changers valued it at 9*d.* or 10*d.* **c.** Since 1795, a silver coin representing the monetary unit of the decimal system; its value was slightly more than 9½*d* in the late 19th c.

c **1386** CHAUCER *Shipman's T.* 201, I wol bringe yow an hundred frankes. *c* **1400** *Sowdone Bab.* 589 Take a thausande pounde of Frankis fyne. **1494** FABYAN *Chron.* VII. 527 A franke is worth .ii.*s.* sterl[g]. **1596** DALRYMPLE tr. *Leslie's Hist. Scot.* IX. 236 Ilk ȝeir how lang he lyuet xxx thousand frankis. **1603** KNOLLES *Hist. Turks* (1638) 223 The yearely tribute of.. eight hundred thousand franks of siluer. **1685** BAXTER *Paraphr. N.T.* Mark vi. 34 *note*, Beza reckoneth the 200 pence, to 35 pound Frank of Tours. **1702** W. J. *Bruyn's Voy. Levant* xxxii. 129 A Chicken of Gold.. which amounts to Seven Francs and half. **1810** *Naval Chron.* XXIV. 300 A piece of silver weighing five grams.. to which has been applied the term *Franc*. **1892** E. REEVES *Homewd. Bound* 227 We had again to turn our pesetas into francs at a loss.

‖**franc-archer** (frɑ̃karʃe). *Fr. Hist.* Pl. **franc(s-archers**. [Fr.; *franc* free (see FRANK *a.*) + *archer* archer.] One of a body of archers established by Charles VII, one man being equipped by each parish, and exempted from taxes in consideration of his service.

1675 tr. *Machiavelli's Prince* (Rtldg. 1883) 293 In every parish in France there is a person called a frank archer. **1852** MISS YONGE *Cameos* (1877) III. ii. 92 Marching all night, he surprised the franc-archers and their leader. **1885** PLUMMER in *Fortescue's Abs. & Lim. Mon.* 197 The francs-archers, abolished by Louis XI after.. Guinegate in 1479.

†**france.** *Obs.* [cf. FRANK *sb.*[3]] = FRANKINCENSE.

14.. *Epiph.* in *Tundale's Vis.* 109 Golde france and myrre thei gaf hym all thre.

†**franch**, **fraunch**, *v.* *Obs.* Also 6 **fraunge**. [? onomatopœic; cf. *craunch*.] *trans.* To devour. *intr.* To feed greedily (*on*). Hence **'franching** *ppl. a.* Also **'francher**, a devourer.

1519 HORMAN *Vulg.* 39 b, He is euer fraunchynge. *Ibid.* 71 Thou arte a rauenar of delicates and a francher. **1541** R. COPLAND *Guydon's Quest. Chirurg.* M iij, People gullyng, fraungyng, and dronkerds. **1563** *Mirr. Mag.*, *Ld. Rivers* lxviii, A Bull and Bore dyd passe, Fraunchyng the fysh and frye, with teeth of brasse. **1575** TURBERVILE *Bk. Venerie* 358 He that.. had yong fleshe to banquet at his fill Were fonde to fraunshe on garbage, graynes or swyll. **1625–6** PURCHAS *Pilgrims* IV. 1579 They cast of them also to flesh fraunching Dogs.

†**franchemyle.** *Cookery.* *Obs.* Also **franchemole**, **frawnchemyle**, **-mul(le**, **fraunchemele**, **fronchemoyle**. [a. F. *franche mulle*, ruminating stomach of a sheep, etc.] A sort of haggis.

c **1420** *Liber Cocorum* 36 For fraunche mele. Take swongene eyrene.. and kreme.. and kremelyd sewet of schepe.. And fylle þy bagge [etc.]. *c* **1430** *Two Cookery-bks.* I. 38 Frawnchemyle. Nym Eyroun [etc.].. & do in the wombe of the chepe, þat is, þe mawe; & seþe hem wel. **1483** *Cath. Angl.* 141 A Franchemole (*v.r.* Frawnchmulle), *lucanica*.

franchisal ('fræntʃɪzəl, -tʃaɪz-), *a.* [f. FRANCHISE *sb.* + -AL.] Of or belonging to the franchise.

1897 F. W. MAITLAND *Domesday Bk.* 80 With feudal justice therefore we contrast 'franchisal' justice. **1954** *Bull. Inst. Hist. Res.* XXVII. 31 There was no court, royal, communal or franchisal, which did not come within the purview of the central courts of common law.

franchise ('frɑːntʃɪz, 'fræn-, -tʃaɪz), *sb.* Forms: 3–6 **fraunchis(e**, **-yse**, 4–6 **franchis**, **-yse**, **-es**, 5–6 **fraunches**, **-schis(se**, (6 **franchese**, **fraunces**, **-chest**, **-chiese**, **-cis**), 3– **franchise**. [a. OF.

franchise freedom, frankness, f. *franc* free, FRANK *a.*[2]

For the history of the pronunciation see ENFRANCHISE.]

I. Freedom, immunity, privilege.

†**1. a.** Freedom as opposed to servitude or subjection. *Obs.*

c **1290** *S. Eng. Leg.* I. 142/1271 And to bi-nime þe kynge is fraunchise. **1297** R. GLOUC. (Rolls) 1091 We wulleþ vor oure franchise fiȝte & vor oure lond. *c* **1386** CHAUCER *Pars. T.* ¶378 þe goodes of body ben hele of body, as strengthe.. beautee, gentrye, fraunchise. **1475** *Bk. Noblesse* 71 Aruns.. assemblid a gret oost ayenst the Romains to have.. put hem in servage out of her fraunchise. **1525** LD. BERNERS *Froiss.* (1812) II. xliii. 140 Ye sholde take all that we haue.. to maynteyne vs and our fraunches. **1648** D. JENKINS *Wks.* 110 The House of Commons by themselves.. have no power to imprison men, or put them out of Franchise.

†**b.** Moral freedom. *Obs.*

a **1300** *Cursor M.* 1637 Al his for-geten nou al þat franches þat I gaue man in paradis. **1477** EARL RIVERS (Caxton) *Dictes* 27 The mooste difficulte in a man.. To knowe hym self, To kepe his fraunchyse or liberte. **1483** CAXTON *Gold. Leg.* 28/2 For where the holy ghoost, is, there is fraunchyse and lyberte.

2. a. A legal immunity or exemption from a particular burden or exaction, or from the jurisdiction of a particular tribunal, granted to an individual, a corporation, an order of persons, etc. In early use also *collect.* or in generalized sense: The immunities, freedom of government, etc., belonging to a municipality, etc.

c **1330** R. BRUNNE *Chron.* (1810) 130, I þe forbede to chalange any clerke In lay courte.. of holy kirke has merke, Ne þe franchise fordo, þat it ouh to halde. **1473** WARKW. *Chron.* 2 He ratyfied.. all the ffraunsches yeve to citeis.. and graunted to many cyteis.. new fraunschesses. **1480** CAXTON *Chron.* cxlvii. Ij, & that holy chyrch shold haue all fraunchises as ferforth as they had in seint Edwards tyme the confessour. **1494** FABYAN *Chron.* VII. 336 This yere the Kynge seasyd the fraunchyse of the cytie of London. **1538** LELAND *Itin.* II. 68 King Eadgar.. bare a gret Zeale to the Towne, and gave very great Frauncheses and Privilges vnto it. **1559** in Strype *Ann. Ref.* I. App. viii. 22 All franchises and liberties of the bisshoppericks.. deryvid from the crowne. **1601** HOLLAND *Pliny* I. 92 A most famous towne.. endowed by Claudius.. with the franchises and right of a Colonie. **1641** *Termes de la Ley* 167 Franchise.. signifies in our Law an Immunity or exemption from ordinary Jurisdiction, as for a Corporation to hold pleas within themselves to such a value, and the like. **1757** BURKE *Abridgm. Eng. Hist.* III. viii. Wks. 1812 V. 684 They had strength enough to oblige him [John] to a solemn promise of restoring those liberties and franchises, which they had always claimed. **1838** PRESCOTT *Ferd. & Is.* (1846) III. xxiii. 334 The city, having first obtained assurance of respect for all its franchises and immunities, surrendered.

b. In wider sense: A privilege or exceptional right granted by the sovereign power to any person or body of persons. In England now chiefly *Hist.* and as a technical term of law; in the U.S. applied *esp.* to the powers conferred on a company formed for some purpose of public utility.

1386 *Rolls of Parlt.* III. 225/1 Noughtwithstondyng the same fredam or fraunchise, Nichol Brembre.. was chosen Mair. **1479** *Bury Wills* (Camden) 53, I beqwethe to Robert myn son, my tenmentes called Calfes and Northes.. w^t the fraunchyse of faldes of ijcc shepe to eche of the seyd tenmentes bylongyng. **1523** LD. BERNERS *Froiss.* I. ccclxxxi. 640 In diuerse countreys.. the noble men hath great fraunches ouer the commons, and kepeth them in seruage. **1557** N. T. (Genev.) *Luke* xxiii. 17 *note*, The Romains had gyuen such franches and liberties to the Iewes [to 'let one lowse vnto them at the feast']. **1596** SPENSER *F.Q.* IV. ix. 37 Ye.. the love of ladies foule defame; To whom the world this franchise ever yeelded, That of their loves choise they might freedom clame. **1598** MANWOOD *Lawes Forest* i. §5 (1615) 24/2 A Forest.. is the most highest franchise of noble, and princely pleasure, that can be insident unto the Crowne and Royall dignitie of a Prince. **1628** COKE *On Litt.* 121 A mannor whereunto the franchise of waife and stray and such like are appendant. **16..** *Act Chas. I*, c. 15 (Manley) 20 And the Lords and owners of Fairs, Markets and other Franchises. **1711** STEELE *Spect.* No. 258 ¶2, I do humbly propose.. that another Theatre of Ease may be erected.. and that the Direction thereof may be made a Franchise in Fee to me, and my Heirs for ever. **1767** BLACKSTONE *Comm.* II. 37 Franchise and liberty are used as synonymous terms: and their definition is, a royal privilege, or branch of the king's prerogative, subsisting in the hands of a subject. **1824** J. MARSHALL *Const. Opin.* (1839) 324 The bill is brought for the purpose of protecting the bank in the exercise of a franchise granted by a law of the United States. **1866** ROGERS *Agric. & Prices* I. ii. 33 The right of having a watermill was a franchise. **1876** DIGBY *Real Prop.* I. App. §1. 268 The rights to have 'waifs, wrecks, estrays, treasure-trove, royal fish, forfeitures, and deodands' are franchises, which must rest on royal grant, or prescription which presupposes a grant. **1888** BRYCE *Amer. Commw.* II. III. lxvi. 500 After the sale by the Board of Aldermen of the Broadway franchise (the right of laying down a tram-way in Broadway), the Aldermanic office was much sought after. *Ibid.* lxvii. 521 The form which corruption usually takes in the populous cities is the sale of 'franchises' (especially monopolies in the use of public thoroughfares). **1892** *Pall Mall G.* 30 Apr. 4/3 The Weights and Measures Bill.. empower[s] municipal and County Councils to purchase 'franchises' of weights and measures.

c. *Marine Insurance.* A percentage below which the underwriter incurs no responsibility.

The term was borrowed from French practice, but the English application differs from the French; cf. **1857** M. HOPKINS *Handbk. Average* 140 In some foreign policies the warranty has a rather different signification. It not only requires that the damage should amount to a certain proportion of the value of the goods insured, but it gives to the assured, in case of Average, only that portion of the loss which exceeds the agreed limit, which is there called the *franchise*, or *affranchisement*.

1895 W. GOW *Marine Insur.* 192 It has been arranged that all claims falling short of a certain amount or percentage should not attach to the policy covering the goods. This amount or percentage is termed the *franchise*. *Ibid.* 195 Nowadays in England when the franchise is once reached, the whole amount of average including the franchise is paid by the underwriter. **1929** V. DOVER *Marine Insur.* (ed. 3) 240 Once the franchise is reached the policy pays in full. *Ibid.* 330 Unless a franchise of 5 *per cent.* is attained. **1962** R. H. BROWN *Dict. Marine Insur. Terms* 103 *Franchise*, an amount or percentage specified in the policy which must be reached before a claim is payable... In some foreign insurances the term may be used to denote a deductible franchise.

d. The authorization granted to an individual or group by a company to sell its products or services in a particular area. Hence ***franchisee***, ***franchiser***, ***franchisor***.

1959 *Listener* 2 Apr. 600/3 Paul had obtained the barber shop franchise in a local hotel. **1966** *Economist* 9 July 148/1 Franchisers, to be successful, must to some degree tell their franchisees what to sell and at what price. **1967** *Times Rev. Industry* Aug. 77/2 In the United States.. some 1,500 franchisors.. handle about 35 per cent of total retail sales. *Ibid.*, The car distributor with the exclusive local franchise. *Ibid.* 77/3 The management, marketing, product and service know-how of the franchise organization. **1970** *Guardian* 31 July 9/7 The endless seekers of franchises on the [pop festival] site. Drinks, hot dogs, records.. are a ready source of cover.

†**3.** Freedom from arrest, secured to fugitives in certain privileged places; right of asylum or sanctuary; privileged character, inviolability, of a place of refuge. Hence *concr.* an asylum, sanctuary.

c **1380** WYCLIF *Sel. Wks.* III. 323 Here men wondren moche whi alle manquelleris shullen have þis fraunchise of þe sche [? *read* seintuarie]. *c* **1450** *St. Cuthbert* (Surtees) 4994 In cuthbert mynster he come forþi, þe fraunchyse to breke of it. **1513** DOUGLAS *Æneis* VIII. vi. 69 The haly schaw, Quilk strang Romulus did reduce and draw In maner of franches or of sanctuary. **1601** HOLLAND *Pliny* I. 121 They forbeare those.. that flie vnto them as to a place of franchise and priuiledge.

attrib. **1525** LD. BERNERS *Froiss.* II. clx. 177 a, Trecte, a fraunches towne for all maner of people.

4. The freedom of or full membership of a body corporate or politic; citizenship.

1579 FULKE *Refut. Rastell* 742 Our franches, freedom, or conuersation is in heauen. **1606** HOLLAND *Sueton.* Annot. 2 Unlesse they might be *donati civitate*. i. enioy the Franchises and Freedome of Rome. **1838** THIRLWALL *Greece* II. 36 Solon.. published an amnesty.. which restored those citizens who had been deprived of their franchise for lighter offences. **1876** FREEMAN *Norm. Conq.* V. xxiii. 305 The men of London.. ranked with the barons of the realm, and many barons of the realm had been admitted to the franchise of their commonalty.

†**5.** The district over which the privilege of a corporation or an individual extends; a territory, domain. Cf. LIBERTY. ***to go*** or ***ride the franchises***: to beat the bounds. *Obs.*

1486 *Surtees Misc.* (1888) 53 Tadcastre brige, being thextremitie of y^s fraunches. **1526** R. WHYTFORD *Martiloge* (1893) 64 In the fraunchest of pontyne. *Ibid.* 174 In the fraunchest of lyngon. **1572** in W. H. Turner *Select. Rec. Oxford* 341 The francheses of this Cytie shalbe ryd according to auncient custom. **1621** BOLTON *Stat. Ireland 36 Hen. VI*, 27 This Statute shall be observed and take place as well within Franchises and liberties as without. **1680** WOOD *Life* (Oxf. Hist. Soc.) II. 493 That day he went the franchises with the mayor and citizens. **1774** E. JACOB *Faversham* 27 The river which separates the franchise of the church of Canterbury down to a place towards the South. **1876** DIGBY *Real Prop.* i. i. §2. 15 The owner of a franchise or liberty or district exempt from the jurisdiction of the hundred.

attrib. **1577** *Nottingham Rec.* IV. 168 Payd for carydg of the olde fraunces crose to the towne. **1587** *Ibid.* 215 Another hole in Wilforth Pasture.. to want frauncis stones.

6. a. The right or privilege of voting at public elections, *esp.* for members of the legislative body.

(Originally a mere contextual application of 2 b; more fully, ***elective franchise***; now the prevailing sense.)

1790 BURKE *Fr. Rev.* Wks. V. 318 It would be too much to tell a man jealous of his equality, that the elector has the same franchise who votes for three members as he who votes for ten. **1819** MACKINTOSH *Parl. Suffrage* Wks. 1846 III. 215 The reasons which make it important to liberty, that the elective franchise should be exercised by large bodies of the lower classes. **1827** HALLAM *Const. Hist.* (1876) III. xiii. 36 New boroughs.. acquired the franchise of election. **1845** McCULLOCH *Taxation* I. ii. (1852) 66 The occupiers of 10*l.* houses have been intrusted with the elective franchise. **1869** RAWLINSON *Anc. Hist.* 128 Citizens in a certain sense, but without franchise.

b. In recent use: One of the various principles of qualification by which the bestowal of the elective franchise may be regulated. ***fancy franchise***: see FANCY C.

1884 GLADSTONE in *Daily News* 29 Feb. 2/4 We propose to establish a new franchise, which I should call—till a better phrase be discovered—the service franchise.

II. As an attribute of character or action.

†**7.** Nobility of mind; liberality, generosity, magnanimity. *Obs.*

13.. *E.E. Allit. P.* B. 750 Ȝif I for-loyne as a fol þy fraunchyse may serue. *c* **1386** CHAUCER *Frankl. T.* 796 A gayns franchise and alle gentillesse. —— *Merch. T.* 743 Heer may ye see, how excellent fraunchise In womman is whan thay narow hem avyse. *c* **1450** *Merlin* 280 And ther-fore remembre vs of pitee and of youre grete fraunchise. *c* **1489** CAXTON *Sonnes of Aymon* xi. 283 Telle Reynawde.. that he take no hede to my trespase & evyll dede, but to his fraunchyse. **1658** J. COLES *Cleopatra* 161 It might be remedied by an action of generosity and franchise.

†**8.** Freedom or licence of speech or manners.

1567 DRANT *Horace's Epist.* II. i. G v, And lo by such like wayes Came firste the fraunchyse Fessentine.

ˈfranchise, *v. Obs.* exc. as vbl. sb. Forms: 4 **fraunchise,** 5 **fraunch(a)yse, fraunches,** 6– **franchise.** [a. OF. *franchiss-*, lengthened stem of *franchir*, f. *franc* free: see FRANK *a.*[2]] *trans.* To make or set free; to invest with a franchise or privilege; = ENFRANCHISE *v.* Const. *from*, *of*.

1390 GOWER *Conf.* I. 269 Thus stonden all men fraunchised. **1393** LANGL. *P. Pl.* C. IV. 114 Hit ys noȝt semly.. þat vsurers.. Be fraunchised for a free man. *c* **1430** LYDG. *Min. Poems* (1840) 3 From other dayes that day whas so devyded, And fraunchesid from mystes and from reyne. **1483** CAXTON *Gold. Leg.* 325 b/2 The kyng.. fraunchysed al England of the trybute. **1494** FABYAN *Chron.* VI. clxxi. 165 He.. fraunchaysed that towne with many great lyberties. **1548** UDALL, etc. *Erasm. Par. Acts* xxii. 28 Before I could be franchisid & made a citizen. **1562** LEIGH *Armorie* (1597) 74 b, Though all the towne were franchised, yet horses are not toll-free to this day. **1605** SHAKS. *Macb.* II. i. 28, I.. still keepe my Bosome franchis'd. **1633** J. DONE *Hist. Septuagint* 24 The summe then of those were franchis'd, mounted unto 400 Talents. **1773** J. ROSS *Fratricide* II. 931 (MS.) Every Soul, when franchis'd from its dust, May quit this life with certain hope in thee. **1793** W. ROBERTS *Looker-on* (1794) II. 432 Franchised by nature.. he [Dryden] felt that he could adventure in poetry beyond any other writer of his age.

Hence **ˈfranchising** *vbl. sb.* (for mod. use cf. FRANCHISE *sb.* 2 d).

1574 tr. *Littleton's Tenures* 43 a, If the Lorde make to him [his villaine] a lease of landes.. thys is no fraunchisinge. **1644** EVELYN *Mem.* (1857) I. 82 Claudius' speech.. concerning the franchising of the town. **1966** *Economist* 9 July 147/3 Congress is listening to arguments that any curbs on franchising would hurt small businessmen. **1967** *Times Rev. Industry* Aug. 77/3 Franchising, as the Wimpy bar idea in Britain illustrates, has become a method of very quickly establishing a distributive network for a product or service.

franchised (ˈfrɑːntʃɪzd, ˈfræn-, -tʃaɪzd), *ppl. a.* [f. FRANCHISE *sb.* and *v.* + -ED.]

†**1.** Of a city, etc.: **a.** Possessing the right of sanctuary. **b.** Invested with municipal or political privileges. *Obs.*

a. **1503–4** *Act 19 Hen. VII*, c. 36 Preamb., Sir Edward kepith hym in such hidelles and other places fraunchesed. **1546** LANGLEY *Pol. Verg. De Invent.* III. viii. 74 b, Moses.. did institute thre franchised tounes.

b. **1451** *Paston Lett.* (1872) I. 194 It was a fraunchised town and within the Duchye. **1538** LELAND *Itin.* (1711) V. 43 There hath beene a Franchisid Toune, now clene decayith. **1641** *Termes de la Ley* 215 Seised of lands in Gavelkind, as in Kent, and in other places franchised.

2. Of persons: Made 'free' of a body politic.

1520 in W. H. Turner *Select. Rec. Oxford* 26 Eny Fraunchesid man sworn unto the fraunches. **1558** *Reg. Gild Corpus Chr. York* (1872) 220 *note*, The mayour's kid-cot, where unto franchised men are used to be commytted for their offens. **1841** W. SPALDING *Italy & It. Isl.* II. 116 The community, composed of all the franchised citizens.

†**3.** Made free, enfranchised. *Obs.*

1650 EARL MONMOUTH tr. *Senault's Man become Guilty* 257 The one was but a franchised slave, and the other a common Player. **1753** L. M. tr. *Du Boscq's Accomplish'd Woman* II. 114 Anicetus. [*Note*] His [Nero's] franchis'd slave.

4. Of a company: possessing special powers or rights conferred on the ground of public utility. Also, possessing a franchise (sense 2 d). *U.S.*

1908 *Munsey's Mag.* Nov. 165/2 His attitude toward the franchised and privileged monopolies of Washington. **1968** *Globe & Mail* (Toronto) 5 Feb. 24/8 (Advt.), For Sale. Franchized dry cleaning plant, operating in busy well located Oshawa Shopping Centre. **1970** *Motoring Which?* Oct. 150/1 Cars were generally serviced better.. at franchised garages.

†**ˈfranchisement.** *Obs.* [a. OF. *franchisement*, *franchissement*, f. *franchir*: see FRANCHISE *v.*]

The action of setting free or investing with a franchise; the state or fact of being enfranchised; = ENFRANCHISEMENT.

1562 LEIGH *Armorie* (1597) 74 b, The franchisement [of Couentrie] was graunted to her vpon condition, that shee should ride naked through the same Citie. **1596** SPENSER *F.Q.* V. xi. 36 Artegall.. went.. to worke Irenaes franchisement. *c* **1611** CHAPMAN *Iliad* V. 375 He could scarce enjoy The benefit of franchisement. **1809** KENDALL *Trav.* I. vi. 49 Till.. the.. superior court shall see cause to restore him to his franchisement or freedom again.

b. A privilege.

1779 *St. Papers* in *Ann. Reg.* 416/1 His Christian Majesty, in making reprisals, would also limit the franchisements of the ships of this state.

ˈfranchiser. *nonce-wd.* [f. FRANCHISE *sb.* + -ER[1].] One possessed of the (elective) franchise.

1843 CARLYLE *Past & Pr.* III. xiii. (1872) 187 O free and independent Franchiser.

Franc hoode: see FRENCH HOOD.

Francic (ˈfrænsɪk), *a.* ? *Obs.* [ad med.L. *Francic-us*, f. *Francus* FRANK *sb.*[1]] = FRANKISH.

1698 *Phil. Trans.* XX. 445 Books written in the Samaritan .. Francic.. and Islandic. **1782** BURNEY *Hist. Music* (1789) II. iv. 261 Lai (lay) seems a word purely Francic and Saxon. **1831** *For. Q. Rev.* VII. 379 He asserts that the language which the Saxons introduced into England must have been

Francic. **1833** G. S. FABER *Recapit. Apostasy* 37 The short-lived Francic Emperorship.

francisc (fran'sɪsk). Also **francesque, -isque.** [ad. med.L. *francisca*, or its adopted form in Fr.] A battle-axe varying in form, used by the Franks.

1801 A. RANKEN *Hist. France* I. 21 One soldier.. raising his francesque or battle-axe, struck the vessel. **1864** KINGSLEY *Rom. & Teut.* vi. (1875) 141 Franks came down ..with.. heavy short-handled double-edged francisc.

Franciscan (fran'sɪskən), *a.* and *sb.* [f. med.L. *Francisc-us* Francis + -AN.]

A. *adj.* Of or belonging to the order of St. Francis; pertaining to the Franciscans.

[**1577** FRAMPTON *Joyful News* I. (1596) 26 A Passenger.. did aduertise mee that a Frauncis Frier, etc.] **1592** SHAKS. *Rom. & Jul.* v. ii. 1 Holy Franciscan Frier, Brother, ho? **1667** MILTON *P.L.* III. 480 They who.. Dying put on the weeds of Dominic, Or in Franciscan think to pass disguised. **1865** PUSEY *Truth Eng. Ch.* 36 The long Franciscan controversy about poverty.

B. *sb.* A friar of the order founded by St. Francis of Assisi in 1209.

1599 SANDYS *Europæ Spec.* (1632) 67 The Franciscans.. in the time of Sixtus Quintus.. are sayd to have beene found by survey to be xxx. thousand. **1677** PLOT *Oxfordsh.* 216 This Learned Franciscan did so far excel the ancient Magicians. **1856** R. A. VAUGHAN *Mystics* (1860) I. 143 Enthusiastic Franciscans who think the end of the world at hand.

Hence **Fran'ciscanism**, the system and practice of St. Francis and the Franciscans.

1855 MILMAN *Lat. Chr.* IV. 275 The first patron of Franciscanism, Gregory IX.

Francis I: see FRANÇOIS PREMIER.

francium ('frænsɪəm). *Chem.* [mod.L. (M. Perey 1946, in *Jrnl. de Chim. phys.* XLIII. 157), f. *Franc(e*: see -IUM.] A radioactive metallic element that is the heaviest member of the alkali-metal series and is chemically similar to cæsium; all its isotopes have short half-lives and only one (francium 223) occurs naturally, being produced by the radioactive decay of actinium 227. Symbol Fr; atomic number 87.

1946 *Jrnl. & Proc. R. Inst. Chem.* Dec. 277 For element 87,.. the name Francium (Fr) has been suggested. **1951** J. R. PARTINGTON *Gen. & Inorg. Chem.* (ed. 2) xii. 323A It was at first called *actinium-K* but has been renamed *francium* (Fr.). **1963** A. G. MADDOCK in *Mellor's Compreh. Treat. Inorg. & Theor. Chem.* II. Suppl. III. II. vi. 2516 Francium-211 may also have a half-life longer than five minutes and there is some evidence that ^{210}Fr and ^{213}Fr may have half-lives near one minute. *Ibid.* 2518 Asimov has calculated that the earth's crust contains 24·5 g. of francium. **1968** C. A. HAMPEL *Encycl. Chem. Elem.* 224/1 Francium exists in aqueous solution as a large singly-charged ion with small tendency to form complex ions.

Francize ('frɑːnsaɪz, 'fræn-), *v.* In 7 **francise.** [ad. F. *franciser*, f. *franç-ais* French.] *trans.* To make French. Hence **Franci'zation** [in F. *francisation*], the action of making French or investing with French nationality, the status thus conferred.

a **1661** FULLER *Worthies* II. (1662) 26 He was an English-man Francised. **1888** *Times* 20 Nov. 5/1 Francisation shall not be too readily accorded. **1888** *Daily Tel.* 21 Nov. 5/2 Why then do Arab boats.. receive francisation?

franckeite ('fræŋkəaɪt). *Min.* [ad. G. *franckeit* (A. W. Stelzner 1893, in *Neues Jahrb. f. Min.* II. 124), f. the name of Carl and Ernest *Francke*, mining engineers: see -ITE[1].] A sulphostannate of lead, $Pb_5Sn_3Sb_2S_{14}$, forming lustrous greyish-black orthorhombic crystals.

1893 *Jrnl. Chem. Soc.* LXIV. II. 576 This new mineral, which is of special interest as indicating the character of the occurrence of tin in the Bolivian mines.. is named franckeite by the author in honour of C. and E. Francke, two mining engineers specially interested in Bolivian mining. **1968** [see CYLINDRITE].

‖**franco** ('fræŋkəʊ), *a.* [It. (*porto*) *franco* free (carriage).] Free of any postal or delivery charge.

1873 *Young Englishwoman* May 256/2 The Malle des Indes sends out patterns by post *franco*. **1962** H. O. BEECHENO *Introd. Bus. Stud.* xii. 113 A *free, franco* or *rendu* quotation includes all costs up to and including delivery to the purchaser's place of business. **1969** J. L. HANSON *Dict. Econ.* (ed. 3) 211/1 *Franco*, a term used in foreign trade transactions, it is a price quotation which includes not only the cost of the commodity but also insurance, freight, and all delivery charges to the importer's ware-house.

Franco- ('fræŋkəʊ), originally med.L., combining form of *Franc-i* the Franks or French; chiefly in combs. signifying 'Frank or French and ..' as ***Franco-American, -Canadian*** adj. and sb., ***-Gallican, -Gauls, -German, -Irish, -negroid, -Prussian, -Roman.*** Cf. ANGLO- 2.

1711 LD. MOLESWORTH tr. *Hotman's Franco-Gallia* (1721) 12 These were Franks, not Gauls, or rather Franco-gauls. *Ibid.* 28 A true History of Francogallican Affairs. **1827** G. S. FABER *Sacred Cal. Prophecy* (1844) II. 182 The Franco-Roman Emperor. **1837** *Niagara Reporter* 24 Sept. 2/3 A meeting.. of the Franco-Canadian clique. **1841** *Montreal Transcript* 30 Oct. 2/4 The vanity of the Franco-Canadians. **1861** J. G. SHEPPARD *Fall Rome* xiii. 740 The Franco-Gallican Church.. would seem to have almost entirely lost the character of a religious institution. **1871** 'E. PERKINS' (*title*) The Franco-Prussian war in a nutshell. **1881** W. J. RATTRAY *Scot in Brit. N. Amer.* II. 404 Under the Constitutional Act of 1791, the Franco-Canadians were, if not quite satisfied, at least tranquil and submissive. **1883** *Harper's Mag.* Feb. 478/1 The Franco-American Claims' Committee decided in favour of the claim. **1885** LADY BRASSEY *The Trades* 285 Hayti, the Franco-negroid portion of San Domingo. **1931** H. S. WEAVER *Let.* 19 July in Joyce *Lett.* (1966) III. 223 A small Franco-Irish contingent of influential people. **1945** R. HARGREAVES *Enemy at Gate* 65 The combined Franco-Irish force. **1966** V. L. LIDTKE *Outlawed Party* iv. 114 Remembering his opposition to the Franco-Prussian War, no one could justifiably accuse him of surrendering to militarism. **1969** *Publ. Amer. Dial. Soc.* LII. 12 Almost all Franco-Canadians learn English.

‖**François Premier** (frɑ̃swa prəmje). Also **Francis I.** The name of Francis I, King of France (reigned 1515–47), used adjectivally to designate the styles in architecture, furniture, etc., characteristic of his reign.

1860 *Dict. Archit.* (Archit. Publ. Soc.) II. 88/2 *Francois Premier* (*Style*). This term properly applies to that portion of *Renaissance* architecture seen at Chenonceaux and Chambord. **1878** MRS. B. PALLISER tr. *Jacquemart's Hist. Furnit.* IV. v. 401 (*caption*) Nef of rock crystal, cut and engraved. Italian workmanship of the Francis I. period. **1910** *Encycl. Brit.* II. 413/2 Between the last phase of Flamboyant Gothic and the introduction of the pure Italian Revival there existed a transitional period, known generally as the 'Francis I. style'. **1923** F. M. ATKINSON tr. *Félice's Fr. Furnit. Middle Ages* II. i. 49 This 'François Ier' art is at bottom truly French, vivid, varied, full of gaiety and fancy. **1961** L. A. BOGER *Compl. Guide Furnit. Styles* vi. 79/2 The Francois I style was essentially a transitional style in furniture design in which Italian Renaissance ornament and detail were found on Gothic forms. **1967** J. PORTER *Chinks in Curtain* iv. 43 The exterior of the château was mock François Premier but the room.. was pure Second Empire.

Francoist ('frænkəʊɪst), *sb.* and *a.* [f. the name of Francisco *Franco* y Bahamonde (1892–1975) (see below) + -IST.] **A.** *sb.* One who supported General Francisco Franco, a leader of the Nationalist revolution in Spain in 1936 and dictator of Spain until his death (see CAUDILLO); one who is sympathetic to Franco's views. **B.** *adj.* Of, pertaining to, or supporting the regime of General Franco, his principles, or policies.

1937 *Sunday Times* 17 Oct. 30 The Franco-ists declare that if they had waited a few weeks longer to rise against the Republic a Bolshevic revolution would have broken out. **1942** S. DE MADARIAGA *Spain* 9 An old Republican.. was in 1936 a convinced 'Nationalist' or Francoist out of his deep disappointment with the mistakes of the Republic. **1962** *Spectator* 10 Aug. 183/1 At bottom, Franco is just a Francoist. **1964** *Economist* 11 Apr. 123/1 Men with Francoist backgrounds. **1976** *Scotsman* 27 Dec. 3/3 The Public Order Tribunal, who try political offences, had been set up under the dictatorship of General Franco and used against anyone opposing the Francoist system. **1985** *Times* 11 Apr. 12/3 Francoist Spain.. did not receive Marshall Aid.

francolin ('fræŋkəlɪn). [a. Fr. *francolin*, ad. It. *francolino*.] A bird of the genus *Francolinus* (sub-family *Perdicinæ* or Partridges), somewhat resembling a pheasant. Also ***francolin partridge***.

[**1594** CAREW tr. *Huarte's Exam. Wits* 304 Partridges and Francolins haue a like substance.] **1653** URQUHART *Rabelais* I. xxxvii, Plovers, francolins, briganders. **1696** tr. *Du Mont's Voy. Levant* 68 Cooks usually stick one of the Feathers of the Wings into the Body of a Francolin. **1808** A. PARSONS *Trav.* i. 4 Hares are plenty.. and the francolin (heathcock) from October to June. **1872** BAKER *Nile Tribut.* xiii. 227 The trees formed a shelter for the black francolin partridge. **1880** P. GILLMORE *On Duty* 380 That splendid bird here denominated a pheasant (but properly speaking a francolin).

francolite ('fræŋkəlaɪt). *Min.* [f. *Franco* (see below) + -LITE.] A variety of apatite found at Wheal Franco in Devonshire in stalactitic masses.

1850 *Philos. Mag.* Ser. III. XXXVI. 311 *Francolite*.

Francomania (fræŋkəʊ'meɪnɪə). [See -MANIA.] A craze or excessive liking for France and for things French. Hence **Franco'maniac**.

1899 *Daily News* 8 May 8/2 From 1750 to the Revolution, Anglo-mania in France was fostered by Franco-mania in England. **1908** *Daily Chron.* 4 Mar. 6/6 That Francomaniac, Frederick the Great. **1930** *Social Sci. Abstr.* 1000 The Francomania of the Restoration.

Franconian (ˌfræŋ'kəʊnɪən), *a.* and *sb.* [f. *Franconia* (see below) + -AN.] **A.** *adj.* Of or pertaining to (the inhabitants of) Franconia, a region of Germany bordering the river Main and in medieval times a duchy. **B.** *sb.* **a.** An inhabitant of Franconia. **b.** (See quot. 1954.)

1805 *Times* 7 Nov. 2/1 An army, consisting of Silesian and Franconian regiments.. is on its march to Franconia. **1812** C. BUTLER *Hist. Rev. Emp. Germany* iii. 59 The principal events in the history of the latter princes of the Franconian line, and of all the princes of the Suabian line, were produced or influenced by the contests between the popes and the emperors. **1847** R. B. PAUL *Hist. Germany* xii. 81 Both were Franconian princes, and grandsons of Conrad. **1849** *Art-Jrnl.* XI. 108/2 The procession is arranged according to the four tribes of Bavarians, Suavians, Franconians and Saxons. **1888** [see GERMANIC *a.*[1] 2]. **1928** J. W. THOMPSON *Feudal Germany* xvi. 607 Carinthia and Styria (which was separated from Carinthia in 1035) were mainly colonized by Franconians and Rhinelanders. **1946** 'O. MARX' tr. *Valentin's German People* i. 6 The East Frisians and the Franconians on the Lower Rhine resemble the Dutch. **1954** PEI & GAYNOR *Dict. Linguistics* 76 *Franconian*, a group of medieval West Germanic dialects, combining the characteristics of Low and High German, and sub-divided into Lower Franconian.. and Middle and Upper Franconian. **1959** *Chambers's Encycl.* II. 165/2 In the 6th century the Bavarians expanded their territory.. to the north beyond the Danube as far as the Franconian Jura.

Francophil(e ('fræŋkəfɪl, -aɪl), *a.* and *sb.* [f. FRANCO- + Gr. φίλος friend. A newspaper word.]

A. *adj.* Characterized by excessive friendliness to the French.

B. *sb.* One who is so affected.

1889 *Pall Mall G.* 10 Jan. 6/2 The Francophil tendencies of the English Court. **1891** *Blackw. Mag.* Oct. 478 Francophobes and Francophiles. **1891** *Times* 15 Aug. 5/3 His admiring Francophile countrymen. **1893** *Rev. Current Hist.* (U.S.) III. 253 Attributed.. to Francophile and Pan-slavist influences in St. Petersburg.

Francophilia (fræŋkəʊ'fɪlɪə). [f. FRANCOPHIL(E *a.* and *sb.* + -IA[1].] Friendliness to France.

1945 *N.Y. Herald-Tribune* (Books) 16 Dec. 3 'The French flu' (Francophilia), a disease which ravages the mind. **1962** *Economist* 9 June 963/2 M. Houphouët-Boigny.. neatly combines Francophilia with power.

Francophobe ('fræŋkəfəʊb), *a.* and *sb.* [f. FRANCO- + Gr. φόβος fear: see -PHOBE.]

A. *adj.* Affected with a morbid fear of the French. **B.** *sb.* One who is so affected.

1891 *Times* 15 Aug. 5/3 In conclusion, observes this.. Francophobe critic. **1891** *Blackw. Mag.* [see FRANCOPHILE].

Francophobia (fræŋkəʊ'fəʊbɪə). [See -PHOBIA.] Dread or dislike of France or the French, tending to become an obsession.

1887 [see -PHOBIA]. **1900** *Fortn. Rev.* May 722 To deny Frenchmen the quality of courage in the face of danger is really to push Francophobia beyond the bounds of common sense. **1928** *Manch. Guardian Weekly* 10 Aug. 104/1 In his indignation M. Jacques Bainville, of the 'Liberté', brings a direct charge of Francophobia. **1961** *Spectator* 20 Oct. 532 Federalist Francophobia led to the passage of the Alien and Sedition Laws.

francophone ('fræŋkəʊfəʊn), *sb.* and *a.* Also with capital initial. [f. FRANCO- + Gr. φωνή voice.] **A.** *sb.* A French-speaking person. **B.** *adj.* French-speaking. Hence **franco'phonia**; **franco'phonic** *a.*

1900 tr. *Deniker's Races of Man* xiii. 508 In Canada two-thirds of the white population are Anglophones, and the rest Francophones. **1962** *Economist* 23 June 1192/1 The steady economic waltz of the general's francophonic clients. *Ibid.* 29 Dec. 1280/2 The theoretically quadrilingual, but in practice largely Francophone, community. **1968** *New Statesman* 12 Jan. 33/3 It is not exactly France's fault.. that the franoophone African states are mostly vast in area but poor in population and in natural resources. **1969** *Daily Colonist* (Victoria, B.C.) 5 July 5/1 The study employs the terms anglophones, francophones and 'others' to denote respectively those who speak English, French or another language in their homes. **1969** *Maclean's* Aug. 1/1 The man behind this sudden surge of Francophonia.. is the paper's new editor-in-chief, Frank Walker. **1971** *Guardian* 5 June 10/6 The 80 million Francophones on whom President Pompidou rests his case for linguistic parity.

‖**franc-tireur** (frɑ̃tirœr). [Fr.; f. *franc* free (see FRANK *a.*) + *tireur* shooter, f. *tirer* to shoot.] One of a corps of light infantry, originating in the wars of the French Revolution, and having an organization distinct from that of the regular army.

1808 W. W. WYNN *Let.* 31 Dec. in R. Leighton *Corresp. Lady Williams Wynn* (1920) xi. 130 He [*sc.* Lord Ebrington] is gone a *franc-tireur* with General Cameron. **1870** *Daily News* 3 Oct., All the volunteers, whether called Francs-tireurs or National Guards.. will.. be embodied in one regular army. **1870** *Daily Globe* 23 Nov. 1/6 Uhlans and Francs-Tireurs. **1910** *Encycl. Brit.* XI. 16 The Germans treated captured francs-tireurs as irresponsible non-combatants found with arms in their hands and usually exacted the death penalty. **1955** J. THOMAS *No Banners* xx. 193 He.. went to meet a *Franc-Tireur* who was on the run after killing several Germans. **1968** *Listener* 15 Feb. 197/3 The *Washington Post*.. has been bombarded with letters expressing horror at that photograph of the Saigon police chief.. executing a Vietcong *franc-tireur*.

frangent ('frændʒənt), *a.* [ad. L. *frangent-em*, pr. pple. of *frangĕre* to break.] Causing fractures.

(WEBSTER 1864 cites H. WALPOLE.)

frangibility (frændʒɪ'bɪlɪtɪ). [ad. F. *frangibilité*, f. *frangible*: see next and -ITY.] The quality of being frangible or breakable.

1783 FOX *Sp. E. India Bills* 1 Dec. *Sp.* (1815) II. 240 He allows the frangibility of charters, when absolute occasion requires it. **1816** P. CLEAVELAND *Mineralogy* 55 *Frangibility* .. This property can be described only in general terms; or by comparing one mineral with another in this respect. *a* **1835** J. MACCULLOCH *Proofs Attrib. God* (1837) II. 454 Steel.. will maintain nearly the same tenacity or strength.. under a frangibility which yields to the slightest impulse.

frangible ('frændʒɪb(ə)l), *a.* [a. OF. *frangible*, as if ad. L. **frangibil-is*, f. *frangĕre* to break.]

Capable of being broken, breakable.

c **1440** *Songs & Carols* (Percy Soc.) 65 An adamant stone, it is not frangebyll With no thyng but with mylke of a gett. *c* **1485** *Digby Myst.* (1882) III. 320 The frangabyll tyn, to Iubyter, yf ȝe can dyscus. **1598** BARRET *Theor. Warres* v. ii. 129 If of hard stone, or of soft, frangible, and easie. **1647** JER. TAYLOR *Lib. Proph.* vi. 121 The Councell is blasphemous in saying that Christs glorified body is passible and frangible by naturall manducation. **1659** D. PELL *Impr. Sea* 383 Your ships..are but made up of..frangible materials. **1796** KIRWAN *Elem. Min.* (ed. 2) I. 223 Hardness from 7 to 9, difficultly frangible. **1865** *Cornh. Mag.* Sept. 259 Whenever ..the housemaid [had] broken any little frangible article. **1883** *Harper's Mag.* Jan. 192/2 The least frangible rays predominate.

b. as *sb.* in *pl.* Things breakable. *nonce-use.*

1824 *Mirror* III. 19/2 Strut around your room..to the manifest terror of all frangibles in your reach.

Hence **'frangibleness.**

1676 H. MORE *Remarks* 100 The lightness and frangibleness of Glass.

frangipane ('frændʒɪpeɪn). [a. F. *frangipane*, said to be from *Frangipani*, the name of the inventor.]

1. A perfume prepared from, or imitating the odour of, the flower of the red jasmine.

1676 SHADWELL *Virtuoso* III. H 4 a, I have choice of good Gloves, Amber, Orangery, Genoa Romane, Frangipand [*sic*]. **1727–41** CHAMBERS *Cycl.*, *Frangipane*, an exquisite kind of perfume. **1858** SIMMONDS *Dict. Trade*, *Frangipane*.

2. = FRANGIPANI.

[**1842** *Curtis's Bot. Mag.* LXVIII. 3952 It is from this circumstance [the white juice], probably, that the French call the species of this Genus 'Franchipanier', *Franchipane* being coagulated milk.] **1866** *Treas. Bot.*, Frangipane, *Plumiera rubra.* **1871** J. SMITH *Domestic Bot.* 292 *P. rubra*, in the West Indies being called Red Jasmine, as also 'Frangipane'—a name also given to the sweet-smelling flowers of *P. acuminata*.

3. In various applications: see quots.

1844 HOBLYN *Med. Dict.*, *Frangipan*, an extract of milk, for preparing artificial milk, made by evaporating skimmed milk to dryness, mixed with almonds and sugar. **1858** SIMMONDS *Dict. Trade*, *Franchipane, Frangipane*, a kind of pastry, a cake of cream, almonds, spice, &c.

attrib. **1892** GARRETT *Encycl. Cookery*, *Frangipane Flawn ..Frangipane paste.* **1895** JUSSERAND *Eng. Ess.* 98 Lafleur, whom he often asked to make frangipane tarts.

frangipani (frændʒɪ'pænɪ, -'pɑːnɪ). Also **-panni.** [See prec.] A fragrant ornamental shrub or tree of the genus *Plumeria*, esp. *P. rubra*. Cf. FRANGIPANE 2.

1864 in WEBSTER. **1882** J. SMITH *Dict. Pop. Names Plants* 180 In the West Indies *Plumeria rubra* and *alba*, shrubs of the Dogbane Family (Apocynaceæ) are called Frangipanni on account of their deliciously-scented flowers. **1898** *Jrnl. R. Hort. Soc.* XXII. 159 Frangipani (*Plumiera* [sic] *rubra, P. alba, P. fragrantissima* &c.).—Commonly planted on graves in Borneo and Malayan islands. **1904** J. CAMERON *Firminger's Man. Garden. India* (ed. 5) IV. 497 P[lumeria] rubra.—The Frangipani Plant. Introduced from Jamaica. **1934** H. B. SHARPE in A. J. Jex-Blake *Gardening E. Afr.* xvii. 252, I planted out everywhere my pink frangipani. **1965** A. THOMAS *Gardening in Hot Countries* vii. 100 Other kinds of *Plumieria* [sic]..have fainter perfumes and may be more pleasing at close quarters than ordinary frangipani.

‖**franglais** (frɑ̃glɛ). [Blend of Fr. *fran(çais* + *an)glais*.] A corrupt version of the French language produced by the indiscriminate introduction of words and phrases of English and American origin. Also *transf.* and as *adj.*

[**1959** M. RAT in R. Etiemble *Parlez-vous Franglais* (1964) ii. 34 Faudra-t-il appeler bientôt *franglais* ce français émaillé de vocables britanniques que la mode actuelle nous impose?] **1964** *Economist* 25 Apr. 354/1 'Franglais'—what the professor [*sc.* Etiemble] sees as French bastardised and ruined by Anglo-Saxon..borrowings. **1964** *Cambr. Rev.* 24 Oct. 45/2 The 'New Britain'..will be a world of tab collars, Mary Quant, and academic *franglais*, no doubt. **1965** *New Statesman* 7 May 735/1 At a time when young English writers and journalists are struggling to strike Gallicisms out of their equipment, the French complain that *le franglais* is taking over theirs. **1967** *Guardian* 8 Feb. 6/5 Upholders of Gallic linguistic purity lament the encroachment of what they call 'franglais'. **1969** N. FREELING *Tsing-Boum* xi. 80 'Alors bye-bye,' she was saying... That awful way French women had on the phone, using idiotic franglais phrases like 'because le job'.

frangulin ('frængjʊlɪn). *Chem.* [f. the mod.Lat. name of the tree (*Rhamnus*) *Frangul a.* + -IN.] (See quot.) Hence **fran'gulic (acid)** *a.*

1864 WATTS *Dict. Chem.* II. 706 *Frangulin*..a yellow crystallisable colouring matter, contained in the bark of the berry-bearing alder. **1872** *Ibid.* Suppl. 623 Frangulic acid.

† **'franion.** *Obs.* Also 6 fronion, frannian. [Of obscure origin.

Cf. OF. *fraignant*, pr. pple. of *fraindre* to break; *fraigneis* uproar. The usual explanation that the word is a corruption of FAINEANT hardly suits the sense.]

A gay reckless fellow; a gallant, paramour. By Spenser applied also to a loose woman.

1571 EDWARDES *Damon & Pith.* in Hazl. *Dodsley* IV. 60 But, my franion, I tell you this one thing. **1587** TURBERVILE *Epitaphs & Sonn.* (1837) 319 Whereby to set their fronions harts on fire. **1589** *Rare Triumphs Love & Fortune* III. i. in Hazl. *Dodsley* VI. 179, I am a gentleman, a courtier, and a merry frank franion. **1596** SPENSER *F.Q.* v. iii. 22 This ladie ..Is not..Florimell..But some fayre franion, fit for such a fere. **1600** HEYWOOD *1st Pt. Edw. IV*, Wks. 1874 I. 44 He's a frank franion..and loues a wench well. **1810** LAMB *Poems, Going or Gone*, Fine merry franions, Wanton companions.

Frank (fræŋk), *sb.*[1] and *a.*[1] Forms: 1 **Franca, Fronca,** 3 **Franke,** 4–7 **Fran(c)k(e,** (8 **Franc**), 7– **Frank.** [ad. L. *Franc-us*, F. *Franc*; a name of Teut. origin, repr. OHG. *Franko* = OE. *Franca*:—prehistoric **Frankon-*.

It is usually believed that the Franks were named from their national weapon, OE. *franca* (:—**frankon-*) javelin; cf. *Saxon* (*Sahson-*), thought to be from **sahso-* (OE. *seax*) knife. The notion that the ethnic name is derived from the adj. meaning 'free' (see FRANK *a.*[2]) was already current in the 10th century; but the real relation between the words seems to be the reverse of this.]

A. *sb.*

1. A person belonging to the Germanic nation, or coalition of nations, that conquered Gaul in the 6th century, and from whom the country received the name of France.

Beowulf 1210 (Gr.) In Francna fæðm. *c* **1205** LAY. 3715 Cordoille þe wes Francene quene. *a* **1300** *Cursor M.* 21081 To þe franckis prechid he. **1776** GIBBON *Decl. & F.* I. x. 259 These Germans..maintained the honourable epithet of Franks or Freemen. **1796** H. HUNTER tr. *St. Pierre's Stud. Nat.* (1799) III. 457 A family of slaves under the Romans risen to Nobility under the Francs. **1844** LD. BROUGHAM *Brit. Const.* iii. (1862) 40 The Franks, who founded the French Monarchy.

2. A name given by the nations bordering on the Levant to an individual of Western nationality. Cf. FERINGHEE.

1687 tr. *De Thevenot's Trav.* II. I. xi. 51 They presently blazed it abroad that I was a Franck. *a* **1734** NORTH *Lives* II. 456 All European nations that live among them..are called Franks. **1808** A. PARSONS *Trav.* iii. 62 Foreign merchants called franks. **1886** *Pall Mall G.* 10 July 4/1 The Greeks.. calling their Roman brethren 'unbaptized dogs' and Franks.

† **3.** With ellipsis of 'language'. A *lingua franca* or mixed language. *Obs.*—[1]

1681 NEVILE *Plato Rediv.* 13 In Germany or Holland.. most of the Hosts speak a certain Franck, compounded of Dutch, Latin, and Italian.

† **B.** *adj.* Belonging to, characteristic of, or customary among the Western nations of Europe. *Obs.*

1632 LITHGOW *Trav.* VI. 245 Beating him most cruelly, and all the rest of the Francke Pilgrimes. **1688** *Lond. Gaz.* No. 2336/5 Two Led Horses, richly furnished, one after the Franke, and the other after the Turkish Fashion.

† **frank,** *sb.*[2] *Obs.* Forms: 4 **frawnke,** 6–7 **franke,** 7 **franck,** 5– **frank.** [a. OF. *franc* in same sense.]

1. An enclosure, *esp.* a place to feed hogs in; a sty. Also, the process of fattening animals.

? *a* **1400** *Morte Arth.* 3248 Alle froytez foddenid was þat floreschede in erthe, ffaire frithed in frawnke appone tha free bowes. *c* **1440** *Promp. Parv.* 177/1 Frank, kepynge of fowlys to make fatte, *saginarium.* **1562** BULLEYN *Def. agst. Sickness* 67 The fatte Oxe, or vglie brauned Bore..can not come out from their frankes or staules. **1621** SANDERSON *Serm.* I. 194 Like boars in a franck, pining themselves into lard. **1736** BAILEY *Househ. Dict.* 115 The Frank should be in form something like a dog kennel, a little longer than the boar. **1823** CRABB *Technol. Dict.*, *Frank*, a place to feed boars in. And in mod. Dicts.

fig. **1563** BECON *Compar. Lord's Supper & Pope's Mass* Wks. III. 110, I may speake nothyng of that most fatte francke of Whoremongers, Adulterers..and suche other idle beastes.

2. *Comb.*: **frank-fed** *a.*, fed in a frank; fatted.

1550 BALE *Image Both Ch.* xiv. H ij b, The frank fed porkelynges of that gredy gulf. **1601** HOLLAND *Pliny* II. 480 These guests of his fared so highly, that a man would haue said they had bin franke-fed.

Hence † **'franky,** *a. nonce-wd.*, looking as if frank-fed; 'stalled'.

1583 STANYHURST *Æneis* III. (Arb.) 77 We view'd grasing heards of bigge franckye fat oxen.

† **frank,** *sb.*[3] *Obs. rare.* [? Short for FRANKINCENSE; cf. FRANCE.]

14.. *Epiph.* in *Tundale's Vis.* 110 Franke. **1502** ARNOLDE *Chron.* (1811) 234 Spycery..Frankke.

† **frank,** *sb.*[4] *Obs.* Also 6–7 **fran(c)k(e.** [f. FRANK *v.*] A name given to the plant Spurry, from its fattening properties; also *frank spurry*.

1578 LYTE *Dodoens* I. xxxviii. 56 This herbe [Spurry] is called in Englishe Francke, bicause of the property it hath to fat cattell. **1640** PARKINSON *Theat. Bot.* 562 Both the Dutch and we in England call it Spurry or Franck Spurry, for the causes aforesaid, but I do a little more explaine the names, in calling it Francking Spurrewort. **1659** TORRIANO, *Spergola*, the hearb Frank, Surrie, or Spurrie: it is good to fatten cattle.

frank (fræŋk), *sb.*[5] [f. FRANK *v.*[2]]

1. The superscribed signature of a person, e.g. a member of Parliament, entitled to send letters post free.

1713 'PHILOPATRIUS' *Refl. Sacheverell's Thanksgiv.-Day* 4 The Franks are now become a Monopoly to one Side. **1776** TWISS *Tour in Ireland* 37 The third custom is that of forging franks. **1812** SCOTT *Let. to Crabbe* in Lockhart *Life* xxv, I must..send this scrawl into town to get a frank..it is not worthy of postage. **1852** RAINE *Mem. Surtees* 92 *note*, The want of a frank for a letter..frequently afforded him an errand.

Comb. **1859** SALA *Gas-light & D.* v. 62 There were regular frank-hunters—men who could nose a member who had not yet given all his franks away.

2. A letter or envelope bearing such a superscription.

1755 WESLEY *Wks.* (1872) XII. 182 Mr. Perronet sends them down to me in franks. **1781** COWPER *Wks.* (1837) XV. 63, I did it to save a frank. **1806** SCOTT *Fam. Lett.* 16 Dec. (1894) I. 62, I cannot employ time or a frank better than by inquiring whether you have got rid of the unlucky typhus. **1838** DICKENS *Nich. Nick.* xvi, To send the manuscript in a frank to the local paper. **1878** SYMONDS *Shelley* 26 Shelley ..would stop to fix his father's franks upon convenient trees and shoot at them.

3. *fig.* Mark of approval; 'stamp'. *rare.*

1876 *World* V. No. 108. 11 Impecuniosity has had the frank of Fashion.

frank (fræŋk), *sb.*[6] *dial.* [app. a rendering of the sound made by the bird; see quots.] A heron.

1823 MOOR *Suffolk Wds.*, *Frank*, the large slow-flying, fish-eating, heron..Our name is probably derived from its monotone—which is supposed to be like *fr a a a nk.* [**1829** COL. HAWKER *Diary* (1893) II. 4 All the flesh and feathers I could see..were 'old Francis' (a heron) and 'the parson' (a cormorant). **1870** *Athenæum* 10 Sept. 332 When danger is apparent, the Heron rises with his peculiar cry of 'frank!']

frank (fræŋk), *sb.*[7] *U.S.* Short for FRANKFURTER.

1936 E. E. CUMMINGS *Let.* 9 May (1969) 145 Sand there shall be with our franks. **1957** J. KEROUAC *On Road* (1958) i. 9 We had a farewell meal of franks and beans. **1959** *Consumer Reports* Sept. 455/3 Slitting the franks may adversely affect the device's ability to cook them properly. **1968** *Washington Post* 5 July A17 (Advt.), Safeway Skinless All Meat Franks. 2 lb. pkg. 99c.

Frank, *a.*[1]: see after FRANK *sb.*[1]

frank (fræŋk), *a.*[2] Forms: 4 **franc,** 5–6 **franke,** 6–7 **franck(e,** (6 **francque**), 5– **frank.** [a. OF. *franc* (= Pr. *franc.* Sp., Pg., It. *franco*):—med.Lat. *francus* free; originally identical with the ethnic name *Francus* (see FRANK *sb.*[1]), which acquired the sense of 'free' because in Frankish Gaul full freedom was possessed only by those belonging to, or adopted into, the dominant people.

Cf. the use of the originally ethnic name SLAVE, and of OE. *wealh*, orig. 'Welshman', to denote a person of servile condition.]

1. = FREE in various applications of the word; often *frank and free.* † **a.** Free in condition; not in serfdom or slavery. *Obs.*

The meaning of the first quot. is doubtful: perh. = 2.

c **1300** *Maximian* 159 (Digby MS.) in *Anglia* III. 280 Of herte ich was wel liȝt..And franc mon of honde. *a* **1470** TIPTOFT *Cæsar* (1530) 13 He was frank & free borne in a free cytye. **1574** tr. *Littleton's Tenures* 40 a, The pleyntyfe sayethe that hee is franke and of free estate and noe vylleyne.

† **b.** Free to come and go; released from captivity. Also *frank and quit*; cf. Fr. *franc et quitte* (Commines), Anglo-L. *liber et quietus. Obs.*

1475 *Bk. Noblesse* 66 He shulde..deliver out of prison a gret nombre of yong men of werre of Cartage.. and he shulde goo frank and quite. *a* **1533** LD. BERNERS *Huon* xliii. 143 He and all his company shall deperte franke and free at there pleasure. **1633** J. DONE *Hist. Septuagint* 25 All the Jewes that..have been taken..shall be sent francke and free.

† **c.** Free from restraint or impediment; unrestricted, unchecked. Const. *of.* Of a wind: Steady (cf. Fr. *vent franc*). *Obs.*

1481 CAXTON *Reynard* (Arb.) 41 He..was all free and franke of alle his enemyes. **1531–2** *Act 23 Hen. VIII*, c. 18 Many shippes..haue..had their franke passages without let impedimente or interruption. **1538** STARKEY *England* I. ii. 53 Euery one of them..are desyrouse of frank lyberty. **1559** in Strype *Ann. Ref.* I. App. viii. 22 When franke election first beganne. **1570** B. GOOGE *Pop. Kingd.* I. i. 46 If any happen to mislike, that they may francke and free appeale unto the Court of Rome. **1579** FENTON *Guicciard.* I. (1599) 30 He offered him..franke power to dispose of him and his armie. **1624** WOTTON *Archit.* in *Reliq.* (1672) 35 A frank light can mis-become no Ædifice whatsoever. **1628** F. FLETCHER *World Encomp.* 45 Being glad..to fall asterne againe, with francke winde [etc.].

† **d.** Free from obligation in respect of payments or other conditions; free of charge; unconditional. *frank traffic* = FREE TRADE. *Obs.*

1525 LD. BERNERS *Froiss.* II. ccxxii. [ccxviii.] 685 Desyre ..that ye may be franke and fre fro all subsydies. **1534** MORE *Treat. Passion* Wks. 1286/2 Landes..franke and free simpliciter and wythout anye condicion. **1581** J. BELL *Haddon's Answ. Osor.* 391 b, Let Pardons be as francke and free as they would seeme to be for me. **1591** SPENSER *M. Hubberd* 531 Thou hast it wonne, for it is of franke gift. **1599** HAKLUYT *Voy.* II. 210 A faire free and franke of al custome. **1659** PEARSON *Creed* (1839) 517 The remission of our sins is the frank forgiving of our debts. **1660** F. BROOKE tr. *Le Blanc's Trav.* 405 All nations..went thither by reason of franck Traffick. **1727** POPE, etc. *Art of Sinking* 122 The court of aldermen..shall all have their places frank.

† **e.** Free from anxiety, unburdened. *Obs.*

c **1477** CAXTON *Jason* 104 The goode shipman began to rowe with a franck corage. **1558** BP. WATSON *Sev. Sacram.* xxvi. 168 With a franke harte and a good wyll.

2. Liberal, bounteous, generous, lavish, *esp.* in dealing with money. Const. †*of.* † *frank house* = 'open house'.

1484 CAXTON *Chivalry* 92 Chyualrye and Fraunchyse accorden to gyder..the knyght must be free and franke. **1582** N. LICHEFIELD tr. *Castanheda's Conq. E. Ind.* iv. 13 Through whose..franke distribution of that he had, many of our men were recouerd. **1587** FLEMING *Contn. Holinshed*

III. 1299/1 My lord Norths..was no whit behind anie of the best for a franke house. **1588** *Marprel. Epist.* (Arb.) 39, I would wish you not to be so francke with your bribes. **1608–11** Bp. Hall *Medit. & Vows* iii. §32 The world, like a frank Chapman, sayes, All these will I give thee. *a* **1633** Wotton in Gutch *Coll. Cur.* I. 217 They have always been frank of their blessings to countenance any great action. **1672** Dryden *Marr. à-la-Mode* Ded., You are endued with that excellent Quality of a frank Nature, to forget the good which you have done. **1676** Etheredge *Man of Mode* v. i, Lose it all like a frank gamester on the square. **1851** Carlyle *Sterling* III. vi. (1872) 219 He..set about improvements.. on a frank scale. **1856** Froude *Hist. Eng.* (1858) I. i. 43 In such frank style the people lived.

†**b.** in bad sense (of a woman).

1735 Pope *Ep. Lady* 71 Chaste to her Husband, frank to all beside.

c. Of a horse: ***frank to the road*** = free *a.* 20 c.

1816 Scott *Antiq.* xl, 'He's very frank to the road.'

3. a. Not practising concealment; ingenuous, open, sincere. Of feelings: Undisguised.

1555 W. Watreman *Fardle Facions* App. 321 The bondeman..lacketh the francque noblenes of minde. **1604** Shaks. *Oth.* I. iii. 38 Bearing with frank appearance Their purposes toward Cyprus. **1656** W. Montague *Accompl. Wom.* 11 Quick and lively humours are readier and franker; but then the Melancholy are the discreeter. **1741** Richardson *Pamela* (1824) I. 146 We dined together in a most..frank manner. **1797** Mrs. Radcliffe *Italian* i, Frank in his temper, ingenuous in his sentiments. **1815** Elphinstone *Acc. Caubul* (1842) I. 323 The manners of the Afghauns are frank and open. **1847–8** H. Miller *First Impr.* v. (1857) 63 The English are by much a franker people than the Scotch. **1873** Black *Pr. Thule* vi. 93 A look of frank gratitude in her eyes.

b. With reference to speech: Candid, outspoken, unreserved.

1548 Udall, etc. *Erasm. Par. Matt.* xi. 10 Whome he folowed also in franke reprouing of kinges. **1599** Shaks. *Hen. V*, I. ii. 244 With franke and with vncurbed plainnesse, Tell vs Dolphins minde. **1660** Ormond *Let. to Cowley* in *Academy* (1893) 7 Oct. 296/2 An ingenuous and frank recantation. **1790** Burke *Fr. Rev.* Wks. V. 251 In their conversation frank and open. **1828** Carlyle *Misc.* (1857) I. 131 How frank and downright in speech. **1849** Thackeray *Pendennis* xvi, The honest frank boy just returned from school. **1870** Mrs. Riddell *Austin Friars* ii, You may as well be frank with me.

c. Avowed, undisguised; downright.

1752 Warburton *Wks.* 1811 IX. vi. 135 The Founders of empires and false religions..were frank Enthusiasts. **1849** Ruskin *Sev. Lamps* iv. §2. 95 Farther than this man's invention could not reach without frank imitation. **1877** *Daily News* 27 Dec. 6/2 What may be effected by frank force remains to be seen. **18..** *Med. News* L. 306 (Cent.) Although there frank peritonitis coexisted.

†**4.** Of plants, trees, etc.: Of superior quality for the purpose to which they are applied; producing good and abundant fruit, or the like. Often applied to cultivated as opposed to wild plants. Of drugs, etc.: Of high quality, valuable. Cf. frankincense. *Obs.*

1486 *Bk. St. Albans* C ij b, Take powder of Canell and the Juce of franke cost. **1572** Mascall *Plant. & Graff.* (1592) 52 Take your Cions of a Peach tree..and graffe them vpon a frank Mulberie tree. **1574** Hyll *Planting* 85 All sortes of franke trees..may be graft with graffes. **1578** Lyte *Dodoens* II. lxxvii. 250 There be two sortes of Sage, the one is small and franke, and the other is great. *Ibid.* VI. lxvii. 743 The seconde kind of Withy called the Franke Ozier hath no great stemme. **1601** Holland *Pliny* I. 369 The greatest price of the garden frank-Myrhh, or that which is set by mans hand is 22 deniers. **1647–8** Cotterell *Davila's Hist. Fr.* (1678) 40 Applied all manner of frank remedies.

†**5.** Luxuriant in growth, lusty, vigorous. *Obs.*

1550 Bale *Image Both Ch.* ix. I iv, When they were ones franke & fatt, they stode vp together proudely againste the Lorde. *Ibid.* K j, I behelde in a visyon the horses, franke, fatte, and fearce. **1555** W. Watreman *Fardle Facions* I. i. 24 The graciousnes of the earth was also abated, and the francke fertilitie therof..withdrawen. **1591** Spenser *Muiopotmos* 148 Over the fields, in his franke lustinesse, And all the champain o're he soared light. **1626** Bacon *Sylva* §540 The Sap is not so frank as to rise all to the Boughs.

6. *Comb.*, chiefly parasynthetic, as †*frank-born*, *-faced*, †*-handed*, *-hearted* (whence *frank-heartedness*) adjs; †*franklike* adv.

1600 Holland *Livy* XLV. xxiv. (1609) 1217 All of us in Rhodes *franke-borne and of free condition. **1873** A. Dobson *Vignettes in Rhyme, Sundial* xii, Blue-eyed, *frank-faced, with clear and open brow. ? *a* **1626** Breton *Mad World* (Grosart) 8 A wench as *franck-handed, as free-hearted, and as liberall for love. **1644** Bulwer *Chirol.* 62 Of a bountifull disposition and franke-handed. *a* **1600** Hooker *Serm. Hab.* ii. 4 Wks. 1888 III. 604 That *frank-hearted wastefulness spoken of in the gospel. **1813** Scott *Trierm.* I. xi, The frank-hearted Monarch. **1571** Golding *Calvin on Ps.* lxviii. 10 Signifieth an unconstreyned willingnesse, or a meere *frankhartednesse. **1587** Turberv. *Trag. T.* (1837) 89 She made a large behest, Of gold that she would *franklike give.

† **frank**, *v.*[1] *Obs.* [f. frank *sb.*[2]]

1. *trans.* To shut up and feed (*up*) in a frank.

c **1440** *Promp. Parv.* 177/1 Frankyd, *saginatus.* **1553** Eden *Treat. Newe Ind.* (Arb.) 29 They..francke them vntyll they be very fat. **1556** Withals *Dict.* (1568) 38 a/2 *Altilia*, all things franked to be made fatte. **1600** Holland *Livy* VI. xvii. (1609) 228 The Commons doe feed and franke up, even for the shambles and butchers knife the fautors and maintainers of their weale and libertie.

2. To feed high; to cram. Also with *up*.

1583 Stanyhurst *Æneis* I. (Arb.) 24 Theyre panch with venison they franck. **1601** Holland *Pliny* I. 539 They.. franke them vp like fat ware, with good corn-meale. **1633** T. Adams *Exp. 2 Peter* ii. 22 When they are saginated and franked, their turn comes to bleed.

fig. **1555** Abp. Parker *Ps.* lxiii. 175 Lo thus my soule full frankt shall bee. **1606** J. Carpenter *Solomon's Solace* i. 5 Israel..franked and pampered with prosperitie. **1633** Ford *Broken H.* III. ii, One that franks his lust In swine-security of bestial incest.

b. *intr.* for *refl.* To feed greedily.

1586 Warner *Alb. Eng.* (1602) 102 That frankes and feedeth daintily, this pines and fareth ill.

Hence †**franked** *ppl. a.*, fattened in a frank or pen. †'**franking** *vbl. sb.*

c **1440** *Promp. Parv.* 177/1 Frankynge, *saginacio.* **1466** *Paston Lett.* No. 549 II. 268, xxvii. frankyd gees, *vis.* viiid. **1574** Hellowes *Gueuara's Fam. Ep.* 98 They set before her ..franked Fesant. **1611** Cotgr., *Engrais de volaille*, the franking or fattening of fowle. **1675** Hobbes *Odyssey* XVII. 171 Fat goats enough they sacrifice, And franked Swine.

frank (fræŋk), *v.*[2] [f. frank *a.*[2], see sense 1 d.]

1. a. *trans.* To superscribe (a letter, etc.) with a signature, so as to ensure its being sent without charge; to send or cause to be sent free of charge (*obs.* exc. *Hist.*). Revived in later use: to mark (a letter, etc.) with a sign (in lieu of an affixed postage stamp) by means of a franking machine.

1708 Hearne *Collect.* 14 June, They'l be frank't at yͤ Posthouse. **1745** *Advt.* in *Swift's Wks.* VIII. 297 It is desired their letters may be either franked, or the post paid. **1764** J. Clayton in Darlington *Mem. J. Bartram, etc.* (1849) 411 Dr. Franklin would be kind enough to frank a small parcel of seeds from you to him. **1804** *Med. Jrnl.* XII. 334 The post-masters-general have had the liberality to frank the correspondence of the Society. **1818** J. Jekyll *Corr.* 7 Dec. (1894) 74 Brougham has just left me; and..I made him frank this cover. *a* **1834** Wirt *Let. to Carr* in J. P. Kennedy *Life* (1860) II. xiv. 228 This is the last letter I shall ever frank to you as Attorney-General. **1855** *Ill. Lond. News* 21 July 70/1 The stamp must be folded outside; and this will frank the paper throughout the United Kingdom for fifteen days. **1887** *Spectator* 29 Oct. 1441 He..has franked masses of letters..with the President's stamp. **1927**, **1928** [implied in franked *ppl. a.* below]. **1971** D. Potter *Brit. Eliz. Stamps* xiii. 141 Letters and packets are franked with a handstamp or machine impression.

b. *absol.* (In quot. 1774 = to obtain franks.)

1774 *Westm. Mag.* II. 600 The trading Cit, whose object was to frank. **1785** Trusler *Mod. Times* III. 231 Many a day have I slipped off my coat, and franked away as for life.

c. *fig.* To facilitate the coming and going of (a person); to furnish with a social passport, secure entrée into society for.

1801 *Spirit. Pub. Jrnls.* IV. 25 A few yards of muslin, &c., and a gig on a Sunday, will frank you for the whole week. **1840** *Fraser's Mag.* XXI. 702 The premier..franks him through England by introducing him to the royal presence. **1864** Burton *Scot Abr.* I. ii. 98 Even some of the best established and most respectable titles have difficulty in franking themselves through all parts of the country. **1887** Stevenson *Mem. & Portraits* i. 2 English..will now frank the traveller through the most of North America.

2. To pay the passage of (a person); to convey gratuitously.

1809 Scott in Smiles *Life J. Murray* (1891) I. vii. 151, I believe I shall get franked, so will have my generosity for nothing. **1851** Thackeray *Lett.* 140, I suppose I could be franked through the kingdom from one grandee to another. **1864** Burton *Scot Abr.* II. ii. 190 He got an opportunity of being franked to Poland.

3. To secure exemption for; to exempt. Const. *against*, *from*. Cf. frank *a.*[2] 1.

1876 Miss Yonge *Womankind* xxix. 260 Most people being in all probability franked against all the common epidemics they have once had. **1881** Saintsbury in *Academy* 15 Jan. 41 The abstract merits..are almost franked from criticism.

Hence **franked** *ppl. a.*, spec. ***franked income*** (see quot. 1965); '**franking** *vbl. sb.* and *ppl. a.*

1727 Berkeley *Let. to Prior* 27 Feb. Wks. 1871 IV. 141 You must take care that no one packet..exceed the limits of franking. **1748** Lady M. W. Montagu *Let. to Wortley M.* 17 July, I begin to suspect my servants put the franking money in their pockets. **1758** J. Blake *Plan Mar. Syst.* 9 The Pay-office shall transmit..a franked order for payment. **1845** McCulloch *Taxation* II. vii. (1852) 321 Franked letters were in most instances addressed to those who could best afford to pay the expense of postage. **1869** W. M. Rossetti *Mem. Shelley* p. xxxiii, In his franking signature outside some of his son's letters. **1880** Disraeli *Endym.* xii, They had never paid postage. They were born and had always lived in the franking world. **1927** *Times* 25 Feb. 10/6 The posting of franked letters at a date subsequent to that marked on the envelope is a violation of the terms of the licence. **1928** M. Rittenberg *Mail-Order made Easy* xiv. 179 Franked or metered mail is accepted under certain conditions. **1955** *Times* 2 July 9/7 Profits tax absorbed £6,000 less, mainly because the proportion of franked income was greater this year. **1965** J. H. Hanson *Dict. Econ.* 188/1 *Franked income*, a term used of a company which derives income from the profits of another company which have been subjected already to profits tax. Such income is said to be 'franked' and so is not liable to profits tax a second time.

frank, *v.*[3] *Build.* (See quot.)

1823 Nicholson *Pract. Builder* 585 *Franking*, in sash-making, is the operation of cutting a small excavation on the side of a bar for the reception of the transverse bar, so that no more of the wood be cut away than may suffice to show a mitre when the two bars are joined together.

frankable ('fræŋkəb(ə)l), *a.* [f. frank *v.*[2] + -able.] That may be franked.

1811 Southey *Lett.* (1856) II. 239 This is a MS. of a frankable size. **1894** *Columbus Disp.* (Ohio) 17 Oct. 7/3 The envelopes, not containing any frankable matter.

frank-almoign, -almoin. *Law.* [a. AF. *fraunke almoigne*: see frank *a.*[2] and almoign.] (See almoign 2.)

†**Frank-arbitrian.** *Obs. rare.* [f. F. *franc arbitre* free-will + -ian.] A free-willer.

1633 W. Struther *True Happines* 19 This is the mother of the Frank-arbitrians pride.

†**frank bank.** *Law. Obs.* Also 6 **frank bench.** [a. AF. *franc banc*, = med.L. *francus bancus*: see frank *a.*[2], bank *sb.*[2]] = free bench.

[**1419** *Liber Albus* I. ii. (Rolls) 68 Quæ habet francum bancum suum.] **1598** Kitchin *Courts Leet* (1675) 202 The Woman..shall have all the Copyhold whereof the Husband died seized for her Franck-bench. **1605–6** *Act 3 Jas. I*, c. 5 §11 The Widowes Estate and Frankbanck. **1651** G. W. tr. *Cowel's Inst.* 59 Tenants in Franck Banck.

'**frank-chase.** *Law.* [f. frank *a.*[2] + chase. *sb.*[1]] Free chase: see quot. 1641 and chase *sb.*[1] 2.

1587 Harrison *England* II. xix. (1877) I. 310 The franke chase..taketh something both of parke and forrest. [**1594** Crompton *Jurisdict.* E. 1. *Trespas* F. 239 Le ley de franke chase est, etc.] **1641** *Termes de la Ley* 167 Francke chase is a liberty of Frank chase, by which all men having land within this compasse are prohibited to cut downe the wood, or discover, &c. without the view of the Forester, although it be his owne. *c* **1645** Howell *Lett.* IV. xvi. (1655) 39 None but the King can have a forest; If he chance to passe one over to a Subject, 'tis no more Forest, but frank Chase.

Frankenstein ('fræŋkənstaɪn). The name of the title-character of Mrs. Shelley's romance *Frankenstein* (1818), who constructed a human monster and endowed it with life. Commonly misused allusively as a typical name for a monster who is a terror to his originator and ends by destroying him. Also *attrib.* Hence **Franken'steinian** *a.*

1838 Gladstone in *Murray's Handbk. Sicily* (1864) p. xlvi, They [*sc.* mules] really seem like Frankensteins of the animal creation. **1889** S. Webb in G. B. Shaw *Fabian Ess.* 38 The landlord and the capitalist are both finding that the steam-engine is a Frankenstein which they had better not have raised. **1907** *Sat. Rev.* 6 Apr. 414/1 Is Great Britain creating for herself something of a Frankenstein monster on the Nile? **1931** R. Campbell *Georgiad* i. 14 No sooner was our Frankenstein set free Than for a name he racks his nimble wits. **1958** I. Asimov *Naked Sun* xiv. 172 Do you know robots started with a Frankenstein complex against them.? They were suspect. Men distrusted and feared robots. **1965** J. Wainwright *Death in Sleeping City* II. 107 Like some Frankensteinian monster, the Police Machine moved forward. **1971** B. Callison *Plague of Sailors* i. 51 The Frankensteinian exhibit in the alcohol bath. **1971** *Daily Tel.* 3 May 1/4 There are now growing indications that the Nationalists in South Africa have created a political Frankenstein which is pointing the way to a non-White political revival.

Frankenthal ('fræŋkəntɑːl). [The name of a town in Germany, in the Bavarian Palatinate.] The designation of a porcelain made at Frankenthal from the middle to the end of the eighteenth century.

1863 W. Chaffers *Marks Pott. & Porc.* 183 The stock and utensils of the Frankenthal manufactory were purchased in 1800 by M. Von Recum. **1887** *Sale Catal. Porc. & Decorative Objects* (*Christie, Manson, & Woods*) 4 Feb. 4 A large Frankenthal group of Chinese figures at an arbour. **1925** W. W. Worster tr. *Hannover's Pott. & Porc.* III. ix. 215 The porcelain body of Frankenthal, which during the best period was brought from Passau, is as a rule of so soft a whiteness as to resemble at times the French soft porcelain. **1947** W. B. Honey *German Porc.* 25 The Frankenthal table-wares and vases of the best period were.. often painted with elaborate figure-subjects of a kind seldom attempted elsewhere in Germany. **1960** H. Hayward *Antique Coll.* 123/1 Frankenthal porcelain figures often have rich pierced, scrolled Rococo bases and sometimes include trellis work.

franker ('fræŋkə(r)). [f. frank *v.*[2] + -er[1].] One who franks a letter. Also, an instrument for franking postal matter.

1784 Mrs. Boscawen *Let.* in *Mrs. Delany's Corr.* Ser. II. III. 228 My son us'd to have the honour to be franker to your ladyship. **1818** Miss Mitford in L'Estrange *Life* (1870) II. 35 He has the worst fault a franker can have; he is un-come-at-able. **1880** *Antiquary* 25/1 The stamp may usually be depended upon to authenticate the autograph of the franker. **1925** *Glasgow Herald* 5 Jan. 8 There are addressers, duplicators,..postal frankers and cheque writers.

'**frank-fee.** *Law.* [f. frank *a.*[2] + fee *sb.* Cf. Anglo-L. *liberum feodum.*] **a.** A tenure of lands in fee-simple, *esp.* as opposed to *ancient demesne*; see demesne 4. **b.** Land so held.

1531 *Dial. Doct. & Stud.* II. ii. 7 a, Whan a plee is remoued out of auncyen demeane for that the lande is franke fee. *a* **1626** Bacon *Max. & Uses Com. Law* ii. (1636) 6 If tenant in ancient demesne bee disseised by the Lord..and the disseisee bring his assize in the Court of the Lord, Francke fee is no plea. **1741** T. Robinson *Gavelkind* v. 70 Yet in his Hands the Land is Frank Fee.

†**frank-ferm.** *Law. Obs.* [a. AF. *franke ferme*: see frank *a.*[2] and farm *sb.*[2]] Freehold tenure at a fixed rent.

1767 Blackstone *Comm.* II. 81 It was thought, in the reigns of both Edward I and Charles II, a point of the utmost importance..to the tenants, to reduce the tenure by knight-service to fraunke ferme or tenure by socage.

ˈ**frankfold.** *Law.* [f. FRANK *a.*[2] + FOLD *v.*[2]] = FALDAGE. Also **frankfoldage** in same sense.

1609 *Patent 7 Jas. I* in *Act 5 Geo. III*, c. 26 Preamb., Rents, pensions, portions, frankfolds. **1628** COKE *On Litt.* 114b, To hold..frank foldage..a man may make title by usage. **1708** *Termes de la Ley* 352 Frankfold is where the Lord hath benefit of folding his Tenants Sheep within his Manor for the manuring of his Land.

Frankfort (ˈfræŋkfət). The name of a German city. *attrib.* in **Frankfort black**, a fine black pigment used in copper-plate engraving.

1823 J. BADCOCK *Dom. Amusem.* 28 The black which is made by sublimation of pitch in dark chambers, and termed lamp-black and Frankfort black. **1853** URE *Dict. Arts, etc.* I. 814 *Frankfort black* is..made by calcining vine-branches, and the other refuse lees of the vinegar vats, in Germany.

frankfurter (ˈfræŋkfɜːtə(r)). Also **frankfurt** (ˈfræŋkfət). [G. *Frankfurter wurst* Frankfurt sausage. Cf. FRANKFORT.] A highly seasoned smoked beef and pork sausage, originally made at Frankfurt am Main.

[**1877** E. S. DALLAS *Kettner's Bk. of Table* 317 In the absence of Chorizos use Frankfort sausages.] **1894** *San Francisco Midwinter Appeal* 17 Feb. 2/1 Four bits for a Frankfurter seems rather steep. **1902** G. H. LORIMER *Lett. Merchant* x. 127 Only last week the head of our sausage department started to put out a tin-tag brand of frankfurts. **1908** —— *J. Spurlock* vii. 147, I told the Major that he had undoubtedly got hold of the hottest dog in the frankfurter can. **1919** F. HURST *Humoresque* 262 Screaming peanut- and frankfurter-stands. **1949** F. MACLEAN *Eastern Approaches* I. vii. 80 We would congregate round a roaring open fire in the *dacha* and Avis would dispense frankfurters and peanut butter. **1964** H. KEMELMAN *Friday the Rabbi slept Late* (1965) vii. 66 They offered..baked beans and frankfurts. **1971** *Sunday Times* (Colour Suppl.) 27 June 50/2 Frankfurters and Viennas are the world's best-known boiling sausages.

frankincense (ˈfræŋkɪnsɛns). Forms: 4 **franke ensens**, 5 **frank encens**, **-ensence**, **-ynsens**, 6 **frankenscence**, **-insence**, (6–7 **fran(c)kumsence**), 6– **frankincense**. [a. OF. *franc encens*: see FRANK *a.*[2] and INCENSE. The special meaning of the adj. in this combination seems to be 'of high quality': see FRANK *a.*[2] 5.]

1. An aromatic gum resin, yielded by trees of the genus *Boswellia*, used for burning as incense; olibanum; occas. the smoke from the same.

a **1387** *Sinon. Barthol.* (Anecd. Oxon.) 42 *Thus album, i. olibanum*, franke ensens. *c* **1450** *Cov. Myst.* (Shaks. Soc.) 8 Kynges iij With gold, myrre, and ffrankynsens. ? *c* **1475** *Sqr. lowe Degre* 849 Cloves that be swete smellyng, Frankensence, and olibanum. **1552** LATIMER *Serm. Gosp.* vi. 188 Franckumsence to signify his priesthoode. **1645** FULLER *Good Th. in Bad T.* (1841) 50 He..sent Leonidas a present of five hundred talents' weight of frankincense. **1718** PRIOR *Pleasure* 904 Curling frankincense ascends to Baal. **1834** LYTTON *Pompeii* IV. iii, Odour of myrrh and frankincense.

2. Resin resembling this, obtained from firs or pines. Also, the tree itself.

1577 HARRISON *England* II. xxii. (1877) I. 342 The firre, frankincense, and pine we doo not altogither want. **1620** J. MASON *Brief Disc. Newfoundland* B iij, Tarre, Tirpintine, Frank-Incense. **1866** *Treas. Bot.*, *Frankincense..European*, a resinous exudation of the spruce fir. The name is also applied to *Pinus Tæda*.

3. *attrib.* as *frankincense-pine*, *-tree*.

1611 BIBLE *Ecclus.* l. 8 As the branches of the frankincense tree in the time of summer. **1671** SALMON *Syn. Med.* III. xxii. 436 Frankincense tree. *c* **1865** LETHEBY in *Circ. Sc.* I. 106/1 The Frankincense pine of Virginia (*Pinus tæda*).

Hence ˈ**frankincensed** *a.*, perfumed with frankincense.

1860 RUSKIN *Mod. Paint.* V. IX. i. 204 No velvet-bound missal, nor frankincensed manuscript.

ˈ**franking machine.** [f. FRANKING *vbl. sb.* + MACHINE *sb.*] An officially authorized machine, introduced by the British Post Office in 1922, used by large concerns for 'stamping' letters, etc., with a sign (in lieu of an affixed postage stamp); it simultaneously records the cost of postage (this being periodically checked and collected by the Post Office). Also **franking stamp**.

1927 *Times* 22 Feb. 10/4 Remembering to have read of a franking machine called a postage meter being recently issued to the public, I wrote to the P.M.G. **1929** *Encycl. Brit.* XVIII. 311/1 Another method of avoiding the use of postage stamps is the employment of postal franking machines, which are now licensed by the post office. These machines impress the correspondence with a red franking stamp which is accepted as the equivalent of a postage stamp. **1961** *Lebende Sprachen* VI. 70/1 *Postage meter machine* (B[ritish] E[nglish]: franking machine).

Frankish (ˈfræŋkɪʃ), *a.* (*sb.*) For earlier forms cf. FRENCH. [f. FRANK *sb.*[1] + -ISH.]

1. Of or pertaining to the ancient Franks.

1802 W. TAYLOR in *Monthly Mag.* XIII. 11 The French, through their Frankish ancestors [have] *hacher*. **1875** J. C. ROBERTSON *Hist. Chr. Ch.* III. 8 Leodegar was..connected with the most powerful families of the Frankish nobility.

2. Of or pertaining to the Western nations.

1594 CAREW *Tasso* I. lxxvi. 41 Onely the King of Trypoli ..Athwart the Frankish army might haue stept. **1862** FAIRHOLT *Up Nile* 52 Frankish gold has overridden religious prejudices.

3. *sb.* The language of the Franks.

1863 MISS SEWELL *Chr. Names* i. 6 France kept Frank names..while ceasing to speak Frankish.

† **frank-law.** *Law. Obs.* [f. FRANK *a.*[2] + LAW.] The condition of a full freeman (*liber et legalis homo*), esp. the liberty of being sworn in courts, as a juror or witness.

1607 in COWEL. **1641** *Termes de la Ley* 78 The party attainted shall lose his Franke Law [AF. *perdera son Frank Ley*], to the intent that hee be not impannelled upon Juries or Assises.

franklin[1] (ˈfræŋklɪn). Forms: 3 **francoleyn**, 4 **fraunkeleyn**, 4–6 **frank(e)le(i)n**, **-(e)leyn**, (4 **fran(c)kelain**, **-layn(e**, 5 **franklon**), 6–9 **fran(c)klin(g**, **-lyn(g**, 6– **franklin**. [First recorded as Anglo-L. *franc-colanus*, *francalanus*, *franchelanus* (12–13th c.); it appears as AF. *fraunclein a* 1307 (Du Cange s.v. *Franchilanus*). The ultimate formation is clearly from med.L. *francus*, OF. *franc* FRANK *a.*[2]; but the process of formation is somewhat obscure.

The suffix is usually supposed to represent the OHG. *-linc*, -LING. This is possible, but the analogy of CHAMBERLAIN is not quite conclusive, as there is no trace of an OHG. **franclinc* or Lat. **franclingus*, nor on the other hand does L. **camerlānus* appear. Possibly *francalānus* may be f. the adj. *francālis* 'having the rights of a freeman', f. *francus*. The earliest spelling *franccolanus* suggests that the word was in 1200 supposed to be a compound.]

† **1.** A freeman. *Obs.*

a **1300** *Cursor M.* 5374 First he was here als our thain Bot now es he for ai franckelain. **1377** LANGL. *P. Pl.* B. XIX. 39 And þo þat bicome crysten, by conseille of þe baptiste, Aren frankeleynes, fre men. *c* **1440** *Promp. Parv.* 177/1 Frankeleyne, *libertinus*.

2. A freeholder; in 14–15th c. the designation of a class of landowners, of free but not noble birth, and ranking next below the gentry.

[**1200** *Rotuli Chartarum* 43/1 Unam carrucatam terrae apud Hamerwich cum villanis et franchelano. *Ibid.* 82/1 Omnia feuda militum et franccolanorum qui tenent de eodem monasterio. *a* **1300** *Vit. Har. Reg.* (1885) 34 A duobus ut fertur mediocribus viris quos francalanos sive agricolas voccant agnitus.] **1297** R. GLOUC. (1724) 36 Wel may a symple Francoleyn in mysese hym so bringe Of lutel lond, wan þen fel such of a kyng. *c* **1330** R. BRUNNE *Chron.* (1810) 239 No oþer lorde stoute, ne fraunkeleyn of toun, Tille holy kirke salle gyue tenement. *c* **1386** CHAUCER *Prol.* 216 Ful wel biloved and famulier was he With frankeleyns over al in his cuntré. *c* **1460** J. RUSSELL *Bk. Nurture* 1071 Marchaundes & Franklonz worshipfulle & honorable..may be set semely at a squyers table. **1528** ROY *Rede Me* (Arb.) 100 One or two ryche francklyngis Occupyinge a dosen mens lyvyngis. **1590** SPENSER *F.Q.* I. x. 6 Entred in, a spatious court they see..Where them does meete a francklin faire and free. **1618–29** *App.* in Rushw. *Hist. Coll.* (1659) I. 17 To make..Francklines, and rich Farmers, Esquires, to precede them, would yield your Majesty also a great sum of money in present. **1655** MOUFET & BENNET *Health's Improv.* (1746) 340 The Franklin's Bread of England is counted most nourishing. **1659** HOWELL *Lexicon*, Proverbs may be called the truest Franklins or Freeholders of a Countrey. **1843** LYTTON *Last Bar.* IV. v, His dress was that of a substantial franklin.

† **3.** Applied allusively to: A liberal host. Cf. FRANK *a.*[2] 2. *Obs.*

1577–87 HOLINSHED *Chron.* II. 31/1 To purchase the name of a sumptuous frankelen or a good viander. **1727** SOMERVILLE *Officious Messenger* 72 No Franklin carving of a Chine At Christide, ever look'd so fine.

Franklin[2] (ˈfræŋklɪn). [f. the name of Benjamin *Franklin* (1706–1790).] † **1.** *U.S.* A lightning-conductor. Also *Franklin's rod*. *Obs.*

1818 J. PALMER *Jrnl. Trav. U.S.* 104 Franklins, or conductors, are a certain safe-guard, and generally used. *a* **1862** S. BRECK *Recoll.* (1877) ii. 71 Our professor of natural philosophy was desirous to erect on the old lofty tower..a lightning-rod, very properly called at that time a 'Franklin'. **1910** *Encycl. Brit.* XI. 30/1 He [*sc.* Benjamin Franklin] planned the lightning-rod (long known as 'Franklin's rod'), which he described and recommended to the public in 1753.

2. *N. Amer.* ***Franklin stove***, a kind of iron fireplace invented by Franklin; also, a free-standing stove for heating a room. Also *ellipt.*

1787 *Massachusetts Centinel* 3 Nov. 3/3 An assortment of Franklin stoves. **1797** *Upper Canada Gaz.* (York, Ont.) 4 Nov. 3/3 For Sale—A Franklin Stove Complete. **1818** J. PALMER *Jrnl. Trav. U.S.* 15 In the best room some have an iron fireplace..called a Franklin; these look very neat, and will much sooner heat a room than the open fire-place. **1897** B. F. TAYLOR *Summer-Savory* x. 95 Within the wide door was the bar-room, with a great hospitable Franklin. **1949** *Los Angeles Times* (Home Mag.) 3 Apr. 20/2 In the living room, an old Franklin stove substitutes for a fireplace. **1954** C. BRUCE *Channel Shore* 28 Anse..threw a cigarette butt at the Franklin stove. **1970** *Globe & Mail* (Toronto) 26 Sept. 13/1 A small Franklin stove..and a number of Canadian antiques add charm.

Franklinian (fræŋˈklɪnɪən), *a.* (*sb.*) [f. the proper name *Franklin* (see prec.) + -IAN.]

A. *adj.* Of or pertaining to Benjamin Franklin; also, following Franklin (in politics).

1767 PRIESTLEY *Hist. Electricity* in *Franklin's Wks.* (1887) II. 65 The Franklinian system. **1808** J. WEBSTER *Nat. Phil.* 133 The Franklinian Theory. **1814** J. Q. ADAMS *Wks.* (1856) X. 90 In politics, Rittenhouse was..Franklinian, democrat, totally ignorant of the world.

B. *sb.* A follower of Franklin; a Franklinist.

1794 G. ADAMS *Nat. & Exp. Philos.* IV. xlvi. 283 You will find the ideas of the Franklinians concerning it quite contradictory.

So **Franˈklinic** *a.* [see -IC], an epithet applied to electricity excited by friction; ˈ**Franklinism** [see -ISM], frictional electricity; ˈ**Franklinist** [see -IST], one who follows Franklin in his theory of electricity.

1767 PRIESTLEY *Hist. Electricity* in *Franklin's Wks.* (1887) II. 65 The terms Franklinism, Franklinist..occur in almost every page. **1772** FRANKLIN *Let.* Wks. 1887 IV. 501 All the rest, who have in any degree acquainted themselves with electricity, are, as he calls them, Franklinists. **1862** GROVE *Corr. Phys. Forces* (ed. 4) 115 What is called Franklinic electricity. **1883** E. C. MANN *Psychol. Med.* 556 (Cent.) It has also been called 'frictional' electricity..or Franklinism.

franklinite (ˈfræŋklɪnaɪt). *Min.* [f. *Franklin*, New Jersey, where it is found + -ITE.] A compound of oxides of iron, manganese, and zinc, found in brilliant black crystals.

1820 *Amer. Jrnl. Sc.* II. 323 The black zinciferous mineral, the Franklinite. **1862** DANA *Man. Geol.* 84 Franklinite, an iron-zinc ore.

Franklinize (ˈfræŋklɪnaɪz), *v.* [f. the proper name *Franklin* (after Benjamin Franklin) + -IZE.] *trans.* To operate on by Franklin's methods. Hence ˈ**Franklinized** *ppl. a.* Also ˌ**Frankliniˈzation** (*Med.*), the therapeutic application of 'Franklinic' or frictional electricity.

1804 J. LARWOOD *No Gun Boats* 27 The Treaty between la-Fayetted France and Franklinised America. **18..** *Med. News* L. 509 (Cent.) Another method that may be applied during the day is general franklinization.

frankly (ˈfræŋklɪ), *adv.* [f. FRANK *a.*[2] + -LY[2].] In a frank manner.

† **1.** Freely; unrestrictedly, without restraint or constraint. *Obs.*

1541 *Act 33 Hen. VIII*, c. 25 All other lawfull thinges.. to do as liberally, frankelie, lawfully..as if they..had been naturally borne within this realme. **1547** *City of London Jrnls.* 317 in *Vicary's Anat.* (1888) App. iii. 132 [To] excercyse the seyd..office..Franklye & frelye. **1626** BACON *Sylva* §544 The Sap..cannot get up, to spread so frankly, as it should do.

2. † **a.** In liberal or abundant measure, bountifully, lavishly (*obs.*). **b.** In a liberal spirit, generously; unconditionally, unreservedly.

1546 BALE *Eng. Votaries* II. (1550) 102 The cattell..was.. frankely fed. **1581** J. BELL *Haddon's Answ. Osor.* 402 They would procure the people to deale their almes some-what more franckly. **1583** STANYHURST *Æneis* II. (Arb.) 48 Wee.. pardon francklye the villeyn. **1600** SURFLET *Countrie Farme* I. xxiii. 130 Oxen are not to be fed so frankely and full in winter. **1602** ROWLANDS *'Tis Merrie when Gossips meet* (1609) 19 His Crownes vpon them frankly he bestowes. **1603** SHAKS. *Meas. for M.* III. i. 106 Were it but my life, I'de throw it downe..As frankely as a pin. **1611** BIBLE *Luke* vii. 42 And when they had nothing to pay, he frankly forgaue them both. **1647** H. MORE *Philos. P.*, *Oracle* 61 Ambrosian streams..Do frankly flow. **1671** *True Non-conf.* 2 I do here fracklie..lay aside all wrath and bitterness. **1683** CLAVERHOUSE 9 June in Mowbray Morris *Life* xii. (1889) 142 All the Justices doe their deuty francly and cheerfully. **1848** C. BRONTË *J. Eyre* xi, The power of meriting the kindness.. so frankly offered. **1877** MRS. FORRESTER *Mignon* I. 50 Sir Tristram accepts the invitation as frankly as it is given.

3. Without concealment, disguise, or reserve; avowedly, openly, plainly. Now freq. with ellipsis of *to speak*.

c **1540** *Fisher's Wks.*, *Life* (E.E.T.S.) p. li, This worthie Byshopp..was..desired to speake his minde frankly and freely. **1625** BACON *Ess.*, *Suspicion* (Arb.) 529 The best Meane..is franckly to communicate them [suspicions]. **1754** CHATHAM *Lett. Nephew* iv. 24 Venture to own frankly that you came to Cambridge to learn what you can. **1847** LYTTON *Lucretia* 27 Frankly, if you can like my niece, win her. **1865** W. ROBERTS *Urin. & Renal Dis.* I. iv. (1885) 185 The deposition of the urates is sufficient evidence that the urine is frankly acid. **1880** L. STEPHEN *Pope* iii. 79 It would be impossible to accept more frankly the theory that lying is wrong when it is found out. **1888** KIPLING *Under Deodars* (1890) 52 *She.*—.. Can you wonder that I'm disinclined for amusement? *He.*—Frankly, I do. **1892** M. DODS *St. John* I. xvi. 248 Frankly open your soul before Him. **1960** L. R. BANKS *L-Shaped Room* xiv. 196 The one [*sc.* board] down his front said, '*Are you ready to meet your maker??*' 'Frankly, yes,' Toby answered it. **1961** A. CHRISTIE *Pale Horse* i. 20 'But you didn't come here to talk to me about my books.' 'Frankly no.'

4. With freedom of artistic treatment.

1851 RUSKIN *Stones Ven.* (1874) I. xix. 198 Frankly completing the arch work and cornice of each. **1885** *Athenæum* 23 May 669/2 Frankly painted, and with much good drawing.

† ˈ**frank-ˌmarriage.** *Law. Obs.* [a. AF. *franc mariage*: see FRANK *a.*[2] and MARRIAGE.] A tenure in virtue of which a man and his wife held lands granted to them by the father or other near relative of the wife, the estate being heritable to the fourth generation of heirs of their bodies, without any service other than fealty.

c **1150** *Newminster Cartul.* (Surtees) 117 Concesserunt eis en fraunkmariage. *c* **1475** *Partenay* 1506 But you wil I gif gentilly, sire, of myne..With my fair doughter in franke mariage. *a* **1647** HABINGTON *Surv. Worcestersh.* in *Worc. Hist. Soc. Proc.* II. 228 Simon his grandfather..had the same in franck mariage by the guyft of Henry Rolland. **1767**

BLACKSTONE *Comm.* II. 115 Estates *in libero maritagio*, or frankmarriage. **1866** ROGERS *Agric. & Prices* I. iv. 68 [He] holds a small amount of land in frank-marriage, and another portion in fee.

frankness (ˈfræŋknɪs). [f. FRANK *a.*² + -NESS.] The quality of being frank.

†**1.** Liberality, bounteousness, generosity. Also, luxuriance. *Obs.*

1591 PERCIVALL *Sp. Dict.*, *Largueza*, franknes. **1597** HOOKER *Eccl. Pol.* v. lxxii. §2 To take downe the frankenesse of nature, and to tame the wildenesse of flesh. **1711** HEARNE *Collect.* (Oxf. Hist. Soc.) III. 124, I requested that you might see it; which, with his usual Frankness, he readyly granted. **1738** *Lucca's Mem.* Pref. vi, Whether it be on account of their Power at Sea, or their Frankness in spending their Money. **1762–71** H. WALPOLE *Vertue's Anecd. Paint.* (1786) III. 64 He..kept a great table, and often pressed the king for money with a freedom which his majesty's own frankness indulged.

2. Freedom of address or manner; absence of disguise, reserve, or suspicion; candour, ingenuousness, openness.

1668 TEMPLE *Let. Sir O. Bridgman* Wks. 1731 II. 55 He would return my Frankness to him with the same to me. **1751** JOHNSON *Rambler* No. 174 ¶7 To expose the levities of frankness. **1816** J. SCOTT *Vis. Paris* (ed. 5) 28 The servants come with an air of frankness to assist him to alight. **1840** ARNOLD *Hist. Rome* II. 346 Fabius had experienced also the noble frankness of Decius' nature. **1858** FROUDE *Hist. Eng.* IV. xviii. 54 The King..implored his nephew to meet his overtures with the frankness with which they were made. **1875** HELPS *Ess.*, *Secrecy* 53 That happy union of frankness and reserve..comes not by studying rules.

b. *esp.* in speech: Outspokenness. More fully, *frankness of speech* (in early use = 'liberty of speech').

1553 BRENDE *Q. Curtius* VIII. 159 All the libertie and franckenes of speache being taken away. **1647** CLARENDON *Hist. Reb.* I. §77 The Other..declared with a very unnecessary Frankness, 'that he would have no Friendship ..with him'. **1729** T. COOKE *Tales, Proposals, etc.* 57 What from the Frankness of your Soul you say The Fool may tattel, and the Knave betray. **1776** GIBBON *Decl. & F.* I. 357 Profound dissimulation under the disguise of military frankness. **1823** LAMB *Elia* (1860) 132 She confessed, with her usual frankness, that she had no sort of dislike to his attentions. **1860** TYNDALL *Glac.* I. xxiv. 168, I shall offend them..by my frankness in stating this. **1886** *Academy* 30 Jan. 83/3 Certain roughnesses and franknesses of expression.

3. Freedom of artistic treatment.

1784 J. BARRY in *Lect. Paint.* vi. (1848) 221 A great work in fresco..requires..spirit, frankness, decision. **1849** RUSKIN *Sev. Lamps* v. §v. 140 Two very distinguishing characters of vital imitation are, its Frankness and Audacity.

ˈfrank-pledge. *O.E. Law. Obs.* exc. *Hist.* Forms: 5 fraunciplegge, 6 frankepledge, 6–8 fran(c)(k)ple(d)ge, 6– frankpledge. [a. AF. *francplege* (Latinized *franciplegium*), f. *franc* FRANK *a.*² + *plege* PLEDGE; app. a Norman mistranslation of OE. *friþ-borh* peace-pledge (see FRITHBORH), *friþ* having been supposed to be connected with *free*.]

1. The system by which every member of a tithing was answerable for the good conduct of, or the damage done by, any one of the other members.

16.. *Act* in Stow *Surv.* (1633) 671 You shall..inquire if any man..abide within your Ward that is not put under frank pledge. **1817** T. J. PETTIGREW *Lettsom* II. 247 Every place must..be a free settlement, where frank-pledge is properly maintained. **1874** GREEN *Short HIst.* iv. §4. 190 The system of 'frank-pledge', or free engagement of neighbour for neighbour, was accepted after the Danish wars.

transf. **1796** BURKE *Let. Noble Ld.* Wks. VIII. 50 The solemn, forensic, constitutional frank-pledge of this nation. **1855** MACAULAY *Hist. Eng.* III. 13 The servants of the Crown were not, as now, bound in frankpledge for each other.

b. *view of frankpledge*: a court held periodically for the production of the members of a tithing, later of a hundred or manor. Cf. COURT-LEET. *Obs.* exc. in formal notices.

[**1292** BRITTON I. i. §13 En cyteez et en burgs et en fraunchises, et en tourns des viscountes, et en vewe de fraung plege.] **1495** *Act 11 Hen. VII*, c. 29 §1 Viewe of fraunciplegge within the purcynct of the seid Manoir. **1588** FRAUNCE *Lawiers Log.* I. xii. 52 b, A generall assembly, yet called the view of Frankepledge..or the Leete court. *c* **1630** RISDON *Surv. Devon* §91 (1810) 88 The town hath a weekly market, and yearly fairs, with toll and view of frank pledge. **1747** CARTE *Hist. Eng.* I. 311 Once a year, (and if necessary twice) there was held an extraordinary assembly of the hundred, called a view of frankpledge or court leet. **1818** [see 2]. **1864** *Notice on Kirkby* (*Yorks.*) *Church Door*, A Court Leet or Law Day, with view of Frankpledge..will be holden.

2. One of the mutually responsible members of a tithing, etc. Occas. the tithing or decenary itself.

1502 ARNOLDE *Chron.* 93 Francpledge. **1523** FITZHERB. *Surv.* xi. (1539) 25 True reue, true frank plege. **1754** HUME *Hist. Eng.* I. ii. 50 These decennaries received the name of the frank-pledge. **1765** BLACKSTONE *Comm.* I. 114 Entire vills sir Henry Spelman conjectures to have consisted of ten freemen, or frank-pledges. **1818** CRUISE *Digest* (ed. 2) III. 266 The view of frankpledge..means the examination or survey of the frankpledges.

†**frankpost.** *Building. Obs.* [f. FRANK *a.*² + POST *sb.*] ? An angle-post in a frame building.

1587 HARRISON *England* II. xii. (1877) I. 233 In the.. champagne countrie they are inforced for want of stuffe to use no studs..but onlie frankeposts, raisins, beames, pricke-posts..whereunto they fasten their splints or radels, and then cast it over with thicke claie.

ˈfrank-ˌtenement. *Law.* [a. AFr.; see FRANK *a.*² and TENEMENT.] = FREEHOLD. So **ˈfrank-ˈtenure** [see TENURE].

[**1292** BRITTON III. ii. §2 Brefs de dreit de mariage ne sount mie fraunc tenement.] **1523** FITZHERB. *Surv.* 14 Yet haue they no franke tenement bycause of the commen lawe. **1592** WEST *1st Pt. Symbol.* §41 B, An estate of franktenement, is where a man hath the freehold of land. **1600** HOLLAND *Livy* XXI. xlv. (1609) 419 To enjoie to them and their heires for ever, as freehold in frank tenure. **1643** SIR J. SPELMAN *Case of Affairs* 6 Yet does not he deprive the Lord of his Lordship in the Copy-hold, nor..devest the Fee and Frank-tenement out of the lord.

fig. **1593** HARVEY *Supererog.* Wks. (Grosart) II. 229 See, how the daggletaild rampalion bustleth for the frank-tenement of the dung-hill.

†**frank-tenementary.** *Sc. Law. Obs.* [See -ARY.] One who possesses freehold lands.

1488 *Acta Dom. Conc.* 92/1 Quharethrow he Intromett wᵗ þe saidis landis bot be his grantschir quhilk wes bot franktenementare alanerly.

†**Frankˈverytie.** *French Feudal Law. Obs.* [ad. F. *franche verité* lit. 'frank truth': see FRANK *a.*² and VERITY.] A feudal court at Calais.

1528 SIR R. WESTON in Dillon *Calais & Pale* (1892) 92 Fynes and amercements presentable every yere at the Court of Frankverytie..Every household ought to pay to the King for the Frankverytie vjᵈ.

frans(e)y, -ical, obs. ff. FRENZY, FRENZICAL.

frantic (ˈfræntɪk), *a.* and *sb.* Forms: α. 4–5 frentik(e, -tyk(e, 6 phrentique, 6–7 fren-, phrenti(c)k(e. β. 4–6 frantyk(e, 6–8 franti(c)k(e, 6 frantycke, -tique, (6 phrantic), 7– frantic. [ME. *frentik, frantik*, a. OF. *frenetique* (mod.F. *frénétique*), ad. late L. *phrenēticus* delirious (see PHRENETIC), a corruption of Gr. φρενιτικός affected with φρενῖτις delirium: see FRENZY.]

A. *adj.*

1. Affected with mental disease, lunatic, insane; in later use, violently or ragingly mad. Now *rare.*

α. **1362** LANGL. *P. Pl.* A. XI. 6 'Wel artou witti', quod heo 'wisdom to telle To fayturs or to fooles that frentik [B. x. 6 frantyk] ben of wittes!' **1401** *Pol. Poems* (Rolls) II. 85, I do the wel to wite, frentike I am not. **1467** J. PASTON in *Paston Lett.* No. 569 II. 299 As for John Appylby, he is half frentyk. **1586** BRIGHT *Melanch.* xi. 52, I..haue obserued..in phrenticke persons the strength doubled vpon them. **1644** DIGBY *Nat. Bodies* (1645) I. 413, I have seene some frenticke persons, that [etc.].

β. **1398** TREVISA *Barth. De P. R.* v. xxiii. (1495) 132 Also by..acorde of musyk seke men and frantyk come ofte to theyr wytte ayen and helthe of body. *c* **1420** *Chron. Vilod.* 587 Frantyke men hadden þer hurre wytte. **1542** BOORDE *Dyetary* xxxvii. (1870) 298 Euery man the whiche is madde, or lunatycke, or frantycke. **1664** H. MORE *Myst. Iniq.* Apol. 562 It makes you look like a Company of Frantick men or Dæmoniacks. **1852** MRS. JAMESON *Leg. Monast. Ord.* 240 His father, believing him frantic, shut him [St. Francis of Assisi] up and bound him in his chamber.

absol. **1787** COWPER *Lett.* 24 Dec., All the frantic who have been restored to their reason.

2. *transf.* **a.** Affected by wild and ungovernable excitement; 'mad' with rage, pain, grief, etc. †Also, in early use, applied as a term of reproach imputing extreme folly (cf. the variation in the shades of the lit. sense 1).

[*c* **1477** CAXTON *Jason* 56 b, He was so angry that he semed better frantyk..thenne other wise. *a* **1547** SURREY *Æneid* II. 410 And thus as phrentik to our gates he ran.] **1561** T. NORTON *Calvin's Inst.* I. xiii. (1634) 56 There be risen up certaine phrenticke men as Servetto and other like. **1697** DRYDEN *Virg. Georg.* III. 420 The furious Mare..is frantick with Despair. **1732** LAW *Serious C.* v. (ed. 2) 73 That they must be grave and solemn at Church, but may be silly and frantick at home. **1822** W. IRVING *Braceb. Hall* xvi. 140 Julia, pale, bleeding..supported in the arms of her frantic lover. *a* **1839** PRAED *Poems* (1864) II. 204 Miss Jonquil was perfectly frantic. **1881** 'RITA' *My Lady Coquette* xii, His Aunt and Cousin are frantic with fear.

fig. **1602** MARSTON *Ant. & Mel.* I. Wks. 1856 I. 17 A heart ..Raging more wilde then is this franticke sea. **1798** FRERE in *Anti-Jacobin* vii. 24 War with herself see frantic Gallia wage. **1870** BRYANT *Iliad* I. v. 176 Fiery, frantic Mars, the unnatural plague Of man.

b. *colloq.* In exaggerated use = 'terrific', 'awful'.

1908 *Punch* 26 Feb. 152/2 I'm working simply most awfully hard for Ireland just now. I've bought a ghastly heap of poplin..and a frantic lot of Limerick lace.

3. †**a.** Of a disease: Attended by frenzy or delirium (*obs.*). **b.** Pertaining to, characterized by, or displaying frenzy; delirious, wild; †insanely foolish.

α. **1565** CALFHILL *Answ. Treat. Crosse* 32 b, Ye shal see it proued in plain words, a frentike part to worship Images. **1576** FLEMING *Panopl. Epist.* 267 It is more grievous then yᵉ phrentique sicknesse of madnesse. **1594** HOOKER *Eccl. Pol.* III. viii. 144 Esteeming in the phrentique error of their mindes the greatest madnes in the world to be wisedome.

β. *a* **1533** FRITH *Disput. Purgat.* Prol. (1829) 93 The ignorant people..was fallen into that frantic imagination that [etc.]. **1586** T. B. *La Primaud. Fr. Acad.* I. 666 There are (as I take it) two causes intermingled, which breede this franticke feaver of our France, the one proceeding from the estate, the other from religion. **1589** COGAN *Haven Health* ccxliii. 264 Strange Agewes arise, raging continuall, burning, phrantike. **1632** LITHGOW *Trav.* IV. 150 For in a franticke piety they cause a Smith to pull forth their eyes. **1781** GIBBON *Decl. & F.* III. xlviii. 47 She displayed a frantic and impotent rage. **1790** BURKE *Fr. Rev.* Wks. V. 142 The royal captives..were slowly moved along, amidst the horrid yells..and frantick dances..of the furies of hell. **1814** SOUTHEY *Roderick* I. 81 He threw his hands aloft in frantic prayer. **1879** DIXON *Windsor* II. xii. 129 His welcome by the citizens was frantic.

†**4.** quasi-*adv.* Frantically. *Obs. rare.*

c **1600** SHAKS. *Sonn.* cxlvii, Past cure I am..And frantic mad with evermore unrest. *a* **1652** BROME *Queene's Exch.* III. i. Wks. 1873 III. 497, I fear he's brain-crack'd, lunatick, and Frantick mad.

5. *Comb.*, as †*frantic-headed*, †*-like* adjs.

1558 PHAER *Æneid* IV. 647 Her golden heare she tare and frantiklyke with moode opprest, She cried, O Iupiter [etc.]. **1640** BP. HALL *Episc.* II. xix. 199 Ærius saith he was a man frantick-headed, proud-minded.

†**B.** *sb.* One who is frantic or frenzied; a lunatic, a delirious patient. *Obs.*

α. *c* **1380** WYCLIF *Serm.* x. Sel. Wks. I. 26 Resoun shulde teche hem þat þei ben worse þan frentikes. **1565** JEWEL *Repl. Harding* (1611) 106 Persons Excommunicate, Infants, Phrentickes, and Mad Men. **1616** B. JONSON *Devil an Ass* IV. vi, You did neuer heare A Phrentick, so in loue with his owne fauour! **1695** WOODWARD *Nat. Hist. Earth* II. 88 The world was little better than a common fold of Phrenticks and Bedlams.

β. **1574** J. JONES *Nat. Beginning Grow. Things* 34 Idiots, Dolts, Lunatikes, Frantikes, and blockheads. **1611** SPEED *Hist. Gt. Brit.* IX. xxiii. §99 He was esteemed as a frantick, and sent to the Marshal-See for a Lunaticke foole. **1669** PENN *No Cross* Wks. 1782 II. 96 Being slighted of them for a ninny, a fool, a frantick [etc.]. **1758** JORTIN *Erasm.* I. 192 The combustions raised by these Frantics.

Hence †**ˈfrantic** *v. intr.*, to move frantically.

1635 QUARLES *Embl.* v. iv. (1818) 270 Like to the arctic needle, that..First frantic's up and down from side to side, And restless heats his crystal ivory case.

frantically (ˈfræntɪkəlɪ), *adv.* [f. FRANTIC *a.* + -AL¹ + -LY².] In a frantic manner.

1749 HURD *Horace's Art of Poetry* Notes §123 She herself ..says, fiercely indeed, but not frantically. **1831** CARLYLE *Sart. Res.* II. v, Our philosopher..was heartily and even frantically in Love. **1859** R. F. BURTON *Centr. Afr.* in *Jrnl. Geog. Soc.* XXIX. 332 Frantically flourishing his spear and agitating his bow.

franticly (ˈfræntɪklɪ), *adv.* [f. FRANTIC *a.* + -LY².] = FRANTICALLY.

1549 BALE *Leland's N. Year's Gift* D i b, Them that so frantycklye on their ale benches do prattle. **1596** *Edward III*, III. v, He lion-like..Franticly rends and bites the woven toil. **1621** G. SANDYS *Ovid's Met.* IX. (1626) 190 Hopelesse, her hated mansion she eschues: And franticklly, her brothers flight persues. **1794** SULLIVAN *View Nat.* I. 8 The one is gloomy and ferociously distracted; the other is merrily, but perhaps not less franticly mad. **1828** SCOTT *F. M. Perth* xix, She cried thus franticly, to ears which she was taught to believe were stopped by death. **1883** *Harper's Mag.* Apr. 687/2 Everything here was..franticly scrubbed.

franticness (ˈfræntɪknɪs). [f. as prec. + -NESS.] The state or condition of being frantic.

a **1529** SKELTON *Sp. Parrot* 411 Of frantycknes and folysshnes, Whyche ys the grett state? **1583** GOLDING *Calvin on Deut.* clxxii. 1568 Men bee driuen with a certaine furie or frentikenesse. **1664** PEPYS *Diary* 15 Aug., Her kinswoman, who it seems is sickly even to frantiqueness sometimes. **1718** *Entertainer* No. 21 ¶6 Frantickness, and a Start of Passion, they deify'd as the Extremity of Courage and Resolution. **1878** MRS. HUNGERFORD *Molly Bawn* (1893) 139 You have all the franticness to yourself.

†**ˈfrantling,** *vbl. sb. Obs. nonce-wd.* Used to express the noise made by peacocks.

a **1693** URQUHART *Rabelais* III. xiii. 107 The barking of Curs..coniating of Storks, frantling of Peacocks.

franzy, dial. form of FRENZY.

†**frap,** *sb. Obs. rare*⁻¹. [echoic: cf. RAP.] A noise made by knocking. In quot. *attrib.*

1583 STANYHURST *Æneis* IV. (Arb.) 120 Mightily rapping Her brest with thumping frap knocks.

frap (fræp), *v.* [a. OF. *fraper* (mod.F. *frapper*) = Pr. *frapar*, It. *frappare* to strike; of obscure origin, but perh. f. the Teut. root *flap-*: see FLAP.

It has been conjectured that the ONorthumb. (*ʒe*)*fræpʒiʒa* meant 'to strike'; it renders (*re*)*verebuntur* (which the glossator may have mistaken for *verberantur*!) and *accusarent*. The two ostensible senses are so irreconcilable that the supposition of a blunder seems justifiable; possibly the ONorthumb. may preserve the Teut. root of the Rom. word.]

1. a. *trans.* To strike; to beat; also *fig. Obs.* exc. *dial.* †**b.** *intr.* To strike (*at, on*). *Obs.*

α. **13..** *Coer de L.* 2513 With myn ax I schal hem frape. *a* **1330** *Syr Degarre* 13 He..frapte his tail with gret miȝt Upon Degarres side. *c* **1400** *Destr. Troy* 10515 Kepis you in couer..Tyll the kyng and his company by comyn within; ffallys on hym fuersly, frap hym to dethe. **1566** PAINTER *Pal. Pleas., Rhom. & Jul.* (1575) II. 197 Who heart was frapped with sutch surpassing woe, as neither teare nor word could issue forth. **1583** STANYHURST *Æneis* III. (Arb.) 88 A seabelch grounting on rough rocks rapfulye frapping Was hard. **1727** BRADLEY *Fam. Dict.* s.v. *Bread*, You may know that the Oven is hot enough, when frapping a Pole against the Hearth..small Sparks arise. **1892** *Northumbld. Gloss.*,

Frap, to strike, to rap. **1896** KIPLING *Seven Seas* 23 Once we frapped a ship, and she laboured woundily.

b. 13.. *Coer de L.* 4546 The Crystene on hem gan fast to frape. ?*a* **1400** *Morte Arth.* 1115 He..frappez faste at hys face fersely þer-aftyr! **1750** ELLIS *Mod. Husb.* IV. iii. 65 (E.D.S.) If [the calf's tail] do not bleed to your desire, frap about it with the handle of a knife.

2. a. *Naut.* To bind tightly. [So also in Fr.]

1548 HALL *Chron., Hen. VIII*, 22b, Thei frapped together xxiiii. greate Hulkes. **1578** BOURNE *Inventions* No. 14. 10 The caske being layd close vnto the ballest, and fraped down close, that it doth not stirre. **1703** [see FRAPE[2] 1.] **1756** *Gentl. Mag.* XXVI. 15 Who..caused the stern-post and standard to be frapped together, and both of them to be frapped to the mizzen-mast. **1769** FALCONER *Dict. Marine* (1789), *Ceintrer*, to frap a ship, or pass turns of a cable round the middle of the hull of a ship, to support her in a storm. **1835** SIR J. ROSS *Narr. 2nd Voy.* iii. 32 It seemed possible to frapp the shrouds and stays in such a way as to secure it from going overboard. **1840** R. H. DANA *Bef. Mast* xxv. 82 We succeeded..in smothering it and frapping it [the sail] with long pieces of sinnet. **1857** S. OSBORN *Quedah* xii. 151 All superfluous branches were lopped off, and the whole well frapped together with cords. **1867** SMYTH *Sailor's Word-bk., Frap*, to secure the falls of a tackle together by means of spun yarn, rope yarn, or any lashing wound round them. **1879** FARRAR *St. Paul* (1883) 714 They could not help in such technical tasks as frapping the vessel. **1882** NARES *Seamanship* (ed. 6) 45 The end is..frapped round all parts. **1962** G. COMPTON *Too Many Murderers* xx. 162 They saw where Jason left his dinghy, and they fraped theirs out on the same line.

b. To brace the cords of a drum by pulling them together.

1874 KNIGHT *Dict. Mech.* I. 914.

†**frapaille.** *Obs.* [a. OF. *frapaille*, collect. f. *frape*: see FRAPE[1].] A contemptuous name given to a body of people; rabble; *esp.* the camp followers of an army.

c **1330** R. BRUNNE *Chron. Wace* (Rolls) 13319 Þer frapaille þat fel nought to be in bataille Vnder an hil he set þem þere.

†'**frapart.** *Obs. rare.* Also in contracted form frap. [a. OF. *frapart*, f. *frapper* to strike.] Only in ***friar frapart*** [F. *frère frappart* 's'est dit d'un moine libertin et débauché' (Littré)].

a **1535** MORE *How Serjeant wolde lerne to be frere* 267 in Hazl. *E.P.P.* III. 129 The frier frap, gate many a swap. **1600** O. E. *Repl. to Libel* Ep. Ded. 3 Be they monarkes, or be they fryer frapartes. *Ibid.* I. i. 5 A..religion..built vpon impious popes, frier fraparts, and massing priests mouthes.

†'**frape.**[1] *Obs.* [? a. OF. *frap* of same meaning, f. *fraper*: see FRAP *v.*]

1. A crowd; a mob, the rabble.

c **1330** R. BRUNNE *Chron.* (1810) 323 Þe þrid day com grete frape, & conged him away. *a* **1400** *Pistill of Susan* 289 Þei be fendes al þe frape. ?*a* **1400** *Morte Arth.* 2091 This gentille.. ffyghttez with alle the ffrappe a furlange of waye. *c* **1430** *Syr Gener.* (Roxb.) 5085 Ther cam of hem a grete frape, Ful like Giauntez thei wer y-shape. **1706** E. WARD *Hud. Rediv.* I. I. 11 Let loose the Frape to shew their Folly. **1710** —— *Brit. Hud.* I. 11 This wild Frape, to Mischief free.

2. ? Tumult, disturbance.

c **1330** R. BRUNNE *Chron.* (1810) 320 In alle þis mykelle frape wex a grete distance Of Boniface þe pape, & þe kyng of France. [**1824–28** *Craven Gloss.*, *Fraps*, noise, tumult.]

frape[2], **frap.** [? f. FRAP *v.* (see quot. 1703).]

1. (See quot. 1867.) Also ***frape-boat***.

1703 DAMPIER *Voy.* III. 20 From which girding them with Ropes, which our Seamen call Fraping, they have the Name of Frape-boats. **1867** SMYTH *Sailor's Word-bk., Frap*, a boat for shipping salt, used at Mayo, one of the Cape de Verde Islands.

2. (See quot. 1963.)

1901 *Pall Mall Mag.* Oct. 183 The boy crept down through the moonlit garden to the dinghy which Billy had left on its frape under the cliff. **1905** 'Q' *Shining Ferry* III. xviii. 186 Through this ring... Mr. Hosken had run a frape, on which he kept his blue boat. **1963** *Amer. Speech* XXXVIII. 299 *Frape*, a rope with blocks for mooring a boat.

†'**fraple,** *v. Obs.* [Cf. FRAP *v.* and OF. *frapillier* to be indignant, murmur.] *intr.* To dispute, wrangle, bluster.

a **1595** KELLEY in Ashm. *Theatr. Chem.* (1652) 324 Then you begin to fraple, Swearing and saying, what a fellow is this? **1609** HOLLAND *Amm. Marcell.* XXVIII. iv. 342 Frapling one against another *pro* and *contra*.

Hence †'**frapling** *vbl. sb.*, †'**frapling** *ppl. a.* Also '**frapler** *sb. arch.*, a blusterer, bully.

1599 B. JONSON *Cynthia's Rev.* IV. iii, Thou art..a frapler, and base. **1600** O. E. *Repl. to Libel* I. ii. 50 This frapling frier. **1600** HOLLAND *Livy* VIII. xxiii. (1609) 297 What frapling is here to no purpose. **1603** —— *Plutarch's Mor.* 47 Idomeneus in frappling prompt, What mean'st thou thus to prate? **1609** BP. W. BARLOW *Answ. Nameless Cath.* 338 Like a vaine & frapling surueyor, who [etc.]. **1863** SALA *Capt. Dangerous* I. ii. 40 Grooms, and porters, and fraplers, and bullies.

‖**frappant** (frapɑ̃), *a.* [Fr.; f. *frapper* to strike.] Striking, impressive.

1797 SCOTT *Fam. Lett.* (1894) I. 10 Her figure is not very *frappant*. [**1812** H. & J. SMITH *Rej. Addr.* x. 60 That ligneous barricado..decorated with frappant and tintinnabulant appendages.] **1823** *Blackw. Mag.* XIV. 576 This is so extraordinarily *frappant*, that the..baronet..only ventured to put it forth once.

‖**frappé** (frape), *a.* and *sb.* [Fr.; pa. pple. of *frapper* in sense of 'to ice (drinks)'.] **A.** *adj.* Iced, cooled. **B.** *sb.* An iced drink, a soft water-ice served in a glass, etc. Also as *v. trans.*, to put (a drink) on ice, to ice (a drink). Also *transf.*

1848 LONGF. in *Life* (1891) II. 121 A warm morning; *frappé* at noon with an east wind. **1870** LOWELL *Study Wind., Good Word for Winter*, The air you drink is *frappé*. **1890** B. HALL *Turnover Club* 230 The guests had rubbed the luckless Agent against the ice-box until he was thoroughly frapped. **1907** J. MASEFIELD *Tarpaulin Muster* xxii. 211 'Put a quart of champagne on ice and bring it up here,' said the boss. 'See you don't *frappé* it too cold.' **1922** *Glasgow Herald* 13 May 6 Besides untold recipes for cobblers, coolers, highballs, frappés, daisies, sangarees. **1936** *Punch* 15 July 70/1 There are Frappés, there are Parfaits, there are Sundaes. **1955** J. G. DAVIS *Dict. Dairying* (ed. 2) 517 *Frappés, soufflés*, etc., are essentially water ices.

†'**frappet.** *Obs. rare*$^{-1}$.

1607 WILKINS *Miseries Enforced Marr.* Hjb, Why my little frappet you, I heard thy Vnckles talk of thy riches.

frapping ('fræpɪŋ), *vbl. sb.* [f. FRAP *v.* + -ING[1].] The action of the vb. FRAP in various senses; an instance of this; also *concr.* a lashing. ***frapping turns*** (see quot. 1867).

1804 A. DUNCAN *Mariner's Chron.* Pref. 8 The opposite ones are braced together under a bowsprit by a frapping. **1859** F. A. GRIFFITHS *Artil. Man.* (1862) 216, 3 takes hold of the tube at the trapping with both hands. **1867** SMYTH *Sailor's Word-bk.* s.v., The frapping increases tension. *Ibid.*, *Frapping turns*, in securing the booms at sea the several turns of the lashings are frapped in preparation for the succeeding turns. **1882** NARES *Seamanship* (ed. 6) 184 Pass a hawser round outside the rigging ready for frapping in a wreck.

†'**frappish,** *a. Obs.* [f. FRAP *v.* + -ISH; cf. *snappish*.] Fretful, peevish.

1631 *Celestina* VII. 82 Hee is frappish, and I cannot beare.

†'**frary.** *Obs.* Also 5 **fray-, freyry**; and see FRIARY. [a. OF. *frairie, frerie*, f. *frere* brother.]

1. A brotherhood, fraternity.

13.. *Seynt Katerine* in *Leg. Kath.* (1840) 196 He hath me to his frari cald That schal be bot of mi bale. *c* **1430** LYDG. *Min. Poems* 171 Swiche a frary requyrithe Goddis curs. *c* **1450** *Cuckold's Dance* 215 in Hazl. *E.P.P.* I. 47 We be all off a freyry; I ame your awne brother. ?*a* **1500** *Mankind* (Brandl) 45/144 Þe numbur of þe demonycall frayry. **1505** *Will of T. Prowde* (Somerset Ho.), I bequeth to seynt Chadde frary.

2. = FRIARY.

1556 *Chron. Gr. Friars* (Camden) 40 All their qwarters.. was burryd at Pardone church yerde in the frary.

attrib. **1514** *Grant* in Wright *Prov. Dict.* s.v. *Frary*, My frary clark.

Frascati (fræ'skɑːtɪ). The name of a district in Latium, SE. of Rome, used for the name of a wine (usu. white) produced there.

[**1908** N. YOUNG *Murray's Handbk. Rome* (ed. 17) 29 The white wine of Frascati is light, sparkling, and rather sweet.] **1935** A. L. SIMON *Wines & Liqueurs from A to Z* 24 *Frascati*, one of the best white wines of the Latium (Italy). **1968** 'A. YORK' *Predator* v. 61 Two tumblers of red Frascati. **1970** *House & Garden* May 140/3 The province of Lazio grows the famous white Frascati, a wine that can be anything from quite dry to very sweet. **1970** 'O. JOHN' *Diamond Dress* xii. 139 I'd been looking forward to some delicious spaghetti alla carbonara and a bottle of Frascati.

frase, var. form of FRAIS, FRAISE.

frase, obs. var. PHRASE *sb.* and *v.*

frasier ('freɪzɪə(r)). *Her.* [ad. F. *fraisier* strawberry plant, f. *fraise* strawberry.] (See quots.)

1828–40 BERRY *Encycl. Her.* I, *Frasier*..used by Scotch heralds in the blazon of the coat of Fraser..but English heralds call it a cinquefoil. **1889** ELVIN *Dict. Her.*, *Frasier, Frases* or *Fraze*, the same as Cinquefoil; sometimes termed a primrose.

‖'**frasilah.** Also 6 **farazuola, frasoll,** 7 **frasslee.** [mod.Arab. *fārsalah*, pl. *farāsulah*; by some scholars thought to be of Romanic origin: cf. PARCEL.] A weight varying from 12 to 35 pounds, used in the East.

1555 EDEN *Decades* 239 The farazuola (which is xxii. poundes and syxe vnces). **1599** HAKLUYT *Voy.* II. I. 273 Which barre..is 20 frasoli, and euery frasoll is 10 manas. **1698** FRYER *Acc. E. Ind. & P.* 211 The Weights by which they are bought, are Baharrs and Frasslees; each Baharr 20 Frasslees, each Frasslee 12*l.* **1866** LIVINGSTONE *Last Jrnls.* (1873) I. ix. 228 An old man..had once carried five trasilahs (= 175 lbs.) of ivory.

†**frask.** *Obs.* [ad. Fr. *frasque*, of same meaning.] A trick.

1524 *St. Papers Hen. VIII*, VI. 328 He shall finde the same but fraskes, cawtelles, and subtelties. **1542** PAGET *Ibid.* IX. 49 We knowe your fraskes wel ynough.

Frasnian ('fræznɪən), *a. Geol.* Formerly also -ien. [ad. F. *Frasnien* (J. Gosselet 1879, in *Ann. Soc. géol. du Nord* VI. 396), f. *Frasne*, var. *Frasnes*, name of a village and commune in southern Belgium.] Name of the lower of the two stages constituting the Upper Devonian in Europe; of or pertaining to this stage or the geological period during which it was deposited. Also *absol.*

1882 A. GEIKIE *Text-bk Geol.* 701 In the Belgian and Eifelian tracts they have been subdivided as under:.. Fammenien..Frasnien. **1894** *Geol. Mag.* Oct. 474 The Frasnien series in the North of France and Belgium. **1963** D. W. & E. E. HUMPHRIES tr. *Termier's Erosion & Sedimentation* xiii. 288 The Frasnian reefs on the edge of the Dinant basin. *Ibid.* 289 The bioherms of the Frasnian form a subsidising series up to 1,300 feet thick.

frass (fræs). [a. Ger. *frasz*, f. root of *fressen* (= FRET) to devour.] The excrement of larvæ; also, the refuse left behind by boring insects.

1854 H. F. STAINTON *Entomol. Comp.* (ed. 2), The half-eaten leaves attest but too surely that some devourer is near. These indications of the presence of a larva are expressed in the German language by the single word 'frass', and we may, without impropriety, use the same word for the purpose of expressing the immediate effect of the larva's jaws, and the more indirect effect of the excrementitious matter ejected by the larva. **1860** E. ADAMS in *Trans. Philol. Soc.* 91, Frass, the rejectamenta found at the entrance of the burrows of wood-boring insects. **18..** *Board of Agric. Leaflet* No. 30. 1 If such apples are split in halves a passage can be seen leading to the ovaries or pip-centres, around which there is usually a mass of 'frass'.

frass, obs. form of FERASH.

frat (fræt), *sb.*[1] *U.S. College slang.*

a. Abbreviated form of FRATERNITY 7. Also *attrib.* **b.** A member of a fraternity.

1895 W. C. GORE in *Inlander* Nov. 64 *Frat*, 1. A fraternity. 2. A member of a fraternity. **1899** A. H. QUINN *Pennsylvania Stories* 186 But any Frat would have wanted Harington. **1902** *Chicago Record-Herald* 7 Sept. 1. 1/3 Alfalfa Eta Fraternity Frat House. **1906** 'N. NEWKIRK' *Recoll. Gold Cure Candidate* 117 The fraternities..have been pointing out that I would never amount to much as a student until I became a Frat man. **1909** *Daily Chron.* 9 Feb. 4/4 The Frat-man is one of a group of about fifteen students... Frat-houses may be expensive or cheap. **1926** *Ladies' Home Jrnl.* Nov. 12 It's a frat house. **1947** *Chicago Tribune* 2 July 19 Too bad he couldn't go to college. He doesn't know what proms and frats an' trig an' hot dates are all about. **1951** M. SHULMAN *Many Loves of Dobie Gillis* (1953) 210 Some frat men say he stole their loving cup. **1967** *Punch* 13 Sept. 377/3 The only Frank Lloyd Wright building on my campus was a frat. house.

frat, *v.* and *sb.*[2]: see FRATTING *vbl. sb.*

fratch (frætʃ), *v.* Now chiefly *dial.* [? onomatopœic.]

†**1.** *intr.* To make a harsh or strident noise; to creak. *Obs.*

c **1440** *Promp. Parv.* 76/1 Cherkyn, or chorkyn, or fracchyn, as newe cartys or plowys, *strideo*.

2. To disagree, quarrel, scold.

1714 D'CHESS MARLBOROUGH in Madresfield *Lett.* (1875) 90, I am intirely of your Mind, that it is not the D. of Marl.'s businesse to fratch. **1764** T. BRYDGES *Homer Travest.* (1797) II. 54 While thus they fratch'd, the Greeks were getting Just finish'd as the sun was setting. **1802** R. ANDERSON *Cumberld. Ball.* (1805) 44 But let them fratch on. **1863** MRS. TOOGOOD *Yorksh. Dial.*, Joseph and his brethren got together fratching, and they put him in a pit. **1868** HOLME LEE *B. Godfrey* xiii. 72 Mr. Godfrey and father can talk together for hours without fratching.

Hence **fratched** *ppl. a.* In quot. *transf.* of a horse: restive, vicious; '**fratching** *vbl. sb.*, a scolding; '**fratching** *ppl. a.* (also '**fratcheous,** '**fratchety,** '**fratchy** *adjs.*), that scolds, quarrelsome. Also **fratch** *sb.*, a disagreement, quarrel; '**fratcher**, one who quarrels, a scold.

c **1746** J. COLLIER (T. Bobbin) *View Lanc. Dial.* Wks. (1862) 52 They'd'n some o' the warst fratchingst company as eer I saigh. **1764** T. BRYDGES *Homer Travest.* (1797) II. 119 Juno, that fratching quean, pretended Her sense of smelling was offended. **1802** R. ANDERSON *Cumberld. Ball.* (1805) 23, I mun heame. Or I's git a deuce of a fratchin. **1803** *Ibid.* 64 He..aye crack'd his thoums for a bit of a fratch. **1807** J. STAGG *Poems* 6 Blackan o' Warton, he was there..An fratcheous Gweordy Barns. **1847** HALLIW., *Fratched*, restive, vicious, applied to a horse. *Ibid.*, *Fratcher*, a scold; one who brags much. *North.* **1854** DICKENS *Hard T.* II. iv, 'I ha' never had no fratch afore sin ever I were born wi' any o' my like.' **1875** WAUGH *Tufts Heather, Old Cronies* vii. Wks. 1881 IV. 285 Come, come, lads; let's ha' no fratchin'! **1875** *Whitby Gloss.* s.v., 'A fratchy body'. **1879** MISS JACKSON *Shropsh. Word-bk.*, *Fratchety*, peevish, irritable.

‖**frate** ('frate). Pl. **frati** (frati). [It.; lit. 'brother'.] A friar.

1722 RICHARDSON *Statues in Italy* 329 A Fine Madonna of the Frate (Fra Bartolomeo is always so call'd). **1823** LADY MORGAN *Salvator Rosa* ii. 48 The rules of the rigid Chartreux oblige the prior and procuratore to flagellate all the frati, or lay brothers. **1875** H. JAMES *R. Hudson* viii. 288 The frate crossed himself, opened his book, and wandered away. **1889** *Athenæum* 27 July 125/3 Every quarter had its child-counsellors..—all children, vigilant, eager, irresponsible instruments of the frate [Savonarola].

frater[1] ('freɪtə(r)). *Obs.* exc. *Hist.* Forms: 3 **freitore,** 4 **freitur, -our,** 4–5 **freytour, frature,** 4–6 **frai-, fraytour,** (5 **freytowre,** 6 **fratour**), 5–7 **frayter,** (5–6 **frai-, fraytre,** 6 **fratre, fratter, froyter**), 5– **frater.** [a. OF. *fraitur*, short for *refreitor*, repr. med.L. *refectōrium* REFECTORY.]

The eating or refreshment room of a monastery; a refectory.

c **1290** *S. Eng. Leg.* I. 286/282 Seint Domenic axede of þe freitore: ȝwat is þi dede þere. *c* **1325** *Poem Times Edw. II*, 171 in *Pol. Songs* (Camden) 331 He shal into the freitur and ben i-mad ful glad. *c* **1420** *Chron. Vilod.* 995 And after in to þe fraytre þo come he. *c* **1430** *Pilgr. Lyf Manhode* IV. xxxii. (1869) 193 Þer was þer inne cloystre and dortour, chirche chapitre and freytour. **1483** CAXTON *Gold. Leg.* 241/2 There cam two yong men of y same habite and forme whiche entrid in to yᵉ refectory or fraitour. **1556** *Chron. Gr. Friars* (Camden) 34 The church was shott in from monday unto thursday, and the servys and masse sayd and songe in the fratter. **1556** WITHALS *Dict.* 64 A fraiter or place to eate meate in, *refectorium.* **1883** *Athenæum* 24 Feb. 255/1 At Westminster..only the frater and the chapel of the infirmary have been formally dismantled.

b. *attrib.* and *Comb.*, as ***frater-wall***; **frater-house** = FRATRY 1.

1546 in W. H. Turner *Select. Rec. Oxford* 183 For takyng downe of the roof of yᵉ fraterhowse of Abynton. **1546** BALE *Eng. Votaries* I. (1550) 69 b, A roode There was upon the frayter wall in the monastery. **1844** F. A. PALEY *Church Restorers* 25 Not less than one hundred brethren dined at once in this noble frater house.

Hence † **'fraterer**, the monk who has charge of the refectory. Also in fem. form and sense.

c **1430** *Pilgr. Lyf Manhode* IV. xlv. (1869) 197 She that hath þe gorgiere is ladi and freytoureere [F. *refecturiere*]. **1483** *Cath. Angl.* 141/2 Frayturer, *refectorarius.*

‖**frater**^{2} ('freɪtə(r)). [L. *frāter* brother.]

† **1.** A friar. *Obs.*

1585 T. WASHINGTON tr. *Nicholay's Voy.* II. xi. 46 The sayd Frater hadde brought with him a great bottle. **1639** LD. G. DIGBY *Lett. Relig.* (1651) 78 As well furnished..as you may imagine some good Fraters closet in Spain..is with the works of Calvin, or Luther.

† **2.** *Cant.* (See quots.) *Obs.*

1561 AWDELAY *Frat. Vacab.* 4 A Frater goeth wyth a like Lisence to beg for some Spittlehouse or Hospital. **1622** FLETCHER *Beggar's Bush* II. i, And these, what name or title e'er they bear, Frater, or abram-man. **1673** R. HEAD *Canting Acad.* 77 Fraters are such, who with a Counterfeit Patent, beg for some Hospital or Spittle-house.

3. A brother, comrade. Also *attrib.*

1794 BURNS *Bard's Epitaph* ii, Is there a Bard of rustic song, Who, noteless, steals the crowds among, O, pass not by! But, with a frater-feeling strong, Here, heave a sigh. **18..** BLACKIE *Death Columba* 38, I am come to bless my people, Faithful fraters, ere I die.

fraternal (frə'tɜːnəl), *a.* and *sb.* [f. L. *frātern-us* (f. *frāter* brother) + -AL^{1}. Cf. F. *fraternel.*]

A. *adj.* **a.** Of or pertaining to brothers or a brother; characteristic of a brother, brotherly.

1494 FABYAN *Chron.* V. cxvi. 90 His vncle Chilperich bare towarde the sayd Guthranus not very fraternall loue. **1526** *Pilgr. Perf.* (W. de W. 1531) 170 Yᵉ prayer that fraternall charite or brotherly loue commendeth before god. **1656** COWLEY *Pindar. Odes* Olympique Ode v, Those kind pious glories do deface The old Fraternal quarrel of thy Race. **1738** GLOVER *Leonidas* I. 247 Sorrows, which fraternal love in vain Hath strove to soothe. **1850** KINGSLEY *Alt. Locke* xxxix, The great new world—new Church I should have said—of enfranchised and fraternal labour. **1874** L. STEPHEN *Hours in Library* (1892) II. i. 8 More than one modern writer has expressed a fraternal affection for Addison.

b. ***fraternal order***, a brotherhood or friendly society. *U.S.*

1889 *Kansas Times & Star* 7 June, The Iron Hall, a western fraternal order, is in session here this week. **1905** D. G. PHILLIPS *Plum Tree* 267 Local machine leaders of Scarborough's party, with corruptible labor and fraternal order leaders.

c. ***fraternal polyandry***, a form of polyandry in which brothers hold a wife in common; ***fraternal twin***, a dizygotic twin.

1896 W. CROOKE *Tribes & Castes N.-W. Prov. & Oudh* II. 445 On this fraternal polyandry, see Westermarck. **1904** H. H. WILDER in *Amer. Jrnl. Anat.* III. 389 Corresponding to this hypothesis..we may designate these two types [of twin] respectively as *Fraternal* and *Duplicate*, thus doing away with the misleading and inapplicable terms 'identical' and 'homologous' as applied to the one type, and furnishing a distinguishing term for the other, which seems thus far to have remained without a name. **1917** H. H. NEWMAN *Biol. of Twins* i. 8 Biologists have for some time recognized at least two distinct types of human twins: *fraternal* and *duplicate. Fraternal* twins may or may not be same-sexed, are usually no more alike than are brothers and sisters, and are believed to be dizygotic, derived from two fertilized eggs. **1921** E. WESTERMARCK *Hist. Human Marriage* (ed. 5) III. xxix. 116 Fraternal polyandry is more or less common in vast districts of the Himalayan region..chiefly among people of Tibetan affinities. *Ibid.* 122 The mountaineers of the Himalayas are not the only people in Northern India that practise fraternal polyandry. **1937** R. H. LOWIE *Hist. Ethnol. Theory* (1938) v. 47 Patrilineal descent results from patrilocal residence with fraternal polyandry. **1938** *Brit. Jrnl. Psychol.* Jan. 356 Comparing the separated identical twins with the fraternal twins it was found that in some of the physical characteristics,..separated identicals were more alike than fraternals. **1941** J. S. HUXLEY *Uniqueness of Man* ii. 48 Fraternal twins of like sex, though as we would expect they show considerably less resemblance than identical twins, are more alike than pairs of brothers or sisters born at different times. **1953** BEALS & HOIJER *Introd. Anthropol.* (1956) xiv. 429 The ideal pattern of marriage in Toda culture is fraternal polyandry, which dictates that when a woman marries a man she becomes, in theory at least, the wife of all his brothers, both the living and those as yet unborn.

B. *sb.* A fraternal twin.

1911 *Jrnl. Morphol.* XXII. 859 Were it possible in a number of cases to determine by examination of the placental relationships of new-born twins whether they were duplicates or fraternals..we would have facts from which we could with confidence draw conclusions. **1935** R. S. WOODWORTH *Psychol.* (ed. 10) vii. 144 The question is whether identical twins are more alike mentally than fraternals or than siblings. **1939** *Nature* 18 Nov. 870/1 The quintuplets were unlike at birth but have become..more similar than fraternals.

Hence **fra'ternally** *adv.*, in a fraternal manner.

1611 COTGR., *Fraternellement*, fraternally, brotherly. **1727** in BAILEY vol. II. **1812** *Examiner* 4 May 284/2 So fraternally gigantick were his imagination and his intellect. **1873** SYMONDS *Grk. Poets* xii. 412 Children of the earth..the Greeks loved all fair and fresh things of the open world fraternally. **1882** SIR R. TEMPLE *Men & Women of My Time* ii. 19 The sitting Director..entreated us..to think kindly, even fraternally, regarding the Natives of India.

fraternalism (frə'tɜːnəlɪz(ə)m). *rare.* [f. prec. + -ISM.] The state or condition of being fraternal.

1893 in J. H. Barrows *Parl. Relig.* II. 1548 Having proclaimed our fraternalism from this national housetop.

† **frater'nality.** *Obs. rare*$^{-0}$. [f. as prec. + -ITY.] (See quot.)

1727–36 BAILEY, *Fraternality*, brotherhood; brotherliness, brotherly Affection.

'fraternate, *v. U.S. rare*$^{-0}$. [f. L. *frātern-us* (see FRATERNAL) + -ATE.] To fraternize.

1846 in WORCESTER (citing JEFFERSON); and in mod. Dicts.

frater'nation. *U.S. rare*$^{-0}$. [f. prec.: see -ATION.] Fraternization.

1846 in WORCESTER (citing JEFFERSON); and in mod. Dicts.

† **'fraterne,** *a. Obs. rare*$^{-1}$. [a. OF. *fraterne*, ad. L. *frātern-us*, f. *frāter* brother.] Fraternal.

c **1470** HARDING *Chron.* LXXXVIII. viii, Austyn..prayed.. Of fraterne loue and due obedience, To helpe hym furth.

'fraternism. *U.S. rare*$^{-0}$. [f. L. *frātern-us* + -ISM.] Fraternization.

1846 in WORCESTER (citing JEFFERSON); and in mod. Dicts.

fraternity (frə'tɜːnɪtɪ). [a. OF. *fraternité*, ad. L. *frāternitāt-em*, f. *frāternus* pertaining to a brother: see FRATERNAL and -ITY.]

1. The relation of a brother or of brothers; brotherhood.

1390 GOWER *Conf.* II. 186 In the virgine, where he [the godhede] nome Oure flesshe and verray man become Of bodely fraternite. **1582** BENTLEY *Mon. Matrones* ii. 22 O my brother what fraternitie! O my child what delectation! **1659** PEARSON *Creed* (1839) 40 If sons, we must be brethren to the only-begotten: but being he came not to do his own will, but the will of him that sent him, he acknowledgeth no fraternity but with such as do the same. **1669** GALE *Crt. Gentiles* I. I. ii. 12 A Phenician Fable touching the Fraternitie of al men made out of the Earth.

2. The state or quality of being fraternal or brotherly; brotherliness.

1470–85 MALORY *Arthur* XVI. iii, Therfor was the round table founden and the Chyualry hath ben at alle tymes soo by the fraternyte whiche was there that she myght not be ouercomen. **1598–9** E. FORDE *Parismus* I. vi. (1636) 34 Those Out-lawes..continued a great fraternity amongst them. **1605** BACON *Adv. Learn.* II. To the King §13 There cannot but be a fraternitie in learning and illumination relating to that Paternitie which is attributed to God. **1793** BURKE *Conduct of Minority* §35 To substitute the principles of fraternity in the room of that salutary prejudice called our Country. **1844** THIRLWALL *Greece* VIII. 255 It was a treaty of friend-ship, fraternity, and alliance. **1875** JOWETT *Plato* (ed. 2) III. 106 Equality and fraternity of governors and governed.

† **3.** A family of brothers. *Obs. rare.*

a **1635** NAUNTON *Fragm. Reg.* (Arb.) 23 When there is an ample fraternity of the bloud Royall, and of the Princes of the Bloud. *Ibid.* 40 Between these two Families, there was.. no great correspondencie..there was a time when (both these Fraternities being met at Court) there passed a challenge between them.

4. A body or order of men organized for religious or devout purposes.

letters of fraternity: letters granted by a convent or an order to its benefactors entitling those named in them to a share in the benefits of its prayers and good works.

c **1330** R. BRUNNE *Chron.* (1810) 188 With [þam] were þe templers, & þer fraternite. **1362** LANGL. *P. Pl.* A. VIII. 179 Thauh thou be founden in fraternite a-mong the foure ordres. *c* **1380** WYCLIF *Wks.* (1880) 12 ȝif þei maken wyues and oþer wymmen hure sustris bi lettris of fraternite. **1401** *Pol. Poems* (Rolls) II. 29 Why be ye so hardie to grant by letters of fraternitie to men and women, that they shall have part and merite of all your good deedes? *a* **1512** FABYAN *Will* in *Chron.* Pref. 5 To the fraternytie of our Lady and seynt Anne, wᵗin the said church xiid. **1653** H. COGAN tr. *Pinto's Trav.* xxvii. 105 Like unto the fraternity of mercy among the Papists, which onely out of charity..do tend those that are sick. **1703** MAUNDRELL *Journ. Jerus.* (1732) 70 Each Fraternity have their Altars and Sanctuary. **1788** PRIESTLEY *Lect. Hist.* IV. xxv. 193 In each mitred abbey of the order of St. Benedict, some persons of the fraternity were appointed to register the most considerable events. **1851** D. WILSON *Preh. Ann.* (1863) II. IV. viii. 398 The first recluses and monks who established religious fraternities in Scotland.

5. A body of men associated by some tie or common interest; a company, guild.

c **1386** CHAUCER *Prol.* 364 An Haberdassher and a Carpenter..clothed in o liveree, Of a solempne and greet fraternitee. **1389** in *Eng. Gilds* (1870) 4 Eche broþer oþer suster þᵗ ben of þe fraternite..schal ȝeue somwhat in maintenance of þᵉ bretherhede. **1433** *E.E. Wills* (1882) 95 The fraternyte of my crafte of cokes. **1483** CAXTON *Cato* 2, I William Caxton..of the fraternyte and felauship of the mercerye. **1611** CORYAT *Crudities* 13 This dooth the fraternity of the shoemakers carry in solemne procession. *a* **1674** CLARENDON *Hist. Reb.* XV. §15 Fraternities enter'd into there for the better carrying on that Plantation. **1762** H. WALPOLE *Vertue's Anecd. Paint.* I. iv. 59 Their first charter in which they are styled Peyntours, was granted in the 6th of Edward IV, but they had existed as a fraternity long before. **1851** D. WILSON *Preh. Ann.* (1863) II. IV. viii. 442 The ancient..fraternity of Free Masons. **1870** YEATS *Techn. Hist. Comm.* 358 Scarcely a town of importance..in Italy was without its fraternity of goldsmiths.

attrib. **1671** EVELYN *Diary* 21 Sept., I din'd in the City, at the fraternity feast in yron-mongers Hall.

6. A body of men of the same class, occupation, pursuits, etc.

1561 AWDELAY (*title*), The Fraternitye of Vacabondes. **1653** WALTON *Angler* i. 5 *Auceps.* Why Sir, I pray, of what Fraternity are you, that you are so angry with the poor Otter! *Pisc.* I am..a Brother of the Angle. **1686** N. COX *Gentl. Recreat.* v. (ed. 3) 44 Some ignorant Grooms..think they are able to give Laws to all their Fraternity. **1712** HENLEY *Spect.* No. 396 ¶2 The Fraternity of the People called Quakers. **1793** BURKE *Conduct of Minority* §25 The French fraternity in that town. **1838** *Murray's Handbk. N. Germany* 91 Calais is one of those places where the fraternity of couriers have a station. **1858** FROUDE *Hist. Eng.* III. xv. 269 [Henry] was..ardently anxious to resume his place in the fraternity of European sovereigns.

7. A social association of the students or alumni of a college or university, usually having a name consisting of three Greek letters, as 'Phi Beta Kappa'. Also *attrib. U.S.*

1777 in F. W. Shepardson *Phi Beta Kappa* (1915) 9 [At the January meeting of 1777..a mode of initiation was reported.] 'I, A. B. do swear..to prove true, just, and deeply attached to this our growing fraternity.' **1844** in A. P. Jacobs *Psi Upsilon Epitome* (1884) 180 Catalogue of the Psi Upsilon Fraternity. **1879** W. R. BAIRD (*title*) Baird's Manual of American college fraternities. **1899** A. H. QUINN *Pennsylvania Stories* 59 He could not help seeing that the Fraternity men were in general the best dressed. **1901** H. D. SHELDON *Student Life* 224 In general, the fraternities dominate the smaller colleges,..although an occasional revolt on the part of the non-fraternity men sometimes occurs. **1902** J. CORBIN *American at Oxford* 54 In Balliol there are three debating clubs, and they are of course in some sense rivals. Like the fraternities in an American college, they look over the freshmen each year pretty closely. *Ibid.* 269 The fraternity houses so widely diffused in America offer almost a counterpart of the halls of the golden age of the mediaeval university. **1905** A. H. RICE *Sandy* 125 Annette counted her fraternity pins. **1927** *Sat. Even. Post* 24 Dec. 19/3 There was heart-breaking rivalry among us to secure fraternity pins from the boys who possessed them. **1967** *Punch* 13 Sept. 377/3 On my own campus, as at many middle-western universities, the fraternity system had great power and prestige.

8. Used by Galton for: the brothers (and sisters) of a family collectively.

1889 F. GALTON *Nat. Inheritance* 234 A Fraternity consists of the brothers of a family, and of the sisters after the qualities of the latter have been transmuted to their Male Equivalents. **1900** K. PEARSON *Gram. Sci.* (ed. 2) xi. 459 The intensity of parental correlation is about .3 to .5, of grandparental about .15 to .3, and of fraternal about .4 to .6, the latter correlation being somewhat reduced when the 'fraternity' consists of members of opposite sexes.

fraternization (ˌfrætənaɪ'zeɪʃən). [a. F. *fraternisation*: see FRATERNIZE and -ATION.]

a. The action of fraternizing or uniting as brothers, the state or condition of fraternity, fraternal association.

1792 *Hist.* in *Ann. Reg.* 2 They..give the kiss of fraternization to negroes. **1827** HARE *Guesses* Ser. I. (1873) 31 The Jacobins, in realizing their system of fraternization, always contrived to be the elder brothers. **1851** L. MARIOTTI *Italy in 1848*, 125 Something even approaching to a fraternisation of the people with the dreaded foreign soldiery.

transf. **1878** T. HARDY *Return of Native* I. i, The obscurity in the air and the obscurity in the land closed together in a black fraternization.

b. *spec.* The cultivation, subject to military discipline, of friendly relations by occupying troops with local inhabitants; relations with local inhabitants that contravene military discipline: used esp. of relations with German women after the war of 1939–45. Also *transf.*

[**1851**: see sense a.] **1944** *New Statesman* 7 Oct. 233/1 The administration of occupied Germany..must necessarily be 'tough'... To judge by his Proclamation No. 1 to the German people, and by his orders forbidding fraternisation, General Eisenhower is going to present his subordinate commanders and staffs with some knotty problems. **1945** *Ibid.* 21 Apr. 252/2 At present it is not clear whether rape [by occupying troops] is a crime to be punished by death, or whether it should be classified as fraternisation, for which the penalty is a fine, or non-fraternisation, which is a laudable act. **1945** *Spectator* 10 Aug. 130/1 'Fraternisation'. .. I write to challenge the implication in 'Serving Officer's' letter that to frequent brothels is to 'be human'. **1946** *Amer. Speech* XXI. 251, I once saw a soldier who had philanthropically sold a prisoner of war a pack of cigarettes for $12 charged with 'fraternization'. **1949** KOESTLER *Promise & Fulfilment* vii. 88 The famous order of the day of the G.O.C. Palestine..which..imposed a ban on fraternization with the Jews. **1969** *Guardian* 29 Aug. 1/6 In Olomouc there are still many girls..whose heads have been shaved for too intimate a fraternisation with their Russian brothers.

fraternize ('frætənaɪz, 'freɪtə-), *v.* [ad. F. *fraterniser*, ad. med.L. *frāterniz-āre*, f. *frāternus*, f. *frāter* brother: see -IZE.]

1. a. *intr.* To associate or sympathize *with* as a brother or as brothers; to form a fraternal friendship.

1611 COTGR., *Fraterniser*, to fraternize, concurre with, be neere vnto, agree as brothers. **1807** SIR R. WILSON *Jrnl.* 1 July in *Life* (1862) II. viii 290 Had Alexander not fraternized with Buonaparte. **1816** SCOTT *Antiq.* v, Too little of a democrat to fraternize with an affiliated society of the *soi-disant* Friends of the People. **1872** BAKER *Nile Tribut.* viii, We fraternised upon the spot.

b. *spec.* To cultivate friendly relations *with* (troops of an opposing army); to practise FRATERNIZATION.

1897 G. B. SHAW *Crude Criminology* in *Doctors' Delusions* (1932) 272 The whole army might..realize that they had no quarrel with the enemy and fraternize with them. **1915** *Sphere* 9 Jan. 31 It has puzzled our French allies..that while we are in a war to the death with the German Empire our soldiers and theirs should have been able to fraternise on Christmas Day... Soldiers of the rival armies exchanged sweets, cigars, and cigarettes, and sang carols and songs in unison. **1928** H. WILLIAMSON *Pathway* x. 228 The German and British staffs both issued orders, about the same time, that any man found fraternizing with the enemy, would be court-martialled. **1937** KOESTLER *Spanish Testament* iii. 72 Soldiers from the rebel ranks fraternising with and discussing the situation with the Government troops. **1944** *New Statesman* 17 June 400/1 The War Office regulation..has laid down that British soldiers must be polite to coloured [U.S.] troops, but not fraternise with them, or offer them drinks. **1946** *Britannica Bk. of Yr.* 832/2 *Fraternize*, to deal socially with members of an enemy nation, especially with women; and, *specifically*, sexually.

2. *trans.* To bring into fraternal association or sympathy; to unite as brothers. Now *rare.*

1656–81 in BLOUNT *Glossogr.* **1793** BURKE *Conduct of Minority* §7 A regular correspondence for fraternizing the two nations had also been carried on. **1794** COLERIDGE *Relig. Musings* vii, To know ourselves Parts and proportions of one wondrous whole! This fraternizes man. **1841** *Tait's Mag.* VIII. 326 Emissaries were soon sent to the West Indies to fraternize the sable citizens of all the French islands. **1856** MRS. BROWNING *Aur. Leigh* 2 It might have..reconciled and fraternised my soul With the new order.

Hence **ˈfraternized** *ppl. a.*, **ˈfraternizing** *vbl. sb.* and *ppl. a.* Also **ˈfraternizer**, one who or that which fraternizes.

1793 *Trial of Fyshe Palmer* 46 Had these fraternizing principles been only heard in France, we might have cared the less. **1795** BURKE *Regic. Peace* iv. Wks. IX. 74, I join issue with the Fraternizers, and positively deny the fact. **1817** *Ann. Reg.* 27 All societies..which extended themselves by fraternized branches. **1837** DE QUINCEY in *Tait's Mag.* IV. 72 All Whigs..all, indeed, fraternisers with French republicanism. **1858** HOGG *Life of Shelley* II. 463 The love of equality, of levelling, and fraternising. **1860** O. W. HOLMES *Prof. Breakf.-t.* ii, The grand equalizer and fraternizer is [wine]. **1880** H. JAMES *Portr. Lady* v, A gentle..old man, who combined consummate shrewdness with a sort of fraternising good humour. **1937** KOESTLER *Spanish Testament* ix. 179 And then ensued a perfect orgy of fraternising and eating. **1945** in *Amer. Speech* (1947) XXII. 147/2 (*heading*) Fraternizing in Germany. **1957** *New Yorker* 26 Oct. 144/2 The fantastic amount of fraternizing with the enemy in the Korean prison camps.

†**fraˈtration.** *Obs. rare*⁻¹. [agent-n. f. L. *frātrāre* expressive of the swelling of the breasts of boys at puberty, f. *frātr-*, *frāter* brother.]

1666 J. SMITH *Pourtract of Old Age* 117 Inflation, and Turgescency of the Seminary vessels both preparatory, and ejaculatory; commonly called Fratration.

fratriage (ˈfreɪtrɪɪdʒ). *Law.* Also **fratrage.** [ad. med.L. *frātriāg-ium*, f. L. *frātr(i)-* brother: see -AGE.] (See quots.)

1730–6 BAILEY (folio), *Fratrage*, the partition among brothers or coheirs, coming to the same inheritance or succession; also that part of the inheritance that comes to the youngest brothers. **1848** WHARTON *Law Lex.*, *Fratriage*, a younger brother's inheritance.

ˈfratriˌcidal, *a.* [f. next + -AL¹.] That kills or has killed his brother; concerned with the slaughter of a brother or of brothers.

1804 LD. TEIGNMOUTH *Mem. Sir W. Jones* (1806) 202 A fratricidal war between the learned. **1809** CAMPBELL *Gertrude Wyom.* vi, Amidst the strife of fratricidal foes. **1850** BLACKIE *Æschylus* II. 202 All gashed and gored, by fratricidal Wounds they die. **1865** KINGSLEY *Herew.* ix, Such a method would give rise to fratricidal civil wars.

fratricide¹ (ˈfreɪtrɪsaɪd, ˈfrætrɪ-). [a. F. *fratricide*, ad. L. *frātricīda*, f. *frāter* brother + *-cīdĕre*: see -CIDE 1.] One who kills his (or her) brother.

c **1450** *Mirour Saluacioun* 3955 Absolon his awen brothere sleere..ffor he a ffratricide is calde. *a* **1685** BP. WOMOCK in Southey *Comm.-pl. Bk.* Ser. II. (1849) 193 For his [Calvin's] bitter speeches Bucer gave him the title of a fratricide. **1779** FRANKLIN *Wks.* (1889) VI. 289 If you will enable the king to reward those fratricides, you will establish a precedent. **1821** BYRON *Cain* III. i, Hence, fratricide! hence-forth that word is Cain.

fratricide² (ˈfreɪtrɪsaɪd, ˈfrætrɪ-). [a. F. *fratricide*, ad. L. *frātricīd-ium*, f. *frāter* brother + *-cīdĕre*: see -CIDE 2.] The action of killing one's brother. (In *Law* also the killing of one's sister.)

1568 GRAFTON *Chron.* 3 For the which fratricide or brother murthering, he [Cain] was by the sentence of Almighty God publyshed for a vagabond. **1687** BOYLE *Martyrd. Theodora* ii. (1703) 25 Fratricide be justly listed among the blackest crimes. **1703** MAUNDRELL *Journ. Jerus.* (1721) 134 The Fratricide..is said to have been committed in this place. **1850** MERIVALE *Rom. Emp.* (1865) II. xxi. 425 The stain of fratricide could never be entirely wiped away.

†**ˈfratruel.** *Obs. rare*⁻¹. [ad. L. *frātruēl-is*, f. *frāter* brother.] (See quot.)

1656 BLOUNT *Glossogr.*, *Fratruels*..brothers children, cousin Germans.

fratry¹, **fratery** (ˈfreɪtrɪ, ˈfreɪtərɪ). Also 9 fratory. [app. f. FRATER¹ + -Y.] = FRATER¹.

1538 LELAND *Itin.* III. 119 This John Chinok buildid the Cloyster, the Dormitor, the Fratery. **1572** R. H. tr. *Lauaterus' Ghostes* (1596) 31 The scroll..at the last they found in the fratry. **1611** COTGR., *Refectouër*, a Refectuarie, or Fratrie: the roome wherein Friers eat together. **1883** *Norfolk Directory* 486 The [Grammar] School was originally kept in the fratory of the Blackfriars.

attrib. **1708** MOTTEUX *Rabelais* v. v. (1737) 18 He led us into a..Refectuary, or Fratrie-room.

b. By some modern writers applied (through etymological association with FRATRY²) as the name of a room in monastic establishments supposed to have served as the common-room of the 'brethren'; also to the chapter-house.

1786 W. GILPIN *Lakes Cumberld.* (1808) II. xx. 95 The fratry, as it is called, or chapter-house in the abbey. **1874** E. SHARPE *Archit. Cistercians* 18 The Fratry, the ordinary day-room of the monks.

ˈfratry². *Obs.* exc. *Hist.* [ad. med.L. *frātria*, *fratreia*, f. *frāter* brother; app. the word was mixed with the adoption of Gr. φρατρεία, f. φράτωρ guild-brother. Cf. FRIARY.] **a.** A fraternity, brotherhood. **b.** A convent of friars, friary.

1532 TINDALE *Exp. Matt.* vi. 16–18 The hypocrisye of the fratrye wher they eate but inuisible flesh. *a* **1571** JEWEL *On Thess.* (1611) 114 He selleth the mercies of God, the blood of the martyrs..the merits of his fratries. **1581** HANMER *Answ. Jesuit's Challenge* 6 a, Here..the merite Cell of orders, Munkry, fratry, and societies is established. **1887** BOASE *Hist. Oxford* 68 Agnellus of Pisa..built a school in the Fratry of Oxford.

fratting, *vbl. sb. slang.* [Short for FRATERNIZING *vbl. sb.*] Friendly relations between British and American soldiers and German women in the occupied parts of Western Germany after the war of 1939–45. Also **frat** *v. intr.*, to FRATERNIZE; **frat** *sb.*², a woman met by 'fratting'; also as short for 'fratting'; **ˈfratter**, one who 'frats'. Also *transf.*

1945 *New Statesman* 14 July 20/3 'Fraternisation' has become a word denoting sexual intercourse ('frats' and 'fratting' are new Army words). **1945** *Manch. Guardian* 18 July 8/4 (*caption*) Frat or Non-frat. **1946** J. IRVING *Royal Navalese* 81 *A piece of Frat*, Wren-language for any attractive young woman—ex-enemy—in occupied territory. **1946** S. SPENDER *European Witness* i. 13 At the messes most of the conversation was about 'fratting'. **1949** G. COTTERELL *Randle in Springtime* I. 8 Then, take my frat I go with, what harm did she ever do? *Ibid.* II. ii. 45 You see all the men here go fratting and it simply isn't fair on us girls... I can't see what they see in these German women. *Ibid.* v. 285 So he's married... I bet she doesn't know what a shameless old fratter you were. **1955** *Times* 11 May 15/3 To an outside observer, brotherly love is not the most striking feature of the Labour Party at this moment—apart, perhaps, from a little 'fratting' with a certain Liberal lady, with an obvious eye to the main chance. **1957** M. K. JOSEPH *I'll soldier no More* (1958) 13 'He was fratting, wasn't he?' 'Sure—dark piece, lives up the Ludwigstrasse.' *Ibid.*, Maybe he'd've rather stayed with his frat. **1965** J. FLEMING *Nothing is Number* II. iv. 78 He did frat, I mean make friends a bit with the people you're thinking of.

‖**frau** (fraʊ). [Ger.] A married woman, wife.

a **1813** A. WILSON *Foresters* Poet. Wks. (1846) 214 Each rugged task his hardy frau partakes. **1818** *Blackw. Mag.* III. 532 Some half a score of Fraus sat round a table. **1880** WEBB *Goethe's Faust* II. vi, You have left the kettle and scorched the frau.

frau, var. form of FROW.

fraud (frɔːd), *sb.* Forms: 4–6 **fraude**, **frawd(e**, 4– **fraud.** [a. OF. *fraude*, ad. L. *fraude-m* (*fraus*) deceit, injury.]

1. The quality or disposition of being deceitful; faithlessness, insincerity. Now *rare.*

? *a* **1400** *Morte Arth.* 3919 Alle for falsede, and frawde. *c* **1430** LYDG. *Min. Poems* 162 Fle doubilnesse, fraud, and collusioun. **1508** DUNBAR *Twa mariit wemen* 255, I semyt sober, and sueit, et sempill without fraud. **1599** SHAKS. *Much Ado* II. iii. 74 The fraud of men was euer so. **1672** MARVELL *Corr.* Wks. 1872–5 II. 408, I do not believe there is any fraud in him. **1718** HICKES & NELSON *J. Kettlewell* II. xxvi. 128 A Person of Simplicity without Fraud. **1827** MACAULAY *Machiav.* Ess. (1854) 36 Vices..which are the natural defence of weakness, fraud and hypocrisy.

personified. **1606** DEKKER *Sev. Sinnes* II. (Arb.) 21 Frawd (with two faces) is his Daughter. **1790** BURKE *Fr. Rev.* Wks. V. 88 The discredited paper securities of impoverished fraud, and beggared rapine.

2. a. Criminal deception; the using of false representations to obtain an unjust advantage or to injure the rights or interests of another.

c **1330** R. BRUNNE *Chron.* (1810) 128 In alle manere cause he sought þe right in skille, To gile no to fraude wild he neuer tille. **1382** WYCLIF *Mark* x. 19 Do no fraude, worschipe thi fadir and modir. **1570** B. GOOGE *Pop. Kingd.* I. (1880) 7 But safely keepes that he hath long, with frawde and lying got. **1667** MILTON *P.L.* I. 646 To work in close design, by fraud or guile, What force effected not. **1726–7** SWIFT *Gulliver* I. vi. 67 They look upon fraud as a greater crime than theft. **1829** LYTTON *Devereux* III. iii, Fraud has been practised.

b. in *Law.* *in fraud of*, *to the fraud of*: so as to defraud; also, to the detriment or hindrance of.

[**1278** *Stat. Glouc. 6 Edw. I*, c. 11 Ou par collusiun ou par fraude pur fere le termer perdre sun terme. **1292** BRITTON I. ii. §11 Ne nule manere de fraude.] **1590** SWINBURNE *Testaments* 151 The condition is reiected, as being made in fraude of mariage. **1596** SPENSER *State Irel.* Wks. (Globe) 622/2 The same Statutes..are often..wrested to the fraud of the subject. **1845** STEPHEN *Comm. Laws Eng.* (1874) II. 268 And shall not have deposited or invested in fraud of his creditors. **1848** WHARTON *Law Lex.*, *Fraud*, all deceitful practices in defrauding or endeavouring to defraud another of his known right, by means of some artful device, contrary to the plain rule of common honesty.

3. a. An act or instance of deception, an artifice by which the right or interest of another is injured, a dishonest trick or stratagem.

c **1374** CHAUCER *Boeth.* I. pr. iv. 9 (Camb. MS.) The iustice Regal hadde whilom demed hem bothe to gon into exil for hir trecheryes and fraudes. *c* **1440** *York Myst.* xxxiii. 131 If ȝe feyne slike frawdis. **1526** *Pilgr. Perf.* (W. de W. 1531) 10 b, Moo than a thousande wayes he hath by his craftly fraudes to deceyue man. **1691** HARTCLIFFE *Virtues* 317 The Pharisees..made great shews of Piety, to cover their Frauds and Rapines. **1751** JOHNSON *Rambler* No. 126 ¶4 Declaiming against the frauds of any employment. **1836** J. GILBERT *Chr. Atonem.* iii. (1852) 72 The fraud of imputing guilt to a known innocent being. **1852** MISS YONGE *Cameos* II. xxix. 312 Most of the Dauphin's followers gloried in their successful fraud and murder.

b. in *Law.* ***statute of frauds***: the statute 29 Chas. II, c. 3, by which written memoranda were in many cases required to give validity to a contract.

1678 *Act 29 Chas. II*, c. 3 *title*, An Act for Prevention of Frauds and Perjuries. **1765** BLACKSTONE *Comm.* I. 362 The frauds, naturally consequent upon this provision..produced [etc.]. **1827** JARMAN *Powell's Devises* II. 29 Which prevents the statute of Frauds from being a bar. **1858** LD. ST. LEONARDS *Handy-bk. Prop. Law* vii. 38 An instance of what is deemed a sufficient fraud to enable equity to relieve.

c. ***pious fraud***: a deception practised for the furtherance of what is considered a good object; *esp.* for the advancement of religion.

[**1563–87** FOXE *A. & M.* (1684) III. 898 Their accustomed lies, which they term Fraudes pieuses, pious beguilings.] **1678** CUDWORTH *Intell. Syst.* 319 There is too much cause to suspect that there have been some Pious Frauds practised upon these Trismegistick Writings. **1712** ADDISON *Spect.* No. 419 ¶5 Pious Frauds were made use of to amuse Man-kind. **1855** MILMAN *Lat. Chr.* (1864) II. III. vii. 143 The pious fraud of a nurse who had substituted her own child for the youngest of the Emperor.

transf. **1868** LOWELL *Willows* xxi, May is a pious fraud of the almanac, A ghastly parody of real Spring.

4. a. A method or means of defrauding or deceiving; a fraudulent contrivance; in mod. colloq. use, a spurious or deceptive thing.

1658 SIR T. BROWNE *Hydriot.* 35 They had an happy fraud against excessive lamentation, by a common opinion that deep sorrows disturbed their ghosts. **1697** DRYDEN *Virg. Georg.* IV. 575 Surprize him first, and with hard Fetters bind; Then all his Frauds will vanish into Wind. **1725** POPE *Odyss.* IV. 597 New from the corse, the scaly frauds diffuse Unsavoury stench of oil. **1782** COWPER *Progr. Err.* 17 Not all..Can..Discern the fraud beneath the specious lure. **1880** MCCARTHY *Own Times* III. 5 Many persons persisted in believing that his supposed suicide was but another fraud. **1890** L. B. WALFORD *Mischief of Monica* i, The whole place is a fraud..we can't live in a villa.

b. *colloq.* of a person: One who is not what he appears to be; an impostor, a humbug; *spec.* *U.S.* (see quot. 1895).

1850 DICKENS *Reprinted Pieces* (1866) 120 The begging-letter writer is one of the most shameless frauds and impositions of this time. **1885** F. B. VAN VOORST *Without a Compass* 12, I had called him an old fraud. **1895** *Standard Dict.*, *Fraud*..specifically..a person, firm, or corporation declared by the Postmaster-general..to be engaged in obtaining money by means of false or fraudulent pretenses, [etc.]..and therefore debarred from obtaining payment of money-orders or the delivery of registered letters.

†**5.** By Milton used in passive sense (as L. *fraus*): State of being defrauded or deluded.

1667 MILTON *P.L.* IX. 643 So glister'd the dire Snake, and into fraud Led Eve. **1671** —— *P.R.* I. 373 To all his Angels he proposed To draw the proud king Ahab into fraud, That he might fall in Ramoth.

6. *Comb.*, as ***fraud squad***; †***fraud-doing*** vbl. sb.; †***fraud-wanting*** adj.; **fraud order** *U.S.*, an official order prohibiting the delivery of letters to a firm or individual suspected of making illegal use of the postal service.

1382 WYCLIF *Dan.* XI. 21 He..shal weelde the rewme in *fraude doynge. **1905** CALKINS & HOLDEN *Art Mod. Advertising* 258 It is often impossible to prosecute the advertisers, and the most the post-office department can do is to issue what is known as a *fraud order. Such an order peremptorily and without redress stops the mail of the advertiser. **1931** C. KELLY *U.S. Postal Policy* 150 Under a 'fraud order' all mail directed to such persons or company is stamped 'Fraudulent' on the outside and returned to the sender. **1967** *Economist* 7 Jan. 49/2 There is also the *Fraud Squad, of gallant lay policemen undertaking (astonishingly well under the circumstances) inquiries that need the most sophisticated legal and financial expertise. **1971** *Times* 27 Sept. 3/3 Post Office investigators and members of Scotland Yard's Fraud Squad are searching for a gang of expert forgers. **1600** NASHE *Summer's Last Will* F 4 *Fraud-wanting honestie.

†**fraud**, *v.* *Obs.* [ad. L. *fraudāre*, f. *fraud-*: see FRAUD *sb.*]

1. *trans.* To defraud, cheat, or deceive (a person).

1551 T. WILSON *Logike* (1580) 16 Muche deceipt used to fraude one an other. **1581** MARBECK *Bk. of Notes* 231 That Christen folkes should not be frauded of the holie Sacrament. **1623** COCKERAM II, To *Deceiue*, Defeate..Fraude, Defraude.

2. To withhold (something) fraudulently.
1382 WYCLIF *Jas.* v. 4 The hijre of ȝoure werkmen, that repiden ȝoure cuntrees, that is fraudid of ȝou. **1502** *Ord. Crysten Men* (W. de W. 1506) IV. xxi. 231 If he hath frauded & retayned taxes.

3. To obtain (something) by fraud.
1573 TUSSER *Husb.* lxii. (1878) 140 Ill husbandrie waies has to fraud what he can.

Hence †**'frauding** *vbl. sb.* Also †**'frauder**, a defrauder.
c **1400** *Apol. Loll.* 54 Fraudars, misdoars, sortylogers, spousbrekars. **1515** BARCLAY *Egloges* iii. (1570) C iij/2 Their dayly murther and forsing of women, Frauding of virgins, pilling of simple men.

†**frau'dation.** *Obs.*—⁰. [ad. L. *fraudātiōn-em*, n. of action f. *fraudāre*: see prec.] 'A deceiving or beguiling' (Blount *Glossogr.* 1656).

†**'fraudelous,** *a. Obs.* [ad. F. *frauduleux, -se.*] = FRAUDULENT.
1483 CAXTON *Gold. Leg.* 313 b/1 This is but temptacion of the deuylle and fraudelous deceyte. **1489** —— *Faytes of A.* IV. i. 230 The frawdylouse deceyuer. **1491** —— *Vitas Patr.* I. l. (1495) 101 b/2 He shall be preserued and kepte from alle frawdelous decepcyons.

Hence **'fraudelously** *adv.*
1481 CAXTON *Godfrey* xcvii. (1893) 148 *heading*, How the vntrew greek latyns departed fraudelously fro the hoost.

fraudful ('frɔːdfʊl), *a.* [f. FRAUD *sb.* + -FUL.] Full of fraud, fraudulent, treacherous.
c **1400** *Apol. Loll.* 112 þus he is a þef & fraudful reuar. *c* **1450** HENRYSON *Fable Dog, Scheip & Wolf* 5 Ane fraudfull Wolf was juge that time. **1500–20** DUNBAR *Poems* xxiv. 39 To pass out of this frawdfull fary. **1602** WARNER *Alb. Eng.* X. lvii. (1612) 251 By forced Warre or fraudfull peace. **1697** DRYDEN *Virg. Past.* VI. 30 By the fraudful God deluded long, They now resolve to have their promis'd Song. **1725** POPE *Odyss* IV. 393 The fraudful horse. *c* **1750** SHENSTONE *Elegies* xxiii. 21 The fraudful maid To these lone hills directs his devious way. **1860** T. MARTIN *Horace* 183 Fraudful Carthage expiring in flame.

Hence **'fraudfully** *adv.*, in a fraudful manner.
c **1375** *Sc. Leg. Saints, Baptista* 497 Til fraudfully scho gert þe kinge..assemble hale his barne. *c* **1470** HENRY *Wallace* XI. 1056 The ayth he maid; Wallace com in his will; Rycht frawdfully all thus schawyt him till. *c* **1610** SIR J. MELVIL *Mem.* (1735) 408 The Chancellor..had left out the Rents of the Abbay of Dunfermling fraudfully. **1876** RUSKIN *Fors Clavig.* VII. lxxiii. 5 In fraudfully writing for the concealment of Fraud.

†**'frauditor.** *Obs. rare.* [badly f. FRAUD *v.*, after *creditor*, etc.] A defrauder, cheat.
1553 T. WILSON *Rhet.* (1580) 204 You have so many Frauditours..and so many Deceivers to get up your money, that thei get all to themselves.

fraudless ('frɔːdlɪs), *a.* Now *rare.* [f. FRAUD *sb.* + -LESS.] Free from fraud.
1580 H. GIFFORD *Gilloflowers* (1875) 103, I which saw such perfect shewes Of fraudlesse fayth in you appeare. **1635** J. HAYWARD tr. *Biondi's Banish'd Virg.* 64 With a sincere and fraudlesse intention. **1652** BENLOWES *Theoph.* XII. xii, I..Forgetting, and forgotten, run to fraudlesse swains.

Hence **'fraudlessly** *adv.*, **'fraudlessness**.
1848 in CRAIG; and in mod. Dicts.

'fraudsman. [f. FRAUD *sb.* + MAN; cf. *tradesman.*] A cheat, a rogue.
1615 T. ADAMS *White Devill* 38 You shall not easily discerne..between a tradesman and a fraudesman. **1958** *Times* 9 Oct. 3/5 In all, the officer questioned 32 witnesses who testified to seeing certain of the 'fraudsmen'. **1966** M. PROCTER *His Weight in Gold* xi. 93 Like nearly all fraudsmen he had a lot of personal charm. **1971** *Daily Express* 22 Mar. 13/3 You cannot..bar your mind against a fraudsman.

fraudster ('frɔːdstə(r)). [f. FRAUD *sb.* + -STER.] One who commits fraud, esp. in a business transaction.
1975 *Financial Times* 22 Dec. 2/4 The conviction of seven persons..and jail sentences on three of the leading fraudsters, disclosed a serious..gap in the criminal law. **1980** *Daily Tel.* 1 Nov. 3/5 The fiddle..collected him the title as the VAT man's biggest individual fraudster. **1985** *Times* 11 June 23/3 Another problem preventing the successful prosecution of computer fraudsters is the current state of English law.

fraudulence ('frɔːdjʊləns). [a. OF. *fraudulence*, f. *fraudulent*: see FRAUDULENT and -ENCE.] The quality or fact of being fraudulent.
1601 HEALEY *St. Aug. Citie of God* 801 Either by his violence or his fraudulence. *a* **1716** SOUTH *Serm.* (1737) V. viii. 340 It was without any fraudulence or injustice on their part. **1812** G. CHALMERS *Dom. Econ. Gt. Brit.* 229 Those who..saw great imprudence, in many, and a little fraudulence, in some. **1891** *Law Times* XC. 464/2 The Customs entry should be held to be sufficient to prove the fraudulence of the trademark.

fraudulency ('frɔːdjʊlənsɪ). ? *Obs.* [f. next: see -ENCY.] = prec.; also an instance of this.
1630 LORD *Banians* 86 The merchants grew full of fraudulency in their dealings. **1659** W. BROUGH *Manual* p. iv, To prevent..all further fraudulencies, He thinks fit to have his Name affixed to it. **1700** S. SEWALL *Diary* 18 Apr. (1879) II. 11, I press'd..that Capt. Checkley should give Daniel a Deed; that so this Fraudulency might not remain to be seen. **1792–7** GEDDES *Crit. Rem. Exod.* xii. 2 (R. Suppl.) The Egyptians were guilty of inexcusable fraudulency.
nonce-use. **1857** *Sat. Rev.* III. 272/1 His Fraudulency Mr. Redpath was visited by the Turnkey this morning.

fraudulent ('frɔːdjʊlənt), *a.* Also 5–6 -elent. [a. OF. *fraudulent*, ad. L. *fraudulent-us*, f. *fraud-*: see FRAUD *sb.* and -ULENT.]

1. Guilty of or addicted to fraud; that wrongs another person by false representations; cheating, deceitful, dishonest.
c **1430** LYDG. *Min. Poems* 197 Dispoosid of kynde for to be fraudelent. **1474** CAXTON *Chesse* 96 He that had be a theef fraudelent was maad afterward a trewe procurour. **1509** BARCLAY *Shyp of Folys* (1874) II. 91 Agayne is the seruaunt fals and fraudelent. *a* **1631** DONNE in *Select.* (1840) 204 Is God so likely to concur with the fraudulent, the deceitful man, as with the laborious, and religious? **1796** BP. WATSON *Apol. Bible* 304 Productions..which were imposed on the world by fraudulent men as the writings of the holy apostles. **1833** HT. MARTINEAU *Berkeley the Banker* I. viii, Fraudulent or careless issuers of convertible paper. **1858** LD. ST. LEONARDS *Handy-bk. Prop. Law* xxi. 163 Parliament has made fraudulent trustees answerable criminally for their acts.

†**b.** Of an animal: Crafty, deceitful. *Obs.*
1608 TOPSELL *Serpents* (1658) 676 A Chamæleon is a fraudulent, ravening and gluttonous Beast.

2. Characterized by, or of the nature of, fraud; serving the purpose of, or accomplished by means of, fraud.
1412–20 LYDG. *Chron. Troy* I. iii, He nought aduertith the menyng fraudulent. *c* **1450** *Mirour Saluacioun* 2923 Abner of Joab was slayne be fraudulent dissymuiling. **1529** MORE *Supplic. Soulys* Wks. 328/2 Their entent is fraudulent and false. **1571** *Act 13 Eliz.* c. 5 Such guylefull covenous or fraudulent Devyses and Practyses. **1646** SIR T. BROWNE *Pseud. Ep.* I. iv. 15 Fraudulent deductions, or inconsequent illations. **1771** *Junius Lett.* li. 262, I cannot..commend him for making patriotism a trade, and a fraudulent trade. **1833** J. HOLLAND *Manuf. Metal* II. 288 The detection of a fraudulent balance. **1891** *Law Times* XC. 460/2 Induced by a fraudulent prospectus to make contracts whereby he was damnified. **1893** SIR J. W. CHITTY in *Law Times Rep.* LXVIII. 429/1 The case set up is one..of fraudulent misrepresentation.

†**3.** *Path.* (After *fraudulentus* in the L. transl. of Avicenna). Deceptive. *Obs.*
1541 R. COPLAND *Guydon's Quest. Chirurg.* Tj, The woundes are somtyme composed with vnnatural mater.. somtyme vyrulent & fraudelent venymous fylthynes [*cum vlceribus sordidis putrefactis & fraudulentis*]. **1588** J. READ *Compend. Method* 101 This auaileth..to all cancrouse and fradulent [*sic*] vlcers of the legges. **1615** CROOKE *Body of Man* 30 These are ψευδοπνεύματα, Bastard, or as Auicen termeth them Fraudulent spirits.

†**4.** used as *sb.* A fraudulent bankrupt. *Obs.*
1796 *Mod. Gulliver's Trav.* 151 A scene where fraudulents may learn to thrive.

'fraudulently, *adv.* [f. prec. + -LY².] In a fraudulent manner, by fraud, with intent to defraud or deceive, dishonestly, wrongfully.
1474 CAXTON *Chesse* 120 Dyuerce offycers accuse the good peple fraudulently. **1523** LD. BERNERS *Froiss.* I. ccxxxv. 330 The kyng my husbande..is taken fraudelently. **1631** GOUGE *God's Arrows* II. vii. 142 What is violently or fraudulently gotten wilbe lavishly spent. **1786** BURKE *W. Hastings* III. ii. §9 The correspondence concerning which the said Hastings hath fraudulently suppressed. **1858** LD. ST. LEONARDS *Handy-bk. Prop. Law* v. 27 The statement must be made fraudulently, that is, with an intention to deceive. **1887** *Times* 26 Aug. 8/6 Deserters and fraudulently enlisted men who have received..a free pardon.

fraudulentness ('frɔːdjʊləntnɪs). *rare.* [f. as prec. + -NESS.] The quality of being fraudulent.
1727 in BAILEY vol. II.

‖**Frauendienst** ('fraʊəndiːnst). [Title of a work by U. von Lichtenstein (d. *c* 1275); f. G. *frauen* pl. of *frau* woman + *dienst* service.] Exaggerated chivalry towards women. Also *transf.*
[**1879** *Encycl. Brit.* X. 525/2 As the expression of all that was fantastic and ridiculous in the age of chivalry, must be mentioned the *Frauendienst* of Ulrich von Lichtenstein, a work which was written about the middle of the 13th century... The author relates the amazing tasks imposed on him by his mistress.] **1932** *Essays & Studies* XVII. 66 Chaucer is emphasizing that parody, or imitation, or rivalry ..of the Christian religion which was inherent in traditional *Frauendienst.* **1941** AUDEN *New Year Let.* III. 69 And his goal The Frauendienst of his weak soul. **1963** —— *Dyer's Hand* 212 We find neither outright sexual passion nor sentimental *Frauendienst.*

fraught (frɔːt), *sb. Obs.* exc. *Sc.* Forms: (? 4 frauh[t]), 4–5 frauȝte, *Sc.* frawcht, 5–6 *Sc.* fraucht, (5, 7 fraght), 5– fraught. [prob. a. MDu. or MLG. *vracht* (also *vrecht*: see FREIGHT *sb.*) freight, cargo, charge for transport; commonly identified with OHG. *frêht* str. fem., earnings:—OTeut. **fra-aihti-z*, f. **fra-*, FOR- *pref.*¹ + **aihti-* (= OE. *ǽht* acquisition, property: see AUGHT), f. root *aig-*: see OWE, OWN.
The irregular vocalism of the Du. word is supposed to point to adoption from Frisian. From Du. or Fris. the word has passed into all Teut. langs., Ger. *fracht*, Da. *fragt*, Sw. *frakt*; the parallel form *vrecht* has given rise to the Rom. forms: see FREIGHT.]

†**1.** The hire of a boat for the transportation of a freight or cargo; the money paid for this; the carriage or transportation of goods, usually by water: = FREIGHT *sb.* 1. *Obs.*
c **1375** *Sc. Leg. Saints, Egipciane* 482 Sad he: 'ȝa, gyf þou has macht to pay þame þi schip fraucht.' 'frawcht haf I nane, bruthyr der.' *c* **1440** *Gesta Rom.* xxiv. 90 (Harl. MS.) My fader had not to pay to the maister of the ship for the fraught. **1443** in Willis and Clark *Cambridge* (1886) I. 388 For fraught of..iij tonne fro London vn to the College at xvj *d.* the tonne. **1535** STEWART *Cron. Scot.* III. 343 In mid water at thame he askit fraucht. **1560** ROLLAND *Crt. Venus* II. 684, I knew not gif he payit fraucht or fie. **1655** GURNALL *Chr. in Arm.* xxii. §1 (1669) 311/1 This is as if the Mariners ..should fill the ship, and leave no stowage for his goods that pays the fraught. **1662** ANN KEITH in J. Russell *Haigs* (1881) 472 For his fraght be sea, 10*s.*
fig. **1637** RUTHERFORD *Lett.* (1862) I. 215 Our souls..are safe over the frith, Christ having paid the fraught.
Proverb.-**1721** KELLY *Scot. Prov.* 318 'Tarry Breeks pays no fraught;'..People of a Trade assist one another mutually.

†**2.** The cargo or lading of a ship: = FREIGHT *sb.* 2. *Obs.*
[*c* **1330** R. BRUNNE *Chron.* (1810) 74 Sir Adinoth þei slouh, & alle þat þei mot hent. Whan þei had frauh [? *read* frauht] inouh, ageyn tille Ireland went.] *a* **1400** *Sir Beues* 507 (MS. E) Marchaundes þai fonde wondyr fale And solde hym for mechel frauȝte [MS. A. auȝte]. *c* **1400** *Destr. Troy* 5384 þan fild þai with fraght all þere fuerse shippes. *c* **1470** HARDING *Chron.* CIII. viii, He had not to his fraught, But fewe persones..vnslayne. *c* **1592** MARLOWE *Jew of Malta* I. i, Bid the merchants and my men despatch, And come ashore, and see the fraught discharg'd. **1624** CAPT. SMITH *Virginia* III. iv. 54 The fraught of this Ship being concluded to be Cedar ..she was quickly reladed. **1685** DRYDEN *Thren. August.* xiii, The Bark..Charg'd with thy Self and James, a doubly Royal fraught.
fig. c **1430** *Hymns Virg.* 76 Ful of synne is my secke; To þe preest y wole schewe þat frauȝte, mi schip is chargid. **1642** MILTON *Apol. Smect.* (1851) 266 To reade good Authors.. till the afternoone be weary, or memory have his full fraught. **1671** —— *Samson* 1075 His habit carries peace, his brow defiance..His fraught we soon shall know, he now arrives.

3. *transf.* A burden, load; also *fig.* **a fraught of water**: 'two pailfuls' (Jam.). *Obs.* exc. *Sc.*
c **1450** *Cov. Myst.* (Shaks. Soc.) 137 As me semyth as be here fraught, 'ffayr chylde, lullay' sone must she syng. **1598** FLORIO, *Soma*..a fraught or charge that a beast doth carie. **1614** C. BROOKE *Ghost Rich. III*, xii, Shee long'd to see, Her burth'nous fraught; at last she brought forth me. **1640** G. SANDYS *Christ's Passion* IV. 343 The Crosses now discharged of their fraught, The People fled. **1773** J. ROSS *Fratricide* (MS.) II. 315 Having disburden'd of its fraught his breast. **1775** PRATT *Liberal Opin.* (1783) I. 41 All load this bosom with a fraught, so sore, scarce can I cater for the daily food. *a* **1810** TANNAHILL *Coggie* Poems (1846) 141 Then, O revere the coggie, sirs!..It warsels care, it fights life's fraughts. **1891** BARRIE *Little Minister* III. 21 To carry a fraught of water to the manse.

4. *Comb.*, as ***fraught money***; ***fraught-free*** adj.
1570 LEVINS *Manip.* 10/34 Fraught money, *naulum.* **1637** RUTHERFORD *Let.* 17 Sept. (1891) 516 To blow our poor tossed bark over the water fraught-free.

fraught (frɔːt), *v. Obs.* exc. in pa. pple.: see next. Forms: 5 fraght, 5–7 *Sc.* fraucht, 6– fraught. *Pa. t.* and *pa. pple.* 6–7 fraught, fraughted. [f. prec. sb.; cf. MDu. *vrachten*, Ger. *frachten*, Da. *fragte*, Sw. *frakta.*]

†**1.** *trans.* To load (a ship) with cargo: = FREIGHT *v.* 1. *Obs.*
c **1400** MAUNDEV. (Roxb.) v. 15 þai wende gladly to Cipre to fraght þer schippes with salt. **1577–87** HOLINSHED *Chron.* I. 30/1 Cesar was constreined to fraught those [ships] that he could get with a greater burden. **1633** T. STAFFORD *Pac. Hib.* II. ii. (1810) 232 Hee provided a Barke, which hee fraught with Hides. **1670** R. COKE *Disc. Trade* 30 If we.. Fraught any Strangers Ship for any of the Trades, it is forfeit with all her Goods.

†**b.** *transf.* and *fig. Obs.*
1611 SHAKS. *Cymb.* I. i. 126 If after this command thou fraught the Court With thy vnworthinesse, thou dyest. **1612** SELDEN *Drayton's Polyolb.* v. 265 note, His wife had.. fraughted her selfe with a yong one. **1637** SUCKLING *Aglaura* I. i, I have so fraught this Barke with hope, that it Dare venture now in any storme or weather.

†**c.** To hire (a vessel) for the carriage of goods or passengers. *Sc. Obs.*
1488 *Sc. Acts Jas. IV* (1814) II. 209/1 And þat naine of oure souerane lordis liegis tak schippis to fraucht vnder colour to defraud oure souerane lord. **1568** *Satir. Poems Reform.* xlvi. 62 Scho [my pynnege] will ressaif na landwart Jok. Thocht he wald frawcht hir for a croun.

†**2.** To carry or convey as freight: = FREIGHT *v.* 2. *Sc. Obs.*
c **1425** WYNTOUN *Cron.* VI. xviii. 228 Quha evyr for his frawcht wald be For caus frawchtyd owre þat se. **1568** *Satir. Poems Reform.* xlvi. 38 Bot, quhair scho findis a fallow fyne, He wilbe frawcht fre for a souss. **1581** *Sc. Act Jas. VI*, c. 120 (1597) 54 That nane of them conduct, fraucht, nor pilot onie stranger, to the said Iles.

3. To store, supply, furnish *with* (a stock of); to equip. *Obs.* exc. *arch.*
1571 GOLDING *Calvin on Ps.* lxxiii. 25 Counterfet Gods with which the comon errour or foly of yᵉ world fraughteth heaven. **1578** T. P. *Gorgious Gallery Gallant Invent.*, With phrases fine they fraught This peereles peece. **1611** SPEED *Hist. Gt. Brit.* IX. iv. §59 His new Parke at Wood-stocke, which he had fraught with all kinde of strange beasts. **1645** BP. HALL *Remedy Discontents* 61 When his better earnings have fraught his trencher with a warm, and pleasing morsell. **1878** *Masque Poets* 27 All these vessels With deadliest poisons had been fraught.

†**b.** with a person as object. *Obs.*
1570 DEE *Math. Pref.* 11 With what feats and Artes, he began to furnish and fraught him selfe. **1630** J. TAYLOR (Water P.) *Descr. Eng. Poetry* Wks. II. 247/2, I haue..found such obseruations as are fit, With plenitude to fraught a barren wit. *a* **1661** FULLER *Worthies* (1840) I. 313 So king Henry full fraught all those with wealth and rewards, whom he retained in that employment.

Hence **'fraughting** *vbl. sb.*; **'fraughting** *ppl. a.*, that forms a freight or cargo.

1598 FLORIO, *Porto*, the cariage, bringing, or fraughting of any thing. **1610** SHAKS. *Temp.* I. ii. 12 The good Ship..and The fraughting Soules within her.

fraught (frɔːt), *pple.* and *ppl. a.* Also **fraughted.** Forms: α. 4 **frauȝt**, 5 **fraght**, (**frawth**, 7 **frought**), 4– **fraught.** β. 6–8 **fraughted.** [pa. pple. of FRAUGHT *v.*]

1. Of a vessel: Laden. Also *full fraught.*

α. **13..** *Coer de L.* 2459 The drowmound was so hevy fraught That unethe myght it saylen aught. **1486** *Bk. St. Albans* L j, A shippe fraght full of hawkis. *c* **1572** GASCOIGNE *Fruites Warre* cvii. Wks. (1587) 136 The ships retire wyth riches full yfraught. **1666** *Lond. Gaz.* No. 106/1 Smaller Vessels that lay fraught for the Streights. **1756** FOOTE *Eng. Fr. Paris* Prol., Our fleets come fraught with every folly home. **1827** MACAULAY *Misc. Poems* (1860) 398 His painted bark of cane Fraught for some proud bazaar's arcades.

β. **1563** SACKVILLE *Induct. Mirr. Mag.* lxxi, And furth we launch ful fraughted to the brinke. **1623** BINGHAM *Xenophon* 113 In the meane time came a Ship from Heraclea fraughted with Barley-meale. **1668** *Lond. Gaz.* No. 261/2 The ships are said to be richly fraughted.

2. *transf.* Stored, supplied, furnished, filled, equipped *with.*

α. **1570–6** LAMBARDE *Peramb. Kent* (1826) 313 This River ..was fraught with these strong and serviceable ships. **1595** SPENSER *Hymn Heavenly Beauty* xxxii, That all the world shold with his rimes be fraught! **1605** BACON *Adv. Learn.* I. iv. § 10 The writings of Plinius..being fraught with much fabulous matter. **1669** W. SIMPSON *Hydrol. Chym.* 137 The Scarborough and Malton water are better fraught and more richly laden with its Minerals. **1671** MILTON *P.R.* III. 336 And Waggons fraught with Utensils of War. **1786** MAD. D'ARBLAY *Diary* 7 Nov., The little princess had excited her curiosity by the full-fraught pincushion. **1801** SOUTHEY *Thalaba* v. iii, A desert Pelican..now, return'd from distant flight, Fraught with the river-stream, Her load of water had disburthen'd there. **1812** CRABBE *Tales, Procrastination* 175 A silver urn with curious work was fraught.

β. **1574** tr. *Marlorat's Apocalips* 32 In these dayes, when the worlde is fraughted with so manye varlettes. **1612** BRINSLEY *Lud. Lit.* 176 For this matter of Theames it is fraughted full of the graue testimonies. **1651** *Raleigh's Ghost* 165 All the books of the Prophets are even fraughted and stored with such predictions.

b. of a person or his attributes.

α. ?**14..** *Cast. Perseverance* 94 in *Eng. Miracle Plays* (1890) 67 With ryche rentes thou schalt be frawth. *c* **1530** H. RHODES *Bk. Nurture* 312 in *Babees Bk.* (1868) 90 Or thou must take it [payne] in thy age, or be fraught full of vyce. **1605** SHAKS. *Lear* I. iv. 241, I would you would make vse of your good wisedome (Whereof I know you are fraught). **1704** SWIFT *Mech. Operat. Spirit*, A large Memory, plentifully fraught with Theological Polysyllables. **1803** S. PEGGE *Anecd. Eng. Lang.* 86 [He] returned to Oxford full fraught with Greek.

β. *a* **1541** WYATT *Poet. Wks.* (1861) 148 My heart above the brink is fraughted full of pain. **1586** J. HOOKER *Girald. Irel.* in Holinshed II. 145/1 The said lawiers..thought themselues so well fraughted with knowledge in the laws. **1647** A. ROSS *Myst. Poet.* xiv. (1675) 367 Such a father is fraughted with more griefs than Pandora's box was with mischiefs. **1798** *Missionary Mag.* No. 24. 224 From these retreats, he often returned fraughted with light.

3. fig. *fraught with*: **a.** attended with, carrying with it as an attribute, accompaniment, etc.; **b.** 'big' with the promise or menace of; destined to produce.

α. **1576** FLEMING *Panopl. Epist.* 178 Such thinges as bee intricate and fraught with difficulties. **1650** T. B. *Worcester's Apoph.* 89 It would in charity (with which it was so fully fraught) do no less. **1755** YOUNG *Centaur* vi. Wks. 1757 IV. 280 Liberty, fraught with blessings as it is, when unabused, has, perhaps, been abused to our destruction. **1840** H. AINSWORTH *Tower of Lond.* (1864) 70 This measure, which, by your own admission, is fraught with danger. **1869** LECKY *Europ. Mor.* I. i. 148 Every event is therefore fraught with a moral import.

β. **1578** *Chr. Prayers* in *Priv. Prayers* (1851) 485 This life of ours is fraughted with adversities. **1643** WITHER *Campo Musæ* 7 Those tedious Declarations, Which with more Wit then Truth, full fraughted came.

4. Distressed; distressing.

1966 *Listener* 3 Mar. 330/3 All that had gone before led me to expect an end more fraught. **1967** P. PURSER *Twentymen* i. 8 Sleep didn't often withhold her favours from me but if she did it was always when the next day was going to be particularly fraught. **1970** D. FRANCIS *Rat Race* ix. 121 Don't look so fraught... They said it was clear there now.

fraughtage ('frɔːtɪdʒ). *arch.* [f. FRAUGHT *v.* + -AGE.]

†**1.** = FREIGHTAGE 1. *Obs.*

1442 in Willis and Clark *Cambridge* (1886) I. 386 For fraughtage of x tonne..fro London vn to yᵉ College at xvj *d.* the tonne.

2. = FREIGHTAGE 2. *Obs.* exc. *arch.*

1590 SHAKS. *Com. Err.* IV. i. 87 Our fraughtage sir, I haue conuei'd aboord. **1670** MILTON *Hist. Eng.* II. Wks. (1851) 38 Broader likewise they were made, for the better transporting of Horses, and all other fraughtage. **1817** *Blackw. Mag.* I. 153 Deep-loaded to the wale with fraughtage rich. **1882** SWINBURNE *Tristram of Lyonesse* 154 But as a merchant's laden be the bark With royal ware for fraughtage.

fig. **1615** JACKSON *Creed* IV. III. vii. § 6 Now where the fraughtage, or furniture of life is precious.

†**3.** The process of lading a vessel. *Obs.*

1683 *Brit. Spec.* 84 Cæsar..ordering them [the Ships] to be low-built for the easier Fraughtage, and better haling ashore.

†**'fraughtsman.** *Sc. Obs.* In 5 frauchtisman. [f. *fraught's*, genitive of FRAUGHT *sb.* + MAN.] A freighter.

1487 *Sc. Acts Jas. III* (1814) II. 178/2 And this to be serchit be þe officiaris of þe burgh, and the heid frauchtismen of þe schip.

‖**fräulein** ('frɔɪlaɪn). [Ger.; dim. of FRAU lady, 'Mrs'.] A young lady, 'miss'. Often applied in England to German governesses.

a **1689** ETHEREDGE *Poems* Wks. (1888) 378 Now sparkling in the Fräulein's hair. **1883** MISS BRADDON *Golden Calf* i, The placid voice of the Fraulein demonstrating to Miss Mullins that..ten words out of every twenty were wrong.

fraunch, fraunge: see FRANCH *v.*

Fraunhofer ('fraʊnhəʊfə(r)). The name of Joseph von *Fraunhofer* (1787–1826), Bavarian optician and physicist, used *attrib.* or in the possessive to designate certain phenomena investigated by him, as ***Fraunhofer('s) diffraction***, diffraction in which the diffraction pattern is a linear function of the variation in phase across the diffracting aperture or object; ***Fraunhofer('s) lines***, the dark lines in the spectra of the sun and other stars; ***Fraunhofer spectrum***, a solar or stellar spectrum containing Fraunhofer lines.

1837 Fraunhofer's lines [see LINE *sb.*² 8 c]. **1840** J. F. W. HERSCHEL in *Phil. Trans. R. Soc.* CXXX. 17 The orange-red rays, or the less refrangible half of the portion from C to D in Fraunhofer's spectrum. **1843** *Phil. Mag.* 3rd Ser. XXII. 361 The spectrum which results is given in great purity, and Fraunhofer's lines are quite apparent. **1888** *Encycl. Brit.* XXIV. 430/1 (*heading*) Fraunhofer's diffraction phenomena. **1905** R. W. WOOD *Physical Optics* vii. 161 (*heading*) Mathematical treatment of Fraunhofer diffraction phenomena. **1937** *Discovery* Apr. 109/2 The Fraunhofer spectrum line, C, of hydrogen in the red at wavelength 6563 Ångström units (also known as Hα). **1963** R. W. DITCHBURN *Light* (ed. 2) viii. 291 A Fraunhofer diffraction pattern is formed in the focal plane of the lens. **1966** *McGraw-Hill Encycl. Sci. & Technol.* XIII. 267 Of the 92 natural elements, 64 are represented in the Fraunhofer spectrum. **1968** R. A. LYTTLETON *Myst. Solar Syst.* iv. 141 When a comet is quiescent,..the detectable light consists of a continuum crossed by the familiar solar Fraunhöfer [*sic*] lines.

fraward, -wart, obs. and Sc. f. FROWARD *a.*

frawn (frɔːn). Also 8 **fraghan**, 9 **frauchan**, **fraun**, **frughan**; 9– **fraughan.** [a. Ir. *fraochan.*] The Irish popular name of the BILBERRY.

1726 THRELKELD *Synopsis Stirp. Hibern.*, *Vaccinia nigra vulgaria*..They grow in wet boggy Ground..the poor Women gather them in Autumn and cry them about the streets of Dublin by the Name of Fraghan. **1859** W. S. COLEMAN *Woodlands* (1862) 92 By the Irish they [Bilberries] are called 'Frawns'. **1869** P. KENNEDY *Evenings on Duffrey* xix. 208 They might..gather..fraughans in the woods. **1878** BRITTEN & HOLLAND *Plant-n.* s.v., Frughans, *Vaccinium Myrtillus*..The old Irish name. **1892** J. BARLOW *Bog-Land Studies* 69 Wee frauns. **1906** *Temple Bar* June 553 They trod the heather and fraughan beneath them. **1914** 'G. A. BIRMINGHAM' *Lost Tribes* xi, Under their shelter fraughan bushes nestled, their black fruit already ripening.

†**'fraxate**, *v. Obs.*⁻⁰ [f. L. *fraxāre*, 'vigiliam circuire' (Festus): see -ATE.] (See quot.)

1623 COCKERAM, *Fraxate*, to goe view the watch.

fraxetin ('fræksɪtɪn). *Chem.* A substance obtained along with glucose by digesting fraxin with dilute sulphuric acid.

1864 in WATTS *Dict. Chem.* **1889** *Watts' Dict. Chem.*, *Fraxetin* $C_{10}H_8O_5$..occurring in horse-chestnut bark.

fraxin ('fræksɪn). *Chem.* [f. L. *frax(inus)* ash + -IN.] (See quot.)

1864 in WATTS *Dict. Chem.* **1889** *Watts' Dict. Chem.*, *Fraxin* $C_{16}H_{18}O_{10}$..A substance occurring in the bark of the common ash, and also, together with æsculin, in the bark of the horse-chestnut.

fraxi'nella. Also 7–8 **fraxinel(l.** [mod.Lat., dim. of L. *fraxinus* ash. Cf. F. *fraxinelle.*] A name for cultivated species of dittany, *esp. Dictamnus Fraxinella.*

1664 EVELYN *Kal. Hort.* (1729) 205 May..Flowers in Prime or yet lasting..Digitalis, Fraxinella. **1688** R. HOLME *Armoury* II. 100 Solomons Seal, of some called St. Johns Seal..or Fraxinell. **1712** tr. *Pomet's Hist. Drugs* I. 41 White Dittany or Fraxinella. **1824** MISS MITFORD *Village* Ser. I. (1863) 122 Old-fashioned durable flowers, jessamine, honeysuckle, and the high-scented fraxinella.

attrib. **1892** SYMONDS in *Pall Mall G.* 15 Aug. 3/1 Amidst the fraxinella bushes and the chestnut copse.

fray (freɪ), *sb.*¹ Also 6 **frai(e**, 7 **frey.** [aphetic f. AFFRAY, EFFRAY. Cf. FRAY *v.*¹]

1. A feeling of fear; alarm, fright, terror. Also in phrase *to take a* or *the fray.* Cf. AFFRAY *sb.* 2. *Obs.* exc. *Sc.*

c **1340** *Cursor M.* 4775 (Trin.) Whenne iacob was moost in fray God him coumfortide. **1398** TREVISA *Barth. De P.R.* XVI. xxix. (Tollem. MS.), It [the stone Crisolitus]..helpeþ nyȝte frayes and dredes. **1432–50** tr. *Higden* (Rolls) I. 243 That theire hertes scholde not be in fray or feere to beholde bloode. **1513** DOUGLAS *Æneis* XI. xii. 51 Al suddanly the Latynis tuke ane fray..and fled away. **1559–66** *Hist. Estate Scot.* in *Wodr. Soc. Misc.* (1844) 61 The Friers takeing the fray—began to dispose the best of their goods. *a* **1649** DRUMM. OF HAWTH. *Sonn.* viii, Nor shepherd hastes (when frays of wolves arise) So fast to fold. **1699** DAMPIER *Voy.* II. I. 148 Thus that Fray was over, and we came ashore again: recovered of the fright we had been in. **1819** W. TENNANT *Papistry Storm'd* (1827) 157 Whan the hail Hellespont reboundit And ky on Ida's taps confoundit Ran down the hills for fray.

†**2.** An assault, attack. Cf. AFFRAY *sb.* 1. *Obs.*

c **1430** *Hymns Virg.* 14 Thou woldist bleede for mannis nede, And suffre manye a feerdful fray. **1432–50** tr. *Higden* (Rolls) II. 95 Hamfare, þat is, a fray made in an howse. *c* **1575** *Durham Depos.* (Surtees) 300 After that Crampton had maid a fraye of the said Martyn, one Robert Johnson cauld for the constable, to carry them to the stoks.

3. A disturbance, *esp.* one caused by fighting; a noisy quarrel, a brawl; a fight, skirmish, conflict.

[**1382** *Durh. Halm. Rolls* (Surtees) 171 De quodam fray in campo de Walleshond per homines de Tynnemouth ad effusionem sanguinis.] *c* **1420** *Chron. Vilod.* 105 And all þe ladyes..Of þis grete fraye þe wheche þye sie and herden, weren Sore agast. **1523** LD. BERNERS *Froiss.* I. xvi. 16 There began a great fraye bitwene some of the gromes and pages of the strangers, and of the archers of Inglande. **1609** ROWLANDS *Knaue of Clubbes* 3 Fleete-street fraies, when Prentices With Clubs did knocke thee downe. **1698** FRYER *E. India & P.* 46 The Vice-Admiral..left not off till Night parted the Fray. **1799** NELSON 12 Sept. in Nicolas *Disp.* IV. 11 The Turks are returned to Constantinople having had a fray with the Sicilians. **1839** THIRLWALL *Greece* VI. 157 He immediately charged into the thickest of the fray. **1878** BAYNE *Purit. Rev.* iv. 126 They were always eager for the fray.

Proverb. a **1631** DONNE *Serm.* xl. (Alford) 306 The first blow makes the Wrong, but the second makes the Fray. **1676** HALE *Contempl.* I. 242 It is a true Proverb, It is the second blow makes the fray.

b. *transf.* (esp. 'a war of words').

1702 C. MATHER *Magn. Chr.* III. II. i. (1852) 356 That fray between that Bishop, and Laud, the Bishop of London. **1851** BRIGHT *Sp. Eccles. Titles Bill* 12 May, The noble Lord ..commenced the fray by his celebrated letter. **1884** RITA *Vivienne* II. iv, I'll wait and see you adorned for the fray.

†**c.** A din, noise, stir. *Obs.*

?*a* **1550** *Dunbar's Poems* (S.T.S.) *Freiris of Berwik* 197 Ȝone is Symone that makis all this fray. **1573** TUSSER *Husb.* lxxvii. (1878) 168 Where window is open, cat maketh a fray. **1632** *Lithgow Trav.* x. 468 The Toune was in Armes, the Bells ringing..people shouting, and Drummes beating..I asked him what the fray was?

†**4.** *to stand at fray*: to 'show fight'. *Obs.*

1727 BRADLEY *Fam. Dict.* s.v. *Badger-hunting*, If the Hounds..undertake the Chase before he Earths, he will then stand at fray, like a Bear, and make most incomparable Sport.

5. *Comb.*, as *fray-maker*, *-making.*

1532 *Act 5 & 6 Edw. VI*, c. 4 § 3 They may be known as *Fray-makers and Fighters. **1643** PRYNNE *Sov. Power Parl.* IV. 28 Constables may by the Law..imprison peace-breakers, fray-makers, riotors, and others. **1884** A. GRIFFITHS *Chron. Newgate* I. vi. 233 Any church brawler.. might be branded with the letter F, as a fraymaker and fighter. *a* **1553** UDALL *Royster D.* I. i. (Arb.) 12 All the day long is he facing and craking Of his great actes in fighting and *fraymaking.

b. Special comb., as †**fray-bell**, an alarm-bell formerly sounded on the occasion of a tumult. Also (perh. f. the verb-stem); †**fray-boggard**, a scarecrow; **fray-bug**, an object of fear; a bogy, spectre (whence *fray-bug* vb. *trans.*, to scare as with a fray-bug; to terrify).

1864 J. RAINE *Priory of Hexham* I. p. cxxiv, The common-bell beginning to peal; and then the great *fray-bell of the monastery boomed in answer. **1535** COVERDALE *Baruch* vi. 69 Like as a *frayboggarde in a garden off Cucumbers kepeth nothinge, euen so are their goddes of wod, of syluer & golde. **1555** SAUNDERS in Foxe *A. & M.* (1563) 1043/2 Howe lothe is this loyteryng sluggard to passe foorth in Goddes pathe. It fantasyeth forsooth much feare of *fray bugges. **1592** STUBBES *Motive Good Wks.* 123 The broching of this fraibugge or scar-crow [Purgatory]. **1671** S. CLARKE *Mirr. Saints & Sinn.* (ed. 4) I. 485 Event proveth that these are no Fray-Bugs. **1546** BALE *Eng. Votaries* II. *Conclusion* (1550) 118 They *fraybugged them with the thunderboltes of their excommunycacyons.

fray, *sb.*² [f. FRAY *v.*²] The result of fraying; a frayed place.

1630 MIDDLETON *Chaste Maid* I. i, Your purest Lawnes haue Frayes, and Cambrickes Brackes. **1648** HERRICK *Hesper.* 91 'Tis like a Lawnie-Firmament as yet Quite dispossest of either fray or fret.

fray (freɪ), *v.*¹ [aphetic f. AFFRAY, EFFRAY *v.*]

1. *trans.* To affect with fear, make afraid, frighten. Cf. AFFRAY *v.* 2. *Obs.* exc. *poet.*

a **1300**, **1330** [see FRAYED *ppl. a.*]. **13..** *E.E. Allit. P.* B. 1553 For al hit frayes my flesche þe fyngres so grymme. **14..** *Sir Beues* 2396 (MS. M.) The dragon kest vp a yelle, That it wolde haue frayed the deuyl of hel. **1531** TINDALE *Exp. 1 John* (1537) 14 That..we shulde exalte our selues ouer you ..frayenge you with the bugge of excommunicacyon. **1604** BP. W. BARLOW *Confer. Hampton Crt.* in *Phenix* (1721) I. 154 A Puritan is a Protestant fray'd out of his Wits. **1742** SHENSTONE *Schoolmistress* 149 And other some with baleful sprig she 'frays. **1832** J. BREE *St. Herbert's Isle* 98 He frayed the monsters with his bugle's sound. **1850** BROWNING *Xmas Eve & Easter Day*, My warnings fray No one, and no one they convert.

absol. **1496** *Bk. St. Albans, Fishing* C j, And when she hath plumyd ynough: go to her softly for frayenge. **1590** SPENSER *F.Q.* II. xii. 40 Instead of fraying they themselves did feare.

2. To frighten or scare away. Also *to fray away, off,* or *out.* Cf. AFFRAY *v.* 4. *Obs.* exc. *arch.*

1526 *Pilgr. Perf.* (W. de W. 1531) 55 God hath ordeyned ..a specyall remedy, wherwith we may fray them away. **1533** TINDALE *Supper of Lord* cv b, Why fraye ye the commen people from the lytteral sense with thys bugge? **1586** MARLOWE *1st Pt. Tamburl.* v. ii, Are the turtles frayed out of their nests? **1613** PURCHAS *Pilgrimage* VI. i. 560 It [the Basilisk]..frayeth away other serpents with the hissing. *a* **1716** SOUTH *Serm.* (1744) X. 232 Can he fray off the vultur from his breast? **1825** SCOTT *Betrothed* xxiii, It is enough to fray every hawk from the perch. **1867** MANNING *Eng. & Christendom* 154 We should have to answer to the Good Shepherd, if so much as one of His sheep were frayed away from the fold by harsh voices.

absol. **1542** BECON *David's Harp* Wks. 1564 I. 147 Exhort unto virtue. Fray away from vice.

b. *simply.* To drive away, disperse.

1635 QUARLES *Embl.* I. xiv. (1718) 57 Thy light will fray These horrid mists. **1655** H. VAUGHAN *Silex Scint.* II. *Death* (1858) 205 Thy shades..Which his first looks will quickly fray.

†**3.** *intr.* To be afraid or frightened; to fear. *Obs.*

a **1529** SKELTON *Image Hypocr.* 509 Yow fray not of his rod. **1535** STEWART *Cron. Scot.* I. 606 Thai had no caus to dreid Nor ȝit to fray. **1638** R. BAILLIE *Lett.* (1775) I. 80 This and the convoy of it make us tremble for fear of division.. Thir thingis make us fray.

†**4.** *trans.* To assault, attack, or make an attack upon; to attack and drive *off*; *rarely* to make a raid on (a place). *Obs.*

c **1400** *Destr. Troy* 5237 The grekys..segh the kyng.. With fele folke vppon fote þat hom fray wold. *a* **1440** *Sir Degrev.* 237 Thus the forest they fray, Hertus bade at abey. *c* **1575** *Durham Depos.* (Surtees) 286 Neither this examinate nor his brother..ever did lay in wayt nor frayd off the said Sir Richard Mylner.

5. *intr.* To make a disturbance; to quarrel or fight. Also, to make an attack *upon*. ***to fray it out***: to settle by fighting. *Obs.* exc. *arch.*

c **1460** *Towneley Myst.* (Surtees) 147 Why shuld we fray? **1465** *Paston Lett.* No. 512 II. 205 My Lord of Suffolks men ..fray uppon us, this dayly. **1494** FABYAN *Chron.* IV. lxxi. (1811) 50 Conan Meridok with a certayne of knyghtes of his affynyte, was purposed to haue frayed with the sayd Maximus, and to haue distressed hym. **1566** DRANT *Horace's Sat.* III. B v b, For foode and harboure gan they fray..with clubbes. **1570** *Song* in *Wit & Sci.* etc. (Shaks. Soc.) 90 The sonne is up with hys bryght beames, As thoughe he woolde with the now fraye, And bete the up out of thy dreames. **1657** HOWELL *Londinop.* 337 A gaol..for such as should brabble, fray, or break the peace. **1889** *Univ. Rev.* Sept. 38 Sooner than fray it out thou wouldst retire.

Hence ˈ**fraying** *vbl. sb.* and *ppl. a.*

c **1450** *Merlin* 339 Arthur was also fallen to grounde with the frayinge that thei hurteled to-geder. **1548** UDALL, etc. *Erasm. Par. John* x. 1 They doe their endeuour to maynteyn their tyrannie with disceytes, frayinges, wiles [etc.]. **1562** J. HEYWOOD *Prov. & Epigr.* (1867) 194 Of fraying of babes. **1577** HANMER *Anc. Eccl. Hist.* (1619) 394 But only avoideth this clause..as a fraying ghost.

fray (freɪ), *v.*^{2} [ad. F. *frayer*:—OF. *freiier* to rub:—L. *fricāre*: see FRICTION.]

I. To rub; to come into collision.

1. *intr.* Of deer: (see quot. 1756). Also *trans.* in ***to fray their heads.***

1576 TURBERV. *Venerie* 69 The old harts do fray their heads upon the yong trees. **1583** STANYHURST *Æneis* I. (Arb.) 23 Chiefe stags vpbearing croches high from the antlier hauted On trees stronglye fraying. **1756** WHALLEY *Notes on B. Jonson's Wks.* V. 103 A deer is said to fray her head when she rubs it against a tree to renew it. **1884** JEFFERIES *Red Deer* vii. 112 Towards the end of July—they are then fraying, rubbing the velvet off their new horns against the trees.

2. *trans.* To rub away, wear through by rubbing; to ravel *out* the edge or end of (something woven or twisted); occasionally, to chafe or irritate by friction.

1710 STEELE *Tatler* No. 245 ¶2 Four striped Muslin Night-Rails very little frayed. **1727** BRADLEY *Fam. Dict.* s.v. *Clear Starching*, Pull out your pinner, holding it by the Edging, with dry and clean hands lest you fray it. **1840** DICKENS *Old C. Shop* xvii, The very bell-rope in the porch was frayed into a fringe. **1873** A. DOBSON *Vignettes in Rhyme*, *Sundial* xii, The frequent sword-hilt had so frayed his glove. **1884** J. F. GOODHART *Dis. Childr.* iv. (1891) 77 The polypus [should be] hooked down, and its pedicle frayed through the nail [of the finger].

fig. **1861** DICKENS *Gt. Expect.* II. 1 The stage coach.. got into the ravel of traffic frayed out about the Cross Keys.

b. *intr.* Of material: To become frayed, to ravel out. Also with *out*.

1721 BAILEY s.v., *To fray*, to fret as Cloth does by Rubbing. **1798** JANE AUSTEN *Northang. Abb.* (1833) I. iii. 14, I do not think it will wash well; I am afraid it will fray.

c. To rub *against*.

1884 JEFFERIES *Red Deer* ii. 29 Dry dark heather continually fraying against my knees.

†**3.** *trans.* To bruise. Also, to deflower. *Obs.*

c **1460** *Play Sacram.* 455 And w^{t} ow^{r} strokys we shalle fray hym as he was on ye rode. **1565** GOLDING *Ovid's Met.* IX. (1593) 220 Whom being then no maid (For why the God of Delos and of Delphos had her fraid).

†**4.** *intr.* To clash, come into collision. *Obs.*

c **1450** *Merlin* 594 Ther myght a man haue sein..many a shafte and shelde frayen to-geder. **1483** CAXTON *Gold. Leg.* 424/2 Whan he sawe..how therthe onelye by frayeng of his staffe was dyched aboute.

II. 5. [A recent adoption from Fr.] *trans.* To clear, cut through, force (a path, way).

1849 E. E. NAPIER *Excurs. S. Africa* II. 81 The narrow thorny paths, frayed by the elephant and the rhinoceros. **1869** BARING-GOULD *Origin Relig. Belief* (1878) I. vii. 135 Man had to fray his road through a wilderness of fable before he could reach the truth.

Hence ˈ**fraying** *vbl. sb.*

1375 BARBOUR *Bruce* x. 653 Thai..Herd bath stering, and ek speking, And [alswa fraying] of armyng.

†**fray**, *v.*^{3} *Obs. rare.* [short f. DEFRAY *v.*] *trans.* To defray; also *absol.*

1450 *Plumpton Corr.* 39 Nothing will they pay, without your said tenants will fray with them. **1631** MASSINGER *Emperor East* IV. iv, The charge of my most curious and costly ingredients frayed..I shall acknowledge myself amply satisfied.

†**fray**, *v.*^{4} *Obs. trans.* ? To fry. Also *absol.*

c **1450** *Two Cookery-bks.* II. 89 Caste hem and the oynons into þat potte with the drawen pesen, and late hem boile togidre..And then take faire oile and fray. **1558–68** WARDE tr. *Alexis' Secr.* 28 a, Havyng frayed and consumed it in hote water, give it to the woman to drinke.

Hence †**frayed** *ppl. a.*

c **1450** *Two Cookery-bks.* II. 93 Take figges..and cast a litull fraied oyle there-to.

fray, obs. f. and Sc. var. of *fra*, FRO.

frayed (freɪd), *ppl. a.*^{1} *arch.* [f. FRAY *v.*^{1} + -ED^{1}.] (The *pple.* passing into *ppl. a.*) Afraid, frightened.

a **1300** *Cursor M.* 5814 A neddir it was, and he was fraid. **1330** [see AFRAID 1]. *c* **1470** HENRY *Wallace* VI. 580 The fute men..On frayt folk set strakis sad and sayr. **1523** LD. BERNERS *Froiss.* I. clxix. 206 All the countre was so frayed, that euery man drue to the fortresses. *a* **1555** LYNDESAY *Tragedy* 185 Be sey and land sic reif without releif, Quhilk to report my frayit hart afferis. **1608** TOPSELL *Serpents* (1658) 795 The Ape is as fraid thereof, as it is of the Snail. **1827** HOOD *Mids. Fairies* vii, Like a fray'd bird in the grey owlet's beak. **1866** G. MACDONALD *Ann. Q. Neighb.* xii. (1878) 238 With a curve in her form like the neck of a frayed horse.

Proverb. **1534** WHITINTON *Tullyes Offices* I. (1540) 36 More frayde than hurte. **1546** J. HEYWOOD *Prov.* (1867) 9 He shall let fall all, And be more fraid then hurt.

b. quasi-*sb.* in phr. *for fraid* = for fear. (Cf. FERD *sb.*^{2})

1536 GRAY in *State P. Hen. VIII*, II. 355 Duetie to my Maister, and force, constraynyth me therto, for frayd of worse to comme herafter. **1889** *N.W. Linc. Gloss.* s.v., *For fraid*..'for fear'.

Hence ˈ**frayedly** *adv.*, ˈ**frayedness**.

1530 PALSGR. 222/2 Fraydnesse, *esmoy*. **1560** ROLLAND *Crt. Venus* II. 347 All for frayitnes he fell in extasie. **1570** *Henry's Wallace* IV. 244 Frayitlie [*MS.* ferdely] thai rais, that war in to thai waynis.

frayed (freɪd), *ppl. a.*^{2} [f. FRAY *v.*^{2} + -ED^{1}.] Rubbed, worn by rubbing, ravelled out. Also with *out*.

1814 SCOTT *Ld. of Isles* v. iii, The ivy twigs were torn and fray'd. **1824** LANDOR *Johnson & Tooke* Wks. 1846 I. 155/1 The leather..will look queerly in its patches on the frayed satin. **1859** TENNYSON *Enid* 296 His dress a suit of fray'd magnificence. **1865** DICKENS *Mut. Fr.* I. xiv, The frayed ends of his dress. **1870** MORRIS *Earthly Par.* III. IV. 107 Not good it is to harp on the frayed string. **1884** *Western Daily Press* 25 Apr. 7/5 The front of the bonnet is composed of frayed silk. **1889** *John Bull* 2 Mar. 149/3 The satin train had a thick ruche of frayed-out silk bordering it all round.

fig. **1896** *Daily News* 11 June 3/1 This novelty is getting just a trifle frayed at the edges. **1934** *Discovery* Dec 345/1 Super-sensitivity to sounds normally arises with frayed nerves due to worry or illness. **1966** J. PORTER *Sour Cream* i. 7 The grandiose schemes of my youth had got more than a bit frayed round the edges.

Hence ˈ**frayedness**, frayed condition.

1893 *Cassell's Fam. Mag.* June 500/2 He hands over [the rope] to us in all its frayedness.

†ˈ**frayer.** *Obs.* [f. FRAY *v.*^{1} + -ER^{1}.] **a.** One who frightens *away*. **b.** One who makes a disturbance; a fighter, rioter.

1494 FABYAN *Chron.* VII. 583 Both frayers were taken & brought vnto the countour in the Pultry. **1543** BECON *Policy War* Wks. 1564 I. 143 They be the aungels of God..the exhorters vnto vertue, the frayers away from vice, &c.

fraying (ˈfreɪɪŋ), *vbl. sb.* [f. FRAY *v.*^{2}]

1. Of a deer: The action of the vb. FRAY. Also that which is rubbed off in fraying; 'peel'.

1576 TURBERV. *Venerie* 243 Then he rubbeth of that pyll and that is called fraying of his head. **1637** B. JONSON *Sad Sheph.* I. ii, For by his Slot, his Entries, and his Port, His Frayings, Fewmets, he doth promise Sport. **1825** SCOTT *Betrothed* xvii, To track mischief from light words, as I would find a buck from his frayings.

b. *Comb.*: **fraying-post**, †**-stock**, the tree or other object against which a deer frays.

1674 N. COX *Gentl. Recreat.* I. (1677) 68 All Stags as they are burnish'd, beat their Heads dry against some Tree or other, which is called their *Fraying-post. **1884** JEFFERIES *Red Deer* vii. 113 A fir, which was used as a fraying post. **1576** TURBERV. *Venerie* 69 When the huntsman hath founde his *frayingstocke, he must marke the heyght where the ende of his croches..hath reached. **1630** J. TAYLOR (Water P.) *Nauy Land Ships* Wks. I. 93/1 Pores, and Entryes, Abatures, and Foyles, Frayen-stockes.

2. Ravellings.

1855 DICKENS *Dorrit* I. xxix, Picking threads and fraying of her work from the carpet.

†ˈ**frayment.** *Obs.* [f. FRAY *v.*^{1} + -MENT.] Disturbance.

1549 CHALONER *Erasm. on Folly* C j, Pan, with his sodaine fraiments and tumults bringeth age over all thyng.

†**frayne**, *sb.*^{1} *Obs.* Also **freyn**. [a. OF. *fraisne*, *fresne* (Fr. *frêne*):—L. *fraxinus*.] An ash.

c **1325** *Lai le Freine* 225 The Freyns of the asche is a freyn After the language of Breteyn. *c* **1380** *Sir Ferumb.* 1035 Vnder a tre of frayne. *c* **1490** CAXTON *Ovid's Met.* x. iv, Lawrers..ffresnes, Cornyliers.

†**frayne**, *sb.*^{2} *Obs.* ? A mark or streak on a horse. Hence †**frayned** *a.*, ? streaked; brindled.

1539 *Richmond Wills* (Surtees) 16, I bequeth to my brother..a great franeid meire. **1550** *Will of R. Maddox* (Somerset Ho.), My frayned gray troting gelding. **1614** MARKHAM *Cheap Husb.* 4 His colour would euer be milke white with red fraynes.

†**frayne**, *sb.*^{3} *Obs. rare*$^{-1}$. [? f. OF. *fraindre* to break; cf. REFRAIN.]

1555 ABP. PARKER *Ps.* A ij, Observe the frayne: the ceasure marke To rest with note in close.

frayne, freyne, *v. Obs.* exc. *dial.* Forms: 1 **freȝnan, friȝnan, frínan**, 3 **fræinen, -ien**, *Orm.* **fraȝȝnenn**, (**frayny**, *south.* **vraini**), 3–5 **frein(e(n**, 4–5 **frain(e, fran(e, -ayn(e, -eyn(e**, (4 **freygne**, 5 **frayen, fraynne**), 9– **frayn**. Also *pa. t.* 4 **frain**. [A Com. Teut. str. vb. inflected in ME. as wk.; OE. *freȝnan*, *friȝnan*, *frínan* (pa. t. *fræȝn*, *frán*, pl. *fruȝnon*, *frúnon*, also wk. (*ȝe*)-*fræȝnade*) = OS. *fregnan* (pa. t. *fragn*), ON. *fregna* (pa. t. *frá*), Goth. *fraihnan* (pa. t. *frah*); the Teut. root **freh-*, *freg-* is found also in OE. *fricȝan* to ask, *fricca* herald, *freht* (= **freoht*, *friht*) oracle, and (with different vowel-grade) in OS. *frâgôn* (Du. *vragen*), OHG. *frâgên*, *frâhen* (MHG. *vrâgen*, mod.Ger. *fragen*); further (with metathesis), OHG. *fergôn* to ask, beg. The OAryan root is **prek-*, *prk-*, found e.g. in L. *precārī* to PRAY; and with *-sk-* suffix in L. *poscĕre* (:—**porksk-*), Ger. *forschen* to demand.]

1. *trans.* To make inquiry of (a person) about (something); = ASK *v.* 2–6 (which see for constructions).

Beowulf (Z.) 1319 (He) fræȝn ȝif him wære æfter neod-laðum niht ȝetæse. *a* **800** *Corpus Gloss.* C 581 (Hessels) *Consulo*, friȝno. *c* **900** tr. *Bæda's Hist.* IV. iii. (1890) 268 Hine fruȝnon and ascodon his ȝeferan, for hwon he þis dyde. *c* **1000** *Ags. Ps.* cxxxviii[i]. 20 þone fælan ȝeþanc frine me syþþan. *c* **1205** LAY. 30734 Brien hine gon fræine of his fare-coste. *a* **1300** *Cursor M.* 7193 Sua lang sco frain him, þat bald, þat suilk a gabing he hir tald. *c* **1325** *Metr. Hom.* (1862) 151 And this ermyt bigan to frain At Satenas, hou he hafd spedde. **1377** LANGL. *P. Pl.* B. VIII. 3 And frayned ful oft of folke þat I mette, If ani wiȝte wiste where dowel was at Inne. *c* **1420** *Sir Amadace* (Camd.) xvii, Sir Amadace franut hur the marchandes name. *a* **1450** *Le Morte Arth.* 678 And sithe he freyned also swithe, 'How fares my lady brighte'? **1501** DOUGLAS *Pal. Hon.* I. xi, I..fast at thame did frane Quhat men thay wer? **1522** SKELTON *Why nat to Court* 397 Of you I wolde frayne Why come ye nat to court. **1555** ABP. PARKER *Ps.* xxviii. 65 Theyr myndes disdayne Gods actes to fraine. **1575–6** *Durham Depos.* (Surtees) 270 The said Umphra frayned the said Thomas. **1592** WARNER *Alb. Eng.* VII. xxxvii. (1612) 181, I, musing, frain'd her meaning. **1703** THORESBY *Let. to Ray* (E.D.S.) *Frayn*, to ask. *Lanc.* **1803** W. S. ROSE *Amadis* 160 Frayn'd by the knight, they told, a beautious maid..Was borne a prisoner.

b. *intr.* To make inquiries; to inquire *at* or *of* (a person); to ask *after* (a person), *of* = about (a thing).

c **900** tr. *Bæda's Hist.* IV. xix. [xxi]. (1890) 316 Swa swa me seolfum frinendum..Wilferþ biscop sæȝde. *c* **1200** ORMIN 19628 þa Farisewwess haffdenn sket Off Cristess dedess fraȝȝnedd. *c* **1275** *O.E. Misc.* 92/73 þagh þu frayny after freond, ne fyndestu non. *a* **1300** *Cursor M.* 3849 þai fran-nid o þar frendes fare. *a* **1420** HOCCLEVE *De Reg. Princ.* 3745 Thus of hir he gan to axe and freyne. *c* **1420** *Sir Amadace* (Camd.) lvi, If he frayne oȝte aftur me..Say him my sute is quite. *c* **1430** *Syr Tryam.* 1099 The kyng at hym can frayne. *c* **1450** HOLLAND *Howlat* 261 He franyt Of thar counsall in this caiss. *c* **1475** *Rauf Coilȝear* 227 He began to frane farther mair. **1568** A. SCOTT *Poems* (S.T.S.) xxxiv. 45 ȝe preiche, ȝe fleich, ȝe frane.

2. a. *trans.* To ask for (a thing); to request (a person) *to* do something. **b.** *intr.* To ask, request. Const. *for*.

13.. *E.E. Allit. P.* A. 129 Fortune fares þer as ho fray-nez. *c* **1425** WYNTOUN *Cron.* VIII. vi. 39 For þis as scho fraynyd fast, He consentyd at þe last. *c* **1430** *Syr Gener.* (Roxb.) 485 He can him frayn Al the sothe him to sayn.

Hence †ˈ**frayning** *vbl. sb.*

a **1300** *Cursor M.* 27371 þe preist bi-gin þan his franyng. *c* **1375** *Sc. Leg. Saints*, *Adrian* 30 þe kynge..one þis wyis mad franyng. *c* **1394** *P. Pl. Crede* 27 By a fraynyng forþan faileþ þer manye. **1536** BELLENDEN *Cron. Scot.* (1821) II. 207 At last, be lang framing of his wife, he schew quhat schame the king had done to him.

frayturer: see FRATERER.

Frazerian (freɪˈzɪərɪən), *a.* Of or pertaining to Sir James George *Frazer*, Scottish anthropologist (1854–1941), or his work. Also as *sb.*, a follower or adherent of Frazer.

1932 *Times Lit. Suppl.* 1 Dec. 915/1 The King of the Shilluk has long been entitled to rank as a classical case of the Frazerian embodiment of the tribal luck whose duty it is to vacate his office by death before the vigour that he must pass on..can suffer diminution. **1937** A. HUXLEY *Ends & Means* v. 38 Two peoples may have what is, according to Frazerian ideas, the same custom. **1962** *Listener* 16 Aug. 258/2 We learnt that an untrained laboratory worm which eats a trained one takes over its responses—though..this principle doesn't apply to human beings, so that any eager Frazerian contemplating a supper of Bronowski *à la mode* had better think again. **1968** *Int. Encycl. Soc. Sci.* V. 552/1 Many anthropologists thus became 'enslaved', as Seligman was and as Malinowski once claimed to have been, by Frazerian anthropology. **1970** E. Leach *Lévi-Strauss* i. 19 The ethnographic observations on which Lévi-Strauss, like his Frazerian predecessors, has chosen to rely.

frazil (freɪ'zɪl). [? A Canadian use of F. *fraisil*, coal-dust, cinders.] In *Canada* and *U.S.* Ice formed at the bottom of a stream, anchor-ice. Also *attrib.*

1888 *Montreal Gaz.* 17 Mar. (Cent.), It has been suggested that it may be due to the accumulation of frazil or anchor-ice. **1893** *Boston* (Mass.) *Youth's Companion* 9 Feb. 71/4 The greater the surface of the swift open water, the greater the quantity of frazil made in a minute, hour, or day. Every open rapid is, in 'zero weather', a frazil-factory.

frazzle ('fræz(ə)l), *v. slang.* or *colloq.* (orig. *dial.*). Also **frazle.** [Cf. FASEL *v.*, and FRAY *v.*[2]] *trans.* To fray, wear out, tear to rags or ribbons. *lit.* and *fig.* Also *intr.* Hence **'frazzled (-*out*)** *ppl. a.*; **'frazzlings,** ravellings.

a **1825** Forby *Voc. E. Anglia, Frazle*, to unravel or rend cloth. *Frazlings*, threads of cloth, torn or unravelled. **1872** *Congress. Globe* 30 May, App. 577/3 The ends of the switches were all frazzled. **1893** *Amer. Missionary* (N.Y.) Dec. 418 One's garments get frazzled in the grass; one's mind and body and spiritual sense sometimes become frazzled, torn to pieces, good-for-nothing. **1895** *Nebraska State Jrnl.* 23 June 3/1 Everyone believed that Thomas would..plant the frazzled banner of the distillers in its place. **1896** J. C. Harris *Sister Jane* 344 He's the genuine article, guaranteed not to rip in the seams or frazzle at the sleeves. **1912** J. H. Moore *Ethics & Educ.* 34 Many a frazzled-out member of society owes his failure in life to no greater misdemeanour than the mere failure to make connection with his calling. **1912** J. London *Son of Sun* viii. 285 Loose ends of rope stood out stiffly horizontal, and, when a whipping gave, the loose end frazzled and blew away. **1912** *Chambers's Jrnl.* Mar. 194/1 For bed a mud *kang* with a frazzled mat on it. **1927** J. Devanny *Old Savage* 43 His fight had left him 'frazzled', as he expressed it. **1960** *Guardian* 6 Jan. 1/7 The insistence of frazzled parents that merry-making and goodwill to men have got to stop somewhere.

frazzle ('fræz(ə)l), *sb.* [f. the vb.] The state of being frazzled or worn out; esp. in phr. (orig. U.S.) *to a frazzle* in fig. expressions denoting complete exhaustion or extinction.

1865 Gordon in W. C. Church *Ulysses Grant* (1897) 318 Tell General Lee, I have fought my corps to a frazzle. **1880** J. C. Harris *Uncle Remus* (1881) xi, Brer Fox dun know Brer Rabbit uv ole, en he know dat sorter game done wo' ter a frazzle. **1894** *Columbus* (Ohio) *Dispatch* 2 Jan., Two years ago his nerves were worn to a frazzle over an attempt made to levy a tax. **1905** *Washington Star* 24 Nov. 22 The Becham machine whipped Blackburn to a frazzle, giving him the first real defeat he had ever experienced. **1908** *Westm. Gaz.* 3 Nov. 7/3 Mr. Roosevelt, when asked for his opinion on the result, said, 'We have got them beaten to a "frazzle".' **1916** *Daily Colonist* (Victoria, B.C.) 29 July 4/4 As a briber and corrupter, Mr. Brewster..has everyone else 'beat to a frazzle'. **1927** *Daily Express* 20 June 3/4 They run motor races on their sea wall at Lowestoft. They..have Canute beaten to a frazzle. **1935** T. E. Lawrence *Let.* 15 Feb. (1938) 856 Some of those lovely worm-driven water hose clips... They beat [*name omitted*] clips to a frazzle. **1937** *Daily Herald* 3 Feb. 15/6 Listens with such inscrutability that he's got the Chinese licked to a frazzle. **1966** C. Bermant *Diary of Old Man* 111 There he goes again, coughing himself to a frazzle.

freak (fri:k), *sb.*[1] [Not found before 16th c.; possibly introduced from dialects, and cognate with OE. *frícian* (*Matt.* xi. 17) to dance.]

1. A sudden causeless change or turn of the mind; a capricious humour, notion, whim, or vagary.

1563 *Mirr. Mag., Jane Shore* ii, Fortunes frekes. **1590** Spenser *F.Q.* I. iv. 50, I feare the fickle freakes..Of Fortune. **1632** Marmion *Holland's Leaguer* II. i, Her I'll make A stale, to take this courtier in a freak. **1661** Cowley *Disc. Govt. O. Cromwell* Wks. 1710 II. 664 Now the Freak takes him and he makes seventy Peers of the Land at one clap. **1712** Steele *Spect.* No. 427 ¶2 Sometimes in a Freak [she] will instantly change her Habitation. **1812** H. & J. Smith *Rej. Addr.* 79 Amid the freaks that modern fashion sanctions, It grieves me much to see live animals Brought on the stage. **1867** Lady Herbert *Cradle L.* vi. 158 Ibrahim Pasha, in a freak of tyrannical fury, turned every Mahometan out of the city. **1891** E. W. Gosse *Gossip Libr.* v. 56 One of the grimmest freaks that ever entered into a pious mind.

2. The disposition of a mind subject to such humours; capriciousness.

1678 R. L'Estrange *Seneca's Mor.* (1702) 54 It is the Freak of many People, they cannot do a good Office, but they are presently boasting of it. **1822** Hazlitt *Table-t.* Ser. II. xviii. 380 Several..have ruined their fortunes out of mere freak. **1848** C. Bronte *J. Eyre* xiii, A decent quiescence under the freak of manner, gave me the advantage.

3. A capricious prank or trick, a caper.

Cf. the earlier synonym REAKS.

1724 Gay *Quidnuncki's*, Thus, as in giddy freaks he bounces, Crack goes the twig, and in he flounces! **1840** Barham *Ingol. Leg., Jackdaw*, The priests, with awe, as such freaks they saw, Said: The Devil must be in that little Jackdaw. **1865** Trollope *Belton Est.* i. 3 Expelled from Harrow for some boyish freak.

4. a. A product of irregular or sportive fancy.

1784 Cowper *Task* v. 130 Thy most magnificent and mighty freak [an ice-palace], The wonder of the North. **1856** Emerson *Eng. Traits, Wealth* Wks. (Bohn) II. 74 Strawberry Hill of Horace Walpole, Fonthill Abbey of Mr. Beckford, were freaks.

b. (More fully ***freak of nature***, = *lusus naturæ*): A monstrosity, an abnormally developed individual of any species; in recent use (*esp.* U.S.), a living curiosity exhibited in a show.

1847 A. M. Gilliam *Trav. Mexico* 230 Many were..the freaks of nature that I beheld in the singular formations of the rocks. **1883** *Daily News* 11 Sept. 2/5 An association of..natural curiosities usually exhibited at booths..called the 'Freaks' Union', the word freaks being an abbreviation of the term 'freaks of nature' by which these monstrosities are described. **1891** C. James *Rom. Rigmarole* 130 The two freaks were retired into private life for purposes of refreshment.

c. One who 'freaks out' (FREAK *v.* 3); a drug addict (see also quots.).

1967 *Atavar* (Boston) 1–14 Sept. 17/1 The life expectancy of the average speed-freak..is less than five years. *Ibid.* Dec. 4/1 Some of us are beginning to wonder who are the 'freaks' in this world and who are the 'straight' people. **1969** R. R. Lingeman *Drugs from A to Z* 79 *Freak*... One who prefers a certain kind of drug, as in *acid freak* or *meth freak*... By extension, one who is obsessed with a certain way of thinking as in 'political freak'. **1970** C. Major *Dict. Afro-Amer. Slang* 55 *Freak*, one who practices socially unaccepted forms of sexual love; strong believer in something. **1971** *Oz* May 7/2 Its hills and valleys are full of hippies, and freaks, camping along the river beds. **1971** *It* 9–23 Sept. 5/5 Power freaks like Ted Heath and union leader Vic Feather. **1971** *Ink* 19 Oct. 7/1 An ideological community of 25 freaks plus guru in Copenhagen. *Ibid.* 7/3 Far from there being any noticeable improvement in the quality of relationships as practised among freaks, I would say there has been a distinct deterioration compared even with the most miserable standards of the straight world.

d. With qualifying word or phrase: one who shows great enthusiasm for the activity, person, or thing specified, as ***health freak, train freak***, etc.; an aficionado. Cf. BUFF *sb.*[2] 6 b and FIEND *sb.* 4 c. *colloq.* (orig. *U.S.*).

1908 *Court of Appeals, State of N.Y.* III. 455 He had a camera. Evidently from the evidence in this case he was one of your kodak freaks. **1946** B. Ulanov *Duke Ellington* xix. 270 'I'm a train freak,' Duke says. **1959** L. Lipton *Holy Barbarians* i. 39 He looked more like one of those beachcomber Nature Boy health freaks than a real hipster. **1967**, etc. [see sense 4 c above]. **1976** *Southern Even. Echo* (Southampton) 18 Nov. 15/7, I'm not a Freud freak, but..you can only stay with them until they are school age. **1977** J. D. MacDonald *Condominium* xxxvi. 354 It's just another one of these so-called scientific studies of doom from another one of the ecology freaks. **1986** P. Booth *Palm Beach* vii. 124 Boy, are you exercise freaks into punishment.

5. *Comb.*, as ***freak-storm***; ***freak-doing*** adj.; also quasi-*adj.* to denote something abnormal or capriciously irregular; **freak show**, at a fair, etc.: a sideshow featuring freaks (sense 4 b).

1862 R. H. Patterson *Ess. Hist. & Art.* 470 The freak-doing Aswins. **1887** E. R. Pennell in *Contemp. Rev.* Mar. 400 *note*, What I should call penny peep, or rather freak, shows. **1898** *Daily News* 17 Mar. 6/5 'The yellow kid', a personification of 'freak' or sensational journalism. **1907** *Westm. Gaz.* 26 Sept. 7/2 The boats which have been built for this race of recent years are freak boats pure and simple. **1907** *Daily Chron.* 5 Oct. 4/4 Conditions in America seem particularly favourable to the propagation of freak religions. **1908** *Westm. Gaz.* 7 Mar. 8/1 The production of freak fruits, such as white blackberries..and seedless oranges. **1928** [see COME *v.* 25 d]. **1939** G. Greene *Lawless Roads* i. 30 A freak show in a little booth. **1951** R. Campbell *Light on Dark Horse* x. 141 These Berghens take a delight in freak-flying. **1963** *Times* 8 May 16/3 The freaker the hands before the goulash the more normal the distribution after the redeal. **1968** A. Taylor *Honour in Shallow Cup* i. 8 They'd been having freak storms there.

Hence **'freakdom**, the region or domain of caprice; **'freakery**, freaks collectively; **'freakful** *a.*, freakish, capricious; **'freaksome** *a.* = prec.

1820 Keats *Lamia* I. 230 By some freakful chance. **1854** *Chamb. Jrnl.* III. 175 The Puck of Fancy, that freaksome, tricksy wight. **1873–4** A. J. Ellis in *Trans. Philol. Soc.* 15 Was it ['scrumptious']..a pure fancy of the moment, with nothing but absurdity and freakdom to generate it? **1876** J. Weiss *Wit, Hum. & Shaks.* i. 5 What a wide range of Nature's curious freakery a forest has!

freak (fri:k), *sb.*[2] [f. FREAK *v.*] A fleck or streak of colour.

1870 Lowell *Study Wind.* (1871) 215 These quaint freaks of russet [in an old book] tell of Montaigne.

freak (fri:k), *v.* [f. FREAK *sb.*[1]; the word (in sense 1) seems to have been formed by Milton.]

1. *trans.* To fleck or streak whimsically or capriciously; to variegate. Usually in pa. pple.

1637 Milton *Lycidas* 144 The pansy freaked with jet. **1726–46** Thomson *Winter* 814 And dark embroun'd, Or beauteous freakt with many a mingled hue. **1834** Beckford *Italy* I. 80 Collecting dianthi freaked with beautifully varied colours. **1880** Swinburne *Studies in Song* 15 The very dawn was..freaked with fire.

fig. **1803** W. Taylor in *Monthly Mag.* XVI. 221 The anxious elaboration of a style freaked with allusions.

2. *intr.* To practise freaks; to sport, gambol, frolic.

1663 [see FREAKING *ppl. a.*]. *a* **1820** J. R. Drake *Culprit Fay* xxvi. 1836 Then glad they left their covert lair, And freaked about in the midnight air.

3. ***to freak out*** (occas. without *out*): to undergo an intense emotional experience, to become stimulated, to rave, esp. under the influence of hallucinatory drugs. Also *trans.*, to cause (a person) to be aroused or stimulated in such a way. (Also in more trivial uses.) So **freaked-out** *a.*, affected thus; **freaking-out** *vbl. sb.*

1965 *Village Voice* (N.Y.) 2/1 (Advt.), Grand Opening!!! Freak with the Fugs!!! The East Side's Most Infinite Hallucination in Person. **1966** *Life* 25 Mar. 33/4 When my husband and I want to take a trip together..I just put a little acid in the kids' orange juice..and let them spend the day freaking out in the woods. **1967** *Oxf. Mail* 3 Mar. 4 'Freak out, baby,' goes the latest rebel war whoop... Frank Zappa ..answers: 'On a personal level, freaking out is a process whereby an individual casts off outmoded and restricted standards of thinking, dress and social etiquette.' **1967** *Atavar* (Boston) 7–13 July 13/2 (*heading*) Freaked-out in the Federal Building. **1968** *It* 1–14 Nov. 8/4 Suppose..that total freedom could be granted now, today. Have you thought of what it would mean? Freedom to freak-out, yes; freedom to do your thing, sure. **1969** *Gandalf's Garden* IV. 9/1 He was the first guy I had ever met who used his music to influence people, to turn them on, or freak them out. **1969** *Daily Tel.* 21 Nov. 4/7 Some 'freaked-out' teenagers cannot move, let alone sit up straight when they attend classes. **1970** *It* 27 Feb.–13 Mar. 11/1 Aage leaps about and shouts at them and freaks them out. **1970** *Times* 5 May 9/3 The full African look..complete with enormous freaked out 'Hair' wig. **1970** *Nature* 23 May 704/1 One question asked the respondents how often they had seen other people 'freak out', that is, have intense, transient emotional upsets.

freak, var. form of FREKE, *Obs.*, man.

† **'freaking,** *ppl. a. Obs.* [f. FREAK *v.*] Addicted to freaks, freakish.

1663 *Flagellum, or O. Cromwell* (1672) 140 After 4 daies time (in which Feak and his Freaking Partisans were almost run from their wits). **1665** Pepys *Diary* 25 Jan., He told me what a mad, freaking fellow Sir Ellis Layton hath been.

freakish ('fri:kɪʃ), *a.* [f. FREAK *sb.*[1] + -ISH.]

1. Full of freaks, characterized by freaks, capricious, whimsical.

1653 H. More *Conject. Cabbal.* (1713) 186 Without any such freakish conceits. **1673** Wycherley *Gentl. Dancing-Master* I. i, An ill-contrived, ugly, freakish fool. **1712** Steele *Spect.* No. 514 ¶4 The most wild and freakish garb that can be imagined. **1784** Cowper *Tiroc.* 605 His freakish thoughts. **1791** W. Bartram *Carolina* 249 We found our companions busily employed in securing the young freakish horses. **1812** W. Tennant *Anster F.* I. viii, Her trees of tinsel kiss'd by freakish gales. **1863** Geo. Eliot *Romola* I. iii, Look at that sketch: it is a fancy of..a strange freakish painter. **1870** Lowell *Study Wind.* (1886) 40 Our freakish climate. **1875** Poste *Gaius* I. (ed. 2) 122 The synthesis of title and right in Civil law may be freakish and capricious.

2. Of the nature of a freak, curious, grotesque.

1805 Scott *Last Minstr.* II. xi, The ozier wand In many a freakish knot had twined. **1827** Hood *Mids. Fairies* lxxxviii, He..had stuck His freakish gauds upon the Ancient's brow.

Hence **'freakishly** *adv.*, **'freakishness.**

1678 *Trans. Crt. Spain* 26 Let us admire the freakishness of worldly affairs. *a* **1714** J. Sharp *Wks.* (1754) V. ii. 48 Such a piece of folly and freakishness. **1727** Bailey vol. II, Freakishly. **1827** Scott *Jrnl.* 27 Apr., That freakishness of humour which made me a voluntary idler. **1873** Symonds *Grk. Poets* vii. 204 But gods intervene mechanically and freakishly, like the magicians in Ariosto or Tasso. **1888** *Repentance P. Wentworth* II. 340 You..are fully persuaded I did it out of sheer freakishness.

'freak-out. [f. the vbl. phr. *to freak out*: see FREAK *v.* 3.] An intense emotional experience, a 'rave-up', esp. one resulting from the use of hallucinatory drugs. (Also in more trivial uses.)

Quot. 1749, an isolated use, is better analysed as a use of the sb. *freak* (sense 3) plus the verbal phr. *to have out* 'to bring to a conclusion' (cf. OUT *adv.* 7 b).

[**1749** J. Cleland *Mem. Woman Pleasure* II. 198 She had had her freak out, and had pretty plentifully drowned her curiosity in a glut of pleasure.] **1966** *Daily Tel.* 10 Aug. 13/3 The tape-recorder picked up the horrifying moans and shrieks of one man who had made 33 pleasurable 'trips' with LSD and was encountering his first 'freakout' or bad LSD experience. **1967** *Spectator* 11 Aug. 158/1 This morning he had got in quick while the others were still half asleep from paper rounds or recovering from Sunday night freak-outs. **1968** L. Deighton *Only when I Larf* iv. 48 That helicopter trip is a futuristic freak-out. **1968** J. Ironside *Fashion Alphabet* 194 *Mop* (also called *Freak-out*)... Introduced in 1967 by the way-out young... A wild looking bush with curls, worn by both girls and boys. **1970** *Toronto Daily Star* 24 Sept. 1/9 They give the impression 'freak outs' happen every week.

freaky ('fri:kɪ), *a.* [f. FREAK *sb.*[1] + -Y[1].]

1. = FREAKISH.

1824 *Blackw. Mag.* XV. 453 Instead of..clipsome hedges and freaky meadows..his faded eye could only fall upon horrid bars and walls. **1891** *Ibid.* CXLIX. 107/2 Theodora was..a slippery, freaky little creature.

2. In senses corresponding to FREAK *v.* 3. Also as quasi-*adv.*

1966 Young & Hixson *LSD on Campus* p. vi, I think it would do everybody good to take LSD. But soon it's gonna get pretty freaky. **1967** A. K. Baer et al. *Study 18 LSD Users on Sunset Strip* 208 Everybody in the car was positive he was on an acid trip. He was freaky. **1969** *Observer* 7 Dec. 25/1 'Live freaky, die freaky,' was the judgment of a neighbour in Benedict Canyon on last August's Sharon Tate massacre. **1969** *Gandalf's Garden* VI. 10/3 *Freaky-straights*, either ordinary-looking people with fanatical ideas on one particular theme, like the 'Flat Earth Society', or people whose appearance is very weird but whose minds are channelled into one usual line of thought... The lack of light in the eyes betrays the freaky-straight.

Hence **'freakiness.**

1886 T. Roosevelt *Hunting Trips* 347 No other species seems to show such peculiar 'freakiness' of character, both individually and locally.

† **fream**, *sb. Obs.*$^{-0}$ 'Arable land worn out of heart, and laid fallow till it recover' (Phillips 1671).

Phillips appends this definition to his explanation of *Freameth* (see next); Kersey 1706 refers it, prob. rightly, to *Fream*. The word is otherwise unknown.

fream (friːm), *v.* Also 6 (? *erron.*) **froam**. [Of uncertain origin.

Perh. an artificial term suggested by L. *fremĕre* to roar (F. *frémir*, to shudder, is too remote in sense). But quot. 1876 suggests that it may, with unexplained irregularity, represent OAngl. *hrēma* = WS. *hrīeman*, to cry out.]

intr. To roar, rage, growl: *spec.* of a boar.

1576 TURBERV. *Venerie* 238 A Bore freameth. **1583** STANYHURST *Æneis* II. (Arb.) 51 Hee freams, and skrawling to the skye brays terribil hoyseth. *Ibid.* IV. (Arb.) 100 Hudge fluds lowdlye freaming from mountayns loftye be trowlling. **1660** HOWELL *Parly of Beasts* viii. 113 He [a man turned into a boar] did..extreamly froam at his own Country-men. **1674** N. COX *Gentl. Recreat.* I. (1677) 11 Terms for their Noise at Rutting time..A Boar Freameth. **1711** PUCKLE *Club* 90 An hart bellows, a buck groyns..a boar freams. [**1876** *Whitby Gloss.*, *Freeam* or *Reeam*, to scream.]

† **frean**, *v. Manège. Obs.* (See quot.)

1607 MARKHAM *Caval.* VI. 28 If he will lie downe and tumble, which horsmen call Freaning, you shall not onely giue him leaue, but..helpe him to wallow ouer and ouer.

† **freare**. *Sc. Obs.* = FRAIL *sb.*^{1}

1565 *Aberd. Reg.* V. 25 (Jam.) Fywe half frearis of feggis. *a* **1575** *Diurn. Occurrents* (1833) 292 Ane frear of feggis. **1582–8** *Hist. James VI* (1804) 166 Quhilk was convoyit to the castell of Edinburgh in a freare of fegges.

freat, obs. form of FRET.

freathe (friːð), *v. Sc.* [? repr. OE. (*á-*)*fréoðan* to foam (pa. pple. *-froðen*: cf. FROTH *sb.*).]

1. *intr.* To froth or foam.

1785 BURNS *Sc. Drink* x, O rare! to see thee fizz an' freath I' th' lugget caup!

2. *trans.* To make to froth or lather.

1725 RAMSAY *Gentle Sheph.* I. ii. song v, We're not yet begun To freath the graith.

freche, obs. form of FRESH.

† '**frechedly**, *adv. Obs. rare*$^{-1}$. [? f. *frech* var. of FRECK + -ED^{1} + -LY^{2}.] Greedily.

c **1450** MYRC 1332 Ete or dronke to frechedely.

freck, frack (frɛk, fræk), *a. Obs.* exc. *Sc.* Forms: α. 1 frec, 3 frech, *south.* vrech, 4 freck, -kk(e, 4–5 frek(e, (5 freik), 8–9 *Sc.* freck. β. *Sc.* 6–7 frak, 6–9 frack. [Com. Teut.: OE. *frec, fric, fræc* = OHG. *freh* covetous, greedy (MHG. *vrech* courageous, Ger. *frech* bold, insolent), ON. *frekr* greedy (Sw. *frack* daring, Da. *fræk*), Goth. (*faihu*) *friks* (fee-)greedy, covetous. Cf. FRIKE *a.*, which seems to have been confused with this word.]

1. Desirous, eager, prompt, quick, ready. Const. *gen.* (OE. only) *to* with *sb.* or *vb.* in *inf. to make freck*: to make ready.

a **1000** *Boeth. Metr.* viii. 15 Hwæt hi firenlusta frece ne wæron. *c* **1205** LAY. 9419 To heo eoden alle afoten & swiðe freche weoren. *a* **1300** *Cursor M.* 5198 To bidd hast now es nan sa frek. **1352** *Pol. Poems* (Rolls) I. 68 Doghty men.. That war ful frek to fight. *c* **1450** *St. Cuthbert* (Surtees) 4441 He was freke his name to frayne. **1560–78** *Bk. Discipl. Ch. Scot.* (1621) Pref., Frack to preach the Gospell in Scotland, as in another Antiochia. *a* **1572** KNOX *Hist. Ref.* Wks. 1846 I. 104 The merchantis maid frack to saill. **1819** W. TENNANT *Papistry Storm'd* (1827) 119 Hae ye your man by acht o'clock, A' frack and furnish't for the shock. **1820** SCOTT *Abbot* xxxiv, You know whether I am so frack as the serving-man spoke him.

b. In bad sense: Greedy, gluttonous; also, keen for mischief.

c **950** *Lindisf. Gosp.* Matt. xi. 19 Heonu monn fric. *a* **1225** *Ancr. R.* 128 þe vox is ec a wrecche vrech best, and fret swuðe wel mid alle. *c* **1275** *O.E. Misc.* 75 Ac sathanas þe frecche þe saule wule drecche, Hwanne he agult habbeþ.

2. Lusty, strong, vigorous.

1500–20 DUNBAR *Poems* liii. 23 On all the flwre thair was nane frackar. **1569** in Napier *Mem.* (1793) 127 Thou art the frackest felow amang them. **1820** SCOTT *Abbot* xxxiv, Unlikely men to stay one of the frackest youths in Scotland of his years.

freck (frɛk), *sb. rare*$^{-1}$. [? Shortened from FRECKLE *sb.*] = FRECKLE.

1866 *Intell. Observ.* No. 53. 349 Burnt-umber spots and frecks.

† **freck, frack**, *v.*^{1} *Sc. Obs.* [f. the adj.] *intr.* To move swiftly or nimbly.

1513 DOUGLAS *Æneis* I. i. 62 As the Troianis frakkis our the fluide. *Ibid.* v. iv. 101.

freck (frɛk), *v.*^{2} [? Shortened from FRECKLE *v.* or var. of FREAK *v.*] *trans.* To mark with spots or freckles; to dapple.

1621 G. SANDYS *Ovid's Met.* II. (1626) 43 There shee a bloodlesse Statue sate, all freckt. **1821** CLARE *Vill. Minstr.* II. 3 Eve put on her sweetest shroud..Freck'd with white and purple cloud. **1869** LOWELL *Cathedr.* Poet. Wks. (1870) 25 The painted windows, frecking [ed. 1890 IV. 47 freaking] gloom with glow.

'**frecken**, *sb. Obs.* exc. *dial.* Forms: 4 frekne, 5 frakyn(e, 5–6 frakene, 6 fracin, frackne, freken, -in, 7 frechon. [a. ON. *freknur* pl. (Sw. *fräkne*, Da. *fregne*).] A freckle.

c **1386** CHAUCER *Knt.'s T.* 1311 A fewe freknes in his face y-spreynd. **14..** *Nom.* in Wr.-Wülcker 680/3 *Hec lenticula*, a frakyn. **1545** RAYNOLD *Byrth Mankynde* IV. vi. (1634) 200 Frekens..may be taken away by often anoynting them with the oyle of Tartar. **1621** BURTON *Anat. Mel.* III. ii. VI. iii. (1651) 562 Redde streeks, frechons, hairs, warts. *a* **1825** FORBY *Voc. E. Anglia*, *Freckens*, freckles.

Hence '**freckened** *ppl. a.*, marked with freckles.

? *a* **1400** *Morte Arth.* 1081 His forhevede alle was it over, As þe felle of a froske, and fraknede it semede. *c* **1440** *Promp. Parv.* 176/1 Fraknyd, *idem quod* Frakny. **1877** in *N.W. Linc. Gloss.*

frecken ('frɛkən), *v. Anglo-Irish*, etc. [mispronunciation of FRIGHTEN.] *trans.* To frighten. Also with *of*.

1847 LE FANU *T. O'Brien* 230 'A whole parish that was freckened beyant all tellin'.' **1894** HALL CAINE *Manxman* 347 'May be it was myself she was freckened of.'

freckle ('frɛk(ə)l), *sb.* Forms: 5–6 fracel, -le, frakel, -il, -le, 6 frekell(e, -le, -yll, 6–7 freck-(e)l, 7 frecle, -lle, 6– freckle. [Alteration of FRECKEN.]

1. A yellowish or light-brown spot in the skin, said to be produced by exposure to the sun and wind.

c **1400** *Lanfranc's Cirurg.* 189 Of cloop þat is clepid fraclis or goute roset. **1544** PHAER *Regim. Lyfe* (1553) B v a, Lac virginis..taketh awaie frekles of yᵉ visage. **1612** WOODALL *Surg. Mate* Wks. (1653) 163 The legs and thighes discoloured into frekels. **1700** DRYDEN *Palamon & A.* III. 76 Some sprinkled freckles on his face were seen, Whose dusk set off the whiteness of the skin. **1775** SHERIDAN *Duenna* II. ii, Her skin..spangled here and there with a golden freckle. **1881** BESANT & RICE *Chapl. Fleet* I. 5 She was running about without thinking of freckles.

fig. *a* **1535** MORE *Wks.* 7 He semed somwhat besprent wᵗ the frekell of negligence.

2. Any small spot or discoloration.

1547 BORDE *Introd. Knowl.* i. (1870) 127 If a man doth cast a cupe..in the well, it wyll be full of droppes or frakils. **1590** SHAKS. *Mids. N.* II. i. 13 In their [Cowslips'] gold coats, spots you see, Those be Rubies, Fairie fauors, In those freckles, liue their sauors. **1693** EVELYN *De la Quint. Compl. Gard.* 3 One would take them at first but for little reddish Frecles and Spots. **1784** COWPER *Task* VI. 241 Not a flower But shows some touch, in freckle, streak, or stain, Of his unrivalled pencil. **1813** T. FORSTER *Atmos. Phænom.* (1815) 78 A sort of cirrostratus like little freckles. **1832** BOWLES *St. John in Patmos* v. 57 Not a freckle stained the firmament High overhead.

transf. **18..** O. W. HOLMES *Good Time Going*, This little speck, the British Isles? 'Tis but a freckle: never mind it!

† **3.** ? A wrinkle. *Obs.*

1519 HORMAN *Vulg.* 169 b, They fille vp theyr frekyllys: and stretche abrode theyr skyn with tetanother.

4. *Comb.*, as *freckle-water*; *freckle-faced* adj.

1688 *Lond. Gaz.* No. 2380/4 Charles Vine..freckle Fac'd ..Run away from his Master. **1856** ANNE MANNING *Tasso & Leonora* 100, I am off to the Barber-surgeon's to buy some freckle-water for Madama Leonora. **1884** *Harper's Mag.* Jan. 307/1 You were freckle-faced.

freckle ('frɛk(ə)l), *v.* [f. the sb.]

1. *trans.* To cover with freckles or spots.

1613 CHAPMAN *Revenge Bussy d' Ambois* Plays 1873 II. 107 The bloud She so much thirsts for, freckling hands and face. **1823** J. BADCOCK *Dom. Amusem.* 68 Persons naturally with brown skins, are blistered or freckled less than those who are fairer. **1844** HOOD *Discov. in Astron.* ii, 'Lord, master..To wonder so at spots upon the sun! I'll tell you what he's done—*Freckled himself!*'

b. *intr.* To appear in spots or patches.

1821 CLARE *Vill. Minstr.* I. 207 The sunbeams, filtering small, Freckling through the branches fall. *Ibid.* II. 201 Where the sunshine freckles on the eye Through the half-clothed branches in the woods.

2. *intr.* To become marked with freckles.

1842 THACKERAY *Fitz-Boodle's Conf.* Wks. 1869 XXII. 220 Those fair complexions, they freckle so. **1889** ANSTEY *Pariah* I. iv, You know I never freckle.

freckled ('frɛk(ə)ld), *ppl. a.* Also 4 y-fracled, 5 y-freklet, fraculd. [f. FRECKLE *sb.* + -ED^{2}.]

1. Marked with freckles.

1440 [see FRECKNY]. **1602** MARSTON *Ant. & Mel.* IV. Wks. 1856 I. 50 She hath a freckled face. **1680** *Lond. Gaz.* No. 1532/4 With pock-holes in his face, and freckled. **1751** GORDON *Another Cordial for Low Spirits* II. 138 One of the Barkin-Tribe, with weather-beaten Countenance and freckl'd Fist. **1885** RUNCIMAN *Skippers & Sh.* 232 The freckled children looked hard and healthy.

2. Spotted; dappled; variegated.

c **1380** *Sir Ferumb.* 3659 Is stede, Al y-fracled wyþ whit & rede. **1422** tr. *Secreta Secret., Priv. Priv.* (E.E.T.S.) 233 Eyen..whit y-freklet, or I-sprotid. *c* **1614** DRAYTON *Quest of Cynthia* Wks. (1748) 227 We'll angle in the brook, The freckled trout to take. **1674** N. COX *Gentl. Recreat.* I. (1677) 41 Their [Hounds'] Legs freckled with red and black. **1821** CLARE *Vill. Minstr.* I. 140 Freckled cowslips are gilding the plain. **1876** ROCK *Text. Fabr.* 63 Velvet..freckled with gold thread sprouting up like loops.

† **3.** Resembling a freckle. *Obs.*$^{-1}$

1611 BIBLE *Lev.* xiii. 39 It is a freckled spot that groweth in the skin.

4. *Comb.*, as *freckled-faced* adj.

1611 SPEED *Theat. Gt. Brit.* (1614) 107/2 When a stout frecled faced King should passe over that ford, then the power of the Welshmen should be brought under. **1687** *Lond. Gaz.* No. 2256/4 They were taken away by a Fellow ..swarthy and freckled Faced. **1885** BLACK *White Heather* ii, The little red-headed, freckled-faced lassie.

Hence '**freckledness**, the state of being freckled.

1611 COTGR., *Canetille*..the frecklednesse of a face.

freckling ('frɛklɪŋ), *vbl. sb.* [f. FRECKLE *v.* + -ING^{1}.] The action of the verb FRECKLE. In quots. quasi-*concr.*, a mark like a freckle. Also *collect.*, a marking with freckles.

1820 KEATS *Lamia* I. 159 A deep Volcanian yellow..Made gloom of all her frecklings, streaks and bars. **1882** *Garden* 28 Jan. 68/3 A white variety without the external freckling is not uncommon.

'**frecklish**, *a. rare*$^{-1}$. [f. FRECKLE *sb.* + -ISH.] Somewhat freckled.

1692 *Lond. Gaz.* No. 2809/4 Timothy Phillips..pale and frecklish..went away..with a..Sum of Money.

freckly ('frɛklɪ), *a.* [f. FRECKLE *sb.* + -Y^{1}.] Full of spots or freckles.

a **1704** T. BROWN *Highlander* 14 He..plumps his Freckly Cheeks with stinking Weed [Tobacco]. **1740** PINEDA *Span. Dict.*, *Sarpullido*, freckly, motly, or full of small Spots. **1935** HUXLEY & HADDON *We Europeans* v. 156 *Skin Colour*. Light, Medium, Swarthy, Freckly.

† '**freckly**, '**frackly**, *adv.* Chiefly *Sc.* [f. FRECK *a.* + -LY^{2}.] **a.** Voraciously, greedily. **b.** Eagerly, with spirit, promptly, lustily.

a. *c* **1205** LAY. 31772 He æt of ane uisce urechliche swiðe. **1375** BARBOUR *Bruce* VII. 166 Thai rostit in hy thair met, And fell rycht frakly for till et.

b. *c* **1440** *York Myst.* xi. 393 Do charge oure charyottis swithe And frekly folowes me. **1513** DOUGLAS *Æneis* VIII. vii. 164 Wonder frakly thai Onto thair labour can thaim all addres. **1600** J. MELVILL *Diary* (1842) 362 The gentilmen offerit tham selves verie fraclie. *a* **1651** CALDERWOOD *Hist. Kirk* (Wodrow Soc.) III. 669 How fracklie, as a perjured and man-sworne person he went forward.

† '**freckny**, *a. Obs.*$^{-1}$ In 5 frakny. [f. FRECKEN *sb.* + -Y^{1}; = Sw. *fräknig*.] Freckled.

c **1440** *Promp. Parv.* 176/1 Frakny, or fraculde (*P.* frekeny) *lentigi(n)osus*.

† '**freddon**, *v. Obs.* Also 6 firdon, friddon, fridoun. [ad. Fr. *fredonner*.] *intr.* To hum, warble, quaver. Hence † '**friddoning** *vbl. sb.*

1584 SOUTHERNE in Puttenham *Eng. Poesie* III. xxii. (Arb.) 260, I will freddon in thine honour. **1588** A. HUME *Triumph Lord* 207 Douce friddoning of flutes. **1599**—— [see FIRDON.] **16..** MONTGOMERIE *Cherrie & Slae* vii (in *Evergreen*,), Compleitly, mair sweitly, Scho fridound flat and schairp.

† **frede**, *v.* Forms: 2–4 frede(n; also 1 ȝefrédan, 3–4 *south.* ivrede(n. [OE. (*ȝe*)*frédan* wk. vb., f. *fród* wise; = MDu. *vroeden*, OHG. *fruotan*.] *trans.* To be sensible of, feel, perceive; with direct *obj.* or with sentence as *obj.* Also *refl.*

c **888** K. ÆLFRED *Boeth.* xli. §4 Sio ȝefrednes hine mæȝ ȝegrapian & ȝefredan þæt hit lichoma biþ. *c* **1000** ÆLFRIC *Hom.* I. 544 Hi swurdes ecȝe ne ȝefreddon. *c* **1000** *Ags. Gosp.* Mark v. 29 Heo on hire ȝefredde [*c* **1160** *Hatton* fredde] ðæt heo of ðam wite ȝehæled wæs. *c* **1205** LAY. 27138 Ah he herm ivredde: his heȝe men he losede. *c* **1275** *Sinners Beware* 197 in *O.E. Misc.* 78 Bute we vs bi-rede þe gost hit schal ivrede. *c* **1315** SHOREHAM 22 3ef that ȝe fredeth ȝou, That he ne be nauȝt digne For te be housled. *c* **1320** *Seuyn Sag.* (W.) 1514 His wife lai warme abedde And solas of hire lemman fredde. **1390** GOWER *Conf.* II. 374 If that I her fredde, Whan I toward offring her ledde.

Frederize, *v. nonce-wd.* [f. *Frederick* + -IZE.] *intr.* To take the part of the Emperor Frederick.

1618 DANIEL *Coll. Hist. Eng.*, *Hen. III.* (an. 1246) 138 Vpon the Popes..dispising the Kings message (who, he said, began to Frederize).

‖ **fredon**. *Obs.* [Fr. *fredon* in similar sense.] A particular sequence of cards: see quot.

1798 *Sporting Mag.* XII. 142 The fredon which is four tens, four aces, four nines, etc.

fred-stole: see FRITHSTOOL.

free (friː), *a.*, *sb.*, and *adv.* Forms: 1 frío, fréo, freoh, frioh, frí, frý, fríȝ, 2–3 fri(e, 3–4 freo, (3 *south.* vreo), 4 fry, frey, *south.* vry, vri, 6 frye, 6–7 (chiefly *Sc.*) frie, 2–6 fre, 4– free. [Com. Teut.: OE. *fréo, frío, fríȝ* corresponds to OFris. *frî*, OS. *frî* (recorded only as sb. and in the compound *frî-lîk*; Du. *vrij*), OHG. *frî* (MHG. *vrî*, mod.Ger. *frei*), ON. **frí-r* (lost exc. in the compound *fríáls*:—**frî-hals* 'free-necked', free; the mod.Icel. *frí*, Sw., Da. *fri* are adopted from Ger.), Goth. *frei-s*:—OTeut. **frijo-* free:—OAryan **priyo-*, represented by Skr. *priyá* dear, Welsh *rhŷdd* free, f. root **pri* to love (Skr. *prî* to delight, endear; OSl. *prijatelĭ* friend, Goth. *frijôn*, OE. *fréon* to love, whence FRIEND).

The primary sense of the adj. is 'dear'; the Germanic and Celtic sense comes of its having been applied as the distinctive epithet of those members of the household who were connected by ties of kindred with the head, as opposed to the slaves. The converse process of sense-development appears in Lat. *līberī* 'children', literally the 'free' members of the household.]

A. *adj.* **I.** Not in bondage to another.

1. a. Of persons: Not bound or subject as a slave is to his master; enjoying personal rights and liberty of action as a member of a society or state.

c **888** K. ÆLFRED *Boeth.* xli. §2 Gif hwylc swiþe rice cyning ..næfde nænne fryne [*MS. Cott.* freone] mon on eallon his rice, ac wæron ealle þeowe. *c* **1000** ÆLFRIC *Exod.* xxi. 2 þeowie he six ȝer and beo him freoh on þam seofoðan. *a* **1300** *Cursor M.* 6708 (Gött.) Qua-so smytes vte his thrales eye.. He sal him make fre and quite. **1535** COVERDALE *Job* iii. 19 The bonde man, and he that is fre from his master. **1606** SHAKS. *Ant. & Cl.* IV. xiv. 81 When I did make thee free. **1610** —— *Temp.* I. ii. 442 Delicate Ariel, I'll set thee free for this. **1657** R. LIGON *Barbadoes* (1673) 16 These are free Negroes, and wear..the badge of their freedom. **1841** LANE *Arab. Nts.* I. 65 It sometimes happens, though rarely, that free girls are sold as slaves.

b. *fig.* (*esp.* in a spiritual sense = not in bondage to sin).

c **975** *Rushw. Gosp.* John viii. 36 Gif forðon sunu iow ȝefrioð soðlice frio ȝe bioðon. *c* **1200** *Trin. Coll. Hom.* 101 He hadde maked hem fre of þe deules þralsipe. **1513** DOUGLAS *Æneis* X. iii. 84 Of the fatis fre [orig. *libera fati*]. **1610** SHAKS. *Temp.* Epil. 20 As you from crimes would pardon'd be, Let your indulgence set me free. **1611** BIBLE *Gal.* v. 1. **1643** DENHAM *Cooper's Hill* 130 Who..free from Conscience, is a slave to Fame. **1695** LD. PRESTON *Boeth.* IV. 194 Everything is by so much the freer from Fate.

c. Of or belonging to free men. ***free labour***: the labour of free men (in contradistinction to that of slaves).

1856 OLMSTED *Slave States* 100 He is satisfied that at present free-labor is more profitable than slave-labor.

d. Colloq. phr. ***to be free, white and*** (***over***) ***twenty-one***: to be a free agent.

1929 J. BUCHAN *Courts of Morning* II. xiv. 346 We're all of us free, white, twenty-one, and hairy-chested, and we know how to be kind to a pretty girl. **1952** D. AMES *Murder, Maestro, Please* xix. 138 She's free, white and—no, I guess she's not twenty-one. **1958** J. CANNAN *And be a Villain* iii. 59 You're free, white and twenty-one. He couldn't *make* you go there. **1962** M. CARLETON *Dread Sunset* (1963) v. 108 What could I do when she insisted?.. She was free, white and, heaven knows, well over twenty-one!

2. a. Of a state, its citizens, institutions, etc.: Enjoying civil liberty; existing under a government which is not arbitrary or despotic, and does not encroach upon individual rights. Also, not subject to foreign dominion.

1375 BARBOUR *Bruce* I. 219 Al[a]s! that folk, that euir wes fre..War tretyt than sa wykkytly. **1382** WYCLIF *1 Macc.* xi. 31 And Jerusalem be holy and free, with his coostis. **1611** SHAKS. *Cymb.* III. i. 49 Till the iniurious Romans did extort This Tribute from vs, we were free. **1667** MILTON *P.L.* I. 259 Here at least We shall be free. **1769** [see PRESS *sb.*[1] 12 f]. **1770** *Junius Lett.* xxxvii. 184 He is king of a free people. **1792** *Residence in France* (1797) I. 155 France is now the freeest country in the world. **1802** WORDSW., *Sonn.*, '*It is not to be thought of that the flood*', We must be free or die, who speak the tongue That Shakspeare spake. **1817–18** COBBETT *Resid. U.S.* (1822) 21 Is it not a mockery to call a man free, who no more dares turn out his tallow into candles for his own use, than he dares rob upon the highway? **1829** W. E. CHANNING *Wks.* (1886) 633/1 Through a free press, all public measures should be brought before the tribunal of the people. **1867** SMILES *Huguenots Eng.* xi. (1880) 187 Holland..became the chief European centre of free thought, free religion, and free industry. **1888** E. BELLAMY *Looking Backward* xv. 229 A free newspaper press..was a redeeming incident of the old system. **1946** *Observer* 10 Feb. 3/3 Britain would have a better chance of recapturing her share of the world markets with a 'free' economy than with nationalised industries. **1948** J. M. MURRY (*title*) The free society. **1951** I. SHAW *Troubled Air* xxi. 347 The benefits of a free society extended from one end of the economic spectrum to the others. **1968** *Guardian* 23 Aug. 9/1 Surprise grew into something like amazement at BBC monitoring stations yesterday as 'free' Czechoslovak broadcasts continued to be transmitted on eight normal wavebands. **1971** P. WORSTHORNE *Socialist Myth* vii. 143 The inevitably fissiparous tendencies of a free society.

b. Colloq. phr. ***it's a free country***: a catch-phrase asserting a person's rights as an individual, implying that the action proposed is not illegal.

1863 [see STEAM *sb.* 7 d]. **1885** 'F. ANSTEY' *Tinted Venus* iv. 51 It's a free country, this is! **1911** A. BENNETT *Card* i. 17 Well, *you* go and do it. It's a free country. **1939** N. STREATFEILD *Luke* 244 Why stop with her if she was always nagging about her soul? That's what gets me. After all it's a free country. **1962** 'H. CALVIN' *System* i. 13 'A girl could do worse,' she said sullenly. 'It's a free country, isn't it?' **1971** R. J. WHITE *Second-hand Tomb* i. 19 'Nuns and photographers.' 'Only one of each,' said Margaret. 'And it's a free country.'

c. In recent specific collocations. (i) Used in titles to denote those who continued resistance to Germany in the 1939–45 war after the capitulation of their respective countries.

1940 *Times* (Weekly ed.) 27 Nov. 11 He dwelt on the importance of the war in the Mediterranean theatre and of the part that Free France could play there in snatching triumph out of defeat. **1941** *Ibid.* 5 Feb. 15 Gen. de Gaulle, leader of the Free French forces. **1941** C. GRAVES *Life Line* 4 To-day we have the scattered remnants of the Free French, Free Dutch, Free Polish, and Free Norwegian Fleets to render certain assistance. **1944** H. G. WELLS *'42 to '44* 150 Vice-Admiral Muselier was appointed Commander of the Free French naval and air forces. **1965** B. SWEET-ESCOTT *Baker St. Irreg.* ii. 52 What the refugees themselves seemed to have in mind was that we should recognize them as a 'Free Rumanian' or a 'Free Bulgarian' movement. **1965** A. J. P. TAYLOR *Eng. Hist. 1914–1945* xiv. 527 German aeroplanes were using air-bases in Syria: Wavell must intervene there also, in cooperation with the Free French.

(ii) ***free world***: a name used of themselves collectively by non-communist countries; so ***free Europe***.

1950 *Time* 17 July 32/3 A branch of the National Committee for a Free Europe founded last year by a group of private U.S. citizens. **1955** *Ann. Reg. 1954* 241 There was the Council of Free Czechoslovakia..the 'rats and jackals' of Radio Free Europe. **1955** *Bull. Atomic Sci.* Feb. 42/3 The Soviet World and the Free World are running neck and neck in the training of scientists. **1957** *BBC Handbk.* 169 Throughout free Europe from Norway to the Turco-Soviet frontier. **1958** *Listener* 7 Aug. 185/2 The scale of human values..which distinguishes the free world from the Communist world. **1963** *Guardian* 19 Apr. 11/2 The free-world countries involved were Britain and Greece.

(iii) In various other collocations, e.g. of or pertaining to subversive movements inside a country.

1968 *N.Y. Rev. Books* 11 July 34/3 We have been unimpressed by the supposedly free universities established on the peripheries of major universities... What is wanted are really new ways of learning, not additional courses taught by Marxists and acidheads. **1969** *Guardian* 16 Sept. 11/3 The absurd romanticism of Free Belfast.

†**3.** Noble, honourable, of gentle birth and breeding. In ME. a stock epithet of compliment. Often in alliterative phr. ***fair and free***. *Obs.*

a **1000** *Cædmon's Gen.* 1642 (Gr.) Ða wearþ Seme suna & dohtra..worn afeded, freora bearna. *c* **1000** *Ags. Ps.* lvi[i]. 9 Ic þe on folcum frine Drihten ecne andete. *c* **1290** *S. Eng Leg.* I. 109/100 þe Amirales douȝter..þat was so fair and fre. **1297** R. GLOUC. (1724) 420 Of fayrost fourme & maners, & mest ȝentyl & fre. *a* **1300** *Cursor M.* 8121 Als milk þair [Ethiopians'] hide becom sa quite And o fre blod þai had þe heu. **13..** *E.E. Allit. P.* A. 795 My joy, my blys, my lemman fre. ? *a* **1366** CHAUCER *Rom. Rose* 633 Mirthe, that is so fair and free. *c* **1384** —— *H. Fame* I. 442 His fader Anchises the free. *c* **1460** *Towneley Myst.* (Surtees) 125 For to wyrship that chyld so fre. *c* **1489** CAXTON *Sonnes of Aymon* ix. 199 They met wyth damp Rambault the free knyght. *c* **1554** *Interlude of Youth* in Hazl. *Dodsley* II. 20 To have a sight I would be fain Of that lady free. **1632** MILTON *L'Allegro* 11 Thou Goddess fair and free.

†**4. a.** Hence in regard to character and conduct: Noble, honourable, generous, magnanimous. *Obs.*

a **1300** *Cursor M.* 25524 þat ilk time þou mistred þe, Suet iesu! wit hert sa fre, To maria magdalene. *c* **1400** *Destr. Troy* 525 'Now frynd', quod þat faire, 'as ye bene fre holden, Will ye suffer me to say, and the sothe telle?' **1559** *Mirr. Mag.*, *Salisbury* xviii, Vertuous life, fre hart and lowly mind. **1594** H. WILLOBIE in *Shaks. C. Praise* 10 You must be secret, constant, free. **1604** SHAKS. *Oth.* III. iii. 199, I would not have your free and noble nature, Out of self-bounty, be abused.

†**b.** Of studies: Liberal; = L. *ingenuæ* (*artes*).

1422 tr. *Secreta Secret., Priv. Priv.* (E.E.T.S.) 150 He sholde make his chyldryn to lerne fre Sciencis of Clergi.

II. Released, loose, unrestricted.

5. a. At liberty; allowed to go where one wishes, not kept in confinement or custody. †***free keeping*** = L. *libera custodia*. Also, released from confinement or imprisonment, liberated. Phr. ***to set free***, ***let go free***, etc. (Also *fig.*)

1483 CAXTON *Gold. Leg.* 206/2 And ii yere he was in free kepyng and disputed ayenst the Jewes. **1585** T. WASHINGTON tr. *Nicholay's Voy.* I. xx. 24 b, He wold..set them at free deliverance. **1608** SHAKS. *Per.* IV. vi. 107 O that the gods Would set me free from this unhallow'd place! **1720** DE FOE *Capt. Singleton* xvi. (1840) 269 We would let them go free. *a* **1721** PRIOR *Love disarmed* 25 Set an unhappy pris'ner free, Who ne'er intended harm to thee. **1824** SYD. SMITH *Wks.* (1859) II. 37/2 We use no compulsion with untried prisoners. You are free as air till you are found guilty. **1871** MORLEY *Voltaire* 2 Calvin..set free all those souls.

b. Of animals: Not kept in confinement, at liberty to range abroad.

1393 LANGL. *P. Pl.* C. XII. 250 Godes foules and hus free bestes. **1697** DRYDEN *Æneid* VI. 889 Their Steeds around, Free from their Harness, graze the flow'ry Ground. **1844** A. B. WELBY *Poems* (1867) 35 The round blue heaven is all thine own, O free and happy bird! **1849** MACAULAY *Hist. Eng.* I. 312 Deer, as free as in an American forest, wandered there by thousands.

6. a. Released from ties, obligations, or constraints upon one's action.

1596 SHAKS. *Tam. Shr.* I. i. 142 Till by helping Baptista's eldest daughter to a husband we set his youngest free for a husband. *a* **1605** MONTGOMERIE *Commend. of Love* 1, I rather far be fast nor frie, Albeit I micht my mynd remove. **1606** SHAKS. *Ant. & Cl.* II. v. 57 Free, madam! no..He's bound unto Octavia. *a* **1721** PRIOR *Song*, '*Phillis, since we*' 18 We both have spent our stock of love, So consequently should be free. **1859** *Autobiog. Beggar-boy* 2 Since I was what may be termed a free man; or, in other words, since I became independent.

b. Released or exempt from work or duty.

1697 DRYDEN *Virg. Georg.* II. 640 The Swain, who, free from Business and Debate, Receives his easy Food from Nature's Hand. **1700** S. L. tr. *Fryke's Voy. E. Ind.* 300 They watch and are free by turns in the day-time, but at night they must all be in the Fort. *a* **1715** BURNET *Own Time* (1766) II. 37 Coleman had a whole day free to make his escape. *c* **1818** SIR R. PEEL in *Croker Papers* (1884) I. iv. 116 A fortnight hence I shall be free as air.

7. Guiltless, innocent, acquitted. Const. *from*, *of* (a crime or offence). ? *Obs.*

1602 SHAKS. *Ham.* III. ii. 252 Your Maiestie and wee that haue free soules, it touches vs not. *Ibid.* v. ii. 343 *Laer.* Mine and my Fathers death come not vpon thee, Nor thine on me. *Ham.* Heauen make thee free of it. **1637** RUTHERFORD *Let.* 23 Sep. (1891) 521, I am free from the blood of all men, for I have communicated to you the whole counsel of God. **1657** R. LIGON *Barbadoes* (1673) 3 A man that hath a free heart, and a good Conscience. **1678** DRYDEN & LEE *Œdipus* III. i. (end), My hands are guilty, but my heart is free.

8. a. Of actions, activity, motion, etc.: Unimpeded, unrestrained, unrestricted, unhampered. Also of persons: Unfettered in their action.

a **1300** *Cursor M.* 13079 þe king þam lete haf fre entre. *c* **1400** *Lanfranc's Cirurg.* 152 þe necke schal nevere have his free mevynge. **1463** *Bury Wills* (Camden) 22 Fre owth goyng and in comyng. **1535** COVERDALE *2 Thess.* iii. 1 That the worde of God maye haue fre passage. **1598** SHAKS. *Merry W.* III. ii. 86 We shall haue the freer woing at Mr Pages. **1613** PURCHAS *Pilgrimage* (1614) 292 That the water may have free passage to all parts. **1655** FULLER *Ch. Hist.* v. iii. §62 Whilst each Bishop in his respective Diocesse, Priest in his Parish, were freer than formerly in execution of their Office. **1664** H. MORE *Myst. Iniq.* Apol. 552 As if one, while his friend was stooping, should fetch a freer stroke at their common Enemy. **1713** BERKELEY *Guardian* No. 49 ¶7 [A] library that I have free access to. **1791** MRS. RADCLIFFE *Rom. Forest* vi, Her dress, which was loosened for the purpose of freer respiration. **1828** LD. GRENVILLE *Sink. Fund* p. viii, Without the free examination of previously received opinion, no branch of human knowledge can ever be advanced. **1851** RUSKIN *Stones Ven.* xvii. (1874) I. 188 They have free admission of the light of Heaven. **1875** JOWETT *Plato* (ed. 2) III. 112 The various passions are allowed to have free play.

b. phr. (***to have*** or ***give***) ***a free hand***: liberty of action in affairs that one has to deal with. So ***to have one's hands free***.

1869 FREEMAN *Norm. Conq.* (1876) III. xiv. 329 Harold thus had his hands free. **1890** J. CORBETT *Drake* ix. 117 He was given a free hand to act against the East and West India convoys. **1895** COL. MAURICE in *United Service Mag.* July 414 No one ever had, in the composition of any history..a freer hand or more ample resources.

c. with *to* and *inf.*: At liberty, allowed, or permitted *to do* something. Also, †permitted by one's conscience, feeling it right *to do* something.

c **1386** CHAUCER *Wife's Prol.* 49, I am free To wedde, a goddes half, wher it lyketh me. **1666** PEPYS *Diary* 1 May, Thomas Pepys did come to me, to consult about..his being a Justice of the Peace, which he is much against..[He] tells me, as a confidant, that he is not free to exercise punishment ..against Quakers and other people, for religion. **1667** MILTON *P.L.* III. 99, I made him just and right, Sufficient to have stood, though free to fall. **1697** DAMPIER *Voy.* I. iii. 31 Privateers are not obliged to any Ship, but free to go ashore where they please. **1812** H. & J. SMITH *Horace in Lond.* 83 He's free to sow discord in German plantations. **1818** SCOTT *Heart Midl.* xix, If ye arena free in conscience to speak for her in the court of judicature. **1840** DICKENS *Old C. Shop* xxxi, She was free to come and go. **1876** SMILES *Sc. Natur.* iii. (ed. 4) 59 Some occupation that would leave him freer to move about.

d. Not fettered in judgement; unbiased, open-minded.

1653 H. MORE *Antid. Ath.* I. xi. (1712) 35, I appeal to any free Judge. *Ibid.* III. xvi. (1712) 141 His own words are so free and ingenuous. **1686** BURNET *Trav.* i. (1750) 60, I wish they had larger and freer Souls.

e. Showing absence of constraint or timidity in one's movements.

1849 JAMES *Woodman* vii, The traveller came forward with a bold, free step.

f. spec. in *Cricket*. Applied to (one who adopts) an unrestrained style of batting.

1851 J. PYCROFT *Cricket Field* iv. 59 In olden time the freest hitter was the best batsman. *Ibid.* x. 203 Many a man ..whose talent lies in defence, tries free hitting, and between the two proves good for nothing. **1860** *Baily's Mag.* Aug. 387 His 45 and 30 were made in a fine free style. **1885** *Punch* 19 Sept. 143/2 Behind the stumps unbeatable, free bat, and slashing field.

9. Of literary or artistic composition, etc.: Not observing strict laws of form; (of a translation, copy, etc.) not adhering strictly to the original.

1813 TYTLER *Ess. Princ. Transl.* (ed. 3) 231 The limits between free translation and paraphrases. **1821** CRAIG *Lect. Drawing* vii. 406 A free and tasteful expression of the minute forms in landscape. **1844** STANLEY *Arnold* I. iii. 142 Any mistake of grammar or construction, however dexterously concealed in the folds of a free translation. **1869** OUSELEY *Counterp.* xv. 97 When..it becomes impossible to follow exactly all the intervals proposed..The imitation is then said to be Free, or Irregular.

10. a. Allowable or allowed (*to* or *for* a person *to do* something); open or permitted *to*.

1576 FLEMING *Panopl. Epist.* 216 If that which we have learned, be free for every man to know. **1618** BOLTON *Florus* To Rdr., Be it free, with reverence and modesty, to note over-sights. **1641** J. JACKSON *True Evang. T.* I. 44 It was free to every one to bastinado a Christian where he met him. **1667** MILTON *P.L.* IV. 747 Defaming as impure what God declares Pure, and commands to some, leaves free to all. **1709** HEARNE *Collect.* 4 Apr., Y^{e} Copy was..free to ye View of any one. **1796** BURKE *Let. Noble Ld.* Wks. VIII. 32 His Grace may think as meanly as he will of my deserts..It is free for him to do so. **1846** TRENCH *Mirac.* xxxii. (1862) 452 The 'twelve legions of Angels', whom it was free to Him to summon to his aid.

b. Open to all competitors; open *for* all. ***free fight***: a fight in which all and sundry engage promiscuously.

1870 LOWELL *Study Wind.* 430 The affair became what they call on the frontier a free fight. **1872** MARK TWAIN *Innoc. Abr.* xvii. 114 The sailors of a British ship.. challenged our Sailors to a free fight. **1887** *Spectator* 4 June 759/2 English riots are mere freefights, begun without special premeditation.

c. *Philol.* Designating a linguistic form that can be used in isolation. Opp. BOUND *ppl. a.*[2] 4 b.

1926, **1957** [see BOUND *ppl. a.*[2] 4 b].

d. *Phonetics*. Of a vowel: not followed by a consonant in the same syllable. Opp. CHECKED *ppl. a.*[1] 1 b.

1895 *Publ. Mod. Lang. Assoc.* X. 306 (*heading*) 'Free' and 'checked' vowels in Gallic Popular Latin. **1946** PRIEBSCH & COLLINSON *German Lang.* (ed. 2) I. iii. 76 Vowels in absolute final position ('free' vowels). **1962** [see CHECKED *ppl. a.*[1] 1 b].

11. Of a space, way, passage, etc.: Clear of obstructions, open, unobstructed. So of air = freely-circulating, in which one breathes freely.

c **1250** *Gen. & Ex.* 3244 On twel doles delt ist ðe se, xii. weiȝes ðer-in ben faiȝer and fre. *a* **1300** *Cursor M.* 5932 (Gött.) Froskis..al þe erde þai couerd sua, A man miht noght fre sett his ta. **1596** SHAKS. *Tam. Shr.* I. ii. 233 Are not the streets as free For me as for you? **1671** NARBOROUGH *Jrnl.* in *Acc. Sev. Late Voy.* I. (1711) 145 They did meet with no Ice, but a free and open Sea. **1697** DRYDEN *Virg. Georg.* I. 47 Where in the Void of Heav'n a Space is free, Betwixt the Scorpion and the Maid for thee. *Ibid.* IV. 424 They stop his Nostrils, while he strives in vain To breath free Air. **1808** SCOTT *Marm.* I. iv, And quickly make the entrance free. **1856** KANE *Arct. Expl.* I. iii. 35 The wind off shore—with much free water. **1878** PATMORE *Tamerton Church-Tower* I. 9 Our weary spirits flagg'd beneath The still and loaded air; We left behind the freër heath.

12. Clear of (something which is regarded as objectionable or an encumbrance). Const. *of*, *from*.

a **1300** *Cursor M.* 5923 Ne was in hus na vessel fre þat watur hild, o stan ne tre, O þis watur þat sua stanc. **1398** TREVISA *Barth. De P.R.* XV. xlii. (1495) 503 Creta is an ylonde free and clene of venyme. **1670** NARBOROUGH *Jrnl.* in *Acc. Sev. Late Voy.* I. (1711) 20 Every Man is commanded to keep himself clean, and free from Lice. **1688** R. HOLME *Armoury* III. 236/2 A Woman all Hairy, no part of her Face free. **1698** FRYER *Acc. E. India & P.* 117 These places are seldom free from Soldiers and Seamen. **1756** C. LUCAS *Ess. Waters* III. 120 There is hardly any mine..free from pyrite. **1854** G. B. RICHARDSON *Univ. Code* v. (ed. 12) 4105, I can keep free with the pumps. **1860** TYNDALL *Glac.* I. xix. 135 [Glacier] Ice, singularly free from air-bubbles. **1885** *Law Times* LXXIX. 176/1 The main travelling ways..had been ..reported free from any accumulation of foul gas.

13. †**a.** Of a bird's flight: Agile, swift. *Obs.*

1657 R. LIGON *Barbadoes* (1673) 4 Her ordinary flying.. is commonly more free than the best Haggard Faulcon. *Ibid.*, A kind of sea Hawk..of a far freer wing, and of a longer continuance.

b. *Naut.* Of the wind: Not adverse (see quot. 1867).

1840 R. H. DANA *Bef. Mast* xxv. 81 We had the wind free ..sail after sail the captain piled upon her. **1867** SMYTH *Sailor's Word-bk.*, s.v. *Freeing*, To be free. Said of the wind when it exceeds 67° 30' from right-ahead. **1880** *Daily Tel.* 7 Sept., She is on the wrong tack, but the last puff was free, and helped her.

14. a. Of material things: Not restrained in movement, not fixed or fastened. *to get free*: to get loose (from something that restrains or encumbers), to extricate.

1590 SPENSER *F.Q.* I. i. 19 And, knitting all his force, got one hand free. **1667** MILTON *P.L.* VII. 464 Now half appeared The tawny lion, pawing to get free His hinder parts. **1861** J. R. GREENE *Man. Anim. Kingd., Cœlent.* 114 The..free zoöids of the *Lucernaridæ*. **1862** H. SPENCER *First Princ.* II. x. §82 (1875) 250 The pennant of a vessel lying becalmed first shows the coming breeze..by gentle undulations that travel from its fixed to its free end. **1878** E. PROUT in Grove *Dict. Mus.* I. 40 The discovery of the free reed. **1884** F. J. BRITTEN *Watch & Clockm.*, *Free Spring*, a balance spring uncontrolled by curb pins. **1890** BOLDREWOOD *Col. Reformer* (1891) 149 The yacht..with courses free.

b. *Physics* and *Chem.* [after G. *frei* in the same sense (P. Drude in *Zeitschr. f. phys. Chem.* (1894) XV. 79, *Ann. d. Physik* (1900) I. 572).] Of an electron: not bound (to an atom, molecule, etc.), and therefore able to move unrestrictedly under the influence of electric and magnetic fields. (Occas. used of other particles, but the sense becomes indistinguishable from sense 16.)

1906 E. E. FOURNIER D'ALBE *Electron Theory* x. 193 They are propagated through space with the velocity of light, and if any matter containing free electrons or positive atoms intervenes, their rate of propagation is lessened. **1907** N. R. CAMPBELL *Mod. Electr. Theory* iii. 70 These 'bound' electrons, as they may be called in distinction to the 'free' electrons which are subject to no restraining force, take no part in electrostatic actions. **1956** N. F. RAMSEY *Molec. Beams* viii. 203 (*heading*) Nuclear and molecular interactions in free molecules. **1958** *Listener* 25 Dec. 1071/1 The number of free electrons in the ionosphere. **1959** *Chambers's Encycl.* V. 127/2 The electron theory of metals..ascribes their conductivity to the presence of free electrons. **1965** PHILLIPS & WILLIAMS *Inorg. Chem.* I. vi. 196 Such a situation corresponds to the so-called 'free-electron theory'.

15. Disengaged from contact or connexion with some other body or surface; relieved from the pressure of an adjacent or superincumbent body. In *Bot.*, not adnate to other organs. ***free-central***: see quot. 1845.

1715 LEONI *Palladio's Archit.* (1742) II. 10 Making over the Architraves..Arches that will bear the weight, and leave the Architraves free. **1830** R. KNOX *Beclard's Anat.* 374 At the free surface of the mucous membrane. **1845** LINDLEY *Sch. Bot.* i. (1858) 16 If it [the placenta] grows in the middle of the ovary, without adhering to its sides..it is called *free central*. **1861** MISS PRATT *Flower. Pl.* I. 8 The anthers remaining separate, and being termed free. **1870** HOOKER *Stud. Flora* 105 Carpels 1 or more, free or connate.

16. *Chem.*, etc. Uncombined. ***free radical***: see FREE *a.* D. 2.

1800 tr. *Lagrange's Chem.* I. 244 The nitric acid remains free in the liquor. **1851** CARPENTER *Man. Phys.* (ed. 2) 51 By the decomposition of the carbonic acid, oxygen is set free. **1862** ANSTED *Channel Isl.* IV. xx. (ed. 2) 464 A silicate of alumina, with some free silica, and a trace of iron. *c* **1865** J. WYLDE in *Circ. Sc.* I. 148/2 A few grains of kaolin..may be added to neutralise an excess of free acid. **1929** *Chem. Abstr.* XXIII. 5159 It is concluded..that the reactive substance in all these expts. is free methyl. **1937** *Discovery* July 199/2 With hydrogen atoms attached to all the free bonds. **1952** *Science News* XXVI. 57 A covalent bond may..break by homolytic fission, each of the electrons separating with one of the atoms, giving two free atoms, e.g.: H–Cl→H– + Cl–, or—if the atoms..have other atoms bound to them —free radicals. **1953** R. W. GURNEY *Ionic Processes in Solution* iv. 64 There will be a dissociative equilibrium in the solution between the free ions and the neutral ion pairs. **1965** PHILLIPS & WILLIAMS *Inorg. Chem.* I. x. 347 Reactions which involved free atoms. **1970** D. F. SHAW *Introd. Electronics* (ed. 2) ix. 181 We thus have a diatomic system with two valence electrons whose energy levels are slightly different from those in the free atomic state.

17. Of power or energy: Disengaged, available for 'work'.

1825 J. NICHOLSON *Operat. Mechanic* 662 The whole power of the engine would be expended in impelling itself and the ship..and no free power would remain for freight. **1837** BREWSTER *Magnet.* 363 The action of the free fluid is in equilibrio with the external force. **1838** *Proc. Amer. Phil. Soc.* I. 6 Free electricity is not under any circumstances conducted silently to the earth.

18. a. Of a material: Yielding easily to operation, easily worked, loose and soft in structure. Also ***free-working***: see D. 1. a below. See also FREESTONE, whence this sense prob. arises.

1573 in Willis & Clark *Cambridge* (1886) I. 174 Item for Ramsey stone free and ragge. **1676** WOOD *Life* (Oxf. Hist. Soc.) II. 353 Many flat stones, but being free and soft, their inscriptions are woren out. **1765** A. DICKSON *Treat. Agric.* (ed. 2) 59 Even that kind of land that is most free and open in its nature, is found to be rendered more fertile by [fallowing]. **1793** SMEATON *Edystone L.* §106 This stone was capable of being thus wrought, and was so free to the tool. **1807** VANCOUVER *Agric. Devon* (1813) 11 It is generally called free, or Dunstone land.

b. Of wood: Without knots. (So ***free-stuff***: see D. 2.)

1678 [see FROUGHY 2]. **1770** KUCKAHN in *Phil. Trans.* LX. 315 Out of any soft free wood, cut an artificial one.

III. Characterized by spontaneity, readiness or profuseness in action.

19. Of a person, his will, etc.: Acting of one's own will or choice, and not under compulsion or constraint; determining one's own action or choice, not motived from without. (See also FREE WILL.)

c **888** K. ÆLFRED *Boeth.* xli. §2 Forþæm he ȝesceop twa ȝesceadwisan ȝesceafta frio [*MS. Cott.* freo], englas & men. *c* **1400** *Rom. Rose* 7441 He knew nat that she was constreyned..But wende she come of wille al fre. **1601**? MARSTON *Pasquil & Kath.* I. 180 Nay, be free, my daughters, in election. **1606** SHAKS. *Tr. & Cr.* II. ii. 170 To make vp a free determination 'Twixt right and wrong. **1662** STILLINGFL. *Orig. Sacr.* III. iii. §5 Considering man as a free agent. **1732** BERKELEY *Alciphr.* VII. §22 A man is said to be free, so far forth as he can do what he will. **1849** MACAULAY *Hist. Eng.* I. 561 From the day when he quitted Friesland.. he had never been a free agent. **1869** FREEMAN *Norm. Conq.* (1876) III. xi. 6 The choice of the electors would be perfectly free.

20. a. Ready in doing or granting anything; acting willingly or spontaneously; (of an act) done of one's own accord; (of an offer, assent, etc.) readily given or made, made with good will.

c **1386** CHAUCER *Prol.* 852 To kepe his forward by his free assent. **1535** COVERDALE *1 Kings* x. 13 And Kynge Salomon gaue vnto yᵉ Quene..all that she desyred and axed, besydes that which he gaue her of a frye hande. **1549** *Bk. Com. Prayer, Collect 20th Sund. Trinity*, That we maye with free hearts accomplyshe those thynges that thou wouldest have done. **1576** FLEMING *Panopl. Epist.* 121 There is no kinde of thing, which Cæsars highnesse..wil not graunt and give of his free bountie. **1607** SHAKS. *Timon* I. ii. 188. **1611** TOURNEUR *Ath. Trag.* I. i, You neede not urge my spirit by disgrace, 'Tis free enough; my Father hinders it. **1618** BOLTON *Florus* (1636) 13 Tarquinius..of his own free courage demanding the Kingdome, had it as freely granted. *a* **1626** BACON *New Atl.* Wks. 1802 II. 132 His noble free offers left us nothing to ask. **1651** C. CARTWRIGHT *Cert. Relig.* I. 206 God doth justifie us (saith he) of his free-goodnes. **1882** OGILVIE s.v., He made him a free offer of his services.

b. with *inf.*: Ready *to do* something; eager, willing, prompt. *Obs.* exc. in phr. ***free to confess***, where the adj. is now apprehended as in 8 c.

1660 *Trial Regic.* 22, I shall be very free to open my Heart. **1699** DAMPIER *Voy.* II. v. 94 He was very free to talk with me, and first asked me my business thither. *a* **1716** BLACKALL *Wks.* (1723) I. 276 To part with anything in this World..and to be free to suffer any temporal Loss..rather than live in a State of strong Temptation to Sin. **1722** SEWEL *Hist. Quakers* (1795) I. III. 191 But they were not free to consent thereto. **1784** *New Spectator* xvi. 6/2 For my own part, I will be free to confess, that, in my opinion, [etc.]. **1821** CLARE *Vill. Minstr.* I. 40 Mark..his generous mind; How free he is to push about his beer. **1824** BYRON *Juan* XVI. lxxiii, He was 'free to confess'—(whence comes this phrase? Is't English? No—'tis only parliamentary) That [etc.]. **1874** RUSKIN *Fors Clav.* xxxvii. 4, I am free to confess I did not quite know the sort of creature I had to deal with.

c. Of a horse: Ready to go, willing.

1477 SIR J. PASTON in *P. Lett.* No. 802 III. 200 It shall never neede to prykk nor threte a free horse. *a* **1592** GREENE *Alphonsus* IV. Wks. (Rtldg.) 242/1 Horses that be free Do need no spurs. **1673** E. BROWN *Brief Acc. Trav.* 71 They [Servian horses] are very free. **1884** *Daily News* 23 July 7/2 'Free horses'—horses that is..that have been working in pairs, and have been too conscientious in their work, and have done more than their share.

21. a. Ready in giving, liberal, lavish. Const. *of*.

a **1300** *Cursor M.* 14397 Sua fre giuer of all-kin gode. *c* **1300** *Ibid.* 27874 (Cott. Galba) Help þe pouer with hert fre. *Ibid.* 28741 (Cott. Galba) What nede es þat þe spenser be nithing of þat þe lord es fre. **1611** BIBLE *2 Chron.* xxix. 31 As many as were of a free heart. **1663** BUTLER *Hud.* I. i. 496 For Saints themselves will sometimes be Of Gifts that cost them nothing, free. **1699** DAMPIER *Voy.* II. I. 84 The Tonquinese in general are very free to their Visitants, treating them with the best cheer they are able to procure. **1719** DE FOE *Crusoe* I. iv, I was not very free of it, for my Store was not great. **1740** GARRICK *Lying Valet* II. Wks. 1798 I. 53 When he's drunk..he's very free, and will give me any thing. **1871** FREEMAN *Norm. Conq.* (1876) IV. xviii. 185 Handsome in person and free of hand.

b. Of a gift: Given out of liberality or generosity (not in return or requital for something else).

c **1380** WYCLIF *Sel. Wks.* III. 312 To fynde goode prestis bi fre almes of þe peple. **1548** UDALL, etc. *Erasm. Par. Matt.* i. 21 The messinger of this free felicitie. **1583** FULKE *Defence* xv. 403 The worde χάρισμα..signifieth..'a free gift', or a gift that is freely giuen..wherof the Prouerbe is, what is so free as gift? **1791** *Gentl. Mag.* LXI. I. 411 Benefices are now, I might almost say never a free gift from a private patron.

22. a. Acting without restriction or limitation; allowing oneself ample measure *in* doing something.

1578 TIMME *Caluine on Gen.* 86 Being convinced..that he was too free in sinning. **1632** J. HAYWARD tr. *Biondi's Eromena* 147 That either too light, or too free feeding hath occasioned you this dreame. **1727** POPE *Th. Var. Subj.* Swift's Wks. 1755 II. I. 224 How free the present age is in laying taxes on the next. **1746** BERKELEY *Lett. Tar-water* ii. §9 The free use of strong fermented liquors. **1791** *Gentl. Mag.* 26/2 Probably no divine made a freer use of the *paronomasia* than Dan. Featley. **1858** HAWTHORNE *Fr. & It. Jrnls.* I. 191 He is..free and careless in displaying his precious wares. **1884** *Manch. Exam.* 4 Apr. 4/5 At the close [of the market] the tone is easy, with free sellers.

b. ***free of*** or ***with***: using or employing without reserve or restraint.

1632 LITHGOW *Trav.* III. 92 He was so free of his stomacke to receive in strong liquor. **1653** BOGAN *Mirth Chr. Life* 80 Grotius, the freest man of his tongue that ever I knew. **1700** S. L. tr. *Fryke's Voy. E. Ind.* 196 He was not free of his Discourse. **1737** BRACKEN *Farriery Impr.* (1757) II. 258 He gives us a Caution not to be too free with such Preparations.

c. Unstinted as to supply, quantity, etc.; coming forth in profusion; administered without stint; abundant, copious. (Used with mixture of sense 8.)

1635 J. HAYWARD tr. *Biondi's Banish'd Virg.* 86 His wounded thigh by its free bleeding gave the..eye occasion to suspect [etc.]. **1707** HEARNE *Collect.* 21 July, After a free glass or two he happen'd to discourse. **1806** *Med. Jrnl.* XV. 217 A free stimulus given to the absorbent system. **1822–34** GOOD *Study Med.* (ed. 4) I. 244 The skin warm, the pulse free and forcible. **1887** BARING-GOULD *Gaverocks* xii, A monthly rose that was a free bloomer.

23. Frank and open in conversation or intercourse, ingenuous, unreserved; also, in bad sense = overfree, forward, 'familiar', ready to 'take liberties'.

1635 QUARLES *Embl.* I. iv. (1718) 18 If thou be free, she's strange; if strange, she's free. **1635** J. HAYWARD tr. *Biondi's Banish'd Virg.* 185 Beeing of a free nature..quite forgot all circumspection. **1671** NARBOROUGH *Jrnl.* in *Acc. Sev. Late Voy.* I. (1711) 132 These Antipodes began to be somewhat bolder, and more free. **1693–4** GIBSON in *Lett. Lit. Men* (Camden) 217 His Grace is very free and open. **1719** DE FOE *Crusoe* II. vi, I pressed him to be free and plain with me. **1775** SHERIDAN *St. Patr. Day* II. ii, Not so free, fellow! **1800** MRS. HERVEY *Mourtray Fam.* II. 171 Daring and free as was this young nobleman, with women whose principles were as free as his own. **1854** HAWTHORNE *Eng. Note-bks.* (1883) I. 464 A very able man, with the Western sociability and free-fellowship.

24. ***to make*** (or *be*) ***free with***: to adopt very familiar terms in one's conversation or dealings with (a person); hence *gen.* and *transf.* to treat unceremoniously, take liberties with. Also *Naut.*, to approach boldly.

1708 SWIFT *Abolit. Chr.* Wks. 1755 II. I. 84 Great wits love to be free with the highest objects; and if they cannot be allowed a God to revile or renounce, they will speak evil of dignities. **1714** ADDISON *Spect.* No. 556 ¶7, I was once like to have run through the Body for making a little too free with my Betters. **1728** N. SALMON in *Lett. Lit. Men* (Camden) 361 The Itinerary of Antoninus I find all authors making free with, condemning it for blunders, and altering figures. **1783** *Hist. Miss Baltimores* II. 79 If I can infuse into Carleton's ear, that Sedly and her ladyship make too free, he may..propose setting me as a watch over his wife's conduct. **1803** NELSON 10 Aug. in Nicolas *Disp.* VIII. 155 You are.. to approach Toulon with great caution and not make too free with the entrance of the harbour. **1826** DISRAELI *Viv. Grey* VI. i, He may with justice make free with our baggage. **1833** HT. MARTINEAU *Vanderput & S.* i. 7 Rebuked him for being so free with the pastor. **1856** READE *Never too late* I, I advise you not to make so free with your servants. **1858** *Merc. Marine Mag.* V. 226 You may make free with the..shore to within half a cable's length.

25. a. Of speech: Characterized by liberty in the expression of sentiments or opinions; uttered or expressed without reserve; frank, plain-spoken.

1611 TOURNEUR *Ath. Trag.* v. ii. Wks. 1878 I. 148 With the free voice of a departing soule, I here protest this Gentlewoman cleare. **1625** BACON *Ess., Counsel* (Arb.) 329 For else Counsellours will but take the Winde of him; And in stead of giuing Free Counsell, sing him a Song of Placebo. **1680** H. MORE *Apocal. Apoc.* 107 Their free rebukes out of the word of God being very disquieting. **1712** STEELE *Spect.* No. 493 ¶1 The Mistress and the Maid shall quarrel, and give each other very free Language. **1794** NELSON 19 Mar. in Nicolas *Disp.* I. 375 Gave Lord Hood my free opinion that 800 troops, with 400 seamen, would take Bastia. **1849** MACAULAY *Hist. Eng.* II. 66 The conversation at table was free; and the weaknesses of the prince whom the confederates hoped to manage were not spared. **1884** L. J. JENNINGS in *Croker Papers* I. viii. 238 Men used rather free expressions to each other.. in the days of the Regency.

b. Not observing due bounds, 'loose', licentious.

1852 THACKERAY *Esmond* III. iii, Where she.. listened to much free talk. **1859** TENNYSON *Enid* 1140 Earl Limours Drank till he jested with all ease, and told Free tales.

IV. Not burdened, not subject or liable, exempt; invested with special rights or privileges.

26. (With const. *from* or *of*): **a.** Released or exempt from, not liable to (e.g. a rule, penalty, payment).

c **1000** *Ags. Gosp.* Matt. xvii. 26 Eornestlice þa barn senden frie. *a* **1300** *Cursor M.* 3240 O þi trout þan mak i þe fre. **1630** *R. Johnson's Kingd. & Commw.* 185 He is free from all tax and imposition.. all his life after. **1694** LOCKE *Hum. Und.* II. xxi. §60 (ed. 2), The will, free from the determination of such desires, is left to the pursuit of nearer satisfactions. **1849** MACAULAY *Hist. Eng.* II. 7 That the Roman Catholic, where the interests of his religion were concerned, thought himself free from all the ordinary rules of morality.

b. Exempt from, having immunity from, not subject to (some circumstances or affection regarded as hurtful or undesirable).

c **1200** ORMIN 16818 þatt Crist wass.. all þwerrt ut off sinne fre. *c* **1230** *Hali Meid.* 5 Freo ouer alle fram alle worldliche weanen. **1581** SIDNEY *Apol. Poetrie* (Arb.) 55 Poetrie.. is the freest from thys obiection. **1594** HOOKER *Eccl. Pol.* IV. ix. §2 The freer our minds are from all distempered affections. **1611** SHAKS. *Wint. T.* I. ii. 264 These.. Are such allow'd Infirmities, that honestie Is neuer free of. **1698** FRYER *Acc. E. India & P.* 35 When they feel themselves freest from Sickness. **1798** FERRIAR *Illustr. Sterne* vi. 179 Our own writers are not free from this error. **1822** LAMB *Elia* Ser. II. *Confess. Drunkard*, I am never free from those uneasy sensations. **1885** *Manch. Exam.* 21 May 5/3 These Highlanders are notoriously free from pulmonary consumption. **1895** SIR N. LINDLEY in *Law Times Rep.* LXXIII. 645/2 The point.. appears to me.. free from any real difficulty.

27. a. Exempt from, or not subject to, some particular jurisdiction or lordship. **b.** Possessed of certain exclusive rights or privileges. Used to designate franchises or liberties, as ***free chapel*** (see CHAPEL *sb.* 3 c); ***free chase*** = FRANK CHASE; ***free fishery*** (see FISHERY 4); ***free marriage*** = FRANK MARRIAGE; ***free warren*** (see WARREN). ***free miner*** (local): see quot. 1883.

1297 R. GLOUC. (1724) 474 Other holi churche was issent, that mid riȝte was so fre. **1375** BARBOUR *Bruce* I. 164 Or as myn eldris forouch me Held it in freyast reawte. *c* **1483** CAXTON *Bk. Trav.* 21 b, A cure of fre chapell. **1535** COVERDALE *Josh.* xx. 2 Giue amonge you fre cities.. yt they may be fre amonge you from the avenger of bloude. **1599** SANDYS *Europæ Spec.* (1632) 170 The Free-Cityes.. have all save some very few, enfreed themselves from the Pope. **1611** SPEED *Hist. Gt. Brit.* IX. iii. §11 Setting to sale the free-rights of the Church. **1641** *Termes de la Ley* 168 Free marriage. **1669** *Sc. Acts Chas. II* 4 Tenements lands and fishings holden in frie burgage. **1697** DAMPIER *Voy.* I. xi. 317 He was a free Merchant.. by that name the Dutch and English in the East Indies, distinguish those Merchants who are not Servants to the Company. **1700** TYRRELL *Hist. Eng.* II. 1107 Their feoffees and Free-Tenants. **1703** *Lond. Gaz.* No. 3950/4 The several Regalties, Free-Fisheries, etc. **1723** *Ibid.* No. 6194/7 Elizabeth Smith.. Free-Dealer. **1726** C. KIRKHAM (*title*), Two Letters.. the First Shewing.. the Rights and Privileges of Pourallees or Free-Hey. **1785** J. PHILLIPS *Treat. Inland Navig.* p. xii, The defection of the Colonies, now the Free and United States. **1810** *Sporting Mag.* XXXVI. 26 The rights of free warren and free chace. **1843** JAMES *Forest Days* v, No free-forester shall ever be arrested by our people, or on our land. **1861** M. PATTISON *Ess.* (1889) I. 44 The free towns of Lübeck, Bremen, and Hamburg. **1883** GRESLEY *Gloss. Coal Mining, Free Miner*.. a man born within the hundred of St. Briavels.. who has worked a year and a day in a mine. **1884** *Law Times* 31 May 78/2 A free miner made an application to the gaveller for a grant to him of one of the two gales.

28. a. Of real property: Held without obligation of rent or service, freehold.

c **1290** *S. Eng. Leg.* I. 52/186 An hondret hidene of guod lond with hire he ȝaf þer þat hous, al-so freo in eche point ase he him-sulf it heold er. *c* **1440** *York Myst.* xxxii. 348 *Armig.* A place here beside lorde wolde I wedde-sette. *Pilat.* What title has þou þer-to? is it þyne awne free? *Armig.* Lorde, fre be my fredome me fallis it. **1465** *Paston Lett.* No. 522 II. 224 Other x acres of fre londe. *a* **1533** LD. BERNERS *Huon* lxxxi. 249 Your landes oughte to be rendred to you franke and fre. **1587** in *Collect.* (Oxf. Hist. Soc.) I. 180 Ladyes Crofte Mr. Losse free. **1601** HOLLAND *Pliny* II. 492 She had conferred frankely vpon the people of Rome, a piece of medow ground ..which was her owne Free-land. **1701** *Lond. Gaz.* No. 3712/4 About 60 Acres of Meadow and Pasture Land, all Free Land.

†**b.** Of property: At one's own disposal. *Obs.*

1808 FORSYTH *Beauties Scotl.* (1808) V. 144 A prohibition existed.. against marriage, unless where the young couple could show they possessed £40 Scots of free gear.

29. a. Invested with the rights or immunities *of*, admitted to the privileges *of* (a chartered company, corporation, city, or the like). Sometimes used simply, without *of*.

1496 *Act 12 Hen. VII*, c. 6 Merchants and Adventurers dwelling and being free within the City of London. **1553** in W. H. Turner *Select. Rec. Oxford* 215 He was made fre in myne yere.. Am not I also a freeman? **1587** FLEMING *Contn. Holinshed* III. 1311/1 Citizen of London, and free of the clothworkers. **1610** B. JONSON *Alch.* I. iii, Free of the Grocers? **1651** *Rec. Carpenters' Co.* 4 Dec. in Jupp *Hist. Acc. Comp. Carpenters* (1887) 160 Whereas the ffree Sawiers have indited a fforreine sawier, etc. **1661** PEPYS *Diary* 3 May, It was in his thoughts to have got me made free of the towne. **1688** *Lond. Gaz.* No. 2317/1 The Company of Free Fishermen of Your River of Thames. **1690** LOCKE *Govt.* II. vi. §59 Is a Man under the Law of England? What made him Free of that Law? **1703** *Lond. Gaz.* No. 3944/4 He is a Free-Burgess of Colchester. **1712** SWIFT *Jrnl. to Stella* 18 Sept., It is necessary they should be made free here before they can be employed. **1719** DE FOE *Crusoe* II. xiii, My horse fell, and made me free of the country, as they call it. **1766** ENTICK *London* IV. 239 The shop-keepers are obliged to be free of the city. **1859** C. BARKER *Assoc. Princ.* ii. 54 Persons not free of the craft.

b. Hence: Allowed the use or enjoyment *of* (a place, etc.).

1687 DRYDEN *Hind & P.* III. 1245 He therefore makes all birds of every sect Free of his farm. **1713** STEELE *Guardian* No. 53 ¶2 Powel of the Bath is reconciled to me, and has made me free of his show. **1818** KEATS *Endymion* III. Poet. Wks. (1886) 139 And I was free of haunts umbrageous. **1840** DICKENS *Barn. Rudge* x, Barnaby's as free of the house as any cat or dog about it.

30. Said of workmen who are not members of a trade-union: also ***free labour*** = the labour of non-unionists.

1890 *Times* 17 Sept. 4/3 A free labour registration for the purpose of securing the services of men.. for work as free men without reference to any other combination. **1891** *Spectator* 17 Jan., The refusal of Union men to work with free-labourers.

31. Exempt from restrictions in regard to trade; allowed to trade in any market or with any commodities; open to all traders; also, not subject to tax, toll, or duty. Freq. as ***free market***, ***port***, both also (hyphened) in *attrib.* use.

1631 WEEVER *Anc. Fun. Mon.* 38 Their Free-martes, or Markets. **1711** SHAFTESB. *Charac.* (1737) I. 64 Nothing is so advantageous to it [trade] as a free-port. **1714** *Fr. Bk. of Rates* 2 The Privileges of Cities, Towns, Persons, Free-fairs, and other Exemptions. **1719** DE FOE *Crusoe* II. xiii, Having gotten a good acquaintance at Manilla, he got his ship made a free ship. **1753** *Scots Mag.* Mar. 110/2 Free ships render the merchandize on board free. **1842** CALHOUN *Wks.* (1874) IV. 105 The act.. increased the list of free articles many-fold. **1862** LATHAM *Channel Isl.* III. xvii. (ed. 2) 400 It became a free port, and throve through its freedom. **1905** *Westm. Gaz.* 8 Sept. 4/1 The great advantage a Free-Port system has over 'Protection'. **1907** *Ibid.* 5 Apr. 3/2 What Preferentialists ask from the masses in England is a price above the free-market price. **1947** V. A. DEMANT *What is happening to Us?* i. 8 The approach to a completely free-market economy began to wreck what any genuine conservative would want to conserve. **1967** *Boston Sunday Herald* 26 Mar. VI. 7/5 (Advt.), Buy silver, china, watches, etc., in our free-port shops right in the hotel.

32. a. (In full *free of cost, charge*, or the like). Given or provided without payment, costless, gratuitous. Of persons: (Admitted, etc.) without payment.

1585 T. WASHINGTON tr. *Nicholay's Voy.* III. xviii. 104 To have free shot and cheare. **1697** DRYDEN *Virg. Georg.* IV. 357 Lazy Drones, without their Share of Pain, In Winter Quarters free, devour the Gain. **1719** DE FOE *Crusoe* I. xvii, You will carry me.. to England, passage-free. **1830** *Blackw. Mag.* XXVIII. 400 Paid.. partly in victuals; and partly in free tickets. **1836** DICKENS *Sk. Boz* vi. (1850) 22/1 Books were bought, all the free-seat people provided therewith. **1852** MACAULAY *Jrnl.* 15 Aug, I got a place among the free seats. **1856** HAWTHORNE *Eng. Note-bks.* (1883) II. 234 We went to the Haymarket Theatre, where Douglas Jerrold is on the free list. **1856** FROUDE *Hist. Eng.* (1858) I. i. 43 To every man.. who chose to ask for it, there was free fare and free lodging. **1894** *Times* (weekly ed.) 9 Feb. 113/2 An.. applicant for a free pass over this company's lines of railway.

b. ***free school***: 'a school in which learning is given without pay' (J.).

It has been denied that this was the meaning of 'free (grammar) school', L. *libera schola grammaticalis*, as the official designation of many schools founded under Edw. VI. The denial rests on the two assertions (both disputable): that the Eng. phrase is a translation of the Latin, not the reverse; and that *liber* could not mean 'gratuitous' in mediæval any more than in classical Latin. Many different interpretations of the adj. have been proposed: (1) exempt from ecclesiastical control; (2) exempted by license from the operation of the statute of mortmain, and hence entitled to hold property (to a limited amount); (3) giving a liberal education; (4) 'privileged' or 'authorized'. We have failed, however, to find any example in which the interpretation 'gratuitous' is inadmissible (though the schools called 'free' were often gratuitous only to a select number or class of scholars); and there is abundant proof that this interpretation was already current *before* the time of Edw. VI.

[**1488** *Will of Sir Edm. Shaw* (Som. Ho.), I woll that the said connyng Preeste kepe a Grammer scole contynually in the said Town of Stopforde [Stockport].. and that he frely without any.. salary asking.. except only my salary.. shall teach, etc.] **1494** FABYAN *Chron.* VI. clxxi. 165 He [King Alfred] ordeyned the firste grammer scole at Oxenforde, and other free scoles. **1500** *Deed Found. Lancaster Grammar Sch.* in *National Observer* (1896) 3 Oct. 578 [The master shall be] a profound grammarian, keping a Fre Scole, teching.. the childer unto the utmost profitt, nothing taking therefor. **1503** *Will of Sir John Percyvale* (Macclesfield 1877) 5, I woll that the said preest shall alway kepe.. in the said Town of Maxfeld a Fre Grammar Scole. *c* **1512** *Ordinance Agnes Mellers* (MS. *c.* 1590) in *Nottingham Rec.* III. 453 [She founds at Nottingham] a Free Schole of one maister and Usher.. [They are forbidden to] take any other gift.. whereby the scollers or their friends should be charged but at the pleasure of the friends of the scholars, save the wages to be paid by the said Guardians. [**1518** *Stat. St Paul's Sch.* in Lupton *Life Colet* 271 John Colet.. in.. 1512 bylded a Scole in the Estende of Paules church for 153 to be taught fre in the same.] **1548** *Chantry Certif.* No. 22 in A. F. Leach *Eng. Schools at Reform.* (1897) 82 The chauntry of Blakebroke.. Founded.. by license obtained of Kinge Henry the Sixt to manteigne a discrete priest.. to kepe a gramer scoole half free, that ys to seye, taking of scolers lerning gramer 8*d.* the quarter, and of others lerning to rede 4*d.* the quarter. **1583** STUBBES *Anat. Abus.* II. (1882) 19 Be there not.. free schooles, where youth may bee brought vp in learning Gratis without any charges to their parents? **1599** *Will of P. Blundell* (founding Tiverton Grammar School) in *Rept. Comm. Char.* 1820 III. App. 136 My meaning is yt shall be for ever a Free Schole and not a Schole of exaction. **1673** *Essex Papers* (Camden) I. 116 There is also a free schoole setled att Carickfergus, which is maintained by the Bishop, Clergy, &c. **1699** *Phil. Trans.* XXI. 441 A State-House, and a Free-School. **1727** *Stat. Bury Gramm. School* (Bury 1863), I have ordered my Free Schole of Bury to be free to all boys born in the parish.. yet my intent is.. not to debar [the masters] from that common priviledg in all Free Scholes of receiving presents, benevolences, gratuities from the scholars. **1759** GOLDSM. *Bee* No. 6 §1 ¶4 The manner in which our youth of London are at present educated is, some in free schools in the city, but the far greater number in boarding schools about town. **1837** HT. MARTINEAU *Soc. Amer.* III. 164 One needs but go from a charity-school in an English county to a free-school in Massachusetts, to see [etc.]. **1838** DICKENS *O. Twist* vii, It's a poor boy from the free-school. **1842** —— *Amer. Notes* (1850) 113/1 Its free-schools, of which it has so many that no person's child among its population can, by possibility, want the means of education.

transf. **1589** R. HARVEY *Pl. Perc.* 10 A free schoole of skolds shalbe set vp for the nonce.

†**B.** *sb. Obs.*

1. The adj. used *absol.*

c **1300** *Beket* 221 The crie was sone wide couth among thue and freo. *c* **1320** *Sir Tristr.* 3153 Þo folwed bond and fre. *c* **1350** *Will. Palerne* 5514 Feiþful.. to fre & to þewe.

2. A person of noble birth or breeding; a knight or lady.

[In OS. poetry *frî* neut. (prob. orig. adj. with ellipsis of *wîf*) is used in the sense of 'lady', or ME. BURD; the same use occurs once in OE. in a passage known to be translated from OS. (quot. *a* **1000** below).]

a **1000** *Cædmon's Gen.* 457 (Gr.) Freo fægroste. *c* **1320** *Sir Tristr.* 3046 Ysonde men calleþ þat fre, Wiþ þe white hand. **13..** *E.E. Allit. P.* B. 929 'Þenne fare forth', quoth þat fre [an angel]. *c* **1350** *Will. Palerne* 505 Whan þe fre was in þe forest founde in his denne. *c* **1380** *Sir Ferumb.* 3441 Þanne saide Roland to þat fry: 'Damesele, þow spekest ful cortesly.' *c* **1460** *Towneley Myst.* (Surtees) 268 Well I wote that it was he My lord Jesu; he that betrayde that fre Sore may he rew. *a* **1549** *Murning Maidin* 14 in *Laneham's Let.* (1871) Pref. 150, I followit on that fre, That semelie wes to se.

C. *adv.* **a.** In a free manner, freely: used in the different senses of the adj. In educated use now only *techn.* or *arch.*, and chiefly in contexts where it admits of being interpreted as adj.

1559 *Mirr. Mag., Worcester* ii, That truth vnshent should speake in all thinges fre. **1613** SHAKS. *Hen. VIII*, II. i. 82, I as free forgiue you As I would be forgiuen. **1681** DRYDEN *Abs. & Achit.* 202 Achitophel.. Disdain'd the golden Fruit to gather free. **1703** MOXON *Mech. Exerc.* 321 So as the Plumb-line play free in the Groove. **1709** STRYPE *Ann. Ref.* I. ii. 61 This subsidy was extreamly free and readily granted. **1776** G. SEMPLE *Building in Water* 105 The Middle of the Current of the River, runs the freest. **1850** MRS. BROWNING *Rom. Page* xxxiv, The knight smiled free at the fantasy. **1885** *Law Times* LXXX. 101/1 An adjoining pulley which ran free.

b. Without cost or payment. Often with *gratis* added, esp. in colloq. phr. ***free, gratis, (and) for nothing***. Phr. ***for free***: see FOR *prep.* 19 g. ***scot free***: see SCOT.

1568 V. SKINNER tr. *Montanus' Inquisit.* 35 b, Escape scotte free. **1682** in Picton *L'pool Munic. Rec.* (1883) I. 252 Hee was admitted free gratis. **1774** *Ibid.* (1886) II. 195 Admitted to the freedom free gratis. **1841** DICKENS *Let.* 30 June (1969) II. 317, I have declined to be brought in, free gratis for nothing and qualified to boot, for a Scotch county that's going a-begging. **1850** KINGSLEY *A. Locke* I. ii. 32 Spittoons, as you see, perwided free gracious [*sic*] for nothing. **1893** E. F. BENSON *Dodo* II. xi. 222 No charge for mixed metaphors. Supplied free, gratis, *and* for nothing. *a* **1898** *Mod.* The gallery will be open free on Saturdays. **1941** H. G. WELLS *You can't be too Careful* III. viii. 146, I was to be sent to France, free gratis and for nothing for six months. **1965** S. JEPSON *Third Possibility* xii. 89 The man you're going to meet can give you more of it free, gratis and for nothing than you can use in a life-time.

c. Naut. (*to sail, go,* etc.) ***free***: i.e. with bowlines slackened and sheets eased; farther from the wind than when close-hauled.

1812 *Examiner* 12 Oct. 649/2 Both keeping up a heavy fire and steering free. **1839** MARRYAT *Phant. Ship* xii, We were going about four knots and a half free. **1883** *Harper's Mag.* Aug. 447/2 A boat.. with ability to fetch to windward and to run free.

D. *Comb.*

1. a. with ppl. adjs. where *free* is either adverbial or enters into parasynthetic combinations, as †***free-bestowed***, ***-bred***, ***-floating***, ***-flowering***, ***-flowing***, ***-flying*** (so ***free-fly*** v., nonce-use), ***-footed***, †***-franchised***,

-garmented, *-growing*, †*-miened*, *-minded*, (*-mindedness*), *-mouthed*, *-moving*, *-ranging*, *-running*, *-spirited*, *-swimming*, *-tongued*, *-working*.

1583 GOLDING *Calvin on Deut.* xiii. 75 Through his owne *freebestowed goodenesse. **1599** MARSTON *Sco. Villanie* II. vi. 201 Oh indignity To my respectless *free-bred poesie. **1921** *Jrnl. Ecol.* IX. 241 A suggestion as to factors influencing the distribution of *free-floating vegetation. **1926** W. MCDOUGALL *Outl. Abnormal Psychol.* xviii. 316 If this accident had not taken place, the free-floating fear would have broken out in a phobia for some other object. **1936** *Discovery* Jan. 3/1 Ultra-microscopic particles of living protoplasm were the germs from which visible free-floating organisms were derived. **1965** *Times Lit. Suppl.* 25 Nov. 1058/3 The more free-floating culture of bohemia. **1824** *Greenhouse Compan.* 68 *Free-flowering plants of different degrees of beauty. **1952** A. G. L. HELLYER *Sanders' Encycl. Gardening* (ed. 22) 223 A large, rounded, free-flowering bush is formed. **1934** WEBSTER, *Free-flowing. **1960** *Farmer & Stockbreeder* 16 Feb. 109 In the Nicholas Liver Fluke Drench, hexachloroethane particles are suspended in a free-flowing liquid and this ensures accurate dosing. **1922** JOYCE *Ulysses* 256 They threw young heads back.. to let *freefly their laughter. **1915** E. R. LANKESTER *Divers. Nat.* 222 Fully-formed *free-flying state. **1961** BANNERMAN *Birds Brit. Isles* X. 290 Only three chicks were reared to the free-flying stage. **1602** SHAKS. *Ham.* III. iii. 26 For we will Fetters put vpon this feare, Which now goes too *free-footed. **1681** COTTON *Wond. Peak* (ed. 4) 28 In these *free franchis'd, subterranean caves. **1848** HARE *Guesses* Ser. II. (1859) 341 The sayings of the *free-garmented folks in Julius Cesar could not have come from the close-buttoned generation in Othello. **1824** LOUDON *Encycl. Gard.* (ed. 2) 396 The species of stocks for fruit-trees are divided into what are called *free-growing and dwarfing stocks. **1902** *Daily Chron.* 1 Apr. 2/1 The free-growing heralds of spring [*sc.* daffodils]. **1952** A. G. L. HELLYER *Sanders' Encycl. Gardening* (ed. 22), *L[ycopodium] Billardieri*, free-growing creeper, New Zealand. **1647** STAPYLTON *Juvenal* 215 They'r *free-mein'd, gallants, and fine gentlemen. **1597** BACON *Ess.*, *Regiment of Health* (Arb.) 58 To be *free minded and chearefully disposed at howers of meate and of sleepe and of exercise. **1834** T. MOORE *Mem.* (1856) VII. 41 As if they were more high and free-minded from having slaves to trample upon. **1579** KNEWSTUB *Confutation* 68 b, Out of the *free mindednes of their heat [? heart]. **1647** H. MORE *Song of Soul* II. iii. III. lviii, Mirth, and Free-mindednesse, Simplicitie. **1862** MERIVALE *Rom. Emp.* (1865) VII. lxii. 403 A vain pretence of *free-mouthed patriotism. **1835–6** TODD *Cycl. Anat.* I. 688/1 The *free-moving young have very well developed eyes. **1942** C. R. CARPENTER in *Jrnl. Compar. Psychol.* XXXIII. 113 (*title*) Sexual behavior of *free ranging rhesus monkeys. **1948** V. MASSEY *On being Canadian* iii. 43 Free-ranging experimentation in ideas. **1958** *Observer* 19 Oct. 17/4 They [*sc.* geese] demand an open-air, free-ranging life. **1963** *Times* 7 Feb. 8/4 The Government.. are anxious that the Commons should work for a free-ranging debate. **1940** *Chambers's Techn. Dict.* 353/2 **Free-running speed*, the speed which a vehicle or train will attain when propelled by a constant tractive effort. **1960** *Farmer & Stockbreeder* 15 Mar. 48/1 (Advt.), Free-running baler and binder twine. **1962** SIMPSON & RICHARDS *Junction Transistors* xvi. 404 The astable circuit is an oscillator whose output is a flat-topped wave... It is often called a free-running multivibrator or.. simply a multivibrator. **1677** GALE *Crt. Gentiles* IV. 429 Princes.. ought to be *freespirited, generose, liberal. **1735** BERKELEY *Def. Free-thinking in Math.* §8 Many free-spirited inquiries after truth. **1894** *Pop. Sci. Monthly* June 272 A pelagic or *free-swimming Ascidian. **1599** MASSINGER, etc. *Old Law* IV. ii, A *free-tongued woman, And very excellent at telling secrets. **1877** DOWDEN *Shaks. Prim.* vi. 141 The free-tongued girls of Cleopatra. *a* **1619** FOTHERBY *Atheom.* I. xiii. §1 (1622) 135 Both wittingly, and willingly, by a *free-working will. **1793** SMEATON *Edystone L.* §98 Portland, or some other free working stone. **1892** J. C. BLOMFIELD *Hist. Heyford* 3 Light or free-working land may be ploughed more easily than that which is stiff and heavy.

b. in derivative combinations based upon some recognized phrase in which the adjective is employed, as *free-agency*, *-citizenship*, *-pressism*, etc. (after *free agent*, *free citizen*, *free press*, etc.).

1754 FIELDING *Voy. Lisbon* (1755) 129, I would rob him of nothing but that *free-agency which is the cause of all the corruption.. of human nature. **1786** BURKE *W. Hastings* Wks. 1842 II. 205 The restoration of the Mogul.. to his free-agency in the conduct of his affairs. **1860** PUSEY *Min. Proph.* 324 He so wills to be freely loved.. that He does not force our free-agency. **1849** GROTE *Greece* II. lxix. (1862) VI. 216 To Xerxes, the conception of *free-citizenship.. was.. incomprehensible. **1856** *Tait's Mag.* XXIII. 698 Our *free pressism is one of our peculiarities.

c. in secondary combination with a verbal or agent noun (where *free* seems partly adverbial, qualifying the action understood), as *free-acting*, *-handler*, *-handling*, *-seeker*, *-speaker*, *-speaking*, *-writer*, *-writing*. So FREE-LIVER, -THINKER, etc.

1738–41 WARBURTON *Div. Legat.* App. 41 'Tis the punishment of *free-acting to fear where no fear is. **1862** F. HALL *Hindu Philos. Syst.* 157 The sanctimonious vocabulary of *free-handlers and secularists. **1875** E. WHITE *Life in Christ* II. xii. (1878) 144 If you will but nullify by criticism and *free-handling the truth on Atonement. **1693** LUTTRELL *Brief Rel.* (1857) III. 56 A new sect is started up here called the *Freeseekers. **1716** ADDISON *Drummer* I. 10 I'm a Free-thinker, Child. *Ab.* I am sure you are a *Free-speaker! **1660** *Trial Regic.* 49 Let there be *free-speaking by the Prisoner and Councel. **1711** SHAFTESB. *Charac.* (1737) I. 65 In the case of many zealots, who have taken upon 'em to answer our modern *free-writers. **1732** BERKELEY *Alciphr.* II. §6 In this most wise and happy age of Free-thinking, Free-speaking, *Free-writing, and Free-acting.

2. In spec. phrases, etc.: **free activity**, used *attrib.* of a type of school or method of teaching in which children learn through their own efforts and experiments and not through instruction by a teacher; also, usu. in *pl.* (not *attrib.*), such activities; †**free alms** = *frank almoign* (see ALMOIGN); **free association** *Psychol.*, in an experiment based on the association of ideas, an association freely made by the person undergoing the test without suggestion or control on the part of the experimenter; hence **free-associational**, **free-associative** *adjs.*; **free-associate** *v. intr.*; **free-chant** *Mus.* (see quot.); **free cinema** (see quots. 1956); so *free film*; **free city**, (*a*) in the Middle Ages, a sovereign city-state in Germany; (*b*) a semi-autonomous city under the authority of an international body; **free companion** (see quot. and cf. FREE LANCE); so **free company**; **free-cutting** *a. Metallurgy*, applied to a metal with good machining properties, esp. when these are due to small quantities of some additional substance; **free diver**, a skin-diver; so **free-diving** *vbl. sb.*, skin-diving; **free drop**, a parachute descent made with a free parachute; **free enterprise**, the freedom of private business from state control; hence **free enterpriser**, an advocate or follower of such a system; **free expression**, the uninhibited expression of one's thoughts, feelings, creative capacities, etc.; **free fall**, the movement, of a body under no forces other than gravity, there being neither thrust nor (appreciable) drag acting on it; as (*a*) the flight of a ballistic missile after the driving power is cut off; (*b*) in a parachute descent, the part of the fall before the parachute opens (drag on the parachutist being neglected); (*c*) the flight of a spacecraft in space when there is no thrust from the engines, and any occupants of it experience weightlessness; phr. ***in free fall***, moving or flying in these conditions; hence **free-fall** *v.*; **free film**, see *free cinema*; †**free fish** (see quot.); **free flight**, *spec.* (*a*) the flight of an unmoored balloon, or of a glider released from its towing-rope; (*b*) flight of an aircraft, missile, etc., in free fall; (*c*) used *attrib.* to designate a wind tunnel in which the model is not mounted but supported by aerodynamic forces like an aircraft in flight; **free food**, food imported free of tax or duty; also *attrib.*; **free-fooder**, a politician who opposes taxes on food; **free-form** *attrib.*, spec. of an irregular shape or structure; also *ellipt.*; **free gift**, *spec.* an object given away without charge to promote sales (cf. sense 21 b); **free gold**, gold occurring naturally in a pure state or uncombined with other substances; **free grace**, the unmerited favour of God (whence †*free gracian*); †**free holly** (see quot.); **free (public) house** (see quot. 1858); **free jump** *Parachuting*, = *free drop*; **free kick** (see KICK *sb.*[1] 1); **free library**: see LIBRARY[1] 1 b; **free list**, a list of persons from whom, or things on which, payment is not required (see also quot. 1870); so **free list** *v. trans.*; **free-loader** *slang* (orig. *U.S.*), one who eats or drinks without expense to himself, a sponger; so **free-loading** *vbl. sb.* and *ppl. a.*, and (as a back-formation) **free-load** *v. intr.*; **free love**, the doctrine of the right of free choice in sexual relations without the restraint of marriage or other legal obligation; whence *free-lover*, *-loving*, *-lovism*, etc.; **free lunch**, a lunch given gratis, esp. by bar-keepers to attract customers; so **free-luncher**; **free-milling** *a. Mining* (of ores) easily reducible; **free paper** *U.S.*, (*pl.*) documents proclaiming the status of a manumitted slave; **free parachute**, one released by the parachutist and not by a static line attached to the aircraft; **free part** *Mus.* (see quot.); **free pass**, authority to travel on a railway, etc., or to enter a place of entertainment without payment; **free path** *Physics*, (*a*) the distance which a molecule or other particle traverses without encountering another particle and without colliding with the walls of the containing vessel; (*b*) the distance a sound wave travels between successive reflections from the walls of an enclosure; usu. as ***mean free path*** (in both senses); **free period** (see quot. 1961); **free place**, a place in a secondary school awarded free to a scholar from an elementary school; also *attrib.*; hence **free-placer**, one who holds a free place; **free radical** *Chem.*, an uncharged atom or group of atoms having one or more unpaired electrons, esp. when these normally form part of a bond; **free range**, (*a*) *U.S.*, free pasturage; (*b*) used esp. *attrib.* of chickens given freedom to range for food (opp. BATTERY 13 c); so *free-range egg*, etc.; **free return** *Astronaut.*, the positioning of a spacecraft on to the correct return flight path by planetary gravitation; **free school**, (*a*) (see sense 32 b); (*b*) an independently-run school based on the principle that children should be allowed to develop without the restrictions imposed by examinations, authority, and other features of traditional education; **free silver** *U.S.*, the free coinage of silver bullion at government mints; also, belief in or advocacy of such a policy; **free skating**, a competitive programme of variable skating figures performed to music; **free speech** (cf. sense 25); **free-standing** *a.*, standing alone; not supported by a structural framework; **Free Stater**, a native or inhabitant of a free state as the Orange Free State or Irish Free State; one supporting such a state; **free stock** (see quot. 1763); plants grown from seed to be used as rootstocks in grafting; **free-stuff** *Building* (see quot.); **free-style** *a.*, = FREE *a.* 9; applied *spec.* to a swimming race in which the style of stroke used is left to the competitor's choice; also *absol.*; †**free suitor**, one of the tenants entitled to attend a manorial court; **free union** [F. *union libre*], cohabitation of a couple without marriage; **free vector** *Math.*, a vector of which only the magnitude and direction are specified, not the position or line of action; **free verse** = VERS LIBRE; so **free-verser**; **free vote**, a Parliamentary vote not made subject to party discipline; †**free ward**, ? = L. *libera custodia*, detention not involving close or ignominious restraint (hence *free-warder*); †**free-work**, ? decorative mason-work.

1941 N. CATTY *Learning & Teaching in Junior School* ii. 34 Other periods are devoted primarily to children's individual work and *free activities. **1942** *Brit. Jrnl. Psychol.* Oct. 140 Four 'experimental' ('free activity') schools were paired with 'control' schools.. in which the teaching was of the formal type. **1965** W. LAMB *Posture & Gesture* viii. 106 'Free activity' methods in the teaching of physical education give scope for much emotional and chaotic work. **1503–4** *Act 19 Hen. VII*, c. 29 Preamb., To hold.. of your Highnesse and of your heyres in *free & perpetuall Almes. **1628** COKE *On Litt.* 97 a, Free almes, (which was free from any limitation of certaintie). **1899** W. JAMES *Talks to Teachers* 219 Stated technically, the law is this: that strong feeling about one's self tends to arrest the *free association of one's objective ideas and motor processes. **1905** E. B. TITCHENER *Exper. Psychol.* II. i. 192 We show him a word; he is to react when the word has suggested something, no matter what. The word *sea* may arouse the idea of land or water or ships or some particular sea or some particular incident at sea,—anything it likes. Associations of this sort are termed, technically, *free* associations. **1964** GOULD & KOLB *Dict. Social Sci.* 557/1 Freud.. induced his patients to disclose their thoughts without censorship, allowing ideas to enter their minds in undirected free association. **1941** *Brit. Jrnl. Psychol.* July 41 The responses given.. were very full and largely *free-associational in content. **1960** *Guardian* 9 Sept. 7/3 A solid chunk of free-associational near-verse. **1958** *Times Lit. Suppl.* 24 Jan. 44/1 A time when literary fantasy of a *free-associative, surrealistic kind was by no means the commonplace that it is today. **1970** *New Yorker* 29 Aug. 24/1 He.. diverted the rest of the hour into a lengthy free-associative screen about certain rhapsodic sexual events. **1941** *Mind* L. 80 If you start *free-associating from any item in consciousness you will be bound to reach a sexual item sooner or later. **1954** *Amer. Jrnl. Psychol.* LXVII. 244, I will read *four* words slowly and.. you are to free-associate to the last word only. **1971** *Daily Tel.* (Colour Suppl.) 2 Apr. 7/1 He is not very interested in probing the subconscious of his patients, or allowing them to free-associate about childhood miseries. **1876** STAINER & BARRETT *Dict. Mus. Terms*, **Free chant* is a form of recitative music for the Psalms and Canticles, in which a phrase, consisting of two chords only, is applied to each hemistich of the words. **1956** *Living Cinema* I. 9 The phrase '*Free Cinema' coined by the National Film Theatre is a happy thought, for it can be used.. to cover words like 'avant-garde' and 'experimental'. *Ibid.*, Free Cinema.. can.. include any film in which the maker has succeeded in breaking the chains.. of financial or ideological control. **1963** *Listener* 14 Feb. 300/1 *Saturday Night and Sunday Morning*, *A Kind of Loving*, and other products of Free Cinema are, at best, admirable documentaries. **1617** *Free city [see IMPERIAL 10]. **1621** P. HEYLYN *Microcosmus* 145 The citties of this country are of 3 sorts... The third sorte are the Free or Imperiall citties... These free citties are in number 60. **1665** Free city [see HANSEATIC *a.*]. **1797** *Encycl. Brit.* VIII. 284/1 [Hamburg] was declared a free imperial city by a decree of the aulic. **1919** *Times* 28 June (Suppl. Treaty Versailles) p. vii/6 (Article 102) The Principal Allied and Associated Powers undertake to establish the town of Danzig.. as a Free City. It will be placed under the protection of the League of Nations. **1958** *Listener* 4 Dec. 936/1 A proposal that.. the western sector [of Berlin] should be made a 'free city' with its own government. **1959** *Chambers's Encycl.* VI. 261 Less secure was the position of the 'free cities' whose autonomy was not protected by imperial privileges. Among them.. were flourishing communities, such as Brunswick, Lüneburg, Magdeburg and Emden. **1965** A. J. P. TAYLOR *Eng. Hist. 1914–1945* iv. 134 Thanks to him [*sc.* Lloyd George], Danzig became a Free City, instead of being annexed to Poland. **1820** SCOTT *Ivanhoe* viii, A knight who rode near him, the leader of a band of *Free Companions, or Condottieri; that is, of mercenaries belonging to no particular nation, but attached for the time to any prince by whom they were paid. **1872** RUSKIN *Fors Clav.* II. xv. 11 A soldier in one of these *free companies. **1927** *Mech. Engin.* XLIX. 163/2 The writer..

asks what is *free-cutting steel, and how does it differ from steel difficult to machine? The latter is tough or ductile, and ..it is often most difficult to cut good threads in such material..but..free-cutting steel is 'free-breaking' steel. 1949 R. T. Rolfe Dict. Metallogr. (ed. 2) 108 Free-cutting quality, the quality possessed by a specific grade of a particular material whereby the machinability..is increased, usually by the addition of a further constituent. 1958 Jrnl. Iron & Steel Inst. CXC. 89/3 In the field of free-cutting steels, special mention is made of leaded steels as a means of improving the machinability of low-carbon, high-nickel carburizing steels. 1963 L. Deighton Horse under Water xxvi. 109 A professional salvage *free-diver. 1963 Harper's Bazaar Jan. 30/2 Breathing in from containers strapped to their backs, experienced 'free divers' can go as deep as 130 ft. for 15 minutes. 1955 Sci. News Let. 2 July 13/1 *Free-diving has given marine biologists a revolutionary method of specimen collecting. 1957 G. Clark Archaeol. & Society (ed. 3) ii. 48 The development of the aqualung and of the technique of free-diving by M. Cousteau and his associates has recently made it possible to envisage submarine archaeology as a field of purposeful research as well as of lucky finds. 1940 War Illustr. 26 Jan. 20/2 Not until 1919 did the first successful '*free' drop take place. 1944 Jane's All World's Aircraft 1943–44 25/1 After seven free drops [the parachutist] qualifies for his parachute badge. 1890 A. Marshall Princ. Econ. I. i. ii. 30 The growth of *free enterprise in England. 1938 Newsweek 3 Oct. 37/3 Management leaders representing the world's democratic countries agreed that free enterprise, not government control, is the key to better times. 1957 L. F. R. Williams State of Israel 103 The so-called middle-class villages—based on free-enterprise farming and hired labour. 1943 Lincoln (Nebr.) Jrnl. 16 Aug., *Free enterprisers in this country include the big industrialists. 1967 Listener 8 June 752/1 Conservatives and free-enterprisers of every colour. 1943 H. Read Educ. through Art v. 109 Play is the most obvious form of *free expression in children and there has been a persistent attempt on the part of anthropologists and psychologists to identify all forms of free expression with play. 1958 Spectator 4 July 14/1 First there were filmed excerpts from the studio, with its presiding talent, Lee Strasberg, analysing free expression exercises. 1967 M. Drabble Jerusalem Golden vi. 149 The efforts of the American teacher at their nursery group to make the children paint with free expression. 1967 D. P. Carew Many Years, Many Girls vii. 140 A 'free expression' afternoon was instituted during which we could please ourselves what we did. 1919 R. D. Goddard Method of Reaching Extreme Altitudes 59 The time of descent [of a rocket] will also be short; but *free fall can be satisfactorily prevented by a suitable parachute. 1920 Flight XII. 210/1 With parachutes having problematical opening..the uncertainty of the free-fall is such that no one ever dreams of making a practice drop with it at less than 2,000 ft. 1930 P. White How to fly Airplane xxii. 304 The usual and safest time to open the parachute is immediately after clearing the ship, unless an emergency arises in which it is necessary to make a long free fall before pulling the rip cord. 1953 Authentic Science Fiction 15 Feb. 49 She wanted me to explain to you that..she was weightless at that point, 'as I'm in free fall'. 1955 Times 25 Aug. 6/3 She claimed a world record for a 'free fall' jump, having descended approximately 26,238 ft. before she pulled the ripcord. 1956 W. A. Heflin U.S.A.F. Dict. 221 Free-fall, to make a free fall. 1958 C. C. Adams et al. Space Flight 142 In the free fall (zero gravity of orbit), telescopes (particularly radio telescopes) of fantastic size could be assembled. 1959 W. Golding (title) Free fall. 1959 Time 17 Aug. 15/3, I free-fell an eternity. 1961 Listener 9 Nov. 765/1 The occupants of the projectile would have been in free fall, and therefore weightless, from the moment of firing. 1962 F. I. Ordway et al. Basic Astronautics viii. 346 An interplanetary vehicle after its freefall back to Earth will have an approach velocity of 25,000 mph or more. 1971 Daily Tel. 16 Aug. 9/7 When he pulled the cord he had been free-falling for 5,000 ft. 1958 R. Hoggart in N. Mackenzie Conviction 137 The '*free' films made by such men as Lindsay Anderson and Karel Reisz. 1602 Carew Cornwall 31 a, After Shell-fish succeedeth the *free-fish, so termed, because he wanteth this shelly bulwarke. 1922 Flight XIV. 147/2 It is probable that the resistance of the supports in *free flight can be cut down to one-half the minimum drag of the wing. 1939 Jrnl. R. Aeronaut. Soc. XLIII. 792 With background experience in development of a free-spinning tunnel..the Committee felt that the attempt to develop a free-flight tunnel was amply justified. 1954 N.Y. Times Mag. 29 Aug. 49/1 The Honest John free-flight artillery rocket is this [pre-set] type of missile. 1959 Listener 12 Feb. 282/1 The condition of weightlessness during free-flight. 1970 R. Turnill Lang. Space 48 An Apollo space-craft is also in 'free flight' all the way to the moon and back once it has been injected into the required trajectory. 1903 Westm. Gaz. 17 June 7/2 The *free food Unionists. 1903 National Rev. Aug. 893 Though calling themselves Free Fooders, they are not in favour of Free Food. 1967 R. S. Churchill Winston Churchill II. ii. 62 Churchill was a prime mover in what was ultimately to be named the Free Food League. 1903 Duke of Devonshire Let. 10 Oct. in J. Amery Life J. Chamberlain (1969) VI. cix. 482, I am not sure whether you and the other *Free Fooders do not wish to take up a more hostile attitude..than I. 1905 Spectator 7 Jan. 13/2 Such a supposition..is surely strange as coming from convinced Free-Fooders. 1969 J. Amery Life J. Chamberlain VI. cxi. 559 This amendment was not one which the 'Free Fooders' would be likely to oppose. 1952 in N. Mailer Advts. for Myself (1961) 157 Sam resents ..the slender coffee table, a *free-form poised like a spider on wire legs. 1957 'P. Quentin' Suspicious Circ. iv. 37, I walked..towards the free-form swimming-pool. 1960 M. Millar Stranger in my Grave xv. 161 A half-finished free-form table which Jim was making. 1968 Economist 17 Feb. 76/1 All these conglomerates have 'free-form' management structures, with a small central staff supervising the profitability of a host of disparate subsidiaries. 1969 Sunday Times (Colour Suppl.) 12 Jan. 15/3 In most of the communities there is free-form music, an uncoordinated bedlam of bells, guitars, drums and oriental chant. 1909 Daily Chron. 28 July 7/6 (Advt.), Make use of the Free Coupon printed here and you will receive..a *free-gift parcel containing a Bottle of Guy's Tonic. 1933 Punch 19 July 61/1 She..collected over a thousand Free Gift coupons which she has exchanged for a portable radio set. 1965 Guardian 19 May 7/1 Gimmicks and the offering of free gifts to promote sales were condemned. 1897 'Mark Twain' Following Equator 687 No way of getting anything out of the rock but the coarser-grained '*free' gold. 1901 Daily Colonist (Victoria, B.C.) 11 Oct. 8/4 The rock is a free-milling quartzite, plentifully impregnated with free gold in specks, plainly visible to the naked eye. 1960 B. Ramsey Barkerville 21 A small vein which showed substantial values and several sizeable fragments of free gold. 1651 C. Cartwright Cert. Relig. i. 108 How many, O Lord, doe with Pelagius fight for Free-will against Thy *Free-grace? 1871 Carlyle in Mrs. Carlyle's Lett. I. 380 [She] was filled with the consciousness of free grace. 1647 Saltmarsh Sparkl. Glory (1847) 141 The *Free-Gracian. They that have discovered up into free-grace or the mystery of salvation [etc.]. 1610 Guillim Heraldry iii. vii. 108 There is a kinde of Holly that is void of these Prickles..and therefore called *Free-holly, which in my opinion is the best Holly. 1858 Simmonds Dict. Trade, *Free public-house, one not belonging to a brewer; the landlord has therefore free liberty to brew his own beer, or purchase where he chooses. 1894 G. Moore Esther Waters xxx. 236 The 'King's Head' ..had..one thing in its favour—it was a free house. 1927 W. E. Collinson Contemp. Eng. 80 Tied houses and free houses. 1930 Daily Express 16 Aug. 10/2 To bring about in large regional areas the compulsory merging of brewery companies, including 'free' houses. 1959 'O. Mills' Stairway to Murder ii. 18 The notification 'Free House' beside the inn-sign. 1930 D. Verrill Aircraft Bk. for Boys xi. 189 A diagram of a '*free jump' from a plane, in which the jumper counts five (or more) before pulling the rip-cord and releasing the parachute. 1806 Let. 26 Dec. in L. Sumbel Mem. (1811) III. 212 He has received Mr. Thomas Sheridan's directions to put her name and friend on the *free-list. 1833 Deb. Congress U.S. 20 Feb. 1749 The gentleman moved to strike the article of cotton out from the free list of imports. 1845 Ann. Rep. Treas. U.S. 6 An adequate revenue will still be produced, and permit the addition to the free list of salt and guano. 1855 M. Thomson Doesticks xxvi. 229 The Bowery Theatre..where they announce a grand 'benefit' five nights in the week, for the purpose of cutting off the free list. 1856 [see free a. 32]. 1870 J. K. Medbery Men & Myst. Wall St. 20 The securities..are divided into two classes, known respectively as the Regular and the Free List. 1909 Daily Chron. 13 Apr. 5/2 Cocoa was free listed on the ground that..it was a common necessity of life. 1969 Listener 13 Nov. 680/3 The Spectator's reviewer..has been dropped from the free list at that theatre. 1967 B. Norman Matter of Mandrake viii. 56 *Free-load, Neddy Masters had said. Get a little drunk. 1968 Word Study Dec. 5/2 A leech is one who attaches himself to another person in order to borrow or to freeload or merely to relieve his loneliness. 1947 Time 24 Mar. 63 Even men who don't frequent saloons would come in to see a hockey game. And *free loaders were no problem; most people bought at least a few beers while they watched. 1948 R. Chandler Let. 20 Sept. (1966) 165 We didn't have this cat seventeen years in order for some freeloader to say God forgive him he'd even take a piece about her for his goddam parish magazine. 1951 N.Y. Times 15 Apr. vii. 23/3 Congressmen are great freeloaders. 1960 News Chron. 12 July 4/4 The weirdest assortment of beatniks, drunks, romantics, poets, free-loaders, millionaires. 1967 Melody Maker 23 Dec. 7 A Freeloader is one who has discovered that you can drink yourself silly for absolutely no expense if you attend all the receptions. 1956 J. Cannon Who struck John? 123 [The art of] *free loading in the fight racket has diminished. 1964 S. Bellow Herzog (1965) 124 My lousy, free-loading bohemian family, all chisellers. 1971 Daily Tel. 1 July 7/3 Since the food cost an average of £1·75 a head, she thought this was freeloading at the taypayers' expense. [1814 Theatr. Inquis. IV. 384 Mr. and Mrs. Kemble, as Freelove and Lady Eliza,..were beyond all praise.] 1822 A. Cunningham Tales Eng. & Sc. Peasantry II. 73 [Her] thoughts had been weaned..from *free love to religion. 1859 Holland Gold F. vi. 96 The free-love doctrines and free-love practices of the day. 1872 Tennyson Last Tournament 275 'Free love—free field—we love but while we may.' 1971 Guardian 23 July 7/2 A young person today was bombarded on all sides by invitations to free love. 1858 Baltimore Sun 28 June (Bartlett), Abolitionists, spiritualists, and *free lovers. 1872 F. Hall Recent Exempl. False Phil. 89 Free-lovers may, with good reason, look up. 1879 Geo. Eliot Theo. Such xviii. 318 Affection which lifts us above emigrating rats and *free-loving baboons. 1864 Realm 17 Feb. 3 Advocates of *free-lovism, who believe the great evil of the world to be the indissolubility of marriage. 1854 Wide West (San Francisco) 26 Nov. 2/3 The excitement during the week on the subject of the '*free lunches' has been of the most intense character. 1889 Kansas Times & Star 25 June, Two..Saloon keepers here were notified by the police department to discontinue the free lunches at their places. 1905 Daily Chron. 9 Sept. 6/7 The free-lunch system in Manchester is dying out. 1908 G. H. Lorimer J. Spurlock v. 82, I had mapped out the most complete little free-lunch route in New York City. 1909 'O. Henry' Roads of Destiny iv. 58 [His] memories of the old hotel are limited to his having been kicked out from its free-lunch counter in 1873. 1927 H. Crane Let. 16 Feb. (1965) 286 If you want the good old beer, the old free-lunch counter and everything thrown in—for 15¢ a glass. 1876 Ventura Free Press (San Buenaventura, Calif.) 8 Jan. 1/6 A healthy *free luncher.. commenced operations with a sandwich. 1898 Daily News 15 July 6/6, I felt flattered myself, a mere free-luncher, when I saw the great Joseph, with the income of a prince, thus deigning to superintend my viands. 1895 City Review 3 July 3/2 *Free milling ores are usually obtained from the auriferous quartz lying near the surface. 1838 in J. S. Buckingham America (1841) I. 282 Henry has relations.. some of them free, and likely he has *free papers. 1881 Century Mag. Nov. 126/1 It was the custom in the state of Maryland to require the free colored people to have what were called free papers. 1933 Flight 30 Mar. 302 (heading) *Free parachute jumping. 1935 C. G. Burge Compl. Bk. Aviation 489/2 Free parachute, a parachute whose pack is secured only to the body of the user, the release of which is dependent on some act on his part other than falling from the aircraft. 1942 A. M. Low Parachutes iii. 39 In the 'free' parachute the airman pulls the rip-cord himself. 1876 Stainer & Barrett Dict. Mus. Terms, *Free-parts, additional parts to a canon or fugue, having independent melodies, in order to strengthen or complete the harmony. 1857 Trans. Ill. Agric. Soc. II. 2 The railroad company sent *free passes over their whole line. 1894 Free pass [see free a. 32]. 1879 English Mechanic 5 Sept. 639/1 This dark space is found to increase and diminish as the vacuum is varied, and is found to be the mean *free path of the molecules of the residual gas. 1940 J. H. Jeans Introd. Kinetic Theory Gases v. 131 Viscosity and conduction of heat can be explained in terms of the collisions of gas molecules, and of the free paths which the molecules describe between collisions. 1947 Proc. Physical Soc. LIX. 536 For rooms of the usual shapes the mean free path of sound is independent of the shape. 1966 McGraw-Hill Encycl. Sci. & Technol. VIII. 187 The types of mean free paths which are used most frequently are for elastic collisions of molecules in a gas, of electrons in a crystal, of phonons in a crystal, and of neutrons in a moderator. 1945 C. V. Good Dict. Educ. 292/1 *Period, free,..designating the time in a regular school day during which a teacher or a pupil has no definitely assigned duties. 1961 Where? Winter 1960–61, 14 Free period, (1) time in a school curriculum for private or unsupervised study. (2) time when a teacher is not allocated a class. 1965 'O. Mills' Dusty Death xx. 196 Old Cowley knows I skive off during that free period. 1968 'P. Hobson' Titty's Dead ii. 22 'So sorry if I'm late. But it's my free period.'.. She taught classics and she was the Senior Mistress. 1907 Hansard, Commons 15 May 1054 These *free places..would be for Public Elementary School children who would not be asked to compete with children outside but who would only be asked to pass a qualifying examination. 1909 Daily Chron. 28 July 5/5 The distinction between fee-paying and free-place scholars. 1920 Rep. Departm. Committee on Scholarships 2 in Parl. Papers (Cmd. 968) XV. 385 To qualify as a 'free place' pupil the child must have attended a Public Elementary School for a certain period previously. Ibid. 35 The existing provision of free places in secondary schools appears to us inadequate. 1926 Rep. Consult. Cttee. Educ. of Adolescent 133 The Free Place Examination is conducted in writing. 1921 G. Sampson English for the English 44 Scholarship children or '*free-placers'. 1961 Economist 16 Dec. 1119/1 These 'free-placers' are sometimes brighter than the fee-payers. [1886 E. F. Smith tr. Richter's Chem. Carbon Compounds 200 The free acid radicals, like all monovalent groups, cannot exist free.] 1900 Jrnl. Amer. Chem. Soc. XXII. 768 We have to deal here with a *free radical, triphenylmethyl. 1948 W. A. Waters Chem. Free Radicals (ed. 2) i. 4 The great chemical activity of the free radicals is to be associated with available combining energy of the odd electron. 1954 Sci. Amer. Sept. 86/3 Fragments of molecules known as free radicals. 1971 Nature 12 Feb. 500/1 The presence of free radicals in cigarette smoke was demonstrated by Lyons et al. 1912 Mulford & Clay Buck Peters 186 Outlying *free range had been thoroughly combed. 1947 Steamboat (Colo.) Pilot 13 Feb. 8/4 Then sheep commenced to come for a share of the free range. 1950 N.Z. Jrnl. Agric. Dec. 550 Pullets are usually given good free range, but frequently cockerels are not so well treated. 1960 Times 2 May 8/6 At least one farmer with a roadside trade knows that increasing numbers of motorist shoppers are looking for eggs produced by free-range hens. Ibid., His blackboard announces two prices which show the premium he expects to be paid for the free-range egg. 1968 Times 29 Nov. 13/1 There seems to be no scientific basis for the commonly held belief that free-range eggs have more flavour and are more nutritious than battery eggs. 1964 R. H. Battin Astronaut. Guidance 392 *Free-return trajectories. 1969 Daily Tel. (Colour Suppl.) 10 Jan. 21 (caption) Moonbug retro-fires to achieve 'free-return' elliptical orbit. 1970 Times 15 Apr. 10/2 As the vehicle travelled round to the back of the moon, the effect of the lunar gravitation field was such as to swing the ship round on to a homeward trajectory. This is what the flight dynamics specialists call a free return trajectory. 1926 A. S. Neill Problem Child xvi. 209 The Germans had a *free school, rather like King Alfred School, in London. A school with co-education, much freedom, no punishments, no rewards. 1968 Time 2 Feb. 60/3 Children who emerge from such a free school tend to be behind in factual knowledge..but they catch up quickly because they are better able to interpret what they read. 1974 D. Head Free Way to Learning i. 19 But free schools wish to be free as a 'free-thinker' is free—free from the authoritarian attitudes, the examinations, the grades, the competition, and all that makes school a mirror of society as it is. 1977 Undercurrents June–July 16/2 Down in West Cork settlers use the local protestant primary schools or none rather than send children to catholic schools. I suppose in due course free schools and play schools will be formed in country areas. 1890 Nation (N.Y.) 1 May 346/1 The latest bill..provides for..the purchase by the Treasury of 4,500,000 ounces of '*free silver' per month. 1895 Chicago Tribune 6 Apr. 1 Free Silver or Ruin, Hinrichsen will force his Fiat Money campaign. 1900 'Mark Twain' Speeches (1910) 192, I am in favor of..the gold standard and free silver. 1942 R. G. Lillard Desert Challenge 50 Free silver was the symbol..of the agricultural West and South against the financial East. 1902 Encycl. Brit. XXXII. 642/2 *Free skating,..affording scope for the performance of dance steps and brilliant individual figures. 1970 Radio Times 29 Jan. 54 Double and treble Axel-Paulsen Jumps are among the most difficult and spectacular manœuvres in free-skating. 1848 N.Y. Weekly Tribune 15 July 3/4 To address the citizens..upon the subject of *Free Soil and Free Speech. 1859 Geo. Eliot Let. 18 Sept. (1954) III. 154, I begin to think silence the only good thing..if the inevitable result of *free speech is, that we must fall..into complaint and accusation. 1943 J. S. Huxley Evol. Ethics vii. 59 The suppression of free speech and inquiry. 1876 J. Fergusson Hist. Indian Archit. i. v. 121 A *free-standing building. 1936 Archit. Rev. LXXIX. 14 (caption) It shows the free-standing structural column which occurs in the hall of each flat. 1951 Good Housek. Home Encycl. 232/1 Both free-standing and built-in models ..are available. 1963 W. F. Grimes in Foster & Alcock Culture & Environment v. 95 A ring of free-standing stones set within or mounted upon a circular bank. 1899 Daily Chron. 27 Sept. 5/3 The sickly sentiment of the *Free Staters. 1940 L. A. G. Strong Sun on Water 206 When the troubles came, it was Johnny..who turned Republican, and Denis a fanatical Free Stater. 1719 London & Wise Compl. Gard. iv. 52 It should be Grafted on a Quince-stock, because on a *Free-Stock the Fruit grows spotted, small, and crumpled. 1763 J. Wheeler Botan. & Gard. Dict. s.v. Pyrus, All the sorts propagated in gardens are produced by budding, or grafting them upon stocks of their own kind; which are commonly called free-stocks. 1852 G. W. Johnson Cottage Gardeners' Dict. 851/2 Free Stocks are such as are raised from the seed, layers, &c., of any of the cultivated varieties of fruit-trees, and others. **1955** R. ATKINSON *Growing Apples* ii. 20 A few seedlings—called 'free' or 'crab' stocks and grown from cider apple or wild crab pips—are still sometimes used. **1823** P. NICHOLSON *Pract. Build.* 223 *Free Stuff, that timber or stuff which is quite clean, or without knots. **1620** WILKINSON *Courts Leet & Baron* 108 Then call the *free suitors and dozonors one after another. *c* **1640** J. SMYTH *Lives Berkeleys* (1883) I. 195 Which in the Court of this Lord in Radclive street shee denyed; whereupon the freesuters there gave judgment vpon his life. **1934** WEBSTER, *Free style. **1950** *Oxf. Jun. Encycl.* IX. 454/2 In free-style and breast-stroke races the competitors start with a dive. **1957** N. FRYE *Anat. Criticism* 91 The free-style allegories. **1958** P. GAMMOND *Decca Bk. Jazz* x. 125 He helped to keep free-style jazz alive with his Clambake Seven. **1960** M. WOODHOUSE *Tree Frog* ii. 10 She ..swam free style for the West of England. **1931** *Times Lit. Suppl.* 1 Oct. 742/4 Marriage, companionate marriage, *free unions, are considered intimately. **1919** L. SILBERSTEIN *Elem. Vector Algebra* i. 2 It is then obviously convenient *not* to include position among the determining characteristics of a vector. Such vectors, in distinction from localized ones, are called *free vectors. **1964** E. Œ. WOLSTENHOLME *Elem. Vectors* i. 2 When the term *vector* is used, it is assumed that it refers to a free vector. **1908** A. NOYES *W. Morris* 119 The so-called '*free-verse' experiments, with abrupt and meaningless jerks or bumps. **1914** C. MACKENZIE *Sinister St.* II. III. ix. 682, I hate Free Thought, Free Love and Free Verse. **1926** W. R. INGE *Lay Thoughts* 31 A cubist or a free-verse writer. **1926** *Glasgow Herald* 1 Feb. 8 Those among the *free-versers who are not purely imbecile are disgruntled, sarcastic, and gloomy. **1931** *Economist* 25 Apr. 885/1 The House was accorded the opportunity of a '*free vote', which it gave..in favour of the Bill. **1955** *Times* 30 June 11/3 In a free vote..the House of Commons signified a desire that legislation should be introduced to improve the financial position of junior Ministers. **1971** *Times* 20 Oct. 1/1 Mr. Heath's dramatic decision on Monday to concede a free vote to Conservative backbenchers placed Opposition leaders in an extremely difficult position. **1637** RUTHERFORD *Let.* 23 Sep. (1891) 523 My spirit also is in *free ward. *Ibid.* 17 Sep. (1891) 516 Jesus hath a backbond of all our temptations, that the free-warders shall come out by law and justice, in respect of the infinite and great sum that the Redeemer paid. *a* **1718** PENN *Tracts* Wks. 1726 I. 726 Sculpture, *Free-work, inlayings and Painted Windows.

free (friː), *v.* Pa. t. and pa. pple. freed. [OE. *fréon*, *fréoȝ(e)an*, = MHG. *vrîjen*, ON. *fría*, *friá*:—OTeut. **frijējan*, f. **frijo-* FREE *a.*]

1. *trans.* To make free; to set at liberty; to release or deliver from bondage or constraint.

c **1000** ÆLFRIC *Lev.* xxv. 10 On þam forȝifenisse ȝeare man sceal freoȝan ælcne þeowan. *c* **1205** LAY. 882 Ich hine wille freoien ȝif he me ȝefeð gersume. *c* **1250** *Gen. & Ex.* 2787 Nu am ic liȝt to fren hem ðeðen, And milche and huniȝe lond hem queðen. *a* **1300** *Cursor M.* 16942 þan war we frehed all. *c* **1470** HENRY *Wallace* VIII. 1580 Thai frede the folk, in Ingland for to gang. **1513** DOUGLAS *Æneis* x. xiii. *heading*, Lausus..Quhilk fred his fader hurt in the bargane. **1572** *Satir. Poems Reform.* xxxi. 108 France will haif hir brocht hame Quene And fred out of Ingland. **1611** BIBLE *2 Macc.* ii. 22 They..freed the citie, and vpheld the lawes. **1639** S. DU VERGER tr. *Camus' Admir. Events* 23 Like a furious Tigres..seeking to free her young ones. **1693** DRYDEN *Persius' Sat.* v. 182 Canst thou no other Master understand Than him that freed thee by the Pretor's Wand. **1841** LANE *Arab. Nts.* I. 64 He who beats his slave without fault..his atonement for this is freeing him. **1865** KINGSLEY *Herew.* xxi. 267 Then he freed one of these four men.

b. Const. *from*, †*of*.

c **1200** *Trin. Coll. Hom.* 103 He ben þanne fried of þe deueles þralshipe. **1340** *Ayenb.* 262 Ac vri ous uram queade. **1613** PURCHAS *Pilgrimage* (1614) 284 The Portugals..not onely freed that their Castle from Turkish bondage, but had meanes to fortifie it better. **1651** HOBBES *Leviath.* III. xl. 250 Till the Israelites were freed from the Egyptians. **1736** BUTLER *Anal.* I. vi. Wks. 1874 I. 116 Freed from the restraints of fear. **1816** J. WILSON *City of Plague* III. i, They all died in ignorance of the plague That freed them from their cells. **1875** JOWETT *Plato* (ed. 2) IV. 234 A philosophy which could free the mind from the power of abstractions.

2. To relieve or deliver *from*, rid or ease *of* (a burden, obligation, inconvenience); to exempt *from* (payment, tribute, etc.), confer immunity upon. †In early use chiefly, to exempt (a church, etc.) from feudal services or exactions.

O.E. Chron. an. 777, Seo kyning freode þa þæt mynstre Wocingas wið cining & wið biscop & wið eorl & wið ealle men. *c* **1205** LAY. 10213 Freoden alle þe chirchen. *c* **1425** *Found. St. Bartholomew's* (E.E.T.S.) 16 Or ony othir chirche yn all Inglonde that is most y-freid. **1530** PALSGR. 558/1, I free a marchandyse or person that shulde paye a somme or tale. *Je quitte.* **1573** *Satir. Poems Reform.* xli. 80 Thocht of this feir thow salbe fred. **1598** HAKLUYT *Voy.* I. 172 The said marchants should be exempted and freed from all custome and imposition of small clothes. **1630** *R. Johnson's Kingd. & Commw.* 95 If it be a blessing..to be freed from corrupt and absurd ceremonies. **1748** *Anson's Voy.* II. ii. 137 We were now freed from the apprehensions of our provisions falling short. **1761** HUME *Hist. Eng.* II. xxvii. 123 He freed their subjects from all oaths of allegiance. **1818** CRUISE *Digest* (ed. 2) III. 314 The lands would be held of nobody, and freed from all feudal services. **1842** A. COMBE *Physiol. Digestion* (ed. 4) 74 From all these inconveniences we are entirely freed. **1866** CRUMP *Banking* ix. 198 That Bank of England notes should be freed from stamp duty. **1874** GREEN *Short Hist.* iv. §2. 171 The towns had long since freed themselves from all payment of the dues ..exacted by the King.

†**b.** intr. *to free with*: = 'To dispense with' (see DISPENSE *v.* 9). *Obs.*

1561 ABP. PARKER *Corr.* (1853) 126 If that this young student had a dispensation for the delay of his orders-taking, yet he were not freed with for his laity and the bishop might repel him at his institution.

†**c.** *trans.* To grant immunity *from* the operation of a thing; to make safe or secure *from*. *Obs.*

1611 SHAKS. *Wint. T.* IV. iv. 444 Thou Churle, for this time (Though full of our displeasure) yet we free thee From the dead blow of it. **1613** PURCHAS *Pilgrimage* (1614) 311 Chederles hereby freed from death. **1659** D. PELL *Impr. Sea* 382 There are but few Trees..that are free'd from the Thunder, save the Lawrel.

d. To relieve or rid of the presence of a person. Const. *from*, *of*.

1580 SIDNEY *Arcadia* II. (1590) 134 Meaning to free him of so serpentine a companion as I am. *a* **1639** SPOTTISWOOD *Hist. Ch. Scotl.* (1677) 74 How soon the Cardinal was freed of the Earl of Lenox, he [etc.] **1821** SCOTT *Kenilw.* ix, Desirous to get her house freed of her guest. **1833** HT. MARTINEAU *Fr. Wines & Pol.* viii. 129 The gentleman soon chose to free the family of his presence. **1844** H. H. WILSON *Brit. India* III. 124 To free his rear from a force which cut off his communication with Rangoon.

†**e.** To clear from blame or stain; to show or declare to be guiltless; to absolve, acquit. *Obs.*

1593 SHAKS. *Lucr.* 1208 My life's foul deed, my life's fair end shall free it. **1611** —— *Wint. T.* III. ii. 112 Mine Honor Which I would free. **1611** BIBLE *Rom.* vi. 7 He that is dead, is freed from sinne.

f. To relieve, unburden (one's mind).

1869 TROLLOPE *He knew, etc.* I. xxvi. 204 'It is a matter in which I am bound to tell you what I think'. 'Very well. If you have freed your mind, I will tell you my purpose!'

3. To clear, disengage, or disentangle (a thing) from some obstruction or encumbrance. Const. *from*, *of*.

1613 PURCHAS *Pilgrimage* (1614) 759 Faire and open grounds, freed from woods. **1697** DRYDEN *Virg. Georg.* III. 835 Nor cou'd their tainted Flesh with Ocean Tides Be freed from Filth. **1796** MRS. GLASSE *Cookery* xvii. 280 Take six pounds of young pork, free it from bone and skin. **1820** KEATS *St. Agnes* xxvi, Of all its wreathed pearls her hair she frees. **1837** GORING & PRITCHARD *Microgr.* 203 For freeing the gases of their impurities. **1886** *Law Times* LXXX. 213/2 Has anyone ever succeeded in freeing a ship at sea in a warm latitude from cockroaches?

b. *Naut.* (See quot. 1627.)

1627 CAPT. SMITH *Seaman's Gram.* vi. 27 Free the Boat is to baile or cast out the water. **1769** FALCONER *Dict. Marine* (1789) S s, There is no resource for the crew, except to free her by the pumps. **1867** SMYTH *Sailor's Word-bk.* s.v., *To free a pump*, to disengage or clear it. **1892** *Law Times Rep.* LXV. 590/1 A ship..fouled her propeller, and it became necessary to put her upon the ground in order to free it.

c. To get (oneself) loose, disengage, extricate.

1659 D. PELL *Impr. Sea* 507 Till you have got up your Anchors, and freed yourselves from the shore. **1665** HOOKE *Microgr.* 37 Its parts will be..agitated, and so by degrees free and extricate themselves from one another. **1852** MISS YONGE *Cameos* I. xxxv. 301 Having freed himself from his difficulties.

†**d.** To open so as to allow free passage. *Obs.*

1690 DRYDEN *Don Sebast.* IV. i, This master Key Frees every Lock, and leads us to his Person. **1700** —— *Cymon & Iphigenia* 285 Hast'ning to his prey, By force the furious lover free'd his way.

†**4.** To remove so as to leave the place clear, banish, get rid of. *Obs.*

1599 DANIEL *Octavia to Antonius* li, Free thine owne torment, and my griefe release. **1605** SHAKS. *Macb.* III. vi. 35 We may againe..Free from our Feasts, and Banquets bloody kniues. **1611** —— *Cymb.* III. vi. 80 *Bel.* He wrings at some distresse. *Gui.* Would I could free't. **1613** HEYWOOD *Brazen Age* II. ii. Wks. 1874 III. 239 By these all his stor'd labours he hath sent To call him home, to free her discontent. **1638** FORD *Fancies* II. ii, Free suspicion.

†**b.** *Naut.* To bale *out* (water) from a ship.

1624 CAPT. SMITH *Virginia* III. v. 56 We kept her [a Barge] from sinking by freeing out the water.

†**5.** To leap or get clear over, clear (a ditch, etc.). Cf. F. *franchir*. *Obs.*

1653 URQUHART *Rabelais* I. xxiii, He..made him [a horse] ..free the ditch with a skip. **1785** BURNS *Death & Dr. Hornbook* iii, I stacher'd whyles, but yet took tent ay To free the ditches. **1799** *Hist.* in *New Ann. Reg.* 299/1 Rallying such of his troops as had been able to free these abysses.

†**6.** To frank (a letter): see FRANK *v.*[2] 1. *Obs.*

1775 JOHNSON *Let. to H. Thrale* Feb., Please to free this letter to Miss L. Porter at Lichfield. **1823** *Mirror* I. 410/2 Those who do not free their letters.

7. *Lead-mining.* To register (a new mine, vein, etc.) by making the customary specified payment to the barmaster. Also, *to free for*.

1601 *High Peak Art.* lii. in Mander *Derbysh. Min. Gloss.* (1824) 131 If any Miner..do free or pay a Meare. **1653** MANLOVE *Lead-Mines* 51 (E.D.S.) First the finder his two meers must free With oar there found, for the Barghmaster's fee. **1747** HOOSON *Miner's Dict.* s.v. *Break-off*, I am obliged to Free for a new Vein, or Forfeit the same to the Lord. **1851** *Act 14 & 15 Vic.* c. 94 Sched. i. §12 If any Miner shall work any Mine or Vein without having duly freed the same.

8. *intr.* (See quot.) ? *U.S.*

1889 *Century Dict.*, *Free, intrans.*, To make free; take liberties: followed by *with*. [Colloq.]

Hence **freed** *ppl. a.*

1710 POPE *Windsor For.* 407 The freed Indians in their native groves. **1837** HT. MARTINEAU *Soc. Amer.* II. 116 The freed slave.

free and easy, *adj. phr.*, (*adv.*) and *sb.*

A. *adjectival phr.* Unconstrained, natural, unaffected; also, careless, slipshod. Hence, easy-going; (morally) lax, permissive.

1699 LISTER *Journ. Paris* 41 In a very free and easie posture. **1711** ADDISON *Spect.* No. 119 ¶3 The fashionable World is grown free and easy. **1756** R. BARON *Pref. Milton's Eikon.*, In the book before us his style is for the most part free and easy. **1861** HUGHES *Tom Brown at Oxf.* viii, I don't think he has ever got back since that day to his original free-and-easy swagger. **1864** NEWMAN *Apologia* 134, I had a lounging free-and-easy way of carrying things on. **1930** MORISON & COMMAGER *Growth of Amer. Republic* xx. 357 The fair, free and easy daughter of the leading publican. *a* **1957** W. S. CAMPBELL in WEBSTER (1961), Too free and easy a community to put up with reformers or longhairs. **1960** K. AMIS *Take Girl like You* iv. 61 'It's just that I don't believe in this—whatever you call it—this free-and-easy way of going on. It—' 'Anticipation of marriage is probably how they put it in your—in the advice columns.' **1981** *Washington Post* 10 Aug. C4 Among the assorted pleasures of the Glen Echo Park summer dance festival is the free and easy atmosphere.

b. quasi-*adv.*

1772 HUTTON *Bridges* 83 Arches..over large waters, which with their navigation pass free and easy under them at the same time.

Hence **free-and-easiness.**

1868 HOLME LEE *B. Godfrey* xxxiv. 184 Belle and Blanche ..were well-bred free-and-easiness personified. **1912** BEERBOHM *Christmas Garland* 36 The general free-and-easiness. **1959** H. HAMILTON *Answer in Negative* i. 9, I came to Fleet Street..and I still like the free-and-easiness of it.

B. *sb.* A convivial gathering for singing, at which one may drink, smoke, etc.

1823 in 'JON BEE' [J. Badcock] *Slang.* **1832** *Examiner* 460/1 The prisoner was a frequenter of Free and Easys. **1878** BESANT & RICE *Celia's Arb.* xxxvi. (1887) 264 The Blue Anchor..where there was a nightly free-and-easy for soldiers and sailors.

'freebase. *slang* (orig. *U.S.*). Also free base. [BASE *sb.*[1] 11.] Cocaine purified by heating with ether, and taken (illegally) by inhaling the fumes or smoking the residue.

1980 *N.Y. Times* 15 June IV. 7 A police lieutenant said Mr. Pryor had told a doctor the accident happened while he was trying to make 'free base', a cocaine derivative produced with the help of ether. **1981** *Daily Tel.* 30 June 15/3 The doctor..began the therapy by showing her photographs of the aggressive behaviour of monkeys who had been fed cocaine 'freebase' in an experiment. **1984** J. LAWTON *All Amer. War Game* i. 12 Football may have..cooked a little 'free-base' stimulation in the dressing-room. **1986** *Q* Oct. 51/2 Crack is the next step on, a sort of fast-food freebase.

Hence as *v. intr.* and *trans.*, to make a 'freebase' of (cocaine); to take (the drug) in this form. Also **'freebasing** *vbl. sb.*

1980 *Courier-Mail* (Brisbane) 18 June 1/1 A police spokesman said Pryor told doctors he was 'free basing',—purifying cocaine by using ether and a flame—when he was burned. **1980** *Time* 23 June 10 The Los Angeles police say Pryor told them that the accident occurred while he was 'free-basing' cocaine. **1981** *Daily Tel.* 30 June 15/3 She recalled that her seven-year-old daughter used to follow her around the house with a deodorant spray because she could not stand the smell of freebasing. **1985** *Times* 21 Jan. 3/2 Cocaine..has traditionally been taken by sniffing but there are reports of 'freebasing', which involves heating the drug to remove impurities and then inhaling the fumes.

free bench. *Law.* Also free bank. (See quot. 1670.)

1670 BLOUNT *Law Dict.*, *Free-bench*..signifies that estate in Copihold Lands which the Wife, being espoused a Virgin, hath, after the death of her Husband, for her Dower, according to the custom of the Mannor. **1714** *Spect.* No. 614 ¶16 The Steward is bound by the Custom to re-admit her to her Free-Bench. **1764** KIRBY *Suffolk Trav.* (ed. 2) 27 To hold in Name of Free-bank. **1818** CRUISE *Digest* (ed. 2) I. 328 If the widow be entitled to the whole of the copyhold, as her free bench, she may enter immediately.

freebie ('friːbɪ), *a.* and *sb.* *U.S. colloq.* Also freebee, freeby. [Arbitrarily f. FREE *a.*]

A. *adj.* Free, without charge. **B.** *sb.* Something that is provided free.

1942 BERREY & VAN DEN BARK *Amer. Thes. Slang* §551/17 *Free*..free gratis for nothing, freebee, freeby, [etc.]. **1946** MEZZROW & WOLFE *Really Blues* xiv. 256 It's the brakeman who throws freebie passengers off. *Ibid.* 373 *Freebie*, handout, something gratis. **1954** L. ARMSTRONG *Satchmo* (1955) vi. 81 That meal was a freebie and didn't cost me anything. **1962** E. LACY *Freeloaders* iv. 83 She'll write 'free' on the slip... They come in for the freebie and end up buying more copies.

free-board ('friːbɔəd). [transl. of AF. *franc bord*: see FREE *a.* and BOARD *sb.* Sense 2 seems to have been suggested by sense 1.]

1. *Law.* In some places the right of claiming a certain quantity of land outside the fence of a park or forest; also, the land thus claimed.

[? *c* **1350** *Carta T. Dom. Moubray* in Dugdale *Monasticon* (1661) II. 241/1 Et totum boscum quod vocatur Brendewode, cum frankbordo duorum pedum & dimidium, per circuitum illius bosci.] **1676** COLES *Free-bord*, a small space beyond or without the fence. **1795** *Epworth* (*Linc.*) *Enclosure Act* 25 Any Freeboard, Screed, or Parcel of Land left outside the fences. **1793** in Chancellor *Hist. Richmond* (1894) 222 The Boundaries of His Majesty's Park at Richmond, and the Free-board thereto belonging. **1894** *Ibid.*, Richmond Park has a free-board of 16½ feet outside the boundary-wall.

2. a. *Naut.* (See quot. 1867.)

1726 G SHELVOCKE *Voy.* (1757) 268 Not having above sixteen inches free board..the water continually ran over us. **1867** SMYTH *Sailor's Word-bk.* s.v. *Plank-sheer*, The space between this [plank-sheer] and the line of flotation has latterly been termed the free-board. **1880** *Times* 6 Aug. 5/3 According to this vessel's construction, she ought to have had 6 ft. freeboard.

b. *transf.* and *fig.*

1896 *McClure's Mag.* Dec. 142/2, I saw Mrs. McPhee swell and swell under her garance-coloured gown. There is no small free-board to Janet McPhee, nor is garance any subdued tint. **1925** J. JOLY *Surface-Hist. Earth* iii. 54 The change of buoyancy of the magma which must arise if the substratum changes from the solid to the liquid state... How will this change affect the 'freeboard' of the continents? When we melt basalt in the laboratory we easily float granite in the fluid rock. It floats with a good free-board, and appears to preserve its buoyancy indefinitely.

Hence **'free-boarded** *a.*

1883 *Harper's Mag.* Aug. 442/2 Low free-boarded, shallow, beamy boats.

†**free-boot,** *sb. Obs.* [f. FREE *a.* + BOOT *sb.*[2]; after FREEBOOTER.] Plunder, robbery.

1647 R. STAPYLTON *Juvenal* 156 The Cilicians, that lived ..upon free boote. **1654** *Vilvain Epit. Ess.* VI. lxxviii, The Swed free boot: Dane Dice and Drink approved.

free-boot, *v.* [back-formation from FREEBOOTER.] *intr.* To act as a freebooter, plunder.

1592 GREENE *Black Bk.'s Messenger* Wks. (Grosart) XI. 17, I came to the credite of a high Lawyer, and with my sword free booted abroad in the country like a Caualier on horse-backe. **1659** GAUDEN *Brounrig* (1660) 104 Jesus.. loves to see his Soldiers not stragling and freebooting in broken parties..but united. **1869** *Echo* 28 Oct., When the conquerors had freebooted thoroughly, they settled. **1879** *N.Y. Tribune* 25 Nov. (Cent.), An ambition to..freeboot it furiously over the placid waters took possession of their bosoms.

Hence **'free-booting** *vbl. sb.* and *ppl. a.*

1596 SPENSER *State Irel.* (Globe) 631 When he goeth abrode in the night on free-booting. **1683** CHALKHILL *Thealma & Cl.* 119 Many a night Had they used this free-booting. **1798** C. SMITH *Young Philosopher* II. 242 The free-booting savage. **1868** MILMAN *St Paul's* iii. 52 The great freebooting rebel. **1876** FOX BOURNE *Locke* II. xi. 162 Where freebooting was terribly rife.

freebooter ('friːbuːtə(r)). Also 6 frebetter, fribooter, 7 frybuter. [ad. Du. *vrijbuiter* (Kilian *vrijbueter*) = Ger. *freibeuter*, f. the equivalents of FREE *a.*, BOOTY or BOOT *sb.*[2], -ER[1]. Cf. also Eng. *flibutor*, s.v. FILIBUSTER.] One who goes about in search of plunder; esp. a pirate or piratical adventurer.

1570 MICHAEL COULWEBER in Burgon *Life Gresham* II. 360 For so much as I was spoyled by the waye in cominge towards England by the Duke of Alva his frebetters, maye it please the Queenes Majestie [etc.]. **1598** HAKLUYT *Voy.* I. To Rdr. *5 They tooke fiue..ships of the Freebooters. **1622** MALYNES *Anc. Law-Merch.* 179 If the ship become assailed by Pirats or Frybuters. *a* **1659** BP. BROWNRIG *Serm.* (1674) I. xxix. 376 The Danites were..Free-booters..and did all by force. **1726** SHELVOCKE *Voy. round World* 12 The ships there..fired several shot at me, mistaking me for a free Booter. **1776** ADAM SMITH *W.N.* IV. vii. (1869) II. 151 St. Domingo was established by pirates and free booters. **1838** THIRLWALL *Greece* V. xlii. 214 Every freebooter was, or might easily become, a pirate. **1856** OLMSTED *Slave States* 314 These rail-road freebooters.

transf. and *fig.* **1600** W. WATSON *Quodlibets Relig. & State* iv. (1602) 100 So..to send abroad his fribooters..against other words and writings. *a* **1656** BP. HALL. *Occas. Medit.* (1851) 20 Those spiritual freebooters, that lie in wait for our souls. **1886** A. WINCHELL *Walks & Talks Geol. Field* 240 The fierce shark is the free-booter of the ocean.

Hence †**'freebooter** *v. intr.* (see quot.); **'free-,bootery,** the practice of freebooters.

1659 TORRIANO, *Vivere à discrettione*..for a souldier to free-booter or free-quarter in any place. **1822** T. L. PEACOCK *Maid Marian* xviii. 273 In the pure principles of freebootery have they excelled all men. **1851** SIR F. PALGRAVE *Norm. & Eng.* I. 448 The Pirate-Kings..agreed unanimously to forego their free-bootery.

†**'free-booty.** *Obs.* [f. FREE *a.* + BOOTY, after FREEBOOTER.]

1. Plunder or spoil (to be) taken by force.

1623 BP. HALL *Serm.* V. 152 If any usurping spirit of error shall have made a free-booty of truth. **1749** FIELDING *Tom Jones* XII. i, Whose property is considered as free-booty by all his poor neighbours.

2. Taking of booty, plundering.

1649 *Depos. Cast. York* (Surtees) 26 To goe to sea as a man of war upon free bootie.

'free-born, *a.* [f. FREE *a.* + BORN *ppl. a.*; cf. Ger. *freigeboren.*]

1. Born free, born to the conditions and privileges of citizenship, inheriting liberty.

c **1340** *Cursor M.* 9497 (Trin.) Fre born to be & not bonde. *c* **1410** *Sir Cleges* 399, I am your man fre born. **1612** ROWLANDS *More Knaues Yet?* (1613) 3 My freeborne Muse is no such seruile baby. *a* **1720** SHEFFIELD (Dk. Buckhm.) *Wks.* (1753) I. 299 That free-born spirits should obey Wretches, who know not to sway! **1794** BLOOMFIELD *Amer. Law Rep.* 14 The Court to adjudge that the said Negro Peter was free-born. **1871** B. TAYLOR *Faust* (1875) II. III. 178 To me a free-born Cretan did that journey bring Imprisonment.

2. Pertaining to or befitting a free-born man.

c **1510** *Robin Hood* 2 in Arb. *Garner* VI. 423 Lithe and listen, Gentlemen, That be of freborn blood. **1605** *1st Pt. Jeronimo* in Dodsley *O. Pl.* (1780) III. 98 A base blush upon our free-born cheeks! **1621** BRATHWAIT *Nat. Emb.* Ded. (1641) A ij, Professed fauorer and furtherer of all freeborne studies. **1781** GIBBON *Decl. & F.* III. lii. 275 They insensibly lost the freeborn and martial virtues of the desert. **1813** SCOTT *Rokeby* I. xvii, The wily priests..damned each free-born deed and thought.

†**free-bound.** *Obs. rare*[−1]. [f. FREE *a.* + BOUND *sb.*[1]] = FREE-BOARD 1.

1639 *Of Nuisance to private Houses* 7 Hee that maketh a Parke, will leave ground..without the pale for the Keeper to walke about it..This is called free-bownd.

†**free burghership.** *Obs. rare.* [f. phrase *free burgher* (FREE *a.* 29) + -SHIP.] Citizenship.

a **1568** COVERDALE *Hope Faithf.* vii. 42 Our conuersation, freburgership or dwelling, is in heauen.

Free Church.

1. *gen.* A church free from state control. In *pl.* a name often given by Nonconformists to the various churches of Congregationalists, Baptists, etc., as distinguished from the Established Church.

1869 SKEATS (*title*) A history of the Free Churches of England from A.D. 1688–A.D. 1851. **1892** *Ch. Q. Rev.* July 355 Their..notion of any number of 'Free Churches'. **1897** FAIRBAIRN in *Oxford Free Ch. Mag.* Jan. 1 (*article*) The Free Churches and the education of their sons.

2. *the Free Church (Kirk) of Scotland*: the organization formed by the ministers who seceded from the established Presbyterian Church in 1843.

1843 [see DISRUPTION 3]. **1874** BLACKIE *Self-Cult.* 47 The Free Church of Scotland.

3. (With small initials.) A church in which the seats are free. *U.S.*

1835 J. MARTIN *Gaz. Virginia* 126 It contains several dwelling houses—one free church—one common school. **1835** A. A. PHELPS in *Life W. L. Garrison* (1885) II. 63 He has since been requested to preach the sermon to the Free Church in Hartford. **1860** *Massachusetts Acts & Resolves* c. 181 An act to incorporate the trustees of the free church of Saint Mary, for sailors.

So **Free-'churchism,** the principles or doctrines of the Free Churches; **Free-'churchman,** a member of a Free Church. Also **Free-'kirker** (*depreciatively*), a member of the Free Kirk of Scotland.

1847 CANDLISH in *Life* xiv. (1860) 402, I feel on this subject far more as a Christian patriot than as a Free Church-man. **1881** *Sat. Rev.* 23 July 116/2 This egregious assumption of the Freekirkers. **1884** *Chr. World* 21 Feb. 135/3 Thus, Freechurchism goes ahead in these colonies. **1897** *Oxford Free Ch. Mag.* Jan. 3 These important bonds of faith between all Free Churchmen.

†**free cost.** *Obs.* In phr. *at, of, on, upon free cost* = cost-free, gratis. (See also COST *sb.*[2] 5 c.)

1563 *Homilies* II. *Agst. Idleness* (1859) 517 Eating other men's bread of free cost. **1627** BP. HALL *Best Bargaine* Wks. 516 An error of free-cost is better than an high-rated veritie. **1655** FULLER *Ch. Hist.* II. iii. §26 If he affirmeth it on free cost, we can confute it as cheap, by denying it. **1676** WYCHERLEY *Pl. Dealer* Ded., A man..had better pay for what he has at an inn than lie on free-cost at a gentleman's house. **1749** LAVINGTON *Enthus. Methodists & Papists* (1820) 172 The Methodists asking her to live upon free-cost. **1764** *Mem. G. Psalmanazar* 134 Considering how well acquainted I was with the way of travelling at free-cost.

b. as adv. phr. without preposition.

1648 HERRICK *Hesper.*, *'Nothing free-cost'* (1869) 189 Nothing comes free-cost here. **1720** OZELL *Vertot's Rom. Rep.* II. IX. 67 That the People might..see the Sports Free-cost.

c. *attrib.* or *adj.* Gratuitous.

1586 T. B. *La Primaud. Fr. Acad.* I. (1594) 136 Such parasites and scrap-gatherers at free-cost feasts.

†**free-denize,** *v. Obs.* = DENIZE.

1577, 1577–87 [see DENIZE 1, 2]. *a* **1628** F. GREVILLE *Sidney* x. (1652) 128 His own subjects free-denized in America. **1630** LENNARD tr. *Charron's Wisd.* I. xxxvii. §10 (1670) 123 The Son of God..being come to secure and free-denize the world.

†**free-'denizen,** *sb. Obs.* = DENIZEN 2, 2 b.

1576 [see DENIZEN 2]. **1587** FLEMING *Contn. Holinshed* III. 1348/2 Peter Moris free denison, having made an engine for that purpose. *a* **1640** JACKSON *Wks.* (1673) III. 619 As often as any good or harm did happen to any Citizen or Free-denizon thereof. *a* **1653** [see DENIZEN 2 b].

†**free-'denizen,** *v. Obs.* = DENIZEN *v.* 1.

1619 T. MILLES tr. *Mexia's Treas. Anc. & Mod. Times* II. 910/2 The Irish language became free-denizened in the English Pale. **1655** BP. HALL *Rem. Wks.* (1660) 202 No worldly respects can free-denison a Christian here.

'freedman. [f. *freed*, pa. pple. of FREE *v.* + MAN *sb.*] A man who has been a slave and is manumitted, an emancipated slave.

1601 HOLLAND *Pliny* I. 245 Optatus his freed man (who sometime had bin a slaue of his). **1794** SULLIVAN *View Nat.* II. 63 the freedman of Tiberius. **1834** LYTTON *Pompeii* I. i, He thinks..to make us forget that he is the son of a freedman. **1870** WHITTIER *Soc. Friends* Pr. Wks. 1889 III. 307 The Freedmen and Indians.

freedom ('friːdəm). Forms: 1 fréodóm, frýdóm, 3–4 freodom, -dam, 4 *south.* vridom, 2–6 fredom(e, 4–5 fre(e)dam, (4 fredame), 6–7 freedome, 7 freedoom, *Sc.* friedome, 4– freedom. [OE. *fréodóm*: see FREE *a.* and -DOM.]

1. a. Exemption or release from slavery or imprisonment; personal liberty. †*letter of freedom*: a document emancipating a slave.

c **1230** *Hali Meid.* 5 Nis ha þenne sariliche..akast & in to þewdom idrahen, þat fram se muchel hehscipe & se seli freodom schal lihte se lahe in to a monnes þeowdom. **1382** WYCLIF *Deut.* xv. 13 And whom with freedam thow ȝyuest, thou shalt not suffre to goon awey voyd. **1596** SPENSER *F.Q.* v. v. 57 Thus he long while in thraldome there remayned.. Untill his owne true love his freedome gayned. **1613** PURCHAS *Pilgrimage* (1614) 295 They will write any thing for monie, as letters of freedome for servants to runne away from their Masters. **1659** D. PELL *Impr. Sea* 298 Taken by the Turks, and..have set their heads on work how to get their freedoms again. **1782** COWPER *Charity* 172 Neither age nor force Can quell the love of freedom in a horse. **1880** E. KIRKE *Garfield* 38 Face to face with the alarming truth that we must lose our own freedom or grant it to the slave.

b. *fig.* Liberation from the bondage of sin.

c **1050** *Byrhtferth's Handboc* in *Anglia* (1885) VIII. 320 Wilniȝende mid þissum þeowdome, cuman to ecum freodome. **1340** *Ayenb.* 86 Þe oþer uridom is þe ilke þet habbeþ þe guodemen..þet god heþ yvryd..uram þe þreldome of þe dyeule. **1526** *Pilgr. Perf.* (W. de W. 1531) 4 b, From the thraldome of the princes of the world to the fredome of glory & kyngdome of god.

2. Exemption from arbitrary, despotic, or autocratic control; independence; civil liberty.

1375 BARBOUR *Bruce* I. 225 Fredome all solace to man giffis. He levys at ese that frely levys! **1606** HOLLAND *Sueton.* 42 They died for the Libertie and Free-dome of their Cittie. **1725** SWIFT *Drapier's Lett.* v. Wks. 1761 III. 97 Freedom consists in a people's being governed by laws made with their own consent. **1780** COWPER *Table Talk* 284 They, that fight for freedom, undertake The noblest cause mankind can have at stake. **1817** BYRON *Beppo* xlvii, I like the freedom of the press and quill. **1850** TENNYSON *In Mem.* cix, A love of freedom rarely felt, Of freedom in her regal seat Of England.

†**3.** The quality of being free or noble; nobility, generosity, liberality. *Obs.*

c **1320** *Cast. Love* 145 He ȝaf Adam..Feirlek, and freodam, and muche miht. *c* **1386** CHAUCER *Monk's T.* 564 He was of knyghthod and of fredam flour. *c* **1430** *Pilgr. Lyf Manhode* I. lxxx. (1869) 47 Nay, but me shulde thinke suich a yifte ful of gret fredom..and of gret curteysye. **1500–20** DUNBAR *Poems* xxi. 28 On fredome is laid foirfaltour. *c* **1530** *Calisto & Melib.* C i a, With grace indewid in fredome as alexandre.

4. a. The state of being able to act without hindrance or restraint, liberty of action.

c **1400** MAUNDEV. xvii. (1839) 193 Fissches, that han fredom to environ alle the Costes of the See, at here owne list, comen of hire owne wille to profren hem to the dethe. **1588** SHAKS. *Tit. A.* I. i. 17 And Romanes, fight for Freedome in your Choice. **1633** BP. HALL *Hard Texts* 513 Alexander of Macedon..shall rule powerfully and with great freedom and absoluteness. **1718** *Freethinker* No. 1 ¶5 Freedom of Thought is like Freedom in Actions. **1878** JEVONS *Prim. Pol. Econ.* 67 It is absolutely necessary to maintain..the freedom of other men to labour if they like. **1885** *L'pool Daily Post* 7 July 4/4 The Government's freedom of action was limited by the fact that they came into negotiations partly concluded.

b. *four freedoms*: those propounded by Franklin D. Roosevelt (see quot. 1941).

1941 F. D. ROOSEVELT in *N.Y. Times* 7 Jan. 4/7 In the future days..we look forward to a world founded upon four essential human freedoms. The first is freedom of speech and expression... The second is freedom of every person to worship God in his own way... The third is freedom from want... The fourth is freedom from fear. **1944** H. G. WELLS *'42 to '44* 69 Our government's good faith in promising mankind a regenerated world, the 'four freedoms' and so forth after the war. **1950** A. HUXLEY *Themes & Variations* 246 To talk about the Rights of Man and the Four Freedoms in connection..with India is merely a cruel joke. **1964** R. CHURCH *Voyage Home* iii. 35 The assumption of the Government..was that..grateful civilians would see to it that the ex-soldiers be eased back with sympathy into an economic way of life supported on the newly-painted pillars of the four freedoms.

5. The quality of being free from the control of fate or necessity; the power of self-determination attributed to the will.

c **888** K. ÆLFRED *Boeth.* xli. §2 Þu seȝist þæt God sylle ællcum frydom [*MS. Cott.* freodom] swa god to donne swa yfel. **1340** *Ayenb.* 86 Uri-wyl huer-by he may chyese and do uryliche oþer þet guod oþer þet kuead. Þerne uridom he halt of god. **1690** LOCKE *Hum. Und.* II. xxi. §27. 123 In this then consists Freedom, (*viz.*) in our being able to act, or not to act, according as we shall choose, or will. **1855** BAIN *Emotions* xi. (1859) 544 The doctrine of Freedom was first elaborated into a metaphysical scheme, implying its opposite Necessity, by St. Augustin against Pelagius. **1884** tr. *Lotze's Metaph.* 420 The freedom which is said to characterise mental life, and is distinguished from the necessity of nature.

†**6.** Readiness or willingness to act. *Obs.*

a **1626** BACON *New Atl.* (1627) 18 We found such humanity, and such a freedome and desire to take strangers as it were into their bosom. **1697** DAMPIER *Voy.* (1729) I. 502, I had been accustomed to hardships and hazards, therefore I did with much freedom undertake it.

7. a. Frankness, openness, familiarity (in intercourse or conversation); outspokenness.

1699 LISTER *Journ. Paris* 67, I had not that freedom of Conversation as I could have wisht with both of them. **1705** ADDISON *Italy* 86 They are generally too distrustful of one another for the Freedoms that are us'd in such kind of Conversations. **1792** BURKE *Corr.* 1844 IV. 32, I talked a great deal to him with the freedom I have long used to him on this and on other subjects. **1887** F. DARWIN *Life & Lett. C. Darwin* I. 18 And laughed and joked with everyone.. with the utmost freedom.

b. The overstepping of due or customary bounds in speech or behaviour; undue familiarity. Phr. *to take the freedom (to do something).*

1618 FLETCHER *Loyal Subj.* II. i, Your eye..Is fix'd upon this captain for his freedom; And happily you find his tongue too forward. **1648** BOYLE *Seraph. Love* (1660) 9 This Love, I have taken the freedom to style 'Seraphic Love'. **1681** OTWAY *Soldier's Fort.* II. i, Let her alone to make the best use of those innocent Freedoms I allow her. **1712** STEELE *Spect.* No. 402 ¶1 The young Women who run into greater Freedoms with the Men. **1854** J. S. C. ABBOTT *Napoleon* (1855) I. xvi. 287 When the officers do not eat or drink, or take too many freedoms with the seamen.

8. Of action, activity, etc.: Ease, facility, absence of encumbrance.

1613 SHAKS. *Hen. VIII*, v. i. 103 You cannot with such freedome purge your selfe. **1705** DE FOE in *Lett. Lit. Men* (Camden) 322, I humbly thank your Lordship for the freedom of access you were pleas'd to give my messenger. **1860** TYNDALL *Glac.* II. iii. 243 The sun's rays penetrate our atmosphere with freedom.

9. Boldness or vigour of conception or execution.

1643 HOWELL *Lett.* I. VI. lvi. (1655) 303, I alwaies lov'd you for the freedom of your genius. **1782** COWPER *Table-talk* 700 Nature.. But seldom.. Vouchsafes to man a poet's just pretence. Fervency, freedom, fluency of thought [etc.]. **1842** ROGERS *Introd. Burke's Wks.* (1842) I. 11 For by knowing.. what was to be done in every figure they designed, they naturally attained a freedom and spirit of outline.

10. a. *Physics.* Capability of motion. ***degree of freedom***: an independent mode in which a body may be displaced.

1867 THOMSON & TAIT *Treat. Nat. Philos.* I. i. 130 A free point has *three* degrees of freedom, inasmuch as the most general displacement which it can take is resolvable into three, parallel respectively to any three directions, and independent of each other... If the point be constrained to remain always on a given surface, *one* degree of constraint is introduced, or there are left but *two* degrees of freedom. **1958** *Van Nostrand's Sci. Encycl.* (ed. 3) 610/2 When heat energy is imparted to a pure diatomic gas, $\frac{3}{5}$ of it goes into each degree of molecular freedom. Three of these degrees of freedom are concerned with motions of translation, so that $\frac{3}{5}$ of the energy takes this form.

b. *Physical Chem.* An independent capability of a system to vary without altering the number of phases and components present.

1899 [see INVARIANT *a.* b]. **1904** A. FINDLAY *Phase Rule* ii. 15 We shall therefore define the number of degrees of freedom of a system as the number of the variable factors, temperature, pressure, and concentration of the components, which must be arbitrarily fixed in order that the condition of the system may be perfectly defined. **1948** GLASSTONE *Physical Chem.* (ed. 2) vi. 475 A system consisting of one phase only, e.g., solid, liquid or gaseous, of water has two degrees of freedom,.. for.. it is necessary to specify both temperature *and* pressure to define completely the state of the system. **1966** TER HAAR & WERGELAND *Elem. Thermodynam.* vi. 82 Gibbs' phase rule... The number of phases plus the number of degrees of freedom exceeds the number of components by 2.

c. *Statistics.* A property of a statistical distribution or of a statistic, in number equal either to the number of values that can be arbitrarily and independently assigned to the distribution, or to the number of independent and unrestricted quantities contributing to the statistic.

1922 R. A. FISHER in *Jrnl. R. Statistical Soc.* LXXXV. 88 We shall show that Elderton's Tables of Goodness of Fit.. may still be applied, but that the value of n' with which the table should be entered is not now equal to the number of cells, but to one more than the number of degrees of freedom in the distribution. **1950** YULE & KENDALL *Introd. Theory Statistics* (ed. 14) xxi. 485 In the quantity $\Sigma(x - m)^2$ there are n independent contributions of the type $(x - m)^2$, and hence we may say that n is the number of degrees of freedom of that estimate; but in the quantity $\Sigma(x - \bar{x})^2$ we have used the data to estimate $\bar{x}$, and hence the number of degrees of freedom is lowered by unity, i.e. equals $n - 1$. **1961** H. JEFFREYS *Theory of Probability* (ed. 3) iii. 145 The estimate of any unknown from the observations directly relating to it may be of very doubtful accuracy on account of the small number of degrees of freedom. **1969** KENDALL & STUART *Adv. Theory of Statistics* (ed. 3) I. xvi. 375 It is thus natural to speak of the number of degrees of freedom, ν, of a function such as χ^2, meaning thereby that it is distributed as the sum of squares of ν independent standardized normal variates.

11. The state of not being affected by (a defect, disadvantage, etc.); exemption *from*.

1606 SHAKS. *Ant. & Cl.* I. iii. 57 Though age from folly could not giue me freedom It does from childishnesse. **1613** PURCHAS *Pilgrimage* (1614) 62 Promising to the doers long life, health.. freedome from losses, and the like. **1756** BURKE *Subl. & B.* I. xiii, The contemplation of our own freedom from the evils which we see represented. **1839** MISS MITFORD in L'Estrange *Life* (1870) III. vii. 99 There is a freedom from cant about the authoresses, which.. I could not have anticipated.

12. a. Exemption *from* a specific burden, charge, or service; an immunity, privilege: = FRANCHISE *sb.* 2 b.

*c***1175** *Lamb. Hom.* 41 We eow wulleð seggen of þa fredome þe limpeð to þan deie þe is iclepeð su sunedei. *c***1205** LAY. 22222 He sette grið he sette frið and alle freodomes. **1386** [see FRANCHISE *sb.* 2 b]. **1387** TREVISA *Higden* (Rolls) III. 61 He graunted hem fredom [*immunitatem*] þat dede þat deede. **1534** WHITTINTON *Tullyes Offices* I. (1540) 24 Many thynges be commune to cytezyns amonge them selfe, as.. fredomes, iudgementes, voyces in elections. **1675** *Essex Papers* (Camden) I. 315 That all yᵉ auntient freemen of yᵉ respective Corporacions should enjoy their former freedoms and Priviledges. **1711** T. MADOX *Hist. & Antiq. Excheq.* 524 K. John.. granted to Robert de Lisieux.. Quittance or Freedom from Tallage. **1719** W. WOOD *Surv. Trade* 9 All Foreigners might freely come and reside in any Part of this Kingdom.. with the like Privileges and Freedoms as our selves. **1839** KEIGHTLEY *Hist. Eng.* I. 332 Freedom from arrest, a privilege at that time necessary for the cause of liberty.

b. A privilege possessed by a city, a corporation, etc. Cf. FRANCHISE *sb.* 2 a.

1596 SHAKS. *Merch. V.* IV. i. 35 If you denie it, let the danger light Vpon your Charter, and your Cities freedome. **1612** DRAYTON *Poly-olb.* xi. 180 The great Freedoms then those kings to these [Universities] did giue. **1673** TEMPLE *Observ. United Prov. Wks.* 1731 I. 9 Cities and Towns; of which the Old had their ancient Freedoms and Jurisdictions confirmed, or others annexed.

†**c.** A city or corporation possessing such immunity. Also, the district over which the immunity extends; the 'liberties'. Cf. FRANCHISE *sb.* 5. *Obs.*

1579 TWYNE *Phisicke agst. Fort.* II. Ep. Ded. 160 b, The actes and lawes of certeine Municipies or freedomes. **1766** ENTICK *London* IV. 306 Passing over Tower-hill, they come again into the freedom.

13. The right of participating in the privileges attached to: **a.** membership *of* a company or trade; **b.** citizenship *of* a town or city; often conferred *honoris causa* upon eminent persons. Also, the document or diploma conferring such freedom.

a. *c***1744** *Parl. Bill* in Hanway *Trav.* (1762) I. v. lxxi. 32 All persons.. should be admitted into the freedom of the said company, upon paying a fine of fifty pounds. **1746** H. WALPOLE *Let. Mann* 1 Aug., It was lately proposed in the city to present him [the Duke of Hamilton] with the freedom of some company.

b. 1579, 1606 [see FRANCHISE *sb.* 4]. **1748** SMOLLETT *Rod. Rand.* (1812) I. 500 The magistrates intended to compliment us with the freedom of their town. **1772** WESLEY *Jrnl.* 28 Apr., They presented me with the freedom of the city. **1864** H. AINSWORTH *John Law* VI. iii, The freedom of his native city of Edinburgh was transmitted to him in a valuable gold box. **1885** *Act 48 & 49 Vict.* c. 29 An Act to enable Municipal Corporations to confer the Honorary Freedom of Boroughs upon persons of distinction.

c. The liberty or right to practise a trade; also the 'fine' paid for this: see *freedom-fine*.

1712 ARBUTHNOT *John Bull* I. iv, Lewis Baboon had taken up the trade of clothier and draper, without serving his time or purchasing his freedom. **1759** GOLDSM. *Bee* No. 5 ¶20 Exclusive of the masters, there are numberless faulty expenses among the workmen,—clubs, garnishes, freedoms, and such like impositions.

d. ***Freedom of the Rule*** (Sc.), liberty granted to a Scotch advocate to plead at the English bar.

1820 SCOTT *Ivanhoe* Introd., Ivanhoe.. may be said to have procured for its Author the freedom of the rules.. since he has ever since been permitted to exercise his powers of fictitious composition in England as well as Scotland.

e. *transf.* Unrestricted use *of*.

1652 NEEDHAM tr. *Selden's Mare Cl.* 155 Hee would not permit Merchants and Sea-men to enjoy a freedom of that Sea.. but at an extraordinarie rate. **1697** DAMPIER *Voy.* I. xix. 528 They having the freedom of our Ship, to go to and fro between Decks. **1862** BURTON *Bk. Hunter* (1863) 48 Having conferred on you the freedom of the library, he will not concern himself by observing how you use it.

14. *Sc.* A piece of common land allotted to a free-man.

1805 FORSYTH *Beauties Scotl.* II. 473 Each of these free-men possesses what is called a lot or freedom, containing about four acres of arable land. **1861** HOWIE *Hist. Acc. Ayr* v. 46 The Newton people divided them [the lands] into 48 portions. These were denominated freedoms.

15. *attrib.* and *Comb.*, as ***freedom-loving*** adj.; **freedom box** (see quot. 1960); **freedom fighter**, one who takes part in a resistance movement against the established political system of a country; also *transf.*; **freedom-fine**, a payment made on being admitted to the freedom of a city, guild, or corporation; **freedom ride** *U.S.*, an organized ride (in buses, etc.) by people demonstrating against racial segregation; so **freedom rider**, one who takes part in such a demonstration of racial protest; similarly ***freedom march, walk***.

1911 C. J. JACKSON *Illustr. Hist. Eng. Plate* II. xxix. 913 Lord Carbery owns an interesting silver-gilt freedom-box.. which was presented by the borough of Bandon-Bridge to George, the third Baron Carbery in 1760. **1960** H. HAYWARD *Antique Coll.* 123/2 *Freedom box*, small circular or oblong box, silver-gilt, when not gold, presented with a script conferring the freedom of a town. Particularly popular in Ireland from the late 18th to the early 19th cent. **1942** J. LEHMANN *40 Poems* 32 Their freedom-fighters staining red the snow. **1958** *Listener* 13 Nov. 786/1 The Hungarian 'freedom fighters'. **1962** *Listener* 20 Dec. 1042/2 The Information Minister [in Jakarta] had urged the press to support the freedom fighters in northern Borneo. **1964** *Ann. Reg. 1963* 113 Mr. Obote had played a prominent part in the Addis Ababa conference.. offering training grounds for 'freedom fighters' against South Africa. **1969** *Daily Nation* (Nairobi) 31 Oct. 16/1 Freedom fighters ring Portuguese territories and Rhodesia with the support of African governments, if not always full acknowledgement. **1969** M. PUGH *Last Place Left* vii. 45 She was a freedom fighter in the sex war. **1882** CASSELL, *Freedom-fine*. **1841** H. S. FOOTE *Texas & Texans* I. 102 The descendants of.. freedom-loving ancestors in Texas nobly resolved to imperil their lives. **1884** MISS HICKSON *Irel. in 17th Cent.* I. Introd. 15 The Ulster of to-day.. filled with the.. freedom-loving men of the mixed race. **1942** W. S. CHURCHILL *End of Beginning* (1943) 122 We shall.. build a sure peace for all freedom-loving peoples. **1965** *Listener* 20 May 755/2 The Alabama freedom march. **1961** *N.Y. Times* 20 Aug. 2E/6 Freedom Rides.. are expected to continue until bus-terminal segregation ends. **1961** *Guardian* 25 May 1/3 Anti-segregation 'freedom riders' arrived here by bus from Montgomery, Alabama. **1961** *Economist* 27 May 890/1 The flow of 'Freedom Riders'—mostly young Negroes, with a few white sympathizers, who are determined to challenge illegal discrimination in the defiant heart of the old South. **1967** *Listener* 17 Aug. 211/2 The old days when Freedom Riders were widely applauded.. have gone. **1967** *Word Study* Dec. 7/2 There were.. 'freedom walks' across Southern states in 1962 and 1963.

Hence †**'freedom** *v. trans.*, to set free. Also **'freedomless** *a.*, without freedom; †**'freedomship**, investiture with a freedom.

1548 GEST *Pr. Masse* 107 Christe mourderd broken, and offered was the meane wherwyth we be fredomed frome yᵉ thraldome of.. yᵉ devyll. **1583** GOLDING *Calvin on Deut.* cxxxvi. 838 Baptisme.. was ministred with such reuerence, that.. the Congregation was assembled together, as if one were to receiue an holy freedomship. **1821** BYRON *Irish Avatar* iii, Famine which dwelt on her freedomless crags.

freedstool: see FRITHSTOOL.

free-for-all, *a.* and *sb.* orig. *U.S.* [FREE *a.* 10 b.] **A.** *adj.* Open to all. **B.** *sb.* A fight, etc., in which anyone may take part.

1881 *Chicago Times* 11 June, The grand free-for-all horse race, open to the world. **1902** S. E. WHITE *Blazed Trail* xxvii. 175 In a free-for-all knock-down-and-drag-out, kicking, gouging, and biting are all legitimate. **1918** C. E. MULFORD *Man fr. Bar-20* vi. 56 From the noise it appeared to be turning into a free-for-all. **1923** L. J. VANCE *Baroque* xiv. 85 The girl quietly lifted the lower sash, letting in.. cacophony of a domestic free-for-all in one of the neighboring flats. **1931** *Amer. Speech* VII. 49 [Lumberjacks'] 'free-for-all' when the 'shanty men' join the 'bull pen boys' around the box stove. **1941** L. A. G. STRONG *Bay* ii. 56 To judge by the sounds, it was a regular free-for-all. **1955** A. L. ROWSE *Expansion Eliz. Eng.* viii. 296 The development of privateering from a promiscuous free-for-all scrimmage.. into a regular business. **1971** *Guardian* 12 July 7/6 The sort of free-for-all tariff system we saw at London Airport in the sixties.

free-hand ('friːhænd), *a.* Of drawing: Done with a free hand, i.e. without guiding instruments, measurements, or other artificial aid. Also *absol.* or quasi-*sb.* = free-hand drawing.

1862 in *Dict. Arch.* (Arch. Publ. Soc.), *s.v.* **1879** *Cassell's Techn. Educ.* I. 48/1 The study and practice of freehand drawing gives accuracy to the eye. **1888** *Nature* XXXVII. 294 The curve was not done by freehand, but by means of engineer's curves.

free-'handed, *a.* [f. FREE *a.* + HAND *sb.* + -ED[2].] Open-handed, generous, liberal.

*a***1656** BP. HALL *Soliloquies* 75 He is freehanded and munificent. **1832** MISS MITFORD *Village* Ser. v. (1863) 325 The free-handed and open-hearted farmer. **1855** MACAULAY *Hist. Eng.* III. 717 A bold, jolly, freehanded English gentleman.

free-'handedness. [f. FREE-HANDED *a.*] Open-handedness, liberality.

1888 J. R. LOWELL *Lit. & Pol. Addresses* (1914) 214 The power of the political boss is built up.. by his free-handedness in distributing the property of other people. **1910** M. S. WATTS *N. Burke* 386 [He] certainly could not be accused of encouraging the Mexicans in their extortionate practices by any particular free-handedness on his own part. **1928** T. J. GRAYSON *Investment Trusts* 68 The facility and freehandedness with which they distribute profits. **1940** K. ROBERTS *O. Wiswell* 192 Here's another thing you'll have to consider, Mr. Wiswell: that's freehandedness with rebels.

free-'hearted, *a.* [f. FREE *a.* + HEART + -ED[2].] Having a 'free heart' in various senses; frank, open, unreserved; unburdened with anxiety, guilt, or suspicion; acting on the spontaneous impulse of the heart; generous, liberal, bountiful.

1398 TREVISA *Barth. De P.R.* XV. lxxix. (1495) 520 Angry of speche and sharpe. Netheles free herted and fayr of speche. *c***1440** *Promp. Parv.* 177/2 Fre hertyd in yeftys.. *liberalis.* **1549** COVERDALE *Erasm. Par.* Ded. 1 They shewed them selues so willing, so glad, so cherefull, and so fre harted, to further the worke. **1571** GOLDING *Calvin on Ps.* xviii. 2 Bound.. with the bond of freeharted and willing love. **1607** SHAKS. *Timon* III. i. 10 That.. Free-hearted Gentleman of Athens. **1684** OTWAY *Atheist* I. i, Come, come, no trifling, be free-hearted and friendly. **1728** GAY *Begg. Op.* II. i, Money was made for the Freehearted and Generous. **1820** W. IRVING *Sketch Bk.* (1859) 43 He.. throws off his habits of shy reserve, and becomes joyous and free-hearted. *a***1853** ROBERTSON *Lect.* ii. (1858) 61 A rigorous proscription of all freehearted mirth.

Hence **free-'heartedly** *adv.* (in mod. Dicts.); **free-'heartedness.**

1607 HIERON *Wks.* I. 389 As for examples, we haue.. the free heartednesse of Cornelius, he gaue much almes. **1686** BURNET *Trav.* i. (1750) 57 They all met with a Kindness and Freeheartedness, that [etc.].

freehold ('friːhəʊld). *Law.* For forms see FREE *a.* [f. FREE *a.* + HOLD *sb.*; a transl. of AF. *fraunc tenement.*]

1. A tenure by which an estate is held in fee-simple, fee-tail, or for term of life; applied also to a corresponding tenure of a dignity or office.

1523 FITZHERB. *Surv.* 12 There be many maner of fre holdes, and holde their landes and tenementes in diuers maner. **1598** MARSTON *Sco. Villanie* I. ii. C 4 When tenure for short yeeres (by many a one) Is thought right good be turn'd forth Littleton, All to be headdie, or free hold at least. *a***1626** BACON *Max. & Uses Com. Law* (1636) 44 Leases for lives are also called freeholds. **1660** R. COKE *Power & Subj.* 25 *Do* or *Dedi* to such a man or woman for term of either of their lives, or to such a man or woman during the life of another, creates a freehold. **1846** PARKE *Moore's P.C. Cases* V. 391 A party cannot be removed from office, in which he has a freehold, but for misconduct. **1858** LD. ST. LEONARDS

Handy-bk. Prop. Law x. 65 An estate for life, or for another man's life, is termed a freehold, less than an inheritance, but still a freehold.

2. An estate or office held by this tenure.

1467 in *Eng. Gilds* (1870) 393 And that he be of frehold yerly, at the leste, xl. *s*. **1495** *Act 11 Hen. VII*, c. 16 Who that hath eny freeholde within the Toun of Caleis. **1542–3** *Act 34 & 35 Hen. VIII*, c. 22 Manours..beinge the inheritaunce or the freholde of his wife. **1691** *Case of Exeter Coll.* 22 He must be turned out by due course of Law; and not frighted from his freehold by the thunder of Excommunication. **1712** PRIDEAUX *Direct. Ch.-wardens* (ed. 4) 25 The Vicar hath the Freehold of the Chancel. **1765** BLACKSTONE *Comm.* I. i. 100 No freeman shall be divested of his freehold. **1856** EMERSON *Eng. Traits, Aristocr.* Wks. (Bohn) II. 81 The great estates are absorbing the small freeholds. **1871** FREEMAN *Norm. Conq.* (1876) IV. xviii. 167 One lordship in Somerset, alone among all the lands of England, became the freehold of the Church of Saint Peter at Rome.

3. *transf.* and *fig.*

1611 BIBLE *Transl. Pref.* 2 He that medleth with mens Religion medleth with their custome, nay, with their freehold. **1631** MASSINGER *Beleive as You List* IV. ii, *Courtezan.* Yf thou wer'et Ten times a Kinge, thou liest. I am a ladie ..*Metellus.* Hee hath touched her free hold. *a* **1882** WHITTIER *My Triumph* 18, I..take by faith, while living, My freehold of thanksgiving.

4. *attrib.* or *adj.* Held by freehold; relating to or of the nature of freehold.

1527 *Test. Ebor.* (Surtees) V. 235 All my landes, as well copiehold as freehold. **1647** WARD *Simp. Cobler* 63, I have observed men to haue two kindes of Wills, a Free-hold will ..or a Copy-hold will. **1827** JARMAN *Powell's Devises* (ed. 3) II. 115 The testatrix having in a former part of her will disposed of all her freehold estate. **1876** DIGBY *Real Prop.* iii. §15. 139 When the rights over the land are given for a period the termination of which is not fixed or ascertained by a specified limit of time, the interest is a freehold interest.

freeholder (ˈfriːhəʊldə(r)). [f. FREE *a.* + HOLDER; rendering AF. *fraunc tenaunt.*]

1. One who possesses a freehold estate.

For the use in *Scots. Law* see quot. 1890.

c **1425** WYNTOUN *Cron.* VIII. xi. 9 In Fyfe þat tyme wes nane Erle, Lord, na Capytane, Ðe Fre-haldarys of þat Land. **1523** FITZHERB. *Surv.* Prol., And than may the lorde of yᵉ sayd maners..haue parfyte knowledge..who is his freholders, copyeholders, customarye tenaunte, or tenaunt at his wyll. **1664** BUTLER *Hud.* II. iii. 1169 He must (at least) hold up his hand, By twelve Free-holders to be scann'd. **1765** BLACKSTONE *Comm.* I. ix. 347 He [the coroner] is still chosen by all the freeholders in the county court. **1876** BANCROFT *Hist. U.S.* III. i. 13 The cultivator of the soil was, for the most part, a freeholder. **1890** *Bell's Dict. Law Scotl.* (ed. 7), *Freeholder*..in modern language, applied to such as, before the passing of the Reform Act of 1832, were entitled to elect or be elected members of Parliament, and who must have held lands extending to a forty shilling land of old extent, or to £400 Scots of valued rent.

fig. **1637** RUTHERFORD *Let.* 9 Sep. (1891) 499 The whole army of the redeemed ones sit rent-free in heaven..we are all freeholders. **1670** BROOKS *Wks.* (1867) VI. 373 Hypocrites are hell's free-holders. **1751** JORTIN *Serm.* (1771) V. ix. 195 God did not make them freeholders; they held their possessions under him.

2. *slang.* (See quot.)

a **1700** B. E. *Dict. Cant. Crew, Freeholder*, he whose Wife goes with him to the Ale-house. **1725** in *New Cant. Dict.*

Hence **ˈfreeholderˌship.**

1810 BENTHAM *Packing* (1821) 247. **1862** ANSTED *Channel Isl.* IV. xxiii. (ed. 2) 544 It began with fiefs, and it has developed a system of practical freeholdership.

†**ˈfreeholding,** *vbl. sb. Obs.* [f. FREE *a.* + HOLDING *vbl. sb.*; after FREEHOLD.] = FREEHOLD.

1591 *Charter of Kilmarnock* in A. McKay *Hist. Kilmarnock* (1864) 359 We have given..to our beloved cousin, Thomas, Lord Boyd, in free-holding or life-rent. **1637** RUTHERFORD *Let.* cciii. (1891) 401 We are but loose in trying our free-holding of Christ. [**1715** M. DAVIES *Athen. Brit.* I. 306 Franktenement..must be the Freeholding of an Estate, either in Fee-simple or Fee-tail.]

ˈfreeholding, *ppl. a. rare.* [f. FREE *a.* + HOLDING *ppl. a.*; after FREEHOLD.] That possesses a freehold; in †early use *absol.* or *sb.* = AF. *fraunc tenaunt*, FREEHOLDER.

13.. *Coer de L.* 1259 To Londoun, to hys somouns, Come ..Serjaunts, and every freeholdande. **1890** *Spectator* 10 May, Freeholding peasants.

freeing (ˈfriːɪŋ), *vbl. sb.* [f. FREE *v.* + -ING¹.] The action of the verb FREE.

1601 *High Peak Art.* l. in Mander *Derbysh. Min. Gloss.* (1824) 130 Such working and freeing of the said new taker. **1620** BRENT *tr. Sarpi's Counc. Trent* I. 6 An absolution or freeing, made by authority of the Prelate. **1631** MASSINGER *Emperor East* V. i, The freeing of an innocent From the emperor's furious jealousy. **1802** MAWE *Mineral Derbysh.* 204 (E.D.S.), *Freeing sb.*, entering a mine or vein in the barmaster's book. **1872** TENNYSON *Lynette* 992 Toward thy sister's freeing.

b. *attrib.* and *Comb.*; **freeing-dish**, the dish or measure of ore with which a Derbyshire lead-miner 'frees' his vein; **freeing-port** (see quot.).

1851 *Act 14 & 15 Vict.* c. 94 Sched. i. §11 Being called the Freeing Dish. **1880** *Times* 23 Oct. 5/4 This inner bulwark is provided at intervals with freeing ports, so that in case a sea breaks over and fills them they may quickly be relieved of the water.

ˈfreeish, *a.* [see -ISH.] Somewhat free.

1820 *Blackw. Mag.* VII. 391 A gay comedy..and a freeish farce.

freel, ? = FRILL *sb.*¹ 2.

1637 T. MORTON *New Eng. Canaan* (1883) 227 Freeles there are, Cockles and Scallopes.

freel(e, obs. form of FRAIL *a.*

ˈfreelage. *Obs.* exc. *Sc. dial.* Forms α. 3 freolac, -aic, -ec, vreoleic. β. 6 frelege, -lige, -lag(e, 7 freledge, 6–7 freelege, 9 freelage. [OE. **fréo-lác*, f. *fréo*, FREE *a.* + *-lác*: see -LOCK (*fréolác* occurs only as a compound of *lác* neut. oblation).

In the later β forms the suffix *-lege* has been substituted for OE. *-lác*, on the analogy of *knowledge*, or possibly by the same process that has led to the substitution in that instance.]

†**1.** = FREEDOM in various senses: *esp.* in later use, a franchise or privilege. *Obs.*

α. *a* **1225** *Ancr. R.* 286 Anker, of oðer freolac, haueð ibeon oðerhwules to freo of hire suluen. *a* **1225** *Leg. Kath.* 2366 Ha ..bisohte..þæt he for his freolec, firstede hire. *c* **1230** *Hali Meid.* 7 Nis þis þeowdom inoh aȝain þat ilke freolaic þat ha hefde.

β. **1513** DOUGLAS *Æneis* IX. iii. 47 Quhat God hes to hym grantit sik frelage? **1535** STEWART *Cron. Scot.* III. 359 In strang presoun, but ransoun or frelag, This nobill man ..[he] maid to die. **1593** B. BARNES *Parthenophil & P.* iv. in Arb. *Garner* V. 341 Whom thou in person guardest! (lest suborners Should work his freelege). **1593** *Rites & Mon. Ch. Durh.* (Surtees) 36 A frelige graunted by God and Sancte Cuthbert for every such offender to flie unto for succour. **1617** in Best *Farm. Bks.* (Surtees) 173 Grace my wife and her mayde to have theire dyet..as they used to have when I was lyveinge, and the freledge of the gardens. **1674** RAY *N.C. Words* 19 *Freelege* (Sheffield), Privilege. *Immunitas.*

2. *Sc. dial.* 'An heritable property, as distinguished from a farm, *Roxb.*' (Jam.)

attrib. **1805–11** A. SCOTT *Poems* 42 (Jam.) Altho' he had a freelage grant O' mony a tree, herb, flower, and plant, Yet still his breast confessed a want.

free lance. Also free-lance, freelance.

1. A term used by writers denoting one of those military adventurers, often of knightly rank, who in the Middle Ages offered their services as mercenaries, or with a view to plunder, to belligerent states; a 'condottiere', a 'free companion'.

1820 SCOTT *Ivanhoe* xxxiv, I offered Richard the service of my Free Lances. **1855** MISS YONGE *Lances of Lynwood* vi. (1864) 95 He..knew a d'Aubricour would be no discredit to his free lances. **1877** MRS. OLIPHANT *Makers Flor.* iii. 77 Those rude German free-lances, ever ready to sell themselves to the highest bidder.

2. *fig.* Applied *esp.* to a politician or controversialist who owns no fixed party allegiance, but from time to time assails one party or the other in a capricious or arbitrary manner; also, to one who in any department of speculation or practice follows the methods of no particular school. In recent usage, a person working for himself and not for an employer; freq. *attrib.*; also of occupations or work performed by free lances.

1864 *Standard* 16 Apr., They may be Free Lances in Parliament so long as the guerilla career suits them. **1882** J. HATTON *Journalistic London* v. 106 The name of Grenville-Murray..might be associated with clever work on many other English as well as French journals. The free lance *par excellence* of journalism was laid to rest..during..1881. **1883** S. C. HALL *Retrospect* II. 135 The band of literary free-lances that..made *Fraser's Magazine* a name of terror. **1889** JESSOPP *Coming of Friars* v. 216 The Friars..were free lances with whom the bishops had little to do. **1901** *Westm. Gaz.* 7 Mar. 9/1 Someone who calls himself a free-lance journalist. **1912** W. OWEN *Let.* 3 June (1967) 139 There entertained my guest, the Preacher—a funny old man who is a free-lance (as he vaunts) and answered the Vicar's advertisement. **1927** CARR-SAUNDERS & JONES *Soc. Struct. Eng. & Wales* 62 Free-lance professional men, doctors and barristers for instance. *Ibid.* 75 When members of a free-lance profession take salaried positions. **1950** *Science News* XV. 7 If they had to rely on the free-lance articles which come in they could close down tomorrow. **1962** MCLUHAN *Gutenberg Galaxy* 74 Leopold Bloom..is a free-lance ad salesman.

Hence **free-lance** *v. intr.*, to act as a free lance; **free-lancer**, a free lance; **free-lancing** *vbl. sb.* and *ppl. a.*

1903 A. BENNETT *Truth abt. Author* v. 60 What in Fleet Street is called 'free-lancing'. **1904** *Westm. Gaz.* 6 May 2/3 Lord Londonderry..has done a bit of free-lancing himself in his non-Ministerial days. **1907** *Ibid.* 27 Mar. 4/2 Some free-lancing Parliamentary iconoclast. **1909** *Daily Chron.* 7 Apr. 4/7 If the clergy were allowed to free-lance in each other's parishes. **1915** W. J. LOCKE *Jaffery* i, He had a terrible time for a dozen years or so, taking pupils, acting, free-lancing in journalism. **1937** *Times* 30 Dec. 6/3 My conviction that one could do more for the general cause of good architecture from within that body [*sc.* the R.I.B.A.] than as a rebel, free-lancing outside it. **1955** L. FEATHER *Encycl. Jazz* i. 28 Mary Lou Williams, free-lancing along the Street. **1966** *New Statesman* 11 Mar. 357/4 (Advt.), *Journalism*: occasional freelancer..seeks full-time position.

†**ˈfreeless,** *a. Obs.*⁻¹ [= ON. *frýju-lauss* blameless, f. *frýja* taunt + *-lauss* -LESS.] Blameless.

13.. *E.E. Allit. P.* A. 431 That freles fleȝe of hyr fasor.

free-ˈliver. One who lives freely; one who gives free indulgence to his appetites.

1711 SHAFTESB. *Charact.* (1737) III. 306 Those naturally honest appellations of free-livers, free-thinkers..or whatever other character implies a largeness of mind and generous use of understanding. **1806** *Culina* 53 This is a good..dish, for free-livers. **1822** W. IRVING *Braceb. Hall* (1849) 87 Free-livers on a small scale.

free-ˈliving, *a.*

1. Living freely and abundantly, given to free indulgence of the appetites.

1818 SCOTT *Hrt. Midl.* xvi, 'He was a gude servant o' the town..though he was an ower free-living man'. **1935** G. GREENE *Basement Room* 40 Any child in those free-living parts might be expected to play truant.

2. *Biol.* Living free from and independent of the parent.

1889 in *Century Dict.* **1912** J. S. HUXLEY *Individ. in Anim. Kingdom* ii. 38 Free-living animals, the Protozoa. **1915** E. R. LANKESTER *Divers. Nat.* 113 It is this change from the life of a free-living shrimp to that of a living lump, adherent by its head to rocks or floating logs. **1967** *Oceanogr. & Marine Biol.* V. 352 (*caption*) Free-living polyzoa.

†**ˈfreely,** *a. Obs.* [OE. *fréolic*: see FREE *a.* and -LY¹.] Free, noble; excellent, goodly, beautiful, lovely. (A stock epithet of compliment in ME. poetry: cf. FREE *a.* 3.)

Beowulf 615 Freolic wif. *a* **1000** *Riddles* xv. 13 Freolic fyrdsceorp. *a* **1225** *Leg. Kath.* 68 A meiden..feir ant freolich o wlite & o westum. *a* **1300** *Cursor M.* 8376 þou freli king, sa ful o bliss. **13..** *E.E. Allit. P.* B. 162 To þis frelych feste þat fele arn to called. *c* **1320** *Sir Tristr.* 193 Sone to deþ þer drewe Mani a frely fode. *c* **1350** *Will. Palerne* 822 Alle freliche foules þat on þat friþ songe. *c* **1460** *Towneley Myst.* (Surtees) 42 Ryse vp now, with thi frely face. ? *c* **1475** *Sqr. lowe Degre* 545 in Hazl. *E.P.P.* II. 44 Vndo thy dore! my frely floure.

b. *absol.* Noble one, fair one. (Cf. FREE B.)

13.. *E.E. Allit. P.* A. 1155 Quen I seȝ my frely I wolde be þere. *c* **1420** *Anturs of Arth.* xxix, That freli..And the kene knyȝte.

Hence **ˈfrelyhede.**

c **1440** *Jacob's Well* (E.E.T.S.) 185 þe vj. spanne in þe handyl of þi confessioun, is frelyhede; þat frely..for loue & deuocyoun to God, þou art schrevyn.

freely (ˈfriːlɪ), *adv.* [OE. *fréolíce*, ME. *freoliche, freliche, frely*, f. FREE *a.* + -LY².]

1. Of one's own accord, spontaneously; without constraint or reluctance; unreservedly, without stipulation; readily, willingly.

c **825** *Vesp. Psalter* xciii. [xciv.] 1 *Libere egit*, freolice dyde. *c* **888** K. ÆLFRED *Boeth.* xviii. §4 Seo sawl færþ swiþe freolice to heofonum. *c* **1205** LAY. 5547 Of Normaundie & of Flaundres freoliche him fulsten. **13..** *Guy Warw.* (A.) 209 Gij him answerd freliche: 'Sir, ichil wel bleþeliche'. *c* **1386** CHAUCER *Frankl. T.* 876–7 And right as frely as he sente hir me, As frely sente I hir to him ageyn. *c* **1460** FORTESCUE *Abs. & Lim. Mon.* xii. (1885) 139 The reaume off Fraunce givith neuer ffrely off thair owne gode will any subsidie to thair prince. **1526** *Pilgr. Perf.* (W. de W. 1531) 11 These..gyftes and graces, he hath gyuen to vs frely. **1586** T. B. *La Primaud. Fr. Acad.* 46 Let us freely forsake all such things [worldly goods]. **1607** SHAKS. *Timon* I. i. 110 Lord Timon, heare me speake. *Tim.* Freely good Father. **1664** EVELYN *Kal. Hort.* (1729) 187 Let none..despise..these short Directions, so freely and ingenuously imparted. **1817** LD. ELLENBOROUGH in Maule & Selwyn *Rep. K. Bench* VI. 316 He does not even ask for [the bills]; but they are freely and voluntarily handed over. **1862** RUSKIN *Unto this Last* 82 He may either give it us freely, or demand payment for it. **1865** R. W. DALE *Jew. Temp.* ix. (1877) 92 He freely forgives the penitent.

b. With freedom of will or choice.

1340 *Ayenb.* 86 Uri-wyl, huer-by he may chyese and do uryliche oþer þet guod oþer þet kuead. **1398** TREVISA *Barth. De P.R.* II. ii. (1495) 28 Angels haue myght and power frely to chese to vnderstonde and to loue. **1667** MILTON *P.L.* V. 538 Freely we serve, Because we freely love, as in our will To love or not.

2. Without constraint or reserve in regard to speech; unreservedly, frankly, openly, plainly.

1596 SHAKS. *Merch. V.* III. ii. 257, I freely told you. **1646** SIR T. BROWNE *Pseud. Ep.* I. viii. 32 To speake freely what cannot bee concealed. **1732** BERKELEY *Alciphr.* I §4 He may speak his mind freely to me without fear of offending. **1766** GOLDSM. *Vic. W.* xxi, We were shewn a room where we could converse more freely. **1849** MACAULAY *Hist. Eng.* II. 69 She well knew that she was not handsome, and jested freely on her own homeliness. **1884** *Leeds Mercury* 24 Oct. 8/2 He..freely criticised the policy of the Government in South Africa.

3. Without restraint or restriction upon action or activity; without let, hindrance, or interference.

a **1300** *Cursor M.* 2238 þat ai quen we se ani chesun, Freli may climbe vp and dun. **13..** *E.E. Allit. P.* B. 1106 Hit ferde freloker in fete in his fayre honde. *c* **1380** WYCLIF *Sel. Wks.* III. 362 For þanne Goddis lawe myȝte freeli renne bi þe lymytis þat Crist haþ ordeyned. **1503–4** *Act 19 Hen. VII*, c. 34 §8 Every suche Woman..[shall] frely enjoye..all hir owne inheretaunce. **1576** BAKER *Jewell of Health* 17 b, To thende the fire maye..burne the freelyer. **1609** SKENE *Reg. Maj.* 38 The woman may frelie marie, against the will of the over-lord. **1695** LD. PRESTON *Boeth.* I. 10, I began to breathe more freely. **1703** MOXON *Mech. Exerc.* 143 That the Light may the freelier play upon the Glass. **1874** MORLEY *Compromise* (1886) 1 The right of thinking freely and acting independently. **1879** *Cassell's Techn. Educ.* VIII. 91/1 These wheels turn freely upon the shaft.

b. Without observance of strict rule; loosely.

1869 PHILLIPS *Vesuv.* vii. 180 Only a freely sweeping line can justly express the form. **1870** MAX MÜLLER *Sc. Relig.* (1873) 122 Translate it somewhat freely.

4. Without stint; plentifully, abundantly; generously, liberally.

a **1300** *Cursor M.* 12332 Iesus tok þis corn for-melt, And freli it a-bute him delt. **13..** *E.E. Allit. P.* C. 20 For þay schal frely be refete ful of alle gode. **1597** SHAKS. *2 Hen. IV*, IV. ii. 75 You would drink freely. **1611** BIBLE *Gen.* ii. 16 Of euery tree of the garden thou mayest freely eate. **1659** D. PELL *Impr. Sea* 100 *note*, Throw your monies away freely in the Alehouse. **1725** DE FOE *Voy. round World* (1840) 260 We ate very freely. **1849** MACAULAY *Hist. Eng.* I. 431 The blood flowed freely. **1879** *Cassell's Techn. Educ.* IV. 23/2 He lived in princely style and spent his money freely. **1883** *Rep. Geol. Explor. N. Zealand* 39 Gold has been found freely. **1892** E. P. DIXON (Hull) *Seed Catal.* 37 *Brachycome Iberidifolia*.. blooms freely, and is useful for bedding.

†**5.** In freedom, with the rights of free birth; without servitude, with absolute possession (of property, franchises, etc.). ***freely begotten*** = lawfully begotten. *Obs.*

c **1205** LAY. 5440 ȝe sculllen.. habben freoliche eoure lond. **1375** BARBOUR *Bruce* I. 228 He levys at ese, that frely levys! *c* **1393** CHAUCER *Mariage* 31 God graunte you youre lyf frely to lede In fredom. **1415** *E.E. Wills* (1882) 24 Hers of his body frelych be-gotun. *c* **1425** WYNTOUN *Cron.* VIII. i. 65 Bot it suld joys all Fredomys, Franchys, Profit, and Customys, Also frely as before. *c* **1430** *Pilgr. Lyf Manhode* I. xlvi. (1869) 27 And that the gouernaunce of heuene longeth freeliche to me. *c* **1500** in Arnolde *Chron.* Index (1811) 11 That citezens of London.. of al their libarteis and fre vsage as holly and fully be restored. As them the tyme of ony our progenitours Kinges frelyest and fullyest they had. **1596** SHAKS. *Merch. V.* III. ii. 252, I must freely haue the halfe of any thing That this same paper brings you. **1601** —— *Twel. N.* I. iv. 40 Thou shalt liue as freely as thy Lord, To call his fortunes thine. *a* **1647** HABINGTON *Surv. Worcestersh.* in *Worc. Hist. Soc. Proc.* II. 255 The Church heald one Hyde freely.

†**6.** Nobly; excellently, beautifully. *Obs.*

c **1205** LAY. 28941 An hundred and sixti þusend freoliche iwapned. *a* **1225** *Juliana* 21 And under hire nebscheft al se freoliche ischapet. *c* **1330** R. BRUNNE *Chron.* (1810) 10 Fulle frely he lyued here. *c* **1350** *Will. Palerne* 2634 On þe fairest on face and frelokest ischapen.

†**7. a.** Without payment or cost, gratis; **b.** without punishment. *Obs.*; = FREE *adv.*

1340 HAMPOLE *Pr. Consc.* 5965 *Quod gratis accepistis, gratis date.* He says, 'þat þat ȝe haf of grace fre And frely resayved, frely gyf ȝe'. **1382** WYCLIF *Isa.* lii. 3 Freeli [Vulg. *gratis*] ȝee ben sold. **1480** CAXTON *Chron. Eng.* cxxxvi. 116 Somme of hem lete he go frelych and somme lete he putte to the deth. **1546** WRIOTHESLEY *Chron.* (1875) I. 163 Which were discharged frelie without paying any fine to the cittie. **1550** CROWLEY *Last Trump* 1411 Let none break such laws freli. **1589** *Act 31 Eliz.* c. 6 §1 Freelye without anye rewarde. **1759** B. MARTIN *Nat. Hist. Eng.* I. 264 For 153 children to be taught freely.

8. *Sc.* †Entirely, completely (*obs.*); also used as an intensive, very.

1500–20 DUNBAR *Poems* xxv. 78 Quhen flude and fyre sall our it frak, And frely frustir feeld and fure. **1873** W. ALEXANDER *Johnny Gibb* xi. (ed. 3) 66, 'I wud like freely weel to see them, man', said the stranger.

freeman ('friːmən). [OE. *fréoman*: see FREE *a.* and MAN *sb.*]

1. a. One who is personally free; one who is not a slave or serf. **b.** In later use often, one who is politically free; one not a subject of a tyrannical or usurped dominion.

a **1000** *Cædmon's Gen.* 2175 (Gr.) Hwæt ȝifest þu me.. freomanna to frofre. *c* **1000** *Laws of Æthelred* I. i. §1 Dæt ælc freoman ȝetreowne borh hæbbe. *c* **1205** LAY. 15577 þu nahtes i nane stude habben freo-monnes ibude. *c* **1275** *Fortune* 3 in *O.E. Misc.* (1872) 86 Wyþ freomen þu art ferly feid. *a* **1300** *Cursor M.* 16022 All þai gedird o þe tun, bath freman and dring. **1382** WYCLIF *Eph.* vi. 8 Whethir seruaunt, whether fre man. *c* **1440** *Promp. Parv.* 178/1 Fremann, made of bonde.. *manumissus.* **1601** SHAKS. *Jul. C.* III. ii. 25 Had you rather Cæsar were liuing, and dye all Slaues; then that Cæsar were dead, to liue all Free-men? **1659** RUSHW. *Hist. Coll.* I. 459 No Free-man shall be imprisoned without due Process of the Law. **1784** COWPER *Task* v. 733 He is the freeman whom the Truth makes free And all are slaves beside. **1793** BURNS *Scots, wha hae* iv, Free-man stand, or free-man fa'. **1850** LYELL *2nd Visit U.S.* II. 98 A coloured free-man. **1875** JOWETT *Plato* (ed. 2) III. 222 Injustice, whether existing among slaves or freemen.

2. One who possesses the freedom of a city, borough, company, etc.

1386 *Rolls of Parlt.* III. 225/1 The eleccion of Mairaltee is to be to the Fre men of the Citee. **1682** *Enq. Elect. Sheriffs* 34 The Rights.. are not only granted to the Mayor, but to the Free-men and Barons. **1705** ADDISON *Italy* Wks. 1721 II. 42 Both having been made Free men on the same day. *c* **1744** *Parl. Bill* in Hanway *Trav.* (1762) I. v. lxxi. 32 The oath to be taken by the freemen of the said company. **1805** FORSYTH *Beauties Scotl.* II. 474 The son and heir of a freeman succeeds to his inheritance within the borough unencumbered by the debts of his father. **1863** H. COX *Instit.* III. ix. 730 The electors [of the Council] are citizens, burgesses, or freemen.

3. In various modern uses. **a.** (See quot.)

1836 W. IRVING *Astoria* I. 194 A class of beaver-trappers and hunters technically called freemen.. They are.. Canadians.. who have been employed.. by some fur company, but their term being expired, continue to hunt and trap on their own account.

b. *Austral.* A 'free-labourer', a non-union man.

1890 *Times* 8 Sept. 3/1 The ships are being loaded by freemen.

4. *Comb.*, as ***freeman-like*** adv.; †**freeman's song**, the name applied in 16th c. to a certain class of vocal compositions of a lively character.

1561 T. NORTON *Calvin's Inst.* III. 273 Children, whiche are more liberally and more freemanlike handled of theyr fathers. *c* **1575** J. HOOKER *Life of Carew* 39 The King would very often use him to sing with him certain songs then called fremen songs, as namely 'By the bank as I lay'. **1609** [T. RAVENSCROFT] *Deuteromelia*: or The Second part of Musicks melodie, or melodius Musicke. Of Pleasant Roundelaies; K.H. mirth, or Freemens Songs. And such delightfull Catches. **1611** COTGR., *Virelay*, a.. Round, freemans Song.

Hence '**freemanship**, the position or status of a freeman, with its rights and privileges.

1869 *Daily News* 31 Aug., The fees payable on taking up freemanship. **1873** MCDOWELL *Hist. Dumfries* xxviii. 315 He had to serve other three years.. before he could aspire to freemanship.

freemartin ('friːˌmɑːtɪn). [Of unknown origin: cf. Ir., Gael. *mart*, heifer.] A hermaphrodite or imperfect female of the ox kind: see quot. 1790.

1681 *Lond. Gaz.* No. 1651/4 The Heifer.. is supposed to be Spaied, or else a Free-Martin. **1779** J. HUNTER in *Phil. Trans.* LXIX. 279 Account of the Free-martin. **1790** BEWICK *Hist. Quadrupeds* (1807) 28 When a Cow happens to bring forth two calves—one of them a male, the other a female,—the former is a perfect animal, but the latter is incapable of propagation, and is well known to farmers under the denomination of a Free Martin. **1856** *Farmer's Mag.* Jan. 56 Freemartins and Spayed Heifers are not qualified.

b. *transf.* Said of a sheep.

a **1722** LISLE *Husb.* (1757) 361 An ewe-sheep, that is a free-martin.. has a.. lanker bearing than other sheep.

Freemason ('friːmeɪs(ə)n). Also **freemason.** [f. FREE *a.* + MASON.

The precise import with which the adj. was originally used in this designation has been much disputed. Three views have been propounded. (1) The suggestion that *free mason* stands for *free-stone mason* would appear unworthy of attention, but for the curious fact that the earliest known instances of any similar appellation are *mestre mason de franche peer*, 'master mason of free stone' (Act 25 Edw. III. st. II. c. 3, A.D. 1350), and *sculptores lapidum liberorum*, 'carvers of free stones', alleged to occur in a document of 1217 (tr. *Findel's Hist. Mas.* 51, citing Wyatt Papworth); the coincidence, however, seems to be merely accidental. (2) The view most generally held is that *free masons* were those who were 'free' of the masons' guild (see FREE *a.* 29). Against this explanation many forcible objections have been brought by Mr. G. W. Speth, who suggests (3) that the itinerant masons were called 'free' because they claimed exemption from the control of the local guilds of the towns in which they temporarily settled. (4) Perhaps the best hypothesis is that the term refers to the mediæval practice of emancipating skilled artisans, in order that they might be able to travel and render their services wherever any great building was in process of construction.]

†**1.** A member of a certain class of skilled workers in stone, in the 14th and following centuries often mentioned in contradistinction to 'rough masons', 'ligiers', etc. They travelled from place to place, finding employment wherever important buildings were being erected, and had a system of secret signs and passwords by which a craftsman who had been admitted on giving evidence of competent skill could be recognized. In later use (16–18th c.) the term seems often to be used merely as a more complimentary synonym of 'mason', implying that the workman so designated belonged to a superior grade. *Obs.*

1376 in Conder *Hole Craft* 51 [A list of the city companies with the number of their representatives on the Council has: Free masons 2, Masons 4. But in the original handwriting the figure for the Masons is altered to 6, and the entry *Free masons* is expunged]. **1396** *Charter Rich. II* (Sloane 4595) in *Masonic Mag.* (1882) 341 Concessimus.. archiepiscopo Cantuar. quod.. viginti et quatuor lathomos vocatos ffre Maceons et viginti et quatuor lathomos vocatos ligiers.. capere.. possit. [**1444** *Act 23 Hen. VI*, c. 12 Les gagez ascun frank mason ou maister Carpenter nexcede pas par le jour iiijd. ovesqe mangier & boier.. un rough mason & mesne Carpenter.. iiid. par le jour.] **1477** NORTON *Ord. Alch.* Proem. in Ashm. (1652) 7 Free Masons and Tanners. **1484** *Churchw. Acc. Wigtoft, Linc.* (Nichols 1797) 80 Paide to Will'm Whelpdale fremason for makyng of the crosse in yᵉ chirchrth. **1495** *Act 11 Hen. VII*, c. 22 §1 A Freemason maister Carpenter Rough mason Brickleyer [etc.] . **1504** *Bury Wills* (Camden) 104 To John Dealtry, fremason, xs. **1526** *Pilgr. Perf.* (W. de W. 1531) 142 The free mason setteth his prentyse first longe tyme to lerne to hewe stones. **1548** *Act 2 & 3 Edw. VI*, c. 15 §3 No Person.. shall.. lett or disturbe any Fre mason, rough mason, carpenter, bricklayer. **1594** BLUNDEVIL *Exerc.* Cont. (ed. 7) A. iv, In free Masons craft, in Joyners craft. **1608** TOPSELL *Serpents* (1658) 650 Who seeth not that it were far better the master work-men, free masons, and carpenters, might be spared, then the true labouring husbandman? **1662** EVELYN *Chalcogr.* (1769) 90 Encountring the difficulties of the free-mason. **1720** *Lond. Gaz.* No. 5907/4 Anthony Ashley.. Free Mason. **1723** *Ibid.* No. 6195/6 John Lane.. Free-Mason.

2. A member of the fraternity called more fully, ***Free and Accepted Masons.***

Early in the 17th c., the societies of freemasons (in sense 1) began to admit honorary members, not connected with the building trades, but supposed to be eminent for architectural or antiquarian learning. These were called *accepted masons*, though the term *free masons* was often loosely applied to them; and they were admitted to a knowledge of the secret signs, and instructed in the legendary history of the craft, which had already begun to be developed. The distinction of being an 'accepted mason' became a fashionable object of ambition, and before the end of the 17th c. the object of the societies of freemasons seems to have been chiefly social and convivial. In 1717, under the guidance of the physicist J. T. Desaguliers, four of these societies or 'lodges' in London united to form a 'grand lodge', with a new constitution and ritual, and a system of secret signs; the object of the society as reconstituted being mutual help and the promotion of brotherly feeling among its members. The London 'grand lodge' became the parent of other 'lodges' in Great Britain and abroad, and there are now powerful bodies of 'freemasons', more or less recognizing each other, in most countries of the world.

1646 ASHMOLE *Mem.* (1717) 15 Oct., [At] 4 Hor. 30 Minutes post merid., I was made a Free-Mason at Warrington in Lancashire, with Colonel Henry Mainwaring. **1686** PLOT *Staffordsh.* 316 Admitting Men into the Society of Free-masons, that in the moorelands of this County seems to be of greater request, than any where else. *Ibid.*, A Fellow of the Society, whom they otherwise call an accepted mason. **1688** R. HOLME *Armoury* III. 393/2, I cannot but Honor.. the Masons.. the more as being a Member of that Society called Free-Masons. **1691** AUBREY *Memorandums* 18 May in Conder *Hole Craft* (1894) 4 This day is a great convention at St. Pauls church of the fraternity of the free [*erased, and* accepted *written above*] Masons; where Sir Christopher Wren is to be adopted a Brother. **1709** STEELE *Tatler* No. 26 ¶3 They have their Signs and Tokens like Free-Masons. **1723** (*title*) The Constitutions of the Free-masons.. for the Use of the Lodges. **1753** *Scots Mag.* Sept. 425/1 The society of free and accepted masons caused a.. triumphal arch.. to be erected. **1816** 'QUIZ' *Grand Master* VII. 174 'I'd turn a Turk, or Methodist—Christian, Freemason, even Jew!'

3. *attrib.* (of or pertaining to freemasons), as ***freemason knock, secret, work.***

1807–8 W. IRVING *Salmag.* (1824) 220, I distinguished his *free-mason knock at my door. **1785** BURKE *Sp. Nabob of Arcot* 33 The true *free-mason secret of the profession of *soucaring.* *a* **1490** BOTONER *Itin.* (Nasmith 1778) 268 De *fremason-work operata.

Hence ˌ**Freema'sonic** *a.*, of or pertaining to freemasons; '**Freeˌmasonism** (*Stand. Dict.*) = FREEMASONRY.

1831 *Westm. Rev.* XIV. 156 A free-masonic order who converse by signs, innuendos, and slang. **1859** THACKERAY *Virgin.* II. xxxviii. 317 That mysterious undefinable freemasonic signal, which passes between women, by which each knows that the other hates her. **1861** SALA *Dutch Pict.* vi. 85 There she is at her post, with a wonderful free-masonic understanding with the doctor.

Freemasonry ('friːmeɪs(ə)nrɪ). [see -RY.]

†**1.** The craft or occupation of a freemason. *Obs.*

1435 in Speth *Freemasonry* 4 [In 1435 'John Wode, masoun', contracted to build the tower of the Abbey Church of St. Edmundsbury] in all mannere of thinges that longe to free masonry.

2. The principles, practices, and institutions of freemasons.

1802 *Edin. Rev.* I. 6 The lodges of Free Masonry. *Ibid.* 14 He denies that the secret of freemasonry consists in liberty and equality. **1825** MACAULAY *Ess., Milton* (1887) 24 Most of their absurdities were mere external badges, like the signs of freemasonry or the dresses of friars.

3. *fig.* Secret or tacit brotherhood, instinctive sympathy.

1810 SCOTT *Fam. Lett.* 30 Mar. (1894) I. vi. 173 There is a freemasonry among kindred spirits.. that always leads them to understand one another at little expense of words. **1847** ALB. SMITH *Chr. Tadpole* vii. (1879) 68 There seemed to be a sort of free-masonry amongst them. **1860** EMERSON *Cond. Life, Culture* Wks. (Bohn) II. 369 The gun, fishing-rod, boat, and horse, constitute among all who use them secret freemasonries. **1886** MRS. CRAIK *K. Arthur* v. 178 The two children with the wonderful freemasonry of childhood.. made friends immediately.

freend, Sc. form of FRIEND.

freeness ('friːnɪs). Now *rare.* [f. FREE *a.* + -NESS.]

1. The quality or state of being free (in different senses of the adj.); freedom.

1435 MISYN *Fire of Love* xx. 46 With frenes truly of þer lyst with grace of god þai ar fulfillyd. **1587** GOLDING *De Mornay* xiii. (1617) 206 According to their freenes.. they work freely. **1642** BP. REYNOLDS *Israel's Petit.* 22 That cometh like water out of a Spring, with a voluntary freenesse. **1647–8** COTTERELL *Davila's Hist. Fr.* (1678) 23 Resolution and freeness of courage. **1656** JEANES *Fuln. Christ* 218 The absolute freenesse of it: It was neither for his advantage, as an end, nor for our deservings, as a motive. **1862** C. DRESSER *Art Decorative Design* 70 The convolvulus winding its way in graceful freeness around the branches.

b. Const. *from.*

1640 BP. REYNOLDS *Passions* xxvi. 260 Freenesse from Enemies, Cleernes from Injuries. **1648** JENKYN *Blind Guide* iii. 36 The freenesse of their writings from.. error.

2. Readiness; generosity, liberality.

c **1300** *Cursor M.* 27861 (Cott. Galba) Frenes of hert and large of gift. **1377** LANGL. *P. Pl.* B. XVI. 88 *Filius*, bi the Fader wille and frenesse of *Spiritus Sancti.* **1611** SHAKS. *Cymb.* v. v. 421 Wee'l learne our Freenesse of a Sonne-in-Law: Pardon's the word to all. **1648** *Petit. Eastern Ass.* 25 Their.. freenesse to assist the Kingdome in a time of need. **1660** FULLER *Mixt Contempl.* (1841) 180 Let us now pay taxes that we may never pay taxes; for, as matters now stand, our freeness at the present may cause our freedom at the future. **1709** *Brit. Apollo* II. No. 37. 1/1 This Comparison displays the Freeness of Remission with regard to the Offending Persons.

3. Unreservedness (in speech, etc.); openness, frankness.

1548 UDALL, etc. *Erasm. Par. Matt.* xvii. 13 Frenesse in reprouyng of kynges. **1553** T. WILSON *Rhet.* 106 b, Freenesse of speache, is when we speake boldely & without feare.. whatsoeuer we please. *c* **1614** CORNWALLIS in Gutch *Coll. Cur.* I. 149 He would requite my kind proceeding with a real freeness. **1633** HEYWOOD *Eng. Trav.* III. Wks. 1874 IV. 57, I am sorry my freenesse should offend you.

free-'quarter. *Hist.* The obligation or impost of having to provide free board and lodging for troops; also, of the troops, the right to be billeted in free quarters, or else the necessity of having to find them for themselves. *to live at free-quarter*: to be maintained without expense to the government.

1648 *Petit. Eastern Ass.* 17 Have not inforced Assessements, and free-quarter grated them as small? **1648** CROMWELL *Lett.* 15 Nov. in *Carlyle*, The Country is.. not able to bear free-quarter; nor well able to furnish provisions if we had moneys. **1655** —— *Sp.* 22 Jan. *ibid.*, These took advantage from.. the stopping of the pay of the army, to run us into Free-quarter. *a* **1680** BUTLER *Rem.* (1759) I. 63 Make Law and Equity as dear, As Plunder and Free-quarter were. **1818** COBBETT in *Pol. Reg.* XXXIII. 524 An army must be sent into Yorkshire; but, they must live at free-quarter then.

Hence †**free-'quarter** *v.*, to live at free-quarter; †**free-'quarterer**, one billeted in free quarters.

1648 PRYNNE *Plea for Lords* C ij, As our free-quarterers doe now. **1654** WHITLOCK *Zootomia* 16 As for evil Things, look on them but as Lodgers, (though as unwelcome as Free-quarterers). **1659** To free-quarter [see FREEBOOTER *v.*].

freer ('friːə(r)). [f. FREE *v.* + -ER[1].] One who frees or sets free.

1610 HEALEY *St. Aug. Citie of God* XIV. xi. (1620) 485 He is the Freer who is the Sauiour. **1638** BAKER tr. *Balzac's Lett.* (1654) III. 142 But the French shall be the freers of all the earth. **1670–98** LASSELS *Voy. Italy* II. 76 It was erected to him.. as to the freer of the city.

freer, obs. and Sc. dial. form of FRIAR.

frees, freese, obs. ff. of FRIEZE, FREEZE.

ˌ**free-se'lector.** *Austral.* One who takes up a block of crown-land under the Land Laws and by annual payments acquires the freehold (Morris). Also called simply *selector*.

1866 *Sydney Morn. Her.* 9 Aug. (Morris), The very law which the free selector puts in force against the squatter. **1881** MRS. C. PRAED *Policy & P.* III. 260 He made a spring at the free-selector. **1883** KEIGHLEY *Who are You* 79 Far apart stood free-selectors' huts.

So **free-se'lect** *v. trans.*, to take up (land) under Government; hence **free-selecting** *vbl. sb.* and *ppl. a.*; **free-se'lection**, the action of the vb.

1870 T. H. BRAIM *New Homes* ii. 87 A man can now go and make his free selection before survey of any quantity of land .. at twenty shillings an acre. **1884** BOLDREWOOD *Melb. Mem.* xix. 134 Had he proceeded to free-select an uninhabited island. *Ibid.* xx. 142 This was years before the free-selection discovery. **1890** —— *Col. Reformer* (1891) 321, I camped.. just below those free-selecting friends of yours. *Ibid.* 401 Free-selecting here might be very well for some people; it didn't suit them.

†**'freeship.** *Obs.* [f. FREE *a.* + -SHIP.]

1. Freedom, liberty.

c **1175** *Lamb. Hom.* 75 He.. gef hom eche frechipe alle þa þet hit alde cunnen. *c* **1205** LAY. 372 Ær we nulleð mid frescipe faren from ure feonden.

2. Liberality, generosity.

a **1225** *Ancr. R.* 386 Luue is heouene stiward, uor hire muchele ureoschipe.

freesia ('friːzɪə, 'friːʒə). [mod.Lat.] A genus of iridaceous bulbous plants of the Cape of Good Hope, allied to *Gladiolus*.

1882 *Garden* 4 Feb. 73/3 Freesias. **1891–6** [In many newspaper quots., often spelt *Freezia*].

free soil, *sb.* and *a. U.S.*

A. *sb.* Territory in which slaveholding was prohibited.

a **1850** CALHOUN *Wks.* (1874) IV. 547 All these, in the slang of the day, were what are called slave territories, and not free soil.

B. *adj.* The epithet of a political party in 1846–56, which opposed the extension of slavery into the territories; pertaining to this party or its principles.

1848 LOWELL *Biglow P.* Poems 1890 II. 143, I went to a free soil meetin' once. **1875** *N. Amer. Rev.* CXX. 69 Mr. Clay was speaking of the antislavery agitators and of the Free-soil party.

So **free-soiler,** (*a*) a politician in favour of free soil and opposed to slavery; (*b*) one who lives on free soil, a free man. **free-soilism**, the principles of the Free-soil party, opposition to slavery.

1849 LONGF. in *Life* (1891) II. 162 Palfrey, Adams, Sumner.. all and several Free-soilers. **1855** *Fraser's Mag.* LI. 675 All the free-soilism of the north will strain its every nerve to [etc.]. **1875** *N. Amer. Rev.* CXX. 73 Tainted with Free-soilism or Abolitionism. **1888** BRYCE *Amer. Commw.* II. III. lv. 355 The abolitionists and Free Soilers.. had for some time previously acted as a group by themselves.

free-spoken, *a.* [cf. *plain spoken*] Accustomed to speak plainly and without reserve. Hence **free-spokenness**.

1625 BACON *Apophthegms* §176 A free-spoken Senatour. **1641** MILTON *Animad. Rem. Def.* Wks. 1738 I. 79 These free-spoken and plain-hearted Men, that are the Eyes of their Country. **1856** GROTE *Greece* II. xcvi. XII. 508 The slaughter of the free-spoken orators. **1863** HAWTHORNE *Our Old Home* 269 In our refined era, just the same as at that more free-spoken epoch. **1882** J. H. BLUNT *Ref. Ch. Eng.* II. 486 The free-spokenness of Queen Elizabeth and King James.

free state.

1. Occasionally = REPUBLIC. Now *rare*.

1646 FULLER *Wounded Consc.* (1841) 330 As all countries are not monarchies governed by kings, but some by free-states, where many together have equal power. **1727–41** CHAMBERS *Cycl.*, *Free State.* **1850** MERIVALE *Rom. Emp.* (1865) I. ii. 54 Names conspicuous in the municipal annals of the free state.

2. *U.S.* Before the Civil War of 1861–5, a state of the Union in which slavery did not exist.

1861 LOWELL *E Pluribus Unum* Prose Wks. 1890 V. 47 He would.. have received the unanimous support of the Free States. **1888** BRYCE *Amer. Commw.* II. III. liii. 334 New States had been admitted substantially in pairs, a slave State balancing a free State.

'free-stone, freestone[1]. Also 4 fre-stane, 6 freese stone, 7 friestane, frise-stone. [f. FREE *a.* + STONE *sb.*; a transl. of OF. *franche pere*, where the adj. means 'of excellent quality'; cf. FRANK *a.*[2] 5.]

1. Any fine-grained sandstone or limestone that can be cut or sawn easily.

c **1320** *Seuyn Sag.* (W.) 3036 The knyght gat masons many ane, And grat them hew ful faire fre-stane. **1463** *Bury Wills* (Camden) 37 An ymage of our lady.. in an howsyng of free stoon. **1577** HARRISON *England* II. iii. (1877) I. 71 Houses builded.. for the most part of hard freestone. **1640–1** *Kirkcudbr. War-Comm. Min. Bk.* (1855) 67 He hes use for certaine friestane for building. **1662** GERBIER *Princ.* 24 As for Free-stone, Portland Stone works well. **1773** BRYDONE *Sicily* xv. (1809) 172 The streets.. are all paved with white free-stone. **1796** KIRWAN *Elem. Min.* (ed. 2) II. 18 The alluminous ore of Whitby is sometimes a grey Freestone. **1878** F. S. WILLIAMS *Midl. Railw.* 367 The handsome embattled tower.. is chequered with flint and freestone.

†**b.** A slab or piece of such stone. *Obs.*

c **1475** *Pict. Voc.* in Wr.-Wülcker 768 *Hec timeria*, a fre-stone. **1626** BACON *Sylva* §570 Toads have been found in the middle of a Freestone. **1712** HEARNE *Collect.* (Oxf. Hist. Soc.) III. 412 A White Free Stone is laid over Mr. Wm. Joyner's Grave.

2. *attrib.* and *Comb.*, as ***freestone house***, †***mason***, ***ornament***, ***passage***, ***quarry***; †**freestone-coloured** *a.*, of the colour of freestone.

1600 SHAKS. *A.Y.L.* IV. iii. 25 She has.. A *freestone coloured hand. **1665–6** WOOD *Life* (Oxf. Hist. Soc.) II. 72 The larg *free-stone house. **1703** in Willis & Clark *Cambridge* (1886) II. 211 Paid the *freestone Mason his bills in full. **1726** AMHERST *Terræ Fil.* xliv. 235 What! are there no living ornaments in Oxford? Are its inanimate, its *free-stone ones its greatest glory? **1766** ENTICK *London* IV. 357 A *free-stone passage. **1776** ADAM SMITH *W.N.* I. xi. III. I. 186 The value of a *freestone quarry.. will.. increase.

'free-stone[2]. A variety of the peach (or nectarine) in which the flesh parts freely from the stone when ripe. Also *free-stone peach*.

1866, 1880 [see CLINGSTONE]. **1889** FARMER *Americanisms*, *Free-stone peach.*

freet, var. of FREIT *Sc.*

free-thinker ('friːˌθɪŋkə(r)). One who refuses to submit his reason to the control of authority in matters of religious belief; a designation claimed *esp.* by the deistic and other rejectors of Christianity at the beginning of the 18th c.

The sect mentioned in the first quot. seems to be identical with the 'free seekers' (quot. 1693 s.v. FREE D. 1 c).

?**1692** S. SMITH (*title*) The Religious Imposter.. dedicated to Doctor S—lm—n, and the rest of the new Religious Fraternity of Free-Thinkers, near Leather-Sellers-Hall.. Printed.. in the first year of Grace and Free Thinking. **1708** SWIFT *Sentim. Ch. of Eng. Man* Wks. (1755) II. I. 56 The atheists, libertines, despisers of religion.. that is to say, all those who usually pass under the name of Free-thinkers. **1836** HOR. SMITH *Tin Trump.* (1876) 170 Freethinker.. has come to be synonymous with a libertine and a contemner of religion. **1874** MORLEY *Compromise* (1886) 151 The modern freethinker does not attack Christianity; he explains it.

transf. **1848** THACKERAY *Van. Fair* xlv, He (who had been .. inclined to be a sad free thinker on these points) entered into poaching and game preserving with ardour.

free-'thinking, *vbl. sb.* The free exercise of reason in matters of religious belief, unrestrained by deference to authority; the adoption of the principles of a free-thinker.

?**1692** [see FREE-THINKER]. **1708** *Brit. Apollo* No. 58. 1/2 Free Thinking (to use the Modish Phrase).. is no better than a Sword in a Child's hand. **1758** GRAY *Let.* Poems (1775) 263 The mode of free-thinking is like that of Ruffs and Farthingales, and has given place to the mode of not thinking at all. **1773** *Gentl. Mag.* XLIII. 122 If, by free-thinking, Deism be meant.

attrib. **1719** *Free-Thinker* 118 ¶2, I proceeded.. to give Assurances of many Free-Thinking Feats, which it was, then, generally suspected I never intended to perform.

free-thinking, *ppl. a.*

1. Holding the principles of a free-thinker.

a **1716** SOUTH *Serm.* (1843) II. 109 Our free thinking and free practising age. **1750** COVENTRY *Pompey Litt.* II. ix. (1785) 66/1 A free-thinking writer of moral essays.

2. Pertaining or relating to free-thinkers or free-thought.

1726 AMHERST *Terræ Fil.* xi. 52 Those heritical, pernicious, and free-thinking tracts. **1848** THACKERAY *Van. Fair* xix, Her shocking free thinking ways. **1882** *Sat. Rev.* 18 Nov. 671/1 Trashy freethinking productions.

free-thought. = FREE-THINKING *vbl. sb.*

1711 SHAFTESB. *Charact.* (1737) II. 116 If it brings along with it any affection opposite to manhood.. or free-thought. **1874** MORLEY *Compromise* (1886) 152 The tendency of modern free thought is [etc.]. **1887** *Academy* 12 Nov. 314 These centres of learning and freethought.

attrib. [**1882** CASSELL, *Free-thought a.* of or pertaining to free-thinking.] *Mod.* A——'s catalogue of free-thought publications.

free trade, free-trade.

1. An open and unrestricted trade.

1606 CHAPMAN *M. D'Olive* I, Wit's become a free trade for all sorts to live by. **1622** MALYNES *Maint. Free Trade* 105 A Remedie, whereby the Kingdome shall enjoy all the three essential parts of Traffique vnder good and Politike Gouernment, which will bee Free Trade effectually or in deed. **1642–3** EARL OF NEWCASTLE *Declar.* in Rushw. *Hist. Coll.* (1721) V. 137 As if they desired not only the free Trade, but even the Monopoly of plundering to themselves. **1670** R. COKE *Disc. Trade* 33 Our Plantations.. would have been much increased and inriched by a Free Trade, more than by this restraint. **1804** *Edin. Rev.* IV. 308 The wisdom of allowing a free trade has been pretty generally allowed in speculation by all statesmen. **1846** MCCULLOCH *Acc. Brit. Empire* (1854) II. 527 The circumstance of our carrying on a great free trade with it.

2. Trade or commerce left to follow its natural course, i.e. without the interference of customs duties designed to restrict imports or of bounties intended to foster home production. Also, the legislative establishment or maintenance of this state of things, and the principles of those who advocate it; opposed to *protection*.

Adam Smith *W.N.* 1776 uses *freedom of trade* in this sense. He has also frequently *a free trade*, in sense 1.

1823 in Cobbett *Rur. Rides* (1885) I. 400 One newspaper says.. he will endeavour to 'inculcate in the mind of the Bourbons wise principles of free trade!' **1825** MCCULLOCH *Pol. Econ.* II. ii. 134 Suppose that, under a system of free trade, we imported a considerable proportion of silks and linens now wholly manufactured at home. **1861** COBDEN in *Times* 18 July, The principles of Free Trade.

b. In various occasional applications (see quots.).

1858 SIMMONDS *Dict. Trade*, *Free-trade*.. unrestricted action in banking operations. **1868** ROGERS *Pol. Econ.* xvii. (1876) 231 Correctly stated, free trade in land consists rather in the removal of the hindrances which the law puts on the conveyance of land.

3. Trade free from the lawful customs duties; smuggling.

1824 SCOTT *Redgauntlet* ch. xiii, 'If you will do nothing for the free trade, I must patronise it myself.' So saying he took a large glass of brandy. **1834** H. MILLER *Scenes & Leg.* xiv. (1889) 211 [He] was engaged.. in the free trade, and had set the officers of the revenue at defiance.

4. *attrib.*

1829 H. HAWTHORN *Visit Babylon* 45 In all this, do you.. discover anything like your free-trade plan? **1877** *Daily News* 5 Oct. 4/4 The free-trade party.

So **free-'trading** *a.*, favouring free-trade; **free-'tradist**, an advocate of free-trade.

1832 GALT in *Fraser's Mag.* VI. 593 To the theory of the free-tradist objections cannot well be made. **1851** LYTTON *Lett. John Bull* 93 To sum up the authorities from Free-trading political economists.

free-'trader.

1. a. One allowed to trade without restriction.

1698 FRYER *Acc. E. India & P.* 86 They permit Free Traders on their Island Bombaim. **1851** MAYHEW *Lond. Labour* I. 375 The pedlar.. was, as it were, the first 'free-trader'.

b. (See quot.)

1867 SMYTH *Sailor's Word-bk.*, *Free Trader*, ships trading formerly under license to India independent of the old East India Company's Charter.

c. A trader not in the service of a company. *U.S.*

1837 W. IRVING *Adv. Capt. Bonneville* (1895) I. 66 Waylaying and dogging the caravans of the free traders, and murdering the solitary trapper. **1902** S. E. WHITE *Conjuror's House* iv. 39 Brooding on his imprisonment the Free Trader forgot his surroundings. **1945** R. W. SERVICE *Ploughman* 429 McTosh is a free trader.. and hates the Company.

2. A smuggler; also, a smuggling vessel.

1815 SCOTT *Guy M.* v, There go the free-traders. **1824** —— *Redgauntlet* ch. xiv, As if.. a free-trader could sail the Solway as securely as a King's cutter!

3. An advocate of free-trade.

1832 *Deb. Congress U.S.* 6 June 3305 He admits a fact which the free traders have always found it difficult to explain, that goods do not usually rise under an increase of duties. **1849** COBDEN *Speeches* 34 If.. there be free-traders who think that free-trade is only an experiment. **1878** *N. Amer. Rev.* CXXVI. 266 They were tariff men and free-traders, conservative Whigs and radical Democrats.

'freeway. orig. *U.S.* [WAY *sb.*[1] 1.]

a. A thoroughfare with restricted access (see quots. 1930, 1936). **b.** An express highway.

1930 *Amer. City* Feb. 95 A freeway is a strip of public land, dedicated to movement, over which the abutting owners have no right of light, air or access. **1935** *Harvard City Planning Studies* VII. 40 Such master plan shall show desirable streets, highways, freeways.. and other planning features. **1936** E. M. BASSETT *Zoning* (new ed.) 83 The increase of freeways, which are thoroughfares to which the abutting owners have no right of direct access, will help to solve the problem of too extensive business districts along main arteries. **1939** *Sun* (Baltimore) 16 Jan. 5/7 Construction of freeways, either elevated or on the ground, would be necessary to facilitate movement of traffic in and out of Washington. **1943** *Life* 22 Nov. 118/2 Almost everybody in Los Angeles has some pet plan for rebuilding large parts of the city after the war and opening up new 'freeways' (express auto highways). **1946** *Archit. Rev.*

XCIX. 127/3 The internal by-pass or 'freeway' is a feature that will demand high technical skill. **1951** *Engineering* 17 Aug. 196/1 Distinction between a freeway and an ordinary highway is in the..access to the freeway... 'Owners of abutting lands have no..or only restricted right..of access.' **1959** *Guardian* 18 Sept. 7/2 The freeways... Mile after mile of smooth, three or four-lane road, unbroken by intersection or traffic lights..minimum permissible speed about 40 m.p.h.

free wheel, free-wheel. [FREE *a.* 14.] The rear wheel of a bicycle arranged so that it can rotate freely while the pedals remain stationary; in a machine other than a bicycle, a wheel, propeller, etc. that can run free of a clutch or other connection with the machine itself; also *attrib.* and *absol.* (= a bicycle with a free wheel).

1899 *Westm. Gaz.* 17 Nov. 7/1 The free-wheel device..is ..*the* novelty of the show. **1900** *Isle of Man Exam.* 3 Nov. 7 The recent free wheel contests. **1901** *Westm. Gaz.* 18 Sept. 8/1 Injuries sustained while riding a free-wheel machine down Knockholt Hill. **1902** A. C. HARMSWORTH et al. *Motors* x. 217 Free-wheel steering gear. **1902** E. NESBIT *Five Children & It* ix. 240 There..stood a bicycle—a beautiful new free-wheel. **1912** W. OWEN *Let.* 6 Feb. (1967) 114 My bicycle is quite disabled now—the free-wheel having worn out. **1930** *Engineering* 7 Feb. 163/1 Free wheels or over-running clutches are referred to. **1958** *Ibid.* 7 Mar. 298/1 There was a free-wheel arrangement between the air turbine and the alternator.

Hence **free-wheel** *v. intr.*, to ride with the wheel that is normally driven rotating freely; to operate as a free wheel; **free-wheeled** *a.*, having a free wheel; **free-wheeler**, a free-wheel bicycle; **free-wheeling** *vbl. sb.* and *ppl. a.* Also *transf.* (of lawn-mowers, etc.).

1900 *Captain* III. 80/2 All these free wheeled machines made a clicking noise. **1903** *Motor Cycle* 31 Mar. 10/2 There is nothing incongruous in the sight of a club of bicyclists.. some of them propelling their bicycles by muscular power at all times, except when free-wheeling downhill. **1905** *Mosquito* Aug. 4 They thoroughly enjoyed the ride coming back and free-wheeled the whole way. **1908** E. M. SNEYD-KYNNERSLEY *H.M.I.* viii. 78 It was the first year of 'free-wheelers'. **1932** *Oxford Times* 23 Sept. 22/3 Free-wheeling and syncro-mesh gears have for some time been almost universal on cars built in the United States. **1935** *Jrnl. R. Aeronaut. Soc.* XXXIX. 1025 The drag of the propeller when locked in position, or free-wheeling. *Ibid.* 1026 Above 13° blade-angle setting the free-wheeling propeller has less drag. **1936** A. BRUNEL *Film Production* 16 Their principal camera developed a strange habit of 'free-wheeling' intermittently. **1970** *Which?* Mar. 83/1 The cutting cylinders of most of the mowers free-wheeled.

fig. **1911** 'I. HAY' *Safety Match* iii. 48 For a moment he was silent—free-wheeling, so to speak, over the pulverised remains of Mr. Winch. **1931** M. DE LA BÉDOYÈRE *Drift of Democracy* iii. 49 Romanticism glides along free-wheeling wheresoever the mood suggests. **1944** AUDEN *Sea & Mirror* (1945) ii. 45 Had you..really left me alone to go my whole free-wheeling way to disorder. **1956** M. STEARNS *Story of Jazz* (1957) vii. 67 In a free-wheeling music such as jazz, a musician is judged by his capacity for sustained and swinging improvisation. **1958** *Times* 24 Nov. p. viii/5 At the other end of the scale from free-wheeling Quebec are its neighbours on the east. **1966** *Listener* 20 Jan. 111/3 He saw drama as something halfway between a poem and a prose narrative, a balance between formalism and free-wheeling. **1967** A. BATTERSBY *Network Analysis* (ed. 2) xiv. 237 He must then ask what is the maximum period for which the project can be allowed to free-wheel without serious departures from the plan occurring.

free will, ˌfree-'will, ˌfree'will. [See FREE *a.* 19.]

1. (Best written as two words.) Spontaneous will, unconstrained choice (to do or act). Often in phr. ***of one's own free will***, and the like. † ***in one's free will***: left to or depending upon one's choice or election.

a **1225** *Ancr. R.* 8 þeos & swuche oþre beoð alle ine freo wille to donne oþer to leten hwon me euer wule. **13..** *Myrour of lewed Men* 4 in *Min. P. Vernon MS.* 407 God send vs thoght to his plesyng In whos fre wil hynges all thyng. *c* **1510** MORE *Picus* Wks. 11/2 Very happy is a christen man, sith that the victorie is..put in his owne frewill. **1590** SPENSER *F.Q.* I. viii. 5 Every dore of freewill open flew. **1611** BIBLE *Ezra* vii. 13 All they..which are minded of their owne free-will to goe vp to Ierusalem. **1694** *Acc. Sev. Late Voy.* II. (1711) 42 Every Ship's master is left to his free will, whether he will sail into the Ice. **1712** STEELE *Spect.* No. 308 ¶ 1 Whether she has not been frightened or sweetned by her Spouse into the Act she is going to do, or whether it is of her own free Will. **1873** SYMONDS *Grk. Poets* vii. 190 Having of her own free-will exposed her life. **1875** JOWETT *Plato* (ed. 2) I. 133 They were allowed to wander at their own free will.

2. a. 'The power of directing our own actions without constraint by necessity or fate' (J.).

a **1300** *Cursor M.* 9408 Wijt and skill he gaf þam till, Might, and fairhid, and frewill. **1340** *Ayenb.* 86 þe uerste is uri-wyl huer-by he may chyese and do uryliche oþer þet guod oþer þet kuead. *c* **1374** CHAUCER *Boeth.* IV. pr. vi. 104 (Camb. MS.) Of the knowynge and predestinacion diuine and of the lyberte of fre wille. **1508** FISHER *7 Penit. Ps.* cxlii. Wks. (1876) 259 He made vs and endued vs with reason and frewyll. **1538** STARKEY *England* I. ii. 28 Frewyl can not be wythout knolege, both of the gud and of the yl. **1654** HOBBES *Liberty, Necess., etc.* (1841) 1 The third way of bringing things to pass, distinct from necessity and chance, namely, freewill. **1700** ASTRY tr. *Saavedra-Faxardo* I. 205 Such variety of Events, as fortune produces, or free-will prepares. **1849** ROBERTSON *Serm.* Ser. I. ii. (1866) 22 Without free-will there could be no human goodness.

b. In a bad sense: Arbitrary or licentious will.

1514 BARCLAY *Cyt. & Uplondyshm.* (Percy Soc.) 34 In stede of vertue, ruleth frewyll & lust! **1547** SALESBURY *Welsh Dict.*, *Mympwy*, Frewyll.

3. a. *attrib.* (in ***free-will offering***) = given readily or spontaneously.

1535 COVERDALE *Ps.* liii[i]. 6 A frewil offeringe wil I geue the. **1611** BIBLE *Ps.* cxix. 108 Accept, I beseech thee, the freewil offrings of my mouth. **1878** BOSW. SMITH *Carthage* 44 The free-will offerings of their golden ornaments by the Libyan women.

b. *attrib.* and *Comb.* (sense 2). ***Free Will Baptist***: a member of a North American sect, of Welsh origin, of Arminian Baptists.

c **1575** FULKE *Confut. Doctr. Purgatory* (1577) 13 The free will men of our time. **1627** S. WARD *Christ All in All* 13 To all..merit and freewill-mongers. **1732** SWIFT *Advantages Repeal. Sacr. Test* 6 Of the three Judges on each Bench, the first may be a Presbyterian, the second a Free-Will Baptist, and the third a churchman. **1816** W. BENTLEY *Diary* 19 May (1914) IV. 389 In Salem, the Free Will Baptists had an Immersion. **1823** *Baptist Mag.* IV. 32 Some who usually assembled with those denominated Free-will Baptists. **1847** H. HOWE *Hist. Coll. Ohio* 348 The village contains..1 Free Will Baptist, 1 Methodist and 1 Universalist church. **1889** 'MARK TWAIN' *Connecticut Yankee* xxxi. 398 My first wife was a Free Will Baptist. **1966** R. G. TORBET *Hist. Baptists* (rev. ed.) x. 285 The Freewill Baptist periodical, *The Morning Star*, became so vocal against slavery that the printing establishment..was twice refused the privilege of incorporation.

Hence **free-'willed** *a.*, having the faculty of free-will; **free-'willer**, a contemptuous term for one who believes in the doctrine of free-will, an Arminian; **free-'willist** *rare*, a believer in free-will, a 'libertarian'; † **free-'willing** *a.* (in Coverdale), spontaneous, giving (or given) freely.

1678 CUDWORTH *Intell. Syst.* 889 Peccability arises from the necessity of imperfect *freewilled beings left to themselves. **1709** PRIOR *Ode to Col. Villiers*, In vain we think that free-will'd Man has pow'r. **1685** BUNYAN *Pharisee & Publ.*, Wks. 1737 II. 681 So again, the *Free-willer, he will ascribe all to God. **1709** STRYPE *Ann. Ref.* I. lii. 562 Using therein the new coined phrase of free-willers. **1732–38** NEAL *Hist. Purit.* (1822) I. 90 Besides these free-willers it seems there were some few in prison for the gospel that were Arians. **1814** *Chron.* in *Ann. Reg.* 534 Freewillers were persecuted as heretics. **1535** COVERDALE *Exod.* xxxv. 29 The children of Israel brought *fre-wyllynge offerynges. —— *1 Chron.* xxx. 9 And y[e] people were glad that they were fre wyllinge: for they gaue it with a good wyll..vnto the Lorde. **1867** BAGEHOT in *Fortn. Rev.* Nov. 522 Every *Freewillist holds that [etc.].

free-woman. A woman who is (personally) free; also, a woman who possesses the freedom of a city. (Cf. FREEMAN.)

1611 BIBLE *1 Macc.* ii. 11 Of a free-woman shee is become a bondslaue. **1635** R. N. *Camden's Hist. Eliz.* I. 3 She was alwaies her owne free woman and obnoxious to none. **1641** HINDE *J. Bruen* li. 168 Are ye not rather the children of the bond woman..than children of the free woman. **1766** ENTICK *London* I. 471 Any freeman or freewoman of this city.

freeze (friːz), *sb.*[1] [f. FREEZE *v.*] **1.** The action of the vb. FREEZE; *lit.* and *fig.* See also FREEZE-OUT; FREEZE-UP.

c **1440** *York Myst.* xiv. 72 þe fellest frese þat euer I felyd. **1630** J. TAYLOR (Water P.) Wks. II. 256/2 The Lord, the Lowne, the Sir, the Swaine Against the freeze, of Freeze make winter suites. **1866** DICKENS *Lett.* 6 Jan. (1880) II. 246, I am charmed to learn that you have had a freeze out of my ghost story. **1882** *Garden* 18 Mar. 177/2 The severe frost of Oct. 5..was an exceptional freeze. **1891** K. FIELD *Washington* IV. 383/2 During a freeze there is no comfort in a southern house.

2. Also in specific *fig.* uses, as: **a.** ***to do a freeze***: to be overlooked or ignored. *Austral.* and *N.Z. slang.*

c **1926** 'MIXER' *Transport Workers' Song Bk.* 23 'I know,' said one, 'I did a freeze Till I tumbled to the lurk.' **1941** BAKER *Dict. Austral. Slang* 30 *Do a freeze*, to be overlooked, ignored.

b. The fixing or establishing of assets, dividends, military strength, etc., at a certain level or figure. Cf. *wage-freeze* and FREEZE *v.* 5 e, f.

1942 *Business Week* 11 Apr. 88/1 In wartime there is much to be said for a general price, wage, and profit freeze. **1948** *Electronics* Nov. 132/1 Television Application Freeze Announced. Recent action by the FCC temporarily halted any further authorization of new television stations... The freeze would remain in effect long enough for the commission to decide whether certain changes should be made. **1951** *Economist* 24 Nov. 1245 In the first twelve months since the end of the so-called freeze, wage rates have increased by 10 per cent. **1959** *Daily Tel.* 23 Mar. 14/4 Mr. Macmillan's plan for a controlled and inspected 'freeze' of forces in a prescribed area. **1962** *Daily Tel.* 26 Oct. 1/3 He has accepted the proposal..for a 'freeze' of two to three weeks. This will involve him in the suspension of all arms shipments to Cuba. **1965** *New Statesman* 9 Apr. 560/3 A socialist government should actively support a new nuclear freeze in Europe.

3. *Cinemat.* and *Television.* A shot in which the movement is arrested by printing the same frame many times. Also **freeze-frame, -shot, frozen-frame.** Cf. FREEZE *v.* 4 f.

1960 O. SKILBECK *ABC of Film & TV* 59 *Freeze frame*, T.V. term meaning a briefly Frozen Shot after the Jingle to allow ample time for Change over at the end of a T.V. 'Commercial'. **1965** L. HALLIWELL *Film-goer's Compan.* 157 *Freeze frame*, a printing device whereby the action appears to 'freeze' into a still, this being accomplished by printing one frame many times. **1966** *New Statesman* 3 June 819/2 Daisy..breaks down but recovers in a frozen-frame finale. (Incidentally, *The Moving Target* ends on a freeze too: perhaps some more conventional way of signing off a story might be returned to.) **1969** *New Yorker* 17 May 127/1 The sound track uses the creak of the prison doors..and, finally, to accompany a freeze-shot of the start of a massacre, the Haydn tune that the Hapsburgs adopted as their anthem. *Ibid.* 20 Dec. 36/3 The freeze-frame of the dream resumes. **1970** A. FOWLES *Dupe Negative* xiv. 190, I crashed berserkly through the door and a freeze frame was stamped obscenely on my mind.

† **freeze,** *sb.*[2] *Obs.* Also **frees.** (See quots.) Also **freeze-water**, water used for diluting wine.

16.. *Songs Lond. Prentices* (Percy Soc.) 155 Let me have but a touch of your ale..Or tinkers frees, Or vintners lees. **1658** tr. *Porta's Nat. Mag.* XVIII. 382 Freeze-water [orig. has *aqua* only] is thinner than new wine, and lighter. **1698** *In Vino Veritas* 8 A Liquid nick-named Freeze, which is..but a hungry, thin, sorry kind of Cyder, which does us a.. kindness in lowering our Wines. **1719** D'URFEY *Pills* III. 104 They had fetched their Frees, And mired their Stomachs quite up to their Knees in Claret and good Cheer.

freeze (friːz), *v.* Pa. t. **froze** (frəʊz). Pa. pple. **frozen** ('frəʊz(ə)n). Forms: *Infin.* 1 **fréosan**, 3–4 **fr(e)osen** 4–6 **fre(e)se(n, frise**, (5 **freys**, 6 **freis, freze**), 6, 8 **frieze**, 7–8 **freez**, (7 **freize**), 6– **freeze.** *Pa. t.* 1 **fréas**, 4 **fre(e)s(e**, 5 **frore, frose**, (9 *dial.* **friz**), 7– **froze**; *weak forms*: 4 **freesed**, 6 **frised**, 9 **freezed.** *Pa. pple.* α. 1 **froren**, 3–5 **froren, -yn**, 5–6, 9 **frorn(e**, 4–9 **frore** (4 **froore**, 5 **froare**) also 3–4 **i-, yfrore.** β. 4–6 **frosen, -yn**, (6 **frose**), 5–9 **froze** (now *vulgar*), (9 *dial.* and *vulgar* **friz**), 6– **frozen**; *weak forms*: 6 **frozed**, 7–8 **freezed.** [A Com. Teut. str. vb.: OE. *fréosan* = MLG. *vrêsen*, Du. *vriezen*, OHG. *friosan* (MHG. *vriesen*, mod.Ger. *frieren*), ON. *friósa* (Sw. *frysa*, Da. *fryse*), Goth. **friusan* (inferred from *frius* frost):—OTeut. **freusan*, f. root **freus-*, *fraus-*, *fruz-*:—pre-Teut. **preus-*, *prous-*, *prus-*; cf. Lat. *pruīna* (:—? **prusvīna* hoar-frost), Skr. *prušva* drop, frozen drop, hoar-frost; less obviously connected in sense are L. *prūrīre* to itch, *prūna* (:—**prusnā*) live coal, Skr. *pluš* to burn; some scholars assume contamination with the Aryan root **qreus*, *qrus* to freeze, whence Gr. κρύσταλλος ice.

The OTeut. conjugation was **freus-*, *fraus*, *fruzum*, *frozono-*, which is accurately represented in the OE. *fréosan*, *fréas*, *fruron*, *froren*. The later Eng. form of the pa. pple. *frosen*, *frozen* (whence pa. t. *froze*) is due to the analogy of the pres.-stem; similarly ON. has *frosenn* (possibly the source of the Eng. form) beside the older *frørenn*, and Du. has pa. t. *vroor*, pa. pple. *vrozen*, as well as the correct *vroos*, *vroren*; the MHG. inf. *vriesen*, pa. t. *vrôs*, have become in mod.Ger. *frieren*, *fror*, through the analogy of the pa. pple. *gefroren*.]

I. intransitive uses.

1. *impers.* ***it freezes***: the local temperature of the atmosphere is such that water becomes ice. †Also quasi-*personal* with a subject (*frost*, etc.).

971 *Blickl. Hom.* 93 Men steorran maȝon ȝeseon swa sutole swa on niht ðonne hit swiðe freoseþ. *a* **1000** *Gnomic Verses* (Bosw.), Forst sceal freosan. *c* **1000** ÆLFRIC *Gram.* xxii. (Z.) 128 *Gelat*, hit fryst. *a* **1250** *Owl & Night.* 620 An his hou never ne vor-lost, Wan hit snuith, ne wan hit frost. *a* **1310** in Wright's *Lyric P.* xxxix. 110 When the forst freseth, muche chele he byd. **1362** LANGL. *P. Pl.* A VIII. 115 Whon the Forst freseth foode hem [the foules] bi-houeth. **1390** GOWER *Conf.* III. 236 If the month of juil shall frese. **1481** CAXTON *Reynard* (Arb.) 82 He shal neuer take harm by colde..thaugh it snowed, stormed or frore neuer so sore. **1548** HALL *Chron.*, *Hen. VIII* (1809) 671 Still it frised. **1649** R. HODGES *Plain. Direct.* 8 If it freez, put on your frees jacket. **1748** F. SMITH *Voy. Disc.* I. 153 It snowed all night, and froze very hard. **1837** W. IRVING *Capt. Bonneville* III. 40 A road in the wet snow, which, should it afterwards freeze, would be sufficiently hard to bear the horses.

2. a. Of a liquid, or liquid particles: To be converted into ice. Of a body of water: To become covered with ice. Occas. with complement, as ***to freeze hard, solid.***

c **1290** *S. Eng. Leg.* I. 317/608 þe dropen bicometh to snowe, And þanne huy freosez adoneward are huy comen here ouȝt lowe. *c* **1330** R. BRUNNE *Chron.* (1810) 121 þe snowe lay in þe feld, þe water frese biside. *c* **1400** MAUNDEV. (1839) xi. 125 Thare ys a nother Ryvere, that upon the nygt freseth wondur faste. *c* **1532** DEWES *Introd. Fr.* in *Palsgr.* 947 To frese, *geller*. **1692** RAY *Creation* II. (ed. 2) 122 The aqueous Humor of the Eye will not freeze. **1694** *Acc. Sev. Late Voy.* II. (1711) 222 The Dutch, who winter'd in Nova Zembla, took notice, that the salt Water freez'd. **1748** F. SMITH *Voy. Disc.* I. 159 Port Wine froze solid. **1816** J. SMITH *Panorama Sc. & Art* II. 41 Some other liquor must be employed, which is not so subject to freeze. **1878** MARKHAM *Gt. Frozen Sea* v. 60 The cold spray flew aft into our faces where it almost froze.

b. To become hard or rigid as the result of cold; *esp.* of objects containing moisture.

1390 GOWER *Conf.* II. 22 Wherof art thou so sore afered, That thou thy tunge suffrest frese. **1694** *Acc. Sev. Late Voy.* II. (1711) 208 Their Tackle was so frozen, and full of Isicles. **1725** POPE *Odyss.* XIX. 238 Snows collected on the mountain freeze. **1748** F. SMITH *Voy. Disc.* I. 21 Our Ropes were now froze with Ice hanging on them.

3. a. To become fixed *to* (something) or *together* by the action of frost.

c **1460** *Towneley Myst.* (Surtees) 99 When my shone freys to my fete It is not alle esy. **1596** SHAKS. *Tam. Shr.* IV. i. 7 Were not I..soone hot; my very lippes might freeze to my teeth. **1860** TYNDALL *Glac.* II. xxiv. 361 Their liquid liberty is destroyed, and the surfaces freeze together. *Mod.* In Canada a child's tongue once froze to a lamp-post he was licking.

b. orig. *U.S.* and *Australian. to freeze* (*on*) *to*: to hold on *to* (a person or thing); to keep tight hold of; also, to become attached *to* (a person), 'take to'. Cf. *to stick to*. Also, *to freeze down*.

1837-40 HALIBURTON *Clockm.* (1862) 377 Do as I do, younker..freeze down solid to it. **1861** LOWELL *Biglow P.* Poet. Wks. 1890 II. 234, I friz right down where I wuz, merried the Widder Shennon. **1876** BESANT & RICE *Gold. Butterfly* xx. 163 No, sir; I am of the children of Israel; and I freeze to that. **1882** SALA *Amer. Revis.* (1885) 193 'Freezing' to him, as the Americans call it—was a tiny fellow of some eight years. **1883** P. ROBINSON *Saints & Sinners* 114 The better the Mormon, the harder he freezes to his religion. **1888** RIDER HAGGARD *Col. Quaritch* xvii, He's a lawyer and he might not freeze on to you. **1890** 'BOLDREWOOD' *Col. Reformer* (1891) 189 Here, Jem!..freeze on to this brute. **1897** *Westm. Gaz.* 23 June 7/1 Londoners, when they get hold of a good thing, like to 'freeze on to' it. **1935** WODEHOUSE *Blandings Castle* i. 25 You won't mind if I freeze on to the two-seater for the nonce? **1960** M. STEWART *My Brother Michael* xv. 188 We'll freeze on to those facts, and let the rest develop as it will.

4. a. To be affected by, or have the sensation of, extreme cold; to feel very chill; to suffer the loss of vital heat; to die by frost. So *to freeze to death*.

1390 GOWER *Conf.* II. 38 Wether that he frese or swete.. He woll ben idel all aboute. **1601**? MARSTON *Pasquil & Kath.* II. 363 Powre wine, sound musicke, let our blouds not freeze. **1613** SHAKS. *Hen. VIII*, I. iv. 21 Nay, you must not freeze. **1681** COLVIL *Whigs Supplic.* (1751) 37 A..passage.. he finds by the north-west, Where Davies freezed to his rest. **1698** FRYER *Acc. E. India & P.* 318 We might sooner have frozen than kept our Innate Heat entire. **1748** F. SMITH *Voy. Disc.* I. 176 By being thus hung in the Air, the Rabbit ..freezes to Death. **1817** COLERIDGE *Three Graves* 22 Her limbs did creep and freeze. **1820** KEATS *Eve St. Agnes* ii, The sculptured dead, on each side, seem to freeze.

b. Of inanimate things: To be extremely cold; to be utterly devoid of heat.

1613 SHAKS. *Hen. VIII*, III. i. 4 Orpheus..made..the Mountaine tops that freeze, Bow themselves. **1700** DRYDEN *Pal. & Arc.* II. 540 Heav'n froze above severe, the clouds congeal. **1823** LAMB *Elia, Old Benchers I.T.*, His kitchen chimney was never suffered to freeze.

c. In non-material or *fig.* sense: To grow intensely cold; to lose warmth of feeling; to be chilled by fear, etc.; to shudder.

a **1557** in *Tottel's Misc.* (Arb.) 169, I frise amids the fire. **1596** SHAKS. *Tam. Shr.* II. i. 340 Gray-beard thy loue doth freeze. **1596** B. L[INCHE] *Diella* (1877) 74 Thou then didst burne in loue, now froz'd in hate. **1607** DEKKER *Whore of Babylon* Wks. 1873 II. 265 Courage, to kill Ten men I should not freeze thus. **1683** CAVE *Ecclesiastici* Introd. 66 Zeal against Paganism did not freeze. **1718** POPE *Iliad* xv. 756 Pale, trembling, tired, the sailors freeze with fears. **1874** MAHAFFY *Soc. Life Greece* ix. 289 If I behold the tiny fish on which they put such a price I freeze with horror.

d. *to freeze out*: (of a plant) to die through freezing. *U.S.*

1872 *Trans. Dep. Agric. Illinois* 73 They [*sc.* strawberry plants] dry out and freeze out worse in a loose and well aerated sand. **1872** *Rep. Vermont Board Agric.* 128 Alsike luxuriates in damp soils, and will not freeze out as red clover.

e. To make oneself suddenly rigid or motionless.

1848 C. BRONTË *J. Eyre* xix, The smile on his lips froze. **1865** *Detroit Tribune* 6 Oct. 3/1 The raiders remained in the back room some minutes without making any demonstration, and Smith in the meantime 'froze' to the door latch. **1908** S. E. WHITE *Riverman* iii. 27 But Orde.. had frozen in an attitude of attentive listening. **1916** H. TITUS *I Conquered* ix. 109 Of a sudden the horse froze, stopped his breathing. **1931** D. L. SAYERS *Five Red Herrings* xxviii. 334 The Chief Constable hurriedly snatched up the rug and froze. **1933** *Brit. Birds* XXVII. 130 It 'froze' here for about five minutes and then started moving its head around. **1959** *Listener* 5 Mar. 414/2 Whenever a sentry appeared, they froze. **1969** I. & P. OPIE *Children's Games* vi. 193 As the person in front turns round, the players 'freeze', for if he sees anyone moving..he sends that player back.

f. *Cinemat.* (See quot. 1960.) Cf. FREEZE *sb.*[1] 3.

1960 O. SKILBECK *ABC of Film & TV* 59 *Freeze*, to arrest movement by successively Printing one Frame of Negative. Done, for instance, to extend a Shot for Optical purposes, as in a Title background; or for comedy effect. **1965** *Movie* Spring 29/1 Oval masking, 'freezing', multiple-image, slow-motion. **1965** [see FREEZE *sb.*[1] 3].

II. Transitive uses.

5. a. Of natural agencies: To change (a fluid) to a solid form by the action of cold; to congeal; to form ice on the surface of (a river, etc.). Also said causatively of personal agents.

1494 FABYAN *Chron.* VII. 609 In this..yere..began a froste that..frose yᵉ Thamys. **1563** W. FULKE *Meteors* (1640) 54 The..Northern winds doe frieze the vapours; and so it becommeth hoare frost. **1570** *Satir. Poems Reform.* x. 325 The froist dois freis vp all fresche watter. **1641** FRENCH *Distill.* v. (1651) 164 It will..forthwith be freezed. **1729** SAVAGE *Wanderer* I. 57 Far hence lies, ever freez'd, the northern main. **1781** CAVALLO in *Phil. Trans.* LXXI. 516, I have froze a quantity of water with an equal weight of good ether. **1835** SIR J. ROSS *Narr. 2nd Voy.* xxxvi. 507 We froze oil of almonds in a shot-mould.

b. With adverbs. *to freeze over*: to cover with a coating of ice. *to freeze in, up*: to set fast in ice. *to freeze up*: to obstruct by frost.

1590 SHAKS. *Com. Err.* v. i. 313 Though..all the Conduits of my blood [be] froze vp. **1601** R. JOHNSON *Kingd. & Commw.* (1603) 146 The rivers and other waters are frozen uppe a yearde or more thicke. **1613** PURCHAS *Pilgrimage* (1614) 433 The Ozera or lake before the toune was frozen over Octob. 13. **1694** *Acc. Sev. Late Voy.* II. (1711) 28 Anvile, Smith's Tongs, and other Tools belonging to the Cookery were frozen up in the Ice. **1719** DE FOE *Crusoe* II. xv, The Baltic would be frozen up. **1748** F. SMITH *Voy. Disc.* I. 105 His Ship..was froze up. *Ibid.* 154 By the ninth the Creek was froze over from Side to Side. **1858** B. TAYLOR *North. Trav.* xvi. 164 Six vessels lay frozen in, at a considerable distance from the town.

c. To congeal (the blood) as if by frost; chiefly as a hyperbolical expression for the effect of terror. Hence with personal obj., to 'make (one's) blood run cold', to horrify intensely.

1398 TREVISA *Barth. De P.R.* VII. lxvi. (1495) 283 The venyme of a scorpion..closyth the herte atte the last and fresyth the blood with his coldenesse. **1579** SPENSER *Sheph. Cal.* Jan. 26 Such rage as winters raigneth in my hart, My life-bloud freesing with unkindly cold. **1602** SHAKS. *Ham.* I. v. 16 A Tale..whose lightest word Would..freeze thy young blood. **1633** FORD *Love's Sacr.* I. ii, Look here, My blood is not yet freez'd. **1639** T. BRUGIS tr. *Camus' Mor. Relat.* 347 The one inflamed me with love, the other freezed me with feare. **1707** *Curios. in Husb. & Gard.* 242 A cool and serious Air, capable of freezing his Readers. **1741** RICHARDSON *Pamela* (1824) I. 102, I should have melted her by love, instead of freezing her by fear. **1755** B. MARTIN *Mag. Arts & Sc.* 79 One Moment's Cold, like theirs, would ..Frieze the Heart's Blood.

d. *fig.* To chill, quench the warmth of (feelings, etc.); to paralyse (one's powers, etc.).

1595 SHAKS. *John* III. iv. 150 This Act..shall coole the hearts Of all his people, and freeze up their zeale. **1750** GRAY *Elegy* 52 Chill Penury repress'd their noble rage, And froze the genial current of the soul. **1793** E. PARSONS *Woman as she should be* III. 133 This paragraph froze his senses. **1842** LYTTON *Zanoni* 25 That recent hiss froze up her faculties and suspended her voice.

e. To make (assets, credits, etc.) unrealizable. Also (*nonce-use*) *intr.*, to become unrealizable.

1922 *Ann. Reg. 1921* II. 71 Credits granted by banks and financial houses to merchants have been frozen in enormous amounts. **1931** *Economist* 1 Aug. 219/1 In so far as the President's plan hints at definite freezing of existing bank credit for an agreed period, it is not acceptable to bankers. **1936** AUDEN *Look, Stranger!* 43 Europe grew anxious about her health, Combines tottered, credits froze. **1941** *Times* (Weekly ed.) 30 July 5/2 The Chinese Government have officially requested the British Government to 'freeze' Chinese assets. **1942** *Ann. Reg. 1941* 63 Great Britain.. promptly 'froze' Japanese assets. **1966** *Listener* 27 Oct. 606/2 They froze his money in the bank.

f. To fix (wages, prices, resources, etc.) at a stated level.

1933 H. L. ICKES *Diary* 12 Oct. (1955) I. 106 This contemplates the freezing of prices at their present level. **1940** *Economist* 16 Mar. 455/2 In addition to the reduction in wages, prices and employment were 'frozen'. **1944** *Ann. Reg. 1943* 287 There should be less political difficulty in 'freezing' wages. **1956** *Ann. Reg. 1955* 135 Military budgets should be 'frozen' at the 1 January 1955 level.

g. To make immobile or inflexible; to arrest at a certain stage of development, etc.

1936 J. GUNTHER *Inside Europe* ix. 142 It would, by 'freezing' the present borders, prevent *Anschluss*, union of Germany and Austria. **1941** *Time* (Air Exp. Ed.) 26 May 22/3 General Electric..had..frozen its models of receivers. **1949** 'G. ORWELL' *Nineteen Eighty-Four* II. 204 The purpose of all of them was to arrest progress and freeze history at a chosen moment. **1958** *New Statesman* 12 Apr. 454/1 Co-op representation is to be 'frozen' at something like the present level of 20 MPs and 10 prospective candidates. **1958** *Spectator* 8 Aug. 185/1 This attempt to freeze frontiers and governments would be absurd coming from anyone. **1969** *Daily Tel.* 18 Jan. 1/6 A Federal Court judge in New York yesterday froze action on the merger of the Atlantic Richfield Company and Sinclair Oil Corporation.

6. To affect with frost; to stiffen, harden, injure, kill, etc. by chilling; to change *into* or *to* (something) and *fig.* to bring *into* a certain state by chilling. Also, *to freeze to death*: rare in active. Occas. to allow to freeze.

1596 SHAKS. *Tam. Shr.* IV. i. 40 My Master and mistris are almost frozen to death. **1634** MILTON *Comus* 449 That snaky-headed Gorgon shield..Wherewith she [Minerva] freezed her foes to congealed stone. **1700** DRYDEN *Pal. & Arc.* III. 839 Sense fled before him [Death], what he touched he froze. **1704** *Ded.* in *Clarendon's Hist. Rep.* III. 4 Severe Winters, that freez..and cut off many hopeful plants. **1748** F. SMITH *Voy. Disc.* I. 163 And if close, the Snow lying there must freeze the Leg. **1855** KINGSLEY *Heroes* II. (1868) 23 Will she not freeze me too into stone? **1878** MRS. STOWE *Poganuc P.* xi. (ed. 3) 91 He [the bird] must have chilled his beak and frozen his toes as he sat there.

7. *to freeze out*: **a.** *lit.* in *pa. pple.* or *ppl. a.*: see FROZEN. **b.** *fig.* (U.S. *colloq.*) To exclude from business, society, etc. by chilling behaviour, severe competition, etc.

1861 G. K. WILDER *Diary* (MS.) 20 July, We finally froze him out. **1867** 'MARK TWAIN' *Amer. Drolleries* (1875) 62 They would let that man go on and pay assessments,..and then they would close in on him and freeze him out. **1869** C. L. BRACE *New West* v. 69 They can..lay assessments to bring a stock down to the lowest point, thus 'freezing out' the unhappy stockholders. **1890** *Daily News* 25 Jan. 2/2 Part of the campaign for 'freezing out' the Rosario Company.

freeze, obs. form of FRIEZE.

freeze-drying, *vbl. sb.* (Stress variable.) [FREEZE *v.*] A method of drying foodstuffs, blood plasma, pharmaceuticals, etc. while retaining their physical structure, the material being frozen and then warmed in a high vacuum so that the ice sublimes. So **freeze-dried** *a.*; (as a back-formation) **freeze-dry** *v. trans.*

1944 *Nature* 22 Apr. 485/2 Many biological materials can be most conveniently preserved..if they are dried from the frozen state. The success of the 'freeze-drying' procedure appears to be chiefly related to the fact that the resulting 'solid state' prevents the concentration and aggregation of the molecules of protein. **1946** *Ibid.* 7 Sept. 349/1 Freeze-dried milk benefited from the addition of cystine. **1949** E. W. FLOSDORF *Freeze-Drying* i. 6 In 1933 in the author's laboratory..the first products for actual clinical use were freeze-dried. **1956** *Nature* 14 Jan. 85/2 Freeze-dried bovine uterine cervical secretions. **1957** *Times* 11 Nov. 13/1 The new 'freeze-dried' BCG tuberculosis vaccine... The virus in this case is live, as opposed to the poliomyelitis virus, which is 'inactivated'. **1959** *Times* 24 Sept. 7/3 Officers sample new freeze-dried foods. **1962** *Engineering* 26 Jan. 133 Freeze-drying, AFD, continues..to hold the imagination with its possibilities for preserving the purity and flavour of perishable foodstuffs. **1962** V. N. OREKHOVICH et al. in A. Pirie *Lens Metabolism Rel. Cataract* 325 The solution was dialysed and then freeze-dried. **1963** *Daily Tel.* 29 Aug. 11/2 The valve came from the body of a man who died..about a month ago... The valve was then 'freeze-dried' and stored. **1967** *New Scientist* 9 Feb. 352/3 More recently, freeze-dried coffee extracts have appeared on the market.

freeze-out. *U.S.* [FREEZE *v.* 7.] **1.** In full *freeze-out poker*. A variety of the game of poker in which the players, as fast as they lose their staked capital, drop out, all the money going to the player last remaining.

1856 *Butte Record* (Oroville, Calif.) 25 Oct. 1/6 He was.. playing 'freeze-out' for the whiskey. **1877** *Harper's Monthly* Oct. 799 (Bartlett), They doant do nuthin' but drink whiskey and play frease aout poker. **1889** FARMER *Americanisms* s.v., In *freeze-out* poker..no player, when his money is exhausted, can borrow, or continue in the game on credit under any circumstances. **1907** B. TARKINGTON *His own People* iv. 61 I'll put it up against that tin automobile of yours, divide chips even and play you freeze-out for it. **1945** R. W. SERVICE *Ploughman* 214 I'll play you for one of them there geese. Stud poker or freeze out.

2. An act of 'freezing' or forcing out.

1883 [J. HAY] *Bread-winners* (U.S.) 144 They organized a freeze-out against him. **1904** F. LYNDE *Grafters* xiv. 190 By that time enough of the stock will have changed hands..and the freeze-out will be a fact accomplished.

†**freeze-pot.** *Obs.* [f. FREEZE *v.*] An epithet applied to January.

1557 TUSSER *100 Points Husb.* (1878) 233 Janeuer fryse pot ..And feuerell fill dyke.

freezer ('fri:zə(r)). [f. FREEZE *v.* + -ER[1].]

1. A machine used for freezing, or for keeping anything extremely cold. Also, a refrigerated room; a compartment in a refrigerator or freezing machine. So in *Comb.*

1847 in *Missouri Hist. Rev.* (1942) XXXVI. 121 An article called a 'Freezer', which consists of a cylindrical jar, made of block tin, and fitted with a close cover [for ice-cream manufacture]. **1860** O. W. HOLMES *Elsie V.* (1887) 74 He had agitated a quantity of..milk in what was called a cream-freezer. **1870** MRS. PRENTISS *Let.* 4 July in *Life* xi. (1883) 350 Papa bought a new fashioned freezer, that professed to freeze in two minutes. **1924** *U.S. Dept. Agric. Dept. Bull.* No. 1246. 9 Most packing and cold-storage plants are also equipped with what are known as 'freezers', which are refrigerating rooms in which the temperature can be lowered to 5° or 10°F.—sometimes lower. **1949** *Gloss. Terms Refrigeration (B.S.I.)* 9 *Freezer*, a low-temperature cold store, normally maintained below 20°F. **1959** *B.S.I. News* Apr. 17/1 The British Standards covering electric refrigerators and food freezers..have now been revised. **1959** *Housewife* June 129 A really big Kelvinator..gives you a roomier freezer compartment. **1961** *Times* 9 Aug. 5/2 The freezer trawler can stay on the fishing grounds until her holds are full. **1970** *Kenya Farmer* Feb. 15/1 A new freezer and chiller block.

2. Anything that freezes.

1845 HOOD *To Adm. Gambier* ix, The Maine—the Weser —or that freezer, Neva.

fig. **1848** DICKENS *Dombey* v, The books..looked..as if they had but one idea among them, and that was a freezer.

3. *N.Z.* A sheep destined, when killed, to exportation in a cold chamber.

1889 WILLIAMS & REEVES *Colonial Couplets* 21 Be they [*sc.* sheep] freezers or crawlers or wethers or ewes. **1893** J. HOTSON *Lect.* in *Age* 30 Nov. 7/2 The breeding of what are in New Zealand known as 'freezers'. **1907** W. H. KOEBEL *Return of Joe* 177 Many were the pressings and pinches bestowed on each indignant animal before he was decided worthy of the honour of becoming a 'freezer'.

4. In *Chasing*, a punch for producing a frosted groundwork. (Cf. FRIEZE *v.*[2] 3.) Also **freezing tool**.

1887 L. L. HASLOPE *Repoussé Work* 23 A small punch, called a freezing tool, which produces a small star. **1898** T. B. WIGLEY *Art Goldsm. & Jeweller* 79 Punches of various shapes, called chasing tools... Freezer. Mat. Dead Mat. Hair Mat.

5. Special Comb.: **freezer-burn**, uneven discoloration of frozen meat or poultry that has been inadequately packaged to prevent surface evaporation.

1929 *Industr. & Engin. Chem.* May 416/2 When certain forms of meats and poultry are sharp-frozen, the extensive drying of the surface, sometimes apparently associated with a partial oxidation of the fats..,causes an effect known as 'freezer-burn'. **1979** *Homes & Gardens* June 154/2 Where inadequate or damaged packaging is used, freezer burn can occur, which shows up as dry discoloured patches on the exposed surface of the food.

freeze-up. [f. the vbl. phr. *to freeze up*: see FREEZE *v.* 5 b.] The condition of being stopped by frost or ice; a period in which land or water is frozen, *esp.* so as to prevent travel; an area so affected: a frozen condition (as of a water tank, engine-cylinder jacket, etc.). Also *transf.* and *fig.*

1876 *Oregon Weekly Tribune* (The Dalles) 29 Jan. 3/2 We hope to see the day when..all the inhabitants east of the Cascades will not be detrimentally affected by any freeze-up which may occur. **1879** *Lumberman's Gaz.* 19 Dec., Most of the saw mills..get as much of their stock into lumber before the freeze-up. **1882** *Golden* (N.M.) *Retort* 28 July 3/2 He says a freeze-up occurred from insufficient fluxing, but thinks the smelter will start up again soon. **1904** J. LYNCH *3 Yrs. Klondike* 129 A couple of steam-engines had been.. brought to Dawson last October just before the freeze-up. **1912** *Motor Man.* (ed. 14) 177 If the motor-house is continually heated..there will be no risk of a freeze-up. **1915** J. LONDON *Lost Face* 116 The freeze-up came on when we were at the mouth of Henderson Creek. **1942** WYNDHAM LEWIS *Let.* 30 Apr. (1963) 320 Meanwhile we are heading for an economic freeze-up. **1948** A. L. RAND *Mammals Eastern Rockies* 2/3 Spreading out over the..forested plains after the freeze-up. **1963** *Daily Tel.* 28 Jan. 18/2 (*headline*) 'Freeze-up' in talks with Treasury. **1964** *Ann. Reg. 1963* p. xvii, One of the longest and most severe winters on record .., with a freeze-up that lasted in Britain well into March.

freezing ('fri:zɪŋ), *vbl. sb.* [f. FREEZE *v.* + -ING[1].]

1. The action of the vb. FREEZE; also, *freezing in*, *out*, etc.: see FREEZE *v.* 5 b, 7. *at freezing* = at freezing-point (see 2).

1398 TREVISA *Barth. De P.R.* XIX. xlvi. (1495) 889 Greys is made faste and harde by fresyng and by colde. **1577** B. GOOGE *Heresbach's Husb.* I. (1586) 29 b, To sowe it..of October, that it may take deepe roote before the freezing and colde in Winter. *c* **1600** SHAKS. *Sonn.* xcvii, What freezings haue I felt. **1665** HOOKE *Microgr.* 91 If you..expose it to a very sharp freezing. **1803** T. BEDDOES *Hygëia* x. 34 The weather was at freezing. **1856** KANE *Arct. Expl.* I. xxxi. 420 Now awaits the freezing-in of her winter cradle. **1891** E. B. HOWELL in *Advance* (Chicago) 25 June, The law permits the unjust 'freezing out' of the small capitalist.

2. *attrib.* and *Comb.*, as ***freezing chamber***; also, **freezing-mixture**, a mixture of two or more substances, e.g. salt and snow, which, while remaining liquid, is cold enough to freeze some other liquid within its influence; **freezing-point**, the point on the thermometer marking the temperature at which a liquid, *esp.* water, freezes; **freezing process** (see quot. 1967); **freezing works** *Austral.* and *N.Z.*, an establishment in which animals are killed and the carcasses prepared and frozen for export.

1889 E. WAKEFIELD *N.Z. after 50 Yrs.* vi. 130 The sheep ..are skilfully slaughtered..and trucked down to the hulk, the whole interior of which is a *freezing chamber. **1896** *Daily News* 28 May 6/3 Delahaeff's body lies in the freezing chamber at the Morgue. **1695** WOODWARD *Nat. Hist. Earth* IV. (1723) 236 A strong *freezing Mixture. **1869** E. A. PARKES *Pract. Hygiene* (ed. 3) 155 The air may also be drawn through tubes cooled by a freezing mixture. **1747** *Phil. Trans.* XLIV. II. 613, 17 degrees above 0 or *freezing Point. **1860** TYNDALL *Glac.* I. xxv. 190 The temperature of the air was 20° Fahr. below the freezing point. **1889** *Science* XIV. 142/1 The Pœtsch *freezing process in mining operations. A brief description of the freezing process devised by Herman Pœtsch for sinking shafts in quicksands and other difficult ground was given. **1905** T. C. FUTERS *Mech. Engin. Collieries* I. 73 (*caption*) Freezing process of shaft sinking. **1967** *Gloss. Mining Terms (B.S.I.)* IX. 9 *Freezing process*, a method of consolidating water-bearing strata, to prepare it for shaft sinking, in which a freezing agent (usually brine) is circulated through suitably disposed boreholes drilled into the strata around the site of the shaft. **1889** E. WAKEFIELD *N.Z. after 50 Yrs.* vi. 130 The solution of all their difficulties ..was found to lie in having *freezing works on shore, near the place of shipment. **1891** R. WALLACE *Rural Econ. Austral. & N.Z.* xxxv. 464 For the shipment of the Queensland supply, freezing works are in process of construction in Brisbane, Rockhampton, and Townsville. **1906** E. W. ELKINGTON *Adrift in N.Z.* v. 72 Cattle and sheep in their thousands..eventually find their way, *via* the freezing works, to our own dinner-tables. **1963** N. HILLIARD *Piece of Land* 28 Within smelling distance of the freezing works and the stock-yards.

freezing ('fri:zɪŋ), *ppl. a.* [f. as prec. + -ING[2].]

1. That freezes, in senses of the vb. Freq. of drizzle, fog, rain, etc.

1611 SHAKS. *Cymb.* III. iii. 39. *c* **1625** MILTON *Death of a fair Infant* 16 Through middle empire of the freezing air. **1697** DRYDEN *Virg. Georg.* IV. 738 By Strymon's freezing Streams he sate alone. **1709** ADDISON *Tatler* No. 100 ¶1 A freezing Night. **1796** KIRWAN *Elem. Min.* (ed. 2) I. 10 In a freezing cold, clay contracts more than any other earth. **1797** *Encycl. Brit.* VII. 460 *Freezing Rain*, or *Raining Ice*, a very uncommon kind of shower. **1940** S. PETTERSSEN *Weather Analysis & Forecasting* i. 40 In the United States weather reports, rain and/or drizzle that produce glazed frost are reported as 'freezing rain'. **1958** *Polar Record* May 92 *Freezing drizzle*, drizzle, the drops of which freeze on impact with the ground or with objects on the earth's surface or with aircraft in flight. **1963** *Meteorol. Gloss.* (*Met. Office*) (ed. 4) *Freezing drizzle, fog, rain*, supercooled water drops of drizzle (or fog or rain) which freeze on impact with the ground (in aviation with an aircraft) to form glazed frost or, in the case of the smaller droplets which comprise fog, rime. **1968** G. R. RUMNEY *Climatol.* v. 76/1 An ice storm, or freezing rain, occurs when liquid drops of rain, having a temperature slightly below freezing, fall upon solid surfaces of the earth..whose temperature is well below freezing.

2. *fig.*; *esp.* of manners: Chilling.

1813 H. & J. SMITH *Horace in Lond.* 95 Oh grant that he may never spread Its freezing influence to my heart. **1849** MISS MULOCK *Ogilvies* iii. (1875) 27 Her sudden burst of enthusiasm met with but a freezing reception. **1850** TENNYSON *In Mem.* cxxiv, A warmth within the breast would melt The freezing reason's colder part. **1855** MACAULAY *Hist. Eng.* IV. 538 Many..had been repelled by his freezing looks. **1886** W. HOOPER *Sk. Acad. Life* 16 To regulate all things with freezing accuracy and precision.

Hence **'freezingly** *adv.*, in a freezing manner.

a **1420** HOCCLEVE *De Reg. Princ.* 1806 Thoght me brenneth and freesyngly keelith. **1798** W. TAYLOR in Robberds *Mem.* (1843) I. 226, I wrote to him very freezingly. **1848** C. BRONTE *J. Eyre* iv. (1873) 31 Her eye of ice continued to dwell freezingly on mine.

freezy ('fri:zɪ), *a. rare.* [f. FREEZE *v.* + -Y[1].] Chilled almost to freezing; freezing cold.

1827 HOOD *Lamia* lx, With blue chilly shades, Showing wherein the freezy blood pervades. **1902** O. WISTER *Virginian* xxiii, Thought it looked pretty freezy out where yu' war riding. **1968** W. GARNER *Deep, Deep Freeze* ix. 111 She said, 'Wow! What's a pretty girl like me doing in a freezy old place like this?'

frefre, var. of FROVER, *Obs.*, to comfort.

freibergite ('fraɪbəgaɪt). *Min.* [f. *Freiberg*, a town in Saxony + -ITE. Named by Kengott in 1853.] A variety of tetrahedrite containing silver.

1856 C. U. SHEPARD *Min.* 347 Freibergite.

freie'slebenite. *Min.* [f. *Freiesleben*, who first described it + -ITE. Named by Haidinger in 1845.] A sulph-antimonide of lead and silver, which crystallizes in striated prisms. Cf. DIAPHORITE.

1850 DANA *Min.* 541 Freieslebenite.

freight (freɪt), *sb.* Also 5 freyte, freyght, 6–7 fraight, 6 frate. [prob. a. MDu. or MLG. *vrecht*, var. of *vracht*: see FRAUGHT *sb.* The word has passed from Du. or LG. into some of the Rom. langs.; F. *fret* hire of a ship (from 13th c.), Sp. *flete*, Pg. *frete*.]

1. a. Hire of a vessel for the transport of goods; the service of transporting goods (originally, by water; now extended, esp. in *U.S.*, to land-transit); the sum of money paid for this. In early use also: Passage-money.

1463 *Mann. & Househ. Exp.* 194 My mastyr toke hym ffor his ffreyte to Caleys..vj. *li.* **1483** CAXTON *Gold. Leg.* 283/2 Whome they receyued in to theyr Shippe gladly and sayd they wold brynge hym thyder without ony freyght or huyr. **1538** STARKEY *England* II. i. 172 Specyally yf to that were joynyd a nother ordynance..wych ys, concernyng the frate of marchandyse. **1580** HOLLYBAND *Treas. Fr. Tong*, *Naulage*, the fraight or fare payed for passage ouer the water. *a* **1687** PETTY *Pol. Arith.* (1690) 19 Those who have the command of the Sea Trade may Work at easier Freight with more profit. **1712** E. COOKE *Voy. S. Sea* 353 Having agreed to pay no Freight there. **1764** BURN *Poor Laws* 180 Let a small deduction be made from the freights of ships, and from seamens wages. **1765** T. HUTCHINSON *Hist. Mass.* I. ii. 257 They purchased a ship-load of masts, the freight whereof cost them sixteen hundred pounds. **1854** HAWTHORNE *Eng. Note-bks.* (1883) II. 123 The captains talk together about..how freights are in America. **1861** GOSCHEN *For. Exch.* 18 The charge for freight acts with the same force as a charge for a commodity actually produced and exported. **1868** ROGERS *Pol. Econ.* ix. (1876) 83 The passage from the East to Europe has been so shortened, that a freight from thence to England is reduced to one-fourth.

†**b.** *to take freight*: to take passage for oneself and goods. *Obs.*

1719 DE FOE *Crusoe* II. xvi, We all took freight with him.

2. a. The cargo or lading (of a ship); a ship-load. Hence, anything carried by sea or land; 'goods' in transit or being transported by rail, road, or sea. Chiefly *N. Amer.* with reference to the carriage of goods by railway. ***fast freight*** (U.S.): see FAST *a.* 11.

1502 ARNOLDE *Chron.* (1811) 229 We..charge you precisely that the forsayd [merchants] wyth their shyp's freight..ye suffer and let go passe. **1540** *Act 32 Hen. VIII*, c. 14 Beyng mynded..to take any freight or ladynge..into any of the saide shyppes. **1694** *Acc. Sev. Late Voy.* II. (1711) 3 When they have their full Fraight of Whales, they put up their great Flag. **1789** BRAND *Hist. Newcastle* II. 255 [A vessel] trading to Newcastle upon Tyne with corn, and returning with a freight of sea coals. **1832** HT. MARTINEAU *Ireland* 131 Do you know that Vessel? You cannot be aware what freight it bears? **1856** KANE *Arct. Expl.* II. xix. 196 They offered to exclude both clothes and food in favor of a full freight of these treasures.

b. *transf.* A load, burden,

1618 CHAPMAN *Hesiod* I. 574 At thy purse's height, And when it fights low, give thy use his freight. **1697** DRYDEN *Virg. Georg.* II. 599 With the ruddy Freight the bending Branches groan. **1805** WORDSW. *Prelude* v. 84, I..looked self-questioned what this freight Which the new comer carried..Could mean. **1878** HUXLEY *Physiogr.* 73 These warm moist winds..deposit their freight of moisture in showers of rain.

c. *fig.*

a **1631** DONNE in *Select.* (1840) 43 Keep up that holy cheerfulness, which Christ makes the ballast of a Christian, and his freight too. **1755** YOUNG *Centaur* v. Wks. 1757 IV. 223 Every moment shall return, and lay its whole freight.. before the Throne. **1812** J. WILSON *Isle of Palms* I. 127 An earthly freight she bears Of joys and sorrows. **1872** HOLLAND *Marb. Proph.* 97 A man who lifted On ready words his freight of gratitude.

†**3.** A journey of a laden vessel. *Obs.*

1716 CHURCH *Philip's War* (1865) I. 157 He made use of Canoo's: But by that time they had made two fraights..the Wind sprung up.

4. orig. *U.S.* Short for *freight-train*: a goods-train. ***by freight***: by the usual means of transportation, as opposed to *by express*.

1861 *Remin. Life Railroad Engineer* 123 He was running the Night Express,..while I was running the through freight. **1881** *Chicago Times* 18 June, A freight of thirty loaded cars..collided with the other train. **1922** M. B. HOUSTON *Witch Man* i. 14 There were four trains a day in Innessburg, not counting the freights. **1955** E. HILLARY *High Adventure* ix. 158 Feeling a little like an express train overhauling a slow freight.

5. *attrib.* and *Comb.*, as ***freight agent***, ***car*** (= goods truck or van), ***carriage***, ***container***, ***depot***, ***elevator***, ***engine***, ***forwarder***, ***house***, ***locomotive***, ***-man***, ***rate***, ***route***, ***shed***, ***steamer***, ***terminal***, ***traffic***, ***train*** (= goods train), ***wagon***, ***yard***; also ***freight-handler***, ***-handling***. Also **'freightliner**, a train carrying goods in containers; †**freight-money**, payment for conveyance of freight.

1843 *Rep. Western R.R.* 17 *Freight-agent. **1875** *N. Amer. Rev.* CXX. 403 He has been promoted to the office of freight-agent. **1944** *Sears, Roebuck Catal.* 900 If there is a freight agent at your station, you pay freight charges when shipment is received. **1833** *Amer. Railroad Jrnl.* II. 325/2, 10 *freight cars. **1856** OLMSTED *Slave States* 55 There were, in the train, two first-class passenger cars, and two freight cars. **1947** *Chicago Daily News* 17 Jan. 4/2 A freight car and caboose were destroyed by fire. **1967** Freight car [see CAR *sb.*[1] 2 a]. **1884** *Pall Mall G.* 25 Sept. 5/2 They will put up their rates on the *freight carriage eastward. **1969** *Jane's Freight Containers 1968–69* 12/1 A *freight container is an article of transport equipment. **1841** *Spirit of Times* 25 Sept. 354/1 *Freight depot. **1904** W. N. HARBEN *Georgians* I The long, brick freight depot. **1906** *Springfield Weekly Republ.* 4 Oct. 7 What the English call a 'railway goods station', and what we call a freight depot. **1903** ADE *In Babel* 18 He had patented certain devices which were used by all makers of passenger and *freight elevators. **1911** *Daily Colonist* (Victoria, B.C.) 21 Apr. 16/3 Expedition combined with safety, can only be secured by means of a freight elevator. **1968** *Globe & Mail* (Toronto) 3 Feb. B5/2 'Do you know that only three apartment buildings in Toronto have freight elevators?' he asked. 'We sometimes have to put furniture on top of elevators to get it into buildings.' **1922** G. T. STUFFLEBEAM *Traffic Dict.* 64 *Freight forwarder*, one who is located at a port, attends to documentation, booking space, securing marine insurance and other detail in connection with export shipments. **1968** *Economist* 14 Sept. p. xxv/1 There is more pressure on the British freight forwarders than there is on their continental counterparts. **1969** *Jane's Freight Containers 1968–69* 28/1 The members of the Canadian International Freight Forwarders Association Inc. **1970** *Times* 2 June (Container Suppl.) p. iv/3 The increasing range of forwarding work, the changing conditions under which it is carried out, and the new physical equipment—containers, in particular—have called for the new and wider description as freight forwarders. **1882** *Pall Mall G.* 12 July 8/2 A riot has occurred [at Jersey city] between the *freight-handlers on strike and the Italian labourers. **1887** *Bureau Statist. Labour* (N.Y.) 327 There was also a great interruption of *freight-handling. **1848** *Hunt's Merch. Mag.* XVIII. 383 The Worcester Railroad.. has a *freight-house in Boston. **1918** *Essex Inst. Hist. Coll.* LIV. 218 They should be run as one road, thus doing away with the expensive separate staffs, repair shops, freight houses, etc. **1948** *Daily Ardmoreite* (Ardmore, Okla.) 28 July 13/2 The car was shunted to a siding near the freight house yesterday afternoon. **1965** *Times* 12 July 14 (*caption*) A typical *Freightliner..will be loaded..by the latest equipment... The container is lifted off the road transport ..and immediately transferred on to the rail wagon. **1966** *Daily Tel.* 11 Aug. 22/7 British Rail is to build 60 refrigerated glass fibre containers to carry meat and perishable goods in its freightliner trains. **1969** *Lebende Sprachen* XIV. 65/2 A grain terminal and a British Railways freightliner terminal are to be built at Tilbury. **1934** WEBSTER, *Freight locomotive. **1935** *Discovery* Nov. 326/1 The freight locomotives were designed to haul considerably heavier trains than the passenger locomotives. **1855** *Gen. Term Rep.*, Goods..should be sent forward by a carrier, or *freightman. **1755** MAGENS *Insurances* II. 189 All Insurances on expected Gain..future *Freight-Monies, Seamens Wages and Mens Lives are universally forbid. **1848** *Hunt's Merch. Mag.* XVIII. 101 *Freight-rates—Iron, 25 cents per 100 pounds. **1881** *Chicago Times* 12 Mar., A freight-rate war between the eastern lines of railroads is regarded..as unavoidable. **1907** *Westm. Gaz.* 20 Nov. 10/2 Startling freight-rate experiments of the German railways. **1943** J. S. HUXLEY *TVA* xii. 114 The inter-territorial freight-rate problem of the U.S.A. **1881** *Chicago Times* 12 Mar., This has been the cheapest *freight route to New York. *Ibid.* 17 June, Between the gas-works and the *freight-sheds of the..railway. **1967** *Economist* 18 Feb. 596/1 The dispute between the railway unions and the management of British Railways over *freight terminals is like an old and hardy sore. **1967** *Punch* 12 July 66/1 A new international freight terminal. **1891** *Pall Mall G.* 3 Dec. 6/2 The St. John's Board of Trade..thinks that the interest of the country would be better served by grants to *freight steamers. **1885** *Ibid.* 10 Sept. 6/1 Goods traffic—called in America '*freight' traffic. **1845** *Ann. Rep. Boston & Worc. R.R.*, *Freight-train. **1872** *Japanese in America* 199 Freight-trains frequently number..one hundred cars. **1887** M. ROBERTS *Western Avernus* 35 We found there was a freight train leaving this town at one o'clock. **1968** B. FOSTER *Changing Eng. Lang.* i. 59 It has recently become fashionable to speak of a goods train as a *freight train* in the American fashion. **1832** *Amer. Railroad Jrnl.* I. 85/3 The snow has not prevented the running of carriages or *freight waggons. **1889** K. MUNROE *Golden Days* ix. 91 Holstead and Thurston soon had their modest outfit..on board an Oregon freight wagon. **1910** J. HART *Vigilante Girl* viii. 122 Behind these were..waiting stage coaches, and behind them freight wagons. **1881** *Chicago Times* 14 May, Twelve days ago the railroad switchmen in all but one of the *freight-yards in this city struck for a slight increase of their wages. **1903** *N.Y. Times* 24 Sept. 5 Two youths..were seen prowling about the freight yards. **1961** L. MUMFORD *City in History* xv. 461 A waste of freight yards and marshalling yards.

freight (freɪt), *v.* Forms: 6-7 **fraight**, (6 **freith**), 7- **freight**. *Pa. t.* and *pa. pple.* 6 **freyghted**, **frayted**, 6-7 **fraighted**, 7- **freighted**. [f. prec. sb.; cf. FRAUGHT *v.*]

1. a. *trans.* To furnish or load (a vessel) with a cargo; to hire or let out (a vessel) for the carriage of goods and passengers. Also with *out* and *to* or *for* (a place).

1485 in Arnolde *Chron.* (1811) 229 For too..lade and freith and cary awaye. **1555** EDEN *Decades* 296 Donco, where the marchauntes..fraight theyr shyppes. **1651** HOBBES *Leviath.* II. xxii. 119 With the Merchandise they buy at home, can fraight a Ship, to export it. **1671** CLARENDON *Dialog.* Tracts (1727) 293 They who freighted them out. **1702** C. MATHER *Magn. Chr.* I. vi. (1852) 84 They build one ship more, which they fraighted for England. **1800** WELLESLEY in Owen *Desp.* 707 The British merchants ..not having obtained the expected permission to freight their ships to the port of London. **1831** SIR J. SINCLAIR *Corr.* II. 223 An opportunity of making immense sums of money, by freighting their ships to the powers at war. **1878** SIMPSON *Sch. Shaks.* I. 120 He proposed to freight as many English vessels as possible by Flemings, Frenchmen, Spaniards, and Italians.

b. *transf.* To load, store. Also *fig.* of a burden: To bear upon as a load.

1829 LYTTON *Devereux* I. vii, Fortune freights not your channel with her hoarded stores. **1838** SPARKS *Biog.* IX. *Eaton* xi. 301 The caravan had been freighted by the Bashaw only to this place. **1892** TALMAGE in *N.Y. Weekly Witness* 13 Jan. 7/5 All the sins of the past and of the present freighting him.

c. *U.S. intr. to freight up*: to take in a cargo. *fig.*

1889 'MARK TWAIN' *Yank. at Crt. K. Arth.* (Tauchn.) I. 128 How to freight up against probable fasts before starting.

2. *trans.* To carry or transport (goods) as freight. Also *absol.*

1540 *Act 32 Hen. VIII*, c. 14 Euery brode wollen cloth freyghted to Daunske. **1697** DAMPIER *Voy.* I. xv. 412 Every man freights his Goods in his own room; and probably lodges there, if he be on board himself. **1855** *N.Y. Weekly Tribune* 6 Jan. 1/2 The Ohio Rail-roads are freighting heavily. **1881** HENTY *Cornet of Horse* xvi. (1888) 160 Van Duyk would have freighted a shipful of presents to Rupert's friends. **1931** *Randolph Enterprise* (Elkins, W. Va.) 8 Jan. 4/5 He lived at Brownsville, Nebraska, and freighted from there to Fort Riley.

Hence **'freighting** *vbl. sb.*

1672 *Essex Papers* (Camden) I. 7, I Incourage all I possibly can buildinge of Ships of our owne (for Fraigtinge of Forringhners distresse us). **1867** SMYTH *Sailor's Word-bk.*, *Freighting*, a letting out of vessels on freight or hire. **1884** L. HAMILTON *Mexican Hand-bk.* 67 The water flowing down from the various ravines..fills the arroyo and renders freighting in wagons difficult.

attrib. **1769** BURKE *Late St. Nat.* Wks. 1842 I. 83 The freighting business revived. The ships were fewer, but much larger. **1856** OLMSTED *Slave States* 396 The roads seemed to be doing a heavy freighting business with cotton. **1830** N. H. BISHOP *4 Months in Sneak-Box* 15 There appears to be no fixed freighting tariff established for boats.

†**freight**, *pple.* and *ppl. a. Obs.* Forms: 5-6 **freyght**, 6-7 **fraight**, 6-8 **freight**. [Contracted pa. pple. of FREIGHT *v.*]

1. Freighted, laden.

1494 FABYAN *Chron.* VII. 494 The ryuer of Loyer, wher at y[t] season certayne shyppes laye freyght with vytall. **1600** HOLLAND *Livy* XXIX. 736 And so [he] dispatched away the ships a second time fraight and laden with the spoiles of enemies. **1649** EVELYN *Mem.* (1857) III. 39 Ships, richly freight with wines and other commodities.

b. *transf.* and *fig.* (Cf. *fret full*, FRET *v.*[6])

1565 JEWEL *Def. Apol.* (1611) 463 It was written by a man of an iron face..and is freight full of most shamelesse lies. **1587** TURBERVILE *Trag. T.* (1837) 214 The jades were fully fraight with heavie burdens. **1600** HOLLAND *Livy* XXIII. xii. (1609) 481 Two strong holds..full and fraight [*plena*] of prizes and victuals. **1711** STEELE *Spect.* No. 134 ⁋2 Each Paragraph is freight either with useful or delightful Notions.

2. Fraught, provided, abounding *with*.

1551 ROBINSON tr. *More's Utop.* (Arb.) 167 This yle is fraight with both bounteously. **1590** SPENSER *F.Q.* I. xii. 35 The king..with suddein indignation fraight Bad on that Messenger rude hands to reach. **1623** WEBSTER *Duchess Malfi* v. i, I'll go in mine own shape, When he shall see it fraight with love and duty.

freightage ('freɪtɪdʒ). [f. FREIGHT *v.* + -AGE.]

1. a. The hire of a vessel for the transport of goods; cost of conveyance of goods (originally, by water; now exended, *esp.* in *U.S.*, to land-transit).

1694 tr. *Milton's Lett. State* July an. 1656 Wks. 1851 VIII. 349 A Sum of Money owing..upon the account of Freightage and Demorage. **1785** J. PHILLIPS *Treat. Inland Navig.* 32 The tonnage, freightage, and tolls, will produce as follow. **1819** SHELLEY *Let. to Peacock* 21 Sept., It costs, with all duties and freightage, about half. **1885** *Law Times* LXXIX. 189/1 The defendants..offered him a steamer called the *Glendevon*..at the rate of 30*s.* freightage. **1885** *L'pool Daily Post* 23 Oct. 4/8 The higher scale of freightage [by railroad] will be maintained.

b. The freighting or hiring of a vessel.

1755 MAGENS *Insurances* II. 282 If a Ship be intirely freighted for a full Cargo..In case the Owner was not informed of the above-mentioned full Freightage.

2. a. That with which a vessel is freighted; freight, cargo; quantity of cargo conveyed.

1803 SYD. SMITH *Wks.* (1859) I. 61/1 The immense increase of their [Danes'] freightage during the wars of this country. **1843** MRS. ROMER *Rhone, etc.* I. 309 The largest vessels can ride at anchor in safety, and unload their freightage close to the very houses. **1860** RUSSELL *Diary India* I. ii. 11 English ships laden with full freightage of gallant soldiers. **1885** *Harper's Mag.* LXXI. 199 Coal as an up freightage is fully as important as the down cargo of grain.

b. *transf.* Burden, load.

1823 *Sismondi's Lit. Eur.* (1846) II. xxix. 282 The wretched freightage of the Atlantic wave. **1825** *Blackw. Mag.* XVIII. 601 The Diligence..discharged its whole freightage into the street.

c. *fig.*

1827 MARY HOWITT *Two Voy.* i, My ship waits but for me ..And all I lack of freightage now is a farewell word from thee. **1859** G. MEREDITH *R. Feverel* xii. (1878) 77 Conscience was beginning to inhabit him, and he carried some of the freightage known to men; though in so crude a form that it overweighed him, now on this side, now on that.

3. Transport of goods.

1872 'MARK TWAIN' *Roughing It* xvii. 137 High freights and bewildering distances of freightage. **1886** *Harper's Mag.* LXXII 216 All travel and freightage are still, as of old, conducted by means of horses, asses, camels and mules.

freighted ('freɪtɪd), *pple.* and *ppl. a.* [f. FREIGHT *v.* + -ED[1].] Laden with cargo.

1553 EDEN *Treat. Newe Ind* (Arb.) 21 Shyppes frayghted wyth gossampine cotton and silke clothes. **1692** LUTTRELL *Brief Rel.* (1857) II. 33 A rich ship from Spain, freighted with pieces of eight. **1703** TATE *Her Majesty's Pict.* xxix, To Western Worlds our Freighted Fleets shall run. **1852** MRS. STOWE *Uncle Tom's C.* xxxi, The boat moved on—freighted with its weight of sorrow. **1855** PRESCOTT *Philip II*, I. IV. v. 455 Their galleys still returned to port freighted with the spoils of the infidel.

b. *transf.* and *fig.*

1567 DRANT *Horace's Epist.* vii. D v, At supper when he had at full Layde out his lauishe mynde At length to bed to take a nap He fraighted, was assynde. **1645** PAGITT *Heresiogr.* (1661) 124 Some persons..being fraighted with many loose, and unsound opinions. **1725** L. WELSTED *Oikogr.* 4 From whence we may..survey, The freighted Thames. **1811** L. M. HAWKINS *C'tess & Gertr.* I. 57 He therefore endured with complacency, her freighted work-basket. **1850** W. IRVING *Goldsmith* xxvi. 257 Just arrived from College..full freighted with academic gleanings. **1860** MOTLEY *Netherl.* (1868) I. i. 2 Epistles which..were freighted with the doom and destiny of countless millions.

freighter ('freɪtə(r)). [f. FREIGHT *v.* + -ER[1].]

1. a. 'One who loads a ship, or one who charters and loads a ship' (W.).

1622 MALYNES *Anc. Law-Merch.* 138 And hereupon C.D. the Merchant and Fraightor, doth likewise couenant with the said Master..that he..will lade or cause to be laden.. the said Ship. **1665** PEPYS *Diary* 22 Mar., Abundance of most ingenious men, owners and freighters of the 'Experiment'. **1727** A. HAMILTON *New Acc. E. Ind.* I. vii. 70 The Freighter, who was a Mahometan, delayed paying the Freight long after it was due by the Tenor of the Charter-party. **1848** ARNOULD *Mar. Insur.* (1866) I. I. iii. 57 It was stipulated by the Charter-party that the freighters should pay for the use of the ship.

b. One who consigns goods for carriage inland.

1872 *Daily News* 2 Oct. 4 It was resolved that a freighters' association be established, having for its object the assimilation and check of railway charges. **1882** *Edin. Rev.* Oct. 458 What the public service demands is, that freighters and manufacturers should be allowed to choose for themselves.

2. One whose business it is to receive and forward freight. Also, one who owns or conducts a freight wagon or train of wagons (*local U.S.*).

1714 MANDEVILLE *Fab. Bees* (1725) I. 205 The Dutch.. are carriers and freighters to the rest of the world. **1852** *Knickerbocker* Mar. 224 The freighters were as impatient of delay as those Æneas saw crowding the shores of Styx. **1874** B. F. TAYLOR *World on Wheels* I. v. 43 You meet now and then a 'freighter', as the ox-expressmen of plain and prairie are called. **1884** *American* IX. 110 Men employed by the freighters to look after the mules..to prevent their straying off. **1907** S. E. WHITE *Arizona Nights* I. xvi. 229 It happened to be..a freighter without the fear of God in his soul.

3. a. A vessel for transporting goods, a cargo vessel.

1839 *Southern Lit. Messenger* V. 5/2 The Great Britain is now sailing as a mere freighter, and larger vessels are sailing as packets. **1878** N. H. BISHOP *Voy. Paper Canoe* 278 Though a freighter and not a royal yacht, the Rurik looked every inch a government vessel. **1893** *Leisure Hour* Apr. 389 Our ships get larger whether they are freighters or expresses.

b. A freight-wagon. *U.S.*

1885 *Century Mag.* Nov. 65/1 Heavily loaded freighters were lurching in. **1921** C. E. MULFORD *Bar-20 Three* xii. 147 Pete Jarvis was proud of his new sixteen-foot freighter. **1929** *Randolph Enterprise* (Elkins, W. Va.) 14 Nov. 1/3 The Conestoga Wagon, known as the freighter, hauled travelers too.

c. A freight-carrying aircraft.

1920 *Flight* XII. 560/1 Owing to increased quantities of heavy and bulky freight being now carried to and from Paris by the Handley Page aeroplanes, a number of specially-constructed freighters will soon be added to the machines employed. **1935** *Ibid.* XXVIII. 657 The D.L.H. freighter, Ju. 52, is just about to leave on its nightly journey to Berlin. **1959** *Listener* 15 Jan. 95/1 The Royal Air Force..is also receiving a 'substantial' number of short-range freighters.

'freightful, *a. rare*[-1]. [perh. f. **freight* dial. = FREIT + -FUL.] ? Of the nature of a charm or incantation.

1716 M. DAVIES *Athen. Brit.* III. *Crit. Hist.* 90 Gnosticks, who all dealt in Magical Medals and freightfull Inscriptions.

freightless ('freɪtlɪs), *a. rare.* [f. FREIGHT *sb.* + -LESS.] Without freight or load.

1791 E. DARWIN *Bot. Gard.* II. 155 Wave after wave rolls freightless to the shore. **1795** A. SEWARD *Lett.* (1811) IV. 94 The age of these freightless, these lonely seas.

†**'freightment.** *Obs.* [f. FREIGHT *v.* + -MENT; after F. *frètement.*] The action of hiring a vessel; the document which records this.

1559 in *Sir R. Sadler's Papers* (1809) II. 235 And if you have advertised me of touching their [shippes'] fretment. **1622** MALYNES *Anc. Law-Merch.* 402 Vpon the ladings of Ships which are to take in the same, or else may incurre a further danger vnto the Charter-partie of fraightment. **1755** MAGENS *Insurances* II. 25 When it can be proved against any one, whether by Charter-Party, Bills of Lading, Freightement..that he has altered the Voyage insured upon.

freik, freir (*Sc.*), var. of FREKE, FRIAR.

freis, var. of FREEZE.

freit (friːt). *Sc.* Forms: 5-6 **frete**, 6-9 **freet**, 7 **freite**, 8 **fret**, 7- **freit**. [a. ON. *frétt* fem., news, inquiry, augury, corresponding to OE. *freht* (for **freoht*, *friht*), oracle (whence *frihtere* diviner, *frihtrian* to divine), from the root of FRAYNE.]

Anything to which superstition attaches; an omen; a superstitious formula or charm; a superstitious observance or act of worship.

a **1300** *Cursor M.* 28310, I..folud wiche-crafte and frete, and charmyng. *c* **1425** WYNTOUN *Cron.* VI. xviii. 362 Makbeth aye In fantown Fretis had gret Fay. **1533** BELLENDEN *Livy* I. (1822) 42 The Albanis hallowit thair fretis, and terribill conjuraciouns. **1597** JAS. I. *Daemonol.* I. iv. 11 All kinde of practicques, freites, or other like extraordinarie actiones. ?**17..** *Adam o' Gordon* xxvii, in Pinkerton *Select. Sc. Ballads* (1783) I. 49 Wha luik to freits, my master deir, Freits will ay follow them. **1768** *Song* in *Ross' Helenore* (1789) 147 Fouk need not on frets to be standing That's woo'd and married and a'. **1868** G. MACDONALD *R. Falconer* III. 70, 'I dream aboot him whiles sae lifelike, that I canna believe him deid. But that's a' freits.'

Hence **'freity** *a.*, superstitious.

1788 J. MACAULAY *Poems* (1790) 122, I..saw a blade fast sticking to my hose, An', being freety, stack it up my nose. **1818** *Edin. Mag.* Sept. 154 Deeply imbued with the superstitious and freitty observances of his native land.

†**freith**, *v. Sc. Obs.* Also 4 **freth**. [Sc. form of FRITH *v.*] *trans.* To set free, liberate. *to freith oneself*: to perform one's promise. *esp.* in *Sc. Law.* To release from an obligation or pecuniary burden.

13.. *Assis. Dav. II* in *Balfour's Practicks* (1754) 18 To freith and releive thair borghis, except thay have a lauchfull essonyie. *c* **1375** *Sc. Leg. Saints*, *Adrian* 290 To freth his borowis & mak fre. **1466** *Acta Dom. Audit.* (1839) 3 To freith the said landis..of the v mercis..that he grantis he promist to pay. *c* **1470** HENRY *Wallace* IX. 1516 Wallace gert freith the wemen, off hys grace. **1535** STEWART *Cron. Scot.* II. 187 That tha had done, and freith [thame] for to go To thair awin land. **1596** DALRYMPLE tr. *Leslie's Hist. Scot.* x. 319 The Protectour denyes ony way to freith the Erle afor the weiris be endet. *Ibid.* 350 Quene mother suld suirlie freith her selfe in al, quhat euir scho had promiste.

†**freke.** *poet. Obs.* Forms: 1 **freca**, 5-6 **freak(e**, **freik(e**, (5 **frecke**, **freeke**, **freyke**), 4- **freke**. [OE. *freca*, properly subst. use of *frec*, FRECK *a.*] Properly, one eager for fight; a warrior, champion; but usually a mere poetic synonym for 'man' (cf. *berne*, *tulk*, *wye*).

Beowulf 1563 He ȝefeng þa fetel-hilt freca scyldinga. **13..** *K. Alis.* 2161 Oure kyng hath this freke y-felde. *c* **1420** *Avow. Arth.* xl, Wele armut and dyȝte, As freke redy to fyȝte. *c* **1450** *Bk. Curtasye* 255 in *Babees Bk.* 305 Go not forthe as a dombe freke. **15..** *Scottish ffeilde* 50 in Furniv. *Percy Folio* I. 214 When his father, that feirce freake, had finished his dayes. *a* **1555** LYNDESAY *Tragedy* 218 Than euery freik thay tuke of me sic feir. *a* **1605** MONTGOMERIE *Commend. of Love* 39 Fy on that freik that can not love.

†**frelan(d, frelange.** *Obs.* (See quot.)

1690 EVELYN *Mundus Muliebris* 6 Place aright..Frelange, Fontange. —— *Fop Dict.*, *Frelan* [ed. 2 *Freland*], Bonnet and Pinner together.

†**frels**, *v. Obs.* Forms: 1 **fréolsian**, 3 *Orm.* **fre(o)llsenn**, 4 **frels(en**. [OE. *fréolsian*, f. *fréols* str. masc., neut. 'freedom, time of freedom, festival', also as adj. 'free'; cf. OFris. *frîhals* freedom, OHG. *frîhals* free man, freedom, ON. *frials* adj. free, Goth. *freihals* freedom; the sb. (adj.) means literally 'free neck': see FREE *a.* and HALS.]

1. *trans.* To keep (a holy day) free from work; to celebrate.

c **1000** ÆLFRIC *Exod.* xxxiv. 21 Wirc six daȝas and freolsa ðone seofoðan. *c* **1200** ORMIN 8895 To frellsenn þær þatt heȝhe tid O þatt Judisskenn wise.

2. To set (a person) free; to free, release.

c **1250** *Lord's Prayer* in *Rel. Ant.* I. 22 Frels us fra alle ivele þinge. *a* **1300** *Cursor M.* 10082 His folk to frels fra sin and scam.

fremail, var. of FERMAIL.

1892 G. LAMBERT *Gold & Silversmiths' Art* 48 Another fremail of gold, garnished with three pearls.

fremd (frɛmd), *a. Obs.* exc. *Sc.* and *north.* Forms: 1 fræmde, frem(e)de, *Northumb.* fremþe, 2–6 fremde, 3 fræmde, *Orm.* fremmde, freomede, *south.* vreomede, 3–5 frem(m)ed(e, (4 fremned, frimmed), 4–5 fremyd, 5–9 *Sc.* frem(m)it, -yt, 4–7 frem(m)e, (7 fremb), 5–7 frem(e)(d, fremb'd(e, 6 frenned, 7, 9 *Sc.* frem, (9 fraim), 6, 8 *Sc.* fram(m)et, (8 fram'd, 9 fraumit), 9 *Sc.* frem't, frem(m)'d. [Com. Teut.: OE. *frę̄mede, frę̄mde, frę̄mþe* = OS. *fremithi* (Du. *vreemd*), OHG. *framadi, fremidi* strange, wonderful (MHG. *vremede, vremde*), Goth. *framaþs* foreign, estranged:—OTeut. **framoþjo-, framiþjo-* f. **fram-*: see FROM.]

1. Foreign: see FOREIGN 8.

a **1000** *Laws of Ine* (Schmid) §20 Gif feorcund mon, oððe fremde, butan weȝe ȝeond wudu gonge. *c* **1386** CHAUCER *Sqr.'s T.* 421 A faukoun peregryn than semed sche Of fremde lond. **1596** DALRYMPLE tr. *Leslie's Hist. Scot.* VII. 4 Ambassadouris thay directe to framit natiounis quha war thair special freinds. ?**17..** in Child *Ballads* II. lii. A. (1884) 450/2, I wish I had died on some frem isle, And never had come hame! **1858** MRS. OLIPHANT *Laird of Norlaw* I. 299 'Dinna bring me a daughter of that land to vex me as the fremd woman vexed Rebecca.' **1864** T. CLARKE *Westmld. Dial.* in *Kendal Merc.* 30 Jan., It mappm mud lead me inta sum fremm'd cuntry.

b. = FOREIGN 4.

1581 MULCASTER *Positions* xli. (1887) 242, I may not at this time prosecute this position, as to fremd for this place.

2. Strange, unknown, unfamiliar. Also *ellipt.* or *absol.* (quasi-*sb.*). ***the fremd***: strangers. Of an incident: Remarkable, surprising.

c **950** *Lindisf. Gosp.* John x. 5 Forðon ne cuðon stefn ðara fremðe. *a* **1225** *Ancr. R.* 106 His deore deciples.. bileueden him alle one, ase ureomede. *a* **1300** *Cursor M.* 28292 Priuetis o fremyd and frende I haue discouerd. *c* **1385** CHAUCER *L.G.W.* 1046 *Dido*, That nevere yit was so fremde a cas. **14..** in *Pol. Rel. & L. Poems* (1866) 249 Euery man, boþe fremyd & kouth, Xul comyn with-outyn ly. **1500–20** DUNBAR *Poems* (1893) 307 The fremmit thairof thair baggis can fill. **1535** *Durham Depos.* (Surtees) 52 Let her take 2 fremde menne, or frendes, and I other 2. **1580** SIDNEY *Arcadia* (1622) 87 Cowards.. With sight of feare from friends to fremb'd doe flie. **1863** MRS. GASKELL *Sylvia's L.* (1874) 184 'There's a fremd man i' t' house, I heerd his voice!' **1871** W. ALEXANDER *Johnny Gibb* xxxv. (1873) 199 Mary Howie needin' to gae awa' to the frem't.

b. Wild, opposed to *tame.*

c **1374** CHAUCER *Troylus* III. 480 (529) Al this world is blynd In this matere, bothe fremed and tame.

3. Like a stranger, estranged, unfriendly. Of the bearing, voice, etc.: Strange, forced, unnatural. Const. in OE. with dat., *with, till.*

a **1000** *Sal. & Sat.* 68 Fracoð he bið ðonne and fremede frean ælmihtigum. *a* **1240** *Ureisun* in *Cott. Hom.* 200 Woa is me þet ich am so freomede wið þe. *c* **1374** CHAUCER *Troylus* II. 199 (248) Lat be to me your fremde maner speche. ?*a* **1400** *Morte Arth.* 3343, I hafe bene frendely, freke, and fremmede tille other. **1508** DUNBAR *Gold. Targe* 225 On syde scho lukit wyth ane fremyt fare. **1580** SIDNEY *Arcadia* III. Wks. 1724 II. 719 And makes them fremb'd, who friends by nature are. **1636** RUTHERFORD *Lett.* (1862) I. 178 He looked fremed and unco-like upon me when I came first here. *a* **1651** CALDERWOOD *Hist. Kirk* (1843) II. 280 The Erle of Murrey was so frem to Mr. Knox, that [etc.]. **1789** BURNS *5 Carlins* xx, Monie a friend that kiss'd his caup, Is now a fremit wight. **1859** J. BROWN *Rab. & F.* 9 Rab called rapidly, and in a fremyt voice.

Proverb. **1721** KELLY *Sc. Prov.* 72 Better my friend think me framet, than fashious. **1823** SCOTT *Quentin D.* vi, 'Better kind fremit, than fremit kindred.'

b. Adverse, unpropitious, hostile.

1423 JAS. I *Kingis Q.* xxiv, So infortunate was we that fremyt day. **1513** DOUGLAS *Æneis* I. i. 58 Scho thame fordrivis.. by fremmit weird full mony ȝeris tharbye. **1535** STEWART *Cron. Scot.* (1858) I. 323 Sayand the Britis fremit war and fals.

4. Not related, of another family or house; opposed to *sib* or *kin.* Often *ellipt.* or *absol.*

a **1200** *Moral Ode* 34 Sone wule hine forȝeten þe fremede and þe sibbe. *a* **1225** *Ancr. R.* 184 Nanmore þen þu woldest beaten a ureomede child þauh hit agulte. *c* **1340** HAMPOLE *Prose Tr.* (1866) 8 Many.. neuer haue halde þe ordyre of lufe ynesche þaire frendys sibbe or ffremede. *c* **1460** *How Goode Wif taught hir Doughter* 17 in Hazl. *E.P.P.* I. 181 Make thou none iangelynge withe fremed ne withe sibbe. *c* **1510** BARCLAY *Mirr. Gd. Manners* (1570) Biij, For thy fremde folke and seruauntes to prouide. **1530** PALSGR. 627, I make of a frenned chylde my sonne by the lawe. *Je adopte.* **1550** COVERDALE *Spir. Perle* xvi. 126 Those children that are nursed by frembd mens fyers. **1611** COTGR., *Affiliation*, adoption, or the conferring on fremme children all aduantages belonging to naturall ones. **1862** HISLOP *Prov. Scot.* 143 Mak friends o' fremit folk.

Hence **'fremdly** *adv.*, strangely, like a stranger; unkindly. **'fremdness**, strangeness, coldness; also personified.

13.. *Gaw. & Gr. Knt.* 714 Fer floten fro his frendez fremedly he rydez. *c* **1500** *Lancelot* 1508 [They] haith no thonk bot fremmytness of the. **1535** STEWART *Cron. Scot.* II. 3 Fra all the Scottis prescribit war ilkone.. So fremmitlie in mony sindrie land. **1560** ROLLAND *Crt. Venus* III. 6 The Iustice Clark, was callit Fremmitnes. **1569–70** KNOX *Let. to Cecil* 2 Jan. in Tytler *Hist. Scot.* (1864) III. 318, I have been fremedly handled. **1807** J. STAGG *Poems* 49 The hand of fate unkeynde Has us'd us fremtly.

†**freme**, *sb. Obs.* Forms: 1 fręmu, freomo, 2–3 freme, 3 freoma, -e, 4 *south.* vreme. [OE. *fręmu* str. fem., noun of quality from *fram* forward.] Advantage, benefit, profit. Cf. FRAME *sb.* 1.

a **700** *Epinal Gloss.* 135 *Beneficium*, fremu. *c* **888** K. ÆLFRED *Boeth.* xiv. §1 Hwelc fremu is ðe ðæt, ðæt þu wilniȝe þissa andweardena ȝesælþa. *c* **1000** *Sax. Leechd.* I. 84 Þonne ys wen þæt hyt him cume to mycelre freme. *a* **1175** *Cott. Hom.* 217 Þat we hine [God] lufie.. naht him to mede ac us to freme and to fultume. *c* **1205** LAY. 674 He deð him selua freoma a helpeð his freondene. **1258** *Charter Hen. III* in Tyrrell *Hist. Eng.* (1700) II. App. 25 Ure treowthe for the freme of the Loande. **1340** *Ayenb.* 69 Yef enye of hare uryendes ham wylleþ rede and hare ureme ssewy naȝt ham nolleþ yhere.

†**freme**, *v. Obs.* Forms: 1–2 fręmian, fręmman, 3 freme(n, -ien, (fremmen, froemen, *south.* vreomien). [OE. *fręmian, fręmman* trans. and intr. = OFris. *fremma*, OS. *fremmian*, OHG. *(gi-)fremen*, ON. *fremja*:—OTeut. **framjan*, f. **fram* forward: see FROM.]

1. *trans.* To help forward, promote the interests of; to benefit; to refresh (with food, etc.). Also, to indulge.

Beowulf 1832 Ic on Hiȝelace wat.. þæt he mec fremman wile weordum ond worcum. *a* **1000** *Andreas* 936 (Gr.) Ðæt ic eaðe mæȝ anra ȝehwylcne fremman and fyrðran freonda minra. *a* **1225** *Leg. Kath.* 2367 Ha.. bisohte.. þæt he for his freolec, firstede hire & fremede. *c* **1250** *Gen. & Ex.* 1245 3he gan fremen ysmael Wið watres drinc and bredes mel.

2. *intr.* **a.** To profit, be of service. **b.** To gain ground, make progress; = FRAME *v.* 1 and 2.

c **1000** ÆLFRIC *Gen.* xxxvii. 20 Ðonne biþ ȝesyne, hwæt him his swefn fremion. *c* **1000** *Ags. Gosp.* Matt. xvi. 26 Hwæt fremað æneȝum menn þeah he [etc.]. *c* **1175** *Lamb. Hom.* 111 Ne ligge nefre on þine heorde, þet hauelese monnam meie fremian. *a* **1225** *Ancr. R.* 284 Gif þu hauest.. eni oðer þing þet ham wolde ureomien. *a* **1300** *E.E. Psalter* lxxxviii[i]. 22 Noghte freme in him sal þe faa.

3. *trans.* To accomplish, effect, perform.

Beowulf 2800 Fremmað ȝe nu [MS. ȝena] leoda þearfe. *a* **1000** *Cædmon's Gen.* 30 (Gr.) Þæs engles mod, þe þone unræd ongan ærest fremman. *c* **1205** LAY. 24010 Heo scullen me monradene mid moscipe fremmen. *c* **1300** *Havelok* 441 Alle haueden sworen.. That he sholden hise wille freme.

†**'fremeful**, *a. Obs.* [OE. *fręmfull*, f. *fręmu*, FREME *sb.* + -FUL.] Advantageous; profitable; beneficial, beneficent.

c **1000** *Sax. Leechd.* I. 152 Ðysse wyrte wos ys swyðe fremful. *c* **1175** *Lamb. Hom.* 109 Ne bið naut his lare fremful. *c* **1200** *Trin. Coll. Hom.* 149 Swich wop is fremful to wassende mide sinnes. **1340** *Ayenb.* 80 Me can todele þri manere guodes, guod worþssiplich, guod lostuoll, and guod uremuol.

Hence **'fremefully** *adv.*, profitably.

c **1200** *Trin. Coll. Hom.* 175 Wat it bitocneð.. fremfulliche to understonden.

†**frement**, *a. Obs.*$^{-0}$ [ad. L. *frementem*, pr. pple. of *fremĕre* to roar.] Roaring.

1656–81 in BLOUNT *Glossogr.*

fremescence (frɪ'mɛsəns). *rare.* [f. next: see -ENCE.] An incipient roaring.

1837 CARLYLE *Fr. Rev.* I. v. iv, Confused tremor and fremescence; waxing into thunderpeals, of Fury stirred on by Fear.

fremescent (frɪ'mɛsənt), *a. rare.* [as if ad. L. **fremescent-em*, pr. pple. of **fremescĕre*, freq. vb. f. L. *fremĕre* to roar.] Murmuring, growing noisy.

1837 CARLYLE *Fr. Rev.* II. VI. vii. (1872) 250 Fremescent clangour comes from the armed Nationals. **1881** *Scotsman* 9 May 4 On either side fremescent crowds jostle and growl.

†**'fremish**, *v. Obs.* [a. OF. and F. *fremiss-* lengthened stem of *frémir*:—pop. L. **fremīre*, L. *fremĕre*.] *intr.* To shudder. Of the ranks in an army: To waver.

c **1425** *Found. St. Bartholomew's* (E.E.T.S.) 5 He fremyshid, and for drede tremelyd. *c* **1450** *Merlin* 162 He.. rode in a-monge hem that alle the renges fremysshed.

‖**fremitus** ('frɛmɪtəs). [L. verbal sb. f. *fremĕre* to roar.] **a.** A dull roaring noise. **b.** *Path.* A palpable vibration or thrill, e.g. of the walls of the chest.

1820 T. MITCHELL *Aristoph.* I. p. lvi, The conviction of Cleinias is followed by a fremitus of applause. **1879** KHORY *Princ. Med.* 47 The fremitus is the movement which can be felt by the hands on making the patient speak.

†**'fremman.** *Obs. rare.* Also 7 frinman. [f. FREMD *a.* + MAN.] A person not related; a stranger.

1568 *Hist. Jacob & Esau* II. ii. C ij, Where is betwene one fremman and an other, Lesse loue found than now betwene brother and brother? *a* **1639** WHATELEY *Prototypes* I. xi. 105, I proceede to Abrahams carriage toward forreiners that were not of his house, whether kinsmen or frinmen as we call them.

fremmit, fremyt, etc.: see FREMD *a.*

fren: see FRENNE.

frenate, *a.*: see FRÆNULUM.

French (frɛn(t)ʃ), *a.* and *sb.* Forms: 1 fręncisc, 3 frenkis, (4 frenkysch), 3–4 frankys, frankis, 3 Frenchis, freinsse, frence, frenchs, frenynch, frensc, (frennssce), frenysch, 3–5 Frensch(e, 3, 6 franch(e, 3–6 frensh(e, 4 freynsch, 4, 6 frenche, 5 frenssh(e, 3– French. [OE. *fręncisc*, f. *franc-a* FRANK *sb.*[1] + *-isc*, -ISH; the suffix produces umlaut. With respect to the contraction, which began in early ME., cf. *Welsh* from OE. *wielisc*, *Scotch* from *Scottish.*

The equivalent continental Teut. *frankisk-*, Latinized as *franciscus*, became in OF. *franceis, -ois*, mod.F. *français*; but the fem. *franceise* instead of *francesche* shows that the termination was very early confused with *-eis*:—L. *-ēnsis* (see -ESE).]

A. *adj.*

1. a. Of or pertaining to France or its inhabitants.

O.E. Chron. an. 1003 (Laud MS.), Her wæs Eaxeceaster abrocen þurh þone Frenciscan ceorl Hugon. *c* **1205** LAY. 3239 Aganippus þe Frennsce king. *c* **1250** *Gen. & Ex.* 81 Ðes frenkis men o france moal, it nemnen 'un jur natural'. *c* **1450** *Cov. Myst.* (Shaks. Soc.) 118 Thi bowe is bent Newly now after the Frensche gyse. *a* **1490** BOTONER *Itin.* (Nasmith 1778) 125 Trewrew, a frensh priorie. **1529** *Supplic. to King* (E.E.T.S.) 52 Nowe the Frenshe fasshyon, nowe the Spanyshe fasshyon. **1592** G. HARVEY *Four Lett.* Wks. (Grosart) I. 174 Such French occurrences.. as the credible relation of inquisitiue frendes.. shall acquaint me withall. **1612** WEBSTER *White Devil* (Rtldg.) 34/2, I have a rare French rider. *a* **1687** PETTY *Polit. Arith.* iv. (1691) 85 The value of the French commodities brought into England. **1712** STEELE *Spect.* No. 350 ¶1 An Engagement between a French Privateer.. and a little Vessel of that Place. **1774** GOLDSM. *Nat. Hist.* (1776) VII. 120 It was eighteen feet and an half, French measure, in length. **1782** COWPER *Truth* 128 An Indian mystic or a French recluse.

¶ Misused for: Gaulish. *Obs.*

1548 W. PATTEN *Exped. Scotl.* Pref. in Arb. *Garner* III. 57 For killing Viridomax the French king in [the] field at the river of Padua. **1616** BUDDEN tr. *Ærodius' Disc. Parent's Hon.* 4 C. Flaminius.. which enacted the law about the partage of some french grounds.

b. with reference to the language, its words or phrases, compositions written in it, etc.

Partly an attrib. use of the sb. ***French class***, a class to which French is taught; so ***French master.***

a **1300** *Cursor M.* 24 Sanges sere of selcuth rime, Inglis, frankys, and latine. *c* **1386** CHAUCER *Pars. T.* ¶174 Thilke newe frenshe song. **1780** COWPER *Progr. Err.* 375 His stock a few French phrases got by heart. **1870** DICKENS *E. Drood* iii, The French class becomes so demoralised that [etc.].

†**c.** ***French Fox***: a game of some kind. *Obs.*

1759 MRS. DELANY *Life & Corr.* (1861) III. 575 How do you think we warmed and amused outselves? Why I taught them French Fox.

d. French-Canadian.

1673 *Hudson's Bay Co. Minutes* (1942) 59 That Mr. Kirke bee desired to treate for provideing Such french goodes as may be necessary. **1842** *Montreal Transcript* 15 Nov. 2/2 The murderer of lieut. Weir.. could be returned as member for any French County in Lower Canada. **1963** W. L. MORTON *Kingdom of Canada* 334 The attitude.. spread to the French element in Red River.

2. a. Having the qualities attributed to French persons or things; French-like.

† ***French fare***: ? elaborately polite behaviour.

13.. *Gaw. & Gr. Knt.* 1116 Syþen with frenkysch fare & fele fayre lotez þay stoden, & stemed & stylly speken. ?*a* **1500** *Chester Pl., Noah's Flood* 100 For all thy frankish fare I will not doe after thy red. **1606** BIRNIE *Kirk-Buriall* (1833) 13 So french hes men beene in their fashions. **1634** W. TIRWHYT tr. *Balzac's Lett.* I. 168 If any place be more French then Paris. **1710** *Acc. Distemp. T. Whigg* I. 6 Their Frowns, French shrugs.. Laughing [etc.]. **1749** LADY LUXBOROUGH *Lett. to Shenstone* 28 Nov., As the French style .. is fashionable. **1784** COWPER *Tiroc.* 670 His address, if not quite French at ease, Not English stiff, but frank, and formed to please. **1794** MRS. RADCLIFFE *Myst. Udolpho* i, Their sprightly melodies, debonnaire steps [etc.].. gave a character to the scene entirely French.

b. With the implication of 'spiciness'. ***French kissing*** (see quot. 1965); so ***French kiss*** *sb.* and *v.*

[**1749** FIELDING *Tom Jones* V. XIII. ix. 75, I am so far from desiring to exhibit such Pictures to the Public, that I would wish to draw a Curtain over those.. in certain French novels.] **1842** R. BROWNING *Bells & Pomegranates* III. 6/2 My scrofulous French novel On grey paper with blunt type! **1850** THACKERAY *Pendennis* II. xxx. 305 Young De Boots.. recognised you as the man who.. did business one-third in money,.. and one-third in French prints. **1922** GALSWORTHY *Windows* III. 28 Mother, I'd no idea you were so—French. **1923** J. MANCHON *Le Slang* 130 *French kiss*, baiser très appuyé. **1926** GALSWORTHY *Silver Spoon* II. viii. 181, I don't advise you to read it; it's very French. **1930** J. DOS PASSOS *42nd Parallel* v. 390 She taught him how to frenchkiss and would stroke his hair. **1931** 'D. STIFF' *Milk & Honey Route* xiv. 152 At one time the hobo enjoyed almost exclusively the 'French post cards' (called 'American cards' in France). **1959** G. ENDORE *Detour through Devon* 166 And in our slang, French means 'perverted'. **1960** V. NABOKOV *Invitation to Beheading* xix. 192 A cursory inspection of the prison collection of French postcards. **1960** J. UPDIKE *Rabbit, Run* (1961) 147 Sometimes just French kissing.., sloppy tongues and nobody can breathe. **1965** W. YOUNG *Eros Denied* xxvii. 271 In England.. we call .. kissing with the tongue in the other's mouth French kissing. **1967** A. WILSON *No Laughing Matter* v. 450, I might give you a nice French kiss.

3. a. In names of things of actual or attributed French origin, as **French barley** (see BARLEY); **French bed** (see quot. 1965); hence ***French bedstead***; **French-bit** (see quot.); **French blue**, (*a*) artificial ultramarine; (*b*) *colloq.* (see quot. 1964); **French-boiler** (see quot.); **French brace**, (*a*) a type of breast-drill; (*b*) in a theatre, a hinged brace (see quot. 1967); **French bread**, a kind of fancy bread; **French brush**, a brush used for rubbing down horses; **French casement** (see quot. and cf. *French window*); **French-chalk**, a variety of steatite, used for making marks on cloth, removing grease-spots, and (in powder) as a dry lubricant for boots and gloves; *v. trans.*, to clean or mark with French chalk; **French clock**, a clock made in France; usu. applied to an elaborately decorated clock of the eighteenth century; **French cricket**, an informal type of cricket without stumps in which a player is out if the 'bowler' succeeds in getting the ball past the bat so that it hits the legs of the batsman; **French curve**, a template used for drawing curved lines; **French defence**, a defence in Chess in which Black replies to an opening move of P-K4 by White with P-K3; also *ellipt.*; **French door** *N. Amer.* = *French window*; **French drain**, a rubble-drain; **French dressing**, a salad-dressing consisting of vinegar and oil, usually with added flavouring; † **French eaves**, eaves provided with a gutter to carry off the water; **French fake**, a variety of the Flemish fake (in Young *Naut. Dict.* 1846); **French 'flu**, excessive fondness for all things French (an expression first used by A. Koestler); **French-flyers** (see quot.); **French fried potatoes**, potato chips (see CHIP *sb.*[1] 2 b); also *French fried(s)*, used *absol.*, and *French fries*; **French-grey** (see quot. 1862); **French hem** (see quot.); **French horn**, a metal wind-instrument (see HORN); **French knot** (see quot. 1964); **French letter** *colloq.*, a contraceptive and disease-preventing sheath, = CONDOM; † **French lock**, ? a kind of shackle for a horse's foot; **French maid**, a lady's maid of French origin, freq. employed in the Victorian and Edwardian eras as a status symbol; † **French panel**, some kind of wainscoting; **French paste** (see quot.); **French pink** (see PINK); **French purple** (see quot.); **French red, rouge** (see quots.); **French Revolution** = REVOLUTION *sb.* 9; **French rice** = AMELCORN; **French roll**: see ROLL; **French roof**, a mansard roof; † **French rowel**, a kind of seton for a horse; **French salt**, ? = bay salt; **French sewing** (see quots.); † **French shroudknot** (see quot.); **French sixth** *Mus.* (see quot.); **French toast**, any of various kinds of toasted bread (see quots.); **French tub, tuning** (see quots.); **French white** (see quot.); **French window**, a long window opening like a folding-door, and serving for exit and entrance.

1661 *Specif. Burneby's Patent* No. 133 That sort of barley commonly called..*French barley. **1770** LATHAM in *Phil. Trans.* LX. 451 He followed the trade of a miller, and maker of French barley. **1825** H. WILSON *Mem.* IV. 38, I pointed ..towards the small *French bed. **1844** B. DISRAELI *Coningsby* II. IV. vii. 77 Under ordinary circumstances a French bed and a brasier of charcoal alone remained for Villebecque, who was equal to the occasion. **1852** RUSKIN *Let.* 25 Mar. in M. Lutyens *Effie in Venice* (1965) II. 288 Tell Mr Snell not to put a four poster—but a large French bed in the bedroom at Herne hill. **1853** C. BRONTË *Villette* I. i. 4 My own French bed in its shady recess. **1965** J. ARONSON *Encycl. Furnit.* (1966) 234/1 *French bed*, roll-end bedstead without posts. **1967** D. MACKENZIE *Death is Friend* 23 The French bed had a velvet padded headboard. **1837** DICKENS *Pickwick* xii. 115 The large man..condensed himself into the limits of a dwarfish *French bedstead. **1842** —— *Amer. Notes* I. iii. 142 Our bedroom was spacious and airy..having no curtains to the French bedstead or to the window. **1868** C. L. EASTLAKE *Hints Household Taste* viii. 185 To the four-poster succeeded..the French bedstead, of which the head and foot-piece were in shape and size alike, and over which two curtains fell, sometimes from a pole fixed at the side, and sometimes from a small circular canopy attached to the ceiling. **1878** H. JAMES *Europeans* I. iv. 131 She can have the large north-east room. And the French bedstead. **1901** MRS. A. PRAGA *How to Furnish* i. 29 We must reserve £2 5s., for ..a black and brass French bedstead,..a double-woven steel wire mattress, a wool mattress, bolster, and two feather pillows. **1874** KNIGHT *Dict. Mech.* I. 915 **French-bit* (Carpentry), a boring tool adapted to use on a lathe-head or by a bow. **1879** ROOD *Chromatics* x. 157 This same tendency ..reached a maximum in *French-blue. **1964** *Lancet* 29 Aug. 452/1 'French blues' (the name for a non-proprietary mixture of amphetamine and a barbiturate). **1967** *Daily Tel.* 21 Feb. 15/7 A schoolgirl of 14 said at Birmingham yesterday that she took 10 'French blue' pep pills she had bought outside the Midnight City dance club in the town. **1968** 'J. WELCOME' *Hell is where you find It* xiv. 166 Some say French blues kill the itch to drink. With me they didn't. **1879** ROSSITER *Dict. Sci. Terms*, **French boiler*, Elephant boiler: one large and two smaller cylinders connected by transverse pipes. **1846** C. HOLTZAPFFEL *Turning* II. xxv. 561 The *French brace..is also constructed in iron, with a pair of equal bevil pinions. **1947** *Gloss. Techn. Theatr. Terms* (*Strand Electr. Co.*) 5 *French brace*, a tall wooden right-angled triangular frame, hinged to the back of a flat or other piece. **1948** H. MELVILL *Designing & Painting Scenery* ii. 18 The brace (called in this instance a 'French brace') can swing out into position, or go flat against the groundrow when not in use. **1967** *Oxf. Compan. Theatre* 912/2 A variant [of the stage brace], composed of a right-angled triangle of wood hinged to the flat, opened out and weighted, is known as a French Brace. **1969** E. H. PINTO *Treen* 380 The more complex French brace or breast drill, came into the English wood-worker's toolchest just before 1900, but it was illustrated in Bergeron more than 100 years earlier. **1686** *Manch. Crt. Leet Rec.* (1888) VI. 246 Short rated *ffrench bread. **1836** *Act 6 & 7 Will. IV*, c. 37 §4 Bread usually sold under the Denomination of French or Fancy Bread or Rolls. **1686** BLOME *Gentl. Recreat.* II. 11 Rub him [Horse] all over with the *French Brush, beginning at his forehead. **1842–59** GWILT *Archit.* Gloss., **French casements*, windows turning upon two vertical edges attached to the jambs. *a* **1728** WOODWARD *Catal. For. Fossils* I. 3 Red *French chalk. **1882** CAULFEILD & SAWARD *Dict. Needlework*, *French Chalk*, a variety of indurated Talc. **1933** P. GODFREY *Back-Stage* xiii. 167 The floor of the stage, which was *French-chalked for dancing to the gramophone. **1963** J. OSBORNE *Dental Mechanics* (ed. 5) iv. 61 The waxed-up model is French-chalked. **1841** *Fraser's Mag.* XXIV. 717/2 On the mantelpiece, huge *French clocks. **1864** J. S. LE FANU *Uncle Silas* I. xxiv. 290 There was a little French clock over the mantlepiece in the school-room. **1964** I. OELLRICHS *Death in Chilly Corner* iv. 30 The little old French clock buzzed three times to indicate three o'clock. **1964** J. SYMONS *End of Solomon Grundy* II. i. 69 She..went to look at the French clock in the sitting-room. **1967** W. EDEY *French Clocks* 9 It is in this capacity, as a decorative art rather than as a work of science, that French clocks excel. **1926** E. BOWEN *Ann Lee's* 221 They went back to the garden and played *French-cricket there with a tennis-ball. [**1935** *Encycl. Sports* 296/2 *French cricket*, game played with a cricket bat and ball in a confined space. It is played by any number, without sides, and there is no scoring. Each batsman plays until he is out, and is then succeded by the next.] **1959** I. & P. OPIE *Lore & Lang. Schoolch.* viii. 137 An informal game of cricket, such as French cricket or Stump cricket. **1885** *Army & Navy Co-op. Soc. Price List* 720 *French Curves, Pear wood, assorted patterns. **1969** R. MAYER *Dict. Art Terms & Techniques* 154 French curves.. are also called irregular curves and drawing curves. **1971** D. CLARK *Sick to Death* i. 18 An artist's drawing-board... A long T-square..a straight edge with a metal ribbon on one side; a french-curve template. **1889** FREEBOROUGH & RANKEN *Chess Openings* v. 239 The *French Defence dates from Lucena (1497). **1895** J. MASON *Art of Chess* 292 The French Defence is often adopted in anticipation of the eternal Lopez, and may be considered one of the best methods of eluding that wearisome game. **1964** *Listener* 1 Oct. 531/2 Peter Lee..specializes in the French Defence. In this game..superior opening knowledge gave him a quick win. **1965** H. EVANS et al. *Korn's Mod. Chess Openings* (ed. 10) 145 The French derives its name from a correspondence game between London and Paris in 1834, even though Lucena had examined it in 1497. **1971** *Oxford Mail* 27 Oct. 16/8 Fischer..opened..with his favourite move and Petrosian went into a French defence. **1923** *Southern Calif. Hardwood Manuf. Co. Catal.* Feb. 97 *French Doors while intended primarily for outside use—porches, sun rooms etc., are now used to good advantage for inter-room use where lighting or heating is a reason for separating two rooms. **1926** *Daily Colonist* (Victoria, B.C.) 18 July 11/5 (Advt.), Thrown wide between two small rooms, French doors allow you the often convenient space of a large room. **1968** *Globe & Mail* (Toronto) 13 Feb. 30/1 (Advt.), Living room with..French doors to screened veranda. **1776** G. SEMPLE *Building in Water* 34 Coarse Rubbish and Stones, which were just like a *French Drain under our Dike. **1884** *Century Mag.* XXIX. 47/1 'Box drains', 'French drains', 'blind drains'. **1900** *Ladies' Home Jrnl.* June 40/3 *French Dressing is a mixture of oil and vinegar in the proportions of six tablespoonfuls of oil to two of vinegar. **1923** H. CRANE *Let.* 5 Dec. (1965) 159, I made some fine lettuce salad with onions and peppers and French dressing. **1945** *La Junta* (Colo.) *Tribune-Democrat* 15 Feb 2/6 French Fried Onions Chef's Salad with French Dressing. **1962** *Woman's Own* 17 Mar. 14/3 Tossed green salad with French dressing. **1634** in Willis & Clark *Cambridge* (1886) II. 699 The *French Eves to keepe the water from the building. **1943** A. KOESTLER in *Yogi & Commissar* (1945) 21 The managerial class on Parnassus.. have lately been affected by a new outbreak of that recurrent epidemic, the *French 'Flu. **1959** *Guardian* 11 Dec. 6/6 Arthur Koestler once diagnosed French 'flu as an unreasoned admiration for everything Gallic. **1966** J. FOWLES *Magus* xv. 83 '*Voila.*' 'Very nice.' I determined to stamp out the French 'flu before it spread. **1874** KNIGHT *Dict. Mech.* I. 915 **French-flyers*..stairs that fly forwards until they reach within a length of a stair from the wall, where a quarter space occurs; the steps next ascend at a right angle, when another quarter space occurs; they then ascend in an opposite flight, parallel to the first direction. **1894** 'O. HENRY' *Rolling Stones* (1916) 150 Our countries are great friends. We have given you Lafayette and *French fried potatoes. **1913** F. H. BURNETT *T. Tembarom* xxii. 287 Beefsteak and French fried potatoes were the favourites. **1944** *This Week Mag.* 18 Mar. 12/2 Sirloin steak I get them, with French frieds and mushrooms. **1956** 'A. GILBERT' *Riddle of Lady* ix. 130 An excellent steak..and what the Nell Gwynn called French fried potatoes and Crook called chips. **1958** G. GREENE *Our Man in Havana* v. iii. 213 Roast turkey, cranberry sauce, sausages and carrots and French fried. **1918** in F. A. Pottle *Stretchers* (1930) 289 After looking around a while we found the Cafe Riche and had a fine steak with *French fries. **1951** C. ARMSTRONG *Black-Eyed Stranger* (1952) ii. 10 Bring me two lamb chops, French fries, cup of coffee. **1862** *Dict. Arch.* (Arch. Publ. Soc.), **French grey*, a tint composed of white with ivory black, Indian red and Chinese blue. **1882** *Garden* 25 Mar. 202/3 The flowers are pale blue, or French grey in colour. **1882** CAULFEILD & SAWARD *Dict. Needlework*, **French Hem*, a description of Hem employed for the finishing of Flounces. *c* **1885**, **1899** *French knot [see KNOT *sb.*[1] 1 b]. **1960** G. LEWIS *Handbk. Crafts* 29 Bumpy stitches like French knots which require great care in pressing to prevent them being flattened are better not used. **1964** *McCall's Sewing* ii. 29/1 *French knot*, decorative hand-stitch in which the thread is twisted around the needle and brought down through the fabric at almost the same spot to form a small dot. *c* **1856** *Paul Pry* in C. Pearl *Girl with Swansdown Seat* (1955) vi. 256 *French letters..prevent the spread of venereal contagion in casual intercourse between the sexes, and in the marriage state, the increase of the family. *c* **1857** *Amours, Intrigues, & Adv. Musical Student* 144 (Advt.), How many industrious men have been crushed by poverty..through ignorance of the existence of French Letters. **1886** R. F. BURTON *Arab. Nts.* X. 239 Of the penis succedaneus..every kind abounds, varying from a stuffed 'French letter' to a cone of ribbed horn. *c* **1888–94** *My Secret Life* III. 324 What Jenny's sister paid for French letters I dont know, I used to pay nine pence each. **1960** B. ASKWITH *Tangled Web* 162, I daresay he would have liked to give me a baby—but he always used a French letter. **1960** M. SPARK *Bachelors* x. 181 They fumble about with their french letters or they tear open their horrible little packets of contraceptives like kids with sweets. **1968** J. R. ACKERLEY *My Father & Myself* vi. 49 My elder brother Peter was the accident. 'Your father happened to have run out of french letters that day.' **1704** *Lond. Gaz.* No. 4067/8 A *French Lock on her off Foot before. **1848** THACKERAY *Vanity Fair* lv. 491 She went up stairs and dressed herself this time without the aid of her *French maid. **1853** DICKENS *Bleak Ho.* xviii. 178, I was conscious of being distressed even by the observation of the French maid. **1899** WILDE *Importance of being Earnest* III. 132 A thoroughly experienced French maid produces a really marvellous result in a very brief space of time. **1905** F. H. BURNETT *Little Princess* ii. 17 One or two of them had even caught a glimpse of her French maid, Mariette, who had arrived the evening before. **1912** A. N. LYONS *Clara* viii. 73 I'm only a little dis'eartened because the motor's broken down and my French maid forgot to air the curling-tongs. **1960** B. KEATON *Wonderf. World of Slapstick* (1967) 55 This little lady carried thirty-six pieces of luggage..and an entourage consisting of a pianist, a chauffeur, a footman, and two French maids. **1556** in Willis & Clark *Cambridge* (1886) II. 564 The backe..vnderneth the turned pilleres of the stalles to be *frenche pannell. **1884** *Chamb. Jrnl.* 15 Nov. 731/2 '*French paste' which imitates the diamond so well, is a kind of glass into which a certain quantity of oxide of lead is introduced. **1873** *Weale's Dict. Archit.* (ed. 3), **French purple*, a beautiful dye prepared from lichens. **1844** HOBLYN *Dict. Med.*, **French red* or *rouge*, genuine carmine. **1791** J. WOODFORDE *Diary* 14 July (1927) III. 285, I hope this Day will be attended with no bad Consequences, this being the Day that the *French Revolution first took Place there last Year. **1819** KEATS *Let.* 18 Sept. (1958) II. 193, I mean that the french Revolution put a temporry stop to this third change, the change for the better. **1907** G. B. SHAW *John Bull's Other Island* p. xxxii, The French revolution would have been a revolution against England and English rule instead of against aristocracy and ecclesiasticism. **1970** R. C. COBB *Police & People* p. xiv, The approach has been throughout to replace the question commonly asked: 'Why did the popular movement fail in the course of the French Revolution?'.. by the question 'How did a popular movement in its own right emerge at all?': for this is perhaps the most astonishing fact about the history of the French Revolution. **1669** in Willis & Clark *Cambridge* (1886) II. 557 The roofe..shalbe a sufficient strong *French roofe to be made after the best manner hipt of[f]. **1883** HOWELLS *Woman's Reason* II. xvii. 118 The row of French-roof cottages. **1703** *Lond. Gaz.* No. 3928/4 A bay Nag..all his Paces, and had lately a *French Rowel in the inside of the near Leg behind above the Hock. **1670** NARBOROUGH *Jrnl.* in *Acc. Sev. Late Voy* I. (1711) 45 Good white Stone-Salt, whiter than *French-salt. **1923** H. A. MADDOX *Dict. Stationery* 31 **French sewing*, a method of sewing small books and pamphlet work without tapes, the cover usually being drawn on. **1963** KENNEISON & SPILMAN *Dict. Printing* 75 *French sewing*, in binding, the method of machine-sewing without tapes, or in hand-sewing, the method of sewing a book without the use of a sewing frame, the sections of the book being sewn at the edge of the bench. **1867** SMYTH *Sailor's Word-bk.*, **French shroud-knot*, the shroud-knot with three strands single walled round the bights of the other three and the standing part. **1841** HAMILTON *Dict. Mus. Terms* App., **French sixth*, the name of a chord composed of a major third, extreme fourth and extreme sixth. **1660** R. MAY *Accomplisht Cook* VI. 162 **French Toasts*. Cut French Bread, and toast it in pretty thick toasts on a clean gridiron, and serve them steeped in claret, sack, or any wine, with sugar and juyce of orange. **1882** F. E. OWENS *Cook Bk.* 128 French toast. Make a batter of two eggs, one-half cup of milk, pinch of salt, and tea-spoon of cornstarch. Dip thin slices of bread in and fry brown in a well-buttered frying pan. **1892** T. F. GARRETT *Encycl. Pract. Cookery* I. 192/1 French Toast. Beat up one egg in a basin with a little salt and 1 teaspoonful of milk, and in this dip some thin slices of Bread..; then plunge the Bread into a frying-pan of boiling fat, and fry to a light brown. Take them out, drain them... Spreading over them with stewed rhubarb, or other fruit in season, is a great improvement. **1924** *Western Daily Press* (Bristol) 20 Mar. 9/5 A piece of bread and butter toasted on the dry side is said to be French toast. **1873** *Weale's Dict. Archit.* (ed. 3), **French tub*, a mixture used by dyers, of the protochloride of tin and logwood. **1876** STAINER & BARRETT *Dict. Mus. Terms*, *Flat tuning*, one of the varieties of tuning on the lute; called also *French tuning or French flat tuning. **1844** HOBLYN *Dict. Med.*, **French white*, the common designation of finely pulverized talc. **1801** *Trans. Soc. Arts* XIX. 291 *French windows and glass doors. **1849** THACKERAY *Pendennis* vi, The Doctor stept out of the French windows of the dining-room into the lawn.

b. of articles of dress, stuffs, etc., as ***French heel, pocket, sleeve, velvet***, etc.; **French cuff**, a double cuff formed by turning back a long cuff band and fastening it with buttons or links; **French pleat**, (*a*) a type of pleat at the top of a curtain (see quot. 1964[1]); (*b*) = *French roll*; **French roll**, a woman's hairstyle, in which the hair is tucked into a vertical roll down the back of the head; **French seam** (see quot. 1968); **French tack** (see quot. 1964); **French twist**, = *French roll*.

1882 CAULFEILD & SAWARD *Dict. Neetlework*, *French canvas*..a description of Grenadine, of a stout wiry character. **1916** *Daily Colonist* (Victoria, B.C.) 22 July 12/5 (Advt.), Each Shirt is finished with French cuffs and separate soft collar. **1964** *McCall's Sewing* xi. 171/1 Apply the French cuff to the lower edge of sleeve. **1967** 'L. EGAN' *Nameless Ones* xv. 187 A fancy sports shirt with French cuffs and gold cuff links. *a* **1706** in *J. Watson's Collect.* I. 30 French-gows cut out and double banded. **1784** COWPER *Task* IV. 546 Her tott'ring form Ill propp'd upon French heels. **1922** JOYCE *Ulysses* 353 With her high crooked

French heels on her. **1928** M. DE LA ROCHE *Whiteoaks* (1929) xii. 157 Four girls approached abreast, wearing French heels and flesh-coloured stockings. **1599** MARSTON *Sco. Villanie* II. vii. 203 Seest thou yon gallant in the sumptuous clothes ..Note his French-herring bones: but note no more. **1812** J. SMYTH *Pract. of Customs* (1821) 127 Cambricks and Lawns, commonly called French Lawns. **1882** CAULFEILD & SAWARD *Dict. Needlework, French Merino*..is manufactured of very superior wool from the Merino sheep. **1948** DERIEUX & STEVENSON *Compl. Bk. Interior Decorating* 147 To simplify making of French pleats two products are available. **1964** *McCall's Sewing* xvi. 284/1 *French pleats.* Divide fullness of pleat fold into three equal, smaller folds. At the bottom of the heading, sew by hand through the three pleats on the right side of the fabric. Pull thread up tight and fasten securely. Top edge of heading is not pressed into pleats. **1964** G. LYALL *Most Dangerous Game* ix. 64 She had..silky fair hair pulled back and coiled in a French pleat. **1966** P. CARLON *Running Woman* viii. 69 Long hair could be worn in a French pleat, a chignon, at times. **1968** R. W. SEMMENS in F. H. Radford *Art & Craft Hairdressing* (ed. 5) I. vii. 116/2 *French Rolls and Pleats.* This is a popular hair style suitable for longer hair. **1675** *Lond. Gaz.* No. 979/4 A strait bodied Coat, with French Pockets. **1882** CAULFEILD & SAWARD *Dict. Needlework, French Point*, a name by which Alençon lace is sometimes called. **1941** F. E. WALL *Princ. & Pract. Beauty Culture* 423 French Roll. This coiffure is particularly becoming to the small woman who wishes to appear taller, but it is equally suitable to a taller woman with a thin face. **1962** in R. Corson *Fashions in Hair* (1965) xii. 630 The bouffant, a hairdo filched from eighteenth-century France, whose tortured variations—mushroom flip, French twist, chemise, French roll..—began sprouting a few years back. **1965** J. CAIRD *Murder Reflected* ii. 19 She had hair of true wheat-gold, worn up in a French roll. **1968** J. IRONSIDE *Fashion Alphabet* 192 With the advent of the 'bouffant' hair-do, the French roll was an easy adaptation, the teased hair being brushed up from the neck and made into a thick roll down the back of the head, thicker at the top. *c* **1890** tr. *T. deDillmont's Encycl. Needlework* 8 For joining such stuffs as fray, use the so-called French seam. **1895** *Montgomery Ward Catal.* 37/1 Ladies' Shirt Waists..all felled French seams. **1956** *And so to Sew* 118/2 Do not use french seams where perfect fitting is necessary or where a flat finish is required. **1967** *Guardian* 23 May 6/5 Bogged down among the plackets and French seams of school dressmaking. **1968** J. IRONSIDE *Fashion Alphabet* 99 *French seam*, a seam made by sewing the two fabrics together on the right side; then turning and sewing on the wrong side, enclosing the raw edges. **1592** GREENE *Def. Conny Catch.* Wks. (Grosart) XI. 96 Blest be the French sleeues and breech verdingales. **1934** *Vogue's Guide Smart Dressmaking* 39 The lining is finished separately from the coat at lower edge, with French tacks at the seams. **1960** *Vogue Pattern Bk.* Early Autumn 57 Catch the seams together near the hemline with loose French tacks. **1964** *McCall's Sewing* ii. 29/1 *French tack*, a thread bar fastening used to hold two pieces of a garment together loosely. Used to attach lining to coat at hemline. **1882** CAULFEILD & SAWARD *Dict. Needlework, French Twill*, although called French this is an English-made dress material—a variety of French Merino. **1877** E. CREER *Lessons in Hairdressing* iii. 48 That [coiffure] which is called a 'French twist' has two different forms and uses. According to some authorities it is made with the back hair, and fixed by means of a comb at the crown of the head... Another 'French twist'..is also known by the names of '*Torsade Dondel*', '*Torsade Repoussée*', '*Torsade Gouffrée*'. It is made with a long, thin strand of hair, and is hollow when completed. **1892** I. MALLON in R. Corson *Fashions in Hair* (1965) xii. 494 Women who wear their hair very plainly part it in the back and turn it over like a French twist, drawing it up to the top of the head. **1962** J. FLEMING *When I grow Rich* viii. 102 She..did her hair up into a French twist at the back. **1966** J. S. COX *Illustr. Dict. Hair-dressing* 61/1 *French twist*,..the same as French Roll. **1603** SHAKS. *Meas. for M.* I. ii. 35, I had as liefe be a Lyst of an English Kersey, as be pil'd..for a French Veluet.

4. In the names of various animals: **French bulldog**, a smaller variety of the English bulldog; **French fly** = CANTHARIDES; **French gurnard, ray, sardine, sole**: see quots.

1894 R. B. LEE *Mod. Dogs* ix. 215, I am surprised that there are show committees who will provide classes for these *French bulldogs to be called 'toys', going up to 23 lb. in weight. **1922** R. LEIGHTON *Complete Bk. of Dog* xx. 308 It was from the English variety of pygmy Bulldogs that the now fashionable French Bulldog was evolved. **1952** E. F. DAVIES *Illyrian Venture* iv. 73 Our shopping expedition produced a French bulldog. **1601** HOLLAND *Pliny* I. 330 The Cantharides or *French greene Flies. **1741** *Compl. Fam.-Piece* I. i. 15 Take French Flies..and a few Drops of Vinegar. **1879** ROSSITER *Dict. Sci. Terms*, *French gurnard, *Trigla lineata*. **1776** PENNANT *Brit. Zool.* III. 77, I met with this species [*Raia fullonica*] at Scarborough, where it is called the *French Ray. **1879** ROSSITER *Dict. Sci. Terms*, **French sardine* = Young pilchard. *Ibid.*, *French sole, *Solea pegusa*.

5. a. In names of various trees and plants; as †**French apple**, some flowering plant; **French-bean** (see BEAN *sb.* 3); **French berry** = AVIGNON BERRY; †**French broom**, *Spartium monospermum*; **French cowslip** (see quot. and COWSLIP 2); **French furze**, *Ulex europæus*; **French grass**, *Onobrychis sativa*; **French heath**, *Erica hibernica*; **French honey-suckle**, *Hedysarum coronarium*; **French lavender**, *Lavandula Stœchas*; **French leek**, *Allium Porrum*; **French lungwort**, *Hieracium murorum*; **French mallow**, a species of *Malva*?; **French marigold**, *Tagetes patula* and other species; **French mercury**, *Mercurialis annua*; **French nut**, the fruit of *Juglans regia* = WALNUT; **French oak**, (*a*) a variety of *Ilex*, (*b*) (see quot. 1829); †**French onion**, *Scilla maritima*; **French pink** *U.S.*, the cornflower, *Centaurea cyanus*, or a species of *Armeria*; **French rose**, the common red rose, esp. as used in the pharmacopœia; **French sage**, a variety of mullein; **French sorrel**, *Oxalis Acetosella* (see also quot. 1829); **French turnip** = NAVEW (*Brassica Napus*); **French walnut** = Common walnut (WALNUT[1] 2 b); **French wheat** = BUCKWHEAT 1; **French willow**, (*a*) *Epilobium angustifolium*, (*b*) *Salix triandra*.

1741 *Compl. Fam. Piece* II. iii. 378 Several annual Flowers, as the *French Apple, Convolvulus..and others. **1552** HULOET, Beanes called *Frenche beanes, *eruilia*. **1719** D'URFEY *Pills* (1872) I. 33 The one thin and lean As a garden French bean. **1861** DELAMER *Kitch. Gard.* 88 French beans may be divided into two classes: the Runners..and the Dwarfs. **1727-51** *French Berry [see AVIGNON BERRY]. **1866** *Treas. Bot., French Berries*, the fruits of *Rhamnus infectorius, saxatilis, amygdalinus, &c.* **1548** TURNER *Names of Herbes* 76 Spartium or spartum..is a bushe called of some gardiners *french broume. **1597** GERARDE *Herbal* II. cclxxv. 663 *Pulmonaria Gallorum*, *French Cowslips of Jerusalem. **1602** CAREW *Cornwall* 21 Great store of furze of which the shrubby sort is called tame, the better growne *French. **1863** PRIOR *Plant-n.* 87 **French grass*, sainfoin. **1871** *Jrnl. Bot.* IX. 52 The beautiful *Erica hibernica*..locally known as *French Heath, is found..to make capital brooms. **1629** PARKINSON *Paradisi in Sole* (1656) 340 The red Sattin flower, although some foolishly call it, the red or *French Honysuckle. **1578** LYTE *Dodoens* II. lxxxvii. 266 It is called in English..*French Lavender. **1597** GERARDE *Herbal* II. clxx. §1. 469 French lauander. **1548** TURNER *Names of Herbes* 65 The one is called..in englishe a *frenche Leke. **1597** GERARDE *Herbal* Table Eng. Names, *French Lungwort. **1796** WITHERING *Brit. Plants* (ed. 3) III. 687 French Lungwort. Golden Lungwort, or Hawk-weed. **1548** TURNER *Names of Herbes* 50 The other kynde..is called in englishe *french Mallowe. **1620** VENNER *Via Recta* vii. 144 The curled Mallow, called of the vulgar sort, French Mallowes. **1548** TURNER *Names of Herbes* 80 *Viola flammea* otherwyse called..in englishe veluet floure or *french Marigoulde. **1578** LYTE *Dodoens* II. xxv. 176 We do call this floure Turkie Gillofers, and French Marygoldes. **1597** GERARDE *Herbal* II. xlvii. 262 It [Mercurialis] is called..in English *French Mercurie. **1398** TREVISA *Barth. De P.R.* XVII. cviii. (1495) 671 The more nottes be *frenshe nottes and the lasse ben Auelanes. **1578** LYTE *Dodoens* VI. lvi. 731 The fruit is called..in Englishe Walnuttes..and of some Frenche Nuttes. **1796** W. MARSHALL *W. England* I. 326 *French nuts*, walnuts. **1597** GERARDE *Herbal* III. xxi. 1161 This Oke [*Ilex*] is named..in English Barren scarlet Oke, or Holme Oke, and also of some *French Oke. **1829** LOUDON *Encycl. Plants* 26 *Catalpa longissima* is..known in the West Indies by the name of French oak. **1548** TURNER *Names of Herbes* 71 Scilla is named..in english a sea Onion, and in some places, a *french Onyon. **1863** S. K. HOLMES *Jrnl.* 12 July (1955) 226 The prairie is a mass of moving purple plumes, '*French Pinks', the natives [*sc.* Texans] call them. **1896** S. O. JEWETT *Country of Pointed Firs* xv. 132 There was little trace of her flower-garden except a single faded sprig of much-enduring French pinks. **1914** L. H. BAILEY *Stand. Cycl. Hort.* II. 711/2 Centaurea..cyanus..Bluebottle. Bluet. Bachelor's Button..Cornflower. Ragged Sailor. French Pink. **1552** HULOET, *French roses, *trachinia*. **1853** *Pereira's Mat. Med.* 1807 *Rosa Gallica*, French or Red Rose ..The dried petals of the unexpanded flowers..constitute the red-rose leaves of the shops. **1882** CASSELL, The petals of the French or Red Rose are astringent and contain a red colouring matter, which is turned green by alkalis. **1597** GERARDE *Herbal* II. ccliii. 625 *Verbascum Mathioli*, *French Sage. **1861** MISS PRATT *Flower. Pl.* IV. 140 Woody Mullein or French Sage. **1829** LOUDON *Encycl. Plants* 1081 The young leaves and shoots of several species of Rumex and Rheum are eaten..under the name of..*French sorrel. **1863-79** PRIOR *Plant-n.* 86 *French Sorrel*, the wood sorrel, *Oxalis acetosella*. **1832** *Veg. Subst. Food* 232 The root of the *French turnip, or naveu, differs from the other varieties. **1841** *Southern Lit. Messenger* VII. 221/1 [I] rode into the yard; found large old *French walnut there. **1966** A. W. LEWIS *Gloss. Woodworking Terms* 107 French Walnut. **1597** GERARDE *Herbal* I. lx. 83 In English *French wheate..and Bucke wheate. **1658** T. MAYERNE *Receipts Cookery* xxxi. 31 Take..a pint of French wheat flower. **1776** WITHERING *Brit. Plants* I. 237 Snakeweed..Buckwheat..Frenchwheat. **1838** LOUDON *Arboretum* III. 1499 *Salix triandra*..The *French willow..cultivated in Sussex and the east parts of England. **1863** PRIOR *Plant-n.* 87 *French Willow* from its leaves somewhat resembling those of the willow, *Epilobium angustifolium* L.

b. †**French pippin, warden**, varieties respectively of apple and pear; **French plum**, the fruit of a variety of *Prunus domestica*, dried and exported from France.

1664 EVELYN *Kal. Hort.* (1729) 191 Golden Pippin, French Pippin, Kirton Pippin. *Ibid.* 226 The..Squib-Pear, Spindle-Pear..and French Wardens. **1838** LOUDON *Arboretum* II. 689 The prune d'Ast..is chiefly used for preparing what are called in England, *French plums.

6. In various names given to venereal diseases.

1503 *Priv. Purse Exp. Eliz. of York* (1830) 105 A Surgeon whiche heled him of the Frenche pox. **1592** GREENE *Disput.* Wks. (Grosart) X. 233 There you shall see men diseased of the French Marbles. **1598** SYLVESTER *Du Bartas* II. i. I. *Eden* 621 His burned stalks, with strong fumosities Of piercing vapours, purge the French disease. **1607** TOURNEUR *Rev. Trag.* I. i. Wks. 1878 II. 10 Like the French Moale. **1612** CHAPMAN *Widowes T.* in Dodsley *O. Pl.* (1780) VI. 229 They shall be burnt..to salve for the french-measles. **1614** J. COOKE *Tu Quoque* ibid. VII. 177 May the french cannibal eat into thy flesh And pick thy bones. **1664** BUTLER *Hud.* II. ii. 456 As no man of his own self catches The Itch, or amorous French aches. **1678** *Ibid.* III. i. 716 Tis hard to say ..who imported the French Goods. **1688** S. PENTON *Guardian's Instruct.* 29 The easie Cure of the French Complement. *a* **1700** B. E. *Dict. Cant. Crew, French Gout*, the Pox. **1740** *Hist. Jamaica* 207 If any Servant..happen to have the French-pox. **1760-72** tr. *Juan & Ulloa's Voy.* (ed. 3) II. 11 It is particularly famous for the cure of the French disease.

7. *Comb.* (chiefly prefixed to ppl. adjs., or objective), as ***French-bred***, ***-built***, ***-heeled***, ***-loving***, ***-speaking*** adjs.; ***French-wise*** adv. Also, esp. in the sense 'French and ——', ***French-American***, ***-British***, ***-Creole***, ***-provincial***, ***-Spanish***, ***-Swiss***. †**French-sick** *a.*, affected with syphilis (cf. 6), also used *punningly*. See also FRENCH CANADIAN *sb.* and *a.*

1915 W. OWEN *Let.* 1 Aug. (1967) 350 The fellow is a Radio-Telegraphist on a *French-American Liner. **1934** DYLAN THOMAS *Let.* 16 Mar. (1966) 96 The French-American Transitionists. **1684** OTWAY *Atheist* III. i, This Man of War, this *French-bred Hero. **1612** W. STRACHEY *Trav. Virginia* (1953) I. x. 121, I haue drunck often of the rath wyne, which..people haue made full as good as your *French-Brittish wyne. **1798** NELSON 28 Sept. in Nicolas *Desp.* (1845) III. 135 The only remaining *French-built Ship of the Line. **1868** G. ROSE *Great Country* 195 The *French Creole ladies. **1956** M. STEARNS *Story of Jazz* (1957) v. 54 The slaves are apparently singing a French-Creole tune in the French-Creole patois. **1915** J. LONDON *Let.* 18 Sept. (1966) 460, I should like to see you in your *French heeled slippers. **1884** *Sat. Rev.* 7 June 731/1 The good *French-loving servants of her English Majesty. **1951** R. CHANDLER *Let.* 5 Feb. (1962) i. 28, I live in a *French Provincial chateau on Mulholland Drive. **1956** 'E. S. AARONS' *Assignment Treason* (1967) x. 78 There was French provincial furniture, softly glowing with centuries of hand polishing. **1970** *Globe & Mail* (Toronto) 25 Sept. 34/1 (Advt.), Lovely 4-bedroom French provincial home with bath, den, family room, [etc.]. **1598** SYLVESTER *Du Bartas* II. i. III. *Furies* 776 Who bear upon their *French-sick backs [*dessus leurs corps du mal François rongez*]..Farms, Castles, Fees. **1772** T. NUGENT tr. *Hist. Friar Gerund* II. 182 Which have made our..idiom so very French-sick..that [etc.]. **1934** WYNDHAM LEWIS *Let.* 3 July (1963) 219 The *French-spanish border. **1865** KINGSLEY *Herew.* Prel., *French-speaking knights. **1921** H. CRANE *Let.* 16 May (1965) 56 There is a *French-Swiss artist here. **1573** BARET *Alv.* F. 1058 Like a frenchman, or *french wise, *Gallicé*.

B. *absol.* and *sb.*

1. a. The French language, or a specified variety of it. ***pedlar's French***: cant, thieves' slang.

1297 R. GLOUC. (Rolls) 7542 Vor bote a man coone frenss, me telþ of him lute. *c* **1320** *Cast. Love* 25 Ne mowe we alle Latin wite..Ne French. *c* **1380** WYCLIF *Wks.* (1880) 429 Þe worþy reume of fraunse..haþ translatid þe bible..out of lateyn in-to freynsch. *c* **1386** CHAUCER *Prol.* 126 For Frensh of Paris was to hir unknowe. *c* **1483** CAXTON *Vocab.* 2 Frenssh and englissh. **1530** PALSGR. 223/1 Frenche spoken in Burgondy, *wallon*. **1533** MORE *Debell. Salem* Wks. 964/1, I..would also be bold in suche frenche as is peculiare to the lawes of this realm, to leaue it with them in wryting too. **1567** HARMAN *Caveat* 24 Pedlers French or Canting. **1642** HOWELL *For. Trav.* (Arb.) 58 Yet since the last Conquest much French hath got in. **1724** DE FOE *Mem. Cavalier* (1840) 12, I could speak but little French. **1888** F. HUME *Mad. Midas* I. Prol., 'So', he said rapidly in French, 'we are in the land of promise'.

b. Used euphemistically for 'bad language', esp. in the phr. ***excuse*** (or ***pardon***) ***my French!***

1895 [see DURNED]. **1909** J. R. WARE *Passing Eng.* 171/1 *Loosing French*, violent language in English. **1922** JOYCE *Ulysses* 446 Bad French I got for my pains. **1936** M. HARRISON *All Trees were Green* II. 104 A bloody sight better (pardon the French!) than most. **1940** *S.P.E. Tract* IV. 181 *Excuse my French!* (forgive me my strong language). **1955** M. MCCARTHY *Charmed Life* (1956) ii. 52 'Damn fool,' he said, vehemently, 'pardon my French.' **1961** J. O'DONOVAN *Middle Tree* ii. 12 A kick in the arse, smartly administered. .. Excuse my French! **1966** A. LA BERN *Goodbye Piccadilly* xxv. 220 Well I'll be buggered. Excuse my French.

2. a. ***the French*** (pl.): the French people. Also (rarely) without article = French persons. †Formerly with inflexion as sb., pl. ***Frenches***.

1595 SHAKS. *John* III. iv. 173 If but a dozen French Were there in Armes, they [etc.]. **1653** URQUHART *Rabelais* I. xlviii, Such is the nature and complexion of the frenches that they are worth nothing, but at the first push. **1664** PEPYS *Diary* 11 Oct., Captain Titus told us the particulars of the French's expedition against Gigery upon the Barbary coast. **1756-7** tr. *Keysler's Trav.* (1760) IV. 434 Germany bravely defended against the French and Bavarians. **1861** M. PATTISON *Ess.* (1889) I. 32 Our island has indeed been conquered by Italians, and conquered by French.

b. ***French and English***: a children's game.

1823 MOOR *Suffolk Words* 238 English and French—French and English (different games)—Frog in the middle [etc.]. **1858** H. MILLER *Sch. & Schm.* (1858) 76 They could play at 'shinty' and 'French and English', almost within hail of their parents' homesteads.

3. Dry vermouth. Usu. in phr. ***gin and French.***

1938 M. ALLINGHAM *Fashion in Shrouds* xxii. 420 There's some gin and French and a little Advocaat..in the cupboard. **1949** A. WILSON *Wrong Set* 208 'How about that gin..?' he asked. 'It's in the shaker,..with some French.' **1967** M. GILBERT *Dust & Heat* 14 He was drinking double gins with single Frenches in them.

4. Fellatio. *slang.*

1958 MURTAGH & HARRIS *Cast First Stone* (Gloss.), *French, Frenchy*, fellatio. **1968** B. TURNER *Sex Trap* vii. 52 You're not queer, are you?.. I just thought you might want a spot of French if you were. *Ibid.* viii. 64 You can be whipped or caned..or you can have French for another pound. **1969** T. PARKER *Twisting Lane* 203 There's two things I won't let her do though, that's French and sadism.

French (frenʃ), *v. rare.* [f. prec. adj.]

1. *to French it*: to speak French. *nonce-use.*

1639 FULLER *Holy Warre* (1647) IV. xvi. 196 The Turks could not French it so handsomely, but that they were discovered.

2. *trans.* To teach (a person) French. *nonce-use.*

1831 *Examiner* 814/1 Where she had been Frenched, danced, and taught to draw. **1861** [see DEPORTMENTED].

3. To render into French or give a French form to.

1887 *Sat. Rev.* 24 Sept. 435 'I love you' (quite correctly Frenched, '*Je vous aime*'). **1890** *Pall Mall G.* 5 Aug. 3/2 Monte Silvio..was Frenched into Mont Cervin.

†**4.** (See FRENCHED *ppl. a.*) *Obs.*

5. *Cookery.* (See quot.) ? *U.S.*

1895 *Standard Dict.*, *French v.* To prepare, as a chop, by partially cutting the meat from the shank and leaving bare the bone so as to fit it for convenient handling.

6. Of tobacco, cotton, or other plants: to become diseased and distorted. (Cf. FRENCHMAN 4.)

1852 G. N. JONES *Florida Plant. Rec.* (1927) 67 My Corn Crop Looks better than it did Last year; this time it have Frenched a Little I see, in Places. **1888** *Congress. Rec.* 17 May 4069 Then [the cotton-plant] begins to blight, then comes frenching and the shedding of squares and formes.

7. *trans.* and *intr.* To practice fellatio or cunnilingus (with). *slang.*

1958 in Partridge *Dict. Underworld* (1968) 821/1 French, *v.* **1965** W. YOUNG *Eros Denied* xxvii. 271 In England..we call..cunt-licking Frenching. *c* **1965** in Partridge *Dict. Slang Suppl.* (1970) 1146 She thought he was asleep, and Frenched him. **1967** WENTWORTH & FLEXNER *Dict. Amer. Slang* 684 *French*, to commit fellatio or cunnilingus.

French Canadian, *sb.* and *a.* **A.** *sb.*

1. A French settler in Canada or a French-speaking descendant of such a settler; a Canadian of French ancestry.

1758 *Descr. Cape Breton* 4 These *French* Canadians..he represents as an indolent People. **1775** J. ADAIR *Hist. Amer. Indians* 153 The French Canadians are highly censurable.. for debauching our peacable northern Indians, with their infernal catechism. **1838** *Westm. Rev.* XXXI. 405 The Hindoos are a more ignorant and more passive people than the French Canadians. **1876** [see CANADIAN *a.* and *sb.*]. **1935** HUXLEY & HADDON *We Europeans* viii. 261 The stock from which the French Canadians sprang. **1967** *Times* 28 Feb. (Canada Suppl.) 24 If a national break-up were to occur, French-Canadians would face a substantial loss. **1968** *Globe & Mail* (Toronto) 17 Feb. 6/2 Sections of the Quebec press have questioned if this is the proper time in our history for a French Canadian to seek the Prime Ministership.

2. The language of this people.

1929 S. BROWN tr. *Constantin-Weyer's Man scans his Past* 203 He hailed me in French Canadian. **1960** *Amer. Speech* XXXV. 229 In French Canadian the high vowels [i y u] are generally unvoiced in unstressed (nonfinal) position.

B. *adj.* (Now usu. with hyphen.) Of or pertaining to the above or to French Canada.

1775 J. ADAIR *Hist. Amer. Indians* 164 The black tribe, the French Canadian priests. **1822** *Kingston* (Ont.) *Chron.* 23 Nov. 3/4 The pages of some French Canadian papers. **1853** S. STRICKLAND *27 Yrs. Canada West* I. 39 One pair of our horses were French Canadian. **1886, 1897** [see *English-Canadian* s.v. ENGLISH *a.* 2 e]. **1930** *Times Lit. Suppl.* 6 Feb. 106/4 The French-Canadian politicians. **1966** *Times* 28 Feb. (Canada Suppl.) p. vi/4 A sharp revival of French-Canadian nationalism. **1969** HALPERT & STORY *Christmas Mumming in Newfoundland* 112 We may contrast this with the French-Canadian pattern of mumming at Lent.

So **French Canadianism**, (advocacy of) the cultural distinctiveness of French Canada or political separatism in Quebec.

1916 A. BRIDLE *Sons of Canada* 33 One might have naively surmised that..he had renounced some of his French Canadianism. **1962** I. FLEMING *Spy who loved Me* ii. 28 My family had belonged to the very innermost citadel of French-Canadianism.

†**French crown.** *Obs.* The English name for the French coin called ECU, ESCU.

1599 B. JONSON *Ev. Man out of Hum.* II. i, You should give him a French crown for it. **1608** TOPSELL *Serpents* (1658) 715 The powder or dust whereof must be the full weight of a golden groat, or as we say a French Crown.

Comb. **1590** SHAKS. *Mids. N.* I. i. 97 Your Frenche-crowne colour'd beard.

b. Punningly, with reference to the baldness produced by the 'French disease'.

1590 SHAKS. *Mids. N.* I. ii. 99.

†**Frenched**, *ppl. a.* [f. FRENCH *v.* + -ED[1].] Dressed in the French fashion.

1762 GOLDSM. *Cit. W.* cv, Mrs. Tibbs in a new sacque, ruffles, and frenched hair.

Frencher ('frɛnʃə(r)). *contemptuous. rare.* [f. FRENCH *a.* + -ER[1].] A Frenchman.

1826 J. F. COOPER *Last of Mohicans* xx, Why did not the grand Frencher [*sc.* Montcalm]..bury the tomahawks of the Hurons? **1845** *Jonathan Sharp* I. 13 Now, these Frenchers, and even the English, do not understand. **1865** KINGSLEY *Herew.* II. i. 3 The mongrel Frenchers who scoff at the tongue of their forefathers.

Frenchery ('frɛnʃərɪ). [See -ERY.] French goods, fashions, characteristics, etc., collectively.

1593 NASHE *4 Lett. Confut.* Wks. (Grosart) II. 224 A cap case full of French occurrences..When that fly-boat of Frenchery is once launcht, your trenchor attendant.. intends [etc.] **1826** H. N. COLERIDGE *West Indies* 149 Bright island; I have a nook in my heart for thee with all thy Frenchery.

French hood. A head-dress worn by women in the sixteenth and seventeenth centuries.

1541 *St. Papers Hen. VIII*, I. 695 To the Quenes Grace ye must appoynte six frenche hoods, with thappurtenaunces. *a* **1553** UDALL *Royster D.* II. iii. (Arb.) 35 We shall go in our frenche hoodes euery day. **1636** JACKSON in *Hygiasticon* To Translator, For these loose times, when a strict sparing food More's out of fashion then an old French hood.

b. ? A head-dress worn by women when punished for unchastity.

1568 *Durham Depos.* (Surtees) 89 A whipe and a cart and a franc hoode, waies me for the, my lasse.

Frenchie, var. FRENCHY *sb.*

Frenchification ('frɛnʃɪfɪ'keɪʃən). [See -FICATION.] The action of Frenchifying.

1834 *New Monthly Mag.* XL. 226 They had assumed all the Frenchifications possible. **1863** LYTTON *Caxtoniana* II. xxv. 265 Where he [Pope] was deemed by his contemporaries to have improved upon Dryden, it was in the more complete Frenchification of Dryden's Style.

Frenchified ('frɛnʃɪfaɪd), *ppl. a.* [f. next + -ED[1].]

1. *contemptuous.* Having French manners or qualities; French-like.

1597 B. JONSON *Ev. Man out of Hum.* I. i. This is one Monsieur Fastidious Brisk, otherwise called the fresh Frenchified courtier. **1606** *Sir G. Goosecappe* I. i. in Bullen *O. Pl.* III. 8 Can yee not knowe a man from a Marmasett, in theis Frenchified dayes of ours? **1717** D. JONES *Secr. Hist. Whitehall* II. 328 Which Procedure thunderstruck the King and his Frenchify'd Council. **1770** J. LOVE *Cricket* 4 The Frenchifi'd Diversion of Billiards. **1819** *Hermit in Lond.* III. 116 Frenchified John Bull is a would-be butterfly, and a positive blockhead. **1861** THACKERAY *Four Georges* ii. (1876) 51 The home satirists jeered at the Frenchified..ways which they brought back.

†**2.** (See quot. 1659). *Obs.*

1655 CULPEPPER, etc. *Riverius* II. viii. 85 One Man.. whom he suspected to be Frenchified. **1659** TORRIANO, *Rinfrancescáre*, to be or become frenchified, or full of the French-pox. *a* **1700** B. E. *Dict. Cant. Crew*, *Frenchified*, in the French Interest or Mode; also Clapt or Poxt. **1725** in *New Cant. Dict.*

Frenchify ('frɛnʃɪfaɪ), *v.* [f. FRENCH *a.* + -FY.]

1. *trans.* To make French in form or character, imbue with French qualities, render French-like.

1592 GREENE *Upst. Courtier* Wks. (Grosart) XI. 247 Or will you be Frenchefied with a loue locke downe to your shoulders? **1605** VERSTEGAN *Dec. Intell.* viii. (1628) 281 Arnoldsonne was Frenchefied into Fitz-Arnold. **1741** RICHARDSON *Pamela* I. Let. to Editor 13 Reduce our Sterling Substance into an empty Shadow, or rather frenchify our English Solidity into Froth and Whip-syllabub. **1761** *Chron.* in *Ann. Reg.* 125/2 They dressed him in a bag-wig..frenchified him up. **1852** MACAULAY in *Life & Lett.* (1883) II. 363 What a quantity of French words have I used! I suppose that the subject Frenchifies my style.

2. *intr.* To become French in ideas, manners, etc.; to have French sympathies.

1775 J. JEKYLL *Corr.* 19 Aug. (1894) 46 'Tis in these domesticated visits one Frenchifies most. **1799** *European Mag.* XXXVI. 60 What astonishes me most is, that this custom of Frenchifying should be so prevalent among us.

Frenchism ('frɛnʃɪz(ə)m). [f. FRENCH *a.* + -ISM.] A French custom, idiom, or characteristic; a Gallicism.

1750 H. WALPOLE *Lett. H. Mann* (1834) II. 306 It is very amusing though very full of Frenchisms.

Frenchize ('frɛnʃaɪz), *v.* [f. as prec. + -IZE.] *trans.* To turn into French.

1887 *Athenæum* 26 Mar. 421/2 Kill-devil (Frenchized into *guildive*). **1887** FURNIVALL *R. Brunne's Chron. Wace* (Rolls) I. 2 *marg.*, Master Wace frenchized all the Latin Brute till Cadwallader's time.

French leave. Originally, the custom (in the 18th c. prevalent in France and sometimes imitated in England) of going away from a reception, etc. without taking leave of the host or hostess. Hence, jocularly, *to take French leave* is to go away, or do anything, without permission or notice.

1771 SMOLLETT *Humph. Clinker* (1895) 238 He stole away an Irishman's bride, and took a French leave of me and his master. **1772** *Town & Country Mag.* 33 She..left Fanny with French leave. **1775** J. JEKYLL *Corr.* (1894) 28 [French etiquettes] are precise to a degree..I will allow that..*taking French leave* (which gains ground even among us at present) is easy and natural. But, on the contrary..there is more formality..in *entering* one assembly here [France] than in taking the round of routs for a whole winter in London. **1775** TRUSLER *Chesterfield's Princ. Politeness* (ed. 4) 72 As the taking what is called a French leave was introduced that on one person's leaving the company the rest might not be disturbed, looking at your watch does what that piece of politeness was designed to prevent. **1821** W. GIFFORD in Smiles *J. Murray* (1891) II. xxi. 55 The few teeth I have seem taking their leave—I wish they would take a French one. **1866** MRS. H. WOOD *St. Martin's Eve* xiii, Her roving son had taken French leave to go back to London.

Frenchless ('frɛnʃlɪs), *a.* [f. FRENCH *sb.* + -LESS.] Having no French.

1818 MOORE *Fudge Fam. Paris* ix. 26 As for me, a Frenchless grub, At Congress never born to stammer. **1894** *Sat. Rev.* 3 Mar. 230 The rest [of the *Romaunt of the Rose*] has to go in double columns of smaller type, Frenchless.

French-like, *adv.* and *a.* [f. as prec. + LIKE.]

A. *adv.* After the manner of the French people; in French fashion.

c **1550** CHEKE *Matt.* xviii. 17 *note*, We folowing y[e] greek calle yis house, as y[e] north doth yet moor truli sound it, y[e] kurk, and we moor corruptli and frenchlike, y[e] church. **1597-8** BP. HALL *Sat.* III. vii. 34 His haire, French-like, stares on his frighted hed. **1632** LITHGOW *Trav.* III. 126 Whatsoever extortion or injury they use against him, he must be French-like contented, bowing his head, and making a counterfeit shew of thankes.

B. *adj.* Like the French.

1848 in CRAIG.

Frenchly ('frɛnʃlɪ), (*a.*) *adv.* [f. FRENCH *a.* + -LY.] †**A.** *adj.* (See quot.) *Obs.*—[0] **B.** *adv.* In a French manner, French-like.

1513 DOUGLAS *Æneis* I. Prol. 269 This wther buik.. Quhilk, ondir colour of sum Franch strang wicht, So frenschlie leis, oneth twa wourdis gais richt. **1530** PALSGR. 313/1 Frenchely belongyng to the countrey of Fraunce *Gaule Gallican.* **1559** *Mirr. Mag.* (1563) *Salisbury* xxxii, And they as frenchly took them selues to flyght. **1599** H. BUTTES *Dyets Dry Dinner* P iv, Go Frenchly: Duchly drink: breath Indianly. **1847** MRS. F. TROLLOPE *Three Cousins* (1866) 33 A word too Frenchly expressive to admit of translation. **1882** MISS WOOLSON *Anne* xxii. 344 He only smiled..and Frenchly shrugged his shoulders!

Frenchman ('frɛnʃmən). [f. FRENCH *a.* + MAN. In early use two words.]

1. a. A man of French birth or nationality.

O.E. Chron. an. 1052 (Laud MS.), þa Francisce menn. *c* **1205** LAY. 7663 Ælc Frensc mon þe wes aht hæfð hine seolfne bi-þoht. *a* **1300** *Cursor M.* 239 Mast es it wroght for frankis man. **1382** WYCLIF *Sel. Wks.* III. 516 Sharper enemys and traitours þan Frensshe men and alle oþere nacIouns. **1480** CAXTON *Chron. Eng.* ccxliv. (1482) 295 The kyng..was wonder sore agreued and right euyll payed toward the frensshmen. **1545** ASCHAM *Toxoph.* (Arb.) 79 The spanyardes, franchmen and germanes. **1607** TOPSELL *Four-f. Beasts* 125 The breast is by the Frenchmen called peculiarly *Hampan.* **1782** COWPER *Truth* 303 The Frenchman first in literary fame. **1841** T. A. TROLLOPE *Summer W. France* I. i. 5 The generality of Frenchmen, too, are naturally averse to travelling.

†**b.** Incorrectly used for: An ancient Gaul.

1387 TREVISA *Higden* (Rolls) III. 271 Afterward he come and brak the siege of Frensche men [*Gallorum*]. **1513** DOUGLAS *Æneis* VIII. xi. 35 How the Franchemen did the ȝet assaill. **1600** HOLLAND *Livy* XXII. lvii. 467 A Frenchman together with a French woman.

2. A (good, etc.) French scholar. *colloq.*

1670 COTTON *Espernon* Pref., The greater part of them being better Frenchmen, than I pretend to be. **1828** BENTHAM Wks. 1843 I. 247 The subject was not without its difficulties; the language French: I am but a sorry Frenchman now; I was, I imagine, not quite so bad an one then.

3. A French ship.

1889 *Daily News* 21 Oct. 6/5 The vessel..proved to be a Frenchman.

†**4.** In Virginian tobacco-raising (see quot. 1688).

1688 J. CLAYTON in *Phil. Trans.* XVII. 948 French-men they call those Plants, whose leaves do not spread and grow large, but rather spire upwards, and grow tall. **1896** P. A. BRUCE *Econ. Hist. Virginia* I. 439 The plants..showed..a tendency to lag in their growth and to take a spiral shape. For this reason they were always referred to as 'Frenchmen', a people who were associated in the Virginian mind with tallness and attenuation in form.

5. A knife used in pointing brickwork.

1885 *Spons' Mechanics' Own Bk.* 591 This Frenchman is simply an old dinner-knife ground to a point, the tip of which is turned down square to form a hook. **1934** T. S. ELIOT *Rock* i. 22 Fancy anyone not knowin' that a Frenchman's a pointin' tool!

6. The French or red-legged partridge, *Alectoris rufa.*

1893 *Baily's Mag.* Oct. 258/1 The red leg, the very much-abused 'Frenchman' of the English fields. **1920** F. M. OGLIVIE *Field Observ. Brit. Birds* 58 A Frenchman..has a loud, combative call. **1965** P. WAYRE *Wind in Reeds* iii. 41 If they are Frenchmen, they may refuse to fly and simply run in front of the dog.

Hence '**Frenchmanlike** *a.* and *adv.*

1807 W. TAYLOR in *Ann. Rev.* V. 560 The character of Orasmane is somewhat too chivalrous and Frenchmanlike for an Eastern sultan. **1827** SOUTHEY *Penins. War* II. 419 Frenchmen like, they had a theatre in their camp.

[**frenchmore**, error for TRENCHMORE.]

Frenchness ('frɛnʃnɪs). [f. FRENCH *a.* + -NESS.] The quality or state of being French or of displaying French characteristics.

1816 SOUTHEY in *Q. Rev.* XIV. 357 The nauseating frenchness (if we may so call it) of the French stage. **1850** *Chamb. Jrnl.* XIV. 257 We are not so much inclined to smile at the Frenchness of the notion.

†**french-peire.** *Obs. rare.* [a. OF. *franche peere*, freestone.] = FREESTONE.

1593 *Rites of Durh.* (Surtees) 5 The two dores in the said French Peire dores.

French polish.

1. A polish for wood-work (see quot. 1874).

1819 *P.O. Lond. Direct.* 367 Wheeler, T., Warehouse for Bentley & Co's French Polish. **1874** KNIGHT *Dict. Mech.* I. 915 *French polish*, a solution of resin or gum resin in alcohol or wood naptha.

2. 'The smooth glossy surface produced on cabinet-work by the application of this substance' (Ogilv.).

Hence **French-polish** *v. trans.*, to make smooth and glossy with French-polish, *lit.* and *fig.*; **French-polished** *ppl. a.* Also **French-polisher**, one who French-polishes (furniture, etc.).

1836 DICKENS *Sk. Boz* (1837) I. 132 You could.. French-polish yourself on any one of the chairs. **1847** ALB. SMITH *Chr. Tadpole* iv. (1879) 40 Houses of rustling brocade and French-polished mahogany. **1858** SIMMONDS *Dict. Trade, French-polisher.* **1863** KINGSLEY *Water Bab.* 144 A shoal of porpoises.. all quite smooth and shiny, because the fairies French-polish them every morning. **1879** *Daily News* 7 Apr. 3/1 Their boat.. has just been left by the French polisher.

punningly. **1886** RUSKIN *Præterita* I. vi. 202 The modern German-plated and French-polished tourist.

'Frenchwoman. A woman of France; also misapplied, †a woman of ancient Gaul.

1593 SHAKS. *2 Hen. VI,* I. iii. 143 Was't I? yea, I it was, prowd French-woman. **1600** [see FRENCHMAN 1 b]. **1870** EMERSON *Soc. & Solit.* vii. 148 As was said of the letters of the Frenchwomen.

Frenchy ('frɛnʃɪ), *a.* (*adv.*) and *sb.* Also **Frenchie.** [f. FRENCH *a.* + -Y.]

A. *adj.* Characteristic of what is French (as opposed to English, etc.); French-like.

1826 H. N. COLERIDGE *West Indies* 148 St. Pierre is a pretty.. town.. it is neat and Frenchy. *a* **1828** D. WORDSWORTH *Tour Continent* in *Jrnls.* (1941) II. 318 A long Village—frenchy in the better style. **1856** EMERSON *Eng. Traits, Lit.* Wks. (Bohn) II. 103 The Englishman.. prefers his hot chop.. to the.. amplest and Frenchiest bill-of-fare. **1950** J. CANNAN *Murder Included* iii. 57 People will suspect Bunny just because she's Frenchy. **1967** C. O. SKINNER *Madame Sarah* viii. 147 Word had gotten about that the plays in her repertoire were 'Frenchy', meaning naughty.

B. *sb.* A disrespectful name for a Frenchman or a French Canadian.

1883 MISS YONGE *Stray Pearls* II. xvi. 267 The squires had begun by calling him Frenchy. **1891** J. OXLEY *Chore-Boy of Camp Kippewa* 74, I wouldn't give him for half a dozen of those *parlez vous* Frenchies. **1895** *Daily News* 27 Dec. 7/3 Of what nationality is he, then?—Witness: Why, I think he's a Frenchy. **1905** BARONESS ORCZY *Scarlet Pimpernel* xii. 117 We seek him here, we seek him there, Those Frenchies seek him everywhere. **1916** 'BOYD CABLE' *Action Front* 89 Now I wonder who it is. A Frenchie by his tunic sleeve. **1955** *Times* 23 May 3/1 Bobbing up now here, now there, he seeks these Frenchies everywhere in Lisbon. **1965** H. GOLD *Man who was not with It.* i. 3 There he is on the midway, Grack the Frenchie, talking for his countstore. **1966** *Maclean's* 2 May 50/4, I was constantly laughed at, pointed at and corrected, as a stupid Frenchy.

Hence **'Frenchily** *adv.*; **'Frenchiness.**

1881 *Lit. World* (Boston) 21 May 179/2 This [book] is an excellent piece of work, true to its title. Its strain is Frenchily enthusiastic. **1890** *Pall Mall G.* 29 Jan. 3/3 This worship of Frenchiness I would brand as.. unworthy of cultured Englishwomen.

frend, obs. form of FRIEND.

†**'frendent,** *a. Obs. rare*⁻¹. [ad. L. *frendent-em*, pr. pple. of *frendĕre* to gnash the teeth.] Gnashing the teeth.

1630 LANE *Cont. Sqr.'s T.* 204 (Ashm. MS.) His frendent horse of manie colors pied.

frenesy, obs. and dial. form of FRENZY, q.v.

frenetic, etc.: see PHRENETIC, etc.

frenge, frenȝe, obs. forms of FRINGE.

†**fre'nigerent,** *a. Obs.*⁻⁰ [L. *frēniger* bridle-bearing: for the termination cf. *belligerent*.]

1656–81 BLOUNT *Glossogr., Frenigerent,* that ruleth the bridle.

†**frenne, fren,** *a.* and *sb. Obs.* [A corrupt form of *frend*, FREMD, influenced by etymologizing association with *forenne*, FOREIGN.]

A. *adj.* Strange, not related. *rare*⁻¹.

1553 GRIMALDE *Cicero's Offices* I. (1558) 21 They conuey those same riches to frenne folke: which it were more reason bothe to bee delt and left to their kinsfolke.

B. *sb.* A foreigner, stranger, enemy.

1579 SPENSER *Sheph. Cal.* Apr. 28 So now his frend is chaunged for a frenne [**1597** fren]. *Gloss., Frenne,* a straunger. The word I thinke was.. poetically put, and afterwarde vsed in common custome of speech for forenne. **1614** DAVIES *Eclogue* in *Browne's Past.*, If frennes forbeare at home hem to inuade, They wry their peace to noy each other.

frenular *a.*, **frenulum:** see FRÆNULUM.

frenum: see FRÆNUM.

†**'frenzic,** *a. Obs. rare.* In 6 frensyke, -icke, -eke. [f. FRENZY *sb.* + -IC.] = FRENZICAL. Hence **'frenzicness.**

1547 RECORDE *Judic. Ur.* 27 But if the pacyent be frensyke.. it doth most commynly betoken death. *Ibid.*, If it be in a burnyng Ague, it is a token of frensycknesse. **1570** LEVINS *Manip.* 54 Frenseke. *Ibid.* 121 Frensicke.

†**'frenzical,** *a. Obs.* Also 6 fransical, 8 phrensical. [f. as prec. + -AL¹.] Affected with, characterized by, or of the nature of frenzy; crazy, mad; wildly enthusiastic.

a **1586** SIDNEY *Wanstead Play* in *Arcadia*, etc. (1629) 619 A certaine fransical maladie they call Loue. **1677** GILPIN *Demonol.* (1867) 50 Their scorns shall have no more impression upon us than the ravings of a frenzical person that knows not what he speaks. **1720** W. GIBSON *Diet. Horses* vii. (1731) 111 When a horse is poisoned.. he will.. sometimes be Phrenzical and delirious. **1748** RICHARDSON *Clarissa* (1811) V. viii. 96 Such a passion.. as might confirm the intimation I had given of a phrensical disorder.

frenzied ('frɛnzɪd), *ppl. a.* [f. FRENZY *v.* + -ED¹.] Affected with or characterized by frenzy; crazy, mad; distracted, frantic; wildly enthusiastic.

1796 JANE WEST *Gossip's Story* I. 156 His troubl'd soul to phrensy'd rage By fancy'd wrong was stung. **1796–7** COLERIDGE *Sonn., To Author of 'The Robbers'*, Wandering at eve with finely frenzied eye. **1808** SCOTT *Marm.* I. xxix, St. Fillan's blessed well, Whose springs can frenzied dreams dispel. **1838** DICKENS *Nich. Nick.* xxviii, He danced in a frenzied manner round the sofa. **1874** L. STEPHEN *Hours in Library* (1892) I. ix. 312 Gatherings of frenzied enthusiasts.

Hence **'frenziedly** *adv.*, in a frenzied manner.

1856 KANE *Arct. Expl.* I. xiv. 158 They bark frenziedly at nothing.

frenzy, phrenzy ('frɛnzɪ), *sb.* and *a.* Forms: α. 4–6 frenesie, -ye, 4 frenesi, frensye, fransie, -ye, (4–5 frenise, 5 frenysye, franesie, 6 frenyse, franzie), 4–7 frenesy, 5–6 fransey, 6–7 frensie, -zie, (7 frensey), 5–9 frensy, (6 frenesi, fransy, -zy, 6–7 frenc(e)y), 7– frenzy. β. 6–7 phrenesie, -ye, phrensie, -zie, 6–9 phrensy, (9 -esy), 7– phrenzy. See also PHRENESIS. [ME. *frenesie*, a. OF. *frenesie* (F. *frénésie*) = Pr. *frenezia*, It. *frenesia*, f. late L. *phrenēsis* (whence directly Pr. *frenezi*, Sp. *frenesí*, Pg. *frenesi*), a pseudo-Gr. formation (on the analogy of pairs of related words in -ησις, -ητικός) after *phrenēticus*, corruption of Gr. φρενιτικός: see FRANTIC.

The spelling with *ph-* is now rare; some writers show a tendency to prefer it when the reference is to prophetic ecstasy or demoniacal possession.]

A. *sb.*

1. Mental derangement; delirium, or temporary insanity; in later use chiefly the uncontrollable rage or excitement of paroxysm of mania. Now somewhat *rare* in lit. sense.

α. *c* **1340** HAMPOLE *Prose Tr.* (1866) 17 A fantasie caused of trubblyng of þe brayne, as a mane þat es in a frensye. **1398** TREVISA *Barth. De P.R.* VII. v. (1495) 225 Frensy is an hote postume in certayn skynnes and felles of the brayne, and therto folowyth wakynge and rauyng. *c* **1440** HYLTON *Scala Perf.* (W. de W. 1494) II. xxii, Thou shalt fall in to syckenes or in to fantasyes or in to frenesyes. **1549** *Compl. Scot.* xv. 124, I may compair them til ane man in ane frenyse, quhilk bytis his auen membris vitht his tetht. **1674** MILTON *P.L.* (ed. 2) XI. 485 Demoniac frenzy, moping melancholy, And moon-struck madness. **1713** SWIFT *Frenzy of J. Denny* Wks. 1755 III. I. 138 An officer of the custom house, who was taken ill of a violent frenzy last April. **1794** COLERIDGE *On a Friend who died of a Fever* 17 Till frenzy.. Darts her hot lightning-flash athwart the brain. **1838** THIRLWALL *Greece* V. 219 He must have been subject to temporary fits of frenzy.

β. **1562** TURNER *Herbal* II. 133 b, Rinning thyme.. is.. good.. for the phrenesye. **1597** HOOKER *Eccl. Pol.* V. iii. §1 They thinke and doe as it were in a phrensie they know not what. *a* **1617** BAYNE *On Eph.* (1658) 82 Through phrenzie out of our right minds. **1793** HOLCROFT tr. *Lavater's Physiog.* i. 8 Should the light by being brought too close to his eyes produce phrensy, he may burn himself. **1835** THIRLWALL *Greece* I. iv. 111 The women of Argos were struck with phrenzy.

2. *fig.* Agitation or disorder of the mind likened to madness; a state of delirious fury, rage, enthusiasm, or the like; also, wild folly, distraction, craziness.

α. [*c* **1386** CHAUCER *Sompn. T.* 501, I hold him in a maner frenesye.] ? *a* **1400** *Morte Arth.* 3827 He felle in a fransye for fersenesse of herte. *c* **1422** HOCCLEVE *Jereslaus' Wife* 715 The Shipman had also the franesie, þat with this Emperice hadde ment ffulfillid his foul lust of aduoutrie. **1532** MORE *Confut. Tindale* Wks. 605/2 Happy were Tindall, if he were as well recouered of his fransies. **1590** SHAKS. *Mids. N.* V. i. 12 The Poets eye in a fine frenzy rolling. **1698** FRYER *Acc. E. India & P.* 266 That the Immortal Gods should be.. pleased with such Wickedness, is the highest Frenzy to believe. **1791** PAINE *Rights of Man* (ed. 4) 8 When the tongue or the pen is let loose in a frenzy of passion. **1837** W. IRVING *Capt. Bonneville* II. 231 The sight inspired almost a frenzy of delight. **1849** MACAULAY *Hist. Eng.* I. 234 Some hot-headed Roman Catholic, driven to frenzy by the lies of Oates. **1871** FREEMAN *Norm. Conq.* (1876) IV. xviii. 112 An act done in the mere frensy of despair.

β. *c* **1665** MRS. HUTCHINSON *Mem. Col. Hutchinson* (1846) 379 *note*, His moderation in a time of phrenzy was surely a sufficient argument. **1795** WINDHAM *Speeches Parl.* 5 Jan. (1812) I. 264 With all the phrenzy and fondness which men usually shew to their most extravagant opinions. **1813** SCOTT *Rokeby* I. xii, I could have laughed.. To see, in phrenesy sublime, How the fierce zealots fought and bled. **1855** H. REED *Lect. Eng. Hist.* ix. 287 The king, probably to save his life from the phrensy of faction, banished him.

b. A crazy notion or wild idea; also, a craze or mania (*for* something).

1632 J. HAYWARD tr. *Biondi's Eromena* 126 A new phrensie being come into his head of getting the Princesse. **1707** *Curios. in Husb. & Gard.* 13 Whom the Frensy of Travelling never carry'd into Foreign Lands. **1761** HUME *Hist. Eng.* III. lx. 291 Accustomed to indulge every chimera in politics, every frenzy in religion.

3. *attrib.* and *Comb.*, as ***frenzy-pointed, -rolling*** adjs.; **frenzy-fever,** a fever attended with delirium, ? brain-fever.

1613 PURCHAS *Pilgrimage* (1614) 903 Had halfe his people on this Coast sicke of shaking, burning, *frenzie-fevers. **1806** *Antid. Mis. Hum. Life* 111 [She] was seized with the scarlet fever, from which she was scarcely recovered when she was attacked by a still more formidable one, a frensy fever. **1835** TALFOURD *Ion* II. iii, The dull groan and *frenzy-pointed shriek Pass them unheard to heaven. **1777** WARTON *Ode* viii. 54 To bid her visions meet the *frenzy-rolling eye.

Hence †**'frenziful** *a.*, affected with frenzy.

1726 DE FOE *Hist. Devil* I. iv, All these pretences of frenziful and fanciful people.

B. *adj.* [? attrib. use of the sb.]

†**1.** Mad, insane, crazy. *Obs.*

1577 tr. *Bullinger's Decades* (1592) 205 He that bindeth a phrensie man, and waketh him that is sick of the lethargie, doth trouble them both, and yet he loueth them both. **1616** S. WARD *Serm.* (1635) 337 All these sharpers have but a frensie mans sleepe. **1647** TRAPP *Comm. Matt.* v. 44 Saunders.. being sent to prison by Stephen Gardner.. (who bad, Carry away this phrensie-fool, etc.).

2. *dial.* Angry; of a violent temper, passionate.

1859 GEO. ELIOT *A. Bede* x, I daresay ye warna franzy, for ye look as if ye'd ne'er been angered i' your life. **1876** *S. Warw. Gloss., Franzy,* passionate. **1884** *Chester Gloss., Franzy,* irritable.

Hence †**'frenzily** *adv.*, †**'frenziness.**

1594 T. B. tr. *La Primaud. Fr. Acad.* II. 310 Vehement anger is often accompanied with frensinesse. *a* **1688** BUNYAN *Wks.* (1692) I. 427/1 How frenzily he imagins!

frenzy ('frɛnzɪ), *v.* [f. FRENZY *sb.*] *trans.* To drive (a person) to frenzy, infuriate.

1810 A. BOSWELL *Edinburgh* 155 A poet.. Frenzied by change of manners and town fashion, Rails at the change. **1857** BUCKLE *Civiliz.* I. vii. 439 The people, frenzied by centuries of oppression, practised the most revolting cruelties. **1872** *Daily News* 18 Mar., The bare thought.. frenzies him to the verge of madness.

Hence **'frenzying** *ppl. a.*

1795 SOUTHEY *Joan of Arc* II. 270 Ever and anon Some mother raised o'er her expiring child A cry of frenzying anguish. **1821** SHELLEY *Prometh. Unb.* I. 267 Rain then thy plagues.. Ghastly disease and frenzying fear.

Freon ('friːɒn). Also **freon.** Proprietary name for any of a group of partially or completely halogenated simple hydrocarbons containing fluorine and usu. chlorine or bromine, used esp. as refrigerants and aerosol propellants.

1932 *Industr. & Engin. Chem.* XXIV. 620 Freon.. was developed in a deliberate attempt to produce, by chemical arrangement, a refrigerant.. which still has properties especially favorable to economic operation. **1941** *Archit. Rev.* XC. 52 Cooling is provided by refrigerating compressors, using Freon gas, a safe and harmless refrigerant. **1945** *Electronic Engin.* XVII. 762 Insulation is provided by freon gas. **1950** J. D. PARK in J. H. Simons *Fluorine Chem.* I. xv. 527 The structures of most of the 'Freons' having from one to five carbon atoms. **1959** *Trade Marks Jrnl.* 25 Feb. 220/2 *Freon,* fluorinated hydrocarbons being chemical substances for use as propellents for aerosols. E. J. Du Pont de Nemours and Company. **1966** *McGraw-Hill Encycl. Sci. & Technol.* V. 501/1 The most popular freons are Freon-11 and Freon-12. **1967** *Jane's Surface Skimmer Systems 1967–68* 106/1 The pilothouse.. and berthing spaces are air-conditioned during the cooling season by a 13 ton capacity freon type compressor system. **1968** *New Scientist* 25 July 197/1 Freons, the halogenated varieties of methane and ethane.. are pretty inert chemically.

freprie, obs. form of FRIPPERY.

frequence ('friːkwəns). [a. F. *fréquence*, ad. L. *frequentia*, f. *frequent-em*: see FREQUENT and -ENCE.].

1. An assembling in large numbers; a crowded state or condition; also *concr.* concourse, crowd, assembled throng. *Obs.* exc. *arch.*

1535 J. AP RICE in *Four C. Eng. Lett.* 33 There was here suche frequence of women commyng and reassorting to this monastery. **1579** FULKE *Confut. Sanders* 542 The great multitude of people in that church, by reason of the frequens of the imperial city. *a* **1656** BP. HALL *Rem. Wks.* (1660) 11, I was encouraged with a sufficient frequence of Auditors. **1671** MILTON *P.R.* I. 128 The Most High who, in full frequence bright Of angels, thus to Gabriel smiling spake. **1835** BROWNING *Paracelsus* II. 242 Hold me before the frequence of Thy seraphs. **1871** —— *Balaust.* 2001 He.. knew the friendly frequence there.

†**2.** Constant use of (something); familiarity, close acquaintance. *Obs.*

1603 FLORIO *Montaigne* II. xxxvii. (1632) 428 [He] submitted himselfe to that arte [medicine].. by reason of the frequence he had in other Sciences. **1617** BP. HALL *Quo Vadis* xx. 79 Besides the ordinary practise of Idolatry, and frequence of oathes. **1624** —— *Rem. Wks.* (1660) 4 Oh ye foolish Israelites with whom too much frequence made the food of Angels contemptible.

3. Frequent occurrence or repetition.

1603 FLORIO *Montaigne* III. v. 522 The long-continued frequence of this accident, should by this time have seasoned the bitter taste thereof. **1641** *Answ. Vind. Smectymnuus* Pref. 1 Bemoaning the frequence of scandalous Pasquins. **1868** BROWNING *Ring & Bk.* VI. 1136 Ever some spiritual witness new and new In faster frequence. **1889** L. KEITH *Hurric. Petticoats* I. x. 212 The granny.. wakes up to tell it [her story] anew with a zest that is never staled by frequence.

†**b.** *Physics.* = FREQUENCY 4 b. *Obs. rare*⁻¹.

1748 HARTLEY *Observ. Man* I. ii. 119 Vibrations of different Kinds, or Frequences.

frequency ('friːkwənsɪ). [ad. L. *frequentia*: see prec. and -ENCY.]

†**1.** The state or condition of being crowded; also *concr.* a numerous assembly, concourse, crowd.

1553–87 FOXE *A. & M.* (1596) 196/1 The king commanded all the.. prelats of the church to be called in a great solemn frequencie. **1570–6** LAMBARDE *Peramb. Kent* (1826) 201 To Pinnendene Heath.. expert men of this Shyre.. came in great frequencie. **1601** R. JOHNSON *Kingd. & Commw.* (1603) 114 Nothing doth better temper the aire of any place than the frequency of inhabitants. **1644** MILTON *Jdgm. Bucer* (1851) 290 He was for two years chief Professor ..with greatest frequency and applause of all learned and pious men. **1723** *State of Russia* I. 209 The frequency of People at Moskow was extraordinary on this Occasion.

†**2.** The fact of occurring at short distances apart; numerousness. *Obs.*

1659 B. HARRIS *Parival's Iron Age* 45 The enemies army could not enter, in regard of the frequency of great rivers.

†**3. a.** The constant use or repetition *of* (something); frequent practice. *Obs.*

1615 J. STEPHENS *Satyr. Ess.* 69 The patronage of Plebeians..The frequencie of which custome made Nobilitie famous. **1682** NORRIS *Hierocles* 14 Neither does this precept of honouring an Oath forbid us Perjury only, but also frequency of Swearing. **1688** S. PENTON *Guardian's Instr.* 59 Oblige him to frequency of Writing Home. **1785** SARAH FIELDING *Ophelia* II. xviii, The frequency of vice had deadened her sense of it.

†**b.** Frequent intercourse, familiarity *with* (a person); constant attendance *at* (a place). *Obs.*

1642 HOWELL *For. Trav.* (Arb.) 21 The greatest bane of English Gentlemen abroad, is too much frequency and communication with their own Countrey-men. **1680** LD. CAPEL *Sp. Ho. Com.* 26 Oct. in *Collect. Poems* 179 Who by his frequency at the Palace, had seemed rather one of the Family.

4. a. The fact of occurring often or being repeated at short intervals. Of the pulse: Rapidity.

1641 LD. J. DIGBY *Sp. Ho. Com.* 19 Jan. 20 The frequencie of Parliament is most essentially necessary. **1696** tr. *Du Mont's Voy. Levant* 226 Earthquakes..there happen'd four in one day..Nor does their frequency make 'em less dreadful. **1732** ARBUTHNOT *Rules of Diet* 272 They increase the Strength and Frequency of the Pulse. **1766** GOLDSM. *Vic. W.* vii, I began..to be displeased with the frequency of his return. **1836** HOR. SMITH *Tin Trumpet* (1876) 271 The diminished frequency of wars. **1883** A. JESSOPP in *19th Cent.* XIII. 259 The ghastly frequency of the punishment of death tended to make people savage and bloodthirsty.

b. *Physics*, etc. The rate of recurrence of any regularly repeated event, *e.g.* a vibration; the number of times that it occurs in a second or other assumed unit of time. In *Telecommunications*, the number of cycles per second of the carrier wave of a transmission; hence *loosely*, a frequency band, a channel. Also, a signal, or a component of a signal, having a frequency of a certain value or in a certain range.

1831 BREWSTER *Nat. Magic* ix. (1868) 287 The pitch or frequency of vibration constituting the note. **1835** *Rep. Brit. Assoc. 1834* 315 The colour of the light is supposed to be determined by the frequency of the ethereal vibrations, or by the length of the wave. **1881** *Nature* No. 616. 359 If the notes *c'* and *d''* are sounded together, their frequencies being in the ratio 8:9. **1893** *Times* 11 May 6/1 Alternating currents of high frequency. **1896** W. G. WOOLLCOMBE *Pract. Work Physics* III. 69 Take the average of these numbers for each fork to represent the ratio of their frequencies. **1943** C. L. BOLTZ *Basic Radio* viii. 133 A succession of such circuits will attenuate the higher frequencies so much that their amplitude is negligible. **1948** P. M. MORSE *Vibration & Sound* (ed. 2) vi. 226 Corresponding to the physical quantities intensity and frequency are the physiological..quantities loudness and pitch. **1958** *Radio Times* 14 Feb. 3/2 To make sure that the BBC keeps strictly to the frequencies (or wavelengths), both in sound and television broadcasting, allotted to it by international agreement. **1958** 'N. SHUTE' *Rainbow & Rose* i. 7 We've been monitoring their frequency. **1962** *Which?* Feb. 41/2 Sound travels in the form of waves—rather like radio waves, but of a far lower frequency. *Ibid.* 42/1 The other VHF radios would reproduce frequencies higher than 4,200 cycles per second, but only at a lower volume. **1971** *Daily Tel.* 7 Jan. 14/6 Enough radio frequencies could be made available on the medium wave to satisfy commercial radio and the existing BBC local stations.

c. *Statistics.* The number of times an event or character occurs in a given sample; also (the ***relative*** or ***proportionate frequency***), this number expressed as a proportion of the total possible number of occurrences.

1854 G. BOOLE *Invest. Laws of Thought* xvii. 268 For if we substitute..we shall form the expression of that event whose probability constitutes the numerator of *c*, and the ratio of the frequency of this event to that of the former one ..will give the value of *c*. **1857** *Phil. Mag.* 4th Ser. XIV. 61, I have commenced collecting statistics showing the relative frequency with which the different simple letters, and various compounds of simple letters, occur in the English language. **1875** F. GALTON in *Ibid.* XLIX. 37 We may work backwards, and, from the relative frequency of occurrence of various magnitudes, derive a knowledge of the true relative values of those magnitudes, expressed in units of probable error. **1937** L. H. C. TIPPETT *Methods of Statistics* (ed. 2) i. 28 Frequencies and proportionate frequencies underlie nearly all methods of statistical representation. **1943** M. G. KENDALL *Adv. Theory Statistics* I. vii. 165 The second approach seeks to define probability in terms of the relative frequency of events. **1950** W. FELLER *Introd. Probability Theory* I. i. 18 The frequency of multiple aces in the hands at bridge. **1955** M. LOÈVE *Probability Theory* i. 5 In a game of dice..'double-six' occurs about once in 36 times, that is, its observed frequencies cluster about 1/36. The number 1/36 is a permanent numerical property of 'double-six' under the conditions of the game, and the observed frequencies are to be thought of as measurements of the property. **1965** A. H. ROBERTS *Statistical Ling. Anal. Amer. Eng.* v. 60 These 8,103 words had a total frequency of 10,503,788 or ⅞ of the total frequencies of occurence.

d. *Ecol.* A measurement of the way individuals of a species are distributed in a community.

1913 C. RAUNKIAER in *Jrnl. Ecol.* I. 24 Each species acquires the same degree of frequency as in a shoot-counting method if the frequency be expressed in whole numbers from 1 to 5. **1921** *Jrnl. Ecol.* IX. 97 If we know the absolute degree of frequency of a species (that is the number of individuals belonging to one species growing on a large area Y) we can calculate the probable occurrence on every area (y) which is smaller than Y. **1932** *Ecol. Monogr.* II. 478 Frequency is concerned with the uniformity with which the plants of a species are distributed throughout a plant community. *Ibid.* 479 The percentage is called the 'frequency index' of the species. **1964** K. A. KERSHAW *Quantitative & Dynamic Ecology* i. 16 The frequency of a species is a measure of the chance of finding it with any one throw of a quadrat in a given area. Thus, if a species has a frequency of 10 per cent then it should occur once in every ten quadrats examined.

5. *attrib.* and *Comb.*, as (sense 4 b) ***frequency characteristic, correction, -dependent*** adj., ***discriminator, divider, doubler, indicator, meter, multiplier, -multiplying*** ppl. adj., ***raiser, range, -selective*** adj., ***teller, transformer***; (sense 4 c) ***frequency-count.***

1926 *Frequency characteristic [see *frequency response*]. **1957** *BBC Handbk.* 49 Sound circuits have to be equalized in frequency characteristic. **1962** A. NISBETT *Technique Sound Studio* i. 17 (*caption*) Between studio, continuity and transmitter there may be..switching centres, boosting amplifers and *frequency correction networks on land-lines, etc. *Ibid.* 254 *Frequency correction*, the change in the frequency characteristics of a signal which is required to restore it to its original form. **1956** J. WHATMOUGH *Language* v. 73 The 20,000 most frequently occurring words (as ascertained by previously made *frequency counts). **1962** W. B. THOMPSON *Introd. Plasma Physics* ii. 14 Thus the plasma appears as a dielectric with a *frequency-dependent dielectric coefficient. **1935** *Frequency discriminator [see DISCRIMINATOR 2 b]. **1943** *Gloss. Terms Telecomm.* (*B.S.I.*) 73 *Frequency discriminator*, a device for producing an output voltage approximately proportional to the deviation of frequency of a signal from a predetermined value. **1944** *Electronic Engin.* XVII. 196 The frequency discriminator.. has only recently been finding its place in commercial radio receivers in this country. **1938** S. R. ROGET *Dict. Electr. Terms* (ed. 3) 141/1 *Frequency divider. **1952** TERMAN & PETTIT *Electronic Measurem.* (ed. 2) v. 196 By means of a chain of subharmonic generators (frequency dividers), one obtains frequencies of 10,000 cycles, 1000 cycles, and 100 cycles which have the same degree of precision as the standard frequency. **1924** S. R. ROGET *Dict. Electr. Terms* 94/2 *Frequency doubler. **1950** P. PARKER *Electronics* xi. 374 A class C amplifier is sometimes used as a frequency doubler, by tuning the tank circuit to the second harmonic of the signal frequency. **1906** J. A. FLEMING *Princ. Electr. Wave Telegr.* i. 42 One well-known form of *frequency indicator is that due to Mr. Campbell. *Ibid.*, In addition to the voltmeters and ammeters..a *frequency meter ought to be provided. **1957** B. L. GINZTON *Microwave Measurem.* viii. 389 The frequency of the unknown signal can be measured with moderate accuracy by an instrument called the heterodyne frequency meter. **1933** K. HENNEY *Radio Engin. Handbk.* xviii. 462 Present practice favors the use of static *frequency multipliers where it is desired to use an alternator of comparatively low frequency. **1966** *McGraw-Hill Encycl. Sci. & Technol.* V. 515/1 A lower frequency is generated in a crystal-controlled oscillator..and a frequency multiplier is employed to obtain the high frequency desired. **1962** SIMPSON & RICHARDS *Junction Transistors* xviii. 457 Using a *frequency-multiplying circuit to increase both the carrier and deviation frequencies. **1893** *Jrnl. Soc. Arts* 5 May 624/1 We want..a *frequency-raiser.., which shall transform the frequency, even as the induction-coil transforms the voltage. **1926** G. G. BLAKE *Hist. Radio Telegr.* 234 The main object of the foregoing frequency raisers has been to obtain an increase of frequency from comparatively low frequency alternators. **1936** *Summ. Doct. Diss. N.W. Univ.* IV. 180 Within any response-band the glottal note was lowered as the supply-tube was lengthened, the successive response-bands, or optima, covering similar *frequency-ranges. **1962** *Which?* Feb. 41/2 We found personal radios had a limited frequency range, from about 220 to 3,900 cycles per second. **1946** *Nature* 23 Nov. 759/1 *Frequency--selective attenuation by interstellar matter. **1962** A. NISBETT *Technique Sound Studio* 245 Marked acoustic colouration in a studio may be due..to frequency-selective excessive absorption of sound. **1906** J. A. FLEMING *Princ. Electr. Wave Telegr.* i. 43 Many other forms of *frequency teller have been developed for practical use in connection with transformer working. **1941** S. R. ROGET *Dict. Electr. Terms* (ed. 4) 144/2 *Frequency teller*, a name used, particularly in radio-communication for a frequency meter. **1893** *Jrnl. Soc. Arts* 5 May 624/1 The *frequency-transformers hitherto used in the laboratory for purposes of research..are not practical for electric-lighting purposes. **1940** *Chambers's Techn. Dict.* 355/2 *Frequency transformer*, a static piece of apparatus (e.g. a transformer or mercury-arc convertor) which receives power at one frequency and delivers it at another frequency.

6. Special comb. **a.** (sense 4 b) **frequency band** = BAND *sb.*[2] 14; **frequency changer**, a machine, circuit, or component that changes an alternating current of one frequency into one of another frequency; *spec.* in a superheterodyne receiver, the circuit or component that combines the incoming signal with that from the local oscillator to produce the intermediate frequency; **frequency converter**, a frequency changer; **frequency distortion**, distortion of a signal in which components of different frequencies are amplified or attenuated to different extents; **frequency diversity**, the use of channels of different frequencies in a diversity system of communication; **frequency response**, the relationship between the output-input ratio of a device or system designed to transform or transmit oscillatory signals and the frequency of the signal; **frequency shift**, used *attrib.* (also *absol.*) to designate a method of radio telegraphy in which the carrier frequency takes either of two approximately equal values according as the signal is a 'space' or a 'mark'; **frequency spectrum**, the entire range of frequencies of electromagnetic waves, sound waves, etc.; also, the distribution of the energy of a wave-form among its different Fourier components. Also FREQUENCY MODULATION.

1922 *Bell Syst. Techn. Jrnl.* July 117 The method consists in analyzing the speech waves as impressed on a condenser transmitter, using a tuned circuit to transmit narrow frequency bands of energy. **1929** J. H. MORECROFT *Elem. Radio Communication* iii. 82 The normal frequency band for broadcasting purposes is..from 550 to 1500 kilocycles. **1956** TIBBS & JOHNSTONE *Frequency Modulation Engin.* (ed. 2) v. 106 Of the three major frequency bands, the v.h.f. band has been developed rapidly. **1902** SHELDON & MASON *A.C. Machines* vii. 157 The synchronous motor necessary to drive the frequency changer. **1965** *BBC Handbk.* 116 For best results on short waves, a receiver should incorporate a tuned radio-frequency amplifier preceding the frequency-changer stage. **1909** *Cent. Dict.* Suppl. I. 292/3 Frequency-converter. **1912** BEDELL & PIERCE *Direct & Altern. Current Man.* (ed. 2) ix. 291 The usual form of frequency changer or frequency converter consists merely of an induction motor and a separate driving motor. **1957** A. C. CLARKE *Deep Range* (1968) xii. 106 This was a simple enough task for the sub's frequency converters; if he wished, Franklin could tune in to any sounds from almost a million cycles a second down to vibrations as sluggish as the slow opening of an ancient, rusty door. **1959** K. HENNEY *Radio Engin. Handbk.* (ed. 5) ix. 9 Semiconductor diodes are used over a very wide frequency range (a-f to microwave) as frequency converters. **1932** F. E. TERMAN *Radio Engin.* v. 121 Frequency distortion tends to be greater as the amplification per stage is increased. **1962** A. NISBETT *Technique Sound Studio* xii. 214 Quite severe frequency distortion can and does go practically unnoticed by 99% of the general public. **1931** *Proc. Inst. Radio Engin.* XIX. 531 Frequency diversity is effective due to the difference of fading times for frequencies differing by as little as several hundred cycles. **1964** *Electronics Weekly* 8 July 7/4 Frequency diversity is a standard feature of most microwave links... If fading occurs in the 'working' channel the telephone traffic..is automatically switched to the other channel. **1926** *Jrnl. Inst. Electr. Engin.* LXIV. 1023/2 Perfect reproduction of the originating wave-form necessitates a system with a uniform frequency response or frequency characteristic at all volume-levels. **1932** C. L. BOLTZ *Everyman's Wireless* xi. 225 The frequency-response curve..shows a very severe resonance at just over 500 cycles. **1971** *Which?* Jan. 19/1 Almost all microphones had at least as good a frequency response as the tape recorders they were to be used with. **1944** *Electronics* Nov. 126/2 The bandwidth required by frequency-shift transmission is no greater than that required by the carrier make and break system. *Ibid.* 127/3 Frequency shift can result in a much lower bandwidth than carrier make-break. **1959** *Chambers's Encycl.* XI. 471/1 A method of keying which is extensively employed with teleprinters is that known as frequency-shift (or carrier shift), in which the sender radiates continously. **1955** F. E. TERMAN et al. *Electronic & Radio Engin.* (ed. 4) xvii. 591 When the instantaneous frequency of a frequency-modulated wave is varied in a more complex manner..the frequency spectrum becomes very complicated. **1962** *Rep. Comm. Broadc. 1960* 5 in *Parl. Papers 1961–2* (Cmnd. 1753) IX. 259 The division by international agreement of the frequency spectrum into bands allocated to particular services forms part of the International Radio Regulations. **1962** A. NISBETT *Technique Sound Studio* 269 *Scale*, division of the audio frequency spectrum by musical intervals (i.e. frequency ratios). **1968** C. W. MCMULLEN *Commun. Theory Princ.* i. 10 The shape and dimensions of the pulse signal determine the frequency spectrum.

b. (sense 4 c) **frequency curve**, a frequency diagram in the form of a continuous curve, with the variable taking any of a continuous range of values for each member of a large population; **frequency diagram**, a diagram in which frequency of occurrence is plotted against the value of the variable; **frequency distribution**, a classification of the members of a population according to the value assumed for each member by some variable; a diagram or table showing the frequency with which a variable takes each of its possible values; **frequency polygon**, a frequency diagram containing a (small) finite number of points that are joined to form a line composed of a number of straight segments.

1893 K. PEARSON in *Nature* 26 Oct. 615/2 The asymmetrical character of certain frequency curves in physical and biological measurements. **1911** G. U. YULE *Introd. Theory Statistics* vi. 76 Such an ideal limit to the frequency-polygon or histogram is termed a frequency-curve. **1932** J. S. HUXLEY *Probl. Rel. Growth* VII. i. 210 The frequency-curve for female body-length is unimodal. **1925** R. A. FISHER *Statistical Methods* ii. 37 Fig. 4 is a frequency diagram illustrating the distribution in stature of 1375 women. **1931** L. H. C. TIPPETT *Methods of Statistics* ii. 23 Frequency diagrams are useful as giving a visual impression of the characteristics of a sample. **1895** K. PEARSON in *Phil. Trans. R. Soc.* A. CLXXXVI. 412 A method is given of expressing any frequency distribution by a series of differences of inverse factorials with arbitrary constants. **1924** WHITTAKER & ROBINSON *Calc. of Observations* viii. 165 The type of frequency distribution which is most familiar to the worker in experimental science is the distribution of the measures obtained by repeated measurements of the same observed quantity. **1948** *New Biol.* IV. 29 We cannot interpret the change in mean until we have examined the type of scatter of the individual heights around the mean, that is what the statistician describes as the frequency distribution of heights. **1965** A. H. ROBERTS *Statistical Ling. Anal. Amer. Eng.* v. 44 Table 3 and Appendix VIII show the joint frequency distribution of word length by syllable and phoneme number. **1897** K. PEARSON *Chances of Death* I. 273 If the tops of these lines be joined we obtain a frequency polygon. **1966** E. B. MODE *Elem. Probability & Statistics* ix. 123 The frequency polygon..gives a picture of the way in which frequency of occurrence varies over the complete gamut of values.

frequency modulation. *Electr.* **a.** Modulation of a wave by variation of its frequency. **b.** The system of transmission of radio waves, etc., using such modulation. Abbrev. F.M. Cf. *amplitude modulation* (AMPLITUDE 6 d).

1922 J. R. CARSON in *Proc. Inst. Radio Engin.* X. 59 It has been proposed..to employ an apparently radically different system of modulation which may be termed frequency modulation as distinguished from amplitude modulation, in the belief that the former system makes possible the transmission of signals by a narrower range of transmitted frequencies. **1943** *Electronic Engin.* XV. 440/1 The ideal detector for frequency modulation is one which not only faithfully reproduces the true form of the f.m. components, but also is unresponsive to amplitude fluctuations of the carrier signal. **1955** *Times* 29 July 5/4 The present system of amplitude modulation in the v.h.f. maritime services should be changed to one of frequency modulation. **1958** *N.Z. Listener* 10 Oct. 21/1 The possibility of introducing FM (frequency modulation), a method of broadcasting that gives high fidelity reception. **1962** *Which?* Feb. 36/2 On the VHF band the FM (frequency modulation) system is used.

Hence **frequency-modulated** *ppl. a.*; (as a back-formation) **frequency-modulate** *v.*

1936 R. GLASGOW *Princ. Radio Engin.* xi. 314 In order for a phase- or a frequency-modulated signal to become audible, it must be converted into an amplitude-modulated signal. **1950** *Gloss. Terms Radar (B.S.I.)* 6 *Frequency-modulated radar*, a form of radar in which the radiated wave is frequency-modulated and the returning echo beats with the wave being radiated, thus enabling the range to be measured. **1962** F. I. ORDWAY et al. *Basic Astronautics* vii. 322 The radio frequency carrier wave is modulated by a group of subcarriers... The subcarriers are frequency-modulated by the characteristics of the intelligence.

† **frequent**, *sb. Obs. rare*$^{-2}$. [f. FREQUENT *v.*] Frequentation, resort.

1631 BRATHWAIT *Whimzies, Decoy* 28 Private alleys are his sanctuaryes in the citie: but places of publike frequent in the countrey. **1635** —— *Arcad. Pr.* II. 162 Private solitary groves Shut from frequent, his contemplation loves.

frequent (ˈfriːkwənt), *a.* [ad. L. *frequent-em* crowded, frequent; cognate with *farcīre* to stuff (see FARCE *v.*^{1}).]

† **1.** Of persons, an assembly, etc.: Assembled in great numbers, crowded, full. Often in *full and frequent. Obs.*

1590 *Disc. conc. Span. Invas.* in *Harl. Misc.* (Malh.) II. 166 There was generally made throughout the whole realm a most frequent assembly of all sorts of people. **1606** HOLLAND *Sueton.* 14 He..in a ful and frequent assemblie.. besought the faithfull helpe and assistance of his soldiers. *c* **1611** CHAPMAN *Iliad* II. 71 As when of frequent bees Swarms rise out of a hollow rock. **1638** BAILLIE *Lett.* (1775) I. 37 To-morrow, in Stirling, is expected a frequent council. **1674** DRYDEN *State Innoc.* I. Wks. 1883 V. 128 'Tis fit in frequent senate we confer. **1725** POPE *Odyss.* XVI. 377 Apart they sate, And full and frequent, form'd a dire debate. **1746** H. WALPOLE *Lett. to Sir H. Mann* (1857) II. 38 One hundred and thirty-nine Lords were present, and made a noble sight on their benches *frequent and full*!

† **b.** Of a place: Filled, full, crowded (with persons, *rarely* with things). Also, much resorted to, frequented. *Obs.*

1536 BELLENDEN *Cron. Scot.* (1821) I. p. xviii, The erd is now mair frequent in pepil than it was. **1555** GRINDAL *Rem.* (1843) 239 Master Scory and certain other..have an English Church there, but not very frequent. **1603** HOLLAND *Plutarch's Mor.* 342 When he was to play upon his harpe, for a prize in some frequent Theater. **1604** R. CAWDREY *Table Alph.*, *Frequent*, much haunted, or goe too. **1673** RAY *Journ. Low C.* 1 The town..seemed frequent and full of people. **1815** SHELLEY *Alastor* 93 Halls, Frequent with crystal column, and clear shrines Of pearl.

2. Found at short distances apart; numerous, abundant. Somewhat *arch.*

1605 CAMDEN *Rem.* (1637) 2 [Britaine is]..beautified with many populous Cities..frequent Hospitals [etc.]. **1607** TOPSELL *Four-f. Beasts* (1658) 343 There is no Beast so frequent as these in all Cilicia. **1657** R. LIGON *Barbadoes* (1673) 2 Pirats and Pickaroones: which are very frequent upon the Coasts of Spain. **1705** ADDISON *Italy* (1766) 149 Through frequent cracks the steaming sulphur broke. **1722** D. COXE *Carolina* 86 The Plant..is very frequent in most of the Southern Parts of this Country. **1816** KEATINGE *Trav.* (1817) I. 217 Walls..flanked and crowned by frequent square towers. **1860** HAWTHORNE *Transform.* II. xvi. 275 It was a wise and lovely sentiment, that set up the frequent shrine and cross along the roadside.

3. Commonly used or practised, well known, common, usual. Now *rare.* †*frequent to*: commonly occurring in.

1531 ELYOT *Gov.* III. vii, Howe frequent and familiar a thynge with euery astate and degre throughout Christendome is this reuerent othe. **1635** A. STAFFORD *Fem. Glory* (1869) 39, I have not..used any one word not frequent and familiar. *a* **1668** DAVENANT *Siege* I. Dram. Wks. 1873 IV. 375 In the epistles Dedicatory..'tis frequent To bely men with praise. **1706** CONGREVE *Disc. Pindaric Ode* Aj, There is nothing more frequent among us, than.. Pindarique Odes. **1762–71** H. WALPOLE *Vertue's Anecd. Paint.* (1786) II. 239 Such enamelled plates being frequent to old watches instead of crystals. **1816** KEATINGE *Trav.* (1817) I. 139 Such we may rely on it was a picture, and a correct one, of frequent life. **1869** *Times* 1 Jan. 4 It is frequent to impute to Radicals the wish to 'Americanize our institutions'.

† **b.** Of a report, etc.: Widely current. Of a book: Widely circulated, popular. *Obs.*

1623 *Crt. & Times Jas. I* (1849) II. 369, I was not then fully persuaded of the prince's going to Spain, though the report were frequent, from London. **1626** MASSINGER *Rom. Actor* I. i, 'Tis frequent in the city he hath subdued The Catti and the Daci. **1628** EARLE *Microcosm., Pot-Poet* (Arb.) 46 His frequent'st Workes goe out in single sheets. **1631** WEEVER *Anc. Fun. Mon.* 62 The story is frequent.

4. Happening or occurring at short intervals; often recurring; coming or happening in close succession. Of the pulse: Faster than is normal or usual (cf. F. *pouls fréquent*).

The prevailing sense, by which all the others, so far as they survive, are more or less coloured.

1604 R. CAWDREY *Table Alph.*, *Frequent*, often, done many times. **1615** J. STEPHENS *Satyr. Ess.* 260 This watch-word will be frequent in his cups. **1662–3** MARVELL *Corr.* xxxvii. Wks. 1872–5 II. 83 Concerning which you may expect frequente letters. **1707** FLOYER *Physic. Pulse-Watch* 43 This Pulse is feverish..and frequenter than the former. **1750** T. NEWTON *Postscr. to Milton's P.L.*, There have been frequent forgeries in the literary world. **1795** *Gentl. Mag.* 539/2 The blights were this year..more frequent, and.. more destructive than usual. **1816** J. WILSON *City of Plague* I. i, These green banks..Brown, when I left them last, with frequent feet. **1860** TYNDALL *Glac.* I. xxiii. 166 The snow was deep..and our immersions in unseen holes very frequent.

5. Addicted *to*, wont to indulge *in* (a practice, course of action); accustomed *to do* (something); given to repetition *in* (a subject). Now *rare.*

1560 ROLLAND *Crt. Venus* II. 911 Bot weill ȝe knaw, thair is na men frequent To enter heir. **1608** DOD & CLEAVER *Expos. Prov.* ix. & xii. 101 The holy Ghost in this booke, is very frequent in this point. **1611** SHAKS. *Wint. T.* IV. ii. 36 He is..lesse frequent to his Princely exercises then formerly he hath appeared. **1616** DONNE *Serm.* cliii. (Alford) VI. 118 The fathers were frequent in comparing..Eve the Mother of Man and Mary the Mother of God. **1649** BP. HALL *Cases Consc.* 7 How frequent the Scripture is in the prohibition of this practice. **1710** STEELE *Tatler* No. 244 ¶5 Fellows of this Class are very frequent in the Repetition of the Words Rough and Manly. **1854–58** NEWMAN *Idea of University* (1873) 329 Milton is frequent in allusions to his own history and circumstances.

6. † **a.** That is often *at* or *in* (a place). *Obs.* **b.** (with an agent-noun): That does a thing often; constant, habitual, regular.

1611 BIBLE *2 Cor.* xi. 23 In prisons more frequent: in deaths oft. **1624** MASSINGER *Parl. Love* I. iv, In suffering such a crew of riotous gallants..to be so frequent Both in your house and presence. **1628** in Picton *L'pool Munic. Rec.* (1883) I. 208 Fyve of the frequentest Comunicants. **1784** COWPER *Task* VI. 306 The timorous hare, Grown so familiar with her frequent guest, Scarce shuns me. **1857** WILLMOTT *Pleas. Lit.* xi. 49 Of course, the frequent writer will in time be quick. **1886** RUSKIN *Præterita* I. vii. 211 The Professor was a frequent guest at my grandmother's tea-table.

† **c.** That is often in company *with* (a person); familiar; conversant *in* (a subject). *Obs.*

c **1600** SHAKS. *Sonn.* cxvii, Accuse me thus..That I haue frequent binne with vnknowne mindes. **1615** J. STEPHENS *Satyr. Ess.* 214 A talkative Barber: with whome he is the more frequent. **1631** HEYWOOD *Eng. Eliz.* (1641) 52 He was ..In the liberall arts so frequent, that they appeared rather innate and born with him, then..acquired. **1632** —— *2nd Pt. Iron Age* To Rdr., Wks. 1874 III. 352 Euery hard name, which may appeare obscure or intricate to such as are not frequent in Poetry.

7. quasi-*adv.* (Also, in illiterate use, as a real adv. = Frequently, often.)

1614 SELDEN *Titles Hon.* 6 Such like more occurre in ancient and later Storie very frequent. **1784** COWPER *Task* II. 61 Th' old And crazy earth has had her shaking fits More frequent. **1810** SCOTT *Lady of L.* I. 490 Nor frequent does the bright oar break The darkening mirror of the lake. **1870** B. HARTE *Truthf. James* ii, But his smile it was pensive and childlike, As I frequent remarked to Bill Nye.

Hence **ˈfrequentness**, the state or condition of being frequent; frequency.

1664 H. MORE *Expos. Seven Churches* c 7 a, The more-then-ordinary frequentness of burning the blessed Protestant Martyrs..in this Period. **1668** —— *Div. Dial.* II. viii. 217 Admit the necessity of dying, what necessity or conveniency of the frequentness of Diseases? **1862** BURTON *Bk. Hunter* 344 The frequentness of saintship among the Irish.

frequent (frɪˈkwɛnt), *v.* [ad. L. *frequentāre*, f. *frequent-em* FREQUENT. Cf. F. *fréquenter* (recorded from 12th c.).]

1. *trans.* To visit or make use of (a place) often; to resort to habitually; to attend (a meeting, etc.).

1555 EDEN *Decades* 320 The nauigation to India was then wel knowen and frequented. **1585** ABP. SANDYS *Serm.* XV. 266 Many..haue frequented sermons with appearance of great deuotion. **1613** PURCHAS *Pilgrimage* (1614) 769 This house is fiftie or threescore yards long, frequented onely by Priests. **1694** GIBSON in *Lett. Lit. Men* (Camden) 227 He constantly frequented the Presbyterian meetings. **1711** STEELE *Spect.* No. 148 ¶4 A Coffee-house which I myself frequent. **1725** DE FOE *Voy. round World* (1840) 193 Some of those ways through the hills were much frequented. **1732** BERKELEY *Alciphr.* I. §11 Proper ideas or materials are only to be got by frequenting good company. **1762–71** H. WALPOLE *Vertue's Anecd. Paint.* (1888) III. 248 Drawing in the academy, which was then frequented, though established only by private contributions among the artists. **1834** L. HUNT *Town* iv. (1848) 191 The Church of St. Clement Danes..was the one most frequented by Dr. Johnson. **1860** *Merc. Marine Mag.* VII. 213 Whales of the species called 'California Greys', frequent this..bay.

2. To visit or associate with (a person); to be frequently with (a person) or in (his company). Now somewhat *rare.*

1477 EARL RIVERS (Caxton) *Dictes* 123 Frequente and haunte the companyes of wysemen and not of the riche. **1576** FLEMING *Panopl. Epist.* 293 If you frequent the companie of Crates, a man indued with rare wisdome. **1580** SIDNEY *Ps.* XXVI. iii, I did not them frequent, Who be to vainesse bent. **1616** in J. Brown *Bunyan* i. (1887) 4 He doth frequent and keep company with Margarett Bennett. **1683** PENN *Wks.* (1782) IV. 307 Nor do their husbands frequent them till that time [their month] be expired. *a* **1734** NORTH *Lives* (1826) II. 192 His Lordship had one friend that used to frequent him much. **1889** LOWELL *Latest Lit. Ess.* (1892) 145 It is for other and greater virtues that I would frequent the Greeks.

† **b.** Of a disease: To attack often. *Obs. rare*$^{-1}$.

1632 tr. *Bruel's Praxis Med.* 59 This disease..doth frequent children.

† **3.** To use habitually or repeatedly; to practise.

1485 CAXTON *Chas. Gt.* 29 Charles..by ardaunt desyre frequented the bookes composed vpon the crysten fayth. **1541** BIBLE (Cranmer) *title-p.*, The Byble in Englyshe..to be frequented and used in everye Churche within this his sayd realme. **1546** LANGLEY tr. *Pol. Verg. de Invent.* I. xi. 226 The Great Prophet Dauid, whiche songe the Misteries of God in Meter frequented Singing. **1576** FLEMING *Panopl. Epist.* Epit. A, Vertue and commendable behaviour, was of them both so frequented and followed. **1614** W. B. *Philosopher's Banquet* (ed. 2) 105 The oyle of Olives they.. frequented..sparingly. **1642** W. BIRD *Mag. Hon.* 55 And after that the word Baron seemeth to be frequented in this Realm in lieu and place of the word Thane. **1665–7** DRYDEN *Ess. Dram. Poesy* (1668) 43 A Play which has been frequented the most of any he has writ.

† **b.** To celebrate (a sacrament, etc.); to honour with observances. Cf. F. *fréquenter. Obs.*

a **1555**, **1669** [see the vbl. sb.]. **1565** JEWEL *Repl. Harding* (1611) 375 He gaue the Image of his Passion to be frequented [*celebrandam*] in the Church. **1579** FULKE *Refut. Rastel* 723 The Christians did solemnelye frequent the memories of the martyrs. **1581** J. BELL *Haddon's Answ. Osor.* 343 b, God did institute in his Church two Sacramentes..If we do not frequent these in that sincerity of Religion..Let us be condemned.

† **c.** *refl.* To busy oneself *about* something. *Obs.*

a **1562** G. CAVENDISH *Wolsey* (1893) 216 He dayly frequentyng hymeself abought suche busynes and deeds of honest charitie.

† **4.** To familiarize *with. Obs.* [Cf. FREQUENT *a.* 6 b.]

1588 *Exhort. to H.M. faithful Subjects* in *Harl. Misc.* II. 93 Ye encounter with them that are rich, hardy, resolute, and frequented with daily victories. **1632** LITHGOW *Trav.* v. 219 [The Armenians practised certain vices] which my conscience commands me to conceale: least I frequent this Northern world with that which their nature never knew.

† **5.** *intr.* To resort *to* or *unto* (a person or place); to associate *with* (a person); to be often *in* or *about* (a place). *Obs.*

1577 HANMER *Anc. Eccl. Hist.* (1619) 96 An infinite multitude..frequented vnto Paulus. **1580** LYLY *Euphues* (Arb.) 467, I frequented more often to Camilla. **1599** SIR R. WROTHE in Ellis *Orig. Lett.* Ser. II. III. 181 Sertaine lewde fellowes..which doe frequente and use aboute Layton heath. **1651** tr. *Life Father Sarpi* (1676) 67 He frequented much with Fra. Antonio da Viterbo. **1660** tr. *Amyraldus' Treat. conc. Relig.* I. vii. 123 Will she frequent in Towns, or will she resort to unhabited places? **1725** POPE *Odyss.* V. 128 Far from all the ways Where men frequent. **1810** SCOTT *Lady of L.* I. xxv, Nor track nor pathway might declare That human foot frequented there.

† **6.** *trans.* **a.** To crowd or pack closely together. **b.** To crowd, fill (a place). **c.** To supply abundantly. *Obs.*

1578 [see FREQUENTED *ppl. a.*]. **1596** DRAYTON *Legends* II. 253 These brimfull Eyes With Tydes of Teares continually frequented. **1667** MILTON *P.L.* x. 1091 With tears Watering the ground, and with our sighs the air Frequenting. **1682** R. BURTON *Admir. Cur.* (1684) 82 Winchester is a City which flourished in the time of the Romans and now indifferently peopled, and frequented by water.

Hence **freˈquenting** *vbl. sb.*

a **1555** RIDLEY in *Confer. betw. Ridley & Latymer* (1556) 16 b, The..institution of our sauior Christe, for the ofte frequenting of the remembrance of his deathe. **1581** J. BELL *Haddon's Answ. Osor.* 138 b, As touchyng Luthers frequentyng of Hyperbolicall speaches. **1669** WOODHEAD *St. Teresa* I. xix. (1671) 119 Here comes in the frequenting of the Sacraments. **1698** FRYER *Acc. E. India & P.* 376 Birds, by whose frequentings he arrives to the top of his hopes. **1870** LUBBOCK *Orig. Civiliz.* v. 163 Which may be known from ordinary snakes by certain signs, such as their frequenting huts, not eating mice [etc.].

frequentable (frɪˈkwɛntəbl), *a. rare.* [f. FREQUENT *v.* + -ABLE. Cf. F. *fréquentable.*] That may be frequented or visited, easily accessible: † **a.** of a person (*obs.*); **b.** of a place.

1580 SIDNEY *Arcadia* (1622) 126 The exercises of that age [youth], and his humour..made him something the more frequentable. **1843** *New Mirror* III. (Cent.), Have made their bookstore more frequentable for facility of purchase.

frequentage (ˈfriːkwəntɪdʒ). *rare*$^{-1}$. [f. FREQUENT *v.* + -AGE.] 'The practice or habit of frequenting' (W.).

1814 SOUTHEY *Roderick* x. 37 To guard them on their flight through upland paths—remote from frequentage.

† **frequentance.** *Obs. rare*⁻¹. [f. FREQUENT *v.* + -ANCE.] ? The fact of being frequented or resorted to.

1593 NASHE *Christ's T.* 79 b, Some one Gentleman generally acquainted, they giue his admission vnto, sans fee, and free priuiledge thence-forward in theyr Nunnery, to procure them frequentance.

frequentation (friːkwən'teɪʃən). [a. F. *fréquentation*, ad. L. *frequentātiōn-em*, n. of action f. *frequentāre* to FREQUENT.]

1. The action or habit of frequenting (a place); a visiting or resorting to frequently; habitual attendance.

1585 T. WASHINGTON tr. *Nicholay's Voy.* II. iii. 33 The principall entrie was..shut with great bushes..which in processe of time and lacke of frequentation, were so growen. **1616** R. C. *Times' Whistle* II. 73 Are these the fruit thy frequentation Of learned sermons yeilds? **1660** WATERHOUSE *Arms & Arm.* 155 Famous it has been for its Trade, and frequentation of forraigners to her. **1748** CHESTERF. *Lett.* (1792) II. cl. 33 The frequentation of courts checks this petulancy of manners. **1775** JOHNSON *Western Isl.* Wks. X. 477 A shop in the islands as in other places of little frequentation. **1807** W. TAYLOR in *Ann. Rev.* V. 571 The art of deserving it [praise] will hardly be attained without some frequentation of the theatre. **1847** GROTE *Hist. Greece* I. xxviii. (1862) III. 46 Reciprocal frequentation of religious festivals was..the standing evidence of friendship.

2. The action or habit of frequenting (a person); familiar intercourse *with*.

? **1520** BARCLAY tr. *Jugurtha* xlv. 63 They dwelled seperat ..farre from the court and frequentation of kynges of numidy. *c* **1610** SIR J. MELVIL *Mem.* (1735) 390 He denied he was a Witch or had any Frequentation with them. **1652** COTTERELL *Cassandra* IV. (1676) 55 Retired from the commerce or frequentation of men. **1882** *Pall Mall G.* 14 Oct. 4 He had however qualities which were derived no doubt from early frequentation with negroes. **1890** *Sat. Rev.* 22 Feb. 216/1 If only frequentation of sovereigns and statesmen could do it, a superficial explanation would be provided.

†**3.** The act of using or making use *of* frequently. Also, in early use, a custom, practice. *Obs.*

1525 LD. BERNERS *Froiss.* II. ccii. [cxcviii.] 620 They be herde people, and of rude engyn and wytte, and of dyuers frequentacyons and vsage. **1578** BANISTER *Hist. Man* VIII. 102 Collumbus reproued such as hitherto haue made description of the eyes, by frequentation of brutish Anathomies. *a* **1678** WOODHEAD *Holy Living* (1688) 56 Frequentation of prayer is an employment more spiritual.

b. Frequent use or celebration (of the sacraments). (So F. *fréquentation*.)

1626 T. H. *Caussin's Holy Crt.* 217 The exercise of the presence of God, ioyned with..frequentation of sacraments. **1887** C. W. WOOD *Marriage* 20 Prayer and the frequentation of the sacraments will be the source of help.

frequentative (frɪ'kwɛntətɪv), *a.* and *sb.* [ad. L. *frequentātīv-us* (in the later L. grammarians), f. *frequentāt-* ppl. stem of *frequentāre*: see FREQUENT *v.* and -IVE. Cf. F. *fréquematif, -ive.*]

A. *adj.*

†**1.** Accustomed, versed *in*. *Obs. Sc. rare*⁻¹.

1560 ROLLAND *Crt. Venus* II. 79 In siclik Actis thay [the Musis] ar frequentatiue, And mair facill ȝour mater will consaif.

2. *Gram.* Of a verb or verbal form: Serving to express the frequent repetition of an action.

1533 UDALL *Flowers Lat. Sp.* 115 *Rescio*..and a verbe frequentatiue of the same: *rescisco*. **1656** HAMMOND *Wks.* (1684) II. 70 There is no such thing in the Greek language, as the variation of frequentative, transitive, and reciprocal. **1711** [see DESIDERATIVE *a.* 2]. **1793** BEATTIE *Moral Sc.* I. i. §3. 58 The verbs called Deponent, Desiderative, Frequentative ..etc. **1845** STODDART in *Encycl. Metrop.* I. 50/1 The termination *so* in *viso*, has a desiderative force, in *pulso*, a frequentative. **1876** BANCROFT *Hist. U.S.* II. xxxvi. 415 An action may be often repeated, and a frequentative conjugation follows.

B. *sb. Gram.* A frequentative verb, verbal form, or conjugation: see prec.

1530 PALSGR. 403 They knowe neyther frequentatyves, nor inchoatyves. **1626** BP. ANDREWES *Serm.* (1856) I. 125 It is not *exiliit* neither, but *exultavit*. And that is a frequentative; and so he did it more than once. **1711** J. GREENWOOD *Eng. Gram.* 193 By the addition of *le*, it becomes a Frequentative, as *Sparkle*. **1870** F. HALL *Hindí Reader* 137 [*Karnā*], following an uninflected past participle, forms a frequentative.

†**b.** ? An adverb expressing frequency. *Obs.*

1635 *Grammar Warre* B viij, Other Adverbs: as Indicatives, Frequentatives, Meditatives.

frequented (frɪ'kwɛntɛd), *ppl. a.* [f. FREQUENT *v.* + -ED¹.] †**a.** Crowded (*obs.*). †**b.** Commonly practised or used (*obs.*). **c.** Of a place: Often resorted to.

1578 BANISTER *Hist. Man* V. 81 Blacke concreted bloud.. packed together with the frequented Fibres. **1586** W. WEBBE *Eng. Poetrie* (Arb.) 56 The most vsuall and frequented kind of our English Poetry. **1601** HOLLAND *Pliny* I. 36 Patales (a most famous and frequented port). **1655** EARL ORRERY *Parthen.* (1676) 1 He invited him into a less frequented walk. **1666** J. SERGEANT *Lett. Thanks* 80 Naturall knowledges imprinted by frequented Sensations. *a* **1677** BARROW *Serm.* (1686) III. 399 The goodness of God is a frequented theme. **1773** *Observ. State Poor* 34 Ghastly countenances..haunting our most frequented avenues. **1863** GEO. ELIOT *Romola* I. xx, It was the least frequented of the bridges. **1875** BEDFORD *Sailor's Pocket-bk.* iv. (ed. 2) 118 In the frequented parts of the North Atlantic.

frequenter (frɪ'kwɛntə(r)). [f. FREQUENT *v.* + -ER¹.] One who frequents or resorts to (a place); also, one who attends (a meeting, etc.).

1613 PURCHAS *Pilgrimage* (1614) To Rdr. ¶iv b, A gratious King, so diligent a frequenter of Sermons. **1634** *Documents agst. Prynne* (Camden) 5 The miserable spectatours and frequenters of these infernall pleasures. **1751** RICHARDSON *Rambler* No. 97 ¶25 What expence of dress..is required to qualify the frequenters for such emulous appearance. **1874** HELPS *Soc. Press.* iii. 56 There are not even seats provided for the frequenters of gin-palaces.

frequentist ('friːkwəntɪst). [f. *frequent-*, stem of adjs., etc., related to FREQUENCY + -IST.] One who believes that the probability of an event should be defined as the limit of its relative frequency in a large number of trials. Also *attrib.* or as *adj.*

1949 M. G. KENDALL in *Biometrika* XXXVI. 104 It might be thought that the differences between the frequentists and the non-frequentists (if I may call them such) are largely due to the difference of the domains which they purport to cover. **1965** I. HACKING *Logic of Statistical Inference* xiii. 227 Neither frequentists nor subjectivists have been right about probability. **1965** D. V. LINDLEY *Introd. Probability & Statistics* II. p. xi, This is not the place to criticize in detail the defects of the purely frequentist approach.

† **fre'quentless,** *a. Obs. rare*⁻¹. [f. FREQUENT *sb.* + -LESS.] Not frequented.

1631 CHETTLE *Hoffman* I b, It semes frequentlesse for the vse of men: Some basiliskes, or poysonous serpents den!

frequently ('friːkwəntlɪ), *adv.* [f. FREQUENT *a.* + -LY².] In a frequent manner.

1. At frequent or short intervals, often, repeatedly.

1531 ELYOT *Gov.* I. xxii. (1880) 245 He had frequently in his mouthe this worde. **1639** MASSINGER *Unnat. Combat* III. ii, These being heaven's gifts, and frequently conferred On such as are beneath them. **1766** GOLDSM. *Vic. W.* xxi, He had been since frequently at my house. **1860** TYNDALL *Glac.* xxvii, I frequently examined the colour of the snow.

†**2.** Numerously, populously. *Obs.*

1615 G. SANDYS *Trav.* IV. 279 The place became frequently inhabited on every side. **1638** R. BAILLIE *Lett.* iv. (1775) I. 34 The noblemen who came in frequently against the afternoon, stayed all that night.

frere, obs. form of FRIAR.

fresadow: see FRISADO.

frescade (frɛ'skɑːd). Also 6 (from It.) freskata. [a. F. *frescade* (Cotgr.), ad. It. *frescata*, f. *fresco* cool, FRESH.] A cool walk; a shady alley.

[**1630** *R. Johnson's Kingd. & Commw.* 7 Nor have those under the Torride Zone so much need of the Romane Grottaes or Freskataes for to coole them.] **1656–81** BLOUNT *Glossogr.*, *Frescades*, refreshments as..light garments, cool air..cool drinks, Bowers or shades over-spread with green boughs. **1759** *Lond. Mag.* XXVIII. 605 They..go in parties to enjoy themselves in their gardens and frescades. **1832** *Fraser's Mag.* IV. 706 The fragrant orangeries,—the grateful frescades,—the many-twinkling fountains.

fresco ('frɛskəʊ), *sb.* Also 6–7 frisco; pl. frescos, -oes. [ad. It. *fresco* cool, FRESH.]

†**1. a.** Cool, fresh air; occas. a fresh breeze. *in fresco*: in the fresh air. *Obs.* Cf. ALFRESCO.

1620 BRENT tr. *Sarpi's Hist. Counc. Trent* (1629) 410 There being a custome amongst the people of Paris, in the Summers euenings, to goe out of the Suburbes of S. German in great multitudes, to take the *fresco*. **1630** B. JONSON *New Inn* IV. ii, Come, let us take in fresco, here, one quart. **1644** EVELYN *Diary* 4 Nov., Here, in summer, the gentle-men of Rome take the fresco in their coaches and on foot. **1698** FRYER *Acc. E. India & P.* 12 We had a promising Fresco, but somewhat chilled by too frequent Calms. *Ibid.* 335 As they sit in Frisco. **1740** GRAY *Lett.* Wks. 1884 II. 82 They..walk about the city, or upon the sea-shore..to enjoy the fresco. **1785** SARAH FIELDING *Ophelia* II. i, I..was.. overtaken by Mrs. Herner, in fresco as before.

attrib. **1742** H. WALPOLE *Let.* 26 May (1857) I. 167 We have as much waterworks and fresco diversions, as if we lay ten degrees nearer warmth.

†**b.** 'It has been sometimes used for any cool refreshing liquor' (T.). *Obs.*⁻⁰

[**1880** C. R. MARKHAM *Peruv. Bark* 7 Fevers, which they treat with *frescos* or cooling drinks.]

2. a. A kind of painting executed in water-colour on a wall, ceiling, etc. of which the mortar or plaster is not quite dry, so that the colours sink in and become more durable. Orig. in phrase (*to paint*) *in fresco*. Also *transf.*

1598 R. H[AYDOCKE] tr. *Lomatius' Artes Paintinge*, etc. III. iv. 99 Which wil cause the colours in Frisco to continue as faire as if they were laid while the chalke is fresh. [**1644** EVELYN *Diary* 21 Oct., The houses..are..excellently painted, *à fresco* on the outer walls.] *Ibid.* 22 Oct., To this church joins a convent, whose cloister is painted in fresco very rarely. **1688** R. HOLME *Armoury* III. 147/1 Frescoe, or Wall Painting; some call it seiling. **1749** STACK in *Phil. Trans.* XLVI. 14 The Paintings..in Herculaneum..are all done in Stucco in Water-colours in Fresco. **1843** RUSKIN *Let.* 21 Sept. in *Atlantic Monthly* LXVIII. 740 It is not the love of fresco that we want. **1870** EMERSON *Soc. & Solit.*, *Domestic Life* Wks. (Bohn) III. 54 The grand sibyls.. painted in fresco by Michel Angelo. **1883** 'OUIDA' (*title*) Frescoes, etc., dramatic sketches. **1899** *Daily News* 28 Mar. 6/1 Florence has often been sketched before, putting Browning aside with his astounding fresco-music. **1933** A. MACLEISH (*title*) Frescoes for Mr. Rockefeller's city. **1966** *Listener* 23 June 924/2 This impressive musical fresco for string orchestra.

b. A painting so executed.

1670 R. LASSELS *Voy. Ital.* I. 238 The Library, painted with a rare *Fresco*, which is yet ravishing and lively after two hundred years. **1717** POPE *Ep. Jervas* 34 A fading Fresco here demands a sigh. **1797** *Monthly Mag.* III. 347 The beautiful frescoes that decorate the walls. **1870** F. R. WILSON *Ch. Lindisf.* 91 This church is represented in one of the famed frescoes at Wallington Hall.

c. *attrib.* and *Comb.*, as *fresco-paint*, *-painting*, *-plaster*, *-wall*; **fresco buono** = BUON FRESCO; **fresco secco** = SECCO B. *sb.*

1843, 1886, *Fresco buono [see *fresco secco* below]. **1842–5** BROWNING *Waring* I. vi, We are on the brink Of something great in *fresco-paint. **1683** EVELYN *Diary* 16 June, The incomparable *fresco painting in St. George's Hall. **1879** SIR G. SCOTT *Lect. Archit.* I. 213 Let us take advantage of the lessons it affords us in..fresco painting. **1843** *Ecclesiologist* II. 19 The use of *fresco-plaister in very early buildings. **1843** W. B. S. TAYLOR *Man. Fresco & Encaustic Painting* vii. 122 Fresco secco..cannot be placed in the same elevated rank as fresco buono. **1886** H. C. STANDAGE *Artists' Man. Pigments* xii. 104 Describe the difference between 'fresco secco' and 'fresco buono'. **1957** *Fresco secco* [see BUON FRESCO]. **1877** M. M. GRANT *Sun-Maid* iv, It was a lofty room with beautiful old *fresco walls and ceiling.

fresco ('frɛskəʊ), *v.* [f. prec. sb.] *trans.* To paint in fresco.

1849 ROCK *Ch. of Fathers* I. iii. 202 The Donation of Constantine, frescoed in the Vatican. **1893** *Pall Mall Mag.* II. 345/2 We do not..fresco our azure ceiling with angels.

Hence **'frescoed** *ppl. a.*, **'frescoing** *vbl. sb.* Also **'frescoer, 'frescoist**, one who paints in fresco.

1849 RUSKIN *Sev. Lamps* i. §7. 15 Have we no..frescoed fancies on our roofs? **1859** *Sat. Rev.* VIII. 73/1 Many a mute inglorious frescoist has only waited his hour. **1882** *Fraser's Mag.* XXVI. 59 The frescoed Parnassus gradually emerges from out of the dark wall. **1882** *Harper's Mag.* Dec. 46/2 Some leisurely prisoner of the frescoer's trade. **1885** *Ibid.* Mar. 609/1 The original frescoing of walls and ceilings.. was the work of a..soldier.

† **'frescour.** ? *nonce-wd.* [ad. pseudo-L. *frescūra*, It. *frescura*, n. of quality f. *fresco* FRESH. Cf. FRAISCHEUR.] Coolness.

1627 tr. *Bacon's Life & D.* (1651) 31 By Cold, and by a kind of Frescour (as we now-a-days speak).

† **frese,** *sb. Obs. north. dial.* Also fres(se. [Of obscure origin.

Stratmann compares OS. *frêsa* str. fem. (MDu. *vrêse*, Du. *vrees*), OHG. *freisa*, fear, danger. The sense is not inappropriate, but the exact OE. equivalent of these words would be **frás*, yielding **frase* in northern ME.]

In phr. *no frese* = 'no doubt'.

a **1400** *Pistill of Susan* (Vernon) 43 To fonge flourus and fruit þouȝt þei no fresse. *c* **1460** *Towneley Myst.* (Surtees) 30 So wold mo, no frese..Of wifes..For the life that thay leyd, Wold thase husbandes were dede. *Ibid.* 291 Putt thi hand in my syde, no fres, ther Longeus put his spere.

† **frese,** *v. Obs. rare*⁻¹. *trans.*

c **1510** *Robin Hood* IV. 42 in Flügel *Lesebuch* 178 Make glad chere sayd lytell Johan And frese our bowes of ewe.

frese, obs. form of FREEZE.

fresh (frɛʃ), *a.*¹, *adv.* and *sb.*¹ Forms: *α.* 1 fersc, 3 fersse, ferchs, *south.* uer(i)sse, 4 fersch(e. *β.* 3 *Orm.* fressh, 3–5 fress(e, 3–6 freche, fres(s)ch(e, 4 fraiche, frechs, 4–5 freys(s(he, freyssche, 4–6 fres(s)h(e, 4 freisch, 5 freisshe, 4– fresh. [The *α.* forms, which are not found later than the 14th c., represent OE. *fersc* (recorded only in senses 4 and 5, opposed to 'salt'), corresponding to Du. *versch*, OHG. *frisc* (MHG. *vrisch*, mod.Ger. *frisch*; used in senses approximately identical with those found in Eng.), ON. *fersk-r* (Sw. *färsk*, Da. *fersk*; chiefly in physical senses; the mod.Icel. *frísk*, Sw., Da. *frisk*, are adopted from Ger.):—OTeut. **frisko-*. As the *β.* forms (with *fre-*) do not occur till the 13th c., it is most likely that they are due to adoption of OF. *freis* masc., *fresche* fem. (mod.F. *frais, fraîche*), = Pr. *fresc*, Sp., Pg., It. *fresco*, a Com. Rom. adoption of OTeut. **frisko-*.

The senses first occurring in ME. coincide substantially with those in OF.; how far they were introduced from that language, and how far they descend from unrecorded OE. uses, cannot be determined.

The ultimate etymology of OTeut. **frisko-* is obscure. Kluge compares OSl. *prěsinŭ* fresh (:—**praiskino*), Lith. *prěskas* unleavened, and Finn. *rieska-* unleavened.]

A. *adj.*

I. New, recent.

1. a. New, novel; not previously known, used, met with, introduced, etc. †Also *absol.* in advb. phr. *of, on fresh* = AFRESH.

a **1340** HAMPOLE *Psalter* Cant. 516 New & freyss goddis come. *c* **1489** CAXTON *Blanchardyn* xliii. 165 The battayl beganne of fresshe to be sore fyers. **1526** *Pilgr. Perf.* (W. de W. 1531) 302 b, Than thy payne began of fresshe to be renewed. **1637** MILTON *Lycidas* 193 To-morrow to fresh woods and pastures new. **1639** FULLER *Holy Warre* (1647) I. xvi. 25 This sight so inspirited the Christians, that coming in on fresh, they obtained a most glorious victorie. **1748** F. SMITH *Voy. Disc.* I. 9 The Fog..presenting continually fresh Objects. **1777** BURKE *Corr.* (1844) II. 162 That fresh concern and anxiety which attends those who [etc.]. **1798** MALTHUS *Popul.* (1878) 3 Very severe labour is requisite to clear a fresh country. **1813** BYRON *Ch. Har.* III. lv. 529 Its [river's] thousand turns disclose Some fresher beauty. **1861** M. Pattison *Ess.* (1889) I. 31 There are few traces of fresh research or new matter produced. **1870** Morris *Earthly Par.* I. I. 384 And with fresh hope came on the fresh May-day. **1888** *Times* 12 Nov. 13/3 The untoward fate of plays that break fresh ground.

b. In weaker sense: Additional, another, other, different, further.

c **1400** Maundev. (1839) xxii. 243 Then thei maken fressche men redye. **1500–20** Dunbar *Poems* xxxvii. 209 Than suld I haif a fresch feir to fang in mynn armes. **1532** More *Confut. Tyndale* Wks. 675 In the conclusion of al that tale, he knitteth it vp with a freshe lusty poynt. **1613** Purchas *Pilgrimage* (1614) 644 In which way having gotten fresh helpe of some other streames. **1674** N. Cox *Gentl. Recreat.* I. (1677) 16 The Hounds..take fresh scent, hunting another Chase. **1709** Steele *Tatler* No. 14 ¶7 The Troops of the Allies have fresh Orders dispatched to them. **1712** Addison *Spect.* No. 452 ¶2 Our Time lies heavy on our Hands till the Arrival of a fresh Mail. **1721** Bailey, *Fresh Spell*..a fresh Gang to relieve the Rowers in the Long-Boat. **1802** Mar. Edgeworth *Moral T.* (1816) I. xiii. 106 Several fresh spectators were yet to see the sight. **1818** Cruise *Digest* (ed. 2) II. 198 Interest was seldom allowed to be turned into principal, except upon the advance of fresh money. **1849** Macaulay *Hist. Eng.* I. 153 One fresh concession..was easily obtained from the restored king. **1896** *Law Times* C. 408/2 We must begin a fresh paragraph.

2. a. Recent; newly made, recently arrived, received, or taken in. Cf. Fr. *frais*.

1340 Hampole *Pr. Consc.* 5307 Woundes..þat fressche sal sem and alle bledand. *c* **1400** *Lanfranc's Cirurg.* 172 So þat þe wounde be freisch and not hold hurt. **1535** Coverdale *1 Sam.* xxi. 6 The Shewbredes..were taken vp before the Lorde, that there might be other freshbredes set therin. **1665** Boyle *Occas. Refl.* Pref. (1845) 11, I was fain..to insert..some of a much fresher date. **1698** Fryer *Acc. E. India & P.* 9 This Morn by fresh Advice he was assured [etc.]. **1704** Swift *T. Tub* Apol., The Author was then young..and his reading fresh in his head. **1748** F. Smith *Voy. Disc.* I. 146 Seeing whether the Marks of their Teeth are fresh or not. **1845** Ford *Handbk. Spain* I. 16 The ministers of Ferdinand VII could not please him more than by laying before him a fresh express or dispatch. **1860** Tyndall *Glac.* I. xxvii. 204 The floor..was covered with snow, and on it were the fresh footmarks of a little animal.

b. Newly come or taken *from*, *out of*.

1699 Dampier *Voy.* II. I. 31 Great yellow Frogs also are admired, especially when they come fresh out of the Pond. **1700** Dryden *Fables, Cock & Fox* 289 The hue and cry of Heaven pursues him at the heels, Fresh from the fact. **1764** Goldsm. *Trav.* 330 By forms unfashioned, fresh from Nature's hand. **1816** Keatinge *Trav.* (1817) I. 45 A..production..fresh from the press. *a* **1839** Praed *Poems* (1864) II. 209 An heiress quite fresh from Bengal. **1867** Freeman *Norm. Conq.* (1876) I. App. 673 The narrative..was fresh from the lips of an Englishman.

c. Law. ***fresh force*** (AF. *fresche force*, Anglo-Lat. *frisca fortia*), ***fresh disseisin***: = 'novel disseisin'; see quots. and DISSEISIN 1 b. ***fresh fine***, ***pursuit***, ***suit***: one made or levied immediately or within a short prescribed interval.

[**1292** Britton I. xix. §6 Deforceours et purprestours par fresche force.] **1419** *Liber Albus* (Rolls) I. 173 Item, de assisis Novæ Disseisinæ, vocatis 'Fresshforce'. **1538** Fitzherb. *Just. Peas* 132 b, Upon any out crie, hute or freshesuit for any felonye. *a* **1626** Bacon *Max. & Uses Com. Law* (1636) 64 But if he [the owner] make fresh pursuit he may take his goods from the thiefe. **1641** *Termes de la Ley* 169 An Assise or Bil of fresh force brought within 40 daies after the force committed, or title to him accrued. *Ibid.* 171 Fresh suit. **1670** Blount *Law Dict.*, *Fresh Disseisin* [see Disseisin 1 b]. **1721** Bailey, *Fresh suit*. **1848** Wharton *Law Lex.*, *Fresh-fine*, a fine which has been levied within a year.

3. Making one's first acquaintance with a position, society, etc.; raw, inexperienced; unsophisticated, 'green'. Also (*University slang*), characteristic of a freshman.

1595 Shaks. *John* III. iv. 145 How green you are, and fresh in this old world. **1724** De Foe *Mem. Cavalier* II. 184 Between two Armies both made up of fresh Men, that have never seen any Service. **1724** R. Falconer *Voy.* (1769) 11 Reserv'd by the old Sailors..must not be touch'd by the fresh Men, as they call 'em. **1815** E. S. Barrett *Heroine* III. 9 If I don't tell the coach-maker what a fresh one he was, to give you his barouche on tick. **1826** Disraeli *Viv. Grey* IV. v, Did you ever fight a duel? No!.. Well! you are fresh, indeed! **1834** *Oxf. Univ. Mag.* I. 101 It is very fresh to walk about in academic costume with a stick in his hand. **1856** Kane *Arct. Expl.* I. xix. 237 He was a perfectly fresh man, not having yet undertaken a journey.

II. Having the signs of newness.

4. a. Of perishable articles of food, etc.: New, in contradistinction to being artificially preserved; (of meat) not salted, pickled, or smoked; (of butter) without salt; (of fruits, etc.) not dried or preserved in sugar or the like.

α. **901–9** *Charter of Eadweard* in *Cod. Dipl.* V. 164 Tu rieðeru oðer sealt oðer fersc.

β. **1388** Wyclif *Num.* vi. 3 Thei schulen not ete freisch grapis and drie [*uvas recentes siccasve*]. *c* **1400** *Lanfranc's Cirurg.* 347 *Adepis porci antiqui sine sale id est* freisch swynys grese molten. *c* **1460** J. Russell *Bk. Nurture* 630 Fresche lamprey bake þus it must be dight. *c* **1483** Caxton *Vocab.* 5 Flesh of bueff saltede shall be good with the mustarde. The fressh with gharlyk. *Ibid.* 6 Fressh hering.. Reede heeryng. **1541** *Act 33 Hen. VIII*, c. 2 No..person..shall..by anie freshe fyshe of anie estraunger in..Flaunders. **1620** Venner *Via Recta* v. 91 There is made a kinde of Iuncket, called in most places a Fresh-Cheese. **1648** Gage *West Ind.* xix. 143 They will buy..a Riall worth of fresh meat to eat on the Lords day. **1697** Dryden *Virg. Georg.* IV. 365 And seek fresh Forrage to sustain their Lives. **1811** A. T. Thomson *Lond. Disp.* (1818) 606 If in the dry state, by pulverization, or, if fresh, by slicing. **1849** Macaulay *Hist. Eng.* I. 314 During several months, even the gentry tasted scarcely any fresh animal food. **1864** Mrs. Carlyle *Lett.* III. 234 Three pounds of fresh butter at twenty pence a pound.

absol. *c* **1330** *Arth. & Merl.* 7290 Made hem at aise with fresche and selt.

¶**b.** (See quot.) *Obs. rare*$^{-1}$. (Perh. some error.)

1530 Palsgr. 313/1 Fresshe or lussyouse as meate that is nat well seasoned, or hath an unplesante swetnesse in it, *fade*.

5. a. Of water: Not salt or bitter; fit for drinking. †Also of a marsh: Containing fresh as opposed to salt water; watered by a river (*obs.*).

[A Com. Teut. sense: prob. an extension of the notion 'without salt' as applied to meat (sense 4).]

α. *c* **893** K. Ælfred *Oros.* II. iv. §6 [Eufrates] is mæst eallra ferscra wætera. *c* **1290** *S. Eng. Leg.* I. 316/597 þe sonne.. makez þe wateres breþi up-riȝt..Boþe þe sees an ferchse wateres.

β. **1398** Trevisa *Barth. De P.R.* XIII. xxii. (1495) 455 For cause of..fresshe waters that come therto the see..is more fresshe. *c* **1440** *Jacob's Well* (E.E.T.S.) 39 Of fysschyng of freschwatyr & of salt watyr, þe tythe owȝte to be payed. *a* **1450** *St. Cuthbert* (Surtees) 2224 A fresche well was þer besyde. **1553** Eden *Treat. Newe Ind.* (Arb.) 26 In this deserte are..founde bytter waters: but more often fresshe and sweete waters. **1576** *Act 18 Eliz.* c. 10 §10 No Acre of fresh Marsh..[shall] be taxed above the Rate of a Penny.. nor of every ten Acres of salt Marsh above the Rate of a Penny. **1582** N. Lichefield tr. *Castanheda's Conq. E. Ind.* vii. 19 Our men quietly landed and tooke in fresh water. **1601** Shaks. *Twel. N.* III. iv. 419 Tempests are kinde, and salt waues fresh in loue. **1670** D. Denton *Descr. N. York* (1845) 19 These woods also every mile..or half-mile are furnished with fresh ponds, brooks, or rivers. *a* **1691** Boyle *Hist. Air* (1692) 154 He always found the ice fresh that floated upon the sea-water. **1697** Dampier *Voy.* I. iii. 34 Sometimes we find them in salt Water, sometimes in fresh. **1708** *Lond. Gaz.* No. 4489/3, 119 Acres of fresh Marsh-Lands. **1775** Romans *Hist. Florida* 267 Another river..is very rich in fresh marsh. **1800** tr. *Lagrange's Chem.* II. 235 Throwing into large quantities of pure fresh water a few drops of volatile oil. **1878** Huxley *Physiogr.* 73 The great stream of fresh water which flows over Teddington Weir.

b. Of or pertaining to such water. †Of fish = FRESHWATER *a.*

1297 R. Glouc. (1724) 1 Engelond ys ful ynow..Of salt fysch and eche fresch, and fayre ryueres þer to. **1467** in *Eng. Gilds* (1870) 396 Fresshe fysshe as Tenches. **1588** Shaks. *Tit. A.* III. i. 128 Till the fresh taste be taken from that cleerenes, And made a brine pit with our bitter teares. **1608–11** Bp. Hall *Medit. & Vows* i. §8, I have oft wondred howe fishes can retaine their fresh taste, and yet live in salt waters. **1881** J. Payn *Hum. Stories* 294 The professional fisherman..whether he be salt or fresh.

6. a. Untainted, pure; hence, possessed of active properties; invigorating, refreshing. Said *esp.* of air (also in attrib. phrases, as ***fresh-air fiend*** or ***maniac***, etc.) and water.

c **1340** *Cursor M.* 11705 (Trin.) A welle out braste wiþ stremes clere fresshe & colde. **1390** Gower *Conf.* III. 16 There sprang a welle fresh and clere. **14..** *Tundale's Vis.* 1071 Sum of hom thei madyn nesche As is the water that is fresche. **1535** Coverdale *Ps.* xxii. 1 He..ledeth me to a fresh water. **1604** Shaks. *Oth.* IV. iii. 45 The fresh Streames ran by her, and murmur'd her moanes. **1611** —— *Cymb.* v. iii. 71 [Death] hides him in fresh Cups, soft Beds, Sweet words. **1648** Gage *West Ind.* xvii. 117 A fruit named Xocotte..it is fresh and cooling. **1667** Milton *P.L.* I. 771 They among fresh dews and flowers Flie to and fro. **1692** Ray *Dissol. World* 82 The inferiour Air..in the Night so very fresh and cold. **1749** Berkeley *Word to Wise* Wks. III. 440 It takes the peasant from his smoky cabin into the fresh air. **1828** Scott *F.M. Perth* xxxii, The desire of fresh air.. had carried her into the..garden. **1855** Bain *Senses & Int.* II. ii. §7 Fresh odours..that have an action akin to pure air. **1882** *N.Y. Tribune* 2 July 7/1 The work of the Fresh Air Fund..sending children for a week or two from poor homes in unhealthy quarters of the city to healthful villages and farms. **1908** *Daily Chron.* 6 July 4/4 The fresh-air cure has been..very much boomed of late years... One result of this has been the evolution of what I may term the fresh-air maniac. **1927** W. E. Collinson *Contemp. Eng.* 39 Before the war we had the fresh air fiends..and the hatless brigade. **1950** N. Cardus *Second Innings* 109 He went rambles all over the lakes—one of the first of the 'fresh-air' fiends.

†**b.** Cool; see COOL *a.* 1 and 1 d. Cf. Fr. *frais*.

In Romanic langs. a very prominent sense; *rare* in Eng.

c **1400** Maundev. (1839) iv. 29 Thei..sytten there [in dyches]..for thei may ben the more fressche. **1412–20** Lydg. *Chron. Troy* II. xi, Fresche alures with lusty hye pynacles. **1580** Frampton *Dial. Yron & Steele* 150 The Porche of the dore is verye freshe. **1697** Dampier *Voy.* I. v. 108 Here is constantly a fresh Sea breeze all Day, and cooling refreshing winds in the Night.

7. a. Retaining its original qualities; not deteriorated or changed by lapse of time; not stale, musty, or vapid. †Formerly often reduplicated ***fresh and fresh*** (cf. 'hot and hot').

c **1330** R. Brunne *Chron.* (1810) 36 þe blode was boþe warme & fresh, þat of þe schankes lete. *c* **1400** *Lanfranc's Cirurg.* 352 An oynement..al freisch leie it þerto, for þe more freisch þat it is þe bettir it is. **1535** Stewart *Cron. Scot.* III. 351 Tua bostis of gude wyne, Baith stark and freche. **1535** Coverdale *Ps.* xci[i]. 10 My horne..shal be anoynted with fresh oyle. **1577** B. Googe *Heresbach's Husb.* IV. (1586) 158 b, See that their nestes bee very cleane, and kept still with freshe cleane strawe. **1632** J. Hayward tr. *Biondi's Eromena* 128 Having restored me with fresh egges. **1699** Dampier *Voy.* II. III. 55 The other Fish we took as we had occasion fresh and fresh. **1805** Dibdin in *Naval Chron.* XIII. 393 Burton ale—fresh or stale. **1823** Lamb *Elia, Distant Correspondents*, As fresh as if it came in ice. **1850** Lyell *2nd Visit U.S.* xxx. 181 Roots of trees and wood in a fresher state than I ever saw them in any tertiary formation. **1859** G. Wilson *Gateways Knowl.* (ed. 3) 71 The.. Mammoth remains fresh as on the day of its death.

b. *transf.* of immaterial things.

14.. *Pol. Rel. & L. Poems* (1866) 233 Trewloue is fress & euere neu. **1712** Addison *Spect.* No. 452 ¶5 By this means my Readers will have their News fresh and fresh. **1758** Johnson *Idler* No. 14 ¶6 To be able to tell the freshest news. **1802** Syd. Smith *Wks.* (1859) I. 6/1 It is only by the fresh feelings of the heart that mankind can be very powerfully affected. **1855** Kingsley *Westw. Ho!* (1861) 350 The genial smile of English mirth fresh on every lip.

8. Not faded or worn; unfading, unobliterated. Said both of material and immaterial things.

c **1384** Chaucer *H. Fame* III. 66 They [i.e. the names] were As fresshe as men had writen hem there the selve day right. **1576** Fleming *Panopl. Epist.* 303 *note*, Wee might still have them, by continual view of their pictures, in freshe remembrance. **1610** Shaks. *Temp.* II. i. 68 Our garments are now as fresh as when we put them on. **1611** Bible *Job* xxix. 20 My glory was fresh in mee. **1626** Bacon *Sylva* §365 These Roses will retaine..their Colour fresh for a yeare at least. **1631** Gouge *God's Arrows* III. lxxvi. 326 By such memorials the memory of Gods mercies is kept fresh. **1641** J. Jackson *True Evang. T.* I. 69 These antipathies..do still remaine..as fresh, as if Adam had but falne yesterday. **1711** *Lond. Gaz.* No. 4867/4 The Small Pox fresh upon him. **1732** Berkeley *Alciphr.* VI. §27 Men..who lived..when the memory of things was fresh. **1837** Disraeli *Venetia* II. i, An incident..as fresh in her memory as if it had occurred yesterday. **1849** Macaulay *Hist. Eng.* I. 447 Samuel Pepys, whose library and diary have kept his name fresh to our time.

9. a. Not sullied or tarnished; bright and pure in colour; blooming, gay.

c **1385** Chaucer *L.G.W.* Prol. 92 Upon the fresshe daysy to beholde. *c* **1386** —— *Knt.'s T.* 260 The fresshe beautee sleeth me sodeynly Of hir that rometh in the yonder place. *c* **1400** *Destr. Troy* 997 Iason..hade fongit þe flese & þe fresshe gold. **1500–20** Dunbar *Thistle & Rose* 55 To luke vpone his [the sun's] fresche and blisfull face. **1526** *Pilgr. Perf.* (W. de W. 1531) 74 Flourysshe the forenoone neuer so fresshe, at the last commeth the euentyde. **1551** T. Wilson *Logike* (1580) 3 Rhetorike..setteth forth those matters with freshe colours. **1667** Milton *P.L.* IX. 1041 Flours were the Couch..Earths freshest, softest lap. **1749** F. Smith *Voy. Disc.* II. 28 The Green of the Pine..now looked fresh and pleasant. **1797** M. Baillie *Morb. Anat.* (1807) 37 He never had a fresh complexion, but it was always dark. **1801** Southey *Thalaba* III. xxxvii, Her cheek Lost its fresh and lively hue. **1860** Tyndall *Glac.* I. xxv. 177 Scarcely less exquisite than the freshest bloom of the Alpine rose.

b. Of personal appearance: Blooming, looking healthy or youthful. Often ***fresh and fair***; also in proverbial phrases ***fresh as paint***, ***as a rose***, etc.

c **1385** Chaucer *L.G.W.* 1191 *Dido*, An huntyng wolde this lusti fresche queene. **1513** Douglas *Æneis* VIII. x. 29 Venus, the fresche Goddes..can draw nere. **1585** Abp. Sandys *Serm.* xv. 267 The freshest Gospeller in appearance, in experience is found not to be the soundest. **1596** Shaks. *Tam. Shr.* IV. v. 29 Hast thou beheld a fresher Gentlewoman. **1635** J. Hayward tr. *Biondi's Banish'd Virg.* 94 A widow fresh and faire. **1800–24** Campbell *Poems, Ritter Bann* iv, 'Twas the Abbot of St. James's monks, A fresh and fair old man. **1815** E. S. Barrett *Heroine* III. 81 Forth they walked..as fresh as an oyster. *Ibid.* III. 155 As fresh as a daisy. **1877** Mrs. Oliphant *Makers Flor.* vi. 172 The fresh country ladies had to be warned against spoiling their natural roses with paint. **1881** *Dr. Gheist* 217 Though nearly seventy years of age, he is still hale and 'fresh as paint'. **1885** Russell in *Harper's Mag.* Apr. 763/2 [They] see him emerge from his carriage, after a long journey, 'fresh as a rose'.

†**c.** Gaily attired, finely dressed. *Obs.*

c **1440** *Generydes* 2037 Ther coursers trappid in the fressest wise. *c* **1460** *Paston Lett.* No. 437 II. 86 Perys of Legh come to Lynne opon Cristynmesse Even in the freshest wise. **1483** Caxton *G. de la Tour* C iij, To array and make me fresshe for them. **1530** Palsgr. 623/2 My maystresse maketh her fresshe, I wene she go out to some feest to daye. *a* **1533** Ld. Berners *Huon* lxviii. 235 They rose & apparelled them in fresshe arraye. **1577–87** Holinshed *Chron.* III. 807/2 With manie a fresh gentleman riding before them.

10. a. Not exhausted or fatigued; full of vigour and energy; brisk, vigorous, active. †Of a country: Of unexhausted fertility.

α. **1297** R. Glouc. (1724) 397 An hondred knyȝtes, pur fersse & sound. *c* **1350** *Will. Palerne* 3633 A fersche ost hem to help hastili þer come.

β. *c* **1205** Lay. 9418 To heo eoden alle afoten: & swiðe freche weoren. **13..** *K. Alis.* 2405 He hadde y-hud..xx. thousand, That scholden come, on fresche steden. *c* **1330** R. Brunne *Chron.* (1810) 103 þe kyng a seknes hent, þe dede him tok alle fresse. *c* **1400** *Melayne* 1528 Oure Britons bolde that fresche come in Thoghte that [etc.]. *c* **1450** *Merlin* 108 Kynge Aguysas..a freisshe yonge knyght, and with hym v C knyghtes. **1523** Ld. Berners *Froiss.* I. cccxxxix. 532 They were nat strong ynough to abyde them that were fresshmen, for theymselfe were sore traueyled. **1538** Starkey *England* I. i. 26 The mornyng, when our wyttys be most redy and fresch. **1632** J. Hayward tr. *Biondi's Eromena* 21 He mounted first on the one fresh horse, and afterwards upon the other, posting on. **1648** Gage *West Ind.* xiii. 74 This Country is very fresh and plentifull. **1843** James *Forest Days* v, Take with you three of your fellows whose horses are the freshest. **1863** Miss Braddon *J. Marchmont* II. i. 3, I never felt fresher in my life. **1882** *Daily Tel.* 3 Jan., Ignition is probably the freshest of all the veterans.

absol. **1594** Daniel *Compl. Rosamond* cii, Or whilst we spend the freshest of our time, The sweet youth in plotting in the ayre; Alas how oft we fall, hoping to clime.

†**b.** Recruited, refreshed, rested. *Obs.*

c **1489** Caxton *Sonnes of Aymon* vii 162 Whan thei shall be fresshe, thenne shall ye mow make werre. **1700** Dryden *Theod. & Honoria* 187 Nor lies she long, but..Springs up to life, and fresh to second pain Is saved to-day, to-morrow to be slain.

c. Of a cow: yielding a renewed or greatly increased supply of milk; coming into milk. *U.S.*

1884 *Vermont Agric. Rep.* VIII. 29 The cows will go dry for a time during the hot weather in summer and be fresh in fall. **1896** *Ibid.* XV. 67 This [inoculating of cream] may be done by using a 'starter' made from cream of the skim-milk of a fresh cow. **1971** *Independent* (Deerfield, Wis.) 23 Sept. 22/4 (Advt.), Fresh, springing, bred back cows and heifers.

†**11. a.** Ready, eager. Const. *to*, also *to* with *inf.*

c **1200** ORMIN 6348 A33 himm birrþ beon fressh þærto [i.e. to worship God]. *c* **1340** *Cursor M.* 18060 (Fairf.), Was nevir ern so fresh to flight. **1340** HAMPOLE *Pr. Consc.* 1254 Enmys thre.. þat, to assayle us here, er ay freshe. **1613** SHAKS. *Hen. VIII*, I. i. 3 Euer since a fresh Admirer of what I saw there.

†**b.** Ready to eat or drink; having an appetite or inclination. Also, *fresh and fasting*. *Obs.*

1613 PURCHAS *Pilgrimage* (1614) 840 Drinking a filthy liquor, whereto they said Tobacco made them fresh. **1698** FRYER *Acc. E. India & P.* 92 They will fresh and fasting, besprinkle themselves with the Stale of a Cow.

12. Of the wind: Having considerable force, strong; †formerly, springing up again (*obs.*). Hence, of the 'way' of a ship: Speedy, steady. Also quasi-*adv.* in *to blow fresh*. Cf. Fr. *frais.*

a **1533** LD. BERNERS *Huon* lxi. 213 They..lyft vp theyr saylles & so had a good freshe wynde. **1582** N. LICHEFIELD tr. *Castanheda's Conq. E. Ind.* xxvi. 66 Uppon a sodayne there came a fresh gale of Winde. **1627** CAPT. SMITH *Seaman's Gram.* x. 46 A fresh Gale is that doth..presently blow after a calme. **1659** D. PELL *Impr. Sea* 322 It is a long time ere a ship can bee put upon the stayes when shee has her freshest way. **1686** *Lond. Gaz.* No. 2181/4 The Wind blowing very fresh..forced into the Downs a Dutch Man of War. **1719** DE FOE *Crusoe* I. x, Not making much fresh Way as I did before. **1766** BRICE in *Phil. Trans.* LVI. 226 The velocity of the wind on May the 6th, when it blew a fresh gale. **1805** NELSON in Nicolas *Disp.* (1846) VII. 77 If it comes on to blow fresh I shall make the signal for Boats to repair on board. **1878** JEVONS *Prim. Pol. Econ.* 29 The miller grinds corn when the breeze is fresh.

13. With regard to the use of drink, in two opposite senses: **a.** Sober. Now only *Sc.*

b. Exhilarated by drink; partially intoxicated; 'half seas over'.

a. *c* **1425** *Seven Sag.* (P.) 1226 He was freche, he was nought dronke. **1628** W. YONGE *Diary* 113 The Lord Denbigh scarce fresh any day after the morning. **1822** SCOTT *Pirate* xxiv, 'Our great udaller is weel eneugh when he is fresh.'

b. 1812 *Sporting Mag.* XL. 174 On his return home, rather fresh. **1829** MARRYAT *F. Mildmay* xiii, I could get 'fresh'.. when in good company. **1849** C. BRONTE *Shirley* iii. 31 For my notion was, they were all fresh.

14. *Sc.* and *north. dial.* Of the weather: **a.** Open, not frosty. **b.** Wet.

1782 SIR J. SINCLAIR *Observ. Sc. Dial.* 49 Fresh weather. Open weather. **1790** GROSE *Prov. Gloss.* (ed. 2) s.v., How's t' weather to-day? Why fresh; i.e. it rains. **1795** *Statist. Acc. Scot., Stirlings.* XV. 319 *note*, Our winters..have been open and fresh, as it is termed. **1827** *Sporting Mag.* XX. 363 What is called in Durham 'fresh weather', *alias* rain. **1880** *Daily News* 29 Dec. 2/1 There were indications of fresh weather.. The fresh became less marked.

15. [Perhaps influenced by G. *frech* saucy, impudent.] Forward, impertinent, free in behaviour. orig. *U.S.*

1848 BARTLETT *Dict. Amer.* App., *Fresh*, forward; as 'don't make yourself too fresh here'; that is to say, not quite so much at home. **1887** F. FRANCIS *Saddle & Mocassin* 136 What's the matter, then? Has Piggy been too 'fresh'? **1902** H. L. WILSON *Spenders* xxiii. 270 And when she goes out and says that isn't right they tell her she's too fresh. **1904** 'A. DALE' *Wanted: a Cook* 199, I smiled, and was about to speak, when she rose, and in a loud voice, cried: 'Say, you're too fresh! Where d'ye think ye are?' **1908** G. H. LORIMER *J. Spurlock* ii. 26 That [remark] was pretty fresh, and my only excuse for doing it was that I couldn't think of anything fresher. **1923** WODEHOUSE *Adv. Sally* xiii. 156 I'm going to show that guy up this afternoon... He's been getting too fresh. **1928** S. VINES *Humours Unreconciled* iii. 41 A woman who does that sort of thing has no business to turn one down as soon as one gets a little bit fresh. **1932** H. NICOLSON *Public Faces* viii. 233 'Those Britishers,' mumbled the President eventually, having taken a large gulp of iced water, 'are getting fresh.' **1953** *Manch. Guardian Weekly* 20 Aug. 7/1 Anybody try any fancy stuff, or they got fresh, ..and they let you have it.

16. *Comb.*, as *fresh-looking*, †*fresh-new* adjs. Chiefly parasynthetic, as *fresh-coloured*, *-complexioned*, *-faced*, *-hearted*, (*-heartedness*), *-leaved*, †*looked*, †*-suited*, *-tinctured* adjs. Similarly *fresh-button*, *-skin* vbs., *fresh-dooring* vbl. sb.

1771 FOOTE *Maid of B.* I. Wks. 1799 II. 213 To turn the lace, and *fresh-button the suit. **1608–11** BP. HALL *Medit. & Vowes* i. §24 *Fresh coloured wares, if they bee often opened, leese their brightnesse. **1848** DICKENS *Dombey* xxxi, With a fresh-coloured face. **1686** *Lond. Gaz.* 2156/4 A Girl of about 11 years of Age..light brown hair, and *fresh Complectioned. **1892** E. REEVES *Homeward Bound* 117 A.. fresh-complexioned, quiet, fair man. **1824** MISS MITFORD *Village* Ser. II. (1863) 250 By dint of whitening, sash-windowing and *fresh-dooring, the old ample farm-house has become a very genteel-looking residence. **1862** H. MARRYAT *Year in Sweden* II. 354 *Fresh-faced girls sit knitting by their myrtles. **1837** HAWTHORNE *Twice-told T.* (1851) II. viii. 123 But I cried the *fresh-hearted New Year. **1870** *Illustr. Lond. News* 29 Oct. 438 The *fresh-heartedness, generosity, and heroism which seagoing has a manifest aptitude to nourish. **1657** COKAINE *Obstinate Lady* I. i, That dost..in *fresh-leaved woods delight! **1714** *Lond. Gaz.* No. 5249/4 One William Williams, a *fresh look'd Boy. **1848** H. ROGERS *Ess.* (1860) III. 314 The *fresh-looking masonry of yesterday. **1608** SHAKS. *Per.* III. i. 41 This *fresh-new sea-farer. **1836** E. HOWARD *R. Reefer* xxii, I had *fresh skinned myself. **1638** FORD *Fancies* I. iii, Enter Livio, *fresh suited. *a* **1743** SAVAGE *Lady Tyrconnel* 43 *Fresh-tinctur'd like a summer-evening sky.

B. *adv.*

1. In a fresh manner, freshly (see senses of the adj.); newly; †clearly; †eagerly; †gaily; †strongly. †Also *Law*, immediately.

c **1386** CHAUCER *Knt.'s T.* 190 Y-clothed was she fresh, for to devyse. *c* **1420** *Anturs of Arth.* iv, Fresche thay folo the fare. *c* **1470** HENRY *Wallace* VIII. 1423 With the small pype, for it most fresche will call. **1500–20** DUNBAR *Poems* lxxxvii. 26 New of thi knop, at morrow fresche atyrit. **1523** SKELTON *Garl. Laurel* 39 A pavylyon..garnysshed fresshe after my fantasy. **1593** SHAKS. *2 Hen. VI*, III. ii. 188 The Heyfer dead, and bleeding fresh. **1622** *Crt. & Times Jas. I* (1849) II. 336 Speak fresh that way. *a* **1626** BACON *Max. & Uses Com. Law* (1636) 64 If fresh after the goods were stolne, the true owner maketh pursuit. **1676** LADY CHAWORTH in *12th Rep. Hist. MSS. Comm.* App. v. 29 There is 4 pound of [comfits] and made fresh for you of the purest sugar. **1684** T. BURNET *Th. Earth* I. 145 When the earth was fresh broken. **1709** tr. *Poncet's Voy. Æthiopia* 11 Thick Beer..being bad to keep, they are forc'd to make it Fresh, almost every Hour. **1737** WHISTON *Josephus' Hist.* I. xiv. §4 Anthony..remembering very fresh the wars he had gone through. **1747** WESLEY *Prim. Physic* (1762) 107 Plantane root fresh digged up. **1777** SHERIDAN *Sch. Scand.* II. ii, *Mrs. Can.* She has a charming fresh colour. *Lady T.* Yes, when it is fresh put on.

2. *Comb.* chiefly with *pres.* and *pa. pples.*, as *fresh-armed*, *-baked*, *-bleeding*, *-blooming*, *-blowing*, *-blown*, *-boiled*, *-born*, *-breaking*, *-caught*, *-coined*, *-comer*, *-cropt*, *-drawn*, *-fallen*, *-forged*, *-killed*, *-made*, *-quilted*, *-rankling*, *-rubbed*, *-slaughtered*, *-thrashed*, *-thrown*, *-turned*, *-watered*; **fresh-find** *v. trans.*, to find (a deer) after the scent has been lost; hence **fresh-found** *ppl. a.*; **fresh-run** *a.*, (a fish, *esp.* a salmon) that has lately run up from the sea.

1535 STEWART *Cron. Scot.* II. 379 Ane new *fresche armit gard. **1849–52** TODD *Cycl. Anat.* IV. 844/2 *Fresh-baked brown bread. **1718** POPE *Iliad* xv. 698 His side, *fresh-bleeding with the dart. **1735** SOMERVILLE *Chase* II. 110 In each smiling Countenance appears *Fresh-blooming Health. **1671** MILTON *Samson* 10 The breath of Heav'n *fresh-blowing, pure and sweet. **1632** —— *L'Allegro* 22 *Fresh-blown roses washed in dew. **1833** MARRYAT *P. Simple* (1863) 243 Looking as red and hot as a *fresh-boiled lobster. **1708** J. PHILIPS *Cyder* II. 438 Can they refuse to usher in The *fresh-born Year with loud Acclaim. **1817** BYRON *Manfred* I. ii, And thou, *fresh breaking Day, and you, ye Mountains, Why are ye beautiful? **1852** MRS. STOWE *Uncle Tom's C.* xx, I thought I would make you a present of a *fresh-caught specimen. **1785** CRABBE *Newspaper* 82 The *fresh-coin'd lie. **1890** *Spectator* 4 Oct., *Fresh-comers from England and elsewhere. **1777** POTTER *Æschylus' Supplicants* 90 Why..fly you to these Gods for refuge, Holding these *fresh-cropt branches crown'd with wreaths? **1872** LEVER *Ld. Kilgobbin* lv, A *fresh-drawn cork. **1885** *Fortn. Rev.* 1 Feb. 170 No doubt the thawing of *fresh-fallen snow is not pleasant. **1856** R. A. VAUGHAN *Mystics* (1860) I. 171 Without loss of time, *fresh-forged anathemas are come. **1780** in C. P. Collyns *Chase Wild Red Deer* (1862) 193 He was *fresh found lying in a rush-bed. **1799** *Ibid.* 209 Here they fresh found him. **1855** in J. Fortescue *Rec. Stag-hunting Exmoor* (1887) 189 Still persevered in hopes of fresh finding him in Haddon. *Ibid.* 190 We had fresh found our deer. **1899** *Westm. Gaz.* 18 Aug. 3/1 A clever huntsman.. usually succeeds in fresh-finding his deer. **1922** JOYCE *Ulysses* 571 After him, freshfound, the hue and cry zigzag gallops. **1700** S. L. tr. *Fryke's Voy. E. Ind.* 238 The Gutts of their Cattle *fresh killed. **1648** HERRICK *Hesper., Corinna's going a Maying* (1869) 69 Aurora throwes her faire *Fresh-quilted colours through the aire. **1763** J. BROWN *Poetry & Mus.* vi. 100 Inward Grief, *fresh-rankling in his Soul. **1896** *Daily News* 2 Apr. 8/5 It had a *fresh-rubbed sore under the collar. **1863** KINGSLEY *Water Bab.* 83 As clean as a *fresh-run salmon. **1718** POPE *Iliad* XVI. 198 Some tall stag, *fresh-slaughter'd in the wood. **1883** *Goole Weekly Times* 7 Sept. 2/6 Very little *fresh-thrashed wheat has been marketed during the past week. **1821** KEATS *Isabella* xlvi, She gazed into the *fresh-thrown mould. **1777** WARTON *First of April* 29 The *fresh-turn'd soil. **1535** COVERDALE *Isa.* lviii. 11 Thou shalt be like a *freshwatred garden. **1744** AKENSIDE *Pleas. Imag.* II. 365 That..verdant lawn, Fresh-water'd from the mountains.

C. *sb.*[1]

1. [The adj. used *absol.* passing into a sb.] The fresh part or period (of a day, year, etc.).

1715 JANE BARKER *Exilius* II. 22 They went to divert themselves in a cool Walk, during the fresh of the Morning. *a* **1734** NORTH *Lives* I. 192 And for that work he took the fresh of the morning. **1883** HOLME LEE *Loving & Serving* I. xv. 288 In the fresh of the morning it is the greatest delight. **1889** LOWELL *Lett.* (1894) II. 381 The robins..keep on pretending it is the fresh of the year.

2. a. A rush of water or increase of the stream in a river; a freshet, flood. Also, a flood of fresh water flowing into the sea; *esp.* an ebb tide, whose force is increased by heavy rains. Freq. in *pl.*

1538 LELAND *Itin.* III. 136 Lichet Village and an Arme out of Pole Water beting with a litle fresch. *c* **1682** J. COLLINS *Making Salt in Eng.* 10 Sometimes there are great freshes in the River of Tyne. **1698** FRYER *Acc. E. India & P.* 25 We met with the Freshes off the Shore caused by the Upland Rains. **1749** F. SMITH *Voy. Disc.* II. 31 And the Freshes or Landwaters, the Snow being mostly dissolved, very much abated. **1764** *Phil. Trans.* LIV. 83 The officers observed the king's boat to float suddenly, which they attributed to a great fresh. **1787** M. CUTLER in *Life, Jrnls. & Corr.* (1888) II. 401 The high freshes..will bear a vessel of any burden..out to sea. **1848** S. W. WILLIAMS *Middle Kingdom* I. i. 18 The banks are not so low as to be injured or overflown to any great extent by the freshes.

b. A sudden increase (of wind); a gust, squall.

1719 DE FOE *Crusoe* I. iii, If I should be taken with a fresh of wind. **1823** SCORESBY *Whale Fishery* 23 In the afternoon we had a fresh of wind.

3. A pool, spring or stream of fresh water.

1571 HANMER *Chron. Irel.* (1633) 63 A small fresh or brook that falleth into the Nure. **1610** SHAKS. *Temp.* III. ii. 75 He shall drinke naught but brine, for I'le not shew him Where the quicke Freshes are. **1612** CAPT. SMITH *Map Virginia* 13 It groweth like a flagge in low muddy freshes. **1791** COWPER *Iliad* II. 952 Brouzed On celery wild, from watery freshes gleaned [ἐλεόθρεπτόν τε σέλινον]. **1817** KEATS *Lett.* Wks. 1889 III. 53, I see Carisbrooke Castle from my window, and have found several delightful wood-alleys.. and quiet freshes.

4. A freshwater stream running out into a tideway; the part of a tidal river next above the salt water; also, the land or lands adjoining this part. Freq. in *pl.* Now *U.S.*

1634 *Relat. Ld. Baltimore's Plantat.* (1865) 12 It runs vp to the North about 20 miles before it comes to the fresh. **1658** R. FRANCK *North. Mem.* (1694) 173 Here the Salmon relinquish the Salts because by the Porposses pursued up the Freshes. **1683** W. PENN *Wks.* (1782) IV. 313 The Swedes [inhabit] the freshes of the river Delaware. —— *Let. to North* in *Pa. Hist. Soc. Mem.* I. 412 We are one hundred and thirty miles from the main sea, and forty miles up the freshes. **1686** *Laws of Maryland* (1765) ii, At Pile's Fresh, on both Sides of the said Fresh. **1689** BANISTER *Virginia* in *Phil. Trans.* XVII. 668, I have sent you what Muscles our Freshes afford. **1693** J. CLAYTON *Acc. Virginia* in *Misc. Cur.* (1708) III. 297 In the Freshes they more rarely are troubled with the Seasonings. **1705** BEVERLEY *Hist. Virginia* II. ii. 6 By running up into the Freshes with the Ship..during the Five or Six Weeks, that the Worm is thus above Water. *Ibid.* iii. 11 Mawborn Hills in the Freshes of James River. **1708** OLDMIXON *Brit. Empire Amer.* I. 151 This part of the Delaware is call'd the Freshes. **1896** P. A. BRUCE *Econ. Hist. Virginia* I. 500 note, His plantation..was situated in the freshes of Rappahannock River.

fresh, *sb.*[2] *Obs.*[−1] [? var. of FRUSH *sb.*[1]] An onset, rush.

c **1400** *Destr. Troy* 4730 The fresshe was so felle of the furse grekes..That [etc.].

fresh, *v.* [f. FRESH *a.*; cf. F. *fraîchir* (OF. *freschir* intr. in the 12th c.).]

1. *trans.* To make fresh. **a.** To refresh, recruit, strengthen; also, to increase. Also with *up*. †**b.** To renew, repair (*obs.*). †**c.** *Naut. to fresh the hawse*: see FRESHEN *v.* 3 (*obs.*).

a. ? *a* **1366** CHAUCER *Rom. Rose* 1513 He thoughte of thilke water shene To drinke and fresshe him wel withalle. **1380** *Lay Folks Catech.* (Lamb. MS.) 119 Crist wolde þat our hope were freschyd in hym. *a* **1420** *Pallad. on Husb.* I. 291 As diuers men han done to fresshe her fame. **14..** *Sir Beues* (1885) 134/77 (MSS. CM.) The watur him freschyd, þat was colde. **1523** LD. BERNERS *Froiss.* I. cxl. 167 They of Calays were often tymes..fresshed by stelth. *c* **1586** C'TESS PEMBROKE *Ps.* CXLVII. iii, [He who] Fresheth the mountaines with such meedfull spring. **1635** QUARLES *Embl.* I. xi. (1718) 45 And fresh their tired souls with strength-restoring sleep. **1835** J. P. KENNEDY *Horse-Shoe Robinson* I. 66 Put a sprinkling of salt in a bucket o' water, ..it sort of freshes the cretur up like. **1890** B. L. GILDERSLEEVE *Ess. & Stud.* 190 Now stay..And fresh your life anon. **1897** KIPLING *Capt. Cour.* 260 The fresh air will fresh Mrs. Cheyne up. **1910** *Westm. Gaz.* 16 Apr. 16/2 The rains have freshed the trout streams.

b. *c* **1420** *Pallad. on Husb.* I. 727 They make Her water thryes fresshed euery day. **1513** *Churchw. Acc., St. Mary hill, London* (Nichols 1797) 107 For freshynge the canopy at the high awter. **1606** SYLVESTER *Du Bartas* II. iv. I. *Tropheis* 325 With fresh assaults freshing their fury so. **1635** QUARLES *Embl.* III. (1857) 268 Groans fresh'd with vows and vows made salt with tears.

c. 1692 *Capt. Smith's Seaman's Gram.* I. xvi. 78 *Fresh the Hawse.*

2. *intr.* †Of the wind: To become fresh, to begin to blow fresh. Also with *up*. Occas. of the sea: To become lively, roughen.

1599 HAKLUYT *Voy.* II. 107 The 16. the winde freshed, and we passed by Mount Carmel. **1659** B. HARRIS *Parival's Iron Age* 282 The wind freshing westwardly, the English bore in..hard among them. *a* **1691** FLAVEL *Sea-Deliver.* (1754) 157 The wind freshed up, and began to blow a brisk gale. **1775** E. WILD *Jrnl.* in *Proc. Mass. Hist. Soc.* Ser. II. II. 267 The wind freshing we got clear after several tacks. **1892** [see *ppl. a.*].

Hence ˈ**freshing** *vbl. sb.*, renewal, refreshment; (of a wound) recrudescence; ˈ**freshing** *ppl. a.*

a **1533** LD. BERNERS *Huon* cxxxii. 488 Thou nedyste not fere of any fresshynge nor of more fourtherynge for me. **1591** SPENSER *Daphn.* 26, I walkt abroad to breath the freshing ayre. **1612** T. TAYLOR *Comm. Titus* iii. 7 Abrahams bosome, wherein the Saints receiue freshing. **1613–16** W. BROWNE *Brit. Past.* I. iv, Her skill in herbs might helpe remove The freshing of a wound which he had got. **1892** *Daily News* 30 Nov. 3/1 He can paint the freshing sea when the tide runs in.

freshen (ˈfrɛʃ(ə)n), *v.* [f. FRESH *a.* + -EN[5].]

1. *intr.* To become fresh. **a.** Of the wind: To begin to blow fresh; to increase in strength. Also with *up*. Const. *into.*

1697 DAMPIER *Voy.* I. iv. 79 The wind came about to the Eastward and freshened upon us. **1760** G. WASHINGTON *Writ.* (1889) II. 143 The Wind freshened up as the Evening came on. **1836** MARRYAT *Midsh. Easy* xvii, The wind now freshened fast. **1884** PAE *Eustace* 197 The wind was again freshening into a gale.

b. To assume a fresh look; to become bright or vivid; to brighten.

1819–20 W. IRVING *Sketch Bk., Christm. Dinner* (1865) 281 How truly is a kind heart a fountain of gladness, making everything in its vicinity to freshen into smiles! **1848** C.

BRONTË *J. Eyre* ix, A greenness grew over those brown beds, which freshening daily, suggested the thought that Hope traversed them at night.

c. To grow fresh; to lose salt or saltness.

1864 in WEBSTER; whence in mod. Dicts.

d. Of a cow: to become fresh (see FRESH *a.* 10c). *U.S.*

1915 J. LONDON *Let.* 26 Jan. (1966) 446 Get Timms'.. number of freshening cows. **1931** *Randolph* (W. Va.) *Enterprise* 9 Apr. 2/2, I have for sale 2 year old Jersey heifers to freshen in April and two Jersey cows,.. one of them fresh now.

e. To wash one's hands and face, tidy one's hair and clothes, etc. Const. *up*. Chiefly *U.S.*

1961 in WEBSTER. **1962** 'A. GILBERT' *No Dust in Attic* vi. 73 She thought she'd run along and freshen up. **1971** 'D. HALLIDAY' *Dolly & Doctor Bird* vii. 92 They all fore-gather ..for drinks before dinner. Would you like to freshen up and we'll take you?

2. *trans.* **a.** To make FRESH, in various senses: *esp.* to recruit, renew, revive, give freshness to; to remove salt or saltness from. Also with *up*.

1749 F. SMITH *Voy. Disc.* II. 14 Water Holes.. were cut in the Ice, for freshening the Meat. **1764** GOLDSM. *Trav.* 246 Freshen'd from the wave the zephyr blew. **1777** ROBERTSON *Hist. Amer.* (1778) I. II. 138 It freshens the ocean many leagues with its flood. **1801** MAR. EDGEWORTH *Belinda* (1833) II. xxi. 90 Let in a little air to freshen the room. **1805** SOUTHEY in *Ann. Rev.* III. 227 [They] get into the suburbs ..and freshen themselves for the confinement of the week to come. **1808** —— *Lett.* (1856) II. 94 He will beat the Austrians, and freshen his popularity in France by so doing. **1856** LOWELL *Lett.* (1894) I. 254 It would freshen up my Italian. **1860–1** FLO. NIGHTINGALE *Nursing* 70 It freshens up a sick person's whole mind to see 'the baby'. **1863** GEO. ELIOT *Romola* I. i, The good wives of the market freshened their utensils. **1871** NAPHEYS *Prev. & Cure Dis.* I. iii. 95 It is freshened with carbonic acid gas. **1874** DEUTSCH *Rem.* 258 And must we again freshen up their memory? **1877** *Goodholme's Dom. Cycl.* 113 (Cent.) Freshen [salt codfish] by leaving it in water an hour.

b. To add fresh wine (spirits, etc.) to a drink which has been standing for some time; to top up (a person's drink). Chiefly *U.S.*

a **1961** in WEBSTER, Freshen the highball with more ice. **1971** M. BUTTERWORTH *Flowers for Dead Witch* xii. 158 You've let your Martini get warm... I'll freshen your glass. **1975** D. LODGE *Changing Places* ii. 67 You might freshen my drink for me. **1986** P. BARKER *Century's Daughter* xv. 262 He ..made himself a cup of coffee and carried the kettle back into the hall. 'Do you want yours freshening?'

3. *Naut.* 'To relieve (a rope) of its strain, or danger of chafing, by shifting or removing its place of nip' (Adm. Smyth). ***to freshen hawse, the nip***: to pay out more cable, so as to change the place of the part exposed to friction (also *fig.*: cf. NIP *sb.*[2] b); ***to freshen ballast***: 'to divide or separate it, so as to alter its position' (Adm. Smyth); ***to freshen way***: of a ship, to increase the speed; also *transf.* of a passenger or traveller.

1827 J. F. COOPER *Red Rover* (1881) iii. 51 Profiting by the occasion 'to freshen his nip', as he quaintly called swallowing a pint of rum and water, he continued his narrative. **1841** *Southern Lit. Messenger* VII. 764/1 After going into the saloon (grog-shop) to 'freshen the nip'—as they professionally called taking a glass of brandy and water —they led me into the upper tier of boxes. **1855** CAPT. CHAMIER *My Trav.* I. xi. 177, I freshened my way, and got home as quickly as possible. **1859** [see NIP *sb.*[1] I c]. **1961** F. H. BURGESS *Dict. Sailing* 98 *Freshen the nip*, veer or haul slightly so that a rope may be moved a little.

Hence **'freshened**, **'freshening** *ppl. adjs.* Also **'freshener**, something that freshens; *spec.* a spell of exercise for 'freshening' a horse.

1794 MRS. RADCLIFFE *Myst. Udolpho* xvi, I..bid the freshen'd waters glide.. Through winding woods and pastures wide. **1817** MOORE *Lalla R.* (1824) 223 Gave her cheeks all the freshened animation of a flower that [etc.]. **1884** *Advance* (Chicago) 13 Mar., Change of method will be a freshener of interest. **1889** MRS. RANDOLPH *New Eve* I. i. 11, I thought of taking the bays out for a freshener on the cliff. **1894** *Westm. Gaz.* 31 Aug. 3/1 The simplest form of this grafting process is the bringing together of 'freshened' edges of flesh.

fresher[1] ('frɛʃə(r)). [f. FRESH *a.* + -ER[1].] One who or that which comes fresh. **a.** *Univ. slang*: = FRESHMAN. **b.** A fresh breeze. Hence **'fresherdom**, the condition of a freshman.

1882 *Society* 14 Oct. 4/2 The entry of freshers is about two hundred under the average. **1891** DUNCAN *Amer. Girl Lond.* 254 According to the pure usage of Oxonian English, he was a 'Fresher'. **1894** *Field* 9 June 836/2 The Britannia took in her flying jib, a fresher from off St. Mary's Marshes laying on until the Prince of Wales's cutter was fairly foaming. **1895** *19th Cent.* Nov. 363 Emergence from the condition of 'fresherdom'.

fresher[2]. *dial.* A young frog.

1823 in MOOR *Suffolk Words.* **1896** *Blackw. Mag.* Mar. 314 He loved to catch 'freshers' and let them hop down his throat.

freshet ('frɛʃɪt). Also 8 *erron.* fresh shot. [f. FRESH *sb.*[1] + -ET[1]; or possibly a. OF. *freschet* adj., dim. of *freis* FRESH *a.* (cf. *fontaine frechette*, 16th c. in Godef.).]

1. A small stream of fresh water. Cf. FRESH *sb.*[1] 3. *Obs.* exc. *poet.*

1598 HAKLUYT *Voy.* I. 113 Freshets distilling from the said mountaines.. do fall into the lake. **1611** SIR T. DALE in A. Brown *Genesis U.S.* (1890) I. 507 A shallop necessarie and propper to discover freshetts, Rivers and Creekes. **1674** JOSSELYN *Voy. New Eng.* 160 Gardens, well watered with springs and small freshets. **1827** CARLYLE *Germ. Romance* IV. xiii. 215 The Traveller.. skirts, on the dry lea, many a little freshet. **1887** BOWEN *Virg. Æneid* I. 168 A cave.. sweet Fountain freshets within it.

2. A stream or rush of fresh water flowing into the sea. Cf. FRESH *sb.*[1] 2.

1596 L. KEYMIS in *Hakluyt's Voy.* (1600) III. 673 The freshets.. grow strong and swift, setting directly off to sea against the wind. **1721** BAILEY, *Fresh Shot*.. is when any great River falls into the Sea. **1871** TYNDALL *Fragm. Sc.* (1879) I. vii. 238 He hugged the cross freshets instead of striking out into the smoother water.

3. A flood or overflowing of a river caused by heavy rains or melted snow.

1654 E. JOHNSON *Wond.-wrkg. Provid.* (1867) 45 Her scituation is neere to a River, whose strong freshet at breaking up of Winter filleth all her Bankes. **1784** M. CUTLER in *Life, Jrnls. & Corr.* (1888) I. 100 The freshet in the river.. was so sudden that cattle.. were in danger of being drowned. **1837** C. T. JACKSON *1st Rep. Geol. Maine* 109 The loose materials.. are deposited along river courses, especially during freshets. **1878** HUXLEY *Physiogr.* 142 In a flood, or freshet, the water is always highly charged with detritus.

transf. and *fig.* **1858** O. W. HOLMES *Aut. Breakf.-t.* (1883) 196 A feast of reason and a regular 'freshet' of soul. **1872** MARK TWAIN *Innoc. Abr.* xvii. 116, I never saw such a freshet of loveliness before. **1886** MRS. PHELPS *Burglars in Par.* ix. 155 Freshets of circulars poured over the land.

attrib. **1865** M. C. HARRIS *St. Philip's* xxiv. 173 Rough bridges.. left gaping from freshet-time to freshet-time. **1875** in Buckland *Log-bk.* 364 It is always in a freshet season that the Channel cuts down the Frampton side. **1895** J. WINSOR *Mississ. Basin* 14 Evans.. puts the ordinary freshet rise at twenty feet.

Hence **'freshet** *v. trans.*, to flood as with a freshet; in quot. *fig.*

1865 MRS. WHITNEY *Gayworthys* II. 179 The winds.. freshetted all the waysides.. with a down-pour of colour.

freshful ('frɛʃfʊl), *a. rare.* [f. FRESH *a.* + -FUL.] Full of freshness; refreshing. Hence **'freshfulness**.

1830 *Fraser's Mag.* I. 426 Fragrant breezes, freshful showers. *a* **1859** L. HUNT *Poems* (1860) 234, I took a long deep draught of silent freshfulness.

'freshhood. *U.S.* = FRESHMANHOOD.

1836 *Harvardiana* III. No. 555. p. 98 When to the college I came in the first dear day of my freshhood.

freshish ('frɛʃɪʃ), *a.* [f. FRESH *a.* + -ISH.] Somewhat fresh; in senses of FRESH *a.*

1741 RICHARDSON *Pamela* I. 170 If the Mould should look a little freshish, it wont be so much suspected. **1798** LADY HUNTER in *Sir M. Hunter's Jrnl.* (1894) 123 All the gales.. are.. a little fresh, or freshish. **1824** *Examiner* 555/2 He was freshish.. neither drunk nor sober. **1862** T. A. TROLLOPE *Marietta* I. i. 6 'It is freshish'.. pulling up the fur collar. **1865** *Examiner* 18 Mar. 163 Sims, a waterman, says there was a freshish wind, but no surf.

†**'fresh-lap.** *Obs.* = DEWLAP I.

1398 [see DEWLAP].

freshly ('frɛʃlɪ), *adv.* [f. FRESH *a.* + -LY[2].] In a fresh manner.

1. Newly; lately; recently. (Now only with ppl. adjs.)

c **1325** *Body & Soul* 255 in *Map's Poems* (Camden) 343 Whoder thou3test thou fere, That were thus freshliche from me gon? **1480** CAXTON *Descr. Brit.* 56 New comen in to Irlonde fresshly after the martirdome of seint Thomas of Caunterbury. **1610** SHAKS. *Temp.* v. i. 236 Where we, in all our trim, freshly beheld Our royall, good, and gallant Ship. **1648** BOYLE *Seraph. Love* xxvi. (1700) 159 As I freshly intimated, I.. fear.. your tir'd Patience.. doth summon me to leave you. **1703** MAUNDRELL *Journ. Jerus.* (1721) Add. 3 The banks were freshly wet. **1812** BYRON *Ch. Har.* I. lxviii, Yells the mad crowd o'er entrails freshly torn. **1856** FROUDE *Hist. Eng.* II. 276 The excommunication of the king was then freshly published.

b. Anew, afresh. Now *rare*.

1613 PURCHAS *Pilgrimage* (1614) 508 He bled freshly. **1617** WITHER *Fidelia* Juvenilia (1633) 458 Downe againe we set And freshly in that sweete discourse went on. **1892** *Bookman* Oct. 27/2 An additional reason for freshly introducing him.. to English readers.

2. With unabated or renewed vigour. †Also fiercely, eagerly (*obs.*).

c **1350** *Will. Palerne* 1190 William ginnes ride fresly toward here fos. **1375** BARBOUR *Bruce* VII. 166 And fell rycht freschly for till ete. **14..** *Fencing w. Two-Handed Sword* in *Rel. Ant.* I. 309 Fresly smyte thy strokis by dene. **1526** *Pilgr. Perf.* (W. de W. 1531) 121 The trees & flowres dyd.. sprynge moost freshly. **1577–87** HOLINSHED *Chron.* III. 818/1 Three score archers shot freshlie at their enimies. **1598** STOW *Surv.* 348 He was.. freshly pursued. **1678** DRYDEN & LEE *Œdipus* IV. Wks. 1883 VI. 205 Fate seemed to wind him up for four score years; Yet freshly ran he on ten winters more. **1849** W. M. W. CALL *Reverberat.* I. 8 Again the life-tree freshlier springs. **1881** SWINBURNE *Mary Stuart* II. ii. 82, I would sleep On this strange news of thine, that being awake I may the freshlier front my sense thereof.

b. With respect to the wind: Briskly; with considerable force.

1399 *Pol. Poems* (Rolls) I. 415 They.. bare a topte saile affor the wynde ffresshely, to make a good ffare. **1850** TENNYSON *In Mem.* xcv,[A breeze] gathering freshlier overhead, Rock'd the full-foliaged elms. **1885** *Manch. Exam.* 10 Sept. 5/5 It has been blowing freshly from W-S-W.

3. With undiminished intensity, purity, distinctness, etc.

c **1369** CHAUCER *Dethe Blaunche* 1228 And love hir alwey freshly newe. **1660** COWLEY *His Majesties Restoration* iv, That name of Cromwell, which does freshly still The Courses of so many Sufferers fill. **1720** POPE *Iliad* XVIII. 621 One held a living foe, that freshly bled With new-made wounds. **1888** BURGON *Lives 12 Gd. Men* I. Pref. 9 While yet the man lives freshly in the memory of his fellows.

4. With fresh appearance, odour, etc.

1600 SHAKS. *A.Y.L.* III. ii. 243 Looks he as freshly, as he did the day he wrastled? **1819** BYRON *Juan* II. clxix, And every morn his colour freshlier came. **1883** STEVENSON *Treas. Isl.* III. xiv, The air.. smelt more freshly than down beside the marsh.

†**5.** Gaily, with magnificence. *Obs.*

c **1400** *Destr. Troy* 6206 A chariot.. Framet ouer fresshly with frettes of perle. **1470–85** MALORY *Arthur* III. i, So they rode freshly with grete royalte. **1523** LD. BERNERS *Froiss.* I. xvi. 16 Ladyes and damozelles freshly apparayled.

6. *Comb.* with pa. pples., as ***freshly-blown, -fallen, -named, -opened*** adjs.

1661 BOYLE *Spring of Air* II. iv. (1682) 49 The one is that freshly-named Mr. Townly and divers ingenious persons, etc. **1860** TYNDALL *Glac.* I. iv. 34 The melting of freshly fallen mountain snow. **1861** L. L. NOBLE *Icebergs* 140 Freshly blown lilacs. **1876** GEO. ELIOT *Dan. Der.* IV. lxi. 216 She.. looked out like a freshly-opened flower.

freshman ('frɛʃmən). [f. FRESH *a.* + MAN.]

1. A new comer; a novice; a 'new hand'. Used by Cheke for †a proselyte.

c **1550** CHEKE *Matt.* xxiii. 15 Ie go about both bi see and land to maak oon freshman. *a* **1627** MIDDLETON *More Dissemblers* II. iv, I'll trust no freshman with such secrets. **1679** BURNET *Hist. Ref.* I. 490 Cranmer was an old and experienced captain, and was not to be troubled by freshmen and novices. **1708** *Royal Proclam.* 26 June in *Lond. Gaz.* No. 4452/2 The Masters of Fishing-Ships.. do neglect to produce Certificates of their Compliments of Green Men or Fresh Men. **1871** B. TAYLOR *Faust* (1875) II. II. i. 89 Shy and unsophisticated I, as honest freshman, waited.

attrib. **1833** WHEWELL in Todhunter *Acct. Whewell's Writ.* (1876) II. 164 We freshman reviewers are too serious for Lockhart.

2. a. A student during his or her first year, *esp.* the first term, at a University. *rare.*

1596 NASHE *Saffron Walden* 4 He was but yet a fresh-man in Cambridge. **1628** EARLE *Microcosm.*, *Gentl. of Univ.* (Arb.) 44 At Tennis.. when hee can once play a Set, he is a Fresh-man no more. **1682** SHADWELL *Lanc. Witches* I. B j b, Your Master of Artship That made you lord it over Boys and Freshmen. **1782** M. CUTLER in *Life, Jrnls. & Corr.* (1888) II. 206 The admission of so large a class of Freshmen the last year.. is matter of agreeable surprise. **1853** 'C. BEDE' *Verdant Green* iii, Freshmen cannot learn the mysteries of college etiquette in a day. **1897–8** *Vassar Coll. Catal.* 90 Freshman Class. Adair, Barbara. Affeld, Antoinette [etc.]. **1971** *Scotsman* 20 May 21/8 The tall, 19-year-old Glasgow University 'freshman' faces her first major test of the season.

b. *Comb.* as **freshman class** *U.S.*, 'the lowest of the four classes in an American college' (Webster 1890); **freshman-sophomore** *U.S.* (see quot. 1851); also shortened ***fresh-soph(omore)***.

1805 D. MCCLURE *Diary* (1899) 8, I.. was examined & admitted into the Freshman Class at Yale College. **1832** *Coll. New H. Hist. Soc.* III. 9 He was.. in 1751.. admitted a member of the freshman class in Harvard University at the age of twelve years. **1842** *Knickerbocker* XIX. 433 From time immemorial a playful animosity has existed between the freshman and sophomore classes. **1847** *Yale Lit. Mag.* XII. 114, I was a Fresh-Sophomore then, and a waiter in the commons' hall. **1851** B. H. HALL *College Words*, *Fresh-soph*, an abbreviation of Freshman-Sophomore. One who enters college in the Sophomore year, having passed the time of the Freshman year elsewhere.

Hence **'freshmanhood**, the condition or state of a freshman; the period during which it lasts; **fresh'manic** *a.*, of or pertaining to a freshman; †**'freshmanly** *a.* = prec.; **'freshmanship** = *freshmanhood*; also *humorous*, the personality of a freshman.

1568 C. WATSON *Polyb.* To Rdr., Thus I put forth this my freshmanly enterprise. **1605** B. JONSON *Volpone* IV. i. (Rtldg.) 195/2 Well, wise sir Pol, since you have practised thus Upon my freshman-ship, I'll try your salt-head, What proof it is against a counter-plot. **1617** HALES *Serm.* 9 This young fencer hath set himselfe vp one of the deepest mysteries of our profession, to practise his freshmanship vpon. *c* **1741** BRAINERD in Edwards *Life* I. (1851) 15 Being much exposed on account of my freshmanship. **1837** LOWELL *Lett.* (1894) I. 21 Those days of Freshmanic innocence. **1848** J. H. NEWMAN *Loss & Gain* 4 What they had in common was freshmanship, etc. **1876** RUSKIN *Fors Clav.* VI. lxvi. 192 That I might not torment Mr. Baker with his freshmanship. **1885** *Macm. Mag.* Nov. 28/1 As it grew in the Freshmanhood of John Henry Newman.

†**'freshment.** *Obs.* [f. FRESH *v.* + -MENT.] Refreshing influence.

1611 J. CARTWRIGHT *Preacher's Trav.* 19 To enioy the freshment of the aire and riuer.

freshness ('frɛʃnɪs). [f. FRESH *a.* + -NESS.] The quality or condition of being fresh in senses of the adj. *spec.* forwardness, impertinence. Also *concr.* (nonce-use) a fresh stream. Cf. FRESH *a.* 15.

1398 TREVISA *Barth. De P.R.* XIII. xxi. (1495) 451 Fressh water rysyth vpwarde for fresshnes and lyghtnes, and salte water fallyth dounwarde for his heuynesse. **1493** *Petronilla* (Pynson) 138 Clad all in floures of spirituall fresshnesse. *a* **1500** *Cuckow & Night.* 155 For therof truly commeth all goodnesse.. Jollitie, pleasaunce, and freshnesse. *a* **1533** LD. BERNERS *Huon* lv. 184 Y[e] fresshenes of his aparyll. **1626** BACON *Sylva* §824 The Kite affecteth not so much the Grossenesse of the Aire as the Cold and Freshnesse thereof.

1683 Boyle in *Phil. Trans.* XVII. 628 My way of examining the Freshness and Saltness of Waters. 1712 Budgell *Spect.* No. 425 ¶1 That I might enjoy the Freshness of the Evening in my Garden. 1768–74 Tucker *Lt. Nat.* I. i. vi. §32 The mind runs after it with..much freshness and eagerness. 1803–6 Wordsw. *Intimations Immort.* i, The glory and the freshness of a dream. *a* 1821 Keats '*I stood tiptoe upon a little hill*', Where the hurrying freshnesses aye preach A natural sermon o'er their pebbly beds. 1844 H. H. Wilson *Brit. India* III. 164 The impression..had already lost much of its freshness. 1870 Morris *Earthly Par.* I. i. 13 The freshness of the open sea Seemed ease and joy and very life to me. 1892 'Mark Twain' *Amer. Claimant* 160 The mob began to take its revenge—for the discomfort..it had brought upon itself by its own too rash freshness. 1901 *Munsey's Mag.* XXIV. 791/1 He had once heartily 'larruped' a new hand who had exhibited an unpleasing 'freshness' when speaking to her. 1928 J. C. Lincoln *Silas Bradford's Boy* 13 The captain's dignity was slightly ruffled by what he considered freshness on the part of his nephew.

'fresh,water, *a.* [f. fresh *a.* + water *sb.*]

1. a. Of or pertaining to, yielding, produced by, or living in water that is fresh or not salt. Also, pertaining to an animal that lives in fresh water. So in names of fishes, as ***freshwater mussel***, etc.

1528 Paynel *Salerne Regim.* O iij, The best freshe water fyshe..is taken in water stonye in the bottum. 1765 T. Hutchinson *Hist. Mass.* I. v. 465 Pearch, and other fresh-water fish. 1768–74 Tucker *Lt. Nat.* (1852) II. 160 The fresh-water polypus. 1774 Goldsm. *Nat. Hist.* (1776) I. 49 Animals..bred in the numerous fresh-water lakes. 1798 *Sporting Mag.* XII. 183 The Bull-head..is in some places called the fresh-water devil. 1828 Miss Mitford *Village* Ser. iii. (1863) 82 Fresh-water flowers of several colours. 1863 Lyell *Antiq. Man* 142 Land and fresh-water shells, are common to both formations. 1875 Croll *Climate & T.* xxix. 485 We suppose those in the western channel to be of freshwater origin.

b. *U.S.* (See quot. 1925.)

1860 O. W. Holmes *E. Venner* vii, A Sophomore from one of the fresh-water colleges. 1881 *Harper's Mag.* Jan. 224/1 'There is enough to send him through college.'.. 'In a fresh-water college?'.. 'Why not, for a fresh-water boy? He will always live in the West.' 1903 C. T. Brady *Bishop* xii. 230 He had just entered the preparatory class of a little Eastern Fresh-water college. 1925 G. P. Krapp *English Lang. in Amer.* I. 135 One speaks also..of regions further inland with the qualifying adjective freshwater, as in *freshwater towns* or *freshwater colleges*, the adjective carrying with it some implication of rusticity and provincialism. 1963 *Punch* 17 Apr. 548/1 A very great improvement in the standard and aims of even quite small 'fresh-water colleges'.

2. a. Unaccustomed to salt water, new to the sea.

1621 *Crt. & Times Jas. I* (1849) II. 215 The French ambassador..being himself such a fresh-water sailor. 1659 D. Pell *Impr. Sea* 515 Fresh-water travellers at Sea. 1719 De Foe *Crusoe* I. i, You're but a fresh-water sailor. 1816 Keatinge *Trav.* (1817) I. 26 A considerable deal of bustle occurs amongst the fresh-water sailors of these countries.

†b. *fig.* Unpractised; unskilled; untrained; raw.

1579–80 North *Plutarch* (1676) 232 [The storm] did marvellously trouble them, and specially those that were but fresh-water Souldiers. 1624 *Crt. & Times Jas. I* (1849) II. 461 Some fresh-water soldiers are preferred to old servitors. 1677 *App. to Spottiswood's Hist. Ch. Scotl.* 15 The Tironenses..are not a distinct Order of Monks, but rather young Novices, or fresh-water Monks. 1727 A. Hamilton *New Acc. E. Ind.* I. xxvii. 338 The..Army was commanded by..Antonio de Figuera, a Freshwater Soldier, but a great Bragadocio. 1754 Fielding *Voy. to Lisbon* Wks. 1882 VII. 11 Ignorant, unlearned, and fresh-water critics.

†3. ***fresh-water soldier***, a name for the plant *Stratiotes aloides* (Gerard, *Herbal*, 1597, ii. ccxcix).

Hence **†fresh-watered** *a.* = prec. 2 b.

1674 S. Vincent *Gallant's Acad.* Ep. Ded. A v b, Commanders will not disdain to instruct even a fresh-watered Souldier in the School-points of War.

'freshwoman. *rare.* The analogue of a freshman in university.

a 1627 Middleton *Chaste Maid* iii. ii, Mother, you do intreat like a fresh-woman. 1871 *Scribner's Monthly* II. 347 To bring them where they can enter as Freshmen, or Freshwomen. 1885 *Academy* 21 Nov. 347 A fresh-woman—if that is the girl-equivalent of fresh-man—is to play the second lady.

freshwood, dial. form of threshold *sb.*

fresison (frɪ'saɪsɒn). *Logic.* A mnemonic word designating the fifth mood of the fourth figure of syllogisms.

1827 Whately *Logic* (ed. 2) 98 Fresison.

Fresnel (freɪ'nɛl). [The name of A. J. *Fresnel* (1788–1827), French physicist and engineer.]

1. Used *attrib.* and in the possessive to designate apparatus, phenomena, and concepts relating to his work in optics, as ***Fresnel biprism*** = biprism; ***Fresnel diffraction***, diffraction in which the diffraction pattern is a non-linear function of the variation in phase across the diffracting aperture or object; ***Fresnel's formulæ***, two formulæ giving the proportion of linearly polarized light reflected from a plane surface in terms of the angles of incidence and refraction (see quot. 1957[1]); ***Fresnel lens***, a lens consisting of a number of concentric annular sections, each of different curvature and so designed that a parallel beam relatively free from spherical aberration can be produced; ***Fresnel's integrals***, the integrals $\int_0^x \cos \frac{1}{2}\pi t^2 dt$ and $\int_0^x \sin \frac{1}{2}\pi t^2 dt$, used in the theory of Fresnel diffraction; ***Fresnel('s) mirror*** or ***mirrors***, two plane mirrors set together at an angle of just less than 180 degrees; ***Fresnel's rhomb***, a glass parallelepiped of such a shape that light can be passed through it to undergo two total internal reflections and emerge parallel to its initial direction.

[1830 D. Brewster in *Phil. Trans. R. Soc.* CXX. 73, I am persuaded that the formulæ of Fresnel are accurate expressions of the phenomena under every variation of incidence and refractive power. *Ibid.* 77 M. Fresnel's general formula has been adapted to this species of rays.] 1835 *Rep. Brit. Assoc.* *1834* 333 M. Poisson applied Fresnel's integral to the case of diffraction by an opaque circular disc. *Ibid.* 370 The parallelopiped thus constructed, and which is known under the name of Fresnel's rhomb, is of essential service in experiments on circular and elliptic polarization. 1848 A. Stevenson *Acc. Skerryvore Lighthouse* ii. 257 The divergence..may be described as the angle which the flame subtends at the principal focus of the lens, the maximum of which, produced at the vertex of Fresnel's great lens.., is about 5° 9′. 1849 G. G. Stokes in *Camb. & Dublin Math. Jrnl.* IV. 9 There are three particular angles of incidence..for which special results are deducible from Fresnel's formulæ. 1854 Fresnel's rhomb [see rhomb 2 b]. 1874 tr. *Lommel's Nature of Light* (1875) xv. 207 (*caption*) Fresnel's mirror. *a* 1884 Knight *Dict. Mech.* Suppl. 356/2 *Fresnel lens*, a lens consisting of a central portion of spherical section and surrounding rings, so adapted as to direct the rays practically parallel. 1890, 1904 Fresnel's biprism [see biprism]. 1905 R. W. Wood *Physical Optics* vii. 195 (*heading*) Fresnel diffraction phenomena. 1937 Jenkins & White *Fund. Optics* viii. 173 Since Fresnel diffraction is the easiest to observe, it was historically the first type to be investigated. 1937 G. S. Monk *Light* x. 129 A much better device for obtaining the interference between two sections of a wave front..is the Fresnel biprism. 1957 *Encycl. Brit.* XIV. 61/1 If *i* is the angle of incidence and *r* that of refraction, the fraction [of light] reflected is $\sin^2(i - r)/\sin^2(i + r)$ or $\tan^2(i - r)/\tan^2(i + r)$, according to the direction of polarization. These expressions are usually called Fresnel's sine and tangent formulae. 1957 *Oxf. Compan. Theatre* (ed. 2) 476/1 The Fresnel lens spotlight or step-lens spotlight seems to have had more development and use in the U.S.A. than in England. 1959 Born & Wolf *Princ. Optics* i. 50 One may also invert the procedure and produce, by means of Fresnel's rhomb, linearly polarized light from elliptically polarized light. 1966 *McGraw-Hill Encycl. Sci. & Technol.* VII. 185 Another way of splitting the light from the source is the Fresnel double mirror.

2. (With lower-case initial letter.) A name occas. used by spectroscopists for a unit of frequency equal to 10^{12} Hz (10^{12} cycles per second).

1939 W. R. Brode *Chem. Spectroscopy* viii. 191 The choice of the fresnel as a unit for recording visible and ultraviolet data is very satisfactory in that the units are not unwieldy. 1951 *Nature* 3 Mar. 367/2 Frequencies expressed in sec.$^{-1}$ involve large powers of ten ($\sim 10^{15}$), while the fresnel ($= 10^{12}$sec.$^{-1}$) has never become popular. 1960 Brode & Corning in W. G. Berl *Physical Methods in Chem. Anal.* (ed. 2) I. 194 The limits of the visible spectrum in frequency are from 750 to 400 fresnel units.

Freson(e; see Frison *Obs.*, Frisian (man or horse).

fres(s)t, var. form of frist, *Obs.*

fret (frɛt), *sb.*[1] Also 4–9 **frette**, 5–6 **frete**, (6 *Sc.* **fratt**). [app. a. OF. *frete* trellis-work, interlaced work (mod.F. *frette*, in the heraldic sense = 2).

This sb. and the related fret *v.*[2] are commonly believed to represent the OE. *frætwe* pl., ornaments, *frætw(i)an* to adorn, but this appears to be phonologically inadmissible, and many of the usual phraseological combinations of the words in ME. are paralleled by similar uses in OF.]

1. Ornamental interlaced work; a net; an ornament (esp. for the hair) consisting of jewels or flowers in a network.

c 1385 Chaucer *L.G.W.* Prol. A 147 A frette of goold sche hadde next hyre her. *Ibid.* B 228 In-with a fret of rede rose leves. 1390 Gower *Conf.* II. 228 With frette of perle upon his hede. 1418 *E.E. Wills* (1882) 36 Wroght wit mapil leues and fret of a iij. foill. ?*c* 1475 *Sqr. lowe Degre* 212 A ladyes head with many a frete. 1488 in Tytler *Hist. Scot.* (1864) II. 392 A frete of the quenis oure set with grete perle. *a* 1500 *Flower & Leaf* 152 On her head A rich fret of gold..full of stately riche stones set. 1516 *Inventories* (1815) 26 Item ane paclott of crammesy satene with ane fratt of gold on it with xii. diamantis. 1603 Drayton *Bar. Wars* vi. xliii, About the Border, in a fine-wrought Fret Emblem's, Empressa's, Hieroglyphics, set. 1867 Morris *Jason* vii. 190 Unto her fragrant breast her hand she set, And drew therefrom a bag of silken fret.

2. *Her.* Originally, a figure formed by two bendlets, dexter and sinister, intersecting; = F. *frette.* (Cf. fretty.) In later use, 'a figure formed by two narrow bands in saltire, interlaced with a mascle' (Cussans).

1572 Bossewell *Armorie* ii. 85 b, The Fret borne in this Cote Armour, is founde borne also of diuerse noble Gentlemen. 1603 Drayton *Bar. Wars* ii. xxiv, In his white Cornet, Verdon doth display A fret of Gueles. 1761 *Brit. Mag.* II. 149 Arms..in the second and third, a fret, or. 1864 Boutell *Her. Hist. & Pop.* xv. 224 Hugh, the head of the family, bears the frette without any difference.

3. †a. *Arch.* Carved ornament, *esp.* in ceilings, consisting of intersecting lines in relief. *Obs.*

1626 Bacon *Sylva* §111 We see in Garden-knots, and the Frets of Houses, and all equall and well answering Figures how they please. 1635 *Althorp MS.* in Simpkinson *Washingtons* App. 71 To Butler and his boye..plastering the fret in the drawinge chamber. 1664 Evelyn *Archit.* 138 Roofs..Emboss'd with Fretts of wonderful relievo.

b. An ornamental pattern composed of continuous combinations of straight lines, joined usually at right angles. Also *attrib.*

1664 Evelyn tr. *Freart's Arch.* ii. ix. 110 The Fret..consists in a certain interlacing of two Lists or small Fillets, which run always in parallel distances equal to their breadth, with this necessary condition, that at every return and intersection they do always fall into right angles. 1665–76 Rea *Flora* 8 A railed fret of twenty-three divisions. 1833 J. Holland *Manuf. Metal* II. 172 The fret, an ornament, either of open filigree work, or cast in bold relief..is placed immediately beneath the lowest bar or fret-rail, and in the best kind of stoves it is made stationary. 1836 H. G. Knight *Archit. Tour Normandy* 199 The most common mouldings are the billet..the zig-zag or embattled frette. 1857 Birch *Anc. Pottery* (1858) II. 4 The fret or herring-bone is of common occurrence on vases of the oldest style. 1879 J. J. Young *Ceram. Art* 209 In the kylix on the right, the rectilinear designs and enclosed squares become the fret.

4. *Comb.*, as **fret-cutting** *vbl. sb.*, the cutting of wood with a fret saw into ornamental designs; also *attrib.*; **fretwood**, wood prepared for fretwork (sense 2). Also fret-saw.

1881 Young *Every Man his own Mechanic* §530 Small pieces of ornamental furniture..can be adorned most effectively by fret-cutting. *Ibid.* §663 A fret-cutting treadle-machine. 1885 *Bazaar* 30 Mar. 1262/3, 12 ft. planed fret-wood.

fret (frɛt), *sb.*[2] Also 6 **frete, freete, freate**, 7 **freat.** [f. fret *v.*[1]]

1. A gnawing or wearing away, erosion. Now *rare.* Also *concr.* †a canker, a fretting sore; a decayed spot (in the wood of a bow or arrow, in a hair).

1545 Ascham *Toxoph.* (Arb.) 120 Freetes be in a shaft as well as in a bowe, and they be muche lyke a Canker, crepynge and encreasynge in those places in a bowe, whyche be weaker then other. 1639 Fuller *Holy Warre* (1647) iv. iv. 173 This string to his bow is so full of gauls, frets, and knots, it cannot hold. 1681 Chetham *Angler's Vade-m.* ii. §6 (1689) 10 Such [hairs] as are..free from Galls, Scabs and Frets. 1822–34 *Good's Study Med.* (ed. 4) II. 82 The fret or erosion which frequently takes place in different parts of the skin. 1830 Tennyson *Poems* 41 Before..the busy fret Of that sharpheaded worm begins.

fig. 1580 Babington *Lord's Prayer* (1596) 6 If thou desirest to be free from the fret of enuie..pray. 1581 J. Bell tr. *Haddon's Answ. Osor.* 391 And now behold how many pumples and fretts lurke under this one skabbe of the popish doctrine. 1603 Drayton *Bar. Wars* iii. xli, Time never toucht him with deforming Fret. 1606 G. W[oodcocke] *Iustine* Gg 6b. He was a diligent repressor of Eunuches and Courtiers, calling them the mothes and frettes of the Pallace.

2. Pain in the bowels, gripes, colic. Also *pl.* Now *dial.* Cf. fret *v.*[1] 4.

1600 Surflet *Countrie Farme* ii. xlix. 316 Oile of [Jesamin]..will..appease the frets of yoong children. 1652 Culpepper *Eng. Physic.* 161 Children..are troubled with winde in the stomach or belly, which they [Nurses] call the Frets. 1681 W. Robertson *Phraseol. Gen.* (1693) 642 The fret, or mouldy-grubs. 1842 Johnson *Farmer's Encycl.*, *Fret* in farriery, a name sometimes applied to gripes or colic in horses or other cattle.

3. Agitation of mind; a ruffled condition of temper; irritation, passion, vexation; also, querulous or peevish utterance. In phr. ***fret of mind, fret and fever, fret and fume.***

1556 J. Heywood *Spider & F.* xliii. 38 This formost spider and flie in furious fret, Frowning ech on other. 1607 Tourneur *Rev. Trag.* i. i. Wks. 1878 II. 6 The thought of that Turnes my abused heart-strings into fret. 1612 *Crt. & Times Jas. I* (1849) I. 184 He is..blamed..as if he had hastened his brother's end by putting him into frets. 1647 Trapp *Comm. 2 Cor.* xii. 5 They make us sick of the fret. 1664 H. More *Myst. Iniq* xx. 77 It were a plague and fret of mind..to the poor credulous Laiety. 1724 De Foe *Mem. Cavalier* (1840) 145 My lord was in as great a fret as I. 1820 Lamb *Elia* Ser i. *South-Sea Ho.*, Situated as thou art..amid the fret and fever of speculation. 1837 Carlyle *Fr. Rev.* II. iii. vii, A fret and fever that keeps heart and brain on fire. 1866 Mrs. Gaskell *Wives & Dau.* xxix. (1867) 290 He heard his wife's plaintive fret. 1885 Spurgeon *Treas. Dav.* Ps. cxxvii. 2 Those whom the Lord loves are delivered from the fret and fume of life.

†4. A sudden disturbance (of weather); a gust, squall (of wind); in early use also, agitation of waves. *Obs.*

1558 W. Towrson in Hakluyt *Voy.* (1589) 130 It [foresaile] was blowen from the yarde with a freat. 1583 Stanyhurst *Æneis* i. (Arb.) 24 Through Sicil his raging wyld frets..you sayled [*Scyllæam rabiem experti*]. 1590 R. Ferris *Voy. Bristow* in Arb. Garner VI. 159 We were in a great fret by reason of the race. 1653–4 Whitelocke *Jrnl. Swed. Emb.* (1772) I. 166 Such frets of weather in twenty howers time..that [etc.]. 1678 Teonge *Diary* (1825) 269 At on this morning roase a frett of wind. *a* 1734 North *Lives* (1826) II. 316 Between Ireland and the height of the Cape, such frets of wind came down.

fig. 1750 Johnson *Rambler* No. 73 ¶10 Frustrated of my hopes by a fret of dotage.

5. Secondary fermentation in liquors. Phr. ***on*** or ***upon the fret.***

1664 Beale *Cider* in *Evelyn's Pomona* 40 Men like or dislike drink, that hath more or less of the fret in it. 1703 *Art & Myst. Vintners* 12 White Wines upon the Frett. 1710 T. Fuller *Pharm. Extemp.* 1 Midling Ale..freshish, and not upon the fret. 1763 S. T. Janssen *Smuggling laid open* 111 The Officer should not dip when any Wines are upon the Fret. 1807 Vancouver *Agric. Devon* (1813) 240 When every symptom of fret is wholly subsided, the cider is racked off. **1890** *Gloucestersh. Gloss.*, *Fret*, a gaseous fermentation of cider or beer.

6. Phr. *on* or *upon the fret* (see senses 3 and 4; perh. partly transf. from sense 5): in a state of agitation, irritation, ill-humour, or impatience.

1679 SHADWELL *True Widow* 6 'Tis some Roring Ranting Play that's upon the fret all the while. **1688** *Vox Cleri Pro Rege* 3 But he fears nothing, when his Zeal and his Discretion are once upon the fret. **1704** ADDISON *Italy* 160 The Surface..cover'd with Froth and Bubbles; for it [River] runs all along upon the Fret. **1705** S. WHATELY in Perry *Hist. Coll. Amer. Col. Ch.* I. 166 Crying out whenever he is put upon the fret, 'Gov[r] Nicholson'. **1782** MISS BURNEY *Cecilia* x. x, The moment you have put him upon the fret, you'll fall into the dumps yourself. **1854** DE QUINCEY *Autobiog.* Wks. II. 280 Flanders..on the fret for an insurrectionary war. **1858** R. S. SURTEES *Ask Mamma* xxv. 94 He was always either on the strut or the fret.

fret (frɛt), *sb.*[3] Also 5-6 freyte. [of uncertain etymology.

Possibly a use of OF. *frete* ring, ferrule (see FRET *sb.*[5]). Another possibility is that it is connected with FRET *v.* to rub (cf. quot. 1606).]

In musical instruments like the guitar, formerly a ring of gut (Stainer), now a bar or ridge of wood, metal, etc. placed on the fingerboard, to regulate the fingering.

c **1500** *Prov.* in *Antiq. Rep.* (1809) IV. 406 In myddest of the body [of Lute], the stryngis soundith best, For, stoppide in the freytes, they abydeth the pynnes wrest. **1565** CALFHILL *Answ. Treat. Crosse* 21 b, If the strings be out of tune, or frets disordered, there wanteth the harmony. **1606** CHAPMAN *M. D'Olive* I. B 3 b, The string soundis euer well, that rubs not too much ath frets. **1698** *Phil. Trans.* XX. 80 The Frets are nearer to one another toward the Bridge. **1788** CAVALLO *ibid.* LXXVIII. 242 In a set of musical keys, pipes, or frets, a temperament is absolutely necessary. **1837** *Blackw. Mag.* XLI. 92 The violin, which once had six strings, with guitar frets, was fortunately relieved from these superfluities.

fig. **1587** *Gascoigne's Wks.*, *Hearbes*, &c., Commend. Verse, Whose cords were coucht on frets of deepe disdaine.

attrib. **1814** CARY *Dante, Parad.* xx. 22 As sound Of cittern, at the fret-board..Is..modulate and tuned.

fret, *sb.*[4] *rare.* [ad. OF. *frete*, *fraite*, *fraicte*, breach.] A breach or passage made by the sea. (Quot. 1884 perh. belongs to FRET *sb.*[2])

1587 FLEMING *Contn. Holinshed* III. 1537/2 They had no entrance at all, vntill the riuer had made a new fret. **1633** T. STAFFORD *Pac. Hib.* III. vi. (1810) 550 Before they could compasse the fret, or cleft rocky ground as aforesaid. **1884** *Times* 15 Aug. 5 The sands had a tendency to accumulate in the Upper Mersey and..it was the 'frets' and erosion of the sand banks which counteracted this tendency.

fret (frɛt), *sb.*[5] *Obs.* exc. *dial.* [a. OF. *frete* (mod.F. *frette*) a ferrule, ring (also *spec.* as below).] (See quots.)

1688 R. HOLME *Armoury* III. 332/1 The Frets..of a Wheel ..are Iron Hoops about the Nave. **1887** *S. Cheshire Gloss.*, *Fret*, the belt of iron which goes round the nave of a wheel. Also called Clam.

†**fret**, *sb.*[6] *Obs.* Also 7 frete. [ad. L. *fretum*. (Perh. confused with FRET *sb.*[4]).] A strait.

1576 SIR H. GILBERT *Disc. passage to Cataia* i, An Islande [America]..hauing on the Southside of it the frete, or strayte of Magellan. **1610** HOLLAND *Camden's Brit.* I. 345 This Sea coast of Britaine is seperated from the Continent of Europe by a frete or streight. **1646** SIR T. BROWNE *Pseud. Ep.* VII. xiii. 364 In this Euripe or fret of Negropont.. Aristotle drowned himselfe, as many affirme. *a* **1661** FULLER *Worthies* (1840) III. 506 A small fret (known by the peculiar name of Menai) sundereth it from the Welch continent.

fret (frɛt), *v.*[1] Pa. t. and pple. fretted. Pr. ppl. fretting. Forms: *Inf.* 1 fretan, 2 freoten, 3-6 frete(n, 3 *south.* vreten, 5 fretyn, freete, 6 freat(e, 6-7 frett(e, 4- fret. *Pa. t.* 1-2 fræt, 3-4 fret(e, *south.* vret, freet, 4 frat(e, frette, 6 fret; also *weak forms*: 5 freted, 6- fretted. *Pa. pple.* 1 freten, 4 freaten, fretyn(e, 5 frete, -ette; *weak forms*: 6- fretted; also 4-7 fret. Also 3-4 i-, yfrete(n, 5- 6 i-, yfret(te. [OE. *fretan* str. vb. (conjugated like *etan* to EAT) = MLG., MDu. *vrēten* (Du. *vreten*), OHG. *frezzan* (MHG. *vrezzen*, mod.G. *fressen*), Goth. *fraitan* (pret. *frêt*), f. OTeut. *fra-* (see FOR- *pref.*[1]) + **etan* to EAT.]

†**1. a.** *trans.* Chiefly of animals: To eat, devour. Also with *up* and to eat *of*. *Obs.*

Beowulf 1582 He..fræt..fyftyne men. *O.E. Chron.* an. 894 Hie..hæfdon miclne dæl þara horsa freten. *c* **1175** *Lamb. Hom.* 133 Sum [sede feol] bi þe weie..and fuȝeles hit freten. *c* **1205** LAY. 274 Let þu þa hundes..eiðer freten oðer. *a* **1225** *Ancr. R.* 66 þe coue..fret al þæt of hwat heo schulde uorð bringen hire cwike briddes. *c* **1250** *Gen & Ex.* 4027 Ðis leun sal oðer folc freten. *a* **1300** *E.E. Psalter* (Horstman) lxxix. 14 A beste frate it and nama. *c* **1315** SHOREHAM 161 Opone thy wombe thou schalt glyde, And erthe frete. **1377** LANGL. *P. Pl.* B. XVIII 194 Adam after-ward aȝeines hus defence Frette of þat fruit. *c* **1385** CHAUCER *L.G.W.* 1951 *Ariadne*, And into a prysoun..cast is he Tyl..he shulde fretyn be. *c* **1394** *P. Pl. Crede* 729 þey freten vp the furste froyt & falsliche lybbeþ.

absol. **1377** LANGL. *P. Pl.* B. II. 95 And in fastyng-dayes to frete ar ful tyme were. **1447** BOKENHAM *Seyntys* (Roxb.) 71 Have of thine own and faste gyne to frete.

†**b.** *transf.* To devour, consume, destroy. *Obs.*

c **1000** ÆLFRIC *Deut.* xxxii. 22 Fyr fryt land mid his wæstme. **13..** *E.E. Allit. P.* B. 404 þat þe flod nade al freten with freȝtande wawez. ? *a* **1366** CHAUCER *Rom. Rose* 387 For alle thing it [tyme] fret and shal. **1388** WYCLIF *Micah* v. 6 Thei shulen frete the lond of Assur bi swerd. *c* **1400** *Destr. Troy* 9691 A tru to be takon..þaire men for to bery, And to frete hom with fyre.

absol. **1583** STANYHURST *Æneis* II. (Arb.) 67 Thee fyre heer on fretting [*ignis edax*] with blaze too rafter is heaued.

2. a. To gnaw; to consume, torture or wear away by gnawing. Now only of small animals: = EAT 9. Also *intr.* (const. *on*, *into*).

a **1200** *Moral Ode* 274 Naddren and snaken..tered and freteð þe uuele speken. *c* **1205** LAY. 166 Heo [fleoȝen] freten þet corn & þat græs. *c* **1275** *XI Pains of Hell* 19 in *O.E. Misc.* 147 Wrmes habbeþ my fleys ifreten. **1340** HAMPOLE *Pr. Consc.* 6570 Vermyn grete..þe synful men sal gnaw and frete. **1340-70** *Alisaunder* 1159 Fayre handes & feete freaten too the bonne. **1387** TREVISA *Higden* (Rolls) V. 171 Wormes ..frate so Julianus his neþer ende þat [etc.]. **1430-40** LYDG. *Bochas* VII. ii. (1554) 166 b, His flesh gan turne to corrupcion Fret with wormes vpon eche partie. *c* **1440** *Gesta Rom.* lxvii. 384 (Add. MS.), I suffere thes todes to frete. *c* **1450** LONELICH *Grail* xlvii. 207 On his hondis he gan to frete. **1547-64** BAULDWIN *Mor. Philos.* (Palfr.) 127 The mothes and soft wormes fret the cloath. **1551** *Psalter* xxxix. 12 Like as it wer a moth fretting a garment. *a* **1577** GASCOIGNE *Flowers* Wks. (1587) 92 The greedie wormes that linger for the nones, To fret vpon her flesh. **1601** HOLLAND *Pliny* I. 198 The Dragons put in their heads into their snout..and withall fret and gnaw the tenderest part. **1826** LAMB *Elia* Ser. II. *Pop. Fallacies, Home is a Home*, etc., We cannot bear to have our thin wardrobe eaten and fretted into by moths. **1864** SWINBURNE *Atalanta* 1423 The..bee Flits through flowering rush to fret White or duskier violet.

fig. **1398** TREVISA *Barth. De P.R.* II. xix. (1495) 45 The fende..purposyth to chew and to frete the clene lyf of gode men.

b. To champ (the bit); also *absol.*

1835 LYTTON *Rienzi* v. ii, Fretting his proud heart, as a steed frets on the bit. **1850** BLACKIE *Æschylus* II. 67 A young colt That frets the bit..Art thou.

3. a. *transf.* of slow and gradual destructive action, as of frost, rust, disease, chemical corrosives, friction, the waves, etc.: = EAT 10. Const. *into*, *to* (the result). Also with *asunder*, *away*, *in pieces*, *off*, *out*.

In this and the following senses this vb. has partly coalesced with FRET *v.*[4]

a **1225** *Ancr. R.* 184 He uret him suluen, weilawei! ase þe uile deð. **13..** *E.E. Allit. P.* B. 1040 þe soyle by þat se halues ..fel fretes þe flesch. **1398** TREVISA *Barth. De P.R.* XVI. vii. (1495) 557 The fome of syluer..fretyth awaye superfluytee of deed flessh. *c* **1430** in *Pol. Rel. & L. Poems* 183 þe rust þat þi siluer duþ freete. **1523** FITZHERB. *Husb.* §20 The thistyll ..freteth away the cornes nygh it. **1567** G. FENNER in Hakluyt *Voy.* (1589) 148 Our cable was fretted in sunder with a rocke. *a* **1577** GASCOIGNE *Flowers* Wks. (1587) 69, I may no praise unto a knife bequeath Wyth rust yfret though painted be the sheath. **1590** R. PAYNE *Descr. Irel.* (1841) 5 The seas fretteth away the Ice and Snowe. **1594** PLAT *Jewell-ho.* III. 37 Inkes that..would corrode or fret the paper in peeces. **1603** FLORIO *Montaigne* (1634) 266 The Barble fishes..will set the line against their backes, and.. presently saw and fret the same asunder. **1640** FULLER *Joseph's Coat* vii. (1867) 182 Some thieves have..fretted off their fetters with mercury water. **1658** W. BURTON *Itin. Anton.* 158 The name of the City [on the coin] fretted out and quite worn away with age. **1660** BOYLE *New Exp. Phys. Mech.* xxii. 166 The Air..is so sharp, that in a short time it frets not only Iron Plates, but..Tiles upon the Roofs of Houses. **1727** W. MATHER *Yng. Man's Comp.* 74 The Copperas in the Ink will fret the Nibs. **1859** KINGSLEY *Misc.* (1860) I. 106 An island fretted by every frost and storm. **1878** HUXLEY *Physiogr.* 134 The river frets away the rocks along its banks.

absol. **1526** TINDALE *2 Tim.* ii. 11 Their wordes shall fret even as doeth a Cancre. **1597** GERARDE *Herbal* I. lxxxiv. 135 The Onions do fret, attenuate or make thin. **1610** MARKHAM *Masterp.* II. clxxiii. 484 Arsnick..eateth, and fretteth, being a very strong corrosiue. **1888** ELWORTHY *W. Somerset Word-bk.* s.v., [Said of a grindstone] Capital stone, it frets (i.e. grinds) well.

b. *fig.* Chiefly of the passions, etc.: To 'devour', 'consume', torment; cf. EAT 10 c. Also, *to fret oneself*. *Obs.* exc. in *fret the heart*, in which use this sense is now hardly distinguishable from 8.

c **1200** ORMIN 16132 Hat lufe towarrd Godess hus me freteþþ att min herrte. **1390** GOWER *Conf.* III. 98 Full of.. wrathfull thought He fret him selven all to nought. **1430-40** LYDG. *Bochas* IV. i. (1554) 101 a, This Manlius was fret in his corage To greater worships sodainly to ascende. *c* **1450** *How good Wife taught Doughter* 80 in Hazl. *E.E.P.* I. 185 Envyouse herte hym selfe fretithe, my dere childe. *a* **1541** WYATT *Poet. Wks.* (1861) 47 So wrathful love..May freat thy cruel heart! *a* **1547** SURREY *Æneid* IV. 126 Dido doth burne with loue, rage fretes her boones. **1600** HOLLAND *Livy* IX. xiv. (1609) 322 Their hearts alreadie fretted and cankered at the very roote, for the last disgrace received. **1711** STEELE *Spect.* No. 260 ¶1 A crafty Constitution, and an uneasy Mind is fretted with vexatious Passions. **1748** RICHARDSON *Clarissa* (1811) III. xli. 241 It did tease me; insomuch that my very heart was fretted. **1849** SAXE *Poems, Proud Miss McBride*, The very sigh That her stately bosom was fretting. **1856** HAWTHORNE *Eng. Note-bks.* (1870) II. 59 So many curiosities drive one crazy, and fret one's heart to death.

†**c.** *to fret out* (time): to waste.

1608 ARMIN *Nest Ninn.* (1880) 50 By the third is cald to question most that musically fret their time out in idle baubling.

†**4.** Said of pains in the stomach or bowels.

c **1275** *XI Pains Hell* 148 in *O.E. Misc.* 151 Gripes freteþ heore Mawen. *c* **1440** *Promp. Parv.* 179/1 Fretyn, or chervyn, *torqueo*.

5. To form or make by wearing away; = EAT 11. With cognate obj. *to fret its way*.

1593 SHAKS. *Rich. II*, III. iii. 167 Till they haue fretted vs a payre of graues, Within the Earth. **1605** —— *Lear* I. iv. 307 Let it stampe wrinkles in her brow of youth, With cadent Teares fret Channels in her cheekes. **1642** FULLER *Holy & Prof. St.* v. xix. 441 As if his eager soul, biting for anger at the clay of his body, desired to fret a passage through it. **1872** C. KING *Mountain. Sierra Nev.* iv. 87 A broad white torrent fretting its way along the bottom of an impassable gorge.

†**6.** *intr.* To make a way by gnawing or corrosion; *lit.* and *fig.*; = EAT 12. Also with *through*. Const. *into*, *to*. *Obs.*

1399 LANGL. *Rich. Redeles* II. 127 The ffresinge ffrost ffreted to here hertis. **1509** HAWES *Past. Pleas.* XXXII. (Percy) 159 With knotted whyppes in the flesshe to frete. **1534** *Act 26 Hen. VIII*, c. 9 The flud and rage of the sea..doth freate ..in dyuers places. **1567** TURBERV. *Epit & Sonn.* (1837) 368 Eche lowering looke of yours, frets farther in my hart. **1614** BP. HALL *Recoll. Treat.* 1126 How dangerous it is, to suffer sinne to lye fretting into the soule! **1635** N. CARPENTER *Geog. Del.* II. vii. 123 The Water..would sooner fret through and cause a passage, then make a stoppage. **1650** FULLER *Pisgah* IV. v. 82 His streams [mouths of the Nile] fret one into another. *Ibid.* 373 Perforations which in process of time might fret in, and indent into the structure itself. **1676** WISEMAN *Surg.* I. xvii. 80 Many Wheals arose, and fretted one into another, with great Excoriation.

†**7.** *intr.* for *refl.* To become eaten, corroded, or worn; to waste or wear away; to decay, become corrupt. Also with *asunder*, *off*, *out*. *Obs.* Cf. FRET *v.*[4] 2.

1486 *Bk. St. Albans* B ij b, And that same penne shalle frete asonder, and fall a way. **1545** ASCHAM *Toxoph.* (Arb.) 121 Bowes moost commonlye freate vnder the hande..for the heete of the hand. **1568** *Jacob & Esau* II. iv. in Hazl. *Dodsley* II. 218 If I had bidden from meat any longer, I think my very maw would have fret asunder. **1593** DRAYTON *Idea* 170 Metals doe waste, and fret with Cankers Rust. **1657** W. RAND tr. *Gassendi's Life of Peiresc* II. 128 When passing through a coloured glasse, they [the Raies of the Sun] fret off, and carry with them some portion of the colour. **1761** HADDINGTON *Forest-trees* (1765) 23 They [Alder trees] fretted at the top and died. **1762** FALCONER *Shipwr.* II. 299 The leather fretting..By friction wore must ever be supply'd. **1804** ABERNETHY *Surg. Observ.* 111 The wound fretted out into a sore.

8. *trans.* To chafe, irritate. Chiefly with regard to the mind: To annoy, distress, vex, worry. Also, *to fret oneself*; and to bring *into* or *to* (a specified condition) by worrying. Cf. FRET *v.*[4] 1.

c **1290** *S. Eng. Leg.* I. 187/95 So þat þe salt scholde is woundene frete. **1535** COVERDALE *Ps.* xxxvi[i]. 1 Frett not thy self at the vngodly. **1546** [see FRETTING *vbl. sb.* 3]. **1594** FORMAN *Diary* (1849) 26 She cam not to me, and I was marvailously freted with yt. **1596** SHAKS. *Merch. V.* IV. i. 77 You may as well forbid the Mountaine Pines To wagge their high tops..When they are fretted with the gusts of heauen. **1658** BROMHALL *Treat. Specters* I. 52 They that stood by mocked him, and he being fretted went away. **1693** W. FREKE *Art of War* ix. 265 Arrows..fret horse doubly more than Guns can. **1709** STEELE & ADDISON *Tatler* No. 160 ¶9, I should have fretted my self to Death at this Promise of a Second Visit. **1768** GOLDSM. *Good-n. Man* I. i, I have tried to fret him myself. **1801** SOUTHEY *Thalaba* XI. iii, The officious hand Of consolation, fretting the sore wound. **1820** W. IRVING *Sketch Bk.* I. 207 The horses were urged and checked until they were fretted into a foam. **1825** LD. COCKBURN *Mem.* iv. (1874) 190 They were fretted into something like contempt by the rejection of a claim. **1859** GEO. ELIOT *A. Bede* 32 The long-lost mother..once fretted our young souls with her anxious humours. **1867** TROLLOPE *Chron. Barset* I. xi. 91 The bishop..fretted himself in his chair, moving about with little movements.

absol. *c* **1400** *Lanfranc's Cirurg.* 173 þe bladdre ne mai not be soudid if it be kutt..for..þe urine fretiþ and þat lettiþ þe souding. **1712** ARBUTHNOT *John Bull* III. v, Injuries from friends fret and gall more.

9. a. *intr.* for *refl.* To distress oneself with constant thoughts of regret or discontent; to vex oneself, chafe, worry. Often with additional notion of giving querulous and peevish expression to these feelings. Also, *to fret and fume*, and *fret it out*, and const. *about*, *after*, *at*, *over*, *upon*.

1551 ROBINSON tr. *More's Utop* I. (1895) 75 He..so fret, so fumed, and chafed at it. **1573** G. HARVEY *Letter-bk.* (Camden) 46 [He] chafid and frettid like a proctor. **1602** MARSTON *Antonio's Rev.* v. III, Another frets, and sets his grinding teeth Foaming with rage. **1631** GOUGE *God's Arrows* III. iii. 188 The more conspicuously are their evill deeds discovered: which makes them the more fret and fume. **1646** J. HALL *Horæ Vac.* 53 Hanniball gallantly frets it out in Silius. **1699** DAMPIER *Voy.* II. I. 81 He fretted to see his inferiours raised. **1709** STEELE *Tatler* No. 9 ¶1 He neither languishes nor burns, but frets for Love. **1768** GOLDSM. *Good-n. Man* v, He only frets to keep himself employed. *a* **1790** B. FRANKLIN *Autobiogr.* (1909) 79 Fretting about the money Collins had got from me. **1802** R. ANDERSON *Cumberld. Ball* 43 Another neet'll suin be here, Sae divvent freet and whine. **1832** TENNYSON *May Queen* Concl. 45 Say to Robin a kind word, and tell him not to fret. **1833** HT. MARTINEAU *Manch. Strike* I. 7 Don't fret, wife, we must do as others do. **1837** E. G. G. HOWARD *Old Commodore* III. 69 Timothy began to fret upon it. **1854** W. COLLINS *Hide & Seek* I. vii. 247 Don't forget the letter, sir, for I shan't fret so much after her, when once I've got that! **1865** M. C. HARRIS *Christine* xi, She went through life.. fretting at her lot. **1874** L. STEPHEN *Hours in Library* (1892) II. v. 150 Englishmen were fretting under their enforced abstinence [etc.]. **1875** W. S. HAYWARD *Love agst. World* 83 In secret, Jasper fretted and fumed. **1899** SKEEL & BREARLEY *King Washington* 224 In vain the captain fretted over the delay.

b. quasi-*trans.* With *away*, *out*.

1605 SHAKS. *Macb.* v. v. 25 A poore Player, That struts and frets his houre vpon the Stage. **1611** BARREY *Ram Alley* III. i. in Hazl. *Dodsley* X. 327 Now let him hang, Fret out his guts, and swear the stars from heaven. **1829** I. TAYLOR *Enthus.* ix. 244 Many who..have fretted away an unblessed existence within..the monastery. **1858** FROUDE *Hist. Eng.*

IV. xviii. 48 She had driven him from his country to fret out his life in banishment. **1879** FARRAR *St. Paul* (1883) 357 The Vibiuses..who..fretted their little hour on the narrow stage of Philippi.

10. a. *intr.* Of liquor: To undergo secondary fermentation. *Obs.* exc. *dial.*

1664 BEALE *Cider* in *Evelyn's Pomona* 36 When it [i.e. the Cider] is bottled it must not be perfectly fine, for if it is so, it will not fret in the bottle. *a* **1680** BUTLER *Rem.* (1759) I. 244 All Love at first, like generous Wine, Ferments and frets, until 'tis fine. **1775** SIR E. BARRY *Observ. Wines* 43 Some of the..more generous kind [of wine]..required great care to prevent them from fretting. **1888** ELWORTHY *W. Somerset Word-bk.* 270 *Fret*, to ferment. **1897** W. J. SYKES *Princ. & Pract. Brewing* 481 Often the secondary fermentation becomes unduly excited; the beer is then said to 'fret' or 'kick up'.

transf. **1804** *Poet Reg.* 470 Beneath these butchers stalls.. Where rankling offals fret in many a heap.

b. *trans.* (*causatively*). Also, *to fret in*: see quot. 1872.

1742 *Lond. & Country Brew.* I. (ed. 4) 66 Without fretting or causing it to burst the Cask for Want of Vent. **1860** O. W. HOLMES *Elsie V* xxii. (1891) 313 Both were..old enough to have all their beliefs 'fretted in', as vintners say,—thoroughly worked up with their characters. **1872** *Cooley's Cycl. Pract. Receipts* (ed. 5) 1185/2 The technical terms 'sweating in' and 'fretting in' are applied to the partial production of a second fermentation, for the purpose of mellowing down the flavour of foreign ingredients (chiefly brandy), added to wine.

11. *intr.* Of a stream, etc.: To move in agitation or turmoil, to flow or rise in little waves; to chafe. Often used with conscious metaphor and mixture of sense 9.

1727-46 THOMSON *Summer* 481 The..brook..fretting o'er a rock. **1803-6** WORDSW. *Intimat. Immort.* xi, I love the brooks which down their channels fret. **1808** SCOTT *Marm.* II. Introd. 104 Scarce can Tweed his passage find, Though much he fret, and chafe, and toil. **1849** C. BRONTE *Shirley* xxi. 307 The mill-stream..fretting with gnarled tree-roots. **1888** BRYCE *Amer. Commw.* I. xiv. 189 Short sharp waves in a Highland loch, fretting under a squall against a rocky shore.

fig. **1822** HAZLITT *Table-t.* Ser. II. iv. (1869) 81 A certain stream of irritability that is continually fretting upon the wheels of life. **1884** W. C. SMITH *Kildrostan* I. iii. 51 The stream of thought, Fretting against its limits and obstructions.

12. *trans.* (*causatively*). To throw (water) into agitation; to cause to rise in waves; to ruffle.

1794 G. ADAMS *Nat. & Exp. Philos.* I. vi. 210 The surface of the water is fretted and curdled into the finest waves by the undulations of the air. **1839** DE QUINCEY *Recoll. Lakes* Wks. 1862 II. 54 Some great river..fretted by rocks or thwarting islands. **1858** LYTTON *What Will He do* I. iv, See ..how the slight pebbles are fretting the wave. **1863** HAWTHORNE *Our Old Home* 272 The surface [of the river].. being fretted by the passage of a hundred steamers. **1871** JOAQUIN MILLER *Songs Italy* (1878) 23 Not one gondola frets the lagoon.

13. *dial.* See quot.; cf. sense 4 and FRET *sb.*[2] 2.

1856 *Jrnl. R. Agric. Soc.* XVII. II. 482 The grassland in this district is peculiarly liable to scour ('fret') the young cattle.

fret (frɛt), *v.*[2] Forms: *Inf.* 4-7 frett(e, (5 freett, 6 freat), 5- fret. *Pa. t.* 5 fret. *Pa. pple.* 4-7 fret(t(e, (5 freit, freyt), 4-5 frettet, -it, -ut, 4- fretted. Also *pa. pple.* 4 ifreted. [Perh. represents several distinct but cognate words. In part this word seems to be a. OF. *freter* (used in pa. pple. *frete*, = Anglo-Lat. *frectatus, frictatus, frestatus*, in the sense 'ornamented with interlaced work, embroidered with gold, etc.', also *Her.* 'fretty'), f. *frete*: see FRET *sb.*[1] In the architectural sense it agrees with FRETISH *v.*[2]; the two forms may be adoptions of the two stems of the OF. vb. **fraitir, fraitiss-*. There may also have been an independent English formation on FRET *sb.*[1]

The common view, that *fret* represents OE. *frætw(i)an*, to adorn, seems inadmissible phonologically; but it is possible that the OE. vb., though not recorded after the 12th c., may have survived in speech, and have been confused with the Romanic vb.]

†**1.** *trans.* To adorn with interlaced work, *esp.* in gold or silver embroidery; in wider sense, to adorn richly with gold, silver, or jewels. *Obs.*

13.. *E.E. Allit. P.* B. 1476 Fyoles fretted with flores & fleez of golde. **1340** HAMPOLE *Pr. Consc.* 9107 Other stanes of gret prys, With fyne gold wyre alle obout frett. **1377** LANGL. *P. Pl.* B. II. 11 Fetislich hir fyngres were fretted with golde wyre. *c* **1400** *Beryn* 3926 A swerd..wyth seyntur Ifreted all with perelis. *c* **1450** *Golagros & Gaw.* 318 Frenyeis of fyne silk, fretit ful fre. **1494** FABYAN *Chron.* IV. lxix. 48 The Emperour..garnysshed the Crosse with many riche stones freit with golde. *a* **1529** SKELTON *Image Hypocr.* 375 Curtle, cope and gowne With golde and perles sett And stones well ifret. **1577-87** HOLINSHED *Chron.* III. 815/1 Ladies all in white and red silke, set vpon coursers trapped in the same sute, freated ouer with gold. *Ibid.* 857/1 The quire..sieled with cloth of gold, and thereon fret ingrailed bent clothes of silke. **1600** FAIRFAX *Tasso* IX. lxxxii. 175 In his Turkish pompe he shone, In purple robe, ore fret with gold and stone. **1607** HIERON *Wks.* I. 74 He could..haue fretted (as it were) the whole volume of the booke with excellencie of words. *a* **1668** DAVENANT *Masque* Wks (1673) 364 His bed-chamber door, and seeling, fretted with stars in Capital Letter.

b. *transf.* To variegate, chequer, form a pattern upon.

1601 SHAKS. *Jul. C.* II. i. 104 Yon grey Lines That fret the Clouds, are Messengers of Day. **1839** LONGF. *Hyperion* III. I (1853) 142 White clouds sail aloft; and vapours fret the blue sky with silver threads.

2. *Arch.* To adorn (*esp.* a ceiling) with carved or embossed work in decorative patterns.

1611 SHAKS. *Cymb.* II. iv. 88 The Roofe o'th Chamber With golden Cherubins is fretted. **1615** SIR R. BOYLE *Diary* (1886) I. 66, I compounded with my plaiserer to ffrett my parlor. **1667** PEPYS *Diary* (1879) IV. 322 The Duke of York's chamber..as it is now fretted at the top, is..one of the noblest and best-proportioned rooms. **1853** KINGSLEY *Hypatia* xix. 218 Against the wall stood presses and chests fretted with fantastic Oriental carving.

transf. and *fig.* **1602** SHAKS. *Ham.* II. ii. 313 This Maiesticall Roofe, fretted with golden fire. **1655** FULLER *Ch. Hist.* VI. v. 336 Simple ignorance not fretted and embossed with malice..caused that desolation of Libraries in England. **1729** SAVAGE *Wanderer* I. 40 The solar fires now faint and wat'ry burn, Just where with ice Aquarius frets his urn! **1796** MORSE *Amer. Geog.* I. 559 Vaulted by magnificent canopies, fretted with a variety of depending petrifactions. **1842** H. MILLER *O.R. Sandst.* viii. (ed. 2) 170 Its shelly armour was delicately fretted with the forms of circular or elliptical scales.

3. *Her.* To interlace.

1572 BOSSEWELL *Armorie* II. 121 b, Hee beareth Or, a Lyon rampaunt d'Ermine, debrused with two Barruletes, and fret with the thirde, Sable. **1828-40** BERRY *Encycl. Her.* I, *Fretting each other*, interlacing each other.

†**fret,** *v.*[3] *Obs. rare.* [ad. OF. *freter* (Fr. *fretter*), f. OF. **frete* (Fr. *frette*) ring, hoop.] *trans.* To bind (properly, with a hoop or ring). Also *fig.*

1401 *Pol. Poems* (Rolls) II. 41 Foxes frettid in fere wasten the cornes. *c* **1430** *Pilgr. Lyf Manhode* IV. xxviii. (1869) 190 She was bounden with hoopes, and faste fretted [*fretee*]. *Ibid.* xxix. 191 She is bounden and bounden ayen; fretted [*F. fretee*] with obseruaunces. *a* **1450** *Fysshynge w. Angle* (1883) 8 Double the lyne and frete hyt fast yn þe top with a nose to fasten an your lyne.

†**fret,** *v.*[4] *Obs.*: merged in FRET *v.*[1] 3-13. [Of difficult etymology.

It might satisfactorily be explained as a. OF. **freiter* = mod.F. dial. *fretter*, Pr. *fretar*, It. *frettare*:—vulgar L. **frictāre*, freq. of L. *fricāre* to rub; but the OF. form has not been found. Cf. the synonymous OF. *froter* (F. *frotter*), which, in spite of phonological difficulties, some scholars connect with this group.]

1. *trans.* To rub, chafe. Also with *away*. Causatively: To make pass by rubbing; to cause (a keel) to graze.

13.. *Minor Poems fr. Vernon MS.* xxxii. 978 Penaunce.. freteþ a-wei þe fulþe of synne. *c* **1375** *Sc. Leg. Saints, Clemens* 283 þai fretyt þare facis þane [*faciem confricantes*] Fore ferly & þis speke be-gane. *c* **1450** *Two Cookery-bks.* 113 Nym appeles, seth hem, let hem kele, frete hem thorwe an her syue. **1483** *Cath. Angl.* 143/1 To Frete; *fricare*..to rubbe. *a* **1547** SURREY in *Tottel's Misc.* (Arb.) 27 Ne by coward dred..On shalow shores thy keel in perill freat. **1653** H. COGAN *Diod. Sic.* 127 The inhabitants..know this tree..by the Elephants rubbing and fretting it. **1705** *Lond. Gaz.* No. 4179/4 The Hair fretted short about the middle of her Mane.

fig. **1581** LAMBARDE *Eiren.* IV. xix. (1588) 602 The one of these Statutes doth not fret the other.

b. Of a bird: To preen (feathers).

1423 JAS. I *Kingis Q.* xxxv, Freschly in thaire birdis kynd arraid Thaire fetheris new, and fret thame In the sonne.

2. *intr.* To rub, produce friction; to fray *out*.

1643 FULLER *Inaug. Serm.* §23 That his curtesies might not unravell or fret out hath bound them with a strong border. **1660** SHARROCK *Vegetables* 147 Such positions, that one [branch] may not easily fret upon another. **1692** *Capt. Smith's Seaman's Gram.* I. xvi. 81 *To Serve a Rope*, is to wind something about it, to keep it from fretting out. **1768-74** TUCKER *Lt. Nat.* (1852) II. 587 Taking off the weight of difficulties, so that they may not fret upon the shoulders.

3. a. ? To have dealings *with* (cf. F. *se frotter avec*). **b.** ? To conflict, offend *against*. *Obs.*

(The interpretation of the words in these passages, and their identity with the present verb, are very doubtful.)

c **1400** *Destr. Troy* 12846 Hetis hom..to haue all hor hert wille, Of ffredom..fret with hom so, And all your will shall ye wyn. **1435** MISYN *Fire of Love* 92 Slike frenschyp is pure naturel, & þerfore meyd ne vnmeyd, bot if it oght freyt [*nisi aliquid moliatur*] agayn godis commament, it is worþi.

fret (frɛt), *v.*[5] [f. FRET *sb.*[3]] *trans.* To furnish (a guitar, etc.) with frets. Hence '**fretted** *ppl. a.*

1600 ROWLANDS *Lett. Humours Blood* 5 While you your selues like musicke sounding Lutes fretted and strunge, gaine them their silken sutes. **1602** SHAKS. *Ham.* III. ii. 388 [Punning use] Call me what Instrument you will, though you can fret me, you cannot play vpon me. **1647** WARD *Simp. Cobler* 39 Instruments may be well made and well strung, but if they be not well fretted, the Musique is marred. **1689** *Lond. Gaz.* No. 2437/4 All sorts of fretted Instruments, especially Lutes and Viols. **1874** KNIGHT *Dict. Mech.* II. 1031 An instrument having the fretted neck of the former [the guitar].

†**fret,** *v.*[6] *Obs. Pa. pple.* fret(t(e; also yfretted. [ad. OF. *freter*, pa. pple. *freté* 'garni' (Godef.); perh. a use of *freter* FRET *v.*[2] Cf. FREIGHT *pple.* 1 b.] *trans.* To furnish, stock, stud, supply. Chiefly in pa. pple. modified by advbs. *full, thick, well.*

13.. *E.E. Allit. P.* B. 339 With alle þe fode þat may be founde frette þy cofer. *c* **1400** *Rom. Rose* 4705 Love, it is an hateful pees..A trouthe [*Thynne and MS.* And through the], fret full of falshede. *c* **1400** MAUNDEV. (Roxb.) xxx. 136 All þir greez er..frette full of perle and oþer precious stanes. *c* **1400** *Ywaine & Gaw.* 3160 A klub..Thik fret with mani a thwang. **1413** *Pilgr. Sowle* (Caxton 1483) IV. xxxii. 81 Armes ..wel frett with senewes and al ful of veynes. **1430-40** LYDG. *Bochas* V. vii. (1554) 127 a, A croune of fresh Laurer Forged of gold, fret full of stones clere.

fret, *ppl. a.* [pa. pple. of FRET *v.*[2]] Of a ceiling: = FRETTED *ppl. a.*[2]

1663 GERBIER *Counsel* (1664) 45 Summers..to be framed in such proportion as may serve to make an Italian fret Seeling. **1720** STRYPE *Stow's Surv.* I. II. xiii. 191/1 This Church..was built in an Octangular Form with a fine fret Cieling.

†**fretchard.** *Obs.*[−1] [f. **fretch*, FRATCH *v.* + -ARD.] A fretful or peevish person.

a **1640** W. FENNER *Sacrifice Faithf.* (1648) 15 The angrie fretchard praies for patience and meeknesse and yet sets downe without it.

†**fretel.** *Obs.*[−1] [a. OFr. *fretel, frestel.*] A sort of flute; a pan-pipe.

1480 CAXTON *Ovid's Met.* XI. iv, And Tymolus..juged by ryghte that the sowne of the lyre was better than the fretel or pype of Cornewaylle.

†**fretewil.** [f. stem of FRET *v.*[1] + *wil* (related to WILL *sb.* and *v.*) desirous. Cf. ME. *drunc-wil, herc-wil, spatwil*, etc.] Voracious.

a **1225** *Ancr. R.* (MS. C) 128 *note*, Fretewil wiðalle.

fretful ('frɛtfʊl), *a.* [f. FRET *v.*[1] + -FUL.]

†**1. a.** Corrosive, irritating, *lit.* and *fig.* **b.** Irritated, inflamed. *Obs.*

1593 SHAKS. *2 Hen. VI*, III. ii. 403 Though parting be a fretfull corosiue, It is applyed to a deathfull wound. **1594** PLAT *Jewell-ho.* I. 56 More sharpe, and fretfull to their fingers than their vsuall morter. **1804** ABERNETHY *Surg. Observ.* 126 The ulcer..was of the size of a shilling, with fretful edges.

2. Disposed to fret, irritable, peevish, ill-tempered; impatient, restless.

1602 SHAKS. *Ham.* I. v. 20 A Tale..whose lightest word would..make..each particular haire to stand on end, Like Quilles vpon the fretfull Porpentine. **1632** J. HAYWARD tr. *Biondi's Eromena* 96 In so much as he became fretfull, and pettish. **1739** CIBBER *Apol.* (1756) II. 34 The fretful temper of a friend. **1774** GOLDSM. *Nat. Hist.* (1776) IV. 209 Impelled by a fretful impetuosity. **1802** *Med. Jrnl.* VIII. 528 The child had become more silly and fretful. **1833** *Regul. Instr. Cavalry* I. 83 A horse continues uneasy and fretful with the bit. **1837** LYTTON *E. Maltrav.* III. ii, Men of second-rate faculties..are fretful and nervous. *a* **1848** ROSSETTI *Blessed Damozel* vi, Where this earth Spins like a fretful midge.

3. a. Of water, etc.: Agitated, troubled, broken into waves. **b.** Of the wind: Blowing in frets or gusts; gusty.

1613-16 W. BROWNE *Brit. Past.* II. iv. 691 Two goodly streames..Whose fretfull waues beating against the hill, Did all the bottome with soft muttrings fill. **1793** SMEATON *Edystone L.* §322 The horizon..was so extremely black, fretful, and hazy, that nothing could be seen. *a* **1849** J. C. MANGAN *Poems* (1859) 122 Bitter blows the fretful morning wind. **1887** *Pall Mall G.* 25 July 2/2 A pretty picture framed by the fretful sea and the cloudless sky.

4. Characterized by or apt to produce fretting.

1737 THOMSON *Mem. Ld. Talbot* 340 The kindred Souls of every Land, (Howe'er divided in the fretful Days Of Prejudice and Error) mingled now. **1798** WORDSW. *Tintern Abbey*, The fretful stir Unprofitable and the fever of the world. **1852** BLACKIE *Study Lang.* 33 To pick words out of a dictionary is fretful. **1890** *Murray's Mag.* June 737 The fearsome, fretful, forest, dank and deep.

Hence '**fretfully** *adv.*, in a fretful manner; '**fretfulness**, the quality or condition of being fretful.

1615 CROOKE *Body of Man* 274 And this we tearme fretfulnesse or pettishnes. **1789** MAD. D'ARBLAY *Diary* Apr., Really frightened at she knew not what, she fretfully exclaimed, [etc.]. **1843** J. MARTINEAU *Chr. Life* (1867) 239 Drives away every trace of fretfulness. **1860** FROUDE *Hist. Eng.* V. 174 The Carews rode fretfully up and down the river banks, probing the mud with their lances to find footing for their horses. **1880** OUIDA *Moths* I. ix. 228 'What is the use of putting off?' said her mother fretfully, 'you will be ill'.

†'**fretish, 'fretize,** *v.*[1] *Obs.* Also 6 fretissh, freatish, 6-7 frettish, -ize. [f. *frediss-* lengthened stem of OFr. *fredir, freidir* (Fr. *froidir*), f. *freid* (Fr. *froid*) cold.] *trans.* To chill, benumb. Only in *pass.*

1523 *St. Papers Hen. VIII*, IV. 52 Many of their horses loste and fretished. **1535** *Ibid.* IX. 147, I could get neither bread, drink, nor fire..till I was fretisshed. **1581** MULCASTER *Positions* xliii. (1887) 265 That foolish fellow was fretished for cold. **1607** WALKINGTON *Opt. Glass* 58 Reviving those remote parts, which without his influence woulde otherwise be frettisht with a chilnes.

Hence '**fretished** *ppl. a.*; '**fretishing,** *vbl. sb.*, a weakness in a horse's feet, the result of a chill, the pinching of a shoe, etc.; '**fretishing** *ppl. a.*, becoming 'fretished'.

1581 MULCASTER *Posit.* vi. (1887) 48 Daunsing.. strengtheneth weake hippes, fainting legges, freatishing feete. **1607** TOPSELL *Four-f. Beasts* (1658) 292 Of the fretized, broken, and rotten lungs. **1610** MARKHAM *Masterp.* II. lxii. 322 If the horse be foundred through the straitnesse of a shoo, which..is not a founder, but a frettizing which is a degree lesse then foundring. **1617** —— *Caval.* VIII. 8 Nowe if his Horse haue beene formerly foundred or frettised vpon his feete. **1639** T. DE GRAY *Compl. Horsem.* 38 We prick the two Toe-veines which do help Frettizing.

†'**fretish, 'fretize,** *v.*[2] *Obs.* In 7 frettish. [Connected with OF. *fraitis* (Godef.), said of

capitals of columns, and app. rendering 'quasi in modum retis' in *1 Kings* vii. 17. Cf. FRET *sb.*[1], *v.*[2] If this be a pa. pple., the Eng. vb. is prob. ad. OF. *fraitiss-, *fraitir. If it be an adj.:—L. type ? *fracticius, the Eng. vb. is prob. formed upon it.]

trans. = FRET *v.*[2] Hence †**'fretized** *ppl. a.*, †**'fretizing** *vbl. sb.*

1579–80 NORTH *Plutarch* (1676) 36 The fretised seelings curiously wrought. **1601** in Willis & Clark *Cambridge* (1886) II. 260 Payde also vnto Cobbe for frettishing the gallerie and the great chamber 30l. **1606** BRETON *Sydney's Ourania* ii, In purple robe with starres yfretized. *Ibid.* xvi, A Carkanet.. Fretized with Carbuncles. **1626** T. H. *Caussin's Holy Crt.* 85 This..beautiful embowed frettizing of the heauenly Orbes. *a* **1693** URQUHART *Rabelais* III. lii. 429 Angiports.. frettized and embowed Seelings. **1703** T. S. *Art's Improv.* I. 43 Frettized work.

fretless ('frɛtlɪs), *a. rare.* [f. FRET *sb.*[2] or *v.*[1] + -LESS.] **a.** Free from fret or annoyance. **b.** Of water: Unruffled.

1878 BROWNING *La Saisiaz* 3 Fretless and free, Soul clap thy pinion! **1894** A. WEBSTER *Mother & Dau.* (1895) 17 A full and crystal lake..strong and fretless, stirs not.

†**'fretly**, *a. Her. Obs.* [a. OF. *fretelé*, occurring in the sense 'bespattered (with mud)', dim. of *freté* FRETTY; cf. the MDu. adapted vb. *freteleeren* to chequer.] = COUNTERFESSED.

1486 *Bk. St. Albans, Her.* B iij a, Fretly is calde in armys whan the cootarmure is counterfesid. **1586** FERNE *Blaz. Gentrie* 207 They called it sometimes Countersesyd, and commonly Frettely.

fretoure, obs. form of FRITTER.

fret-saw. [f. FRET *sb.*[1] + SAW *sb.*] A saw used for fret-cutting. So **fret-sawing** *vbl. sb.*, fret-cutting with such a saw.

1865 *Specif. J. Kennan's Patent* No. 926. 1 Oscillating frame in which the fret-saw is strained. **1875** W. E. A. AXON *Mechanic's Friend* 15 Vibrating fret-saw.

'fretsome, *a. rare.* [f. FRET *v.*[1] + -SOME.]

a. Causing to fret; annoying. **b.** Given to fretting.

1834 J. WILSON in *Blackw. Mag.* XXXVI. 586 Incessant refilling of plates is fretsome. **1870** MRS. PHELPS *Hedged In* xviii. 273 Been aye too busy and poor an' fretsome.

frettage[1] ('frɛtɪdʒ). [a. Fr. *frettage*, f. *fretter* to ring, f. *frette* FRET *sb.*[5]] **a.** The process of shrinking on rings of metal about the breech of a gun to give additional strength. **b.** The collection of rings thus employed.

1882 *Rep. Chief of Ordnance* 244 (Cent.) The gun.. ordinarily receives an exterior frettage.

frettage[2] ('frɛtɪdʒ). [f. FRET *v.*[1] + -AGE.] = FRETTING *vbl. sb.*[1] 1 c; ***frettage corrosion***, fretting corrosion.

1938 *Times* 29 June 11/3 The Engineering Department itself is attacking the puzzling problem of 'frettage corrosion', which, when vibration is present, causes a fine reddish-brown dust to appear between surfaces usually regarded as fitting so tightly that no relative movement is possible. **1960** U. R. EVANS *Corrosion & Oxidation of Metals* xviii. 738 In aircraft, frettage has been found between plates of bolted or riveted assemblages. *Ibid.*, The presence of oxygen..increases damage due to frettage, which in presence of oxygen is called fretting oxidation or fretting corrosion.

frettation (frɛ'teɪʃən). *rare*⁻¹. [f. FRET *v.*[1] + -ATION.] Annoyance; discomposure.

1779 MAD. D'ARBLAY *Diary* (1842) I. iv. 163 She heard of my infinite *frettation* upon occasion of being pamphleted.

†**frette.** *Obs. rare.* [app. ad. med.L. *fretum*, adapted form of the Teut. **friþu-* FRITH *sb.*, peace.] A composition, agreement.

c **1330** R. BRUNNE *Chron.* (1810) 290 Barons..Suld com þer he was, & with him mak þer frette, Or [etc.]. **1480** CAXTON *Chron. Eng.* cxciii. 169 No man must speke with the Kyng, but he had made with hym [the chamberlain] a frette for to done his nede.

frette, var. of FRET *sb.*[1]

fretted ('frɛtɪd), *ppl. a.*[1] [f. FRET *v.*[1] + -ED[1].]

1. Eaten or worn into holes, chafed.

1545 ASCHAM *Toxoph.* (Arb.) 121 To make the freated place as stronge or stronger then any other. **1649** G. DANIEL *Trinarch., Hen. IV*, ccclxxxii, His Raigne was All one thin Much-fretted veile of Loyaltie. **1821** JOANNA BAILLIE *Met. Leg., Lady G. B.* xxxi, Through fretted hose and garment rent.

2. Worried, vexed, chafed, distressed.

1756 C. LUCAS *Ess. Waters* I. Pref., The fears of these fretted philosophers will by and by subside. **1797–1803** FOSTER in *Life & Corr.* (1846) I. 203 Feelings are rather fretted than melancholy. **1864** E. A. MURRAY *E. Norman* I. 7 Mrs. Townshend's..countenance..bore that fretted expression which [etc.]. **1876** BLACKIE *Songs Relig. & Life* 136 Like ruffled plumes upon a fretted bird.

3. Of water: Raised in small waves, ruffled.

1855 H. REED *Lect. Eng. Hist.* III. 416 The sentiment of filial piety, which ought to flow in a placid current, is changed into a broken and fretted tide.

fretted ('frɛtɪd), *ppl. a.*[2] [f. FRET *v.*[2] + -ED[1].]

1. Adorned with carving in elaborate patterns; carved or wrought into decorative patterns.

1552 HULOET, s.v. *Beame*, Beame of a rouffe, not beynge inbowed or fretted. **1667** PEPYS *Diary* 3 May, The Duke of York's chamber..is now fretted at the top. **1711** POPE *Temp. Fame* 138 Wide vaults appear, and roofs of fretted gold. **1750** GRAY *Elegy* 39 Thro' the long-drawn isle and fretted vault The pealing anthem swells the note of praise. **1813** BYRON *Br. Abydos* II. v, And round her lamp of fretted gold Bloom flowers in urns of China's mould. **1872** RUSKIN *Eagle's Nest* §92 The fretted pinnacles of Rouen.

b. *transf.* and *fig.* in various senses.

c **1420** *Pallad. on Husb.* IV. 725 His necke in many a ruge Yfretted grete. **1784** COWPER *Task* v. 118 Embossed, and fretted wild The growing wonder takes a thousand shapes Capricious. **1809** PINKNEY *Trav. France* 205, I..watched.. the moon ascending in the fretted vault. **1856** CAPERN *Poems* (ed. 2) 11 The antler'd oak, the fretted thorn. **1860** TYNDALL *Glac.* I. xi. 78 The slope..its termination being the fretted coping of the precipice.

2. *Her.* Interlaced. Cf. FRETTY *a.*[1]

1586 FERNE *Blaz. Gentrie* 177 Burley beareth palee of 6 parts A and B, fretted with a barrulet in fesse G, chiefe and baste of the same. **1610** GUILLIM *Heraldry* IV. iii. 195 The Field is Pearle, a Purse open, the long strings thereof pendant, Fretted, Nowed, Buttoned and Tasselled.

†**'fretten.** *Obs.* Also 5 freton. [ad. Fr. *fretin* broken pieces, ultimately f. L. *fractus* broken.] (See quots.)

1477 NORTON *Ord. Alch.* vi. in Ashm. (1652) 96 The harder stuffe is called Freton, Of clipping of other Glasses it come. **1688** R. HOLME *Armoury* III. 385/2 Fretten is waste cut and broken Glasse fit for noe worke. Castaway glasse.

fretter[1] ('frɛtə(r)). [f. FRET *v.*[1] + -ER[1].] One who or that which frets.

1. † **a.** A devourer (*obs.*). **b.** That which gnaws, eats away, or corrodes. *Obs.* exc. in ***vine-fretter***: see quot. 1608.

1523 FITZHERB. *Husb.* § 43 Terre..is a fretter, and no healer, without it be medled with some of these [oil, butter, etc.]. **1568–9** *Act 11 Eliz.* in Bolton *Stat. Irel.* (1621) 298 The fretter of our lives and substance. **1608** TOPSELL *Serpents* 666 Vine-fretters, which are a kind of Caterpillers, or little hairy wormes with many feet, that eat vines when they begin to shoot. **1610** MARKHAM *Masterp.* II. cxxx. 432 Other Farriers vse the powder of Risagallo, or Risagre, but it is a great deale too strong a fretter. **1611** COTGR., *Tavelliere*, the little worme called a Wood-fretter. **1771** *Misc.* in *Ann. Reg.* 172/2 Reaumur has proved that vine fretters do not want an union of sexes for the multiplication of their kind. **1895** *Dublin Rev.* Oct. 444 He considered the generation of vine fretters from a new point of view.

2. a. One who or something which irritates or chafes. **b.** One who gives way to fretting or ill-temper.

a. 1503 HAWES *Examp. Virt.* viii. (Arb.) 38 So that fraylte to hym be no freter. *a* **1625** BEAUM. & FL. *Bloody Bro.* II. ii, Give me some drink, this fire's a plaguy fretter. **1790** WOLCOTT (P. Pindar) *Advice to Fut. Laureat* Wks. 1812 II. 341 Thou plague of Post Office, the teaser, fretter.

b. 1649 FULLER *Just Man's Fun.* 19 The first are the fretters. *a* **1732** T. BOSTON *Serm.* (1850) 120 This doctrine reproves murmurers and fretters.

fretter[2] ('frɛtə(r)). [f. FRET *v.*[4] + -ER[1].] A branch that rubs.

1615 W. LAWSON *Orch. & Gard.* III. xi. (1668) 38 Fretters are when..two or more parts of the tree, or of divers trees, as arms, boughs..grow so near and close together, that one of them by rubbing doth wound one another. **1664** EVELYN *Sylva* (1776) 472 This is of great importance and so is the sedulously taking away of Suckers, Water-boughs, Fretters, etc. **1670** J. SMITH *England's Improv. Reviv'd* 72.

fretting ('frɛtɪŋ), *vbl. sb.*[1] [f. FRET *v.*[1] + -ING[1].] The action of FRET *v.*[1] in various senses.

1. a. A slow gnawing or eating away; erosion, corrosion; also, the process of decaying or wasting.

1382 WYCLIF *1 Kings* viii. 37 If that hungre were growen vp on the erthe, or..fretynge or locust. **1398** TREVISA *Barth. De P.R.* XVI. xlv. (1495) 568 Rust is..done awaye..by.. fretyng of a sawe or a fyle. *c* **1440** *Gesta Rom.* lxiv. 278 (Add. MS.) And the thirde day after she died, as by fretyng of the addres. **1545** ASCHAM *Toxoph.* (Arb.) 108 Buckles and agglettes at vnwares, shall race hys bowe, a thinge..perilous for freatynge. **1599** HAKLUYT *Voy.* II. 161 No Wooll is lesse subiect to Mothes, or to fretting in presse, then this. **1793** G. WHITE *Selborne* v. (1853) 22 These roads are by..the fretting of water worn down through the first stratum of our freestone. **1878** *Masque Poets* 106 The fretting of worms on withered wood.

†**b.** A gnawing or pain (in the bowels). *Obs.*

c **1440** *Promp. Parv.* 73/1 Chervynge, or fretynge in þe wombe, *torcio.* **1533** ELYOT *Cast. Helthe* 24 [Fennel seed] mytigateth freatynges of the stomake and guttes. **1578** LYTE *Dodoens* v. lxxviii. 646 Gripings and frettings of the belly.

c. Damage suffered by two metal surfaces when clamped or otherwise held together, owing to slight relative motion to and fro; ***fretting corrosion***, fretting accompanied by a chemical change of the surfaces.

1939 G. A. TOMLINSON et al. in *Proc. Inst. Mech. Engineers* CXLI. 235/2 It appears desirable to denote the present action by the term 'fretting corrosion'. *Ibid.* 223/1 Although..chemical action accompanies fretting corrosion, the process nevertheless is almost certainly not one of corrosion as ordinarily understood. **1948** H. H. UHLIG *Corrosion Handbk.* III. 590 Increasing trouble from fretting corrosion can be expected as machine parts are operated at higher stresses. **1960** *New Scientist* 22 Sept. 776/3 This variety is termed fretting corrosion, and is differentiated from simple fretting by the fact that the abraded particles undergo chemical change, generally as a result of oxidation.

2. Of fermented liquors: The process of undergoing a second and inactive fermentation.

a **1700** B. E. *Dict. Cant. Crew, Parell*..poured into a Vessel of Wine to Cure it's Fretting. **1745** NEEDHAM *Microsc. Disc.* vii. 76 The fretting of Wine in the Spring Time..may be owing to a Fermentation. **1846** J. BAXTER *Libr. Pract. Agric.* (ed. 4) I. 171 Singing must be carefully distinguished from fretting. The former is the result of active, the latter of inactive, fermentation.

3. The action of irritating or chafing.

1546 PHAER *Bk. Childr.* (1553) T v b, Some haue an ytch and a fretting of the skynne as yf it hadde bene rubbed with nettels. **1638** BAKER tr. *Balzac's Lett.* (vol. II) 194 The onely Medicine that..cleanseth without fretting.

4. Vexation, worrying: an instance of this.

1526 *Pilgr. Perf.* (W. de W. 1531) 115 Turment not thy selfe (my hert) with afflicoyon & frettynge for that thynge that thou can not haue. **1583** STANYHURST *Æneis* II. (Arb.) 46 With choloricque fretting I dumpt. **1607** TOPSELL *Four-f. Beasts* (1658) 83 They fall into passions, frettings, sweating, pulling off their hats, and trembling fearfully. *a* **1716** BLACKALL *Wks.* (1723) I. 46 By their continual Peevishness and Frettings, they become ten times more uneasy. **1860** EMERSON *Cond. Life, Fate* Wks. (Bohn) II. 325 In age, we put out another sort of perspiration,—gout, fever, rheumatism..fretting, avarice.

fretting ('frɛtɪŋ), *vbl. sb.*[2] [f. FRET *v.*[2] + -ING[1].] The action of covering (a ceiling, etc.) with frets or fretwork, the ornamentation so produced. Also *transf.*

1614 SIR R. BOYLE *Diary* (1886) I. 49, I agree to paie the plaisterers for fretting of my gallery at Yoghall 40 marks. **1624** WOTTON *Archit.* (1672) 63 Of this plastick Art, the chief use with us is in the graceful fretting of Roofs. **1801** SOUTHEY *Thalaba* IV. x, The lovely Moon, O'er whose broad orb the boughs A mazy fretting framed. **1858** G. MACDONALD *Phantastes* xiv. 185 The arches intersected intricately, forming a fretting of black upon the white. **1880** WATSON in *Jrnl. Linn. Soc.* XV. No. 84. 227 The peculiar microscopic spiral fretting of the genus.

†**'fretting**, *vbl. sb.*[3] *Obs.* [f. FRET *v.*[4] + -ING[2].]

c **1400** *Lanfranc's Cirurg.* 179 If þou wolt kepe þe eendis of þe heeris fro fretynge. **1552** HULOET s.v. *Bolster*, Bolsters whyche bearers of burdens, as porters, etc. do weare for freatynge, *thomices.* **1578** BANISTER *Hist. Man* I. 13 [A] Gristle..maketh the motion..more easie, and swift, without metyng and frettyng of the Bones. **1600** HAKLUYT *Voy.* (1810) III. 128 They kindle their fire with..fretting one sticke against another. **1657** AUSTEN *Fruit Trees* I. 65 Trees planted a good distance one from another are freed from frettings and gallings.

fretting ('frɛtɪŋ), *ppl. a.* [f. FRET *v.*[1] + -ING[2].] That frets, in senses of the vb.

1. Gnawing, corroding, consuming, wasting.

a. in material sense. *Obs.* or *arch.*

1393 LANGL. *P. Pl.* C. XXI. 158 Of alle fretynge venymes þe vilest is þe scorpion. *c* **1400** *Lanfranc's Cirurg.* 203 Eruginosa is lijk þe rust of copur. & þis maner of colre is miche freting & scharp. **1570** G. ELLIS *Lament. Lost Sheep* lxxvii, Thou drankest freting vineger with gall, To make their bitter waters hunny-sweet. **1578** LYTE *Dodoens* III. lvi. 223 Cast into fretting and devouring ulcers..it stayeth the same. **1603** SHAKS. *Meas. for M.* IV. iii. 151 Command these fretting waters from your eies. **1665–6** *Phil. Trans.* I. 257 Some other thing that will not be injured by the fretting Brine. **1676** D'URFEY *Mad. Fickle* IV. i, *Dor.* Now has he a fretting Feaver on him. **1685** BOYLE *Salub. Air* 65 The Liquor..by its fretting quality corrodes and dissolves Gold. **1769** J. BROWN *Dict. Bible* s.v., A fretting leprosy is one which by prickling and rankling wastes the flesh. **1813** T. BUSBY *Lucretius* I. 361 To watery drops the hardest marbles yield, And lessening ploughshares own the fretting field. **1873** FARRAR *Silence & V.* iii. (1875) 61 All these gifts combined saved her not from being eaten away by that fretting leprosy of her favourite sins.

b. in immaterial sense.

1413 *Pilgr. Sowle* (Caxton 1483) III. iii. 51 Ye ben lene Caitifs withouten flesshe and that is of youre owne fretyng hertes. *c* **1450** LYDG. & BURGH *Secrees* 1573 The sharp Corosye of fretyng detraccioun. *Ibid.* 1971 And delyuer in the heed, ffrom fretyng malencolye. *c* **1586** C'TESS PEMBROKE *Ps.* LXXVIII. iii, These memories, in memory enrold, By fretting time may never thence be worn. **1652** R. BOREMAN *Countr. Catech.* x. 28 Sinne, which is of that fretting nature, that wasting power [etc.]. **1682** O. N. *Boileau's Lutrin* IV. 332 Exiling fretting Care, that kills a Cat! **1751** JORTIN *Serm.* (1771) I. iv. 75 By industry we shut out ..many fretting desires. **1878** MORLEY *Vauvenargues* 7 If poverty means pinching and fretting need of money.

c. *intr.* for *refl.* Decaying.

1821 CLARE *Vill. Minstr.* I. 46 Curiosity his steps hath led To gaze on some old arch or fretting wall.

2. Chafing, fretful. Of a horse: Impatient. Also *transf.*

1587 TURBERV. *Trag. T.* (1837) 43 Full sore she feard her flanks, and thought shee sawe Her friende pursue her on his fretting steed. **1594** HOOKER *Eccl. Pol.* IV. ix. §2 When wee are in a fretting moode at the Church of Rome. **1864** SIR F. PALGRAVE *Norm. & Eng.* IV. 179 Familiar and friendly conversation with the angry fretting king. **1883** *Pall Mall G.* 30 Nov. 4/2 Slow barges..move on more speedily behind a fretting tug.

3. a. Agitated, frothing. Of wine or beer: That is undergoing a second fermentation.

1567 TURBERV. *Epit. & Sonn.* (1837) 342 No force of fretting fome. **1733** CHEYNE *Eng. Malady* III. iv. (1734) 300 Just as a Bottle of..fretting Wine, when the Cork is pull'd out, will fly up, fume, and rage. *a* **1764** J. CLUBBE *Physiognomy* 38 Anger is a kind of yeast in lumpish constitutions, that ferments, and gives a frothy, fretting volatility to the sluggish matter. **1940** H. L. HIND *Brewing* II. xxxv. 870 Some of the smaller types of wild yeast are.. very resistant to fining, which entirely fails to remove them from a fretting beer.

b. Of the wind: Blowing in frets or gusts.

1628 DIGBY *Voy. Medit.* (1868) 51 It was a maine storme, and a furious fretting wind, and in gustes there came most violent flawes.

Hence **'frettingly** *adv.*, in a fretting manner.

1649 DRUMM. OF HAWTH. *Hist. Jas. V.* Wks. (1711) 107 In musical instruments, if a string jar and be out of tune, we do not frettingly break it, but leisurely veer it about to a concord. **1866** MRS. M. J. PRESTON *Beechenbrook*, Like a mettled young war-horse that.. frettingly champs at the bit.

fretty ('frɛtɪ), *a.*[1] Also **fretté(e**. [ad. OFr. *fretté*, f. *frete* trellis-work: see FRET *sb.*[1]]

1. *Her.* 'Covered with a number of narrow bars or sticks, usually eight, lying in the directions of the bend and bend-sinister, interlacing each other' (Cussans). † Of a charge: Fretted or interlaced *with*.

1562 LEGH *Armory* 158b, If there be mo then viii Peces, then shall it be blazed frette and neuer tell the pices. **1572** BOSSEWELL *Armorie* II. 36b, This Cheuron may be borne frettie with an other. **1705** HEARNE *Collect.* 24 Nov., [He] bore for his Armes Or frettè gules, with a Besant on each joynt of yᵉ Frettè. **1844** PAGE *Suppl. Suff. Trav.* 159 Willoughby: or; fretty, azure. **1850** MRS. JAMESON *Leg. Monast. Ord.* (1863) 109 Morville bears the Fretty fleurs-de-lis.

absol. quasi-*sb.* **1687** *Long. Gaz.* No. 2217/4 The following Coats of Arms.. viz. A Frettee of Six Barrs, and a Party-par-pale Indented Quarter'd Coat upon the one Pair. **1869** W. S ELLIS *Antiq. Her.* x. 236 The Lord Audley as a special favour.. allowed four of his esquires to bear his own fretty in their coat armour.

†**2.** *transf.*

a **1618** J. DAVIES *Sonnet Oxf. Univ.* 16 Oxford, o I praise thy situation..Thy Bough-deckt-dainty Walkes, with Brooks beset Fretty, like Christall Knots, in mould of Iet.

fretty ('frɛtɪ), *a.*[2] [f. FRET *v.*[1] + -Y[1].] Inclined to fret. **a.** Of persons: Fretful; irritable. **b.** Of a sore: Inflamed, festering.

1844 DICKENS *Let. to Forster* in Forster *Life* (1873) II. 110 O'Connell's speeches are the old thing: fretty, boastful, frothy. **1890** *Life's Remorse* II. 136 I have been rather fretty about it. **1894** *Catholic News* 16 June, The book is a literary running sore, fretty, stenchsome and repulsive. **1895** R. KIPLING in *Pall Mall G.* 26 June 2/1 It is a curious thing that if you call his name aloud in public after an Englishman you make him hot and fretty.

c. Of beer: characterized by fretting or secondary fermentation (see FRET *v.*[1] 10, FRETTING *vbl. sb.*[1] 2).

1897 W. J. SYKES *Princ. & Pract. Brewing* 382 Beers produced from such contaminated waters show a great tendency, especially marked in hot weather, to become 'fretty', go turbid, turn sour.

†**'fretwise, -ways**, *adv. Obs.* [f. FRET *sb.*[1] + -WISE.] In the form of a fret; so as to interlace.

1423 JAS. I *Kingis Q.* xlvi, In fret-wise couchit [was] with perleis quhite. **1610** GUILLIM *Heraldry* III. xxii. 169 Sometimes you shall find Fishes borne fret-waies, that is to say fretted or interlaced one ouer another. **1717** TABOR in *Phil. Trans.* XXX. 558 Some [bricks] had one of their Sides wav'd.. some Fretwise.

'fretwork. [f. FRET *sb.*[1] + WORK *sb.*]

1. *Arch.* Carved work in decorative patterns consisting largely of intersecting lines, *esp.* as used in the decoration of ceilings.

1601 HOLLAND *Pliny* XXXVI. xxiv. II. 595 Plastre serveth passing well to white wals or seeling; also for to make little images in fretworke, to set forth houses. *c* **1710** C. FIENNES *Diary* (1888) 144 Yᵉ Church is new and very handsome, good frettworke on yᵉ top. **1768** GRAY in *Corr. w. N. Nicholls* (1843) 81 The wooden fretwork of the north isle you may copy, when you build the best room of your new Gothic parsonage. **1823** BYRON *Juan* XII. lxii, The gale sweeps through its fretwork. **1852** MISS YONGE *Cameos* (1877) II. xiv. 149 A tomb rich in fretwork and imagery.

transf. and *fig.* **1693** W. FREKE *Sel. Ess.* Apol. 6 If.. the.. sincerity of my Work has been full and just.. I may well leave the Fretwork.. to an after part. **1712** ADDISON *Spect.* No. 414 ¶2 The curious Fret-work of Rocks and Grottos. **1820** LAMB *Elia* Ser. I. *South Sea Ho.*, Moths.. making fine fret-work among their single and double entries. **1855** MACAULAY *Hist. Eng.* III. 353 Some party of pleasure banqueting on the turf in the fretwork of shade and sunshine.

attrib. **1634** WITHER *Emblemes* 222 Hee that in his hall or parlour dines Which fret-worke roofes, or costly cedar lines. **1799** R. WARNER *Walks* (1800) 43 The magnificent cathedral of Wells, with its fret-work towers. **1807** WORDSW. *White Doe* VII. 343 And floors encumbered with the show Of fret-work imagery laid low. **1841** T. J. OUSELEY *Eng. Melodies* 146 To gaze upon the leafy fret-work screens. **1878** M VITTIE *Ch.-Ch. Cathedral* 75 A fret-work string course under the triforium arcade.

2. Wood-work cut with a fret-saw into ornamental designs.

1881 YOUNG *Every man his own Mechanic* §39 Better adapted for back-grounds than for sawing as fret-work. *Ibid.* §633 Fret-work consists chiefly in cutting out an open and elaborate design in thin wood.

3. *Her.*

1864 BOUTELL *Her. Hist. & Pop.* vii. 32 This Frette-Work is supposed to be in relief upon the field.

4. (See quot.)

1859 GWILT *Encycl. Arch.* II. iii. (ed. 4) 586 Fretwork is the ornamental part of lead-light work, and consists in working ground or stained glass into different patterns and devices.

Hence **'fretworked** *ppl. a.*

1875 J. H. BENNET *Winter Medit.* IV. xix. 607 The sand-stone rocks.. are.. fretworked into every conceivable shape.

freuch, Sc. form of FROUGH *a.*, weak, frail.

Freudian ('frɔɪdɪən), *a.* (*sb.*) [See -IAN.] Of or pertaining to Sigmund *Freud* (1856–1939), Austrian specialist in neurology and founder of psychoanalysis, or his teaching; spec. ***Freudian censor*** = CENSOR *sb.* 4; ***Freudian slip***, an unintentional mistake that seems to reveal a subconscious intention. Also *sb.*, a follower or adherent of Freud. Hence **'Freudianism**, **'Freudism**, the teaching or system of Freud; a characteristic specimen of this; **'Freudianly** *adv.*, in a Freudian manner.

1910 *Amer. Jrnl. Psychol.* Apr. 289, I recently dreamt that I was travelling to Italy on my way to the next Freudian Congress (which is to be held in March). **1912** [see CENSOR *sb.* 4]. **1914** A. A. BRILL tr. *Freud's Psychopathol. Everyday Life* iii. 44 The Freudians will continue looking for the causes of mental diseases. **1915** E. B. HOLT *Freudian Wish* p. vi, The idea has gone abroad that the term 'Freudian' is somehow synonymous with 'sexual'. **1920** B. LOW *Psycho-Anal.* 10 The Freudian theory and technique, and these alone, constitute Psycho-Analysis. **1921** *19th Cent.* Mar. 477 The attitude of the new school towards Freudism. **1922** R. S. WOODWORTH *Psychol.* xix. 505 The Freudian would shake his head at our interpretation of the lightning dream. **1923** *Times Lit. Suppl.* 12 Apr. 245/2 Once or twice he strains us with a Freudianism. **1924** E. & C. PAUL tr. *Wittels' Sigmund Freud* 225 Able thinkers who have no intimate connexion with Freudianism. **1927** A. HUXLEY *Proper Studies* 95 The Freudian censor is a real person with lodgings inside the skull. **1943** *Mind* LII. 78 He distinguishes very properly between the psycho-analytical technique.. and what he calls: 'Freudism'—the hypotheses and 'philosophy' which has been built up on the revelations for which the technique is responsible. **1955** M. MCCARTHY *Charmed Life* (1956) ii. 37 He did not see quite how it worked Freudianly. **1958** *Times Lit. Suppl.* 19 Sept. 533/4 M. Sartre's own existentialism.. making it, potentially at least, much more nourishing than the other two forms of *Weltanschauung* which have divided the mind and heart of Europe.. Marxism and Freudianism. **1959** *Listener* 13 Aug. 257/2 A Freudian slip of the tongue at a dinner party. **1963** 'N. BLAKE' *Deadly Joker* iii. 51 It was an odd little slip of the tongue.. They call them Freudian slips nowadays. **1964** A. BOROWIK *How Many Miles?* xv. 95 A girl friend of mine.. is married to a strict Freudian-type analyst. **1966** *Guardian* 25 Mar. 8/2 We think we can explain these flaws nowadays, Freudianly or otherwise. **1971** *New Yorker* 27 Feb. 57/1 It is such a primitive kind of Freudianism that.. it hardly seems Freudian at all now.

freure, var. of FROVER, *Obs.*, comfort.

frevol(l, -wall, -ell, -ill, var. ff. FRIVOL, *Obs.*

frey, obs. form of FRY *sb.*, young fish.

freyne, var. of FRIAN, *Obs.*

freytoureere: see FRATERER.

frezel, var. of FRIZZLE, *sb.*[2]

friability (fraɪə'bɪlɪtɪ). [ad. F. *friabilité*: see FRIABLE and -ITY.] The quality of being friable.

1620 VENNER *Via Recta* iv. 73 Codfish for.. friability of substance is commended. **1690** LOCKE *Hum. Und.* IV. vi. (1695) 337 Its Malleableness too.. would be changed into a perfect Friability. **1792** A. YOUNG *Trav. France* 289 In some states the particles.. recede and melt with friability. **1858** GEIKIE *Hist. Boulder* viii. 153 From their friability they are most easily decomposed.

friable ('fraɪəb(ə)l), *a.* Also 7–8 **fryable**. [a. F. *friable*, ad. L. *friābilis*, f. *friāre* to crumble into small pieces.] Capable of being easily crumbled or reduced to powder; pulverizable, crumbly.

1563 T. GALE *Treat. Gonneshot* 2 The spume of Nitre is Judged best, which is most lyghte, fryable. **1614** RALEIGH *Hist. World* Pref. 17 Stone Walls, of matter moldring and friable, have stood two or three thousand years. **1684–5** BOYLE *Min. Waters* 48 Lightly calcin'd.. till it became.. friable between the Fingers. **1793** G. WHITE *Selborne* iv. (1853) 21 Balls of a friable substance like rust of iron called rust balls. **1845** G. E. DAY tr. *Simon's Anim. Chem.* I. 288 The clot is soft, friable.. and is very rarely covered with a buffy coat. **1870** EMERSON *Soc. & Solit., Farming* Wks. (Bohn) III. 61 These tiles.. drain the land, make it sweet and friable.

Hence **'friableness**.

1667 BOYLE *Orig. Formes & Qual.* (ed. 2) 317 In Vitriol the friableness.. need not be attributed to the compositum as such. **1852** JOHNSTON in *Jrnl. R. Agric. Soc.* XIII. I. 21 The natural fertility and friableness of its soils.

‖**friagem** ('friːəʒɛm). [Pg., cold spell.] A spell of unusually cold weather in Brazil, caused by the presence of Antarctic air.

1922 W. G. KENDREW *Clim. Cont.* xl. 327 On the middle Amazon there is usually a cool spell of 5 or 6 days in May or June, brought by a south wind called 'friagem' [ed. 3 (1937), a south wind; it is called 'friagem']. **1931** A. A. MILLER *Climatology* vi. 130 Cold waves known as 'friagems'. **1944** HAURWITZ & AUSTIN *Climatology* x. 225 Throughout the world, invasions of markedly cold air into equatorial regions are usually rare, and consequently the *friagem* is a very interesting meteorological phenomenon. **1968** G. R. RUMNEY *Climatology* xiv. 288 Occasional outbursts of unusually cold, relatively dry air.., originating over the expanded frozen surfaces around Antarctica, make their way much farther north than is normal and sometimes actually cross the equator... Such weather in Brazil is called a friagem.

†**frian, freyne.** *Cookery. Obs.*

c **1500** *For to serve a Lord* in *Babees Bk.* 376 Chese, freynes, brede hote, with a cake. **1597** *Bk. Cookerie* F, How to make Frians.

†**'friand**, *a.* (*sb.*) *Obs.* [a. F. *friand* dainty; according to Hatz.-Darm. an alteration of *friant*, pa. pple. of *frire*, the primary sense being 'qui grille (d'impatience)'.] **A.** *adj.* Dainty; delicious to the palate; fond of delicate food. **B.** *sb.* A person of dainty taste in food, an epicure.

1598 FLORIO, *Leccardo*, a glutton, a friand, a gurmand. **1599** A. HUME *Hymns* (1832) 11 The little friand fish in flude, and dentie volatil. **1603** FLORIO *Montaigne* III. xiii. (1632) 622, I am very friand and gluttonous of fish. **1792** BENTHAM *Wks.* (1838–43) X. 276 The good family wanted something friand for a side dish. **1818** T. MOORE *Fudge Family* 22 The land of Cocaigne, That Elysium of all that is friand and nice.

†**friandise.** *Obs.* [a. F. *friandise*, f. *friand* dainty.]

1. Something dainty to the taste, a delicacy.

1483 CAXTON *G. de la Tour* B vij, She.. gaf to them flesshe and other fryandyses delycyous.

2. Daintiness, fondness for delicate fare.

1603 FLORIO *Montaigne* III. xiii. (1632) 620 Whosoever remooveth from a child a certaine.. obstinate affection.. to bakon, or to garlike, taketh friandize from him. **1604** E. G. *D'Acosta's Hist. Indies* IV. xvi. 255 They have invented.. (for friandise and pleasure) a certaine kinde of paste.

friar (fraɪə(r), 'fraɪə(r)), *sb.* Forms: 3–6, 9 *arch.* **frere**, 3–5 **frer**, 5–6 **freer(e**, 6 *Sc.* **freir**, (**freyr**), 6 **freare**, **freaȝour**, **frir**, 6–7 **fryer**, 6–8 **frier**, **fryar**, 9 *Sc. dial.* **freer**, **freir**, 5, 7– **friar**. [ME. *frere*, a. OF. *frere* (mod.F. *frère*), earlier *fredre*:—Lat. *frātrem*, BROTHER.

In Fr. and Pr. the words for brother and friar are the same; in the other Rom. langs. they are different. It. *frate* (as a prefixed title *fra*) is ad. L. *frāter*; Sp. *fraile* (as prefix *fray*), earlier *fraire*, is ad. Pr. *fraire*, regularly repr. L. *frātrem*: Pg. has *frei* from the Sp. *fray*.

For the change of *frere* into *friar*, cf. *quire* (= choir) from *quere*, *briar* from *brere*, *entire* from *entere*.]

†**1.** = BROTHER, in fig. applications; *esp.* in OFr. phrase *beu frere* 'fair brother'. *Obs.*

c **1290** *Beket* 1348 in *S. Eng. Leg.* I. 145 'Certes, beu frere' quat þe pope: 'I-nelle nouȝt take on so'. *c* **1290** *St. Brendan* 121 *Ibid.* 223 'Beau freres' quaþ seint brendan: 'ȝe neþore noþing drede'. *c* **1330** *Amis & Amil.* 17 How yong the[y] become frere, In courte whereas thei were. *c* **1530** *Hickscorner* E ij, What Frewyll myne owne frere Arte thou out of thy minde. **1821** JOANNA BAILLIE *Met. Leg., Lady G. B.* xix, Her jealous Frere, oft on her gazing.

2. a. In the *Roman Cath. Ch.*: A brother or member of one of certain religious orders founded in the 13th c. and afterwards, of which the chief were the four mendicant orders: the Franciscans († ***Friars minors, Minorites***, or ***Grey Friars***); the Augustines (***Austin Friars***); the Dominicans (***Friars Preachers, Black Friars***); and the Carmelites († ***Frirs carims*** = F. *frères carmes*; ***White Friars***).

c **1290** *Beket* 1170 in *S. Eng. Leg.* I. 140 Forth rod þis holi man As þei it were a frere and let him cleopie frere cristian. **1297** R. GLOUC. (Rolls) 10105 & þer.. þe ordre bigan of frere prechors. *a* **1310** in Wright's *Lyric P.* 110 He leneþ on is forke ase a grey frere. *c* **1325** *Poem Times Edw. II*, 163 in *Pol. Songs* (Camden) 331 Freres of the Carme, and of Seint Austin. *c* **1400** MAUNDEV. (Roxb.) xxxi. 139 Twa frere meneours of Lombardy. *c* **1400** *Rom. Rose* 7462 Sakked Freres. *c* **1460** *Towneley Myst.* (Surtees) 91 Geder up, lo, lo, Ye hungre begers frerys. *c* **1500** *God speed the Plough* 55 Then commeth the blak freres. *a* **1502** in Arnolde *Chron.* (1811) p. xxi, This yere.. frirs carims began first.. A°. Dni. M.ij.C.xx. **1526** *Pilgr. Perf.* (W. de W. 1531) 140 Though the frere minor gyue great example of holynes. **1529** MORE *Dyaloge* III. Wks. 223/2 Frere Hierom geuing vp his order of the frere obseruants came to hym. **1537** in Brand *Hist. Newcastle* (1789) I. 130 *note*, Prior of the Freaȝours Preachours of Newcastell. *a* **1596** in Shaks. *Tam. Shr.* IV. i. 148 It was the Friar of Orders gray As he forth walked on his way. **1628** COKE *On Litt.* 132 The Order of Friers Minors and Preachers. **1647** TRAPP *Comm. 1 Tim.* iv. 2 It was grown to a common Proverb, *A Frier, a lier.* **1673** RAY *Journ. Low C., Spain* 492 A great Convent of Dominican Freres. **1691** WOOD *Ath. Oxon.* I. 19 Johan. de Coloribus.. by Profession a Black Frier, was a Reader of Divinity. **1703** MAUNDRELL *Journ. Jerus.* (1732) 7 Some Itinerant Fryars. **1797** MRS. RADCLIFFE *Italian* vi, These friars had left the convent. **1812** BYRON *Ch. Har.* I. xxix, Lordlings and freres—ill-sorted fry I ween! **1816** SCOTT *Antiq.* xxvii, 'He might be a capechin freer for fat I kend.' **1874** GREEN *Short Hist.* iii. §6. 145 To the towns especially the coming of the Friars was a religious revolution.

b. Sometimes loosely applied to members of the monastic or of the military orders.

c **1330** R. BRUNNE *Chron.* (1810) 197 þe freres of þe hospital, & þe temple also. **1653** URQUHART *Rabelais* II. vii. (1884) 139 The brimborions of the cælestine friars. **1801** A. RANKEN *Hist. France* I. 225 In ordinary occurrences of difficulty he [the Abbot] may consult with the older friars.

c. *pl.* The quarters or convent of a particular order; hence often used as a proper name for the part of a town where their convent formerly existed.

1375 BARBOUR *Bruce* II. 33 He.. with Schyr Ihone the Cumyn met, In the freris, at the hye Awter. **1479** in *Eng. Gilds* (1870) 426 They shall here sermonde at the ffrere menors. **1480** CAXTON *Chron. Eng.* cxcvii. 173 The barons token counceyll bytwene hem at Frere prechours at pountfret. **1536** BELLENDEN *Cron. Scot.* XIV. vii, He wes in þe freiris of Dunfreis. **1655** FULLER *Ch. Hist.* VI. i. 270 A place.. still retaining the name of Black Fryers. **1822** SCOTT *Nigel* xxv, You are about to leave the Friars? I will go with you. **1897** *Oxf. Times* 13 Feb. 5/8 Houses in the.. Friars have been invaded by the flood-water.

†**3.** Some vessel, etc. made in the similitude of a friar. *Obs.*

1463 *Bury Wills* (Camden) 41 To Kateryne Druy my best gay cuppe of erthe kevvryd, or ellys oon of the frerys, to chese of bothe.

†**4.** Some kind of fly (see quot.) *Obs.*

1661 Lovell *Hist. Anim. & Min.* 48 The long flye called a Frier..which is counted poysonsome.

5. A name given to various fishes.

1603 Owen *Pembrokesh.* (1891) 123 The frier [named in a list of fish]. **1889** *Century Dict.*, *Friar*, a fish of the family *Atherinidæ*. An Irish name of the angler, *Lophius piscatorius*. **1892** Simmonds *Dict. Trade* Suppl., *Friar*, a name for the silversides, a North American fish, *Chirostoma notatum*.

6. An Australian bird of the genus *Philemon*. Now usually *friar-bird*.

1798 D. Collins *Acc. Eng. Col. N.S. Wales* 615 Vocab., *Wirg-an*, Bird named by us the Friar. **1848** J. Gould *Birds Austral.* IV. *Descr.* pl. 58 *Tropidorhynchus Corniculatus*.. Friar Bird.

7. *Print.* (See quots.)

1683 Moxon *Mech. Exerc.* II. 377 *Fryer*, when the Balls do not Take, the Un-taking part of the Balls that touches the Form will be left White, or if the Press-men Skip over any part of the Form, and touch it not with the Balls, though they do Take, yet in both these cases the White place is cal'd a Fryer. **1824** J. Johnson *Typogr.* II. 524 That corner untouched by the ball [of printer's ink]..is technically termed a *friar*. **1871** *Amer. Encycl. Print.* (ed. Ringwalt), *Friars*, light patches caused by imperfect inking of the form.

8. *white friars*: 'a small flake of light-coloured sediment floating in wine'.

a **1745** Swift *Direct. Serv.* i. Wks. 1824 XI. 396 If the cork be musty or white friars in your liquor.

9. *attrib.* and *Comb.* **a.** attributive (of or pertaining to the friars), as *friar-house*, *-kirk*, *-lands*; appositive, as *friar-beggar* (and see under sense 2).

1480 Caxton *Chron. Eng.* ccxxxvii. 262 The iiij ordres of the *frere beggers. **1525** Fitzherb. *Husb.* 58 b, Chyrches, abbeys, *frere houses. **1535** Stewart *Cron. Scot.* III. 488 He..Syne bureit was..In the *freir kirk at the hie altar end. **1681** in Southey *Comm.-pl. Bk.* IV. 379 They likewise renounce all chapels..monk-land, *frier-lands..and dice.

b. Special comb.: **friar's balsam**, tincture of benzoin compound used as an application for ulcers and wounds; also inhaled and used internally as an expectorant; **friar-bird**: see sense 6; **friar's cap(s**, the Monkshood, *Aconitum Napellus*; **friar's chicken**, 'chicken-broth with eggs dropped in it' (Jam.); **friar's cowl**, the Cuckoo-pint or Wake Robin, *Arum maculatum*; **friar's crown**, *Carduus eriophorus*; †**friar-fly**, an idler; **friar's goose**, *Eryngium campestre*; **friar's grey**, grey worn by the Franciscans; **friar's-hood** = *friar's cowl*; **friar('s knots**, in goldsmith's work, knots made in imitation of the knotted cords of the Franciscans; **friar's lantern** = *ignis fatuus*; **friar-skate**, the *Raia alba*; **friar's thistle** = *friar's crown*.

1753 W. Lewis *New Dispensatory* 427/2 *Balsamum commendatoris*... This balsam has been inserted..in some foreign pharmacopœias..under the titles of..Balsam of Berne, Wade's balsam, *Friar's balsam, Jesuit's drops, &c. **1772** [see Mohock 2]. **1831** R. Cox *Adv. Columbia River* vi. 78 The wound was dressed with friar's balsam and lint. **1844** Hoblyn *Dict. Med.*, *Friars' balsam*. **1959** W. Golding *Free Fall* i. 30 Then they realized of course that they had given him poison instead of friar's balsam... They had pulled and pulled but the spoon wouldn't come out [of his mouth]. **1963** *Brit. Pharm. Codex* 1261 Tincture of benzoin, compound... Friar's balsam. **1967** *Listener* 28 Sept. 419/2 For congested noses, Friar's Balsam... You inhale this—remember that nostalgic paraphernalia of cloths and steam? **1830** *Withering's Brit. Plants* (ed. 7) (Brit. & H.), **Friars caps.* **1861** Miss Pratt *Flower. Pl.* I. 46 Monk's-hood, *Aconitum Napellus*..Had the old names of Helmet-flower and Friar's-cap. **1782** Sir J. Sinclair *Observ. Sc. Dial.* 150 *Fried chickens*, (properly) **Friars chickens.* A dish invented by that luxurious body of men. **1815** [see crappit-head]. **1597** Gerarde *Herbal* ii. ccxci. 686 Of *Friers Coule, or hooded Cuckowpint. **1688** R. Holme *Armoury* ii. 90 Wake Robin or Cuckow Pintle..is of some called Friers Coule, because of the hooding of the Pestle, when it is springing forth. **1597** Gerarde *Herbal* ii. cccclxii. 990 The downe Thistle..is thought of diuers to be that..report[ed] to be called *Corona fratrum* or *Friers Crowne. **1577** Northbrooke *Dicing* (1579) 11 b, Idlers & wanderers were wont to be called *friers flees [the Lat. above is *fratres muscas*] that do no good. **1861** Mrs. Lankester *Wild Flowers* 62 Another British species, *Eryngium Campestre*, called by John Ray *Friar's Goose. **1594** Hooker *Eccl. Pol.* iv. xiii. §6 As one family is not abridged of liberty to be clothed in *friar's-grey for that another doth wear clay-colour, so neither are all churches bound to the self-same indifferent ceremonies which it liketh sundry to use. **1597** Gerarde *Herbal* ii. ccxci. 686 *Friers hood is of two sorts, the one broad leafed, the other narrow leafed. **1488** in *Ld. Treas. Acc. Scotl.* (1877) I. 83 A chenȝe of gold maid in fassone of *frere knottis. **1529** M. Parr in *Wills Doct. Comm.* (Camden) 18, xviij. diamontes sett with fryers knottes. **1632** Milton *L'Allegro* 104 And he, by *Friar's Lantern led, Tells how [etc.]. **1810** Neill *List Fishes* 28 (Jam.) Sharp-nosed Ray..*Friar-skate.

†**friar**, *v.* *Obs.* [f. prec. sb.]

1. *intr.* To act as a friar, play the friar.

a **1535** More *How Serjeant would be Frere* 156 in Hazl. *E.P.P.* III. 125 His heart for pride lept in his side, to see howe well he freered. *c* **1645** Howell *Lett.* (1892) II. 571 A rich Boor's Son, whom his Father had sent abroad a Fryaring, that is, shroving in our Language.

2. *trans.* To make (a person) a friar.

1599 Sandys *Europæ Spec.* (1632) 232 There remaines nothing for a Iew converted, but to bee Friered.

†**'friarage.** *Obs.* In 6 **frerage.** [f. friar *sb.* + -age.] The system of the orders of friars.

1555 Ridley *Farew. Let.* in *Cert. Godly Lett. Saints* (1564) 100 b, Her false counterfayte religion in her monkery and frerage, and her traditions, whereby [etc.].

'friarhood. [f. friar *sb.* + -hood.] = fraternity.

1726 Ayliffe *Parergon* 259 By the Canon-Law..Abbots ..may excommunicate their Monks for Disobedience..and if they become incorrigible thereby, they may be expell'd and turn'd out of the Society of the Fryar-hood.

†**'friarish**, *a.* *Obs.* [f. as prec. + -ish.] Of or pertaining to friars, friar-like.

1581 Hanmer *Answ. Jesuit's Challenge* To Rdr. 2 In weede monkish, frierish, priestly and Pharisaicall. *Ibid.* 25 b, This is right Frierish, Limitor like.

'friar-like, *a.* Like a friar; of or pertaining to friars.

1600 O. E. *Repl. to Libel* i. viii. 189 All honest men detest this frierlike fashion. **1603** Knolles *Hist. Turks* (R.), Their friar like general would the next day make one holy-day in the Christian calendars in remembrance of 30,000 Hungarian martyrs slain of the Turks. **1646** P. Bulkeley *Gospel Covt.* i. 24 The idle toyes, and frier-like conceits about Purgatory drawn from hence, I passe by.

†**'friarling.** *Obs. rare*$^{-1}$. [f. as prec. + -ling.] A young friar, a disciple in friarhood.

1563-87 Foxe *A. & M.* (1596) 381, I..will that all my frierlings shall labor, and liue of their labor.

friarly ('fraɪəlɪ), *a.* (*adv.*) Now *rare*. [f. as prec. + -ly[1] and [2].]

A. *adj.* Of or pertaining to friars; resembling a friar; friar-like.

1549 Latimer *5th Serm. bef. Edw. VI* (Arb.) 151 Thys is a fryerly fassion that wyll receyue no monye in theyr handes but wyll haue it put vpon theyr sleues. **1583** Golding *Calvin on Deut.* lxxxiv. 518 These frierly flatterers. **1609** Bp. W. Barlow *Answ. Nameless Cath.* 247 In his Friarly garments (habits of peace and pietie). *a* **1661** Fuller *Worthies* iii. (1662) 125 He never set his name to his Books, but it may (according to the Frierly-Fancy) be collected out of the Capital Letters of his severall works. **1817** T. L. Peacock *Melincourt* II. 33 In life three ghostly friars were we And now three friarly ghosts we be. **1885** G. Meredith *Diana Crossways* II. vii. 159 We will..send you back sobered and friarly to Caen.

B. *adv.* In friarly fashion, after the manner of the friars.

a **1631** Donne *Lett. to Sir R. H.* (Alford) VI. 337, I never fettered nor imprisoned the word Religion, not straightening it Friarly, *ad religiones factitias*.

†**Friar Rush.** The proper name (Ger. *Rausch*) of the hero of a popular story, which tells of the adventures of a demon disguised as a friar. Hence used as the name of a Christmas game.

1603 *Declar. Popish Impost.* 33 Fitting complements for ..*coale vnder candlesticke*: *Frier Rush*: and *wo-penny hoe.*

¶ Confused by Scott (? after Milton *L'Allegro* 104) with *Ignis fatuus*.

1808 Scott *Marm.* iv. i, Better we had..Been lanthorn-led by Friar Rush.

'friarship. *nonce-wd.* [f. friar *sb.* + -ship.] A mock title applied to a friar or monk.

1708 Motteux *Rabelais* iv. lxvi. (1737) 272 As if every one was a Monk, like his Fryarship.

friary ('fraɪərɪ), *sb.* [f. friar *sb.* + -y[2]; see the earlier frary.]

1. A convent of friars.

1538 Latimer *Let. to Cromwell* 6 Oct., Rem. (Parker Soc.) 403 If the kings grace..would vouchsafe to bestow the two frieries, Black and Grey, with their appurtenance, upon this his poor, ancient city. *a* **1659** Cleveland *Wks.* (1687) 217 Not a poor loop-hole, Error could sneak by, No not the Abbess to the Friery. **1759** B. Martin *Nat. Hist. Eng.* I. 156 Near Guildford is the Friery. **1824** Miss Mitford *Village* Ser. i. (1863) 122 The remains of an old friary. **1884** *Catholic Times* 10 Oct. 4/8 The foundation-stone of the new Friary.. the first of the kind established since the Reformation.

2. A fraternity or brotherhood of friars.

1631 Weever *Anc. Fun. Mon.* 423 A Friery or Brotherhood founded by Raph Hosiar. **1697** *Lond. Gaz.* No. 3312/3 A Bill for Suppressing Fryeries was presented this day to the House of Lords. **1762** tr. *Busching's Syst. Geog.* II. 216 He proposed also to found a convent, to be dedicated to the poorest friary in the Kingdom.

†**3.** The institution or practices of friars. *Obs.*

1655 Fuller *Ch. Hist.* vi. 272 When John Milverton.. began (in favour of Friery) furiously to engage against Bishops and the Secular Clergy. *a* **1661** —— *Worthies* iv. (1662) 9 A Secular Priest, betwixt whose Profession and Fryery, there was an ancient Antipathy.

4. *attrib.* (of or pertaining to a friary or friaries), as *friary-cart*, *-chapel*, *-church*.

1598 Stow *Surv.* 357 This was called the frery cart..and had the priueledge of sanctuary. **1774** Warton *Hist. Eng. Poet.* I. ix. 293 It was fashionable for persons of the highest rank to bequeath their bodies to be buried in the friary churches. **1872** *Daily News* 22 May, The Friary Chapel, where the ceremony was to be held.

†**'friary**, *a.* *Obs.* [f. friar *sb.* + -y[1].] Of or pertaining to the friars.

1589 Cooper *Admon.* 224 Hypocrites..which will haue these preceptes perpetuall, and builde thereon frierie and monkish superstition. **1605** Camden *Rem.* (1636) 165 Francis Cornefield..invented to signifie his name, Saint Francis with his Friery kowle in a cornefield.

†**fri'ation.** *Obs.* [as if ad. L. **friātiōn-em*, n. of action f. *friāre* to rub into small pieces.] The action of rubbing or crumbling into small pieces.

1656 Blount *Glossogr.*, *Frication* or *Friation*, a rubbing or fretting together. **1657** R. Turner *Paracels. Chym. Transmut.* 43 The first beginning of its Resolution is not Friation. **1743** *Lond. & Country Brew.* ii. (ed. 2) 139 By such Friation they are put into a Condition of imparting their Essence more freely to the Wort.

frib: see fribby *a.*

fribble ('frɪb(ə)l), *sb.* and *a.* [f. next vb.]

A. *sb.*

1. A trifling, frivolous person, one not occupied in serious employment, a trifler.

1664 J. Wilson *Cheats* i. iii, A Company of Fribbles, enough to discredit any honest House in the World. **1771** J. Giles *Poems* 161 A nymph who can for me forego The fop, the fribble, and the beau. **1865** Merivale *Rom. Emp.* VIII. lxiv. 128 The criminals they lash were at least no milksops in crime, no fribbles in vice. **1874** M. Clarke *His Natural Life* (1875) I. i. xi. 162 Flirt, fribble, and shrew as she was. **1881** Besant & Rice *Chapl. Fleet* ii. iii, Yonder little fribble ..is a haberdasher from town, who pretends to be a Templar. **1912** D. H. Lawrence *Let.* 14 Nov. (1932) 76 William gives his sex to a fribble.

2. A trifling thing; also, a frivolous notion, idea, or characteristic.

1832 W. Stephenson *Gateshead Poems* 24 To supply his horse's rack He deem'd it but a fribble. **1874** Blackie *Self-Cult.* 83 The fribbles, oddities, and monstrosities of humanity.

3. Frivolity, nonsense.

1881 E. Mulford *Republic of God* ii. 31 *note*, This life, that is not that of fribble or of crime, is not ephemeral.

4. *Comb.*, as *fribble-like* adj.; **fribble-frabble**, nonsense.

1822 T. Mitchell *Aristoph.* II. 239 He with legs planted wide in this fashion, Fribble-like, swings his frame. **1859** Sala *Tw. round Clock* (1861) 77 The innumerable whim-whams and fribble-frabble of fashion.

B. *adj.* Trifling, frivolous, ridiculous.

1798 *Brit. Critic* Jan. 96 The superficial, trivial and frigid manner in which that fribble minister (*Ministre de Boudoir*) treated this important branch of administration. **1839** Thackeray *Crit. Rev.* Wks. 1886 XXIII. 128 An illustration of some wretched story in some wretched fribble Annual. **1840** —— *Catherine* i, Lovely woman!..what lies and fribble nonsense canst thou make us listen to.

Hence **'fribbledom**, the spirit or behaviour of a fribble; **'fribbleism**, the quality characteristic of a fribble, frivolity.

1758 *Phanor* in *Goldsmith's Wks.* (ed. Gibbs) IV. 429 He [Shakespear] disdained the fribleism of the French, in adopting the blemishes with equal passion as the beauties of the ancients. **1844** *Blackw. Mag.* LV. 557 Such as the Quarterly informed us last year, in a fit of fribbledom, were worthy the neat little crowquills of lady-authors.

fribble ('frɪb(ə)l), *v.* [onomatopœic; prob. influenced in sense by association with frivol.]

†**1. a.** *trans.* To falter, stammer (*out*); also *intr.* with *through*. **b.** *intr.* To falter, totter in walking. *Obs.*

a **1627** Middleton *Mayor of Queenborough* v. i, They speak but what they list of it, and fribble out the rest. **1640** Brome *Antipodes* ii. Wks. 1873 III. 257 If he [the actor] can frible through, and move delight In others, I [the author] am pleas'd. *a* **1652** —— *Mad Couple* ii. ibid. I. 26 You haue often muttered and fribled some intentions towards me. **1709** Steele *Tatler* No. 49 ¶8 The poor Creature fribles in his gate. **1848** Craig, *Fribble*..to totter like a weak person.

2. *intr.* In early use, to act aimlessly or feebly, to busy oneself to no purpose; to 'fiddle'. Now (exc. *dial.*) only in strongly contemptuous sense: To behave frivolously, trifle.

1640 Brome *Sparagus Garden* ii. ii, As true as I live he fribles with mee sir Hugh. **1664** Butler *Hud.* ii. iii. 36 Though Cheats yet more intelligible Than those that with the Stars do fribble. **1748** Richardson *Clarissa* (1811) VI. lxxviii. 378 He fribbled with his waistcoat buttons, as if he had been telling his beads. **1855** Thackeray *Newcomes* II. 27 Not as you treat these fools that are fribbling round about you. **1892** I. Zangwill *Bow Myst.* 60 Who's fribbling now, you or me, Cantercot? **1895** *E. Anglian Gloss.*, *Fribble*, to fuss about.

b. *trans.* *to fribble away*: to throw away or part with lightly, fool away. *to fribble out* (nonce-use): to portray with purposeless minuteness.

1633 Shirley *Witty Fair One* iv. ii, Here is twenty pieces; you shall fribble them away at the Exchange presently. *a* **1834** Lamb *Final Mem.* viii. To B. Barton, Rembrandt has painted only Belshazzar, and a courtier or two..not fribbled out a mob of fine folks. **1879** McCarthy *Own Times* I. x. 205 While Lord Melbourne and his Whig colleagues..were fribbling away their popularity. **1887** Fenn *Master of Ceremonies* xii, Don't fribble away the season.

3. To frizz or frizzle (a wig). *Sc.*

1756 [see fribbled *ppl. a.*]. **1822** Galt *Steamboat* xii. 297 The minister had a blockhead whereon he was wont to dress and fribble his wig.

Hence **'fribbled** *ppl. a.*, **'fribbling** *vbl. sb.* and *ppl. a.* Also **'fribbler**, a trifler; **'fribblery**, frivolity.

1654 Whitlock *Zootomia* 474 The gingling Eare, or Fancy..may have Patterns exceeding ordinary Imitation, or Fribling of Wit. **1656** R. Fletcher *Martiall* iii. 63 He then that's pretty's but a fribbling fool. *a* **1680** Earl of

ROCHESTER *Poems* (1702) 129 And fribling for free speaking does mistake. **1706** PHILLIPS (ed. Kersey), A Fribbling Question. **1712** STEELE *Spect.* No. 288 ¶2 A Fribbler is one who professes Rapture and Admiration for the Woman to whom he addresses, and dreads nothing so much as her Consent. **1756** TOLDERVY *Two Orphans* III. 106 It was a severe punishment to the fribbled jessamy waiter. **1873** H. KINGSLEY *Oakshott* xli. 278 He had been writing fribbling poetry. **1889** T. WRIGHT *Chalice of Carden* xxxiii. 227 Why this waste of time, this wronging of self, this reduction to a condition of fribblery?

fribblish (ˈfrɪblɪʃ), *a.* [f. FRIBBLE *sb.* + -ISH.] Characteristic of or suited to a fribble; frivolous, trifling.

1768 MRS. DELANY *Lett.* Ser. II. I. 176 His library is indeed as fribblish as himself. *c* **1770** T. ERSKINE *Barber* in *Poet. Reg.* (1810) 329 No longer England owns your fribblish laws. **1803** S. PEGGE *Anecd. Eng. Lang.* 153 You may perhaps be puzzled..to discover how, instead of our received preterite *fought* he should obtain such a maidenly and fribblish substitute as *fit.* **1830** J. WILSON in *Blackw. Mag.* XXVIII. 848, I love to be candid, fribbleish and feeble.

fribby (ˈfrɪbɪ), *a.* (*sb.*) *Austral.* and *N.Z.* [Origin unknown.] Applied to small short locks of wool. Also as *sb.* (usu. *pl.*), such locks. Also **frib** (usu. *pl.*), short wool pieces and second cuts.

1900 A. HAWKESWORTH *Austral. Sheep & Wool* 180 A fleece is said to be fribby when a great number of second cuts or fribs fall out when it is shaken or in the process of rolling. **1915** J. R. MACDONALD *N.Z. Sheep-farming* xxvi. 69 When the fleece is placed on the table..the stained and fribby pieces should be taken off the edges. **1929** H. B. SMITH *Sheep & Wool Industry Austral. & N.Z.* (ed. 3) 209 *Fribby*, short locky pieces of wool such as second cuts and small black yolky locks from crutch and under fore-legs of sheep. **1951** L. G. D. ACLAND *Early Canterbury Runs* 379 *Fribby*. Perhaps more a wool trade term than a station one. The yolky locks round the points taken off by the roller from a decently skirted fleece.

friborgh, -burgh: see FRITHBORH, *Hist.*

†**fricace**, *sb. Obs.* Forms: 6 fricasie, -ye, 6–7 fricacie, 7 fricace. [ad. L. *fricātio* FRICATION; for the form cf. *conspiracy*.] = FRICATION, FRICTION I.

1533 ELYOT *Cast. Helthe* (1541) 47 a, Of fricasies or rubbynges preceding exercise. **1605** B. JONSON *Volpone* II. ii, Applying only a warme napkin to the place, after the vnction, and fricace. *a* **1643** W. CARTWRIGHT *Love's Convert* II. ii, Some Grooms o' the Teeth, and others of the hair; Mistres o' th' Fricace, one, one of the Powders.

†ˈ**fricace**, *v. Obs.* In 6–7 fric(c)ase. *trans.* To rub; to subject to friction. Hence ˈ**fricacing** *vbl. sb.*

1579 J. JONES *Preserv. Bodie & Soule* I. xxiii. 44 Fricasing the bodie first emptied of the common excrements. **1607** TOPSELL *Four-f. Beasts* (1658) 143 First rub and friccase the wart violently, and afterward anoint it with Salt. *Ibid.* 504 [The powder] rubbed upon the teeth, although they be loose ..yet, Pliny saith, they will be recovered by that friccassing.

fricandeau (frɪkænˈdəʊ). Pl. fricandeaux. Also 8 fricando(e. [a. F. *fricandeau*.] A slice of veal or other meat fried or stewed and served with sauce; a collop; a fricassee of veal.

1706 PHILLIPS (ed. Kersey), *Fricandoe*, a sort of Scotch Collops made of thin slices of Veal, well larded and stuff'd. **1725** BRADLEY *Fam. Dict.* s.v., To make farced Fricandoes or Scotch Collops. **1769** MRS. RAFFALD *Eng. Housekpr.* (1778) 115 A Fricando of Beef. **1812** COMBE *Picturesque* XXVI, 'That dish', he cried, 'I'd rather see, Than *fricandeau* or *fricassee*'. **1829** LYTTON *Devereux* IV. vii, I think her very like a fricandeau—white, soft, and insipid. **1884** *Girls' Own Paper* June 491/1 For birds, hares and fricandeaux the bacon should be two inches long.

Hence **fricanˈdeau** *v. trans.*, to make into fricandeaux.

1769 MRS. RAFFALD *Eng. Housekpr.* (1778) 132 To fricando Pigeons.

fricandel, -elle (frɪkænˈdɛl). Also fricadelle. [quasi-Fr. form of prec.] (See quot. 1892.)

1872 *Warne's Every-day Cookery* 155 Ragout, Fricandelles, Sweetbreads. **1892** GARRETT *Encycl. Cookery*, *Fricadelles*, These are also erroneously called Fricadilloes and Fricatelles. They are hashed meat made into balls and fried.

fricassee (frɪkəˈsiː, ˈfrɪ-), *sb.* Forms: 6–7 **fricase, fricacy, -ie,** 6–8 **fricasy,** (7 **frycase, fricace, fregacy**), 7 **fricassie, (frigasie),** (8 **fricasey, frigacy, frigusee**), 7–9 **fricassé,** 7–9 **fricasee,** 7– **fricassee.** [a. F. *fricassée*, f. *fricasser* to mince and cook in sauce; of unknown origin.]

1. Meat sliced and fried or stewed and served with sauce. Now usually a ragout of small animals or birds cut in pieces.

1568 NORTH tr. *Gueuara's Diall Pr.* (1619) 624 That hee coulde make seuen manner of fricasies. **1597** *2nd Pt. Gd. Hus-wiues Jewell* B ij, For fricasies of a lambes head and purtenance. **1656** *Perfect Eng. Cooke* 3 To make a Fregacy of Lamb or Veal. **1678** J. PHILLIPS *Tavernier's Trav., Persia* III. i. 101 Little Birds..of which we caught enow to make a lusty Fricassie. **1772–84** COOK *Voy.* (1790) I. 263 A duck, which was hot at dinner, was brought cold in the evening, the next day served up as a fricassee. **1858** HAWTHORNE *Fr. & It. Jrnls.* (1872) I. 25 A fowl, in some sort of delicate fricasee.

fig. *a* **1657** LOVELACE *Lucasta* (1659) 80 Hotter than all the rosted Cooks you sat To dresse the fricace of your Alphabet. **1861** THORNBURY *Turner* I. 300 His confused and unequal picture of the 'Field of Waterloo'..a perfect fricassee of ill-drawn lumps of figures.

†**2.** (See quot. 1611.) *Obs. rare*⁻¹.

c **1575** *Life Ld. Grey* (Camden) 30 It was resolved..to make a fricoisie within the bullckwarck, and prezently too withdrawe all from thence..and then too have blowen it up whoale. [**1611** COTGR., *Fricassee*.. a kind of charge for a Morter, or murdering peece, of stones, bullets, nailes, and peeces of old yron closed together with grease, and gun-powder.]

†**3.** A kind of dance: see quot. *Obs. rare*⁻¹.

1775 MRS. HARRIS in *Priv. Lett. Ld. Malmesbury* (1870) I. 294 A new dance at the Festino, called the Fricasée..begins with an affront, then they fight and fire pistols, then they are reconciled, embrace, and so ends the dance.

fricassee (frɪkəˈsiː, ˈfrɪ-), *v.* [f. prec. sb. Cf. F. *fricasser*.] *trans.* To make a fricassee of; to dress as a fricassee. Also *transf.*

1657 R. LIGON *Barbadoes* (1673) 10 The Sun..did so scald us without, as we were in a fitter condition to be fricased for the Padres dinner, than to eat any dinner our selves. **1671** EACHARD *Observ. Answ. Cont. Clergy* (1696) 63 Common sense and truth will not down with them unless they be hash'd and fricassed. **1724** *Compl. Fam. Piece* I. ii. 127 You may fricasy it, or fry it as you do Veal. **1788** LD. AUCKLAND *Diary* Corr. 1861 II. 76 They are all fried and fricasseed by the sun at Madrid. **1817** KEATS *Lett.* Wks. 1889 III. 72, I would have..fricaseed..her radishes.. ragouted her onions. **1859** THACKERAY *Virgin.* viii, We cannot afford to be both scalped by Indians or fricasseed by French. **1874** COOKE *Fungi* 98 *Sparassis crispa*..In Austria it is fricasseed with butter and herbs.

fig. **1719** D'URFEY *Pills* II. 2 He Trills, and Gapes, and Struts, And Fricassee's the Notes.

Hence **fricasseed** *ppl. a., lit.* and *fig.*

1672 R. WILD *Declar. Lib. Consc.* 9 All manner of Rost, boyl'd..friggassi'd, carbonado'd sinners of both sexes. **1768** STERNE *Sent. Journ.* (1775) I. 4 By three I had got sat down to my dinner upon a fricassee'd chicken. **1859** JEPHSON *Brittany* v. 54 A breakfast of..fricasseed chicken [etc.].

fricasseer (frɪkæˈsiːə(r)). [f. prec. + -ER¹. Cf. F. *fricasseur*.] One who makes fricassees.

1791–1823 D'ISRAELI *Cur. Lit.* (1866) 268/1 Call we this plodding fricasseer a Cook?

†**fricate**, *v. Obs. rare*⁻¹. [f. L. *fricāt-* ppl. stem of *fricā-re* to rub.] *trans.* To rub (one body *on* another).

1716 NEWTON *Let. to Law* 15 Dec. in *Nature* (1881) 12 May, A piece of Amber or resin fricated on Silke clothe.

†**friˈcation.** *Obs.* Also 6 fricacion. [ad. L. *fricātiōn-em*, n. of action f. *fricāre* to rub.]

1. The action or process of chafing or rubbing (the body) with the hands. Cf. FRICACE and FRICTION I.

1533 ELYOT *Cast. Helthe* (1541) 75 b, Then increase fricacions and exercise by litel & litel. **1626** BACON *Sylva* §58 Gentle Frication draweth forth the Nourishment, by making the Parts a little Hungry. **1661** K. W. *Conf. Charac., Detracting Empiric* (1860) 65 This quackroyall is..never so happy as when he's..telling them..how many humours he hath asswaged by frication. **1694** R. BURTHOGGE *Reason* 85 By..a strong Frication of the eye from without.

2. The action of rubbing the surface of one body against that of another; friction.

1631 JORDAN *Nat. Bathes* v. (1669) 29 Some woods that are unctuous..which yield fire by frication. **1664** POWER *Exp. Philos.* III. 156 A well polished Stick of hard Wax (immediately after frication) will..move the Directory Needle. **1725** BRADLEY *Fam. Dict.* s.v. *Shrouding*, They [trees] need no fence..as standing in no Danger of the Brousings and Frications of Cattle or Conies.

fricative (ˈfrɪkətɪv), *a.* and *sb.* [ad. mod.L. *fricātīv-us*, f. L. *fricāre* to rub: see -ATIVE.]

A. *adj.*

1. Of a consonant-sound: Produced by the friction of the breath through a narrow opening between two of the mouth-organs.

1860 MARSH *Eng. Lang.* 489 The *b*..showing no tendency to the more explosive articulation of some of the German dialects, or the more fricative of the Spanish. **1875** WHITNEY *Life Lang.* iv. 61 A sound of very different character, a fricative consonant. **1883** [see FAUCAL *sb.*].

2. 'Sounded by friction, as certain musical instruments' (*Cent. Dict.*).

B. *sb.* A fricative consonant.

1863 LEPSIUS *Standard Alphabet* 68, H belongs, therefore, to the unvocalised strong fricatives.

fricatory (ˈfrɪkətərɪ), *a. nonce-wd.* [f. L. type **fricātōri-us*, f. *fricātor* one who rubs: see -ORY.] *fig.* That rubs or 'rubs down'.

1819 MOORE *Diary* 6–7 Apr., One of those fricatory letters with which we asses of literature rub each other.

fricatrice (ˈfrɪkətrɪs). [ad. L. **fricātrīc-em*, fem. agent-n. f. *fricāre* to rub.] A lewd woman.

1605 B. JONSON *Volpone* IV. ii, [A patron] To a lewd harlot, a base fricatrice. **1708** MOTTEUX *Rabelais* v. v. 165 Ingles, Fricatrices, He-Whores. **1871** R. ELLIS *Catullus* xcix. 10 Like slaver abhorr'd breath'd from a foul fricatrice.

fricht, Sc. form of FRIGHT *v.*

†**frickle.** *Obs.*⁻⁰

1681 BLOUNT *Glossogr.*, *Frickle*, a Basket (for fruit) that holds about a bushel.

fricollis: see FRIJOLES.

frictile (ˈfrɪktɪl), *a. Obs. rare*⁻¹. [f. L. type **frictilis*, f. *fricāre* (pa. pple. *frict-us*): see -ILE.] Obtained by friction.

1883 J. S. STALLYBRASS tr. *Grimm's Teut. Mythol.* II. 610 There is water boiled on the frictile fire.

friction (ˈfrɪkʃən), *sb.* [a. F. *friction*, ad. L. *frictiōn-em*, n. of action from *fricāre* to rub.]

1. a. The action of chafing or rubbing (the body or limbs). (Formerly much used in medical treatment.) Cf. FRICATION.

1581 MULCASTER *Positions* xxxiv. (1887) 122 Gouerning the body after exercise, and his frictions to rubbe it and chafe it. **1629** MASSINGER *Picture* IV. ii, If he but hear a coach ..The friction with fumigation, cannot save him From the chine-evil. **1704** F. FULLER *Med. Gymn.* (1711) 35 The Solids..must be treated..by Frictions, Exercise of the Body..and the like. **1800** *Med. Jrnl.* IV. 369 Observations on the Effects of Acetic Ether applied by Friction in Rheumatic Complaints. **1843** CARLYLE *Past & Pr.* I. vi, Hoping to have got off by..a little blistery friction on the back! **1875** HAMERTON *Intell. Life* x. v. 388 A cold bath, with friction and a little exercise.

b. *Hairdressing.* A massage of the scalp.

1931 G. A. FOAN *Art & Craft Hairdressing* ii. 114/2 Frictions are very popular in the gentleman's saloon, and may be considered as invigorating and beneficial in that they tone up the debilitated scalp. **1948** *Hairdressing & Beauty Culture* i. 10 A friction is a service which is greatly beneficial to the scalp and hair, particularly after an oil or a wet shampoo. **1966** J. S. COX *Illustr. Dict. Hairdressing* 61/2 *Friction*, a massage movement in which the fingers press and rub the scalp surface, imparting their effect in depth.

2. The rubbing of one body against another; attrition.

1704 NEWTON *Optics* III. i. (1721) 314 Whether that agitation be made by Heat, or by Friction, or Percussion, or Putrefaction, or by any vital Motion. **1796** MORSE *Amer. Geog.* I. 481 The rocks below..are worn many feet deep by the constant friction of the water. *a* **1800** COWPER *Mischievous Bull* iii, The sheep here smooths the knotted thorn With frictions of her fleece. **1845** DARWIN *Voy. Nat.* xviii. (1852) 409 A light was procured by rubbing a blunt-pointed stick in a groove made in another..until by friction the dust was ignited.

3. *Physics* and *Mech.* The resistance which any body meets with in moving over another body.

angle of friction, the maximum slope at which one body will rest upon another without sliding down. ***centre of friction***: see CENTRE 16. ***coefficient of friction***, the ratio between the force necessary to move one surface horizontally over another and the pressure between the two surfaces; cf. COEFFICIENT *sb.* 2 b. ***friction at rest***, the amount of friction between two touching bodies that are relatively at rest. ***friction of motion***, 'the power required to keep a moving body in motion' (*Lockwood*). ***friction of repose***, 'the power necessary to set a body moving from a state of quiescence' (*Lockwood*).

1722 CHESELDEN *Anat.* vii. (ed. 2) 39 This Contrivance is always found necessary by Mechanics, where the Friction of the Joynts of any of their Machines is great. **1755** JOHNSON, *Friction*, the resistance in machines caused by the motion of one body upon another. **1822** IMISON *Sc. & Art* I. 57 Polished substances..have less friction than rough ones. **1859** RANKINE *Steam Engine* §13 That excess, however, of the friction of rest over the friction of motion, is instantly destroyed by a slight vibration. **1868** E. J. ROUTH *Rigid Dynamics* 110 When one part of a body rests on another a force is called into play tending to prevent slipping. This force is called friction. **1875** NYSTROM *Elem. Mech.* 88 *Rolling-friction* is the resistance of uneven surfaces rolling on one another, like that of a wheel rolling on a road.

4. *fig.*; *esp.* of the jarring or conflict of unlike opinions, temperaments, etc.

1761 STERNE *Tr. Shandy* III. iii, Souls..by long friction and incumbition, have the happiness..to get all be-virtu'd. **1768–74** TUCKER *Lt. Nat.* (1852) II. 531 When memory began to lay in her stores, their frictions among one another struck out the first sparkles of judgment and forecast. **1792** MAD. D'ARBLAY *Let. to A. Young* 18 June, You find by a little approximation and friction of tempers and things that they are mortal. **1834** H. MILLER *Scenes & Leg.* xvi. (1857) 239 The fears of the people, exposed to so continual a friction, began to wear out. **1875** H. JAMES *R. Hudson* (1879) I. 25 He felt the friction of existence more than was suspected. **1884** J. HALL *Chr. Home* 151 In this case friction between parent and child is out of the question.

5. *Comb.*, chiefly *Mech.*, as ***friction-brush***; **friction-ball**, one of the balls used to lessen the friction of bearings, etc.; **friction-block**, a block which is pressed against a revolving body to arrest its motion by friction; **friction-brake**, see quots.: also, a brake operating by means of friction; **friction-breccia** *Geol.* = *fault-rock* (see FAULT 11); **friction-clutch, -cone, -coupling, -disc**, contrivances for transmitting motion by frictional contact; **friction-drive**, a transmission of power by means of friction-gearing; **friction drum** (see quot. 1960); **friction-fire**, fire obtained by means of a fire-drill; **friction-fremitus** *Path.* = *friction-sound*; **friction-fuse** = *friction-tube*; **friction-gear, -gearing**, gear or gearing for transmitting motion by frictional contact; **friction-glazing**, the process of producing a high polish on paper by passing it through calender rollers that are revolving at unequal speeds; also *attrib.*; hence **friction-glazed** *a.*, **-glazer**; **friction head** [HEAD *sb.* 17 b], the head that goes to overcome the frictional resistance of a liquid flowing in a pipe;

friction-machine (see quot. 1884); **friction-match**, a match that ignites by friction; **friction-powder** (see quot.); **friction-primer**, the name used in the U.S. for *friction-tube*; **friction-roller**, (*a*) a roller placed so as to lessen the friction of anything passing over it; (*b*) see quot. 1888; **friction-sound** *Path.* (see quot.); **friction-tight** *a.*, fitting so tightly that the desired amount of friction is obtained; **friction-tube** (see quots.); **friction welding**, a welding technique in which the necessary heat is produced by first rotating one component mechanically while pressing it against the other, which is held stationary; hence, any bonding of surfaces as a result of frictional heating; **friction-wheel**, (*a*) see *friction-roller*; (*b*) see quot. 1888.

1813 *Niles' Weekly Reg.* IV. 111/2 The wheels of both boats and carriages are provided with double ratchets reversed, or *friction cups and balls. **1842** FRANCIS *Dict. Arts, Friction balls.* **1874** KNIGHT *Dict. Mech.* I. 915/2 **Friction-brake*, a form of dynamometer invented by Prony, in which a pair of *friction-blocks are screwed to a journal rotating at a given speed. **1879** THOMSON & TAIT *Nat. Phil.* I. I. §436 White's friction brake measures the amount of work actually performed in any time by an engine or other 'prime mover', by allowing it during the time of trial to waste all its work on friction. **1884** KNIGHT *Dict. Mech.* IV. 357/1 *Friction Brake*..2 A measurer of the lubricity of oils. **1895** *Montgomery Ward Catal.* 103/2 Superior *friction brushes made from select bristles. **1939–40** *Army & Navy Stores Catal.* 104/3 Body friction brush... Healthy exercise for the skin. **1842** FRANCIS *Dict. Arts*, **Friction-clutch. Ibid.*, **Friction-cones.* **1888** *Lockwood's Dict. Mech. Engin.*, **Friction Disc.* **1907** *Motor Boat* 19 Sept. 190/2 The cargo winch should have a *friction drive and a good brake for lowering. **1927** T. WOODHOUSE *Artificial Silk* 54 By these means, and a suitable combined belt, wheel, and friction drive, the trough can be tilted, when desired. **1957** *Times* 18 Nov. 11/1 An electric friction-drive car for which no key is required for 16s. 11d. **1909** *Westm. Gaz.* 4 Feb. 4/1 What.. had Islam to do with bull-roarers and *friction-drums? **1960** C. WINICK *Dict. Anthropol.* 177/2 *Friction drum*, a drum with a string or stick attached to the center of the membrane. The fingers are rosined or moistened and drawn along the string or stick and the resulting vibrations are transmitted to the membrane. Friction drums are often used ceremonially. **1865** TYLOR *Early Hist. Man.* ix. 257 The flint and steel has superseded the ancient *friction-fire. **1877** ROBERTS *Handbk. Med.* (ed. 3) II. 7 The presence of any cardiac thrill or pericardial *friction-fremitus. **1879** KHORY *Princ. Med.* 47 Friction fremitus may be felt while the patient is taking deep breath. **1860** *Illustr. Lond. News* 25 Feb. 191/2 The old plan of a touch-hole on the top is disused, and the *friction-fuse substituted. **1874** KNIGHT *Dict. Mech.* I. 916/2 **Friction-gear.* **1888** *Lockwood's Dict. Mech. Engin., Friction Gearing*..gearing, whose driving force is produced by the friction only of the peripheries of the wheels. **1907** CROSS & BEVAN *Text-bk. Paper-Making* (ed. 3) x. 271 The '*friction-glazed' or burnished surface..is used chiefly for certain kinds of strong wrapping papers, and for certain coated papers. **1962** F. T. DAY *Introd. to Paper* vi. 65 These body papers may vary considerably from plain writings and printings, to coated friction-glazed papers, such as enamels, chromos and metallics. **1963** R. R. A. HIGHAM *Handbk. Papermaking* viii. 213 *Friction glazers are used to produce a very high finish on single-sided coated papers which contain wax in the coating. **1878** *Paper Makers' Handbk.* 10 **Friction-glazing calenders*, a machine consisting of several rolls of unequal diameter working on one another and kept in position by very strong upright frames. **1888** CROSS & BEVAN *Text-bk. Paper-Making* xi. 169 Another method, known as 'friction-glazing', employed for giving a very high finish to paper, generally on one side only, is to pass it between a very large paper roll and a smaller iron one, the latter revolving at a much greater speed than the former. **1962** F. T. DAY *Introd. to Paper* v. 52 The finishing is then carried out by..friction glazing in the case of flint and enamel papers. **1889** M. MERRIMAN *Treat. Hydraulics* vii. 201 *Y* is the *friction-head consumed in the large main. **1963** A. C. TWORT *Textbk. Water Supply* x. 274 (*caption*) Friction head loss through various fittings, etc. **1802** *Med. Jrnl.* VIII. 478 An isolated electric pile, or a *friction machine of Nairn, positive and negative, and also isolated. **1884** KNIGHT *Dict. Mech.* IV. 357/2 *Friction Machine*, an electric machine, generating electricity by contact with amalgamated silk. **1847** EMERSON *Repr. Men, Montaigne* Wks. (Bohn) I. 337 Thus, the men of the senses..believe that mustard bites the tongue, that..*friction-matches are incendiary. **1864** WEBSTER, **Friction powder*, a composition of chlorate of potash and antimony, which readily ignites by friction. **1874** KNIGHT *Dict. Mech.* I. 916/2 **Friction-primer*, a small brass tube filled with gunpowder, and having a smaller tube containing friction composition inserted at right angles near the top. **1793** WOLLASTON in *Phil. Trans.* LXXXIII. 150 *Friction-rollers were applied to take off some of the weight. **1875** R. F. MARTIN tr. *Havrez' Winding Mach.* 91 The movement of this valve is produced by a cam with bosses, by means of a lever and a friction-roller. **1888** *Lockwood's Dict. Mech. Engin., Friction Rollers*, or *Friction Wheels*, small rollers which revolve in bearings, and sustain an axle in the depression formed by the contiguity of the upper portion of their peripheries. **1860** FOWLER *Med. Voc.*, **Friction sound*, the auscultatory sound heard when the pleuræ or pericardium are roughened by inflammation and effused lymph. **1864** WEBSTER, **Friction tube*, (Mil.), a tube used for firing cannon by means of friction. **1867** SMYTH *Sailor's Word-bk., Friction-tube*..ignition is caused by the friction on sudden withdrawal of a small horizontal metal bar from the detonating priming in the head of the tube. **1946** *Trans. Inst. Welding* IX. 52/3 *Friction welding in its simplest form was one of the first methods used by the Germans for the welding of thermo-plastic pipes. **1964** *Ann. Reg. 1963* 388 Another new way of treating metals, friction-welding, was announced as a commercial process in 1963. **1967** M. CHANDLER *Ceramics in Mod. World* vi. 173 (*caption*) Silicon powder (A) is isostatically pressed, causing weak friction-welding at junctions (B). **1772** *Phil. Trans.* LXXII. 476 Their axes..rested on *friction wheels of four inches diameter. **1826** J. ADAMSON *Railroads* 23 A large fixed pulley or friction-wheel. **1888** *Lockwood's Dict. Mech. Engin., Friction Wheel*, any wheel which drives or is driven by friction.

friction ('frɪkʃən), *v.* [f. prec. sb.] **a.** *intr.* To move *about* with friction; *to friction away*, to go on rubbing. **b.** *trans.* To chafe or rub (the body or limbs). **c.** *intr.* To sustain friction (see quot. 1855).

1842 *Mech. Mag.* XXXVI. 61 Did not the earth perform its motions as regularly before the creation of man, as now it does with 800,000,000 of human beings on its surface incessantly frictioning about. **1855** *Tait's Mag.* XXII. 186 If it [an oil-painting] will 'friction' as the term is—that is, if he can raise the varnish by rubbing with finger or thumb, he accounts himself happy; and, laying it flat on his dining-table, he frictions away till his hands are tender and blistered. **1856** KANE *Arct. Expl.* I. xxvii. 361, I reached the ice-floe, and was frictioned by Hans with frightful zeal.

frictionable ('frɪkʃənəb(ə)l), *a. rare.* [f. FRICTION *sb.* + -ABLE.] Liable to undergo friction.

1847 *Jrnl. R. Agric. Soc.* VIII. II. 338 An agricultural steam-engine being much exposed to the weather, and consequently the frictionable parts liable to corrosion.

frictional ('frɪkʃənəl), *a.* [f. FRICTION *sb.* + -AL[1].] Of or pertaining to friction, moved or produced by friction.

frictional electricity, electricity developed by friction (see ELECTRICITY 1). *frictional escapement* in *Watch and Cl.-making*, an escapement receiving and transmitting motion by friction. *frictional gearing (-wheels)*, wheels which transmit motion by friction instead of by teeth. *frictional resistance*, the resistance of surfaces due to friction; *esp.* the resistance to slipping of riveted joints by the contraction of the rivets (*Lockwood*).

1850 GROVE *Corr. Phys. Forces* (ed. 2) 23 The deflection of the magnetic needle..when resulting from frictional electricity. **1870** TYNDALL *Lect. Electr.* 17 By linking cells together we cause the voltaic current to approach more and more to the character of the frictional current. **1871** PROCTOR *Sun* iv. 211 The frictional impulses of circulating planetary matter in process of subsidence into..the larger body. **1879** THOMSON & TAIT *Nat. Phil.* I. I. §275 No relative motion can take place without meeting with frictional or other forms of resistance. **1884** F. J. BRITTEN *Watch & Clockm.* 107 The Cylinder, Verge, and Duplex are the best known examples of frictional escapements for watches. **1886** A. WINCHELL *Walks & Talks Geol. Field* 101 Daily motions adequate to develop a large amount of frictional heat.

Hence **'frictionally** *adv.*, 'as regards friction' (Cassell 1882); by means or by way of friction.

1882[see above]. **1927** T. WOODHOUSE *Artificial Silk* 90 These vertical discs impart motion frictionally to horizontal discs.

frictionary ('frɪkʃənərɪ), *a. nonce-wd.* [f. FRICTION *sb.* + -ARY.] = FRICTIONAL *a.*

1839 LADY LYTTON *Cheveley* (ed. 2) I. xii. 281 He considerably endangered Frump's frictionary equilibrium, and nearly reduced her to a horizontal position.

frictionize ('frɪkʃənaɪz), *v.* [f. FRICTION *sb.* + -IZE.] *trans.* To subject to friction; to rub.

1853 KANE *Grinnell Exp.* xxxiv. (1856) 301 By the aid of a hard towel—he goes over his entire skeleton, frictionizing. **1859** SALA *Tw. round Clock* (1861) 376 Their principal recreation is to scrub, polish, tickle, and frictionise the brass and wood work of the fire-engines.

frictionless ('frɪkʃənlɪs), *a.* [f. FRICTION *sb.* + -LESS.] Free from or without friction.

1848 in CRAIG. **1875** CROLL *Climate & T.* viii. 136 Unless water be frictionless, a thing which it is not. **1887** EWING in *Encycl. Brit.* XXII. 597/2 The joints and bearings of all the levers are made frictionless.

fig. **1848** LOWELL *Fable for Critics* Poet. Wks. 1890 III. 53 It gives you a cool brain, quite frictionless, quiet. **1884** *Kendal Mercury* 19 Dec. 5/2 The..frictionless speed with which the Boundary Commission are proceeding.

Hence **'frictionlessly** *adv.*, in a frictionless manner; without friction.

1879 THOMSON & TAIT *Nat. Phil.* I. I. §319 A system in which any number of fly wheels..are pivoted frictionlessly on any moveable part of the system.

Friday ('fraɪdeɪ, -dɪ). Forms: 1 **fríȝedæȝ, fríȝdæȝ**, 3 **fridæi**, 2–3 **fridai**, 3 *south.* **vridei, vridawe, vryday**, 3–7 **fryday**, 4–6 **frydaye**, (4 **fredaye**), 6 **fridaie**, 3– **friday**. [OE. *fríȝedæȝ*, 'day of (the goddess) *Fríȝ*'; a Com. WGer. translation of the late L. *dies Veneris*, day of (the planet) Venus. Cf. OFris. *frigendei* (where however the name of the goddess is of the weak declension), MDu. *vrīdag* (Du. *vrijdag*), OHG. *frîatag* (MHG. *vrîtac*, mod.Ger. *freitag*); the ON. *friádagr* (Sw., Da. *fredag*) seems to be of Ger. origin.

The OE. *Fríȝ* str. fem. occurs only in this name and as a common noun in pl. = Lat. *veneres*; it corresponds to ON. *Frigg*, name of the wife of Odin (not, as often said, to *Freyja*, though the latter goddess corresponds more nearly in character to Venus), and is the fem. of the OTeut. adj. **frijo-*, originally 'beloved, loving': see FREE. The more exact transl. of 'Dies Veneris', *Freyjudagr*, occurs *Hist.* in some Icel. writers.]

1. The sixth day of the week.

Black Friday (*a*) †*School slang* (see quot. 1611); (*b*) applied to various historic dates of disastrous events which took place on Friday, as Dec. 6, 1745, when the landing of the Young Pretender was announced in London; May 11, 1866, when a commercial panic ensued on the failure of Overend, Gurney, & Co. *Golden Friday*, the Friday in each of the Ember weeks. †*the three Golden Fridays*, humorously for Good Friday: see quot. 1532. *Good Friday*, the Friday before Easter-day, observed as a holy day to commemorate Christ's crucifixion; also †*Long Friday* (see quot. 1891).

a **1000** *Laws Eth.* v. §17 Fæstan ælce Friȝe-dæȝ. *c* **1050** *Byrhtferth's Handboc* in *Anglia* (1885) VIII. 302 Friȝedæȝ, wodnesdæȝ, sæternes dæȝ. *a* **1123** *O.E. Chron.* an. 1106 On þon Friȝedæȝ..ætywde an unȝewunelic steorra. **1154** *O.E. Chron.* an. 1137 (Laud MS.), & on lang fridæi him on rode hengen for ure Drihtines luue. *c* **1205** LAY. 13932 Freon heore læfdi heo ȝiuen hire fridæi. **1297** R. GLOUC. (1724) 229 Þer uore þe Englysse clupede..after Frye, Fryday. [*c* **1330** *Ann. Lond.* an. 1305 in Stubbs *Chron. Edw. I & II* (Rolls) I. 136 Die qui dicebatur bonus dies Veneris.] **1393** LANGL. *P. Pl.* C. xix. 168 This by-fil on a Fryday, a litel by-fore Paske. *c* **1400** MAUNDEV. (1839) vii. 76 And on the Gode Fryday it [the Lampe] gothe out be him self. *c* **1485** *Digby Myst.* (1882) III. 1513 On þe fryday, god mad man. **1526** *Pilgr. Perf.* (W. de W. 1531) 303 b, The sixth chapiter sheweth a meditacyon for Fryday. **1532** MORE *Confut. Tindale Wks.* 651/2 The .iii. golden frydayes, that is to wit, the frydaye nexte after Palme sundaye, and the frydaye next afore easter day, and good fryday. **1584** R. SCOT *Discov. Witchcr.* II. viii. 24 Above all other times they [witches] confesse upon fridaies. **1611** BOYS *Exp. Epist. & Gosp.* (1630) 203 Let me tell them of another schoole-tricke; at the world's end there is a blacke-friday, a generall examination. *a* **1618** RALEIGH *Mahomet* (1637) 19 And because his [Mahomet's] creation hapned upon a friday, that day was ordayned by him to be their Sabbaoth. **1850** NEALE *East Ch.* IV. i. I. 750 The Friday after Pentecost is called Golden Friday, and is a high Festival. **1868** CAMPION & BEAUMONT *Prayer-bk. Interleaved* (1876) 115 The term Good Friday is peculiar to the English Church. **1891** BENHAM *Dict. Relig.* 476 Among the Saxons it [the Friday in Holy Week] was called Long Friday—probably on account of the long fasts and offices used on this day.

2. A reception or entertainment given on that day.

1836 C'TESS GRANVILLE *Lett.* (1894) II. 209 Not a Genoese appeared there, or at my Friday. **1871** M. COLLINS *Mrq. & Merch.* I. ii. 73 Happy the man who was admitted to the Marchioness's Fridays.

3. *attrib.* and *Comb.*, as ***Friday morning***. Also †**Friday-face**, a grave or gloomy expression of the countenance: whence †**Friday-faced** *a.*, sad-looking; **Friday-fare**, food for a fast-day; †**Friday-feast**, a fast-day meal, a fish dinner; †**Friday-look**, a solemn look = *Friday-face*.

1592 GREENE *Groatsw. Wit* (1617) C iv b, The Foxe made a *Fridayface, counterfeiting sorrow. **1681** W. ROBERTSON *Phraseol. Gen.* (1693) 1092 What makes you look so sad, and moodily? with such a Friday face. *c* **1600** DAY *Begg. Bednall Gr.* III. ii. (1881) 57 No, you *Friday-fac't-frying-pan. **1606** *Wily Beguiled* in Hawkins *Eng. Drama* (1773) III. 356 What a friday-fac'd slave it is! I think..his face never keeps holiday. **1649** G. DANIEL *Trinarch., Hen. V*, xlix, That he might haue his Capons, *fryday fare. **1864** TENNYSON *En. Ard.* 100 The lonely Hall, Whose Friday fare was Enoch's ministering. **1649** BP. HALL *Cases Consc.* 56 Invites his friends to a *friday feast. *a* **1716** SOUTH *Serm.* (1717) VI. 109 If he steps forth with a *Friday-look and a Lenten Face.. Oh! then he is a Saint upon Earth. **1633** ROWLEY *Match Midnight* I, A plague of *Friday mornings!

fridge (frɪdʒ), *v.* Also FRIG. [App. onomatopœic; cf. FIDGE, FIG.]

†**1.** *intr.* To move restlessly (*about* or *up and down*); to fidget. Cf. FIDGE *v. Obs.*

a **1550** *Hye way to Spyttel-ho.* 394 in Hazl. *E.P.P.* IV. 44 At euery doore there they foot and frydge. **1617** MARKHAM *Caval.* v. 23 Whilest you currie your Horse, if hee keepe a fridging vp and downe..it is a signe your Currie-combe is too sharpe. **1642** H. MORE *Song of Soul* II. ii. III. xxii, So must it..rub against the Stars, surround the Sun..Then swiftly fridge about the pallid Moon. **1681** HALLIWELL *Melampronoea* 3 The little Motes or Atoms that fridge, and play in the Beams of the sun.

†**2.** To chafe, rub, scrape (*against* or *upon*). *Obs.*

1617 MARKHAM *Caval.* III. 70 His spurs also must needes fridge vpon his sides. **1651** H. MORE *Second Lash* (1655) II. 213 The parts fridge one against another uncessantly.

3. *trans.* To rub, fray, chafe; to wear away by rubbing. Also with *off*. Now chiefly *dial.*

1617 [see the vbl. sb.] **1761** STERNE *Tr. Shandy* III. iv, You might have..fretted and fridged the outside of them all to pieces. **1781** J. HUTTON *Tour to Caves* Gloss., *Fridge*, to rub in pieces. **1788** MARSHALL *Rural Econ., E. Yorks.* (E.D.S.), *Fridge*, to chafe, to wear or injure by friction. **1848** A. B. EVANS *Leicestersh. Words, etc., Fridge*, To fray, chafe, or 'rough up'..'These stockings won't fridge you so much as coarse ones'. **1857** MRS. GATTY *Parables fr. Nat.* (1859) II. 33 The Spruce-fir next him had come so close that its branches fridged off little pieces of his..bark.

†**4.** ? To jerk or scrape *out*. *Obs.*[−1]

1676 H. MORE *Remarks* xxxiii. 132 The immersion of the Tube may be made so obliquely and leasurely as neither to press out nor fridge out any mercurial *effluvia*.

Hence **'fridging** *vbl. sb.*

1617 MARKHAM *Caval.* II. 79 Yet when you strike, to strike firmly and soundly, for the tickling or fridging of a horse with the spurre is a grosse fault. **1668** H. MORE *Div. Dial.* I. x. (1713) 19 By the mutual fridging of those Particles one against another. **1678** CUDWORTH *Intell. Syst.* 831 The meer Fridging up and down, of the Parts of an Extended Substance, changing their Place. **1737** BRACKEN *Farriery Impr.* (1756) I. 333 By the Fridging, etc. in Riding, the Serum or watery Part of the Blood is gathered between the two Skins.

fridge (frɪdʒ), *sb.* Also frig. Colloq. abbrev. of REFRIGERATOR 2.

The proprietary name *Frigidaire* may also have contributed to the currency of the shortened form *frig.* Cf. also *frigerator* in *D.A.* (quots. 1886, 1909).

1926 E. F. SPANNER *Broken Trident* xvi. 181 Best part of our stuff here is chilled, and with no 'frig plant working, the mercury will climb like a rocket. **1935** C. BROOKS *Frame-Up* xix. 243 Do you mean that you keep a dead body in a fridge waiting for the right moment to bring her out? **1939** M. DICKENS *One Pair of Hands* xii. 198 Your frig is out of order and the trifle hasn't got cold. **1946** *News Chron.* 25 Feb. 3/7 (*heading*) A Communal 'Frig.' with 300 Lockers. **1954** I. MURDOCH *Under Net* vi. 90 In the fridge was salmon, raspberries and considerable quantities of butter, milk and cheese. **1955** G. GREENE *Quiet American* 90 We haven't a frig—we send out for ice. **1960** [see BLINK *sb.*[2] 1 d]. **1971** *Islander* (Victoria, B.C.) 21 Mar. 2/2 We usually landed more than could be eaten fresh and having no fridge, dressed the surplus fillets with smoked salt and hung them up to dry.

b. fridge-freezer, an upright unit comprising a refrigerator and a freezer, each self-contained; **fridge-heater**, a machine that uses the heat extracted by a refrigerator to provide hot water.

1971 *Homes & Gardens* Aug. 84/2 Two-door *fridge-freezers are becoming ever more popular. **1985** *Times* 9 Aug. 11/3 The prize.. is well worth winning and calls for a strong effort by big companies if, as with fridge-freezers and vacuum cleaners, they [*sc.* British firms] have firm evidence to offer. **1957** *Archit. Rev.* CXXI. 459/2 Also on the ground floor is a demonstration larder for the new Ferranti '*fridge-heater' with an adjacent tea-kitchen that serves the entire premises; the fridge-heater cools the larder and at the same time produces hot water for the tea-kitchen.

†**frie**, *v. Obs.*$^{-1}$ [ad. ON. *frýja* to challenge.] *trans.* To blame. Cf. FREELESS.

c **1300** *Havelok* 1998 And ther nis he nouth to frie, For other sholde he make hem lye Ded.

fried (fraɪd), *ppl. a.* Also 4 i-friȝet. [pa. pple. of FRY *v.*] **1. a.** Cooked by frying.

1362 LANGL. *P. Pl.* A. VII. 298 Bote hit weore fresch flesch or elles fisch i-friȝet. *c* **1460** J. RUSSELL *Bk. Nurture* 500 Off Fryed metes be ware, for þey ar Fumose in dede. **1598** *Epulario* H j b, Cut it on both sides like a fried fish. **1771** GOLDSM. *Haunch of Venison*, At the top a fried liver and bacon was seen. **1860** TYNDALL *Glac.* I. xii. 86 Roast mutton and fried potatos were our incessant fare.

fig. **1624** CAPT. SMITH *Virginia* VI. 208 Who would have sought for wealth amongst those fried Regions of blacke brutish Negars.

b. *fried-fish shop*, a shop that sells fried fish, usually with fried (chipped) potatoes. Also, formerly, *fried-fish warehouse*.

1838 DICKENS *O. Twist* II. xxvi. 92 Field Lane.. has its barber, its coffee-shop.. and its fried-fish warehouse. **1898** J. D. BRAYSHAW *Slum Silhouettes* 215 I've just seed Liz Dukeson, the donah at the fried-fish shop. **1939** 'G. ORWELL' *Coming up for Air* IV. vi. 275 Flats, pubs, fried-fish shops, picture-houses, on and on for twenty miles.

2. Drunk. *slang.*

1926 in WENTWORTH & FLEXNER *Dict. Amer. Slang* (1960) 201/1 Princeton has completed the idiom of the cuisine by adding *fried* to *boiled* and *stewed*, meaning intoxicated. **1954** N. COWARD *Future Indefinite* IV. 195 After a gay reunion party.. I retired to be slightly fried, blissfully happy. **1966** 'D. SHANNON' *With a Vengeance* (1968) vi. 82, I don't know nothin' about how he got took off... I also heard he was fried that night.

Friedel-Crafts (ˌfriːd(ə)l 'krɑːfts, -æ-). *Chem.* The names of Charles *Friedel* (1832–99), French chemist, and J. M. *Crafts* (1839–1917), American chemist, used *attrib.* with reference to a method, discovered by them, of alkylating or acylating aromatic hydrocarbons or ketones by the use of anhydrous aluminium chloride (or a similar substance) as a catalyst.

1892 *Jrnl. Chem. Soc.* LXII. I. 337 Friedel-Crafts' synthesis. **1900** *Ibid.* LXXVII. 1006 The Friedel-Crafts reaction is among all synthetical methods the one most commonly used. **1927** *Industr. & Engin. Chem.* XIX. 1063 The summer of 1927 marks the fiftieth anniversary of the announcement of the Friedel-Crafts reaction. **1937** *Jrnl. Chem. Soc.* 504 Three main possibilities in the Friedel-Crafts mechanism. **1961** *New Scientist* 16 Mar. 686/1 Mixtures of the compounds containing 17–32 per cent of chlorine can be polymerized with heat and a Friedel-Crafts catalyst. **1964** N. G. CLARK *Mod. Org. Chem.* xix. 386 Friedel-Crafts acylation differs from the alkylation in a number of important aspects.

Friedmanite ('friːdmənaɪt), *sb.* and *a.* [f. the name of Milton *Friedman* (b. 1912), American economist + -ITE[1].] **A.** *sb.* An adherent of the theories of Friedman. **B.** *adj.* Of or pertaining to Friedman or his theories, esp. regarding regulation of the economy by control of the money supply.

1970 *Times* 13 Mar. 10/1 Debate has raged passionately in the United States for years between the Friedmanites and the Keynesians. **1977** I. GILMOUR *Inside Right* (1978) III. vi. 230 Mr Patrick Hutber of the *Sunday Telegraph* is now an uncompromising if entertaining Friedmanite. **1979** LD. ROBBINS *Against Inflation* xvi. 80, I am not a Friedmanite monetarist. **1985** *Washington Post* 25 Sept. A15/5 Today the movement accommodates both tolerant libertarianism and strict fundamentalism, free-market Friedmanites and devout Falwellites.

Also **Fried'manian** *a.*; **'Friedmanism**.

1969 Friedmanian [see MONETARISM]. **1980** *Listener* 1 May 561/1 The BBC were right to buy and show the bulk of the Friedman series.. because 'Friedmanism' has become a central—perhaps *the* central—issue in British domestic political debate. **1985** *Christian Science Monitor* 23 Aug. 22/2 The Fed has permitted money-supply growth above its earlier targets, braving the wrath of the Friedmanian monetarists.

Friedreich ('friːdraɪk, -aɪç). The name of Nikolaus *Friedreich* (1825–82), German neurologist, used *attrib.* and in the possessive to designate: **a.** Hereditary locomotor ataxia, an inherited disease of the central nervous system marked by an unsteady gait and an inability to co-ordinate voluntary movements; also its accompanying deformity, ***Friedreich('s) foot***.

1883 *Brit. Med. Jrnl.* 31 Mar. 627/2 The term 'hereditary ataxy' is, therefore, a misnomer. 'Family ataxy', although more correct, does not sound well; and, under these circumstances, we may provisionally accept Browne's [? *an error for* Brousse's] proposal to call the malady in question 'Friedreich's disease'. **1890** *Brain* XIII. 503 Tabes is an affection of adult age; Friedreich's ataxy a disease of childhood. **1940** S. A. K. WILSON *Neurology* II. xlix. 950 Time of appearance is variable for the 'Freidreich [*sic*] foot' may have been present from the outset. **1964** S. DUKE-ELDER *Parsons' Dis. Eye* (ed. 14) xxxiv. 545 In Hereditary Ataxia (Friedreich's Disease) optic atrophy and paralyses of the ocular muscles are very rare. **1970** *Sunday Times* 13 Dec. 34/6 (Advt.), Friedreich's ataxia is a crippling disease of the Nervous System which starts in childhood or adolescence.

b. *Paramyoclonus multiplex*, a rare disease characterized by involuntary twitching of the muscles, esp. of the limbs.

1889 *Brain* XI. 417 Friedreich's paramyoclonus, a fibrillar twitching insufficient to move the limb. **1903** *Jrnl. Nerv. & Mental Dis.* XXX. 365 In his opinion, the distinguishing feature of myoclonus of the Friedreich type was the occurrence of contractions of individual muscles not under the control of the will. **1967** *Brain* XC. 673 Similar families have been reported previously, often under the title of Friedreich's paramyoclonus multiplex.

friend (frɛnd), *sb.* and *a.* Forms: 1 fréond, fríond, (*dat.* fríend, frýnd), 2–3 friend, 4 *south.* vriend, 2–7 frend(e, 4 *south.* vrend(e, 3–4 freond, (3 *south.* vreond), 3–7 freind(e, 4 *south.* vrind, vryend, 4–6 freend(e, freynd, 5–7 frind(e, 5–6 frynd(e, (6 *Sc.* freyind), 6– friend. *Pl.* 1 fríend, frýnd, fréond, fréondas, fríondas, 2–3 frend, friend(e, 3 frond, 3–4 freond; otherwise *regular*. [Com. Teut.: OE. *fréond* str. masc. = OFris., OS. *friund*, *friond* (Du. *vriend*), OHG. *friunt* (MHG. *vriunt*, mod.Ger. *freund*), ON. (with change of declension in sing.) *frǽnde* (Sw. *frände*, Da. *frænde*), Goth. *frijōnds*; the pr. pple. of the OTeut. vb. **frijôjan* to love (OE. *fréoȝan*, *fréon*, Goth. *frijôn*; the Ger. *freien*, Du. *vrijen* to woo, and the rare ON. *friá* to caress, are prob. not identical, though from the same root), f. pre-Teut. **priyo-* dear: see FREE *a.*]

A. *sb.*

1. a. 'One joined to another in mutual benevolence and intimacy' (J.). Not ordinarily applied to lovers or relatives (but cf. senses 3, 4).

Beowulf 1018 (Gr.) Heorot innan wæs freondum afylled. *a* **1000** *Cædmon's Gen.* 2025 þa þæt inwitspell Abraham sæȝde freondum sinum. *c* **1200** ORMIN 17960, & whase iss þatt bridgumess frend, He stannt wiþþ himm. *c* **1205** LAY. 703 Ȝe sculen.. beon mine leofe freond. *c* **1305** *Pilate* 98–9 in *E.E.P.* (1862) 114 Gode freond hi were For tuei schrewen wolleþ freond beo. *c* **1400** *Destr. Troy* 8523 Ho was vnkyndly to knaw of hir kyd frendis. **1484** CAXTON *Fables of Æsop* III. xiii, A trewe frend is oftyme better at a nede than a Royalme. **1557** *Tottel's Misc.* (Arb.) 185 A faythfull frende is thing most worth. *c* **1651** HOBBES *Rhet.* (1840) 455 A friend is he that loves, and he that is beloved. **1768–74** TUCKER *Lt. Nat.* (1852) II. 310 If we observe the common discourses of mankind, we shall find a friend to be one we frequently visit, who is our boon companion, or joins with us in our pleasures and diversions, or [etc.]. **1801** SOUTHEY *Thalaba* VIII. i, The sound of his dear native tongue May be like the voice of a friend. **1881** BESANT & RICE *Chapl. Fleet* I. 91 The doctor is a private friend of the dean.

b. In various proverbial expressions. † ***but a friend's friend***: ever so remotely connected.

1340 *Ayenb.* 186 þanne he yziȝþ his niede: uor ate niede me yziȝþ huet þe urend is. *c* **1468** *Paston Lett.* No. 582 II. 313 Better ys a frende unknow then knowen. *c* **1489** CAXTON *Sonnes of Aymon* xix. 433 It is sayd, that at the nede the frende is knowen. **1539** TAVERNER *Erasm. Prov.* (1552) 32 A frende is more necessary than either fyer or water. **1546** J. HEYWOOD *Prov.* (1867) 37 Many kynsfolke and few freends, some folke saie. **1562** —— *Prov. and Epigr.* (1867) 132 Proue thy freende er thou neede. **1599** PORTER *Angry Wom. Abingd.* (Percy) 82 No, by lady, a friend is not so soone gotten as lost. **1642** JER. TAYLOR *Episc.* Pref., I am confident you will owne any thing that is but a friends friend to a cause of Loyalty. **1816** 'QUIZ' *Grand Master* v. 100 'A friend in need' Is, certainly, 'a friend in deed'.

c. *friend of God*: a person eminent for piety, and presumed to enjoy God's special favour. Now only with express reference to *Jam.* ii. 23.

O.E. Chron. an. 654 He wæs swyðe Godes freond. *c* **1205** LAY. 9145 þat scolde beon i-haten Hælend & helpen his freondes. *c* **1230** *Hali Meid.* 7 þus hauen godes freond al þe fruit of þis world. *c* **1375** *Sc. Leg. Saints, Berthol.* 41 Of mychty god.. þe frende he is.

d. Used in subscribing a letter.

1529 WOLSEY in *Four C. Eng. Lett.* 11 Youre olde brynger up and lovying frende. **1650** CHAS. II in *Hamilton Papers* (Camden) 254 Your most affectionate frende, Charles R. **1661** JER. TAYLOR in *Hatton Corr.* (1878) 27 Your Lorp[s] most endeared, as most obliged, freind and servant.

e. Applied to a second in a duel.

1800 MAR. EDGEWORTH *Belinda* (1832) I. iv. 72 Miss Honor O'Grady would be her *friend* upon the occasion. **1874** E. B. DE FONBLANQUE *Life A. Fonblanque* 16 The matter was at this point referred to two 'friends', by whom a hostile meeting was arranged.

2. Used *loosely* in various ways: e.g. applied to a mere acquaintance, or to a stranger, as a mark of goodwill or kindly condescension on the part of the speaker; by members of the 'Society of Friends' adopted as the ordinary mode of address (cf. 7). Also often *ironically*.

Similarly in parliamentary language, 'my honourable friend' is often used by members in referring to each other; so also 'my learned friend' is applied in the law courts by counsel to each other. Cf. 6.

c **1290** *S. Eng. Leg.* I. 21/83 'Mine leue frend', seide þis holie Man. *a* **1300** *Cursor M.* 3229 'Frend', he said, 'þou wend in hij vntil mesopotani'. *c* **1375** *Lay Folks Mass Bk.* (MS. B.) 369 Oure sib men and oure wele-willandes, Oure frendes, tenandes, & seruandes. **1382** WYCLIF *Matt.* xxii. 12 Frend, hou entridist thou hidir, nat hauynge brijd clothe? *Ibid.* xxvi. 50 Frend, wherto art thou comen? *c* **1470** HENRY *Wallace* II. 89 Gud freynd, pray I the, The schireffis serwand thow wald lat him be. **1508** FISHER 7 *Penit. Ps.* i. Wks. (1876) 2 Frendes this day I shall not declare vnto you ony parte of the epystle. **1710** STEELE *Tatler* No. 204 ¶6 A Quaker.. with an Air of good Nature and Charity calls you Friend. **1802** MAR. EDGEWORTH *Moral T.* (1813) II. 195 'Nay, keep it, friend, keep it', said Dinah Plait. **1859** GEO. ELIOT *A. Bede* ii, Dear friends, come and take this blessedness. **1890** BOLDREWOOD *Col. Reformer* (1891) 321 Those free-selecting friends of yours.

3. A kinsman or near relation. Now only in *pl.* (one's) relatives, kinsfolk, 'people'.

This is the only sense of the word in the Scand. langs., where sense 1 is expressed by ON. *vinr* (Sw. *vän*, Da. *ven*); similarly in many HG. dialects, *freund* is 'kinsman', the sense of 'friend' being expressed by *guter freund* (Kluge).

O.E. Chron. an. 1135 þa namen his sune & his frend & brohten his lic to Englelande. *c* **1200** *Vices & Virtues* xvii. (1888) 41 Of his aȝene wiue and ec of his auene frienden. *a* **1300** *Cursor M.* 3016 For þe birth of ysaac, gret ioi can his frendes mak. *c* **1489** CAXTON *Sonnes of Aymon* ix. 225 For who that betraieth.. his frende carnall ought not to lyve nor have ever ony worshyp. **1502** *Ord. Crysten Men* (W. de W. 1506) II. viii. 104 All the sones & doughters of Adam & of Eue the whiche were our fyrst frendes. **1591** SHAKS. *Two Gent.* III. i. 106 She.. is promis'd by her friends Vnto a youthfull Gentleman of worth. **1721** KELLY *Sc. Prov.* 103 Friends agree best at a distance. By Friends here is meant Relations. *Mod.* The prisoner will be handed over to the care of his friends. His friends are well-to-do people.

4. A lover or paramour, of either sex.

1490 CAXTON *Eneydos* xviii. 67 Playse the, thenne to haue mercy of this poure desolate frende [Dido], that shalle be sone broughte to the poynte mortalle. **1588** SHAKS. *L.L.L.* v. ii. 405 O! neuer will I.. come in vizard to my friend, Nor woo in rime like a blind-harpers songe. **1603** —— *Meas. for M.* I. iv. 29 He hath got his friend with childe. **1765** FOOTE *Commissary* I. Wks. 1799 II. 16 When a gentleman wanted a friend, I could supply him with choice in an hour. **1961** PARTRIDGE *Dict. Slang* Suppl. 1097/2 *Friend*, the man who keeps a harlot as his mistress. **1967** *Guardian* 11 Dec. 1/8 The boy's mother.. was joined.. by a man described as her 'friend'. The mother is apparently divorced.

5. a. One who wishes (another, a cause, etc.) well; a sympathiser, favourer, helper, patron, or supporter; *spec.* a supporter of an institution or the like, contributing help, money, etc. Const. *of*, *to*. Usu. in *pl.*

c **1205** LAY. 1615 In to France he ferde þer he freond funde. *a* **1300** *Cursor M.* 14569 To iurselem rede we þou wende For þar es communli þi freind. **1382** WYCLIF *Prov.* xxii. 11 Who loueth clennesse of herte, for the grace of his lippis shal han the king frend. *a* **1550** *Christis Kirke Gr.* ix, With that a freynd of his cry'd, fy! And up ane arrow drew. **1609** BIBLE (Douay) *1 Macc.* vii. 7 Let him punish al his frends and ayders. **1612** PEACHAM *Graphice* II. iv, Shee is a friend to all studies, especially poetry. **1710** SHAFTESB. *Advice to Author* (1757) 143 The Minister who was no friend to the young nobleman. **1782** PRIESTLEY *Corrupt. Chr.* II. IX. 206 The Gnostics.. were no friends to marriage. **1876** J. PARKER *Paracl.* II. xviii. 341 Physical science has a friend in every theologian. **1878** MORLEY *Carlyle* Crit. Misc. Ser. I. 198 These who should only have been friends of order. **1926** (*title*) Friends of the Bodleian. First Annual Report 1925–26. *Ibid.* title-p. *verso*, In presenting this first Annual Report of the Friends of the Bodleian, the Secretary would like to point out that a considerable part of the year has.. been spent in launching the Society... However, the Friends are now a considerable body. **1927** *Times* 20 July 17/6 The Dean and Chapter of Canterbury are forming a society of men and women to be known as 'The Friends of Canterbury Cathedral'. *Ibid.*, The Prince of Wales, on the special ground of the link between Canterbury Cathedral and Edward the Black Prince, is the first Friend entered on the roll. **1963** *Guardian* 22 Apr. 7/3 The twenty more or less aristocratic Friends of the Tate Gallery. **1963** *Times* 3 June 10/4 He also initiated 'The Friends of Bristol Cathedral', of which Queen Mary became the first Friend-in-Chief. **1971** *Guardian* 7 July 24 The Friends of the Lake District, a conservationist body which has already fought Manchester Corporation over its water extraction plans.

b. Said of God or Christ.

c **1325** *Metr. Hom.* 23 Criste warnes us ful fair als frend. *c* **1460** *Towneley Myst.* (Surtees) 14 Cain, I reyde thou so teynd That God of heven be thi freynd. **1500–20** DUNBAR *Poems* xx. 43 Hald God thy freind, evir stabill be him stand. **1754** CHATHAM *Lett. Nephew* iv. 26 His never-failing Almighty Friend.

c. *friend in* or *at court*: one who has ability and disposition to help another by his influence in high quarters.

c **1400** *Rom. Rose* 5541 For freend in court ay better is Than peny in [his] purs [*orig.* Qu'ades vaut miex amis en voie Que ne font deniers en corroie]. **1539** TAVERNER *Erasm.*

Prov. (1552) 14 A frend in court is worth a peny in purse. **1655** Dickson *On Ps.* cv. 16 When the Lord was to bring his people into Egypt He provided so as they should have a friend at court before they came. **1848** Dickens *Dombey* xxxviii, I shouldn't wonder—friends at court you know—but never you mind, mother, just now. **1886** *Pall Mall G.* 23 Sept. 11/2 Despite the activity of the squatters' friends 'at court' (that is, in the public land offices at Sydney).

d. *transf.* Anything helpful.

*c***1400** *Lanfranc's Cirurg.* 150 Wherfore spiritus exaliþ þe whiche þat ben freendis boþe to þe body and also to þe soule. **1611** Shaks. *Wint. T.* i. ii. 458 Good Expedition be my friend. **1671** Narborough *Jrnl.* in *Acc. Sev. Late Voy.* i. (1711) 186 Here Brandy was our best Friend, for it kept them always Fox'd.

6. a. As opposed to *enemy* in various senses: One who is on good terms with another, not hostile or at variance; one who is on the same side in warfare, politics, etc.

*a***1000** *Elene* 953 (Gr.) Se feond & se freond. *a***1175** *Cott. Hom.* 231 Wa..him were frend oðer fend. **13..** *K. Alis.* 122 He disgysed him anon, That him no kneow freond neo fon. *c***1400** *Destr. Troy* 7853 To beri þe bodys of hor bold frendys. *c***1440** *York Myst.* xx. 173 For frende or foo. **1508** Dunbar *Flyting w. Kennedie* 85 My freyindis thow reprovit with thy pen? Thow leis, tratour! **1596** Shaks. *Merch. V.* v. i. 26 *Lor.* Who comes so fast in silence of the night? *Mes.* A friend. **1696** tr. *Du Mont's Voy. Levant* 175 The French, whom they call Friends and Allies. **1717** Bolingbroke *Let. to Windham* Wks. 1809 I. 7 From our enemies we expect evil treatment..but when our friends abandon us..the firmest mind finds it hard to resist. **1782** Priestley *Corrupt. Chr.* I. Pref. 20 Whether it be by a friend or an enemy, I shall be glad. **1816** Scott *Old Mort.* xlii, 'I hae been willing to save the life o' friend and foe.'

b. Phrases: *to be, †hold, keep, make friends with, † to make friends to*: to be or get on good terms with; also absol. *to be friends. † to have,* etc. *to (at) friend*, i.e. as a 'friend', on one's side.

1590 Spenser *F.Q.* i. i. 28 So forward on his way (with God to frend) He passed forth. **1596** Shaks. *1 Hen. IV*, iii. iii. 203, I am good Friends with my Father, and may do any thing. **1599** —— *Much Ado* i. i. 91 *Mess.* I will hold friends with you Lady. **1601** —— *Jul. C.* iii. i. 143, I know that we shall haue him well to Friend. **1603** —— *Meas. for M.* i. iii. 182 Implore her..that she make friends To the strict deputie. **1605** —— *Macb.* iv. iii. 10 As I shall finde the time to friend; I wil. **1611** —— *Wint. T.* v. i. 140 From him Giue you all greetings, that a king (at friend) Can send his Brother. **1647** Clarendon *Hist. Reb.* vii. §24 The King had no Port to Friend, by which he could bring Ammunition to Oxford. **1651** N. Bacon *Disc. Govt. Eng.* ii. xxxix. (1739) 173 The people..had God to Friend in all. **1657** R. Ligon *Barbadoes* (1673) 108 By his own Industry, and activity (having youth and strength to friends) raise his fortune. **1697** Dampier *Voy.* I. ii. 23 A party of 500, or 600 men.. may do it without asking leave of the Indians; though it be much better to be friends with them. **1715–20** Pope *Iliad* viii. 230 Sole should he sit, with scarce a god to friend. **1823** J. Wilson *Trials Marg. Lyndsay* xxiii. 190 Will you be friends with me again, Mary? **1873** Black *Pr. Thule* xvi. 255 You will never make friends with me by speaking ill of my husband. **1884** W. E. Norris *Thirlby Hall* v, You must keep friends with her, or she may do you an ill turn one of these days.

†**c.** *heavy friend, small friend*: an enemy. Cf. backfriend 1.

1606 Holland *Sueton.* 182 His Aunt Lepida..hee deposed against..thereby to gratifie his mother her heavie friend, and who followed the suite hotly against her. **1767** Wesley *Wks.* (1872) III. 270 So hitherto all the bad labour of my small friends is lost.

7. A member of the Society of Friends, a Quaker.

1679 *Establ. Test* 24 He passes for one of their *Friends*. **1708** Whiting (*title*), A Catalogue of Friends Books; Written by many of the People, called Quakers. **1796** T. Twining *Trav. Amer.* (1894) 67 It is probable that his name is held in respect by the 'Friends' of Pennsylvania. **1870** Whittier *Pr. Wks.* (1889) III. 307, I am not blind to the shortcomings of Friends.

8. *attrib.* and *Comb.*, as *†friend-foe, -killer, -maker, -spectator; friend-betraying, -finding, -making, †-pretending, †-seeming adjs.* Also **†friend-pipe**, the calumet; **friend-stead** *a. Sc.*, 'possessing a friend' (Jam.), befriended; **friend-strong** *a.*, having many friends.

1645 Quarles *Sol. Recant.* i. 37 Where..*friend-betraying treasure May passe in barter for repented Pleasure. **1846** Browning *Soul's Trag.* i. 63 Luitolfo was the proper *Friend-making, everywhere *friend-finding soul. *a***1618** Sylvester *Miracle Peace* Wks. (Grosart) II. 42 The *friend-foe strangers, With us, against us. **1586** J. Hooker *Girald. Irel.* in *Holinshed* II. 182/2 He received his just reward of..a *friend killer. **1580** Lupton *Sivqila* 118 The chiefe friende and *friendmaker is money. **1775** Adair *Amer. Ind.* 167 Indian methods of making peace..They first smoke out of the *friend-pipe, and eat together. *a***1661** Fuller *Worthies* (1840) III. 274 His *friend-pretending foes. **1620** Melton *Astrolog.* 74 In fawning and *friend-seeming shewes. **1632** Brome *North. Lasse* Prol., Gallants and *Friends-spectators will yee see A strain of Wit that is not Poetry? **1637** Rutherford *Lett.* (1862) I. 462, I am sure that while Christ lives, I am well enough *friend-stead. *a***1618** Sylvester *Sonn.* vii. Wks. (Grosart) II. 322 Our *friend-strong Muse shall use the helpe of Strangers.

†**B.** *adj.* Well-disposed, friendly, not hostile. (Cf. enemy *a.*) *Obs.*

1398 Trevisa *Barth. De P.R.* xvii. lxvii. (Tollem. MS.) Fresche bred and clene, made of whete, is moste frende and acordynge to kynde. *c***1400** *Lanfranc's Cirurg.* 69 A fisician þat was frend to þe freendis of þe pacient. **1574** Hellowes *Gueuara's Fam. Ep.* 28 The citie of Sagunto was alwayes friend and allied with the Romanes. **1600** E. Blount tr. *Conestaggio* (ed. 2) 33 They were in a strong lodging, ioyning to a friend towne. **1601** Shaks. *Jul. C.* v. iii. 18 That I may rest assur'd Whether yond Troopes are Friend or Enemy. **1623** Bingham *Xenophon* 36 Passe you not with much labour many plaines, that are friend to vs? **1690** S. Sewall *Diary* 10 Mar. (1878) I. 315 The present settlement of the Friend-Indians.

friend (frɛnd), *v.* Forms: 3 **vreonden**, 4–6 **fre(e)nde**, 9 *Sc.* **freend**, 6– **friend**. [f. friend *sb.*]

†**1.** *trans.* To gain friends for. *Obs. rare*$^{-1}$.

*a***1225** *Ancr. R.* 420 Ne makie none purses, uorte ureonden ou mide.

†**2.** To make (persons) friends or friendly; to join in friendship; to join (a person) *to* or *with* another in friendship. Chiefly in pass. *to be friended. Obs.*

1387–8 T. Usk *Test. Love* iii. ix. 109 Charitie is love, and love is charity. God graunt us al[le] therin to be frended! *c***1425** Wyntoun *Cron.* vii. vi. 196 And eftyr swne frendyt were The Kyng Dawy of Scotland And Stewyn Kyng þan of Ingland. **1585** Earl Leycester in *Corr. Dudley* (1844) 33 Yf the man be as he now semeth, hit were petty to loose him, for he is in dede mervelously frended. **1587** Fleming *Contn. Holinshed* III. 1346/2 What freendship he had shewed.. both by his owne purse, as also by freending them to some of the popes chamber. *a***1598** Rollock *Serm.* Wks. 1849 I. 363 Thou sall never get regeneratioun befoir God be friended with thee: thou is his enemie, thou mon be friended with him. **1604** T. Wright *Passions* i. x. 37 Others you have, soone angrie. soone friended.

3. To act as a friend to, befriend (a person, cause, etc.); to assist, help. *arch.* or *poet.*

1562 J. Heywood *Prov. & Epigr.* (1867) 89 Freende they any, That flatter many? **1581** Savile *Tacitus' Hist.* iv. xxxix. (1591) 198 Kings which frended the cause. **1600** Holland *Livy* xxxi. xi. 779 They had undertaken the warre upon king Philip, because he had friended and aided [*auxiliis juvisset*] the Carthaginians. *a***1618** Sylvester *Maiden's Blush* 967 Shee all the gods requires To friend her love, and further her desires. **1676** W. Row *Contn. Blair's Autobiog.* xii. (1848) 434 Reports came that the King would friend Lauderdale. **1855** Singleton *Virgil* I. 27 Do thou but at his birth the boy..O chaste Lucina, friend.
absol. **1606** Shaks. *Tr. & Cr.* i. ii. 84 Well, the Gods are aboue, time must friend or end.

b. *fig.* of things.

1598 Barret *Theor. Warres* v. ii. 143 If they be not friended with hedge, ditch, or some such place of aduantage. **1599** Shaks. *Hen. V*, iv. v. 19 Disorder that hath spoyl'd vs, friend vs now. **1622** Drayton *Poly-olb.* xxii. (1748) 343 But friended with the flood the barons hold their strength. **1721** Southerne *Spartan Dame* i. i, There the street Is narrow, and may friend our purpose well. **1867** M. Arnold *Poems, St. Brandan*, That germ of kindness..outlives my doom, And friends me in the pit of fire.

4. *to friend it*: to act the friend. *rare.*

1849 Clough *Dipsychus* i. iii, To herd with people that one owns no care for; Friend it with strangers that one sees but once.

Hence †**'friending** *vbl. sb.*, friendliness; the action of befriending or favouring one's friends.

1602 Shaks. *Ham.* i. v. 185 T'expresse his loue and friending to you. **1642** *Compl. Ho. Com.* 10 There is notable friending there in causes.

†**'friendable**, *a. Obs. rare.* [f. friend *sb.* + -able. Cf. *amicable*.] Friendly.

*c***1570** *Pride & Lowl.* (1841) 83 Sleepe to nature so friendable.

friended ('frɛndɪd), *ppl. a.* [f. friend *sb.* and *v.*]

a. Having a friend; possessed of or supplied with friends. Usually qualified by an adv. as *ill, well,* etc. *friended.* **b.** In sense 3 of the vb.: Befriended (*rare*).

1530 *St. Papers Hen. VIII*, VII. 243 Cassalis and other be so frendyd abought Yowr Grace, that they have avyses of al the tenour off yowr mooste honorable lettres writen hyther. **1568** Tilney *Disc. Mariage* E iv, What avayleth it a man to have his wife of..good parentage, and wel friended, if [etc.]. **1580** Sidney *Arcadia* iii. (1605) 292 The curteous Amphialus..ranne ouer the head of his therein friended enemie. **1581** Mulcaster *Positions* iv. (1887) 19 Who is so ill freinded, as he hath not one, with whom to conferre. **1603** Knolles *Hist. Turks*, Although he was a man mightily frended, yet was he..banished. **1824** Scott *Redgauntlet* let. xi, 'He was weel-freended and at last he got the haill scraped thegither.' **1884** Edna Lyall *We Two* xl, I have been well 'friended' all my life, he said.
Prov. **1538** Starkey *England* i. iii. 86 For (as hyt ys commynly and truly also sayd) materys be endyd as they be frendyd. **1605** Camden *Rem.* (1637) 292 As a man is friended, so the law is ended. **1610** Heywood *Gold. Age* i. i. Wks. 1874 III. 6 Causes best friended haue the best euent.

†**'friendess.** *Obs.* In 4 **frendesse**. [f. friend *sb.* + -ess.] A female friend.

1382 Wyclif *Prov.* vii. 4 Clepe thou prudence thi frendesse. **1388** —— *Song Sol.* i. 8.

†**'friendful**, *a. Obs.* [f. friend *sb.* or *v.* + -ful.] Friendly, well-disposed, loving.

*c***1375** *Sc. Leg. Saints, Vincencius* 173 þar-for so frendful ma nane be to me as þu. *c***1470** Henry *Wallace* ix. 1383 A hous, quhar..A wedow duelt was frendfull till our men. *a***1509** Hen. VII in *Antiq. Rep.* (1808) II. 321 *note*, The dedly corrupcion did utterly overcom the pure and frendfull blod. **1570** Buchanan *Ane Admonitioun* Wks. (1892) 36 Remember yat he schew him self neuir mair freindfull and succurabill to na people yan he hes done to ȝow.

Hence †**'friendfully** *adv.*, in a friendly manner.

*c***1375** *Sc. Leg. Saints, Placidas* 659 He hyme met, &..ful frendfyly hym gret. *c***1450** *Golagros & Gaw.* 1173, I mak you request, Freyndfully, but falsset, or ony fenyeing, That ye wald to me..Tell your entent. **1535** Stewart *Cron. Scot.* III. 329 Thir governouris to purpois than tuke Richt freindfullie to deliuer this duke To his fredome.

'friendism. *nonce-wd.* [f. friend *sb.* + -ism.]

1820 Coleridge *Lit. Rem.* II. 174 Shakspeare meant to represent Richard as..a man with a wantonness of spirit in external show, a feminine friendism, an intensity of woman-like love of those immediately about him.

friendless ('frɛndlɪs), *a.* [f. friend *sb.* + -less.]

1. Destitute of friends. †*friendless man*: in OE. law a frequent designation for an outlaw.

*c***950** *Lindisf. Gosp.* John xiv. 18 Ne forlet ic iuih freondleasa ic cymmo to iuih. *a***1035** *Laws of Cnut* ii. §35 (Schmid) Gif freondleas man ȝeswenced weorþe. *c***1290** *S. Eng. Leg.* I. 331/292 So freondlese ase huy were. *c***1330** *Amis & Amil.* 1559 A frendleser man than he was. *c***1400** *Beryn* 1721 For now ful frendlese, yee mowe wel sey that ye been. **1552** Abp. Hamilton *Catech.* (1884) 31 Ane freindles man or woman. **1613** Shaks. *Hen. VIII*, iii. i. 81 Alas, I am a Woman frendlesse, hopelesse. **1664** South *Serm.* (1737) II. ii. 68 Woe to him that is alone, is verified upon none so much as upon the friendless person. **1847** Longf. *Ev.* ii. i, Friendless, homeless, hopeless, they wandered from city to city.
absol. *a***1035** *Laws of Cnut* ii. §35 (Schmid) Be freondleasan. **1526** Tindale *Jas.* i. 27 To vysit the frendlesse and widdowes in their adwersite. *a***1777** Fawkes *Nathan's Parable* 29 To recompense the friendless and the poor.

2. Used by Shelley = unfriendly.

1818 Shelley *Rev. Islam* iii. xiii, One bare A lighted torch, and four with friendless care Guided my steps the cavern-paths along.

Hence **'friendlessness**.

1812 Byron *Ch. Har.* ii. vii, The seeming friendlessness of him who strove To win no confidence. **1854** J. S. C. Abbott *Napoleon* (1855) I. iv. 72 She experienced the most afflictive reverses of friendlessness..and penury.

†**'friendlihood.** *Obs.* Forms: 4 **frendelyhede**, 5 **frendle-, frendlihede, frendlyhead, -hed(e, -hode**. [f. friendly + -head, -hood.] Friendliness, friendship.

1390 Gower *Conf.* II. 286 As by way of frendelyhede. *a***1420** Hoccleve *De Reg. Princ.* 958 In mukke is alle this worldes frendlyhede. *c***1440** *Generydes* 5170 Telle me doughter, of very frendlehede, What sygrem seid. **1481** Earl Worcester *Tulle on Friendsh.* (1530) A v, I truste that the frendlyhode of Scipio with Lelyus shalle be knowen to all them whiche shal come aftir us.

friendlike ('frɛndlaɪk), *a.* [f. friend + -like.] Like a friend or friends, friendly.

1559 W. Cunningham *Cosmog. Glass* 171 The nature of the people more ciuill, frindlyke, wise. **1596** Drayton *Leg. Matilda* lviii, But soone my Soule had gath'red vp her Powers, Which in this need might, friendlike, giue her ayd. *a***1721** Prior *Erle Robert's Mice* 35 Reply'd the friendlike Peer, I weene, Matthew is angred on the Spleene.

friendlily ('frɛndlɪlɪ), *adv.* [f. friendly *a.* + -ly^{2}.] In a friendly manner, like a friend.

1680 *Earl Rochester's Will* in *Wills Doctor's Comm.* (Camden) 140 Soe long as my wife shall..friendlily live with my mother. *c***1728** Earl of Ailesbury *Mem.* (1890) 651 We discoursed friendlily on several subjects. **1829** S. Turner *Mod. Hist. Eng.* II. ii. xi. 356 She sent the two nobles..to persuade him..to come back friendlily to him. **1883** Miss Broughton *Belinda* i. vii, Nodding friendlily to the powdery miller as they pass.

friendliness ('frɛndlɪnɪs). [f. friendly *a.* + -ness.] The quality or condition of being friendly; rarely *pl.*, manifestations of friendliness.

1490 Caxton *Eneydos* vii. 31 They began to treate wyth theym curtoysly, wyth all gre and frendlynes. *a***1500** *Chaucer's Dreme* 814 She had whole richesse Of woman-head, and friendlinesse. **1570** Dee *Math. Pref.* 10 His humblenes, and frendelynes to all men. **1650** Jer. Taylor *Holy Living* i. §4 (1680) 7 Let all the intervals..be employed in prayers..charity, friendliness, and neighbourhood. **1790** G. Walker *Serm.* II. xxi. 127 All the engaging, the heart-rejoicing friendlinesses of a human being. **1807** Southey *Let.* 8 Dec. in *Life & Corr.* III. xiii. 124 Fully sensible of your friendliness. **1863** Geo. Eliot *Romola* i. xvi, The keen eyes were bright with hope and friendliness.

friendly ('frɛndlɪ), *a.* (*sb.*) and *adv.* [OE. *fréondlic* adj., *-líce* adv.: see friend *sb.* and -ly^{1,2}.] **A.** *adj.*

1. Having the qualities or disposition of a friend, disposed to act as a friend, kind.

*c***900** tr. *Bæda's Hist.* v. xiii. (1891) 440 Oðþe ðurh ða freondlican ænglas oðþe ða feondas. *c***1374** Chaucer *Troylus* ii. 106 (155) He is the frendliest man Of so grete astate, that ever I saw in my lyve. **1402** Hoccleve *Let. of Cupid* 302 How frendely was Medea to Jason. **1477** Earl Rivers (Caxton) *Dictes* 8b, The enuyous man is frendely to him that is present. **1584** Burleigh in Fuller *Ch. Hist.* ix. v. 159 Your Graces as friendly as any Will. Burley. **1766** Goldsm. *Vic. W.* vi, I knew him to be friendly as far as he was able. **1871** G. Meredith *H. Richmond* xlii, No one could be friendlier.

2. a. Characteristic of or befitting a friend or friends; manifesting friendship.

*c***1385** Chaucer *L.G.W.* Prol. 251 Hyde Jonathas al thyn frendely manere. **1525** Ld. Berners *Froiss.* II. ccxli. 312 The grayhounde..made to hym the same frendly countinaunce and chere as he was wonte to do to the kyng. **1606** Shaks. *Ant. & Cl.* ii. vi. 47 Your Mother came to Cicelie, and did finde Her welcome Friendly. **1683** *Pennsylv. Archives* I. 72 And first, I congratulate wth a friendly Joy. **1709** Steele & Swift *Tatler* No. 67 ¶12 To tell People of their Faults in a friendly and private Manner. **1785** J. C. Lettsom *Let.* 8 Apr. in T. J. Pettigrew *Life* (1817)

II. 425, I was sorry to perceive by your last friendly letter that you have failed in procuring a loan for my friend Mr. W. **1868** Miss Braddon *Run to Earth* I. i. 9 Jernam acknowledged their courtesy with a friendly nod.

b. ***friendly lead***, among the poorer classes in London, an entertainment given by friends for the benefit of a person in distress, etc.

1886 Besant *Childr. Gibeon* II. xxxii, The great table dented..with a thousand hammerings of pewter pots at friendly leads. **1895** *Daily Tel.* 26 Sept. 3 He went to a 'friendly lead' for the benefit of a man who had just come out of the hospital.

3. a. Not hostile or at variance; on amicable terms. Const. *to*, *with*.

1595 Shaks. *John* II. i. 481 Why answer not the double Maiesties, This friendly treatie of our threatned Towne. **1607** —— *Timon* V. i. 122 Nothing but himselfe, which lookes like man, Is friendly with him. **1613** Purchas *Pilgrimage* (1614) 695 The Inhabitants whereof..have shewed themselves friendly to the Portugals. **1671** Narborough *Jrnl.* in *Acc. Sev. Late Voy.* I. (1711) 135 The People were friendly..but..very theevish. **1798** Nelson 22 July in Nicolas *Disp.* (1845) III. 47 The King's flag is insulted at every Friendly Port we look at. **1849** Macaulay *Hist. Eng.* I. 399 The wits and the Puritans had never been on friendly terms. **1860** *Ann. Reg.* 21 Sowing suspicion and distrust, calculated to bring about a total rupture with a neighbouring and friendly country.

b. Not proceeding from or attended with hostility; amicable. Of an action at Law: Brought between parties not really at variance, in order to obtain a decision on some point.

c. Of a match at football, etc.: Played simply for the honour of the thing and not in competition for a cup, etc. Usually *ellipt.* (quasi-*sb.*).

1894 *Athletic News* 5 Nov. 4 The Sunderland and Woolwich Arsenal match was a friendly. **1895** *Westm. Gaz.* 7 Nov. 3/2 When an inter-club match is called a 'friendly', the inference as to what a league match means is fairly easy. **1903** Wodehouse *Tales of St. Austin's* 18 Merevale's were playing a 'friendly' with the School-House, and..Harrison had been pressed into service as umpire. *Ibid.* 22 Lucky the game was only a friendly. **1963** *Times* 11 May 3/6 He has appeared in a number of first-team friendlies. **1971** *Daily Tel.* 2 Aug. 3/7 Fighting broke out on the terraces during the Port Vale 'friendly' match against Manchester City at Vale Park.

4. Favourably disposed, well-wishing; inclined to approve, help, or support.

1535 Coverdale *Ps.* xxiv. [xxv.] 8 O how frendly & rightuous is the Lorde. **1601** Shaks. *Jul. C.* V. i. 94 The Gods to day stand friendly. **1826** Foster in *Life & Corr.* (1846) II. 79 A letter..which contained a most friendly reference to me. **1878** J. C. Morison *Gibbon* 72 The side of his history from which a friendly biographer would most readily turn away.

5. a. Of things, influences, etc: Disposed or likely to be helpful or serviceable; kindly, propitious, favourable, salutary. Const. *to*, †*unto*.

c **1391** Chaucer *Astrol.* II. §4 He is in dignite & conforted with frendly aspectys of planetes. **1592** Shaks. *Rom. & Jul.* V. iii. 163 O churle, drinke all? and left no friendly drop, To helpe me after. **1659** Hammond *On Ps.* cvii. 23–30 By the friendliest gales. **1683** Tryon *Way to Health* 192 The more simple..sorts of Food and Drink, as Bread, Cheese..are both mild and friendly. **1821** Lamb *Elia* Ser. I. *Mackery End*, As words written in lemon come out upon exposure to a friendly warmth. **1850** Prescott *Peru* II. 341 He bent down his head to kiss it, when a stroke, more friendly than the rest, put an end to his existence.

b. Suitable to one's comfort, convenient.

1697 Dryden *Virg. Georg.* IV. 33 Neighb'ring Trees, with friendly Shade invite The Troops. **1713** Addison *Cato* I. iv, At th' approach of Night On the first friendly Bank he throws him down. **1885** J. Payn *Talk of Town* II. 196 A friendly pillar brought Dennis himself to anchorage.

†**6.** Of things: 'Disposed to union' (J.); not jarring or conflicting. *Obs.*

1717 Pope *Ep. to Jervas* 15 Like friendly colours [we] found them both unite. **1793** Smeaton *Edystone L.* §272 To bring all the parts into their most friendly state of contact.

7. Of or pertaining to the Society of Friends.

1886 *American* XII. 155 Whose family are Friendly people.

8. Friendly Society. Originally, the name of a particular fire-insurance company. In later use, one of numerous associations, the members of which pay fixed contributions to insure pecuniary help in sickness or old age, and provision for their families in the event of death.

1703 *Lond. Gaz.* No. 3910/4 All Persons who have any Demands upon the Undertakers of the Friendly Society, by reason of the late Fire..may..Receive the money, due on any Policy of Insurance. **1720** *Ibid.* No. 5909/3 The Friendly Society (or Sheaf or Arrows) give Notice, That they assure Losses from Fire. **1819** *Gentl. Mag.* 529 He placed the property of Friendly Societies under the protection of the laws. **1863** Fawcett *Pol. Econ.* II. ix. (1876) 240 A Trades'-Union performs the ordinary functions of a Friendly Society.

9. *Comb.*, as ***friendly-fiendly***, ***-seeming*** adjs.

1709 E. Holdsworth *Muscipula* (1749) 51 With friendly-seeming wellcome. **1877** Tennyson *Harold* III. i, With that friendly-fiendly smile of his.

B. *sb.* (See also A. 3 c.) A member of a people that is 'friendly', esp. to whites. Usually *pl.*

1861 *Let.* 18 May in *Richmond-Atkinson Papers* (1960) I. xii. 707 No natives about except the 'friendlies' at Poutoko and Hauranga. **1869** B. Y. Ashwell *Let.* 8 May IV. 554, 200 Friendlies went with Heta. **1870** *Pall Mall G.* 19 Apr., They were friendlies returning home. **1885** *Ibid.* 17 Mar. 8/1 Our Arab 'friendlies' declare that [etc.].

C. *adv.* In a friendly manner or spirit, like a friend, with friendship.

Beowulf 1027 Ne ȝefræȝn ic freondlicor feower madmas. *c* **1205** Lay. 14845 We scullen an londe..godes folc uroæfrien & freondliche hit halden. *a* **1300** *Cursor M.* 15294 Forwit his disciplis fete Ful freindli he fell. **1362** Langl. *P. Pl.* A. XI. 171 Was neuer gome vppon grounde..Feirore vndurfonge ne frendloker maad at ese. *c* **1440** *York Myst.* xxxiii. 76 So frendly he fared. *c* **1475** *Rauf Coilȝear* 281 Than spak he freindly. **1549** Coverdale, etc. *Erasm. Par. Jas.* i. 27 Euen so muste we agayne bee bothe mercyfull and frendely liberall towardes our neighbour. **1608** Rowlands *Humors Looking Glasse* 9 Vnles he friendly drew his purse. **1705** Hearne *Collect.* 21 Nov., W^ch [he] was friendly told of. **1772–84** Cook *Voy.* (1790) V. 1672 Some of the men marry three wives, who in general live friendly together. **1807** P. Gass *Jrnl.* 255 The natives used us friendly and with kindness. **1869** Freeman *Norm. Conq.* (1876) III. xii. 157 He tended him friendly in his castle for three days.

† **'friendman.** *Obs.* [f. friend *sb.* + man.] An intimate friend; also, a relative.

c **1200** *Trin. Coll. Hom.* 183 Among þat þe sowle witeð þe licame worpeð hewe and þe frendmen him biwepeð gef þar anie ben. *a* **1300** *Cursor M.* 20242 Hir freind-men til hir scho cald. [**1884** J. Parker *Apost. Life* III. 4 Man looks for man—not any man, but the friend-man.]

† **'friendrede.** *Obs.* [OE. *fréondrǽden*: see friend *sb.* and -red.] Friendship.

c **888** K. Ælfred *Boeth.* xxi, þæt hie ȝetreowlice heora.. freondrædenne healdaþ. **13..** *K. Alis.* 1488 To beon of his freondrede. **1340** *Ayenb.* 149 þise urendrede ous ssewede Iesu crist þe zoþe urend.

friendship ('frɛndʃɪp). Forms: 1–3 **fréondscipe**, (1 **-scype**, 3 **freond-**, **freontschipe**, **freonscipe**), 2–3 **frendshipe**, 3–4 **frenscip**, **-scep**, **freinschip**, 3–5 **frendscip**, **-schip**, **frenschip(e**, (4 **frendischipe**, **frencipp**, **-s(c)hepe**, 5 **-chepe**), 4–5 **frendeship**, (**freendshippe**), **frenship(pe**, **-shyp**, 4–6 **frendship(pe**, (4 **frendshepe**, 6 **-shype**, 4 *Sc.* **freyndschip**, 6 *Sc.* **freindship**, 6– **friendship**. [OE. *fréondscipe*: see friend *sb.* and -ship.]

1. The state or relation of being a friend; association of persons as friends.

Beowulf 2069 þy ic Heaðobeardna hyldo ne telȝe.. freondscipe fæstne. *c* **1175** *Lamb. Hom.* 33 Alre erest þu most habben mine freonscipe. *a* **1225** *Ancr. R.* 98 Uor no freondschipe nis so vuel ase is fals freondschipe. **1297** R. Glouc. (1724) 35 þat bi nom þe myn frenschipe for þi soþnesse al clene. **1398** Trevisa *Barth. De P.R.* XVI. iii. (1495) 553 It is sayd that alabastre..gendryth and kepyth frendshypp. *c* **1440** *York Myst.* xxxiii. 76 He fest me to his frenschippe, so frendly he fared. **1553** Eden *Treat. Newe Ind.* (Arb.) 36 Wilde menne, which could by no gentilnes be allured to frendshippe. **1612** Bacon *Ess., Friendship* (Arb.) 160 Without friendship, society is but meeting. **1733** Swift *Life & Char. Dean S—t* 43 True friendship in two breasts requires The same aversions, and desires. **1875** Manning *Mission H. Ghost* v. 125 The love of friendship is..the most perfect form of love.

b. A friendly relation or intimacy.

c **1000** *Sax. Leechd.* III. 210 Freondscipas niwe. **1536** Bellenden *Cron. Scot.* (1821) I. 7 Knawing weill, na thing micht bring the pepill sonar under ane freindschip and band than sic doingis. **1664** Evelyn *Kal. Hort.* (1729) 85 The learned and choice Friendships that you enjoy. **1697** Dampier *Voy.* I. vii. 182 To endeavour a Friendship with those Indians; a thing our Privateers had long coveted. **1842** Tennyson *Will Waterproof* 40 And softly, thro' a vinous mist, My college friendships glimmer. **1871** Morley *Voltaire* (1886) 361 His friendship with two of the chief actors may have biassed his judgment.

†**c.** *collect.* Friends. *Obs.*

c **1400** *Beryn* 3526 And lokid..with a rewful cher..on othir frendshipp and neyȝbours he had ther. *a* **1440** *Sir Degrev.* 1274 The duke rekyvered aȝyne, Hys frenchepys were fayn. **1480** Caxton *Chron. Eng.* c. 80 Cadwalyn in playne batayll slowe Edwyn and al his frendshippes.

2. Friendly feeling or disposition felt or shown by one person for or towards another; friendliness. † ***in friendship***: on friendly terms.

a **1300** *Cursor M.* 14359 Mikel frenscip has þou him kidd. **1375** Barbour *Bruce* I. 84 For that at the King off Ingland Held swylk freyndschip and cumpany To thar King. *c* **1400** Maundev. (Roxb.) ii. 7 þat was giffen me for grete frenschepe. **1596** Spenser *State Irel.* (Globe) 661 Such rawe captaynes as are usuallye sent out of England, being therto preferred onely by frendship, and not chosen by sufficiencye. **1644** South *Serm.* (1737) II. ii. 45 We have here..an account of Christ's friendship to his disciples. **1723–4** in *Swift's Lett.* (1766) II. 277, I could never impute it to want of friendship in one, whose goodness to me has always been abundantly more than I could deserve. **1861** M. Pattison *Ess.* (1889) I. 38 To renew the assurance of his friendship, which was not diminished by the sorrowful event.

†**3.** A friendly act; a favour; friendly aid. *Obs.*

1535 Coverdale *Prov.* xviii. 24 A frende that delyteth in loue, doth a man more frendshipe, and sticketh faster vnto him then a brother. **1605** Shaks. *Lear* III. ii. 62 Hard by heere is a Houell, Some friendship will it lend you 'gainst the Tempest. **1613** Beaum. & Fl. *Coxcomb* II. i, You have done to me friendships infinite, and often.

†**4.** 'Conformity, affinity, correspondence, aptness to unite' (J.). Cf. friendly 6. *Obs. rare*$^{-1}$.

1695 Dryden tr. *Dufresnoy's Art Paint.* Observ. 175 This rule obliges us to know those Colours which have a Friendship with each other, and those which are incompatible.

† **'friendsome**, *a.* *Obs.* [f. friend (? *sb.* or *a.*) + -some.] Friendly, kindly, benign.

a **1300** *E.E. Psalter* lxviii. 20 [lxix. 16] Here me, lauerd, witterli, For frendsome es þi merci. **1375** Barbour *Bruce* I. 88 Thai trowyt that he..as freyndsome compositur, Wald hawe Iugyt in lawte.

Hence † **'friendsomeness**.

a **1300** *E.E. Psalter* lxiv. 12 [lxv. 11] Blisse saltou þe croune þat es Of yhere of his frendsomnes. *Ibid.* lxxxiv. 13 [lxxxv. 12] Sothlike frendsomnes lauerd giue sal.

frienge, obs. form of fringe.

frier, var. of fryer; obs. form of friar.

†**Friese**, *a.* and *sb.* *Obs.* [The native name: see Frisian.] = Frisian *a.* and *sb.*

1481 Caxton *Reynard* (Arb.) 42 Pater symonet the friese was woned to make there false money. **1675** tr. *Camden's Hist. Eliz.* IV. (1688) 592 They [Spaniards] were received by the Friese Musketiers with a Volley of small Shot.

Hence **'Friesic** *a.*, † **'Friesish** *a.* [see -ic, -ish], = Frisian.

1864 Webster, *Friesish* (rare). **1887** Cummins (*title*) A Grammar of the Old Friesic Language.

Friesian ('friːzɪən, -ʃən), *sb.* and *a.* [Var. of Frisian *a.* and *sb.*] **A.** *sb.* (One of) a breed of usu. black and white large dairy cattle, orig. from Friesland. **B.** *adj.* Of or pertaining to this breed.

1923 R. Wallace *Farm Live Stock* (ed. 5) 222 The general type of the Friesian is that of a large dairy animal. *Ibid.* Index, Friesian (or Fresian) British cattle. **1955** *Times* 6 July 7/1 The British Friesians are good. **1969** *Listener* 30 Jan. 159/1 Friesian cows have been found more profitable than others.

frieze (friːz), *sb.*[1] Forms: 5–6 **fres(s)e**, 5–7 **fryce**, **fryse**, 6 **friese**, **fryze**, 6–8 **frees(e**, **-z(e**, 5–9 **frise**, 6–9 **frize**, 7 **friese**, **-ze**, 6– **frieze**. [a. Fr. *frise* (from 15th c.), f. *friser* (16th c.) to curl (hair, etc.): see frizz *v.*[1]]

1. A kind of coarse woollen cloth, with a nap, usually on one side only; now *esp.* of Irish manufacture. Also **frieze-cloth**, †**frieze-ware**.

1418 *E.E. Wills* (1882) 37 Also a gowne of grene frese. **1462** *Mann. & Househ. Exp.* 150 Item, payd ffor iij. ȝerdys off blakke ffryce ij. *s.* ob. **1483** *Act 1 Ric. III*, c. 8 §18 The making..of any Cloth called *Frise Ware.* *a* **1529** Skelton *Wks.* (Dyce) I. 121 In dud frese ye war schrynyd With better frese lynyd. **1561** T. Norton *Calvin's Inst.* III. xix. (1634) 407 For this is truly said, that oftentimes in freese and course cloth dwelleth a purple heart. **1611** Speed *Theat. Gt. Brit.* vi. (1614) 11/1 A home-spun freeze-cloth. **1627** *Lisander & Cal.* v. 89 His wast-coate of redde fryse. **1683** *Brit. Spec.* 43 A thick Covering made of course Wool, having a Nap on both sides like Freez, worn by the Gauls and better sort of Britains to keep out the Cold. **1765** Sterne *Tr. Shandy* VII. xxi, An old calash..lined with green frize. **1803** *Ann. Rev.* I. 416 In the county of Wicklow a kind of frize and ratteen of pretty good quality, is very generally made for domestic uses. **1827** Miss Sedgwick *H. Leslie* (1872) II. 187 His dress was an overcoat of coarse frieze cloth. **1856** Mrs. Browning *Aur. Leigh* IV. 540 Half St. Giles in frieze Was bidden to meet St. James in cloth of gold.

†**2.** The nap or down on a plant; a tuft of the same. *Obs.*

1640 Parkinson *Theat. Bot.* 255 Nine leaves, three whereof fall downe, having a freeze neere the bottomes. **1657** W. Coles *Adam in Eden* 110 Round Leaves..thicker and greener than those of the Butter-burr, with a little Down or freese. **1688** R. Holme *Armoury* II. 109/1 Dittany hath..a Tassel in the middle..with a little Freez or Thrum.

3. In *Leather-manuf.* An imperfection in leather, consisting in a bruising or abrasion of the grain.

1885 C. T. Davis *Leather* IV. xiii. 239 'Frieze' is principally caused in the subsequent step of sweating when the grain of the hide is inclined to be tender and has the appearance of being scraped off.

4. *attrib.* and *Comb.* Chiefly simple *attrib.* or quasi-*adj.* = 'made of frieze', as in ***frieze coat*** (whence ***frieze-coated*** adj.). Also **frieze-coat**, a designation applied to an Irish peasant; † **frieze-leather** = frizzed leather.

1531 in Weaver *Wells Wills* (1890) 29 Wm Wey *als.* Smyȝth my old ffryse cotte. **1535** *Ibid.* 28 Sir John Sherman my ffryce gowne. *c* **1550** W. S. *Disc. Common Weal Eng.* II. (1893) 82 In a kendall cote in somer or in a frese cote in winter. **1563** Foxe *A. & M.* 1365 I Maister Latimer.. wearing an olde threade-bare Bristowe fryse gowne gyrded to his bodye with a peny lether gyrdell. **1594** Plat *Jewell-ho.* III. 72 A peece of freese-leather. **1598** Florio, *Marrochino*, Spanish lether, frizeleather. **1610** Rowlands *Martin Mark-all* A ij, Vp starts an old cacodemicall Academicke with his frize bonnet. **1640** W. M. *Wandering Jew* (1857) 22 A poore Ale-house is your Inne, an old Freeze Jerkin in Summer your Sonday-suit. **1775** Sheridan *Duenna* II. iii, As ridiculous as gold lace on a frize coat. **1796** Coleridge *Observ. Blossom 1st Feb.*, This dark, frieze-coated, hoarse, teeth-chattering Month. **1845** Disraeli *Sybil* (Rtldg.) 295 'Poor Ireland!' said Gerard. 'Well, I think the frieze-coats might give us a helping hand now, and employ the troops at least.' **1886** Hall Caine *Son of Hagar* II. xvi, Paul had thrown on a long frieze ulster.

fig. **1589** *Pappe w. Hatchet* (1844) 39 Such frize jestes upon fustian earnest.

frieze (friːz), *sb.*[2] *Arch.* Forms: 5 **fres**, 6 **frise**, **fryse**, 6–7 **frese**, 6–9 **frize**, 7 **freese**, 7–8 **freeze**, 8 **freze**, 7– **frieze**. [a. Fr. *frise* fem., which (with Sp. *friso* masc.) is prob. related in some way to the synonymous It. *fregio* masc., also 'border, fringe, ornament':—L. *Phrygium* (sc. *opus*) a Phrygian work (cf. *Phrygiæ vestes* embroidered garments).]

1. That member in the entablature of an order which comes between the architrave and cornice. Also in extended sense (see quot. 1850).

1563 SHUTE *Archit.* Divb, The Architraue, frise, and Cornish.. Zophorus, which we cal yᵉ frese. **1644** EVELYN *Mem.* (1857) I. 110 The room.. is tapestried with crimson damask.. the frieze above rarely painted. **1656** DAVENANT *Siege of Rhodes* I. Dram. Wks. 1873 III. 259 In the middle of the freese was a compartiment, wherein was written Rhodes. **1726** LEONI *Designs* Pref. 2/1 Makes the projection of the Architrave.. hide the Freze. **1762-71** H. WALPOLE *Vertue's Anecd. Paint.* (1786) II. 57 *note*, The.. frieze adorned in stucco with sea-monsters. *a* **1774** GOLDSM. *Descr. Author's Bed. Chamb.* 17 With beer and milk arrears, the frieze [of a mantel-piece] was scored. **1812-16** J. SMITH *Panorama Sc. & Art* I. 158 Stiffly ornamented friezes. **1850** PARKER *Gloss. Archit.* (ed. 5) 221 Any horizontal broad band which is occupied by sculpture may be correctly termed a frieze (and is so by architectural writers), whether it form part of an entablature or be placed in any other position. **1852** MRS. JAMESON *Leg. Madonna* (1857) 148 A frieze of angelic boys ornaments the alcove.

b. A band of painted or sculptured decoration.

1847 DISRAELI *Tancred* I. vi, They entered the ball-room .. the walls of looking-glass, enclosing friezes of festive sculpture. **1851** LAYARD *Pop. Acc. Discov. Nineveh* xiii. 344 A thin coat of plaster, on which were painted figures and ornamental friezes.

2. a. In a column (also *frieze of the capital*) = HYPOTRACHELIUM. **b.** In a cannon: The encircling ring immediately behind the cornice-ring (see CORNICE 4).

1569-91 SPENSER *Vis. Bellay* iv, The chapters Alablaster, the fryses christall. **1663** GERBIER *Counsel* 32 The Freese, Gul or Throat. **1692** *Capt. Smith's Seaman's Gram.* II. vi. 94 C is the Freeze [of a cannon]. **1711** POPE *Temp. Fame* 142 The freezes gold, and gold the capitals.

3. *attrib.* and *Comb.*, as *frieze-work*. Also †**frieze-orders** *pl.*, those in which a frieze is always a part of the entablature; **frieze-panel**, (*a*) one of the uppermost panels of a six-panelled door; (*b*) the lower part of a gun-port (Adm. Smyth); **frieze-rail**, the rail below the frieze-panels.

1663 GERBIER *Counsel* 31 Any of the *Frese orders. **1678** MOXON *Mech. Exerc.* I. 106 The *Friese Pannel above the *Friese Rail. **1859** GWILT *Encycl. Arch.* (ed. 4) 568 In-doors, the upper rails are called *top rails*; the next in descending, *frize rails*.. The panels are also named from their situations on the door; thus CC, being the uppermost, are called *frize panels*. **1772-84** COOK *Voy.* (1790) V. 1773 Nothing is to be seen without a kind of *freeze-work, or a representation of some animal upon it.

Hence **friezed** *ppl. a.* [-ED²], furnished with a frieze; **friezeless** *a.*, having no frieze.

1819 WIFFEN *Aonian Hours* (1820) 76 Night's shrieking bird Flaps the friezed window with her wing. **1852** WILLIS *Summer Cruise in Medit.* xl. 244 Some friezeless portico.

frieze (fri:z), *v.*¹ Forms: see FRIEZE *sb.*¹ [ad. F. *friser* or Sp. *frisar*; perh. identical with the vb. of the same form represented by FRIEZE *v.*²: see FRIZZ *v.*¹]

1. *trans.* To cover with a nap; = COTTON *v.*¹ 1. *Obs.* exc. *Hist.*

1509, 1557 [see FRIEZED *ppl. a.*¹]. **1541** *Act 33 Hen. VIII*, c. 15 Many poore people haue ben well set a worke.. with dressing & frising of the said cottons. **1591** [see COTTON *v.*¹ 1]. **1601** [see FRIEZED *ppl. a.*¹ 1]. **1685** *Lond. Gaz.* No. 2009/8 For Beautifying of Cloth.. by Napping and Freezing the same without Honey. **1885** *Fortn. in Waggonette* 61 There were mills for scouring, fulling, and friezing cloth.

†**2.** = FRIZZ *v.*¹ (q.v. for examples in the forms *freeze, frize*). *Obs.*

†**3.** To brush lightly *over*. (= F. *friser* 'effleurer', Littré.) Cf. FRIZZLE *v.*¹ 3. *Obs.*

1622 PEACHAM *Compl. Gent.* 115 For Leather.. take yellow Oker.. and where you will have it darker, by degrees, mix Umber with it, and when you have wrought it over, take a broad Pencil and frieze it over with Umber.

4. *Comb.*, †**frieze-board** (see quot.).

1688 R. HOLME *Armoury* III. 348/1 The [Clothiers] Frise Board is that by which the Cloth after it is sheared hath a Nap or Curl put upon it.

Hence **ˈfriezing** *vbl. sb.*¹; also *attrib.*

1565 *Act 8 Eliz.* c. 7 §4 No Person.. shall use or exercise the Faculty of Frizing or Cottoning. **1694** *Lond. Gaz.* No. 2985/4 A new built Water-Mill.. containing.. a Fryzing Mill, a Raising Mill for Cloth.

frieze (fri:z), *v.*² [ad. F. *friser*, related to *frise* FRIEZE *sb.*²; chiefly in pa. pple. *frisé*, whence med.L. *frisātus* embroidered (with gold).]

1. *trans.* To embroider with gold; to work (gold) into arabesques, etc. Now *rare.*

1577-87 [see FRIEZED *ppl. a.*²]. **1881** *Academy* 28 May 400/2 A magnificent screen—golden in hue and patterned and friezed in exquisitely delicate arabesque.

2. *Naut.* (See quots.)

1769 [implied in FRIEZING *vbl. sb.*²]. **1771** REAR ADMIRAL J. MONTAGU *To Secretary of Admiralty* 15 Apr., An order to the Navy Board 'for his Majesty's ship Captain to be freezed on the quarters'.

3. To cover (a silver plate) with chased patterns.

Now used by workmen with reference to 'frosted work', and associated with FREEZE *v.*

1678 *Lond. Gaz.* No. 1301/4 Lost.. A round Gold Watch .. the Dial plate freezed with a little knot in the middle. **1683** *Ibid.* 1800/4 A round Silver Watch.. with a Freiz'd Dial-Plate. **1684** *Ibid.* 1938/4 A Silver Watch with.. long frized Hours on the Dyal Plate.

frieze, friezeadow: see FREEZE, FRIZADO.

friezed (fri:zd), *ppl. a.*¹ *Obs.* exc. *Hist.* [f. FRIEZE *v.*¹ and *sb.*¹ + -ED.]

1. Of cloth: Having a nap; = COTTONED 1.

1509 *Bury Wills* (Camden) 112, I wyll yᵗ euery poor man and woman dwellyng in my almesse howsyn have.. a ffrysed rosat gown. **1557** *Act 4 & 5 Phil. & Mary* c. 5 §12 Upon Pain of Forfeiture for every Welsh Cotton or Lining frised or cottoned to the contrary, vj. *s.* viij. *d.* **1601** HOLLAND *Pliny* I. 227 About Istria and Liburnia, the sheeps fleece resembleth haire rather than wooll, nothing at all good for to make frized clothes with a high nap. **1721** C. KING *Brit. Merch.* I. 291 Pennistones freized. **1865** DIRCKS *Mrq. Worc.* iv. 37 The term being applied to garments having long wool, then said to be friezed.

2. Of a plant: Downy; = COTTONED 2.

1578 LYTE *Dodoens* III. x. 328 Rha (as it is thought) hath great broade leaues.. white and fryzed underneath. **1597** GERARDE *Herbal* I. xxxvi. §1. 51 A fringe.. downe the middle of the lower leaves.. tipped or frized.

†**friezed**, *ppl. a.*² *Obs.* In 6 frised, frized. [See FRIEZE *v.*²] Of gold: Wrought into ornamental patterns. Of cloth: Embroidered or otherwise adorned with patterns in gold.

1577-87 HOLINSHED *Chron.* III. 805/2 Fret with frised gold. *Ibid.* 807/1 A tree of gold, the branches and boughes frised with gold. **1587** FLEMING *Contn. Holinshed* III. 1338/1 A canopie of cloth of gold frized.

friezer (ˈfri:zə(r)). Forms: 6 friser, 6-9 frizer. [f. FRIEZE *v.*¹ + -ER¹.] One who friezes cloth.

1557 [see COTTONER 1]. **1565** *Act 8 Eliz.* c. 7 §1 Six hundred Persons of the Art or Science of Sheermen or Frizers. **1871** *Gd. Words* 608 The drapers, cottoners, and frizers of Shrewsbury.

ˈfriezing, *vbl. sb.*² [f. FRIEZE *sb.*² or *v.*²] Frieze-work. Also *attrib.*

1769 FALCONER *Dict. Marine* (1776), *Freezing*, a sort of ornamental painting on the upper part of a ship's quarter, stern or bow. It consists generally of armour, instruments of war, marine emblems, etc. *c* **1850** *Rudim. Navig.* (Weale) 120 *Friezing*, ornamental carving or painting above the drift-rails, and likewise round the stern or bow. **1899** *Westm. Gaz.* 17 May 5/2 The large amount of window space will contrast pleasingly with the plain friezing above. **1909** WEBSTER, *Friezing machine*, a machine for making edge moldings on woodwork.

ˈfriezy, *a.* [f. FRIEZE *sb.*¹ + -Y¹.] **1.** Clad in frieze.

1849 ALB. SMITH *Pottleton Leg.* 35 A rough, friezy man brought in some uncouth leathern bags. **1855** *Chamb. Jrnl.* IV. 153 Friezy hairy groups.. wondering at us.

2. Resembling frieze.

1891 J. H. PEARCE *Esther Pentreath* I. iii, Covering him over with Tom's freezy coat. **1892** R. O. HESLOP *Northumbld. Words* s.v., A friezy coat is made of a kind of rough home-spun yarn. **1901** *Westm. Gaz.* 25 July 3/1 The Highwayman coat,.. formed of a friezy tweed or homespun.

frig (frɪg), *v.* Also frigg. [? Onomatopœic alteration of FRIKE *v.*; cf. FRIDGE, FIG, FIDGE *vbs.*]

†**1.** *intr.* To move about restlessly; to agitate the body or limbs. Cf. FRIDGE *v.* 1. *Obs.*

c **1460** *Towneley Myst.* (Surtees) 313 A welle blawen bowke thise frygges as frogges. **1598** E. GILPIN *Skial.* (1878) 51 Marke how Seuerus frigs from roome to roome. **1653** URQUHART *Rabelais* I. xi, He would.. be often in the dumps, and frig and wriggle it. **1658** ROWLAND *Moufet's Theat. Ins.* 955 How ridiculously the barbarous people when they are bitten will frig and frisk. **1719** D'URFEY *Pills* IV. 124 O! how they do frig it, Jump it and Jigg it.

†**2.** *trans.* To rub, chafe: = FRIDGE *v.* 3. *Obs.*

a **1529** SKELTON *E. Rummyng* 178 The bore.. His rumpe .. he frygges Agaynst the hye benche. *a* **1605** POLWART *Flyting w. Montgomerie* 724 Except I were to frig thee with whin stanes. **1674** N. FAIRFAX *Bulk & Selv.* Ep. Ded., As long as the Summers warmth holds on to cocker them, and the days heat to frigge and chafe them [flowers and insects].

3. Freq. used with euphemistic force. **a.** *trans.* and *intr.* = FUCK *v.* 1. **b.** To masturbate.

1598 FLORIO *Worlde of Wordes* 139 *Fricciare*, to frig, to wriggle, to tickle. **1680** ROCHESTER *Poems on Several Occasions* (1950) 14 Poor pensive Lover, in this place, Would Frigg upon his Mothers Face. **1680** OLDHAM in *Ibid.* 131 There Punk, perhaps, may thy brave works rehearse, Frigging the senseless thing, with Hand, and Verse. *c* **1684** *Sodom* IV. 120, I caught one frigging with a curs bob tayle. *a* **1749** A. ROBERTSON *Poems* (1751) 83 So to a House of Office.. a School-Boy does repair, To.. fr—— his P—— there. **1858** H. SILVER *Diary* 21 Oct. in G. Ray *Thackeray* (1955) I. 452 Thackeray says one of the first orders he recᵈ [at Charterhouse] was 'Come & frig me'. **1865** E. SELLON *New Epicurean* (1875) 11, I frigged and kissed their fragrant cunnies. *Ibid.* 22 The next minute I had flung her back on the hay, and was frigging away at her maidenhead. *c* **1888-94** *My Secret Life* II. 268, I have frigged myself in the streets before entering my house, sooner than fuck her. *Ibid.*, I got up,.. frigged my prick, probed her. *a* **1935** T. E. LAWRENCE *Mint* (1950) II. x. 128 'If you ask me, Sir,' replied Taffy unabashed 'like a pack of skeletons frigging on a tin roof.' **1946** MEZZROW & WOLFE *Really Blues* 380 *High-pressure romancing* (find 'em, fool 'em, frig 'em and forget 'em).

c. *fig.* Also used as a coarse expletive. Cf. FUCK *v.* 2.

1905 S. JOYCE in *Lett. J. Joyce* (1966) II. 104 Cosgrave says it's unfair for you to frig the one idea about love, which he had before he met you. **1936** S. KINGSLEY *Dead End* I. 33 *Spit*: Frig you! **1958** 'E. MCBAIN' *Killer's Choice* (1960) 10 'He's telling us politely to go to hell.' 'Well, frig him,' Monoghan said. **1970** L. MEYNELL *Curious Crime of Miss Julia Blossom* xi. 153 'And what about the rent?' 'Frig the rent.'

d. [cf. sense 1 and FUCK *v.* 3.] Const. *about, around*: to muck about, fool around (*with*). Const. *off*: to go away, make off.

1933 J. MASEFIELD *Conway* 211 *Frig about*, to fool around. **1940** HEMINGWAY *For whom Bell Tolls* xx. 272 We do not let the gypsy nor others frig with it [*sc.* a gun]. **1943** *Penguin New Writing* XVII. 87 You get an order, and you're frigging around like a pack of schoolgirls for five blinking minutes. **1955** N. BALCHIN *Fall of Sparrow* 166 So we've got to *move* people. See? Not keep them about here frigging around being tested for things. **1960** D. FEARON *Murder-on-Thames* xx. 188 It's not so easy to frig about with a stiff corpse and not leave bruise marks. **1965** H. C. RAE *Skinner* IV. xiii. 261 'Frig off,' he said, swinging towards the door. **1967** 'J. PALMER' *Above & Below* iv. 44 He asked to be sent to a fighting unit where he could do something more useful.. than frig about with papers.

4. *Comb.*, as †**frig-beard**.

1708 MOTTEUX *Rabelais* V. v. 164 Shavers and Frig-beards.

Hence **ˈfrigging** *vbl. sb.* (also *ppl. a.* and quasi-*adv.*); **ˈfrigger**¹.

In quot. 1736 Friga is a proper name applied to a hermaphodite lover, but the pun is transparent.

c **1560** A. SCOTT *Poems* (S.T.S.) 21 Sum luvis lang trollie lolly, And sum of frigging fane. **1598** FLORIO, *Menamenti*, stirrings, friggings. **1659** TORRIANO, *Frugatoio*.. a frigger, a clown, a wriggler up and down. **1707** *Indictment J. Marshall for publ. School of Love* (P.R.O. 6 Anne KB 28/24/9) My lovely Phil. is.. so well versed in the various manners of fucking and frigging as the captain of the virtuosas. **1736** 'F. SCHEFFER' *Toast* IV. 177 And surpriz'd (well-a-day!) the great Friga and Frow In a Posture—the Muse must not venture to shew! *Ibid.* 180 Ill presage! And had Friga but made a right Use Of a Hint so instructive, and op'd her own Sluice; Swelling high the Imp's Pool in a Torrent had run. *c* **1888-94** *My Secret Life* I. 93 Having come to the conclusion.. that frigging makes people mad. **1922** JOYCE *Ulysses* 725 Doing that frigging drawing out the thing by the hour. **1930** J. DOS PASSOS *42nd Parallel* Newsreel v. 63 Station agent's so friggin' tough in this dump. *Ibid.* 77 When does the friggin' boat go? **1944** J. B. PRIESTLEY *Daylight on Saturday* xii. 78 This shunting frigging new arrangement.. has got every flaming thing foxed up. **1951** E. MITTELHOLZER *Shadows move among Them* I. xv. 145 'You have the right spirit—and that's no frigging pun.' 'Hendrik! Please! No obscenity!' **1953** W. R. BURNETT *Vanity Row* xiv. 100 I'm god-damned frigging tired of getting shoved around by you. **1959** K. WATERHOUSE *Billy Liar* 40 *Take* your frigging mucky hands off my pullover. **1962** *Observer* 4 Mar. 1/6 We cannot go on with this piecemeal frigging around... Now we want to see finality brought about.

frig (frɪg), *sb.* [f. the vb.] In senses corresponding to the verb (sense 3).

c **1888-94** *My Secret Life* V. 171, I pulled out my prick and with two or three frigs spent in a spasm of pain and pleasure. **1941** BAKER *Dict. Austral. Slang* 30 *Frigg-up*, a confusion, muddle. **1955** M. MCCARTHY *Charmed Life* (1956) iii. 70, I don't give a frig about Sinnott's heredity.

frig: see FRIDGE.

frigate (ˈfrɪgət). Forms: 6-7 **fregate, -att, -ot, frig(g)ot(e, -tt, 6-9 frigat,** (6 **frygatte**, 7 **fricket, friggatt, -ett**), 6- **frigate.** Also 6 in It. form **fragatta** [ad. Fr. *frégate*, ad. It. *fregata, fragata*, = Sp., Pg., Cat. *fragata*.

The ultimate etymology is unknown, the hypothesis of Diez, that it represents a late L. *fabricāta* in the sense 'building' (cf. F. *bâtiment* building, ship), being generally rejected by recent scholars.]

1. A light and swift vessel, orig. built for rowing, afterwards for sailing. *Obs.* exc. *poet.*

1585 T. WASHINGTON tr. *Nicholay's Voy.* I. ii. 2b, With a frigat to accompany us and to bring backe newes from us. **1588** PARKE tr. *Mendoza's Hist. China* 151 All which people were embarked in small ships and two frygattes [*printed* foygattes]. **1599** HAKLUYT *Voy.* II. I. 111 And toward Sunne set, the castle sent a Fragatta vnto vs, to giue vs warning of three Foistes comming after vs. **1613** SHERLEY *Trav. Persia* 8 Perceiving a Fregat a farre off, rowing towards vs. **1698** FRYER *Acc. E. India & P.* 106 The other are Frigats fit to Row or Sail. **1732** LEDIARD *Sethos* II. VIII. 171 He promis'd .. to furnish him.. with a frigat to carry him.. to the port. **1810** SCOTT *Lady of L.* I. xxiv, Permit me.. to guide Your fairy frigate o'er the tide.

2. Applied to a vessel of larger size. †**a.** A merchantman. Also *galleon-frigate*. *Obs.*

1624 CAPT. SMITH *Virginia* V. 180 They sent one of the two Frigats last left with them for England. *a* **1674** CLARENDON *Hist. Reb.* IX. §115 They.. had at that time another Frigat of Mr. Hasduncks. **1723** *Lond. Gaz.* No. 6142/2, $\frac{1}{16}$ of the Craggs Frigate. **1800** *Naval Chron.* II. 237 Two more galleon frigates were expected. **1894** C. N. ROBINSON *Brit. Fleet* 229 Among the merchant-men serving against the Armada.. was a frigate.

fig. **1642** MILTON *Apol. Smect.* (1851) 298 He must cut out large docks.. to unlade the foolish frigate of his unseasonable autorities.

b. A war-vessel. In the Royal Navy, formerly a vessel of the class next in size and equipment to ships of the line, carrying from 28 to 60 guns on the main deck and a raised quarter-deck and forecastle. As subsequently used, the term no longer denoted a distinct class of vessels, being often applied to ships of much larger size than those that were so designated early in the nineteenth century. Since 1943, a naval escort vessel, a large corvette.

1630 *R. Johnson's Kingd. & Commw.* 224 There are continuall fights with the Portugall Frigats. **1641** EVELYN *Mem.* (1857) I. 41 The packet-boat..a pretty frigate of six guns. **1774** GOLDSM. *Nat. Hist.* (1776) I. 264 Being with one of the king's frigates in the Baltic. **1825** J. NEAL *Bro. Jonathan* III. 43 Without a single ship of war, frigate or sloop, to encounter a powerful navy. **1867** SMYTH *Sailor's Word-bk., Donkey-frigate*, those of 28 guns, frigate-built; that is, having guns protected by an upper deck, with guns on the quarter-deck and forecastle. **1877** W. THOMSON *Voy. Challenger* I. i. 11 She has all the accommodation of a frigate with the handiness and draught of water of a corvette. **1955** *Times* 10 May 7/1 The Leopard, a multi-purpose frigate with a heavy anti-aircraft armament, has an extreme length of 340 ft. and a beam of 40 ft. **1959** *Chambers's Encycl.* VI. 88/1 *Frigate*... The name was reintroduced during the second world war for a new type of convoy-escort vessel.

3. A large swift-flying raptorial bird (*Fregata aquila* or *Tachypetes aquilus*), found near land in the tropical and warmer temperate seas. Also ***frigate-bird, -petrel***.

1738 ALBIN *Nat. Hist. Birds* III. 75 The Frigate Bird. The Indians call it so, because of the Swiftness of its Flight. **1756** *Phil. Trans.* XLIX. 627 The sea-birds, called frigates ..quit the air, and seek the shore. **1837** MRS. CAULFEILD *Deluge* 94 At his side The kingly eagle, frigat, pelican. **1859** DARWIN *Orig. Spec.* vi. (1878) 142 No one except Audubon has seen the frigate-bird..alight on the surface of the ocean. **1895** *Daily News* 16 Sept. 6/2 The Frigate Petrel..a specimen was washed up dead on the shore of Walney Island in November 1890.

4. *attrib.* and *Comb.*, as ***frigate-almshouse*** (nonce-wd.), ***-fashion***; ***frigate-like*** adj. and adv. Also **frigate-built** *a.*, having 'a descent of some steps from the quarter-deck and forecastle into the waist' (Adm. Smyth); **frigate-bird, -petrel** (see 3); **frigate mackerel**, *Auxis rochei* or *A. thazard*, fishes of the family Scombridæ, found in warm seas.

a **1657** LOVELACE *Poems* (1864) 201 Have you not seen a charact lie A great cathedral in the sea, Under whose Babylonian walls A small thin *frigot almshouse stalls? **1676** *Lond. Gaz.* No. 1130/4 *Viva Oranga* of St. Malo's, Burthen 50 Tuns..*Frigat built. **1725** DE FOE *Voy. round World* (1840) 213 A small frigate-built vessel. **1863** P. BARRY *Dockyard Econ.* 75 A ship of more than usually heavy scantling, and with a variety of foreign timber judiciously distributed in all its parts, might have fairly claimed to be frigate-built. **1641** EVELYN *Mem.* (1857) I. 18 Phineas Pett, inventor of the *frigate-fashion of building. **1676** *Lond. Gaz.* No. 1077/4 A small Bark, called the Castle Frigat of Falmouth, burthen 25 to 30 Tun, built *Frigat like. **1708** *Ibid.* No. 4398/3 Captain Haddock..got Sight..of two Frigat-like Ships. **1884** G. B. GOODE *Nat. Hist. Aquat. Anim.* I. III. 306 It is not unusual in the Bermudas, where it is called the '*Frigate Mackerel', a name not inappropriate for adoption in this country [*sc.* the U.S.]. **1902** JORDAN & EVERMANN *Amer. Food & Game Fishes* I. 277 The only species of this genus is the frigate mackerel. **1933** *Bulletin* (Sydney) 19 Apr. 20/4 The rare capture on the coast of Otago..of a fish known in Australia as the frigate mackerel. **1965** A. J. MCCLANE *Standard Fishing Encycl.* 374/1 Frigate mackerels are generally small, seldom reaching a length of 2 feet.

frigatoon (frɪgəˈtuːn). [ad. It. *fregatone*, augmentative of *fregata* FRIGATE.] (See quot.) 'Also applied to a ship sloop-of-war' (Adm. Smyth).

1721 BAILEY, *Frigatoon*, a Venetian Vessel, built with a square Stern without any Fore-mast, having only a Main-Mast, Mizen-Mast and Bow-sprit. [Hence in mod. Dicts.]

†**ˈfrigefact**, *v.* *Obs.*$^{-1}$ [ad. L. *frīgĕfact-āre*, f. *frīgē-re* to be cold + *fact-* ppl. stem of *facĕre* to make.] *trans.* To chill. So †**ˈfrigefacted** *ppl. a.* [see -ED[1]], made frigid; †**frigeˈfaction** [see -ION[1] or -TION], the action or process of chilling; †**frigeˈfactive** *a.* [see -IVE], chilling.

1599 A. M. tr. *Gabelhouer's Bk. Physicke* 21/2 If it be a Foote or a Legge which is in this sorte frigefacted, I then take my beginning of circumoulutione at the knees to the bodye vpwardes. **1651** BIGGS *New Disp.* ¶ 192 Frigefactive and positive power. *c* **1656** USSHER *Ann.* vi. (1658) 279 Taking a huge draught of frigifacted wine. **1656** BLOUNT *Glossogr., Frigefaction*, a making cool. **1660** H. MORE *Myst. Godliness* VII. xv. 340 Saturn..is in an high degree frigefactive, as also exsiccative. **1673** *Phil. Trans.* VIII. 6132 All these to be further examined by Contusion, Agitation, Frigefaction. **1684** *Ibid.* XIV. 769 The severity of the Air's frigefactive power.

†**ˈfrigefy**, *v.* *Obs.* Also frigify. [ad. med.L. **frīgĕficāre*, f. *frīgēre* to be cold: see -FY.]

1. *trans.* To make cold; to cool.

Hence **ˈfrigefied, ˈfrigefying** *ppl. adjs.*

1599 A. M. tr. *Gabelhouer's Bk. Physicke* 44/1 Then infuse her in frigefyed water. *Ibid.* 226/1 She must eschewe..of Onions, Apples, Peares, Oranges, and of all other frigifyinge fruictes. **1604** R. CAWDREY *Table Alph., Frigifie*, coole, make cold. **1657** TOMLINSON *Renou's Disp.* 153 When any want a Medicament that califies or frigifies.

2. *intr.* To become cold.

1599 A. M. tr. *Gabelhouer's Bk. Physicke* 2/1 Let them seeth sufficiently in water, and then let it somwhat frigifye.

†**ˈfrigerate**, *v.* *Obs.*$^{-0}$ [f. L. *frīgerāt-* ppl. stem of *frīgerāre* to cool, f. *frīgus*: see FRIGID and -ATE.] *trans.* To make frigid; to cool. So †**frigeˈration** *Obs.*$^{-1}$ [see -ATION], the action or process of cooling; †**ˈfrigeratory** *Obs.*$^{-0}$ [see -ORY], see quot.

1656–81 BLOUNT *Glossogr., Frigerate*, to cool. *Frigeratory*, a Cooling-house, or place. *a* **1691** BOYLE *Hist. Air* xl. (1692) 248 Which wonderful Change I should not so much ascribe to a Frigeration of the Air..as to some nitrous..Exhalations.

frigger[2] (ˈfrɪgə(r)). [Etym. unknown.] A small glass ornament or testing sample.

1923 H. J. POWELL *Glass-Making in England* vii. 100 'Friggers' may be seen as chimney-piece ornaments in glass-blowers' homes in every glass-making district. **1938** A. FLEMING *Scott. & Jacobite Glass* ix. 107 Friggers have ever been a feature among East Coast glass-blowers who can produce whole 'Zoos' of little glass animals. **1964** *Punch* 29 July 175/1 The best 'glassmakers' frigger' of all—a flip-flop.

friggle (ˈfrɪg(ə)l), *v.* [frequentative of FRIG.] *intr.* †**a.** To jerk oneself about; to wriggle. **b.** *dial.* To fribble, to fuss. Hence **ˈfriggling** *ppl. a.*

1621 S. WARD *Happin. Pract.* (1627) 44 Is it harder for vs to cut off the friggling taile of that Hydra of Rome? **1626** J. YATES *Ibis ad Cæs.* I. 6 Though the head of this Hydra was cut off, yet it had still a frigling taile. **1848** A. B. EVANS *Leicestersh. Words, etc., Friggle*, to be tediously particular over a thing..She *friggles* so long at it.

fright (fraɪt), *sb.* Forms: 1 fyrhto, -u (*Northumb.* fryhto, fyrihto), 3–4 friȝt, 5 fryȝt, frey(h)t(e, -th, 7– fright. [OE. *fryhto*, a metathetic form (recorded only in Northumb.) of *fyrhto*, *-u* = Goth. *faurhtei*:—OTeut. **furhtîn-* wk. fem., noun of state or quality from **furhto-*, *forhto-* adj., afraid (Goth. *faurhts*, OS. *foroht*, *for(a)ht*, OHG. *foraht*, OE. *forht*). The other WGer. langs. have a synonymous derivative of the same root; OFris. *fruchta*, OS. *for(a)hta* (MDu. *vrucht(e*, *vrocht*), OHG. *for(a)hta* (MHG. *vorhte*, mod.Ger. *furcht*):—OTeut. **(furhtâ*, *-ôn-) forhtâ*, *-ôn-* str. and wk. fem.]

1. †**a.** In OE.: Fear in general (*obs.*). **b.** In ME. and in mod. use: Sudden fear, violent terror, alarm. An instance of this. Phr. *to take fright*.

c **825** *Vesp. Hymns* xii. 13 Ðylæs fiondes ðes efestgan facne fyrhtu stille awecce. *c* **1000** *Ags. Ps.* liv. 20 [lv. 19] Ne him Godes fyrhtu ȝeorne ondrædað. *c* **1250** *Gen. & Ex.* 1234 His moder wurð neȝ dead for friȝt. *c* **1325** *Body & Soul* in *Map's Poems* (Camd.) 338 Ne thorte us have friȝt ne fer, that God ne wolde his blisse us sent. *c* **1425** *Seven Sag.* (P.) 948 Tho the knave hadde a fryȝt. *c* **1440** *Promp. Parv.* 177/2 Freyhte, or feer..*timor, pavor, terror*. **1604** SHAKS. *Oth.* II. iii. 232 Least by his clamour..The Towne might fall in fright. **1609** HOLLAND *Amm. Marcell.* XXIX. xii. 369 The Mazices..thus beaten down in sundry slaughters, in a foule fright, brake their arraies. **1654** SIR E. NICHOLAS in *N. Papers* (Camden) II. 96 The greate advance made into this countrye had noe other ende then by giving a generall fright. **1770** *Junius Lett.* xxxviii. 189 *note*, The minister took fright. **1791** MRS. RADCLIFFE *Rom. Forest* iv, In my fright..I forgot to take the roundabout way. **1837** W. IRVING *Capt. Bonneville* III. 221 The antelopes, nearly exhausted with fatigue and fright.. made no effort to break through the ring of the hunters. **1847** TENNYSON *Princ.* VI. 351 An echo started up..and died of fright in far apartments.

2. †Anything that causes terror (*obs.*). Hence (*colloq.*) a person or thing of a shocking, grotesque, or ridiculous appearance.

1634 W. TIRWHYT tr. *Balzac's Lett.* I. 8 Hide my selfe here with your good favour..than to beare a shew there with their frights and soure lookes. **1661** BOYLE *Style of Script.* (1675) 27 As a skilful fowler..catches..some with frights, as black-birds with a sparrow-hawk or a low-bell. **1751** MRS. DELANY *Let. to Mrs. Dewes* in *Life & Corr.* 50 A friend ..who is working a fright of a carpet! **1809** MISS MITFORD in L'Estrange *Life* (1870) I. 76 The present race of young men are such a set of frights. **1832** *E. Ind. Sketch Bk.* II. 174 To be sure..the women are sad frights, very yellow, and mostly so lean. **1864** H. AINSWORTH *John Law* III. iii, 'You mustn't marry that ridiculous old fright', she whispered.

¶**3.** ? Misused for FRET *sb.*

1668 in Boyle *Hist. Air* xv. (1692) 85 The Storm had seven Paroxysms or Exacerbations, which the Seamen call Frights of Weather.

fright (fraɪt), *v.* Forms: 1 fyrhtan (*Northumb.* fyrhta, fryhta), 3 friȝten, 5, 9 *Sc.* fricht, 6 frite, 6– fright. *Pa. pple.* 9 *dial.* frit. [OE. **fryhtan* (Northumb. *fryhta*), metathetic var. of *fyrhtan*, corresp. to OFris. *fruchta*, OS. *forhtian* (MDu. *vruchten*), OHG. *forhten*, *furhten* (MHG. *vürhten*, mod.Ger. *fürchten*), Goth. *faurhtjan* :—OTeut. **furhtjan* to fear, f. **furhto-* (*forhto-*) afraid. (OE. had also *forhtian* = OS. *forhtôn*, of the same meaning but differing conjugation). The factitive sense 'to terrify' is peculiar to Eng.]

†**1.** *intr.* To be afraid, to fear. *Obs.*

c **1000** *Durham Rit.* (Surtees) 102/21 Ðu doest ða fyrhta, *facis eam tremere*. *c* **1250** *Gen. & Ex.* 1861 Oc michil he friȝtede for-ði boðen symeon and leui. *Ibid.* 3978 Ðhoȝ ðe asse spac, friȝtede he noȝt.

2. *trans.* To affect with fright; to scare, terrify. Now *rare* exc. *poet.* and *dial.*; in ordinary language its place has been taken by *frighten*.

c **900** tr. *Bæda's Hist.* IV. iii. (1890) 268 Gif..þunorrade eorðan and lyfte brægden and fyrhten. **1423** JAS. I *Kingis Q.* clxii, I ne wist quhat to done, so was I fricht. **1580** SIDNEY *Ps.* IX. xiii, With terrors greate, O Lord, doe thou them fright. **1628** HOBBES *Thucyd.* (1822) 23 The likelihood of the war wherewith the Corcyreans frighting you go about [etc.]. **1700** PENN in *Pa. Hist. Soc. Mem.* IX. 9 Those that fired upon the Indians, and frighted them. **1773** GOLDSM. *Stoops to Conq.* I. i, Frighting the maids, and worrying the kittens. **1821** CLARE *Vill. Minstr.* II. 196 The coy hare squats nestling in the corn, Frit at the bow'd ear tott'ring o'er her head. **1850** TENNYSON *In Mem.* lxxxii, No lower life that earth's embrace May breed with him, can fright my faith. **1869** C. GIBBON *R. Gray* iv, 'Ye needna be frichted, mither, he's just got himsel hurt'. **1908** D. H. LAWRENCE *Let.* 31 Dec. (1962) I. 44 The woman is..a wee bit frit. **1960** *Oxford Mail* 4 Aug. 1/5 When I heard he was dead I got frit. **1970** *New Society* 19 Nov. 897/3, I was frit, cold and bored.

absol. **1748** JOHNSON *Vanity of human Wishes* 148 Should no..difficulty fright.

b. With complement: To scare *away*, etc.

1592 SHAKS. *Rom. & Jul.* IV. v. 11 Heele fright you vp yfaith. **1637** B. JONSON *Sad Sheph.* I. ii, Except Love's fires the vertue have To fright the frost out of the grave. *a* **1643** SUCKLING *Acc. Relig.* Ep. (1646) 1, I send you that Discourse which frighted the Lady into a cold sweat. **1651** HOBBES *Leviath.* IV. xlvi. 373 Would fright them from Obeying the Laws. **1667** MILTON *P.L.* XI. 121 Of a Sword the flame Wide waving, all approach farr off to fright. **1678** WANLEY *Wond. Lit. World* v. i. §97. 468/1 Charles the fifth ..frighted Solyman the Turk from Vienna. **1697** DRYDEN *Virg. Georg.* IV. 167 The God..who frights away, With his Lath Sword, the Thieves and Birds of Prey. **1697** BP. PATRICK *Comm. Exod.* ix. 27 A Man distracted and frighted out of his Wits. **1705** STANHOPE *Paraphr.* (1709) IV. 558 A Refractory People might be frighted into good Manners. **1719** WATTS '*There is a land of pure delight*', Not Jordan's stream, nor death's cold flood, Should fright us from the shore. **1779–81** JOHNSON *L.P., Thomson* Wks. IV. 170 He accompanied the players by audible recitation, till a friendly hint frighted him to silence. **1821** KEATS *Lamia* I. 5 Before King Oberon's bright diadem..Frighted away the Dryads and the Fauns From rushes green.

Hence **ˈfrighting** *vbl. sb.* and *ppl. a.*

1631 DENISON *Heav. Banq.* 188 Frightings and terrors. **1648** GAGE *West Ind.* xxi. 188 How did I sometimes look upon Deaths frighting visage? **1650** W. BROUGH *Sacr. Princ.* (1659) 16 Their triviall and frighting argument. **1663** J. SPENCER *Prodigies* (1665) 29 God hath now, in a great measure, left frighting of men to Heaven by visible terrors. **1674** J. B[RIAN] *Harv. Home* iii. 19 Frighting fearfull terrors.

frightable (ˈfraɪtəb(ə)l), *a.* *rare*$^{-1}$. [f. FRIGHT *v.* + -ABLE.] Capable of being frightened.

1832 CARLYLE *Let.* 31 Aug. in Froude *Life* (1882) II. 306 Medical men can do nothing except frighten those that are frightable.

frighted (ˈfraɪtɪd), *ppl. a.* [f. FRIGHT *v.* + -ED[1].] Affected with fright, scared.

1647 TRAPP *Mellif. Theolog.* in *Comm. Epist.* 727 As a frighted worme wriggles into its hole. **1650** W. BROUGH *Sacr. Princ.* (1659) 480 The sinner..must be [penitent] not from a frighted phansie. **1700** DENNIS *Iphigenia* 49 Frighted Wolves, with dreadful Howl, Her dire approach declare. **1748** RICHARDSON *Clarissa* (1811) II. x. 61 The man must think he has a frighted fool to deal with. **1839** LONGF. *Hesperus* vii, She shuddered..like a frighted steed. **1870** BRYANT *Iliad* II. XXII. 311 Driven within the city walls Like frighted fawns.

¶**b.** Of a region or space: Pervaded with fear.

Milton's ***frighted deep*** is echoed by later writers.

1667 MILTON *P.L.* II. 994 Such a numerous host Fled not in silence through the frighted deep. **1715–20** POPE *Iliad* XIV. 446 Like lightning flashing through the frighted Skies. *a* **1780** BLAKE *Tiriel* vii. 1 She..led him over mountains and through frighted vales. **1808** J. BARLOW *Columb.* II. 207 Ere Rome's first Eagle clave the frighted air.

Hence **ˈfrightedly** *adv.*, in a frighted manner.

1748 RICHARDSON *Clarissa* (1811) IV. lix. 395 An accent rather frightedly and hoarsely inward than shrilly clamorous.

frighten (ˈfraɪt(ə)n), *v.* [f. FRIGHT *sb.* + -EN[5]. A late formation, which has taken the place of the earlier FRIGHT *v.*] **a.** *trans.* To throw into a fright; to terrify; = FRIGHT *v.* 2.

1666 PEPYS *Diary* 4 Sept., Which at first did frighten people more than any thing. **1697** DAMPIER *Voy.* I. x. 280 But even that was a Voyage enough to frighten us, considering our scanty Provisions. **1791** MRS. RADCLIFFE *Rom. Forest* x, I am sorry I frightened you so last night. **1842** ABDY *Water Cure* (1843) 206 These lunatics..never frighten women or children. **1883** FROUDE *Short Stud.* IV. I. vi. 65 In fearing that England would go into schism the pope was frightened by a shadow.

b. With complement: To scare *into*, *out of*, *off* (adv. and prep.), etc.

1691 W. NICHOLLS *Answ. Naked Gospel* 47 They were frightened to it by the Arms and Threats of the Souldiers. **1700** S. L. tr. *Fryke's Voy. E. Ind.* 278 [They] thought by Fire and Sword..to frighten him out of his Kingdom. **1726** SHELVOCKE *Voy. round World* (1757) 116 They frighten them into the most laborious submission. **1806–7** J. BERESFORD *Miseries Hum. Life* XXI. xv, Paying handsomely ..to be canted out of your saddle, and frightened out of your wits. **1861** GEO. ELIOT *Silas M.* xiv. 261 If you can't bring your mind to frighten her off touching things, you must.. keep 'em out of her way. **1883** FROUDE *Short. Stud.* IV. II. i. 168 The French Revolution had frightened all classes out of advanced ways of thinking. **1890** *Spectator* 1 Nov. 583/1 Manufacturers..are frightened to death at the..rise in prices. **1891** *Daily News* 23 Nov. 2/6 There are no stocks to frighten down prices. **1892** *Law Times* XCII. 394/2 Evidently the idea was to frighten and terrorise the lady into paying. **1904** L. T. MEADE *Love Triumphant* IV. x, I frightened those fellows off, didn't I, Beaufort?

Hence **ˈfrightenable** *a.*, capable of being frightened.

1812 COLERIDGE *Lit. Rem.* (1836) I. 362 Man as..a frightenable being. **1850** MRS. F. TROLLOPE *Petticoat Govt.* 32 You do not look so frightenable as my Aunt does.

frightened ('fraɪt(ə)nd), *ppl. a.* [f. prec. + -ED¹.] That is put into a fright; affected with fright. Also *fig.*

a **1721** PRIOR *Lady's Looking-glass* 16 Big waves lash the frighten'd shores. **1828** SCOTT *F.M. Perth* xi, He suffered the frightened girl to spring to the ground. **1863** GEO. ELIOT *Romola* I. xx, Her face wore a frightened look, as if she dreaded the effect of her boldness. **1885** *Athenæum* 2 May 561/3 The police..turn the frightened inmates out of their beds.

b. Const. *at.* In recent colloquial use *frightened of* (cf. 'afraid of') is common; *frightened for* in the same sense is Sc.

1827 CARLYLE *Germ. Romance* II. 123, I saw thee running ..but thou wert frightened for our little dog. **1830** WHEWELL in Todhunter *Acct. Whewell's Writ.* (1876) II. 108, I cannot but be vexed that..you should set seriously about being frightened of my own worshipful self. **1858** *Sat. Rev.* VI. 310/2 It is not usual for educated people to perpetrate such sentences as..'I was frightened *of* her'. **1881** MRS. MOLESWORTH *Herr Baby* 113 Baby was at first terribly frightened of him. **1890** [see the vb.]. **1897** *Daily News* 8 Apr. 11/1 What were you frightened at?

Hence **'frightenedly** *adv.*

1884 E. FAWCETT *Rutherford* xxiv. 294 She was on the verge of drawing away from her frightenedly. **1891** H. HERMAN *His Angel* 10 Looking out..not in the least frightenedly, but inquiringly.

frightener ('fraɪt(ə)nə(r)). [f. FRIGHTEN *v.* + -ER¹.] One who or that which frightens; *spec.* a member of a criminal gang who intimidates the victims of its activities, esp. in phr. *to put the frighteners in, on*: to intimidate (*slang*).

1841 COL. HAWKER *Diary* (1893) II. 195 A bird frightener from Southampton. **1958** F. NORMAN *Bang to Rights* i. 23 Spud Murphy gave him a very strong pull, and put the frighteners on him. **1962** R. COOK *Crust on its Uppers* ii. 18 They were just slag punters and couldn't pay even when we put the frighteners in. **1962** *Daily Tel.* 19 Dec. 15/6 Soho 'frighteners'—gangsters who try to extort money from club owners—were told..at the Old Bailey..that they faced severe punishment. **1966** A. PRIOR *Operators* vi. 64 His job had been to put the frighteners on various shopkeepers. *Ibid.*, The other man and himself had got a quid a piece out of it, the traditional ten per cent always paid to the frighteners. **1971** R. BUSBY *Deadlock* ix. 146 Some firm's trying to put the frighteners on, so I give him a bit of protection.

frightening ('fraɪt(ə)nɪŋ), *vbl. sb.* and *ppl. a.* [f. FRIGHTEN *v.* + -ING².] That frightens. Hence **frighteningly** *adv.*

1715 BURNET *Hist. Ref.* III. 390 *note*, I do not find there was any frightning Threatnings. *c* **1854** FABER *Hymn, Predestination* vi, And still the frightening echoes grow, As it goes sounding on. —— *Divine Favours* v, Why didst Thou come so frighteningly. **1865** *Englishman's Mag.* Oct. 298 The number and variety of living things is positively frightening. **1906** W. J. LOCKE *Beloved Vagabond* xi, The backward vista down the years is too frighteningly long. **1921** GALSWORTHY *To Let* I. ii, She was frighteningly self-willed. **1922** A. S. M. HUTCHINSON *This Freedom* IV. i. 251 Her mother had scalded her hand and had cried out to her, frighteningly. **1952** E. HOBSBAWM in *Granta* 15 Nov., Most of us—at any rate the frighteningly large number which gets into print—specialise in the tedium of telling you how mistaken we were about politics.

† **'frighter.** *Obs.* [f. FRIGHT *v.* + -ER¹.] One who or that which causes fright or scares away. *fever-frighter*: = FEBRIFUGE.

c **1611** CHAPMAN *Iliad* XIII. 279 And is of such strength that in war the frighter he affrights. **1683** SALMON *Doron Med.* II. 586 The Fever 'frighter' of Dr. Riverius. **1693** —— *Bate's Pharm.* (1713) 277/2 'Tis a famous Ague Frighter, seldom or never failing the Cure at some few Doses taking.

frightful ('fraɪtfʊl), *a.* [f. FRIGHT *sb.* + -FUL.]

† **1.** *subjectively.* Full of terror; timid; alarmed.

c **1250** *Gen. & Ex.* 3459 ðis friȝ[t]ful [folc] ðus a-biden, Quiles ðis daiȝes for[ð] ben gliden. **1612** DRAYTON *Poly-olb.* xiii. 215 The wild and frightfull Heards..Feed fairely on the Launds. **1677** GILPIN *Demonol.* (1867) 168 The heart is apt to be startled with threatenings..especially those that are of a more tender and frightful spirit. **1765** FOOTE *Commissary* II. Wks. 1799 II. 24 These Bourgois are so frightful. **1802** MRS. J. WEST *Infidel Father* III. 332, I am so frightful at being in a murderer's house.

Comb. **1718** ROWE tr. *Lucan* 245 Ghastly, and frightful-pale her Face is seen.

2. *objectively.* **a.** Tending to cause fright; alarming. Const. *to.* ? *Obs.*

1607 TOURNEUR *Rev. Trag.* II. ii. Wks. 1878 II. 64 It fell so without fright-full word. **1690** J. MACKENZIE *Siege London-Derry* 31/1 It was then a little more frightful to our people than afterwards. **1725** DE FOE *Voy. round World* (1840) 349 Any..ravenous creature..which..were frightful to the deer. **1812** SHELLEY *Addr. Irish People* 8 Is danger frightful to an Irishman who speaks for his own liberty?

b. Horrible to contemplate, shocking, dreadful, revolting. Often hyperbolically applied to bad or annoying things; cf. *awful, fearful, terrible*, etc.

'A cant word among women for anything unpleasing' (J.).

1700 S. L. tr. *Fryke's Voy. E. Ind.* 295 Sea-Devils or Sand-Creepers are 5 or 6 yards long, with a frightful Head. **1733** POPE *Ep. to Cobham* 250 One would not, sure, be frightful when one's dead. **1752** HUME *Ess. & Treat.* (1777) I. 199, I need not recount the frightful effects of jealousy. **1756** NUGENT *Gr. Tour, Germany* II. 301 A high tower, from whence he sounds a frightful horn. **1827** MACAULAY *Macchiav.* Ess. (1850) 33 The annals of France and England present us only with a frightful spectacle of poverty, barbarity and ignorance. **1879** FROUDE *Cæsar* xii. 162 The Clodius business had been a frightful scandal.

† **3.** quasi-*sb.* (*pl.*) = frightful adjuncts or accessories.

1727 DE FOE *Secrets Invis. World* (1735) xiii. 329 If he [the Devil] will come in all his Formalities and Frightfuls, he would not be capable of half so many Cozenings and Cheatings as he now puts upon us.

frightfully ('fraɪtfʊlɪ), *adv.* [f. FRIGHTFUL + -LY².] In a frightful manner; to a frightful degree.

† **1.** *subjectively.* In a manner indicating fright; timidly. *Obs.*

1621 LADY M. WROTH *Urania* 237 She, as if her enemy had been at hand, amazedly and frightfully answered [etc.]. **1653** H. MORE *Antid. Ath.* II. xii. (1712) 82 To run away from a snail, and very ruefully and frightfully to look back. **1674** BREVINT *Saul at Endor* 55 [He] cryed out frightfully, Who art thou?

2. *objectively.* † **a.** qualifying a vb.: Like a 'fright'; hideously. *Obs.*

1729 SWIFT *Lady's Jrnl.* 48 Then to her glass; and, 'Betty, pray Don't I look frightfully to-day?' **1752** JOHNSON *Rambler* No. 193 ¶8 The Beauty remarks how frightfully she looks.

b. To a frightful extent or degree. Often hyperbolically as a mere intensive with adjs. of unfavourable connotation. Now freq. without depreciatory reference, but merely = 'awfully', greatly, very (*colloq.* or *slang*). Cf. FRIGHTFUL 2.

1817 J. SCOTT *Paris Revis.* (ed. 4) 350 Their reverses made one feel the place frightfully unsafe. **1828** LADY GRANVILLE *Lett.* 22 Nov. (1894) II. 36 His thirst for knowledge is frightfully minute. **1855** MACAULAY *Hist. Eng.* IV. 252 His cheeks..grew frightfully livid. *Ibid.* 275 His features were frightfully harsh. **1870** DICKENS *E. Drood* ii, You look frightfully ill. **1875** *Punch* 24 July 31/1 Everything is..'How deliciously frightful!' 'How frightfully charming!' **1880** MRS. FORRESTER *Roy. & V.* I. 65 We English are frightfully wanting in tact. **1928** GALSWORTHY *Swan Song* I. v. 39 With more jaw, and deeper set eyes, but frightfully like Jon! *Ibid.* III. vii. 308, I don't know that I approve of it frightfully. **1958** P. KEMP *No Colours or Crest* ii. 14, I say, you know, it's frightfully nice of you chaps to go on with this show.

frightfulness ('fraɪtfʊlnɪs). [f. as prec. + -NESS.] The quality or state of being frightful.

1. The state of being filled with fright.

1621 LADY M. WROTH *Urania* 401 Her face sad and perplexed, shewing frightfulnesse so perfectly. **1633** BP. HALL *Hard Texts* 453 Express a frightfulness and an amazed suspicion of the approach of an enemy. **1684** tr. *Bonet's Merc. Compit.* IX. 333 Is Wormwood good for frightfulness?

2. a. The quality of causing fright; hideousness.

1713 NELSON *Dr. Bull* Introd. (1840) 7 All this serveth chiefly to cover the frightfulness of mortality.

b. Used during the war of 1914–18 to render G. *schrecklichkeit* (see SCHRECKLICHKEIT), implying a deliberate policy of terrorizing the enemy (esp. non-combatants) as a military resource. Also *transf.*

1914 R. BROOKE *Let.* 11 Nov. (1968) 632 Belgium is..the country where three civilians have been killed to every one soldier. That damnable policy of 'frightfulness' succeeded for a time. **1915** D. O. BARNETT *Lett.* 115 We are having a quiet time to-day, without any frightfulness for a change. **1915** P. GIBBS *Soul of War* 155 It was only when special orders for 'frightfulness' had been issued,..that the rank and file of the enemy's army committed its brutalities. **1924** J. S. C. BRIDGE *Hist. France* II. 119 Attributing to the French the deliberate pursuit of a policy of 'frightfulness'. **1945** R. HARGREAVES *Enemy at Gate* 70 The impression persists..that his preference was for the methods of 'frightfulness'. But if terrorisation was the besiegers' object, their sanguine hopes were doomed to condign disappointment. **1968** G. JONES *Hist. Vikings* III. iii. 212 Ragnar attacked the smaller Frankish force..and took 111 prisoners. These as a deliberate exercise in 'frightfulness' he hanged..in full view of the second Frankish division.

frightless ('fraɪtlɪs), *a.* [f. FRIGHT *sb.* + -LESS.] Free from fright, without fear.

1606 MARSTON *Sophonisba* IV. i, I speake all frightles.

† **'frightly,** *adv. Obs.* [f. **fright*, contracted pa. pple. of FRIGHT *v.* + -LY². Cf. FRIGHTILY under FRIGHTY.] In a frighted manner.

c **1250** *Gen. & Ex.* 3870 Ic wene friȝtlike ðat he do. *c* **1460** *Towneley Myst.* (Surtees) 152, I was castyn in care so frightly afrayd.

frightment ('fraɪtmənt). *rare.* [f. FRIGHT *v.* + -MENT.] **a.** The state of being in a fright. **b.** Something that causes fright.

1607 DEKKER *Westw. Hoe* Wks. 1873 II. 338 All these frightments are but idle dreames. **1647** W. BROWNE tr. *Polexander* III. II. 62 Bellerophon came on for all the turbulency and furious frightments of his horse. **1649** DRUMM OF HAWTH. *Poems* Wks. (1711) 46 Sighs, plaints, horrors, frightments,..Invest these mountains. **1831** J. WILSON *Unimore* vi. 259 Remorse there sends her frightments, Conscience hers.

† **'frightness.** *Obs.* [f. **fright* (see FRIGHTLY) + -NESS.] The state of being in a fright, panic.

c **1425** *Eng. Conq. Irel.* (E.E.T.S.) 16 Whan the host was in so gret frightnes.

frightsome ('fraɪtsəm), *a.* [f. FRIGHT *sb.* + -SOME.] **a.** Causing fright; frightful. **b.** Feeling fright, full of fear.

c **1817** HOGG *Tales & Sk.* II. 94 How lonely and frightsome—to be left by herself. **1827** CARLYLE *German Romance* I. 306 Edwald and Froda had their own almost frightsome thoughts on the matter.

† **'frighty,** *a.* In 3 friȝti. [f. FRIGHT *sb.* + -Y¹.] **a.** Causing fright, formidable. **b.** Suffering from fright; fearful. Hence † **'frightihead**, fearfulness; **'frightily** *adv.*

c **1250** *Gen. & Ex.* 984 Of him kumen folc friȝti. *Ibid.* 1617 Iacob abraid, & seide friȝtilike. *Ibid.* 2222 Al he it listnede in friȝtihed. *Ibid.* 2849 Sephora..gret, and wente friȝti a-gen.

frigid ('frɪdʒɪd), *a.* [ad. L. *frīgid-us*, f. *frīgēre* to be cold, f. *frīgus* cold.]

1. a. Intensely cold, devoid of heat or warmth, of a very low temperature.

1639 CHAPMAN & SHIRLEY *Ball* IV. ii, Your eye Will make the frigid region temperate, Should you but smile upon't. **1665** GLANVILL *Scepsis Sci.* vii. 35 If..in a Winter-night, we expose the liquor to the frigid air. **1800** *Med. Jrnl.* IV. 4 Frigid applications, would..have induced a spontaneous separation. **1820** SCORESBY *Acc. Arctic Reg.* I. 340 In these frigid regions, the scurvy becomes a very alarming disease. *Ibid.* 362 Frigid winds (or winds blowing over an extensive surface of ice). **1849** LONGF. *Christmas Carol* v, Nuns in frigid cells At this holy tide. **1878** M. A. BROWN *Nadeschda* 47 Like snow on the mountains, So white but yet so frigid.

b. *frigid zone*: each of the two regions of the globe which lie within the north and south polar circles respectively.

[**1597** HARTWELL *Pigafetta's Congo* (Title-page), The two Zones, *Torrida & Frigida*.] **1622** MASSINGER & DEKKER *Virg. Mart.* v. i, I'll..hang thee In a contorted chain of icicles In the frigid zone. **1764** GOLDSM. *Trav.* 65 The shudd'ring tenant of the frigid zone, Boldly proclaims that happiest spot his own. **1860** MAURY *Phys. Geog. Sea* i. 15 It conveys heat away from the torrid zone and ice from the frigid.

2. *transf.* Wanting in sexual vigour; impotent. Now usu. applied to women who are sexually unresponsive.

1660 R. COKE *Power & Subj.* 78 If either party were precontracted, or frigid; these necessarily preceding the matrimony do dissolve the bond. *a* **1700** B. E. *Dict. Cant. Crew, Frigid*, a weak disabled Husband, cold, impotent. **1732** SWIFT *Beasts' Confession* Wks. 1755 IV. I. 268 He was not much inclin'd To fondness for the female kind..Not from his frigid constitution, But through a pious resolution. **1893** J. A. SYMONDS *Life Michelangelo* II. 384 The whole weight of argument..leaves the impression on our mind that he was a man of physically frigid temperament, extremely sensitive to beauty of the male type. **1927** W. M. GALLICHAN *Sexual Apathy* i. 11 The frigid wife sheds an unconscious influence upon her children and those around her. **1953** J. S. VAN TESLAAR tr. *Stekel's Frigidity in Woman* v. 96 (*heading*) Psychology of the frigid woman. *Ibid.* 97 On their part they remain frigid during the act. **1962** C. ALLEN *Textbk. Psychosexual Disorders* v. xiv. 279 Women who are frigid frequently show great fear of snakes and often dream of them.

3. *fig.* **a.** Destitute of ardour or warmth of feeling, lacking enthusiasm or zeal; cold, indifferent, apathetic; formal, stiff.

1658 SIR T. BROWNE *Hydriot.* v. 27 To be content that times to come should onely know there was such a man, not caring whether they knew more of him, was a frigid ambition in Cardan. *a* **1661** FULLER *Worthies* (1840) III. 363 His faint and frigid expressions thereof manifested his mind rather to betray than defend it. **1750** JOHNSON *Rambler* No. 18 ¶3 The most frigid and inexorable judge. **1751** *Ibid.* No. 149 ¶5 Our reception was rather frigid than malignant. **1807–8** W. IRVING *Salmag.* (1824) 353 Charms that might warm even the frigid heart of a dervise. **1862** MERIVALE *Rom. Emp.* (1865) IV. xxxviii. 321 The nobles..let matters take their course with frigid indifference. **1880** T. HARDY *Trumpet Major* III. 224 Anne went home with her, bidding Loveday a frigid adieu.

absol. **1762** FOOTE *Orators* II. Wks. 1799 I. 219 You will have at one view, the choleric..the frigid, the frothy..and the clamorous.

b. Said of things: Chilling, depressing.

1844 ALB. SMITH *Adv. Mr. Ledbury* vi. (1886) 18 The frigid respectability and dilapidated grandeur of the Faubourg St. Germain. **1888** F. HUME *Mad. Midas* I. iv, Placed, not amid the frigid splendours of the drawing room, but..in his own particular den.

c. That leaves the imagination cold; that does not stir the fancy; lacking fire or spirit; dull, flat, insipid. †Formerly also (as L. *frigidus*), of a reason, argument, etc.: Lacking force or point, senseless, absurd.

1643 MILTON *Divorce* ix. (1851) 46 The pretended reason of it [is] as frigid as frigidity it self. **1699** BENTLEY *Phalaris* 112 Was ever any thing so forced, so frigid, so unworthy of refutation? **1713** PARNELL *Styles Poetry* 65 Bleak level Realm, where Frigid Styles abound, Where never yet a daring thought was found. **1729** SWIFT *On burning a dull Poem* Misc. 1735 V. 48 Methought..No Vessel but an Ass's Head Such frigid Fustian could contain. **1839** H. ROGERS *Ess.* II. iii. 138 The one shall impart the most frigid, and the other the most vivid conception of the meaning. **1855** MACAULAY *Hist. Eng.* IV. 273 He..gave vent to his feelings in a hundred and sixty lines of frigid bombast.

Hence **'frigidly** *adv.*, **'frigidness.**

1647 TRAPP *Comm. Mark* i. 22 And not as the Scribes. Frigidly and jejunely. **1697** BATES *Harmony Div. Attrib.* xvii. 322 If in the Platonical Philosophy there are some things directing to it, yet they are but frigidly exprest. **1727** BAILEY vol. II, *Frigidness*, coldness. **1777** *Nat. Hist.* in *Ann. Reg.* 89/1 Lands doomed by nature to perpetual frigidness.

1844 HOOD *Bridge of Sighs* xv, Ere her limbs frigidly Stiffen too rigidly. **1883** BLACK *Shandon Bells* xxvi, 'What I have is quite enough', said the..lady, somewhat frigidly.

Frigidaire (frɪdʒɪˈdɛə(r)). [Quasi-Fr., ad. L. *frigidarium*.] The proprietary name of a brand of refrigerator. (In quot. 1929 *fig.*)

1926 *Publishers' Weekly* 18 Sept. 964/2 Vacuum cleaners, frigidaires, radios. **1929** *Melody Maker* Jan. 25 We'd make a lovely pair If you would only care But you're a Frigidaire. **1930** *Morning Post* 17 June 20/3 Frigidaire fitments. **1931** *Trade Marks Jrnl.* 16 Dec. 1644/1 *Frigidaire*. Refrigerating machines and parts thereof.. Frigidaire Corporation.. City of Dayton, State of Ohio, United States of America. **1940** AUDEN *Another Time* 96 And had everything necessary to the Modern Man, A gramophone, a radio, a car and a frigidaire. **1946** A. CHRISTIE *Come, tell me how you Live* 9 But I was thinking of a plan To kill a millionaire And hide the body in a van Or some large Frigidaire.

† **ˈfrigidal**, *a. Obs. rare*$^{-1}$. [f. FRIGID + -AL[1].] = FRIGID.

1651 BIGGS *New Disp.* ¶ 171 Of a frigidal temper.

‖ **frigidarium** (frɪdʒɪˈdɛərɪəm). [L., f. *frīgid-us* cold.] The cooling-room in a Roman bath.

1706 in PHILLIPS (ed. Kersey). **1832** GELL *Pompeiana* I. vi. 95 Here was certainly the frigidarium. **1840** HOOD *Up Rhine* 244 Grown men and women were wading up to their chins in a sort of Frigidarium.

b. *transf.* A room kept at a low temperature.

1892 *Q. Rev.* Apr. 400 The chief rooms with all their ample fire-places were but miserable frigidaria. **1892** *Pall Mall G.* 14 Apr. 2/2 Room.. for fourteen in the frigidarium [of the Morgue].

† **ˈfrigidate**, *v. Obs. rare*$^{-1}$. [f. ppl. stem of L. *frīgid-āre*, f. *frīgid-us* FRIGID: see -ATE[3].] *trans.* To make frigid. (Cf. *infrigidate*.)

1691 *New Discov. Old Intreague* xxxi, Who Frigidated by Distemper'd Hams, His Fiery Zeal for Slavery proclaims.

† **ˈfrigidative**, *a. Obs. rare*$^{-1}$. [f. L. *frīgidāre*: see prec. and -ATIVE.] Cooling.

1659 MACALLO *Can. Physick* 87 The frigidative or cooling remedy.

† **friˈgidious**, *a. Obs. rare*$^{-1}$. [irreg. f. FRIGID + -(I)OUS.] Frigid, intensely cold.

1630 J. TAYLOR (Water P.) *Anagrams & Sonn.* Wks. II. 257/1 Frigidious Janus twofold frozen face, Turnes moyst Aquarius into congeal'd yce.

frigidite (ˈfrɪdʒɪdaɪt). *Min.* [f. *Frigid-o* the place where found + -ITE.] (See quot.)

1887 DANA *Man. Min. & Lith.* 150 Frigidite is a nickeliferous variety [of Tetrahedrite] from the Apuan Alps.

frigidity (frɪˈdʒɪdɪtɪ). [a. F. *frigidité*, ad. L. *frīgiditāt-em*, f. *frīgidus*: see FRIGID and -ITY.]

1. a. The state or condition of being frigid; intense coldness.

c **1420** *Pallad. on Husb.* IV. 124 And in frigiditie [L. *locis frigidis*] Of seed and bayes make the semynary. **1630** J. TAYLOR (Water P.) *Fight at Sea* Wks. III. 37 Neither the parching heat of Lybia.. or the benumming frigiditie of Groenland. **1659** D. PELL *Impr. Sea* 274 There is such an intolerable frigidity in some parts under the Poles, as that they cannot bee discovered. **1795** *Gentl. Mag.* 539/2 It had seemed probable that the intense frigidity of the winter would have destroyed the animalculæ.

b. In old Physiology: The quality of being frigid or producing frigidness: = COLDNESS 1 b.

1574 NEWTON *Health Mag.* 44 The great frigiditie and coldnesse of it [Purselayne].. maye be tempered and qualefied with Minte. **1610** HEALEY *St. Aug. Citie of God* 438 Our Astronomicall divines say that Saturns frigidity proceedeth from these waters. **1634** T. JOHNSON *Parey's Chirurg.* XXVI. vii. (1678) 633 If to the same frigidity remaining in Fruits, a certain humidity accrew. **1750** tr. *Leonardus' Mirr. Stones* 100 As it is of an exceeding cold nature, it does, with its frigidity, convert the air.. into water.

c. Lack of natural heat or warmth (of the body).

1631 GOUGE *God's Arrows* II. i. 131 Before David died, such frigidity fell upon him, as with cloathes they could not keepe him warme. **1665** GLANVILL *Scepsis Sci.* xiv. 82 The frigidity of decrepit Age is as much its enemy.

2. *transf.* Want of generative heat; impotence. Now usu. lack of sexual response in a woman.

1586 FERNE *Blaz. Gentrie* II. 58 His I. wife.. was deuorced from him for cause of frigiditye. *c* **1645** HOWELL *Lett.* (1650) I. 4 His articulate lady, called so, for articling against the frigidity and impotence of her former Lord. **1645** MILTON *Colast.* Wks. 1738 I. 299 Why are we suffered to divorce Adulteries, Desertions, or Frigidities? **1658** ROWLAND *Moufet's Theat. Ins.* 992 Forasmuch as Eunuchs.. make most noise and greater than young persons that are more hot, therefore frigidity cannot be the cause. **1897** H. ELLIS *Stud. Psychol. Sex* I. v. 113 The lad in this case.. has recently consulted me for *impotentia coeundi*, manifesting a frigidity for women. **1903** *Ibid.* III. 162 In dealing with the characteristics of the sexual impulse in women.. we have also to consider the prevalence of frigidity, or sexual anæsthesia. **1963** A. HERON *Towards Quaker View of Sex* 65 But 'frigidity'.. implies more than failure to have orgasm: it is the inability to enjoy love-making and penetration. **1970** *N. & Q.* Dec. 450/2 This relation between sexual frigidity and wrath does not seem to occur in the standard popular treatments of the Sins.

3. *fig.* **a.** Want of warmth of feeling or enthusiasm; apathy, coldness, indifference.

a **1631** DONNE in *Select.* (1840) 220 This heat may overcome my former frigidity and coldness. **1771** JOHNSON *Lett. to Mrs. Thrale* 20 July, I dare neither write with frigidity nor with fire. **1841** MYERS *Cath. Th.* III. xlv. 173 There is need that the frigidity of the Scholar be exchanged for the genial nature of the dweller in the open sunshine of heaven. **1860** HOLLAND *Miss Gilbert* xvii. 318 'She is not, sir', replied Fanny with excessive frigidity. **1870** EMERSON *Soc. & Solit., Success* Wks. (Bohn) III. 128, I seek one who shall make me forget or overcome the frigidities.. into which I fall.

b. Lack of imagination; deficiency in fire or spirit; flatness, insipidity; also quasi-*concr.*

1642 MILTON *Apol. Smect.* vi. 33 Having begun loftily.. he falls downe to that wretched poorenesse and frigidity as to talke of *Bridge street in heav'n*. **1646** SIR T. BROWNE *Pseud. Ep.* I. ix. 37 Driving at these as at the highest elegancies, which are but the frigidities of wit. **1763** FORDYCE in *Four C. Eng. Lett.* 286 The polite frigidity of the French drama. **1846** HAWTHORNE *Mosses* I. i. 17 The frigidity of modern productions was characteristic.

frigidize (ˈfrɪdʒɪdaɪz), *v. rare*$^{-1}$. [f. FRIGID *a.* + -IZE.] *trans.* To depress (a person) by frigidity of manner; to make frigid.

1868 D. RICE. *Gowers of Glenarne* I. 105 Lady Gower.. tried at first to frown her down and frigidize her.

† **friˈgiferous**, *a. Obs. rare*$^{-1}$. In 7 frigiverous. [badly f. L. *frīg-us* cold + -(I)FEROUS.] Bearing or bringing cold; cold.

1664 EVELYN *Sylva* (1776) 26 Not exposed to Sulphurous exhalations or Frigiverous winds.

† **ˈfrigitate**, *v. Obs. rare*$^{-1}$. [irregularly f. L. *frīgus* cold.] *intr.* To freeze.

1635 *Voy. Foxe & James to N. West* (Hakluyt Soc.) 427 The sea doth keepe it selfe from frigitating.

† **frigor**. *Obs. rare.* [a. L. *frīgor*, noun of state from *frīgēre* to be cold.] Extreme coldness.

1599 A. M. tr. *Gabelhouer's Bk. Phys.* 183/1 Ther will approach on him a vehement frigor, or coulde. **1603** OWEN *Pembrokesh.* (1891) 121 To avoyde the frigor of the frozen seas.

frigoric (frɪˈgɒrɪk), *sb.* and *a.* [f. L. *frīgor-*, *frīgus* cold + -IC. Cf. F. *frigorique* sb. (Littré *Suppl.*).]

† **A.** *sb.* An imagined 'imponderable' substance supposed to be the cause of cold. Cf. CALORIC *sb.*

1812 *Monthly Mag.* XXXIV. 297 If.. water has decreased in temperature, and dilated by the presence of frigoric, why should frigoric.. produce a contrary effect [in mercury]?

B. *adj.* 'Pertaining to or consisting in the application of cold' (*Cent. Dict.*). *rare.*

1887 *Sci. Amer.* N.S. LVI. 178 The conditions under which the frigoric service was to be introduced into the morgue.

frigorific (frɪgəˈrɪfɪk), *a. Physics.* [a. F. *frigorifique*, ad. L. *frīgorific-us* cooling: see prec. and -FIC.] Producing cold, freezing; cooling.

1667 BOYLE in *Phil. Trans.* II. 608 A strongly frigorifick mixture of Ice and Salt. **1685** —— *Effects of Mot.* iv. 41 The Atomists ascribe the freezing of water to the ingress of multitudes of frigorifick corpuscles. **1789** *Chron.* in *Ann. Reg.* 195/1 Quicksilver was again completely frozen.. in a frigorific mixture. **1820** SCORESBY *Acc. Arctic Reg.* I. 364 Data for determining the frigorific effect of the ice on the temperature of the Pole. **1863** TYNDALL *Heat* x. 277 Rumford maintained with great tenacity the existence of 'frigorific rays'.

b. *fig.*

1751 JOHNSON *Rambler* No. 159 ¶ 7 Knowledge and virtue remain too long congealed by this frigorifick power. **1810** SHELLEY *Zastrozzi* xiv, A frigorific torpidity of despair chilled every sense. **1867** BUSHNELL *Mor. Uses Dark Th.* 195 Their moral nature wants the true frigorific tension of a well-wintered life and experience.

† **frigoˈrifical**, *a. Obs.*$^{-0}$ [see -AL[1].] = prec.

1656 in BLOUNT *Glossogr.* **1721** in BAILEY.

‖ **frigorifico** (frigoˈrifiko). [Amer. Sp. *frigorífico*, lit. refrigerator.] In S. America, a meat-packing plant, esp. one concerned with the freezing of carcasses for export.

1917 L. E. ELLIOTT *Brazil Today & Tomorrow* v. 210 Opened in 1913, the *frigorifico* first supplied chilled meat to the city of S. Paulo. **1928** *Daily Tel.* 20 Mar. 10/7 He [*sc.* Lord Bledisloe] found.. that except in the frigorificos and in the corrales.. adjoining them there was little or no systematic attempt to control the dissemination of the [foot-and-mouth] disease. **1931** *Discovery* July 218/1 We passed several cattle barges on our journey up the river, most of them taking cattle to the frigorificos near Rosario. **1960** H. S. FERNS *Brit. & Argentine* xiii. 417 In 1884 the Sansinena brothers converted their *saladero* to a *frigorifico*.

frigorify (frɪˈgɒrɪfaɪ), *v.* [f. L. *frīgor-*, *frīgus* cold + -(I)FY.] *trans.* To cool or make cool. Hence **friˈgorifying** *ppl. a.*

1851 CARPENTER *Man. Phys.* (ed. 2) 74 Cold-blooded animals.. are provided with a frigorifying rather than with a calorifying apparatus.

† **ˈfrigot**. *Obs. rare*$^{-1}$. [? arbitrarily f. FRIGID, after *bigot*, etc.] A person of frigid temperament.

1683 KENNETT tr. *Erasm. on Folly* 26 It is much better patiently to be such a hen-peckt frigot than always to be wrack'd and tortured with.. suspicion and jealousie.

frijoles (in Sp. friˈxoles), *sb. pl.* Also 6 frisoles, frysoles, 7 frixoles, frizoles, 9 fricollis. A kind of kidney-bean grown and much used in Mexico. Cf. FASELS.

1577 FRAMPTON *Joyful News* 66 b, I doe sende you.. certaine Frisoles, that you maie commaunde to bee sowen in the beginning of Marche. **1613** PURCHAS *Pilgrimage* (1614) 803 Three boyes sate by eating tosted Mais, with sodden Frizoles in a little pan. **1648** GAGE *West Ind.* xv. 99 A dish of Frixoles.. being black and dry Turkey or French beanes boyled with a little biting Chille. **1832** *Veg. Subst. Food* 222 The small black beans called *fricollis*, which are in general demand all over Mexico, are no doubt a kind of kidney-bean. **1840** R. H. DANA *Bef. Mast* xiv. 35 Living upon beef, hard bread, and frijoles, (a peculiar kind of bean, very abundant in California). **1854** J. L. Stephens *Centr. Amer.* 27 He.. set before us chocolate and what he called the national dish, frijoles, or black beans fried.

† **frike**, *a. Obs.* [a. OF. *frique* (13th c.), regarded by some scholars as the earlier form of *frisque* (see FRISK *a.*); it is perh. a. Teut. **freko-* FRECK *a.* In ME. the adjs. *frike* and *freck* seem to have been somewhat confused.]

1. Lusty, strong, vigorous.

13.. *Fest. Church in Holy Rood* 221 The egle is frikest fowle in flye. *c* **1400** *Destr. Troy* 2204 My floures bene fallen, & my frike age. *c* **1400** *Sowdone Bab.* 104 Barons, Admyralls, and Dukes frike. *c* **1430** LYDG. *Min. Poems* (Percy) 230 When thou art fryke and in thy flowres, Thou werest purpure, perreye, ore palle. *c* **1440** *Promp. Parv.* 179/1 Fryke, or craske, or yn grete helthe, *crassus*. *c* **1475** *Partenay* 2803 The body welle made, frike in ioly plite.

2. Joyful.

c **1430** *Hymns Virg.* (1867) 23 Loue is hetter þan þe cole To hem þat of it is fayn & frike [*rime* lijke].

Hence † **ˈfrickly** *adv.*, † **ˈfrikeness**.

c **1400** *Destr. Troy* 6120 Lest þi friknes so furse.. Brynge þe to bale. *Ibid.* 9880 All ffrickly his fos fled at the last. *c* **1440** *Promp. Parv.* 179/1 Frykenesse, *crassitudo*.

† **frike**, *v. Obs. rare.* [OE. *frícian* (only once).] *intr.* To dance, move briskly.

c **1000** *Ags. Gosp.* Matt. xi. 17 We sungun eow & ʒe ne fricudun [*c* **1175** *Hatton Gosp.* fricodon]. *c* **1200** *Trin. Coll. Hom.* 211 Al hit is idel þat me at pleʒe bihalt.. þih and shonkes and fet oppieð.. armes and hondes frikieð.

frikkadel (ˈfrɪkəˌdɛl). *S. Afr.* Also fricadel, frickadel, frik(k)adel, frikkadelle, frikkedel. [Afrikaans. Cf. FRICANDEL, -ELLE.] A ball of minced meat, fried or baked; a rissole.

1870 [see BOBOTIE]. **1913** PETTMAN *Africanderisms* 178 *Frikadels* or *Frikadeletjes*, balls of minced meat and vegetables either fried or baked. **1926** O. SCHREINER *From Man to Man* 330 He bent low over his plate, shovelling in the frikkedel and gravy with his knife. **1946** *Cape Times* 5 Oct. (Week-end Mag.) 2/5 Fish frikkadel. **1966** E. PALMER *Plains of Camdeboo* vii. 122 Eating frikkadelle laced with rosemary and drinking coffee.

† **frilal**. *Obs.*$^{-1}$ [? f. FRILL *sb.* after the analogy of FALLAL.] A border of ornamental ribbon.

1690 EVELYN *Mundus Muliebris* 6 Frilal next upper Pinner set, Round which it does our Ladies please To spread the Hood call'd Rayonnés. **1846** in FAIRHOLT *Gloss.*

frill (frɪl), *sb.*[1] [This and the related FRILL *v.*[1] are of uncertain origin. The common view is that FRILL *v.*[3], to shiver, gave rise to a sb. (see FRILL *sb.*[3]) meaning 'the ruffling of a hawk's feathers when shivering', and that the word as applied to an article of costume is a transferred use of this. But this hypothesis finds no support in the rare early instances of the words; and there is no proof that the sb. ever had the alleged sense. Sense 2 of the vb. suggests that it may be a metathetic form of FURL; but this is app. peculiar to Knolles, and should perh. be regarded as an unconnected word. The sb. as used by butchers (sense 3 below) is commonly regarded as a transferred sense from the 'frill' of a shirt; but the analogy of CHITTERLING and of F. *fraise* (mesentery of a calf, 14th c.; ruff, frill, 16th c.) suggests the possibility that the butchers' sense may be the original (though not recorded until quite recently). Godef. has one quot. for an OF. pple. *freolé* (v.r. *freioleit*) = 'frilled' (said of a shirt); and it is noteworthy that in the 17th c. the F. equivalent of FURL *v.* (cf. FRILL *v.*[1] 2) was *fresler*, which seems to belong to OF. *freseler* to frill, adorn, f. *fresel*, *-ele*, dim. of *fraise* ruff; but it is not easy to see how Eng. *frill* can be connected with these words.]

1. a. An ornamental edging made of a strip of any woven material, of which one edge is gathered and the other left loose so as to give it a wavy or fluted appearance. *Toby-frill*, such as appears on the figure of Toby in the frontispiece of *Punch*.

(The sense in the first quot. is doubtful; '*borrowed* frills' suggests rather false curls or the like than what is defined above; cf. FRILL *v.*[1] 2.)

1591 R. TURNBULL *Expos. Jas.* 95 b, Their flaunting ruffes .. their borowed frilles, and such like vanities. **1801** MASON *Suppl. to Johnson, Frill*, an edging of fine linen on the bosom of a shirt. **1812** J. NOTT *Dekker's Gvlls Horne-bk.* 90 note, What we now call the frill or chitterling of the shirt. **1841** LYTTON *Nt. & Morn.* II. iii, What have you been at? You have torn your frill into tatters. **1882** MISS BRADDON *Mt. Royal* II. x. 210 Mopsy and Dopsy, their long limbs sheathed in sea-green velveteen, Toby-frills round their necks.

b. *transf.* A similar article of cut paper or net put round the knuckle of a ham, etc. when brought to table.

1866 Geo. Eliot *F. Holt* (1868) 33 His eyes fixed abstractedly on the frill of a ham before him.

c. Anything resembling such an edging; e.g. a fringe of feathers round the neck of a bird (esp. in pigeons; hence, a pigeon having a frill: cf. *frill-back* in 5); a process like this on an invertebrate animal, a ring on a fungus, a tuft on the neck of a dog, etc.

1860 B. P. Brent *Pigeon Bk.* 53 The eye..is of a pearl or gravel colour..very different from the Turbit's,..and the frill is rarely so long. **1878** Bell *Gegenbaur's Comp. Anat.* 122 They consist of 4 or 8 frills, curved in a semilunar form. **1879** L. Wright *Pract. Pigeon Keeper* xiv. 165 The fourth and last property is frill. *Ibid.*, If the frill, or group of re-curved feathers on the breast is to extend [etc.]. **1883** G. Stables *Our Friend the Dog* vii. 60 Frill—The mass of feather on a long-coated dog's chest. **1890** *Daily News* 8 Jan. 2/4 Oriental frills, imported 20 years ago from Turkey and Smyrna. **1957** C. Osman *Racing Pigeons* i. 24 The same family [*sc.* the Git group of pigeons] occasionally has frills, feathers running across the breast of the bird and curling over backwards.

d. *fig.* (*colloq.*, orig. *U.S.*). An affectation of dress or manners, an air. Usually *pl.*

a **1845** Sydney Smith in S. Holland *Mem.* (ed. 3, 1855) I. ix. 407 Mr. —— has great good sense, but I never met a manner more entirely without frill. **1865** 'Mark Twain' in Harte & 'Twain' *Sks. Sixties* (1926) 189 You put on as many frills and make as much fuss..as if it were..a first-class power among nations. **1870** *Sacramento paper* (De Vere), I can't bear his talk, it's all frills. **1871** Schele de Vere *Americanisms* (1872) 603 *Frills*, denotes, in California and the West generally, any assumption of style. **1885** 'Mark Twain' *Huck. Finn* v, You've put on considerable many frills since I been away. *Ibid.*, He cussed me for putting on frills, and trying to be better than him. **1889** *Century Dict.* s.v., He puts on too many frills. **1891** E. Kinglake *Austral. at Home* 157 Do not put on what the Americans call 'frill'. **1892** Kipling *Barrack-R. Ballads* 12 It's the commissariat camel puttin' on 'is bloomin' frills! **1900** G. Bonner *Hard-Pan* vi. 194 She suffered from none of that rancor which the boarder who is suspected of 'putting on frills' is liable to arouse. **1928** Galsworthy *Swan Song* iii. 23 The first book was born too still for anything. A sort of 'African Farm', without the spiritual frills—if you remember it.

e. *fig.* A thing or feature which is merely ornamental; an embellishment. Usually in a derogatory sense.

1893 Farmer *Slang*, *Frills*, swagger; conceit; also accomplishments (as music, languages, etc.); and culture; *cf.*, Man with no frills. **1904** *N.Y. Tribune* 13 Oct. 6 The Board of Education should be encouraged in its tendency to lop off a few 'frills' from the curriculum and add the time saved to the substantial parts of the course. **1909** *Westm. Gaz.* 4 Aug. 4/1 A full-fledged Parliament.., a Speaker, a Mace, and all the frills and furbelows still considered essential to Parliamentary Government. **1916** A. Quiller-Couch *Art of Writing* vii. 133 The editor of a mining paper in Denver, U.S.A., boldly the other day laid down this law, that niceties of language were mere 'frills'. **1919** L. F. Cody *Buffalo Bill* 21 There were no frills about Will Cody's story as he told it to me. **1949** F. Swinnerton *Doctor's Wife comes to Stay* 121 A simple, good-natured soul, who wants to be painted just as he is...'No frills.' **1962** Parker & Allerton *Courage of Convictions* iv. 168 He was a pig-headed authoritarian without frills.

2. A kind of scallop-shell. See freel.

1803 Montagu in Gosse *Year at Shore* (1865) 25 *note*, [This Pecten] is known by the name of Frills or Queens. **1865** Gosse *ibid.*, The term 'frill' obviously refers to the form of the shell.

3. Used by butchers for: The mesentery of an animal.

1879 Miss Jackson *Shropsh. Word-bk.*, *Frill*, a piece of fleshy fat surrounding the entrails of a pig; it has the appearance of being puckered like a frill, whence its name. **1884** *Chesh. Gloss.*, *Frill*, the puckered edge of the fat which is stripped from the entrails of a pig.

4. *Photography.* [From the vb.] The irregular rising of a gelatine film at the edges of a plate, so as to present the semblance of a frill.

5. *attrib.* and *Comb.*, as *frill-like* adj.; **frill-back** (see quot.); **frill-lizard**, an Australian lizard of the genus *Chlamydosaurus* whose neck is encircled by a broad membrane, erectile at pleasure.

1765 *Treatise Dom. Pigeons* 144 The Frill-back..what is remarkable in them is the turn of their feathers, which appear as if every one distinctly had been raised at the extremity with a small round-pointed instrument, in such a manner as to form a small cavity in each of them. **1895** *Westm. Gaz.* 17 Aug. 3/3 The extraordinary frill-like appendage which encircles it neck.

Hence **'frillless** *a.* [-less], having no frill.

1883 D. Wingate *Lost Laird* xvi, Over her grey hair she wore a frillless 'mutch'.

†**frill**, *sb.*² *Obs.* (See quot.)

1611 Cotgr., *Maie*, the greatest kind of sea-Crab, round, long-legd, and verie rough-shelled; some call her, a Frill.

frill, *sb.*³ *rare*⁻⁰. [f. frill *v.*³; but the word seems to be an etymologizing figment: see note on frill *sb.*¹] (See quot.)

1846 Worcester, *Frill*..the ruffling of a hawk's feathers when frilling with cold.

frill (frɪl), *v.*¹ [See frill *sb.*¹]

1. *trans.* To furnish or decorate with a frill. (In the first quot. the meaning may be 'to curl the hair'; cf. sense 2 and frill *sb.*¹ 1, quot. 1591.)

1574 Hellowes *Gueuara's Fam. Ep.* 296 The goode townse-like craftsman, needes no daughter in lawe that can fril and paint her selfe [*que sepan affeytar*]. **1766** Smollett *Trav.* I. vii. 105 When I see one of those fine creatures, sailing along, in her taudry robes of silk and gauze, frilled, and flounced, and furbelowed. **1831** Sir F. B. Head *Bubbles of Brunnen* 114 Next came a row of women in caps, frilled and bedizened. **1866** Geo. Eliot *F. Holt* (1868) 53 A dainty work-basket frilled with blue satin.

absol. **1766** Goldsm. *Vic. W.* xi, They can pink, point, and frill, and know something of music.

b. To serve as a frill for.

1887 Fenn *Master of Ceremonies* iii, The great mob of lace that frilled her night-cap.

†**2.** To furl *up*; to twist *back*. *Obs. rare.*

1603 Knolles *Hist. Turks* (1621) 516 His long mustachoes on his vpper lip, like bristles, frild back to his neck..did so expresse his martiall disposition..that [etc.]. *Ibid.* 1256 To depart whither they would, with their ensignes frilled vp. *Ibid.* 1288 Ensignes..frilled vp.

3. *Photography.* **a.** *trans.* (*causatively.*) To raise (a film) in flutes like a frill. **b.** *intr.* Of the film: To rise in flutes like a frill.

1891 *Anthony's Photogr. Bull.* IV. 57 The drops of perspiration would sometimes splash on a plate, you know, and sort of frill the film.

†**frill**, *v.*² *Obs. rare.* [prob. echoic.] *intr.* Of the eagle: To scream.

1677 Wittie *Gout Raptures* lviii. (1681) 103 The Goat did blare, squeak did the Hare, And there the Eagle frilled. **1688** R. Holme *Armoury* II. 310/2 The Eagle Frilleth, or Scriketh.

Hence **frill** *sb.*, the cry of an eagle.

1847 in Halliwell.

†**frill**, *v.*³ *Obs.*⁻⁰ [ad. OF. *friller.*] *intr.* To shiver with cold.

1671 Skinner *Etymol. Ling. Angl.* Ttij, The hawk Frilleth, *a* Fr. G. *Friller, Horrere, Rigere, Tremere.* **1721** Bailey s.v., The Hawk frills. **1755** in Johnson. **1847** in Halliwell. Hence in mod. Dicts.

frilled (frɪld), *ppl. a.* [f. frill *sb.*¹ or *v.*¹ + -ed¹ or ².] Having, wearing, or adorned with a frill, or something like a frill. Of a photographic plate: Raised in flutes at the edges. *frilled lizard* = *frill-lizard.* Hence **'frilledness.**

1825 Ld. Cockburn *Mem.* i. (1856) 37 The polite ruffled and frilled gentlemen of the olden time. **1827** in Hone *Everyday Bk.* II. 190 A delicate frilled hand. **1863** Wood *Illustr. Nat. Hist.* III. 87 The Frilled Lizard is a native of Australia. **1865** *Sat. Rev.* 21 Oct. 513/2 In America the legs of tables have been seen by travellers encased in frilled trousers. **1867** W. B. Tegetmeier *Pigeons* ix. 82 Some of the flying birds seen in this country are frilled very much like an Owl or a Turbit. **1889** *Anthony's Photogr. Bull.* II. 302 The very beggar or fakir in the streets, whose face has more lines of humiliation and dejection than a frilled negative.

frillery ('frɪlərɪ). [f. frill *sb.*¹ + -ery.] An arrangement or mass of frills; frills collectively.

1887 A. Sterry *Lazy Minstr.* (1892) 85 A wealth of snowy frillery and lace. **1889** *Daily News* 13 July 3/3 Many of the frills were silk as well; in one case a thick ruching of white silk having been substituted for the more orthodox sort of frillery.

frilling ('frɪlɪŋ), *vbl. sb.* [f. frill *v.*¹ + -ing¹.]

1. a. The action of putting a frill to (a garment); also *concr.* frilled edging; frills collectively.

1815 E. S. Barrett *Heroine* II. 149 Here was no..seaming, or frilling, or flouncing. **1861** Dickens *Gt. Expect.* viii, The frillings and trimmings on her bridal dress looking like earthy paper. **1886** J. K. Jerome *Idle Thoughts* (1889) 153 [They] mourn with one another over the decadence of cambric frilling. **1896** *Daily News* 7 Mar. 6/3 Accordeon-pleated frilling lavished on hats, toques, and capes.

attrib. **1887** *Daily News* 7 Nov. 2/5 The ruching and frilling department is dull.

b. *fig.*

1899 C. J. C. Hyne *Further Adv. Capt. Kettle* vi, Great masses of foliage growing to the crown of the splintered heights, with a surf frilling. **1903** *Westm. Gaz.* 2 Mar. 8/2 A mid-day meal of stewed steak and frillings.

2. *Photography.* The rising of a gelatine film in flutes along the edge.

1880 *Athenæum* 11 Dec. 782/1 'Frilling' was prevented by the same means. **1890** Abney *Treat. Photogr.* (ed. 6) 136 'Frilling' of the plate takes place in the hyposulphite of soda solution.

†**frillock.** *Obs. rare*⁻¹. ? = fillock.

1647 G. W. *Grand Pluto's Progress through Gt. Brit.* 15 Madge my deare and bonny Frillock Set we downe beside this hillock.

frilly ('frɪlɪ), *a.* and *sb.* [f. frill *sb.*¹ + -y¹.]

A. *adj.* Furnished with a frill; full of frills; resembling frills. Also *fig.*

1843 Hood *To Henrietta* ii, With..a pair of frilly trousers, like a little bantam cock. **1890** E. Custer *Following Guidon* xiv. 202 Our opera-glasses looked just a little 'frilly' in such a place, but they were really useful. **1896** *Punch* 21 Mar. 133/3 Blossoms flounced and frilly. **1899** *Westm. Gaz.* 21 Sept. 3/2 Fluffy, frilly wraps. **1900** *Ibid.* 19 July 3/1 Capelines..more or less frilly and floppy. **1902** *Ibid.* 20 Nov. 3/1 The effect was delightfully rippling and frilly. **1904** B. von Hutten *Pam* I. iii, Pamela in a frilly nightgown. **1911** H. S. Harrison *Queed* vi. 75, I am a clerk,..and office girl. My official title of course, is a little more frilly. **1922** *Glasgow Herald* 22 Mar. 10 [He] insisted upon the need for a thorough elementary education..even if less attention were paid to the 'frilly' subjects than at present.

B. *sb. pl.* Frilled undergarments. *colloq.*

1900 E. Glyn *Visits Eliz.* 16 Lady Doraine and that horrid Smith creature made a place for me in the empty hammock between them, and, as I knew my 'frillies' were all right, I hammocked too. **1917** H. Jenkins *Bindle* vi. 87 In the bed was a figure..rising up from a foam of frillies. **1927** *Daily Express* 27 June 13/4 There are bargains to be found from fur coats to 'frillies'. **1970** S. J. Perelman *Baby, it's Cold Inside* 97, I am..shopping for some feminine 'frillies'.

Hence **'frilliness**, frilly character; also *fig.*

1909 *Westm. Gaz.* 3 July 15/1 Once more everything is tending towards paniers, frilliness, flounces, and full skirts. **1927** *Daily Express* 27 Apr. 3/2 There was..more coy frilliness..about the evening dresses than last year. *Ibid.* 23 Sept. 3/3 The food was nourishing and English—..none of your Frenchified frillinesses.

frim, *a. Obs.* exc. *dial.* Forms: 1 freme, 4 frym, 6–7 frimm(e, (7 frime, 8 frem), 7– frim. [OE. *freme*:—prehistoric *frami-, cognate with *fram* adj., forward, advanced, bold.]

a. Vigorous, flourishing; after OE. only in physical sense (or *fig.* of this), luxuriant in growth, plump, full-fleshed. **b.** Abundant in sap, juicy, full of moisture; rarely in unfavourable sense. Also of sap: Abundant, rich. **c.** Easily melting, soluble, fusible.

Beowulf 1932 Mod þryðo wæᵹ fremu folces cwen. *c* **1000** *Cædmon's Gen.* 2328 (Gr.) Ic þam magorince mine sylle godcunde gife gastes mihtum, freondsped fremum. **13..** *E.E. Allit. P.* A. 1078, & twelue syþez on ȝer þay beren ful frym [fruits]. *c* **1420** *Liber Cocorum* (1862) 5 Cast on þe powder of hare I wot; Hit is so frym, ren hyt wylle An malt as sugur. **1589** *Mar Martine* 3 Abbots were fat and friers frimme. **1600** Holland *Livy* VI. vii. (1609) 221 Those nations that by long peace were most frimme and lustie [*ex integerrimis*]. **1601** —— *Pliny* I. 348 Many are so frim and free of milke, that [etc.]. *Ibid.* 463 The timber also is more frim and soft. **1604** Drayton *Owle* 5 The frim sap..From the full root, doth swell the plenteous rynde. **1613** —— *Poly-olb.* xiii, My frim and lusty flank Her bravery then displays. **1622** *Ibid.* xxvii, Her deare daughter Dale, which her frim Cheeke doth lay To her cleere mothers Breast. **1657** Austen *Fruit Trees* I. 136 Seede plants are commonly more frim straight and handsome, then wood-stocks. **1669** Worlidge *Syst. Agric.* (1681) 224 If May and June prove wet Months, it causes a Frimm and Frothy Grass. **1712** Morton *Northamptonshire* 51 The fremmest..that is the richest feeding land we have. **1736** W. Ellis *New Exp. Husb.* 54 The shorter and younger the grass, the frimmer is the Sap. **1747** Hooson *Miner's Dict.* O j b, Potter's Ore..is so frim and fusible that a great deal of this sort is sold. **1750** W. Ellis *Mod. Husb.* IV. i. 151 A frim growing time. **1888** *Sheffield Gloss.* s.v., This lettuce is very frim.

Hence **'frimness.**

c **1714** T. Bates in *Athenæum* No. 1982 (1865) 535/3 The frimness of the grass. **1736** W. Ellis *New Exp. Husb.* 64 We ..sow a Mixture of Clover..to allay its Frimness.

‖**Frimaire** (frimɛr). [Fr., f. *frim-as* hoar-frost.] The third month of the French revolutionary calendar (from Nov. 21 to Dec. 20).

1838 Nicolas *Chron. Hist.* 171 Frimaire (Sleety Month).

frim fram, var. of flim-flam.

1693 *Sc. Presbyt. Eloq.* (1738) 131 Criticks with their frim frams and whytie waities.

fringe (frɪndʒ), *sb.* Forms: 4–7 frenge, (5 freny(e, 6 *Sc.* frenȝe, 6–7 fryi(y)ng, frienge), (7 frindge), 6– fringe. [ME. *frenge*, a. OF. *frenge* (1316 in Douët d'Arcq *Comptes de l'Arg. des Rois de France* 60), also (Walloon) *fringe* (mod.Fr. *frange*) = Pr. *fremja, fermja*:—popular L. **frimbia*, metathetic alteration of class. Lat. *fimbria* border, fringe. The change of ME. (ɛ) to mod.Eng. (ɪ) before (ndʒ) is normal: cf. *hinge*, *singe*.]

1. a. An ornamental bordering, consisting of a narrow band to which are attached threads of silk, cotton, etc., either loose or formed into tassels, twists, etc. (Occas. *spec.* that worn by the Hebrews in accordance with the command in Num. xv. 38.)

13.. *Gaw. & Gr. Knt.* 598 A sadel, þat glemed ful gayly with mony golde frenges. **1407** *Nottingham Rec.* II. 52 Pro uno riben frenge de cirico, xvij *d.* *c* **1540** *Pilgr. T.* 175 in *Thynne's Animadv.* (1865) App. i, With a blak fryng hemyd al about. **1602** Marston *Ant. & Mel.* III. Wks. 1856 I. 39 The fringe of your sattin peticote is ript. *a* **1714** M. Henry *Exp. Judges* xix. 22 What did it avail them that they had..God's Law in their Fringes, but the Devil in their Hearts. **1762–71** H. Walpole *Vertue's Anecd. Paint.* (1786) IV. 70 Another Dutch painter..faithfully imitating the details of lace, embroidery, fringes, and even the threads of stockings. **1861** Miss Yonge *Stokesley Secret* ii. (1862) 42 Drab alpaca frocks..not a coloured bow nor handkerchief, not a flounce nor fringe, to relieve them.

b. *collect.* A manufactured article of this kind which may be cut into lengths.

1327 *Wardr. Acc. Edw. III* 33/2, 14 uln. frenge, serico nigro, per uln', 3*d.* **1461–83** *Wardr. Acc. Edw. IV* (Nicolas) 117 For frenge of gold of Venys at vj*s.* the ounce. **1466** *Paston Lett.* No. 549 II. 270 For grey lynen cloth and sylk frenge for the hers. **1589** *Nottingham Rec.* IV. 226 For fustyan and frenge..trymminge vpp of the townes pikes. **1660** *Goostrey Churchw. Acc.* in Earwaker *Sandbach* (1890) 248 Pd. for cloth, silke, thread, and frinje, for a pulpit chussin

1 li. **1708** J. CHAMBERLAYNE *St. Gt. Brit.* I. III. iii. (1743) 168 An earl may also have a cloth of State without pendants, but only Fringe. **1814** JANE AUSTEN *Mansf. Park* II. i. 184 She had..made many yards of fringe. **1815** JANE TAYLOR *Display* xiii. 167 Pray do you sell silk fringe?

2. a. Anything resembling this; a border or edging, esp. one that is broken or serrated.

1649 JER. TAYLOR *Gt. Exemp.* Pref. §11 Little distances neere the centre make larger figures, then when they part neere the fringes of the circle. **1649** G. DANIEL *Trinarch., Hen. V*, cxc, A Curled Cloud, whose Top With golden frindge, Spreads Glorie. *a* **1687** COTTON *Song*, Poems (1689) 354 Light..Beautifies The rayie fringe of her fair Eyes. **1711** ADDISON *Spect.* No. 85 ¶1 A friend of mine..has converted an Essay of a Man of Quality into a kind of fringe for his candlesticks. **1720** GAY *Poems* (1745) II. 107 Some works come forth at noon and die at night In blazing fringes round a tallow light. **1815** BYRON *Siege Cor.* xvi, The fringe of the foam may be seen below. **1852** CONYBEARE & H. *St. Paul* (1862) I. i. 8 Asia Minor..was bordered by a fringe of Greek colonies. **1856** LD. COCKBURN *Mem.* i. (1874) 46 [He] detected the dying man peeping cautiously through the fringes of his eyelids. **1857** LIVINGSTONE *Trav.* v. 96 A rim or fringe of ancient rocks. **1864** C. CLARKE *Box for Season* I. 95 His whiskers met in what is commonly known as a Newgate fringe. **1866** GEO. ELIOT *F. Holt* (1868) 5 The handlooms made a far-reaching straggling fringe about the great centres of manufacture. **1871** L. STEPHEN *Playgr. Eur.* iii. (1894) 85 A broad fringe of snow ending in a bergschrund. **1890** BOLDREWOOD *Col. Reformer* (1891) 221 A grand-looking sheet of fresh water..a thin fringe of timber surrounding its margin.

b. *fig.* occas. in sense of an appendage or sequel; also (*slang* or *colloq.*), irrelevant matter. In wider use: an outer edge or margin of any kind, material or immaterial; an outer limit of a country, area, or population. Also *attrib.* = existing on the edge or margin of an area or region. Cf. also CELTIC *a.* 2.

1642 [see FACING 4 b]. **1651-3** JER. TAYLOR *Serm. for Year* (1678) 357 In..the confines of Grace and the fringes of Repentance. *a* **1734** NORTH *Lives* I. 322 There followed the horrid conspiracy, called the Rye plot, and, as fringes to these, other minor plots. **1874** H. R. REYNOLDS *John Bapt.* i. §5. 47 A fringe of Gentile forces and influences had surrounded the sacred institutions of Judaism. **1875** EMERSON *Lett. & Soc. Aims, Greatness* Wks. (Bohn) III. 272 Depth of intellect relieves even the ink of crime with a fringe of light. **1886** *Police Report*, As to what had taken place in the park, he (the magistrate) considered it simple fringe, and he would not go into that. **1898** Q. VICTORIA in *Daily News* 20 Dec. 5/4 All these people ask is to be allowed to do their daily task in peace..and to have a little fringe of play. **1902** D. G. HOGARTH *Nearer East* 162 The density of this Fringe population depends on fertility. *Ibid.* 181 It is necessary to detach the Arabs, who are found in the Arabian and Mesopotamian Fringe, from the central Semitic group. *Ibid.* 185 The outer desert ring has up to now proved effective to separate this loose unity from the Fringe populations. *Ibid.* 221 This system of railways..will serve to neutralise the immemorial tendency of this Fringe to display upon a superficial area..a *congeries* of human groups bitterly antagonistic in tradition and hope. **1903** [see MARGINAL *a.* 3]. **1926** J. GEDDIE (*title*) The Fringes of Edinburgh. **1935** *Amer. Speech* X. 10/2 Information.. regarding the language spoken on the fringes of society. **1943** *Times* 21 Dec. 2/3 Altogether 35 sneak-raiders were destroyed in 'fringe target' attacks alone during the first half of the year. **1947** in *Amer. Speech* (1950) XXV. 65/1 'Fringe' Parking. **1951** *Electronic Engin.* XXIII. 262 He is resident in a fringe area. **1958** *Spectator* 14 Feb. 195/3 It may have won him a few fringe votes in Rochdale. **1958** *Times* 11 Nov. 4/3 Certain 'fringe' events arranged in Bath during the festival, notably the Festival Ball, [etc.]. **1960** *Guardian* 23 June 8/1 This is not part of the festival, but one of the 'fringe' entertainments. **1960** G. MURRAY in *Spectator* 28 Oct. 639, I have..adopted the term 'fringe' to indicate those medical practices which are not available to the patient in the NHS as a matter of course. **1962** *Guardian* 4 July 7/1 The posturings of a bunch of fringe-lunatics. **1966** *Times* 9 Nov. 13/5 Fringe Londoners like to keep the odd pig or two in their outbuildings. **1971** *Ink* 12 June 12/4 Events include discussions, rock groups, fringe theatre.

c. A portion of the front hair brushed forward and cut short. Cf. BANG. Also ***Grecian fringe***.

1876 *Queen* 29 July (Advt.), Curled or waved fringes for the front hair. **1878** *Cassell's Fam. Mag.* IV. 175/2 None of that affected 'Grecian fringe' with which modern 'girls of the period' strive to hide what little forehead they possess. **1883** MRS. OLIPHANT *A Lover & his Lass* (ed. 2) III. iv. 84 Jean was not too old to indulge in..fringes and curls on her forehead. **1884** BESANT *Childr. Gibeon* 49 The 'fringe' was never intended to darken and disfigure the face. **1887** *Daily News* 2 May 7/2 Wanted, at once, a young person..who understands house and parlour work..No fringe.

d. In plants.

1601 HOLLAND *Pliny* II. 217 The said root is full of strings or fringes. **1796** WITHERING *Brit. Plants* (ed. 2) III. 330 *Splachnum*..fringe with 8 teeth. **1846** J. BAXTER *Libr. Pract. Agric.* (ed. 4) I. 363 Calyx magnified, showing the fringes. **1856** CAPERN *Poems* (ed. 2) 136 Why its [the daisy's] fringe ..Is thrown o'er mosses mellow. **1862** DARWIN *Fertil. Orchids* v. 207 If these fringes are placentae, they are more largely developed than in other Orchids. **1879** LUBBOCK *Sci. Lect.* i. 17 Small flies..when they have once entered the tube, are imprisoned by the fringe of hairs.

e. In animals.

1665 HOOKE *Microgr.* 174 The whole edge of the wing is cover'd with a small fringe, consisting of short and more slender brisles. **1811** A. T. THOMSON *Lond. Disp.* II. (1818) 279 A black substance on the fringe or fin [of oysters]. **1828** STARK *Elem. Nat. Hist.* II. 327 Elytra and wings..without fringes. **1841-71** T. R. JONES *Anim. Kingd.* (ed. 4) 107 A delicate contractile arborescent fringe. **1848** CARPENTER *Anim. Phys.* 248 In Fishes the gills are composed of fringes.

f. *Anat.* = FIMBRIA.

1857 BULLOCK *Cazeaux' Midwif.* 65 One of these fringes ..attaches itself to the extremity of the ovary.

g. *Optics.* A band or strip of contrasting brightness or darkness produced by the diffraction or interference of light and usually seen as one of a series.

1704 NEWTON *Optics* III. i. (1721) 293 These Shadows have three parallel Fringes, Bands or Ranks of colour'd Light adjacent to them. **1827-8** J. F. W. HERSCHEL in *Encycl. Metrop.* IV. 468 On the whole, the lamina would appear marked all over with dark and bright alternating fringes, just as we see it actually does. **1831** BREWSTER *Optics* iv. 32 A bright light..separated from the faint light by a coloured fringe. **1837** GORING & PRITCHARD *Microgr.* 76 When I obtained the light of the prism..obliquely, the coloured fringes instantly appeared. **1866** E. ATKINSON tr. *Ganot's Elem. Treat. Physics* (ed. 2) VII. viii. 491 From the fact that the dark fringes disappear when one of the beams is intercepted, it is concluded that they arise from the interference of the two pencils which cross obliquely. *Ibid.* 493 A series of alternate dark and light bands or fringes are seen parallel to the line of shadow. **1923** GLAZEBROOK *Dict. Appl. Physics* IV. 144/2 The simplest application of interference fringes is the testing of optical surfaces by means of test plates. **1963** R. W. DITCHBURN *Light* (ed. 2) v. 127 Coloured fringes are often seen when a thin film of transparent material is viewed by reflected light. The film may be a layer of oil on water or on the surface of a road. **1966** W. J. SMITH *Mod. Optical Engin.* xiv. 416 The accuracy of the fit between work and gage is described in terms of the number of fringes seen when the gage is placed in contact with the work.

h. A strip of false colour between regions of contrasting brightness in an optical image, or surrounding the representation of an object on a colour film or in a projected colour picture (cf. FRINGING *vbl. sb.* b).

1891 H. T. WOOD *Light* vii. 105 Newton..arrived at the conclusion..that an achromatic object-glass, or a glass not showing these coloured fringes, was impossible. **1936** A. B. KLEIN *Colour Cinematogr.* 322 A fringe may be caused by parallax, error in printing registration, or by movement in the object which has taken place between the exposure of color-separation negatives. **1943** A. COX *Optics* 220 When there is any appreciable amount of lateral chromatic aberration present one side of the image has a red fringe, and the other has a deep blue fringe. **1963** R. W. DITCHBURN *Light* (ed. 2) vii. 259 When white light is used, coloured fringes appear at the boundaries between light and dark regions in an image.

3. *attrib.* and *Comb.*, as ***fringe-maker***; ***fringe-making*** vbl. sb.; ***fringe-backed***, ***-finned***, ***-hung***, ***-lipped*** adjs. Also **fringe benefit** orig. *U.S.*, a perquisite or benefit of some kind provided by an employer to supplement a money wage or salary; also *transf.*; **fringe-flower** = *fringe-tree*; **fringe-gloves**, fringed gloves, gloves ornamented with a fringe; **fringe-loom** (see quot.); **fringe medicine**, a collective term for systems of treatment of disease, etc., that are not regarded by the medical profession as part of orthodox treatment or whose efficacy and underlying premises are disputed; **fringe-moss**, a name for various species of moss (see quot.); **fringe-myrtle** (see quot.); **fringe-net**, a net intended to confine a fringe (2 c) of hair; hence **fringe-netted** *ppl. a.*; **fringe-pod**, a name given in California to *Thysanocarpus laciniatus*; **fringe-tree**, *Chionanthus virginica*; **fringe-variation** *Chess* (see quot. 1907).

1952 *Newsweek* 18 Feb. 74/2 For its 650,000 members it had asked..several cents' worth of *fringe benefits. **1955** *Times* 6 June 10/3 Many of the gains that labour has been getting through new contracts are not so much increases in money wages as in so-called 'fringe' benefits—such as larger pensions and welfare payments. **1962** *Times* 12 Nov. 11/3 The term 'fringe benefit' was apparently first recorded..in an announcement by the United States War Labour Board during the Second World War. **1969** *Times* 30 Apr. 24/4 (Advt.), Successful candidates can expect to receive salaries based on their experience and ability and fringe benefits which include 18 working days holiday a year, generous contributory pension scheme, free life insurance to the value of two years salary and car purchase at reduced rates. **1872** NICHOLSON *Palæont.* 321 A division of Ganoids called.. Crossopterygidæ, or *fringe-finned. **1882** JOHN SMITH *Dict. Pop. Names Pl.* *Fringe-Flower (*Chionanthus virginica*) a shrub..of the Olive family. **1589** *Acc.-bk. W. Wray* in *Antiquary* XXXII. 55 A dosse' *fringe gloves. **1670** WOOD *Life* (Oxf. Hist. Soc.) II. 208 A rich pair of fring-gloves. **1827** HOOD *Hero & Leander* lxxvi, Picture one..Who slowly parts the *fringe-hung canopies. **1836** YARRELL *Brit. Fishes* (1859) I. 19 The *Fringe-lipped Lampern. **1874** KNIGHT *Dict. Mech.*, **Fringe-loom*, one in which the weft-thread is carried and detained beyond the limit of the warp, which has thus a series of loops beyond the selvage. **1679** BEDLOE *Popish Plot* 11 French-*fring-maker. **1712** STEELE *Spect.* No. 478 ¶2 Fringe-makers, lace-men. **1713** *Lond. Gaz.* No. 5086/4 The Employment..of *Fringmaking. **1960** G. MURRAY in *Spectator* 28 Oct. 639, I have not attempted to assess the merits of the treatments that *fringe medicine can provide. **1964** B. INGLIS *Fringe Medicine* 264 The distinction between orthodox and fringe medicine today is that orthodox treatment relies mainly on fighting disease with the help of drugs or surgery, whereas unorthodox treatment concentrates on stimulating the patient's constitution to fight on its own behalf, on the assumption that this is safer and more effective. **1980** *Conc. Med. Dict.* 248/1 Among the more reputable of systems of fringe medicine are osteopathy, acupuncture, homeopathy, naturopathy, and chiropractic. **1983** *Guardian* 15 Apr. 15/4 Herbalism and other forms of fringe medicine attracted him. **1818** WITHERING *Brit. Plants* (ed. 6) III. 1058 Toothed Hoary *Fringe-Moss, *Bryum hypnoides*. **1868** TRIPP *Brit. Mosses* 124 *Ptychomitrium polyphyllum*, Many-leaved Fringe Moss. **1866** *Treas. Bot.*, **Fringe-Myrtles*, a name given by Lindley to the Chamælanciaceæ. **1899** *Westm. Gaz.* 10 June 2/1 She was now engrossed with a refractory *fringe-net. **1909** M. B. SAUNDERS *Litany Lane* I. vi, Her round face, tightened up in a stiff frame of fringe-nets. **1966** J. S. COX *Illustr. Dict. Hairdressing* 61/2 *Fringe net*, a net of human hair or, exceptionally, of silk or nylon used to confine a fringe of hair. **1909** M. B. SAUNDERS *Litany Lane* I. x, Provincial mayoress..with *fringe-netted hair. **1775** A. BURNABY *Trav.* 7 The woods are beautified with *fringe-trees, flowering poplars, etc. **1863** S. L. J. *Life in South* I. vi. 85 The fringe-tree. **1898** *Brit. Chess Mag.* 472 It would not be very difficult to find quite a goodly collection of two-movers in which every specimen contained the weakness of a '*fringe' variation. **1907** S. BLACKBURNE *Terms & Themes Chess Probl.* I. 54 A variation which does not spring naturally from the position, but has been tacked on by the employment of men which have otherwise no effect upon the solution, is known as a 'Fringe Variation'.

Hence **'fringeless** *a.*, having no fringe; **'fringelet**, a small fringe.

1837 COOPER *Recollect. Europe* II. 78 The present cropped and fringeless, bewhiskered and laceless generation of France. **1868** TRIPP *Brit. Mosses* 71 *Anodus Donianus*.. Fringeless Bristle Moss. **1887** *Pop. Sci. Monthly* XXXI. 747 Each fringelet is a tube made of firm elastic membrane.

fringe (frɪndʒ), *v.* [f. FRINGE *sb.*]

1. *trans.* To furnish, adorn, or encircle with a fringe or something resembling a fringe. Chiefly in pa. pple.

1480 *Wardr. Acc. Edw. IV* (1830) 143 An other sperver.. frenged with frenge of silk. **1555** EDEN *Decades* 315 They so rychely frynge and byset the same with perles. **1665** HOOKE *Microgr.* 174 Nor is this edge onely thus fring'd. **1698** FRYER *Acc. E. India & P.* 37 Curtains fringed with Battlements from one to the other. **1717** LADY M. W. MONTAGU *Let. to Lady Rich* 1 Apr., They are covered..with..cloth..very often richly embroidered and fringed. **1821** CLARE *Vill. Minstr.* II. 164 Day's first rays..Fring'd the blue clouds with gold. **1846** J. BAXTER *Libr. Pract. Agric.* (ed. 4) II. 9 The wheat fly itself is very small..with rounded wings, fringed with short hairs. **1850** HAWTHORNE *Scarlet L.* vii. (1883) 125 A pair of gloves, which she had fringed and embroidered to his order. **1870** E. PEACOCK *Ralf Skirl.* II. 165 A long tract of moorland, fringed with villages. **1888** F. HUME *Mad. Midas* 1 Prol., Fringing the wet sands with many coloured wreaths of sea-weed and delicate shells.

fig. **1613** PURCHAS *Pilgrimage* (1614) 250 When he hath set downe some wicked Doctrine, presently to lace and fringe it with Precepts of Fasting, Prayer, or Good manners. *c* **1645** HOWELL *Lett.* (1650) II. II. 20 The transaction..was fringd with such cautelous restraints that he was sure to keep the better end of the staff still to himself. **1828** *Sporting Mag.* XXII. 233 The old Gentleman's memory is fringed with exemplary characteristics.

2. To serve as a fringe to; to present the appearance of a fringe upon.

1794 W. HUTCHINSON *Hist. Cumberld.* I. 188 The wood that fringes the border of the rivers. **1813** H. & J. SMITH *Rej. Addr.* 65 Why, beautiful nymph, do you close The curtain that fringes your eye? **1859** W. S. COLEMAN *Woodlands* (1866) 84 The Alder loves also to fringe the margins of our lakes and pools. **1865** TYLOR *Early Hist. Man.* xii. 342 Close upon the Esquimaux who fringe the northern coast. **1873** TRISTRAM *Moab* viii. 153 Camels in scattered order..fringed the horizon. **1884** BOWER & SCOTT *De Bary's Phaner.* 338 A narrow band, fringing the lateral edge of the bundle.

3. To fritter or trifle *away*. *rare.*

1863 G. ELIOT in Cross *Life* (1885) II. 367 Such fringing away of precious life, in thinking of carpets and tables, is an affliction to me.

4. *intr.* To spread like a fringe *away*, *off*, *out*, *over*, etc.

1858 GEO. ELIOT *Sc. Cler. Life* II. III. iv. 113 The Bridge Way was an irregular, straggling street, where the town fringed off raggedly into the Whitlow Road. **1875** 'MARK TWAIN' in *Atlantic Monthly* Mar. 286/2 Do you see where the line fringes out at the upper end and begins to fade away? **1877** *Ibid.* Nov. 591 Its [*sc.* the town's] borders fringed off and thinned away among the cedar forest. **1899** C. P. ALLEN *What is Liberalism?* viii. 48 Its limits fringe away from it like a huge penumbra. **1901** *Westm. Gaz.* 15 Aug. 2/1 Exmoor ..is for the most part in the west of Somerset, but it fringes over into the north-eastern part of Devon.

fringed (frɪndʒd), *ppl. a.* [f. FRINGE *sb.* or *v.* + -ED.] Furnished with a fringe; adorned with or as with a fringe.

1495 *Wills Doct. Com.* (Camden) 4 Twoo curteyns of whit sarcenet fringed. **1552** *Church Goods* in Dillon *Calais & Pale* (1892) 97 Foure quesshinges, one of reede fryngRed silke. **1610** SHAKS. *Temp.* I. ii. 408 The fringed Curtaines of thine eye aduance. **1654-5** in *12th Rep. Hist. MSS. Comm.* App. VII. (1890) 22, 4*s.* for a black fringed belt. **1667** MILTON *P.L.* IV. 262 The fringed Bank with Myrtle crownd. *a* **1775** *Hobie Noble* in Child *Ballads* clxxxix. 2/1 He has pulld out his fringed grey. **1776** WITHERING *Brit. Plants* (1796) II. 380 Flowers 3 or 4 together, included in a membranaceous fringed sheath. **1828** STARK *Elem. Nat. Hist.* II. 369 The margin of their wings is fringed. **1882** *Garden* 24 June 437/2 The old and pretty Fringed Pink.

fringent ('frɪndʒənt), *a.* *rare*$^{-1}$. [? formed to correspond with *friction*, on the supposed analogy of *fraction*, *frangent*.] Exercising friction.

1847 EMERSON *Poems* (1857) 104 A shower of meteors..lit by fringent air, Blaze near and far.

fringer ('frɪndʒə(r)). [f. FRINGE *sb.* + -ER[1].] One who is on the fringe (sense 2 b).

1938 *Times Lit. Suppl.* 26 Feb. 139/3 Picked up a bit of a living by introducing snob-conscious bourgeois to social fringers. **1952** J. MASEFIELD *So Long to Learn* 100 There were so many ways, cliques and coteries; there were..Celtic fringers. **1962** *Spectator* 26 Jan. 97, I knew he would denounce even the most casual approach to a 'fringer'.

fringi'llaceous, *a.* [f. L. *fringilla* finch + -ACEOUS.] Pertaining to the finches (Webster 1864). **frin'gillide** [anglicized sing. form of mod.L. *fringillidæ*], a bird of the finch family. **frin'gilliform** *a.*, [-(I)FORM], finch-like (*Cent. Dict.*). **frin'gilline** *a.*, [-INE], of or pertaining to the finches.

1853 KANE *Grinnell Exp.* xlii. (1856) 390 That familiar little fringillide, the snowbird. **1874** COUES *Birds N.W.* 163 The Lark Bunting is one of the most singularly specialized of all our fringilline forms. **1893** W. H. HUDSON *Idle Days in Patagonia* I. 15 The finest voiced of all the fringilline birds.

fringing ('frɪndʒɪŋ), *vbl. sb.* [f. FRINGE *v.* + -ING[1].] **a.** The action of the vb. FRINGE; in quots. *concr.* = FRINGE 1 a. Also *transf.*

1598 FLORIO, *Smancerie*..any trimming, lacing, fringing, or such ornament. **1843** CARLYLE *Past & Pr.* II. i, With much plumage and fringing. **1864** —— *Fredk. Gt.* IV. 576 Some fringing of light horse. **1892** E. REEVES *Homeward Bound* 306 Simulated pearls of transparent radiance..adorn it round about with a fringing of copper.

b. The appearance of fringes of false colour in a projected colour picture as a result of imperfect registration of component images.

1912 F. A. TALBOT *Moving Pictures* xxvi. 298 Another disconcerting feature..is the apparent duplication of the outlines of figures near the camera... 'Fringing', as this defect is called, is difficult to eliminate. **1921** *Conquest* Oct. 511/2 The moment motion of any rapidity occurs the objectionable defect of 'fringing' makes itself apparent. **1936** A. B. KLEIN *Colour Cinematogr.* iv. 244 The writer has photographed the ripples on a stream without obvious signs of fringing. **1969** *Focal Encycl. Film & Telev.* 301/1 Fringing is particularly objectionable in colour synthesis, since the fringes will then be of different colours from adjacent parts of the images.

c. The spreading of magnetic or electric lines of force at the edge of a region in which they otherwise form a simple pattern amenable to calculation.

1893 D. C. JACKSON *Text-bk. Electro-Magn.* I. v. 145 To this should be added about 10 per cent to allow for the 'fringing' of the lines of force at the corners of the pole pieces. **1943** *Electronic Engin.* XVI. 254 As we approach the edge of the plates the field becomes non-uniform and we have wide curvature of the lines of force. This is technically known as 'fringing'. **1957** AMOS & BIRKINSHAW *Television Engin.* (ed. 2) I. x. 262 The expression is approximate because it was assumed that the field between the plates was parallel whereas in fact it tends to spread at the edges... This effect is known as fringing. **1963** B. FOZARD *Instrumentation Nucl. Reactors* iii. 26 Fringing effects in the electric field at the ends of the electrodes tend to cause the magnitude of the sensitive volume to vary with applied voltage.

'fringing, *ppl. a.* [f. FRINGE *v.* + -ING[2].] That fringes. ***fringing forest***: see quot. 1926; ***fringing reef***: see quot. 1878.

1845 DARWIN *Voy. Nat.* xx. (1873) 465 The three great classes of coral-reefs, Atolls, Barrier, and Fringing-reefs. **1878** HUXLEY *Physiogr.* xv. 253 Rocky ridges which fringe a shore in the manner just described, are known as fringing-reefs. **1888** BRYCE *Amer. Commw.* I. xxiii. 339 The American Constitution..with the mass of fringing decisions which explain it. **1895** *Daily News* 26 Aug. 3/2 Its blue sea, and fringing islands. **1903** W. R. FISHER tr. *Schimper's Plant-Geogr.* II. i. 177 We find the banks of rivers and lakes stocked with woods as far as infiltration extends. These are often mere brush-woods, but not unfrequently developed as luxuriant forests (fringing forests) not inferior to those of the best forest climate. **1926** TANSLEY & CHIPP *Study of Vegetation* x. 208 Fringing forest..occurs as a fringe of forest or woodland along the banks of perennial rivers. **1960** N. POLUNIN *Introd. Plant Geogr.* xiv. 439 There often occur, along rivers, 'fringing forests' which are evergreen and otherwise reminiscent of the rain forest.

fringy ('frɪndʒɪ), *a.* [f. FRINGE *sb.* + -Y[1].]

1. Of the nature of or resembling a fringe.

c **1750** SHENSTONE *Elegies* xxi. 10 My devious path I bend, Through fringy woodland, or smooth-shaven lawn. **1822–34** *Good's Study Med.* (ed. 4) IV. 327 The fringy termination of the Fallopian Tubes. **1853** KANE *Grinnell Exp.* xxxv. (1856) 321 A fimbriated or fringy series of purple cirri. **1880** 'MARK TWAIN' *Tramp Abroad* I. 75 The gracefullest little fringy films of lace.

2. Furnished or adorned with a fringe or fringes; covered with fringes.

1831 T. L. PEACOCK *Crotchet Castle* xiv. (1887) 149 All that surrounded their [eyes'] fringy portals was radiant as 'the forehead of the morning sky'. **1852** *Meanderings of Mem.* I. 206 Fluttering as the mantle's fringy rim. **1865** CARLYLE *Fredk. Gt.* XVII. v. VII. 48 Green, shaggy or fringy mountains looking down on it to rearward. **1886** RUSKIN *Præterita* I. vi. 203 Any sort of people in conical hats and fringy caps.

Comb. **1860** RUSKIN *Mod. Paint.* V. IX. iii. §21 The dog..is one of the little curly, short-nosed, fringy-pawed things.

Fringy, var. of FERINGHEE.

†**Fri'night.** *Obs. rare.* [= ON. *friá-nótt*; cf. OE. *frige-æten* Thursday evening.] **a.** The night before (Good) Friday. **b.** The night of (Good) Friday.

a **1225** *Ancr. R.* 122 Efter alle þe schendfule pinen þet he þolede oðe longe uriniht, me ledde him amorwen uorte hongen o waritreo. *c* **1440** *Jacob's Well* (E.E.T.S.) 177 On good fryȝ-nyȝt..þe chanoun lay be þe iewys dowter. On þe satyrday [etc.].

‖**fripier** ('frɪpɪə(r), fripje). Also 9 frippier. [Fr. *fripier*: see FRIPPER.] A dealer in old clothes.

1826 *Blackw. Mag.* XX. 242 Men..turn their principles inside out, as a frippier does a garment. **1847** JAMES *J. Marston Hall* xxi, The house of the well-known fripier Martin, where every sort of dress..was to be procured.

†**'fripler.** *Obs.* [transformation of Fr. *fripier*: see next.] = FRIPPER.

1589 NASHE *Ep. to Greene's Menaphon* (Arb.) 8 Those and these are..bought at the deerest though they smell of the friplers lauander halfe a yeere after. **1596** —— *Saffron Walden* 72 When hee first began to be a fripler or broker in that trade.

‖**'fripon.** *Obs.* [Fr.] A rogue.

1691 *Satyr agst. French* 19 (Stanf.) Attended by a young *petit Garçon*, Who from his Cradle was an arch *Fripon*. **1724** RAMSAY *Evergreen* (1824) II. 70 (Dunbar's Flyting) And help to hang Fripons for half a Frank [*original* and help to hang the pece for half a frank].

‖**fri'pon(n)erie.** *rare.* Also fripp-. [Fr. *friponnerie*, f. *fripon* (see prec.).] Roguery.

1708 tr. *Petronius Arbiter* Key 1 Associates in all sorts of Friponeries and Debocheries. **1747** WALPOLE *Let. H. Mann* 26 June, Lett. 1857 II. 90 The shortest way to prevent any *frippomnerie*. **1818** R. PETERS in *J. Jay's Corr. & Publ. Papers* (1893) IV. 424 Most of the articles went through my hands ..and a more complete piece of fripponerie never was seen.

†**'fripper.** *Obs.* [ad. Fr. *fripier*, f. *friper* to tear to rags, f. OF. *frepe*, *ferpe*, *felpe* rag.] = next.

1598 FLORIO, *Barattiere*..a trucker, a marter..a fripper. **1605** BACON *Adv. Learn.* II. xvii. §14. 66 Like a Frippers or Brokers Shoppe; that hath ends of euerie thing, but nothing of worth. **1657** HOWELL *Londinop.* 81 Frippers or Upholders, that sold Apparel. **1697** *View Penal Laws* 31 Goods wrongfully gotten, and sold to Brokers, Frippers or Pawn-takers.

fripperer ('frɪpərə(r)). [extended form of prec.: see -ER[1] 3.] A dealer in cast-off clothing.

1584 WHETSTONE *Mirr. Mag.* 33 b, They upon their owne or maisters apparell..finde Brokers or fripperers. **1641** *Termes de la Ley* 171 b, Friperer is one that uses to dresse old clothes to sell againe. **1805** W. TAYLOR in *Ann. Rev.* III. 619 To see his fripperer..reminds him of his meanness. **1860** *All Year Round* No. 76. 614 Birchover-lane, where the fripperers, or sellers of old clothes, dwell.

frippery ('frɪpərɪ), *sb.* Forms: 6 freprie, fripperie, (7 thripperie), 7 fripery, 7– frippery. [a. or ad. OF. *freperie*, *ferperie*, *felperie* (Fr. *friperie*), f. *frepe*, *ferpe*, *felpe* rag.]

In all senses, more or less collective.

†**1.** Old clothes; cast-off garments. *Obs.*

1568 *Satir. Poems Reform.* xlviii. 74 Thoᵗ it be awld, and twenty tymis sawld, ȝit will the freprie mak ȝow fane With vlis to renew it and mak it weill hewit. **1606** HOLLAND *Sueton.* 241 Which extendeth also to slaves and old wares or thripperie. **1638** FORD *Fancies* I. iii, Some frippery to hide nakedness. **1700** CONGREVE *Way of World* III. v, I'll reduce him to frippery and rags. **1790** BURKE *Fr. Rev.* Wks. V. 409 An old huge full-bottomed perriwig out of the wardrobe of the antiquated frippery of Louis the Fourteenth. **1824** W. IRVING *T. Trav.* I. 199 The old garments and frippery that fluttered from every window.

fig. **1638** BAKER tr. *Balzac's Lett.* To Rdr. (1654) 3 And makes a great shew of the frippery and brokage of other Authors. **1742** H. WALPOLE *Lett. H. Mann* (1834) I. xxv. 112 Old Sarah's Memoirs..are nothing but remnants of old women's frippery.

2. Finery in dress, *esp.* tawdry finery; an example of this, an article of fashionable attire. Also, *transf.* tawdry ornamentation in general.

1637 SIR E. BURKE in *Dk. of Rutland's MSS.* (1888) I. 498 Such a cuning peti larceny of fripery as amazes us all. **1681** CROWNE *Hen VI*, I. 10 A little Pinke Laden with toyes and fripperies from France. **1773** GOLDSM. *She Stoops to Conquer* I, She is as fond of gauze and French frippery as the best of them. **1833** HT. MARTINEAU *Manch. Strike* i. 16, I will..send my wife with a cloak..to hide the child's frippery. **1856** MISS MULOCK *J. Halifax* x, With no fripperies or fandangos of any sort. **1864** KNIGHT *Passages Wrkg. Life* I. v. 220 We obtained one of this class of Churches..at a preposterous cost for Bath stone and corresponding frippery.

b. Applied to a showily-dressed person.

1877 BLACK *Green Past.* iv. (1878) 34 The painted fripperies you meet at every woman's house in London.

c. Articles of small value; trifles.

1803 JANE PORTER *Thaddeus* xxiv. (1831) 203 Boxes, baskets, and other frippery. **1831** TRELAWNY *Adv. Younger Son* II. 241 Modern frippery of combs, razors, brushes [etc.].

d. *fig.* Empty display, *esp.* in speech or literary composition; showy talk; ostentation.

1727 SWIFT *To Yng. Lady* Wks. 1755 II. II. 47 You will gather more advantage by listening to them, than from all the nonsense and frippery of your own sex. **1764** GRAY *Lett.* Wks. 1884 III. 187, I can stay with great patience for anything that comes from Voltaire. They tell me it is frippery, and blasphemy, and wit. **1871** FREEMAN *Hist. Ess.* Ser. I. v. 114 Throwing aside all the fopperies and fripperies of chivalry. **1877** MRS. OLIPHANT *Makers Flor.* ix. 237 A noble young gentleman amid all his frippery of courtier and virtuoso.

†**3.** A place where cast-off clothes are sold. *Obs.*

1598 FLORIO, *Recateria*, a fripperie or brokers shop. **1610** SHAKS. *Temp.* IV. i. 225 Oh, ho, Monster; wee know what belongs to a frippery. *a* **1635** CORBET *Poems* (1807) 98 For learning, th' Universitie; And for old clothes, the Frippery. [**1830** JAMES *Darnley* xxix. 128/2, I will get the three dresses this very night, from a frippery in Poole Street.]

fig. **1616** B. JONSON *Epigr.* I. lvi, Whose Workes are eene the frippery of wit. **1649** OWEN *Serm.* Wks. 1851 VIII. 236 Ireland was termed by some in civil things a frippery of bankrupts. *a* **1680** BUTLER *Rem.* (1759) I. 364 A Frippery of common Places of Pulpit Railing, ill put together.

†**4.** A stand or horse for dresses, etc.; a wardrobe. *Obs.*

a **1616** [see FLIPPERY: Dyce prints *frippery*]. **1632** MASSINGER *City Madam* I. i, He shews like a walking frippery. *c* **1645** SIR R. VERNEY *Inv. Claydon* in Lady Verney *Mem. Verney Fam.* I. 6 The little and greate Fripperies, etc.

†**5.** Trade or traffic in cast-off clothes. *Obs.*

1599 SANDYS *Europæ Spec.* (1632) 131 The Iewes..have generally not any other trades than frippery and usury. **1606** CHAPMAN *Mons. D'Olive* III. i, *D'Ol.* Now your profession, I pray? *Frip.* Fripperie, my Lord, or as some tearme it, Petty Brokery.

6. Tawdry style; frivolity. *rare.*

1802 MAD. D'ARBLAY *Diary* 5 May, His manly air carried off the frippery of his trappings. **1855** CHAMIER *My Travels* I. xviii. 310 The frippery of fashion might not have caused a Roman to strut about with an eye-glass.

7. *attrib.* and *Comb.*

c **1645** HOWELL *Lett.* VI. 24 Yet by that base and servile way of Frippery trade, they grow rich. **1744** *Ess. Acting* 18 Macbeth's..Night Gown..ought to be a Red Damask, and not the frippery-flowered one of a Foppington.

Hence **'fripperied over**, *pa. pple.*, showily tricked out.

1858 MISS MULOCK *Thoughts Women* 323 Flimsy, light-coloured dresses, fripperied over with trimmings.

frippery ('frɪpərɪ), *a.* [developed from the attrib. use of the sb.] Trifling; frivolous; contemptible; trumpery.

a **1625** FLETCHER *Chances* II. ii, A frippery cause. **1739** GRAY *Lett.* Wks. 1884 II. 49 That city..made so frippery an appearance, that instead of spending some days there..we only dined, and went on to Parma. **1768** FOOTE *Devil on 2 Sticks* I, In spite of the frippery French Salick laws, a woman is a free agent. **1795** *Jemima* I. 161 His dress..is so frippery. **1844** *Blackw. Mag.* LV. 200 Neither will they be persuaded by the frippery tomes which load the counters. **1859** JEPHSON *Brittany* v. 55 Numbers of frippery and vulgar ornaments on the table. **18..** M. PATTISON *Mem.* ii. (1885) 89 Betake themselves..to the frippery work of attending boards.

frippet ('frɪpɪt). *slang.* [Origin unknown.] A frivolous or showy young woman.

1908 D. H. LAWRENCE *Let.* 15 May (1962) I. 11 The girl will have a soul—she will not be a frippet. **1927** *Blackw. Mag.* May 673/2 'Frippets—three in number,' was the.. diagnosis. **1933** W. CHETHAM STRODE *Sometimes Even Now* III. ii. 89 I'll invite him—and he can bring all his 'lovelys' and 'frippets' with him. **1945** E. TAYLOR *At Mrs. Lippincote's* xxiii. 196 'Mistress!' he thought... It was like the swine of a man to use such a word for what he and Edwards would have called a bit of a frippet. **1960** W. SHEED *Middle Class Education* (1961) 50 Did you have a rewarding life experience last night with that rather enticing bit of frippet? **1971** D. CLARK *Sick to Death* vi. 123 Quite a nice bit of frippet. But too young for me. I like a mature woman.

†**frippish**, *a.* *Obs.* *rare*[−1]. [f. FRIPP-ERY + -ISH.] Tawdry, gaudy.

1787 *Generous Attachment* I. 156 Let them erect their pompous edifices with all the frippish grandeur of modern architecture.

†**'fripple**, var. of FRIBBLE *sb.*

1610 HEALEY *St. Aug. Citie of God* 355 Do but leave your fripples and sticke to the fathers.

frisado: see FRIZADO.

Frisbee, frisbee ('frɪzbɪ). Also frisby. [See quot. 1970.] The proprietary name of a concave plastic disc which spins when thrown into the air and is used in a catching game.

1957 *Newsweek* 8 July 85 The object of the game is simply for one player to toss the Frisbee, or disk, into the air and try to keep it from his opponent's grasp. **1959** *Official Gaz.* (U.S. Pat. Office) 26 May TM 168/2 Frisbee. 679,186. Wham-O Mfg. Co. For: Toy Flying Saucers for Toss Games in Class 22. **1967** *Wanganui* (N.Z.) *Photo News* 11 Feb. 35 Frisbees are plastic dishes which perform all manner of gyrations when tossed in the air. **1969** *Guardian* 5 July 9/2 The frisbee..is a plastic disc about the size of a frying pan that in the hands of the experts out boomerangs the boomerang. **1970** *Sports Illustrated* 3 Aug. 48/1 Thirteen years ago the Wham-O Manufacturing Company of San Gabriel, Calif...brought out the first Frisbee. Wham-O purchased the rights from a Los Angeles building inspector named Fred Morrison, who in turn had been inspired by the airworthy pie tins of the Frisbie bakery in Bridgeport, Conn. (which went out of business in March of 1958). He changed the spelling to avoid legal problems. **1971** *Islander* (Victoria, B.C.) 27 June 6/3 Gunny-sacked racers hobble about and frisbee circles form.

†**fri'scado.** *Obs.*[−1] [f. FRISCO + -ADO.] = FRISCO.

1634 W. WOOD *New Eng. Prosp.* II. xv, Fearefull to approach neere the friscadoes of her Iron heeles.

†**frisca'joly**, *a.* *Obs.* [? f. *frisca*, FRISCO + JOLLY.] Used as a refrain for jovial songs; also *attrib.*

1519 *Interl. 4 Elem.* (1848) 17 Synge fryska joly, with hey troly loly. *a* **1529** SKELTON *Replyc.* Wks. 1843 I. 209 Stoicall studiantes, and friscaioly yonkerkyns. **1538** BALE *Thre Lawes* 1794 Now shall I be able to..make frowlyke chere, with hey now fryska Jolye. [**1580**: see FRISK *a.*]

†'**friscal.** *Obs.* Also 6-7 friscol, -oil, 7 friskal, -kle. [f. FRISK *sb.* or FRISCO; perh. on the analogy of *caracole*.] = FRISCO.

c **1570** *Marr. Wit & Science* IV. ii. D ij, These friscoles shal not serue your tourne for al your vauntes so braue. **1611** *Coryat's Crudities* Panegyr. Verses, His treadings were but friscals of a poppet. **1612** SHELTON *Quixote* I. IV. iii. 315 And saying so, he gaue two or three friskles in the ayre with very great signes of contentment. **1622** MABBE tr. *Aleman's Guzman d'Alf.* II. 175 Their beds..wherein they were like to..fetch..friscalls in the ayre.

transf. **1613** WITHER *Epithal.* Juvenilia (1633) 360 Comets and Meteors..shew their fiery Friscoils in the ayre.

friscay, obs. form of FRISKY.

†'**frisco.** *Obs.* Also 6 frysca, frischo, 7 friska, friskoe; *pl.* -os, -oes, -as. [? Pseudo-It. form of FRISK *sb.*]

1. A brisk movement in dancing; a caper.

1519 *Interl. 4 Elem.* (1848) 45 That shall both daunce and spryng..With fryscas and with gambawdes round. **1566** J. PARTRIDGE *Plasidas* B iij, With fetching frischoes here and there. **1598** BARCKLEY *Felic. Man* I. (1603) 38 Hee fetched at the last such a frisco, that he fell downe and brake his neck. **1608** ARMIN *Nest. Ninn.* (1880) 56 Shee longed to heare his friscoes morallized, and his gambals set downe. **1634** FORD *P. Warbeck* III. ii, Observe the friska, be enchanted With the rare discord of bells, pipes, and tabours. **1675** TEONGE *Diary* (1825) 50 Having taken their frisco, returnd as they cam.

2. Applied to a person as a term of endearment. (Cf. FRISKIN 2.)

a **1652** BROME *New Acad.* I. Wks. 1873 II. 3 Where's my Boykin? my Friskoe? my Delight?

frisco(i)l, var. of FRISCAL.

frise (fri:z), *sb.* [short for CHEVAL DE FRISE.] = CHEVAL DE FRISE I. Also *transf.*

1809 CAMPBELL *Gertr. Wyom.* III. xxv, Each bold and promontory mound With..armour crown'd, And arrowy frize. **1856** LEVER *Martins of Cro' M.* 145 A low wall, coped with a formidable 'frize' of broken bottles.

‖**frisé** (frize), *a.* [Fr. *frisé* in similar sense, pa. pple. of *friser*: see FRIEZE, FRIZZ *vbs.*] (See quot. 1884.)

1884 *West. Daily Press* 20 June 7/5 Frisé materials are everywhere, frisé meaning a raised design..in silk, looking as if it had been woven over pins, and the pins withdrawn. **1892** *Daily News* 24 Oct. 3/1 A raised frisé stripe in black silky wool.

frise, obs. form of FREEZE, FRIEZE.

friseado, var. of FRIZADO.

Frisesomorum (,fraısεsə'mɔərəm). *Logic.* [Formed by the letters signifying the propositions of the syllogistic mood.] The mnemonic term for that indirect mood of the first figure of syllogisms in which the major premiss is particular and affirmative, the minor universal and negative, and the conclusion particular and negative. Also called **Frisesmo.**

1599 BLUNDEVIL *Logike* 121 Celantes: Dabitis: Fapesmo: Frisesomorum. **1685** tr. *Arnauld & Nicole's Logic* III. viii. 35 These five modes are generally denoted by these words, Baralipton, Celantes, Dabitis, Fapesmo, Frisesomorum [printed Trisesomorum]. **1849** H. L. MANSEL *Aldrich* 65 The five indirect moods of the first figure were called Baralip, Celantes, Dabitis, Fapesmo, Frisesmo. **1884** J. N. KEYNES *Formal Logic* 199 Similarly, *Fapesmo* and *Frisesomorum* (the *Fesapo* and *Fresison* of Figure 4) have no corresponding direct moods. **1937** I. CHOQUETTE tr. *Maritain's Introd. Logic* iii. 189 When these conventional words have more than three syllables, *e.g.*, *Frisesomorum*, the extra syllables are but stopgaps, and have no symbolic meaning. **1960** J. ROLAND et al. tr. *Dopp's Formal Logic* viii. 172 The moods similar to *Dabitis* and *Frisesomorum* (4th figure)..cannot, therefore, be valid.

frise stone, var. of FREESTONE.

frisette (frı'zεt). Also frisett, frizette. [a. Fr. *frisette*, f. *friser* to FRIZZ.] A band or cluster of small curls, usually artificial, worn on the forehead.

1818 LADY MORGAN *Fl. Macarthy* IV. §vi. 239 The one appeared without his stays, and the other without her frizette. **1858** O. W. HOLMES *Aut. Breakf.-t.* ii. (1891) 30 A ..middle-aged female, with a parchment forehead and a dry little 'frisette' shingling it. **1868** *Daily News* 10 Aug., The sixpenny frisett sold to fill out the sparse locks of the servant-of-all-work.

‖**friseur** (frizœr). Also frizeur. [Fr. *friseur*, f. *friser* to FRIZZ] A hairdresser; now *rare*.

1750 CHESTERF. *Lett.* (1774) II. 60 Let your man learn of the best *friseur* to do your hair well. **1777** FRANKLIN *Lett.* Wks. 1889 VI. 69, I wish every lady and gentle-man in France would..dismiss their friseurs, and pay me half the money they paid to them. **1816** *Sporting Mag.* XLVII. 306 By mercers, frizeurs, mantua-makers press'd. **1831** JEKYLL *Corr.* (1894) 279 The sister, a romp, married a sort of friseur, the son of old Viscount Fitzwilliam. **1866** R. W. PROCTER *Barber's Shop* vii. (1883) 35 He was surpassed by..a conscientious frizeur of an older school.

Frisian ('frızıən), *a.* and *sb.* [f. L. *Frisi-ī* pl. (ad. the native name: OFris. *Frise*, *Frese*, MDu. *Vriese* (Du. *Vries*), OHG. *Friaso*, *Frieso*, OE. *Frísa*, *Frésa* wk. sb., a Frisian) + -AN.]

A. *adj.* Of or pertaining to the people of Friesland. **B.** *sb.* **a.** An inhabitant of Friesland. **b.** The language of Friesland.

1598 GRENEWEY *Tacitus' Ann.* XI. vi. 147 The Frisian nation..rebelled after the ouerthrow of L. Apronius. **1601** HOLLAND *Pliny* II. 212 The Frisians, neere vnto whom we lay incamped, shewed our men this herb. **1875** WHITNEY *Life Lang.* x. 181 English literary monuments go back to the seventh century..and Frisian literature from the fourteenth. **1882-3** SCHAFF *Encycl. Relig. Knowl.* II. 1472 The rigorous party was again divided into Vlamingen and Frisians.

†'**Frisic,** *a. Obs.* In 7-8 -ick. See FRIESIC. [f. as prec. + -IC.] Of or pertaining to Friesland.

1677 HALE *Prim. Orig. Man.* II. iv. 163 Divers other [Languages] seem to be much derived from them, namely, the Greek..Frisick, Illyrian [etc.]. **1763** JOHNSON *Let. to Boswell* 8 Dec. in *Life*, It will be a favour if you can get me any books in the Frisick language.

frisk (frısk), *sb.* [f. FRISK *v.*]

†**1.** A brisk and lively movement in horsemanship or dancing; a caracole or curvet; a caper, a jig. *to fetch a frisk*: see FETCH *v.* 9. *Obs.*

1525 LD. BERNERS *Froiss.* II. lxxviii. [lxxiv.] 234 Eche of them [knyghtes] a good dystaunce fro other made theyr tournes and fryskes fresshly. **1563-87** FOXE *A. & M.* (1684) III. 145 He leapt, and set a frisk or twain, as men commonly do in dauncing. **1596** SPENSER *F.Q.* IV. x. 46 Then doe the salvage beasts begin to play Their pleasant friskes. **1610** ROWLANDS *Martin Mark-all* 36 Diuers..can now for ioy.. fetch friskes about the house. **1640** SHIRLEY *Arcadia* III. i, The new frisk we danced at Enispe to-day. **1696** AUBREY *Misc.* (1721) 79 When he had done his Message he gave a Frisk. **1780** COWPER *Table T.* 237 Give him [the Frenchman] his lass, his fiddle and his frisk. **1842** C. WHITEHEAD *Richard Savage* (1845) I. vii. 89 He favoured me with a frisk as I left him at his own door.

2. *transf.* and *fig.* A brisk sportive movement; a frolic; also, a freak, whim. †*frisk of nature* = *freak of nature*: see FREAK *sb.* 4.

1665 HOOKE *Microgr.* 186 If they do by a frisk get below that superficies, they presently ascend again. *a* **1677** BARROW *Serm.* Wks. 1716 III. 79 New objects..excite the spirits into a pleasant frisk of motion. **1752** JOHNSON in Boswell (1848) 80/1 I'll have a frisk with you. **1801** FOSTER in *Life & Corr.* (1846) I. 133 The frisks of a company of summer flies. **1809** *Ann. Reg.* 754* There is scarcely a nobleman..who is not possessed of one or more of these frisks of nature. **1819** SCOTT *Fam. Lett.* 17 Apr. (1894) II. xv. 43, I wish you would all take a frisk down here this summer. **1825** —— *Jrnl.* 22 Dec., Can't say what made me take a frisk so uncommon of late years, as to write verses of free-will. **1852** DICKENS *Bleak Ho.* xx, When you and I had a frisk down in Lincolnshire. **1889** H. F. WOOD *Englishman of Rue Cain* iv, The married frumps come over for a frisk.

†**frisk,** *a. Obs.* Also 6 friske, fryske, frixe. [a. OFr. *frisque*, of uncertain origin; by some viewed as ad. Teut. **frisk-*, FRESH *a.*; by others as an altered form of *frique*: see FRIKE *a.*] Full of life and spirit; brisk, lively, frisky.

1528 PAYNEL *Salerne Regim.* H b, Wyne muste be friske & sprynkelynge. *c* **1540** BOORDE *The boke for to Lerne* B ij b, The Est wynde is temperat fryske and fragrant. **1580** SIDNEY *Arcadia* III. 401 Thou seest how friske and jolly now he is. **1597-8** BP. HALL *Sat.* VI. i. 294 Fayne would she seeme all frixe and frolicke still. **1611** COTGR. s.v. *Asne*, Asses discharged of their burthens, vnsadled, and set at libertie, are the friskest creatures aliue.

b. Of a horse's tail: Constantly in motion; jerky. Cf. FLISK, FLICKY, FLIGGY, FLETCH.

1694 *Lond. Gaz.* No. 3017/4 A brown bay Mare with a.. frisk Tail. **1705** *Ibid.* No. 4148/4 A black Gelding..with a long frisk Tail.

frisk (frısk), *v.* Also 6-7 friske, frysk(e, 7 frisque. [f. prec. adj.]

1. *intr.* Of living beings: To move briskly and sportively; to dance, frolic, gambol, jig. Also with *about*, *away*, *in and out*, *off*, and *to frisk it*.

1519 *Interl. 4 Elem.* (1848) 49 And I can fryske it freshly. **1583** STANYHURST *Æneis* I. (Arb.) 34 Nymphs a thowsand do frisk with Princelye Diana. **1601** R. JOHNSON *Kingd. & Commw.* (1603) 64 Sholes of fish frisking and playing hard under the wals of the citie. **1611** SHAKS. *Wint. T.* I. ii. 67 We were as twyn'd Lambs, that did frisk i' th' Sun. **1664** POWER *Exp. Philos.* I. 2 He [the Flea]..will frisk and curvet so nimbly. **1679** E. BROWN *Let. to Blythe* in *2nd Rep. Hist. MSS. Comm.* App. 114/2 The gallants are frisquing and making merry in Hyde Park. *c* **1704** PRIOR *Simile* 14 Those merry blades, That frisk it under Pindus' shades. **1730** FIELDING *Temple Beau* I. i, For your heart is like a coffee-house, where the beaus frisk in and out, one after another. **1764** GOLDSM. *Trav.* 253 The gay grandsire, skilled in gestic lore, Has frisked beneath the burden of threescore. **1785** BURNS *To Jas. Smith* xv, Cold-pausing caution's lessons scorning, We frisk away. **1821** T. W. CROKER *Diary* 8 June, To-day he has frisked off to Windsor. **1891** SMILES *J. Murray* II. xxv. 177 He..rejoiced at seeing the children frisking about in the happiness of youth.

transf. and *fig.* **1626** BACON *Sylva* §9 It will make the Water friske and sprinkle up in a fine Dew. *a* **1716** SOUTH *Serm.* (1717) V. 492 The Proclamation of a Prince never frisks it in Tropes. **1779** A. HAMILTON *Wks.* (1886) VII. 586 Did I mean to show my wit?.. Did I only intend to frisk? **1823** LAMB *Elia, Oxford in Vacation*, The enfranchised quill ..frisks and curvets..over the flowery carpet-ground of a midnight dissertation.

2. *trans.* **a.** To move (*up*, *out*, *about*, etc.) in a sportive or lively manner. **b.** *to frisk away*: to squander on freaks or caprices.

? **16..** *A Cap, etc.* (N.), To frisk away much of thy time and estate. **1665** HOOKE *Microgr.* 187 It would by frisking out of its tail..sink itself below the surface. *a* **1693** URQUHART *Rabelais* III. xvii. 140 A pair of Yarn Windles, which she..veered, and frisked about. **1862** R. H. PATTERSON *Ess. Hist. & Art* 109 The tail is frisked up into the air in the liveliest manner possible.

†**3.** To render sprightly, enliven. *Obs.*

1802 FENTON *Wks.* 63, I look'd for sparkling lines, and something gay To frisk my fancy with.

4. *slang.* **a.** To search (a person or place); esp. to run the hand rapidly over (a person or his clothing), in a search for a concealed weapon, stolen goods, etc. **b.** To hoax.

1789 G. PARKER *Life's Painter* xv. 179 They *frisk* him, that is, search him. **1812** J. H. VAUX *Flash Dict.*, *Frisk*, to search; *to frisk a cly* is to empty a pocket of its contents; to stand *frisk* is to stand search. **1825** C. M. WESTMACOTT *Eng. Spy* I. 150 Has Tom been frisking you already with some of his jokes? **1920** I. OSTRANDER *How Many Cards?* 65 When you frisk this man Hill at Headquarters, if you find a pair of gloves on him keep them aside till I get there. **1929** C. E. MERRIAM *Chicago* 289 To take the police away from the task of frisking hip pockets and inspecting refrigerators. **1930** E. V. KNOX in *Punch* 26 Feb. 236 His arm was twisted during the course of the interview, and his person was frisked on the chance of finding a gun. **1937** 'N. BLAKE' *There's Trouble Brewing* iii. 52 'Frisk him, Sergeant.'..The cleaner had to submit to a thorough examination of his pockets and person. **1940** R. STOUT *Over my Dead Body* xiii. 13 The place has been frisked by someone in a hurry. **1955** *Times* 25 June 6/4 At a local exhibition several similar discs were handed to members of the public to hide in their clothing before being 'frisked' with a geiger counter. **1959** 'A. GILBERT' *Death takes Wife* xv. 198 Put down money for a joint you didn't frisk in advance. **1970** *New Statesman* 23 Oct. 520/2 Showing his teeth in a vicious snarl as they frisk him and open his jacket to feel under his arm.

friskal, var. of FRISCAL.

frisker ('frıskə(r)). Also frysker. [f. FRISK *v.* + -ER[1].] One who or that which frisks. Also *slang* (see the *vb.* 4 a), a pilferer.

1547 BOORDE *Introd. Knowl.* (1870) 117 Now I am a frysker, all men doth on me looke. **1633** MARMION *Fine Companion* G ij, He tells thee right, my brave Frisker. **1719** D'URFEY *Pills* II. 20 Such Fraysters and Friskers as these Lads and Lasses. **1842** BROWNING *Pied Piper*, Grave old plodders, gay young friskers. **1892** *Star* 6 Feb. 3/4 A dangerous gang of 'till friskers'.

†'**frisket**[1]. *Obs rare*[−1]. [Meaning and origin doubtful: cf. OF. *friquet* a small lively sparrow.]

c **1602** in Nichols *Progr. Q. Eliz.* III. 586 The chatting of pyes, and the chirkinge of the friskets.

frisket[2] ('frıskıt). *Printing.* [ad. Fr. *frisquette*, of unknown origin.] A thin iron frame hinged to the tympan, having tapes or paper strips stretched across it, for keeping the sheet in position while printing. *to fly the frisket*: see FLY *v.*[2] 2.

1683 MOXON *Mech. Exerc.* II. 55 Which..serves for the Frisket to move truly upon. **1777** HOOLE *Comenius' Vis. World* (ed. 12) 118 The pressman beateth it over with printers ink..spreadeth upon it the papers put in the frisket. **1824** J. JOHNSON *Typogr.* II. 526 To catch the bottom of the sheet when the frisket rises and conveys it quickly and gently to the catch. **1884** *West. Morn. News* 23 Apr. 5/2 A press frisket was thrown down.

attrib. **1683** MOXON *Mech. Exerc.* II. 55 From the Fore-end or Frisket-joynt. **1825** J. NICHOLSON *Operat. Mechanic* 308 The clerk now inks the type with a printer's ball, opens the frisket sheet..on its hinges, and places the note..against the tympan. **1880** *Printing Times* 15 Mar. Advt., Frisket forks are so arranged that, etc.

friskful ('frıskfʊl), *a. rare.* [f. FRISK *sb.* or *v.* + -FUL.] Apt to frisk, frolicsome.

1728-46 THOMSON *Spring* 836 His sportive lambs..in friskful glee, Their frolics play. **1876** F. LOCKER *Bramble-Rise* viii. in *Lond. Lyr.*, My little friskful daughter.

†'**friskin.** *Obs.* Also 6 fruskin, 7 frisquin. [f. FRISK *sb.* or *v.* + *-in* (? for -ING[1]).]

1. A brisk lively action; a frolic, playful encounter. *to try a friskin*: to have a brush (see BRUSH *sb.*[3] 1). Also *to dance friskin*.

1570 LEVINS *Manip.* 133 Fruskin, *saltus*. **1599** NASHE *Lenten Stuffe* To Rdr. (1871) 18 This is a light friskin of my wit. **1612** *Two Noble K.* IV. iii, The pranks And friskins of her madness. **1621** BURTON *Anat. Mel.* III. ii. III. iii. (1651) 472 It was the custome of some lascivious queans to dance friskin in that fashion. **1675-93** CROWNE *Country Wit* I. Dram. Wks. 1874 III. 34 Yes, Betty Frisque and you shall try a frisquin for him,—you shall duel it, you shall.

2. A gay frisky person.

1596 NASHE *Saffron Walden* 143 His Wench or Friskin was footing it aloft on the greene. **1602** DEKKER *Satirom.* Dram. Wks. 1873 I. 217 *Sir Q.* I gaue thee this chaine, manlie Tucca. *Tuc.* I, sayst thou so, Friskin.

frisking ('frıskıŋ), *vbl. sb.* [f. FRISK *v.* + -ING[1].] In senses of the vb.

1553 tr. *Beza's Admonit. Parl.* (1566) G iij b, The Lords Supper..is transformed into..olde stagelike frisking and horrible Idol gadding. **1611** COTGR. s.v. *Gambade*, Old peoples frisking doth presage their ending. **1725** BRADLEY *Fam. Dict.* s.v. *Nose*, If it [the Blood] proceeds from a Vein, it is thicker and redder, and runs without any frisking. **1867** SMYTH *Sailor's Word-bk.*, *Frisking*, the wind freshening. **1890** *Spectator* 3 May 624/1 And the lambs bleat!.. And their friskings, and their races! **1913** H. A. FRANCK *Zone Policeman 88* v. 140 We..gave them and their baggage such a 'frisking' as befalls a kaffir leaving a South African diamond mine. **1938** M. ALLINGHAM *Fashion in Shrouds* xix.

342 She only admitted one person at a time into the room, and then only after a keen visual 'frisking'. **1958** S. ELLIN *Eighth Circle* II. xviii. 141 It was a professional frisking, down to the way his wrist watch..and pen were removed and examined. **1968** *New Scientist* 9 May 288/3 These [uses] included alarm devices in the entrances to banks and aircraft and as a police tool for the 'frisking' of the public. **1971** *Times* 7 May 2/3 (*headline*) Judge rejects protest over frisking.

frisking (ˈfrɪskɪŋ), *ppl. a.* [f. FRISK *v.* + -ING[2].] That frisks, in senses of the vb. †Of wine: Sparkling.

1566 DRANT *Horace's Sat.* I. F ij, Fragrant friskyng wyne. **1610** *Dr. Dodypoll* III. i. in Bullen *O. Pl.* III. 122 A fine frisking usher in a dauncing schoole. **1697** DRYDEN *Virg. Georg.* III. 105 The quick Motions of the frisking Tail. **1725** POPE *Odyss.* XIII. 296 The bounding goats and frisking heifers rove. **1827** CARLYLE *Misc.* (1857) I. 21 A certain snappishness—a frisking abruptness.

Hence ˈ**friskingly** *adv.*, in a frisking or frisky manner.

In mod. Dicts.

friskle, var. of FRISCAL.

frisky (ˈfrɪskɪ), *a.* Also 6 **frysky, friscay**, [f. FRISK *sb.* + -Y[1].] Given to frisking; lively; playful.

?*a* **1500** *Ragman Roll* 132 in Hazl. *E.P.P.* I. 75 And your foot ye tappyn, and ye daunce, Thogh hit the fryskyst horse were in a towne. **1525** LD. BERNERS *Froiss.* II. clx. [clvi.] 279 a, The lorde of Clary..was a frisca, and a lusty knyght. **1743** J. DAVIDSON *Æneid* VII. 203 By the Heat in Frisky Bells the Liquors dance. **1780** MAD. D'ARBLAY *Lett.* July, She was as gay, flighty, entertaining, and frisky as ever. **1812** BYRON *Waltz* vii, His Sancho thought The knight's fandango friskier than it ought. **1861** L. L. NOBLE *Icebergs* 291 Away they trip it, like so many frisky buffalo calves. **1875** J. H. BENNET *Winter Medit.* III. xv. 500 The Negroes ..of all ages, from frisky merry little children to decrepit old men. **1885** *Manch. Exam.* 2 May 6/2 The dogs, at once sagacious and frisky, have been admirably drawn.

Hence ˈ**friskily** *adv.*, in a frisky manner; ˈ**friskiness**, the quality or state of being frisky.

1727 BAILEY, *Friskiness*. **1778** MAD. D'ARBLAY *Diary* 3 Aug., I left him..to make his own comments upon my friskiness. **1862** LYTTON *Str. Story* II. 74 The white bear gambols..friskily after his meal on human flesh. **1865** *Sat. Rev.* 5 Aug. 172 An outpouring of intellectual friskiness. **1894** *Daily News* 20 Mar. 3/1 The brims to hats are friskily curved.

†ˈ**frislet.** *Obs. rare*$^{-1}$. [? f. OF. *fresel*, dim. of *fraise* ruff + -ET[1].] 'A kind of small ruffle' (Halliwell).

1607 BREWER *Lingua* IV. vi, Partlets, Frislets, Bandlets.

frisole, var. of FRIJOLE.

†ˈ**Frison**[1]. *Obs.* Forms: 4 **frysoun**, 5 **freson(e, -un.** [a. OF. *frison*, ad. late L. *frison-em* a Frisian.] **a.** A native of Friesland. **b.** A Friesland horse.

1303 R. BRUNNE *Handl. Synne* 10663 A frysoun ȝe shul vndyrstande To a marchaunde of fryslande. ?*a* **1400** *Morte Arth.* 1365 A freke..Come forthermaste on a fresone in flawmande wedes. *c* **1420** *Anturs of Arth.* xxxi, The freson was afrayet, and ferd of that fare.

†**frison**[2]. *Obs.* [a. F. *frison* (1474 in Godef.); Littré and Hatz.-Darm. derive it from *friser* FRIEZE *v.*[1]] ? Some kind of woollen stuff. Also ***frison-stuff***.

1562 *Stanford Churchw. Acct.* in *Antiquary* (April 1888) 168 For ij lodes of ffrysons ijs. **1714** *French Bk. Rates* 69 Frizon-Stuffs, 13 Ells.

†**frisoneer.** *Obs.* ? = prec.

1700 CONGREVE *Way of World* V. i, Go, hang out an old Frisoneer-gorget.

frisque, frisquin, obs. ff. FRISK, FRISKIN.

‖**frisson** (frisɔ̃). [Fr., shiver, thrill.] An emotional thrill.

1777 H. WALPOLE *Let.* 8 Oct. (1904) X. 130, I tore open the sacred box with..little reverence... No holy *frisson*, no involuntary tear warned me. **1903** A. BENNETT *Truth abt. Author* xii. 156 The cult of the literary *frisson*. **1920** *Public Opinion* 24 Sept. 290/1 There had been a frisson of horror because the enemy was over the Marne. **1956** B. RUSSELL *Portraits from Memory* 203 They rather enjoyed the *frisson* that its horrors gave them. **1967** *Times* 24 May 8/4 She provides that indescribable *frisson* which is the prerogative of only a few singers in each generation. **1971** *Observer* 31 Oct. 11/4 The dramatist seemed to have projected him on stage first to grip the audience with a frisson of alarm and impending melodrama.

frist, *sb. Obs.* exc. *arch.* Forms: 1 **first, fyrst, frist**, 2–4 **first(e**, *south.* **virst**, (3 **ferst, feorst, forst**), 3–4 **furst (y)**, 3–5 **fres(s)t**, (4 **freist**), 4 **friste**, 5 **fryst**, 5– **frist.** [OE. *first, fyrst, frist* masc. Cf. OFris. *first, ferst* neut., OS. *frist*, OHG. *frist* fem. (neut.) (MHG. *vrist*, Ger. *frist* fem.), ON. *frest* neut. pl. (fem. sing.).]

1. A space of time, time; a certain time.

Beowulf 134 Næs hit lengra fyrst. *O.E. Chron.* an. 918 Oþ þone first þe hie wurdon swiþe metelease. *a* **1175** *Cott. Hom.* 229 Furtie daȝen firste [he] ham mid wnede. *c* **1205** LAY. 12242 Wið innen ane ȝere, nes þer first na mare, iwrað þe king Gracien gumene forcuðest.

2. Delay, respite; also, a truce. *to do in* or *a* (= *on*) *frist*: to delay, procrastinate, give respite of. *of* or *on frist*: (*Sc.*) in the future, at a distance. *to frist*: on loan or credit.

c **1175** *Lamb. Hom.* 71 Ure deð he do in firste ȝet. *c* **1200** *Moral Ode* 38 Ne scholde nomon don a virst ne slakien wel to donne. *a* **1300** *Cursor M.* 19225 þe penis..he broght, witvten frest. *c* **1300** *Beket* 890 For-to þe nexte daie we biddez furst. **1375** BARBOUR *Bruce* II. 277 At to morn, but langar frest, ȝe sall isch furth. **1387** TREVISA *Higden* (Rolls) VII. 49 First of ten dayes were i-graunted. **14..** *Tundale's Vis.* 60 He wold gyve dayes for his best But he sold the derur for the fryst. *c* **1440** *Promp. Parv.* 178/2 Freste, or to frest yn byynge or borowynge, *mutuum*. ?*c* **1450** *How goode wif taught doughter* 161 in Hazl. *E.P.P.* I. 191 Borow nought blethely, ne take nought frest. *a* **1555** LYNDESAY *Peder Coffeis* 43 Ane dyvour coffe..Takis gudis to frist fra fremmit men. **1888** *Murray's Mag.* Apr. 497 My time is short, my frist is o'er, and I have much to say.

attrib. **1387** TREVISA *Higden* (Rolls) VII. 49 þe firste dayes.

Proverb. (*Sc.*) *c* **1565** LINDESAY (Pitscottie) *Chron. Scot.* (1814) I. 238 All thir lordis war verrie blyth, thinking that all evil was guid of frist. **1808–80** JAMIESON *s.v.*, All ills are good a frist.

†**frist**, *v. Obs.* Forms: see the sb. [f. the sb.; cf. OFris. *fersta*, OHG. *fristen, fristôn* (MHG. *vristen*, mod.Ger. *fristen*), ON. *fresta*, (Sw. *frista*, Da. *friste*).]

1. *intr.* To delay, grant respite. Also *to frist it*.

a **1225** *St. Marher.* 15 þæt ha ne firsten hit nawiht to schawen hit ischrifte. *a* **1225** *Leg. Kath.* 2331 Nawiht, King, ne kepe ich þæt tu hit fir firsti. **13..** *E.E. Allit. P.* B. 743 þaȝ faurty forfete ȝet fryst I a whyle. **1535** STEWART *Cron. Scot.* (1858) I. 162 Thairof wald delay no langar nor frist.

2. a. with *dat.* passing into *trans.* To grant delay to (a person); to respite. **b.** *trans.* To put off, delay (a thing); to postpone the enjoyment of.

a **1225** *Leg. Kath.* 2399 þæt he, for his freolec firstede hire. **1340** *Ayenb.* 173 And naȝt ne uerste uram daye to daye. **1570** *Satir. Poems Reform.* xvi. 71 Thocht he be fristit at this tyme, He will not be forgeuin. **1637** RUTHERFORD *Lett.* clxxx. (1848) 345, I would frist heaven for many years.

3. *trans.* **a.** To lend or give (a thing) on credit. **b.** To give (a debtor) credit or time for payment. **c.** To grant time for payment of (a debt).

c **1440** *Promp. Parv.* 178/2 Frestyn, or lende to freste. **1549** *Compl. Scot.* xv. 124 Quhen I laubyr..be mecanik craftis, I am compellit to len and to fyrst it to my tua cruel briethr. **1632** RUTHERFORD *Lett.* lxxxix. (1848) 165 That debt is not forgiven, but fristed. **1637** *Ibid.* cv. 202 Frist Christ; He is an honest debtor. *Ibid.* cclxvii. 527, I am content; my faith will frist God my happiness. **1691** RAY *N.C. Words, Frist*, to trust for a Time.

absol. **14..** *Rel. Ant.* I. 316 Kype and save, and thou schalle have; Frest and leve, and thou schall crave.

Proverb. **1718** RAMSAY *Christis Kirke Gr.* III. iii, What aft fristed's no forgien. **1824** SCOTT *Redgauntlet* ch. xi, What is fristed is not forgiven.

Hence ˈ**fristed** *ppl. a.*, ˈ**fristing** *vbl. sb.*

14.. *Tundale's Vis.* 55 For frystyng wold he ocur take And nothyng leyn for Goddis sake. *a* **1605** MONTGOMERIE *Misc. Poems* v. 45 Sen fristed goods ar not forgivin, Quhen cuppe is full, then hold it evin. **1637** RUTHERFORD *Lett.* ccxxvi. (1848) 443 A suspension and a fristing of my heaven. *Ibid.* ccxi. 413 Few know the pain and torment of Christ's fristed love.

frist(e, obs. form of FIRST.

†ˈ**fristel(l)e.** *Obs.* [a. OF. *frestel(e.)*] A flute.

c **1400** *Ywaine & Gaw.* 1396 Damysels danceand ful wele, With trompes, pipes, and with fristele. **1483** *Cath. Angl.* 143 Fristelle, *fistula*.

†ˈ**frister.** *Obs. rare*$^{-1}$. [a. Du. *vrijster* = *vrijdster* 'amasia, virgo nubilis' (Kilian), f. *vrij(d)en* to woo, court.] A sweetheart.

1640 GLAPTHORNE *Wallenstein* I. iii, A short coat frister, That as she milkes each morning, Bedews the coole grasse with her Virgin moisture.

ˈ**frisure.** Also **frizure.** [a. Fr. *frisure*, f. *friser*: see FRIZZ.] Mode or fashion of curling the hair.

1755 *Lond. Mag.* July 343 Let an artificial flow'r Set the frisure off before. **1771** SMOLLETT *Humph. Cl.* II. 18 July Let. i, She was most remarkable for the frisure of her head. **1773** GRAVES *Spirit. Quixote* v. vii. 285 Though it had not received the fashionable frizure, it was grown..long enough to curl. **1790–1811** COMBE *Devil upon 2 Sticks in Eng.* (1817) IV. 23 The immense expanding frisure of 1780. **1927** *Daily Express* 4 Oct. 9/6 Other resolutions declared that bobbed and shingled heads should have a higher frisure than formerly.

†**frit**, *sb.*[1] [a. Fr. *frit*, pa. pple. of *frire* to fry.] ? Toast.

14.. *Anc. Cookery* in *Househ. Ord.* (1790) 449 Daryolus, and leche-fryes, made of frit and friture.

frit (frɪt), *sb.*[2] Also 7–9 **fritt.** [ad. (directly or through F. *fritte*) It. *fritta*, fem. pa. pple. of *friggĕre* to FRY.]

1. *Glass-making.* A calcined mixture of sand and fluxes ready to be melted in a crucible to form glass.

1662 MERRETT tr. *Neri's Art of Glass* 17 Fritt is nothing else but a calcination of those materials which make glass. **1773** FRANKLIN *Lett.* Wks. 1840 V. 461 The globe in question was of this frit. **1800** tr. *Lagrange's Chem.* I. 415 The product is a kind of vitreous frit, soluble in water. **1853** URE *Dict. Arts* I. 908 The founding-pots are filled up with these blocks of frit. **1870** T. W. WEBB in *Eng. Mech.* 21 Jan. 448/1 Specks of 'frit' (unmelted material in the substance of the glass).

2. *Ceramics.* The vitreous composition from which soft porcelain is made.

1791 E. DARWIN *Bot. Gard.* I. Notes 39 The frit of the potters..is liable to crack in drying. **1832** G. R. PORTER *Porcelain & Gl.* 43 A frit compounded of nitre, soda, alum and selenite. **1875** FORTNUM *Majolica* i. 2 A loose frit or body, to which an enamel adheres.

3. *attrib.* and *Comb.*, as ***frit-brick, -mixer, -powder***. Also **frit-porcelain** (see quot.).

1853 URE *Dict. Arts* I. 908 These frit-bricks are afterwards piled up in a large apartment for use. **1874** KNIGHT *Dict. Mech.* I. 917 A *frit-mixer* is a horizontal cylinder with oblique beaters, or a box with semi-cylindrical bottom and a rotating shaft with beaters or stirring arms. **1881** *Porcelain Works, Worcester* 15 This fritt powder is used along with borax and other materials. **1889** *Century Dict., Frit procelain*, a name given to the artificial soft-paste English porcelain.

frit (frɪt), *v.* [f. FRIT *sb.*[2]] *trans.* To make into frit; to fuse partially; to calcine. Hence ˈ**fritted** *ppl. a.*, ˈ**fritting** *vbl. sb.*; also *attrib.*

1805–17 R. JAMESON *Char. Min.* (ed. 3) 295 *Fritting*, when single parts of the mass are melted, while others remain unaltered. **1832** G. R. PORTER *Porcelain & Gl.* vi. 199 The sand, lime, soda, and manganese, being properly intermingled, are fritted in small furnaces. **1853** URE *Dict. Arts* I. 908 When the fourth hour has expired the fritting operation is finished. **1879** RUTLEY *Stud. Rocks* xiv. 291 Porcelain jasper has a fused or fritted appearance. **1881** RAYMOND *Mining Gloss., Fritting*, the formation of a slag by heat with but incipient fusion. **1881** *Harper's Mag.* Feb. 364 These..are fritted or melted in an oven till they run like molasses.

frit, *a.* Dial. and colloq. pa. pple. of FRIGHT *v.* 2 a.

ˈ**frit-fly.** A small fly of the genus *Oscinis*, destructive to wheat.

1881 MISS E. A. ORMEROD *Injur. Insects* (1890) 92 The Frit Fly is a small, black, shining, two-winged fly. **1893** *Jrnl. R. Agric. Soc.* Dec. 827 Some other pests..are wire-worms, crane-fly, frit-fly..and winter-moth.

frith, *sb.*[1] *Obs.* exc. *Hist.* [Com. Teut.: OE. *friðu, frioðu, freoðu* str. masc. and fem., *frið* str. neut., = OFris. *fretho, frede, ferd*, OS. *frithu* masc. (MDu. *vrēde, verde*, Du. *vrede* masc.), OHG. *fridu* (MHG. *vride*, mod.G. *friede*), ON. *frið-r* (Sw., Da. *fred*), Goth. **friþu-s* (in comb. *Friþareiks* = Frederick); f. OTeut. root **fri-* to love: see FRIEND.]

1. Peace; freedom from molestation, protection; safety, security.

c **893** K. ÆLFRED *Oros.* v. ii. §8 He ȝenom friþ wiþ þæt folc. *c* **950** *Lindisf. Gosp.* Matt. x. 34 Ne cuom ic frið sende ah suord. *O.E. Chron.* an. 1011 (Laud MS.), þonne nam man grið & frið wið hi. *c* **1175** *Lamb. Hom.* 13 Londe þet bið on griðe and on friðe under mire onwalde. *c* **1250** *Gen. & Ex.* 681 Euerilc man he gaf lif and frið ðat to ðat likenesse soȝte grið. *c* **1330** R. BRUNNE *Chron.* (1810) 90 þat bataile was hard, fo men has no frith. *c* **1380** WYCLIF *Wks.* (1880) 289 ȝif þes poscessioneris toke freþis in here lond. **1874** GREEN *Short Hist.* i. §5. 45 Their leader was bound by a solemn peace or 'frith'.

†**2. a.** A game-preserve, deer-park. **b.** *water frith*: a place where the fishing is preserved. *Obs.*

OE. had *déor-frið* in the abstract sense 'protection of game' (*OE. Chron.* an. 1086).

c **1205** LAY. 1432 ȝe huntieð i þes kinges friðe [*c* **1275** parc]. **1584** in Binnell *Descr. Thames* 63 Places inhibited to fish in, called Water Friths.

3. *Comb.*: **frith-guild**, a guild established for the maintenance of peace; also *attrib.*; **frith-silver**, ? some feudal payment (see quots.); **frithsoken** *OE.* and *Hist.*, an asylum, a sanctuary (the later explanations seem to be baseless conjectures).

a **1000** *Law of Æthelstan* VI. c. 8 §9 (Schmid), Gif ure hlaford..us æniȝne eacan ȝeþæncean mæȝe to urum *friðgildum. **1861** PEARSON *Early & Mid. Ages Eng.* 128 The frank-pledge or frith-guild system had been vigorously enforced under Edward. **1874** GREEN *Short Hist.* iv. §4. 190 The tendency to unite in such 'Frith-gilds' or Peace-clubs became general throughout Europe. **1669** in E. Salt *Hist. Standon* (1888) 114 It was agreed..that John Hardinge shall sett a gate..he payinge yearly the *frith selver of the towne. **1863** *N. & Q.* Ser. III. IV. 477 *Frith-silver*, up to the last fifteen or twenty years, a payment, chargeable on the poor rates of the parish [Alrewas, Lichfield], was annually made to Lord Somers, and bore the above name. **1014** *Laws of Ethelred* VIII. c. 1 (Schmid), Ðæt he *friðsocne..ȝesece. *c* **1250** *Gloss. Law Terms* in *Rel. Ant.* I. 33 *Frithsocne*, Franchise de francplege. *a* **1342** HIGDEN *Polychr.* (Rolls) II. 94 Frithsoken, id est, tutatio in jurisdictione; Gallice, seurte en defence.

frith (frɪθ), *sb.*[2] Forms: 1 **(ȝe)fyrhðe, fyr(h)ð**, 4 **friht, fryht**, 5 **freth**, 9 *Kent.* **fright** (-*wood*, 6 **fryth(e**, 3– **frith.** Also FIRTH *sb.*[1] [OE. *(ȝe)fyrhðe* str. neut. (also *fyrhð* str. fem.):—OTeut. type **(ga)furhiþjo*^{m} (see below). In ME. and in mod.E. the word seems to have been confused with others of similar sound: see the remarks under senses 1 and 4 below.

The OTeut. type **(ga)furhiþjo*^{m} would appear to be a collective f. **furhā* FIR; but there is no trace in Eng. of the etymological sense 'fir-wood', and as firs seem to have been not very abundant in early times in this country, the development of the general sense 'wooded or waste land' must have taken place on the continent. Cf., however, the mod.Ger. *forchdistel*, *forchgras*, *forchheide* (Grimm), which seem to contain a word that may be the source of med.L. *frocus* (OF. *frou*) waste land; if so *fyrhðe* may be derived from it.

With regard to the form-history in Eng., the reduced form *fyrðe* is represented by FIRTH *sb.*[1], and with metathesis by *frith*. The fuller form *fyrhðe* is represented, with metathesis, by ME. *friht*, mod.Kentish *fright-wood*.

The Welsh *ffridd*, *ffrith*, often given as the etymon, are adopted forms of the Eng. word.

To the scanty evidence for the OE. *fyrhð(e* must be added the place-name Pirbright in Surrey, which in documents of 13th and 14th c. appears as Pirifirith, Pirifright, Pirifrith, Purifright:—OE. **piriȝ-fyrhðe* pear-'frith': see *Cal. Close Rolls* 1326 p. 622, Manning & Bray *Surrey* I. 145, *Surrey Fines* (Surrey Archæol. Soc.) 22.]

1. With uncertain meaning, denoting a wood of some kind, or wooded country collectively, *esp.* in poet. phrases associated with *fell*, *field*.

In the later quots. the word occurs only as a poetical archaism of vague meaning. In the earlier quots. it may have had the more definite sense explained under 2. In senses 1, 2 there may be confusion with FRITH *sb.*[1] 2 a.

?**826** *Charter of Ecgberht* in Birch *Cart. Sax.* I. 545 þonne on þone haȝan to witan fyrðe. **898** *Charter of Ælfred* (Farleigh, Kent) ibid. II. 220 Ðonne is ðæt suð land ȝemære ðæs cinges west andlang ðæs fyrhðes oð ðone bradan weȝ. ?**956** *Charter of Eadwig* ibid. III. 120 Of þan stapole on accan ȝefyrhðe. **973–4** (MS. 12th c.) *Charter of Eadgar* (Hants) ibid. III. 632 On ðet wot treow æt ðere baran fyrhðe. *a* **1300** *Cursor M.* 7697 In feild and tun, in frith and fell. *a* **1310** in Wright's *Lyric P.* x. 36 In a fryht . . y founde a wel feyr fenge to fere. *c* **1320** *Kyng & Hermit* 20 in Hazl. *E.P.P.* I. 13 The grete herte for to hunte, In frythys and in felle. *c* **1350** *Will. Palerne* 2216 þei trauailed al a niȝt, out of forest & friþes & alle faire wodes. **1377** Langl. *P. Pl.* B. xii. 219 And of the floures in the fryth and of her feire hewes. **1562** Phaer *Æneid* ix. Aa iij, A Pynetree frith I had [Lat. *pinea silva mihi*]. **1573–80** Golding *To Rdr.* in *Baret's Alv.* A v/1 In plant, or tree, By natures gift abroad in frith and feeld. **1612** Drayton *Poly-olb.* xi. 174 As over Holt and Heath, as thorough Frith [*margin*, high wood] and Fell. **1855** Bailey *Mystic* 83 Where now stretch Forest and upland frith.

2. A piece of land grown sparsely with trees or with underwood only. Also, a space between woods; unused pasture land (see quots.). Now only *dial.*

1538 Leland *Itin.* (ed. 2, 1745) II. 3 From Maidenhedde Town a 2 Miles by narow wooddy Way to the Frithe, and so thorough the Frithe 3 Miles. *Ibid.* (*margin*), *Fruticea Sylva*, Angl. Frithe. **1628** Coke *On Litt.* 5 b, Frythe is a plain between woods. **1641** *N. Riding Rec.* IV. 216 The inhabitants of Sheriff Hutton presented for not repairing the high-way leading to le Frith. **1790** Mrs. Wheeler *Westmld. Dial.* (1840), *Frith*, unused pasture land. **1869** in *Lonsdale Gloss.* **1887** *Kentish Gloss.*, *Frith* . . a thin, scrubby wood, with little or no timber, and consisting mainly of inferior growths. **1892** *Northumbld. Gloss.*, *Frith*, a clearing in a forest.

3. Brushwood, underwood; sometimes forming a hedge, hedgewood.

1605 *Rec. Chippenham* 194 in *Wilts Gloss.* (1893) s.v., Itm to James Smalwood for an Acre and halfe of hedginge frith out of Heywood . . Item for felling the same frith. **1631** Markham *Weald of Kent* ii. i. (1668) 2 It will grow to frith or wood, if it be not continually . . laboured with the plough. **1668** Worlidge *Dict. Rust.*, *Frith*, underwood, or the shroud of Trees. **1670** J. Smith *England's Improv. Reviv'd* 27 A dead Hedge . . made of dead wood, as Bushes and Frith, which is all sorts of small wood that are not Thorns. *Ibid.* 31 Frith . . is all small lops or shreadings of trees, as also all Under-woods. **1796** W. Marshall *W. England* I. 326 *Frith*, brush-wood. **1813** T. Davis *Agric. Wilts* 267 *Frith*, thorns or bush underwood. **1853** W. D. Cooper *Sussex Gloss.* (ed. 2), *Frith*, young underwood growing by the side of hedges. **1863** Wise *New Forest* 183 Frith, too, still means copse-wood.

4. A hedge; *esp.* one made of wattled brushwood; also, a hurdle.

[Although this sense appears to be chiefly a development of sense 3, it may partly belong to other words of similar form but etymologically unconnected. (1) The sense 'hedge', and the related FRITH *v.*[2] 1, might without difficulty be regarded as special uses of FRITH *sb.*[1] and *v.*[1]; cf. MHG. *vride* (= FRITH *sb.*[1]) used in the senses of 'fence, fenced place', mod.Ger. *einfriedigen* to fence in. (2) As in S.W. dialects both *fr-* and *wr-* are represented by *vr-*, it is possible that *frith* in the sense of 'wattled work' may be partly a literary rendering of a dialectal *vrith*, *vreath* connected with OE. *wríðan* (see WRITHE, WREATHE).]

[*c* **1430** *Durh. MS. Cell. Roll*, Item in fridys, vj*d.* Item in cirpis, vj*d.*] **1511–1647** *MS. Acc. St. John's Hosp., Canterb.* in *Kent. Gloss.* s.v., To enclose the vij acres wt. a quyk fryth before the Fest of the Purification. **1810** *Voc. Dev. & Cornw.* in *Monthly Mag.* XXIX. 466 *Frith*, *writh*, wattles or hurdles, placed in a gap. **1864** T. Q. Couch *E. Cornwall Wds.* in *Jrnl. Roy. Inst. Cornw.* Mar., *Freath*, or *Vreath*, a wattled gap in a hedge. **1884** *Blackw. Mag.* CXXXVI. 785/1, I was getting over a frith [*foot-note*, hurdle] by Nicholls's cow-house. **1887** *Kent. Gloss.*, *Frith*, a hedge.

†**b.** The same used as a fish-weir. *Obs.*

1602 Carew *Cornwall* 30 The Weare is a frith, reaching slope-wise through the Ose, from the land to low water marke, and hauing in it, a bunt or cod with an eye-hooke, where the fish entering, vpon their comming backe with the ebbe are stopped from issuing out againe . . and left drie on the Ose.

5. *attrib.* and *Comb.*, as †***frith-copse***, †***-man***, ***-wood***; †**frith-pear**, the name of a kind of pear; **frith-work** (*dial.*), wattling.

1583 Stanyhurst *Æneis* i. (Arb.) 32 In this greene *frith-cops a new sight newly repressed Long feareful dangers. *a* **1400–50** *Alexander* 5597 Fiue thousand olifants in fere þa *frithmenn him broȝt. **1664** Evelyn *Kal. Hort.* (1729) 217 **Frith-Pears, Arundel-Pears* (also to bake). **1887** *Kent. Gloss.* s.v. *Frith*, Though some of the old woods bearing this name may now, by modern treatment, have been made much thicker and more valuable, they are also still called, as of old, *fright-woods, as the Fright Woods, near Bedgebury. **1807** Vancouver *Agric. Devon* (1813) 134 The *frithe-work or wattling was made upon willow or sallow stakes.

frith (frɪθ), *sb.*[3] [Metathetic form of FIRTH *sb.*[2]; possibly suggested by the form FRITH *sb.*[2] = FIRTH *sb.*[1], or by the once commonly supposed derivation from L. *fretum.*] = FIRTH[2].

1600 Holland *Livy* 1375 The Tyber . . brake out many times, and having found a frith or creeke, it beat upon the foot of the Aventine. **1667** Milton *P.L.* ii. 919 The warie fiend Stood . . Pondering his Voyage; for no narrow frith He had to cross. *a* **1698** Temple *Hist. Eng.* (1699) 37 The Neck of Land between the two Fryths about Sterling and Glasco. **1722** De Foe *Col. Jack* (1840) 243 Waiting to go up the frith with the flood. **1784** Cowper *Task* ii. 16 Lands intersected by a narrow frith Abhor each other. **1806** *Gazetteer Scotl.* Introd. 7 The Friths of Forth and Clyde. **1850** Tennyson *In Mem.* Concl. 115 The friths that branch and spread Their sleeping silver thro' the hills.

†**frith**, *v.*[1] *Obs.* Also 3 **fruðie**, 4 *south.* **vreþie**, 5 **frethe**. [OE. *friðian*, *freoðian*, f. FRITH *sb.*[1]; cf. OFris. *frethia*, *ferdia*, OS. *frithôn*, OHG. *(ga-)fridôn*, ON. *friða* (Sw. *freda*, Da. *frede*). Cf. FREITH *v.*]

1. *trans.* To keep in peace, make peace with; to secure from disturbance, defend, help, preserve, protect.

c **893** K. Ælfred *Oros.* iv. i. §9 Angunnan þa herȝean & hienan þa þe hie friþian sceoldon. *O.E. Chron.* an. 921 þæt hie . . eall þæt friþian woldon þæt se cyng friþian wolde. *c* **1175** *Lamb. Hom.* 15 Eower lond ic wulle friþian. *c* **1205** Lay. 16804 ȝif . . þu me wult fruðien we þe wulleð to teon. *a* **1300** *Cursor M.* 24133 þou frith me noght als freind. *c* **1330** R. Brunne *Chron. Wace* (Rolls) 8733 þeyr buryels he þoughte for to honure Wyþ som þyng þat ay myght dure, & ffryþe þe stede þer þey lay. **1340** *Ayenb.* 7 Me ssel hine loky and ureþie zo holyliche. ?*a* **1400** *Morte Arth.* 656 Fannde my fforestez be ffrythede . . That nane werreye my wylde.

2. To free, liberate. Cf. FREITH *v.*

c **1250** *Gen. & Ex.* 3094 Bi-sek ȝet god, ðis one siðe, ðat he vs of ðis pine friðe. **1470** Harding *Chron.* clxix. v, Then was Vmfrey erle of Herford frethed clene, And enterchaungid for Kyng Robertes wife.

frith (frɪθ), *v.*[2] *Obs.* exc. *dial.* Also 4 **frethe**, 9 *dial.* **freath**. [f. FRITH *sb.*[2] (senses 3, 4); but perh. of mixed derivation: see note under FRITH *sb.*[2] 4.]

1. *trans.* To fence in. Also *fig.*

1377 Langl. *P. Pl.* B. v. 590 He is frithed in with floreines. ?*a* **1400** *Morte Arth.* 3247 Froytez . . ffaire frithed in frawnke appone tha free bowes. *c* **1400** *Beryn* 292 The sauge & the Isope, I-frethid & I-stakid. **1541** *Old Ways* (1892) 110 Walter was cuttyng off a hagge to frithe a corne.

2. *intr.* **a.** To form a hedge of wattled brushwood; to wattle. **b.** To cut underwood. **c.** (See quot. 1893.)

1807 Vancouver *Agric. Devon* (1813) 132 Frithing, or wattling with willow-stakes, or any other hardy wood. **1847–78** Halliwell, *Frith*, to plash a hedge. *Devon.* **1866** Blackmore *C. Nowell* l, A labourer . . had been frithing: that is to say, cutting underwood in one of the forest copses. **1893** *Wiltsh. Gloss.*, *Frith*, to make a brushwood drain.

Hence '**frithing**, material for fencing; brushwood, underwood.

1429 *Durh. MS. Cell. Roll*, In ij Draghtrapis et iij frethyng', xix*d.* **1866** Blackmore *C. Nowell* xlv, The frithings have not been cut for ten years.

†'**frithborh**. *Law.* Only *OE.* and *Hist.* Also **frithborg, -burg, frichborgh, fridburgh, friborg(h, -burg(h, -bourg, freoborg, freeborgh**. [OE. **friðborh* lit. 'peace-pledge': see FRITH *sb.*[1] and BORROW *sb.*; the word, though found in no document earlier than the spurious 'Laws of Edward the Confessor' (app. the source of all the later statements on the subject), is certainly genuine. A mistranslation of the corrupt form *friborg*, *freoborg* gave rise to the later name FRANKPLEDGE.] The Old English name for FRANKPLEDGE.

a **1200** *Laws of Edw. Conf.* c. 20 Preamble (Schmid) Alia pax maxima est, per quam omnes firmiori statu sustentantur; scilicet fidejussionis stabilitate, quam Angli vocant frið-borgas, præter Eboracenses, qui vocant eam tenmanne tale. *Ibid.* c. 20. §3 and caps. 21, 29 [other texts read *fri-*, *freo-*]. *c* **1290** Fleta i. xlvii. §10 (1647) 62 Frichborgh. **1607** [see DECENER 2]. *a* **1641** Spelman *Anc. Govt. Eng.*, *Reliq.* (1723) 51 Every Hundred was divided into many Freeborgs or Tithings . . which stood all bound one for the other. **1747** Carte *Hist. Eng.* I. 311 Appeals from the decisions of particular friborghs. **1754** Hume *Hist. Eng.* (1761) I. ii. 49 A tithing, decennary, or fribourg. **1874** Stubbs *Const. Hist.* §41 I. 87 The association of ten men in common responsibility legally embodied in the frithborh or frankpledge.

†'**frithburgher**. *Obs. local.* [Interpreted as f. FRITH *sb.*[2] + BURGHER; but perh. originally connected with FRITHBORH.]

1587 in *Chambers' Bk. Days* I. 728 The Lord Bailiff . . issued his summons . . to choose four 'Frith Burghers' . . to act as jurymen. **1769** *De Foe's Tour Gt. Brit.* III. 151 If the Offence was committed . . within the Bounds of the Forest, then there were Frithbourgers also to judge of the Fact, who were to be summoned out of the Forestholders, as they are called, who were to hold of that Frith, that is of the Forest. **1825** Hone *Every-day Bk.* I. 145 This officer summoned a jury of frith-burghers to try him.

'**frithles**, *sb. pl. dial.* [f. FRITH *sb.*[2] or *v.*[2]; but cf. OE. *wríþels* band.] A flexible branch or twig used for wattling.

1881 Blackmore *Christowell* (1882) II. iv. 79 To lash it, with stout oak frithles, to a pair of stout ash-saplings.

†**frith-stool**. *Obs.* exc. *Hist.* Also 1 **frith-, frythstól**, 7 **freedstool**, 9 **fridstool**. [OE., f. *frið*, FRITH *sb.*[1] + *stól* chair, seat: see STOOL.] **a.** OE. only. A place of safety; a refuge. **b.** A seat, usually of stone, formerly placed near the altar in some churches, which afforded inviolable protection to those who sought privilege of sanctuary.

c **1000** *Ags. Ps.* (Th.) lxxxix. 1 þu eart frið-stol us fæste, Drihten. *a* **1016** *Laws of Ethelred* vii. c. 16 And ȝif forworht man frið-stol ȝesece. **1610** Holland *Camden's Brit.* i. 712 This seat of Stone is called Freedstool, that is, The chaire of Peace. **1662** Ray *Three Itin.* ii. 137 At the upper end of the choir, on the right side of the altar stands the Freed stool. **1829** G. Poulson *Beverley* 687 The Fridstool is . . hewn out of a solid stone, with a hollow back. **1871** Freeman *Norm. Conq.* (1876) IV. xviii. 288 Inviolable sanctuary . . was afforded . . by the frithstool of the saint.

†**frithy**, *a. Obs. rare*$^{-1}$. [f. FRITH *sb.*[2] + -Y[1].] Of the nature of 'frith' or brushwood.

a **1529** Skelton *Garl. Laurell* 22 In the frytthy forest of Galteres.

‖**Fritillaria** (frɪtɪ'lɛərɪə). Also 7 **frit(t)ell-**. [mod.L. *fritillāria*, f. *fritillus* dice-box.

According to Clusius *Rariorum aliquot Stirpium per Pannon. etc. observ. Hist.* (1583) 172, the name was given by Noel Capperon, a druggist of Orleans, to the Common Fritillary, 'quod ejus areolæ versicolores fritillum quodammodo æmulentur'. Unless this refers to some chequered pattern with which dice-boxes were painted, Gerarde's explanation below would seem to be correct, though the Lat. dicts. of the 16th c. and still earlier give the correct explanation of *fritillus*. In any case the name refers to the chequered markings of the corolla, not to its shape as is usually stated.]

A genus of liliaceous plants, the best known species of which are the CROWN IMPERIAL (*F. imperialis*), and the Common Fritillary or Snakeshead (*F. Meleagris*) found locally in moist meadows.

1578 Lyte *Dodoens* ii. lii. 214 The third [Tulipa] is called . . *Flos Meleagris* . . some do also cal this flower *Fritillaria*. **1597** Gerarde *Herball* 123 It hath been called Frittillaria, of the table or boord vpon which men plaie at chesse, which square checkers the flower doth very much resemble, some thinking that it [the chess-board] was named Frittillus. **1611** *Tradescant's bill* in A. Amherst *Gard. Eng.* (1895) 170 Fortye fritellarias at 3 pence the peece. **1625** Bacon *Ess.*, *Gardens* (Arb.) 556 Camaïris, Frettellaria. **1664** Evelyn *Kal. Hort.* (1729) 198 *March* . . Violets, *Fritillaria*. **1741** *Compl. Fam. Piece* ii. iii. 378 Bulbous-rooted Flowers . . such as the . . Fritillaria's, and Colchicum. **1881** Miss Braddon *Asph.* xii. 137 Primroses; anemones; hyacinths; and the rare fritillaria.

fritillary (frɪ'tɪlərɪ). [Anglicized form of prec. Cf. Fr. *fritillaire*.]

1. Any plant of the genus *Fritillaria*, esp. *F. Meleagris* (see prec.).

1633 *Gerarde's Herball* i. lxxxix. 151 In English we may call it Turky-hen or Ginny-hen Floure, and also Checquered Daffodill, and Fritillarie, according to the Latine. **1668** Wilkins *Real Char.* 74 Fritillary. **1688** R. Holme *Armoury* ii. 74/1 The sullen Lady . . some call it the black Fritillary. **1767** J. Abercrombie *Ev. Man his own Gard.* (1803) 47 Fritillaries, crown imperials, or any other kind of bulbous flower-roots. **1828** Miss Mitford *Village* Ser. iii. (1863) 531 The chequered fritillary or the tinted wood anemone. **1867** M. Arnold *Thyrsis*, I know what white, what purple fritillaries The grassy harvest of the river-fields Above by Ensham, down by Sandford yields.

2. A name for several species of butterfly, e.g. the Silver-washed Fritillary (*Argynnis paphia*) and the Queen of Spain Fritillary (*A. lathonia*).

1857 Kingsley *Two Y. Ago* III. 132–3 The 'white admirals' and silver washed 'fritillaries' flit round every bramble bed. **1866** Blackmore *C. Nowell* xxx, Off dashed Bob after a Queen of Spain fritillary.

†**fri'tiniency**. *Obs.*$^{-1}$ (In the first ed. spelt *fritiniancy*; the mod. Dicts. spell *fritinancy*.) [f. L. *fritinnī-re* to twitter + -ANCY.] Twittering.

1646 Sir T. Browne *Pseud. Ep.* v. iii. 236 The note or fritiniancy [of the Cicada] is far more shrill then that of the Locust. **1656–81** Blount *Glossogr.*, *Fritiniancy*, *Fritiniency*.

fritt: see FRIT *sb.*[2]

†**fri'ttado**. *Obs.* [ad. It. *frittata*, f. *frittare* to fry, f. *fritto*, pa. pple. of *friggere*: see FRY *v.*] A fritter.

1635 J. Hayward tr. *Biondi's Banish'd Virg.* 46 Making her a frittado of egges and milke he set it before her.

fritter ('frɪtə(r)), *sb.*[1] Forms: 5 **fretoure, -ure, frutter, fruyter, frytour, -owre, (freature)**, 5–6 **frit-, frut-, -er, -eur, -our(e, -ur(e**, 6 **frither, frytter**, 7 **frittar**, 5– **fritter**. [a. Fr. *friture* = Sp. *fritura*, It. *frittura*:—Lat. type **frīctūra*, f. *frīgĕre* to FRY.]

1. Usually *pl.* A portion of batter, sometimes containing slices of apple, meat, etc., fried in oil, lard, etc. Often preceded by some qualifying word, as ***apple-***, ***oyster-***, ***rice-fritter***; also, in 15–16th c., in some semi-anglicized French terms, as †*fritter-bounce*, *-pouch*, *-sage*, *-viant* (meat) (*obs.*).

c **1420** *Liber Cocorum* (1862) 55 Tarts and daryels and custan dere, Rysshene and pome dorres, and frutur in fere. *c* **1460** J. RUSSELL *Bk. Nurture* 501–2 O fruture viant, Frutur sawge, byn good, bettur is Frutur powche; Appulle fruture is good hoot, but þe cold ye not towche. **1494** FABYAN *Chron.* VII. 600 Frytour of sunne facion, with a floure delyce therin. **1502** ARNOLDE *Chron.* (1811) 240 Fresshe storgion, quynces in paste, tarte poleyn, fritour bounce. **1634** J. TAYLOR (Water P.) *Gt. Eater Kent* 12 Pancake or fritter or flap-iacke. **1664** PEPYS *Diary* 19 Aug., Home to supper to a good dish of fritters. **1769** MRS. RAFFALD *Eng. Housekpr.* (1778) 161 Batter, made as for common fritters. **1835** W. IRVING *Tour Prairies* 72 A paste made of flour and water, and fried, like fritters, in lard. **1859** *All Year Round* No. 36. 222 The fritter refuses to imbibe any more oil. **1861** SALA *Dutch Pict.* xix. 301, I have heard much of the rice fritters and savoury soups of the Lancashire vegetarians.

fig. **1580** SIDNEY *Arcadia* (1622) 276 O Clinias..the very fritter of fraud, and seething pot of iniquitie.

†**2.** ? A species of apple. *Obs.*⁻¹

1591 LYLY *Endym.* III. iii, For fruit these, fritters, medlers, hartichokes and lady longings.

3. *pl. Whaling* = FENKS.

[Perh. a transferred use of F. *friture* fat in which something is fried.]

1631 PELLHAM *Preserv. 8 Englishm. in Green-land* 22 We agreed..to keepe Wednesdayes and Fridayes Fasting dayes; excepting from the Frittars or Graves of the Whale. (*marg. note.* These be the Scraps of the Fat of the Whale, which are flung away after the Oyle is gotten out of it.) **1813** *Chron.* in *Ann. Reg.* 488 Extracting the oil from the fritters. **1820** SCORESBY *Acc. Arctic Reg.* II. 176 The finks or fritters were always sufficient to boil the remainder without any other fuel.

4. *attrib.* and *Comb.*, as ***fritter-barrow***, ***-pan***, ***-seller***; ***fritter-filled*** ppl. a.

1820 SCORESBY *Acc. Arctic Reg.* II. 176 A '*fritter barrow' being furnished with a grating..drained the oil from the fritters. **1619** *Pasquil's Palin.* (1877) 152 When every paunch till it can hold no more, Is *Fritter-fild, as well as heart can wish. **1625** B. JONSON *Staple of N.* II. i, My face dropt like the skimmer in a *fritter-pan. **1636** DAVENANT *Witts* I. i, Hans van Holme, *fritter seller of Bombell.

fritter (ˈfrɪtə(r)), *sb.*² [app. an altered form of FITTERS; perh. due to the influence of prec.; but cf. OF. *freture*, *fraiture*:—L. *fractūra* FRACTURE.]

1. *pl.* Minute pieces, fragments, shreds. Also, articles of trifling size, trifles. Now *rare.*

In Johnson's quots. (BACON, **1626**; BUTLER, **1678**) the correct reading is *fitters*; in SHAKS. *Merry W.* v. v. 151 the word is prob. FRITTER *sb.*¹

1755 in JOHNSON. **1767** H. BROOKE *Fool of Qual.* (1792) I. iv. 94 Trimmings hanging in fritters and tattars. ?*c* **1890** in *Daily News* 12 Oct. (1895) 6/3 A huge collection of ornamental fritters huddled together.

attrib. **1686** GOAD *Celest. Bodies* II. ii. 168 There appears these differences, Flaxen Clouds, Fleec'd Clouds, some which I call Fritter Clouds, all from their likeness.

2. [From the vb.] Excessive subdivision (by which the general effect is lost).

1803 REPTON *Landscape Gard.* (1805) 56 Producing variety without fritter, and continuity without sameness. **1848** RICKMAN *Archit.* 201 This window is a series of small panels..and these..throw the building into fritter.

fritter (ˈfrɪtə(r)), *v.* Also 8 fretter. [f. prec.]

1. *trans.* To break or tear into pieces or fragments; to subdivide minutely. Now *rare.*

1772–84 COOK *Voy.* (1790) IV. 1243 Having our main-top-gallant yard carried away in the slings, and the sail frittered in a thousand pieces. **1780** BURKE *Sp. Œcon. Reform* Wks. III. 285 Frittering and crumbling down the attention by a blind unsystematick observance of every trifle. **1784** J. BARRY in *Lect. Paint.* i. (1848) 83 The no less mischievous fragments into which they [northern hordes] were frittered. **1803** T. JEFFERSON *Writ.* (1830) III. 508 Perverting the simple doctrines he taught..and frittering them into subtleties. **1806–7** J. BERESFORD *Miseries Hum. Life* (1826) XX. ix. 268 The kernel to be..frittered among the parties cracking. **1816** KEATINGE *Trav.* (1817) II. 236 France was once frittered into subdivisions, as Spain still is. **1822–34** *Good's Study Med.* (ed. 4) I. 359 When they [i.e. hydatids] die, the bags and cysts are often broken up and become frittered into minute tatters and filaments. **1866** ALGER *Solit. Nat. & Man* IV. 366 That throng of women whose attention is frittered on trifles.

b. *intr.* for *refl.* †To become broken into pieces or subdivided (*obs.*). *rarely*, To dwindle.

1796 KIRWAN *Elem. Min.* (ed. 2) I. 79 Small pieces of it fritter between the fingers. *a* **1828** H. NEELE *Lit. Rem.* (1829) 18 The canvass fritters into shreds and the column moulders into ruin. **1876** J. PARKER *Paracl.* II. Epil. 374 Minuteness never fritters into pettiness.

2. a. With *away*, *down*: To do away with piecemeal; to attenuate, wear down, whittle away; to spend (energy, time) on trifles, to waste.

1728 POPE *Dunc.* I. 232 How prologues into prefaces decay And these to notes are fritter'd quite away. **1777** BURKE *Let. to Mrq. Rockingham* Wks. IX. 170 To break the continuity of your conduct, and thereby to weaken and fritter away the impression of it. **1799** HAN. MORE *Fem. Educat.* (ed. 4) I. 73 They had..frittered down delicacy into frivolousness. **1803** WELLINGTON *Let. to Close* in Gurw. *Desp.* II. 88 To fritter away the small force which his Highness has produced. **1820** LD. DUDLEY *Lett.* 26 Sept. (1840) 266 Our unpunctuality..fritters away so large a part of the..day in wearisome waiting. **1846** MCCULLOCH *Acc. Brit. Empire* (1854) I. 537 The whole country would be frittered down into potato gardens. **1846** THACKERAY *Crit. Rev.* Wks. 1886 XXIII. 96 He frittered away in fugitive publications time and genius. **1868** MISS BRADDON *Run to Earth* III. vi. 87 You know what Sheridan said about frittering away his money in paying his debts.

†**b.** With *out*. To bring out, utter piecemeal.

a **1764** LLOYD *Poetry Professors* 42 What pretty things imagination Will fritter out in adulation.

Hence **ˈfrittered** *ppl. a.*, **ˈfrittering** *vbl. sb.* and *ppl. a.*

1778 BOSWELL in *Johnson* (1791) II. 216 He could put together only curt frittered fragments of his own. **1795** MASON *Ch. Mus.* ii. 136 The frittering of one syllable into almost half a century of semiquavers is perhaps the best and only expedient for shewing its executive powers. **1803** REPTON *Landscape Gard.* (1805) 47 If too many trees be introduced..the effect becomes fritter'd. **1816** J. SCOTT *Vis Paris* (ed. 5) 77 Broken mass of small windows, unequal stories, frittered compartments. **1853** ROBERTSON *Serm.* Ser. II. 337 A foolish, frivolous, disgraceful, frittered past. **1889** *Spectator* 9 Nov., This frittering away of feeling on the scenes of an opera.

fritterer (ˈfrɪtərə(r)). [f. FRITTER *v.* + -ER¹.] One who fritters or wastes (time).

1837 LOWELL *Lett.* (1894) I. 14 On this day..have I, erst the most incorrigible of time's fritterers, learned..twenty (!) pages in Cicero. **1892** *Welsh Rev.* Feb. 351 The unawakened but happy fritterer.

†**ˈfrittle**, *a. Obs.* ? Fickle.

1579 TOMSON *Calvin's Serm. Tim.* 612/1 We are so frittle, that though the way be plaine and beaten before vs, yet can we hardly lift vp one foote. **1638** FARLEY *Emblems* xxxix, Then to the frittle people he doth stinke.

‖**fritto misto** (ˈfritto ˈmisto). [It., mixed fry (FRY *sb.*² 2).] A mixed grill.

1903 N. NEWNHAM-DAVIS *Gourmet's Guide to Europe* ix. 158 The *Minestrone* of Milan and Genoa differ and so does the *Fritto Misto* of Rome and Turin. **1933** H. G. WELLS *Bulpington of Blup* vii. 277 They were eating a fritto misto..in the *Isola Bella*. **1958** A. WILSON *Middle Age of Mrs. Eliot* II. 220 Well cooked escalopes, or fritto misto. **1961** M. HOWARD *Surgeon's Dilemma* ii. 48 'What are you thinking about?' '*Spaghetti Bolognese* and *Fritto misti della Mare*.'

friture, obs. form of FRITTER *sb.*¹

Fritz¹ (frɪts). German nickname for *Friedrich* (= Frederick). Hence, esp. in the 1914–18 war, used for: a German, *esp.* a German soldier (as typical of the German army); also, a German shell, aircraft, submarine, etc. Also *attrib.*

[**1883** G. MEREDITH *Let.* 1 Feb. (1970) II. 684 Many of your friends have bitterly deplored the German Inundation...But..let each have his time—Fritz after Alphonse.] **1915** D. O. BARNETT *Let.* 11 June 174 By that time, of course, Fritz had made himself scarce. **1915** *Sphere* 28 Aug. 229/1 'Fritz' is the name our men have given to the latest air creation of Germany. **1916** *Daily Mail* 1 Nov. 4/4 An effective bombardment of the enemy's lines or a successful trench raid [is] described by Tommy as 'strafing the Fritzes'. **1919** G. K. ROSE *2/4th Oxf. & Bucks Lt. Infty.* 54 At night it seemed probable that a patrol of a few brave men could crawl right up to the German wire and listen, or by setting foot in them enquire whether 'Fritz' was at home in his trenches or no. **1919** J. B. MORTON *Barber of Putney* xiv. 228 Anyone'd think you was the first bloke that ever done a Fritz in. **1932** J. DOS PASSOS *Nineteen Nineteen* 377 The Fritz officer..shouted in English. **1955** J. THOMAS *No Banners* xxvi. 261, I gathered he was more of a *collaborateur* than anything else. He praised you Fritzes up to the skies.

fritz² (frɪts). *slang* (orig. and chiefly *U.S.*). [Origin unknown.] Phr. ***on the fritz***: out of order, defective, unsatisfactory; ***to put on the fritz*** (also ***to put the fritz on***): to spoil, destroy, put a stop to.

1903 R. L. MCCARDELL *Conversat. Chorus Girl* 15 They gave an open air [performance] that put our opera house show on the Fritz. **1906** H. GREEN *At Actors' Boarding House* 359 What with me ketchin' 'em cookin' spaghetti on the gas an' tearin' up the bedspreads to use fur makeup towels, they're puttin' the place on the fritz! **1924** WODEHOUSE *Bill the Conqueror* v. 122 Everything's on the fritz nowadays. **1962** *Guardian* 11 Apr. 9/2 It appeared, for an awful moment, that a cue had failed, that the teleprompter was on the fritz. **1968** R. H. R. SMITHIES *Shoplifter* (1969) vii. 151 It's Mother's plan to put the fritz on shoplifting.

Friulian (frɪˈuːlɪən), *a.* and *sb.* [f. *Friuli*, a district in N.E. Italy: see -AN.] **A.** *adj.* Of or pertaining to Friuli or its inhabitants. **B.** *sb.* A native or inhabitant of Friuli; the Rhæto-Romance dialect spoken by the people of Friuli.

1880 *Encycl. Brit.* XIII. 492/2 *Eastern Section or Friulian Region.*—Here there still exists a flourishing 'Ladinity', but at the same time it tends towards Italian. **1910** C. HULTON tr. *Villari's Mediæval Italy* i. 4 In Italy the Friulian Marches, eventually extending to the Adige, were constituted. **1959** *Chambers's Encycl.* VI. 89/2 Friuli is rich in both maize and wine, and its inhabitants..are mostly Italians, but some speak Slovenian and some Friulian, a Romansch dialect. **1963** *Times* 12 Feb. 8/6 The Friulians can hardly have been happy that Trieste is to be the regional capital. **1966** *Listener* 2 June 814/3 The recent *Elegie* for voice, violin, clarinet, and guitar (1962) on the Friulian poems of Franco Gironcoli. **1968** *Encycl. Brit.* XVIII. 1101/1 The RR dialects are spoken in three major areas: (1) In Friuli, the region between the Alps and the head of the Adriatic sea... This idiom is called Friulian.

†**ˈfrivol**, *a.* and *sb.* Chiefly *Sc. Obs.* Forms: 5 frewall, -ill, 5–6 -ell, -oll, 5–6 frivole, 7 -oll, fryvol(l)e, 6 frevol(l, fruell, 7 frival(l. [a. F. *frivole*, ad. L. *frīvol-us*: see FRIVOLOUS.]

A. *adj.*

1. Fickle, unreliable.

c **1470** HENRY *Wallace* II. 144 Frewill [*v.r.* freuoll] fortoun thus broucht him in the snar. *Ibid.* v. 646 The obserwance Quhilk langis luff, and all his frewill [*v.r.* freuoll] chance.

2. Frivolous, of little account, paltry, trumpery, flimsy, absurd. (In quot. 1894 merely a nonce-use.)

1492 *Acta Dom. Conc.* (1839) 246/1 Nain vther frewell exceptioune. **1497** BP. ALCOCK *Mons Perfect.* Biij, Whiche all ben but fryvole excuses. **1501** DOUGLAS *Pal. Hon.* II. xxiii, My friwoll actioun. **1573** *Satir. Poems Reform.* xlii. 883 Thair friuole foches to repeit. **1605** CHAPMAN *All Fooles* Plays 1873 I. 134, I did (to shift him with some contentment) Make such a frivall promise. **1609** SKENE *Reg. Maj., Stat. Robt. II* 49 The saidis frivoll and dilatour exceptions being omitted. [**1894** *Sat. Rev.* 9 June 615/2 That wearyful transition from the novel simply frivol to the novel frivol-philosophic.]

B. *sb.* A frivolous thing, a trifle.

c **1450** tr. *De Imitatione* III. xxvii. 97 Wiþouten þe all þinges are friuoles. *c* **1489** CAXTON *Blanchardyn* xii. 44 Put out of your ymaginacyon suche casuall fryuolles.

†**ˈfrivol**, *v.*¹ *Sc. Obs.*⁻¹ [f. prec. adj.] *trans.* To declare frivolous; to quash, set aside.

1533 BELLENDEN *Livy* I. (1822) 45 Gif thir jugis frivole his appellacioun, and convict him.

frivol (ˈfrɪv(ə)l), *v.*² Not in dignified use. Also frivel, frivvle. [Back-formation from FRIVOLOUS.] *intr.* To behave frivolously, to trifle. Also, *to frivol away* (money, time): to spend foolishly.

1866 MRS. WHITNEY *L. Goldthwaite* iv. (1873) 56 They will come, and frivel about the gates, without ever once entering in. **1883** BLACK in *Illustr. Lond. News* 251 If you want to frivvle..I shut my door on you. **1885** L. WINGFIELD *Barbara Philpot* II. v. 152 Had he not drawn 5,000*l.* a year ..which his Duchess frivolled away?

Hence **ˈfrivolling** *vbl. sb.* and *ppl. a.* Also **ˈfrivoller**, one who 'frivols'.

1882 *Tales Mod. Oxf.* vii. 183 So between cricket and boating and frivoling at the vicarage, the sunny summer days sped along. **1883** *Athenæum* 31 Mar. 405/3 We fear that very little confidence could be felt in the frivolling princes of Simla. **1889** A. SERGEANT *Esther Denison* II. IV. xxxii. 268, I am a born trifler—a flâneur—a 'frivoller', as we call it in our modern slang.

ˈfrivolism. ? *Obs.* [f. FRIVOL *a.* + -ISM.]

1. A frivolous occupation.

1778 APTHORPE *Preval. Chr.* 179 Botany, entomology, and other frivolisms.

2. Frivolity.

In dicts. citing PRIESTLEY.

frivolist (ˈfrɪvəlɪst). [f. as prec. + -IST.] One who gives his time to frivolity.

1884 *Chr. World Pulpit* XXV. 138/2 Look on the frivolist. He is endowed with capacity for thought and will and aspiration, but he lives making life a laugh.

frivolity (frɪˈvɒlɪtɪ). [ad. F. *frivolité*: see FRIVOL *a.* and -ITY.]

1. The quality of being frivolous; disposition to trifle, frivolous behaviour, levity.

1796 BURKE *Regic. Peace* i. Wks. VIII. 86 When frivolity and effeminacy had been..acknowledged as their national character by the good people of this kingdom. **1816** SCOTT *Antiq.* xii, Musing upon the frivolity of mortal pursuits. **1841–4** EMERSON *Ess., Exper.* Wks. (Bohn) I. 189 A preoccupied attention is the only answer to the importunate frivolity of other people.

2. A frivolous act or thing.

1838 DICKENS *Nich. Nick.* iii, Mr. Nickleby glanced at these frivolities with great contempt. **1845** MAURICE *Mor. & Met. Philos.* in *Encycl. Metrop.* II. 625/1 Pithy maxims of conduct..entering into the lowest details and frivolities.

frivolize (ˈfrɪvəlaɪz), *v.* [f. FRIVOL *a.*, FRIVOL(OUS) + -IZE.] *trans.* To render frivolous.

1821 *Examiner* 662/2 The mode in which the King is spoken of..is improved through a French strainer, which frivolises it most admirably. **1849** ROBERTSON *Serm.* Ser. I. *Sower*, Human presence, if frivolous, in such moments frivolizes the soul. **1878** C. STANFORD *Symb. Christ* vii. 195 You are allowing some levity to frivolize your life.

frivolous (ˈfrɪvələs), *a.* Forms: 6 frivolus, fryvolous(e, (7 frivoulous), 6–7 frivelous, (6 fryvlous) 7 frivilous, 6– frivolous. [f. L. *frīvol-us* + -OUS. Cf. FRIVOL *a.*]

1. Of little or no weight, value, or importance; paltry, trumpery; not worthy of serious attention; having no reasonable ground or purpose.

1549 BALE *Leland's N.Y. Gift* Div, We fynde for true hystoryes, most fryuolouse fables and lyes. **1578** TIMME *Caluine on Gen.* 25 It is too frivolous and vaine to expound this worde. **1624** LD. KENSINGTON in Ellis *Orig. Lett.* Ser. I. III. 172 In their frivolous delayes, and in the unreasonable conditions which they propounded. **1648** GAGE *West Ind.* xx. 169 His answers seeming frivolous. *c* **1670** WOOD *Life* (O.H.S.) I. 398 The warden..did put the college to unnecessary charges, and very frivolous expences. **1770** *Junius' Lett.* xxxix. 198 They voted his information frivolous. **1776** ADAM SMITH *W.N.* I. xi. (1869) I. 184 The other frivolous ornaments of dress and furniture. **1828** SCOTT *F.M. Perth* vii, The slight and frivolous complaints unnecessarily brought before him. **1871** DIXON *Tower* III. xxv. 280 He was arrested on a frivolous charge.

b. *Law.* In pleading: Manifestly insufficient or futile.

1736 in *Swift's Lett.* (1766) II. 249 The decree was affirmed most unanimously, the appeal adjudged frivolous.

1883 SIR H. COTTON in *Law Rep.* 11 Q. Bench Div. 532 Unless the counter-claim is frivolous and unsubstantial.

2. Characterized by lack of seriousness, sense, or reverence; given to trifling, silly.

1560 tr. *Fisher's Treat. Prayer* F ij, Eschewyng all vayne, friuolus, and vnfruitfull thoughtes. **1575** G. HARVEY *Letter-bk.* (Camden) 101 Frivolous boyishe grammer schole trickes. **1687** WOOD *Life* 21 Apr., The duke of Bucks is dead ..many frivolous things extant—'Bays', a comedy. **1711** STEELE *Spect.* No. 156 ¶6 From reading frivolous Books, and keeping as frivolous Company. **1783** JOHNSON 18 Apr. in *Boswell*, He may be a frivolous man, and be so much occupied with petty pursuits, that he may not want friends. **1862** MISS BRADDON *Lady Audley* ix. 63 Lady Audley amused herself in her own frivolous fashion.

absol. **1836** EMERSON *Nat., Idealism* Wks. (Bohn) II. 160 The frivolous make themselves merry with the Ideal theory, as if its consequences were burlesque.

Hence **'frivolously** *adv.*, **'frivolousness.**

1611 COTGR., *Vainement*, vainely, friuolously, to no purpose. **1624** DONNE *Serm.* (Alford) V. cxxx. 330 If Abraham had any such doubts, of a Frivolousness in so base a Seal. **1712** STEELE *Spect.* No. 448 ¶2 The frivolously false ones. **1768–74** TUCKER *Lt. Nat.* (1852) I. 119 To..judge of the weight or frivolousness of objections. **1812** G. CHALMERS *Dom. Econ. Gt. Brit.* 396 This argument..has been found to have, at least, the pertinacity of faction, if it have not the frivolousness of folly. **1885** LD. BLACKBURN in *Law Rep.* 10 Appeal Cases 223 The bankrupt being held to be acting frivolously and vexatiously.

frixe, obs. form of FRISK *a.*

†**'frixion.** *Obs.* [as if ad. L. **frīxiōn-em*, n. of action f. *frīgĕre* (ppl. stem *frīx-*) to roast.] (See quots.)

1612 WOODALL *Surg. Mate* Wks. (1653) 271 Frixion is the preparation of some medicaments, with oyl, butter, [etc.]. **1657** TOMLINSON *Renou's Disp.* 66 Assation and Frixion differ thus.

†**'frixory.** *Obs.* [ad. L. *frīxōrium*, f. as prec.] A frying-pan.

1657 TOMLINSON *Renou's Disp.* 472 That same supellex is necessary..as Pottengers, Frixories, etc.

friz, variant of FRIZZ.

†**fri'zado**, *sb.* *Obs.* Forms: 6–8 fris(e-, frysado(w(e, (6 fres-, frisc-, friz-, 7 friez(e)ado(w), 7– frizado. [a. Sp. *frisado* (obs.), explained to mean 'silk plush', f. *frisar* = Fr. *friser* to curl (hair), raise a nap on (cloth); see FRIZZ, FRIEZE *vbs.*] A fine kind of frieze. Also *attrib.*

1542 *Nottingham Rec.* III. 220 One Spaynes cloke of frysado. **1546** O. JOHNSON in Ellis *Orig. Lett.* Ser. II. II. 175 Untill I have made sale of the frisados and lynnen cloeth. **1600** VAUGHAN *Direct. Health* (1633) 165 In Winter, your upper garment must be of Cotton or Friezeadow. **1630** J. TAYLOR (Water P.) *Praise Hempseed* Wks. III. 64/1 Our cottons, penistones, frizadoes, baze. **1719** D'URFEY *Pills* III. 272 And an old Frysadoe Coat to cover his Worship's trunk Hose.

Hence †**fri'zado** *v. intr.*, to produce the appearance of frizado. In quot. *transf.*

1598 SYLVESTER *Du Bartas* II. i. IV. *Handie-crafts* 591 A cleer Brook..Whose gurgling streams frizado'd on the gravell.

frize, obs. form of FREEZE, FRIEZE.

frizel, var. of FRIZZLE *sb.*[2]

frizette, frizeur, vars. of FRISETTE, FRISEUR.

†**frizi'lation.** *Obs.*[−1] [f. FRIZZLE *v.*[1] + -ATION.] The action of frizzling (hair).

1567 FENTON *Trag. Disc.* 141 Her chief and comon exercise, was, to force a frizilacion of her haire.

frizon, frizure, var. ff. FRISON[2], FRISURE.

frizz, friz (frɪz), *sb.* Also 7 frizze. [f. next vb.] The state of being frizzed or curled; *concr.* frizzed hair; a row or wig of crisp curls.

1668 ETHEREDGE *She would if she could* III. iii, Draw a Comb through him, there is not such Another Frizz in Europe. **1685** *Lond. Gaz.* No. 2075/4 Her hair brown of a natural Frizze or Curl about the forehead. **1704** ADDISON *Italy* (1733) 189 A little Friz, like a Tower, running round the Edges of the Face. **1802** SYD. SMITH in *Edin. Rev.* I. 18 Dr. Parr's wig..swells out into boundless convexity of frizz. **1827** T. HAMILTON *Cyril Thornton* (1845) 277 His golden locks were spread out in the utmost amplitude of friz. **1861** WYNTER *Soc. Bees* 517 Clustering glossy curls, which were sometimes made soft and semi-transparent by a peculiar friz.

fig. **1848** HARE *Guesses* Ser. II. (1867) 478 A similar full-bottomed well-curled friz of words.

b. *attrib.*

1646 in Thornbury *Haunted London* (1865) 383 Gave to old Friz-wig..o. 6. o. **1713** STEELE *Englishm.* No. 40. 260 A Head..with a friz Wig and plenteous Cravat-string.

frizz, friz (frɪz), *v.*[1] Also 7 freeze, 7–8 frize, 8 frieze. [ad. Fr. *friser*, = Sp. *frisar*, to curl (hair), raise a nap on (cloth); in the latter of these senses the Fr. vb. was adopted earlier; see FRIEZE *v.*[1] The Eng. word seems to have been originally pronounced (friːz), but to have afterwards undergone assimilation to the older FRIZZLE *v.*

The origin of the Rom. vb. is disputed. There seems to be no good ground for the common view that it is of Teut. etymology (the interpretation of the ethnic name of the *Frisians* as 'curly-haired' being a mere assumption); quite possibly it may be a mere special use of the homophonous F. *friser* FRIEZE *v.*[1]]

1. *trans.* To curl or crisp (the hair); to form into a mass of small, crisp curls.

1660 PEPYS *Diary* 22 Nov., Dressing of herself with her haire frized short up to her eares. **1750** F. COVENTRY *Hist. Pompey* II. iii. (1785) 53/2 People who frize their hair in the newest fashion. **1771** SMOLLETT *Humph. Clinker* (1895) 378 This machine [a tye-periwig] has been in buckle ever since, and now all the servants in the family were employed to frizz it out for the ceremony. **1777** W. WHITEHEAD *Goat's Beard* 32 Is't not enough you read Voltaire, While sneering valets frizz your hair? **1820** LAMB *Elia* Ser. I. *South-Sea Ho.*, He wore his hair..powdered and frizzed out. **1862** H. MARRYAT *Year in Sweden* II. 41 Grayish hair, frizzed, in short crêpé curls.

2. *intr.* Of hair: To stand up in short crisp curls. Also *trans.* To set up (hair) on end; to erect.

1696 [see FRIZZING *ppl. a.*]. **1791** W. BARTRAM *Carolina* 501 [The hair] at the crown of the head..is about two inches broad..and stands frized upright. **1810** *Sporting Mag.* XXXV. 246 The lion roaring and frizzing his shaggy crest.

3. *trans.* To raise a bur on (the nap of cloth). = FRIEZE *v.*[1]

1806 WEBSTER *Compend. Dict.*, *Friz*, to form nap into small burs.

4. In *Leather-dressing*: To rub (wash-leather, etc.) with pumice-stone or a blunt knife, so as to remove the grain, soften the surface, and give a uniform thickness.

1697 [see FRIZZED *ppl. a.*]. **1726** *Dict. Rust.* (ed. 3) s.v. *Wet-glover*, Frizing is the working the Skin woolly on one side. **1853** C. MORFIT *Arts of Tanning* 434 The skins, after having been brought to a state of pelt..are subjected to what is technically termed frizing, which is a rubbing with a pumice stone, or working under the round edge of a blunt knife. **1885** C. T. DAVIS *Leather* xlii. 681 The treatment with the scraping-knife being generally not sufficient for complete frizzing, the remaining portions of the grain are removed with another sharp knife.

Hence **frizzed** *ppl. a.*, **'frizzing** *vbl. sb.* and *ppl. a.*

c **1620** Z. BOYD *Zion's Flowers* (1855) 117 Freez'd Minions all, most brave in vaunts and vowes. **1689** *Lond. Gaz.* No. 2459/4 Black short frized Hair. **1696** W. MOUNTAGUE *Delights Holland* 52 Fellows, with black frizzing Hair and great Whiskers. **1697** *View Penal Laws* 60 To use dry, curried and frized Leather. *c* **1770** ERSKINE *Barber* in *Poet. Reg.* (1810) 327 Ruin seize thee, scoundrel Coe! Confusion on thy frizzing wait. **1787** *Generous Attachm.* I. 28 His hair wears the flourishes of the most skilful of the frizzing tribe. **1822** W. IRVING *Braceb. Hall* (1845) 309 The barber would thrust out his frizzed head, with a comb sticking in it. **1856** R. W. PROCTER *Barber's Shop* xxi. (1883) 204 He..walked about London in his well-combed wig, frizzed and three tailed. **1874** KNIGHT *Dict. Mech.* I. 917 *Frizzing-machine*, a machine on which the nap of woolen cloth is formed into a number of little prominences or tufts.

frizz (frɪz), *v.*[2] [f. FRY *v.* with echoic termination.] **a.** *intr.* To make a sputtering noise in frying. **b.** *trans.* (See quot. 1891.)

1835 MARRYAT *Jac. Faithf.* ix, What's that frizzing in your frying-pan? **1891** *Hartland Gloss.*, *Frizz* or *Frizzle*, to scorch or dry up.

frizziness ('frɪzɪnɪs). [f. FRIZZY *a.* + -NESS.] Frizzy style or character.

1906 W. J. LOCKE *Beloved Vagabond* iii. 36, I criticised her straight Teutonic fringe and fanfaronaded on the captivating frizziness of Janna's hair. **1912** L. A. HARKER *Mr. Wycherly's Wards* xvii, Your type is severe and classical; 'frizziness' would be quite dreadful and incongruous. **1955** *N.Y. Times* 14 Aug. III. 11 Some domestic supplies [of hair] ..proved unsatisfactory because of frizziness.

frizzle ('frɪz(ə)l), *sb.*[1] [See FRIZZLE *v.*[1]]

1. Frizzled hair; a short crisp curl.

1613 PURCHAS *Pilgrimage* (1614) 650 They curle and fold the haire of their head, making a hill in the midst like a hat, with frizzles round about. **1641** MILTON *Animadv.* (1851) 191 To rumple her laces, her frizzles, and her bobbins. *a* **1845** HOOD *Hymeneal Retrosp.* I. vii, Though now they look only like frizzles of wool, By a bramble torn off from a sheep. **1879** BROWNING *Ned Bratts* 32 Some blue fly Which punctured a dewy scalp where the frizzles stuck awry.

transf. **1865** CARLYLE *Fredk. Gt.* XVIII. xiii, Bald crown of the landscape, girt with a frizzle of firwoods all round.

†**b.** A frizzled wig. *Obs.*

1628 BP. HALL *Righteous Mammon* Wks. 720 When his eyes should meet with a poudred frizle.

2. [f. the vb.] The state of being frizzled.

1850 HAWTHORNE *Scarlet L.*, *Custom Ho.* (1851) 39 A wig of majestic frizzle.

3. *attrib.* and *Comb.*, as †*frizzle-frize*, *-head*; *frizzle-headed*, *-topped* adjs.

1565 GOLDING *Ovid's Met.* VIII. (1593) 208 The frizzle topped wench in coorse and sluttish geere. **1778** MISS BURNEY *Evelina* lxxxii, Pray what do you do with that frizle-frize top of your own? **1840** LADY C. BURY *Hist. Flirt* iv, Fancy him bowing his little frizzle head. **1891** T. HARDY *Tess* I. 19 A frizzle-headed brawny damsel.

frizzle ('frɪz(ə)l), *sb.*[2] *dial.* Also 7 frezel, 9 friz(z)el. [Cf. FLEERISH, FURISON.] See quot. 1892.

1629 Z. BOYD *Last Battell Soule* 1266 He is euer readie to strik fyre with his frezell and his flint. *c* **1817** HOGG *Tales & Sk.* III. 192 Putting down the frizzel, and making it spring up again with a loud snap. **1892** *Northumbld. Gloss.* 305 *Frizzle*, in flint and steel guns the piece of iron acted on by the flint to produce the explosion.

frizzle ('frɪz(ə)l), *v.*[1] Forms: 6 frisel, frysle, 6–8 frisle, frizel(l, frizle, (7 frez-, frizil), 7– frizzle. [This and the related FRIZZLE *sb.* are of obscure origin; they occur much earlier than FRIZZ *v.* to curl (hair) from which they might be supposed to be derived; the verb to FRIEZE cloth, however, which is etymologically identical, is older, and may have given rise to *frisel* as a frequentative formation. Cf. OFris. *frisle*, *fresle*, head of hair, curls, North Fris. *friessle*, *fressle* head of hair, lock of hair, mod.Fris. *frisseljen*, *frislen* to plait (*esp.* the hair); but the origin of these words, and their relation to the Eng. words, is uncertain; cf. also OF. *fresel* a comb worn in the hair.]

1. *trans.* To curl (hair) in small crisp curls.

1565–73 COOPER *Thesaurus*, *Calamistratus*, trimmed: crisped: or frisled. **1573** TWYNE *Æneid* Llj, Lockes with bodkins frisled fine. **1631** BRATHWAIT *Eng. Gentlew.* (1641) 283 A long lock he has got, and the art to frizle it. **1707** *Curios. in Husb. & Gard.* 277 'Tis enough only that her Hair be not frizzled. **1766** [ANSTEY] *Bath Guide* xi. 41 A prodigious rough black Head of Hair That is frizzled and curl'd o'er her Neck that is bare. **1822** W. IRVING *Braceb. Hall* iv. 34 Her hair..is frizzled out and put up with pins. **1869** TROLLOPE *He Knew* vii, Her grey hair was always frizzled with the greatest care.

absol. **1576** GASCOIGNE *Steele Gl.* Epil. 15 They.. bumbast, bolster, frisle, and perfume. *a* **1613** OVERBURY *A Wife* (1638) 180 Hee studies by the discretion of his Barber, to frizle like a Baboone.

†**b.** ? *transf.* To adorn with frills or ruffles. *Obs.*

[But possibly a distinct word. Cf. OF. *freselé* frilled, ruffled, f. *fresel* frill; also FRISLET.]

1753 *Songs Costume* (Percy) 231 Frizzle your elbows with ruffles sixteen. **1755** *Lond. Mag.* July 343 Circling round her iv'ry neck, Frizzle out the smart Vandike.

2. *intr.* for *refl.* To form into crisp curls; to curl or twist *up.*

1607 TOPSELL *Four-f. Beasts* (1658) 505 The dust of the same mixed with oyl..doth cause the hair to frisle and curl. **1727** BRADLEY *Fam. Dict.* s.v. *Crown-Scab*, A..malignant Matter, that breaks forth at the Roots of the Hair, where it sticks to the Skin, and makes it frizzle and stare. **1886** *Law Times* LXXXI. 84/1 The smoke and the noxious gases caused the leaves of the plants, etc., to curl and frizzle up.

†**3.** *trans.* To brush or touch lightly. Cf. FRIEZE *v.*[1] 3.

1634 PEACHAM *Gentl. Exerc.* I. xxvi. 93 For a feather, Lake frizled with red lead. **1652** WRIGHT tr. *Camus' Nature's Paradox* 134 The agreeable noise, which the Leaves of the Neighbouring Trees did make, when frizled by the Zephyr's welcome Wings.

Hence **'frizzling** *ppl. a.* Also **'frizzler**, one who frizzles.

1779 FORREST *Voy. N. Guinea* 95 Their comb..with which they now and then combed their frizzling locks. **1779–80** COOK *Voy.* (1785) I. 183 In some it [hair] was of a frizzling disposition. **1816** J. GILCHRIST *Philos. Etym.* 263 Musicians, dancing-masters, perfumers, frizzlers, gilders.

frizzle ('frɪz(ə)l), *v.*[2] [f. FRIZZ *v.*[2]: see -LE.]

a. *intr.* = FRIZZ *v.*[2] a. **b.** *trans.* To fry, toast, or grill (with a sputtering noise).

a. 1839 THACKERAY *Fatal Boots* (1869) 362 A nice fresh steak was frizzling on the gridiron. **1863** *Confess. Ticket-of-Leave Man* 77 Jack dropped the candle, and set some of the wigs frizzling. **1874** DASENT *Tales Fjeld* 187 He heard the molten lead bubbling and frizzling in our clerk's throat.

b. 1858 HAWTHORNE *Fr. & It. Jrnls.* II. 134 When the sun had the fairest chance to frizzle me. **1888** BURGON *Lives 12 Gd. Men* I. iv. 388 To pull a herring daily from the string, and to frizzle it..for breakfast.

Hence **'frizzled, 'frizzling** *ppl. adjs.* Also **'frizzle** *sb.*, the action of the vb.

1852 MRS. STOWE *Uncle Tom's C.* iv, Aunt Chloe.. presiding..over certain frizzling items in a stewpan. **1860** *All Year Round* 460 My frizzling brains. **1891** *Rutland Gloss.* s.v. 'The doctor says as how he's to hev some frizzled mutton.' **1894** CROCKETT *Raiders* (ed. 3) 35 Flounders.. with their tails jerking Flip, flap, in the frizzle of the pan.

frizzled ('frɪz(ə)ld), *ppl. a.* [f. FRIZZLE *v.*[1] + -ED[1].] In senses of the vb.: **a.** of hair. Also, of a wig, the head: Consisting of or covered with crisp curls. Of a fowl: see quot. 1885.

1567 DRANT *Horace's Art Poetrie, etc.* C iij a, Mecænas, if I meete with the without my frisled top, Not notted fyne and fashion lyke. **1573** G. HARVEY *Letter-bk.* (Camden) 103 A gallant friseld pate. **1598** BARCKLEY *Felic. Man* III. (1603) 272 You shall have a halter in place of your frizeled haire. **1650** BULWER *Anthropomet.* ii. 58 The frizled and over-powdered Gallants of our times. **1660** F. BROOKE tr. *Le Blanc's Trav.* 250 Displumed geese, as likewise most part of the ducks were, the rest frizeled. **1725** BRADLEY *Fam. Dict.* s.v. *Poultry*, Frisled Hens..may also be put into the Yard. **1779** FORREST *Voy. N. Guinea* 6 He called it New Guinea, from the frizzled locks of the inhabitants. **1817** LADY GRANVILLE *Lett.* June (1894) I. 101 A fine, courteous-looking seigneur, with a grey frizzled head. **1847** LD. LINDSAY *Chr. Art* I. 126 Cain is represented with frizzled hair. **1885** TEGETMEIER in *Encycl. Brit.* XIX. 645 Frizzled fowls are birds in which each feather curls outwards away from the body. They are common in India.

fig. **1577** HARRISON *England* Pref. (1877) 111, I hope that this foule frizeled Treatise of mine will prooue a spur to others better learned. **1652** BENLOWES *Theoph.* v. vii. 68, I will Neglect curl'd Phrases frizled skill.

b. of other objects.

1596 R. L[INCHE] *Diella* (1877) 66 All tapistred with Natures mossie greene, Wrought in a frizled guise. **1599** THYNNE *Animadv.* (1875) 33 *note*, *Aurifrisium* frisled cloth of gold. **1601** HOLLAND *Pliny* I. 396 Those [citron tables] that are frisled with small spots standing thicke. **1613–16** W. BROWNE *Brit. Past.* II. v. 158 The frizled coates which doe the mountaines hide. **1667** MILTON *P.L.* VII. 323 The..

Bush with frizl'd hair implicit. **1746-7** HERVEY *Medit.* (1818) 101 The parsley, with her frizzled locks. *a* **1803** BEATTIE *Hares* 34 O'er their head The furze its frizzled covering spread. **1784-1815** *Annals of Agric., Suff.* V. 251 (E.D.S.) *Frizled.* 'The straw [of the potatoes] being frizled (curled) as they call it here.'

frizzling ('frɪzlɪŋ), *vbl. sb.* [f. FRIZZLE *v.*[1] + -ING[1].] The action of the vb. FRIZZLE in various senses; an instance of this. Also *attrib.*

1592 T. TIMME *Ten Eng. Lepers* F iij, The divell himselfe was the first inventer of..frizling. **1611** CORYAT *Crudities* 261 A frisling or crisping pinne of iron. **1633** PRYNNE *Histriom.* I. VI. i. 303 Meretricious Paintings, Frizlings, Pouldrings, Attyrings, and the like. **1862** SALA *Accepted Addr.* 128 No frizzling tongs had ever been heard of in their vicinity.

frizzly ('frɪzlɪ), *a.* [f. FRIZZLE *sb.*[1] + -Y[1].] Full of frizzles or crisp curls.

1707 J. STEVENS tr. *Quevedo's Com. Wks.* (1709) 370 Frizly black..Hair. **1782** ELPHINSTON tr. *Martial* II. xxxvi. 103 Nor with frizzly shock, nor frowsy hair. **1833** LONGF. *Outre-Mer* Prose Wks. 1886 I. 264 The crisping, frizzly waves glide in snaky folds. **1882** *Day of Rest* 206 The under steward—whose frizzly unkempt head of hair stood out.. round his head like a halo.

frizzy ('frɪzɪ), *a.* [f. FRIZZ *sb.* + -Y[1].] Of, pertaining to, or resembling a frizz.

1870 DASENT *Annals* (ed. 4) I. 339 A thing with frizzy hair all down her neck. **1876** GEO. ELIOT *Dan. Der.* I. 217 Mr. Lush's..strong black grey-besprinkled hair of frizzy thickness. **1881** TYLOR *Anthropol.* 72 The Africans show the woolly or frizzy kind [of hair].

†**fro**, *sb. Obs.*[−1] [? a. ON. *fró* in the same sense.] Comfort, relief.

c **1310** in Wright's *Lyric P.* xxxvi. 100 Of myne deden fynde y non fro.

fro (frəʊ), *Sc.* **frae** (fre), *prep.* (*adv.*, *conj.*). Forms: *α.* (chiefly *north.* and *Sc.*) 2-7 **fra**, 5-6 **fray**, (6 **fre**, **frea**), 8-9 **frae**; *β.* 2- **fro**, (4-5 **froo**, 7 **frow**). [a. ON. *frá*, corresp. to OE. *fram*, FROM.]

A. *prep.* (Now only *Sc.* and *dial.*)

1. = FROM in all its senses.

α. *c* **1200** ORMIN 211 Fra þiss daȝȝ þu shallt ben dumb. *Ibid.* 1265 Swa ferr fra Godess riche. *a* **1300** *Cursor M.* 479 (Gött.) Lucifer..fell For his pride fra heuen to hell. *c* **1400** MAUNDEV. (Roxb.) Pref. 1 To..delyuer vs fra deed withouten end. **1563-7** BUCHANAN *Reform. St. Andros* Wks. (1892) 9 Euery Satterday fra ane efter none to four houris. **1558** KENNEDY *Compend. Tractiue* in *Wodr. Soc. Misc.* (1844) 103 To discerne the rycht understanding of the Scripture fra the wrang. **1588** A. KING tr. *Canisius' Catech.* 163 To abstein fra flesh. **1788** BURNS *Naebody*, I'll borrow frae nae-body. **1803** WORDSW. *Yarrow Unv.* v, Fair hangs the apple frae the rock. **1816** SCOTT *Antiq.* ix, After his walk frae the manse. **1876** J. WILSON *Noct. Ambr.* Wks. 1855 I. 174 You canna tell a tree frae a tether. **1877** *N.W. Linc. Gloss.*, *Fra*, from.

β. *c* **1200** *Trin. Coll. Hom.* 111 þis longe weie þe he ferde fro heuene to helle. *c* **1250** *Gen. & Ex.* 89 God ledde hem fro helle niȝt to paradises leue liȝt. *c* **1374** CHAUCER *Compl. Mars* 256 Whan hit was fro his possession. *c* **1380** WYCLIF *Serm.* Sel. Wks. I. 138 And þus semen oure religious to be exempte fro charite. **1382** —— 2 *Sam.* xxiv. 15 Fro Dan vnto Bersabee. *c* **1386** CHAUCER *Reeve's T.* 1 At Trumpington, nat fer fro Cantebrigge. **1393** LANGL. *P. Pl.* C. I. 54 Cloþede hem in copis, to be knowe fro oþere. **1423** JAS. I *Kingis Q.* iii, Fro this day forth. *c* **1449** PECOCK *Repr.* I. i. 7 Fro al resonyng. **1480** CAXTON *Chron. Eng.* xliv. 29 They went fro toune to toune. **1526** *Pilgr. Perf.* (W. de W. 1531) 15 [He] gyueth fro hymselfe frely. **1581** SIDNEY *Astr. & Stella* ix, Where you may haue some defence Fro the storms in my breast breeding. **1611** SHAKS. *Cymb.* v. v. 261 Why did you throw your wedded Lady fro you? *a* **1631** DONNE *Poems* (1650) 29 Can cal vow'd men fro cloysters, dead from tombs. **1884** *Cheshire Gloss.*, *Fro*, from.

†**b.** In verse frequently placed after its sb. (*esp.* as a rime-wd.). *Obs.*

a **1300** *Cursor M.* 16814 + 20 Or þai parted hom froo. **1362** LANGL. *P. Pl.* A. II. 34 When heo was me fro, I loked and byhelde. *c* **1400** *Rom. Rose* 4120 That I mote goo So fer the fresh floures fro. *c* **1460** *Towneley Myst.* (Surtees) 258 That no tratur stylle his cors you fray. *c* **1470** HENRY *Wallace* VIII. 837 Bot othir dede, or ellis fled thaim fray. **1549-62** STERNHOLD & H. *Ps.* xxx. 13 The mourning weede thou tookest me fro. **1580** SIDNEY *Arcadia* (1622) 87 Pas thought it hell, while he was Cosma fro. **1805** SCOTT *Last Minstr.* III. xvi, Well could he hit a fallow-deer Five hundred feet him fro.

†**c.** *fro oneself*: 'beside oneself', out of one's wits. *clean fro*: quite contrary to. (Cf. FROM 8 b.)

1483 *Vulgaria abs Terentio* 18 b, I am fro my selfe for angyre. **1483** CAXTON *G. de la Tour* B iij, She bycam al frantyke and fro herself. **1525** LD. BERNERS *Froiss.* II. ccxix. [ccxv.] 676 They had spyces ynoughe, and bredde made of mylke, clene fro the nature of Fraunce. *c* **1530** —— *Arth. Lyt. Bryt.* (1814) 111 He was so sore dyspleased, that he was nye therwyth fro him selfe.

2. Followed by other prepositions. (Cf. FROM 16.)

a **1300** *Cursor M.* 14407 Fra amang þat cursed ledd. *c* **1340** *Ibid.* 25596 (Fairf.) þou was tane fra of þe crosse. **1382** WYCLIF *Josh.* viii. 11 Fro aȝens of the citee [Vulg. *ex adverso civitatis*]. **1382** —— *Luke* i. 78 He spryngynge vp fro an hiȝ hath visytid vs. *c* **1400** *Gamelyn* 803 Tho come Gamelyn fro under þe wode-rys. *a* **1592** MARLOWE & NASHE *Dido* III. (Rtldg.) 262/2 But I will tear thy eyes fro forth thy head. **1813** HOGG *Queen's Wake* 70 Than up there rase ane wee wee man Franethe the moss-gray stane.

†**3.** With an adverb in place of a sb.-object. (Cf. FROM 15.) *fro ðan ðat*: from the time that. *froforth*: ? = from this time forth. *Obs.*

c **1200** ORMIN 17970 He þatt fra bibufenn comm. *c* **1250** *Gen. & Ex.* 188 Fro ðan ðat he sinȝen bi-gan. *a* **1300** *Cursor M.* 932 Eue fra þan hir cald adam. *Ibid.* 10976 þou sal be dumb fra nu. *Ibid.* 20078 For quam i com dun fra o-bouen. *c* **1340** HAMPOLE *Wks.* (Horstman) I. 187 Sothely fra thythene Inryses a gret lufe. **1377** LANGL. *P. Pl.* B. III. 109 Cam late fro biȝunde. *c* **1449** PECOCK *Repr.* I. xii. 63 Be waar therfore frohens forthward. *Ibid.* II. ix. 197 Whanne he were departid frothens. *a* **1533** LD. BERNERS *Huon* lxxxi. 243 Ye may go fro hens forth where ye lyst. **1536** in Strype *Eccl. Mem.* (1721) I. xxxv. 271 It is to trust..that party will also froforth..own to law all other abusions.

†**4.** Of, concerning. Cf. ON. *frá*. *rare*[−1].

c **1300** *Harrow. Hell* 28 More wo Then i con ou telle fro.

B. *adv.* In a direction or position that is remote or apart; away. Now only in phr. *to and fro* (see TO); for which rarely *fro* (*fra*) *and till*. †*to do fro*: to remove. Also, contrary, against. *of or fro*: for or against.

a **1300** *Cursor M.* 8927 þar was a stank bot littel fra Hight piscina probatica. *Ibid.* 11937 þat water moght rin fra and till, Vte of þe flum al atte will. *c* **1420** *Pallad. on Husb.* XII. 197 Whan they come vp the smallest fro they do, So that the saddist faster may ascende. *c* **1450** HOLLAND *Howlat* 270 Sum said to and sum fra, Sum nay and sum ȝa. **1562** *Child-Marriages* (E.E.T.S.) 204 He sais he cannot say anythinge of his honesty, of nor fro. **1576** FLEMING *Panopl. Epist.* Epit. A iij b, Passage to, fro, and through without danger.

†**b.** *Comb.*, as *fro-leader* = ABDUCTOR 1. *Obs.*

1615 CROOKE *Body of Man* 749 Called the Fro-leader or the muscle of Indignation or the Wayward muscle.

†**C.** *conj.* (Chiefly *north.*) *Obs.*

1. From the time that, from the moment when; as soon as, when. Also, *fra that*.

13.. *E.E. Allit. P.* B. 1325, & al þurȝ dome of Daniel, fro he deuised hade, þat alle goudes com of god. **1375** BARBOUR *Bruce* I. 141 And fra he wyst quhat charge thai had, He buskyt hym, but mar abad. *Ibid.* 581 Fra at the Brwce to dede war brocht. *c* **1375** *Sc. Leg. Saints, Petrus* 536 And fra Marcellus þis cane se, He had þarof rycht mekil wondir. *c* **1400** MAUNDEV. (Roxb.) xxiv. 109 And, fra I come þare, I knewe wele þat it was oþerwise. *c* **1450** *St. Cuthbert* (Surtees) 39 Fra he was eght ȝers ald. *Ibid.* 3435 Fra þat god my saule will haue. **14..** *Plumpton Corr.* (1839) 28, I am siker he will thank you full hartely, fro I lett him witt. **15..** [DUNBAR] *Gif ȝe wald lufe* 14 Poems (1893) 312 And he that is of hairt vntrew, Fra he be kend, fair weill, adew. **1513** DOUGLAS *Æneis* VI. x. 1 Fra that the ancyant nun of Dan Phebus Thir wordis endit had.

2. In a logical sense: Since, seeing that.

1535 STEWART *Cron. Scot.* II. 701 Syne efter him Alexander his bruther..After his deid succeidit in his steid, Fra this Edgair withoutin child wes deid. **1585** JAS. I *Ess. Poesie* (Arb.) 43 Then, fra I saw (as I already told) How men complaind. **1609** SKENE *Reg. Maj.* 102 Fra the follower haue founden borgh lawfullie.

†**fro** (frəʊ), *v.* [? f. FRO *adv.*] †**1.** *intr.* ? To go frowardly or untowardly, be unsuccessful. *Obs.* **b.** As **'froing** *vbl. sb.* (See TO AND FRO *phr.* E.)

1559 *Mirr. Mag., Dk. York* xxiii, God that causeth thinges to fro or frame.

fro, obs. form of FROW, Dutchwoman.

froam, ? erron. form of FREAM.

froat, **froath**, vars. of FROT, FROTH.

frob, obs. var. of THROB.

Fröbel ('frøːbəl). Also **Froebel**. The name of F.W.A. *Fröbel* (1782–1852), German teacher, used *attrib.* or in the possessive to designate the system of child education introduced by him, or a school following this system. (Cf. KINDERGARTEN.) Hence **Froe'belian** *a.*, of or pertaining to his system; as *sb.*, an adherent of his system; **'Froebelism**, the system of education introduced by Fröbel.

1873 *Jrnl. Women's Educ. Union* I. 144/2 Those who are interested in the Froebelian system of education will be glad to know that the Ecole Normale..will be re-opened in September. **1875** *Ibid.* III. 31 Frobel Society for the Promotion of the Kindergarten System.—An Association has been formed with the object of promoting.. Kindergarten work. **1876** E. SHIRREFF *Kinder-Garten* v. 40 It is..an object of the Fröbel method to hinder the ripening of the reasoning and critical faculty without corresponding practical activity. **1879** *Encycl. Brit.* IX. 794/1 The uncle and nephew [*sc.* F.W.A. and Karl Froebel] differed so widely that the new 'Froebelians' were the enemies of the old. *Ibid.* 795/1 The late Joseph Payne advocated Froebelism in a pamphlet, *Froebel and the Kindergarten System.* **1881** H. BARNARD (*title*) Papers on Froebel's Kindergarten. **1904** G. S. HALL *Adolescence* I. iii. 171 Froebelian influence in manual training reaches through the eight school years. **1958** *Observer* 23 Feb. 8/4 If anything distinguishes Montessori from the Froebelians..it is the fact that she stands definitely for work and not for play. **1959** *Chambers's Encycl.* VI. 90/2 The central organizing body for Froebel education in England is the National Froebel Foundation. **1969** L. C. SCHILLER in M. Ash *Who are Progressives Now?* 154 In the middle of the [nineteenth] century a new influence arrived in England, the Froebel Kindergarten. *Ibid.* 155 In Froebel Colleges..the principles and practice of Friedrich Froebel were expounded.

frock (frɒk), *sb.* Forms: 4-5 **frokke**, 5 **frogge**, 4-6 **frok(e**, *Sc.* or *north.* **frog**, 6-7 **frocke**, 6- **frock.** [a. F. *froc* (recorded from 12th c.); of uncertain origin.

Cf. Pr. *floc* frock, med.L. *froccus*, *floccus*. Some scholars regard the *fl-* forms as the original, and identify the word with L. *floccus*, OF. *floc* FLOCK *sb.*[2] Others regard *froc* as adopted from a Teut. word, OHG. *hroch* (once), OS. *hroc* (once), OFris. *hrokk* (rare); but in these forms it is believed by many Germanists that the *hr-* is a misspelling without phonetic significance, the usual forms being OHG. *roch* (mod.Ger. *rock*), OFris. *rokk*, OE. *rocc*.]

1. A long habit with large open sleeves; the outer and characteristic dress of a monk. *Rarely*, a cassock (of an Anglican clergyman). Hence, the priestly office which it indicates. Cf. UNFROCK *v.*

1350 *Durh. MS. Cha. Roll*, In xj pannis..præter ij frokkes. **1362** LANGL. *P. Pl.* A. v. 64 Of a freris frokke were the fore-sleuys. *c* **1440** *Promp. Parv.* 179/2 Froke, monkes habyte..*cuculla.* **1466** *Paston Lett.* No. 549 II. 270 For a cope called a frogge of worsted for the Prior of Bromholm xxvi *s.* viii *d.* **1548** UDALL *Erasm. Par. Luke* xix. 3-4 An other poynteth to some one of the pharisaical sort, clad in a blacke frocke or cope. **1683** TEMPLE *Mem.* Wks. 1731 I. 465 A French Monk, who some time since had left his Frock for a Petticoat. **1762** H. WALPOLE *Vertue's Anecd. Paint.* I. iii. 51 As the frock of no religious order ever was green, this cannot be meant for a friar. **1810** SCOTT *Lady of L.* III. iv, The Hermit by it stood, Barefooted, in his frock and hood. **1887** W. GLADDEN *Parish Problems* 333 It was the utterance of such words as these that cost the great Carmelite preacher [Father Hyacinthe] his frock.

2. a. An upper garment worn chiefly by men; a long coat, tunic, or mantle.

13.. *E.E. Allit. P.* B. 1742 þe kyng comaunded anon to cleþe þat wyse, In frokkes of fyn cloþ. **1375** BARBOUR *Bruce* x. 375 With blak froggis all helit thai The Armouris at thai on thame had. *c* **1425** WYNTOUN *Cron.* VIII. xxxviii. 57 Ilkane a gud Burdowne in hand, And royd Frogis on þare Armyng. *c* **1460** *Towneley Myst.* (Surtees) 241, I wold be fayn of this frog [Christ's coat] myght it fall vnto me. **1500-20** DUNBAR *Poems* li. 3 To giff a doublett he is als doure, As it war off ane futt syd frog. **1527** *Lanc. Wills* I. 6 And also that he geiff to Richard Fene a jakett called my frocke. **1611** BIBLE *Ecclus.* xl. 4 From him that weareth purple, and a crown, vnto him that is clothed with a linnen frocke. **1649** G. DANIEL *Trinarch., Hen. V*, clxxix, Another girds his Frock, wth a sure Thonge. **1700** DRYDEN *Sigism. & Guisc.* 144 Yet (for the wood perplexed with thorns he knew) A frock of leather o'er his limbs he drew. **1848** W. H. KELLY tr. *L. Blanc's Hist. Ten Years* II. 559 Kings at arms covered with long frocks of cloth of gold.

fig. **1604** SHAKS. *Ham.* III. iv. 164 (Qo. 2) That monster custome..to the vse of actions faire and good..giues a frock or Liuery That aptly is put on to refraine night.

b. *frock of mail*: a defensive garment, armour. Cf. *coat of mail*.

1671 MILTON *Samson* 133 Samson..Made arms ridiculous, useless the..frock of mail Adamantean proof. **1835** BROWNING *Paracelsus* III. 715, I have addressed a frock of heavy mail, Yet may not join the troop of sacred knights.

fig. **1841-4** EMERSON *Ess., Politics* Wks. (Bohn) I. 244 The gladiators in the lists of power feel, through all their frocks of force and simulation the presence of worth.

3. a. A loose outer garment worn by peasants and workmen; an overall; more fully *smock-frock*.

a **1668** DAVENANT *News from Plymouth* IV. i, *Cable.* Come your affair, Squire of the Frock! Briefly Dispatch! Where is this courteous Damsel? *Porter.* At my House, Sir. **1698** FRYER *Acc. E. India & P.* 95 Flesh-coloured Vests, somewhat like our Brickmakers Frocks. **1724** DE FOE *Mem. Cavalier* (1840) 237, I had pistols under my grey frock. **1777** WATSON *Philip II* (1839) 525 Three officers..disguised like the peasants of that country with long frocks. **1840** R. H. DANA *Bef. Mast* xxxvi. 136 The duck frocks for tarring down rigging. **1883** C. WALFORD *Fairs* 153 Dealers in haubergs, or waggoners' frocks.

b. A wearer of a smock-frock; a poor person.

1612 W. PARKES *Curtaine-Dr.* (1876) 25 The rich and the poore, euen from the furd gown to the sweating frock. **1625** B. JONSON *Staple of N.* v. ii, *Porter.* Sir, I did give it him. *P. sen.* What..A frock spend sixpence!

c. A woollen 'guernsey' or 'jersey' worn by sailors; *esp.* in *Guernsey* or *Jersey frock*.

1811 W. THOM *Hist. Aberd.* vi. 150 Besides stockings, they make frocks, mitts, and all sorts of hosiery. **1825** JAMIESON, *Frock*, a sort of worsted netting worn by sailors, often in lieu of a shirt. **1856** EMERSON *Eng. Traits, Voy. Eng.* Wks. (Bohn) II. 13 The sailors have dressed him in [a] Guernsey frock. **1867** SMYTH *Sailor's Word-bk.*, *Frog*, an old term for a seaman's coat or frock. *Ibid.*, *Jersey frocks*, woollen frocks supplied to seamen.

4. The outer garment, for indoor wear, of women and children, consisting of a bodice and skirt; a gown, dress.

The word is now applied chiefly to the garment worn by children and young girls, cf. *short frock*; that worn by women is commonly called a *dress*; *gown* is also current, though (exc. in the U.S.) less generally. (But in the language of fashionable society the use of *frock* for 'dress' has within the last few years been revived.)

1538 *Bury Wills* (Camden) 134, I wyll my goddowter and seruant, shall haue my wosted kyrtell..and my froke. **1550** CROWLEY *Way to Wealth* 325 Let youre wiues therefore put of theire fine frockes and Frenche hoodes. **1613** DRAYTON *Poly-olb.* xviii. 284 And on her loynes a frock with many a swelling pleate. **1705** *Lond. Gaz.* No. 4117/4 Cloathed with a red Damask Coat, with blue Flowers, and over it a white Holland Frock. *Ibid.* No. 4149/4 James Smith, upwards of 4 years of Age, in a hanging Sleeve Coat, and a painted Frock ..is missing. **1755** JOHNSON s.v. *Frock*, A kind of gown for children. **1818** *La Belle Assemblée* XVII. No. 108. 87/2 The newest ball-dress is composed of a frock of tulle, over a rose-coloured slip of satin. **1833** HT. MARTINEAU *Three Ages* III. 108 Striving to patch up once more the girl's frock and the boy's coat. **1867** TROLLOPE *Chron. Barset* II. xlv. 9, I don't think I've ever been in London since I wore short frocks. **1882** MISS BRADDON *Mt. Royal* II. vii. 143 Fishky..looked lovely in her white satin frock and orange-blossoms. **1884** *Girl's Own Paper* 28 June 618/3, I think 'frock' seems to be applied to the morning costume, and 'dress' to that of evening only. **1889** BARRIE *Window in Thrums* 172 There could never be more than a Sabbath frock and an everyday gown for her.

5. a. A coat with long skirts. In mod. quots. = FROCK-COAT.

1719 DE FOE *Crusoe* II. vi, A light coat like a frock. **1748** SMOLLETT *Rod. Rand.* (1812) I. 387 A gentleman dressed in a green frock came in. **1770** RICHARDSON *Anecd. Russian Emp.* 325 A light blue frock with silver frogs. **1839–40** W. IRVING *Wolfert's R.* (1855) 162, I observed the Duke of Wellington.. He was alone, simply attired in a blue frock. **1855** THACKERAY *Newcomes* I. 128 Dine in your frock..if your dress-coat is in the country. **1876** BESANT & RICE *Gold. Butterfly* III. 194 The coat..a comfortable easy old frock, a little baggy at the elbows.

b. A coat of a similar 'cut' used as a military uniform; *spec.* see quot. 1881.

1753 HANWAY *Trav.* (1762) I. VII. xcii. 422 He..appears ..always in his regimentals, which are a blue cloth frock with silver brandenburgs. **1881** WILHELM *Milit. Dict.*, *Frock*, in the British service, the undress regimental coat of the guards, artillery, and royal marines. **1890** *19th Cent.* Nov. 842 The stable jacket will retain its freshness, as its owner drills in his 'service frock'.

c. *transf.* A *député* or politician.

[**1917** H. WILSON *Diary* 24 Apr. (1927) I. xviii. 342 It makes it all the more necessary to put off the next meeting of the Frock Coats till after that date.] **1919** *Ibid.* 28 Mar. II. xxvii. 177, I think the Frocks have gone mad. They sit and talk all day. **1921** W. ORPEN *Onlooker in France* xiv. 100 A little mass of black frock-coated figures—'frocks' as we called them. **1926** *Blackw. Mag.* Oct. 455/2 These deputies were not as the 'frocks' of 1914–18, remarkable only for their ignorance of matters military. **1928** *Observer* 26 Aug. 5 Contemptible as a soldier, Lord George was impossible as a 'frock'.

6. *attrib.* and *Comb.*, ***frock-body***; ***frock-like*** adj.; †**frock-clothes** = *frock-dress*; **frock-dress** (*rare*), (*a*) dress of which a frock-coat is a part: so **frock-suit**; (*b*) a form of court dress (see quot. 1875); †**frock-man** = 3 b; **frock-uniform**, undress uniform (see 5 b).

1862 F. WILFORD *Maiden of our own day* 97, I can make this *frock-body while you are making the skirt. **1769** *Public Advertiser* 1 June 3/2 Silk Cloths..for Gentlemens Dress and *Frock Cloaths. **1854** J. BUCHANAN in *Harper's Mag.* Jan. (1884) 256/1, I was invited 'in *frock dress' to the dinner. **1875** *Dress worn by Gentlemen at Court* 3 Frock Dress is worn at Dinners and Evening Parties, where uniform is not worn, and consists of Dress Coat lappelled, Waistcoat, Breeches or Pantaloons, with white Cravat. **1903** *Westm. Gaz.* 17 Nov. 1/1 'Windsor Uniform—Frock dress' is the order for evening attire at Court this week. **1886** W. J. TUCKER *E. Europe* 183 From beneath his vest there hung ..the *frock-like 'gatya' (drawers) of the Magyar peasant. **1657** REEVE *God's Plea for Nineveh* II. 46 If ye fight for the wall, let not the *frokman take the right hand of you in worth. **1810** WELLINGTON in Gurw. *Desp.* VI. 591 We.. shall be highly flattered by your company..whether in full or in *frock uniforms.

Hence **'frockhood**, the state of being dressed in a (short) frock; †**'frockified** *ppl. a.*, clad in a (monk's) frock.

1708 MOTTEUX *Rabelais* IV. xlvi. (1737) 186 A frockify'd Hobgoblin. **1861** WYNTER *Soc. Bees* 124 How many Billies and Bobbies, revelling in all the glorious ease of frockhood, have you not reduced to the cruel purgatory of breeches.

frock (frɒk), *v.* [f. FROCK *sb.*] *trans.* To provide with or dress in a frock; *lit.* and *fig.* **b.** To invest (a person) with priestly office or privilege. Cf. UNFROCK *v.*

1828 W. S. LANDOR *Wks.* (1846) I. 535/2 A gentleman whom perhaps nothing but the hope of gratifying his amiable passions had cowled and frocked. **1860** *All Year Round* No. 54. 79, I have seen baby London short-coated, and frocked, and breeched. **1878** BROWNING *Poets Croisic* xcv, I'll..femininely frock, Your poem masculine that courts La Rocque. **1896** FAIRBAIRN in *Contemp. Rev.* Mar. 315 Founding a Jerusalem bishopric and frocking its new bishop.

'frock-'coat. A double-breasted coat with skirts extending almost to the knees, which are not cut away but of the same length in front as behind.

1823 *Spirit Pub. Jrnls.* (1824) 60 A regularly built green frock coat, not forgetting the velvet collar. **1835** WILLIS *Pencillings* II. xliv. 46 He sat on a divan, cross-legged, in a military frock-coat. **1836–7** DICKENS *Sk. Boz* (1850) 192/1 He usually wore a brown frock-coat, without a wrinkle. **1886** HALL CAINE *Son of Hagar* II. xvi, There was John Proudfoot, the blacksmith, uncommonly awkward in a frock coat.

Hence **frock-'coated** *ppl. a.*, wearing a frock-coat.

1852 R. S. SURTEES *Sponge's Sp. Tour* (1893) 205 The people..could hardly recognise the frock-coated, fancy-vested, military-trousered swell as Lord Scamperdale.

frocked (frɒkt), *pple.* and *ppl. a.* [f. FROCK *sb.* and *v.* + -ED.] Dressed in a frock.

?*c* **1550** *Robin Consc.* 167 in Hazl. *E.P.P.* III. 238, I will goe frocked and in a french hood. **1830** TENNYSON *Poems* 146 Both in bloomwhite silk are frockèd. **1860** HAWTHORNE *Marb. Faun* xxi. (1883) 226 Frocked and hooded skeletons. **1868** GEO. ELIOT *Sp. Gipsy* 318 The Father came bare-headed, frocked, a rope Around his neck.

frocking ('frɒkɪŋ). [f. FROCK *sb.* + -ING[1]. Cf. COATING.] Material for (smock-)frocks.

1864 LOWELL *Moosehead Jrnl.*, *Fireside Trav.* 112 Enormous cowhide boots, over which large blue trousers of frocking strove in vain to crowd themselves.

frockless ('frɒklɪs), *a.* [f. FROCK *sb.* + -LESS.] Without a frock.

1880 *Daily News* 1 Nov. 2/5 Brissac privately orders a guard to be set over the frockless friars.

†**'frodils.** *Obs.* Also 7 **frodels.** [shortened ad. Fr. *afrodille*: see AFFODILL.] = AFFODILL 1.

1674 N. COX *Gentl. Recreat.* I. (1677) 146 Two pound of the Roots of Frodels. **1725** BRADLEY *Fam. Dict.* s.v. *Mange*, The Roots of Frodils two Pounds.

froe, frow (frəʊ). Now chiefly *U.S.* Also 6–7 **frower,** 7 **frowe, frau,** 8 **fro.** [The synonymous FROMWARD suggests that the earliest form *frower* represents a subst. use of FROWARD *a.* in the lit. sense 'turned away', the reference being to the position of the handle.]

1. A wedge-shaped tool used for cleaving and riving staves, shingles, etc. It has a handle in the plane of the blade, set at right angles to the back.

1573 TUSSER *Husb.* xvii. (1878) 36 A frower of iron, for cleauing of lath. **1616** J. LANE *Cont. Sqr.'s T.* ix. 63 Incastinge stooles, ropes, froes, chaines..and all trassh whatsoever. **1624** CAPT. SMITH *Virginia* IV. Wks. (Arb.) 608 Tooles [required]..5 frowes to cleaue pale. **1668** WORLIDGE *Dict. Rust.*, A *Frower*, an Edge-tool used in cleaving Lath. **1685** R. BURTON *Eng. Emp. Amer.* x. 149 A set of Wedges and Fraus..to every family. **1775** ROMANS *Hist. Florida* 182 A river or splitter, who rives them [trees] with the fro. **1851** S. JUDD *Margaret* xvi. (1871) 137 With froe in one hand and mallet in the other. **1874** KNIGHT *Dict. Mech.* I. 918 *Frow* (Coopering).

†**2.** (See quot.; perh. a distinct word.) *Obs.*

1594 PLAT *Jewell-ho.* III. 20 Those warming pinnes.. which of some are called Froes, and being put into their cases, and those cases wrapped in linnen bagges, doe serve to heate beddes.

froe, obs. form of FROW, Dutchwoman.

Froebel: see FRÖBEL.

frog[1] (frɒg). Forms: 1 **frogga,** 2–7 **frogge,** 4 **frock,** 5 **froke,** (4 **froge,** 5 **frugge**), 7 **frogg,** 5– **frog.** *Pl.* 2 **froggen,** 3 **wroggen.** [OE. *frogga* wk. masc.; a hypocoristic formation (peculiar to Eng.), from the root contained in the various Teut. synonyms, of which there are three different types: (1) OE. *frox*, (**frosc*). *forsc* str. masc. (see FROSH) = Du. *vorsch*, OHG. *forsk* (MHG. *vorsch*, mod.G. *frosch*), ON. *frosk-r*:—OTeut. **frosko-z*; (2) ME. *frūde*, FROUD, frog or toad, related by ablaut to ON. *frauð-r*, OSw. pl. *frødhir* (Da. *frö*); cf. OF. *froit*, *frot* toad, which is perh. of Scandinavian origin; (3) ON. *frauke*, whence perh. the ME. *froke*, given among the forms of the present word.

The etymological relation between the various Teut. words involves some unsolved difficulties. Some scholars, on the ground of OE *frogga*, and ON. *frauke*, assume a root ending in a guttural, and explain OTeut. **frosko-* as = **froh-sko-*. This does not account for the ME. *frūde*, ON. *frauð -r*, and hence it has been suggested that the common root of all the words is *frud-* (*frod-*), *fraud-*, *frūd-*; OTeut. *frud-* + suffix *-ko-* would by phonetic law become **frosko-*; the ON. *frauke* appears to be for **frauðke*. With regard to OE. *frogga* it may be remarked that the ending *-gga* occurs in several other names of animals: cf. *stagga*, *docga*, *wicga*. It is possible that *frogga* may owe its form to the analogy of other animal names with this termination.]

1. a. A tailless amphibious animal of the genus *Rana*, or, in wider sense, of the family *Ranidæ*.

The *Promp. Parv.* (Norfolk, *c* 1440) explains *frogge*, *frugge* as meaning 'toad' (*bufo*), while the forms *froke* and *frosche* are said to mean 'frog' (*rana*). It is not known whether this distinction was recognized in the Norfolk dialect of the time; modern East Anglian glossaries do not mention it.

c **1000** ÆLFRIC *Gloss.* in Wr.-Wülcker 122/10 *Rana*, frogga. *c* **1000** —— *Hom.* II. 192 He afylde eal heora land mid froggum. *c* **1175** *Lamb. Hom.* 51 þer wunieð in-ne ..ȝeluwe froggen and crabben. **1297** R. GLOUC. (1724) 69 For it alles com forþ, yt was a foul frogge. *a* **1300** *Vox & Wolf* 256 Wroggen haueth his dou iknede. **13..** *M.E. Glosses* in *Rel. Ant.* I. 80 Frock, *reyne.* **1387** TREVISA *Higden* (Rolls) IV. 397 þey..made hym unwitynge drinke a frogge. *c* **1440** *Promp. Parv.* 180/1 Froke or frosche..*rana.* **1486** *Bk. St. Albans* C iv b, Yeue hir a frogge for to eete. **1555** EDEN *Decades* Pref. (Arb.) 53 Leaste..thou bee lyke vnto Isopes frogges. **1605** SHAKS. *Macb.* IV. i. 14 Eye of Newt, and Toe of Frogge. **1653** WALTON *Angler* vii. 145 The Pike will eat venemous things (as some kind of Frogs are). **1698** G. THOMAS *Pennsylv.* (1848) 16 There is another sort of Frog that crawls up the Tops of Trees. **1774** GOLDSM. *Nat. Hist.* (1776) VII. 73 The frog..can live several days under water, without any danger of suffocation. **1802** BINGLEY *Anim. Biog.* (1813) II. 389 The Edible Frog. **1840** HOOD *Up the Rhine* 129 Amongst the fossils is a complete series of frogs.

b. In various proverbial expressions.

1548 UDALL, etc. *Erasm. Par. John* Pref. 4 The whiche peraduenture will..saye y[t] I geue frogges wine, as the Greke prouerbe speaketh. *a* **1555** LATIMER in Foxe *A. & M.* (1684) III. 413 Well, I have fished and caught a Frog; brought little to pass with much ado. **1603** DEKKER *Grissil* v. i, Old M[aster] you haue fisht faire and caught a frog. **1823** LOCKHART *Reg. Dalton* VI. i. (1842) 345 Whose coat was as bare of nap as a frog's is of feathers.

2. Applied to certain animals more or less resembling frogs, e.g. the FROG-FISH or ANGLER 2.

1769 PENNANT *Zool.* (1776) III. 106, I have changed the old name of Fishing Frog to the more simple one of Angler. **1855** OGILVIE Suppl., *Frog, Frog-fish*, names sometimes applied to..(*Lophius piscatorius*) the angler. **1885** T. ROOSEVELT *Hunting Trips* vi. 191 The horned frog is not a frog at all, but a lizard.

3. a. As a term of abuse applied to a man or woman. Also, †a Dutchman.

c **1330** R. BRUNNE *Chron. Wace* (Rolls) 1782 Formest was sire Gogmagog, He was most, þat foule froge. **1535** LYNDESAY *Satyre* 2136 Ane Frog that fyles the winde. **1626** L. OWEN *Spec. Jesuit.* (1629) 54 These infernall frogs [Jesuits] are crept into the West and East Indyes. **1652** *Season. Exp. Netherl.* 2 Neither had I ever wished the charming of those Froggs [the Dutch].

b. = FROGGY *sb.* 2. Also, the French language. Also *attrib.* or as *adj.*

1778 F. BURNEY *Evelina* I. xiv. 79 Hark you, Mrs. Frog.. you may lie in the mud till some of your Monsieurs come to help you out of it. **1845** F. A. KEMBLE *Let.* 15 Dec. in *Rec. Later Life* (1882) III. 110 Surely I shall always be able, go where I will, among frogs or maccaronis, to procure *sucre noir*, or *inchiostro nero.* **1914** R. BROOKE *Let.* July (1968) 601 Could we go on Friday to the Frog-Art show at Grosvenor House? From the First Frog to Cézanne. **1932** J. DOS PASSOS *Nineteen Nineteen* 55 Even the dogs looked like frog dogs. **1938** S. V. BENÉT *Thirteen O'Clock* 234 But there'd be the nuisance of learning frog-talk and the passage there and back. **1955** W. FAULKNER *Fable* 333 Ask him... You can speak Frog. **1962** I. MURDOCH *Unofficial Rose* viii. 84 Not that I want you to marry a frog, but she sounded quite a nice girl. **1970** *Private Eye* 27 Mar. 16, I dunno about the no hard feeling's bit—from what I hear about them frog sheilahs!

4. a. A name given to certain diseases of the throat or mouth.

1656 RIDGLEY *Pract. Physick* 174 The Frog—It is a swelling under the Tongue that is common to children. **1748** tr. *Renatus' Distemp. Horses* 235 Little Frogs, Pushes or Swellings in the Tongues of Oxen. **1876** *Mid-Yorksh. Gloss.*, *Frog-i-t'-mouth*, a popular name for the complaint known as the thrush. **1885** *Syd. Soc. Lex.*, *Frog*, the thrush, or aphthous stomatitis, of infants.

b. Colloq. phr. ***frog in the throat***: (temporary) hoarseness; an irritation in the throat.

1909 in *Cent. Dict.* Suppl. **1933** F. RICHARDS *Old Soldiers never Die* xvii. 223 One was speaking very thickly and the other lost his temper and told him to pull the bloody frog out of his throat. **1962** A. NISBETT *Technique Sound Studio* vii. 125 If the speaker has a frog in his throat..it will not do any harm to leave in the cough which clears it.

5. = *frog-stool.*

1398 TREVISA *Barth. De P.R.* XVII. cviii. (Tollem. MS.), Yf it is doo amonge frogges [**1535** frogge stoles: Lat. *fungos*] & venemouse meetes, it..quencheþ all þe venym.

6. *Brickmaking.* (See quot.)

1876 SIR E. BECKETT *Bk. Build.* 162 Making bricks with a hollow in one or both faces which I have heard absurdly called a frog.

7. *attrib.* and *Comb.* **a.** attributive, as ***frog-colour, -concert, -green, -kind, -pit, -spear, -tribe***; ***frog-like*** adj.; **b.** objective, as ***frog-fishing***; **c.** parasynthetic, as ***frog-coloured, -hearted, -voiced*** adjs.

1836 B. D. WALSH *Aristoph.*, *Knights* I. iii, Died himself *Frog-colour. **1817** COLERIDGE *Biog. Lit.* 238 Many of the faces round me assumed a very doleful and *frog-coloured appearance. **1837** HT. MARTINEAU *Soc. Amer.* II. 184 We were being treated with a *frog-concert. **1889** *Century Dict.*, **Frog-fishing*, the act or practice of fishing for frogs with hook, line, and rod; frogging. **1890** *Daily News* 20 Nov. 2/1 The small bonnet..is in *frog-green velvet. **1846** E. FITZGERALD *Lett.* (1894) I. 201 A *frog-hearted wretch. **1774** GOLDSM. *Nat. Hist.* (1776) VI. 97 The *Frog kind. **1561** DAUS tr. *Bullinger on Apoc.* (1573) 225 b, By their complaintes..and disputations altogether *frogge-lyke and fenlyke, they be hatefull both to God and men. **1842** S. LOVER *Handy Andy* xix. 176 As loud as his frog-like voice permitted. **1615** J. STEPHENS *Satyr. Ess.* A viij b, They that take From puddles or dull *Frog-pits, never make Themselves nor others happy. **1891** *Fur, Fin & Feather* Mar. 196 If the tourist likes frogs' legs..a *frog spear is handy but not necessary. **1849–52** TODD *Cycl. Anat.* IV. 1213/1 The larva, resembling in appearance a *frog-tadpole. **1851** CARPENTER *Man. Phys.* (ed. 2) 396 The *Frog tribe, which forms the lowest order of Reptiles. **1799** COLERIDGE *Lett.* (1895) 308 You ill-looking *frog-voiced reptile!

8. a. Special comb.: **frog-back,** a 'back' at leap-frog; **frog-catcher** (see quot.); **frog-clock,** ? = *frog-hopper*; **frog-crab,** a member of the crustaceous genus *Ranina*; **frog-dance,** ? a kind of hornpipe in which the performer crouches down in a frog-like attitude; **frog-eater,** one who eats frogs, a term contemptuously applied to Frenchmen; so **frog-eating** *ppl. a.*; **frog eye,** a fungal disease of plants indicated by spots on the leaves, *esp.* a tobacco disease caused by *Cercospora nicotianæ* or an American disease of apple and other trees caused by *Physalospora obtusa*; also *attrib.*; also **frog's eye; frog-face,** (*a*) a face like that of a frog; (*b*) *Path.*, a type of facial deformity usu. caused by a tumour in the region of the nose; **frog-hopper,** a group of homopterous insects of the family *Cercopidæ*, so called from their shape and leaping powers; **frog's hornpipe** (see *frog-dance*); †**frog-paddock,** a large kind of frog; **frog-pecker,** a heron; **frog-pike, frog-plate, frog-shell** (see quots.); **frog-spit, -spittle,** (*a*) = CUCKOO-SPIT[2] 1: (*b*) = *frog-spawn*; **frog-tongue** (see quot.).

a **1861** MRS. BROWNING *Lett. R. H. Horne* (1877) II. 258 Everybody was bound to run at the '*frog-back' given, and do his best. **1796** MORSE *Amer. Geog.* I. 212 Quaw bird or *Frog Catcher, *Ardea clemata.* **1653** W. LAUSON *Comm. J. D[ennys] Secr. Angling* in Arb. *Garner* I. 196 Washing down worms, flies, *frog-clocks, etc. **1879** ROSSITER *Dict. Sci.*

Terms, **Frog crab*, Ranina: can climb trees, etc. **1895** *Westm. Gaz.* 30 Oct. 1/2 A '*frog-dance', cleverly executed by a budding barge-builder of seventeen. **1863** G. KEARLEY *Links in Chain* viii. 179 M. de Lacépède was a *frog eater. **1889** *Century Dict.*, **Frog-eating*. **1914** *Jrnl. Agric. Res.* II. 57 Enlargements, which give to the disease the common name of '*frog-eye', are usually in alternating rings or zones of brown and gray. *Ibid.* 66 (*caption*) Typical spots of the frog-eye disease. **1926** F. D. HEALD *Man. Plant Dis.* xxii. 585 The leaf attacks [of *Physalospora cydoniæ*] are referred to as leaf spot, leaf blight, brown spot and frog eye. **1950** C. WESTCOTT *Plant Dis. Handbk.* iv. 308 Frog-eye leaf spot, general on apple, [etc.]. **1971** K. M. GRAHAM *Plant Dis. Fiji* 210 Frog eye is common on tobacco wherever it is grown... The frog eye fungus persists in crop refuse. **1872** GEO. ELIOT *Middlem.* IV. xxxiv. 189 A little round head with bulging eyes—a sort of *frog-face. **1884** M. MACKENZIE *Man. Dis. Throat & Nose* II. 385 The most marked symptoms [of enchondromata of the nose] are obstruction of the nasal passages, and deformity in advanced cases amounting to 'frog-face'. **1948** *Ann. Surg.* CXXVII. 522 As the growth expands and advances, the floor of the orbit is elevated (unilateral or bilateral), producing 'frog-face' deformity. **1711** *Phil. Trans.* XXVII. 351 The remaining *Ranatræ*, or *Froghoppers. **1857** LIVINGSTONE *Trav.* (1861) 281 Our own 'frog-hopper' (*Aphrophora spumaria*) or 'cuckoo-spit'. **1844** DICKENS *Mart. Chuz.* xi, A dancing step ..commonly called the *Frog's Hornpipe. **1653** WALTON *Angler* vii. 151 The green Frog..is by Topsel taken to be venemous; and so is the Padock, or *Frog-Padock, which usually keeps or breeds on the land. **1825** SCOTT *Betrothed* xxiii, I will shew you one of these *frog-peckers. **1867** SMYTH *Sailor's Word-bk.*, **Frog-pike*, a female pike, so called from its period of spawning being late, contemporary with the frogs. **1867** J. HOGG *Microsc.* I. ii. 110 A *Frog-plate for viewing the circulation of the blood in the web of a frog's foot. **1911** *Encycl. Brit.* XXVI. 1038/1 '*Frog's eye', or 'leaf spot', denotes the occurrence of small white specks on the leaf. This disease is probably bacterial in origin. **1855** OGILVIE Suppl., **Frog-shell*, the name applied to various species of shells of the genus Ranella. *a* **1825** FORBY *Voc. E. Anglia*, **Frog-spit*. **1855** OGILVIE Suppl., Cuckoo-spittle or *frog-spittle (*Aphrophora spumaria*). **1822–34** *Good's Study Med.* (ed. 4) I. 94 The Ranula or *frog-tongue, is a tumour under the tongue.

b. In various plant-names, as **frog-bit**, (*a*) *Hydrocharis Morsus-ranæ*, an aquatic plant; (*b*) *Limnobium Spongia*, a similar plant of America; **frog-cheese**, (*a*) (see quot. 1866); (*b*) *Malva sylvestris* (cf. CHEESE *sb.*[1] 5); **frog('s-foot**, duckweed (*Lemna*); **frog-grass**, (*a*) = CRAB-GRASS 1; †(*b*) *Juncus bufonius*; **frog's lettuce**, water caltrops, *Potamogeton densus*; **frog-lily** *U.S.*, the American yellow water-lily, *Nuphar advena*; also called SPATTERDOCK and cow-lily; **frog-orchis** (see quots.); †**frog-parsley**, some plant (? = *fools' parsley*); **frog-stool** = TOADSTOOL *sb.*; **frog-wort**, a name given to species of *Orchis*.

1578 LYTE *Dodoens* I. lxxi. 106 The thirde [kind of floating weeds]..is called..*Frogge bitte. **1741** *Compl. Fam.-Piece* II. iii. 374 The..Spearwort, and Frogbits. **1866** *Treas. Bot.*, Frog-bit, American, *Limnobium*. **1868** *Nat. Encycl.* I. 659 One of the Frogbit tribe of plants. **1818** *Withering's Brit. Plants* (ed. 6) IV. 453 *Lycoperdon*..*Frogcheese. **1866** *Treas. Bot.*, *Frog-cheese*, a name applied occasionally to the larger puff-balls when young. **1529** *Grete Herbal* cclix. Pi, Lentylles of the water ben called *frogges fote. **1863** PRIOR *Plant-n.* 87 Frog-foot, *lemna*. **1597** *Frog grasse [see CRAB-GRASS 1]. **1640** PARKINSON *Theat. Bot.* Index 1738 Frogge grasse or Toadegrass. *Ibid.* II. lviii. 281 The people that dwell neare it by the Sea side, call it Frogge grasse or Crab grasse. **1861** MISS PRATT *Flower. Pl.* IV. 385 Glass-wort is sometimes called..Frog-grass. **1597** GERARDE *Herbal* II. ccxcviii. 824 Small water Caltrops or *Frogs lettuce. **1869** J. G. FULLER *Flower-Gatherers* 204 It flourishes best in dull, stagnant pools, and is often called the **Frog-lily*. **1931** W. N. CLUTE *Common Names of Plants* 111 The frog lily (*Nymphaea advena*) is better named, for frogs delight to rest on its round floating leaves. **1840** PAXTON *Bot. Dict.*, **Frog-orchis*, see *Gymnadenia viridis*. **1861** MISS PRATT *Flower. Pl.* V. 214 Green Habenaria..sometimes called..Frog Orchis. **1651** J. F[REAKE] *Agrippa's Occ. Philos.* xviii. 41 Sheep fly from *Frog-parsley as from some deadly thing. **1535** *Frogge stoles [see **1398** quot. in FROG *sb.*[1] 5]. **1661** LOVELL *Hist. Anim. & Min.* 144 The dung helps against Frogstooles with wine and vineger. **1865** *Science Gossip* 1 Nov. 258 In Dorsetshire poisonous fungi are often called 'Frogstools'. *a* **1824** HOLDICH *Ess. Weeds* (1825) 65 Man-orchis, Red-lead and *Frogwort are the only English names we have heard given to these weeds in damp pastures.

c. In names of games, as ***frog-in-the-middle***, ***frog over an old dog***. Also LEAP-FROG *sb.*

1801 STRUTT *Sports & Past.* IV. iv. 293 Another [game] equally..well known with us, and called Frog in the middle. **1847–78** HALLIWELL *Frog over an old dog*, leap-frog, list of games, Rawl. MS.

frog[2] (frɒg). [Of doubtful origin.]

Perh. a use of prec., suggested by some resemblance in sound between this word and the It. name *forchetta*, or some dialectal variant of F. *fourchette*.

a. An elastic, horny substance growing in the middle of the sole of a horse's hoof.

1610 MARKHAM *Masterp.* II. ci. 384 The Frush, which of some is called the Frogge of the foot, is the tenderest part of the hoofe towards the heele. **1727** SWIFT *Gulliver* IV. ix, They have excellent medicines..to cure..cuts in the pastern or frog of the foot. **1840** YOUATT *Horse* xviii. 376 In the space between the bars, and accurately filling it is the frog.

b. *Comb.*: **frog-band**, a band running from above the wall below the coronary band to join the frog; **frog-pad** = CUSHION *sb.* 4 b; **frog-stay** (see quot.).

1829 B. CLARK *Hippodon.* (ed. 2) 61 This cell or cleft of the frog is..prevented from rupturing inwards towards the quick by a stout considerable cone of horn passing directly from it into the sensitive frog..This cone commences nearly opposite to the termination of the heels of the coffin-bone.. This part..being without even a name, I gave it the epithet frog-stay..from its closing the frog, and holding more firmly its halves together. **1831** W. YOUATT *Horse* p. vi, The Anatomy of the Foot... The coronary ligament: the coronary ring: the frog-band. **1908** *Animal Managem.* 217 A firm, soft cushion, sometimes called the 'frog pad' or 'cushion of the heels'.

frog[3] (frɒg). [Of obscure origin; perh. ad. Pg. *froco* (repr. L. *floccus* FLOCK *sb.*), which has much the same sense.]

1. An attachment to the waist-belt in which a sword or bayonet or hatchet may be carried.

1719 DE FOE *Crusoe* I. xv, A belt with a frog hanging to it, such as..we wear hangers in. **1725** —— *Voy. round World* (1840) 150 Every man a hatchet, hung in a little frog at his belt. **1876** VOYLE & STEVENSON *Milit. Dict.*, *Frog*..that part of a soldier's accoutrements which is attached to the waist-belt for holding the bayonet. **1879** RUTLEY *Study Rocks* v. 40 A small leathern frog with a flap.

2. An ornamental fastening for the front of a military coat or cloak, consisting of a spindle-shaped button, covered with silk or other material, which passes through a loop on the opposite side of the garment.

1746 BERKELEY *Let.* Wks. 1871 IV. 306 Laces, frogs, cockades..are so many..obstacles to a soldier's exerting his strength. **1770** W. RICHARDSON *Anecd. Russian Emp.* 325 In a light blue frock with silver frogs. **1796** J. ANSTEY *Pleader's Guide* (1803) 181 The coat..With tabby lin'd and frogs complete. **1836** DICKENS *Sk. Boz* vii, He wore a braided surtout with frogs behind. **1846** *Hist. Rec. 3rd Light Dragoons* 39 The buttons set on three and three upon yellow frogs or loops. **1848** CRAIG, *Frog*..a small barrel-shaped silk ornament with tassels, used in the decoration of mantles, etc. **1896** *Daily News* 19 Mar. 6/5 Serge suits and tweed costumes are better adapted than any other to this style of ornamentation. Frogs are sold in sets to accompany the braiding.

3. *Comb.*, as ***frog-belt***, ***-button***.

1719 DE FOE *Crusoe* II. iv. (1840) II. 68 He drew a hatchet out of a frog-belt. **1827** HONE *Every-day Bk.* II. 190 A coat with frog-buttons. **1867** SMYTH *Sailor's Word-bk.*, *Frog-belt*, a baldrick.

frog[4] (frɒg). (See quot. 1860.)

1847 *Rep. U.S. Comm. Patents 1846* 95 Frogs are used having guards or grinders on their outsides, and double inclined planes up and down, by which the wheels are guided to the right track. **1860** WORCESTER (citing Williams), *Frog* (Railroads), a grooved piece of iron placed at the junction of the rails where one track crosses another. **1889** *Scott. Leader* 30 Apr. 5 The accident..would appear to have been caused by the train suddenly leaving the rails at a 'frog'.

frog-fish. A name given to various fishes, *esp.* to the Angler or Fishing-frog (*Lophius piscatorius*). Other varieties belong to the genera *Batrachus* and *Chironectes*.

1646 SIR T. BROWNE *Pseud. Ep.* III. xxiv. 169 The..Frog-fish. **1769** PENNANT *Zool.* (1776) III. 105 Toad-fish, Frog-fish, or Sea-Devil. **1835–6** TODD *Cycl. Anat.* I. 114/2 The œsophagus of the frog-fish leads to a large globular stomach. **1879** ROSSITER *Dict. Sci. Terms*, *Frog fishes*, Chironectes.

frogged (frɒgd), *ppl. a.* [f. FROG[3] + -ED[2].] Of a coat, etc.: Fastened or ornamented with frogs.

1774 W. COLE in *J. Granger's Lett.* (1805) 370 Coat with frogs, and slashed sleeves frogged also. **1796** J. ANSTEY *Pleader's Guide* (1803) 181 Which coat, so trimmed, so frog'd, said Gull Did spoil. **1812** H. & J. SMITH *Rej. Addr.* ii. (1873) 13 *note*, Young Betty..clad in a furred and frogged surtout. **1861** THACKERAY *Four Georges* iv. (1862) 188 A frogged frock-coat with a fur collar.

froggery ('frɒgərɪ). [f. FROG[1] + -ERY.]

1. An assemblage of frogs, frogs collectively.

1785 SARA FIELDING *Ophelia* II. ii, The concert, of which the froggery made the bass. **1842** *Blackw. Mag.* LI. 47 A thrush, who is watching the froggery from above.

2. A place where frogs are kept or abound.

1763 ELIZ. CARTER in *Pennington's Memoirs* (1808) I. 335 A very high causeway, with a perpendicular descent on each side to the toaderies and frogeries below. **1854** *Tait's Mag.* XXI. 695 He had what he called a Froggery and Toadery at the bottom of his orchard. **1871** *Echo* 14 Jan., Mr... confesses to have actually kept a 'froggery' for his own private consumption.

frogging ('frɒgɪŋ), *vbl. sb.*[1] [f. FROG[1] + -ING[1].] Catching frogs, fishing for frogs. Also *attrib.*

1651–7 T. BARKER *Art of Angling* (1820) 25 Pikes go a frogging. **1884** G. W. SEARS *Woodcraft* (Cent.), When.. fishing is very poor, try frogging. **1893** J. A. BARRY *S. Brown's Bunyip, etc.* 78 A thumping, lively carpet snake, whose frogging ground he had intruded on. **1895** K. GRAHAME *Golden Age* 182 Nor had he gone frogging by himself.

frogging ('frɒgɪŋ), *vbl. sb.*[2] [f. FROG[3] + -ING[1].] The ornamentation on a frogged coat.

1888 *Times* 20 Jan. 5/3 A Bohemian costume, made up of a long, frogged coat—this frogging being, by the way, an essentially Hungarian ornament.

froggish ('frɒgɪʃ), *a.* [f. FROG *sb.*[1] + -ISH.] Frog-like.

a **1861** T. WINTHROP *John Brent* (1883) xxii. 194 Thanks La Grenouille, rover of the wilderness, for thy froggish instinct. *a* **1889** J. G. WOOD (Cent.), The froggish aspect.

froggy ('frɒgɪ), *sb.* [f. FROG[1] + -Y.]

1. A playful designation for a frog.

1840 HOOD *Up the Rhine* 129 A series of frogs, from the full-grown froggy..down to that minute frogling or tadpole.

2. *slang.* Also **froggee.** A term of contempt for a Frenchman, from their reputed habit of eating frogs.

1872 S. DE VERE *Americanisms* 82 As when Frenchmen were dubbed Froggies. **1883** *Referee* 15 July 7/3 While Ned from Boulogne says '*Oui, mon brave*, The Froggies must answer for Tamatave.' **1887** W. S. GILBERT *Ruddigore* I. 11 Froggee answers with a shout As he sees us go about. **1894** ASTLEY *50 Years Life* I. 203 With the assistance of 'Froggy', we succeeded in filling all our bottles. **1955** G. GREENE *Quiet American* IV. ii. 241 Don't go, Fowler... I can't talk to those Froggies. **1965** *Guardian* 3 Sept. 9/6 A group of stage-type Limeys spend a weekend in France where they mix with a series of stage-type Froggies.

froggy ('frɒgɪ), *a.* [f. FROG[1] + -Y[1].]

1. Having or abounding in frogs.

1611 COTGR., *Grenouillere*, a froggie place. **1823** *Blackw. Mag.* XIII. 458 A..slimy, froggy pool. **1882** EDNA LYALL *Donovan* xxiv, Why are you wandering up and down the very froggiest and toadiest path in the garden?

2. Frog-like, such as a frog would have.

1837 GEN. P. THOMPSON *Exerc.* (1842) IV. 223 The little Whigs..are puffing out their froggy sides to the dimensions of the ox. **1883** R. F. BURTON & CAMERON *Gold Coast* I. iii. 59 Froggy faces.

3. *slang.* French.

1937 in PARTRIDGE *Dict. Slang.* **1953** G. KERSH *Brighton Monster* 187 We specialised in French brandy: stopped the Froggy boats in mid-Channel, grabbed the cargo. **1959** *Listener* 24 Dec. 1108/2 Where is this froggy speech of mine? **1962** I. MURDOCH *Unofficial Rose* viii. 84 What about that froggy girl, the one you met in Singapore?

froghood ('frɒghʊd). [f. FROG[1] + -HOOD.] Quality or standing as a frog.

a **1770** C. SMART *Duellist* 32 Too hard for any frog's digestion, To have his froghood call'd in question. **1888** G. ALLEN in *Gd. Words* 230 In the accomplished dignity of perfect froghood.

frogland ('frɒglænd). [f. FROG[1] + LAND *sb.*[1]] Marshy land in which frogs abound, as the Fens, Holland, etc. In quots. *attrib.* only.

1721 RAMSAY *Tartana* xxxiii, May she be curst to starve in frogland fens. **1830** SCOTT *Auchindrane* I. i, A Netherlander, One of our Frogland friends.

So '**froglander**, *slang*, a Dutchman.

a **1700** B. E. *Dict. Cant. Crew*, *Frog-landers*, Dutch-men. **1867** in SMYTH *Sailor's Word-bk.*

froglet ('frɒglɪt). [See -LET.] A small or young frog.

1907 W. DE MORGAN *Alice-for-Short* xxi, Just one chirp of a nightingale or trill of a flute from a froglet. **1926** J. S. HUXLEY *Ess. Pop. Sci.* xvii. 196 The brusque transformation of tadpole into froglet. **1956** *Nature* 18 Feb. 342/2 By August..the froglets from this spawn were approximately 1½ cm. long.

frogling ('frɒglɪŋ). [dim. of FROG[1]: see -LING.] A little frog; also, a tadpole.

1742 JARVIS *Quix.* I. III. iv. (1749) 107 He does not fail.. the wormlings of the earth, nor the froglings of the water. **1831** CARLYLE in *For. Q. Rev.* VIII. 365 A Frog with Frogling by his side Came hopping through the plain. **1840** HOOD *Up the Rhine* 129 That minute frogling, or tadpole.

'**frogman.** [FROG[1] I.] A man wearing a close-fitting suit of rubber or the like, with goggles and flippers, and equipped with a self-contained supply of oxygen to enable him to swim and operate under water; so '**frogwoman. b.** (See quot. 1962.)

1945 *Sphere* 22 Sept. 359/3 (*caption*) The complete apparatus worn by the 'frog-men'. **1947** *Nature* 18 Jan. 88/2 An attempt to obtain samples of blood and tissues from the whale carcase..will be made by a scientific man working in a self-contained oxygen swim-suit ('frog man suit'). **1949** *N.Y. Times* 25 Dec. E7/5 'Frogmen', as they are called, wear self-contained breathing apparatus and web-like rubber shoes, used in the war, and swim like fish without stirring up mud, so that fish can be stalked with cameras. **1955** *Times* 6 June 4/2 Royal Navy frogmen flown by helicopter from Gosport searched the wreckage and recovered the four bodies. **1962** D. E. BARNES *Newnes Conc. Encycl. Nucl. Energy* 266/1 Frogmen is the name given to those who work in completely enclosing rubber suits, known as frogsuits, which are used to give protection against airborne radioactive material. *Ibid.* 266/2 (*caption*) Frogman suit. **1963** *Daily Tel.* 22 July 11/8 Teams of frogmen and frogwomen from all parts of Britain searched the sea and two lakes yesterday for a trail of clues leading to three sunken 'treasure' chests.

frog-march, frog's-march, *sb.*

1. A movement forward in frog fashion.

1880 SIR S. LAKEMAN *Kaffir-land* iv. 26 He had had a frog's march—that is to say, on hands, belly, and knees.

2. *slang.* The method of carrying a drunken or refractory prisoner face downwards between four men, each holding a limb.

1871 *Evening Standard* 18 Apr. 5/4 They did not give the defendant the 'Frog's March'. **1882** *Daily Tel.* 20 Nov. 3/2 Treating a refractory toper to the frog's-march, by carrying him, face downwards, to the station. **1885** in *West. Morn. News* 2 Jan. 7/3 What is known as the 'frog's-march'.

Hence **frog-march, frog's-march** *v. trans.*, to carry (a prisoner) face downwards; now usually, to hustle (a person) forward after seizing him from behind and pinning his arms together; **frog-marching** *vbl. sb.*

1884 *B'ham Weekly Post* 15 Nov. 3/7 Deceased was 'frog's-marched'—that is, with face downwards—from Deal to Walmer. **1894** *Times* 8 May 13/6 Death was accelerated by the 'frog-marching'. **1931** J. FERGUSON *Death comes to Perigord* viii. 97 Cæsar slewed him round, and forcing both arms behind his back, got ready to frog-march him to the door. **1935** D. L. SAYERS *Gaudy Night* xxi. 446 Someone seized her round the neck from behind and frog's-marched her off to the cellar. **1952** B. HAMILTON *So Sad, so Fresh* xii. 84 We took complete charge.. frogs-marching Marya to the piano. **1965** *Times Lit. Suppl.* 19 Aug. 715/4 When I was at school in Yorkshire to be frog-marched meant that one's arms were secured behind one's back by a heftier fellow than oneself and one was propelled forward by the tormentor's knee being applied regularly and forcibly to one's behind. **1969** R. F. DELDERFIELD *Come Home Charlie* viii. 89 He.. took me by the collar and the seat of my pants and frogmarched me the length of the café.

frog-mouth, frog's mouth.

1. A name given to the Snapdragon (see quot.).

1851 S. THOMSON *Wild Fl.* III. (ed. 4) 252 The great snapdragon or frog's-mouth (*Antirrhinum majus*).

2. A bird of the family *Podargidæ*.

1888 *Riverside Nat. Hist.* IV. Birds 387 The frog-mouths (*Batrachostomus*) are confined to southern India [etc.].

frog-spawn, frogs' spawn.

1. The ova, spawn, or young of frogs.

1621 BURTON *Anat. Mel.* I. iii. II. ii. (1651) 200 He had.. swallowed frogs-spawn. **1718** QUINCY *Compl. Disp.* 228 Frog's Spawn. **1833** J. RENNIE *Alph. Angling* 11 Carp.. will devour small eels, frog-spawn, and the roe or the young of fishes. **1885** *Syd. Soc. Lex.*, *Frog's spawn*, the ova of the common frog.. Once used in medicine.

attrib. **1710** STEELE *Tatler* No. 245 ¶2 A Collection of Receipts to make.. Frog Spawn Water.

2. a. The popular name for certain freshwater algæ, which form green and slimy masses floating on the surface of ponds and ditches.

1864 *Realm* 15 June 546 Cities to which Genoa is a cob-web on a wall and Venice mere frog-spawn in a puddle. **1884** *Public Opinion* 5 Sept. 299/1 Slime and frog-spawn are the chief products of these holes.

fig. **1895** J. SMITH *Message of Exodus* xix. 297 God in whom his fathers trusted was different from the frog-spawn of superstition.

b. *colloq.* Tapioca or sago pudding.

1959 I. & P. OPIE *Lore & Lang. Schoolch.* ix. 163 Tapioca or sago is.., very commonly, 'frog spawn'. **1963** *New Society* 22 Aug. 5/1 The well-known fly cemetery and frogspawn are still o.k.-descriptions of currant puddings and tapioca.

3. *Sugar-manuf.* A fungus destructive to saccharine solutions.

1887 tr. *De Bary's Fungi* 469 *Leuconostoc mesenterioides*, the 'frog-spawn' of sugar-factories.

Fröhlich ('frøːlɪç). Also **Froelich**. The name of Alfred *Fröhlich*, Austrian neurologist (1871–1953), used *attrib.* and in the possessive to designate a syndrome characterized esp. by obesity and sexual infantilism and caused by a tumour in the pituitary gland.

1909 *Jrnl. Amer. Med. Assoc.* 24 July 255/1 Delayed adolescence of the Fröhlich type. **1912** H. CUSHING *Pituitary Body* 337 (*index*) Fröhlich's syndrome. **1964** A. GROLLMAN *Clin. Endocrinol.* vi. 89/2 The chief symptoms observed in Fröhlich's syndrome are obesity, faulty skeletal development and genital hypoplasia.

froise, fraise (frɔɪz, freɪz). Forms: 4–7 froyse, froyze, 5 froys, 7 frois, (froyes), 7–9 froize, 4– froise, 8– fraise. [The twofold spelling with *ai*, *oi* would seem to point to a Fr. etymon, OF. **freis*, **freise*, repr. popular Lat. **frīxum*, *-a*, var. of *frixum*, *-a*, pa. pple. neut. and fem. of *frīgĕre* to FRY; but the word has not been found.] A kind of pancake or omelette, often containing slices of bacon.

1338 *Durh. MS. Cell. Roll*, In Carnibus porc' pro froys, ijd. **1390** GOWER *Conf.* II. 93 He routeth with a slepy noise And brustleth as a monkes froise Whan it is throwe into the panne. **14..** *Nom.* in Wr.-Wülcker 741/29 *Hoc frixum*, a froys. **1579** TWYNE *Phisicke agst. Fort.* II. cxvi. 310b, Eschue puddinges, sausages, froyses, and al manner confected and mengled meates. **1651** RANDOLPH, etc. *Hey for Honesty* v. Wks. (1875) 475 They'd make me froises and flapjacks too. **1672** T. B. *Let. to Author Vind. Clergy* 79 To smell a Fanatick as far as another man shall do broil'd Herrings, or a burnt froise. **1755** JOHNSON, *Fraise*, a pancake with bacon in it. **1819** W. TAYLOR in *Monthly Mag.* XLVII. 133 The general.. threw the froize out of the window. **1879** MISS JACKSON *Shropsh. Word-bk.*, *Fraise*, a kind of pancake eaten with sweet sauce: it was thicker than the ordinary pancake, and made with a 'stiffer' batter.

froit, Sc. var. FROT; obs. form of FRUIT.

† **'frokin.** *Obs.* [a. Du. †*vrouwken* (Kilian), dim. of *vrouw*: see FROW and -KIN.] A little Dutch woman; a Dutch child.

1603 DEKKER *Wonderfull Yeare* D iv b, A little Frokin (one of my Dutch runnawayes children). **1620** MIDDLETON *Courtly Masque* Wks. (Bullen) VII. 169 You, blue-ey'd frokin, looks like fire and brimstone. **1738** *Common Sense* (1739) II. 58 My Neighbours learn nothing but to be so proud they won't darn their own Linnen, and all their Talk is of nothing but Mantelets, Frokins, Farinelli, and London Midwives.

frolic ('frɒlɪk), *sb.* [f. FROLIC *v.* or *a.*]

1. An outburst of fun, gaiety, or mirth; a prank. Also, †a flourish (on the drum). *on the frolic*: on the 'spree'.

a **1635** CORBET *To Ld. Mordaunt* 110 Whiles the bold Drum Strikes up his Frolick, through the Hall they come. **1654** WHITLOCK *Zootomia* 311 Thou and I will enjoy our selves in uncontrouled Frolicks, and Discourse. **1681** DRYDEN *Sp. Friar* III. iii, I was upon the frolic this evening, and came to visit thee in masquerade. **1700** CIBBER *Love makes Man* v. iii, What, is my deary in her frolics already? **1784** FRANKLIN *Autobiog.* Wks. 1840 I. 101, I spent no time in taverns, games, or frolics of any kind. **1828** SCOTT *F.M. Perth* xxx, But mark you, it shall be the last of my frolics. **1873** LOWELL *Among my Bks.* Ser. II. 176 He.. often filled whole pages.. with the gay frolics of his pencil.

b. Fun, merriment, sportive mirth.

1676 D'URFEY *Mad. Fickle* III. i, There's mirth and frolick in 't. *a* **1715** BURNET *Own Time* (1766) I. 282 To such a madness of frolick and intemperance. **1774** GOLDSM. *Retal.* 52 Alas, that such frolic should now be so quiet! *a* **1839** PRAED *Poems* (1864) I. 276 Those who meet as we have met, In frolic and in laughter. **1875** JOWETT *Plato* (ed. 2) V. 39 All young creatures are full of motion and frolic.

c. = WHIM.

1711 SWIFT *Jrnl. to Stella* 5 Apr., If the frolic should take you of going to Bath, I here send you a note on Parvisol.

2. A scene or occasion of gaiety or mirth; a merry-making; a party. In *U.S.* = BEE 4. Also preceded by some modifying word, as *reaping-*, *water-frolic*.

c **1645** HOWELL *Lett.* VI. 37, I intend to wait on you, and give you a frolik. **1663** COWLEY *Cutter Coleman St.* v. x, We hit upon this Frolick, Colonel, only for a kind o' Mask.. to celebrate your Nuptials. **1770** MAD. D'ARBLAY *Early Diary* 20 Apr., I told him of my frolick for Friday. **1817** J. BRADBURY *Trav. Amer.* 292 This operation is almost always the subject of what they term a frolic, or in some places, a bee. **1833** HT. MARTINEAU *Briery Creek* i. 18 They meant to have a reaping frolic when the corn should be ripe. It should be a pic-nic. **1895** *E. Anglia Gloss.*, *Frolic*, water-frolic, a gala, regatta, or water-picnic.

†**3.** ? Humorous verses circulated at a feast. *Obs.*

1616 B. JONSON *Devil an Ass* II. viii, To see him.. drinke vnto 'hem; And then talke baudy: and send frolicks! O! **1631** R. H. *Arraignm. Whole Creature* xiv. §2. 244 Moveable as Shittlecockes.. or as Frolicks at Feasts, sent from man to man, returning againe at last, to the first man.

†**4.** A plaything; toy. *Obs.*

1650 FULLER *Pisgah* IV. vii. 136 Apples were dedicated unto her, and her image commonly made with such fruit, as a frolick in her hand.

Hence **'frolicful** *a.*; **'frolicky** *a.*, full of frolic, frolicsome.

1848 CRAIG, *Frolicful.* **1748** RICHARDSON *Clarissa* V. xxiv. 209 A little too frolicky that air—Yet have I prepared my Beloved to expect.. great vivacity and quality-freedom. **1751** *Ibid.* (ed. 4) V. x. 68 Yet may we.. make a good frolicky half-day with them. **1883** E. W. NYE *Baled Hay* 88 They was just frolicky and gay because they felt good.

frolic ('frɒlɪk), *a.* Forms: 6–8 frol(l)i(c)k(e, (6 fralicke, fro(w)lyke), 6–9 frolique, (7 frœlich), 6– frolic. [a. Du. *vrolijk* (in Kilian *vrolick*), = OS. **frôlîc* (whence *frôlîco* adv.), OHG. *frôlîch* (MHG. *vrôlich*, *vrœlic*, mod.Ger. *fröhlich*); f. MDu. *vrô* = OHG. *frô* (MHG. *vrô*, mod.G. *froh*) glad, joyous.]

1. In early use: Joyous, merry, mirthful. In later use with sense derived from the vb.: Frolicsome, sportive, full of merry pranks.

1538 BALE *Thre Lawes* 1794 And make frowlyke chere, with hey how fryska jolye! *c* **1600** DAY *Begg. Bednall Gr.* II. i. (1881) 30 Fair Love, be frolick; talk no more of death and care. **1632** MILTON *L'Allegro* 18 The frolic wind that breathes the spring. **1647** CLARENDON *Hist. Reb.* I. §74 The Nature and Education of Spain restrain'd men from.. Gayety, and Frolique humour. **1676** ETHEREDGE *Man of Mode* IV, i, Then sparkling champagne.. Makes us frolic and gay. **1791** E. DARWIN *Bot. Gard.* II. 140 Galantha.. prints with frolic step the melting snows. **1844** DISRAELI *Coningsby* VII. iv, Her voice was rich and sweet; the air she sang.. fantastically frolic. **1873** HOLLAND *A. Bonnic.* iii. 60 A thousand forms of frolic life.

absol. *a* **1656** BP. HALL *Rem. Wks.* (1660) 182 Blessed are the frolick and joviall. **1711** STEELE *Spect.* No. 176 ¶6 You may find Instances of the Haughty, the Proud, the Frolick, the Stubborn, who are each of them in secret downright Slaves. **1779–81** JOHNSON *L.P.*, *Addison* Wks. III. 54 The Tatler and Spectator.. taught the frolic and the gay to unite merriment with decency.

†**b.** *transf.* of colours, wine, etc. *Obs.*

? **1606** DRAYTON *Eclog.* iv, *Poems*, etc., E j b, She ware a frock of frolicke green. **1644** QUARLES *Barnabas & B.* 2 Eat thy bread with a merry heart, and gulp down care in frolic cups of liberal wine. **1648** HERRICK *Hesper.*, *Ode for B. Jonson*, And yet, each Verse of thine Out-did the meat, out-did the frolick wine.

†**2.** Free; liberal. Const. *of*. *Obs.*[−1]

1593 *Pass. Morrice* 79 Shee began to perceave that Master Anthonie was changed, being nothing so frolick of his kindness as he had been.

3. quasi-*adv.* or *interjectional.*

1594 LODGE *Wounds Civ. War* (1883) 19 Frolike braue Souldiers wee must foote it now. **1596** SHAKS. *Tam. Shr.* IV. iii. 184 Therefore frolicke, we will hence forthwith.

4. *Comb.*, as *frolic-hearted* adj.

1646 QUARLES *Judgemt. & Mercy* Wks. (Grosart) I. 73/2 The vacant houres of frolique-hearted youth.

Hence †**'frolickish** *a.*, somewhat sportive; †**'frolickness**, the state of being frolic.

1617 HIERON *Wks.* II. 104 Dost thou maruell at his frollikenesse and iollitie. **1660** *Charac. Italy* To Rdr. A iv, The more frolickish Genius, who no doubt is freer from intended mischief then the thoughtful man, will disgest it. *a* **1679** T. GOODWIN *Wks.* (1704) V. 199 Mirth, Jollity, Frolickness of youth, as you call them. **1681** GLANVILL *Sadducismus* II. (1726) 453 Frolickness of Fancy.

frolic ('frɒlɪk), *v.* Inflected **frolicked, frolicking.** [f. the adj.; cf. Flem. *frolicken* (Kilian), also Ger. *frohlocken* (where the second element is of obscure origin).]

1. *intr.* To make merry; in later use, to play pranks, gambol, caper about. Also, *to frolic it.*

1593 *Tell-Troth's N.Y. Gift* 29 They frolique both in glory. **1601** ? MARSTON *Pasquil & Kath.* I. 52 'Tis Whitson-tyde, and we must frolick it. **1624** FORD *Sun's Darling* v. i, I come to frolic with you, and to cheer Your drooping souls by vigour of my beams. *a* **1677** BARROW *Wks.* (1687) I. xiv. 201 Those who can devise no other subjects to frollick upon beside these. *Ibid.* 205 It would not be seemly to frolick it thus. **1770** GOLDSM. *Des. Vill.* 257 Lightly they frolic o'er the vacant mind. **1780** JOHNSON *Lett.* 11 Apr., My mistress.. laughs, and frisks, and frolicks it all the long day. **1823** BYRON *Island* III. iii, Its bounding crystal frolick'd in the ray. **1841–4** EMERSON *Ess.*, *Poet* Wks. (Bohn) I. 158 Talent may frolic and juggle; genius realizes and adds. **1886** RUSKIN *Præterita* I. vi. 181 Horses.. frolicking with each other when they had a chance.

quasi-*trans.* **1798** *Spirit Pub. Jrnls.* (1799) II. 194 'Twas theirs.. To laugh, intrigue, and frolic life away.

2. *trans.* †**a.** To make joyous or merry (*obs.*) **b.** [from the sb.] To give 'frolics' or parties to.

1583 STANYHURST *Æneis* III. (Arb.) 81 Also mye companions in country cittye be frollickt. **1627–77** FELTHAM *Resolves* I. lxxv. Wks. 115 Virtue.. gives such Cordials, as frolick the heart, in the press of adversity. **1807–8** W. IRVING *Salmag.* (1824) 137 By dint of dinners, of feeding and frolicking the town, the Giblet family worked themselves into notice.

Hence **'frolicking** *vbl. sb.* and *ppl. a.* Also **'frolicker**, one who frolicks; **'frolickery** ? *nonce-wd.* [see -ERY], buffoonery.

1676 TEONGE *Diary* (1825) 165 All the day following they spend in frollikeing with their women. *c* **1741** BRAINERD in Edwards *Life* i. (1851) 3 Addicted to young company or frolicing (as it is called). **1786** MAD. D'ARBLAY *Diary* Nov., In the midst of this frolicking.. the King entered. **1801** in D. L. Leonard *Papers Ohio Ch. Hist. Soc.* (1894) V. 48 Swearers and Sabbath-breakers, frolickers and dancers were pricked and crying for mercy. **1829** COBBETT *Adv. to Lover* §147 Winter is the great season for jaunting and dancing (called frolicking) in America. **1851** SIR F. PALGRAVE *Norm. & Eng.* I. 408 He took to the trade in frolickery. **1872** 'MARK TWAIN' *Innoc. Abr.* i. 11 A long summer day's laborious frolicking. **1887** BOWEN *Virg. Eclog.* ii. 64 Frolicking she-goat roves to the cytisus flower to be fed.

† **'frolicly**, *adv. Obs.* Also **frolickly**. [f. FROLIC *a.* + -LY[2].] In a frolic manner; mirthfully.

1592 GREENE *Upst. Courtier* G ij, A mad merrie crue.. leping ouer the field, as frolikly as if they ought not all the world two pence. **1658** ROWLAND *Moufet's Theat. Ins.* 1102 The Fox.. very froliquely being delivered from their [fleas'] molestation.. swims to land. *a* **1674** CLARENDON *Hist. Reb.* IX. §14 But, after some days frolickly spent at Bath, he return'd to his former temper.

frolicsome ('frɒlɪksəm), *a.* Also **frolicksom(e.** [f. FROLIC *v.* or *sb.* + -SOME.] Full of frolic; gay, merry, mirthful.

1699 SHAFTESB. *Virtue* II. II. iii, A gay and frolicksome Delight in what is injurious to others. **1724** R. FALCONER *Voy.* (1769) 86 Instead of coming on board to be frolicksome and merry, we should have given Thanks. **1791** BOSWELL *Johnson* Ded., Dr. Clarke.. was unbending himself.. in the most playful and frolicksome manner. **1807–8** W. IRVING *Salmag.* (1824) 147 In their frolicsome malice the Fates had ordered that a French boarding-house.. should be established directly opposite my aunt's residence. **1863** GEO. ELIOT *Romola* I. x, Mingled with the more decent holiday-makers there were frolicsome apprentices.

Hence **'frolicsomely** *adv.*, **'frolicsomeness.**

1727 BAILEY, *Frolicksomness.* **1835** *Blackw. Mag.* XXXVIII. 23 They gave way.. to the.. mischievous frolicsomeness.. of advanced boyhood. **1874** T. HARDY *Madding Crowd* I. xiii. 163 'Capital!' she exclaimed, throwing down the letter frolicsomely. **188.** R. G. H[ILL] *Voices in Solitude* 195 The fresh breeze.. frolicsomely flaps them on her breast.

† **'froligozene, -one.** *Obs.* [? suggested by Du. *vrolijk zijn* 'to be jolly': see FROLIC *a.*]

1599 PORTER *Angry Wom. Abingd.* (Percy) 50 Ha, my resolued Nicke, froligozene! **1634** HEYWOOD & BROME *Lanc. Witches* I. B 2, What all lustick, all froligozone?

from (frɒm), *prep.* (*adv.*, *conj.*). Forms: 1–6 fram, 3–4 *south.* vram, vrom, 4 fromme, 5 frome, 1– from. [OE. *fram*, *frǫm*, = OS. *fram*, OHG. *fram* (MHG. *vram*), Goth. *fram*, ON. *frá* (see FRO). The primary sense is 'forward'; cf. ON. *fram*(*m* (Sw. *fram*, Da. *frem*):—**framz* = Goth. *framis* (comparative) 'forward', adv.; cf. also the adj. OE. *fram*, *from*, ON. *fram-r* forward, valiant; further cognates are cited under FORME, FRAME. From the sense 'forward' were developed those of 'onward', 'on the way', 'away', whence the transition to the prepositional use is easy.]

A. *prep.*

1. Denoting departure or moving away: governing a sb. which indicates a point of departure or place whence motion takes place. Also with advbs. prefixed (e.g. *away*, *down*, *out*).

O.E. Chron. an. 874 Her for se here from Lindesse to Hreopedune. *c* **1175** *Lamb. Hom.* 79 A mon lihte from ierusalem in to ierico. **1297** R. Glouc. (1724) 325 Hardeknout hys broþer þo þen wey sone nome Fram Denemarch in to Engelond. *c* **1320** *Sir Tristr.* 349 Out of hauen þai rade ..Fram þe brimes brade Gun flete. *c* **1386** Chaucer *Prol.* 128 She leet no morsel from hir lippes falle. **1563** W. Fulke *Meteors* (1640) 4 Lifteth them up very high from the earth into the aire. **1611** Bible *Gen.* iv. 16 And Cain went out from the presence of the Lord. **1660** Barrow *Euclid* iii. Prop. xxviii, From the centers *G*, *H* draw *GA*, *GC*, and *HD*, *HF*. **1719** De Foe *Crusoe* i. iv, I came down from my apartment in the tree. **1762** Goldsm. *Cit. W.* xiii, I am just returned from Westminster Abbey. **1811** L. M. Hawkins *C'tess & Gertr.* IV. lxxxv. 328, I should chuse to have her buried from her own house. **1838** Arnold *Hist. Rome* (1845) I. xi. 200 He..leapt down from his seat. **1875** Jowett *Plato* (ed. 2) I. 399 During the voyage of the sacred ship to and from Delos.

b. *from*..*to*, used with repeated sb. to denote succession, change of place. Similarly in proverb. phr. ***from post to pillar***, and the like.

1530 Palsgr. 818/2 From towne to towne, *de ville en ville*. **1563** W. Fulke *Meteors* (1640) 24 When the Exhalation is driven from side to side of that cloud. **1583** Golding *Calvin on Deut.* c. 615 Certaine others of the faithfull whome God tossed from post to piller. **1583** Stubbes *Anat. Abus.* ii. (1882) 27 To beg their breade from doore to doore. **1631** Weever *Anc. Fun. Mon.* 262 How often the body of Saint Augustine was tost from porch to pillar. **1821** Keats *Lamia* 27 From vale to vale, from wood to wood, he flew. **1849** Sir J. Stephen *Eccl. Biog.* I. 215 Xavier's name was repeated from mouth to mouth with cries of vengeance.

2. Indicating the starting-point or the first considered of two boundaries adopted in defining a given extent in space.

971 *Blickl. Hom.* 5 Ac se ȝeleafa sceal beon fram eorþan up to heofonum areaht. *c* **1200** *Trin. Coll. Hom.* 179 Þe sæ is biter, swo is ec þis woreld fram ende to oðer. *c* **1400** *Lanfranc's Cirurg.* 2 Techinge þe anotomie of alle lymes from þe heed to þe foot. **1535** Coverdale *2 Sam.* xxiv. 15 So that there dyed of the people from Dan vnto Berseba, thre score and ten thousande men. **1590** Spenser *F.Q.* iii. i. 3 Full many Countreyes they did overronne, From the uprising to the setting Sunne. **1727** Gay *Fables, Barley-Mow & Dunghill* 2 How many saucy airs we meet, From Temple-bar to Aldgate-street! **1806–7** J. Beresford *Miseries Hum. Life* (1826) vi. *Miseries Stage Coaches* iv, The whole machine..groaning under its cargo from the box to the basket. **1845** M. Pattison *Ess.* (1889) I. 16 Neustria.. extended from the Meuse almost to the present southern limits of France. **1884** *Illustr. Lond. News* 20 Dec. 603/1 From title to colophon all is sound and whole.

b. Indicating the starting-point in a series or statement of limits.

Expressions like 'from four to ten' are treated grammatically as simple numerals, and may qualify the subject of a sentence, or the obj. of a vb. or prep.

c **1000** Ælfric *Gen.* vi. 7 Ic adiliȝe þone mannan..fram þære eorðan ansine fram þam men oð þa nytenu, fram þam slincendum oð þa fuȝelas. **1526** *Pilgr. Perf.* (W. de W. 1531) 25 b, From yᵉ begynnynge to yᵉ ende. **1662** Stillingfl. *Orig. Sacr.* i. vi. §3 The Sicyonian Kingdom..from which Varro began his history. **1699** Dampier *Voy.* II. i. 75 They are rowed with from 16 or 20 to 24 Oars. **1789** G. White *Selborne* (1813) I. xviii. 286 The swallow lays from four to six white eggs. **1866** Crump *Banking* ix. 207 Many bankers are always below their authorised issues by from 25 to 20 per cent. **1872** Ellacombe *Ch. Bells Devon* ix. 269 The whole alphabet..is not unfrequently met with as an inscription, from the fourteenth, or fifteenth, to the seventeenth century.

3. Indicating a starting-point in time, or the beginning of a period. (The date *from* which one reckons may be either inclusive or exclusive). Also in idiomatic phrases like ***from a child*** = from (his) childhood (cf. Gr. ἐκ παιδός, ἐκ παίδων).

c **1050** *Byrhtferth's Handboc* in *Anglia* (1885) VIII. 300 Fram easter tide þæt he eft cume. **1340** *Ayenb.* 12 Alle þon þet uram þe ginningge of þe wordle storue in zoþ & guode byleaue. *c* **1386** Chaucer *Prol.* 324 In termes hadde he caas and domes alle, That from the tyme of king William were falle. **1535** Coverdale *Neh.* xiii. 21 From that tyme forth came they nomore on the Sabbath. **1579** Fulke *Confut. Sanders* 593 Images were vsed from the Apostles, and Christ him selfe. **1611** Bible *2 Tim.* iii. 15 From a childe thou hast knowen the holy Scriptures. *a* **1616** Beaum. & Fl. *Thierry & Theod.* v. i, We are thieves from our cradles, and will die so. **1748** Smollett *Rod. Rand.* (1792) II. 275 Here I absconded from five o'clock in the morning to six in the evening. **1795** *Gentl. Mag.* 545/1 The scenes to which we have been accustomed from our infancy. **1816** Keatinge *Trav.* (1817) I. 99 An unaltered smile, and an inflexible seat, were preserved from first to last. **1836** W. Irving *Astoria* III. 257 A succession of adverse circumstances..beset it almost from the outset. **1844** *Regul. & Ord. Army* 3 Officers ..are to take Rank and Precedence from their Commissions as Colonels in the Army, not from the dates of their Appointments as Brigadiers. **1848** C. Bronte *J. Eyre* xxxvi, I knew him from a boy. **1885** *Law Rep.* 10 Appeal Cases 379 The gate was erected in 1846, and the public were effectually excluded from that year.

b. *from*..*to*, used with repeated sb. to denote succession or recurrence at regular intervals.

c **1325** *Lai le Freine* 229 This Frein thriued fram yer to yer. **1530** Palsgr. 808/2 From hour to hour, *de heure en heure*. **1600** Shaks. *A.Y.L.* ii. vii. 26 And so from houre to houre, we ripe, and ripe. **1621** Bolton *Stat. Irel.* 37 (*an.* 5 *Edw. IV*) On paine of two pence a man from moneth to other. **1675** tr. *Machiavelli's Prince* (1883) 285 Having received a new policy from three months to three months. **1711** Addison *Spect.* No. 63 ¶1 The Thoughts will be rising of themselves from time to time. **1790** Cowper *Stanzas for* 1790, He who sits from day to day Where the prisoned lark is hung. **1895** A. F. Warr in *Law Times* XCIX. 547/1 The..examination is in special books set from time to time.

4. Indicating a place or object which is left at a distance or left behind by an object which withdraws or goes away. Formerly also with ellipsis of verb.

O.E. Chron. an. 755 Ond him cyþdon þæt hiera mæȝas him mid wæron, þa þe him from noldon. **971** *Blickl. Hom.* 47 Þonne flyhþ þæt deofol fram us. *c* **1290** *Beket* 340 in *S. Eng. Leg.* I. 116 Sire henri, þe kingus sone..bi-lefde euere in is warde, fram him nolde he nouȝt. *c* **1340** *Cursor M.* 20308 (Br. Mus. Add. MS.) Hit rewiþ me, that I schal—Iohan—parte fram þee. **1579** Spenser *Sheph. Cal.* Aug. 107 Yet should thilke lasse not from my thought. **1593** Shaks. *3 Hen. VI*, v. iv. 21 We will not from the Helme, to sit and weepe. **1697** Dryden *Virg. Georg.* iii. 49 And, spurring from the Fight, confess their Fear. **1709** Swift & Addison *Tatler* No. 32 ¶2 She shrinks from the Touch like a Sensitive Plant. **1838** Thirlwall *Greece* II. 304 He withdrew from the council unobserved. **1843** *Fraser's Mag.* XXVIII. 714, I recoiled from the murderous instrument.

b. Indicating a place or object which is left on one side by an object which deflects or turns away. †Rarely used *simply* = 'averted from'.

1597 Hooker *Eccl. Pol.* v. xxx. §1 Whether it be a thing allowable or no that the minister should..turn his face at any time from the people. *a* **1616** Beaum. & Fl. *Knt. of Malta* i. i, Why speak'st thou from me? **1732** Berkeley *Alciphr.* vii. §2 Mankind are generally averse from thinking. **1812–16** J. Smith *Panorama Sc. & Art* I. 422 The ray being bent towards the perpendicular on entering another medium of greater density, and from the perpendicular, on entering a medium of less density.

5. Denoting (statically) distance, absence, remoteness: **a.** after words indicative of the extent of distance, also after *away*, *absent*, *apart*, etc.

O.E. Chron. an. 893 Hi tuȝon up hiora scipu oþ þone weald .iiii., iv mila fram þæm muþan ute weardum. **971** *Blickl. Hom.* 43 Sæȝde..þæt he ȝesawe naht feor from þæs mæsse-preostes sidan..oþerne ealdne man. **1340** *Ayenb.* 270 Lyȝt ne is naȝt awaye: ac ye byeþ awaye uram lyȝte. **1506** Guylforde *Pilgr.* (Camden) 47 Sydon is but right lytell from the citye of Tyre. **1588** J. Udall *Demonstr. Discipl.* (Arb.) 26 How can he feed them from whom he is absent. *Ibid.* 27 If the priests might not dwell farre from the temple. **1653** Holcroft *Procopius' Gothick Wars* iv. 124 The Ocean being far distant from these mountains. **1766** Goldsm. *Vic. W.* xxv, We were now got from my late dwelling about two miles. **1820** Keats *St. Agnes* xvi, Alone with her good angels, far apart From wicked men like thee. **1838** Arnold *Hist. Rome* (1845) I. xii. 211 Veii lay about ten miles from Rome. **1847–9** Helps *Friends in C.* Ser. i. (1851) I. 179, I am far from saying that merit is sufficiently looked out for.

b. used *simply* = away from, apart from, absent from, etc. Now only in ***from home***. (Cf. 8 b.)

c **1340** *Cursor M.* 10413 (Fairf.) When he hym held from home. *c* **1374** Chaucer *Troylus* iv. 738 (766) What is Criseyde worth, from Troilus? **1562** J. Heywood *Prov. & Epigr.* (1867) 206, I dwell from the citee in subbarbes. **1571** in W. H. Turner *Select. Rec. Oxford* 339 Noe freman of the Cytie..shall grynde from the said milles any kynd of grayne. **1584** R. Scot *Discov. Witchcr.* xv. x. (1886) 341 Go to a faire parlor or chamber..and from people nine daies. **1607** Tourneur *Rev. Trag.* ii. ii. Wks. 1878 II. 64 'Tis now good policie to be from sight. **1738** Johnson *London* 225 Sign your will, before you sup from home. **1761** Mrs. F. Sheridan *Sidney Bidulph* I. 318 Whatever your designs may be, it will be less to my dishonour, if you prosecute them from under your husband's roof. *Ibid.* II. 118 Mrs. Arnold was from under her husband's protection. **1796** Moser *Hermit of Caucasus* I. 238 He was continually from home, running from one house to another. **1802** Mrs. E. Parsons *Myst. Visit* IV. 203 Georgina she could not bear a moment from her sight.

6. Denoting removal, abstraction, separation, expulsion, exclusion, or the like: **a.** Governing a sb. or pron. expressing a concrete object.

971 *Blickl. Hom.* 67 Maria hire ȝeceas þone betstan dæl, se ne bið næfre fram hire afyrred. *c* **1000** *Ags. Gosp.* Matt. xxv. 32 Swa swa se hyrde asyndraþ ða scep fram tyccenum. **1377** Langl. *P. Pl.* B. xiii. 446 For to saue thi soule fram Sathan thin enemy. **1585** T. Washington tr. *Nicholay's Voy.* i. xviii. 21 Which gave occasion unto a brother of his to take away his life from him. **1590** C. S. *Right Relig.* 26 From the determination of a counsell there can be no appellation. **1610** Shaks. *Temp.* Epil. 9 But release me from my bands. **1697** Dryden *Virg. Georg.* iii. 513 Some bending Valley.. Clos'd from the Sun, but open to the Wind. **1807** Crabbe *Par. Reg.* i. 194 There hungry dogs from hungry children steal. **1821** Keats *Isabella* xvii, Paled in and vine-yarded from beggar-spies. **1841** Elphinstone *Hist. Ind.* I. 439 The narrow tract..separated from Mékrán..by the range of hills which form Cape Arboo. **1891** *Law Times* XCII. 18/2 Will there be an appeal to the Court of Appeal from a refusal to certify?

b. Denoting privation, separation, abstention, freedom, deliverance, etc. (*from* a state, condition, action, etc.).

c **950** *Lindisf. Gosp.* Matt. vi. 13 Ah ȝefriȝ usich from yfle. **971** *Blickl. Hom.* 25 Men..nellaþ ablinnan from heora unrihtum ȝestreonum. **1340** *Ayenb.* 86 Þe guodemen..þet god heþ yvryd..uram þe þreldome of þe dyeule. *c* **1400** *Lanfranc's Cirurg.* 70 Noon oþer wey þat myȝte save þe sike man from deeþ. *c* **1449** Pecock *Repr.* v. xiii. 553 Refreynyng from yuel. **1548–9** (Mar.) *Bk. Com. Prayer* Litany, From battaile and murther, & from sodain death: Good lorde deliuer us. **1576** Fleming *Panopl. Epist.* 400 *note*, Greedines of vayne glorie an impediment from keeping due order. **1647** Ward *Simp. Cobler* 51 To keep their Kings from devillizing. **1710** Steele *Tatler* No. 176 ¶1 After a little Ease from the raging Pain caused by..an aking Tooth. **1732** Berkeley *Alciphr.* i. §3 Lysicles could hardly refrain from laughing. **1807** Crabbe *Par. Reg.* i. 507 When thy rich master seems from trouble free. **1845** M. Pattison *Ess.* (1889) I. 18 To vindicate himself from the charge of treason. **1847–9** Helps *Friends in C.* Ser. i. (1851) I. 206, I did not attempt to dissuade Milverton from his purpose.

†**c.** followed by inf. instead of the vbl. sb. *Obs.*

1591 Spenser *Ruins of Time* 429 Not to haue been dipt in Lethe lake Could saue the sonne of Thetis from to die. **1596** —— *F.Q.* iv. v. 7 He sau'd the victour from fordonne.

7. Indicating a state, condition, etc., which is abandoned or which is changed for another. Often used before an adj., or a sb. that denotes a person, as if with ellipsis of *being*.

1340 *Ayenb.* 7 Oure lhord aros uram dyaþe to lyue þane zonday. **1399** Langl. *Rich. Redeles* i. 5 Ȝe were lyghtlich y-lyfte ffrom that ȝou leef thouȝte And ffrom ȝoure willffull werkis ȝoure will was chaungid. **1595** Shaks. *John* v. iv. 25 Euen as a forme of waxe Resolueth from his figure 'gainst the fire. **1641** *Ariana* 328 From a slave she became to be a Princesse. **1700** Dryden *Pal. & Arc.* iii. 750 Meanwhile, the health of Arcite still impairs; From bad proceeds to worse. **1741** Richardson *Pamela* I. 55 You have made our Master, from the sweetest-temper'd Gentleman in the World, one of the most peevish. **1771** Goldsm. *Hist. Eng.* II. 203 From being attacked, the French now in turn became the aggressors. **1823** F. Clissold *Ascent Mt. Blanc* 23 The western arc of the misty circle kindled, from a rosy to a deep reddening glow. **1856** Froude *Hist. Eng.* (1858) I. iv. 312 It became necessary to increase the penalty..from banishment to death. **1870** Rogers *Hist. Gleanings* Ser. ii. 51 From villains they became prosperous and independent yeomen. **1872** Browning *Fifine* cx. 6 Temples..which tremblingly grew blank From bright.

8. Used after words which signify distinction, difference, unlikeness, etc.

Formerly more widely used than at present; we now say 'inferior *to*', 'other *than*', and (usually) 'foreign *to*'; but verbs of distinguishing, differing, etc. still take *from*; so also *different* (but see that word), *difference*, *distinct*, etc.

1377 Langl. *P. Pl.* B. Prol. 56 Clotheden hem in copis to ben knowen fram othere. **1553** Eden *Treat. Newe Ind.* (Arb.) 15 The Elephant is a beast..little inferiour from humaine sense. *a* **1656** Hales *Tract* (1677) 170 Others from themselves. **1828** Whately *Rhet.* i. ii. §2 Quite foreign from all their experience. **1849** Macaulay *Hist. Eng.* I. 82 The extreme Puritan was at once known from other men by his gait. **1861** M. Pattison *Ess.* (1889) I. 47 The Corporation had its constitution, not materially differing from those of other guilds. *a* **1881** Rossetti *House of Life* v, Thy Soul I know not from thy body. **1887** L. Carroll *Game of Logic* iv. 94 You can't tell one flower from another.

†**b.** used *simply* to denote qualitative remoteness, unlikeness, incongruity, etc.: = away from, apart or aside from, out of, alien to. ***from oneself*** = beside oneself, out of one's wits. *Obs.* (Cf. 5 b.)

c **1050** *Martyrology* (Cockayne) 118 Þæt ic for þe sprece from minre ȝecynde. **1490** Caxton *Eneydos* xvii. (heading) As a woman disperate and from herselfe. **1531** Elyot *Gov.* iii. xxi, Thou art all inflamed with wrathe, and clene from the pacience which thou so much praysest. **1579** Fulke *Heskins' Parl.* 58 M. Heskins collections are vaine, and from the authors meaning. **1580** Sidney *Arcadia* iii. (1605) 298 He was quite from himself. *c* **1600** Shaks. *Sonn.* cxlvii, My thoughts and my discourse as mad mens are, At random from the truth vainely exprest. **1607** Tourneur *Rev. Trag.* v. i. Wks. 1878 II. 132 O pardon me to call you from your names! *a* **1616** Beaum. & Fl. *Knt. of Malta* iii. iv, A very hard thing, Sir, and from my power. **1632** Massinger *Maid of Hon.* iii. i, *Ast.* But this is from the purpose. *Rod.* To the point then. *a* **1637** B. Jonson tr. *Horace's Art Poet.* 159 If now the phrase of him that speaks shall flow In sound quite from his fortune [*fortunis absona*].

9. Indicating the place, quarter, etc. whence something comes or is brought or fetched; often = out of; also after words denoting choice, selection, or distinction out of a number or mass of individuals.

1621 Burton *Anat. Mel.* iii. ii. vi. i. (1651) 545, I light my Candle from their Torches. **1697** Dryden *Virg. Georg.* iv. 793 From his Herd he culls, For Slaughter, four the fairest of his Bulls. **1712–14** Pope *Rape Lock* iii. 128 Clarissa drew ..A two-edged weapon from her shining case. **1808** Scott *Marm.* v. Introd. 145 Such notes as from the Breton tongue Marie translated. **1838** Arnold *Hist. Rome* I. vii, She drew a knife from her bosom. **1843** *Fraser's Mag.* XXVIII. 565 Jenny gathers cranberries from the neighbouring wood. **1864** *Law Times Rep.* X. 718/2 A labourer..employed..to dig ballast from a pit. **1879** Church *Spenser* ii. 29 He came from Cambridge. **1885** *Law Times* LXXX. 37/2 The following, extracted respectively from *The World* and *Truth*. **1897** F. Hall in *Nation* (N.Y.) LXIV. 163/1 This list I could amplify from my own verbal stores.

b. with ellipsis of a verb or participle: = coming from, taken from, etc.

1745 *De Foe's Eng. Tradesman* xxvi. (1841) I. 266 Serge from Taunton and Exeter. **1771** R. Henry *Hist. Gt. Brit.* I. i. vi. 378 The Phœnicians from Cadiz were the only persons who traded to these islands. **1849** Macaulay *Hist. Eng.* II. 3 Zealous Cavaliers from the country. **1895** *Bookman* Oct. 26/2 The history has been..distorted by stock quotations from the fathers.

10. Indicating a place or position where action or motion is originated which extends beyond that place, while the originator remains fixed there (e.g. a place whence a person directs his vision, and *fig.* a 'point of view'). Similarly after words which express 'hanging', 'depending', and the like.

1592 Shaks. *Rom. & Jul.* iii. v. 228 *Jul.* Speakest thou from thy heart? *Nur.* And from my soule too. **1619** Daniel *To Henry Wriothesly* 42 He..doth from a patience hie Looke onely on the cause [etc.]. **1658** *Hist. Q. Christiana's Progress to Rome* 246 Gay ornaments hanging from the window's and balcons. **1667** Milton *P.L.* xii. 227 God from the mount of Sinai..will himself..Ordain them laws. **1697** Dryden *Virg. Georg.* iv. 615 The sultry Dog-star from the Sky Scorch'd Indian Swains. **1771** R. Henry *Hist. Gt. Brit.* I. i. v. 338 Those who fought from chariots. **1801** Southey *Thalaba* viii. ix, The Cryer from the Minaret, Proclaim'd the midnight hour. **1844** *Huc's Tartary* I. 150

Each of us hung a bag from his shoulders. **1867–76** G. F. Chambers *Astron.* 685 When observations are made from the deck of a ship. **1887** L. Carroll *Game of Logic* i. §3. 35 From their point of view they are perfectly right.

11. Indicating a person as a more or less distant source of action, *esp.* as a giver, sender, or the like. In OE. also indicating the agent = by.

971 *Blickl. Hom.* 27 þæt he wære costod from deofle. *Ibid.* 45 þonne onfoþ hi from Gode maran mede þonne hi from ænigum oþrum lacum don. *c* **1205** Lay. 20 Æfter þan flode þe from drihtene com. *a* **1240** *Ureisun* 86 in *Cott. Hom.* 195 Uor þere gretunge þet Gabriel ðe brouhte urom ure heouen kinge. *c* **1489** Caxton *Sonnes of Aymon* vii. 159 Ye shall telle the emperour from my behalve, that [etc.]. **1585** T. Washington tr. *Nicholay's Voy.* I. ii. 2b, With a frigat to accompany us and to bring backe newes from us. **1605** Shaks. *Macb.* I. iii. 105 He bad me, from him, call thee Thane of Cawdor. **1608** —— *Per.* I. i. 164 An arrow shot From a well-experienced archer. **1611** Bible *John* vii. 29 For I am from him, and he hath sent me. **1662** Stillingfl. *Orig. Sacr.* II. iii. §1 Moses tells them as from God himself. **1664** Marvell *Corr.* Wks. 1872–5 II. 159 On the third [day] ..he had audience from his Majesty. **1790–1811** Combe *Devil upon Two Sticks in Eng.* (1817) I. 263 In this business, as in every other, she acted from herself. **1843** *Fraser's Mag.* XXVIII. 328 You shall hear from my attorney. **1844** Thirlwall *Hist. Greece* VIII. 303 Dionysodorus, an envoy from Attalus. **1849** Macaulay *Hist. Eng.* I. 405 Independence, veracity, self-respect, were things not required by the world from him. **1883** *Century Mag.* XXVI. 919/1 He..still holds his place from the trustees. **1883** *Daily News* 22 Sept. 4/6 Virulent abuse from that class of men.

12. Denoting derivation, source, descent, or the like: **a.** in regard to material things.

1399 *Rolls of Parlt.* III. 423/1, I Henry of Lancaster..am disendit by right lyne of the Blode comyng from the gude lord Kyng Henry therde. **1595** Shaks. *John* I. i. 124 This Calfe, bred from his Cow. **1646** Sir T. Browne *Pseud. Ep.* v. v. 239 Eve, who..anomalously proceeded from Adam. **1667** Milton *P.L.* v. 480 So from the root Springs lighter the green stalk, from thence the leaves More aerie. **1697** Dryden *Virg. Georg.* IV. 481 Clio and Beroe, from one Father both. **1736** W. Stukeley in *Mem.* (Surtees) III. 169 Ebulus or wild elder, fancyed to spring from the Danes blood. **1771** R. Henry *Hist. Gt. Brit.* I. I. vi. 371 The greatest rivers sometimes flow from the smallest fountains. **1807** Crabbe *Par. Reg.* I. 739 Bequeathed to missions money from the stocks. **1821** Keats *Lamia* I. 334 A real woman, lineal indeed From Pyrrha's pebbles or old Adam's seed. **1870** Anderson *Missions Amer. Bd.* II. ix. 68 Dangerous cuts from a sabre.

b. in regard to things immaterial; *esp.* 'noting progress from premisses to inferences' (J.).

1585 T. Washington tr. *Nicholay's Voy.* Ded. ¶3 An argument drawen from the greatnesse of the labors. **1658** J. Robinson *Eudoxa* ii. 23 The Argumentation is from a Similitude, therefore not Apodictick. **1712–14** Pope *Rape Lock* I. 1 What dire offence from am'rous causes springs. **1795** *Gentl. Mag.* 541/1 You will be astonished at the logick which could draw such an inference from that address. **1821** Keats *Isabella* xiv, Enriched from ancestral merchandise. **1838** Thirlwall *Hist. Greece* IV. 223 Several very pernicious consequences arose from this bent of mind. **1839** G. Bird *Nat. Philos.* 40 From these facts the following laws have been deduced. **1849** Macaulay *Hist. Eng.* I. 320 His chief pleasures were commonly derived from field sports and from an unrefined sensuality. **1887** L. Carroll *Game of Logic* i. §2. 21 Let us try to draw a Conclusion from the two Premisses.

13. Indicating a model, rule, copy; also, a person or thing after which another is named.

1596 Shaks. *Tam. Shr.* III. i. 53 For sure Æacides Was Aiax, cald so from his grandfather. **1655** Stanley *Hist. Philos.* I. (1701) 42/2 Cleobulus..had a Daughter whom he named Eumetis, but was called commonly from her Father Cleobulina. **1697** Dryden *Æneid* III. 28, I lay the deep Foundations of a Wall; And Enos, nam'd from me, the City call. **1703** Moxon *Mech. Exerc.* 127 You are to consider what Apartments..to make on your Ground-plot..and to set them off from your Scale. **1800** H. Wells *Const. Neville* III. 266, I am..to take charge of a younger brother, who was named from him. **1811** L. M. Hawkins *C'tess & Gertr.* III. lix. 259 She sketched objects; she colored from nature. **1875** *Knight's London* (Walford) I. xi. 195 The Birdcage walk.. was so named from the cages of an aviary disposed among the trees which bordered it.

14. Denoting ground, reason, cause, or motive: Because of, on account of, owing to, as a result of, through. Now replaced in some uses by *for*.

1611 Shaks. *Cymb.* I. v. 24 Your Highnesse Shall from this practise but make hard your heart. **1622** Fletcher *Sp. Curate* III. iii, For what I now do is not out of spleen..but from remorse of conscience. **1663** Cowley *Pindar. Odes* 2nd Olympique, Argt., He is commended..from his Hospitality, Munificence and other Virtues. **1710** Norris *Chr. Prud.* ii. 99 His Cunning is the more odious from the resemblance it has to Wisdom. **1762** Goldsm. *Cit. W.* xi, From such a picture of nature in primeval simplicity..are you in love with fatigue and solitude? **1764** Foote *Mayor of G.* I. Wks. 1799 I. 165 Whether from the fall or the fright, the Major mov'd off in a month. **1776** *Trial of Nundocomar* 32/2 The man could not be brought here..without imminent danger of expiring from fatigue. **1796** *Hist.* in *Ann. Reg.* 8 They spoke and acted from principle. **1844** Disraeli *Coningsby* IV. iii, Remarkable from the neatness.. of its architecture. **1849** Macaulay *Hist. Eng.* II. 232 That weak apostle who from fear denied the Master. **1851** *Illustr. Lond. News* 11 Jan. 23 Nine children died from want of breast milk. **1863** Whyte Melville *Gladiators* I. 264 The mighty fabric..was beginning..to sink and crumble from its own enormous size and weight. **1883** *Manch. Exam.* 29 Oct. 5/4 The firm had to suspend payment, not from any fault of their own, but from their connection with another firm. **1883** *Law Rep.* 11 Q. Bench Div. 597 The censure had been made injuriously and from motives of private malice. **1885** T. Raleigh in *Law Q. Rev.* Apr. 151 A person suffering from senile dementia is not a lunatic.

b. indicating the ground of a judgement, belief, or the like.

c **1000** *Ags. Gosp.* Matt. vii. 16 Fram hyra wæstmun ȝe hi underȝytað. **1673** Ray *Journ. Low C.* (1738) I. 7 That the rain doth continually wash down earth from the mountains ..is manifest from the Lagune or flats about Venice. **1855** J. W. Croker in *C. Papers* (1884) III. xxix. 328 From your silence I fear the fact is so. **1891** M. R. Haselden in *Law Times* XCII. 107/1 From the language of the preamble you might perhaps fancy that [etc.]. **1894** *Solicitor's Jrnl.* XXXIX. 2/2 It is clear from these decisions that [etc.].

15. Used in certain of the above senses (esp. 1, 2, 3, 9, 10) with an adverb or a phrase (prep. + sb. or pron.) as object. **a.** With obj. an adverb (of place or time), as ***from above***, ***afar***, etc. Also, more or less pleonastically, before *hence*, *thence*, *whence*, *henceforth*, etc.: see those words.

c **1340** *Cursor M.* 7505 (Trin.), I hadde no helpe but from aboue. *Ibid.* 16749 (Fairf.) From then [*Gött.* fra þan. *Trin.* fro þenne]. **1362** Langl. *P. Pl.* A. III. 105 Com late from biȝonde. *a* **1553** Philpot *Exam.* (1842) 403 A destiny which from ever hath been, is, and shall be true. **1625** Bacon *Ess.*, *Plantations* (Arb.) 534 That the Plantation may spread into Generations, and not be euer peeced from without. **1685** Dryden *Thren. August.* 169 They mined it near, they battered from afar. **1748** Thomson *Cast. Indol.* II. 391 And from beneath was heard a wailing sound. **1770** Goldsm. *Des. Vill.* 116 The mingling notes came softened from below. **1821** Keats *Isabella* xxxii, The breath of Winter comes from far away. **1837** Carlyle *Fr. Rev.* I. II. vii, From of old, Doubt was but half a Magician.

b. Followed by a preposition indicating a static condition, as ***from amidst***, ***beneath***, etc.

c **1000** *Ags. Gosp.* Matt. iv. 25 Fram beȝeondan iordanen. **1388** Wyclif *Luke* xxiv. 49 Til that ȝe be clothid with vertu from an hiȝ. **1588** Shaks. *Tit. A.* IV. i. 44 She culd it from among the rest. **1637** Milton *Lycidas* 16 The sacred well That from beneath the seat of Jove doth spring. **1671** —— *Samson* 1691 His fiery virtue roused From under ashes into sudden flame. **1667** Sir R. Moray *Let.* 10 Dec. in *Lauderdale Papers* (1885) II. 88 There is a Damned book come hither from beyond sea called Naphtali. **1710** Steele *Tatler* No. 170 ¶4, I thought it better to remove a studious Countenance from among busy ones. **1719** De Foe *Crusoe* II. vi, That they might feast on fresh meat from on shore, as we did with their salt meat from on board. **1761** [see 5b]. **1786** Mackenzie *Lounger* No. 56 (1787) II. 197, I see my grandmother..looking at me from under her spectacles. **1835** Lytton *Rienzi* I. i, A body of horsemen..dashed from amidst the trees.

c. Followed, more or less pleonastically, by a prep. of similar meaning, as *out*, *out of*, *forth*, *off*, where each prep. serves to strengthen or supplement the sense of the other.

c **1592** Marlowe *Massacre Paris* II. iii, His soul is fled from out his breast. **1594** Hooker *Eccl. Pol.* I. viii. §5 [A principle] drawn from out of the very bowels of heaven and earth. **1607** Shaks. *Timon* I. i. 138, I will choose Mine heyre from forth the Beggers of the world. **1632** G. Hughes *Saints Losse* 51 Know ye not that God hath taken away your captaine from off your heads this day? **1700** Dryden *Pal. & Arc.* III. 514 Knights unhorsed may rise from off the plain. **1789** G. White *Selborne* (1813) I. xiv. 256 From out of the side of this bed leaped an animal. **1820** Keats *St. Agnes* xxx, While he from forth the closet brought a heap [etc.]. **1887** A. Birrell *Obiter Dicta* Ser. II. 150 Ready to engage with all comers on all subjects from out the stores of his accumulated knowledge.

†**B.** quasi-*adv.* = away. (Cf. fro B.) Only in phr. ***to and from*** (= to and fro), ***from and back***.

a **1450** *Knt. de la Tour* (1868) 60 The synner that gothe ofte to and from in his foule plesaunce. **1608** Topsell *Serpents* (1658) 608 A sliding snake..Gliding along the altar, from and back.

†**C.** quasi-*conj.* = from the time when. (Cf. fro C. 1.) *Obs.*

? *a* **1366** Chaucer *Rom. Rose* 850 From she was twelve yeer of age, She of hir love graunt him made. *c* **1500** *Lancelot* 1432 Euery gilt..Done frome he passith the ȝeris of Innocens. **1583** Babington *Commandm.* ix. Applic. Wks. (1637) 92 From morning to night, from wee rise till we goe to bed. **1602** Warner *Alb. Eng.* XI. lxvi. (1612) 282 From Elizabeth to Raigne, and I to liue begunne.

frome, fromenty: see frume, frumenty.

fromple, var. of frumple.

†**fromshapen**, *ppl. a. Obs.* Also 6 **frameshapen**. [f. from + shapen; ? in imitation of L. *dēformātus*.] Deformed, misshapen.

1581 J. Bell tr. *Haddon's Answ. Osor.* II. 75b, This extraordinarie Jurisdiction of the Pope, is a most.. deformed frameshapen chaungelyng. **1594** Carew *Huarte's Exam. Wits* xv. §4. 307 How from-shapen this philosophy is, which Aristotle bringeth in.

ˈfromward, *sb. dial.* Also **frommard**. [app. subst. use of next: see froe.] = froe.

1883 *Hants Gloss.*, *Fromward* or *Frommard*, a tool used in lath-rending or cleaving. **1890** *Glouc. Gloss.*, *Frommard*.

†**ˈfromward**, *a.*, *adv.*, *prep. Obs.* Forms: 1 **frǫmweard** (*adj.*), 3 **frommard**, *south.* **vrommard**, 3–4 **framward**, 4–6 **fromwarde**, 3– **fromward**. [f. from + -ward.]

A. *adj.* = Turned from or away. (See also B. 1 *attrib.*)

1. Departing, about to depart. (Only OE.)

c **888** K. Ælfred *Boeth.* xi. §2 Ælc þara þe þas woruld ȝesælþa hæfþ oþer tweȝa oþþe he wat þæt he him fromwearde beoþ oððe he hit nat. *c* **1000** *Seafarer* 71 Adl oþþe yldo oþþe ecȝhete fæȝum fromweardum feorh oðþringeð.

2. Froward.

c **1275** *Luue Ron* 45 in *O.E. Misc.* 94 þeo luue þat ne may her abyde..hit is fals and mereuh and frouh And fromward in vychon tide. **1576** Peterson tr. *Della Casa's Galateo* 25, I call them Fromward people, which will in all things be ouertwart to other men.

B. *adv.*

1. In a direction which leads from, or is turned from, a given place or object.

a **1547** Surrey *Ps.* lv. 1 Give ear to my suit, Lord! fromward hide not thy face. **1552** Huloet s.v. *Becke* .. Wyth a becke fromwarde or to warde. **1591** Sylvester *Du Bartas* I. iv. 354 They from-ward turn. **1711** *Lond. Gaz.* No. 4917/4 The forepart of his Mane longest, the one part being short, lies toward, the other fromward.

attrib. **1645** Wither *Vox Pacif.* 41 Who can unite again a Broken-bone, Whose parted ends, are set the fromward way.

2. Of time: Onward from a given date.

c **1400** Maundev. (1839) xviii. 197 And fro thens fromward, thei ben alle obeyssant to him.

3. *fig.* In a different or diverse way, contrarily.

a **1225** *Ancr. R.* 134 Heo makieð frommard hore nest—softe wiðuten & þorni wiðinnen. *Ibid.* 248 Lo! nu, hu urommard beoð þe ontfule to ure Louerd!

C. *prep.*

1. In a direction which leads from or is turned from (an object), away from.

c **1205** Lay. 1899 Geomagog..þudde Corineum frommard [**1275** framward] his breoste. *a* **1225** *Ancr. R.* 112 þe hole half & te cwike dole drowen þet vuele blod ut frommard þe unhole. *c* **1300** *Beket* 886 And kniȝtes that were ek with him al framward him drowe. **1398** Trevisa *Barth. De P.R.* XIV. ii. (Tollem. MS.), Mounteynes ben..rered fromwarde þe erþe towarde þe heuen. **1493** *Festivall* (W. de W. 1515) 50b, All his steppes towarde and fromwarde the holy churche. **1551** Recorde *Cast. Knowl.* (1556) 93 To go wyth their feet the one against the other, and their heddes the one fromwarde the other. **1580** Sidney *Arcadia* (1622) 127 As cheerefully going towards, as Pyrocles went frowardly fromward his death. **1651** Hobbes *Leviath.* I. vi. 23 When the Endeavour is fromward something, it is generally called Aversion. **1673** *Phil. Trans.* VIII. 5194 Shooting it self forth into several points or striæ..fromward its Center. **1713** Derham *Phys. Theol.* IV. xii. 221 The Feathers being placed fromward the Head toward the Tail.

b. with tmesis, ***from..ward***.

1565–73 Cooper *Thesaurus* s.v. *Auersus*, *Auersis ..cornibus*,..with the corners from the sunne warde. **1603** J. Davies *Microcosm.* (Grosart) 22/2 Sol..makes vs heavie going from-vs-ward. **1633** T. James *Voy.* 13 The Ice had broken from the Ship-ward. **1703** T. N. *City & C. Purchaser* 29 To signifie that a Wall..doth not stand up right, but leans from-you-ward, when you stand before it.

2. Contrary to, different from.

a **1225** *Ancr. R.* 100 Hercneð nu..al an oðer speche, & frommard tisse vorme.

So **ˈfromwards** *adv.* and *prep.*

c **1000** *Sax. Leechd.* II. 142 Gif hunta ȝebite mannan, sleah þry scearpan neah fromweardes. **1634–5** Brereton *Trav.* (1844) 109 Those are also called to account that are met walking fromwards the Church. **1664** *Relat. Proc. at Hertford Assize* Aug. 7 With his face from-wards the place where they usually met. **1674** N. Fairfax *Bulk & Selv.* 119 A pend or earnest strift fromwards. **1713** Derham *Phys.-Theol.* v. i. 316 Towards or fromwards the Zenith. **1855** Morton *Cycl. Agric.* II. 723 *Fromward* (West Eng.), land is ploughed 'framwards' when the horses are turning to the right. **1880** Jefferies *Gt. Estate* 159 The carters..saying 'toward' for anything near or leaning towards you, and 'vrammards' for the reverse.

†**ˈfroncle.** *Obs. rare.* [a. OF. *froncle*, ad. L. *fūrunculus* furuncle.] A furuncle or boil.

1543 Traheron *Vigo's Chirurg.* (1586) 53. **1547** Boorde *Brev. Health* lxxiii. 26b, A froncle is a lytle impostume ingendred of a gross bloud.

frond (frɒnd), *sb.*[1] [ad. L. *frond-*, *frōns* leaf, applied by Linnæus in a specific sense, in contradistinction to *folium* leaf.]

1. *Bot.* The leaf-like organ formed by the union of stem and foliage in certain flowerless plants. Formerly (and still in loose popular language) applied also to the large compound leaves, e.g. of the palm, banana, etc.

[**1753** Chambers *Cycl. Supp.* s.v. *Leaf*, *Frondes* expresses leaves consisting of several other leaves and forming the whole plant.] **1785** Martyn *Rousseau's Bot.* xxxii. 489 Our common species..may be known by the frond or leaf being ovate. **1791** W. Bartram *Carolina* 478 The lower larger fronds were digitated, or rather radiated. **1840** E. Newman *Brit. Ferns* Introd. (1844) 31 The fronds of ferns are generally much divided. **1858** T. R. Jones *Aquar. Nat.* 14 One or two fragments of stone with fronds of green sea-weed growing thereon. **1874** C. Geikie *Life in Woods* vi. 110 The broad fronds of the pine trees. **1877** —— *Christ* liv. (1879) 661 Cutting fronds..from the palm-trees, that lined the path. **1878** Huxley *Physiogr.* 235 A frond differs from an ordinary leaf in usually bearing fructification.

attrib. **1877** F. Heath *Fern W.* 112 One of the latter contains a frond-bud or imperfect germ.

2. *Zool.* A leaf-like expansion found in certain animal organisms.

1846 Dana *Zooph.* (1848) 323 Small, foliaceous, fronds solitary. **1876** Harley *Mat. Med.* (ed. 6) 370 The fronds are mucilaginous when young.

frond (frɒnd), *sb.*[2] *Surg.* [ad. F. *fronde* lit. 'sling'. The *Syd. Soc. Lex.* gives, as obsolete, a latinized form *frondium*.] (See quot.)

1848 Craig, *Frond*..a bandage employed principally in wounds and diseases of the nose and chin, and more especially in cases of fracture or dislocation of the lower jaw.

frond (frɒnd), *v. nonce-wd.* [f. FROND *sb.*[1]] *intr.* To wave with fronds.
1866 BLACKMORE *Cradock Nowell* i, A massive wood.. crisping, fronding, feathering.. here and there.

frond, obs. form of FRIEND.

frondage ('frɒndɪdʒ). [f. FROND *sb.*[1] + -AGE.] The fronds (of a tree or plant) collectively. Sometimes improperly used as a synonym of foliage.
1842 SIR A. DE VERE *Song of Faith* 21 Cedarn woods with shadowy frondage cool. **1871** SWINBURNE *Songs bef. Sunrise, Hertha*, The tree many-rooted.. With frondage red-fruited. **1885** LADY BRASSEY *The Trades* 475 Jamaica, with its tree-ferns and flowerless frondage.

frondaille, var. of FRUNDEL. *Obs.*

†**'frondated**, *a. Obs. rare.* [f. L. *frondāt-us* leaved (f. *frond-*, *frōns* leaf) + -ED[1].] 'Leaved, having leaves' (1727 Bailey vol. II).

†**fron'dation.** *Obs. rare*⁻¹. [ad. late L. *frondātiōn-em*, f. *frond-*, *frōns* leaf.] (See quot.)
1664 EVELYN *Sylva* xxviii. 77 Lastly, Frondation or the taking off some of the luxuriant branches and sprays, of such Trees.. is a kind of pruning.

‖**Fronde** (frɔ̃d). *Fr. Hist.* [F. *fronde* sling.] The name given to the party which rose in rebellion against Mazarin and the Court during the minority of Louis XIV; hence, a malcontent party; also, violent political opposition.
1798 J. Q. ADAMS *Wks.* (1854) IX. 206 The history of France during the periods of the League and the Fronde. **1808** *Edin. Rev.* XII. 493 Was there ever a mixed constitution without a *fronde*? **1831** DISRAELI *Yng. Duke* III. x. 136 A *fronde* was formed but they wanted a De Retz. **1889** *Athenæum* 20 Apr. 507/2 His chance came in the *fronde* against the Second Empire when its day was waning.

†**'fronded,** *ppl. a.*[1] [ad. L. *frondātus*: see FRONDATED.] Having leaves or foliage.
1640 HOWELL *Dodona's Gr.* i. 19 The Clustre of Diadems which begirt her high fronded forehead.

fronded ('frɒndɪd), *ppl. a.*[2] [f. FROND *sb.*[1] + -ED[2].] Having fronds.
1882 WHITTIER *Eternal Goodness* 20, I know not where His islands lift Their fronded palms in air. **1883** W. WESTALL *Ralph Norbreck's Trust* III. xiv. 186 She was sitting.. under the fronded roof of the mighty palms.

frondent ('frɒndənt), *a.* [ad. L. *frondent-em*, pr. pple. of *frondēre* to put forth leaves.] Full of fronds or leaves, leafy.
1677 T. HARVEY tr. *Owen's Epigr.* III. No. 118, I, Phœbus Tree, still frondent, flourishing. **1727** BAILEY vol. II, *Frondent*, bringing forth Leaves. **1837** CARLYLE *Fr. Rev.* I. VII. vi, That broad frondent *Avenue de Versailles*. **1864** —— *Fredk. Gt.* XI. i. (1865) IV. 12 A real Newspaper, frondent with genial leafy speculation. **1863** *Reader* 7 Nov. 537 The.. broad frondent banana-like leafage.

frondesce (frɒn'dɛs), *v.* [ad. L. *frondescĕre* (see FRONDESCENT).] *intr.* To put forth leaves.
a **1816** STAUGHTON *Eulogy Dr. Rush* in Pickering *Vocab.* (1816) s.v., His powers began now to frondesce and blossom. [Hence **1846** in WORCESTER.]

frondescence (frɒn'dɛsəns). [ad. mod.L. *frondescentia*, f. L. *frondescent-em*: see next and -ENCE.] **a.** The process or period of coming into leaf. **b.** The conversion or development of other organs into leaves. **c.** Fronds or leaves collectively.
[**1793** MARTYN *Lang. Bot.*, *Frondescentia*, leafing season.. the time of the year when plants first unfold their leaves]. **1841** MAUNDER *Sci. & Lit. Treas.*, *Frondescence*.. the precise time of the year and month in which each species of plant unfolds its leaves. **1888** *Harper's Mag.* July LXXVII. 216 Nearly as bright are the masses of pomme-cannelle frondescence, the groves of lemon and orange.

frondescent (frɒn'dɛsənt), *a.* [ad. L. *frondescent-em*, pr. pple. of *frondescĕre*, freq. of *frondēre* to put into leaves, f. *frond-*, *frōns* leaf.] Springing into leaf; expanding into fronds.
1828 STARK *Elem. Nat. Hist.* II. 435 Polypiferous masses sub-stony, with crustaceous or frondescent expansions. **1846** DANA *Zooph.* (1848) 125 Frondescent or papillose appendages. **1858** J. MARTINEAU *Stud. Chr.* (1873) 411 A young frondescent life would show itself again.
Hence **fron'descently** *adv.*
1846 DANA *Zooph.* (1848) 125 Tentacles papillose or frondescently lobed.

‖**Frondeur** (frɔ̃dœr). [F. *frondeur*, f. *fronde* (see FRONDE).]
1. *Fr. Hist.* A member of the Fronde.
1798 *Anecd. Dist. Persons* IV. 333 Would to Heaven that the late Frondeurs in that Country had been as harmless.
2. *transf.* A malcontent, an 'irreconcilable'.
1847 LONGF. in *Life* (1891) II. 93 All Americans who return from Europe malcontent with their own country, we call Frondeurs. **1880** *Daily Tel.* 22 Sept., Are the French, then, incurable frondeurs? incorrigible revolutionists, who must attack a Minister simply because he is 'in'?

frondiferous (frɒn'dɪfərəs), *a.* [f. L. *frondifer* bearing leaves (f. *frond-*, FROND *sb.*[1]: see -(I)FEROUS).] Bearing leaves or fronds.
1599 R. LINCHE *Anc. Fiction* M iij, Ouershadowed with frondiferous boughes. **1656** BLOUNT *Glossogr.*, *Frondiferous*, that beareth leaves or branches. **1825** HAMILTON *Handbk. Terms*, *Frondiferous* in Botany, bearing leaves. **1885** *Syd. Soc. Lex.*, *Frondiferous*, leaf-bearing; applied to flowers which produce leaves. Also applied to plants, like ferns, which bear fronds.

frondiform ('frɒndɪfɔːrm), *a.* [f. L. *frond-*, FROND *sb.*[1] + (I)FORM.] Having the shape of a frond.
1885 in *Syd. Soc. Lex.*

frondigerous (frɒn'dɪdʒərəs), *a.* [f. L. *frond-*, FROND *sb.*[1] + -(I)GEROUS.] Bearing fronds.
1885 in *Syd. Soc. Lex.*

frondiparous (frɒn'dɪpərəs), *a.* [f. L. *frond-*, FROND *sb.*[1] + *par-ĕre* to bring forth + -OUS.] Producing leaves instead of fruit.
1866 *Treas. Bot.*, *Frondiparous*, a monstrosity, consisting in the production of leaves instead of fruit. **1885** *Syd. Soc. Lex.*, *Frondiparous*, leaf producing; applied to flowers which produce leaves.

frondivorous (frɒn'dɪvərəs), *a.* [f. L. *frond-*, FROND *sb.*[1] + *-vor-us* devouring + -OUS.] Eating or feeding on leaves.
1828 SOUTHEY *Lett.* (1856) IV. 126 Graminivorous, frondivorous, carnivorous.

frondlet ('frɒndlɪt). [f. FROND *sb.*[1] + -LET.] A little frond.
1862 *Jrnl. R. Dublin Soc.* Apr. 348 The first young frondlet was seen to be protruded from the nipple end of the sporangia. **1881** G. ALLEN *Evolutionist at Large* xxii. 213 Each frondlet.. is separately symmetrical as well.

frondose (frɒn'dəʊs), *a.* [ad. L. *frondōs-us*, f. *frond-*, FROND *sb.*[1]] Covered with fronds; having the form or appearance of a frond. In early use, †Leafy, leaf-like.
1721–92 BAILEY, *Frondose*, leavy or full of leaves. **1793** MARTYN *Lang. Bot.*, A frondose stem; applied to Palms. **1807** J. E. SMITH *Phys. Bot.* 493 Liverworts. Of these the herbage is commonly frondose. **1831** LOUDON *Encycl. Agric.* §3987 (ed. 2) 648 The branches of frondose trees. **1890** H. M. STANLEY *Darkest Africa* II. xxviii. 260 Banana groves.. extended out in deep frondiose [*sic*] groves far into the Semliki Valley.
b. *Comb.*, **frondose-branched** *a.*, having flat branches spread horizontally like the fronds of a fern.
1831 LOUDON *Encycl. Brit.* §3987 (ed. 2) 648 Resinous or frondose-branched trees.
Hence **fron'dosely** *adv.*, **fron'doseness**.
1727 BAILEY vol. II, *Frondoseness*, leafiness. **1882** CROMBIE in *Encycl. Brit.* XIV. 561/2 Thallus frondosely dilated.

†**fron'dosity.** *Obs.* [f. as prec. + -ITY.]
1. Leafiness.
1656 BLOUNT *Glossogr.*, *Frondosity*, leaviness, or aptness to bear leaves. **1772** NUGENT tr. *Hist. Fr. Gerund* I. 330 In the frondosity of a pleasant meadow.
2. (See quot.)
1658 PHILLIPS, *Frondosity*, a flourishing with green leaves, being just under the architrave.

†**fron'dosous,** *a. Obs.*⁻⁰ [badly f. L. *frondōs-us* (see FRONDOSE) + -OUS.] (See quot.)
1623 COCKERAM, *Frondosous*, full of leaues.

frondous ('frɒndəs), *a.* [ad. L. *frondōs-us*; see FRONDOSE and -OUS.] Leafy (see quots.).
1828 WEBSTER (citing Milne) s.v., A frondous flower is one which is leafy, one which produces branches charged with both leaves and flowers. **1864** SIR K. JAMES *Tasso* XVI. xii, Among the frondous boughs. **1885** *Syd. Soc. Lex.*, *Frondous*, having branches bearing both leaves and flowers. Also, a term applied to flowers parts of which develop into leafy structures.

frondule ('frɒndjuːl). [dim. of FROND *sb.*[1]: see -ULE.] A small frond (*Syd. Soc. Lex.* 1885).

‖**frons** (frɒnz). [Lat.] = FRONT *sb.* 1 c.
1856–8 W. CLARK *Van der Hoeven's Zool.* I. 290 Polyzonium Brandt. Two series of 3 small eyes in the frons.

front (frʌnt), *sb.* (and *a.*) Forms: 3–7 fount(e, frunt(e, 4 *Sc.* froynt(t, 4–6 fronte, 4, 6 frownt, (4 frond), 3– front. [a. OF. and Fr. *front*, ad. L. *front-em*, *frōns* the forehead.]
I. Forehead, face.
1. a. = FOREHEAD 1. Now only *poet.* or in highly rhetorical language.
c **1290** *S. Eng. Leg.* I. 169/2176 Bote fram þe riȝt half of is frount. *c* **1375** *Sc. Leg. Saints, Machor* 1547 þe takine of þe cors to mak, one þar froyntis. **1390** GOWER *Conf.* I. 47 A sterre whit Amiddes in her front she [the hors] hadde. *c* **1450** *St. Cuthbert* (Surtees) 405 þe calf is rede I undertake, With a white sterne in þe fronte. **1481** CAXTON *Myrr.* II. v. 71 Peple ther.. haue only but one eye, and that standeth right in the myddys of the fronte or forhede. **1585** T. WASHINGTON tr. *Nicholay's Voy.* I. vi. 4 b, On theyr heads a Saracoll of Crymson velvet, and before the front the bande, a silver socket set with long feathers. **1602** SHAKS. *Ham.* III. iv. 56 See what a grace was seated on his Brow, Hyperions curles, the front of Ioue himselfe. **1671** MILTON *Samson* 496 The mark of fool set on his front! **1735** SOMERVILLE *Chase* III. 513 Soon he rears Erect his tow'ring Front. **1777** SHERIDAN *Sch. Scand.* A Portrait 13 Ye matron censors.. Whose peering eye and wrinkled front declare, etc. **1814** SCOTT *Ld. of Isles* VI. xxxvii, And bore he.. Such noble front, such waving hair? **1847** LYTTON *Lucretia* (1853) 227 Her nostrils dilated, and her front rose erect. **1884** W. ALLINGHAM *Blackberries* (1890) 88 Blear eyes, huge ears, and front of ape.
b. in fig. phrases, after Shakspere.
1604 SHAKS. *Oth.* I. iii. 80 The verie head, and front of my offending. *Ibid.* III. i. 52 (Qq.) To take the safest occasion by the front. **1816** KEATINGE *Trav.* (1817) I. 15 This was the whole front of his offending. **1878** MORLEY *Condorcet* 37 Placing social aims at the head and front of his life.
c. *rarely* used *techn.*, e.g. in *Entomology*.
1826 KIRBY & SP. *Entomol.* (1828) III. xxxiv. 483 The front of insects may be denominated the middle part of the face between the eyes.
2. By extension: The whole face. Cf. Fr. *front*. ***front to front*** (arch.) = *face to face*: see FACE 2 d.
1398 TREVISA *Barth. De P.R.* IX. ix. (1495) 354 Januarius is paynted wyth two frontes to shewe and to teche the begynnynge and ende of the yere. *c* **1450** *Mirour Saluacioun* 791 Nor hire nekke nor hire front vsed sho to bere vppright. **1508** DUNBAR *Flyting w. Kennedie* 84 Fy! feyndly front, far fowlar than ane fen. *a* **1605** POLWART *Flyting w. Montgomerie* 784 Jock Blunt, thrawin frunt! **1605** SHAKS. *Macb.* IV. iii. 232 Front to Front, Bring thou this Fiend of Scotland and my selfe. **1654** WHITLOCK *Zootomia* 82 Brazen Impudence.. hath two fronts, its boasting one, and bold one: with the one they look back.. the other looketh forward. **1697** CREECH *Manilius* I. ix, They stand not front to front, but each doth view The others Tayl, pursu'd as they pursue. **1698** FRYER *Acc. E. India & P.* 292 Antelopes.. guarding their Fronts, scampering with their Heads to the Earth, to avoid the.. Enemy aloft. **1767** SIR W. JONES 7 *Fountains* Poems (1777) 50 Till thrice the sun his rising front has shown. **1802** BEDDOES *Hygëia* II. 39 Those.. have the courage to treat it, front to front, in a manner corresponding to the enormity of the consequences [etc.]. **1855** TENNYSON *Maud* II. i. 28 For front to front in an hour we stood.
3. †**a.** The face as expressive of emotion or character; expression of countenance (*obs.*). **b.** Bearing or demeanour in confronting anything; degree of composure or confidence in the presence of danger, etc. Also outward appearance or aspect; façade; *spec.* a bluff. Also *fig.* Cf. sense 7 g.
c **1374** CHAUCER *Boeth.* II. pr. viii. 47 (Camb. MS.) Whan she [fortune] descoeuereth hir frownt and sheweth hir maneres. *c* **1477** CAXTON *Jason* 104 b, [Medea] commanded that her ladies.. shold put on the fayr fronte in entencion to make feste solempne. **1637** HEYWOOD *Royall King* I. Wks. 1874 VI. 17 That face.. beares the selfe-same front. **1711** STEELE *Spect.* No. 20 ¶ 3 A Fellow that is capable of shewing an impudent Front before a whole Congregation. **1762** FALCONER *Shipwr.* II. 347 Who, patient in adversity, still bear The firmest front. **1800–24** CAMPBELL *Poems, Visiting Scene in Ayrshire* iv, Through the perils of chance.. May thy front be unalter'd. **1821** SCOTT *Kenilw.* vi, The.. unclouded front of an accomplished courtier. **1873–4** DIXON *Two Queens* IV. XXII. ix. 221 Kildare.. resolved to.. meet his accusers with a brazen front. **1900** 'FLYNT' & WALTON *Powers that Prey* 181 It riles a bloke's sense o' justice to be accused false an' helps him to put up a front. **1934** J. O'HARA *Appointment in Samarra* (1935) 27 There was dancing and a hat-check girl and waiters in uniform and all that front. **1949** E. COXHEAD *Wind in West* vii. 193 While he still put a good front on the affair, she said nothing. **1952** A. BARON *With Hope, Farewell* 124 It was only a front. He was scared stiff. **1953** R. LEHMANN *Echoing Grove* 136 Will you kindly assist me to preserve a front till Monday?.. My parents have been through enough—we've got to put a face on it.
transf. **1855** PRESCOTT *Philip II*, I. II. xiv. 309 The league, which had raised so bold a front against the government, had crumbled away. **1860** TYNDALL *Glac.* I. xi. 76 The limestone bastions.. preserved a front of gloom and grandeur.
4. Effrontery, impudence. Cf. FACE 7, FOREHEAD 2. Now *rare.* So, †***man of front***. ***to have the front***: to be sufficiently impudent.
1653 H. MORE *Antid. Ath.* III. ix. (1712) 170, I.. wonder how any man, except one of the most hardened front, can [etc.]. **1709** STEELE *Tatler* No. 168 ¶ 3 Men of Front carry Things before 'em with little Opposition. **1717** DE FOE *Mem. Ch. Scot.* (1844) 5 With what Front the Absurdities charg'd on her could be broach'd in the World. **1849** MACAULAY *Hist. Eng.* II. 293 None of the commissioners had the front to pronounce that [etc.].
II. Foremost part.
5. *Mil.* **a.** The foremost line or part of an army or battalion. Also, †a rank (*obs.*), and in words of command; e.g. ***files to the front***, ***right in front***.
c **1350** *Will. Palerne* 3584 In sexe semli batailes.. al be fore in þe fronde he ferde þan him-selue. *c* **1400** *Destr. Troy* 1278 þan.. ffrochit into þe frount & a fray made. **1470–85** MALORY *Arthur* II. x. 87 But alweyes kyng Lot helde hym in the formest frunte. **1598** BARRET *Theor. Warres* Gloss. 250 Fronte, a French word, is the face or foreparte of a squadron or battell. **1607** SHAKS. *Cor.* I. vi. 8 Both our powers, with smiling Fronts encountring. **1625** MARKHAM *Souldiers Accid.* 6 The Rankes are called Frunts, because they stand formost.. but in truth none can properly be called the Frunt, but the ranke which standeth formost. **1667** MILTON *P.L.* VI. 105 Front to Front Presented stood in terrible array. **1697** DRYDEN *Virg. Georg.* II. 378 As Legions in the Field their Front display. **1700** S. L. tr. *Fryke's Voy. E. Ind.* 61 Commanded Captain Jochem, who led the Blacks, to march in the Front. **1775** R. KING in *Life & Corr.* (1894) I. 9 They.. began their march, with a very wide Front. **1838–43** ARNOLD *Hist. Rome* III. xliii. 141 The.. Gaulish horse charged the Romans front to front. **1859** F. A. GRIFFITHS *Artil. Man.* (1862) 7 Files to the front. *Ibid.* 18 A column Left in front will bring its rear companies to the front. *Ibid.* 19 Open column, right in front—right about face.
b. Line of battle.

1375 BARBOUR *Bruce* XVII. 569 The Ingliss men com on sadly..Richt in a frount vith a baner. *c* **1400** *Destr. Troy* 10869 And all fore to þe fight in a frunt hole. **1607** TOPSELL *Four-f. Beasts* (1658) 249 They used to terrifie the Barbarians, setting their Horses in a double front, so as they appeared headed both wayes. **1623** BINGHAM *Xenophon* 78 If we aduance in a large Front..if in a narrow Front. **1667** MILTON *P.L.* I. 563 Advanc't in view they stand, a horrid Front Of dreadful length. **1710** *Lond. Gaz.* No. 4744/2 Our ..Army..marched..to Attack the Enemy in full Front. **1838** THIRLWALL *Greece* III. 349 The Spartans..preserving an even and unbroken front. **1886** *Daily News* 13 Sept. 5/7 The troops marched past, the infantry in company fronts and the cavalry by half squadrons.

c. The foremost part of the ground occupied, or in wider sense, of the field of operations; the part next the enemy.

1665 MANLEY *Grotius' Low C. Warres* 440 Not onely the Front as heretofore, but the backside also..rendred unsafe. **1781** GIBBON *Decl. & F.* II. xli. 504 Belisarius protected his front with a deep trench. **1810** WELLINGTON in Gurw. *Desp.* VI. 367, I propose to move up the infantry of the army to the front again. **1844** H. H. WILSON *Brit. India* III. 320 One division..was sent to take the stockades in rear, while another..threatened them from the front. **1879** FIFE-COOKSON *Armies of Balkans* i. 6 To see him before his departure for the front next day. **1889** R. KIPLING *Willie Winkie* 72 British Regiments were wanted—badly wanted—at the Front. **1944** *Hutchinson's Pict. Hist. War* 27 Oct. '43–11 Apr. '44 237 A 20-mile advance on the south of the bulge which opened up a 'breakthrough' front 60 miles in width. **1967** J. MARSHALL-CORNWALL *Napoleon* iv. 50 Only 25,000 were available as a mobile field force, and these were extended..on a front of about 30 miles.

fig. **1846** GREENER *Sci. Gunnery* 54 The present state of our artillery requires an advance to the front, to be in a line with the march of science.

d. The direction towards which the line faces when formed. ***change of front***: see CHANGE *v.* 9 b; in quot. *fig.* ***to make front to***: to face in the direction of; in quot. *fig.*

1832 in *Prop. Regul. Instr. Cavalry* III. 46. **1833** *Regul. Instr. Cavalry* I. 14 The whole will face, as accurately as possible, to their former front. **1837** CARLYLE *Fr. Rev.* III. I. i. (1872) 9 The improvised Municipals make front to this also. **1879** LUBBOCK *Addr. Pol. & Educ.* iv. 92 This change of front seems to be founded on the report of the Board of Education for Scotland. **1891** *Daily News* 28 Nov. 5/6 The eventuality of a war with two fronts—that is to say, with France and Russia—was foreseen.

e. ***front of fortification***: see quot. 1859.

1851 J. S. MACAULAY *Field Fortif.* 23 The outline above traced is called a Front of Fortification. **1859** F. A. GRIFFITHS *Artil. Man.* (1862) 261 A Front of Fortification consists of two half bastions, and a curtain.

f. *transf.* With preceding epithet, an organized sector of activity, as ***domestic front, home front***, etc.

1919 *Punch's Hist. Gt. War* 19 The trials..on the home front. **1929** *Nation* 4 Dec. 696/1 Gleb's victory on the economic front is somewhat spoiled by his partial defeat on the 'domestic front'. **1934** A. HUXLEY *Beyond Mexique Bay* 6 The amusement front had its duly appointed commissar. **1938** *Ann. Reg. 1937* 67 Sir A. Sinclair complained that the Government was concentrating its energies too much on preparations for attack, to the neglect of what was commonly known as 'the home front'. **1941** *Punch* 3 Sept. 211/3 My sister..writes..of the many..economical dishes she is now able to prepare as a result of the B.B.C. talks on the Kitchen Front. **1959** *Encounter* July 79/2 Myths of Soviet home-front propaganda. **1969** *Times* 6 Jan. 7/8 But the industry is fighting back on the marketing as well as the political front.

g. *transf.* An organized body of political forces.

1926 D. L. SAYERS *Clouds of Witness* vii. 157 A woman.. looking like a personification of the United Front of the 'Internationale'. **1934** *Ann. Reg. 1933* II. 171 A uniform National-Socialist organisation embracing all German workers was called into existence under the designation 'The German Workers' Front'. **1936** E. A. PEERS *Spanish Tragedy 1930–36* iv. 188 And combine under him [*sc.* Sr. Azaña] they did—Republican Left, Republican Union, Socialists, Syndicalists, Anarchists, Marxists and Communists—forming, for the purpose of the election campaign, a united phalanx, a 'Popular Front', as they called it: *Frente Popular*. **1940** *Amer. Speech* XV. 453/2 He [*sc.* Dimitrov]..urged members of the Communist Party to organize 'Popular Fronts' in the democracies. **1968** *Listener* 15 Aug. 195/2 The Popular Front for the Liberation of Palestine.

6. *Arch.* 'Any side or face of a building, but more commonly used to denote the entrance side' (Gwilt); occas. *collect.* in *sing.*, and *pl.* = 'the four sides' (of a mansion). Also ***back-, rear-front.***

1365 *Durham Halm. Rolls* (Surtees) 41 Non fecit clausuram tenementi sui de le front. **1382** WYCLIF *Ezek.* xl. 9 He metide..the frount therof in two cubitis. *c* **1440** *Promp. Parv.* 181/1 Frownt, or frunt of a churche, or oþer howsys. **1624** WOTTON *Archit.* (1672) 16 And the contrary fault of low distended Fronts, is as unseemly. **1703** MOXON *Mech. Exerc.* 265 A Building, which is 25 Feet, both in the Front and Reer Front. **1760–72** tr. *Juan & Ulloa's Voy.* (ed. 3) II. 32 The fronts being of stone. **1806** *Gazetteer Scotl.* (ed. 2) 144 The Town-house, an elegant structure, with a handsome front. **1841** W. SPALDING *Italy & It. Isl.* III. 150 Monastic cloisters with their dark length of front. *Ibid.* 166 One of the back-fronts of the old palace. **1888** BURGON *Lives 12 Gd. Men* II. xii. 355 The garden front was most inconveniently embowered..in forest trees. **1893** W. P. COURTNEY in *Academy* 13 May 413/1 The fronts of the mansion were decorated with statues by skilled sculptors.

7. a. *gen.* The part or side of an object which seems to look out or to be presented to the eye; the fore-part of anything, the part to which one normally comes first. Opposed to *back*, *esp.* in objects that have only two sides. Cf. BACK *sb.* 3.

c **1400** *Destr. Troy* 10814 In þe frunt of þat faire yle, Was a prouynse of prise. **1555** EDEN *Decades* 85 We found the fyrst front of this land to bee broader. **1577** B. GOOGE *Heresbach's Husb.* I. (1586) 41 b, A lowe kinde of Carre with a couple of wheeles, and the Front armed with sharpe Syckles. **1605** SHAKS. *Macb.* v. viii. 47 Had he his hurts before? I, on the Front. **1705** ADDISON *Italy* 5 The Front to the Sea is not large, but there are a great many Houses behind it built up the Side of the Mountain. **1788** GIBBON *Decl. & F.* I. (Milman) V. 2 The southern basis presents a front of a thousand miles to the Indian Ocean. **1823** H. J. BROOKE *Introd. Crystallogr.* 287 The opposite angles, edges, and planes, which are supposed to form the back of the engraved figure, are respectively similar to those which appear on its front. **1851** CARPENTER *Man. Phys.* (ed. 2) 398 The sternum itself being so largely developed, as to cover almost the entire front of the body. **1893** F. W. MAITLAND *Mem. de Parl.* Introd. 92 The skin being thin, the writing on the front could be seen upon the back.

b. *transf.* With reference to time: The first period; the beginning. *poet.*

c **1600** SHAKS. *Sonn.* cii, Philomel in summer's front doth sing. **1842** TENNYSON *Gard. Dau.* 28 More black than ashbuds in the front of March. **1883** STEVENSON *Silverado Sq.* 237 A hawthorn in the front of June.

†**c.** = FRONTIER *sb.* 4. *Obs.*

1589 GREENE *Sp. Masquerado* Wks. (Grosart) V. 256 When the Sarasens..had inuaded Germanie, and the frontes of France. **1593** HOLLYBAND *Fr. Dict.* P 2 b, *Les frontieres d'vn pais*, the frontiers of a countrey: the front or marches.

d. *Mining.* = FACE 20 a.

1717 tr. *Frezier's Voy. S. Sea* 183 A Mine, which is 40 Varas, or Spanish Yards in Front. **1867** W. W. SMYTH *Coal & Coal-mining* 140 Let us now turn our attention to the 'face' or front of the working.

e. Land facing a road, river, the sea, etc.; a frontage. *spec.* with *the*: the promenade of a seaside resort, often with adjoining gardens. Cf. SEA-FRONT 2.

1766 *Laws of N. Carolina* (1791) 234 The Water Fronts of the Lots herein before mentioned. **1769** *Bp. Wilton Inclos. Act* 2 Occupiers of ancient messuages, cottages, houses or fronts. **1904** *Ward, Lock's Guide Isle of Man* 44 The Queen's Promenade..is the part of the Front most favoured by visitors with a taste for quiet. **1920** *Glasgow Herald* 17 July 7 For them the 'front', palpitating with cheerful humanity, is Elysium. **1938** G. GREENE *Brighton Rock* I. i. 20 A blow along the front'll do you good. *Ibid.* iii. 42 I'd like to have asked them why he left me like that, to go scampering down the front in that sun.

f. *Theatrical.* (See quots.) Also ***front-of-(the-)house*** attrib. phr.

1806 G. F. COOKE *Diary* 6 Dec. in W. Dunlap *Mem. G.F.C.* (1813) I. 328 Went to the theatre..passed Mr Rae into the front of the house. **1810** SCOTT *Fam. Lett.* 30 Mar. (1894) I. 174 There was fine work in the front, as they call the audience part of the house. **1894** *Evening News* 18 Oct. 2/6 Generally speaking, the 'front of the house' means the audience; but among theatrical employés the 'front of the house' means everybody engaged to work before the curtain. **1930** C. H. RIDGE *Stage Lighting* iv. 62 Front-of-the-house lighting tends to flatness. **1935** RIDGE & ALDRED *Stage Lighting* viii. 73/2 The following notes may serve to sum up the subject of Front-of-House Lighting. **1961** BOWMAN & BALL *Theatre Lang.* 149 *Front of house; front-of-house; front of the house*; abbreviation, *F.O.H.* 1. The parts of the theatre in front of the proscenium arch. Hence, said of equipment placed therein, as, *a front of house light*... 4. The personnel and operations of the business staff, including the ushers, as, *the front of house staff*. **1985** *Financial Times* 20 July p. xiii/5 The ICA itself provides the performing space and front of house facilities.

g. A person, organization, etc., that serves as a cover for subversive or illegal activities. So ***front man, organization.*** orig. *U.S.*

1905 *McClure's Mag.* XXIV. 346 For Brayton was the front, not the head of the System. **1926** J. BLACK *You can't Win* iv. 27 The store was but a 'front' or blind for a poker game and dice games in the back room. **1934** H. N. ROSE *Thesaurus of Slang* 25/1 Representative Who Poses as the 'Big Shot' of a Gang (n. phr.): *the front man.* **1938** H. ASBURY *Sucker's Progr.* 345 Their agent and front man was the Chief of Police. **1940** in *Amer. Speech* (1941) XVI. 146/2 Foreign 'isms'..masquerading behind 'front' organizations. **1940** *Time* 29 Jan. 23/3 Department of Justice investigators believe that Earl Browder is a mere front-man. **1949** M. MILLER *Sure Thing* (1950) 67 It's a front; the Commies control it. *Ibid.* 70 'I attended a camp of the Youth League of America.' 'You knew..that was merely a front for the Communist Party.' **1951** J. CORNISH *Provincials* 213, I dare say it was all a 'front' for spy activities. **1959** 'M. ERSKINE' *House of Enchantress* ix. 130 He was..respectable-looking and meek,..just the type to make an excellent front for Madame Rosario. **1960** *Spectator* 16 Sept. 408 He becomes the nark and front-man for an unscrupulous white landlord in a slum-house area. **1965** *Ibid.* 19 Feb. 220/1 A Communist 'front' organisation formed and financed by the Communist régime in North Vietnam.

h. *Meteorol.* A bounding surface or a transition zone between two air masses at different temperatures; also, the line on the ground that marks the lower edge of this surface; so ***cold, warm front***: the forward boundary of a mass of advancing cold, or warm, air.

1921 BJERKNES & SOLBERG in *Geofysiske Publikationer* II. III. 12 In the first case, the boundary line at the ground will be the front of advancing cold air, or, to introduce a shorter expression, a '*cold front*'. In the latter case, the boundary line will be the front of advancing warm air, or simply a '*warm front*'. **1923** N. SHAW *Air & its Ways* vii. 74 The polar front is regarded as being a bank of air with stream lines..over which the equatorial air is advancing gradually upward by motion directly transverse to the line of motion in the front. **1938** *Nature* 29 Oct. 804/1 Any pressure system, such as a cyclone, an anticyclone, a trough or a front. **1956** *Weather* May 147 The front is not a surface but a zone of rapid temperature transition between air masses. **1957** *Times* 11 May 7/1 A depression near Ireland will be slow moving and associated weak fronts will move slowly N.E. to E. districts. **1970** R. W. LONGLEY *Elem. Meteorol.* x. 223 A frontal surface is the bounding surface between two air masses... The front is the intersection of such a frontal surface with the ground.

†**8. a.** The first part or line of anything written or printed. ***in the front***: at the head. *Obs.*

1576 FLEMING *Panopl. Epist.* 435, I could not but in ye very front and beginning of my letter, use this. **1594** BLUNDEVIL *Exerc.* III. I. xx. (ed. 7) 324 Six Columnes, every front or head whereof is noted with three great letters, D.M.S. signifying degrees, minutes, and seconds. **1654** WHITLOCK *Zootomia* 94 A Catalogue of above three hundred Advisers, and his name in the Front. **1697** DRYDEN *Virg. Past.* VI. 17 Thy Name..Shall in the front of every Page be shown.

†**b.** = FRONTISPIECE *sb.* 3 or 4. *Obs.*

1647 CRASHAW *Poems* 128 If with distinctive eye and mind you look Upon the front, you see more than one book. *a* **1718** PENN *Life* Wks. 1726 I. 147 Which the Reader may find in the Front of the Books they [the Prefaces] were designed for.

9. a. A fore-part or piece having some particular use or function.

1847 A. M. GILLIAM *Trav. Mexico* 152 The body of the wagon is about equally balanced over the axletree, the front resting upon the tongue. **1851** *Offic. Catal. Gt. Exhib.* I. 467 Pianoforte..in newly designed case with sliding front. *Ibid.* II. 526 Boots and shoes..with elastic fronts and sides.

†**b.** = FRONTAL *sb.* 2. *Obs.*

1533 in Weaver *Wells Wills* (1890) 148 To the gyltyng of the ffrownt at the hye auter. **1539** *Peterboro' Inv.* in *N. & Q.* 3rd Ser. IV. 459 In the Rood Loft..one front of painted cloth. **1552–3** *Inv. Ch. Goods Staffs.* in *Ann. Lichfield* IV. 66 One fronte for an alter of yelowe and grene satten.

c. A band or bands of false hair, or a set of false curls, worn by women over the forehead.

1687 CONGREVE *Old Bach.* IV. iv, I undertook the modelling of one of their fronts, the more modern structure. **1837** THACKERAY *Ravenswing* i, Mamma means her front! **1865** TROLLOPE *Belton Est.* xvii, The graces of her own hair had given way to a front. **1886** *Pall Mall G.* 24 Aug. 13/2 A ..black velvet band..to keep her auburn front..in its place.

d. That part of a man's shirt which covers the chest and is more or less displayed; a shirt-front; also, a 'dicky'; also, a similar article of silk, etc. serving as a cravat.

1844 DICKENS *Mart. Chuz.* xvii, What a very few shirts there are, and what a many fronts. **1851** *Offic. Catal. Gt. Exhib.* II. 579 Gentlemen's fronts and stocks.

e. The front part of a woman's garment.

1801 JANE AUSTEN *Let.* 5 May (1932) I. 125 It is to be a round gown, with a jacket and a frock front..to open at the side. *Ibid.*, The front is sloped round to the bosom and drawn in. **1889** *Daily News* 23 July 7/2 The travelling mantle..buttons the whole way down the front, and is provided with over-fronts which fall straight from the shoulders. *Ibid.*, These fronts are lined with yellow and pink ..surah. **1932** E. BOWEN *To North* iv. 38 One wore frills down her front, she was going to have a baby.

10. A position or place situated before something or towards a spectator; forward position or situation. Only in phrases with prefixed prep.

a. ***in (the) front of*** (prep. phr.): at a position before, in advance of, facing, or confronting; at the head of (troops). ***in his, our,*** etc. ***front***: in front of or facing him, us, etc.

The article is now omitted, exc. in expressions like ***in the (very) front of (danger*** etc.) = 'in the position most exposed to', 'bearing the brunt of'.

1698 FRYER *Acc. E. India & P.* 144, I saw..a pragmatical Portugal..in the front of 40 men marching to the Governor's. **1712** W. ROGERS *Voy.* 174 We..fir'd..at the Men in Arms in the front of the Church. **1777** WATSON *Philip II* (1839) 143 Behind him there was a little wood and the walls of a convent; and in his front, the morass above mentioned, which was almost impassable. **1816** KEATINGE *Trav.* (1817) I. 225 The standards were faced about, and formed in our fronts. **1847** A. M. GILLIAM *Trav. Mexico* 256, I was particular to make my servants keep in front of me. **1853** SIR H. DOUGLAS *Milit. Bridges* (ed. 3) 144 Forcing a passage across the river in his front. **1855** MACAULAY *Hist. Eng.* III. 1 The proclamation was repeated..in front of the Royal Exchange.

fig. **1609** TOURNEUR *Funeral Poeme on Sir F. Vere* 172, I the front Of danger where he did his deedes advance. **1817** CHALMERS *Astron. Disc.* v. (1852) 124 Those holy..men..in the front of severest obloquy, are now labouring in remotest lands. **1848** W. H. KELLY tr. *L. Blanc's Hist. Ten Y.* II. 345 In the very front of danger. **1892** *Spectator* 12 Mar. 353/1 His majesty will speedily be in front of a new difficulty. **1896** *Westm. Gaz.* 28 July 9/2 The shares had nothing in front of them—no preference or debenture capital.

b. ***in (†the) front*** (advb. phr.): in an advanced or forward position; on the side that meets the eye; in a position facing the spectator.

1613 PURCHAS *Pilgrimage* (1614) 380 With his whole forces, in front, [he] assailed. **1700** T. BROWN tr. *Fresny's Amusem. Ser. & Com.* 21 By comes a Christning, with the Reader and the Midwife strutting in the Front. **1748** F. SMITH *Voy. Disc.* I. 133 The upper Story had the two Captains Cabins in Front. **1821** G. W. MANBY *Voy. Greenland* (1823) 134 Determined..to attack him [a bear] in front, I got upon the ice. **1847** A. M. GILLIAM *Trav. Mexico* 76 These dirt hovels presented a bold contrast with the city behind, and the wealthy church in front. *Ibid.* 99 A kind of shawl [which] by being crossed in front, obscures the bosom. **1879** HARLAN *Eyesight* ix. 129 The most injurious direction for light to come from is that directly in front. **1895** *Scot. Antiq.* X. 78 Setting an old press in front so as to conceal the door.

c. *to the front* (*of*): to a position in front (of).

1820 Scoresby *Acc. Arctic Reg.* I. 235 Being removed to the front of a brisk fire, a strong ebullition commenced. **1887** Bowen *Virg. Æneid* v. 150 Far to the front shoots Gyas.. Gliding ahead on the water.

d. *to come to the front*: to become conspicuous, be revealed, emerge into publicity; to make oneself or itself manifest. So (*to be*) *to the front* = 'to the fore' (*rare*).

1871 *Archæol. Assoc. Jrnl.* Sept. 323 Another saint came to the front. **1876** Trevelyan *Macaulay* II. ix. 132 When subjects came to the front on which his knowledge was great. **1878** *Scribner's Mag.* XVI. 184/2 At such a time his true boastful self would come to the front. **1885** Mrs. Lynn Linton *Chr. Kirkland* III. vi. 231 Underneath in the hidden depths lurked other matters than those which came to the front. **1886** *Daily News* 6 Jan. 5/1 The year has gone, however, and the aged Emperor is still to the front.

11. *ellipt.* (quasi-*adj.* or *adv.*) **a.** *spec.* = *front-pipe* (see 14).

1667 Primatt *City & C. Build.* 36 Suppose that same be 25 foot Front, and forty foot deep, it may be let for to be built, for forty shillings the foot Front. *c* **1680** Hickeringill *Wks.* (1716) II. 512 The Enemy..had beset them Front and Rear. **1698** Fryer *Acc. E. India & P.* 8 The biggest of them [buildings] had not four yards Front. **1845** *Florist's Jrnl.* 25 A little shed, open back and front. **1879** *Organ Voicing* 12 Zinc is frequently used for basses and 'fronts'. **1892** I. Zangwill *Bow Myst.* 127 It's the key of my first-floor front.

b. *front of*: in front of. *U.S.*

1843 'R. Carlton' *New Purchase* xv. 110 Front of the fire-place was the parlour. **1871** Mrs. Stowe *Sam Lawson* 45 Wall, she was a standin' front o' this. **1896** S. Jewett *Country of Pointed Firs* 107 He used to..throw a little bundle 'way up the green slope front o' the house.

c. As a command: to the front, forward.

1907 *N.Y. Even. Post* (semi-weekly ed.) 13 May 6 The register clerk [at a Shanghai hotel] assigns you to a room, and instead of 'Front!' he shouts 'Boy!'

†**12.** [from the vb.] Encounter, onset; = affront *sb.* 3. *Obs.*

1523 Ld. Berners *Froiss.* I. ccccxxxii. 760 The men of armes..at the first front ouerthrue many.

III. *attrib.* and *Comb.*

13. *attrib.*, passing into *adj.* **a.** = Of or pertaining to the front, situated in front. (The comb. of adj. + sb. is itself often used *attrib.*) Freq. in various more or less technical uses.

1600 Holland *Livy* xxxvii. 957 They had raunged their ships broad in a front-ranke. **1709** Steele *Tatler* No. 145 ¶2 She in a Front Box, he in the Pit next the Stage. **1710** *Brit. Apollo* III. No. 106. 4/1 The Front side of a good House, is to be Lett. **1718** *Freethinker* No. 57 ¶3, I shall be next Saturday at the Play, in a Front Row. **1770** G. White *Selborne* let. xxviii. 80 The horn of a male moose, which had no front-antlers. **1832** *Prop. Regul. Instr. Cavalry* II. 33 The leading front-rank man advances two horses' lengths. **1838** Lytton *Alice* 64 The front entrance is kept locked up. **1843** Sir C. Scudamore *Med. Visit Gräfenberg* 2 The small-pox, and the loss of some front teeth from an accident, impair his good looks. **1851** *Offic. Catal. Gt. Exhib.* I. 467 A front and side elevation of the Elizabethan pianoforte. **1860** Tyndall *Glac.* II. x. 275 A straight pinnacle of ice, the front edge of which was perfectly vertical. **1883** *Expositor* VI. 434 He [St. Peter] was naturally quick, mobile, a front-man. **1884** *Milit. Engin.* I. II. 43 The front ditch party are extended at 5 feet apart. **1897** *Encycl. Sport* I. 267/2 It ruins the tyres, and, if applied to the front wheel, puts a great strain on the front forks. *Ibid.* 493/1 It often happens in heavy shooting that the recoil of the second barrel causes the front trigger to cut the first joint of the fore-finger. **1902** *Captain* VII. 474 Crabb front rim brake. **1907** *Daily Chron.* 11 Nov. 7/4 The front axle being..used for both steering and driving alike. **1908** *Westm. Gaz.* 18 Jan. 7/2 Front-pressure over the area of a railway carriage must be from 25lb. to 35lb. per sq. foot before the stability of the train is imperilled. **1908** *Daily Chron.* 3 July 6/4 This front-cover picture. **1925** *Morris Man.* 68 When the front axle is off the ground, the pedal should be depressed. **1967** *Gloss. Mining Terms* (*B.S.I.*) xi. 8 Front abutment pressure.

b. *Phonetics.* Applied to sounds in the formation of which the fore-part of the tongue touches or is raised towards the hard palate.

1867 A. M. Bell *Vis. Speech* 52 Front. The Front of the Tongue contracting the oral passage between it and the roof of the mouth. *Ibid.*, Front-Mixed. The Front and the Point of the Tongue both raised. *Ibid.* 58 The 'Front-divided' Consonant has its side apertures within the palatal arch. **1888** H. Sweet *Hist. Eng. Sounds* 2 Front vowels are rounded by the lips only. **1918**, **1962** [see clear *a.* 13 b]. **1933**, **1965** [see central *a.* 1 d].

14. In special comb. and phrases: **front-action** *a.* (see quots.); **front bench**, the foremost bench on either side of the Houses of Lords and Commons, occupied by ministers and ex-ministers respectively; **front-bencher**, an occupant of a front bench, a leading member of the Government or Opposition; **front brake** = *front-wheel brake*; **front burner**: a boiling ring or plate at the front of a cooking stove; freq. used *fig.* in colloq. phr. *on the front burner* (orig. *U.S.*): of an issue, etc., in the state of being urgently considered; in the forefront of attention; of a plan, that receives priority; cf. *to cook on the front burner* s.v. cook *v.*[1] 1 b; opp. to *back burner* s.v. back- B; **front cloth** *Theatr.*, a painted cloth before which a scene is played while the stage is set for another scene behind it; **front door**, the principal entrance-door of a house; **front driver** (see driver 6 b); **front-fastening** *a.*, that fastens in front; **front flight** = first flight (see flight *sb.*[1] 8 d); also *attrib.*; **front foot**, a linear foot along the front of a plot of ground (cf. *foot front* in 11); **front-handed** *a.*, done with a forward movement of the hand; **front line** = front *sb.* 5; also *spec.* the musicians in a jazz band other than the rhythm section; freq. *attrib.*, of, pertaining to, or situated on the front-line or at the front; also *transf.* and *fig.*; ***front-line state***, (usu. in *pl.*) a state bordering on a country to which it is actively hostile; *spec.* a Black state lying on the border of the Republic of South Africa; **front-loader**, a machine, esp. a washing-machine, designed to be loaded from the front, as distinct from one loaded from the top, etc.; also **front-loading** *ppl. a.*; (as a back-formation) **front-load** *v. trans.*, (*a*) *U.S.*, to concentrate a load at the front of (a vehicle); (in quots. *fig.*); (*b*) to load (a washing-machine, etc.) from the front; also *transf.*; **front man** *spec.* (orig. *U.S.*), (*a*) see sense 7 g; (*b*) the leader of a band; (*c*) one who represents an organization, etc., publicly; *spec.* a television presenter; **front matter** *Printing* (orig. *U.S.*), all matter (title-page, preface, table of contents, etc.) in a book that precedes the text; the prelims; **front money** orig. *U.S.*, money paid in advance or at the beginning of a business transaction, esp. to secure additional finance or co-operation; cf. upfront *adv.* and *a.*; **front name** *U.S.* (*jocular* or *vulgar*), a Christian name; **front office** orig. *U.S.*, a main or head office; *spec.* police headquarters; **front page**, the front outside page of a newspaper; often *attrib.* to indicate an important or striking piece of news; so ***front-page*** v. trans. (orig. and chiefly *U.S.*), to feature on the front page; **front-pager**, one who is worthy of being featured on the front page; a celebrity; **front-piece** *Theatr.*, a small play acted in front of the curtain; **front-pipe**, each of the row of pipes which form the front of an organ, often gilded or otherwise decorated; **front rank**, the first or foremost rank; also *attrib.*; **front-ranker**, a person (ship, etc.) of the highest class or of leading position; **front room**, a room situated at the front of a house, esp. a sitting-room; *spec.* one kept as the best room in the house; **front-runner** (orig. *U.S.*), '(i) a contestant who runs best when in the lead; also, one who can set his own fast pace; (ii) the leading contestant in a competition' (Webster 1961); so **front-running** *a.*; (as a back-formation) **front-run** *v. intr.*; **front-stall**, an appendage to the bridle covering the horse's forehead; †**front-tickled** *a.* (? *nonce-wd.*), ? flattered; **front trench** *Mil.*, the trench nearest the enemy; **front-ways, -wise** *advbs.*, in a position or direction facing to the front; **front wheel**, the foremost or either of the foremost wheels upon which a vehicle runs; also *attrib.*, as ***front-wheel brake, drive***.

1881 W. W. Greener *Gun* 209 Back-action locks..tend to weaken the stock at the grip more than *front-action locks. **1907** *Ibid.* (ed. 8) 144 If the mainspring [of the lock]..is placed before the tumbler, it is 'front action' or 'bar'. **1891** *Daily News* 28 July 3/4 To have seen the motion carried on the strength of the two *Front Bench speeches. **1907** *Westm. Gaz.* 31 Aug. 1/3 Each Unionist *Front-Bencher will have to do a double or treble turn. **1919** G. B. Shaw *Heartbreak House* p. ix, Where were our front benchers to nest if not here? **1968** *Listener* 30 May 694/3 Would you say that to be in opposition as a backbencher, or indeed even as a frontbencher, is virtually a role of impotence? **1925** *Morris Man.* 68 From the points near the ends of the front number plate to the *front brake assemblies. **1959** *Motor Man.* (ed. 36) v. 137 (*caption*) Details of a Lockheed hydraulic two-leading-shoe front brake. **1945**, etc. *Front burner [see cook *v.*[1] 1 b]. **1970** *Times* 26 Sept. 7/2 The whole issue is now on the front burner with the flame turned up high. **1978** *Guardian Weekly* 4 June 16/4 Meany's agreement..that inflation has indeed superseded employment as the key problem..was remarkable for the most influential man on the labor scene, who for obvious reasons normally keeps the jobs picture on the front burner. **1884** J. Hatton *Irving's Impressions of America* II. xi. 268 Every scene is a set, except two, and they are *front cloths. **1896** G. B. Shaw *Our Theatres in Nineties* (1932) II. 32 Long enough to allow the carpenters time to set the most elaborate water-scene behind the front cloth. **1958** B. Nichols *Sweet & Twenties* 141 Those most precious of all items to the revue writer, the 'front-cloth numbers', which can be played without props or scenery. **1812** *Examiner* 31 Aug. 552/1 At the *front door. **1858** O. W. Holmes *Aut. Breakf.-t.* (1883) 110 The front-door is on the street. **1871** *Figure Training* 88 A *front-fastening corset. **1899** *Westm. Gaz.* 1 Dec. 4/2 The field gradually tailed off and only the *front-flight men were able to keep on terms. **1902** *Daily Chron.* 5 Dec. 3/4 A department of the chase upon which front-flight men of the shires may be inclined to look down. **1812** *Deb. Congress U.S.* 4 May (1853) 2288 [The city of Washington] shall have power to cause [street improvements] to be done at any expense not exceeding two dollars and fifty cents per *front foot. **1865** *Harper's Mag.* Aug. 319/1 Men bought town lots for $400 a front foot. **1925** B. Snyder *Real Estate Handbk.* 341 The land value map is designed to show the value of the land per front foot. *Ibid.*, These front-foot values are called unit values. **1843** *P. Parley's Ann.* IV. 74 He..made a quick *front-handed plunge in the direction from which the attack came. **1899** R. Whiteing *No. 5 John St.* xiv. 148 Tuesday, put you in the *front line gents, and do you well..our luncheon tent's goin' to beat creation. **1915** 'I. Hay' *First Hundred Thousand* xviii. 248 That sudden disturbance in the front-line trench. *Ibid.* 251 Our front-line parapet. **1917** F. M. Ford *Let.* 1 Jan. (1965) 81, I hope to get to Mesopotamia as I am not fit for the front line. **1920** G. K. Rose *2/4th Oxf. & Bucks Lt. Infty.* 36 My company supplied parties to carry wire and stakes up to the front line. **1927** W. Deeping *Kitty* xxi. 268 You've got a front line face. It's the March wind. **1931** *Times Lit. Suppl.* 12 Feb. 116/4 From a vast mass of published diaries..by officers and men whose duties brought them constantly into the front line, Professor Cru, himself a front-line soldier, has studied the fundamental nature of war. **1936** *Economist* 8 Feb. 291/1 The Government's declared programme of enlarging the Air Force to a strength of 2,100 'front line machines'. **1955** *Jazzbook 1955* 18 A coloured front line..and a mixed white and coloured rhythm section. **1959** J. S. Wilson *Collector's Jazz: Modern* 49 Brown makes some adept front-line uses of his bass on *Bass Hit*, Verve 8022. **1962** A. Nisbett *Technique Sound Studio* xiii. 225 This front-line audience can be of immense value to him in cross-checking his calculation or intuition. **1965** G. Melly *Owning-Up* vi. 72 The front line were blowing through their mouth pieces to warm them up sufficiently to play in tune. **1975** *Economist* 15 Feb. 72/3 The $1 billion military aid to Egypt and other front-line states given by Arab Opec members in 1973 and 1974. **1976** *Guardian Weekly* 19 Sept. 6/2 In Tanzania, Mozambique, and Botswana, the so-called 'front-line states', there is a mood of caution and pessimism. **1985** *Times* 21 Mar. 42/3 (Advt.), These opportunities hold..the immediate satisfaction of knowing that you will be making a tangible contribution to front-line marketing. **1977** *New Yorker* 26 Sept. 85/1, I decided to *frontload the court system instead of backloading it as before, by settling minor cases at the time of arraignment, the first step in the court process. **1984** *Listener* 15 Mar. 5/1 He was planning to 'front-load' his campaign with successes in Iowa, New Hampshire and on 'Super Tuesday'. **1984** *Which?* Aug. 384/2 For front-loading automatics, eczema sufferers may find ordinary automatic washing powders less of a problem than biological ones. **1960** *Farmer & Stockbreeder* 12 Jan. 84 (Advt.), Independent operation of *front-loaders, dozers, etc. **1970** *Guardian* 17 Nov. 9/2 The best laundromat machines..are the front-loaders. **1960** *Farmer & Stockbreeder* 8 Mar. 25/1 Taper ditching bucket and.. hydraulic *front-loading shovel. **1937** *Amer. Speech* XII. 46/1 **Front man*, the leader of the band. **1946** R. Blesh *Shining Trumpets* (1949) xii. 279 To hire New Orleans players and then leave them free to play jazz, never occurred to the natty swing 'front men'. **1959** 'F. Newton' *Jazz Scene* xi. 186 A good and permanent band is normally run by a martinet, or a 'natural' front man with an eye to the public. **1977** *TV Times* (Brisbane) 3 Sept. 18/2 Its producers faced another crisis. They met this..by casting about for another compere... They imported another frontman, David Frost, albeit briefly. **1985** *Washington Post* 25 Oct. C3/1, I hate to sound like a front man for the Network of Bill Cosby. **1909** *Cent. Dict.* Suppl., *Front matter. **1920** *Publishers' Weekly* 4 Oct. 1660/2 We have cast-off your manuscript and estimate it will make 8 pages of front-matter and 248 pages of text. **1966** H. Williamson *Methods Bk. Design* (ed. 2) xii. 176 American designers sometimes use the terms 'front matter' and 'end matter'. **1931** W. L. Stoddard *Financial Racketeering* i. 4 **Front Money*, money advanced to a salesman before commissions are earned. Money paid by companies for the purpose of securing finances, such money being paid to so-called 'financial engineers' on their promise to secure finances, which promises are seldom carried out. **1964** *Times Rev. Industry & Technol.* Feb. 11/1 His [*sc.* a film distributor's] guarantee is the necessary security on which the producer can borrow money from a bank. The amount borrowed constitutes what is known as front money and has absolute priority of repayment. **1977** H. Fast *Immigrants* v. 307 It's an investment. We call it front money, seed money. When the studio picks up, the money is repaid. **1877** Bartlett *Dict. Amer.* (ed. 4), **Front name*, Christian name. 'The familiar manner in which the telegraph handles my front name', i.e. in calling him Ben. **1895** *Pall Mall Mag.* Mar. 511 'What's your front name?' asked Roy boldly. **1900** 'J. Flynt' *Notes Itinerant Policeman* 73 The capture dwindles down to a request on the part of the chief or his officer that the man shall go to the '*front office'. **1935** Wodehouse *Blandings Castle* xii. 302 The Front Office has just sent out a communication to all writers. **1966** *Punch* 1 June 818/1 This is the sort of thing that can happen when the 'front office' is dubious about a film's popular appeal. **1902** *Out West* Jan. 39 Bearing on its *front page a picture of the murderer, and the 'story'. **1917** *Writer's Bulletin* Mar. 56/2 He pounds the typewriter keys And in the distance clearly sees A front page story and a raise. **1917** Wodehouse *Uneasy Money* xii. 134 'Why, we may all be murdered in our beds!' he cried. 'Front page stuff!' said Roscoe Sherriff, with gleaming eyes. **1929** *Times* 4 Feb. 13/5 The recent serious illness of the King has been 'front page news' from the beginning. **1929** M. Lief *Hangover* 54 Most of these society dames front-paged their fed-uppance with tea-fights and garden soirées. **1957** *N.Z. News* 17 Dec. 2/1 *The New York Times* front-paged Labour's victory. **1958** *Times Lit. Suppl.* 4 July 377/3 It is most gratifying to see a front-page article ..devoted to an intelligent and knowledgeable discussion of contemporary Russian poets. **1970** *Daily Tel.* 1 Jan. 5/8 Mr Barber is too good a journalist not to give the whole story breathless front-page excitement. **1899** *Daily News* 28 Feb. 4/7 A dazzling array of eminent '*front-pagers'. **1934** A. Huxley *Beyond Mexique Bay* 3 The gay and charming front-pagers who go on winter cruises are, in the main, elderly people. *a* **1889** *Evening News* (Barrère & Leland), At the Gaiety..a farce, 'Lot 49', by Mr. Fisher, as a *front piece to 'Frankenstein'. **1907** *Daily Chron.* 9 Nov. 4/4 Thirty-four full-length plays and seven front-pieces. **1855** E. J. Hopkins *Organ* 73 Tin does not soon become tarnished; hence its peculiar appropriateness for ungilded '*front pipes'. **1905** T. Elliston *Organs & Tuning* 393 The front pipes to be of stout V.M. zinc silvered with aluminium leaf. **1954** *Grove's Dict. Mus.* (ed. 5) VI. 290/2 The front pipes were made of tin, those inside of lead. **1872** G. MEREDITH *Let.* 15 Nov. (1970) I. 472 The suspicion that Burton did not do what he said is unworthy, considering the things he has undoubtedly accomplished, and which place him in the *front rank of adventurous travellers. **1897** *Sears, Roebuck Catal.* 579 This rifle..stands in the 'front rank' with the very best target rifles of this and other countries. **1899** *Westm. Gaz.* 10 Mar. 4/3 Mr. Fox, another front-rank costumier. **1935** *Discovery* Nov. 321 British manufacturers are in the front rank in this branch of scientific industry. **1905** *Westm. Gaz.* 25 Mar. 15/1 The eagerness which was displayed by some '*front-rankers' to get a 'line' of the Ceylon Pearl Syndicate's underwriting. **1914** in E. C. Barnes *Alfred Yarrow* (1923) xxvii. 260 The *Firedrake* and *Lurcher* were looked upon as two front-rankers. **1928** *Manch. Guardian Weekly* 7 Dec. Suppl. p. vi/1 It is a long time since a year's verse list was led by so many front rankers. **1963** *Times* 9 Feb. 10/5 London's light operatic conductors, at a time when Ivan Caryll, Herman Finck, Jimmy Glover, and Alfred Dove were front-rankers. **1679** MOXON *Mech. Exerc.* I. vii. 133 If your Shop stand in an eminent Street, the *Front Rooms are commonly more Airy than the Back Rooms. **1827** A. ROYALL *Tennessean* ii. 12 What were you doing in this front room? I was sweeping it. **1922** JOYCE *Ulysses* 690 He..reascended the stairs, reapproached the door of the front room, hallfloor, and reentered. **1976** T. SHARPE *Wilt* ii. 11 She got the washing-up done and the front room vacuumed. **1986** *N.Y. Times* 23 Feb. I. 18/4 Mr. Tutuola sits in the front room of his apartment, tugging constantly on his metal-stemmed pipe. **1940** *Time* 4 Nov. 71 He has won most of his subsequent newspaper clippings by *front-running for the U.S.'s No. 1 anti-Wall Street financier. **1958** *Times* 24 Oct. 17/6 Eldon tried to front-run without the necessary strength and experience. **1914** *Automobile* 27 Aug. 390/2 Always a *front-runner, he soon opened a gap on the field which looked to be a safe one. **1952** *Birmingham* (Ala.) *News* 5 May 12/1 Not a front runner, he is a dark horse who might come in first should Taft and Eisenhower cancel each other out. **1960** *Times* 29 June 17/7 There can be no doubt that the emergence of a few brave front-runners has lifted the middle distance running out of the doldrums. **1970** W. SMITH *Gold Mine* vii. 18 He had joined C.R.C. a mere twelve years previously..and now he was the front runner. **1950** *N.Y. Times* 11 June 53/2 Wade beat Pearman by nine yards in the 880 with a *front-running race. **1951** *Life* 1 Oct. 32/1 Taft is the strongest single Republican and the front-running candidate for the '52 nomination. **1601** HOLLAND *Pliny* II. 631 The KK. of the East had their horses set out therewith [cochlides]..in their *frontstals. **1653** URQUHART *Rabelais* II. xii. 83 A barbed horse furnished with a frontstal. **1825** SCOTT *Talism.* i, The front-stall of the bridle was a steel plate, with apertures for the eyes and nostrils. **1649** G. DANIEL *Trinarch., Hen. V*, ciii, But faire pretence leads on; and the Dull Heard *Front-tickled, yeild themselves into his hand. **1916** 'BOYD CABLE' *Action Front* 143 The stretcher-bearers carried their burden into the *front trench. **1863** R. H. GRONOW *Remin.* II. 46 The cocked hat he always wore, placed *frontways on his head, like that of the Emperor Napoleon. **1774** GOLDSM. *Nat. Hist.* V. III. ii. (*Venom. Serpents*), It has..a mark of dark brown on the forehead, which, when viewed *frontwise, looks like a pair of spectacles. **1885** MIDDLETON in *Encycl. Brit.* XIX. 612/1 Though the faces are nearly always represented in profile, the eyes are shown frontwise. **1897** *Front wheel [see sense 13 above]. **1902** A. C. HARMSWORTH et al. *Motors* x. 218 The automobilist should frequently jack up the front of his car so that the front wheels are free of the ground. **1878** *Design & Work* IV. 218/1, 52 in. Wolverhampton..with lamp and pouch, *front wheel brake. **1900** *Captain* III. 463/2 Gamage's Holborn front wheel rim brake. **1904** GOODCHILD & TWENEY *Technol. & Sci. Dict.* 147/2 The front wheel brake usually carries two blocks on a horseshoe-shaped clip. **1908** *Westm. Gaz.* 3 Nov. 4/1 The Allen-Liversidge system of *front-wheel braking. **1928** *Daily Mail* 13 Aug. 12/6 Will the new principle of *front wheel drive prove a success? **1968** N. FLEMING *Counter Paradise* iii. 42 'Great heap,' Jake grinned... 'Yes..and it's got front-wheel drive.' **1971** *Guardian* 18 Feb. 2/6 The Renault 17..is a front-wheel drive model.

front (frʌnt), *v.*[1] [ad. OF. *front-er* in same sense, f. *front* FRONT *sb.*; it may however in some uses be an independent formation on the Eng. sb.]

1. a. *intr.* To have the front in a specified direction; to face, look. Const. *on, to, towards, upon.*

1523 LD. BERNERS *Froiss.* I. li. 73 The french king..purueyed suffyciently for all the forteresses frontyng on Flanders. **1583** STANYHURST *Æneis* III. (Arb.) 88 Tarent..to which heunlye Lacinia fronteth. **1660** F. BROOKE tr. *Le Blanc's Trav.* 297 A countrey..fronts upon another Nation. **1703** MAUNDRELL *Journ. Jerus.* (1732) 143 Having a few small Rooms fronting outward. **1762** H. WALPOLE *Vertue's Anecd. Paint.* II. ii. 48 This room was erected..fronting westward to the privy-garden. **1864** TENNYSON *Enoch Arden*, Philip's dwelling fronted on the street. **1894** HALL CAINE *Manxman* III. iii. 134 The rooms fronted to Athol Street.

†**b.** *trans.* To set the front of (a building) in a specified direction. *Obs.*

1665 J. WEBB *Stone-Heng* (1725) 105 Temples..should be so fronted, as that Travellers passing by might behold them. *a* **1817** T. DWIGHT *Trav. New Eng.* (1821) II. 97 Mr. G. has erected a large elegant mansion, fronted towards the river.

2. *trans.* **a.** To have the front towards; to 'face', stand opposite to.

1606 SHAKS. *Tr. & Cr.* III. iii. 122 Like a gate of steele, Fronting the Sunne. **1696** tr. *Du Mont's Voy. Levant* 2 All the Houses..which fronted the Bishop's Palace. **1749** FIELDING *Tom Jones* v. v, This enclosed place exactly fronted the foot of the bed. **1823** F. CLISSOLD *Ascent Mt. Blanc* 11 Fronting us, rose the summit of Mont Blanc. **1835** URE *Philos. Manuf.* 109 The perspective picture which fronts the title-page represents a cotton factory.

b. Of a building: To have its front on the side of (a street, etc.).

1698 FRYER *Acc. E. India & P.* 38 Opposite to this, one [Gate] more stately fronts the High-street. **1741** RICHARDSON *Pamela* (1883) I. 323 This alcove fronts the longest gravel-walk in the garden. **1833** *Act 3 & 4 Will. IV*, c. 46 §90 The proprietor or proprietors of any buildings fronting any of the streets. **1847** A. M. GILLIAM *Trav. Mexico* 166 The church..was to have fronted the Plaza.

3. a. To stand face to face with, meet face to face, look straight at, face, confront; *esp.* to face in defiance or hostility, present a bold front to, oppose. *lit.* and *fig.*

1583 STANYHURST *Æneis* II. (Arb.) 55 Of Greeks thee first man with a gallant coompanye garded Fronted vs. **1596** SPENSER *State Irel.* (Globe) 660/1 He dare now to fronte princes. **1601** SHAKS. *Twel. N.* I. iii. 59 Front her, boord her, woe her, assayle her. *c* **1618** FLETCHER *Q. Corinth* IV. iii, Amazed..at your..impudence, That dare thus front us. **1697** DRYDEN *Disc. Epic Poetry* D 4, When Æneas and Turnus stood fronting each other before the altar. **1701** W. WOTTON *Hist. Rome, Marcus* iv. 65 Some fell upon the Rear, some fronted them directly. **1837** HAWTHORNE *Amer. Note-bks.* (1883) 104 Here you fronted the ocean, looking at a sail. **1839** CARLYLE *Chartism* (1842) 98 Evil, once manfully fronted, ceases to be evil. **1852** ROBERTSON *Serm.* Ser. III. xvii. 222 Soldiers can be hired..to front death in its worst form. **1864** KIRK *Chas. Bold* I. i. 22 The brazen pride with which he fronted accusation and reproach.

b. said of things.

1602 W. WATSON *Decacordon* 265 Would God such things ..never had fronted our native shores! **1606** SHAKS. *Ant. & Cl.* II. ii. 61 Those Warres Which fronted mine owne peace. **1637** HEYWOOD *Royall King* II. iv. Wks. 1874 VI. 26, I am arm'd with innocence, And that dares front all danger. **1873** BLACK *Pr. Thule* (1874) 6 At length, the boat..fronted the broad waters of the Atlantic.

4. To set face to face *with*, confront *with*.

1617 COLLINS *Def. Bp. Ely* II. ix. 351 The Cardinall had fronted him with one such false place out of Chrysostome. **1625** BACON *Ess., Seditions* (Arb.) 411 Which kinde of Persons, are..to be fronted, with some other, of the same Party, that may oppose them. **1853** ROBERTSON *Serm.* Ser. III. xxi. 275 Fronting his patron and his prince with the stern unpalatable truth of God.

5. To adorn in front; to furnish with a front. (So in comb. *new-front.*) Also, to face (with some specified material); = FACE *v.* 13.

1635 DAVENANT *Prince d'Amour* Wks. (1673) 396 The Scæne was discovered with a Village consisting of Ale-houses and Tobacco shops, each fronted with a red Lettice. **1742** W. COLE in Willis & Clark *Cambridge* (1886) I. 228 They have..new Fronted the east front. **1762–71** H. WALPOLE *Vertue's Anecd. Paint.* (1786) IV. 231 He new fronted his house in Piccadilly. **1772** J. G. W. DE BRAHM *Hist. Georgia* (1849) 45 The Savannah Bay is nearly fronted with contiguous Wharfs. **1782** COWPER *Let.* Wks. 1837 XV. 116 My green-house..is fronted with myrtles, and lined with mats. *a* **1817** T. DWIGHT *Trav. New Eng.* (1821) II. 31 The Presbyterian church..is fronted with two towers. **1824** *Ann. Reg.* 87 The whole building was proposed to be fronted with stone.

†**6. a.** To introduce (a tale, etc.) *with* (the mention of or reference to something); to preface. *Obs.*

1592 GREENE *Art Conny Catch.* III. 9 The wily Treacher ..coyned such a smooth tale vnto them both, fronting it with the Gammon of Bacon and the Cheese sent from their maides Father. **1599** *Broughton's Let.* v. 15 You..haue fronted your Libell with this inscription. **1654** WHITLOCK *Zootomia* 109 Hippocrates did wel to front his Axiomaticall Experiments..with the grand Miscariages in the practice of Physitians. *a* **1732** T. BOSTON *Crook in Lot* (1805) 73 Solomon..fronts his writings, in the beginning of the Proverbs, with most express gospel.

b. To place in front as a frontispiece. *Obs.*$^{-1}$

1609 BP. W. BARLOW *Answ. Nameless Cath.* 305 Pindarus would haue in the beginning of a Treatise..some glorious personage fronted.

7. a. To be or stand in front of, to serve as a front to.

1591 SPENSER *Vis. Bellay* ii, I saw a stately frame..With hundreth pillours fronting faire the same. **1606** SHAKS. *Tr. & Cr.* IV. v. 219 Yonder wals that pertly front your Towne ..Must kisse their owne feet. **1791** MRS. RADCLIFFE *Rom. Forest* v, She came to the lawn which fronted the fabric. **1845** DARWIN *Voy. Nat.* xiv. (1879) 296 The coast..is fronted by many breakers. *a* **1847** MRS. SHERWOOD *Lady of Manor* II. x. 3 A..mansion..fronted by a garden abounding with fruits and flowers. **1884** *Law Times Rep.* LI. 228/1 The damage done to the sea wall fronting Curry Marsh Farm.

b. To serve as a 'front' (see FRONT *sb.* 7 g). *slang* (orig. *U.S.*).

1932 J. SAYRE *Rackety Rax* vii. 55 You'll have to front for us, knowin' the collegiate racket and all. **1939** R. CHANDLER *Big Sleep* xxvi. 232 Why should I front for that twist? **1939** *Nation* 5 Aug. 134/2 *America*, accusing us of 'fronting' for the Semites and Communists. **1951** *Manch. Guardian Weekly* 1 Mar. 3 Mr. Churchill agreed to 'front' for the quick pride of the Royal Navy. **1959** M. AINSWORTH *Murder is Catching* vii. 90 Was he merely doing his job..? Or was he fronting for Pender? **1971** N. FREELING *Over High Side* I. 41 To..help him out occasionally I have fronted for him—a telephone call. And I'm bound to say he helped me.

c. To lead (a band). Also *intr.* orig. *U.S.*

1936 *Amer. Mercury* May p. x/2 *Baton weaver*, the joe personality who fronts the band. **1937** *Amer. Speech* XII. 46/2 Ted is fronting for Smith's old band. **1946** P. FISCHER in *Jazzways* 48/2 Hampton was with the Les Hite Orchestra, occasionally 'fronted' by Louis Armstrong. **1949** L. FEATHER *Inside Be-Bop* iii. 26 Coleman Hawkins, who was fronting Clarke's band, copyrighted the tune. **1958** P. GAMMOND *Decca Bk. Jazz* x. 128 The remnants of Isham Jones's Orchestra were taken over..by Woody Herman, a clarinet player with a taste for jazz and a talent for fronting a band.

8. Chiefly *Mil.* †**a.** *intr.* To march in the front or first rank. *Obs.*$^{-1}$

1613 SHAKS. *Hen. VIII*, I. ii. 42, I..front but in that File Where others tell steps with me.

b. To turn the front or face in a specified direction; = FACE *v.* 9 b. Also, as word of command.

1635 J. HAYWARD tr. *Biondi's Banish'd Virg.* 122 Upon this the third fronting to their flanckward spurr'd towards him. **1833** *Regul. Instr. Cavalry* I. 14 He fronts to the left. **1847** *Infantry Man.* (1854) 5 Upon the word *Front*, if he has faced to the right, he fronts to the left.

c. To form a front or extended line.

1802 C. JAMES *Milit. Dict.* s.v., When the battalion is marching by files..the word *front* is always practised to restore it to its natural situation in line. **1807** PIKE *Sources Mississ.* III. (1810) 258 The Spanish troops..were remarkably polite, always fronting and saluting when I passed. **1883** *Army Corps Orders* in *Standard* 22 Mar. 3/2 It will halt, front, and march past.

d. *to front about*: to turn round so as to face in another direction.

1886 STEVENSON *Dr. Jekyll* 23 Mr. H...fronted about with an air of defiance.

e. *trans.* (causatively, from *front!* as a word of command): To cause to form a front or line.

1796 *Instr. & Reg. Cavalry* (1813) 74 He then *Halts, fronts!* it, and dresses and closes it to its pivot marker on the line. **1832** *Prop. Regul. Instr. Cavalry* II. 14 In the movement of Threes to a flank, the squadron should occupy but little more ground than when fronted. **1859** F. A. GRIFFITHS *Artil. Man.* (1862) 25 Each company in succession will be halted, and fronted.

†**9.** (See quot.) *Obs.*

1530 PALSGR. 559/1, I fronte up, as a woman dothe the heare of her heed with a fyllet. *Je effronte.* I wene you be bydden to some bridale to daye, you be so well fronted up.

10. *Sc.* and *dial.* (See quots.)

1808–18 JAMIESON, *To front*, applied to meat, when it swells in boiling. **1887** *S. Cheshire Gloss.*, *Front*, of tender meat which swells in cooking; of meal which swells under boiling water; of the full feeling supervening after a hearty meal, etc.

11. *Phonetics.* To pronounce with the tongue in a front position, i.e. touching or raised towards the hard palate; to palatalize. Also *intr.*

1888 H. SWEET *Hist. Eng. Sounds* 36 The fronting is carried out most fully with the point nasals and stops. *Ibid.*, These fronted consonants again in their turn influence a preceding sound. *Ibid.* 37 [This sound] fronts the preceding ʃ. **1907** H. C. WYLD *Hist. Study Mother Tongue* viii. 160 A natural inference is that..*e* being a front vowel, fronted the preceding consonant. **1929** *Encycl. Brit.* I. 1/2 These [changes] are due to fronting..or to rounding. **1939** *Trans. Philol. Soc.* 1939 89 In OE, Germ *a* appears as *æ*. Some dialects have *e*, but..the fronting first produced *æ*. **1964** *Language* XL. 31 Perhaps we can see a reason why /a/ should front.

†**front**, *v.*[2] *Obs.* In 4–5 **frunt**, pa. t. **frunt.** [ad. OF. *fronter* to ill-treat.]

1. *trans.* To strike, kick, drive *back.*

13.. *E.E. Allit. P.* C. 187 Þe freke hym frunt with his fot. *c* **1400** *Destr. Troy* 6923 He..frunt hym in þe fase a full fel wond. *Ibid.* 8327 Polidamas..ffaght with hom felly, frunt hom abacke.

2. *intr.* **a.** To rush, make a rush. **b.** To fall plump.

c **1400** *Destr. Troy* 6887 Þe freke, with a felle spere frunt vnto Ector. *Ibid.* 6890 He frunt of hys fol flat to þe ground.

frontage (ˈfrʌntɪdʒ), *sb.* [f. FRONT *sb.* + -AGE.] Not in Johnson or Todd.

1. Land which abuts on a river or piece of water, or on a road. Also, the land between the front of a building and the road, etc.

1622 CALLIS *Stat. Sewers* (1647) 87 Frontage is where the grounds of any man do joyn with the brow or front thereof to the Sea, or to great or royal streams. **1813** *Examiner* 17 May 319/2 They have obliged proprietors of houses situated at a short distance from the road to purchase their frontage. **1831** *Drakard's Stamford News* 4 Feb. Advt. 1 Two Frontages with two cottages upon the same. **1861** M. PATTISON *Ess.* (1889) I. 46 One corner of the Thames Street frontage [of the Steelyard] was occupied by a wine-house. **1870** *Daily News* 16 Feb., The remainder of the establishment consisting chiefly of the river frontage, will then be sold in plots. **1875** *Spectator* (Melbourne) 15 May 16/1 It might be bought and sold in the market any day, like a Collins-street frontage.

2. Measurement of front-line, extent of front.

1844 *Port Phillip Patriot* 18 July 3/7 The run has four miles frontage to the Yarra Yarra. **1863** HINCHLIFF *Trav. S. Amer.* 24 Shopkeepers in the best quarters pay enormous rents, but get very little frontage to display their goods. **1867** SMYTH *Sailor's Word-bk.*, *Frontage*, the length or face of a wharf. **1873** GEIKIE *Gt. Ice Age* v. 66 The..glacier.. shedding icebergs along its whole vast extent of frontage. **1887** *Times* (weekly ed.) 1 July 20/4 The substantial old Family Mansion..extensive frontage of 35 ft.

3. The front face or part of a building. Also *collect.*

1861 *Times* 16 Aug., There is a breadth of roadway and a grandeur of frontage that would not disgrace the neighbourhood of Piccadilly. **1875** MERIVALE *Gen. Hist. Rome* lxxix. (1877) 669 The august capitals of Egypt and Syria, with their long columnar frontages, and marked horizontal lines of architecture. **1875** M. PATTISON *Casaubon* 400 Savile was just finishing the fine frontage towards the meadows. **1877** M. M. GRANT *Sun-Maid* ii, The frontage of the Château looked southward. **1894** *Daily News* 5 Sept. 5/3 A municipal law requires the frontages of Paris houses to be painted or scraped every six or seven years.

4. *Mil.* 'The ground troops of line occupy either on parade or in camp' (Voyle).

1893 *Times* 15 June 12/1 The battalion commander 'instructs the captains as to the frontage of their companies.'

5. The action of fronting in a certain direction; the fact of facing a certain way; exposure, outlook.

1859 R. F. BURTON *Centr. Afr.* in *Jrnl. Geog. Soc.* XXIX. 183 The breeze is..excluded by careless frontage. **1867** D. G. MITCHELL *Rural Stud.* 286 But it has no wide and open frontage to the sun. **1871** *Daily News* 22 Sept., We had changed front left back to meet his flank attack; now we had still to maintain that frontage.

¶ An alleged sense 'part of a woman's head-dress', given in some Dicts., is based on a blundered version of a passage of Addison: see quot. 1711, s.v. FONTANGE.

6. *attrib.*, as ***frontage-foot***, ***-owner***, ***-rate***, ***-system***; **frontage-claim**, a portion of land of a definite measurement in front, but of indefinite length towards the rear.

1869 R. B. SMYTH *Goldf. Victoria* 612 Frontage-claim—A claim, the lateral boundaries of which are not fixed until the lead has been traced through it. **1877** BLACK *Green Past.* xli. (1878) 325 We would cover every frontage foot with gold. **1889** *Spectator* 14 Dec. 843 The small affair of a frontage rate. **1890** BOLDREWOOD *Miner's Right* viii. 81 The frontage system..was considered..to afford a highly needful guarantee for capital invested in mining enterprise. **1896** *Star* 15 Dec. 2/6 Charging the frontage owners 9*s.* in the pound.

frontage ('frʌntɪdʒ), *v.* [f. the sb.] *trans.* To face; to have the front towards.

1914 N. MUNRO *New Road* ii. 17 Narrow, broken lanes with all the gable-ends of the abutting buildings frontaging the thoroughfare. **1958** *Times* 15 Mar. 7/5 His ratable value increased because he now frontages a made-up road.

frontager ('frʌntɪdʒə(r)). [f. FRONTAGE *sb.* + -ER[1].]

1. An owner of land or property adjoining:

a. the sea-shore.

1622 CALLIS *Stat. Sewers* (1647) 25 The Frontagers have claimed those grounds so left, by a pretended Custome of Frontagers. **1866** *Pall Mall G.* 4 Dec., The free use and enjoyment of the sea-shore..giving to the frontager..such a title as may not be inconsistent with those rights. **1885** *Law Rep.* 14 Q. Bench Div. 570 The liability of a frontager to repair a sea-wall..can only be ascertained by usage.

b. a roadway.

1739 *Bewholm Inclos. Act* 6 Messuagers, cottagers and frontagers. **1880** LD. THESIGER in *Law Rep.* Exch. Div. V. 206 Several frontagers called upon to pay the expenses of paving a street. **1890** *Sat. Rev.* 10 May 559/2 Mr. Forbes would willingly carry a new line along the proposed route.. with the permission of the frontagers and owners.

2. One who lives on a frontier. *rare*$^{-1}$.

1893 S. L. POOLE *Auranzeb* vi. 115 Mir Junda's disastrous campaign in Assam was typical of many attempts to subdue the North-east frontagers of India.

frontal ('frʌntəl), *sb.* Forms: 4–5 **fro(u)ntel(l**, 5–6 **fruntall(e**, **-telle**, 6–7 **frontall**, 6–8 **frontale**, (6 **frontayle**), 7– **frontal**. [ME. *frountel*, a. OF. *frontel*:—late L. *frontāle*, f. *front-*, *frōns*: see FRONT *sb.* and -AL[1]. OF. had also the form *frontal* (still preserved in some senses); in mod.F., by confusion of suffixes, *frontail* and *fronteau* (cf. med.L. *frontellum* in *Promp. Parv.*) are used in various specific applications of the general sense.]

†**1.** Something applied to the forehead. *Obs.*

a. A band or ornament worn on the forehead.

c **1320** *Pol. Songs* (Camden) 154 The bout and the barbet wyth frountel shule feȝe. **14..** *Voc.* in Wr.-Wülcker 585/2 *Frontale*, a frontell. **1552** HULOET, Frontayle for a womans head, some call it a fruntlet. **1603** HOLLAND *Plutarch's Mor.* 416 His brother foorthwith tooke the roiall frontall called a diademe, and did it about his owne head. **1611** BP. HALL *Serm.* v. 52 Look how much difference there is between.. the frontal of the high priest and the bells of the horses.

b. A piece of defensive armour for a horse's head; = *front-stall.* (Cf. Fr. *frontail*, *fronteau.*)

1587 UNDERDOWN tr. *Heliodorus* IX. 126 They arme their horses too; about his legges they tie bootes, and couer his head with frontals of steele.

c. *Med.* A medicament applied to the forehead to cure headache. (Cf. Fr. *frontal*, *fronteau.*)

1601 HOLLAND *Pliny* II. 75 It cureth the head-ach, if it be applied as a frontall to the forehead and temples. **1710** T. FULLER *Pharm. Extemp.* 172 A Frontal with Mastic. **1753** SMOLLETT *Ct. Fathom* (1784) 154/1 The frontal prescribed by Fathom was applied.

d. A knotted cord, wound tightly round the forehead as a means of torture. (Cf. Fr. *frontal.*)

1653 H. COGAN tr. *Pinto's Trav.* xv. 48 To make your brains fly out of your heads with a frontal of cord.

2. A movable covering for the front of an altar, generally of embroidered cloth, silk, etc., but sometimes of metal.

1381 in *Eng. Gilds* (1870) 233 An altar-cloth, with a frontel, for the great feast-days. **1459** *Paston Lett.* No. 336 I. 489 Item, j. auter clothe, withe a frontell of white damaske. **1536** BELLENDEN *Cron. Scot.* (1821) II. 394 The goldin and silkin claithis..war distribute amang the abbays of Scotland to be vestamentis and frontallis to thair altaris. **1566** *Eng. Ch. Furniture* (Peacock 1866) 49 A girdell a fruntall and 3 albes. **1874** MICKLETHWAITE *Mod. Par. Churches* 305 The frontal, or coloured altar-cloth, should hang separately from the altar. **1877** J. D. CHAMBERS *Div. Worship* 268 Frontals may be..formed of gold and silver plates.

†**b.** ? A hanging for the front of a bed. *Obs.*

1539 in *Inv. R. Wardrobe* (1815) 47 Rufis of beddis.—Item ..thre curtingis..with ane frontale. **1542** *Ibid.* 98 The nether frontale of the samyne bed.

c. A decorated front for a tomb.

1881 *Academy* 5 Mar. 177/3 The whole frontal is enriched in a..somewhat tawdry manner by numerous false gems.

3. The façade of a building.

1784 HENLEY *Beckford's Vathek* (1868) 136 *note*, We are told of a strange fortress..whose frontal presented the following inscription. **1827** LYTTON *Pelham* xxiii, Vast hotels, with their gloomy frontals, and magnificent contempt of comfort. **1893** M. E. FRANCIS *N.C. Village* 202 Not a very imposing building..with its low frontal and irregular architecture.

†**4.** *Arch.* (See quot. 1730–6.) *Obs.*

1578 T. N. tr. *Conq. W. India* 36 It hath foure windowes with frontals and galleries. **1730–6** BAILEY (folio), *Frontal*, a little fronton or pediment sometimes placed over a little door or window.

†**5.** = FRONTIER *sb.* 3 (where see quot. 1412–20).

frontal ('frɒntəl; in sense 2 often 'frʌntəl), *a.* [ad. mod.L. *frontālis*, f. *front-*, *frōns*: see FRONT and -AL[1]. Cf. Fr. *frontal* adj.]

1. Of or pertaining to the forehead, or to the corresponding part in the lower animals. Frequent in anatomical applications, as ***frontal artery***, ***bone***, ***sinus***, ***vein***, etc. ***frontal tonsure***: see quot. 1894.

1656 BLOUNT *Glossogr.* s.v. *Vein*, *Frontal-vein*, the forehead vein, a third branch of the outward throat vein, whence, mounting by the bottom of the nether jaw, it comes into the lips and nose, and thence ascends by the inside of the eye to the middle of the fore-head. **1741** MONRO *Anat. Bones* (ed. 3) 87 The frontal Bone serves to contain, defend and sustain the anterior Lobes of the Brain. **1746** PARSONS in *Phil. Trans.* XLIV. 6 The true Frontal Muscle arises fleshy from the Process of the *Os Frontis.* **1826** KIRBY & SP. *Entomol.* (1828) IV. xlv. 258 He conjectures the seat of this sense [smell] to reside in certain frontal organs. **1840** G. V. ELLIS *Anat.* 2 The frontal artery, a branch..of the ophthalmic. **1879** CALDERWOOD *Mind & Br.* ii. 16 The front of the brain..is known as the Frontal Lobe. **1894** J. T. FOWLER *Adamnan* Introd. 41 The tonsure was made by shaving off all the hair in front of a line drawn from ear to ear, and is called the frontal tonsure.

2. a. Of or pertaining to the forepart or foremost edge. ***frontal hammer***: see quot. 1881.

1860 TYNDALL *Glac.* I. xxvii. 217 From the summit descended by a glissade to the frontal portion of the cavern. **1863** LYELL *Antiq. Man* xv. 300 The frontal or terminal moraine. **1881** RAYMOND *Mining Gloss.*, *Frontal hammer* or *Frontal helve*, a forge-hammer lifted by a cam, acting upon a 'tongue' immediately in front of the hammer-head.

b. Of an attack, etc.: Directed against or delivered upon the front.

1884 *Milit. Engin.* I. II. 63 A magazine exposed to frontal fire only. **1886** N. L. WALFORD *Parl. Gen. Civ. War* 43 With the aid of a frontal attack by the infantry.

c. [after Da. *frontal* (J. Lange 1892 as in next).] Of or pertaining to the façade of a building; also in *Gr. Art*, pertaining to front or full-face view of a sculptured object (see FRONTALITY); similarly of a naked human body.

1893 *Funk's Stand. Dict.* s.v., The frontal effect of a fine building. **1905** P. GARDNER *Gram. Gr. Art* v. 57 One finds figures stooping, or kneeling, or in a variety of other attitudes; but the frontal law still holds. **1971** W. J. BURLEY *Guilt Edged* iii. 46 Full frontal nudity on the stage. **1971** *Times* 12 Aug. 8/2 His [*sc.* Linnæus's] sketch..of *Andromeda polifolia* shows a naked virgin in full frontal exposure. **1971** *Times* 23 Aug. 10/4 The many publications which print explicit colour photographs of full frontal female nudes..and in some cases male nudes.

3. quasi-*sb.* = *frontal bone.*

1854 OWEN *Skel. & Teeth* in *Circ. Sc.* I. 193 The frontals ..rest by descending lateral plates, representing connate orbitosphenoids. **1857** BULLOCK *Cazeaux' Midwif.* 218 The frontal, forming the forehead, as well as the superior-anterior part of the face. **1858** LYTTON *What will he do* II. iv, This was, indeed, a horse of great power..and such a head! the ear, the frontal, the nostril?

†**'frontal**, *v. Obs.*$^{-1}$ [f. FRONTAL *sb.*] *trans.* To be a frontal or prelude to; to precede.

1652 URQUHART *Jewel* Wks. (1834) 177 Serving in this place to frontal a Vindication of the honour of Scotland.

frontality (frʌn'tælɪtɪ). [tr. Da. *frontalitet* (J. Lange, *Billedkunstens Fremstilling græske Kunst* (1892) 54), f. FRONTAL *a.* + -ITY: so G. *frontalität*, F. *frontalité.*] A principle in sculpture, according to which the figure is carved or moulded as seen from the full front.

In the strictest style, the figure is divided by an imaginary plane into two symmetrical halves, with no bending to either side.

1905 P. GARDNER *Gram. Gk. Art* v. 56 Lange has expounded in detail his theory of frontality in early art. **1910** E. A. GARDNER *Six Greek Sculptors* 34 The bold modelling of the figure, and the skill with which the twist of the body is rendered, make it worthy of notice in its departure from the rigid 'frontality' of early art. **1920** *Q. Rev.* July 39 A new decorative style of portraiture, of which the leading characteristic was a return to the frontal view of primitive Greek art. That is to say, 'frontality' became, as in the archaic periods, the basic principle of composition. **1938** *Burlington Mag.* June 307/2 Rousseau found in frontality a compositional device used by the primitives. **1958** *Times Lit. Suppl.* 21 Mar. 148/4 The well-known panels in San Vitale at Ravenna depicting Justinian and Theodora with their retinues (which illustrate the replacement of the Hellenistic three-quarter pose of the head by full-faced frontality).

frontally ('frʌntəlɪ), *adv.* [f. FRONTAL *a.* + -LY[2].] By a frontal attack. Also *fig.*

1900 *Westm. Gaz.* 2 Feb. 7/1 Thus Buller, in order to relieve Ladysmith, must frontally force a tremendous position held by 10,000 or 12,000 of the best riflemen in the world. **1961** M. HOWARD *Franco-Prussian War* iv. 152 While his 5th Division attacked the enemy frontally from the south, 6th Division was to sweep round to the west. **1971** *Listener* 5 Aug. 181/1 The political impact of student discontent is touched on, rather than tackled frontally.

†**'frontary.** *Obs.* [f. FRONT *sb.* + -ARY[1].] = FRONTAL *sb.* 1 c.

1564–78 BULLEYN *Dial. agst. Pest.* (1888) 27, I haue appoincted..in what order that your frontary should bee applied to your forehed to cause you to sleape quietly.

frontate ('frɒnt-, 'frʌnteɪt), *a. Bot.* [ad. mod.L. *frontāt-us*, f. *front-*, *frōns*: see FRONT and -ATE[2].] = next.

1855 in OGILVIE Suppl.

†**'frontated**, *a.* [f. as prec. + -ED[1].] (See quot.)

1719 QUINCY *Lex. Physico-Med.* 161 *Frontated*, in Botany expresses the Leaf of a Flower growing broader and broader, and at last..terminating in a right Line.

frontayle, **-el(l**, obs. forms of FRONTAL.

fronted ('frʌntɛd), *ppl. a.* [f. FRONT *sb.* or *v.* + -ED.] Furnished with or having a front; formed with a front. With qualifying adverb: Having a front or countenance with a specified expression.

1615 J. STEPHENS *Satyr. Ess.*, *Impudent Censurer* (1857) 133 Hee is so fronted with striving to discountenance knowlege, by the contempt of it, as you would think him borne to insolence. **1667** MILTON *P.L.* II. 532 Part curb thir fierie Steeds, or shun the Goal With rapid wheels, or fronted Brigads form. **1873** A. DOBSON *Vignettes in Rhyme*, *Sundial* xii, So kindly fronted that you marvelled how The frequent sword-hilt had so frayed his glove.

front end (frʌnt ɛnd; *attrib.* 'frʌntɛnd). [f. FRONT *sb.* (and *a.*) + END *sb.*] **1.** *Electronics.* The part of a radio or television receiver to which the aerial signal goes first; *esp.* the tuner, local oscillator, and mixer of a superheterodyne.

1938 G. E. STERLING *Radio Man.* (ed. 3) iv. 171 Thus improved 'front end' selectivity is indicated, and while this can be provided by merely adding more front-end tuned circuits, such a procedure wastes some of the wanted signal. **1956** *Proc. IRE* XLIV. 1871/2 Fig. 30 is a simplified diagram of the uhf front end. **1970** J. EARL *Tuners & Amplifiers* ii. 32 The f.m. front-end determines the noise performance of the tuner and to some extent determines the sensitivity. **1980** *Philips Technical Rev.* XXXIX. 260/1 The function of the receiver front-end is to pick up the 12 GHz signal from space..and to convert it into a signal at a lower frequency which can be subjected to a conversion from the frequency modulation of the satellite signal into the standard television signal.

2. The forward part of a motor vehicle or railway train. *colloq.*

1954 *Amer. Speech* XXV. 96 *Dropped front end*, a front-end suspension whereby the front of the vehicle sits lower than..on the 'stock' model. **1970** *Toronto Daily Star* 24 Sept. 12/5 Mediators reported acceptance in principle of a plan to combine the job of firemen with front-end brakemen ..on diesel freight locomotives. **1986** *Truck* July 8/2 A new 7·5 tonne front axle..gives very generous front end capacity.

3. Applied *attrib.* (usu. with hyphen) to money paid or charged at the beginning of a transaction, esp. as ***front-end charge***, ***fee***; also, of transactions which involve such arrangements; **front-end load(ing)**, the practice or result of arranging the repayments of a loan so that service charges and other fees relating to the whole period of the loan are recovered in the early payments. orig. *U.S.*

1962 *Wall St. Jrnl.* 14 May 26/1 Under the so-called 'front-end load' system, a mutual fund concentrates its service charges for the entire contractual term into the opening years of the contract. **1970** *Times* 12 Feb. 24/1 He also criticized 'front-end loading' in the form of substantial legal, survey and administration fees. **1972** *Real Estate Rev.* Winter 21/1 The reasons for this phenomenal growth were manifold. Chief among them were that..condominium development required minimum front-end capital from the developer. **1977** *Time* 5 Sept. 49/3 Smaller banks rushed to make loans to Turkey because they could charge 'front-end' fees of 6% to 10% in addition to high regular interest rates. **1983** *Times* 23 July 13/6 Annual management charges..are between ½ and 1 per cent for the single currency funds. There is no 'front-end load'. **1985** *Times* 9 Mar. 14 Why pay the five per cent front end charge, plus an annual management charge for something you can do yourself.

4. a. An electronic device or computer system that supplies input or provides access to another device; the part of a computer system that a user deals with directly; *spec.* (in full ***front-end processor***), a computer that processes or routes input for a central computer, e.g. in a multi-terminal system. Usu. *attrib.*, as ***front-end machine***, ***system***, etc.

1971 N. CHAPIN *Computers* xii. 313 Some subcenters are sufficiently extensive to be substantially free-standing complete computers, as suggested by the names given some types, such as peripheral or front-end processors. **1972** *Sci.*

Amer. Sept. 126 The role of the communication-control unit varies with the system. It can act essentially as a computer and perform several functions, including routing commands and messages, checking errors and converting one data format to another. The unit is often called a front-end processor. **1975** *Nature* 16 Oct. 559/2 If that mini can also be connected in to a large mainframe computer as a 'front-end machine', then the tasks which can be carried out (particularly 'number crunching') can be that much more sophisticated and complex. **1976** *Proc. 1975 IFAC-IFIP Workshop Real-Time Programming* 165/1 The logical restructuring of the network which will accompany the replacement of the existing front-end by a twin-processor Interdata 85 system is described. **1979** J. E. ROWLEY *Mechanised In-House Information Syst.* I. 66 A minicomputer can be used in any one of the following three modes: a) in a stand-alone system .. b) in a front-end system, where the minicomputer exerts control over the communications between several remote terminals and the main frame computer; and c) as part of a network. **1981** *Electronics* 24 Mar. 175/1 Designed primarily as a front-end system for a 32- or 48-channel logic analyzer, it can also operate as a stand-alone emulator. **1981** *ABA Banking Jrnl.* May 61/2 Virtually all major brokers have automated their order entry process. Many have also developed the ability to interface these front-end systems with clearing banks. **1983** *Austral. Microcomputer Mag.* Nov. 45/1 The university computering services centre..has..models from the PDP-11/40 to 11/70 as front ends to the larger processors. **1986** *Pract. Computing* Oct. 107/1 There are no trimmings in the form of a neat front end, and a proper menu and linking arrangement would much improve the package.

b. *attrib.* (usu. with hyphen). Involving direct computer input by a journalist, cashier, etc., as a work activity otherwise done at a later stage.

1976 *National Observer* (U.S.) 19 June 11/1 Fifty-four U.S. supermarkets now use the UPC technology, which is variously called 'computer assisted check-out', 'electronic front-end check-out' or 'front-end automation'. **1979** *Spectator* 27 Oct. 3/1 The critical issue is 'front-end' setting, or 'single-keystroking', that is whether journalists and advertising clerks should be able to set copy directly, rather than type it for re-setting by a printer. **1980** *Times* 26 June 2/2 The agreement excluded new technology typesetting, known as front-end system, for at least three years.

5. Special Comb.: **front end loader,** a tractor or haulage vehicle which has a shovelling or loading implement attached to the front; **front-end processor**: see sense 4 above.

1959 C. OGBURN *Marauders* (1960) iii. 92 Bulldozers, power shovels, earth-movers and front-end loaders. **1960** *Farmer & Stockbreeder* 8 Mar. 76/3 They had mounted a cutter-bar driven by hydraulic motor, on to a tractor front-end loader. **1969** *Jane's Freight Containers 1968–69* 83/2 Stevedoring contractors' equipment at Port Brownsville includes approximately..14 front end bulk loaders, [etc.]. **1986** *New Yorker* 17 Mar. 55/1 Men 'muck it out' with front-end loaders.

fronter, var. of THRINTER *Sc.* (= a ewe in her fourth year).

frontier ('frɒn-, 'frʌntɪə(r)), *sb.* and *a.* Forms: 5 **frounter(e, -teere, -tier, -tor, fron-, frowntere, 5–6 frontyer, 5–7 fronter, 6 frontour, 6–7 frontire, 6– frontier.** Also FRONTURE (*obs.*). [a. OF. *frontier* masc., *frontiere* fem. (mod.Fr. *frontière*), f. *front* FRONT *sb.* Cf. Pr. *fronteira* forehead, It. *frontiera*, Sp. *frontera*, Pg. *fronteira* frontier.]

A. *sb.*

†**1. a.** The front side; the forepart. *Obs.*

c **1430** LYDG. *Min. Poems* (Percy) 16 Att ffrountor of thees welles clere, Ther whas a scripture commendyng ther lycour. **1538** LELAND *Itin.* I. 107 The fronter of which Ward in the entering is exceeding stronge with Toures and Portecoleces. **1551** ROBINSON tr. *More's Utop.* II. (1895) 116 The forefrontes or frontiers of the ii corners [of the haven] ..be very..daungerous.

†**b.** The side that fronts in a specified direction. *Obs.*[−1]

1599 HAKLUYT *Voy.* I. 95 The principal wife placeth her court on the West frontier.

†**c.** The forehead. *Obs. rare*[−1].

1583 STUBBES *Anat. Abus.* I. (1877) 67 Their bolstred heir ..standeth crested round about their frontiers.

†**2.** = FRONTLET 4. *Obs.*

1440 in *Eng. Ch. Furniture* (Peacock 1866) 182 Item syx alter towelles of lynnen cloth the first with a frounter pailed read white and black..the 5th with a frountier of burde Alisander.

†**3.** The front line or foremost part of an army. Hence 'attack, resistance' in phr. ***to make frontier*** (tr. OF. *faire frontière*). *Obs.*

?*a* **1400** *Morte Arth.* 2898 Frykis one the frowntere welle a fyve hundreth. **1412–20** LYDG. *Chron. Troy* I. ix. (1555) In the frounter [**1513** frountell] many manly man With sharpe speres first together ran. **1523** LD. BERNERS *Froiss.* I. cclv. 378 He sent them into Poicters to kepe the citie, and to make fronter there agaynst the frenchemen.

4. a. *sing.* and *pl.* The part of a country which fronts or faces another country; the marches; the border or extremity conterminous with that of another.

1413 *Pilgr. Sowle* (Caxton 1483) IV. xxx. 80 To kepe the frounters of the reame fro perille of enemyes. **1489** CAXTON *Faytes of A.* III. xxii. 215 The fronteres of Caleys. **1540** *Act 32 Hen. VIII*, c. 48 On yᵉ east partes and frontours of this his realm. **1601** R. JOHNSON *Kingd. & Commw.* 171 Vpon another frontire lie the Spaniards. **1648** GAGE *West Ind.* xx. 157 After the two daies we drew neer unto the Heathens Frontiers. **1711** ADDISON *Spect.* No. 129 ¶8 A Country Church upon the Frontiers of Cornwall. **1781** GIBBON *Decl. & F.* III. 126 It might be dangerous to weaken the defence of the frontier. **1838** LYTTON *Calderon* i. 64 He..received an order to join the army on the frontiers. **1853** J. H. NEWMAN *Hist. Sk.* (1873) II. I. ii. 84 He found a difficulty in defending his frontier towards Persia. **1956** E.-J. FINBERT *Israel* 2 [Israel's] land frontiers are spread over 951 k. (591 miles). **1964** *Ann. Reg. 1963* 306 A U.N. observer would be sent to the Yemen-Saudi frontier.

transf. and *fig.* **1672–3** MARVELL *Reh. Transp.* I. 39 Those Churches which are seated nearer upon the Frontire of Popery. **1738** *Tom King's, or Humours Cov. Garden* 3 A spacious Plain..Whose large Frontiers with Pallisados bound From Trivia's Filth inshrines the hallow'd Ground. **1768** W. WILKIE *Rake & Hermit* 65 Faith in the utmost frontier stands. **1839** MURCHISON *Silur. Syst.* I. xxvii. 350 Along this portion of their frontier, the Upper Silurian Rocks [etc.]. **1855** MACAULAY *Hist. Eng.* IV. 150 A few seditious persons..had gone very near to the frontier of treason. **1870** MAX MÜLLER *Sci. Relig.* (1873) 391 Even in this more general study of mankind, the frontiers of language and race ought never to disappear.

b. *U.S.* 'That part of a country which forms the border of its settled or inhabited regions: as (before the settlement of the Pacific coast), the western frontier of the United States' (*Cent. Dict.*). Also in specific use (see quot. 1894 and D.A.).

1676 W. BERKELEY *Let.* 1 Apr. in W.E. Washburn *Governor & Rebel* (1957) 184 We have now such a strength on the frontiers of al our Plantations that we cannot feare them [*sc.* the Indians] if they were ten times more in number then they are. **1756** [see FRONTIER B. *adj.* 1]. **1842** *Amer. Pioneer* I. 226 Of all the men I ever knew he was the best qualified to live on a frontier where there were savages..to contend with. **1870** EMERSON *Soc. & Solit., Civiliz.* Wks. (Bohn) III. 8 'Tis wonderful how soon a piano gets into a log-hut on the frontier. **1894** F. J. TURNER *Frontier in Amer. Hist.* 3 What is the frontier?.. In the census reports it is treated as the margin of that settlement which has a density of two or more to the square mile.

†**5. a.** A fortress on the frontier; a frontier town.

1604 SHAKS. *Ham.* (Qº. 2) IV. iv. 16 Goes it against the maine of Poland, sir, Or for some frontire? **1641** EVELYN *Mem.* (1857) I. 22 Gorcum, a very strong and considerable frontier. **1725** DE FOE *Voy. round World* (1840) 222 It [Baldivia] was a fortification and a frontier. **1796** MORSE *Amer. Georg.* I. 721 [Natchitoches in Louisiana] was a frontier on the Spanish settlements.

†**b.** A barrier against attack. *Obs.*

1589 IVE *Fortif.* 1 A Forte not placed where it were needefull, might skantly be accompted for frontier. **1648** GAGE *West Ind.* xv. 105 This Province..which is a Frontier against those Heathens. **1664** MARVELL *Corr.* Wks. 1872–5 II. 122 His Navies do carry a moveable Frontire to all the habitable world. **1690** W. EDMUNDSON *Jrnl.* (1715) 133 Three Hundred Firelocks, as a Frontier, to intercept the English Soldiers.

†**6.** A settler on the frontier; a frontier-man.

1677 W. HUBBARD *Narrative* 51 The Frontiers discerning Indians in..the Swamp, fired immediately upon them.

B. *adj.*

1. Of or belonging to the frontier of a country; situated on the frontier, bordering; const. *to*. Also, characteristic of people living at a frontier; pioneering; primitive.

1523 LD. BERNERS *Froiss.* I. cxiii. 135 The erle..departed his people into dyuers garysons, to kepe fronter warre. **1530** PALSGR. 34 The dyuersite of pronuncyacion of the other frontier countreys. **1611** CORYAT *Crudities* 638 This Bommel is the farthest frontier towne westward of Gelderland. **1615** G. SANDYS *Trav.* 43 Diuers frontier Cities and Castles. **1647** W. BROWNE tr. *Polexander* III. 87 A desert which is frontire betweene Guinea and Senega. *a* **1648** LD. HERBERT *Life* (1886) 240 Held their way towards Bayonne, a city frontier to Spain. **1667** MILTON *P.L.* I. 466 Dreaded through..Gaza's frontier bounds. **1701** *Col. Rec. Pennsylv.* II. 20 Leaving that most ffronter part..Denuded of.. Defence. **1756** G. WASHINGTON *Lett.* Writ. 1889 I. 360 The intent of sending men hither was to protect the frontier inhabitants. **1827** J. F. COOPER *Prairie* I. xiv. 209 If you come a foot nigher, you shall have frontier punishment. **1840** J. S. MILL in *Westm. Rev.* XXXIV. 489 The comparatively petty interest of some frontier dispute. **1852** MISS YONGE *Cameos* I. xxxiii. 281 A few of the frontier castles had fallen into his hands. **1854** THOREAU *Walden* 14 It would be some advantage to live a primitive and frontier life, though in the midst of an outward civilization, if only to learn what are the gross necessaries of life. **1902** S. WEYMAN *In Kings' Byways* I. 137 In the summer of 1706..one of the Austrian captains sat down before the frontier town of Huymonde, in Spanish Flanders, and prepared to take it. **1958** *Spectator* 14 Feb. 206/3 The connection in him between his 'frontier' mentality and his secret craving for respectability. **1960** *Guardian* 8 Dec. 8/2, I don't know about university education. In 'frontier' societies it is perhaps not a good thing. **1963** A. HERON *Towards Quaker View of Sex* 64 In frontier conditions or settled agricultural societies children represent an economic asset. **1968** MRS. L. B. JOHNSON *White House Diary* 2 Oct. (1970) 714 There ..came into being today the North Cascades National Park in the State of Washington—an area that's called the American Alps and is still very much frontier.

†**2.** Fronting; opposite. *Obs.*

1609 HOLLAND *Amm. Marcell.* 106 With readie minds.. they breake through the frontier bankes over-against them.

frontier ('frɒn-, 'frʌntɪə(r)), *v.* [f. prec. sb.]

†**1.** *intr.* To be a frontier, or as a frontier; to border *on* or *upon*. *Obs.*

1599 HAKLUYT *Voy.* II. 15 The countrey called Suet.. frontering vpon the countrie of the Damascenes. **1652–62** HEYLIN *Cosmogr.* II. (1682) 166 As far Westward as the River Tibiscus, where it frontiered on the Jazyges Metanastæ.

2. *trans.* **a.** To look upon the frontier, boundary, or coast of; to face; now *rare*. †**b.** To stand in front of; to bar, oppose. *Obs.*

1579 FENTON *Guicciard.* (1618) 270 They saw the armie so hardie, as to incampe in that valley which was frontired with troublesome mountaines, and in the midst of the enemies countrey. **1586** FERNE *Blaz. Gentrie* II. 32 Being that part of the country a frontering the sea. **1589** IVE *Fortif.* 29 So small Forts may well serue to hinder the courses of a small number, but not to frontier a forcible enemie. **1596** SPENSER *State Irel.* (Globe) 621/2 Now that it is noe more a border, nor frontyerd with enemyes. *a* **1849** J. C. MANGAN *Poems* (1859) 227 The bridge that, bounding Life's domain, frontiers the wold of death.

Hence †'**frontiering** *ppl. a.*, occupying the frontier or border; neighbouring.

1600 DYMMOK *Ireland* (1843) 35 His Lordship..repared the breaches of the castle, and placed such a garrison in the same as might anoy the fronteringe rebells.

'**frontierism.** *rare*[−1]. [See -ISM.] A mode of expression current on the (U.S.) frontier.

1890 *Harper's Mag.* Aug. 383/1 A shallow 'cooley' (frontierism for gully) that led down through the bluff.

'**frontierless,** *a.* [See -LESS.] Having no frontier or dividing line.

1925 *Inner Life* ix. 165 The English layman as he comes to receive the Holy Communion in his parish Church, finds himself caught up into a Fellowship which is frontierless. **1935** G. GREENE *England made Me* iv. 131 One believed in a new frontierless world.

'**frontierman,** '**frontiersman.** Chiefly *U.S.* [f. FRONTIER *sb.* + MAN; for the second form cf. *draughtsman, tradesman.*] **1.** One who lives on the frontier of a country, or on the outlying districts of civilization. ***Legion of Frontiersmen***, an organization intended to enrol for irregular service men with colonial or frontier experience.

1782 ST. JEAN DE CRÈVECŒUR *Lett. Amer. Farmer* xii. 270 (*heading*) Distresses of a frontier man. **1813** *Sporting Mag.* XLII. 209 Somewhat in the manner of our frontier men's leggins. **1814** BRACKENRIDGE *Views Louisiana* 116 There seems to prevail a rage amongst the frontiers-men, for emigration to that quarter. **1851** MAYNE REID *Scalp Hunt.* xx. 142 They were all, or nearly all, natives of the Mexican border, frontier-men. **1877** W. MATTHEWS *Ethnogr. Hidatsa* 22 The whites they had seen were mostly rude Canadian frontiersmen. **1883** B. MITFORD *Zulu Country* iii. 45 A burly frontiersman..strides along in all the glory of wideawake and corduroy. **1905** *Times* 11 Apr. 8/1 A corporation to be called the 'Legion of Frontiersmen'. **1906** *Daily Chron.* 21 May 7/1 Mr. Roger Pocock, founder and hon. secretary of the Legion of Frontiersmen. **1930** *Times* 8 Nov. 8/7 A movement has been set on foot for the formation of a Maritime Command of the Legion of Frontiersmen.

2. *transf.* and *fig.*

1912 A. CONAN DOYLE *Lost World* ii. 24 I'm a frontiersman from the extreme edge of the Knowable. **1963** *Guardian* 13 Mar. 13/1 Thanks to these four men, and many another British literary frontiersman who has followed in their pioneering footsteps.

frontignac (frɒntɪ'njæk), *sb.* Often *attrib.* or quasi-*adj.* Forms 7–9 **frontiniac(k, (7 frantiniak, -ick, frontineacke), 8 frontigniac, 8– frontignac.** [erroneous form of next; the substitution of *-ac* for *-an* is perh. due to a reminiscence of the many southern Fr. names in *-ignac*.]

1. A muscat wine made at Frontignan, in the department of Hérault, France.

1629 WELDON in Chambers *Life Jas. I* (1830) II. v. 148 His drinks..were frontiniac, canary, high country wine. **1636** DAVENANT *Witts* v. i, Nothing could please your haughty Pallat but The Muskatelli, and Frantiniak Grape! **1670** W. HUGHES *Compl. Vineyard* (1683) 73 Frantinick is a very pretty pleasant Wine. **1765** BROWNRIGG in *Phil. Trans.* LV. 221 Those long vials, in which Frontiniac wine is usually kept. **1826** POLWHELE *Trad. & Recoll.* II. 377 The Coniac-brandy, Claret and Frontiniac were excellent.

2. The grape from which this is made.

a **1641** SUCKLING *Lett.* (1646) 55 Mistresse and Woman differ no otherwise than Frontiniack and ordinary Grapes. **1725** BRADLEY *Fam. Dict.* s.v. *Exposition*, Muscats (the grapes) they call Frontiniacks. **1769** MRS. RAFFALD *Eng. Housekpr.* (1778) 363 The Frontiniac grape is the best.

†**frontignan.** *Obs.* = prec.

1756 NUGENT *Gr. Tour, France* IV. 36 Frontignan excellent for a glass or two. **1777** G. FORSTER *Voy. round World* I. 78 French plants of burgundy, muscade, and frontignan have likewise been tried.

fronting ('frʌntɪŋ), *vbl. sb.* [f. FRONT *v.*]

1. The action of the vb. FRONT in various senses.

1581 MULCASTER *Positions* xxxix. (1887) 212 In some desperate cases, fantasie is froward, and wil bide no fronting. **1659** TORRIANO, *Facciata*..any fronting or facing. **1796** *Instr. & Reg. Cavalry* (1813) 183 The fronting every two hundred yards is prescribed to prevent the breaking or falling into file of the line. **1832** *Prop. Regul. Instr. Cavalry* III. 86 The halting and fronting of each line may..be regulated. **1883–4** J. G. BUTLER in *Bible-Work* II. 65 This bold fronting of danger for the preaching of Christ. **1895** *Daily News* 1 June 5/6 It was..determined to achieve the new fronting without disturbing it [the Dutch cannon ball].

2. *concr.* A superficial coat or layer; a facing.

1886 *Athenæum* 22 May 686/3 The bath..reaching to the marble semicircular fronting of the western mosaic. **1891** *Daily News* 26 Dec. 5/5 The..town has everywhere a thin fronting of sparkling white.

fronting ('frʌntɪŋ), *ppl. a.* [f. FRONT *v.* + -ING[2].] That fronts (in senses of the vb.).

1597 SHAKS. *2 Hen. IV*, IV. iv. 66 Oh, with what Wings shall his Affections flye Towards fronting Perill, and oppos'd Decay? *a* **1711** KEN *Hymns Evang.* Poet. Wks. 1721 I. 82 They made supernal Waves asunder start, And into fronting liquid Bastions part. **1797** COLERIDGE *This Lime-Tree Bower, etc.* 54 Those fronting elms. **1816** KEATINGE *Trav.* (1817) I. 192 Their military [infantry] is formed in a long..lane of two fronting ranks. **1844** MRS. BROWNING *Lady Geraldine's Courtship* 68 She, with level fronting eyelids. **1846** LD. HOUGHTON *Men of Old* iv, Content, as men-at-arms, to cope Each with his fronting foe.

Hence, **frontingly** *adv.*

1859 *Chamb. Jrnl.* XI. 128 Hostile armies..On dimly tented fields, stand frontingly.

†**'frontish,** *a. Obs. rare.*⁻¹ [f. FRONT *a.* + -ISH.] Only in *frontish-door* = *front-door.*

1703 T. N. *City & C. Purchaser* 128 Frontish doors in great Buildings, with their Ornaments, as Pilasters, etc.

frontispiece ('frʌntɪspiːs), *sb.* Forms: 7 frontispice, -peece, (frontespice, frontice-piece, frontispeice), 6- frontispiece. [a. Fr. *frontispice*, ad. med.L. *frontispicium* lit. 'looking at the forehead', metoposcopy, hence physiognomy, countenance, face or façade of a building, f. L. *front(i)-* (see FRONT *sb.*) + *spicium*, f. early Lat. *specĕre* to look. In English the spelling was very early assimilated to that of *piece*.]

1. The principal face or front of a building; 'but the term is more usually applied to the decorated entrance of a building' (Gwilt).

1597-8 BP. HALL *Sat.* v. ii. 62 But if thou chance cast vp thy wondring eyes, Thou shalt descerne vpon the Frontispice, *ΟΥΔΕΙΣ ΕΙΣΙΤΩ* grauen vp on hye. **1630** BRATHWAIT *Eng. Gentlem.* (1641) 8 An indiscreet builder, who preferreth the care of his frontispice before the maine foundation. **1689** BURNET *Tracts* I. 45 The French King gives 10000 Livres for the Frontis-peice. **1753** HANWAY *Trav.* (1762) I. VII. xcv. 440 The ornaments of the architecture, and the relievo in the frontispiece, are after the chinese and japan manner. **1797** HOLCROFT *Stolberg's Trav.* (ed. 2) II. lvi. 302 The temple..was of white marble. On the frontispiece was the..chariot of the Sun. **1855** FERGUSSON *Handbk. Arch.* II. 772 As a frontispiece..it [the three-gabled front of the Cathedral of Orvieto] is not without considerable appropriateness and even beauty. **1874** SYMONDS *Italy & Greece* 102 The façade [of the Cathedral of Orvieto] is a triumph of decorative art. It is strictly what Fergusson has styled a 'frontispiece'; for it bears no relation whatever to the construction of the building.

transf. and *fig.* **1607** WALKINGTON *Opt. Glass* i. (1664) 3 He had his celestial sentence..engraven on the frontispeece of his Heart. *a* **1678** MARVELL *Poems, Appleton House* 23 A stately frontispiece of poor Adorns without the open door. **1690** LOCKE *Hum. Und.* III. xi. §20 Who is it has inform'd us, that a rational Soul can inhabit no Tenement, unless it has just such a sort of Frontispiece. **1728** GLOVER *On Sir Isaac Newton* 207 The ev'ning on the frontispiece of heav'n His mantle spreads with many colours gay.

†**b.** The summit of a building. *Obs.* [So sometimes med.L. *frontispicium*.]

1600 HOLLAND *Livy* x. xxiii. 368 The image of Jupiter..in the lanterne or frontispice [L. *culmine*] of the Capitoll.

2. The pediment over a door, gate, etc. Also, a sculptured or engraved panel.

1601 HOLLAND *Pliny* II. 580 The very frontispiece and maine lintle-tree which lay ouer the jambes or cheekes of the great dore of the said temple. **1637** HEYWOOD *Royal Ship* 41 Upon the upright of the Upper Counter, standeth Victory, in the middle of a Frontispiece. **1667** MILTON *P.L.* III. 506 A Kingly Palace Gate, With Frontispice of Diamond and Gold Embellisht. **1686** BURNET *Trav.* iii. (1750) 168 The great Dome is a magnificent Building, but the Frontis-piece to the great Gate is not yet made. **1819** SHELLEY *To Peacock* 25 Feb., Columns..supporting a perfect architrave, and two shattered frontispieces. **1850** LEITCH tr. *Müller's Anc. Art* §109. 76 An Ionic portico on the outside, and on each side a Doric frontispiece.

fig. **1622** MISSELDEN *Free Trade* (ed. 2) 2 When God himselfe setteth these duties in the frontispice or top of both the Tables of the Decalogue.

†**3.** The first page of a book or pamphlet, or what is printed on it; the title-page including illustrations and table of contents; hence, an introduction or preface. *Obs.*

1607 R. C. tr. *H. Estienne's World of Wonders* Ep. Ded., I could see none..fitter to be placed in the Frontispice of this worke..then your two Lordships. **1614** SELDEN *Titles Hon.* 226 In the Frontispice of Ina's laws, he saith he made them with the assent and help of his Bishops. **1618** BOLTON *Florus* To Rdr., Hee figures the whole people of Rome, in the person of a Man (as the frontis-pice sheweth). **1646** BURGESS in *Presbyt. Rev.* (1887) 317 This speech..a scoffing Remonstrant takes, and sets it forth odiously in the Frontispice of his Book. **1647** CLARENDON *Hist. Reb.* v. §1 A Declaration (which he caused to be printed, and, in the Frontispiece, recommended to the consideration of all his loving Subjects). **1712** STEELE *Spect.* No. 296 ¶1 Your prefixing Greek Motto's to the Frontispiece of your late Papers. **1721** BAILEY, *Frontispiece*..the Title or first Page of a Book done in Picture.

fig. *c* **1640** J. SMYTH *Lives Berkeleys* (1883) II. 409 His face was the frontispice of his mind; he knew not how to dissemble a thought. **1651** JER. TAYLOR *Serm. for Year* I. v. 57 Godly sorrow is but the frontispiece or title page. **1673** *Lady's Call.* I. ii. 12 Nature..never meant a serene and clear forehead should be the frontispiece to a cloudy tempestuous heart. **1704** S. WESLEY *Def. Let. conc. Educ. Dissenters* 23 Stephen Marshall, the very Frontispiece of Smectimnuus.

4. An illustration facing the title-page of a book or division of a book. (The current sense.)

The 'Frontis-piece' of the first quot. faces the title-page. **1682** *Lithgow's Trav.* III. 120 And lo in the Frontis-piece is my Effigies affixed with my Turkish habit..even as I travelled. **1748** LADY LUXBOROUGH *Lett. to Shenstone* 28 May, I grudge six shillings for Herveys Meditations..but I want to see the frontispieces. **1753** GRAY *Let.* Poems (1775) 225 If I had received such a book, with such a frontispiece..it would have given me a palsy. **1820** SCORESBY *Acc. Arctic Reg.* II. 368 The engraving which forms the frontispiece to this volume..is illustrative of this accident. **1878** H. H. GIBBS *Ombre* 8 One of them appears in the Frontispiece which is taken from Seymour's 'Compleat Gamester'.

fig. **1691** J. WILSON *Belphegor* I. ii, In a word, a thing made up of so many several parishes, that you'd have taken him at first sight for a frontispiece of the resurrection.

5. The front piece or forepart of anything.

a. The face or forehead. Chiefly *jocular.*

a **1625** *Grobian's Nuptialls, MS. Bodl.* 30, lf. 17a, That fayre frontispeece of yours. **1754** HUME *Hist. Eng.* (1761) I. i. 26 It were a pity that..so beautiful a frontispiece should cover a mind destitute of internal grace. **1772** NUGENT tr. *Hist. Fr. Gerund* I. iv. 120 A smart little father, with a bit of toupet on his frontispiece. **1821** *Sporting Mag.* VIII. 233 Hammering his frontispiece to the appearance of a pudding-stone. **1872** BROWNING *Fifine* xcv, No face-shape, beast or bird..but some one had preferred From out its frontispiece..To make the vizard whence himself should view the world.

†**b.** In a theatre: The front scenery; also, the forepart of the stage. *Obs.*

1651 J. WILSON *Astræa* A viij, The Shepherdess avanceth to the Frontispiece of the Scene. **1667** DAVENANT & DRYDEN *Tempest* I. i, The curtain rises, and discovers a new frontis-piece, joined to the great pilasters.

frontispiece ('frʌntɪspiːs), *v.* [f. prec. sb.] *trans.* **a.** To furnish *with* as a FRONTISPIECE (senses 3, 4), put a frontispiece to. **b.** To represent on the frontispiece. **c.** To put as a frontispiece.

1715 M. DAVIES *Athen. Brit.* I. Pref. 12 Those two Clementin Epistles..wherewith..Cotelerius frontispiec'd his Collection of Apostolick Remains. **1716** *Ibid.* II. 297 His insolent Sermon, Sawcily frontispiec'd, *Non-Resistance without Priestcraft*, &c. *c* **1821** BYRON in Dowden *Shelley* (1887) II. 364, I have advised him to frontispiece his book with his own head, Capo di Traditore, the head of a traitor. **1831** *Fraser's Mag.* III. 201 [He] is frontispieced most abominably, in a sort of caricature of the Freischutz. **1836** *Ibid.* XIII. 34 Poole's Sketches..are frontispieced with an engraving. **1894** *Speaker* 19 May 560/2 Let him frontispiece a good map.

Hence **'frontispiecer,** one who supplies a frontispiece.

1828 LAMB *Let. to Barton* 5 Dec., I esteem thy verses..honour thy frontispicer, and..reverence thy..dedicatee.

frontisterion, -um: see PHRONTISTERY.

frontless ('frʌntlɪs), *a.* Also 7 frontles(se. [f. FRONT *sb.* + -LESS.] Having no front.

1. *fig.* Unblushing, shameless, audacious, daring; = FOREHEADLESS *a.* Now *rare.*

1605 B. JONSON *Volpone* IV. v, The most prodigious, and most frontlesse piece Of solid impudence. **1615** CHAPMAN *Odyss.* I. 425 Command to towns of their nativity These frontless wooers. **1633** T. ADAMS *Exp. 2 Peter* ii. 10 The whelps of that Roman litter have thus cast frontless imputations upon them. **1739** CIBBER *Apol.* (1756) I. 99 As if the author had impos'd upon them the most frontless..absurdity. **1791** BOSWELL *Johnson* 10 Sept. an. 1773 The duchess had not superior parts, but was a bold frontless woman. **1823** *Blackw. Mag.* XIV. 464 We have..editors frontless enough to advocate them. **1850** L. HUNT *Autobiog.* II. xi. 79 The repulsiveness of a republic..with its frontless love of money. **1886** SWINBURNE *Miscell.* 297 A brainless and frontless trafficker in scandal.

2. Of a house: That has had its front destroyed.

1887 *Pall Mall G.* 1 Mar. 12/1 Diano Marina is a wreck..The passengers in the trains look into frontless houses.

Hence **'frontlessly** *adv.*, **'frontlessness.**

1618 CHAPMAN *Hesiod* 143 The worse depraving the better; and that frontlessly. **1631** BRATHWAIT *Whimzies, Ruffian* 83 Hee will intrude most frontlesly into any company. **1698** R. FERGUSSON *Ecclesiastick* 5 Without a strange frontlessness, they can neither deny [etc.]. **1709** J. LOGAN in *Pa. Hist. Soc. Mem.* X. 370, I cannot persuade myself that any man will be so frontlessly base.

frontlet ('frʌntlɪt). Forms: 5-6 frontlett(e, (6 frountlett, 7 frontilet), 6- frontlet. [a. OF. *frontelet*, dim. of *frontel, fronteau* FRONTAL *sb.*: see -LET.]

1. Something worn on the forehead.

a. An ornament or band; also, a bandage worn at night to prevent or remove wrinkles.

1478 in *Rolls of Parlt.* VI. 289 Frontlettes of blak velvet. **1502** *Priv. Purse Exp. Eliz. of York* (1830) 68 A frontlet of golde for the Quene. *c* **1540** J. HEYWOOD *Four P.P.* B j b, And they be masked in many nettes As frontlettes, fillettes, partlettes, & braceletes. **1613** PURCHAS *Pilgrimage* (1614) 837 They weare also frontlets of feathers: in their eares they weare bones. **1641** J. JACKSON *True Evang. T.* III. 206 Holinesse to the Lord is found written..upon the high Priests frontlet. *a* **1717** PARNELL *To an Old Beauty* 2 To please our youthful sight You sleep in cream and frontlets all the night. **1755** YOUNG *Centaur* vi. Wks. 1757 IV. 255 The Centaurs..wearing frontlets of brass on their foreheads. **1807** WORDSW. *White Doe* I. 260 That Dame of haughty air..wears a frontlet edged with gold. **1866** J. G. MURPHY *Comm. Ex.* xiii. 9 The fillet or frontlet encircles the head.

fig. **1605** SHAKS. *Lear* I. iv. 208 How now Daughter? what makes that Frontlet on? You are too much of late i'th'frowne. **1791** COWPER *Odyss.* XIII. 469 As when we loosed Her radiant frontlet from the brows of Troy. **1876** SWINBURNE *Erechtheus* 1396 To bind on the brows of thy godhead a frontlet of night.

b. In *Exod.* xiii. 16, *Deut.* vi. 8, or phrases referring thereto: = PHYLACTERY.

1578 BIBLE (Genev.) *Exod.* xiii. 16 It shalbe as a token upon thine hande, and as frontlets betwene thine eyes. **1670** L. STUCLEY *Gossip-Glass* xl. 481 Let it be as Frontlets between thine eyes day and night. **1732** SWIFT *Lett.* Wks. 1841 II. 674 His [Clarendon's] books had frontlets of Scripture to recommend and sanctify all their venom. **1825** MACAULAY *Milton* Ess. (1854) 27 That sublime treatise which every statesman should wear as a sign upon his hand and as frontlets between his eyes.

†**c.** A cloth or bandage containing some medicament; also, the medicament itself. *Obs.*

1600 SURFLET *Countrie Farme* I. xii. 57 To cause them to sleepe..it is good to make a frontlet with the seede of poppie, [etc.]. **1607** TOPSELL *Four-f. Beasts* (1658) 401 To put them all together into a Frontlet or fore-head cloth. **1621-51** BURTON *Anat. Mel.* II. v. I. vi. 396 Frontlets are well known to every good wife, Rose water and Vinegar..applied to both temples. **1725** BRADLEY *Fam. Dict.* s.v. *Eye*, You are to apply to the Temples a Frontlet made with Provence Roses.

d. = FRONT 9 c. *rare*⁻¹.

1785 CRABBE *Newspaper* 375 These flaxen frontlets with elastic springs.

e. = FRONTAL 1 b, *front-stall* (see FRONT *sb.* 15).

1805 SCOTT *Last Minstr.* I. v, Thirty steeds..Barbed with frontlet of steel. **1873** OUIDA *Pascarel* II. 89 The bullocks went on their slow ways with flowers in their leathern frontlets.

†**f.** A coronet. *Obs.*

1610 GUILLIM *Heraldry* VI. Concl. (1611) 283 Twixt an Earle and Vicounts Frontilets The ods is like: so needlesse to be learn'd.

2. = FOREHEAD 1. Now only of animals.

1659 D. PELL *Impr. Sea* 378 Like the smooth-faced *fontes, fluvia, stagna,* and *lacus's* of a land, that lyes with never a wrinckle upon their frontlets. **1758** DYER *Fleece* I. 203 A fairer species..Of shorter limb, and frontlet more ornate. **1810** SCOTT *Lady of L.* I. ii, The antlered monarch of the waste..Tossed his beamed frontlet to the sky. **1851** MAYNE REID *Scalp Hunt.* xxxix. 299 We can recognise the horns and frontlets of the elk. **1878** G. MACDONALD *Phantastes* vi. 88 From frontlet to tail the horse likewise shone red. **1890** BOLDREWOOD *Col. Reformer* (1891) 228 A very evil-looking beast..with a development of horn remarkable even in that forest of frontlets.

b. *Ornith.* The margin of the head, behind the bill, of birds, generally clothed with rigid bristles.

1874 COUES *Birds N.W.* 89 The differences..are found in every sufficient series of the North American bird; thus, of two specimens, both shot at Washington, D.C., one has a whitish and the other a brown frontlet.

3. The façade of a building: = FRONT *sb.* 6. Also *transf.*

1808 SCOTT *Marm.* V. xx, The antique buildings, climbing high, Whose Gothic frontlets sought the sky. **1830** W. PHILLIPS *Mt. Sinai* I. 338 Fair east he turn'd him, and anon attain'd The beetling frontlet of the mountain.

4. A superfrontal or cloth hanging over the upper part of an altar frontal; also, an ornamental border to an altar-cloth.

1536 *Reg. of Riches* in *Antiq. Sarisb.* (1771) 199 A purpure cloth, with an ymage of the Crucifix..with a divers frontlet, having in every end two white Leopards. **1549** *Eng. Ch. Furniture* (Peacock 1860) 246 Item on corporaxe cloth & ij tasslys. Item one lyttell frountlett of ffustyan. **1874** MICKLETHWAITE *Mod. Par. Churches* 305 One frontlet may serve with a variety of frontals. **1877** J. D. CHAMBERS *Div. Worship* 269 Frontlets may be sewn on the front of these linen cloths so as to hang over the edge.

†**frontly,** *adv. Obs.* [f. FRONT *sb.* + -LY².] ? With a bold front, bravely.

1375 BARBOUR *Bruce* XVI. 174 Thai..frontly with thar fayis can ficht.

fronto- ('frɒntəʊ), used in scientific nomenclature for *fronti-*, the combining form of L. *front-em, frōns* FRONT, chiefly in anatomical and surgical combs. signifying 'pertaining to the front or forehead and to something else'; as in *fronto-auricular, -ethmoid, -malar, -mental* (see MENTAL *a.*²), *-nasal, -occipital, -orbital, -parietal, -sphenoidal, -squamosal, -temporal,* for which see the word forming the second member of the combination.

1857 BULLOCK *Cazeaux' Midwif.* 221 The fronto-mental, or the facial, extends from the frontal boss to the point of the chin. **1864** *Reader* No. 85. 204/1 The fronto-nasal protuberance. **1866** HUXLEY *Preh. Rem. Caithn.* 99 The basi-cranial line is from the anterior margin of the *foramen magnum* to the fronto-nasal suture. **1872** MIVART *Elem. Anat.* 100 The parietal may be one with the frontal, forming a fronto-parietal bone. **1886** F. H. H. GUILLEMARD *Cruise Marchesa* I. 214 Thus causing the fronto-orbital edge to be very sharp.

frontogenesis (ˌfrʌntəʊ'dʒɛnɪsɪs). *Meteorol.* [ad. G. *frontogenese* (T. Bergeron *Über die dreidimensional verknüpfende Wetteranalyse* (1928) I. 15), f. FRONTO- + GENESIS.] The formation or development of fronts.

1934 D. BRUNT *Physical & Dynamical Meteorol.* xviii. 333 Bergeron has suggested the name *frontolysis* to denote the smoothing out of a front from discontinuity to continuity, and the name *frontogenesis* to denote the reverse process. **1939** *Geogr. Jrnl.* XCIV. 145 The primary factor in the formation of fronts (called frontogenesis) consists of the air movements which bring cold and warm masses into juxtaposition and form a diffuse front. **1967** *Jrnl. Atmospheric Sci.* Nov. 627/1 The time scale for the fronto-genesis process must be small since fronts often form in less than 24 hr.

Hence ˌ**frontoge'netic** *a.*

1966 *Jrnl. Atmospheric Sci.* Sept. 455/2 A paper.. presented with the purpose of determining the frontogenetic potentialities of deformation fields.

fronton (ˈfrʌntən). Also 9 frontoon. [a. Fr. *fronton*, ad. It. *frontone*, f. *fronte* FRONT.]

1. *Arch.* A pediment.

1698 M. LISTER *Journ. to Paris* (1699) 42 There are two Stones in the Fronton of the South East Facade of the Louvre. **1721** BAILEY, *Fronton* [in Architecture] is a Member which serves to compose an Ornament, raised over Doors, Cross-works, Nitches, etc. **1802** W. TAYLOR in Robberds *Mem.* I. 417 Every architrave and window-sill of the long and regular palace of the Tuileries was thickly dotted with these arches,—every frontoon and arch regularly framed with them. **1850** LEITCH tr. *Müller's Anc. Art* §284. 314 It stands more upright over the fronton and inclines forward more above the side-walls. **1894** *Daily News* 9 Oct. 5/3 One of the curiosities of Paris is the bas-relief on the fronton of the east side of the Louvre over the colonnade.

2. Of an altar: = FRONTAL *sb.* 2.

1749 U. AP RHYS *Tour Spain & Portugal* (1760) 83 An exceeding rich Altar, the Fronton of which is of Brass gilt.

‖**3.** [Sp.] A building where pelota is played.

1896 *Westm. Gaz.* 23 Apr. 7/1 The great objection to the popularity of pelota over here is the expense of the fronton or court. **1896** *Daily Chron.* 16 May 9/4 A fronton epidemic broke out in Madrid.

ˈfrontsman. [f. FRONT *sb.* + MAN.] A salesman who stands on the pavement in front of a shop.

1896 *Daily Chron.* 25 Aug. 9/4 Butchers.—Young man, 22, seeks Situation as cutter and frontsman.

ˈfrontstead. [f. FRONT *sb.* + STEAD *sb.*] A piece of ground between the front of a house and the road or street; a fore-court, a front garden. Now *dial.* only.

1688 *Depos. Cast. York* (Surtees) 285 He would make a bonefire on his own frontstead. **1769** *Aclome Inclos. Act* 11 Houses, frontsteads, garths, gardens, and orchards. **1825** *Brighton Commissioners Act* §76. **1876** *Whitby Gloss.*, *Frontstead*, a front site in the line of a street.

†**ˈfronture.** *Obs.* Also 5 frunture. [altered form (after words with suffix -URE) of FRONTIER.] = FRONTIER.

1417 LD. FURNYVAL in Ellis *Orig. Lett.* Ser. II. I. 58 A bridge..sett in the fronture of the borders of the Irish enimies. *c* **1430** LYDG. *Min. Poems* (Percy) 18 And last was wryten in the ffrontures 'I schalle ffullefille him withe joy' [etc.]. **1452** *Paston Lett.* I. 237 Charlys Nowel, Otywell Nowell, Robert Ledeham..kepe a frunture and a forslet at the hows of the seid Robert Ledeham, and issu ought at her pleser. **1611** SPEED *Hist. Gt. Brit.* VI. xvii. §7. 97 Placed in the fronture of this Chapter.

frontward, -wards (ˈfrʌntwəd, -z), *adv.* (*a.*, *sb.*) [f. FRONT *sb.* + -WARD(S.]

1. Towards or in the direction of the front; also, to the front *of*.

1865 G. MEREDITH *Rhoda Fleming* xxvi, She spoke, gazing frontward all the while. **1876** S. LANIER *Poems* (1884) 133 Run each road that frontward leads. **1877** —— *Hard Times in Elfland* 6 Drew More frontward of the mighty fire.

b. quasi-*adj.* Of or pertaining to the front.

1865 CARLYLE *Fredk. Gt.* XX. xi. IX. 208 Burkersdorf, Ludwigsdorf..are frontward posts.

†**c.** quasi-*sb.* The direction towards the front.

1553 BRENDE *Q. Curtius* (1570) 90 b, Suche as stode in yᵉ hinder partes of the battailles, were ordered to turne their faces from yᵉ frontwards.

2. With the front or face in a specified direction. Const. *to. rare*⁻¹.

1856 MRS. BROWNING *Aur. Leigh* VII. 310 Men define a man The creature who stands frontward to the stars.

front yard. *U.S.* [FRONT *sb.* (*a.*) 13.] A piece of ground or garden in front of a house.

1767 J. BROWNE *Diary* 122 My pump in the front yard froze. **1835** J. H. INGRAHAM *South-West* II. 114 Southerners, with the exception of the cultivation of a few plants in a front yard, pay little regard to horticulture. **1897** 'MARK TWAIN' *Following Equator* xxix. 282 There cannot be another town in the world that has no..weed-grown front-yards of the poor. **1908** *Westm. Gaz.* 29 May 1/3 'The front-yard', as my old farming friend in the train informed me, was mostly grass. **1916** H. L. WILSON *Somewhere in Red Gap* ii. 69 The Piedmont Queen dahlia bulbs I'd ordered for the front yard.

†**ˈfronysate,** *a. Obs.* [app. connected with Gr. φρόνησις thought, intelligence.]

1541 R. COPLAND *Guydon's Quest. Chirurg.* Pref., Your scyentycall beneuolence and clere fronysate intellygence.

†**froofe.** *Obs. rare*⁻¹. App. used by Chapman for 'the handle of an auger' (Nares).

1615 CHAPMAN *Odyss.* IX. 530 And as you haue seene A ship-wright bore a nauall beame; he oft Thrusts at the Augurs Froofe; works still aloft; And at the shanke, helpe others; with a cord Wound round about, to make it sooner bor'd.

†**ˈfroppish,** *a. Obs.* Also fropish. [? f. *frop, var. of FRAP *v.* + -ISH.] Froward, fretful, peevish.

1659 J. ALLEINE in *Life* (1838) Let. I. 140 As a man would give a thing to a froppish child. **1709** *Brit. Apollo* II. No. 77. 2/2 A fropish, froward..Perverse Wife. **1754** RICHARDSON *Grandison* (1781) IV. xxxvii. 260 So, once, he was as froppish as a child, on my calling him *the man*. **1784** R. BAGE *Barham Downs* I. 138, I was a giddy headed girl, too proud and froppish to take up with my sister's leavings.

Hence †**ˈfroppishness.**

1688 S. PENTON *Guardian's Instr.* 75 Whenever you find the Child in an Extravagant fit of Froppishness and Anger. **1754** RICHARDSON *Grandison* (ed. 7) V. 112 If my Lord will ask pardon for his froppishness, as we say of children.

frore (frɔə(r)), † **froren,** †**frorn(e,** *pa. pple.* and *ppl. a.* [pa. pple. of FREEZE *v.* (q.v. for Forms).]

1. With distinctly participial sense: Frozen. *Obs.* exc. *dial.*

c **1250** *Gen. & Ex.* 97 Of waters froren, of yses wal, ðis middel werld it luket al. **1297** R. GLOUC. (1724) 265 þe water yfrore hys. **1398** TREVISA *Barth. De P.R.* XVIII. xcii. (1495) 840 Salamandra quenchyth the fyre that he towchyth as yse dooth and water frore. **1477** NORTON *Ord. Alch.* I. in Ashm. (1652) 19 Plenty of water that was therein froare. **1542** HEN. VIII *Declar. Scots* 197 Our bloud is..frorne with the cold ayre of Scotlande. **1880** SHARP *Sword of Damocles* III. 74 The lake..was soon 'frorn', as they say in Suffolk.

absol. *c* **1430** *Pilgr. Lyf Manhode* II. xc. (1869) 108, I hatte Peresce..the foollich, the founded, the froren.

2. Intensely cold, frosty, frost-like. Now only *poet.* in the form *frore* (after Milton's use).

1483 CAXTON *Gold. Leg.* 130 b/1 After longe tyme saynt Julyen slepte aboute mydnyght..and it was frorn and moche colde. **1667** MILTON *P.L.* II. 595 The parching Air Burns frore, and cold performs th' effect of Fire. **1708** J. PHILIPS *Cyder* II. 74 Th' aged Year Inclines, and Boreas' Spirit blusters frore. **1764** CHURCHILL *Gotham* I. Poems II. 19 Frore January, Leader of the Year. **1821** SHELLEY *Prometh. Unb.* I. 121 Snow-fed streams now seen athwart frore vapours. **1829** SOUTHEY in *Anniversary* 9 *Epistle*, Time upon my head Hath laid his frore and monitory hand. **1850** MRS. BROWNING *Poems* II. 415 The Loves..lie, Frore as taken in a snow-storm. **1887** BOWEN *Virg. Æneid* IV. 251 His beard is with icicles frore.

frory (ˈfrɔərɪ), *a.* Also froarie, -y. [f. FRORE *ppl. a.* + -Y¹. Cf. OE. *fréoriȝ*.]

1. Frozen; frosty; extremely cold.

a **1555** ABP. PARKER *Ps.* cxxi. 368 The moone by night shall serue thy turne: Her frory hornes shall thee not fray. **1590** SPENSER *F.Q.* III. viii. 35 Her up betwixt his rugged hands he reard, And with his frory lips full softly kist. **1691** DRYDEN *Arthur* III. 31 There the pale Pole Star in the North of Heav'n Sits high and on the frory Winter broods. **1855** SINGLETON *Virgil* II. 271 Her son within a vale retired afar, Sequestered by the frory flood, she saw.

†**2.** Covered with foam or froth. *Obs.*

1600 FAIRFAX *Tasso* II. xl, While..yong, she vs'd with tender hand The foming steed with froarie bit to steare.

†**froˈsender.** *Obs.*⁻¹ [f. FRO *adv.* + SENDER.] One who sends forth. So **froˈsent** *ppl. a.* [SENT *ppl. a.*], that is sent forth; in quot. *absol.*

c **1550** CHEKE *Matt.* ix. 5 *note*, Even as yᵉ servant is to yᵉ Mʳ..so is yᵉ frosender, and yᵉ frosent.

frosh¹, frosk. *Obs.* exc. *dial.* Forms: 1 frox, forsc, 3–4 frosse, 3–5 frosk(e, 3, 5–6 frosche, 4–5 frossh(e, 5–7 frosh, 8–9 *dial.* frosk. *Pl.* 3 frosse. [See FROG *sb.*¹] A frog.

c **1000** ÆLFRIC *Exod.* viii. 4 To þe and to þinum folce and in to eallum þinum þeowum gað þa froxas. *a* **1240** *Sawles Warde* in *Cott. Hom.* 251 Neddren ant eauraskes [*v. rr.* eaureskes, eafroskes]. *c* **1250** *Gen. & Ex.* 2969 Ðo cam ðor up swilc froskes here ðe ðede al folc egipte dere. *a* **1300** *Cursor M.* 5928 þat toþer on-com þat him fell Was frosse þat na tung moght tell. **1382** WYCLIF *Ps.* lxxvii. 45 He sente in ..a frogge [*v.r.* frosshe], and it destroȝede them. ? *a* **1400** *Morte Arth.* 1081 His frount and his forheuede, alle was it ouer, As the felle of a froske. **1481** CAXTON *Reynard* (Arb.) 37 The frosshis..complayned that they had none lorde. **1565** GOLDING *Ovid's Met.* xv. (1593) 356 The mud hath in it certaine seed whereof greene froshes rise. **1674–91** RAY *N.C. Words* (E.D.S.), *Frosh*, a frog. **1690** in Picton *L'pool Munic. Rec.* (1883) I. 288 It is order'd in Councel yᵗ no allowance be given him to slutch yᵉ frosse lake. **1781** HUTTON *Tour to Caves* Gloss., *Frosk*. **1821** MRS. WHEELER *Cumbld. Dial.* App. 7 Thou cuddent tell me be a frosk, at hed been hung up beeth heels ith' sunshine, an dryt to deeth. **1869** *Lonsdale Gloss.*, *Frosg*, *Frosk*. **1873** *Swaledale Gloss.*, *Frosk*.

frosh² (frɒʃ). *N. Amer. slang.* Also †frosch. [Modified shortening of FRESHMAN, perh. under influence of Ger. *frosch* frog, (*dial.*) grammar-school pupil.] A college freshman; a member of a freshman sports team. Also freshmen *collect.*, and *attrib.*

1915 *Univ. Oklahoman* 29 Oct. 1/5 Some of the more advanced among the Frosch are holding out for 'Back to Nature' garb. **1915** *Dialect Notes* IV. 236 *Frosh*, freshman. **1942** BERREY & VAN DEN BARK *Amer. Thes. Slang* §636/32 *Member of freshman team*, frosh, papoose, peagreener, yearling. **1947** *Chicago Daily News* 29 Nov. 3/1 Dr. Snyder followed her dutifully, after donning the frosh cap she had brought for him. **1973** *Tucson (Arizona) Daily Citizen* 22 Aug. 57 The 6-4, 205-pound frosh split end came up with a knee injury. **1985** *Univ. Waterloo* (Ontario) *Gaz.* 11 Sept. 5 (*heading*) Wright gives frosh audience views on funding. *Ibid.* 5/1 'A university is a very special kind of place,' Wright told the 2,000 frosh.

†**froshell.** *Obs.* In 5 freshell (? *incorrectly*), frosshell. [app. a corruption of OF. *fourchelle*, *forcel*: see FORCEL.] The furcula of a bird.

1486 *Bk. St. Albans* C iij b, Yeue hir a chekyn..and take the tenderist of the brest withe the ffreshell [**1496** frosshell] bone and let hir eate it.

ˈfrosling. *Obs.* exc. *dial.* [? for *frostling, f. FROST *sb.* + -LING.] (See quot. 1823.)

a **1529** SKELTON *E. Rummyng* 460 Another brought two goslynges, That were noughty froslynges. **1823** MOOR *Suffolk Words*, *Froslin*, a lamb, a goslin, a chicken, an apple, &c., nipped, or pinched, or injured by frost.

frost (frɒst, -ɔː-), *sb.* Forms: 1 frost, forst, 2–5 forst(e, 3 *south.* vorst, 5 froste, (4 wrost, froist, 7 froast), 4– frost. [Com. Teut.: OE. *frost*, usually *forst*, str. masc., corresponds to OFris. *frost*, *forst*, OS. *frost* (MDu. *vorst* masc. and fem., mod.Du. fem. only), OHG. *frost* (MHG. *vrost*, mod.Ger. *frost*) str. masc., ON. *frost* neut. (Sw., Da. *frost* masc.):—OTeut. **frusto-*, f. weak-grade of the root of **freusan* to FREEZE.]

1. a. The act or state of freezing or becoming frozen; the temperature of the atmosphere when it is below the freezing-point of water; extreme cold. Often used with qualifying adj. as ***hard***, ***sharp***, etc. ***frost***. ***black frost***: frost not accompanied by rime; opposed to *white frost* (see sense 2). Also *personified* in *Jack Frost*.

†*below frost*: below freezing-point (*obs.*). (*ten*, etc.) *degrees of frost*: degrees below freezing-point.

a **700** *Epinal Gloss.* 485 *Gelum*, frost. *a* **1000** *Phoenix* 58 Se hearda forst. *a* **1123** *O.E. Chron.* an. 1110 Treow wæstmas wurdon þære nihte þurh forste swiðe for numene. *c* **1175** *Lamb. Hom.* 35 Ic walde fein pinian and sitten on forste and on snawe up et mine chinne. *a* **1250** *Owl & Night.* 524 Wane niȝtes cumeth longe, And bringeth forstes starke an stronge. **1382** WYCLIF *Dan.* iii. 69 Byndynge frost [**1388** Blac forst] and colde, bless ȝe to the Lord. *c* **1450** *Merlin* 149 Thei cloded hem warme as thei myght, for the froste was grete. **1523** LD. BERNERS *Froiss.* I. cclxxxvi. 428 They went a seuyn leages afote..and it was harde frost, wherby they cutte their fete. **1576** FLEMING *Panopl. Epist.* 395 The Winter Frostes doe not alwayes indure: no more should your greefe. **1647** COWLEY *Mistress*, *Bathing in the River* iv, When rigorous Winter binds you [river] up with Frost. **1694** *Acc. Sev. Late Voy.* II. (1711) 207 The Days in Summer being excessive hot, and the Nights sharp Frosts, even to an inch thickness in the Ponds. **1715** DESAGULIERS *Fires Impr.* 47 The Liquor subsided to 18 degrees, which was two Degrees below Frost. **1804** J. GRAHAME *Sabbath* 214 As when a waveless lake..Is sheeted by a nightly frost with ice. **1847** A. M. GILLIAM *Trav. Mexico* 9 Welcome Jack Frost had visited the city of New Orleans..that hoary benefactor. **1851** HAWTHORNE *Twice-told T.* Ser. II. *Shaker Bridal*, The hoarfrost, and the blackfrost, hath done its work on Brother Adam.

b. viewed as an agent which penetrates and freezes the contained moisture of a porous substance, *esp.* the ground.

1694 *Acc. Sev. Late Voy.* II. (1711) 27 The frost cannot penetrate far into such Ground. **18..** C. D. WARNER *Spring in New Eng.* (Cent.), In the shade there is still frost in the ground. **1891** S. C. SCRIVENER *Our Fields & Cities* 139 Frost will penetrate eight inches, sometimes more. **1894** *Westm. Gaz.* 5 Apr. 3/2 A sheep's carcass is small; you can get the frost out of it as soon as you require it.

†**c.** *Proverb.* (Cf. *farewell fieldfare*.) *Obs.*

c **1590** *Play Sir Thomas More* (1844) 52 Why, farewell, frost. **1599** PORTER *Angry Wom. Abingd.* (Percy Soc.) 43 Farewell, frost. **1670** RAY *Eng. Prov.* 174 Farewel, frost; nothing got, nor nothing lost.

2. a. Frozen dew or vapour. More fully ***hoar(y***, ***rime***, or ***white frost***.

a **1000** *Riddles* lxxxviii. 8 (Gr.) Hwilum hara scoc forst of feaxe. *a* **1300** *Cursor M.* 6520 Manna..fel fra lift sa gret plente, Als a grideld frost to se. *a* **1340** HAMPOLE *Psalter* lxxvii. 52 þaire mours [Vulg. *moros*]..he sloghe in ryme froist. **1382** WYCLIF *Dan.* iii. 68 Dewis and whyt frost, blesse ȝe to the Lord. **1563** W. FULKE *Meteors* (1640) 54 Hoare frost or white frost is nothing else, but dew congealed by over much cold. **1667** MILTON *P.L.* XI. 899 Seed-time and Harvest, Heat and hoary Frost, Shall hold their course. **1704** POPE *Winter* 9 Behold the groves that shine with silver frost. **1739** T. SMITH *Jrnl.* (1849) 268 Last night there was a very white frost, that killed the tops of our potatoes. **1832** TENNYSON *New Year's Eve* iv, There's not a flower on all the hills: the frost is on the pane.

†**b.** Frozen water, ice. *Obs.*

c **1400** MAUNDEV. (Roxb.) xiv. 61 Anoþer water þat on nyghtes fresez hard, and on days es na frost sene þeron. **1580** FRAMPTON *Dial. Yron & Steele* 169 Waters which doe proceed of snow and of frost. *Ibid.* 170 With a piece of frost, chewing it continually.

3. *fig.*

c **1200** ORMIN 12655 To shridenn uss þærwiþþ onnȝæn þe frosst off fakenn trowwþe. **1595** in *Caxton's Blanchardyn* (E.E.T.S.) 214 A frost of cares [began] to ouer runne their summers blisse. **1769** SIR W. JONES *Pal. Fortune* Poems (1777) 22 A reverend sage, Whose beard was hoary with the frost of age. **1851** RUSKIN *Stones Ven.* (1874) I. xx. 225 The Renaissance frosts came, and all perished.

b. *esp.* Of a person: Coldness of behaviour or temperament, frigidity; also *slang*, a 'coolness'.

1635 J. HAYWARD tr. *Biondi's Banish'd Virg.* 141 The difference betweene a woman of frost and one of fire. **1720** *Humourist* 99 But with all this Shyness, Frost, and Virtue.. my Friend finds her as willing a Tit [etc.]. **1815** SCOTT *Guy M.* lv, One of those moments of intense feeling when the frost of the Scottish people melts like a snow wreath. **1886** MALLOCK *Old Order Changes* II. 256 He could not..keep a slight frost from his manner. **1891** S. J. DUNCAN *Amer. Girl Lond.* 196 There's a frost on—we don't play with each other any more.

c. *Sc.* (See quot. 1825–80.)

a **1757** *Gil Morrice* x. in Child *Ballads* IV. lxxxiii. (1886) 272 Sen ye by me will nae be warnd, In it ye sall find frost. **1825–80** JAMIESON, *Frost*, difficulty; *to fin' frost*, to meet with difficulties, Banffs.

4. *slang* (originally *Theatr.*). A failure.

1886 *Stage Gossip* 70 When a piece 'goes' badly, it is called, a 'frost'. **1891** I. ZANGWILL *Bachelors' Club* 209 This last book..is a regular frost. **1896** *Q. Rev.* Oct. 538 The Randt mines would, in mining phrase, 'turn out a frost'.

†**5. a.** A colour like that of hoarfrost; silver-grey. **b.** Gold or silver frost-work; cf. *frost-button*. *Obs.*

1657 R. LIGON *Barbadoes* (1673) 83 The colour for the most part, frost upon green. 1702 *Lond. Gaz.* No. 3810/8 All Gold and Silver Plate shall be spun close on well boiled and light died Silk only, (Frost excepted).

†**6.** ? = CALK *sb.*[1] 2. *Obs.*

1718 S. SEWALL *Diary* 19 Jan. (1882) III. 161 Great Rain, and very Slippery: was fain to wear Frosts. *Ibid.* 5 Feb. III. 165 Had like to have fallen grievously, by reason of my Frosts, on the Steps in the night. (*Note*, Probably the caulks or mocassins of those days, which were in use till quite recently by aged people.)

7. *attrib.* and *Comb.* **a.** simple attrib., as ***frost-diamond, -giant, -mark, -power, -scene, -time, -wind, -wound, -wreath***; also ***frost-free, -like, -proof*** adjs.

1868 LD. HOUGHTON *Select. fr. Wks.* 215 *Frost-diamonds twinkle on the grass. 1926 *Nat. Geogr. Mag.* May 513/1 (*heading*) Over mountain roads to a *frostfree thermal belt. 1946 *Nature* 20 July 78/1 Most suitable frost-free sites are gentle slopes. 1889 R. B. ANDERSON tr. *Rydberg's Teut. Mythol.* 134 Thor, the divine foe of the *frost-giants. 1832 TENNYSON *Palace Art* xiii, From shadow'd grots of arches interlaced, And tipt with *frost-like spires. 1856 KANE *Arct. Expl.* II. xix. 193 Not an icicle or even a *frost-mark was to be seen on the roof. 1889 R. B. ANDERSON tr. *Rydberg's Teut. Mythol.* 138 The *frost-powers led by Thjasse's kinsmen. 1896 T. W. SANDERS *Encycl. Gardening* (ed. 2) 1 Lift tubers ..& store in *frost-proof place. 1960 *Farmer & Stockbreeder* 23 Feb. 72/2 The store was made frost-proof by lining the inner wall with glass-fibre. 1709 STEELE *Tatler* No. 182 ¶1 We shall not shortly have so much as a Landskip or *Frost-Scene to refresh ourselves. 1387 TREVISA *Higden* (Rolls) IV. 467 Longe aftirward, in frosty time [*v.r.* *frost tyme], Iulian was wery, and reste hym aboute mydnyȝt. 1818 SCOTT *Rob Roy* xxxiii, A sharp *frost-wind, which made itself heard and felt from time to time. 1820 KEATS *St. Agnes* xxxvi, The frost-wind blows. 1856 KANE *Arct. Expl.* II. iii. 45 One [suffering] from *frost-wounds. 1872 BRYANT *Little People of Snow* 349 Around that little grave, in the long night, *Frost-wreaths were laid.

b. instrumental, as ***frost-beaded, -bound, -burnt, -chequered, -concocted. -congealed, -fettered, -firmed, -kibed, -rent, -riven, -tempered*** adjs.

1842 FABER *Styrian Lake, etc.* 122 The white *frost-beaded grass. 1785 COWPER *Task* v. 155 Materials..*frost-bound Firm as a rock. 1848 KINGSLEY *Saint's Trag.* IV. i, I came..Among the Alps, all through one frost-bound dawn. 1770 ARMSTRONG *Misc.* I. 152 Whipping the *frost-burnt villagers to the bones. *a* 1847 ELIZA COOK *To the Robin* vii, The *frost-chequer'd pane. 1726-46 THOMSON *Winter* 707 The *frost-concocted glebe Draws in abundant vegetable soul. 1877 LONGF. *Wapentake*, Voiceless as a rivulet *frost-congealed. 1811 E. LYSAGHT *Poems* 1 The *frost-fettered rivers no longer can flow. 1591 SYLVESTER *Du Bartas* I. v. 875 For when her Troops of wandring Cranes forsake *Frost-firmèd Strymon. 1848 KINGSLEY *Saint's Trag.* I. iii, Proud of your *frost-kibed feet, and dirty serge. 1806 J. GRAHAME *Birds Scotl.* 84 A *frost-rent fragment. 1873 J. GEIKIE *Gt. Ice Age* v. 58 A heap of *frost-riven débris. 1856 KANE *Arct. Expl.* II. i. 16 My thoughts recal the *frost-tempered junks of this pachydermoid amphibion.

c. Special comb.: **frost-bearer** = CRYOPHORUS; **frost-bird** (see quot.); **frost-blite**, the plant *Chenopodium album* (see quot.); **frost blue** (see quot.); **frost-bow** (see quot.); †**frost-brained** *a.*, dull, stupid; **frost-button**, a button with a frosted surface; **frost-cog** (see quot.); **frost-crack**, a vertical split in a tree-trunk caused by the stress created as the wood freezes; **frost-dew**, hoar-frost, rime; **frost-fall** (see quot.); **frost-fern**, a fern-like figure produced by the freezing of a moist surface; **frost-fish**, (*a*) the Tomcod, *Microgadus tomcodus*, so called from its appearing on the coast of N. America as the frost sets in; (*b*) the scabbard-fish, *Lepidopus caudatus*; **frost-fix** *v.*, to fix with frost; **frost-flower**, an ice-crystal resembling a flower; **frost-fog** = *frost-mist*; **frost-grape**, an American species of the vine *Vitis cordifolia* or *riparia*; **frost-heave, -heaving**, uplift of soil surface caused by expansion of water beneath the surface on freezing; so **frost-heaved** *a.*; **frost-hoar** *a.*, covered with hoar frost; **frost-hollow** (see quots.); **frost-itch, -lamp** (see quots.); **frost-line** (after *snow-line*), the limit of frost; **frost-mist**, mist caused by the freezing of vapour in the atmosphere; **frost-nail** *sb.*, a nail driven into the shoe to prevent slipping in frosty weather; so **frost-nail** *v.*, to put frost-nails in the shoes; **frost-piece**, a person of cold behaviour or disposition; **frost pocket**, a small low-lying area affected by frost (cf. POCKET *sb.* 8 c); **frost-rime** = *frost-smoke*; **frost-ring**, a ring-shaped zone of tissue damaged by frost in the trunk of a tree; **frost-root**, the common fleabane of the U.S., *Erigeron philadelphicus* (*Cent. Dict.*); **frost-shod** *pple.*, shod with frost-nails; also *fig.*; **frost-smoke** (see quot. 1867); **frost-split** (see quot.); **frost-stud** = *frost-nail* sb.; **frost-thrust** *Geol.*, (*a*) *sb.* = *frost-thrusting*; (*b*) *adj.*, that results from or has been subjected to frost-thrusting; **frost-thrusting** *Geol.*, movement of soil during freezing, often with consequent lateral or vertical movement of partly buried rocks; **frost-valve** (see quot.); **frost-weed, -wort**, the plant *Helianthemum canadense*, sometimes used as an astringent or aromatic tonic; so called because, late in autumn, crystals of ice shoot from the cracked bark at the root (W.). Also FROST-BITE, -BITTEN, FROST-NIP, -NIPPED, FROST-WORK.

1826 *Frost-bearer [see CRYOPHORUS]. 1848 H. W. HERBERT *Field Sports in U.S.* II. 58 The American Golden Plover..is better known to our gunners by the name of *'Frost Bird', so called from being more plentiful during the early frosts in autumn. 1835 BOOTH *Analyt. Dict.*, **Frost-blite.* 1863 PRIOR *Plant-n.*, *Frost-blite*, a blite whitened as by hoar-frost, *Chenopodium album.* 1873 *Weale's Dict. Arch.* (ed. 4), **Frost blue*, a coarse variety of smalt. 1863 *Home Walks* 20 A *frostbow appeared, resembling in all respects a rainbow, except that it was of a lustrous white. 1592 *Nobody & Someb.* in Simpson *Sch. Shaks.* (1878) I. 300 But he, *frost-braind, will not be obtaind To take upon him this Realmes government. 1686 *Lond. Gaz.* No. 2192/4 A good cloth Coat..trim'd with a silver and silk *frost Button. 1711 *Ibid.* No. 4912/4 A dark Grey Suit of Cloaths, trim'd with Gold Frost Buttons. 1884 KNIGHT *Dict. Mech.* IV. 358/2 **Frost Cog*, a toe or projection on a horse shoe to keep the animal from slipping. 1894 T. LASLETT *Timber & Timber Trees* (ed. 2) iv. 61 An expansion may result at a certain stage of the freezing of the inner woody cylinder, and the consequence is a *frost-crack. 1960 KRAMER & KOZLOWSKI *Physiol. Trees* xvi. 490 Frost cracks are more common in forest trees than in orchard trees. 1826 SCOTT *Woodst.* xxviii, My pumps are full of this *frost-dew. 1879 MISS BIRD *Rocky Mount.* I. 295 That curious phenomena [*sic*] called *frost-fall..in which, whatever moisture may exist in the air, somehow aggregates into feathers and fern-leaves. 1871 TYNDALL *Fragm. Sc.* (1879) II. xiv. 358 When it [water] runs into *frost-ferns upon a window pane. 1634 W. WOOD *New Eng. Prosp.* (1865) 36 Th' *Frost fish and the Smelt. 1795 J. SULLIVAN *Hist. Maine* 21 The people have tom cod, or what they call frost fish..in great plenty. 1880 GÜNTHER *Introd. Study Fishes* 435 The Scabbard-fish (*Lepidopus caudatus*) is well known in New Zealand, where it is called 'Frost-fish'. 1890 J. HABBERTON *Out at Twinnetts* 50 A string of frost-fish in one hand, and a lighted pipe in the other. 1800 HURDIS *Fav. Village* I. 15 When did the God.. Congeal and *frost-fix your [mountain's] prodigious limbs. 1847 C. BRONTË *J. Eyre* I. iv. 47, I fell to breathing on the *frost-flowers with which the window was fretted. 1923 E. SITWELL *Bucolic Comedies* 78 The frost-flowers upon the window-panes. 1813 SCOTT *Trierm.* I. iii, The sun was struggling with *frost-fog grey. 1789 *Trans. Amer. Philos. Soc.* I. 261 The *frost or winter grape is known to every body. 1859 BARTLETT *Dict. Amer.*, *Chicken Grape*, the River Grape, or *Vitis riparia*; also called *Frost Grape.* 1946 *Amer. Jrnl. Sci.* CCXLIV. 623 Thus the general use by geologists of..'*frost-heave' and '*frost-heaved' is not completely supported by dictionary definitions. 1957 J. K. CHARLESWORTH *Quaternary Era* I. xxvii. 567 Geologically, it [*sc.* permafrost] is most important in giving rise to frost thrust..and frost heave. 1967 F. A. COOK in Hamelin & Cook *Illustr. Gloss. Periglacial Phenomena* ix. 193 Frost-heaved congelifracts, involutions and injection plugs. 1929 *Jrnl. Geol.* XXXVII. 430 The maximum amount of *frost heaving that occurs during cold winters..is not known. 1930 *Ibid.* XXXVIII. 303 (*title*) The mechanics of frost heaving. 1853 C. BRONTË *Villette* iv, The ice-bound waters and *frost-hoar fields. 1895 W. R. FISHER *Schlich's Man. Forestry* IV. iv. 431 Damp, low-lying places with stagnating air..termed *frost-hollows. 1953 H. L. EDLIN *Forester's Handbk.* v. 75 Valley bottoms and slight depressions of the ground in which cold air collects on still, cloudless nights..are known as frost-hollows. 1894 DUANE *Student's Dict. Med.*, *Pruritus hiemalis*, winter itch, *frost-itch. 1874 KNIGHT *Dict. Mech.* I. 918/2 **Frost-lamp*, an oil-lamp placed beneath the oil-tube of an Argand lamp to keep the oil in a flowing condition. 1865 WHITTIER *Snow-Bound* 160 While the red logs before us beat The *frost-line back with tropic heat. 1814 SCOTT *Wav.* xlvi, A *frost-mist rising from the ocean, covered the eastern horizon. 1611 COTGR., *Ferré a glace*, shod with *frost-nayles. 1874 KNIGHT *Dict. Mech.* I. 918/2 *Frost-nail*, a roughing nail driven into a horse's shoe in slippery weather. 1594 PLAT *Jewell-ho.* II. 26 If I slip, you shall see how I will *frostnayle my selfe the nexte time that I ride abroade. 1673 *Lond. Gaz.* No. 753/3 His Highness hath caused all the Horse of his Guard to be Frost-nailed. 1748 RICHARDSON *Clarissa* xxxi, The little hold I have in the heart of this charming *frost-piece. 1828 SCOTT *F.M. Perth* xxxi, Away, villain, and marshal in this fair frost-piece. 1931 *Forestry* V. 118 The leaders of Norway Spruce in small low-lying areas, '*frost pockets', are killed back. 1932 FULLER & CONARD tr. *Braun-Blanquet's Plant Sociol.* v. 86 The frost pockets (*Frostlöcher*) of the southwestern Swiss Jura are well known and shunned. 1968 R. AMBERLEY *Incitement to Murder* ii. 29 Is the more exposed land, farther down..also yours?.. There is a frost pocket there, no doubt. 1820 SCORESBY *Acc. Arctic Reg.* I. 434 *Frost-rime or frost-smoke..consists of a dense frozen vapour, apparently arising out of the sea or any large sheet of water. 1929 T. THOMSON tr. *Büsgen's Struct. & Life Forest Trees* v. 146 The *frost rings did not extend beyond the fourth year. 1960 KRAMER & KOZLOWSKI *Physiol. Trees* ii. 16 Frost rings are most often found near the center of a tree because young shoots are more susceptible to frost injury than are old stems. 1603 FLORIO *Montaigne* II. xiii. 354 To say truth, it [self murder] is a meate a man must swallow without chewing, vnlesse his throate be *frost-shod [Fr. *ferré à glace*]. 1765 SMOLLETT *Trav.* xxxviii. (1766) II. 216 The mules..were frost-shod for the occasion. 1774 GOLDSM. *Nat. Hist.* (1862) I. xxi. 136 In those forlorn regions round the poles..the sea smokes like an oven, and a fog arises which mariners call the *frost smoke. 1867 SMYTH *Sailor's Word-bk.*, *Frost-smoke*, a thick mist in high latitudes, arising from the surface of the sea when exposed to a temperature much below freezing; when the vapours as they rise are condensed either into a thick fog, or, with the thermometer about zero, hug the water in eddying white wreaths. 1753 CHAMBERS *Cycl. Supp.*, **Frost split*, a phrase used by our farmers to express such trees as have large cracks in their trunks and branches. 1895 *Times* 21 Jan. 13/6 The sudden change in the weather has checked the demand for skates, *frost studs, and heating apparatus. 1946 K. BRYAN in *Amer. Jrnl. Sci.* CCXLIV. 625 There is no common expression for the lateral thrust resulting from expansion although horizontal as contrasted with vertical *frost-thrust would sufficiently carry the meaning. 1951 [see *frost-thrusting*]. 1957 [see *frost-heave*]. 1951 *Jrnl. Geol.* LIX. 65 The writer has found no terms descriptive of these particular phenomena. Consequently the following terminology is used: **Frost-thrusting* is used for the process whereby large blocks of rock have been raised, commonly vertically, or have changed position with respect to the rest of the outcrop, owing to the frost action. *Frost-thrust blocks* refers to the blocks of rock which have been moved by frost-thrusting. 1954 *Amer. Jrnl. Sci.* CCLII. 55 From their structures we conclude that frost thrusting—lateral soil movement during freezing—plays a major role in their development. 1884 KNIGHT *Dict. Mech.* IV. 358/2 **Frost Valve*, a valve which opens to allow water to escape from the portion of the pipe or pump where it is liable to be frozen. 1866 *Treas. Bot.*, **Frost-weed, Helianthemum canadense.* 1859 BARTLETT *Dict. Amer.*, **Frostwort* (*Cistus canadensis*), a medicinal plant prepared by the Shakers, and used for its astringent and tonic properties.

frost (frɒst, -ɔː-), *v.* [f. prec. sb.]

1. *trans.* To freeze, frost-bite, nip with frost. *to frost off*: to cause to drop off with frost. Chiefly *fig.*

1807 [see FROSTED 1]. 1818 KEATS *Endym.* III. 188 At this, a surprised start Frosted the springing verdure of his heart. 1871 BLACKIE *Four Phases* i. 49 Individuals whose social sympathies have been frosted in early life. 1884 TENNYSON *Becket* I. iv, The golden leaves, these earls and barons, that clung to me, frosted off me by the first cold frown of the King. 1887 *S. Chesh. Gloss.*, *Frost*, to spoil by the frost, of potatoes.

2. To cover with or as with rime; also with *over*. Chiefly *fig.*

1635 J. HAYWARD tr. *Biondi's Banish'd Virg.* 153 Such beauties as Aurora takes oft-times pleasure, in first frosting over with her canded dewes. 1787-9 WORDSW. *Evening Walk*, The rising moon, While with a hoary light she frosts the ground. 1791 E. DARWIN *Bot. Gard.* I. 73 Nitre..frosts with branching plumes the mouldering walls. 1861 *Times* 22 Oct., These camps increase in number and in size till the white canvass frosts every knoll. 1890 C. DIXON *Stray Feathers* ii. 26 He frosts the feathers of some with gold and silver.

3. To give a frosted surface to (glass or metal); to make (glass) to resemble ice.

1832 [see FROSTING 1]. 1849 [see FROSTED 5 b].

4. To treat (a horse's shoes) by the insertion of frost-nails, roughing, etc., as a protection against slipping in frosty weather; to shoe (a horse) in this way.

1572 in Gage *Hist. Hengrave* (1822) 192 For frosting the cart-horses at Thetford..vd. 1665 PEPYS *Diary* 26 Nov., I ..set out, after my horses' being frosted, which I know not what it means to this day. 1752 J. MACSPARRAN *America Dissected* (1753) 39 With a Horse well caulk'd and frosted, 'tis fine Travelling. 1831 SIR J. SINCLAIR *Corr.* II. 189, I could not get the shoes of my horses frosted. 1877 *N.W. Linc. Gloss.*, *Frost*, to turn up the hinder part of a horse's shoes, or to put frost-nails in them to hinder the animal from slipping on ice.

'frost-,bit, *pple.* and *ppl. a. rare.* = FROST-BITTEN.

1749 F. SMITH *Voy. Disc.* II. 13 The Weather was so sharp as several of the People were Frost-bit. 1851 D. JERROLD *St. Giles* i. 7 There's some poor devil outside that's frost-bit and going to die.

fig. 1823 BYRON *Age Bronze* x, A Calmuck beauty with a Cossack wit, And generous Spirit, when 't is not frost-bit.

'frost-,bite, *sb.* 'The inflamed or gangrenous condition of the skin and adjacent parts produced by exposure to severe cold. The milder forms constitute chilblain; the severe form, or gangrene, may be either dry or moist, usually the latter' (*Syd. Soc. Lex.* 1885).

1813 J. THOMSON *Lect. Inflam.* 57 Inflammation accompanying the state which is usually denominated frost-bite. 1823 SCORESBY *Jrnl. Whale Fishery* 44 Some of the sailors suffered considerably from partial frost-bites. 1876 A. ARNOLD in *Contemp. Rev.* June 42 One does not look for frostbite in Ispahan.

'frost-,bite, *v.* Also 7 **frost-bit**. *trans.* †To injure with intense cold, also *fig.*; to invigorate by exposure to the frost (*obs.*); to get (oneself or one's limbs) frost-bitten.

1611 *Coryat's Crudities* Panegyr. Verses G iij b, Emilia faire thou didst frost-bit, And shee inflamed thy melting wit. 1667 PEPYS *Diary* 2 Jan., My wife up, and with Mrs. Pen to walk in the fields to frost-bite themselves. 1856 KANE *Arct. Expl.* I. xxix. 403 Morton has frost-bitten both his heels.

b. *fig.* To whiten.

a 1618 J. DAVIES *Wittes Pilgrim.* xcvii. Wks. (Grosart) 19 Many winters haue Frost-bit my Haires.

So **frost-biting** *vbl. sb.*; **frost-biting** *ppl. a.*, intensely cold. *lit.* and *fig.*

1593 *Tell-Troth's N.Y. Gift* 23 His frost-biting words should nippe her. 1633 EARL MANCH. *Al Mondo* (1636) 28 The graine cast into the earth, after a frost-biting, comes up the fairer. 1635 L. FOXE *N.W. Foxe* 171 Such as had been upon those Frost-biting voyages. 1711 SWIFT *Lett.* (1767) III. 243 Pray walk when the frost comes, young ladies, go a frost-biting. 1817-8 COBBETT *Resid. U.S.* (1822) 202 If the cold be such as to produce danger of frost-biting, you must take care not to drink strong liquors. 1895 C. MARKHAM in *Westm. Gaz.* 5 Sept. 7/1 The only effect of this was to stop the circulation and make frost-biting all the easier.

'frost-,bitten, *pple.* and *ppl. a.* Injured by exposure to frost.

1593 NASHE *Christ's T.* Wks. (Grosart) IV. 181 Farre poorer then poore frost bitten Snakes. 1594 —— *Terrors of Night* Ibid. III. 267 [He] like a lanke frost-bitten plant looseth hys vigor. 1665 PEPYS *Diary* 21 Dec., A good chine of beef..being all frost bitten, was most of it unroast. **1669** WORLIDGE *Syst. Agric.* (1681) 93 The Leaves also gathered ..somewhat before they are much frost-bitten. **1824** W. IRVING *T. Trav.* I. 250 Some fruits become mellower..from having been bruised and frost-bitten. **1865** DICKENS *Lett.* 1 Mar. (1880) II. 226, I have been laid up here with a frost-bitten foot.

fig. **1622** MABBE tr. *Aleman's Guzman d'Alf.* II. 34 The Captaine, when hee heard me say so, was frost-bitten. **1634** FORD *P. Warbeck* IV. v, Lady, I return But barren crops of early protestations, Frost-bitten in the spring of fruitless hopes. **1891** C. JAMES *Rom. Rigmarole* 60 'She's 'ad what I may call a frost-bitten life of it.'

b. ***frost-bitten asphyxy*** (see quot.).

1822-34 *Good's Study Med.* (ed. 4) III. 435 Frost-bitten Asphyxy, or that produced by intense cold.

frosted ('frɒstɪd, -ɔː-), *ppl. a.* [f. FROST *sb.* and *v.* + -ED.]

1. Injured by frost, frozen, frost-bitten.

1807 WILKINSON in Pike *Sources Mississ.* (1810) II. App. 29 Two more of my men got badly frosted. **1871** BLACKIE *Four Phases* i. 13 Socrates..trod the frosted ground with his bare feet. **1884** ROE *Nat. Ser. Story* ii, Why does sudden heat..destroy a frosted plant? **1892** *Times* (weekly ed.) 2 Feb. 89/3 Slightly frosted wheat is reduced for flour making purposes perhaps 30 per cent. in value, what is called frozen wheat 50 per cent.

2. Covered (*over*) with rime or hoar-frost.

1720 GAY *Poems* (1745) I. 164 Hoary Thames with frosted oziers crownd. **1842** MOTLEY *Corr.* (1889) I. iv. 115 The trees were frosted all over with silver. **1858** HAWTHORNE *Fr. & It. Jrnls.* (1872) I. 9 The windows were already frosted with French breath. **1873** SYMONDS *Grk. Poets* x. 313 Tall tree-heaths that wave their frosted boughs above your head.

fig. **1847-8** H. MILLER *First Impr.* ii. 25 Picturesque incidents..frosted over with the romance of history.

3. Covered with a fine powder or coating resembling rime. Also with *over*. ***frosted cake***: cake covered with concreted sugar or 'icing'.

1698 FRYER *Acc. E. India & P.* 318 Entering upon the Plains..we found it all frosted with Salt. **1734** FIELDING *Old Man taught Wisdom* Wks. 1874 III. 122 His head is..done all down upon the top with sugar, like a frosted cake. **1796** KIRWAN *Elem. Min.* (ed. 2) I. 128 Its [Fluor's] surface mostly smooth, and frosted over with minute crystals. **1856** EMERSON *Eng. Traits, Lit.* Wks. (Bohn) II. 114 Pope and his school wrote poetry fit to put round a frosted cake. **1887** *Lady* 20 Jan. 37/1 The younger [lady] was attired in frosted tulle and snowdrops.

b. *spec.* in *Zool.* and *Bot.* Covered with glistening particles, silvery hairs or scales, etc.

1796 WITHERING *Brit. Plants* (ed. 3) IV. 279 Pileus.. when fresh gathered, beautifully frosted over with distinct globular pellucid particles. **1829** LOUDON *Plants* 1099 *Frosted*, covered with glittering particles, as if fine dew had been congealed upon it. **1861** MISS PRATT *Flower. Pl.* IV. 279 Frosted Sea Orache.

c. Of the hair: Hoary, white.

1645 G. DANIEL *Poems* Wks. 1878 II. 64 'Twould trouble me, when I, with frosted hairs, Should look at what I was. *a* **1717** PARNELL *Gift of Poetry* Poet. Wks. (1758) 35 Helpless Age with hoary frosted head.

4. Of glass, silver, etc.: Having a surface roughened or finely granulated so as to resemble a coating of hoar-frost.

1689 *Lond. Gaz.* No. 2429/4 The 5th had a Silver Box and pinn'd Case, long Hours of the Dial Plate, and Frosted. **1711** *Ibid.* No. 4916/4 A..Cloth Suit trim'd with frosted Buttons. **1793** SMEATON *Edystone L.* §211 Being of a dead frosted surface on breaking. **1825** T. COSNETT *Footman's Directory* 31 The parts [of silver salvers, etc.] which are rough, or what is called frosted. **1852** R. S. SURTEES *Sponge's Sp. Tour* (1893) 156 A large jug..between two frosted tumblers. **1883** *Hardwick's Photogr. Chem.* (ed. Taylor) 123 The Salts of Iron..produce a sparkling precipitate, resembling what is termed frosted silver. **1889** *Times* (weekly ed.) 20 Dec. 7/4 This office had frosted glass windows.

5. Made to resemble rough ice: **a.** *Arch.* Resembling a cluster of icicles or ice formed by irregular drops of water.

1790 W. WRIGHTE *Grotesque Archit.* 7 The arcades to be ice or frosted work. **1859** GWILT *Archit.* Gloss., *Frosted*, a species of rustic-work, imitative of ice formed by irregular drops of water. **1868** G. STEPHENS *Runic Mon.* II. 507 The single lines slightly roped or twisted or frosted, or whatever we may call it.

b. ***frosted glass***: a kind of Venetian glass (see quot.).

1849 A. PELLATT *Curios. Glass-making* 116 Frosted glass ..has irregularly veined, marble-like projecting dislocations, with intervening fissures. *Ibid.* 139 Fig. 2 Ancient Venetian frosted vase..The satyr heads have been impressed..after the vase was frosted. The frosting manipulation and the Vitro di Trino are explained at pages 113 and 114.

frostify ('frɒstɪfaɪ, -ɔː-), *v.* [f. FROST *sb.* + -(I)FY.] *intr.* To become frosty. Implied in ˌ**frostifi'cation**, *jocular*, the process of becoming frosty; '**frostified** *ppl. a.*, *dial.*, frosty.

1831 J. WILSON in *Blackw. Mag.* XXX. 543 A certain frostification in progress among most elaborately tended whiskers. **1854** MISS BAKER *Northhants. Gloss.*, *Frostified*.

frosting ('frɒstɪŋ, -ɔː-), *vbl. sb.* [f. FROST *v.*]

1. The action of the vb. FROST; exposure to the influence of frost or frosty air (gerundially † *a* or †*on frosting*).

1617 BP. HALL *Quo Vadis?* §3 Fond mothers vse to send forth their daughters on frosting, early in cold mornings. **1647** TRAPP *Comm. Heb.* xii. 10 Aloes kils worms, and stained clothes are whitened by frosting. **1667** PRIMATT *City & C. Build.* 51 Mould that was digged up in the winter, and laid a frosting. **1832** G. R. PORTER *Porcelain & Gl.* 310 The grinding of glass, or frosting it, in order to lessen its transparency. **1849** [see FROSTED 5 b].

2. *concr.* **a.** A substance powdered to resemble frost and used for 'frosting' purposes; *esp.* pulverized white sugar used for 'icing' cake. **b.** A 'frosted' surface: see quot. 1892.

1756 C. LUCAS *Ess. Waters* III. 64 A kind of stoney concrete..like a sort of frosting. **1858** SIMMONDS *Dict. Trade, Frosting*, loaf-sugar prepared to coat plum cakes with. **1892** F. J. BRITTEN *Watch & Clockm.* (ed. 8), *Frosting*, (1) the grey surface produced on steel work for watches, etc.; (2) the granular or 'matted' surface given to brass pieces prior to gilding. **1894** *Times* 16 Aug. 6/2 Lakes, crayons, smalts and frostings.

frostless ('frɒstlɪs, -ɔː-), *a.* [f. FROST *sb.* + -LESS.] Without frost.

1711 SWIFT *Jrnl. to Stella* 14 Jan., Did you ever see such a frostless winter? **1851** *Jrnl. R. Agric. Soc.* XII. II. 358 A wet or frostless winter.

frostling. *Building.* (See quot.)

1823 P. NICHOLSON *Pract. Build.* vii. 337 It is this crystallization which is observed by the workmen when a heap of lime is mixed with water, and left for some time to macerate. A hard crust is formed upon the surface, which is ignorantly called *frostling*, though it takes place in summer as well as in winter.

'**frost-**ˌ**nip**, *sb. rare*⁻¹. = FROST-BITE *sb.*

1869 BLACKMORE *Lorna D.* xli, Two of his toes had been lost by frost-nip.

'**frost-**ˌ**nip**, *v. rare*⁻¹. *trans.* To nip or injure with frost. Cf. FROST-BITE *v.*

1642 FULLER *Holy & Prof. St.* IV. i. 241 They..will not so much as frostnip their souls with a cold thought of want hereafter.

'**frost-**ˌ**nipped**, *pple.* and *ppl. a.* = FROST-BITTEN.

1773 *Phil. Trans.* LXIII. 129 Its other branches were.. frost-nipt. **1796** *Campaigns 1793-4* II. 122 A pair of naked frost-nipt legs. **1817** SCOTT *Harold* II. ii, Frost-nipt leaves. **1886** HALL CAINE *Son of Hagar* II. xiv, Sheep were bleating high up on the frost-nipped side of the fell.

fig. **1684** Z. CAWDREY *Certainty Salvat.* 28 The first warm ..Spring-beam to the Frost-nipt Loyalty of the Nation. **1695** CONGREVE *Love for L.* IV. xv, Honesty will go as it did, frost-nipped in a summer suit. **1797** M. ROBINSON *Walsingham* II. 219 Its expanding wings had been frost-nipped by disappointment.

frost-work.

1. Work produced by frost; *esp.* the delicate tracery formed on the surface of glass, etc. by frost.

1729 SAVAGE *Wanderer* III. 65 In Frost-work now delight the sportive kind [Fairies]. **1827** *Gentl. Mag.* XCVII. II. 483, I peeped through the chamber window externally beautified by the glittering frost-work. **1862** M'COSH *Supernat.* II. i. §4. 153 The frostworks on our flag-stones, and windows, so like the tree in their ramifications.

fig. **1792** S. ROGERS *Pleas. Mem.* II. 438 Lo, Fancy's fairy frost-work melts away. **1853** C. BRONTE *Villette* xix. 188 These few warm words..breathed on that frail frost-work of reserve.

attrib. **1822** SHELLEY *Hellas* 416 Ye who strike To dust the citadels of sanguine kings..And thaw their frostwork diadems like dew. **1832** J. BREE *St. Herbert's Isle* 4 The frost-work palace of an April night.

2. Ornamentation in imitation of this.

1648 E. SPARKE in *J. Shute's Sarah & Hagar* (1649) Pref. b 1 a, Many others set but their slight Frost-works upon Sattin. **1664** POWER *Exp. Philos.* I. 7 Her body looks like Silver in Frost-work. **1872** RUSKIN *Eagle's Nest* §174 The feathers like frost-work of silver.

attrib. **1703** MOXON *Mech. Exerc.* 59 Like frost work Silver.

Hence '**frost-worked** *ppl. a.*, ornamented with frost-work, frosted.

1710 *Lond. Gaz.* No. 4748/4 A small silver Milk Pot frost worked.

frosty ('frɒstɪ, -ɔː-), *a.* [f. FROST *sb.* + -Y[1]; OE. had the equivalent *fyrstiȝ*; cf. Du. *vorstig*, OHG. *frostag* (MHG. *vrostec, -ic*, mod.Ger. *frostig*).]

1. Affected with or characterized by frost; reduced to a temperature at or below freezing-point; ice-cold.

c **900** tr. *Bæda's Hist.* III. xiv. [xix.] (1890) 217, & se winter wære grim & cald & fyrstig. *c* **1374** CHAUCER *Anel. & Arc.* 2 In the frosty contrey called Trace. *c* **1400** *Lanfranc's Cirurg.* 79 Whanne a bodi breþiþ wiþ þe mouþ in frosty wedir..þou myȝt se þe breeþ. **1557** *Tottel's Misc.* (Arb.) 171 The sparrow in the frosty nyght, May shroude her in the eaues. **1626** BACON *Sylva* §231 In Frosty weather, Musick within doors soundeth better. **1710** SWIFT *Lett.* (1767) III. 45 It has been fair two or three days, and is this day grown cold and frosty. **1765** AKENSIDE *Pleas. Imag.* II. 339 The frosty moon Glittering on some smooth sea. **1860** TYNDALL *Glac.* II. v. 251 If the winter set in with clear frosty weather. **1864** TENNYSON *Boädicea* 75 The noise of frosty woodlands, when they shiver in January.

†**b.** Belonging to the winter-season. *Obs.*

c **1381** CHAUCER *Parl. Foules* 364 The throstel old; the frosty feldefare.

2. *transf.* and *fig.* Cold as frost; chilling; without ardour or warmth of feeling, frigid.

c **1385** CHAUCER *L.G.W.* 173 *Thisbe*, How kysseth she his frosty mouthe so colde? **1592** SHAKS. *Ven. & Ad.* 36 She red and hot..He red for shame, but frosty in desire. **1599** B. JONSON *Ev. Man out of Hum.* Dram. Pers., *Asper*..One whom no..frosty apprehension of danger, can make to be a parasite. **1605** *Tryall Chev.* II. iii. in Bullen *O. Pl.* III. 295 Her father..is frosty in my fervent suite. **1726** *Adv. Capt. R. Boyle* 83 Death still bore to me a frosty Sound. **1833** CARLYLE in Froude *Carlyle* (1882) II. xvi. 381 He [Jeffrey] now writes to Jane in the frostiest..manner. **1871** PALGRAVE *Lyr. Poems* 77 Fenced from the frosty gales of ill.

3. Covered with or consisting of hoar-frost.

1577 B. GOOGE *Heresbach's Husb.* III. (1586) 141 The frostye Grasse..fils their bellies full of water. *c* **1586** C'TESS PEMBROKE *Ps.* LXXIV. xvi, The winters frosty gowne. **1856** KANE *Arct. Expl.* I. xxxi. 424 The dormitory decked itself on the instant with a frosty forest of feathers [when the cold outside air was let in].

4. Having the appearance of being covered with frost. **a.** Of the hair: Hoary, white.

14.. *Circumcision* in *Tundale's Vis.* 85 Janus bifrons.. With frosty berd. **1579** E. K. in *Spenser's Sheph. Cal.* Feb. Embleme, So the old man checketh the rash-headed boy for despysing his gray and frostye heares. **1625** HART *Anat. Ur.* II. ix. 117 Where was old frostie father gray-beard (Saturne I meane)? **1794** BURNS *John Anderson my Jo*, Your locks are like the snaw; But blessings on your frosty pow, John Anderson my jo.

b. Hence, Characteristic of old age.

1588 SHAKS. *Tit. A.* v. iii. 77 If my frostie signes and chaps of age..Cannot induce you to attend my words. **1863** HAWTHORNE *Our old Home* 257 That dreary picture of Lear, an explosion of frosty fury.

c. *spec.* in *Entom.* Of a glistening white colour. Also ***frosty white***.

1698 J. PETIVER in *Phil. Trans.* XX. 396 The Sides are grey or frosty. **18..** PACKARD (Cent.), When seen laterally the surface appears frosty white.

5. *Comb.* **a.** adverbial, as †***frosty cold***; **b.** parasynthetic, as ***frosty-natured***, ***-spirited***, ***-whiskered***; **frosty-face** *slang* (see quot. 1785); also *attrib.*

1413 *Pilgr. Sowle* (Caxton 1483) IV. xx. 67 Now thou art *frosty cold, now fyry hote. **1753** A. MURPHY *Gray's-Inn Jrnl.* No. 48 ⁋11 My Friend's Wife damned ugly in a Morning—A *frosty Face Devil. **1785** GROSE *Dict. Vulgar Tongue, Frosty face*, one pitted with the small pox. **1618** DEKKER *Owles Almanacke*, Men are so *frosty natur'd. **1596** SHAKS. *1 Hen. IV*, II. iii. 21 What a *Frosty-spirited rogue is this? **1852** R. S. SURTEES *Sponge's Sp. Tour* (1893) 35 His old brandy-nosed, *frosty-whiskered trumpeter of a groom.

Hence '**frostily** *adv.*, '**frostiness**. Also †'**frosty** *v.*, to make to look frosty, cover with ice.

1596 LODGE *Marg. Amer.* C ij, But when againe her morrow-gathered Ice The morne displaies, and frostieth drouping leaues. **1616** B. JONSON *Epigr.* lii, I rather thou should'st utterly Dispraise my work, than praise it frostily. **1720** WELTON *Suffer. Son of God* I. vi. 118 The Pinching Cold and Frostiness of the Night! **1830** E. B. PUSEY *Hist. Enquiry* II. 239 The iciness of the state, the chillness of letters, the frostiness of the people. **1851** HAWTHORNE *Snow Image, etc.* (1879) 31 The stars glimmering frostily. **1859** *Life E. Henderson* vi. 392 Volumes chargeable with somewhat of frostiness. **1885** *Harper's Mag.* Mar. 593/1 Her mother met them frostily.

frot (frɒt), *v.* Forms: 4-7 frote, (4 froote, *Sc.* froit), 6-7 frott(e, 7 froat(e, 4- frot; *pa. pple.* 4 ifroted, 5 yfrote. [a. OF. *froter* (mod.Fr. *frotter*), of unknown origin.]

†**1.** *trans.* To rub, chafe; *spec.* to polish (a precious stone); to rub (a garment) with perfumes; in early use, to stroke, caress (an animal). *Obs.*

a **1225** [see FROTTING *vbl. sb.*]. *c* **1320** *Orfeo* 77 She froted hur hondys and hur fete. **13..** *Gaw. & Gr. Knt.* 1919 Her [dogs'] hedez þay fawne & frote. **1340-70** *Alisaunder* 1174 Hee raught forthe his right hand & his [Bucephalus'] rigge frotus. *c* **1375** *Sc. Leg. Saints, Pelagia* 71 For-þi he one þe cause fel..& one þe erde froittit his face. **1387** TREVISA *Higden* (Rolls) II. 17 ȝif he [a stoon] is i-froted and i-het, he holdeþ what hym neiȝheþ. *Ibid.* (Rolls) IV. 25 ȝongelynges ..frotede þe oliphauntes in þe forhedes wiþ horns combes. *c* **1440** *Partonope* 1927 Embrowded with peerle wele y-frote. *c* **1450** *Merlin* 76 Frote youre visage with this herbe, and youre handes. **1561** HOLLYBUSH *Hom. Apoth.* 2 Let him frot the head sore therewyth. **1562** LEIGH *Armorie* (1597) 52 The Hart..froteth his hornes to make them sharpe. **1600** B. JONSON *Cynthia's Rev.* (1616) v. iv, I assure you, sir, pure beniamin..I frotted a jerkin, for a new-reuenu'd gentleman, yeelded me three score crownes but this morning, and the same titillation. **1608** MIDDLETON *Trick, etc.* IV. iii, A sweet debt for froating your doublets. **1688** R. HOLME *Armoury* II. 239/1 [To] Frott or Rub themselves as Hawks will do..to rub her eyes on her Wings.

absol. *c* **1430** *Pilgr. Lyf Manhode* II. cxxxiii. (1869) 127 On that oon side [i can] frote and enoynte.

fig. *a* **1340** HAMPOLE *Psalter* cxxxi. 5 Wiþ þis thoght frote þi for heuyd.

2. *Tanning.* To work or render supple by rubbing.

1853 [see FROTTING *vbl. sb.*].

Hence †'**froterer**, one who rubs.

1607 MARSTON *What you will* III. i. E iv b, I am his froterer or rubber in a Hot-house.

froth (frɒθ, -ɔː-), *sb.* Forms: 4 frooth, froþe, 5-6 frothe, 6-8 froath, 4- froth. [Not found in OE.; perh. a. ON. *froða* wk. fem. (Da. *fraade*; the relation of Sw. *fradga* is obscure), related to the synonymous ON. *frauð* neut.; the root (OTeut. **freuþ-, frauþ-, frud-*) appears in OE. *á-fréoðan* to froth.

Possibly the Eng. word represents both ON. *frauð* and *froða*; for the later shortening cf. *cloth*.]

1. a. The aggregation of small bubbles formed in liquids by agitation, fermentation, effervescence, etc.; foam, spume; = FOAM *sb.* 1.

1382 WYCLIF *Hos.* x. 6 Samarie made his king for to passe, as frooth on the face of water. *c* **1440** *Promp. Parv.* 180/2 Frothe, *spuma.* **1530** PALSGR. 223/1 Frothe of an egge, *glette.* **1589** GREENE *Menaphon* (Arb.) 24 Venus was feigned by the Poets to spring of the froathe of the Seas. **1648** GAGE *West Ind.* xvi. 106 Untill it bubble and rise into a froath. **1672–3** GREW *Anat. Roots* I. iii. §4 The Froth of Beer or Eggs. **1725** DE FOE *Voy. round World* (1840) 333 The water was all a white foam of froth. **1795** SIR J. DALRYMPLE *Let. to Admiralty* 4 It would prevent the Yeast, or, as it is commonly called, the Froth, from bubbling over. **1806** *Gazetteer Scotl.* (ed. 2) 132 This second caldron is always covered with a foam or froth. **1886** *Tip Cat* xxii. 300 She.. had shaken the bottle so vigourously that its contents were more than half froth.

transf. and *fig.* **1581** J. BELL *Haddon's Answ. Osor.* 108 Through the resistyng of the froath and enticementes of sinne. **1635** SWAN *Spec. M.* i. §3 (1643) 24 The doting froth of a wittie brain. **1676** DRYDEN *Aurengz.* v. (1685) 71 Forgive those foolish words—They were the froth my raging folly mov'd When it boil'd up. **1692** WAGSTAFFE *Vind. Carol.* Introd. 11 My end is.. to blow off that Froth, that has been thrown on his Memory. **1824** LANDOR *Imag. Conv.* Wks. 1846 I. 3 Society is froth above and dregs below. **1878** MORLEY *Carlyle* 194 The lees and froth of common humanity.

b. *spec.* Foaming saliva issuing from the mouth.

13.. *Gaw. & Gr. Knt.* 1572 þe froþe femed at his mouth vnfayre bi þe wykez, Whettez his whyte tuschez. **1601** HOLLAND *Pliny* xxxv. x. 542 The froth which fell from his [a dog's] mouth as hee panted and blowed almost windlesse with running. **1753** CHAMBERS *Cycl. Supp.*, *Froth*.. is a moist white matter that oozes from a horse's mouth. **1885** *Syd. Soc. Lex.*, *Froth, bronchial*, the tenacious frothy secretion expectorated in some cases of asthma.. and other affections of the respiratory organs.

c. Extraneous or impure matter rising to the surface of liquids during boiling, etc.; scum.

1533 ELYOT *Cast. Helthe* II. xviii. (1541) 134 That [water], wherof commeth least skimme or froth, whan it doth boyle. **1648** GAGE *West Ind.* xvi. 107 In wine which is in the Must ..a thinner substance, which is the flower, and may be called the scum, or froath. **1846** J. BAXTER *Libr. Pract. Agric.* (ed. 4) I. 170 To skim off the froth collected on the surface. **1878** HUXLEY *Physiogr.* 193 Its name recalling its origin as the froth or scum of lava. **1883** *Hardwick's Photogr. Chem.* (ed. Taylor) 363 A mixture is made of Gelatine, Albumen, [etc.].. the ingredients being well beaten together; when the froth has settled down the mixture is filtered.

2. a. Something comparable to 'froth' as being unsubstantial or of little worth.

1593 SHAKS. *Lucr.* 212 What win I if I gaine the thing I seeke?.. a froth of fleeting ioy. **1604** EARL STIRLING *Darius* i, Chorus, Drunke with frothes of pleasure. **1612** BRINSLEY *Lud. Lit.* 210 Nothing but froth, childishnesse and vncertanetie. **1686** HORNECK *Crucif. Jesus* xxii. 629 When thou hast delighted in froth, and idle talk. **1702** C. MATHER *Magn. Chr.* III. iii. (1852) 547 It was food and not froth, which in his publick sermons he entertained the souls of his people with. **1783** H. BLAIR *Rhet.* (1812) II. xviii. 23 There is no froth nor affectation in it.

†**b.** Applied to what is tender or immature.

a **1420** HOCCLEVE *De Reg. Princ.* 2270 We Romayns þat þey han in prison loke, Ben but ȝonge froth, vnlernèd in batayle, And othir feble folk with age I-broke. **1557** TUSSER *100 Points Husb.* lix, Eate vp thy veale, pig and lambe being froth.

3. Applied contemptuously to persons. Cf. SCUM.

1598 SHAKS. *Merry W.* I. i. 167 Froth, and scum thou liest. **1603** DEKKER *Grissil* III. ii. Wks. (Grosart) V. 168 Out, you froth, you scumme. **1678** MARVELL *Growth Popery* 22 The Froath of the town, and the Scum of the University. **1887** HALL CAINE *Deemster* xv, That his son should consort with all.. the dirtiest froth of the sea.

4. *attrib.* and *Comb.* **a.** attributive, as ***froth-flake***; ***froth-like*** adj.; **b.** instrumental and originative, as ***froth-becurled***, ***-born***, ***-clad***, ***-faced***, ***-foamy*** adjs.; **c.** special comb., as **froth-blower** *joc.*, a beer-drinker: adopted as the title of a certain charitable organization; **froth-spit** = CUCKOO-SPIT 1; **froth-stick**, a stick for whipping cream, etc. Also in many names given to the frog-hopper (*Aphrophora spumaria*) or cuckoo-spit insect, as **froth-fly**, **-frog-hopper**, **-insect**, **-worm**.

1624 MILTON *Ps.* cxiv. 8 That saw the troubled sea and shivering fled And sought to hide his *froth-becurled head. **1905** *Daily Chron.* 25 Mar. 6/4 The quaintly-named '*Froth Blowers'.. are a little group of twenty-four working men. **1927** *Times* 25 June 9/7 A company limited by guarantee under the title of 'Ye Ancient Order of Froth-Blowers, Limited', has been registered to take over all or part of the property and liabilities of the incorporated Ancient Order of Froth-Blowers. **1928** *Times* 8 Feb. 5/3 In 1924 Mr. Herbert Temple.. desired to benefit certain charities. He invented the name 'Ancient Order of Frothblowers'. **1928** 'SAPPER' *Female of Species* xvii, Now then, boys, once again—and all together—Froth Blowers for ever. **1931** E. WAUGH *Remote People* i. 12 He had Froth Blowers' cuff-links, and a Rotarian wheel in his buttonhole. *a* **1649** DRUMM. OF HAWTH. *Poems* Wks. (1711) 19/2 The *froth-born goddess of the sea. **1769** HOME *Fatal Discov.* v, The *froth-clad pool. **1625** W. HARBERT *Poems* (Grosart) 81 *Froth-faced Neptune. **1841** BROWNING *Pippa* Introd. 6 Not a *froth-flake touched the rim Of yonder gap in the solid gray Of the eastern cloud. **1864** *Frothfly [see FESCUE 4]. **1590** SPENSER *F.Q.* I. xi. 23 The nimble thyes Of his *froth-fomy steed. **1816** KIRBY & SP. *Entomol.* (1843) II. 10 The *Froth-frog-hoppers.. entered the room in such numbers as to cover the table. **1774** GOLDSM. *Nat. Hist.* (1776) VII. 355 Of the Earwig, the *Froth Insect, and some others. **1860** O. W. HOLMES *Elsie V.* (1861) 257 A very shallow crape bonnet frilled and *froth-like. **1753** CHAMBERS *Cycl. Supp.*, **Froth spit* or cuckow spit. *a* **1706** *Country Wedding* in *Watson's Collect.* III. (1706) 47 My bairn has tocher of her awn.. A *Froath-stick, a Can, a Creel, a Knock. **1774** GOLDSM. *Nat. Hist.* VII. II. v. 358 To this order of insects we may also refer the Cuckow Spit, or *Froth Worm.

froth (frɒθ, -ɔː-), *v.* Also 5–6 (? *erron.*) frote, 7–8 froath. [f. prec. sb.; ON. had *frøyða.*]

1. *intr.* To emit froth or foam; to foam at the mouth. Of liquids: To gather or throw up froth; to run foaming *away*, *by*, *over*.

1382 WYCLIF *Mark* ix. 17 The which.. hirtith him, and he frothith, or vometh. *c* **1386** CHAUCER *Knt.'s T.* 801 As wilde bores.. That frothen whyte as foom for ire wood. *c* **1425** *Found. St. Bartholomew's* (E.E.T.S.) 36 The mayde begane greuously to be turmentyd, and sorer than she was woonnte to be vexid, frotyng at the moweth. **1529** MORE *Supplic. Soulys* 13 These folk.. fume, frete, frote and fome as fyerce and as angerly as a new huntyd sow. **1603** HOLLAND *Plutarch's Mor.* VI. ix. 607 When oyle doth froath or fome. **1641** HINDE *J. Bruen* xlvii. 148 Hee would.. froth and fome like a Boare. **1712–14** POPE *Rape Lock* II. 136 The sea that froaths below. **1821** CLARE *Vill. Minstr.* I. 45 They.. call for brimming tankards frothing o'er. *a* **1839** PRAED *Poems* (1864) II. 50 Grief soon would bid the beer to run, Because the squire's mad race was done, Not less than now it froths away, Because 'the squire's of age to-day'. **1855** BROWNING *Childe Roland* xix, This, as it frothed by, might have been a bath For the fiend's glowing hoof. **1876** T. HARDY *Ethelberta* (1890) 370 His lips frothing like a mug of hot ale. **1880** 'OUIDA' *Moths* I. 12 The cutlets duly frothing in their silver dish.

fig. **1824** *Blackw. Mag.* XV. 594 For this the demagogue spouts—the newspaper froths—the liberal in Parliament proses. **1873–4** DIXON *Two Queens* III. XIII. x. 55 The leaguers of Cambrai were frothing at each other, and preparing for a future fight.

2. *trans.* To emit or send forth in or like froth or foam. Now only with *out*.

1382 WYCLIF *Jude* ii. 13 Frothinge out her confusiouns. **1388** —— *Wisd.* xi. 19 Ether beestis frothinge heete of firis. **1859** TENNYSON *Vivien* 765 Is your spleen froth'd out, or have ye more?

3. To cause to foam; to make froth rise on the surface of; to pour *out* in such a manner as to make frothy. Also to ***froth up***.

1621 FLETCHER *Pilgrim* III. vi, Fill me a thousand pots, and froth 'em, froth 'em. **1715** PRIOR *Down-Hall* 120 The wine was froth'd out by the hand of mine host. **1773** JOHNSON in Boswell 30 Sept., She.. made his coffee, and frothed his chocolate. **1806** *Culina* 79 Judiciously beating and frothing the eggs. **1832** TENNYSON *Death Old Year* iii, He froth'd his bumpers to the brim. **1864** MRS. CARLYLE *Lett.* III. 227 A tumbler of milk warm from the cow, and all frothed up.

absol. **1598** SHAKS. *Merry W.* I. iii. 15 Let me see thee froth and liue.

4. To bespatter or cover with or as with froth or foam. Also, *to froth over* (something). *fig.*

1771 SMOLLETT *H. Clinker* Wks. 1806 VI. 122 He suddenly bolted out.. his face frothed up to the eyes with soap lather. **1801** SOUTHEY *Thalaba* VI. v, The foam froth'd his limbs. **1856** KANE *Arct. Expl.* I. xxx. 415 Foam pours out from his jaws till it froths his beard. **1885** O. W. HOLMES *Mort. Antip.* Introd. (1886) 4 A certain amount of sentiment ..somewhat frothed over by his worldly experiences.

5. *Comb.* †**froth-can**, the trick of frothing the can.

1624 *Skelton's Ghost, E. Rumming* Prol. 19 Our pots were full quarted, We were not thus thwarted, With froth-canne and nick-pot.

Hence **'frothed** *ppl. a.*, **'frothing** *vbl. sb.* and *ppl. a.*

13.. *E.E. Allit. P.* B. 1721 þat froþande fylþe. **1613–16** W. BROWNE *Brit. Past.* II. iii, His hasty waves among The frothed Rocks, bearing the tender song. **1628** *Robin Goodfellow* II. (1638) D iij a, A Tapster.. with his pots smalnesse, and with frothing of his drinke, had got a good summe of money together. **1673** R. HEAD *Canting Acad.* 186 By brewing Rebellion, Micking, and Frothing. **1753** *Scots Mag.* July 318/2 Which she.. threw back with some frothed phlegm. **1795** A. SEWARD *Lett.* (1811) IV. 102 A frothing brook leaps and clamours over the rough stones. **1798** FERRIAR *Of Genius* in *Illustr. Sterne, etc.* 285 Alexander learnt the art of frothing at the mouth. **1807** T. THOMSON *Chem.* (ed. 3) II. 484 The frothing might.. be ascribed to the emission of this oxygen on the application of heat. **1820** L. HUNT *Indicator* No. 23 (1822) I. 177 That frothed glass of porter. **1873** 'OUIDA' *Pascarèl* I. 47 Florio was perpetually in and out.. with some frothing cup of chocolate.

'frothery. *nonce-wd.* [f. FROTH *sb.* + -ERY.] Mere froth, empty display, triviality.

1851 CARLYLE *Jrnl.* in Froude *C.'s Life in Lond.* II. xix. 79 'All nations' crowding to us with their so-called industry or ostentatious frothery.

frothless ('frɒθlɪs, -ɔː-), *a.* [f. FROTH *sb.* + -LESS.] Having no froth, free from froth.

1848 in CRAIG; and in later Dicts.

frothsome ('frɒθsəm, -ɔː-), *a.* [f. FROTH *sb.* + -SOME.] Full of froth, frothy.

1880 BLACKMORE *Mary Anerley* III. ix. 127 The sea.. weltered in a sadly frothsome state.

frothy ('frɒθɪ, -ɔː-), *a.* [f. FROTH *sb.* + -Y[1].]

1. a. Full of, covered with, or accompanied by froth or foam; foamy.

1533 FRITH *Disput. Purgat.* (1829) 157 Their.. frothy waves. **1592** SHAKS. *Ven. & Ad.* 901 The hunted boar Whose frothy mouth.. A second fear through all her sinews spread. **1613** *Uncasing of Machivils Instr.* C ij b, Beare with a Tapster though his Cans be frothie. **1615** LATHAM *Falconry* (1633) 117 When you do finde your Hawkes mouth and throat to bee continually frothy and furred. **1700** DRYDEN *Palamon & A.* II. 205 Two boars.. With rising bristles, and with frothy jaws. **1740** SOMERVILLE *Hobbinol.* III. 281 Wanton Joy Lavish had spilt the Cyder's frothy Flood. **1822–34** *Good's Study Med.* (ed. 4) II. 450 A frothy cough ensues. **1846** G. E. DAY tr. *Simon's Anim. Chem.* II. 311 The urine.. was turbid and of a reddish colour, very frothy [etc.]. **1871** B. TAYLOR *Faust* (1875) II. II. iii. 124 Back the frothy wave is flowing.

†**b.** ***frothy poppy***, the bladder campion.

So called because it was supposed that cuckoo-spit was more frequently found on this than on other plants.

1597 GERARDE *Herbal* II. ccxiv. 551 Called.. in English Spatling Poppie, frothie Poppie, and white Ben. **1878** in BRITTEN & HOLLAND *Plant-n.*

2. a. Consisting of froth or light bubbles, of the nature of or resembling foam, spumous.

1605 TIMME *Quersit.* I. vii. 32 The flower of salt.. is frothy. **1646** SIR T. BROWNE *Pseud. Ep.* v. iii. 237 That spumous frothy dew or exudation. **1697** DRYDEN *Virg. Georg.* III. 400 About his churning Chaps the frothy Bubbles rise. **1799** *Med. Jrnl.* II. 140 His saliva was remarkably frothy. **1839** MURCHISON *Silur. Syst.* I. xxv. 320 The frothy breccia on one side. **1882** VINES *Sachs' Bot.* 454 The tapetum becomes disorganised and forms a frothy mucilage.

†**b.** Soft, not firm or solid, flabby. *Obs.*

1626 BACON *Sylva* §740 You need not fear that Bathing should make them [the Turks' bodies] frothy. **1658** ROWLAND *Moufet's Theat. Ins.* 1070 She hath a frothy body.

c. Used to describe very light, tenuous dress-material.

1901 *Westm. Gaz.* 10 Jan. 3/2 In evening frocks and teagowns there is still a very marked liking for frilled frothy edges. **1930** [implied in FROTHINESS below].

3. *fig.* Vain, empty, unsubstantial, trifling. Also, of a person: Having no depth of character, conviction, knowledge, etc.; shallow.

1593 NASHE *4 Lett. Confut.* 16 The abiectest and frothiest forme of Diuinitie. **1622** WITHER *Mistr., Philar.* Wks. (1633) 686 Such frothy Gallants. *a* **1652** J. SMITH *Sel. Disc.* iii. 54 Contentious disputes, and frothy reasonings. **1661** BOYLE *Style of Script.* (1675) 189 Our frothy censurers. **1707** *Reflex. upon Ridicule* 66 Most young People are too frothy. **1742** RICHARDSON *Pamela* III. 412 Adding, in his frothy Way, Now can I say, I have saluted an Angel. **1831** CARLYLE *Sart. Res.* II. viii. (1871) 123 With.. much frothy rant. **1884** EDNA LYALL *We Two* xvi, A mere ranter, a frothy mob orator. **1885** *Mag. of Art* Sept. 450/2 Much frothy fine writing.

absol. **1762** FOOTE *Orators* II. Wks. 1799 I. 219 You will have at one view.. the frothy, the turgid, the calm, and the clamorous.

4. *Comb.*, as ***frothy-looking*** adj.

1880 MISS BIRD *Japan* I. 133 A frothy-looking silk crêpe.

Hence **'frothily** *adv.*, **'frothiness.**

1615 CROOKE *Body of Man* 259 The humidity, heate, frothinesse and whitenes. *a* **1716** SOUTH *Serm.* (1737) VIII. ix. 264 The profaneness and frothiness of his discourse. **1727** BAILEY vol. II, *Frothily*, with Froth; also emptily, not solidly or substantially, lightly. **1823** LAMB *Elia, On some Old Actors*, The.. face.. that looked out so formally flat in Foppington, so frothily pert in Tattle. **1846** G. E. DAY tr. *Simon's Anim. Chem.* II. 5 A limpid fluid.. unobscured by frothiness. **1890** *Longm. Mag.* Nov. 109 Persons who frothily declaim about genius. **1930** *Times* 13 Mar. 11/6 The outstanding feature is the frothiness of the dresses made from perishable materials with their innumerable frills, flounces, and furbelows.

†**'frotion.** *Obs. rare*[−1]. [? a. Du. *vrouwtje(n* = *vrouwken*: see FROKIN.] ? A maiden.

1587 TURBERV. *Trag. T.* 12 a, Athwart the wood With cruell curres an armed knight there went, That had in chace a frotion fresh of hewe.

‖**frottage** (frɔtaʒ). [a. F. *frottage* rubbing, friction, f. *frotter* to rub (see FROT *v.*).]

1. *Psychiatry.* (See quot. 1933.)

1933 H. ELLIS *Psychol. Sex* ii. 37 The special perversion of frottage.. consists in a desire to bring the clothed body, and usually though not exclusively the genital region, into close contact with the clothed body of a woman. **1939** G. R. SCOTT *Encycl. Sex* s.v., Like fetichism, too, frottage is evidently a morbid development of the normal sexual excitatory effects of touching or contact with the opposite sex. **1955** H. T. MOORE in D.H. Lawrence *Sex, Lit. & Censorship* 27 The entire day's catalogue of voyeurism, frottage, and various other kinds of aberrant gratification.

2. *Art.* The technique or process of taking a rubbing from an uneven surface, e.g. grained wood or sacking, as a point of departure for a work of art.

1935 [see COLLAGE]. **1959** H. READ *Conc. Hist. Mod. Painting* iv. 138 Max Ernst.. also invented the 'frottage'—that is to say, designs composed of 'rubbings' of various rough surfaces. **1961** *Spectator* 29 Sept. 428 Evolved his own special techniques of frottage (a process not unlike brass-rubbing) and collage. **1967** G. H. HAMILTON *Painting & Sculpture in Europe* vii. 265 The discovery of.. *frottage* (rubbing), occurred on the rainy evening of 10 August 1925 in a room by the sea.

frotting ('frɒtɪŋ), *vbl. sb.* [f. FROT *v.* + -ING[1].] The action of the vb. FROT in various senses.

a **1225** *Ancr. R.* 284 þe caliz.. þuruh so monie duntes & frotunges, to Godes biheue.. so swuðe ueire afeited. **1387** TREVISA *Higden* (Rolls) I. 417 Frotinge of iren and whestones þou schalt hire. *c* **1400** *Lanfranc's Cirurg.* 195 Froting wiþ squillis is good þerfore. **1853** C. MORFIT *Tanning, etc.* 157 The working, or frotting is solely to remove the wrinkles and stiffness of the dry skins.

†**'frotting,** *ppl. a. Obs.* [f. FROT *v.* + -ING[2].] Rubbing; (of language) grating, harsh.

1387 TREVISA *Higden* (Rolls) II. 163 þe longage of þe Norþhumbres.. is so scharp, slitting, and frotynge. **1567** TURBERV. *Epitaphes, etc.* 70 b, It frets the Culter keene that cuts the froting soyle.

‖**frottola** (ˈfrɒtələ). *Mus.* Pl. frottole. [It.] A form of Italian popular song common esp. in the 15th and 16th centuries.

1854 R. BROWN tr. *Giustiniano's Despatches* I. 83 The.. word..'Frottola'..is used by the novellist Sachetti,..and applied to certain compositions of his in verse... The word is now merely employed to signify a comic song. **1875** A. W. WARD *Hist. Eng. Dram. Lit.* I. ii. 128 The *frottola* (literally a comic ditty) marks a step in advance. Here types take the place of abstractions. **1900** *Grove's Dict. Mus.* I. 566/1 The words of the Frottole were often comic (in fact the word is a synonym for a joke) but still oftener extremely sentimental. **1960** *Times* 2 Sept. 13/6 Second came the more complete Hispanization of the *villancio* (the equivalent of the Italian frottola). **1970** *Computers & Humanities* V. 109 The thematic indices of printed sources of the frottola and the Palestrina repertory.

‖**frotton** (frɔtɔ̃). [Fr., f. *frotter* to rub. The termination *-on* denotes a tool or implement.] In early block-printing, a dabber or burnisher used to press the damp sheet upon the inked block.

1876 T. L. DE VINNE *Invention of Printing* 83 How were these images printed? Almost every author who has written on printing has said that they were printed by friction, with a tool known as the frotton, which has been described as a small cushion of cloth stuffed with wool. **1893** E. G. DUFF *Early Printed Bks.* 17 It consists of three sheets of paper, each of which contains an impression from a block... They are printed by means of the frotton in light-coloured ink. **1911** *Encycl. Brit.* XXVII. 511/2 Then a sheet of damp paper was laid upon it [*sc.* the block], and the back of the paper was carefully rubbed with some kind of dabber or burnisher, usually called a *frotton*, till an impression from the ridges of the carved block had been transferred to the paper. **1960** G. A. GLAISTER *Gloss. Bk.* 149 *Frotton printing*, a method of taking an impression from type by rubbing the verso of a leaf laid upon it. This method was used before the invention of the press.

†**froud.** *Obs.* Also 2 frude, -te, 3 frode, 5 frowde. [ME. *frūde* (riming with *prūde*); see FROG *sb.*[1]] A frog or toad.

a **1200** *Moral Ode* 271 Þeor beð naddren and snaken eueten and frude [*v. rr.* fruden, frute]. *a* **1240** *Sawles Warde* in *Cott. Hom.* 251 Þe laðe helle wurmes, tadden ant froggen [*v.r.* froden] Þe freoteð ham ut te ehnen. *c* **1440** *Jacob's Well* (E.E.T.S.) 209 He openyd his cofere in presence of his confessour, & fonde þer-in as manye frowdys as he putt þer-in almessis. Þe preest seyde: 'here þou seest how almes of euyl getyn good plesyth god!' þat man seyde..syth I falsly haue deuouryd þe peple of here good, þerfore þise frowdys schal deuowre my body qwyk. **1496** *Dives & Paup.* (W. de W.) I. xlvi. 87/1 Some man hadde leuer for to mete with a froude or a frogge in the waye than to mete with a knyght or a squyre.

frou-frou (fruː fruː), *sb.* [Fr.; of echoic formation.] A rustling, *esp.* the rustling of a dress.

1870 *Athenæum* 4 June 734 The modern *frou-frou* of satin and gros-de-Naples skirts is nothing to the rustling of brocaded silks. **1871** M. COLLINS *Mrq. & Merch.* III. v. 155 With a frou-frou of soft silk she arose. **1891** *Speaker* 2 May 527/1 The rustle of the dresses, the frou-frou of the fans. *fig.* **1876** BESANT & RICE *Gold. Butterfly* vi, The frou-frou of life was lost to her. **1883** 'OUIDA' *Wanda* II. 4 The Princess fretted for some little frou-frou of the world to break its solemn silence.

frou-frou, *v.* [f. the sb.] *intr.* To move about with a rustle of draperies. Only in *frou-frouing.*

1905 *Truth* 18 May 1289/2 Frou-frouing femininities. **1909** M. B. SAUNDERS *Litany Lane* II. xvii, She found herself floating and frou-frouing up Majorson's monastic stairs. **1958** A. WILSON *Middle Age of Mrs. Eliot* II. 166 Up those stairs should have come frou-frouing skirts.

frough, frow, *a. Obs.* exc. *dial.* Forms: 3 frouh, 4 frouȝ, 5 frogh, 5, 6, 9 *Sc.* freuch, (6 frewch, 8 freugh), 4, 7- frow, 8 frowe, 5, 7- frough. [Of obscure origin: the forms point back to OE. **frōh*, or possibly **prōh*; a word of the latter form is represented by *prōȝum* 'rancidis', *prōn* 'rancida' (Napier *OE. Gll.* VII. 193, 210); for the meaning cf. FROUGHY.]

1. Liable to break or give way, not to be depended on, frail, brittle. *lit.* and *fig.*

c **1275** *Luue Ron* 44 in *O.E. Misc.* (1872) 94 Hit is fals and mereuh and frouh. **1303** R. BRUNNE *Handl. Synne* 2305 Þoghe Þe prest be fals or frow. *c* **1420** *Pallad. on Husb.* III. 671 Ek thike ysowe is frough [L. *sectilis*] And rare ysowe is heded grete & tough. *c* **1475** *Rauf Coilȝear* 525 Oft fair foullis ar fundin faynt, and als freuch. **1501** DOUGLAS *Pal. Hon.* I. vii, Quha suld haue firm esperance in this, Whilk is alace sa ffreuch and variant? **1568** *Bannatyne Poems* (1770) 185 This warld is verry frewch. **1664** EVELYN *Sylva* (1679) 18 Timber..which grows in Gravel is subject to be Frow (as they term it) and brittle. **1674-91** RAY *N.C. Words* 28 *Frough*, loose, spungy. *Frough wood*, brittle. *a* **1722** LISLE *Husb.* (1757) 37 The arms of an ash-tree are commonly put in if they be not too frowe. **1787** GROSE *Prov. Gloss.*, *Frough-wood*, brittle wood. **1785** *Jrnl. fr. Lond.* in *Poems Buchan Dial.* 5 The swingle-trees flew in flinders, as gin they had been as freugh as kail-castacks. **1825** BROCKETT *N.C. Words*, *Frough*, loose, spungy, easily broken.

2. Crisp or 'short' to the taste.

c **1420** *Pallad. on Husb.* III. 662 To make hem frough, kitte of the bladys longe.

3. *Sc.* (See quot.)

1808-80 JAMIESON, *Freuch*..2. dry; applied to corn, that has recovered from the effects of rain in the time of harvest.

froughy, frowy (ˈfraʊɪ), *a.* Now *dial.* [? f. FROUGH *a.* + -Y[1].]

1. Musty, sour, stale, not sweet.

1579 SPENCER *Sheph. Cal.* July 111 They..like not of the frowie fede. *a* **1825** FORBY *Voc. E. Anglia*, *Frowy*, stale, on the point of turning sour from being over kept. **1866** MRS. STOWE *Lit. Foxes* 117 Mrs. D. is a decent housekeeper, and so her bread be not sour, her butter not frowy [etc.].

2. Of wood: Spongy, soft-textured, brittle. ***frowy-stuff*** (see quot. 1858).

1641 BEST *Farm. Bks.* (Surtees) 32 The best stricles are those that are made of froughy, unseasoned oake. **1677** MOXON *Mech. Exerc.* (1703) 67 If your Wood be soft, and your Stuff free, and frowy, that is, evenly temper'd all the way. **1750** W. ELLIS *Mod. Husb.* VII. ii. 43 (E.D.S.) Such an ash..grows frowy, short and spungy. **1858** SIMMONDS *Dict. Trade*, *Frowy-stuff*, a builder's name for short, or brittle and soft, timber. **1889** FARMER *Americanisms*, *Froughy*, spongy, brittle, or, in fact, applied to anything that is of inferior quality.

frounce (fraʊns), *sb.*[1] Also 5-7 frownce. Cf. the altered form FLOUNCE *sb.* [a. OFr. *fronce*, *fronche* (Fr. *fronce*), = Sardinian *frunza*.

According to some scholars a vbl. noun f. the Rom. **frontire* (OF., Pr., OSp. *froncir*, Sp. *fruncir*, Cat. *frunsir*, Sard. *frunziri*), to wrinkle the brow, to wrinkle, f. L. *front-em* brow, FRONT. Others consider the Rom. sb. to be adopted from OHG. (**wrunza*), *runza*, modG. *runze* wrinkle.]

†**1.** A wrinkle. *Obs.*

1390 GOWER *Conf.* III. 27 He seeth her front is large and pleine, Withoute frounce of any greine. **1430-40** LYDG. *Bochas* I. xx. (1494) e vij b, Their reueled skyn abrode to drawe and streyne Frowarde frouncis to make theym smoth & pleyne. **1527** ANDREW *Brunswyke's Distyll. Waters* C iv, The same water taketh awaye the frounces in the face whan it is rubbed therwith. **1616** BULLOKAR, *Frownce*, a wrinkle. **1721** BAILEY, *Frounce*, a Plait, a Wrinkle. Hence in mod. Dicts.

†**2.** A fold, crease; a pleat. Also *fig.*, duplicity.

c **1374** CHAUCER *Boeth.* I. pr. ii. 5 (Camb. MS.) With the lappe of hir garnement I-plited in a frounce she dryede myn eyen. **1377** LANGL. *P. Pl.* B. XIII. 318 'Bi Criste', quod Conscience tho, 'thi best cote..hath many moles and spottes'..'ȝe, who so toke hede'.. Men sholde fynde many frounces and many foule plottes. **1390** GOWER *Conf.* I. 173 So that he pronounce A plein good word withouten frounce. **1721** [see 1].

†**3.** The ornamented edge of a cup. *Obs.*

c **1440** *Promp. Parv.* 180/2 Frownce of a cuppe, *frontinella* (Pynson *frigium*).

†**4.** = FLOUNCE *sb.*[2] 1. *Obs.*[−1]

1619 FLETCHER *M. Thomas* III. ii, Farthingals, and frounces.

5. With allusion to Milton's use of FROUNCE *v.*: A piece of foppish display.

1881 DUFFIELD *Don Quix.* II. 397 With these [dresses] he made so many frounces and tricks. **1887** SAINTSBURY *Ess. Eng. Lit.* (1891) 153 A rather plain and straightforward writer, with few tricks and frounces of phrase and style.

Hence †ˈ**frounceless** *a.*, without a frounce or wrinkle, unwrinkled.

? *a* **1366** CHAUCER *Rom. Rose* 860 Hir forheed frounceles.

†**frounce,** *sb.*[2] *Obs.* Forms: 5 frounch, 5 fronse, 6 fronce, frounze, 6-8 frownce, 5- frounce. [Of obscure origin; no similar word of like meaning is known in Fr.

Perhaps it may be etymologically identical with prec., or due to some mistake; cf. FRONCLE and FORMICA 2.]

1. A canker or sore in the mouth of a hawk.

a **1450** *Fysshynge w. Angle* (1883) 3 With mysfedyng þen schall sche haue the frounce. *c* **1450** *Bk. Hawkyng* in *Rel. Ant.* I. 301 Of the f[r]ounches it is drede for it is a noyous sekenes. **1486** *Bk. St. Albans* C vj b, Blaynis in haukes mouthes cald frounches. **1587** TURBERV. *Trag. Tales* 183 The frounce consume the flesh of her, that feedes vpon my bones. **1674** N. COX *Gentl. Recreat.* II. (1677) 249 The Frownce proceedeth from moist and cold Humours which descend from the Hawk's Head to the Palate. **1725** BRADLEY *Fam. Dict.* s.v. *Rye*, It..causes the Frownce, or a perpetual dropping Humour, very hard to be cur'd. **1820** SCOTT *Abbot* iv, 'Twere the ready way to give her the frounce.

2. A disease in the mouth of a horse: see quot. 1587. Cf. CAMERY.

1587 MASCALL *Govt. Cattle, Horses* (1627) 131 The frounce is a disease soone cured, and they are smal pimples or warts in the midst of the pallat of his mouth aboue, and they are soft, and they will let him to eat his meat. **1610** [see CAMERY]. **1725** BRADLEY *Fam. Dict.*, *Camery* or *Frounce*, a Distemper in Horses. In mod. Dicts.

frounce (fraʊns), *v.* Forms: 3-4 fronce, 4-6 frounse, 6-7 frounze, frownce, -se, 4- frounce. [ad. OF. *froncier*, *froncir* (Fr. *froncer*), f. *fronce* FROUNCE *sb.*[1]]

†**1.** *trans.* To gather in folds or wrinkles, to wrinkle; to knit, purse (the brows or lips); occas. to knit the brows of. Also with *up.* *Obs.*

The first quot. perhaps belongs to 1 b.

a **1300** *Cursor M.* 3571 Þe front it fronces þat was scene. **13..** *Gaw. & Gr. Knt.* 2306 Þenne tas he hym strype to stryke, & frounses boþe lyppe & browe. **1390** GOWER *Conf.* I. 95 With that she frounceth up the browe. *c* **1572** GASCOIGNE *Fruites Warre* (1831) 209 The frolicke fauour frounst and foule defast. **1587** HUGHES *Misfort. Arthur* IV. ii. in Hazl. *Dodsley* IV. 321 All fury-like, frounc'd up with frantic frets. **1628** LE GRYS tr. *Barclay's Argenis* 143 That he may not seeme merveyle, hee will frounce his browes.

†**b.** *intr.* To knit the brows; to look angry. Also of the face or forehead: To fall into wrinkles, become wrinkled. *Obs.*

c **1450** HENRYSON *Test. Cress.* 155 in Thynne's *Chaucer* Qq iiij, His face frounsed..His teth chattred. *c* **1530** LD. BERNERS *Arth. Lyt. Bryt.* (1814) 489[He] frounsed and glared with his eyen as though he had ben wode. **1583** STANYHURST *Æneis* II. (Arb.) 63 Grislye faces frouncing, dyd I see. **1600** HOLLAND *Livy* VII. vi. 253 They frounced and tooke on most insolently for this unhappie expedition.

2. *trans.* To frizz, curl (the hair, a wig, etc.); also, to curl the hair of.

1526 SKELTON *Magnyf.* 1532 Schall frounce them in the foretop. **1559** AYLMER *Harborowe* N j b, Ladies..with their heares frownsed and curled. *a* **1592** GREENE *Mamillia* II. Wks. (Rtldg.) 316/1 A periwig frounc'd faste to the front. **1632** MILTON *Penseroso* 123 Not trick'd and frounc'd as she was wont. **1819** H. BUSK *Vestriad* II. 102 Some..scatter'd o'er the silver margin stood, To frounce their braids.

b. *fig.* [Echoing Milton: see quot. 1632 in 2.]

1891 SAINTSBURY *Scherer's Ess.* Pref. 9 Not only unnecessary, but in bad taste, to trick or frounce him in English.

†**3.** To gather (a piece of cloth, a garment, etc.) into creases or pleats; to pleat. *Obs.*

a **1533** LD. BERNERS *Gold. Bk. M. Aurel.* (1546) Cc vj, Their shurts frounced. **1559** *Mirr. Mag.*, *Mowbray's Banishm.* xxv, All iagde and frounst with diuers coloures dekt. **1610** GUILLIM *Heraldry* VI. v. (1611) 266 A piece of cloth..that is iagged and frowneed after the manner of our now commonly recieued Mantlings. **1805** SCOTT *Last Minstr.* IV. xviii, Buff coats, all frounced and broidered o'er.

†**b.** *intr.* To fall into creases or pleats. *Obs.*

c **1400** *Rom. Rose* 7259 Shoos knopped with dagges That frouncen lyke a quaile pipe. **1548** HALL *Chron.*, *Hen. VIII* (1809) 691 It bossed out and frounced very stately to behold.

Hence **frounced** *ppl. a.*, †(*a*) of the forehead: Wrinkled; (*b*) of the hair, the head, etc.: Curled, frizzed; ˈ**frouncing** *vbl. sb.*, †(*a*) knitting of brows; (*b*) frizzing; also *attrib.*

1422 tr. *Secreta Secret.*, *Priv. Priv.* (E.E.T.S.) 221 A sharpe straght farred, noght gretly lene ne al full, nethyr al frouncet. *c* **1450** HENRYSON *Fables*, *Paddok & Mous* 43 Her fronsit face. *a* **1529** SKELTON *P. Sparowe* 1337 The ferryman of hell, Caron..with his frownsid foretop. **1530** PALSGR. 223/2 Frounsyng, *froncement*. *a* **1568** ASCHAM *Scholem.* (Arb.) 54 An ouerstaring frounced hed, as though out of euerie heeres toppe, should suddenlie start out a good big othe. **1593** NASHE *Christ's T.* (1613) 148 Thy flaring frounzed Periwigs. **1600** HOLLAND *Livy* XXXIII. xxxix. (1609) 846 There was frounsing, and their bloud was up. **1603** H. CROSSE *Vertues Commw.* (1878) 76 Fye vpon these frownsing Irons. **1656** W. D. tr. *Comenius' Gate Lat. Unl.* §203 The Temples..in those that are angry frowneed or furrowed. **1835** in *Gentl. Mag.* Feb. (1836) 135 And her hair was all frizzled and frounc'd like a nigger.

frount(e, frountel(l, frounter, obs. ff. of FRONT, FRONTAL, FRONTIER.

†ˈ**frousshure.** *Obs.*[−1] [ad. OF. *froisseure* (Fr. *froissure*), f. *froisser* to rub violently, to crush.] A bruise, contusion.

c **1477** CAXTON *Jason* 138 b, Renewing to him the dolour and grete payne of his woundes and frousshures.

frouzy: see FROWZY.

†ˈ**frover,** *sb. Obs.* Forms: 1 frófer, -or, -ur, 2-3 frofer, 3 frofre, froure, frowere, frover(e, *south.* vroure. [OE. *frófor*, str. fem. and masc. = OS. *fróbra*, *frófra*, OHG. *fluobara*.]

1. Comfort; a means of comforting.

Beowulf 698 Him dryhten forgeaf..frofor ond fultum. *c* **1000** ÆLFRIC *Hom.* I. 136 He ȝe-andbidode ðone frofer. *c* **1200** ORMIN 8786 Forr þatt he ȝifeþþ her hiss þeoww Hiss frofre o seofenn wise. *a* **1225** *Ancr. R.* 92 Þeonne schullen ȝe iseon hu al þe world nis nout, & hu hire uroure is fals. *a* **1240** *Ureisun* in *Cott. Hom.* 185 We..buggeþ worldles froure wiþ moni sori teone.

b. applied to God, the Holy Ghost.

a **1225** *Juliana* 11 Ʒef þu wult..leuen..i þe hali gast folkene froure. *c* **1250** *Hymn to God* 5 in *Trin. Coll. Hom.* App. 258 Vroure & hele folkes fader. *c* **1250** *Gen. & Ex.* 54 Hali froure welt oc ðat miȝt. *c* **1275** LAY. 387 Fader he his on heuene and alle man his frouere.

2. *attrib.*, as *Frover-Ghost* [= OHG. *fluobargeist*]; also in syntactical form *Frovre Ghost*, the Comforter, the Holy Ghost.

c **1000** *Ags. Gosp.* John xiv. 26 Se haliȝa frofre gast. *c* **1000** ÆLFRIC *Hom.* I. 322 Se Halga Gast..is ȝehaten on Greciscum ȝereorde, Paraclitus, ðæt is, Frofor-gast. *c* **1175** *Lamb. Hom.* 97 Þe frofre gast. *c* **1200** ORMIN 10554 Þe Faderr, & te Frofre Gast Himm hafenn sett to demenn.

†ˈ**frover,** *v. Obs.* Forms: 1 fréfran, -ian, fróf(e)rian, 2-3 fréfrian, -en, 2-3 freuren, -in, 2-4 frou(e)ren, -in, *south.* vrouren, vroæfrien, (3 froðeren). Also 1-2 ȝefréfran, -ian, 2 ifréfran, 3 ifrófren. [OE. *fréfrian*, *frófrian*, also *ȝefréfran*, *ȝefréfrian*, f. *frófor*, FROVER *sb.* Cf. OS. *fróbrean*, OHG. *fluobiren*.]

trans. To comfort, console. Const. *for*, *of*.

c **900** tr. *Bæda's Hist.* V. v. (1890) 396 Cwæð he þæt ȝewune-lice word þæra frefrendra. *c* **1000** *Ags. Gosp.* John xi. 19 Hiȝ woldon hi frefrian for hyra broðor þingon. *c* **1175** *Lamb. Hom.* 97 He ifrefrað þa droriȝan. *c* **1200** ORMIN 150 Forr þatt he wollde himm frofrenn. *c* **1200** *Trin. Coll. Hom.* 119 Bidde we nu þe holigost..þat he..freure us of alle soreȝe. *c* **1205** LAY. 19545 Þat [ich] on þissen felde mote beon ifroured. *c* **1290** *S. Eng. Leg.* I. 465/104 Pouere Men þare-with to freueri. *c* **1315** SHOREHAM 7 Frevereth thorwe his body man. *c* **1320** *Cast. Loue* 889 Of þulke [grace] þat alle [con] frouere.

Hence †ˈ**frovering** *vbl. sb.*

c **1200** *Trin. Coll. Hom.* 117 Ich wile ȝiu senden þe heuenliche frefringe wið-innen a lit daȝes. *c* **1300** *Harrow.*

Hell 166 We hopeth wel thourh thy comyng Of oure sunnes haven froryng.

frow (fraʊ), *sb.* Forms: 4, 6–8 frow(e, 6–8 fro(e, (7 frau, phraw), 7– frow. [ad. Du. *vrouw* = Ger. *frau* lady, woman, wife.]

1. A Dutchwoman.

1390 *Will of M. Quellyngbourgh* (Comm. Crt. Lond.), Margareta Quellyngbourgh Frowe. **1477** *Paston Lett.* No. 792 III. 181 The frowys of Broggys, with there hye cappes. **1605** *Lond. Prodigal* v. i, By this light a Dutch frow; they say they are called kind. **1617** MIDDLETON & ROWLEY *Fair Quarrel* III. ii. 1 [To a Dutch nurse] Sweet fro, to your most indulgent care Take this my heart's joy. *c* **1681** *Roxb. Ball.* (1891) VII. 490 In Holland a Phraw he did wed, a couple he marri'd in Cailes. **1796** *Campaigns 1793–4* I. I. ii. 7 The skippers and frows flocked in crowds to the pier.

2. A woman, a lady; a wife. Chiefly of Dutch or German women, or of others compared to them.

1587 HARRISON *England* II. ix. (1877) I. 189 Saxon princes began to ioine in matrimonie with the British ladies, as the British barons did with the Saxon frowes. **1639** GLAPTHORNE *Wallenstein* III. ii, I've known him.. for all this heat 'Gainst woman-hood, pursue a sutlers froe. **1666** tr. *Horace's Odes* VIII. ii, The sun-burnt froe Of him that was chose Consul from the plough. **1708** E. COOK *Sot-weed Factor* (1865) 21 We scarce had play'd a Round about, But that these Indian Froes fell out. **1831** TRELAWNY *Adv. Younger Son* I. 168 Old Saboo there keeps himself, and frow, and half a score of young ones.

†3. Applied to the Mænads or Bacchantes of classical paganism; also *transf.*

1567 TURBERV. *Ovid's Ep.* 114 The frantike fro, Whome fell Erichtho hath in chase. **1589** *Pasquil's Ret.* D, Some gadded vppe and downe the streetes, like Bacchus Froes. **1606** CHAPMAN *M. D'Olive* Plays 1873 I. 208 The Ladies of this land would teare him peece-meal (As did the drunken Froes, the Thratian Harper). **1612** DRAYTON *Poly-olb.* viii. 117 The frantick British Froes, their hair disheuelled With fire-brands ran about. *a* **1616** BEAUM. & FL. *Wit at Sev. Weapons* v. i, They are now Buxsome as Bachus Froes—revelling, dancing.

4. *dial.* (See quot.)

1781 J. HUTTON *Tour to Caves* Gloss. *Frow* sb., an idle, dirty woman. *c* **1795** [? PORSON] *Horace* Odes I. xxvii. in *Spirit Publ. Jrnls.* (1799) I. 142 And were your girl the dirtiest drab.. Out with it.. What? is it she? the filthy frow.

†frow, *adv. Obs. rare*⁻¹. [Cf. ON. *frá-r* adj., quick.] Hastily.

c **1325** *Earth* i. in *E.E.P.* (1862) 150 Erþ vp erþ falliþ fol frow [glossed *festine*].

frow: see FROE, FROUGH.

froward (ˈfrəʊwəd), *a.*, *adv.*, *prep.* Forms: α. 2–5 fraward, 3 *Orm.* frawarrd, 4–5 frawarde, -werd, frauward, 5–6 *Sc.* frawart, 6 frauwerde; β. 2– froward, 4–5 frowerd, 4–6 frowarde. [Early ME. f. *fra*, FRO + -WARD. Cf. FROMWARD.]

A. *adj.* (Not now in colloquial use.)

1. Disposed to go counter to what is demanded or what is reasonable; perverse, difficult to deal with, hard to please; refractory, ungovernable; †also, in a wider sense, bad, evilly-disposed, 'naughty'. (The opposite of *toward.*)

a **1300** *Cursor M.* 7302 'Parfai', þan answard samuel, 'Yee ar to fraward [*Trin.* frowarde] wit to dele'. **1340** HAMPOLE *Pr. Consc.* 5854 If man be til God frawarde. **1382** WYCLIF *Deut.* xxi. 18 If a man gete a rebel sone, and a fraward. **1387** TREVISA *Higden* (Rolls) IV. 319 To chaste froward men and sturne men. *c* **1430** LYDG. *Min. Poems* 141 How may this be that thou art froward To hooly chirche to pay thy dewtee. **14..** *Why I can't be a Nun* 317 in *E.E.P.* (1862) 146 For sum bene devowte, holy, and towarde.. And sum bene feble, lewde, and frowarde. **1548** UDALL, etc. *Erasm. Par. Matt.* vi. 13 Ye shall be safe.. agaynste the frowarde temptour. **1577** B. GOOGE *Heresbach's Husb.* IV. (1586) 167b, The Cocke of this kinde, is a frowarde and mischievous Birde. **1585** ABP. SANDYS *Serm.* ii. 28 Samuel, reiected.. by this froward & rebellious people. **1625** BACON *Ess., Innovations* (Arb.) 527 A Froward Retention of Custome, is as turbulent a Thing, as an Innouation. **1689–90** TEMPLE *Ess., Poetry* Wks. 1731 I. 249 When all is done, Human Life is, at the greatest and the best, but like a froward Child, that must be play'd with and humour'd a little to keep it quiet till it falls asleep. **1703** *Clarendon's Hist. Reb.* II. Ded. 5 That this Remark may not look froward or angry. *a* **1716** BLACKALL *Wks.* (1723) I. 45 Such froward and touchy People as these. **1775** JOHNSON 14 Apr. in *Boswell*, A judge may become froward from age. **1820** HAZLITT *Lect. Dram. Lit.* 270 In the infancy of taste, the froward pupils of art took nature to pieces, as spoiled children do a watch. **1848** LYTTON *Harold* v. vii, 'Speak on' said Hilda, calmly as a nurse to a froward child. **1855** MACAULAY *Hist. Eng.* IV. xix. (1858) 291 Russell had always been froward, arrogant, and mutinous.

absol. **1535** COVERDALE *Ps.* xvii[i]. 26 With the frowarde thou shalt be frowarde. **1661** BRAMHALL *Just Vind.* iii. 47 They may remove the froward from their offices. **1842** J. H. NEWMAN *Par. Serm.* VI. 346 If you bear with the froward.

2. Of things: **†a.** Adverse, unfavourable, untoward; difficult to deal with, refractory. Of shape (cf. B. 2): Ill-formed, ugly (*obs.*). **b.** In later use only as *fig.* of sense 1 (said, e.g., of fortune): Perverse, ill-humoured.

a **1300** *Cursor M.* 8104 Bi-halden vs inogh has þou Vr fraward scapp al ses þou hov. **13..** *Seuyn Sag.* (W.) 2622 The weder was cold & froward. **1430** LYDG. *Min. Poems* 103 By froward chaunce my hood was gone. **1513** DOUGLAS *Æneis* III. ii. 149 Syryus, the frawart star. **1523** SKELTON *Garl. Laurel* 1450 This delycate dasy, With froward frostis, alas was all to-fret. **1541** R. COPLAND *Galyen's Terap.* 2 Diij, Curacyon of frowarde and rebel vlceres. **1576** FLEMING *Panopl. Epist.* 120 To take his froward fortune and untoward luck with.. patience. **1756** C. LUCAS *Ess. Waters* III. 213 It has been my froward fate to have too much. **1793** SMEATON *Edystone L.* §270 During this month of froward weather. **1805** WORDSW. *Prelude* v. 348 The froward chaos of futurity. **1880** MISS BROUGHTON *Sec. Th.* II. vii, The froward May month.

†3. quasi-*sb.* A froward person or thing. *Obs.*

a **1529** SKELTON *P. Sparowe* 779 Our language is so rusty, So cankered, and so full Of frowardes. **1581** J. BELL *Haddon's Answ. Osor.* 266b, Through the cankerd peevishnes of wayward frowardes.

†B. *adv. Obs.*

1. In a direction that leads away from the person or thing under consideration; = FROMWARD.

O.E. Chron. an. 1127 Eall þæt þa beon drazen toward swa frett þa drane & drazað fraward. **1426** AUDELAY *Poems* 68 3if thou to the cherche go, Toward, froward, or ellis cum fro. **1494** FABYAN *Chron.* v. cxxvii. 108 He myghte goo or ryde frowarde or sydewarde, but towarde the chapell myght he in no wyse atteygne. **1540–54** CROKE *Ps.* (Percy Soc.) 34 Thy face allwey thus wilt thou let Be turned froward? **1596** SPENSER *F.Q.* VI. x. 24 And eeke them selves so in their daunce they bore, That two of them still froward seem'd to bee, But one still towards shew'd her selfe afore.

2. *fig.* Untowardly; perversely. ***froward shapen*** = misshapen (cf. FROM-SHAPEN).

a **1300** *Cursor M.* 8076 Sagh man neuer for-wit þat hore, Sua fraward scapen creature. **1580** LYLY *Euphues* (Arb.) 465 Thou knowest howe frowarde matters went, when thou tookest shippe.

†C. *prep.* (In a direction) away from; = FROMWARD. Also in form *frowards*. *Obs.* (or *arch.*)

c **1200** ORMIN 4672 þa turrnesst tu þe frawarrd Godd, & towarrd eorþlic ahhte. *c* **1250** *Gen. & Ex.* 3322 At euen cam a fuзel-fliзt, fro-ward arabie to hem riзt. **1398** TREVISA *Barth. De P.R.* II. viii. (1495) 36 The angels slake neuer.. nother tornyth theyr entent frowarde god. *c* **1400** *Melayne* 1314 The Sowdane.. sawe the Cristen in the felde Frowarde the Cite ride. *c* **1470** HENRY *Wallace* v. 786 Frawart the south thaim thocht it best to draw. **1470–85** MALORY *Arthur* x. xxx, And euer sire Tristram tracyd and trauercyd and wente froward hym here and there. **1513** DOUGLAS *Æneis* I. i. 57 Scho thame fordrivis, and causis oft ga will Frawart Latium. *Ibid.* IV. Prol. 130 Thy self or thame thou frawartis God remouis. *a* **1850** ROSSETTI *Dante & Circ.* I. (1874) 106 He only is a pilgrim who goeth towards or frowards the House of St. James.

b. with tmesis *fro..ward.*

c **1220** *Bestiary* 719 And wende we neure fro him-ward.

†ˈfroward, *v. Obs.* [f. prec. adj.] *trans.* To make froward.

1627–47 FELTHAM *Resolves* I. xxxvi. 119 Vexations when they daily billow upon the minde, they froward even the sweetest soul, and.. turn it into spleen and testinesse.

ˈfrowardhede. *Obs.* [*-hede*, -HEAD.] = FROWARDNESS.

c **1470** HARDING *Chron.* CCIX. ix, The prynce of wrath and wilfull hede Agayne hym made debate and frowardhede.

frowardly (ˈfrəʊwədlɪ), *adv.* [f. FROWARD *a.* + -LY².] In a froward manner; perversely; adversely. (Now chiefly *arch.* in Biblical phrases.)

a **1300** *Cursor M.* 7317 (Gött.) 'Mi folk', said godd, 'full frawarly [*Trin.* frowardly] þai seke and wirke full grett enuy. **14..** LYDG. *Secrees* 1032 Avaryce and gadering frowardly. **1435** MISYN *Fire of Love* I. v. 11, & luf of þe endeles lufar for fals luf frawardly þai haue lost. **1509** HAWES *Past. Pleas.* XIV. ii, Afrycus, Auster bloweth frowardly. **1526** TINDALE *1 Cor.* xiii. 4 Love doth not frowardly. **1588** A. KING tr. *Canisius' Catech.* 145 Quhilk glaidlie or frawartlie dois præsume to speik agains the halie decrees of the fathers. **1645** MILTON *Tetrach.* Wks. (1847) 211 Finding the misbeliever not frowardly affected. **1688** S. PENTON *Guardians Instr.* 71, I once dealt with him very Frowardly, and ask'd him plainly, How [etc.]. **1845–6** TRENCH *Huls. Lect.* Ser. II. vii. 263 He deals frowardly in the land of uprightness.

frowardness (ˈfrəʊwədnɪs). [f. as prec. + -NESS.] Froward quality or condition; perversity; untowardness; an instance of this.

a **1300** *Cursor M.* 27617 O pride bicums vnbuxumnes, strif and strutt, and frawardnes. *a* **1340** HAMPOLE *Psalter* liv. 22 Dwelland in frawardnes of þaire witt. *c* **1440** *Jacob's Well* (E.E.T.S.) 155 Frowardnes comyth fro þe herte, but þe tunge schewyth it out thrugh ouer-thwerte woordys. *c* **1555** HARPSFIELD *Divorce Hen. VIII* (Camden) 223 He did it not for any self-will or frowardness. **1576** FLEMING *Panopl. Epist.* 393 The frowardnesse of my fortune. **1647** CLARENDON *Hist. Reb.* VI. §21 The pride, frowardness, and perverseness of the Rebels. **1712** BERKELEY *Pass. Obed.* §42 We should not.. shew a frowardness or impatience of those transient sufferings. *a* **1716** SOUTH *Serm.* II. 78 How many Frowardnesses of ours does he smother, how many Indignities does he pass by. **1775** BURKE *Sp. Conc. Amer.* Wks. (1808) III. 62 It is nothing but a little sally of anger, like the frowardness of peevish children, who, when they cannot get all they would have, are resolved to take nothing. **1848** W. H. KELLY tr. *L. Blanc's Hist. Ten Y.* I. 188 Giving way to one of his occasional fits of boyish frowardness, he dashed his sword on the floor.

†ˈfrowardship. *Obs.* [see -SHIP.] = prec.

14.. *Burgh Laws* c. 34 (*Sc. Stat.* I.), Throuch frawartschyp [*contrarietate*] of hym selff.

frowde, var. of FROUD, *Obs.*, frog or toad.

frower: see FROE *sb.*

frowie, var. of FROUGHY *a. Obs.*

ˈfrowish, *a.*¹ *Obs. rare.*⁻¹ [? f. *frow*, FRO + -ISH, after *froward.*] ? Unfavourably disposed, froward.

1589 GREENE *Tullies Love* (1609) D b, Were you but as fauourable as you are frowish.

†ˈfrowish, *a.*² *Obs.* [f. *frow*, FROUGH *a.*, + -ISH.] Frowzy, stale-smelling, fetid.

1608 *Withals' Dict.* 286 He that is rank or frowish in savour, *hircosus.* **1688** BUNYAN *Solomon's Temple* xvii, Covetousness makes a minister smell frowish.

frown (fraʊn), *sb.* [f. next; but cf. the equivalent OF. *froigne.*]

1. A wrinkled aspect of the brow; a look expressive of disapprobation or severity, occas. of deep thought or perplexity. Also, the habit of frowning.

1605 SHAKS. *Lear* I. iv. 209 You are too much of late i' th' frowne. **1625** in Ellis *Orig. Lett.* Ser. I. III. 206 With one frown, divers of us being at White Hall to see her.. she drave us all out of the Chamber. **1710** STEELE & ADDISON *Tatler* No. 253 ¶8 May a Man knit his Forehead into a Frown. **1801** SOUTHEY *Thalaba* I. viii, His brow in manly frowns was knit. **1863** MISS BRADDON *Eleanor's Vict.* III. i. 3 The lawyer.. walked away from his wife with a frown upon his face. **1872** DARWIN *Emotions* ix. 223 He encounters some obstacle in his train of reasoning.. and then a frown passes like a shadow over his brow.

fig. **1783** MASON *Du Fresnoy's Art Paint.* 341 Beneath the frown of angry Heav'n.. The guilty Empire sunk. **1808** J. BARLOW *Columb.* III. 636 Ere darkness shroud you in a deeper frown.

2. A manifestation of disapprobation.

1581 MULCASTER *Positions* v. (1887) 27 Dissuaded from the worse, by misliking and frowne. *a* **1627** SIR J. BEAUMONT *Ausonius* xvi. 33 Peruerting crimes he checkes with angry frownes. **1721–2** WODROW *Suffer. Ch. Scot.* (1838) I. I. ii. §2. 112/1 To this no answer was given, but frowns. **1722** DE FOE *Relig. Courtsh.* I. iii. (1840) 104 The father's frowns are a part of correction. **1849** MACAULAY *Hist. Eng.* II. 205 He tried the effects of frowns and menaces. Frowns and menaces failed. **1868** E. EDWARDS *Raleigh* I. ix. 140 Ralegh .. was still.. under the frown of his royal mistress.

Hence **ˈfrownful** *a.*, full of frowns; **ˈfrownless** *a.*, devoid of frowns; **ˈfrowny** *a.*, having a habit of frowning.

1771 LANGHORNE *Laurel & Reed* 52 The murderer's burning cheek to hide, And on his frownful temples die. *a* **1861** SIR F. PALGRAVE (Ogilvie), Her frowny mother's ragged shoulder. **1890** *Univ. Rev.* 15 June 262 Planted with virtues, frownless gravity And sober elegance.

frown (fraʊn), *v.* Forms: 4–6 froun(e, (5 frownyn), 6–7 frowne, 4– frown. [ME. *froune*, ad. OF. *froignier*, *frongnier* (mod.F. only in the compound *refrogner*), of obscure origin.]

1. *intr.* To knit the brows, especially by way of expressing displeasure or (less frequently) concentration of thought; to look sternly. Said also of the brow. †Also (*rarely*), to sneer.

c **1386** [see FROWNING *ppl. a.*] *c* **1430** LYDG. *Min. Poems* 17 Wiche ought of resone the devise to excuse To alle tho that wold ageyn it ffroune or musee. *c* **1440** *Promp. Parv.* 181/1 Frownyn wythe the nose, *nasio.* *c* **1477** CAXTON *Jason* 52 He frowned in this wise and bote on his lippe a grete while. **1574** *Mirr. Mag., Sabrina* xxix, When Fortune most doth smile: Then will she froune: she laughes but euen a while. **1602** MARSTON *Ant. & Mel.* III. Wks. 1856 I. 32 Fortunes browe hath frown'd, Even to the utmost wrinkle it can bend. **1667** MILTON *P.L.* II. 106 He ended frowning, and his look denounc'd Desperate revenge. **1777** SHERIDAN *Sch. Scand.* A Portrait, She frowns no goddess, and she moves no queen. **1858** LYTTON *What will he do* II. xii, Had I been your father, I should have taken alarm, and frowned. **1872** DARWIN *Emotions* ix. 223 A man who joined us, and who could not conceive what we were doing, when asked to listen, frowned much, though not in an ill temper.

b. Of inanimate things: To present a gloomy or threatening aspect.

1642 ROGERS *Naaman* 118 They saw the times to frowne and trouble to come. **1659** D. PELL *Impr. Sea* 480 And will you not bee in the like fear, when the Heavens frown above you? **1764** GOLDSM. *Trav.* 85 And though the rocky-crested summits frown. **1794** MRS. RADCLIFFE *Myst. Udolpho* i, And sometimes frowned with forests of gloomy pine. **1839** YEOWELL *Anc. Brit. Ch.* i. (1847) 7 That wild architecture, whose gigantic stones.. are still to be seen frowning upon the plains of Stonehenge. **1854** J. S. C. ABBOTT *Napoleon* (1855) II. xv. 283 The cannon of the Prussians frowned along the rugged eminences of their left. **1868** MILMAN *St. Paul's* i. 9 A rude Saxon temple may have frowned down from the height above the Thames.

2. To express disapprobation or unfriendliness by a stern look. Const. *at*, *on*, *upon.* Also in *indirect passive.*

1576 FLEMING *Panopl. Epist.* 395 You are not the first upon whom fortune hath frowned. **1590** SHAKS. *Mids. N.* I. i. 194, I frowne vpon him, yet he loues me still. **1648** GAGE *West Ind.* iv. 13 Much were wee frowned at by the Dominicans our chiefest friends. **1709** ADDISON *Tatler* No. 24 ¶11 Frontlet not only looks serious, but frowns at him. **1794** MRS. RADCLIFFE *Myst. Udolpho* xix, Montoni frowned upon him. *a* **1859** MACAULAY *Hist. Eng.* V. 152 That they should be.. frowned upon at Kensington for not going farther.

b. attributed to inanimate objects.

1611 SHAKS. *Wint. T.* III. iii. 6 The heauens with that we haue in hand, are angry, And frowne vpon 's. **1816** KEATINGE *Trav.* (1817) II. 32 Robat and Sallee seem to frown at each other across this fine river.

3. quasi-*trans.* **a.** To drive or force with a frown *away*, *back*, *down*, *off*; also *from*, *into* (something).

1678 DRYDEN *All for Love* II. i, Ventidius fix'd his Eyes upon my Passage Severely, as he meant to frown me back. **1712** BLACKMORE *Creation* 315 Despairing wretch, he'll frown thee from his throne. **1741** WATTS *Improv. Mind* I. iii. §2 Nor should such an enquiring temper be frowned into silence. *c* **1800** K. WHITE *Lett.* (1837) 274 The fear of singularity frowns me into the concealment of it. **1805** BYRON *To Dorset* v, Peace, that reflection never frown'd away. **1806** WEBSTER in Scudder *Life* vi. (1882) 231, I will be neither frowned nor ridiculed into error. **1831** LYTTON *Godolph.* 66 You would not frown a great person like Lady Delville into affection for us. **1840** DICKENS *Barn. Rudge* ii, And the cold black country seemed to frown him off. **1870** BALDW. BROWN *Eccl. Truth* 261 A new order of society in which..judges [should] no more frown down the poor.

b. To enforce, express, produce, etc. by a frown.

1775 SHERIDAN *Rivals* Epil., She smiles preferment, or she frowns disgrace. **1798** W. TAYLOR in *Monthly Rev.* XXV. 518 Among us, however, the present statue of the prophet would seem to frown restraint on levity and mirth. **1871** L. STEPHEN *Playgr. Eur.* iii. (1894) 72 In 1861 the Schreckhorn..still frowned defiance upon all comers.

Hence † **frowned** *ppl. a.*, covered with a frown; made to look frowning. Also **'frowner**, one who frowns.

1598 FLORIO, *Inarcato*, a frowned or scouled countenance. **1630** BRATHWAIT *Eng. Gentlem.* (1641) 138 Such..friends or acquaintance as are neither..Fawners nor Frowners. *a* **1763** BYROM *Christ among Doctors* 10 That meek old Priest, with placid Face of Joy, That Pharisaic Frowner at the Boy. **1872** DARWIN *Emotions* ix. 223 Some persons are such habitual frowners that the mere effort of speaking almost always causes their brows to contract. **1892** *Idler* June 590 A handful of frowners against thirty million laughers!

frownce, obs. form of FROUNCE.

frowning ('fraʊnɪŋ), *vbl. sb.* [f. FROWN *v.* + -ING[1].] The action of the vb. FROWN; an instance of the same.

c **1400** *Rom. Rose* 4062 With that the cherl his clubbe gan shake, Frouning his eyen gan to make, And hidous chere. *c* **1440** *Promp. Parv.* 181/1 Frownynge. **1548** UDALL *Erasm. Par. Luke* iii. 9 E vj, For bittur frounyng, godly ioye and lightenesse of herte. **1592** WYRLEY *Armorie* 145 With frownings dume, downe are his smilings cast. **1616** J. LANE *Cont. Sqr.'s T.* x. 478 Turnes him fro, and nought but frowninges gave. **1713** SWIFT *Frenzy of J. Dennis* Wks. 1755 III. I. 146 He read a page or two with much frowning. **1821** CLARE *Vill. Minstr.* I. 16 How pinch'd with winter's frownings he has been. **1872** DARWIN *Emotions* ix. 224 We may conclude that frowning is not the expression of simple reflection..but of something difficult or displeasing encountered.

frowning ('fraʊnɪŋ), *ppl. a.* [f. FROWN *v.* + -ING[2].] That frowns; gloomy; stern; disapproving, threatening.

c **1386** CHAUCER *Clerk's T.* 300 And eke whan I say ya, ye say not nay, Neither by word ne frouning countenance: Swere this, and here I swere our alliance. *c* **1430** LYDG. *Min. Poems* 245 Now frownyng cheer, now fressh of visage. **1567** TURBERV. *To a Gentlewoman from whome he tooke a Ring* 1 What needes this frowning face? **1659** D. PELL *Impr. Sea* 377 A frowning, raging, and rowling storm. **1736** NEAL *Hist. Purit.* III. 520 The General Assembly..sent at the same time two frowning letters. **1822** B. CORNWALL *Poems, Modena*, And o'er her many a frowning fold Of crimson shades her closed eyes. **1847** A. M. GILLIAM *Trav. Mexico* 20 The frowning guns of the Castle. **1862** H. MARRYAT *Year in Sweden* II. 402 A deep ravine of frowning rocks.

b. *attrib.* in †*frowning cloth*, an imaginary frontlet supposed to be worn by a person when displeased.

1580 LYLY *Euphues* (Arb.) 285 The gallery, where shee was solitaryly walking, with her frowning cloth, as sick lately of the solens.

frowningly ('fraʊnɪŋlɪ), *adv.* [f. FROWNING *ppl. a.* + -LY[2].] In a frowning manner.

1556 J. HEYWOOD *Spider & F.* lxxvi. 22 Such flies as erst had frowninglie faste him: Louinglie they then, on him did smothlie smile. **1617** HIERON *Wks.* (1619–20) II. 270 With the eye of his soule he saw the Lord looke frowningly vpon him. **1797** MRS. RADCLIFFE *Italian* xxvi, 'You shall know me hereafter', said the stranger, frowningly. **1870** MISS BRIDGMAN *Ro. Lynne* II. ii. 21 Four rows of dark houses that frowningly faced one another.

frownt, obs. form of FRONT.

frowst, froust (fraʊst), *v.* ? *dial.* [Of unknown origin; see FROWST *sb.* 1.] *intr.* To take pleasure in staying in a warm, close, 'fuggy' atmosphere. Hence **'frowster**.

1884 *Standard* 5 May 4/4 A generation that frousts over the fire. **1889** B. WHITBY *Awakening M. Fenwick* II. 182, I hate..frowsting over a fire. **1917** 'I. HAY' *Carrying On* iii. 68 In winter it is much warmer below the earth than upon its surface, and Thomas Atkins is the most confirmed 'frowster' in the world. **1929** 'A. BERKELEY' *Wychford Poisoning Case* xxiii. 280 'Hallo, you frowsters!' cried Sheila, bursting without warning into the room.

frowst (fraʊst), *sb. colloq.* Also froust. [Back-formation from FROWSTY *a.*]

1. At Harrow School: see quots.

1880 *Hugh Russell at Harrow* 12 Can't you let a fellow take his frowst the very second morning? *Ibid.*, Gloss., *Frowst*, extra time in bed on Sundays, saints' days and whole holidays. **1905** H. A. VACHELL *Hill* v. 113 Lying in bed in the morning when there is no First School is a 'frowst'. By a subtle law of association, an armchair is also a 'frowst'. **1923** GALSWORTHY *Captures* 60 Ruding..looked right down on me in my old 'froust', as we called arm-chairs.

2. The close and fusty air of a room, etc., which is over-warm or over-crowded and without adequate ventilation.

1907 'J. HALSHAM' *Lonewood Corner* 130 For the manufacture of froust trust the elementary schools! **1921** *Blackw. Mag.* Apr. 453/1 Poor Colin..had to listen in candle-lit frowst [in a dug-out] to the banalities talked by the Brigadier. **1929** D. COKE *Monkey Tree* vii, He liked the cheap room and its genial frowst. **1946** H. CROOME *Faithless Mirror* 70 Inside, a magnificently fruity frowst greeted them, strongly flavoured with wood smoke.

frowstiness ('fraʊstɪnɪs). [f. FROWSTY *a.* + -NESS.] Frowsty quality; fustiness, stuffiness.

1923 *Daily Mail* 21 June 10 To clear his lungs of their over-night 'frowstiness'. **1926** W. J. LOCKE *Old Bridge* III. ix, The old frowstiness of dirt had given place to the fragrance of cleanliness. **1960** *Guardian* 24 Feb. 12/6 The froustiness of last night's supper at breakfast-time.

frowsty ('fraʊstɪ), *a.* orig. *dial.* [Of obscure origin; cf. OF. *frouste* ruinous, decayed; also FROUGHY, FROWISH, FROWZY.] Fusty; having an unpleasant smell. (In Berks., Oxf., Leic., and Glouc. glossaries.) Also in *Comb.*

1865 *Athenæum* No. 1960. 678/1 Use it on his frowsty head. **1881** E. J. WORBOISE *Sissie* xvii, When it is not only humble, but *frowsty*..you are apt to wish you were anywhere else than at home! **1922** D. H. LAWRENCE *Aaron's Rod* xiv. 195 A frowsty-looking man. **1924** F. HURST *Lummox* §3. 10 She was kind enough in a frowsty way. **1927** *Manch. Guardian Weekly* 28 Jan. 75/2 The frousty, self-conscious hedonism of the swagger music-hall. **1958** P. KEMP *No Colours or Crest* iii. 25 Neither daylight nor fresh air could penetrate to lighten the frowsty atmosphere of our dormitories.

frowy: see FROUGHY *a.*

† **frowze**, *sb. Obs.* Also (? 6 frowes), 6–7 frowse, 7–8 fruz, 8 frouze. [Of uncertain origin; possibly an alteration of FROUNCE, with assimilation to FRIZ, FUZZ.] ? A wig of frizzed hair worn by women. Also *frowze-*, *fruz-tower*.

1563 FOXE *A. & M.* 919/2 Her two gentlewomen..helped her of therwith [her gowne] and also with her frowes paste and neckerchefe. **1670** LADY M. BERTIE in *12th Rep. Hist. MSS. Comm.* App. v. 21 Some ware all small ribban, others brode ribbans..and all frowzes of their owen haire. **1676** ETHEREGE *Man of Mode* I. i. Wks. (1888) 245 This fine woman, I'll lay my life..has adorned her baldness with a large white fruz. **1687** CONGREVE *Old Bach.* IV. viii, The mother [bought] a great fruz-tower and a fat amber-necklace. **1710** *Brit. Apollo* II. No. 101. 3/2 This filthy Fruz I ne'er shall brook. **1724** [see BULL-TOUR].

frowze, *v. Obs.* exc. *dial.* In 7 frouze. Also FRUZ *v.* [related to prec. sb.] *trans.* To curl, frizz, ruffle, rumple.

1611 FLORIO, *Increspare*, to crispe, to curle, to frouze. Also to wrimple. **1881** *Isle of Wight Gloss.*, *Frowze*, to rumple.

frowzled ('fraʊz(ə)ld), *ppl. a.* Rumpled, tousled, dishevelled, frowzy. Also **frowzly** ('fraʊzlɪ) *a.* (in quots. *frowsly*), in similar sense.

1808 M. WILMOT *Jrnl.* 20 Sept. (1934) III. 376 [His] enthusiasm caught fire & made him..rub his frouzled Crop till every hair stood erect. **1872** S. HALE *Lett.* (1919) 111 Both these Fräuleins had short frowsly hair. **1901** *Harper's Mag.* CII. 665/1 Look at the poor thing's hair! Only see how frowsly it is.

frowzy ('fraʊzɪ), *a.* Also 7–9 frouzy, 8–9 frowsy, (9 frousy). [Perh. cognate with FROWSTY, or with some of the other words there referred to. Cf. also FROWZE *sb.*]

1. Ill-smelling, fusty, musty; having a 'close' unpleasant smell from being dirty, unwashed, ill-ventilated, or the like.

1681 OTWAY *Soldier's Fort.* IV. i, An overgrown Deputy of the Ward, tho a frouzy Fellmonger. *a* **1700** DRYDEN quoted in *Faction Displ.* (1704) 15 With Frowzy Pores, that taint the ambient Air. **1773** FRANKLIN *Lett.* Wks. 1840 VI. 400 It is the frouzy corrupt air from animal substances. *a* **1802** STRUTT *Bumpkin's Disaster* (1808) 19 Is pinching frowzy wenches in their bed Fit sport for spirits? **1838** DICKENS *Nich. Nick.* xvi, By the steams of moist acts of Parliament and frowsy petitions. **1857** HUGHES *Tom Brown* I. ix, In his weeks my study was so frowsy I couldn't sit in it. **1871** L. STEPHEN *Playgr. Eur.* iv. III. 252 Another Greek convent, said to be frowzier, if possible, than that of Csalho.

2. Having a dirty, untidy, soiled, neglected appearance (like e.g. unkempt hair); dingy, rusty, slatternly, unkempt. Of the complexion: Red and coarse, blowzy.

1710 *Apparition* 7 A frowzy high-crown'd Hat his face did hide. **1716** SWIFT *Progr. Beauty* Wks. 1755 III. II. 163 A frowzy dirty-colour'd red Sits on her cloudy wrinkled face. **1752** J. SPENCE [Sir H. Beaumont] *Crito* 53 His Woman of a..sun-burnt frowsy Complexion. **1807** CRABBE *Par. Reg.* I. 214 See! on the floor, what frowzy patches rest! **1823** *Blackw. Mag.* XIV. 530 The frowzy hostess would complain. **1840** DICKENS *Old C. Shop* iii, Hair..hanging in a frowzy fringe about his forehead. **1848** —— *Dombey* vi, There were frowzy fields, and cowhouses..at the very door of the Railway. **1857** W. COLLINS *Dead Secret* II. ii, [He] produced from the pocket..three frowsy acidulated drops. **1882** *Chamb. Jrnl.* 90 A pony would be shoving its frowzy brow against its master's shoulder. **1895** *Gloss. E. Anglia*, *Frouzy*, with disordered and uncombed hair.

fig. **1821** BYRON *Juan* III. xciv, A drowzy frowzy poem, call'd the ' Excursion', Writ in a manner which is my aversion. **1859** LANG *Wand. India* 245 Even the frowsy military board—composed of several very old and feeble Company's officers of the last century—was frightened into something like activity.

3. *Comb.*, as *frowzy-headed* adj.

1860 HOLLAND *Miss Gilbert* iv. 53 Frowzy-headed men passed him in the yard. **1875** HOWELLS *Foregone Concl.* 60 A frowsy-headed woman.

Hence **'frowziness**.

1714 MANDEVILLE *Fab. Bees* II. (1733) 41 The Frowsiness of the Place, and the ill Scents of different kinds, are a perpetual Nuisance. **1835** BECKFORD *Recoll.* 106 That species of high conventual frowziness which monastic habits and garments are not a little apt to engender. **1881** *Daily News* 7 Dec. 5/3 They regard..the frowziness of our [railway-carriage] accommodation with contempt. **1893** *Temple Bar Mag.* XCIX. 197 He loves to have his room reeking with heat and frowsiness.

froynt, obs. Sc. form of FRONT.

froyter, var. of FRATER, *Obs.*

frozen ('frəʊz(ə)n), *ppl. a.* Forms: see the verb. [pa. pple. of FREEZE *v.*]

1. a. Congealed by extreme cold; subjected or exposed to extreme cold; *spec.* of food: preserved by refrigeration to below freezing point.

a **1340** HAMPOLE *Psalter* cxxv. 5 þe south blawand frosyn strandis lesis & rennys. *a* **1400–50** *Alexander* 3063 Sir Dary ..fande it [the burne] frosyn hym byfore. **1555** EDEN *Decades* Contents, The nauigation by the frosen sea. **1667** MILTON *P.L.* II. 587 Beyond this flood a frozen Continent Lies dark and wilde. **1698** FRYER *Acc. E. India & P.* 3 Warmth adds Spirits to our frozen Limbs. **1833** N. ARNOTT *Physics* (ed. 5) II. I. 90 A piece of frozen mercury..thrown into a little water at 32°. **1872** YEATS *Techn. Hist. Comm.* 224 In Canada..frozen meat is a common article of commerce. **1891**, etc. [see CHILLED *ppl. a.* 2 b]. **1893** *Times* (weekly ed.) 2 Feb. 89/3 Allowance must be made in the North-West [of Canada] for a proportion of frozen wheat. **1933** *Discovery* Apr. 127 The authors described some new experiments designed to retain the full flavour and colour of frozen fruit. **1950** *Archit. Rev.* CVIII. 142/3 A 'Kelvinator' dual freeze unit— i.e., for ordinary refrigeration and frozen food storage. **1957** *Daily Mail* 5 Sept. 9/4 Frozen-food producers came to the rescue with frozen fried fish and now the latest, frozen chips. **1967** *Listener* 20 Apr. 533/3 The same frozen scampi and vegetables.

b. *fig.* and of immaterial things. Of facts, truth (*U.S.*) = HARD, SOLID. ***the frozen limit*** (colloq.): the hard and fast limit; the *ne plus ultra* of what is objectionable or unendurable; see LIMIT *sb.*

1576 FLEMING *Panopl. Epist.* 367 Is that olde acquaintance..frozen..in you? **1641** MILTON *Ch. Govt.* vi. (1851) 125 But farre worse then any frozen captivity is the bondage of Prelates. **1697** DRYDEN *Virg. Past.* VIII. 99 Verse fires the frozen Veins. **1760** T. HUTCHINSON *Hist. Mass.* 146 They hoped to see..christian charity, then frozen, wax warm. **1814** BYRON *Corsair* I. xv, The tender blue of that large loving eye Grew frozen with its gaze on vacancy. **1858** HAWTHORNE *Fr. & It. Jrnls.* II. 62 This frozen sisterhood of the allegoric family. **1867** M. ARNOLD *Sonn., West London*, The rich she had let pass with frozen stare. **1884** *Boston* (Mass.) *Herald* 25 Sept., 'Frozen Facts' is a purely American expression. *Ibid.* 22 Oct. 2/2 We were simply stating the frozen truth. **1917** W. H. L. WATSON *Adv. Despatch Rider* x. 216, I don't mind their machine-guns, but their Minnenwerfer are the frozen limit! **1920** 'SAPPER' *Bull-Dog Drummond* i. §1, Only his eyes redeemed his face from being what is known in the vernacular as the Frozen Limit.

c. *Billiards.* Used to designate a ball at rest in close contact with another ball or a cushion.

1904 S. A. MUSSABINI *Mannock's Billiards* II. 275 When the object is frozen to the side cushion. *Ibid.* 287 Here we have the red ball 'frozen' or 'tight up' against an end cushion. *Ibid.* 293 A ball 'frozen' on a cushion. **1961** J. S. SALAK *Dict. Amer. Sports* 188 When object balls are frozen they remain in play as they are.

d. Of credits, assets, etc.: impossible to liquidate or realize at maturity or some other given time. Also *fig.* (Opp. LIQUID *a.* 6; cf. FREEZE *v.* 5 e.)

1922 *Daily Mail* 16 Dec. 9 Germany has an immense quantity of 'frozen credits' locked up in this country. **1923** *Ibid.* 9 Jan. 7 A large part of British assets..were temporarily 'frozen'. **1929** *Encycl. Brit.* IX. 876/2 *Frozen credit*, credit (generally bank-loans) which has been extended but which the creditors find it impossible or highly inexpedient to collect at maturity or at any given time... In such a case the bank will often renew or extend the loan, and this credit is said to be *frozen*, a term signifying the opposite of 'liquid' as applied to credit, capital or assets. **1930** *Times* 24 Mar. 23/5 The opportunity to accomplish this liquidation of over $10,000,000 of frozen assets. **1937** WODEHOUSE *Ld. Emsworth & Others* iv. 158 Angus McTavish was the sort of man who, just by going about looking like a frozen asset, takes all the edge and zip out of a girl's game. **1959** *Daily Tel.* 2 May 6/2 Property sequestrated or, to use the current jargon, 'frozen'.

2. *frozen-out*: cut off or excluded by frost. *frozen-up*: closed or stopped by frost.

1885 G. ALLEN *Babylon* iii, On the stray chance of catching a frozen-out racoon. **1890** *Daily News* 31 Dec. 3/2 'All froze-out poor working men who've got no work to do-o-o'..The carrying of water to frozen-up householders has become almost a..recognised industry. In many of the suburbs there has been..a mellifluous sing-song telling of frozen-up pipes. **1893** *Ibid.* 23 Feb. 7/4 The frozen-up German seed is still delayed.

3. *Comb.*, as *frozen-faced*, *-hearted* adjs.

1654 tr. *Scudery's Curia Pol.* 26 They are not men, but cold statues, and such as the frozen hearted Venetians. **1921** S. ADAMS *Success* vii. 212 Old frozen-faced Willis Enderby. **1925** T. DREISER *Amer. Trag.* (1926) II. III. ix. 150 His frozen-faced terror. **1964** *Daily Tel.* 6 Jan. 1/2 Even the most frozen-faced Cardinals in Vatican City were taken by surprise in viewing..the overpowering..enthusiasm the Pope encountered.

Hence **'frozenly** *adv.*, in a frozen manner; with a cold look or action; (*U.S.*) stubbornly; **'frozenness**, frozen condition.

1653 GAUDEN *Hieraspistes* 486 For however people have now and then a warm fit of giving..they soon returne to that frozenness, which is hardly dissolved by any mans warmest breathings. **1725** BRADLEY *Fam. Dict.* s.v. *Towering*, The Signs of which are, they look frozenly on their Sides. **1851** D. JERROLD *St. Giles* xv. 151 He..looked frozenly at the prisoner, rebuking him [etc.]. **1864** LOWELL *Fireside Trav.* 150, I..began to hack frozenly at a log.

† **frub**, *v. Obs. rare.* [Short f. FRUBBISH, perh. influenced by RUB.] *trans.* To furbish or polish.

1611 FLORIO, *Amolare*, to frub or furbish. **1656** W. D. tr. *Comenius' Gate Lat. Unl.* §415. 119 The Frubber or Furbisher frubbeth or furbisheth.

† **'frubber.** *Obs.* [f. prec. + -ER[1]. Cf. FURBER.] A furbisher, burnisher, or polisher.

1612 CHAPMAN *Widowes T.* Plays 1873 III. 73 [To a maid-servant] Well said frubber, was there no Souldier here lately? **1659** TORRIANO, *Frugatoio*, also a burnisher or a frubber.

† **'frubbish**, *v. Obs.* Also **frobish.** [var. of FURBISH.] *trans.* To furbish or polish by rubbing.

1570 LEVINS *Manip.* 144/20 To Frubbish, *fricando polire*. **1601** HOLLAND *Pliny* II. 466 When it is well scoured and clensed with sand, and knowne by the brightnesse and lustre thereof that it hath bin sufficiently frobished and purified. *a* **1625** FLETCHER *Cust. Country* III. iii, I'll make you young again, beleeve that Lady, I will so frubbish you.

Hence † **'frubbisher**, a furbisher.

1526 SKELTON *Magnyf.* 1074 The frubyssher hath my sword.

fruct(e, obs. var. of FRUIT *sb.* and *v.*

fructan ('frʌktæn). *Chem.* [f. FRUCT(OSE + *-an*, as in *glucosan.*] Any of a group of polysaccharides that are composed of fructose residues and occur widely in plants, esp. as reserve foods; a fructosan.

1953 WHISTLER & SMART *Polysaccharide Chem.* i. 17 The polysaccharides termed fructosans in the literature are hence incorrectly named. The preferred name fructans is employed in this book. **1957** WHISTLER & CORBETT in W. Pigman *Carbohydrates* xii. 683 Dahlia tubers and the tubers of the Jerusalem artichoke are rich in fructans. **1964** D. D. DAVIES et al. *Plant Biochem.* iii. 145 Most fructans also contain very small amounts of glucose.

fructed ('frʌktɪd), *a. Her.* [f. L. *frūct-us* fruit + -ED[2].] Of a tree or plant: Having fruit (of a specified tincture).

1610 GUILLIM *Heraldry* III. vii. (1611) 105 He beareth argent a pine apple tree Fructed proper. **1688** R. HOLME *Armoury* II. 5/1 A Garland of Vine leaves fructed (that is with Bunches of Grapes) about his Temples. **1708** [see ERADICATED b.] **1828–40** BERRY *Encycl. Her.*, A pear tree erased, fructed ppr. that is, with its fruit in the natural colour. **1868** CUSSANS *Her.* (1893) 103 An Oak-tree is fructed of its Acorns; and a Pine, of its Cones.

† **'fructerist.** *Obs. rare.* (See FRUCTSTER.)

fructescence (frʌk'tɛsəns). [ad. mod.L. *fructescentia*, f. *fructescent-em*: see FRUCTESCENT and -ENCE.] (See quot.)

1793 MARTYN *Lang. Bot.*, *Fructescentia*..Fructescence, or the fruiting season, is the time when vegetables scatter their ripe seeds. **1848** in CRAIG.

fructescent (frʌk'tɛsənt), *a.* [ad. mod.L. *fructescent-em*, pr. pple. of *fructescĕre* to produce fruit, f. L. *frūctus* fruit.] Beginning to bear fruit.

1862 F. HALL *Hindu Philos. Syst.* 30 Works are of three descriptions, technically designated as accumulated, current, and fructescent.

fructicist ('frʌktɪsɪst). Also FRUCTIST. [f. L. *frūct-us* FRUIT + -IC + -IST.] One who classifies plants by their fruit.

1837 WHEWELL *Hist. Induct. Sc.* (1857) III. 253 Linnæus ..began by being a fructicist. **1886** THOMPSON in *Encycl. Brit.* XX. 301/1 He [Ray] was no longer a fructicist but a corollist.

[**fructiculose**, spurious word in mod. Dictionaries: see FRUTICULOSE.]

‖**Fructidor** (fryktidɔr). [Fr.; f. L. *frūct-us* fruit + Gr. δῶρον gift.] The twelfth month of the French revolutionary calendar (from Aug. 18 to Sept. 16); the revolution which took place in that month in 1797. Hence **Fructidorian**, *a.*, belonging to the party that came into power in Fructidor.

1793–97 *Spirit Publ. Jrnls.* (1799) 35 *note*, The explosion of the 18th Fructidor. **1884** J. R. SEELEY in *Encycl. Brit.* XVII. 199 The catastrophe came on 18th Fructidor (September 4, 1797)..Such was Fructidor, which may be considered as the third of the revolutions which compose the ..French Revolution..The circle of Madame de Staël was strongly Fructidorian.

fructiferous (frʌk'tɪfərəs), *a.* [f. L. *frūctifer* (f. *frūctus* fruit + *-fer* bearing) + -OUS.] Bearing or producing fruit; fertilizing.

1632 LITHGOW *Trav.* III. 85 All other fructiferous trees. **1660** F. BROOKE tr. *Le Blanc's Trav.* 217 Inundations which fertilize all Egypt, and serve instead of fructiferous rains. **1823** J. BADCOCK *Dom. Amusem.* 61 The finely divided, loamy or fructiferous part of the soil. **1857** H. MILLER *Test. Rocks* xi. 433 None of its branches yet found bear the fructiferous stalk or spike.

Hence **fruc'tiferously** *adv.*

1626 A. SPEED *Adam out of E.* xvi. (1659) 134 You may sometimes cast the water that drayneth from the Muck, upon the muck heaps again, which will..desend to the former receptacle more fructiferously. **1635** HEYWOOD *Hierarch.* II. Comm. 98 Neither more fructiferously can any thing be found than the holy Trinitie.

† **'fructi̦fiable**, *a. Obs. rare*[−1]. [f. FRUCTIFY + -ABLE.] Capable of bearing fruit.

1623 T. ADAMS *Barren Tree* 37 The Fig-tree does not beare so soone as it is planted..but now it is growne fructifiable.

fructification (ˌfrʌktɪfɪ'keɪʃən). [ad. L. *frūctificātiōn-em*, f. *frūctificāre* to FRUCTIFY.]

1. The action or process of fructifying or producing fruit (now *rare* exc. *Bot.*). Also fecundation, fertilization (? *obs.*).

1615 JACKSON *Creed* IV. II. vi. §3 When the first seeds of that faith, which..by fructification..becomes salvifical, are first sown in our hearts. **1632** MARMION *Holland's Leaguer* IV. i, Wholly given To the deeds of fructification. **1635** SWAN *Spec. M.* vi. §4 (1643) 236 The sprouting, springing, and fructification of the earth. **1650** SIR T. BROWNE *Pseud. Ep.* III. xxi. (1658) 198 As may be discovered from several Insects generated in rain water, from the prevalent fructification of plants thereby. *a* **1665** J. GOODWIN *Filled w. the Spirit* (1867) 483 They may indeed be sowed too thick with seed of another nature, which may hinder the fructification thereof. **1759** tr. *Duhamel's Husb.* I. xv. 91 The organs of fructification. **1822–34** *Good's Study Med.* (ed. 4) IV. 10 The plants of the feeblest structure die, as soon as fructification has taken place. **1846** J. BAXTER *Libr. Pract. Agric.* (ed. 4) II. 73 At the time of fructification, watch the plants daily.

fig. **1604** T. WRIGHT *Passions* v. §4. 253 Giving is a free translation of the right or title, of dominion..or fructification of anything to any man. **1721** R. KEITH tr. *T. à Kempis Solil. Soul* xvi. 229 Temptation is wont to be very helpful..to the Fructification of Virtues. **1892** *Pall Mall G.* 13 Sept. 3/3 As regards the fructification of their estate, there is all the difference in the world between the value of arable as distinguished from mere grazing land.

2. *concr.* in *Bot.* **a.** The fruit of a plant; **b.** *collect.* the organs of fruiting or reproduction, *esp.* the reproductive parts of ferns and mosses.

1764 GRAINGER *Sugar Cane* I. *note* 6 That part of the Cane which shoots up into the fructification, is called by planters its Arrow. **1767** P. COLLINSON in *Darlington's Mem.* (1849) 292 The Wild Lime is a singular plant. Dr. Solander wishes for its fructifications. **1791** E. DARWIN *Bot. Gard.* II. Pref., The families or Genera are characterized by the analogy of all the parts of the flower or fructification. **1864** T. MOORE *Brit. Ferns* 11 Collectively, these cases and their contents are called the fructification. **1877** F. HEATH *Fern W.* 294 Nearly the whole under side of the frond is covered with the fructification. **1882** VINES *Sachs' Bot.* 95 This is usually the case..with many Lichens and the fructifications of Fungi.

fructificative ('frʌktɪfɪˌkeɪtɪv), *a.* [f. L. *frūctificāre*: see FRUCTIFY and -ATIVE.] Capable of fructifying; produced by fructification.

1887 tr. *De Bary's Fungi* iv. 125 Where fructificative and purely propagative generations of bions proceed alternately from one another.

fructiform ('frʌktɪfɔːm), *a.* [f. L. *frūct-us* fruit + -(I)FORM.] Having the form of a fruit.

1816 SIR J. SINCLAIR in *Monthly Mag.* XLII. 298 The fructiform productions which were found upon the same stalks often remained fixed together.

fructify ('frʌktɪfaɪ), *v.* Also 6 **frutyfye.** [a. F. *fructifier*, ad. L. *frūctificāre*, f. *frūctus* fruit: see -FY.]

1. *intr.* To bear fruit, become fruitful.

a **1325** *Prose Psalter* li[i]. 8 Ich am in Godes hous as oliue fructifiand. **1340** *Ayenb.* 234 Þet zed..fructefide of one half to þe þrittaȝte, of oþer half to zixtiaȝte. *c* **1400** MAUNDEV. (1839) v. 50 Elles it [the Bawm] would not fructify. *c* **1450** *Mirour Saluacioun* 1065 Aarons ȝerde fructified without plantacionne. **1538** BALE *Thre Lawes* 141 Hys wyfe shall encreace, hys land shall frutyfye. **1561** DAUS tr. *Bullinger on Apoc.* (1573) 304 The tree of lyfe..doeth fructifie, or bring forth fruite twelue tymes in the yeare. **1665** BOYLE *Occas. Refl.* IV. xv. (1845) 260 Those Soils wherein they will afterwards Flourish and Fructifie. **1709** *Brit. Apollo* II. No. 7. 2/2 Saffron..needs no adventitious moisture to make it Fructify. **1794** G. ADAMS *Nat. & Exp. Philos.* III. xxvi. 84 Causing it [the perfect animal] to fructify and renew the species. **1874** COOKE *Fungi* 13 Species of lichens which in many countries do not fructify.

fig. *c* **1393** CHAUCER *Scogan* 48 Thenke on Tullius kindenesse, Minne thy frend, ther it may fructifye! *c* **1422** HOCCLEVE *Learn to Die* 17 Y shal teche thee Thyng þat shal to thy soule fructifie. **1483** CAXTON *Gold. Leg.* 422 b/1 So moche grewe and fructefyed the chylde in resplendour or lyghte of alle good vertues. **1502** *Ord. Crysten Men* (W. de W. 1506) I. iii. 24 And desyreth not to fructefye neyther to encrease with the goodes of the erthe. **1699** DAMPIER *Voy.* II. I. 96 It seems very improbable that Christianity should fructify there. **1847** C. G. ADDISON *Contracts* II. iii. §1 (1883) 591 This description of pledge..was constantly fructifying and paying off the debt. **1875** HAMERTON *Intell. Life* XI. iv. 420 Each has caused to fructify the talent which the Master gave.

2. *trans.* To make fruitful, cause to bear fruit; to fecundate, impregnate.

1583 STUBBES *Anat. Abus.* II. (1882) 66 To fructifie and increase the earth. **1611** BEAUM. & FL. *King & No K.* II. i, Let a man..fructify foreign countries with his blood. *c* **1630** RISDON *Surv. Devon* (1810) 4 The red marle hath this property to fructify the barrenest ground. *a* **1711** KEN *Christophil* Poet. Wks. 1721 I. 441 To fructify the Seed he sow'd. **1822–34** *Good's Study Med.* (ed. 4) I. 654 On the mucous surface of which..it [exhalation of yellow fever].. fructifies a like harvest of contagious matter. **1865** W. KAY *Crisis Hupfeldiana* 6 Many a plant has been fructified by means of pollen..brought to it unwittingly by an insect.

fig. **1768–74** TUCKER *Lt. Nat.* (1852) I. 204 It fructifies our knowledge by making it practical. **1769** BURKE *Late St. Nat.* Wks. 1842 I. 85 Floods of treasure would..have fructified an exhausted exchequer. **1860** SMILES *Self-Help* xi. 282 The facility with which young people are made to acquire knowledge..fills, but does not fructify the mind.

Hence **'fructified** *ppl. a.*, in senses of the vb.; also †*Her.* = FRUCTED; **'fructifying** *vbl. sb.*, the action of the vb.; **'fructifying** *ppl. a.* Also **'fructifier**, one who or that which fructifies.

c **1374** CHAUCER *Boeth.* I pr. i. 3 (Camb. MS.) Affeccyons whiche þat ne ben nothing fructefiynge nor profytable. **1532** Fructyfyed [see FRUCTIVE]. **1594** PLAT *Jewell-ho.* I. 3 The vegetatiue & fructifying Salt of Nature. **1638** WILKINS *New World* I. (1684) 128 It is not necessary there should be the same means of Growth and Fructifying in both these Worlds. **1649** HAMMOND *Serm. Chr. Oblig. Peace* 10 The growths and fructifyings of his Graces. **1681** T. JORDAN *London's Joy* 5 An Almond-tree Leav'd, Blossom'd, and Fructified. **1708** MOTTEUX *Rabelais* v. Prol. (1737) p. lvii, These merry and fructifying..Books. **1816** SCOTT *Old Mort.* viii, An able and fructifying preacher. **1825** COLERIDGE *Aids Refl.* (1848) I. 261 A fructifying of the corrupt seed, of which death is the germination. **1835** *Fraser's Mag.* XII. 39 Think you..that one of our great financiers I mean the Thomsonian fructifier..would be scared from his presidency by apprehension of a general bankruptcy? **1879** B. TAYLOR *Stud. Germ. Lit.* 263 His ideas still retain their fructifying character.

fructiparous (frʌk'tɪpərəs), *a.* [f. L. *frūct-us* fruit + *par-ĕre* to produce + -OUS.] (See quot.)

1866 in *Treas. Bot.* **1885** *Syd. Soc. Lex.*, *Fructiparous*, producing fruit in excess of the normal quantity.

fructist ('frʌktɪst). [ad. mod.L. *fructist-a*, f. L. *frūctus* fruit: see -IST.] (See quot.)

1775 ASH, *Fructist*, a botanist who endeavours to distinguish the several kinds of plants by the fruit or seeds which they produce.

† **'fructive**, *a. Obs. rare*[−1]. [irreg. f. L. *frūct-us* fruit + -IVE.] Fruitful.

14.. LYD. *Commend. Our Lady* 38 Fructif [**1532** *Thynne's Chaucer*, Fructyfyed] olyue, of foyles faire and thikke, And redolent cedre.

fructivorous (frʌk'tɪvərəs), *a.* [as if f. L. **frūctivor-us* (f. *frūct-us* fruit + *-vorus* devouring) + -OUS.] Eating or feeding on fruit.

1688 R. HOLME *Armoury* II. 310/1 Fructivorous Birds such as feed upon Fruit. **1845** *Zoologist* III. 912 Fructivorous animals will sometimes feed on flesh. **1947** J. STEVENSON-HAMILTON *Wild Life S. Afr.* xxxi. 261 Being already both fructivorous and insectivorous, the species [*sc.* the baboon] may be at the early beginning of becoming carnivorous also. **1970** *Watsonia* VIII. 67 Red berries for fructivorous birds.

fructolysis (frʌk'tɒlɪsɪs). *Biochem.* [f. FRUCTO(SE + LYSIS.] (See quot. 1943.)

1932 DICKENS & GREVILLE in *Biochem. Jrnl.* XXVI. 1252 For the sake of brevity, we shall use the following terms. *Glycolysis.* General expression denoting the break-down of carbohydrate to lactic acid... *Glucolysis.* The glycolysis in the presence of added glucose. *Fructolysis.* The glycolysis in the presence of added fructose. **1943** *Thorpe's Dict. Appl. Chem.* (ed. 4) VI. 74/1 'Glucolysis' has been the name given to the phenomenon of glucose breakdown to lactic acid, and 'fructolysis' has been applied when the sugar in question has been fructose.

fructosan ('frʌktəʊsæn). *Chem.* [f. FRUCTOS(E + *-an*, as in *glucosan.*] = FRUCTAN.

1928 *Chem. Abstr.* XXII. 4480, 9 g. of a yellow trifructosan..is obtained. *Ibid.* 4481 Heating inulin for 6 hrs. at 140° produces 51% of a difructosan. *Ibid.*, A monofructosan. *Ibid.* 5849 (Index), Fructosans, and acetates. **1931** E. C. MILLER *Plant Physiol.* viii. 412 The hexosans may be further classified according to the type of hexose that they yield on hydrolysis into the dextrosans (glucosans), the levulosans (fructosans), the mannans, and the galactans. **1940** *New Phytologist* XXXIX. 185 While the term fructosan should properly apply to the whole group of fructose polymers including inulin, it is frequently used to designate only this second class of polymers found in monocotyledons. **1953** [see FRUCTAN]. **1966** P. MCDONALD et al. *Anim. Nutrition* ii. 18 Many grasses contain appreciable quantities of fructosans.

fructose ('frʌktəʊs). *Chem.* [f. L. *fruct-us* fruit + -OSE.] 'Fruit sugar or lævulose. Also applied to the sugar found in fruit, which consists of variable proportions of lævulose and dextrose' (*Syd. Soc. Lex.* 1885).

1864 in WEBSTER. **1893** P. F. FRANKLAND *Secr. Friends & Foes* 104 One of the principal artificial sugars prepared by Fischer is called fructose. **1894** GOULD *Illustr. Dict. Med.*, *Fructose*, $C_6H_{12}O_6$ Fruit-sugar, formerly called levulose.

† **'fructster.** *Obs. rare*[−1]. [Cf. FRUITESTER.]

1688 R. HOLME *Armoury* II. 86/1 Fructster a Fruit-seller; of some Fructerist or Fruterer.

† **ˈfructuage.** *Sc. Obs.* [f. L. *frūctu-s* FRUIT + -AGE. Cf. FRUITAGE.] Fruits collectively, fruit.
1637–50 Row *Hist. Kirk* (1842) 141 Their Moondayes mercatt, occasioning necessarlie the carieing of loads on the Lord's day; Item, Selling of flours and fructuages that day.

† **ˈfructual,** *a. Obs. rare.* [f. as prec. + -AL¹.] Fruitful.
1528 LYNDESAY *Dream* 818 The haboundance of fyschis in our seis, And fructuall montanis for our bestiall. **1629** T. ADAMS *Serm.* Wks. I. 274 It is fructuall: let it be so to vs in operation. It giues vs the fruite of life, let vs returne it the fruits of obedience.

fructuary (ˈfrʌktjuːərɪ), *a.* and *sb.* [ad. L. *frūctuāri-us*, f. *frūctus* FRUIT: see -ARY.]
A. *adj.* in *Roman Law.* Of or belonging to usufruct; usufructuary. Only in ***fructuary stipulation.***
1875 POSTE *Gaius* IV. §166 Provided that he gives his opponent security by the fructuary stipulation.
† B. *sb. Obs.*
1. One who enjoys the 'fruits' or profits (of something); a usufructuary.
1643 PRYNNE *Sov. Power Parl.* App. 168 A fructuary can dispose or give the profits at his pleasure. **1687** DR. SMITH in *Magd. Coll. & Jas. II* (O.H.S.) 162 Of which we are but the fructuaries.
2. Something enjoyed by usufruct. *rare*⁻¹.
1651 W. G. tr. *Cowel's Inst.* 63 In fructuaries and in those things whereof we have the use but not the property.

† **ˈfructuate,** *v. Obs.*⁻¹ [f. L. *frūctu-s* FRUIT + -ATE³.] *intr.* To bear fruit; to fructify.
1663 *Flagellum, or O. Cromwell* (ed. 2) 5 Those ill qualities which fructuated in him [Cromwell] at this age.
Hence **ˈfructuated** *ppl. a. Her.* = FRUCTED. Also **fructuˈation,** the action of bearing fruit; †*concr.* a crop of fruit (in quot. *fig.*).
1782 T. POWNALL *Antiquity* 60 Knowing..with what superabundant population the first fructuation of an advancing society is loaded. **1809** J. HOME in *Naval Chron.* XXIV. 193 An oak tree vert..fructuated or. **1885** *Syd. Soc. Lex., Fructuation,* the development or production of fruit.

fructule (ˈfrʌktjuːl). [a. F. *fructule*, f. L. *frūctus* + -ULE.] (See quot.)
1885 *Syd. Soc. Lex., Fructule,* one of the parts or simple fruits of which a compound fruit is made up.

† **fructuose,** *a. Obs.* Also 5 frut-. [ad. L. *frūctuōs-us*: see FRUCTUOUS and -OSE.] = FRUCTUOUS.
c **1440** *Promp. Parv.* 181/2 Frutuose or full of frute ..*fructuosus.* *c* **1450** tr. *De Imitatione* I. xv. (1893) 17 What euer be doon of charite..is fructuose. **1524** *St. Papers Hen. VIII*, VI. 317 He may perceve the Kinges recommendations ..to be unto him fructuose and to good purpose. **1727–36** in BAILEY.

† **fructuˈosity.** *Obs.*⁻⁰ [ad. F. *fructuosité*, f. L. *frūctuōs-us*: see next and -ITY.] The condition or quality of being fructuous.
1727–36 in BAILEY.

fructuous (ˈfrʌktjuːəs), *a.* Also 5 fructuowse, 6 fructuus, -eous. [a. OF. *fructuous* (mod.F. *fructueux*), ad. L. *frūctuōs-us*, f. *frūctus* FRUIT: see -OUS.]
1. Full of, abounding with, or producing fruit.
1382 WYCLIF *Jer.* xi. 16 An olyue plenteous, fair, fructuous. *c* **1400** MAUNDEV. (1839) v. 42 That Lond..is drye and nothing fructuous. **1413** *Pilgr. Sowle* (Caxton 1483) IV. ii. 58 That graf was taken fro a free appel tree and a fructuous. **1513** DOUGLAS *Æneis* I. viii. 68 Ane..fructuus grund, plenteous of victall. **1535** STEWART *Cron. Scot.* II. 106 Thair follouit ȝeiris thre So fructuous with sic fertilitie. **1614** T. ADAMS *Devil's Banquet* 310 It was as populous as fructuous; and at once blessed with pregnancie both of fruits for the people, and of people for the fruits. **1627–77** FELTHAM *Resolves* I. xix. 33 As fruits..trans-earth'd..haue vigour enough in themselves to be fructuous according to their nature. **1853** G. JOHNSTON *Nat. Hist. E. Bord.* I. 106 It leads us..to woods and fructuous plains. **1855** BROWNING *Old Pict. Florence* xxxiv, Contrast the fructuous and sterile eras. **1886** B. ROOSEVELT *Copper Queen* I. ii. 23 Did not fruit come from St. Joseph, and every other fructuous town from east, west, north, or south?
† **b.** Promoting fertility. *rare.*
1603 HOLLAND *Plutarch's Mor.* 991 If water were of the oune nature fructuous, it must needs follow, that it selfe alone, and at all times, should be able to produce fruit. **1708** J. PHILIPS *Cyder* I. 35 So rich the soil, So much does fructuous moisture o'erabound.
2. *fig.* Productive of 'fruits' or results; advantageous, beneficial, profitable.
c **1386** CHAUCER *Pars. Prol.* 73 Telleth quod he youre meditacioun..Beth fructuous and that in litel space. *c* **1410** LOVE *Bonavent. Mirr.* xl. 88 (Gibbs MS.) After þat worthy sopere was done: and þat noble and fructuouse sermon endet. **1528** ROY *Rede Me* (Arb.) 115 Goddis worde..The fructeous fode of oure faythfull trust, Thou hast condempned. **1879** A. W. WARD *Chaucer* ii. 123 The even more improbable, but..infinitely more fructuous tale of patient Griseldis. **1884** *Law Times* 14 June 119/1 The execution must be fructuous if poundage is to be payable.
Hence **ˈfructuously** *adv.*, **ˈfructuousness.**
1382 WYCLIF *Ecclus.* viii. 10 Of hem [wise prestis] forsothe thou shalt lerne wisdam..and fructuousli vse grete men withoute pleynt. *c* **1450** *Gesta Rom.* lii. 233 (Harl. MS.) Who so euer prechithe fructuovslye the worde of god. **1530** *Proper Dyaloge* (Arb.) 150 Old writinges..do include The pithe of a matter most fructuously. **1855** OGILVIE Suppl., *Fructuously*, fruitfully, fertilely. *Fructuousness*, fruitfulness, fertility.

† **ˈfructure.** *Obs. rare*⁻⁰. [a. OF. *fructure*, ad. med.L. *fructūra*, f. *fruī* (ppl. stem *fruct-*) to enjoy.] The use or enjoyment of the fruits (of something).
1611 COTGR., *Fructure*, the fructure, vse, fruition, possession, or enjoyment of.

frude, var. of FROUD, *Obs.*, frog, toad.

frug (frʌg, fruːg). [Origin unknown.] A modern dance. Hence as *v. intr.*
1964 in *Amer. Speech* (1965) XL. 143 Discotheque dresses make dancing the frug..and the Watusi a delight because they move with the beat. **1965** *Daily Express* 27 Sept. 3/5 Other guests..were wearing themselves out with the latest dance craze, the Frug. **1965** J. PHILIPS *Twisted People* I. i. 10 The frug, the Watusi, the surf, the monkey—strange dances in which the partners do not touch, do not talk. **1965** *Punch* 22 Dec. 930/2 They were frugging around to a new Who waxing. **1967** *Spectator* 29 Sept. 350/1 Mr. George Brown went to New York to dance the frug and tell the United Nations about Vietnam. **1968** J. C. HOLMES *Nothing More to Declare* 11 Energetic kids, with their guitars and placards, who frug and demonstrate so indefatigably everywhere these days. **1968** J. UPDIKE *Couples* (1969) iv. 365 Bernadette..heard a frug record put on the phonograph and held wide her arms. **1971** *Courier Mail* (Brisbane) 1 Feb. 16/8 They frugged and danced.

frugal (ˈfruːgəl), *a.* [ad. L. *frūgālis*, f. *frūgī* used as indecl. adj. = 'frugal, economical, useful', originally the dat. of *frux* profit, utility, fruit (chiefly in pl. *frūgēs* fruits): see -AL¹. Cf. F. *frugal.*]
1. Careful or sparing in the use of food, goods, etc.; economical. Const. *of* (? *obs.*).
1598 SHAKS. *Merry W.* II. i. 28, I was then Frugall of my mirth. **1656** COWLEY *Pindar. Odes, 2nd Olymp. Ode* xi, 'Tis now the cheap and frugal fashion, Rather to Hide than Pay the Obligation. **1758** J. S. *Le Dran's Observ. Surg.* (1771) 51 Observation had taught me to be frugal of the Teguments. **1761** HUME *Hist. Eng.* II. xxvii. 120 Few had borne a greater part in the frugal politics of the late king. **1782** COWPER *Gilpin* viii, Though on pleasure she was bent She had a frugal mind. **1841** ELPHINSTONE *Hist. Ind.* II. 457 The mere husbandmen are sober, frugal, and industrious. **1875** JOWETT *Plato* (ed. 2) III. 685 The frugal life of the true Hellenic citizen.
b. Of things, *esp.* food: Sparingly supplied or used; of small cost; opposed to *luxurious.*
1603 HOLLAND *Plutarch's Mor.* 616 Captaine Timotheus having upon a time beene at a sober and frugall scholars supper. **1697** DRYDEN *Virg. Georg.* IV. 194 Pot-herbs.. bruis'd with Vervain, were his frugal Fare. **1762** GOLDSM. *Cit. W.* xlvi. (1837) 267 A frugal meal, which consisted of roots and tea. **1783** CRABBE *Village* I. 324 The glad parish pays the frugal fee. **1868** BROWNING *Ring & Bk.* II. *Half-Rome* 460 A frugal board, bare sustenance, no more. **1894** MRS. H. WARD *Marcella* I. 9 The uncovered boards with their frugal strips of carpet.
2. *Comb.*, as ***frugal-feeding*** adj.
1814 *Edin. Rev.* XXIII. 51 The frugal-feeding goat supplied a competency of milk.
Hence **ˈfrugally** *adv.*, in a frugal manner; **ˈfrugalness.**
1597 HOOKER *Eccl. Pol.* V. lxxix. §1 For worldly goods it sufficeth frugally and honestly to vse them to our owne benefit. **1658** SIR T. BROWNE *Hydriot.* iii. 37 Plato seemed too frugally politick, who allowed no larger Monument then would contain four Heroick Verses. **1721** BERKELEY *Prev. Ruin Gt. Brit.* Wks. III. 198 That sum..frugally and prudently laid out in workhouses. **1727** BAILEY vol. II, *Frugalness.* **1779–81** JOHNSON *L.P.* Wks. 1816 IX. 338 He seldom lives frugally who lives by chance. **1871** CARLYLE in *Mrs. Carlyle's Lett.* I. 373 His frugally elegant small house and table. **1886** RUSKIN *Præterita* II. ix. 328 The bunch of grapes or stalk of garlic they frugally dined on.

frugalist (ˈfruːgəlɪst). [f. FRUGAL *a.* + -IST.] One who lives frugally.
1864 *Daily Tel.* 12 Oct., Unless the colleges could be enlarged, residence within the walls for the 'frugalists' would be impossible.

frugality (fruːˈgælɪtɪ). [a. F. *frugalité*, ad. L. *frūgālitāt-em*, f. *frūgālis*: see FRUGAL and -ITY.]
The quality of being frugal; moderate or sparing expenditure or use of provisions, goods, etc.
1531 ELYOT *Gov.* III. xxi, The auncient temperaunce, and moderation in diete, called sobrietie, or in a more general terme, frugalitie. *a* **1568** ASCHAM *Scholem.* (Arb.) 136 Frugalitie in diet was priuately misliked: Towne going to good cheare openly vsed. **1651** HOBBES *Govt. & Soc.* xii. §9. 183 Riches are gotten with industry, and kept by frugality. **1758** JOHNSON *Idler* No. 13 ¶2 A family remarkable for domestic prudence and elegant frugality. **1807** CRABBE *Par. Reg.* I. 445 The wise frugality that does not give A life to saving, but that saves to live. **1881** P. BROOKS *Candle of Lord* 128 In this miracle..there is a meeting of generosity and frugality which is striking.
b. Const. *of* (? *obs.*).
1700 DRYDEN *Fables* Ded. (1721) 8 In this frugality of your praises there are some things which I cannot omit.
c. Occasional uses: The product of frugality, wealth gathered by economy; also in *pl.* frugal ways of living, frugal fare.
1725 POPE *Odyss.* II. 62 Thro' my court the noise of Revel rings, And wastes the wise frugality of Kings. **1842** KINGSLEY *Lett.* (1878) I. 61 A temporary sharer in the frugalities of my farm house lodging.

frugardite (ˈfruːgɑːdaɪt). *Min.* Also -it. [f. *Frugard* in Finland, where found + -ITE. Cf. F. *frugardite.*] (See quots.)
1823 H. J. BROOKE *Introd. Crystallogr.* 467 Frugardit, reddish idocrase containing magnesia. **1884** DANA *Min.* 277 The mineral from Gokum..and that from Frugard, Frugardite, have been denominated magnesian.

fruggan (ˈfrʌgən). *dial.* Also 7 fruggin. [var. of FURGON.] (See quots.)
1611 COTGR., *Fourgon*, an Ouen-forke (tearmed in Lincolnshire, a Fruggin) wherewith fuell is both put into an Ouen, and stirred when it is (on fire) in it. **1652** *Inv. T. Teanby of Barton-on-Humber* (*N.W. Linc. Gloss.*), In the kitchen..on fruggin. **1788** W. MARSHALL *Yorksh. Gloss.* (E.D.S.), *Fruggan*, an oven-poker. **1868** ATKINSON *Cleveland Gloss.*, *Fruggan*, a curved iron scraper or rake to stir ashes in an oven with, or on the hearth. **1892** in *Northumb. Gloss.*

† **fruˈgiferent,** *a. Obs.*⁻⁰ [ad. L. *frūgiferent-em* f. as next: see -ENT.] = next.
1656 BLOUNT *Glossogr.*, *Frugiferent*, bringing forth fruit, profitable.

frugiferous (fruːˈdʒɪfərəs), *a.* [f. L. *frūgifer* (f. *frūgi-, frux* fruit + *-fer* bearing) + -OUS.] Fruit-bearing, fruitful. Hence **fruˈgiferousness** (Bailey 1727–36).
1633 T. ADAMS *Exp. 2 Peter* iii. 18 All trees are not frugiferous, Christians are. **1653** H. MORE *Conject. Cabbal.* (1713) 4 And God said, Behold, I give you every frugiferous Herb, which is upon the face of the Earth.
fig. **1671** J. WEBSTER *Metallogr.* xxvi. 318 We never accounted the Experiment either so luciferous or frugiferous, to make it our business to attend rivals.

frugivorous (fruːˈdʒɪvərəs), *a.* [f. L. *frūgi-, frux* fruit + *-vorus* devouring + -OUS.] Eating or feeding on fruit. Hence **fruˈgivorousness** (Bailey 1727–36).
1713 DERHAM *Phys.-Theol.* VII. ii. 384 Suited to various Foods, some Membranaceous, agreeable to the frugivorous or carnivorous kind. **1791** W. BARTRAM *Carolina* 302 This bird having a remarkable thick, strong bill, more like the frugivorous tribes. **1809** SYD. SMITH in *Edin. Rev.* Apr. 147 Philippics against frugivorous children after dinner, are too common. **1873** E. SMITH *Foods* 86 A small monkey and a frugivorous bat are eaten as delicacies in Zanzibar.

† **fruibly,** *adv. Obs.*⁻¹ [f. **fruible* (ad. med.L. **fruibilis*, f. *fruī*: see next) + -LY².] Enjoyingly; in a state of enjoyment.
c **1450** tr. *De Imitatione* II. i. 41 A louer of ihesu..may frely..lifte himself aboue himself in spirit, and þere reste fruibly [L. *fruitive*].

† **fruish,** *v. Obs.* In 5 fruisshe. [ad. OF. *fruiss-* lengthened stem of *fruir* to enjoy, ad. pop. L. **fruīre* (classical L. *fruī* deponent vb.).] *trans.* To enjoy. Hence ***fruishing** *ppl. a.*, **fruishingly** *adv.*
c **1450** tr. *De Imitatione* III. xxiii. 92, I may not fruisshe tho iocunde clippinges that are redy to holy spirites. *Ibid.* III. xviii. 86, III. lvi. 133. *Ibid.* III. lxiii. 147 Gone all & hool into þe loue of me, in whom þei reste fruisshingly.

fruit (fruːt), *sb.* Forms: α. 2–6 frut, 3–6 fruyt(e, 4–5 froyte, (4 frot(t, fryt(e), 4–6 frute, -tt(e, *north.* and *Sc.* froit(e, (4 freut, frou(i)t, fruȝt, 5 fret, fruth), 4–7 fruite, (4 fruyȝte, 6 frught, *Sc.* frw(i)t), 3– fruit. β. 4–6 fruct(e, 6 fruict. [a. OFr. *fruit* (later often spelt *fruict*):— L. *frūctus* (*u*-stem), f. **frugv-* root of *fruī* to enjoy.]
The form *fruct(e* in 14–15th c. English use, and still later in Sc. writers, appears to be merely a variety of spelling (of course after the L.); but it is possible that in the few English 16th c. uses of this form, which seem to be confined to immaterial senses, the writers intended the word to be taken as a direct adaptation of the Latin, with the *c* pronounced.
1. Vegetable products in general, that are fit to be used as food by men and animals. Now usually in *pl.* Also ***fruits of the earth*** or ***the ground.***
α. *c* **1175** *Lamb Hom.* 135 Me saweð sed on ane time and gedereð þet frut on oðer time. *c* **1300** *Cursor M.* 28833 (Cott. Galba) Þe pouer man es like þe felde, þat mekill fruit es wont to yelde. *c* **1375** *Lay Folks Mass Bk.* (MS. B.) 392 Þo froytes of þo erthe make plentuus. **1389** in *Eng. Gilds* (1870) 111 We schal beseke for yᵉ frutte yᵗ is on yᵉ herthe. **1486** *Bk. St. Albans* E v, Booth in wodys and feldis corne and oder frute. **1538** STARKEY *England* I. iii. 73 Yf hyt were dylygently laburyd hyt wold bryng forth frute for the nuryschyng of man. **1549** *Bk. Com. Prayer*, Litany, That it may please thee to give and preserve to our use the kindly fruits of the earth. **1648** GAGE *West Ind.* xii. 43 The answer of our Queene Elizabeth..to some that presented unto her of the fruits of America. **1665** *Ord. Mayor Lond.* in De Foe *Plague* (1840) 46 That no..musty corn, or other corrupt fruits..be suffered to be sold. **1725** WATTS *Logic* I. vi. §3 If the husk or seeds are eaten, they are called the fruits of the ground. **1791** NEWTE *Tour Eng. & Scot.* 196 At Aberdeen, turnips, carrots, and potatoes, pass, among the common people, by the name of fruit. **1859** JEPHSON *Brittany* ii. 20 The Breton peasant can turn all the fruits of the earth to account.
β. *c* **1374** CHAUCER *Former Age* 3 They helde hem paied of the fructes þat þey ete. **1500–20** DUNBAR *Poems* xiv. 63 Quhilk slayis the corne and fruct that growis grene.
fig. *c* **1374** CHAUCER *Boeth.* I. pr. i. 3 (Camb. MS.) Thise ben tho that..destroyen the corn plentyuous of fruites of resone. **1559** *Mirr. Mag., Hen. VI*, xxxix, See here the pleasant fruytes that many princes reape. **1707** WATTS *Hymn, 'Come, we that love the Lord'* viii, Celestial Fruits on earthly Ground From Faith and Hope may grow. **1783**

WATSON *Philip III* (1793) I. II. 233 The only fruit which he could reap from a victory.

2. The edible product of a plant or tree, consisting of the seed and its envelope, *esp.* the latter when it is of a juicy pulpy nature, as in the apple, orange, plum, etc. †*tree of fruit* = *fruit-tree*.

As denoting an article of food, the word is popularly extended to include certain vegetable products that resemble 'fruits' in their qualities, e.g. the stalks of rhubarb.

a. *collect.* in *sing.*

a **1225** *Ancr. R.* 150 Figer is ones kunnes treou þet bereð swete frut, þet me clepeð figes. **13..** *E.E. Allit. P.* B. 1044 Þe fayrest fryt þat may in folde growe, As orenge & oþer fryt. *c* **1380** WYCLIF *Serm.* Sel. Wks. I. 69 Al oþer trees of fruyte. *c* **1400** *Lanfranc's Cirurg.* 75, I ne apreve nouȝt almaundis ne noon oþer vaperous fruyt: as notis eiþir walnotis eiþer avellanes. *c* **1483** CAXTON *Vocab.* 6 b, Of fruyt shall ye here named Peres, apples, plommes. **1577** B. GOOGE *Heresbach's Husb.* II. (1586) 62 The berries, which is the fruite, are redde. **1626** BACON *Sylva* §432 The lowness of the Bough, where the Fruit cometh, maketh the Fruit greater. **1677** GREW *Anat. Fruits* v. §1 (1682) 186 The Fruit, strictly so called, is, A Fleshy Uterus, which grows more moist and Pulpy, as the Seed ripens. **1706** POPE *Let. to Wycherley* 10 Apr. Lett. (1735) 26 We take Branches from a Tree, to add to the Fruit. **1837** *Penny Cycl.* VII. 27 [Bats] devouring indiscriminately every kind of fruit.

fig. *a* **1225** *Ancr. R.* 276 Mon, þi flesch, hwat frut bereð hit? **1697** DRYDEN *Virg. Georg.* III. 57 Heroes, whose Etherial Root Is Jove himself, and Cæsar is the Fruit. **1771** *Junius Lett.* lix. 304 [He] sees the fruit of his honest industry ripen beyond his hopes.

b. with *a* and *pl.*, as denoting a kind of fruit.

α. *c* **1250** *Gen. & Ex.* 216 Ðat he sulde him ðer loken fro A fruit, ðe kenned wel and wo. *a* **1300** *Cursor M.* 11667 (Gött.) Scho..sau a frout..Men clepes palmes in þat land. **1375** BARBOUR *Bruce* x. 191 The treis..Chargit vith froytis on syndri viss. *c* **1400** *Lanfranc's Cirurg.* 261 Þou schalt purge colre wiþ a decocioun of fretis. *c* **1460** J. RUSSELL *Bk. Nurture* 667 Speke..For frutes a-fore mete to ete þem fastyngely. **1527** R. THORNE in Hakluyt *Voy.* (1589) 252 Our fruites and graines be Apples, Nuts, and Corne. **1650** FULLER *Pisgah* I. iv. 11 Dates, Almonds..Nuts..Pomegranates and other severall fruits. **1795** *Gentl. Mag.* 540/1 The glow of ripe fruits and declining leaves mark the autumn. **1842** TENNYSON *Gard. Dau.* 190 Fruits and cream served in the weeping elm. **1858** HOMANS *Cycl. Commerce* 886 This fruit [currants] is of a violet colour, and hangs in long loose bunches.

β. **1475** *Bk. Noblesse* 70 Planted withe treis of verdure of divers fructis. **1585** JAS. I *Ess. Poesie* (Arb.) 14 To taste, and smell..Delicious fruictis, whilks in that tyme abound. **1596** DALRYMPLE tr. *Leslie's Hist. Scot.* I. 6 Excepte spice and Vine, and sum fructes.

c. An individual product of a tree. *rare.*

1873 C. ROBINSON *N.S. Wales* 26 The Mandarin has borne 4,200 fruits in the year.

d. *Proverbs.*

α. *a* **1300** *Cursor M.* 38 (Gött.) Wers tre wer frouit it beris. *c* **1530** R. HILLES *Common-pl. Bk.* (1858) 140 Often tymys provyth the frught affore The stok that hyt cometh off. **1596** SHAKS. *Merch. V.* IV. i. 115 The weakest kinde of fruite Drops earliest to the ground. **1640** J. DYKE *Worthy Commun.* 176 No roote no fruite.

β. **1535** STEWART *Cron. Scot.* (1858) I. 165 Sindrie tymes we se That rycht gude fruct cumis of ane gude tre.

e. *old* (*tin of*) *fruit*: a term of familiar address. (Cf. *old bean.*) *slang.*

1923 *Daily Mail* 8 Feb. 6 Was she simply bursting to address him Gaily as her 'dear old tin of fruit'? **1928** *Ibid.* 25 July 10/6 Then their politeness. No slapping a friend on the back with a 'What cheer, old fruit?' **1951** T. RATTIGAN *Who is Sylvia?* I. 212 You don't mind me asking, did you, old fruit? **1968** K. BIRD *Smash Glass Image* xiii. 162 *Adiós*, old fruit. *Hasta luego.* Go and jump in the nearest lake.

†**3.** A fruit-tree; also a food-plant. *Obs. rare.*

a **1300** *Cursor M.* 8239 All frutes he plantede in þat place. **1577** B. GOOGE *Heresbach's Husb.* II. (1586) 84 b, About the tenth of June, both the Vine, and Wheate, the two noble fruites, do flowre. **1767** A. YOUNG *Farmer's Lett. People* 313 Many of our fruits and most useful plants are the natural inhabitants of much warmer countries.

†**4.** A course of fruit; the dessert. *to be in one's fruits*: to be at dessert. *Obs.*

1577–87 HOLINSHED *Chron.* III. 915/2 The officers being at dinner, and the cardinall not fullie dined, being then in his fruits. **1602** SHAKS. *Ham.* II. ii. 52 My Newes shall be the fruite to that great Feast.

5. The seed of a plant or tree, regarded as the means of reproduction, together with its envelope; *spec.* in *Bot.* 'the ripe pistil containing the ovules, arrived at the state of seeds' (Lindley); also, the spores of cryptogams.

1794 MARTYN *Rousseau's Bot.* i. 21 In Botany, by fruit, in herbs as well as in trees, we understand the whole fabric of the seed. **1796** WITHERING *Brit. Plants* (ed. 3) II. 194 Its flower is that of Plantago, but..its fruit distinguish[es] it from that genus. **1813** SIR H. DAVY *Agric. Chem.* (1814) 140 Fruits..contain a certain quantity of nourishment laid up in their cells for the use of the Embryon plant. **1870** HOOKER *Stud. Flora* 210 Hypochæris..Fruits striate, scabrous. **1886** A. WINCHELL *Walks & Talks Geol. Field* 174 The low rank of these plants [in the coal-formation] is evinced also by the absence of flowers and fruit.

6. Offspring, progeny. Also, an embryo, fœtus. Orig. a Hebraism. Now *rare*, exc. in Biblical phraseology. More fully ***fruit of the body, loins, womb.***

a **1300** *Cursor M.* 5445 Þi frut i se bi-for mi nei. *a* **1340** HAMPOLE *Psalter* cxxxi. 11 Of þe froite of þi wambe i sall sett on þi seat. **1382** WYCLIF *Acts* ii. 30 God hadde sworn to him, of the fruyt of his leende for to sitte on his seete. **1398** TREVISA *Barth. De P.R.* XVII. lxxiv. (1495) 647 We speke vnproperly somtyme and call the brode of the beestys frute. *c* **1425** *Found. St. Bartholomew's* (E.E.T.S.) 42 Stondyng neyr the tyme that the fruyt shulde be proferid forth. *c* **1500** *Melusine* xxx. 218 Duchesse, take good heede of your fruyte that groweth in your blood. **1533** GAU *Richt Vay* (1888) 12 Thay quhilk takis avay the frwtis of thair nichtburs beistis. **1535** COVERDALE *Deut.* xxviii. 4 Blessed shalbe the frute of thy body. **1578** LYTE *Dodoens* II. lxxvii. 252 It closeth the Matrice, causeth the fruite to live. **1593** SHAKS. *3 Hen. VI*, IV. iv. 24 Least with my sighes or teares I blast or drowne King Edwards Fruite. **1607** TOPSELL *Four-f. Beasts* (1658) 463 There is..another excellent medicine..whereby the fruit in a womans womb may be brought forth either dead or putrified. **1611** BIBLE *Exod.* xxi. 22 If men striue, and hurt a woman with child, so that her fruit depart from her. **1641** HINDE *J. Bruen* i. 2 The Lord with-held the fruit of the womb..so that by her he had no issue. **1822–34** *Good's Study Med.* (ed. 4) IV. 128 Risking the loss of the uterine fruit.

7. Anything accruing, produced, or resulting from an action or effort, the operation of a cause, etc.

a. Material produce, outgrowth, increase; *pl.* products, revenues.

α. *c* **1440** *Jacob's Well* (E.E.T.S.) 202 Þe fruyte & þe profyȝte of þat lande & of beeste in þi tyme. **1523** FITZHERB. *Surv.* 36 S. B. occupyeth the sayd personage him selfe, withall the glebe landes, medowes, tythes, and all other frutes. **1611** BIBLE *2 Esdras* viii. 10 Milke..which is the fruit of the breasts. **1715–20** POPE *Iliad* XVII. 6 Round her new-fallen young the heifer moves, Fruit of her throes. **1726** SHELVOCKE *Voy. round World* 86 A dozen of hams..the fruit of this country. **1849** MACAULAY *Hist. Eng.* I. 311 The produce of the soil far exceeded the value of all the other fruits of human industry.

β. *a* **1500** *Colkelbie Sow* iii. 763 Quhilk for þe tyme no fruct nor proffeit did. **1563** ABP. PARKER *Articles*, Ani patron that ..taketh the tythes and other fructes to him selfe.

b. An immaterial product, a result, issue, consequence. *sing.* and *pl.*

α. *a* **1300** *Cursor M.* 19230 Was neuer þe fruit o suilk bot ill. *c* **1375** *Sc. Leg. Saints, Baptista* 268 Dois worthy froite of pennance ay. *c* **1386** CHAUCER *Knt.'s T.* 424 Of al oure strif, God woot, the fruyt is thin. **1413** *Pilgr. Sowle* (Caxton) v. xiv. (1859) 80 Alle the wyde world is fulfylled with the fruyte of theyr good labour. *c* **1460** FORTESCUE *Abs. & Lim. Mon.* iii. (1885) 116 Sumwhat now I haue shewid the frutes of both lawes. **1548–9** (Mar.) *Bk. Com. Prayer* Post-Communion, The fruite of good liuing. **1601** SHAKS. *Twel. N.* II. v. 216 If you will then see the fruites of the sport, mark his first approach before my lady. **1659** HAMMOND *On Ps.* 1 All these Psalms are not the fruit or product of one inspired brain. **1668** TEMPLE *Let. to Ld. Arlington* Wks. 1731 II. 108 The Fruits of our Conferences your Lordship will find in the Enclosed. **1712** ADDISON *Spect.* No. 287 ¶ 6 Riches and Plenty are the natural Fruits of Liberty. **1786** COWPER *Let. to Churchey* Wks. 1837 XV. 189 The most effectual spur to industry in all such exertions, is to lay the fruit of them before the public. **1853** J. H. NEWMAN *Hist. Sk.* (1873) II. I. ii. 64 Zingis swept round the sea of Aral, and destroyed the fruits of a long civilization. **1858** CARLYLE *Fredk. Gt.* II. vi. (1865) I. 85 His going on the Crusade..was partly the fruit of the life she led him.

β. *a* **1568** ASCHAM *Scholem.* (Arb.) 23, I wishe..that yong M. Rob. Sackuille, may take that fructe of this labor. **1585** M. W. *Commend. Verses to Jas. I's Ess. Poesie* (Arb.) 10 Lo, heir the fructis, Nymphe, of thy foster faire.

c. Advantage, benefit, enjoyment, profit.

α. *c* **1230** *Hali Meid.* 7 Þus hauen godes freond al þe fruit of þis world þat ha forsaken habbeð. **1484** CAXTON *Curiall* 3 Thou shalt haue labour wythoute fruyt and shalt vse thy lyf in perylle. **1559** *Mirr. Mag., Worcester* v, The fruite Of reading stories, standeth in the suite. **1588** J. UDALL *Diotrephes* (Arb.) 17 You shold preach foure times euery weeke, with more fruit than you can doe now foure times euery yeere. **1602** SHAKS. *Ham.* II. ii. 145 She tooke the Fruites of my Aduice. **1630** *R. Johnson's Kingd. & Commw.* 384 The greatest fruit which the Emperour reapeth by the Crowne of Hungarland, ariseth by the benefit of Mines. **1698** J. HOWE in H. Rogers *Life* x. (1863) 219, I read thy lines with fruit and delight. **1858** F. HALL in *Jrnl. Amer. Orient. Soc.* (1862) VII. 31 Whosesoever..at any time, has been the soil, his, at that time, has been the fruit of even the previous bestowment thereof.

β. **1500–20** DUNBAR *Poems* xxiv. 22 Off warldis gud and grit richess, Quhat fruct hes man but miriness?

8. a. A dupe, an 'easy mark'. **b.** A male homosexual. *slang* (orig. *U.S.*).

1895 W. C. GORE in *Inlander* Dec. 111 *Fruit*, one who can be easily deceived. **1913** *Punch* 22 Jan. 72/2 It was a flaw in the new play that its mugs were such 'easy fruit'. **1931** G. IRWIN *Amer. Tramp & Underworld Slang* 81 *Fruit*, an 'easy mark'. A girl or woman willing to oblige. Probably..from the fact that they are 'easy picking'. **1935** N. ERSINE *Underworld & Prison Slang* 38 *Fruit*, a sexual pervert. **1957** K. MARTIN *Aubade* v. 79 The way I'm acting anyone would think I was a fruit. Gary probably is. He looks like one. **1970** *Guardian* 13 Feb. 9/5 He is a fruit, which means..that he is a queer. **1971** *Rolling Stone* 24 June 3/2 John Mendelsohn did an excellent job acting like a fruit.

9. *attrib.* and *Comb.* **a.** simple attrib., as ***fruit-barrow, -basket, -branch, -broker, -close, -dealer, -dish, -farm, -garden, -grove, -industry, -juice, -loft, -lot, -pulp, -shop, -sort, -stall, -stand, -stone, -tart, -time, -year***; also ***fruitwise*** adv.

1801 *Spirit Publ. Jrnls.* (1802) V. 187 *Fruit-barrows and the hunger-giving cries Of vegetable venders fill the air. **1803** *Gentl. Mag.* Ibid. (1804) VII. 44 Look at..the fillagree tea-caddies, the *fruit-baskets, &c., &c. **1719** LONDON & WISE *Compl. Gard.* xv. 123 If a *Fruit Branch should chance to be join'd with the two Wood Branches it may be preserv'd. **1844** DICKENS *Mart. Chuz.* ix, Several *fruit-brokers had their marts near Todger's. **1882** SHORTHOUSE *J. Inglesant* II. xxvi. 317 Inheritance of *fruit-closes, and olive-grounds. **1810** *Sporting Mag.* XXXV. 39 The defendant is a *fruit-dealer. **1603** SHAKS. *Meas. for M.* II. i. 95 We had but two in the house, which..stood, as it were in a *fruit dish. **1872** *Trans. Dep. Agric. Illinois* IX. 65 The first consideration in the establishment of a *fruit farm is accessibility to market. **1911** E. M. CLOWES *On Wallaby* iv. 92 Some neighbouring station, dairy, or fruit-farm. **1712** J. JAMES tr. *Le Blond's Gardening* 3 Kitchen and *Fruit-Gardens. **1725** POPE *Odyss.* IV. 974 The faithful slave Whom to my nuptial train Icarius gave, To tend the *fruit-groves. **1894** *Daily News* 5 Apr. 5/5 Will the *fruit industry of this country find another £100 towards it? **1880** *Jrnl. Chem. Soc.* XXXVIII. 354 Behaviour of *fruit-juices of different ages with reagents. **1951** AUDEN *Nones* (1952) 64 The unamerican survivor Hears angels drinking fruit-juice with their wives. **1552** HULOET, *Fruite loft, or place to lay fruite in, or to kepe fruite, *oporotheca*. **1604** *Office B.V.M.* 277 Ps. lxxviii. 1 They haue made Hierusalem a frute loft. **1912** *Chambers's Jrnl.* Mar. 173/2 It is very beautiful up behind the *fruit-lot among the rocks and the pine-trees. **1887** *Colon. & Indian Exhib., Rep. Col. Sect.* 131 Importing a large quantity of fresh fruit, and what is called '*fruit-pulp' from Tasmania. **1887** C. A. MOLONEY *Sk. Forestry W. Afr.* 339 The fruit-pulp is eaten and also prepared into a pleasant beverage. **1906** *Westm. Gaz.* 28 Aug. 6/1 To avail themselves of any cheap and defective fruit-pulp for the making of jam. **1650** HOWELL *Giraffi's Rev. Naples* I. (1664) 10 He went up and down the *fruit-shops that were in that quarter. **1842** BROWNING *Soliloquy Sp. Cloister* vi, How go your flowers? None double? Not one *fruit-sort can you spy? **1858** SIMMONDS *Dict. Trade*, **Fruit stall*, a stand on the pavement where fruit is sold in the streets. **1800** *Morn. Chron.* in *Spirit Publ. Jrnls.* (1801) IV. 40 Nor do we ever see him..riding backwards over *fruit-stands. **1845–6** G. E. DAY tr. *Simon's Anim. Chem.* II. 465 Their nucleus is usually a foreign body, a *fruit-stone, a splinter of bone, a needle, or woody fibre. **1568** NORTH *Gueuara's Diall Pr.* IV. (1619) 624/1 Hee coulde make..twelue sorts of sawces and ten of *fruit tartes. **1552** HULOET, *Fruite tyme, when fruite is ripe, *vindemia*. **1712** ADDISON *Spect.* No. 477 ¶ 1, I do not suffer any one..to drive them [the birds] from their usual haunts in fruit-time. **1864** SWINBURNE *Atalanta* 214 *Fruit-wise upon the old flower of tears. **1742** W. ELLIS *Timber-Tree* (ed. 3) II. II. xl. 192 When they sell well, as they do in plentiful *Fruit-years. **1811** R. SUTCLIFF *Trav. N. Amer.* ii. 27 This was likely to be a very abundant fruit year.

b. objective, as ***fruit-bearer, -culture, -eater, -evaporation, -farmer, -giver, -grower, -keeper, -monger, -picker, -seller, -vendor***; ***fruit-bearing, -candying, -farming, -growing, -packing, -raising*** vbl. sbs.; ***fruit-bearing, -bringing, -eating, -growing, -producing*** ppl. adjs.

1726 LEONI *Alberti's Archit.* I. 24/2 Trees..especially *Fruit-bearers. **1883** H. DRUMMOND *Nat. Law in Spir. W.* (ed. 2) 271 *Fruit-bearing without Christ is not an improbability, but an impossibility. **1629** PARKINSON *Paradisi* Title-p., An Orchard of all sorte of *fruit-bearing Trees. **1863** BERKELEY *Brit. Mosses* i. 4 We have the fruit-bearing branches more distinct. **1853** HICKIE tr. *Aristoph.* (1872) II. 546 Ceres, the *fruit-bringing queen. **1889** *Daily News* 31 May 5/4 *Fruit-candying establishments. **1483** *Cath. Angl.* 144 A *Frute eter, *xirofagus*. **1848** CRAIG, *Ampelidæ*, Chatterers or fruit-eaters. **1883** G. ALLEN in *Knowl.* 25 May 304/1 The blackcap..is a confirmed fruit-eater. **1884** *Littell's Living Age* 688 The shambling, *fruit-eating, bear. **1895** *Daily News* 13 Dec. 5/4 *Fruit evaporation would pay British fruit-growers. **1872** *Trans. Dep. Agric. Illinois* IX. 66 The *fruit farmer can raise cheap pork in his apple and peach orchards. **1890** W. BOOTH *In Darkest Eng.* II. iii. 133 *Fruit farming affords a great opening for female labour. **1888** *Epictetus* II. x. 74 He will be Raingiver and *Fruitgiver. **1825** G. BLISS (*title*) The *fruit grower's instructor. **1854** *Trans. Illinois Agric. Soc.* I. 70 The fruit and fruit growers of seven states were represented. **1884** *Harper's Mag.* Mar. 602/2 The..fruit-grower may..be made independent of the weather. **1850** *Rep. U.S. Comm. Patents Agric. 1849* 106 This perhaps is the best *fruit-growing district of the State. **1854** *Trans. Illinois Agric. Soc.* I. 135 Fruit growing..has not increased any faster than the growing of other agricultural produce. **1872** *Trans. Dep. Agric. Illinois* IX. 66 A soil adapted to the growth of forest trees is..the best for fruit growing. **1894** *Pop. Sci. Monthly* XLIV. 487 Our neighbors of northern Europe are..removed from fruit-growing regions. **1905** J. F. FRASER *Canada* iii. 32 This jut of land is as rich for fruit growing as Kent itself. **1623** COCKERAM II, A *fruit keeper, *epicarpean*. **1721** BRADLEY *Virtue Coffee* 28 As our *Fruit-mongers do for Cherries. **1894** *Daily News* 22 Jan. 6/3, I am not going to reply in 'The Daily News' to the three letters on *fruit-packing. **1880** *Libr. Univ. Knowl.* I. 164 For harvesting, we have mowing, reaping and binding machines, shellers, *fruit-pickers, etc. **1895** *Daily News* 27 Sept. 2/3 Great Britain has to be seriously reckoned with as a *fruit-producing country. **1854** *Trans. Illinois Agric. Soc.* I. 500 The fact that *fruit raising here is attended by drawbacks. **1891** *Harper's Mag.* Jan. 168/2 California has much to learn about fruit-raising. **1552** HULOET, *Fruite seller, *fructuarius*. **1887** *Spectator* 25 Mar. 412/2 The Italian *fruit-vendor or organ-grinder is often a retired workman.

10. Special comb.: **fruit bark beetle** = *fruit tree* (*bark*) *beetle*; **fruit bat**, a member of the sub-order Megachiroptera, which includes the flying-foxes (*Pteropus*) and other fruit-eating bats; **fruit-body**, the part of a fungus that bears the spores and spore-producing organs; **fruit-bud**, a bud containing a fruit germ, in opposition to *leaf-bud*; **fruit-button** = *fruit-bud*; **fruit-cake**, (*a*) a cake containing fruit; (*b*) (see quot.); (*c*) *slang* (orig. *U.S.*), a crazy or eccentric person; one who is insane; cf. *nutty as a fruit-cake* s.v. NUTTY *a.* 3 b; **fruit-clipper**, a fast-sailing ship, built for the conveyance of fruit; **fruit cocktail**, a preparation of fruit used as an appetizer or refreshment; **fruit-crow** (see quot.); **fruit cup**, a preparation of fruit used as an appetizer or dessert; **fruit-dot**, *Bot.*, the sorus of ferns; **fruit drop** [DROP *sb.* 10 e], a fruit-flavoured sweet; **fruit-fly** (see quot.); **fruit-frame** (see quot.); **fruit-gatherer**, an implement for gathering fruit from tall trees; **fruit-girl**, a girl who sells fruit; **fruit gum** [GUM *sb.* 1 h], a fruit-flavoured gum; **fruit-house**, a house for storing fruit; **fruit-jelly**, a fruit-flavoured table-jelly; **fruit-knife**, a knife for cutting fruit, with a blade of silver or other material not affected by the acids of the fruit; **fruit machine**, a coin- or token-operated gaming machine which pays out according to the combination of symbols (often representations of fruit) appearing on the edges of wheels spun by the operation of a lever; also *transf.* in various *slang* uses; **fruit-meter**, a person officially appointed to examine all fruit brought into a market (Cassell); **fruit-mill** (see quot.); †**fruits-paying**, the payment of annates or 'first-fruits'; **fruit-piece**, 'a pictured or sculptured representation of fruit' (*Cent. Dict.*); **fruit-pigeon**, a general name given to the pigeons of the genera *Carpophaga* and *Treron*; **fruit-press**, an apparatus for extracting the juice from fruit by pressure; **fruit salad**, (*a*) fruits, usually uncooked, cut up and mixed together, often served with sugar, cream, etc.; (*b*) an array of service ribbons and decorations (*Services' slang*); **fruit salts**, effervescent health salts (also formerly in *sing.*); **fruit-spur**, a small branch whose growth is stopped to ensure the development of fruit-buds; **fruit-stalk**, a stalk that bears fruit; *spec.* = PEDUNCLE; also occas. = CARPOPHORE; **fruit-sugar** = GLUCOSE or LEVULOSE; **fruit-tree**, a tree cultivated for its fruit; **fruit tree (bark) beetle**, *Scolytus rugulosus*, which burrows beneath the bark of fruit-trees; †**fruit-trencher**, a wooden tray, formerly used as a dessert-plate; †**fruit-user** = USUFRUCTUARY *sb.*; **fruit-wall**, a wall against which fruit-trees are trained; **fruit-wife**, **fruit-woman**, a woman who sells fruit; also, †a bawd; **fruitwood**, the wood of fruit-trees, esp. pear, used to make furniture; †**fruit-yard**, an orchard.

1892 *Insect Life* IV. 293 The topics treated are the *Fruit Bark-beetle (*Scolytus rugulosus*); [etc.]. **1951** *Dict. Gardening* (R. Hort. Soc.) II. 843/1 Fruit-bark Beetle, *Scolytus rugulosus*, attacks a number of fruit trees, especially Apple and Plum. **1877** W. S. DALLAS in *Cassell's Nat. Hist.* I. 269 The young African *Fruit Bats born in the Zoological Gardens were covered with short, smooth hair. **1883** *Chamb. Jrnl.* 22 Dec. 810/1 That curious species of bats known as the fruit-bat or flying-fox. **1905** *Westm. Gaz.* 8 Nov. 10/2 The Indian fruit bat..is not a novelty in the menagerie. **1936** *Discovery* Oct. 307/1 Before the advent of the white man and his cultivated fruits, these great fruit bats lived on scrub figs, berries, ti-tree and gum blossoms for the honey they contained. **1966** V. SERVENTY *Continent in Danger* iv. 86 Some of the 'batteries' or camps of the fruit bats..number hundreds of thousands of individuals. **1912** C. THOM in C. E. Marshall *Microbiol.* i. 13 The systems of classification used are largely based upon the types of sexual *fruit bodies produced. **1927** GWYNNE-VAUGHAN & BARNES *Struct. & Developm. Fungi* 1 In relation to the fruit bodies of higher forms, they [*sc.* the hyphae] become woven into a dense mass. **1968** *Gloss. Terms Timber Preservation* (*B.S.I.*) 10 *Fruit(ing) body*, in wood-destroying fungi, a structure that bears the spore-producing organs and spores, commonly a conspicuous bracket, toadstool or compacted sheet, with pores, gills, spines, etc., bearing the spores. **1969** *New Scientist* 27 Nov. 451/1 Only when fruitbodies are formed does the maximum conversion of compost nutrients into edible food take place. **1664** EVELYN *Kal. Hort.* (1729) 190 [When] the Sap begins to stir..one then best discerns the *Fruit-buds. **1707** *Curios. in Husb. & Gard.* 147 The Graft very seldom fails..provided it..have *Fruit-Buttons. **1854** E. RUSKIN *Let.* 27 Feb. in M. Lutyens *Millais & Ruskins* (1967) 143 At night Old Anne gets out wine and *fruit cake and they sit and gossip. **1885** LANKESTER in *Encycl. Brit.* XIX. 841/2 The cysts [of the *Endosporeæ*] may be united side by side in larger or smaller groups..These composite bodies are termed 'fruit-cakes' or 'æthalia', in view of the fact that the spore-cysts of Fuligo, also called Æthalium—the well-known 'flowers of tan'—form a cake of this description. **1960** WENTWORTH & FLEXNER *Dict. Amer. Slang* 203/2 Fruitcake [*citing* 1952 *film*]. **1967** 'T. WELLS' *Dead by Light of Moon* iii. 39 Everett Johns is part fruitcake. Goes around in thong sandals when it's warm enough, practices Yoga. **1967** J. POTTER *Foul Play* xiii. 153 Through a mouthful of fruit cake he congratulated her crumbily. **1977** *Rolling Stone* 19 May 69/3 There is some fear that he has made 'talking to the president a viable goal for every fruitcake in the country'. **1982** *Observer* 29 Aug. 7/3 To be considered as a candidate you must first get onto the Panel, which is a sort of index designed mainly to exclude fruitcakes. **1864** BLACKMORE *C. Vaughan* lxxi, The 'Lily-flower'..could exhibit her taffrail to the smartest *fruit-clipper. **1922** *N.Y. Hotel Rev.* 18 Mar. 62 *Fruit cocktail. **1928** *Sat. Even. Post* 12 May 107/1 Mr. Montgomery had taken a morsel of fruit cocktail. *c* **1938** *Fortnum & Mason Catal.* 32/1 Fruits in syrup..Fruit Cocktail..per tin 1/8. **1968** C. DRUMMOND *Death & Leaping Ladies* i. 22, I ended up with eighteen fruit cocktails and..was left with eleven sure-fire hits. **1856** W. S. DALLAS *Nat. Hist. Anim. Kingd.* 552 The Gymnoderinæ, or *Fruit Crows. **1931** *N. & Q.* 4 Apr. 241/2 Where *fruit-cup, ices and wonderful cakes were served. **1959** N. MAILER *Advts. for Myself* (1961) 358 You Americans always eat the last course first... Fruit cup with sherbet, if you please. **1880** GRAY *Struct. Bot.* 433/2 The clustered *fruit-dots of ferns. **1907** *Yesterday's Shopping* (1969) 50 Acidulated *fruit drops. **1935** G. GREENE *Basement Room* 40 A sticky fruit drop in his hand. **1959** I. & P. OPIE *Lore & Lang. Schoolch.* ix. 166 'Lollies' is becoming a general term..for..humbugs, large aniseed balls, and fruit drops. **1971** *Guardian* 18 Aug. 4/3 Fruit-drops, lollipops, a stick of chewing-gum. **1753** CHAMBERS *Cycl. Supp.*, **Fruit-flies*, a name given by gardeners, and others, to a sort of small black flies, found in vast numbers among fruit trees, in the spring season. **1874** KNIGHT *Dict. Mech.*, **Fruit-frame*, *Hort.* a trellis or espalier. **1847** *Rep. U.S. Comm. Patents 1846* 19 A *fruit-gatherer, of very ingenious and simple construction, has been patented. **1910** *Daily Chron.* 10 Feb. 1/5 A fruit-gatherer attached to a pole and armed with cutting teeth. **1750** H. WALPOLE *Let. to G. Montagu* 23 July (1857) II. 213 She had brought Betty, the *fruit-girl, with hampers of strawberries and cherries. **1812** COMBE *Picturesque* XXIII, A fruit-girl's barrow strikes his shin. **1938** G. GREENE *Brighton Rock* VII. vii. 328 The packets of *fruit gums came dropping out. **1960** E. W. HILDICK *Boy at Window* xiv. 108, I asked him for a box and he simply tipped the rolls of fruit gum out of this. **1971** *Times Educ. Suppl.* 25 June 20/3 A skyver..offered the teacher a fruit gum. **1794** LD. SPENCER in *Ld. Auckland's Corr.* (1862) III. 255, I am going with Caroline to the *fruit-house. **1846** A. SOYER *Gastronomic Regenerator* p. xxi, All *fruit jellies [should be] as near as possible to the colour of the fruit. **1875** *Encycl. Brit.* I. 172/1 Jams, marmalades, and fruit jellies. **1855** H. CLARKE *Dict.*, **Fruit-knife*. **1933** *Times* 7 Apr. 4/2 Committed to trial..on a charge of receiving 20 automatic '*fruit' machines..knowing them to be stolen. **1943** HUNT & PRINGLE *Service Slang* 33 *Fruit machine*, an anti-aircraft predictor. **1957** *Economist* 30 Nov. 781/2 Permission to install the minor gambling devices known as 'fruit machines'..is by county option. **1959** G. JENKINS *Twist of Sand* vii. 110 The 'fruit machine' fed by information from two officers, gave the course and speed of the warships. **1965** *Listener* 2 Sept. 342/3 There are three juke boxes; pin tables; fruit machines. **1881** *Daily News* 5 Aug. 2/7 In long past days the Corporation *fruitmeters claimed a sample of fruit from each package entering the Port of London. **1874** KNIGHT *Dict. Mech.*, **Fruit-Mill*, a mill for grinding grapes for must or apples for cider. **1709** STRYPE *Ann. Ref.* I. vi. 97 To pray the Queen..to be discharged of their own subsidies the first year of their *fruits-paying. **1865** *Athenæum* No. 1954. 494/3 A rare *fruit-pigeon from the Seychelles. **1861** MRS. BEETON *Bk. Househ. Managem.* 798 *Fruit salads are made by stripping the fruit from the stalks, piling it on a dish, and sprinkling over it finely-pounded sugar. **1943** HUNT & PRINGLE *Service Slang* 33 *Fruit salad*, a large collection of medal ribbons which runs to three or more rows. **1955** 'N. SHUTE' *Requiem for Wren* iii. 74 A red-faced old gentleman with..a fruit salad of medal ribbons on his chest. **1961** *Times* 19 Apr. 13/3 The ribbons worn on the chest and colloquially called 'fruit salad'. **1964** B. FALK *Peacock Cookery Bk.* 136 A fruit salad can be made from any mixture of fresh fruit in season together with some tinned fruit, or from fresh fruit alone. **1889** *Illustr. London News* 31 July 33 (Advt.), For health and longevity, use Eno's '*Fruit Salt'. **1892** E. LYTTON *Let.* 18 Nov. in E. Lutyens *Blessed Girl* (1953) ix. 179 When he comes down cured..Sir Augustus puts it down to Eno's Fruit Salts. **1939** D. L. SAYERS *In Teeth of Evidence* 64 Mr. Loveday had gone in to borrow a dose of fruit salts from Mr. Turnbull. **1823** in Cobbett *Rur. Rides* (1885) I. 325 [A] great number of these shoots have *fruit-spurs, which will have blossom, if not fruit, next year. **1796** WITHERING *Brit. Plants* (ed. 3) II. 17 Leaf-stalks, shorter than the *fruit-stalks. **1846** J. BAXTER *Libr. Pract. Agric.* (ed. 4) II. 301 [Strawberries] Every runner is, in its incipient state of formation, capable of becoming a fruit-stalk. **1898** E. A. ORMEROD *Handbk. Insects Injur. Fruits* 197 (*heading*) *Fruit-tree Bark Beetle. **1921** T. W. SANDERS *Fruit Foes* I. 30 Fruit Tree Beetle (Scolytus rugulosus).—Both the beetle and the larvæ are injurious to fruit trees. **1577** B. GOOGE *Heresbach's Husb.* II. (1586) 72 *Fruite trees and Vines. **1667** MILTON *P.L.* v. 213 Where any row Of Fruit-trees..reached too farr Thir pamperd boughes. **1846** J. BAXTER *Libr. Pract. Agric.* (ed. 4) II. 379 Three modes of pruning..first, the fruit-tree method. **1642** MILTON *Apol. Smect.* 28 He greets us with a quantity of thum-ring posies. *He has a fortune therefore good, because he is content with it.* This is a piece of sapience not worth the brain of a *fruit-trencher. **1883** *Oxf. Guide-book* [The picture-gallery of the Bodleian contains] Queen Elizabeth's fruit-trenchers. *c* **1449** PECOCK *Repr.* 411 But thei ben *Fruyte Users of the godis. **1699** (*title*) *Fruit Walls improved by inclining them to the Horizon. **1773** MRS. GRANT *Lett. fr. Mount.* (1807) I. x. 78 She has built a fruit wall, a thing before unheard of here. **1611** COTGR., *Fruictiere*, a *Fruit-wife; or woman that selleth fruits. **1672** DRYDEN *Assignation* III. i. Wks. 1883 IV. 416 She's as arrant a *fruit-woman as any is about Rome. **1849** MACAULAY *Hist. Eng.* I. 358 Fruit women screamed. **1927** MACQUOID & EDWARDS *Dict. Eng. Furnit.* III. 29 In common with other *fruit woods, it [*sc.* pear wood] has been used from a very early period. **1939** E. WENHAM *Old Furnit. for Mod. Rooms* i. 7 Bobbin-turned chairs of oak, or of some fruitwood. **1947** J. C. S. BROUGH *Timbers for Woodwork* xvi. 134 One of several 'fruitwoods' it [*sc.* apple wood] was in former days employed largely for domestic commodities. **1964** J. GLOAG *Englishman's Chair* ix. 194 Elm seats, ash or yew bows, with arms and turned work in fruit wood or yew. **1971** *Times* 19 June 12/5 The marquetry of flowers, birds and grotesque masks is in ivory and fruitwood. **1555** W. WATREMAN *Fardle Facions* II. ix. 205 The Gelonites, occupienge tilthe: liue by corne, and haue their *frute yardes.

fruit (fru:t), *v.* Also α. 4–5 **frute, -yn**; β. 5 **fruct.** *Pa. pple.* 4 **y-fruited.** [f. prec. sb.]

1. *intr.* To bear fruit.

α. **1377** LANGL. *P. Pl.* B. XVI. 39, I saue it til I se it.. somdel y-fruited. *c* **1440** *Promp. Parv.* 182/1 Frutyn, or brynge forþe frute, *fructifico*. **1712** J. PETIVER in *Phil. Trans.* XXVII. 424 It Fruits yearly in Chelsey Garden. **1793** *Trans. Soc. Arts* (ed. 2) IV. 220 They have fruited, and are now propagated in almost all the West-India islands. **1854** HOOKER *Himal. Jrnls.* II. xxvii. 253 But few of them fruit. **1882** MRS. RIDDELL *Daisies & B.* I. 114 The scarlet-runners fruiting and blooming at the same time.

β. *a* **1500** *Colkelbie Sow* iii. 766 How suld a penny fruct contrair nature.

fig. *c* **1440** *Jacob's Well* (E.E.T.S.) 259 Mysgouernaunce.. frutyth noȝt in goodnesse to þe soule. **1851** *Beddoes' Poems* Mem. 113 Interchanging knowledge, as it..fruited daily in every branch of science. **1883** BALDW. BROWN *Home* iii. 50 We can see the passions and the forces working, which fruit in bane or blessing.

2. *trans.* (*causatively*) To make bear fruit; to cultivate to the point of bearing fruit. *lit.* and *fig.*

1640 J. DYKE *Worthy Commun.* 177 He is rooted in Christ, and therefore fruited by Christ. **1851** *Beck's Florist* Jan. 8, I have not fruited those sorts [of Strawberries]. **1862** THOREAU *Excurs.*, *On Wild Apples* (1863) 291 Their 'Favorites' [apples]..when I have fruited them turn out very tame. **1882** W. B. WEEDEN *Soc. Law Labor* 25 For Capital is Labor fruited, saved and preserved.

†**3.** In various obsolete uses: **a.** To produce as fruit. **b.** To flavour with fruit-juice. *Obs.*

1382 WYCLIF *Ecclus.* xxiv. 23, I as a vyne frutede [Vulg. *fructificavi*] swotnesse of smel. **1736** BAILEY *Househ. Dict.* 359 Fill tin iceing pots with any sorts of cream you please, either plain or sweetened, or you may fruit it.

fruitage ('fru:tɪdʒ). Also 6–8 **frutage**, (7 **-idge**). [a. OF. *fruitage*, f. *fruit* FRUIT.]

1. The process, season, or state of bearing fruit.

1578 BANISTER *Hist. Man* VIII. 102 Plantes: which onely florish in growyng, and frutage. **1610** W. FOLKINGHAM *Art of Survey* I. iii. 6 In Grouth, the thriuage, verdure, fruitage ..&c., of particular Vegetables are regardable. **1816** COLERIDGE *Biog. Lit.*, *Lay Serm.* 317 A tree transplanted from Paradise, with all its branches in full fruitage. **1871** LYTTON *Coming Race* xvii, Fruit-bearing plants after fruitage either shed or change the colour of their leaves.

fig. **1892** *Ch. Q. Rev.* Jan. 444 Many have commented on the late fruitage of Swift's genius.

2. Fruit collectively; a crop of fruit.

1610 W. FOLKINGHAM *Art of Survey* I. vi. 13 What Trees, Plants, Shrubs: what Frutage, Mastage, Gummage. **1613** CHAPMAN *Masque of Inns of Court* Plays 1873 III. 117 Freely earth her fruitage bearing. **1667** MILTON *P.L.* x. 561 Greedily they pluck'd The Frutage fair to sight. **1708** J. PHILIPS *Cyder* I. 3 Whoeer expects his lab'ring trees should bend With frutage. **1808** J. BARLOW *Columb.* II. 215 The wide domain, with game and fruitage crown'd, Supplied their food. **1883** MRS. ROLLINS *New Eng. Bygones* 180 Much of the plumpest fruitage found its way into the hoards of thieving boys.

fig. **1652** BENLOWES *Theoph.* IV. l. 58 When me Thou shalt impregn'd with Vertues make A fruitful Eden, all the frutage take. **1749** SMOLLETT *Regicide* IV. iii, I come..To claim the promis'd fruitage of my love. **1883** S. C. HALL *Retrospect* II. 39 His genius was yet in the bud—with the promise of glorious fruitage.

†**b.** *pl.* Various sorts of fruit. *Obs.*

a **1693** URQUHART *Rabelais* III. xiii. 110 Men do more copiously in the Season of Harvest feed on Fruitages then at any other time.

c. *transf.* Offspring. *rare*$^{-1}$.

1850 BLACKIE *Æschylus* I. 195 Yet should she By her own body's fruitage have been slain?

†**3.** A decorative arrangement of fruits; a representation of this in embroidery, painting, carving, etc. *Obs.*

1600 *Q. Eliz. Wardr.* in Nichols *Progr.* (1823) III. 509 One peticoate..with a verie faire border of pomegranetts, pyne aple trees, frutidge. **1604** DEKKER *King's Entertainm.* Wks. 1873 I. 309 Pomona—attirde in greene, a wreath of frutages circling her temples. **1645** EVELYN *Diary* 29 Jan., The vines, climbing to the summit of the trees, reach in festoons and fruitages from one tree to another. **1688** R. HOLME *Armoury* II. 115/2 Fruitage is the hanging of several sorts of Fruit together in husks with strings. *c* **1710** C. FIENNES *Diary* (1888) 238 The most exactest workmanship in yᵉ wood carving..both in figures, fruitages, beasts, birds, flowers. **1719** LONDON & WISE *Compl. Gard.* 37 A glorious Embroidery of Festoons, and Frutages, depending from the yielding Boughs.

Hence '**fruitaged** *ppl. a.*, abounding in fruitage.

1846 C. G. PROWETT *Æschylus' Prometh. Bound* 22 Flowery spring Or fruitaged summer.

fruitarian (fru:'tɛərɪən), *sb.* (and *a.*) *rare.* [f. FRUIT *sb.* + -ARIAN; cf. *vegetarian.*] One who lives on fruit. Also as *adj.*

1893 *Nat. Food Mag.* Feb., Even at 3*d.* a lb...the economical fruitarian would gain on the economical cerealist. **1896** *Westm. Gaz.* 4 May 10/1 He became 'fruitarian'..He believed in nothing but fruit. **1902** H. BEGBIE *Adv. Sir John Sparrow* x. 150 The form of eating which I practise..is not vegetarian, but fruitarian. **1903** *Sci. Amer.* 10 Oct. 255/2 Fruits contain little protein, and nuts are relied on in the fruitarian plan of eating to balance the ration.

Hence **frui'tarianism**, the principles or practice of fruitarians.

1902 H. BEGBIE *Adv. Sir John Sparrow* xiv. 221 We flee from before the face of vegetarianism, fruitarianism, theosophy, and religious manias. **1908** *Practitioner* Mar. 401 Vegetarianism, fruitarianism, and even zomotherapy may suit a few. **1930** E. T. THURSTON *Man in Black Hat* viii. 149 The medical profession at the moment approves of fruitarianism.

fruited ('fru:tɪd), *ppl. a.* [f. FRUIT *v.* + -ED[2].]

†**1.** Having fruit of a certain kind. *Obs.*

1612 T. JAMES *Jesuits' Downf.* 4 Fie on such Fatherhood, so rooted, so fruited.

2. a. Of a branch, tree, etc.: Having fruit upon it. **b.** Abounding in or laden with fruit.

1784 BURNS '*Now Westlin Winds*' iv, Let us..view..The rustling corn, the fruited thorn, And ev'ry happy creature. **1850** BLACKIE *Æschylus* II. 122 Mighty Jove, the gracious giver..Crown the fruited year! **1864** BOUTELL *Her. Hist. & Pop.* xiii. (ed. 3) 124 A wreath of peach-branches fruited. **1885** *Manch. Exam.* 14 July 4/5 The plant..though small is unusually heavily fruited. **1888** MORRIS *Burghers' Battle* in *Athenæum* 16 June 761/2 The shadows of the fruited close Dapple the feast-hall floor.

fruiten ('fruːt(ə)n), *v.* [f. FRUIT *sb.* + -EN[5].]

†**a.** *trans.* To make fruitful (*obs.*). **b.** *intr.* To become full of fruit. Hence '**fruitening** *ppl. a.* (*rare*[−1]).

1633 BP. HALL *Hard Texts* 84, I will give you seasonable rains..to supple and fruiten the earth. **1839** BAILEY *Festus* (1848) 11/2 Fanning the fruitening plains.

fruiter ('fruːtə(r)). [orig. a. F. *fruitier*, f. *fruit*; later prob. independently f. FRUIT *sb.* or *v.* + -ER[1].] †**a.** One who deals in, or has the care of fruit. **b.** A vessel engaged in the fruit-trade. **c.** A tree that produces fruit. **d.** A fruit-grower.

a **1483** *Liber Niger* in *Househ. Ord.* (1790) 22 Besides the fruter and waferer. *c* **1500** *Cocke Lorell's B.* (Percy) 9 Fruyters, chese-mongers, and mynstrelles. **1667** *Canterbury Marriage Licences* 31 July (MS.) William Settertree of Brooke..fruiter. **1860** A. CUMMING in *Merc. Marine Mag.* VII. 102 Let them swing to one anchor..(as the fruiters do at St. Michael's). **1870** *Harper's Mag.* XLI. 864 A man can't bring into port..a fruiter from the Levant, with Portuguese and Greeks before the mast. **1882** *Gard. Chron.* No. 421. 79 The former is a handsome variety of medium growth, and a sure fruiter. **1887** J. E. MCGOWAN *Chattanooga & Tennessee* 35 The fruiter, farmers and truckers have now more capital for their business.

fruiterer ('fruːtərə(r)). [extended form of prec.: see -ER[1] 3.]

1. A dealer in fruit; a fruit-seller.

1408 *Close Roll* 9 *Hen. IV* b, Thomas Sebeche, ffruterer. **1556** J. HEYWOOD *Spider & F.* Ss j b, The frewte..on the frewterers hande lying. **1597** SHAKS. *2 Hen. IV*, III. ii. 36 The very same-day did I fight with one Sampson Stock-fish, a Fruiterer. **1650** HOWELL *Giraffi's Rev. Naples* I. (1664) 12 Telling the fruiterers that they should pay the gabell. **1720** GAY *Poems* (1745) I. 167 Walnuts the fruiterer's hand, in autumn stain. **1815** ELPHINSTONE *Acc. Caubul* (1842) I. 75 Amongst the handsomest shops were the fruiterers'. **1875** HAMERTON *Intell. Life* IX. i. 301 Careful as a fruiterer is of the bloom upon his grapes.

†**2.** A fruit-grower. *Obs.*

1612 DRAYTON *Poly-olb.* xviii. 298 The Pear-maine.. Which carefull frut'rers now have denized our owne. **1615** W. LAWSON *Orch. & Gard.* III. i. (1668) 1 Whosoever desireth..to have a pleasant and profitable Orchard, must provide himself of a fruiterer..Skilful in that faculty. **1813** SIR H. DAVY *Agric. Chem.* (1814) 255 Most of our best apples are supposed to have been introduced into Britain by a fruiterer of Henry the Eighth.

fruiteress ('fruːtərɪs). Also 8 **fruitress.** [f. as prec. + -ESS.] A female seller of fruit.

1713 STEELE *Guardian* No. 87 ¶1 The hawker-women, fruitresses, and milk-maids. **1809** *Sporting Mag.* XXXIV. 244 The fair fruiteress, it seems was jealous of her neighbour. **1823** LAMB *Elia, My First Play*, The fashionable pronunciation of the theatrical fruiteresses then was 'Chase some oranges'..chase *pro* chuse.

fruitery ('fruːtərɪ). Also 7 frut(e)ry. [ad. Fr. *fruiterie*, f. *fruit* FRUIT.]

†**1.** A place for growing or storing fruit. *Obs.*

1609 *Patent* 7 *Jas. I* in *Act* 5 *Geo. III*, c. 26. Preamble, Dove-houses, orchards, fruiteries, gardens, lofts, cottages. **1725** BRADLEY *Fam. Dict.* s.v., You must be careful in cleaning and sweeping your Fruitery often. **1816** KIRBY & SP. *Entomol.* (1843) I. 161, I must next conduct you from the garden into the orchard and fruitery.

2. Fruit collectively; a crop of fruit. Now *rare.*

16.. SYLVESTER *Du Bartas* (N.), He sowde and planted in his proper grange (Upon som savage stock) som frutry strange. **1612** DRAYTON *Poly-olb.* xiv. 229 Where full Pomona seems most plentiously to flowe, And with her fruitery swells by Pershore in her pride. **1656** S. HOLLAND *Zara* (1719) 27 Indeed she had manifested a prodigious prodigality, and she afforded a Shambles to her Frutery. **1708** J. PHILIPS *Cyder* II. 35 Oft, notwithstanding all thy Care To help thy Plants, when the small Fruit'ry seems Exempt from Ills, an oriental Blast Disastrous flies. **1828** MISS MITFORD *Village* Ser. III. (1863) 491 Dealing with him in all sorts of fishery and fruitery for..her shop.

†**fruitester.** *Obs. rare*[−1]. [f. FRUIT *sb.* + -STER.] = FRUITERESS. (Cf. quot. 1672 for *fruit-woman* in FRUIT *sb.* 10.)

c **1386** CHAUCER *Pardoner's T.* 16 Than comen tombesteres Fetys and smale, and yonge frutesteres [*v. rr.* fruytesteres, fruytsters].

fruitful ('fruːtfʊl), *a.* Forms: α. (see FRUIT *sb.*). β. 4–7 **fructfull,** (5 **fructufulle**), 6 **fruictfull.** [f. FRUIT *sb.* + -FUL.]

1. Productive of fruit. Of trees, etc.: Bearing plenty of fruit. Of soils, etc.: Fertile. Of rain, etc.: Causing fertility.

a **1300** *E.E. Psalter* cxlviii. 9 Tries fruitefulle and cedres alle. *c* **1400** MAUNDEV. (Roxb.) xiv. 61 Þir hilles er riȝt fruytfull. **1535** COVERDALE *Neh.* ix. 25 Vynyardes, oylgarden, and many fruitfull trees. **1563** W. FULKE *Meteors* (1640) 63 Clay..is not so fruitfull as marle. **1594** SHAKS. *Rich. III*, v. ii. 8 The..Boare (That spoyl'd your Summer Fields, and fruitfull Vines). **1601** HOLLAND *Pliny* XIX. vii, Such seeds..must be all throughly dried before they be.. fruitfull. **1649** JER. TAYLOR *Gt. Exemp.* III. xiv. 49 The fruitfull Nilus..filling all the trenches to make a plenty of corn and fruits. **1697** DAMPIER *Voy.* I. x. 293 The Tree hath usually 3 fruitfull Branches. **1697** DRYDEN *Virg. Georg.* I. 236 Heav'n invok'd with Vows for fruitful Rain. **1739** LADY POMFRET *Let.* I. xxii. 84 A very steep but fruitful hill..the vineyards.. crown the very summit. **1859** THACKERAY *Virgin.* xxiv, His estate..was as large as Kent; and.. infinitely more fruitful.

2. Productive of offspring; not barren; producing offspring in abundance, prolific.

c **1520** L. ANDREWE *Noble Lyfe* in *Babees Bk.* 229 A Bremon is a fruteful fisshe that hathe moche sede. **1526** *Pilgr. Perf.* (W. de W. 1531) 153 b, Lya was the more fruytfull, and had more chyldren than Rachel. **1577** B. GOOGE *Heresbach's Husb.* IV. (1586) 162 Some [hens] are so fruitfull, as they kill them selves with laying. **1611** BIBLE *Gen.* i. 22 God blessed them, saying, Be fruitfull, and multiply. **1667** D'CHESS NEWCASTLE *Life Dk. Newcastle* (1886) 87 A young woman that might prove fruitful to him. *a* **1715** BURNET *Own Time* (1766) II. 225 The fruitfullest marriage that has been known in our age. **1774** GOLDSM. *Nat. Hist.* (1776) VIII. 43 Nature..has rendered some animals surprizingly fruitful. **1841–71** T. R. JONES *Anim. Kingd.* (ed. 4) 367 The queen bee, when deprived of her wings before any communication with the male has taken place, will nevertheless lay fruitful eggs. **1869** FREEMAN *Norm. Conq.* (1876) III. xii. 111 That marriage proved happy and fruitful.

b. *Astrol.* Favourable to fecundity.

1721 BAILEY, *Fruitful Signs*, [in Astrology] are the Signs Gemini, Cancer and Pisces.

†**3.** Of a harvest, a crop, hence of a reward, a meal, etc.: Abundant, copious. Chiefly in Shaks.

1602 SHAKS. *Ham.* I. ii. 80 The fruitfull Riuer in the Eye. **1603** —— *Meas. for M.* IV. iii. 161 One fruitful Meale would set mee too't. **1607** —— *Timon* V. i. 153 With a recompence more fruitfull Than their offence can weigh downe. **1697** DRYDEN *Virg. Georg.* II. 197 Harvests heavy with their fruitful weight, Adorn our fields.

4. *transf.* and *fig.* †**a.** Productive *of* (material things), abounding *in. Obs.*

1629 *S'hertogenbosh* 1 This Boscage was..fruitfull of wild Deere. **1698** FRYER *Acc. E. India & P.* 328 The whole Region is very fruitful of Barren Mountains.

b. With reference to immaterial things: Prolific; abundantly productive. Const. *in, of.*

1535 COVERDALE *Col.* i. 10 To be frutefull in all good workes. **1667** MILTON *P.L.* III. 337 Golden days, fruitful of golden deeds. **1674** WOOD *Life* (O.H.S.) II. 284 Martock in com. Somerset, ever fruitfull in good wits. **1774** ARMSTRONG *Preserv. Health* II. 457 We curse not wine: The vile excess we blame; More fruitful than th' accumulated board Of pain and misery. **1826** T. I. WHARTON in *Pa. Hist. Soc. Mem.* I. 134 His travels are fruitful of information. **1843** PRESCOTT *Mexico* VI. i. (1864) 335 His fruitful genius suggested an expedient. **1844** H. H. WILSON *Brit. India* II. 406 A fruitful subject of contention. **1876** TREVELYAN *Macaulay* I. v. 289 The main incidents of that Session, so fruitful in great measures. **1885** *Public Opinion* 9 Jan. 37/2 Prince Albert Victor..has probably a long and fruitful career before him.

5. Productive of good results; beneficial, profitable, remunerative. Now only of actions, qualities, or the like; formerly also of concrete things.

c **1386** CHAUCER *Pars. T.* ¶36 And this is fruitful penance ayenst tho three thinges, in which we wrathen our Lord Jesu Christ. *c* **1440** *Jacob's Well* (E.E.T.S.) 228 Ydelnesse & ese wyth-oute fruytfull occupacyoun. **1504** ATKYNSON tr. *De Imitatione* I. xxv. 178 Holye redynge of frutefull doctrine. **1616** SURF. & MARKH. *Country Farme* 316 The fruitfullest thing that can be kept about a Countrie-house is Bees. **1640** YORKE *Union Hon.* 4 Robert with his followers obtained a fruitfull possession in those parts. **1712** ADDISON *Spect.* No. 303 ¶4 Instances of the same great and fruitful Invention. **1867** A. BARRY *Sir C. Barry* ix. 303 It had the opportunities of rapid and fruitful exercise.

β. **1475** *Bk. Noblesse* 56 The noble and fructufulle examples of the noble cenatours. **1547–8** *Ordre of Communion* 4 His mooste fruictfull and glorious Passion. **1552** LYNDESAY *Monarche* 4788 Lat thay y[t] fructfull fysche [*i.e.* the Kirk] eschaip thare handis.

†'**fruitfulhead.** *Obs.* In 5 **fruȝtfulhed.** [f. FRUITFUL + -HEAD, -HOOD.] = FRUITFULNESS.

c **1440** *Jacob's Well* (E.E.T.S.) 238 Wetched softhed & neschhed, fruȝtfulhed.

fruitfully ('fruːtfʊlɪ), *adv.* [f. FRUITFUL + -LY[2].] In a fruitful manner.

1. So as to produce good results; with good effect, beneficially, profitably, edifyingly.

c **1450** tr. *De Imitatione* I. xviii. 20 Euery tyme þei spendid fruytfully. **1597** HOOKER *Eccl. Pol.* V. lxv. §19 Our very nature doth hardly yeeld to destroy that which may bee fruitefully kept. **1643** BURROUGHES *Exp. Hosea* ix. 311 That you may be helped fruitfully to read much Scripture. **1658** C. CARTWRIGHT (*title*) A Practical and Polemical Commentary..on the Whole Fifteenth Psalm. Wherein the Text is learnedly and fruitfully explained. **1894** *Advance* (Chicago) 29 Apr., It is the mission of others to illustrate and to show how to think, wisely, deeply, fruitfully.

†**2. a.** Copiously, fully. **b.** In such a manner as to be prolific. *Obs. rare.*

1601 SHAKS. *All's Well* II. ii. 73 *La.* You vnderstand me. *Clo.* Most fruitfully. **1605** —— *Lear* IV. vi. 270 If your will want not, time and place will be fruitfully offer'd. *a* **1684** EARL ROSCOMMON *Virgil's Sixth Eclogue* 45 How scatter'd Seeds of Sea, and Air, and Earth, And purer Fire..did fruitfully unite.

fruitfulness ('fruːtfʊlnɪs). [f. FRUITFUL + -NESS.] The quality, fact, or state of being fruitful, in senses of the adj.

1. Fertility in crops; exuberant production.

1398 TREVISA *Barth. De P.R.* XVII. lxi. (1495) 637 The fygge tree..hath that name of fruitfulnesse, for it is more fruytfull than other trees. **1561** T. NORTON *Calvin's Inst.* I. xvi. (1634) 85 As though the fruitfulnesse of one yeare were not the singular blessing of God. **1601** WEEVER *Mirr. Mart.* B ij, A ground Which thrice a yeere her fruitfulnes did show. **1695** LD. PRESTON *Boeth.* I. 18 *note*, Named Felix..famous for its Fruitfulness and Number of Cities. **1775** ADAIR *Amer. Ind.* 184 The vine was..a symbol of fruitfulness. **1879** *Cassell's Techn. Educ.* I. 245 Some idea of its [banana's] fruitfulness may be gathered from the statement [etc.].

concr. **1649** ROBERTS *Clavis Bibl.* 80 And plentifully he did eate The fruitfulnesses of the field.

2. Fertility in offspring; fecundity.

1624 GATAKER *Transubst.* 138 By that blessing hee bestowed fruitfulnesse upon them. **1647** FULLER *Good Th. in Worse T.* (1841) 120 That water..proved like the spa unto her, so famous for causing fruitfulness. **1702** ADDISON *Dial. Medals* ii. 93 The Cornu-copiæ in her hand is a type of her fruitfulness. **1846** MCCULLOCH *Acc. Brit. Empire* (1854) I. 420 The increase..must..be attributed to an increased fruitfulness of the female sex.

3. Productiveness in general:

a. of material things. ? *Obs.*

1630 *R. Johnson's Kingd. & Commw.* 237 The fruitfulnesse of the Mines is no whit diminished. **1641** J. JACKSON *True Evang. T.* II. 103 The milkie fruitfulnesse of the Cow.

b. of immaterial things. Also, profitableness, utility; occas. †liberality.

1509 HAWES *Past. Pleas.* XI. xxxvii, He shal attaste the well of frutefulness Which Vyrgyl claryfied. **1551** BIBLE *Ps.* xxxvi. *note*, The fertilitie and fruitfulnes of the holy Ghoste. **1576** FLEMING *Panopl. Epist.* 266 To heale that up by the fruitfulnesse of physicke. **1604** SHAKS. *Oth.* III. iv. 38 This argues fruitfulnesse, and liberal heart. *a* **1661** FULLER *Worthies* (1840) III. 87 It [woad] giveth them [colours] truth and fruitfulness. **1702** ADDISON *Dial. Medals* ii. 52 Shows at the same time the great fruitfulness of the Poet's fancy. **1833** LAMB *Elia, Product. Mod. Art*, To the lowest subjects..the Great Masters gave loftiness and fruitfulness. **1881** J. R. ILLINGWORTH *Serm. Coll. Chapel* 150 The fruitfulness of the fragmentary lives of old.

fruiting ('fruːtɪŋ), *vbl. sb.* [f. FRUIT *v.* + -ING[1].] The action of the vb. FRUIT; the process of bearing fruit. †In early use *concr.*: Offspring.

a **1300** *Cursor M.* 12257 (Gött.) þat þe geld þair fruiting find. **1862** ANSTED *Channel Isl.* IV. xxi. (ed.2) 488 A..white frost, will..check the fruiting of the trees for several years. **1871–2** H. MACMILLAN *True Vine* iii. 115 The period of.. fruiting is accelerated..by grafting.

fruiting ('fruːtɪŋ), *ppl. a.* [f. FRUIT *v.* + -ING[2].] Bearing fruit; **fruiting body** = *fruit-body*; also occas. applied to spore-producing bacteria.

1778 COWPER *Let.* 3 Dec., He has presented me with six fruiting pines. **1870** HOOKER *Stud. Flora* 178 *Galium uliginosum*..fruiting pedicels erect. **1872** OLIVER *Elem. Bot.* II. 289 [Of Horsetail] The fertile or fruiting stem is unbranched. **1894** FLORA A. STEEL *Potter's Thumb* (1895) 161 A shingled hut, hung with flowering, fruiting gourds. **1918** HAWLEY & HAWES *Man. Forestry Northeast. U.S.* vii. 125 These fruiting bodies are the only part of the fungus visible to the naked eye. **1944** *Proc. Soc. Exp. Biol. & Med.* LVI. 18 The production of fruiting bodies in aqueous media is a new observation. **1962** W. P. K. FINDLAY *Preservation of Timber* ii. 16 A fruiting body of one of the larger bracket fungi may produce over eight hundred million spores per hour.

fruition (fruː'ɪʃən). Forms: 5–6 **fruicion, -yon, fruycion,** (5 **fruycon**), **fruyssyon,** 6 **fruitioun, fruytion,** 6– **fruition.** [a. OF. *fruission, fruition, fruycion*, ad. L. *fruitiōnem*, n. of action f. *fruī* to enjoy: see FRUIT *sb.*]

The action of enjoying; enjoyment, pleasurable possession, the pleasure arising from possession. †*in the fruition of* = in the possession of.

1413 *Pilgr. Sowle* (Caxton 1483) IV. xxviii. 75 An aungel hath that knowynge of his creatour by very fruycion. *c* **1450** *Cov. Myst.* (Shaks. Soc.) 86 Contryssyon, Compassyon, and Clennes, And that holy mayde Fruyssyon. **1554** LATIMER in Strype *Eccl. Mem.* III. App. xxxv. 98 If we live by hope let us desire the end and fruition of our hope. **1600** HAKLUYT *Voy.* (1810) III. 57 We had when so disposed, the fruition of our bookes. **1632** LITHGOW *Trav.* V. 179 Solyman entred the Toune as conquerour..It is ever since in the fruition of Turkes. *c* **1655** A. SIDNEY *Treat. Love* in *19th Cent.* Jan. (1884) 61 It is very certaine that all desire is for fruition. **1711** ADDISON *Spect.* No. 256 ¶7 An Object of Desire placed out of the Possibility of Fruition. **1855** THACKERAY *Newcomes* I. 20 Repaid by such a scant holiday and brief fruition. **1883** *19th Cent.* May 854 In the contemplation and fruition of the Uncreated Good.

2. Erroneously associated with FRUIT, in the sense: the state or process of bearing fruit, esp. in phr. ***to come to*** (***reach,*** etc.) ***fruition*** or ***full fruition.*** Freq. *transf.* and *fig.* (Now a standard usage.)

(The blunder was not countenanced by 19th-cent. Dictionaries in this country, nor by Webster or Worcester though it was somewhat common both in England and in the U.S.)

1885 *Harper's Mag.* May 906 The greenish nuts, ripened as always from the flowers of the previous year and now in their full fruition. **1889** *Century Dict.*, *Fruition*, a coming into fruit or fulfilment. **1895** *Standard Dict.*, *Fruition*, the bearing of fruit; the yielding of natural or expected results; realization, fulfilment. **1936** G. B. STERN *Monogram* III. 202 The words you have written for publication..should be a fastidiously selected portion of your mind and experience which has slowly grown to fruition and importance. **1958** *Times Lit. Suppl.* 8 Aug. 447/3 Sir Edmund Chambers's monumental labours on Shakespeare and the Shakespearian stage were based largely on the resources of the London Library, without which they could never have been brought to fruition, even if they had been attempted. **1959** *Times* 7 July 3/6 This process..has now reached full fruition with the standardization of body shells for a whole range of models [of motor cars]. **1968** *Times* 28 Nov. 14/1 A project for revealing the undiscovered burial chambers thought to exist within the pyramid of Khephren at Giza, Cairo, is shortly to come to fruition.

fruitist (ˈfruːtɪst). [f. FRUIT *sb.* + -IST.] One who cultivates fruit.

1824 B. MAUND (*title*) Fruitist: a Treatise on Orchard and Garden Fruits. **1848–61** (*title*) The florist, fruitist and garden miscellany. **1849** *Florist* 52 Our space prevents our doing more than warmly recommending such of our readers as are fruitists to procure this work.

fruitive (ˈfruːɪtɪv), *a.* [ad. med.L. *fruitīvus*, in *unio fruitiva* (Thomas à Kempis); f. L. *fru-ī* (see FRUITION).] Consisting of, arising from, or producing fruition or enjoyment; having the faculty or function of enjoying.

1635 ROUS *Myst. Marr.* (1653) 263 A spiritual conjunction & the excesses of a fruitive union. **1648** BOYLE *Seraph. Love* xxvi. (1700) 154 To whet our Longings for Fruitive (or experimental) knowledge. **1668** HOWE *Bless. Righteous* (1825) 77 This vision is fruitive, unites the Soul with the blessed object. *a* **1866** J. GROTE *Treat. Mor. Ideals* (1876) 293 Utilitarianism..looks upon man as fruitive, or enjoying, in the first instance, and active only in the second instance.

fruitless (ˈfruːtlɪs), *a.* [f. FRUIT *sb.* + -LESS.] Devoid of fruit.

1. Not producing fruit; barren, sterile. †*Rarely* of animals: Not producing offspring, unfruitful.

1513 BRADSHAW *St. Werburge* (1887) 806 With whom this lady lyued a longe season Barrayn and fruyteles of generacion. **1546** *Supplic. Poore Commons* (E.E.T.S.) 92 Rotton and fruyteles trees. **1596** *Edw. III*, I. ii. 151 The ground..seemes barrayne, sere, vnfertill, fructles [ed. 1599 fruitles], dry. **1601** HOLLAND *Pliny* I. 224 Such begotten in this maner..are themselues barren and fruitles, vnable either to beare or beget yong. **1615** CROOKE *Body of Man* 230 We see some women which haue conceyued to become fruitlesse for a space. **1634** RAINBOW *Labour* (1635) 3 Christ ..had power..to turne the fruitlesse desarts into kitchins. **1725** BRADLEY *Fam. Dict.* s.v. *July*, Diligently removing, either by Pinching or the Knife, all weak and fruitless Shoots. **1800** STUART in Owen *Wellesley's Desp.* 571 The part that does not belong to us is savage and fruitless. **1851** RUSKIN *Stones Ven.* II. iv. §17. 69 The root of a fruitless tree.

2. Yielding no profit or advantage; producing no effect or result; inefficacious, ineffectual, unprofitable, useless; empty, idle, vain.

1340 HAMPOLE *Pr. Consc.* 5666 Ilk idel worde, spoken in vayne, þat es to say, þat war fruytles. **1500–20** DUNBAR *Poems* lxvi. 2 This waverand warldis wretchidness, The failȝeand and frutless bissiness. **1580** SIDNEY *Arcadia* I. (1605) 44 The basest and fruitlessest of al passions. **1590** SHAKS. *Mids. N.* III. ii. 371 When they next wake, all this derision Shall seeme a dreame, and fruitlesse vision. **1611** BIBLE *Wisd.* xv. 4 An image spotted with diuers colours, the painters fruitlesse labour. **1697** DAMPIER *Voy.* I. ix. 251 Our search was..fruitless. **1751** JORTIN *Serm.* (1771) V. iii. 49 Vows which often end in fruitless regrets. **1849** MACAULAY *Hist. Eng.* I. 298 The liberality of the nation had been made fruitless by the vices of the government. **1878** MORLEY *Crit. Misc., Carlyle* 202 It is fruitless to go to him for help in the solution of philosophic problems.

3. a. Of persons: Not attaining one's object; unsuccessful. **b.** Const. *of.* Unable to produce or utter (words). *rare.*

1843 CARLYLE *Past & Pr.* II. vi, The Devil and the Dream both fled away fruitless. **1858** —— *Fredk. Gt.* IV. v. (1865) I. 309 He storms and rages forward..but..has to retire fruitless, about daybreak, himself wounded. **1869** LOWELL *Under the Willows* Poet. Wks. (1880) 195 Dumbly felt with thrills Moving the lips, though fruitless of the words.

Hence **ˈfruitlessly** *adv.*, **ˈfruitlessness.**

1612–15 BP. HALL *Contempl.*, *O.T.* XI. v, Then she had griefe from her own fruitlesnesse. **1626** MASSINGER *Rom. Actor* IV. i, You have but fruitlessly laboured to sully A white robe of perfection. **1727** W. MATHER *Yng. Man's Comp.* 72 Time fruitlesly pass'd away, will in the end cause an aking Heart. **1791** MRS. RADCLIFFE *Rom. Forest* xi, She saw the inconvenience and fruitlessness of opposition. **1858** FROUDE *Hist. Eng.* IV. xviii. 55 Policy had laboured for a union, and had laboured fruitlessly. **1872** LIDDON *Elem. Relig.* v. 184 If by 'God' is meant only [etc.]..we need not read Spinoza to convince ourselves of the fruitlessness of prayer.

fruitlet (ˈfruːtlɪt). [f. FRUIT *sb.* + -LET.] A little fruit; *Bot.*, a single member of an aggregate fruit: see AGGREGATE *a.* 5.

1882 VINES *Sachs' Bot.* 495 If the carpels do not cohere, each forms a part of the fruit, or a fruitlet. **1883** G. ALLEN *Col. Clout's Cal.* xxi. 119 The blackberry and raspberry; where the individual fruitlets grow soft, sweet, and pulpy.

fruitling (ˈfruːtlɪŋ). [f. FRUIT *sb.* + -LING.] A small fruit; in material and immaterial sense.

1876 J. ELLIS *Caesar in Egypt* 247 Time lost! in acquiring some fruitlings of error. **1891** *Chamb. Jrnl.* Feb. 107/2 A mango tree with two small green fruitlings on it.

†**fruituously**, *adv. Obs.*[−1] Altered form of FRUCTUOUSLY, after FRUIT.

c **1450** tr. *De Imitatione* I. xiv. 16 Euere he laboriþ fruytuously.

†**ˈfruiture.** *Obs.*[−1] [As if ad. L. *fruitūra, f. *fruī* to enjoy: see FRUIT.] Fruition.

a **1653** G. DANIEL *Idyll* i. 99 To give the fruiture of each desire.

fruity (ˈfruːtɪ), *a.* [f. FRUIT *sb.* + -Y[1].]

1. Of or pertaining to or resembling fruit.

1657 R. LIGON *Barbadoes* (1673) 72 A fruity taste. **1817** L. HUNT *Let. to C. C. Clarke* in *Gentl. Mag.* May (1876) 600 All that is fine, floral, and fruity. **1850** BLACKIE *Æschylus* I. 81 The flowery calix, full surcharged With fruity promise. **1858** BUSHNELL *Nat. & Supernat.* iv. (1864) 91 The succulent peach gathers its fruity parts..about the nut or stone. *a* **1861** MRS. BROWNING *Lett. R. H. Horne* (1877) II. 131, I never saw a blooming girl of sixteen with a more fruity hopefulness in her countenance.

2. Of wine: Having the taste of the grape.

1844 DICKENS *Mart. Chuz.* xii. 151 Whether he would wish to try a fruity port with greater body. **1851** D. JERROLD *St. Giles* xxvii. 281 A glass of good fruity port—and yours is capital. **1855** *Athenæum* 13 Oct. 1194 Genuine Masdeu is a very fine fruity wine.

3. *colloq.* Full of rich or strong quality; highly interesting, attractive, or suggestive. Cf. JUICY *a.* 2, SPICY *a.* 7.

1900 T. HOPKINS *Silent Gate* ii. 45 When pulled up short, his language was of the Dials, fruity. **1915** T. BURKE *Nights in Town* 337 A popular murder, fruity, cleverly done, and with a sex interest. **1921** WODEHOUSE *Indiscretions of Archie* 299 It's here now. The dickens of a fruity picture. **1925** *Weekly Westminster* 19 Sept. 522/3 Mr. John Garside's Young Launcelot is more intelligent, even if it is like the work of a fruity comedian without his fruitiness. **1928** S. VINES *Humours Unreconciled* xv. 201 An unusually 'fruity' political scandal connected with bribery. **1938** G. HEYER *Blunt Instrument* xi. 204 It might strike him as a pretty fruity idea to do in his victims as clumsily as he could. **1958** WODEHOUSE *Cocktail Time* xviii. 151 Some minutes later, a fruity voice caressed his ear. Albert Peasemarch's mentor, Coggs, had advised making the telephone-answering voice as fruity as possible in the tradition of the great butlers of the past. **1959** *Oxf. Mag.* 4 June 452/1 Angela Pedlar would have been wonderful if she could have been twice as fruity and three times as loud; she sounded exciting but far away. **1969** *Country Life* 25 Dec. 1697 A design as robust as it is ostentatious; Renaissance at its fruitiest, Elizabethan at its most exuberant, are gaily mixed together.

Hence **ˈfruitiness.**

1869 *Contemp. Rev.* XI. 357 Appreciating critics who write about its [a picture's] fruitiness, and juiciness, and pulpiness. **1895** *Daily News* 10 Apr. 4/7 The wines of the last vintage..are wanting in ripeness and fruitiness.

†**frumberdling.** *Obs.* [OE. *frumbierdling*, *frumbyrdling*, f. *frum-a* first + *beard* beard (with umlaut of *ea* to *ie*) + -LING.] A youth.

c **1000** *Supp. Ælfric's Voc.* in Wr.-Wülcker 171/22 *Pube tenus*, frumbyrdling. *c* **1200** *Trin. Coll. Hom.* 41 He frumberdlinges binimeð unðeawes and gode techeð.

†**frume.** *Obs.* Also 1 fruma, 3–4 frome. [OE. *fruma* wk. masc.: see FORME *a.*] Beginning.

Beowulf 2309 Wæs se fruma egeslic. *c* **1000** *Ags. Gosp.* Matt. xix. 4 Se þe on fruman worhte, he worhte wæpmann ænd wif-mann. *c* **1205** LAY. 13265 þe frume wes vnhende: & al swa wes þe ænde. *a* **1250** *Owl & Night.* 476 Hit is gode monne i-wone, An was from the worlde frome, That [etc.]. **13..** *Sir Beues* 3197 (MS. A.) Ich bidde the at the ferste frome That [etc.]. *c* **1380** *Sir Ferumb.* 1104 Speke we atte frome Of Erld Olyuer & his felawes.

†**ˈfrument.** *Obs.* [ad. L. *frūment-um* corn, f. *frugv-* root of *fruī* to enjoy.]

1. Corn.

c **1440** LYDG. *St. Albon* (1534) Aiij, Grayne of this frument was this man Albon. *c* **1510** BARCLAY *Mirr. Gd. Manners* (1570) Ciij, Fulsome fieldes habundaunt of frument. **1601** HOLLAND *Pliny* XVIII. vii. 560 When the Bruers steep their wheat or frument in water.

2. = FRUMENTY 1.

1494 FABYAN *Chron.* VII. 599 Frument with venyson. **1677** GALE *Crt. Gentiles* II. III. 173 Bread, and Fruments [orig. *pultes*] and Wine.

frumentaceous (fruːmənˈteɪʃəs), *a.* [f. late L. *frūmentāce-us* (f. L. *frūmentum* corn) + -OUS.] Of the nature of or resembling wheat or other cereals. *Bot.* (see quot. 1841).

1668 WILKINS *Real Char.* 70 Frumentaceous; Such whose seed is used by men for food. **1721–92** BAILEY, *Frumentaceous plants.* **1841** MAUNDER *Sci. & Lit. Treas.*, *Frumentaceous*, in botany an epithet for plants that have their stalks pointed, and their leaves like reeds, bearing their seed in ears, like corn.

†**frumental**, *a. Obs. rare.* [ad. L. *frūmentāl-em*, f. *frūmentum* corn: see -AL[1].] Of or pertaining to corn or grain.

1670 R. WITTIE in *Phil. Trans.* V. 1076 Any Vinous or Frumental Spirit.

†**frumenˈtarian**, *a. Rom. Ant. Obs. rare.* [f. L. *frūmentāri-us*, f. *frūmentum* corn + -AN.] = next. Only in ***frumentarian law***, i.e. a law providing for the distribution of corn at low rates.

1652 *Observ. Forms Govt.* 31 They..humoured the Commons by the Agrarian and frumentarian Laws.

frumentarious (fruːmənˈtɛərɪəs), *a. rare.* [f. as prec. + -OUS.] Of or pertaining to corn.

1670–81 in BLOUNT *Glossogr.* **1806** SYD. SMITH in *Mem.* (1855) II. 24 Horner, the frumentarious philosopher.

†**ˈfrumentary**, *a. Obs. rare.* [ad. L. *frūmentāri-us*: see prec.] = FRUMENTARIAN *a.*

1656 EARL MONM. *Advt. fr. Parnass.* 10 Those seditious Frumentary, and Agrarian Laws.

frumentation (fruːmənˈteɪʃən). *Rom. Ant.* [ad. L. *frūmentātiōn-em*, f. *frūmentārī* to furnish with corn, f. *frūmentum* corn.] (See quot. 1861.)

1623 in COCKERAM. **1721–92** in BAILEY. **1861** J. G. SHEPPARD *Fall Rome* i. 28 The third class..lived upon the 'frumentations', or public largesses of corn.

†**frumenˈtose**, *a. Obs. rare.* [as if ad. L. *frūmentōs-us, f. *frūmentum* corn: see -OSE.] 'Full of corn' (1727 BAILEY, vol. II).

frumenty (ˈfruːməntɪ), **furmety** (ˈfɜːmɪtɪ). Forms: α. 4 frumentee, 5 frumyte, 6–7 frumentie, -tye, 7 frummetry, 7, 9 fromenty, 7–9 frumet(t)y, 8 frumentary, 9 fromety, frumerty, -arty, frummaty, -ety, 5– frumenty. β. 4–5 furmente, 5, 6, 9 -ty, 6 fermeté, fer-, fir-, four-, fur-, fyrmentie, -ye, 7 fir-, formity, formety, 8–9 fu(r)metry, furmetree, -etty, 7–9 furmety, -ity. [ME. *frumentee*, *furmente*, a. OF. *frumentée*, *fourmentee*, f. *frument*, *fourment* (mod.F. *froment*):—late popular L. *frŭmentum = class. L. *frūmentum* corn.]

1. A dish made of hulled wheat boiled in milk, and seasoned with cinnamon, sugar, etc.

? *a* **1400** *Morte Arth.* 180 Flesch fluriste of fermysone with frumentee noble. *c* **1460** J. RUSSELL *Bk. Nurture* 383 Fatt venesoun with frumenty. **1483** *Cath. Angl.* 144/2 Frumyte, *frumenticium.* **1562** TURNER *Herbal* II. Ee b/1 Frumentie made of sodden wheate. **1732** *Acc. Workhouses* 11 Dinner.. Frumetty and Beer at 3 o'clock. **1820** W. IRVING *Sketch Bk.* II. 68 The Squire made his supper of frumenty, a dish made of wheat cakes boiled in milk with rich spices. **1860** GEO. ELIOT *Mill on Fl.* II. 153 Mothers..who made their butter and their fromenty well.

β. ? *c* **1390** *Form of Cury* in Warner *Antiq. Culin.* 15 Make furmente as before. *c* **1483** CAXTON *Vocab.* 6 b, Furmente whiche is made of whete. **1544** PHAER *Regim. Life* (1560) G v, Peasen, beanes, mylke, cheese, ryse, and firmentie. *a* **1616** BEAUM. & FL. *Bonduca* I. ii, He'll finde you out a food that needs no teeth nor stomack; a strange formity Will feed ye up as fat as hens i'th forehead. **1796** *Sporting Mag.* VIII. 220 John Gawston, eat such a quantity of what is called furmety..that he actually burst! **1827** CLARE *Sheph. Cal.* 56 The high bowl..Fill'd full of furmety. **1859** MRS. GASKELL *Round the Sofa* 42 We had..furmenty on Mothering Sunday. **1864** KNIGHT *Passages Wrkg. Life* I. 28 On that fourth Sunday in Lent, I regularly feasted on Furmety.

†**2.** A kind of wheat or spelt. *Obs.*

1600 SURFLET *Country Farme* v. xvii. 687 Furmentie is that which the Latines call *Alica* or *Chondrus*, and it is a kind of wheate, whereof..is made a kinde of grosse meale, resembling oatmeale. **1601** HOLLAND *Pliny* XVIII. xxiii. 582 After the Frumentie or Spike corn be taken off, there be pulse sowed three times, one after another.

3. Wheat mashed for brewing. *rare* (? *nonce-use*).

1882 tr. *Thausing's Beer* iv. 197 The wheat is crushed and mixed with water. This frumenty is allowed to ferment.

4. *Comb.*, as ***frumenty-*** or ***furmety-corn***, ***-kettle***, ***-pot***, ***-seller***. Also **frumenty sweat** (see quot. 1847).

1535 COVERDALE *2 Sam.* xvii. 19 The woman..strowed firmentye corne theron. *c* **1550** *Wyl Bucke His Test.* (Halliw.) 43, I bequeth my grece to..the fermeté potte. **1623** MASSINGER *Bondman* I. iii, Licking his lips Like a spaniel o'er a furmenty-pot. **1668** R. L'ESTRANGE *Vis. Quev.* (1708) 127 Simpering like a Frumety-Kettle. **1847** HALLIWELL s.v., A person in a dilemma is said to be in a frumenty sweat. **1889** T. HARDY *Mayor of Casterbridge* i, The furmity seller decided to close for the night.

frumious (ˈfruːmɪəs), *a.* A factitious word introduced by 'Lewis Carroll' (see quot. 1871), and subsequently explained by him as a blend of *fuming* and *furious* (*Hunting of Snark*, pp. x–xi). Cf. BANDERSNATCH.

1871 'L. CARROLL' *Through Looking-Glass* i. 22 Beware the Jubjub bird, and shun The frumious Bandersnatch! **1876** —— *Hunting of Snark* 72 While those frumious jaws Went savagely snapping around. **1960** 'J. WINTON' *We saw Sea* iii. 54 'How peaceful it all is,' he said, 'now we've curbed the frumious Goldilocks.' **1966** *New Statesman* 14 Jan. 59/2 In each revue-type episode, an increasingly glazed Michael Graham Cox is confronted with Peter Bayliss, splendidly frumious in each incarnation of shamed authority, gnashing on a marvellous repertoire of sobbing animal snarls. **1985** *N.Y. Times* 21 Apr. VII. 24/3 (*heading*) Shun the frumious ziz.

†**frumkenned**, *ppl. a. Obs.* [OE. *frumcęnned*, f. *frum-a* first + *cęnned*, pa. pple. of *cęnnan* to bear.] First-born.

c **893** K. ÆLFRED *Oros.* I. vii. §1 Ealle ða cnihtas and ealle ða mædena þe on þæm lande frumcennede wæron. *c* **1000** *Ags. Gosp.* Matt. i. 1 Heo cende hyre frum-cennedan [*c* **1160** *Hatton* kennede] sunu. *c* **1175** *Lamb. Hom.* 87 Godes engel ..acwalde on elche huse..frumkenede childe.

†**ˈfrummagemed**, *ppl. Cant. Obs.* (See quots.)

a **1700** B. E. *Dict. Cant. Crew*, *Frummagem'd*, choaked. **1785** GROSE *Dict. Vulg. Tongue*, *Frummagem'd*, choak'd, strangled, or hanged.

†**ˈfrummer.** *Obs. rare.* [? var. of FRUMPER.]

1659 TORRIANO, *Taccagnatore*, a chuff, a caviller, a frummer, a niggardly wretch.

frump (frʌmp), *sb.* [Of unknown origin; possibly shortened from FRUMPLE.]

†**1.** ? A sneer, ? a derisive snort. *Obs.*

1589 R. HARVEY *Pl. Perc.* 4 You vse the nostrils too much, and to many vnseasoned frumps [to a man, as if he were a horse]. **1592** GREENE *Disput.* 24, I gaue him slender thankes, but with such a frump that he perceiued how light I made of his counsayle. **1650** TRAPP *Comm. Deut.* xxiii. 4 As God takes notice of the least courtesie shewed to his people..so he doth of the least discourtesie, even to a frown or a frump.

†**2.** A mocking speech or action; a flout, jeer. *Obs.*

1553 T. WILSON *Rhet.* (1580) 188 You brought a shillyng to ninepence.. and so gave hym a frumpe euen to his face. **1598** BARCKLEY *Felic. Man* (1631) 99 Esteeming those things as the frumps of fortune, which ye exalt above the skies and take for felicitie. **1616** BEAUM. & FL. *Scornf. Lady* II. iii, Sweet Widow leave your frumps, and be edified. **1651** HOWELL in *Cartwright's Poems* b 8 b, They dash thee on the Nose with frumps and rapps. *a* **1700** B. E. *Dict. Cant. Crew, Frump*, a dry Bob, or Jest.

†**3.** A derisive deception, a hoax. *Obs.*

1593 HOLLYBAND *Fr. Dict.* (Halliw.), To tell one a lie, to give a frumpe. **1668** DAVENANT *Man's the Master* II. i, These are a kind of witty frumps of mine like selling of bargains. **1791** PEGGE *Derbicisms* Ser. II. (E.D.S.), *Frump*, an untruth, a story.

4. *pl.* Sulks, ill-humour. Now *dial.*

1668 DRYDEN *Evening's Love* IV. i, Not to be behind hand with you in your Frumps, I give you back your Purse of Gold. **1678** —— *Kind Kpr.* I. i, Why should you be in your frumps, Pug, when I design only to oblige you? **1823** SCOTT *Peveril* xl, When the Duchess of Portsmouth takes the frumps. **1823** MOOR *Suffolk Words* s.v., If insolent withal, she [a cross old woman] would be said to be *frumpy* or *frumpish* or 'in her frumps'.

5. A cross, old-fashioned, dowdily-dressed woman. Also *rarely*, said of a man.

1817 GODWIN *Mandeville* I. xi. 261 They voted me a prig, a frump, a fogram. **1840** BARHAM *Ingol. Leg., Hamilton Tighe* 97 All the best trumps Get into the hands of the other old frumps. **1859** G. MEREDITH *R. Feverel* xlii, I looked a frump. **1888** RIDER HAGGARD *Col. Quaritch* I. 231 'Hang me ..if she has not taken up with that confounded old military frump'.

b. said of a dowdy dress.

1886 G. R. SIMS *Ring o' Bells, &c.* ix. 229 She taught me ..how to make pretty dresses..for half what my ugly old frumps of gowns..used to cost me.

frump (frʌmp), *v.* [Connected with FRUMP *sb.*]

1. *trans.* To mock, flout, jeer; to taunt, insult, browbeat, snub. ***to frump off***: to put off with jeering answers. *Obs.* or *arch.*

1577–87 HOLINSHED *Chron.* II. 34/1 He taketh the man to be overlavish of his pen in frumping of his adversaries with quipping taunts. **1606** HOLLAND *Sueton.* 149 Whom..Caius was wont to frump and flout in most opprobrious termes as a wanton and effeminate person. *a* **1625** FLETCHER *Chances* III. i, Was ever Gentlewoman So frumpt off with a foole? **1655** GURNALL *Chr. in Arm.* I. 116 God suffers somtimes the infirmities of his people to be known by the wicked (who are ready to check and frump them for them). **1753** *School of Man* 288 How can your spirit bear that Aglae shall daily be frumping you.

¶ ?*erron.* **1841** *Tait's Mag.* VIII. 561 Conceiting himself, when he is only frumping the face of his own whim, to be beating..a whole world of buckramed giants into jelly.

†**2.** *intr.* To scoff, mock. Const. *at. Obs.*

1566 DRANT *Horace's Sat.* III. B iij b, One Mevius did frumpe and floute at Nevie then awaye. **1583** GOLDING *Calvin on Deut.* xiv. 81 These skoffers which are alwayes frumping. **1611** DEKKER *Roaring Girle* Wks. 1873 III. 202 We are but frumpt at and libell'd vpon. **1662** *Rump Songs* II. 60, I do not love for to frump. [**1851** S. JUDD *Margaret* xvii. (1871) 148 The riders screamed, cross-bit, frumped and hooted at each other.]

†**3.** To sulk, be in a bad temper. *Obs.*

1693 SOUTHERNE *Maid's Last Prayer* III. i, My wife frump'd all the while and did not say one word.

4. *trans.* To put in a bad humour, vex.

1862 H. MARRYAT *Year in Sweden* II. 59 Gustaf, frumped at the non-arrival of the Garter, placed the portrait of Charles Edward..opposite his own in the palace.

Hence **'frumping** *vbl. sb.* Also **'frumper**, one who 'frumps'.

1598 FLORIO, *Motteggiatore*, a frumper, giber or iester, a quipper. **1611** COTGR., *Mocquerie*..a mocking, flowting, scoffing, frumping. *Ibid., Mocqueur*, a mocker, flowter, frumper. **1664** COTTON *Poet. Wks.* (1765) 31 Pray young Man leave off your Frumping. **1677** HOLYOKE *Lat. Dict.*, A frumper, *sannio.*

†**'frumpery.** *Obs.* [f. FRUMP *sb.* + -ERY.] Abuse, mockery; also, a flout, mock, or sneer.

1583 STANYHURST *Æneis, etc.* (Arb.) 145 With bitter frumperye taunting. **1653** URQUHART *Rabelais* I. xl, Which is the cause wherefore he hath of all men mocks, frumperies and bastonadoes.

frumpiness ('frʌmpɪnɪs). [f. FRUMPY *a.* + -NESS.] The quality or condition of a frump.

1912 C. N. & A. M. WILLIAMSON *Heather Moon* I. v. 59 Aline tried to think that she was the weirdest frump in the world... The thing was to hurry her away in all her frumpiness. **1924** *Sunday at Home* Feb. 258/1, I am going to take you up and save you from frumpiness and spinsterhood.

frumping ('frʌmpɪŋ), *ppl. a.* [f. FRUMP *v.* + -ING².] That frumps; mocking, scoffing, jeering.

1577 HOLINSHED *Chron.* (1807–8) II. 24 This frumping speech so moued the king, that, [etc.]. **1609** HOLLAND *Amm. Marcell.* xxx. iv. 387 Æsops frumping scoffes or fables. *a* **1652** BROME *Damoiselle* II. Wks. 1873 I. 403 The frumping Jacks are gone.

Hence **'frumpingly** *adv.*

1576 FLEMING tr. *Caius' Dogs* in Arb. *Garner* III. 267 [Dogs] which some, frumpingly, term Fisting Hounds.

frumpish ('frʌmpɪʃ), *a.* [f. FRUMP *sb.* + -ISH.] Disposed to mock or flout; jesting, sneering; also, cross, ill-tempered.

1647 WHARTON *Pluto's Progr. Gt. Brit.* 15 Thy lowring scowling makes me dumpish, For to see my Love so frumpish. *a* **1668** DAVENANT *Play-House to be Let* Wks. (1673) 116 When Fortune frumpish is, who e're withstood her? **1757** FOOTE *Author* II. Wks. 1799 I. 155 Methought she looked very frumpish and jealous. **1820** KEATS & HUNT *Keats' Wks.* (1889) III. 35 Such a frumpish old fellow. **1882** MISS BRADDON *Mt. Royal* I. ii. 47 The companion sour and frumpish.

frumpishly ('frʌmpɪʃlɪ), *adv.* [-LY².] In a frumpish manner; like a frump or dowdy.

1927 *Daily Tel.* 23 Aug. 8/5 The middle-aged matron refuses definitely to take a back seat. She does not feel a frump. Why, then, should she dress frumpishly?

†**'frumple,** *sb. Obs.* Also 5 **fromple**. [f. next vb.] A wrinkle.

c **1440** *Promp. Parv.* 181/2 Frumpylle, *ruga.* **1490** CAXTON *Eneydos* xxviii. 111 Grete ryueles and fromples that putte oute the beaulte of the playsaunte vysage.

'frumple, *v. Obs.* exc. *dial.* Also 5–6 **fromple**, 5 **frompel**, 6 **frompill**. [? ad. Du. *verrompelen* (Kilian) of same meaning, f. *ver-* = FOR- + *rompelen* to RUMPLE.]

1. *trans.* To wrinkle, crumple.

1398 TREVISA *Barth. De P.R.* v. l. (1495) 168 The flesshe in the buttockes is fromplyd and knotty. *c* **1489** CAXTON *Sonnes of Aymon* i. 48 He frompeled his forhede and knytted his browes. **1493** *Festivall* (W. de W. 1515) 112 b, She founde all his clothes frompled. **1578** LYTE *Dodoens* VI. iv. 660 The leaves are not smoth, but crompled or frompled. **1611** COTGR., *Plionner*, to wrinkle, crumple, frumple. **1825–80** JAMIESON, *Frumple*, to crease, to crumple. **1828** *Craven Gloss.* (ed. 2), *Frumple*, to wrinkle, to ruffle or disorder.

2. ? To rumple, tumble.

a **1529** SKELTON *Manerly Margery* 16 What wolde ye frompill me? now fy!

Hence **'frumpled** *ppl. a.*

c **1440** *Promp. Parv.* 181/2 Frumplyd, *rugatus.* **1896** *Warwicksh. Gloss.* s.v., A frumpled pinafore.

frumpy ('frʌmpɪ), *a.* [f. FRUMP *sb.* + -Y¹.] Cross-tempered; also, like a frump, dowdy.

1746 *Clan Ronaldsmen* in *Jacobite Songs* (1887) 238 The frumpy forward Duke. *a* **1825** FORBY *Voc. E. Anglia, Frumpy*, having a sour and ill-humoured look. *c* **1840** J. MITFORD in *C. M.'s Lett. & Remin.* (1891) 181 He is as old-fashioned and frumpy as if he had never been out of college. **1845** *Blackw. Mag.* LVII. 243 An old, faded, frumpy bonnet. **1849** DICKENS *Dav. Copp.* xliv, I have been a grumpy, frumpy, wayward sort of a woman, a good many years. **1882** MISS BRADDON *Mt. Royal* xxvii, She was frumpy and dowdy.

†**'frumrese.** *Obs.* In 3 **frumræs**. [f. OE. *frum-a* first + *rǽs* rush.] A first attack, onslaught.

c **1205** LAY. 8655 Æt þon frum ræsen; he feolde..feowerti hundred.

†**'frumschaft.** *Obs.* [OE. *frumsceaft*, f. *frum-a* first + *sceaft* creation, f. *sciеppan* to SHAPE.] First formation, creation.

Beowulf 91 Sæʒde, se þe cuþe frumsceaft fira feorran reccan. *c* **900** tr. *Bæda's Hist.* IV. xxv. [xxiv.] (1890) 344 þa cwæð he: Hwæt sceal ic singan? Cwæð he: Sing me frumsceaft. *a* **1225** *Juliana* 3 In ure lauerdes luue þe feader is of frumscheft. *a* **1225** *St. Marher.* 20 þu folckes feder of frumschaft schuptest al the ischapen is.

†**frumth.** *Obs.* Forms: 1 **frymð** (? *erroneously* **frumð**), **frymðo**, 2 **fremð**, 2–3 **frumð**, *south.* **vrumð**, *Orm.* **frummþ**. [OE. *frymð*, Northumb. *frymðo*, fem. f. *frum* adj., original.] Beginning.

c **950** *Lindisf. Gosp.* Matt. xxv. 34 From frymðo middanʒeardes. *a* **1000** *Elene* 345 (Gr.) Frumða god. *a* **1000** *Boeth. Metr.* xi. 75 Hi..sculon þone ilcan ryne eft ʒecyrran þe æt frymðe. *c* **1200** ORMIN 18555 þiss wass i frummþe wiþþ soþ Godd. *a* **1225** *Ancr. R.* 104 Ich seide..iðe frumðe of þis tale. **12..** *Duty Chr.* 30 in *O.E. Misc.* 142 He [Crist] hit haued al biþouht þe frumðe to þon ende.

†**'frundel.** *Obs.* Forms: 6 **frondaille, frundle**, 6–7 **frundel(l**, 7 **frundele**. [app. a var. of *farundell*, FARTHINGDEAL.] A dry measure; by Ray said to be equal to two pecks.

Quot. 1641 seems to identify the *frundel* and the peck. This appears more probable than Ray's statement, if the word means etymologically 'quarter' (of a bushel); but the discrepancy may admit of being explained, as Ray mentions the existence of a 'bushel' twice as large as the standard bushel.

c **1550** *Bottesford Manor Rec.* (N.W. Linc. Gloss.), From martyngmes to mydsomer i frondaille off malt. **1557** in *Antiquary* Dec. (1888) 20, i frundell of barlye. **1641** BEST *Farm. Bks.* (Surtees) 68 Many will putte to a pecke or frundell of malte..to make it both stronge and likewise to keepe well. **1673** *Yorksh. Dial.* 6 in 9 *Specim.* (E.D.S.) 111 You s' ge m'a frundel o' yar grains. **1674–91** RAY *N.C. Words* 28 A Frundele: Two pecks.

frunt(e, obs. form of FRONT.

fruntall(e, -elle, obs. forms of FRONTAL.

frunter, var. of THRINTER *Sc.* (a ewe in her fourth year).

frunture, var. of FRONTURE, *Obs.*

frush (frʌʃ), *sb.*¹ *Obs.* exc. *Sc.* Also 4–5 **frusche**, 4–6 **frusshe**, (5 **frushe**, 9 *arch.* **frusch**). [a. OF. *fruis, frois*, n. of action f. *fruissier, froissier*: see FRUSH *v.*]

†**1.** A rush, charge, onset, collision. *Obs.*

1375 BARBOUR *Bruce* XIII. 292 He and all his cumpany.. In-till a frusche all tuk the flycht. *c* **1400** *Melayne* 268 Righte at the firste frusche thay felde Fyve thowsande knyghtis. **1412–20** LYDG. *Chron. Troy* II. xxi, All in a frushe in all the haste they may They ran. *a* **1533** LD. BERNERS *Huon* cxxx. 474 So they aprochyd, and al at a frusshe of both partyes dasshed together.

b. The noise caused by this; the crash of breaking weapons, etc.

1375 BARBOUR *Bruce* XII. 545 Men mycht her, that had beyn by, A gret frusche of the speres that brast. **1805** SOUTHEY *Madoc* II. xix, With horrible uproar and frush Of rocks that meet in battle. **1875** J. VEITCH *Tweed* 144 Of mingling spears a shivering frusch.

2. *collect.* Fragments, splinters.

1583 STANYHURST *Æneis* I. (Arb.) 18 Al the frushe and leauings of Greeks. **1819** W. TENNANT *Papistry Storm'd* (1827) 190 Some brak in sma' The carvit wark..Sending the glory o' the wa' In fritter't frush about.

frush (frʌʃ), *sb.*² *Obs.* exc. *dial.* [Of uncertain origin; Topsell's suggestion (quot. 1607) seems not impossible. It might be plausibly regarded as a subst. use of FRUSH *a.*; but that word has not been found earlier than the nineteenth century.] = FROG *sb.*² Also (more fully ***running frush***) a disease which attacks this part of a horse's foot; thrush.

1607 TOPSELL *Four-f. Beasts* (1658) 324 The frush is the tenderest part of the hoof towards the heel..and because it is fashioned like a forked head, the French men call it 'Furchette' which word our farriers..perhaps for easiness sake of pronuntiation, do make it a monosyllable, and pronounce it the 'frush'. **1639** T. DE GRAY *Compl. Horsem.* 9 Let her shooes be taken off, her feet pared well, the Frush and heeles opened. **1688** R. HOLME *Armoury* II. 152/2 The running of the Frush; which is a rotten corrupt humour, that comes out of his [a horse's] Leg. **1725** BRADLEY *Fam. Dict.* s.v. *Hoof*, When the Frush is broad, the Heels will be weak. **1737** BRACKEN *Farriery Impr.* (1757) II. 32 A large Coronet is often accompanied with a tender Heel and running Frush. **1754** *Dict. Arts & Sc.* II. 1350 *Frush*, or Frog, among farriers, a sort of tender horn which arises in the middle of a horse's sole. **1892** *Northumbld. Gloss., Frush*, the thrush, or tender part of a horse's foot.

frush (frʌʃ), *a. Sc.* and *north. dial.* [? f. FRUSH *v.*; but cf. the synonymous FROUGH *a.*]

1. Liable to break; brittle, dry, fragile. Cf. FRUSHY *a.*

1802 in Scott *Minstr. Scott. Bord.* II. 142 O wae betide the frush saugh wand! **1826** *Blackw. Mag.* XIX. 243 Frush becomes the whole cover in a few seasons; and not a bird can open its wing..without scattering the straw like chaff. **1834** M. SCOTT *Cruise Midge* (1863) 200 The bottom of the pulpit being auld and frush the wooden tram flew crash through. **1878** *Cumberld. Gloss., Frush*, very brittle; crumbly. **1880** *Antrim & Down Gloss., Frush*, brittle, as applied to wood, &c.: said of flax when the 'shoughs' separate easily from the fibre.

fig. **1823** GALT *Entail* I. 59 When we think o' the frush green kail-custock-like nature of bairns.

2. Soft, not firm in substance.

1848 T. AIRD *Frank Sylvan* Poet. Wks. 302 They..peel the foul brown film of rind [of the earth-nut] away To the pure white, and taste it soft and frush. **1889** *Daily News* 12 Nov. 2/1 Beef that is in the flabby, unwholesome-looking condition that the butchers call 'frush'.

3. Frank, forward. *Aberd.* (Jam.) ? *Obs.*

1779 in *J. Skinner's Misc. Poetry* (1809) 183 Ye're unco frush At praising what's nae worth a rush.

frush (frʌʃ), *v.* Forms: 4–6 **frusch(e, frus(s)he**, (4 **frussche, fruyshe, froche**), 6– **frush**. Also (sense 5) 8 **frust**. [a. OF. *fruissier, froissier* (mod.F. *froisser*):—popular L. **frustiāre* to shiver in pieces, f. L. *frustum* fragment: see FRUSTUM.]

†**1.** *trans.* To strike violently so as to crush, bruise, or smash. *Obs.*

13.. *K. Alis.* 1814 To frusche the gadelyng, and to bete, And none of heom on lyve lete. *c* **1380** WYCLIF *Serm.* Sel. Wks. I. 201 Lest þei frushen her owne brest at þe hard stoone. *c* **1477** CAXTON *Jason* 138 They frusshed his helme and made him a meruaillous wounde in his hede. **1588** GREENE *Pandosto* (1607) 10 High Cedars are frushed with tempests, when lowe shrubs are not toucht with the wind. **1609** HEYWOOD *Brit. Troy* XI. lxv, With fury each invades His opposite their mutual armour frushing.

†**b.** with *adv.* or advb. phrase. *Obs.*

c **1375** *Sc. Leg. Saints, Petrus* 588 Harnise and sched & body all Fruschit in peciss vndir small. *c* **1500** *Lancelot* 1201 Thei fond his scheld was fruschit al to nocht. **1534** MORE *On the Passion* Wks. 1275/1 Enmyty wil I put betwene thee and the woman..she shal frushe thyne head in peeces. **1569** STOCKER tr. *Diod. Sic.* III. ii. 107 He was..frushed and brused to death. **1609** BIBLE (Douay) *Judg.* v. 11 The chariottes were frushed together.

†**c.** To dash (a person) *aback, down*, etc. *Obs.*

c **1380** WYCLIF *Serm.* Sel. Wks. II. 204 Where evere þis spirit takiþ him he fruyshiþ him doun. *c* **1400** *Destr. Troy* 3225 þai..frusshit hom abake. *Ibid.* 5931 He frusshet so felly freikes to ground.

†**d.** *fig.* To crush, disable. *Obs.*

c **1470** HENRY *Wallace* III. 197 The Sothroune part so fruschet was that tide, That in the stour thai mycht no langar bide. *c* **1510** MORE *Picus* Wks. 9/1 Refreshing all his membres that were bruised and frushed with that feuer. **1577** STANYHURST *Descr. Irel.* in *Holinshed* (1807–8) VI. 38 They are sore frusht with sicknesse.

†**2.** *intr.* To rush violently; also with *in, out, together.* Also in comb. ***again-frushe***: see AGAIN- 2.

1375 BARBOUR *Bruce* XVI. 161 Horss com thair fruschand, hed for hed. *c* **1400** *Destr. Troy* 11893 þan the freike shuld frusshe out, & a fyre make. *Ibid.* 11927 The grekes.. Frushet in felly at the faire yates. *c* **1400** *Melayne* 469 A fire þan fro þᵉ crosse gane frusche. *c* **1400** MAUNDEV. (1839) xxii. 238 Thei frusschen to gidere fulle fiercely. *c* **1430** *Syr Gener* (Roxb.) 3831 He com frushing, and leid on, And sleugh ther many a worthie mon. *c* **1450** *Merlin* 208 Thei frussht bothe on an hepe, the horse and his maister.

3. *trans.* To rub harshly, scratch. *Obs.* exc. *dial.*

c **1400** *Destr. Troy* 13940 He..ffowle frusshet his face with his felle nailes. *c* **1430** LYDG. *Min. Poems* (Percy) 39 With his berde he frusshed hir mouthe un-mete. [**1877** *N.W. Linc. Gloss.*, *Frush*, to rub, to rub bright, to polish.]

†**4.** *intr.* To break, snap; to break or become broken under pressure; to become crushed. *Obs. rare.*

1489 *Barbour's Bruce* XII. 57 (Edin. MS.) The hand-ax-schaft..fruschit..in twa. **1665** J. WEBB *Stone-Heng* 219 Timber-Work..to keep the Arras from frushing.

†**5.** *trans.* The technical expression for: **a.** To carve (a chicken); cf. BREAK *v.* 2 b. **b.** To dress (a chub). *Obs.*

c **1430** LYDG. *Hors, Shepe & G.* (Roxb.) 33 A chekyn [is] frusshed. **1513** *Bk. Keruynge* in *Babees Bk.* (1868) 265 Termes of a Keruer..frusshe that chekyn. **1708** W. KING *Cookery* 33 Persons of some Rank, and Quality, say, Pray cut up that Goose: Help me to some of that Chicken..not considering how indiscreetly they talk, before Men of Art, whose proper Terms are, Break that Goose, frust that Chicken. **1726** *Gentleman Angler* 149 *Frushed* is a Term used for a Chub or Chevin when it is dressed; as to Frush, *i.e.* to Dress. **1787** BEST *Angling* (ed. 2) 168 *Frush a chub*, dress him.

6. To straighten, set upright (the feathers of an arrow). *Obs.* exc. *Hist.*

1548 HALL *Chron.* (1809) 418 How quikly the Archers bent their bowes and frushed theire feathers. **1611** SPEED *Hist. Gt. Brit.* IX. xix. §56 The Archers stript vp their sleeues, bent their Bowes, and frushed their feathers. **1877** MISS YONGE *Cameos* Ser. III. xx. 189 The archers strung their bows and 'frushed' their arrows.

Hence † **'frushing** *vbl. sb. Obs.*

1375 BARBOUR *Bruce* XII. 504 At the assemble thair, Sic a frusching of speris wair That fer avay men mycht it her. *c* **1530** LD. BERNERS *Arth. Lyt. Bryt.* (1814) 18 Than began great..frusshyng of speres, & bateryng of harneys w[t] swerdes. **1562** BULLEYN *Dial. Soarnes & Chir.* 39 b, Euery riuyng, or frushyng of mannes fleshe, whiche maie be..by meanes of a wounde, and without a wounde. **1589** FLORIO, *Ammaccatura*..a frushing together.

† **'frushing,** *ppl. a. Obs. rare.* Also 5 *Sc.* **fruschand.** [f. FRUSH *v.* + -ING[2].] That breaks or is liable to break; brittle.

c **1470** HENRY *Wallace* II. 190 O wareide suerd, of tempyr neuir trew, Thi fruschand blaid in presoune sone me threw. *Ibid.* III. 147 The shafft to schonkit off the fruschand tre.

Hence † **'frushingly** *adv. Obs.*

1659 TORRIANO, *Affrústo*, by shivers, frushingly, piece-meal.

† **'frushy,** *a. Obs.* Also 8 **frushey.** [f. FRUSH + -Y[1].] Liable to break, brittle, fragile. Cf. FRUSH *a.* 1.

1610 W. FOLKINGHAM *Art of Survey* 7 The large and loose grained timber of the old Oake and frusshie Ash. **1776** G. SEMPLE *Building in Water* 86 Bog Oak Timber is always found to be frushey.

fruskin, var. of FRISKIN, *Obs.*

† **frust** (frʌst). *Obs. rare.* [ad. L. *frust-um* a piece.] A fragment.

1765 STERNE *Tr. Shandy* VII. xxxi, Such a story affords more *pabulum* to the brain than all the Frusts, and Crusts, and Rusts of antiquity, which travellers can cook up for it. **1820** *Sporting Mag.* (N.S.) VI. 165 The top is a mere frust.

† **'fruster,** *a.* and *sb. Sc. Obs.* Also **frustar, -ir, -yr.** [? Back-formation from FRUSTER *v.* or FRUSTRATE.]

A. *adj.* Fruitless, ineffectual, meaningless, vain; empty *of* (deeds). Also *absol.* **in fruster**: in vain.

c **1470** HENRY *Wallace* IV. 345 In frustyr termys I will nocht tarry long. **1500–20** DUNBAR *Poems* xlvi. 53 He of natur that wirker wes and king, Wald no thing frustir put. *Ibid.* lxv. 21 To ws..in our darkness be lampis in schyning: Or than in frustar is [all] ȝour lang leirning. **1508** —— *Tua Mariit Wemen* 190 He has a forme without force, And fair wordis but effect, all fruster of dedis.

B. *sb.* Frustration, disappointment.

c **1470** HENRY *Wallace* I. 313 Quhat suld I spek of frustir?

† **'fruster,** *v. Obs.* [ad. Fr. *frustrer*, ad. L. *frustrārī*: see FRUSTRATE *v.*]

1. *trans.* To balk or defraud *of* something due or expected. Also, to falsify (a prediction).

1490 CAXTON *Eneydos* xii. 45 Pygmalyon the wolde haue frustred of the grete tresours and Rychesses that he awayteth to haue of thy somtyme husbande. *Ibid.* xxii. 80 Prenostycatures..that to her were frustred.

2. To bring to nought, render useless; to frustrate (an enterprise); to destroy, lay waste, ruin. Also *intr.* for *refl.*

1500–20 DUNBAR *Poems* xxi. 78 Quhen flude and fyre sall our it frak, And frely frustir feild and fure. **1535** STEWART *Cron. Scot.* (1858) I. 45 [This] wald be caus sone efterwart perchance The commoun weill to fruster and to faill. **1570** *Satir. Poems Reform.* xviii. 50 Bot God, that hes thy Maiestie in cure, Will fruster all thair fulische Interprysis. *c* **1611** SYLVESTER *Du Bartas* II. iv. IV. *Decay* 1127 Have these..Withstood your Fury, and repulst your Powrs, Frust'red your Rams, fired your flying Towrs?

† **frusti'llation.** *Obs.* [f. L. *frustill-um* a small piece + -ATION.] A breaking into small pieces. In quot. quasi-*concr.* something fragmentary.

1653 J. HALL *Paradoxes* 53 All pleasures here are but petty frustillations.

† **'frustrable,** *a. Obs. rare.* [ad. late L. *frustrābilis*, f. *frustrārī*: see FRUSTRATE *v.*] Capable of being frustrated or rendered ineffectual.

1674 HICKMAN *Quinquart. Hist.* (ed. 2) 176 The Dominicans, from whom it is likely he got nothing agreeable to the Jesuits notion of respective Decrees, and frustrable grace. **1677** GALE *Crt. Gentiles* IV. 404 The Divine Wil is universally efficacious, insuperable..nor impedible and frustrable in any manner.

† **fru'straneous,** *a. Obs.* Also 7 *erron.* **frustaneous.** [f. L. type **frustrāne-us* (f. *frustrā* in vain) + -ous. Cf. It. and Sp. *frustraneo.*]

Vain, useless, ineffectual, unprofitable.

a **1643** J. SHUTE *Judgem. & Mercy* (1645) 4 Though hee saw how frustranious [*sic*] and empty all his intendments and purposes were. **1649** MILTON *Eikon.* 53 A most insufficient and frustraneous meanes. **1653** GAUDEN *Hierasp.* 74 Frustaneous and vain desires. **1665** G. HARVEY *Advice agst. Plague* 25 This, if frustraneous, is fortified with *Diascord.* or *Laud. Op.* *a* **1711** KEN *Hymns Festiv.* Poet. Wks. 1721 I. 317 Their real Substance to evade, And have their Force frustraneous made. **1780** J. HOWIE *Faithf. Contend.* Pref. 10 It were frustraneous to insist upon a portrait of that here.

Hence † **fru'straneously** *adv.*, vainly.

1689 G. HARVEY *Curing Dis. by Expect.* 2 From which the Patient day by day frustraneously expecting relief.

frustrate ('frʌstreɪt), *pa. pple.* and *ppl. a. arch.* Forms: 5–7 **frustrat,** (6 **frustraite**), 5– **frustrate.** [ad. L. *frustrāt-us*, pa. pple. of *frustrārī*, *frustrāre*: see next.] Equivalent to the later FRUSTRATED.

† **A.** *pa. pple.* In various senses of the vb. *Obs.*

In recent archaistic use the word is prob. viewed by the writers as adj.; see the examples under B.

1447 BOKENHAM *Seyntys* (Roxb.) 100 So the abbot frustrat went home sory. **1471** RIPLEY *Comp. Alch.* v. in Ashm. (1652) 148 That thy labor therfore be not frustrate. **1500–20** DUNBAR *Poems* xxxv. 40 Sleipand and walkand wes frustrat my desyr. **1504** ATKYNSON tr. *De Imitatione* III. iii. 197 They be ofte frustrate of that that they truste vpon. **1528** GARDINER in Pocock *Rec. Ref.* I. l. 103 The said Commission might be..frustrate and letted. **1529** MORE *Dyaloge* III. Wks. 236/1 Because the cumming together of the Lordes from Grenewiche..shoulde not bee frustrate. **1540–1** ELYOT *Image Gov.* 24 Noble Germanicus, who shoulde have succeded Tiberius in the empyre, if the treason of Fiso hadde not frustrate the truste of the People. **1555** EDEN *Decades* 66 Beinge thus frustrate of the increase of theyr seedes. **1606** SHAKS. *Ant. & Cl.* v. i. 2 Go to him, Dolla-bella, bid him yeeld, Being so frustrate, tell him, He mockes the pawses that he makes. **1642** MILTON *Apol. Smect.* (1851) 270 He who would not be frustrate of his hope to write well hereafter in laudable things, ought him selfe to be a true Poem. *a* **1693** URQUHART *Rabelais* III. Prol. 13 He was altogether frustrate and disappointed.

B. *ppl. a.*

1. a. Bereft or deprived *of*, or of the chance *of*; destitute *of*. *Obs.* exc. *arch.* Cf. Fr. *frustré*.

1576 FLEMING *Panopl. Epist.* 3 Death..leaveth the body frustrate of feeling. **1587** A. DAY *Daphnis & Chlor.*, Frustrate was his body of garments. **1602** FULBECKE *1st Pt. Parall.* Introd. 1 Such a profitable thing should [not] be altogether frustrate of attempt, howsoeuer voide of effect. **1616** J. HAIG in J. Russell *Haigs* vi. (1881) 140, I am frustrat of money, so that I cannot come to Newmarket myself. **1632** LITHGOW *Trav.* IV. 149 Returne againe from whence they came frustrate of power, and robbed of obedience. **1868** BROWNING *Ring & Bk.* IV. 141 The face Of Pietro frustrate of its ancient cheer. **1878** —— *La Saisiaz* 364 At what moment did I so advance Near to knowledge as when frustrate of escape from ignorance.

† **b.** Balked, disappointed *of*. *Obs.*

1563 *Homilies* II. *Sacrament* II. (1859) 439 That the same most merciful worke might..not be frustrate of his end and purpose. **1675** HOBBES *Odyssey* x. 412 But of that intent I was made frustrate by the Company. **1703** A. B. *Law Success. Benefices* 34 The great Work..becomes frustrate of its End.

2. Failing of effect; ineffectual, fruitless, unavailing, useless. ? *Obs.*

1529 MORE *Dyaloge* I. Wks. 144/1 And finally, then wer these wordes frustrate where he said: Lo, I am w[t] you al y[e] dayes to y[e] worldes ende. **1600** *Maides Metam.* III. i. in Bullen *O. Pl.* I. 131 We wish you to forbeare this frustrate mone. **1651** STANLEY *Poems* 34 And doth relate His frustrate sport. **1715–20** POPE *Iliad* v. 237 Some guardian of the skies, Involved in clouds..turns unseen the frustrate dart away. **1785** MARTYN *Rousseau's Bot.* x. (1794) 103 The florets..of the ray are imperfect, and therefore abortive or frustrate. **1847** R. W. HAMILTON *Disq. Sabbath* i. (1848) 20 Else were creation a frustrate thing.

† **b.** Of a legal document, enactment, or proceeding: Invalid, null, unavailing. *Obs.*

1497 BP. ALCOCK *Mons Perfect.* C iij, Without they be kept in dewe obedyence ben voyde & frustrate. *c* **1555** HARPSFIELD *Divorce Hen. VIII* (Camden) 46 Whether all marriages made against that prohibition were void and frustrate it is not very certain. **1590** SWINBURNE *Testaments* 263 The later testament doth make frustrate the former. **1638** SIR R. COTTON *Abstr. Rec. Tower* 6 Thus the Parliament continued..untill the King was out of debt, making frustrate the grant. **1664** *Flodden F.* I. 6 The league therefore and peace is vain And frustrate.

3. Of a desire, hope, purpose, etc.: Balked, defeated, disappointed, futile.

1588 Q. ELIZ. in Ellis *Orig. Lett.* Ser. II. III. 138 That purposse which we doubte not but by godes goodnes, shall prove frustrate. **1647** MAY *Hist. Parl.* II. v. 91 Though that expectation were made frustrate by the Earl of Warwick. **1700** DRYDEN *Fables*, *Meleager & Atalanta* 164 And multitude makes frustrate the design. **1740** SOMERVILLE *Hobbinol* III. 348 His frustrate Hopes, and unavailing Pains. **1863** I. WILLIAMS *Baptistery* II. xxiv. (1874) 93 Men..in their frustrate longings still again The weary round of earthly things pursue! **1876** FARRAR *Marlb. Serm.* xxxix. 395 To all of you pain must come..and many frustrate hopes.

† **4.** Idle, vain, purposeless. *Obs.*

1500–20 DUNBAR *Poems* ix. 107, I knaw me vicious, Lord, and right culpable..Of frustrat speiking in court, in kirk, and table. **1529** MORE *Comf. agst. Trib.* I. Wks. 1143/1 So were it vndoutedlye frustrate to laye spirituall causes of coumforte, to hym that hath no faythe. **1535** *Act 27 Hen. VIII*, c. 3 Without frustrate or wilful delay.

Hence † **'frustrately** *adv.*, in vain.

1632 VICARS *Virgil's Æneid* XI. 812 Great Tuscane dames, as she their towns past by, Wisht her their daughter in law, but frustrately.

frustrate (frʌ'streɪt, 'frʌstreɪt), *v.* Pa. pple. 6– **frustrated;** 5–7, 9 *arch.* (see FRUSTRATE *pple.*). [f. L. *frustrāt-* ppl. stem of *frustrārī* to disappoint, f. *frustrā* in vain. Cf. Fr. *frustrer.*]

1. *trans.* To balk, disappoint (a person).

1447, 1606 [see FRUSTRATE *pa. pple.*]. **1663** WOOD *Life* (O.H.S.) I. 509 And soe they were frustrated in their designes. **1766** GOLDSM. *Vic. W.* xiii, To improve their good sense, in proportion as they were frustrated in ambition. **1847** JAMES *Convict* iii, He had been seldom frustrated in life. **1876** GEO. ELIOT *Dan. Der.* IV. xxviii, Gwendolen he would certainly not have been sorry to frustrate a little.

b. Const. *of* (a desired object). Now *rare.*

1548 UDALL, etc. *Erasm. Par. Matt.* vi, They frustrate and defeact themselues of that blessed rewarde, whiche [etc.]. **1571** HANMER *Chron. Irel.* (1633) 119 Being frustrated of your long desired presence and promises. **1697** DAMPIER *Voy.* I. ii. 17 Being frustrated of getting over the River this way, we look'd about for a Tree to fell across the River. **1754** EDWARDS *Freed. Will* II. xi. 115 God, after he had made the World, was liable to be wholly frustrated of His End in the Creation of it. **1865** *Pall Mall G.* 30 Dec. 1 Frustrating them [Americans] of what they consider their 'destiny'.

2. To deprive of effect, render ineffectual; to neutralize, counteract (an effort or effect).

1471 [see FRUSTRATE *pa. pple.*]. **1553** EDEN *Treat. Newe Ind.* (Arb.) 14 To bewray poisons and to frustrate th[e] opperacion therof. **1613** PURCHAS *Pilgrimage* (1614) 762 They are heartlesse, if they see defence to frustrate their arrowes. **1671** J. WEBSTER *Metallogr.* vi. 108 Yet they not lying near enough the superficies of the earth, may frustrate its effects. **1703** J. BARRETT *Analecta* 50 Is not such a Course likely to frustrate to them all means of Conversion? **1841** ELPHINSTONE *Hist. Ind.* II. 23 He endeavoured to frustrate the effects of it by imposing many humiliating ceremonies on Bakarra Khán. **1875** SCRIVENER *Lect. Text N. Test.* 9 The worst effects of the enemy's malice were frustrated.

b. To make null and void; to annul, abrogate (a law, etc.); to do away with (a right). Now somewhat *rare.*

1528 [see FRUSTRATE *pa. pple.*]. **1601** R. JOHNSON *Kingd. & Commw.* (1603) 67 The Ordinances of these diets cannot bee frustrated, but by another diet. **1660** R. COKE *Power & Subj.* 205 Nor [ought] the Laws and Statutes of this Realm [to be] by him frustrated. *a* **1848** R. W. HAMILTON *Rew. & Punishm.* vi. (1853) 239 A moral system is not frustrated, so long as it can enforce its sanctions. **1852** SIR W. HAMILTON *Discuss.* 411 The fellows frustrated the common right of graduates to the Office of Tutor.

3. To render vain; to balk, disappoint (a hope, expectation, etc.); to baffle, defeat, foil (a design, purpose, etc.). (The current use.) Also, †to prevent the fulfilment of (a prophecy).

1500–20, 1540–1 [see FRUSTRATE *pa. pple.*]. **1605** SHAKS. *Lear* IV. vi. 64 'Twas yet some comfort When misery could beguile the Tyrants rage And frustrate his proud will. **1613** PURCHAS *Pilgrimage* (1614) 116 Julian..sent for worke-men from all places, thinking to frustrate Christs prophecie concerning the Temple. **1700** S. L. tr. *Fryke's Voy. E. Ind.* 17 But our hopes were strangely frustrated: for we quite lost our course. **1732** LEDIARD *Sethos* II. IX. 339 He was..thoughtful of..frustrating Anteus's unjust design. **1769** BLACKSTONE *Comm.* IV. 14 The innocent has a chance to frustrate or avoid the villany. **1809** ROLAND *Fencing* 67 You have the power frequently to frustrate your adversary's intended motion. **1844** H. H. WILSON *Brit. India* II. 155 Sastri's enemies..had come from Baroda to frustrate his negotiation. **1858** BUCKLE *Civiliz.* (1873) II. viii. 548 His plan was frustrated, owing to its premature announcement by his friends in Paris.

Hence **frustrating** *vbl. sb.* Also † **frustrater,** one who frustrates.

1640 G. WATTS tr. *Bacon's Adv. Learn.* VI. 298 The frustrating of that vaine conceit makes it seem longer than the truth. **1648** *Eikon Bas.* v. 31 Let thy grace teach Mee wisely to enjoie as well the frustrateings, as the fulfillings of My best hopes. *a* **1665** DIGBY *Priv. Mem.* (1827) 117 To continue too long in such a school is a frustrating of the intent of it. **1676** *Packet Adv. Men of Shaftesbury* 39 Continual Frustrater of the Parliamentary Constitution. **1681** BAXTER *Answ. Dodwell* 149, I would have endeavoured to avoid the common frustraters of Disputes. **1843** LYTTON *Last Bar.* IV. i, I shall know how to advise Edward to the frustrating all your schemes.

frustrated (frʌ'streɪtɪd, 'frʌstreɪtɪd), *ppl. a.* [f. FRUSTRATE *v.* + -ED[1].] **1.** In senses of the vb.; disappointed, balked, etc.; *spec.* of persons.

1641 J. SHUTE *Sarah & Hagar* (1649) 155 A frustrated name is an hainous crime. **1661** BOYLE *Style of Script.* 48 Our By-acquists do richly recompense our frustrated (or rather unsucceeding) pains. **1799** R. WARNER *Walk West. Counties* (1800) 143 The two ravens..returned to accomplish their frustrated purpose. **1828** CARLYLE *Misc.*

(1857) I. 128 With a frustrated, nay terrified aspect. **1854** EMERSON *Lett. & Soc. Aims, Comic* Wks. (Bohn) III. 204 The frustrated expectation..in the intellect is comedy. **1866** GEO. ELIOT *F. Holt* xxiv, Now he felt weary, frustrated and doubtful of his own temper. **1877** *Daily News* 5 Nov. 5/2 There must surely be..a good many frustrated careers. **1943** J. S. HUXLEY *Evol. Ethics* iii. 22 The individual if not grossly frustrated or oppressed, can adjust himself..to the ethical standards of his society. **1957** *Times Lit. Suppl.* 1 Nov. 651/1 A whole class of discontented and frustrated young men who, after returning from the war, found inadequate scope for their energies.

2. Of goods, etc.: delayed or prevented from being dispatched.

1941 *Times* (Weekly ed.) 30 July 17/3 We have recently had the unsatisfactory business of 'frustrated exports'... Exports to several South American countries were 'frustrated' by official decree. **1952** *Economist* 31 May 612/1 The 'frustrated exports' that are already individually licensed for sale at home.

frustration (frʌˈstreɪʃən). [ad. L. *frustrātiōn-em*, n. of action f. *frustrārī* to FRUSTRATE.] The action of frustrating; disappointment; defeat; an instance of this.

c **1555** HARPSFIELD *Divorce Hen. VIII* (Camden) 184 That he should..with crafty secret frustrations dally with him. **1598** HAKLUYT *Voy.* I. 175 The perpetuall frustration and reuocation of the foresayd priuiledges. **1646** SIR T. BROWNE *Pseud. Ep.* III. xii. 135 This were..a frustration of that seminall power committed to animalls at the creation. **1676** SOUTH *Serm.* (1823) I. 247 The authors..having missed of their mighty aims, are fain to retreat with frustration and a baffle. **1776** G. HORNE *Comm. Ps.* lxxxix. 46 The frustration of the divine counsels concerning man. **1852** GROTE *Greece* II. lxxvii. X. 101 *note*, Aristeides ascribes the frustration of this attack to the valour of two Athenian generals. **1863** GEO. ELIOT *Romola* I. ii, He thrust his hand into a purse..and explored it again and again with a look of frustration. **1884** *Law Rep.* 12 Q. Bench Div. 548 There may be cases of acts absolutely inconsistent with, and amounting to an entire frustration of the main object of the deed.

frustrative (ˈfrʌstrətɪv), *a. rare.* [f. L. *frustrāt-* (see FRUSTRATE *v.*) + -IVE. Cf. OF. *frustratif.*] Tending to frustrate, balk, or defeat; disappointing.

1730 in BAILEY (folio). **1755** in JOHNSON. **1839** L. BLANCHARD in *New Monthly Mag.* LVII. 418 The exposition..would have been utterly frustrative of its intention.

†ˈ**frustratory**, *a. Obs.* Also 5 frustratoire, 6–7 frust(r)atorie, (6 frustatery, frustratarie, 7–8 frustatory). [ad. OF. *frustratoire* and late L. *frustrātōrius*, f. *frustrārī* to FRUSTRATE.] Tending to frustrate, balk, defeat, or make void. In early use also: Resulting in disappointment, disappointing.

1490 CAXTON *Eneydos* xxii. 78 Many goynges & comynges were there made of the sayd anne..that fynably were all frustratoire. **1529** *Act 21 Hen. VIII*, c. 5 With convenyent spede without any frustratory delay. **1592** *Conspir. Pretended Ref.* 60 Then would he..by frustratorie kindes of answeres goe about to put off such interrogatories. **1650** GENTILIS tr. *Malvezzi's Considerat.* 144 If this be not true, that was frustratory, and of no availment to Socrates. **1681** HICKERINGILL *Vind. Naked Truth* II. 26 Without Frustatory Delay. **1726** AYLIFFE *Parergon* 75 Bartolus restrains this to a Frustatory Appeal.

frustule (ˈfrʌstjuːl). [a. F. *frustule*, ad. late L. *frustulum*, dim. of FRUSTUM.] The siliceous two-valved shell of a diatom, with its contents.

1857 BERKELEY *Cryptog. Bot.* §103. 130 The frustules which are long and slender, slip over each other, yet so as always to adhere. **1867** J. HOGG *Microsc.* II. i. 278 Each frustule is however a perfect unicellular plant. **1876** PAGE *Adv. Text-bk. Geol.* iii. 67 Diatomaceae..whose frustules are also of silex.

frustulent (ˈfrʌstjʊlənt), *a.* [ad. L. *frustulentus*, f. FRUSTUM.] Full of small pieces.

1656–81 in BLOUNT *Glossogr.* Hence in later Dicts.

frustulose (ˌfrʌstjʊˈləʊs), *a. Bot.* [f. L. *frustulum* + -OSE.] (See quot.)

1866 *Treas. Bot.*, *Frustulose*, consisting of small fragments. **1880** in GRAY *Struct. Bot.* 412/2.

‖ˈ**frustulum.** *Obs.* Pl. frustula. [L. *frustulum* small piece.] **a.** A fragment, an atom. **b.** *Math.* A small frustum.

1700 S. PARKER 6 *Philos. Ess.* 109 Nor yet could each such Frustulum have been so modify'd and temper'd as we find, unless by the same. **1785** HERSCHEL in *Phil. Trans.* LXXV. 241 Suppose a rectangular cone cut into frustula by..planes perpendicular to the axis.

frustum (ˈfrʌstəm). Pl. -a, -ums. Also *erron.* 7–9 frustrum. [a. L. *frustum* piece broken off.]

1. *Math.* The portion of a regular solid left after cutting off the upper part by a plane parallel to the base; or the portion intercepted between two planes, either parallel or inclined to each other.

1658 SIR T. BROWNE *Gard. Cyrus* iii. 57 In the parts thereof [plants] we finde..frustums of Archimedes. **1669** *Phil. Trans.* IV. 960 The Axis of a Pyramid..and of a Figure of different Bases, which he calls a Frustrum of a Prisme. **1706** W. JONES *Syn. Palmar. Matheseos* 265 The.. Frustrums of Spheres, cut by parallel Planes, are equal to the corresponding Surfaces of the Sphere's Circumscr. Cylinder. **1779** FORREST *Voy. N. Guinea* 49 We could see within the straits a hill with a flat top, like what is called the frustum of a cone. **1812–6** PLAYFAIR *Nat. Phil.* II. 291 This proposition is easily proved of pyramids, and frusta of pyramids, of which the solid angle is indefinitely small. **1828** J. M. SPEARMAN *Brit. Gunner* (ed. 2) 378 The difference between the two piles thus found will be the number in the frustum or incomplete pile. **1860** MAURY *Phys. Geog. Sea* iv. §218 We may..liken this belt of winds which encircles the earth..to the frustum of a hollow cone.

b. Applied to the sections of the shaft of a column.

1835 WILLIS *Pencillings* II. xl. 23 We were directed to it by thirteen or fourteen frustra of enormous columns. **1850** LEITCH tr. *Müller's Anc. Art* §286. 316 A truncated pillar, or frustum of a column.

2. *gen.* A portion or fragment of anything material or immaterial. *rare.*

1721 BAILEY, *Frustum*, a Fragment, a broken Piece. *a* **1733** R. NORTH *Examen* III. viii. (1740) 624 This Frustum of a Libel is grafted into his pious History. **1812** CRABBE *T. in Verse* vii. Wks. 1834 IV. 288 She minced the sanguine flesh in frustrums fine. **1812** KNOX & JEBB *Corr.* II. 94 What I would deprecate is, putting into people's hands the frusta of a system.

frutage, obs. form of FRUITAGE.

frute, var. of FROUD, *Obs.*, frog, toad.

frutescence (fruːˈtɛsəns). [f. next: see -ENCE.] Shrubbiness.

1882 *N. Y. Tribune* 28 June, The earlier this is done after the first appearance of frutescence the better.

frutescent (fruːˈtɛsənt), *a. Bot.* [Incorrectly f. FRUT-EX + -ESCENT. The correct form would be **fruticescent.*] Becoming shrubby; having the appearance or habit of a shrub.

1709 *Phil. Trans.* XXVI. 469 Our Frutescent Herbs, such as Lavenders, Abrotonums, Rue, Tyme. **1775** MASSON *ibid.* LXVI. 288 Evergreen shrubs, both frutescent and succulent. **1801** BARROW *Interior S. Africa* I. i. 26 The frutescent or shrubby plants. *Ibid.* 38 A tall, elegant, fruitescent [*sic*] plant. **1830** LINDLEY *Nat. Syst. Bot.* 185 Stems..in the frutescent species leafy. **1859** R. F. BURTON *Centr. Afr.* in *Jrnl. Geog. Soc.* XXIX. 142 The fruitescent [*sic*] produce of the mountains.

frutex (ˈfruːtɛks). *Bot.* In 7 pl. frutexes. [a. L. *frutex.*] A plant having a woody stem, but smaller than a tree; a shrub.

1664 EVELYN *Sylva* (1776) 67 What is meant by trees, frutexes, &c. **1727** in BAILEY II. **1880** in GRAY *Struct. Bot.*

†ˈ**frutical**, *a. Obs.* [f. L. *frutic-* FRUTEX + -AL[1].] Having the nature of a shrub, shrubby.

1597 GERARDE *Herbal* III. xiv. 1129 This shrubbie or fruticall plant. **1657** TOMLINSON *Renou's Disp.* 396 The ferulaceous Plants can scarce be called fruticall.

†ˈ**fruticant**, *a. Obs.*[−1] [ad. L. *fruticant-em* pr. pple. of *fruticāre* to sprout.] Putting forth shoots, sprouting. Also †ˈ**fruticate** *v. Obs.*[−1] *intr.* To shoot, sprout. †**fruti'cation.** *Obs.*[−0] [L. *fruticātiōn-em.*] (See quot.)

1656 BLOUNT *Glossogr.*, *Frutication*, sprouting out of young sprigs, a springing forth. **1657** TOMLINSON *Renou's Disp.* 148 In which..Soyl, many of the same kind fruticate. **1664** EVELYN *Sylva* (1679) 2 These [trees] we shall divide into the greater and more deciduous, fruticant, and shrubby. **1740** TULL *Suppl. Horse-hoing* 260 The other Fields..being planted late, could not be ho'd till after the time of Frutication (i.e. Tillering) was past.

†**fruˈticeous**, *a. Obs.* [f. L. *frutic-* FRUTEX + -EOUS.] Shrubby, bushy.

a **1682** SIR T. BROWNE *Tracts* 34 Of a low and fruticeous growth.

fruticetum (fruːtɪˈsiːtəm). [a. L. *fruticetum* a place full of shrubs or bushes, f. *frutex* shrub, bush.] A collection of shrubs; cf. ARBORETUM.

1824 J. C. LOUDON *Encycl. Gardening* (ed. 2) 1059 There should..have been three grand parts:..a circumference, displaying the arboretum, fruticetum, and ornamental flowers. **1936** *Discovery* Mar. 86/1 There is no separate arboretum, fruticetum, and herbaceous garden.

fruticose (ˌfruːtɪˈkəʊs), *a. Nat. Hist.* Also 9 *erron.* fructicose. [ad. L. *fruticōs-us*, f. *frutic-* FRUTEX.]

1. Of the nature of a shrub; having woody stalks.

1668 WILKINS *Real Char.* II. iv. §4. 81 Fruticose, having stalks of a hard woody consistence. **1721** BAILEY, *Fruticose Stalks*, stalks of a hard woody Substance. **1870** HOOKER *Stud. Flora* 120 The fruticose Rubi. **1882** VINES *Sachs' Bot.* 475 The main shoots..may..climb, or may form the stems of arborescent and fruticose plants.

2. Resembling a shrub in external appearance; said *e.g.*, of certain minerals, zoophytes, and lichens.

1805–17 R. JAMESON *Char. Min.* (ed. 3) 95 The whole when viewed from above has a fructicose aspect, not unlike the appearance of cauliflower. **1846** DANA *Zooph.* (1848) 432 The mode of growth..arborescent, and clustered (fruticose). **1857** BERKELEY *Cryptog. Bot.* §56. 70 The species which are most fruticose in habit consist of a single cell. **1882** VINES *Sachs' Bot.* 319 The Fruticose Lichens are attached only at one spot and with a narrow base, and rise from it in the form of small much-branched shrubs.

fruticous (ˈfruːtɪkəs), *a. rare*[−0]. [f. L. *frutic-em* FRUTEX + -OUS.] = prec.

1828 in WEBSTER. Hence in mod. Dicts.

fruticulose (fruːtɪkjʊˈləʊs), *a.* [as if ad. L. **fruticulōs-us*, f. **fruticul-us*, dim. of FRUTEX.] Resembling a small shrub. Also in comb. form **fruticuˈloso-.**

1830 LINDLEY *Nat. Syst. Bot.* 331 In the fruticulose or foliaceous species [of Lichens] the medulla is distinctly floccose. **1846** DANA *Zooph.* (1848) 611 Carnose Alcyonidæ, fruticuloso-ramose.

ˈ**frutify**, *v. nonce-wd.* A comic blunder attributed to an illiterate person; the word meant is *notify*, which is confused with *fructify*.

1596 SHAKS. *Merch. V.* II. ii. 142 The Jew hauing done me wrong, doth cause me as my Father being I hope an old man shall frutifie unto you.

fruycion, -ssyon, -tion, obs. ff. FRUITION.

†**fruz**, *sb.* [onomatopœic; cf. FRIZ, FUZZ: see also FROWZE.] A collection of short and small branches, producing a frizzy appearance.

1693 EVELYN *De la Quint. Compl. Gard.* II. 53 The Second cut all those Branches within three or four Eyes, or Buds, and by that means occasion abundance of Fruz.

fruz, *v. Obs.* exc. *dial.* [Cf. prec.] *trans.* To spread out (hair) in a frizzy mass; to ruffle, rumple.

1703 MRS. CENTLIVRE *Beau's Duel* IV. i, Mercy on me, what a bush of hair is there fruz'd out. **1705** ROWE *Biter* I. i, She has as much..black Hair fruz'd out as any Toast of 'em all. **1713** *Lond. Gaz.* No. 5171/4 Short fruz'd brown Hair. **1873** *Yorksh. Mag.* May 378 (in *N.W. Linc. Gloss.* s.v.) He could..smooth the place down, and fruzz it up from beneath so deftly, that no one could tell that any hay had been taken. **1889** *N.W. Linc. Gloss.*, *Fruz*, to rub the hair the wrong way on, to entangle.

fry (fraɪ), *sb.*[1] Also 7 frey. [a. ON. *frió, freó, fræ* neut., seed = Goth. *fraiw* seed, offspring. Cf. ON. *frió-r, fræ-r* adj., fertile. The F. *frai* masc., used in sense 3, is believed to be unconnected.]

1. Offspring, progeny, seed, young (of human beings); a man's children or family; *rarely*, a child. Now *obs.* exc. as transf. from sense 3.

c **1375** *Sc. Leg. Saints, George* 867 Fourty thousand wane to þe fay, outakine wemene & ȝung fry. *c* **1460** *Towneley Myst.* (Surtees) 24 *Deus.* Noe, to the and to thi fry My blyssyng graunt I. **1508** DUNBAR *Tua mariit Wemen* 403, I ..maid bot fulis of the fry of his first wif. **1564–78** BULLEYN *Dial. agst. Pest.* (1888) 13 Commaunde your folkes to departe out of the chamber and your yonge frie also. **1605** SHAKS. *Macb.* IV. ii. 83 What you Egge? Yong fry of Treachery. **1624** QUARLES *Sion's Elegies* I. 5 Thy tender frie Whom childhood taught no language, but their crie T' expresse their infant griefe.

2. The roe (of a female fish).

c **1430** *Two Cookery-bks.* I. 16 Take fayre Frye of Pyke, and caste it raw on a morter. *c* **1440** *Anc. Cookery* in *Househ. Ord.* (1790) 469 Take frye of female pike, and pille away the skyn. [**1869** *Lonsdale Gloss.*, *To shoot one's fry*, to make a last effort without success. Derived from the analogy of a female herring, who having shot her fry, has done all she can do in the course of nature.]

3. Young fishes just produced from the spawn; *spec.* the young of salmon in the second year, more fully ***salmon fry.***

1389 *Act 13 Rich. II*, c. 19. §1 Stalkers..par les quelles le frie ou brood des salmons laumpreis..pourra estre pris. **1462** *Mann. & Househ. Exp.* (Roxb.) 562 Grete carpes and many oare smale and myche ffrye. *c* **1475** *Rauf Coilȝear* 682 Fyne foullis in Fyrth, and Fischis with fry. **1531–2** *Act 23 Hen. VIII*, c. 18 Broode and frie of fisshe in the saide riuer ..be commonly therby distroied. **1565** J. SPARKE in *Hawkins' Voy.* (1878) 61 An innumerable yonge frie of these flying fishes. **1635** SWAN *Spec. M.* v. §2 (1643) 141 The force of winds may suddenly sweep away little frey out of ponds. **1677** JOHNSON in *Ray's Corr.* (1848) 128 In Cumberland, the [salmon] fishers have four distinctions of yearly growth (after the first summer, when they call them free, or frie, as we smowts, or smelts)..young fry of other fishes. **1766** PENNANT *Zool.* (1776) III. 297 They feed..sometimes on their own fry. **1807** VANCOUVER *Agric. Devon* (1813) 75 The young salmon fry, or gravellers. **1861** *Act 24 & 25 Vict.* c. 109. §4 Fish of the genus salmon, whether known by the names..salmon..burntail, fry, samlet, [etc.].

b. Applied to the young of other creatures produced in very large numbers, *e.g.* bees, frogs.

1577 B. GOOGE *Heresbach's Husb.* (1586) 903 Combs.. which contain the young spawn or fry of the Bees. **1609** C. BUTLER *Fem. Mon.* (1634) 135 The Bees, specially the young fry (being loaded and weary with their labour)..are beaten down. **1622** MASSINGER *Virg. Mart.* II. ii, A bed of snakes.. whose poisonous spawn Ingenders such a fry of speckled villainies. **1784** COWPER *Task* II. 832 A race obscene, Spawned in the muddy beds of Nile..And the land stank —so numerous was the fry. **1854** WOODWARD *Mollusca* (1856) 10 The fry of the aquatic races are almost as different from their parents as the caterpillar from the butterfly.

c. *fig.*

1600 HEYWOOD *1st Pt. Edw. IV* (1613) C ij a, This hedge-bred rascall this filthy fry of ditches, A vengeance take you all. **1607** HIERON *Wks.* I. 442 They come from the sea of Rome..to beget a new spawne and frie of catholikes. **1613** PURCHAS *Pilgrimage* (1614) 459 The Sunne..together with his frie (whole armie of Gnats). **1806** SURR *Winter in Lond.* (ed. 3) II. 199 It was reserved for the present day to bring forth a fry of young critic imps.

4. Hence, as a collective term for young or insignificant beings: now chiefly in phrase *lesser, small* or *young fry.* **a.** The smaller kinds of fish or other animals.

1666 DRYDEN *Ann. Mirab.* 811 The huge Leviathans.. attend their prey And give no chase, but swallow in the frie. **1674** PULLEYN in *Flatman's Poems* 2/2 Let your eye Wander, and see one of the lesser frie.. Ruffle his painted feathers, and look big. **1674** N. Cox *Gentl. Recreat.* I. (1677) 56 We bring out not onely Pike and Carp, but lesser Fry. **1697** DAMPIER *Voy.* I. xvi. 465 This small Fry I take to be the top of their Fishery: they have no Instruments to catch great Fish. **1718** PRIOR *Knowledge* 108 Of fishes next.. From the small fry that glide on Jordan's stream.. To that Leviathan. **1845** DARWIN *Voy. Nat.* vii. (1879) 137 A lake.. which.. swarmed with small fry. **1873** G. C. DAVIES *Mount. & Mere* xiii. 101 One of the small fry.. is hopping about on the grass.

b. Young or insignificant persons (collectively or in a body); a 'swarm' or crowd of such persons.

a **1577** GASCOIGNE *Herbs, Weeds, etc.* Wks. (1587) 303 To make their coine a net to catch yong frie. **1590** SPENSER *F.Q.* I. xii. 7 Them before, the fry of children yong.. did play. **1607** BEAUM. & FL. *Woman-Hater* III. iii, The whole frie in a Colledge, or an Inn of Court. **1641** MILTON *Prel. Episc.* 2 To that indigested heap, and frie of Authors. **1689** SWIFT *Ode to Temple* Wks. 1755 IV. I. 242 As in a theatre the ignorant fry, Because the cords escape their eye, Wonder to see the motions fly. **1738** BIRCH *Milton* M.'s Wks. 1738 I. 27 A public School to teach all the young Fry of a Parish. **1799** *Morn. Post* in *Spirit Publ. Jrnls.* (1800) III. 122 The fresh fry so constantly emerging from the scholastic trammels of Eton. **1852** MRS. STOWE *Uncle Tom's C.* ix, Mrs. Bird.. followed by the two eldest boys, the smaller fry having by this time been safely disposed of in bed. **1878–82** C. FLEET *Ancestors in Sussex* Ser. I. 122 Chambermaids, and all the fry who feed on the little weaknesses of humanity. **1885** J. PAYN *Talk of Town* II. 99 Compared with [Sheridan], all other managers were small fry.

c. of inanimate things.

1587 *Mirr. Mag., Bladud* xvi, An heape of hurtes.. a fry of foule decayes. **1650** tr. *Hotham's Introd. Teut. Philos.* Pref., Few have attained its height in this last frie of books. **1652–62** HEYLIN *Cosmogr.* III. (1682) 220 South of Japan, lyeth a great fry of Islands. *a* **1797** H. WALPOLE (Ogilvie), We have burned two frigates, and a hundred and twenty small fry. **1859** JEPHSON *Brittany* iv. 38 Having sold his eggs, rags, and other small fry. **1861** *Sat. Rev.* 7 Dec. 591 The smaller fry of Christmas Books.

Hence **'fryhood**, the state of being 'fry'.

1884 *Longm. Mag.* III. 531 An abdominal pouch, where they [the eggs] are.. nourished during their early fryhood.

fry (fraɪ), *sb.*[2] [f. FRY *v.*[1]]

†**1.** Excessive heat. *Obs. rare*⁻¹.

1634 SIR T. HERBERT *Trav.* 187 Their colour is blacke (living in the scorching frie of the Torrid Zone).

2. Food cooked in a frying-pan; fried meat.

1639 MAYNE *City Match* III. ii, This came from The Indies, and eats five Crownes a day in frye, Oxe livers, and browne past. **1848** DICKENS *Dombey* xviii, Cook promises a little fry for supper. *a* **1850** ROSSETTI *Dante & Circ.* I. (1874) 226, I get my dinner, you your supper, free; And, if I bite the fat, you suck the fry.

b. *dial.* Applied locally to various internal parts of animals, usually eaten fried.

1847–78 HALLIWELL, *Fry*, the pluck of a calf. *North.* **1877** *Holderness Gloss., Fry*, the viscera of a pig, or other animal, generally cooked in a frying-pan. **1879** *Cumbld. Gloss., Fry*, pig's liver. 'Mudder sent us a fry o't' killin' day.' **1888** ELWORTHY *W. Somerset Word-bk.* s.v., The products of lambs' castration are called lamb's fries. **1894** BLACKMORE *Perlycross* 110 A dish of lamb's fry reposing among its parsley.

†**fry**, *sb.*[3] *Obs. rare*⁻¹. [? cf. FLY *sb.*[2] 5 d.] 'A kind of sieve' (J.).

1707 MORTIMER *Husb.* 270 He dresseth the Dust from it [Malt], by running it thro' a Fan or Frie.

fry (fraɪ), *v.*[1] Inflected fried, frying. [a. F. *fri-re* (= Pr. *frir*, Sp. *freir*, Pg. *frigir*, It. *friggere*):—L. *frīgĕre* to roast, fry, cogn. with Gr. *φρύγειν*, Skr. *bhrajj*, of the same meaning.]

1. a. *trans.* To cook (food) with fat in a shallow pan over the fire. With *up*: to 'hot up' (cold food) in a frying-pan.

c **1290** [see FRYING *vbl. sb.*]. **1340** *Ayenb.* 111 Þet ilke bread.. wes ymad of oure doȝe.. and yfryd ine þe panne of þe crouche. **1398** TREVISA *Barth. De P.R.* XVIII. i. (1495) 747 Flesche of bestys is sometyme rostyd and somtyme fryed. *c* **1420** *Liber Cocorum* (1862) 21 Take onyons and.. Frye hom in grece. **1486** *Bk. St. Albans* C iij a, Take a blacke snake.. and fry it in an erthyn potte. **1530** PALSGR. 158 *Vne póylle*, a fryeng pan to frye any meate in. **1579** LANGHAM *Gard. Health* (1633) 95 Frie it with sheeps suet, and apply it to bruses. **1769** MRS. RAFFALD *Eng. Housekpr.* (1778) 71 A very good way to fry Beef Steaks. **1805** *Med. Jrnl.* XIV. 65 The tender leaves are very commonly.. fried with other herbs. **1875** MARY JEWEL *Model Cookery* 21/1 Frying being actually boiling in fat instead of water. **1899** G. B. BURGIN *Bread of Tears* I. v, 'What are you cooking there, Fenella? It smells good.' 'Frying up the cold fowl,' said Fenella.

b. Phrases: ***fry your eggs***: mind your own business. ***to have other fish to fry*** (see FISH *sb.* 4 c).

1841 JAMES *Brigand* ii, Fry your eggs, Gandelot, and leave other people to fry theirs. **1864** *N. & Q.* 3rd Ser. VI. 495/1 Cornish Proverbs.. Fry me for a fool and you'll lose your fat in frying.

2. *transf.* and *fig.* †**a.** *trans.* To torture (a person) by fire; to burn or scorch (anything) with effects analogous to those of frying; sometimes *hyperbolically*, of the heat of the sun, etc. *Obs.*

1382 WYCLIF *Jer.* xxix. 22 As Achab whom friede [Vulg. *frixit*] the king of Babiloyne. *c* **1440** *Jacob's Well* (E.E.T.S.) 11 Þou schalt be rostyd and fryed in þe fyir of helle! *c* **1526** FRITH *Disput. Purgat.* (1829) 112 He will not fry us in the fire of purgatory for our sins. **1588** A. KING tr. *Canisius' Catech.* Prayers 27 My banes as it ver in ane frying panne ar fried. **1628** WITHER *Brit. Rememb.* VIII. 2700 When we were boyld and fryde, in blood and fire. **1695** BLACKMORE *Pr. Arth.* IV. 925 Raging Sirius fries the thirsty Land. **1697** DRYDEN *Æneid* VII. 644 So when with crackling Flames a Cauldron fries, The bubbling Waters from the Bottom rise.

†**b.** ***to fry a faggot***: see FAGGOT *sb.* 2. *Obs.*

1563–87 FOXE *A. & M.* (1684) III. 124 Master Hooper.. said.. must we two take this matter in hand, and begin to frie these faggots. **1577–87** HOLINSHED *Chron.* III. 946/2 A great manie of them.. had died for it in Smithfield, in frieng a faggot.

c. To execute in the electric chair; also *intr.*, to be executed thus. *U.S. slang.*

1929 *Flynn's* 17 Aug. 702/2 I'll fry for it, I suppose—that's the law, Doc. **1934** A. MERRITT *Burn Witch Burn!* v. 68 They'll laugh themselves sick an' fry us at Sing Sing. **1956** 'J. WYNDHAM' *Seeds of Time* 107 You'll hang or you'll fry, every one of you.

3. *intr.* To undergo the operation of cooking with fat in a pan. *rare* in lit. sense. ***to fry in one's own grease*** (also †in *passive*): originally *transf.*, said *e.g.* of persons burning alive, and *fig.* to be tormented by one's own passions; now only, to suffer the consequences of one's own folly.

13.. *Coer de L.* 4409 Beter it is that we out renne, Thenne as wrehches in house to brenne, And frye inne oure owne gres! *c* **1386** CHAUCER *Wife's Prol.* 487 In his owene grece I made him frye For angre, and for verray Jalousye. *a* **1415** LYDG. *Temp. Glas* (1891) 14 Thus is he fryed in his owene gres, To-rent & torn with his owene rage. **1546** J. HEYWOOD *Prov.* (1867) 37 She is as fierce as a Lyon of Cotsolde. She fryeth in hir owne grease. **1684** T. BURNET *Th. Earth* II. 78 Let.. the woods and forests blaze away, and the fat soyl of the earth fry in its own grease; these things will not affect us [the rocks and mountains].

4. *transf.* **a.** To undergo the action of fire or intense heat, with effects resembling those of frying; to frizzle, burn with a sputter or exudation of juices. †Formerly often of persons tormented by fire; also *hyperbolically*.

c **1526** FRITH *Disput. Purgat.* (1829) 136 Thinkest thou to be justified by frying in purgatory? **1570** *Satir. Poems Reform.* xii. 117 Luke gif ȝour partie prydis yame in thair spurring, Keipand the feildis, and fryis not in thair furring. **1583** LYLY *Pref. Ep.* in *T. Watson's Poems* (Arb.) 29 A sworde frieth in the fire like a blacke ele. **1596** DRAYTON *Legends* iii. 147 Fuell to that fire, Wherein He fry'd. **1601** B. JONSON *Poetaster* I. i, Earth and seas in fire and flame shall fry. **1647** TRAPP *Comm. Matt.* vii. 6 The Smiths forge fries, when cold water is cast upon it. **1656** COWLEY *Mistress, Incurable* ii, As well might men who in a feaver fry, Mathematique doubts debate. **1664** WALLER *Late War Spain* 84 Spices and Gums about them melting fry. *a* **1711** KEN *Imitat.* Poet. Wks. 1721 IV. 529 Tho' frying where the Sun all Day Shoots perpendicular fierce Ray. **1715** BENTLEY *Serm.* x. 358 What Heart could bear that his dead Father should fry in the flames of Purgatory? **1886** A. WINCHELL *Walks & Talks Geol. Field* 152 Caking-coals, when ignited, seem to fry with an exudation of a fluid petroleum.

b. with advbs. *up*, *out* expressing the result of heating.

1630 MAY *Lucan* v. 471 The metalls melted by the Sunne, fry'd vp. **1694** *Acc. Late Voy.* II. (1711) 177 When the Fat is well tryed or fryed out. **1816** *Chron.* in *Ann. Reg.* 1 The heat of the stove made the rosin in the wood to fry out.

c. *fig.* Of a person: To burn with strong passion or emotion. Also *refl.* in same sense.

1573 *Satir. Poems Reform.* xl. 163 Thay fryit in furie that he schaipit quick. **1583** STANYHURST *Æneis* I. (Arb.) 19 Thus she frying fretted, thus deepely plunged in anger Æolian kingdoom shee raught. **1591** LYLY *Endym.* v. iii, In the moment that I feared his falshood and fried myself most in mine affections. **1646** SIR R. FANSHAWE tr. *Guarino's Pastor Fido* (1676) 192 The happiest Pair that this day fry Under the torrid Zone of Love. **1648** JOS. BEAUMONT *Psyche* I. ccxviii, Whether she walks, or sits, or stands, or lies, Her wretched self still in her self she fries. **1767** *Babler* I. 97, I sat frying the whole time, from a conscious incapacity to please. **1771** SMOLLETT *Humph. Cl.* (1815) 62 My uncle, frying with vexation, cried, [etc.]. **1842** T. MARTIN in *Fraser's Mag.* Dec. XXVI. 652/2, I lay frying with impatience to hear the clatter of cups.

†**d.** said of a feeling, passion, etc. *Obs.*

1563 B. GOOGE *Eglogs* (Arb.) 83 Here fyre and flames by Fancie framde, In brest doo broyle and frye. **1581** T. HOWELL *Deuises* (1879) 176 Thus loue at once doth frye, freeze, ryse and fall. *a* **1632** FAIRFAX (Ogilvie), What kindling motions in their breasts do fry.

†**5. a.** Of water: To be agitated, boil, seethe, foam. *Obs.*

1590 SPENSER *F.Q.* II. xii. 45 Ye might have seene the frothy billowes fry Vnder the ship. **1697** DRYDEN *Æneid* VII. 737 Thus, when a black-brow'd gust begins to rise, White foam at first on the curl'd ocean fries.

b. To ferment; to seethe (in the stomach). Of lime: To slake. *Obs.*

1624 CAPT. SMITH *Virginia* III. ii. 44 As much barley boyled with water for a man a day, and this having fryed some 26 weekes in the ships hold, contained as many wormes as graines. **1626** BACON *Sylva* §52 To keep the Oyle from frying in the Stomach, you must drinke.. Milde Beere after it. **1647** TRAPP *Mellificium Theol.* in *Comm. Ep.* 619 Cast water upon this lime, it will fry the faster.

Hence **'frying** *ppl. a.*

1587 TURBERV. *Trag. T.* (1837) 128 Whose frying hartes With Cupids coles did melte. **1592** GREENE *Mamillia* II. Wks. (Grosart) II. 175 So discontinuance should be of sufficient force to quench out yᵉ frying flames of loue.

fry (fraɪ), *v.*[2] *rare*⁻¹. [f. FRY *sb.*[1]] *intr.* To swarm.

1816 L. HUNT *Rimini* II. 171 Plashy pools with rushes, About whose sides the swarming insects fry, Opening with noisome din, as they go by.

†**fryberry.** *Obs. rare*⁻¹. A raspberry.

c **1532** DEWES *Introd. Fr.* in Palsgr. 1073 Fruites, as cheres.. strauberis, fryberis [F. *framboises*].

fryce, obs. form of FRIEZE *sb.*[1]

fryer, frier ('fraɪə(r)). [f. FRY *v.*[1] + -ER[1].]

1. One who fries (fish); also a vessel used in frying (fish). More fully ***fish-frier***: see FISH *sb.*[1] 6 d.

1859 SALA *Tw. round Clock* (1861) 18 Offal [fish] is bought only by the 'fryers'. **1884** *Health Exhib. Catal.* p. lvii/2 Four Large Fish Fryers.

2. *pl.* Fish for frying.

1851 MAYHEW *Lond. Labour* I. 166 This supply is known in the trade as 'friers', and consists of the overplus of a fishmonger's stock.

3. A chicken suitable for frying. *U.S.*

1923 *Dialect Notes* V. 207 *Frier*, a chicken of frying size. **1940** C. MCCULLERS *Heart is Lonely Hunter* (1943) I. iii. 41 They haves [*sic*] a mule and.. from twenty to twenty-five laying hens and fryers. **1957** J. STEINBECK *Short Reign of Pippin IV* 67 H.W... was selling eggs and fryers to the Army and Navy.

frying ('fraɪɪŋ), *vbl. sb.* [f. FRY *v.*[1] + -ING[1].]

1. The action of the vb. FRY.

c **1290** *S. Eng. Leg.* I. 187/86 Þat grece of him orn a-brod: ase þei it frijnge were. **1340** *Ayenb.* 23 Þis zenne is þe dyeules panne of helle huerinne he makeþ his friinges. **1535** COVERDALE *1 Chron.* xxv. 29 For the pannes, for yᵉ fryenge. **1633** P. FLETCHER *Contemnenti* 2 Chill icie frosts in midst of Summer's frying. **1829** MARRYAT *F. Mildmay* ii, The frying of beef-steaks and onions. **1840** DICKENS *Barn. Rudge* ii, There stole upon him from the distant kitchen a gentle sound of frying.

2. *attrib.* and *Comb.*, as ***frying-piece***; **frying-basket**, a vessel of metal basket-work used for frying fish, etc. See also FRYING-PAN.

1877 E. S. DALLAS *Kettner's Bk. Table* 490 Put them [*sc.* whitebait] into a wire frying-basket. **1890** *19th Cent.* Nov. 838 The orderly corporal slices off a frying piece and has it cooked for his breakfast. **1951** *Good Housek. Home Encycl.* 393/2 Put the balls into a frying basket and fry in deep fat.

'frying-ˌpan. [f. FRYING *vbl. sb.*]

1. A shallow pan, usually of iron, with a long handle, in which food is fried.

1382 WYCLIF *1 Chron.* xxiii. 29 The prestis.. to the fryinge panne [Vulg. *ad sartaginem*]. **1398** TREVISA *Barth. De P.R.* XIX. cxxviii. (1495) 936 Sartago the fryenge panne hath that name of the noys that is therin whan oyle brennyth therin. **1481–90** *Howard Househ. Bks.* (Roxb.) 129 Item, for a frying pane x.d. **1545** RAYNOLD *Byrth Mankynde* III. iii. (1634) 167 That that remaineth, fry it together in a Frying panne with Suger. **1624** CAPT. SMITH *Virginia* III. v. 58 For want of nets.. we attempted to catch them [fish] with a frying pan. **1719** D'URFEY *Pills* (1872) V. 38 Frying-Pans they do use for Ladles. **1806** *Culina* 218 Melt a piece of butter in a frying-pan.. pour in the above preparation. **1865** LIVINGSTONE *Zambesi* xxvii. 564 Which.. resembled the noise of fifty fryingpans in active operation.

fig. **1602** *Narcissus* (1893) 643 O frieng panne of all fritters of fraud. **1616–61** HOLYDAY *Persius* (1673) 296 This hissing frying-pan of speach.

b. Phrase (*to jump, leap*, etc.) ***out of the frying-pan into the fire***: to escape from one evil only to fall into a greater one.

1532 MORE *Confut. Tindale* Wks. 488/2 [He] featly conuayed himself out of the frying panne fayre into the fyre. **1546** J. HEYWOOD *Prov. & Epigr.* (1874) 126 Leape out of the frying pan into the fyre; and change from il paine to worse. **1613** PURCHAS *Pilgrimage* I. vi. (1614) 32 Like.. the foolish fish that leapeth out of the frying pan into the fire. **1705** HICKERINGILL *Priest-cr.* I. (1721) 32 Priest-craft got the Ascendant at Rome, and then Men were—out of the Frying Pan into the Fire. **1890** *Guardian* 1 Oct. 1507/3 If they thought they could get away from the State by disestablishment, they would find that they were jumping out of the frying-pan into the fire.

2. *attrib.* and *Comb.*, as ***frying-pan maker***; **frying-pan brand** (*Austral.*), 'a large brand used by cattle-stealers to cover the owner's brand' (Morris); **frying-pan plate**, ? a piece of tin-plate cut out to be made into a frying-pan.

1686 PLOT *Staffordsh.* ix. 335 Nine fryingpan-plates being commonly laid upon one another and claspt together by turning up 4 Labells. *Ibid.* 336 There are but two Master Frying-pan makers.. in the whole Kingdom. **1857** F. DE B. COOPER *Wild Adv. Austral.* 104 This person.. got into some trouble.. by using a 'frying-pan brand'.

†**fry money.** *Obs.* ? = *frith silver* (see FRITH *sb.*[1] b).

1530 in Weaver *Wells Wills* (1890) 115 *Debts*.. Rob ffarmer, and Jone Portyn wedowe, of fry mony iijli. vjs. viijd.

'fry-pan. [f. FRY *v.*[1]] = FRYING-PAN.

1832 *Chambers's Edin. Jrnl.* I. 130/1 To the ropes.. are attached fry-pans, children's toys, and other light articles. *a* **1862** THOREAU *Maine Woods* (1864) 323 Three tin plates, a fry-pan. **1918** H. BINDLOSS *Agatha's Fortune* xxi. 192 Two fry pans stood upon the logs. **1959** *Sunday Times* 30 Aug. 14/4 Sunbeam are bringing out a new deep lid for their plug-in frypan. **1963** *Amer. Speech* XXXVIII. 210 The term *fry pan* rarely occurs before the 1950s. When it does, it is often as the *double fry* or *omelette pan*... But the advent of the electric fryers marks a revival of *fry pans*. **1970** *Toronto Daily Star* 24 Sept. 8/3 (Advt.), Toastess electric frypan.

fryse, obs. form of FRIEZE *sb.*[1]

fryst, fryze, obs. forms of FIRST, FRIEZE *sb.*[1]

fry-up ('fraɪʌp). [f. *to fry up* (see FRY *v.*[1] 1).] An easily prepared and quickly cooked dish of fried food, esp. of cold food heated up in a frying-pan; also, the preparation of such a dish.

1967 'M. Erskine' *Case with Three Husbands* vii. 96 The two men decided finally on a mixed grill..and a fry-up of cold potatoes. **1968** 'E. Trevor' *Place for Wicked* xix. 258 Are you hungry?.. We'll have a fry-up, shall we? **1969** J. Wainwright *Take-Over Men* xii. 203 Then lunch. More often than not a 'fry-up'—I became a dab hand with a frying-pan.

fuage, var. of feuage, *Obs.*, hearth-tax.

1765 [see fumage].

fuants, var. of fiants, *Obs.*

1674 N. Cox *Gentl. Recreat.* i. (1677) 12 Of a Fox, the Billiting; and all other such Vermin, the Fuants.

fub, *vb.*, var. of fob *v.*, to cheat, impose upon, put *off* deceitfully (in quot. 1619, ? to reject with scorn).

1597, 1602, 1647 [see fob *v.*[1]]. **1619** Fletcher *M. Thomas* ii. ii, My letter fubb'd too, And no access without I mend my manners! **1639** Massinger *Unnat. Combat.* iii. i, Well, I must not Be fubb'd off thus. **1889** Stevenson *Master of B.* 74 Our Albanian fubbed us off with a thousand delays.

fub(b, fub(b)s. [onomatopœic: suggested by *full*, *chub*, etc.]

†**1.** A small chubby person. Chiefly used as a term of endearment. *Obs.*

1614 T. Freeman *Rub & Great Cast* xliv, Caspia, that same fowle deformed Fubs. **1678** Otway *Friendship in F.* iii. i, So farewell Fubb. **1681** —— *Soldier's Fort.* i. i, Dead, my poor Fubses! **1685** Crowne *Sir C. Nice* v. 48 'Tis he that I told you is to marry my Indian Fubs of a Sister. **1694** Echard *Plautus, Rudens* ii. viii, Here's the Water, my little Fubs ye! **1721** Bailey, *Fub*, as a fat Fub, a little plump Child.

2. (See quots.)

1807 *Public Char., Ld. Somerville* 213 It is the custom in Spain and adopted here with our Merino wool, to divide or sort the fleece into three portions of different qualities, namely into rafinos, finos, and terceros; or superfine, fine, and fubs or refuse. **1882** *Lanc. Gloss.*, *Fub*, long withered grass on old pastures or meadows.

†**'fubbery.** *Obs. rare.* Cf. fobbery. [f. fub *v.* + -ery.] Cheating, deception.

1604 Marston & Webster *Malcontent* i. i, O heaven! O fubbery, fubbery!

†**'fubble**, *v. Obs. rare*[−1]. [onomatopœic: cf. *fumble*.] *trans.* ? To jumble (*up*).

1611 Cotgr., *Entretouillé*..intangled, fubbled, confounded. *Entretouiller*, to mingle, intangle, confound, fubble vp things together.

fubby ('fʌbɪ), *a. rare.* [f. fub *sb.* + -y[1]. Cf. fobby.] = fubsy.

1790 J. Williams *Shrove Tuesday* (1794) 12 Th' Idalian urchin and his fubby crew. **1815** Nichols *Lit. Anecd. 18th C.* IX. 339 *note*, The Sculptors and Painters apply this epithet to children, and say for instance of the boys of Fiammengo, that they are *fubby*. **1867** R. S. Hawker *Prose Wks.* (1893) 144 A ruddy-visaged widow..fubby and interjectional in figure.

'fubsical, *a. rare*[−1]. [f. fubsy + -ic + -al[1].] = fubsy.

1834 Beckford *Italy* II. 51 A fubsical, squat wife.

fubsy ('fʌbzɪ), *a.* Also 8 **fubsey**, 9 **fubzy**. [f. fub(s + -y[1].] Of the figure, limbs, etc.: Fat and squat.

1780 Mad. D'Arblay *Diary* Apr., Her daughter, a fubsy, good-humoured..merry old maid. **1826** J. Wilson *Noct. Ambr.* Wks. 1855 I. 261 Fat and fubzy fellows of colleges. **1829** Dk. Buckhm. *Priv. Diary* III. vii. 159 A fat, fubsy foot, as unsentimental as could be. **1879** Sala *Paris herself again* (1880) II. iv. 57 She was a squat, fubsy little old woman. **1895** *Spectator* 23 Nov. 723 To hold and confess the opposite opinion is to announce oneself a fubsy Philistine.

transf. **1837** Marryat *Dog-fiend* viii, He was..cosily..seated upon the..little fubsy sofa.

fucaceous (fjuːˈkeɪʃəs), *a.* [f. mod.L. *fūcāce-æ* (f. L. *fūcus*: see fucus) + -ous.] Of or belonging to the group *Fucaceæ* of seaweeds.

1891 *Athenæum* 21 Mar. 382/3 The Fucaceous Genus Turbinaria.

†**'fucal**, *a. Obs. rare*[−1]. [f. fuc-us + -al[1].] Of the nature of 'fucus'; specious, fair-seeming.

1619 H. Hutton *Follies Anat.* (Percy) 53 Joves constant Daphne, timorous, perplext, His fucall arguments doth still confute.

†**'fucate**, *a. Obs.* [ad. L. *fūcāt-us*, pa. pple. of *fūcāre* to paint, rouge, f. *fūcus* fucus.] Artificially coloured, beautified with paint; hence, falsified, disguised, counterfeit.

1531 Elyot *Gov.* iii. iv. (1883) 221 In vertue may be nothing fucate or counterfayte. **1583** Stubbes *Anat. Abus.* i. (1877) 183 What setting foorth of fucate and deceiuable wares. **1621** Burton *Anat. Mel.* iii. i. ii. iii, Virtue and honesty are great motives..especially if they be sincere and right, not fucate.

†**fucate**, *v. Obs.*[−0] [f. L. *fūcāt-*, ppl. stem of *fūcāre*: see prec.] *trans.* To paint, counterfeit.

1535 [see next]. **1656** in Blount *Glossogr.* **1721** in Bailey.

†**fucated**, *ppl. a. Obs.* [f. prec. + -ed[1].] = fucate *a.*

1535 Joye *Apol. Tindale* 20 For the trowth knoweth no fucated, polesshed and paynted oracion. **1755** in Johnson.

†**fu'cation.** *Obs. rare.* [n. of action f. L. *fūcāre*: see fucate and -ation.] The action of painting the face; hence, the giving of a false semblance or appearance, counterfeiting.

1612 J. Cotta *Dang. Pract. Phys.* i. v. 46 Apothecaries..that..use faithfull industrie in fitting wholesome and incorrupt remedies..without fucation, adulteration or deceit. **1638** Nabbes *Covent Garden* i. iii, They [balconies] set off a Ladies person well, when she presents her selfe to the view of gazing passengers. Artificial fucations are not discern'd at distance. **1721** Bailey, *Fucation*, a Colouring, Painting, or Counterfeiting.

†**fu'catious**, *a. Obs. rare.* [f. prec.: see -ous.] Of the nature of 'fucation', fair-seeming, specious, deceitful.

1654 Vilvain *Theorem. Theol.* ii. 78 To offer a courtesy under impossible condition, is frivolous or fucatious. **1660** Waterhouse *Arms & Arm.* 38 Varnished over with fucatious semblances of truth.

†**'fucatory**, *a. Obs.* [f. L. *fūcāt-* (see fucate) + -ory.] Relating to painting or artificial colouring.

1657 Tomlinson *Renou's Disp.* 737 This Fucatory Art..is exercised by none but some Juglers, and vafrous Knaves.

fucher, fuchez, obs. pl. ff. fitchew, polecat.

c **1450** *Bk. Hawkyng* in *Rel. Ant.* I. 305 That no fucher no volymare enter in. **1467** in *Ripon Ch. Acts* (Surtees) 235 Unam togam de crymysin, pænulatam cum fuchez.

fuchsia ('fjuːʃ(ɪ)ə). [mod.L. f. the name of the German botanist Leonhard Fuchs (16th c.).]

a. A genus of ornamental shrubs (N.O. *Onagraceæ*) with drooping flowers; a plant of this genus.

1753 in Chambers *Cycl. Supp.* **1789** *Curtis' Bot. Mag.* III. 97 *Fuchsia coccinea*..Scarlet Fuchsia..was introduced to the royal gardens at Kew in the year 1788. **1837–9** Hallam *Hist. Lit.* I. ix. i. §20. 471 Leonard Fuchs..has secured a verdant immortality in the well-known *Fuchsia.* **1861** Whyte Melville *Good for Nothing* II. 169 The pendant fuchsias drooped in their last loveliness. **1868** *Less. Mid. Age* 316 Pretty bow-windows, with the crimson fuchsias climbing up them.

b. (See quots.)

1866 *Treas. Bot.*, *Fuchsia*, Australian or native. A colonial name for *Correa.* **1880** L. A. Meredith *Tasm. Friends & Foes* iii. 23 *note*, *Correa speciosa*—native fuchsia of Colonies.

c. *attrib.*, as ***fuchsia-red***, ***-tree***.

1873 Black *Pr. Thule* (1874) 47 The girl..turned to a fuchsia-tree, pretending to pick some of its flowers. **1895** *Daily News* 16 Jan. 7/4 Bright fuchsia-red has become..a favourite.

d. A red colour like that of the fuchsia flower, fuchsia-red.

1923 *Daily Mail* 5 Mar. 13 Colours: Peach, Apple, Apricot, Mauve, Fuchsia, Periwinkle. **1930** *Times* 29 Nov. 16 A colour scheme of fuchsia and gold predominates. **1963** *New Yorker* 29 June 64/1 (Advt.), Mandarin Coat—or Dress..Red, Black, Fuchsia.

fuchsine ('fuːksɪn). [f. fuchs-ia + -ine. Named from its resemblance to the colour of the flower.] A salt of rosaniline, crystallizing in iridescent green tablets, soluble in water and forming a deep red liquid; used as a dye.

1865 *Reader* 23 Sept. 354/1 An alcoholic solution of aniline red and fuchsine. **1883** *West. Daily Press* 22 Oct., Apple, foreign seeds, and currants well mixed, and tinctured with fuchsine, are frequently palmed off as..raspberry jam.

fuchsinophil, -phile (fuːk-, fjuːkˈsɪnəfɪl, -faɪl), *a. Biol.* [f. fuchsin(e + -o + -phil, -phile.] Readily stained with fuchsine; produced by staining with fuchsine. Also ˌ**fuchsino'philic** *a.*, in the same sense. Hence ˌ**fuchsino'philia**, affinity for fuchsine.

1900 Dorland *Med. Dict.* 268/1 Fuchsinophil. **1904** *Jrnl. R. Microsc. Soc.* 639 (*heading*) The fuchsinophile granules of spinal ganglia cells. **1910** H. W. Armit tr. *Ehrlich & Lazarus' Anæmia* I. i. iii. 102 The fact that these cells cannot possibly be lymphocytes is proved by the complete absence of fuchsinophile granules. **1931** *Amer. Jrnl. Anat.* XLVIII. 165 Many of the fuchsinophilic or eosinophilic necrotic cells have disappeared. **1936** H. D. Rolleston *Endocrine Organs* vi. 310 In female foetuses this fuchsinophil reaction did not last so long. *Ibid.*, The suppression of the fuchsinophil stain in female foetuses may be due to inhibition exerted by the pituitary. **1940** *Amer. Jrnl. Anat.* LXVII. 190 After Orth's fixation the fuchsinophilia varies considerably from gland to gland. **1967** *Pathol. & Microbiol.* XXX. 402 A marked fuchsinophilia lasting up to 30 minutes was observed in the heart muscle fibers. **1970** H. Selye *Exper. Cardiovasc. Dis.* II. iv. 665 Fuchsinophilic degeneration is a pre-necrotic change affecting certain myocardial fibers in damaged areas. *Ibid.*, The fuchsinophilic fibers or fiber segments. *Ibid.*, Fuchsinophilic staining.

fuchsite ('fuːksaɪt). *Min.* [Named in 1842 after the mineralogist J. N. von Fuchs: see -ite.] A variety of muscovite containing chromium, which gives it a green colour.

1844 Dana *Min.* 321 Fuchsite is a chrome mica from the Zillerthal.

fucidin ('fjuːsɪdɪn). *Pharm.* Also **Fucidine** (proprietary name). [Formed by alteration of fusid(ic *a.* + -ine[5].] The sodium salt of fusidic acid, used as an oral antibiotic esp. against staphylococci. Also used *loosely* for *fusidic acid.*

1961 *Trade Marks Jrnl.* 30 Aug. 1189/2 Fucidine. **1962** *Lancet* 8 Sept. 478/1 A small controlled trial of the new antibiotic 'Fucidin'..in patients whose burns were colonised by *Staph. aureus.* **1966** Dunlop & Alstead *Textbk. Med. Treatm.* (ed. 10) 73 The use of fucidin should only be seriously considered for a patient with severe staphylococcal disease who is able to swallow and who is known to be hypersensitive to penicillin. **1968** Garrod & O'Grady *Antibiotic & Chemotherapy* (ed. 2) xi. 200 Fucidin is active against species of Gram-positive bacteria and the Gram-negative cocci. **1970** *To-day's Drugs* (Brit. Med. Assoc.) 21 It is very rare to find a fucidin-resistant staphylococcus.

fucivorous (fjuːˈsɪvərəs), *a.* [f. L. *fūc-us* fucus + *-vor-us* devouring + -ous.] Eating, or subsisting on, seaweed.

1860 in Fowler *Med. Voc.* **1864** Webster cites Dana.

fuck (fʌk), *v.* Also 6 fuk, 7- f—k, etc. [Early mod.E *fuck, fuk*, answering to a ME. type **fuken* (wk. vb.) not found; ulterior etym. unknown. Synonymous G. *ficken* cannot be shown to be related.]

For centuries, and still by the great majority, regarded as a taboo-word; until recent times not often recorded in print but frequent in coarse speech.

1. *intr.* To copulate. *trans.* (Rarely used with female subject.) To copulate with; to have sexual connection with.

a **1503** Dunbar *Poems* lxxv. 13 Be his feiris he wald haue fukkit. **1535** Lyndesay *Satyre* 1363 Bischops..may fuck thair fill and be vnmaryit. **1535–36** —— *Answer to Kingis Flyting* 49 Ay fukkand lyke ane furious Fornicatour. **1598** Florio *Worlde of Wordes* 137/1 *Fottere*, to iape, to sard, to fucke, to swive, to occupy. *c* **1650** in Hales & Furnivall *Percy's Folio MS.* (1867) 90 Which made him to have a mighty mind To clipp, kisse, & to ffuck. **1680** Rochester *Poems on Several Occasions* (1950) 14 Much Wine had past with grave discourse, Of who Fucks who, and who does worse. *c* **1684** *Sodom* II. 30 Hee Fucks to please his will, but I for need. **1707** 'Madam B[ran]le' *Fifteen Plagues of Maidenhead* 4 But I poor Virgin never shall be F—. *a* **1750** A. Robertson *Poems* (1750) 256 But she gave proof that she could f—k. *c* **1800** Burns *Merry Muses* (1911) 71 You can f—k where'er you please. *c* **1863** Philo cunnus *Festival of Passions* II. 54 That female nation who being encamped near their enemies were fucked, during a truce, by the hostile party. **1869** Rossetti *Let.* 15 Sept. (1965) II. 743 If Byron f—d his sister he f—d her and there an end. *c* **1888–94** *My Secret Life* IV. 64 Then a dread came over me. I had fucked a common street nymph. **1922** Joyce *Ulysses* 765 His wife is fucked yes and damn well fucked too. **1928** D. H. Lawrence *Lady Chatterley* iv. 44 Fellows with swaying waists fucking little jazz girls. **1967** D. Wright tr. *R. Queneau's Between Blue & Blue* v. 48 'Well, Lamélie,' says Cidrolin, 'while you're waiting to get married, do you want to be entertained or educated?' 'No, Dad, what I want to do is to fuck.' **1971** *Ink* 19 Oct. 15/3, I don't want to fuck anyone, and I don't want to be fucked either.

2. Used profanely in imprecations and exclamations as the coarsest equivalent of damn *v.* 5.

1922 Joyce *Ulysses* 587 God fuck old Bennett! **1929** F. Manning *Middle Parts of Fortune* II. xv. 379 'Fuck the bloody thing!' he said fiercely under his breath. **1955** S. Beckett *Molloy* 69 Fuck the son of a bitch. **1959** F. King *So Hurt & Humiliated* 151 'Suppose any of the neighbours were to look out and see them.' 'Oh, f— the neighbours!' 'Really, Henry!' **1969** 'J. Morris' *Fever Grass* ii. 24 Why don't you..tell whoever it is to go fuck themselves?

3. Const. with various adverbs: ***fuck about***, to fool about, mess about; ***fuck off***, to go away, make off; ***fuck up***: (*a*) *trans.*, to ruin, spoil, mess up; (*b*) *intr.*, to blunder, to make a (serious) error; to fail; cf. screw *v.* 12 c.

1929 F. Manning *Middle Parts of Fortune* I. ii. 31 They kept 'em fuckin' about the camp, while they sent us over the bloody top. *Ibid.* iii. 37 As soon as a bit o' shrapnel comes their way, [they] fuck off 'ome jildy, toot sweet. **1944** *Amer. Speech* XIX. 108 Go on, now, fuck off! **1958** S. Beckett *Malone Dies* 116 She wants to know if you're the one in charge. Fuck off, said Lemuel. **1967** R. Shaw *Man in Glass Booth* (1969) xvi. 114 'Can't be too specific,' answered the old man. 'Don't want to fuck up my case.' **1968** J. Updike *Couples* iv. 294 This fucks up our party, doesn't it? **1969** *It* 11–24 Apr. 12/3 The..neatly planned plot to fuck up their transport scene. **1971** E. E. Landy *Underground Dict.* 84 *Fuck up*, *v.* 1. Make a gross error... 2. Fall completely under the influence of a drug or alcohol. **1977** *Rolling Stone* 13 Jan. 13/2 We fucked up in New York. **1980** *Maledicta* Summer 85 The RSV translates 'They were well-fed lusty stallions' but the King James [Bible] totally fucked up here and confused Hebrew *maškīm* 'well-balled' (where the *-īm* is the marker of the plural) with Hebrew *maškīm* 'rising early in the morning' (where the *-īm* is part of the root).

Hence '**fucking** *vbl. sb.* Also as ***ppl. a.*** and ***adv.***, used esp. as a mere intensive.

a **1568** A. Scott *Poems* iv. 55 Thir foure, the suth to sane, Enforsis thame to fucking. **1680** Rochester *Poems on Several Occasions* (1950) 30 Through all the Town, the common Fucking Post, On whom each Whore, relieves her tingling Cunt. **1707** [see frigging *vbl. sb.*]. *c* **1888–94** *My Secret Life* III. 228 This house had but eight rooms, and two mere closets to let out for fucking. *Ibid.* VIII. 307 She was..a magnificent bit of fucking flesh, but nothing more. **1893** Farmer & Henley *Slang* III. 80/2 *Fucking*..Adj., A qualification of extreme contumely. Adv. Intensitive and expletive; a more violent form of *bloody.* **1922** Joyce *Ulysses* 580 I'll wring the neck of any bugger says a word against my fucking king. **1929** F. Manning *Middle Parts of Fortune* I. ii. 23 Blown to fuckin' bits as soon as we got out of the trench, poor bugger. **1930** J. Dos Passos *42nd Parallel* 94 It was a fucking shame it was Freddy hit you. **1938** Dylan

THOMAS *Let.* 31 Aug. (1966) 208 None using obscene words, none..to do with fucking. **1939** —— *Let.* 29 Sept. (1966) 240 I'll give Dent the whole fucking works. **1960** D. LESSING *In Pursuit of English* 12 'What the f--ing hell's that for?' my father said. **1969** AUDEN *City without Walls* 49 I'm so bored with the whole fucking crowd of you I could scream! **1971** *It* 2-16 June 18/3 The Youngbloods..are so fucking good they can do spontaneous albums.

fuck (fʌk), *sb.* [f. prec.] **1.** An act of copulation.
1680 ANON. in *Rochester's Poems on Several Occasions* (1950) 37 Thus was I Rook'd of Twelve substantial Fucks. *c* **1684** *Sodom* (Epilogue spoken by Fuckadilla) l. 19 A little fuck can't stay our appetite. *c* **1800** BURNS *Merry Muses* (1911) 68 When maukin bucks, at early f—ks, In dewy glens are seen, sir. *c* **1888–94** *My Secret Life* III. 139, I was dying with want of a fuck. **1928** D. H. LAWRENCE *Lady Chatterley* xviii. 342 A lily-livered hound with never a fuck in him. **1965** E. J. HOWARD *After Julius* iii. 38 Eat well, don't smoke, and a fuck was equal to a five-mile walk.

b. *concr.* A person (usu. a woman) considered in sexual terms.
1874 *Lett. fr. Friend in Paris* II. 168, I had always held that dear mamma was the best fuck in the family, and in every way a most desirable and splendid creature. **1969** S. GREENLEE *Spook who sat by Door* ix. 77 An aborted marriage to a favourite fuck. **1969** 'J. MORRIS' *Fever Grass* ii. 26 She was a good fuck... She was great in bed.

2. Phr. ***not to give*** (or ***care***) ***a fuck***: not to care in the slightest.
1929 F. MANNING *Middle Parts of Fortune* I. v. 87 'They don't care a fuck 'ow us'ns live,' said little Martlow bitterly. **1934** H. MILLER *Tropic of Cancer* (1948) 37 Nobody gives a fuck about her except to use her. **1962** I. MURDOCH *Unofficial Rose* vi. 63 Not that I care a fuck. **1971** *Ink* 12 June 3/2 We don't give a fuck if we have to stand around all day doing nothing.

3. Various other casual, intensive, etc., uses.
1959 W. BURROUGHS *Naked Lunch* 63 How in the fuck should I know? *Ibid.* 96 You may be a tedious old fuck yourself some day. **1966** D. HOLBROOK *Flesh Wounds* 129 Driver speed up. Come on, for fuck's sake. **1968** *Anarchy* Oct. 314 A lad of 13 who has had his hand up for some time trying to attract the chairman's attention says 'Oh, for fuck's sake.' **1969** *Oz* May 13/1 (Advt.), Pete Quesnal, late of St. Nicholas, where the fuck are you. **1970** G. LORD *Marshmallow Pie* xv. 136 What the fuck do you think you're doing?

4. ***fuck-all***, (absolutely) nothing, esp. in phr. ***to know fuck-all***. Cf. ALL *a.* 8 f.
1960 C. MACINNES *Mr. Love & Justice* 50 The customers ..just mean sweet f--k-all to me. **1971** *Ink* 12 June 15/2 It's a speech about the Mediterranean..about the 'flat-bellied Mediterranean ideology we know fuck all about'. **1978** J. KRANTZ *Scruples* x. 280 Maggie..had always been smart enough to have a suspicion, a disturbingly insecure inkling that maybe she didn't know fuck-all about clothes. **1985** A. LURIE *Foreign Affairs* ix. 221 You don't know fuck-all about life.

5. **'fuck-up**, a mess, muddle.
1958 J. O'HARA *From Terrace* (1959) 257 Such a Goddam fuck-up. **1968** M. RICHLER *Cocksure* iv. 29 I'm sorry about this fuck-up, Mr Griffin.

'fucker. [f. FUCK *v.* + -ER[1].] One who copulates. Also in extended use as a general term of abuse.
1598 FLORIO *Worlde of Wordes* 137/1 *Fottitore*, a iaper, a sarder, a swiver, a fucker, an occupier. **1893** FARMER & HENLEY *Slang* III. 80/2 *Fucker*. 1. A lover. 2. A term of endearment, admiration, derision, etc. **1922** JOYCE *Ulysses* 584 I'll wring the bastard fucker's bleeding blasted fucking windpipe! **1928** D. H. LAWRENCE *Lady Chatterley* xviii. 334 I'm not just my lady's fucker, after all. **1929** F. MANNING *Middle Parts of Fortune* II. xii. 268 'Laugh, you silly fuckers!' he cried in vehement rage. **1961** A. WILSON *Old Men at Zoo* v. 276 'We'll get you, you fucker!' Barley was shouting.

fuck-up: see FUCK *v.* 3 and FUCK *sb.* 5.

fuck-wind, *sb.*: see WINDFUCKER.

†**fuco'd**, *ppl. a. Obs. rare*[−1]. Beautified with fucus, painted.
1652 BENLOWES *Theoph.* I. xii, Frequent are fuco'd Checks; the Virtuosa's rare.

fucoid ('fjuːkɔɪd), *a.* and *sb.* [f. FUC-US + -OID. Cf. F. *fucoïde.*]
A. *adj.* **a.** Resembling or belonging to seaweeds, *esp.* those of the group *Fucaceæ.* **b.** Characterized by or containing impressions of such seaweeds or markings similar to them.
1839 ROBERTS *Dict. Geol.*, *Fucoïd*, a term applied to several fossil plants. There is a fucoïd shale, so called from the abundance of fuci it contains. **1854** MURCHISON *Siluria* vi. 136 In the cliffs at Ludlow, the chief rocks are surmounted by what I termed the fucoid bed. This is a greenish-grey argillaceous sandstone, almost entirely made up of a multitude of small, wavy, rounded, stem-like forms, which resemble entangled sea-weeds. **1871** LYELL *Student's Elem. Geol.* xxvii. 473 These sandstones have been called in Sweden 'fucoid sandstones'.

B. *sb.* **a.** A seaweed of the group *Fucaceæ.* **b.** A fossil marine plant resembling these.
1848 CRAIG, *Fucoid*, a fossil plant belonging to the order Fucaceæ. **1857** H. MILLER *Test. Rocks* i. 17 The fucoids, or kelp-weeds. **1859** PAGE *Handbk. Geol. Terms* s.v., Fucoids or fucus-like impressions occur in strata of every epoch. **1860** HARTWIG *Sea & Wond.* iii. 30 The feathery sertularia, the delicate fucoid. **1860** *All Year Round* No. 50. 562 Little fucoids, progenitors of the kelp-weeds. **1872** NICHOLSON *Palæont.* 477 The Lower Cambrian Rocks have yielded many so-called 'fucoids'.

fucoidal (fjuː'kɔɪdəl), *a.* [f. prec. + -AL[1].] = FUCOID A. b.
1849 MURCHISON *Siluria* viii. 177 Fucoidal sandstones. **1857** H. MILLER *Test. Rocks* xi. 465 They seemed fucoidal, and might of course belong to any age. **1872** NICHOLSON *Palæont.* 477 The 'Fucoidal Sandstone' of Sweden.

†**fu'cose**, *a. Obs.*[−0] [ad. L. *fūcōsus*, f. FUCUS.]
1727 BAILEY vol. II, *Fucose*, painted, feigned, counterfeited.

†**'fucous**, *a. Obs.* [f. L. *fūcōs-us*: see prec. and -OUS.] Of the nature of fucus or 'paint'.
1660 R. COKE *Power & Subj.* Pref. 4 It is Vice which.. hath such specious shewes and pretences put upon it, to make it seem Virtue, which fucous and false paint continues no longer then the present Faction.

fucoxanthin (ˌfjuːkəʊ'zænθɪn). *Chem.* Also 9 -ine. [f. FUC(US + -O + XANTHINE.] A brown carotenoid pigment, $C_{42}H_{58}O_6$, occurring in and generally characteristic of the brown algæ.
1873 H. C. SORBY in *Proc. R. Soc.* XXI. 461 *Fucoxanthine.* This is the name I propose for the principal colouring-matter of *Fuci* and other olive *Algæ.* **1917** HAAS & HILL *Introd. Chem. Plant Products* (ed. 2) v. 229 Carotin, Xanthophyll, and Fucoxanthin..are known collectively as the Carotinoids. **1949** *New Biology* VII. 90 The masking pigment [of chlorophyll] in the brown algae is called fucoxanthin, and in the case of the reds phycoerythrin. **1965** T. W. GOODWIN *Chem. & Biochem. Plant Pigments* iv. 133 Three main classes of the division Phaeophyta all characteristically synthesize fucoxanthin.

‖**fucus** ('fjuːkəs). Pl. ‖fuci ('fjuːsaɪ); also 7–8 fucus(s)es, 7 fucus's, fucos, fucu's; also anglicized *β.* fukes. [a. L. *fūcus* rock-lichen, red dye, rouge, false colour: cf. Gr. φῦκος (neut.).]
†**1.** Paint or cosmetic for beautifying the skin; a wash or colouring for the face. Frequent in 17th c. writers. *Obs.*
α. **1599** B. JONSON *Cynthia's Rev.* v. ii, What are the ingredients to your fucus? **1607** DEKKER *Westw. Hoe* Wks. 1873 II. 285 Heere is..an excellent Fucus to..weede out Freckles. **1672** CAVE *Prim. Chr.* II. iii. (1673) 66 Leaving fucus's and paintings..to those that belong to Plays and Theatres. **1675** COCKER *Morals* 59 Virtue hates Fucos, Patches and perfumes. *a* **1711** KEN *Urania* Poet. Wks. 1721 IV. 496 The loathsome Fucus..Which fill'd and glaz'd her furrow'd Skin. **1757** *Phil. Trans.* L. 76 Bella-donna..came into credit as a fucus among the Italian ladies.
β. **1600** SURFLET *Countrie Farme* III. lxix. 592 These compound waters are..for fukes and painting, as ornaments to the body. **1601** HOLLAND *Pliny* (1634) Words of Art, *Fukes*, paintings to beautify the face in outward appearance.
†**b.** *fig. Obs.*
1640 J. HOLLIS in Rushw. *Hist. Coll.* III. (1692) I. 168 Whatsoever Fucus or Artifice they be slighted over with, I do not like their Countenance. **1681–6** J. SCOTT *Chr. Life* III. (1696) 390 God..sees through all the Dawbings and Fucu's of Hypocrisie. **1701** COLLIER *M. Anton.* (1726) 155 Pull off its mask and fucus, and view it in its naked essence. **1742** YOUNG *Nt. Th.* VIII. 462 Of fortune's fucus strip them, yet alive.
β. **1657** REEVE *God's Plea* 108 If not a Penitent, what will all his Church tinctures do him good? No, Jerusalem had all these fukes to Admiration.
†**c.** *gen.* Any dye or colouring. *Obs.*
1676 R. DIXON *Nat. two Test.* 2 To give Poyson a gusto of Honey, and colour over a Leaden Cause with a Fucus of Gold. **1698** J. FRYER *Acc. E. Ind. & P.* 332 We..have hardly given the Potter his handful of White Marle to form into Vessels without Fucus.
2. A genus of seaweeds with flat leathery fronds. Formerly applied more widely.
1716 DERHAM *Physico-Theol.* 415 *note*, The first that discovered the Seeds in *Fuci*, was the before commended Dr. Tancred Robinson. **1756** *Gentl. Mag.* XXVI. 63 The whole rock..was covered with that curious kind of fucus. **1778** LIGHTFOOT *Flora Scot.* (1789) 996 In basons of water left by the tides, and often adhering to Fucuses. **1813** SIR H. DAVY *Agric. Chem.* (1814) 282 The common fucus, which is the sea-weed usually most abundant on the coast. **1838** T. THOMSON *Chem. Org. Bodies* 945 *Laminaria digitata.* This fucus is olive-coloured. **1857** WOOD *Com. Obj. Seashore* 30 The slimy and slippery fuci make the rock-walking exceedingly dangerous.
Hence **'fucused** *ppl. a.*, beautified with paint, painted (also *fig.*); **'fucusing** *vbl. sb.*
a **1680** EARL OF ROCHESTER in *D'Urfey's Pills* (1719) III. 343 With butter'd Hair, and fucus'd Breast. **1681** GLANVILL *Sadducismus* II. (ed. 2) 34 How did the Jugglers do this with Painting and Fucussing. **1684** PHILLIPS tr. *Plutarch's Mor.* (1691) III. VII. 199 The Sibyl..uttering Sentences altogether thoughtful and serious, neither fucus'd nor perfum'd. **1855** KINGSLEY *Westw. Ho!* (1861) 180 A painted, patched, fucused, perriwigged, bolstered, Charybdis.

fud (fʌd). *Sc.* and *north. dial.* [Of uncertain origin; perh. a. or cognate with ON. *fuð* neut., cunnus, = MHG. *vut* (mod.Ger. *hundsfott* used as a term of abuse); formally identical with Skr. *putau* dual, buttocks.]
1. 'The backside or buttocks' (Jam.).
1785 R. FORBES *Poems in Buchan Dial.* 5 He..turn'd to us his fud. **1804** TARRAS *Poems* 99, I..wad yir heavy fud gie A piercin pike.
2. The tail or 'scut' of a hare, rabbit, etc.
1787 BURNS *Tam Samson* vii, Ye maukins cock your fud fu' braw, Withouten dread. **1833** M. SCOTT *Tom Cringle* xvii. (1859) 459 Do you cock your fud at me, you tiny thief you?—he struck at it with his stick. Tip the duck dived and did not rise again. **1847** in HALLIWELL; and in various dial. glossaries.

3. *Woollen-manuf.* [Perh. a different word. Cf. FOOD 4 b.]
1873 *Weale's Dict. Archit.* (ed. 3), *Fud*, woollen waste. **1892** *Labour Commission* Gloss., *Fudd*, the refuse or dirt cleaned out of the materials during the processes of scribbling and carding.

fud(d)e, obs. form of FOOD.

fudder ('fʌdə(r)). Also 7–8 fooder. [ad. Ger. *fuder* (= FOTHER) used in the same sense.] A tun (of wine).
1679–88 *Secr. Serv. Money Chas. & Jas.* (Camden) 118 5 fooder of Rhenish wine, containing 37——, and 40[ty] gallons. *a* **1767** *Sir Aldingar* xli. in Child *Ballads* III. lix. (1885) 46 Thou seemust as bigge as a ffooder. **1839** BURCKHARDT *German Dict.*, *Fuder*, fudder, tun (of wine). **1851** LONGF. *Gold. Leg.* IV. *Convent of Hirschau* 100 A benison rest on the Bishop who sends Such a fudder of wine as this to his friends! [**1884** *St. James's Gaz.* 11 Aug. 5/2 Eight fuders of wine.]

fudder, Sc. var. of FOULDRE.
c **1590** BUREL *Pass. Pilgr.* in *J. Watson's Collect.* (1706) II. 24 To fle the flichts, of fudder.
attrib. **1819** W. TENNANT *Papistry Storm'd* (1827) 219 Thunder-vollies..And fudder-flashes mixt wi' hail.

fudder, obs. form of FODDER, FOTHER.

fuddle ('fʌd(ə)l), *sb. slang* or *colloq.* [f. next vb.]
†**1.** Drink, liquor, 'booze'. *Obs.*
1680 R. L'ESTRANGE *Colloq. Erasm.* 124 They have taken their Dose of Fuddle. *c* **1680** *Roxb. Ball.* (1890) VII. 78 With a cup of fuddle. *a* **1700** B. E. *Dict. Cant. Crew, Fuddle*, Drink. **1706** E. WARD *Hud. Rediv.* I. v, We sipp'd our Fuddle, As Women in the Straw do Caudle.
2. A drinking bout. ***on the fuddle***: out for a lengthened spell of drinking.
a **1813** A. WILSON *My Landlady's Nose* Poet. Wks. (1846) 301 Old Patrick M'Dougherty when on the fuddle, Pulls out a cigar, and [etc.]. **1832–53** *Whistle-binkie* (Scot. Songs) Ser. III. 111 For a ance-a-year fuddle I'd scarce gie a strae. **1865** B. BRIERLEY *Irkdale* I. 61 At th' height of a wakes fuddle. **1891** *Newcastle Even. Chron.* 29 Jan. 3/1 She usually provided food in the house when she was not on the 'fuddle'.
3. Intoxication; an intoxicated state.
1764 *Low Life* 24 In order to take large Morning Draughts, and secure the first Fuddle of the Day. **1890** *Yoshiwara Episode* 67 If he were only in his senses, instead of in a fuddle.
4. *transf.* The state of being muddled, confused, or the like.
1827 R. H. FROUDE *Remains* (1838) I. 219 My notions about it have been..very fuddled and bewildered; and, I suppose, if I were to attempt to analyse and explain them, I might raise my fuddle to the nth power. **1880** WEBB *Goethe's Faust* II. v, He rushed about—Vain was his frenzied fuddle.

fuddle ('fʌd(ə)l), *v.* [Of obscure origin; cf. Du. *vod* soft, slack, loose, Ger. dial. *fuddeln* to swindle.]
1. *intr.* To have a drinking bout; to tipple, booze. Also, ***to fuddle it***.
1588 *Acc.* in Morris *Chester* (1895) 328 John Wright, for fuddleing and drinkinge with other leters and molestationers, just nothing. **1659** D. PELL *Impr. Sea* 116 *note*, See a Captain of a ship sending for this, and the other shandy fellow..to fuddle it in their cabbins. **1696** W. MOUNTAGUE *Delights Holland* 184 The Men..sit up Gaming and Fuddling greatest part of Night. **1713** *Pol. Ballads* (1860) II. 137 Here Barons may talk, and Squires may fuddle. **1821** *Joseph the Book-Man* 33 No man might drink That could not fuddle till he wink. **1863** BATES *Nat. Amazon* iii. (1864) 53 He is going to fuddle in honour of St. Thomé.
b. quasi-*trans.* with *away.* †Also, to empty (a pot) by drinking.
c **1680** *Roxb. Ball.* (1890) VII. 77 She calls up her Neighbors, for to go and fuddle a Pot. **1756** *Gentl. Mag.* XXVI. 431 They fuddle away the day with riot and prophaneness.
2. *trans.* To confuse with or as with drink, intoxicate, render tipsy.
c **1600** *Timon* II. v. (1842) 37 Ile giue thee ale pragmaticall indeede Which, if thou drinke, shall fuddle thee hande and foote. **1633** MAY *Heir* I. in Hazl. *Dodsley* XI. 523 Did you never come in half fuddled? **1706** E. BAYNARD *Cold Baths* II. (1709) 362, I made my Man give him a Cup of Ale..under a Pint, yet it almost fuddled him. **1771** SMOLLETT *Humph. Cl.* (1815) 233 After all the other females were fuddled with dram-drinking. **1809** W. IRVING *Knickerb.* (1861) 241 The inhabitants..get fuddled with mint-julep and apple-toddy. **1837** DICKENS *Pickw.* l, Bob Sawyer and Ben Allen, both slightly fuddled. **1890** *Spectator* 27 Dec. 938/1 It [hypnotism] fuddles the will, in fact, but does not destroy it.
absol. **1725** BRADLEY *Fam. Dict.* s.v. *Strawberry*, The Wine made of them will Fuddle. **1826** J. WILSON *Noct. Ambr.* Wks. 1855 I. 130 The toddy having lost all taste and all power o' fuddlin.
b. ***to fuddle one's cap*** or ***nose***: to get drunk.
1663 COWLEY *Cutter of Colman St.* II. ii, We'll fuddle our Noses together. **1719** D'URFEY *Pills* (1872) IV. 106 If their Caps be fuddled with Ipse. **1724** in Ramsay *Tea-t. Misc.* (1729) 15 Come, let us fuddle all our Noses. *c* **1793** *Spirit Pub. Jrnls.* (1799) I. 9 No Persian of old, till he fuddled his nose, Any measure in Senate was wont to propose.
c. *transf.* (See quots.)
1825 BROCKETT *N.C. Words*, *Fuddle*, to intoxicate fish. **1835** S. OLIVER *Rambles in Northumb.* 83 What they call fuddling the fish, by liming the water, or throwing into the pools a preparation of Coculus Indicus.
3. *transf.* and *fig.* To stupefy, muddle, confuse (also † with *up*). Formerly also of delight, etc.: To 'intoxicate'. (In quots. 1617, 1678 perh. = FUBBLE.)

1617 tr. *De Dominis on Rom.* xiii. 12 Nor would they suffer themselues to be any longer deceiued, and fuddled up in that darke cloud, and night of infolded faith. **1678** CUDWORTH *Intell. Syst.* I. iii. 157 Nature is..Reason immersed and plunged into Matter, and as it were fuddled in it, and confounded with it. **1694** CROWNE *Married Beau* v. Wks. 1874 IV. 325 Now she will fuddle me with every kiss. **1745** LADY S. COWPER *Let. to Mrs. Dewes* 5 June in *Mrs. Delany's Life & Corr.* (1861) II. 356 He was quite fuddled with joy. **1803** *Edin. Rev.* II. 398 He is fuddled with animal spirits. **1854** H. ROGERS *Ess.* (1860) II. 6 To impair and fuddle the intellect.

4. *Comb.*: †**fuddle cap** [see 2 b], a tippler, sot.

1666 tr. *Horace's Odes* I. i, The Fuddlecap whose God's the Vyne. **1708** MOTTEUX *Rabelais* v. vi. (1737) 21 Here's to thee, old Fuddlecap.

fuddled ('fʌd(ə)ld), *ppl. a.* [f. FUDDLE *v.* + -ED¹.] Intoxicated; also, muddled.

1656 H. MORE *Enthus. Triumph.* 7 They would consider of it first both welnigh fuddled and sober. **1693** DRYDEN *Juvenal* vi. 420 Full Brimmers to their Fuddled Noses thrust. **1730–46** THOMSON *Autumn* 537 The table floating round, And pavement, faithless to the fuddled foot. **1830** *Boston Gaz.* 26 Oct. 4, I was not drunk, I was only fuddled. **1865** LIVINGSTONE *Zambesi* v. 117 Our men soon pacified the fuddled but good-humoured medico.

fuddler ('fʌdlə(r)). [f. FUDDLE *v.* + -ER¹.] One who fuddles, a tippler.

1699 BENTLEY *Phal.* iii. 125 What Present could be more proper to such a Fuddler than..one of the biggest of Cups? **1764** *Low Life* 32 For the Use of..conceited Fudlers. **1812** W. TENNANT *Anster F.* I. xix, I'll not have you, thou fuddler.

'fuddling, *vbl. sb.* [f. FUDDLE *v.* + -ING¹.]

1. The action of the vb. FUDDLE.

1665 J. WEBB *Stone-Heng* (1725) 225 His other Fables, of Electing, Feasting, Fudling, Fidling, they are beneath us. **1670** J. FURLY *Test. to True Light* 24 Go not a Fudling, but fear the Lord. **1871** C. GIBBON *Lack of Gold* xxx, The fuddling commenced in earnest.

2. *attrib.* and *Comb.*, as *fuddling-bout*, *-cap*, *-liquor*, *-table*, *-tent*; **fuddling-crib**, **-school**, a drinking den.

1708 MOTTEUX *Rabelais* v. ix, We went back to have t'other *fuddling Bout. *c* **1600** *Songs Costume* (Percy) 119 The *fuddling cap, by Bacchus' might, Turns night to day, and day to night. **1738** *Gentl. Mag.* VIII. 80 The Parson hath lost his Fuddling-cap. **1856** *Househ. Words* XIII. 544 Saunders's *fuddling crib was a double hovel. **1707** SLOANE *Jamaica* I. p. xxix, The common *fuddling liquor..is Rum-punch. **1680** MORDEN *Geog. Rect.* (1685) 333 The Greeks..keep *Fudling Schools for the Mariners. **1708** T. WARD *Eng. Ref.* (1716) 37 Transform'd the..Altars into *Fuddling Tables. **1683–4** *Frost of 1683–4* (Percy) 6 Where ships and barges used to frequent Now may you see a booth or *fuddling tent.

fuddling ('fʌdlɪŋ), *ppl. a.* [f. as prec. + -ING².] That fuddles, tippling.

1654 R. WHITLOCK *Zootomia* 93 Fudling Gossips. **1662–3** PEPYS *Diary* 24 Mar., A fuddling, troublesome fellow. **1852** THACKERAY *Esmond* I. xi, Fuddling squires from the country round.

'fuddydud. Used occas. as a shortened form of next.

1914 *Dialect Notes* IV. 72 *Fuddydud*.., fussy person. **1952** M. MCCARTHY *Groves of Academe* (1953) ix. 167 'You old fuddydud,' she finally teased him. **1967** *Listener* 2 Nov. 584/2 The Robust Individualist is too often a whimsical fuddydud born out of his time.

fuddy-duddy ('fʌdɪdʌdɪ). *slang.* [Origin unknown.] An old-fashioned person; an ineffectual old fogy. Also *attrib.* or as *adj.*

[**1899** W. DICKINSON *Cumberland Gloss.* 106/2 *Duddy fuddiel*, a ragged fellow.] **1904** in H. WENTWORTH *Amer. Dial. Dict.* (1944) 236/2. **1907** *Dialect Notes* III. 244 Fuddy-duddy, n. and adj. **1938** D. MOFFAT *Mott Family in France* xvii. 191 Mr. Mott wandered along the Promenade.. looking at the damned old fuddy-duddies who cluttered it up. **1940** *Harper's* Dec. 1 a A great many people..believe its [American army] officer class is caste-ridden and fuddy-duddy. **1951** 'N. SHUTE' *Round Bend* 310 People may call the Sheikh of Khulal an old fuddy-duddy, but he's an important man in these parts. **1957** *Times* 23 Aug. 9/4 What was once called prudish and is now sneered at as being 'fuddy-duddy'. **1958** *Observer* 23 Mar. 14/4 Deserted country-house with fuddy-duddy owner. **1964** L. NKOSI *Rhythm of Violence* II. ii. 30 Some priests can be..more militant than some fuddy-duddies who pass as politicians! **1970** D. BALSDON *Oxford Now & Then* 134 So much for 'a straight run to the grave'. How fuddy-duddy they all were.

fude, obs. form of FEUD *sb.*¹, FOOD.

fudge (fʌdʒ), *int.* and *sb.* [Origin obscure.

The int. as used by Goldsmith (quot. 1766) seems from the context merely to represent an inarticulate expression of indignant disgust, though later writers who adopted it from him use it with a more definite meaning. The sb. appears to have been developed partly from the int., and partly from FUDGE *v.* The etymology suggested in the annexed quot. 1700 can hardly be correct, though Captain Fudge, 'by some called Lying Fudge', (*Letter* of 1664 in Crouch *Posthuma Christiana* 1712, p. 87) was a real person (the surname is still common in Dorset). The nautical phrase 'You fudge it', associated in 1700 with the name of the mendacious captain, prob. belongs to FUDGE *v.* 1. In a dialogue of 1702, 'The Present Condition of the English Navy', one of the interlocutors is called 'Young Fudg of the Admiralty', perh. with allusion to the same verb.

1700 *Remarks on the Navy* in D'Israeli *Cur. Lit.*, *Neology* (1841), There was, sir, in our time one Captain Fudge..who ..always brought home his owners a good cargo of lies, so much that now aboard ship the sailors, when they hear a great lie told, cry out, 'You fudge it'.]

A. *int.* Stuff and nonsense! Bosh!

1766 GOLDSM. *Vic. W.* xi, The very impolite behaviour of Mr. Burchell, who..at the conclusion of every sentence would cry out Fudge! *c* **1818** PEEL in *Croker Papers* (1884) I. iv. 116 To all the latter part of your letter I answer..Fudge. **1842** BARHAM *Ingol. Leg.*, *Bloudie Jacke*, But others cry 'fudge'. **1876** F. E. TROLLOPE *Charming Fellow* I. xv. 200 Anything of consequence to say? Fudge! He is coming begging.

B. *sb.*

1. Contemptible nonsense, 'stuff', bosh.

1791 MRS. RADCLIFFE *Rom. Forest* x, That is all fudge to frighten you. **1838** LOWELL *Lett.* (1894) I. 28 As for my dependence on my own powers, 'tis all fudge. **1865** E. C. CLAYTON *Cruel Fortune* II. 105, I only hope your marriage will cure you of your silly fudge.

2. A made-up story, a deceit.

1797 MRS. A. M. BENNETT *Beggar Girl* (1813) III. 112 But that must be all a fudge; because, you see, he did not overtake you. **1841** LYTTON *Nt. & Morn.* II. vii, Very genteel young man—prepossessing appearance—(that's a fudge!) highly educated. **1878** EMERSON *Misc. Papers, Fort. Republ.* Wks. (Bohn) III. 399 'Tis a wild democracy; the riot of mediocrities and dishonesties and fudges.

3. An impostor, humbug.

1794 MRS. A. M. BENNETT *Ellen* III. 132 What an old fudge! You won't give her up, I hope, Charles.

4. A patch of print, esp. a piece of late news, inserted in a newspaper page; also, a machine or cylinder for inserting such patches. Also *attrib.*, as *fudge-cylinder*, *-plate*, *-shaft*, *-space*, *-unit*; **fudge-box** (see quot. 1929).

1899 *Daily News* 23 Sept. 5/1 The blank space left for 'fudge' while the evening paper is being printed off is caused by the presence of the empty fudge-box. **1902** *Daily Mail* 27 June 7/5 After the paper has passed through the big cylinders that print the entire sheets, it goes past the small cylinder which prints the contents of the 'fudge box' in the vacant space. **1910** E. WALLACE *Nine Bears* vi. 45 'Issued at 4.10,' he said, glancing at the 'fudge' space, where the result of a race had been printed. **1929** *Encycl. Brit.* XVIII. 508/1 This late news is printed into the blank spaces by a contrivance called a 'fudge box' which is circular in form and into which are secured linotype slugs. The 'fudge' is fastened on to an auxiliary cylinder equipped with inking mechanism. **1964** *Gloss. Letterpress Rotary Print. Terms* (*B.S.I.*) 13 Fudge cylinder, plate, shaft, unit. **1967** *Evening News* 13 July 4/4 (*caption*) You must excuse me while I break off to stamp-in the 20th lap positions for our 3.30 fudge.

5. A soft-grained sweetmeat prepared by boiling together milk, sugar, butter, etc. orig. *U.S.*

1896 W. C. GORE in *Inlander* Jan. 147 *Fudges*, a kind of chocolate bonbons. **1902** *Queen* 3 May 763/1 The greatest 'stunt' among college students is to make *Fudge*. *Ibid.*, Nut Fudges... Fruit Fudge. **1905** *Buffalo Express* 16 Jan. 2 The overturning of an alcohol lamp over which some girls were cooking fudge. **1960** *Good Housek. Cookery Bk.* (ed. 5) 431/1 The fudge is poured into an oiled tin or caramel bars and cut up as soon as it is firm. **1971** *Islander* (Victoria, B.C.) 18 July 2/1 A batch of fudge which all enjoyed.

fudge (fʌdʒ), *v.* [app. an onomatopœic alteration of FADGE *v.*, with vowel expressive of more clumsy action.]

1. *trans.* To fit together or adjust in a clumsy, makeshift, or dishonest manner; to patch or 'fake' *up*; to 'cook' accounts. Often in schoolboy language: To make (a problem) look as if it had been correctly worked, by altering figures; to conceal the defects of (a map or other drawing) by adjustment of the parts, so that no glaring disproportion is observed; and in other like uses. Cf. FADGE *v.* 3. Often with *up*.

The first quot. is open to doubt, as the word may be a misprint for *fridged*.

1674 N. FAIRFAX *Bulk & Selv.* Ep. Ded., They may..be ..fudged up into such a smirkish liveliness, as may last as long as the Summers warmth holds on. **1771** LUCKOMBE *Printing* 498 *Fudge*, to contrive without necessary Materials or do Work in a bungling Manner. **1861** SALA *Dutch Pictures* xvi. 255 Do they go to chapel in surplices, and fudge impositions? **1867** MISS BRADDON *Birds of Prey* I. ii, Any one who can fudge up the faintest pretence of a claim to it. **1879** F. POLLOK *Sport Brit. Burmah* II. 99 They fudged their accounts so as to give little or no trouble to the almighty control department. **1886** C. D. WARNER *Their Pilgrim.* xiv. 297 A stout resolute matron..with a lot of cotton lace fudged about her neck. **1890** W. WESTCOTT in *Brit. Med. Jrnl.* 15 Mar. 620 The root of the white bryony..is sometimes fudged up by dealers to imitate the mandrake root.

absol. **1888** RYE *Record-searching* 9 Straining coincidences, presuming identities, and fudging judiciously.

b. To thrust *in* awkwardly or irrelevantly; to foist *in*.

1776 FOOTE *Bankrupt* III. Wks. 1799 II. 128 That last suppose is fudged in. **1824** *Blackw. Mag.* XVI. 708 This adjected part of the plan, which has been fudged in with so much unnecessary haste.

c. *Naut. to fudge a day's work*: to work a dead reckoning by rapid 'rule of thumb' methods.

1830 MARRYAT *King's Own* viii, He could *fudge* a day's work. **1836** —— *Midsh. Easy* xviii, Before they arrived at Malta, Jack could fudge a day's work.

2. *intr.* To fit in with what is anticipated, come off; also, to turn out, result; = FADGE *v.* 4.

Is *fadge* the true reading in these passages?

1615 CHAMBERLAIN *Let.* 15 June in *Crt. & Times Jas. I* (1849) I. 366 Sir Fulk Greville is once more in speech to be made a baron..but, if that fudge not, the Bishop of Winchester is in the way to be lord privy seal. **1829** SCOTT *Jrnl.* 2 Feb., We will see how this will fudge. **1831** *Ibid.* 20 Jan., We will see how the matter fudges.

3. [f. FUDGE *int.* or *sb.*] To talk nonsense, tell 'crams'. Also quasi-*trans.*

1834 *Tait's Mag.* I. 205 The Duchess..feeds, flatters and fudges them into allegiance. **1884** *Chester Gloss.*, *Fudge*, to talk nonsense; especially with the intent to *cram* another person.

Hence **fudged** *ppl. a.*, **'fudging** *vbl. sb.*

1860 R. F. BURTON *Centr. Afr.* I. v. 132 He had..an addiction to 'fudging', which rendered the severest overseeing necessary. **1885** RYE *Hist. Norfolk* 226 A lot of fudged heraldry. **1895** *Edin. Rev.* Apr. 465 A circular dome can easily be raised with only a little fudging of the surfaces.

fudge-wheel. [? f. FUDGE *v.* + WHEEL *sb.*] (See quot.)

1874 KNIGHT *Dict. Mech.* I. 921 *Fudge-wheel* (Shoemaking), a tool to ornament the edge of a sole.

fudgy ('fʌdʒɪ), *a.* [? f. FUDGE *v.* + -Y¹.]

1. Fretful, irritable, uneasy.

1819 *Blackw. Mag.* V. 677 [He] kept running to and fro like a wasp without a sting, very fierce and fudgy. **1883** *Hants Gloss.* s.v., They young cows are apt to be fudgy in milking.

2. *U.S.* Botched, bungling, awkward.

1872 C. D. WARNER *Saunterings* (1883) 156 There is some fashion, in a fudgy quaint way, here in Munich.

Fuegian (fuː'iːdʒɪən, 'fweɪdʒɪən), *a.* and *sb.* [f. the name Tierra del *Fuego*, lit. 'land of fire' + -IAN.] **A.** *adj.* Of or pertaining to Tierra del Fuego, or its inhabitants. **B.** *sb.* One of a primitive people inhabiting this S. American archipelago.

1825 J. WEDDELL *Voy. towards S. Pole* vi. 148 It was not long before the Fuegians arrived within hearing; and soon made themselves known by a singing noise. *Ibid.* 161 According to the Fuegian mode of salutation, they soon commenced shouting. **1871** C. M. YONGE *Pioneers & Founders* x. 273 The Fuegians are as degraded a people as any on the face of the earth. *Ibid.* 274 The poor little ship.. drifting near the Fuegian coast. **1890** W. JAMES *Princ. Psychol.* II. xix. 110 The Fuegians, in Darwin's voyage, wondered at the small boats,..but took the big ship as a 'matter of course'. **1900** J. G. FRAZER *Golden Bough* (ed. 2) I. i. 120 Fuegian wizards throw shells against the wind to make it drop. **1918** G. B. SHAW in *W.E.A. Educ. Yearbk. 1918* 22 A certificate classing you with a Fuegian or with Plato or Shakespear. **1931** *Times Lit. Suppl.* 5 Mar. 167/2 Tasmanian or Fuegian equivalents of eternity, omniscience and so on. **1969** *Nature* 6 Dec. 974/1 Once round the Horn, the three pathetic Fuegians who had spent a year or so in Britain..landed.

Fuehrer: see FÜHRER.

fueillemort(e: see FEUILLEMORTE, FILEMOT.

fuel ('fjuːəl), *sb.* Forms: 4–5 fewaile, 5–6 -all, 5–8 -el(l, 4–5 fowayle, 5 -aly, -el(l, 4 *Sc.* fwaill, 4–7 fuell(e, 8 feuel, 7– fuel. [a. OF. *fowaille*, *feuaile*:—popular L. *focālia*, neut. pl. of *focālis* adj., f. *focus* fire: see FOCUS. In the mediæval Lat. of France and England *focalia* pl., *focale* or *focalium* sing., frequently occur in charters with reference to the obligation to furnish or the right to demand supplies of fuel.]

1. a. Material for burning, combustible matter as used in fires, etc.

1398 TREVISA *Barth. De P.R.* xv. cix. (1495) 528 In many places the grounde is glewy: and of it they make good fuell. *c* **1400** MAUNDEV. (Roxb.) xxvii. 126 Men..driez bestez dung and brynnez for defaute of fewaile. *c* **1450** *Bk. Curtasye* 385 in *Babees Bk.* 311 Fuelle þat schalle brenne In halle. **1548** FORREST *Pleas. Poesye* 347 Meate, clothe, and fewell withe the same to bye. **1632** LITHGOW *Trav.* x. 497 Divers kinds of Coale, and earth fewell. **1727** SWIFT *Gulliver* III. i. 180 Dry grass and sea-weed which I intended for feuel. **1815** ELPHINSTONE *Acc. Caubul* (1842) I. 381 Shrubs, which ..serve for fuel. **1827** FARADAY *Chem. Manip.* iv. 98 The fuel to be used in furnaces..coal, coke, and charcoal.

¶ In the poem of *Coer de Lion*, which contains the earliest known examples of the word in Eng., it seems to be used for 'victuals, provisions', perh. by a misinterpretation of the OF. phrase *bouche et fouaille* 'meat and fuel', which seems to have been current as a general expression for the necessaries of life; cf. the quots. from Barbour below.

13.. *Coer de L.* 1471 No man selle hem no fowayle. *Ibid.* 1545 ' Swylk fowayle as we bought yistyrday, For no catel get I may.' Rychard aunsweryd..'Off froyt here is gret plentе!'. **1375** BARBOUR *Bruce* IV. 64 The castell weill vittalit thai, With met and fwaill can purvay. *Ibid.* 170 [Thai] na wittaill na fwaill had.

b. *fig.*; *esp.* something that serves to feed or inflame passion, excitement, or the like.

c **1580** C'TESS PEMBROKE *Ps.* cxlvii. 3 [He] Fuell of life to mountaine cattaile yieldes. **1596** DRAYTON *Legends* iii. 147 My blandishments were Fuell to that fire. **1641** J. JACKSON *True Evang. T.* III. 206 They foment, and adde fuell to their inimicitious qualities. **1681** TEMPLE *Mem.* III. Wks. 1731 I. 339 Lord Shaftsbury had been busie in preparing Fewel for next Session. **1709** STEELE *Tatler* No. 150 ¶6 Where each Party is always laying up Fuel for Dissention. **1818** JAS. MILL *Brit. India* II. IV. viii. 273 This elevation added fuel to the ambition of Hyder. **1835** THIRLWALL *Greece* I. viii. 299 Enjoyments which could supply fuel to private cupidity. **1855** BAIN *Senses & Int.* III. iii. §13 Difficulty adds fuel to the flame.

2. (With *a* and *pl.*) A kind of fuel. †Also *pl.* in collective sense, articles serving as fuel.

1626 BACON *Sylva* §775 Turf, and Peat, and Cow-sheards are cheap Fewels, and last long. *a* **1694** M. ROBINSON *Autobiog.* (1856) 60 That none should be troublesome to their neighbours by cutting their wood or breaking their fuels. **1776** ADAM SMTH *W.N.* I. xi. II. (1869) I. 176 Coals are a less agreeable fuel than wood. **1858** LARDNER *Hand-bk. Nat. Phil.* 386 This fuel, like coal, consists principally of carbon and hydrogen in various proportions. **1894** *Daily News* 25 May 2/6 Mr. G. Stockfleth read a paper on 'Liquid Fuels'.

3. Specific senses, related more or less closely to senses 1 and 2.

Senses b and c below are properly regarded as uses of senses 1 and 2 in specific contexts. Senses a and d represent two extensions in sense, more or less corresponding to similar extensions in the meaning of *burn* vb. and *combustion*.

a. Food, regarded as that which supplies the body with energy; those constituents of food which are utilized by the body to produce energy. (Usu. as a conscious metaphor.)

1876 A. H. CHURCH *Food* I. i. 1 In the case of the human body we likewise have, first, a material structure; secondly, fuel, in the form of our daily rations of food. **1902** W. G. THOMPSON *Pract. Dietetics* (ed. 2) I. 9 If water is withheld, preventing the transportation of the fuel and oxygen to various parts of the body, death follows in about two to seven days or more. **1949** L. J. BOGERT *Nutrition & Physical Fitness* viii. 121 Calorie values are especially useful in thinking or talking of food as body fuel. **1952** MCLESTER & DARBY *Nutrition & Diet* (ed. 6) iii. 39 In the calculation of fuel requirements, the physician will not go far astray if he adds to the physiologic basal metabolism some 10 per cent to cover the cost of the specific dynamic action of the ingested food. **1964** A. Z. BAKER *Dietetics & Nutrition* ii. 21 When other energy-releasing foods are lacking, as in starvation, body proteins are used as fuel. **1968** PASSMORE & ROBSON *Compan. Med. Studies* I. iv. 2 The fuels of the body are carbohydrate, fat, protein and ethyl alcohol, taken in the diet. **1970** FISHER & BENDER *Value of Food* i. 19 When fuel, for example glucose, is burned oxygen is used and carbon dioxide is formed.

b. (A kind of) liquid or other material which by its combustion with air in an internal combustion engine provides power.

1886 D. CLERK *Gas Engine* i. 23 The fuel..is, in the gas engine, introduced directly to the motive cylinder and burned there. It is indeed part of the working fluid. **1902** A. C. HARMSWORTH et al. *Motors* xii. 243 Instead of the combustible or fuel being burned..in the cylinder of the engine, as in the internal combustion engine of the petrol car, it is burned under a boiler. *c* **1915** *Autocar Handbk.* (ed. 6) iii. 61 The function of the carburetter is to convert the liquid fuel (petrol in most cases) into a gas. **1918** V. W. PAGÉ *Aviation Engines* v. 110 The power obtained from the gas-engine depends upon the combustion of fuel in the cylinders. **1955** *Times* 26 Aug. 4/5 In a conventional jet engine all the air is compressed and then heated by the injection of burning fuel. **1963** C. CAMPBELL *Sports Car Engine* iv. 61 The commercial motor fuels sold to-day are all blended to conform to a very narrow specification.

c. (A kind of) material which reacts with an oxidizer to produce thrust (in a rocket engine) or electricity (in a fuel cell). Also *loosely*, a propellant.

1922 *Trans. Faraday Soc.* XVII. 467 If..natural fuel consisted of metallic zinc—not coal—it could be burnt in primary cells to give electrical power directly. **1929** R. H. GODDARD *Papers* (1970) II. 662 Construction and tests of rocket having same fuel capacity as large rocket previously used in tests of lifting power. *Ibid.* 675 The ascent [of the rocket] was about 100 feet, the horizontal distance being much greater, but there was fuel enough to last about half a minute. **1947** W. LEY *Rockets & Space Travel* (1948) x. 238 For the more distant future one may speculate on monatomic hydrogen as a rocket fuel. **1952** E. BURGESS *Rocket Propulsion* i. 14 Essentially then, the rocket consists of two tanks containing a fuel and an oxidiser and these two propellants are forced into a combustion chamber. **1962** A. SHEPARD in *Into Orbit* 97 At 3:30 A.M., with the liquid oxygen fuel already loaded aboard the booster, the technicians..declared a hold. **1966** *McGraw-Hill Encycl. Sci. & Technol.* V. 551/2 Modern fuel cells use gaseous fuels, either H_2 or CO or mixtures of these gases. The oxidizer is normally oxygen or air. **1970** C. M. BEIGHLEY et al. in G. A. Partel *Space Engin.* 167 Current operational propellants are based on hydrogen and hydrogen-rich compounds of carbon and nitrogen as fuels and oxygen or oxygen-based oxidizers.

d. *Nuclear Sci.* (A kind of) material used as a source of energy in a nuclear reactor; material that can support a self-sustaining chain reaction.

1946 *Edison Electric Inst. Bull.* Jan. 23/3 Large power and heating plants using atomic fuel. **1948** *Nature* 28 Aug. 318/1 Uranium 235, the only naturally occurring, or 'primary', nuclear fuel must be made to breed 'secondary' fuel from more abundant materials: either plutonium from uranium 238 or U233 from thorium. **1950** GLASSTONE *Sourcebk. Atomic Energy* xiv. 402/2 In the construction of a breeder reactor, the fertile material..may form a blanket or reflecting shield surrounding the core of fuel. **1962** F. I. ORDWAY et al. *Basic Astronautics* x. 421 Less than 1 percent of the uranium fuel will be fissioned in present rocket engine reactors. **1963** B. FOZARD *Instrumentation Nucl. Reactors* xiii. 158 For a given core arrangement the reactivity depends upon the balance between the amount of neutron-producing material (fuel) and the amount of neutron-absorbing material (absorber).

4. a. *attrib.* and *Comb.*, as ***fuel consumption, economy, -forest, -house, -log, tank, -wood; fuel economic*** adj.

1890 W. ROBINSON *Gas & Petroleum Engines* i. 6 The total *fuel consumption..was only 1·2 lb. per indicated horse-power per hour. **1907** WOODWARD & PRESTON tr. *Sorel's Carbureting & Combustion in Alcohol Engines* i. 18 It is probable that for any given engine the fuel consumption is also affected by the quantity and temperature of cooling water used. **1971** *Selling Today* Sept. 4/2 Devices for cutting fuel consumption are frequently advertised as bringing about substantial savings in motoring costs. **1975** *Aviation Week & Space Technol.* 10 Nov. 87/1 Laminar flow control ..is one technology—which NASA separates from the *fuel economic aircraft studies. **1983** *Punch* 27 Apr. 69/2 These are incorporated in the full range of Pirelli tyres, from the highly successful P4 and P6 to the fuel-economic P8. **1904** BOOTH & KERSHAW (*title*) Smoke prevention and *fuel economy. **1932** *Economist* 2 Jan. 9/2 Continental makers had no advantage over Great Britain in coal. But that undoubtedly stimulated European pursuit of important methods of fuel economy. **1979** *Washington Post* 12 Aug. A2/1 More efficient and durable products and buildings, automobiles with higher fuel economy, [etc.]. **1895** *Daily News* 16 May 6/5 A French *fuel forest. **1807** VANCOUVER *Agric. Devon* (1813) 473 *Fuel-house. **1897** MARY KINGSLEY *W. Africa* 126 One half of her deck is dedicated to *fuel logs. **1900** A. H. GOLDINGHAM *Oil Engines* i. 13 The oil is stored under pressure in the *fuel-tank. **1935** *Economist* 7 Dec. 1144/2 The adoption of fuel pressure systems..has enabled the fuel tank to be located in a non-vulnerable position. **1959** *Observer* 1 Mar. 21/5 Twin fuel tanks in the rear wings leave space for a big, deep trunk. **1668** WILKINS *Real Char.* 330 Hay, Straw, *Fewel wood. **1823** in Cobbett *Rur. Rides* (1885) I. 361 There is a good deal of fuel-wood.

b. Special comb.: †**fuel-bear** (see quot. and BIER); **fuel cell**, a primary cell which consumes fuel continuously and converts its chemical energy directly into electrical energy; **fuel-economizer**, a contrivance for saving fuel in an engine or furnace; **fuel efficiency**, the efficient use of fuel in an engine or other system; the capacity of an engine to obtain energy from fuel; also **fuel-efficient** *a.*; **fuel element**, an assemblage of nuclear fuel with other materials to form a unit for use in a reactor; also ***fuel rod***; **fuel-feeder** (see quot.); **fuel food**, food that is rich in fats or carbohydrates and therefore provides the body with energy, in contrast to food that is of value chiefly because of the vitamins or trace elements it contains; **fuel-gas**, gas intended for use as fuel; **fuel injection**, the direct introduction of fuel under pressure into the combustion chamber or its intakes in an internal combustion engine; so **fuel injector**, the nozzle through which the fuel is forced, with its associated valve mechanism; **fuel oil**, oil used as fuel in an engine or furnace; **fuel-value**, (*a*) the value of a combustible article as fuel; (*b*) the value of food as a source of energy; the amount of energy obtained by the body from a given quantity of food.

1612 STURTEVANT *Metallica* (1854) 117 The *Fewell-beare is a generall part of a Furnace which beareth and holdeth the fewell and fire. **1922** *Trans. Faraday Soc.* XVII. 482 *Fuel cells may be classified as—(1) Direct fuel-cells burning solid fuel... (2) Semi-direct fuel-cells burning gaseous fuel... (3) Indirect cells of (*a*) Oxidation-reduction Type... (*b*) Metal Anode Type. **1956** *Engineer* 20 July 93 (*heading*) High-pressure hydrogen-oxygen fuel cell. **1969** *New Scientist* 13 Nov. (Energy Suppl.) 16/2 Both the *Gemini* and *Apollo* programmes relied on fuel cells of different kinds for their power. **1880** *Engineering* 2 Apr. 262 An arrangement of *fuel economiser. **1974** *Science* 19 Apr. 265/1 The present concern with *fuel efficiency in industry follows a wave of unprecedented oil price increases. **1978** *Newsweek* (Atlantic ed.) 25 Sept. 39/2 The EPA fuel-efficiency standards have left their mark on every automaker. **1982** *Gloss. Terms Solid Mineral Fuels* (Standards Assoc. Austral.) VI. 5 *Fuel efficiency*, the proportion of the potential heat of a fuel converted into a required form of energy. **1986** *Financial Times* 6 Aug. 8/2 This in turn leads to lower weight, improved fuel efficiency and quieter operation. **1975** *Business Week* 20 Jan. 82/1 Detroit must learn to build cars that are both *fuel-efficient and reasonably priced. **1979** *Time* 2 Apr. 21/2 With only two engines and a 'supercritical' wing that cuts aerodynamic drag, it is the most fuel-efficient commercial jet flying today. **1951** *Nucleonics* Nov. 20/1 The fission products gradually build up inside these sealed *fuel elements. **1970** *Nature* 26 Dec. 1245/2 Among the recent innovations is the introduction of fuel elements in the form of large blocks of graphite with machined holes to carry tubular pins. **1874** KNIGHT *Dict. Mech.* I. 921 **Fuel-feeder*, a device for feeding fuel in graduated quantities to a furnace. **1905** *Daily Chron.* 14 July 4/4 At the present period of year there is comparatively little demand for *fuel-food. **1944** J. S. HUXLEY *On Living in Rev.* xiii. 134 The civilian population ..will have been going short of vitamins and fuel-foods. **1886** *Jrnl. Franklin Inst.* CXXI. 311 Some form of *fuel-gas will be manufactured to take its place. **1900** A. H. GOLDINGHAM *Oil Engines* 53 This method of *fuel injection forms the subject-matter of U.S. patent 650,583, granted to the writer May 29, 1900. **1941** *Nature* 26 July 105/1 The Minister of Aircraft Production..mentioned that where the British aero engine industry uses the carburettor, the Germans have adopted the fuel injection system. **1966** *McGraw-Hill Encycl. Sci. & Technol.* V. 555/2 In engines with continuous combustion, such as gas turbines and liquid-fueled rockets, fuel injection is necessary because the pumping action of piston-type engines is unavailable to draw fuel into the combustion chamber. **1914** HISCOX & PAGÉ *Gas, Gasoline & Oil-Engines* (ed. 21) xvii. 458 The *fuel injectors are of the orthodox pattern with oil-spreading plates. **1962** F. I. ORDWAY et al. *Basic Astronautics* x. 401 The combustion chamber contains the fuel injectors, spark plugs, flame holder, and the exhaust nozzle. **1893** *Power* Mar. 6 A contract..for the supply of all *fuel oil required during 1893. **1957** 'N. SHUTE' *On Beach* i. 4 He had returned to Williamstown in *Anzac* on the last of her fuel oil. **1947** C. GOODMAN *Sci. & Engin. Nuclear Power* I. 319 Solid *fuel rods, clad with a non-corrosive metallic coating. **1886** *Lett. fr. Donegal* 36 Bog once 'cut out' does not grow again, and the *fuel-value is permanently lost to the land. **1902** W. G. THOMPSON *Pract. Dietetics* (ed. 2) I. 13 A day labourer requires 0·28 pound of protein per diem plus enough fat and carbohydrate to yield a total fuel value of 3,500 calories. **1928** A. B. CALLOW *Food & Health* 18 Water cannot be burnt in the body, and therefore has no fuel-value. **1949** L. J. BOGERT *Nutrition & Physical Fitness* viii. 122 In general, the foods with high fuel value will be seen to be those which are either rich in fat or low in water content. **1964** H. H. MITCHELL *Comp. Nutrition Man & Dom. Anim.* II. xviii. 480 In terms commonly used in human nutrition, the fuel value or available energy in the diet would be 2745 cal.

fuel ('fjuːəl), *v.* [f. prec. sb.]

1. *trans.* To feed or furnish with fuel. *lit.* and *fig.*

c **1592** MARLOWE *Massacre Paris* I. i, The native sparks of princely love..May still be fuell'd in our progeny. **1609** W. M. *Man in Moone* (1849) 12 Five chimnies, well fewel'd, vent not more smoake then his mouth and nostrils. **1647** COWLEY *Mistress, Despair* ii, That dreadful Name, Which fewels the infernal Flame. *a* **1711** KEN *Hymnarium* Poet. Wks. 1721 II. 130 Wealth fuel'd Sin. **1733** CHEYNE *Eng. Malady* II. viii. §8 (1734) 204 Neglecting the Means, or fuelling the Disease by a Mal-regimen. **1811** W. R. SPENCER *Poems* 120 Whose fires are not lighted and fuel'd by Love. **1817** COLERIDGE *Sibyl. Leaves* (1862) 129 The magic cauldron of a fervid and ebullient fancy, constantly fuelled by an unexampled opulence of language. **1859** LD. LYTTON *Wanderer* 169 We fuel ourselves, I conceive, The fire the Fiend lights. **1869** BLACKMORE *Lorna D.* xvi, I would not put a trunk of wood on the fire in the kitchen, but let Annie ..fuel it. **1950** F. GAYNOR *Encycl. Atomic Energy* 62 The Los Alamos fast-neutron reactor..is 'fuelled' by plutonium. **1950** *Sci. Amer.* Mar. 11/2 In the President's first announcement of the Hiroshima atomic bomb, it was stated that the bomb drew its energy from the same source that fuels the sun and the stars. **1962** A. SHEPARD in *Into Orbit* 99 The crews started fuelling the Redstone with liquid oxygen shortly after midnight. **1970** *Guardian* 15 Apr. 5/6 Students who raided administrative files discovered that outside complaints had been recorded... This fuelled suspicion at other universities.

2. *intr.* To get fuel.

1880 DIXON *Windsor* IV. ii. 14 Poor people had enjoyed the right of fuelling in the park.

†'**fuelist.** *Obs. rare.* [f. FUEL + -IST.] One who supplies fuel.

1664 EVELYN *Sylva* (1776) 538 First that our Fuelist begin with the Underwood. **1736** in BAILEY (folio).

fuellage, obs. form of FOLIAGE.

fuelled ('fjuːəld), *ppl. a.* [f. FUEL + -ED[1].] Furnished with fuel.

1624 WOTTON *Elem. Arch.* in *Reliq.* (1651) 203 Some [of the precepts for well-building] are plainly Oeconomicall; as that the seat be well-watered and well fuelled. **1667** MILTON *P.L.* I. 234 Thundring Ætna, whose combustible And fewel'd entrals, etc. **1730–46** THOMSON *Autumn* 502 The fuel'd chimney blazes wide. **1772** MURPHY *Grecian Dau.* IV. ii, The fuelled entrails [of mount Ætna] summon all their rage.

fueller ('fjuːələ(r)). Now *rare.* [f. FUEL *v.* + -ER[1].] One who or that which supplies fuel for fires. Also, the domestic who makes the fires, and *fig.*

14.. *Nom.* in Wr.-Wülcker 688/32 *Hic focarius*, a fewyller. **1483** *Cath. Angl.* 145/1 Fueller (*A.* Feweller), *focarius.* **1591** PERCIVALL *Sp. Dict.*, *Leñador*, a fueller, a wood carrier. **1601** CHETTLE & MUNDAY *Death Earl of Huntington* I. in Hazl. *Dodsley* VIII. 235 See the fueller Suffer the cook to want no wood. *a* **1603** T. CARTWRIGHT *Confut. Rhem. N.T.* (1618) 738 Let vs see what fine fuellers they be in the Popes kichen that they can make the Purgatorie fire so cunningly. **1647** C. HARVEY *Sch. Heart* (Grosart) 122 See how hell's fueller his bellowes plies Blowing the fire that burnt too fast before. **1720** STRYPE *Stow's Surv.* (1754) II. v. xiv. 313/2 The Carmen..were incorporated with the people called Fuellers by the name of woodmongers. **1892** *Columbus* (Ohio) *Dispatch* 5 May, The fuelers..desire to help the cargo loaders.

fuelless ('fjuːəllɪs), *a.* [f. FUEL *sb.* + -LESS.] Destitute of fuel.

1897 *Sat. Rev.* LXXXIII. 251/2 The party entered the fuelless wastes of the Barren Land.

fuelling ('fjuːəlɪŋ), *vbl. sb.* [f. FUEL *v.* + -ING[1].] The action of laying in, or furnishing with, fuel; supply or storage of fuel. Also *attrib.* and *transf.*

1921 *19th Cent.* June 1063 At each port, facilities for fuelling and for receiving the various supplies which a fleet requires must..be forthcoming. *Ibid.* 1068 There are numerous minor ports available as temporary fuelling bases. **1927** *Glasgow Herald* 14 July 11 The broad Imperial development of the science of fuelling. **1949** W. G. MOORE *Dict. Geogr.* (1950) 67 *Fuelling station*, a port, or a repository within a port, which supplies fuel in the form of coal or oil to ocean-going vessels, which are unable to carry enough in their bunkers for their complete voyage. **1971** *Sunday Times* (Johannesburg) (Business Section) 28 Mar. 6/7 The outlook for commerce is delicately poised between dampening factors..and the fuelling factors—salary increases and expected price rises.

†'**fuellize**, *v. Obs.* [f. FUEL *sb.* + -IZE.] *trans.* To supply with fuel, feed.

1631 R. H. *Arraignm. Whole Creature* v. 33 Whom the ordinary Creatures cannot content in fuellizing and refreshing Nature. *Ibid.* xiii. §2. 203 Imagining to satisfie Lust, by fuellizing and feeding it.

fuerse, obs. form of FIERCE.

fuff (fʌf), *sb.* Chiefly *Sc.* [f. next vb.]

1. A puff of wind; also a sound resembling this; the 'spit' of a cat; a whiff (of tobacco-smoke).

1535 LYNDESAY *Satyre* 2137 Ane fistand flag; a flagartie fuffe. **1804** TARRAS *Poems* 67 Something hin' her wi' a skyte, Gat up, an' gied a fuff. **1816** SCOTT *Antiq.* ix, 'The ghaist..

then disappeared like a fuff o' tobacco.' **1881** STEVENSON *Thrawn Janet* in *Cornhill Mag.* XLIV. 443 'There cam' a clap o' wund, like a cat's fuff.' **1895** *United Presb. Mag.* Apr. 167 The stillness was unbroken save by the cheerful fuff of the fire.

2. A burst of ill temper; 'huff', 'fume'.

1834 CARLYLE *Let.* 28 Jan. in Froude *Remin.* (1882) II. 410 What a miserable fuff thou gettest into, poor old exasperated politician! **1838** MRS. CARLYLE *Lett.* (1883) I. 102, I have put the Stimabile in a great fuff. **1893** STEVENSON *Catriona* 235 The causelessness of all this fuff stirred my own bile.

3. ? A soft feathery mass. (Cf. *fluff*.)

1700 S. L. tr. *Fryke's Voy. E. Ind.* 47 The Leaves [of the coco-nut tree] spread themselves all in a fuff, and the Nutts under them.

fuff (fʌf), *v. Sc.* and *dial.* [echoic. Cf. FAFFLE, *faff* dial.]

1. *intr.* To puff. Said of a breeze, fire, etc.; also, of a person in anger or out of breath. Also, ***to fume and fuff, fuff and pegh.***

1513 DOUGLAS *Æneis* VIII. vii. 120 The hait fyr Dois fuf and blaw in blesis byrnand schyr. **1721** RAMSAY *Elegy Patie Birnie* iii, When strangers landed..Fuffin an peghing, he wad gang, And crave their pardon that sae lang He'd been a coming. **1756** MRS. CALDERWOOD *Jrnl.* vii. (1884) 204 She fuffed and kindled, if they but opened their mouth. **1819** W. TENNANT *Papistry Storm'd* (1827) 160 For ane that gat in o' that rout, Ten fuffin' stood a while thairout. **1822** HOGG *Perils of Man* II. 39 He brings me in mind o' a barrel o' beer, fuming and fuffing. **1864** *Athenæum* No. 1928. 456/2 It was a smithy, fuffing, glowing. **1876** *Whitby Gloss.*, *Fuff*, to puff, as a breeze does.

b. To go *away* or *off* with a puff. *lit.* and *fig.*

1822 GALT *Sir A. Wylie* III. xviii. 150 'He fuffed awa wi a' his gowd and gear to Miss Jenny'. **1892** *Northumbld. Gloss.* s.v., The poother fuffed off iv a jiffy.

2. Of a cat or tiger: To 'spit'.

a **1693** [see the vbl. sb.]. **1840** MRS. CARLYLE *Lett.* (1883) I. 124 Coiled up and fuffing like a young tiger about to spring.

3. *trans.* To puff (a tobacco-pipe). Also, to send *out* (steam) with a fuff.

1787 BURNS *Halloween* xiii, She fuff't her pipe wi' sic a lunt. **1818** SCOTT *Hrt. Midl.* xlv, 'Reuben Butler isna the man I take him to be, if he disna learn the Captain to fuff his pipe some other gate than in God's house.' **1894** CROCKETT *Raiders* 240 The pot boiled and fuffed out little puffs of steam.

Hence **'fuffing** *vbl. sb.* and *ppl. a.*

1687 COLVIL *Whigs Supplic.* (1751) 151 Batrons..Doth fall a fuffing, and a mewing, While monkeys are the chesnuts chewing. *a* **1693** URQUHART *Rabelais* III. xiii. 107 Mioling of Tygers, bruzzing of Bears, sussing [*read* fuffing (Jam.)] of Kitnings. **1822** HOGG *Perils of Man* II. 231, 'I should hae said something in return, but..I was like to fa' to the fuffing and greeting.' **1895** CROCKETT *Men of Mosshags* 165 'Them that steals..burns in muckle hell—bleezin' up in fuffin' lowes.'

fuff (fʌf), *int. Sc.* **a.** Used to imitate a sound. **b.** An exclamation of contempt.

1780 MAYNE *Siller Gun* II. xli, Fuff play'd the priming—heels owr ither, They fell in shairn! **1804** TARRAS *Poems* 4 Fuff, Robie man! chear up your dowie saul!

fuffle ('fʌf(ə)l), *v. Sc. rare.* [onomatopœic.] *trans.* To throw into disorder; to jerk about; to hustle, treat with contumely. Hence **'fuffled** *ppl. a.* Also **'fuffle** *sb.*, violent exertion, fuss.

1536 LYNDESAY *Answ. Kingis Flyting* 54 That feynd, with fuffilling of hir roistit hoch, Caist doun the fat. **1635** D. DICKSON *Pract. Writ.* (1845) I. 177 Thou must be content instead of favour to be fuffled. **1801** HOGG *Sc. Pastorals* 14 When muckle Pate, wi' desp'rate fuffle, Had at Poltowa won the scuffle. **1819** W. TENNANT *Papistry Storm'd* (1827) 66 He saw the Vicar..In fuffel'd garb, and plicht ungainly.

fuffy ('fʌfɪ), *a. Sc.* and *north. dial.* [f. FUFF *sb.* + -Y[1].]

1. Light and soft.

1824 in *Craven Gloss.* **1851** S. JUDD *Margaret* xvii. (1871) 147 She mounted the high, white, fuffy plain [of snow]. **1876** *Whitby Gloss.*, *Fuffy*, light, soft, and fraught with dust, like a fuzz-ball.

2. 'Huffy', 'touchy'.

1858 M. PORTEOUS *Souter Johnny* 30 Nocht invites Your fuffy bardship, mair nor see His Satellites.

‖**fufu** ('fu:fu:). *West African.* (See quots.) (See also FOO-FOO.)

1740 C. LESLIE *New Hist. Jamaica* ii. 33 And boil it with beaten Maiz or Indian Corn, (which they call Fu Fu). **1863** *Wand. W. Africa* II. 144 'Fufu' is composed of yam, plaintain, or casava; it is peeled, boiled, pounded and made into balls. **1888** *Daily News* 17 July 5/3 Plantains..form the staple of food with the natives, who beat them up into fufu. **1930** *Discovery* Mar. 99/1 The various vegetables used for making the soups or sauces which flavour their *fu-fu*, a kind of porridge. **1959** *Guardian* 24 Oct. 4/5 Quantities of jollof rice and fufu were placed round about.

fug (fʌg), *sb. colloq.* (orig *dial.* and *School slang*). [? Related to FOGO. Cf. FUGGY *a.*] A thick, close, stuffy atmosphere, esp. that of a room overcrowded and with little or no ventilation. Also **fug-footer, -soccer, -socker** *School* and *University slang*, indoor football.

1888 E. F. BENSON *Sks. fr. Marlborough* i. 16 Seating himself in the most comfortable chair, as a consolation for the prevailing fug. **1905** C. RANGER-GULL *Harvest of Love* i. 10 He met a group of school-house boys carrying a round football. They had been playing 'fug-soccer' in the racquet courts. **1914** C. MACKENZIE *Sinister St.* II. III. viii. 663 Nigel had booked himself to play fug-socker with three hearty Trindogs of Trinity. **1915** 'BARTIMEUS' *A Tall Ship* iv. 78 We get up quite a good fug in our case-mate at night. *Ibid.* ix. 171 'Pouf!' he exclaimed. 'What a fug!' And elevated his nose with a sniff. **1923** U. L. SILBERRAD *Lett. J. Armiter* x. 214 Can you smell the cold damp fug of those wet Sunday afternoons..? **1925** *Chambers's Jrnl.* 556/1 The 'fug' that could be got up inside these huts was sheer bliss to many a trench-weary soldier during the war. **1927** W. DEEPING *Kitty* xvii, It [*sc.* a sickroom] smelt like a greenhouse, full of soft fug. **1940** M. MARPLES *Pub. Sch. Slang* 85 *Fug-footer* (Harrow, 1884 +), indoor football. **1948** G. H. JOHNSTON *Death takes Small Bites* i. 29 The fug of the room. **1968** J. E. MATTHEWS *Brew's Youth & Youth Groups* (ed. 2) x. 149 There are only three necessities—light, ..warmth, and if we cater for boys this often means a 'fug'—and comradeship.

Hence **fug** *v. intr.*, to stay in a stuffy atmosphere. Also with *up*. Hence **fugged** *ppl. a.*, stuffy, thick.

1889 BARRÈRE & LELAND *Dict. Slang* I. 387/2 *To fug* (Shrewsbury), to stay in a close, stuffy room. **1919** W. T. GRENFELL *Labrador Doctor* (1920) ii. 35 Others were 'fugging' in the house or had gone to bed. **1921** A. S. M. HUTCHINSON *If Winter Comes* II. v. 122, I like it a jolly sight better than fugging up in those carriages with all that gassing crowd. **1971** H. C. RAE *Marksman* I. v. 45 The room was stuffy, fugged with tobacco smoke.

fug, Sc. form of FOG *sb.*[1]

fugacious (fju:'geɪʃəs), *a.* Also 7 **-atious.** [f. L. *fugāci-, fugax* (f. *fugĕre* to flee) + -OUS.]

1. Apt to flee away or flit. **a.** Of immaterial things: Tending to disappear, of short duration; evanescent, fleeting, transient, fugitive.

1634 RAINBOW *Labour* (1635) A ij, Fugatious words, which escape the eares pursuit. *a* **1677** BARROW *Serm.* Wks. 1716 III. 53 A thing most fugacious and slippery. **1722** WOLLASTON *Relig. Nat.* ix. 206 With at best only a few deceitful, little, fugacious pleasures interspersed. **1774** WARTON *Hist. Eng. Poetry* xli. III. 433, I owe this information to the manuscript papers of these fugacious anecdotes. **1817** W. TAYLOR in *Monthly Mag.* XLIV. 234 There is in the affection of poetic readers a something very fugacious. **1855** HT. MARTINEAU *Autobiog.* (1877) II. 226 The fugacious nature of life and time. **1865** MILL *Exam. Hamilton* 203 Colours, tastes, smells..being, in comparison, fugacious.

b. Of persons: †Ready to run away. Also *humorously* (of persons), fleeing; (of things) slippery. *rare.*

1651 J. F[REAKE] *Agrippa's Occ. Philos.* 557 The most fugatious of all the Gods. **1872** HOWELLS *Wedd. Journ.* 81 The oily slices of fugacious potatoes slipping about in the dish. **1885** *Harper's Mag.* Feb. 367/1 Aunt..chuckled away to herself at the retrospect of her own fugacious figure.

c. Of a material substance: Volatile.

1671 J. WEBSTER *Metallogr.* viii. 126 This *primum ens*..is a fugacious spirit. **1684** tr. *Bonet's Merc. Compit.* VI. 198 The fugacious poison departs as the Serum breaks out. **1794** G. ADAMS *Nat. & Exp. Philos.* I. xi. 433 No one..has analyzed the fugacious element of air with more success. **1823** *Mechanic's Mag.* No. 10. 160 From the highly fugacious nature of that part of coffee on which its fine flavour depends.

2. *Bot.* and *Zool.* Falling or fading early; soon cast off. Cf. CADUCOUS 1.

1750 G. HUGHES *Barbadoes* 35 An immoderate use of crude fugacious fruits..will likewise occasion a Diarrhœa. **1796** WITHERING *Brit. Plants* (ed. 3) IV. 288 Curtain white, delicate, fugacious, hanging in fragments at the edge of the pileus. **1796** C. MARSHALL *Garden.* ii. (1813) 16 Seed..may be extremely fugacious by its slight adhesion to the plant. **1874** COOKE *Fungi* (1875) 18 In some Agarics the ring is very fugacious or absent altogether. **1877–84** F. E. HULME *Wild Fl.* Ser. I. p. xiv, Petals..very fugacious.

Hence **fu'gaciously** *adv.*, **fu'gaciousness**.

1664 EVELYN *Kal. Hort.* Introd. 56 Well therefore did..Columella put his Gard'ner in mind of the fugaciousness of the Seasons. **1811** A. T. THOMSON *Lond. Disp.* (1830) 1011 Sulphuretted hydrogen is known to be contained in water..by its reddening the infusion of litmus fugaciously. **1821** *New Monthly Mag.* I. 160 The utter inanity and fugaciousness of all mortal grandeur. **1875** H. C. WOOD *Therap.* (1879) 116 The volatility of ammonia and the extreme fugaciousness of its action.

fugacity (fju:'gæsɪtɪ). [f. as prec. + -TY.] The quality of being fugacious; instability; transitoriness. Of a material substance: Volatility.

1656 BLOUNT *Glossogr.*, *Fugacity*, a readiness to run away, inconstancy, an inclination to flight. **1666** BOYLE *Orig. Formes & Qual.* 190 By our Experiment, its Fugacity is so restrain'd, that..the *Caput mortuum*..endured a good fire in the Retort. **1751** JOHNSON *Rambler* No. 143 ¶3 The deceitfulness of hope, the fugacity of pleasure, the fragility of beauty. **1807** F. WRANGHAM *Serm. Transl. Script.* 31 Considerations of the fugacity of time. **1830** LINDLEY *Nat. Syst. Bot.* 288 The acrid principle..notwithstanding its fugacity, has been lately obtained pure. **1841–44** EMERSON *Ess., Poet* (1876) II. 321 The accidency and fugacity of the symbol. **1868** BUSHNELL *Serm. Liv. Subj.* 281 The fugacities are left behind us.

Comb. **1894** *Brit. Jrnl. Photog.* XLI. 68 The fugacity-producing quality of this bath.

†**'fugacy.** *Obs.* [as if ad. L. **fugācia*, f. *fugax.*] Flight; also, the fact of being a fugitive slave.

c **1600** NORDEN *Spec. Brit., Cornw.* (1728) 2 Upon the fugacie of the conquered Britons. **1610** W. FOLKINGHAM *Art of Survey* III. iv. 71 All goods and chattels, which being stolne, are left or forsaken by the thiefe in his fugacie. *a* **1641** BP. MONTAGU *Acts & Mon.* (1642) 15 That earthly City, built up by Cain in the Land of his Banishment, and Fugacy from God. *a* **1661** HOLYDAY *Juvenal* 261 They were branded to express their fugacy with Φ or F.

fugade, var. of FOUGADE.

1687 J. RICHARDS *Jrnl. Siege Buda* 18 Those that went to the Left were..beaten off, by the springing of a Fugade.

fugal ('fju:gəl), *sb. Australian.* [short f. CENTRIFUGAL.] A centrifugal machine for drying wool.

1895 *Australian Pastoralist Rev.* 15 Aug. p. xii, Will dry more Wool at less cost than any other Fugal made.

fugal ('fju:gəl), *a.* [f. FUGUE + -AL[1].]

1. *Music.* Of, pertaining to, or of the nature of fugues.

1854 *Cherubini's Counterpoint* 7 He will be able to form himself in the style which befits the fugal art. **1875** OUSELEY *Mus. Form* ii. 23 This is..common in fugal works. **1881** *Mus. Trades Rev.* 15 Feb. 7/1 It is in B minor *allegro*, and opens with a fugal figure.

2. *Psychiatry.* Of or pertaining to a fugue state (see FUGUE 2).

1940 C. S. MYERS *Shell Shock* iii. 66 When the 'shock' is severe, it may be followed by..fugal automatism, or stupor, on recovery from..which the patient can recall none of the acts performed by him.

Hence **'fugally** *adv.*, in a fugal manner.

1892 *Daily News* 4 Nov. 2/1 The various themes are properly developed, and in at least two instances are even treated fugally.

†**'fugate**, *v. Obs. rare.* [f. L. *fugāt-* ppl. stem of *fugāre* to put to flight, f. *fuga* flight.] *trans.* To put to flight.

1603 HARSNET *Pop. Impost.* 67 It hath not the qualities of Stygian fire..to..fugate the devil. **1653** J. MAYER *Comm. Job, etc.* 236 Singing Psalmes fugates Devils.

†**fu'gation.** *Obs.* [ad. med.L. *fugātiōn-em*, n. of action f. L. *fugāre*: see prec.] **a.** A chase; privilege of hunting. **b.** A 'run' for cattle.

a **1483** *Liber Niger* in *Househ. Ord.* (1790) 62 This Clerk owght to have a booke of Remembraunces of all manner pourveyaunces of beefe and motons..that the pasture and fugations take trewe allowance. **1502** ARNOLDE *Chron.* (1811) 2 That they haue their fugacions and huntyngis lyke as they had the tyme of King Harry the Second. **1526** *Househ. Ord.* (1790) 196 Item, Fugation of beefs, muttons, and veales.

‖**fugato** (fu'gato), *adv.*, *a.* (and *sb.*) *Music.* [It. *fugato* fugued, f. *fuga* FUGUE.] **A.** *adv.* In the fugue style, but not in strict fugue form. **B.** As *sb.*, music composed in this style (Stainer & Barrett 1876). Also *attrib.* or as *adj.*

1866 ENGEL *Nat. Mus.* iii. 104 The motive is treated fugato at the commencement of the allegro. **1876** STAINER & BARRETT *Dict. Mus. Terms*, *Fugato*, in the fugue style; a composition containing fugal imitation, but which is not in strict fugue form. **1891** E. PROUT *Fugue* §358 Passages of imitation, provided that all the voices take part in them, will very often be also fugato passages. *Ibid.* §359 The freedom allowed in fugato. **1903** *Trawl* May 28 A fugato entry for the lower strings. **1906** *Grove's Dict. Mus.* II. 118/1 Beethoven was particularly fond of the fugato. **1968** *Listener* 26 Sept. 418/3 The least satisfying section of the movement is a long *fugato* in the middle.

†**fu'gator.** *Obs. rare*[−1]. In 7 **fugatour.** [a. late L. *fugātor*, agent-n. f. *fugāre*: see FUGATE.] That which puts to flight or drives away.

1657 TOMLINSON *Renou's Disp.* 300 It is a most solemn fugatour of Pestilence.

†**fuge**, *sb. Obs.*[−1] [? ad. L. *fuga* flight.] ? Flight.

1436 in *Pol. Poems* (1859) II. 198 Assaute was there none; No sege, but fuge, welle was he that myght gon.

†**fuge**, *v. Obs.*[−1] [ad. L. *fugĕre* to flee.] *intr.* To flee.

1566 G. GASCOIGNE *Supposes* Wks. (1587) 34, I to fuge and away hither as fast as I could.

-fuge (fju:dʒ), *suffix*, occurring in words (adj. and sb.) f. mod.L. types in *-fugus*. According to classical L. analogy, this ending should be connected with *fugĕre* to flee (cf. *profugus*), and should have the sense 'fleeing from' (cf. *lucifugus*, *erifuga*). In the medical words *febrifugus*, lit. driving away fevers, *vermifugus* expelling worms, however, the ending derives its sense from L. *fugāre*, to put to flight. In imitation of the anglicized forms of these, nonce-wds. in *-fuge* have occasionally been formed; chiefly on Lat. stems, as DEMONIFUGE (q.v.), **dolorifuge**, something to drive away pain; but occasionally on Eng. words, as ***mendacity-fuge***.

1802–12 BENTHAM *Rationale of Judic. Evid.* (1827) V. IX. iv. 429 In all purely pecuniary cases, to which the virtue of the mendacity-fuge diaphoretic does not extend. **1891** T. HARDY *Tess* I. 86 The children..had made use of this idea as a species of dolorifuge after the death of the horse.

†**'fugeand**, *a. Obs.*[−1] [Belongs to the spurious Sherwood dialect of the piece; it may be an alteration of FIGENT.]

1637 B. JONSON *Sad Sheph.* II. i, Shew your sell In all the shepherds bauldly; gaing amang 'em, Be mickel in their eye, frequent and fugeand.

†**fuger**¹, **fugo.** *Obs.* [cf. AF. *satayn fugeree*, in *Stat. Edw. IV* (Godefr.).]

1465 in *Paston Lett.* III. 436 The polronds of a payre bryganders of rede sateyn ffugr. **1596** *Unton Invent.* (1841) 11 One cover of a fielde bedde of fuger satten yellowe and redde. **1638** *Lanc. Wills* III. 206 And a petticoate of fugo satten layd on wth silver and gold lace and spangled.

†**fuger**². *Obs.*⁻¹

1681 MRS. BEHN *Rover* II. Epil., Right Worshipfuls and Squires: Who laugh, and cry Ads Nigs, 'tis woundy good When the fuger's all the Jest that's understood.

†**fugeratta.** *Obs.* [quasi-It. deriv. of FUGER¹.]

1638 *Proclam.* 5 Sep. in Rymer *Fœd.* (1735) 271/1 Silk Mohair, Barratine Silk, Rash Silk.. Fugeratta.

fuggle ('fʌg(ə)l). Also Fuggle's. A variety of hops.

1898 *Westm. Gaz.* 5 Sept. 7/3 All good sound hops suitable for copper use, such as the fuggle. **1902** *Times* 5 Sept. 2/5 Bramblings that are picked are small.. but fuggles have developed most. **1908** *Westm. Gaz.* 25 Sept. 9/2 The growers of 'Fuggles' and other comparatively hardy kinds. **1910** *Encycl. Brit.* XIII. 679/2 The variety known as Fuggle's, a heavy-cropping though slightly coarse hop, has been much planted in the Weald of Kent.

fuggy ('fʌgɪ), *a. colloq.* (orig. *dial.* and *School slang*). [f. FUG *sb.* + -Y¹; or FUG may be a back-formation from this. Cf. FOG *sb.*² and FOGGY *a.*] Of the air in a room: close, stuffy, and smelly, from want of ventilation. Of persons: addicted to living in such an atmosphere.

1888 E. F. BENSON *Sks. fr. Marlborough* i. 15 How beastly fuggy this place is. *Ibid.* vi. 58 He was rude enough to say that I was a fuggy beast. **1889** BARRÈRE & LELAND *Dict. Slang, Fuggy* (Shrewsbury), stuffy. **1900** *Globe* 12 Jan. 3/1 They missed the warm, and it must be owned often 'fuggy' heat of their old cabins. **1921** *Chambers's Jrnl.* 19 Feb. 189/1 In the fuggy comfort of the engineer's mess. **1923** U. L. SILBERRAD *Lett. J. Armiter* iv. §3. 102 He came up to the window and I opened it—the artists are rather a fuggy lot indoors.

fuggy, Sc. form of FOGGY *a.*³

†**fugh**, *int. Obs.* Variant of *fough*, FAUGH.

1690 DRYDEN *Don Sebast.* II. ii, A very filthy Fellow: how odiously he smells of his Country garlike! fugh, how he stinks of Spain! **1755** in JOHNSON. Hence in mod. Dicts.

fughetta (fju:'gɛtə). *Mus.* [It., dim. of *fuga* FUGUE. Cf. G. *fughette.*] A short, condensed fugue. Also *attrib.*

1876 in STAINER & BARRETT *Dict. Mus.* **1891** E. PROUT *Fugue* §351 In the form most frequently met with, a fughetta is an abridged fugue. *Ibid.* §356 Another variety of the fughetta form. **1898** *Westm. Gaz.* 19 Dec. 10/2 The Finale, ..with..its fughetta based..on the first subject of the first movement. **1947** A. EINSTEIN *Mus. Romantic Era* viii. 77 His [*sc.* Schumann's] Seven Pieces in Fughetta Form, Op. 126 (1853). **1959** *Times* 21 Sept. 5/5 The *fughetta* was particularly well played.

fughist, obs. form of FUGUIST.

'**fugie.** *Sc. Obs.* exc. *Hist.* Also 8 fugee. [perh. f. *fugæ* in the Law Lat. phrase *in meditatione fugæ* 'contemplating flight', occurring in the 'fugie-warrant' (see 2).]

1. A cock that will not fight; a runaway. Hence as a term of abuse, a coward.

1777 BRAND *Pop. Antiq.* (1813) I. 61 The School-masters were said to preside at the Battle, and claimed the run-away Cocks, called Fugees, as their perquisites. **1785** R. FORBES *Poems in Buchan Dial.* 29 How foul's the bibble he spits out, Fan he ca's me a fugee! **1834** H. MILLER *Scenes & Leg.* xxviii. (1857) 418 The birds..were converted into droits, under the ill-omened name of fugies. **1876** GRANT *Burgh Sch. Scotl.* II. xiv. 478 The master..enjoyed the perquisite of all the runaway cocks, called fugies.

2. *Comb.*: **fugie-warrant**, a warrant granted against a debtor, on a sworn information that he intends to flee.

1816 SCOTT *Antiq.* xxxix, 'Ay', said Ochiltree, 'that will be what they ca' the fugie-warrants'.

†'**fugient**, *a. Obs.*⁻¹ [ad. L. *fugient-em*, pr. pple. of L. *fugĕre* to flee.] Fleeing.

1650 ASHMOLE *Chym. Collect.* 60 Lest the fugient should first fly away, before the Fire could any way bring forth the persequent thing.

†'**fugill.** *Obs.*⁻¹ [ad. med.L. *fugilla.*] A glandular swelling.

1543 TRAHERON *Vigo's Chirurg.* 129 Scruphules and fugilles ben often engendred vnder the arme holes. [**1706** PHILLIPS (ed. Kersey) *Fugile*, an Impostume in the Ears.]

†'**fugitable**, *a. Obs. rare*⁻¹. [f. L. *fugit-* (see FUGITIVE) + -ABLE.] = FUGITIVE.

1628 FELTHAM *Resolves* II. xlvii. 139 Devoting thee to pleasure, and the fugitable [**1631** fugitiue] toyes of life.

'**fugitate**, *ppl. a. Sc. Law.* [ad. L. *fugitāt-us*, pa. pple. of *fugitāre*: see next.] Outlawed.

1752 J. LOUTHIAN *Form of Process* (ed. 2) 235 Such of the Pannels as were absent, were fugitate.

fugitate ('fju:dʒɪteɪt), *v.* [f. L. *fugitāt-* ppl. stem of *fugitāre*, frequentative vb. f. *fugĕre* to flee, but as used in *Sc. Law* f. FUGIT-IVE + -ATE³.]

1. *trans. Sc. Law.* To declare fugitive, to outlaw.

1721 WODROW *Sufferings Ch. Scot.* I. 11 On the 10th of October [1660] the Committee fugitate Sir Archibald Johnstoun of Waristoun [and others]. **1766** *Chron.* in *Ann. Reg.* 63/1 The offenders were both fugitated for non-appearance.

2. *intr.* To run away. *rare*⁻¹.

1830 *Fraser's Mag.* I. 182 My valet..had edged to the door, and was on the point of fugitating.

Hence '**fugitated** *ppl. a.*, put to flight, expelled.

1824 J. MCCULLOCH *Highlands Scotl.* IV. 171 Many manuscripts were carried to Douay, Rome, and Ratisbon, by the fugitated monks.

fugitation (fju:dʒɪ'teɪʃən). [n. of action from prec.: see -ATION.]

1. *Sc. Law.* A judicial sentence, declaring a person to be a fugitive from justice, and inflicting the penalty of outlawry and confiscation of goods.

1752 J. LOUTHIAN *Form of Process* (ed. 2) 144 The Sentence of Fugitation is pronounced by the Clerk to the Macer..thus: 'The Lords Justice-Clerk and Commissioners of Justiciary, Decern and adjudge—, —and—— to be Out-laws and Fugitives..and ordain..all their moveable Goods..to be escheat. **1820** *Edin. Rev.* XXXIV. 192 Pronounce sentence of outlawry and fugitation. **1880** MASSON *Milton* VI. I. i. 134 On the 10th of October there was a decree of fugitation or outlawry against Sir Archibald Johnstone [etc.].

b. *transf.* Exclusion from society.

1837 *Blackw. Mag.* XLII. 516 Their ladyships know well that..instant fugitation [would] be the inevitable reward of too much candour.

2. The action of fleeing.

1823 *Blackw. Mag.* XIV. 14 The bustle of fugitation and war. **1881** MASSON *De Quincey* 110 With all allowance for his wanderings and fugitations.

fugitive ('fju:dʒɪtɪv), *a.* and *sb.* Forms: 4-6 fugit-, fugyt-, -if(e, -yf(e, -yve, (5 fegetyff), 6- fugitive. [a. F. *fugitif, fugitive*, ad. L. *fugitīvus*, f. *fugit-* ppl. stem of *fugĕre* to flee.]

A. *adj.* (Formerly sometimes with inflected plural, esp. in legal phrases after AF.)

1. Apt or tending to flee; given to, or in the act of, running away.

1606 SHAKS. *Ant. & Cl.* III. i. 7 Whilst yet with Parthian blood thy Sword is warme, The Fugitiue Parthians follow. **1625** K. LONG tr. *Barclay's Argenis* III. xv. 200 Hee was not much pleased with this fugitive course. *a* **1704** T. BROWN *Pleas. Ep.* Wks. 1730 I. 110 Call back our fugitive mercers from Covent-garden. **1871** R. ELLIS *Catullus* lxiv. 68 His oars with fugitive hurry the waters beat.

fig. **1627-77** FELTHAM *Resolves* I. xx. 87 Fugitive Divines, that like cowards..run away from their Text. **1644** MILTON *Areop.* (Arb.) 45 A fugitive and cloister'd vertue..that never sallies out and sees her adversary.

b. That has taken flight, *esp.* from duty, an enemy, justice, or a master. †Also, of a debtor: Intending flight.

1467 in *Eng. Gilds* (1870) 376 That no citezein be attached by his body as fugityf. **1495** *Act 11 Hen. VII*, c. 48. §2 Catalles of felons fugitif. **1527** R. THORNE in Hakluyt *Voy.* (1589) 255 That none should receiue the others subiects fugitiues. **1535** COVERDALE *Judg.* xii. 5 Now whan one of ye fugityue Ephraites dyd saye [etc.]. **1576** FLEMING *Panopl. Epist.* 139 If it be my lucke to recover the fugitive fellowe [a slave]. **1597** SKENE *De Verb. Sign.* 120 Malefactoures quha are fugitive fra the law. **1600** HOLLAND *Livy* XXIV. XXX. (1609) 530 There were scourged and beheaded of fugitive traitours, to the number of two thousand. **1613** SIR H. FINCH *Law* (1636) 78 In London, if the debtor be fugitive, that the creditor before the day of payment may arrest him to find better surety. **1667** MILTON *P.L.* IX. 16 The wrauth Of stern Achilles on his Foe pursu'd Thrice Fugitive about Troy Wall. **1748** RICHARDSON *Clarissa* III. xxxi. 168 To countenance a fugitive daughter, in opposition to her parents. **1753** GLOVER *Boadicea* I. i, Come from your hills, ye fugitive remains Of shattered cohorts. **1796** H. HUNTER tr. *St. Pierre's Stud. Nat.* (1799) III. 99 To implore the pardon of a poor fugitive negress. **1855** MACAULAY *Hist. Eng.* III. 224 The fugitive Englishry found in England.. munificent relief. **1880** E. KIRKE *Garfield* 19 This was the first instance in which a Union officer refused to return a fugitive slave.

fig. **1551** ROBINSON tr. *More's Utop.* I. (Arb.) 56 By what crafte..the kynge maye..drawe to him againe fugitiue Naples. **1704** *Addr. Glamorgan* in *Lond. Gaz.* No. 4064/6 For him it was reserved to reduce fugitive Victory to her former Mistriss's Land.

†**c.** Of a substance (*e.g.* the metal mercury): Escaping from or eluding the grasp, slippery. *Obs.*⁻¹

c **1485** *Digby Myst.* (1882) III. 318 þe fegetyff mercury [perteynyng] on-to mercuryus.

†**2.** Driven out, banished, exiled. Const. *from*, *of*.

c **1384** CHAUCER *H. Fame* I. 146 That first came thorgh his destanee ffugityfe of Troy Contree In Italye. **1513** DOUGLAS *Æneis* I. i. 4 The man..that fugitive By fait to Itale coyme. **1549** *Compl. Scot.* ix. 81 He vas fugitiue fra al cuntreis. *c* **1560** R. MORICE in *Lett. Lit. Men* (Camden) 25, I became fugityve frome myn awne house. **1598** GRENEWEY *Tacitus' Ann.* 34 The Armenians..receiued the fugitiue Vonones.

3. Moving from place to place; flitting, shifting, vagabond. Also *fig.* Fickle.

1481 CAXTON *Godfrey* cxxxi. 195 *heading*, How guyllem de grateuylle and his felaws fugytyfs cam in to Allexandrye the lasse. **1490** —— *Eneydos* ii. 16 This noble companye..now vacabonde and fugytyf by the feeldes dardanike. **1563-87** FOXE *A. & M.* (1596) 266/2 The Pictavians..fugitiue and unstable. **1615** J. STEPHENS *Satyr. Ess.* 277 His helpe extends farre and neere to fugitive Raga-muffins. **1621** BURTON *Anat. Mel.* I. iii. I. ii. (1651) 185 Restless..fickle, fugitive, they may not abide to tarrie in one place long. **1662** R. MATHEW *Unl. Alch.* §114. 186, I pity thy fugitive mind, and pray for thee, when I see thee hunt from one man to another, and from one Medicine unto another. **1883** MACFADYEN in *Congreg. Year Bk.* 72 Fugitive preachers make fugitive congregations. **1893** *Daily News* 26 Apr. 2/3 With fugitive securities, which move between London and foreign stock markets.

4. a. Of immaterial things: Evanescent, fleeting, of short duration.

c **1510** BARCLAY *Mirr. Gd. Manners* (1570) B iv, This shorte life present as shadowe fugitiue. **1635** R. BOLTON *Comf. Affl. Consc.* v. 127 Fugitive follies and fading pleasures. **1697** DRYDEN *Virg. Georg.* III. 109 In Youth alone, unhappy Mortals live; But, ah! the mighty Bliss is fugitive. **1743** R. BLAIR *Grave* 568 Bless'd as the pleasing dreams of holy men; But fugitive like those. **1816** L. HUNT *Rimini* iv. 7 The woe was earthly, fugitive, is past. **1863** MARY HOWITT *F. Bremer's Greece* I. vi. 162 A fugitive gleam lit up the Vales of Athens and Sparta. **1877** DOWDEN *Shaks. Prim.* iv. 41 The latter—the weak endings—are more fugitive and evanescent in character.

b. Of impressions, colours, etc.: Quickly fading or becoming effaced. Less correctly of material substances: Perishable.

1678 R. R[USSELL] *Geber* I. v. 12 For the Fire..consumes every Fugitive and inflammable Substance. **1695** WOODWARD *Nat. Hist. Earth* VI. (1723) 296 The more tender and fugitive Parts, as the Leaves. **1822** IMISON *Sc. & Art* II. 188 The colour is extremely fugitive. **1842** BISCHOFF *Woollen Manuf.* II. 81 The materials used in the fugitive dyes. **1879** FARRAR *St. Paul* I. 574 *note*, Letters written on fugitive materials. **1879** *Print. Trades Jrnl.* No. 26. 30 Cerise, like most aniline colors, is fugitive.

c. Of a chemical substance: Volatile. *rare.*

1666 BOYLE *Orig. Formes & Qual.* (1667) 48 Quicksilver ..may be turn'd into..a Fugitive Smoak. **1684-5** —— *Min. Waters* 76 Spirituous and Fugitive Exhalations. **1850** DAUBENY *Atom. Th.* x. (ed. 2) 324 A fixed carbonate.. heated along with an ammoniacal compound of a less fugitive description.

d. *Bot.* Of flowers and petals: Soon falling.

1830 LINDLEY *Nat. Syst. Bot.* 151 [Of the Rock-rose Tribe] Petals 5, hypogynous, very fugitive. *Ibid.* Their beautiful fugitive flowers.

5. Of a literary composition (occas. of a writer): Concerned or dealing with subjects of passing interest; ephemeral, occasional.

1766 ANSTEY *Bath Guide* ii. (1832) 15 At least when he chooses his book to increase I may take a small flight as a fugitive piece. **1820** BYRON *Blues* II. 95 You're a fugitive writer, I think, sir, of rhymes? **1823** J. BADCOCK *Dom. Amusem.* p. vii, Various fugitive publications of the day. **1864** *Spectator* 9 Apr. 423 The greater part of periodical literature is meant to be, and ought to remain, fugitive.

B. *sb.*

1. One who flees or tries to escape from danger, an enemy, justice, or an owner. Cf. A. 1. Occas. one who intends flight. ***to declare a person a fugitive*** (Sc. Law): to pronounce sentence of FUGITATION upon.

1382 WYCLIF *Num.* xxxv. 11 Fugityues that not wilnyng sheeden blood. *c* **1400** MAUNDEV. (1839) vi. 66 Men resceyved there all manere of Fugityfes of other places. **1467** *Eng. Gilds* 405 Though it so be the seid fugitif fynd suerte to answer to the accion comencyd ayenst hym. **1489** CAXTON *Faytes of A.* I. vii. 16 To fugityues vnneth or with grete payne cometh agayn the herte to fighte. **1576** FLEMING *Panopl. Epist.* 128 Your clearke or Secretarie, hath plaide the fugitive or runnagate. **1667-1708** *Termes de la Ley* 357 Fugitives Goods are the proper goods of him that flies upon felony, which, after the Flight lawfully found, do belong to the King. [The AF. version has *fugitives biens*, as if the word were an adj.; but the passage of Coke referred to (*Rep.* v. 109 b) has *bona fugitivorum*.] **1672** WILKINS *Nat. Relig.* 252 That man (saith he [Antoninus]) is to be esteemed a fugitive and an apostate, who runs away from his master. **1752** J. LOUTHIAN *Form of Process* (ed. 2) 147 The Persons contained in the Criminal Letters, and formerly declared Fugitives. **1845** S. AUSTIN *Ranke's Hist. Ref.* III. 473 The approach of the Turks filled the town with crowds of fugitives. **1887** BOWEN *Virg. Æneid* I. 340 Dido..a fugitive here Fled from a brother.

†**b.** A deserter. *Obs.*

1553 BRENDE *Q. Curtius* v. 94/1 It was there shewed him by fugitiues that came out of Darius camp, that he was fled with al spede into Bactria. **1606** SHAKS. *Ant. & Cl.* IV. ix. 22 But let the world ranke me in Register A Master leauer, and a fugitiue. **1611** BIBLE *2 Kings* xxv. 11 The fugitiues that fell away to the king of Babylon. **1659** PEARSON *Creed* (1839) 293 The Romans themselves accounted it a servile punishment, and inflicted it upon their slaves and fugitives.

c. One who quits or is banished from his country; an exile, refugee.

1591 SHAKS. *1 Hen. VI*, III. iii. 67 Who then, but English Henry, will be Lord, And thou be thrust out, like a Fugitive? **1630** *R. Johnson's Kingd. & Commw.* 48 Rome..is the Seminary and Nursery of English Fugitives. **1692** WASHINGTON tr. *Milton's Def. Pop.* M.'s Wks. 1738 I. 510 This is what that herd of Fugitives and Vagabonds hired you to write. **1788** PRIESTLEY *Lect. Hist.* v. xxxvi. 265 The Greek fugitives from Constantinople promoted a taste for eloquence. **1836** W. IRVING *Astoria* II. 58 Fugitives from the Spanish and American frontiers. **1855** MILMAN *Lat. Chr.* II. i. (1864) I. 137 The fugitives from Rome were found in all parts of the world.

†**d.** One that abandons a monastic life. *Obs.*⁻¹

1482 *Monk of Evesham* (Arb.) 84 Religyous persons that were fugytyuys that is to say that ranne oute of her order.

2. One who shifts about or moves from place to place; a vagabond, wanderer. Applied also to the lower animals.

1563-87 FOXE *A. & M.* (1684) III. 747 If thou wert an honest Woman, thou wouldest not..run about the Country like a Fugitive. **1688** R. HOLME *Armoury* II. 239/1 [A]

Fugitive..is a Hawk that rangleth and wandreth abroad. **1697** DRYDEN *Virg. Georg.* IV. 159 When the Swarms..idly Stray, Restrain the wanton Fugitives.

3. Something fugitive; something fleeting, or that eludes the grasp. *Obs.* exc. with personification.

1683 PETTUS *Fleta Min.* I. (1686) 242 They [light ores] cannot well be brought into compass, for they rise for the most part in the Water, and are fugitives. **1690** EVELYN *Mem.* (1857) III. 316 You would not exchange your inward consolation, for the return of all those external fugitives you once enjoyed. *a* **1774** HARTE *Vis. Death* Introd. 48 What Muse but his can Nature's beauties hit, Or catch that airy fugitive, called wit. **1847** EMERSON *Poems, Ode to Beauty*, Thou eternal fugitive, Hovering over all that live.

Hence **'fugitive** *v.* (*nonce-wd.*) *trans.*, to make fugitive, drive into exile; **'fugitively** *adv. rare*$^{-0}$, in a fugitive manner (Webster 1864); **'fugiti,vism**, the condition of a fugitive; **fugi'tivity**, the quality or state of being fugitive.

1843 W. S. LANDOR *Let.* 16 Apr. in R. R. Madden *Life C'tess Blessington* (ed. 2) II. 411 What fugitivities in this lower world of ours! **1864** GREENSHIELD *Ann. Lesmahagow* vi. 116 Her son Thomas was fugitived in the persecution. **1877** D. M. WALLACE *Russia* xxix. 468 This change in the position of the peasantry..naturally increased fugitivism and vagrancy.

fugitiveness ('fju:dʒɪtɪvnɪs). [f. FUGITIVE *a.* + -NESS.] The quality or condition of being fugitive (see the adj.).

a **1661** FULLER *Worthies* I. (1662) 38 The Ficklenesse and Fugitivenesse of such Servants, justly addeth a valuation to their constancy, who are Standards in a Family. **1664** H. MORE *Antid. Idol.* 2 The Ludicrousnesse and Fugitivenesse of our wanton Reason. **1680** BOYLE *Scept. Chem.* v. 318 That also divers Salts..are very Volatile, is plain from the fugitiveness of Salt. **1822** HAZLITT *Table-t.* Ser. II. i. (1869) 2 The suddenness and fugitiveness of the interest taken in them. **1833** LAMB *Elia, Superann. Man* II, What with my sense of its fugitiveness, and over-care to get the greatest quantity of pleasure out of it.

† **'fugitour.** *Sc. Obs.* Also 6 fug(i)atour. [ad. L. *fugitor*, f. *fugĕre* to flee.] A fugitive.

1533 BELLENDEN *Livy* II. (1822) 124 The Hethruschis war advertist be ane fugitoure of this huge nowmer of bestial liand utouth the portis. **1535** STEWART *Cron. Scot.* II. 355 All fugatouris als far fra the law that fled, Siclyke for rebell to thame bayth be hed.

'fugle, *v.*[1] *slang* or *dial. trans.* To cheat, trick.

1719 D'URFEY *Pills* I. 126 Who fugell'd the Parson's fine Maid. **1883** *Almondbury Gloss.*, Fugel, or Fugle, to cheat, deceive, or trick; used actively.

fugle ('fju:g(ə)l), *v.*[2] [back-formation from FUGLEMAN.]

1. *intr.* To do the duty of a fugleman; to act as guide or director; to make signals. *lit.* and *fig.*

1837 CARLYLE *Fr. Rev.* III. v. vii. (1871) 207 Wooden arms with elbow-joints are jerking and fugling in the air, in the most rapid mysterious manner! **1863** DE MORGAN in *From Matter to Spirit* Pref. 35 The case..fugles admirably for a very large class of the philosophical principles.

b. *trans.* To give an example of (something) *to*.

1868 *Pall Mall G.* 29 June 12/2 The cost of keeping a few thousand good men to fugle all the public and domestic virtues to the benighted millions of Roman Catholics.

2. *Comb.*

1837 CARLYLE *Fr. Rev.* III. v. iv. (1871) 191 The French nation is of gregarious imitative nature; it needed but a fugle-motion in this matter. **1842** MIALL in *Nonconf.* II. 377 The fugle-word [Martyrdom] of our present article, is a venerable expression.

Hence **'fugling** *vbl. sb.*

1858 CARLYLE *Fredk. Gt.* II. ii. (1868) I. 81 No Czech blows into his pipe in the woodlands, without certain precautions, and preliminary fuglings of a devotional nature. *Ibid.* IV. viii. 468 A certain handy and correct young fellow..who already knew his fugling to a hair's-breadth, was Drill-master. **1863** *Reader* 5 Dec. 656 What the author calls, metaphorically, 'Fugling', or the representation of a corporate process of mind by some single exaggerated instance of the same process stationed in front of it.

fugleman ('fju:g(ə)lmən). Also **fugelman, fugal man, flugleman, flugelman.** [ad. Ger. *flügelmann* leader of the file, f. *flügel* wing + *mann* MAN.]

a. A soldier especially expert and well drilled, formerly placed in front of a regiment or company as an example or model to the others in their exercises.

1804 *Morn. Chron.* in *Spirit Publ. Jrnls.* (1805) VIII. 117 Time has utterly deprived these stiffening limbs of mine of all power to spring through the rapid motions of the fugleman. **1809** W. IRVING *Knickerb.* (1861) 143 Several times was Antony obliged to stand forth like a fugleman and repeat the sign. **1814** W. TAYLOR in *Monthly Rev.* LXXIV. 271 Like the flugelman of a regiment, he over-acts the movements which he would excite in others. **1858** CARLYLE *Fredk. Gt.* I. v. v. 579 This Hohmann was now *Flügelmann* ('fugleman' as we have named it, leader of the file). **1886** H. F. LESTER *Under two Fig Trees* 229 With the captain as volunteer fugleman the colony quickly enrolled.

b. *transf.* and *fig.*

1814 J. GILCHRIST *Reason* 44 After the example of some great gardener who has been made flugle-man to all generations. **1827** SYD. SMITH *Wks.* (1859) II. 120/2 We propose Lord Nugent as a political flugelman. **1845** MIALL in *Nonconf.* V. 33 What! must the state be fugleman to God's worshipers, that all may assume the same posture and bow alike? **1847** ALB. SMITH *Chr. Tadpole* xliv. (1879) 388 Acting as fugleman for the approbation, which was judiciously thrown in from time to time. **1855** E. FORBES *Lit. Papers* vi. 168 Popular guides to public collections are seldom of more value than the explanations of the fugleman of a raree-show. **1875** F. HALL in *Lippincott's Mag.* XV. 342/1, I picked out their fugleman, a well-grown boar, and fired.

Hence **'fuglemanship**, the office and duties of a fugleman. Also by substitution, **'fuglewoman**, a woman who gives a signal.

1845 CARLYLE *Cromwell* (1871) I. 37 Not the smallest regularity of fuglemanship or devotional drill-exercise. **1868** *Daily Tel.* 27 May, Miss Tickletoby..well acting as fuglewoman to her eight-and-twenty boarders, waves her virtuous pocket-handkerchief in response to the salutations from a drag full of roystering young guardsmen.

fugue (fju:g), *sb.* Forms: 6–8 fuge, (7 fug), 7–8 feuge, 7– fugue. [a. F. *fugue*, ad. It. *fuga* lit. 'flight':—L. *fuga*, related to *fugĕre* to flee.] **1.** 'A polyphonic composition constructed on one or more short subjects or themes, which are harmonized according to the laws of counterpoint, and introduced from time to time with various contrapuntal devices' (Stainer and Barrett). ***double fugue*** (see quot. 1880).

1597 MORLEY *Introd. Mus.* 76 We call that a Fuge, when one part beginneth and the other singeth the same, for some number of notes (which the first did sing). **1626** BACON *Sylva* § 113 The Reports and Fuges have an Agreement with the Figures in Rhetorick, of Repetition, and Traduction. *a* **1646** J. GREGORY *Posthuma* (1649) 48 The Contrapunctum figuratum, consisting of Feuges, or maintaining of Points. **1667** PEPYS *Diary* 15 Sept., The sense of the words being lost by not being heard, and especially as they set them with Fuges of words, one after another. **1667** MILTON *P.L.* XI. 563 His volant touch Instinct through all proportions low and high Fled and pursu'd transverse the resonant fugue. **1795** MASON *Ch. Mus.* i. 59 The Fugue is indeed come into disrepute with Modern Masters. **1875** OUSELEY *Mus. Form* ii. 4 The art of Fugue can be mastered thoroughly by dint of laborious application. **1880** GROVE *Dict. Mus.* I. 459 *Double Fugue*, a common term for a fugue on two subjects, in which the two start together.

transf. **1863** GEO. ELIOT *Romola* I. i, Elderly market-women..contributed a wailing fugue of invocation.

Comb. **1869** OUSELEY *Counterp.* xviii. 150 Of all kinds of musical composition none perhaps is so important as the art of fugue-writing. **1876** STAINER & BARRETT *Dict. Mus. Terms* 181/1 The simplest form of diatonic fugue-subject is that which lies in a compass of a fifth. **1959** D. COOKE *Lang. Mus.* i. 8 A typical contrapuntal point or fugue-subject has no real significance until it takes its place in the construction as a whole.

2. *Psychiatry.* A flight from one's own identity, often involving travel to some unconsciously desired locality. It is a dissociative reaction to shock or emotional stress in a neurotic, during which all awareness of personal identity is lost though the person's outward behaviour may appear rational. On recovery, memory of events during the state is totally repressed but may become conscious under hypnosis or psycho-analysis. A fugue may also be part of an epileptic or hysterical seizure. Also *attrib.*, as ***fugue state***.

1901 C. R. CORSON tr. *Janet's Mental State Hystericals* 422 Those long flights (*fugues*),..those strange excursions, accomplished automatically, of which the patient has not the least recollection. **1923** OGDEN & RICHARDS *Meaning of Meaning* vi. 220 'The Unconscious' is what causes dreams, fugues, psychoses, humour and the rest. **1925** J. LAIRD *Our Minds & Their Bodies* iv. 86 There is a palpable difference between man's behaviour in somnambulism, or in a fugue, or in masked epilepsy, and ordinary human conduct. **1946** LANDIS & BOLLES *Textbk. Abnormal Psychol.* vii. 94 A middle-aged embezzler recalled events that had occurred during a fugue state more than twenty years earlier, although he had not been able to remember them during the entire twenty years. **1961** *Lancet* 29 July 240/1 She had also been a voluntary patient in a mental hospital..once after an epileptic fugue. **1965** ROSEN & GREGORY *Abnormal Psychol.* II. xii. 241 A fugue is a combination of amnesia and physical fright. The individual flees from his customary surroundings; what he is really trying to escape is his own fear. **1969** ULLMANN & KRASNER *Psychol. Approach to Abnormal Behavior* II. xv. 289/2 Two days before the fugue, an anonymous letter advised him that he was in danger.

fugue (fju:g), *v.* [f. prec. sb.] *intr.* To compose, or perform, a fugue. (Nonce-use, ***to fugue it.***)

1834 BECKFORD *Italy* I. 4 Half-a-dozen squeaking fiddles fugued and flourished away in the galleries. **1894** DU MAURIER *Trilby* i. 41 They fugued and canoned and counterpointed it.

So **'fuguing** *vbl. sb.*; **'fuguing** *ppl. a.* (= FUGUED *ppl. a.*).

1694 PURCELL *Playford's Skill Mus.* (1697) 98 The third sort of Fugeing is called a Double Fuge. **1731** *Rules for Thorow-Bass* in *Holder's Harmony* 200 Short Lessons by way of Fugeing. **1795** MASON *Ch. Mus.* ii. 104 Dr. Tudway..had the boldness to declare, 'that the practice of fuguing in vocal music obscured the sense.' **1862** W. W. STORY *Roba di R.* iv. (1864) 48 The fuguing chants of the Papal choir sound..down the aisles. **1878** MRS. STOWE *Poganuc P.* vii. 56 Those old fuguing tunes were like the same [calm] ocean aroused by storming winds.

fugued (fju:gd), *ppl. a.* [f. FUGUE *sb.* and *v.* + -ED. Cf. F. *fugué*.] Composed in the form of a fugue.

1856 *Sat. Rev.* I. 319/2 The first part is brought to a close by a fugued chorus. **1871** H. B. FORMAN *Living Poets* 369 A sort of fugued movement. **1878** E. PROUT in Grove *Dict. Mus.* I. 307 Pieces written..in a fugued style, though not strict fugues.

fuguist ('fju:gɪst). Also 8 fughist, 9 fugueist. [f. FUGUE *sb.* + -IST.] A composer of fugues.

1789 BURNEY *Hist. Mus.* III. ii. 110 Handel was perhaps the only great Fughist exempt from pedantry. **1829** LAMB *Lett.* (1888) II. 233 Dear Fugueist, or hear'st thou rather Contrapuntist? **1841** H. F. CHORLEY *Mus. & Mann.* (1844) III. 246 Classical preluders and steady fuguists will come in time.

fuhel, -wel, obs. forms of FOWL *sb.*

Führer ('fy:rə(r)). Also **Fuehrer.** [G., leader.] Part of the title (*Führer und Reichskanzler*) assumed by Adolf Hitler (see HITLER) in 1934 as head of the German Reich, after the model of DUCE. Also *transf.* and *attrib.*

1934 *N. & Q.* CLXVII. 254/1 Since the Führer refuses permission for this, it is thought probable the German stamps will show the swastika. **1936** A. HUXLEY *Eyeless in Gaza* viii. 91 Stupidity has come back, as a king—no; as an emperor, as a divine Führer of all the Aryans. **1937** —— *Ends & Means* v. 34 They yet persist in taking the same roads as are taken by the Duces and Fuehrers. **1943** 'G. ORWELL' in *Partisan Rev.* July–Aug. 347 Some..declare that he has a 'fuehrer complex' and..would split it rather than share authority. **1944** H. G. WELLS *'42 to '44* 183 Galton had the mental disposition of a Fascist and was all for fuehrers and duces. **1948** E. E. CUMMINGS *Let.* 24 Sept. (1969) 186 Presently a smallish mob of muckers..materialized, & their führer-commissar suggested a friendly snowfight. **1959** *Sunday Times* 14 June 22/5 The cold and pointless ferocity of the gang fights came out vividly in interviews..with two or three young fuehrers. **1967** *Spectator* 29 Dec. 819/3 Mr. Gordon Walker..issued his führer order that the Bloomsbury site be scrapped.

Hence **Führer-prinzip** (or **principle**): see quot. 1950.

1937 AUDEN *Let.* in Auden & MacNeice *Lett. fr. Iceland* v. 57 The Teutonic Führer-Prinzip would have appealed to you. **1940** *Ann. Reg. 1939* 148 The tendency to adopt the 'führer' principle would threaten religious life and freedom. **1950** THEIMER & CAMPBELL *Encycl. World Politics* 176/2 The *Fuehrer Prinzip* was the principle that the fuehrer had the right to command and the people the duty to obey him. **1959** *Chambers's Encycl.* XI. 51/2 Fascism was inherently militaristic and anti-democratic, with the 'Führer-principle' as its dominant political idea.

fuid(e, obs. form of FEUD *sb.*[1]

fuil-de-mort, corrupt f. FEUILLEMORTE *a.*

1687 A. LOVELL tr. *Bergerac's Com. Hist.* I. 138 And contents himself with an old Fuil-de-mort Cloak.

fuilȝie, var. of FULYIE, *Sc.*

fuir-days. *Sc.* Also foor-, fure-, fuor-. [Somewhat obscure; the sense would suggest identification of the first element with FORE *adv.*, but the phonology is in that case abnormal.]

a. Late in the day: = *far days, forth days* (see FAR *adv.* 3 c, FORTH A. 4 b). **b.** Broad daylight.

1535 STEWART *Cron. Scot.* II. 517 The king..left his sueit that tyme, and tuke gud rest, Sleipand rycht sound quhill all the nycht wes past, And on the morne, quhill it wes neir fuir-dais. **1718** RAMSAY *Christ's Kirk Gr.* III. 17 Be that time it was fair foor days. **1807** J. STAGG *Poems* 17 At last 'twas gitten wheyte fuor days, The lavrocks shrill war whuslin'.

fuisum, -un, obs. forms of FOISON.

† **fuite.** *Obs. rare.* In 5 fuyte. [a. F. *fuite* flight, f. *fuir* to flee.] Flight.

1499 CAXTON *Eneydos* vii. 31 Semed to theym that they oughte to make an ende of their fuyte or fleeynge.

† **fuk.** *Obs.* Also 5 fukke, 6 fuck(e, fouke. [Proximate source uncertain; the word, with such variety of application as is not uncommonly found in nautical terms (cf., e.g., MIZEN), occurs in many mod. European langs.: F. *foc* jib; Du. *fok* (MDu. *fokke*) foremast; Ger. *fock(e*, Sw. *fock*, Da. *fok* foresail. The origin is usually sought in ON. *fok*, action of driving, f. root of *fúka* to drive; possibly the nautical word was originally a shortening of various compounds of this.] Some kind of sail; ? a jib, a stay-sail (but prob. used loosely in quots.). Also in Comb. ***fukmast*** (in quot. 1598 = 'foremast'), ***fuksail, fuksheet.***

1465 *Mann. & Househ. Exp.* (Roxb.) 200 Item, my mastyr paid for a ffukke maste, iiij.*s.* iiij.*d.* **1535** STEWART *Cron. Scot.* (1858) I. 20 Tha salit fast..befoir the wynd With fuksaill, topsaill, manesaill, musall, and blynd. *Ibid.* 100 It is..Sax houris saling bayth with fuk and blind. **1568** *Satir. Poems Reform.* xlvi. 30 Plum weill the grund quhat evir ȝe doo, Haill on the fukscheit and the blind. **1598** W. PHILLIPS tr. *Linschoten* I. 165 The chiefe Boteson hath..gouernement ouer the Fouke mast, and the fore sayles.

transf. **1500–20** DUNBAR *Poems* xiv. 74 So mony fillok with fuck sailis Within this land was nevir hard nor sene. *a* **1529** SKELTON *Col. Cloute* 399 Set up theyr fucke sayles To catch wynde.

fuke (fju:k). *Obs.* exc. *dial.* Also 5 fuike, -yke. A lock of hair.

1483 *Cath. Angl.* 145/1 Fuike (*A.* Fuyke), *lanigo.* **1674** RAY *N.C. Words* 19 *Fukes*: Chesh. Locks of Hair. **1688** R. HOLME *Armoury* II. 154/1 The Topping, or fore-top [of a horse]; Fuke. **1879** in MISS JACKSON *Shropsh. Wordbk.*

fukes: see FUCUS.

ful, obs. form of FOUL.

-ful, *suffix*, originally identical with FULL *a.*

1. Forming adjs. In OE. the adj. *full*, like its equivalent in the other Teut. langs., was used in composition with a preceding sb., forming adjs., the etymological sense of which (= 'full of...') is usually somewhat weakened, so that the words may be rendered 'having', 'characterized by' (the attribute denoted by the sb.); the meaning of the suffix thus differs little from that of L. *-ōsus*, -OUS. In ME. and in mod.E. many new formations of this type have arisen, some of them from Romanic sbs., as *beautiful*, *graceful*; and the suffix is still to some extent productive. In the 14th c. a few new forms arose in which the suffix had the force of 'possessing the qualities of'; e.g. *masterful*, *manful*. In OE. *-full* was not ordinarily appended to adjs.; an instance occurs in *deorcfull*, DARKFUL, used to render L. *tenebrosus*, and prob. formed in imitation of it. In the 16th and 17th c. a few new words appear f. adjs. or L. adj. stems + *-ful*, e.g. *direful*, *grateful*, *tristful*, *fierceful*; prob. these were due to the analogy of older synonyms having this suffix, though it is possible that they may have been in part suggested by It. words like *gratevole* (*gradevole*), the ending of which has an accidental resemblance to the Eng. suffix. As the sbs. to which *-ful* is appended are often nouns of action or state coincident in form with the stems of related vbs., it happens frequently that a word really f. a sb. + *-ful* is associated in ordinary apprehension rather with the vb. than the sb. (For this there are sometimes special causes; e.g. the sb. *thank* being obsolete in the sing. while *thank* vb. is current, the adj. *thankful* is naturally viewed as a derivative of the latter.) Hence in mod.Eng. adjs. in *-ful* are sometimes formed directly on verb-stems, the sense of the suffix being 'apt to', 'able or accustomed to', as in *assistful*, *distractful*, *crossful*, *mournful*; an example of a passive sense (= *-able*) occurs in *bashful*.

2. Forming sbs. In the Teut. langs. the form of expression in which a sb. denoting a receptacle is followed by the adj. FULL in concord with it and governing a genitive (e.g. 'a hand full of corn') was used, not only in its proper sense, but in the transferred sense of 'the quantity that fills or would fill' (the receptacle): see FULL *a.* 1 b. The ambiguity thus arising is partly obviated by a differentiation of form; the sb. and adj. are treated as independent words when they retain their proper sense, but as forming a compound when the sense is transferred. This differentiation has not been carried out to an equal extent in the various langs. In Ger., *handvoll* 'handful', *mundvoll* 'mouthful' are written as single words, but this makes no real difference in their syntactical value; the gender of the quasi-compound is determined by that of its first element, and there is no inflexion. In OE. the development had proceeded a step further in the case of *handfull*, which, although retaining the fem. gender of *hand*, was so completely one word as to be declinable (accus. *-fulle*, pl. *-fulla*, after the prevailing declension of feminines); in the 14th c. the pl. was *handfullis*. No other compound of this class is found in OE.; commonly the notion was expressed in the original Teut. manner by the adj. *full* in concord with the sb. This continued also in ME.; but owing to the practice of using the sing. of a noun of quantity instead of the pl. after a numeral, there is seldom any evidence to show whether the ME. antecedent of a word like *dishful* is to be regarded as a syntactical combination or as a single word. In mod.Eng. *-ful* has become a suffix forming derivatives with the general sense 'quantity that fills or would fill' (something), and may be attached at pleasure to any sb. denoting an object that can be regarded as holding or containing a more or less definite quantity of anything; thus we have not only *bottleful*, *boxful*, *canful*, *spoonful*, etc., but *bookful*, *churchful*, *houseful*, *worldful*, etc. The plural forms *spoonsful*, *cupsful*, etc., which are still sometimes heard, represent either a survival of, or (much more probably) a return to, the older grammatical view; but though they have thus some appearance of historical justification, they are contrary to good modern usage, and are objectionable on account of their ambiguity.

The ON. *-fyllr* (*handfyllr* handful, *munnfyllr* mouthful, etc.) is not identical with the Eng. suffix, but is the sb. *fyllr* fem. = FILL *sb.*[1], and the compounds are therefore all fem., whatever the gender of the first element.

Fulah ('fuːlə), *sb.* and *a.* Also Foulah, Ful, Fula. **A.** *sb.* **a.** One of a Sudanese people of partly non-Negro extraction. **b.** The language of this people. **B.** *adj.* Of or pertaining to this people or their language. Also called **Fulbe, Fullatah**, etc. Cf. next.

1832 *Jrnl. R. Geogr. Soc.* II. 283 The principal internal trade is maintained with the Foulahs. **1854** E. NORRIS *MacBrair's Gram. Fulah Lang.* 1 The pronunciation of the Fulah language is rather guttural. *Ibid.* 4 Terminations expressing the size of objects are very common in Fulah. **1875** *Encycl. Brit.* I. 263/1 The *Foulahs* or *Fellatas* occupy the central parts of the Soudan. **1884** *Ibid.* XVII. 318/1 Nor is it possible to regard the..Fulah, and many other Soudanese tongues as fragments or offshoots of Bantu. **1887** *Ibid.* XXII. 278/2 Recent research has shown..that the Fulahs and Nubians differ fundamentally in speech and physique, the former being of Caucasic and the latter of Negro type. **1901** *Ibid.* XXIX. 234/1 Most of the kings and of the ruling class are not Hausas, but belong to a tribe variously called Fulah, Fulani, Fulbe, or Fullatah. Whilst the Hausas are a quiet commercial people, the Fulahs are a race of soldiers and rulers. **1921** E. SAPIR *Lang.* 75 Ful, an African language of the Soudan. **1938** J. CARY *Castle Corner* 351 The Emir was a high bred Fulbe. **1957** M. BANTON *W. Afr. City* ii. 34 After the French colonies had joined the Allies, Fula traders appeared in greater numbers.

Fulani ('fuːlənɪ, fuː'lɑːnɪ), *sb.* and *a.* [Native name.] = FULAH *sb.* and *a.*; *spec.* the Fulah of northern Nigeria and adjacent territories.

1855 S. CROWTHER *Jrnl. Exped. Niger* 147 We had not seen a real Filani, till we came to the neighbourhood of Hamaruwa. **1860** R. CAMPBELL *Pilgr. Motherland* ix. 105 Every person in Ilorin is said to speak both the Aku and Fulanee languages. **1901** [see FULAH *sb.* and *a.*]. **1931** *Times Lit. Suppl.* 26 Feb. 145/1 The Fulani form perhaps the one group that is really of ambiguous status. **1932** J. CARY *Aissa Saved* i. 6 A half-bred Fulani girl with big soft eyes and a fine golden skin. **1957** *Encycl. Brit.* I. 312/1 The most important non-Negro group to be found in the region is the Fulani (Fula, Peul), a people of white Mediterranean race closely related to the Berbers. **1960** *Guardian* 15 July 14/3 Although the ruling classes [in northern Nigeria] are still Fulani, they early on became assimilated with the Hausas. **1960** G. DURRELL *Zoo in my Luggage* vi. 150 A herd of the long horned Fulani cattle..surrounded us... They were huge, beautiful beasts of a dark chocolate brown, with enormous melting eyes and a massive spread of white horns, sometimes as much as five feet from tip to tip.

Fulbright ('fʊlbraɪt). The name of Senator William *Fulbright*, of Arkansas, U.S.A., designating the *Fulbright* Act (Public Law 584 of the 79th Congress), of 1 August 1946, which authorized agreements with foreign countries by which local currencies acquired by the American government from the sale of surplus war property might be used for financing higher learning; hence applied *attrib.* to a grant, etc., awarded by virtue of such agreements, or to a person holding such a grant or position, as ***Fulbright professor***, ***scholar***. Also *ellipt.* Hence **'Fulbrighter** *colloq.*, the holder of a Fulbright grant.

1951 *Times Educ. Suppl.* 23 Mar. 229/2, 23 visiting American lecturers and 20 research scholars are..here with Fulbright awards. **1952** M. MCCARTHY *Groves of Academe* (1953) x. 197 Percy copped a Fulbright to lecture on Amiel in Lebanon. **1957** *Times Lit. Suppl.* 8 Nov. 680/1 Professor Jayne's year of research in England, supported by Fulbright and Guggenheim funds. **1958** *Times* 22 Sept. 11/6 A party of some 200 Americans disembark... If you..asked who they were, you might well be given the laconic reply: 'Fulbrighters.' **1958** S. ELLIN *Eighth Circle* (1959) II. i. 28 He went to Oxford on a Fulbright. **1959** *Encounter* Oct. 38/2 Some stranded Fulbrights, a Mexican pundit, a Lapp. **1959** *Times Lit. Suppl.* 6 Nov. 647/1 A Fulbright scholar.

†**'fulcible**, *a. Obs.*[−0] [f. L. *fulcīre* to support: see FULCRUM and -BLE.] That may be propped up.

1623-6 in COCKERAM; whence in later Dicts.

†**'fulciment.** *Obs.* [ad. late L. *fulcīmentum*, f. *fulcīre*: see FULCRUM and -MENT.] A prop or support; usually *spec.* a fulcrum.

1648 WILKINS *Math. Magic* I. xii. 80 If we conceive the same dis-proportion betwixt their several distances in the former faculties, from the fulciment, or center of gravity, they would both equiponderate. **1657** TOMLINSON *Renou's Disp.* 258 Boughs which without fulciments would lay along the ground. **1695** ALINGHAM *Geom. Epit.* 54 The *fulciment* or point of bearing comes nearer the middle of the Oar. **1710** *Brit. Apollo* III. No. 56. 2/1 In this Position of the Body the Fulciment..is the Legs. **1759** tr. *Duhamel's Husb.* I. vii. (1762) 17 And a weight, or fulciment, as he calls it.

fig. **1796** W. TAYLOR in *Monthly Rev.* XIX. 518 A fulciment is wanting to the lever of revolution.

fulcne(n, var. of *fulhtne*, early ME., to baptize, q.v. under FULLOUGHT.

fulcra: pl. of FULCRUM.

fulcraceous (fʌl'kreɪʃəs), *a. Bot.* [f. FULCR-UM + -ACEOUS.] Of or pertaining to the fulcra of plants.

1866 in *Treas. Bot.*

fulcral ('fʌlkrəl), *a. rare.* [f. FULCR-UM + -AL[1].] Relating to the fulcra of a fish.

1872 NICHOLSON *Palæont.* 323 Fin borders generally with fulcral scales.

fulcrant ('fʌlkrənt). *Ent.* (See quot.)

1826 KIRBY & SP. *Entomol.* IV. 346 *Fulcrant*, when the trochanter merely props the thigh below at the base, but does not at all intervene between it and the coxa.

fulcrate ('fʌlkreɪt), *a. Bot.* [f. FULCR-UM + -ATE[2].] Supported by or provided with fulcra.

1760 LEE *Introd. Bot.* III. iv. 166 Fulcrate, propt; when their Branches descend to the Root; as in *Ficus*. **1860** FOWLER *Med. Voc.*, *Fulcrate*, in *Bot.*, having branches descending to the earth; having fulcres. **1880** GRAY *Struct. Bot.* 412/2.

fulcre. Englishing of FULCRUM (in sense 2 a).

1860 in FOWLER *Med. Voc.*

fulcrum ('fʌlkrəm, 'fʊl-). Pl. fulcra. Also 7 fulchrum. [a. L. *fulcrum* (in class.L. 'the post or foot of a couch'), f. root of *fulc-īre* to support, prop.]

1. a. A prop or support; now only *spec.* in *Mech.* the point against which a lever is placed to get purchase or upon which it turns or is supported.

1674 PETTY *Disc. Dupl. Proportion* 41 Square Rods.. whose Ends let be supported with convenient Blocks or Fulcra. **1690** BOYLE *Med. Hydrostat.* ix. 60 The Ballance hangs on a stable Fulcrum. **1774** GOLDSM. *Nat. Hist.* (1776) VII. 182 They [serpents] entirely want a *fulcrum*, if I may so express it, from whence to take their spring. **1802** PALEY *Nat. Theol.* viii. §2 The same spine was also..to afford a fulcrum, stay or basis for the insertion of the muscles which are spread over the trunk of the body. **1803** J. WOOD *Princ. Mech.* iv. 50 The Lever is an inflexible rod, moveable upon a point which is called the fulcrum or center of motion. **1832** DE LA BECHE *Geol. Man.* (ed. 2) 40 If the centre of gravity of the mass chances to be high and far removed from the perpendicular of its fulcrum, the stone falls from its elevation. **1855** HOLDEN *Hum. Osteol.* (1878) 141 The use of the scapula is to afford a movable fulcrum for the motions of the arm. **1869** GILLMORE *Reptiles & Birds* ii. 59 They hook themselves on to a tree, which gives them the power of a double fulcrum.

b. *fig.*

1678 CUDWORTH *Intell. Syst.* 472 The most excellent Fulcrum of the Soul, the perswasion of the Everliving God. *a* **1679** T. GOODWIN *Wks.* (1682) II. IV. 335 Our Hearts will need a most special strong fulchrum, support and susteiner (as the word imports). **1804** W. TAYLOR in *Ann. Rev.* II. 334 This..should have been selected as the fulcrum of indignation. **1850** MERIVALE *Rom. Emp.* (1865) I. iv. 172 The consulship was the fulcrum from which the whole Roman world was to be moved. **1853** SIR H. DOUGLAS *Milit. Bridges* (ed. 3) 222 A footing once gained is a fulcrum which should never be lost.

2. (Chiefly *pl.*) **a.** *Bot.* Accessory organs or appendages of a plant; e.g. bracts, stipules, tendrils, etc.

1785 MARTYN *Rousseau's Bot.* xxxi. 485 The parts I now allude to, are what he [Linnæus] calls *Fulcra*, props or supports of the plant. **1807** J. E. SMITH *Phys. Bot.* xvii. 218 Of the several kinds of Fulcra, or Appendages to a plant. **1874** COOKE *Fungi* 62 In an exotic genus..the fulcra, or appendages..are black.

b. *Ichth.* (*pl.*) The small osseous scales arranged in a row and situated on the anterior ray of the fins of many ganoid fishes.

1880 GÜNTHER *Fishes* 360 Vertical fins with a single series of fulcra in front. **1885** tr. *Claus' Zoöl.* II. 164 The spine-like splints known as *fulcra*.

c. *Zool.* The stem or median part of the incus of the mastax of certain rotifers.

1856 [see RAMUS 3]. **1886** C. T. HUDSON *Rotifera* I. 118 The trophi consist mainly of two ribbed rami, attached to a long narrow plate (the fulcrum). **1896** *Cambr. Nat. Hist.* II. 210 In the ventral wall of the gizzard of most Ploima is a median piece, the *fulcrum*, from which run forwards and upwards two pieces, the *rami*, which are hinged on the fulcrum. The Y-shaped structure formed of these three pieces is called the *incus* (anvil). **1951** L. H. HYMAN *Invertebrates* III. xiii. 88 The fulcrum, the median, usually posterior piece, is commonly a thin plate lying in the sagittal plane of the body. **1967** P. A. MEGLITSCH *Invert. Zool.* viii. 261/1 The fulcrum and rami together form the incus.

d. In trilobites (see quot. 1909).

1900 C. R. EASTMAN tr. *Zittel's Text-bk. Palaeontol.* I. 612 The distal portion [of the pleura], beginning at the fulcrum, may continue of equal thickness. **1909** *Cambr. Nat. Hist.* IV. 234 At some distance from the axis the pleurae are bent downwards and backwards. The point where this bend occurs is called the 'fulcrum'; it divides the pleura into an internal and an external part. **1953** SHROCK & TWENHOFEL *Princ. Invert. Paleontol.* (ed. 2) xiii. 583 (*caption*) Fulcrum.

e. *Ent.* In Diptera, a chitinous portion of the pharynx.

1910 C. G. HEWITT *House-Flies* 12 The Fulcrum.—This chitinous portion of the pharynx..lies on the lower part of the head and in the rostrum. **1925** A. D. IMMS *Gen. Textbk. Ent.* 597 Situated within this region is a complex framework of chitin known as the *fulcrum*, which forms a kind of case enclosing the pharynx, and is present in almost all Diptera. **1951** L. S. WEST *Housefly* iii. 51 Its [*sc.* the rostrum's] internal support consists chiefly of a large stirrup-shaped sclerite, the fulcrum.

fulder, Sc. var. of FOULDRE, *Obs.*, a thunderbolt.

1513 DOUGLAS *Æneis* XII. xiv. 88 Nor fulderis dynt..With sik a rummyll com bratland on sa fast.

fule, Sc. form of FOOL; obs. form of FOWL.

fulfil (fʊl'fɪl), *v.* Pa. t. and pa. pple. fulfilled (fʊl'fɪld). Forms: 1–7 (see FULL *a.* and FILL *v.*), 8–9 fullfill, 3–9 fulfill, 4– fulfil. [OE. *fullfyllan*, f.

FULL *a.* + *fyllan* to FILL. Cf. *to fill full*: see FILL *v.* I.]

1. *trans.* To fill to the full, fill up, make full. Const. *of*, *with*. Now only *arch.*

a. in material sense.

c **1000** ÆLFRIC *Gram.* xxvi. (Z.) 153 *Compleo*, ic fullfylle. *c* **1250** *Old Kent. Serm.* in *O.E. Misc.* (1872) 29 Þo serganz uuluelden þo faten of watere. *c* **1350** *Will. Palerne* 4319 Al þat huge halle was hastili fulfulled. **1382** WYCLIF *Gen.* i. 28 Growe ȝe and be ȝe multiplied and fulfille ȝe the erthe. *c* **1400** *Lanfranc's Cirurg.* 102 Aftirward I fulfillide þe wounde with hoot oile of rosis. **1483** CAXTON *Gold. Leg.* 79 b/2 All the londe therof shal be fulfyllid with deserte. ? *a* **1500** *Chester Pl.* (E.E.T.S.) ii. 68 All Beastes I byd yow multeply..the earth to fulfill. **1548–77** VICARY *Anat.* ii. (1888) 22 Simple and pure fleshe, which fulfylleth the concauities of voyde places. **1875** JOWETT *Plato* (ed. 2) III. 676 The world has received animals..and is fulfilled with them.

b. in immaterial applications.

a **1300** *Cursor M.* 852 (Gött.) God..fulfild þis world al wid his grace. **1413** *Pilgr. Sowle* (Caxton) v. xiv. (1859) 80 The Apostles were fulfylled with the holy ghoost. **1480** *Robt. Devyll* 5 Hys hearte was fullfylled all with thought. **1529** MORE *Comf. agst. Trib.* I. Wks. 1151/2 Theyr owne conscience..may fulfil their heartes wyth spirituall ioy. **1563** *Homilies* II. *Rogation Week* I. (1859) 475 He..fulfilleth both heaven and earth with his presence. **1612** T. TAYLOR *Comm. Titus* ii. 12 Be not drunke with wine, but be fulfilled with the spirit. **1825** SCOTT *Talism.* xxiv, I have never known knight more fulfilled of nobleness. **1830** TENNYSON *Poems* 35 Her subtil, warm, and golden breath Which mixing with the infant's blood Fullfills him with beatitude. **1864** SWINBURNE *Atalanta* 2120 Filling thine eyes And fulfilling thine ears With the brilliance of battle. **1870** MORRIS *Earthly Par.* I. I. 313 When he was fulfilled of this delight.

†**c.** To spread through the whole extent of; to pervade. *Obs.*

1382 WYCLIF *Jer.* xxiii. 24 Whether not heuene and erthe Y fulfille? seith the Lord. **1535** COVERDALE *Dan.* ii. 35 The stone..became a greate mountayne which fulfylleth the whole earth. **1581** MARBECK *Bk. of Notes* 436 The glorie of the Lord fulfilling the house.

†**2.** To furnish or supply to the full with what is wished for; to fill as with food; to satisfy the appetite or desire of. *Obs.*

a **1300** *E.E. Psalter* ciii[i]. 16 Be fulefilled sal trees ofe felde ilkan. *c* **1340** *Cursor M.* 6842 (Fairf.) Þe seyuende ȝere lete hit ly stille þe pouer men hunger for to fulfille. **1382** WYCLIF *Matt.* xv. 33 Therfore wherof so many loouys to vs in desert, that we fulfille so grete a cumpanye of peple? **1430–40** LYDG. *Bochas* III. i. (1554) 70 b, Thyne empty wombe eche day to fulfill, If thou mightest haue vittayle at thy will. *c* **1450** tr. *De Imitatione* I. i. 3 Þe eye is not fulfilled wiþ þe siȝt nor þe ere wiþ heringe. *c* **1500** *Lancelot* 941 Your plesance may ye wel fulfill Of me. **1592** TIMME *Ten Eng. Lepers* F ij, Not to sustaine nature..but to fulfill insaciable gurmandize. **1601** HOLLAND *Pliny* I. 114 To fulfill his greedy and endlesse appetite.

3. a. To fill up or make complete; to supply what is lacking in; †formerly sometimes with *forth*. Also, to fill up or supply the place of (something); to compensate for (a defect). *Obs.* exc. *arch.*

a **1175** *Cott. Hom.* 219 Al swa fele þe me mihte þat tioðe hape fulfellen. *c* **1290** *S. Eng. Leg.* I. 305/214 Þare-fore man is i-wrouȝt, To fulfulle þe teoþe ordre þat was out of heouene i-brouȝt. *c* **1380** WYCLIF *Last Age Chirche* p. xxvii, Cristen men hauen xxi lettris..and ȝeuynge to eche c. þe newe Testament was endid whanne þe noumbre of þes assingned lettris was fulfilled. **1382** —— *Phil.* ii. 2 Fulfille ȝe my joye. *c* **1400** *Lanfranc's Cirurg.* 29 Þo .ij. defautis þe medlynge of þe ligament fulfilliþ. *c* **1440** *Promp. Parv.* 182 Fulfyllyn or make a-cethe in thynge þat wantythe, *supleo.* **1473** in *Ld. Treas. Acc. Scotl.* (1877) I. 30 Item iij quarteris of blak to fulfill furth the lynyng of the Queynis goone. **1533** BELLENDEN *Livy* II. (1822) 107 The new Faderis chosin..to fulfill the auld nowmer of Faderis afore minist. **1556** ROBINSON tr. *More's Utop.* (ed. 2) II. (Arb.) 90 Then they fulfyll and make vp the numbre with cytezens. **1850** MRS. BROWNING *Poems* I. 9 Glory and life Fulfil their own depletions.

†**b.** *absol.* or *intr.* To supply what is wanted.

1390 GOWER *Conf.* III. 138 Where lacketh good the word fulfilleth To make amendes for the wronge.

†**4.** To fill, hold, or occupy (a position that has been vacant); to take (the place of something). *Obs.*

c **1200** *Trin. Coll. Hom.* 33 Man sholde fuluullen englene sete. *c* **1400** *Lanfranc's Cirurg.* 221 Þat it miȝte fulfille þe place of þe prote. **1432–50** tr. *Higden* (Rolls) I. 289 Whiche gete turfes..to fullefille the stede of woode. **1509** BARCLAY *Shyp of Folys* (1570) 168 His wretched Carcas shall the voyde graue fulfill. **1548–77** VICARY *Anat.* ii. (1888) 18 Some [bones] to fulfyll the hollowe places, as in the handes and feete.

5. To carry out or bring to consummation (a prophecy, promise, etc.); to satisfy (a desire, prayer). *refl.* Of a person: to work out one's destiny; to develp one's gifts and character to the full. (A development of Tennyson's use:)

In origin a Hebraism: a literal transl. of the Vulgate *adimplere, implere*, Hellenistic Greek πληροῦν, used in an unclassical sense after Heb. *ml'*, literally 'to fill'.

c **1290** *S. Eng. Leg.* I. 104/119 Ȝuit it scholde bi-foren eov alle bi fulfolid bi me her. *a* **1300** *Cursor M.* 26254 His flexs lust to ful-fill. *c* **1320** *Cast. Love* 1201 The profecye of Symeon Wes fulfylled thon. *c* **1385** CHAUCER *L.G.W.* 694 *Cleopatra*, Thilke comenant..I wele fulfille. **1400** G. AP DAVID in Ellis *Orig. Lett.* Ser. II. I. 6 Other thinges he behiȝt me the qwich he fulfylled nat. **1514** BARCLAY *Cyt. & Uplondyshm.* (Percy Soc.) 9 Fulfill thy promise, I praye the now begynne. *a* **1633** AUSTIN *Medit.* (1635) 43 His purpose was onely to get money: but God's purpose was (thereby) to bring Mary to Bethlehem. Hee, to fill full his Coffers, God, to fulfill the Prophecies. **1769** J. BROWN *Dict. Bible* (1818) s.v., To fulfil requests and desires is to grant the things desired. **1837** CARLYLE *Fr. Rev.* I. IV. i. (1872) 101 The universal prayer therefore is to be fulfilled. **1860** TYNDALL *Glac.* I. xvi. 112, I fulfilled to the letter my engagement..to ask no help. **1864** BRYCE *Holy Rom. Emp.* ix. (1875) 145 Full of bright promise never fulfilled. **1883** H. SPENCER in *Contemp. Rev.* XLIII. 15 Nature leads men by purely personal motives to fulfil her ends.

refl. **1842** TENNYSON *Gard. Dau.* 233 My desire..By its own energy fulfill'd itself. **1847** —— *Princ.* VII. 121 If you be, what I think you, some sweet dream, I would but ask you to fulfil yourself. **1920** R. MACAULAY *Potterism* III. i. §8. 117 In what place, under what conditions, would Oliver Hobart now fulfil himself, now carry on the work so faithfully begun on earth? *Ibid.* VI. v. §8. 259 Jane would, no doubt, fulfil herself in the course of time, make an adequate figure in the world she loved. **1971** *Times* 16 Oct. 8/7 The belief that a degree is evidence of 'ability' and that without one you..have not 'fulfilled' yourself.

6. a. To carry out, perform, execute, do (something enjoined); to obey or follow (a command, the law, etc.).

c **1250** *Gen. & Ex.* 1222 To fulfillen godes reed. *a* **1300** *Cursor M.* 9736 Þi will i sal euermar full-fill. **1390** GOWER *Conf.* III. 264 That thing may he nought fulfille. **1484** CAXTON *Fables of Æsop* II. xvi, My mayster..whiche constrayneth me to fulfylle his wylle. **1526** *Pilgr. Perf.* (W. de W. 1531) 2 So to study this present treatyse, that they may fulfyll it in theyr lyuyng. **1645** MILTON *Colast.* Wks. (1851) 353 Let not therfore under the name of fulfilling Charity, such an unmercifull..yoke, bee padlockt upon the neck of any Christian. **1667** —— *P.L.* XII. 402 The Law of God exact he shall fulfil. **1777** BLAIR *Serm.* I. iv. 111 Let us carry on our preparation for heaven..by fulfilling the duties and offices of every station in life. **1781** COWPER *Expost.* 644 To praise him is to serve him, and fulfil..his unquestioned will. **1835** J. H. NEWMAN *Par. Serm.* (1837) I. v. 76 In what sense do we fulfil the words of Christ? **1871** R. ELLIS *Catullus* lxiv. 310 Still each hand fulfilled its pious labour eternal.

†**b.** To perform, execute, accomplish (a deed).

a **1225** *Ancr. R.* 288 Ȝif þer were eise uorto fulfullen þe dede. *c* **1400** MAUNDEV. (1839) v. 53 Thei fulfillen first the more longe Pilgrymage, and after retournen aȝen be the nexte Weyes. **1582** A. MUNDAY *Discov. E. Campion* in Arb. *Garner* VIII. 205 The deaths of these noble personages should be presently fulfilled. **1593** SHAKS. *Lucr.* 1635 Where you did fulfil The loathsome act of lust.

c. To fill the requirements of, answer (a purpose), comply with (conditions).

1784 COWPER *Tiroc.* 93 If all..Fulfill the purpose, and appear design'd Proofs of the wisdom of th' all-seeing Mind. **1793** SMEATON *Edystone L.* §304 Every stone fulfils its place inside and out. **1834** LYTTON *Pompeii* I. ii, The numerous haunts which fulfilled with that idle people the office of cafés and clubs at this day. **1840** LARDNER *Geom.* 112 If in two triangles, either of the conditions of similarity be fulfilled, the other condition must also be fulfilled. **1860** MILL *Repr. Govt.* (1865) 1/1 To inquire what form of government is best fitted to fulfil those purposes. **1862** H. SPENCER *First Princ.* II. iv. §53 (1875) 174 Before a truth can be known as necessary, two conditions must be fulfilled. **1870** M. D. CONWAY *Earthw. Pilgr.* xxvii. 320 A street speaker and his audience fulfilling the condition of moving on. **1875** JOWETT *Plato* (ed. 2) V. 200 The Cretan laws..fulfil the object of laws, which is to make those who use them happy.

7. To bring to an end, finish, complete (a period, portion of time, a work, etc.).

c **1290** *S. Eng. Leg.* I. 5/145 Ȝwane þe time were folfuld. **1340** *Ayenb.* 262 Þis boc is uolueld ine þe eue of þe holy apostles Symon an Iudas. *c* **1400** *Lanfranc's Cirurg.* 168 Þere is fulfillid þe firste digestioun of þe guttis. *c* **1400** tr. *Secreta Secret., Gov. Lordsh.* (E.E.T.S.) 71 Turne þe vpon þy left syde, and fulfylle þy sleepe vpon þat syde. **1413** *Pilgr. Sowle* (Caxton) v. i. (1859) 72 A thynge that is infynyte maye not be fulfilled. **1526–34** TINDALE *Acts* xiii. 25 When John had fulfylled his course, he sayde, whome ye thinke that I am the same am I not. **1535** COVERDALE *2 Sam.* vii. 12 Whan thy tyme is fulfylled yͭ thou shalt slepe with thy fathers. **1784** COWPER *Task* VI. 786 Six thousand years of sorrow have well-nigh Fulfilled their tardy and disastrous course Over a sinful world. **1814** SCOTT *Ld. of Isles* II. xxix, Whose ill-timed speed Fulfill'd my soon-repented deed.

Hence **ful'filled** *ppl. a.*

1649 MILTON *Eikon.* xxvii. Wks. (1847) 329/1 All our past and fulfill'd miseries.

fulfiller (fʊl'fɪlə(r)). [f. FULFIL *v.* + -ER¹.] One who fulfils, in various senses of the vb.

1413 *Pilgr. Sowle* (Caxton 1483) v. xiv. 108 The hooly ghoost that is the ender and the fulfiller. **1545** BRINKLOW *Lament.* 24 b, Christ wolde not breake the lawe, but was the fullfiller of the lawe. **1692** SOUTH *Serm.* (1718) II. 102 God himself is first the author, and then the fulfiller of them. **1752** LAW *Spirit of Love* II. (1816) 138 A fulfiller of all righteousness. **1843** HOOD *Forge* I. xiii, Of his duty so true a fulfiller. **1860** PUSEY *Min. Proph.* 110 The faithful Fulfiller of His promises.

fulfilling (fʊl'fɪlɪŋ), *vbl. sb.* [f. FULFIL *v.* + -ING¹.] The action of the vb. FULFIL in various senses; an instance of this; also *concr.* that which fulfils. Cf. FULFILMENT, now usually substituted.

1340 *Ayenb.* 260 God þet is þe ende and þe uoluellinge and þe somme of his wylninges. **1382** WYCLIF *Rom.* xiii. 10 Therfore loue is the plente, or fulfillinge, of the lawe. **1480** CAXTON *Chron. Eng.* ccxxxviii. 263 For vnmesurable fulfylling of his lust his lyf shorted the souner. **1526** *Pilgr. Perf.* (W. de W. 1531) 43 The accomplysshynge or fulfyllynge of his commaundementes. **1628** J. GAULE *Pract. Theories* (1629) 22 He could haue indured any thing rather then a Prophecies not fulfilling. **1671** MILTON *P.R.* II. 109 With thoughts Meekly compos'd awaited the fulfilling. **1715** DE FOE *Fam. Instruct.* I. i. (1841) I. 29 The fulfilling of Old Testament types, and Old Testament promises.

fulfilling (fʊl'fɪlɪŋ), *ppl. a.* [f. as prec. + -ING².] That fulfils, in senses of the vb.; †hence, complementary or suitable *to* (*obs.*).

1340 *Ayenb.* 113 Þaȝ ha leuede an hondred year..he ne miȝte naȝt do uoluellinde penonce of one dyadliche zenne. **1452** in Willis & Clark *Cambridge* (1886) I. 282 A Batylment by nethe with a Crest above and a Casement fulfyllyng to the werk. **1606** SHAKS. *Tr. & Cr.* Prol. 18 With massie Staples And corresponsiue and fulfilling Bolts.

fulfilment (fʊl'fɪlmənt). [f. FULFIL *v.* + -MENT.] The action or an act or process of fulfilling; accomplishment, performance, completion. (Not in Johnson 1755.)

1775 in ASH. **1777** BLAIR *Serm.* I. v. 141 With what entire confidence ought we to wait for the fulfilment of all his other promises, in their due time. **1786–1805** J. H. TOOKE *Purley* (1860) 586 Gage. By which a man is bound to certain fulfilments. **1830** HERSCHEL *Stud. Nat. Phil.* I. iii. (1851) 42 There are consequences and fulfilments of the laws of nature. **1849** JAMES *Woodman* ii, She exacted a fulfilment of all prescribed duties from her nuns. **1891** *Law Rep.* Weekly Notes 76/2 The fulfilment of the condition literally became impossible.

† **'fulgence.** *Obs.* [f. as next: see -ENCE.] = next.

? *a* **1500** *Chester Pl.* (E.E.T.S.) i. 180 And here were now the Trynitie, We sholde him pass by our fulgence. *a* **1645** HEYWOOD *Epil.* Wks. 1874 VI. 343 May Venus and the Moones bright constellations, With their best fulgence smile on all your Nations. **1652** BENLOWES *Theoph.* v. lvii, Sols radiant Fulgence in meridian Skies Seem'd shade unto those Clarities.

† **'fulgency.** *Obs.* [f. next: see -ENCY.] Fulgent quality; brightness, splendour.

1659 D. PELL *Impr. Sea* 480 A flower that will constantly expose itself unto the fulgency of the Sun. **1794** SULLIVAN *View Nat.* II. 412 The great fulgency and clearness of the sun's light.

fulgent ('fʌldʒənt), *a.* [ad. L. *fulgent-em*, pr. pple. of *fulgēre* to shine: see -ENT.] Shining brightly; brilliant, glittering, resplendent. Now *poet.* or *rhetorical.*

1432–50 tr. *Higden* (Rolls) I. 13 Asches or sonde, whiche semenge as thynges impure and wontenge ly3hte be wonte to yelde pure materes and fulgent. ? *a* **1500** *York Myst.*, *Inholders* (1885) 514 Hayle! fulgent Phebus. **1615** CROOKE *Body of Man* 563 It doth lesse hinder the fulgent brightnes of the christaline. **1636** HEYWOOD *Loves Mistress* 2nd Prol. Wks. 1874 V. 88 Liquid Gold Of fulgent beautie. **1667** MILTON *P.L.* x. 449 At last, as from a Cloud, his fulgent head And shape Starr-bright appeer'd. **1770** GLOVER *Leonidas* IV. 518 Other Thracians..fulgent morions wore, With horns of bulls in imitating brass Curv'd o'er the crested ridge. **1807** WORDSW. *Gipsies* 16 Then issued Vesper from the fulgent west. **1835** *Blackw. Mag.* XXXVIII. 401 Brighter..than the stream Which in Pirene shed its fulgent gleam.

fig. **1879** G. MEREDITH *Egoist* II. ii. 32 The studious mind ..throws off acids and crusty particles in the piling of the years, until it is fulgent by clarity.

b. *Her.* (See quot.)

1828–40 BERRY *Encycl. Her.* I, *Fulgent*, having rays, as a star fulgent.

Hence **'fulgently** *adv.*, **'fulgentness**.

1727 BAILEY vol. II, *Fulgentness.* **1880** G. MEREDITH *Trag. Com.* (1881) 36 Her hero faced about and stood up, looking at her fulgently.

fulgid ('fʌldʒɪd), *a.* [ad. L. *fulgid-us*, f. *fulgēre* to shine.]

1. Flashing, glittering, shining.

1656–81 BLOUNT *Glossogr.*, *Fulgid*, shining, glistering, bright. **1678** R. R[USSELL] *Geber* II. I. III. vi. 74 Of most.. fulgid Splendor. **1715–20** POPE *Iliad* x. 547 Through the brown shade the fulgid weapons shined. **1773** WILSON in *Phil. Trans.* LXIV. 16 This beauteous substance is at the surface, most fulgid. **1791** W. BARTRAM *Carolina* 51 The fulgid sunbeams spread abroad their animating light. **1822** T. TAYLOR *Apuleius* XI. 261 A very black robe fulgid with a dark splendour. **1870** EMERSON *Soc. & Solit.* viii. 163 Demons with fulgid eyes.

2. *Nat. Hist.* (See quot.)

1826 KIRBY & SP. *Entomol.* IV. 279 *Fulgid*, a bright fiery red.

Hence **ful'gidity**, fulgid state or condition.

1656–81 in BLOUNT *Glossogr.* **1755** in JOHNSON; and in mod. Dicts.

fulgor, fulgour ('fʌlgə(r), -ɔː(r)). *arch.* [a. L. *fulgor*, f. *fulgēre* to shine.] A brilliant or flashing light; dazzling brightness, splendour.

1602 MARSTON *Ant. & Mel.* I. Introd., By the resplendent fulgor of this steele, I will defende the feminine to death. **1646** SIR T. BROWNE *Pseud. Ep.* III. x. 128 Glowewormes alive, project a lustre in the darke, which fulgour notwithstanding ceaseth after death. **1665** SIR T. HERBERT *Trav.* (1677) 302 Chains of burnished Gold or Brass, whose fulgor they delighted in. **1791** W. BARTRAM *Carolina* 13 The fulgour and rapidity of the streams of lightning..exhibited a very awful scene. **1837** CARLYLE *Fr. Rev.* II. v. iv, There had risen..quite another variegated Glitter and nocturnal Fulgor. **1877** L. MORRIS *Epic Hades* II. 103 Leaped up the hot red sun above the sea, And lit the horrid fulgour of his scales.

fig. **1635** HEYWOOD *Hierarch.* v. 278 Those Mindes and Essences diuine By nature with Miraculous Fulgor shine. **1668** H. MORE *Div. Dial.* I. xiv. (1713) 28 *Hyl.* There shines from them such an intellectual fulgor. **1834** *Fraser's Mag.* X. 699 Their influence shall enable us to make this article.. glow with a fulgour not otherwise its own.

fulgorid ('fʌlgərɪd), *sb.* and *a. Ent.* [ad. mod.L. *Fulgoridæ*, f. the generic name *Fulgora*, a. L. *Fulgora* goddess of lightning, f. *fulgur* lightning:

see -ID[3].] A. *sb.* An insect of the homopterous family Fulgoridæ which includes the lantern-flies. B. *adj.* Belonging to this family.

1893 in *Funk's Stand. Dict.* **1899** *Cambr. Nat. Hist.* VI. 576 The wax of Fulgorids is used by the Chinese for candles. **1913** *Zoologist* 4th Ser. XVII. 281 Some notes on a Luminous South African Fulgorid Insect (Rhinortha Guttata). *Ibid.* 289 With approach of cold weather all signs of the Fulgorid parasites disappeared. **1923** H. M. LEFROY *Man. Ent.* 259 Some Fulgorids are quite small, others are very large: the Lantern-flies are included in this family; they were so called because the front of the head, extending into a bladder-like structure, was believed to be luminous. **1926** E. O. ESSIG *Insects Western N. Amer.* 218 The date fulgorid ..is 4–6 mm. long, reddish-brown in the nymphal stage and very dark brown in the adult stage. **1954** BORROR & DELONG *Introd. Study Insects* xx. 260 None of the fulgorids is known to be luminescent.

fulgorous (ˈfʌlgərəs), *a. rare.* [f. FULGOR + -OUS.] Flashing, brilliant, lustrous. *lit.* and *fig.*

1772 NUGENT tr. *Hist. Fr. Gerund* I. 204 Their waxen wings desolving at the inflamed and sparkling rays of so fulgorous and resplendent a defender. **1833** CARLYLE *Diderot* Misc. 1857 III. 194 He heard him [Diderot] talk one day..with a fulgorous impetuosity almost beyond human.

‖ **ˈfulgur.** *Obs.* [L., f. *fulgēre* to lighten.] Lightning, a flash of lightning.

1563 W. FULKE *Meteors* (1640) 27 Fulgur is that kinde of lightning which followeth thunder. **1695** D'URFEY *Gloriana* ix. 2 Till by some Flashes of Ætherial Fire, And fatal Fulgur glimmering Light was lent.

fig. **1665** SIR T. HERBERT *Trav.* (1677) 175 The King..by the fulgur of his eye can dart them dead.

fulgural (ˈfʌlgjʊərəl), *a. rare.* [a. F. *fulgural*, ad. L. *fulgurālis*, f. *fulgur* lightning: see -AL[1].] Of or pertaining to lightning. ***fulgural science*** (Fr. *science fulgurale*): divination by lightning.

1656–81 BLOUNT *Glossogr.*, *Fulgural*, belonging to lightning. **1813** T. BUSBY tr. *Lucretius* VI. Comm. iv, The Romans, it is well known, derived from the Tuscans the system of their fulgural superstition. *Ibid.* v. Comm. v, Their skill in fulgural divination. **1891** tr. *De la Saussaye's Man. Sc. Relig.* xvi. 139 This fulgural science was considered of Etruscan origin.

† **ˈfulgurance.** *Obs. rare.* [f. next: see -ANCE.] Dazzling brilliance (as of lightning).

1652 BENLOWES *Theoph.* VI. xxiv, Who, like a full-orb'd Moon, our stars out-shin'd In glorious Fulgurance of minde. *Ibid.* VII. xxviii, From this Fulgurance such splendors fly.

fulgurant (ˈfʌlgjʊərənt), *a.* [ad. L. *fulgurant-em*, pr. pple. of *fulgurāre* to lighten, f. *fulgur* lightning: see -ANT.] Flashing like lightning.

1647 H. MORE *Resolution* Poems 175 [Though] Nature play her fiery games In this forc'd Night, with fulgurant flames. **1840** BROWNING *Sordello* v. 43 Careful Jove's face be duly fulgurant. **1868** —— *Ring & Bk.* VI. 1600 That erect form, flashing brow, fulgurant eye.

Hence **ˈfulgurantly** *adv.*

1873 DOWDEN in *Contemp. Rev.* July 193 This eruption [in V. Hugo's *Châtiments*], which is meant to overwhelm the gewgaw Empire goes on fulgurantly, resoundingly, and not without scoriæ and smoke.

ˈfulgurate, *v.* [f. L. *fulgurāt-* ppl. stem of *fulgurāre* to lighten, f. *fulgur* lightning: see -ATE[3].] *intr.* To emit vivid flashes like lightning.

1677 *Phil. Trans.* XVIII. 867 [It] doth now and then fulgurate, and sometimes also raise it self as 'twere into waves of light. **1686** GOAD *Celest. Bodies* II. iii. 179 As soon would we have believed that two Diamonds could Fulgurate. **1756** [see FLAGRATE *v.*]

Hence **ˈfulgurating** *ppl. a.*; also *transf.* (of pains) darting like lightning through the body.

1677 *Phil. Trans.* XVIII. 867 This fulgurating substance carries its light alwaies with it. **1709** F. HAUKSBEE *Phys. Mech. Exp.* ii. (1719) 36 A brisk Fulgurating Light was produc'd. **1878** A. M. HAMILTON *Nerv. Dis.* 276 The individual may first notice the commencement of the disease by fulgurating pains which dart from the feet up the legs and thighs.

fulguration (fʌlgjʊəˈreɪʃən). [ad. L. *fulgurātiōn-em*, n. of action f. *fulgurāre*: see FULGURATE and -ATION. Cf. F. *fulguration*.]

1. The action of lightning or flashing like lightning; chiefly in *pl.* flashes of lightning. Now *rare* in literal sense.

1633 J. DONE *Hist. Septuagint* 57 Your Eyes..were so incountred with the order and splendor of the workes..so as you should be forced to turn them elsewhere or not too stedfastly behold their Fulguration. **1642** HOWELL *For. Trav.* (Arb.) 12 Though thunder be first in Nature being by the violent eruption it makes out of the cloud the cause of such fulgurations. **1684** T. BURNET *Th. Earth* II. 93 These signs are chiefly..the fulgurations of the air, and the falling of stars. **1813** T. FORSTER *Atmosph. Phaenom.* (1815) 76 The vespertine fulgurations, called summer lightning, are not followed by any thunder at all.

fig. **1874** H. R. REYNOLDS *John Bapt.* ii. 88 Angels are the fulgurations of His power. **1877** E. CAIRD *Philos. Kant* v. 86 The continual fulgurations of deity.

2. In *Assaying.* (See quots.) Cf. BLICK.

1676 COLES, *Fulguration*, a reducing metals into vapours by the help of lead (in a copel) and a violent fire. **1758** REID tr. *Macquer's Chym.* I. 323 The surface of that metal will at once dart out a dazling splendour: but, if the fire be strong enough to keep the Silver in fusion..this change of colour, which is called its fulguration, will not be so perceptible, and the Silver will appear like a bead of fire. **1853** URE *Dict. Arts* I. 98 When the lead is wasted to a certain degree, a very thin film of it only remains on the silver, which causes the iridescent appearance, like the colours of soap-bubbles; a phenomenon, called by the old chemists, fulguration.

3. *Med.* [a. F. *fulguration* (S. Pozzi 1907, in *Bull. de l'Acad. de Méd.* 30 July 193).] The destruction of tissues, esp. tumours, by means of electric sparks.

1907 *Daily Chron.* 11 Oct. 5/6 Dr. Hart [*sc.* de Keating-Hart] treats cancer by ordinary surgical means, utilising fulguration as a valuable healing agent. **1962** *Lancet* 31 Mar. 693/1 Fulguration [of the bladder neck] aims at destroying infected glands and pseudo-polyps but may cure by destroying part of the internal sphincter.

‖ **ˈfulgurator.** *rare.* [L. *fulgurātor*, f. *fulgur* lightning.] A priest who interprets lightning.

1813 T. BUSBY tr. *Lucretius* VI. Comm. v, The Tuscan fulgurators..were induced..to direct sacrifices which they knew would be unacceptable to the Gods.

† **ˈfulgure.** *Obs. rare.* [a. OF. *fulgure*, f. L. *fulgur* lightning.] = FULGOR.

a **1633** AUSTIN *Medit.* (1635) 88 The Light or fulgure in it [star] was purely Supernaturall. **1661** MORGAN *Sph. Gentry* I. iii. 34 Noble by reason of fulgure and transparencie.

fulˈgureous, *a. rare*[−1]. [f. L. *fulgureus* (f. *fulgur* lightning): see -EOUS.] Of the nature of lightning.

1865 TYLOR *Early Hist. Man.* viii. 224 Generated in the sky by a fulgureous exhalation.

fulgurite (ˈfʌlgjʊəraɪt). [f. L. *fulgur* lightning + -ITE.]

1. *Geol.* (See quot. 1865.) Also written (less correctly) ***fulgorite***.

1834 MRS. SOMERVILLE *Connex. Phys. Sc.* xxvii. (1835) 312 Dr. Fiedler exhibited several of these fulgorites in London..dug out of the sandy plains of Silesia and Eastern Prussia. **1845** DARWIN *Voy. Nat.* iii. (1852) 60 At Paris MM. Hachette and Beudant succeeded in making tubes in most respect similar to these fulgurites. **1865** PAGE *Handbk. Geol. Terms*, *Fulgurite*, *Fulgorite*, any rocky substance that has been fused or vitrified by lightning. More strictly applied to a bore or tube produced by the passage of lightning into a sandy soil. **1884** *Cornh. Mag.* Nov. 526 In sand or rock, where lightning has struck, it often forms long hollow tubes, known to the calmly discriminating geological intelligence as fulgurites.

2. An explosive substance (see quot. 1889).

1882 H. S. DRINKER *Tunnelling* (ed. 2) 102. **1889** CUNDILL *Dict. Explosives*, *Fulgurite* consists of nitro-glycerine mixed with some coarsely ground farinaceous substance. **1894** *Daily News* 22 Jan. 5/5 At Geneva a trial has been made in a quarry with the new explosive, 'fulgurite', under the direction of the inventor, Raoul Pictet.

† **fulˈgurity.** *Obs.*[−0] (See quots.)

1623 COCKERAM, *Fulguritie*, lightening. [In eds. 1631–2 printed *Fulgurite*, in 1637–9 *Fulgurie*.] **1721** BAILEY, *Fulgurity*, Shining, Glistering.

fulgurous (ˈfʌlgjʊərəs), *a.* Also 7 fulgrous. [f. L. *fulgur* lightning + -OUS.] Resembling lightning; full of or charged with lightning. Also *fig.*

1616 J. LANE *Contn. Sqr.'s T.* VIII. 217 The pitchie clowdes of fulgrous heavn. **1865** CARLYLE *Fredk. Gt.* XIX. viii. VIII. 261 The angry similitude had shot, slightly fulgurous and consolatory, athwart the gloom of one's mood. **1876** LOWELL *Ode* Poet. Wks. 1890 IV. 94 Of Rome, fair quarry where those eagles crowd Whose fulgurous vans about the world had blown Triumphant storm and seeds of polity.

fulham (ˈfʊləm). *slang.* Forms: 6 fullan, 6–7 fullam, 6–8 fullom, (7 fullum), 7– fulham. [Of uncertain origin: by some conjectured to be derived from the place-name *Fulham*, once a noted haunt of gamesters. Another conjecture is that the oldest form *fullan* = 'full one', which would suit the sense.] A die loaded at the corner. (A ***high fulham*** was loaded so as to ensure a cast of 4, 5, or 6; a ***low fulham***, so as to ensure a cast of 1, 2, or 3.)

c **1550** *Dice-Play* C iiij a, Fullans..be square outward. Yet being within at the corner with lead, or other pondorus matter stopped, minister as great an aduantage as any of the rest. **1592** *Nobody & Someb.* in Simpson *Sch. Shaks.* (1878) I. 337 Those are called high Fulloms. **1598** SHAKS. *Merry W.* I. iii. 94 Let Vultures gripe thy guts: for gourd, and Fullam holds: & high and low beguiles the rich & poore. **1605** *Lond. Prodigal* I. i, Two bale of false dice, videlicet, high men and low men, fulloms..and other bones of function. **1674** COTTON *Compl. Gamester* 12 This they do by false Dice, as High-Fullams 4, 5, 6. Low-Fullams 1, 2, 3. **1711** PUCKLE *Club* 21 At dice they have The Doctors, the fulloms. **1801** *Sporting Mag.* XVIII. 100 A bale of fulhams. **1889** DOYLE *Micah Clarke* xxx. 316 There is no loading of the dice, or throwing of fulhams.

fig. **1644–7** CLEVELAND *Char. Lond. Diurn.* (1677) 108 Now a Scotch-man's Tongue runs high *Fullams*. There is a Cheat in his Idiom. **1664** BUTLER *Hud.* II. i. 642 One cut out to pass your tricks on, With Fulhams of Poetick fiction.

† **fuˈliginated,** *a. Obs. rare.* [f. L. *fūlīgināt-us* (f. *fūlīgo* soot) + -ED[1].] Of a sooty colour, as if powdered black.

1634 SIR T. HERBERT *Trav.* 193 Such the misery of these fuliginated creatures, who as they use all Ceremonies of devotion usually on the nights and not at daytime, tis they say because the Devill is then sole Ruler. **1796** KIRWAN *Elem. Min.* (ed. 2) II. 310 It is formed either by the union of the Yellow Calx with an excess of Volalkali, and this may be called the Fuliginated Calx.

† **fuligiˈnose,** *a. Obs.*[−0] [ad. L. *fūlīginōs-us*: see FULIGINOUS and -OSE.] = FULIGINOUS 1 and 3.

1721–36 in BAILEY. **1866** in *Treas. Bot.*

fuliginosity (fjuːˌlɪdʒɪˈnɒsɪtɪ). [ad. F. *fuliginosité*, f. L. *fūlīginōs-us* (see next) + -ITY.] The condition or quality of being fuliginous or sooty; sooty matter, soot.

1758 REID tr. *Macquer's Chym.* I. 185 A short tapering funnel..which will serve for a chimney to carry off all fuliginosities. **1799** KIRWAN *Geol. Ess.* 471 All fuliginosities arising from combustion on the surface of the earth are finally carried into the sea.

fig. **1837** CARLYLE *Mirabeau*, *Ess.* (1840) V. 136 In the old Marquis there dwells withal..a latent fury and fuliginosity very perverting. **1895** *Expositor* Nov. 350 This might be due to intentional fuliginosity—(if I may coin a word) but it cannot be the case that the whole of the Talmud has been wilfully obscured.

fuliginous (fjuːˈlɪdʒɪnəs), *a.* Also 7 -enous, -inus. [ad. L. *fūlīginōs-us*, f. *fūlīgo* soot: see -OUS. Cf. F. *fuligineux*, *-euse*.]

1. Pertaining to, consisting of, containing, or resembling soot; sooty.

1621 BURTON *Anat. Mel.* I. ii. II. v, It offends commonly if it be to..fuligenous, cloudy, blustering, or a tempestuous Aire. **1638** WILKINS *New World* I. (1684) 73 This Fuliginus matter, which did thus obscure the Sun, must needs be very near his Body. **1646** SIR T. BROWNE *Pseud. Ep.* VI. xii. 334 A sootish and fuliginous matter proceeding from the sulphur of bodies torrified. **1684** EVELYN *Diary* 24 Jan., London..was so filled with the fuliginous steam of the sea-coal, that hardly could one see across the streets. **1731** HALES *Stat. Ess.* I. 260 In great cities where the air is full of fuliginous vapours. **1822** LAMB *Elia* Ser. I. *Praise of Chimneysweepers*, The fuliginous concretions, which are sometimes found (in dissections) to adhere to the roof of the mouth in these unfledged practitioners. **1842** DE QUINCEY *Pagan Oracles* Wks. VIII. 222 A huge octagon lamp, that apparently never had been cleaned from smoke and fuliginous tarnish.

fig. c **1645** HOWELL *Lett.* (1650) II. 107 Prayer compar'd with praise, is but a fuliginous smoak issuing from the sense of sin. **1761** STERNE *Tr. Shandy* III. xix, His ideas..all obfuscated and darkened over with fuliginous matter! **1845** CARLYLE *Cromwell* (1871) IV. 3 A very fuliginous set of doctrines. **1860** TROLLOPE *Cast. Richmond* II. 80 The debate went on..with many sparks..of eager benevolence, and some few passing clouds of fuliginous self-interest.

b. Covered or blackened with soot. Chiefly in humorously bombastic use.

a **1763** [see FULIGINOUSLY]. **1843** CARLYLE *Past & Pr.* III. xv, To that dingy fuliginous Operative, emerging from his soot-mill. **1865** *Dublin Univ. Mag.* II. 32 A fuliginous suburb of factories. *a* **1876** M. COLLINS *Pen Sketches* (1879) I. 59 The pleasant gardens..are a delight and a luxury to the Londoner escaped from some close fuliginous domicile. **1884** *Pall Mall G.* 16 Oct. 1/1 All the world is peering down the fuliginous chimney.

† **2.** In old physiology applied to certain thick 'vapours' or 'exhalations' said to be formed by organic combustion, and noxious to the head and vital parts. *Obs.*

1574 NEWTON *Health Mag.* 53 Those apples..repel and drive away all fuliginous moyste vapours which trouble the harte and strike up into the head. **1621** BURTON *Anat. Mel.* II. v. I. iv, It is not amiss to bore the scull with an instrument to let out the fuliginous vapours. **1664** POWER *Exp. Philos.* I. 57 The grosser Steams that continually perspire out of our own Bodies..are the fuliginous Eructations of that internal fire, that constantly burns within us. **1725** BRADLEY *Fam. Dict.* s.v. *Bath*, It will be attended with these two Advantages, viz. the Dissipation of the fuliginous Excrements, and drawing out the superfluous Humours.

3. (Chiefly *Nat. Hist.*) Soot-coloured, dusky.

[**1688** R. HOLME *Armoury* II. 290 The upper part of the Body is brown, or Fuligineous (*sic*).] **1822–34** *Good's Study Med.* (ed. 4) I. 339 A morbid deep-coloured bile, fulvous, greenish, or fuliginous. **1826** KIRBY & SP. *Entomol.* IV. 282 *Fuliginous*, the opaque black of soot. **1869** O. W. HOLMES *Cinders from Ashes* in *Old Vol. Life* (1891) 247 An older and much bigger boy, or youth, with a fuliginous complexion. **1874** COUES *Birds N.W.* 642 Entire plumage deep sooty or fuliginous blackish.

Hence **fuˈliginously** *adv.*, **fuˈliginousness.**

1576 NEWTON *Lemnie's Complex.* (1633) 222 When this sinke of Melancholy is once exhausted, and all fuliginousnesse banished. **1652** FRENCH *Yorksh. Spa* ii. 27 According to the fuliginousness of vapours more or less recoiling, the fire is more or less choaked. *a* **1763** SHENSTONE *Wks.* (1764) I. 114 To rear some breathless vapid flow'rs Or shrubs fuliginously grim. **1837** CARLYLE *Fr. Rev.* II. II. iii, Military France is everywhere full of sour inflammatory humour, which exhales itself fuliginously, this way or that.

‖ **fuligo** (fjuːˈlaɪgəʊ). [L.] Soot. (See also quot. 1727.)

1646 SIR T. BROWNE *Pseud. Ep.* VI. xii. 335 Thus Camphire of a white substance, by its fuligo affordeth a deepe black. **1693** EVELYN *De la Quint. Compl. Gard.* Advt. to Curious 4 Wax, or Oyl-Olive (for such it ought to be, to avoid the intollerable smell and fuligo's of gross and cheaper Materials). **1727** BAILEY vol. II, *Fuligo*, sulphureous, foul and thick Vapours, breath'd out at the Mouth, or thro' the Pores of the Body. **1830** *Westm. Rev.* XII. 387 The book before us smells pestilently of orange peel and the lamp..nor is the *fuligo* wanting.

fulimart, obs. form of FOUMART.

fulk (fʊlk), *v. dial.* Also fullock. [Of obscure origin; cf. FULKAT.] (See quots.) Hence **ˈfullocking** *vbl. sb.*

a **1784** in MILLES *MS. Gloss.* (Halliw.). **1796** GROSE *Dict. Vulg. Tongue* (ed. 3), *Fulk*, to use an unfair motion of the hand in plumping at taw. *Schoolboy's term.* **1843** *P. Parley's*

Ann. IV. 311 Come, down with your taw—no fulking... I like to see boys manly, even in their boyhood. **1874** HALLIWELL, *Fulk*, a phrase made use of by boys playing at taw, when they slily push the hand forward to be nearer the mark. *Fullock*, to jerk the hand unlawfully. A term at marbles. **1869** *Lonsdale Gloss.*, *Fullock*, to jerk the hand and arm unlawfully at marbles, instead of shooting from the thumb-joint with the hand perfectly steady. **1875** *Whitby Gloss.*, *Fullock*, to fire a marble..from the hand by a jerk of the bent thumb. 'That was well fullock'd.'

fulk, obs. form of FOLK.

†**fulkat**, *v. Obs. rare*$^{-1}$. (See quot.)

1688 R. HOLME *Armoury* III. 263/1 Fulkat, or Fulkating over hand [in the Game of Truck] is to make your Ball jump over his through the Argolis, when his Ball lies directly in the way before you.

†'**fulker**. *Obs. rare*$^{-1}$. [Corruption of Ger. *fucker, fugger*: cf. FOGGER, FOOKER, FOWKER.] 'A pawnbroker or usurer' (Halliwell).

1566 GASCOIGNE *Supposes* ii. iii, A prety paune, the fulkers will not lend you a farthing upon it.

†**full**, *sb.*[1] *Obs.* [OE. *ful* = OS. *ful*, ON. *full*, str. neut.; perh. originally the neuter of the adj.] A cup, goblet; a bumper.

Beowulf 616 þa freolic wif ful ȝe-sealde ærest Eastdena eþel-wearde. *c* **1000** *Sax. Leechd.* I. 88 Drince ðonne þreo ful fulle..nistiȝ. *c* **1205** LAY. 14325 Oder uul me þider fareð ..þenne þat uul beoð icumen þenne cusseoð heo þreoien.

†**full**, *sb.*[2] *Obs. rare.*$^{-1}$ [Identical with Sc. *fow* (see quot. 1673 below) of which FOOSE seems to be the plural, and FOUAT a derivative or compound.

It is not clear whether Bullen's *full* is the original form (? from FULL *a.*, with reference to the fleshy leaves), or due to his own conjectural identification of the sb. *fow* with *fow* = full.]

Houseleek.

1562 BULLEIN *Bk. Simples* (1579) 35 It is called Houslike ..in the South parts of England, but in the North it is called Full. **1673** WEDDERBURN *Vocab.*, *Sedum majus*, Fow.

full (fʊl), *a.*, *sb.*[3], and *adv.* Forms: 1–7 ful, 3–5 fol(le, *south.* vol(le, 4–5 fulle, 6 *Sc.* fow, 8 *Sc.* fou, 1– full. [Com. Teut.: OE. *full* = OFris. *fol, ful*, OS. *ful(l* (Du. *vol*), OHG. *fol(l* (MHG. *vol*, mod.Ger. *voll*), ON. *full-r* (OSw. *fuld-er*, mod.Sw. *full*, Da. *fuld*), Goth. *full-s*:—OTeut. **follo-*, *fullo-*:—OAryan **pl̥-nó*, represented also in Lith. *pilna-s*, OSl. *plŭnŭ*; cf. also the synonymous Skr. *pūrṇá*, L. *plēnus*, OIr. *lán*, Welsh *llawn*(:—pre-Celtic **plāno-*, *plōno-*), which though not formally identical contain the same root and suffix. From the Aryan root **pel-*, *pol-*, *-pl̥*, and its extended forms *plē-*, *plō-*, etc. are derived many words expressing the notion of abounding, filling, etc., as Skr. *puru*, Gr. πολύς (see FELE *a.*); Gr. πιμπλάναι to fill, πλήρης full, πλῆθος multitude, L. (*com-*, *im-*, *op-*, *re-*, *sup-*) *plēre* to fill, *plūs* more.

In this and in several other words (Sievers *Ags. Gr.* §55), the OE. *u* represents WGer. *o*; when this is the case a labial consonant is almost always present, but the precise conditions have not been determined.]

A. *adj.*

1. a. Having within its limits all it will hold; having no space empty; replete. Const. *of* (in OE. with *genitive*). Often with intensive phrases, as ***full as an egg, full to the brim*** (see BRIM *sb.*[2] 4b), ***full to overflowing, full up*** (colloq.), etc. For advbl. phrase ***full mouth***: see MOUTH.

a **1000** *Judith* 19 þær wæron bollan steape boren..swylce eac bunan and orcas fulle flettsittendum. *c* **1290** *S. Eng. Leg.* I. 193/45 A fat þare stod fol of baþe-water. *a* **1300** *E.E. Psalter* cxliii. 14 Cleues ofe þa fulle ere yhite [*promptuaria eorum plena*]. *c* **1400** *Lanfranc's Cirurg.* 41 Heelde into þe hoole..hoot oile of roses.. til al þe wounde be ful. *c* **1483** CAXTON *Vocab.* 12 Hit is of a fulle fatte. **1563** W. FULKE *Meteors* (1640) 56 The ignorant in Philosophy must be admonished, that all things are full, nothing is empty, for nature abhorreth emptinesse. **1590** NASHE *Pasquil's Apol.* I. C ij b, To preache to Gods people vpon a full stomach. **1597** SHAKS. *2 Hen. IV*, II. iv. 68 Can a weake emptie Vessel beare such a huge full Hogs-head? **1648** GAGE *West Ind.* vi. 19 Filling them [boats] so fast and so full, that some sunke. **1694** *Acc. Sev. Late Voy.* II. (1711) 175 When many Whales float on the Sea, they [birds] have their Bellies full. **1698** FRYER *Acc. E. India & P.* 112 A Board plastered over, which with Cotton they wipe out, when full, as we do from Slates. **1711** BUDGELL *Spect.* No. 77 ¶9 When he is playing at Backgammon, he calls for a full glass of Wine and Water. **1712** ARBUTHNOT *John Bull* III. iv. 49 When she came into any full assembly. **1764** FOOTE *Patron* III. Wks. 1799 I. 353 Full..As an egg. **1786** BURNS *Dream* 131, I hae seen their coggie fou. **1823** SCORESBY *Whale Fishery* 126 An ancient flying, a signal indicative in the whale fishery of a full-ship. **1866** G. MACDONALD *Ann. Q. Neighb.* iii. (1878) 32 A few full sacks, tied tight at the mouth. **1870** L'ESTRANGE *Miss Mitford* I. ii. 37 The coach was completely full. **1891** E. PEACOCK *N. Brendon* I. 131 All the stables were full. **1892** *Daily News* 18 Oct. 5/3 Because they [cemeteries] are full up ..this additional one is required.

b. Locutions in which *full* is in concord with a preceding sb. denoting a receptacle are sometimes used *transf.* to signify either (1) the contents viewed with respect to quantity, or (2) a quantity equal to the capacity of the receptacle. In the latter of these applications, this usage is now almost superseded by the practice of forming derivatives ad libitum with the suffix -FUL 2.

c **1000** *Sax. Leechd.* II. 268 Sele þonne cælic fulne to drincanne. *c* **1205** LAY. 1285 In þære sæ heo funden vtlawen ..fifti scipen fulle. *Ibid.* 6470 A kene sweord and enne koker fulne flan. **1563** W. FULKE *Meteors* (1640) 52 He that hath seene an egges shell full of dew drawn up by the Sunne..in a May morning. **1884** G. MOORE *Mummer's Wife* (1887) 179 A theatrefull of people.

c. *fig.* (see 2c); *esp.* of the heart: Overcharged with emotion, ready to overflow.

c **1300** *Cursor M.* 19404 (Edin.) Steuin of strenþe and godis grace was fillid ful in ilk a place. **1604** SHAKS. *Oth.* V. ii. 175 Speake, for my heart is full. **1719** DE FOE *Crusoe* I. i, His heart was so full, he could say no more. **1797** MRS. RADCLIFFE *Italian* xii, My heart was never so full in my life.

†**d.** Of an office: Occupied, not vacant. Const. *of*. *Obs.*

1574 tr. *Littleton's Tenures* 38b, Where a villeyne purchasethe the avowson of a Church full of an incumbent. *a* **1734** NORTH *Lives* (1826) II. 11 He laid his eye on the place of Chief Justice of Chester, which was full of Sir Job Charleton.

e. Of an animal: Pregnant. Of a fish: Charged with roe. †***full of (foal)***: big with.

a **1618** *Rates Merchandize* G i b, Hearings white, full, or shotten, the barrell viijs. iiijd. **1722** *Lond. Gaz.* No. 6120/4 A large Black Mare..very full of Foal. **1864** MITCHELL *Herring* 114 If the herrings are assorted, namely, the full herrings (herrings full of milt and roe) separated from *matjes* (herrings with the milt and roe of a small size), and these separated from 'ylen', empty or shotten herrings, the fishery officer has authority to apply a brand with the word 'full' to the first, and the word 'maties' to the second description.. in addition to the crown brand.

†**f.** Having the outline filled in; solid, not open. ***full flower*** (= F. *fleur pleine*) = 'double flower'.

1597 MORLEY *Introd. Mus.* Annot., There were..foure maners of pricking, one al blacke, which they tearmed blacke full, another which we vse now which they called black void, the third all red, which they called red ful [etc.]. **1683** ROBINSON in *Ray's Corr.* (1848) 137 It hath no full, or double flower. **1715** DESAGULIERS *Fires Impr.* 118 Make three openings in it..the space *lm*, which is 6 Inches wide, must be left full..leave *qc* open 6 Inches wide, *bc* and *qy* full, being of 6 Inches each.

absol. **1703** T. N. *City & C. Purchaser* 128 Let the Doors ..be right over one another, that the void may be upon the void, and the full upon the full.

2. a. Containing abundance *of*; plentifully charged, crowded. †Rarely const. *with*.

a **1000** *Sal. & Sat.* 174 (Gr.) Hateþ ðonne heahcyning helle betynan, fyres fulle. **1297** R. GLOUC. (Rolls) 11 Engelonde is vol inoȝ of frut and ek of tren. **1340** *Ayenb.* 28 þet corn..is uol of frut and al ripe. *c* **1386** CHAUCER *Knt.'s T.* 1288 A wrethe of gold..set ful of stones brighte. *c* **1400** *Lanfranc's Cirurg.* 53 But if þe membre þat was brusid be ful of senewis, as þe hand ouþer þe foot. **1519** HORMAN *Vulg.* xxxi. 257a, The fylde was strowed full of caltroppis. **1582** N. LICHEFIELD tr. *Castanheda's Conq. E. Ind.* xl. 94 Great adders, which are very full of poison. **1613** PURCHAS *Pilgrimage* (1614) 341 Which the people take with boords bored full of holes. **1621** LADY M. WROTH *Urania* 229 As full of spite and ill nature as a Spider with poyson. **1737** BRACKEN *Farriery Impr.* (1757) II. 147 Some Horses will be too full of flesh. **1849** MACAULAY *Hist. Eng.* I. 436 His bedchamber is full of Protestant clergymen. **1878** SMILES *Robert Dick* vii. 76 The sky was full of fire.

†**b.** Formerly sometimes of a surface: Covered (with). Const. *of*. *Obs.*

1563 W. FULKE *Meteors* (1640) 36b, The lidde will be all full of small drops of water. **1579** GOSSON *Sch. Abuse* (Arb.) 54 We..turne him away with his backe full of stripes. **1583** HOLLYBAND *Campo di Fior* 133 Here be the dice. How full of dust they be. **1657** R. LIGON *Barbadoes* (1673) 75 The rind of a pure ash colour, full of wrinkles.

c. In non-material sense: Abounding (in), abundantly characterized (by). Const. *of*, occas. †*with* (in OE. with *genit.* or *instrumental*).

a **1000** *Cædmon's Gen.* 1292 (Gr.) He..ȝeseah unrihte eorðan fulle. *c* **1200** ORMIN 1784 Crisstnedd þed..iss All full off haliȝdomess. *c* **1250** *Gen. & Ex.* 110 Ouer ðat..An oðer heuene ful o blis. *c* **1320** *Sir Tristr.* 1917 A loghe þai founden made, Was ful of gamen and play. **1340** HAMPOLE *Pr. Consc.* 551 þus may a man his bygynnyng se Ful of wrechednes and of caytifté. **1397** *Rolls of Parlt.* III. 379/2 He that hathe ever bene ful of mercy and of grace to all his lyeges. **1513** DOUGLAS *Æneis* III. Prol. 13 Of uncouth dangeris this nixt buik hail is full. **1569** TURBERV. *Trag. T. etc.* (1587) 199, I found him full of amours euery where. **1611** BIBLE *Acts* xiii. 10 O full of all subtilty and all mischiefe. **1650** TRAPP *Comm.* Deut. vi. 12 Full with Gods benefits. **1682** NORRIS *Hierocles* 24 The fuller it is of labour & slavery. **1715** LADY M. W. MONTAGU *Lett.* (1837) II. 12 Your whole letter is full of mistakes. **1754** SHEBBEARE *Matrimony* (1766) I. 150 Mr. Sharply being retired, full with Self-applause of his deep Cunning. **1857** LD. HOUGHTON in *Life* (1891) II. xii. 18 M. Guizot is..full of political and literary gossip. **1878** MORLEY *Carlyle* Crit. Misc., Ser. I. 200 The Protestant cause remained full of vitality.

d. ***a full man***: (After Bacon) one whose mind is richly stored.

1597–8 BACON *Ess.*, *Studies* (Arb.) 10 Reading maketh a full man. **1868** LOWELL *Dryden* Pr. Wks. 1890 III. 105 For, like Johnson, Burke, and the full as distinguished from the learned men, he was always a random reader.

3. Engrossed with or absorbed in; fully occupied with the thought of (something). Now only with const. *of*. †Formerly also with *that* or *infinitive*.

1607 FENTON in *Lismore Papers* Ser. II. (1887) I. 116 We are now so full to prouide for the daungers which the tyme doth threaten on all sides, that [etc.]. **1633** BP. HALL *Hard Texts* 403 Those that are most full, and most conscious of their owne infirmities. **1657** R. LIGON *Barbadoes* (1673) 26, I could not go my self about it, being full of other business. **1669** PEPYS *Diary* 24 Jan., The king seemed mighty full that we should have money to do all that we desired. **1737** BRACKEN *Farriery Impr.* (1757) II. 79 These Sort of *Petit Maitres* are so full of themselves, that they reject all wise Counsel. **1765** REID *Let.* in Wks. I. 43/1 Your friend..was very full of you when he was here. **1853** MRS. CARLYLE *Lett.* II. 238, I am full of business, owing to the sudden movements. **1866** ALGER *Solit. Nat. & Man* III. 130 The lonely man, if full, is quite likely to be full of himself.

4. a. Having eaten or drunk to repletion. (Cf. FOU.) Also ***full of food, wine***, etc. Now *arch.* (and *vulgar*).

c **1000** *Ags. Ps.* lviii[i]. 15 Gif hi fulle ne beoð [hi] fela gnorniað. **1382** WYCLIF *Acts* ii. 13 Thei ben ful of must. *c* **1400** *Lanfranc's Cirurg.* 229 And he schal not, whanne he is ful, slepe anoon þerupon. **1576** FLEMING *Panopl. Epist.* 290 Full of wine, and intoxicated with Bacchus berries. **1583** HOLLYBAND *Campo di Fior* 43 Hast thou no liste to eat? Art thou full? **1611** BIBLE *Prov.* xxvii. 7 The full soule loatheth an honie combe. **1710** SWIFT *Jrnl. to Stella* 7 Dec., I..have eaten cold pie..and I am full. **1737** RAMSAY *Scot. Prov.* (1776) 33 He's unco fou in his ain house that canna pike a bane in his neighbour's. **1787** 'G. GAMBADO' *Acad. Horsemen* (1809) 26 Horses full of grass are very subject to scourings. **1875** DASENT *Vikings* III. 176 So they ate and drank and drained the mead-horn once more, and, when they were all full, they made a raft.

b. Having one's needs or appetite satisfied; having 'had one's fill' of anything. *Obs.* exc. in the Hebraisms ***full of days, years, children***.

c **1175** *Lamb. Hom.* 103 Heo [Auaricia] is helle iliche, forðon þet hi ha habbeð unafillendliche gredinesse, þet hi nefre ne beoð fulle. *c* **1230** *Hali Meid.* 39 Upo hwas nebschaft þe engles ne beoð neauer fulle to bihalden. **1382** WYCLIF *Job* xlii. 17 He diede old, and ful of daȝis. **1585** T. WASHINGTON tr. *Nicholay's Voy.* Ded. ¶iij, An example of Jacob, an old man, and ful of yeres. **1611** BIBLE *Ps.* xvii. 14 They are full of children. **1715** TICKELL *Iliad* I. 292 Full of Days was He; Two Ages past, he liv'd the Third to see. **1852** THACKERAY *Esmond* I. ii, The first Viscount Castlewood died full of years.

c. †Sated, weary *of* (*obs.*). Similarly in mod. colonial slang, ***full up*** (*of*).

1297 R. GLOUC. (1724) 32 Heo [Regan] was al ful of hym [Lear] er þe ȝeres ende. *c* **1320** R. BRUNNE *Medit.* 993 Ȝyf ȝe be ful of my der sone. *c* **1477** CAXTON *Jason* 21 Anone..ye shal be wery and full of her. **1555** W. WATREMAN *Fardle Facions* App. 322 He maye waxe full of the lawe, and vtterly contempne it. **1603** HOLLAND *Plutarch's Mor.* 418 The Athenians being full of him, tooke pleasure to raise slanders and contumelious reproches of him [Themistocles]. **1611** BIBLE *Isa.* i. 11, I am full of the burnt offerings of rammes. **1625** BACON *Ess.*, *Masques*, The Alterations of Scenes..feed and relieue the Eye, before it be full of the same Obiect. **1890** BOLDREWOOD *Miner's Right* xxiii. 213 She was 'full up' of the Oxley..a rowdy, disagreeable gold-field. **1891** E. REEVES *Homeward Bound* 33 The men..get tired, or as the colonial slang goes, 'full up', soonest.

d. ***as full as a tick*** (see TICK *sb.*[1]). Also, in this and similar comparisons, extremely drunk. *Austral.* and *N.Z. slang*.

1892 *Dialect Notes* I. 210 *Full as a tick*, drunk. **1915** *Bulletin* (Sydney) 11 Mar. 44/2 We both got full as ticks. **1930** *Ibid.* 2 Apr. 51/4 'I met Mace down at Cafferty's,' he told his father... 'Full as an egg, and inclined to be nasty!' **1947** P. NEWTON *Wayleggo* (1949) ix. 103 By the time the dance was under way I was as 'full as a bull' and ripe for anything. **1949** D. M. DAVIN *Roads from Home* I. v. 74 Wasn't he in here this afternoon and as full as a tick? **1960** N. HILLIARD in C. K. Stead *N.Z. Short Stories* (1966) 237, I noticed he was full as a bull in no time.

†**5.** Abounding in wealth; amply supplied with means; also in weaker sense, having sufficient for one's needs. *Obs.*

1585 T. WASHINGTON tr. *Nicholay's Voy.* II. iii. 74b, To have a new [emperor] ful, and ready to give. **1611** BIBLE *Phil.* iv. 18, I haue all, and abound. I am full. **1681** W. ROBERTSON *Phraseol. Gen.* (1693) 651 He is a full man, *omnium rerum affluentibus copiis ditatur*. **1683** SALMON *Doron Med.* I. 118 Of the Poor and Needy no recompence can be expected, as of the Rich and Full.

6. a. Abundant, amply sufficient, copious, satisfying, satisfactory. Said both of material and immaterial things.

c **1000** *Ags. Gosp.* Luke vi. 38 Syllað and eow byþ ȝeseald God ȝemet and full. **1052–1067** *Charter of Eadweard* in *Cod. Dipl.* IV. 211 Ic wille habban fullne dom of ðam menn. *a* **1300** *Cursor M.* 9560 His witherwin him wroght ful wa. *c* **1400** *Lanfranc's Cirurg.* 37 Of þese mundificatyves þou schalt have a ful techinge in þe laste tretis. **1576** FLEMING *Panopl. Epist.* 342 *note*, He had full experience and proofe of his qualities in freendship. **1630** *R. Johnson's Kingd. & Commw.* 53 Of diets..that of Germany is full, or rather fulsome. **1638** BAKER tr. *Balzac's Lett.* (vol. III.) 9 Thus I doe but tast of that whereof you make full meales. **1655** STANLEY *Hist. Philos.* I. (1701) 31/2 They who want means Believe themselves of full estates possest. **1697** DRYDEN *Virg. Georg.* II. 756 The falling Mast For greedy Swine provides a full Repast. **1707** FLOYER *Physic. Pulse-Watch* 316, I want a full Experience in these low Pulses. **1732** BERKELEY *Alciphr.* II. §7 Suppose you saw a fruit of a new untried kind; would you recommend it to your own family to make a full meal of? **1884** CHURCH *Bacon* ii. 29 He turned his studies to full account.

b. Of an account or report, hence of a writer, etc.: Complete or abundant in detail.

1656 DENHAM *Destr. Troy* Pref., Where my expressions are not so full as his. **1662** STILLINGFL. *Orig. Sacr.* I. ii. §8 They who were so famed for wisdom and antiquity, should be able to give a full and exact account of themselves through all the ages of the world. **1712** BERKELEY *Pass. Obed.*

Wks. III. 139, I have endeavoured to be as full and clear as the usual length of these discourses would permit. **1845** GRAVES *Rom. Law* in *Encycl. Metrop.* 778/1 For the basis of his Greek text, Contius took, as the best and fullest, the edition of Scrimger. **1866** LORD BLACKBURN in *Hurlstone & Coltman's Rep.* IV. 275 The case is reported..by Lord Raymond, whose report is the fullest. **1871** FREEMAN *Hist. Ess.* Ser. I. iv. 90 We might have expected him [Roger] to be very full on that part of his history. **1882** PEBODY *Eng. Journalism* xx. 152 You will find in its columns all the latest and fullest telegrams from every part of the world. **1884** SIR E. E. KAY in *Law Times Rep.* 26 Apr. 257/2 The audience are quite at liberty to take the fullest notes they like for their own personal convenience.

7. a. Complete, entire, perfect. † (to be) ***in full will to***: quite ready, eager *to*. Also ***full point, stop***, for which see those words.

O.E. Chron. an. 917 Þa land leode..ȝebrohton hie on fullum fleame. *a* **1000** *Boeth. Metr.* xxi. 8 Sece him eft hræðe fulne friodom. *c* **1205** LAY. 29047 We wulleð mid þe uehten mid fullere strenðen. **1340** HAMPOLE *Pr. Consc.* 2611–2 Þe bodys sal..outher þan have full ioy togyder, Or ful sorow. *c* **1380** WYCLIF *Wks.* (1880) 22 Þei were..in fulwille to suffre ..for þe love of ihesu Crist. **1399** *Rolls of Parlt.* III. 424/1 Whiche States..gafen hem full auctorite and power. **1417** *E.E. Wills* (1882) 28 This testament is my volle & hole wille. **1551** RECORDE *Pathw. Knowl.* II. xlii, Foure longsquares.. and one full square. **1563** W. FULKE *Meteors* (1640) 17 Seen only in the morning and evening, when the light of the Sunne is not in his full force. **1576** FLEMING *Panopl. Epist.* 240 Taking a view of ourselves by this looking glasse to make full and just account. **1582** N. LICHEFIELD tr. *Castanheda's Conq. E. Ind.* lxxvi. 156b, He gaue them for ful answere, that [etc.]. **1590** SHAKS. *Com. Err.* v. i. 399 We shall make full satisfaction. **1622** SPARROW *Bk. Com. Prayer* (1661) 313 For our fuller perswation of this. **1631** GOUGE *God's Arrows* IV. xiii. 391 In his time the Gospell shined out in her full brightnesse. **1638** BAKER tr. *Balzac's Lett.* (vol. III.) 115 When a comely personage comes in place..you shall have all husht..onely to take a full view. **1652** C. B. STAPYLTON *Herodian* II. 21 To make the matter full, there souldiers came Unknown unto Perennus. **1669** STURMY *Mariner's Mag.* I. 20 That the Prize may receive our full Broadside. **1701** SWIFT *Contests Nobles & Com.* Wks. 1755 II. I. 33 Entering the scene in the time of a full peace. **1717** tr. *Frezier's Voy. S. Sea* 14 When it was full Day [we spy'd] a very high Land. **1732** BERKELEY *Alciphr.* I. §5 We assured him, he was at full liberty to speak his mind. **1822–34** *Good's Study Med.* (ed. 4) II. 132 Full vomiting..has also been very advantageously employed. **1838** THIRLWALL *Greece* III. xx. 131 They received each a full suit of armour. **1843** LEFEVRE *Life Trav. Phys.* I. I. i. 10, I was introduced to him in full form. **1845** *P. Parley's Ann.* VI. 36 White batenbrier often in full flower. **1849** MACAULAY *Hist. Eng.* I. 439 When he declared himself a Roman Catholic, he was in full possession of his faculties. **1849** CLARIDGE *Cold Water-cure* (1869) 211 The rabbit is now in full health and vigour. **1874** GREEN *Short Hist.* iv. §4 192 A seven years' apprenticeship formed the necessary prelude to full membership of any trade-gild. **1875** FORTNUM *Majolica* xii. 113 The Gubbio fabrique was in full work previous to 1518.

b. Answering in every respect to a description; possessed of all the qualifications, or entitled to all the privileges implied in a designation. ***full brother, sister***: born of the same father and mother (opposed to HALF-BROTHER). ***full man***: see quot. 1867.

O.E. Chron. an. 1036 He wæs þæh full cyng ofer eall Engla land. **1508** KENNEDIE *Flyting w. Dunbar* 33 Belzebub thy full brothir will clame To be thyne air. **1570** *Bury Wills* (Camden) 156 Agnes my wyfe I doo ordeine and make my full executrix. **1604** SHAKS. *Oth.* II. i. 36 For I haue serv'd him, and the man commands Like a full soldier. **1606** —— *Ant. & Cl.* III. xiii. 87 One that but performes The bidding of the fullest man. **1634** CANNE *Necess. Separ.* (1849) 238 Their deacons are not to administer the sacraments, neither any of those which are full priests, but according to a popish liturgy. **1738** SWIFT *Corr.* Wks. 1841 II. 803 He proved the fullest rogue..in either kingdom. **1760** R. HEBER *Horse Matches* ix. 143 Chub is full brother in blood to Mirza. **1810** *Naval Chron.* XXIII. 94 The term 'full passenger' is explained..Every person above 16 years of age falls under that description. *a* **1825** *Fair Annie* xxxi. in Child *Ballads* III. lxii. (1885) 73/2 'Then I'm your sister, Ann', she says, 'And I'm a full sister to thee'. **1867** SMYTH *Sailor's Word-bk.*, *Full man*, a rating in coasters for one receiving whole pay, as being competent to all his duties; able seaman. **1883** *American* VI. 125 Mr. Frank Holl has been elected a full Royal Academician. **1891** D. MACRAE *G. Gilfillan* 78 One full sister of Dr. Anderson and three full brothers died in youth. **1894** DOYLE *S. Holmes* 148 A gallant veteran, who started as a full private.

†**c.** Of a foe: Avowed, open. Of a friend: Thorough, trusty. (Cf. ENTIRE 3 c.) *Obs.*

972 *Will of Ælflæd* in Birch *Cartul. Sax.* III. 603 Þæt he beo..min fulla freo[n]d & forespreca. *c* **1275** *Passion* 174 in *O.E. Misc.* 42 Þer him cumeþ iudas, þat is my fulle i-vo. *a* **1300** *Cursor M.* 14780 Þai him held þair ful fa. *c* **1374** CHAUCER *Troylus* I. 1059 Pandarus..desirous to serve His fulle freend, than seyde in this manere.

8. a. Complete in number, quantity, magnitude or extent; reaching the specified or usual limit. Of the moon: Having the disc completely illuminated; cf. FULL MOON. Of the face, or front: Entirely visible to the spectator; advb. phr. (*in*) ***full face***. ***full pay*** (see quot. 1867).

c **1000** ÆLFRIC *Gen.* l. 10 Ðar hiȝ wæron seofon daȝas fulle. *a* **1123** *O.E. Chron.* an. 1013 Bead þa Sweȝen full ȝild. *Ibid.* an. 1031 Whenne þæt flod byþ..ealra fullost. *Ibid.* an. 1106 Wæron ȝesewen tweȝen monan..beȝen fulle. *c* **1205** LAY. 1632 Fulle seouen nihte heo somenede cnihtes. *c* **1315** SHOREHAM 45 So thes beth ordres folle sevene. *c* **1350** *Will. Palerne* 2745 At þe fulle flod þei ferden to sayle. *c* **1410** *Chron. Eng.* 416 in Ritson II. 287 Ahte ant tuenti folle yer. **1463** *Bury Wills* (Camden) 16 Alle other that hath take the ful ordir of preesthod. *c* **1477** CAXTON *Jason* 76b, The whiche deyde assone as it was born for it had not his full time. **1535** COVERDALE *1 Chron.* xxii. 22 For yᵉ full money shalt thou geue it me. **1599** W. CUNNINGHAM *Cosmogr. Glasse* 98 Whan as the mone unto the world..shining with face both full and round. **1610** SHAKS. *Temp.* I. ii. 250 Thou did promise To bate me a full yeere. **1613** PURCHAS *Pilgrimage* (1614) 401 And over ten thousands, which made a full regiment. *Ibid.* 740 One of their ships..happened to strike on a great Whale with her full stemme. **1648** GAGE *West Ind.* xii. 43 To visit Mexico (which was not two full miles from us). **1655** STANLEY *Hist. Philos.* (1701) 38/2 He lived to a full Age, about Seventy Years, or (following the account of Suidas for his Birth) Eighty. **1671** MILTON *P.R.* I. 287, I knew the time Now full, that I no more should live obscure. **1700** S. L. tr. *Fryke's Voy. E. Ind.* 6 The full and regular pay begins only after they are passed the Tonnen. **1701** *Lond. Gaz.* No. 3756/15 Irish Usquebagh..to be sold in full Quart Bottles. **1702** ADDISON *Dial. Medals* Wks. 1721 I. 538 The head of a Roman Emperor drawn with a full face. **1710** In full Front [see FRONT *sb.* 5 b]. **1715** *Lond. Gaz.* No. 5351/3 He will be..pleased to allow Full-Pay to such Half-Pay Officers. **1723** SIR R. BLACKMORE *Hist. Conspiracy* 36 His Lieutenant Colonel, Major, and Captains, being named, and the Troops almost full. **1742** *Lond. & Country Brew.* I. (ed. 4) 11 The Flour of the Grain will remain in its full Quantity. **1750** BEAWES *Lex Mercat.* (1752) 250 When the Sea is full, the Admiral hath Jurisdiction there. **1753** *Scots Mag.* Feb. 100/1 The moon was..full. **1784** HERSCHEL in *Phil. Trans.* LXXIV. 262 Measure..of the polar diameter 21″ 15‴ full measure, that is, certainly not too small. **1805** T. LINDLEY *Voy. Brasil* (1808) 102 A concert of sacred music was performed by a full band, with vocal parts. **1817** W. SELWYN *Law Nisi Prius* (ed. 4) II. 1252 The plaintiff shall have full costs. **1853** KINGSLEY *Hypatia* xxix. 360 There Philammon waited a full half-hour. **1855** MACAULAY *Hist. Eng.* III. 355 The muster was not a very full one. **1867** SMYTH *Sailor's Word-bk.*, *Full pay*, the stipend allowed when on actual service. **1876** VOYLE *Milit. Dict.* 153 *Full Charges*, in artillery, are the ordinary charges used with rifled projectiles. **1876** HUMPHREYS *Coin Coll. Man.* vi. 54 The head of Apollo on the gold coin..appears in full face. **1895** M. R. JAMES *Abbey St. Edmund at Bury* 51 At top is Christ in a mandorla seated full-face with a book.

b. Of an assembly, council, etc.: One from which none or few of the members are absent.

1557 *Order of Hospitalls* Civ, Item That no Lease, alienation..be..done, of Lands or Tenements except at a Full Court. **1604** SHAKS. *Oth.* IV. i. 275 Is this the Noble Moore, whom our full Senate Call all in all sufficient? **1834** WALLACE in Mackintosh *Hist. Rev.* p. viii, He..kept the academic senate waiting for him in full conclave. **1849** MACAULAY *Hist. Eng.* II. 78 James..in full council declared it to be his pleasure that [etc.].

†**c.** Of a point in the compass: Exact, due (east, etc.). Cf. C. 3 b. *Obs. rare.*

1630 *R. Johnson's Kingd. & Commw.* 77 The Island is situated almost full North. *Ibid.* 122 On the full East doe the Alps divide it [France] from Italie.

d. In various phraseological combinations: as ***full flood, sea, tide*** (*lit.* and *fig.*) indicating the greatest height of the water, or the time when it is highest. Also ***full tide***, used *attrib.* and as *adv.* ***full summer***: the height of summer. Cf. B. 4 b.

c **1450** *St. Cuthbert* (Surtees) 5174 It was full se. *Ibid.* 5178 And so it was full flode. **1574** BOURNE *Regiment for Sea* 7 b, The Moone dooth make a full Sea at that place. **1576** FLEMING *Panopl. Epist.* 395 Thinke you..that your ebb is so lowe, that you are never like to have a ful tyde? **1648** JOS. BEAUMONT *Psyche* XIV. 83 Although the courteous Sun With free and ful-tide Raies about it flows. **1699** DAMPIER *Voy.* II. I. 16 Not so swift near full Sea as at other times. **1708** MRS. CENTLIVRE *Busie Body* II. ii, Such Swi-m-ing in the Brain..carries many a Guinea full-tide to the Doctor. **1845** G. MURRAY *Islaford* 78 Fortune's full-tide flowing Shall bring him back to me. **1865** TROLLOPE *Belton Est.* I. 5 It was full summer at Belton. **1867** SMYTH *Sailor's Word-bk.*, *Full sea*, high water. **1875** W. MCILWRAITH *Guide Wigtownshire* 140 The surf breaking over the rock at full flood. **1887** *Spectator* 25 June 859/2 At this Jubilee-time, when the whole nation is in the full tide of rejoicing.

9. a. Possessed of, delivered with, or exerting the utmost force. † ***with a full arm, eye, mouth, soul***: with the utmost strength of (the arm, etc.).

c **1290** *S. Eng. Leg.* I. 86/93 Loude he gradde with folle Mouth. *c* **1489** CAXTON *Sonnes of Aymon* xvi. 392 He..toke hym wyth a full arme..in lyke wyse in maner of wrastelyng. **1509** BARCLAY *Shyp of Folys* (1570) 99 It neuer loketh on man with eyes full But euer his heart by furious wrath is dull. *a* **1533** LD. BERNERS *Huon* lxvii. 230 Whom so euer he strake a full stroke neded after no surgyon. **1583** HOLLYBAND *Campo di Fior* 121 Was better fixed in the memorie..if I did speake with a full voice. **1609** BIBLE (Douay) *Isa.* ix. 12 The Philisthims..shal devoure Israel with ful mouth. **1610** SHAKS. *Temp.* III. i. 44 For seuerall vertues Haue I lik'd seuerall women, neuer any With so full soule, but [etc.]. **1632** J. HAYWARD tr. *Biondi's Eromena* 28 Rush't into the chamber..and..thrust at him a full *stocada*. **1634–5** BRERETON *Trav.* (Chetham) 124 Presently favouring us..with a full gale of wind. **1657** R. LIGON *Barbadoes* (1673) 29 Bread..has not here that full taste it has in England. **1694** *Acc. Sev. Late Voy.* II. (1711) 38 If in a brisk Gale of a full Wind the Sails are all full and Round. **1700** S. L. tr. *Fryke's Voy. E. Ind.* 207 The Javians set up a full Huzza. **1783** J. C. SMYTH in *Med. Commun.* I. 142 Pulse 68, full and strong. **1805** T. LINDLEY *Voy. Brasil* (1808) 21 His pulse full and regular.

b. Of light: Intense. Of colour: Deep, intense.

1657 R. LIGON *Barbadoes* (1673) 66 These leaves being.. of a full green. **1664** POWER *Exp. Philos.* I. 26 View her with a full light transmitted through a Burning-glass. **1791** HAMILTON *Berthollet's Dyeing* I. I. I. i. 19 The colour of the wool will be much more full and intense. **1842** TENNYSON *Locksley Hall* 17 In the spring a fuller crimson comes upon the robin's breast. **1869** PHILLIPS *Vesuv.* xi. 303 Under the application of heat, amounting to a full red in iron.

c. In various phraseological combinations: as ***full butt, cry, drive, gallop, jump, pack, pelt, pitch, retreat, sail, scent, speed, stretch, swing, tilt***, etc.: for which see the words.

10. a. Having a rounded outline; large, swelling, plump, protuberant.

c **1000** *Sax. Leechd.* III. 268 Ealle eorþlice lichaman beoþ fulran on weaxendum monan. **1577** B. GOOGE *Heresbach's Husb.* III. (1586) 115 The hoofe that is ful and fleshy, is not to be liked. **1627** CAPT. SMITH *Seaman's Gram.* xi. 54 The longer a ship is, the fuller should be her Bow. **1674** N. COX *Gentl. Recreat.* II. (1677) 178 A round Head, somewhat full on the top. **1688** *Lond. Gaz.* No. 2320/1 This Sultan Soliman is of a long, lean and pale Visage, with a full black Eye. **1697** DAMPIER *Voy.* I. iii. 32 Full round Faces, small black Eyes..full Lips, and short Chins. *Ibid.* vi. 131 It is a high bluff, or full point of Land. **1698** FRYER *Acc. E. India & P.* 53 Where we took in fuller and larger Pepper than any yet. **1726** *Adv. Capt. R. Boyle* 125 The Women..fine large full Eyes, round Faces, and every Feature exact. **1803** *Med. Jrnl.* IX. 36 In proportion as the patient was full, robust and vigorous. **1840** MISS MITFORD in L'Estrange *Life* (1870) III. vii. 109 She is..full enough to prevent the haggard look which comes upon women who grow thin at fifty. *c* **1850** *Rudim. Navig.* (Weale) 152 Its use is to take out the snying edge occasioned by a full bow. **1894** J. E. HUMPHREY in *Pop. Sci. Monthly* XLIV. 494 The fruit is cut as soon as it is 'full'.

b. Of portions of dress: Containing a superfluity of material which is arranged in gathers or folds.

1789 MRS. PIOZZI *Journ. France* I. 306 White silk petticoat, exceedingly full and short. **1824** MISS MITFORD *Village* Ser. I. (1863) 213 An open gown..whose very full tail..would have formed an inconvenient little train. **1862** MISS YONGE *Stokesley Secret* ii. 42 Alpaca frocks, rather long and not very full. **1891** *Leeds Mercury* 27 Apr. 4/7 Velvet sleeves, full and high on the shoulders.

11. *Naut.* (with mixed notion of 1 and 10). Of a sail: Filled. Of the ship: Having her sails filled with wind; and in phrase ***keep*** (***her***, i.e. the ship) ***full***. ***full and by***: see BY *adv.* 1 d; also *fig.* ***full for stays***: see quot.

1627 [see BY *adv.* 1 d]. **1697** *Occasional Conformity* 10 'Tis like a Ship with her Sails hal'd some back, and some full. **1769** FALCONER *Dict. Marine* (1789) Zziij, You are all in the wind; keep her full! **1805** ADM. STIRLING in *Naval Chron.* XV. 80 We..had our main-top-sail full. **1838** POE *A. G. Pym* Wks. 1864 IV. 15 We..kept full, and started boldly out to sea. **1867** SMYTH *Sailor's Word-bk.*, *Full for Stays!* The order to keep the sails full to preserve the velocity, assisting the action of the rudder in tacking ship. **1882** NARES *Seamanship* (ed. 6) 148 When the fore sail is full, 'Let draw'. **1930** *New Statesman* 5 July 412/1 And, take it full and bye, it is one of the very few things to be honoured in our nature.

12. *Comb.* **a.** with sbs. forming combinations used attrib.; as ***full-cream, -draught, -dug, -hand, -page, -plate, -power, -scale, -size, -term, -top, -value, -way, -weight***.

1881 *Chicago Times* 16 Apr., The *full-cream cheese manufactured in the states of Wisconsin and Illinois. **1856** KANE *Arct. Expl.* II. iii. 46, I have manufactured a *full-draught pipe for our smoky stove. **1852** *Meanderings of Mem.* I. 79 Where *full-dug foragers at evening meet In Cow-bell concert. **1593** NASHE *Christ's T.* 22 The..profuse sacrificatory expences of *ful-hand oblationers. **1889** *Spectator* 14 Dec. 849 We may select for notice the *full-page illustrations of 'Dundee' and 'Stirling'. **1911** A. BENNETT *Card* xi. 245 The only hotel in the Five Towns seriously pretending to be 'first-class' in the full-page advertisement sense. **1954** M. RICHERT *Painting in Brit.: Middle Ages* iv. 81 The few uncoloured full-page miniatures which precede a copy of the gospels. **1884** F. J. BRITTEN *Watch & Clockm.* 108 A *full plate watch has a top plate.. of a circular form. **1890** *Times* 18 Sept. 4/2 The Skipjack.. left Sheerness yesterday for the *full-power official trial of her machinery. **1933** *Discovery* Aug. 257/1 *Full-scale experiments in flight are of necessity difficult and take a long time. **1957** *Times Lit. Suppl.* 20 Dec. 778/1 Since Alexander Henderson..there has been no full-scale monograph on the wines of antiquity. **1832** in A. Adburgham *Shops & Shopping* (1964) iv. 40 *Full-size Paper Patterns. **1957** *Times Survey Brit. Aviation* Sept. 7 A full-size mock-up of the Vanguard's cockpit. **1907** W. J. MALONEY tr. Budin (*title*) The nursling: the feeding and hygiene of premature and *full-term infants. **1949** M. MEAD *Male & Female* viii. 179 They smother in economic details the memory of their miscarriages, as if these had been full-term children. **1723** *Lond. Gaz.* No. 6206/9 He is..pale fac'd, a *full-top Wig. **1896** *Daily News* 31 Mar. 9/3 Any *full-value gold pieces in circulation will have to be called in. **1882** *Worc. Exhib. Catal.* iii. 49 Excelsior *full-way hot water valves. **1884** KNIGHT *Dict. Mech.* IV, *Full Way Valve*, a pipe valve which lifts entirely out of the current. Also called a clear-way valve. **1866** CRUMP *Banking* x. 234 The Bank..would supply new and *full-weight coin.

b. with pres. and pa. pples. forming combinations in which *full* stands as a complement; as ***full-built, -charged, -crammed, -farced, -fed, -flowering, -flowing, -fraught, -freight, -freighted, -gorged, -made, -opening, -pulsing, -resounding, -stuffed, -swelling***; also ***full-feeding*** vbl. sb.

1709 *Lond. Gaz.* No. 4510 The Hoy Burthen 9 or 10 Tun, very *full built forward. **1613** SHAKS. *Hen. VIII*, I. ii. 3, I stood i' th' leuell Of a *full-charg'd confederacie. **1827** KEBLE *Chr. Y.* 1st Sund. in Lent, Thy full-charg'd vial standing by. **1613** WITHER *Satir. Ess.* II. ii. Pj a, Emptying their *full cram'd bags. **1879** HUXLEY *Hume* i. 56 Unknown to this full-crammed and much-examined generation. **1578** TIMME *Caluine on Gen.* 189 The place..so *full-farssed and stuffed up. **1593** SHAKS. *Lucr.* 594 The *full-fed hound or gorged hawk, Make slow pursuit. **1887** *Spectator* 5 Mar. 320/1 We..have a notion that full-fed authors do bad work. **1382** WYCLIF *Gen.* xli. 20 Other seuen oxen..the whiche.. no merke of *fulfedyng ȝouun. **1577** *St. Aug. Manual* (Longm.) 12 The place of fulfeedyng by the plentifull running streames. **1821** KEATS *Lamia* I. 44 The taller grasses and *full-flowering weed. **1605** SHAKS. *Lear* v. iii.

74 Lady I am not well, else I should answere From a *full flowing stomack. **1832** TENNYSON *Œnone* 67 While I look'd And listen'd.. the fullflowing river of speech Came down upon my heart. *c*1606 FLETCHER *Woman Hater* I. ii, His tables are *full fraught with most nourishing food. **1694** ECHARD *Plautus* 103 I'll teach her how t' act..and send her *full-fraight with my Tricks. **1740** SOMERVILLE *Hobbinol* III. 356 A full-freight Ship, Blest in a rich Return of Pearl, or Gold. *a*1711 KEN *Hymnotheo* Poet. Wks. 1721 III. 319 His *full-freighted Thought, Back on his Tongue, Hymn and Heroick brought. **1596** SHAKS. *Tam. Shr.* IV. i. 194 She [my Faulcon] must not be *full gorg'd, For then she neuer lookes vpon her lure. **1781** COWPER *Hope* 509 The full-gorged savage. **1790** *Pol. Misc.* 58 With *full-made sleeves and pendant lace. **1730–46** THOMSON *Autumn* 421 The pack *full-opening various. **1878** MORLEY *Carlyle* 189 No feeling for broad force and *full-pulsing vitality. **1737** POPE *Hor. Epist.* II. i. 268 Dryden taught to join the *full-resounding line. **1613** DRAYTON *Poly-olb.* XIV. 118 When twixt their burly Stacks and *full-stuft Barnes they stand. **1748** THOMSON *Cast. Indol.* I. 297 Each spacious room was one *full-swelling bed.

c. parasynthetic, as ***full-bagged, -banked, -bellied, -bloomed, -blossomed, -bosomed, -bowed, -brained, -busted, -buttocked, -cheeked, -chested, -clustered, -eared, -feathered, -flanked, -fleshed, -flocked, -foliaged, -formed, -fortuned, -fronted, -fruited,*** †***-gaskined, -haired, -handed, -happinessed, -haunched, -headed, -hipped, -jointed, -leaved, -licensed, -limbed, -lipped, -measured, -minded, -natured, -necked, -paunched, -personed, -powered, -proportioned, -rayed, -rigged, -roed, -sailed*** (lit. and fig.), ***-shouldered, -sized, -skirted, -souled,*** †***-speeched, -sphered, -statured*** (lit. and fig.), ***-stomached, -streamed, -throated, -timed, -toned, -tushed, -uddered, -voiced, -weighted, -whiskered, -winged, -witted, -wombed.***

1613 DRAYTON *Poly-olb.* XIV. 227 The *full-bagd Cow. **1630** J. TAYLOR (Water P.) *Wks.* 15 No full bag'd man would euer durst haue entered. **1622** DRAYTON *Poly-olb.* XXVIII. 205 Many a *full-bankt Flood. **1681** *Lond. Gaz.* No. 1638/8 Stolen..a dark Brown Nag..pretty *full-bellied, and reasonable fat. **1909** *Daily Chron.* 2 June 5/6 The full-bellied barges of 600 tons freightage. **1937** N. COWARD *Present Indicative* VIII. 333 A full-bellied roar of laughter. **1646** CRASHAW *Steps to Temple* 21 Lo! a mouth, whose *full-bloom'd lips At two deare a rate are roses. **1840** LONGF. *Sp. Stud.* I. iii, The *full-blossomed trees filled all the air with fragrance. **1603** DRAYTON *To Maiestie K. James* A iv, The fruitfull and *ful-bosom'd Spring. **1883** *Harper's Mag.* Aug. 376/2 The *full-bowed schooners lean over on the beach at low tide. **1596** FITZ-GEFFRAY *Sir F. Drake* (1881) 26 Whose *ful-braind temples deck't with laurell crowne. **1864** TENNYSON *En. Ard.* 539 Her *full-busted figure head Stared o'er the ripple feathering from her bows. **1672** *Lond. Gaz.* No. 657/4 A Bay Mare..with..a black List down the Buttock, and *full Buttockt. **1686** *Ibid.* No. 2145/4 Elizabeth Tildel..short and black, *full-cheek'd. *a*1711 KEN *Preparatives* Poet. Wks. 1721 IV. 92 It chanc'd, just as the full-cheek'd Moon Reach'd her nocturnal Noon. **1681** *Lond. Gaz.* No. 1620/4 A black brown Gelding..short Neck, *full Chested. **1645** QUARLES *Sol. Recant.* vii. 19 *Full clusterd Vineyards. **1635** —— *Emblems* I. ii. Epig. 2 A *full-ear'd Crop, and thriving. **1845** MRS. NORTON *Child of Islands* (1846) 107 Whose mass of full-eared sheaves the reapers bind. **1806** SURR *Winter in Lond.* (ed. 3) II. 254 Barton is a *full-feathered pigeon. **1612** DRAYTON *Poly-olb.* III. 298 Many a plump-thigh'd moor & *ful-flank'd marsh. **1832** MOTHERWELL *Poet. Wks.* (1847) 48 In *full-fleshed pride, Bright roses burst in June. **1622** DRAYTON *Poly-olb.* XXVI. 38 The large, and goodly *full-flockd Oulds. **1807–8** W. IRVING *Salmag.* (1824) 187 The whispers of the *full-foliaged grove fall on the ear of contemplation. **1727–46** THOMSON *Summer* 823 The *full-formed maids of Afric. **1606** SHAKS. *Ant. & Cl.* IV. xv. 24 Th' Imperious shew Of the *full-Fortun'd Cæsar. **1895** *Daily News* 20 Mar. 7/1 A *full-fronted coat. **1853** HICKIE tr. *Aristoph.* (1872) II. 543 Shaking the *full-fruited chaplet about your head. **1682** *Lond. Gaz.* No. 1768/4 A white grey Roan Gelding..well Crested..*full gascoign'd. **1689** *Ibid.* No. 2513/4 A grey Mare..only gallops and trots, and a *full haired bob Tail. **1643** [ANGIER] *Lanc. Vall. Achor* 35 Mercies..have been granted..with *full-handed favours. **1815** LAMB. *Lett.* (1888) I. 294 My *full-happinessed friend is picking his crackers. **1685** *Lond. Gaz.* No. 2019/8 Stolen..a brown bay Nag..*full Haunched, and small Bodied. **1816** KEATINGE *Trav.* (1817) I. 152 *Full-headed trees..have been left at judicious intervals. **1882** O'DONOVAN *Merv Oasis* I. 343 The..slovenly-looking *full-hipped tunic. **1688** *Lond. Gaz.* No. 2355/4 A dapple grey..*full jointed in both his hinder Legs. **1630** DRAYTON *Muses Elysium* 199 With *full leav'd lilies I will stick Thy braided hair. **1864** G. M. HOPKINS *Poems* (1948) 131 Now while the full-leaved hursts unalter'd stand. **1917** J. MASEFIELD *Lollingdon Downs* 74 The full-leaved summer bore no fruit. **1883** *Goole Weekly Times* 14 Sept. 5/3 To be let, the 'Royal Oak Inn'..a *full-licensed House. **1859** TENNYSON *Guinevere* 43 Those whom God had made *full-limb'd and tall. **1859** BAGEHOT in *National Review* IX. 383 Lancelot, the great knight of many exploits and *full-lipped enjoyment. **1932** E. HEMINGWAY *Death in Afternoon* ix. 244 He had a full-lipped face. *a*1711 KEN *Hymnarium* Poet. Wks. 1721 II. 114 God oft makes Thunder, Lightning, Storm, Hail, Snows, Pour on full-measur'd Sin, *full-measur'd Woes. **1627–77** FELTHAM *Resolves* I. xxxiv. 58 To be poor, is to be made a pavement for the tread of the *full-minded man. **1823** LAMB *Elia* Ser. II. *Child Angel*, Those *full-natured angels tended it by turns. **1670** NARBOROUGH *Jrnl.* in *Acc. Sev. Late Voy.* I. (1694) 59 They are *full-necked, and headed and beaked like a Crow. **1607** TOPSELL *Four-f. Beasts* (1658) 332 To be ministered..when the horse is not altogether *full-panched, but rather empty. **1873** HOWELLS *Chance Acquaint.* i. 14 The *full-personed good-humored looking gentleman. **1742** YOUNG *Nt. Th.* II. 317 To-day is yesterday return'd ..*Full-pow'r'd. **1631** WEEVER *Anc. Fun. Mon.* 762 Two *full proportioned figures in brasse. **1879** GEO. ELIOT *Coll. Breakf. P.* 762 *Full-rayed sensibilities which blend Truth and desire. **1830** N. S. WHEATON *Jrnl.* 342 A *full-rigged [French] bagage waggon is a curious spectacle. **1884** E. INGERSOLL in *Harper's Mag.* May 869/2 Full-rigged foreign ships. **1895** *Daily News* 26 Jan. 5/5 The *full-roed Norway herrings. **1594** NASHE *Unfort. Trav.* A 3 Mercenarie attendants on his *ful-sayld fortune. **1622** DRAYTON *Poly-olb.* XIX. 178 Arthur's full-sail'd Fleet. **1629** MASSINGER *Picture* II. ii, Such is my full-sailed confidence in her virtue. **1808** J. BARLOW *Columb.* I. 623 The fullsail'd ship..Dash'd into fragments by the floating rock. **1838** DICKENS *O. Twist* xxxix, A *full-sized wine-bottle carefully corked. **1689** *Lond. Gaz.* No. 2416/4 A *full skirted Leather Saddle. **1882** OGILVIE, **Full-souled*, magnanimous; of noble disposition. **1692** *Lond. Gaz.* No. 2809/4 Timothy Phillips..*full speech'd, in a light grey..Suit..went away..with a..Sum of Money. **1833** TENNYSON *Poems* 84 *Fullsphered contemplation. **1691** *Lond. Gaz.* No. 2631/4 A Black named Johanna..*full Statured. **1844** MRS. BROWNING *Lady Geraldine's Courtship* lxvii, And my soul..sprang, full-statured in an hour. **1593** NASHE *Christ's T.* 63 Grosse *full-stomacht tautology. **1611** TOURNEUR *Ath. Trag.* II. i. Wks. 1878 I. 40 The full-stomack'd Sea. **1593** NASHE *Christ's T.* 38 b, Hearing riche London was the *full-streamed wel-head. **1806** J. GRAHAME *Birds Scot.* 72 And joins, with opened banks, the full-streamed Clyde. **1820** KEATS *Ode to Nightingale* 10 Thou, light-winged Dryad of the trees.. Singest of summer in *full-throated ease. **1889** *Daily News* 5 June 6/7 Just preceding or at the time of her death she had been delivered of a *full-timed child. **1827** KEBLE *Chr. Y.* SS. Simon and Jude, Mild As evening blackbird's *full-ton'd lay. **1611** COTGR., *Miré*..long-tusked, *full-tushed, as a full-growne Boare. **1727–46** THOMSON *Summer* 222 The *full-uddered mother lows around The cheerful cottage. **1632** MILTON *Penseroso* 162 There let the pealing organ blow, To the *full-voiced quire below. **1888** *Daily News* 5 Oct. 5/2 The Bank of Germany does not refuse *full-weighted gold to those who can demand it. **1838** DICKENS *Nich. Nick.* xvii, Such a *full-whiskered dashing young man. **1611** SHAKS. *Cymb.* III. iii. 21 The *full-wing'd Eagle. *c*1630 DRUMMOND OF HAWTH. *Poems* Wks. (1711) 41/1 Full-winged argoses. **1957** BANNERMAN *Birds Brit. Isles* VI. 251 There has been a mixed flock of *full-winged* snow and blue geese at Woburn for fifty years at least. **1884** *American* VIII. 251 Any *full-witted American. **1630** DRAYTON *Noah's Flood* 34 The *full-womb'd Women very hardly went Out their nine months.

d. Special comb.: **full-back** (*Football*), position in the field behind the other 'backs'; a player in this position; also *attrib.*; †**full-belly**, one who has or makes a point of having his belly full; **full board**, (*a*) [BOARD *sb.* 2 d] *Austral.* and *N.Z.*, a full complement of shearers on the board; (*b*) the provision of a bed and all meals: an arrangement offered by hotels, boarding houses, etc.; **full-bodied** *a.*, having a full body (*esp.* of wine: see BODY *sb.* 25); also *fig.*; **full-bound** *a. Book-binding*, bound entirely in leather; **full-breasted** *a.*, having a full breast; also *transf.*; **full-brimmed** *a.*, full to the brim, overflowing; **full-cell process**, Bethell's process (cf. BETHELL); **full-centre arch** [Fr. *arc à plein-cintre*] (see quot.); **full character** (see quot.); †**full-charge** *v.*, to charge to the full (cf. *full-charged* in 12 b); **full-choke**, a gun or gun-barrel with the maximum amount of choke-boring; **full-circle** *adv.*, with the form of a full circle or disc; **full-cream** *attrib.*, consisting of or made from unskimmed milk; **full employment** (see quot. 1948); **full-eyed**, †(*a*) perfectly visible; seen in the front; (*b*) having full eyes; **full-flavoured** *a.*, having a full or strong flavour (said esp. of cigars); also *fig.*; **full-forward**, in Australian National Football, one of three players (esp. the centrally positioned one) who constitute the front forward line and stand closest to the opposing goal; **full-front** *v.*, to present a full front to; **full-frontal** *attrib. phr.*, (*a*) ***full-frontal nudity***, complete nudity, in which a person's body is seen from the front; cf. FRONTAL *a.* 2 c; (*b*) *fig.*, that reveals everything or holds nothing back; explicit, unequivocal; open, honest; **full hand** *Poker* = FULL HOUSE 2; **full-mouth**, (*a*) one whose mouth is full (of words), a chatterer; also *attrib.* = FULL-MOUTHED; (*b*) a full-mouthed animal; **full-orbed** *a. poet.* (of the moon), having its disc completely illuminated; also *fig.*; (hence *full-orbedness*); **full pitch, toss** *Cricket*, a ball pitched right up to the batsman; also as *advb. phr.*, without the ball having first touched the ground; so **full-pitched** *a.*; **full professor** orig. *U.S.*, a professor with the highest ranking position on the staff of a university or college; **full score** *Mus.*, a score in which the parts for all voices and instruments are given on separate staves; **full snipe**, a popular name for the common snipe, *Gallinago gallinago*; †**full-trussed** *a.* (of a horse), having full hind-quarters; **full word** *Linguistics*, a word that has an independent meaning; also *attrib.*; *spec.* in *Chinese Grammar* (see quot. 1954).

1887 SHEARMAN *Athletics & Football* 324 Last but not least comes the *full back..Two things only are required of him, that he should be an admirable and accurate drop, and a safe and strong tackler. **1893** A. H. HARRISON in *Assoc. Football Handbk.* 18 Let the full-backs keep close to their halves. **1896** *Daily News* 29 Oct. 9/4 A splendid little bit of full-back work. **1637** R. HUMPHREY tr. *St. Ambrose* I. 30 Lazy lubbers, and *full bellyes, drowned in worldly delights. **1894** E. WILSON *In Land of Tui* xv. 242 At one side [of the shearing shed], down the whole length of the building, the shearers work, thirteen of whom are called a '*full board'. **1910** *Bradshaw's Railway Guide* Apr. 1149/2 Very comfortable rooms from 3/-, and full board from 7/6. **1941** BAKER *N.Z. Slang* v. 39 The use of *board* for the floor of a shearing shed is also slang. Whence comes *a full board.* **1971** *Oxford Mail* 11 Oct. 11/4 (Advt.), Accommodation urgently reqd for daughter aged 15. North Oxford preferred, bed and breakfast or full board. **1686** *Lond. Gaz.* No. 2162/4 He is about 21 years of age..broad-shoulder'd, *full-bodied. **1688** R. HOLME *Armoury* II. 336/2 A Bleke.. is a full bodied little Fish..with red eyes. **1710** J. CLARKE *Rohault's Nat. Phil.* (1729) 177, I put in a Quart of full-bodied Red Wine. **1835** WILLIS *Pencillings* I. ix. 60 It is a ripe, rich, full-bodied liquor. **1890** *Standard* 10 Mar., To the full-bodied humour of..Hogarth. **1880** J. W. ZAEHNSDORF *Art of Bookbinding* 171 When the sides and back of a volume are covered with leather it is said to be *full-bound. **1946** H. WHETTON *Pract. Printing & Binding* xxxi. 381 The book may be full-bound..that is, the leather may fully cover the boards. **1611** SPEED *Theat. Gt. Brit.* (1614) 125/1 A provident and *full-breasted mother. **1657** R. LIGON *Barbadoes* (1673) 51 The men, they are..full breasted, well filletted. **1677** YARRANTON *Eng. Improv.* 120 Our Wheat is large, full-brested, and thin-rined. **1622** DRAYTON *Poly-olb.* XXIX. 110 Two faire and *full-brim'd Floods. *a*1845 HOOD *To Mrs. Fry* xiii, I like the pity in your full-brimmed eye. **1915** H. F. WEISS *Preserv. Struct. Timber* v. 57 The Bethell or *full-cell process is considered the standard process of treating timber with creosote. **1940** H. TROTTER *Man. Indian Forest Utiliz.* ix. 202 The full-cell process has been known for over 80 years. **1962** Full cell process [see BETHELL]. **1874** KNIGHT *Dict. Mech.*, **Full-centre Arch*, a semi-circular arch or vault. One describing the full amount of 180°. **1863** J. EDKINS *Gram. Chinese Lang.* (ed. 2) II. iii. 105 They call significant words..*full characters, while the auxiliary words or those which are non-significant, they term..empty characters. **1766** SPRY *Locked Jaw* in *Phil. Trans.* LVII. 89, I now..several times *full-charged her with the electric matter. **1881** W. W. GREENER *Gun* 387 A *full choke is constricted to the extent of 30 to 40,000ths of an inch. **1892** —— *Breech-loader* 134 The 16-bore full-choke, with barrels 30 inches in length. **1895** *Outing* (U.S.) XXVII. 65/1, I have ruined too many fine birds with the full-choke to want to use it any more. **1964** H. L. PETERSON *Encycl. Firearms* 52/1 Full chokes are used for long-range shooting, modified chokes or cylinder bores for upland birds and skeet shooting. **1879** BROWNING *Pheidippides* 39 The moon, half-orbed, is unable to take *Full-circle her state in the sky! **1881** *Full-cream [see FULL *a.* 12 a]. **1929** *Punch* 8 May p. viii, Fresh, full-cream milk. **1970** *Guardian* 14 Apr. 10/3 We needed full cream milk powder for the babies. **1835** J. LOUDON *Philanthropy* 107 If the self same cause which gives cheap food, gives *full employment to labour [etc.]. **1846** LD. BEAUVALE in C'tess of Airlie *Lady Palmerston* (1922) II. xvi. 102 By God's blessing there is full employment with high wages. **1940** *Economist* 20 Jan. 88/1 Optimistic assumptions of the effect that the attainment of 'full employment' will have on the revenue. **1948** G. CROWTHER *Outl. Money* (ed. 2) v. 138 'Full employment' does not necessarily mean that every man and women has a job. It means only that there are no more supplies of idle labour or idle capital of the sorts that are actually being demanded. **1633** G. HERBERT *Temple, Glance* iii, What wonders shall we feel when we shall see Thy *full-ey'd love. **1688** *Lond. Gaz.* No. 2318/4 One of the persons a little Man, full eyed, in a cinnamon colour'd Coat. **1891** DUNCAN *Amer. Girl in Lond.* 231 A very frank and *full-flavoured criticism. **1965** *Austral. Encycl.* IV. 135 The *full-forward of each team, in particular, is chosen for his ability to take the ball high in the air. **1969** *Sun-Herald* (Sydney) 13 July 48/1 Hawthorn full-forward Peter Hudson kicked five goals although heavily guarded by Essendon's defenders. **1855** BROWNING *Saul*, Perfection, no more and no less, In the kind I imagined, *full-fronts me. **1970** *Private Eye* 22 May 5/3 Despite outraged reaction from..the Scottish establishment..*full frontal nudity in the theatre will soon strike north of the border for the first time. **1971** *New Scientist* 4 Feb. 272/1 Full frontal facts of life for the pre-pubertal child..is fair enough. **1976** R. QUIRK in *Style & Communication in Eng. Lang.* (1982) vii. 92 It could even be argued that dictionaries are now merely pandering to current waves of full-frontal fashion. **1984** *Times* 18 Dec. 17/1 The Chancellor of the Exchequer made a full frontal attack on the Bank of England's competence. **1850** *Bohn's Handbk. Games* 382 *Full hand. **1950** *Hoyle's Games* (ed. 20) I. 118 With Full Hands the higher threes win, e.g. 3 threes and 2 fours are better than 3 twos and pair aces. **1589** GREENE *Menaphon* (Arb.) 54 Some propheticall *full mouth. **1646** CRASHAW *Music's Duel* 156 A full-mouth Diapason swallowes all. **1950** *N.Z. Jrnl. Agric.* Oct. 351/1 No sheep are carried beyond full mouth; at this age the cast ewes are disposed of privately. **1959** S. J. BAKER *Drum* II. 111 *Full-mouth*, an eight-tooth sheep. **1667** MILTON *P.L.* v. 42 Now reigns *Full-orbed the moon. **1851** MAYNE REID *Scalp Hunt.* xxxiv. 260 The moon, full-orbed, is sweeping up towards the zenith. **1871** R. B. VAUGHAN *Life Thomas Aquinas* II. 644 The steady full-orbed revelation of Jesus Christ. **1895** *United Presbyt. Mag.* 259 We confess to the impression that he lacks somewhat of *fullorbedness. **1843** 'WYKEHAMIST' *Pract. Hints Cricket* 15 The player being *enticed* to play to it as to a *full-pitch. **1895** H. G. HUTCHINSON *P. Steele* i. 29 One or two [balls] went over the wicket altogether, and were taken, full pitch, by the wicket-keeper. *Ibid.*, He..sent..ball after ball full-pitched. **1929** Full-pitch [see CARRY *v.* 9 b]. **1934** J. W. BURGESS *Reminisc. Amer. Scholar* iii. 42 The faculty of the college was at that time a strong body of teachers, most of them being *full professors of long experience and high standing. **1947** *Partisan Rev.* XIV. 474 The academic hierarchy, from instructor up to full professor, enforces caution on the imaginative or adventurous thinker. **1966** P. GREEN tr. *Escarpit's Novel Computer* ix. 116 Statisticians..do a numerical break-down of the full professors..and various other species of academic fauna. **1971** *Nature* 4 June 275/1 Even Berkeley is only able to boast that two per cent of its full professors were women in 1970. **1876** STAINER & BARRETT *Dict. Mus. Terms*, *Full score. **1946** *Penguin Music Mag.* Dec. 15 Purcell never saw an Italian opera... He may just possibly have read a full score—we know that Pepys possessed one. **1885** F. S. MITCHELL *Birds Lancs.* 185 Common Snipe... Local names.—*Full Snipe, Lady Snipe. **1887** A. C. SMITH *Birds Wilts.* 431 The provincial names of these three species accurately describe their relative size; the Jack or Half Snipe weighing about 2 ozs., the Common, Whole, or Full Snipe 4 ozs., and the Great or Double Snipe 8 ozs. **1913** H. K. SWANN *Dict. Eng. & Folk-Names Brit. Birds* 90 The Common Snipe is also sometimes termed Full Snipe to distinguish it from the Jack (or Half) Snipe. **1965** *Jrnl. Lancs. Dial. Soc.* Jan. 15 *Snipe*,.. full snipe, scape snipe: Heywood. **1826** *Manch. Guardian* 5 Aug. 4/3 Barker, the Nottingham bowler,.. so far lost his temper, as to give a *full toss, as we thought, at the face of the player, instead of his wicket. **1906** A. E. KNIGHT *Compl. Cricketer* iii. 113 Over-pitch the ball and it presents the easiest of full tosses. **1683** *Lond. Gaz.* No. 1846/4 A *full trust Nag, a good Trot, short Rack. **1892** H. SWEET *New Eng. Gram.* I. 22. §58 When a form-word is entirely devoid of meaning, we may call it an *empty word*, as opposed to **full words* such as *earth* and *round*. **1929** GRATTAN & GURREY *Our Living Lang.* 98 Words which have an independent meaning of their own. These are known as Full-words. **1933** BLOOMFIELD *Lang.* xii. 199 The parts of speech [in Chinese] are *full words* and *particles*. **1934** PRIEBSCH & COLLINSON *German Lang.* iii. 249 Other full-word suffixes are *-bar*, *-haft*. **1954** PEI & GAYNOR *Dict. Linguistics* 78 *Full word*, in Chinese grammar, any word which expresses a concept or idea or designates a person, object, quality, etc.—i.e., verbs, substantives and adjectives. **1966** J. E. BUSE in C. E. Bazell *In Memory of J. R. Firth* 53 Full-words consist of a single free morpheme.. with or without one or more of the following affixes.

B. quasi-*sb.* and *sb.*

1. The *adj.* used *absol.*, passing into *sb.* In various adverbial phrases.

a. at (the) full: †(*a*) In various uses, now chiefly expressed by the other phrases below: Fully, completely; at full length; to the full extent (*obs.*). (*b*) At the position or moment of fullness; in the state of fullness (cf. 4 c).

c **1340** *Cursor M.* 4008 (Trin.) But who so god helpe wol May sauely go at þe fol. *c* **1380** WYCLIF *Church & Members* Sel. Wks. III. 347 Lord! where he were not charged at the fulle as apostlis weren. **1398** TREVISA *Barth. De P.R.* XV. cxxvii. (1495) 536 A penne maye not wryte at full the praysynge of this kyngdom. **1413** *Pilgr. Sowle* (Caxton 1483) IV. xxxii. 81 They ben wel ioynted and myghtely boned so that they ben strong at the fulle. **1563** *Homilies* II. *Agst. Gluttony* (1859) 299 They that use to drinke deeply and to feed at full. **1632** J. HAYWARD tr. *Biondi's Eromena* 171 Satisfying..the rest of his demands at full. **1662** GERBIER *Princ.* 35 Eight Foote in length, being at full the space which the Horse doth possess when.. he lyeth stretcht on his Litter. **1667** MILTON *P.L.* I. 641 His regal state Put forth at full. **1705** HEARNE *Collect.* 22 Nov., Giving his Reasons at full. **1742** YOUNG *Nt. Th.* v. 878 He drops his mask; Frowns out at full. **1790** BURKE *Fr. Rev.* 66 The power of the house of commons.. is.. great; and long may it be able to preserve its greatness..at the full. **1874** MICKLETHWAITE *Mod. Par. Churches* 186 Having certain jets turned on at full.

b. in (†the) full: (*a*) with reference to a statement, etc.: At full length, in extenso; (*b*) Of payments, receipts, etc.: To the full amount. ***in full of***: in full discharge or satisfaction of. †***a leg in the full***: one that is plump and well rounded.

1552 J. CAIUS *Sweating Sickness* 4 A woorke of Erasmus.. I dyd geue..not in the ful as the authore made it, but abbreuiate. **1602** MARSTON *Ant. & Mel.* III. Wks. 1856 I. 36, I have a good head of haire..a legge, faith, in the full. **1679–88** *Secr. Serv. Money Chas. & Jas.* (Camden) 35, 37^{li} 5^{s} 9^{d}, in full of a former bill for that service. **1704** J. PITTS *Acc. Mahometans* 23 The Cause..may be for not paying in full to two or three Shillings. **1741** RICHARDSON *Pamela* II. 368 To assign her Five Hundred Pounds, in full of all her Demands upon her Family. **1754–62** HUME *Hist. Eng.* (1806) IV. liv. 177 Eight hundred and fifty pounds a day, in full of their subsistence. **1781** COWPER *Convers.* 201 A satisfactory receipt in full. **1879** *Law Rep.* 14 Q. Bench Div. 814 A sufficient sum to pay the trade-creditors of my aforesaid sons in full. **1885** *Manch. Exam.* Nov. 3/2 Reproducing in full instead of simply summarising the.. documentary material.

c. to the full (also †*to full*): to the utmost extent, completely, fully, quite. Also †to satiety.

1393 LANGL. *P. Pl.* C. XXI. 413 May no..presiouse drynkes Moyst me to þe fulle. *c* **1430** *Freemasonry* 682 The angele Gabryelle, Wol kepe hem to the ful welle. **1577** *St. Aug. Manual* (Longm.) 114 Although I cannot do it to the full in this lyfe: yet let me profite from day to day untill it may come to the full. **1611** BIBLE *Exod.* xvi. 3 When we did eate bread to the full. **1628** GAULE *Pract. Theorists Paneg.* 60 Done, Done to full, whatsoe're he came to doe. **1648** GAGE *West Ind.* xxi. 190 We thought our money had satisfied them ..to the full. **1701** PENN in *Pa. Hist. Soc. Mem.* IX. 53, I must expect my right to the full. **1798** G. WASHINGTON *Lett.* Writ. 1893 XIV. 73 To keep them out of it; or which is to the full as likely, to direct them into another course. **1885** *L'pool Daily Post* 1 June 5/4 The University match promises to illustrate to the full the delightful uncertainty of cricket.

2. a. = FILL *sb.*[1] 1. Now *rare*.

1377 LANGL. *P. Pl.* B. VI. 266 Arise vp ar appetit haue eten his fulle. **1607** TOPSELL *Four-f. Beasts* (1658) 187 If they eat Walnuts (and not to their full) unripe. **1648** GAGE *West Ind.* xiii. 76 Here is now enough, drink thy full of it. **1862** MERIVALE *Rom. Emp.* (1871) V. xliv. 281 These flies, he said, have nearly sucked their full. **1874** DASENT *Tales fr. Fjeld* 152 Tom Toper had eaten his full. *Ibid.* 178 They had all stared their full.

†**b.** The quantity that fills (a receptacle). *Obs.* [app. evolved from -FUL 2.]

1799 *Spirit Publ. Jrnls.* (1800) III. 7 The full of his hat is the standard of his corn measures.

3. Complete scope, entire range; entire amount or sum total; completeness, fullness. †In adverbial phrase, ***all the full***: in all its fullness or completeness (*obs.*). Now *rare*.

c **1330** *Arth. & Merl.* 8433 What þou se al þe fulle, Wiche socour don we schulle. *c* **1400** *Destr. Troy* 13855 When the freike had the fulle of xv^{tene} yeres. **1523** LD. BERNERS *Froiss.* (1812) I. 689 They shulde playnly shewe the full of his entencyon and mynde. **1592** DANIEL *Delia* Poems (1717) 409 Her tender Bud doth undisclose That Full of Beauty, Time bestows upon her. **1670** COTTON *Espernon* I. II. 49 The Lords of Guise had the full of their own demands. **1720** DE FOE *Capt. Singleton* x. (1840) 172, I should not be able to recollect the full..of the great variety. **1734** SNELGRAVE *Guinea & Slave Trade* 55 Afterwards we experienced the full of what he told us. **1843** J. H. NEWMAN *Apologia* (1864) 358 With my opinions, to the full of which I dare not confess. **1890** W. C. RUSSELL *Ocean Trag.* II. xix. 134 Sleeping as he did, right in the 'eyes', he got the very full of the motion.

4. a. The period, point, or state of the greatest fullness or strength.

1398 TREVISA *Barth. De P.R.* VII. lxix. (1495) 287 One manere medicyne nedyth in the begynnynge of the euyll, and a nother in the fulle, and a nother in passynge therof. *c* **1400** *Destr. Troy* 12560 [The] stones at the full of the flode [were] flet all aboue. **1611** SPEED *Hist. Gt. Brit.* VII. xxxi. 317 Empires..haue their risings, their fuls, and their fals. **1613** PURCHAS *Pilgrimage* (1614) 399 Their [the Romanes'] Empire was growing to the full. *c* **1621** S. WARD *Life of Faith* (1627) 97 Whiles he was..in the full of his prosperity.

b. Of a month or season: The height, the middle.

1658 EVELYN *Fr. Gard.* (1675) 143 The perfect season to sow Melon-seeds, is in the full of february. **1855** BROWNING *Another Way of Love* i, June was not over Though past the full. **1858** MOTLEY *Corr.* (1889) I. 327 The highest circles of London in the full of the season.

c. ***the full of the moon*** (also ellipt. ***the full*** and in phr. ***at full***): the period or state of complete illumination of the moon's disc.

c **1386** CHAUCER *Frankl. T.* 341 Thanne shal she [the moon] been euene atte fulle alway. **1398** TREVISA *Barth. De P.R.* v. lviii. (1495) 174 Beestes and trees haue passynge plente of humours and of marowe in the fulle of the mone. **1559** W. CUNNINGHAM *Cosmogr. Glasse* 149 Before the Full, and after the change, she shineth presently, the sonne being set. **1598** YONG *Diana* 309 The fuls and wanes of the Moone. *a* **1652** BROME *Queene's Exch.* II. i. Wks. 1873 III. 473 Bright Cynthia in her full of Lustre. **1664** BUTLER *Hud.* II. iii. 262 He made an Instrument to know If the Moon shine at full or no. **1686** PLOT *Staffordsh.* 431 The Paschal Moone, whose Full fell..next after the Vernal Equinox. **1720** DE FOE *Capt. Singleton* vii. (1840) 123 The moon was near the full. **1794** *Trans. Soc. Arts* XII. 245 Every full and change of the moon. **1818** M. G. LEWIS *Jrnl. W. Ind.* (1834) 28 She is to be at her full to-morrow. **1840** DICKENS *Barn. Rudge* i, The moon is past the full, and she rises at nine.

fig. **1590** NASHE *Pasquil's Apol.* I. C, Heere his wit is at the fullest, and presentlie it beginneth to wane againe.

5. The full grasp (of the hand).

1833 *Regul. Instr. Cavalry* I. 59 The bridoon rein..to be held in the full of the bridlehand.

6. ***crown fulls***: Herrings of the best brand (see quot. 1864 in A. 1. e).

1892 *Berwick Advertiser* 16 Sept. 3/6 Not a single barrel of crown fulls has been branded this summer.

†**7.** A set (of kettles). *Obs.* (? Another word.)

1466 *Mann. & Househ. Exp.* 206 My mastyr paid..for iij. kettelles calde a ffulle, iij.s vj.d. **1502** ARNOLDE *Chron.* (1811) 237 Fullis off ketellis redy bownde, the full, at iij.s'. iiij.d'. **1528** SIR R. WESTON in Dillon *Calais & Pale* (1892) 91 Item, of every fulle [*printed* fulte] of kettles j^{d}. **1660–1** *Newcastle Merch. Advent.* (Surtees) 202 Railph Fell.. petitioned for a full of battery seized on.

C. *adv.*

1. Simply intensive: Very, exceedingly.

a. with adjs. of quality. Now only *poet.*

c **888** K. ÆLFRED *Boeth.* xi. §1 Maneȝe beoþ þeah æȝþer ȝe full æþele ȝe full weliȝe and beoþ þeah full unrote. *c* **1000** *Ags. Ps.* (Th.) lxxxviii[i]. 3 [4] Ic..ȝeworhte ful sefte seld, þæt hi sæton on. *a* **1200** *Moral Ode* 75 in *Trin. Coll. Hom.* 222 Heuene and erðe he ouersihð his eien beð ful brihte. *c* **1300** *Cursor M.* 21061 (Edin.) Ful elde [quen þat] he seich his endedai him neiȝand neich. *c* **1380** WYCLIF *Wks.* (1880) 309 Ȝee, ful deer breþeren. *c* **1400** *Lanfranc's Cirurg.* 110 Þese boonys in oon partie ben ful hard. *c* **1420** *Sir Amadace* (Camd.) xxvii, Sir Amadace toke leue atte alle, Un-semand with fulle glad chere. **1450–1530** *Myrr. our Ladye* 7 Praye for oure right poure and full wretched soulle. **1461** *Paston Lett.* No. 416 II. 51 To my full worshipfull..maister. **1482** *Inv. of W. Pelle* (Somerset Ho.) The Full Reverend Fadur in God John Archepysshop of Canterbury. *a* **1550** *Christis Kirke Gr.* I. iii, Fou ȝellow ȝellow wes hir heid. **1590** SPENSER *F.Q.* I. viii. 17 Came hurtling in full fierce. **1613** SHAKS. *Hen. VIII*, I. i. 133 Anger is like A full hot Horse. **1640** J. DYKE *Worthy Commun.* 56 Full faine wilt thou be to have Christ Jesus to receive thy soule. **1741** RICHARDSON *Pamela* I. 70 And I suppose too, she'll say, I have been full pert. **1869** JEAN INGELOW *Lily & Lute* II. 104 O, full sweet, and O, full high, Ran that music up the sky.

b. with adjs. of quantity or indefinite numerals. Now only *arch.* in ***full many***.

a **1300** *Cursor M.* 17288 + 39 Ful litel while it was þat he in ioy wald bee. **13..** *E.E. Allit. P.* C. 18 For þay schal comfort encroche in kyþes ful mony. *c* **1330** R. BRUNNE *Chron.* (1810) 40 Fulle fo [*printed* so] frendes he had. *c* **1400** MAUNDEV. (1839) xviii. 198 In that Lond is full mochelle waste. *c* **1450** *Mirour Saluacioun* 1278 [She] lete falle fulle many a tere. **1477** NORTON *Ord. Alch.* Proem in Ashm. (1652) 10 Full few Clerks. **1557** NORTH *Gueuara's Diall Pr.* *ij a, Gen. Prol., Q iv b, Ful few are the pleasures which Princes enioy. **1750** GRAY *Elegy* xiv, Full many a gem of purest ray serene. **1820** KEATS *St. Agnes* v, Old dames full many times declare. **1853** KINGSLEY *Hypatia* xiv. 168 Philammon would have gone hungry to his couch full many a night.

c. with advbs. Now *arch.*, chiefly in ***full well***.

c **888** K. ÆLFRED *Boeth.* xxxviii. §5 Þa men þe habbaþ unhale eaȝan, ne maȝon ful eaþe locian onȝean þa sunnan. *a* **1000** *Byrhtnoth* 311 (Gr.) He ful baldlice beornas lærde. *c* **1175** *Lamb. Hom.* 29 Þa iuguleres and þa oðer sottes alle heo habbeð an þonc fulneh. *a* **1225** *Ancr. R.* 90 'Vbi amor, ibi oculus'; wite þu fulewel. *a* **1300** *Cursor M.* 1800 (Gött.) Allas! fule late þai þaim began. *c* **1300** *Harrow. Hell* 100 Jesu, wel y knowe the! That ful sore reweth me. **1382** WYCLIF *1 Macc.* vi. 62 The kyng..brake fulsoone the ooth that he swore. *c* **1450** *Merlin* 25 Full euell haue ye sped that thus haue slayn youre kynge. *c* **1489** CAXTON *Sonnes of Aymon* i. 35 He thenne kyssed his childe alle bloody full often. **1529** FRITH *Wks.* (1573) 98 Christ full lowly and meekely washed his disciples feete. **1600** HOLLAND *Livy* VIII. xxxviii. (1609) 310 Let them buy it full deerly. **1635** J. HAYWARD tr. *Biondi's Banish'd Virg.* 206 Full litle slept the Duke that night. **1667** MILTON *P.L.* I. 536 The imperial ensign..full high advanced, Shone like a meteor. *a* **1711** KEN *Christophil* Poet. Wks. 1721 I. 523 Full well I know my Jesus present there. **1782** COWPER *Gilpin* 79 Full slowly pacing o'er the stones. **1818** WORDSW. *Had this effulgence* iv, Full early lost, and fruitlessly deplored. **1875** HELPS *Ess., Transact. Business* 73 Those who can seem to forget what they know full well.

2. Completely, entirely, fully, quite.

a. with adjs., *esp.* numerals. Also ***full due*** (see quots. 1867 and 1895).

a **1000** *Boeth. Metr.* xxvi. 33 Aulixes..sæt longe þæs tyn winter full. *c* **1340** *Cursor M.* 9227 (Trin.) Siþ þis world bigon to be Is foure þousonde six hundride fol. *c* **1374** CHAUCER *Troylus* I. 378 Thus argumentyd he, in his bygynnyng, Ful unavysed of his wo cominge. **1552** *Bk. Com. Prayer, Ordination*, Full .xxiiii. yeres olde. **1577** B. GOOGE *Heresbach's Husb.* I. (1586) 27 It waxeth greater, and ..is within fourtie dayes after ful ripe. **1610** SHAKS. *Temp.* I. ii. 396 Full fadom fiue thy Father lies. **1653** SIR E. NICHOLAS in *N. Papers* (Camden) II. 6 Being now not full 13 years of age. *c* **1710** C. FIENNES *Diary* (1888) 11 We were full an hour passing that hill. **1812** *Examiner* 5 Oct. 634/1 New Beans are full 6*s.* per quarter lower: but old ones fully support their price. **1825** COBBETT *Rur. Rides* 245 A hill of full a mile high. **1863** KINGSLEY *Water Bab.* 9 He weighed full fifteen stone. **1867** SMYTH *Sailor's Word-bk.*, *Full due* , for good; for ever; complete; belay. **1871** PALGRAVE *Lyr. Poems* 35 She..Blushed like a full-ripe apple. **1874** STUBBS *Const. Hist.* I. iii. 50 As being a full-free member of the community. **1884** READE in *Harper's Mag.* Mar. 637/2 'I condemned it ten years ago'. 'Full that..,' said Pierre. **1895** *E. Anglian Gloss.*, *Full due*, final acquittance, for good and all.

b. with advbs. Now *rare*.

1382 WYCLIF *Josh.* vi. 5 And the wallis of the cyte [Jericho] shulen fuldoun falle. **1523** LD. BERNERS *Froiss.* I. clxii. 200 Kynge Johan was that day a full right good knyght. ? *a* **1550** *Frere & Boye* 134 in Ritson *Anc. P.P.* 40 Than drewe it towarde nyght, Jacke hym hyed home full ryght. **1746** CHESTERF. *Lett.* (1792) I. cv. 288 He articulated every word..full loud enough to be heard the whole length of my library. **1833** H. MARTINEAU *Tale of Tyne* vi. 116 Adam, as I told you, I saw full enough of.

c. with advbl. phrases. Also in ***full as***, ***full as*** (or †*so*)...*as*.

1529 MORE *Comf. agst. Trib.* III. Wks. 1215/2 Though menne shoulde neuer stande full out of feare of fallynge. **1670** NARBOROUGH *Jrnl.* in *Acc. Sev. Late Voy.* I. (1711) 52 Some Swans but not full so large as ours. **1698** FRYER *Acc. E. India & P.* 215 The Topaz is a Stone very hard, full as hard as the Saphire. **1719** DE FOE *Crusoe* II. vi, They lived, though..concealed, yet full at large. **1752** YOUNG *Brothers* III. i, To mount full rebel-high. **1762** FOOTE *Lyar* II. Wks. 1799 I. 302 You will be full as useful to it by recruiting her subjects at home. **1796** MRS. GLASSE *Cookery* v. 53 Butter put into the dripping-pan does full as well. **1825** in Cobbett *Rur. Rides* (1885) II. 38, I should get full as much by keeping it [the story] to myself. **1837** HT. MARTINEAU *Soc. Amer.* III. 92 To the English reader they are full as interesting as to Americans.

†**d. ful iwis, fuliwis, to fuliwis**: full certainly, for certain, assuredly. *Obs.*

c **1200** ORMIN 2529 Þatt witt tu fuliwiss. *c* **1205** LAY. 26841 Ich wulle bitachen þe ful iwis minne castel inne Paris. *c* **1220** *Bestiary* 563 Fro ðe noule niðerward ne is ȝe no man like, Oc fis to fuliwis. *c* **1300** *Harrow. Hell* 55 Fore Adames sunne, fol y wis, Ich have tholed al this.

e. full out: to the full, fully, out and out, quite, thoroughly; now esp., at full power, at top speed; also *attrib.* or as *adj.*

1382 WYCLIF *Isa.* xii. 6 Ful out ioȝe, and preise, thou dwelling of Sion. *c* **1400** *Prymer, Litany* in Maskell *Mon. Rit.* (1846–7) II. 106 Lord, make saaf the king: and ful out heere thou us in the dai that we shulen inclepe thee. *a* **1500** *Chaucer's Dreme* 2138 Archbishop and archdiacre Song full out the servise. **1600** ABP. ABBOT *Exp. Jonah* 624 This number must definitely be taken for so many thousands full out, that [etc.]. **1615** BP. ANDREWES *Serm.* (1629) 485 Sacrilege the Apostle rankes with Idolatrie; as being full out as evill. **1676** HALLEY in Rigaud *Corr. Sci. Men* (1841) I. 226 Mr. Mercator is full out as obscure in his treatise of Mars. **1699** T. C[OCKMAN] *Tully's Offices* (1706) 201 And Lucius Crassus..was full-out as generous. **1869** in *Lonsdale Gloss.* **1917** 'CONTACT' *Airman's Outings* 46 With nose down and engine full out, we raced towards the lines and safety. **1933** *Jrnl. R. Aeronaut. Soc.* XXXVII. 877 On its official trials the machine did a full-out speed, while flying level at 19,000 ft., of 121 m.p.h., its cruising speed. **1938** *Times* 2 Feb. 14/5 It sounded as if the engine was 'full out' when the machine struck the ground. **1938** *Sunday Express* 13 Nov., Alvis was working *full out* to supply the demand. **1942** *Ann. Reg. 1941* 120 The Government [of Canada] had pledged themselves to a full-out war effort. **1971** *Financial Mail* (Johannesburg) 26 Feb. 652/3 A dedicated Mr Botha himself runs the Department full out.

3. a. Of position and direction: Exactly, directly, straight.

1582 N. LICHEFIELD tr. *Castanheda's Conq. E. Ind.* lxvii. 137 Our Ordinance beeing shot off, did all light full amongst the enimies. **1584** R. SCOT *Discov. Witchcr.* II. v. (1886) 20 [They] dare not looke a man full in the face. **1632** LITHGOW *Trav.* VI. 248 An olde Arch of stone..standing ful in the high Way. **1674** N. COX *Gentl. Recreat.* III. (1677) 13 Always..shoot..rather side-ways, or behinde the Fowl, than full in their faces. **1698** FRYER *Acc. E. India & P.* 25 For which the Winds served them well enough, though full in our Teeth. **1702** POPE *Jan. & May* 456 Full in the centre of the flow'ry ground A crystal fountain spreads its streams around. **1801** SOUTHEY *Thalaba* x. xvii, Full in his face the lightning-bolt was driven. **1832** H. MARTINEAU *Demerara* ii. 16 With these principles full in his mind, he began to observe all that surrounded him. **1883** E. INGERSOLL in *Harper's Mag.* Jan. 196/1 A sudden escape from curtaining oak branches brought us full upon the summit.

b. With reference to the points of the compass: Due. See DUE B. 2. ? *Obs.*

1559 W. CUNNINGHAM *Cosmogr. Glasse* 146 Untill she commeth to the Meridian Circle, and is full South. **1601** HOLLAND *Pliny* I. 79 Before Zacynthus 35 miles full East, are the two Strophades. **1670** EACHARD *Cont. Clergy* Pref. A school that stands full south. **1708** *Brit. Apol.* No. 93. 2/1 The.. Wind is.. Full East. **1720** DE FOE *Capt. Singleton* ix. (1840) 154 The one [way] was to travel full west.

†**4.** With vbs. or pples.: Fully, completely, entirely, quite, thoroughly. *Obs.*

c **900** tr. *Bæda's Hist.* II. xiv. [xvi.] (1890) 144 Bi fulcuðum strætum. **1154** *O.E. Chron.* an. 1083 Hi comon into capitulan on uppon þa munecas full ȝewepnede. **1340** *Ayenb.* 107 Huer-by we ssolle by zuo uol dronke of þine loue þet [etc.]. **1430-40** LYDG. *Bochas* I. ix. (1544) 17 a, He was brought forth and recured And full made hole of his woundes sore. **1529** MORE *Comf. agst. Trib.* II. 1182/2 Then he feareth that he bee neuer full confessed, nor neuer full contrite. **1611** BIBLE *John* vii. 8 My time is not yet full come. **1613** PURCHAS *Pilgrimage* (1614) 508 Our Reader.. being before full cloyed with our tedious Narrations. **1697** DRYDEN *Virg. Georg.* III. 319 When once he's broken, feed him full and high. **1807** *Med. Jrnl.* XVII. 237 He had the small-pox.. again very full.

5. *Comb.* †**a.** with vbs.: **full-bring** [cf. OFris. *ful-branga*, Ger. *vollbringen*] *trans.*, to accomplish; **full-burn** *intr.*, to blaze forth, follow hotly; **full-forth** [+ FORTH *v.*] *trans.*, to accomplish, complete; **full-make** *trans.*, to complete, perfect; **full-serve** *trans.*, to serve fully; **full-sound** *intr.*, to sound loudly; **full-thrive** *intr.*, to thrive to the full; **full-timber** *trans.*, to build completely; **full-work** [OE. *full-wyrcan* = OHG. *fol(l)awurchan*] *trans.*, (*a*) OE. to perpetuate; (*b*) to complete. *Obs.*

c **1200** ORMIN 16335 Ʒure temmple timmbredd wass, & all *fullbrohht till ende. **1382** WYCLIF *Gen.* xxxi. 36 For what my synne, has thow thus *fulbrent [Vulg. *exarsisti*] after me. *a* **1175** *Cott. Hom.* 237 His ȝiaf miht and strencþe þurl þe gief of his gaste his hesne to *fulforðie. *c* **1200** ORMIN 15597 Ær þann þiss temmple mihhte ben Fullwrohht & all fullforþedd. *a* **1300** *E.E. Psalter* xvi[i]. 5 *Ful-make mi steppes in sties þine. **1490** CAXTON *Eneydos* xxvii. 104 Fulmake thoblacyon to pluto. **1340** *Ayenb.* 33 And me kan zigge huo þet serueþ and naȝt *uol-serueþ his ssepe he lyest. **1382** WYCLIF *Judg.* vii. 18 Whanne the trompe *fulsowneth in myn hoond. *c* **1200** ORMIN 5130 Swa *fullþrifenn þatt itt nohht Ne maȝȝ na mare waxxenn. *Ibid.* 16321 Godess temmple.. wass i sexe ȝeress all and fow-werrtiȝ *fulltimmbredd. *a* **1035** *Cnut's Laws* II. c. 61 (Schmid) Gif hwa on fyrde griðbryce *fulwyrce. *c* **1200** Fullwrohht [see quot. for *fullforth* above].

b. with pres. and pa. pples. (cf. A. 12 b, to which some of these might be referred), as ***full-accomplished***, ***-acorned***, ***-adjusted***, ***-armed***, ***-assembled***, ***-assured***, ***-beaming***, ***-bearing***, ***-born***, ***-bound***, ***-buckramed***, ***-descending***, ***-digested***, ***-distended***, †***-drive(n***, ***-exerted***, ***-extended***, †***-fast***, ***-fatted***, ***-fledged***, ***-glowing***, †***-greased***, †***-knowing***, †***-known***, ***-levelled***, ***-manned***, ***-nerved***, ***-plumed***, ***-ripened***, ***-spread***, ***-strained***, ***-trimmed***, ***-tuned***, †***-waxen***; †**full-begotten**, lawfully begotten, legitimate; **full-blown**[1], filled with wind, puffed out (*lit.* and *fig.*); see BLOW *v.*[1] 22; **full-blown**[2], in full bloom (*lit.* and *fig.*); see BLOW *v.*[2] 1; **full-fashioned** = *fully-fashioned* adj.; **full-stated** (see quot.).

1726-46 THOMSON *Winter* 668 Indulge her fond ambition ..To mark thy various *full-accomplished mind. **1611** SHAKS. *Cymb.* II. v. 16 Like a *full Acorn'd Boare. **1730-46** THOMSON *Autumn* 835 The *full-adjusted harmony of things. **1776** MICKLE tr. *Camoens' Lusiad* 31 *Full-arm'd they came, for brave defence prepared. **1735** THOMSON *Liberty* III. 260 Her *full-assembled Youth innumerous swarm'd. **1839** BAILEY *Festus* xix. (1848) 220 The *full-assured faith. **1735** SOMERVILLE *Chase* II. 142 Had not her Eyes, With Life *full-beaming, her vain Wiles betray'd. **1896** *Daily News* 17 June 4/5 The thousand acres is never all *full-bearing altogether. **1636** RUTHERFORD *Lett.* (1862) I. 182 Your Father counteth you not a bastard: *full-begotten bairns are nurtured. **1615** J. STEPHENS *Satyr. Ess.* 3 With cheeks *full blowne Each man will wish the case had beene his owne. *a* **1635** NAUNTON *Fragm. Reg.* (Arb.) 15 A time in which (for externals) she was full blown. **1635-56** COWLEY *Davideis* II. 735 Some did the Way with full-blown Roses spread. **1693** DRYDEN *Persius* I. 254 Who at enormous Villany turns pale, And steers against it with a full-blown Sail. **1699** BENTLEY *Phal.* 414 Full blown with the opinion of his wonderfull Acuteness. **1749** JOHNSON *Vanity Hum. Wishes* 99 In full-blown dignity, see Wolsey stand. **1878** BROWNING *La Saisiaz* 20 Flower that's full-blown tempts the butterfly. **1821** KEATS *Lamia* I. 172 Whither fled Lamia, now a lady bright, A *full-born beauty new and exquisite. **1766** W. GORDON *Gen. Counting-ho.* 319, 45 barrels *full bound mess-beef. **1851** *Offic. Catal. Gt. Exhib.* II. 545 Bible, 8vo., full-bound in maroon Turkey morocco. **1833** HT. MARTINEAU *Berkeley the Banker* I. i. 7 The *full-buckramed fancy dresses of the young gentlemen. **1715-20** POPE *Iliad* xx. 460 The impatient steel with *full-descending sway Forced through his brazen helm its furious way. **1768-74** TUCKER *Lt. Nat.* (1852) I. 419 We shall.. partake in the expertness and *full-digested remembrance belonging to that. **1728-46** THOMSON *Spring* 185 The *full-distended clouds Indulge their genial stores. *c* **1386** CHAUCER *Frankl. T.* 502 This bargayn is *ful dryue, for we been knyt. **1726-46** THOMSON *Winter* 171 Before the breath Of *full-exerted heaven they wing their course. **1730-46** —— *Autumn* 1119 The long lines of *full-extended war In bleeding flight commixed. **1883** *Glasg. Weekly Her.* 21 Apr. 8/2 Ladies' *full-fashioned black Lisle thread hose. **1927** T. WOODHOUSE *Artificial Silk* 92 Originally, the spring beard needles were used in full-fashioned (flat) machines. *Ibid.* 95 Needles have to be taken out of action when it is desired to decrease the width of any part of the full-fashioned fabric... This possibility of effecting various changes in the width according to the amount of material required for various parts of the human body, gave rise to the term 'full-fashioned'. **1937** *Times* 29 Nov. 38/2 'What does "full-fashioned" mean?'.. 'It means that a stocking is made to fit the contours of the leg.' *c* **1175** *Lamb. Hom.* 61 þa odre weren *fulfeste sone. **1382** WYCLIF *Deut.* xxxii. 15 Ful fat maad is the loued, and aȝen wynsed; *ful-fattid, fulgresid, outlargid. **1883** 'MARK TWAIN' *Life on Mississippi* 246, I was a pilot now, *full-fledged. **1884** *Times* (weekly ed.) 7 Nov. 8/2 A tutor's pay is only about a third of that of a full-fledged professor. **1895** SIR W. HARCOURT *Sp. in Ho. Com.* 14 May, A full-fledged butterfly. **1961** *Brno Studies* III. 92 A 'full-fledged' verb. **1863** I. WILLIAMS *Baptistery* I. viii. (1874) 89 The sun.. Blending them in the golden blazonry Of his *full-glowing orb. **1382** *Ful-gresid [see *full-fatted*]. **1612** SELDEN *Drayton's Poly-olb.* To Rdr., What the Verse oft with allusion, as supposing a *full knowing Reader, lets slip. **1386** *Rolls of Parlt.* III. 225/1 Nichol Brembre.. with stronge honde, as it is *ful knowen.. was chosen Mair. **1701** NORRIS *Ideal World* I. i. 6 This is.. staring, with a *full-levelled eye, the great luminary of spirits in the face. **1606** SHAKS. *Ant. & Cl.* III. vii. 52 Our ouer-plus of shipping will we burne, And with the rest *full mann'd, from th' head of Action Beate th' approaching Cæsar. **1839** BAILEY *Festus* vii. (1848) 70 Dare with *fullnerved arm the rage of all. *c* **1630** DRUMM. OF HAWTH. *Elegy on G. Adolphus* Wks. (1711) 54 With *full plum'd wing thou faulkon-like could fly. **1861** THORNBURY *Turner* (1862) I. 58 He will be a full-plumed Royal Academy Student. **1878** *Masque Poets* 214 Brings to northern shores *full-ripened tropic fruits. **1660** DRYDEN *Astræa Redux* 64 With *full-spread sails to run before the wind. **1748** THOMSON *Castl. Indol.* I. 209 Slow from his bench arose A comely full-spread porter, swol'n with sleep. **1867** SMYTH *Sailor's Word-bk.*, *Full spread*, all sail set. **1746** *Exmoor Scolding* 405 (E.D.S.) Ya know es kep Challacomb-Moor in Hond; tes *vull stated. *Ibid.*, *Full-stated*, spoken of a Leasehold Estate that has Three Lives subsisting thereon. **1757** DYER *Fleece* III. 169 Sinewy arms of men, with *full strain'd strength, Wring out the latent water. **1826** SCOTT *Mal. Malagr.* ii. 59 A *full-trimmed suit of black silk, or velvet. **1842** TENNYSON *Love & Duty* 40 When thy low voice, Faltering, would break its syllables, to keep My own *full-tuned. *c* **1200** ORMIN 10890 He wass *full-waxenn mann.

full, *sb.*[4] *local* (Kent). [Prob. a use of FULL *sb.*[3]] A ridge of shingle or sand pushed or cast up by the tide. So **full** *v.*[4] *trans.*, to form such a ridge on (the beach).

1846 F. DREW *Geol. Folkestone & Rye* 16 The beach is gradually 'fulled', that is pebbles are heaped up in front of the breaker, generally forming a small ridge. **1847** *Proc. Inst. Civil Engin.* VI. 476 No certain record has ever been kept of the increase of the coast line; but from the best existing data, it appears to be about two yards annually, and allowing the accumulation to have been rather more rapid at first, say three yards per annum, a period of about nineteen hundred years will have elapsed, since the sea first left the original 'Full' at Lydd. **1864** *Ibid.* XXIII. 195 The spit.. is formed of parallel 'fulls' of beach. **1902** LD. AVEBURY *Scenery of Eng.* 163 It [*sc.* North Weir Point] consists of a series of curved concentric ridges or 'fulls'.. forming a projecting cape or 'Ness'. **1964** V. J. CHAPMAN *Coastal Veget.* viii. 205 At Dungeness the ridges, known as 'fulls', generally bear Curled dock.

†**full**, *v.*[1] *Obs.* Forms: 1 ful(l)wian, fullian, 3-4 folle(n, 3 *south.* volle(n, 3 fulhe(n, vulȝen, fulewen, folewen, 2-4 fulwe(n, fulȝe, 2 fule(h)ȝen, 4 folwen, fologhe, 5 folowe, 4-6 fulle, (4 fully). [OE. *fullian*, *fullwian*, f. FULL *adv.* + OTeut. **wîhêjan*, *wîhjan* (OHG. *wîhen*, mod.Ger. *weihen*) to consecrate, f. **wîho-* (OS., OHG. *wîh*, Goth. *weihs*) holy.

The word thus means 'to consecrate *fully*'. A convert who was deemed not sufficiently instructed for baptism, or who shrank from assuming the responsibilities which it involved, was frequently *prime-signed*, i.e. marked with the sign of the cross only, the 'full consecration' by baptism being deferred till a later period.]

trans. To baptize.

c **900** tr. *Bæda's Hist.* I. xv. [xxvi.] (1890) 62 Ongunnon heo somnian & singan.. & men læran & fulwian. *a* **1000** *Martyrol.* (E.E.T.S.) 80 He wæs ȝefullwad æt Rome. *c* **1000** *Ags. Gosp.* John i. 33 Se þe me sende to fullianne on wætere. *c* **1175** *Lamb. Hom.* 101 Heo setteð heoran handan ofer ifulȝede men. *c* **1205** LAY. 2402 þe king heo lette fulwen æfter þon lawen. *a* **1225** *Leg. Kath.* 1391 Hwi ne hihe we for to beon Ifulhet [*v.r.* ifulhtnet] as he het his. **1297** R. GLOUC. (1724) 239 As ȝoure fader dude, do, And be yuolled in holy water. **13..** *E.E. Allit. P.* B. 164 Alle arn laþed luflyly.. þat euer wern fulȝed in font þat fest to haue. *c* **1380** *Sir Ferumb.* 5697 He wolde fully.. þan Amyral þat was þere. *c* **1430** *Chev. Assigne* 369 The sixte was fulwedde cheuelere assigne. *c* **1450** MYRC 85 To folowe the chylde ȝef hyt be nede. **1483** *Festivall* (W. de W. 1515) 32 b, Cryste.. was fulled in water.

full (fʊl), *v.*[2] Also 4 follen, fulle(n. [f. FULL *a.* OE. had *fullian* to fulfil (*Cædmon's Gen.* 2317), but continuity is doubtful; in the early ME. *fullen* the *u* prob. represents (y), so that the examples belong to FILL *v.*]

†**1. a.** *trans.* To make full. Cf. FILL *v.* 1. *Obs.*

1362 LANGL. *P. Pl.* A. v. 184 In couenant that Clement schulde the cuppe fulle. *a* **1400** *Prymer* (1891) 39 Thanne is oure mouth fulled of joye. **1484** CAXTON *Fables of Æsop* (1889) 72 He was.. fulled with sorowe. **1627-47** FELTHAM *Resolves* I. lxxxvii. 270 Surely travail fulleth the man.

b. *intr.* To be or become full. Const. *of*. *Obs.* exc. *dial.* and in U.S. of the moon and the tide.

1362 LANGL. *P. Pl.* A. XI. 44 Thei.. demeth god in-to the gorge whon heore gottus follen. *c* **1450** *Cov. Myst.* (Shaks. Soc.) 343 Myn heed dullyth Myn herte ffullyth Of sslepp. **1794** E. DRINKER *Jrnl.* 9 Sept. (1889) 237 The moon fulled this morning about 8 or 10 o'clock. **1864** WEBSTER, The moon fulls at midnight. **1878** B. F. TAYLOR *Between Gates* 40 It is as if a poor little aster should full like the moon and be a dahlia. *a* **1898** Suffolk dial. (F. Hall) 'The moon will full to-night'. **1912** L. J. VANCE *Destroying Angel* xix, He should be able to catch the tide just as it was nearing high water. Allowing it to swing him north-west until it fulled, he ought to be a third of the way across by the time it slackened. **1938** W. DE LA MARE *Memory* 32 Fulling moon aloft doth ride.

†**2.** *trans.* To fulfil, complete. *Obs.*

1380 [see FULLING *vbl. sb.*]. **1492** *Acta Dom. Conc.* (1839) 247/1 þe saidis persons sall mak na payment of the said soume quhill the poyntis of þe said decrett be fullit efter the forme of þe samyn. **1640** BROME *Antipodes* III. viii. Wks. 1873 III. 290 Before he has given her satisfaction I may not full my suit.

3. *Dressmaking.* To make full; to gather or pleat. Also with *on*.

1831 *Westm. Rev.* XIV. 424 The milliner with her fulling, and quilling, and puckering, come[s] in to supply the retiring graces of nature. **1832** *E. Ind. Sketch Bk.* I. 261 A petticoat fulled and stiffened into the dignified rotundity of a hoop. **1884** *West. Daily Press* 2 June 7/2 Plastrons.. are composed of a straight piece, fulled into a small band at the top. **1890** *Daily News* 4 Dec. 3/4 Many pretty little jackets .. are composed of black lace fulled on over a foundation of silk or gold gauze.

b. *intr.* To draw up, pucker, bunch.

1889 *Century Dict.*, The skirt fulls too much in front.

Hence **fulled** *ppl. a.*, gathered or pleated; arranged in folds; ˈ**fulling** *vbl. sb.*, the action of the vb.; †(*a*) the action of fulfilling; (*b*) the action of gathering or pleating; in quots. *concr.*

c **1380** WYCLIF *Sel. Wks.* III. 257 Her matere schulde be truþe and fullynge of Goddis lawe. **1760** MRS. DELANY *Life & Corr.* Ser. II. III. App. 504 There was very little fulling, but the whole design was to be seen without many folds. **1877** BLACKMORE *Cripps* I. ii. 24 She gathered in the skirt of her frock and the fulling of her cloak. **1892** *Daily News* 16 Feb. 6/5 Coats.. finished off at the neck with a fulled shoulder cape.

full (fʊl), *v.*[3] Also 5 ful(le. [ad. OF. *fuler* (F. *fouler*): see FOIL *v.*[1]]

1. *trans. spec.* To tread or beat (cloth) for the purpose of cleansing and thickening it; hence, to cleanse and thicken (cloth, etc.).

1377 LANGL. *P. Pl.* B. xv. 445 Cloth that cometh fro the weuyng is nouȝt comly to were, Tyl it is fulled vnder fote or in fullyng-stokkes. *c* **1440** *Prompt. Parv.* 182/1 Fulle clothe, *fullo*. *c* **1483** CAXTON *Vocab.* 15 b, Colard.. Can well fulle cloth. **1511-2** *Act 3 Hen. VIII*, c. 6 §1 The Walker and Fuller shall truely walke fulle thikke and werke every webbe of wollen yerne. **1598** FLORIO, *Follare*, to full, as clothes in a presse. **1643** PRYNNE *Open. Gt. Seale* 20 One.. man should be assigned.. to seale the Clothes that shall be wrought and fulled in London. **1695** *Lond. Gaz.* No. 3086/4 A new Invented Engine, which Fulls all sorts of Stuffs by Hand or Mans Labour. **1812** SOUTHEY in *Q. Rev.* VII. 63 In this manner a girl can full twenty pair of hose in four or five hours. **1872** YEATS *Techn. Hist. Comm.* 147 English cloths, at the outset were sent to be fulled and dyed in the Netherlands. **1884** J. PAYNE *Tales fr. Arabic* I. 233, I shall .. weave for her and full her yarn.

†**2.** *gen.* To beat or trample down; also, to destroy. *Obs.*

c **1400** *Rowland & O.* 112 Fulle the under my horse fete. *c* **1440** *York Myst.* xi. 118 Nowe kyng Pharo fuls thare childir ful faste. **1641** BEST *Farm. Bks.* (Surtees) 78 Hee threw his hey abroad a nights afore hee lette them in, because then they did not runne over it and full it so much.

†ˈ**fullage.** *Obs.* [a. OF. *foullage* (F. *foulage*), f. *fouler* to FULL.]

1. Money paid for the fulling of cloth.

1611 in COTGR. s.v. *Foullage*. **1706** in PHILLIPS (ed. Kersey). **1755** in JOHNSON. Hence in mod. Dicts.

2. [Cf. FULYIE *sb.*[2]; the lit. sense is 'what is trampled under foot'.] Refuse, street-sweepings, filth.

1689 T. PLUNKET *Char. Gd. Commander* 51 Some storm or other must be near at hand, To sweep away the fullage of the Land. **1780** A. YOUNG *Tour. Irel.* I. 9 They go much to Dublin for fullage of the streets to lay on their hay grounds.

full age.

Adult or mature age, esp. (in opposition to *nonage*) the age of 21 years. Cf. AGE *sb.* 3.

1622 BACON *Holy War* (1629) 129 That after full Age the Sonnes should Expulse their Fathers and Mothers out of their Possessions. **1675** BROOKS *Gold. Key* Wks. 1867 V. 320 God had a respect to the non-age and full-age of his people. **1818** CRUISE *Digest* (ed. 2) V. 428 Those.. who are of full age and sufficient understanding, should have power to suffer a common recovery. **1885** GLADSTONE in *Chr. World* 15 Jan. 37/1 The anniversary.. which will to-morrow bring your Royal Highness to full age.

attrib. *a* **1659** CLEVELAND *Poor Cavalier* 11 E'er ripe Rebellion had a full-age Power.

Hence †**full-aged** *ppl. a.*, being of full or mature age. Of a horse: Exceeding the age of 6 years (now simply, *aged*). *Obs.*

1631 QUARLES *Div. Poems, Samson* xiii. 31 A full ag'd Lyon, who had sought.. his long-desired prey. **1682** *Lond. Gaz.* No. 1737/4 A chesnut sorrel Nag, with a bob Tail, full aged. **1712** STEELE *Spect.* No. 514 ¶4 There stood by her a man full-aged, and of great gravity. **1724** *Lond. Gaz.* No. 6310/3 A sorrel Horse.. full aged.

full-blood, *a.* and *sb.* **A.** *adj.* **a.** Of a brother or sister: Born of the same parents (opposed to

HALF-BLOOD 1. *attrib.*). **b.** Qualifying an ethnic designation: Of pure or unmixed race.

1812 *Niles' Weekly Reg.* II. 408/1 His full blood merino ram lamb. **1850** *Rep. U.S. Comm. Patents Agric. 1849* 88 Sheep..ranging in quality from half to full-blood merino. **1882** A. MACFARLANE *Consanguin.* 17 Brother, full-blood = male child of male and female parents. **1888** *Harper's Mag.* Mar. LXXVI. 602 The full-blood [Cherokee] is always present in the national Legislature. **1893** *Columbus* (Ohio) *Disp.* 2 Oct., His mother [was] a full-blood Potawatomie squaw.

B. *sb.* A pure-bred person or animal.

1846 R. B. SAGE *Scenes Rocky Mts.* xx. 166 They [*sc.* half-breed children] were more beautiful..than the same number of full-bloods,—either of whites or Indians. **1864** *Ret. Agric. Soc. Maine* 9 Those [sheep] exhibited were mostly Spanish Merinos..most full bloods. **1873** J. H. BEADLE *Undevel. West* xix. 358 One may travel for days in the Territory, and never see a full-blood. **1888** *Vermont Agric. Rep.* X. 38, I breed Jerseys; have no full-bloods but high grades. **1964** *Observer* 12 Jan. 6/8 Gathering opinion throughout Australia that the nation's 20,000 full-bloods cannot be indefinitely treated as a lesser breed.

Similarly **full-'blooded** *a.* = FULL BLOOD, *lit.* and *fig.*; also, having plenty of blood. Hence **full-'bloodedly** *adv.*, forcefully, whole-heartedly; **full-'bloodedness** *lit.* and *fig.*

1774 P. V. FITHIAN *Jrnl.* 8 Jan. (1900) I. 89 Balantine, either to shew himself a true full-blooded Buck, or out of mere wantonness..turned the Bones..into many improper and indecent postures. **1786** *Maryland Jrnl.* 31 Mar. (Th.), A number of full-blooded Colts and Fillies. **1801** *Steele Papers* I. 218 The present Secy. altho' a full blooded Yankee, as we call him in these parts, knows the importance of this place. **1810** *Massachusetts Spy* 25 Apr. 3/1 Forty-five full-blooded Merino Sheep. **1825** J. NEAL *Bro. Jonathan* II. 68 A full-blooded republican 'driver'. **1841** CATLIN *N. Amer. Ind.* (1844) II. lvii. 220 His general appearance and actions, those of a full-blooded and wild Indian. **1884** *Century Mag.* XXVIII. 42 The full-bloodedness, the large feet and hands. **1894** *Athenæum* 5 May 571/3 His unquestioned ability has not the roundness, the ripeness, the mellow full-bloodedness of the style of 'The Heptameron'. **1931** *Times Lit. Suppl.* 19 Feb. 137/4 The story is full-bloodedly crowded with sudden deaths. **1958** *Listener* 18 Dec. 1050/1 The difficulty of putting Lorca across full-bloodedly.

'full-bottom. [f. FULL *a.* + BOTTOM *sb.*] A full-bottomed wig.

1713 GAY *Guardian* No. 149 ¶5 Little master will smile when you..thrust its little knuckles in papa's full-bottom. **1759** *Chron.* in *Ann. Reg.* 169/2 A flaxen full bottom suitable to the age between forty and fifty. **1822** T. MITCHELL *Aristoph.* II. 296 Full-bottom, tie, perriwig, curl, or toupee.

'full-bottomed, *a.* [f. as prec. + -ED².]

1. Of a wig: Having a full or large bottom.

1711 BUDGELL *Spect.* No. 150 ¶7 My Banker ever bows lowest to me when I wear my full-bottom'd Wig. **1797** *The College* 15 A huge full-bottom'd wig, and college gown. **1878** *N. Amer. Rev.* CXXVI. 52 Their hero..wore a Greek helmet over a full-bottomed wig.

2. *Naut.* (See quot.)

1867 SMYTH *Sailor's Word-bk., Full-bottomed*, an epithet to signify such vessels as are designed to carry large cargoes.

†fullcome, *v. Obs.* [f. FULL *adv.* + COME *v.* Cf. Ger. *volkommen* adj., perfect.] *trans.* To finish; to perfect.

c **1477** CAXTON *Jason* 16 An other spere that he [Jason] had taken of his esquyer for to fulcome his emprise. *c* **1483** —— *Vocab.* 47 *Dieu leur laisse leur voye Bien employer*, God late them theyr waye Well fulcome.

†,full'do, *v. Obs.* [f. FULL *a.* + DO.] *trans.* To accomplish, fulfil, complete.

a **1225** *Ancr. R.* 372 Me schal fuldon flesches pine ase uorð ase euere efne mei þolien. **1340** *Ayenb.* 28 To destrue..alle guod by hit lite by hit lesse by hit uoldo. *c* **1483** CAXTON *Vocab.* 23 Whiche make very confession. And theyr penaunce fuldoo. *c* **1500** *Melusine* i. 1 He wyl helpe me to bring vnto a good ende & to fuldoo it att hys glorye & praysyng. **1605** VERSTEGAN *Dec. Intell.* ii. (1628) 29 Willing to full-doe their too-falne lot.

Hence **†'full-do** *sb.*, completion, finish. (Perh. the source of the Naut. phrase *for a full due*: see DUE *sb.* 8.)

1631 [see DO *sb.*¹ 2].

full dress. a. See DRESS *sb.* 2 a. Also *fig.*

1790 COWPER *Lett.* 17 June, Here am I at eight in the morning in full dress. **1875** LOWELL *Poet. Wks.* (1879) 465 The habitual full-dress of his well-bred mind. **1887** *Spectator* 4 June 764/2 A crown that could be worn, like a tiara of diamonds, as an adjunct of full dress.

b. *attrib.* as in *full-dress coat, dinner, rehearsal, suit*, etc.; also *fig.*, as in ***full-dress debate***, a formal debate in which important speeches are delivered on each side.

1761 *Ipswich Jrnl.* 24 Jan. 4/1 (Advt.), I have laid in an entire fresh Stock in the Peruke Way, and..will make..full-dress Bobs, from one Pound ten to one Pound fifteen. **1812** J. NOTT *Dekker's Gvlls Horne-bk.* 41 *note*, Not a full-dress coat is made without it. **1834** T. MOORE *Mem.* (1856) VII. 47 A Tory of the full dress school. **1851** *Illustr. Catal. Gt. Exhib.* II. 526 Pair of full-dress boots. **1879** F. W. ROBINSON *Coward Consc.* I. viii, A rusty, black, full-dress suit. **1888** BRYCE *Amer. Commw.* III. VI. cxi. 600 At present the 'full-dress debates' in the Senate are apt to want life. **1893** *Times* 8 July 12/2 Mr. Heneage's amendment is not the best possible text for a full-dress debate. **1926** FOWLER *Mod. Eng. Usage* 155/2 Those who like a full-dress word better than a plain one continue to use..it. **1942** *Amer. Speech* XVII. 271/1 It amounted to a full-dress war before it was finished. **1963** J. JOESTEN *They call it Intelligence* II. viii. 72 By 1923 Rudolf [Abel] had become a full-dress member of the Communist Party.

full-dressed, *a.* Fully dressed; wearing full dress. †Of a coat: = prec. b.

1752 A. MURPHY *Gray's-Inn Jrnl.* No. 14 ¶2 In a full-dressed Coat, with long Skirts. **1806** SURR *Winter in Lond.* (ed. 3) III. 161, I have no objection in the world to full-dressed assemblies. **1824–9** LANDOR *Imag. Conv.* Wks. 1846 I. 206/2 There are hours and occasions when she needs not be full-dressed.

†fu'llend, *v. Obs.* [OE. *fullendian* (= Ger. *vollenden*): see FULL *adv.* and END *v.*] *trans.* To end fully, accomplish, complete, fulfil.

c **900** tr. *Bæda's Hist.* III. xxiii. (MS. B in Smith 554 *note*), He bæd Cynebill..þæt he ða arfæstan ongunnennesse fullendode and ȝefylde. *a* **1200** *Moral Ode* 239 in *O.E. Misc.* 66 Þeo þat gode werc by-gunne and ful-endy hit nolden. *c* **1200** *Trin. Coll. Hom.* 61 We hauen ure penitence fulended. *c* **1300** *Beket* 2322 If he ful in feble stat, that he ne miȝte hit ful ende. **1382** WYCLIF *Ecclus.* xxxiv. 8 With oute lesing shal be ful endid the word of the lawe. **1398** TREVISA *Barth. De P.R.* IX. iv. (1495) 349 The Cycle and the Course of the Mone is fullended in the nintenth yere. *c* **1425** *Eng. Conq. Irel.* (E.E.T.S.) 134 He that al thynge fulle endet.

fuller ('fʊlə(r)), *sb.*¹ Forms: 1–4 fullere, 3 follare, 4 *south.* vollere, 4–6 fullar(e, (6 fullor, furler, 7 fullner), 4– fuller. [OE. *fullere*, ad. L. *fullō* (of unknown origin), assimilated to agent-nouns in *-ere*, -ER¹. If there existed an OE. **fullian* vb., ad. late L. *fullāre* to FULL, the agent-noun may have been derived from it.]

1. One whose occupation is to full cloth.

c **1000** *Ags. Gosp.* Mark ix. 3. *c* **1290** *S. Eng. Leg.* I. 366/53 Mid one follares perche; þat men tesieth opon cloth. *a* **1327** *Pol. Songs* (Camden) 188 The webbes ant the fullaris assembleden hem alle. **1340** *Ayenb.* 167 Mochel is defouled mid þe uet of uolleres þe robe of scarlet. **1511–2** [see FULL *v.*² 1]. **1583** STUBBES *Anat. Abus.* II. (1882) 24 Compounding with the Fuller to thicke it [wool] very much. **1645** BP. HALL *Remedy Discontents* 118 The Fuller treads upon that cloth which he means to whiten. **1764** BURN *Poor Laws* 156 Three weavers..six spinners, one fuller and burler. **1866** ROGERS *Agric. & Prices* I. iv. 103 There are twelve clergymen..six fullers and six girdlers. **1885** *Instructions to Census Clerks* 66 (In list of workers in textile fabrics). Fuller.

2. In the names of various materials, plants, etc. used in the process of fulling; as **fuller's clay** = FULLER'S EARTH; **fuller's grass, herb, weed,** (*Saponaria officinalis*); **fuller's teazel, thistle** (*Dipsacus fullonum*); **fuller's thorn** ? = prec.

1776 ADAM SMITH *W.N.* IV. viii. (1869) II. 238 *Fuller's earth or fuller's clay. **1876** PAGE *Adv. Text-bk. Geol.* v. 101 Fuller's clay or earth. **1526** *Grete Herball* ccclxxxiiij, Saponaria..is called..*fullers grasse. **1601** HOLLAND *Pliny* II. 262 The *Fullers herb in wine honied. **1607** TOPSELL *Four-f. Beasts* (1658) 486 There is an herb called Fullers-herb which doth soften wool. **1578** LYTE *Dodoens* IV. lx. 522 This kinde of Thistel is called..*Fullers Teasel. **1653** CULPEPER *Eng. Phys.* 356 *Fullers Thistle, or Teasel. **1626** BACON *Sylva* §661 An Herbe called Hippophæston [that groweth] vpon the *Fullers Thorne. **1706** PHILLIPS (ed. Kersey), **Fullers-Weed*, or Fullers-thistle, an Herb.

'fuller, *sb.*² [? f. FULL *v.*² (sense 3) + -ER¹.]

1. *Blacksmithing*, etc. A grooved tool on which iron is shaped by being driven into the grooves.

1864 WEBSTER, *Fuller*, a die, a half-round set-hammer. **1896** *Farrier's Price List*, Best Cast Steel, for Fullers, Stamps, &c.

2. A groove made by a fuller.

1855 MILES *Horse-shoeing* 9 The 'fuller' should be carried quite round the shoe to the heels, and the fullering iron should have both sides alike. **1867** SMYTH *Sailor's Word-bk., Fuller*, the fluting groove of a bayonet. **1889** *Daily Tel.* 1 Mar. 5/8 The present pattern is too thin in the 'fuller'.

Hence **'fuller** *v.*, to stamp with a fuller; to groove by stamping; also *dial.* to goffer (linen). **'fullered** *ppl. a.* **'fullering** *vbl. sb.*, the action of the vb.; also *concr.* the groove thus formed.

1820 BRACY CLARK *Descr. New Horse Shoe* 14 Our old English custom of fullering. **1831** J. HOLLAND *Manuf. Metal* I. 170 The shoes being fullered or grooved near the outer edge to receive the heads. **1841** HARTSHORNE *Salopia Antiq.* Gloss. 434 *Fullaring*, a groove into which the nails of a horse's shoe are inserted. **1855** Fullering iron [see sense 2 above]. **1868** *Regul. & Ord. Army* ¶573 The horse's Shoe is not to be grooved or fullered. **1880** BLACKMORE *Mary Anerley* I. xi. 159 His linen clothes are dry, and even quite lately fullered—ironed you might call it. *Mod. Advt.*, Sandal horse shoe..made of plain, fuller'd, or Rodway bar.

fullerphone ('fʊləfəʊn). [f. name of Major A. C. *Fuller* + *-phone* in *telephone*.] A telegraphic instrument used in war-signalling.

1920 *Glasgow Herald* 2 Mar. 7 The claim of Major A. C. Fuller in respect of the 'Fullerphone'. **1922** *Encycl. Brit.* XXXII. 491/2 The fullerphone is a telegraph instrument, the essential point of which is the changing at the receiving end of a steady current into an intermittent current of audible frequency, while at the same time the current in the line remains steady. **1928** BLUNDEN *Undertones of War* xxvi. 253 The mechanism of the 'fullerphone' or 'power buzzer'.

,fuller's 'earth. A hydrous silicate of alumina, used in cleansing cloth; also *Geol.* a group of strata characterized by the presence of this earth.

1523 FITZHERB. *Surv.* 31 Mynes of tynne, leed, ore, cole..lymestonne, chalke, furlers [*sic* **1526**; ed. **1534** fullers] erthe, Sande, cley. **1601** HOLLAND *Pliny* XXXV. xvii. II. 560 This Fullers earth Cimolia, is of a cooling nature. **1667** E. CHAMBERLAYNE *St. Gt. Brit.* I. (1684) 7 Fullers Earth is no where else produced in that abundance and excellency as in England. **1738** CHESTERF. *Comm. Sense* 11 Nov. (1739) II. 238 Fuller's-Earth, the Exportation of which is strictly prohibited by our Laws. **1836** HOR. SMITH *Tin Trump.* I. 9 Like fuller's earth, defiling for the moment but purifying in the end. **1854** F. C. BAKEWELL *Geol.* 50 The bed of clay called fuller's earth..may be considered merely local. **1878** HUXLEY *Physiogr.* 36 This Fuller's earth forms a thick bed of clay which retains the water that reaches it.

fig. **1670** EACHARD *Cont. Clergy* 56 The blots of sin will be easily taken out by the soap of sorrow, and the fullers-earth of contrition. **1727** GAY *Beggar's Opera* I. ix, Money, Wife, is the true Fuller's Earth for Reputations, there is not a Spot or a Stain but what it can take out.

attrib. **1816** W. SMITH *Strata Ident.* 31 The Fuller's Earth Rock..in many places is imperfectly lapidified.

†'fullery. *Obs.*⁻⁰ [f. FULLER *sb.*¹ + -Y³.] A place where the process of fulling is carried on.

1730–6 in BAILEY (folio). **1755** in JOHNSON. Hence in mod. Dicts.

full-face. [f. the advb. phr. (*in*) *full face* s.v. FULL *a.* 8 a.]

1. *attrib. phr.* = FULL-FACED *a.* 2.

1909 *Daily Chron.* 4 Mar. 1/3 The Halcyon was struck a heavy full face blow on the port quarter. **1927** R. H. WILENSKI *Mod. Movement in Art* 133 The full-face eye in profile heads in Egyptian art.

2. *Printing.* A full-faced letter or fount of such letters (cf. next).

1892 *N.Y. Nation* 25 Feb. 155/3 The page is divided into triple columns, and the leading word of each column is in full-face. **1923** *J.J. Little Bk. Types*, etc. (N.Y.) 409 Bold Face.—A fullface letter similar to the roman, containing both hair lines and heavy strokes. **1963** KENNEISON & SPILMAN *Dict. Printing* 77 *Full face*, a fount of capitals designed to occupy the complete body size, as there are no descenders to provide for.

,full-'faced, *a.* [f. FULL *a.* + FACE + -ED².]

1. a. Having a full face; *esp.* of persons, having a full or plump face.

1622 MABBE tr. *Aleman's Guzman d'Alf.* I. 31, I was a yong Lad, ruddy-cheek't, full-fac't, and plumpe withall. **1675** *Lond. Gaz.* No. 980/4 Stolen..a large silver Cup..by a Lodger..a Full-fac'd man. **1796** *Hull Advertiser* 3 Sept. 2/2 David Hallett..stout made, of a low stature, and full faced. **1824** MISS MITFORD *Village* Ser. I. (1863) 230 One side consisting of a full-faced damask rose.

b. said of the moon at full.

1647 H. MORE *Song of Soul* III. II. xxvii, Not from full-faced Cynthia.

2. Having the face turned fully on the spectator or in some specified direction.

1610 GUILLIM *Heraldry* VI. v. 265 The full faced Helmet doth signifie direction or command. **1832** TENNYSON *Œnone* 79 When all the full-faced presence of the Gods Ranged in the halls of Peleus. **1894** J. P. HOPPS in *Westm. Gaz.* 7 Feb. 2/1 As full-faced to the sunshine as you are to-day.

3. *Printing.* Designating letters, chiefly capitals, which have a face occupying the complete body size.

1824 J. JOHNSON *Typogr.* II. i. 10 Being cast in all the various sizes, both Full-faced and Open. **1841** W. SAVAGE *Dict. Art Printing* 247 A full faced letter is considerably larger in proportion than a letter of the regular face upon the same body. **1888** C. T. JACOBI *Printers' Vocab.* 49 *Full-faced letter*, a fount of capitals which has no beard on the top of the shank, occupying the whole depth of the body.

†full'freme, *v. Obs.* Also 5 full-ferm. [OE. *ful(l)fremian, -fremman*: see FULL *adv.* and FREME *v.*] *trans.* To accomplish, fulfil, perfect.

Hence **†full'fremed** *ppl. a.*; **†full'fremedly** *adv.*, perfectly; **†full'fremedness**, perfection.

c **888** K. ÆLFRED *Boeth.* vii. §5 þinre unriht gitsunga ȝewill to fulfremmanne. *c* **900** tr. *Bæda's Hist.* III. xix. [xxvii.] (1891) 244 Lifde he his lif in micelre eaðmodnesse..and in fulfremednesse. **971** *Blickl. Hom.* 35 Gif we þa daȝas fulfremedlice for Gode liſȝeaþ. *c* **1000** *Ags. Gosp.* John iv. 34 þæt ic full fremme [*c* **1160** *Hatton* fulfremie] his weorc. *a* **1175** *Cott. Hom.* 219 Ne meȝ nan iscefte ful-fremedlice smeaȝan ne understonden embe god. *c* **1200** ORMIN 2530 Fullfremedd herrsummnesse. *Ibid.* 5135 þatt te birrþ eȝȝþerr lufess mahht Fullfremeddlike fillenn. *Ibid.* 6083 þatt mann þatt tiss Fullfremeddnesse follȝheþþ. **1486** *Bk. St. Albans* A viij b, Thos same barris shall telle you whan she is full summed or full fermyd.

'full-'grown. [f. FULL *adv.* + GROWN.] Fully grown; having attained full size or maturity.

1667 MILTON *P.L.* VII. 456 Innumerous living Creatures ..Limb'd and full grown. **1724** DE FOE *Mem. Cavalier* (1840) 30 Wickedness presented itself full-grown. **1767** HUNTER in *Phil. Trans.* LVIII. 43 Fig. II. The same view of the same bone in a full-grown Elephant. **1859** DARWIN *Orig. Spec.* iii. (1873) 52 In a state of nature almost every full-grown plant annually produces seed. **1871** BLACKIE *Four Phases* I. 151 He had two sons, one full-grown.

transf. **1856** STANLEY *Sinai & Pal.* x. (1858) 374 Four springs pour their almost full-grown rivers through the plain.

Hence **full-'growner** *colloq.* or *slang*, a full-grown person.

1867 P. FITZGERALD 75 *Brooke St.* III. 251 A full growner: no 'Miss' at all in the case.

†'fullhead¹. *Obs.* In 4–5 fulhed(e. [f. FULL *a.* + -HEAD.] Fullness.

a **1300** *E.E. Psalter* xxxv. 9 [xxxvi. 8] þai sal be drunken, als of wine, Of þe fulhed of house þine. **1340** *Ayenb.* 119 Alsuo wes he..zuo uol of grace..þet of his uolhede we nimeþ al. *c* **1440** HYLTON *Scala Perf.* (1494) III. xxii, In hyr was fulhede of all vertues without wem of synne.

† **'fullhead**². *Obs.* [f. FULL *a.* + HEAD *sb.*] A castrated stag.

1803 J. SLEIGHT in *Ann. Agric.* XXXIX. 556 The full-heads..always herd with the bucks, excepting in the rut.

'full-'hearted, *a.* [f. FULL *a.* + HEART + -ED².] Having a full heart. **a.** Full of courage and confidence; hence of a work: Carried on with zeal. **b.** Full of feeling; indicative of strong emotion. Hence **,full-'heartedly** *adv.*

1611 SHAKS. *Cymb.* v. iii. 7 The Enemy full-hearted, Lolling the Tongue with slaught'ring. **1851** MRS. BROWNING *Casa Guidi* 31 The sky above..seemed to..palpitate in glory, like a dove Who has flown too fast, full-hearted. **1859** SMILES *Self-Help* xii. (1860) 323 The most effective work is always the full-hearted work. **1876** GEO. ELIOT *Dan. Der.* IV. lxiii. 240 Full-hearted silence. **1882** J. L. LUDLOW in *Homilet. Monthly* May 451 For you he lived ..and sends his Holy Spirit as full-heartedly as if there were no other human being.

full house. 1. An assembly or audience which fills the building in which a performance is given or a meeting is held; also in extended use. Also, a session of a legislative or deliberative body, in which all or most of the members are present in their usual capacity (*Funk's Stand. Dict.* 1893).

[**1662–3** s.v. HOUSE *sb.*¹ 4g]. **1710** STEELE *Tatler* No. 187 ¶5 The full House which is to be at Othello on Thursday. **1764** D. E. BAKER *Compan. Playhouse* I, *Minor*... It brought full Houses for thirty-eight Nights. **1828** *Olio* 22 Mar. 164/1 A party of itinerant Maromeros (or rope dancers) held their exhibition in the large walled yard.., to about eight hundred people; which was considered as a very 'full house'. **1961** *Times* 28 Aug. 3/1 It should be a full-house..when Spurs visit Old Trafford.

2. *Poker.* A hand containing three of a kind and a pair (next in value below four of a kind). Also *fig.*

1887 *Puck* (U.S.) 7 Sept. 21/2 Noah drew to pairs and got a full house [in the ark]. **1908** C. E. MULFORD *Orphan* xxi. 267 You two make a pair of aces what can beat any full-house ever got together. **1922** —— *Tex* iii. 33 Tex wondered what the crowd would say if he should lean over and pull a royal flush out of Williams' ear, or a full-house from the nephew's nose. **1929** E. LINKLATER *Poet's Pub* xxv. 274 He had filled the kitty roof-high, bluffed the four-ace-players, scared the full-house-holders. **1963** G. F. HERVEY *Handbk. Card Games* 238 If the 3 of Diamonds is discarded, the odds against improving to a full house is about 11 to 1.

fullimart, obs. form of FOUMART.

† **'fulling**, *vbl. sb.*¹ *Obs.* Also 5 folowynge. [f. FULL *v.*¹] Baptizing.

1387 TREVISA *Higden* (Rolls) IV. 257 Som acounteþ from þe fullynge of Crist. **1393** LANGL. *P. Pl.* C. xv. 207 Ther is follyng of font and follyng in blod-shedynge. *c* **1450** MYRC 146 Eghte dayes they schullen abyde That at the fonte halowynge They mowe take here folowynge. **1483** *Festivall* (W. de W. 1515) 48 This trynyte was knowen in the fullynge of Cryst as the gospel setteth.

fulling, *vbl. sb.*²: see after FULL *v.*²

fulling ('fʊlɪŋ), *vbl. sb.*³ [f. FULL *v.*³ + -ING¹.]

1. The process of cleansing and thickening cloth by beating and washing; also called *milling*.

1688 R. HOLME *Armoury* III. 348/2 This trade of Milling or thickning Cloth is termed Fulling. **1791** HAMILTON tr. *Berthollet's Dyeing* I. I. II. i. 127 He has explained the effects of fulling by the external conformation of the hair or wool of animals. **1812** SOUTHEY in *Q. Rev.* VII. 63 The women perform the work of fulling by treading the cloth in a tub.

transf. **1894** GOULD *Illustr. Dict. Med., Fulling*, in massage, a valuable method of kneading, named from the motion used by fullers in rubbing linen between their hands.

2. *attrib.* as ***fulling-boy, -hammer***, †***-mace, -stone***; †**fulling-clay**, †**-earth** = *fuller's earth*; **fulling-mill**, a mill in which cloth is fulled or milled by being beaten with wooden mallets, which are let fall upon it (or in modern use, by being pressed between rollers) and cleansed with soap or fuller's earth; †**fulling-stocks**, wooden mallets worked by machinery, used for fulling cloth.

1677 YARRANTON *Eng. Improv.* 109, If I had not been an old Clothier, and a *Fulling-Boy when I was young. **1688** *Lond. Gaz.* No. 2338/1 We do..streightly Charge..that no manner of..*Fulling Clay, be..exported. **1720** *Ibid.* No. 5853/1 Any Fuller's-Earth, or Fulling-Clay. **1563–87** FOXE *A. & M.* (1684) III. 591 A certain poor man..went to the Sea, minding to have gone into Kent for *Fulling Earth. **1796** KIRWAN *Elem. Min.* (ed. 2) I. 186 Some fulling Earths, it is said, effervesce slightly with acids. **1712** MOTTEUX *Quixote* III. vi. (1749) I. 160 Let the six *fulling-hammers be transform'd into so many giants. **1612** SHELTON *Quixote* III. vii. 175 Without being able to attribute it to the little knowledge of the *fulling Maces or the darkenesse of the night. **1417–18** *Abingdon Acc.* (Camden) 88 *note*, The reparacions done this yere at yᵉ *Fullingmilles. **1523** FITZHERB. *Surv.* 9b, Fullyngmylnes, sythe mylnes, cutlersmylnes. **1612** in *Naworth Househ. Bks.* 8 The wholl yeares rent of the fulling mill. **1748** SMOLLETT *Rod. Rand.* xvi. (1804) 97 My heart went knock, knock..like a fulling-mill. **1805** LUCCOCK *Nat. Wool* 161 Nor will the cloth.. endure without injury the violent strokes of the fulling mill. **1876** HOLLAND *Sev. Oaks* i. 2 Below this two or three saw-mills..and a fulling-mill. **1377** *Fullyng-stokkes [see FULL *v.*³ 1]. **1879** *Cassell's Techn. Educ.* IV. 342/2 The 'fulling-stocks'..consist of heavy wooden mallets. **1884** J. PAYNE *1000 Nts. & One Nt.* VIII. 135 Making the ship fast to one of the *Fulling-Stones.

fullish ('fʊlɪʃ), *a.* [f. FULL *a.* + -ISH.] Somewhat full.

1822 *Blackw. Mag.* XI. 164 Rather pompous and dullish; of falsetto, too, fullish. **1871** G. MEREDITH *H. Richmond* (1886) 206 Her nose firm, her lips fullish. **1889** *National Rev.* XIII. 686 The most noticeable features of the face are the rather prominent nose and fullish lips.

¶ app. misused for *fulliche*, FULLY *adv.*

c **1500** *Melusine* xxvi. 208 It is not fullyssh a moneth complet syn that we departed thens.

full length. The entire length or extension of any object.

1. In advbl. phrase, ***(at) full length.***

1709 STEELE & ADDISON *Tatler* No. 93 ¶4, I have..drawn at full Length, the Figures of all sorts of Men. **1844** DICKENS *Mart. Chuz.* vi, By constructing..a temporary sofa of three chairs..and lying down at full-length upon it. **1855** SINGLETON *Virgil* I. 47 Of polished marble thou full-length shalt stand.

2. *attrib.*, as ***full-length figure, portrait***, etc. Also *ellipt.* ***a full-length.***

1760 STERNE *Tr. Shandy* I. xxiii. 171 One of these you will see drawing a full-length character *against the light*. **1782** T. PENNANT *Journ. Chester to London* 383 In the hall is a full-length of the unfortunate Mary Queen of Scots. **1850** L. HUNT *Autobiog.* II. xiv. 141 A full-length portrait..of a little girl. **1894** A. D. WHITE in *Pop. Sci. Monthly* XLIV. 722 A full-length woodcut showing the Almighty in the act of extracting Eve. **1896** *Westm. Gaz.* 1 May 1/2 Just above the line, hangs a full-length of the German Emperor. **1897** *Daily News* 8 Apr. 8/1 This is, we under-stand, the first full-length novel he has written.

fig. **1822–34** *Good's Study Med.* (ed. 4) I. 296 What may be called a close and full-length portrait [of a disease].

full moon.

1. The moon with its entire disc illuminated.

a **1000** *Boeth. Metr.* xxviii. 81 Hwa is on weorulde þæt ne wundriȝe fulles monan. **1530** PALSGR. 223/2 Full moone, *plaine lune*. **1681** OTWAY *Soldier's Fort.* IV. i, 'Twas a Full-moon, and such a Moon, Sir! **1812–16** J. SMITH *Panorama Sc. & Art* I. 597 The full moon rises at sun-set. **1883** OUIDA *Wanda* I. 58 The full moon was rising above the Glöckner range.

2. The period at which this occurs (= L. *plenilunium*).

a **1300** *Cursor M.* 17288 + 72 þese thre thinges a-bod our lord, or he to ded wald goo, Vre leuedy day & friday als and ful moyne als-soo. *c* **1475** *Pict. Voc.* in Wr.-Wülcker 800 *Hoc plenilunium*, fulmone. **1563** W. FULKE *Meteors* (1640) 61 b, From the new moone, to the full, all humors do encrease and from the full to the new Moone, decrease againe. **1676** WISEMAN *Wounds* v. ix. 393 Towards the Full-moon, as he was coming home one morning, he felt his Legs faulter. **1796** H. HUNTER tr. *St.-Pierre's Stud. Nat.* (1799) III. 34 They [tides] exhibit no sensible rise till the second or third day after the full Moon.

3. *attrib.*

1780 COWPER *Progr. Err.* 282 The breach, though small at first, soon opening wide, In rushes folly with a full-moon tide. **1797** SOUTHEY in J. Cottle *Remin.* (1847) 211 A very brown-looking man of..full-moon cheeks. **1894** G. MEREDITH *Lord Ormont* I. iii. 91 Howling like full-moon dogs all through their lives.

,full-'mouthed, *a.* [f. FULL *a.* + MOUTH *sb.* + -ED².] Having a full mouth.

1. Of cattle: Having the mouth full of teeth; having the full complement of teeth.

1577 HARRISON *England* I. iv, Now forasmuch as in such as bee full mouthed, eche chap hath 16 teeth at the least. **1685** *Lond. Gaz.* No. 1998/4 A brown bay Mare above 14 hands high, full Mouth'd. **1709** *Ibid.* No. 4521/4 Stoln..a blood-bay Mare..full mouth'd. **1846** J. BAXTER *Libr. Pract. Agric.* (ed. 4) II. 93 These six teeth tolerably developed.. probably misled Mr. Parkinson.. to say that at four years old cattle were full-mouthed. **1892** *Salisbury Jrnl.* 6 Aug. 4/1, 100 grand full-mouthed ewes.

†**2.** Having the mouth filled with food; hence, Festive. *transf.* Of a sail: Filled with wind. Also *fig.* *Obs.*

1635 QUARLES *Embl.* v. vii. Epig. 271 Cheare up, my soule: call home thy spir'ts, and beare One bad Good-Friday; Full-mouth'd Easter's neare. **1645** G. DANIEL *Poems* Wks. 1878 II. 12 Where, where resides content? 'Tis neither in Extent Of Power, nor full-mouth'd gaine. **1645** QUARLES *Sol. Recant.* iv. 39 Force and bold-fac'd Wrong May hap to roar upon thy full-mouth'd Sailes. *a* **1701** SEDLEY *Poems* Wks. 1722 I. 16 Like murm'ring full-mouth'd Isra'lites we stand.

3. a. Having a loud voice or sound; sounding or talking loud. Of dogs: Baying loudly. **b.** Produced or uttered with a loud voice or with violence.

a. 1648 JOS. BEAUMONT *Psyche* II. 161 Whom both the full-mouth'd Elders hastened To catch th' Adulterer. **1698** FRYER *Acc. E. India & P.* 314 He came to me full mouth'd in the King's Name. **1735** SOMERVILLE *Chase* III. 410 The full-mouth'd Pack With dreadful Consort thunder in his Rear.

b. 1605 *Narr. Murthers Sir J. Fitz* (1860) 6 The fulmouth'd report of infamous rumour. **1620** QUARLES *Jonah* Kj b, Had Boreas blown His full-mouth'd blast. *c* **1645** HOWELL *Lett.* (1655) II. 76 A full-mouth'd Language she [German] is, and pronounc'd with that strength as if one had bones in his tongue instead of nerfs. **1708** MOTTEUX *Rabelais* IV. lxvii. (1737) 276 With a full mouth'd laugh. **1856** KANE *Arct. Expl.* I. xxii. 279 These faithful servants generally bayed their full-mouthed welcome from afar off.

Hence **full'mouthedly** *adv.*, with a full mouth; uncompromisingly.

1887 SAINTSBURY *Hist. Elizab. Lit.* iv. (1890) 154 The earlier Satires..denounce lewd verses most fullmouthedly.

fullness, fulness ('fʊlnɪs). [f. FULL *a.* + -NESS. OE. had *fyllnes* = OHG. *folnissi*:—OTeut. **fullinassu-z*; but as the existing word does not appear before the 14th c. it was prob. a new formation rather than a refashioning of the older word.

The spelling *fullness*, though less common (exc. in the U.S.) than *fulness*, is here adopted as more in accordance with analogy: see the remarks s.v. DULLNESS.]

The quality or condition of being full.

1. a. The condition of being filled so as to include no vacant space.

1577 B. GOOGE *Heresbach's Husb.* II. (1586) 80 b, The equall medley of heat and cold, drieth and moisture, fulnesse and emptinesse. **1632** LITHGOW *Trav.* VI. 254 How commeth it to passe..that the Lake it selfe never diminisheth, nor increaseth, but alwayes standeth at one fulnesse. **1692** BENTLEY *Boyle Lect.* vii. 223 If the presence of this æthereal Matter made an absolute Fulness. *a* **1716** SOUTH *Serm.* (1737) II. iv. 145 Like water in a well, where you have fulness in a little compass.

b. *fig.* Of the 'heart': The state of being overcharged with emotion.

1625 BACON *Ess., Friendship* (Arb.) 165 A principall Fruit of Frendship, is the Ease and Discharge of the Fulnesse and Swellings of the Heart. **1797** MRS. RADCLIFFE *Italian* xx. (1824) 636 He yielded to the fulness of his heart. **1885** R. BUCHANAN *Annan Water* vi, Father only speaks out of the fulness of his heart.

2. a. The condition of containing (something) in abundance, or of abounding in (a quality, etc.).

a **1340** HAMPOLE *Psalter* xviii. 2 Fulnes of wisdom & gastly sauour. **1651** HOBBES *Leviath.* III. xxxiv. 215 That Fulnesse [of the Holy Ghost] is not to be understood for Infusion of the substance of God. **1878** L. P. MEREDITH *Teeth* 19 He.. died in consequence of fulness of blood.

b. *concr.* All that is contained in (the world, etc.). A Hebraism.

a **1325** *Prose Psalter* xlix. [l.] 13 þe world and þe fulnes of it is myn. **1535** COVERDALE *1 Chron.* xvii. 32 Let the See make a noyse, and the fulnesse therof. **1738** WESLEY *Ps.* xxiv. i, The Earth and all her Fulness owns Jehovah for her sovereign Lord!

3. a. Completeness, perfection; complete or ample measure or degree.

c **1320** *Cast. Love* 283 Of oone volnes they were ful ryȝht. **1548–9** (Mar.) *Bk. Com. Prayer* Offices 8 b, The fulnesse of thy grace. **1593** SHAKS. *2 Hen. VI*, I. i. 35 Such is the Fulnesse of my hearts content. **1610** BP. CARLETON *Jurisd.* 2 They yeeld to the Pope a fulnesse of power as they tearme it, from whence all Spirituall Iurisdiction must proceed to others. **1611** BIBLE *Ps.* xvi. 11 In thy presence is fulnesse of ioy. **1667** MILTON *P.L.* III. 225 The Son of God, In whom the fulness dwels of love divine. *a* **1704** T. BROWN *Two Oxford Scholars* Wks. 1730 I. 10 Houses where I shall be entertained with such fulness of delight..that [etc.]. **1843** MIALL in *Nonconf.* III. 401 Christianity is distinguished by ..a fulness of generosity. **1855** MILMAN *Lat. Chr.* IV. VII. ii. 44 The papacy in the fullness of its strength.

b. Phrases. ***the fullness of time*** (= Gr. πλήρωμα τοῦ χρόνου): In Biblical language, the proper or destined time. ***in its fullness***: in its full extent, without exceptions or qualifications.

1560 BIBLE (Genev.) *Gal.* iv. 4 When the fulnes of time was come, God sent forthe his Sonne. **1640** HOWELL *Dodona's Gr.* (1645) 41 And this work was done in a fulness of time. **1751** JORTIN *Serm.* (1771) I. i. 4 Which in the fulness of time should be made manifest. **1842** MRS. BROWNING *Grk. Chr. Poets* (1863) 134 Admitting the suggestion in its fulness. **1867** FREEMAN *Norm. Conq.* (1876) I. App. 728 That tale he adopts in its fulness.

c. Copiousness or exhaustiveness (of knowledge, statement, or expression).

1860 PUSEY *Min. Proph.* 410 The words, with a Divine fulness, express [etc.]. **1875** WHITNEY *Life Lang.* i. 5 To illustrate the principles of linguistic science..with as much fullness as the limited space at command shall allow. **1885** *Manch. Exam.* 8 May 5/2 The study of the ancient languages is one which peculiarly demands fullness of knowledge to make it fruitful. **1887** *Spectator* 3 Sept. 1188 The interesting matters which he describes with more or less fullness.

†**4.** The condition of being satisfied or sated; satiety, repletion; the condition of having indulged to excess. *Obs.*

1382 WYCLIF *Isa.* lvi. 10 Vnshamefast doggus knewen not fulnesse. *c* **1440** *Promp. Parv.* 182/1 Fulnesse of mete, *sacietas*. *c* **1560** A. SCOTT *Poems* (S.T.S.) ii. 109 Thair wes nowdir lad nor [*pr.* not] loun Mycht eit ane baikin loche For fowness. **1576** FLEMING *Panopl. Epist.* 115 As for me, if I may enjoy the fulnesse of my desyres, the residue of my lyfe will I lead in Rhodes. *c* **1600** SHAKS. *Sonn.* lvi. 6 Although today thou fill Thy hungry eyes even till they wink with fullness. **1666** STILLINGFL. *Serm.* (1696) I. i. 43 When God hath made us smart for our fulness and wantonness, then we grew sullen and murmured and disputed against providence. **1682** NORRIS *Hierocles* 93 In the third place he puts Exercise, as that which corrects the fulness of diet.

†**5.** The condition of being well supplied with what one needs. Hence, of things, abundance, plenty. *Obs.*

c **1440** *Promp. Parv.* 182/2 Fulnesse or plente, *habundancia, copia*. **1611** SHAKS. *Cymb.* III. vi. 12 To lapse in Fulnesse Is sorer, then to lye for Neede. **1648** *Eikon Bas.* ix. 57 The Houses; to whom I wished nothing more then Safetie, Fulness, and Freedom. **1698** FRYER *Acc. E. India & P.* 225 Amidst this Fulness of every thing. **1722** DE FOE *Col. Jack* (1840) 180 Before I revelled in fulness, and here I struggled with hard fare.

6. Of sound, colour, etc.: The quality of being full; 'volume', 'body'.

1440 *Promp. Parv.* 182/2 Fulnesse of sownde, *sonoritas*. **1622** BACON *Hen. VII*, 7 The..Applauses of the People..

were true and vnfeigned, as might well appeare in the very Demonstrations and Fulnesse of the Crie. *a* **1744** POPE *Pastorals* I. *note*, This sort of poetry [pastoral] derives almost its whole beauty from a natural ease of thought and smoothness of verse; whereas that of most other kinds consists in the strength and fulness of both. **1851** *Illustr. Catal. Gt. Exhib.* I. 131 Ochres..Exhibited on account of their clearness, fulness of colour, body. **1879** *Cassell's Techn. Educ.* I. 230/2 A subtle mingling of colour, an exquisite delicacy and refinement of treatment, a fulness such as always results from a rich mingling of hues. **1881** *Standard* 18 Oct. 3/4 The wort is..passed into a copper with 20 per cent. of malt-flour, to impart fullness and flavour.

7. a. Full habit of body; roundness or protuberance of outline.

1613 PURCHAS *Pilgrimage* (1614) 505 Crabbes heere with us have a sympathy with the Moone, and are fullest with her fulnes. **1638** BAKER tr. *Balzac's Lett.* (vol. III.) 173 To heare of your health, and that you keepe your bodie in that reasonable fulnesse of flesh, which contributes something to your gravitie. **1698** FRYER *Acc. E. India & P.* 378 Most of them by a Fulness of Body are subject to the Hemorrhoids. **1798** FERRIAR *Illustr. Sterne* i. 7 A certain degree of fulness improves the figure. *a* **1822** SHELLEY *Pericles* Ess. & Lett. (Camelot) 140 The face is of an oval fulness. **1841** BREWSTER *Mart. Sc.* III. ii, In a family notorious for fulness, she is considered superfluously fat.

b. A feeling of internal pressure or distension.

1800 *Med. Jrnl.* IV. 364, I perceived a sense of fulness in the head, and throbbing of the arteries. **1807** *Ibid.* XVII. 528 'Internal distress, a sense of fulness and aching' may be felt.

8. *Dressmaking.* The condition of being 'full'. Also *concr.* the portion of material arranged in folds to produce this.

1801 JANE AUSTEN *Let.* 5 May (1952) 125 No fulness appears either in the body or the flap; the back is quite plain. **1884** *West. Daily Press* 2 June 7/2 An ordinary short skirt.. trimmed with flounces, or other fulnesses. **1897** *Globe* 18 Feb. 6/3 The fulness of this blouse effect is drawn in close at the waist.

fullock: see FULK *v. dial.*

† **fu'llonical**, *a. Obs.*—[0] [f. L. *fullōnic-us* (f. *fullōn-*, *fullō*, a fuller) + -AL[1].] 'Belonging to a fuller' (Bailey 1721).

† **'fullought.** *Obs.* Forms: 1 ful(l)wiht, 1–2 fulluht, 2–3 fuluht, ful(e)ht, 3 fulleht, 4 fullaut, fullouȝt, folloȝt, fullauȝt, fullou(g)ht, 5 folghthe. [OE. *ful(l)wiht*, noun of action f. *fulwian* (prehistoric *-wīhan*): see FULL *v.*[1]] Baptism.

c **1000** *Ags. Gosp.* Matt. xxi. 25 Hwæðer wæs iohannes fulluht þe of heofonum þe of mannum. *c* **1175** *Lamb. Hom.* 91 Underfoð fuluht on cristes nome. *c* **1205** LAY. 9617 þa þe time wes ifulled þæt hit [þet child] fulleht sculde habben. *a* **1225** *Ancr. R.* 160 He was Godes baptiste—þe muchele heihnesse þet he heold, ine fuluhte under his honden. *a* **1330** *Otuel* 316 þou nost what follaut is. *a* **1375** *Joseph Arim.* 682 þenne com Seraphes and fullouȝt furst askes. **1393** LANGL. *P. Pl.* C. XVIII. 76 Follouht is trewe. *c* **1450** MYRC 177 Alle these be cosynes to hym for ay..The preste þat foloweþ..þe godfader & hys Wyf knowe be-fore folghthe.

Hence in early ME. **'ful(e)htles** *a.* [see -LESS], without baptism. **'fulhte** *v.*, also **'fulhtne (fulcne)**, *v.* [see -EN] *trans.* to baptize. **'fulhtninge, fulcninge**, *vbl. sb.* **'fulcnere** [see -ER[1]], (John the) Baptist.

c **1175** *Lamb. Hom.* 73 Mon scule childre fulhten. *Ibid.*, þa weren monie childre dede fulhtles. *c* **1200** *Trin. Coll. Hom.* 15 Ðre þing..þat on is rihte bileue, þat oðer is fulohtninge, þe þridde þe faire liflode. *Ibid.* 131 Iohan þe fulcnere. *Ibid.* 139 Seint iohan baptiste was send into þis midden erd to donde þrefolde wike, an is to kiðen cristes to cume, oðer is bodien fulcninge, þat þridde is fulcnen. *c* **1200** ORMIN 9149 Siþþenn toc he þær þe follc To spellenn & to fullhtnenn. *c* **1205** LAY. 29769 þeo he alle fullehteð and to gode fuseoð. *a* **1225** *Leg. Kath.* [see FULL *v.*[1]].

full-'rigger. [See RIGGER[1] 4.] A full-rigged vessel. Also *fig.*

1899 C. J. C. HYNE *Further Adv. Captain Kettle* vii, Image nodded towards the deserted vessel. 'Fine full-rigger, hasn't she been?' **1907** *Daily Chron.* 27 Dec. 3/2 A well-found full-rigger of 600 tons. **1908** *Ibid.* 17 Dec. 3/3 Instead of being the fine fullrigger that it might have been, it is, comparatively, only a topsail schooner.

full-summed, *a.*

1. *Falconry.* Of a hawk or its wings: In full plumage.

1486 [see FULLFREME]. **1562** J. HEYWOOD *Prov. & Epigr.* (1867) 169 Byrdes wynges once full sumd byrdes wyll hardly be catcht. **1640** HOWELL *Dodona's Gr.* 72 The King of Birds ..with fullsummd wings fastning his Talents East and West. **1671** MILTON *P.R.* I. 14 Inspire..my prompted song ..And bear through highth or depth of Nature's bounds, With prosperous wing full summed.

2. *nonce-use.* Fully developed or accomplished.

1847 TENNYSON *Princ.* VII. 272 These twain, upon the skirts of Time, Sit side by side, full-summ'd in all their powers.

full time. The total number of hours normally allotted to daily or weekly work, etc. Chiefly *attrib.* (hyphened) and advb., esp. in sense 'that occupies all one's time, that engages one to the exclusion of other activities'.

1898 *Daily News* 13 Dec. 5/7 The half-time system..does irretrievable hurt to the full-time scholars as well. **1911** *Rep. Labour & Social Conditions in Germany* III. 89 Full-time employment. *Ibid.* 97 Full time is worked all the year round. *Ibid.* 104 All the factories we visited were running full time. **1921** *Act 11 & 12 Geo. V* c. 51 §77 (2) Any young person..shown..to be under suitable and efficient full-time instruction. *a* **1926** in Fowler *Mod. Eng. Usage* 737/2 That motherhood is a full-time job all worth-while mothers will readily admit. **1927** BOWLEY & STAMP *Nat. Income 1924* 31 The general average increase in weekly full-time wages. **1930** A. FLEXNER *Universities* 87 So-called 'full-time' units, consisting of groups on salary devoting themselves solely to teaching, research, and the care of hospital patients. **1955** *Times* 15 July 9/6 But though the universities will probably be able to satisfy most of the demand for full-time degree-courses they will certainly not be able to supply industry with all the technologists it requires. **1959** *Manch. Guardian* 6 Aug. 3/5 Mr. Wesker will become a full-time professional writer. **1968** *Time* 17 May 66 The Institute..now employs 575 full-time civilian analysts. **1971** *Engineering* Apr. 55/2 It is the full-time business of these agencies.

,full-'timer. [f. phrase *full time* + -ER[1].]

1. A child that attends school during the whole of the school hours; opposed to HALF-TIMER b.

1870 *Morning Post* 2 June 2/1 There is no uniform rule as to the period either of age or knowledge when the 'full-timer' shall become the 'half-timer'. **1895** *Westm. Gaz.* 6 June 2/2 He [the half-timer] needn't read so well, write so well, draw so well, cipher so well as the full timer at school.

2. One who works full-time.

1868 *Fortn. Rev.* Oct. 430 At thirteen the boy 'passes the doctor' (*i.e.*, obtains a medical certificate of age), and becomes a 'full-timer',..amenable to the same rules, and subject to the same hours of labour, as the adult operative. **1877** H. E. MANNING *Misc.* II. ii. 96 Is it possible for a child to be educated who becomes a full-timer at ten or even twelve years of age? **1934** *Times Lit. Suppl.* 21 June (Ital. Suppl.) p. v/4 If a full-timer, he began his duties before the lady rose, when he might have to air her linen.

† **'fully**, *a. Obs.* [f. FULL *a.* + -Y[1].] Complete, perfect, thorough, without defect. Also, of a full or rounded form.

a **1300** *E.E. Psalter* cxxxviii[i]. 22 With fulli hatereden hated I þa. *a* **1300** *Cursor M.* 9862 All es fulli þat he wroght. **1505** in *Mem. Hen. VII* (Rolls) 232 The said queen's [Joanna, of Naples] breasts be somewhat great and fully.. they were trussed somewhat high..the which causeth her grace to seem much the fullyer, & her neck to be the shorter. **1513** BRADSHAW *St. Werburge* I. 1366 Well byloued father this is my fully mynde.

Hence † **'fullily** *adv.*, completely, fully; † **'fulliness**, fullness.

a **1300** *Cursor M.* 10404 (Cott.) þe takening of a hundret tale Al fullines it takens hale. **1375** BARBOUR *Bruce* II. 424 And haid till erd gane fullyly, Ne war he hynt him by his sted. *c* **1375** *Sc. Leg. Saints, Baptista* 207 Al þe lafe..of his gret fullyness has tane. **1535** STEWART *Cron. Scot.* III. 127 All the laif..wes..with the said bischop fullelie remittit. **1588** A. KING tr. *Canisius' Catech.* 174 S. Johne..is fullalie occupied in commending vnto vs brotherlie charitie.

fully ('fʊlɪ), *adv.* Forms: see FULL *a.* and -LY[2]. [OE. *fullíce*, f. FULL *a.* + *líce* -LY[2] = OS. *fullíko*, OHG. *follicho* (MHG. *volliche*).]

a. In a full manner or degree; to the full, without deficiency; completely, entirely; thoroughly, exactly, quite. † **fully and by** (*Naut.*) = *full and by*: see BY B. 1 d; **fully-fashioned** *a.*, of a garment (esp. a stocking): shaped to fit closely to the body; also *transf.*; **fully-fledged** *a.* = full-fledged (see FULL *adv.* 5 b).

c **900** tr. *Bæda's Hist.* II. iii. (1890) 104 Heo [the church] þa ȝyta næs fullice ȝeworht ne ȝehalȝod. *c* **1050** *Byrhtferth's Handboc* in *Anglia* VIII. 306 þæt he fullice ȝefrætwod sy mid feower & twentiȝ tidum. *c* **1175** *Lamb. Hom.* 73 He nis noht fulliche cristene mon þet [etc.]. *c* **1205** LAY. 14150 Ich beo i þine londe fulliche at-stonde. *c* **1230** *Hali Meid.* 11 Meidenhad is te blosme þat beo ha eanes fulliche forcoruen, ne spruteð ha neauer eft. *c* **1290** *S. Eng. Leg.* I. 29/6 þat fulliche so holi man nas. **1340** HAMPOLE *Pr. Consc.* 476 Unnethes es a child born fully That it ne bygynnes to goule. **1389** in *Eng. Gilds* (1870) 50 We fulliche vndirstondend ȝour lettres. *c* **1440** *Lanfranc's Cirurg.* 87 Him nediþ his medicyn I-maad nouȝt fulliche so drie. *c* **1440** *Douce MS.* 55 ch. xx, Lete it nat buille fully. *c* **1440** *Gesta Rom.* ii. 5 (Harl. MS.) Whenne the candell was liȝt, þey sawe fully the toode sitting on his brest. **1482** *Monk of Evesham* (Arb.) 26 More opynner and fullyor than he knewe afore. **1526** *Pilgr. Perf.* (W. de W. 1531) 230 b, All the powers & desyres of mannes soule shall be fully contented & quyeted. **1611** BIBLE *Rev.* xiv. 18 Gather the clusters of the vine of the earth, for her grapes are fully ripe. **1630** *R. Johnson's Kingd. & Commw.* 187 Italian, Spanish, and Greek, who fully pronounce every letter in the word. **1633** BP. HALL *Hard Texts* 275 His eyes..are so fully placed as is most comely. **1653** BAXTER *Chr. Concord* 19 The things that we thought should be fullier expressed then in the ancient Creed, are these. **1695** LD. PRESTON *Boeth.* II. 63, I know that thou art one who hast been fully perswaded. **1727** A. HAMILTON *New Acc. E. Ind.* I. i. 15 Sheeps Wooll, that is fully as hard and coarse as Hogs Hair. **1766** GOLDSM. *Vic. W.* iii, In this I satisfied him fully. **1769** FALCONER *Dict. Marine* (1789) E ee, Fully and by! **1791** MRS. RADCLIFFE *Rom. Forest* i, And introduced the strangers more fully to each other. **1845** M. PATTISON *Ess.* (1889) I. 17 Inferior Franks..posted themselves, fully armed, outside. **1848** C. BRONTË *J. Eyre.* v, By the time that exercise was terminated, day had fully dawned. **1891** *law times* XC. 441/2 Both sides should be heard, and heard fully. **1906** *Daily Chron.* 23 Mar. 4/4 This suggestion that unions should be compulsorily converted into fully-fledged corporate bodies. **1923–4** *Army & Navy Stores Catal.* 649 Cashmere hose, fully fashioned. **1936** *Discovery* Aug. 262/1 It was thought that a gap intervened between the Old and the New Stone Ages, during which man retreated from Northern Europe to return fully-fledged as neolithic man. **1945** R. DIMBLEBY in L. Miall *R.D., Broadcaster* (1966) 41 A woman friend.. wearing what looked to me like fully-fashioned silk stockings. **1946** *Picture Post* 11 May 17/2 Pure silk stockings cost about 25s. a pair, and fully-fashioned 'mixtures' from 15s. to about 6s. **1957** C. HUNT *Guide to Communist Jargon* xxvi. 92 Fully-fledged nations..possessing a common language, territory, economic life and national character. **1959** *Times* 28 May 13/4 More fully-fashioned stockings are being sold in Britain to-day than ever before. **1963** A. J. HALL *Textile Sci.* iii. 149 Use must be made of a fully-fashioned knitting machine. **1971** *Engineering* Apr. 27/2 Management and marketing are now fully-fledged subjects in their own right.

b. With numerals and expressions of quantity. Also (*to eat, feed*) *fully* = to satiety.

a **1300** *Cursor M.* 488 þar he badd noght fullik an vre. **1340** HAMPOLE *Pr. Consc.* 4570 Anticrist..Sal regne thre yhere and a half fully. *c* **1380** *Sir Ferumb.* 2092 Fuliche ne is he noȝt now fram þe vj fet y-mete in brede. *c* **1386** CHAUCER *Knt.'s T.* 111 Ne take his ese [wolde he] fully half a day. *c* **1425** *Craft Nombrynge* (E.E.T.S.) 26 By twene an hundryth and a thowsande, so þat it be not a þowsande fully. **1480** CAXTON *Chron. Eng.* ccvii. 189 The kyng had not yet fullych eten. **1552** *Bk. Com. Prayer, Ordination* Pref., Fully thyrtie yeres of age. *c* **1586** C'TESS PEMBROKE *Ps.* cxxxii. x, The poore..with store of bread Shall fully all be fedd. **1720** POPE *Iliad* XXIII. 220 Behold Achilles' promise fully paid. **1863** KINGLAKE *Crimea* (1877) II. ii. 25 Hesitation lasting fully two days.

fully ('fʊlɪ), *v. slang.* [f. the adv., in phr. 'fully committed for trial'.] *trans.* To commit (a person) for trial. Hence **'fullied** *ppl. a.*

1849 *Sessions Papers* 1 Feb. 324 The prisoner said..he expected either to be *turned up* or *fully'd*..—those are *cant* expressions, meaning either to be discharged, or committed for trial. **1859** MATSELL *Vocabulum*, *Fullied*, committed for trial. **1926** E. WALLACE *More Educated Evans* iv. 97 We found a lot of stolen property in his house, and he is certain to be fullied. **1936** J. CURTIS *Gilt Kid* xxix. 281 They'll fully me to the Old Bailey, I reckon.

fullymart, obs. form of FOUMART.

fulmar ('fʊlmə(r)). [originally belonging to the dialect of the Hebrides, and so prob. of Norse origin; perh. f. ON. *fúl-l* FOUL (referring to the disgusting odour of the bird) + *má-r* MEW, gull.

That the word is, as commonly said, a transferred use of *fulmar*, FOUMART, seems unlikely. The Gael. *fulmair* and the scientific Latin *fulmarus* are from Eng.]

A sea-bird of the petrel kind (*Fulmarus glacialis*), about the size of the common gull. Also called *fulmar petrel*.

1698 M. MARTIN *Voy. St. Kilda* 55 The Fulmar, in Bigness equals the Malls of the Second Rate. **1742** *De Foe's Tour Gt. Brit.* IV. 275 Another Bird..called Fulmar, about the Size of a Moor-hen. **1766** PENNANT *Zool.* (1768) II. 431 The Fulmar supplies them with oil for their lamps, down for their beds. **1823** SCORESBY *Whale Fishery* 126 In consequence of a fulmar's darting upon its back, and plunging its beak in the skin. **1863** BARING-GOULD *Iceland* 406 Still and ghost-like buoyant Fulmars wing their way.

fulmar(d(e, -mart, obs. form of FOUMART.

‖ **fulmen** ('fʌlmɛn). [L.; = 'lightning that strikes or sets on fire, a thunderbolt'.] A thunderbolt; thunder, esp. as the attribute of Jupiter.

1684 I. MATHER *Remark. Provid.* 79 The fulmeen or thunder-bolt is the same with the lightning. **1747** J. SPENCE *Polymetis* II. vi. 49 In his right hand..he grasps his fulmen; his thunder, as we are used to translate that word, improperly enough. **1812** *Examiner* 25 May 328/1 We recognise the..god..by his fulmen.

fig. *a* **1856** SIR W. HAMILTON (Ogilv.), Reasoning cannot find such a mine of thought, nor eloquence such a fulmen of expression.

fulmer(d(e, -mert, obs. forms of FOUMART.

fulminancy ('fʌlmɪnənsɪ). *rare.* [f. next: see -ANCY.] Fulminant character.

1858 CARLYLE *Fredk. Gt.* I. v. (1865) I. 46 The new King noticed her, and hurled back a look of due fulminancy.

fulminant ('fʌlmɪnənt), *ppl. a.* and *sb.* [a. F. *fulminant*, or ad. its original L. *fulminant-em*, pr. pple. of *fulmināre*: see FULMINATE *v.*]

A. *adj.*

1. = FULMINATING, in various senses.

1602 FULBECKE *Pandectes* 78 Let..his fulminant foolish deity..bee measured by the law of God. **1681** H. MORE *Exp. Dan.* ii. 46 Who..had power over Purgatory and Hell, thither to strike innocent Souls by his fulminant Excommunications. **1693** SALMON *Bates' Dispens.* (1713) 319/1 This Fulminant Gold. **1818** MOORE *Fudge Fam. Paris* vii. 99 Fierce was the cry and fulminant the ban. **1872** BLACKIE *Lays Highl.* 117 From whom the fulminant Frenchman knew defeat.

2. *Path.* Developing suddenly.

1876 tr. *Wagner's Gen. Pathol.* 104 The fulminant forms of anthrax. **18..** *Med. News* L. 41 (Cent.) The glandular alterations were especially pronounced in fulminant cases.

B. *sb.* Something that thunders or explodes; a thunderbolt, an explosive. *rare.*

1808 J. BARLOW *Columb.* VIII. 557 He bids conflicting fulminants expire The guided blast, and holds the imprison'd fire. **1891** *Chambers' Encycl.* s.v. *Mandeville*, This book was a pothouse fulminant, levelled against the ethical theories of Shaftesbury.

fulminate ('fʌlmɪneɪt), *sb.* [f. FULMIN(IC) + -ATE.] A compound of fulminic acid with a base, detonating by percussion, friction, or heat.

1826 HENRY *Elem. Chem.* I. 456 A class of salts, to which they have given the name of fulminates. **1860** PIESSE *Lab. Chem. Wonders* 25 Fulminate is prepared with nitric acid.. alcohol..and mercury. **1864** WATTS *Dict. Chem.* II. 732

Fulminate of Copper is obtained in green crystals. *Ibid.*, *Fulminate of mercury*, *Mercuric fulminate*, *Fulminating Mercury*. *Ibid.*, 737 *Fulminates of Zinc*. The neutral salt, also called fulminating zinc, was first obtained by Liebig.

fulminate ('fʌlmɪneɪt), *v.* Pa. t. and pa. pple. 5-6 **fulminat**, 6-8 (pa. pple.) **fulminate**. [f. L. *fulmināt-* ppl. stem of *fulmināre* to lighten, strike with lightning, f. *fulmen* lightning.]

I. In physical senses.

1. *intr.* To thunder and lighten. *rare.*

1610 J. DAVIES *Wits Pilgrim* I iv b, With a firy Wreathe bind thou my Brow That mak'st the Muse in Flames to fulminate. **1656** S. HOLLAND *Zara* (1719) 60 It tonitruated horribly, fulminating promiscuously from all parts of the troubled Hemisphere. [Meant for ludicrous bombast.] **1742** YOUNG *Nt. Th.* IX. 490 Loud Ætnas fulminate in love to man.

2. To issue as a thunderbolt.

1861 J. G. SHEPPARD *Fall Rome* iv. 164 It was on the latter body that the bolt of Roman vengeance first fell, and it was as sudden and as terrible in its effects as if it had really fulminated from the throne of Capitolian Jove.

†**3.** *Metallurgy.* Of gold: To become suddenly bright and uniform in colour. *Obs.*

1727 P. SHAW tr. *Boerhaave's Chem.* (1741) I. 71 *note*, Till ..the gold have fulminated, as the refiners call it.

†**4.** *trans.* To strike with lightning. *Obs. rare.*

1666 SANCROFT *Lex Ignea* 40 Shall our Mountain..be fulminated, and thunder-strook.

5. To flash forth like lightning.

1630 RANDOLPH *Panegyr. to Shirley's Gratef. Serv.* A iij, I cannot fulminate or tonitruate words..nor make a iusiurand, that [etc.]. **1863** MRS. C. CLARKE *Shaks. Char.* ii. 46 The one [Beatrice's wit] is fulminated in brilliant coruscations..the other [Rosalind's wit] shines with gentle, genial radiance.

6. †**a.** *trans.* To cause to explode with sudden loud report (? *obs.*). **b.** *intr.* To explode with a loud report, detonate, go off.

1667 HENSHAW in Sprat *Hist. R. Soc.* 275 If you fulminate it [salt-petre] in a Crucible. **1799** G. SMITH *Laboratory* I. 235 The nitre and tartar will soon begin to fulminate. **1853** W. GREGORY *Inorg. Chem.* (ed. 3) 255 A dark powder is formed, which fulminates violently when heated.

II. *fig.*

[Originally a rendering of med.L. *fulminare*, the technical term for the formal issuing of condemnations or censures by the pope or other ecclesiastical authority; afterwards used with wider application and with reference to the literal sense.]

7. *trans.* To 'thunder forth'; to utter or publish (a formal condemnation or censure) upon a person.

c **1450** HENRYSON *Tale of Dog* 80 The Arbiteris..The sentence gaif, and proces fulminat. **1532-3** *Act 24 Hen. VIII*, c. 12 §2 Notwithstandynge.. it should happen any Excommengement..to be fulminate, promulged, declared, or put in Execucion. **1560** ROLLAND *Crt. Venus* III. 17 The mater was to be fulminat. **1682** *News fr. France* 37 The Pope sent..a Bull of Excommunication, which he required him.. to fulminate in his Name against all the Assembly. **1726** AYLIFFE *Parergon* 157 All Ecclesiastical Persons..to whom an Ordinary Jurisdiction is given..may fulminate these Church-Censures. **1750** WARBURTON *Doctr. Grace* II. v. Wks. 1811 VIII. 339 Judgments..fulminated with the air of one who had the divine Vengeance at his disposal. **1816** J. SCOTT *Vis. Paris* (ed.5) Pref. 27 The maledictions he [Napoleon] fulminated against our Island. **1832** tr. *Sismondi's Ital. Rep.* xii. 272 The pope fulminated a bull against him..for having hanged an archbishop. **1871** NAPHEYS *Prev. & Cure Dis.* I. iii. 112 Kings have fulminated their decrees against it.

8. To strike with the 'thunderbolts' of ecclesiastical censure; hence *gen.* to denounce in scathing terms, condemn vehemently.

1687 DRYDEN *Hind & P.* II. 584 For all of ancient that you had before..Was Errour fulminated o'er and o'er. **1688** T. BROWNE *Reasons Bays Changing Relig.* 15, I fulminated Johnsons affected Style. **1760** HURD in *Lett. late eminent Prelate* (1809) 311, *Burnet's Exposition* I find was fulminate; and, had the Convocation been as busy, twenty years ago, as Dr. Atterbury would have it, I should have been in pain for the *Divine Legation*. **1773** BURKE *Sp. Prot. Diss. Bill* Wks. X. 37, I would have the Laws rise in all their majesty of terrours, to fulminate such vain and impious wretches. **1806** W. TAYLOR in *Ann. Rev.* IV. 263 The catholic church.. fulminates without hesitation a Julian or an Elizabeth.

9. *intr.* Of the pope, etc.: To issue censures or condemnations (*against*); *gen.* to 'thunder', inveigh violently *against*.

1639 FULLER *Holy War* III. xxx. (1647) 162 Before his time the Imperiall majesty..was never fulminated against with excommunication. **1660** R. COKE *Power & Subj.* 215 Pope Paul..after he had fulminated so dreadfully against him, proposed him for an Example to be imitated. **1768** BOSWELL *Corsica* ii. (ed. 2) 65 The Vatican from whence the holy father used..to fulminate with serious effect against the greatest powers in Europe. **1792** *Bar. Munchausen's Trav.* xxxiv. 159, I..seized the Speaker, who was fulminating against the Aristocrats. **1849** SIR J. STEPHEN *Eccl. Biog.* (1850) I. 466 Pulpits fulminated, presses groaned. **1852** GLADSTONE *Glean.* (1879) IV. xxii. 157 It will be the duty of the Pope himself to fulminate against them.

10. *Path.* Of a disease: to develop suddenly and severely. (Cf. FULMINATING *ppl. a.* 3.)

1910 *Practitioner* June 744 A gland presumably tuberculous... Sooner or later such a gland almost always fulminates, that is to say, rapidly bursts its capsule and allows the broken-down contents to invade the surrounding lymphoid tissues.

Hence **'fulminating** *vbl. sb.*, the action of the vb.

1693 W. SALMON *Bates' Dispens.* (1715) 537/1 You need not fear its fulminating in the drying.

†**'fulminate,** *ppl. a. Obs. rare.* [ad. L. *fulmināt-us*, pa. pple. of *fulmināre* (see FULMINATE *v.*).] Fulminated, emitted as a thunderbolt.

1659 BAXTER *Key Cath.* xlv. 315 They [the Jesuits] were the only cause that incensed the Pope to send so many fulminate Breves to these Kingdoms.

fulminating ('fʌlmɪneɪtɪŋ), *ppl. a.* [f. FULMINATE *v.* + -ING².] That fulminates.

1. a. Detonating, violently explosive.

fulminating gold, mercury, platinum, silver, various fulminates or salts of fulminic acid. ***fulminating pane*** (see quot. 1879). ***fulminating powder***, formerly, a mixture of nitre, potash, and sulphur; now sometimes applied to other violently explosive powders, chiefly containing fulminate of mercury.

1646 SIR T. BROWNE *Pseud. Ep.* II. v. 89 These afford no fulminating report. **1665** HOOKE *Microgr.* 35 These I found to have quite lost all their fulminating or flying quality. **1691** RAY *Creation* I. (1704) 80 For fulminating Engines. **1695** WOODWARD *Nat. Hist. Earth* IV. (1723) 227 The Fulminating Damp will take Fire at a Candle. **1794** J. HUTTON *Philos. Light, etc.* 210 This fulminating composition. **1804** T. G. FESSENDEN *Terrible Tractoration* 142 Sound Discord's jarring tocsin louder, Than Howard's fulminating powder. **1807** T. THOMSON *Chem.* (ed. 3) II. 12 This powder is fulminating gold, which is composed of five parts of yellow oxide of gold and one part of ammonia. *Ibid.* 423 Mr. Howard..has given it the name of fulminating mercury. **1858** GREENER *Gunnery* 22 Nothing can resist the exceeding intensity of the action of fulminating powder. **1879** ROSSITER *Dict. Sci. Terms*, *Fulminating pane*, glass plate coated on each side with tin-foil, which, when electrified, can be discharged with a spark. **1879** *Cassell's Techn. Educ.* IV. 146/2 Fulminating silver, even when moist, will explode by percussion.

b. Producing a brilliant flash when ignited.

1676 LISTER in *Ray's Corr.* (1848) 124 The fulminating powder, which the spikes of *Muscus Lycopod.* yield.

2. *fig.* That thunders or hurls forth censures, denunciations, or the like; also, that is thundered forth.

1626 T. H[AWKINS] *Caussin's Holy Crt.* 127 Rome, from whence came all the fulminating thunders, and bloudy Edicts agaynst Christians. *a* **1693** URQUHART *Rabelais* III. xii. 93 A powerful and fulminating Goddess. **1734** tr. *Rollin's Anc. Hist.* (1827) II. II. 91 This fulminating decree. **1790** BURKE *Fr. Rev.* 16 All things in this his fulminating bull are not of so innoxious a tendency. *a* **1839** PRAED *Poems* (1864) II. 273 Hits Sent slyly out by little wits, A fulminating breed.

3. *Path.* Of a disease: coming on suddenly with intense severity; foudroyant; = FULMINANT *a.* 2.

1875 R. B. CARTER *Pract. Treat. Dis. Eye* xi. 413 The 'fulminating' form [of glaucoma] differs from the acute only in the extreme degree of tension, [etc.]. **1900** in DORLAND *Med. Dict.* **1908** *Brit. Med. Jrnl.* 22 Aug. 477/1 Two cases of fulminating pyorrhœa alveolaris specifica. **1910** *Practitioner* Feb. 204 Fulminating cases of infection with virulent organisms. **1964** M. HYNES *Med. Bacteriol.* (ed. 8) x. 135 A fulminating gastro-enteritis which is commonly fatal. **1970** R. M. GOODMAN *Genetic Disorders Man* xvii. 871/2 The disease [*sc.* galactosemia] may be fulminating and result in early death.

fulmination (fʌlmɪ'neɪʃən). [ad. L. *fulminātiōn-em*, n. of action f. *fulmināre* (see FULMINATE *v.*).]

1. The bursting forth of thunder and lightning. In quots. only *fig.*: cf. 4.

1623 COCKERAM, *Fulmination*, thundring. **1650** BULWER *Anthropomet.* 126 Like wicked Outlawes despising the fulmination of divine Anger. **1868** BROWNING *Ring & Bk.* IX. 606 St. Paul..Deplored the check o' the puny presence, still Cheating his fulmination of its flash. **1869** GOULBURN *Purs. Holiness* 96 He beats down with His fulminations the old idols of prejudice.

2. The action of fulminating or detonating; loud explosion.

1667 HENSHAW in Sprat *Hist. R. Soc.* 275 The Volatile part that was seperated from it in the fulmination. **1765** HAMILTON in *Phil. Trans.* LV. 176 Mariotte..calls these bubbles [in boiling water] fulminations. **1794** J. HUTTON *Philos. Light, etc.* 232 Another species of explosion, which has been termed fulmination. **1885** *Syd. Soc. Lex.*, *Fulmination*, an explosion with noise, resulting from the sudden decomposition of a chemical substance.

†**3.** *Metallurgy.* (See FULMINATE *v.* 3.) *Obs.*

1612 WOODALL *Surg. Mate* Wks. (1653) 271 Fulmination ..is a metallicall gradation, with excoction to an absolute perfection in Cinerition, whose purity is declared by an effulgent splendor.

4. The formal emission of an ecclesiastical condemnation or censure (see FULMINATE *v.* II). Subsequently with a more general sense: Violent denunciation or threatening; an instance of this, a terrific explosion of indignation.

1502 *Ord. Crysten Men* (W. de W. 1506) IV. viii. 191 For the twenty fulminacyons that they make at this day comenly. **1532-3** *Act 24 Hen. VIII*, c. 12 §3 The sayde fulminacions of any of the same interdictions. **1606** *Crt. & Times Jas. I* (1849) I. 63 Their protestation against the Pope's fulmination. **1726** AYLIFFE *Parergon* 132 These Fulminations from the Vatican were turn'd into Ridicule. **1809** KNOX & JEBB *Corr.* I. 556 Gross vice is not, in the first instance, to be encountered with menaces and fulminations. **1845** H. ROGERS *Ess.* I. iii. 122 Awaiting the fulmination of the bull. **1858** *Times* 6 Aug. 11/2 His..generals were more strictly bound down by great fulminations never to attack without permission. **1861** MISS C. FOX *Jrnls.* II. 280 John Bright is great fun, always ready for a chat and a fulmination.

fulminatory ('fʌlmɪnəˌtərɪ), *a.* [ad. F. *fulminatoire*, f. L. *fulmināre*: see FULMINATE *v.* and -ORY.] Sending forth fulminations, thundering.

1611 COTGR., *Fulminatoire*, fulminatorie, thundering, lightening, destroying, terrible. **1656-81** in BLOUNT *Glossogr.* **1721-92** in BAILEY. **1820** *Examiner* No. 641. 475/2 One of the framers of the fulminatory preamble. **1837** CARLYLE *Fr. Rev.* II. v. ii, Its speculatory Height or Mountain, which will become a practical fulminatory Height. **1840** J. QUINCY *Hist. Harvard Univ.* I. 134 Their violent and fulminatory measures.

fulmine ('fʌlmɪn), *v.* [ad. L. *fulmin-āre*: see FULMINATE *v.*]

1. *trans.* To send forth (lightning or thunder).

1590 SPENSER *F.Q.* III. ii. 5 As it had beene a flake Of lightning through bright heven fulmined. **1830** W. PHILLIPS *Mt. Sinai* IV. 381 A sound As 'twere of thunder fulmined nigh at hand, O'erwhelm'd his hearing.

b. *fig.* To 'fulmine' or flash *out*.

1847 TENNYSON *Princ.* II. 118 She fulmined out her scorn of laws Salique And little-footed China.

2. *intr.* To 'thunder', speak out fiercely or energetically. Now chiefly in echoes of Milton's use (quot. 1671).

1623 tr. *Favine's Theat. Hon.* II. xiii. 276 He had interdicted and fulmined against the Emperour. **1671** MILTON *P.R.* IV. 270 Whose resistless eloquence Wielded at will that fierce Democratie, Shook the Arsenal and fulmined over Greece. *c* **1820** S. ROGERS *Italy, Luigi* 35 How unlike him who fulmined in old Rome! **1870** LOWELL *Study Wind.* 384 Listening to him who fulmined over Greece.

fulmineous (fʌl'mɪnɪəs), *a.* ? *Obs.* [f. L. *fulmine-us* (f. *fulmin-* FULMEN) + -OUS.] Pertaining to thunder or lightning.

1727 in BAILEY vol. II. **1744** *J. Claridge's Shepherd of Banbury's Rules* 31 The fulmineous matter in the air is set on fire. **1766** G. CANNING *Anti-Lucretius* IV. 318 Than the flame fulmineous fiercer far.

ful'minic (fʌl'mɪnɪk), *a. Chem.* [f. L. *fulmin-* (with sense derived from FULMINATE *v.*) + -IC.] In ***fulminic acid***: $C_2H_2N_2O_2$, nitro-acetonitril, an acid (not yet isolated) forming explosive salts with some metals.

1825 HAMILTON *Dict. Terms*, *Fulminic Acid*, in Chemistry, an acid capable of combining in different proportions, with different bases, and thus forming as many detonating salts. **1850** DAUBENY *Atom. The.* vii. (ed. 2) 215 Cy 2 + oxygen 2 + Aq. 1 forms fulminic acid. **1864** H. SPENCER *Biol.* I. 8 The various fulminating salts are all formed by the union with metals, of a certain nitrogenous acid called fulminic acid.

fulminous ('fʌlmɪnəs), *a.* [f. L. *fulmin-* FULMEN + -OUS.] Of or pertaining to thunder and lightning; fulminating.

1635 HEYWOOD *Hierarch.* II. 63 In his hand a Trisulc thunderbolt or Fulminous brand. **1665** SIR T. BROWNE *Wks.* (1835) IV. 354 The like fulminous fire killed a man in Erpingham church. **1876** F. HARRISON *Choice Bks.* (1886) 122 Sad as those fulminous imprecations on mankind, when Lear bows his head to the storm.

fulminurate (fʌlmɪ'njʊəreɪt). *Chem.* [f. as next + -ATE: see URATE.] A salt of fulminuric acid.

1864 WATTS *Dict. Chem.* II. 739 *Fulminurates.* Fulminuric acid appears to be monobasic; at all events all the fulminurates hitherto obtained contain only 1 at. metal in place of hydrogen.

fulminuric (fʌlmɪ'njʊərɪk), *a. Chem.* [f. FULMIN-IC + URIC.] Only in ***fulminuric acid*** (see quots.); ***fulminuric ether***.

1864 WATTS *Dict. Chem.* II. 738 *Fulminuric Acid* $C^3H^3N^3O^3$ Isocyanuric acid. An acid isomeric with cyanuric acid. *Ibid.* 741 *Fulminuric Ether*: see Fulminurate of Ethyl. **1879** ROSSITER *Dict. Sci. Terms*, *Fulminuric acid*.. an anhydrous crystalline substance obtained from fulminic acid.

fulness: see FULLNESS.

†**ful'samic,** *a. Obs. rare*⁻¹. [? corruptly f. FULSOME + -IC.] = FULSOME.

1694 CONGREVE *Double Dealer* III. x, O filthy Mr. Sneer; he's a nauseous figure, a most fulsamick Fop, Foh!

†**'fulsion.** *Obs. rare*⁻¹. [as if ad. L. **fulsiōn-em*, f. *fulgēre* to shine.] The action of shining forth; an instance of this.

1690 W. LEYBOURN *Cursus. Math.* 782 Fourteen of the Extream Fulsions, or of the brightest shinings of Mars.

fulsome ('fʌlsəm), *a.* Forms: 3-5 **fulsum**, 4-8 **fulsom**, 5 **fulsome**; also 5 **folsome**, 6 **fulsoom**, 7 **fullsome**, (9 **foulsome**), 6 *Sc.* **fowsum**, 7, 9 *Sc.* **fousome**. [f. FULL *a.* + -SOME.

It is possible that there may have been a ME. *fūlsum* (f. *fūl*, FOUL *a.*) which has coalesced with this; but the supposition is not absolutely necessary to account for the development of senses.]

†**1.** Characterized by abundance, possessing or affording copious supply; abundant, plentiful, full.

c **1250** *Gen. & Ex.* 2153 Ðe .vii. fulsum ȝeres faren. ? *a* **1412** LYDG. *Lyfe our Ladye* (Caxton) A v, For alwey God gaf hyr to her presence So fulsom lyght of heuenly influence. *Ibid.* B v b, Like as a fulsum welle Shedyth his stremys in to the ryuere. *c* **1440** —— *Secrees* 723 At Ellyconys welle This philisoffre by fulsom habundance Drank grettest plente. **1481** EARL WORCESTER *Tulle on Friendsh.* B vii b, Though he

..were sette in moost folsom plente. *c* **1510** BARCLAY *Mirr. Gd. Manners* (1570) Ciij b, Folowe fulsome fieldes habundaunt of frument. **1515** —— *Egloges* IV. (1570) Ciij a, Suche fulsome pasture made him a double chin. **1571** GOLDING *Calvin on Ps.* lxxiii. 26 Much more fulsome is Davids confession [orig. *Longè plenior est Dauidis confessio*]. **1583** —— *Calvin on Deut.* xcii. 571 Likewise of their first fruites insteede of making good fulsome sheaues and bundels vnto God, they gelded them, and made them verie thinne and lanke. [**1868** HELPS *Realmah* II. xi. 80 My complaint of the world..is this—that there is too much of everything.. and so I could go on enumerating..all the things which are too full in this fulsome world. I use fulsome in the original sense.]

†**b.** Growing abundantly, rank in growth. *Obs.*

1633 *Costlie Whore* IV. i. in Bullen *O. Pl.* IV, Plucke up the fulsome thistle in the prime.

†**2.** Of the body, etc.: Full and plump, fat, well-grown; in a bad sense, over-grown. *Obs.*

1340–70 *Alex. & Dind.* 497 Wiþ þe siht clene We ben as fulsom i-founde as þouȝ we fed were. *c* **1400** *Destr. Troy* 3068 With a necke..Nawþer fulsom, ne fat, but fetis & round. **1565** GOLDING *Ovid's Met.* VII. (1567) 85 a, His leane, pale, hore, and withered corse grew fulsome, faire, and fresh. **1593** RICH *Greene's Newes* G iij b, A chuffe-headed Cardinall with a paire of fulsome cheekes. **1628** WITHER *Brit. Rememb.* VI. 637 For either arme in such a mould is cast As makes it full as fulsome as their waste. **1664** H. MORE *Myst. Iniq.* 238 A fulsome and over-grown and unwholesome Flesh. **1678** OTWAY *Friendship in F.* II. i, 'Tis such a fulsom overgrown Rogue!

†**b.** Overfed, surfeited. Also *fig. Obs.*

1642 ROGERS *Naaman* 24 Lazy, Laodicean temper of a fulsome, carelesse, surfeted spirit. *Ibid.* 346 Doth he not deserve at our hands more then a faint fulsome grant with Martha, thou canst doe all things. **1805** A. SCOTT *Poems* 40 (Jam.) Nor fall their [? read *they*] victims to a fulsome rift.

†**c.** App. used for: Lustful, 'rank'. *Obs.*

1596 SHAKS. *Merch. V.* I. iii. 87 The fulsome Ewes. [Cf. *rancke* in line 81.]

†**3.** Of food: Satiating, 'filling', tending to cloy or surfeit; also, coarse, gross, unsuited to a dainty palate. *Obs.*

c **1410** LOVE *Bonavent. Mirr.* lxiii, It shulde so soone be fulsome and not comfortable deynte. **1555** W. WATREMAN *Fardle Facions* I. vi. 94 This kinde of meate onely, serueth them all their life tyme..and neuer waxeth fulsome vnto theim. **1577** HARRISON *England* II. vi. (1877) I. 160 Our ale ..is more thicke, fulsome and of no continuance. **1594** CAREW *Huarte's Exam. Wits* xii (1596) 198 Though the same were a meat of such delicacie and pleasing rellish, yet in the end, the people of Israell found it fulsome. **1614** BP. HALL *Recoll. Treat.* 488 A little honie is sweet; much, fulsome. **1655** MOUFET & BENNET *Health's Improv.* (1746) 229 A gross and fulsome Nourishment, unless they meet with a strong and good Stomach. *a* **1668** DAVENANT *News fr. Plym.* (1673) 3 Their gross feedings On fulsome Butter, Essex Cheese. **1735** POPE *Donne Sat.* II. 118 Carthusian fasts, and fulsome Bacchanals. **1742** YOUNG *Nt. Th.* VII. 263 Why starv'd, on earth, our angel-appetites; While brutal are indulg'd their fulsome fill? **1770** WILKES *Let.* 29 July in *Corr.* (1805) IV. 76, I dined with the lord-mayor..We had two turtles, and a fulsome great dinner.

†**b.** Having a sickly or sickening taste; tending to cause nausea. *Obs.*

1601 HOLLAND *Pliny* I. 434 The oile..is very fulsome and naught to be eaten. **1614** BP. HALL *Recoll. Treat.* 248 The very sight of that cup, wherein such a fulsome potion was brought him, turnes his stomacke. **1694** WESTMACOTT *Script. Herb.* 6 The common Anise-Seed-Water..is the most fulsom and insalubrious of Strong-waters. **1743** *Lond. & Country Brew.* II. (ed. 2) 107 A certain sour, fulsome Quality that the former Wort left behind.

†**c.** *fig.* Cloying, satiating, wearisome from excess or repetition. (Cf. sense 7.) *Obs.*

1531 ELYOT *Gov.* I. xxi, Lest in repetyng a thinge so frequent and commune, my boke shulde be..fastidious or fulsome to the reders. **1601** SHAKS. *Twel. N.* V. i. 112 If it be ought to the old tune, my Lord, It is as fat and fulsome to mine eare As howling after Musicke. **1605** CAMDEN *Rem.* (1637) 43 The Spanish majesticall, but fulsome, running too much on the O. **1633** ROGERS *Treat. Sacram.* I. 163 Who then wonders if the Supper of Christ..be as a fulsome thing unto you? **1694** ADDISON *Eng. Greatest Poets* Misc. Wks. 1726 I. 36 The long-spun allegories fulsom grow, While the dull moral lyes too plain below. **1709** STEELE *Tatler* No. 70 ¶4 As too little Action is cold, so too much is fulsome.

†**4.** Offensive to the sense of smell: **a.** Strong-smelling, of strong, rank, or overpowering odour. **b.** Foul-smelling, stinking. *Obs.*

1583 STANYHURST *Æneis* II. (Arb.) 66 Eech path was fulsoom with sent of sulphurus orpyn. **1606** *Sir G. Goosecappe* I. ii. in Bullen *O. Pl.* III. 14 Heres such a fulsome Aire comes into this Chamber. **1626** BACON *Sylva* §507 They are commonly of rank and fulsome smell; as May-Flowers and White Lillies. **1683** TRYON *Way to Health* 119 That is the reason why fryed, baked and stewed Food does send forth a stronger and fulsomer scent than other Preparations. **1725** BRADLEY *Fam. Dict.* s.v. *Malt*, The Kiln ought to have convenient Windows, that your gross Steams, fulsom Damps, and stupifying Vapours may pass freely away.

†**5.** Offensive to the senses generally; physically disgusting, foul, or loathsome. *Obs.*

? **1507** *Communyc.* (W. de W.) A ij, Man is but fulsome erthe and claye. **1579** LYLY *Euphues* (Arb.) 130 Whereby they noted the great dislyking they had of their fulsome feedinge. **1595** SHAKS. *John* III. iv. 32, I will..stop this gap of breath with fulsome dust. **1621** BURTON *Anat. Mel.* I. ii. I. ii. (1651) 53 She vomited some 24 pounds of fulsome stuffe of all colours. *Ibid.* II. ii. I. i. 232 Calis..would use no Vulgar water; but she died..of so fulsome a disease that no water could wash her clean. **1627** DRAYTON *Agincourt* etc. 199 A thousand silken Puppets should haue died, And in their fulsome Coffins putrified, Ere [etc.]. **1642** DAVENANT *Unfort. Lovers* iv, Who once departed, know this fulsome world So much unfit to mingle with their pure Refined ayre, that they will returne. **1720** T. BOSTON *Hum. Nat. in Fourfold St.* (1797) 152 They cleave fondly to these fulsome breasts. [**1849** *Tait's Mag.* XVI. 120/2 Hundreds of dogs.. are annually committed to the abysses of these foulsome waters.]

6. Offensive to normal tastes or sensibilities; exciting aversion or repugnance; disgusting, repulsive, odious. ? *Obs.* exc. as in sense 7.

c **1375** *Sc. Leg. Saints, Julian* 496 Of his wykytnes þat fulsume til al gud-men wes. ? *a* **1400** *Morte Arth.* 1061 There thow lygges, ffor the fulsomeste freke that fourmede was euere! **1532** MORE *Confut. Tindale* Wks. 713/2 Tindall ..with hys fulsome feeling fayth. **1579** TOMSON *Calvin's Serm. Tim.* 464/2 It is a foule and fulsome thing, whiche shee must leaue off. **1611** COTGR. s.v. *Robin*, A filthie knaue with a fulsome queane. **1635** QUARLES *Embl.* III. ii. (1718) 133 Seest thou this fulsom ideot? *c* **1645** HOWELL *Lett.* (1650) I. 188 A phlegmatic dull wife is fulsome and fastidious. **1680** OTWAY *Orphan* I. i. (1691) 3 Now half the Youth of Europe are in Arms, How fulsome must it be to stay behind, And dye of rank diseases here at home? **1684** SIR C. SCROPE *Misc. Poems* 112 Let not his fulsome armes embrace your waste. **1702** POPE *Wife of Bath* 173 Fulsom love for gain we can endure. **1780** COWPER *Progr. Err.* 291 And lest the fulsome artifice should fail, Themselves will hide its coarseness with a veil. **1819** W. TENNANT *Papistry Storm'd* (1827) 29 Have at a fousome kirk, and batter Her lustfu' banes until they clatter! **1826** SCOTT *Woodst.* iii, In a booth at the fulsome fair.

†**b.** Morally foul, filthy, obscene. *Obs.*

1604 SHAKS. *Oth.* IV. i. 37 Lye with her: that's fullsome. **1630** DRYDEN *Pref. to Ovid's Epist.* (1683) A iij b, A certain Epigram, which is ascrib'd to him [the emperour]..is more fulsome than any passage I have met with in our Poet. **1682** SHADWELL *Medal* 3 Thy Mirth by foolish Bawdry is exprest; And so debauch'd, so fulsome, and so odd. **1719** D'URFEY *Pills* (1872) I. 327 And earn a hated living in an odious Fulsome way. **1726** AMHERST *Terræ Fil.* xxvi. 144 What followed was too fulsome for the eyes of my chaste readers.

7. Of language, style, behaviour, etc.: Offensive to good taste; *esp.* offending from excess or want of measure or from being 'over-done'. Now chiefly used in reference to gross or excessive flattery, over-demonstrative affection, or the like.

1663 BP. PATRICK *Parab. Pilgr.* 201, I never heard anything so fulsome from the mouth of man; and found my self..impatient of such silly stuff. **1692** BENTLEY *Boyle Lect.* vi. 189 They were puffed up with the fulsome Flatteries of their Philosophers and Sophists. **1702** ROWE *Tamerl.* III. i. 1081 Bear back thy fulsom Greeting to thy Master. **1762** GOLDSM. *Cit. W.* xviii, Concealed disgust under the appearance of fulsome endearment. **1782** J. WARTON *Ess. Pope* II. xii. 338 This fawning and fulsome court-historian. **1784** COWPER *Task* VI. 289 The fulsome cant And pedantry that coxcombs learn with ease. **1802** MAR. EDGEWORTH *Moral T.* (1816) I. 226 The fulsome strains of courtly adulation. **1873** SYMONDS *Grk. Poets* vi. 169 Pindar was never fulsome in his panegyric. **1874** HELPS *Soc. Press.* xiii. 778 This fulsome publicity I have described.

b. quasi-*sb.*

1742 H. WALPOLE *Lett. H. Mann* (1834) I. xxiv. 104 Some choice letters from Queen Anne, little inferior in the fulsome to those from King James to..Buckingham.

†'**fulsomehead.** *Obs.* [f. FULSOME + -HEAD.] Plentifulness, abundance.

c **1250** *Gen. & Ex.* 1548 Heuene dew and erðes fetthed, Of win and olie fulsum-hed. *Ibid.* 2128 Ðo .vij. ȝer ben ȝet to cumen In al fulsum-hed sulen it ben numen.

fulsomely ('fʌlsəmlɪ), *adv.* [f. FULSOME + -LY[2].] In a fulsome manner.

†**1.** Abundantly, plentifully, fully. *Obs.*

a **1300** *Cursor M.* 17805 (Gött.) Ga we þan fulsumli þeder. *c* **1350** *Will. Palerne* 4325 þann were spacli spices spended al a boute fulsumli at þe ful to eche freke þer-inne. **1412–20** LYDG. *Chron. Troy*, The foyson and plente Of kyngly fredom unto hye and lowe So fulsomly gan there to reygne and snowe. *c* **1440** HYLTON *Scala Perf.* (W. de W. 1494) II. xxvii, He that woll..fulsomly fele the loue of Jhesu in his sowle.

2. In a way that causes surfeit or nausea; in a way that offends the senses; cloyingly, sickeningly; disgustingly, loathsomely.

1536 BELLENDEN *Cron. Scot., Cosmogr. & Descr. Albion* iv. (1541) B ij b, Thow sall fynd thaym throw thair intemperance and surfet diet sa fowsumlie growin. **1563** *Homilies* II. *Repairing Ch.* (1859) 274 Suffered Gods House to bee in ruine and decay, to lye uncomely, and fulsomely. **1572** J. JONES *Bathes Buckstone* 10 b, Neyther with such [euill ayre] as commeth of houses fulsomely kept. **1599** NASHE *Lenten Stuffe* (1871) 91 The very embers whereon he was singed..fumed most fulsomely of his fatty droppings. **1620** VENNER *Via Recta* (1650) 34 It is nauseous and fulsomely sweet. **1708** *Brit. Apollo* No. 78. 3/1 Who but in the Lushious delight, Which fulsomely Cloys.

3. In a way that is offensive to good taste (see FULSOME 7). †Also, coarsely, obscenely (*obs.*).

1677 SEDLEY *Ant. & Cl.* IV. i, Your slighted love..Can you forget? and fulsomely pursue The man with kindness who despises you? **1678** CUDWORTH *Intell. Syst.* 553 Apuleius also..grosly and fulsomely imputes the same to Plato. **1693** DRYDEN *Juvenal* Ded. (1697) 34 The Act of Consummation fulsomly describ'd in the very Words of the most Modest amongst all Poets. **1700** CONGREVE *Way of World* IV. v, That nauseous cant, in which men and their wives are so fulsomely familiar. **1748** RICHARDSON *Clarissa* (1811) III. lxv. 377 Mr. Belford seems..although very complaisant, not so fulsomely so as Mr. Tourville. **1849** MACAULAY *Hist. Eng.* I. 225 The language of these compositions was..fulsomely servile. **1861** PEARSON *Early & Mid. Ages Eng.* 444 Praising a king fulsomely during his lifetime.

fulsomeness ('fʌlsəmnɪs). [f. as prec. + -NESS.] The quality or state of being fulsome.

†**1.** Abundance, plentifulness, fullness. *Obs.*

c **1386** CHAUCER *Sqr.'s T.* 397 The knotte, why that every tale is told, If it be taryed til that lust be cold..The savour passeth ever lenger the more, For fulsomnes of his prolixité. *a* **1400** *Prymer* (1891) 95 Y seyde in my fulsumnesse [*in abundantia mea*]. *c* **1430** LYDG. *Min. Poems* (Percy) 14 Bochous schewed ther his fulsomnes Off holsome wynes to every maner wighte. **1447** BOKENHAM *Seyntys* (Roxb.) 274 Of wych ioye kyng dauyd þus seyde expresse, I lord with þi fulsumnesse sacyat shal be.

†**2.** The quality of cloying, surfeiting, or nauseating the palate; grossness, sickliness, or offensiveness of savour. Also, the state of being cloyed or surfeited. Also *fig. Obs.*

1481 EARL WORCESTER *Tulle on Friendsh.* C iij a, Ther is not suche fulsomnesse in frendship, as ther is in other thynges, ffor frendship fareth as wine which may be kepte many yeres. **1576** NEWTON *Lemnie's Complex.* 156 a, The body lacking exercise, gathereth fulsomnes & pestilent sauours. **1594** CAREW *Huarte's Exam. Wits* xii. (1596) 191 Our soule hath a fulsomnesse at this slight meat. **1620** VENNER *Via Recta* viii. 169 They induce fulsomenesse, and subuert the stomacke. **1621** BURTON *Anat. Mel.* II. ii. II. (1651) 238 To absterge belike that fulsomeness of sweet, to which they are there subject. **1656** H. MORE *Enthus. Tri.* 20 Quickned and actuated..(as the fulsomnesse of sugar is by the acrimony of Lemons). **1688** CLAYTON in *Phil. Trans.* XVII. 979 A strong sort of Tobacco, in which the Smoakers say they can plainly taste the fulsomness of the Dung. **1876** TRENCH *Synon. N.T.* lxi. 219 By 'fulsomeness' is indicated the disgust and loathing from over-fulness of meat as well as of wine.

†**3.** The quality of being offensive or disgusting to the senses; foulness, loathsomeness. *Obs.*

1563 *Homilies* II. *Repairing Ch.* (1859) 277 All these abominations they..have cleansed and purged the churches of England of, taking away all such fulsomeness and filthiness as [etc.]. **1610** PRICE *Creat. Prince* B j b, Others haue described them by some diseases, to manifest the fulsomness and loathsomnesse thereof.

4. The quality of being offensive to good taste (esp. by over-adulation or the like). †Also, coarseness, obscenity (*obs.*). (See FULSOME 6–7.)

1693 DRYDEN *Juvenal* Ded. (1697) 60 No Decency is consider'd, no Fulsomness omitted. **1699** BENTLEY *Phal.* Pref. 50 How a man may commend himself, without Envy or Fulsomness. **1845** LD. CAMPBELL *Chancellors* (1857) I. lviii. 179 Rather a proof of the bad taste in pulpit oratory prevailing..than of any peculiar servility or fulsomeness. **1881** *Times* 13 Mar. 9/3 Adulation became an art, and was carried to a pitch of fulsomeness beyond modern conception.

fulsun, var. of FILSEN *v. Obs.*, to aid.

13.. *Gaw. & Gr. Knt.* 99 As fortune wolde fulsun hom þe fayrer to haue.

fulth. *Obs.* exc. *dial.* Also *Sc.* FOUTH. [f. FULL *a.* + -TH[1]; cf. *length, depth.*] Fullness. Also = FILL *sb.*[1], in ***to eat one's fulth.***

c **1325** *Metr. Hom.* 7 Ar the fulthe of tim was comen. *c* **1375** *Sc. Leg. Saints, Paulus* 863 Quhare hele beis ay but seknes..fulth but hungir. *a* **1400–50** *Alexander* 2171 þare his forrayouris fand þe fulth of vitaill. *c* **1425** WYNTOUN *Cron.* I. xiii. 12 Fra fwlth of mete. **1641** BEST *Farm. Bks.* (Surtees) 5 A lambe will fall..to eatinge of grasse, when it is aboute a moneth..olde; yett if it have its fulth of milke it will forbeare the longer. **1855** ROBINSON *Whitby Gloss.* s.v., Take and eat your fulth on 't. **1881** *Leicestersh. Gloss., Fulth*, fulness, full growth, perfection, as applied to flowers, &c.

fulthe, early ME. form of FILTH.

†'**fultum.** *Obs.* Also 1 fultéam, 3 foltom. [OE. *fultum, fultéam*, f. **fulltéon* (= OHG. *follaziohan*) to assist, f. FULL *adv.* + *téon* to draw, TEE *v.* Cf. TEAM f. the root of the simple vb. With regard to the sense-development see the remarks s.v. FOLLOW *v.*] Help, assistance, support; also *concr.* one who or something which helps.

Beowulf 698 Ac him dryhten for-ȝeaf..frofor and fultum. *a* **800** *Erfurt Gloss.* 360 *Emolomentum*, fulteam [*Corpus Gloss.* fultum]. *c* **1175** *Lamb. Hom.* 105 þurh drihtnes fultum. *c* **1205** LAY. 417 þat Troynisce folc mid his fulle fultume nomen..Brutus & makeden hine to duke. *c* **1250** *Gen. & Ex.* 2824 Of me sal fultum ben ðe broȝt.

†**fulve**, *a. Obs. rare*[−1]. [ad. L. *fulv-us*: see FULVOUS.] = FULVOUS.

1657 TOMLINSON *Renou's Disp.* 252 Whose surcles are very slender, fulve, odorate.

fulvescent (fʌl'vɛsənt), *a.* [f. L. *fulv-us* (see FULVOUS) + -ESCENT.] Passing into a fulvous tint, somewhat tawny.

1816 KIRBY & SP. *Entomol.* (1828) II. xix. 124 *note*, The ventral segments are fulvescent. **1819** G. SAMOUELLE *Entomol. Compend.* 287 Those of a fulvescent colour.

fulvid ('fʌlvɪd), *a.* Now *rare.* [ad. med.L. *fulvid-us*, f. L. *fulvus* reddish-yellow.] = FULVOUS.

1599 A. M. tr. *Gabelhouer's Bk. Physicke* 40/1 Take a fulvide or blewe woollen cloth. **1642** H. MORE *Song of Soul* I. I. iii, The fulvid Eagle with her sun-bright eye. **1681** —— *Exp. Dan.* 27 A Beast of a fulvid or Golden colour. **1860** *Sir Rohan's Ghost* vi. 133 Something in the softened light, through the fulvid noon, was moving here.

Hence '**fulvidness**.

1685 H. MORE *Illustration* 304 The fulvidness of the Sand of the Sea.

† **'fulvify,** *v. Obs. rare.* [f. L. *fulv-us* (see FULVOUS *a.*) + -(I)FY.] *trans.* To make fulvous.
1599 A. M. tr. *Gabelhouer's Bk. Physicke* 142/2 Fulvefye, or make it yellow with the poulder of pomegranate shelles.

fulvo-, used as combining form of FULVOUS *a.*, meaning 'having a reddish-yellow hue'.
1879 W. A. LEIGHTON *Lichen-flora Gt. Brit.* (ed. 3) 512 *Fulvo-testaceus*, tawny-yellow-brown. **1887** W. PHILLIPS *Brit. Discomycetes* 256 Exterior fulvo-rufous. **1943** H. A. DADE *Colour Terminol. Biol.* 5 Armeniacus: apricot colour; lightly greyed orange-scarlet; = Fries's terms fulvo-cinnamomeus and helvelo-alutaceus.

fulvous ('fʌlvəs), *a.* Chiefly *Nat. Hist.* [f. L. *fulv-us* reddish-yellow + -OUS.] Reddish-yellow, dull yellowish-brown or tawny.
1664 BEALE *Aphor. Cider* xxxix. in Evelyn *Pomona* 26 A more fulvous or ruddy colour. **1688** R. HOLME *Armoury* II. 246/1 A Thistle-finch..hath..Neck & Back of a fulvous or reddish Ash colour. **1828** STARK *Elem. Nat. Hist.* I. 93 Fur shining fulvous brown. **1839** G. RAYMOND in *New Monthly Mag.* LVI. 312, I now clearly distinguished an expansive eagle..on the fulvous panel of the hinder boot. **1848** LOWELL *Biglow P.* Poems 1890 II. 8 A Nemean lion, fulvous, torrid-eyed.

‖**fulwa** ('fʊlwə). [corruptly ad. Bengali *phulwara*, the native name of *Bassia butyracea*.] (See quots.) Also ***fulwa-butter***.
1835 *Penny Cycl.* IV. 2 *Bassia butyracea*, the Indian butter-tree, also the *Fulwa*, or *Phulwara-tree*..This phulwara butter will keep many months. **1866** *Treas. Bot.*, *Fulwa*, a solid buttery oil obtained from Bassia butyracea. **1885** *Syd. Soc. Lex*, *Fulwa butter*, the concrete oil of the seeds of *Bassia butyracea*.

fulyie ('fuljɪ), *sb.*[1] *Sc.* Also 5–9 fulye, 6 fulȝe, 9 fulzie, foolyie. [var. of FOIL *sb.*[1]]
†**1.** A leaf. *Obs.*
1513 DOUGLAS *Æneis* XII. Prol. 89 Euery faill Ourfret with fulȝeis of figuris full diuers. **1819** W. TENNANT *Papistry Storm'd* (1827) 113 Sae thick they [Bees] owr the fulȝies stalk.
2. Gold-leaf.
c **1450** *Golagros & Gaw.* 939 The fulye of the fyne gold fell in the feild. **1488** in *Ld. Treas. Acc. Scotl.* (1877) I. 85 A buke with levis of gold, with xiij levis of gold fulȝe. **1808–80** JAMIESON, *Fulye* 2. Leaf gold.. We still use fulye in the same sense, without the addition of the term gold.

fulyie, fulzie, *sb.*[2] *Sc.* Also 5–6 fulye, 8 foulyie, 9 foulzie, fuilzie. [app. f. next vb.; the primary sense appears to be 'what is trampled underfoot'. Cf. FULLAGE.
The prevailing spelling in official documents and newspapers is *fulzie*, which often receives the anglicized pronunciation ('fʌlzɪ). The *z*, however, historically represents ȝ = *y*, and the purely popular pronunciation is ('fuljɪ) or ('fulɪ).]
1. The sweepings or refuse of the streets.
1538 *Extr. Aberd. Reg.* (1844) 154 Assis nor fulze. **1692** *Act Sederunt* 4 Aug., The muck and fulzie of the towne. **1826** J. WILSON *Noct. Ambr.* Wks. 1855 I. 174 When towns' bodies..are pestilential wi' filth and foulzie. **1833** *Act 3 & 4 Will. IV*, c. 46 §111 Scavengers..to remove the dung or fuilzie thereof. **1863** *Daily Rev.* 22 Oct., They received about £7000 for the fulzie of the town.
2. Manure.
1492 *Acta Dom. Conc.* 289/2 þe tatht & fulye of þe said nolt & scheip. **1721** KELLY *Sc. Prov.* 308 The Master's Foot is the best Foulzie.
3. *Comb.*: **fulyie-man,** a scavenger.
1826 J. WILSON *Noct. Ambr.* Wks. 1855 I. 197 A ginshower aneuch to sicken a fulzie-man.

† **'fulyie,** *v. Sc. Obs.* [Sc. var. of FOIL *v.*] *trans.* in various senses of FOIL. **a.** To trample on. **b.** To injure, destroy. **c.** To defeat, overcome. **d.** To dishonour, violate (a woman).
c **1450** *Golagros & Gaw.* 928 He..Pertly put with his pith at his pesane, And fulyeit of the fyne maill ma þan fyfty. *c* **1470** HENRY *Wallace* IV. 456 Sone wndir feit fulȝeid was men of wer. *Ibid.* XI. 22 Hagis, alais, be laubour that was thar, Fulȝeit and spilt. **1535** STEWART *Cron. Scot.* III. 350 Seand his men so fulȝeit in that fecht. **1536** BELLENDEN *Cron. Scot.* (1821) I. 165 He, with unbridlit lust, fulyeit his anttis. *a* **1807** *Christmas Ba'ing* xxvi. in J. Skinner *Misc. Coll. Poet.* (1809) 131 Tam Tull.. Saw him sae mony fuilzie [ed. **1805** foolyie].
Hence **'fulyeit** *ppl. a.*, exhausted, worn out. Also **'fulyear,** one who dishonours (women).
1508 DUNBAR *Tua mariit wemen* 63 Birdis..lattis thair fulȝeit feiris flie quhair thai pleis. *Ibid.* 86 Nothir febill, nor fant, nor fulȝeit in labour. **1536** BELLENDEN *Cron. Scot.* (1821) II. 20 He wes ane..fulyear of matronis.

fum (fʌm), *sb.* Also fung. [corruption of Chinese *fung* (*hwang*).] A fabulous bird (by Europeans commonly called the phœnix), one of the symbols of the imperial dignity in China.
1820 MOORE *Fum & Hum* Wks. VI. 132 One day the Chinese Bird of Royalty, Fum, Thus accosted our own Bird of Royalty, Hum. **1825** C. M. WESTMACOTT *Eng. Spy* I. 332 The fum or Chinese bird of royalty.

† **fum,** *v. Obs.* [echoic.]
1. *intr.* To play (on a guitar) with the fingers. Cf. STRUM, THRUM *vbs.*
1607 DEKKER & WEBSTER *Westw. Hoe* v. Wks. 1873 II. 349 Follow me, and fum as you goe. **1672** DRYDEN *Assignation* II. iii, He fums on the Guittar.
2. *trans.* ? To thump, beat. (The quot. is negro-Eng.; but cf. FUM-FUM b.)
1790 J. B. MORETON *W. Indies* 154 Then missess fum me wid long switch.. Me fum'd when me no.. me fum'd too if me do it.
So with reduplication **fum-fum,** (*a*) expressing the sound of a stringed instrument; (*b*) a thumping or beating.
1656 EARL MONM. *Advt. fr. Parnass.* 326 Trivial Fidlers, who play fum fum in the meanest Assemblies. **1885** *Blackw. Mag.* Oct. 522/2 He got fum-fum for purloining again.

fu'macious, *a. rare*[−0]. [f. L. *fūmāre* to smoke, after the analogy of Lat. adjs. in *-āc-em*: see -ACIOUS.] Fond of smoking.
1864 in WEBSTER.

fumade (fjuː'meɪd). Also 6–9 fumado, (7 fumatho). Also corruptly FAIR MAID. [app. ad. Sp. *fumado* (fu'maðo) pple., smoked; the spelling *fumatho* seems to indicate retention of the original pronunciation.] A smoked pilchard.
1599 NASHE *Lenten Stuffe* (1871) 61 Cornish pilchards, otherwise called Fumados. *c* **1600** NORDEN *Spec. Brit.*, *Cornw.* (1728) 23 The dryed ware they carrye into Spayne, Italie, Venice..and in those partes tooke name Fumados, for that they are dryed in the smoake. **1602** CAREW *Cornwall* 33 a. *a* **1661** FULLER *Worthies, Cornwall* I. (1662) 194 Then (by the name of Fumadoes), with Oyle and a Lemon, they [Pilchards] are meat for the mightiest Don in Spain. *c* **1682** J. COLLINS *Making of Salt* 105 This sort [of salted Herrings] are commonly called Fumathos. **1859** WALCOTT *Guide Devon & Cornw.* 525 Pilchards, which elsewhere are known as 'Fair maids', are here called Fumados.

'fumage[1]. *Hist.* [ad. med.L. *fūmāgium*, f. *fūm-us* smoke.] Hearth-money.
1755 in JOHNSON. **1765** BLACKSTONE *Comm.* I. vii. 323 As early as the conquest mention is made in domesday book of fumage or fuage, vulgarly called smoke farthings; which were paid by custom to the king for every chimney in the house. **1876** S. DOWELL *Taxes in Eng.* (1888) I. I. 10 A fumage, or tax of smoke farthings, or hearth tax.. ranges among those of the Anglo-Saxon period.

† **'fumage**[2]. *Obs.*[−0] [a. F. *fumage*, f. *fumer* to dung.] (See quot. 1725.)
1676–1732 COLES, *Fumage*, manuring with dung. **1725** BRADLEY *Fam. Dict.*, *Fumage*, a Term in Agriculture signifying Dung, or manuring with Dung.

fumagillin (ˌfjuːmə'dʒɪlɪn). *Biochem.* [f. mod.L. *Aspergillus fumigatus* (see def.) by rearrangement of some of its elements: see -IN[1].] An unstable colourless crystalline compound, $C_{26}H_{34}O_7$, which is produced by the growth of the fungus *Aspergillus fumigatus* and which has antibiotic activity against some viruses and protozoa.
1951 EBLE & HANSON in *Antibiotics & Chemotherapy* I. 54 The present paper concerns the isolation and properties of the active crystalline compound which we call fumagillin. **1967** E. PARYSKI tr. *Korzybski's Antibiotics* II. III. 1296 Encouraging results were achieved during the treatment with fumagillin of chronic intestinal amoebiasis of man.

fumagine ('fjuːmədʒɪn, -iːn). *Bot.* [Fr., f. FUMAGO.] A black superficial mould on plants, caused by fungi once grouped under the name *Fumago*, and associated with the honey-dew produced by certain insect pests.
[**1879** G. B. BUCKTON *Monogr. Brit. Aphides* II. 20 Passerini remarks that *Rhopalosiphum dianthi* is one of the most destructive Aphides in foreign greenhouses. They there give rise to a kind of mould on the plants they infest, to which the French give the name *Fumagine*.] **1913** D. GRANT tr. *Bourcart's Insecticides* 393 Fumagine is the term applied to the black coating which appears on certain plants infested by plant lice or cochineals (scale insects). This coating is formed by the black mycelium of a fungus which lives solely on the saccharine liquid, the honey-dew, which the insects project on the leaves.

‖**fumago** (fjuː'meɪgəʊ). [mod.L., f. *fūm-us* smoke.] (See quot.)
1887 *Jrnl. Soc. Arts* 2 Sept. 918/1 The soot dews, or fumagos, are a genus of fungi which are mainly epiphytes.. The fumago settles upon the upper sides of leaves.

fumant ('fjuːmənt), *a. Her.* [a. F. *fumant* pr. pple. of *fumer* to smoke.] (See quot.)
1828–40 BERRY *Encycl. Her.* I, *Fumant*, emitting vapour or smoke. **1889** in ELVIN *Dict. Her.*

fumarin ('fjuːmərɪn). *Chem.* [f. mod.L. *Fumaria* FUMITORY.] (See quot. 1864.) So **fu'maric acid** (see quot); **'fumarate,** a salt of this acid.
1864 WATTS *Dict. Chem.* II. 741 *Fumaric acid.* $C^4H^4O^4$.. An acid isomeric with maleic acid.. It is produced by the dehydration of malic acid. *Ibid.* 743 Some of the fumarates are crystalline, others pulverulent, and most of them have a mild taste. *Ibid.* 747 *Fumarine*, an organic base, contained in fumitory (*Fumaria officinalis*). **1876** HARLEY *Mat. Med.* 362 The lichen contains.. a little fumaric acid.

fumaroid ('fjuːmərɔɪd), *a. Chem.* [f. FUMAR(IC *a.* + -OID.] Resembling fumaric acid in having a *trans* configuration in geometrical isomerism.
1895 *Bloxam's Chem.* (ed. 8) 595 Many cases of stereoisomerism are believed to be explicable by formulæ resembling those given above, so that the expressions maleinoid and fumaroid structure are used. **1938** A. J. MEE tr. *Karrer's Org. Chem.* xvii. 256 It thus became common to call *cis*-ethylenic compounds, malenoid, and *trans*-ethylenic derivatives, fumaroid forms. **1964** *Internat. Encycl. Chem. Sci.* 480/1 *Fumaroid form*, the axial symmetric or *trans*-form of ethylene geometrical isomers, named from fumaric acid.

fumarole ('fjuːmərəʊl). Also fumarol, fumerole. [ad. F. *fumerolle* (*fumarolle*): see FEMERELL.] A hole or vent through which vapour issues from a volcano; a smoke-hole.
1811 PINKERTON *Petral.* II. 548 A more proper name for these ignited hills and spots would be fumarols. **1830** LYELL *Princ. Geol.* I. 342 Fumeroles or small crevices in the cone through which hot vapours are disengaged. **1852** *Blackw. Mag.* LXXI. 522 Cracks..are produced in the solid rocks; smoking fumeroles appear. **1881** W. G. MARSHALL *Thro. Amer.* xv. 315 The Californian Geysers are rather fumaroles —an immense collection of vents from which hot air is emitted.

fumarolic (fjuːmə'rɒlɪk), *a.* [f. FUMAROLE + -IC.] Of or belonging to a fumarole; formed by a fumarole.
1903 *Science* 3 Apr. 543 The placing of various ore deposits of many well-known districts in such classes as fumarolic, solfataric, pneumatolytic, etc...seemed to the speaker to be premature. **1944** C. A. COTTON *Volcanoes* xii. 203 In this case the fumarolic activity continued for ten years. **1965** G. J. WILLIAMS *Econ. Geol. N.Z.* xiv. 220/2 Fleming showed the gypsum to be prominent in altered deposits at the sites of extinct or dying fumarolic activity.

fumaroyl ('fjuːmərəʊɪl). *Chem.* [f. as FUMARYL + -OYL.]
A bivalent radical, –CO·CH:CH·CO–, derived from fumaric acid.
1952 *Chem. Abstr.* XLVI. 13043/1 (Index), Fumaroyl chloride. **1965** *Nomencl. Org. Chem.* (*I.U.P.A.C.*) C. 236 Fumaroyl (preferred to *trans*-butenedioyl). **1970** R. W. MCGILVERY *Biochem.* xvii. 387 Another oxidase..cleaves the ring to form the *cis*-unsaturated compound, C-maleoylacetoacetate. An isomerase converts this to the *trans*-compound, C-fumaroylacetoacetate.

fumart, var. of FOUMART.

fumaryl ('fjuːmərɪl, -aɪl). *Chem.* [f. FUMAR(IC *a.* + -YL.] = FUMAROYL.
1864 WATTS *Dict. Chem.* II. 747 Chloride of Fumaryl. **1963** *Jrnl. Pharmaceut. Sci.* LII. 1168 There are marked differences in biological potency between maleyl and fumaryl dicholines compared with succinyl dicholine.

fumatho, obs. form of FUMADE.

† **fu'matic.** *Obs. rare*[−1]. [f. L. *fūm-us* smoke; ? a derisive parody of PNEUMATIC.]
1641 *True Char. Untrue Bishop* 7 He hateth his enthusiastick fumaticks, who talk so much of the Spirit.

fumatory ('fjuːmətərɪ), *sb.* Also incorrectly fumitory. [f. Lat. type **fūmātōrium*, f. *fūmāre*: see next and -ORY.]
†**1.** A censer. *Obs. rare*[−1].
c **1530** in Gutch *Coll. Cur.* II. 318 The mending of a Fumitory waying more then it dyd before by d. oz.
2. A place set apart for smoking or fumigating purposes.
a **1704** T. BROWN *Wks.* (1730) II. 179 To sot away your time in Mongo's fumitory among a parcel of old smoak-dry'd cadators. **1842** *Fraser's Mag.* XXVI. 361 The great united talent of the age..had alighted..on this great 'fumatory' [Manchester]. **1851** S. JUDD *Margaret* II. v. (1871) 238 We have erected a Fumitory for the more complete cleansing of all that pass this way.

fumatory ('fjuːmətərɪ), *a.* [f. L. type **fūmātōri-us*, f. *fūmāre* to smoke, f. *fūmus*: see FUME *sb.* and -ORY.] Of or pertaining to (tobacco-) smoking.
1847 *Blackw. Mag.* LXI. 744 This fumatory process proceeded for some time almost in silence.

† **fumay,** *v. Hunting. Obs. rare.* Also 5 femay, femy, fymay. [? ad. AF. **fu-*, *femeiier*; cf. OF. *femeis* and *femier*, *fumier* dunghill, *femer* (mod.F. *fumer*) to manure; the ultimate source is L. *fimus* dung.] *intr.* Of certain animals, esp. the hare: To evacuate excrement.
1486 [see CROTEY *v.*, FEN *v.*[1]].

fumble ('fʌmb(ə)l), *v.* Also 6 fomble. [Of obscure origin: equivalent forms exist in other Teut. langs.; cf. Du. *fommelen*, LG. *fummeln*, *fommeln*, Sw. *fumla*, to fumble, grope; prob. onomatopœic; cf. *bumble*, *jumble*, *mumble*, *stumble*, also FAMBLE, FIMBLE *vbs.* Possibly the formation of the word may have been in part suggested by the sb. which appears as OE. *folm(e*, OS. **folm* (pl. *folmos*, OHG. *folma* hand; cf. ON. *falma* (Icel. *fálma*) to grope, with which Sw. *famla*, Da. *famle* (= FAMBLE *v.*) are commonly regarded as identical.]
1. a. *intr.* To use one's hands or fingers awkwardly or ineffectually; to grope about. ***to fumble at***: to make clumsy attempts at doing or handling (something). ***to fumble for*** or ***after***: to make clumsy attempts to reach or grasp. Also ***to fumble about***.
1534 MORE *On the Passion* Wks. 1293/1 The dyuel.. should not be able to reache hys [Christe's] heade.. but only to fumble about his foote. **1563–87** FOXE *A. & M.* (1596)

1858/2 She desired him to looke in his Testament. Then he fumbled and sought about him for one. 1599 Shaks. *Hen. V*, ii. iii. 14 For after I saw him fumble with the Sheets, and play with Flowers.. I knew there was but one way. 1602 Dekker *Satirom.* Wks. 1873 I. 219 What made these paire of shittle-cockes heere? What doe they fumble for? *a* 1680 Butler *Rem.* (1759) II. 108 Those, that cannot play, delight to fumble on Instruments. 1739 R. Bull tr. *Dedekindus' Grobianus* 251 He vainly fumbles at the fatal Door. 1768–74 Tucker *Lt. Nat.* (1852) I. 288 If you set a man with gloves on, or a rustic whose hands are hard by labour to take off a single sheet, he will fumble about a long while. 1809 W. Irving *Knickerb.* (1861) 169 Seeing him lay down his pipe and begin to fumble with his walking-staff. 1855 Macaulay *Hist. Eng.* III. 361 The soldiers were still fumbling with the muzzles of their guns.. when the whole flood of Macleans, Macdonalds, and Camerons came down. 1859 Kingsley *Misc.* (1860) II. 139 He.. fumbled for the bible in his boot. 1874 Burnand *My Time* xiv. 119 'Let me see' said [he].. fumbling about in all his pockets.

b. *transf.* and *fig.*

1612 T. Taylor *Comm. Titus* iii. 5 He will be nibling and fumbling at all these as far as he dare. 1656 H. More *Enthus. Tri.* (1662) 1 The foulness of his Mind makes him fumble very dotingly in the use thereof. 1678 Cudworth *Intell. Syst.* 683 Our Mechanick or Atomick Theists, will have their Atoms, never so much as once to have Fumbled, in these their Fortuitous Motions. 1686 N. Cox *Gentl. Recreat.* v. (ed. 3) 47 If he [horse] fumbles with his Corn, then give him no more at that time. 1784 J. Barry in *Lect. Paint.* vi. (1848) 223 Any artist.. fumbling through three or four strata of colour before he can find them. 1870 M. D. Conway *Earthw. Pilgr.* xxiii. 267 Englishmen are still fumbling about Mount Sinai in the East.

c. ? quasi-*trans.* with complement.

1864 Lowell *Fireside Trav.* 110 A hostler fumbled the door open. 1887 *Punch* 19 Mar. 143/2 Dizzy, then Premier, fumbled his eyeglass into position.

2. a. *trans.* To handle awkwardly or with nervous clumsiness. Also with *on*, *out*, *over*.

1606 Shaks. *Tr. & Cr.* i. iii. 174 And with a palsie fumbling on his Gorget, Shake in and out the Riuet. *a* 1658 Cleveland *To T.C.* 17 A Nut which when thou'st crack'd and fumbled o'er Thou'lt find the Squirrel has been there before. 1681 Dryden *Spanish Friar* i. i, His greasy bald-pate choir Came fumbling o'er the beads, in such an agony, They told 'em false for fear. 1756 *Connoisseur* No. 134 (1774) IV. 228 The old women.. fumbling over their tattered testaments till they have found the text. 1801 Gabrielli *Myst. Husband* I. 235 The fugitives.. having fumbled out their bundles in the dark, first handed them to him. 1840 Thackeray *Bedford-Row Conspir.* i, [He] came forward, looking very red, and fumbling two large kid gloves. 1894 Sala *Things I have seen* II. xx. 254 The coin.. I very soon tarnished by fumbling it.. between my hot, moist little fingers.

fig. 1895 *Westm. Gaz.* 30 May 3/1 His incident must come to him naturally or he fumbles it.

b. *spec.* In games with a ball, *to fumble the ball*: to fail to take it 'cleanly'; to stop or catch it clumsily.

c. *to fumble one's way*: to find it by groping.

1801 Gabrielli *Myst. Husb.* III. 80 She started up, and fumbled her way down the dark stairs. 1879 G. W. Cable *Old Creole Days* 13 Late that night a small square man.. fumbled his way into the damp entrance.

3. To wrap up clumsily, huddle together. Also with *up*.

c 1572 Gascoigne *Fruites Warre* (1831) 212 Constreynd to sit.. Close in a corner fumbled vp for feare. 1588 Shaks. *Tit. A.* iv. ii. 58 What dost thou wrap and fumble in thine armes? 1606 —— *Tr. & Cr.* iv. iv. 48 As many farwels as be stars in heauen, With distinct breath, and consign'd kisses to them, He fumbles vp into a loose adiew. 1621 Molle *Camerar. Liv. Libr.* iii. xiii. 189 They send them [their women] forth so couered, vailed, and fumbled up. 1647 Fuller *Good Th. in Worse T.* (1841) 140 So many fumble this, last and next weeks devotion all in a prayer. 1681 [see fumbling *ppl. a.* d]. 1830 *Fraser's Mag.* I. 342 The attenuated, sham, filagree work.. wherewith Mr. Thomas Moore has thought fit to fumble up the personages of his 'Lalla Rookh'.

4. *slang.* (Cf. fumbler b, fumbling *ppl. a.* c.) Also *absol.* or *intr.*

1508 Dunbar *Tua mariit wemen* 134 3it leit I neuer that larbar.. fumyll me, without a fee gret. *c* 1690 *Sat. on Lawyers* in *Collect. Poems* 18 Old Maynard.. Who mumbles all Day, and fumbles all Night. 1754 Shebbeare *Matrimony* (1766) II. 239 The old Man.. rejoicing to see her return in Good-Humour, fumbled away the Night. 1762 Goldsm. *Nash* 180 Impotent posterity would in vain fumble to produce his fellow.

5. a. *intr.* To hesitate in speaking; to speak haltingly or indistinctly; to mumble, mutter.

1563 *Homilies* ii. *Agst. Gluttony* (1859) 305 A drunkard.. fumbleth and stammereth in his speech. 1591 *Troub. Raigne K. John* ii. (1611) 110 He fumbleth in the mouth, His speech doth faile. 1600 Holland *Livy* xlii. xxvi. (1609) 1130 Being.. found fumbling in their answere [*hæsitantibus in responso*] they were commaunded to void out of the Counsel-chamber. 1611 [see famble *v.*]. 1647 Trapp *Comm. Matt.* xxvii. 38 His tongue did so fumble and falter in his head. 1704 Cibber *Careless Husb.* i. i, How silly a man fumbles for an excuse, when he is a little ashamed of being in love. 1828 Scott *F.M. Perth* viii, Never lose time fumbling and prating about it.

b. *trans.* To speak (words, etc.) indistinctly or hesitatingly. Also with *out*, *up*.

1555 Eden *Decades* 46 He fumbeleth certeyne confounded woordes with hym selfe. 1579 Fulke *Heskins' Parl.* 370 M. Heskins fombleth out the matter with a foolish caueat. 1583 Stanyhurst *Æneis* iii. (Arb.) 74, I.. With stutting stamering at length thus fumbled an answer. 1584 Fenner *Def. Ministers* (1587) 121 He blameth vs for fumbling vp those things, which we answered distinctlie inough. 1602 Marston *Antonio's Rev.* iv. iii. Wks. 1856 I. 127 She fumbled out, thanks good, and so she dide. 1749 Chesterf. *Lett.* (1792) II. ccxiii. 319 As soon as I had fumbled out this answer.

6. Forming combs., as ***fumble-fisted***, ***-footed*** adjs.

1847 Halliwell, *Fumble-fisted*, very awkward in handling things. *Suffolk.* 1877 A. Sewell *Black Beauty* xxxi. 149, I don't know what is the matter with this horse, he goes very fumble-footed. 1926 A. B. Smith *Studies & Caprices* 150 Music which even the most fumble-fisted can play with pleasure.

Hence **'fumbled** *ppl. a.* Also **'fumble** *sb.*, a piece of fumbling, a bungling attempt at something; *spec.* in ball games, a clumsy handling of the ball; †also, confused utterance, mumbling.

1647 Ward *Simp. Cobler* 84 The world's a well strung fidle, mans tongue the quill, That fills the world with fumble for want of skill. *c* 1831 J. Wilson in Lang *Life & Lett. Lockhart* (1897) II. 109 He [Wilson] called Lockhart's remarks 'a feeble fumble of falsehood'. 1884 F. D. Millet in *Harper's Mag.* Dec. 134/1 The newspapers grew sticky, fumbled, and worn at the hands of the frequent readers. 1895 *Daily Chron.* 17 Jan. 6/4 At the first fumble of a Surrey back, Maturin rushed round.

fumbler ('fʌmblə(r)). Also 6 fumblar, *Sc.* fumler. [f. fumble *v.* + -er[1].] One who fumbles, in senses of the vb. ***cake fumbler***: see cake *sb.* 9.

1519 Horman *Vulg.* 31 No man shulde rebuke.. a stuttar or fumblar. *c* 1800 K. White *Rem.* II. 49 The work of, Sir, your humble Servant (Who, though I say't, am no such fumbler). 1826 J. Wilson *Noct. Ambr.* Wks. 1855 I. 92, I must not let down the character of the work, to flatter a few feckless fumblers. 1879 Geo. Eliot *Theo. Such* viii. 145 A man.. may be a mere fumbler in physiology and yet show a keen insight into human motives.

b. *slang.* (See quot. *a* 1700.)

1640 Brome *Sparagus Garden* ii. ii, What stay we for, can you tell fumbler? 1679 Oldham *Sat. Woman* 129 Wks. (1698) i. 147. *a* 1700 B. E. *Dict. Cant. Crew*, *Fumbler*, an unperforming Husband, one that is insufficient. 1719 D'Urfey *Pills* V. 349 Wench Fumblers give ear ev'ry Man. 1748 Smollett *Rod. Rand.* xi. (1804) 56 In the mean-time give me a kiss, you old fumbler. 1818 Southey *Lett.* (1856) III. 90 A married couple, who have had no children, after a certain number of years, are compelled by their neighbours to give what we call a Fumbler's Feast.

fumbling ('fʌmblɪŋ), *vbl. sb.* [f. fumble *v.* + -ing[1].] The action of the vb. fumble.

1562 J. Heywood *Prov. & Epigr.* (1867) 217 This man in his breech feelyng such fumblyng. 1601 Weever *Mirr. Mart.* C ij, Now are we dwarfs, they [our issue] will be pismires then, This is the fumbling of our aged men. 1645 Milton *Colast.* Wks. (1851) 351 Your second Argument, without more tedious fumbling is briefly thus. 1762 Stevenson *Crazy Tales* 49 There's a disorder we call Fumbling, Amongst the men call'd Fighting shy. 1875 Kinglake *Crimea* (1877) V. i. 366 That impotent fumbling after carbines or pistols. 1892 Jessopp *Stud. by Recluse* Pref. (1893) 15, I do not call these stray papers Essays, but mere Studies—fumblings if you will.

'fumbling, *ppl. a.* [f. as prec. + -ing[2].]

a. That fumbles or gropes about; also, characterized by fumbling.

1847 Emerson *Poems* (1857) 62 The frost-king ties my fumbling feet. 1848 Dickens *Dombey* xxxiv, She attired herself, with fumbling fingers. 1865 Max Müller *Chips* (1880) II. xxv. 286 The fumbling efforts of gentlemen in removing their gloves before shaking hands. 1889 H. F. Wood *Englishm. of Rue Caïn* v, A spare individual.. entered.. after a fumbling rap at the door.

b. *fig.* That does something clumsily or awkwardly; also, hesitating in speech, mumbling.

1532 More *Confut. Tindale* Wks. 698/1 Not anye true feelynge faythe, but a false fumblyng fantasye. *a* 1577 Gascoigne *Herbs, Weedes*, etc. Wks. (1587) 114 Wyth hollow voice and fumbling toong thus spoke. 1597 Hooker *Eccl. Pol.* v. lxii. §14 Such are their fumbling shifts. 1602 Marston *Antonio's Rev.* i. i. Wks. 1856 I. 75, I could eate Thy fumbling throat, for thy lagd censure. 1638 Baker tr. *Balzac's Lett.* (vol. III) 258 He hath.. but a very fumbling speech. 1681 Hickeringill *Vind. Truth* ii. 36 A fibling.. fumbling Arch-Deacon. 1848 Kingsley *Saint's Trag.* v. iii, There are wrongs The fumbling piecemeal law can never touch.

c. Sexually impotent. Cf. fumble *v.* 4 and fumbler b.

1576 Newton *Lemnie's Complex.* 81 b, They be vnto carnall coiture fumbling, slow, and not greatly therto addicted. *a* 1703 Pomfret *Poet. Wks.* (1833) 17 Dull old age, with fumbling labour, cloys Before the bliss. 1710 *Brit. Apollo* III. No. 77. 3/2 Their Fumbling Neighbours.. cannot Enjoy The Pleasure of getting a Girl, or a Boy. 1786 Burns *Scotch Drink* xii, How fumblin cuifs their dearies slight.

fig. *a* 1577 Gascoigne *Gardninges* 32, *Herbs* (1587) 164 If barreyn soyle, why then it chaungeth hewe, It fadeth faste, it flits to fumbling yeares. 1684 Otway *Prol. Lee's Constantine*, Fumbling, itching Rhimers of the town [proud] T' adopt some base-born Song that's not their own. 1689 Hickeringill *Ceremony-Monger* Introd. *Wks.* (1716) II. 500 Impotency is supply'd by Fumbling Registers.

d. (See fumble *v.* 3.)

1681 Crowne *Hen. VI*, i. 3 Pox o' these fumbling robes! How came my warlike spirit wrapt in these Formalities, that hold my hands from blood?

Hence **'fumblingly** *adv.*

1598 Florio, *Palpegone*, gropingly, fumblingly. 1636 B. Jonson *Discov.*, *Perspicuitas* (Rtldg.) 760/2 Many good scholars speak but fumblingly. 1870 *Daily News* 9 Nov., He is obliged to put on his spectacles fumblingly.

fume (fjuːm), *sb.* Also 5 feum, 6 fewme. [a. OF. *fum* masc. = Pr. *fum*, Sp. *humo* (earlier *fumo*), Pg., It. *fumo*:—L. *fūmus* smoke; also OF. *fume* fem. in the same sense, a derivative (like *fumée*, which has been retained in mod.F.) of *fumer*, fume *v.* The Eng. sb. may be in part a direct adaptation from the Latin.]

I. 1. a. The volatile matter produced by and usually accompanying combustion; smoke. Also with *a* and in *pl.* *Obs.* or *arch.*

? *a* 1400 *Pety Iob* 279 in *Hampole's Wks.* (Horstm.) II. 384 As frome the fyre departeth fume, So body and sowle a-sundre goth. 1447 Bokenham *Seyntys* (Roxb.) 56 Wyth the fume he [angel] toke to heven his flyht. 1549–62 Sternhold & H. *Ps.* xxi. 9 Like an Oven burn them, Lord, in fiery flames and fume. 1618 Bolton *Florus* iii. iv. 176 By this kinde of mockage defiling death as well with fire as fume. 1703 Pope *Thebais* 600 While yet thin fumes from dying sparks arise. 1783 Priestley in *Phil. Trans.* LXXIII. 403 A copious black fume came from it. 1854–6 Patmore *Angel in H.* ii. Epil. (1879) 259 A fresh-lit fire Sends forth to heaven great shows of fume.

b. Odorous smoke (*e.g.* that of incense, tobacco). † ***Indian fume***: tobacco smoke.

c 1400 *Sowdone Bab.* 681 Thai brente Frankensense That smoked up so stronge The Fume in her presence. 1483 Caxton *Gold. Leg.* 34 b/1 It hath vertue tascende by the lightnes of the fume [of encence]. *c* 1550 Lloyd *Treas. Health* (1585) C i, Fume made of Roes lether, doth myghtyly sterre hym vp. 1555 Eden *Decades* 138 Whose fume is holsome ageynst reumes and heauynesse of the heade. 1621 G. Sandys *Ovid's Met.* xi. (1626) 230 Meanewhile Alcyone holy fumes presents To all the Gods. 1627 Drayton *Moon Calf* Poems (1748) 172 In some six days journey, doth consume Ten pounds in suckets, and the Indian fume. 1697 Bp. Patrick *Comm. Exod.* xxx. 35 One of the most antient Ways of worshipping God; the first Men making a Fume, by burning parts of Trees, and Shrubs. 1784 Cowper *Task* iv. 473 Curling clouds Of Indian fume. 1838 Dickens *Nich. Nick.* ii, And the fumes of choice tobacco scent the air.

†c. Something used or prepared for producing aromatic vapour. *Obs.*

1540–1 Elyot *Image Gov.* 41 Duryng the time of his execucion the Emperour commaunded the beedile to crie, With fume shall he die, who fumes hath sold. 1656 Ridgley *Pract. Physick* 219 Rulandus makes a fume of one dram of white Amber to take at the Mouth. 1665 Pepys *Diary* 4 Nov., They suspect by their sending for plaister and fume, that it may be the plague. 1679 Wood *Life* (O.H.S.) II. 451 A julep, 3*s.* 6*d.*; a fume 2*s.* 1722 De Foe *Plague* (1884) 207 They had burnt a great variety of Fumes and Perfumes in.. the Rooms.

2. Odour or odorous exhalation (either fragrant or offensive) emitted from a substance, flower, etc.

c 1400 *Lanfranc's Cirurg.* 251 Breke hem [braunchis of fenel] a litil wiþ þi teeþ, and þan þou schalt blowe in his iȝe.. þat þe fume of þe fenel mowe entre into his iȝe. 1483 Caxton *Gold. Leg.* 10 b/1 The fume & stenche of donge. 1509 Hawes *Past. Pleas.* iv. iv, Aromatyke lycoure, Fragraunt of fume. 1599 *Life More* in Wordsw. *Eccl. Biog.* (1853) II. 47 The fume of hilicampana is very pleasing. 1610 Fletcher *Faithf. Shepherdess* v. ii, Send a fume, and keep the air Pure and wholesome. 1658 A. Fox *Wurtz' Surg.* ii. xiv. 115 When these [poultesses] are taken off.. there comes a great fume from the Wound. 1718 *Freethinker* No. 92 ¶6 She.. cannot bear the Fumes of the Table. 1739 R. Bull tr. *Dedekindus' Grobianus* 17 A horrid Fume shall straight your Crime proclaim To ev'ry Nose. 1865 Swinburne *Hymn to Proserpine* 96 And the wind falls faint as it blows with the fume of the flowers of the night.

3. †a. Vapour or steam given out by bodies when heated. *Obs.*

c 1400 *Lanfranc's Cirurg.* 278 Stoppe it [þe vessel] faste, þat þer mowe come out þerof no fume. 1544 Phaer *Regim. Lyfe* (1553) C iv b, Receyuing the fume of the sayd decoccyon wythin the eyes. 1607 Topsell *Four-f. Beasts* (1658) 93 The liver of a Roe sod in salt water, and the eyes of a purblinde man held over the fume or reek thereof, are cured of their blindeness. 1695 Woodward *Nat. Hist. Earth* iv. (1723) 236 Flowing out of the Mouth in Form of a Fume, or crasser Vapour.

b. The vapour given off by acids and volatile substances; said esp. of exhalations or vapours which are irritant, stifling, or the like. Rare in *sing.*

1665 Hooke *Microgr.* 229 Looking at bodies through the fumes of *Aqua fortis.* 1680 Boyle *Scept. Chem.* i. 87 The Predominant Fire will Carry up all the Volatile Elements Confusedly in one Fume. 1774 Goldsm. *Nat. Hist.* (1776) I. 319 The fumes of hot iron, copper, or any other heated metal. 1800 *Med. Jrnl.* IV. 467 The nitrat of pneum.. discharges the acid in red fumes. 1834 J. Forbes *Laennec's Dis. Chest* (ed. 4) 65 The inhalation of acrid fumes.. sometimes gives rise to pulmonary catarrh. 1879 Geo. Gladstone in *Cassell's Techn. Educ.* IV. 17/1 The fume when given off from the furnace appears as a dense white smoke.

c. An exhalation or watery vapour rising from the earth, the sea, etc.

1549 *Compl. Scot.* vi. 38 Al corrupit humiditeis, ande caliginus fumis.. that hed bene generit in the sycond regione of the ayr. 1602 Marston *Ant. & Mel.* i. Wks. 1856 I. 11, I descry a fume Creeping from out the bosome of the deepe. 1635 N. Carpenter *Geog. Del.* ii. i. 12 The vpper face of the Earth.. sendeth forth many times certaine hot fumes and vapours. 1755 B. Martin *Mag. Arts & Sc.* xv. 103 A prodigious Quantity of Fume and Vapours flying off from the Body of the Comet. 1828 J. H. Moore *Pract. Navig.* (ed. 20) 127 The sun's rays upon the earth cause vapours or fumes to be continually rising from it. 1875 M. McIlwraith *Guide Wigtownshire* 62 The fissure is filled with fume and spray.

4. A vapour or exhalation produced as an 'excrement' of the body; *esp.* a noxious vapour supposed formerly to rise to the brain from the stomach (now chiefly as the result of drinking 'strong' or alcoholic liquors).

c **1400** *Lanfranc's Cirurg.* 163 þe lungis drawiþ eir into þe herte, for to do awei þe fume and þe untemprid heete of þe herte. *a* **1420** HOCCLEVE *De Reg. Princ.* 3880 Whan the paunch is fulle, A fume clymbethe up into the hede. **1548–77** VICARY *Anat.* ii. (1888) 24 The Nayles..are a superfluitie of members, engendred of great earthly smoke or fume. **1667** MILTON *P.L.* IX. 1050 Grosser sleep, Bred of unkindly fumes. **1697** POTTER *Antiq. Greece* II. xiii. (1715) 309 Dreams were believ'd to proceed from the Fumes of the last Night's Supper. **1719** DE FOE *Crusoe* II. viii, The wine ..raise[d] disagreeable fumes from the stomach into the head. **1806** *Gazetteer Scotl.* (ed. 2) 203 The fumes of the whisky had taken possession of his brain. **1844** THIRLWALL *Greece* VIII. lxiii. 240 The fumes of the wine at length thawed their reserve.

II. Figurative senses.

5. Something comparable to smoke or vapour as being unsubstantial, transient, imaginary, etc.

When used with reference to flattery, the word has often a mixture of the notions of 'incense' (1 b), and of sense 6.

1531 ELYOT *Gov.* II. i, Fainte praise that is goten with feare or by flaterars gyuen..is but fume whiche is supported by silence prouoked by menacis. **1592** SHAKS. *Rom. & Jul.* I. i. 196 Loue, is a smoake made with the fume of sighes. **1605** BACON *Adv. Learn.* II. i. §6. 10 Such Naturall Philosophie..shall not vanish in the fume of subtile, sublime, or delectable speculation. **1613–18** DANIEL *Coll. Hist. Eng.* (1626) 4 Claudius..hauing much of the fume of glory, and little fire to raise it otherwhere. **1621** BURTON *Anat. Mel.* Democr. to Rdr. (1651) 34 To smother him with fumes and eulogies. **1648** MILTON *Observ. Art. Peace* Wks. (1851) 566 As if the known and try'd Constancy of that valiant Gentleman were to be bought with Court fumes. **1784** COWPER *Task* III. 172 Great pity too..That..They should go out in fume and be forgot. **1843** LEFEVRE *Life Trav. Phys.* I. I. ix. 198 The fumes of philosophical reasoning were dissipated by more material..ingredients. **1871** R. ELLIS *Catullus* liv. 3 Libo's airs to a fume of art refine them.

6. Something which 'goes to the head' and clouds the faculties or the reason.

1574 *Mirr. Mag., Sabrine* viii, For gelouzie..With frensies fume, enragde hir restles braine. **1610** SHAKS. *Temp.* v. i. 67 Their rising sences Begin to chace the ignorant fumes that mantle Their cleerer reason. **1691** HARTCLIFFE *Virtues* 391 Vertue doth refine and purifie our Minds, by stifling the fumes and steams of every Vice and Passion. **1712** ADDISON *Spect.* No. 281 ¶14 It dissipated the Fumes of Sleep and left me in an Instant broad awake. **1761–2** HUME *Hist. Eng.* (1806) IV. lx. 517 The fumes of enthusiasm presently dissipate. **1865** M. ARNOLD *Ess. Crit.* ii. 75 Sometimes his head gets a little hot with the fumes of patriotism.

7. a. A fit of anger, an irritable or angry mood. Chiefly in phrase ***in a fume***.

1522 SKELTON *Why not to Court* 421 In a fume or an hete Wardeyn of the Flete Set hym faste by the fete. **1535** JOYE *Apol. Tindale* (Arb.) 27 Softe & pacient, good wordis Tindale: and no furiouse fumes. **1539** TAVERNER *Gard. Wysed.* I. 27 b, He was in suche a fume, that he ranne vpon the yonge man, to haue beaten him. **1602** MARSTON *Antonio's Rev.* I. v. Wks. 1856 I. 88 Tis not true valors pride ..To stab in fume of blood. **1654** TRAPP *Comm. Neh.* iii. 20 He burst out in a heat, being angry both at himself and others..and in an holy fume, finished quickly. **1775** JOHNSON *Lett. to Mrs. Thrale* 13 June, Every now and then a lady in a fume withdraws her name. *a* **1839** PRAED *Poems* (1864) II. 96 There's Serjeant Cross, in fume and fret. **1865** CARLYLE *Fredk. Gt.* XXI. vi. X. 103 Kaiser Joseph, in a fume at this, shot-off an express to Bohemia.

b. One who is apt to 'get into a fume'. *rare*$^{-1}$.

1768 STERNE *Sent. Journ.* (1775) II. 123 The notary's wife was a little fume of a woman.

III. 8. *attrib.* and *Comb.*, as ***fume-black***, ***-blind***; **fume-chamber**, **-cupboard**, **-hood**, **-pipe**, ventilation contrivances for getting rid of noxious gases generated in laboratory work; †**fume-gallant** (humorously), a smoker; **fume-worts**, a book-name for plants of the N.O. *Fumariaceæ* (Lindley *Veg. K.* 1846, p. 435).

1573 *Art of Limming* 6 To make a fume blacke called Sable. *a* **1618** SYLVESTER *Du Bartas, Panaretus* 791 A rash Excesse of Courage boiling fell; whose fume-blind force.. Resembles right a sightlesse Polyphem. **1905** *Strand Mag.* Apr. 422/1 It is..fitted up with..'muffles'..fume chambers, [etc.]. **1913** *Oxf. Univ. Gaz.* 4 June 943/2 [Apparatus of the pharmacological laboratory] Fume chamber. **1921** A. E. MUNBY *Laboratories* 35 Fume cupboards or draught closets..consist of a wood-framed glazed case in which the experiment is performed, with some special means of ventilation. **1938** *Jrnl. R. Aeronaut. Soc.* XLII. 744 The bath is placed in a fume cupboard with forced ventilation. **1621** VENNER *Tobacco* C 4 b, Let these fume-gallants enioy their vanity. **1921** A. E. MUNBY *Laboratories* 34 Fume hoods on the benches are sometimes provided in the form of a metal or wood tube or boxing with a small hood 9 or 10 ins. square attached to a ventilating trunk in the bench. **1965** *Economist* 25 Dec. 1437/3 (*caption*) Fume hood. **1921** A. E. MUNBY *Laboratories* 44 Fume pipe for benches or lecture table.

Hence **'fumeless** *a.*, free from fumes.

1864 in WEBSTER; and in later Dicts.

fume (fjuːm), *v.* Also 7 feum. [a. F. *fumer* = Pr., Sp., Pg. *fumar*, It. *fumare*:—L. *fūmāre*, f. *fūm-us*: see prec. sb.]

1. a. *trans.* To apply smoke or fumes to; to fumigate.

c **1400** *Lanfranc's Cirurg.* 179 Herwiþ anoynte hise heeris, and firste þou schalt fumie hem wiþ sulphur. **1544** PHAER *Pestilence* (1553) L vj a, The Egipcyans were wont to fume their houses..with turpentine or rosin. **1612** WOODALL *Surg. Mate* Wks. (1653) 74 *Succinum*..is good..to fume a ship or house in time of infectious aires. **1669** WORLIDGE *Syst. Agric.* (1681) 217 Fuming the holes with Brimstone, Garlick, and other unsavoury things, will drive them out. **1741** *Compl. Fam.-Piece* I. v. 267 First fume the Vessel with Brimstone.

b. To perfume with incense; to burn incense before or offer incense to.

1641 MILTON *Reform.* I They hallowed it, they fumed it, they sprinkled it. **1700** DRYDEN *Fables, Ceyx & Alcyone* 241 She fum'd the temples with an od'rous flame. **1849–53** ROCK *Ch. of Fathers* IV. xii. 186 The celebrant..went up to the altar, and..fum'd it all about with incense.

fig. **1784** COWPER *Task* v. 266 They demi-deify and fume him so.

†**c.** To perfume. *Obs.*

a **1483** *Liber Niger* in *Househ. Ord.* (1790) 40 That the kings robes, doublettes, shetes & sheortes be fumyd, by all the yere, of the yeoman pothecary. **1592** GREENE *Poems* 113 Crisps and scarfs, worn a la morisco, Fumed with sweets. **1607** MARSTON *What You Will* III. i, Now are the Lawne sheetes fum'd with Vyolets. **1680** SHADWELL *Woman-Captain* II. Wks. 1720 III. 361 Let me have costlier scents, and fume the room. **1740** DYER *Ruins of Rome* 501 Chian Wines with Incence fum'd.

†**d.** To preserve by smoking; to smoke-dry (provisions). *Obs.*

1602 CAREW *Cornwall* I. (1723) 33 Those [fish] that serue for the hotter Countries of Spaine and Italie, they vsed at first to fume, by..drying them with the smoake of a soft and continuall fire. **1661** EVELYN *Fumifugium* Misc. Writ. (1805) I. 228 If one hang up gammons of bacon, beefe, or other flesh to fume, and prepare it in the chimnies.

e. *Photogr.* To expose to the fumes of ammonia.

1890 ABNEY *Treat. Photogr.* (ed. 6) 164 By fuming the film with the vapour of ammonia..increased vigour is imparted to the print. **1890** *Anthony's Photogr. Bull.* III. 68 Some say fume ten minutes, and some say an hour.

2. a. *intr.* To emit fumes, smoke, or vapour.

c **1532** DEWES *Introd. Fr.* in *Palsgr.* 946 To fume, *fumer*. **1600** FAIRFAX *Tasso* VIII. 74 Like boyling liquor..That fumeth, swelleth high and bubbleth fast. **1613** PURCHAS *Pilgrimage* (1614) 539 A Censer is there left fuming all the day and night. **1621** G. SANDYS *Ovid's Met.* II. (1626) 29 The Poles aboue At either end do fume. **1743** *Lond. & Country Brew.* IV. (ed. 2) 306 It will make the Drink fret and fume at the Bung. **1784** COWPER *Task* v. 56 A short tube That fumes beneath his nose. **1791–1823** D'ISRAELI *Cur. Lit.* (1859) II. 259 On other occasions, they put burnt old shoes to fume in the censers. **1853** W. GREGORY *Inorg. Chem.* (ed. 3) 119 The acid appears as a very volatile liquid ..fuming in the air. **1878** C. D. WARNER *In the Wilderness* vi. 143 The fire sputters and fumes.

fig. **1620** in Farr *S.P. Jas. I* (1848) 74 Lust's a fire.. Lighting never, ever fuming. **1633** G. HERBERT *Temple, Nature* ii, If thou shalt let this venome lurk, And in suggestions fume and work. **1840** DICKENS *Barn. Rudge* iv, The spiritual essence or soul of Sim would sometimes fume within that precious cask, his body.

†**b.** *trans.* To cause to emit fumes. *Obs. rare.*

1652 GAULE *Magastrom.* 248 Frankincense being fumed, and candles being lighted. **1666** W. BOGHURST *Loimographia* (1894) 62 Burning or fuming vinegar and rose water. **1681** [see FUMING *vbl. sb.*].

3. a. *intr.* Of smoke, a vapour, etc.: To issue, rise, pass off; to rise and pass *away*.

1593 SHAKS. *Lucr.* 1043 As smoke..which from discharged cannon fumes. **1595** SPENSER *Col. Clout* 720 Even such is all their vaunted vanitie, Nought else but smoke, that fumeth soone away. **1620** VENNER *Via Recta* (1650) 309 The vapours..do slowly fume and ascend to the head. **1643** WITHER *Campo Musæ* 17 Whence, may fume Into thy nostrils, that sweet-smelling savour. **1667** MILTON *P.L.* VII. 600 Incense Clouds Fuming from Golden Censers, hid the Mount. **1870** BRYANT *Iliad* II. XIV. 67 From it fumes A stifling smell of sulphur.

†**b.** Of food, wine, etc.: To rise as fumes (*to* or *into* the head). Also with *up*. *Obs.*

1571 GOLDING *Calvin on Ps.* lxxv. 9 Stronge wyne fuminge quickly and strongly into the brayne. **1603** HOLLAND *Plutarch's Mor.* 407 One of them when the wine had a little fumed up into the head, began both to speake and doe foolishly. **1610** BARROUGH *Meth. Physick* I. ii. (1639) 3 He must abstaine from milke, and meates that fume into the head. **1626** BACON *Sylva* §782 They haue a manner to prepare their Greek-Wines, to keepe them from Fuming and Inebriating. **1703** *Art & Myst. Vintners* 9 To prevent their fuming up to the head and inebriating.

c. To pass *away* or *off* in fumes or vapour. *rare.*

1705 CHEYNE *Philos. Princ. Relig.* I. §38. 78 Their parts are kept from fuming away by their fixity. **1866** MRS. WHITNEY *L. Goldthwaite* x. 253 They..did something to it—applied heat, I believe—to drive away the sulphur. That fumed off, and left the rest as promiscuous as before.

fig. **1728–46** THOMSON *Spring* 244 Their light slumbers gently fum'd away, And up they rose. **1751** JOHNSON *Rambler* No. 172 ¶4 The madness of joy will fume away. **1852** JAMES *Agnes Sorel* (1860) II. 2 The Gamin spirit fumed off in a metaphor. *a* **1859** DE QUINCEY *Post. Wks.* (1891) I. 73 Yet all this marvellous learning fumes away in boyish impertinence.

†**4.** *trans.* To send forth or emit as vapour, disperse in vapour. Also with *away*, *forth*, *out*. *Obs.*

1563 HYLL *Art Garden.* (1593) 38 The snake and Adders ..be driuen away with euery sharpe and stincking sauour fumed abroad. **1627** CAPT. SMITH *Seaman's Gram.* xiv. 67 Some..will..fume out a most stinking..smoke. **1647** TRAPP *Comm. Matt.* xxvii. 36 That golden censer, Christ's body; which through the holes that were made in it..fumed forth a sweet savour. **1700** T. BROWN tr. *Fresny's Amusem. Ser. & Com.* 116 Which being Foppishly fumed into their Noses, Eyes, and Ears, has the Vertue to make them Talk. **1707** MORTIMER *Husb.* Bees 213 Otherwise the heat will fume away most of the Scent.

fig. **1606** WARNER *Alb. Eng.* XIV. xci. (1612) 369 An Indian weede, That feum'd away more wealth than would a many thousands feed. **1742** YOUNG *Nt. Th.* VII. 1370 How vicious hearts fume phrensy to the brain! **1866** G. MACDONALD *Ann. Q. Neighb.* xv. (1878) 320 The worship of one's own will fumes out around the being an atmosphere of evil.

†**5.** *intr.* Of the head or brain: To be 'clouded' with fumes (of liquor). *Obs.*

1606 SHAKS. *Ant. & Cl.* II. i. 24 Tye vp the Libertine in a field of Feasts, Keepe his Braine fuming.

6. *fig.* **a.** To give way to or exhibit anger or irritation. Often in phrase ***fume and chafe***, ***fret and fume***. Also with *up*.

1522 MORE *De quat. Noviss.* Wks. 85/1 As the fire of the burnyng hyl of Ethna burneth only it self, so doth the enuious parson, fret, fume, & burne in his owne hert. **1535**, **1581** [see CHAFE *v.* 10]. **1551**, **1631**, **1875** [see FRET *v.*[1] 9]. **1676** HOBBES *Iliad* 187 He..fum'd Both for the loss of the good spear he brake, And of the victory he had presum'd. **1768–74** TUCKER *Lt. Nat.* (1852) II. 313 How much he will fret and fume when he comes to discover the roguery. **1838** DICKENS *Nich. Nick.* xxxii, Nicholas, who had been fuming and chafing until he was nearly wild. **1839–40** W. IRVING *Wolfert's R.* (1855) 211, I walked up and down the bar-room, fuming with conscious independence and insulted dignity. **1859** GEN. P. THOMPSON *Audi Alt.* II. lxxxii. 44 People who would fume up at any intimation that they were indifferent. **1872** BLACK *Adv. Phaeton* v, The Lieutenant.. was fuming about the yard to rout out the ostler's assistants. **1878** MISS BRADDON *Open Verd.* I. i. 9 Your wisely selfish man knows his own interest too well to fret and fume about trifles.

b. quasi-*trans.* with a sentence or words as obj.: to utter irritatedly. Also with *away*: to pass or spend (time) fuming.

1897 W. W. JACOBS *Skipper's Wooing* xii, Glover fumed the afternoon away. **1907** *Munsey's Mag.* Dec. 392/1 'What are you doing—guying us?' fumed Bailey. **1908** *Smart Set* Sept. 76/2 'Good Gad, Titcomb,' fumed Parmalee,.. 'it's a chamber of horrors.'

Hence **fumed** *ppl. a.*; ***fumed oak***, oak which has been darkened by exposure to ammonia vapour (cf. FUMÉ *a.* b and FUMIGATED *ppl. a.*).

1612 WEBSTER *White Devil* v. iv, Isabella..was impoisoned By a fumed picture. **1617** MORYSON *Itin.* III. II. iv. 96 They exported..pickeld and fumed Herrings. **1890** WOODBURY *Encycl. Photogr.* 308 Fumed paper should be used within a day or two after fuming. **1902** *Idler* Nov. 255 Bookcase in Fumed Oak. **1910** *Encycl. Brit.* XI. 301/1 'Fumigated' or 'fumed' oak. **1915** T. BURKE *Nights in Town* 110 There is one of those ubiquitous fumed-oak bookcases. **1936** *Punch* 23 Dec. 726/2 But Mrs. Twankey and her son Jack now live..in a semi-detached villa, where their fumed-oak sideboard and brown plush drawing-room suite are the envy of all their neighbours. **1936** N. COWARD *To-night at 8.30* II. 33 (*title*) Fumed oak. A comedy in two scenes. *Ibid.* 35 There is a fumed oak dining-room suite consisting of a table, and six chairs. *Ibid.* 61 They knew there was a bit more to it [*sc.* life] than refinement and fumed oak and lace curtains. **1958** B. WHITE *Remodelling Old Furniture* vi. 140 Fumed oak should be coated with clear polish.

‖**fumé** (fyme), *a.* [Fr.; pa. pple. of *fumer* to smoke.] **a.** Of glass: Having a smoky tint. **b.** Of oak: Subjected to the process of fuming. (See FUMING *vbl. sb.* b.)

1883 *Fisheries Exhib. Catal.* 79 Venetian Blown Glass..in ..opal, avventurino, fumé, corniola. **1895** *Daily News* 15 Nov. 6/6 The case is of solid oak, fumé, relieved by scrolls.

†**fumee.** *Obs. rare.* [a. F. *fumée*, f. *fumer* to FUME.] Smoke, a cloud of smoke.

1481 CAXTON *Myrr.* II. viii. 85 They sette by them fyre and encence. And they wene certaynly that their thoughtes goo vp vnto our lord in this fumee. **1483** —— *Gold. Leg.* 302 a/2 He vanysshed awey as a fumee or smoke.

fumer ('fjuːmə(r)). [f. FUME *v.* + -ER[1].]

†**1.** A perfumer. *Obs.*

1611 BEAUM. & FL. *Triumph Time* i, An endless troop of tailors, Mercers, embroiderers..fumers.

2. One who fumes or 'gets into a fume'.

1894 *Advance* (Chicago) 29 Mar., Fumers and fanatics who do nothing but talk about corrupt politics.

fumerel(l, -ill, obs. forms of FEMERELL.

fumerole, var. FUMAROLE.

†**'fumet**[1]. *Obs.* or *arch.* Chiefly *pl.* Also 5 *pl.* fumes, 7 *pl.* fumers, 6–9 fewmet. [app. a. AF. **fumets* (**fumez*) pl., f. *fumer* (repr. L. *fūmāre*) to dung. The continental Fr. word in this sense was *fumées*, of parallel formation.] The excrement (of a deer). *rare* in *sing.*

14.. *Maystre of the Game* MS. Bodl. 546 (Halliw.) And ȝif men speke and aske hym of the fumes, he shal clepe fumes of an hert. **1576** TURBERV. *Venerie* 66 There is difference betweene the fewmet of the morning and that of the evenyng. **1598** [see FUMISHING]. **1637** B. JONSON *Sad Sheph.* I. ii, By his..fewmets, he doth promise sport. **1668** DAVENANT *Rivals* IV, That [Game] both his Slote and Fumers do proclaim. **1741** *Compl. Fam.-Piece* II. i. 290 Take up the Fewmet, as well made in the Evening Relief, as in the Morning. **1774** GOLDSM. *Nat. Hist.* (1862) I. II. v. 324 The stag's tail is called the single; his excrement the fumet. **1871** TENNYSON *Last Tourn.* 371 The..fewmets of a deer.

fumet[2], **fu'mette** (fymɛ, -ɛt). [a. F. *fumet*, f. *fumer* to FUME.] The scent or smell of game when high; game flavour. Also, a concentrated fish stock used for flavouring.

1723 SWIFT *Stella at Wood Park* 14 A haunch of ven'son made her sweat, Unless it had the right fumette. **1753** SMOLLETT *Ct. Fathom* (1784) 64/1 A roasted leveret very strong of the fumet. **1755** JOHNSON, *Fumette*, a word introduced by cooks, and the pupils of cooks, for the stink of meat. **1786** MACKENZIE *Lounger* No. 89 ¶11 [He] gave the venison a reprieve to a certain distant day, when it should acquire the exact proper *fumet* for the palate of a connoisseur. **1877** E. S. DALLAS *Kettner's Bk. of Table* 340 Pheasant..requires to be kept till the *fumet* is fully developed. **1906** MRS. BEETON *Househ. Managem.* lxii. 1660 *Fumet*, the flavour or essence of game, fish..used to impart a rich flavour to certain dishes. **1936** LUCAS & HUME *Au Petit Cordon Bleu* 173 *Fish fumet*, fish stock. **1939** [see CONCENTRATE *sb.* c]. **1965** *House & Garden* Dec. 84/3 Fumet ..is the very highly concentrated stock of, usually, game or fish, used to flavour other dishes or sauces.

transf. **1796** *Mod. Gulliver's Trav.* 109 The rest were cramming every crevice they could find with paper, to exclude the fumette arising from the well-dressed field.

† **'fumid**, *a. Obs.* Also 7 fumide. [ad. L. *fūmid-us*, f. *fūmus* FUME *sb.*] Fuming, vaporous.

1597 LOWE *Chirurg.* (1634) 210 The cause..is..drinking of strong and fumide drinke. **1634** T. JOHNSON *Parey's Chirurg.* I. ix. (1678) 14 Every smell, or fumid exhalation breathing out of bodies. **1661** EVELYN *Fumifugium* II. 16 Two or three of these fumid vortices are able to whirle it about the whole City. **1686** GOAD *Celest. Bodies* I. ix. 31 The Vegetable Spirit is of the same Nature with the Plant..the Fumid Spirit with the Odour. **1797** *Encycl. Brit.* II. 445/2 The comet..appeared like..a rude mass of matter illuminated with a dusky fumid light. **1889** ELVIN *Dict. Her.*, *Fumid*, emitting smoke.

Hence †**fu'midity**, †**'fumidness**, the condition or quality of being fumid.

1623 COCKERAM, *Fumiditie*, smoake. **1656-81** BLOUNT *Glossogr.*, *Fumidity*, smoakiness. **1727** BAILEY vol. II, *Fumidness.*

'fumiduct. *rare.* Also fumeduct. [f. L. *fūmus* smoke; after AQUEDUCT.] A passage for smoke.

1854 *Chamb. Jrnl.* I. 106 He would have all the smoke led downwards by a series of fumiducts. **1867** *Morn. Star* 26 Dec. 7 The smoke from the stoves is conveyed by what may be called a fumeduct to a further distance, and there passed into an ordinary chimney.

† **'fumier.** *Obs. rare.* In 5 fumyer. [a. OF. *fumier*:—L. *fūmārium* (in class. Lat. a chamber for smoking wines), f. *fūm-us* smoke.] Smoke.

c **1500** *Melusine* xxxvi. 278 He shuld conduyte the vanwarde, puttyng fyre vpon the way where he went to thentent he shuld not fayll to fynd hym by the trasse of the fumyer.

† **fu'miferous**, *a. Obs. rare*$^{-1}$. [f. L. *fūmifer* producing smoke (f. *fūmus* FUME *sb.* + *-fer* bearing) + -OUS.] Bearing or producing fumes or smoke.

1656-81 in BLOUNT *Glossogr.* **1721** in BAILEY. **1742** *Lond. & Country Brew.* I. (ed. 4) 12 This Malt..being very much impregnated with the fiery Fumiferous Particles of the Kiln.

† **fu'mific**, *a. Obs.*$^{-0}$ [ad. L. *fūmific-us*, f. *fūmus* smoke + *-ficus*: see -FIC.] (See quot.)

1727-36 BAILEY, *Fumifick*, making Smoak, Perfuming.

† **'fumificate**, *v. Obs.*$^{-0}$ [f. L. *fūmificāt-* ppl. stem of *fūmificāre*: see FUMIFY.] To make or cause smoke. Hence **'fumificated** *ppl. a.*, **,fumifi'cation.**

1721-92 BAILEY, *Fumificate.* **1721** *Ibid.*, *Fumification*, a Perfuming. **1727** *Ibid.* vol. II, *Fumificated*, incensed.

fu'mifugist. *rare*$^{-0}$. [f. L. *fūm-us* smoke + -FUGE + -IST.] 'One who or that which drives away smoke or fumes'.

1846 in WORCESTER. **1864** in WEBSTER.

fumify ('fju:mɪfaɪ), *v. rare*$^{-1}$. [ad. L. *fūmificāre*, f. *fūmific-us*: see FUMIFIC.] *trans.* (*jocularly*) To fumigate.

a **1704** T. BROWN *Wks.* (1760) II. 190 We had every one ramm'd a full charge of sot-weed into our infernal guns, in order to fumify our immortalities.

fumigacin (fju:mɪ'geɪsɪn, fju:'mɪgəsɪn). *Biochem.* [f. mod.L. *fūmigā-tus* (see FUMIGATIN) + *-cin* as in *actinomycin*: see -IN^1.] **a.** An antibiotic produced by the fungus *Aspergillus fumigatus*, now considered to be a mixture of the antibiotics helvolic acid and gliotoxin. **b.** = *helvolic acid.*

1942 [see CLAVACIN]. **1944** *Jrnl. Biol. Chem.* CLII. 429 The crystalline material formerly described as fumigacin is a mixture of fumigacin and gliotoxin. Pure fumigacin.. appears to be identical with the helvolic acid recently isolated. **1949** H. W. FLOREY et al. *Antibiotics* I. vii. 333 Fumigacin..appeared to differ..from helvolic acid. Further investigations.. showed that fumigacin was, in fact, a mixture of helvolic acid and gliotoxin. **1953** J. RAMSBOTTOM *Mushrooms & Toadstools* xxiii. 289 Fumigacin (helvolic acid)..has all the necessary qualities except that bacteria readily acquire resistance to it. **1959** [see CLAVACIN].

† **fumigal**, *a. Obs. rare*$^{-1}$. [? Badly f. L. *fūmigāre* to FUMIGATE.] ? Productive of fumes.

1477 NORTON *Ord. Alch.* v. in Ashm. (1652) 70 Pleasant Odours ingendered be shall Of cleane and Pure substance and fumigale [fumigall, *MS. margin*] As it appeareth in Amber, Narde, and Mirrhe.

fumigant ('fju:mɪgənt), *a.* and *sb.* [ad. L. *fūmigant-em*, pr. pple. of *fūmigāre*: see next.]

† **A.** *adj.* That fumes. *Obs.* **B.** *sb.* That which fumigates.

1727-36 BAILEY, *Fumigant*, smoaking, fuming. **1890** *Scott. Leader* 7 Feb. 7 The production of the fashionable little fumigant [cigarette] has trebled in the last two years. **1940** *Chambers's Techn. Dict.* 359/1 Examples of fumigants are hydrogen cyanide and ethylene oxide. **1952** *Oxf. Jun. Encycl.* VI. 327/1 The farmer and gardener have a number of methods of control they can use against pests, apart from ..spraying with..Fumigants. **1971** *Listener* 15 Apr. 493/2 Dr Bannerman had put microbes in the privy to test the fumigant.

fumigate ('fju:mɪgeɪt), *v.* [f. L. *fūmigāt-* ppl. stem of *fūmigāre* to smoke, f. *fūmus* FUME *sb.*]

1. *trans.* To apply smoke or fumes to; *esp.* to disinfect or purify by exposure to smoke or fumes.

1781 COWPER *Let. to Newton* (1884) 69 You never fumigate the ladies, or force them out of company. **1791** HAMILTON *Berthollet's Dyeing* I. I. II. i. 136 The silks..are fumigated with sulphur. **1803** *Med. Jrnl.* IX. 460 Acid fumigations bid fair to stop the progress of the complaint.. though it might not always have been proper to fumigate the apartments of the sick. **1845** *Florist's Jrnl.* 170 Let them [plants] be frequently well fumigated.

fig. **1876** GEO. ELIOT *Dan. Der.* II. xix. 7 These fine words with which we fumigate..unpleasant facts.

b. To scent with fumes; to perfume.

1530 PALSGR. 559/2, I fumygate a place with a swete fumygacion, *je enfume* or *je parfume*. Let the place be well fumygate, or ever they come. **1610** B. JONSON *Alch.* I. i, You must be bath'd and fumigated first. **1697** DRYDEN *Virg. Georg.* IV. 350 With fragrant Thyme the City fumigate. **1836** LANE *Mod. Egypt.* I. v. 171 The Egyptians take great delight in perfumes, and often fumigate their apartments. **1860** MOTLEY *Netherl.* (1868) I. v. 259 The Cathedral had been thoroughly fumigated with frankincense.

† **c.** 'To medicate or heal by vapours' (J.). *Obs.*

1713 SWIFT, etc. *Frenzy of J. Dennis* Wks. 1755 III. I. 142 Fumigate him, I say, this very evening, while he is relieved by an interval.

† **2.** To extract in fumes, vaporize. *Obs. rare.*

1663 [see FUMIGATED *ppl. a.*].

3. To darken (oak) by the process of fuming. See FUMING *vbl. sb.* b.

Hence **'fumigated** *ppl. a.*

1663 BOYLE *Usefuln. Nat. Phil.* II. v. vii. 183, I shall only subjoyn this secret, which a friend of mine practises in preserving the fumigated Juyces of Herbs. **1727** in BAILEY vol. II. **18..** *Beck's Jrnl. Dec. Art* II. 346 (Cent.) A high dado, 8 ft. high, of fumigated oak.

fumigatin (fju:mɪ'geɪtɪn). *Biochem.* [f. mod.L. *fūmigāt-us*, specific epithet of the fungus *Aspergillus fumigatus*, f. L. *fūmigāt-* ppl. stem of *fūmigāre* (see FUMIGATE *v.*) + -IN^1.] A maroon crystalline compound, $C_8H_8O_4$, with antibiotic activity, obtained synthetically and from *Aspergillus fumigatus.*

1938 ANSLOW & RAISTRICK in *Biochem. Jrnl.* XXXII. 695 A hitherto undescribed mould metabolic product fumigatin, $C_8H_8O_4$,..[has] been isolated from cultures of *Aspergillus fumigatus* Fresenius. **1946** *Nature* 17 Aug. 241/1 Fumigatin, spinulosin, helvolic acid, and gliotoxin are the four metabolic products of *A. fumigatus* which show considerable antibiotic activity. **1967** E. PARYSKI tr. *Korzybski's Antibiotics* II. III. 1273 Fumigatin, $C_8H_8O_4$, is a quinone containing one methoxyl and one methyl group: 3-hydroxy-4-methoxytoluquinone.

fumigating ('fju:mɪgeɪtɪŋ), *vbl. sb.* [f. FUMIGATE *v.* + -ING^1.] The action of the vb. FUMIGATE.

1881 M. A. LEWIS *Two Pretty G.* I. 40 Washings, fumigatings, and burnings.

attrib. **1801** *Med. Jrnl.* V. 218, I applied the nitrous gas.. by means of a tube from the top of a patent fumigating lamp. **1869** E. A. PARKES *Pract. Hygiene* (ed. 3) 332 Fumigating-room. **1881** *Daily News* 13 Sept. 6/6 The fumigating walking sticks carried by physicians when visiting plague and fever cases.

fumigation (fju:mɪ'geɪʃən). [ad. L. *fūmigātiōn-em*, n. of action f. *fūmigāre* to FUMIGATE. Cf. F. *fumigation.*]

1. The action of generating odorous smoke or fumes, *esp.* as one of the ceremonies of incantation; the action of perfuming with aromatic herbs, perfumes, etc. Also *concr.* the preparation used to produce this, or the fumes resulting from it.

c **1384** CHAUCER *H. Fame* III. 174 Olde wicches, sorceresses, That use exorsisaciouns, And eek thise fumigaciouns. *a* **1483** *Liber Niger* in *Househ. Ord.* (1790) 40 These ij wardrobers have all theyre fumygations. **1522** SKELTON *Why not to Court* 696 It was by necromansy Under a certeyne constellacyon, And a certayne fumygacyon. **1547-64** BAULDWIN *Mor. Philos.* (Palfr.) 148 Perfect deuotion & the knowledge of Gods law..smelleth far more sweetly before Him, then any earthly fumigation..doth pleasantly smell in the nose of man. **1599** B. JONSON *Cynthia's Rev.* v. ii, It is the sorting, and the dividing, and the mixing..that makes the fumigation and the suffumigation. *a* **1680** BUTLER *Rem.* (1759) II. 235 These Spirits they use to catch by the Noses with Fumigations. **1758** JOHNSON *Idler* No. 35 ¶9 She keeps the rooms always scented by fumigations. **1856** R. A. VAUGHAN *Mystics* (1860) I. 36 A divine efficacy is attributed to rites and formulas, sprinklings or fumigations. **1867** PARKMAN *Jesuits N. Amer.* viii. (1875) 91 On these the sorcerer threw tobacco, producing a stifling fumigation.

b. *jocularly.* Tobacco-smoking.

1800 *Freemason's Magazine* in *Spirit Publ. Jrnls.* (1801) IV. 157 Taciturnity and fumigation are now two essential requisites in a candidate..Every member of this society must, immediately after supper, take a pipe.

2. The action or process of fumigating or applying fumes or smoke, esp. as a disinfectant.

1572 MASCALL *Plant. & Graff.* (1592) 49 Defend them from the frost (if there come any) with fumigations or smokes, made on the winde side of your Orchards. **1658** ROWLAND *Moufet's Theat. Ins.* 956 You may make a Fumigation or Perfume of Pomegranat Pills..Sulphur, and Vitriol, which will drive them away. **1757** DARWIN in *Phil. Trans.* L. 252 The fumes of boiling water were conveyed upon this ball..and, after a fumigation for thirty seconds, it shewed signs of electricity. *a* **1777** FAWKES *Argonautics* II. *note* (1780) 347 It was the custom of the ancients to force bees out of their hives by fumigation. **1813** J. THOMSON *Lect. Inflam.* 489 The day after the fumigation not the slightest vestige of any offensive odour could be perceived. **1892** *Times* (weekly ed.) 21 Oct. 2/4 The vessel is detained for fumigation.

† **b.** *spec.* (See quots.) *Obs.*

1612 WOODALL *Surg. Mate* Wks. (1653) 271 Fumigation is calcination of metals, by the sharp corroding vapour of Mercury, Philosophers Lead. **1641** FRENCH *Distill.* iii. (1651) 80 Calcine it by fumigation i.e. by the fume of some very sharp Spirit as of *Aqua fortis.* **1683** PETTUS *Fleta Min.* II. 21 There are other ways of Calcination especially of Metals; viz. by..Fumigations.

3. *Med.* 'Exposure to fumes, especially the exposure of the body or a part of it, such as the skin or the respiratory mucous membrane, to fumes in order to produce a therapeutic effect' (*Syd. Soc. Lex.* 1885). Also *concr.* the fumes generated for this purpose.

c **1400** *Lanfranc's Cirurg.* 256 Make him a fumigacioun to his eere wiþ hoot watir. *Ibid.* 291 Drie hem with fumygaciouns maad of pulpa coloquintida. **1527** ANDREW *Brunswyke's Distyll. Waters* T ij b, A fumygacyon made of the same water is good for hering. **1629** MASSINGER *Picture* IV. ii, The friction with fumigation, cannot save him From the chine-evil. **1655** CULPEPPER, etc. *Riverius* I. i. 3 Fumigations if they be not too strong, do well to consume moisture. **1713** SWIFT, etc. *Frenzy of J. Dennis* Wks. 1755 III. I. 142 Let fumigations be used to corroborate the brain. **1801** *Med. Jrnl.* V. 219, I also applied the nitrous fumigation in cases of synochus. **1876** BARTHOLOW *Mat. Med.* (1879) 129 In..maladies of the respiratory organs, it [arsenic] is used with advantage by the process of fumigation.

4. *Comb.*: **fumigation-lamp** (see quot.).

1815 *Falconer's Dict. Marine* (ed. Burney), *Fumigation Lamps*, a recent invention for the purpose of expelling foul air from the holds and other confined places of ships. **1867** in SMYTH *Sailor's Word-bk.*

fumigative ('fju:mɪgeɪtɪv), *a.* and *sb.* [ad. mod.L. *fūmigatīv-us*, f. L. *fūmigāre*: see FUMIGATE *v.* and -IVE.]

† **A.** *adj.* That is used in (medicinal) fumigation. *Obs.* **B.** *sb.* (*nonce-wd.*) = FUMIGANT *sb.*

1599 A. M. tr. *Gabelhouer's Bk. Physicke* 200/2 Cause the loyncte, or the whole bodye, to sweate in a fumigative bath. **1897** *Daily News* 13 Feb. 6/4 Whether he uses tobacco thus openly as a friendly fumigative only I know not.

fumigator ('fju:mɪgeɪtə(r)). [agent-n. f. L. *fūmigāre*: see FUMIGATE *v.* and -OR. Cf. F. *fumigateur.*] One who or that which fumigates; *spec.*, see quot. 1874.

1872 'MARK TWAIN' *Innoc. Abr.* xxi, *We* feel no malice toward these fumigators. **1874** KNIGHT *Dict. Mech.* I. 924/2 *Fumigator*, an apparatus for applying smoke, gas, or perfume. **1888** *Sci. Amer.* N.S. LIX. 177 A corps of physicians and fumigators..thoroughly disinfected and fumigated the room.

fumigatorium (,fju:mɪgə'tɔərɪəm). *U.S.* [f. FUMIGAT(E *v.* + -ORIUM.] An air-tight container or building in which fumigation, esp. of plants, takes place.

1902 W. G. JOHNSON *Fumigation Methods* xi. 97 *A fumigatorium* is a house or room constructed or adapted for the fumigation of nursery stock or other materials. **1903** *Florida Experiment Station Bull.* LXIII. 651 To kill the white fly larvae in an air-tight fumigatorium, I commenced by using one gramme of KCN to 15 cubic feet of space. **1909** *U.S. Dept. Agric. Bur. Ent. Bull.* LXXXIV. 24 A larger fumigatorium was constructed. **1919** *U.S. Dept. Agric. Farmers' Bull.* MXXIX. 36 A fumigatorium is a container in which anything can be fumigated.

fumigatory ('fju:mɪgə,tərɪ), *a.* and *sb. rare.* [f. mod.L. type **fūmigātōri-us* (med.L. *fūmigātōrium* censer) f. L. *fūmigāre*: see FUMIGATE *v.* and -ORY. Cf. F. *fumigatoire.*]

A. *adj.* Having the quality of fumigating; concerned with fumigation. **B.** *sb.* 'A room or an apparatus used for fumigation' (*Syd. Soc. Lex.* 1885).

1799 W. TOOKE *View Russian Emp.* II. 224 The commission for quelling the contagion caused three receipts for making fumigatory powders to be published. **1852** *Fraser's Mag.* XLV. 675 A brother-officer..sitting down to join in our fumigatory conclave.

fuming ('fju:mɪŋ), *vbl. sb.* [f. FUME *v.* + -ING^1.] The action of the vb. FUME in various senses.

1529 MORE *Comf. agst. Trib.* II. Wks. 1172/2 Rather of his pacyence to take both ease and thanke, then by frettynge and fumynge to encrease hys presente payne. **1578** *Mirr. Mag.*, *Harold* xvi, O Fancy fonde, thy fuminges hath mee fed. **1620** DEKKER *Dream Christ's Coming* Wks. (Grosart) III. 22 Learning burnt bright, without Contentious fuming.

1681-6 J. Scott *Chr. Life* (1747) III. vii. 197 This fuming of the Incense by the Priests..was nothing but a mystical Oblation of those Prayers to God. **1693** Salmon *Bates' Dispens.* (1713) 712/1 They are used for the fuming of the Bed Chambers of sick People. **1870** R. W. Dale *Week-day Serm.* ii. 40 No fuming and fretting will make any difference.

b. The treatment of oak with fumes of ammonia in order to give it an antique appearance.

1893 *Westm. Gaz.* 27 Feb. 8/1 Oak..shaded to the..tint of the antique work by the process known as 'fuming'.

c. *Photogr.* (See quot. 1890.)

1889 *Anthony's Photogr. Bull.* II. 347 Paper must be thoroughly dried before fuming. **1890** Woodbury *Encycl. Photogr.*, *Fuming*, a process of subjecting albuminised paper to the fumes of ammonia.

d. *Comb.*: **fuming-box**, †(*a*) 'a pastile-burner' (Halliwell 1847); (*b*) (*Photogr.*), an apparatus in which the sensitive paper is exposed to the fumes of ammonia; **fuming-pot**, 'a brazier or censer' (*Cent. Dict.*).

1874 Knight *Dict. Mech.* I. 925/1 *Fuming-box.* **1890** *Anthony's Photogr. Bull.* III. 68 If paper is..dry when put in the fuming box, long fuming does no harm.

fuming ('fjuːmɪŋ), *ppl. a.* [f. as prec. + -ing².]

1. That emits smoke, steam, or vapour; that rises in fumes. Of acids: Emitting fumes on exposure to the air. ***fuming liquor of Boyle*** (see quot. 1807).

1575 Turberv. *Faulconrie* 309 A fumyng heate that ascendeth up from the liver to theyr [hawks'] heads. *c* **1586** C'tess Pembroke *Ps.* cxliv. 3 Lord..make the stormes arise From mountane's fuming crown. **1615** J. Stephens *Satyr. Ess.* 282 He doth sophisticate his fuming Beere, to breed a skirmish the sooner. **1725** Pope *Odyss.* viii. 474 The fuming waters bubble o'er the blaze. **1735** Somerville *Chase* I. 347 Fuming Vapours rise And hang upon the gently purling Brook. **1791** W. Nicholson tr. *Chaptal's Elem. Chem.* (1800) III. 55 The fuming nitric acid immediately turns the fixed oil black. **1807** T. Thomson *Chem.* (ed. 3) II. 10 Hydrogureted sulphuret of ammonia, known formerly by the name of fuming liquor of Boyle, because it was first described by that philosopher. **1853** W. Gregory *Inorg. Chem.* (ed. 3) 233 Terchloride of Arsenic..is a colourless, volatile, fuming liquid. **1862** Goulburn *Pers. Relig.* v. (1873) 286 A fuming caldron. **1871** R. Ellis *Catullus* lxiv. 393 All Delphi's city..Blithely receiv'd their god on fuming festival altars.

fig. **1820** Wordsworth *Sky Prosp.*, All the fuming vanities of Earth.

b. Applied to foaming or seething water; also to waves perh. with allusion to sense 3. *Obs.* or *poet.*

1598 Marston *Pygmal.* iv. 151 So haue I seene the fuming waues to fret. **1667** Milton *P.L.* v. 6 Th' only sound Of leaves and fuming rills. **1731** Swift *Strephon & Chloe* Wks. 1755 IV. i. 155 Strephon who heard the fuming rill. **1805** W. Richardson *Poems & Plays* I. 28 By the brooks and fuming rills Come, Smiling Health.

2. That emits odorous fumes, aromatic.

1601 Holland *Pliny* (1634) I. 380 The fume and smoke of the Cedar and the Citron trees onely, the old Troianes were acquainted with when they offered sacrifice: their fuming and walming steame..they vsed. **1607** Topsell *Four-f. Beasts* (1658) 244 They make a burning fire with sticks, putting therein certain fuming herbs.

3. That fumes, angry, raging. Also, characterized by or exhibiting anger.

1583 Stanyhurst *Æneis* ii. (Arb.) 46 With fuming fustian anger..I vowd to be kindlye reuenged. **1615** J. Stephens *Satyr. Ess.* 44 He will raile..For I have often heard such fuming stuffe Presented to an Audience. **1820** W. Irving *Sketch Bk.* (1859) 113 The baron..was naturally a fuming bustling little man. **1889** *Pall Mall G.* 4 Jan. 1/1 His fuming protests against English occupation.

Hence **'fumingly** *adv.*, in a fuming manner; manifesting 'fume' or rage.

1597 Hooker *Eccl. Pol.* v. xxii. §7 They answere fumingly, that they are ashamed to defile their pennes with making answere to such idle questions. **1611** Cotgr., *Fumeusement*, smoakily, fumingly. **1709** Strype *Ann. Ref.* I. xxxviii. 441 Hereupon he departed fumingly. **1894** *Argosy* May 356 It was an insult—as he fumingly told himself.

†**'fumish**, *a. Obs.* [f. fume *sb.* + -ish.]

1. Emitting smoke or vapour. Of a chimney: Smoky. Of waves: = fuming *ppl. a.* 1 b.

1574 Hellowes *Gueuara's Fam. Ep.* (1577) 63 Little chimneyes alwayes be somewhat fumishe or smokie. **1599** Nashe *Lenten Stuff* Wks. (Grosart) V. 204 Firmely piled and rampierd against the fumish waues battry.

2. Of the nature of fume, vapour, or smoke.

1613 Purchas *Pilgrimage* i. viii. 43 The fumish and dryer part of the cloude yeelding a purplish, the waterie, a greenish sea colour. **1619** Bainbridge *Descr. late Comet* 39 Who may not from these smoakie parents feare a fumish generation?

3. Belonging to or of the nature of fumes which rise in the body or stomach. Of meat or wine: Causing or emitting fumes.

1519 Horman *Vulg.* 28 b, Heare is genderd of superfluous humours and fumysshe vapours. **1528** Paynel *Salerne's Regim.* F iij b, White wyne..is lesse fumishe and lesse vaperous than other. **1544** Phaer *Regim. Lyfe* (1560) G v, The paciente oughte..to abstaine from..poudred meates and fumyshe. **1547** Boorde *Brev. Health* cclxxxv. 94 This infirmitie [pleurisy] doth come of a fumyshe bloud. **1562** Turner *Baths* 12 a, If it be to fumish, then lay..a peace of bread in the wine. *a* **1693** Urquhart *Rabelais* iii. xiii. 109 The fumish Steam of Meat.

4. *fig.* Inclined to fume, hot-tempered, irascible, passionate; also, characterized by or exhibiting anger or irascibility.

1523 Ld. Berners *Froiss.* I. cccxlvi. 547 He was a fumisshe man and malincolyous. **1539** Cranmer in Strype *Life* (1694) II. 248 Wee go not about..to abate our fumish and rancorous stomacks. *c* **1546** Joye in Gardiner *Declar. Art. Joye* (1546) 92 b, Let him..not dispute with poore men in his fetters and presons with his fumisshe threatis. **1567** Drant *Horace Ep.* ii. *To Lollius* C iij, Of foolishe kinges..a fumishe flame. **1576** Newton *Lemnie's Complex.* 133 a Yet is nothing more noysome and preiudiciall then..fumish anger and testynesse. **1608** Topsell *Serpents* (1658) 650 A more fumish, testy, angry, Waspish..generation.

Hence **'fumishly** *adv.*, **'fumishness**.

1519 Horman *Vulg.* 71 Fury and fumysshnes is the blynde snare of right iugement. **1528** Paynel *Salerne's Regim.* H j a, Be ware howe they drinke stronge wyne..For the fumishenes therof hurteth yᵉ heed. **1540-7** Coverdale *Fruitf. Less. Passion* (1593) P j a, O driue thou out of vs all fumishnesse, indignation, and selfe will. **1563-87** Foxe *A. & M.* (1684) I. 661/1 So wildly he writeth, so fumishly he fareth. **1608** Topsell *Serpents* (1658) 652 Their naturall inclination to anger, and the hasty fumishness of Wasps.

†**'fumishing.** *Obs.* Also 6-7 **fewmishing**, (6 **femysshyng, femishing**), 7-8 **fimashing**. [app. f. OF. *femer, fumer* to dung (see fumet²), + *-ish* (on the analogy of vbs. a Fr. vbs. in *-iss-, -ir*) + -ing¹.] The excrement (of a deer). Cf. fumets.

1527 *St. Papers Hen. VIII*, VI. 598 The scantlyn and femysshyng of such deir. **1575** [see crotey *sb.*]. **1596** Harington *Metam. Ajax* 32 Doth not the keeper..shew you his femishing? **1598** Manwood *Lawes Forest* iv. §6 (1615) 45 Of all Deere, the ordure is called fewmets or fewmishing. **1726** *Dict. Rust.* (ed. 3), *Fimashing* (among Hunters), the Dunging of any sort of wild Beasts.

†**'fumist.** *Obs. rare*⁻¹. [a. F. *fumiste*, f. L. *fūmus* smoke.] One who 'cures' smoky chimneys; a chimney-doctor.

1785 Franklin *Wks.* (1840) VI. 526 The nostrums of pretending chimney doctors and fumists.

fumitory ('fjuːmɪtərɪ). Forms: α. 4-5 **fumeter(e**, 4, 6 **-terre**, 4-7 **fumiterre**, 4-5 **-ytere**, (5 **fumtere, fymterre**), 6 **femiter, -ar**. β. 6 **fume(n)torie, femetary, fumitarie, -orie**, (**fumyterry, -tory**), 7 **fume-, fumitery**, 8 **fumetory**, 6- **fumitory**. [a. OF. *fumeterre*, ad. med.L. *fūmus terræ* lit. 'smoke of the earth'; so called because 'it spryngyth...out of the erthe in grete quantyte as smoke dooth other fumosyte that comyth of the erthe' (Trevisa, tr. *Barth. De P.R.* xvii. lxix). In the 16th c. the ending was confused with -ary, -ory.

The med.L. name is also represented by Pr. *fumterra*, and corruptly by It. *fummosterno*; translated forms are Ger. *erdrauch*, Sw. *jordrök*, Eng. *earth-smoke*; cf. the Sp., Pg. *fumaria*, whence the mod.L. botanical name.]

A plant of the genus *Fumaria* (or the related *Corydalis*), usually *F. officinalis*.

α. *c* **1386** Chaucer *Nun's Pr. T.* 143 Of lauriol, centaure, and fumeterre. *a* **1387** *Sinon. Barthol.* (Anecd. Oxon) 22/1 *Fumus terre*, fumeter. *c* **1440** *Promp. Parv.* 161 Fymterre, herbe, *fumus terre*. *c* **1450** *M.E. Med. Bk.* (Heinrich) 158 Take þe jus..of fumtere, [etc.]. **1549** *Compl. Scot.* vi. 67, I sau fumeterre, that tempris ane heyt lyuyr. **1578** Lyte *Dodoens* i. xv. 23 There is two kindes of Fumeterre. **1601** Holland *Pliny* II. 247 Fumiterre the herb whosoeuer do eat, shal purge choler by vrine.

β. **1516** *Grete Herball* K vj a, De Fumo terre, Fumyterry. **1533** Elyot *Cast. Helth* (1541) 58 a, Wylde hoppes: Wormewode: Centorie: Fumitorie. **1548** Turner *Names of Herbes* (E.D.S.) 23 Capnos called in latin Fumaria, and in englishe Fumitarie..in frenche fumiterre. **1573** Tusser *Husb.* xci. (1878) 182 Get water of Fumentorie, Liuer to coole. **1650** H. Brooke *Conserv. Health* 53 Whey with Fumitery. **1670** Ray *Catal. Plant. Angl.* 122 Climbing-Fumitory. **1736** Bailey *Househ. Dict.* 295 Fumitory is good to cure the itch, scurf and tetters. **1794** Martyn *Rousseau's Bot.* xxiv. 346 Fumitory has two filaments, each..terminated by three anthers. **1802-3** tr. *Pallas' Trav.* (1812) I. 90 The *Fumaria bulbosa*, or great bulbous fumitory. **1861** Delamer *Fl. Gard.* 88 Fumitory—*Fumaria* of the old botanists, *Corydalis* of the moderns..The Tuberous Fumitory, *C. bulbosa*.

b. *attrib.*

1576 Baker *Jewell of Health* 199 b, Taken with Fumyterre water..it cureth the Leprie.

fumitory, incorrect form of fumatory.

†**'fumity.** *Obs. rare*⁻¹. = fumosity.

1572 J. Jones *Bathes Buckstone* 15 b, It diminisheth the fumity, or juyce hurtfull.

fumivorous (fjuː'mɪvərəs), *a. nonce-wd.* [as if f. L. **fūmivor-us* (f. *fūm-us* smoke + *-vorus* devouring) + -ous.] Feeding or living on smoke.

1824 *New Monthly Mag.* XI. 316 Citizen.—A fumivorous being, much given to making money.

fummel: see funnel², sort of mule.

fummerel(l, obs. form of femerell.

fumose (fjuː'məʊs), *a.* [ad. L. *fūmōs-us*, f. *fūmus* smoke.]

1. Full of fumes, giving off fumes, vaporous, flatulent.

c **1400** *Lanfranc's Cirurg.* (MS. B.) 25 To entempren þe fumose hete of þe same herte. **1436** *Pol. Poems* (Rolls) II. 162 To feche the fumose wine. *c* **1460** J. Russell *Bk. Nurture* 354 Y pray yow for to telle me Certenle of how many metes þat ar fumose in þeire degre. **1861** *Wheat & Tares* 199 The 'Publican and Sinner' wafted its praises aloft on a cloud of fumose panegyric.

2. Smoky, thick with smoke, like smoke.

1432-50 tr. *Higden* (Rolls) I. 319 He..seyde ofte tymes when wyndes scholde folowe by fumose vapores ascendenge. **1727** Bailey vol. II, *Fumose*. **1833** *Fraser's Mag.* VIII. 733 What fumose volume comes from the sheets!

3. *Bot.* (See quot.)

1866 *Treas. Bot.*, *Fumous, Fumose*, grey, changing to brown, smoke-coloured.

†**fu'mosity.** *Obs.* [ad. F. *fumosité* or med.L. *fūmōsitās*: see fumose, fumous, and -ity.]

1. The quality of being full of fumes or vapours.

1398 Trevisa *Barth. De P.R.* xvii. vi. (1495) 607 For fumosyte of the stomacke greuyth the heed and makyth it ake. *c* **1570** *Pride & Lowl.* (1841) 5 Engendering in the head fumositie. **1652** J. Wadsworth tr. *Colmenero's Chocolate* 19 Benzoin the Head frees from Fumosity.

2. The flatulent quality of various articles of food; the heady quality of wine, etc.

c **1460** J. Russell *Bk. Nurture* 105 ȝiff dyuerse drynkes of theire fumosite haue þe dissesid. *Ibid.* 350 Ye must thus know..þe fumositees of fysch, flesche, & fowles. **1542** Boorde *Dyetary* x. (1870) 254 Bycause wyne is full of fumosyte.

b. Ill-smelling breath; smell of food or drink in the breath.

c **1530** H. Rhodes *Bk. Nurture* 230 Belche thou neare to no mans face with a corrupt fumosytye. **1558** Warde tr. *Alexis' Secr.* 83 b, Rubbe your teeth wel..to take awaye the fumositie of the meate.

3. Vaporous humour rising into the head from the stomach.

c **1386** Chaucer *Sqr's T.* 358 Ful were hir hedes of fumositee. *c* **1400** *Lanfranc's Cirurg.* 74 Þis drynke is alteratijf..and it lettiþ fumosite to arise to þe brayn. **1601** Holland *Pliny* II. 325 The fumosities that trouble and dim the eiesight. **1678** R. R[ussell] *Geber* ii. i. iii. 28 Their Brain repleat with many Fumosities cannot receive the true Intention.

4. a. The state of fuming or giving off fumes.

b. *concr.* A fumy or vaporous exhalation from anything, a fume; the volatile part given off from a mineral or the like.

1477 Norton *Ord. Alch.* v. in Ashm. (1652) 65 Infused with a thick Fumosity congregate Of Water, and alsoe of Erth succended. **1563** W. Fulke *Meteors* (1640) 58 That water receiveth the fumosity of brimstone, and other minerals, thorow which it runneth. **1598** Sylvester *Du Bartas* ii. i. i. *Eden* 620 His burnèd stalks with strong fumosities Of piercing vapours, purge the French disease. **1650** Ashmole *Chym. Collect.* 132 So that Mercury be made hot even to Fumosity. **1688** R. Holme *Armoury* ii. 31/2 Rain is..an Earthly humor, or fumosities drawn up out of the Water and Earth. **1726** Leoni tr. *Alberti's Archit.* I. 3/1 Whether the Wind be occasioned by a dry Fumosity of the Earth. **1750** tr. *Leonardus' Mirr. Stones* 37 The Red colour happens in perspicuous stones, when a lighted fumosity and a tender fire is infused in a perspicuous light.

fumous ('fjuːməs), *a.* [f. L. *fūm-ōsus* (f. *fūmus* smoke) + -ous. Cf. F. *fumeux*.]

†**1.** Giving off fumes; *esp.* tending to generate wind or gas in the stomach, flatulent. *Obs.*

1477 Norton *Ord. Alch.* v. in Ashm. (1652) 73 Fumous things alone. **1543** Traheron *Vigo's Chirurg.* iii. i. iv. 90 If it [an aposteme] came of to muche eatynge of fumous meates. **1610** Barrough *Meth. Physick* i. xxiv. (1639) 40 He must abstaine from Garlick, Onions..and such like fumous things. **1688** R. Holme *Armoury* iii. 430/2 The Stopple, which hath a large Head..contains the fumous Medicine. **1706** Phillips (ed. Kersey), *Fumous*, apt to fume up, that sends Fumes into the Head, heady.

†**2.** Consisting of fumes; vaporous, windy. *Obs.*

1534 Elyot *Cast. Helthe* iv. xii. 94 b, Let them abstein from meate, that ingender botches..fumouse ructuacions or vapours. **1548-77** Vicary *Anat.* ii. (1888) 21 That Artere bringeth with him from the lunges ayre to temper the fumous heate that is in the harte. **1604** Jas. I *Counterbl.* (Arb.) 98 Since the Subiect is but of Smoke, I thinke the fume of an idle braine, may serue for a sufficient battery against so fumous and feeble an enemy. **1612** Woodall *Surg. Mate* Wks. (1653) 21 The Glister Instrument, fit for the exact giving of a vaporous, fumous, or dry Glister, &c. **1678** R. R[ussell] *Geber* ii. i. ii. ii. 41 The subtile fumous Humidity.

3. Pertaining to smoke or smoking. Now *jocular*.

1661 Evelyn *Fumifugium* i. 7 Those fumous Works many of them were either left off or spent but few Coales. **1830** Lytton *Paul Clifford* II. iv. 100 As soon as the revellers had provided themselves with their wonted luxuries, potatory and fumous.

†**4.** Full of passion, angry, furious. *Obs.*

1430-40 Lydg. *Bochas* vii. ii. (1554) 166 b, Hasty, fumous, with furies infernal Of wilful malice innocentes blood to shede. **1460** *Paston Lett.* No. 349 I. 514 Here hevedy and fumows langage. *c* **1526** Frith *Disput. Purgat.* (1829) 88 A man's enemy..gathereth together all that he can imagine, and so accuseth a man more of a fumous heat than of any verity. **1560** Rolland *Crt. Venus* i. 617 With fax and face fumous. **1684** H. More *Answer* 84 Each maintaining their cause with like fumous Animosity.

5. *Bot.* = fumose *a.* 3.

1866 [see fumose *a.* 3].

Hence **'fumously** *adv.*; in quots. †angrily, furiously.

1460 *Paston Lett.* No. 349 I. 512 Whan he seyd so fumowsly, 'Who so ever sey that of me, he lyeth falsly in hise hede, &c.' **1526** Skelton *Magnyf.* 2522 And fumously addresse you. **1553** T. Wilson *Rhet.* (1580) 151 An other beyng sore offended . . said fumouslie unto hym, dooest thou heare me? *a* 1652 BROME *Covent Garden* I. Wks. 1873 II. 17 Some have by the phrensie of despair Fumously run into the sea to throw Their wretched bodies.

fumrell, obs. form of FEMERELL.

fumy (ˈfjuːmɪ), *a.* [f. FUME *sb.* + -Y[1].]

Composed of, or full of, fumes, vapours, or smoke; of the nature of fume or fumes.

1570 LEVINS *Manip.* 101/40 Fumye, *fumosus.* 1591 SYLVESTER *Du Bartas* I. ii. 1006 Blent With fumie mixture of grosse nourishment. 1605 TIMME *Quersit.* I. ix. 36 Ashes . . have in them partly that which is earthie, and partly that which is fumie. 1635 SIR H. WOTTON in *Lismore Papers* (1888) Ser. II. III. 219 This fumie Citie [London]. 1703 ROWE *Ulyss.* II. i. 953 The fumy Vapours And mounting Spirits of the deep-drunk Bowl. 1794 MATHIAS *Purs. Lit.* (1803) 368 The fumy tint [of a smoked glass]. 1871 G. MACDONALD *Parable* in *Wks. Fancy & Imag.* IV. 71 Through the fumy, thickened air. 1885 G. MEREDITH *Diana* I. i. 4 It knows enough for its fumy dubiousness.

†**b.** ***fumy ball***: ? 'a puff-ball' (Halliw.); ? a bubble.

1598 HALL *Sat.* IV. iv, All soft as is the falling thistledown, Soft as the fumy ball, or *Morrians* crowne.

Hence ˈ**fumily** *adv.*, smokily.

1855 in OGILVIE *Supp.*

fun (fʌn), *sb.* [prob. f. FUN *v.*]

†**1.** A cheat or trick; a hoax, a practical joke.

a 1700 B. E. *Dict. Cant. Crew*, *Fun*, a Cheat or slippery Trick. 1719 D'URFEY *Pills* (1872) V. 259 A Hackney Coachman he did hug her, And was not this a very good Fun?

2. a. Diversion, amusement, sport; also, boisterous jocularity or gaiety, drollery. Also, a source or cause of amusement or pleasure.

(Johnson 1755 stigmatizes it as 'a low cant word'; in present use it is merely somewhat familiar.)

1727 SWIFT *Misc. Epit. By-words*, Tho' he talk'd much of virtue, his head always run Upon something or other she found better fun. 1749 FIELDING *Tom Jones* IX. vi, Partridge . . was a great lover of what is called fun. 1751 E. MOORE *Gil Blas* Prol. 25 Don't mind me tho', for all my fun and jokes. 1767 H. BROOKE *Fool of Qual.* I. 99 Vindex . . looked smilingly about him with much fun in his face. 1768–74 TUCKER *Lt. Nat.* (1852) II. 313 It is fun to them to break off an ornament, or disfigure a statue. 1790 BURNS *Tam o' Shanter* 144 The mirth and fun grew fast and furious. 1837 DICKENS *Pickw.* ii, 'What's the fun?' said a rather tall thin young man. 1845 S. C. HALL *Bk. Gems* 90 His wit and humour delightful, when it does not degenerate into 'fun'. 1849 E. E. NAPIER *Excurs. S. Africa* II. 331 Being better mounted than the rest of his troop, [he] pushed on to see more of the fun. 1887 SHEARMAN *Athletics & Football* 325 Most footballers play for the fun and the fun alone. 1889 J. K. JEROME *Idle Thoughts* 42 There is no fun in doing nothing when you have nothing to do. 1891 BARING-GOULD *In Troubadour-Land* iv. 50, I do not see the fun of going to hotels of the first class. 1934 *Punch* 9 May 526/1 A Rector in an unapostolic fury is rather fun. 1954 *Economist* 20 Mar., His book has all the charm of science fiction; it is enormous fun. 1958 *Listener* 25 Dec. 1085/1 The clothes were Jacobean, and fun to wear.

b. Phr. ***to make fun of***, ***poke fun at*** (a person, etc.): to ridicule. ***for*** or ***in fun***: as a joke, sportively, not seriously. (***he, it is***) ***good, great fun***: a source of much amusement. ***like fun***: energetically, very quickly, vigorously. ***what fun!*** how very amusing! ***for the fun of the thing***: for amusement; ***to have fun*** (***with***): to enjoy (a process); *spec.* to have sexual intercourse.

1737 H. WALPOLE *Corr.* (1820) I. 17, I can't help making fun of myself. 1833 C. A. DAVIS *Lett. J. Downing* (1834) 24 And began to laugh like fun. 1840 HOOD *Up Rhine* 157 The American . . in a dry way began to poke his fun at the unfortunate traveller. *a* 1847 MRS. SHERWOOD *Lady of Manor* III. xxi. 250 Then you won't make fun of me, will you? 1848 LOWELL *Biglow P.* Ser. I. IV. 98 Stickin' together like fun. 1848 MRS. GASKELL *M. Barton* I. v. 73 Carsons' mill is blazing away like fun. 1849 LYTTON *Caxtons* 19 You would be very sorry if your mamma were to . . break it for fun. 1857 HUGHES *Tom Brown* II. iii, The bolts went to like fun. 1860 GEN. P. THOMPSON *Audi Alt.* III. cxxvi. 82 Who knows but Volunteer Rifles may make a campaign in the Holy Land, and mount guard over the production of the holy fire at Easter? 'What fun!' 1875 JOWETT *Plato* (ed. 2) I. 151 He may pretend in fun that he has a bad memory. 1877 M. M. GRANT *Sun-Maid* iii, The races are great fun. 1877 *Independent* 19 July 15/2 Little Tad commissioned lieutenant by Stanton, 'just for the fun of the thing'. 1891 N. GOULD *Double Event* 1 He's such good fun, and he's so obliging. 1893 FARMER & HENLEY *Slang* III. 86/2 *To have* (or *do*) *a bit of fun*, to procure or enjoy the sexual favour. 1895 H. A. KENNEDY in *19th Cent.* Aug. 331, I suppose the wood-carver was poking fun at him? 1903 BEERBOHM *Around Theatres* (1924) I. 425 Amateur mimes . . go in for private theatricals . . just for the fun of the thing. 1958 *Times Lit. Suppl.* 7 Feb. 73/4 The clerks . . get their own back by unmasking frauds and . . having fun with the low standard of French commercial honesty. 1961 M. DICKENS *Heart of London* II. 198 Ambrosia had pushed Edgar and the girl in there with the admonition to have some fun, dears.

c. Exciting goings-on. Also ***fun and games***, *freq.* used ironically; *spec.* amatory play. *colloq.*

1879 [see CHINKEY, etc.]. 1897 *Daily News* 13 Sept. 7/1 The engineer officers who are engaged in carrying out some of the Sirdar's plans get much more than their fair share of 'the fun' . 1898 *Westm. Gaz.* 28 Oct. 3/1 It is possible that there may be rare fun by-and-by on the Nile. 1920 'SAPPER' *Bull-Dog Drummond* vi. 155 We've had lots of fun and games since I last saw you. 1940 N. MITFORD *Pigeon Pie* iii. 66 Farther on, however, you come to jolly fun and games—great notices. 1948 PARTRIDGE *Dict. Forces' Slang* 78 *Fun and games*, any sort of brush with the enemy at sea. 1948 'N. SHUTE' *No Highway* iii. 70 'Fun and games,' he said. 'The boffin's going mad.' 1952 E. GRIERSON *Reputation for Song* xxix. 260 Beneath the orderly conduct of her bar there was always present the possibility of 'fun and games'. 1954 C. ARMSTRONG *Better to Eat You* ii. 22 If it happened because somebody is having fun-and-games with Miss Sarah Shepherd, somebody is going to be sorry. 1966 J. PORTER *Sour Cream* v. 59, I headed the car in the direction of the coast road. We had the usual fun and games with the local drivers. 1970 *Globe & Mail* (Toronto) 26 Sept. B3/3 Mr. Brown also expects the fun and games of tax haven subsidiaries to disappear with the new legislation.

3. a. *Comb.*, as ***fun-loving*** adj. Also *attrib.*, passing into *adj.* with the sense 'amusing, entertaining, enjoyable'.

1775 PRATT *Liberal Opin.* (1783) II. 119 This fun-loving Alicia. *a* 1846 B. R. HAYDON *Autobiogr.* (1927) III. xvii. 358 There was a room at Holly House called the 'fun-room', without chair or table. It was for dancing and romping. 1853 N. P. WILLIS (*title*) Fun jottings; or, Laughs I have taken pen to. 1892 *Daily News* 14 July 5/1 A fun-loving, jolly, prankish elf of a woman. 1908 *Daily Chron.* 26 Dec. 4/4 The side-show is blossoming out again at all points of the compass in 'fun towns' and the like. 1959 J. OSBORNE *World of Paul Slickey* I. vii. 61 You'll always be a Fun Person. 1962 *Sat. Even. Post* 13 Oct. 69 Some fur coats are, however, just for fun. The 'fun fur' coat has given a big boost to the industry. 1962 *Sunday Express* 16 Dec. 18/5 Nowadays you can't rustle up enough fun people for a small party any more. 1965 *New Statesman* 7 May 712/3 Millions have sampled the delights of St Tropez and St Moritz and a lot more of the so-called 'fun places' for themselves. 1965 *Punch* 18 Aug. 254/3 The cheap 'fun furs' acclaimed as so young and amusing. 1968 A. DIMENT *Bang Bang Birds* x. 186, I was remembering Marianne and the fun times we have had. 1968 J. IRONSIDE *Fashion Alphabet* 151 The young have taken to 'fun' furs which may be rabbit dyed to any colour under the sun. 1969 *Listener* 13 Feb. 221/3 Much better to give St Katharine Docks to Joan Littlewood for a fun palace. 1971 *New Yorker* 8 May 107 We have the Osborns, the Beals, the Hartungs, the Falmers, and us. Now let's think of someone fun.

b. Special comb., as **fun fair**, a fair (or that part of a fair) which is devoted to amusements and side-shows; **funfest** [FEST] chiefly *U.S.*, a gathering for the purposes of amusement; **fun-maker**, a comedian, humorist, jester; **fun run** orig. *U.S.*, an organized and largely uncompetitive long-distance run, esp. characterized by the mass participation of occasional (often sponsored) runners; also **fun runner**, one who takes part in a long-distance run for fun, rather than competitively; **fun running**.

1925 A. HUXLEY *Those Barren Leaves* II. iii. 106, I cannot claim to bring every attraction of the Fun Fair into your place of labour—only the switchback, the water-shoot and the mountain railway. 1951 A. BARON *Rosie Hogarth* 16 Fun fairs discharge their screech and blare upon the passer-by. 1955 *Times* 18 July 5/3 The fun fair at the Festival Gardens, Battersea, opened bashfully . . for its first Sunday session yesterday. There was no music. Nor was there any beer. 1918 in *Dialect Notes* V. 11 (*headline*) Lincoln High invites to fun-fest. 1922 S. LEWIS *Babbitt* xiii. 172 You will get 111% on your kale in this fun-fest. 1962 J. D. MACDONALD *Key to Suite* x. 140 The convention . . wasn't . . a fun-fest, a week of broads and bottles. 1963 *Punch* 4 Dec. 803/1 A riotous funfest. 1904 *Daily Chron.* 12 Nov. 5/6 Mr. James Welch to be Prominent Fun-maker at Drury Lane. 1906 R. L. RAMSAY *Skelton's Magnyf.* p. xcvii, The two fun-makers of the morality are the brothers Fancy and Folly. 1936 *Variety* 15 July 14/2 At last those three ace fun makers . . get a chance to go to town in a big time laugh hit of their own. 1976 *Runner's World* Mar. 11/1 Fun running is about to take off nationwide... The following cities and towns report having events of the *Fun Run type,—in brief, regularly scheduled, timed runs over accurate courses. 1977 *Sunday Times* 23 Oct. 29/6 Coming: Report of a Fun Run for everyone. It starts from Gateshead Stadium next Saturday, and Brendan Foster hopes to popularise this American mass participation idea. 1980 *Sunday Times* 23 Mar. 28/1 The £11,700 raised for the British Heart Foundation by last year's *fun runners will support . . an important study which is attempting to establish blood-pressure patterns in infants. 1985 *Athletics Today* Dec. 26/1, I was really about 50th overall, but I did win the Fun Run... The Mansfield Half Marathon consists of two races at once—one for affiliated athletes and one for unaffiliated, or Fun Runners. 1986 *N.Y. Times* 21 Apr. c6/1 Thousands of fun runners and disabled competitors pounded the same rain-soaked course as the stars.

fun (fʌn), *v.* [Perh. a dialectal pronunc. of FON *v.*, to befool (not recorded after 15th c.).]

1. *trans.* To cheat, hoax; also, to cajole. Const. *of*, *out of*. *Obs.* exc. *dial.*

1685 *Roxb. Ball.* VII. 473 She had fun'd him of his Coin. *a* 1700 B. E. *Dict. Cant. Crew* s.v., What do you Fun me? Do you think to Sharp or Trick me? 1744 OZELL tr. *Brantome's Sp. Rhodomontades* (ed. 2) 44 He that funs me out of her, may boldly say, he has fun'd the best Sword in France. 1785 GROSE *Dict. Vulg. Tongue* s.v., Do you think to fun me out of it. 1812 *Sporting Mag.* XL. 86 Sure your lordship wouldn't be funning me. 1847–78 HALLIWELL, *Fun*, to cheat, to deceive, *Somerset*. 1886 ELWORTHY *W. Somerset Word-bk.* s.v., He've a-fun me out o' vower poun.

2. [from the sb.] *intr.* To make fun or sport; to indulge in fun; to fool, joke.

1833 M. SCOTT *Tom Cringle* x, If it be . . Christian-like . . to be after funning and fuddling, while a fellow-creature . . stands before you, all but dead. 1853 W. JERDAN *Autobiog.* III. vii. 83 In later days he was often funning—I can find no other word to express it—in 'Blackwood'. 1886 E. L. BYNNER *A. Surriage* vi. 77 'Ye must be funnin', sir-r', she almost gasped.

Hence ˈ**funning** *vbl. sb.*

1728 GAY *Begg. Op.* II. Air xix, Cease your funning, Force or Cunning Never shall my Heart trapan. 1850 T. A. TROLLOPE *Impress. Wand.* xxv. 377 He took upon him to furnish amusement during the . . journey by a succession of funning. 1879 SEGUIN *Black For.* xiii. 222 He generally contrives that his victims shall not materially suffer from his funning.

fun, obs. and dial. pa. pple. of FIND.

†**fuˈnambulant.** *Obs.* [as if ad. L. **fūnambulant-em*, pr. pple. of an assumed vb. **fūnambulāre* to walk on a rope, f. *fūnambulus* (see FUNAMBULE) or its elements.] A rope-walker, a funambulist. So **fuˈnambulate** *v.*, to walk on a stretched rope (in mod. Dicts.). **fuˈnambulation**, the action of walking on a rope. **fuˈnambulator**, a rope-walker. **fuˈnambulatory** *a.*, pertaining to rope-walking; that walks on a rope.

1606 SYLVESTER *Du Bartas* II. iv. IV. *Decay* 911 Hee's fain to stand like the *Funambulant Who seems to tread the air. 1623 COCKERAM II, A Rope walker, *Funambulante.* 1721–92 BAILEY, **Funambulation.* 1797 E. DARWIN *Cond. Fem. Educ.*, Skating on the ice in winter, swimming in summer, funambulation or dancing on the straight rope. 1676–1732 COLES, **Funambulator* . . a dancer on the Ropes. 1883 SALA in *Illustr. Lond. News* 11 Aug., The apprenticeship of young children to acrobats and funambulators. 1682 SIR T. BROWNE *Chr. Mor.* I. §1 Tread softly and circumspectly in this *funambulatory Track and narrow Path of Goodness. 1727–41 CHAMBERS *Cycl.* s.v. *Funambulus*, In the floralia . . held under Galba, there were funambulatory elephants. 1880 J. H. INGRAM in *Academy* 28 Feb. 153/2 Funambulatory labours.

†**fuˈnambule**, *sb.* *Obs.* In 7 **funamble.** [ad. L. *fūnambul-us*, f. *fūn-is* rope + *ambul-āre* to walk. Cf. F. *funambule.*] A rope-walker.

1697 EVELYN *Numism.* 277 The late Famous Funamble Turk.

Hence **fuˈnambulic** *a.*, of or pertaining to rope-walkers or rope-walking.

1867 *Lond. Rev.* 27 Apr. 480 M. Blondin created, as we are told, an era in the funambulic art.

†**fuˈnambule**, *v.* *Obs.*[-0] [f. FUNAMBULE *sb.*] *intr.* To walk on a stretched rope.

Hence †**fuˈnambuling** *vbl. sb.*, the action of the vb. Also †**fuˈnambuler**, a rope-walker.

1650 B. *Discolliminium* 5 Now go I a funambuling, I wish I may go steady lest I tumble. 1659 TORRIANO, *Artegatóre*, a tumbler, a funeambuler, a dancer on ropes.

funambulist (fjuːˈnæmbjʊlɪst). [f. as prec. + -IST.] A performer on the tight (or slack) rope, a rope-walker, a rope-dancer.

1793 *Looker-on* No. 80 ¶3 What man will withhold from the funambulist the praise of justice, who considers his inflexible uprightness? 1824 HEBER *Jrnl.* (ed. 2) II. xx. 334 Tricks which proved him to be a funambulist of considerable merit. 1847–8 DE QUINCEY *Protestantism* Wks. VIII. 95 That would be a sad task for the most skilful of funambulists or theological tumblers. 1896 *Daily News* 1 Sept. 3 A Funambulist is a gentleman who . . on a rope . . turns sommersaults, leaps thro' a ring, and plays on a fiddle while whirling like a Catharine wheel.

So **fuˈnambulism** [see -ISM], rope-walking.

1824 DE QUINCEY *Conversation* Wks. 1890 X. 280 A sort of monster hired to play tricks of funambulism for the night. 1886 A. JESSOPP in *Athenæum* 20 Feb. 264 Horrible lessons of ghastly grammar and dreary funambulism yclept analysis of the sentence.

‖**fuˈnambulo.** *arch.* [Sp. or It., ad. L. *fūnambulus*: see FUNAMBULE.] A funambulist.

1605 BACON *Adv. Learn.* II. xv. §2. 58 The Trickes of Tumblers, Funambuloes, Baladynes. *a* 1626 —— *Let. & Disc. H. Saville* in *Resuscitatio* (1657) 227 We see the Industry, and Practise, of Tumblers, and Funambulo's. 1895 *N. & Q.* 8th Ser. VIII. 251 The conjurors and funambuloes of our adventurously impudent century.

†**fuˈnambulous**, *a.* *Obs. rare.* [f. L. *fūnambul-us* (see FUNAMBULE *sb.*) + -OUS.] Of or pertaining to a rope-walker.

1672 SIR T. BROWNE *Lett. Friend* (1690) 9 Tread softly and circumspectly in this funambulous Track and narrow Path of Goodness [cf. quot. 1682 s.v. FUNAMBULATORY].

‖**fuˈnambulus.** *Obs.* Pl. **funambuli.** [L.: see FUNAMBULE *sb.*] A rope-dancer.

a 1614 JAS. MELVILL *Diary* (1842) 487, I saw a funambulus, a Frenchman, play strang and incredible prattiks upon stented takell in the Palace-close. *a* 1639 WOTTON in *Reliq.* (1651) 484 Walking not like a Funambulus upon a Cord, but upon the edge of a rasor. 1650 BULWER *Anthropomet.* xxii. 240 Our Funambuli and Tumblers. 1686 PLOT *Staffordsh.* vii. 239 Spiders . . will winde up the thred shorter till it is very straight, as the Funambuli strain their roaps.

function (ˈfʌŋkʃən), *sb.* Also 6 funccion. [a. OF. *function* (F. *fonction*, cf. It. *funzione*, Sp. *funcion*), ad. L. *functiōn-em*, n. of action f. *fungī* (*fungor*) to perform.]

†**1.** In etymological sense: The action of performing; discharge or performance *of* (something).

1597 DANIEL *Civ. Wars* VI. xciii, His hand, his eye, his wits all present, wrought The function of the glorious Part he beares. 1656–81 in BLOUNT *Glossogr.* 1701 SWIFT *Contests Nobles & Com.* Wks. 1755 II. I. 50 A representing commoner in the function of his publick calling. **1755** in JOHNSON. Hence in mod. Dicts.

†**2.** Activity; action in general, whether physical or mental. Of a person: Bearing, gestures. *Obs.*

1579 LYLY *Euphues* (Arb.) 142 A trifold kinde of life, Actiue, which is about ciuil function, and administration. **1602** SHAKS. *Ham.* II. ii. 582 Teares in his eyes..A broken voyce, and his whole Function suiting With Formes, to his Conceit. **1605** —— *Macb.* I. iii. 140 Function is smother'd in surmise.

3. The special kind of activity proper to anything; the mode of action by which it fulfils its purpose. Also in generalized application, esp. (*Phys.*) as contrasted with *structure*.

a. of a physical organ; in early use of animal organisms only; later of vegetable. Often preceded by some defining word, as *animal*, *organic*, *vital*, etc.

1590 SHAKS. *Mids. N.* III. ii. 177 Dark night, that from the eye his function takes, The eare more quicke of apprehension makes. **1664** H. MORE *Myst. Iniq.*, *Apol.* 500 The Earth..modified into a frame fit for the functions of life. **1692** BENTLEY *Boyle Lect.* viii. 284 If our Air had not been a springy Elastical Body, no Animal could have exercised the very Function of Respiration. **1704** F. FULLER *Med. Gymn.* (1711) 22 Animal Spirits..serve to execute other Functions besides that of Motion. **1797** M. BAILLIE *Morb. Anat.* (1807) 285 There is little disadvantage to the animal functions produced by this variety. **1808** *Med. Jrnl.* XIX. 386 Before we can..understand the functions of the nerves, we must understand those of the brain. **1813** SIR H. DAVY *Agric. Chem.* (1814) 34 The same..law..is..essential to the functions of vegetable life. **1831** BREWSTER *Nat. Magic* iii. (1833) 51 Some accidental and temporary derangement of the vital functions. **1838** T. THOMSON *Chem. Org. Bodies* 988 The functions of the leaves during the day are very different from what they are during the night. **1862** DARWIN *Fertil. Orchids* ii. 65 These points of structure and function. **1882** VINES *Sachs' Bot.* 730 If the..limits mentioned..are exceeded, the functions of the plant may..simply come to rest. **1886** A. WINCHELL *Walks & Talks Geol. Field* 260 They [Pterosaurs] foreshadowed birds ..in the flying function.

b. of the intellectual and moral powers, etc.

1604 SHAKS. *Oth.* II. ii. 354 As her Appetite shall play the God, With his weake Function. **1671** MILTON *Samson* 596 Nature within me seems In all her functions weary of herself. **1809–10** COLERIDGE *Friend* (1837) III. 192 The functions of comparison, judgment, and interpretation. **1868** FARRAR *Silence & V.* ii. (1875) 33 The first function of the conscience is to warn.

c. of things in general; *spec.* in *Philology*; so **function word** (see quot. 1940).

1541 R. COPLAND *Galyen's Terap.* 2 Cj, There be two fyrste dyfferences of the functions and actions of medycyne. **1776** ADAM SMITH *W. N.* I. iv. (1869) I. 25 These rude bars, therefore, performed at this time the function of money. **1805–17** R. JAMESON *Char. Min.* (ed. 3) 189 The letters are placed as if all the angles and edges had different functions. **1854** BREWSTER *More Worlds* v. 93 The sun has a great function to perform in controlling the movements of the whole system. **1862** H. SPENCER *First Princ.* I. i. §2 (1875) 8 They assert that the sole function of the State is the protection of persons against each other, and against a foreign foe. **1872** RUSKIN *Eagle's N.* §210 The function of historical painting. **1894** O. JESPERSEN *Progress in Lang.* v. 135 Syntax is nothing but the theory of the functions, *i.e.*, meanings, of the grammatical forms. **1919** E. CLASSEN *Outl. Hist. Eng. Lang.* ii. 35 One of the consequences of the fixing of the word order was that each word in the sentence had its particular syntactic function according to its exact position, and that the survivals of free word order which were to be found in Old English disappeared in Middle English. **1926** L. BLOOMFIELD in *Language* II. 159 The positions in which a form occurs are its *functions*. **1933** —— *Lang.* xvi. 265 The lexical form in any actual utterance, as a concrete linguistic form, is always accompanied by some grammatical form: it appears in some function, and these privileges of occurrence make up, collectively, the grammatical *function* of the lexical form. *Ibid.*, Lexical forms which have any function in common, belong to a common form-class. **1940** C. C. FRIES *Amer. Eng. Gram.* 109 By a function word I mean a word that has little or no meaning apart from the grammatical idea it expresses. **1963** F. T. VISSER *Hist. Syntax* I. iii. 189 The verb is not a content-word, but a function-word, and is traditionally called 'copula'. **1967** [see FUNCTOR 2].

d. *Computers.* Any of the basic operations in a computer, esp. one that corresponds to a single instruction.

1947 D. R. HARTREE *Calculating Machines* 11 Consider, therefore, the functions required in the operation of a digital calculating machine. *Ibid.* 12 The components carrying out these functions may not all be physically distinct; for example a single unit may act both as an adding unit and a memory unit. **1952** *Math. Tables & other Aids to Computation* VI. 170 A 'left-shift' function is available. This shifts the entire product one place to the left and may be called by a digit impulse supplied to its function gate. **1962** *Gloss. Terms Autom. Data Processing (B.S.I.)* 37 *Function part* (operation part, function digits, function number), that part of an instruction which specifies the operation to be performed. **1964** F. L. WESTWATER *Electronic Computers* i. 10 A calculation can be carried out if the necessary functions are carried out in the correct order.

4. a. The kind of action proper to a person as belonging to a particular class, *esp.* to the holder of any office; hence, the office itself, an employment, profession, calling, trade.

1533 MORE *Confut. Barnes* VIII. Wks. 761/1 [Barnes values his own prayers above those of Our Lady and the saints] because the sayntes be al departed hence..and be no lenger of our funccion. **1564** *Brief Exam.* *****, Garmentes make not the person known by name, but his common function. **1574** *Ord.* in D. Irving *Hist. Scot. Poetry* (1861) 451 The contraveners hereof, if they be ministers, to be secludit fra the function. **1612** BRINSLEY *Lud. Lit.* i. (1627) 1 A Discourse betweene two Schoolemasters, Concerning their function. **1662** *Bk. Com. Prayer* Prayer Ember Week, To those which shall be ordained to any holy function. **1706** ESTCOURT *Fair Examp.* IV. i, If I don't succeed here, I'll renounce the Honour of my Function. **1725** DE FOE *Voy. round World* (1840) 210 Exercise no other function than that of a physician. **1791** BURKE *App. Whigs* Wks. VI. 85 With perfidy to their colleagues in function. **1795** —— *Regic. Peace* i. Wks. IX. 81 One of the very first acts, by which it auspicated its entrance into function. **1811** LAMB *Good Clerk* Misc. Wks. (1871) 385 The quill, which is the badge of his function, stuck behind his dexter ear. **1862** STANLEY *Jew. Ch.* (1877) I. xix. 369 The Jewish Prophets..included within their number functions so different as those of king and peasant. **1871** PALGRAVE *Lyr. Poems* 118 Then at thy noble function toil. **1878** R. W. DALE *Lect. Preach.* viii. 252 It is our function as ministers to satisfy the wants..of the higher life of man.

†**b.** *collect.* The persons following a profession or trade; an order, class. *Obs.*

*c***1580** in Rye *Cromer* (1870) p. lxiii, The Peere..will yealde further meanes of trade and wourke to every function. **1613** PURCHAS *Pilgrimage* (1614) 146 The Scribes are not a Sect, but a function. **1647** CLARENDON *Hist. Reb.* III. §145 The Earl of Essex was rather Displeased with the Person of the Arch-Bishop..than Indevoted to the Function. *a***1713** ELLWOOD *Autobiog.* (1765) 19, I went..to hear the Minister of Chinner; and this was the last time I ever went to hear any of that Function. **1725** POPE *Odyss.* XXI. 177 Thy coward function ever is in fear [said to a priest]. **1732** FIELDING *Miser* III. iv, Never was a person of my function so used.

c. *pl.* Official duties.

1550 BALE *Apol.* 105 b, Preferrynge vyrgynyte as..more free to all godly funccions. **1596** BP. W. BARLOW *Three Serm.* ii. 71 Eyther Prince or Subiect fayling in their seuerall functions and places. **1703** MAUNDRELL *Journ. Jerus.* (1732) 71 More..exact in their functions than the other Monks. **1774** J. BRYANT *Mythol.* I. 335 They were in some particular functions the most accurate..of any creatures upon earth. **1792** J. BARLOW *Const. of 1791*, 5 The quantity of prejudice with which their functions called them to contend. **1845** FORD *Handbk. Spain* I. 44 The mule performs in Spain the functions of the camel in the East. **1868** HELPS *Realmah* iii. (1876) 43 Ministers are worked to death by their double functions—parliamentary and official. **1874** FARRAR *Christ* 86 Caiaphas and Annas were dividing the functions of a priesthood which they disgraced.

5. a. A religious ceremony; orig. in the Roman Catholic Church. (Cf. It. *funzione.*)

1640 in *Trans. St. Paul's Eccles. Soc.* I. 46 Wee have had neyther prayers nor any other function her thes two yers. **1670–98** LASSELS *Voy. Italy* II. 33 A cross set with Diamonds and Pearls which the Pope wears at his breast in great functions. **1741** MIDDLETON *Cicero* I. VI. 416 The dedication was not performed with any of the solemn words and rites which such a function required. **1789** MRS. PIOZZI *Journ. France* I. 83 The Christmas functions here were showy. **1818** H. V. ELLIOTT *Let.* in Bateman *Life* iv. (1870) 70 These were the finest parts of the 'Function' as it is called. **1855** THACKERAY *Newcomes* xi, The function over, one almost expects to see the sextons put brown hollands over the pews. **1868** BROWNING *Ring & Bk.* IV. 439 After function's done with, down we go. **1884** *Sat. Rev.* 7 June 745/2 On Wednesday and Thursday last week there were functions in two adjacent Cathedrals.

b. [? after Sp. *funcion*: see quot. 1858.] A public ceremony; a social or festive meeting conducted with form and ceremony.

[**1858** W. STUART *Let.* in Hare *Story Two Noble Lives* (1893) II. 431, I hope that Char. s journal will have done justice to the Rajah of Mysore and his function along the road to receive her.] **1864** KINGSLEY *Rom. & Teut.* 123 Then was held a grand function. Dietrich..had Italy ceded to him by a 'Pragmatic' sanction. **1878** BESANT & RICE *Celia's Arb.* xxxvii, There was a Function of some kind—a Launch—a Reception—a Royal Visit—going on in the Dockyard. **1884** *Manch. Exam.* 11 Nov. 5/2 The American people are fond of functions. **1894** DU MAURIER *Trilby* (1895) 333 A prandial function which did not promise to be very amusing.

6. *Math.* A variable quantity regarded in its relation to one or more other variables in terms of which it may be expressed, or on the value of which its own value depends; **function space**, a topological space the elements of which are functions.

[This use of the L. *functio* is due to Leibnitz and his associates. A paper in the *Acta Eruditorum* for 1692, pp. 169–170, signed 'O.V.E.', but prob. written by Leibnitz, uses *functiones* in a sense hardly different from its ordinary untechnical sense, to denote the various 'offices' which a straight line may fulfil in relation to a curve, viz. its tangent, normal, etc. In the same journal for 1694, p. 316, Leibnitz defines *functio* as 'a part of a straight line which is cut off by straight lines drawn solely by means of a fixed point, and of a point in the curve which is given together with its degree of curvature'; the examples given being the ordinate, abscissa, tangent, normal, etc. As the *functiones* (in Leibnitz' sense) of a curve are variable quantities having a fixed mutual relation, this use of the word easily developed into the modern sense, which occurs in the writings of the Bernoullis early in the 18th c. A somewhat peculiar use occurs about 1713, in Leibnitz' *Hist. et Origo Calc. Diff.* (*Math. Schriften* ed. Gerhardt V. 408), where he says that just as constant quantities have their 'functions', viz. powers and roots, so variables have also 'functions' of a third kind, viz. differentials.]

1779 *Chambers' Cycl.* (ed. Rees) s.v., The term *function* is used in algebra, for an analytical expression any way compounded of a variable quantity, and of numbers, or constant quantities. **1789** WARING in *Phil. Trans.* LXXIX. 184 Let a quantity P be a function of x, or the fluent of a function of $x \times \dot{x}$. **1816** BABBAGE, etc. tr. *Lacroix's Diff. & Int. Calc.* 2 Let us take a function a little more complicated, $u = ax^2$. **1837** BREWSTER *Magnet.* 145 Whether the quantity and deviation at any point could be expressed by any function of the latitude and longitude of that point. **1885** WATSON & BURBURY *Math. Th. Electr. & Magn.* I. 242 The functions ϕ_a and ϕ_b may be positive or negative. **1892** J. EDWARDS *Diff. Calculus* i. §6 (ed. 2) 2 When one quantity depends upon another or upon a system of others, so that it assumes a definite value when a system of definite values is given to the others, it is called a function of those others. **1893** FORSYTH *Theory of Functions* 8 A complex quantity w is a function of another complex quantity z when they change together in such a manner that the value of $\frac{dw}{dz}$ is independent of the differential element dz. This is Riemann's definition. **1931** H. P. ROBERTSON tr. *Weyl's Theory of Groups & Quantum Mech.* i. 32 The totality of such functions $\psi(s)$ therefore constitute a linear 'function space' of continuously infinite dimensions. **1961** R. A. SILVERMAN tr. *Smirnov's Linear Algebra & Group Theory* v. 218 So far, we have considered the space H, where a vector is defined as an infinite set of numbers... We now consider a function space F, where continuously varying functions of one or several variables play the role of vectors. **1968** E. T. COPSON *Metric Spaces* iv. 57 The simplest function space consists of all functions $x(t)$ continuous on a closed interval $[a, b]$.

transf. **1876** L. TOLLEMACHE in *Fortn. Rev.* Jan. 110 A man's fortitude under given painful conditions is a function of two variables.

7. Special Comb.: **function key** *Computing*, a key that initiates an operation or sequence of operations, usu. other than the selection or transmission of one character.

1964 TROLLHANN & WITTMANN *Dict. Data Processing* 72/2 Function key. **1968** *IBM Systems Jrnl.* VIII. 148 The cathode-ray tube display with its attendant function keys, light pen..and typewriter keyboard is assumed as the device for the transfer of information between user and computer. **1984** J. HILTON *Choosing & Using your Home Computer* 83 The BASIC word PRINT can be produced by simply pressing the special function key and the key for the letter P together. **1985** *Which Computer?* Apr. 35/2 A special function key on the keyboard will produce a screen dump of whatever is currently on the screen.

Hence **'functioned** *ppl. a.*, furnished with or having a function.

1882 *Athenæum* 18 Nov. 657/2 Imagine a spiritual being so placed, so surrounded, and so functioned.

function ('fʌŋkʃən), *v.* [f. prec. sb. Cf. F. *fonctionner.*]

1. a. *intr.* To fulfil a function; to perform one's duty or part; to operate; to act. (In mod. use influenced by F. *fonctionner.*)

1856 MASSON *Chatterton* II. iv. (1874) 227 Debt, though negative property, still is a kind of property, and functions as such to the advantage of its possessor. **1862** MARSH *Eng. Lang.* 40 When played upon by an expert operator it functioned, as the French say, very well. **1876** MAUDSLEY *Physiol. Mind* v. 328 The mind will function along certain definite lines or paths. **1889** *Edin. Rev.* Oct. 533 No instrument of despotism..has ever functioned with so little noise. **1894** H. DRUMMOND *Ascent Man* 257 In the higher groups the nutritive system is..the first to function, and the last to cease its work. **1897** G. ALLEN *Evol. Idea of God* iii. 46 We..know..consciousness ceases altogether at death, when the brain no longer functions. **1907** *Daily Chron.* 21 Aug. 4/7 This joy does not 'function', as the French so charmingly say, over the present sample of autumnal weather in a month that should strictly be August. **1918** *Times* 18 Apr. 8/3 The agencies of obstruction and party intrigue which will immediately begin to function in every section of the political arena. **1924** GALSWORTHY *White Monkey* I. viii, There are rules of the game which must be observed, if society is to function at all. **1965** M. SPARK *Mandelbaum Gate* iii. 50 Freddy functioned on with his letter, as he had done for thirty years of his natural history, a letter a week.

b. *Phys.*

1878 BELL *Gegenbaur's Comp. Anat.* 7 We..know Vertebrata in which the clefts function only for a time as respiratory organs. **1887** *Athenæum* 29 Oct. 572/1 Groups.. having the nephridia functioning as efferent ducts for the gonads. **1896** *Life & Lett. G. J. Romanes* 16 But in no case had it been shewn that they [nerves] functioned as such.

2. To hold a 'function' (see FUNCTION *sb.* 5 b) or ceremonial meeting. ? *nonce-use.*

1890 *Sat. Rev.* 10 May 554/1 Two other Societies ..'functioned' on the same day.

Hence **'functioning** *vbl. sb.* and *ppl. a.*

1881 W. S. TUKE tr. *Charcot's Clin. Lect.* 232 Disturbances resulting from the abnormal functioning of the affected organ. **1894** *Westm. Mag.* 8 May 2/3 The mere show, the social functioning and ceremony, remains, although everyone knows that the life of the metropolis no longer expresses itself through the City Corporation. **1894** H. DRUMMOND *Ascent Man* ii. 117 The still functioning muscles of the forehead.

functional ('fʌŋkʃənəl), *a.* and *sb.* [f. FUNCTION *sb.* + -AL[1].]

A. *adj.* **1. a.** Of or pertaining to some function or office; official. In weaker sense: Formal.

1631 J. BURGES *Answ. Rejoined* 205 The title of holines is not alwaies personall, but often functionall..thus..the Levites and Priests..were stiled holy. **1860** S. WILBERFORCE *Addr. Ordin.* 23 The validity..of..functional acts..is not affected by the unworthiness of the appointed agent. **1874** H. R. REYNOLDS *John Bapt.* v. §3. 351 He had certain national..offices to fill, for which He needed specific and functional introduction. **1889** *Pall Mall G.* 23 May 5/1 Some..functional speeches followed.

b. Relating to the system which specializes and divides the functions of managers, workers, or employees in a business, factory, etc. *U.S.*

1903 F. W. TAYLOR *Shop Management* §234 'Functional management' consists in so dividing the work of management that each man from the assistant superintendent down shall have as few functions as possible to perform. *Ibid.* §240 The four functional bosses who are a part of the planning department. *Ibid.* §245 Functional Foremanship. **1911** —— *Princ. Sci. Management* 65 It is necessary, therefore, to provide teachers (called functional foremen) to see that the workmen both understand and carry out these written instructions. Under functional management, the old-fashioned single foreman is superseded by eight different men, each one of whom has his own special duties. **1930** M. CLARK *Home Trade* 198 Foremen are of the type termed 'functional'.

c. As related to the arts, esp. to architecture: designating work executed with a view to its utilitarian purpose; also, of artists, builders, etc.: concerned with the use intended for their product, not with traditional or other theories of design.

1928 G. H. EDGELL *Amer. Archit. To-day* iv. 301 These.. stand for the two types of daring engineering with architectural beauty and of pre-eminent monumentality with perfect functional fitness. **1931** C. H. REILLY in W. Rose *Outl. Mod. Knowl.* 997 Their buildings are in the first and last place functional and..with them form follows function both within and without. **1937** H. READ *Art & Society* vii. 261 (*heading*) Functional Art. **1938** *Encycl. Brit. Bk. of Yr.* 54/2 Even before the World War..structural requirements, *i.e.* 'functional' plan, more often conflicted than harmonized with the 'architectural' design of a building. **1956** A. WILSON *Anglo-Saxon Att.* I. iii. 81 Light industry was embodied in a splendid compromise between functional and more conventional English taste. **1957** J. BRAINE *Room at Top* vii. 72 It [*sc.* the house] was 1930 functional in white concrete, with a flat roof. **1966** *Illustr. London News* 30 July 29/1 The outside of this building is functional and severe.

2. *Phys.* **a.** Of or pertaining to the functions of an organ. Of diseases: Affecting the functions only, not structural or organic. Also of a mental disorder: having no discernible organic cause. **b.** Of an organ: Serving a function (oppposed to *rudimentary*).

1843 SIR C. SCUDAMORE *Med. Visit Gräfenberg* 53 It seems probable that more than functional error in the membranes of the brain and spinal marrow exists in this case. **1872** DARWIN *Emotions* vi. 164 It would appear..that the lachrymal glands do not..come to full functional activity at a very early period of life. **1874** MAUDSLEY *Respons. in Ment. Dis.* ii. 44 It is with so-called functional diseases such as epilepsy, chorea, neuralgia. **1884** *Cassell's Family Mag.* Feb. 143/2 Functional disease of the heart. **1920** *Proc. R. Soc. Medicine* XIII. III. *Psychiatry* 32 Functional disorders of particular systems and communities of neurones. **1926** W. McDOUGALL *Outl. Abnormal Psychol.* i. 1 There are two great classes of disorders of our mental life, those that are directly due to organic lesions of the nervous system and those which seem to imply no such lesion, no gross injury to the structure of the brain, and which are therefore called 'functional disorders'. **1960** HINSIE & CAMPBELL *Psychiatric Dict.* 310/2 A functional mental disorder is one which, insofar as knowledge permits, stems from the psyche. **1962** *Listener* 21 June 1082/3 The patient complains of, and suffers, the appropriate pains; but there are no, or inadequate, physiological grounds for them; in current medical jargon they are 'functional'. **1971** *Brit. Med. Bull.* XXVII. 77/1 The term 'functional psychosis' has no precise meaning.

c. *Social Sciences.* Of or pertaining to a particular mental or social function. Applied to an approach to the study of the interrelations of particular phenomena within a given framework or structure, freq. in contrast to a structural approach.

1884 W. JAMES in *Mind* IX. 19 The contrast is really between two *aspects*, in which all mental facts without exception may be taken; their structural aspect, as being subjective, and their functional aspect as being cognitions. **1898** *Philos. Rev.* VII. 451 There is, however, a functional psychology, over and above this psychology of structure. **1921** *Amer. Jrnl. Psychol.* XXXII. 519 Functional psychology, in this sense, is especially American, and the psychology of act especially German. *Ibid.* 533 If the view of my book is accepted, both 'functional' and 'structural', as qualifications of 'psychology', are now obsolete terms. **1926** B. MALINOWSKI in *Encycl. Brit.* Suppl. I. 132/2 *The Functional Analysis of Culture.*—This type of theory aims at the explanation of anthropological facts at all levels of development by their function, by the part which they play within the integral system of culture, by the manner in which they are related to each other within the system, and by the manner in which this system is related to the physical surroundings. **1937** G. W. ALLPORT *Personality* (1938) v. 133 The boundaries between the functional systems are weak in infancy, causing the child to react as a whole. *Ibid.* vii. 191 For convenience of discussion this new principle [of growth] may be christened the functional autonomy of motives. **1944** B. MALINOWSKI *Sci. Theory of Culture* x. 115 The cogency of the functional approach consists in the fact that it does not pretend to forecast exactly how a problem posed for a culture will be solved. **1948** T. G. ANDREWS *Methods of Psychol.* i. 10 Experiments of the functional type are designed to answer the question *how*. **1951** R. C. SHELDON in Parsons & Shils *Toward Gen. Theory of Action* I. 35 Such difficulties are at the bottom of the dissatisfaction that many social scientists feel with the functional approach in social science, which assumes that every action has the function of promoting the maintenance of a system. **1951** E. E. EVANS-PRITCHARD *Social Anthropol.* iii. 56 Functional anthropology, with its emphasis on the concept of social system and hence on the need for systematic studies of the social life of primitive peoples as they are today,..not only separated..social anthropology from ethnology; it also brought together the theoretical study of institutions and the observational study of primitive social life. **1968** *Encycl. Soc. Sci.* VI. 21/2 Structural-functional analysis is not new in either the social or the natural sciences... The only new aspect of it is its formidable new name, structural-functional analysis. *Ibid.* 23/2 What general conditions must be met (i.e. functional requisites) if the unit is to persist in its setting without change.

d. Pertaining to or serving a function (opp. *functionless*). Also, practical, utilitarian.

1864 *Reader* 24 Dec. 792/2 The stage never needed a tonic more. There are many indications of returning health, amid all its symptoms of weakness and functional derangement. **1875** BLAKE *Zool.* 25 The hoofs may be..2 functional and 2 rudimental, as in the greatest number of ruminant types. **1879** SIR G. SCOTT *Lect. Archit.* II. 190 My last lecture brought the subject of vaulting to its full functional development. **1890** W. JAMES *Princ. Psychol.* I. x. 401 If there be such a meaning..it alone can make clear to us why such finite human streams of thought are called into existence in such functional dependence upon brains. **1943** *Mind* LII. 360 The whole point is to discover unexpected functional dependences, and this can only be done by operating in unusual conditions and with unusual material. **1950** *Times Lit. Suppl.* 13 Jan. 26/2 In a good poem imagery and rhythm are functional, not merely decorative. **1960** C. WINICK *Dict. Anthropol.* 535/1 The instability in human speech is caused by the varying needs of society. These needs are manifest in functional changes of the elements, eventually resulting in modifications of the linguistic structure. **1961** E. NAGEL *Structure of Sci.* iv. 73 The more sophisticated modern notions of cause as invariable functional dependence. **1962** J. GLENN in *Into Orbit* 40 It was an extremely difficult vehicle to build... It was not perfect; but it was functional.

3. *Math.* Of or pertaining to a function: see FUNCTION *sb.* 6.

1806 GOMPERTZ in *Phil. Trans.* XCVI. 176 This theorem evidently supposes that the functional values of *pz* are distinct in the general expression for the sum of the series. **1815** BABBAGE *Ibid.* CV. II. 390 A functional equation is said to be of the first order, when it contains only the first function of the unknown quantity. *Ibid.*, α, β, γ, &c. are known functional characteristics. **1860** BOOLE *Finite Diff.* xi. 218 The most general definition of a functional equation is that it expresses a relation arising from the forms of functions; a relation therefore which is independent of the particular values of the subject variable.

4. *Logic.* **functional calculus** = *predicate calculus.*

1933 M. BLACK *Nature of Math.* 63 These new symbols are both primitive in the functional calculus. **1951** *Mind* LX. 265 The basic notions of the lower functional calculus.

B. *sb. Math.* [ad. F. *fonctionnelle* in same sense (M. Fréchet 1906, in *Rendiconti del Circ. matem. di Palermo* XXII. 38; Fréchet ascribes the word to Hadamard (1903), who, however, used it only as an adj., in *opération fonctionnelle*).] A function the value of which depends on the whole form of another function; **functional analysis**, the analysis of functionals.

1917 *Proc. Nat. Acad. Sci.* III. 640 (*heading*) On bi-linear and *n*-linear functionals. **1918** G. C. EVANS *Functionals & their Applications* i. 1 The maximum of a function is a functional of that function. **1945** E. T. BELL *Devel. Math.* (ed. 2) xxii. 535 Volterra used the terminology 'functions depending on other functions', and the special case of 'functions of lines', for what were subsequently called functionals..by Hadamard. *Ibid.*, $F[x(t)]$ is called a functional of $x(t)$ when its value depends on all the values assumed by $x(t)$. **1948** E. HILLE (*title*) Functional analysis and semi-groups. **1966** R. STONE *Math. in Soc. Sci.* i. 11 Often when taking a decision..what we have to maximize (or minimize) is a functional rather than a function. **1968** E. T. COPSON *Metric Spaces* Pref., The theory of the topology of metric spaces..is not only the basis of functional analysis but also unifies many branches of classical analysis.

Hence **functio'nality**, functional character; in *Math.*, the condition of being a function.

1871 EARLE *Philol. Eng. Tongue* §252 The old native Latin, whose vitality and functionality was all but purely flectional. **1879** CAYLEY in *Encycl. Brit.* IX. 818/1 Functionality in Analysis is dependence on a variable or variables.

'functionalism. [f. FUNCTIONAL *a.* + -ISM.]

1. *Social Sciences.* The method of studying, or the theory of, the functional interactions and adaptations of particular phenomena within a given framework or structure.

1914 J. B. WATSON *Behavior* i. 9 We advance the view that behaviorism is the only consistent and logical functionalism. **1932** *Encycl. Social Sci.* VI. 524/1 The reason is probably the fact that the whole trend of the social process since Darwin has been in the direction of functionalism and might be described as its verification and validation. **1933** P. RADIN *Method & Theory Ethnol.* vi. 176 Why a new term like functionalism should be applied to it is not at all evident. **1937** R. H. LOWIE *Hist. Ethnol. Theory* xiii. 235 Malinowski's functionalism is avowedly antidistributional, antihistorical, and treats each culture as a closed system except insofar as its elements correspond to vital biological urges. **1944** B. MALINOWSKI *Sci. Theory of Culture* x. 117 The type of criticism levelled against functionalism, to the effect that it never can prove why a specific form..of table implement or theological concept, is prevalent in a culture, derives from the prescientific craving for first causes. **1951** R. B. MACLEOD in Rohrer & Sherif *Social Psychol. at Crossroads* 224 Functionalism..has settled down to the 'middle of the road' American psychology. **1956** J. H. M. BEATTIE in A. Pryce-Jones *New Outl. Mod. Knowl.* 259 But basic to all forms of functionalism is the view that the facts of social life may not usefully be thought of as a collection of separate elements. **1963** C. JACOBSON tr. *Lévi-Strauss's Struct. Anthropol.* v. xv. 290 Therefore, historico-geographical concerns should not be excluded from the field of structural studies, as was generally implied by the widely accepted opposition between 'diffusionism' and 'functionalism'.

2. Regard for the function and purpose of a building as regulating its shape and style. Also in extended use.

1930 *Observer* 29 June 20 Sugar-cube architecture, or to be impressively abstract 'Functionalism'. *Ibid.* 5 Oct. 19 This is what is called the architecture of functionalism. The architectural form arises purely out of the purpose of the building. **1935** *Fortnightly* Apr. 410 We are now told that 'Functionalism' is the one and only test of art. **1941** *Burlington Mag.* Feb. 66/2 His definition of modern 'Functionalism' will not satisfy all readers, though it will make many of them chuckle: 'The theory that any building which could be made to stand up at all was All Right.' **1955** S. SPENDER *Making of Poem* i. 18 Functionalism is the philistinism of people who talk about a work of art as a 'well-done job' like any other piece of plumbing. **1957** E. H. GOMBRICH *Story of Art* xxvii. 421 The theories for which the Bauhaus stood are sometimes condensed in the slogan of 'functionalism'—the belief that if something is only designed to fit its purpose we can let beauty look after itself.

'functionalist, *sb.* (and *a.*) [f. FUNCTIONAL *a.* + -IST.]

1. *Social Sciences.* An adherent or advocate of the functional approach (see FUNCTIONAL *a.* 2 c). Also *attrib.* or as *adj.*

1914 J. B. WATSON *Behavior* i. 8 The difference between functional psychology and structural psychology, as the functionalists have so far stated the case, is unintelligible. *Ibid.*, The terms sensation, perception, affection, emotion, volition are used as much by the functionalist as by the structuralist. **1931** R. S. WOODWORTH *Contemp. Schools Psychol.* iii. 48 This attempt of the functionalists to revise the definition of psychology by lining it up with biology. **1933** P. RADIN *Method & Theory Ethnol.* ii. 24 The so-called functionalist school of Radcliffe-Brown and Malinowski. **1937** R. H. LOWIE *Hist. Ethnol. Theory* xiii. 236 There is only one natural unit for the ethnologist—the culture of all humanity at all periods and in all places; only when the functionalist has..defined his particular culture within that frame of reference, does he know what he is talking about. **1951** R. B. MACLEOD in Rohrer & Sherif *Social Psychol. at Crossroads* 224 For the functionalist perceiving is also a function, one of the organism's ways of adjusting itself. **1952** W. J. H. SPROTT *Social Psychol.* 221 The 'Functionalists'—such as Malinowski and Radcliffe-Brown—come to our aid. At least every society must provide means of satisfying the basic needs of its members, and we can therefore explain many of their institutions in terms of the function they perform to this end. **1961** *Oxf. Mag.* 1 June 387/1 Professor Evans-Pritchard's criticisms of 'functionalist' (i.e. unhistorical) anthropology have been made on earlier occasions. **1970** E. LEACH *Lévi-Strauss* i. 7 Most..social anthropologists..claim to be 'functionalists'; broadly speaking they are anthropologists in the style and tradition of Malinowski. In contrast, Claude Lévi-Strauss is a social anthropologist in the tradition of Frazer.

2. An adherent of functionalism in design. Also *attrib.* or as *adj.*, exhibiting functionalism.

1932 H. ROBERTSON *Mod. Archit. Design* iv. 140 The functionalist, in theory at any rate, seeks in design only the most effective expression of the *use* of any object, whether it be a house to live in, or a chair to sit on. **1934** *Archit. Rev.* LXXV. 9 Having been first designed as a quasi 'free classic' building, it was, as it were, driven to re-designing itself in a more functionalist fashion by sheer pressure of circumstances. **1939** O. LANCASTER *Homes Sweet Homes* 78 Recent compliance on the part of the insular British with the extreme dictates of the continental functionalists.

functionalize ('fʌŋkʃənəlaɪz), *v.* [f. FUNCTIONAL *a.* + IZE.] *trans.* To place or assign to some function or office (Webster 1864); *U.S.* in the theory of business management: to distribute or assign (work) with due regard to the special function of the individual worker. Hence **,functionali'zation**, the system governing such assignment of work.

1923 R. H. LANSBURGH *Industr. Management* 55 Functionalization has brought with it basic changes in the structure of industrial organizations. *Ibid.* 60 These functionalized foremen. *Ibid.* 63 Functionalized departments working through one foreman. **1925** W. H. LEFFINGWELL *Office Management* 108 As business grows ever larger and becomes increasingly functionalized and specialized. *Ibid.* 118 The functionalization of all industrial departments. **1958** *Times Lit. Suppl.* 4 Apr. 186/3 Collectivization and functionalization, in short, are facts: or rather, series of events, because they have happened historically and uncritically.

functionally ('fʌŋkʃənəlɪ), *adv.* [f. FUNCTIONAL *a.* + -LY².] In a functional manner; with respect to the functions; in the discharge of the functions.

1820 W. LAWRENCE *Lect.* ii. 163 The organ is said to be functionally disordered. **1846** OWEN *Brit. Fossil Mamm.* 433 The horned Ruminants, for example, manifest transitorily in the embryo-state the germs of upper incisors and canines, which disappear before birth, but which were retained and functionally developed in the cloven-footed Anoplothere. **1854** WOODWARD *Mollusca* (1856) 256 Its muscle becomes (functionally) an adductor. **1879** H. SPENCER *Data of Ethics* xi. 188 Functionally produced modifications. **1882** VINES *Sachs' Bot.* 919 The male organs of species-hybrids are functionally weak to a higher degree than the female organs. **1927** E. A. SONNENSCHEIN *Soul of Grammar* 3 Two cases might differ functionally without differing morphologically. **1934** H. READ *Art & Industry* 11 C. 91/1 For sitting upright, actually the stool or the bench is all that is functionally necessary. **1951** E. E. EVANS-PRITCHARD *Social Anthropol.* ii. 22 [Montesquieu] had the idea of everything in a society and its ambient being functionally related to everything else. **1971** *Nature* 30 Apr. 578/3 The indications are clear that the ancestral middle Miocene hominoids were structurally and functionally advanced in this locomotor style.

functionarism ('fʌŋkʃənərɪz(ə)m). [f. FUNCTIONARY + -ISM.] The system of administration by means of functionaries; the characteristic bearing and manner of functionaries: officialism.

1842 *Tait's Mag.* IX. 177 That new power which in this country is termed official patronage, and which Mr. Laing calls Functionarism. **1851** HT. MARTINEAU *Hist. Peace* (1877) III. IV. xiii. 121 By a rapid and perpetual extension of functionarism..he was casting a net over France. **1880** *Contemp. Rev.* Mar. 432 Functionarism is one of the most characteristic phenomena in Germany. **1885** *Sat. Rev.* 3 Oct. 463 What Mr. Newmarch called 'functionarism' in opposition to individualism—the State undertaking the functions of the individual.

functionary ('fʌŋkʃənərɪ), *sb.* [f. FUNCTION *sb.* + -ARY[1], after F. *fonctionnaire.*] One invested with a function; one who has certain functions or duties to perform; an official.

1791 BURKE *Th. Fr. Affairs* Wks. VII. 19 Their republick is to have a first functionary (as they call him) under the name of king, or not, as they think fit. **1816** J. SCOTT *Vis. Paris* (ed. 5) Pref. 61 Several houses have been burnt, and an unfortunate functionary cut to pieces. **1844** DICKENS *Mart. Chuz.* (C.D. ed.) 195 A female functionary, a nurse. **1879** FROUDE *Cæsar* xviii. 303 Legitimate functionaries to carry on the government.

'**functionary**, *a.* [f. FUNCTION *sb.* + -ARY[2].]

1. = FUNCTIONAL 2.

1822–34 *Good's Study Med.* (ed. 4) III. 59 The disease may..commence in some structural or functionary affection of the abdominal organs.

2. Official; = FUNCTIONAL 1.

1862 MERIVALE *Rom. Emp.* (1865) VI. xlix. 118 In order that these offices should be adequately filled..it was necessary to maintain this functionary reservoir constantly at the same exalted level. **1882–3** *Schaff's Encycl. Relig. Knowl.* II. 1310 The functionary duties of the Levites. **1895** *Westm. Gaz.* 23 Aug. 2/3 Let us have done with these fictions of functionary superiority.

functionate ('fʌŋkʃəneɪt), *v.* Somewhat *rare.* [f. as prec. + -ATE[3].] *intr.* To perform one's function; to work, operate; to officiate. Hence '**functionating** *vbl. sb.*, in quot. *attrib.*

1856 LEVER *Martins of Cro' M.* 149 The worst of the class is, they'll only functionate for your grand dinners, and they leave your every-day meal to some inferior in the department. **1869** *Daily News* 11 June, The reflective faculty remains in undisturbed repose. As the French say, it does not 'functionate'. **1873** E. H. CLARKE *Sex in Educ.* 40 The muscles and the brain cannot functionate in their best way at the same moment. **1891** D. WILSON *Right Hand* 187 The existence, then, of greater nutrition and greater functionating ability in the left hemisphere might well be assumed.

functionize ('fʌŋkʃənaɪz), *v. rare.* [f. FUNCTION *sb.* + -IZE.] = FUNCTION *v.* 1.

1868 N. PORTER *Human Intellect* Introd. IV. §41. 55 A soul that is self-conscious is not so singular as a brain functionizing about itself and its own being.

functionless (fʌŋkʃənlɪs), *a.* [f. as prec. + -LESS.] Having no function: chiefly in physiological sense. Cf. FUNCTION *sb.* 3 a.

1836 FONBLANQUE *Eng. under Seven Admin.* (1837) III. 296 Its nominal functionless minister. **1839–47** TODD *Cycl. Anat.* III. 238/1 Clavicles..almost obsolete and functionless. **1871** DARWIN *Desc. Man* I. i. 29 The os coccyx in man, though functionless as a tail, plainly represents this part in other vertebrate animals. **1879** A. W. BENNETT in *Academy* 32 A fifth stamen, which however is functionless, so far as the ordinary purpose of stamens is concerned. **1889** *Pall Mall G.* 13 Nov. 6/2 These organs are quite functionless as wings. **1894** J. R. ILLINGWORTH *Personality* ii. (1895) 52 Capabilities..which we cannot conceive ultimately frustrated and functionless.

functor ('fʌŋktə(r)). [f. FUNCT(ION *sb.* + -OR, after type *factor.*] **1.** *Logic.* A function or operator.

1937 A. SMEATON tr. *Carnap's Logical Syntax Lang.* §3. p. 14 In order to express properties or relations of position by means of numbers, we shall use functors. *Ibid.*, Besides such descriptive functors, we make use also of logical functors. For example: 'sum (3, 4)' has the meaning: '3 plus 4'. **1947** H. REICHENBACH *Elem. Symb. Logic* §54. p. 312 Among the functors, the unique mathematical functions are of particular importance. **1951** J. ŁUKASIEWICZ *Aristotle's Syllogistic* iv. 78 The principle of my notation is to write the functors before the arguments. In this way I can avoid brackets. **1956** E. H. HUTTEN *Lang. Mod. Physics* vi. 232 Newton's first law..finds a 'natural' translation as, e.g. (x)(Rx v Ux ⊃ ~ Fx), if the functors R, U, and F mean 'being at rest', 'being in uniform motion', and 'being acted upon by a force', respectively. **1963** *Med. Ævum* XXXII. 144 One should have '*can* exist of itself'; this modal functor ..is vital to the course of the..exposition.

2. *Linguistics.* = *form-word*; also used more widely, to include similar affixes, etc.

1958 C. F. HOCKETT *Course in Mod. Ling.* xxxi. 264 There are at least three types of grammatical forms which are to be classed as functors. **1964** R. A. HALL *Introd. Ling.* iii. 15 These elements which indicate grammatical functions are termed 'function-words' or 'functors'. **1965** *Listener* 17 June 903/2 In themselves prepostions (which may be described as structure-words or functors) have no lexical meanings. **1967** R. A. WALDRON *Sense & Sense Devel.* ii. 45 Even individual words like *and, but, or,*..(which are variously known as function words, form words, operators, functors, or kenemes)..are defined grammatically rather than, or as well as, lexically.

Hence **func'torial** *a.*

1951 J. ŁUKASIEWICZ *Aristotle's Syllogistic* v. 132 All these may be called functorial propositions, since in all of them there occurs a propositional functor, like 'if—then', 'or', 'and'. **1955** A. N. PRIOR *Formal Logic* I. iv. 94 If quantifiers and functorial variables are introduced, we may obtain just as rich a system.

fund (fʌnd), *sb.* [ad. L. *fund-us* the bottom; also, a piece of land. Cf. FOND *sb.*

Fund and *fond* were used indiscriminately in the 17th c.; in the 18th c. *fond* went out of use. The senses represent those of F. *fond, fonds,* rather than those of L. *fundus.*]

†**1. a.** The bottom; in various application; occas. *Phys.* = FUNDUS. ***in the fund*** (= F. *dans le fond, au fond*): at bottom. ***fund of grass***: a low-lying grass-plat. Cf. BOTTOM *sb.* 4 b. *Obs.*

1677 GALE *Crt. Gentiles* II. IV. 36 An adventitious joy, which hath no funde or bottome. **1682** H. MORE *Annot. Glanvill's Lux O.* 18 Objects of Sight, whose Chief, if not onely Images, are in the fund of the Eye. **1705** VANBRUGH *Confed.* IV. Wks. (Rtldg.) 431/2 In the fund she is the softest, sweetest, gentlest lady breathing. **1709** *Brit. Apollo* II. No. 77. 2/1 A Glass-Bubble..fix'd..to the Fund of a Vessel. **1712** J. JAMES tr. *Le Blond's Gardening* 61 Bowling-Greens, or hollow Funds of Grass. **1737** BRACKEN *Farriery Impr.* (1757) II. 281 So that the Wound may be closed in its whole Length, from the Fund to the outward Orifice. *a* **1761** LAW *Comf. Weary Pilgr.* (1809) 58 This depth is called the center, the fund or bottom of the soul.

†**b.** A coach-seat. (Cf. F. *carrosse à deux fonds.*) *Obs.*

1699 M. LISTER *Journ. Paris* 12 The Coaches..of the great Nobility..have two Seats or Funds.

c. of a medal.

1697 EVELYN *Numism.* vi. 214 Moulding Medals..in case they polish the Fund with any Tool, 'twill seem to have been trimm'd with more Niceness and Formality than is Genuine.

†**2.** Foundation, groundwork, basis; only in immaterial sense; = FOND *sb.* 1. ***upon one's own fund***: on one's own account. *Obs.*

1677 GALE *Crt. Gentiles* II. III. 143 A secret desire of Independence..is graven on the very fund of our corrupt nature. **1699** BENTLEY *Phal.* 75 The only Fund for this Conjecture is Hermippus's Relation of Pythagoras's Death. **1729** BUTLER *Serm.* Wks. 1874 II. 12 Weak ties indeed, and what may afford fund enough for ridicule. **1745** DE FOE *Eng. Tradesman* Introd. (1841) I. 3 The..British product, being the fund of its inland trade. **1748** H. WALPOLE *Corr.* (1837) II. cxciii. 239, I took to him for his resemblance to you; but am grown to love him upon his own fund.

3. Source of supply; a permanent stock that can be drawn upon:

†**a.** of material things. Rarely *pl. Obs.*

1695 WOODWARD *Nat. Hist. Earth* I. (1723) 52 The Matter it self [being] restored to its original Fund and Promptuary, the Earth. **1716** R. COTES in *Phil. Trans.* XXXI. 69 For let A B, represent the plane of the Horizon..E F, a fund of Vapours or Exhalations at a considerable height above us. **1725** *Wodrow Corr.* (1843) III. 231, I know not what funds they have of the papers of those times. **1757** A. COOPER *Distiller* I. xviii. (1760) 79 Nor is this the only Fund of their Brandies. **1793** N. VANSITTART *Refl. Propriety Peace* 127 An inexhaustible fund of recruits may be drawn from Hungary. **1796** MORSE *Amer. Geog.* I. 757 The northern parts are covered with wood, among which is an inexhaustible fund of large timber.

b. of immaterial things; = FOND *sb.* 2; sometimes with mixture of sense 2. †***out of one's own fund*** [= F. *de son propre fonds*]: from one's own stock of knowledge, out of one's own head.

a **1704** T. BROWN *Wks.* (1707) I. II. 81 The translating most of the French letters gave me as much trouble as if I had written them out of my own fund. **1723** DE FOE *Col. Jack* (1840) 185 Nor had I a fund of religious knowledge. **1769** *Junius Lett.* xvi. 73 There is a fund of good sense in this country, which cannot be deceived. **1770** LANGHORNE *Plutarch* (1879) I. 400/1 Learning..ought not to be considered as mere pastime and an useless fund for talk. **1832** HT. MARTINEAU *Life in Wilds* vi. 80 When we get such a fund of labour as this at our command. **1863** MRS. C. CLARKE *Shaks. Char.* xii. 300 Beatrice possesses a fund of hidden tenderness beneath her exterior gaiety and sarcasm. **1877** A. B. EDWARDS *Up Nile* vi. 134 The Painter..brings a fund of experience into the council.

4. a. *sing.* A stock or sum of money, *esp.* one set apart for a particular purpose. Cf. FOND *sb.* 3. ***sinking fund***: see SINKING *vbl. sb.*

1694 *Massachusetts Law* 27 Oct., A fund for the repayment of all such sums. **1726–7** SWIFT *Gulliver* I. vi, Or, if that fund be deficient, it is largely supplied by the crown. **1764** GOLDSM. *Trav.* 202 And e'en those ills, that round his mansion rise, Enhance the bliss his scanty fund supplies. **1795** *Gentl. Mag.* 544/2 The principal projector of the fund for decayed musicians. **1838** DICKENS *Nich. Nick.* xvi, A small fund raised by the conversion of some spare clothes into ready money. **1868** G. DUFF *Pol. Surv.* 25 There is a reserve fund, valued at from two to three times the amount of the yearly expenditure.

b. *pl.* Money at a person's disposal; pecuniary resources. (***to be*** or ***put***) ***in funds***: in possession of money.

1728 YOUNG *Love Fame* I. (1757) 86 By your revenue measure your expence; And to your funds and acres join your sense. **1798** Picton *L'pool Munic. Rec.* (1886) II. 225 Your Committee has little doubt of its bringing into the Corporation Funds a sum of money. **1848** MILL *Pol. Econ.* I. v. §2. (1876) 41 Funds which have not yet found an investment. **1849** THACKERAY *Pendennis* (1885) II. 17 When he had no funds he went on tick. **1873** C. ROBINSON *N.S. Wales* 93 An additional guarantee from the public funds of one-half the cost of building. **1879** MISS BRADDON *Clov. Foot* II. i. 11 When he was in funds he preferred a hansom. **1895** BUDD in *Law Times* XCIX. 545/1 With a view to putting the society in funds to pay its out-of-pocket disbursements.

5. † **a.** *sing.* A portion of revenue set apart as a security for specified payments. *Obs.*

a **1700** B. E. *Dict. Cant. Crew* s.v., *A Staunch Fund*, a good Security. *a* **1715** BURNET *Own Time* (1734) II. 209 The parliament went on slowly in fixing the fund for the Supplies they had voted. **1726–31** TINDAL *Rapin's Hist. Eng.* (1743) II. XVII. 135 Some good fund should be assigned her for the payment of what was due. **1740** W. DOUGLASS *Disc. Curr. Brit. Plant. Amer.* 13 The 500,000*l.* lately proposed without Fund or Period. **1776** ADAM SMITH *W.N.* v. iii. (1869) II. 513 The first general mortgage or fund, consisting of a prolongation to the first of August 1706, of several different taxes which would have expired within a shorter term.

fig. **1819** J. MARSHALL *Const. Opin.* (1839) 152 Industry, talents and integrity constitute a fund which is as confidently trusted as property itself.

b. ***the (public) funds***: the stock of the national debt, considered as a mode of investment.

(The origin of this sense may perh. be illustrated by phrases like 'to invest in *securities*'.)

1713 STEELE *Englishm.* No. 55. 353 Methought my Mony chink'd..for joy of the Safety of the rest I have in the Funds. **1783** COWPER *Let.* 23 Nov., If he be the happiest man who has least money in the funds. **1809** R. LANGFORD *Introd. Trade* 52 Funds is a general term for money lent to government, and which constitutes the national debt. **1848** THACKERAY *Van. Fair* xx, Look what the funds were on the 1st of March. **1875** W. S. HAYWARD *Love agst. World* ii. 10 He..must have close on a hundred and fifty thousand in the funds.

†**6.** In sense of L. *fundus*: A farm. *Obs.*[−1]

1708 MOTTEUX *Rabelais* (1737) V. 230 You to your..rural Fund migrate.

7. *Printing.* = FOUNT[2]. Also *attrib.*

1683 [see FOUNT[2]]. **1695** *Specimen of Let. to Univ. by Dr. John Fell*, 5 Pair of Fund Cases. **1709** TANNER *Let.* 3 Oct. in Hearne *Collect.* II. 458 They can have a new fund of Letter from Holland.

8. *Comb.*, as ***fund-raising*** adj. and sb.; so ***fund-raiser***; **fund-holder**, one who has money invested in the public funds; so ***fund-holding*** ppl. adj.; **fund-lord** (formed by Cobbett after *land-lord*), a magnate whose position is due to wealth invested in the funds; **fund-monger**, one who speculates in the public funds; whence ***fund-mongering*** vbl. sb.

1797 FOX *Sp. Assessed Tax Bill* 14 Dec. *Sp.* (1815) VI. 375 Would you tax the property of the *fund-holder? **1812** H. CAMPBELL in *Examiner* 25 May 333/1 In 1688..the fundholder received about 80 quartern loaves for his pound sterling annuity. **1878** F. HARRISON in *Fortn. Rev.* Nov. 697 If the Sovereign State borrows money at 3 per cent., it..confers on the fundholder a legal right. **1825** COBBETT *Rur. Rides* (1830) I. 81 The taxes being, in fact, tripled by Peel's Bill, the *fundlords increase in riches. **1888** *Pall Mall G.* 18 Apr. 3/1 The Rothschild family..those land-absorbing Fund-lords. **1862** *N.Y. Tribune* 12 June (Cent.) Importing that the present civil war has been got up jobbers, swindlers and *fund-mongers. **1886** *N. Amer. Rev.* Sept. CXLIII. 210 Thoroughly imbued with its hostility to perpetual debt and *fund-mongering. **1957** V. PACKARD *Hidden Persuaders* i. 8 A great many advertising men, publicists, *fund raisers, personnel experts, and political leaders..still do a straightforward job. **1961** *Guardian* 26 Jan. 22/6 Money should..be available for a..memorial..if the Press gave the fund-raisers its backing. **1940** *Struct. Amer. Econ.* (Nat. Resources Planning Board) II. 39/1 The entire present contributory basis of the social security system could be reexamined with a view..to merging *fund-raising for social security with fund raising for all other governmental purposes. **1954** KOESTLER *Invis. Writing* xx. 224 Willy asked me to..write a fund-raising pamphlet about it. **1959** *Times* 30 Dec. 9/1 A worldly young Rabbi who is more interested in fund-raising than in religious rites. **1964** A. WYKES *Gambling* x. 242 The fund-raising potentials of the state lottery. **1970** *New Yorker* 14 Nov. 44/2 Marriage and fatherhood eventually nudged him into public relations and fund-raising.

fund (fʌnd), *v.* [f. prec. sb.]

1. *trans.* Originally, to provide a 'fund' (see FUND *sb.* 5) for the regular payment of the interest on (an amount of public debt); hence, to convert (a floating debt) into a more or less permanent debt at a fixed rate of interest.

1776 [see FUNDED *ppl. a.*]. **1789** T. JEFFERSON *Writ.* (1859) II. 584 If they fund their public debt judiciously..I believe they will be able to borrow any sums they please. **1802** ADDINGTON in G. Rose *Diaries* (1860) I. 513 Exchequer bills, which he says he shall..fund. **1845** MCCULLOCH *Taxation* III. ii. (1852) 454 Had it been funded in a six and a quarter or six and a half per cent. stock, the interest might have been reduced five and twenty years ago to 4 or 4½ per cent.

2. To put into a fund or store (see FUND *sb.* 3 b); to collect; to store (immaterial things).

1806–7 J. BERESFORD *Miseries Hum. Life* (1826) VII. Introd., I have been little in a humour for..noting them down in my tablets;—I have funded a few loose agonies, however. [? Allusion to sense 1.] **1845** FORD *Handbk. Spain* I. 50 Every day and everywhere we are unconsciously funding a stock of treasures and pleasures of memory. **1879** *Family Herald* XLIII. 109 A reserve of lion-like courage was funded ready for use in that dull mass of matter.

3. To put (money) in the 'funds' (see FUND *sb.* 5 b); to invest.

1855 THACKERAY *Newcomes* II. 48, I. R. sent a hundred pounds over to his father..who funded it in his son's name.

4. intr. ***to fund up***: to 'pay up', provide funds.

1888 FENN *Man with Shadow* II. xix. 223 You will have to fund up among the rest, if you don't want to see your poor parson in rags.

5. *trans.* To supply with funds, pay (a person); to finance (a position or enterprise).

1900 *Westm. Gaz.* 6 July 6/3 The War Office had..given the London Scottish commander to understand that they..would 'fund'..the 320 men who were in readiness to join the emergency camp. **1966** *New Statesman* 7 Jan. 27/4 (Advt.),

These posts are funded from a Hayter Committee Grant. **1970** *Sci. Jrnl.* Jan. 28/4 We work in a system in which research projects are funded by grants. **1970** *Sunday Times* 8 Mar. 60/8 An average local radio station..costs £80,000 a year to run. Eventually all will be funded wholly by the BBC, at an annual cost..of some £3,200,000.

Hence **'funding** *ppl. a.*, in sense 1.

a **1852** MOORE *Country Dance & Quad.* 98 [John Bull] unfleeced by funding block heads.

fund, fund-: see FOUND, FOUND-.

fundable ('fʌndəb(ə)l), *a.* [f. FUND *v.* + -ABLE.] Capable of being funded.

1884 *Pall Mall G.* 30 Apr. 11/2 As for the Ten-Forties, they are now selling at their fundable value.

fundaco, obs. form of FONDACO.

fundal ('fʌndəl), *a.* [f. FUND-US + -AL[1].] Relating to the fundus or base of an organ.

1889 J. M. DUNCAN *Lect. Dis. Wom.* x. (ed. 4) 59 Inflammation..of the fundus uteri, fundal endometritis.

†**fun'dality.** *Obs. Feudal Law.* [ad. med.L. *fundālitas*, f. *fundālis*, f. L. *fundus* an estate. Cf. F. *fondalité*.] (See quot.)

1611 COTGR., *Fondalité*, fundalitie; right of, or interest in, the soyle; the title or estate of the Lord of a soyle.

‖**fun'damen.** *Obs. rare.* [L., f. *fundāre* to FOUND.] Foundation, basis.

1677 GALE *Crt. Gentiles* II. IV. 168 Plato makes Religion to be the principal Fundamen of a Republic. **1678** *Ibid.* III. 131 The fundamen of clearing God from being the Author of sin is [etc.].

fundament ('fʌndəmənt). Also †**foundment.** Forms: 3-6 **fond(e)-, found(e)-, fund(e)-ment,** (4-5 occas. in pl. **-mens**), 4, 7 **fonda-**, 5-7 **foundament,** 5, 7 **fundamente,** 4- **fundament.** [ME. *fondement*, a. OF. *fondement*:—L. *fundāment-um*, f. *fundāre* (see FOUND *v.*[2]), f. *fundus* bottom: see FUND *sb.* The form *fundament* is directly from the Lat., and is therefore strictly a distinct word from *foundment*, but it is convenient to treat them together on account of the occurrence of mixed forms.]

I. †**1. a.** The foundation or base of a wall, building, etc. *Obs.*

1297 R. GLOUC. (1724) 131 Lat delue vnder þe fundement, & þou schalt bi neþe fynde A water pol. **13..** *Seuyn Sag.* 2112 (W.) Thai to-rent ston fram ston, The fondement to-brast anon. **1377** LANGL. *P. Pl.* B. XIX. 322 Þere-with grace bigan to make a good foundement, And watteled it and walled it with his peynes & his passioun. **1426** AUDELAY *Poems* 23 3if the fondment be false, the werke most nede falle. **1481** CAXTON *Godfrey* 248 The fondementes of it ben in the holy montaynes. **1535** STEWART *Cron. Scot.* II. 261 Ane castell..Quhairof the fundament restis 3it to se. **1558** KENNEDY *Compend. Tract.* in *Wodr. Soc. Misc.* (1844) 160 Thyse did big firmelye on that sure roke and fundament.

transf. and *fig.* *a* **1300** *Cursor M.* 21739 It [þe croice] es.. Fondement of ur clergi. *c* **1375** *Sc. Leg. Saints, Petrus* 9 For-þi cane criste apone hym lay þe fundament of haly kirk. **1377** LANGL. *P. Pl.* B. XIV. 199 Elles is al owre labour loste ..if fals be þe foundement. **1382** WYCLIF *Prov.* viii. 29 Whan he heeng vp the foundemens of the erthe. *c* **1449** PECOCK *Repr.* 438 It [Cephas] is also a word of Sire tunge in which it is as miche to seie as fundament or ground or stable. **1521** FISHER *Serm. agst. Luther* Wks. (1876) 321 That grete foundament of the chirche and most stable stone. **1678** BUTLER *Hud.* III. ii. 1598 As in Bodies Natural The Rump's the Fundament of all.

†**b.** A surface on which to stand, footing. *Obs.*

c **1418** *Pol. Poems* (Rolls) II. 243 Ther fete failen fondement.

c. *Geogr.* Any landscape before colonization by man in general or by any particular group of men.

1928 J. B. LEIGHLY in *Univ. Calif. Publ. Geogr.* III. 3 The forces which condition and shape a cultural landscape are many and of varied origin, each fluctuating in intensity through time... The natural fundament which they modify, on which they erect their proper structures, is similarly varied from place to place, itself changing through natural processes. **1934** *Ann. Assoc. Amer. Geogr.* XXIV. 80 By an extension of its dictionary meaning, fundament is used to indicate the foundation on which the works of man have been built. Fundament may be defined as the face of the earth as it existed before the entrance of man into the scene. **1954** *Ibid.* XLIV. 248 What the fundament or 'natural' Calumet originally looked like.

†**2.** *fig.* = FOUNDATION 6. *Obs.*

c **1374** CHAUCER *Boeth.* IV. pr. iv. 100 (Camb. MS.) The which thing sustenyd by a stronge fowndement of resouns. **1474** CAXTON *Chesse* 71 The first fondement of Justyce is that no man shold noye ne greue other. **1481** —— *Myrr.* II. xxv. 117 The sonne is the foundement of alle hete and of alle tyme. **1533** GAU *Richt Vay* (1888) 27 Articulis..as thay ar contenit in the creid quhair thay haiff thair grund and fundment prowine be the halie writ. **1536** BELLENDEN *Cron. Scot.* (1821) II. 105, I think it expedient..to preche first the foundment of the Cristin faith. **1554** KNOX *Godly Let.* Cj, The fundament and reason, why, he wil neither offer sacrefice to Idols, neither yet defyle hys mouthe with their names. **1677** GALE *Crt. Gentiles* II. IV. 45 There is nothing in Moralitie but has some relation to..human nature as its subject and fundament.

3. a. The lower part of the body, on which one sits; the buttocks; also, the orifice of the intestines, the anus. In birds, the vent.

1297 R. GLOUC. (Rolls) 6340 þe luþer þef..smot him þoru þe fondement. *c* **1340** *Cursor M.* 22395 (Fairf.) Alle þe filþ of his magh salle breste out atte his fondament for drede. **1480** CAXTON *Chron. Eng.* cxcvii. 174 He..with a spere smote the noble knyght in to the foundament soo that his bowels comen oute there. **1486** *Bk. St. Albans* Cv, Anoynt hir fundement with Oyll. **1533** ELYOT *Cast. Helthe* (1539) 56 b, It amendeth the affectes of..the fundement. **1607** TOPSELL *Four-f. Beasts* (1658) 148 The falling of the fundament. **1656** RIDGLEY *Pract. Physick* 35 Cock chickens made bare at the Fundament. **1698** SIR R. SIBBALD in *Phil. Trans.* XX. 266 He hath passed Three by the Fundament. **1727** SWIFT *Gulliver* III. v, The orifice of the fundament. **1754** *Connoisseur* No. 5 ¶12 Applying his foot directly to my fundament. **1871** NAPHEYS *Prev. & Cure Dis.* II. iv. 546 The end may be attained by the pressure of a warm cloth against the fundament.

b. *Comb.*, as **fundament-bot** (see quot.).

1836 *Penny Cycl.* V. 261 The *Œstrus hæmorrhoidalis*, or fundament-bot.

4. (See quot.)

1894 GOULD *Illustr. Dict. Med.* etc., *Fundament*, in embryology, the rudiment.

†**II. 5.** The action of founding or establishing; also, something that is founded, an institution. *Obs.*

c **1394** *P. Pl. Crede* 250 Our foundement was first of þe oþere. **1513** DOUGLAS *Æneis* III. i. 37 Begouth I first set wallis of a citie Allthocht my fundment was infortunate. **1536** BELLENDEN *Cron. Scot.* (1821) II. 6 Thay..maid the first foundement of the nobil realme of France.

fundamental (fʌndə'mɛntəl), *a.* and *sb.* [ad. mod.L. *fundāmentālis*, f. *fundāmentum*: see FUNDAMENT and -AL[1]. Cf. F. *fondamental*.]

A. *adj.*

†**1. a.** Of or pertaining to the foundation or base of a building. *Obs.*

1611 CORYAT *Crudities* 503 Conrade..placed the first fundamentall stone with his owne handes. **1632** LITHGOW *Trav.* III. 123 The fundamentall walls yet extant. *c* **1650** Z. BOYD in *Zion's Flowers* (1855) Introd. 50 Christ the fundamental stone. **1769** *Middlesex Jrnl.* 12-14 Sept. 2/2 Near 300*l.* expended in fundamental repairs [of a tavern].

b. Having a foundation, fixed, not temporary. *Obs. rare*[−1].

1633 T. ADAMS *Exp. 2 Peter* i. 18 'Let us build here three tabernacles', movable tilts? No; fundamental and constant habitations.

2. Of or pertaining to the foundation or ground-work, going to the root of the matter.

c **1449** PECOCK *Repr.* III. xix. 413 Aftir sure fundamental encerche. **1658** A. FOX *Wurtz' Surg.* I. vi. 25 The true signs, whereby you may have a fundamental information of a wounds condition. **1659** PEARSON *Creed* (1839) 5 If there be any fundamental distinction in the authority of the testimony. **1781** J. MOORE *View Soc. It.* (1790) I. viii. 80 Before they could submit to such a fundamental change. **1860** TYNDALL *Glac.* II. i. 227 The fundamental analogy of sound and light is thus before us. **1868** M. PATTISON *Academ. Org.* v. 120 The consideration involves the fundamental question of what is a University.

3. a. Serving as the foundation or base on which something is built. Chiefly and now exclusively in immaterial applications. Hence, forming an essential or indispensable part of a system, institution, etc. Const. *to* (rarely *of*).

1601 SHAKS. *All's Well* III. i. 2 Now haue you heard The fundamentall reasons of this warre. **1641** *Vind. Smectymnuus* iv. 56 Fundamentall laws are not subject to alteration. **1649** BLITHE *Eng. Improv. Impr.* (1653) 223 The Sheath and plough-head, which is the materiall fundamentall peece in the Plough, must be made of heart of Oak. **1650** FULLER *Pisgah* II. xi. 235 Samson applied himself to the two pillars most fundamentall to the roof of Dagons Temple. *a* **1705** HOWE in Spurgeon *Treas. Dav.* Ps. lxxxix. 2 Former mercies are fundamental to later ones. **1718** PRIOR *Power* 217 Their ills all built on life, that fundamental ill. **1771** *Junius Lett.* lix. 304 The fundamental principles of christianity may still be preserved. **1785** REID *Int. Powers* 608 The fundamental rules of poetry and music and painting, and dramatic action, and eloquence, have always been the same, and will be to the end of the world. **1835** J. HARRIS *Gt. Teacher* (1837) 87 The existence of the Deity is a truth fundamental of every other. **1863** GEO. ELIOT *Romola* III. xx, The ideas of strict law and order were fundamental to all his political teaching. **1876** MOZLEY *Univ. Serm.* iv. (1877) 88 How low down in a man sometimes..lies the fundamental motive which sways his life!

b. Primary, original; from which others are derived.

c **1449** PECOCK *Repr.* III. xii. 350 Noon fundamental cronicler or Storier writith therof saue Girald. **1868** CARPENTER in *Sci. Opin.* 6 Jan. 174/2 Of the most varied shapes, apparently referrible to the *Astrorhiza limicola* as their fundamental type. **1874** SAYCE *Compar. Philol.* vii. 262 In the noun the nominative was regarded as the fundamental case. **1879** tr. *Semper's Anim. Life* 11 To show ..how such a change in the organ might be effected side by side with permanence of the fundamental form. **1881** WESTCOTT & HORT *Grk. N.T.* Introd. §15 The fundamental editions were those of Erasmus..and of Stunica.

c. esp. *Math.* and *Cryst.*

1570 DEE *Math. Pref.* 30 Diuide the side of your Fundamentall Cube into so many æquall partes. **1669** STURMY *Mariner's Mag.* II. 47 Therefore we will demonstrate the fundamental Diagram of the Mathematical Scale. **1706** PHILLIPS (ed. Kersey), *Fundamental Diagram*, a Projection of the Sphere in a Plane &c. **1721-92** in BAILEY. **1805-17** R. JAMESON *Char. Min.* (ed. 3) 120 A fundamental figure is said to be acuminated when [etc.]. **1875** EVERETT *C.G.S. Syst. Units* ii. 7 The quantities commonly selected to serve as the fundamental units are—a definite length, a definite mass, a definite interval of time. **1882** MINCHIN *Unipl. Kinemat.* 235 In virtue of the fundamental equations (2) of No. 2, we have [etc.]. **1888** *Lockwood's Dict. Mech. Engin.*, *Fundamental Circle* or *Base Circle*, a curve which is rolled over by a generating circle in the production of cycloidal curves. **1893** FORSYTH *Th. Functions* 591 There is considerable freedom of choice of an initial region of reference, which may be called a fundamental region. *Ibid.* 603 It is a circle being the inverse of a line; it is unaltered by the substitutions of the new group, and it is therefore called the fundamental circle of this group.

4. Of strata: Lying at the bottom. ***fundamental complex*** (see quot. 1961).

1799 KIRWAN *Geol. Ess.* 42 Mr. Eversman..tells us that the fundamental rock of Scotland is a mass of the granitic kind. **1830** LYELL *Princ. Geol.* I. 202 The fundamental rock ..is a black slate. **1861** W. FAIRBAIRN *Addr. Brit. Assoc.*, He has proved the existence of a fundamental gneiss, on which all the other rocks repose. **1893** A. GEIKIE *Text-bk. Geol.* (ed. 3) II. VI. I. 715 The pre-Cambrian rocks..may be divided into two great series. At the base lies a vast mass of gneisses, schists, and eruptive rocks, which, known as the 'Fundamental Complex', is regarded as the oldest of the whole. **1910** *Encycl. Brit.* II. 361/1 The so-called 'fundamental complex', an assemblage of acid, basic and intermediate irruptive rocks, associated together in a complex of extraordinary intricacy. **1961** L. D. STAMP *Gloss. Geogr. Terms* 202/2 *Fundamental complex*, in geology the rocks of the 'original' crust of the earth formerly applied to the great areas of pre-Cambrian crystalline rocks. It is still used although it is now recognized that probably no part represents the 'original' crust of the earth.

5. *Biol.* and *Bot.* (See quots.)

1856 HENSLOW *Dict. Bot. Terms*, *Fundamental-organs*, the nutritive organs absolutely essential to the existence of the individual. **1866** *Treas. Bot.*, *Fundamental*, constituting the essential part of anything; in a plant, the axis and its appendages. **1882** VINES *Sachs' Bot.* 155 Epidermal and fundamental tissues. **1885** *Syd. Soc. Lex.*, *Fundamental organs*, term applied by von Baer to the primary structures which directly issue from the blastoderm in the form of tubes, and from which the permanent organs or structures are developed. **1894** GOULD *Illustr. Dict. Med., etc.*, *Fundamental Tissue*, in biology, unspecialized parenchyma; those tissues of a plant through which the fibro-vascular bundles are distributed.

6. *Mus.* Applied to the lowest note of a chord, considered as the foundation or 'root' of it; also to the tone produced by the vibration of the whole of a sonorous body, as distinguished from the higher tones or HARMONICS produced by that of its parts.

fundamental bass, a low note, or series of low notes, forming the root or roots of a chord or succession of chords. ***fundamental chord***, an old name for the common chord; now extended to any chord formed of harmonics of the fundamental tone.

1752 tr. *Rameau's Treat. Mus.* ii. 9 Of the Fundamental Bass. *Ibid.* x. 28 Any one of the Notes contained in the fundamental Chords. **1825** DANNELEY *Encycl. Mus.*, *Fundamental Movement*, progression or movement of that species of bass. *Ibid.*, *Fundamental Sound*, the gravest sound or generator. **1828** BUSBY *Mus. Man.*, *Fundamental Bass*, that bass on which the superincumbent harmony is founded; or of which the superior parts of the accompanying chord constitute the third, fifth, and eighth. *Ibid.*, *Fundamental Chord*, a chord consisting of the third, fifth and eighth, of the fundamental bass. **1831** BREWSTER *Nat. Magic* viii. (1833) 181 This sound is called the fundamental sound of the string. **1876** tr. *Blaserna's Sound* i. 18 The note is the lowest that the pipe can give, for which reason it is called the fundamental note of the pipe. **1876** STAINER & BARRETT *Dict. Mus. T.*, *Fundamental tones*, the tones from which harmonics are generated. **1889** E. PROUT *Harmony* iii. §61 Our 'fundamental chord'—that is, a chord composed of the harmonics of its fundamental tone, or generator. *Ibid.* ix. §197 We here meet..with a 'fundamental discord'.

¶**7.** *jocularly.* Of or pertaining to the fundament or 'seat', posterior.

1767 A. CAMPBELL *Lexiph.* (1774) 65, I lingered behind, detained by my fundamental malady. **1828** *Blackw. Mag.* XXIV. 184 He fixes his fundamental feature upon the outer edge of a chair.

B. *sb.*

1. a. A leading or primary principle, rule, law, or article, which serves as the groundwork of a system; an essential part. Chiefly in *pl.*; the sing. is *obs.* or *arch.*

1637 *Crt. & Times Chas. I* (1848) II. 263 They have composed a symbol of fundamentals, which both the Lutherans and Calvinists do hold without interfering one with another. **1641** *Vind. Smectymnuus* iv. 60 How then is Episcopacie one of the fundamentals of the kingdome? **1650** H. BROOKE *Conserv. Health* 24 A Fundamentall in Physic. *a* **1652** J. SMITH *Sel. Disc.* VI. v. (1821) 228 Relying upon this known fundamental, viz. That there is no prophecy revealed but by one of these two ways. **1704** NELSON *Fest. & Fasts* vii. (1739) 540 The same Apostle mentions as a Fundamental, not only..Baptism but also the laying on of Hands. **1862** MERIVALE *Rom. Emp.* (1865) IV. xxxix. 373 They permitted little deviation..from these great fundamentals. **1864** BURTON *Scot Abr.* I. i. 16 There is an odd tenacity of life in the fundamentals of..legends. **1878** MORLEY *Vauvenargues* 11 Very faint and doubtful as to even the fundamentals—God, immortality, and the like.

b. *pl.* Fundamental requisites. ? *nonce-use.*

1864 E. BURRITT *Walk fr. Lond. to John o' Groats* 378 Bread, bacon, and butter. Their stock of these fundamentals was exhausted.

2. *Mus.* Short for *fundamental tone* or *note*: see A. 6. (Formerly = *key-note.*)

1727-41 CHAMBERS *Cycl.*, *Fundamental*, in music, denotes the principal note of a song or composition, to which all the rest are in some measure adapted, and by which they are swayed. **1825** DANNELEY *Encycl. Mus.*, *Fundamental*, the principal note or root of a harmony, concordant or discordant.

Hence **funda'mentalness.**

1727 in BAILEY vol. II.

fundamentalism (fʌndəˈmɛntəlɪz(ə)m). [f. FUNDAMENTAL *a.* + -ISM.] **a.** A religious movement, which orig. became active among various Protestant bodies in the United States after the war of 1914–1918, based on strict adherence to certain tenets (e.g. the literal inerrancy of Scripture) held to be fundamental to the Christian faith; the beliefs of this movement; opp. *liberalism* and *modernism*.

1923 *Daily Mail* 24 May 8 Mr. William Jennings Bryan.. has been exerting the full force of his great eloquence in a campaign on behalf of what is termed 'Fundamentalism'. **1925** K. LAKE *Relig. Yesterday & To-morrow* 63 There has been in America some surprise at the sudden rise of Fundamentalism in the last five years. **1927** *Observer* 5 June 5/3 Fundamentalism and the Klux Klan are signs of alarm on behalf of the older ideals. **1955** *Times* 25 Aug. 14/1 'Fundamentalism'..appears to have been used first in connexion with the (American) Northern Baptist Convention of 1920 to describe the more conservative delegates who desired 'to restate, reaffirm, and re-emphasize the fundamentals of our New Testament faith'. *Ibid.*, Now 'fundamentalism'..appears to describe the bigoted rejection of all Biblical criticism, a mechanical view of inspiration and an excessively literalist interpretation of scripture.

b. In other religions, esp. Islam, a similarly strict adherence to ancient or fundamental doctrines, with no concessions to modern developments in thought or customs.

1957 L. BINDER in *Middle East Jrnl.* XI. 391 Fundamentalism in religion and the Hinduization of the national historical myth were made possible [in India]..by the historical and religious work of Europeans. **1961** —— *Relig. & Politics in Pakistan* ii. 52 These same circumstances determined that the Congress act as midwife at the birth of Islamic fundamentalism in the Khilafat movement. **1981** *Observer* 27 Sept. 32/1 The new, or rather very old, Islam, the dangerous fundamentalism revived by the ayatollahs and their admirers. **1984** *Church Times* 2 Mar. 6/1 The newly-revived Western Christian awareness of 'Islamic fundamentalism', whose symbolic figure is Ayatollah Khomeini. **1984** *Times* 27 Apr. 13/2 It is this very process that has helped ignite the fires of Sikh fundamentalism, rather as Shiite fundamentalism was sparked off by the forces of modernization in Iran.

So **fundaˈmentalist**, an adherent of fundamentalism; also, an economic or political doctrinaire. Also *attrib.* or as *adj.*, and *transf.*

1922 *Contemp. Rev.* July 20 The fundamentalist creed. *Ibid.* 21 The Fundamentalists have been fortunate in their non-ministerial leader [*sc.* W. J. Bryan]. **1925** K. LAKE *Relig. Yesterday & To-morrow* 60 The most energetic.. group, but the least well educated, is the Fundamentalist. *Ibid.* 62 The Fundamentalists have zeal, but it is certainly not according to knowledge. **1926** H. F. OSBORN *Evol. & Relig. in Educ.* 12 The fundamentalist movement..sought to re-establish the Biblical literalism of the time of Cromwell, Milton, and the Puritans. **1955** *Times* 25 Aug. 14/1 The dangers of the new fundamentalist movement. One of the encouraging developments for Christian teachers to-day is the new relationship which is growing up between scientific and religious thought. **1957** *Middle East Jrnl.* XI. 391 Less well known is their [*sc.* Europeans'] part in the development of non-Christian fundamentalist movements through their translations..of the ancient sources. **1961** L. BINDER *Relig. & Pol. in Pakistan* xiii. 378 The fundamentalist movement is a lower middle-class movement..oriented to the institutions of a..passing age. **1961** WEBSTER, *Fundamentalist*, an extreme conservative; *esp*: one who attacks any deviation from certain doctrines and practices he considers essential (as to a religious, political, or educational system). **1969** *New Yorker* 14 June 45/1 I've never been a flashy stylist, like Arthur. I'm a fundamentalist. Arthur is a bachelor. I am married and conservative. **1973** *Economist* 15 Dec. 106/2 The fundamentalists look at a company's product, balance sheet, record and management before deciding whether the stock market has put the right value on the shares. **1981** *Times* 26 Sept. 4/2 The measures are designed mostly to curb the influence of Muslim fundamentalists. **1985** *Daily Tel.* 29 Mar. 22/4 Fundamentalist Jews are limbering up to oppose the plan on the grounds that it will depict scenes from the New Testament as well as the Old.

fundamentality (ˌfʌndəmənˈtælɪtɪ). [f. FUNDAMENTAL *a.* and *sb.* + -ITY.] The quality or state of being fundamental.

1721–92 BAILEY, *Fundamentality*, the belonging to the Foundation. **1816** W. TAYLOR in *Monthly Rev.* LXXX. 367 More of fundamentality in the research. **1840** GLADSTONE *Ch. Princ.* 301 The fundamentality of a given proposition in religion.

fundamentally (fʌndəˈmɛntəlɪ), *adv.* [f. as prec. + -LY².] In a fundamental manner.

†**1.** From the foundation or bottom upwards, thoroughly. *Obs.*

1602 F. HERING *Anat.* 21 Fundamentally learne the Noble Art of Physicke. **1658** A. FOX *Wurtz' Surg.* I. iii. 7 It is undeniable, that wounds ought to be cured fundamentally, not superficially. **1662** PETTY *Taxes* 27 Men..cobble up old houses, until they become fundamentally irreparable.

2. In fundamental or essential matters or points, as regards fundamentals, essentially.

1628 T. SPENCER *Logick* 236 To conclude this point of Connext axiomes; I hope it doth now appeare, that, they are fundamentally, and indeed no other but simple. **1664** H. MORE *Myst. Iniq.* 110 There can be nothing more fundamentally Antichristian than it. **1701** J. LAW *Counc. Trade* (1751) 5 Such as fundamentally, at least understand arithmetic and accompts. **1748** CHESTERF. *Lett.* 16 Feb. (1870) My health..though not fundamentally bad, yet.. wanted some repairs. **1790** BURKE *Fr. Rev.* Wks. V. 125 The simple governments are fundamentally defective. **1827** YEATS *Techn. Hist. Comm.* 325 Fundamentally, the process consists in [etc.]. **1880** H. JAMES *Diary of Man of Fifty* 324, I was fundamentally not the least addicted to thinking evil.

¶**3.** *jocularly.* At the fundament or 'seat'.

1836 E. HOWARD *R. Reefer* v, Oh! those floggings, how deceptive they were, and how much I regretted them when I came to understand the thing fundamentally. **1842** [see DEPHLOGISTICATE *v.* 2].

†**fundamentive**, *a. Obs. rare.* [f. FUNDAMENT + -IVE.] Original.

1593 NASHE *Christ's T.* (1613) 58 There were in Ierusalem three factions, Eleazers..was the fundamentiue and first.

fundamentum. Short for FUNDAMENTUM RELATIONIS.

[**1599** BLUNDEVIL *Logike* 33 Here note that of the schoolemen the thing from which the application is made, is called in latine *fundamentum*, in English the foundation.] **1883** F. H. BRADLEY *Princ. Logic* II. II. i. 295 What is the fact or phenomenon constituting the *fundamentum* of this relation? **1907** W. JAMES *Meaning of Truth* (1909) vii. 163 This relation, like all relations, has its *fundamentum*. *Ibid.*, In the case of the relation between 'heir' and 'legacy' the *fundamentum* is a world in which there was a testator, and in which there is now a will and an executor.

‖**fundamentum divisionis** (fʌndəˈmɛntəm dɪvɪʒɪˈəʊnɪs). *Logic.* Pl. **-menta** (-ˈmɛntə). [L., = foundation or basis of division.] The principle or basis of logical division of a genus into its constituent species.

1849 W. THOMSON *Outl. Laws of Thought* (ed. 2) 134 The division must be made according to one principle (*fundamentum divisionis*). **1870** W. S. JEVONS *Elem. Lessons Logic* xii. 105 The size of the books is in this case the ground, basis, or principle of division, commonly called the *Fundamentum Divisionis*. **1906** H. W. B. JOSEPH *Introd. Logic* v. 104 The *fundamentum divisionis*, the principle or basis of a division, is that aspect of the genus, in respect of which the species are differentiated. **1956** J. O. URMSON *Philos. Analysis* v. 68 The distinction 'positive-negative' has a different *fundamentum divisionis* from the distinction 'particular-general'.

fundamentum relationis (fʌndəˈmɛntəm rɪleɪʃɪˈəʊnɪs). *Logic.* [L., = foundation of the relation.] Those elements of the objective world that constitute the terms of a relation. (See also FUNDAMENTUM.)

1843 MILL *Logic* I. ii. §7. I. 55 The series of events may be said to *constitute* the relation; the schoolmen called it the foundation of the relation, *fundamentum relationis*. **1906** J. N. KEYNES *Formal Logic* (ed. 4) I. iv. 64 The fact or facts constituting the ground of both correlative names is called the *fundamentum relationis*. For example,..in the case of husband and wife, the facts which constitute the marriage tie. **1907** W. JAMES *Let.* 4 Aug. in R. B. PERRY *Tht. & Char. W.J.* (1935) II. 540 The *fundamentum relationis* of the fact that the idea may mean and point to that reality, and know it truly, is to be found in the enveloping experiences and nowhere else.

†**ˈfundative**, *a. Obs.* [f. L. type **fundātīvus*, f. *fundāre*: see FOUND *v.*¹ and -ATIVE.] Tending to found or originate.

1677 GALE *Crt. Gentiles* II. IV. 14 The Divine Bonitie..is ..constitutive and fundative of althings.

fundatorial (fʌndəˈtɔərɪəl), *a. rare.* [f. L. type **fundātōri-us* (see next) + -AL¹.] Pertaining or proper to a founder.

1892 FREEMAN *Hist. Ess.* Ser. II. xvi. 305 The Queen issues the document by virtue of her 'fundatorial' powers.

†**ˈfundatory**, *a. Obs.* [f. L. type **fundātōrius*, f. *fundāre*: see FOUND *v.*¹ and -ORY.] Having the function or effect of founding (an institution).

1635 PAGITT *Christianogr.* III. (1636) 67 The Fundatory Letters, or Statutes of the Foundation of the said Monastery.

fundatrix. [mod.L. *fundātrix*, fem. of L. *fundātor*, agent-n. f. *fundāre*: see FOUND *v.*²]

†**1.** *Obs.* = FOUNDRESS¹.

1549 RIDLEY in *Bradford's Wks.* (1853) II. 371 The fundatrix purpose was wondrous godly, her fact was godly.

2. *Ent.* The founding female of a colony of aphids, which produces young parthenogenetically.

[**1875** G. B. BUCKTON *Monogr. Brit. Aphides* I. 76 This hibernation of the foundress of a colony..is somewhat exceptional.] **1907** W. R. FISHER *Schlich's Man. Forestry* (ed. 2) IV. 362 The wingless parthenogenetic ♀, stem-mother or *fundatrix*, hibernates alone on spruce buds. **1923** H. M. LEFROY *Entomol.* 272 These first females are known as fundatrices, or stem-mothers. **1936** *Forestry* X. 134 A primary [host], on which the fundatrix vera or foundress,.. and the gallicolae or gall-dwellers are reared. **1952** ESSIG & ABERNATHY *Aphid Genus Periphyllus* 41 The mature fundatrix is wingless, small, dark brown. **1971** *Nature* 2 July 14/1 Each fertilized female..lays one egg which later hatches to give the fundatrix—the first wingless female of the cycle.

funded (ˈfʌndɪd), *ppl. a.* [f. FUND *v.* + -ED¹.]

1. a. Of a debt or stock: That has been made part of the permanent debt of the state, with provision for the regular payment of interest at a fixed rate.

1776 ADAM SMITH *W.N.* v. iii. (1869) II. 522 The publick debts of Great Britain funded and unfunded. **1797** *Monthly Mag.* III. 199 Besides the said four funded stocks, a national bank is established at Philadelphia. **1820** SYD. SMITH *Plymley's Lett.* Wks. 1859 II. 166/2 Ireland now supports a funded debt of about 64 millions. **1866** CRUMP *Banking* ix. 183 The permanent debt due to the Bank..which was included in the national debt accounts as funded debt.

b. Of property: Invested in 'the funds'.

1848 MILL *Pol. Econ.* Prelim. Remarks I. 9 Funded property therefore cannot be counted as part of the national wealth. **1858** LD. ST. LEONARDS *Handy-bk. Prop. Law* xx. 152 In bequeathing your stock, give it generally, as all your funded property.

2. Stored up. Cf. FUND *v.* 2.

1841–4 EMERSON *Ess.*, *Manners* Wks. (Bohn) I. 208 The class of power, the working heroes..see that..fashion is funded talent. **1888** T. W. HIGGINSON *Women & Men* xv. 77 The traditions and habits of society are to a great extent what might be called funded and accumulated good feeling.

fundi (ˈfʌndɪ). [Native African name.] A West African grass, *Digitaria exilis*, cultivated for its seed, which resembles millet; hungry rice.

1858, **1877** [see HUNGRY *a.* 4]. **1915** *Nature* XCVI. 350/2 Fundi, *Digitaria exilis*, has been known for some time as a cultivated cereal... It is cooked by being thrown into boiling water or used like porridge. **1957** M. BANTON *W. Afr. City* iii. 45 *April...* Farms are prepared for fundi, ginger and groundnuts.

†**ˈfundible**, *a. Obs.*$^{-0}$ [as if ad. L. **fundibilis*, f. *fundĕre* to pour.] That may be poured.

1775 in ASH.

fundie, var. of FOUND *v.*⁵ (In quot. *trans.* = to benumb.)

1591 JAS. I. tr. *Du Bartas' Furies* 240 The Moone doth deaze and fundie him, Her brother rosts him quite.

fundiform (ˈfʌndɪfɔːm), *a. Anat.* [ad. mod.L. *fundiform-is* (A. Retzius 1841, in *Arch. f. Anat., Physiol. und wiss. Med.* 499, translating G. *schleuderförmig* shaped like a sling), f. L. *funda* sling: see -FORM.] ***fundiform ligament***: a ligament having the shape of a sling; *spec.* (*a*) a ligament on the front of the ankle which encloses the tendons of two extensor muscles of the leg; (*b*) a ligament which forms a loop enclosing the root of the penis and partly supports the weight of the latter.

1854 E. WILSON *Anatomist's Vade Mecum* (ed. 6) iv. 305 The tendons of the extensor longus digitorum and peroneus tertius have also a separate loop connected with the cruciform ligament, the sling ligament (fundiforme) of Retzius. **1900** DORLAND *Med. Dict.* 356/2 *Fundiform ligament*, a portion of the anterior annular ligament of the ankle. **1962** *Gray's Anat.* (ed. 33) 1530 The fundiform ligament..springs from the lower side of the linea alba and splits into two lamellae which pass one on each side of the penis and unite below with the septum of the scrotum.

funding (ˈfʌndɪŋ), *vbl. sb.* [f. FUND *v.* + -ING¹.] The action of the vb. FUND (sense 1); conversion of a floating debt into a permanent one.

1776 ADAM SMITH *W.N.* v. iii. (1869) II. 521 We had recourse to the ruinous expedient of perpetual funding. **1792** A YOUNG. *Trav. France* 517 It remains a subject of infinite curiosity, to see how far the infatuated and blind spirit of funding will now be pursued. **1845** MᶜCULLOCH *Taxation* III. ii. (1852) 447 Funding is now effected in France as in England, by granting interminable annuities redeemable at pleasure.

attrib. **1790** M. CUTLER in *Life Jrnls. & Corr.* (1888) I. 463 Congress..ought to pay no regard to this matter in their establishment of a funding system. **1846** MᶜCULLOCH *Acc. Brit. Emp.* (1854) II. 428 In the infancy of the funding system it was customary to borrow upon the security of some tax, or portion of a tax, set apart as a fund for discharging the principal and interest of the sum borrowed. **1892** *Daily News* 29 June 2/3 The directors protest against the receipt of funding bonds instead of the cash guarantee.

fundless (ˈfʌndlɪs), *a.* [f. FUND *sb.* + -LESS.] Without funds.

1891 *Sat. Rev.* 7 Mar. 278/1 The unhappy anti-Parnellites, bookless, fundless, branchless, denounced him.

funduck, obs. form of FONDUK.

‖**fundus** (ˈfʌndəs). [L. *fundus* bottom.]

1. *Anat.* The base or bottom of an organ; the part remote from the external aperture. ***fundus of the eye***: 'the back part of the globe of the eye behind the crystalline lens' (*Syd. Soc. Lex.* 1885).

1754–64 SMELLIE *Midwif.* I. 96 The Uterus..is divided into neck and Fundus. **1804** *Med. Jrnl.* XII. 236 The uterus was united with the fundus of the bladder, and projected very little above it. **1840** G. V. ELLIS *Anat.* 608 The upper part or fundus is convex, and covered by peritonæum. **1871** HAMMOND *Dis. Nerv. Syst.* p. xii, This process gives a very satisfactory view of the fundus with the optic disk and retinal vessels. **1877** HUXLEY *Anat. Inv. Anim.* x. 604 The œsophageal opening looks backwards to the fundus of the sac. **1887** G. T. LADD *Physiol. Psychol.* x. §16 549 Prolonged work with the microscope will cause the images seen in its focus to 'live in the fundus of the eye'.

2. Foundation, groundwork. *rare*$^{-1}$.

1840 DE QUINCEY *Style* in *Blackw. Mag.* July XLVIII. 1 Want of principle and want of moral sensibility compose the original *fundus* of southern manners.

fune, var. of FOIN *sb.*¹ *Obs.*

funebrial (fjuːˈniːbrɪəl), *a.* Now *rare.* Also 7 funebriall, 7–8 funebral. [f. L. *fūnebri-s* (f. *fūnus* funeral) + -AL[1].] Of or pertaining to funerals, funereal. Hence, gloomy, sad, melancholy.

1604 T. WRIGHT *Passions* v. §2. 163 What are funebriall accents, but ruthful lamentations for our friends eclipsed? **1645** EVELYN *Mem.* (1857) I. 174 Here I heard a Spanish sermon, or funebral oration. **1664** —— *Sylva* (1776) 291 We have most of our pot-ashes of this wood together with the torch or Funebral Staves. *a* **1682** SIR T. BROWNE *Tracts* (1684) 91 Their funebrial Garlands had little of beauty in them beside Roses. **1790** PENNANT *London* (1813) 507 A shroud..he dressed himself in that funebrial habit. **1830** SOUTHEY *Let.* 10 July in *Life & Corr.* VI. 108 An air of book-making..which is not lessened by the funebrial verses that it contains. **1865** L'ESTRANGE *Yachting round W. Eng.* 100 By some they are considered to have been funebrial, and originally covered with mounds of earth. **1866** G. MACDONALD *Unspoken Serm.* (1884) 237 Those pagans who in their Elysian fields could hope to possess only such a thin, fleeting, dreamy, and altogether funebrial existence.

† **fu'nebrious**, *a. Obs.* Also funebrous. [f. as prec. + -OUS. With *funebrous* cf. OF. *funebreux.*] = prec.

1653 SIR G. WHARTON *Disc. Comets* Wks. (1683) 159 Comets are certain Funebrious Appearances. **1654** COKAINE *Dianea* III. 217 At so funebrous a spectacle I could not refraine from griefe. **1669** R. B. *Life T. Morton* Pref. 16 Funebrious sickness of the plague. **1708** OZELL *Boileau's Lutrin* iii. 42 Here Ravens and Funebrous Birds resort. **1721** BAILEY, *Funebrous.* [In mod. Dicts.]

† **funel.** *Obs. rare*[−1]. Also 3-4 fonel. [a. OF. *funel*:—L. *fūnāle*, f. *fūnis* rope.] A rope.

a **1300** *Cursor M.* 3306 Wantes vs here na uessell, Ne mele, ne bucket, ne funell [*v.r.* fonel].

funeral ('fjuːnərəl), *a.* and *sb.* Forms: 5-7 funerall, (5 fynerall, 6 funyralle), 4- funeral. *Plural.* 5-7 funeralles, (5 funerales, funeralx, fyneralles, 6 funirals), 6- 7 funeral(l)s. [The adj. is a. OF. *funeral*, ad. med.L. *fūnerāl-is*, f. *fūner-, fūnus*, funeral, death, dead body. The sb. is ad. OF. *funeraille* (1406 Hatz.-Darm.), collect. fem. sing., ad. med.L. *fūnerālia*, neut. pl. of the adj. Like many other OF. sbs. in *-aille* of similar derivation, the word was used in the pl. with the same sense as in the sing. (mod.F. has only the pl. *funérailles*); this usage was originally followed in English, and continued until the end of the 17th c.]

A. *adj.*

1. Of or pertaining to the ceremonial burial (or cremation) of the dead; used, observed, delivered, etc. at a burial. Now usually apprehended as an attributive use of the *sb.* Cf. B. 6.

funeral-ale (? nonce-wd.) = ARVAL. ***funeral column*** (see quot. 1862). ***funeral-house***: (*a*) the house from which a funeral has started; (*b*) a mortuary. ***funeral pall***: the pall used to cover the coffin, also *fig.* ***funeral pile, pyre***: the pile of wood and other combustibles on which a dead body is burned. †***funeral pot*** = funeral urn. †***funeral ring***: a ring given at or in remembrance of a funeral; a mourning ring. ***funeral-toll***: the tolling of a bell at a funeral. ***funeral urn***: the urn in which the ashes were placed after cremation.

c **1386** CHAUCER *Knt's T.* 2006 He wolde make a fyr, in which thoffice Funeral he mighte al accomplice. **1439** *E.E. Wills* (1882) 115 My byryng..& expenses funeralx. **1529** MORE *Supplic. Soulys* Wks. 328/1 There wer in the funeral seruice at the burying of the corps, the selfe same psalmes songen. **1548** UDALL, etc., *Erasm. Par. Mark* v. 38-9 The syngyng men that synge vayne funerall songes vnto the deade bodie. **1579-80** NORTH *Plutarch* (1676) 315 [The people] came..to touch the Funerall-pot of his ashes. **1583** STUBBES *Anat. Abus.* II. (1882) 84 Is it not lawfull for him to take monie in his cure for preaching funerall sermons? **1593** SHAKS. *3 Hen. VI*, II. v. 117 My sighing brest, shall be thy Funerall bell. **1601** WEEVER *Mirr. Mart.* D vj b, My Swans last funerall dirgee to the king. **1604** DEKKER *Honest Wh.* Wks. 1873 II. 4 Funerall griefe loathes words. **1629** J. COLE *Of Death* 164 After any buriall, the neerest friends returne to the Funerall house. **1638** BAKER tr. *Balzac's Lett.* I. (vol. II.) 76 You have had the pleasure to heare your owne Funerall Oration. **1648** *Bury Wills* (Camden) 211 That noe funerall pompe be bestowed at my buriall. **1658** SIR T. BROWNE *Hydriot.* Bp. Ded., The Funeral Pyre was out and the last Valediction over. **1683** *Lond. Gaz.* No. 1789/4 All Persons who shall have occasion for Funeral Rings for time to come. *a* **1693** URQUHART *Rabelais* III. lii. 423 The Fuel of the Funeral and bustuary Fire. **1719** DE FOE *Crusoe* II. i, The flattery of a funeral sermon. **1756-7** tr. *Keysler's Trav.* (1760) II. 315 They were equal as to fame and funeral honours. *a* **1771** GRAY *Desc. Odin* 70 Hoder's corse.. Flaming on the fun'ral pile. **1797** MRS. RADCLIFFE *Italian* vi, She repaired first to the convent to attend the funeral service. **1804** J. GRAHAME *Sabbath* 191 The funeral-toll, announces solemnly The service of the tomb. **1818** CRUISE *Digest* (ed. 2) VI. 339 After payment of my just debts and funeral expences. **1827** POLLOK *Course T.* IX. 1180 Thousands that sleep Forgotten beneath the funeral pall of Time. **1838** THIRLWALL *Greece* III. 131 The praises of Athens were the main topic of every funeral harangue. **1850** *Ecclesiologist* X. 339 Vague terms as Burial-House, or Rest-House, or Funeral-House, will never come into vogue. **1854** C. F. ALEXANDER *Burial of Moses* v. Poems (1896) 84 But when the warrior dieth, His comrades in the war, With arms reversed and muffled drum, Follow his funeral car. **1862** *Dict. Arch.* (Arch. Publ. Soc.), *Funeral column*, the name applied by some writers to a pillar raised instead of a cenotaph; or over a place of sepulture. **1875** *Edin. Rev.* July CXLII. 208 It is far more likely..that the vow was made at his [Harold Harfagr's] father's funeral-ale.

2. = FUNEREAL.

1651 JER. TAYLOR *Holy Dying* iii. §6 To converse with his friends and standers by so as may do them comfort, and ease their funeral and civil complaints. **1678** CUDWORTH *Intell. Syst.* 226 Many of the Religious Rites and Solemnities, observed by the Pagan Priests, were Mournful and Funeral. **1771** SMOLLETT *Humph. Cl.* III. 8 Aug., The firs..look dull and funeral. **1814** BYRON *Corsair* II. xvi, O'er which the raven flaps her funeral wing.

B. *sb.* **1.** The ceremonies connected with the burial (or cremation, etc.) of the body of a dead person; obsequies; a burial (or its equivalent) with the attendant observances.

a **1512** FABYAN *Will* in *Chron.* Pref. 6, I will that after my funerall..that .xii. of the foresaid torches be bestowed as after foloweth. **1526** *Pilgr. Pref.* (W. de W. 1531) 257 b, At complyn where shold be remembred the funerall or buryall of that most holy corps. **1601** SHAKS. *Jul. C.* III. i. 233 Do not consent That Antony speake in his Funerall. **1667** EVELYN *Diary* 3 Aug., Went to Mr. Cowley's funeral, whose corpse ..was conveyed to Westminster Abbey in a hearse with six horses. **1712** ADDISON *Spect.* No. 416 ¶2 Melancholy Scenes and Apprehensions of Deaths and Funerals. **1794** MRS. RADCLIFFE *Myst. Udolpho* ii, On his return from the funeral, St. Aubert shut himself in his chamber. **1820** W. IRVING *Sketch Bk.* I. 300 Funerals in the country are solemnly impressive. **1858** LD. ST. LEONARDS *Handy-bk. Prop. Law* xxi. 168 You must be careful in your expenditure on the funeral.

fig. **1885** TENNYSON *To Princess Beatrice*, The Mother weeps At that white funeral of the single life, Her maiden daughter's marriage. **1894** *Westm. Gaz.* 29 Aug. 5/2 Next election would see the funeral of party government.

† **b.** pl. with sing. sense. *Obs.*

1543 GRAFTON *Contn. Harding* 475 The duke of Gloucestre kepte the kyng his brothers funeralles. *a* **1553** UDALL *Royster D.* (Arb.) 88 Some parte of his funeralls let vs here beginne. **1645** QUARLES *Sol. Recant.* xii. 58 Mourners come to meet Thy tear-bedabled fun'rals in the Street. **1691** WOOD *Ath. Oxon.* I. 280 On the 5 of Sept. following his Funerals were solemnized. **1711** LD. MOLESWORTH tr. *F. Hotman's Franco-Gallia* (1721) 22 Lewis..celebrated his Funerals.

fig. **1589** R. HARVEY *Pl. Perc.* (1590) 23, I..drinke to the funerals of your Enimitie. **1684** *Scanderbeg Rediv.* iii. 45 Behold, I say, the time which is the Funerals of my Glory.

c. ***none of your*** (***our***, etc.) ***funeral***: no affair of yours (ours, etc.), nothing to do with you (us, etc.); ***your*** (etc.) ***funeral***: your (etc.) affair or concern (often with an implication of unpleasant consequences). orig. *U.S. slang.*

1854 *Oregon Weekly Times* 25 Nov. (Th.), A boy said to an outsider who was making a great ado during some impressive mortuary ceremonies, 'What are you crying about? it's none of your funeral.' **1867** *Trans Ill. Agric. Soc.* VI. 167 As this was 'none of our funeral', of course the party of the other part was provided with all the regalia of the occasion. **1870** *Congress. Globe* 12 Apr. 2780/3 Mr. Painter then addressing you said, 'This is not my funeral.' **1877** *Hartford Times* 17 Oct. (Farmer), Oh, that isn't my funeral, I want you to understand. **1895** *Century Mag.* Sept. 674/1 We don't know for certain it was them, and it's none of our funeral, anyhow. **1908** S. E. WHITE *Riverman* vii. 60 However, it's your funeral. Come on, if you want to. **1917** S. GRAHAM *Priest of Ideal* i, But although we go into black it is not *our* funeral. **1921** A. S. M. HUTCHINSON *If Winter Comes* IV. i. 254 However his wife was his funeral, not mine, and I said nothing. **1930** SAYERS & 'EUSTACE' *Documents in Case* 72 But how he can ever imagine that it will sell... But that's his funeral. **1948** *Sat. Even. Post* 26 June 82/4, I assured LaGuardia that it was 'his funeral, and not mine'. **1952** G. W. BRACE *Spire* (1953) xii. 114, I refuse to involve myself. It is your problem and your funeral.

† **2.** *pl.* The expenses attending a funeral. *Obs.*

1496 *Will of Cely* (Somerset Ho.), After that my funerales and dethe be paied. **1590** SWINBURNE *Testaments* 104 The lawe of this lande..leaueth all the residue to the disposition of the testator, funeralles and debts deducted. *a* **1626** BACON *Max. & Uses Com. Law* (1635) 71 If the Executor or Administrator pay debts, or funeralls, or Legacies of his owne money.

3. *sing.* and *pl.* A funeral sermon; a funeral service. Now only *U.S.*

1641 TRAPP *Theol. Theol.* 193 The fiend..preacht Sauls funerall, as one calls it. **1655** FULLER *Ch. Hist.* IX. iii. §2 In the absence of Doctor Humfreys designed for that service, Mr. Giles Laurence preached his Funeralls. *a* **1661** —— *Worthies, Hereford* (1662) 41, I could learn little from the Minister which preached his funeral. **1853** in N. E. Eliason *Tarheel Talk* (1956) 273 Was her funeral preached at the burying, if not, I would like to know when it will be. **1871** SCHELE DE VERE *Americanisms* (1872) 238 This led to the custom, still prevailing in densely-settled districts, and especially among the freed-men of the South, to have *funerals*, i.e. special funeral sermons preached some time after the death of the person. **1905** *N.Y. Even. Post.* 9 Mar. 8 An official funeral will be held in the Senate chamber to-morrow at two o'clock, and the body will be taken to Tennessee to-morrow evening. **1922** M. B. HOUSTON *Witch Man* xi. 131 The cemetery to which Wilda had fared as much as twice for many of the graves within it, first when the sleeper was laid there and later—sometimes there was the lapse of a year—when his funeral was preached.

fig. **1621** *Crt. & Times Jas. I* (1849) II. 245, I send you here the funerals of the Bohemian affairs, if that be true which the enclosed reporteth.

4. A burial procession.

a **1745** SWIFT *Direct. Servants, Chambermaid* Wks. 1824 XI. 443 You are sometimes desirous to see a funeral..As they pass by in the street [etc.]. **1812** J. WILSON *Isle of Palms* II. 103 A city bell Wailed for a funeral passing to the tomb. **1824-9** LANDOR *Imag. Conv.* Wks. 1846 I. l. 320 There is no funeral so sad to follow as the funeral of our own youth. **1877** BRYANT *Poems, Among the Trees* 45 The funeral goes forth; a silent train Moves slowly from the desolate home.

5. In various indefinite applications: **a.** death; **b.** grave; **c.** monument.

1575 R. B. *Appius & Virginia* in Hazl. *Dodsley* IV. 149 Which hast the seed of thine own loin thrust forth to funeral! **1590** SPENSER *F.Q.* II. v. 25 Him deeming dead..[he] Fledd fast away to tell his funerall Unto his brother. **1591** —— *Ruins of Rome* 37 Rome now of Rome is th' onely funerall. **1608** SHAKS. *Per.* II. iv. 32 He lives to govern us, Or dead, give's cause to mourn his funeral. **1668** DENHAM *Pass. Dido* 199 May he..find his funeral I' th' Sands, when he before his day shall fall. **1705** STANHOPE *Paraphr.* II. 316 Those Funerals which come by gentle and leisurely decays.

6. *attrib.* and *Comb.*, as ***funeral-biscuit, -boat, -cake, -cup, director*** (orig. *U.S.*), ***home*** (orig. *U.S.*), ***parlour*** (orig. *U.S.*), ***-party, undertaker.***

1882 MCQUEEN in *Macm. Mag.* XLVI. 163, I have already referred to what was called the '*funeral biscuit'. **1884** *Contemp. Rev.* Aug. 329 'Funeral biscuits' are baked expressly for those who visit the house on the day of interment. **1843** S. C. HALL *Ireland* III. 187 And all in that *funeral-boat repeated 'why—why— why'. **1884** *Chesh. Gloss.*, **Funeral-cakes*, long, narrow, sponge cakes used at funerals. *Ibid.*, **Funeral cups*, drinking vessels used at funerals. **1886** J. A. PORTER *New Stand. Guide Washington* 178 General Furnishing Undertaker and *Funeral Director. **1963** *New Statesman* 12 Apr. 516/3 'The reason why we have changed the name,' said Peter Beaty, secretary of the National Association of Funeral Directors, 'is for the services rendered.' **1964** *English Studies* XLV. (Suppl.) 23 Britain's 4,400 undertakers, or funeral directors, as they prefer to call themselves. **1936** MENCKEN *Amer. Lang.* (ed. 4) vi. 287 When it [*sc.* the mortician's business] is achieved the patient is put into a *casket* and stored in the *reposing room* or *slumber-room* of a **funeral-home*. **1968** *Globe & Mail* (Toronto) 17 Feb. 53/5 (Advt.), Hallowell Funeral Home. **1927** *Sat. Even. Post* 12 Mar. 6/3 Rows of wooden folding chairs, often rented from *funeral parlors. **1938** AUDEN & ISHERWOOD *On Frontier* I. i. 24 Our doctors will see to your health, and our funeral parlours will bury you. **1963** J. MITFORD *Amer. Way Death* i. 29 The nomenclature has gradually changed. From 'undertaker' *tout court* to 'funeral parlor' to 'funeral home' to 'chapel' has been the linguistic progression. **1832** *E. Ind. Sketch Bk.* II. 124, I watched the *funeral-party as they stood..in all the pride of their military array. **1707** EARL OF BINDON in *Lond. Gaz.* No. 4339/3 Divers Abuses..have been committed..by Painters, *Funeral-Undertakers.

† **funeral**, *v. Obs.*[−1] [f. prec. sb.] *trans.* To bury. Also (? nonce-use), ***to funeral it***: to mourn for the dead.

1595 HUNNIS *Joseph* 76 The purchase of the field and caue; and all that therein stood Of Heth his children purchast was, to funerall the good. **1641** R. HARRIS *Abners Funerall* 1 'Tis an hard thing to Funerall it well..God.. helps us here by David. He has the art of mourning.

† '**funeralize**, *v. Obs.*[−1] [f. FUNERAL *a.* + -IZE.] *trans.* To render sad or melancholy.

1654 COKAINE *Dianea* II. 119 It transfixes my soule, that the first day in which I have had the fortune to reverence you should be funeralized with things most molestfull.

† '**funerally**, *adv. Obs.* [f. as prec. + -LY[2].] In a funeral manner; with funeral ceremonies.

1658 SIR T. BROWNE *Hydriot.* i. 3 For when even crows were funerally burnt, Poppæa the wife of Nero found a peculiar grave enterment.

funerary ('fjuːnərərɪ), *a.* [ad. late L. *fūnerārius*, f. *fūner-, fūnus*: see FUNERAL. Cf. F. *funéraire.*] Of or pertaining to a funeral or burial.

a **1693** URQUHART *Rabelais* III. xxiii. 185 Those Funerary and Obsequial Festivals. *a* **1822** SHELLEY *Pr. Wks.* (1880) III. 62 It was probably an altar to Bacchus, possibly a funerary urn. **1866** *Daily Tel.* 16 Jan. 7/3 The deciphering of Egyptian funerary rolls. **1890** A. B. EDWARDS in *Century Mag.* Jan. XXXIX. 328 The sacred cats..had their funerary bronzes laid beside them in the grave.

† '**funerate**, *v. Obs.* Pa. pple. 6 funerat, funerated. [f. L. *fūnerāt-* ppl. stem. of *fūnerāre*, f. *fūner-, fūnus*: see FUNERAL.] *trans.* To bury with funeral rites.

1548 *Richmond Wills* (Surtees) 66 My body to be funerat within the churcheyerd of Fyngell. **1568** *Ibid.* My bodye to be funerated or buried within the churche of Est Witton.

So **fune'ration** [late L. *fūnerātiōn-em*], the performance of funeral rites.

1625 USSHER *Answ. Jesuit* 311 To the..funeration belongeth the imbalming of the dead body. **1693** KNATCHBULL *Difficult Texts* 41 The rites of funeration.

funereal (fjuː'nɪərɪəl), *a.* [f. L. *fūnere-us* (f. *fūner-, fūnus*: see FUNERAL) + -AL[1].] Of or pertaining to a funeral; appropriate to a funeral. Hence, gloomy, dark, dismal, melancholy, mournful.

1725 POPE *Odyss.* IV. 740 You timely will return a welcome guest, With him to share the sad funereal feast. *c* **1750** SHENSTONE *Elegies* iv. 2 Near some lone fane, or yew's funereal green. **1791** COWPER *Iliad* II. 725 Cyparissa veiled With broad redundance of funereal shades. **1818** SCOTT *Rob Roy* xxxv, A chill hung over our minds, as if the feast had been funereal. **1841** THACKERAY *2nd Funer. Napol.* i, A car ..decked with funereal emblems, had been prepared. **1871** L. STEPHEN *Playgr. Eur.* iv. 111. 239 We marched at a funereal pace through the forest. **1875** RENOUF *Egypt. Gram.* 66 The funereal papyri.

Hence **fu'nereally** *adv.*, in a funereal manner.

1860 *All Year Round* No. 39. 294 Strangely and funereally suggestive of a mausoleum. **1886** W. J. TUCKER *E. Europe* 332 The hearse..was drawn by four black funereally-draped horses.

† '**funerous**, *a. Obs.*[−0] [f. L. *fūner-, fūnus* FUNERAL.]

1656 in BLOUNT *Glossogr.* **1676** in COLES.

funest (fjuː'nɛst), *a.* Now *rare.* Also 7 funeste. [ad. F. *funeste*, ad. L. *fūnestus*, f. *fūnus*: see

FUNERAL.] Causing or portending death or evil; fatal, deadly, disastrous; deeply deplorable.

1654 tr. *Scudery's Curia Pol.* 96 How funest and direfull must my conceptions be, looking upon her prison all hanged with black. **1671** *True Non-conf.* 418 This execution was.. one of the funeste effects of the war. **1727** SWIFT *God's Rev. agst. Punning* Wks. 1755 III. I. 169 Scarce had this unhappy nation recovered these funest disasters. **1865** LONGF. *To Italy* 3 The dower funest of infinite wretchedness.

Hence †**fu'nestal**, †**fu'nestous** *adjs.* [see -AL, -OUS] = FUNEST. †**fu'nestate** *v.* [f. L. *fūnestāt-*: see -ATE³.] *trans.* To make funest or disastrous (Cockeram 1623). †**fune'station** [see -ATION], 'pollution by touching a dead body' (Coles 1676).

1555 EDEN *Decades* 151 A court or yarde nere vnto this funestal place. **1647** W. BROWNE tr. *Polexander* I. 90 Have pity on a wretch to whom both life and death are equally funestous. **1650** HOWELL *Giraffe's Rev. Naples* 69 With such funestous preparatifs. **1689** *Myst. Iniq.* 10 That funestous War betwixt Charles the First and the Parliament.

fung (fʌŋ). *rare.* Anglicized form of FUNGUS.

1882 [see ALG].

fungaceous (fʌŋ'geɪʃəs), *a.* [f. L. *fung-us* + -ACEOUS.] Of the nature of a fungus or fungi.

1874 COOKE *Fungi* (1875) 270 Circumstances which cause the destruction of the primitive fungaceous vegetation.

fungal ('fʌŋgəl), *a.* and *sb.* [ad. mod.L. *fungālis*, f. L. *fungus* FUNGUS.]

A. *adj.* Of or pertaining to a fungus; of the nature of a fungus. ***Fungal Alliance***: Lindley's name for the group of fungi.

1835 LINDLEY *Introd. Bot.* (1848) II. 119 The Fungal Alliance. **1874** COOKE *Fungi* (1875) 16 Unnatural union between a captive algal damsel and a tyrant fungal master. **1882** *Quain's Med. Dict.* 523 Assuming the filaments to be of undoubted fungal origin. **1887** *Pall Mall G.* 16 June 5/2 The peculiar parasite or fungal formation, for the removal of which he has had to undergo an operation.

B. *sb.* A fungus.

1845 LINDLEY *Sch. Bot.* 156 Fungi—Fungals. **1849** SIDNEY in *Jrnl. Roy. Agric. Soc.* X. II. 382 Fungals most commonly grow upon animal or vegetable substances in a state of decomposition. **1874** COOKE *Fungi* 36 Many of them are now proved to be imperfect in themselves, and only forms or conditions of other fungals.

†'**fungate**, *sb. Obs.* [f. FUNG-US + -ATE¹. Cf. F. *fongate.*] *Chem.* A salt formed by the combination of 'fungic acid' with a base.

1821 URE *Dict. Chem.*, *Fungates*, the saline compounds of a peculiar acid, which M. Braconnot has lately extracted from mushrooms. **1838** T. THOMSON *Chem. Org. Bodies* 941 Fungate of potash.

fungate ('fʌŋgeɪt), *v. Path.* [f. FUNG-US + -ATE³.] *intr.* To grow up with a fungous form or appearance; to grow rapidly like a fungus (Gould *Illust. Dict. Med.* 1894): see FUNGUS *sb.* 2. Hence '**fungating** *ppl. a.*

1847-9 TODD *Cycl. Anat.* IV. 132/1 The fungating sore produced in the tongue or cheek by a carious tooth. **1878** T. BRYANT *Pract. Surg.* I. 107 An irregular, fungating, bleeding surface. *Ibid.* I. 124 It may fungate, crack, fissure, or ulcerate.

fungation (fʌŋ'geɪʃən). *Path.* [f. as FUNGATE *v.*: see -ATION.] The formation of a fungus-like growth.

1908 *Practitioner* Sept. 395 These palliative operations are performed to prolong life, to prevent fungation, to give relief to pain. **1910** *Ibid.* June 764 Owing to the fungation, this was the most unfavourable of the cases. **1949** *Year Bk. Gen. Surg.* 187 In special circumstances, such as fungation or a large tumor, simple mastectomy may be indicated.

†**funge.** *Obs.* [a. OF. *funge, fonge, ad. L. *fungus* FUNGUS.]

1. A mushroom or fungus.

?*c***1390** *Form of Cury* in Warner *Antiq. Culin.* 5 Take Funges and pare hem clene and dyce hem. **1398** TREVISA *Barth. De P.R.* XVII. cxxiv. (1495) 686 Asshen of wylde perys dronken helpyth ayenst Funges: todestoles.

2. A soft-headed fellow. [After L. *fungus.*]

1621 BURTON *Anat. Mel.* I. ii. III. xiv. (1651) 123 Whenas indeed, in all wise mens judgments..they are mad empty vessels, funges, beside themselves. *Ibid.* II. ii. VI. iii. (1651) 306 Drink drowns more than the sea (meer Funges and Casks).

b. ? *attrib.*

1556 J. HEYWOOD *Spider & F.* xxviii. 3 There liueth not thy lyke (for a flie) I trow, For funge wit: thou arte the fly for the nonse.

†'**fungeous**, *a. Obs.* Also 6 fungious. [ad. OF. *fongeux*, f. *fonge* FUNGUS.] = FUNGOUS.

1597 GERARDE *Herbal* I. lvi. §2. 78 Blew Panick hath a reddish stalke..full of a fungious pith. **1682** T. GIBSON *Anat.* 34 They are soft and fungeous.

†'**fungiate.** *Obs.* [f. FUNGI-C + -ATE¹.] = FUNGATE *sb.*

1848 in CRAIG. **1864** in WEBSTER.

fungible ('fʌndʒɪb(ə)l), *a.* and *sb. Law.* [ad. med.L. *fungibilis* ('*res fungibiles*' Du Cange), f. *fungī* (with sense as in *fungi vice*, to take the place, fulfil the office of).

The adj. belongs to Civil Law and to the general theory of Jurisprudence; the sb. is in addition a current term of the law of Scotland.]

A. *adj.* (See quot. 1832.)

1818 H. T. COLEBROOKE *Oblig. & Contracts* I. 64 In the instance of money and other fungible articles. **1832** AUSTIN *Jurispr.* (1879) II. xlvi. 807 When a thing which is the subject of an obligation..must be delivered in specie, the thing is not fungible, i.e. that very thing, and not another thing of the same or another class in lieu of it must be delivered. Where the subject of the obligation is *a* thing of a given class, the thing is said to be fungible, i.e. the delivery of any object which answers to the generic description will satisfy the terms of the obligation. **1886** *Sat. Rev.* 25 Dec. 853 A certain number of persons..do not..regard books as 'fungible', but exercise a choice as to the books they read.

B. *sb.* A fungible thing.

a **1765** ERSKINE *Inst.* III. i. §18 (1773) I. 418 Grain and coin are fungibles, because one guinea, or one bushel or boll of sufficient merchantable wheat, precisely supplies the place of another. **1865** M. LENNAN *Prim. Marriage* i. in *Stud. Anc. Hist.* (1887) 8 The Libripens with his scales, officiating at a will or act of adoption..illustrates the sources whence all ideas of formal dispositions were derived—the sale of fungibles. **1874** *Act 37 & 38 Vict.* c. 94 §15 Casualties..paid in money or in fungibles at fixed periods or intervals. **1880** MUIRHEAD *Gaius* Digest 489 If he..had been guilty of immorality, he was punished by being required to restore fungibles at once.

'**fungic**, *a.* [f. FUNG-US + -IC. Cf. F. *fongique.*] Of or pertaining to fungi or mushrooms. ***fungic acid*** (see quot. 1885).

1819 J. G. CHILDREN *Chem. Anal.* 275 M. Braconnot has discovered another acid in fungi, which..he has named fungic acid. **1864** WATTS *Dict. Chem.* II. 747 *Fungic acid*.. According to Dessaignes..the acid in question is nothing but a mixture of citric, malic, and phosphoric acids. **1883** *Sword & Trowel* Sept. 480 A John Chinaman was passing the Consulate just then, and was soon introduced to the fungic fare.

fungicidal (fʌndʒɪ'saɪdəl), *a.* [f. FUNGICID(E + -AL.] Of the nature of, or acting as, a fungicide; characteristic of a fungicide.

1905 G. F. STRAWSON *Insects & Fungi Injurious to Plants* II. 60 The quantity of copper sulphate decomposed is small and not wasted, as the resulting precipitate has fungicidal qualities. **1909** B. M. DUGGAR *Fungous Dis. Plants* vi. 87 In the case of some of the powdery mildews the use of any fungicidal sprays or dusts may be beneficial. **1930** *Nature* 13 Dec. 921 The fungicidal power of wood preservatives. **1942** [see FUNGISTATIC *a.*]. **1969** B. E. J. WHEELER *Introd. Plant Dis.* xx. 333 In recent years a number of heterocyclic nitrogen compounds have been developed with marked fungicidal and bactericidal activity.

fungicide ('fʌndʒɪsaɪd). [f. *fungi-* FUNGUS + -CIDE 2.] Something used for destroying fungi.

1889 *Voice* (N.Y.) 6 June, Paris Green, being composed in part of sulphate of copper, may act to a limited extent as a fungicide. **1894** *Times* 10 Dec. 10/2 The latest improvements in..appliances for the distribution of.. fungicides upon growing crops.

†**fun'giferous**, *a. Obs.* [f. *fungi-* FUNGUS + L. *-fer* bearing + -OUS.] Bearing fungi; covered with fungi.

1765 *Univ. Mag.* XXXVII. 76/2 The Fungiferous Stone.

fungiform ('fʌndʒɪfɔːm), *a.* [f. *fungi-* FUNGUS + -FORM. Cf. F. *fongiforme.*] Having the form of a fungus; having a termination resembling the head of a mushroom. Said esp. of papillæ on the tongue.

1823 PHILLIPS *Mineral.* p. lxxxviii, *Fungiform*, certain subtances..are occasionally met with having a termination similar to the head of a fungus; whence they are said to be fungiform. **1831** R. KNOX *Cloquet's Anat.* 589 Fungiform Papillæ. Their number is indeterminate. **1868** WRIGHT *Ocean World* v. 120 Happalimus.—Mass fungiform, pedicillate below, expanding conically. **1881** MIVART *Cat* 172 The fungiform papillæ are much smaller and more numerous than the circumvallate ones.

†'**fungify**, *v. Obs. rare.* [f. L. *fung-ī* to perform + -(I)FY.] *trans.* To fulfil or perform (an office).

1650 T. BAYLY *Herba Parietis* 109 Bending the severall parts of the body in a devout posture to fungifie their severall offices. **1651** C. CARTWRIGHT *Cert. Relig.* I. 62 Every Minister of the Church..should be in a capacity of fungifying his office in preaching the Gospel.

‖**fungillus** (fʌn'dʒɪləs). [mod.L. *fungillus*, dim. of L. *fungus* FUNGUS.] A little fungus. Hence **fun'gilliform** *a.* [-FORM.] = FUNGIFORM.

1830 LINDLEY *Nat. Syst. Bot.* 13 Embryo fungilliform, seated at the base of firm somewhat fleshy albumen. **1885** P. MACOWAN *Rep. Cape Town Bot. Gard.* 12 Our specimens of the fungillus being decayed.

fungin ('fʌndʒɪn). (Incorrectly fungine). [f. FUNG-US + -IN. Cf. F. *fongine, fungine.*] The substance which forms the cell-walls of a mushroom or fungus.

1819 J. G. CHILDREN *Chem. Anal.* 299 Fungin is to the fungi, what woody fibre is to trees. **1869** *Eng. Mech.* 17 Dec. 333/1 The nutritive part is in the fungin.

funginous ('fʌndʒɪnəs), *a.* [f. L. *fungin-us*, f. *fungus* + -OUS.] Of or belonging to a fungus.

1866 in *Treas. Bot.* Hence in mod. Dicts.

fungistasis (fʌndʒɪ'steɪsɪs). [f. *fungi-*, combining form of FUNGUS *sb.* + Gr. στάσις stopping.] Inhibition of the growth of fungi.

1930 *Arch. Dermatol. & Syphilol.* XXII. 225 (*heading*) Fungistasis in ringworm of the toes and of the feet. **1970** *Nature* 14 Mar. 1071/1 Fungistasis is usually considered to result from biological activity in soil.

fungistatic (fʌndʒɪ'stætɪk), *a.* [f. as prec. + STATIC *a.* and *sb.*] Inhibiting the growth of fungi. Hence **fungi'statically** *adv.*

1922 *Arch. Dermatol. & Syphilol.* VI. 754 We have endeavored by a fungistatic (restraining) test and a fungicidal (killing) test to determine the affinities of various commonly employed medicaments and of certain laboratory stains for three different, pathogenic molds. **1941** *Experiment Station Record* Feb. 161 A branched chain acid, in general, proved less effective fungistatically than the corresponding straight chain acid. **1942** *Contrib. Boyce Thompson Inst.* XII. 451 Protective fungicides can function in their initial action fungistatically though in time the effect may be lethal or fungicidal. **1946** [see ACETYLENIC *a.*]. **1971** *Times* 25 Oct. 12/8 It [*sc.* a new paint] comprises a fungistatic high polymer with mycologically active reagents.

†'**fungite.** *Obs.* [f. FUNG-US + -ITE.] A kind of fossil coral.

1691 RAY *Creation* (1701) 102 Fungites, which grow upon the rocks like Shrubs. **1756** *Phil. Trans.* XLIX. 514 The.. most remarkably shaped fungites I ever saw.

fungitoxicity (fʌndʒɪtɒk'sɪsɪtɪ). [f. as FUNGISTATIC *a.* + TOXICITY.] Toxicity to fungi. So **fungi'toxic** *a.*, toxic to fungi; **fungi'toxicant**, any substance with fungitoxic action.

1951 *Contrib. Boyce Thompson Inst.* XVI. 332 The fungitoxicity of phenothiazone. *Ibid.*, Many of them are quite fungitoxic. **1953** *Nature* 1 Aug. 199/1 The finding by Neilson-Jones of some fungitoxicity in the more normal Oxshott Heath soil is also significant. **1958** V. W. COCHRANE *Physiol. of Fungi* xiv. 461 Sulfanilamide is, however, not strongly fungitoxic. *Ibid.* 463 None of these four types of reaction is certainly known to be responsible for the action of fungitoxicants. **1970** *Nature* 19 Sept. 1267/2 There is.. no correlation between the therapeutic effect of the compounds *in vivo* and their fungitoxicity *in vitro*.

fungivorous (fʌn'dʒɪvərəs), *a.* [f. L. *fungi-*, *fungus* + *-vor-us* devouring + -OUS.] Feeding on mushrooms or fungi.

1826 KIRBY & SP. *Entomol.* let. xlix. (1828) IV. 492 Among the phytiphagous insects the fungivorous ones form about a twentieth. **1849** HARDY in *Proc. Berw. Nat. Club* II. No. 7. 361 Other species whose larvæ are considered..to be either fungivorous or saprophagous.

†'**fungo.** *Obs.* Also 6 **funga.** [? a. It. or Sp. *fungo* FUNGUS.] A mushroom or fungus.

1562 BULLEYN *Bk. Simples* 3 b, Rotten Moushrimpes called Fungas. **1647** R. STAPYLTON *Juvenal* 73 Pure fungo's, such as Claudius eate, before His wife's came, after which he ne're eate more. **1682** *Loyal Satirist* in Somers *Tracts* (Scott) VII. 68 Are frogs, fungos, and toadstools the chiefest dish in a spiritual collation?

fungoid ('fʌŋgɔɪd), *a.* and *sb.* [f. FUNG-US + -OID. Cf. F. *fongoïde.*]

A. *adj.* Resembling a fungus or its qualities; of the nature of a fungus.

1836 *Penny Cycl.* V. 252/3 *Fungoid*, resembling a fungus; that is, irregular in form and fleshy in texture. **1853** KANE *Grinnell Exp.* xlv. (1856) 411 The familiar mushroom or fungoid appearance which is shown in many of the plates. **1861** S. THOMSON *Wild Fl.* II. (ed. 4) 133 Minute fungoid moulds. **1874** COOKE *Fungi* 100 Peziza venosa has the most decided nitrous odour, and also fungoid flavour. **1875** DARWIN *Insectiv. Pl.* xi. 272 Yeast and other low fungoid forms flourish in solutions of ammonia.

b. *Path.* (See FUNGUS 2.)

1844 DUFTON *Deafness* 89 An inert substance in the ear.. surrounded by fungoid growths. **1845** TODD & BOWMAN *Phys. Anat.* I. 100 Cancer, or fungoid disease. **1875** B. W. RICHARDSON *Dis. Mod. Life* 30 The malignant growths include fungoid tumour. **1878** HABERSHON *Dis. Abdomen* 42 The diphtheritic membrane is fungoid in character.

B. *sb.* A fungoid plant. Also *attrib.*

1861 H. MACMILLAN *Footn. fr. Page Nat.* 211 The highest development of fungoid life. **1891** *Daily News* 3 Nov. 6 1 They lived on a spoonful or two of arrowroot, with such fungoids as they could gather in the forest.

fungology (fʌŋ'gɒlədʒɪ). [f. FUNG-US + -(O)LOGY.] The science or study of fungi. Hence **fungo'logical** *a.* [+ -IC + -AL], of or pertaining to fungology. **fun'gologist** [+ -IST], one who studies or is learned in fungology.

1860 BERKELEY (*title*), Outlines of British Fungology. **1865** *Athenæum* No. 1980. 463/3 A philanthropic fungologist. **1882** *Gard. Chron.* XVIII. 73 The seeker after fungological knowledge. **1885** GRAY *Lett.* (1893) 769 Harkness..is absorbed in fungology. **1885** *Leeds Mercury* 26 Aug. 3/2 The fungologist may not be altogether unwilling to part with a group which has always been a source of some perplexity to him.

fun'gose, *a.* [ad. L. *fungōsus*, f. *fungus.*] = FUNGOUS 1.

1713 J. PETIVER in *Phil. Trans.* XXVIII. 217 The welted Bark or Fungose excrescencies which grow to its Branches. **1880** GRAY *Struct. Bot.* 412/2 *Fungose*, spongy in texture, fungus-like.

fungosity (fʌŋˈgɒsɪtɪ). [f. prec. + -ITY.] The quality or condition of being fungous; in quots. *concr.* a fungous growth.

1720 S. PARKER *Biblioth. Bibl.* I. 292 Certain little Pustulæ and Fungosities on its Surface. **1815** W. TAYLOR in *Monthly Rev.* LXXVIII. 107 A fibrous, excrescent, and feeble fungosity. **1861** BUMSTEAD *Ven. Dis.* (1879) 404 An extensive cavity is exposed, covered with fungosities of a bluish color.

fungous (ˈfʌŋgəs), *a.* [ad. L. *fungōsus*, f. *fungus*: see FUNGUS and -OUS. Cf. F. *fongueux*.]

1. Of or pertaining to fungi; having the nature of a fungus. †Also, formerly, Resembling a fungus in texture; spongy.

c **1420** *Pallad. on Husb.* IX. 42 And chaf is bettir for hem than is donge, For they therof wol be right fungous stronge. **1578** BANISTER *Hist. Man* I. 8 The tables of the bones of yᵉ head whiche shut betwene them the Fungous substaunce. **1601** HOLLAND *Pliny* XVIII. xxxv. I. 613 We may be sure of raine, in case wee see a fungous substance or soot gathered about lamps and candle snuffs. **1661** LOVELL *Hist. Anim. & Min.* Introd., Their lungs are single, fibrous, divided by pipes, very long and fungous. **1712** tr. *Pomet's Hist. Drugs* I. 27 Rhubarb is a thick fungous Root. **1780** A. YOUNG *Tour Irel.* I. 397 Twenty-five acres of spungy fungous bog. **1781** COWPER *Conversat.* 54 The sapless wood, divested of the bark, Grows fungous. **1799** J. ROBERTSON *Agric. Perth* 274 There is a deep soil, with a crust of fungous moss. **1830** LINDLEY *Nat. Syst. Bot.* 221 *Placentæ* either single and fungous, or double and thin. **1855** O. W. HOLMES *Poems* 237 No fungous weeds invade thy scanty soil. **1876** T. HARDY *Ethelberta* (1890) 84 An afternoon which had a fungous smell out of doors.

transf. and *fig.* **1652** J. HALL *Height Eloq.* p. vi, Fungous and empty inflations are evill in an Oration, as well as in a naturall body. **1853** RUSKIN *Stones Ven.* II. vii. §47. 269 The base principles of modern building..some fungous wall of nascent rottenness that a thunder-shower soaks down. **1859** HAWTHORNE *Fr. & It. Jrnls.* II. 267 Antiquity, with merely the natural growth of fungous human life upon it.

b. *Path.* (Cf. FUNGUS 2.)

1667 R. LOWER in *Phil. Trans.* II. 614 What the cause may be of that fungous Excressence, or why Horses are peculiarly obnoxious to it. **1725** BRADLEY *Fam. Dict.* s.v. *White honey Charge*, Verdigrease or Vitriols keep down the growth of proud fungous Flesh. **1803** *Phil. Trans.* XCIII. 207 The following case of fungous excrescence from the tongue. **1834** J. FORBES *Laennec's Dis. Chest* (ed. 4) 669 Desault mistook a fungous tumour of the bladder for a calculus. **1877** ROBERTS *Handbk. Med.* (ed. 3) I. 275 This form of cancer may produce very vascular fungous growths.

2. Growing or springing up suddenly like a mushroom, not durable or substantial.

1751 HARRIS *Hermes* III. v. (1765) 424 That fungous growth of Novels and of Pamphlets. **1782** V. KNOX *Ess.* (1819) I. xiv. 86 The fungous production of the common novel-wright will be too insignificant to attract his notice. **1816** T. L. PEACOCK *Headlong Hall* vii, Those manufactories, which have suddenly sprung up, like fungous excrescences. **1829** W. G. MEREDITH *Mem. Chas. K. of Sweden* Introd. §33. 89 One of the mushroom monarchs of Napoleon, fortunate in not being as evanescent as his fungous brethren. **1874** H. R. REYNOLDS *John Bapt.* i. §6. 59 These temporary elements have been fungous in their growth.

Hence **ˈfungousness**, fungous quality.

1730–6 in BAILEY (folio).

fungus (ˈfʌŋgəs), *sb.* Pl. fungi (ˈfʌndʒaɪ), funguses. Also 7 fungous. [a. L. *fungus*, commonly believed to be cognate with or ad. Gr. σφόγγος, σπόγγος SPONGE; in sense 2 prob. through OF. *fungus* (F. *fongus*).]

1. a. A mushroom, toadstool, or one of the allied plants, including the various forms of mould. In *Bot.*, a cryptogamous plant, characterized by the absence of chlorophyll, and deriving its sustenance from dead or living organic matter. Also *collect.* in *sing.*

1527 ANDREW *Brunswyke's Distyll. Waters* E vj b, Water of fungus..The beste parte and tyme be the whyte tode stoles or muscheroms whan they be full rype. **1601** HOLLAND *Pliny* II. 132 Those excrescenses in manner of Mushromes, which be named Fungi. **1665** HOOKE *Microgr.* 115 Cork seems to be by..the pores, a kind of Fungus or Mushrome. **1694** *Acc. Sev. Late Voy.* II. (1711) 152 Like unto the Fungus that grows on Elder, which we call Jews-ears. **1804** *Med. Jrnl.* XII. 385 Case of Poison from a Vegetable Fungus. **1838** T. THOMSON *Chem. Org. Bodies* 947 This black matter is a species of small fungus, which draws its nourishment from the wheat. **1847** BADHAM *Escul. Funguses* p. xiii, No country is perhaps richer in esculent Funguses than our own. **1882** VINES *Sachs' Bot.* 243, I shall..treat separately the forms which contain chlorophyll (so-called Algæ) from those destitute of chlorophyll (so-called Fungi).

b. *transf.* and *fig.* Often used *fig.* for something of rapid growth.

1750 WARBURTON *Julian* Introd. (1751) 45 Exsuding from her [the Church's] sickly Trunk a number of deform'd Fungus's. **1757** FOOTE *Author* II. Wks. 1799 I. 156 The offspring of a dunghill! born in a cellar..and living in a garret; a fungus, a mushroom. **1791** PAINE *Rights of Man* (ed. 4) 107 They began to consider aristocracy as a kind of fungus growing out of the corruption of society. **1862** *Fraser's Mag.* Nov. 631 Nor, when criticising this architectural fungus [Exhibition Building], must its cost be forgotten. **187.** SPURGEON *Treas. Dav.* Ps. lxxviii. 36 A mere unsubstantial fungus of unabiding excitement. **1881** G. W. CABLE *Mme. Delphine* i. 2 That significant fungus, the Chinaman.

c. A beard. Also *face-fungus* s.v. FACE *sb.* 27. *slang.*

1925 WODEHOUSE *Sam the Sudden* xiii. 89 Where did you get the fungus? **1936** [see BEAVER³]. **1937** 'R. CROMPTON' *William—the Showman* x. 240 'Is it to be me or that ass with the fungus on his cheeks?' demanded Richard belligerently. **1959** H. HOBSON *Mission House Murder* ii. 14 In addition to the chin-fungus he'd put on a little weight.

2. a. *Path.* A spongy morbid growth or excrescence, such as exuberant granulation in a wound.

1674–7 MOLINS *Anat. Obs.* (1896) 17 An old Man having a Contusion upon his Skin there threw out such Fungous that all the Escharotticks signified nothing. **1721** BAILEY, *Fungus* [in Surgery], soft spungy, Flesh which grows upon Wounds. **1748** HARTLEY *Observ. Man* I. ii. 152 Bitters and Acids applied to Funguses of the Brain. **1804** ABERNETHY *Surg. Obs.* 91 It is no uncommon circumstance to meet with wens, that have burst spontaneously, and have thrown out a fungus. **1844** DUFTON *Deafness* 41 Sometimes small vegetations can be observed on its surface, and the commencing existence of polypus or fungus.

fig. **1711** SHAFTESB. *Charac.* (1737) I. 248 The comick genius was apply'd as a kind of caustick, to those exuberances and fungus's of the swoln dialect, and magnificent manner of speech.

b. A skin disease in fish.

1892 *Daily News* 12 Jan. 5/4 Though the disease of the skin of fish known as 'fungus' is common..they never had a better supply of salmon in the river than at present.

†**3.** An excrescence of lamp-black or charred fibre on the wick of a candle or lamp. *lit.* and *fig.* (So in Latin.) *Obs.*

1775 FLETCHER *Last Check* §18 Wks. 1795 VI. 243 Is a spiritual lamp trimmed when its flame is darkened by the black fungus of indwelling sin? **1813** T. FORSTER *Atmosph. Phænom.* (1815) 150 The excrescence of fungi about the wicks of lamps and candles; the flaring and snapping of the flame.

4. The vegetable growth employed as tinder.

[**1664** EVELYN *Sylva* (1679) 27 Nor may we here omit to mention the..fungus's to make Tinder.] **1831** BREWSTER *Nat. Magic* xiii. (1833) 320 The heat of the wire is always sufficient to kindle a piece of German fungus.

5. *attrib.* and *Comb.*, as ***fungus disease*** (see 2 b above), ***-eater***, ***-flora***, ***growth***, ***-hunt***, ***-hunter***, ***production***, ***-ring***, ***tree***; ***fungus-covered***, ***-eating***, ***-like***, ***-plagued***, ***-proof*** adjs.; **fungus-garden** (see quot.); **fungus-gnat**, **-midge** *Ent.*, a fly of the dipterous family Mycetophilidæ.

1880 BURTON *Q. Anne* III. xvii. 169 *Fungus-covered cabins. **1888** *Pall Mall G.* 3 Sept. 9/1 Fish affected with *fungus disease. **1899** G. H. CARPENTER *Insects* 304 *Fungus-Eaters... A considerable number of small Beetles together with the grubs of many Flies and Midges find their sustenance in fungi. *Ibid.* Index 397/1 *Fungus-eating insects. **1892** G. MASSEE (*title*) British *fungus-flora. **1924** J. A. THOMSON *Science Old & New* xvi. 88 The *fungus-gardens of the termites are seen at their best in Ceylon, and the characteristic feature is the construction of a maze of chewed wood with labyrinthine passages, on the walls of which the fungi grow. **1884** J. S. KINGSLEY *Stand. Nat. Hist.* (1888) II. 407 The family *Mycetophilidæ*, commonly called *Fungus Gnats. **1955** *Sci. Amer.* May 104/3 In caves of the Great Smokies in Tennessee and North Carolina, there is a large fly, the fungus gnat (*Platyura fultoni*), which is luminous in its larval stage. **1899** BURNAND in *Pall Mall Mag.* XVIII. 536 We espied the Professor..evidently enjoying a *fungus-hunt. **1886** P. ROBINSON *Valley of Teetotum Trees* 134 A common object of the country in 'the fall of the year'..is the fungus. And scarcely less familiar, in wooded districts especially, the *fungus-hunter. **1899** G. H. CARPENTER *Insects* 256 The *Mycetophilidæ* or *Fungus-midges. **1918** W. BEEBE *Jungle Peace* (1919) viii. 178 Light-starved and *fungus-plagued, the shrub and saplings are stunted and weak. **1826** DISRAELI *Viv. Grey* IV. i, The Literature of the present day, a *fungus production which has flourished from the artificial state of our Society. **1887** DARWIN in *Life & Lett.* (1887) III. 348 Raising *fungus-proof varieties of the potato. **1907** WOODRUFFE-PEACOCK *Pasture & Meadow Anal.* 5 The flora of *fungus-rings.. should always be most carefully noted the season through. **1963** *Field Archæol.* (Ordnance Survey) (ed. 4) 7 The fungus rings which suggest barrow circles. **1848** DICKENS *Dombey* xxiii, *Fungus trees grew in corners of the cellars.

Hence **ˈfungus** *v. intr.*, to grow *out* rapidly like a fungus; **ˈfungused** *pa. pple.*, grown over or covered with fungus.

1841 LYTTON *Nt. & Morn.* (1851) 167 From that little boss has fungused out a terrible hump. **1862** *Sat. Rev.* XIII. 209/1 From a celebrated cellar, cobwebbed and fungused with the dirt and dust of half-a-century of neglect.

fungusy (ˈfʌŋgəsɪ), *a.* Also **fungousy**. [f. FUNGUS + -Y¹.] **a.** Covered with a fungous growth. **b.** Of a fish: Affected with a fungous disease.

1856 CANNING in Hare *2 Noble Lives* (1893) II. 89 Despatch-boxes not opened for some time assume the appearance of a bottle of curious old port—white and fungus-y. **1880** F. BUCKLAND in *Scotsman* (1883) 10 Nov. 6/6 He received a pike..which after a while became fungousy.

†**ˈfungy**, *a.* *Obs.* [f. FUNGE + -Y¹.] Like a fungus in texture, cellular, spongy.

1578 BANISTER *Hist. Man* I. 7 The Bones of the Head are neither altogether Solid, nor yet wholly fungie. **1721** BAILEY s.v. *Funk*, A fungy Excrescence of some Trees.

†**funible.** *Obs.* = FUNNEL 1. (The orig. has *trächter*.)

1658 A. FOX *Wurtz' Surg.* III. vi. 234 The fume..which the party took down at his mouth going to-bed, in a funible or pipe.

funic (ˈfjuːnɪk), *a.* [f. FUN-IS + -IC.] Pertaining to the funis or umbilical cord.

1857 in DUNGLISON *Med. Lex.* **1876** PLAYFAIR *Treat. Midw.* I. II. iv. 159 One of these [sounds heard in auscultation] is the so-called *umbilical* or *funic souffle*.

†**ˈfunical**, *a.* *Obs.*⁻¹ [f. FUN-IS + -IC + -AL¹.] Of or pertaining to the funis or umbilical cord; supplied through the funis.

1753 N. TORRIANO *Midwifry* 13 The Opinion of the funical Nourishment is also defensible from another Circumstance.

funicle (ˈfjuːnɪk(ə)l). [Anglicized form of FUNICULUS.] In various senses of FUNICULUS, *esp.* **a.** = FUNICULUS 2. **b.** *Bot.* = FUNICULUS 3.

1664 POWER *Exp. Philos.* II. 134 The uppermost Surface of the Quicksilver being sliced off, is dilated into a tenuous Column or Funicle. **1840** PAXTON *Bot. Dict.*, *Funicle*, a little stalk, by which the seed is attached to the placenta. **1860** FOWLER *Med. Voc.*, *Funicle*, in Anat., an aggregation of fibres into a little round cord. **1870** HOOKER *Stud. Flora* 87 Cytisus, Broom..seeds with a tumid funicle.

c. *Ent.* = FUNICULUS 4.

1881 L. O. HOWARD in *Rep. U.S. Dept. Agric. 1880* III. 361 The club is rather large..as long as or longer than the last four funicle joints together. **1888** J. H. COMSTOCK *Introd. Ent.* ii. 11 The funicle is that part of the clavola between the club and the ring-joints; or, when the latter are not specialized, between the club and the pedicel. **1923** A. D. MACGILLIVRAY *Guide Ext. Insect Anat.* iii. 79 In those species..where the distal end of the flagellum is clavate, the enlarged segments are known as the club and the segments between the club and the ring-segments as the funicle. **1925** A. D. IMMS *Gen. Textbk. Ent.* 14 In some insects, particularly among Hymenoptera, the flagellum is divisible into the ring-joints, the funicle, and the club... The funicle comprises those joints which intervene between the ring-joints and the club,..or between the latter and the pedicel in cases when the ring-joints are not differentiated. **1937** [see FUNICULUS 4 b].

‖**funiculaire** (fynikylɛr). [Fr.: see FUNICULAR *a.*] A funicular railway.

1907 *Westm. Gaz.* 9 Oct. 2/1 We never go up anything except by funiculaire. **1927** *Observer* 18 Dec. 9/4 Every attention is paid to the comfort of travellers, even in the funiculaires.

funicular (fjuːˈnɪkjʊlə(r)), *a.* and *sb.* [f. L. *fūnicul-us* + -AR. Cf. F. *funiculaire*.]

A. *adj.* **1.** Of or pertaining to a funiculus in various senses. †***funicular hypothesis***: see FUNICULUS 2.

1664 POWER *Exp. Philos.* II. 138 A Confutation of this Funicular Hypothesis of Linus. **1709** F. HAUKSBEE *Phys. Mech. Exp.* iii. (1719) 89 The Objections of the Favourers of Suction, and the Funicular Hypothesis. **1866** A. FLINT *Princ. Med.* (1880) 735 The name *funicular sclerosis* is given to sclerosis following certain definite columns of the cord, such as lateral and posterior spinal sclerosis.

2. Of or pertaining to a rope or its tension; depending on or worked by a rope. ***funicular machine***: an arrangement of a cord, pulleys, and suspended weights, designed to illustrate statical principles. ***funicular polygon***: the figure assumed by a cord supported at its extremities, and having weights suspended from it at various points. ***funicular railway***: one worked by a cable and stationary engine; a cable railway.

1828 J. M. SPEARMAN *Brit. Gunner* (ed. 2) 296 The whole is called the Funicular Machine. **1837** WHEWELL *Hist. Induct. Sc.* (1857) II. 13 Stevin..applies his principle of equilibrium to cordage, pullies, funicular polygons. **1886** *Pall Mall G.* 24 June 14/1 The ascent..will be by means of a funicular railway. **1892** *Tablet* 3 Sept. 365 A funicular railway runs up the mountain's side.

3. Resembling a cord; *spec.* in *Anat.* and *Bot.*

1835–6 TODD *Cycl. Anat.* I. 702/1 Small muscles..to which Poli has given the name of funicular muscles. **1845** TODD & BOWMAN *Phys. Anat.* I. 70 Funicular, rounded cords of white fibrous tissue. **1851** D. WILSON *Preh. Ann.* (1863) I. II. vi. 465 The knotted funicular torc. **1856** HENSLOW *Dict. Bot. Terms*, *Funicular chord*, a cord-like appendage, by the intervention of which..the seeds are attached, instead of being seated immediately on the placenta.

4. Pertaining to the funis or umbilical cord.

1873 KENNEDY in Leishman *Syst. Midwif.* ix. 179 Except under such circumstances, it must be very difficult to discover the funicular soufflet.

B. *sb.* A funicular railway (Webster 1909).

1911 A. BENNETT *Card* xi. 280 He had been to Montreux and missed the funicular back. *Ibid.* 284 We all saw the Countess off in the funicular at three o'clock. **1926** H. BENNETT tr. *Leroux's Adv. Coquette* vi, A number of travellers set down by the funicular gazed from a respectful distance at the actress's enthusiasm. **1957** P. KEMP *Mine were of Trouble* x. 187 The disused funicular that climbed La Rhûne, a prominent mountain nearby. **1971** *Daily Tel.* 30 Jan. 7/2 The resort has..four funiculars and one chairlift.

fuˈniculared, *ppl. a.* [f. FUNICULAR *sb.*] Provided with a funicular railway.

1933 *Times Lit. Suppl.* 30 Mar. 211/2 The Arctic figures as going the way of Africa and funiculared mountains.

funicularize (fjuːˈnɪkjʊləraɪz), *v.* [f. FUNICULAR *a.* + -IZE.] *trans.* To provide with a funicular railway.

1927 R. CAPELL in H. J. Foss *Heritage of Music* 216 The Alps..are now mostly funicularised. **1936** *Times Lit. Suppl.* 9 May 397/3 The Alps before they were funicularized for Winter Sports.

funiculate (fjuːˈnɪkjʊleɪt), *a.* *Bot.* and *Zool.* [f. FUNICUL-US + -ATE².] Having a funiculus.

1826 KIRBY & SP. *Entomol.* IV. 349 *Funiculate*, when it [the postfrænum] forms a narrow ridge. In mod. Dicts.

‖**funiculus** (fjuːˈnɪkjʊləs). [L. *fūniculus*, dim. of *fūnis* rope.]

†**1.** A little rope. *Obs. rare*⁻⁰.

1706 in PHILLIPS (ed. Kersey).

†**2.** A hypothetical 'string' or filament of extremely rarefied matter, imagined to be the agent operating in the suspension of the mercury in the Torricellian experiment. *Obs.*

The hypothesis was propounded by Franciscus Linus (the Jesuit F. Line or Hall) in his book *De Corporum Inseparabilitate* 1661, which attempts to refute the correct explanation of the phenomenon that had been given by Boyle.

1662 BOYLE *Spring of Air* II. i. (1682) 18 That the things we ascribe to the weight or spring of the air are really performed by neither, but by a certain Funiculus, or extremely thin substance provided by Nature..which.. does violently attract bodies whereunto it is contiguous if they be not too heavy to be removed by it. **1669** —— *Contn. New Exp.* I. (1682) 5 Who attribute the suspension of the Quicksilver in the Torricellian experiment to a certain rarified matter, which some call a Funiculus.

3. The umbilical cord; = FUNIS. Hence *transf.* in *Bot.*, a little stalk by which a seed or ovule is attached to the placenta.

1830 LINDLEY *Nat. Syst. Bot.* 111 Ovules ascending from the axis, attached to a short funiculus. **1854** MAYNE *Exp. Lex.*, *Funiculus*, a name for the umbilical cord. **1870** BENTLEY *Bot.* 326 The funiculus is parallel to the ovule, instead of being at right angles to it. **1882** VINES *Sachs' Bot.* 492 The nucellus..is seated on a stalk, the Funiculus.

4. *Ent.* **a.** 'A term for the part of the antenna which lies between the scape and the club in certain insects' (*Syd. Soc. Lex.*).

1877 W. THOMSON *Voy. Challenger* I. iv. 262 Lamellar appendage of the outer antennæ reaching to the middle of the second joint of the funiculus.

b. (See quots.)

1826 KIRBY & SPENCE *Introd. Entomol.* III. xxxiii. 389 The Funiculus, a small cartilaginous cord, passing through a minute orifice of the *Postfrœnum*, just above the point where the footstalk is fixed, to an opposite hole above it. **1895** *Cambr. Nat. Hist.* V. I. 492 The petiole, besides articulating..with the propodeum by means of certain prominences and notches, is also connected there-with by means of a slender ligament placed on its dorsal aspect and called the funiculus. **1923** A. D. MACGILLIVRAY *Guide Ext. Insect Anat.* iii. 79 When the ring-segments are wanting and the antenna is geniculate, the segments between the club and the scape are known as the funiculus. **1937** J. R. DE LA TORRE-BUENO *Gloss. Ent.* 110 Funicle, funicule, funiculus, in the insect antenna, that part of the clavola between the club and the ring-joints (Comstock).

5. *Anat.* 'Applied to the primitive cord or bundle of nerve fibres, bound together in a sheath of connective tissue, called the perineurium or neurilemma' (*Syd. Soc. Lex.*).

6. In *Polyzoa*. (See quot.)

1877 HUXLEY *Anat. Inv. Anim.* viii. 455 Very generally, the gastric division of the alimentary canal is connected with the parietes of the body by a sort of ligament, the funiculus, or gastro-parietal band.

funiform (ˈfjuːnɪfɔːm), *a.* [f. L. *fūni-s* rope + -FORM.] Having the form of a cord or rope.

1865 PAGE *Handbk. Geol. Terms* (ed. 2), *Funiform*, cord-like, rope-like. **1877** W. JONES *Finger-ring* 61 The whole is overlaid with funiform wire ornaments.

funiliform (fjuːˈnɪlɪfɔːm), *a. Bot.* [as if f. L. **fūnīli-s* adj. (f. *fūnis* rope) + -FORM.] (See quot.)

1856 HENSLOW *Dict. Bot. Terms*, *Funiliform*, tough, cylindrical, and flexible, like a chord; as the roots of arborescent monocotyledones.

funipendulous (ˌfjuːnɪˈpɛndjʊləs), *a.* [f. L. *fūni-s* rope + *pendul-us* hanging + -OUS.] Hanging from a rope; connected with a hanging rope.

1706 W. JONES *Syn. Palmar. Matheseos* 290 The greater the Funipendulous Body is, the less does the Medium Resist it. **1829** T. L. PEACOCK *Misfort. Elphin* vi. 92 The exhibition of some half-dozen funipendulous forgers might have shocked..his humanity. **1863** DE MORGAN *Budget* (1872) 386 And so, having shown how the reviewer has hung himself, I leave him funipendulous.

funipotent (fjuːˈnɪpətənt), *a. nonce-wd.* [f. L. *fūni-s* rope + *potent-em* POTENT.] Playing tricks with ropes.

1880 F. POLLOCK *Spinoza* 60 Believers in table-moving, slate-writing, funipotent and other goblins.

‖**funis** (ˈfjuːnɪs). *Anat.* [L. *fūnis* rope.] †**a.** Short for *funis brachii*, 'an old name for the median vein' (*Syd. Soc. Lex.*). **b.** The umbilical cord.

c **1400** *Lanfranc's Cirurg.* 159 þis veyne..is eftsoones dyvydid, and þe oon partie is spred bi þe arm manye weies wiþoute forþ, þat is clepid funis. **1753** N. TORRIANO *Midwifry* 8 The Funis, the Placenta, with its Amnion and Chorion, and Allantoides. **1800** *Med. Jrnl.* IV. 323 With the other [hand] we take hold of the funis and make a gentle distension. **1855** RAMSBOTTOM *Obstetr. Med.* 64 One coil of the funis is seen twisted round the neck, and another round the left ancle.

†**funk**, *sb.*¹ *Obs.* Also 4 **fonk**, 4–7 **funke**, 7 **founck**. [Corresponds to MDu. *vonke* (Du. *vonk*), OHG. *funcho* (MHG. *vunke*, mod.Ger. *funke*) wk. masc., spark; the Eng. word may have been adapted from Du., or it may represent an OE. **funca*. The existence of the ablaut-var. MHG. *vanke*, mod.Ger. dial. *fanke*, renders it unlikely that the word is a diminutive of the sb. represented in Goth. by *fôn* (gen. *funins*) fire.]

1. A spark. (The sense in the quots. from R. Brunne is quite uncertain.)

c **1330** R. BRUNNE *Chron.* (1810) 172 Þat was not worth a fonk. *Ibid.* 211 Þe kyng an oth suore, He suld him venge on Steuen..& of þo fourtene monkes..Be beten alle fonkes. **1390** GOWER *Conf.* III. 18 Of lust that ilke firy funke Hath made hem as who saith half wode. **1393** LANGL. *P. Pl.* C. VII. 335 For al the wrecchednesse of this worlde and wicked dedes Fareth as a fonk of fuyr that ful a-myde Temese. *c* **1440** *Promp. Parv.* 182/2 Funke or lytylle fyyr, *igniculus, foculus*.

2. Touch-wood. Cf. PUNK, SPUNK.

1673 [see 3]. **1704** E. WARD *Dissenting Hypocrite* 35 Burn it as Funk, or keep't as Fodder. **1721** BAILEY, *Funk*, a fungy Excrescence of some Trees dress'd to strike Fire on. **1754** GOOCH in *Phil. Trans.* XLVIII. 817 They gather an excrescence, growing..upon oaks, and call it Funk, which impregnated with nitre, is used as a match to light pipes. *a* **1825** in FORBY *Voc. E. Anglia*, *Funk*, touch-wood.

3. *Comb.*, as **funk horn**, ? a horn case containing touchwood.

1673 CHANNON in *Col. St. Papers, Amer. & W. Ind.* (1889) 538 A flint and 'founck horn,' which a man had put in his pocket the day before to strike fire in the night.

funk, *sb.*² [f. FUNK *v.*¹] **1.** A strong smell or stink: also, tobacco smoke. *Obs.* exc. *U.S. dial.*

1623 W. CAPPS in P. A. Bruce *Econ. Hist. Virginia* (1896) I. 136 Betwixt decks there can hardlie a man fetch his breath by reason there ariseth such a funke in the night that it causes putrefaction of bloud. *a* **1700** B. E. *Dict. Cant. Crew*, *Funk*, Tobacco Smoak; also a strong Smell or Stink. **1725** *New Cant. Dict.* s.v., What a Funk here is! What a thick Smoak of Tobacco is here! Here's a damn'd Funk, here's a great Stink. **1917** *Dialect Notes* IV. 412 Open up the door and let the funk out. **1937–40** in WENTWORTH *Amer. Dial. Dict.* (1944) 237/2.

fig. **1659** D. PELL *Impr. Sea* 491 *note*, I would either run out of the stinke of swearing, or make them to run out of the ship that should..make such a filthy funke in it.

2. Music that is 'funky' (see quots. and FUNKY *a.*³ 2). *slang* (orig. *U.S.*).

1959 *Jazz* Fall 292 You can even try to put too much 'funk' in a thing. **1960** *Melody Maker* 31 Dec., The American jazz public is 'funk'-crazy. **1961** *Sunday Times* 5 Feb. 36/5 The contemporary jazz cult of 'blues roots'—otherwise described as 'soul' or 'funk'. **1962** *Radio Times* 10 May 42/2 *Funk*, basically, 'smelly'—signifies return of modern jazzmen to earthy roughage of blues and New Orleans, but rephrased with modern techniques; similar to soul, only more extrovert. **1970** C. MAJOR *Dict. Afro-Amer. Slang* 56 *Funk*, 'soul' quality in black music, melancholy mood of the blues.

funk (fʌŋk), *sb.*³ *slang.* [First mentioned as Oxford slang; possibly, as Lye suggests, a. Flemish *fonck* (Kilian), the origin of which is unknown.]

1. Cowering fear; a state of panic or shrinking terror. ***blue funk***: see BLUE *a.* 3.

1743 LYE in *Junius' Etymologicum* s.v., Funk vox Academicis Oxon. familiaris . *to be in a funk* . vett. Flandris *fonck* est Turba, perturbatio . *in de fonck siin*, Turbari, tumultuari, in perturbatione versari. **1765** E. SEDGWICK in *10th Rep. Hist. MSS. Comm.* App. I. 390 Poor Todd..is said to be in a violent funk. **1785** GROSE *Dict. Vulg. Tongue* s.v., I was in a cursed funk. **1827** DE QUINCEY in *Blackw. Mag.* XXI. 204 The horrid panic or 'funk' (as the men of Eton call it) in which Des Cartes must have found himself. **1839** SIR C. NAPIER 9 Apr. in W. N. Bruce *Life* iv. (1885) 127 *Funk* is the order of the day. **1861** HUGHES *Tom Brown at Oxf.* xliv, There is no sign of anything like funk amongst our fellows. **1874** M. COLLINS *Transmigr.* II. xi. 183 With all my heroism, I was in a frightful funk.

2. One who funks; a coward.

1860 in BARTLETT *Dict. Amer.*, *Funk*..2 a coward. **1888** *Daily Tel.* 13 Apr. 5/2 The public opinion among youth would..dub a 'fellow' a 'funk'.

funk (fʌŋk), *sb.*⁴ *Sc.* and *north.* [f. FUNK *v.*³]

1. A kick.

1808–80 in JAMIESON. **1838** J. HALLEY in *Life* (1842) 145 He placed his hand..unluckily just on the spot where Mr. Pony is rather touchy. Sundry vehement funks..were the immediate consequence.

2. Ill-humour, passion.

1808–80 JAMIESON s.v., In a funk, in a surly state, or in a fit of passion. *Loth.* **1892** *Northumbld. Gloss.* s.v., 'The gaffer's in a fine funk'.

funk (fʌŋk), *v.*¹ *slang.* [perh. a F. dial. *funkier* = OF. *funkier*, *fungier*:—L. **fūmicare* (It. *fumicare*), *fūmigāre*, f. *fūmus* smoke. (FUNK *sb.*², though app. f. this vb., is recorded earlier.)]

1. *trans.* To blow smoke upon (a person); to annoy with smoke.

1699 W. KING *Furmetry* iii. 56 What with strong smoke, and with his stronger breath, He funks Basketia and her son to death. **1719** D'URFEY *Pills* VI. 303 He..with a sober Dose Of Coffee funks his Nose. **1753** SMOLLETT *Ct. Fathom* (1784) 119/1 He proposed that we should retire into a corner, and funk one another with brimstone. **1785** GROSE *Dict. Vulg. Tongue* s.v., To funk the cobbler, a school boy's trick, performed with assa fœtida and cotton, which are stuffed into a pipe..and..the smoke is blown..through the crannies of a cobler's stall. **1835** MARRYAT *Jac. Faithf.* xxv, Do look how the old gentleman is funking Mary, and casting sheep's eyes at her through the smoke. **1840** BARHAM *Ingol. Leg.*, *Spectre Tappington*, An arrangement happily adapted for the escape of the noxious fumes up the chimney, without that unmerciful 'funking' each other, which a less scientific disposition of the weed would have induced.

b. To smoke (a pipe, tobacco). †Also, to blow (tobacco smoke) *on* (a person).

a **1704** T. BROWN *Inscript. Tobacco-box* Wks. 1730 I. 65 Since Jove..Gives us the Indian weed to funk. **1733** *Revolution Politicks* II. 67 When the King was upon his Trial, did not the Soldiers funk Tobacco in on the King as he sat, to offend him. **1764** T. BRYDGES *Homer Travest.* (1797) II. 54 Where a round dozen pipes they funk, And then return to town dead drunk. **1791** HUDDESFORD *Salmag.* 114 A pipe I did funk.

c. *intr.* To smoke.

1829 H. MURRAY *N. Amer.* I. iv. 211 The grain having funked for six and twenty weeks in the ship's hold. **1832** W. STEPHENSON *Gateshead Local Poems* 29 At Jenny Brown's she'd smoke and funk. **1855** BROWNING *Fra Lippo* 174 My straw-fire flared and funked. **1860** BARTLETT *Dict. Amer.* s.v., When the smoke puffs out from a chimney place or stove, we say 'it funks'.

2. To cause an offensive smell.

1708 MOTTEUX *Rabelais* IV. xxxii. 92 **1829** BROCKETT *N.C. Words*, *Funk*, to smoke or rather to cause an offensive smell.

Hence ˈ**funking** *ppl. a.*

1700 S. PARKER *Six Philos. Ess.* 54 Many a funking Poor may have had his Pipe lighted by a Flash.

funk (fʌŋk), *v.*² *slang.* [Belongs to FUNK *sb.*³]

1. *intr.* To flinch or shrink through fear; to 'show the white feather', try to back out of anything. Also const. *at*.

1737–9 H. WALPOLE *Lett.* (1886) I. 15 The last time I saw him here [Eton], was standing up funking over against a conduit to be catechised. **1813** LD. CAMPBELL *Let.* Apr. in *Life* (1881) I. 295, I funk before Ellenborough as much as ever. I almost despair of ever acquiring a sufficient degree of confidence before him to put me in possession of my faculties. **1841** *Punch* 13 Nov. 213/2 Funking at the rejection of a clever man,..determining to take prussic acid in the event of being refused.., the student finds his first ordeal approach. **1847** *Illustr. Lond. News* 27 Nov. 360/2 It occurred to me that the change of temperature would be disagreeable, and I rather funked. **1848** LOWELL *Biglow P.* Ser. I. ix. Poems 1890 II. 137 To Funk right out o' p'lit'cal strife aint thought to be the thing. **1857** T. HOOD *Pen & Pencil Pict.* 144, I have seen him out with the governor's hounds: he funked at the first hedge. **1859** *Punch* 23 July 34/2 Louis Napoleon, who had gone to war on a pledge that the Austrians should be driven out of Italy, had 'funked' at the Quadrilateral. **1863** READE *Hard Cash* xxv, I began to funk again at his knowing that;..I was flustered, ye see. **1885** RUNCIMAN *Skippers & Sh.* 79, I hope you will not think I am funking.

2. *trans.* To fight shy of, wish or try to shirk or evade (an undertaking, duty, etc.). Also, ***to funk it***.

1857 KINGSLEY *Two Y. Ago* III. 103 He'll have funked it, when he comes to the edge, and sees nothing but mist below. **1881** H. JAMES *Portr. Lady* xlv, Not that he liked good-byes—he always funked them.

3. To fear, be afraid of (a person).

1836–48 B. D. WALSH *Aristoph.*, *Knights* 154 The rich men fear him, And he is funked by all the poorer class. **1849** ALB. SMITH *Pottleton Leg.* 385, 'I rather funk the governor' replied, in turn, Mr. Spooner.

4. To frighten or scare.

1819 *Sporting Mag.* IV. 197 The Frenchman, funked at the superiority of his antagonist. **1831** SCOTT *Jrnl.* 20 May, Jeffrey is fairly funked about it. **1892** *Sat. Rev.* 30 Apr. 496/2 The jury, 'funked' by the Anarchists, returned extenuating circumstances in the miscreant's case.

5. *Comb.*, as **funkstick** (*Hunting*), one who 'funks' the 'sticks' or fences; *transf.*, a coward.

1889 *Univ. Rev.* III. 76 The 'funksticks' immediately slacken rein. **1897** R. BADEN-POWELL *Matabele Campaign* xvii. 438 A nervous man is forty thousand times worse than a frightened woman, especially when..he has any number of drink-fuddled 'funk-sticks' ready to echo his alarm. **1916** *National Rev.* No. 382. 527 The rising predicted by Bernhardi and feared by all funksticks. **1930** A. E. W. MASON *Dean's Elbow* vi. 68 She thought of William Mardyke and his timidities. 'He'll never do that. What did you call him?' 'A funkstick.'

Hence ˈ**funking** *vbl. sb.* Also ˈ**funker**.

a **1845** HOOD *Jack Hall* xi, Funking, indeed. was quite a thing Beside his function. **1857** HUGHES *Tom Brown* I. viii, While he [Flashman] was thrashing them, they would roar out instances of his funking at football. **1864** C. CLARKE *Box for Season* II. 115 Martyr and Dickenson are both funkers. **1875** WHYTE MELVILLE *Riding Recoll.* iv. (1879) 64 Of all riders 'the hard funker' is the most unmerciful to his beast.

funk (fʌŋk), *v.*³ *Sc.* and *north.* [app. onomatopœic; a variant *fung* is common (see Jamieson).] *trans.* and *intr.* To kick.

c **1709** *Auld Grey Mare* i. in *Jacobite Songs* (1887) 56 You've curried the auld mare's hide, She'll funk nae mair at you. *Ibid.* v, The good auld yaud Could nowther funk nor fling. **1821** *Blackw. Mag.* Nov. X. 393 The horse funkit him aff into the dub. **1823** J. WILSON *Trials Marg. Lyndsay* xxxv. 294 The beast's funking like mad. **1834** M. SCOTT *Cruise Midge* (1859) 375 The quadruped funking up her heels and tossing the dry sand with her horns. **1892** *Northumbld. Gloss.*, *Funk*, to kick, to kick up the heels as a horse or donkey does. 'To funk off' is to throw the rider.

Hence ˈ**funking** *vbl. sb.* Also ˈ**funker**.

1823 *Blackw. Mag.* Mar. XIII. 313 It's hard to gar a wicked cout leave off funking. **1825–80** JAMIESON s.v., Dinna buy that beast, she's a funker. **1852** R. S. SURTEES *Sponge's Sp. Tour* (1893) 219 The move of the hounds caused a rush of gentlemen to their horses, and there was the usual scramblings up, and fidgetings, and funkings.

funk-hole. *slang.* [f. FUNK *sb.*³] A place of safety into which one can retreat; esp. in war, as a dug-out. Also *transf.* and *fig.*, e.g. an employment which is used as a pretext for evading military service.

1900 *Daily News* 20 Nov. 3/2 The Funk Holes which the besieged residents had mined in the river bank. **1914** *Daily Mail* 4 Dec. 8/3, I am sitting in my 'funk hole' lined with straw. **1918** W. J. Locke *Rough Road* xx. 245 'J. M. T. and I have looked Death in the face many a time—and really he's a poor raw-head and bloody-bones sort of Bogey; don't you think so, old chap?' 'It all depends on whether you've got a funk-hole handy.' **1920** *Blackw. Mag.* May 608/1 Grain-pits that afford excellent ready-made funk-holes. **1922** C. E. Montague *Disenchantment* xiv. 188 Some of our higher commanders would use their A.D.C. rooms as funk-holes to shelter..their distant cousin the marquis. **1928** *Sunday Dispatch* 20 Sept. 2/2 Jim might have stayed! A few hours away from the office wouldn't matter. Lovely funk-holes, offices! **1932** 'A. Bridge' *Peking Picnic* v. 48 This place was one of her favourite funk-holes. **1946** R. Campbell *Talking Bronco* 15 To jobs in ministries they'll fly, And funk-holes in the B.B.C. **1959** J. D. Clark *Prehist. S. Afr.* ix. 219 Deep, dark caves were never occupied except very occasionally as refuges or 'funk holes'.

funkia ('fʌŋkɪə). Also **funckia.** [mod.L., ad. *funckia* (K. Sprengel 1817, in *Anleitung zur Kenntnis d. Gewächse* (ed. 2) I. 246), f. the name of H. C. *Funck* (1771–1839), Prussian botanist + -ia[1].] A member of the genus of liliaceous plants from Japan once so named, but now called *Hosta*, having racemes of drooping white or lilac bell-shaped flowers; a plantain-lily.

1839 *Curtis's Bot. Mag.* LXV. 3657 This interesting species of Funckia was received from Belgium. **1883** W. Robinson *Eng. Flower Garden* 132/2 The bold and striking foliage of some of the strongest plain-leaved section of Funkias renders them very effective as edging plants for large beds. **1927** E. H. M. Cox *Evol. Garden* v. 78 Funkias, or Plantain Lilies, are among the best foliage plants of the herbaceous border. **1970** *Countryman* LXXV. 291 We tend to think of hostas as recent introductions, but this variety [sc. *Hosta undulata variegata*] was brought from Japan as long ago as 1834... But then, of course, they were called funkias.

funkite ('fʌŋkaɪt). *Min.* [Named by Dufresnoy in 1837, presumably after some person surnamed *Funk*.] A variant of pyroxene containing ten per cent. or more of iron.

1850 Dana *Min.* 268 Funkite is a green coccolite.

funky ('fʌŋkɪ), *a.*[1] [f. funk *sb.*[3] + -y[1].] In a state of 'funk', frightened, nervous, timid.

1837 Dickens *Pickw.* [The nervous junior counsel in Bardell v. Pickwick is named 'Mr. Phunky'.] **1845** S. Naylor *Reynard* 46, I do feel somewhat funky. **1871** G. Meredith *H. Richmond* lii. (1889) 501 If he did not give up to you like a funky traveller to a highwayman.

Hence **'funkiness.**

1896 *Punch* 22 Aug. 88/2, I subdued my native funkiness so far as to make the revolution of the great wheel.

funky ('fʌŋkɪ), *a.*[2] *Sc.* [f. funk *sb.*[4]] 'Given to kick, as a horse' (Ogilvie *Supp.* 1855).

'funky ('fʌŋkɪ), *a.*[3] [f. funk *sb.*[2] + -y[1].] **1.** Mouldy, old, musty; smelling strong or bad. Now *U.S. dial.*

1784 Twamley *Dairying* 11 [Faults in Cheese] Sweet or Funkey Cheese. *Ibid.* 30 A means of preventing Sweet, or Funkey Cheese. **1906** *Dialect Notes* III. 118 This butter's funky. **1909** *Ibid.* 396 This room smells funky. **1929** T. Wolfe *Look Homeward* iv. 41 [A Negress's] strong smell, black and funky. *a* **1938** —— *Web & Rock* (1947) 25 Breathe in the funky nigger stench. **1962** J. Baldwin *Another Country* (1963) I. i. 12 They knew..why his hair was nappy, his armpits funky.

2. Of jazz or similar music: down-to-earth and uncomplicated; emotional; having the qualities of the blues. Also in extended use: 'in', 'swinging', fashionable. *slang* (orig. *U.S.*).

1954 *Time* 8 Nov. 42 *Funky*, authentic, swinging. **1957** [see bop *sb.*[2]]. **1959** 'F. Newton' *Jazz Scene* vi. 119 Critics are on the search for something a little more like the old, original, passion-laden blues: the trade-name which has been suggested for it is 'funky' (literally: 'smelly', i.e. symbolising the return from the upper atmosphere to physical, down-to-earth, reality). **1960** *Melody Maker* 31 Dec., Horace [Silver] recalls that the use of the word funk in the modern sense goes back to his composition 'Opus de Funk'. 'When you put a lot of little blues inflections in the solos, people would say you were really funky, by which they just mean bluesy, and that is how I came up with the title. So the critics started to talk about me as funky.' **1962** *John o' London's* 10 May 457/1 He has a strong blues feeling and he doesn't overdo the fashionable 'funky' business. **1969** *Sat. Rev.* 27 Sept. 25/1 You can't hype kids into buying things they don't want, even with people in funky clothes soft-selling them. **1970** *Sunday Times* 8 Feb. 15/1 John and Yoko: a life-style that's getting funkier all the time. **1971** *Frendz* 21 May 17/1 *Brown Sugar* and *Bitch* are Jagger at his foxy, dirty, funky best.

funnel ('fʌnəl), *sb.*[1] Forms: 5 fonel(le, 6–7 funell, 6–8 funnell, (6 fonnell, funnelle), 7– funnel. [ME. *fonel* (15th c.; a supposed earlier example belongs to funel, rope), app. a. OF. **founil* (whence Breton *founil*). Mod.Pr. dialects have *founil*, *enfounilh*, which are probably corrupted adoptions of L. *infundibulum*, f. *infundĕre* to pour in (the Lat. word may have been familiar from its use in pharmacy); the unrecorded OF. form, and the Sp. *fonil*, Pg. *funil*, may be adoptions from Pr.]

1. a. A cone-shaped vessel usually fitted at the apex with a short tube, by means of which a liquid, powder, or the like, may be conducted through a small opening.

1402–3 *Durh. MS. Alm. Roll.*, j funell. *c* **1430** *Pilgr. Lyf Manhode* III. xxxvii. (1869) 155 A gret old oon..þat a foul sak, deep and perced, heeld with hire teeth, and hadde with inne it a fonelle [F. *entonnour*]. *c* **1440** *Promp. Parv.* 170/1 Fonel, or tonowre, *fusorium.* **1578** Lyte *Dodoens* I. xii. 20 The parfume..taken into the mouth through the pipe of a funnell, or tunnell. **1630** B. Jonson *New Inn* I. i, With a funnel, I make shift to fill The narrow vessel. **1739** 'R. Bull' tr. *Dedekindus' Grobianus* 202 To ev'ry Mouth by Turns the Funnel guide, Let Streams of Wine, thro' pewter Channels, glide. **1799** G. Smith *Laboratory* I. 179 Make a paper funnel, and put it in the hole of the globe. **1854** Ronalds & Richardson *Chem. Technol.* (ed. 2) I. 221 The whole fire-box is then filled up with fuel by means of a funnel. **1866** Rogers *Agric. & Prices* I. xxi. 549 The juice being poured into the tun by means of a funnel. **1878** Huxley *Physiogr.* 49 A circular metallic funnel for catching the rain, and a vessel for storing it.

fig. **1711** Steele *Spect.* No. 228 ¶2 The Inquisitive are the Funnels of Conversation..They are the Channels through which all the Good and Evil that is spoken in Town are conveyed. **1886** *Pall Mall G.* 3 June 2/1 If they..become the 'animated funnels' of the executives of their associations. **1890** *Spectator* 16 Aug., The funnel through which legislation can trickle down to the country is..nearly blocked up.

b. *spec.* in *Casting.* The hole through which the metal is poured into a mould. Cf. gate, ingate, tedge.

1874 in Knight *Dict. Mech.* I. 925/1.

c. *Anat.* and *Zool.* A funnel-shaped organ or limb; an infundibulum.

1712 Blackmore *Creation* vi. 493 Some [muscles] the long Funnel's curious Mouth extend Thro' which ingested Meats with Ease descend. **1839** Johnston in *Proc. Berw. Nat. Club* I. No. 7. 200 Funnel [of cuttle-fish] white. **1841–71** T. R. Jones *Anim. Kingd.* (ed. 4) 623 The surrounding element being alternately drawn into the branchial cavity..and again expelled in powerful streams through the orifice of the funnel.

2. a. A tube or shaft for lighting or ventilating purposes; also, the metal chimney of an engine, steamboat, etc. †Formerly also, the soil-pipe of a privy.

1555 Eden *Decades* 333 A funell or trunke of woodde or such other open instrument wherby the ayer maye be conueyed into the caue. **1612** Sturtevant *Metallica* xiii. 92 Priuy Funnels or Vaults may also bee made by the Press-ware Art so close and so sweete that there can no annoyance or vnsauory smels euapoure out..Many houses..are much annoyed by the leaking and sincking through the funnels of Brick. **1698** Fryer *Acc. E. India & P.* 39 Admitting neither Light nor Air, more than what the Lamps, always burning, are by open Funnels above suffered to ventilate. **1701** Luttrell *Brief Rel.* (1857) V. 36 Sir Christopher Wren has made this day 4 funnells on the top of the house of commons, to lett out the heat, in case they sitt in the summer. **1719** De Foe *Crusoe* II. xv. The funnel to carry the smoke. **1748** *Anson's Voy.* III. viii. (ed. 4) 506 These funnels served to communicate the air to the hold. **1773** *Gentl. Mag.* XLIII. 480/2 There are..eight funnels for letting out the steam through windows. **1833** Marryat *P. Simple* xxix, Mr. Chucks slapped his fist against the funnel. **1839** R. S. Robinson *Naut. Steam Eng.* 127 The chimney, or funnel, is made of sheet iron, and rivetted on to the uptake. **1868** *Lessons Mid. Age* 315 All this while the steam has been fiercely chafing through the funnel.

b. The flue of a chimney, somewhat resembling an inverted funnel (see quot. 1859).

1688 J. Clayton in *Phil. Trans.* XVII. 787 The Funnel of the Chimney. **1715** Desaguliers *Fires Impr.* 51 The outward Hole of the Funnel ought to be small, always less than the Bore of the Funnel. **1859** Gwilt *Archit.* (ed. 4) 949 The cavity or hollow [of a chimney] from the fireplace to the top of the room is called the funnel.

3. Applied to a funnel-shaped opening, shaft, or channel in rocks, etc.

1774 Goldsm. *Nat. Hist.* (1776) I. 102 The sides of the funnel are actually often burst with the great violence of the flame. **1791** W. Bartram *Carolina* 246 The ground..presenting to view, those funnels, sinks and wells in groups of rocks..as already recited. **1812** Brackenridge *Views Louisiana* (1814) 106 The number of funnels, or sink holes, formed by the washing of the earth into fissures of the lime-stone rock. **1836** W. Irving *Astoria* II. 137 A narrow gap or funnel in the mountains through which the river forces its way between perpendicular precipices. **1867** Smyth *Sailor's Word-bk.*, *Funnel*, the excavation formed by the explosion of a mine. **1869** Phillips *Vesuv.* iv. 105 The crater now became a funnel which was accessible to the bottom.

4. Applied to anything of conical shape with an extension at the apex.

1871 Tyndall *Fragm. Sc.* (1879) I. iv. 108 This [cloud] gradually changed into a filmy funnel, from the narrow end of which the 'cord' extended to the cloud in advance. **1897** Hall Caine *Christian* x, He lay back, sent funnels of smoke to the ceiling.

5. A cylindrical band of metal; esp. that fitted on to the head of the topgallant and royal masts, to which the rigging is attached.

1694 *Acc. Sev. Late Voy.* II. (1711) 161 The Wooden Stick is fastened within the Iron Coller or Funnel of the Harpoon, with Packthread wound all about. *c* **1860** H. Stuart *Seaman's Catech.* 74 The head is round to receive the funnel. **1882** Nares *Seamanship* (ed. 6) 31 The rigging of a royal mast, topgallant mast and topmast, is placed upon a copper funnel fitting the mast head.

6. A channel, leading from a pond, over which a net is spread forming a 'pipe', broad at the mouth but narrowing to a point, into which wild fowl are decoyed.

1774 Goldsm. *Nat. Hist.* (1776) VI. 138 This little animal [dog]..keeps playing among the reeds, nearer and nearer the funnel, till they [wild fowl] follow him too far to recede.

7. *attrib.* and *Comb.*: **a.** simple attrib., as *funnel-pipe, tube*; similative, as *funnel-fashioned, -formed, -like* adjs.; *funnel-wise* adv.

1753 Chambers *Cycl. Supp.*, **Funnel-fashioned flowers.* **1831** T. L. Peacock *Crotchet Castle* xviii. (1887) 176 The smoke was caught and carried back under a *funnel-formed canopy into a hollow central pillar. **1836–9** Todd *Cycl. Anat.* II. 757/2 The fibrous *funnel-like sheath. **1846** *Daily News* 21 Jan. 6/5 Narrow, up-hill, funnel-like streets. **1827** Faraday *Chem. Manip.* 13 A piece of *funnel-pipe fitted loosely into the hole. **1853** W. Gregory *Inorg. Chem.* (ed. 3) 231 Through one aperture in the cork passes the *funnel tube. **1840** Dickens *Old C. Shop* xviii, The landlord..applied himself to warm the same in a small tin-vessel shaped *funnel-wise.

b. Special comb., as **funnel-beaker** *Archæol.*, a type of beaker with a narrow neck; also *attrib.* of a culture characterized by the use of beakers of this type; **funnel-casing(s** (see quot. 1883); **funnel-form** = *funnel-shaped*; **funnel-hood** (see quot.); **funnel-net**, the net of a funnel (sense 6); **funnel polype** (see quot.); **funnel-shaped** *a.*, shaped like a funnel, infundibuliform, *esp.* in *Bot.*; **funnel-stays** (see quot.); **funnel-top** (see quot.); **funnel web**, a funnel-shaped spider's web; **funnel-web spider**, (*a*) *U.S.*, a spider of the family Agelenidæ; (*b*) *Austral.*, a poisonous spider of the family Dipluridæ; also *ellipt.*; **funnel-web tarantula** = *funnel-web spider* (b); **funnel-web weaver** = *funnel-web spider* (a).

[**1929** V. G. Childe *Danube in Pre-History* vii. 117 A relatively closed group is constituted by collared flasks, funnel-necked beakers, and amphorae.] **1954** R. W. Ehrich *Rel. Chronol. Old World Archeol.* viii. 118 There is a penetration southward from the northern European plain of various groups of people who had..*funnel beakers,..and the like. **1955** *Proc. Prehist. Soc.* XXI. 120 It does not seem that they have expanded west of the Vistula in the territory occupied by the Funnel-Beaker population. **1957** V. G. Childe *Dawn Europ. Civilization* (ed. 6) ix. 159 A herding group who sometimes decorated their funnel-beakers..with cord imprints had cleared tracts of Denmark and Southern Sweden for pasture in Late Atlantic times. *Ibid.* x. 176 The sub-division of Early Neolithic was originally based on the typology of the funnel-beaker—the most distinctive vase in the dominant culture which is usually called after it..the Funnel-Beaker culture. **1877** W. Thomson *Voy. Challenger* I. i. 18 An excellent drying-room has been discovered in a space in the *funnel-casings. **1883** W. C. Russell *Sailor's Lang.*, *Funnel-casing*, a portion of the funnel of a steamer extending from the smoke-box to some distance upwards. **1880** Gray *Struct. Bot.* vi. §5. 249 Infundibuliform, or *Funnel-form, such as the corolla of common Morning-Glory, denotes a tube gradually enlarged upwards from a narrow base into an expanding border or limb. **1883** W. C. Russell *Sailor's Lang.*, **Funnel-hood*, a projected portion of or protection to the funnel, raised some feet above the deck. **1774** Goldsm. *Nat. Hist.* (1776) VI. 138 The decoy-ducks never enter the *funnel-net with the rest. **1753** Chambers *Cycl. Supp.* s.v. *Polype*, The *funnel polype nearly resembles a funnel, from which it has its name. *Ibid.*, *Infundibuliform*..There are properly two species of the *funnel-shaped flowers. **1823** J. Badcock *Dom. Amusem.* 147 Over this a kind of funnel-shaped supplier is to be made fast. **1860** W. G. Clark *Vac. Tour* 77 The surface is honeycombed throughout with circular, funnel-shaped holes. **1846** Young *Naut. Dict.* s.v. *Funnel*, This [funnel] is secured by ropes or chains, called the *funnel-stays, leading from eye-plates near the top of the funnel to the ship's sides. **1854** Mayne *Exp. Lex.*, **Funnel-Top*, common name for the genus *Peziza*. **1895** J. H. & A. B. Comstock *Man. Stud. Insects* ii. 30 The greater number of the webs seen at such times [*sc.* in the early morning] are of the form we term *funnel-webs. **1912** J. H. Comstock *Spider Bk.* iv. 193 The principal part of a funnel-web is sheet-like in structure. **1949** W. J. Gertsch *Amer. Spiders* x. 216 The funnel web of the agelenids is little changed from the silken cell of their forebears. **1912** J. H. Comstock *Spider Bk.* vii. 582 The members of this family [*sc.* Agelenidæ] spin sheet-like webs, which are usually furnished with a tubular retreat; this suggests the common name *funnel-web spiders for the family. **1933** *Bulletin* (Sydney) 15 Mar. 21 Three people have been killed recently from the bite of a spider, known as the atrax or funnel-web spider. **1954** Borror & DeLong *Introd. Study Insects* xxx. 797 The web of the funnel-web spiders is somewhat sheetlike, but is shaped like a funnel. *Ibid.* 805 The Agelenidae, or funnel-web spiders, are a large group. **1956** S. Hope *Diggers' Paradise* xxii. 203 The funnel-web lives almost exclusively in the Greater Sydney zone. **1970** *Times* 30 Dec. 4/5 She was bitten yesterday by a funnel web spider about an inch long. **1912** J. H. Comstock *Spider Bk.* vi. 247 The *funnel-web tarantulas resemble the two preceding families. **1954** Borror & DeLong *Introd. Study Insects* xxx. 798 The Dipluridae are the funnel-web tarantulas. **1895** J. H. & A. B. Comstock *Man. Stud. Insects* ii. 31 The *funnel-web weavers..are long-legged, brown spiders.

Hence **'funnelled** *a.*, funnel-shaped; also *fig.*; in *Bot.* infundibuliform.

1793 W. Roberts *Looker-on* No. 67 ¶14 The auditory passage was extremely narrow, and not funnelled as in other subjects. **1849** *Florist* 194 [A pelargonium] too funnelled, and the blotch on upper petals not even. **1883** D. Pidgeon in *Nature* 23 June, The double funneled stem of whirling mist [of a waterspout]. **1894** Blackmore *Perlycross* 130 Quivering to the swell of funneled uproar.

funnel ('fʌnəl), *sb.*² *dial.* Also **fummel.** (See quots.; the form *fummel* seems of doubtful genuineness.)

1835 BOOTH *Analyt. Dict.* 323 The Little Mule, or Hinny ..the produce of a Stallion and a She-ass..In some counties, it is called a Fummel. **1847** HALLIWELL, *Funnel*, a mare mule produced by an ass covered by a horse. *Linc.* **1866** BROGDEN *Linc. Gloss.*, *Funnel*, a mule whose sire is an ass.

funnel ('fʌnəl), *v.* [f. FUNNEL *sb.*¹] †**1. a.** *intr.* Of smoke: to issue *out* or rise *up* in a funnel-shaped cloud. **b.** *trans.* To feed with a funnel.

1594 NASHE *Unfort. Trav.* Wks. (Grosart) V. 125 Before a gun is shot off, a stinking smoake funnels out. **1596** —— *Saffron Walden* 102 A dampe (like the smoake of a Cannon) ..would strugglingly funnell vp. **1739** 'R. BULL' tr. *Dedekindus' Grobianus* 202 To ev'ry Mouth by Turns the Funnel guide, Let Streams of Wine, thro' pewter Channels, glide Adown the Throats..[*Note*] Whenever this Comedy is represented, the Gentlemen of the upper Gallery are exceedingly delighted with seeing Teague funnel Obadiah.

2. *trans.* and *intr.* To guide or move through a funnel. Also *transf.* and *fig.*

1901 KIPLING *Kim* xiii. 330 Jammed into a corner between cliffs that funnelled and focused every wandering blast. **1923** —— *Land & Sea* 182 That wind's funnelling badly in the valley. **1936** L. C. DOUGLAS *White Banners* x. 214 Crowds like swollen rivers funnelled through station exits. **1958** *Sunday Times* 12 Oct. 1/3 All the data is funneled into the Air Force Data Reduction Centre at Englewood, near Los Angeles. **1961** *Times* 20 Feb. 14/3 [soccer] They made less impression..on Vowels and his colleagues, funnelling back. **1964** W. MCCORD in I. L. Horowitz *New Sociol.* 431 The popular policy of funneling resources into primary education must be viewed with some caution. **1971** *Sci. Amer.* June 65/1 Three magnetic spectrometers, which funnel the electrons into a system of detectors.

funniment ('fʌnɪmənt). *jocular.* [f. FUNNY *a.* + -MENT. Cf. *merriment.*] Drollery, humour; also, a joke, a comicality.

1845 ALB. SMITH *Fort. Scatterg. Fam.* xix. (1887) 65 His first funniment took place amongst the macaws. **1861** MAYHEW *Lond. Labour* III. 138 A man with heaps of funniment and plenty of talk. **1878** E. YATES *Wrecked in Port* xxviii. 319 I'll take care to repay you that little funniment on the first convenient opportunity.

funniosity (fʌnɪ'ɒsɪtɪ). *jocular.* [f. FUNNY *a.* + -OSITY.] Comicality, jocularity; also, something comical, a comicality.

1890 in W. T. Vincent *Recoll. F. Leslie* (1894) II. xxiv. 117 Then the conversation reverted for a brief space to that very choice mixture of funniosities. **1900** *Westm. Gaz.* 5 July 3/2 There is no end to the freaks and funniosities of the cricket field. **1920** S. GRAHAM *Childr. of Slaves* xiv. 271 The mind stocked with music-hall funniosity and pseudo-cynicism. **1921** —— *Europe* x. 138 Shylock's cleverness and intellectual assurance was obscured by funniosities.

funny ('fʌnɪ), *sb.* [perh. f. next adj.] A narrow, clinker-built pleasure-boat for a pair of sculls. Also loosely, any light boat.

1799 *Caldron or Follies Camb.* 9 While others woo The well-oar'd funney or the slim canoe. **1808** *Ann. Reg.* 109 A young couple..took a sail in a funny off Fulham. **1843** ATKINSON in *Zoologist* I. 293, I was in a 'funny'—as the small boats at Cambridge are called. **1870** DASENT *Annals Eventful Life* (ed. 4) I. 140 The funnies, cutters, wherries.. that thronged the river daily.

funny ('fʌnɪ), *a.* and *sb. pl.* [f. FUN *sb.* + -Y¹.]

A. *adj.* **1. a.** Affording fun, mirth-producing, comical, facetious.

1756 TOLDERVY *Two Orphans* II. 151 Tom Heartley and Richmond said a great many funny things. **1762** FOOTE *Orators* I. i, Is it damn'd funny and comical? **1787** BURNS *Halloween* xxviii, Unco tales, an' funnie jokes. **1827** DE QUINCEY *Murder* Wks. 1862 IV. 22 He became very sociable and funny. **1849** THACKERAY *Pendennis* xiii, Popping in his little funny head.

absol. **1820** PRAED *Eve of Battle* 297 A mixture of the grave and funny.

b. *funny business*, action (on the part of a clown or actor) intended to excite laughter; hence, jesting, nonsense; also *slang*, fooling or monkeying about; deceitful or underhand practices; similarly *funny stuff*, *funny dope*; *funny column*, *paper*, a (section of a) newspaper containing humorous matter or illustrations. orig. *U.S.*

1860 W. HANCOCK *Emigrant's Five Years Free States Amer.* iv. 93 The 'funny' column of any American journal. **1874** in L. Hearn *Amer. Miscellany* (1924) I. 20 The said *Giglampz* is not a funny paper. **1888** E. W. NYE *Baled Hay* 38 There was no funny business in his nature. **1890** *Century Mag.* Dec. 303 She even ventured on the funny column, for it was not Sunday. **1891** E. S. ELLIS *Check No. 2134* xiv. 93, I hope we'll get through without any more funny business. **1915** FROEST & DILNOT *Crime Club* x, The blue barrel of a revolver showed in the electric light. 'No funny business!' he warned them. 'You guys can't play it on me.' *Ibid.* xii, Especially if you try to put any of the funny dope over on me. **1930** *London Mercury* Feb. 324 He'll be out and about in a fortnight. Till then we will visit him together—and no funny stuff! **1936** 'I. HAY' *Housemaster* xv. 191 She seemed to be labouring under the idea that he, Victor, was trying to start some funny business with her. **1946** WODEHOUSE *Money in Bank* xii. 105 He is far too scared of our hostess to try any funny stuff on her. **1960** O. MANNING *Great Fortune* III. xviii. 210 Our permits..are issued on the understanding that we do not get mixed up in any funny business. **1968** *Globe & Mail Mag.* (Toronto) 13 Jan. 15/3 Despite an early apprenticeship to the funny papers McArthur was a subtle humorist. **1971** D. POTTER *Brit. Eliz. Stamps* iii. 44, 1968 was even quieter. Only four sets, no strange se-tenant strips or funny business.

2. a. Curious, queer, odd, strange. *colloq.*

1806 METCALFE in Owen *Wellesley's Desp.* 809 This study to decrease our influence is funny. I cannot understand it. **1838** JAMES *Robber* i, That was a funny slip of mine. **1852** MRS. STOWE *Uncle Tom's C.* xix, 'What funny things you are making'..'I'm trying to write to my poor old woman.' **1855** LD. HOUGHTON in *Life* (1891) I. xi. 527 Lady Ellesmere was very funny about Mrs. Gaskell, wanting very much to see her, and yet quite shy about it. **1889** *N.W. Linc. Gloss.* (ed. 2) s.v., 'To keap fun'rals waaitin' time efter time is a straange funny waay for a parson to go on.'

b. *funny-peculiar*, a colloquialism introduced to distinguish sense 2 from sense 1 (*funny-ha-ha*), the two antithetic expressions freq. appearing together.

1938 'I. HAY' *Housemaster* III. 78 *Chris.* That's funny. *Button.* What do you mean, funny? Funny-peculiar, or funny ha-ha? **1942** *Horizon* July 69 He says, 'Funny-haha or funny-peculiar?' and I says, 'Funny-peculiar.' **1946** S. GIBBONS *Westwood* vii. 95 You said her *conscience* forced her into being a you-know-what. It sounds awfully funny-peculiar. **1955** M. MCCARTHY *Charmed Life* (1956) iii. 58 His art-school training rendered him funny ha-ha to the cognoscenti. **1959** J. VERNEY *Friday's Tunnel* xxv. 227 John Gubbins leant forward, smiling in a funny-peculiar not funny-ha-ha way. **1965** *Times Lit. Suppl.* 8 Apr. 281/3 Whether it is also amusing or merely funny-peculiar will depend upon the reader. **1970** 'D. SHANNON' *Unexpected Death* (1971) ii. 24 He thought the blonde was rather funny ..in the sense of funny-peculiar.

†**3.** *slang.* Tipsy. *Obs.*

1756 TOLDERVY *Two Orphans* I. 62 More brandy was drank, and, Tom Throw beginning to be what is called funny, the house was full of uproar and confusion.

4. *Comb.*, as *funny-looking* adj.; **funny-bone**, the popular name for that part of the elbow over which the ulnar nerve passes, from the peculiar sensation experienced when it is struck; also *fig.*; **funny-face**, a *joc.* and *colloq.* form of address; **funny farm** *slang*, a mental hospital; **funny-man**, a professional jester; **funny party** *Naut.*, a ship's concert party.

1840 BARHAM *Ingol. Leg.*, *Bloudie Jacke*, And they smack, and they thwack, Till your '*funny bones' crack. **1867** *Pall Mall G.* 30 Jan. 4 It is like rapping a man..over the funny-bone. **1881** BLACKMORE *Christowell* xv, Even the fiddlers three..worked their funny-bones more gently. **1902** *Daily Chron.* 12 June 3/3 Two principal figures and a few carefully careless scratches—that is all Mr. Raven-Hill uses in the pointing of his joke, but he hits the universal funny-bone with his pencil. **1965** G. MCINNES *Road to Gundagai* x. 161 Kennedy..hit our funny-bones because he was a man who used long words with an extremely sober face. **1927** I. GERSHWIN (*song title*) *Funny face. **1930** SAYERS & 'EUSTACE' *Documents in Case* 38 Ever and ever yours, funny-face, old dear. **1943** A. CHRISTIE *Moving Finger* v. 52 'It's all right, funny face,' I said. **1963** J. N. HARRIS *Weird World Wes Beattie* v. 61 Before Baldwin Ogilvy agrees to locking his client away in the *funny farm, he might like to investigate the whole bang shoot. **1969** E. AMBLER *Intercom Conspiracy* (1970) ix. 173 *Intercom* was described as 'the Batman of the funny-farm set' and its editor as 'the Lone Ranger of the lunatic fringe'. **1895** M. E. FRANCIS *Frieze & Fustian* 283 'Yon's a *funny-lookin' lass. Let's chase her!' **1861** MAYHEW *Lond. Labour* III. 119 What I've earn'd as clown, or the *funnyman, with a party of acrobats. **1911** 'GUNS' & 'THEELUKER' *Middle Watch Musings* 137 Nearly every ship has a '*funny' party. **1917** 'TAFFRAIL' *Sub* vii. 178 Once a year came the squadron regatta and sports, while at intervals our 'Funny Party', or pierrot troupe, gave an entertainment.

B. *sb. pl.* Comic illustrations, etc.; *spec.* comic strips, or the section of a newspaper devoted to these (D.A.). Hence, funny persons, books, etc.; jokes. *rare* in *sing.* orig. *U.S.*

1852 *Lantern* (N.Y.) II. 114/1 Keeping our dear public advised of all operations in the 'Funnies'. **1920** C. SANDBURG *Smoke & Steel* 33 About the funnies in the papers. **1922** —— *Slabs of Sunburnt West* 35 Turning among headlines, date lines, funnies, ads. **1925** A. HUXLEY *Those Barren Leaves* I. i. 8 The funnies and the fuzzy-wuzzies—in a word, the artists. **1936** WODEHOUSE *Laughing Gas* xxvi. 272 We've only read the movie section and the funnies. **1941** BELLOC *Silence of Sea* v. 33 What some modern funnies call 'wish-fulfilment'. **1952** in WENTWORTH & FLEXNER *Dict. Amer. Slang* (1960) 205/2 Cut the funnies an' git a can-opener. **1959** *Punch* 30 Dec. 682/2 Makers of pantomimes engaged the ripest music-hall funnies they could find. **1961** *John o' London's* 14 Sept. 307/1 The best bet would have been to ship this Mexican funny [*sc.* a film] straight out on circuit. **1961** 'B. WELLS' *Day Earth caught Fire* viii. 118 No funnies, Dave. Something's going on. **1970** *New Yorker* 17 Oct. 148/2, I hear he's a lawyer now, restricted, I suppose, to sneaking in a funny now and then in his summation to the jury.

Hence '**funnily** *adv.*, in a funny manner; '**funniness**, the quality or state of being funny; a funny saying or joke. Also '**funnyism** *nonce-wd.*, a joke.

1814 LADY GRANVILLE *Lett.* 18 Nov. (1894) I. 51 [He] says she..talks so funnily and sweetly. **1839** CAROLINE FOX *Mem. Old Friends* (1882) 37 His stories and funnyisms of all descriptions. **1856** LD. COCKBURN *Mem.* 317 *note*, It was funnily done; which was not always the case, for it was often with bitter gravity. **1857** GEN. P. THOMPSON *Audi Alt.* I. xi. 57, I did hear one or two members..make a kind of school-boy titter at the funniness of a man's not being seconded. **1865** *Daily Tel.* 8 Dec. 4/6 Marching..to the sound of their own..irrepressible funninesses. **1882** J. BROWN *Horæ Subs.* Ser. III. 35 A man..whose absolute levity and funniness became ponderous.

funny ('fʌnɪ), *v.* *Sc.* [mod. form of *fundy*, FOUND *v.*⁵] *intr.* To become stiff with cold, to be benumbed. Hence '**funnied** *ppl. a.*

1721 KELLY *Sc. Prov.* 52 An eating Horse never funnied. **1785** *Jrnl. fr. Lond.* 3 in *Poems Buchan Dial.*, The wile limmer was sae dozen'd an' funied wi' cauld. **1845** *Whistle-Binkie* (Scot. Songs) Ser. III. (1890) I. 418 The funneit tod cam forth.

funster ('fʌnstə(r)). *jocular.* [f. FUN *sb.* + -STER after PUNSTER.] One who makes fun.

1788 *Gentl. Mag.* LVIII. 4/1 Mr. T—ffe, a Fellow of the same college, and a *fellow-funster* also,..arrived when the Dr. was out upon his visits. **1887** *Through the Long Day* I. 234 Punster is universally recognised as a permissible and legitimate word, and why not 'funster'? **1892** *Dram. Opin.* 13 Jan. 3/1 The greatest punster since Hood, and greatest funster of his age.

fuor, mistake for, or var. FUR *sb.*¹ (sense 7).

1858–9 WEALE *Dict. Arch.* (ed. 2) *Fuor*, among carpenters, a piece nailed upon a rafter to strengthen it when decayed.

fur (fɜː(r)), *sb.*¹ Forms: 4–7 furre, 7–9 furr, 8 fir, 6– fur. [f. FUR *v.*

The OF. *forre, fuerre*, sheath, case, is commonly given as the immediate source; but it does not appear to have had the sense of the Eng. sb., though the derived vb. *forrer* (mod.F. *fourrer*), originally to encase, developed the sense 'to line', and 'to line or trim with fur.' The Fr. word for fur is *fourrure* (OF. *forrure*): see FURRURE.]

I. 1. a. A trimming or lining for a garment, made of the dressed coat of certain animals (as the ermine, beaver, etc.: see 2); *hence*, the coat of such animals as a material for trimmings, linings, or entire garments (worn either for warmth or for ornament). Also a garment made of, or trimmed or lined with, this material; now chiefly *pl.*, exc. as denoting a piece of fur to be worn about the neck.

?*a* **1366** CHAUCER *Rom. Rose* 228 A burnet cote..Furred with no menivere, But with a furre rough of here, Of lambe-skinnes. **1387** TREVISA *Higden* (Rolls) VII. 401 þei schal were no manere furres. **1418** *E.E. Wills* (1882) 34, I bequethe..my ffurre of Calabre. *c* **1460** *Towneley Myst.* (Surtees) 163 Thay are so gay in furrys fyne. **1551** in Strype *Eccl. Mem.* (1721) II. xxxiii. 539 A fur of black Irish lamb. **1602** MARSTON *Antonio's Rev.* II. iii, Thou wrapt in furres.. Forbidst the frozen zone to shudder. **1681** WOOD *Life* (O.H.S.) II. 525 Blak gownes, fac'd with furr. **1774** GOLDSM. *Nat. Hist.* (1776) II. 231 The inhabitants go.. cloathed in furs or feathers. **1814** SCOTT *Ld. of Isles* II. vi, The costly furs That erst had deck'd their caps were torn. **1886** HALL CAINE *Son of Hagar* II. xvi, Greta had returned to the parlour, muffled in furs.

fig. **1621** MOLLE *Camerar. Liv. Libr.* v. xiv. 374 Ill will, envie, grudgings, the right linings and furres of the soule.

b. worn as a mark of office or state, and as a badge of certain degrees at the Universities.

1634 MILTON *Comus* 707 Those budge doctors of the Stoic fur. **1675** OTWAY *Alcibiades* I. i, Heavy Gown-men clad in formal Furrs. **1729** WATERLAND *Let.* Wks. 1823 X. 320 The picture of Sir William Cecil..in his gown and furs. *a* **1763** SHENSTONE *Economy* I. 148 And add strange wisdom to the furs of Pow'r.

2. a. The short, fine, soft hair of certain animals (as the sable, ermine, beaver, otter, bear, etc.) growing thick upon the skin, and distinguished from the ordinary hair, which is longer and coarser. Formerly also, †the wool of sheep.

c **1430** LYDG. *Hors, Shepe & G.* 49 in *Pol. Rel. & L. Poems* 16 The shepe..berythe the furres blake and whyte. **1579** SPENSER *Sheph. Cal.* Sept. 165 Thy Ball is a bold bigge curre, And could make a iolly hole in theyr furre. **1608** SHAKS. *Lear* III. i. 14 (Qo. 1) This night, wherin..The Lyon, and the belly pinched Wolfe Keepe their furre dry. **1732** POPE *Ess. Man* I. 176 To want the strength of Bulls, the fur of Bears. **1748** F. SMITH *Voy. Disc.* I. 189 Leave the Hair on Skins, where the Fleece or Fir is soft and warm, as Beaver, Otter, &c. **1812** J. SMYTH *Pract. Customs* (1821) 310 Coney Wool, or Rabbits' Fur..principally used by Hatters. **1847** LONGF. *Ev.* I. ii. 10 Cold would the winter be, for thick was the fur of the foxes. **1868** DARWIN *Anim. & Pl.* I. i. 46 All the cats are covered with short stiff hair instead of fur.

b. *fig.* in phr. ***to stroke the fur the wrong way*** (i.e. to cause irritation); ***to make the fur fly*** (orig. U.S. slang: see quot. 1848); also ***the fur flies***, etc.

[**1663** BUTLER *Hud.* I. iii. 184 I'le make the fur Flie 'bout the eares of the old Cur.] **1814** *Niles' Reg.* VI. 67/2 Smugglers look out, or you will soon see 'the fur fly'. **1834** D. CROCKETT *Narr. Life* ii. 11, I knew very well that I was in a devil of a hobble, for my father had been taking a few horns, and was in a good condition to make the fur fly. **1848** BARTLETT *Dict. Amer.*, *To make the fur fly*. To claw; scratch; wound severely. Used figuratively. **1870** MISS BRIDGMAN *Ro. Lynne* I. vii. 100 He stroked all the fur the wrong way. **1888** *Denver Republican* 29 Feb. (Farmer), 'Wait until the National Committee assembles..and you will see the fur fly from the Cleveland hide'. **1955** M. GILBERT *Sky High* v. 70 There was a slip-up... There was some fur flew about *that*, I can tell you. **1963** V. GIELGUD *Goggle-Box Affair* viii. 73 A good deal of fur's always flying about Gargantua.

3. *pl.* Skins of such animals with the fur on them.

1555 EDEN *Decades* 214 In this lande are many excellent furres as marterns, sables. *c* **1645** HOWELL *Lett.* (1655) I. vi. iii. 9, I shall be carefull to bring with me those Furres, I had instructions for. **1748** F. SMITH *Voy. Disc.* I. 156 The Skins of those Beasts, which are killed in Winter being only of Value, and what we call Firs. **1828** SCOTT *F.M. Perth* xxvii, This his old host and friend, with whom he had transacted many bargains for hides and furs. **1836** W. IRVING *Astoria*

III. 168 Mr. Clarke accordingly packed all his furs on twenty-eight horses.

4. *Her.* A tincture representing tufts upon a plain ground, or patches of different colours supposed to be sewn together.

The eight principal furs are ermine, ermines, erminois, pean, vair, countervair, potent, and counterpotent.

1610 GUILLIM *Heraldry* I. iv. (1660) 20 Furres (used in Armes) are taken for the Skins of certain beasts stripped from the bodies and artificially trimmed for the furring, doubling, or lining of Robes and Garments. **1708** [see DOUBLING *vbl. sb.* 2]. **1725** BRADLEY *Fam. Dict.*, *Furs*, in Heraldry are used in the Doublings of Mantles pertaining to a Coat of Arms, and sometimes to the Coat itself: They are usually of two Colours. **1766** [see DOUBLE *v.* 6 a]. **1882** CUSSANS *Her.* iii. (ed. 3) 55 Furs are known by the name of Doublings, when used in the linings of mantles; but when coming under the denomination of Tinctures, they are called each by their respective name.

5. *collect.* Furred animals. Also in phrase ***fur and feather***. See FEATHER *sb.* 4.

1827 POLLOK *Course T.* v. 1025 Hunted thence the fur To Labrador. **1875** 'STONEHENGE' *Brit. Sports* I. I. vii. §7. 106 They will readily hunt fur when nothing else is to be had. **1884** *St. James's Gaz.* 7 Aug. 4/2 Farmers..find it somewhat difficult to carry on their coursing meetings because of the scarcity of fur.

6. a. Applied to something resembling fur or adhering to a surface like fur; e.g. a coat or crust of mould, of deposit from wine, etc.

1843 LEVER *J. Hinton* vi. (1878) 38 The ill-omened fur one sees on an antiquated apple-pie. **1852** MRS. C. MEREDITH *Home in Tasmania* I. ix. 134 Projecting ridges [in shells], fringed beneath like the fur of a mushroom. **1855** DICKENS *Dorrit* I. v, Empty wine-bottles with fur and fungus choking up their throats. **1864** WEBSTER, *Fur*..the soft, downy covering on the skin of a peach. **1877** BLACK *Green Past.* xix, Covered the thick top-coats of the two men with a fur of wet.

b. *esp.* A coating formed on the tongue in certain diseased conditions of the body.

1693 DRYDEN tr. *Persius* III. 172 My Pulse unequal, and my Breath is strong; Besides, a filthy Furr upon my Tongue. **1783** S. CHAPMAN in *Med. Commun.* I. 277 Her tongue had a whitish fur on it. **1801** *Med. Jrnl.* V. 508 Her tongue, teeth, and lips were covered with a black fur. **1849–52** TODD *Cycl. Anat.* IV. 1139/2 Variation in the quantity of fur on the tongue from day to day.

c. A coating or crust formed by the deposit of carbonate of lime on the interior surface of a kettle, boiler, etc.

1805 W. SAUNDERS *Min. Waters* 38 Boiling..drives off the excess of carbonic acid, and thus causes the chalk to be precipitated; hence the earthy crust, or furr, on kettles. **1837** *Mech. Mag.* XXVIII. 96 An invention for dissolving the 'fur' which collects in kettles and boilers. **1865** *Pall Mall G.* 7 July 7/2 For the purpose of removing the fur from the steam boiler.

7. *Carpentry.* (See quot.) Cf. FURRING *vbl. sb.* 3 b, FUR *v.* 6.

1703 T. N. *City & C. Purchaser* 146 When Rafters are.. sunk hollow in the middle, and pieces (cut thickest in the middle, and to a point at each end) are nail'd upon them to make them straight again..those pieces so put on are call'd Furrs. [**1858–9**: see FUOR.]

II. *attrib.* and *Comb.*

8. *attrib.* or as *adj.* Made of fur.

1597 SKENE *De Verb. Sign* s.v. *Bullion*, Ilk serplaith of furfelles, con. 4000 .iiij. ounce. **1713** WARDER *True Amazons* 58 A Velvet Cape or Fur Gorget about her Shoulders. **1792** *Descript. Kentucky* 49 Fur-muffs and tippets. **1884** *Chamb. Jrnl.* 5 Jan. 10/1 The dogs..should then be protected by fur-boots. **1885** *Girl's Own Paper* Jan. 202/1 Fur balls, fur fringe, and fur tails seem the most usual finish on all mantles.

9. General comb., as ***fur company***, ***-farm***, ***-farmer***, ***-farming***, ***-hunting***, ***-sewer***, ***trade***, ***-trader***, ***-trading***; objective, as ***fur-dressing*** vbl. sb.; instrumental, as ***fur-bordered***, ***-bound***, ***-clad***, ***-lined***, ***-muffled***, ***-topped***, ***-trimmed***, ***-wrapped***, ***-wrought*** ppl. adjs.; parasynthetic, as ***fur-capped***, ***-collared***, ***-cuffed***, ***-gowned*** ppl. adjs.

1903 *Westm. Gaz.* 8 Oct. 4/2 The *fur-bordered, serrated lace collar. **1898** *Ibid.* 18 Nov. 3/2 A *fur-bound coat. **1887** J. A. STERRY *Lazy Minstr.* (1892) 68 Here comes a stout, *fur-capped Mossoo. **1784** COWPER *Task* v. 129 Imperial mistress of the *fur-clad Russ! **1842** MACAULAY *Lays, Proph. Capys* xxxi, Where fur-clad hunters wander Amidst the northern ice. **1856** LEVER *Martins of Cro' M.* 136 A grey cloth spencer being drawn over his coat, *fur-collared and cuffed. **1818** *Niles' Reg.* XV. 19/2 A small canal has been opened..by the North West *fur company. **1880** *Scribner's Monthly* May 125/1 Trappers and hunters for the fur companies would have thought themselves in paradise could they have seen our stores in '74. **1888** *Daily News* 21 Sept. 7/2 A *fur-dressing patent. **1914** *Outing* (U.S.) Dec. 345/1 A manager of a *fur farm must have a liking for animals. *Ibid.* 343/1 The trade must look to the *fur-farmer for a considerable portion of its supply. **1961** *New Scientist* 23 Feb. 460/3 Many types of animals being bred at fur-farms are particularly sensitive to the..noise created by subsonic aircraft, and the sudden nature of sonic bangs might cause still greater losses than the fur-farmers have so far experienced. **1911** *Daily Colonist* (Victoria, B.C.) 12 Apr. 5/4 This is nothing less than *fur farming on an extensive scale, the breeding of marten being specialized. **1923** J. C. SACHS *Furs & Fur Trade* 92 Fur farming..is one of the oldest of occupations. **1757** J. G. COOPER *Apol. Aristippus* iii. 160 The..*fur-gown'd Pedants' bookish Rules. **1819** L. A. ANSPACH *Hist. Newfoundland* xiv. 378 This *fur-hunting employs a great number of persons. **1919** W. T. GRENFELL *Labrador Doctor* (1920) xiii. 238 The only trouble with.. fur-hunting is that its very nature limits its supply. **1886** W. J. TUCKER *E. Europe* 202 He muffled himself in his *fur-lined cloak. **1905** *Westm. Gaz.* 16 Jan. 2/1 Sleighs with *fur-muffled occupants. **1896** MRS. H. WARD *Sir G. Tressady* xi. 227 Tailoresses and shirtmakers and *fur-sewers. **1928** *Daily Express* 11 Oct. 5/5 Russian boot..*fur-topped, fleece-lined. **1732** L. ARMSTRONG *Let.* 11 Sept. in *Calendar of State Papers, America & W. Indies* (1939) 255 They.. engross the whole management of the *fur trade. **1807** P. GASS *Jrnl.* 65 This and Hudson's Bay Company..carry on almost the whole of the fur trade in that extensive country. **1837** W. IRVING *Capt. Bonneville* I. 42 People connected with the fur trade. **1911** *North Amer. Rev.* Mar. 396 Astor's experience in the fur trade..enabled him to plan on a vast scale. **1815** *Kingston* (Ontario) *Gaz.* 8 July 1/3 Conveying goods for the *fur traders. **1848** THOREAU *Maine W.* (1894) 14 One small leaden bullet, and some colored beads, the last to be referred, perhaps, to early fur-trader days. **1841** G. CATLIN *Indians* II. 29 St. Louis..is the great depot of all the *Fur Trading Companies to the Upper Missouri and Rocky Mountains. **1911** FLETCHER & KIPLING *School Hist. Eng.* ix. 169 We had a whale-fishing and fur-trading station in Hudson Bay. **1860** G. A. SPOTTISWOODE *Vac. Tour* 98 Long, straight, *fur-trimmed coats. **1898** *Westm. Gaz.* 4 Nov. 3/1 The Common Councillors..in their fur-trimmed robes. **1895** KIPLING *2nd Jungle Book* 151 He and his master ..hunted together,..*fur-wrapped boy and savage,.. yellow brute. **1731** GAY *Rur. Sports* i. 270 Let me, less cruel, cast the feather'd hook..And with the *fur-wrought fly delude the prey.

10. Special comb.: **fur-bearer**, an animal that yields a fur of (commercial) value; so ***fur-bearing*** adj.; **fur-cloth, -fabric** (see quot. 1928); **fur felt**, a felt fabric, deeply napped to give a fur-like effect; **fur-fever, -moth** (see quots.); †**fur-man** *slang* (see quot.); **fur-puller** (see quot.); so ***fur-pulling*** vbl. sb.; **fur seal**, the seal which affords the valuable fur known as seal-skin.

1906 E. INGERSOLL *Life Anim.*: *Mammals* 162 The *Fur Bearers..the martens, weasels, badgers, ratels, skunks, otters and their kin of the family Mustelidæ. **1941** J. S. HUXLEY *Uniqueness of Man* viii. 186 Direct destruction may be for commercial gain, as with whales, egrets, or fur-bearers. **1876** J. BURROUGHS *Winter Sunshine* (1883) iv. 91 The fox..furnishes, perhaps, the only instance..of a *fur-bearing animal..that actually increases in the face of the means that are used for its extermination. **1936** *Discovery* Jan. 30/2 To slaughter fur-bearing animals for Broadway shops. **1928** *Daily Express* 23 June 5/1 *Fur-cloth is specially made to imitate fur, and can be used for all furry animals. **1944** M. LASKI *Love on Supertax* v. 57 Four little boys in everyday clothes topped by fur-cloth Cossack hats. **1938** *Decorative Art* 57/1 Armchairs with imitation *fur fabric upholstery. **1952** *Vogue* Dec. 126 (Advt.), For coats: velours, fancy and check tweeds, fur fabrics. **1968** *Guardian* 22 Oct. 7/3 Gabardine coats lined with a light-weight fur fabric. **1897** *Sears, Roebucks Catal.* 232/1 The newest shape, black stiff, *fur felt hat. **1971** *Guardian* 4 Jan. 7/3 When Mr. Patey's firm makes an Ascot hat it is a proper 'pullover'— grey fur felt pulled over a gossamer frame. **1905** *Pearson's Mag.* July 102/2 Bronchial catarrh, and '*fur fever'..are both caused by inhaling this 'fluff' and dust. *a* **1700** B. E. *Dict. Cant. Crew*, **Fur-men*, Aldermen. **1725** in *New Cant. Dict.* **1842** T. W. HARRIS *Insects Injur. Veget.* 360 The *fur-moth (*Tinea pellionella*). **1938** L. HUNTER *Domestic Pests* xvii. 154 The case-bearing clothes-moth (*Tinea pellionella*), sometimes called the fur moth or the single spotted clothes-moth. **1891** *Labour Commission* Gloss., **Fur-pullers*, those who scrape the loose down off rabbit and other skins, and do various minor parts of fur-making. **1886** *Daily News* 13 Dec. 5/5 A widow, working at *fur pulling. **1775** CLAYTON in *Phil. Trans.* LXVI. 102 The *furr seal has its name from its coat, which is a fine soft furr, and is thinner skinned than any of the others. **1883** *Fisheries Exhib. Catal.* (ed. 4) 191 Group of Fur Seals..stuffed Ribbon Seal..cast of Harbour Seal.

fur, *sb.*[2] ? *Obs.* [? Cf. OF. *forre* sheath, case.] = BOX *sb.*[2] 16.

1740 *Lond. Mag.* 382/1 While a Wheel is turning round once, all the Parts of the Fur or Box in the Nave, rub against the Axletree..The Fur or Box in the hinder Wheels, is no bigger than the Fur or Box in the fore Wheels. Now, if the hind Wheels be as high again as the fore ones..the rubbing round the Fur or Box in the hind Wheels, will carry the Load twice as far as the fore Wheels.

fur, *sb.*[3] *dial.* Also 5 fyre, firre (fyir, fyyre), 6 fyrre, furre, 9 furr. [See FURZE.] = FURZE. Chiefly in Comb., as ***fur-bill***, ***-bush*** (***-busk***), ***-stack***; **fur chuck**, the bird furze-chat.

1440 *Promp. Parv.* 162/1 Fyyre, sharpe brusche (*K.* firre, whynne, *P.* fyir or qwynne), *saliunca*. *c* **1540** R. MORICE in *Lett. Lit. Men* (Camden) 24 A gentilman..toke a fyrre bushe on..a pitche-fork, and being all sett on fyer thruste it into his moth. **1562** W. BULLEYN *Bk. Simples* 69 a, The Brome and the Whin or Furre bushe. **1606** BRYSKETT *Civ. Life* 22 He that shooteth at a starre, aimeth higher then he that shooteth at a furbush. **1870** E. PEACOCK *Ralf Skirl.* II. 13 We are guarding the place now with duck-guns, fur-bills, and other spears. **1885** SWAINSON *Prov. Names Birds* 11 Whinchat (*Pratincola rubetra*)..Furr chuck (Norfolk). **1889** *N. W. Linc. Gloss.*, *Fur-bill*, a bill-hook: perhaps a furze-bill. *Fur-busk*, a bush of gorse. *Fur-stack*, a stack of gorse.

fur (fɜː(r)), *v.* [a. OF. *forre-r* (mod.F. *fourrer*) to line, envelop, encase, sheathe, = Sp., Pg. *forrar*, It. *foderare*, a Com. Rom. vb. f. **fod(e)ro* case, sheath (OF. *fuerre*, *forre*, Sp., Pg. *forro*, It. *fodero*), a. Teut. **fôðro-* (Goth. *fôdr*, OE. *fóddor*, OHG. *fuotar*, mod.Ger. *futter*). In all senses exc. 6 and 7 the Eng. vb. is closely connected with FUR *sb.*[1], of which it is commonly apprehended as a derivative. Cf. FOTHER *v.*]

1. *trans.* To line, trim, or cover (a garment) with fur.

13.. *K. Alis.* 5474 The kyng dude of his robe, furred with meneuere. ? *a* **1366** [see FUR *sb.*[1] 1]. *a* **1450** *Knt. de la Tour* (1868) 30 Y wolle furre her gowne, coleres, sleues, and cotes, the here outwarde. *a* **1533** LD. BERNERS *Huon* xlviii. 160 They gaue her..a mantell furryd with ermyns. **1599** HAKLUYT *Voy.* I. 98 The rich Tartars sometimes fur their gowns with pelluce or silke shag. **1696** tr. *Du Mont's Voy. Levant* 266 In Winter 'tis furr'd with a Skin, call'd *Samour*. **1841** MOTLEY *Corr.* (1889) I. iv. 73 A pair of fur boots (furred on both sides). **1842** H. AINSWORTH *Tower Lond.* II. i, A robe of violet-coloured velvet, furred with powdered ermine.

fig. **1648** GAGE *West Ind.* xiv. 96 A Supper, that should strongly support our empty stomacks, and furre and line them well for the next foure and twenty houres.

b. To serve as a lining or trimming for.

1576 TURBERV. *Venerie* 198 His [Raynard's] case will serue to fur the Cape of Master huntsmans gowne. **1631** T. POWELL *Tom All Trades* 165 As many Fox-skins as will furre his Long-lane gowne.

2. To clothe or adorn (a person) with fur.

? **1370** *Robt. Cicyle* 56 The aungelle..clad them alle in clothys of pryse, And furryd them with armyne. *a* **1450** *Knt. de la Tour* (1868) 30 She shalle be better purfiled and furred thanne other ladies and gentille women. *a* **1533** LD. BERNERS *Gold. Bk. M. Aurel.* (1546) I j, I am furred with the furres that thou hast sent me. **1812** *Examiner* 12 Oct. 652/2 So to ribband, to fur, to tassel, and to fringe..men is..degrading their humanity. **1815** SCOTT *Guy M.* xx, Miss Mannering was furred and mantled up to the throat. **1886** *Tinsley's Mag.* July 49 It was the 29th May..and still the fair were furred.

b. *pass.* Of an animal or his skin: To be covered with fur. Also *fig.*

1651 *Fuller's Abel Rediv.*, *J. Fox* 383 Rare Fox (well furr'd with patience). **1823** SCORESBY *Whale Fishery* 109 The skin which was very white, and well furred.

3. To coat or cover with fur or morbid matter. ***to fur up***: to stop up or 'clog' with this.

1593 NASHE *Christ's T.* 31 a, Her Alablaster walls were all furred and fome-painted, with the bespraying of mens braines. **1601** ? MARSTON *Pasquil & Kath.* I. 34 Yee shall haue me an emptie caske that's furd With nought but barmie froth. **1669** W. SIMPSON *Hydrol. Chym.* 354 A rejected Sordes of the blood, which furs up the Orifices. **1700** ADDISON *Eneid* III. Misc. Wks. 1726 I. 60 The walls On all sides furr'd with mouldy damps. **1792** S. IRELAND *Views Thames* II. 89 This water has the property of not furring any vessel it is boiled in. **1839** STONEHOUSE *Axholme* 25 It [the water]..furs every thing in which it is kept. **1863** TYNDALL *Heat* xi. 375 The surface of the vessel..is now white-furred all over with hoar-frost.

fig. **1641** MILTON *Animadv.* (1851) 220 We..after all these spirituall preparatives, and purgations have our earthly apprehensions so clamm'd and furr'd with the old levin. **1684** J. LACY *Sir H. Buffoon* IV. iii, Thy love to her is furred all over like a sick man's tongue. **1863** *Hants.* (*Otterbourn*) *Dial.*, One can't do nothing, one's so furred up with things.

4. *intr.* To become furred or coated with morbid matter. Also, to collect as fur. ***to fur up***: to become 'clogged' with fur.

1550 BECON *Fortr. Faithf.* Prol. A vij b, Nowadayes yᵉ archedecons aske not for yᵉ pore..but whether yᵉ hosts be wel kept in yᵉ pyxe from moulding & furring. **1601** HOLLAND *Pliny* II. 520 Take it forth, and scrape from it the mouldinesse or vinewing that doth furre or gather about it. **1615** CROOKE *Body of Man* 401 A little skill to cleere and dresse the wheeles may keepe this watch of his life [the heart] in motion, which otherwise will furre vp and stand in his dissolution. **1648** HERRICK *Hesper.*, *Upon Glasco* (1869) 46 Teeth..Which though they furre, will neither ake or rot. **1649** BLITHE *Eng. Improv. Impr.* (1653) 71 The better will they [Spades] rid off work by far..and not fur and clog with Earth. *a* **1706** E. BAYNARD *Health* (1740) 6 For too much Meat the Bowels fur. **1743** *Lond. & Country Brew.* III. (ed. 2) 245 Their rough Inside, that is sooner apt to furr, taint and leak. *Mod.* This kettle soon furs.

†**b.** ***to fur up***: to become fluffy. *Obs.*

1825 J. NICHOLSON *Operat. Mechanic* 395 The thread is slightly twisted, in order to enable it to bear the action of the hot liquor without the fibres separating or furring up.

5. *trans.* To clean off the fur of (a boiler).

1867 SMYTH *Sailor's Word-bk.*, *Furring the boilers*, in a steamer, cleaning off the incrustation or sediment which forms on their inner surfaces.

6. *Carpentry.* To fix strips of wood to (floor-timbers, rafters, etc.) in order to bring them to a level, or to the required surface. Also with *off.* (Cf. FUR *sb.*[1] 7.)

1678, **1703**, **1823** [Implied in FURRING *vbl. sb.* 3 b]. **1842** GWILT *Archit.* 977 The timbers of a floor, though level at first, oftentimes require to be furred. **1852** *P. Nicholson's Encycl. Archit.* I. 436. **1891** *Scribner's Mag.* Sept. 312/1 Some sod walls are furred off, lathed, and plastered.

¶ **7.** (? *nonce-use* after F. *fourrer*). To foist or thrust *in.*

1592 BACON *Disc. in Praise of Sovereign* in Spedding *Life* I. 134 But only by furring in audacious persons into sundry governments.

fur, obs. or dial. f. FAR, FIR, FIRE, FURROW.

furacious (fjʊˈreɪʃəs), *a.* Now *pedantic* or *humorous*. [f. L. *fūrāci-* (nom. *fūrax*), f. *fūrāri* to steal + -OUS.] Given to thieving, thievish.

1676 in COLES. **1702** C. MATHER *Magn. Chr.* II. App. (1852) 194 There could be no stop given to his furacious exorbitancies any way but one. **1831** GEN. P. THOMPSON *Exerc.* (1842) I. 393 How like is man in one place, to man everywhere; equally prosing, fraudulent, and furacious. **1842** DE QUINCEY *Pagan Oracles* Wks. VIII. 208 *note*, Greece was *mendax*, *edax*, *furax* (mendacious, edacious, furacious).

Hence **fuˈraciousness**, **fuˈracity**, the quality of being furacious; inclination or tendency to steal.

1623–6 COCKERAM, *Furacity*. **1644** BULWER *Chirol.* 134 In their way of Hieroglyphique when they figured furacity or theft by a light fingered left hand. **1727** BAILEY vol. II, *Furaciousness*. **1790** UMFREVILLE *Hudson's Bay* 36 They [Indians] glory in every species of furacity and artifice.

furaldehyde (fjʊˈrældɪhaɪd). *Chem.* [Abbrev. of FURFURALDEHYDE.] Either of the two aldehyde isomers of the compound $C_4H_3O{\cdot}CHO$ derived from furan, *esp.* 2-furaldehyde or FURFURAL.

1916 *Chem. Abstr.* X. 3508/1 (*index*) 2-Furaldehyde. **1953** DUNLOP & PETERS *Furans* i. 22 The aldehyde (VII) related to furoic acid would be named 2-furaldehyde, or simply furaldehyde. Its common name is furfural.., a non-systematic name, yet one so widely used that it would be unwise to make a change.

furan (ˈfjʊəræn). *Chem.* Also **furane** (-eɪn). [Abbrev. of FURFURAN.] **a.** A heterocyclic compound having a five-membered ring, $(CH)_4O$, and isolated as a colourless liquid with an ethereal odour. **b.** Any compound derived from furan that contains a furan ring. Also *attrib.*, as **furan nucleus** or **ring**, a ring of four carbon atoms and one oxygen atom; so ***furan-ringed*** adj.; **furan resin**, any of various resins that are polymers of a furan, esp. of furfuryl alcohol or furfural.

1894 G. MCGOWAN tr *Bernthsen's Text-bk. Org. Chem.* (ed. 2) xv. 329 The furfurane derivatives are frequently termed 'furane' derivatives for shortness' sake. **1899** *Jrnl. Chem. Soc.* LXXV. II. 1201/2 (*index*) Furfuran (furan). **1907** *Ibid.* XCII. I. 146 (*heading*) Reduction of the furan nucleus. **1930** *Jrnl. Amer. Chem. Soc.* LII. 1697 Glyco-sides which possess the furan ring are very readily hydrolyzed. *Ibid.*, The furan-ringed methylglycosides. **1935** C. ELLIS *Chem. Synthetic Resins* II. 1516/2 (*index*) Furan resins. **1951** R. S. MORRELL in Morrell & Langton *Synthetic Resins & Allied Plastics* (ed. 3) xiii. 409 Furanes may be used in fungicides and fly-repellent preparations. **1953** DUNLOP & PETERS *Furans* i. 3 Furans substitute with greater ease than their benzene analogs. **1969** J. A. BRYDSON *Plastics Materials* (ed. 2) xxiv. 511 The furan resins have never achieved importance for mouldings or laminates but.. have found value in anti-corrosion applications.

furanose (ˈfjʊərənəʊz, -s). *Chem.* [f. FURAN + -OSE[2].] A structure containing a furan ring thought to be sometimes assumed by monosaccharide sugars that contain four or more carbon atoms; also, a sugar having this structure. Freq. *attrib.*, as ***furanose form, ring,*** etc.

1927 GOODYEAR & HAWORTH in *Jrnl. Chem. Soc.* II. 3140 (*caption*) Furanose (a tetrose). *Ibid.* 3141 The corresponding labile or γ-isomerides may be described as arabo-furanose, xylo-furanose etc. **1948** W. W. PIGMAN *Chem. Carbohydrates* ii. 52 The basic types of the furanoses are the pentoses. **1957** E. V. MILLER *Chem. Plants* i. 6 Glucose and other hexoses may exist in the form of a pyranose ring or a furanose ring, the former being the more stable form. **1963** E. PERCIVAL in Florkin & Stotz *Comprehensive Biochem.* V. i. 24 Furanose forms of unsubstituted sugars have never been isolated although in solution they are considered to exist in equilibrium with the open-chain and pyranose ring forms.

furanoside (fjuːˈrænəsaɪd). *Chem.* [f. FURANOS(E + -IDE.] Any glycoside in the furanose form.

1932 *Jrnl. Chem. Soc.* 2255 The crystalline furanosides are reasonably stable to neutral aqueous permanganate. **1934** E. F. & K. F. ARMSTRONG *Carbohydrates* (ed. 5) XVI. 193 Haworth compares the relative velocity constant values for the hydrolysis of sucrose and furanosides with certain pyranosides, proving that sucrose is a typical furanose in this characteristic. **1966** C. A. MARSH in G. J. Dutton *Glucuronic Acid* i. 43 The electrophoretic mobilities on paper of the pyranoside and furanoside forms of both 2-naphthyl β-D-glucoside and 2-naphthyl β-D-glucosiduronic acid.

furbelow (ˈfɜːbɪləʊ), *sb.* Forms: 7–8 furbelo(e, 8 furbellow, (furbolo, furbuloe), 8– furbelow. [An alteration of FALBALA.]

1. A piece of stuff pleated and puckered on a gown or petticoat; a flounce; the pleated border of a petticoat or gown. Now often in *pl.* as a contemptuous term for showy ornaments or trimming, esp. in a lady's dress.

1706 MRS. CENTLIVRE *Basset Table* IV. H 2 b, Lady Revel .. Discovers a purse in the Furbeloes of her Apron. *c* **1710** C. FIENNES *Diary* (1888) 15 Their peticoates silke y[t] were with furbellows one above another with Ribons. **1711** ADDISON *Spect.* No. 15 ¶4 A Furbelow of precious Stones, an Hat buttoned with a Diamond. **1760** C. JOHNSTON *Chrysal* (1822) I. 275 Here, Jane, settle the furbellows of my scarf. **1827** PRAED *Poems* (1865) II. 355 The Baron bows low to a furbelow, If it be not my Lady's dress. **1862** MISS BRADDON *Lady Audley* xxxiii. 249 My lady smiled as she looked at the festoons and furbelows which met her eye upon every side.

fig. **1883** D. G. MITCHELL *Bound Together* i, Rhetorical furbelows or broidery that belong to the wardrobes of the past.

2. Anything resembling a flounce.

1742 H. BAKER *Microsc.* II. xxvi. 203 Its Wings are encompassed with a Furbelow of long Feathers. **1875** CARPENTER *Microscope* xi. §481. 584 The beautiful *Chrysaora* remarkable for its long 'furbelows' which act as organs of prehension.

3. A name for *Laminaria bulbosa*, a seaweed with a large wrinkled frond.

1846–51 HARVEY *Phycologia Britannica* III. Plate ccxli, This is the largest British species of the Laminarieæ.. Its common name is Furbelows. **1864** TENNYSON *Sea Dreams* 257 You.. made The dimpled flounce of the sea-furbelow flap.. to please the child.

†**4.** *Conchol.* (See quot.) ? *Obs.*

1776 tr. *Da Costa's Conchol.* 289 The Furbelow from Falkland Island; Baccinium Fimbriatum.

5. *attrib.* passing into *adj.*; chiefly in the sense 'having furbelows', pleated. †Also as the name of a kind of pear.

c **1680** *Crys of London* in *Bagford Ballads* I. 116 Will you buy any Furbeloe Pears. **1705** *Lond. Gaz.* No. 4177/4 Lost .. a blue Furbelow Coach-Box Cloth. **1706** FARQUHAR *Recruit. Officer* IV. i, I'll buy you a furbelow scarf. **1712** ARBUTHNOT *John Bull* III. i, Crimpt ribbons in her head-dress, furbelo-scarfs, and hooped-petticoats. **1803** MARY CHARLTON *Wife & Mistress* III. 221 If you were to put round you a heap of furbelow veils, you would look picturesque enough.

furbelow (ˈfɜːbɪləʊ), *v.* [f. prec. sb.] *trans.* To ornament with a furbelow, or with something resembling a furbelow.

1701 *Lond. Gaz.* No. 3743/4 Lost.. a Deal Box.. having in it a rich Scarf forbulo'd with a rich Gold Lace. **1731–7** MILLER *Gard. Dict.* s.v. *Chelone*, Many flat Seeds, that are furbelow'd on the Edges. **1760–72** tr. *Juan & Ulloa's Voy.* (ed. 3) I. 157 It is furbeloed with a richer stuff, near half a yard in depth. **1840** DICKENS *Barn. Rudge* (1849) 74/2 Many a private chair too, inclosing some fine lady, monstrously hooped and furbelowed. **1865** L. OLIPHANT *Piccadilly* (1870) 222 Trains of daughters, furbelowed and flounced by the same dressmakers.

fig. **1709–10** ADDISON *Tatler* No. 116 ¶2 Very florid Harangues, which they did not fail to set off and furbelow (if I may be allowed the Metaphor) with many periodical Sentences. **1717** PRIOR *Alma* II. 44 To break their points, you turn their force, And furbelow the plain discourse.

absol. **1784** R. BAGE *Barham Downs* I. 171 They could trim, flounce, and furbelow to admiration.

Hence **ˈfurbelowed** *ppl. a.*

1703 FARQUHAR *Inconstant* II. i, Have you got home your furbelowed smocks yet? **1713** STEELE *Guardian* No. 142 ¶5, I am now rearing up a set of fine furbelowed dock-leaves. **1835** BECKFORD *Recoll.* 104 Under a most sumptuously fringed and furbelowed canopy of purple velvet. **1861** J. R. GREENE *Man. Anim. Kingd., Cœlent.* 123 It terminates in four furbelowed lips.

†**ˈfurber.** *Obs.* Also 5 fourbour, forbyer, 6 forborer, 7 forbere. [a. OF. *forbere, forbeor,* agent-n. f. *forbir* to FURBISH.] = FURBISHER.

c **1415** in Davies *York Rec.* (1843) 233 Coupers,.. Fourbours. **1492** *Nottingham Rec.* III. 24, j. forbyer pretii vj d. *c* **1515** *Cocke Lorell's B.* (Percy) 9 Gyrdelers, forborers, and webbers. **1609** D. ROGERS in *Digby Myst.* (1882) p. xxi, Smythes, forberes, Pewterers.

furbery, var. FOURBERY, *Obs.*

furbish (ˈfɜːbɪʃ), *v.* Forms: 4–6 furbusshe, 4–7 furbush, (4 forbisch, fourbosh, 5 forbesh, foorbush, 6 furbisshe, 7 forbush), 5 forbysch(yn, 5–7 f(o)urbyssh(e, 4– furbish. [ad. OF. *forbiss-* lengthened stem of *forbir* (= Pr. *forbir*, It. *forbire*), ad. OHG. *furban* in the same sense.]

1. *trans.* To remove rust from (a weapon, armour, etc.); to brighten by rubbing, polish, burnish. Also with *up*.

1382 WYCLIF *Ezek.* xxi. 9 The swerd is whettid and furbishid. *c* **1483** CAXTON *Vocab.* 16 A swerde, Whiche me ought to furbysshe. *c* **1530** LD. BERNERS *Arth. Lyt. Bryt.* (1814) 327 Varlettes were furbusshynge.. of theyr maysters harneys. **1647** WARD *Simp. Cobler* 70 In heaven.. your swords are furbushed and sharpened, by him that made their metall. **1719** DE FOE *Crusoe* I. xii, I.. furbished up one of the.. cutlasses. **1791** COWPER *Iliad* XIII. 415 Corslets furbish'd bright. **1852** HAWTHORNE *Tanglewood T., Golden Fleece* (1879) 215 As soon as they could furbish up their helmets. **1863** GEO. ELIOT *Romola* II. xxi, Old arms duly furbished.

absol. **1624** QUARLES *Div. Poems, Job* III. li, Or if, by forbushing, he [the potter] take more paine To make it fairer, shall the Pot complaine?

fig. *c* **1380** WYCLIF *Serm.* Sel. Wks. I. 224 Men shulden not holde al gold þat shyneþ as gold, for many þingis ben fourboshid ful falseli. **1581** J. BELL *Haddon's Answ. Osor.* 134 b, He hath somewhat furbushed the old rusty Argumentes of other raynebeaten souldiours. **1593** SHAKS. *Rich. II*, I. iii. 76 With thy blessings steele my Lances point, That it may enter Mowbrayes waxen Coate, And furbish new the name of John a Gaunt. **1654** TRAPP *Comm. Job* xxix. 25 He had so fourbished the sword of Justice with the Oyle of Mercy.

2. To brush or clean up (anything faded or soiled); to give a new look to (an object either material or immaterial); to do or get up afresh, renovate, revive. Chiefly with *up*, occas. *over*.

1587 GOLDING *De Mornay* xvii. (1617) 304 The soule, which must be fain to be, as it were, new furbished. **1598** E. GILPIN *Skial.* (1878) 65 Thei'le flowt a man behind his backe, if he Be not trim furbish'd and in decencie. **1629** N. CARPENTER *Achitophel* III. (1640) 131 He shewed himselfe ambitious to file and furbish over the staine of his shamefull life. **1642** FULLER *Holy & Prof. St.* V. iv. 397 This infection [Pelagianisme] was to come to this Iland in after-ages, furbished up under a new name. **1687** DRYDEN *Hind & P.* III. 582 Their ancient houses, running to decay, Are furbish'd up. **1691** WOOD *Ath. Oxon.* II. 28 The University Statutes.. were afterwards corrected, methodized, and furbisht over with excellent Latine. **1715** ROWE *Lady Jane Gray* III. i, They furbish up their Holy Trumpery. **1774** J. Q. ADAMS in *Fam. Lett.* (1876) 5, I might be furbishing up my old reading in Law and History. **1837** SOUTHEY *Doctor* IV. cxxiii. 228 Some part of the furniture was to be furbished, some to be renewed. **1844** DISRAELI *Coningsby* VIII. iii, What we want.. is not to.. furbish up old baronies, but to establish great principles.

†**b.** *intr.* for *refl.* *Obs. rare*[−1].

1697 DENNIS *Plot & no Plot* I. 12 Go, get you gone and furbish, you little young Dog.

Hence **ˈfurbished** *ppl. a.*; **ˈfurbishing** *vbl. sb.*; also *attrib.* and used gerundially with the omission of *in*. Also **ˈfurbish** *sb.*, the action of the vb.

c **1430** *Pilgr. Lyf Manhode* I. iii. (1869) 2 A foorbushed swerd wel grownden. **1463** *Mann. & Househ. Exp.* 226 My mastyre payd to Robyn the armerere.. ffor xij. dayis werke in fforbeshynge, iij. s. **1605** SHAKS. *Macb.* I. ii. 32 The Norweyan Lord.. With furbusht Armes, and new supplyes of men, Began a fresh assault. *a* **1640** BALL *Answ. J. Can* I. (1642) 90 A new furbishing over of the same broken staffe. **1713** STEELE *Englishm.* No. 40. 264 These.. are lately furbishing up to shine out at some favourable Conjuncture. **1775** S. J. PRATT *Liberal Opin.* II. 159 For all the furbish'd up stuff it contains. **1839** COL. HAWKER *Diary* (1893) II. 171 Had a general furbish of all the gear and stores. **1875** JOWETT *Plato* (ed. 2) IV. 438 To this the arts of fulling and.. furbishing attend in a number of minute particulars. **1862** *Lond. Rev.* 30 Aug. 188 The tarnished lace having been subjected to a furbishing process.

†**ˈfurbishable**, *a.* *Obs.*[−0] Capable of being furbished or polished.

1611 COTGR., *Polissable*, burnishable, furbishable.

furbisher (ˈfɜːbɪʃə(r)). [f. FURBISH *v.* + -ER[1]. Cf. F. *fourbisseur.*] One who furbishes.

c **1440** *Promp. Parv.* 470/1 Foorbyschowre, *eruginator*. *c* **1483** CAXTON *Vocab.* 16 Denis the fourbysshour Hath of me a swerd. **1594** *Mirr. Policy* (1599) 257 The which Armourers, Fourbushers, Cutlers, and such like doe furnish. **1653** URQUHART *Rabelais* II. xxx. 199 Ogier the Dane was a Furbisher of armour. **1766** ENTICK *London* IV. 344 Wherein are.. employed about 14 furbishers, in cleaning, repairing, and new-placing the arms. **1840** COL. HAWKER *Diary* (1893) II. 172 About getting Long the appointment of furbisher at the Tower. **1881** J. EVANS *Anc. Bronze Implem.* 5 A furbisher of every cutting instrument in those metals.

fig. **1617** J. MOORE *Mappe Mans Mortal.* II. v. 126 As furbushers, to varnish vs from the rust and canker of our corruption.

furbishment (ˈfɜːbɪʃmənt). [f. FURBISH *v.* + -MENT.] The action of the vb. FURBISH.

1850 BLACKIE *Æschylus* I. Pref. 8 Every sort of fine flourishing and delicate furbishment.

‖**furca** (ˈfʊrkə). [L.]

1. *Rom. Ant.* (and *allusively*). A gallows.

1653 JER. TAYLOR *XXV Serm. Gold.-Grove* xii. 162 They shall escape the *furca* and the *wheel*. **1779** *Gentl. Mag.* XLIX. 460 The American General deserved a *furca* rather than a *mischianza*.

2. *Ent.* **a.** An apodeme or process in the thorax of many insects.

1895 *Cambr. Nat. Hist.* V. I. 103 Entothorax (apophysis or furca). **1910** C. G. HEWITT *House Fly* 9 The theca rests on a triradiate chitinous sclerite—the furca, which consists of a median, slightly convex rod. **1925** A. D. IMMS *Gen. Textbk. Ent.* 47 The endosternites (apophyses of some writers) are commonly represented by the *furcæ*; each furca is a median apodeme, unpaired at its base, with two free distal arms. *Ibid.* 598 The *theca*.. articulates distally with a short rod or *furca*. **1969** R. F. CHAPMAN *Insects* viii. 131 In higher insects the two apophyses arise together in the midline and only separate internally, forming a Y-shaped furca.

b. = FURCULA 3.

1939 H. WOMERSLEY *Prim. Insects S. Austral.* 81 In most species [of Collembola], the fourth ventral segment carries a pair of large, partially fused, appendages which form the characteristic spring or furca. **1969** R. F. CHAPMAN *Insects* ix. 154 The jump is produced by the sudden release of the furca.

3. *Zool.* A pair of divergent processes on the last abdominal segment of certain crustaceans.

1903 J. S. KINGSLEY tr. *Hertwig's Man. Zool.* 420 The terminal abdominal segment [of the *Copepoda*] is two-forked, forming the 'furca'. **1932** BORRADAILE & POTTS *Invertebrata* xii. 303 On the telson [of Crustacea] usually.. is a pair of caudal rami forming the caudal furca. **1956** *Nature* 11 Feb. 289/2 In the arrangement of the setæ on uropods and furca the new species is similar to *Th*[*ermobathynella*] *leleupi*.

furcal (ˈfɜːkəl), *a.* *Zool.* [f. L. *furca* fork + -AL.] Forked, furcate; esp. of or pertaining to a furca.

1851 *Trans. Linn. Soc.* XX. 434 Some traces of the entrances into these furcal bones exist in the sternal plates of *Perla*. **1895** *Cambr. Nat. Hist.* V. I. 399 [In Perlidæ] the metasternum.. has on each side a peculiar slit; similar orifices exist on the other sterna... Newport.. says that they are blind invaginations of the integument; he calls them the sternal or furcal orifices. **1969** R. F. CHAPMAN *Insects* ix. 154 It is probable that the mechanism of furcal extension is not the same in all Collembola.

furcate (ˈfɜːkeɪt, -ət), *a.* [ad. med.L. *furcātus* (of a hoof) cloven, f. L. *furca* fork.] Formed like a fork; forked or branched.

1819 G. SAMOUELLE *Entomol. Compend.* 248 Converted into a furcate tail. **1826** KIRBY & SP. *Entomol.* (1828) III. xxix. 149 The furcate horn of the caterpillar of Parnassius Apollo. **1841–71** T. R. JONES *Anim. Kingd.* (ed. 4) 729 The insect, being seized by its furcate extremity, is.. brought between the jaws of its destroyer. **1870** BENTLEY *Bot.* 148 A variety of venation may be therefore called Furcate or forked.

Hence **ˈfurcately** *adv.* Also **furˈcato-**, used as combining form = forkedly-.

1846 DANA *Zooph.* (1848) 163 Segregato-gemmate, furcately ramose. *Ibid.* 511 Glomerate or furcato-ramose. *Ibid.* 669 Furcato-dichotomous, two feet high, axils arcuate.

furcate (ˈfɜːkeɪt), *v.* [f. ppl. stem of assumed L. **furcāre*, f. *furca* FORK *sb.*] *intr.* To form a fork; to divide into branches.

1846 DANA *Zooph.* (1848) 79 These lines frequently furcate or give out lateral branches. *Ibid.* 198 Stems straight, furcating. **1852** —— *Crust.* I. 142 Another small fissure, which furcates a short distance above.

furcated (ˈfɜːkeɪtɪd), *ppl. a.* [f. med.L. *furcāt-us* + -ED[1].] = FURCATE *a.*

1828 STARK *Elem. Nat. Hist.* II. 426 Ramuli furcated at the apex. **1847–9** TODD *Cycl. Anat.* IV. 401/1 Chætonotus and Ichthydium possess a furcated foot. **1859** W. H. GREGORY *Egypt* I. 174 The dôm-palm.. invariably divides at a certain height into two branches, and these again.. become furcated. **1874** COOKE *Fungi* 52 Each of these.. branch out into a furcated form.

furcation (fɜːˈkeɪʃən). [f. L. *furca* fork; see -ATION.] A forking or branching; hence, a fork-like division or branch.

1646 SIR T. BROWNE *Pseud. Ep.* III. ix. 124 When they [deer] grow old, they.. first doe lose their.. brow Antlers or, lowest furcations next the head. **1846** DANA *Zooph.* (1848) 71 There are two modes of branching:—1. By a simple furcation of the extremity of a branch. **1862** —— *Man. Geol.* 36 Another furcation of it passes by Eastern Borneo. **1874** COOKE *Fungi* 52 The furcations being made in such a manner that the ends of the branch at last so stand together that their surface forms a ball.

furch (fɜːtʃ). Also FOUCH. [ad. F. *fourche* FORK *sb.*]

†**1.** = FOUCH 2. *Obs.*

1491 in *Ld. Treas. Acc. Scotl.* (1877) I. 181 Item.. till a man of the Chanslaris that brocht a furche of venyson to the King v *s.* **1693** URQUHART *Rabelais* III. xi, My heart like the furch of a hart in rut doth beat within my breast.

2. *Vet. Surg.* = FRUSH, FROG. Also *attrib.* in *furch-stay*.

[App. introduced by B. Clark, as a more etymologically correct substitute for the current forms. The Fr. equivalent is *fourchette*.]

1842 BRACY CLARK *On Running Frush* (ed. 3) 2 The part diseased, and which in my Treatise on the Foot of the Horse published in 1809, I called the Furch-stay, as being the part which held the base of the Furch together. *Ibid.* 3 This remarkable part was without any name and very little noticed, till I gave it the epithet Frog-stay or Furch-stay.

furch, obs. form of FURROW.

furchur(e, var. of FORCHURE, *Obs.*

13.. *K. Alis.* 4995 Another folk there is bisyde That habbeth furchures swithe wide.

furciferine (fɜːˈsɪfəraɪn), *a. Zool.* [f. L. *furcifer* (see FURCIFEROUS) + -INE[1].] Of or pertaining to western South American deer of the genus *Hippocamelus*, which have forked antlers and were formerly grouped in the genus *Furcifer*.

1891 FLOWER & LYDEKKER *Introd. Stud. Mammals* 329 The Furciferine group includes *Cervus chilensis.* **1966** *Punch* 25 May 775/3 Chile should also be all right with its *huemal*, an elusive furciferine deer which only exists in the high mountains of the country.

furciferous (fɜːˈsɪfərəs), *a.* [f. L. *furcifer* (f. *furca* FORK *sb.* + *-fer* bearing) fork-bearer, hence (with reference to the 'fork' or yoke placed on the necks of criminals) rascal, jail-bird + -OUS.]

1. *Ent.* Bearing a forked process; said of the larvæ of certain butterflies (*Cent. Dict.*).

2. Rascally. *rare* (somewhat *jocular*).

1823 *Monthly Mag.* LV. 222 Long addicted to furciferous practices. **1835** DE QUINCEY in *Tait's Mag.* II. 81 Observe the dilemma into which these furciferous knaves must drop.

furcræa (fɜːˈkriːə). Also four-, crœa, -croya. [mod.L. (A. Ventenat 1793, in *Bulletin des Sciences de la Société Philomathique* I. 65), f. the name of the French chemist A. F. de *Fourcroy* (1755–1809).] A tropical American plant of the genus so named, closely related to *Agave* and belonging to the family Amaryllidaceæ.

1821 *Curtis's Bot. Mag.* XLVIII. 2250 (*heading*) Gigantic Furcræa. **1900** L. H. BAILEY *Cycl. Amer. Hort.* s.v., As a rule, Furcræas bear fruit not more than once, and then die without producing suckers. **1901** *Westm. Gaz.* 3 July 7/1 Poles of the furcroea aloe for the construction of recreation-rooms and school houses. **1963** ROBERTSON & GOODING *Bot. Caribbean* v. 45 (*caption*) Bulbil of *Furcraea*. *Ibid.* xxiii. 213 Other members [of the Agavaceæ] familiar in the West Indies are.. *Furcraea* spp. (Maypole) with creamy white flowers.

‖**furcula** (ˈfɜːkjʊlə). [L. *furcula*, dim. of *furca* fork.] **1.** *Ornith.* A forked bone below the neck of a bird, consisting of the two clavicles and an inter-clavicle; the merry-thought or wish-bone.

1859 DARWIN *Orig. Spec.* i. (1878) 16 Relative size of the two arms of the furcula. **1868** —— *Anim. & Pl.* I. v. 175 The sternum, scapulæ, and furcula are all reduced in proportional length. **1903** J. S. KINGSLEY tr. *Hertwig's Man. Zool.* 605 Clavicles and furcula are united directly or by ligaments to the broad sternum. **1954** G. C. KENT *Compar. Anat. Vertebrates* viii. 253 The two clavicles unite in the midline to form a furcula (wishbone).

2. *Embryol.* A process from which the epiglottis is developed.

1887 A. C. HADDON *Introd. Study Embryol.* vi. 183 Behind this [projection] are a pair of folds (furcula), which eventually will form the epiglottis. **1926** JORDAN & KINDRED *Textbk. Embryol.* xv. 196 The crest of the furcula becomes elevated and develops into the epiglottis.

3. *Ent.* A forked appendage at the end of the abdomen in springtails.

[**1871** *Amer. Naturalist* V. 10 The spring consists of a pair of three-jointed appendages.. forming a fork.] **1906** J. W. FOLSOM *Entomology* ii. 68 *Appendages*... In Collembola.. those of the fourth segment form the characteristic leaping organ, or furcula. **1909** *Jrnl. Econ. Bot.* IV. 9 Furcula somewhat broader than in *S*[*minthurus*] *aureus*. **1932** BORRADAILE & POTTS *Invertebrata* xiv. 408 By contraction of the extensor muscles of the furcula the latter is pulled down out of contact with the hamula and the animal is propelled forwards into the air. **1964** J. T. SALMON *Index to Collembola* I. 111 Re-examination showed this species to have a well developed furcula.

furcular (ˈfɜːkjʊlə(r)), *a.* Also 6 furculare. [ad. OF. *furculaire*, f. L. FURCULA; in later use f. FURCULA + -AR.] Of or pertaining to the furcula; in early use, to the collar-bone.

1541 R. COPLAND *Guydon's Quest. Chirurg.* F 4 b, Howe many bones are in y[e] sholdre?.. the bone sholdre blade and the bone furculare. **1856–8** W. CLARK *Van der Hoeven's Zool.* II. 609 Two clavicles, a coracoid and a furcular.

†ˈ**furcule.** *Obs.* Also 6 furculle, furkle. [ad. L. *furcula*: see FURCULA.] = FORCEL. Also *attrib.*

1541 R. COPLAND *Guydon's Quest. Chirurg.* D 3 b, Some be proprely lacertes that brede nyghe the eares tyll they come to the furcules or forkes of the brest. **1548–77** VICARY *Anat.* vii. (1888) 56 In the vpper ende of Thorax is an hole .. in which is set the foote of the Furklebone or Canel bone.

‖**furculum** (ˈfɜːkjʊləm). *Ornith.* [mod.L. *furculum*, incorrectly formed dim. of *furca*.] = FURCULA 1.

1833 SIR C. BELL *Hand* (1834) 54 The furculum or fork bone, which in carving, we detach after removing the wings of the fowl, corresponds with the clavicle. **1863** LYELL *Antiq. Man* xxii. 451 The furculum, or merry-thought.. marks the forepart of the trunk. **1873** J. GEIKIE *Gt. Ice Age* App. 525 The furculum of a gull was found in brick-clay at the Bridge of Johnston, near Paisley.

†ˈ**furdel, ˈfurdle,** *v. Obs.* [var. of FARDEL, *v.*] *trans.* To furl or fold. Also with *up*.

1594 GLENHAM *News fr. Levane Seas* 16 Their sayles furdeld. **1630** J. TAYLOR (Water P.) *Peace France* Wks. III. 114/1 The Colours furdled vp, the Drum is mute. **1635** *Fox's Voy. N.-W. Pass.* (Hakluyt Soc.) 496 We strooke all our sayles and furdeld them up. *a* **1682** SIR T. BROWNE *Tracts* (1684) 34 Which being a drie and ligneous Plant.. though crumpled and furdled up, yet, if infused in Water, will swell and display its parts.

Hence ˈ**furdled** *ppl. a.*, †ˈ**furdling** *vbl. sb.*

1658 SIR T. BROWNE *Gard. Cyrus* iii. 128 To urge the thwart enclosure and furdling of flowers, and blossomes before explication.

furder, obs. form of FURTHER.

†**fure,** *v. Obs. Sc.* [f. **fure*, Sc. form of FORE a journey.]

1. *trans.* To bear, carry.

c **1470** HENRY *Wallace* III. 222 With flour and wyne als mekill as thai mycht fur. **1487** *Sc. Acts Jas. III* (1814) II. 178/2 That na gudis be furit be þe master apoun his ouerloft. *c* **1560** A. SCOTT *Poems* (S.T.S.) xvi. 1 How suld my febill body fure The dowble dolour I indure? **1609** SKENE *Reg. Maj.* 141 Na gudes sould be fured vpon the over-loft of the shippes.

2. To lead, conduct. Also *absol.*

1536 BELLENDEN *Cron. Scot.* (1821) I. Proheme p. vi, So far as laboure and his wisdome furis. **1637** MONRO *Exped.* I. 45 To his Master the Kings Majesty or Generall, that fuers or leades the warre.

Hence ˈ**furing** *vbl. sb.*, freight.

1535 STEWART *Cron. Scot.* II. 246 For birth and wecht hir furing wes so hie, With thame ilkane scho sank into the se.

fure, obs. form of FIRE.

†**furel.** *Obs.* [Possibly a mistake of some kind: cf. FORCHE.] ? A gallows.

1587 HARRISON *England* II. xix. (1877) I. 310 It is not lawfull for anie subiect.. to.. set vp furels, tumbrell, thew or pillorie.. within his owne soile without his [the king's] warrant and grant.

furel, obs. var. FOREL, sheath.

furen, var. FIREN *a.*, *Obs.*, fiery.

furfur (ˈfɜːfə(r)). *Path.* Pl. furfures. Also 7 furfaire, 9 *arch.* furfair. [a. L. *furfur* bran.] Dandriff, scurf; *pl.* particles of epidermis or scurf; also, a bran-like sediment in the urine.

1621 BURTON *Anat. Mel.* I. i. ii. iii. (1651) 7 Grievances, which.. are inward or outward.. belonging to the brain, as baldness, falling of haire, furfaire. *Ibid.* II. i. IV. iii. 231 Leprosie, Ulcers, Itches, Furfures, Scabs, etc. **1754** *Dict. Arts & Sc.* II. 1358 Those excrementitious particles which are evacuated with the urine, are also called furfures. **1798–1808** R. WILLAN *Cutaneous Dis.* in *Cullen's Nosol. Method.* App. (1820) 320 *note*, Furfur (scruf), small exfoliations of the cuticle which occur after slight inflammation of the skin. **1835** BROWNING *Paracelsus* IV. 117 My outward crust Of lies, which wrap as tetter, morphew, furfair, Wrap the sound flesh. **1885** *Syd. Soc. Lex.*, *Furfur*, a term applied, especially in France, to the layers of cuticle, like to bran, which are detached from the skin in such diseases as pityriasis.

furfuraceous (fɜːfjʊəˈreɪʃəs), *a.* Also 7 *erron.* -acerous, 8 -acious. [f. late L. *furfurāce-us* (f. *furfur* bran) + -OUS.] Resembling bran; scurfy, scaly; in *Bot.* covered with bran-like scales.

1650 BULWER *Anthropomet.* 101 The furfuracerous excrements of the Temples. **1735** J. MOORE *Columbarium* 26 The upper Chap of the Bill is half cover'd.. with a naked, white, tuberous, furfuraceous Flesh. **1822–34** *Good's Study Med.* (ed. 4) I. 674 The urine is peculiarly distinguished by a natural furfuraceous separation. **1860** BERKELEY *Brit. Fungol.* 177 Stem somewhat flexuous, brittle, furfuraceous, then smooth. **1876** *Clin. Soc. Trans.* IX. 45 The epidermis, on being scratched, was raised in furfuraceous scales.

furfural (ˈfɜːfjʊəræl). *Chem.* [f. FURFUR(OL + -AL[2].] An aldehyde of furan, $C_4H_3O{\cdot}CHO$, a colourless liquid which darkens in air and which is used chiefly as a solvent and in the manufacture of furan derivatives and synthetic resins; 2-furaldehyde; = FURFUROL; **furfural resin** = *furan resin*.

1879 H. WATTS *Dict. Chem.* (ed. 2) VIII. I. 832 Furfural or furfurol, $C_5H_4O_2$. Pyromucic aldehyde. **1901** *Daily Chron.* 11 May 2/2 In the case of whisky the chief cause of mischief is furfural, from which old matured whisky is free. **1939** H. R. SIMONDS *Industr. Plastics* (1940) iii. 74 The furfural resins are dark in color and therefore are used only with great difficulty for producing light colored plastics. **1960** *Times Rev. Industry* May 82/3 By the hydrolysis of the waste products [from the manufacture of cellulose] furfural—an important raw material for the oil processing industries and an intermediate in the manufacture of nylon—may be obtained. **1969** J. A. BRYDSON *Plastics Materials* (ed. 2) xxiv. 511 Furfural occurs in the free state in many plants but is obtained commercially by degradation of hemi-cellulose consitutents present in these plants.

furfuraldehyde (fɜːfjʊəˈrældɪhaɪd). *Chem.* [f. FURFUR(OL + ALDEHYDE.] = prec.

1879 *Jrnl. Chem. Soc.* XXXVI. 137 A preparation of glacial acetic acid.. which had been observed.. to give a deep red coloration with aniline.. he finds to contain furfuraldehyde. **1969** L. K. ARNOLD *Introd. Plastics* xvi. 172 Furfural (furfuraldehyde) is used in phenol-furfural resins and as an intermediate in nylon 6,6.

furfuramide (ˈfɜːfjʊərəmaɪd). Also furfuˈrolamide. [f. FURFUR(OL + AMIDE.] A white crystalline substance produced by the action of ammonia on furfurol.

1845 Furfurolamide [see FURFUROL]. **1864** WATTS *Dict. Chem.* II. 747 Furfuramide [see FURFURINE].

furfuran (ˈfɜːfjʊəræn). *Chem.* Also -ane. [a. G. *furfuran* (A. Baeyer 1877, in *Ber. d. Deut. Chem. Ges.* X. 1361), f. FURFUR(OL + -AN, -ANE.] = FURAN.

1877 *Jrnl. Chem. Soc.* II. 745 The author [*sc.* A. Baeyer] proposes for the group C_4H_4O (Limpricht's *Tetraphenol*) the name 'furfuran'. **1895** *Bloxam's Chem.* (ed. 8) 744 Furfurane, C_4H_4O, is found in the first runnings of the distillation of wood-tar. **1899** [see FURAN]. **1923** C. ELLIS *Synthetic Resins & Plastics* xi. 202 The cyclic compound, furfurane, may be looked upon as a member of the ethylene oxide series. **1958** PACKER & VAUGHAN *Org. Chem.* XXVII. 937 Furan (furane, furfuran) is a colourless liquid.

furfuration (fɜːfjʊəˈreɪʃən). *rare*[−0]. [f. L. *furfur* bran + -ATION.] 'The shedding of the skin in small branny particles'. (*Syd. Soc. Lex.*)

1706 PHILLIPS (ed. Kersey), *Furfuration*, the falling of Dandriff or Scurf from the Head, when it is comb'd. **1721** in BAILEY. **1854** in MAYNE *Exp. Lex.*

furfurine (ˈfɜːfjʊərɪn). [f. L. *furfur* bran + -INE.] (See quot. 1864.)

1845 [see FURFUROL]. **1864** WATTS *Dict. Chem.* II. 747 *Furfurine*.. an organic base, isomeric with furfuramide, and produced therefrom under the influence of caustic potash, or simply of heat.

furfurol (ˈfɜːfjʊərɒl). [f. L. *furfur* + -OL.] A volatile oil obtained by distilling bran with dilute sulphuric acid.

1845 FOWNES in *Phil. Trans.* CXXXV. 261 The following .. will be the provisional nomenclature:—Oil produced by the action of sulphuric acid on bran, &c.. termed 'furfurol' .. Product of the action of ammonia on furfurol or 'furfurolamide'.. Vegeto-alkali, 'furfurine,' produced by the duplication of the elements of furfurolamide.

†**furfuˈrose**, *a. Obs.*[−0] [ad. L. *furfurōs-us*, f. *furfur* bran.] Full of bran.

1727 in BAILEY vol. II.

furfurous (ˈfɜːfjʊərəs), *a.* [f. L. *furfur* bran + -OUS.] Resembling bran; containing bran or bran-like particles; made of bran.

1547 BOORDE *Brev. Health* lxxiii. 23 A furfurouse water or urine that is lyke as branne were in it. **1744** MITCHELL in *Phil. Trans.* XLIII. 144 Furfurous Desquammations. **1822** SYD. SMITH *Wks.* (1867) I. 359 Furfurous bread and the water of the pool constitute his food.

furfuryl (ˈfɜːfjʊərɪl, -aɪl). *Chem.* [f. FURFUR(OL + -YL.] **a.** The univalent radical $C_4H_3O{\cdot}CH_2$-containing a furan ring. **furfuryl alcohol**, a colourless liquid, $C_4H_3O{\cdot}CH_2OH$, darkening in air and used industrially as a solvent and in the manufacture of synthetic resins. †**b.** = FURYL. *Obs.*

1873 *Jrnl. Chem. Soc.* XXVI. 626 Furfuryl alcohol, $C_5H_6O_2$, is produced, together with pyromucic acid, by the action of alcoholic potash and furfurol. **1884** ROSCOE & SCHORLEMMER *Treat. Chem.* III. II. 614 Constitution of the Furfuryl Compounds.—These contain the group C_4H_3O, which in accordance with Baeyer's suggestion is termed 'furfur'. **1958** *Spectator* 20 June 804/3 The stuff which, apparently, gives coffee its flavour—a chemical called furfuryl mercaptan.

furgon ('fɜːgən). Also 6 furgone, 9 furgen, *dial.* FRUGGAN. [ad. F. *fourgon* poker.] †**a.** An oven-fork, a poker (*obs.*). **b.** (See quot. 1881.)

14.. *Tundale's Vis.* 1059 The turmentowris com rennand With furgons and with tongis glowand. **1530** PALSGR. 223/2 Furgone for an ovyn, *uavldree*. **1534** *Eng. Ch. Furnit.* (1866) 211, iij furgons of yron. **1881** RAYMOND *Mining Gloss.*, *Furgen*, a round rod used for sounding a bloomary fire.

†**'furial**, *a. Obs.* [a. OF. *furial*, ad. L. *furiāl-is*, f. *furia* FURY.] Furious, raging.

c **1386** CHAUCER *Sqr.'s T.* 440 This furial pyne of helle. **1640** J. GOWER *Ovid's Fest.* 43 Meanwhile, the young Prince, furiall lust doth move.

furiant ('fʊərɪənt, 'fjʊərɪənt). *Mus.* [Czech.] A type of Bohemian dance, or its music, in quick triple time with frequently-shifting accents.

1881 GROVE *Dict. Mus.* III. 614/2 Bohemia is preeminently rich in dances (such as the *beseda, dudik, furiant*, [etc.]). **1902** *Encycl. Brit.* XXVII. 554/1 The fiddlers who scraped out their 'furiants' and other wild dances. **1943** *Times* 11 Nov. 6/5 The ballet,..with Miss Sasha Machov to teach them the authentic style in polka and furiant. **1967** *Listener* 13 Apr. 505/2 An example of just that sort of thing is Dvořák's *Czech Suite* of 1879. Its five movements include a polka, a bucolic minuet, and a *furiant* finale.

furibund ('fjʊərɪbʌnd), *a.* Also 5 furybound, 6 *Sc.* furebund, 8–9 foribond. [ad. L. *furibund-us* (f. *furĕre* to rage); the earlier forms through F. *furibond.*] Furious, raging, mad.

1490 CAXTON *Eneydos* xix. 72 As a persone furybounde and furyous. **1535** STEWART *Cron. Scot.* II. 610 All in ane mynd and will, Richt furebund. **1601** B. JONSON *Poetaster* v. iii. M 3 b, [In a list of affected words] Oblatrant—Obcæcate —Furibund—Fatuate. **1669** W. SIMPSON *Hydrol. Chym.* 78 Enragements of that furibund animal the Matrix. **1755** T. H. CROKER *Orl. Fur.* XIV. cxix, Brutal, superb, audacious, furibond. **1837** CARLYLE *Fr. Rev.* I. IV. iv. (1872) 120 A waste energy as of Hercules not yet furibund. **1855** R. R. MADDEN *Life C'tess Blessington* II. 104 Strangely jocular in his furibond movements. **1880** *Standard* 16 Jan. 4 The furibund utterances of Ultramontane journalism.

†**'furibundal**, *a. Obs. rare*⁻¹. [f. as prec. + -AL¹.] = prec.

1592 G. HARVEY *Pierce's Super.* Wks. (Grosart) II. 17 The furibundall Champion of Fame.

furicane, -cana, -cano: see HURRICANE.

†**'furie**, *v. Obs.*⁻¹ [ad. OF. *furrer, fourrer* to forage.] *intr.* To search.

c **1290** *S. Eng. Leg.* I. 377/26 To furie after a Carpenter.

furied ('fjʊərɪd), *a. rare.* [f. FURY + -ED².] Having fury, furious.

1878 P. W. WYATT *Hardrada* 6 The fight Unbroken raged in its first furied might.

†**'furifuff**. *Obs. rare*⁻¹.

1689 T. PLUNKET *Char. Gd. Commander* 14 Timon Misantropos (though churl enough) I think, was better than this Furifuff.

furify ('fjʊərɪfaɪ), *v. rare.* [f. FURY + -(I)FY.] *trans.* To render furious.

1872 BROWNING *Fifine* lxxix, Some real man..must thwart And furify and set a-fizz this counterpart O' the pismire.

furi'osant, *a. Her.* [? f. FURIOUS *a.* + -ANT.] (See quot.)

1828–40 BERRY *Encycl. Her.* I, *Furiosant*, is a term applicable to the bull..and other animals, when depicted in a rage, or madness: it is also termed *rangant.*

furiosity (fjʊərɪ'ɒsɪtɪ). [ad. late L. *furiōsitāt-em*, f. *furiōsus* FURIOUS: see -ITY.]

1. The quality or state of being furious; fury; an instance of this. Now *rare.*

1509 BARCLAY *Shyp of Folys* (1570) 69 His owne madnes and cruell furiositie. **1560** ROLLAND *Crt. Venus* III. 578 We reid greit furiositie Of slauchter maid be Leui and Simeon. **1727** BAILEY vol. II, *Furiosity*, furiousness. **1894** PHIL. ROBINSON in *Monthly Packet* Feb. 152 His furiosities do not count for much.

2. Madness, *esp.* in *Sc. Law* (see quot. 1882). ***brieve of furiosity***: a BRIEVE directing an inquiry as to a person's sanity.

1432–50 tr. *Higden* (Rolls) IV. 371 After the dethe of whom, Claudius..as in furiosite, wolde say oftetymes, and inquire..why Messalina his lady come not to table. **1475** *Sc. Acts Jas. III* (1814) II. 112 þat in tyme tocum þe said brefe be reformit and a clauss put þarin to Inquere of þe foly and furiosite. **1557–75** *Diurn. Occurr.* (Bannatyne) 75 The quenis grace commandit him to pas to the castell of Edinburgh induring hir will, to appeis the furiositie foirsaid. **1707** in *Athenæum* 1 Feb. (1896) 143/1 A person, because of her Furiosity, unfitt to be dealt with according to Discipline. **1752** J. LOUTHIAN *Form of Process* (ed. 2) 286 Services of Idiotry and Furiosity to pay as General Services. **1814** SCOTT *Wav.* xii, As it is expressed in the breves of furiosity. **1868** *Act 31 & 32 Vict.* c. 100 §101 The brieves of furiosity and idiotry hitherto in use are hereby abolished. **1882** *W. Bell's Dict. Law Scotl.*, *Furiosity*, or madness, by which the judgment is prevented from being applied to the ordinary purposes of life.

‖**furioso** (furioso), *a.*, (quasi-*adv.*), and *sb.* [It.:—L. *furiōsus*: see FURIOUS *a.*]

A. *adj.* (*Music.*) See quot. 1825. Also quasi-*adv.*

1823 CRABB *Technol. Dict.*, *Furioso* (Mus.) or *con furia*, Italian, signifying furiously or with vehemence. **1825** DANNELEY *Encycl. Mus.*, *Furioso* denotes a quick movement, but principally that species of movement which requires a wildness of character in the execution.

B. *sb.* A furious person. (Also furiosa fem.)

Presumably suggested by the title of Ariosto's *Orlando Furioso.*

a **1670** HACKET *Abp. Williams* II. §202 (1693) 218 A violent Man, and a Furioso. **1710** *Age of Wonders* vi. in Wilkins *Pol. Ball.* (1860) II. 69 The furiosas of the Church Come foremost like the wind. **1726** DE FOE *Hist. Devil* II. viii. (1840) 290 He gave Oliver the protectorship, but would not let him call himself king, which stuck so close to that furioso, that the mortification spread into his soul. **1784** *Lett. to Honoria & Marianne* I. 74, I have heard one of these pitiful furioso's raving to a most amiable woman.

furious ('fjʊərɪəs), *a.* Also 4 furyus, 5–6 *Sc.* -ius, 5 *Sc.* furiouss, -eous, 5–6 furyous, 6 furiouse. [a. OF. *furieus* (mod.F. *furieux*), ad. L. *furiōsus*, f. *furia* FURY.]

1. a. Of a person, an animal, etc.: Full of fury or fierce passion; mad with anger, zeal, or the like; raging, frantic. Also of actions, attributes, utterances: Proceeding from or exhibiting fury; fierce, raging, destructively or menacingly violent.

c **1374** CHAUCER *Compl. Mars* 143 Now wol I speke of Mars, furious and wood. *c* **1430** LYDG. *Min. Poems* 157 Whan he [the lioun] is moost furious in his myhte, Ther comyth a quarteyn. **1535** COVERDALE *Ps.* vii. 6 Lift vp thyself ouer the furious indignacion of myne enemies. **1582** N. LICHEFIELD tr. *Castanheda's Conq. E. Ind.* xxxvi. 87 a, Heerevppon, they began in a furious outrage, running out of their dores like madde men. **1611** BIBLE *Ezek.* v. 15 When I shall execute iudgments in thee in anger and in furie, and in furious rebukes. **1641** in Hearne *Collect.* 15 Aug. (1706) (O.H.S.) I. 285 Yᵉ furiousest Presbyterians. **1645** MILTON *Tetrach.* To Parlt., Wks. (1847) 175/2 The furious incitements which have been us'd. **1697** DRYDEN *Virg. Georg.* III. 419 The furious Mare, Barr'd from the Male, is frantick with Despair. **1752** HUME *Ess. & Treat.* (1777) I. 62 Parties of religion are more furious. *a* **1853** ROBERTSON *Lect.* ii. (1858) 58 Furious against every one whose words make them tremble at their own insecurity. **1855** MOTLEY *Dutch Rep.* I. iii. (1866) 112 The King, already enraged, was furious at the presentation of this petition. **1863** F. A. KEMBLE *Resid. Georgia* 14, I cannot help being astonished at the furious and ungoverned execration.

b. *transf.* Of the elements: Moving with or as if moved by fury, violent, raging.

1585 T. WASHINGTON tr. *Nicholay's Voy.* III. vii. 80 If the water be too furious and deepe. **1611** SHAKS. *Cymb.* IV. ii. 259 Feare no more..the furious Winters rages. **1700** S. L. tr. *Fryke's Voy. E. Ind.* 126 It got a head after so furious a manner, that it set fire on the Ship itself. **1774** PENNANT *Tour Scotl. in 1772*, 119 From the top is a view of the furious Stream. **1799** COWPER *Castaway* iv, The furious blast. **1853** KANE *Grinnell Exp.* xxiv. (1856) 196 Blowing a furious gale.

†**c.** Of pains, diseases, evil influences: Raging, cruel. *Obs.*

c **1386** CHAUCER *Frankl. T.* 373 In langour and in torment furyus. **1430–40** LYDG. *Bochas* I. viii. (1544) 14 Folke were there blent with furious darkenes. *c* **1470** HENRY *Wallace* II. 211 In fureous payne. **1597** GERARDE *Herbal* II. li. 270 Furious agues. **1627** ABP. ABBOT *Narr.* in Rushw. *Hist. Coll.* (1659) I. 434 Some furious infirmities of Body.

d. ***fast and furious***: (of mirth) eager, uproarious, noisy. Also *advb.*, rapidly, uproariously, noisily.

1790 [see FUN *sb.*2]. **1820** SCOTT *Ivanhoe* xviii, Fast and furious grew the mirth of the parties. **1851** H. MELVILLE *Moby Dick* II. xlii. 284 He swam so fast and furious. **1859** A. ROBERTSON *Let.* 10 Feb. in R. Fulford *Dearest Child* (1964) 162 The dancing was resumed, and..they were going on at it 'fast and furious'. **1899** *Tit-Bits* 29 Apr. 103/1 Pictures came fast and furious. **1931** *Week-end Rev.* 21 Nov. 654/2 The fun is fast and furious.

2. *Hyperbolically* (after Fr. use): Excessive, extravagant. *rare.*

1668 DRYDEN *Evening's Love* III. i, What a furious indigence of ribbons is here upon my head! *Ibid.* v. i, I will do my best to disingage my Heart from this furious Tender which I have for him. **1822–56** DE QUINCEY *Confess.* (1862) 7 Without a suspicion of his own furious romancing.

3. Mad, insane. *Obs.* exc. in *Scots Law.*

1475 *Sc. Acts Jas. III* (1814) II. 112 The Inquest fyndis þat he was ouder fule or furiouss. **1564** *Child Marriages, etc.* (1897) 135 She, beinge seruaunt with the testatrix, did neuer knowe that euer she was Lunatike or furiouse. **1597** HOOKER *Eccl. Pol.* v. lxiv. §4 Neither furious persons nor children may receive any ciuill stipulation. **1609** SKENE *Reg. Maj.*, *Stat. Robt. I*, 33 Fvrious men sould be taken, and keiped be their friends. **1642** *View Print. Book int. Observat.* 10 Except the King be Captive, furious, or in his infancy. **1754** ERSKINE *Princ. Sc. Law* (1809) 66 Idiots..and furious persons cannot marry.

†**4.** Foolish, absurd. *Obs.*

1526 *Pilgr. Perf.* (W. de W. 1531) 253 b, In theyr moost furyous & false opinyon they iudged hym a dissembler and an ypocryte. **1608–11** HALL *Medit. & Vows* I. §62, I have ever found, that to strive with my superiour is furious, with my equall doubtfull.

5. *Comb.*, as ***furious-curious***, ***-faced*** adjs.; ***furious-wise*** adv.

1598 SYLVESTER *Du Bartas* II. i. iv, *Handie-Craftes* 630 Dauncing, foaming, rowling furious-wise. **1614** —— *Little Bartas* 407 The furious-curious Spell Of those Black-Artists. **1636** RUTHERFORD *Lett.* (1862) I. 174 To go through a furious faced death to life eternal!

furiously ('fjʊərɪəslɪ), *adv.* [f. prec. + -LY².]

1. With fury, in a mad or frantic manner, to an irrational degree, madly.

1555 EDEN *Decades* 2 They furiousely cryed out againste him. *c* **1610** *Women Saints* (E.E.T.S.) 46 The king raging at these wordes and full of concupiscence, furiouslie sayd vnto her [etc.]. **1611** BIBLE *Ezek.* xxiii. 25 They shall deale furiously with thee. **1751** WARBURTON *Julian* (ed. 2) I. v. 99 An inference so furiously sceptical, as would overturn the whole Body of civil history. **1849** MACAULAY *Hist. Eng.* I. 362 His scheme was..furiously attacked. **1873** BLACK *Pr. Thule* (1874) 18 To see how furiously jealous you would become. **1890** *Spectator* 11 Oct., Furiously interested classes.

2. With impetuous or boisterous motion or agitation; swiftly, violently, vehemently.

a **1577** GASCOIGNE *Dan Barthol.*, *Reporters Concl.* xix, So staies the streame, when furiouslie it flouth. **1611** BIBLE *2 Kings* ix. 20 Iehu..drieueth furiously. **1686** tr. *Chardin's Trav.* 391 The water..is furiously hot. **1700** S. L. tr. *Fryke's Voy. E. Ind.* 72 The Piece recoiled so furiously. **1758** REID tr. *Macquer's Chym.* I. 279 The Phosphorus took fire, burnt furiously, and burst the vessels. **1797** MRS. RADCLIFFE *Italian* xvi, Perceiving his master beset, he came furiously to his aid. **1840** DICKENS *Barn. Rudge* vi, Before the words had passed my lips, he rode upon me furiously. **1860** MAURY *Phys. Geog.* vi. §312 Here..the sea-breeze blows furiously. **1877** LADY BRASSEY *Voy. Sunbeam* xv. (1878) 269 Where the molten lava dashed up furiously against the rocks.

3. Excessively, 'awfully'. Cf. F. *furieusement.*

1822–56 DE QUINCEY *Confess.* (1862) 35 The lady of 1752 if living in 1800 must be furiously wrinkled.

furiousness ('fjʊərɪəsnɪs). [f. as prec. + -NESS.] The quality or state of being furious; madness, fury.

c **1500** *Melusine* xlvi. 321 Makyng..by her furyousnes suche horryble crye & noyse that it semed al thayer to be replete with thundre & tempeste. **1535** COVERDALE *Ps.* lxxvii[i]. 49 He sent vpon them yᵉ furiousnesse of his wrath. **1628** WITHER *Brit. Rememb.* III. 1125 Unlesse God had, in mercy, curb'd their furiousnesse. **1746–7** HERVEY *Medit.* (1818) 180 Instead of discharging the furiousness of his wrath upon this guilty head. **1840** in SMART; and in later Dicts.

'furison. *Obs.* exc. *Her.* [a. MDu. *vuurijzen* (Kilian *vierijzer*), f. *vuur* FIRE *sb.* + *ijzen, ijzer*, IRON. (Perh. FLEERISH is a corruption of this.)] (See quot. 1889.)

1536 BELLENDEN *Cron. Scot.* (1821) I. p. lvii, He that was found in the army but flint and furisine, or but his swerd. **1889** ELVIN *Dict. Her.*, *Furisons*, the steel used for striking fire from a flint.

furl (fɜːl), *sb.* [f. next vb.]

1. A roll, coil, or curl of any furled body.

1643 WITHER *Campo Musæ* 17 [Who] Hath taken downe, one furle of his proud sailes. **1746–7** HERVEY *Medit.* (1818) 180 Ye vernal Clouds, furls of finer air, folds of softer moisture.

2. The action of furling or state of being furled, the manner in which a sail is furled.

1836 E. HOWARD *R. Reefer* xxxii, That part of the sail.. was wanted to be rolled in with the furl. **1840** R. H. DANA *Bef. Mast* xxiii. 70 Every sailor knows that a vessel is judged of, a good deal, by the furl of her sails.

furl (fɜːl), *v.* [prob., as Prof. Skeat suggests, an alteration of FURDLE *v.*

This cannot, however, be considered certain, as *furdle* may have been due to a mixture of *furl* and *fardle*. Cf. the synonymous F. *ferler* (by Littré regarded as adopted from Eng.), also early mod.F. *fresler* (cited s.v. FRILL).]

1. *trans.* 'To roll up and bind (a sail) neatly upon its respective yard or boom' (Adm. Smyth); to roll or gather up (a flag) into small compass. Also with *up.* ***to furl in a body, the bunt*** (see *vbl. sb.* 1).

1556 W. TOWRSON in Hakluyt *Voy.* (1589) 113 Offering vs, if wee woulde, to furle his Flagges, and to be at our commaundement in all things. **1626** *Sir F. Drake revived* in Arb. *Garner* V. 500 A ship..which..had not yet furled her sprit-sail. **1647** WARD *Simp Cobler* 33 By furling up all the Ensignes. **1712** W. ROGERS *Voy.* 24 A Sailor going up to furl the Main-Top-Gallant Sail, fell. **1720** *Lond. Gaz.* No. 5917/3 They furled their Colours and began to fly. **1748** *Anson's Voy.* III. ii. (ed. 4) 413 We were full five hours in furling our sails. **1775** *Tender Father* II. 142 The method of furling up a pair of colours. **1842** TENNYSON *Locksley Hall* 127 Till..the battle-flags were furl'd In the Parliament of man. **1876** SAUNDERS *Lion in Path* vii, The fisherman furls his sail.

b. *transf.* and *fig.*

a **1657** LOVELACE *Poems* (1864) 232 All the hopes of your reward you furl. **1659** D. PELL *Impr. Sea* 318 When providence has been pleased to furle up the foggy curtains of the Heavens. **1713** *Guardian* No. 11 ¶8 She on a sudden.. furl'd her fan. **1742** *Lond. & Country Brew.* I. (ed. 4) 65 This Paper must be furled or twisted round the Bung. **1801** SOUTHEY *Thalaba* III. v, Moath furl'd the tent. **1816** SCOTT *Old Mort* xi, I hope my sister-in-law is well—furl up the bed-curtain. **1847** ALB. SMITH *Chr. Tadpole* viii. (1879) 84 The umbrella was directly furled. **1861** LYTTON & FANE *Tannhäuser* 15 But, furl'd beneath that florid surface, lurk'd A vice of nature, breeding death, not life. **1863** FR. A. KEMBLE *Resid. Georgia* 69 The eagle..furled his great wings.

†**2.** To twist or curl (hair). In quot. *absol.* Cf. FRILL *v. Obs.*

1606 SYLVESTER *Du Bartas* II. iv. II. *Magnif.* 742 One.. Combs out at length her goodly golden locks..Th'other.. Frizzles and Furls in Curls and Rings a-part.

†**b.** Of a lion: To ruffle (its mane). *Obs.*

1682 TATE *Abs. & Achit.* II. 837 [The lion] Disdaining furls his mane and tears the ground.

†**3.** To make undulations on (a surface); to furrow, wrinkle. *Obs.*

1681 CHETHAM *Angler's Vade-m.* x. §1 (1689) 98 Cloudy and windy day that furls the Water. **1742** SHENSTONE *Schoolmistr.* 261 He..furls his wrinkly front, and cries, 'What stuff is here!' *a* **1763** —— *Odes*, etc. (1765) 206 Nor bite your lip, nor furl your brow.

4. To swathe or envelope *in* or *with* something twisted or folded. Now *rare*.

1712 STEELE *Spect.* No. 53 ¶8 A Purple Canopy furled with curious Wreaths of Drapery. **1806** A. DUNCAN *Nelson's Funeral* 29 His staff tipped with silver, and furled with sarsnet. *a* **1850** ROSSETTI *Dante & Circ.* I. (1874) 184 When its flesh is furl'd Within a shroud.

5. *intr.* To become furled: to be rolled or gathered up in a spiral or twisted form; to curl *up*.

1676 *Lond. Gaz.* No. 1130/4 Her Foresail and Foretopsail furling aloft. **1686** GOAD *Celest. Bodies* I. ii. 2 It [a fog] sometimes casts it self into Threds or Ropes, and by the warmth of the Sun furls up into Gossamere. **1816** BYRON *Siege Cor.* xi, The banners drooped along their staves And as they fell around them furling. **1821** —— *Juan* III. lxxii, Her..Turkish trousers furl'd Above the prettiest ankle in the world.

b. (with *from*, *off*.) To roll away (like passing clouds). Also (*nonce-use*) of the sky, *to furl asunder*.

1814 *Prophetess* III. v, The Trojan ruins burning, and the skies Furling asunder, that the Gods may view Their dreadful warrants rig'rously fulfill'd. **1844** LOWELL *Poems, Forlorn* viii, And years of misery and sin Furl off, and leave her heaven blue. —— *Captive* v, The dread, like mist in sunshine, Furled serenely from her mind. **1859** MISS MULOCK *Romant. T.* 206 The clouds furled off from the sky.

¶**6.** Misused for *unfurl*.

1798 PENNANT *Hindoostan* II. 153 A lady..laid hold of an umbrella, and furling it full in the animal's face, terrified it so that it instantly retired.

Hence **furled** *ppl. a.* Also **'furler**, one who furls: only in comb., as *sail furler*.

a **1659** CLEVELAND *May Day* i, Why shroud Ye up your selves in the furl'd Sails of Night? *c* **1860** H. STUART *Seaman's Catech.* 45 The sailfurlers go below. **1867** SMYTH *Sailor's Word-bk.*, *Gasket*, a cord..to secure furled sails to the yard.

†**'furlength.** *Sc. Obs.* [= *furrow-length*, q.v. under FURROW.] = FURLONG.

a **1400-50** *Alexander* 2898 ȝit hase þe flode, as I fynd a furelenth of brede. *c* **1450** *Golagros & Gaw.* 1279 Ane furlenth before his folk, on feildis so faw.

furless ('fɜːlɪs), *a.* [f. FUR *sb.*[1] + -LESS.] Having no fur.

1855 GEO. ELIOT *Jrnl.* in *Life* (1884) I. 301 Though he was wrapped in fur; and we, all fur-less as we were, pitied him. **1882** MISS WOOLSON *Anne* 7 The degeneracy of the furless times.

furlet, -ot, obs. forms of FIRLOT.

furling ('fɜːlɪŋ), *vbl. sb.* [f. FURL *v.* + -ING[1].]

1. The action of the vb. *furling in a body*, *in the bunt* (see quot. 1867).

1836 E. HOWARD *R. Reefer* xxxii, That they might practise furling. **1865** MASSON *Rec. Brit. Philos.* iv. 345 The instinctive furling off..of a conceived external world of possibilities from a conscious and persisting personality. **1867** SMYTH *Sailor's Word-bk.*, *Furling in a body*, a method of rolling up a topsail..by gathering all the loose part of the sail into the top, about the heel of the topmast, whereby the yard appears much thinner and lighter than when the sail is furled in the usual manner, which is sometimes termed, for distinction sake, furling in the *bunt*.

2. *Comb.*, as *furling-system*; **furling-line**, a line or cord used in furling sails.

1626 CAPT. SMITH *Accid. Yng. Sea-men* 15 The..gassits or furling lines. **1627** —— *Seaman's Gram.* v. 22 Furling lines are small lines made fast to the top saile, top gallant saile, and the missen yards armes. **1860** *Merc. Marine Mag.* VII. 114 Captain Finlay intended to confine his furling system..to schooners. **1867** SMYTH *Sailor's Word-bk.*, *Furling-line*, a generally flat cord called a *gasket*.

furlong ('fɜːlɒŋ). Forms: 1 furlang, -ung, 2 -eng, 3-5 fur(e)lang(e, 4 ferlong, fourlonge, 4-5 for(e)lang(e, 4-6 -long(e, 4-5 fur(e)longe, 4- furlong. *Pl.* 4-5 for-, furlong. [OE. *furlang* str. neut., f. *furh*, FURROW + *lang*, LONG *a.*]

1. Originally, the length of the furrow in the common field, which was theoretically regarded as a square containing ten acres. As a lineal measure, the furlong therefore varied according to the extent assigned at various times and places to the ACRE, but was usually understood to be equal to 40 poles (rods, perches). As early as the 9th c. it was regarded as the equivalent of the Roman *stadium*, which was ⅛ of a Roman mile; and hence *furlong* has always been used as a name for the eighth part of an English mile, whether this coincided with the agricultural measure so called or not. The present statute furlong is 220 yards, and is equal both to the eighth part of a statute mile, and to the side of a square of 10 statute acres.

a. as a measure in current use. (Early examples are wanting.)

c **1330** *Arth. & Merl.* 6693 .V. forlong he dede hem recoile. **1377** LANGL. *P. Pl.* B. v. 5 Er I hadde faren a fourlonge feyntise me hente. **14..** *Sir Beues* 752 (MS. M.) Ther was no hors in the world so stronge That myght ffolowe hym a fur longe. *a* **1400-50** *Alexander* 3856 A foure furelange or fyue it was of full brede. **1470-85** MALORY *Arthur* IX. xi, Thenne he..departed his waye a furlonge. **1559** W. CUNNINGHAM *Cosmogr. Glasse* 56 There is also diversitie what a Furlong should conteine in length. **1627** CAPT. SMITH *Seaman's Gram.* x. 48 Fifteene furlongs, that is, a mile and ⅞ parts. **1653** WALTON *Angler* v. 128 For Gesner observes, the Otter smels a fish forty furlong off him in the water. **1703** MAUNDRELL *Journ. Jerus.* (1732) 15 About two furlongs out of Town. **1753** CHAMBERS *Cycl. Supp.* s.v., In Scotland the furlong is equal to forty falls. **1789** G. WHITE *Selborne* xvi. (1853) 68 This noise may be heard a furlong or more. **1814** SCOTT *Ld. of Isles* VI. xxix, The fresh and desperate onset bore The foes three furlongs back. **1847** EMERSON *Poems, Monadnoc*, His day's ride is a furlong space.

b. *Antiq.* as a rendering of L. *stadium* or Gr. *στάδιον*.

c **900** tr. *Bæda's Hist.* I. xxv. (1890) 56 Se is þreora furlunga brad. *c* **1000** *Ags. Gosp.* Luke xxiv. 13 Syxtiȝ furlanga fram hierusalem. **13..** *E.E. Allit. P.* A. 1030 Twelue [thousand] forlonge space. **1382** WYCLIF *Luke* xxiv. 13 A castel, that was fro Jerusalem in space of sixty furlongis. **1550** BALE *Image Both Ch.* III. xxi. Hhiij, A furlonge is the eyght parte of a myle and contayneth a hundreth and xxv. paces, which is in length vi. hundreth and xxv. fote. **1625-35** N. CARPENTER *Geog. Del.* I. viii. (ed. 2) 195 A Furlong contains according to Herodotus 600 feet. **1760** FAWKES *Hero & Leander* 23 *note*, The narrowest Part of the Channel is about seven Stadia, or Furlongs.

†**c.** *furlong way*: a short distance, hence the time taken in walking this, a brief space. *Obs.*

c **1384** CHAUCER *H. Fame* III. 974 Or hyt a forlonge way was olde. *c* **1386** —— *Miller's T.* 451 They sitten stille wel a furlong way. *c* **1450** *Two Cookery-bks.* II. 91 þenne take hem downe..and lete stonde a forlonge wey or ij. **1470-85** MALORY *Arthur* V. v, I had leuer..that I hadde ben a forlonge way to fore hym.

†**2.** Used (on the analogy of 1 b) to render L. *stadium* in the sense of 'the course for foot-races'. (Chiefly *fig.*) *Obs.*

The course for runners at Olympia was a stadium in length; hence the use of *στάδιον*, *stadium* in this sense.

c **1374** CHAUCER *Boeth.* IV. pr. iii. 93 (Camb. MS.) Yif a man renneþ in the stadie or in the forlong for the corone. *c* **1380** WYCLIF *Serm.* Sel. Wks. II. 258 þei þat rennen in þe ferlong for þe pris. **1450-1530** *Myrr. our Ladye* 328 After the forlonge of thys presente lyfe. **1526** *Pilgr. Perf.* (1531) 62 b, For every relygyous persone sholde renne in the forelonge of perfeccyon.

3. An area of land a 'furlong' each way, containing ten acres.

1819 REES *Cycl.* s.v., The furlong as a superficial measure, is generally 10 acres, according to the acre of different counties.

†**b.** The eighth part of an acre. *Obs.*[−0]

Perh. only a blunder of Minsheu.

1617 MINSHEU *Ductor*, *Furlong*..is otherwise the eight part of an acre. **1656-81** in BLOUNT *Glossogr.*

4. The headland of a common field. *Obs.* exc. *dial.*

?**854** *Charter of Æthelwolf of Wessex* in *Cod. Dipl.* V. 111 Of twelf æceran ut forð bufon scortan hlince æt ðæs furlanges ende. **1649** BLITHE *Eng. Improv. Impr.* (1652) 10 One Furlong butting or Hadlanding upon other Furlongs. **1877** *N.W. Linc. Gloss.*, *Furlong*, the road or boundary upon which the separate lots abut in an 'open field' or piece of unenclosed ground divided into several occupations.

5. An indefinite division of an unenclosed field.

12.. *Newminster Cartul.* (1878) 122 Usque ad Gauelok furlang. **1377** LANGL. *P. Pl.* B. v. 424, I can fynde in a felde or in a fourlonge an hare. **1438** *Nottingham Rec.* II. 170 Quinta acra jacet super eundem furlong. [But is this 4?] **1523** FITZHERB. *Surv.* 38 b, At a furlong called Dale furlong yᵉ whiche furlong conteyneth .xxx. landes and two heed landes. **1637** HARRISON in *Sheffield Gloss.*, A piece of land enclosed lying in furlongs. *a* **1825** FORBY *Voc. E. Anglia*, *Furlong*, a division of an uninclosed cornfield. **1839** STONEHOUSE *Axholme* 302 Two selions of land containing one acre, lying in a furlong called Foxholes. **1854** MISS BAKER *Northampt. Gloss.*, *Furlong*, an indefinite number of lands or leys, running parallel to each other.

6. = LAND. (See quot. 1893.) *Obs.* exc. *dial.*

1660 SHARROCK *Vegetables* 97 The land must be cast into furlongs, that the furrows may convey the water one to another into a general trench. **1893** *Wiltsh. Gloss.*, *Furlong*.. the strip of newly-ploughed land lying between two main furrows.

7. 'The line of direction of plowed lands' (Marshall).

1787 W. MARSHALL *Norfolk* I. (1795) 131 Endeavouring to lay their 'furlongs' north-and-south, that the sun may have an equal influence on either side the narrow ridges.

furlough ('fɜːləʊ), *sb.* Forms: 7 vorloffe, foreloofe, forloff, furloff, -ogh, 7, 9 furlo, 8 furloe, foreloff, 7-9 furlow, 7- furlough. [a. Du. *verlof*, app. formed in imitation of Ger. *verlaub*, f. *ver-* FOR- *pref.*[1] + root *laub-*: see BELIEVE *v.*, LEAVE *sb.*[1] Cf. Da. *forlov*, Sw. *förlof*. The Eng. word, having from the beginning been stressed on the first syll., seems to show influence of the synonymous Du. *oorlof*, = Ger. *urlaub* (OHG., MHG. *urloup*), abstract noun corresp. to the OTeut. vb. **izlaubôjan*, *-laubjan* to give leave, allow (Goth. *uslaubjan*, OHG. *irloubôn*, mod.G. *erlauben*, OE. *āliefan*): see A- *pref.*[1] and LEAVE *sb.*[1]]

1. Leave of absence, esp. a permit or licence given to a soldier (or more rarely, an official) to be absent from duty for a stated time.

1625 B. JONSON *Stable of N.* v. i, The deed..is a thing of greater consequence, Then to be borne about in a blacke boxe, Like a Low-Countrey vorloffe, or Welsh-briefe. **1637** R. MONRO *Exped.* I. 34 The Lievetenant Colonell taking a fore-loofe, did go unto Holland. **1649** G. DANIEL *Trinarch.*, *Hen. V*, clxxxii, They'd feigned Furloghs, of Sloth, or Feare. **1707** FARQUHAR *Recruiting Officer* I. i, Enter him a grenadier..absent on furlow. **1749** *MS. Desp.* 14 Nov., *Bd. of Trade, S. Carolina* T. 68 In Charlestown living on the license of your Excellency's third foreloff. **1772** *Ann. Reg.* 198/1 Maclauchlan..was sent off upon a furlow for three months. **1804** WELLINGTON in Gurw. *Desp.* III. 41 Officers not on furlough..are to join their corps without delay. **1835** MARRYAT *Jac. Faithf.* xxxvi, My uncle James came home on furlough, for he held a very high and lucrative situation under the Company. **1893** FORBES-MITCHELL *Remin. Gt. Mutiny* 71 Over fifty men..were found to have furloughs, or leave-certificates..in their pockets.

attrib. **1845** STOCQUELER *Handbk. Brit. India* (1854) 51 The salaries are large..the furlough allowance and retiring annuity handsome and all-sufficient. **1876** *Voyle's Milit. Dict.* (ed. 3) s.v. *Furlough*, The furlough pay is as follows.

fig. **1816-7** COLERIDGE *Lay Serm.* 378 One of those short furloughs from the service of the body, which the soul may sometimes obtain even in this, its militant state.

b. extended to general use.

1763 COWPER *Let.* 9 Aug. Wks. (1876) 5 My destination is settled at last, and I have obtained a furlough. **1793** MAD. D'ARBLAY *Lett.* 22 Feb., You..could not refuse to her request the week's furlough. **1843** LEFEVRE *Life Trav. Phys.* I 1. vii. 158, I..demanded a furlough of a fortnight, to enable me to see my friends in England. **1848** KINGSLEY *Saint's Trag.* I. i, Would but her saintship leave her gold behind, We'd give herself her furlough.

†**2.** A passport; a licence, or permit.

a **1659** CLEVELAND *Wks.* (1687) 7 The greatest Honours on the aged hurl'd Are but gay Furlows for another World. **1826** SCOTT *Woodst.* ii, Or what else will your uncle Everard do for us? Get us a furlough to beg?

furlough ('fɜːləʊ), *v.* Chiefly *U.S.* [f. prec.]

1. *trans.* To grant (a person) a furlough; to give leave of absence to.

1783 N. GREENE in Sparks *Corr. Amer. Rev.* (1853) IV. 38 The Northern Army does not choose to be furloughed. **1799** G. WASHINGTON *Lett.* Writ. 1893 XIV. 208 The practice of furloughing officers, and then renewing the furloughs from time to time. **1867** EMERSON *May-Day & Other Pieces* Wks. (Bohn) III. 423 Amid the hue and cry Of scholars furloughed from their tasks. **1869** LOWELL *Cathedral* 236 With outward senses furloughed.

2. *intr.* To spend a furlough.

1892 *Black & White* Christm. No. 31/2 The unsteady white gaiters of two Grenadiers furloughing in the village.

furloughed ('fɜːləʊd), *ppl. a.* [f. FURLOUGH *sb.* or *v.* + -ED.] Having a furlough or leave of absence; hence, unoccupied, inactive.

1811 W. R. SPENCER *Poems* 5 Ten thousand furlow'd Heroes. **1848** LOWELL *Biglow P.* Poems 1890 II. 23 She.. Patted the furloughed ferule on her palm. **1864** *Daily Tel.* 26 Nov., All furloughed officers and men have been ordered to return immediately.

†**'furmage.** *Obs. rare.* [a. OF. *fourmage* (mod.F. *fromage*):—popular L. **formāticum*, f. *forma* mould, FORM.] Cheese.

14.. HENRYSON *Two Myss* 124 Bannatyne MS. VII. (1881) 963 Furmag full fyne scho brocht in steid of geill.

furme, obs. form of FORM.

furmente, -ty, furmety, -ity: see FRUMENTY.

furnace ('fɜːnɪs), *sb.* Forms: 3 furneise, 4-5 f(o)urneys(e, fo(u)rnays(e, fournas, fornayce, fornes, (5 fornas, furnasee), 4-6 forneys(e, f(o)urneis, furnes(s, (5 furnoys, 6 furneyse, fournes), 6-7 fornace, (6 fournace, furnise), 6- furnace. [a. OF. *fornais*, masc. (= Pr. *fornatz*, *fornaz*, It. *fornace*), also *fornaise* (mod.F. *fournaise*, = Sp. *hornaza*), repr. L. *fornāc-em*, *fornax*, fem., f. *forn-us*, *furn-us*, oven.]

1. a. An apparatus consisting essentially of a chamber to contain combustibles for the purpose of subjecting minerals, metals, etc. to the continuous action of intense heat.

In modern use it chiefly denotes a building of masonry lined with firebrick, used for metallurgical operations, the baking of pottery, or the like; but it is also applied to smaller apparatus (usually constructed of iron) used in chemistry, assaying, etc.

a **1225** *Juliana* 32 As þu..te þreo children..biwistest unwemmet from þe ferliche fur of þe furneise. *a* **1340** HAMPOLE *Psalter* xvi. 4 þe fournas þat purges metall. **1382** WYCLIF *Matt* vi. 30 The heye of the feeld, that to day is, and to morwe is sente in to the fourneyse. **1413** *Pilgr. Sowle* (Caxton 1483) III. vii. 55 With fyre pykes they cast them in the forneis. **1535** COVERDALE *Prov.* xvii. 3 Like as syluer is tried in the fire and golde in the fornace. **1544** PHAER *Regym. Lyfe* (1553) I iij b, Baken or dryed as clay is in the fourneis. **1600** SHAKS. *A.Y.L.* II. vii. 148 The Louer, Sighing like Furnace. **1664** EVELYN *Kal. Hort.* (1729) 229 A plain single Furnace, (such as Chymists use in their Laboratories for common Operations). **1725** DE FOE *Voy. round World* (1840) 272 Running like liquid metal out of a furnace. **1837** WHITTOCK, etc. *Bk. Trades* (1842) 130 The furnaces, retorts and other apparatus are too numerous to be described. **1872** ELLACOMBE *Ch. Bells Devon* i. 11 On the signal being given, the furnaces were tapped, and the metal flowed.

b. *transf.* The fire of a volcano; the volcano itself.

1660 F. BROOKE tr. *Le Blanc's Trav.* 376 One of the most conspicuous furnaces of the Indies..for the hill..hath five mouths..for casting out fire. **1796** H. HUNTER tr. *St. Pierre's Stud. Nat.* (1799) I. 344 Volcanos must have emitted their fiery currents more frequently in the earlier ages, when..the Ocean, loaded with it's vegetable spoils, supplied more abundant matter to their furnaces. **1804** C. B. BROWN tr. *Volney's View Soil U.S.* 99 The existence of this furnace agrees with all the traces of earthquakes hitherto mentioned.

c. *fig.*, esp. used to express any severe test or trial. Also, a place of excessive heat; a 'hotbed'.

1340 *Ayenb.* 131 þise wordle þet ne is bote..a fornays anhet mid uer of zenne and of zorȝe. **1382** WYCLIF *Deut.* iv. 20 The Lord took ȝow, and ladde ȝow oute fro the yren forneys of Egipte. **1497** BP. ALCOCK *Mons Perfect.* C iij, He lyved here in purgatory and in the fornays of temptacyon. **1600** FAIRFAX *Tasso* xv. l, He..open set Of his broad gaping iawes the fornace wide. **1611** BIBLE *Isa.* xlviii. 10, I haue chosen thee in the fornace of affliction. **1727–46** THOMSON *Summer* 962 Breathed hot From all the boundless furnace of the sky..A suffocating wind the pilgrim smites With instant death. **1844** KINGLAKE *Eöthen* xxiv. 320 Nablous is the very furnace of Mahometan bigotry.

†**2.** Applied to an oven or chamber for producing a moderate continuous heat; in quots. an incubating chamber. *Obs.*

c **1400** MAUNDEV. (1839) v. 49 There is a comoun Hows in that Cytee, that is alle ffulle of smale Furneys; and thidre bryngen Wommen of the Toun here Eyren of Hennes, of Gees and of Dokes, for to ben put in to tho Furneyses. **1585** T. WASHINGTON tr. *Nicholay's Voy.* I. viii. 7 b, Furnaces, made in maner like unto..stoves of Germanie in the whiche with a small heate they do..hatch their egges. **1616** [see FURNER 1].

3. A closed fireplace for heating a building by means of hot-air or hot-water pipes; also, 'the fireplace of a marine boiler' (Adm. Smyth).

1691 EVELYN *Diary* 28 Dec., Saw the effect of my greenhouse furnace. **1881** FAWKES *Horticult. Build.* 218 Stoke-holes, furnaces, and boilers, should always be protected by an enclosed shed from rain and wind.

4. A boiler, cauldron, crucible. *Obs.* exc. *dial.* (See quots. 1884 and 1886.)

c **1290** *S. Eng. Leg.* I. 295/61 A forneis he let maken of bras: and fullen it ful of led. **13..** *E.E. Allit. P.* B. 1011 As a fornes ful of flot þat vpon fyr boyles. *c* **1400** *Lanfranc's Cirurg.* 171 Þe heete of þe lyvere makiþ þe stomac to seþe as fier makiþ a furneis to seþe. **1494** *Nottingham Rec.* III. 30 Unum fornes de plumbo. **1540** *Yatton Churchw. Acc.* (Som. Rec. Soc.) 154 To sawyng yᵉ quyrbys to yᵉ Furnes of Chyrche howse vjᵈ. *a* **1661** FULLER *Worthies* (1840) III. 486 Seethe all these [herbs] (being well washed) in a furnace of fair water. **1884** *Upton on Severn Gloss.*, *Furnace*, a large boiler set in brickwork, for brewing, making soup, &c. **1886** *W. Somerset Gloss.*, Galvanized iron Furnace, 27 gals...11*s.* 9*d.*

5. *attrib.* and *Comb.*, as ***furnace air-pipe, -chink, -coke, -feeder, -filler, -fire, -firer, -glow, -heat, -house, -smoke; furnace-burning, -like*** adjs.; ***furnace-ward*** adv. Also **furnace-bar** = *fire-bar* (see FIRE B. 5); **furnace-bridge** (see quot.); **furnace cadmia** or **cadmium** (see quot.); **furnace-drift**, †**-earth** (see quots.); **furnace line**, a line in a furnace spectrum; **furnaceman**, one who tends a furnace; **furnace-pumice** *Metall.*, 'a slag often produced in smelting pisolitic iron ores, having the cellular appearance of pumice-stone' (Cassell); **furnace spectrum**, the spectrum of the light emitted by a substance when heated in an electric furnace; **furnace-tube** (see quot.).

1664 EVELYN *Kal. Hort.* (1729) 231 The *Furnace Air-pipes..are placed to pass through the Fire and Brick-work. **1888** *Lockwood's Dict. Mech. Engin.*, **Furnace Bars.* **1874** KNIGHT *Dict. Mech.* I. 926/2 **Furnace-Bridge*, a barrier of fire-bricks or of iron plates containing water thrown across the furnace at the extreme end of the fire-bars, to prevent the fuel being carried into the flues, and to quicken the draft by contracting the area. **1593** SHAKS. *3 Hen. VI*, II. i. 80 All my bodies moysture Scarse serues to quench my *Furnace-burning hart. **1881** RAYMOND *Mining Gloss.*, **Furnace cadmium* or *cadmia*, the oxide of zinc which accumulates in the chimneys of furnaces smelting zinciferous ores. *a* **1849** MANGAN *Poems* (1859) 35 That the flame, with subtle flood, Through the *furnace-chink may fly. **1889** *Daily News* 16 Dec. 2/7 This week *furnace coke has been selling at 22*s.* 6*d.* to 23*s.* per ton at the ovens. **1892** *Northumbld. Gloss.*, **Furnace-drift*, a passage leading into an 'upcast' pit provided with a furnace for the purpose of ventilating the mine. **1612** STURTEVANT *Metallica* (1854) 114 *Furnace-earths..where-withall you build up your Furnaces. **1858** SIMMONDS *Dict. Trade*, **Furnace-feeder*, a stoker or fireman; one who supplies fuel to the furnace. **1892** *Labour Commission* Gloss., **Furnace Fillers*, men who remain at the top of the furnace and empty therein the loaded barrows sent up from the bottom. *c* **1645** HOWELL *Lett.* I. xxix. 41 If this small *furnace-fire hath vertue to convert such a small lump of Dark Dust and Sand into such a precious clear Body as Crystal. **1889** *Daily News* 4 Dec. 5/6 A *furnace firer..stated that [etc.]. **1863–65** J. THOMSON *Sunday at Hampstead* vi, The East resumes its *furnace-glow. **1849** E. E. NAPIER *Excurs. S. Africa* II. 407 Alternate *furnace heat and chilly dampness. **1882** OUIDA *In Maremma* I. 62 A *furnace-house to make the salt that was raked upon the beach. **1577** B. GOOGE *Heresbach's Husb.* II. (1586) 77 b. The Furrow must be made *Furnase like, straight aboue, and broade in the bottome. **1825** HEBER *Narrative* (1828) III. 33 Such a furnace-like climate. **1911** *Contribs. Mt. Wilson Solar Observ.* III. 6 The quality of the *furnace lines for measurement is in general good. **1922** A. S. EDDINGTON in *Encycl. Brit.* XXX. 298/2 The 'enhanced lines' of strontium 4077 and 4215 are relatively strong in stars of high luminosity; whereas the 'furnace lines' of strontium 4607 and calcium 4455 behave in the reverse manner. **1883** GRESLEY *Gloss. Coal Mining*, **Furnaceman.* **1884** *B'ham Daily Post* 23 Feb. 3/5 Wanted two little Mill Furnacemen. **1797** *College* 20 Like *furnace-smoke in volumes rolling down. [**1905** *Astrophys. Jrnl.* XXI. 256 The oven spectrum shows new groups of bands in the spectra of Ca, Sr, Ba, and Cu.] **1911** *Contribs. Mt. Wilson Solar Observ.* 16 The..strong lines..are given by the core of the arc, and appear in the *furnace spectrum very faintly at the highest temperatures. **1943** *Astrophys. Jrnl.* XCVIII. 33 For the furnace spectrum, dysprosium was vaporized in the carbon-tube vacuum furnace at a temperature near 2600°C. **1888** *Lockwood's Dict. Mech. Engin.*, **Furnace-tube*, the tube within which the fuel is enclosed in an internally fired boiler. *c* **1420** *Pallad. on Husb.* I. 1087 First floore hit ij feet thicke enclynynge softe The *fourneis ward.

furnace ('fɜːnɪs), *v.* [f. prec. sb.]

1. a. *trans.* To exhale like a furnace. **b.** *intr.* To issue as from a furnace.

1598 CHAPMAN *Achilles Shield* Ep. Ded. A iv b, That raging vlcer, which..Furnaceth the vniuersall sighes and complaintes of this transposed world. **1607** SHAKS. *Cor.* I. vi. 66 He furnaces The thicke sighes from him. **1624** QUARLES *Div. Poems, Sion's Sonn.* xx, Represse those flames, that furnace from thine eye.

2. *trans.* To subject to the heat of a furnace.

1612 [see the vbl. sb.]. **1842** T. GRAHAM *Chem.* v. 474 It has been proposed, instead of furnacing the sulphate of soda, to decompose it by caustic barytes. **1876** *Catal. Sci. App. S. Kens.* No. 2726 This mixture is furnaced during a period of 5⅝ hours.

fig. **1790** J. WILLIAMS *Shrove Tuesday* (1794) 33 The faithful must be damn'd before they die, And, like th' asbestos, furnac'd to be white. **1848** LOWELL *Fable for Critics* Poet. Wks. 1890 III. 50 Every word that he speaks has been fierily furnaced In the blast of a life that has struggled in earnest.

3. To make a furnace in.

1833 [see CHIMNEY *v.* 1].

Hence **'furnaced** *ppl. a.*, in quot. *fig.*; **'furnacing** *vbl. sb.*, also *attrib.* Also **'furnacer**.

1612 STURTEVANT *Metallica* (1854) 58 All kinde of ouens, lamps, stoues, kilnes, hearths, all which we generally comprehend vnder the name of Furnacing. *Ibid.* 59 Furnacing may be briefly touched as being a necessarie instrument in most Inuentions. **1853** URE *Dict. Arts* II. 680 The dexterous management of this transposition characterizes a good soda-furnacer. **1862** H. C. KENDALL *Fainting by Way* 5 Poems 20 Furnaced waste lands..like to stony billows rolled. **1869** —— *Glen of Arrawatta* 167 In soft Australian nights; And through the furnaced noons. **1880** J. LOMAS *Alkali Trade* 4 The manufacturer should be..able..to..perform the furnacing operation himself.

'furnage. *Obs.* exc. *Hist.* Forms: 4–8 **fornage**, (6 **firnage**), 5– **furnage**. [a. OF. *fornage* (F. *fournage*), f. OF. *forn* (F. *four*):—L. *furn-us* oven.] **a.** The process of baking; the price paid for baking. **b.** *Feudal Law.* (See quot. 1753; the interpretation is justified by the med.Lat. quots. in Du Cange s.v. *Furnagium.*)

1468 in *Stow's Surv. Lond.* (ed. Strype 1754) II. 443/1 The Baker shall be allowed..two Lofis for Fornage. *a* **1470** TIPTOFT *Cæsar* v. (1530) 7 They shulde haue no corne to furnage. **1572** in Nichols *Progr. Q. Eliz.* II. 48 Wood for firnage of breed by the yere. **1601** F. TATE *Househ. Ord. Edw. II*, §43 (1876) 26 This serjant shal take for fornage of pain de main for the kinges mouth. **1676–1732** in COLES. **1753** CHAMBERS *Cycl. Supp.*, *Fornage*, the fee taken by a lord from his tenants, bound to bake in the lord's oven, or for a permission to use their own. **1875** *Sussex Gloss.*, *Furnage*, a sum formerly paid by the tenants of the Lord of the manor for right to bake in his oven. **1882** A. W. ALEXANDER *Preston Guilds* 6 A burgess may make an oven upon his grounds, and bake for his furnage for one horse load of flour or meal, one halfpenny.

attrib. **1851** TURNER *Dom. Archit.* II. iii. 112 A seignorial oven in which all the tenants were obliged to bake their bread and pay furnage dues.

furner ('fɜːnə(r)). *Obs.* exc. *dial.* Also 5–6 furnour, 7 furnar. [late ME. *furnour*, ad. OF. *fornier*:—late L. *furnārius*, f. *furn-us* oven.]

1. One who has charge of an oven; a baker.

a **1483** *Liber Niger* in *Househ. Ord.* (1790) 70 One yoman furnour also in this office [the Bakehouse] making the weyght of brede. **1555** *Will of T. Clayton* (Somerset Ho.), To Christofer Strongman my furnour xx*s.* **1612** STURTEVANT *Metallica* (1854) 117 Glasse windowes..so that thereby the Furnar may continually see and behold his Rawe-matters..and how his fire and Furnace worketh upon them. **1616** *Trav. Eng. Pilgr.* in *Harl. Misc.* I. 338 The country people bring their eggs..to this place, where there is an oven, or furnace, purposely kept temperately warm; and the furner, or master thereof standeth ready at a little door, to receive the eggs. **1736** LEWIS *Hist. Isle Tenet* (ed. 2) 36 *Furner*, a baker. **1887** *Kent Gloss.*, *Furner*, a baker.

2. (See quots.)

1598 FLORIO, *Bisciere*, a furner or a maulkin. **1847–78** HALLIWELL, *Furner*, a malkin for an oven. *Linc.*

†**'furney,** *v. Obs.* In 4 **furneye**. [ad. OF. *furni-r*: see next.] *trans.* To procure.

13.. *Coer de L.* 5517 Furneye a tree, styff and strong.

†**'furniment.** *Obs.* Also 6 **f(o)urnyment**, (**furnament**). [ad. OF. *fourniment*, f. *fournir* to FURNISH.] **a.** The state or condition of being furnished. **b.** *pl.* Accoutrements, decorations, fittings.

1553 BRENDE *Q. Curtius* III. 14 Neither the men nor the horse..glistered..with golde nor precyous furnymentes. **1561** T. HOBY tr. *Castiglione's Covrtyer* (1577) S ij a, I wyll not haue the Courtier bereaued from hys due honoure and the fournymentes whiche you youre selfe promised hym yesternyght. **1596** SPENSER *F.Q.* IV. iii. 38 They spyde with speedie whirling pace One in a charet of straunge furniment.

furnish ('fɜːnɪʃ), *sb.* [f. next vb.] †**a.** A furnishing or providing; *concr.* a provision or stock of anything (*obs.*). †**b.** The state of being furnished or fitted (*obs.*). **c.** *colloq.* A setting off or embellishing.

1500 *Will of Treffry* (Somerset Ho.), A Furnyssh of bras. **1604** DANIEL *Funeral Poem Earl Devonsh.*, That furnish perfect held. **1613–21** —— *Hist. Eng.* 169 He sends him a whole Furnish of all Vessels for his Chamber of cleane gold. **1617** *Greene's Groat's W. Wit* A 3, To lend the world a furnish of witte, she lays her owne to pawne. **1633** J. DONE *Hist. Septuagint* 115 Very liberall..chiefly to have in regard the Furnish for these grave and reverent Persons. *Ibid.* 179 Furniture for the whole furnish of a chamber. **1896** *Daily News* 7 Mar. 6/3 The chin..is often the better for the 'furnish' of the strings.

d. The materials from which paper is manufactured.

1920 CROSS & BEVAN *Paper-Making* 374 The characters of these sorted rags are taken into account in the composition of the paper-maker's furnish. **1929** *Penrose's Ann.* XXXI. 99 A good proportion of cotton and/or linen in the furnish of a paper, as well as high chemical purity, are essential for durability. **1969** M. KILBY *Write on Both Sides* i. 31 'Depends what furnish you're working to.' 'Furnish?' 'That's what we call the formula of a paper.'

furnish ('fɜːnɪʃ), *v.* Forms: 5–6 **fourn-, furnis(s)he, -ys(s)he**, (6 **fornyssh, furnesshe, -ice**), 6–7, 9 *Sc.* **furneis, -ess, -ich, -ise, -yse**. [a. OF. *furniss-* lengthened stem of *furnir*, also *fornir*, *fournir* (F. *fournir*) = Pr., Sp., Pg. *fornir*, It. *fornire*, app. a Com. Rom. alteration of an earlier **formire*, **fromire* (Pr. *formir, furmir, fromir*), ad. WGer. **frummjan* (OS. *frummian*, OHG. *frummen*, MHG, *vrümen*) to further, promote, accomplish, supply, f. **frum-* (as in OHG., OS. *fruma* fem., profit, advantage) ablaut-var. of **fram-* forward: see FROM.]

†**1.** *trans.* To accomplish, complete, fulfil. Also with *that* and obj. clause: To bring about, ensure.

c **1477** CAXTON *Jason* 87, I shall not departe me but that I shal furnisshe myn auowe. *c* **1489** —— *Blanchardyn* ix. (1890) 39 The knyght..shewed hym the waye that he muste holde for to furnysshe his entrepryse. *Ibid.* xxxiv. 126 For to see and furnysshe that this were doon. **1494** FABYAN *Chron.* lxxxiv. 62 To furnysshe or perfourme the Story of Vortiger. *c* **1500** *Melusine* xx. 111 Behighte no thing but that ye may fournysshe & hold it. *a* **1533** LD. BERNERS *Huon* lxxxi. 245, I sawe that I hadde furnysshed your message. **1551** ROBINSON tr. *More's Utop.* I. (1895) 212 A man maye see..furnished..those thinges whiche husbande-men doo commenly in other countreys.

†**2. a.** To fill, occupy, garrison (a place, etc.). Const. *of, with*, also simply. *Obs.*

c **1500** *Three Kings' Sons* (E.E.T.S.) 33 The houses were all fornyssht with folkes. **1523** LD. BERNERS *Froiss.* I. xxxviii. 52 The cyte was strong, and well furnysshed of men a warr. **1526** *Househ. Ord.* 153 There shall be a boord..furnished with lords spirituall and temporal. **1533** CRANMER in Furniv. *Ballads fr. MSS.* I. 384 Four rich charettes, one of them empty, & three other furnished with divers ancient old ladies. **1596** DALRYMPLE tr. *Leslie's Hist. Scot.* x. 278 The Gouernour commandes to furnice the castell of Edʳ. be al meines. **1692** RAY *Dissol. World* Pref. (1732) 11 A World already filled & furnished.

b. To fill, occupy (a position); also with *out*.

1576 FLEMING *Panopl. Epist.* 257 There is a place voide and to be furnished. **1583** GOLDING *Calvin on Deut.* xviii. 108 That they haue neede to be instructed or els that they cannot furnish out the place to performe their dutie.

†**3.** To supply, provide for (needs, occasions, expenses). *Obs.*

1496 in *Ld. Treas. Acc. Scotl.* (1877) I. 304 Item..giffin..to furnys Margret Drummondis costis in Linlithquho. **1555** L. SAUNDERS in Coverdale *Lett. Mart.* (1564) 191 My need concerning bodely necessaryes is..furnyshed by Gods provision. **1666** MARVELL *Corr.* lii. Wks. 1872–5 II. 192 The House is much in earnest to furnish his Majestye's present occasions.

4. a. To provide or supply *with* (something necessary, useful, or desirable, either material or immaterial). †Also const. *in* (cf. FIND *v.* 19), *of*.

1529 WOLSEY in *Four C. Eng. Lett.* 10 Of evry thyng mete for houssold vnprovydyd and furnyshyd. *a* **1533** LD. BERNERS *Huon* xlvi. 154 Whan the shyppe was fournyshyd with vytaylles, than he put therin his horses. **1550** CROWLEY *Way to Wealth* 326 Let your wiues..furnishe them selues with al pointes of honest housewifery. **1553** BRENDE *Q. Curtius* x. 5 To furnish them of iron, hemp and sails. **1596** DALRYMPLE tr. *Leslie's Hist. Scot.* v. 301 Scotland had furnist Jngland in all necessaries to the Weiris. **1610** SHAKS. *Temp.* II. ii. 147 Come, sweare to that: kisse the Booke: I will furnish it anon with new Contents. **1625** PURCHAS *Pilgrims* II. IX. xv. §9. 1600 Parmezan, of which the Bailo of Venice doth alwayes furnish them. **1674** N. COX *Gentl. Recreat.* III. (1677) 38 Ending at May, at which time the Trees begin to be furnished with leaves. **1700** WALLIS in *Collect.* (O.H.S.) I. 319 A man may be furnished with genteel accomplishment. **1754** ERSKINE *Princ. Sc. Law* (1809) 18 An inhabitant..who has furnished one..in meat, clothes, or other merchandise. **1772** MACKENZIE *Man World* II. iv. (1823) 470 There was too much innocence in the breast of Lucy, to suffer it to be furnished with disguise. **1849** MACAULEY *Hist. Eng.* I. 638 The officers..had orders to furnish him with whatever military aid he might require. **1875** JOWETT *Plato* (ed. 2) V. 192 He [Plato] has furnished us with the instruments of thought.

†**b.** *intr.* for *refl.* To provide oneself *with* (something). *Obs.*

1631 NATH. WARD *Let.* in *Simp. Cobler* (1843) 93. I expect measure hard enough and must furnish apace with proportionable armour.

c. (Chiefly in *pass.*) To provide (an instrument, organ, etc.) *with* (some appendage subsidiary to its function).

1799 G. SMITH *Laboratory* I. 15 Rockets may be both within and without furnished with crackers. **1816** J. SMITH *Panorama Sc. & Art* II. 352 Each of the bladders should be furnished with a stopcock. **1830** R. KNOX *Béclard's Anat.* 19 Bones..which..are furnished with a great mass of muscles. **1886** A. WINCHELL *Walks & Talks Geol. Field* 252 The..tail of this bird..is furnished with proper quills.

5. †**a.** *simply.* To supply with what is necessary.

1596 SHAKS. *Merch. V.* II. iv. 9 'Tis now but foure of clock, we haue two houres To furnish vs. **1611** BIBLE *Ps.* lxxviii. 19 Can God furnish a table in the wildernes? **1633** J. DONE *Hist. Septuagint* 76 It is succoured and furnished by the neerenesse of the Port of Ascalon [etc.]. **1668** CULPEPPER & COLE *Barthol. Anat.* Man. II. iii. 318 The outer [branch]..furnishes the Cheeks and Muscles of the Face. **1688** R. HOLME *Armoury* III. 185/1 The Abbots Table must be furnished for Strangers. **1743** *Lond. & Country Brew.* II. (ed. 2) 93 The English..thinking themselves compleatly furnished by Barley and Oat-Malt-Liquors, have supinely neglected the Improvement of the best of all others.

†**b.** To decorate, embellish. *Obs.*

1599 SHAKS. *Much Ado* III. i. 103 Ile shew thee some attires, and haue thy counsell, Which is the best to furnish me tomorrow. **1690** HALIFAX *Epist. Earl Dorset* 185 The wounded Arm wou'd furnish all their Rooms, And bleed for ever Scarlet in the Looms.

c. in *Hop-growing.* (See quot.)

1848 *Jrnl. R. Agric. Soc.* IX. II. 555 It is not..necessary for the hop-tiers to wait until there are three bines for every pole long enough to tie, that is, for the hills to furnish, as they term it..When every pole furnished with three bines pull the remainder out of the hills. *Ibid.* 556, I have known bine that has been kept back..by cold weather..so as not to furnish the poles before the middle of June.

†**6.** *esp.* To prepare for work or active service; to equip (a person), caparison, harness (a horse), fit up (a weapon, etc.), fit out (a ship). *Obs.*

1548 *Privy Council Acts* (1890) II. 197 Hand-goones furnesshed, cc. **1577** HANMER *Anc. Eccl. Hist.* v. ix. (1619) 494 Chosroes, being now furnished to battell. **1591** SHAKS. *1 Hen. VI*, IV. i. 39 He then, that is not furnish'd in this sort, Doth but vsurpe the Sacred name of Knight. **1596** DALRYMPLE tr. *Leslie's Hist. Scot.* IX. 242 How sune the schip was now furniched, sayle thay lous. **1598** BARRET *Theor. Warres* II. i. 18 He shall not suffer any souldier to come thither without his Armes fully furnished. **1607** TOPSELL *Four-f. Beasts* (1658) 244 Bucephalus..being sadled and furnished..could endure none but Alexander. **1657** R. LIGON *Barbadoes* (1673) 22 Far better..to purchase a Plantation there ready furnish'd. **1684** BUNYAN *Pilgr.* II. 34 There is sufficient to furnish them against all attempts whatsoever. **1703** MAUNDRELL *Journ. Jerus.* (1732) 127 Six led Horses, all of excellent shape, and nobly furnish'd. **1725** DEFOE *Voy. round World* (1840) 2 Every sailor is able to do it if his merchants are but qualified to furnish him for so long a voyage.

7. To fit up (an apartment, a house) with all requisite appliances, including a supply of movable 'furniture' (see FURNITURE 7), which in mod. use is the predominant notion.

[**1611** BIBLE *Luke* xxii. 12 He shall shew you a large vpper roume furnished. (Strictly to sense 5)] **1650** EVELYN *Mem.* (1857) I. 270 A stately chamber furnished to have entertained a prince. **1762** H. WALPOLE *Vertue's Anecd. Paint.* I. i. 2 The apartments are lofty and enormous and they knew not how to furnish them. **1838** THIRLWALL *Greece* V. xli. 159 He had taken more pains to furnish his house, than his mind. **1874** MICKLETHWAITE *Mod. Par. Churches* 342 A church may be furnished, as well as built, by degrees.

absol. **1837** HOOK in *Life* I. 407 My lady is very busy a-furnishing.

8. To provide, contribute, afford, supply, yield.

The general currency of this sense appears to date from the 18th c., and is perh. due to mod. Fr. influence. The Sc. instances (16–17th c.) quoted below may belong to 6.

[**1563** WINȜET *Wks.* (1890) II. 6, I may nocht furnise to this excellent werk euery kind of necessar waippin. **1640–1** *Kirkcudbr. War-Comm. Min. Bk.* (1855) 142 The Committie finding that Johne Wilsone, runaway, in Crocemichael, is unable to goe upon service..ordaines the said paroche of Crocemichael to furneis ane uther in his place.] **1754** SHERLOCK *Disc.* (1759) I. iii. 110 Philosophy has furnished Difficulties on every Side. **1759** GOLDSM. *Bee* No. 5 *Unfort. Merit* ¶9 The host..refused to furnish him a dinner without previous payment. **1790** BURKE *Fr. Rev.* Wks. V. 78 The idea of inheritance furnishes a sure principle of conservation. **1809** *Med. Jrnl.* XXI. 390 The exhalents..furnish a fluid similar in use to the secretion of the lachrymal gland. **1849** RUSKIN *Sev. Lamps* iv. §29. 119 The pinnacles furnish the third term to the spire and tower. **1875** JOWETT *Plato* (ed. 2) I. 453 The proof which you desire has been already furnished. **1888** BRYCE *Amer. Commw.* I. iii. 25 *note*, Rhode Island..has furnished the most abundant analogies to the Greek republics of antiquity.

9. *dial.* = BURNISH *v.*[2] Hence in *Stable slang*, of a horse: To fill out, gain in strength and 'condition'. (Cf. FURNISHED 2 b.)

1862 H. KINGSLEY *Ravenshoe* II. x. 103 The horse had furnished so since then. **1883** *Standard* 19 May 3/3 Being a big horse he is not quite furnished yet. *Mod.* (Suffolk) 'She is tall for age, and thin; now, it is to be hoped, she will begin to furnish'.

10. With adverbs.

a. furnish forth. Used by Shaks. with the sense = 5, 6 above; echoed by later writers (by Scott in the more recent sense 8).

1597 SHAKS. *2 Hen. IV*, I. ii. 251 Will your Lordship lend mee a thousand pound, to furnish me forth? **1602** —— *Ham.* I. ii. 181 The Funeral Bake-meats Did coldly furnish forth the Marriage Tables. **1810** SCOTT *Lady of L.* I. xxii, Our broad nets have swept the mere, To furnish forth your evening cheer. **1825** COBBETT *Rur. Rides* 188, I got myself well furnished forth as a defence against the rain. **1850** F. E. SMEDLEY *F. Fairlegh* iv, Clayton had..slain a sufficient number of victims to furnish forth pies for the supply of the whole mess. **1860** GEO. ELIOT *Bro. Jacob* ii, What housewife..would not think shame to furnish forth her table with articles that were not home-cooked? **1903** R. LANGBRIDGE *Flame & Flood* xvi, So she would..order..the best that the 'cuiseen'..could furnish forth.

b. furnish out. (*a*) To supply what is lacking in; to complete. (*b*) To supply adequate materials or provision for. (*c*) To send out with proper equipment or training. Now *rare.*

1577 B. GOOGE *Heresbach's Husb.* IV. (1586) 18 b, When..you are to furnish out the number, you must [etc.]. **1581** MULCASTER *Positions* ii. (1887) 5 To furnish out all knowledge in the cunning, and all iudgement in the wise. **1607** SHAKS. *Timon* III. iv. 116 There's not so much left to furnish out a moderate Table. **1639** FULLER *Holy War* v. v. (1647) 236 They..improved their interest with all their benefactours, to furnish out a fleet. **1662** H. MORE *Philos. Writ.* Pref. Gen. (1712) 22 Whose great example..furnished out many undaunted Champions of the Christian Faith. **1702** ADDISON *Dial. Medals* i. 16 How many Heroes would Moor-fields have furnished out in days of old. **1750** JOHNSON *Rambler* No. 1 ¶15 He may yet have enough to furnish out an essay. **1847** L. HUNT *Men, Women, & B.* I. xiv. 268 Modern customs..often leave to the imagination the task of furnishing out the proper quantity of beauty.

†**c. furnish up.** (*a*) To supply the necessary material for, make up, bring into a complete form. (*b*) To fit up with proper equipment. *Obs.*

1573 G. HARVEY *Letter-bk.* (Camden) 9 Here was stuf gud plente to furnish up a trim tragedi. **1593** ABP. BANCROFT *Daung. Posit.* III. xiii. 115 Before a Nationall Synode be celebrated, let it be called three monethes afore, that they may prepare and furnish vp those thinges, that belong vnto it. **1606** G. W[OODCOCKE] tr. *Hist. Ivstine* 26 a, With al dilligence..he furnished vp his Nauy to the sea. **1785** CRABBE *Newspaper* 221 As many rows, as furnish up a sheet.

furnishable ('fɜːnɪʃəb(ə)l), *a.* [f. FURNISH *v.* + -ABLE.] Capable of being furnished.

1831 CARLYLE *Sart. Res.* (1858) 121 Hast thou not a Brain..furnishable with some glimmerings of Light?

furnished ('fɜːnɪʃt), *ppl. a.* [f. FURNISH *v.* + -ED.[1]] In senses of the vb.

†**1.** Possessed of one's faculties physical and mental. *Obs.*

1473 *Writ* 10 Nov., *Patent Roll* 13 Edw. IV, I. m. 3 Oure deerest sone..whom it hath pleased God to yeve unto us hool and fornissed in nature.

2. Generally preceded by a qualifying adverb, and often only with the force of the *pass. pple.*

†**a.** Provided or stocked *with* (something, material or immaterial). *Obs.*

1570 *Satir. Poems Reform.* xxii. 34 A wylie wicht..With warldly wit weill furnissit at will. **1670** D. DENTON *Descr. New York* (1845) 5 These Rivers are very well furnished with Fish. **1674** PLAYFORD *Skill Mus.* I. xi. 56 Our own Nation was never better furnished with able and skilful artists. **1697** DAMPIER *Voy.* I. viii. 231 It was plentifully furnished with groves of Green Trees. **1751** J. STUART in *Lett. Lit. Men* (Camden) 382 Gentlemen..abundantly furnished with Literature. **1756** C. LUCAS *Ess. Waters* III. 237 The city is plentifully furnished with a very excellent coal.

b. Covered with flesh, filled out. [= F. *bien fourni.*]

a **1533** LD. BERNERS *Arthur* (1814) 258 He was byg, and mighty..with byg armes and longe, wel furnisshed.

c. Equipped; formerly in material sense, †Accoutred, dressed, provided with necessaries; now only in immaterial sense, Informed, instructed, prepared. †Of a tree: Clothed with foliage.

1553 T. WILSON *Rhet.* Epist. A ij, Some other not so well-furnished as your Lordeshypp is. **1566** PAINTER *Pal. Pleas.* (1569) 150 b, The sight of his sonne richly furnished..did more astonne him. **1576** FLEMING *Panopl. Epist.* 83 Readie furnished against all manner of misfortunes. **1585** T. WASHINGTON tr. *Nicholay's Voy.* I. i. 1 b, Two Gallies of the best and best furnished that were within the haven of Marseillie. **1596** SHAKS. *1 Hen. IV*, v. iii. 21 A gallant Knight he was..Semblably furnish'd like the King himselfe. **1596** DALRYMPLE tr. *Leslie's Hist. Scot.* v. 263 The Scotis sal rais ane furnist armie, nochtwithstanding vpon the French expenses. **1611** BIBLE *2 Tim.* iii. 17 That the man of God may be perfect, throughly furnished vnto all good workes. **1647** tr. *Malvezzi's Pourtract* 47 The English-men were expected with so furnished a preparation, that [etc.]. **1712** J. JAMES tr. *Le Blond's Gardening* 148 This Shrub grows very well furnish'd. **1869** GOULBURN *Purs. Holiness* Pref. 9 For the composition of which its writer is by no means furnished. **1875** HAMERTON *Intell. Life* I. i. (1876) 4 A remarkably clear, and richly furnished intellect.

d. Of a house or apartment: Stocked with furniture: e.g. in phr. ***to let, furnished.***

1703 *Lond. Gaz.* No. 3905/4 The Three Colts Inn..is to be let..furnished. **1734** BERKELEY *Let. to Prior* 2 Apr. Wks. 1871 IV. 220 We would..have a furnished house to ourselves. **1801** WINDHAM *Speeches Parl.* 4 Nov. (1812) II. 45 A ready-furnished lodging. **1846** MCCULLOCH *Acc. Brit. Empire* (1854) II. 519 Their cottages are, for the most part, comfortable and well furnished. **1848** DICKENS *Dombey* vii, At this other private house..apartments were let Furnished.

e. *Her.* (See quot.)

1828–40 BERRY *Encycl. Her.* I, *Furnished* is a term used when a horse is borne bridled, saddled, and completely caparisoned; in blazon he is then said to be furnished or completely furnished..It is, likewise, applicable to..the attire of a stag, furnished with six antlers. &c.

furnisher ('fɜːnɪʃə(r)). [f. FURNISH *v.* + -ER[1].]

1. a. One who furnishes, in senses of the vb.; *spec.* one who supplies furniture. **b.** *Austral. Mining* (See quot. 1869.)

1611 COTGR., *Fournisseur*, a furnisher. **1632** LITHGOW *Trav.* VI. 269 Their victuals are brought dayly..each furnisher ringing the Bell, giveth warning to his friends, to come receive their necessars. **1694** *Acc. Sev. Late Voy.* II. (1711) 158 The Line-furnisher, or the Man that doth look after the Ropes. **1759** FOUNTAINHALL *Decis.* I. 303 Some gave out the Duchess of Lauderdale as a..furnisher of him with money. **1869** R. B. SMYTH *Goldf. Victoria* 612 *Furnisher*, a capitalist who by erecting machinery for, or otherwise assisting a party of miners working a claim, becomes entitled to a share of the profits. **1881** *Daily News* 8 Nov. 5/2 The furnishers of pantomine properties. **1894** *Westm. Gaz.* 16 Aug. 3/1 Diversity is the aim of the modern furnisher.

2. In textile printing, a revolving brush or roller that supplies the colour.

1897 C. F. S. ROTHWELL *Printing Textile Fabrics* I. 29 The furnisher generally revolves the same way as the printing roller, and consists then of the ordinary cloth-covered wooden roller; but when pigment colours, or any colour that has a tencency to stick in the engraving, are being printed it is usual to use a brush furnisher and to work it in the opposite way. **1898** F. H. THORP *Outl. Industr. Chem.* I. 495 The color is fed to the print roll from the color box by a revolving cylindrical brush called the 'furnisher', which dips into the color paste. **1961** BLACKSHAW & BRIGHTMAN *Dict. Dyeing* 29 The Brush Furnisher is used for print pastes containing a high solids content of heavy density ingredients such as zinc oxide.

furnishing ('fɜːnɪʃɪŋ), *vbl. sb.* [f. FURNISH *v.* + -ING[1].]

1. a. The action of the vb. FURNISH, in senses of the vb.; an instance of this. Also gerundial with omission of *in.*

1496–7 *Act 12 Hen. VII*, c. 13 *Preamble*, The behoufull chargis and expencis for the fornysshyng and contynuaunce of the same armyes. **1523** LD. BERNERS *Froiss.* I. cclxxxi. 421 For yᵉ furnysshyng of his vowe. **1668** *Lond. Gaz.* No. 237/2 The Queen of Swadeland..for whom a Palace is already furnishing. **1691** T. HALE *Acc. New Invent.* 35 Rudder-Irons..of this Company's furnishing. **1851** CARLYLE *Sterling* I. x. (1872) 61 Due furnishings began to be executed in it [a ship]. **1861** M. PATTISON *Ess.* (1889) I. 47 A complete furnishing for war.

attrib. **1833** *Knickerbocker* I. 157 Gardiner's magnificent furnishing establishment already totters on its base. **1848** E. BRYANT *California* i. 14 These I obtained at reasonable rates, of Messrs. Wilson & Clarke, who keep a general furnishing store for these expeditions. **1860** GEO. ELIOT *Let.* 20 Dec. in J. W. Cross *Life* (1885) II. xi. 282 Our curtains are not up and our oil-cloth is not down. Such is life, seen from the furnishing point of view! **1887** *Daily News* 7 Feb. 2/5 General furnishing goods. **1967** E. SHORT *Embroidery & Fabric Collage* i. 18 Colours which shocked a few years ago are now accepted, and commonly found on furnishing and dress fabric.

b. *concr.* A sum of money furnished; a supply.

1833 ALISON *Hist. Europe* (1849–50) II. lxxvi. §22. 432 The war..cost..in subsidies or furnishings to foreign powers, ten millions four hundred thousand pounds.

2. Decoration.

1594 CAREW *Tasso* (1881) 63 Those two who thus in one conioyned goe and parrell white, white haue their furnishing. **1882** *Garden* 3 June 394/3 The Fruiting Duckweed..is now largely used in London for what is termed 'furnishing'. **1895** *Daily News* 8 Apr. 6/7 Hats provided for young girls have a floral furnishing.

3. *pl.* †**a.** Unimportant appendages; mere externals. **b.** Articles of furniture; apparatus, etc. **c.** (See quot. 1892.)

1605 SHAKS. *Lear* III. i. 29 Something deeper, Whereof (perchance) these are but furnishings. **1858** CARLYLE *Fredk. Gt.* II. v. (1865) I. 76 Now a Penitentiary, with treadmill and the other furnishings. **1877** M. M. GRANT *Sun-Maid* ii, The furnishings were small and dainty. **1885** *Law Times* LXXX. 113/1 All the furnishings of an hotel. **1891** *Daily News* 23 Jan. 5/5 Carpets from Fontainebleau, furnishings from Saint Cloud. **1892** *Labour Commission* Gloss., *Furnishings*, Scotch term, equivalent to the English term 'grindery'; that is, rivets, sprigs, &c., used by the men to fasten the bottoms of boots to the uppers; and also the materials used in the process of finishing.

furnishment ('fɜːnɪʃmənt). [f. FURNISH *v.* + -MENT. Cf. F. *fournissement.*]

1. The action of furnishing or supplying; the state of being furnished or supplied.

1563 MAN *Musculus' Commonpl.* 43 b, They bestow a great deal upon the furnishment of images. **1592** DANIEL *Epist. Bp. Winchester* Poems (1717) 426 Yet, Rev'rend Lord, vouchsafe me Leave to bring One Weapon more unto your Furnishment. *a* **1627** HAYWARD *Four Y. Eliz.* (Camden) 96 He sent Briguemant into England to deal with the Queen for some furnishment of men. **1631** WEEVER *Anc. Funeral Mon.* 12 A feast of magnificent furnishment. *a* **1639** WOTTON in *Reliq. Wotton.* (1651) 317 The culture and furnishment of the mind. **1644** VICARS *Jehovah-Jireh* 68 Cambridge Countie also petitioning the Parliament for furnishment of Armes. *a* **1670** BP. HACKET *Abp. Williams* I. (1692) 176 Yet with all this furnishment, out of a custom which modesty had observed, Sir Thomas deprecated the burthen. **1895** *Daily News* 11 Jan. 3/1 The grannies had no real cause for complaint of the furnishment of the tea table.

2. *pl.* Supplies in general; munitions (of war). Now *rare.*

1558–9 ABP. PARKER *Corr.* (Parker Soc.) 58 And as for other furnishments I am too far behind. **1617** DANIEL *Hist. Eng.* 93 No other thing was thought or talked on, but onely preparations, and furnishments for this businesse. **1619** tr. P. Mexia *Treas. Anc. & Mod. T.* II. III. xxi. 345 The Castle..was munited with Artillery of all sorts, and other furnishments for warre, in great plenty. **1880** L. WALLACE *Ben-Hur* 346 Purveyor for the army..vastly rich; grown so as contractor of furnishments which he never furnishes.

†**'furnitor.** *Obs. rare*$^{-1}$. = FURNER 1.

1601 *Househ. Ord.* (1790) 294 The Yeoman furnitor hath for his fee all the burnt coales drawne out of the oven.

furniture ('fɜːnɪtjʊə(r)). Forms: 6 forniture, (furnature, furnitury), 6–7 furnyture, 6– furniture. [ad. F. *fourniture* (*forneture*, 13th c.), f. *fournir* to FURNISH. Cf. Sp., It. *fornitura.* (Many of the applications, including the important sense 7, have been developed in Eng.)]

†**1.** The action of furnishing: **a.** The action of fitting out or equipping, of accomplishing (a design), or of providing *with* (supplies); occas. *furniture forth. Obs.*

1529 WOLSEY in *Four C. Eng. Lett.* 11 Appoyntyng such thyngs as shuld be convenient for my furniture. **1531** ELYOT *Gov.* I. xvi, Exercises, apt to the furniture of a gentilemannes personage. **1540** *Act 32 Hen. VIII*, c. 14 The said owners shalbe more charged for the furniture of their shippes..with vitailes. **1550** in Strype *Eccl. Mem.* (1721) II. xxxiv. 282 The King..granted 200 mark..toward the charge of the said Earls furniture. **1563** SHUTE *Archit.* B iij b, You must deuide all your seuerall places of offices appartayning to the furniture of your house. **1577–87** HOLINSHED *Chron.* III. 855/2 That he should be at so great charges for his furniture foorth at this time. **1581** LAMBARDE *Eiren.* II. iv. (1588) 172 For the more complete furniture of the Iustice of the Peace in this seruice. **1596** SHAKS. *1 Hen. IV*, III. iii. 226 There shalt thou know thy Charge, and there receiue Money and Order for their Furniture. **1611** SPEED *Hist. Gt. Brit.* IX. xii. (1632) 711 Toward the furniture of his hostile designs hee had extraordinary Subsidy granted. **1668–83** OWEN *Exp. Heb.* (1790) IV. 33 The furniture of the Lord Christ..to the discharge of his work of mediation, was the peculiar act of the Father. **1699** BENTLEY *Phal.* 359 For a hundred years after the beginning of the Thurian Government, the Expense and Furniture of Tragedy was very moderate.

b. The action of decorating or embellishing; a means of doing this. Hence *concr.* a decoration, an embellishment; also *collect. Obs.*

1548 GEST *Pr. Masse* 132 As they [the gospell and epystell] be inserted and placed in the pryvee masse to the furniture, worship, and commendation therof. **1549** COVERDALE, etc. *Erasm. Par. Jas.* 25 Nothing wanting..that perteyneth to the perfite absolute furniture of the godlynes of the Gospell. *Ibid.*, *1 Cor.* xi. 15 It is to a womanne a furniture to haue long heare. **1561** HOBY tr. *Castiglione's Courtyer* (1577) X 6 a, Laughters, gestures, and all the other pleasaunte furnitoures of beautye. **1601** R. JOHNSON *Kingd. & Commw.* (1603) 138 They adorne themselves with plumes and feathers of eagles ..These and such like furnitures do cause them to be discerned of their fellowes. **1613** SHAKS. *Hen. VIII*, II. i. 99 See the Barge be ready; And fit it with such furniture as suites The Greatnesse of his Person. **1633** G. HERBERT *Temple, Affliction* ii, I looked on thy furniture so fine. *a* **1677** BARROW *Serm.* Wks. 1716 II. 21 That God..should erect this stately fabrick of heaven and earth decked with so rich and goodly furniture.

c. The action of supplying, affording, or yielding. *Obs.*

1646 EVELYN *Diary* (1889) I. 227 Passing by the Euganean hills, celebrated for the furniture of rare simples, which we found growing about them. *a* **1649** DRUMM. OF HAWTH. *Jas. V*, Wks. (1711) 93 They..stop all furniture of food and victuals. **1690** E. GEE *Jesuit's Mem.* 141 The provision and furniture of Vestments.

2. a. The condition of being equipped whether in body or mind; equipment in dress or armour; preparedness for action; mental cultivation, culture. *Obs.* exc. *arch.* †*furniture of* (*arts*): the being equipped with or accomplished in. Cf. 5.

1560 DAUS tr. *Sleidane's Comm.* 260 b, They..through their [cities'] force, & furniture, haue gotten the landes & possessions of others. **1571** GOLDING *Calvin on Ps.* ii. 4 David hath reherced..the furniture and powers..of his enemies. **1594** CAREW *Huarte's Exam. Wits* (1616) 129 The perfection of pleading required the notice and furniture of all the arts in the world. **1596** SHAKS. *Tam. Shr.* IV. iii. 183 Neither art thou the worse For this poore furniture, and meane array. **1603** KNOLLES *Hist. Turks* (1621) 662 Souldiers..differing..in language, countenance, and manner of furniture. *a* **1656** HALES *Gold. Rem.* (1688) 17 Great defect of inward Furniture and Worth. **1657** EVELYN *Mem.* (1857) III. 83 You will inform yourself of the.. furniture of the French on the Mediterranean Seas. **1748** J. MASON *Elocut.* 8 A Thing that hath been often attempted by Men of mean Furniture. **1846** URWICK *Life Howe* in *H.'s Wks.* p. ii, The Gospel had to grapple with antagonists of no common nerve, furniture and skill.

†**b.** The condition of being occupied (by persons); complement of occupants. *Obs.*

1526 *Househ. Ord.* (1790) 153 There shall be a boord.. furnished with lords spirituall and temporal..being above the degree of a barron; and lacking such furniture to supply and fulfill the same boord with barrons.

3. †**a.** That with which one is provided; a provision, stock, or supply of anything (whether material or immaterial); stores in general, provisions; necessaries. *Obs.*

1549 SOMERSET *Let. to Hoby* in Strype *Eccl. Mem.* II. App. FF. 106 Their victuals and other provisions, wherof they had gotten large furniture. **1570** BILLINGSLEY *Euclid* II. i. 62 Great increase and furniture of knowledge. **1577–87** HOLINSHED *Scot. Chron.* (1805) II. 210 He left..his own treasurie not emptie, but abundantly stored with gold, silver and other furniture. **1632** LITHGOW *Trav.* v. 235 Wee were particularly searched, to the effect wee carried in no Furniture of Armes, nor Powder with us. **1670** NARBOROUGH *Jrnl.* in *Acc. Sev. Late Voy.* I. (1711) 95 Ships ..which come from Lima with Furniture for the People. **1683** CAVE *Ecclesiastici, Chrysostom* 528 Having thus ransack'd the Sacred Treasuries, and carried away a noble Furniture of Divine Learning. **1725** WATTS *Logic* III. iv. §2 Enlarge your general acquaintance with things daily, in order to attain a rich furniture of topics. **1787** BEST *Angling* (ed. 2) 4 Fishes considered as a food, make a considerable addition to the furniture of the table.

b. That with which something is or may be stocked; something to fill or occupy (a receptacle, etc.), contents. Now *rare.*

1612 T. TAYLOR *Comm. Titus* i. 15 For first, whose are the heauens and earth, and the furniture of them? **1692** RAY *Dissol. World* III. xi. (1732) 415 The Earth remaining without any Furniture or Inhabitants. **1788** COWPER *Let. to Mrs. Hill* 17 Mar., I am likely to be furnished soon with shelves..but furniture for these shelves I shall not presently procure, unless by recovering my stray authors. **1828–31** MISS BERRY *Soc. Life Eng. & Fr.* 107 The modern furniture of a circulating library. **1851** D. JERROLD *St. Giles* xi. 109 The furniture of his pocket, and his outside chattels in no way harmonising together.

4. Means of equipment.

†**a.** Apparel, dress, outfit, personal belongings. Also *pl.* in the same sense. *Obs.*

1566 PAINTER *Pal. Pleas.* I. 52 His wife sitteth vpon the ground, apparelled with those furnitures that he did weare. **1605** VERSTEGAN *Dec. Intell.* x. (1628) 322 The office of prouiding furniture for the armie. **1633** MASSINGER *Guardian* II. iv, How shall we know them?..if horsemen, by short boots, And riding furniture of several counties. **1672–3** MARVELL *Reh. Transp.* I. 111 The king would find himself incommoded with all that furniture upon his back. **1748** SMOLLETT *Rod. Rand.* (1760) I. viii. 44 My companion being charged with the furniture of us both, crammed into one knapsack.

†**b.** Armour, accoutrements, weapons, munitions of war. Also, a suit of armour. *Obs.*

1569 in Strype *Ann. Ref.* I. lv. 603 They shall want furniture; your self shall have abundance. **1570–6** LAMBARDE *Peramb. Kent* (1826) 301 Sallet, shield, sword, and..many other partes of defensive and invasive furniture. **1582** N. LICHEFIELD tr. *Castanheda's Conq. E. Ind.* lxxviii. 158 b, The Boates went verye heauie laden with theyr furniture. **1601** R. JOHNSON *Kingd. & Commw.* (1603) 77 It is thought that there is inough to arme 70,000, of which may be som x or 12,000 furnitures for horsemen. **1603** KNOLLES *Hist. Turks* (1621) 214 Caused..most part of his furniture to be convaied by the Caspian Sea. **1626** *Impeachm. Dk. Buckhm.* (Camden) 63 Two warlike furnitures and their bandeliers. **1648** *Bury Wills* (Camden) 209 My horse and horse armo^r, pistolls, and the other furniture belonging thereto. **1678** BUNYAN *Pilgr.* I. 62 They showed him all manner of furniture which their Lord had provided for Pilgrims.

fig. **1576** FLEMING *Panopl. Epist.* To Rdr., Sufficient furniture to arme..them against ignoraunce. **1581** J. BELL *Haddon's Answ. Osor.* 207 He armed hym with sufficient furniture agaynst sinne.

c. The harness, housings, trappings, etc. of a horse or other draught animal; rarely in *pl.* a single article of this kind. Similarly, the hood, bells, etc. of a hawk.

1553 EDEN *Treat. Newe Ind.* (Arb.) 15 Precious stones.. wherewith ye trappers, barbes and other furnitures of his horse are couered. **1577–87** HOLINSHED *Chron.* III. 1171/1 He kept in his stable..twentie great horsse..and had in a readinesse furniture for them all to serue in the field. **1601** HOLLAND *Pliny* I. 127 They are able..to set out with furniture 300 Elephants. **1611** BIBLE *Gen.* xxxi. 34 Rachel had taken the images, and put them in the camels furniture. **1674** N. COX *Gentl. Recreat.* II. (1677) 180 A Hawk newly taken ought to have all new Furniture. **1716** B. CHURCH *Hist. Philip's War* (1865) I. 20 They provided him a Horse and Furniture. **1781** GIBBON *Decl. & F.* II. xxxv. 299 The saddles and rich furniture of the cavalry were collected. **1806** A. DUNCAN *Nelson's Funeral* 35 Six led horses, in elegant furniture. **1851** D. WILSON *Preh. Ann.* (1863) II. III. vi. 159 Bridle-bits and other portions of horse furniture. **1862** STANLEY *Jew. Ch.* (1877) I. iii. 53 The seats and furniture of the camels stowed within the covering of the tents.

d. Hangings and ornamental drapery; also, the coverlets and linen for a bed.

1576 FLEMING *Panopl. Epist.* 245 His bed, and the necessarie furniture thereunto belonging. **1683** TRYON *Way to Health* 586 Most People take care that their Furnitures are daily brushed and rubbed. **1705** STANHOPE *Paraphr.* I. 34 The way before him not covered with Tapestry or rich Furniture. **1728** NEWTON *Chronol. Amended* ii. 241 Menes taught them to adorn their beds and tables with rich furniture. **1791** MRS. RADCLIFFE *Rom. Forest* viii, She..perceived a broken bedstead, with some decayed remnants of furniture. **1855** BROWNING *Fra Lippo* 64 Curtain and counterpane and coverlet, All the bed-furniture.

5. Apparatus, appliances, or instruments for work. **a.** material: Implements, tools, utensils; rigging, stores, and tackle of a ship; military engines and defensive works. Now chiefly *Naut.*

1577 B. GOOGE *Heresbach's Husb.* I. (1586) 11 Hesiodus would have a husbande have all his furniture redy. **1582** N. LICHEFIELD tr. *Castanheda's Conq. E. Ind.* xxix 73 b, The tackling with the other furniture of the Shippes..made such a terrible noyse. **1590** SPENSER *Muiopot.* 56 Yong Clarion.. did cast abroad to fare; And theretoo gan his furnitures prepare. **1600** SURFLET *Countrie Farme* I. xxiii. 125 A cow is not of so great charge to maintaine and keepe..neither yet of her handling..neither yet in furniture. **1601** R. JOHNSON *Kingd. & Commw.* 30 Ladders, bridges, shot, powder, and other furnitures. **1602** SEGAR *Hon. Mil. & Civ.* 173 A Fained fortresse, with Trenches, Baracadoes, and other furniture of defence was erected. **1652** NEEDHAM tr. *Selden's Mare Cl.* 77 It was provided that Antiochus should surrender his long ships and their warlike furniture. **1667** MILTON *P.L.* IX. 34 Tilting Furniture, emblazon'd Shields, Impreses quaint, Caparasons and Steeds. **1680** H. MORE *Apocal. Apoc.* 125 Images or Idols, and such gross furniture of their worship. **1795** in Nicolas *Disp. Nelson* (1846) VII. p. xxvii, The yawl astern swamped, and was lost with all her furniture. **1800** *Med. Jrnl.* IV. 182 A very useful and commendable piece of furniture. **1867** SMYTH *Sailor's Word-bk.*, *Furniture*, the rigging, sails, spars, anchors, cables, boats, tackle, provisions, and every article with which a ship is fitted out.

b. immaterial; *esp.* Of intellectual faculties, or aptitudes; now only with *mental* or some equivalent defining expression.

In the quots. the sense borders closely on 2.

1561 T. NORTON *Calvin's Inst.* II. 146 He now refuseth and abhorreth the sacrificing of beastes, and al that furniture of the Leuiticall Presthode, wherwith in the olde time he was delited. **1609** DEKKER *Guls Horne-bk.* vii. 32 That qualitie.. is the onely furniture to a Courtier thats but a new beginner, and is but in his A B C of Complement. **1677** GILPIN *Demonol.* (1867) 52 All the malice, power, cruelty, and diligence of which we have spoken..are but his furniture and accomplishment which fit him for his subtle contrivances of delusion. **1788** REID *Aristotle's Log.* ii. §2. 26 Thus the whole furniture of the human mind is presented to us at one view. **1833** I. TAYLOR *Fanat.* I. 21 His faculty and furniture of mind would have been employed in defending himself. **1887** LOWELL *Democr.*, etc. 52 Impressed with the statesmanlike furniture of his mind. **1894** *Daily News* 5 Mar. 5/8 Lord Russell..had a mental furniture fit for repose.

6. a. Accessories, appendages. (Formerly also *pl.* in the same sense.) Now only *techn.* in specific applications; used, e.g., for the finger-plates, handles, locks, etc. of a door; the plates and handles, etc. of a coffin; and the like; *spec.* the mountings of a rifle.

1568 *Wills & Inv. N.C.* (Surtees 1835) I. 282 One syde sadle wth the furnitury. **1578** TIMME *Caluine on Gen.* 52 The woman..was nothing else but the addition and furniture of the man. **1615** *Nottingham Rec.* (1889) IV. 339 16 musketts or bastard musketts, and furnytures to them. *a* **1718** PENN *Tracts* Wks. 1726 I. 870 A plain Coffin, without any Covering or Furniture upon it. **1729** SHELVOCKE *Artillery* III. 149 To force up the Rocket and all its Furniture. **1774** GOLDSM. *Nat. Hist.* (1776) III. 125 The stag and fallow deer. Alike..in the superb furniture of their heads. **1808** *Beverley Lighting Act* 20 The posts, irons, cover, or other furniture of any such lamp. **1810** *Sporting Mag.* XXXV. 299 The two competitors for the enemy's furniture [fox's brush]. **1852** *Househ. Words* 13 Mar. 582/1 Such close fittings as those of the furniture of guns to the stocks. **1859** GWILT *Archit.* Gloss., *Furniture*, the visible brass work of locks, knobs to doors, window-shutters, and the like. **1866** ROGERS *Agric. & Prices* I. xxi. 544 Sometimes the cart with the whole furniture..is bought. **1881** YOUNG *Every Man his own Mechanic* §1493 The new kind of door-handle or 'furniture' as it is technically called. **1886** *Pall Mall G.* 10 Aug. 8/2 A massive oak coffin, with heavy brass furniture. **1892** W. W. GREENER *Breech-Loader* 14 The furniture of the stock consists of the heel-plate, trigger-guard, &c.

†**b.** *pl.* Adjuncts or condiments of a salad. Cf. F. *fourniture. Obs.*

1693 EVELYN *De la Quint. Compl. Gard.* Dict., Furnitures, are all hot and spicy Herbs, mixed with..cold Herbs in Sallets to temper and relish them. **1719** LONDON & WISE *Compl. Gard.* 196 Melesse, is an odoriferous Herb, whose Leaf, when tender, makes a part of Sallad-Furnitures. **1727** S. SWITZER *Pract. Gard.* I. iii. 19 Tarragon, basil, burnet, mint, and other sallet furnitures.

c. *Printing.* (See quot. 1874.)

1683 MOXON *Mech. Exerc.* II. viii. 28 By Furniture is meant the Head-sticks, Foot-sticks, Side-sticks, Gutter-sticks, Riglets, Scabbords and Quoyns. **1824** J. JOHNSON *Typogr.* II. xv. 534 If letters, quadrats, or furniture, rise up and black the paper, they should be put down with the bodkin. **1874** KNIGHT *Dict. Mech.*, *Furniture* (*Printing*), the wooden inclosing strips and quoins which surround the matter in the chase.

d. (See quot.)

1704 HARRIS *Lex. Techn.*, *Furniture of a Dial*, are such Lines as are drawn thereon for Ornament; as the Parallels of Declination, Length of the Day, Azimuths, &c.

7. a. (The prevailing sense.) Movable articles, whether useful or ornamental, in a dwelling-house, place of business, or public building. Formerly including also the fittings. (†Occas. const. as *pl.*)

1573 TUSSER *Husb.* viii. (1878) 16 Be house or the furniture neuer so rude. **1582** N. LICHEFIELD tr. *Castanheda's Conq. E. Ind.* [x]xii. 78 b, All the furniture for his Chamber and Kitchin. **1637** *Documents agst. Prynne* (Camden) 99 My interest in the lease of Swanswick, and my hangings, pictures, and furniture there. **1705** ADDISON *Italy* 86 Their Furniture is not commonly very Rich, if we except the Pictures. **1768–74** TUCKER *Lt. Nat.* (1852) I. 412 He might..take some sly opportunity to slit holes in our furniture. **1797** MRS. A. M. BENNETT *Beggar Girl* (1813) V. 197 The furniture were all in their places. **1816** J. SCOTT *Vis. Paris* (ed. 5) p. lv, The groups of poor peasants flocking in, with cart-loads of furniture..present very distressing spectacles. **1866** GEO. ELIOT *F. Holt* (1868) 10 There was a great deal of..dinginess on the walls and furniture of this smaller room.

b. Applied in the book trade to well-bound volumes and 'standard' sets which serve to fill and adorn the shelves of a private library. (Cf. *furniture-picture* in 10.)

1928 *Periodical* No. 143. 25 Its [*sc.* the O.E.D.'s] claims as 'furniture' are not despicable. **1928** *Times Lit. Suppl.* 5 Apr. 260/3 The big 'furniture' books in folio and quarto which long formed the most conspicuous feature of private libraries. **1928** *Publishers' Circular* 6 Oct. 461 Much of it just furniture, and yet there were many very nice items.

c. *part of the furniture*, something familiar enough to be regarded as a permanent feature (and therefore taken for granted). *colloq.*

1910 E. M. FORSTER *Howards End* xxx. 250, I want to tell you the story... You must do exactly what you like—treat it as part of the furniture. **1936** G. B. SHAW *Simpleton* II. 78, I am part of the furniture of your house. I am a matter of course... Was I that in the childhood of our marriage? **1974** M. FORSTER *Seduction of Mrs Pendlebury* xi. 117 The sight of Mrs P. complete with black fur hat and garish make-up might have proved irresistible. As it was, she was accepted as part of the furniture, at least until the grown-ups came at the end to collect their offspring.

8. *Music.* (See quots. and cf. F. *fourniture*.)

1690 *Specif. Organ Magd. Coll., Oxf.* in Grove *Dict. Mus.* II. 594/2 Furniture of 3 ranks. **1776** SIR J. HAWKINS *Hist. Mus.* IV. I. x. 147 The compound stops are the Furniture, and sundry others. **1876** STAINER & BARRETT *Dict. Mus. Terms*, *Furniture*, the name of one of the mixture stops in an organ.

9. *Bell-founding.* (See quot.) ? *Obs.*

1756 *Dict. Arts & Sc.* s.v. *Bell*, The waist or furniture viz. the part of the Bell, which grows always wider or thicker by a supply of metal, which is larger and larger quite to the brim.

10. *attrib.*, as ***furniture-broker***, ***-polish***, ***-remover***, ***-shop***, ***-van***; and in names of fabrics used for covering furniture, as ***furniture-plush***, ***-print***, ***-silk***. Also **furniture beetle**, a small wood-boring beetle of the family Anobiidæ, esp. *Anobium punctatum*; **furniture cream**, a creamy substance or preparation used for polishing furniture; **furniture-pad** (see quot.); **furniture-picture** (see quot.); **furniture-pin**, a pin for fixing the furniture (see 6) of a gun; **furniture-stop** *Music* (see 8); †**furniture-tree**, ? an ornamental tree.

1915 *Proc. R. Phys. Soc. Edinb.* XIX. 220 The *Furniture beetles are comprised in the two families Anobiidæ and Lyctidæ. **1938** L. HUNTER *Domestic Pests* xvi. 121 The common furniture beetles emerge from the pupal stage just beneath the surface of the wood. **1959** E. F. LINSSEN *Beetles Brit. Is.* II. 62 The most annoying of all household Furniture Beetles is *Anobium punctatum*. **1971** *Times* 28 Jan. 12/5 He can point to the exact spot where the furniture beetle may be found at work on a damaged specimen beech. **1842** DICKENS *Amer. Notes* (1850) 80/1 The small shops.. occupied..by *furniture-brokers. **1873** E. SPON *Workshop Receipts* 86/2 **Furniture Cream*.—1. Yellow wax, 4 oz.; yellow soap, 2 oz.; water, 50 oz.; boil and add boiled oil and oil of turpentine, each 5 oz. **1904** J. VAIZEY *More about Pixie* viii. 90 Sukey mixed the lettuce with furniture cream instead of salad-dressing. **1962** G. BUTLER *Coffin in Oxford* x. 138 A smell of furniture cream, lightly scented with lavender. **1874** KNIGHT *Dict. Mech.*, **Furniture-pad*, a piece of india-rubber or similar thing attached to a piece of furniture to prevent rubbing or striking against objects. **1889** BARRÈRE & LELAND *Dict. Slang.*, **Furniture pictures*, pictures painted by the dozen for the trade. Of the same class as 'pot-boilers'. **1881** GREENER *Gun* 262 After having removed the *furniture-pins, the trigger-plate and triggers may be taken from the stock. **1884** KNIGHT *Dict. Mech.* IV. 363 **Furniture Plush* (*Fabric*), also known as Utrecht velvet. **1833** J. NEAL *Down-Easters* I. 15 Plastering the foot all over with his *furniture polish and wrapping it up. **1891** KIPLING *Light that Failed* iv. 59 If they want furniture-polish, let them have furniture-polish, so long as they pay for it. **1951** *Good Housek. Home Encycl.* 222/2 *Liquid Furniture Polish.* ½ pint turpentine. ¼ pint linseed oil. ⅛ pint methylated spirit. ⅛ pint vinegar. **1895** MASKELYNE in *Daily Chron.* 29 Oct. 3/5 She has more methods of lifting a table than any *furniture remover has ever dreamt of. **1866** MRS CARLYLE *Lett.* III. 337, I saw in an old *furniture-shop window..a copy of the Frederick picture. **1664** EVELYN *Sylva* (1776) 310 Those.. gardeners who..expose their tender *Furniture-trees of the green-house too early. **1858** C. M. YONGE *Christmas Mummers* i. 7 A large scarlet vehicle, painted in yellow letters, with the words, 'Postlethwayte's *Furniture Van'. **1889** H. F. WOOD *Englishm. of Rue Caïn* iv, A dismal furniture-van.

furnitureless (ˈfɜːnɪtjʊəlɪs), *a.* [f. FURNITURE + -LESS.] Having no furniture.

1887 W. JAMES *Let.* 5 Feb. (1920) I. 262 My heart was heavy in my breast that so rich a nature..should have nothing but that furnitureless cabin within and snow and sky without, to live upon. **1890** W. BOOTH *In Darkest Eng.* II. v. 167 We found them both out of work, home furnitureless, in debt. **1927** *Glasgow Herald* 8 Nov. 11 Marlborough House is still furnitureless, and is a place of ladders and dust-sheets.

fur-nut. [? f. *fur* FURROW + NUT.] = EARTH-NUT I.

1804 *Med. Jrnl.* XII. 361 Earth, kipper, pig, hawk or fur-nut.

‖**furole.** ? *Obs.* [F. *furole*, earlier *fuirole*.] = CORPOSANT.

1656–81 BLOUNT *Glossogr.*, *Furole* (Fr.), a little blaze of fire, appearing by night on the tops of Souldiers Launces or at Sea on Sayl-yards, where it whirles and leaps in a moment from one place to another. **1706** PHILLIPS (ed. Kersey), *Furole*, a kind of little Meteor appearing amidst the Sails of a Ship, especially upon an approaching Storm. **1867** SMYTH *Sailor's Word-bk.*, *Furole*, the luminous appearance called the *corpo santo*.

‖**furor** (ˈfjʊərɔː(r)). Forms: 5 fourour, fureur, 5–6 furour(e, 6– furor. [L.; originally a. F. *fureur*, ad. L. *furōr-em*, n. of state f. *furĕre* to rage, be mad.]

1. Fury, rage, madness, anger, mania.

c **1477** CAXTON *Jason* 22 b, Considerest thou not the strenghe and force of my body and the furour of my swerde? **1489** —— *Faytes of A.* III. xxi. 219 A madde man duryng his fourour may not be reputed nor taken for enemye. **1509** BARCLAY *Shyp of Folys* (1570) 70 Where.. wrath doth reigne with his furours. **1525** LD. BERNERS *Froiss.* II. xlvii. 162 Some oppressed..with the furoure of the see. *a* **1541** WYATT *To his unkind love* Poet. Wks. (1861) 46 What rage is this? what furor? of what kind? **1561** T. NORTON *Calvin's Inst.* III. 191 Hoping that the Lord mighte be..turned from the furor of hys wrath. **1603** SIR C. HEYDON *Jud. Astrol.* ii. 85 The furors of Nero. **1758** H. WALPOLE *Catal. Roy. Authors* (1759) II. 122 A Lord, who with..some derangement of his intellects was so unlucky as not to have his furor of the true poetic sort. **1801** FUSELI in *Lect. Paint.* iii. (1848) 413 The enthusiastic furor of the God of War. **1837** CARLYLE *Fr. Rev.* II. II. vi, In mixed terror and furor. **1862** MAURICE *Mor. & Met. Philos.* IV. vi. §5. 209 The anti-papal furor of the king's youth.

2. The inspired frenzy of poets and prophets; in weaker sense, a 'glow', excited mood.

1589 PUTTENHAM *Eng. Poesie* I. i. (Arb.) 20 This science in his perfection can not grow, but by some diuine instinct, the Platonicks call it furor. **1757** FOOTE *Author* I. 13, I am afraid the poetic Furor may have betray'd me into some Indecency. **1837** CARLYLE *Fr. Rev.* I. IV. i. (1872) 102 Rises into furor almost Pythic. **1856** R. A. VAUGHAN *Mystics* (1860) I. 218 Of these two kinds of divining..the latter is [characterized] by a fervency and elevation such as the ancients styled furor. **1860** GEO. ELIOT in *Life* (1885) II. 159 They [the pages] were written in a furor; but I dare say there is not a word different from what it would have been, if I had written them at the slowest pace.

3. Great enthusiasm or excitement, a 'rage' or craze which takes every one by storm. Now chiefly *N. Amer.* (Cf. next.)

1704 SWIFT *Mech. Operat. Spirit* Misc. (1711) 301 He seldom was without some female Patients among them, for the furor. **1865** *Cornh. Mag.* July 100 Like most old churches, Earndale had suffered under the beautifying furor of the eighteenth century. **1868** M. PATTISON *Academ. Org.* v. 316 The mastery which the athletic furor has established over all minds in this place.

4. Sometimes with L. adj. added to define the nature of the 'frenzy', as ***furor academicus***, ***biographicus***, ***papisticus***, ***poeticus***, ***teutonicus***. Also ***furor scribendi***.

1850 KINGSLEY *A. Locke* I. xx. 278 Mackaye grumbled at my writing so much, and so fast, and sneered about the *furor scribendi*. *a* **1873** MILL *Ess. Relig.* (1874) 33 The fire of London, which is believed to have had so salutary an effect on the healthiness of the city, would have produced that effect just as much if it had been really the work of the 'furor papisticus' so long commemorated on the Monument. **1922** A. HUXLEY *Let.* 8 June (1969) 207 His parents-in-law elect are extremely averse to being anything more than elect—on the score, I gather, of poor Robert's..furious *furor poeticus*. **1928** *Daily Tel.* 11 Sept. 12/1 Once upon a time Macaulay complained of the furor biographicus or lues Boswelliana which makes biographies an orgy of praise. **1960** *Times* 2 Dec. 20/6 From the early *furor teutonicus* to the present mood of lyric vitality, the achievement..is impressive. **1963** P. H. JOHNSON *Night & Silence* v. 27 The man was obviously wild with excitement, with *furor academicus*. **1964** F. BOWERS *Bibliogr. & Textual Crit.* v. iv. 151 A balance that is sometimes neglected in the *furor poeticus* of textual speculation. **1964** *Economist* 31 Oct. 507/1 The obsessive *furor scribendi* which..drove him to proliferate lectures, addresses and prefaces.

‖**furore** (fuˈrore, fjʊəˈrɔːrɪ). [It. form of prec.]

1. Enthusiastic popular admiration; a 'rage', 'craze'.

1790 E. WYNNE *Diary* 15 Feb. (1935) I. ii. 34 Went to the opera... They made a great furore for Mrs Banti. **1831** J. C. YOUNG *Diary* 16 June in *Mem. C. M. Young* (1871) I. vi. 208, I heard Paganini. The *furore* there has been about this man has bordered on fatuity. **1851** CARLYLE in Froude *Life* (1884) II. 83 This blockhead..is..making quite a furore at Glasgow. **1864** LEWINS *H.M. Mails* 263 It was little thought that..they would excite such a furore among stamp collectors. **1867** DICKENS *Lett.* 25 Nov., If we make a furore there.

2. Uproar, disturbance, fury.

1946 H. MILLER *Let.* 7 Oct. in Durrell & Miller *Private Corr.* 231 Girodias, Gallimard and Denoël will all be brought to trial in a few months for publishing French versions of the *Tropics* and *Black Spring*. A real shindig!.. A tremendous furore. They now talk about 'Le Cas Miller', as they talked once of the Dreyfus affair. **1947** I. BROWN *Say Word* 54 Consider Furore. Nowadays, especially in the Press, it often has a totally incorrect meaning. We read that so-and-so's speech caused a furore, i.e. an uproar of resentment. **1948** H. ACTON *Mem. Aesthete* v. 114 My 'Conversazione of Musical Instruments', which was to create a furore when I recited it at Oxford. **1970** E. O'BRIEN *Pagan Place* II. 124 Your father laughed recalling fist-fights about such issues as the best goalie in the county... One thing he always made a point of was to stand a round of drinks after the furore had died down.

furphy (ˈfɜːfɪ). *Austral. slang.* [Associated with *Furphy carts*, water and sanitary carts used in the 1914–18 war, manufactured at a foundry established by the Furphy family at Shepparton, Vict.] A false report or rumour; an absurd story. Also *attrib.*

1916 *Anzac Bk.* 56/1 These furphies are the very devil. *Ibid.*, Furphy was the name of the contractor which was written large upon the rubbish carts that he supplied to the Melbourne camps. The name was transferred to a certain class of news item, very common since the war, which flourished greatly upon all the beaches. **1916** C. J. DENNIS *Moods of Ginger Mick* 122 Soljerin's me game. That's no furphy. **1919** W. H. DOWNING *Digger Dial.* 25 *Furphy-king*, a retailer of rumours. **1933** *Bulletin* (Sydney) 12 Apr. 21 The persistent rumour that they were introduced to check ragwort is a furphy. **1942** C. BARRETT *On Wallaby* iv. 70 Tim broke the..news... It was no furphy this time. We really were going..to somewhere in Sinai. **1945** L. GLASSOP *We were Rats* III. xlv. 247 We did not believe it when they told us... 'Mick,' [Eddie] said earnestly, 'it's a furphy. It's the same old furphy..an'..it's not funny any more.' **1960** 'J. WYNDHAM' *Trouble with Lichen* xii. 153 The furphy round the House is that *they* believe in the thing so solidly that they've convinced their husbands.

furred (fɜːd), *ppl. a.* [f. FUR *sb.* and *v.* + -ED.]

1. Made of fur, lined or trimmed with fur.

c **1325** *Poem Times Edw. II*, 148 in *Pol. Songs* (Camden) 330 But if he have hod and cappe furred, he nis noht i-told. **1375** BARBOUR *Bruce* XVI. 485 The richmond commonly Wes wount that furrit hat to wer. **1377** LANGL. *P. Pl.* B. xx. 175 A Fisicien with a forred hood. **1480** CAXTON *Chron. Eng.* cc. 181 He lete hym vnclothe of his furred taberd and of his hode and of his furred cotes. **1514** BARCLAY *Cyt. & Uplondyshm.* (Percy) p. lxi, His furred mittens were of a curres skin. **1634–5** BRERETON *Trav.* (1844) 57 Prince of Orange, in a furred and almost like alderman's gown. **1762–71** H. WALPOLE *Vertue's Anecd. Paint.* (1786) I. 216 The original painted by himself with a black cap and furred gown. **1856** LD. COCKBURN *Mem.* i. (1874) 43 He generally wore the furred greatcoat even within doors.

2. Of an animal: Provided with or having fur.

1545 BRINKLOW *Compl.* 61 As thou maist know a foxe by his furred tayle. **1651** DAVENANT *Gondibert* II. vi, Man.. Whom, when his Furr'd and Horned Subjects knew, Their sport is ended. **1816** KEATINGE *Trav.* (1817) I. 218 The furred, the provident, and the torpid tribes. **1879** JEFFERIES *Wild Life in S. Co.* 179 A map..showing the routes and resorts of furred and feathered creatures.

b. *Ent.* (See quot.)

1826 KIRBY & SP. *Entomol.* IV. 278 *Furred*, when shorter decumbent hairs thickly cover any space.

3. Wearing fur; wrapped up or clothed in furs.

1593 WARNER *Alb. Eng.* VII. xxxvii. (1612) 186 Empson and Dudley, fur'd Esquiers. **1642** EGLISHAM *Forerunner Revenge* in *Select. fr. Harl. Misc.* (1793) 276 Buckingham came out muffled and furred in his coach. **1798** S. ROGERS *Epist. to Friend*, The furred Beauty comes to winter there. **1809** HEBER in *Q. Rev.* II. 295 The furred and muffled nobles. **1891** *Daily News* 7 Jan. 3/4 You..will pass in graceful sweep many a furred damsel.

fig. *c* **1596–1603** in Hargrave *Coll. Tracts Law Eng.* I. 314 For heretofore in 5. R. 2. there was a complaint exhibited against them in parliament, that they were over fatt, both in boddie and purse, and over well furred in ther benefices.

4. Covered or coated with morbid matter, incrusted; *esp.* of the tongue: 'Covered with a more or less thick substance consisting of epithelial scales, granular matter, food particles, and often fungoid growths' (*Syd. Soc. Lex.* 1885).

1509 HAWES *Past. Pleas.* XXXII. (Percy) 159 Right anone a lady gan to scrape His furred tonge. **1634** PEACHAM *Gentl. Exerc.* I. xxiii. 72 Take a torch or linke, and hold it under the bottome of a latten basen, and as it groweth to be furd and blacke within strike it with a feather into some shell or other. **1707** J. STEVENS tr. *Quevedo's Com. Wks.* (1709) 149 My.. Teeth were..all firr'd. **1743** R. BLAIR *Grave* 16 Musty vaults, Furr'd round with mouldy damps. **1803** *Med. Jrnl.* IX. 510 Teeth furred, and throat sore. **1878** HABERSHON *Dis. Abdomen* 16 A furred tongue is generally caused by the excessive formation of the epithelial coat.

†**b.** *transf.* of the voice: Husky. *Obs.*

1666 PEPYS *Diary* 12 Oct., Her voice, for want of use, is so furred that it do not at present please me.

c. Of a boiler: Encrusted.

1873 R. WILSON *Steam Boilers* vii. 118 The objection..is their liability to become furred up when the water contains a considerable quantity of lime salts.

†**5.** (See quot.) *Obs.*

1697 EVELYN *Numism.* vi. 213 Monetaries have melted old Coins, and taking a slight Proportion of Silver, cover'd the Copper, and new stamp'd it; these among Medalists are called Plated, or Furr'd Medals.

furrene, var. FERREN, *Obs.*

†ˈ**furrer.** *Obs.* [? aphetic form of *afurer*, AFFEEROR. Cf. FEEROR.] ? = AFFEEROR.

1486 *Ord. Lichfield Gild* (Stanley) 12 The presentment by the xij men, and the furrers of the court, vnto my lord reservedd notwithstondinge.

furres, obs. form of FURZE.

‖**furriel.** *Obs.* [Sp. (obsolete); perh. a corruption of F. *fourrier*.] = FURRIER[1], FORAYER 2.

1598 R. BARRET *Mod. Warres* 150 All the furriels, maiors, or chiefe Harbingers of the Tertios of the Infantery. **1599** MINSHEU *Span. Dial.* 59/2, I would to God such were the health of the Furriel which gaue it vs.

†ˈ**furrier**[1]. *Obs.* Also 6 furiour, furrior, -yer, 7 furriour. See also FORAYER, FOURRIER. [ad. F. *fourrier*, OF. *forier*, f. *feurre* FORAGE.]

One who went in advance of an army, etc. to secure and arrange accommodation, etc.; a purveyor, quarter-master; hence also a courier, harbinger. *Comb.*, as ***furrier-major***.

1525 LD. BERNERS *Froiss.* II. clix. [clx.] 456 The nexte day [the Erle of Foiz] departed fro Tholous, and lefte his furriers behynde hym to paye for euery thyng. **1581** STYWARD *Mart. Discipl.* I. 18 Ther must by him be appointed, a furrior or harbinger, who shall..lodge ye whole companie. **1606** BIRNIE *Kirk-Buriall* (1833) 4 Our two faithful furriours Enoch and Elias. **1637** R. MONRO *Exped.* I. 33 The Furriers sent before, to divide the Quarters. **1704** *Lond. Mag.* No. 4022/4 Deserted..Jacob Fulk..a Furrier.

furrier[2] ('fʌrɪə(r)). [f. FUR *sb.* + -IER; cf. *clothier*. Fr. has *fourreur*, agent-n. f. *fourrer* FUR *v.*] A dealer in or dresser of fur or furs.

[*c* **1330**: see FURROUR.] **1576** TURBERV. *Venerie* 12 Skynnes sent to the furryers and pellytours of Fraunce. **1598** HAKLUYT *Voy.* I. 156 Certaine Furriers of London..haue had a great part of the sayd goods, namely of the Furres. **1774** GOLDSM. *Nat. Hist.* (1776) III. 323 Of this [skin] the furriers make a covering that is warm and durable. **1836** W. IRVING *Astoria* (1849) 28 Mr. Astor became acquainted with a countryman of his, a furrier by trade. **1859** DARWIN *Orig. Spec.* v. (1872) 107 It is well known to furriers that animals of the same species have thicker fur the further north they live.

furriered ('fʌrɪəd), *pa. pple.* [-ED[1].] Made or treated by a furrier.

1923 *Daily Mail* 2 July 4 This regal looking garment.. Lined and Furriered beautifully. **1927** *Observer* 20 Nov. 20 French fur productions. Furriered from hundreds of perfect pelts. **1929** *Daily News* 5 Oct. 1, 8 Fitch Skins.. furriered in Paris.

furriery ('fʌrɪərɪ). [f. FURRIER[2]: see -ERY.]

†**1.** *pl.* Furs collectively. *Obs.*

1784 KING in King & Cook *Voy.* III. VI. vi. 340 No labour can ever be turned to so good account as what is employed upon their furrieries. The animals, therefore, which supply these, come next to be considered. **1799** W. TOOKE *View Russian Empire* III. 51 For smaller furrieries and edgings, the skins of the Marten, the Squirrel, the Ermine, the Rabbit and the Marmotte are the choicest. [**1828–32** WEBSTER, *Furriery*, furs in general. *Tooke*.]

2. The art of dressing and making up furs; furrier's work; the trade or business of a furrier.

1920 C. J. ROSENBERG *Furs & Furriery* p. v, There was no work obtainable dealing with the practical side of Furriery. **1929** *Daily News* 5 Oct. 1 A stole which cannot fail to please —the quality and furriery are *sans reproche*. *Ibid.*, The finest points of furriery are embodied in this charming Coat. **1959** *Chambers's Encycl.* VI. 127/2 The Rex coat is ideal for furriery, being produced in a variety of colours.

furrin ('fʌrɪn), *a.* Humorous or dialectal perversion of *foreign*.

1895 MRS. H. WARD *Story of Bessie Costrell* iii. 52 'Ee's a bishop, they ses—someun from furrin parts. **1915** F. H. BURNETT *Lost Prince* vi. 60 It'd be likely to be in some o' these furrin places. England'd be too far. **1950** L. DURRELL *Spirit of Place* (1969) 104 Dear Anne, I have been owing you a letter From furrin parts. **1969** E. MCGIRR *Entry of Death* vii. 145 May I present Sergeant Griffid. I'll spell it on account of it being hard on furrin ears.

furriner ('fʌrɪnə(r)). Humorous or dialectal perversion of *foreigner*.

1849 C. BRONTË *Shirley* I. vii. 191 As a furriner,..you have not that understanding of huz and wer ways. **1852** E. TWISLETON *Let.* 29 Oct. (1928) iv. 61 This is what it is to have married a 'furriner' and left one's sisters. **1924** J. BUCHAN *Three Hostages* xvii. 242 The worst of them furriners..is that you can't never be sure what they thinks of you. **1968** D. HOPKINSON *Incense-Tree* ii. 17 They left the beaches to 'furriners' like ourselves.

furring ('fɜːrɪŋ), *vbl. sb.* [f. FUR *v.* + -ING[1].]

1. a. The action of clothing or adorning with fur. **b.** *concr.* A lining or trimming of fur. Also *collect.*

c **1386** CHAUCER *Pars. T.* ¶ 344 Þer is also costlewe furring in here gownes. *c* **1394** *P.P. Crede* 604 Hem faileþ no furrynge ne cloþes at full. **1536** BELLENDENE *Cron. Scot.* (1821) I. xxxiii, Mony martrikis, bevers, quhitredis and toddis; the furringis and skinnis of thaim ar coft with gret price amang uncouth marchandis. **1554** T. MARTIN *Bk. Priests' Marriages* (R.), Their whole life is spent..in providing for furring of their backs. *a* **1577** GASCOIGNE *Flowers*, etc. Wks. (1587) 38 Their garments..fret for lack of furring. **1585** *T. Washington* tr. *Nicholay's Voy.* II. xxiii. 62 He shall have the whole furring of a long gowne..for fourescore or a 100 ducats. *c* **1610** SIR J. MELVIL *Mem.* (1735) 209 He sent me his own Night-Gown furred with rich Furrings. **1708** J. CHAMBERLAYNE *St. Gt. Brit.* II. III. vi. (1743) 416 None might wear Silk or costly Furring except Knights & Barons. **1849** ROCK *Ch. of Fathers* II. vi. 53 Among the clergy of the lower grade in a cathedral, there was a distinction marked by the furring of the amys. **1886** *Sci. Amer.* N.S. LV. 129/2 A sort of hedgehog with heavy furring and short legs.

2. The process of becoming furred or incrusted; the state of being furred; also, a coating of fur.

1601 HOLLAND *Pliny* XX. xiv. II. 59 With Honie it [Mint] cureth the roughnes & furring of the toung. **1612** WOODALL *Surg. Mate* Wks. (1653) 217 The furring of the mouth and the throat in fevers. **1831** BREWSTER *Newton* (1855) I. i. 9 Their chief inconvenience arose from the furring up of the small hole through which the water passed. **1885** W. L. CARPENTER *Soaps & Candles* 212 The lime salts are deposited in an insoluble form, such as the 'furring' in a tea-kettle or boiler.

3. a. *Shipbuilding.* The action or process of double planking a ship's side; also, a piece of timber used for this. Cf. DOUBLING 3 b.

1622 R. HAWKINS *Voy. S. Sea* (1847) 120 Another manner is used with double plankes as thicke without as within after the manner of furring. **1627** CAPT. SMITH *Seaman's Gram.* xi. 52 Ripping off the plankes two or three strakes vnder water and as much aboue, and put other Timbers vpon the first, and then put on the planks vpon those timbers, this.. is called Furring. *a* **1642** SIR W. MONSON *Naval Tracts* III (1704) 346/2 Another Sheathing is with double Planks..like a Furring. **1867** SMYTH *Sailor's Word-bk.*, *Furring*, doubling planks on a ship. Also, a furring in the ship's side.

b. *Building.* The nailing on of thin strips of board in order to level or raise a surface for lathing, boarding, etc. Also, the strips thus laid on.

1678 MOXON *Mech. Exerc.* I. 167 Furrings, the making good of the Rafters Feet in the Cornice. **1703** T. N. *City & C. Purchaser* 146 When Rafters are..sunk hollow in the middle, and pieces (cut thickest in the middle, and to a point at each end) are nail'd upon them to make them straight again; the putting on of those pieces is call'd Furring the Rafters. **1823** P. NICHOLSON *Pract. Build.* 223 Furrings, slips of timber nailed to joists or rafters, in order to bring them to a level. **1850** PARKER *Gloss. Archit.* (ed. 5), *Furrings*, or Shreadings, short pieces attached to the feet of the rafters of a roof. **1859** GWILT *Archit.* Gloss., *Furring*, the fixing of thin scantlings or laths upon the edges of any number of timbers in a range, when such timbers are out of the surface they were intended to form. **1883** *Harper's Mag.* Nov. 884/2 The only combustible material..is the wood used in the floors and their furrings.

c. *Building.* 'A lining of scantling and plaster-work on a brick wall, to prevent the dampness of the latter reaching the room' (*Cassell*).

4. The business of collecting furs or hunting furred animals; fur-trading. Also *attrib.*

1778 G. CARTWRIGHT *Jrnl.* (1792) II. 373, I fitted out Joseph Tero for a furring voyage to White-bear River. **1849** *Jrnl. Bp. Newfoundland's Voy.* 67 Sixty miles within that bay the Hudson's Bay Company have a furring establishment. *Ibid.*, The settled inhabitants..are supported by the salmon fishery, by furring, and by killing seals. **1856** W. E. CORMACK *Narr. Journey Newfoundland* (1874) VIII. 73 The extent of their salmon and cod fisheries, and of their furring, was noticed when speaking of the occupation collectively of the inhabitants of St. George's Bay. **1920** GRENFELL & SPALDING *Le Petit Nord* (1921) 62 In the winter the northern people move up the bays and go 'furring'.

†**furrour.** *Obs.* Also forrour. [a. OF. *forreor* (mod.F. *fourreur*), agent-n. f. *forrer* to FUR.] A furrier.

c **1330** R. BRUNNE *Chron. Wace* (Rolls) 12453 Til a pane, as a furour [*v.r.* forrour], he did hem tewe.

furrow ('fʌrəʊ), *sb.* Forms: α. 1 furh, fyrh (*dat.*), 3 furȝ, 3–4 furgh(e, 3–5 forw(h, 4 fo(o)rew, forwe, forȝ, furch, 4–5 forgh(e, 4–6 for(r)ough(e, for(r)ow(e, (6 furrough, furrowe, 7 forrwe), 6– furrow. β. 4–5 fore, *south.* vore, 5 fure, (foure, fowre), 6 feure, 7 furr(e, 9 furr, 4– *Sc.* fur. [Com. Teut.: OE. *furh* str. fem. (gen. *fyrh*, *fure*, dat. *fyrh*) = MDu. *vōre* (Du. *voor*, *vore*), OHG. *furuh* (MHG. *vurch*, mod.Ger. *furche*) furrow, ON. *for* trench, drain:—OTeut. **furh-*:—pre-Teut. **pr̥k-*; cf. L. *porca* ridge between furrows, OIr. *rech*, Welsh *rhych* (:—**pricâ*, *priccâ*).

Some scholars connect this word with L. *porcus*, Eng. FARROW, assigning to the common root the sense 'to root like a swine'.]

1. A narrow trench made in the earth with a plough, esp. for the reception of seed. ***to sow under the furrow*** (see quot. 1523).

† ***to spare neither ridge nor furrow***: a proverbial phrase in ME. poems expressive of reckless speed on the part of a rider.

α. *c* **888** K. ÆLFRED *Boeth.* v. §2 Þonne dysegaþ se þe þonne wile hwilc sæd oþfæstan þam drium furum. **955** *Charter of Eadred* in Birch *Cartul. Sax.* III. 70 Andlang weȝes to ðære ȝedrifonan furh, andlang fyrh oþ hit cymð [etc.]. *c* **1220** *Bestiary* 398 [This der] goð o felde to a furȝ, and falleð ðar-inne..forto bilirten fuȝeles. *c* **1374** CHAUCER *Former Age* 12 No man yit knew the forwes of his lond. **14** .. *Tretyce* in *W. of Henley's Husb.* (1890) 47 Yeff [ye] sowe your lande vnder þe foroughe let it be ereyd. *c* **1440** *Bone Flor.* 746 He stroke the stede with the spurrys, He spared nodur rygge nor forows. **1523** FITZHERB. *Husb.* §34 Wheate is mooste commonlye sowen vnder the forowe, that is to saye, caste it vppon the falowe, and than plowe it vnder. **1583** STUBBES *Anat. Abus.* II. (1882) 77 A man..shuld take his plow, and go draw a furrow in a field. **1697** DRYDEN *Virg. Georg.* III. 797 The lab'ring Swain Scratch'd with a Rake, a Furrow for his Grain. **1728–46** THOMSON *Spring* 37 The well-us'd plough Lies in the furrow. **1807** CRABBE *Par. Reg.* I. 658 The straightest furrow lifts the ploughman's heart. **1831** *Sir J. Sinclair's Corr.* II. 365 The chief furrows, which conduct the choaked-up water, are always laid out by the agriculturist himself. **1883** MACFADYEN in *Congregat. Year Bk.* 47 The furrow is uneven because an ox and an ass draw the plough.

β. *c* **1380** *Sir Ferumb.* 1565 Þay..Ne spared rigges noþer vores; til þay mette þat pray. *c* **1470** HENRY *Wallace* I. 405 The suerd flaw fra him a fur breid on the land. **1513** DOUGLAS *Æneis* VII. iv. 20 A lityll fur, To mark the fundment of his new citie. **1600** DYMMOK *Ireland* (1843) 42 Men..hidd themselves lyke fearefull hares in the furres. **1641** BEST *Farm. Bks.* (Surtees) 44 The furre on your lefte hande is the best for the fore-furre; for then the corne falleth the fittest for the hande. **1765** A. DICKSON *Treat. Agric.* (ed. 2) 238 The plough will..go upon the points of the irons, which will make her..make a bad fur. **1816** SCOTT *Old Mort.* xiv, 'I wad..turn sic furs on the bonny rigs o' Milnwood holms, that it wad be worth a pint but to look at them.' **1877–89** *N.W. Linc. Gloss.*, *Fur*, a furrow. 'Th' furs was all full o' watter on pag-rag daay, an' soa th' taaties rotted.'

b. *transf.* and *fig.*, *esp.* in allusion to the track of a vessel over the sea.

1382 WYCLIF *Ecclus.* vii. 3 Sowe thou not eueles in the foorewes of vnriȝtwisnesse. **1535** COVERDALE *Ps.* cxxviii[i]. 3 The plowers plowed vpon my backe, and made longe forowes. **1589** *Pasquil's Ret.* C b, God shall..punish euery forrow they haue plowed vpon his backe. *c* **1600** SHAKS. *Sonn.* xxii, When in thee times forrwes I behould. **1814** CARY *Dante, Par.* II. 15 Marking well the furrow broad Before you in the wave. **1842** TENNYSON *Ulysses* 59 Push off ..smite The sounding furrows. **1887** BOWEN *Virg. Æneid* v. 157 Each with her long keel ploughing in lengthened furrows the brine.

c. *poet.* Used *loosely* for arable land, a piece of ploughed land, the cornfields.

α. *c* **1380** *Sir Ferumb.* 5593 Ac sone sterte he vp of þe forȝ. **1610** SHAKS. *Temp.* IV. i. 135 You Sun-burn'd Sicklemen of August weary, Come hether from the furrow, and be merry. **1634** MILTON *Comus* 292 What time the laboured ox In his loose traces from the furrow came. **1735** SOMERVILLE *Chase* II. 130 See how they thread The Brakes, and up yon Furrow drive along.

β. **1500–20** DUNBAR *Poems* xvii. 12 Barronis takis..All fruct that growis on the feure.

d. (In form *fur.*) A ploughing. Now only *Sc.*

1610 W. FOLKINGHAM *Art of Survey* I. xi. 43 Their seuerall orders and seasons for fallowing, twifallowing, trifallowing and seed-furre. **1743** MAXWELL *Trans. Soc. Improv. Agric. Scotl.* 21 It is advised to plow it with all convenient Haste, that so it may have got three Furs betwixt and the latter End of April or Beginning of May; the first to be cloven, the second a cross Fur, the third to be gathered.

†**2.** In extended sense: A trench, drain. *Obs.*

c **1330** *Arth. & Merl.* 3460 Þe kniȝt fel ded in a forwe. *Ibid.* 8184 He cleued thurch..king Beas doun in a furch. **1382** WYCLIF *1 Kings* xviii. 32 And he made a water cundid, as by two litil forwis in envyroun of the auter. *c* **1420** *Pallad. on Husb.* VI. 36 A forgh iij footes deep thy landes thorgh. **1561** T. NORTON *Calvin's Inst.* IV. 121 Out of a fountaine water is somtime dronk..somtime by forrowes is conueied to the watering of groundes. **1577** B. GOOGE *Heresbach's Husb.* II. (1586) 72 If you will needes plante the same yeere..let the furrowes be made at least two moneths before. **1611** BIBLE *Ezek.* xvii. 7 That hee might water it by the furrowes of her plantation. **1626** BACON *Sylva* §600 Carrying it [Water] in some long Furrowes; And from those Furrowes, drawing it trauerse. **1765** A. DICKSON *Treat. Agric.* (ed. 2) 144 The soil ..will not give it a passage into the furrows or drains. **1884** *Chr. World* 21 Feb. 134/3 Fortunately, our water furrow is a swift-flowing stream.

†**3.** A quantity (of land) having the length or breadth of a furrow. *Obs.*

c **1300** *Havelok* 1094 Ne shulde he hauen of Engelond Onlepi forw in his hond. **1377** LANGL. *P. Pl.* B. XIII. 372 Þat a fote londe or a forwe fecchen I wolde. **1390** GOWER *Conf.* III. 245 Til they have with a plough to broke A furgh of lond. *c* **1425** WYNTOUN *Cron.* IX. v. 135 Ðat nowþir Fure na Fute of Land Wes at þaire Pes þan of Ingland. *c* **1470** HENRY *Wallace* VIII. 22 Off him I held neuir a fur off land.

4. Anything resembling a furrow; **a.** generally, e.g. a rut or track, a groove, indentation, or depression narrow in proportion to its length.

c **1374** CHAUCER *Boeth.* v. metr. v. 132 (Camb. MS.) Som of hem..drawen after hem a traas or a forwh I-kountynued. **1398** TREVISA *Barth. De P.R.* XIX cxxix. (1495) 938 Orbita is the forough of a whele that makyth a depe forough in the wyndynge and trendlynge abowte. **1513** DOUGLAS *Æneis* II. xi. 32 Thair followis [the sterne] a streme of fire, or a lang fur. **1607** TOPSELL *Four-f. Beasts* (1658) 282 The first furrow of the mouth—I mean that which is next unto the upper fore-teeth. **1665** HOOKE *Microgr.* 4 There were several great and deep scratches, or furrows. **1712** ADDISON *Spect.* No. 416 ¶2 The different Furrows and Impressions of the Chisel. **1774** GOLDSM. *Nat. Hist.* (1776) I. 205 The middle waters..sink in a furrow. **1813** J. THOMSON *Lect. Inflam.* 615 This ligature produced a slight furrow in the arm.

b. on the face: A deep wrinkle.

1589 GREENE *Tullies Loue* Wks. (Grosart) VII. 204 If it [my brow] once proue full of angrie forrowes. **1609** DEKKER *Guls Horne-bk.* i. 7 Now those furrowes are fild vp with Ceruse and Vermilion. **1797** MRS. RADCLIFFE *Italian* vi, Habitual discontent had fixed the furrows of their cheeks. **1859** HELPS *Friends in C.* Ser. II. II. iv. 86 They make.. furrows in the cheeks of the sufferers.

c. *Milling.* One of the grooves in the face of a millstone. ***furrow and land*** (see quot. 1880).

1825 J. NICHOLSON *Operat. Mechanic* 144 When the furrows become blunt and shallow by wearing, the running stone must be taken up, and both stones new dressed with a chisel and hammer. **1870** *Eng. Mech.* 28 Jan. 485/2 Cutting all the short furrows into the master furrow. **1880** *Antrim & Down Gloss.*, *Furrow and Land*, the hollows and heights on the surface of a mill-stone.

d. *Anat.*, *Zool.*, etc. (= L. *sulcus*).

1807–26 S. COOPER *First Lines Surg.* (ed. 5) 301 The lateral sinuses..occupy the deep transverse furrows in the middle of the inner surface of the os occipitis. **1832** DE LA BECHE *Geol. Man.* (ed. 2) 327 Whorls..divided by eight or ten furrows into as many imbricating joints. **1846** ELLIS *Elgin Marb.* II. 26 A furrow which forms the line of contact with the forehead. **1868** DARWIN *Anim. & Pl.* I. v. 140 The external orifice or furrow of the nostrils was also twice as long. **1874** LUBBOCK *Orig. & Met. Ins.* iii. 45 The median furrow easily discerned. **1879** CALDERWOOD *Mind & Br.* ii. 12 The soft mass [of the brain] being arranged alternately in ridges, and in grooves or furrows.

e. *Bot.*

1725 BRADLEY *Fam. Dict.*, *Furrow*, among Botanists.. signifies a Ridge or Swelling on the Sides either of a Tree, Stalk, or Fruit. **1776** WITHERING *Brit. Plants* (1796) I. 151 Seed single..marked with a furrow lengthways. **1862** DARWIN *Fertil. Orchids* iii. 118 If the furrow he touched very gently by a needle..it instantly splits along its whole length. **1882** VINES *Sachs' Bot.* 396 The arrangement of.. projecting longitudinal ridges, and depressions or furrows, is exactly repeated.

5. *attrib.* and *Comb.*, as ***furrow-water***; ***furrow-cloven***, ***-like*** adjs. Also **furrow-board** = MOULD-BOARD; **furrow-drain** (see quot.), hence ***furrow-drain*** vb., ***-draining***; †**furrow-face**, one who has a wrinkled face; **furrow-faced**, **-fronted** *a.*, having furrows or wrinkles on the face or forehead; **furrow-** (*dial.* **fur-**) **side**, the side of the plough towards the furrows already made; **furrow-slice**, the slice of earth turned up by the mould-board of the plough; **furrow-**

weed, a weed that grows on the 'furrow' or ploughed land.

1649 *Furrow-board [see EARTH-BOARD]. **1847** TENNYSON *Princess* vii 192 The firths of ice That huddling slant in *furrow-cloven falls. **1858** SIMMONDS *Dict. Trade*, **Furrow-drain*, a deep open channel made by a plough to carry off water. **1846** MCCULLOCH *Acc. Brit. Empire* (1854) I. 593 The new practice of *furrow-draining has been the most important of the recent improvements in Scotch agriculture. **1621** BURTON *Anat. Mel.* I. ii. III. iv. 130 b, Pale, and leane, *furrow-faces. **1605** B. JONSON *Volpone* I. i, I.. expose no ships To threat'nings of the *furrow-faced sea. **1640** RAWLINS *Rebellion* II. i, The *furrow-fronted Fates have made an Anvill To forge diseases on. **1879** D. M. WALLACE *Australas.* xi. 225 The loose surface.. sometimes forming hilly undulations, at others *furrow-like ripples. **1765** A. DICKSON *Treat. Agric.* (ed. 2) 215 This lessons the resistance from the *furrow-side. *Ibid.* 235 If the beam points to the fur-side, the plough will have too much land; and if it points to the land-side, the plough will have too little land. **1805** R. W. DICKSON *Pract. Agric.* (1807) I. 5 The perfect turning over of the *furrow-slice. **1862** J. WILSON *Farming* 206 In ploughing for a seed-bed the furrow-slice is usually cut about 5 inches deep. **1679** DRYDEN *Tr. & Cr.* II. iii, *Furrow Water Is all the Wine we taste. **1605** SHAKS. *Lear* IV. iv. 3 He was met euen now As mad as the vext Sea, singing alowd, Crown'd with ranke Fenitar and *furrow weeds.

furrow ('fʌrəʊ), *v.* Also 5 forow, 6 furow, 7 furr. [f. prec. sb.]

1. *trans.* To make furrows in (earth) with a plough; to plough.

1576 FLEMING *Panopl. Epist.* 354 They [oxen] drawe the plough, they furrowe the soyle. **1607** TOPSELL *Four-f. Beasts* (1658) 48 They furrow the earth like a draught of Oxen with a plow. **1894** T. ROOSEVELT in *Forum* (U.S.) Apr. 202 Fields already fifty times furrowed by the German ploughs.

fig. **1847** JAMES *Convict* v, Heaven.. furrows the heart with griefs to produce a rich crop of joys hereafter.

b. *transf.* To make a track or tracks in (water); to cleave; to plough.

c **1425** *Found. St. Bartholomew's* (E.E.T.S.) 43 Certeyne shypmen at sandwyche, glad and mery with a prosperous cowrse forowid the dowtable see. *a* **1547** SURREY *Æneid* II. 1038 Long to furrow large space of stormy seas. **1583** STANYHURST *Æneis* III. (Arb.) 76 With wooddden vessel thee rough seas deepelye we furrowe. **1632** J. HAYWARD tr. *Biondi's Eromena* 39 Prince Meleneone furrowed the surging waves. **1662** STILLINGFL. *Orig. Sacr.* III. i. §10 They pass down the strong current of Time with the same facility that a well built ship.. doth furrow the Ocean. **1814** SCOTT *Lord of Isles* IV. xiii, Now launch'd once more, the inland sea They furrow with fair augury. **1845** DARWIN *Voy. Nat.* iii. 39 The whole sea was in places furrowed by them [porpoises]. **1876** R. F. BURTON *Gorilla L.* I. 171 We.. saw sundry shoals of fish furrowing the water.

2. To make furrow-like depressions, indentations, or channels in. Also with *up*.

1609 HOLLAND *Amm. Marcell.* XXIX. i. 354 When.. they began to.. varie in their words, after their sides were throughly furrowed [L. *fodicatis*]. **1692** BENTLEY *Boyle Lect.* viii. 298 Furrowed from Pole to Pole with the Deep Channel of the Sea. **1697** DRYDEN *Virg. Georg.* III. 656 The chapt Earth is furrow'd o'er with Chinks. **1732** LEDIARD *Sethos* II. VII. 83 They furrow'd their bodies with sharp stones. **1774** GOLDSM. *Nat. Hist.* (1776) VII. 328 After furrowing up the sand, it hides itself under it, horns and all. **1834** J. FORBES *Laennec's Dis. Chest* (ed. 4) 287 A hard and irregular surface, furrowed by linear marks. **1863** BARING-GOULD *Iceland* 116 Then [the wind] rolls onward to furrow the snows on Eiriks Jokull. **1879** BROWNING *Ivan Ivanovitch* 225 O God, the feel of the fang furrowing my shoulder! see! It grinds—it grates the bone.

b. To make wrinkles in.

1593 SHAKS. *Rich. II*, I. iii. 229 Thou canst helpe time to furrow me with age. **1627–77** FELTHAM *Resolves* I. xiii. 20 Another lives hardly here, with a heavy heart, furrowing of a mournful face. **1661** *Sir A. Haslerig's Last Will & Test.* Supp. 6 The inraged Tygre.. furrowed his Front. **1729** T. COOKE *Tales, Proposals*, etc. 595 Sev'nty years have furrow'd o'er her Face. **1838** LYTTON *Leila* I. v, The lordly features.. furrowed by petty cares. **1870** MORRIS *Earthly Par.* I. I. 5 Their brows seem furrowed deep with more than years.

c. *fig.* Said of the action of tears.

1523 HYRDE tr. *Vives' Instr. Chr. Wom.* I. ix. I ij a, Howe can she weep for her sinne, y[t] muste bare her skynne there with, and forowe her face? *a* **1656** BP. HALL *Rem. Wks.* (1660) 184 We may furrow our cheekes with our tears. **1816** BYRON *Ch. Har.* III. xx, Fair cheeks were furrowed with hot tears. **1871** MACDUFF *Mem. Patmos* ix. 113 The Apostle.. with a tear.. furrowing his cheek.

d. To gather *up* in folds or wrinkles. *rare*$^{-1}$.

1853 DALE tr. *Baldeschi's Ceremonial* 66 *note*, Cotta, the short surplice worn in Rome.. is usually furrowed up in a full and tasteful manner.

3. *intr.* To make furrows or grooves; to make wrinkles.

1576 FLEMING *Panopl. Epist.* 356 Let us catche the ploughe by the handle, and fall to furrowing. *a* **1577** GASCOIGNE *Flowers*, etc. Wks. (1587) 45 We furrowing in the foaming floods to take our best availes. **1863** J. L. W. *By-gone Days* 2 Where the ploughshare furrows in spring.

b. quasi-*trans.*, as in *to furrow* (*out, up*) *one's way*. Of a river: to excavate (a channel), to force *itself* along a channel.

1613 PURCHAS *Pilgrimage* (1614) 820 Maragnon is far greater, whose waters having furrowed a Channell of six thousand miles, in the length of his winding passage [etc.]. *a* **1639** WOTTON *Ps.* civ. in Farr *S.P. Jas. I* (1848) 248 There go the ships, that furrow out their way. **1647** W. BROWNE tr. *Polexander* III. 241 Let thy choler furrow up and make a way to that Island whereto none can arrive. **1791** COWPER *Odyss.* v. 492 And I have pass'd, Furrowing my way. **1883** F. M. CRAWFORD *Dr. Claudius* vi, The circular wrinkle slowly furrowed its way round Barker's mouth. **1890** H. M. STANLEY *Darkest Africa* II. xxviii. 259 The Rami-lulu had eventually furrowed and grooved itself deeply through.

Hence **'furrowing** *vbl. sb.* and *ppl. a.* Also **'furrower**, one who or that which furrows.

1611 COTGR., *Canelure*, a channelling, or furrowing in stone, or in timber; a fluting. **1612** DRAYTON *Poly-olb.* i. 3 Vpon the utmost end of Cornwall's furrowing beake. *Ibid.* xviii. 78 She learn'd.. To steele the coulters edge, and sharpe the furrowing share. **1841–3** *Anthon's Class. Dict.* 380 Gyes (the part of the plough to which the share is fixed) is the Furrower. **1891** *Athenæum* 17 Oct. 523/1 The greater number of them have been crushed and broken by the deep furrowing of the steam cultivator.

furrow, obs. form of FORAY.

furrow (cow): see FARROW *a.*

furrowed ('fʌrəʊd), *ppl. a.* [f. FURROW *v.* + -ED[1].] In senses of the vb.; *spec.* in *Masonry* (see quots. 1904, 1929); †*furrowed-grass*: see CHAMELEON *sb.* 6 c, and quot. 1598 there.

1599 SHAKS. *Hen. V.* III. Prol. 12 The threaden Sayles.. Draw the huge Bottomes through the furrowed Sea. **1615** J. STEPHENS *Satyr. Ess.* 18 Another doth conceale The furrowed wrinkles of his tawny skinne. **1632** MILTON *L'Allegro* 64 While the ploughman, near at hand, Whistles o'er the furrowed land. **1646** GAULE *Sel. Cases Consc.* 4 Every old woman with a wrinkled face, a furr'd brow.. is.. pronounced for a witch. **1713** ADDISON *Guardian* No. 114 ⁋1 The features are strong and well furrowed. **1810** SCOTT *Lady of L.* II. xvi, The furrowed bosom of the deep. **1828** STARK *Elem. Nat. Hist.* II. 305 Thorax furrowed and crenated on the margin. **1855** KINGSLEY *Heroes, Theseus* II. 205 The furrowed marble walls. **1904** C. F. MITCHELL *Brickwork & Masonry* 128 *Furrowed Work*... This labour, used to accentuate quoins, consists in sinking a draught about the four sides of the face of a stone, leaving the central portion projecting about ⅛ inch, in which a number of vertical grooves about ⅜ inch wide are sunk. **1929** E. G. WARLAND *Mod. Pract. Masonry* 24 *Furrowed Surfaces.*— Small flutings, from ½ to ⅝ in. wide, are worked vertically or horizontally across the surface.

furrowless ('fʌrəʊlɪs), *a.* [f. FURROW *sb.* + -LESS.] Having no furrows, grooves, or wrinkles.

a **1847** ELIZA COOK *River Thought* v, The furrowless brow. **18..** LOWELL *Pioneer* Poet. Wks. (1890) I. 248 When all before him stretches, furrowless and lone.

furrowy ('fʌrəʊɪ), *a.* [f. FURROW *sb.* + -Y[1].] Full of furrows or wrinkles.

1611 COTGR., *Rayonner*, to furrow; make furrowes, or make furrowie. **1818** MILMAN *Samor* 267, I should have known, though furrowy, sunk and wan, That face. **1829** *Blackw. Mag.* XXV. 71 We view their furrowy track. **1847** TENNYSON *Princess* III. 158 A double hill ran up his furrowy forks Beyond the thick-leaved platans of the vale.

†**'furrure.** *Obs.* Also 4 for(r)-, furrour(e, 5 forer, forur(e, furure, furrur. [a. OF. *forrëure, fourrëure* (mod.F. *fourrure*), f. *forrer, fourrer*, FUR *v.*] Fur; a trimming, lining, or adornment of fur.

1387 TREVISA *Higden* (Rolls) VII. 373 He usede forours of symple prys. *c* **1400** MAUNDEV. (1839) xxiii. 247 The folk of that Contree usen alle longe Clothes with outen Furroures. **1420** *E.E. Wills* (1882) 54 Also I will þat all þ[e] ffurrurs þat I haue, be sould and doon for my saule. **1439** *Ibid.* 118 All my .. clothis of silke, with-oute ffurrereur [*sic*]. **1463** *Mann. & Househ. Exp.* 151 Item, he owyth ffor the forer off the same gowne, x. li. **1480** CAXTON *Chron. Eng.* ccxxv. 229 No clothe that was wrought oute of Englond.. ne furrur of beyonde the see.

attrib. **1387** TREVISA *Higden* (Rolls) VI. 475 Furrour skynnes.

furry ('fɜːrɪ), *a.* (and *sb.*[1]) [f. FUR *sb.* + -Y[1].]

A. *adj.*

1. Of or composed of fur; consisting of furs.

a **1674** MILTON *Hist. Mosc.* ii. (1851) 483 The Furs which clothe them; the furry side in Summer outward. **1725** POPE *Odyss.* XVII. 40 Euryclea spreads With furry spoils of beasts the splendid beds. **1881** R. ROUTLEDGE *Hist. Sc.* i. 1 Man is even unprotected from the vicissitudes of the seasons by the furry coat which covers the beasts of the field.

2. Of animals: Covered with fur; furred.

1687 DRYDEN *Hind & P.* III. 25 The time When all her furry sons in frequent senate met. **1823** BYRON *Juan* X. xxvi, Bear-skins black and furry. **1873** G. C. DAVIES *Mount. & Mere* viii. 59 A furry little water-rat swimming along by the edge of the bank.

fig. **1865** *Pall Mall G.* 22 June 11 He is one of those sleek 'furry' little men who are met with in all close religious communities.

3. Of persons: Wearing fur, clad in furs.

1717 FENTON *Ode Ld. Gower* 36 From Volga's Banks, th' imperious Czar Leads forth his Furry Troops to War.

4. Made of fur, lined or trimmed with fur.

1865 KINGSLEY *Herew.* vi, His furry cloak shewed him to be no common man. **1872** BRYANT *Poems, Little People of Show* 97 With ample furry robe Close-belted round her waist.

b. *transf.* and *fig.*

1691 DRYDEN *K. Arthur* III. ii, Awake, awake, And winter from thy furry mantle shake. **1716** ROWE *Ode for N. Year* 1717 i, Winter! thou hoary, venerable Sire, All richly in thy furry Mantle clad. **1835** SIR J. ROSS *Narr. 2nd Voy.* xlvi. 591 We wrap ourselves up in a sort of furry contentment.

5. Resembling fur, fur-like, soft.

1876 T. HARDY *Ethelberta* (1890) 88 An open space.. floored at the bottom with.. cushions of furry moss.

6. Of the nature of, or coated with, fur or morbid matter.

1739 'R. BULL' tr. *Dedekindus' Grobianus* 222 Laughter misbecomes Foul furry Teeth. **1836** T. HOOK *G. Gurney* III. i. 31 Two foggy decanters, half full of the remnants of yesterday's libation, with a sort of furry rim just over the surface. **1856** CANNING in Hare 2 *Noble Lives* (1893) II. 89 One's shoes get furry with mildew in a day. **1871** NAPHEYS *Prev. & Cure Dis.* III. ii. 624 Yellowish furry coating [of the tongue].

†**B.** *sb.* A hairy caterpillar. *Obs.*

1598 FLORIO, *Millepiedi*, a worme having manie feete, called a furrie or a palmer.

furry ('fʌrɪ), *sb.*[2] *dial.* [Perh. in some way connected with FAIR *sb.*, L. *fēria*.] A festival observed at Helston, Cornwall, on the eighth of May; also, a peculiar dance used on that occasion. (The *W. Cornwall Gloss.* gives *faddy* and *flora* as synonyms.) Also *attrib.*

1790 in *Gentl. Mag.* LX. I. 520 At Helstone.. it is customary to dedicate the 8th of May to revelry.. It is called the Furry-day. **1848** C. A. JOHNS *Week at Lizard* 225 A large party of ladies and gentlemen.. commence a peculiar kind of dance, called 'the furry'. **1872** HARDWICK *Trad. Lanc.* 87 A spring festival.. annually celebrated at Helston.. named the 'Furry', or gathering.

†**'furry**, *v. Obs. rare.* [? back-formation from FURRIER[1].] *trans.* To quarter (soldiers).

1579 FENTON *Guicciard.* II. 89 The armie being furried in many partes of the realme.. lived in such vnbrideled incontinencie [etc.].

Fursday, Sc. var. of THURSDAY.

furse, obs. form of FIERCE.

†**'fursell.** *Obs.* [dim. of FURZE.] = FURZE.

1639 T. DE GREY *Compl. Horseman* 5 Underwoods, Bushes, Fursells, Broome.

†**'furshe**, *a. Her. Obs. rare.* [a. F. *fourchée*: see FORCHE *a.*] = FORCHE *a.*

1572 BOSSEWELL *Armorie* II. 136 Beareth party per pale Sable and Argent, a crosse Furshe of the one and the other.

furst, var. of FRIST and obs. f. of FIRST, THIRST.

[**furt**, in Dicts. explained 'theft', is a misprint in the later edd. of Tomkis's *Albumazar* for *furie*.]

furth, obs. and Sc. form of FORTH.

†**'further**, *sb. Obs.* [f. FURTHER *v.*] The action of the vb. FURTHER; = FURTHERANCE.

1526 Q. MARGT. (Scotl.) *Let. Wolsey* (MS. Caligula B. viii. 160) in M. A. Everett Wood *Lett. R. & Illustr. Ladies* II. 9 The said bearer, whom pleaseth you, my Lord, cause have good further and expedition of his errands. **1535** STEWART *Cron. Scot.* I. 522 Commending him that he had done sic thing, In so greit forder of the commoun weill. **1641** HINDE *J. Bruen* xxviii. 87 For the increase of Religion and further of the Gospel. **1785** BURNS *3rd Ep. to J. Lapraik* 1 Guid speed and furder to you, Johnny.

further ('fɜːðə(r)), *a.* Forms: 1 furðra (*Northumb.* forðora), 2 furþur, 4–5 furþer(e, 3–7 forþer(e, -ther, *Orm.* forrþerr, (5 forthre), 6–7 furder, 4–7 forder, 6 forthir, 6– further. See also FARTHER. [OE. *furðra* = OFris, *fordera*, OS. *forthoro* (MLG. *vordere*), OHG. *ford(e)ro*, *fordaro, fordoro* (MHG. *vordere*, mod.G. *vorder*):—OTeut. **furþeron-* wk., f. **furþero-* str. (the acc. neut. of which appears in FURTHER *adv.*):—pre-Teut. *pr̥-tero-*, f. root of FORE *adv.* + comparative suffix as in *af-ter, o-ther*.

On this assumption the Eng. *further* adj. and adv. have nothing but their ultimate root in common with the Goth. *faurþis* adv:—OTeut. **furþ-iz* or **furþ-joz*, f. the stem of FORTH + comparative suffix = -ER[3]. A different hypothesis (Kluge in Paul's *Grdr.*, ed. 2, I. 483) is that *further* and its cognates are f. the stem of FORTH + compar. suffix (not *-izon-* but) *-eron-, -uron-*, as in *inner, outer* (see -ER[3] A. 2). The OHG. *furdir* adv. is explained by Kluge as repr. a locative **furþirî*.]

†**1. a.** That is before another in position, order, or rank; *esp.* of an animal's limbs or a part of the body: Front. *Obs.* (Cf. FARTHER B. 1.)

c **1000** *Ags. Gosp.* John xiii. 16 Soþlice ic eow secȝe nys se ðeowa furðra þonne his hlaford. *a* **1300** *Cursor M.* 28169 He was for-þer mar þen j. **1387** TREVISA *Higden* (Rolls) VII. 187 A wounde receyved in þe furþer partie of his body [*in anteriori parte corporis*]. *c* **1400** *Lanfranc's Cirurg.* 113 Brood twoward þe forþere side of þe heed & scharpere twoward þe hyndere syde. **1486** *Bk. St. Albans* E ij b, The ij. forther legges the hede layde by twene. **1539** *Invent. R. Wardrobe* (1815) 36 Lynit the forthir quarteris with blak taffiteis. **1609** SKENE *Reg. Maj.* 134 Gif ane horse slayes ane man passand before him, with his forther feete.

b. With reference to time: Former. Also in comb. *further-ealdefader* (cf. L. *proavus*): great grandfather. *Obs.*

1155 *Proc. Henry II*, in *Anglia* VII. 220 þæt hi beon ælc þare lande wurþa þe hi eafdon in Edwardes kinges deȝe & on Willelmes kinges mines furþur ealdefader. **1557** N.T. (Genev.) *Jas.* v. 7 The forther and the latter rayne. **1561** CHRIST. HINDALL *Depos.* in *Bp. Chester Eccl. Crt.* 1561–6, lf. 10 b, Mr. Holden did knowe of his forther wief beynge on lyve. **1562** *Child Marriages*, etc. (1897) 192 She was temptid by daily sute of the said Dilon, & did forget her forther promesse.

2. More extended, going beyond what already exists or has been dealt with; additional, more. †*further age*: advanced age. †*further way*: a further-continued road. ***further education***, formal education organized for adults, or for young people who have left school; also *attrib.* (Cf. FARTHER B. 2.)

a **1300** *Cursor M.* 10327 Child to gett, Bituix and þair forþer eild. **1495** in *Yorksh. Archæol. Soc.* (Record Ser. 1895) XVII. 127 Oure forthre pleasir in that behalf. **1526** *Pilgr. Perf.* (W. de W. 1531) 50b, For a forther knowledge of this tree, you must vnderstande that [etc.]. **1582** N. LICHEFIELD tr. *Castanheda's Conq. E. Ind.* xxiii. 58 Without any further delay, the King sent them away. **1609** SKENE *Reg. Maj., Forme of Proces* 22 He..judicially renunces all forder probation. **1634** W. TIRWHYT tr. *Balzac's Lett.* 44 Without further ambiguity. **1667** MILTON *P.L.* IV. 174 To th' ascent of that..Hill Satan had journied on..But further way found none. **1711** ADDISON *Spect.* No. 65 ¶2 Without further Preface, I am going to look into some of our most applauded Plays. **1794** PALEY *Evid.* (ed. 2) I. v. 97 We find ..two of them..seized.. and threatened with further punishment. **1838** DE MORGAN *Ess. Prob.* 201, I now proceed to some further instances. **1861** BUCKLE *Civiliz.* II. iv. 315 This was a further stimulus to Scotch industry. [**1898** G. BALFOUR *Educ. Syst. Gt. Brit. & Ireland* p. xxii, No adequate system of intermediate schools exists to receive, as a matter of routine, those elementary pupils who are fitted for further education.] **1913** J. H. WHITEHOUSE *Nat. Syst. Educ.* ii. 6 The writer suggests..the conferring on local authorities of the power to enforce further education compulsorily for children between the ages of 14 and 18. **1937** G. A. N. LOWNDES *Silent Social Revolution* II. 95 The growth of our modern system—or rather systems—of technical and further education drawing their strength both from the secondary and (since 1926) the Hadow senior schools. **1944** *Act 7 & 8 Geo. VI* c. 31 §7 The statutory system of public education shall be organised in three progressive stages to be known as primary education, secondary education, and further education. **1962** J. BRAINE *Life at Top* i. 11 Now he was dead and Sindram Grange had been taken over by the County as a Further Education Centre. **1970** *Daily Tel.* 28 Aug. 2/2 The establishment and development of polytechnics as bridges between further and higher education.

3. More distant, remoter, esp. the remoter of two. Of a horse: The off (side). (Cf. FARTHER B. 3.)

1578 in W. H. Turner *Select. Rec. Oxford* (1880) 396 One grey..mare, crapped on the further yeare. **1611** BIBLE *2 Esdras* xiii. 41 They would..goe foorth into a further countrey. **1675** A. BROWNE *Ars Pict.* 90 Work your further Mountains so that they should seem to be lost in the Air. **1678** BUTLER *Hud.* III. iii. 58 With kicks and bangs he ply'd The further and the nearer side [of a horse]. **1821** JOANNA BAILLIE *Metr. Leg., Wallace* lvi, In the further rear. **1869** TENNYSON *Coming of Arthur* 396 Not ever to be question'd any more Save on the further side.

†**4.** *absol.* ***further of the day***: a later hour.

1546 LANGLEY *Pol. Verg. de Invent.* ix. 113b, Fyrst at mydnight..the seconde in the mornyng..the thyrd at further of the day.

further ('fɜːðə(r)), *adv.* Forms: 1–2 **furð-, furþor,** 1 *Northumb.* **forðer, -ur, -or,** 2–4 **furð-, furþer** (**furthir**), 3–5 **forðere, -ðre, -þer(e, -þir, -thir(e,** 3–6 **forther(e,** (3 **forer**), 4–5 **furþere,** 4–7 **furder,** 5 **forder,** (6 **fourther**), 6– **further.** See also FARTHER *adv.* [OE. *furðor* = OS. *furthor* (early mod.Du. *voorder*); for the formation, and the relation to Goth. *faurþis*, OHG. *furdir*, etc.: see FURTHER *a.*]

1. To or at a more advanced point of progress: **a.** of space; *lit.* and *fig.*; occas. with omission of *go*. Proverb, ***to go further, and fare worse.*** (Cf. FARTHER A. 1 a.)

c **1000** ÆLFRIC *Josh.* x. 12 Ne gang þu mona onȝean Achialon anne stæpe furþor. *c* **1050** *O.E. Chron.* an. 1039 Eode se sæster hwætes to lv penega and eac furðor. *c* **1205** LAY. 4880 He furðer lað, to Seguine duc. *a* **1240** *Ureisun* in *Cott. Hom.* 203 Nere þe heorte so cold þat ne schulde neuer sunne habben for-ðer in-ȝong þer þis brune were. *a* **1250** *Prov. Ælfred* 128 in *O.E. Misc.* 110 Nere he for his weole neuer þe furþer. *c* **1330** R. BRUNNE *Chron. Wace* Prol. 182 Vnto þe Cadwaladres; No forer, þer makes he ses. **1340** HAMPOLE *Pr. Consc.* 440 Þarfor I wille, ar [I] forthir pas, Shew yhou what a man first was. *c* **1340** *Cursor M.* 10156 (Fairf.) As furthir in this boke we rede. *c* **1400** *Lanfranc's Cirurg.* 221, I lete make a pipe of silvir and putte it in at her mouþ & passede forþere þan þe wounde was. **1494** FABYAN *Chron.* (1811) I. cxxvii. 107 Forthere then ye chapell dore noon of them wold enter. **1535** COVERDALE *Job* xxxviii. 11 Hither to shalt thou come, but no further. **1546** J. HEYWOOD *Prov.* (1867) 51 You..might haue gone further, and haue faren wurs. **1559** W. CUNNINGHAM *Cosmogr. Glasse* 60 But or we further proced, marke this figure. **1593** SHAKS. *2 Hen. VI*, III. ii. 169 His eye balles further out, than when he liued. **1615** J. STEPHENS *Satyr. Ess.* 26 Go tell a trades-man he deceives..And he will answere..Go further on, you will be cheated worse. **1641** MILTON *Animadv.* (1851) 187 Ere a foot furder we must bee content [etc.]. **1655** SIR E. NICHOLAS in *N. Papers* (Camden) II. 336 Taken out of their bedds..and carryed on shipboard, and whence further is vnknowen. **1719** DE FOE *Crusoe* II. v, They kept out of sight further and further. **1771** FOOTE *Maid of B.* I. Wks. 1799 II. 214 Folks may go further and fare worse, as they say. **1813** SHELLEY *Q. Mab* IX. 182 Whose stingings bade thy heart look further still. **1855** MACAULAY *Hist. Eng.* IV. 1 It was not thought safe for the ships to proceed further in the darkness.

b. of time. (Cf. FARTHER A. 1 b.)

c **1290** *Beket* 2321 in *S. Eng. Leg.* I. 173 So þat forþere in þe ȝere: it was wel onder-stonde..In ȝwat manere he was a-slawe. **1896** *Act 59 & 60 Vict.* c. 39 §1 The acts..shall..be continued until the 31st day of December 1897 and shall then expire unless further continued.

2. To a greater extent; more. (Cf. FARTHER A. 2.)

c **1050** *Byrhtferth's Handboc* in *Anglia* (1885) VIII. 299 Nu wille we furðor geican þurh godes mihta. *a* **1225** *Juliana* 47, & ȝef ich mahte [wurche his wil] forðre ich walde beo þe feinre. *a* **1300** *Cursor M.* 28869 (Cott.) And for þer mater es gode to knau, Of almus sal i for-þer drau. *c* **1340** *Ibid.* 858 (Trin.) Leue we now of þis spelle Of oure story furþere to telle. *a* **1400–50** *Alexander* 523 And if ȝow likis of þis lare to lesten any forthire. **1552–3** *Inv. Ch. Goods, Staffs.* in *Ann. Lichfield* IV. 2 There saffeli to be kepte untill the kinges majesties pleasure be therin furder knowen. **1559** HETHE in Strype *Ann. Ref.* I. App. vi. 7 That the doinges of this honourable assembly may..be allwayes fourther honourable. **1641** MILTON *Ch. Govt.* II. iii. Wks. (1847) 48/2 To the intent of further healing man's deprav'd mind. **1734** BERKELEY *Analyst* §7 Men who pretend to believe no further than they can see. **1749** F. SMITH *Voy. Disc.* II. 90 All the western Merchants declined..from being further Adventurers. **1862** STANLEY *Jew. Ch.* (1877) I. xiii. 252 When we inquire further into the worship.

3. In addition, additionally; moreover. (Cf. FARTHER A. 3.)

c **1200** *Vices & Virtues* (1888) 57 Ȝiet hie seið furðer. **1450** W. SOMNER in *Four C. Eng. Lett.* 4 Forther the maister desyryd to wete yf the shipmen would holde with the duke. **1559** W. CUNNINGHAM *Cosmogr. Glasse* 22, I do furder perceive that [etc.]. **1560–78** *Bk. Discipl. Ch. Scot.* (1621) 40 And furder we think it expedient [etc.]. **1582** N. LICHEFIELD tr. *Castanheda's Conq. E. Ind.* vii. 16b, What further than followed. **1749** F. SMITH *Voy. Disc.* II. 58 What further keeps the Cold from the Arm-pits is, that [etc.]. **1875** MANNING *Mission H. Ghost* iv. 100 And, further, God is the only end that can..satisfy the soul with bliss. **1879** *Cassell's Techn. Educ.* IV. 92/2 The sketching-case may be..further provided with a cover.

4. At a greater distance in space; sometimes with mixture of sense 1. Also † ***more further, further off.*** (Cf. FARTHER A. 4.)

c **1400** MAUNDEV. (1839) xxxi. 306 Oþer Yles þat ben more furþere beȝonde. **1578** WHETSTONE *Promos & Cass.* II. iv, The furder off I wretched finde both comfort and reliefe. **1601** SHAKS. *Jul. C.* II. ii. 125 So neere will I be That your best Friends shall wish I had beene further. **1630** *R. Johnson's Kingd. & Commw.* 68 Island disjoyned no further than a ship in one day may saile unto. **1710** *Tatler* No. 254 ¶7 The Dutch Cabbin, which lay about a Mile further up into the Country. **1812–16** J. SMITH *Panorama Sc. & Art* I. 572 It was calculated to be 18,000 times further from us than the sun. **1875** JOWETT *Plato* (ed. 2) IV. 156 There is nothing further from his thoughts than scepticism.

b. Phrases. † ***to be further***: to get on. † ***I'll be further, if*** (etc.); ***I'll see you further (first)***: strong forms of refusal. ***to wish any one further***: i.e. to wish him away. See also FARTHER A. 4.

1526 DARRELL *Let.* 1 Aug. in Ellis *Orig. Lett.* Ser. III. II. 163, I..intende to be further and doo. **1621** LADY M. WROTH *Urania* 16 She..wished the beast further, yet taking her wonted strength of heart..she said thus. **1741** RICHARDSON *Pamela* II. 320 And so that I must not wish to incur [his Displeasure] to save any body else. I'll be further if I do. *Ibid.* 377, I bow'd to him, but I could have wish'd him further, to make me sit so in the Notice of every one. **1873** *Punch* 3 May 185/1 He'll see me further first.

†**c.** Used as the comparative of *far*, as in ***further-fetched***, compar. of *far-fetched*.

1680 BAXTER *Cath. Commun.* (1684) 23 But God being infinitely more perfect then man, the phrase is further fetcht, and less proper of God then of man.

further ('fɜːðə(r)), *v.* Forms: *α.* 1 **fyrðran, -ian,** 2–4 **furðrien,** 3 *Orm.* **firrþrenn,** *north.* **firther,** 4 **ferthren, -ther, furthren,** 4, 6 *Sc.* **furthir,** (6 **furthur**), 6–8 **furder,** 4– **further.** *β.* 3–4 **forthren,** 4 **forþer, -thor,** 4–6 **forther, -ire,** 5, 8 **forder.** See also FARTHER *v.* [OE. *fyrðr(i)an*, f. *furðor*, *-ðra* FURTHER *adv.* and *a.*; equivalent forms are OHG. *furdiren* (MHG. *vürdern*, mod.G. *fördern*); cf. also OHG. *fordarôn* (MHG. *vordern*, mod.G. *fordern*) to further, call forth, demand.]

1. *trans.* To help forward, assist (usually things; less frequently †persons); to promote, favour (an action or movement). Cf. FARTHER *v.* †Also ***to further forth, on.***

c **888** K. ÆLFRED *Boeth.* xxxix. §2 Þæt hi maȝen henan ða yflan and fyrþrian þa godan. *c* **1200** *Trin. Coll. Hom.* 11 Ac alle þo þe leueð þat swilch þing hem muȝe furðrie oðer letten, ben cursed of godes muðe. *c* **1200** ORMIN 1250 Ȝiff þu firrþresst fremmde menn. *a* **1225** *Ancr. R.* 156 Ðet tet swuðest auaunceð & furðreð hit, þet is onlich stude. *a* **1300** *Cursor M.* 27918 Sua vr flexs to firþer and fede, þat it fale in na dedli dede. *a* **1310** in Wright *Lyric P.* xxxvi. 99 God, that deȝedest on the rod, Al this world to forthren ant fylle. *c* **1374** CHAUCER *Boeth.* II. pr. iv. 41 (Camb. MS.), I haue sumwhat auaunced and forþered þe, quod she. **1412–20** LYDG. *Chron. Troy* II. x, For me to further Clio came to late. **1477** EARL RIVERS (Caxton) *Dictes* 18 Ire..furthereth all euyl. **1513** DOUGLAS *Æneis* V. xiii. 112 And furthir hym eik sall I Ontil Avern, clepit the loch of hell. **1566** in Keith *Hist. Ch. Scotl.* (1734) 331 The saids Rebels..promittit they should forder him to the Crown Matrimoniall. **1577** B. GOOGE *Heresbach's Husb.* IV. (1586) 158 You must..further their laying, by giving them meates for the purpose. **1603** KNOLLES *Hist. Turks* (1621) 877 Furthered with a faire gale of wind. **1664** POWER *Exp. Philos.* Pref. 20 A more wary Builder may be very much further'd by it. **1715** M. DAVIES *Athen. Brit.* I. 172 Barnevelt's hard Fate was occasion'd or further'd on by Maurice. **1777–1808** MAYNE *Siller Gun* III. xxv, Here Discord strave new broils to forder. **1816** SCOTT *Old Mort.* xi, To remain together in arms for furthering the covenanted work of reformation. **1866** GEO. ELIOT *F. Holt* ix, I came to see..if you had any wishes that I could further. **1869** ROGERS *Pref. to Adam Smith's W.N.* I. 6 The necessity of furthering a general system of school training.

absol. **1560–78** BIBLE (Genev.) To Chr. Rdr. 52 Some notable worde..which may greatly further..for memorie. **1607** S. HIERON *Defence* I. 160 Wheras the addition of 2 or 3 wordes oftentimes furthereth to the meaning.

†**2.** To honour. *Obs. rare.*

c **1374** CHAUCER *Anel. & Arc.* 273 And thenken yee that ferthered be your name To love a newe. *c* **1400** *Destr. Troy* 11170 To forther þat fre with fynerall seruys.

3. *intr.* To go on, continue; to advance, make progress. *Obs.* exc. *Sc.*

c **1200** *Trin. Coll. Hom.* 107 Eft sone sum godes giue is bigunnen alse rihte leue and furðreð alse trust. *c* **1350** *Will. Palerne* 5397 And touche we ferre as þis tale forþeres. **1560** ROLLAND *Crt. Venus* II. 378 Wald thow further and prosper in thy wais. **1789** D. DAVIDSON *Seasons, etc.* 182 Wha fastest rides does aft least forder. **1794** BURNS *Hee Balou* 10 Thro' the Lawlands, o'er the border, Weel, my babie, may thou furder.

†**4.** *trans.* To put (an event) further; to defer, postpone. *Obs.*

1529 WOLSEY *Let. to [Crumwell]* in *St. Papers* (1830) I. 351 The ferderyng and puttyng ovyr of your commyng hyther hath..increasyd my sorowe.

furtherance ('fɜːðərəns). Forms: *α.* 5–7 **forþ-, fortheraunce, -ans, forderance,** (5 **firtherance, foderance**), 6 **fordraunce,** 7 **fortherance.** *β.* 5–7 **furtheraunce,** (7 **-ence**), 6–7 **furderance, -aunce, -auns,** 5– **furtherance.** See also FARTHERANCE. [f. FURTHER *v.* + -ANCE.]

1. The fact or state of being furthered or helped forward; the action of helping forward; advancement, aid, assistance. Also *concr.* a means or source of help.

c **1440** *York Myst.* xxvi. 48 Yf þat false faytor Your fortheraunce may fang. **1494** FABYAN *Chron.* an. 1448 (1559) II. 446 For the furtheraunce of this purpose. **1551** RECORDE *Pathw. Knowl.* II. Pref., All suche..shall finde greate ease and furtheraunce by this simple..forme of writinge. **1606** *Sc. Acts Jas. VI* (1814) IV. 286 For the greater forderance and better executioun of justice. **1610** HEALEY *St. Aug. Citie of God* I. xi. (1620) 19 The pompes of the funeralls are rather solaces to the liuing then furtherances to the dead. **1640–1** *Kirkcudbr. War-Comm. Min. Bk.* (1855) 72 Expecting your fortherance in all. **1748** F. SMITH *Voy. Disc.* I. 89 Thinking of the many Furtherances this Voyage received from that honourable Knight. **1831** CARLYLE *Sart. Res.* (1858) 4 Issuing..with every external furtherance, it is of such internal quality as to set Neglect at defiance. **1844** H. H. WILSON *Brit. India* III. 422 In furtherance of this project, she kept her son in a state of ignorance and vice. **1875** HELPS *Ess., Organ. Daily Life* 174 Some few furtherances have been shown.

2. *Coal-mining.* (See quot. 1883.)

1851 in GREENWELL *Coal-trade Terms* 27. **1883** GRESLEY *Gloss. Coal Mining, Furtherance* (North), an additional sum of money paid per score to hewers, putters, &c. as an allowance in respect of inferior coal, a bad roof, a fault, &c.

Hence † '**furtherancer** *Obs.* *rare*$^{-1}$. One who gives furtherance to (anything).

1599 HAYWARD *1st Pt. Hen. IV*, 6 A dissolute and dishonest life, which findeth some followers when it findeth no furtherancers.

furtherer ('fɜːðərə(r)). Also 5 **furtherar,** 6 **ford-, fortherer.** See also FARTHERER. [f. FURTHER *v.* + -ER[1].] One who or that which furthers or helps forward; a helper, promoter, supporter; an aid or encouragement.

1390 GOWER *Conf.* III. 111 The brighte sonne..furtherer of the daies light. *c* **1465** *Eng. Chron.* (Camd. 1856) 23 He was our furtherar and promoter. **1555** ABP. PARKER *Ps.* E iij, The Psalme..is a furtherer to them which go forwarde to vertue. **1594** BLUNDEVIL *Exerc.* III. I. i. (ed. 7) 278 Leaving to speak of the first inventers, or of the furtherers of these Sciences. **1630** LORD *Banians* 32 Making the profits..the furtherers of ryot and excesse. **1691** WOOD *Ath. Oxon.* I. 297 He was a continual favourer and furtherer of learning. **1828** LANDOR *Imag. Conv.* Wks. 1846 I. 315 Ploughs and oxen are not instruments and furtherers of disobedience. **1867** *Sat. Rev.* 26 Oct. 535/1 The fate which seems to turn men..into furtherers of a cause which they know to be evil.

† '**further,forth**, *adv.* *Obs.* [f. FURTHER *adv.* + FORTH *adv.*] Further on; to a greater distance or extent.

a **1541** WYATT *Poet. Wks.* (1861) 182 Further-forth he starts With venom'd breath. **1583** GOLDING *Calvin on Deut.* vi. 33 Not to be inquisitiue of Gods trueth furtherfoorth than it is vttered in the holy scriptures. **1587** —— *De Mornay* xxi. (1617) 355 Open the booke furtherfoorth at all aduenture wheresoeuer you list.

† '**furtherhead.** *Obs.* In 4 **forþer-, furþerhed(e, -heed.** [f. FURTHER *a.* + -HEAD.] Priority.

c **1380** WYCLIF *Sel. Wks.* I. 75 Joon spekiþ of forþerhede of manhede of Crist bifore Ioon in grace, and also in worþynes. *Ibid.* III. 78 Þe first furþerheed is forþerhed of comynge forþ and þe toþir forþerheed is furþerheed of kynde.

furthering ('fɜːðərɪŋ), *vbl. sb.* *Obs.* exc. *arch.* [OE. *fyrðrung* furtherance, f. *fyrðrian*: see FURTHER *v.* and -ING[1].] The action of the vb. FURTHER.

c **1000** *Sax. Leechd.* III. 208 Sæ smylte ȝesihð ceapas fyrðrunge ȝe[tacnað]. *c* **1384** CHAUCER *H. Fame* II. 128 Thou ..ever mo of love enditest..in his folkes furtherynges. **1390** GOWER *Conf.* I. 182 Take a newe faith, Which shall be forthringe of thy life. *c* **1440** *Promp. Parv.* 174/1 Fortherynge, *promocio*. **1526** TINDALE *Phil.* i. 12 The gretter furtherynge off the gospell. **1623** WHITBOURNE *Newfoundland* 8 They are a great furthering to diuers Ships voiages. **1864** CARLYLE *Fredk. Gt.* XVI. i, There is eager Furthering of the Husbandries.

† **'furthering**, *ppl. a. Obs.* [f. FURTHER *v.* + -ING².] That furthers, aids, or helps; helpful. Of a gale: Favourable.

1418 *E.E. Wills* (1882) 38 Y pray hem þat þey be well wyllet and forderyng to here. **1494** FABYAN *Chron.* VII. 486 Y mayre..was nat quyk or fortherynge in that mater. **1599** HAKLUYT *Voy.* II. I. 102 The winde..blew a furthering gale.

'furtherly, *a.* and *adv.* [f. FURTHER *a.* and *adv.* + -LY¹ and ².]

A. *adj. Obs.* exc. *dial.*

a. Adapted to further, favourable. **b.** In a forward condition, advanced. **c.** *dial.* (see quot. 1855.)

1513 MORE *Rich. III* Wks. 38/1 He..thought that their deuision shoulde bee..a fortherlye begynnynge to the pursuite of his intente. **1571** *Durham Depos.* (Surtees) 238 The matter was so furtherlye bytwix them 2, that neither his frends nor hir frends can hynder the same. **1855** ROBINSON *Whitby Gloss.*, *Furtherly*, forward and flourishing.

†**B.** *adv.* **a.** In an onward direction, in advance; hence, completely, thoroughly. **b.** = FURTHER *adv.*

c **1200** ORMIN 14812 He [Faraon] comm swa forrþerrliȝ þatt all hiss follc was inne. *a* **1225** *Ancr. R.* 236 þet oðer is, þet he furðerluker echeð his pine. *a* **1300** *Cursor M.* 1585 þe find wend..þat..Man kind war til his wil bekend Sua forþerli þat [etc.]. *c* **1400** MAUNDEV. (Roxb.) xxxi. 141 þir husband sall hafe his actioun agaynes him before þe iusticez of þe land, als fortherly as he had bene aboute for to slae him. **1494** FABYAN *Chron.* v. cxl. 127 To the correccyon of suche as be lerned, & not oonly to Englysshe reders as there is fortherly declared. **1523** *Act 14 & 15 Hen. VIII*, c. 5 §2 That it pleas your Highnes with th' assent..furtherlie to enacte ordeign and stablisshe that [etc.].

furthermore ('fɜːðəmɔə(r)), *adv.* See also FARTHERMORE. [f. FURTHER *adv.* + MORE *adv.*]

†**1.** To a more advanced point of progress, still further; = FURTHER *adv.* 1 a. Occas. with omission of *go*. *Obs.*

c **1200** ORMIN 7338 þe sterrne comm riht till þatt hus & flæh itt ta na forrþerr mar. *a* **1300** *Cursor M.* 6543 þar-wit forþer-mar he yede. **1375** BARBOUR *Bruce* VII. 8 [Bruce] said he mycht no forthirmar. **14..** *Tundale's Vis.* 991 Com furder more and folow me. *c* **1425** *Craft Nombrynge* (E.E.T.S.) 8 Do away þe cifer & þat 1. & sette þere 8. þan go forthermore. **1552** LYNDESAY *Monarche* 4401 Father, or we passe forther more, Quhen did begyn thare temporall glore?

†**2.** To a greater extent, more; = FURTHER *adv.* 2.

a **1300** *Cursor M.* 27958 Forthermar o þis lecheri agh i þe noght to specifie. **1340** HAMPOLE *Pr. Consc.* 2892 Now wille I rede forthermare, And shew yhow of sum paynes þat er þare. *c* **1450** *St. Cuthbert* (Surtees) 7247 ȝit forthir mare of þe same.

3. Besides, also, moreover; = FURTHER *adv.* 3.

c **1275** *XI Pains of Hell* 67 in *O.E. Misc.* 149 A hwel of stele is furþer mo. **1411** *Rolls of Parlt.* III. 650/2 Further-more, the forsaid Lord the Roos..schall forgevyn the forsaid Robert. **1483** CAXTON *Gold. Leg.* 400 b/1 Yet he sayd furthermore who so compleyneth is no monke. **1555** SPURGE in Strype *Eccl. Mem.* III. App. xl. 110 Furthermore..we humbly beseech thee. **1614** RALEIGH *Hist. World* I. iv. §3 Furthermore..the leaues, body, and boughes, of this Tree ..exceede all other Plants. **1730** BOLINGBROKE in *Swift's Lett.* (1766) II. 109 And furthermore, I think myself in honour bound to acknowledge, that [etc.]. **1820** KEATS *Isabella* lviii, And, furthermore her brethren wonder'd much Why she sat drooping. **1871** SMILES *Charac.* ii. (1876) 55 Furthermore, to direct the power of the home aright, women..need [etc.].

†**4.** Of time: Henceforth, subsequently. *Obs.*

a **1300** *Cursor M.* 28677 þis man sais..þat him reuys his sinnes sare, and will for-bere þam forþire mare. *c* **1430** *Two Cookery-bks.* I. 29 Rede Rose—Take þe same, saue a-lye it with þe ȝolkys of eyroun & forþer-more as vyolet.

furthermost ('fɜːðəməʊst), *a.* Also 4 forthirmaste. See also FARTHERMOST. [f. FURTHER *a.* + -MOST.]

†**1.** Foremost, first. *Obs.*

?*a* **1400** *Morte Arth.* 3331 The forthirmaste was..The faireste of fyssnamy þat fourmede was euer. *c* **1400** *Melayne* 721 One the forthirmaste daye of Auerille.

2. Most distant or remote.

1765 FOOTE *Commissary* I. Wks. 1799 II. 16 The furthermost cushion in the window. **1786** S. HASWELL *Victoria* I. 51 We were sitting in an arbour at the furthermost part of the garden. **1860** PUSEY *Min. Proph.* 266 He instantly sets himself to flee to the then furthermost West.

† **'furtherous**, *a. Obs.* [f. FURTHER *v.* + -OUS.] = FURTHERSOME 1.

1597 J. PAYNE *Royal Exch.* 3 Vessells for his glorie, furtherouse to his churche. **1620** tr. *Boccaccio's Decameron* 6 b, Wee may very well hope that Fortune will be furtherous to our purposed journey.

†**,furthe'rover**, *adv. Obs.* [f. FURTHER *adv.* + OVER *adv.*] Besides, moreover.

c **1386** CHAUCER *Pars. T.* ⁋231 Forther ouer contricion moste be continueel. **1623** LISLE *Ælfric on O. & N. Test.* Pref. 16 Furtherover, these monuments of reverend antiquitie..will in many places convince of affected obscurity some late translators.

furthersome ('fɜːðəsəm), *a.* Also 9 *Sc.* for-, furdersome. [f. FURTHER *v.* or *adv.* + -SOME.]

1. Adapted to further or help forward, advantageous, helpful. Const. *to.*

1626 W. SCLATER *Expos. 2 Thess.* (1629) 3 That state, that is most furthersome to Gods seruice. **1637** *Declar. Pfaltzgrave's Faith* 19 It is most comfortable and furthersome vnmeasurably to the believers. **1827** CARLYLE *Germ. Rom.* IV. 242 A principle which he had often..perceived for himself to be furthersome and reasonable. **1832** *Fraser's Mag.* VI. 387 So furthersome an instrument Honorio would never leave behind. **1845** CARLYLE *Cromwell* (1871) I. 68 Two little pieces of advice which may prove furthersome to him. **1880** *Academy* 23 Oct. 301/1 An interesting performance, highly furthersome to the interests of the drama.

2. Inclined to go forward; rash, venturous.

1862 HISLOP *Prov. Scot.* 195 They are eith hindered that are no fordersome. **1896** 'IAN MACLAREN' *Kate Carnegie* (ed. 2) 118 He's young and fordersome (rash), but gude stuff for a' his pliskies (frolics).

†**'furtherward**, *adv. Obs.* [f. FURTHER *adv.* + -WARD.] Forward; straight on. Of time: Henceforth.

a **1300** *Cursor M.* 5480 In egipt held he þam sa hard, Als i sal tel yow forþer-ward. *Ibid.* 7525 Ne forþerward ne yeitt o bake. *Ibid.* 13958 Ai fra þis dai fortherward þe Iues..soght ihesu at do to ded.

furthest ('fɜːðɪst), *a.* and *adv.* Also (? 4) 5 **fyrthest, fertherest, forthest(e, 6 furdest.** See also FARTHEST. [superl. formed (app. in the 14th c.) to correspond to the comparative FURTHER.

The instances in the 14th c. are somewhat doubtful (at least with regard to the precise form of the word), owing to the absence of contemporary MSS.]

A. *adj.*

1. Most advanced in any direction. Also as the superl. of FAR *a.* (now usually superseded by FARTHEST): Situated at the greatest distance, most remote. *lit.* and *fig.*

c **1374** CHAUCER *Boeth.* IV. pr. vi. (Skeat) 86 þilke [cercle] þat is outterest..is unfolden by larger spaces in so moche as it is forthest [*MS. C. and ed. Thynne* fertherest] fro þe middel simplicitee of þe poynt. **1390** GOWER *Conf.* I. 108 When I wende next have be..Than was I furthest ate laste. **1559** W. CUNNINGHAM *Cosmogr. Glasse* 60 Portsmouth, whiche is the furdest place on the south shore of Englande. **1599** SHAKS. *Much Ado* II. i. 275, I will fetch you a tooth-picker now from the furthest inch of Asia. **1725** SWIFT *Corr.* Wks. 1841 II. 576 The furthest corner of Naboth's vineyard. **1779** BURKE *Corr.* (1844) II. 293 Those who are the furthest in the world from you in religious tenets. *a* **1881** ROSSETTI *House of Life* x, He who seeks her beauty's furthest goal.

2. †**a.** In past time: Earliest, first (*obs.*). **b.** In future time: Latest. *Obs.* exc. *absol.* in ***at (the) furthest.***

1552 EDW. VI *Jrnl.* 25 Oct., That they might be in such place..by Christmas or Candlemas at the furdest. **1599** HAKLUYT *Voy.* II. I. 85 He should take the towne in fifteene dayes, or a moneth at the furthest. *a* **1648** LD. HERBERT *Life* (1886) 30 When I came to talk, one of the furthest inquiries I made was, how I came into this world? **1653** H. COGAN tr. *Pinto's Trav.* i. 2 The funeral pomp of King Emanuel was celebrated at Lisbon, namely..December 1521, which is the furthest thing I can remember.

B. *adv.* To or at the greatest distance, farthest.

c **1374** CHAUCER *Boeth.* IV. pr. vi. (Skeat) 91 Thilke thing that departeth forthest [*MSS. A and C* fyrthest] fro the first thoght of god. **1559** W. CUNNINGHAM *Cosmogr. Glasse* 156 Th'other part furdest Weast, noted wyth F. *a* **1577** GASCOIGNE *Hearbes, Weedes*, etc. Wks. (1587) 185 The stiffe and strongest arme..shootes furdest stil. **1729** BUTLER *Serm.* Wks. 1874 II. 192 Ideas..the furthest removed from anything sensual. **1886** D. C. MURRAY *Aunt Rachel* II. 68 Even when his thoughts wandered furthest, he was mechanically accurate.

Comb. **1880** GLADSTONE in *Daily News* 28 Feb. 3/2 From the highest Tory to the furthest-going Home Ruler.

'furthy, *a. Sc.* Var. of FORTHY *a.* Hence **'furthiness.**

a **1658** J. DURHAM *Exp. Commandm.* (1675) 360 There is a gadding, and a so called furthiness, especially in women.. which is exceedingly offensive. **1777–1808** MAYNE *Siller Gun* II. xliv, Less furthy dames (wha cou'd resist them!) Th' example take. *a* **1810** TANNAHILL *Poems* (1846) 58 Thy furthy, kindly, takin' gait.

furtive ('fɜːtɪv), *a.* [a. F. *furtif, furtive*, ad. L. *furtīvus*, f. *fūr* thief; cf. *furtum* theft, *furtim* adv., by stealth.]

1. Done by stealth or with the hope of escaping observation; clandestine, surreptitious, secret, unperceived.

1490 [implied in FURTIVELY]. **1612** WOODALL *Surg. Mate* Wks. (1653) 301 In wounds, where no Gangrena may be suspected..nor furtive hemorrhage, &c. **1635** J. HAYWARD tr. *Biondi's Banish'd Virg.* Stolen embraces and furtive births prov'd to be ever the best. **1656** *Artif. Handsom.* 96 By a furtive simulation. **1787–9** WORDSW. *Evening Walk* 423 Tender cares and mild domestic loves With furtive watch pursue her as she moves. **1824** W. IRVING *T. Trav.* I. 106, I noticed the same singular, and, as it were, furtive glance, over the shoulder. **1855** THACKERAY *Newcomes* II. 128 The proprietor of the house cowered over a bed-candle, and a furtive tea-pot in the back drawing-room. **1877** GLADSTONE *Glean.* IV. xx. 354 It does not at once appear how the Canal could be secured against the furtive scuttling of ships.

b. *Hebrew Gram.* (See quot.)

1852 tr. *Gesenius' Hebr. Gram.* 42 [Between a strong and unchangeable vowel and a final guttural] there is involuntarily uttered a hasty *ă* (*Pathach furtive*).. Analogous to this is our use of a *furtive e* before *r* after long [vowels]; e.g. *here* (sounded *hēer*), *fire* (*fier*).

2. Of a person, etc.: Stealthy, sly.

1858 LYTTON *What will he do* II. xiv, There was something furtive and sinister about the man. **1865** DICKENS *Mut. Fr.* III. i, Eyeing him with furtive eyes. **1867** M. ARNOLD *St. Brandan*, That furtive mien, that scowling eye.

3. Obtained by theft, stolen; also in milder sense, taken by stealth or secretly.

1718 PRIOR *Solomon* I. 500 Do they [planets]..Dart furtive beams, and glory not their own? **1729** SAVAGE *Wanderer* I. 293 He clear'd, manur'd, enlarg'd the furtive ground. **1864** KIRK *Chas. Bold* I. i. 25 The patches from which a furtive harvest was thus gathered. **1894** J. T. FOWLER *Adamnan* Introd. 53 Columba's furtive copy from St. Finnian's psalter.

4. Thievish, pilfering.

1816 KIRBY & SP. *Entomol.* (1843) II. 30 Ants whose employment is to mine for gold and from whose vengeance the furtive Indian is constrained to fly on the swift camel's back. **1873** BURTON *Hist. Scot.* VI. lxx. 208 The Highlander could not be absolutely trusted to withhold his furtive hand from the flocks of his chief's friend. **1885** *That Very Mab* viii. 129 The farmers were so much plagued by the furtive bird.

Hence **'furtively** *adv.*, **'furtiveness.**

1490 CAXTON *Eneydos* xix. 69, I wold not haue departed furtyuely out of thy land. **1765** STERNE *Tr. Shandy* VIII. xxiv, One lambent delicious fire, furtively shooting out from every part of it. **1838** DICKENS *Nich. Nick.* xxvi, Sir Mulberry..had been furtively trying to discover whence Kate had so suddenly appeared. **1862** MISS BRADDON *Lady Audley* viii. 55 My lady's pale-faced maid, who looked furtively under her white eye-lashes at the two young men. **1884** tr. *Lotze's Metaph.* 211 The implied idea by which, whether furtively or explicitly, we console ourselves. **1896** *Westm. Gaz.* 4 Aug. 1/3 Strolling, as we do..through the press and bustle, we can sometimes capture a small hasty furtiveness.

† **furtu'ose**, *a. Obs. rare.* [ad. med.L. *furtuōs-us*, f. L. *furtum* theft: see -OSE.] 'Much given to theft or stealing' (Bailey, vol. II. 1727).

furuncle ('fjʊərʌŋk(ə)l). [ad. L. *fūruncul-us*, orig. 'little thief', dim. of *fūr*. Cf. F. *furoncle* FRONCLE.] A boil or inflammatory tumour.

1676 WISEMAN *Chirurg. Treat.* I. vii. 43 Sorely afflicted with a Furuncle within his Nostrils. **1743** tr. *Heister's Surg.* 195 A Boil or Furuncle is a small resisting Tumor. **1856** KANE *Arct. Expl.* II. xx. 204, I had relieved her from much suffering by opening a furuncle. **1872** F. G. THOMAS *Dis. Women* 105 The peculiar blood state which results in the development of furuncles and carbuncles.

furuncular (fjʊ'rʌŋkjʊlə(r)), *a.* [f. L. *fūruncul-us* (see FURUNCLE) + -AR.] Of, pertaining to, or characterized by furuncles or boils.

1844–57 G. BIRD *Urin. Deposits* (ed. 5) 457 Furuncular disease of cellular tissue. **1847–9** TODD *Cycl. Anat.* IV. 438/1 The scapular region is sometimes the seat of furuncular inflammation. **1875** H. C. WOOD *Therap.* (1879) 569 A most painful furuncular eruption.

So **fu'runculoid** *a.* [-OID], resembling a furuncle or boil.

1860 R. FOWLER *Med. Vocab.*, *Furunculoid.*

furunculosis (fjʊrʌŋkjʊ'ləʊsɪs). *Path.* [mod.L., f. L. *furunculus* FURUNCLE: see -OSIS.]

1. A diseased condition marked by the appearance of a crop of boils.

1886 *Med. & Surg. Reporter* LV. 609 (*heading*) Furunculosis. **1908** *Practitioner* June 858 Eczema, with complicating furunculosis. **1946** MACKEE & CIPOLLARO *Skin Dis. Children* (ed. 2) ii. 25 Localized recurrent furunculosis is best treated with roentgen rays. **1968** NAYLOR & ROOK in A. Rook et al. *Textbk. Dermatol.* I. xx. 607/1 Epidemics of furunculosis attributable to specific strains of staphylococci have occurred.

2. [ad. G. *furunkulose* (Emmerich & Weibel 1894, in *Archiv für Hygiene* XXI. 5).] A disease of salmonid fishes caused by the bacterium *Aeromonas salmonicida.*

1912 MASTERMAN & ARKWRIGHT *Rep. Epidemic Salmonidæ 1911* 13 The epizootic disease which occurred amongst the salmon and trout in the south-west of England during the summer of 1911 presented the same symptoms as the disease which occurs in Germany, especially Bavaria, and in France, and is called Furunculosis of the Salmonidae. **1930** *Discovery* Aug. 268/2 'Furunculosis'..affects salmon and trout rivers where it may cause great havoc among the fish. The disease is caused by a bacterium, which cannot survive in absolutely pure water but arises in water polluted by organic matter. **1959** J. W. JONES *Salmon* 165 One of the most important factors in causing epidemics of furunculosis is water temperature.

furunculous (fjʊ'rʌŋkjʊləs), *a.* [f. L. *fūruncul-us* FURUNCLE + -OUS.] = FURUNCULAR.

1861 HULME tr. *Moquin-Tandon* II. VII. vii. 367 A furunculous tumour produced by a Filaria. **1890** GOULD *New Dict. Med.*, *Furunculous*, pertaining to the continuous production of furuncles.

fury ('fjʊərɪ), *sb.* Forms: 5 furey, 4–6 furye, 4–7 -ie, 5– fury. [a. F. *furie* (14th c. in Littré), ad. L. *furia*, related to *furĕre* to rage, be mad. (OFr. had originally *fuire*).]

1. Fierce passion, disorder or tumult of mind approaching madness; *esp.* wild anger, frenzied rage; also, a fit or access of such passion.

The pl. is sometimes used in imitation of F. *furies* or L. *furiæ.*

c **1374** CHAUCER *Troylus* IV. 817 (845) Anoy, smert, drede, fury and eek siknesse. *Ibid.* v. 212 To bedde he goth and weyleth there and torneth In furie, as dooth he, Ixion, in helle. *c* **1430** LYDG. *Min. Poems* 206 Sobre and appeese suche folk as falle in furye. **1491** *Act 7 Hen. VII*, c. 15 Certeyn persones..murdred..in an outrageous hedy furey ..John Mountagu late Erle of Sarum. **1564** *Child Marriages*, etc. (1897) 123 Biecause the wordes were spoken in a furye. **1611** BIBLE *Gen.* xxvii. 44 Tary with him a few dayes, vntill thy brothers furie turne away. **1621** BURTON *Anat. Mel.* III. iv. I. i. 706 As Plato doth in his Conuiuio make mention of two distinct furies; and amongst our Neotericks, Hercules de Saxonia.. doth expressly treat of it [religious melancholy] in a distinct Species. *a* **1683** SIDNEY *Disc. Govt.* I. xix. (1704) 46 A Poison that would fill the gentlest Spirits with the most violent Furys. **1692** DRYDEN *St. Evremont's Ess.* 351 He.. fell into such strange furies, that [etc.]. **1704** F. FULLER *Med. Gymn.* (1705) 159 (*Hypochondria*), 'Tis the first Fury that is the most Dangerous and Violent. **1713** SWIFT, etc. *Frenzy J. Dennis* Wks. 1755 III. I. 146 He flung down the book in a terrible fury. **1756** BURKE *Vind. Nat. Soc.* Wks. I. 37 When Alexander had in his fury inhumanly butchered one of his best friends. **1866** CONINGTON *Æneid* XII. 410 Such furies in his bosom rise. **1879** FARRAR *St. Paul* (1883) 118 He could hardly have addressed them in words more calculated to kindle their fury.

b. of beasts.

1592 SHAKS. *Rom. & Jul.* III. iii. 111 Thy wild acts denote The vnreasonable Furie of a beast. **1611** BIBLE *Wisd.* vii. 20 The natures of liuing creatures, and the furies of wilde beasts. **1698** FRYER *Acc. E. India & P.* 298 A large Camel raging with Lust for the Female.. This Fury lasts Forty Days. **1727** SWIFT *Gulliver* II. vii, Unable to defend himself from.. the fury of wild beasts. **1774** GOLDSM. *Nat. Hist.* (1776) IV. 288 In such a case, there was no method of appeasing its fury, but by giving it something to eat.

2. Fierce impetuosity or violence; *esp.* warlike rage, fierceness in conflict, attack, or the like. †Rarely, fierce cruelty.

1534 ELYOT tr. *Isocrates' Doctr. Princes* 9 b, Dooe thou nothyng in furie, sens other men knowe what time and occasion is meetest for the. **1553** BRENDE *Q. Curtius* IV. 42 b, Two thousand whome the furye of the slaughter had lefte on lyue. **1601** R. JOHNSON *Kingd. & Commw.* (1603) 41 In assaulting of tounes and fortresses, I confesse furie to be of great moment. **1630** *Ibid.* 13 If ever your eares heard of more hellish furies than those which these Princes have put in execution. **1712** POPE *Spect.* No. 408 ¶7 'Tis fit the Fury of the Coursers should not be too great for the Strength of the Charioteer. **1726** *Adv. Capt. R. Boyle* 155 The Fight continu'd half an Hour with the utmost Fury. **1769** *Junius Lett.* xv. 65 The extremes of alternate indolence or fury.. have governed your whole administration. **1805** SCOTT *Last Minstr.* I. vii, The furies of the Border war. **1856** EMERSON *Eng. Traits, Race* Wks. (Bohn) II. 31 To hunt with fury.. all the game that is in nature.

b. *Hist.* ***the (Spanish) Fury***: the massacre perpetrated by the Spaniards at Antwerp in Oct.–Nov. 1576.

1576 HETON *Let.* 10 Nov. in Arb. *Garner* VIII. 166 To answer and content the Spanish soldiers and others who, in the Fury, entered our said House. **1855** MOTLEY *Rise Dutch Repub.* III. 116 It was called the Spanish Fury, by which dread name it has been known for ages.

3. *transf.* of things (e.g. of a tempest, the wind, a raging malady, etc.).

1585 T. WASHINGTON tr. *Nicholay's Voy.* II. xi. 46 b, In despite of the rayne, wind, and furye of the sea. **1599** R. LINCHE *Anc. Fiction* V ij a, Those places which, by the ardent furie of the sunnes vertue, become drie. **1662** STILLINGFL. *Orig. Sacr.* III. iv. §5 These waters falling down with so much fury and violence. **1697** DAMPIER *Voy.* I. xiii. 348 Before the Winds abated of their fury. **1698** FRYER *Acc. E. India & P.* 235 Had not the late unusuall Rain something allayed the Fury of the Heats. **1726** *Adv. Capt. R. Boyle* 127 Leaving their naked Bodies expos'd to the Fury of the Storm. **1742** *Lond. & Country Brew.* I. (ed. 4) 51 For retarding and keeping back any Drink that is too much heated in working.. it may be broke into several other Tubs, where, by its shallow Lying, it will be taken off its Fury. **1756** C. LUCAS *Ess. Waters* I. 217 All his former complaints rage with more than double fury. **1887** BOWEN *Virg. Æneid* I. 69 Arm with fury the winds.

b. phr. ***like fury***: furiously, 'like mad'. *colloq.*

1840 LONGF. in *Life* (1891) I. 359 The last eighteen miles it rained like fury.

4. Inspired frenzy, as of one possessed by a god or demon; esp. poetic 'rage'. Now *rare.*

1546 LANGLEY *Pol. Verg. de Invent.* I. xix. 33 b, When they prophesie in manner of furie, and rauishinge of mynde. **1563** B. GOOGE *Eglogs* i. (Arb.) 32 O Cupyde kynge of fyerye Loue.. with Furye fyll my brayne, That I may able be to tell, the cause of Louers payne. **1581** SIDNEY *Apol. Poetrie* (Arb.) 72 They are so beloued of the Gods, that whatsoeuer they write, proceeds of a diuine fury. **1597** MORLEY *Introd. Mus.* 35 This hath been a mightie musicall furie, which hath caused him to shewe such diuersitie in so small bounds. **1604** SHAKS. *Oth.* III. iv. 72 A Sybill.. In her Prophetticke furie sow'd the Worke. **1676** HOBBES *Iliad* Pref. (1686) 5 The Sublimity of a Poet, which is that Poetical Fury which the Readers for the most part call for. **1703** POPE *Thebais* 3 A sacred fury fires My ravish'd breast, and all the Muse inspires. **1707** *Curios, in Husb. & Gard.* 74 All that Enthusiasm or poetick Fury could inspire.

5. One of the avenging deities (L. *Furiæ*, *Diræ*, Gr. *Ἐρινύες*, *Εὐμενίδες*), dread goddesses with snakes twined in their hair, sent from Tartarus to avenge wrong and punish crime: in later accounts, three in number (Tisiphone, Megæra, Alecto). Hence *gen.* an avenging or tormenting infernal spirit.

c **1385** CHAUCER *L.G.W.* 2252 *Philomela*, The furies three with aile hir mortel brond. *c* **1386** —— *Knt.'s T.* 1826 Out of the ground a furie [*v.rr.* fyr(e, fir(e] infernal sterte. From Pluto sent, at requeste of Saturne. **1574** *Mirr. Mag.*, *Cordila* xxiv, Art thou some fury sent? My wofull corps with paynes to more tormente? **1596** SPENSER *F.Q.* IV. i. 26 For she at first was borne of hellish brood And by infernall furies nourished. **1614** BP. HALL *Recoll. Treat.* 111 Thou shalt neuer want furies so long as thou hast thy selfe. **1667** MILTON *P.L.* x. 620 Had not the folly of Man Let in these wastful Furies. **1709** STEELE *Tatler* No. 137 ¶3 Thunder, Furies, and Damnation! I'll cut your Ears off. **1737** WHISTON *Josephus' Hist.* VI. iii. §4 Be thou a fury [*orig.* Ἐρινύς] to these seditious varlets. **1838** ARNOLD *Hist. Rome* (1846) I. vii. 106 All prayed that the furies of her father's blood might visit her with vengeance. **1840** MACAULAY *Ess.*, *Clive* (1865) II. 104/1 He [Surajah Dowlah] sat gloomily in his tent, haunted, a Greek poet would have said, by the furies of those who had cursed him with their last breath in the Black Hole.

b. Used for: One of the three 'Fates' or *Parcæ.*

1637 MILTON *Lycidas* 75 Comes the blind Fury with the abhorred shears And slits the thin-spun life.

6. *transf.* One who is likened to an infernal spirit or minister of vengeance; *esp.* a ferociously angry or malignant woman.

c **1374** CHAUCER *Troylus* v. 1498 And of the holy serpent, and the welle, And of the furies, al she gan him telle. *a* **1611** BEAUM. & FL. *Philaster* II. iv, Come, sir, you put me to a woman's madness, The glory of a fury. **1611** BIBLE *2 Macc.* vii. 9 Thou like a fury takest vs out of this present life. **1676** DRYDEN *Aurengz.* II. Wks. 1883 V. 224 Remember, sir, your fury of a wife. **1687** T. BROWN *Saints in Uproar* Wks. 1730 I. 73 Here's a termagant fury, St. Ursula by name. **1719** DE FOE *Crusoe* I. xvi, He flew upon his murderers like a fury. **1768** GOLDSM. *Good-n. Man* I. i, There was the old deaf dowager, as usual, bidding like a fury against herself. **1843** MACAULAY *Ess. Mad. D'Arblay* (1865) II. 307/1 The card-table of the old Fury to whom she was tethered. **1873–4** DIXON *Two Queens* IV. XXI. v. 149 When the King's confessor went to Oxford, he was stoned by female furies in the Market Place.

b. *humorously*, of things.

1856 KANE *Arct. Expl.* I. xv. 167 Facing the little lobster-red fury of a stove.

7. *attrib.* and *Comb.*, as ***fury-form***, ***rage***; ***fury-haunted***, ***-moving*** adjs; ***fury-like*** adj. and adv. †Also **fury fire**, app. a technical term for a white heat.

1644 DIGBY *Nat. Bodies* I. iii. 21 When the smith and the glassemender driue theire white and *fury fires (as they terme them). **1866** CONINGTON *Æneid* VIII. 282 There Catiline Hangs poised above the infernal deep With *Fury-forms behind. **1735** SOMERVILLE *Chase* III. 468 So the poor *Fury-haunted Wretch.. still seems to hear The dying Shrieks. **1600** FAIRFAX *Tasso* XVI. lviii, My angrie soule ..*furie like in snakes and fire brands drest, Shall aie torment thee. **1711** KEN *Hymns Evang.* Poet. Wks. 1721 I. 49 All dream'd that Herod Fury-like appear'd. *a* **1748** THOMSON *Song*, Come, gentle God of soft desire, Come, and possess my happy breast; Not, fury-like, in flames and fire, In rapture, rage, and nonsense, drest. **1597** DANIEL *Civ. Wars* IV. xlv, Forth-with, began these *fury-mouing sounds. **1513** DOUGLAS *Æneis* XII. ii. 129 With sykkin *fury rage catchit is he.

† **'fury**, *v. Obs. rare*$^{-1}$. [f. prec. sb.] *refl.* To drive oneself to fury, become infuriated.

1628 FELTHAM *Resolves* I. x. (1631) 29 As I would not neglect a suddaine good opportunity; so I would not fury my-selfe in the search.

So **'furying** *ppl. a.*, raging, moving with fury.

a **1861** CLOUGH *Life & Duty* vii, The wild sea's furying waters.

fury, obs. form of FIERY.

furyl ('fjʊərɪl, -aɪl). *Chem.* [Abbrev. of FURFURYL.] The univalent radical C_4H_3O-based on furan. Cf. FURFURYL.

1916 *Chem. Abstr.* X. 3400 Organic radicals... Furyl (2-, 3-),

O·CH:CH·CH:C–

1963 F. M. DEAN *Naturally Occurring Oxygen Ring Compounds* i. 3 Furyl carbinols behave as allylic alcohols in suffering hydrogenolysis to alkyl furans. **1966** *Nomenclature Org. Chem.* (I.U.P.A.C.) (ed. 2) 67 Univalent radicals derived from heterocyclic compounds by removal of hydrogen from a ring are in principle named by adding 'yl' to the names of the parent compounds... The following exceptions are retained: furyl, [etc.].

furze (fɜːz). Forms: 1 **fyrs**, 4–6 **firse**, (5 **virse**), 4, 6–7 **furs(e**, 5 **fyrrys**, 6 **fyrs**, 6–7 **firr(e)s**, **firze**, (6 **fyrze**), **furres**, 7–9 **furz**, 7–9 *dial.* **fuz**, 8 **fuzz**, 6– **furze**. Also pl. 4 **firsen**, **fursyn**, 5 **fyrsyn**, 6 **fursen**, 6–7, 9 *dial.* **furzen**, (7 **-on**), 9 *dial.* **fuzzen**. See also FUR *sb.*[3] [OE. *fyrs* str. masc.; no connexions are known; the Gr. *πράσον*, Lat. *porrum*, leek, might be cognate so far as the form is concerned, but the difference of sense is unfavourable to this supposition. The disyllabic forms *fyrrys*, *firres*, etc. seem to have been apprehended as plural, and a new sing. was formed from them: see FUR *sb.*[3]]

1. The popular name of *Ulex europæus*, a spiny evergreen shrub with yellow flowers, growing abundantly on waste lands throughout Europe. Also named *gorse*, *whin*; ***common***, ***great*** or ***French furze***. †Sometimes, a bush or piece of this.

c **888** K. ÆLFRED *Boeth.* xxiii, Swa hwa swa wille sawan westmbære land atio ærest of þa þornas & þa fyrsas. *c* **1000** *Ags. Voc.* in Wr.-Wülcker 324 *Ramnus*, fyrs. **1362** LANGL. *P. Pl.* A. v. 195 All that herde.. weschte that hit weore i-wipet with a wesp of firsen. **1382** WYCLIF *Micah* vii. 4 A palyure, that is, a sharp bushe, or a thistil or frijse [*v.r.* firse]. **1436** *Rolls of Parlt.* IV. 498 Pasture, Wode, Hetthe, Virses, and Gorste. **1523** FITZHERB. *Surv.* 6 b, All the wode, brome, gorse, fyrs, braken. **1573** TUSSER *Husb.* liii. (1878) 119 With whinnes or with furzes thy houell renew. **1610** SHAKS. *Temp.* IV. i. 180 Tooth'd briars, sharpe firzes, pricking gosse. *a* **1626** BRETON *Daffodils & Primr.* (Grosart) 23 Forrestes full of furres and brakes. **1647** COWLEY *Mistress, Discovery* ii, The humble Furzes of the Plain. *a* **1701** SEDLEY *Virgil's Past.* Wks. 1722 I. 296 May I to thee more bitter seem than Rue, More course than Fuz. **1735** SOMERVILLE *Chase* III. 42 Thick with entangling Grass, or prickly Furze. **1770** GOLDSM. *Des. Vill.* 192 With blossom'd furze unprofitably gay. **1832** LYTTON *Eugene A.* IV. ii, A broad patch of green heath, covered with furz. **1887** SIR R. H. ROBERTS *In the Shires* i. 3 The hounds are making the furze crack and shake in their eager efforts.

b. *transf.* and *fig.*

1602 MARSTON *Ant. & Mel.* v. Wks. 1856 I. 60 Oh, to have a husband.. with a bush of furs on the ridge of his chinne. **1705** ELSTOB in Hearne *Collect.* 30 Nov. (O.H.S.) I. 107 From Fuzz and Bramble to the downy beard He whisk'd them off.

2. In popular names of other plants, as **dwarf furze** (*Ulex nanus*); **ground furze**, the Rest-harrow (*Ononis arvensis*); **needle furze** (*Genista anglica*).

1578 LYTE *Dodoens* VI. x. 669 This herbe is called.. in Englishe Rest Harrow, Cammocke, Whyn, Pety Whyn, or ground Furze. **1650** *Phytologia Brit.* 45 Genistella.. Needle Furze or Petty Whin. *Ibid.*, Creeping Dwarfe Furze or Whins. **1738** C. DEERING *Catal. Stirp.* 89 Needle Furze.

3. *attrib.* and *Comb.*

a. chiefly attributive, as ***furze-bed***, ***-brake***, ***-cover***, ***-croft***, ***-cutter***, ***-down***, ***-faggot***, ***-flower***, ***-hill***, ***-lea***, ***-top***, ***-toppings*** (*pl.*); ***furze-clad*** adj.

1644 VICARS *Jehovah-Jireh* 133 His *Furze-bed was the best bed that ever he lay on. **1711** BUDGELL *Spect.* No. 116 ¶5, I saw a Hare pop out from a small *Furze-brake. **1807** VANCOUVER *Agric. Devon* (1813) 38 The higher sides of the hills.. are advantageously appropriated for furze-brakes. **1795–1814** WORDSW. *Excurs.* VIII. 370 Upon the skirts Of *furze-clad commons. **1795** *Gentl. Mag.* June 462 The custom of setting fire to the *furze-covers on midsummer-day. **1857** KINGSLEY *Two Y. Ago* I. 63 A green down stretches up to bright yellow *furze-crofts far aloft. **1882** OUIDA *Maremma* I. 45 Here and there a *furze cutter. **1865** KINGSLEY *Herew.* I. v. 157 Flat and open *furze-downs. *c* **1555** in Strype *Cranmer* 392 One load of *Furs-Fagots. **1686** PLOT *Staffordsh.* 355 Laying at the bottom.. a range of furse-faggots. **1793** COLERIDGE *Songs of Pixies* ii, We sip the *furze-flowers' fragrant dews. **1800** HURDIS *Fav. Village* 174 How elegant yon *furze-hill clothed in gold. **1794** *Act Inclosing S. Kelsey* 1 *Furze Leas, and Waste Grounds. **1859** W. S. COLEMAN *Woodlands* (1866) 126 The action of which effectually bruizes the *Furze-tops intended for Fodder. **1865** KINGSLEY *Herew.* II. xx. 347 Who was often glad enough.. to rob his own ponies of their *furze-toppings and boil them down for want of kale.

b. *esp.* in ***furze-bush***, also (*obs.* and *dial.*) **furzen bush.**

1530 PALSGR. 220/2 Fyrsbusshe, *jovmarin.* **1600** HEYWOOD *1st Pt. Edw. IV*, II. ii, So many men in the moon, And every one a furzen bush in his mouth. **1644** VICARS *Jehovah-Jireh* 133 Many other young Gentlemen.. lay all that night.. upon Furze-bushes on the ground. **1668** J. WHITE *Rich Cab.* (ed. 4) 51 If you will graft a white rose upon a Broom-stalk, or on a furzon bush. **1738** C. DEERING *Catal. Stirp.* 89 Genista spinosa minor.. The lesser Furze Bush. **1882** BLACK *Shandon Bells* xxiii, Miss Patience asked me if I had combed it [my hair] with a furze-bush.

4. Special comb.: †**furze cat**, a name given to the hare; **furze-huck** *dial.*, a heap or stack of furze; **furze-owl**, a cockchafer; **furze-pig**, the hedgehog.

a **1325** *Names of Hare* in *Rel. Ant.* I. 133 The *furse-cat. **1869** BLACKMORE *Lorna D.* xiii, The *furze-hucks of the summer-time, were all out of shape in the twist of it. **1847–78** HALLIWELL, **Furze-owl*, a cockchafer. Somerset. **1865** *Cornh. Mag.* July 40 As in Gloucestershire, *'furse-pig' for hedgehog.

b. In popular names of various birds, as **furze-chat**, the whinchat (*Pratincola rubetra*); **furze-chirper**, **-chucker**, the mountain finch or brambling (*Fringilla montifringilla*); **furze-hacker** = *furze-chat*; **furze-** (*dial.* **fuz-**) **kite** (see quots.); **furze-lark**, the tit-lark (*Anthus pratensis*); **furze-wren** = FURZELING.

1839–43 YARRELL *Hist. Birds* I. 249 The Whinchat, or *Furzechat. **1847–78** HALLIWELL, **Furze-chirper*, the mountain finch. It is also called the *furze-chucker. **1862** J. R. WISE *New Forest* (1863) 270 The whinchat, known.. from its cry, as the '*furze hacker'. **1635** BRATHWAIT *Arcad. Princesse* 237 Where choughs and *fuskites built their nest. **1880** *W. Cornw. Gloss.*, *Fuz'-kite*, the ring-tailed kite. **1886** ELWORTHY *W. Somerset Word-bk.*, *Vuz-kite*, a kestrel. *a* **1854** CLARE *MS. Poems* in Miss Baker *Northants. Gloss.*, I wept to see the hawk severe Murder the *furze-lark whistling nigh. **1839–43** YARRELL *Hist. Birds* I. 313 The *Furze Wren.

Hence **furzed** *a.* [-ED[2]], made or covered with furze. Also **'furzeling** [-LING], the Dartford Warbler (*Melizophilus undatus*).

1855 OGILVIE Supp., Furzeling, Furze-wren, *Melizophilus provincialis.* **1873** *Daily News* 21 May 5/5 There are a ditch, a bank with a drop, a kind of furzed fence, and a low wall of turf and stones. **1885** W. ALLINGHAM *Flower Pieces* (1887) 14 Harbours the wren, the furzeling, and the coney.

furzery ('fɜːzərɪ). [f. FURZE *sb.* + -ERY.] A mass of furze, furze collectively.

1866 BLACKMORE *Cradock Nowell* i, A heavy-browed crest of furzery.

furzy ('fɜːzɪ), *a.* Also 7 **fursy**. [f. FURZE *sb.* + -Y[1].]

1. Of or pertaining to furze; composed of furze; covered or overgrown with furze.

1613–16 W. BROWNE *Brit. Past.* II. iv, No furzy tuft.. shall harbour Wolfe. **1686** PLOT *Staffordsh.* 344 Their broomy, gorsy or fursy, hot sandy land. **1781** P. BECKFORD *Hunting* (1802) 249 Where the cover is thick.. particularly if it be furzy. **1845** TALFOURD *Vac. Rambles* (1847) I. 127 We crossed an angle of furzy common. **1869** BLACKMORE *Lorna D.* xli, All things had..a kind of furzy colour.

2. Fuzzy, fluffy.

1719 H. BARHAM in *Phil. Trans.* XXX. 1037 When the loose furzy Substance is taken off. **1880** SENIOR *Trav. & Trout in Antip.* 127 The old fellow is very furzy in the matter of hair.

b. Fuzzy, indistinct, blurred.

1825 MOORE *Sheridan* 664 Those painters, who endeavour to disguise their ignorance of anatomy by an indistinct and furzy outline.

fus, var. of FOUS *a. Obs.*, eager, ready.

‖**fusain** (fyzɛ̃). **1. a.** A charcoal crayon made of the wood of the Spindle Tree (F. *fusain*); also *attrib.*, as in ***fusain drawing***. **b.** A drawing executed with this.

1870 *Eng. Mech.* 11 Mar. 638/3 Fontanesi, of Geneva, is well known for his fusain drawings. I have seen some admirable drawings in fusain (charcoal). **1884** *Gd. Words* Feb. 91/1 Good as Lalanne's etchings are, his fusains are better.

2. Anglicized as (ˈfjuːzeɪn). A friable, porous type of coal that occurs as dull layers or masses in bituminous seams; 'mineral charcoal'.

1883 *Jrnl. Chem. Soc.* XLIV. 941 Fusain is a variety of coal, resembling wood-charcoal in appearance. Some stalks, the interior of which is composed of fusain, are covered with a bark which has been converted into coal. **1913** *Proc. Amer. Philos. Soc.* LII. 89 The unaided eye can discern many features of coal in the bed; it can group types into glance, matt, cannel, fusain. **1919** [see CLARAIN]. **1935** *Nature* 23 Nov. 818/2 Quite moderate variation in the amount of fusain in the coal has important effects on its utility. **1961** W. FRANCIS *Coal* (ed. 2) v. 296 Fusain differs very considerably in constitution and properties from the remaining ingredients of coal. *Ibid.*, The proportion of fusain in most coals is small, generally less than 3%.

fusarole (ˈfjuːzərəʊl). *Arch.* Also 7 **fuserole**, 9 **fusurole**. [a. F. *fusarolle*, ad. It. *fusaruola*, later *fusajuola*, alteration of *fusaruolo* (*fusajuolo*) spindle-whorl, f. L. *fūsus* spindle.] (See quots.)

1664 EVELYN tr. *Freart's Archit.* 128 A smaller Bracelet again which incircles the Capital under the Voluta in the Composita, taken for the Fuserole. **1704** in HARRIS *Lex. Techn.* [**1715** LEONI *Palladio's Archit.* (1742) I. 23 The Composite Order has..the Voluta, Ovolo, and Fusarolo, or Fuse, which are Members of the Ionick Capitel.] **1852** *P. Nicholson's Dict. Archit.*, *Fusurole, Fusarole.* **1859** GWILT *Archit.* Gloss., *Fusarole*, a member whose section is that of a semicircle carved into beads. It is generally placed under the echinus, or quarter round of columns in the Doric, Ionic, and Corinthian orders.

fusate (ˈfjuːseɪt), *a. rare*$^{-0}$. [f. L. *fūs-us* spindle + -ATE.] = FUSIFORM.

1889 in *Century Dict.*

fusball, obs. form of FUZZBALL.

ˈfusby. ? *Obs.* [? = FUBSY.] A contemptuous designation applied to women. Also *attrib.*

1719 D'URFEY *Pills* V. 108 With that the Flat-capt Fusby smiled. **1845** *Punch* 29 Nov. 240 A fusby woman who has indulged in the vulgar weakness of giving her children fine names.

fusc: see FUSK *a.*

†**fuˈscation.** *Obs.*$^{-0}$ [agent-n. f. L. *fuscāre* to darken, f. *fuscus* dark, dusky: see -ATION.] 'A darkening; obscurity; obfuscation' (W.).

1656–81 BLOUNT *Glossogr.*, *Fuscation*, a darkning or clouding. **1727** in BAILEY, vol. II. **1755** in JOHNSON.

fuscescent (fʌˈsɛsənt), *a. rare*$^{-1}$. [f. L. *fusc-us* (see FUSCOUS) + -ESCENT.] Passing into a dark or dusky hue; 'brownish; approaching to darkish brown in colour' (*Syd. Soc. Lex.* 1885).

1881 JOHNSON in *Jrnl. Bot.* No. 220. 113 Their colour is fuscescent.

fuscin (ˈfʌsɪn). *Chem.* Also **-ine**. [f. L. *fusc-us* (see FUSCOUS) + -IN.] 'A brown substance obtained by Unverdorben from the animal oil of Dippel after exposure to the air' (*Syd. Soc. Lex.* 1885).

1864 WEBSTER, *Fuscine*.

†**fuscite** (ˈfʌsaɪt). *Min.* [f. L. *fuscus* (see FUSCOUS) + -ITE.] Obs. synonym of WERNERITE.

1808 T. ALLAN *Alphabet. List* 32 Fuscite..a mineral from Arendal resembling the Pinite.

†**ˈfuscity.** *Obs.*$^{-0}$ [ad. late L. *fuscitās*, f. *fuscus*: see FUSCOUS.] 'Darkness, dimness' (Bailey, vol. II. 1727).

fusco- (ˈfʌskəʊ), used as combining form of L. *fuscus* 'dusky', in certain adjs., as **fusco-ferruginous**, dull rust-coloured; **fusco-piceous**, dull reddish-black; **fusco-testaceous**, dull reddish-brown.

1847 HARDY in *Proc. Berw. Nat. Club* II. No. 5. 237 Antennæ black, fusco-piceous at the apex. *Ibid.* 244 Elytra ..with nearly parallel sides, flat, black, or fusco-testaceous.

fuscous (ˈfʌskəs), *a.* [f. L. *fuscus* dark, dusky + -OUS.] Of a dark or sombre hue; dusky, swarthy. (Chiefly *Nat. Hist.*)

1662 RAY *Itin.* in *Rem.* (1760) 247 The 5 or 6 first Feathers of the Wing above of a dark or fuscous Colour, near Black. **1671** J. WEBSTER *Metallogr.* xvi. 235 A fuscous or darkish redness. **1756** BURKE *Subl. & B.* II. xvi, Sad and fuscous colours, as black, or brown, or deep purple. **1826** KIRBY & SP. *Entomol.* IV. 282 *Fuscous*, a dull brown. **1828** STARK *Elem. Nat. Hist.* II. 210 Back fuscous brown, with four lines of white spots. **1848** J. GOULD *Birds Austral.* Descr. pl. 44 *Ptilotis fusca*, Fuscous Honey-eater. **1853** DE QUINCEY *Wks.* (1862) XIV. 390 The other sad, fuscous, begrimed with the snuff of ages. **1870** HOOKER *Stud. Flora* 57 Seeds fuscous acutely tubercled.

fig. **1855** DE QUINCEY *Lett.* 31 July in H. A. Page *Life* (1877) II. xviii. 106 Some confused remembrance I had that we were or ought to be in a relation of hostility, though *why* I could ground upon none but fuscous and cloudy reasons.

†**fuse**, *sb.*[1] *Obs. rare.* [perh. ad. OF. *fuies*, pl. of *fuie*:—L. *fuga* flight.] The track of an animal. Also *fig.*

1611 COTGR., *Foulée*, the Slot of a Stag, the Fuse of a Bucke. *a* **1670** HACKET *Abp. Williams* I. (1692) 14 There wants a Scholar like a Hound of a sure Nose, that would not miss a true Scent..to trace those old Bishops in their fuse.

fuse (fjuːz), *sb.*[2] Also 8 **feuze**, 9 **fuze**. [ad. It. *fuso* (:—L. *fūsus*) spindle, hence applied to the spindle-shaped tube originally used as a 'fuse' for a bomb, etc. Cf. FUSEE[2] 3.]

1. A tube, casing, cord, etc., filled or saturated with combustible material, by means of which a military shell, the blast of a mine, etc. is ignited and exploded.

1644 NYE *Gunnery* (1670) 63 Every Ball hath a hole, left to put in a Fuse or piece of wood just like a Faucet for a spigot ..made taper. **1692** *Capt. Smith's Seaman's Gram.* II. xxxi. 145 It is far more certain to fire a Morter-piece with Fuses then with Match. **1769** FALCONER *Dict. Marine* (1789) Cciv, The fuse..is generally a conical tube, formed of beech, willow, or some dry wood, and filled with a composition of sulphur, salt petre, and mealed powder. **1863** KINGLAKE *Crimea* (1876) I. xiv. 240 The other was the man standing by with a lighted match and determined to touch the fuse. **1869** R. B. SMYTH *Goldf Victoria* 612 *Fuse, Fuze*, a small cylindrical cord filled with powder or other combustible matter used for igniting the powder in a bore-hole. **1879** FIFE-COOKSON *Armies of Balkans* ii. 25 The shrapnel..did execution around us, the time fuzes acting well.

b. Prepared material of which fuses may be made by cutting it into lengths.

1767 H. BROOKE *Fool of Quality* (1792) II. x. 86 Having bound some feuze round..the extremity of each of their tails. **1884** [see quot for *fuse-bag* in 2].

c. fig. ***short fuse***: see SHORT *a.* 26 a.

2. *attrib.* and *Comb.*, as ***fuse-bag***, ***-composition***, ***-hole***. Also **fuse-cutter**, **-extractor**, **-gauge**, **-saw**, **-setter**, **-tape** (see quots.).

1884 *Mil. Engin.* I. II. 109 Each *fuze bag to contain eight pieces of Bickford fuze. **1846** GREENER *Sc. Gunnery* 49, I therefore venture to suggest the possibility of the *fuse composition becoming altered in its properties, by the action of time and moisture. **1874** KNIGHT *Dict. Mech.* I. 920/2 **Fuse-cutter*, an implement for gaging time-fuses to the desired seconds and fractions..The cutter for paper fuses for rifled guns..is more usually called a fuse-gage. It is a block of wood with a graduated brass gage let into one side, and having a hinged knife..by which the fuse..is cut off so as to burn any required length of time. *Ibid.* 930/1 **Fuse-extractor*, this implement is designed for extracting fuses from shells. **1874** *Fuse-gage [see *fuse-cutter*]. **1692** *Capt. Smith's Seaman's Gram.* II. xxxi. 146 Try your Shells ..by putting in a little Powder, and firing it, immediately stopping the *Fuse-hole with Clay. **1858** GREENER *Gunnery* 83 A light cast-iron hollow ball, with a fuse hole. **1874** KNIGHT *Dict. Mech.* I. 930/2 **Fuse-saw*, a tenon-saw used by artillery-men. *Ibid.*, **Fuse-setter*, an implement for driving home wooden fuses. *Ibid.*, **Fuse-tape*, a flat form of fuse, coated externally with pitch or tar.

†**fuse, fuze**, *sb.*[3] *Obs. rare.* [alteration of FUSEE, assimilated to prec.] = FUSEE[2] 2. Also ***fuse-wheel***.

1674 PETTY *Disc. Dupl. Proportion* 119 In the Fuze of a Watch, the greatest Strength of the Spring is made to work upon the shortest Vectis. **1701** GREW *Cosm. Sacra* II. vi. §86. 61 Thinking Men considered how it [a clock] might be made portable..and so..put the Spring and Fuse-wheel, which make a Watch.

†**fuse**, *sb.*[4] *Obs. rare*$^{-1}$. = FUSAROLE.

1715 [see FUSAROLE].

fuse (fjuːz), *sb.*[5] *Electr.* [f. FUSE *v.*[2]] In full ***safety fuse***. A strip or wire of easily fusible metal (or a device containing this) inserted in an electric circuit, which melts (or 'blows') and thus interrupts the circuit when the current increases beyond a certain safe strength. Also *fig.* (see BLOW *v.*[1] 19 c).

1884 R. HAMMOND *Electr. Light* v. 56 Conductor Joined with Fuse. *Ibid.* 58 Showing Safety Fuses in Circuit. **1890** J. W. URQUHART *Electr. Light Fitting* 160 The main object, then, of a safety fuse or cut-out..is to prevent accidental overheating. *Ibid.* 165 [see b]. **1923** WODEHOUSE *Inimitable Jeeves* ii. 28 That scheme of yours..has blown out a fuse. **1969** *Which?* Sept. 282/2 When you buy a plug, it will normally have a 13-amp fuse inside.

b. fuse-block, **-board**, **-box**, **-carrier**, **-holder**, **-mounting**, **-plate**, **-plug**, various contrivances for holding a fuse or a number of fuses; **fuse-wire**, wire used to make fuses.

1885 J. DREDGE *Electr. Illum.* II. 325 A fuse box containing six fuses. **1890** J. W. URQUHART *Electr. Light Fitting* 162 The fuse plate may easily be removed and replaced by others. *Ibid.* 165 In such cases it is considered safer to assemble all the fuses upon a fuse board. **1891** H. E. SWIFT *U.S. Patent 455,366*, Fuse-wire cut outs or 'fuse-blocks', as they are commonly called, have also been used in connection with incandescent lamps, said fuse-blocks being located on the ceiling. **1892** F. C. ALLSOP *Pract. Electr. Light Fitting* 57 The reason why lead or lead-tin alloy is preferred for the fuse-wire of a cut-out. **1893** W. P. MAYCOCK *Electr. Lighting* III. xv. §220. 384 A S.P. fuse block. *Ibid.* 386 The fuse wire is fitted in what is called a fuse plug. **1894** D. L. SALOMONS *Electr. Light Install.* (ed. 7) II. 219 Another improvement..is that of placing under the fuse binding-screw a washer carrying a steady pin, which passes loose into the fuse block. *Ibid.* III. 162 It is almost impossible to remove the fuse-box cover or replace the fuse without removing this box completely. **1899** W. P. MAYCOCK *Electr. Wiring* 185 The removable fuse carrier is of porcelain. *Ibid.* 245 The fuse-holders are of porcelain. **1899** H. M. LEAF *Internal Wiring* 85 A guide for determining..the sizes of fuse wires that may be employed for cut-outs. **1914** S. C. BATSTONE *Electr.-Light Fitting* 104 Porcelain Tubular Fuse Carrier. **1936** M. KENNEDY *Together & Apart* I. 47 She snipped off lengths of fuse wire. **1964** R. F. FICCHI *Electrical Interference* vi. 78 The fuse-mounting and relay assembly is usually mounted close to the power source.

†**fuse**, *a. Obs. rare*$^{-1}$. [ad. L. *fūs-us* lit. 'poured out', pa. pple. of *fundĕre* to pour.] = DIFFUSE.

1724 *Wodrow Corr.* (1843) III. 160 His style is fuse, and reasonings..pretty magisterial.

†**fuse**, *v.*[1] *Obs.* Forms: 1 *fȳsan*, 3 *fusen* (y). Also 3 *fouse* (see under FOUS *a.*). [OE. *fȳsan*, f. *fús* FOUS *a.* (Not identical with FEEZE.)]

1. *intr.* To hasten, set out hastily. Also *refl.*

a **1000** *Cædmon's Gen.* 2860 (Gr.) He..sona ongann fysan to fore. *a* **1000** *Andreas* 1698 (Gr.) He..Ongan hine þa fysan & to flote ȝyrwan. *c* **1205** LAY. 1865 Forð com Corineus & fusde hine sulfne. *Ibid.* 13534 Alle we mote fusen.

2. *trans.* To forward or send forth speedily; to dispatch.

a **1000** *Byrhtnoth* 269 (Gr.) He fysde forð flan ȝ enehe. *c* **1000** *Lamb. Ps.* li. 7 (Bosw.) He fysþ ðe of ȝetelde. *c* **1205** LAY. 1511 Brutus nom al his ȝunge folc & hem to scipe fusede.

fuse (fjuːz), *v.*[2] [f. L. *fūs-* ppl. stem of *fundĕre* to pour, melt, FOUND *v.*]

1. a. *trans.* To make fluid by means of intense heat; to liquefy, melt. Also with *apart*, *together*.

1681 tr. *Willis' Rem. Med. Wks.* Vocab., *Fuse*, to melt as metals. **1800** tr. *Lagrange's Chem.* I. 321 If it be still exposed to heat, it..becomes fused into a transparent glass. **1816** J. SMITH *Panorama Sc. & Art* II. 756 As soon as the colours are fused, the intensity of the fire should be abated. **1863** TYNDALL *Heat* xiv. §113 A quantity of silver which had been fused in a ladle was allowed to solidify. **1866** LIVINGSTONE *Last Jrnls.* (1873) I. iv. 85 The strata fused together by heat. **1878** B. TAYLOR *Deukalion* II. i. 58 As by fierce heat, the chains be fused apart.

absol. **1831** *Fraser's Mag.* III. 134 The volcanic fire that smoulders and fuses in secret. **1879** *Cassell's Techn. Educ.* IV. 359/2 Collect the crystals, dry, and fuse.

b. Of a flux: To facilitate the fusion of.

1796 KIRWAN *Elem. Min.* (ed. 2) I. 6 They [fluxes] fuse lime without effervescence. **1800** tr. *Lagrange's Chem.* I. 378 Ammoniacal phosphate of soda fuses this matter perfectly.

c. *fig.* Often with the sense: To blend intimately, amalgamate, unite into one whole, as by melting together.

1817 COLERIDGE *Biog. Lit.* 149 He diffuses a tone and spirit of unity, that blends, and (as it were) fuses, each into each. **1851** ROBERTSON *Serm.* Ser. III. xi. 136 The threat of foreign invasion had fused down and broken the edges of conflict and variance. **1857** H. REED *Lect. Brit. Poets* iv. 136 Fused by the heat of poetic genius and poured out in one glowing and glittering flood. **1860** TYNDALL *Glac.* I. xxii. 159 To fuse myself amongst them as if I had been an old acquaintance. **1867** GOLDW. SMITH *Three Eng. Statesmen* (1882) 12 The Scotch nation, nobles and commons, ministers and people, wonderfully fused together by fiery enthusiasm, poured like a lava torrent on the aggressor. **1869** FARRAR *Fam. Speech* iv. (1873) 121 A Chinese grammar cannot..be fused into the moulds of our Aryan logic.

d. *transf.* To liquefy, attenuate, thin (the blood).

1704 F. FULLER *Med. Gymn.* (1711) 111 They fuze and divide [the Blood] and break its Globules. **1733** CHEYNE *Eng. Malady* II. iv. §4 (1734) 147 Purgatives are either..to cleanse the *Primæ Viæ*, or to fuse and thin the Blood. **1822–34** [see FUSED *ppl. a.*].

2. a. *intr.* To become fluid or liquefied with heat; to melt.

1800 tr. *Lagrange's Chem.* I. 167 A mixture of these three substances fuses much easier. **1838** T. THOMSON *Chem. Org. Bodies* 16 The crystals..fuse into a liquid. **1858** FROUDE *Hist. Eng.* III. 74 They were to fret and chafe till the dust was beaten off, and the grains of gold could meet and fuse. **1881** YOUNG *Every Man his own Mechanic* §1500. 678 By hard solder is meant one that only fuses at a high temperature.

b. *fig.*

1840 DICKENS *Barn. Rudge* xxxvii, Eyes so small and near together, that his broken nose alone seemed to prevent their meeting and fusing into one of the usual size. **1873** DIXON *Two Queens* I. III. iii. 131 These passions fused and centred in one radiant point.

c. Of an electric light, appliance, etc.: to fail or be extinguished owing to the melting of a fuse. Also *trans.*, to cause (a circuit, etc.) so to fail.
1887 *Fire Offices Rules for Electr. Light Installations* 7 The cut-outs may be arranged to fuse at a higher per-centage. **1930** *Daily Express* 6 Nov. 2/2 Two minutes before he arrived..the lights in the building fused. **1940** G. D. H. & M. Cole *Murder at Munition Works* xx. 192, I was in his shop once when the light fused. **1951** *Good Housek. Home Encycl.* 80/2 A heater should never be run from a lighting plug, as this is apt to fuse the circuit.

3. *Anat.* Of contiguous vessels, bones, etc.: To coalesce.
1870 Rolleston *Anim. Life* Introd. 56 There are two systemic aortæ which either fuse, or anastomose. **1872** Mivart *Elem. Anat.* 39 In Tortoises all the trunk vertebræ are fused. **1878** Bell *Gegenbaur's Comp. Anat.* 456 In the Anura these fuse together on either side to form a fronto-parietal.

Hence **'fusing** *ppl. a.*
1817 Coleridge *Biog. Lit.* II. xxii. 171 The blinding, fusing power of Imagination and Passion. **1873** Symonds *Grk. Poets* i. 10 The fire of moulding, fusing and controlling genius.

fuse, fuze (fjuːz), *v.*[3] [f. fuse *sb.*[2]] Also fuze. *trans.* To furnish with a fuse.
1802 Wellington *Jrnl.* 30 Nov. in Gurw. *Desp.* I. 382 Ordering..2500 four and half inch shells, 600 to be filled, fused, etc. **1823** P. Nicholson *Pract. Build.* 396 Slate is extracted..by making perforations between its beds, into which gunpowder is placed and fused. **1869** *Daily News* 3 July, The projectiles can be fuzed and adjusted.

Hence **fused** *ppl. a.*, **'fusing** *vbl. sb.*
1869 *Daily News* 3 July, The Horse Artillery..obtained 265 impressions with the Shrapnell; 323 with the segment, double fuzed. **1884** *Mil. Engin.* I. ii. 104 Each man will throw four fuzed grenades across the ditch. **1895** *Daily News* 23 July 6/1 They failed in one important point—the correct fuzing of the shells.

fuse (fjuːz), *v.*[4] [f. fuse *sb.*[5]] *trans.* To insert a fuse in (a circuit), to furnish with a fuse.
1894 D. Salomons *Electr. Light Installations* (ed. 7) II. vi. 234 The idea of fusing the plug is probably due to Mr. Massey. **1914** D. C. Shafer *Harper's Everyday Electricity* ix. 90 The method of fusing a house circuit is best shown in Fig. 12. **1954** F. Wiseman *Penguin Handyman* (ed. 3) i. 11 A circuit supplying this [current] should be fused with a 5-amp fuse wire.

Hence **fused** *ppl. a.*
1934 C. Haslett *Electr. Handbk. for Women* ix. 183 Fused plugs are available and are often found very useful. **1962** *B.S.I. News* Mar. 24/2 Socket-outlets requiring fused plugs must not accept unfused plugs. **1967** *Do It Yourself* Nov. 1283/2 Feed the circuit from a fused spur box situated in a conspicuous position on the landing.

fused (fjuːzd), *ppl. a.* [f. fuse *v.*[2] + -ed[1].]
a. Liquefied by heat, melted.
1699 Salmon *Pharm. Bateana* (1713) 144/1 Fine cleanly powder'd fus'd Salt. *a* **1763** Byrom *Verses intended to have been Spoken* v. 10 The Forge wherein his fused Metals flow'd. **1837** Brewster *Magnet.* 135 He used a cylindrical needle of fused steel. **1878** Huxley *Physiogr.* 213 The fused rocks in the depths of the earth which are vomited forth by volcanoes.
fig. **1855** H. Spencer *Princ. Psychol.* (1870) I. ii. ii. 178 The fused set of sounds we call a word. **1876** Douse *Grimm's L.* §30. 63 If the dialects..again become completely fused.

b. Of the blood: Attenuated, thin.
1822–34 *Good's Study Med.* (ed. 4) IV. 372 How are we to account for that crude, fused, or dissolved state of the blood?

c. ***fused participle***: a participle regarded as being joined grammatically with a preceding noun or pronoun, rather than as a gerund that requires the possessive, or as an ordinary participle qualifying the noun (see quot. 1926).
1906 H. W. & F. G. Fowler *King's Eng.* ii. 119 The mistake is caused by certain types of sentence in which a real, not a fused participle is so used that the noun and its (unfused) participle give a sense hardly distinguishable from a possessive noun and a gerund. *Ibid.* 120 Long fused-participle phrases are a variety of abstract expression, and as such to be deprecated. **1926** Fowler *Mod. Eng. Usage* 205/2 *Fused participle* is a name given to the construction exemplified in its simplest form by 'I like *you pleading* poverty'... The name was invented..for the purpose of labelling & so making recognizable & avoidable a usage considered by the inventor to be rapidly corrupting modern English style. **1942** Partridge *Usage & Abusage* 124/2 Idiomatically, the *excuse me doing* form is generally understood to be positive; but it is much rarer than the *excuse my doing* form, especially since ca. 1920, when the fused participle doctrine began to ravage the land. **1954** E. Gowers *Compl. Plain Words* ix. 157 What they are not agreed about is whether it is also correct to..write 'the Bill getting a second reading surprised everyone'. If that is a legitimate grammatical construction, the subject of the sentence, which cannot be *Bill* by itself, or *getting* by itself, must be a fusion of the two. Hence the name 'fused participle'.

fusee[1], **fuzee** (fjuː'ziː). *Obs.* exc. *Hist.* [a. F. *fusil* (pronounced (fyzi)): see fusil[2].] A light musket or firelock.
1661 Evelyn *Mem.* (1857) I. App. 430 Horsemen well appointed with..carabines, musquetoons, or fuzees. **1705** S. Sewall *Diary* 26 Mar. (1879) II. 127 A souldier from Deerfield accompanied us with his Fusee. **1760** *Chron.* in *Ann. Reg.* 82/1 A handsome double barrell'd fuzee valued at twelve or fifteen guineas. *a* **1813** A. Wilson *Foresters* Poet. Wks. (1846) 211 His light fuzee across his shoulder thrown.

†b. One who is armed with a fusee; a fusilier.
1650 A. B. *Mutat. Polemo* 29 That brave Gallant number of Fusees were squandred all to peices, knockt o' the head, or starved.

fusee[2], **fuzee** (fjuː'ziː). Also 7 fus(s)ie, fusey, phusee, 8 fusy. [a. F. *fusée*, primarily, spindleful of tow (:—med.L. *fūsāta*, f. L. *fūsus* spindle); hence used for spindle, and in senses 2–4 below. Sense 5 is an Eng. development from 3.]

†1. A spindle-shaped figure: = fusil[1] 1. *Obs.*
1589 Puttenham *Eng. Poesie* (Arb.) 105 The Fuzie or spindle, called Romboides.

2. A conical pulley or wheel, *esp.* the wheel of a watch or clock upon which the chain is wound and by which the power of the mainspring is equalized.
1622 in *Naworth Househ. Bks.* 199 Making a fussie to my Lords cloke. **1658** S. Crooke *Div. Char.* i. ix. 82 This is the first wheele, yea, the Phusee, the inward spring that moves his watch so swiftly. **1677** Hale *Prim. Orig. Man.* i. ii. 50 In the Watch..the reason of the motion of the Ballance is by the motion of the next Wheel, and that by the motion of the next, and that by the motion of the Fusee. **1713** *Lond. Gaz.* No. 5155/4 A Gold Watch..going with a Spring, without Fusey, Chain or String. *c* **1790** Imison *Sch. Art* II. 284 From the fusy to the balance the wheels drive the pinions. **1824** R. Stuart *Hist. Steam Engine* 146 Chains acting on a spiral in the manner of a fusee. **1827** Faraday *Chem. Manip.* iv. 112 The mouth at this time represents the going fuzee of a chronometer. **1884** F. J. Britten *Watch & Clockm.* 108 In modern watches and clocks the fusee is furnished with maintaining power to drive the train while the fusee is being turned backwards during the process of winding.

3. = fuse *sb.*[2] 1.
1704 *Lond. Gaz.* No. 4062/7 The Enemy..set Fire to great quantities of Powder, with Intent to spring their Mines; which..was prevented from taking Effect, by cutting off the Fusees. **1769** Falconer *Dict. Marine* (1789), *Secret d'un brulot*, that part of the train of a fire-ship where the match or fusee is laid. **1809** *Naval Chron.* XXII. 287 Cones, containing..12 lbs. of powder, to burst by fuzees. **1858** Greener *Gunnery* 139 The aperture [of the shell] is securely screwed up: fusees not being necessary in this arrangement.

4. *Farriery.* An exostosis upon one of the cannon-bones.
¶Some modern Dicts, by an obvious misapprehension, define it as 'a kind of splint applied to the legs of horses'.
1720 Gibson *Farrier's Guide* ii. lxxviii. (1738) 233 Sometimes a double Splent is formed which is called by the French a Fuzee. **1727** Bailey, vol. II, *Fuzee* [in Horses] two dangerous Splents joining above and downwards. **1753** Chambers *Cycl. Supp. s.v.*, Commonly a fuzee rises to the knee and lames the horse. Fuzees differ from screws or thorough splents in this, that the latter are placed on the two opposite sides of the leg.

5. A kind of match with a large head of combustible material tipped with brimstone for ignition by friction; a lucifer, vesuvian.
1832 *Specif. Jones' Patent* No. 6335. 2, Fuzees for the purpose of lighting cigars, pipes, etc. **1851** Mayhew *Lond. Labour* I. 433 The 'fuzees', as I most frequently heard them called..are chiefly German made. **1888** Rider Haggard *Col. Quaritch* xxiv, It was one of those flaming fusees, and burnt with a blue light.

6. *attrib.* and *Comb.*, as *fusee-maker*, *-wheel*. Also **fusee-engine, -machine**, a machine for cutting fusees for watches; **fusee-piece, -sink, -snail, -windlass** (see quots.).
1858 Simmonds *Dict. Trade*, *Fusee-engine, a clock-maker's machine for cutting and shaping fusees. **1874** Knight *Dict. Mech.* I. 930/1 **Fusee-machine*, a machine for cutting the snail-shaped or spirally grooved wheel on which the chains of certain descriptions of watches are wound. **1858** Simmonds *Dict. Trade*, **Fuzee-maker*, a manufacturer of parts of watch-work. **1884** F. J. Britten *Watch & Clockm.* 110 *Fusee Piece..the circular plug screwed to the top plate in which the upper pivot of the fusee works. *Ibid.*, *Fusee Sink..the sink cut in the top plate of a watch to give space for the fusee. *Ibid.* 247 The *fusee snail, a projecting nose on the end of the fusee. **1838** *Penny Cycl.* XII. 303 (art. *Horology*) The spring..gives motion to the fusee, and with it the *fusee-wheel and the rest of the train. **1874** Knight *Dict. Mech.* I. 930/1 **Fusee-windlass*, a pump-windlass with a conical barrel.

fusel ('fjuːzəl). [a. Ger. *fusel* bad brandy or other spirits; formerly applied in LG. dialects also to bad tobacco. Cf. Ger. *fuseln* to bungle (see foozle).] *attrib.* in *fusel oil*, 'a term for a mixture of several homologous alcohols, chiefly amylic alcohol, and especially applied to this when in its crude form' (*Syd. Soc. Lex.* 1885).
1850 Daubeny *Atom. Th.* vii. (ed. 2) 227 Being abundantly obtained during the distillation of potatoes..the name of oil of potato spirit, or fusel oil, has been assigned to it. **1859** *All Year Round* No. 32. 128 Fusel oil..makes oil of pear, used in perfumery and the so-called 'jargonelle pear drops'. **1868** *Q. Rev.* No. 248. 350 A peculiarly fœtid oil, termed 'fusel' oil, is formed in making brandy and whisky.

fuselage ('fjuːzɪlɑːʒ, -ɪdʒ). [Fr., f. *fuseler* to shape like a spindle, f. *fuseau* spindle: see fusil[1] and -age. So called from its spindle-like shape.] The elongated body of an aeroplane, to which the wings and tail unit are attached and which (in modern aircraft) contains the crew and the passengers or cargo. (In early use given slightly varying meanings: see quots.)
1909 *Flight* 19 June 366/2 The aeroplane itself was considerably damaged, the *fuselage* which carries the elevating-plane in front..being completely broken. **1910** R. Ferris *How it Flies* xx. 461 *Fuselage*, the framework of the body of an aeroplane. **1913** A. E. Berriman *Aviation* 249 Another French word at present in common use is *fuselage*, meaning the girder-like backbone employed in modern aeroplane design. This member also forms the body of the machine. **1913** *Times* 14 Apr. 4/1 The number of machines which have broken their fuselage—to say nothing of their wings. **1913** A. H. Verrill *Harper's Aircraft Bk.* xi. 120 The parts of an aeroplane are mainly the frame, or 'chassis'; the body, or 'fuselage'; the wings, or 'planes'; [etc.]. **1918** Cowley & Levy *Aeronautics* vii. 141 The fuselage connecting the body and the tail system exists purely to provide support for the latter. **1932** E. Bowen *To North* xvii. 175 Catching the full summer sun on its wings and fuselage.., the plane evenly passed to the coast. **1960** C. H. Gibbs-Smith *Aeroplane* i. xvi. 129 The construction of a large conventional all-metal aeroplane of today..is stressed skin, with (in the fuselage) the metal skin laid over a multiple system of ring-line formers.

fushionless: see foisonless.

fusht (fʌʃt), *intr.* [Sc. dial. pronunciation of whisht.] Hush!
1816 Scott *Antiq.* xxvii, 'Fusht, fusht,' said Francie.

fusibility (fjuːzɪ'bɪlɪtɪ). [ad. F. *fusibilité*, f. *fusible*: see next.] The quality of being fusible.
1624 Wotton *Archit.* (1672) 20 Observing in that Material..a Fusibility. **1756** C. Lucas *Ess. Waters* I. 3 Metals..lose their metallic splendor, fusibility, ductility and other properties. **1846** G. E. Day tr. *Simon's Anim. Chem.* II. 433 Its fusibility is proportionate to the amount of the magnesian salt present. **1880** W. C. Roberts *Introd. Metallurgy* 29 Carbon, it is well known, gives to iron fusibility.

fusible ('fjuːzɪb(ə)l), *a.* Also 7 fusable. [a. F. *fusible*, ad. mod.L. **fūsibilis*, f. L. *fūs-*, ppl. stem of *fundĕre* to pour, melt, fuse.] Capable of being fused or melted. ***fusible metal*** (see quot. 1853). ***fusible plug*** (see quot. 1874).
c **1386** Chaucer *Can. Yeom. Prol. & T.* 303 Also of hir induration, Oiles, ablucions, and metal fusible To tellen al, wolde passen any bible. **1605** Timme *Quersit.* ii. i. 104 Salt is fusible. **1615** G. Sandys *Trav.* iii. 203 Sand..becoming fusable with the heate of the fornace. **1685** Boyle *Effects of Mot.* iv. 36 The burning fluid..may be made..to melt..the more fusible metals. **1747** Hooson *Miner's Dict.* O j b, That called Potter's Ore..is so frim and fusible that [etc.]. **1812** Sir H. Davy *Chem. Philos.* 297 These mixtures are more fusible than either of their constituents. **1844–57** G. Bird *Urin. Deposits* (ed. 5) 472 The most contorted and irregularly figured calculus is the triple or fusible. **1853** Ure *Dict. Arts* I. 46 The fusible metal consisting of 8 parts of bismuth, 5 of lead, and 3 of tin..melts at the heat of boiling water or 212° Fahr. though the melting point deduced from the mean of its components should be 514°. **1874** Knight *Dict. Mech.*, Fusible plug, one placed in the skin of a steam-boiler, so as to be melted and allow the discharge of the contents when a dangerous heat is reached. **1884** *Manch. Exam.* 1 Dec. 5/4 The explosion..was partly due..to a defective fusible plug.

Hence **'fusibleness**, the quality of being fusible.
1684 Boyle *Porousn. Anim. & Solid Bod.* viii. 130 He had reduced..real Gold, to that degree of Fusibleness and subtlety, that..the finer part of the Metal would sweat through his Glasses.

fusidic (fjuː'sɪdɪk), *a. Biochem.* [f. mod.L. *Fusid-ium* (see def.), f. L. *fūs-us* spindle + con)idium: see -ic.] ***fusidic acid***: a steroid, $C_{31}H_{48}O_6$, with antibiotic properties, orig. isolated from a strain of the fungus *Fusidium coccineum* and esp. effective against *Staphylococcus aureus.*
1962 W. O. Godtfredsen et al. in *Nature* 10 Mar. 987/1 From the fermentation broth of a strain of *Fusidium* a hitherto unrecorded antibiotic, for which the name 'fusidic acid' is proposed, has been isolated. **1962** *Lancet* 15 Dec. 1278/1 Success with fusidic acid in a highly resistant case of staphylococcal septicæmia. **1967** Gottlieb & Shaw *Antibiotics* II. 144 Fusidic acid, $C_{31}H_{48}O_6$, a metabolite of *Fusidium coccineum* and *Cephalosporium lamellaecola. Ibid.* 145 Fusidic acid, sometimes called 'Antibiotic ZN-6', is identical with 'Ramycin' from *Mucor ramannianus.*

†**fusie**, var. of fowsie. *Obs.*
1617 *Sc. Acts Jas. VI* (1814) IV. 536/2 Ditches and fusies.

fusiform ('fjuːzɪfɔːm), *a.* [f. L. *fūs-us* spindle + -(i)form. Cf. F. *fusiforme.*] Spindle-shaped; tapering from the middle towards each end; esp. in *Bot.*, *Entom.*, and *Zool.*
1746 Da Costa in *Phil. Trans.* XLIV. 404 The cylindric, fusiform, and other Belemnites, of which the two Ends or Extremes terminate pointed. **1805** J. Galpine *Brit. Bot.* (1806) 311 Root caulescent, fusiform. **1826** Kirby & Sp. *Entomol.* (1828) IV. xxxvii. 14 The great ganglion of the rhinoceros-beetle is fusiform. **1830** Lindley *Nat. Syst. Bot.* 154 Seeds indefinite, very minute, fusiform. **1854** Woodward *Mollusca* (1856) 108 Shell fusiform, elongated. **1877** Huxley *Anat. Inv. Anim.* ii. 79 Each of these elongates, and surrounds itself with a delicate, fusiform, silicious case. **1881** Geikie in *Nature* XXV. 2 A genus of Palæoniscid fishes, possessing a fusiform body. **1887** *Scribner's Mag.* I. 427/2 This torpedo..is fusiform, or cigar-shaped.

fusil[1] ('fjuːzɪl). *Her.* Forms: 5–6 fusille, 7 fusile, -ll, 7– fusil. [ad. OF. *fu(i)sel* (F. *fuseau*):—popular L. **fūsell-us*, dim. of *fūsus* spindle.
The mod. Fr. heraldic term is *fusée*; but the adj. *fuselé*, = fusilly, seems to show that *fusel* was formerly used in this sense.]
A bearing in the form of an elongated lozenge; understood to have been originally a representation of a spindle covered with tow.

1486 *Bk. St. Albans, Her.* E ij a, It is calde fusillit for it is made all of fusillis. **1572** BOSSEWELL *Armorie* II. 34 b, Fusilles, whiche are so termed, for that they be made like Spindles. **1602** SEGAR *Hon. Mil. & Civ.* II. xiv. 79 Embrodered round about with a border of flames, fusils and fleeces. **1653** A. ROSS *Πανσεβεια* (1658) 351 The great Collar was made of double Fusiles enterwoven with Stones and Flints, sparkling flames of fire. **1765–87** in PORNY *Her.* Gloss. **1828–40** BERRY *Encycl. Her.* I. s.v., The fusil nearly resembles the lozenge in shape, but is longer.

Comb. **1860** J. HEWITT *Anc. Arm.* II. 235 Fusil-shaped spikes [of a Rowel-spur].

Hence †**'fusilled** *ppl. a.* (see quot. 1486 above).

fusil² ('fju:zɪl). Also 6 fusill, 8–9 fuzil; and see FUSEE¹. [a. F. *fusil* (OF. *fuisil*) = It. *focile*:—late L. **focīle*, f. *focus* hearth (in pop. Lat. fire).]

†**1.** A fire steel for a tinder-box. *Obs.*

1580 HOLLYBAND *Treas. Fr. Tong, Vn Fusil*, a Fusill to strike fire in a tinder boxe.

2. A light musket or firelock.

1680 *Eng. Milit. Discipl.* I. 20 The Mousqueton is not so long as the Fusil or Fire-Lock. **1682** *Lond. Gaz.* No. 1684/1 Six Men of the tallest Stature, with long Fusils. **1719** DE FOE *Crusoe* I. xx, We were..armed with a fusil..each man. **1762–71** H. WALPOLE *Vertue's Anecd. Paint.* (1786) V. 137 The dew..had made his fusil rusty, and..he was scraping and cleaning it. **1847** *Infantry Man.* (1854) 28 Seize the fusil with the left hand. **1876** BANCROFT *Hist. U.S.* IV. xxxii. 555 The sentry snapped a fusil at him.

fusile ('fju:zɪl), *a.* Also 7–9 fusil. [ad. L. *fūsil-is*, f. *fūs-* ppl. stem of *fundĕre* to pour: see FOUND *v.*³, FUSE *v.*² and -ILE.]

1. Capable of being melted. Now *rare.*

1605 TIMME *Quersit.* II. i. 105 Metall is nothing else but a certaine fusil salt. **1660** R. COKE *Power & Subj.* 162 We teach, that every Cup in which the Eucharist is consecrated be Fusil. **1758** A. REID tr. *Macquer's Chem.* I. 358 Mix with this powder.. one part of fusile glass. **1875** JOWETT *Plato* (ed. 2) III. 641 Water, again, admits in the first place of a division into two kinds; the one liquid and the other fusile.

2. Running or flowing by the force of heat; made liquid by heat. Now *rare.*

a **1631** DONNE in *Select.* (1840) 220 Metal may be soft, and yet not fusile. **1639** FULLER *Holy War* II. xii. (1647) 59 The glassie sand..could not be made fusile till it was brought hither. **1708** J. PHILIPS *Cyder* II. 70 A fusil sea That in his furnace bubbles sunny red. **1725** POPE *Odyss.* VI. 278 And o'er the silver pours the fusil gold.

fig. **1839** *Blackw. Mag.* XLV. 461 The fusile capacity of a language for running into ready coalitions of polysyllables aids this tendency.

3. Formed by melting or casting.

1398 TREVISA *Barth. De P.R.* XVI. xxxvi. (1495) 564 Bras that is wroughte wyth hamour is callid Regular, and bras that oonly is meltyd hyghte Fusile. **1667** MILTON *P.L.* XI. 573 He formd First, his own Tooles; then, what might else be wrought Fusil or grav'n in mettle. **1796** MORSE *Amer. Geog.* II. 490 The fusile or moveable types were undoubtedly Dutch or German inventions. **1837** WHITTOCK, etc. *Bk. Trades* (1842) 386 To Peter Schoeffer belonged the honor of inventing 'fusil' types.

fig. **1624** DONNE *LXXX Serm.* xlvi. (1640) 460 S. Paul was borne a man, an Apostle, not carved out, as the rest, in time; but a fusile Apostle, an Apostle powred out, and cast in a Mold.

fusilier (fju:zɪ'lɪə(r)). Forms: 7–8 fuzil(l)eer, (7 fuseleer, phusilier), 8–9 fusileer, (8 fuzeleer), 7– fusilier. [a. F. *fusilier*, f. *fusil* FUSIL².] Originally, a soldier armed with a fusil (see FUSIL² 2). In the British army, the designation of 'Fusiliers' is still retained by certain regiments which are distinguished from the other regiments of the line only by wearing a kind of busby and by some small peculiarities of costume.

1680 *Eng. Milit. Discipl.* IV. 132 The Fusiliers have for Arms the Sword, the Bayonet, and Fusil or Fire-lock. **1686** *Lond. Gaz.* No. 2135/1 His Majesties Company of Fuseleers of this City, Commanded by Captain Graham. **1753** HANWAY *Trav.* (1762) I. VII. xciii. 429 Some of the fuzileers, who are smaller bodied men, have their arms proportioned. **1813** *Examiner* 26 Apr. 272/2 Lieut. Brownson, of his Majesty's 23d Regiment Royal Welch Fusileers. **1858** J. B. NORTON *Topics* 128 Her [Madras] illustrious Fusiliers.. have been dispatched bodily to Calcutta.

attrib. **1802** C. JAMES *Milit. Dict.* s.v., All officers belonging to fusileer corps have two epaulettes. **1868** *Regul. & Ord. Army* ¶854 All grenadier and fusilier Regiments are ..to march to the tune of the British Grenadiers.

fusillade (fju:zɪ'leɪd), *sb.* Also 9 fusilade. [a. F. *fusillade*, f. *fusiller* to shoot, f. *fusil* FUSIL².] A simultaneous discharge of fire-arms; a wholesale execution by this means.

1801 *Times* in *Spirit Publ. Jrnls.* (1802) V. 53 From hence were shot those diavolinis and cardamoms, which have been so much admired for their happy illustration of the mitraille and fusillades. **1813** WELLINGTON in Gurw. *Desp.* XI. 359 The enemy have a considerable force..and are keeping up a fusillade. **1835** MACAULAY *Ess., Mackintosh's Hist. Rev.* (1887) 336 Then came..revolutionary tribunals, noyades, fusillades. **1863** KINGLAKE *Crimea* (1876) I. xiv. 283 This wanton fusilade must have been the result of a panic. **1885** *Times* (weekly ed.) 16 Oct. 6/2 Notwithstanding the fusillade, no one..appears to have been hurt.

transf. and *fig.* **186.** B. HARTE *Sanitary Message* i, I heard the welcome rain, A fusillade upon the roof, A tattoo on the pane. **1863** LONGF. *Wayside Inn, Birds of Killingw.* xxiii, O'er woodland crests, The ceaseless fusillade of terror ran. **1881** GEIKIE in *Macm. Mag.* Oct. 429 The men found relief in fusillades of swearing. **1884** *Pall Mall G.* 7 Nov. 1/1 The din of controversy, the fusillade of personalities.

fusillade (fju:zɪ'leɪd), *v.* [f. prec. sb.] *trans.* To assault (a place), to shoot down (persons) by a simultaneous discharge of fire-arms.

1816 SOUTHEY in *Q. Rev.* XV. 56 A whole corps..were marched apart by one of Stofflet's officers and fusilladed. **1851** CARLYLE *Sterling* I. xiii. (1872) 77 Give them shriving if they want it; that done, fusillade them all. **1884** *Century Mag.* XXVIII. 560 The Mahdi's adherents fusilladed his palace at Khartoum.

Hence **fusi'llading** *vbl. sb.* Also **fusi'llader**.

1839 CARLYLE *Chartism* v. 141 Lyons fusilladings..these ..were but a new irrefragable preaching abroad of that. **1878** H. M. STANLEY *Dark Cont.* II. iv. 119 The butcher of women and fusillader of children.

fusillation (fju:zɪ'leɪʃən). *rare.* [n. of action f. F. *fusiller* to shoot: see FUSILLADE *sb.* and -ATION.] Capital punishment by shooting.

1859 SALA *Gas-light & D.* vii. 83 The black cutty [pipe].. was with him when under sentence of fusillation for sketching a droschky in the Nevski Perspective.

fusilly ('fju:zɪlɪ), *a. Her.* Also 6 fusile, 7 fusillee, 8 fusiley, 9 fusilé. [a. OF. *fuselé*, f. *fusel*: see FUSIL¹.] Of a field: Covered with fusils (see FUSIL¹ 1).

1572 BOSSEWELL *Armorie* II. 116 Two Pillers in pile fusile Dargent. **1634** PEACHAM *Gentl. Exerc.* III. 149 Fusillee is like unto Masculy, but your fusils must be made long and small in the middle. **1711** HEARNE *Collect.* (O.H.S.) III. 165 The old Manner of Ingrailing in Arms is like Fusiley. **1825** *Gentl. Mag.* XCV. I. 309 The Tabley family, whose armorial ensign was; Argent, a pale fusilè Sable. **1864** BOUTELL *Her. Hist. & Pop.* viii. 35 In a Field Fusilly..the divisions are narrower than in Lozengy.

b. Fusil-shaped.

1860 HEWITT *Anc. Arm.* II. 235 The rowels..may be divided into three kinds—the star shaped, the indented, and the fusilly.

fusimotor ('fju:zɪməʊtə(r)), *a. Physiol.* [f. L. *fūs-us* spindle + MOTOR *a.* 2]. Of, pertaining to, or designating the motor neurones with fibres of small diameter which innervate the intrafusal fibres (spindles) of muscle.

1958 HUNT & PAINTAL in *Jrnl. Physiol.* CXLIII. 195 The motor fibres to the spindle have been designated γ efferents by Leksell (1945) and small motor fibres by Kuffler et al. (1951). Both designations have possible ambiguity... We therefore propose the term fusimotor with reference to neurones that are motor to the muscle spindle. **1962** P. B. C. MATTHEWS in *Q. Jrnl. Exper. Physiol.* XLVII. 327 There exist fusimotor fibres of two functionally distinct kinds, which for the purposes of the present description, and for the want of better terms, will be called static and dynamic fusimotor fibres. **1968** *Jrnl. Physiol.* CXCV. 420 It has been proposed that voluntary movement may be initiated and sustained by the activation of fusimotor neurones.. operating the muscle spindles and monosynaptic reflex as a follow-up length servo. **1969** *Proc. R. Soc.* B. CLXXIII. 162 It is difficult to see how such a segmental motor apparatus could allow the cortex to initiate precise movements of the hand, employing only the fusimotor route.

fusing ('fju:zɪŋ), *vbl. sb.* [f. FUSE *v.*² + -ING¹.] The action or process of fusing (see FUSE *v.*²), *lit.* and *fig.*

1832 G. R. PORTER *Porcelain & Gl.* 192 This, in fusing, was converted into a black glass. **1886** *Athenæum* 22 May 684/1 A little fusing into harmony would do wonders for this picture.

b. *attrib.*, as ***fusing point*** or ***temperature***, the point or temperature at which fusion takes place.

1860 TYNDALL *Glac.* II. xxxi. 409 The fusing point has been elevated by the pressure. **1863** —— *Heat* vi. §240 (1870) 188 The fusing-point of cast iron is 2,000° F. **1886** A. WINCHELL *Walks & Talks Geol. Field* 101 The fusing temperature now existing within [the earth].

fusion ('fju:ʒən). [ad. L. *fūsiōn-em*, n. of action f. *fundĕre* to pour. Cf. FOISON and F. *fusion.*]

1. a. The action or operation of fusing or rendering fluid by heat; the state of flowing or fluidity in consequence of heat. Also in phrases †***of easy, hard fusion***: melted with ease or difficulty. †***watery fusion***: the melting of certain crystals by heat in their own water of crystallization.

1555 EDEN *Decades* 327 To brynge it to fusion or meltynge. **1594** PLAT *Jewell-ho.* I. 14 Although some sortes of them [Ashes] bee of harder fusion or melting than others. **1646** SIR T. BROWNE *Pseud. Ep.* II. i. 51 Flints and pebbles are subject unto fusion. **1683** PETTUS *Fleta Min.* I. (1686) 5 Oars..of an easier Fusion. **1718** QUINCY *Compl. Disp.* 12 This Operation is..seldom perform'd without Melting or Fusion. **1807** T. THOMSON *Chem.* (ed. 3) II. 53 When exposed to the heat of boiling water, they undergo the watery fusion; that is to say, the water which they contain becomes sufficient to keep the barytes in solution. **1812–16** J. SMITH *Panorama Sc. & Art* I. 5 The texture of steel is rendered more uniform by fusion. **1832** G. R. PORTER *Porcelain & Gl.* 70 That degree of heat must be employed which will give perfect fusion to the glaze. **1878** HUXLEY *Physiogr.* 199 It [the earth] existed at one time in a state of fusion.

fig. **1850** MRS. JAMESON *Leg. Monast. Ord.* (1863) 227 That wonderful religious movement which..threw men's minds into a state of fusion.

b. *concr.* A fused mass.

1823 J. BADCOCK *Dom. Amusem.* 138 The fusion is to be raised to the tempering height. **1863** FR. A. KEMBLE *Resid. in Georgia* 61 Clouds, which appeared but a fusion of the great orb of light. **1882** T. COAN *Life in Hawaii* 330 Drawing out small lumps of the adhering fusion, they moulded it, before it had time to cool, into various forms.

†**2.** *Path.* and *Phys.* **a.** Thinning, attenuation (of the blood). Cf. FUSE *v.*² 1 d. **b.** In etymological sense: A pouring; pouring forth (of the blood); ? = CIRCULATION. *Obs.*

1710 T. FULLER *Pharm. Extemp.* 54 A Decoction of Burdock..keeps the blood in a due mixture, and hinders its Fusion. **1725** N. ROBINSON *Th. Physick* 114 The Arteries, on whose Forces the Division and Fusion of the Blood entirely depend.

3. a. The union or blending together of different things (whether material or immaterial) as if by melting, so as to form one whole; the result or state of being so blended. Const. *into, with.*

1776 ADAM SMITH *W.N.* I. iv. (1869) I. 24 By fusion of the parts they can easily be reunited. **1830–3** LYELL *Princ. Geol.* (1875) II. III. xxxviii. 353 There seems to have been a partial fusion of the mammalia at some remote period. **1831** LAMB *Elia* Ser. II. *Ellistoniana*, That harmonious fusion of the manners of the player into those of everyday life. *a* **1834** COLERIDGE *Shaks. Notes* (1849) 10 The fusion of the sensual into the spiritual. **1841** MYERS *Cath. Th.* IV. l. 434 A fusion of nations..and an assimilation of races. **1855** MILMAN *Lat. Chr.* (1864) IV. VII. vi. 206 This absolute fusion of the religion of peace with barbarous warfare. **1856** EMERSON *Eng. Traits, Race* Wks. (Bohn) II. 22 Everything English is a fusion of distinct and antagonistic elements. **1875** MAINE *Hist. Inst.* xiii. 398 He argues for a fusion of law and equity. **1880** BASTIAN *Brain* 28 Fusions of ganglia may occur during the development of some animals. **1882** VINES *Sachs' Bot.* 582 The embryo-sac is formed by the fusion of two cells equivalent to spore-mother-cells.

b. *Politics.* The coalition (of parties or factions).

1845 DISRAELI *Sybil* (1863) 22 Political conciliation became the slang of the day, and the fusion of parties the babble of clubs. **1861** MAY *Const. Hist.* (1863) I. i. 8 A new reign was favorable..to the fusion of parties. **1879** GREEN *Read. Eng. Hist.* vi. 33 Their union was the result of no direct policy of fusion.

attrib. **1864** GREELEY *Amer. Confl.* I. xxii. 328 The refusal of part of the Douglas men to support the Fusion ticket (composed of three Douglas, two Bell, and two Breckinridge men). **1896** *Daily News* 27 July 7/5 Great difficulties are inevitable in making a fusion ticket in the various States.

c. (i) *Psychol.* and *Physiol.* [tr. G. *verschmelzung* (J. F. Herbert *Psychol. als Wiss.* (1824) I. 200).] A blending together of separate simultaneous sensations into a new complex experience or qualitative perception; the process whereby a succession of similar stimuli produces a continuous response or the sensation of a continuous stimulus.

1892 W. JAMES *Text-bk. Psychol.* 57 The so-called Fusion of Sensations in Hearing. **1903** G. F. STOUT *Groundwork Psychol.* 45 They [*sc.* sensations] may combine..like the bitterness, sweetness, and aroma of a cup of coffee... The first of these modes of union is called *fusion* or blending... Fusion is characterised by the absence of any definite order among the constituents of the sensation complex. **1911** E. B. TITCHENER *Text-bk. Psychol.* II. 351 The classical instance of the qualitative perception is the tonal fusion. **1946** D. P. C. LLOYD in J. F. Fulton *Howell's Textbk. Physiol.* (ed. 15) ii. 37 The frequency of stimulation necessary to promote full mechanical fusion of the contraction response is..different for different muscles. **1952** H. H. EMSLEY *Visual Optics* (ed. 5) I. i. 29 The final meticulous adjustment of the eyes is carried out under the compelling desire for fusion of the two uniocular images into a single perceptual image in the cortex.

(ii) *Psychiatry.* [tr. G. *mischung* (Freud *Das Ich und das Es* (1923) iv. 50).] In Freudian theory, the union and balance of life and death instincts which exist in normal persons.

1927, **1946** [see DEFUSION]. **1953** *Hibbert Jrnl.* July 332 Freud noted how masochism and sadism both arise from fusion of the life and death instincts. *Ibid.*, This peculiar fusion, with the death instinct preponderating, lies at the base of the desires..for sexual self-mutilation.

d. *Nuclear Sci.* The formation of a heavier, more complex nucleus by the coming together of two or more lighter ones, usu. accompanied by the release of relatively large amounts of energy; also, the utilization of this process as a source of energy.

1947 *Sci. News Let.* 7 June 358 (*heading*) Atom fusion gives energy. **1952** *Economist* 22 Nov. 541/1 This may have been a hybrid bomb, part atom, part hydrogen, but enough to prove that the scientists have solved the problem of releasing energy by nuclear fusion. **1957** *Rev. Mod. Physics* XXIX. 565/1 It has been suggested..that the fusion of helium plays an important role in energy generation and element synthesis in the red-giant stage of the star's evolution. **1958** *Engineering* 21 Feb. 227/3 Fission and fusion, at least in the initial stages, may well be complementary, both being necessary for a properly integrated nuclear power programme. **1964** R. H. BAKER *Astron.* (ed. 8) xvi. 479 The fusion of hydrogen into helium in the cores of these more massive stars may be principally by means of the carbon cycle. **1968** M. S. LIVINGSTON *Particle Physics* i. 5 Another special type of interaction is the fusion of lightweight nuclei such as H^2..into the more stable He^4 nuclei plus extra neutrons, with the release of several million electron volts per particle. **1969** J. DOUGALL tr. *Born's Atomic Physics* (ed. 8) x. 356 The only example of a man-made thermonuclear fusion process is in the form of the hydrogen bomb, where the high temperatures are produced by means of an initiating atomic (i.e. fission) explosion.

4. *attrib.* and *Comb.*, as ***fusion energy***, ***reaction***, ***reactor***, ***weapon***; **fusion bomb**, a bomb in which the energy released is derived from an uncontrolled process of nuclear fusion; *spec.* a hydrogen bomb; **(critical) fusion frequency** [tr. G. *verschmelzungsfrequenz* (J. v. Kries 1903, in *Zeitschr. f. Psychol. u. Physiol. d. Sinnesorgane* XXXII. 115)] *Physiol.* = *flicker-fusion frequency*; **fusion nucleus** *Biol.*, a cell nucleus that results from the fusion of two or more nuclei; **fusion welding**, a welding technique in which the metal is melted and joined without the application of pressure; so **fusion weld** *sb.*, **-welded** *ppl. a.*

1950 *Sci. Amer.* Mar. 13/2 The designer of a fusion bomb clearly would start with a fission bomb of uranium or plutonium, the explosion of which would produce the high temperatures required for the thermonuclear fusion reaction. **1955** *Sci. News* XXXVIII. 8 He [*sc.* Dr. Bhabha] predicted that a way would be found 'for liberating fusion energy in a controlled manner within the next two decades'. **1924** J. P. C. Southall tr. *Helmholtz's Treat. Physical Optics* II. 374 Porter compared the fusion frequencies for a series of different intensities of illumination. **1970** T. Cornsweet *Visual Perception* xiv. 393 If the frequency of flashing of a light is gradually increased from a low rate, there will be some frequency for which the light will just look steady.., and this is called the critical fusion frequency, or CFF. **1904** *Ann. Bot.* XVIII. 345 The fusion-nucleus then increased in size. **1928** E. B. Wilson *Cell* (ed. 3) v. 400 The pronuclei conjugate immediately after the entrance of the sperm and apparently fuse completely to form a fusion-nucleus. **1941** Johannsen & Butt *Embryol. Insects* ii. 9 The zygote, or fusion nucleus, in which the diploid number of chromosomes has been restored. **1950** F. Gaynor *Encycl. Atomic Energy* 129 Fusion reactions go on constantly in the interiors of the stars..and form the basic principle of the hydrogen bomb. **1957** O. Frisch in *Atlantic* Oct. 76 The fusion reaction—as far as we can see at present—will have to be operated at a temperature of many million degrees, and the production, control, and containment of such temperatures..is a stupendous problem. **1955** *Time* 25 July 62/3 If a fusion reactor works with reasonable efficiency it would have great advantages. **1955** *Bull. Atomic Sci.* Mar. 94/1 The presence of fission or fusion weapons in another major conflict seems inevitable. **1965** H. Kahn *On Escalation* vi. 96 'Clean' fusion weapons, leaving little or no residual fallout. **1930** *Engineering* 14 Mar. 364/1 With fusion welds, there is no difficulty in obtaining metal stronger than the plate. *Ibid.*, It has been customary to express the strength of a fusion-welded butt joint as a percentage of the plate strength. **1959** *B.S.I. News* Nov. 7/2 Fusion-welded pressure vessels. **1918** *Nature* 11 Apr. 105/2 The oxy-acetylene flame is most generally used for fusion welding, owing to its high temperature. **1958** *Engineering* 18 Apr. 501/1 The equipment includes an a.c./d.c. set for fusion welding under argon..and a resistance welding machine.

fusion, -ou(n)n(e, obs. forms of foison.

fusional ('fju:ʒənəl), *a.* [f. fusion + -al.] Of or pertaining to fusion; *spec.* designating a class of languages (see quots.).

1921 E. Sapir *Lang.* vi. 144 'Fusional' and 'symbolic' contrast with 'agglutinative', which is not on a par with 'inflective' at all. What are we to do with the fusional and symbolic languages that do not express relational concepts in the word but leave them to the sentence? *Ibid.* 148 By a 'fusional-agglutinative' language we would understand one that fuses its derivational elements but allows a greater independence to those that indicate relations. **1932** W. L. Graff *Lang.* ix. 333 When the union of radical and nonradical parts [of a word] is so great that a considerable alteration of either or both occurs, we obtain another structural type altogether, namely the *fusional* one. **1957** *Encycl. Brit.* XIII. 700/2 Fusional languages (the term inflected is also used) are the languages of the classical European tradition, such as Latin or Greek. Here grammatical endings are numerous, but it is not easy to isolate out the separate functions fused in each. **1964** R. H. Robins *Gen. Ling.* 322 Words in which several grammatical categories are marked by word forms in which it is difficult ..to assign each category to a specific and serially identifiable morphemic section are instances of fusional word structure (the term *inflecting*, or *inflectional*, is the older and traditional name for the typological class here called fusional..). **1964** S. Duke-Elder *Parsons' Dis. Eye* (ed. 14) xxviii. 451 The involuntary reflexes which depend on vision (fixation, fusional movement, convergence, etc.).

fusionism ('fju:ʒənɪz(ə)m). [f. fusion *sb.* + -ism.] The principle or practice of supporting a coalition or coalitions between political parties.

1851 *Fraser's Mag.* XLIII. 683 Fusionism means..a renunciation of the Revolution of July, 1830, its deeds and principles [etc.].

fusionist ('fju:ʒənɪst). [f. fusion *sb.* + -ist. Cf. F. *fusionniste.*] One who strives to promote fusion or coalition between differing associations, parties, or opinions.

1851 *Fraser's Mag.* XLIII. 683 The man..now comes forward as a fusionist. **1856** *Westm. Rev.* XXI. 479 Its [the French Academy's] elections are pitched battles between the Imperialists and the Fusionists. **1884** *Century Mag.* Jan. 399/1 Ready to break a lance one day for the Orleanists, another for the fusionists.

b. *attrib.* passing into *adj.*

1858 J. W. Donaldson *Lit. Greece* III. 41 Neglecting the reactionary or fusionist schemes of Philo or Antiochus. **1873** *Daily News* 22 Aug., The Fusionist negotiations have suddenly and finally ended in failure. **1875** M. Pattison *Casaubon* 504 After a short period of irresolution..he settled down in the attitude which we may call fusionist. **1882** *Pall Mall G.* 19 Apr. 6 Among Canadian Railway Securities there is the fusionist conflict with its ups and downs of prices.

fusionless: see foisonless.

†**'fusitive,** *a. Obs.* [irregularly f. L. *fūs-* ppl. stem of *fundĕre* to pour.] Of or pertaining to fusing or melting.

1657 Tomlinson *Renou's Disp.* 75 Whereby the liquative or fusitive Art is enriched.

†**'fusive,** *a.* and *sb. Obs. rare.* [f. L. *fūs-* ppl. stem of *fundĕre* to pour + -ive.] **A.** *adj.* Tending to fuse; in quot., tending to thin (the blood). Cf. fuse *v.*[2] 1 d. **B.** *sb.* Something which fuses.

1657 Tomlinson *Renou's Disp.* 262 Esula is..sharp, incisive, tenuative, fusive, apertive and siccative. **1678** R. R[ussell] *Geber* iii. ii. ii. xii. 197 The special fusive of it [i.e. Iron] is Arsnick of every kind.

fusk, *a. rare.* Also fusc. [ad. L. *fusc-us* in same sense.] Dark brown, dusky, fuscous. Hence †**'fuskish** *a. Obs.*, somewhat dark or dusky; †**'fusky** *a. Obs.*$^{-1}$ = fusk.

1563 Hyll *Art Garden.* (1593) 13 The seeds be then ripe to be gathered, when the grapes bee full ripe, which ripenesse of them by their fuskish and browne colour..may be knowen. **1577** Dee *Relat. Spir.* i. (1659) 75 That about the center is of fuskish or leadish colour. **1599** A. M. tr. *Gabelhouer's Bk. Physicke* 56/1 Till such time as the fuscke coloured oyle come therout. **1610** Tofte *Hon. Acad.* ii. 44 The dreadfull lodge of the fuskie daughters of blacke Night. **1657** Tomlinson *Renou's Disp.* 715 Verdigrease makes it sometimes citreous, sometimes fusk. **1669** Sir R. Paston in *Sir T. Browne's Wks.* (1848) III. 513, I found it, from itts fuscye red color, looke licke white lead ground with oyle. **1829** Lamb *Let. to H. C. Robinson* 27 Feb., Your strange-shaped present, while yet undisclosed from its fusc envelope.

†**'fuskin.** *Obs. rare*$^{-1}$. [ad. L. *fuscina* in same sense.] A three-pronged spear.

1575 Laneham *Let.* (1871) 52 A one syde, Neptune wyth hiz Tridental Fuskin.

fusle, var. of fuzzle *v.*, *Obs.*

†**fusoe.** *Obs.*$^{-1}$ [Anglicized spelling of Fr. *fuseau.*] A spindle.

c **1710** C. Fiennes *Diary* (1888) 119 People both in Suffolk and Norfolk knitt much and spin, some wth ye Rock and fusoe as the French does, others at their wheeles.

fusoid ('fju:zɔɪd), *a.* [f. L. *fūs-us* spindle + -oid.] = fusiform 2.

1889 in *Century Dict.*

†**'fusory,** *a. Obs.* $^{-1}$ [ad. L. *fūsōri-us*, f. *fūs-* ppl. stem of *fundĕre* to pour.] Adapted or tending to fuse or melt.

1678 R. R[ussell] *Geber* v. v. 276 The Fusory Furnace is that in which all Bodies are easily melted by themselves.

fusoun, obs. form of foison.

†**fuss,** *sb.*[1] *Obs.* = fussock 1, fustilugs.

1667 Dryden & Davenant *Tempest* iii. iii, This [his Bosen's Whistle]..is a Badge of my Sea-Office; my fair Fuss, thou dost not know it. **1675** Cotton *Burlesque on B.* 113 That great ramping Fuss, thy Daughter. **1702** Steele *Funeral* iii. (1734) 51 O' Sunday Morning at Church I curtsied to you; and look'd at a great Fuss in a glaring light dress next Pew.

fuss (fʌs), *sb.*[2] [Perh. echoic of the sound of something sputtering or bubbling, or expressive of the action of 'puffing and blowing'. Cf. also *fuss*, fuzz (= *fuzzball*). The common view that the word is connected with fous *a.*, 'eager, ready,' is baseless; the adj. is not found later than the 15th c., and has little affinity of sense with the sb.]

1. a. A bustle or commotion out of proportion to the occasion; a needless or excessive display of concern about anything; ostentatious or officious activity. Phrases: † ***to keep a fuss with*** = the later ***to make a fuss about***; ***to make a fuss of*** or ***over*** (†***with***): to pamper; to treat with an excessive display of affection or attention.

1701 Farquhar *Sir H. Wildair* iii. i, Ah! I hate these Congregation-women. There's such a fuss and such a clutter about their Devotion. **1726** Swift *To a Lady* in Johnson *Eng. Poets* XLIII. 79 Come to use and application; Nor with senates keep a fuss. *c* **1730** Ld. Lansdowne *Wild Boar's Def.* Wks. 1732 I. 140 With your Humanity you keep a Fuss; But are in truth worse brutes than all of us. **1783** Mad. D'Arblay *Diary* Jan., I felt so fagged with the preceding day's fuss. **1806–7** J. Beresford *Miseries Hum. Life* (1826) xi. 271 You have both been making a great fuss about nothing. **1814** Jane Austen *Mansf. Park* III. xiv. 267, I thought little of his illness at first. I looked upon him as the sort of person to be made a fuss with..in any trifling disorder. **1840** R. H. Dana *Bef. Mast* xxiii. 71 She got under weigh with very little fuss. **1850** Lowell *Lett.* (1894) I. 175 It is only foolish little men that are fond of mysteries and fusses. **1879** Dixon *Brit. Cyprus* vi. 58 They were to ask no leave, and make no fuss. **1888** Bryce *Amer. Commw.* III. ci. 424 There is a good deal of fuss about trotting-matches. **1928** *Daily Mail* 13 Aug. 19/2 He asked her if she were not going to let him make a fuss of her before he went. **1931** E. O'Neill *Mourning becomes Electra* i. iii. 71 His mother was stern with him, while Marie, she made a fuss over him and petted him. *a* **1953** —— *Long Day's Journey* (1956) i. 37 You like to get us worried so we'll make a fuss over you. *Ibid.* ii. ii. 78 You want to be petted and spoiled and made a fuss over.

b. ***fuss-and-feathers***, bustle and display; hence ***fuss-and-featherdom***.

1866 *Temple Bar* May 198 Their [hen-women's] fuss and featherdom have..a different direction. **1891** Wolseley in *Pall Mall G.* 23 Sept. 7/2 It was no fuss-and-feathers and gold-lace army.

2. A state of (more or less ludicrous) consternation or anxiety.

1705 Vanbrugh *Confed.* iv. Wks. (Rtldg.) 431/1 Why, here's your Master in a most violent Fuss, and no mortal Soul can tell for what. **1746** Hawley in Albemarle *50 Yrs. of my Life* (1876) I. 114, I could not tell you..the fusse the battalions of Guards are in upon this sudden embarcation. **1813** Lady Burghersh *Lett.* (1893) 74 Madame Legoux.. had been in a fine fuss about us.

3. [f. the vb.] One who fusses.

1875 Howells *Foregone Concl.* 98, I am a fuss, and I don't deny it.

4. *Comb.*, as **fuss-box, -budget, -pot**, a person who fusses.

1901 R. Meinertzhagen *Army Diary* 30 Apr. (1960) 22 Major Mainwaring..is..a grumpy old fuss-box. **1939** D. L. Sayers *In Teeth of Evidence* 236 What an old fuss-box you are, darling. **1904** *Dialect Notes* II. 397 *Fuss-budget*, a nervous, fidgety person. **1936** M. Mitchell *Gone with Wind* xxviii. 476 Her husband was old fuss-budget Frank. **1966** *Punch* 30 Nov. 823/2 The two Mrs. Oswalds are viable characters, the younger played very artfully by Sarah Miles and the elder, on its terms of chatterbox fussbudget, vividly impersonated by Bessie Love. **1921** G. O'Donovan *Vocations* i. 16 You *are* a fuss-pot. First you won't and then you will. **1951** J. B. Priestley *Festival at Farbridge* ii. ii. 249 In the woman's opinion, the gentleman was a fusspot but wonderfully free with his money. **1966** M. R. D. Foot *SOE in France* iii. 50 Some were foolhardy, some were fusspots.

fuss (fʌs), *v.* [f. prec. sb.]

1. *intr.* To make a fuss; to be in a bustle; to busy oneself restlessly about trifles; to move fussily (*about, up and down*, etc.).

1792 *Elvina* II. 132 The Thorntons were among the first, Sir Gilbert fussing about, with his large white wig and gouty legs, as happy as any of them. **1797** Polwhele *Old Eng. Gentl.* 62 She fuss'd to form arrangements with the cook. **1852** R. S. Surtees *Sponge's Sp. Tour* xv. 78 He had been fussing about it not long before..dusting the portrait of himself. **1859** *Blackw. Mag.* Apr. 456/2 Forth would fuss Achmet, with a huge crowd of staff. **1871** Dixon *Tower* IV. iv. 34 Sir John..fussed and fumed about the Court. **1876** Mrs. F. E. Trollope *Charming Fellow* I. xi. 143 His wife liked to be fussing about in kitchen and store-room. **1883** J. Parker *Tyne Ch.* 11 But the more he was fussed over the more he infidelled. **1887** T. A. Trollope *What I remember* I. xiv. 293, I remember the host fussing in and out of the room during the quarter of an hour before dinner. **1889** *The County* vi. in *Cornh. Mag.* Feb., They may be fussed over as novelties.

transf. **1847** Lytton *Lucretia* 114 By the coal fire, where, through volumes of smoke, fussed and flickered a pretension to flame. **1862** H. Marryat *Year in Sweden* I. 340 Little stream gondolas with onion-funnels, puffing and fussing like busy water-beetles in a microscope.

2. *trans.* To put into a fuss; to agitate, worry; to bother about trifles. Also ***to fuss up*** (? dial.): to flatter, treat with fussy politeness.

1816 T. Moore *Mem.* (1853) II. 98 Safe arrived,—quite well, but more pulled about, fussed, and bustled than ever. **1820** Clare *Rural Life* (ed. 3) 14 Since Hope's deluding tongue inclin'd me To fuss myself. **1821** —— *Vill. Minstr.* I. 157 Since he fuss'd me so up in the grove. **1876** Miss Yonge *Womankind* xxviii. 245 It is generally the safest way to take care to be in time ourselves, but to guard against fussing other people. **1885** Mrs. Walford *Nan*, etc. II. 163 The going in and out..always fusses me.

Hence **fussed** *ppl. a.*, in a fuss; agitated, disconcerted; **fussing** *vbl. sb.* and *ppl. a.* Also **fu'ssation** [see -ation], the action, habit, or practice of fussing; **'fusser** [see -er[1]], one who fusses.

1775 Mad. D'Arblay *Let.* Nov. in *Early Diary*, She dispelled all sort of ceremony, distance, or fussation. **1826** Miss Mitford *Village* ii. (1863) 317 She was addicted to a fussing and fidgetty neatness. **1832** Scott *St. Ronan's* Introd. 9 The character of the traveller, meddling, self-important, and what the ladies call fussing. **1847** Bushnell *Chr. Nurt.* ii. i. (1861) 245 His obstinacy is but the fussing of his weakness. **1860** Miss Yonge *Stokesley Secr.* v. (1880) 228 David is taking up his slate, and looking a little fussed because there is a scratch in the corner. **1869** Lady Barker *Station Life N. Zealand* xv. (1874) 108, I have finished all my little fussings about the house. **1884** A. A. Putnam *10 Yrs. Police Judge* xv. 161 Every witness, affiant, loafer, fusser, and teazer of this jurisdictional region. **1890** *Pall Mall G.* 2 May 2/3 The *Standard* with its fellow fussers and fogies abroad sits down and waits the event. **1895** *World* Christm. No. 61/2 That idiotic fussation..all the excitement, and all those people staring at her.

fuss, fuss-ball: see fuzz, fuzz-ball.

†**fusse.** *Her. Obs.* [ad. F. *fosse* a ditch.] A foss, ditch, or pool represented as a charge on a shield.

1523 Ld. Berners *Froiss.* I. cclxxxi. 171 b, The blasure of his armes was goules, two fusses sable [*a deux fosses noires*] a border sable.

‖**'fussefall.** *Obs.*$^{-1}$ [Ger. *fuszfall*, f. phrase (*einem*) *zu fuszc* or *zu füssen fallen* to fall at one's feet.] Prostration before a sovereign.

1547 Thirlby in *St. Papers Hen. VIII*, XI. 402 The Commissaries of the Duke of Wyrtenberghe have made theyr fussefall and kneled before thEmperour.

fusses: see FUST *sb.*[2]

fussify (ˈfʌsɪfaɪ), *v.* [f. FUSS *v.* + -(I)FY.] *intr.* To make a fuss, to go about fussily. So **ˌfussifiˈcation** [-(I)FICATION], the action of making a fuss.

1834 BECKFORD *Italy* II. 311 How to escape formal fussifications. **1868** *Q. Rev.* Apr. 317 Johnson was constantly fussifying about the brewery with an ink-horn in his button-hole. **1883** MISS BRADDON *Phantom Fort.* xli, Fussification about her carriage.

fussily (ˈfʌsɪlɪ), *adv.* [f. FUSSY *a.* + -LY[2].] In a fussy manner.

1817 BYRON *Beppo* lxxiii, Who..getting but a nibble at a time, Still fussily keeps fishing on. **1864** J. FORSTER *Life Sir J. Eliot* I. 114 He had to make answer by fussily quoting his own book against Bellarmine. **1883** F. M. PEARD *Contrad.* I. 33 He had acted, a little fussily perhaps, but nobly.

fussiness (ˈfʌsɪnɪs). [f. FUSSY *a.* + -NESS.] The quality or habit of being fussy; restless or ostentatious activity about trifles.

1851 HELPS *Comp. Solit.* xi. (1874) 192 That freedom from small fussiness. **1876** GREEN *Stray Stud.* 316 Her religious exhortations are backed by scoldings and fussiness. **1884** *Manch. Exam.* 20 May 5/2 The fussiness of Thiers, who would have a finger in every pie that was being made.

† **ˈfussle.** *Obs.*

1607 BREWER *Lingua* IV. vi, Such stirre with..Muffes, Pussles, Fussles..Fillets, Croslets..and so many lets, that yet shee is scarse drest to the girdle.

ˈfussock, fuzzock. Also 7 fussocks. [Cf. FUSS *sb.*[1]; also *fuss*, FUZZ *sb.*[1], FUZZ-BALL.]

1. A fat, unwieldy woman. *dial.* or *slang.*

a **1700** B. E. *Dict. Cant. Crew* s.v., *A Fat Fussocks*, a Flusom, Fat, Strapping Woman. *c* **1746** J. COLLIER (Tim Bobbin) *View Lanc. Dial.* Wks. (1862) 55 This broddling Fussock lookt feaw os Tunor [a dog] when id done. **1868** WAUGH *Sneck Bant* ii. 40 'Nay,' cried Billy; 'thae'rt noan beawn to run off thi bargain becose o' this fuzzock makin' her din, arto?'

2. *Sc.* A fluffy mass (of cotton).

1882 G. MACDONALD *Castle Warlock* xxiv. (1883) 153 A fussock o cotton-'oo' rowed roon a bit o' stick.

Hence † **ˈfussock** *v. Obs. intr.*, to roll about in an unwieldy way. Implied in † **ˈfussocking** *ppl. a.* ? *Obs.*

1782 CHARLOTTE BURNEY in *Mad. D'Arblay's Early Diary* (1889) II. 297 Mrs. Percy is a vulgar, fussocking, proud woman; but very civil to us. **1847–78** HALLIWELL, *Fussocking*, large and fat.

fussy (ˈfʌsɪ), *a.* [f. FUSS *sb.*[2] + -Y[1].]

1. Of persons, their habits and actions: Fond of fuss, moving and acting with fuss; habitually busy about trifles.

1831 T. MOORE *Mem.* (1854) VI. 201 Lucky for him that he is so little of an irritable or fussy nature. **1850** *Fraser's Mag.* XLI. 163 She is fussy and fidgetty (if there be such words). **1854** LOWELL *Cambridge 30 Y. Ago* Prose Wks. 1890 I. 46 Foreign travel may..make them, if not wiser, at any rate less fussy. **1866** MISS BRADDON *Lady's Mile* iii. 41 The fussy dowager..swooped down upon her nephew. **1877** OWEN *Wellesley's Desp.* p. xlv, The fussy charlatanism ..of ambitious sciolists. **1892** JESSOPP *Stud. Recluse* Pref. (1893) 11 There were no schools then; no fussy visiting of the poor.

transf. **1871** L. STEPHEN *Playgr. Eur.* ix. (1894) 212 The butterfly..is much too fussy an insect to enjoy himself properly. **1895** *Daily News* 5 July 9/1 The fussy little Conservancy tug.

2. *dial.* and *U.S.* Of places: Full of bustle, bustling.

1848 A. B. EVANS *Leicestersh. Words, etc.* s.v., The shops will be quite full and fussy. **1853** MOTLEY *Corr.* (1889) I. vi. 161 A populous, busy, fuming, fussy, little world like this.

3. Of dress, etc.: Full of petty details. Also, in dressmaking language, without depreciatory implication; With many flounces, puffs, pleats, etc.

1858 HOLLAND *Titcomb's Lett.* i. 92 Let every garment be well fitted..fussy in no point. **1881** *Queen* 1 Oct. Advt., The skirt..puffed more or less fussy, according to figure. **1895** *Daily Chron.* 15 Jan. 7/3 The latter [medal] had been withheld, the designs being fussy and of doubtful construction. **1896** *Westm. Gaz.* 7 May 3/1 The fussy sunshade is much beflounced with lace-edged chiffon.

† **fust,** *sb.*[1] *Obs.* Also 6 foust. [a. OF. *fust* (mod.F. *fût*): see FOIST *sb.*[2]]

I. 1. A wine-cask.

1481–90 *Howard Househ. Bks.* (Roxb.) 85, xxx. pipes bere, and a toon wyn x.*s.*, the bere x.*li.* and for the fustes xxx.*s.* **1601** *Househ. Ord.* (1790) 295 The Serjant..hath for his fee, all the empty foustes of wine.

2. 'A strong smell, as that of a mouldy barrel' (Johnson 1755).

Whence in mod. Dicts.

II. 3. (See quot. 1819.) [So F. *fût*, It. *fusto*.]

1665 J. WEBB *Stone-Heng* (1725) 35 The Column.. diminishing (from the third Part of the Fust upwards). **1682** WHELER *Journ. Greece* I. 48 They were neither Channell'd, nor altogether plain; but their Fusts cut into Angles. **1717** BERKELEY *Jrnl. Tour Italy* 27 Jan. Wks. 1871 IV. 550 The wreaths along the fusts of the columns. **1819** NICHOLSON *Dict. Archit.*, *Fust*, the shaft of a column, or trunk of a pilaster.

† **fust,** *sb.*[2] *Obs.* In *pl.* 6–7 fusses, fusts. [ad. It. *fusto* lit. 'stick'. Cf. F. *fût de girofle.*

With the plural form *fusses* cf. dial. *fisses* for *fists.* It is somewhat doubtful whether the first quot. belongs to this word.]

(See quot. 1657.)

1422 tr. *Secreta Secret., Priv. Priv.* (E.E.T.S.) 240 Moche worth is the lytwary y makyd of fuste and aloes, for that fuste confortyth the stomake..Then sethe he fuste in wynne, and drynke hit erly. **1597** GERARDE *Herbal* III. cxliv. 1352 Those grosse kinde of Cloues..which of the ancients are called Fusti, whereof we haue englished them Fusses. **1657** W. COLES *Adam in Eden* cxxxiv. 199 Those [Cloves] that do abide longer on the trees..being called by most Fusses, yet some call the stalks of the Cloves Fusses. *Ibid.*, Table.. Fusses or Fusts.

fust, *sb.*[3] *Obs.* exc. *dial.* [var. of FIRST *sb.*] The ridge of the roof of a house: see quot. 1819.

1703 MOXON *Mech. Exerc.* 142 The Fust of the House. **1819** NICHOLSON *Dict. Archit.*, *Fust*, a term used in Devonshire, and perhaps in some other counties, for the ridge of a house.

† **fust,** *sb.*[4] *Obs.* [short f. FUSTIC.] = FUSTIC.

1682 WHELER *Journ. Greece* IV. 307 There groweth Fust also, or Yellow-wood, used to dye with.

fust, *a.* (*sb.*[5]) and *adv.* Dial. and U.S. dial. var. of FIRST. Also redundantly as superl. fustest, esp. in phr. ***to get there fustest with the mostest*** (see quot. 1925).

1851 J. J. HOOPER *Widow Rugby's Husband* 45 The fust I know'd of it, tho', was when I was 'bout ten years old. *Ibid.* 47 We had a fust-rate time of it. **1862** H. MAYHEW *London Labour* Extra vol. 418/2 The fust thing as I remember was the river side (the Thames), and running in low-tide to find things. **1865** DICKENS *Mut. Fr.* II. III. xi. 99 It would be a wonder if I did not, being by the Chris'en name of Roger, which took it arter my own father,..though which of our fam'ly fust took it nat'ral I will not..mislead you by undertakin' to say. **1896** A. V. CULBERTSON *Lays of Wandering Minstrel* 179 An' honey, yo'n's de fustes' fren'ly face I've seed. **1905** [see MOSTEST *a.* (*sb.*) and *adv.*]. **1907** G. B. SHAW *Major Barbara* II. 214 Fust: I'm intelligent... Second, an intelligent bein needs a doo share of appiness. **1925** F. MAURICE *Robert E. Lee* 21 To one who once asked him to what he attributed his victories he [*sc.* Lieut.-General N. B. Forrest] answered, 'I get there fustest with the mostest men.' **1939** JOYCE *Finnegans Wake* 49 This stage thunkard is said..to have solemnly said—as had the brief thot but fell in till his head like a bass dropt neck fust in till a bung crate (cogged!): Me drames, O'Loughlins, has come through! **1940** *Time* 4 Nov. 12/3 One of the most popular inhabitants of the train was Porter Foley, who could get there fustest with the mostest drinks. **1983** *Outdoor Life* June 130 Fust thang anybody know'd he'd gone crazy.

fust (fʌst), *v. Obs.* exc. *dial.* Also FOIST *v.*[2] [f. FUST *sb.*[1] 1, 2.] *intr.* To become mouldy or stale-smelling; *esp.* **a.** Of corn: To become mouldy; also *fig.* **b.** Of wine: To taste of the cask; also *fig.*

a **1592** H. SMITH *Serm.* (1637) 440 As the Manna which the Jewes gathered over an Homer did them no good, but mould and fust. **1604** SHAKS. *Ham.* IV. iv. 39 (Qo. 2) He that made vs..gaue vs not That capabilitie and god-like reason To fust in vs vnvsd. **1755** JOHNSON, *Fust*, to grow mouldy; to smell ill. **1799** G. SMITH *Laboratory* I. 429 To prevent wine from fusting, otherwise tasting of the cask. **1869** *Lonsdale Gloss.*, *Fust*, to mould as corn does.

Hence **ˈfusted** *ppl. a.* = FUSTY 1.

1597–8 BP. HALL *Sat.* IV. v. 117 Of fusted hoppes now lost for lack of sale. **1621–51** BURTON *Anat. Mel.* I. ii. I. vi. 63 If the spirits of the brain be fusted..the children will be fusted in the brain; they will be dull..all their lives. **1799** G. SMITH *Laboratory* I. 432 To restore a wine fusted, or tasting of the cask. **1897** G. MACDONALD *Salted with Fire* 203 To me it was like the fuistit husks o' the half-faimisht swine!

fust, obs. f. of FIST *sb.*[1], var. of FOIST *sb.*[1] *Obs.*

fustage (ˈfʌstɪdʒ). *Cape Colony.* [f. FUST *sb.* + -AGE.] 'The vats, tubs, and all the wooden utensils used in making wine' (*MS. Let.* Nov. 1865).

1868 *Cape & Natal News* 7 Dec. 18 A large vintage in prospect, and no fustage in which to store it.

fustanella (fʌstəˈnɛlə). Also fustinella, fustanelle, (badly) fustanelli. [a. It. lingua franca *fustanella*, dim. of the name by which the garment is known in Greece and Turkey: mod.Gr. φουστανι, Albanian *fustan*, believed to be a. It. *fustagno* FUSTIAN.] A stiff full petticoat of white cotton or linen worn by men in Modern Greece.

1849 CURZON *Visits Monast.* 266 Gentlemen in dirty white jackets and fustanellas. **1854** B. TAYLOR *Lands of Saracen* 359 The spruce young Greeks, whose snowy fustanelles were terribly bespattered, came off much worse. **1866** FELTON *Anc. & Mod. Gr.* II. II. vii. 407 The Pellecaria.. walking jauntily along the Street of Æolus..in tasselled fez, embroidered jacket, snowy fustanelli. **1882** G. F. ARMSTRONG *Garl. fr. Greece, Brigand Parnass.* 10 You see him yonder..his fustinella white and bright as it should be.

Hence **fustaˈnellaed** *a.*, wearing a fustanella.

1853 FELTON *Fam. Lett.* xli. (1865) 310 He was a fustinellied fellow, with a villainous..look. **1883** A. J. EVANS in *Archaeol.* (1884) XLIX. 24 These fustanella'd peasants.

fuste, obs. form of FIST *sb.*[1]

† **ˈfuster.** *Obs.* Also 5 fuystour, 6 fustar, 6–7 foystor. [a. AF. *fuster*, *fuyster*, f. *fust* (mod.F. *fût*) piece of wood. In continental OF. *fustier* had the wider sense of worker in wood, carpenter, etc.] A saddle-tree-maker.

[**1309** *Lib. Custum. Lond.* (Godef.), Que nul fuster face arzons de seles, sinoun de quarter.] **1415** in *York Myst.* Introd. 26 Fuystours. **1530** PALSGR. 223/2 Fustar that maketh saddell trees, *bastier.* **1598** STOW *Surv.* (1603) 542 Foystors, the wardens and two persons, one messe. **1609** D. ROGERS *Harl. MS.* 1944 lf. 26 in *Digby Myst.* (1882) Forewords 22 Sadlers, fusters. **1611** *Canterbury Marriage Licences* (MS.) 7 Oct., Joh'em Morcetur de Challock, ffuster.

† **ˈfusterer.** *Obs. rare*[−1]. = prec.

1600 *Chester Pl.* (E.E.T.S.) I. 7 Saddlers and ffusterers.

fusteric (ˈfʌstərɪk). [f. FUST-ET, after *turmeric.*] The colouring matter of fustet. Cf. FUSTIN.

1860 *Ure's Dict. Arts* II. 318 This wood contains a large quantity of yellow colouring matter, named fusteric.

fustet (ˈfʌstɪt). [a. F. *fustet*, ad. Pr. *fustet* = Sp. *fustete*, an etymologizing corruption (as if dim. of Pr. *fust*, Sp. *fuste* stick, piece of wood) of the Arab. source of FUSTIC.] A small European shrub (*Rhus Cotinus*), from which a yellow dye is extracted; called also *young fustic.* (See quots.)

1821 URE *Dict. Chem.*, *Fustet*, the wood of the *rhus cotinus*, or Venus's sumach, yields a fine orange colour, but not at all durable. **1828** in WEBSTER. **1853** URE *Dict. Arts* I. 834 *Fustet*, the wood of the *rhus cotinus*, a fugitive yellow dye. *Ibid.* I. 837 *Fustic*, the old fustic of the English dyer, as the article fustet is their young fustic.

fustian (ˈfʌstɪən), *sb.* and *a.* Forms: 3 fustane, 4–5 fustain, 4 fustayn, 4–6 fustiane, -yan(e, fusten(e, (5 fustien, fustyn, 6 fustin, fuschain, fustheyn, fushtyayne, fustyam, fusteen, fosten, *Sc.* fustean), 5–7 fustion, -yon, 4– fustian. [a. OF. *fustaigne*, *-aine*, mod.F. *futaine* fem. = Pr. *fustani*, Sp. *fustan*, Pg. *fustão*, It. *fustagno*, repr. med.L. (*pannus*) *fustāneus*, (*tela*) *fustānea*; conjecturally derived from *Fostat*, the name of a suburb of Cairo where cloth was manufactured.]

A. *sb.*

1. Formerly, a kind of coarse cloth made of cotton and flax. Now, a thick, twilled, cotton cloth with a short pile or nap, usually dyed of an olive, leaden, or other dark colour.

c **1200** *Trin. Coll. Hom.* 163 Ðe meshakele of medeme fustane [*or perh.* fustani]. *c* **1386** CHAUCER *Prol.* 75 Of fustyan he wered a gepoun. *c* **1450** *Merlin* 279 His clothinge was blakke fustyan with bendes on the sleues. **1502** *Privy Purse Exp. Eliz. of York* (1830) 16, ij yerdes of white fustyan for sokkes for the Quene. **1558** *Wills & Inv. N.C.* (Surtees 1835) 162, ij blanketts of fustheyn. **1586** SHAKS. *Tam. Shr.* IV. i. 49 Where's the Cooke..the seruingmen in their new fustian. **1658** A. FOX *Wurtz' Surg.* II. xxix. 149 Commonly I used..some pieces of fustions, cutting them of two fingers breadth. **1696** J. F. *Merchant's Ware-ho.* 8 Dimetty..which is called Pillus Fustian, is of great use to put Feathers in for Pillows. **1860** *All Year Round* No. 44. 418 Fustian and corduroy that was neither sound nor fragrant.

† **b.** A blanket made of this material. *Obs.*

1424 *E.E. Wills* (1882) 56, I wull he haue to þe oone bed a peyre fustyans. *c* **1460** J. RUSSELL *Bk. Nurture* 922 Fustian and shetis clene by sight and sans ye tast. **1494** *Househ. Ord.* (1790) 121 Then shall the yeoman of the stuffe take a fustian ..& caste it upon the bedd..& the sheete likewise..then lay on the other sheete..then lay on the over fustian above. **1500** *Inv.* in *Ann. Reg.* (1768) 134 A paire of old Fustians.

† **c. fustian of Naples.** Also 6 ***fustian in naples*** or ***aplis***, ***fustyan(e aples*** or ***n)apes***, ***fwstinaples***, ***fustianapes***, ***fustniapes***, 6–7 ***fustian anapes*** or ***an apes***. App. a kind of cotton velvet. Cf. A-NAPES. *Obs.*

1465 *Rolls of Parlt.* V. 505 Fustian, bustian, nor fustian of Napuls. **1534** in *Eng. Ch. Furniture* (Peacock 1866) 207 A new cusshion of fustian in naples. **1594** BLUNDEVIL *Exerc.* V. iii. (ed. 7) 533 Fustianapes of Vellures, and of Wool, Bayes, Silke, Parchment lace, Sarcenet and Inkle. **1575**, **1611**, *a* **1627** [see A-NAPES].

2. *fig.* Inflated, turgid, or inappropriately lofty language; speech or writing composed of high-sounding words and phrases; bombast, rant; in early use also †jargon, made-up language, gibberish. For the development of sense cf. BOMBAST.

c **1590** MARLOWE *Faust.* iv. 76 *Wag.* Let thy left eye be diametarily fixed upon my right heel, with *quasi vestigiis nostris insistere. Clown.* God forgive me, he speaks Dutch fustian. **1599** B. JONSON *Ev. Man out of his Humour* III. i, Prithee let's talk fustian a little, and gull them. **1621** BURTON *Anat. Mel.* II. iii. II. (1651) 316 If he can..wear his clothes in fashion..talk big fustian. **1651** CLEVELAND *Poems* 41 With humble service, and such other Fustian. **1681** DRYDEN *Sp. Friar* Ded., I am much deceiv'd if this be not abominable fustian, that is, thoughts and words ill sorted, and without the least relation to each other. **1735** POPE *Prol. Sat.* 187 And he, whose fustian's so sublimely bad, It is not Poetry, but prose run mad. *a* **1797** H. WALPOLE *Mem. Geo. III* (1848) I. viii. 111 Glover..uttered a speech in most heroic fustian. **1822** HAZLITT *Table-t.* Ser. II. v. (1869) 123 They flounder about between fustian in expression, and bathos in sentiment. **1884** *Fortn. Rev.* June 838 It was all nonsense, and the basest kind of political fustian.

b. *occas.* Clap-trap.

1880 BEACONSFIELD *Endymion* xci, Sensible Englishmen ..looked upon the whole exhibition as fustian.

3. (See quot.)

1832 HONE *Year Bk.* 62 Rum fustian is a 'night-cap', made precisely in the same way [as egg-flip].

4. *Comb.*, as ***fustian-maker***; ***fustian-clad***, ***-suited*** adjs. Also **fustian-cutting**, the action or process of cutting the surface-threads of weft of fustian; so **fustian-cutter**, one who performs this; † **fustian-man**, a fustian-maker; **fustian-picker**, a workman who dresses fustian.

1876 C. M. DAVIES *Unorth. Lond.* 54 *Fustian clad men. **1884** *Chesh. Gloss.*, **Fustian cutter*, one who finishes off fustian by cutting it to a sort of velvetty pile. **1855** MRS. GASKELL *North & S.* xvii, Where is your sister? Gone *fustian-cutting. **1704** *Lond. Gaz.* No. 3987/4 Robert Dunn, of Bolton in Le Moors..*Fustian-maker. **1720** *Ibid.* No. 5909/8 William Nabbs, late of Hallifax, *Fustianman. **1865** *Public Opinion* 21 Jan. 55/1 If the makers of lucifer-matches are not henceforth to be poisoned..nor *fustian-pickers to be rendered deformed by bad conditions of work. **1891** *Daily News* 26 Dec. 5/5 A gardener..assisted by one of his *fustian-suited fellows, is staking and pruning a tree.

B. *adj.*

1. [attrib. use of the sb.] Made of fustian.

1537 *Bury Wills* (Camden) 128 Item I geve to Wylliam Boloʳ my fosten doblett. **1554** *Ibid.* 144 A paier of fustian blankets. **1611** CORYAT *Crudities* 465 For my clothes being but a threadbare fustian case were so meane. **1712** STEELE *Spect.* No. 498 ¶3 A lively young fellow in a fustian jacket. **1753** SMOLLETT *Ct. Fathom* (1781) 63/2 For all my bit of a fustian frock..I have more dust in my fob, than all these powdered sparks put together. **1826** KIRBY & SP. *Entomol.* (1828) IV. 538 The plain fustian jacket used by English sportsmen. **1859** THACKERAY *Virgin.* xxii, He wore a plain fustian cloak.

fig. **1589** *Pappe w. Hatchet* (1844) 39 Botching in such frize iestes vppon fustion earnest. **1592** G. HARVEY *Pierce's Super.* 158, I could smile at a frise jest when the good man would be pleasurable and laugh at fustion earnest when the merry man would be surly. **1885** E. W. LIGHTNER in *Harper's Mag.* Mar. 533/1 To gain some individuality which will remove the impression that it is a fustian counter-part of a genuine and admirable fabric.

b. *dial.* (See quot., and cf. FUSTIANY.)

1750 W. ELLIS *Mod. Husb.* III. I. 66 There are four several sorts [of Marl], viz.—the Fustian, the Cowshit, the Black-steel, and the Shale: The Fustian Sort is an Earth composed of a fat Loam and Sand, of a reddish Colour.

2. Of language: Of the nature of fustian; ridiculously lofty in expression; bombastic, high-flown, inflated, pompous. †Also, belonging to cant or made-up jargon.

1592 GREENE *Upst. Courtier* (1871) 37 Then comes he out ..with his fustian eloquence. **1598** FLORIO, *Monêlle*, a roguish or fustian word, a word in pedlers French, signifying wenches. **1610** B. JONSON *Alch.* IV. ii, Haue 'hem vp, and shew 'hem Some fustian booke, or the darke glasse. **1623** COCKERAM *Premon.*, The fustian termes, vsed by too many who study rather to bee heard speake, than to vnderstand themselves. **1660** HOWELL *Lex. Tetragl.*, *Fustian Language*, Barra-goüin; la lingua furbesca; Jerigonça. **1670** COTTON *Espernon* II. VII. 329 The Queen.. writ a Letter to the Duke..in a fustian style. **1748** *Anson's Voy.* III. vii. 482 Notwithstanding the fustian eulogiums bestowed upon them by the Catholic Missionaries. **1838–9** HALLAM *Hist. Lit.* II. v. II. §73. 229 Pope censures the haste, negligence and fustian language of Chapman. **1884** J. SHARMAN *Hist. Swearing* ii. 26 The fustian ornament of somewhat spirited talk.

†**b.** Hence of a writer or speaker. *Obs.*

[**1597**: see 3.] **1693** DRYDEN *Persius* v. 9 Let Fustian Poets with their Stuff be gone. **1782** J. WARTON *Ess. Pope* II. x. 149 *note*, Ridiculing the false pomp of fustian writers.

†**c.** ***fustian fume***: a great display of anger. So ***fustian anger***. *Obs.*

1553 BALE *Vocacyon* 30 b, The Treasurer, beynge in hys fustene fumes, stoughtely demaunded a determinate answere. **1583** STANYHURST *Æneis* II. (Arb.) 46 With fuming fustian anger. **1626** L. OWEN *Spec. Jesuit.* (1629) 3 Vpon this the Monke in a Spanish fustian-fume, cryed out. **1682** N. O. *Boileau's Lutrin* IV. 173 The Chanter netled heard in fustian fume Rejoyning Girard thus sawcily presume.

3. Worthless, sorry, pretentious.

1523 SKELTON *Garl. Laurel* 1206 This fustian maistres and this giggishe gase. **1597** SHAKS. *2 Hen. IV*, II. iv. 203 Thrust him downe stayres, I cannot endure such a Fustian Rascall. **1600** *Dr. Dodypoll* I. i. in Bullen *O. Pl.* III. 103 A fustie Potticarie ever at hand with his fustian drugges. **1632** LITHGOW *Trav.* III. 108 Now what a selfe Losungeous fellow hath this fustian companion proved. **1861** K. H. DIGBY *Chapel St. John* (1863) 325 The fustian rascal and his poor lack-linen mate.

†**b.** 'Made up', imaginary. *Obs.*

1600 B. JONSON *Cynthia's Rev.* (1692) Induction, The scene Gargaphie; which I do vehemently suspect for some fustian country.

†**4.** *Sc.* ? Coarse, plain, homely. *Obs. rare*$^{-1}$.

1549 *Compl. Scot.* vi. 43 Thai hed na breyd bot ry caikis and fustean skonnis maid of flour.

Hence **ˈfustianed** *a.*, clothed in fustian; **ˈfustianist**, one who writes fustian; **ˈfustianize** *v. intr.*, to write fustian; **ˈfustiany** *a. dial.* (see quot., and cf. FUSTIAN B. 1 b).

1642 MILTON *Apol. Smect.* viii, Preferring the gay rankness of Apuleius, Arnobius, or any modern Fustianist, before the native Latinisms of Cicero. **1830** O. W. HOLMES *Poet's Lot* 4 To get a ring, or some such thing, And fustianize upon it. **1849** ALB. SMITH *Pottleton Leg.* 62 The fustianed keeper winked at the gorgeous Roman warrior. **1883** T. HARDY *Wessex T.* in *Longm. Mag.* I. 572 Hob-nailed and fustianed peasantry. **1884** *Chesh. Gloss.*, *Fustiany*, applied to sand with a good deal of earth (the colour of fustian) in it, that prevents its being used for mortar.

fustic (ˈfʌstɪk). Also 6–7 fusticke, (7 fustwick, 8 fustoc, -uc), 7–9 fustick. [a. F. *fustoc*, a. Sp. *fustoc*, a. Arab. *fustuq*, ad. Gr. πιστάκη PISTACHIO. The name was transferred from the pistachio to the closely-allied sumach-tree (*Rhus Cotinus*), and thence to another tree which resembles the latter in yielding a yellow dye.]

1. The name of two kinds of wood, both used for dyeing yellow. **a.** The wood of the Venetian sumach (*Rhus Cotinus*). Now only with defining word, ***young*** or ***Zante fustic***. **b.** The wood of the *Cladrastis* (*Chlorophora*, *Maclura*) *tinctoria* of America and the West Indies. Sometimes called for distinction ***old fustic***.

1545 ASCHAM *Toxoph.* (Arb.) 123 Steles [of arrows] be made of dyuerse woodes, as..Fusticke [etc.]. **1646** *Royalist Composition Papers* (Yorksh. Archæol. Soc.) II. 47 In goods viz. Oyles, Mathers, Gales, Copperis, Retwood, ffustwick. **1652** *Perfect Account* No. 101. 2071, 2 Cannestrees of Cochinele, a good quantity of Fustick. **1719** DE FOE *Crusoe* I. xvi, It was very like the Tree we call Fustic. **1757** DYER *Fleece* (1807) 97 The snowy web is steep'd, with grains of weld, Fustic, or logwood, mix'd, or cochineal. **1812** J. SMYTH *Pract. of Customs* (1821) 290 Fustick imported from the Greek islands is in very small sticks, and is denominated by the trade young Fustick. **1838** T. THOMSON *Chem. Org. Bodies* 414 Before fustic can be employed as a dye-stuff, it must be cut into chips. **1870** YEATS *Nat. Hist. Comm.* 218 Fustic is brought to market in long pieces or logs.

2. A yellow dye extracted from the wood of the fustic trees.

1858 CARPENTER *Veg. Phys.* §367 The dye termed Fustic ..is extracted from the wood of a species of Mulberry tree. **1863** *Life in South* II. 306 Fustic, and copal, with other dyes and varnishes.

3. *attrib.*, as ***fustic-tree***, ***-wood***.

1630 CAPT. SMITH *Trav. & Adv.* xxvi. 56 Fusticke trees are very great and the wood yellow, good for dying. **1712** tr. *Pomet's Hist. Drugs* I. 70 The People of Provence and Italy, after they have peel'd off the Bark, sell the Fustick Wood. **1756** P. BROWNE *Jamaica* 339 The Fustic tree. This is a fine timber wood, and a principal ingredient in most of our yellow dyes.

fustied (ˈfʌstɪd), *a.* [f. FUSTY + -ED[1].] Made fusty; deprived of brightness or freshness.

1576 NEWTON *Lemnie's Complex.* II. vi. 141 b, Affections and perplexities..making him to loke lyke syluer al fustyed wyth chimney soote.

fustigate (ˈfʌstɪgeɪt), *v.* Now *humorously pedantic.* [f. L. *fūstigāt-* ppl. stem of *fūstigāre* to cudgel to death, f. *fūstis* cudgel.] *trans.* To cudgel, beat.

1656–81 BLOUNT *Glossogr.*, *Fustigate*, to beat with a staff, to cudgel. *a* **1661** FULLER *Worthies* (1662) 136 Falling out with his Steward..and fustigating him for his faults. **1837** CARLYLE *Fr. Rev.* III. III. viii. (1872) 131 These serpent-haired Extreme She Patriots do now..shamefully fustigate her. **1851** R. F. BURTON *Goa* 168 Our panting steeds, whom the Vetterino was fustigating. **1879** *Brit. Med. Jrnl.* 31 May 813 She may now leave the business to the small patient himself, provided he be old and sensible enough to fustigate himself systematically.

fig. (*absol.*) **1888** *Sat. Rev.* 2 June 667 He brands, he bruises, he fustigates; he stamps his victims ridiculous.

Hence **ˈfustigated** *ppl. a.* Also **ˈfustigator**, one who fustigates or beats (another).

1727 BAILEY vol. II, *Fustigated*, beaten with a Cudgel. **1865** *Pall Mall G.* 8 Nov. 9 We shall hear by an early mail of the magistrate himself having been assaulted..as soon as the gallant fustigator is liberated on bail.

fustigation (fʌstɪˈgeɪʃən). [ad. L. *fūstigātiōn-em*, n. of action f. *fūstigāre* to FUSTIGATE. Cf. F. *fustigation*.] The action of cudgelling or beating.

1563–87 FOXE *A. & M.* (1596) 609/2 This penance..to be done..that is to say, six fustigations or displings about the parish church of Aldborough. **1614** SELDEN *Titles Hon.* 64 That punishment of Fustigation was it seems, instituted by Antoninus and Commodus. **1667** EARL OF BRISTOL *Elvira* II. in Hazl. *Dodsley* XV. 32 Heaven send him a light hand To whom my fustigation shall belong. **1715** tr. *C'tess D'Aunoy's Wks.* 205 Don Pedro cry'd so loud at that fustigation. **1837** CARLYLE *Fr. Rev.* II. IV. i, Martyrdom not of massacre, yet of fustigation. **1860** J. C. JEAFFRESON *Bk. about Doctors* I. 7 For many centuries fustigation was believed in as a sovereign remedy for bodily ailments.

fig. **1858** MOTLEY *Corr.* (1889) I. 249 Lord Clarendon in the Lords administered a most serious fustigation.

†**fustiˈlarian.** *Obs.* (? *nonce-wd.*) [? Comic formation on next.] ? = next.

1597 SHAKS. *2 Hen. IV*, II. i. 66 (Qo. 1600) Away you scullian, you rampallian, you fustilarian [**1623** Fustillirian], ile tickle your catastrophe.

fustilugs (ˈfʌstɪlʌgz). *Obs.* exc. *dial.* [? f. FUSTY *a.* + LUG in the sense of something heavy or slow.] A person, esp. a woman, of gross or corpulent habit; a fat, frowzy woman.

1607 R. C. tr. *Estienne's World of Wonders* Pref. 10 The country swains contenting themselues though they haue not the fairest, take the woodden-fac'd wenches and the ill-fauourd-foule-fustilugs for a small summe. **1621** BURTON *Anat. Mel.* III. ii. IV. i. (1651) 519 Every lover admires his mistress, though she be..a vast virago, or..a fat fustylugs. **1639** tr. *Junius' Sin Stigmat.* xv. 39 You may dayly see such fustilugs walking in the streets, like so many Tunnes, each moving upon two pottle pots. **1746** *Exmoor Scolding* 118 (E.D.S.) Ya gurt Fustilugs! **1778** *Ibid.* Gloss., *Fusty-lugs*, —spoken of a big-boned Person,—a Great foul Creature. **1867** W. F. ROCK *Jim an' Nell* lxii. (E.D.S. No. 76) 'Nell isn't a gurt fustilugs O' cart-hoss heft, an' hulking dugs.'

fustin (ˈfʌstɪn). *Chem.* [f. FUST-IC or FUST-ET + -IN.] 'The name given by Preisser to the colouring matter of *Rhus Cotinus*' (Watts *Dict. Chem.* 1864). Cf. FUSTERIC.

fustle (ˈfʌs(ə)l), *sb.* *Sc.* and *dial.* Also fussle. [onomatopœic; cf. FUSS, BUSTLE.] (See quots.) So **ˈfustle** *v. dial.*, to make a fuss; **ˈfustling** *ppl. a. dial.*, fussing, fussy.

1832–53 J. BALLANTYNE in *Whistle-Binkie* (Scot. Songs) Ser. II. 116 Thou jaggy, kittly, gleg wee thing..Soon scamper aff, hap stap an' fling, Wi' couring fustle. **1847–78** HALLIWELL, *Fussle*, a slight confusion. *Suffolk. Fustle*, a fuss, or bustle. *Warw.* **1867** W. F. ROCK *Jim an' Nell* cxxxiv. (E.D.S. No. 76), Zum foreward, fustling youth. **1891** *Hartland Gloss.*, *Fustle*, to make a fuss.

†**ˈfustler.** *Obs. rare*$^{-1}$. ? = FUSTER.

1605 *Depos.* in *Wells Depos.* (MS.), Johannes Webb, de Brushford in comite Somerset, Fustler.

fusty (ˈfʌstɪ), *a.* Also 6 **fewsty**; and see FOISTY. [f. FUST *sb.*[1] 2.]

1. That has lost its freshness, stale-smelling, musty. **a.** Of a wine-cask or vessel. Also of the wine: Tasting of the cask. *Obs.* exc. *dial.*

1398 TREVISA *Barth. De P.R.* III. xii. (1495) 57 Wyne and other licour takyth infeccion of a vessell that is fusty. **1520** WHITINTON *Vulg.* (1527) 15 The wyne bottell is somwhat fusty. **1601** HOLLAND *Pliny* II. 152 To renue their wines, and make them seem fresh and new, after they haue by long lying gotten a fusty rotten tast. **1616** SURFL. & MARKH. *Country Farme* 617 To restore againe into his former and sound estate, the Wine that is growne fat, fustie, and hath taken winde. **1877** *Holderness Gloss.*, *Fusty*, musty; fetid; stale: generally applied to malt liquors, or vessels containing them.

fig. **1645** MILTON *Colast.* (1851) 375 His farewell, which is to be a concluding taste of his jabberment in law, the flashiest and the fustiest that ever corrupted in such an unswill'd hogshead.

b. Of bread, corn, meat, etc.: Smelling of mould or damp.

1491 CAXTON *Vitas Patr.* (1495) 6 He..founde brede.. the whyche was not fayre, but fusty and spotted. **1545** ASCHAM *Toxoph.* I. (Arb.) 76 If a feaste..had fewsty and noughty bread, all the other daynties shulde be vnsauery. **1596** BP. W. BARLOW *Three Serm.* ii. 59 Who had rather the corne should waxe fustie in their garners then to sell it out. **1606** SHAKS. *Tr. & Cr.* II. i. 111 If he knocke out either of your braines, he were as good cracke a fustie nut with no kernell. **1655** MOUFET & BENNET *Health's Improv.* (1746) 339 You must not presently mould up your Meal after grinding..nor keep it too long, lest it prove fusty. **1884** *J. Bull's Neighb. in True Light* xii. 88 He will take a piece of diseased horse or fusty beef, and make a *ragoût* that will cause you to smack your lips.

fig. **1650** TRAPP *Comm. Numbers* ix. 11 That fusty, swelling, sowring, spreading corruption of nature and practice.

2. Of persons, places, etc.: Having an unpleasant, 'close', or 'stuffy' smell such as arises from dirt, dust, or damp.

a **1529** SKELTON *Agst. Garnesche* 77 Fusty bawdyas. **1601** B. JONSON *Poetaster* III. iv, Hang him, fustie Satire, he smells all goat. **1602** *2nd Pt. Return fr. Parnass.* V. iv. 2233 Farewell musty, dusty, rusty, fusty London. *c* **1648–50** BRATHWAIT *Barnabees Jrnl.* X v a, Ins are nasty, dusty, fustie. **1798** A. SEWARD *Lett.* (1811) V. 147 Old fusty stuff-beds. **1840** LADY GRANVILLE *Lett.* Jan. (1894) II. 299 Intense heat in the mild, fusty weather. **1842** DICKENS in Forster *Life* III. 101 Dirty clothes-bags musty, moist and fusty. **1848** KINGSLEY *Saint's Trag.* IV. iv, Stifling her with fusty sighs. **1861** HUGHES *Tom Brown at Oxf.* iv, A fusty old gown which had been about college probably for ten generations.

3. *fig.* That has lost its freshness and interest; bearing marks of age or neglect; of old-fashioned appearance or behaviour, 'fogeyish'.

1606 SHAKS. *Tr. & Cr.* I. iii. 161 At this fusty stuffe, The large Achilles..laughes out a lowd applause. **1609** W. M. *Man in Moone* (1857) 84 True is the proverbe, though fustie to fine wits. **1674** J. D. *Mall* I. i. in *Dryden's Wks.* 1884 VIII. 513 All pretty Ladies will shun thee for a fusty Husband. **1728** CAREY *Song* in Vanbr. & Cib. *Prov. Husb.* IV, If I stay 'till I grow gray, They'll call me old Maid, and fusty old jade. **1743–4** MRS. DELANY *Let. to Mrs. Dewes* in *Life & Corr.* 249 Old fusty physicians, you know, are full of ceremony. **1782** MISS BURNEY *Cecilia* X. x, What could ever induce you to give up your charming estate for the sake of coming into his fusty old family! **1833** TENNYSON *Poems* 153, I forgave you all the blame, Musty Christopher; I could *not* forgive the praise, Fusty Christopher. **1842** MRS. GORE *Fascin.* 164 Létorière is too good a rider..to lose his time with fusty Latin and Greek. **1883** *Gd. Words* 183 The doctors say we get musty and fusty if we stay in one place.

†**b.** ? Ill-humoured, peevish, dull. *Obs. rare*$^{-1}$.

1668 PEPYS *Diary* 18 June, My wife still in a melancholy, fusty humour, and crying, and do not tell me plainly what it is.

†**c.** Used as *sb.*: A 'seedy' person. *Obs.*

a **1732** GAY *Distress'd Wife* II. v, If Mr. Forward calls, I think—Yes—You may let him in..But, be sure you let in no Fusties.

4. *Comb.*, as ***fusty framed***, ***-looking***, ***-rusty*** adjs.

1593 *Tell-Troth's N.Y. Gift* 4 After the finishinge of whose fustie framed speech. **1782** COWPER *Let. to Unwin* 5 Jan. in *Life* 1804 III. 110 But what shall we say of his [Johnson's] fusty-rusty remarks upon Henry and Emma? **1877** M. M. GRANT *Sun-Maid* i, A fusty-looking old personage with a large umbrella.

Hence **ˈfustily** *adv.*, **ˈfustiness**; also (jocular nonce-wds.) **ˈfusticate** *v. trans.*, to make fusty;

intr., to stay in a close stuffy atmosphere. **'fustified** *a.* = FUSTY *a.* 3.

1526 *Househ. Ord.* (1790) 218 Item, that the Brewers doe brew good and seasonable stuff without Weevell or Fustines. *a* **1661** FULLER *Worthies* (1840) III. 333 If any fustiness be found in his writings, it comes not from the grape, but from the cask. *a* **1722** LISLE *Husb.* (1752) 169 'Tis not only the loss of those grains that actually grow, but a foulness and fustiness also. **1835** BECKFORD *Recoll.* 150 This most consequential of equerries..invited us..to screen ourselves from the meridian heats..Preceded by the right pompous and fustified equerry, we diverged from the mended track. **1839** *Blackw. Mag.* XLVI. 734 When there was a sort of golden age..and shepherds had nothing to do but pipe..The country pipes now-a-days, are terribly fusticated with tobacco. **1864** *Realm* 18 May 8 We have so long associated him [an actor] with Melter Moss, that rustiness and fustiness seemed a normal part of his being. **1874** BLACKIE *Self-Cult.* 30 A student, and smells fustily of books, as an inveterate smoker does of tobacco. **1883** J. PAYN *Thicker than Water* 151 The one is fustiness, the other is skimpiness. In the former case..the air is rather difficult to breathe. Flue is everywhere. **1923** U. L. SILBERRAD *Lett. J. Armiter* iv. 102 'Are you going to stop—' (I feel sure he meant 'fusticating', though he was too polite to say it) 'in here all afternoon?' he asked.

fusula ('fjuːzjʊlə). *Zool.* Also fusule. Pl. -æ. [mod.L., incorrectly f. L. *fūsus* spindle.] (See quots.)

1909 A. E. SHIPLEY in *Cambr. Nat. Hist.* IV. 325 These spinnerets..are movable turrets on which are mounted the 'fusulae' or projections where the tubes from the spinning glands open. *Ibid.* 326 In some spiders the fusulae are all much alike, but usually a few very much larger than the rest are noticeable under the microscope, and these are often alluded to as 'spigots'. **1928** T. H. SAVORY *Biology of Spiders* ii. 41 The smaller ones [*sc.* tubes], called spools or fusulae, consist either of a cylindrical basal portion traversed by a long thin tube or of a slightly conical base with a curved thin tube. **1951** LOCKET & MILLIDGE *Brit. Spiders* I. 28 The *fusules* from which the silk is produced are situated on the tips or on the apical segments of the spinners.

‖**fusuma** ('fuːsuːma, ‖husuma). [Jap.] A sliding screen, covered with paper on both sides, used to separate room from room in a Japanese house.

1880 I. L. BIRD *Unbeaten Tracks Japan* I. ix. 88 The large tea-houses contain the possibilities for a number of rooms which can be extemporised at once by sliding paper panels, called *fusuma*, along grooves in the floor and in the ceiling or cross-beams. **1886** E. S. MORSE *Jap. Homes* 126 The *fusuma* forming the movable partitions between the rooms are covered on both sides with thick paper. **1890** B. H. CHAMBERLAIN *Things Japanese* 24 The rooms are divided from each other by opaque paper screens, called *fusuma* or *karakami*, which run in grooves at the top and bottom. **1905** *Westm. Gaz.* 23 Sept. 10/2 Sliding the fusuma, the screen of opaque paper separating the living- from the sleeping-room, Sada entered the chamber.

fusun, obs. form of FOISON.

'fusure. *rare*$^{-0}$. [ad. L. *fūsūra* founding, f. *fundĕre* to found (metals).] Fusing, smelting.

1727 BAILEY vol. II, *Fusure*, a flowing or melting of Metals. Hence in mod. Dicts.

†**fut**, *int. Obs.* [? an instinctive exclamation; but cf. FOOT *sb.* 1 b.] Used to express surprise.

1602 MARSTON *Ant. & Mel.* II. Wks. 1856 I. 23 Fut, how he tickles yon trout under the gilles. *Ibid.* III. 35.

fut, obs. and Sc. form of FOOT.

fut, var. of PHUT.

‖**futah** ('fuːta). Also footah, fotah, futu. [ad. Arab. *fūṭa* cloth used as a waist-wrapper.] A kind of material orig. imported to Arab countries from India; hence, an article or garment made from this material, *spec.* a kind of loin-cloth or short skirt worn by Arabs.

[**1616** B. FARIE *Let.* 26 May in W. Foster *Lett. Received by E. India Co.* (1900) IV. 306 As for the sales of the Surratt clothing you sent along in the Sea Adventure, I refer you to the advice of Mr. Sairs, entreating you that if you have..lunges and footaes of all sorts that will not vend in Japon, to ship them away for this place.] **1738** T. SHAW *Travels or Observations Barbary & Levant* 293 But when the Women are at Home and in Private, then they lay aside their Hykes and sometimes their Tunicks, and, instead of Drawers, find only a Towel about their Loyns... This is called both in Barbary and the Levant, a Footah. **1836** E. W. LANE *Mod. Egyptians* I. 175 A napkin ('footah') is given to each person **1853** J. RICHARDSON *Mission to Cent. Afr.* I. v. 67 A few [of the Touaregs] sport a red *fotah*, or turban. **1923** *Other Lands* Oct. 17/1 The fūtah is tied round the waist, and reaches nearly to the knees. **1936** F. STARK *S. Gates Arabia* iii. 32 They wore their futahs (loin-cloths) as long as a kilt or even a skirt. **1962** *Times* 12 Jan. 12/6 The tribesmen in their kilts, or *futas* as they call them. **1966** 'S. HARVESTER' *Treacherous Road* x. 90 A knee-length *futah*, a sort of kilt, of printed or white cotton.

futchel(l ('fʌtʃəl). [Of obscure origin.

Possibly repr. some compound of FOOT; cf. *pole-foot*, 'the hind end of a pole which goes into the cleaves of the futchels' (Knight).]

One of the pieces of timber carrying or supporting the shafts, or pole, or splinter-bar of a carriage.

1794 W. FELTON *Carriages* (1801) I. 50 The futchels are 2 light timbers fixed in The fore axeltree bed. **1851** *Illustr. Catal. Gt. Exhib.* I. 260 Friction plates attached to futchells. **1853** URE *Dict. Arts* (ed. 4) II. 940 The futchel or socket for the pole of the carriage, must also be jointed to the middle of the fore-axletree bed and splinter bar. **1876** VOYLE *Mil. Dict.* (ed. 3), *Futchels* are strong pieces of wood or iron, three in number, uniting the splinter-bar and the axle-tree bed of a gun-carriage or limber.

†**fute**, *v. Obs.*$^{-1}$ [? echoic.] *intr.* To whistle.

c **1650** *Robin Hood* 52 in Furniv. *Percy Folio* I. 29 Now fute on, fute on thou cutted fryar..it is not the futing in a fryers fist that can doe me any ill.

fute, obs. Sc. form of FOOD, FOOT.

fute, futerer, var. FEUTE, FEWTERER, *Obs.*

futher, -ir, obs. forms of FOTHER *sb.*

futhorc ('fuːθɔːk). Also futhark, -ork. [Named from the first six letters, *f, u, þ, o* or *a, r, k*.] The Runic alphabet.

1851 D. WILSON *Preh. Ann.* (1863) II. IV. iv. 285 The name futhork is applied to all systems of phonetic signs of the Teutonic Stock, for the same reason as those of classical derivation are called alphabet. **1865** LUBBOCK *Preh. Times* App. (1878) 618 We possess no less than 61 Runic Futhorcs. **1868** G. STEPHENS *Runic Mon.* I. p. vii, Shown by a couple of the later futhorcs.

futile ('fjuːtɪl, -aɪl), *a.* [a. F. *futile* or ad. L. *fūtilis* (more correctly *futtilis*) that easily pours out, leaky, hence untrustworthy, vain, useless, usu. supposed to be f. *fud-* stem of *fundĕre* to pour out.]

1. Incapable of producing any result; failing utterly of the desired end through intrinsic defect; useless, ineffectual, vain.

c **1555** HARPSFIELD *Divorce Hen. VIII* (Camden) 252 How weak and futile it is..we have already shown. *c* **1750** SHENSTONE *Elegies* ix. 31 Disdaining riches as the futile weeds. **1758** JOHNSON *Idler* No. 13 ¶8 Half the rooms are adorned with a kind of futile tapestry. **1792** BURKE *Pres. St. Affairs* Wks. VII. 113 Render it as futile in its effects, as it is feeble in its principle. **1802** SYD. SMITH *Wks.* (1867) I. 12 All complaint is futile which is not followed up by appropriate remedies. **1853** C. BRONTE *Villette* xvii, These struggles with the natural character..may seem futile and fruitless, but in the end they do good. **1875** JOWETT *Plato* (ed. 2) I. 112 An inference that Protagoras evades by drawing a futile distinction between the courageous and the confident. **1875** E. WHITE *Life in Christ* Pref. (1878) 13 This is indeed an appeal which is made by every futile dreamer.

2. Occupied with things of no value or importance, addicted to trifling, lacking in purpose. ? *Obs.*

1736 BOLINGBROKE *Patriot.* (1749) 112 These judgments and these reasonings may be expected in an age as futile and as corrupt as ours. **1751** CHESTERF. *Lett.* (1792) III. 152 The polite conversation of the men and women of fashion at Paris, though not always very deep, is much less futile and frivolous than ours here. *Ibid.* 192 Frivolous futile people. **1791** BOSWELL *Johnson* 27 Mar. an. 1775 'Davy has some convivial pleasantry about him; but 'tis a futile fellow.'

†**3.** Unable to hold one's tongue, addicted to talking, loquacious. *Obs.* [From the etymological sense, 'leaky'.] Cf. FUTILITY 3.

1612 BACON *Ess., Counsell* (Arb.) 320 One futile person, that maketh it his glory to tell, will do more hurt, then manie that know it their dutie to conceale. **1625** —— *Simulation* (Arb.) 508 Talkers and Futile Persons.

4. quasi-*sb.* A futile person.

1892 T. DUNCAN *Canaanitish Woman* x. 130 After all, why should he remain for ever among the futiles?

Hence **'futilely** *adv.*, **'futileness.**

1727 BAILEY vol. II, *Futileness, Futility*, Blabbing, Silliness, Lightness, Vanity. **1812** J. J. HENRY *Camp. agst. Quebec* 80 Being without arms, and in an unknown country, my inconsequence and futileness lay heavy on my spirit. **1881** *Harper's Mag.* LXIII. 353 Regnault met his death, futilely in almost the last engagement of the war. **1888** MRS. M. HUNGERFORD *Hon. Mrs. Vereker* I. xvii. 232 The Chinese lanterns that so liberally, but so futilely, sought to light the pleasure grounds.

futili'tarian, *a.* and *sb.* [A humorous coinage, f. FUTILITY, after UTILITARIAN.]

A. *adj.* Devoted to futility or futile pursuits. **B.** *sb.* One who is devoted to futility.

1827 SOUTHEY in C. C. Southey *Life & Corr.* V. 290 If the Utilitarians would reason and write like you, they would no longer deserve to be called Futilitarians. **1834** —— *Doctor* xxxv. (1848) 85 The whole race of Political Economists, our Malthusites, Benthamites, Utilitarians, or Futilitarians. **1873** F. HALL *Mod. Eng.* 19 *note*, The word *international*, introduced by the immortal Bentham, and Mr. Carlyle's *gigmanity*..are significantly characteristic of the utilitarian philanthropist and of the futilitarian misanthropist, respectively.

futilitarianism (ˌfjuːtɪlɪ'tɛərɪənɪz(ə)m). [f. FUTILITARIAN + -ISM.] Futilitarian policy.

1921 *Glasgow Herald* 3 Feb. 8 To associate the activities of the Church with the Labour Party would be one more example of the Higher Futilitarianism with which ecclesiastics in all ages have been tempted to experiment. **1924** C. E. MONTAGUE *Right Place* x. 153 At least for some eager and absorbed hours your true rambler has washed all that futilitarianism out of his soul.

†**fu'tilitous**, *a. Obs. rare*$^{-1}$. [irreg. f. FUTILIT-Y + -OUS.] = FUTILE.

1765 STERNE *Tr. Shandy* VIII. xiii, Love is..one of the most Agitating, Bewitching..Futilitous..of all human passions.

futility (fjuː'tɪlɪtɪ). [ad. F. *futilité* or L. *fūti-, futtilitātem*, f. *futtilis*: see FUTILE and -ITY.]

1. The quality of being futile; triflingness, want of weight or importance; *esp.* inadequacy to produce a result or bring about a required end, ineffectiveness, uselessness.

1623 COCKERAM, *Futilitie*, vanitie. **1654** WHITLOCK *Zootomia* 477 Divine Poems..might well absolve Poetry of its objected Futility, and Levity. **1732** BERKELEY *Alciphr.* v. §19 Whatever futility there may be in their notions. **1777** PRIESTLEY *Disc. Philos. Necess.* 204 Shew the futility of these replies, if you can. **1845** McCULLOCH *Taxation* II. vi. (1852) 253 We have already seen the futility of all attempts to assess taxes proportionally to real profits. **1875** JOWETT *Plato* (ed. 2) I. 117 The manifest futility and absurdity of the explanation. **1879** M. ARNOLD *Mixed Ess., Irish Cathol.* 104 We should recognize the futility of contending against the most rooted of prejudices.

2. Disposition to trifle or be occupied with trifles, incapacity for serious affairs or interests, lack of purpose, frivolousness.

1692 BENTLEY *Boyle Lect.* iii. 28 The same trifling futility appears in their xii Signs of the Zodiack. **1748** CHESTERF. *Lett.* (1792) II. clvi. 57 If they [diversions] are futile and frivolous, it is time worse than lost, for they will give you an habit of futility. **1758** JOHNSON *Idler* No. 25 ¶11 Leave foppery and futility to die of themselves. **1856** MRS. C. CLARKE *Shaks. Char.* xx. (1863) 507 If they go wrong, it is from utter futility and incapacity to keep out of harm's way. **1866** GEO. ELIOT *F. Holt* II. xxiii. 128 The noisy futility that belongs to schismatics generally.

†**3.** Talkativeness, loquacity, inability to hold one's tongue. Cf. FUTILE *a.* 3. *Obs.*

1640 WATTS tr. *Bacon's Adv. Learn.* VIII. ii. 383 The Futility of vaine Persons, which easily utter, as well what may be spoken, as what should be secreted. **1692** R. L'ESTRANGE *Fables* ccccxxvii, This Fable does not strike so much at the Futility of Women in General, as at the Incontinent Levity of a Prying Inquisitive Humour.

4. Something that is futile.

1667 BP. S. PARKER *Free & Impart. Censure* 100, I am sure that those Notions..were but grand and pompous Futilities. **1840** CARLYLE *Heroes* iii. (1841) 163 *He* was but a loud-sounding inanity and futility; at bottom, he *was* not at all. **1843** —— *Past & Pr.* I. i, His mouth full of loud futilities. **1870** LOWELL *Study Wind.* 222 A patchwork of second-hand memories is a laborious futility, hard to write and harder to read. **1871** MORLEY *Voltaire* (1886) 8 To reduce the faith to a vague futility.

futilize ('fjuːtɪlaɪz), *v. rare.* [f. FUTILE + -IZE.] *trans.* To make futile.

1766 H. BROOKE *Fool of Qual.* II. ix. 119 Her whole soul and essence is futilized and extracted into shew and superficials. **1867** R. M. PHILLIMORE tr. *Dupanloup's Stud. Wom.* vi. (1869) 35 Not to futilize (if I may be allowed the word) the mind of men, who are already too much inclined to futility.

†**'futilous**, *a. Obs.* [irreg. f. L. *fūti-, futtil-is* FUTILE + -OUS.] = FUTILE.

1607 S. HIERON *Defence* I. 171 These arguments..are futilous. **1631** R. BYFIELD *Doctr. Sabb.* 11 A futilous distinction of *of* and *to*. **1643** *True Informer* 30 The Authors ..were worthlesse and meane futilous persons. **1647** WARD *Simp. Cobler* 26 It is a most unworthy thing, for men, to spend their lives in making fidle-cases for futilous womens phansies. **1692** WASHINGTON tr. *Milton's Def. Pop.* viii. (1851) 201 Which is enough to discover how futilous you are, to say, as you have done, that it was a Pope. **1703** BP. PATRICK *Comm. 2 Sam.* vi. 20 Not with a futilous, lascivious, and petulant joy, but with a pious and moderate.

‖**futon** ('fuːtɒn, ‖huton). [Jap.] A Japanese bed-quilt.

1876 *Trans. Asiatic Soc. Japan* IV. 172 Those..who..are tired of tinned meats and live *futons*. **1886** E. S. MORSE *Jap. Homes* 212 The *futons*, or comforters, are..hung over the balcony rail to air. **1891** CHAMBERLAIN & MASON *Handbk. Japan* 8 Beds are still rare; but good quilts (*futon*) are laid down on the mats. **1959** *Encounter* Jan. 20/2 Their *futon* —the wadded quilt stuffed with cotton-wool which serves the Japanese for a bed.

futra: see FOUTRE.

futtah ('fʌtə). *N.Z.* Also futter, whata, etc. Early spellings representing the pronunciation of Maori *whata*, a food-store raised on posts.

1834 E. MARKHAM *N.Z. or Recollections of It* 37, I have seen a Wutter or Platform 80 feet above ground in an immense Tree all the Branches cut off And a Platform well secured, and the Potatoes on it and thatched over. **1878** E. S. ELWELL *Boy Colonists* 100 Walker..afterwards gave him another pair of trousers from the futtah. **1888** A. H. DUNCAN *Wakatipians* iii. 22 The buildings at the home-station..were represented by a 'futter' and a long narrow hut. **1891** *Rep. Austral. Assoc. Advancem. Sci.* III. 378 The men gathered the food and stored it in *whatas* or store-rooms, which were attached to every chief's compound, and built on tall posts to protect the contents from damp and rats. **1892** *N.Z. Alpine Jrnl.* I. ii. 95 Our second [camp] was in George's Creek, where we built a 'futtah' for the provisions. **1954** E. C. STUDHOLME *Te Waimate* (ed. 2) III. v. 260 Most stations..had a futtah—a corruption of the Maori word, whata, meaning 'a raised store-house in which food is kept'.

futtling ('fʌtlɪŋ). *Naut.* = FOOT-WALING (see FOOT *sb.* 35).

c **1850** *Rudim. Navig.* (Weale) 119 *Footwaling*, or *Futtling*, or *Ceiling*, the inside plank of the ship's bottom.

futtock (ˈfʌtək). *Naut.* Also 8 foot-hook. [prob., as already suggested in quot. 1644, a pronunciation of *foot-hook* (see quot. 1769).]

1. One of the middle timbers of the frame of a ship, between the floor and the top timbers.

1611 COTGR., *Cour-baston*..(in a ship) a crooked peece of tymber, tearmed a Knee, or Futtocke. **1644** MANWAYRING *Sea-mans Dict.*, *Futtocks*, this word is commonly pronounced but I thinke more properly it should be called Foote-hookes; for the Futtocks are those compassing timbers, which give the bredth and bearing to the ship, which are scarfed to the ground-timbers. **1769** FALCONER *Dict. Marine* (1776), *Futtocks*, the middle division of a ship's timbers: or those parts which are situated between the floor and the top-timbers..As the epithet *hooked* is..applied..to several crooked timbers in a ship, as the breast-hooks, fore-hooks, after-hooks, &c., this term is evidently derived from the lowest part or *foot* of the timber and from the shape of the piece. **1789** G. KEATE *Pelew Isl.* 94 The jolly-boat was dispatched to..fetch some timbers for futtocks. **1832** MARRYAT *N. Forster* iii, Several of the lower futtocks and timbers still hung together. **1846** ADDISON *Contracts* II. vii. §2 (1883) 998 The twenty-two broken futtocks of the vessel were concealed only by the ballast. *c* **1850** *Rudim. Navig.* (Weale) 120 Futtocks..are named according to their situation, that nearest the keel being called the first futtock; the next above, the second futtock, etc.

2. *Comb.*, as ***futtock-mould, -rigging, -timber.*** Also **futtock-head, -hole, -hoop** (see quots.); **futtock-plank**, = LIMBER-STRAKE; **futtock-plate**, one of the iron plates crossing the sides of the top-rim perpendicularly, to which the futtock-shrouds are secured; **futtock-rider** (see quot. 1867); **futtock-shroud**, one of the small shrouds which secure the lower dead-eyes and futtock-plates of top-mast rigging to a band round a lower mast; **futtock-staff, -stave** (see quots.).

1867 SMYTH *Sailor's Word-bk.*, **Futtock-head*, in ship-building, is a name for the 5th, the 7th, and the 9th diagonals. **1846** YOUNG *Naut. Dict.* s.v. *Futtock-shrouds*, They are often formed by a continuation of the topmast rigging coming down through holes in the top, called *futtock-holes. **1867** SMYTH *Sailor's Word-bk.*, *Futtock-holes*, places through the top rim for the futtock-plates. **1874** KNIGHT *Dict. Mech.* I. 931 **Futtock-hoop*, a hoop encircling the mast at a point below the head, and serving for the attachment of the shackles of the futtock-shrouds. **1664** E. BUSHNELL *Compl. Shipwright* 19 The..*futtock-Mould is hauled downward. **1846** YOUNG *Naut. Dict.*, *Limber-strake*..sometimes called the **futtock-plank*. **1769** FALCONER *Dict. Marine* (1789) M m ij, An iron band, called the *foot-hook-plate. **1841** R. H. DANA *Seaman's Man.* 106 *Futtock-plates.* **1769** FALCONER *Dict. Marine* (1789), *Eguillettes*..the *futtock-riders. **1867** SMYTH *Sailor's Word-bk.*, *Futtock-riders* when a rider is lengthened by means of pieces batted or scarphed to it and each other, the first piece is termed the first futtock-rider, the next the second futtock-rider, and so on. *c* **1860** H. STUART *Seaman's Catech.* 17 What is the name of the rigging from the necklace to the top rims? *Futtock-rigging. **1769** FALCONER *Dict. Marine* (1789) M m ij, A rope called the *foot-hook-shroud. **1840** R. H. DANA *Bef. Mast* vi. 13 He fell from the star-board futtock shrouds. **1861** H. KINGSLEY *Ravenshoe* vi, Clinging to the futtock shrouds. **1841** R. H. DANA *Seaman's Man.* 106 **Futtock-staff*, a short piece of wood or iron, seized across the upper part of the rigging, to which the catharpin legs are secured. **1794** *Rigging & Seamanship* I. 166 **Futtock-stave*, a short piece of rope served over with spun-yarn, to which the shrouds are confined at the catharpins. **1841** R. H. DANA *Seaman's Man.* 107 **Futtock-timbers*, those timbers between the floor and navel timbers and the top timbers.

† **ˈfuturable**, *a.* *Obs.*⁻¹ [f. FUTURE + -ABLE.] That may happen in the future.

1655 FULLER *Ch. Hist.* XI. iii. §51. 175 What the issue..would have been, is only known to him..whose prescience extends not only to things future, but futurable, having the certain cognisance of contingents, which might, yet never actually shall, come to passe.

futural (ˈfjuːtjʊərəl), *a.* [ad. med.L. *futūrālis* (see FUTURALITY).] Of or pertaining to the future; spec. *Gram.*, having a future sense.

1906 J. H. MOULTON *Gram. N.T. Gk.* I. 120 Futural presents..have no lack of durativity about them. **1953** *Jrnl. Philos.* 27 Aug. 553, I suppose positive results for all possible tests, present as well as futural.

† **futuˈrality.** *Obs.*⁻¹ [f. med.L. *futūrāl-is* (f. *futūr-us* future: see -AL[1]) + -ITY.] Futurity; the future (of a person).

1666 G. ALSOP *Maryland* (1869) 101 What the futurality of my days will bring forth, I know not.

future (ˈfjuːtjʊə(r), ˈfjuːtʃə(r)), *a.* and *sb.* Also 4 futur. [a. OF. and F. *futur* masc., *future* fem., ad. L. *futūrus*, fut. pple. of *esse* to be, f. stem *fu-* (see BE etym. 3).]

A. *adj.*

1. a. That is to be, or will be, hereafter. Often qualifying a sb., with the sense: The person or thing that is expected to be (what the sb. denotes).

c **1374** CHAUCER *Troylus* v. 748 Futur tyme, er I was in the snare, Coude I not seen. *c* **1440** *Gesta Rom.* xxviii. 105 (Harl. MS.) Vyneger was gode, and that is for þe preterit tyme; wyne is gode, and þat is for the presente tyme; and muste shalle be gode, and that is for the future tyme. **1600** HAKLUYT *Voy.* III. 860 There is no likelihood of future sedition..in any of the kingdoms. **1641** MILTON *Ch. Govt.* I. vii, The trifling doubts and jealousies of future sects. **1725** WATTS *Logic* II. v. §7 We attain the greatest assurance of things past and future by divine faith. **1816** M. GREENLEAF *Distr. Maine* 136 Like every thing future, all speculations on this subject must..be in a measure uncertain. **1838** LYTTON *Alice* 25, I wish I were the future Lady Vargrave. **1841–71** T. R. JONES *Anim. Kingd.* (ed. 4) 228 The little embryo bears no resemblance whatever to the future animal. **1860** TYNDALL *Glac.* I. xxvi. 374 To help future observers to place this point beyond doubt, etc. **1882** J. H. BLUNT *Ref. Ch. Eng.* II. 428 The series of events which the future Cardinal thus indicated in outline. **1884** tr. *Lotze's Metaph.* 264 If to one and the same consciousness that is to become Present which was previously Future to it. **1895** *Law Times* XCVIII. 280/1 The injury..blighting the plaintiff's whole future career.

b. In certain contexts used *spec.* with reference to the condition of the soul after death. ***a future state, life***: existence after death, esp. as an object of belief.

1733 POPE *Ess. Man* I. *Contents*, It is partly upon this Ignorance of future Events, and partly upon the Hope of a Future State, that all his Happiness in the Present depends. **1776** GIBBON *Decl. & F.* I. xv. 450 The doctrine of a future life, improved by every additional circumstance which could give weight and efficacy to that important truth. **1799** WILLES & DURNFORD *Comm. Pleas Cases* 550 Supposing an infidel who believes a God..but does not believe a future state, be examined on his oath. **1814** J. KENRICK (*title*) The necessity of revelation to teach the doctrine of a future life. **1879** *Psychol. Rev.* I. 335 Those who believe in God and a Future Life. **1883** GILMOUR *Mongols* xvii. 207 The theory of a man's future state depending simply on the preponderance of his good or bad actions. **1945** B. RUSSELL *Hist. Western Philos.* II. ii. 330 As regards the doctrine of a future life, in the West it was first taught by the Orphics and thence adopted by Greek philosophers.

c. *absol.* or *ellipt.*; esp. in phr. ***in future.***

1607 SHAKS. *Timon* I. i. 141 Three Talents on the present; in future, all. **1650** WELDON *Crt. Jas. I.* 155 It utterly cast him out of all favour from the King in future. **1667** MILTON *P.L.* III. 78 Him God beholding from his prospect high, Wherin past, present, future he beholds. **1808** T. LINDLEY *Voy. Brasil* 28, I shall be obliged to..endure a dark room in future.

d. (*Philos.*) ***future contingent***: a proposition which is neither true nor false, because it is about the future; sometimes, the future event itself, that may or may not occur. Also *attrib.*

1623, 1788 [see CONTINGENT *sb.* 2]. **1885** J. VEITCH *Institutes* §463 This happens especially in future contingents. **1957** A. N. PRIOR *Time & Modality* 120 We assign to future contingents a third truth-value. **1969** N. RESCHER *Many-Valued Logic* ii. 148 The so-called future-contingent propositions..involve the outcome of free human choices.

2. Of or pertaining to time to come; esp. in *Gram.* of a tense: Relating to time to come; describing an event yet to happen. Also *ellipt.* (= *future tense*).

future perfect (*tense*): expressing an event or action viewed as past in relation to a given future time.

1530 PALSGR. 84 The future tens, as *je parleráy*. **1579** FULKE *Refut. Rastell* 768 Hee maketh them..plainer by chaunging the pretertence into the future. **1612** BRINSLEY *Pos. Parts* (1669) 34 What time speaks the Future Tense of? *A.* Of the time to Come. **1633** EARL MANCH. *Al Mondo* (1636) 32 Man is a future creature, the eye of his soule lookes beyond this life. **1708** *Brit. Apollo* No. 51. 1/2 Tho' the first Aorist be..used for the second future. **1824** L. MURRAY *Eng. Gram.* (ed. 5) I. 124 The first Future Tense..The second Future.

¶**3.** Loosely used for: Subsequent (to a specified past epoch).

1600 J. LANE *Tom Tel-troth* 120 Since those times by future times were changed. **1630** *R. Johnson's Kingd. & Commw.* 114 Scotland..in times past began at the Mountaine Grampius..But in future times, by the extinguishment of the Picts, it reached also unto Tweed. **1664** POWER *Exp. Philos.* II. 107 Prognosticks..made good by the future event of the Experiments. **1858** W. L. SARGANT *Soc. Innov.* 27 This rhapsody will not be intelligible to those unacquainted with St. Simon's future history.

B. *sb.*

† **1.** *pl.* Future events. *Obs.*

c **1374** CHAUCER *Boeth.* v. vi. 133 (Camb. MS.) It..procedith fro preteritz in to futuris. *Ibid.* 134 It ne hath nat the futuris þat ben nat yit. **1654** WHITLOCK *Zootomia* 476 Providence against all sorts of Futures that fall under our Care.

2. ***the future.*** **a.** Time to come; future time. Phr. ***for the future***: in all future time.

c **1400** *Rom. Rose* 5015 Aforn hir she may see In the future som socour. **1601** SHAKS. *All's Well* IV. ii. 63 That what in time proceeds, May token to the future, our past deeds. **1693** *Hum. & Conv. Town* 63 All the Fury of Minor Criticks follow..all his Opinions for the future. **1796** *Campaigns* 1793–4 II. viii. 52 I'll..teach him to take better care for the future. **1822** HAZLITT *Table-t.* I. iii. 52 The future is like a dead wall or a thick mist hiding all objects from our view. **1878** MORLEY *Crit. Misc.* Ser. I. *Carlyle* 197 The industrial organization of the future.

personified. **1821** SHELLEY *Adonais* i, Till the Future dares Forget the Past.

b. What will happen in the future.

1607 SHAKS. *Timon* II. i. 157 The future comes apace. **1732** POPE *Ess. Man* I. 81 Oh blindness to the future! Kindly giv'n. **1759** JOHNSON *Rasselas* xxix. (1787) 85 The future [is the object] of hope and fear. **1820** LAMB *Elia, Oxf. in Vac.*, The mighty future is as nothing, being every-thing! **1866** GLADSTONE in *Pall Mall G.* 28 July (1892) 1/2 You cannot fight against the future..time is on our side.

3. a. A condition in time to come different (esp. in a favourable sense) from the present.

1852 H. ROGERS *Ecl. Faith* (1853) 61 Every little present has its little future for which we live. **1879** E. ARNOLD *Lt. Asia* v. 132 Making all futures fruits of all the pasts. **1891** C. JAMES *Rom. Rigmarole* 86, I would soon carve out a new future for us both.

b. The prospective condition (of a person, country, etc.); *spec.* a prospective condition of success, prosperity, etc.; (***there is***) ***no future in*** (something): there is no prospect of success or advancement in (it).

1858 LYTTON *What will he do?* II. viii, My sacrifice to Jasper's future might not have been in vain. **1863** MARY HOWITT tr. *F. Bremer's Greece* I. viii. 263–4 See every-thing which belongs to the future of Greece. **1882** PEBODY *Eng. Journalism* xx. 152 Its future is a future which..is likely to add fresh lustre to the Newspaper Press. **1891** WILDE *Pict. Dorian Gray* xv. 268, I like men who have a future, and women who have a past. **1921** [see FUTURISTIC *a.*]. **1926** GALSWORTHY *Silver Spoon* II. x. 199 No future in it! **1932** *Week-end Rev.* 7 May 586/2 Miss Stone certainly has a future as a novelist. **1948** 'N. SHUTE' *No Highway* ii. 40 We can't hide things up. There's no future in that. **1960** L. COOPER *Accomplices* I. vi. 62 You can't rob a bank or bash a chap's head in and then say to the police, Oh it doesn't matter I'm leaving here next week. (You can, I suppose, if you feel that way, but there's no future in it.) **1968** *Listener* 28 Nov. 714/2 I've known Lowry since 1919, when we were both working in the life class in Manchester School of Art, and I predicted a future for Lowry. **1971** 'H. CARMICHAEL' *Most Deadly Hate* v. 62 There's no future in being an accessory after the fact in a murder case.

4. *Gram.* = *future tense*: see A. 2.

1881 RUTHERFORD *New Phrynichus* 405 It affords the necessary authority to supply deponent futures to a group of verbs..of which by a singular fatality no future form has been preserved.

5. One who is affianced in marriage, one's betrothed. [After F. *futur, future.*]

1827 T. MOORE *Mem.* (1854) V. 196 Lord Charles took his pretty future to Church this morning to receive the sacrament.

6. *Comm.* in *pl.* Goods (esp. corn, cotton and other produce) and stocks sold on an agreement for future delivery. Also, contracts to sell or buy on these terms. Also *attrib.*, as in ***future system.***

1880 *Daily News* 10 Nov. 3/8 American futures are in better demand. **1883** *Manch. Exam.* 6 Nov. 4/4 Amongst the new developments of the cotton trade, the buying of futures may be looked upon as the most prominent. **1888** *Times* 26 June 12/1 Coffee very dull on the spot and not much done in futures. **1896** *Daily News* 22 Sept. 8/4 The question on the programme was that of 'futures'. **1897** *Westm. Gaz.* 5 Jan. 9/1 The future system had created..in New York..an enormous market.

7. *attrib.*, as **future(s) research, study** = FUTUROLOGY; **future shock**: see SHOCK *sb.*[3] 4 d (b).

1969 *New Scientist* 18 Dec. 588/2 A conflict about the conduct of futures research in West Germany has blown up among the futurologists themselves. **1971** *Observer* 10 Jan. 21/4 'The Institute for the Future'..is trying to get futures study out of the gee-whiz stage and give it a much more intellectually solid basis. **1971** *Sunday Times* (Johannesburg) (Business Section) 28 Mar. 10/2 (Advt.), Duties will include so called 'future' research into the implications of rapid technological change for *Man.*

† **ˈfuture**, *v.* *Obs.* [f. FUTURE *a.*; cf. med.L. *futūrāre* in the same sense.] *trans.* To make future, put off to a future day. Also *absol.*

1642 R. HARRIS *Serm.* 15 And who knows but that therefore God hath futured other hopes, and frustrated other means, to the intent that he might honor this ordinance? **1646** TRAPP *Comm. John* xii. 35 So they trifle, and by futuring, fool away their own salvation. **1647** —— *Matt.* xxv. 11 Trifling..with Christ and their souls, futuring their repentance. **1650** —— *Gen.* xx. 8 So [they] are shut out, with the foolish Virgins, for their lingring and futuring.

ˈfutureless, *a.* [f. FUTURE *sb.* + -LESS.] Without a future, having no future before one.

1863 *All Year Round* July 477/1 An animal, a brute beast, soulless and futureless. **1879** HOWELLS *L. Aroostook* (1882) I. 141 The ordinary, futureless young girl.

† **ˈfuturely**, *adv.* *Obs.* [f. FUTURE *a.* + -LY[2].] In future, at a future time, hereafter. Also *loosely*, at a time later than a certain epoch, thereafter.

c **1611** CHAPMAN *Iliad* VI. 201 This field the Lycians futurely..the Errant call'd. **1628** STRAFFORD in Browning *Life* (1891) 293 A distinction by which I shall futurely govern my self. **1649** JER. TAYLOR *Gt. Exemp.* III. xv. 78 Jesus..foretold great sadnesses..futurely contingent to it. **1673** GARROWAY in *Debates Ho. of C.* (Grey) II. 213 As for Duncombe's argument of building ships futurely, Money may be had. **1793** G. READ in *Life & Corr.* 1870) 547 That I may not be thought concluded from asking for an increase of allowance futurely.

ˈfutureness. [f. FUTURE *a.* + -NESS.] The quality of being future.

1829 JAS. MILL *Hum. Mind* (1869) II. xiv. §5. 118 You have pastness, presentness, and futureness. **1875** MCCOSH *Scot. Philos.* li. 386 Time is pastness, presentness, and futureness joined by association.

futurism (ˈfjuːtjʊərɪz(ə)m, -tʃər-). [f. FUTURE *a.* + -ISM, after It. *futurismo*, F. *futurisme.*] An art-movement, originating in Italy, characterized by violent departure from traditional forms, the avowed aim being to express movement and growth in objects, not their appearance at some particular moment. Also applied to similar tendencies in literature and music.

1909 *Daily Chron.* 5 May 6/6 'Futurism' is the declaration of the new school of literature grounded by the International Review 'Poesia'. **1915** W. H. WRIGHT *Mod. Painting* 276

Marinetti, a poet, is the spiritual (and monetary) father of Futurism. **1921** Galsworthy *To Let* II. ii, Paul Post—that painter a little in advance of Futurism. **1937** N. Slonimsky *Mus. since 1900* (1938) p. xviii, Futurism was proclaimed in a manifesto published in the Paris *Figaro* on 20 February 1909. It aimed at complete annihilation of all accepted forms in favor of a future music created according to some imagined law of machine-like perfection. **1963** *Cambr. Rev.* 4 May 405/1 Voznesensky perpetuates..one specific trend in Russian poetry—the school of futurism, represented by Khlebnikov and Mayakovsky, Tsvetayeva, and Pasternak. **1967** E. Short *Embroidery & Fabric Collage* iv. 89 In a comparatively short time Fauvism, Cubism, Expressionism, Dadaism, Futurism, and Surrealism threw new light on the treatment of subject matter.

futurist (ˈfjuːtjʊərɪst), *sb.* (*a.*) [f. FUTURE *sb.* + -IST.] **1.** *Theol.* **a.** One who believes that the Scripture prophecies, esp. those in the Book of Revelation, are still to be fulfilled in the future.

1842 G. S. Faber *Prov. Lett.* (1844) I. 88 *note*, Dr. Todd and Mr. Mac-Causland..are alike stanch Antiprotestant Futurists. **1854** D. S. Desprez *Apocal. Fulfilled* i. 2 We have Præterists and Futurists—one class of interpreters believing that the Apocalypse was fulfilled in the first three or four centuries of the Christian æra; another class maintaining that, with the exception of the three first chapters, none of it is fulfilled. **1882** Farrar *Early Chr.* II. 227.

b. *attrib.* passing into *adj.*

1878 H. G. Guinness *End of Age* Pref. (1880) 5 The futurist school of prophetic interpreters. **1881** *Ch. Times* 25 Feb. 121 To give themselves up..to idle futurist speculations.

2. One who has regard to or studies the future; a believer in human progress.

1846 in Worcester. **1936** G. K. Chesterton *Autobiogr.* 25 The one thing forbidden to such futurists was Looking Backwards. **1956** A. Toynbee *Historian's Approach to Religion* vi. 79 The futurists are revolutionaries who consciously and deliberately set out to break with a disintegrating social past in order to create a new society. **1964** E. M. Forster in *Granta* 15 Feb. 9/1 *Traction Engine*: I shall pass often enough in the future. *Punt*: A Futurist! Better and better. **1971** *Observer* 10 Jan. 21/7 A man whose name had often been mentioned respectfully by other futurists.

3. [After It. *futuristo*, F. *futuriste*.] An adherent of futurism. Also *attrib.* or as *adj.*

1911 W. J. Locke *Clementina Wing* xxii. 278 After that they had gone to see the New Futurists. **1914** *Star* 16 Dec. 6/2 Small bullet-proof shields,..painted in cubist patterns in futurist colours. **1915** W. H. Wright *Mod. Painting* 272 The famous Futurist statement that 'a running horse has not four legs, but twenty'. **1916** 'Boyd Cable' *Action Front* 128 Erratic daubs of bright colours laid on after the most approved Futurist style. **1924** C. Hamilton *Prisoners of Hope* 129 The walls..were covered with the raw and confused handiwork of the people who called themselves futurists because they had never been taught how to paint. **1958** *Times Lit. Suppl.* 31 Jan. 58/1 Trotsky writes superbly on the literary 'fellow-travellers', Alexander Blok, and the Futurists in particular.

futuristic (fjuːtjʊəˈrɪstɪk, -tʃər-), *a.* [f. prec. + -IC.] **1.** Having the characteristics of futurism; avant-garde; ultra-modern.

1915 W. H. Wright *Mod. Painting* 257 His [*sc.* Gleizes'] well-known L'Homme au Balcon appears to us today almost Futuristic in conception. **1921** *Queen* 10 Sept. 326 Quaint futuristic or jazz embroidery. **1921** Galsworthy *To Let* I. i, What was the use of going in to look at this crazy, futuristic stuff with the view of seeing whether it had any future? **1928** *Melody Maker* Feb. 182/2 Some pretty futuristic harmony. **1968** J. Ironside *Fashion Alphabet* 16 Garments, both futuristic and yet based on armour and chain-mail.

2. Of or pertaining to the future; predicted for the future.

1958 *Listener* 18 Dec. 1021/2 It may well be that only when optical telescopes can be carried in earth satellites or erected on the moon will it be possible to look back into the past to this extent. Before the advent of such futuristic enterprises it seems likely that the great radio telescopes will give us the answer we require. **1969** *N.Y. Rev. Books* 16 Jan. 32/4 Goldbloom has merely invented a novel kind of anachronism that might be called 'futuristic' or 'projective'.

futuritial (fjuːtjʊˈrɪʃəl), *a. Obs.*$^{-0}$ [f. FUTURIT-Y + -(I)AL.] Relating to what is to come; pertaining to future time or events.

1846 in Worcester (citing Hamilton); hence in mod. Dicts.

futurition (fjuːtjʊˈrɪʃən). *Philos.* [ad. med.L. *futūritiōn-em*, irreg. f. *futūr-us* FUTURE.

As a metaphysical term the med.L. word is used e.g. by St. Bonaventura *Opera* ed. Peltier 1864 II. 65 b, in discussions relating to God's foreknowledge of events. A different sense, = 'the act of forecasting the future', occurs in a letter of Bp. Jewel, 1 Aug. 1559, in *Zurich Lett.* ser. 1 (Parker Soc.) App. 22. The Parker Soc. translator renders Jewel's *valde deditum futuritionibus* by 'mightily addicted to futuritions'; but the sense is not otherwise authenticated either in Lat. or Eng.]

1. Existence or occurrence in the future; future existence or accomplishment. Now *rare*.

1641 D. Cawdrey *3 Serm.* 72 In the one there shall be a succession of punishments, and so there shall be a respect of futurition or time to come. **1654** Vilvain *Theorem. Theol.* ii. 64 A certainty of divine Prescience touching the precise period of every mans life, as also the order or maner of its futurition. **1659** Pearson *Creed* (1682) I. 115 In which words is clearly expressed the futurition of salvation certain by him. **1684–5** South *Serm.* (1823) I. 207 Is it imaginable, that the great means of the worlds redemption..should hang so loose in respect of its futurition as [etc.]. **1824** L. Murray *Eng. Gram.* (ed. 5) I. 147 The word *shall*..does not mean, to promise..in the third person, but the mere futurition of an event. **1882–3** in Schaff *Encycl. Relig. Knowl.* III. 2524/1 While foreknowledge may insure the certain futurition of a volition.

b. quasi-*concr.* A future event or existence; a futurity.

1668 Shiells *Naphtali* Pref. 49 Let us not be anxious about futuritions. *a* **1670** Hacket *Cent. Serm.* (1675) 996 There is a futurition of glory for the Soul. **1684** T. Burnet *Th. Earth* I. 107 Seeing thorough the possibilities and futuritions of each [world]. **1840** *Blackw. Mag.* XLVIII. 144 Some mere futurition, as metaphysicians love to speak, some event in futurity.

2. The quality, attribute, or fact of being future; the fact or circumstance that (something specified) will be.

1666 Spurstowe *Spir. Chym.* (1668) 79 Futurition in respect of existency of things, is no prejudice to the Eye of Faith, in the beholding of them as present. **1699** Burnet *39 Art.* xvii. (1700) 153 When God decrees that anything shall be, it has from that a certain futurition. **1754** Edwards *Freed. Will* IV. viii. 251 The Acts and State of the Wills of moral Agents, which had a fix'd Futurition from Eternity. **1839** *Blackw. Mag.* XLV. 462 The Romans..had..forms expressing futurition and desire. **1847** Bushnell *Chr. Nurt.* vii. (1861) 166 If there is any law of futurition.

futurity (fjuːˈtjʊərɪtɪ). [f. FUTURE + -ITY.]

1. The quality, state, or fact of being future; = FUTURITION 2. *rare*.

1637 Bastwick *Litany* I. 11 The hope of my blessednes is not here: the futurity of which doth no way mitigate my comfort. **1660** Glanvill *Sceps. Sci.* viii. 74 The bare Possibilities, which never commence into a Futurity. **1864** Burton *Scot Abr.* II. i. 56 The comforting elements of futurity and uncertainty.

2. Future time; the future; a future space of time.

1604 Shaks. *Oth.* III. iv. 117 Nor present Sorrowes, Nor purpos'd merit in futurity. **1664** Power *Exp. Philos.* I. 60 A white Spot..which in futurity proves the Heart with its Veins and arteries. **1741** Richardson *Pamela* (1824) I. 159 Involved in the dark bosom of futurity. **1792** S. Rogers *Pleas. Mem.* II. 58 Futurity's blank page. **1819** Scott *Leg. Montrose* i, These events were still in the womb of futurity. **1841** Myers *Cath. Th.* IV. xxxiii. 346 The particular events and personages of a distant futurity. **1876** Mozley *Univ. Serm.* iii. (1877) 64 Throwing forward into the darkness of futurity an image of himself here.

3. What is future.

a. What will exist or happen in the future; future events as a whole. Also †those that will live in the future, posterity (*obs. rare*).

1664 Power *Exp. Philos.* Pref. 17 And perhaps not out of the reach of futurity to exhibit. **1713** Berkeley *Guardian* No. 35 ¶5 A wretch racked..with..a secret dread of futurity. **1738** Swift *Let.* 24 Aug., I will..contrive some way to be known to futurity, that [etc.]. **1754** Sherlock *Disc.* (1759) I. i. 19 We must have no Share or Lot in the Glories of Futurity. **1781** Gibbon *Decl. & Fall* III. 60 An Egyptian monk, who possessed..the knowledge of futurity. **1884** J. S. C. Abbott *Napoleon* (1855) I. xxiv. 389 The caprices of fate and the uncertainty of futurity.

b. *pl.* Future events.

1651 Biggs *New Disp.* ¶304 In the futurities of our performances. **1694** J. Howe in H. Rogers *Life* x. (1863) 285 Such sad futurities God, in mercy to us, hides from us. *a* **1703** Burkitt *On N.T.* Luke xxi. 7 What an itching curiosity there is in the best of men, to know futurities. **1779** Franklin *Lett.* Wks. 1889 VI. 420, I must one of these days go back to see him..but futurities are uncertain. **1850** Mrs. Browning *Poems* II. 177 O centuries That roll, in vision, your futurities My future grave athwart. *a* **1859** De Quincey *Posthum. Wks.* (1891) I. 85 *note*, The reader whose scholarship is still amongst his futurities.

c. State or condition in the future. Also, existence after death.

1741 Middleton *Cicero* I. iii. 166 The expectation of a futurity. **1748** Hartley *Observ. Man.* I. iii. 355 Rules..which teach Mankind how to secure a happy Futurity. **1775** Johnson *Tax. no Tyr.* in Boswell an. 1775, This futurity of Whiggism. **1836** Hor. Smith *Tin Trump.* (1876) 173 Futurity..what we are to be, determined by what we have been. **1860** Mill *Repr. Govt.* (1865) 39/1 The practical dangers to which the futurity of representative governments will be exposed.

futurize (ˈfjuːtjʊəraɪz), *v. rare.* [f. FUTURE + -IZE.] *intr.* To form the future tense; to express the idea of futurity.

1859 J. Hadley *Ess.* (1873) 194 But it is in the Romance languages that this mode of 'futurizing' (if we may so call it) has shown itself on the largest scale.

futurology (fjuːtjʊəˈrɒlədʒɪ, -tʃər-). [f. FUTURE *sb.* + -OLOGY.] The forecasting of the future on a systematic basis, esp. by the study of present-day trends in human affairs. Hence **futuˈrologist**.

1946 A. Huxley *Let.* 29 Mar. (1969) 542 Thank you for..the interesting enclosure on 'Teaching the Future'. I think that 'futurology' might be a very good thing. **1967** *Listener* 23 Mar. 397/1 Futurology, the systematic study of trends which enable us to forecast the shape of things to come. *Ibid.* 397/2 Here we are with the automation process which, according to well-known futurologists, will lead to enforced leisure for a large part of the population. **1969** *New Scientist* 11 Dec. 570/2 Futurology..cannot be turned into a respectable 'hard' science merely by getting the economists and the technologists to put some numbers to it. **1970** *Financial Times* 13 Apr. 7/1 American futurologist Herman Kahn is wrong in seeing the 21st century as belonging to Japan.

futz (fʌts), *v. U.S. slang.* [Origin uncertain; perh. alteration of Yiddish *arumfartzen* (*Amer. Speech* (1943) XVIII. 43).] *intr.* To loaf, waste time, mess *around*.

1932 J. T. Farrell *Studs Lonigan* (1936) iii. 56 Studs kept futzing around until Helen Shire came out with her soccer ball. **1941** B. Schulberg *What makes Sammy Run?* vii. 114 Sammy said, '..Maybe you ought to write a play too.'.. 'I've been working on one for a couple of years,' I said. 'Don't futz around with it too long,' Sammy said. **1968** N. Benchley *Welcome to Xanadu* vi. 130 It's bad for your blood pressure to futz around like this.

fuxl, -ol, -ul, obs. forms of FOWL *sb.*

fuyl, obs. Sc. form of FOOL.

1533 Gau *Richt Vay* To Rdr. (1888) 3 As sum fuyl or munk maid.

fuyle, obs. form of FILE *v.*[2] or FOIL *v.*[1]

c **1340** *Cursor M.* 882 (Trin.) She haþ me fuyled wiþ her synne.

fuyt, var. FEUTE, *Obs.*

fu yung (fuː jʌŋ). Also fooyong, foo yong, yoong, fu-yung, etc. [a. Chinese (Cantonese) *fúyúng*, lit. 'lotus'.] A Chinese sauce made with eggs mixed and cooked with a variety of other ingredients. Usu. in the name of the dish with which the sauce is served, as ***egg fu yung***, etc.

1917 V. Galster *Chinese Cook Bk.* 5 (*heading*) Eggs fo yung with shrimp, lobster or chicken. **1928** *Mandarin Chop Suey Cook Bk.* 6 With the aid of the *Mandarin Chop Suey Cook Book*, however, Chop Suey, Chow Mein, Egg Foo Young..now can..be prepared in every American household. **1934** G. Ross *Tips on Tables* 119 The varieties of chow mein and the egg Foo Yung are well-prepared. **1935** M. Morphy *Recipes of All Nations* 722 Foo Yong Hy (crab omelet). **1948** R. W. Dana *Where to eat in N.Y.* 66 The theater and night-club performers drop in late for chicken egg foo yong. **1952** D. Y. H. Feng *Joy of Chinese Cooking* iv. 90 Foo Yoong Daahn—Rich Egg Omelet. **1956** B. Y. Chao *How to cook & eat in Chinese* II. xiii. 160 (*heading*) Egg *fu-yung* (with meat shreds). **1965** P. Robinson *Pakistani Agent* viii. 113 I'll have a prawn fooyong and chicken chow mein. **1972** K. Lo *Chinese Food* I. 30 One of the favourite Chinese white sauces for vegetables is the *fu-yung* sauce, which is made from minced chicken mixed with broth, egg white, cornflour, and some milk or cream. *Ibid.* 44 Classically, the term *fu-yung* should only apply to egg white and cornflour mixed with minced chicken (a completely white mixture). **1974** *N.Y. Times* 4 Oct. 34 With a gusto once reserved for chow mein and egg foo yong New Yorkers are now dipping their chopsticks into another Oriental taste treat. **1979** *Tucson Mag.* Mar. 73/1 The Chinese dishes Americans know best—egg roll, egg foo yung, roast pork.

fuzil: see FUSIL.

fuzz (fʌz), *sb.*[1] In sense 2 also 7 **fuss.** [Perh. imitative of the action of blowing away light particles. Cf., however, FOZY and the cognate words there cited.]

1. Loose volatile matter; a mass of fine, light, fluffy particles.

1674 N. Fairfax *Bulk & Selv.* 125 A Snayl..which is..to our feeling, very cold, is fain to brood its as cold sweatty eggs..bespiewing them about with the fuzze of a cold clammy froth. *c* **1720** Prior *Pontius & Pontia* ii. Misc. Wks. (1740) 107 One ask'd, if that high fuzz of hair Was, bona fide, all your Own. **1840** Smart, *Fuzz*, volatile matter. **1854** Hawthorne *Eng. Note-bks.* II. 319 Blankets with the woollen fuzz upon them. **1865** Miss Cary *Ball. & Lyrics* 61 Your hair! why, you've only a little gray fuzz! **1881** *Sat. Rev.* No. 1320. 203 The expensive valentines are gaudy chromolithographic objects, fluttering in a fuzz of paper-lace.

†2. = FUZZ-BALL. *Obs.*

1601 Holland *Pliny* II. 7 Puffes, Fusbals or Fusses. **1656** Ridgley *Pract. Physick* 45 The most conservent is that Toadstool which is called a Fuss. **1701–2** De la Pryme *Diary* (Surtees) 249 The bottom part of a great cup mushroom or fuz.

3. *Photogr.* = FUZZINESS.

1889 *Anthony's Photogr. Bull.* II. 370 The importance of knowing beforehand by what standard (focus or fuzz) we are to be judged.

4. *Comb.*: **fuzz-type**, a jocular name for a photograph with (intentional) blurred effect; **fuzz-wig**, a wig of crisp curls; so ***fuzz-wigged*** adj.

1848 Thackeray *Bk. Snobs* xi, A shovel-hatted fuzz-wigged Silenus. **1854** —— *J. Leech's Pict.* (1869) 327 There was Rowlandson's..Doctor Syntax in a fuzz-wig. **1893** *Brit. Jrnl. Photogr.* XL. 750 However tolerable a 14 × 12 fuzztype (as they have been jocularly called) may be.

† fuzz, *sb.*[2] *Obs. rare.* [cf. FUZZ *v.*[3]] A fuddled or muddled state.

1711 Swift *Lett.* (1767) III. 155, I think I'm in a fuzz, and don't know what I say.

fuzz (fʌz), *sb.*[3] *slang* (orig. *U.S.*). [Origin uncertain.] A policeman or detective (see also quot. 1931); freq. *collect.*, the police.

1929 E. Booth *Stealing through Life* xii. 301 Don't run, and rank yourself—the fuzz don't know what's doin' yet. **1931** G. Irwin *Amer. Tramp & Underworld Slang* 81 *Fuzz*, a detective; a prison guard or turnkey. Here it is likely that 'fuzz' was originally 'fuss', one hard to please or over-particular. **1938** D. Runyon *Take it Easy* ii. 33 A race-track fuzz catches up with him. **1959** *Observer* 1 Nov. 7/5 'Fuzz broke up two of my poetry readings last night.'.. Fuzz means police. **1961** Wodehouse *Ice in Bedroom* x. 75 The society of coppers, peelers, flatfeet, rozzers and what are known in the newest argot of her native land as 'the fuzz' always affected her with an unpleasant breathlessness. **1964**

E. Ambler *Kind of Anger* iii. 76 If the fuzz get excited we may have to produce her. **1969** *Times* 25 July 5/2 (*heading*) Fuzz sock it to the mean cats. **1971** Wodehouse *Much Obliged, Jeeves* xv. 165 If the fuzz search my room, I'm sunk.

† **fuzz**, *v.*[1] *Obs.* [echoic; cf. *buzz, fizz*.] *intr.* To buzz. Hence **'fuzzing** *vbl. sb.*

1676 T. Mace *Musick's Mon.* II. iv. 57 You may discover the least Crack or Looseness of any Barr, by the shattering or Fuzzing it will make.

fuzz (fʌz), *v.*[2] *slang.* (See quot. 1754; it is doubtful whether the later explanations represent a change of sense or a misunderstanding.)

1753 E. Moore in *World* No 41 ¶7 As to shuffling, fuzzing, changing of seats..he was an absolute ideot. **1754** Chesterf. *Ibid.* No. 101 ¶5, I was also a witness to the rise and progress of that most important verb, to *fuzz*; which, if not of legitimate birth, is at least of fair extraction..it means no less than dealing twice together with the same pack of cards, for luck's sake, at whist. **1755** *Connoisseur* No. 60 ¶3 They can scarce tell what is meant by..fuzzing the cards. **1796** Grose *Dict. Vulg. Tongue* (ed. 3), To *Fuzz*, to shuffle cards minutely; also, to change the pack.

† **fuzz**, *v.*[3] *Obs.*[−1] [Perh. connected with fuzz *sb.*[1], *v.*[4] through the notion of blurring or confusing.] *trans.* To make drunk, fuddle.

1685 Wood *Life* (O.H.S.) III. 152 The University troop dined with the Earl of Abendon at Ricot, and came home well fuz'd.

fuzz (fʌz), *v.*[4] [f. fuzz *sb.*[1]]

1. *intr.* (See quots.) Also *to fuzz out.*

1702 in J. K. *Dict.* **1706** Phillips (ed. Kersey), To *Fuzz*, to ravel or run out, as some sorts of Stuff and Silk do. **1753** Mrs. Delany *Let. to Mrs. Dewes* in *Life & Corr.* (1862) 258 Have you begun the shade for your toilette? If not, I believe you must do it to wash, for the catgut in time grows very limp, and the silk fuses. **1840** Smart, *Fuzz*, to fly out in small particles. **1862** Miss Yonge *C'tess Kate* ix. (1881) 93 A flounced frock of dark silk figured with blue, that looked slightly fuzzed out.

2. *trans.* To cover with fine or minute particles.

1851 S. Judd *Margaret* xvii, The fine grail glancing in her eyes and fuzzing her face.

Hence **'fuzzing** *ppl. a.*

1775 Ash, *Fuzzing*, flying off in small parts, fretting out in small particles.

fuzz-ball ('fʌzbɔːl). Forms: 6–7 fus(se)bal(l, 7, 9 fuss-, 7–9 fuz-, 7– fuzz-ball. [f. fuzz *sb.*[1] + ball.]

A popular name of the fungus *Lycoperdon Bovista*, puff-ball.

1597 Gerarde *Herbal* III. clxii. 1386 Puffes Fistes & Fusse-bals. **1598** R. Bernard tr. *Terence, Adelphi* II. ii, He hath made..my head as soft as a fusball with buffets. **1616** Surfl. & Markh. *Country Farme* 328 With a Fusse-ball, or some sharpe smoake, smoake them to death. **1648** Sanderson *Serm.* II. 245 As soon as touched..[they] like a fuss-ball, resolve all into dust and smoak. **1755** *Gentl. Mag.* XXV. 585 The spungey internal part of the common fuz-ball. **1825** Waterton *Wand. S. Amer.* I. i. 107 Tread on it, and like the fuss-ball it will break into dust. **1863** Mrs. Whitney *F. Gartney's Girlhood* iv. 25 Short, sandy hair standing up about the temples like a fuzz-ball.

transf. and *fig.*

1664 Power *Exp. Philos.* I. 7 The Gray or Horse-Fly. Her legs..slit at the ends into two toes, both which are lined with two white sponges or fuzballs. **1679** Dryden *Troilus* II. iii, You empty fuzz-balls, your heads are full of nothing else but proclamations. **1698** Fryer *Acc. E. India & P.* 291 When they [Hedge Hogs] fear any harm towards them, gather themselves into a round Fuz-ball.

attrib. **1648** Herrick *Hesper., Oberon's Feast* (1869) 126 A little fuz-ball pudding stands By.

fuzze. ? *Obs.* [dial. var. fuse *sb.*[2]] (See quot.)

1802 Mawe *Min. Derbysh.* 204 *Fuzze*, straws, or hollow briars, reeds, &c., filled with powder. *Fuzze-borer*, an iron made red hot to bore a fuzze to hold powder.

fuzzen, obs. f. foison, and dial. f. furze.

fuzzily, fuzziness: see under fuzzy.

† **fuzzle** ('fʌz(ə)l), *v. Obs.* In 7 fusle. [cf. fuzz *v.*[3], fuddle.] *trans.* To intoxicate, make drunk, confuse, muddle.

1621 Burton *Anat. Mel.* I. ii. I. vi, If the spirits of the brain be fusled..at such a time, their children will be fusled in the brain. **1632** Sherwood, To fuzzle, *enyvrer*.

fuzzword ('fʌzwɜːd). orig. and chiefly *U.S.* [f. fuzz(y *a.* + word *sb.*, after *buzzword* s.v. buzz *sb.*[1] 5.] A deliberately confusing or imprecise term; a piece of jargon, used more to impress than to inform.

1983 *Washington Post Mag.* 23 Jan. 14/3 Fuzzifying, the larger field within which fuzzwords operate, is the presentation of data, concepts, programs or goals in what appear to be precise terms while permitting a flexibility of future interpretation. **1983** *Washington Post* 30 Oct. (Book World) 12/2 Stamaty creates a Washington world..where 'perceptual engineers' string together fuzzwords and buzzwords to sell their candidates. **1984** *National Jrnl.* 14 Apr. 730/1 In the often emotional arms control debate, there may be no more common fuzzword than 'verification'.

fuzzy ('fʌzɪ), *a.* [f. fuzz *sb.*[1] + -y[1]. Cf. fozy.]

1. Not firm or sound in substance; spongy. *Obs.* exc. *dial.* (Cf. fozy.)

1616 Surfl. & Markh. *Country Farme* IV. iv. 498 If your ground be subiect to anie filthie soft mosse, or fuzzie grasse, which is both vnsauourie and vnwholesome for beasts. **1664** Power *Exp. Philos.* I. 5 A fuzzy kinde of substance like little sponges. **1725** Kelly in *Phil. Trans.* XXXIV. 122 A fuzzy sort of Earth, that we call Moss. **1728** T. Sheridan *Persius* (1739) 21 As dry and fuzzy as an old Branch spread over with Spungy Cork. **1824** *Craven Gloss.*, *Fuzzy*, light and spungy. **1869** in *Lonsdale Gloss.*

2. Frayed into loose fibres; covered with fuzz; fluffy, downy.

1713 Steele *Englishm.* No. 40. 259 Their Linnen of the same Hue, and so fuzzy that it was not easy to distinguish. **1823** Moor *Suffolk Words* s.v., The fine ends of silk or cotton..when they appear make the article 'wear fuzzy'. **1857** Hughes *Tom Brown* I. v, Those fuzzy, dusty, padded first-class carriages. **1860** *All Year Round* No. 46. 460 Nine pennyworth of muslin with gilt fuzzy ends. **1885** *Century Mag.* XXX. 808 Seen through a magnifying glass, rough or plain paper has a surface..made up of fuzzy elevations and depressions, not unlike that of cotton cloth, but on a smaller scale. **1894** *Times* 9 Feb. 8/3 There are so many fuzzy politicians who have not hearts but only cotton wool in the place of them.

3. Blurred, indistinct.

1778 *Phil. Trans.* LXVIII. 401 Venus appeared very dim and fuzzy. **1832** G. Downes *Lett. Cont. Countries* I. 30 The fuzzy glass. **1871** *Daily News* 20 Dec. 2/4 It makes the picture more 'fuzzy'. **1884** *Gd. Words* Dec. 819/2 His drawing is rougher and fuzzier.

b. Of thought, etc.: imprecisely defined; confused, vague. Also of persons: inexact in thought or expression.

1937 [see blurriness]. **1939** *Canad. Forum* Aug. 166/1 There is also a deplorable display of fuzzy moralizing which is distinctly out of place. **1955** *Time* 5 Dec. 16/2 What an appalling display of fuzzy thinking in some of the world's leading editorial comment! **1958** J. K. Galbraith *Affluent Society* xxiv. 347 Since these achievements are not easily measured, as a goal they are 'fuzzy'..a fatal condemnation. **1968** N. Chomsky in *Listener* 30 May 690/3 It seems to me that empiricists have been a bit fuzzy on this. **1974** A. Lurie *War between Tates* iii. 51 Encouraging each other in escapism and fuzzy thinking; absorbing bogus ideas. **1977** *Time* 19 Sept. 23/1 The line between using a plane legitimately to build good will for a corporation and using it illegally seems fuzzy.

c. *Computing* and *Logic.* (Of a set) defined so as to allow for imprecise membership criteria and for gradations of membership; pertaining or belonging to such a set; ***fuzzy logic***, the logic of fuzzy sets and fuzzy concepts; ***fuzzy matching***, (the facility for) matching items which are similar but not identical.

1964 L. A. Zadeh et al. *Memorandum* (Rand Corporation) RM-4307-PR 1 The notion of a 'fuzzy' set..extends the concept of membership in a set to situations in which there are many, possibly a continuum of, grades of membership. **1969** *IEEE Trans. Computers* XVIII. 348/2 In the digital field, pattern recognitions and classification are..potential users of fuzzy logic. **1973** *Jrnl. Philos. Logic* II. 491 Fuzzy concepts have had a bad press among logicians. **1976** J. H. Conway *Numbers & Games* vii. 79 We say that G and H are confused or that G is fuzzy against H. **1979** Kandel & Lee *Fuzzy Switching & Automata* ii. 46 Definitions, theorems, proofs, etc., of fuzzy set theory always hold for non-fuzzy sets. **1982** *IEEE Internat. Conf. Acoustics, Speech & Signal Processing* II. 1162/1 One of the key problems in Image Understanding is the matching of two symbolic structures, a model and the result of a segmentation...We present..a formalism which can deal with the inexact or fuzzy matching of such structures in a highly parallel fashion. **1985** *Computer Bull.* Mar. 35/1 De Mori's work on acoustic phonetics is based on knowledge representation by the production rules of grammars, and reasoning by parsing, with fuzzy logic introduced at every stage. **1985** *Computer Newslet.* Mar. 2/1 There is a 'fuzzy matching' between what is requested and what is obtained from the system, in that they are only approximately related.

4. Of hair: Frizzy, fluffy.

a **1825** Forby *Voc. E. Anglia*, *Fuzzy*, rough and shaggy. **1856** F. E. Paget *Owlet Owlst.* 171 A..black man, with thick lips and fuzzy hair. **1870** Thornbury *Tour Eng.* II. xxi. 83 Fuzzy red wigs, stuck with jewels.

5. *Comb.*, as ***fuzzy-headed, -legged, -minded*** adjs.; **fuzzy-ball** = fuzz-ball; **fuzzy-wuzzy**, a soldier's nickname for the typical Sudanese warrior, from his method of dressing his hair; hence as a slang term for a coloured native of other countries, such as Fiji and New Guinea.

c **1850** *Denham Tracts* (1895) II. 48 The dust of a *fuzzy ball cast in the eyes will cause blindness. **1885** *Spectator* 8 Aug. 1043/1 They were..*fuzzie-headed. **1833** T. Hook *Widow & Marquess* xii, A couple of *fuzzy-legged hens. **1983** P. Kurth *Anastasia* (1985) III. xii. 366 The world press rediscovered her in the early fifties—'a *fuzzy-minded, ageing woman', as *Time* magazine reported. **1892** R. Kipling *Barrack-r. Ballads* 10 So 'ere's to you, *Fuzzy-Wuzzy, at your 'ome in the Soudan. **1940** N. Mitford *Pigeon Pie* iii. 41 There are Chinks and Japs and Fuzzy Wuzzies and Ice Creamers and Dagos, and so on. *Ibid.* xiii. 208 You brutish Hun... Savage—Kaffir—fuzzy-wuzzy. **1965** *Listener* 30 Dec. 1067/1 England came up against a tough opponent after a series of easy victories against Tibetans, Zulus, and other relatively speaking unarmed fuzzy-wuzzies.

Hence **'fuzzily** *adv.*, **'fuzziness**. Also **'fuzzyism** [-ism], *Photogr.*, the studied production of 'fuzzy' pictures.

1613 Markham *Eng. Husbandman* H ij, A little paire of round wheeles, which..doth so certainly guide the Plough ..that it can neither..drownd through the easie lightnesse of the earth, nor runne too shallow through the fussinesse of the mould. **1866** *Athenæum* No. 2042. 801/1 A certain 'fuzziness', as artists say, appears in many examples. **1867** Miss Broughton *Not Wisely* (1869) 10 They [locks of hair] ..thence went off crisply, fuzzily, in a most unaffected wave. **1874** M. Collins *Transmigr.* II. xiv. 221 Her hair was a bunch of fuzziness. **1886** *Century Mag.* XXXI. 477 Tomentose appearance of stem or fuzziness of stem. **1894** *Brit. Jrnl. Photogr.* XLI. Supp. 5 A prelude to a descent into Fuzzyism. **1973** *Jrnl. Philos. Logic* II. 468 We have been employing a many-valued logic in an attempt to provide an initial explication of fuzziness in natural language. **1983** *Nature* 15 Dec. 637/2 Such a way of tackling the problem of AI seems to have inspired the now fashionable concern with what is called fuzziness, the attempt to build imprecision into programs.

fuzzy ('fʌzɪ), *sb. slang.* = *fuzzy-wuzzy* (fuzzy *a.* 5).

1890 Kipling *Barrack-r. Ballads* (1892) 10 The Fuzzy was the finest o' the lot. **1923** —— *Land & Sea T.* 11 A wounded Sudanese—what our soldiers used to call a 'fuzzy'. **1926** R. Macaulay *Crewe Train* II. iii, Those infernal fuzzies of yours have upset the lamas.

fwde, obs. Sc. form of food.

† **fy**, *v. Obs.* [aphetic form of defy *v.*[2]] *trans.* To digest.

13.. *Knowe þi self* 65 in E.E.P. (1862) 131 Þi flesche foode þe wormes wol fye. *c* **1440** *Promp. Parv.* 159/2 Fyin, or defyin mete and drynke..*digero*.

fy, obs. form of fie.

fy-: see also fi-.

-fy (faɪ), *suffix*, forming *verbs*. The older Eng. vbs. in *-fy* are adoptions of Fr. vbs in *-fier*, which are either adapted from Lat. vbs. in *-ficāre* or formed on the analogy of vbs. so originating. (The form *-fier* was used as the representative of L. *-ficāre* on the analogy of words like *saintefier*:—*sanctificāre*.) The Lat. vbs. in *-ficāre* were originally derivatives of adjs. in *-fic-us* (see -fic), though subsequently the suffix could be used to form vbs. without the intervention of an adj. They may be divided into three classes (corresponding to three classes of adjectives in *-ficus*: see -fic), all of which are represented by adapted words in Eng.: (1) vbs. f. sbs., with the sense 'to make, produce', as *pācificāre* (orig. *intr.* to make peace) pacify, *ædificāre* edify, or 'to make or convert into something', as *deificāre* deify; (2) f. adjs., with the sense 'to bring into a certain state', as *santificāre* sanctify; (3) f. vb.-stems, with causative sense, as *horrificāre* horrify. In med.L. there was a tendency to substitute *-ficāre* for *-facĕre* in the few Lat. vbs. so ending, and hence Fr. and Eng. vbs. in *-fier*, *-fy* sometimes correspond to Lat. vbs. in *-facĕre*; e.g. F. *stupéfier* (but in pa. pple. *stupéfait* as well as *stupéfié*) stupefy, OF. *satisfier* (but mod.F. *satisfaire*) satisfy, F. *liquéfier* liquefy, F. *rubéfier* rubefy, med.L. *caleficare* calefy. Exc. in the case of these few vbs. the ending has normally the form *-ify* (for the reason see -fic). It is now used as the regular rendering of *-ficāre* in new words adopted from Lat. or formed on assumable Lat. types, and is also freely added to Eng. adjs. and sbs. to form vbs., mostly somewhat jocular or trivial, with the senses: 'to make a specified thing', as *speechify*; 'to assimilate to the character of something' (chiefly in pa. pple., as *countrified*); 'to invest with certain attributes', as *Frenchify*. (A large proportion of these vbs are from sbs. and adjs. ending in *-y* or *-ey*, the suffix then having the form *-fy* instead of the usual *-ify*. An early example is *beautify*, but the analogy on which this word was formed is not clear.) In a few cases the suffix has been quite irregularly added to vb. stems, but the words are either obsolete, as *dedify*, *hindrify*, *ornify*, or merely jocular or illiterate, as *argufy*. The noun of action related to vbs. in *-ify* normally ends in *-ification*, though, by confusion of suffix, *petrifaction* is used in Eng. where Fr. has more correctly *pétrification*. The words in which *-fy* represents L. *-facĕre* having their corresponding nouns of action ending in *-faction*.

The following examples illustrate the freedom with which this suffix has been used in the formation of nonce-words.

1602 Dekker *Satiromastix* L iv a, Nay by Sesu you shall bee a Poet, though not Lawrefyed, yet Nettlefyed so. **1647** Trapp *Comm. Ephes.* iv. 15 But speaking the truth..Doing the truth..Truthifying. **1775** S. J. Pratt *Liberal Opin.* (1783) II. 260 Not that I would have you suppose I am bigotted to frippery, even though you now see me so apefied. **1790** A. Seward *Lett.* (1811) II. 381 Though fashion has now bullified us all. **1834** Southey *Doctor* II. Inter-ch. vi. 119 Either of these misfortunes would have emasculated his mind, unipsefying and unegofying the *Ipsissimus Ego*. **1844** Haliburton *Sam Slick in Eng.* I. viii. 135 He might have knowed how to feel for other folks, and not funkify them so peskily. **1872** [Earl Pembroke & G. H. Kingsley] *S. Sea Bubbles* viii. 206 The boom of the pigeon is wondrous pleasant and drowsyfying.

fyall, var. filiole[1], *Obs.*

fyar, obs. form of FIRE.

fyble, -bull, obs. forms of FEEBLE.

fych(e, obs. form of FISH, FITCH *sb.*[2]

fyciscien, obs. form of PHYSICIAN.

fye, obs. form of FAY *v.*[1], FIE.

fyell, var. FILIOLE[1], *Obs.*

fyen, -ene, obs. forms of FAY *v.*[2], FAIN.

fyers(e, fyest, obs. ff. FIERCE, FIST *sb.*[2]

'fying, *vbl. sb.* [f. FIE *v.* + -ING[1].] The action of saying FIE!

1662 *Rump Songs* (1874) II. 63 Which put pretty Maids to pishing and fying.

fyke (faɪk), *sb. U.S.* Also **fike**. [a. Du. *fuik.*] **a.** A bag-net used for catching fish, esp. shad.

1832 in T. F. De Voe *Market Assistant* (1867) 197 They discovered a sea-dog stealing bass from a fuik of a bass-net. **1860** BARTLETT *Dict. Amer.*, Fyke..the large bow-nets in New York harbor, used for catching shad, are called shad-fykes. **1871** *Game Laws N.Y.* in *Fur, Fin & Feather* (1872) 28 It shall not be lawful for any person to take eels in fikes or pots. **1942** C. WEYGANDT *Plenty of Pennsylvania* 45 They set fykes for the up-stream run of suckers in March.

b. *Comb.*, as ***fyke-net***; also **fyke-fisherman**, one who fishes with a fyke (*Cent. Dict.*).

1842 *Nat. Hist. N.Y., Zool.* I. 54 Mr. Everson..has taken them..in the fyke-nets. **1891** W. K. BROOKS *Oyster* 181 The shores..are now so lined by fyke nets..that the number of shad which reach the spawning grounds at all is proportionally much less than it was in 1880.

fyld(e, fylet(te, obs. forms of FIELD, FILLET.

fylfot ('fɪlfɒt). [The sole authority on which this word has been accepted by modern antiquaries as the name of the mark in question is the passage from the Lansdowne MS. quoted below. The context in which the word there occurs seems to favour the supposition that it is simply *fill-foot*, meaning a pattern or device for 'filling the foot' of a painted window. There is nothing to show whether the word denoted specifically this device as distinguished from others used for the same purpose, and it is even possible that it may have been a mere nonce-word.] A name for the figure called also a cross cramponnee (see CRAMPONNEE), and identical with the SWASTIKA of India, the *gammadion* of Byzantine ecclesiastical ornament; it has been extensively used as a decoration (often, apparently, as a mystical symbol) in almost all known parts of the world from prehistoric times to the present day. Also ***fylfot cross.***

a **1500** *Instruct. Memorial Wind.* in *MS. Lansdowne* 874 lf. 190 Let me stand in the medyll pane..a rolle abo[ve my hede] in the hyest..[pane] vpward, the fylfot in the nedermast pane vnder ther I knele. [The words defaced or torn off are supplied conjecturally. In the sketch, below the effigy of the writer, is a 'fylfot' composed of broad fillets, with tricking app. intended for 'ermine'.] **1842** J. G. WALLER *Brasses*, Priest & Franklin, This device is denominated ' the fylfot' on the authority of some ancient directions for the execution of two figures in painted glass.. preserved in Lansdowne MS. 874. **1852** PLANCHÉ *Pursuiv. Arms* 135 The Fylfot is a mystic figure, called in the Greek Church, Gammadion. It is very early seen in Heraldry. **1861** HAINES *Mon. Brasses* p. cix, The Fylfot, a kind of cross potent rebated, or cross cramponeé. **1868** BARING-GOULD *Curious Myths* Ser. II. iii. 89 Bells were often marked with the 'fylfot', or cross of Thorr. **1887** *Athenæum* 20 Aug. 249/2 It comprises a fylfot cross set with studs.

fym(e)rel, -elle, obs. forms of FEMERELL.

fymterre, obs. form of FUMITORY.

fynd(e, fyne, obs. ff. FIEND, FIND *v.*, FAIN.

fynerall, obs. form of FUNERAL.

fynt, obs. form of FIEND.

fyrble, obs. form of FIMBLE *sb.*[1]

fyrd (fɜːd, fɪəd). *Hist.* [OE. *fyrd*: see FERD.] The military array of the whole country before the Conquest; also, the obligation to military service.

1832 J. BREE *St. Herbert's Isle* 99 'The..fyrd!' cried Edwal, 'raise the fyrd.' **1839** KEIGHTLEY *Hist. Eng.* I. 83 A threefold obligation lay on all the holders of land in the Kingdom. This consisted of the Bricgbote, Burhbote, and Fyrd. **1861** FREEMAN *Norm. Conq.* (1876) IV. xviii. 147 When the king summoned his fyrd to his standard. **1895** MEIKLEJOHN *Hist. Eng.* I. 105 In 1181 a regulation called the Assize of Arms was issued for the Fyrd or National Militia.

fyre, obs. form of FIR, FIRE.

fyrette, obs. form of FERRET *sb.*[1]

fyrmentie, -mete: see FRUMENTY, FIRMITY[2].

fyrrys, fyrs, obs. forms of FURZE.

fyrst, var. FRIST, and obs. form of FIRST.

fyry, -ie, -e, obs. forms of FIERY.

fysegge, fysel(l, obs. ff. VISAGE, FIZZLE *v.*[1]

fysnomye, obs. form of PHYSIOGNOMY.

fysoun, fysyke, obs. ff. FOISON, PHYSIC.

fytch, obs. form of FITCH *sb.*[1] = VETCH.

fythal, -el(e, -il, -ylle, obs. ff. FIDDLE.

fytlo(c)k, obs. form of FETLOCK.

fyton, var. FITTEN, *Obs.*, untruth.

fytte: see FIT *sb.*[1] *Obs.*

fyver(e, obs. form of FEVER.

fyxyll, var. THIXEL, *Obs.*, pole of a wagon.

1411 *Nottingham Rec.* II. 86, j. fyxyll ij*d.*

fyz, obs. form of FITZ.

G

G (dʒiː), the seventh letter of the Roman alphabet, was originally a differentiated form of C; for its early history see that letter. In Latin G represented the voiced guttural stop; but in the later period of the language it must have been pronounced before front vowels as a palatal, its representation in the Rom. langs. being precisely the same as that of Lat. I consonant (J); hence in OF. G before *e*, *i* was pronounced like J, viz. as the assibilated (dʒ).

In OE. the letter stood for four different sounds, viz. the voiced guttural and palatal stop (in this Dictionary represented by g, *g*), and the voiced guttural and palatal spirant (here printed ᵹ, *ᵹ*). The precise distribution of these sounds is much disputed, but if we confine our view to the very end of the OE. period the following statements may be made. Initial G before back vowels was a guttural stop (g), developed from an earlier spirant. Initial G before front vowels was a palatal spirant (j). Medially and finally, G represented a guttural or a palatal, according to the nature of the associated sounds; in the combinations *ng* and *gg* (written *cg* when palatal, rarely when guttural) it was a stop, and in other positions a spirant. In early ME., or perh. in late OE., the palatal stop developed into the complex sound (dʒ), thus coinciding with the power of G before *e*, *i*, in contemporary French.

In early ME. the continental form of G (approximately 𝔤) was used for the two sounds which the letter had in French, (g) and (dʒ), while the OE. form ᵹ was used for the sounds peculiar to native words, viz. the guttural and palatal spirants (ɣ, j). Ormin attempted to differentiate the symbol 𝔤 into two, 𝔤 = (dʒ), and ꝩ = (g); but his example was not followed. The symbol ᵹ gradually came to assume a form indistinguishable from that used for Z in contemporary MSS.; in this Dictionary the form ȝ is employed for ME. words. This symbol was commonly used in ME. for the sound of (j) initial and final, for the guttural and palatal unvoiced spirant final or before *t* (as in *inouȝ*, *auȝt*, *niȝt*, OE. *ᵹenóh*, *áht*, *niht*), and, so long as the sound remained in the language, for the guttural voiced spirant. From the 13th c., however, the ȝ was by some scribes wholly or partially discarded for *y* or *gh*; a few texts have *yh*. In the 15th c. vocabularies the words beginning with ȝ are at the end of the alphabet. Caxton uses the symbol sparingly, chiefly before final *t*. The English printers of the 16th c. scarcely use it at all; but in Scotland it survived longer, and has left a trace in the use of *z* for *y* in the spelling of surnames like *Menzies* and *Dalziel*, and of such words as *capercailzie*, *gaberlunzie*.

In modern English G has the so-called 'hard' sound (g) at the end of a word, before a consonant or *a*, *o*, *u*, (exc. in *gaol*, *gaoler*), and in words of Teutonic etymology before *e* and *i*, as in *give*, *get*; also in Hebrew proper names, as *Gedaliah*, *Gideon*. In words from Lat. or Romanic it has the 'soft' sound (dʒ) before *e*, *i*, *y*; and at the end of a syllable, in words of whatever origin, the sound (dʒ) is represented always by *dge* or *ge*, the letter J not being used in this position. The combination *gn* is sounded *n* initially or at the end of a syllable. When the combination *ng* occurs in one syllable, the *g* is now silent, serving only to give to the *n* the value of (ŋ). With regard to the pronunciation of *ng* in the middle of a disyllable, modern usage is somewhat inconsistent: in the inflexions and derivatives of verbs the *g* is silent, as in *singer*, *singeth*, *singing* ('sɪŋə(r), 'sɪŋɪθ, 'sɪŋɪŋ), but is sounded in the comparatives and superlatives of adjs., as in *younger*, *longer* ('jʌŋgə(r), 'lɒŋgə(r)), and the other words generally, as *finger* ('fɪŋgə(r)).

The combination *gh* is in a few words (*aghast*, *ghastly*, *ghost*) a mere capricious substitute for *g* (cf. Caxton's frequent *ghoos*, *ghoot*, *gherle* = goose, goat, girl). Elsewhere it chiefly represents the older guttural or palatal spirant (OE. ᵹ or *h*), which in modern pronunciation is either dropped, as in *high*, *night*, *through*, *plough*, or replaced by (f), as in *laugh*, *rough*, *tough*; a special development has taken place in *hough* (hɒk).

II. Used as a symbol, with reference to its place (7th) in the alphabet

1. G. g, *g* is used to denote anything occupying the seventh place in a series. (Cf. A, B, C, etc.)

2. In *Music* G is the name of the 5th note of the diatonic scale of C major; called G in Germany, *sol* in France and Italy. Also the scale or key which has that note for its tonic. *G clef*: the treble clef (see CLEF[1]) placed on the line in the stave appropriated to the note G.

1596 *Pathw. to Mus.* A iv b, Note also that what is vnder G *sol re vt*, the same is vnder *Gamma-vt*, and what is aboue E *la mi*, the same is aboue ee *la*. **1609** DOULAND *Ornithop. Microl.* 7 Keyes .. are 22 in number. The first is of Capitall Letters .. viz. Γ. A. B. C. D. E. F. G. **1806** CALLCOTT *Mus. Gram.* iii. 6 The G Clef is a compound character of the letters G and S, for the Syllable, Sol. **1881** *Scribner's Mag.* XXI. 75/2 [He] burst forth with a high *G* of astounding volume. **1891** S. MOSTYN *Curatica* 106 The curate .. after waiting in vain for his G [note on the organ], was obliged at last to start without it.

III. Abbreviations.

a. G. = various proper names, as George, Gertrude. **b.** In *Physics g* (or *G*) is the symbol for the acceleration due to gravity = about 9·8 m. (32 ft.) per second per second at sea level; also used to denote gravity generally, or the associated forces. Also *attrib.*, as ***g-force***, ***-stress***; G-SUIT. **c.** *Math.* G.C.F. or G.C.M. = Greatest Common Factor or Measure. **d.** *Comm.* G.M.B.: see quot. **e.** In the order of Freemasons, G.M. = Grand Master.

1785 T. PARKINSON *Syst. Mech.* xiv. 244 If *G* be the force of gravity, the axis and all diameters of the parabola, are perpendicular to the horizon. **1806** G. GREGORY *Dict. Arts & Sci.* I. 870/2 M. Krafft gives a formula for the proportion of gravity in different latitudes on the earth's surface, which is this: $y = (1 + 0.0052848 \text{ sine}^2 \lambda)g$; where *g* denotes the gravity at the equator, and *y* the gravity under any other latitude λ. **1825** *Phil. Mag.* LXVI. 110, *l* denotes the height of the homogeneous atmosphere in feet, and *g* the gravitating force. **1869** *Ibid.* 4th Ser. XXXVIII. 83, M is the mass of a unit volume of a fluid, and *g* the accelerating force of gravity. **1884** *Pall Mall G.* 21 Feb. 5/2 'G.M.B.' means a good merchantable brand of iron; but a small proportion .. which is neither good nor merchantable, has been deposited in the stores as 'G.M.B.' **1928** N. MACMILLAN *Art of Flying* x. 138 Sustained high manœuvre loadings .. are referred to for brevity as 1G, 2G, or 6G. The question of G affects the pilot as well as the aeroplane. **1931** *Jrnl. R. Aeronaut. Soc.* XXXV. 1042 A figure of 3 or 4g is common in fast turns and in loops. **1938** *Lancet* 31 Dec. 1508/1 This was seen especially during looping, the maximal *g* stress occurring at the point of pulling up from the dive. **1945** [see ANTI-G *a.*]. **1959** *Daily Tel.* 23 Feb. 11/7 Protective clothing, or 'space suits' will be needed to help guard a man against the heavy G forces imposed on him because of the great thrust upwards that a space vehicle will develop. **1959** KAYE & LABY *Tables of Physical & Chem. Constants* (ed. 12) 9 A standard value for the gravitational acceleration *g* at the Earth's surface is necessary for fixing the values of certain derived units and standards in the C.G.S. and M.K.S. systems.

f. Miscellaneous abbreviations. (Abbreviations given here with the full stop are frequently found without it.) **G**, general: denoting films which are classified as suitable for viewing by audiences of any age-group (*U.S.* and *Austral. Cinemat.*); cf. U 4 a; **G** = GIGA-; **G.** = GRAND *sb.* 8 (*U.S. slang*); **G**, group: **G5** (*U.S.* **G-5**), Group of Five; **G10** (*U.S.* **G-10**), Group of Ten (see GROUP *sb.* 3 g); **𝔤**, the 'general factor' of intelligence (see quots.); **𝔤**, Ger. *gerade*, 'even', used in *Physics* in the designation of functions (especially wave-functions) which do not change sign on inversion through the origin, and of atomic states, etc., represented by such functions; **𝔤.**, gram(me); **G-agent**, a type of nerve-gas (orig. *U.S.*); **G.A.W.**, guaranteed annual wage (*U.S.*); **G.B.**, **𝔤.b.**, grand bounce, *i.e.* dismissal, ejection (*U.S. colloq.*, *obs.*); **G.B.**, Great Britain (esp. as a sign carried on a motor vehicle to indicate that it is registered in Britain); **G.B.E.**, Grand Cross of the British Empire; **G.B.H.**, grievous bodily harm; **G.B.P.**, **𝔤.b.p.**, great British public; **G.C.**, George Cross; **G.C.E.**, General Certificate of Education; **GCSE**, General Certificate of Secondary Education; **G.C.I.**, ground-control(led) interception; **G.C.I.E.**, Grand Commander of the Indian Empire; **G.C.M.G.**, Grand Commander of St. Michael and St. George; **G.D.P.**, gross domestic product; **G.D.R.**, German Democratic Republic; **GeV** [f. G(IGA- + *electron volt*], a thousand million (10^9) electron volts; **G.F.S.**, Girls' Friendly Society; **G.H.**, growth hormone; **G.H.Q.**, general headquarters; **G.L.C.**, Greater London Council; **G.M.**, **𝔤.m.** [shortening of G.M.T.], humorous substitute for *a.m.* or *p.m.*; **G.M.T.**, Greenwich mean time; **G.N.P.**, gross national product; **G.O.C.**, General Officer Commanding; **G.O.M.**, Grand Old Man, a name given to W. E. Gladstone; also *transf.*; **G.O.P.**, (see GRAND OLD PARTY 2); **G.P.**, general practitioner; **G.P.**, grand(e) passion; **G.P.I.**, **𝔤.p.i.**, general paralysis of the insane; **G-plan** [f. the initial letter of the manufacturer's name + PLAN *sb.*], the proprietary trademark of a type of furniture manufactured by Messrs. E. Gomme, Ltd.; **G.P.O.**, General Post Office; **G.P.U.** = OGPU; **G.S.**, general service; **G.S.R.** = *galvanic skin response* or *reflex*; **G.T.**, *gran turismo*; **G.T.T.** (orig. **G.T.**), gone to Texas; absconded (*U.S.*); **GUT** (gʌt) *Physics* = ***grand unified theory*** s.v. GRAND *a.* 12; **G.V.** (*slang*), governor; **G.W.(R.)**, Great Western (Railway). See also G.A.T.T., G.I., G-MAN, G STRING.

1915 E. WEBB in *Brit. Jrnl. Psychol.* Monogr. Suppl. III. iv. 38 The marks for these tests together with the above coefficients of their 'saturation' by the general factor (**g*) ought to furnish a measure of '*g*' itself. **1927** C. SPEARMAN *Abilities of Man* vi. 75 The 'general factor' .. denoted by the letter *g* .. is so named because, although varying freely from individual to individual, it remains the same for any one individual in respect of all the correlated abilities. **1966** *N.Y. Times* 8 Oct. 49/1 The rating system, which goes into effect on films released after Nov. 1, will classify movies in four categories: *G—acceptable for general audiences. **1974** [see PG s.v. P II]. **1985** *Washington Post* 7 May A14/2 On-campus movies are censored to the equivalent of a G rating. **1930** R. S. MULLIKEN in *Physical Rev.* 2nd Ser. XXXVI. 617 The subscripts **g* (German *gerade*) for even terms and *u* (German *ungerade*) for odd terms are recommended. **1962** R. E. DODD *Chem. Spectroscopy* iv. 220 In homo-nuclear diatomic molecules there is also a prohibition against g-g or u-u transitions. **1885** A. MACFARLANE *Physical Arithmetic* iv. 142 The authorized abbreviation for gramme is **g.*, but it is customary with English writers to use *gm.*, in order to distinguish between gramme and grain. **1902** *Encycl. Brit.* XXXIII. 808/2, 1 gramme (g.) = 15.4323564 grains or 0.7716 scruple. **1928** J. O'CONNOR *Broadway Racketeers* xvii. 182 They had me in the bag for nearly ten *G's before I pulled the string and let the joint go blooey. **1937** D. RUNYON *More than Somewhat* ii. 35, I am going to stake them to a few G's. **1971** A. CURRY *Shack-up* vi. 86 He'd probably drop me a few G's for the names of the guys in London. **1977** *N.Y. Times* 8 May III. 14/1 Without *G-5 there would have been no economic summit today in London. **1985** *Economist* 26 Jan. 68/2 Finance ministers from America, Japan, Britain, West Germany and France —the so-called G5 countries—had hoped that .. they could halt or reverse the rise of the dollar. **1986** *Times* 20 Jan. 21/1 In the past G5 has gone to some pains to hide its meetings from public view... The G5 then blew its own cover. **1980** *Amer. Banker* 30 Sept. 9/2 Earlier this year, the central bank Governors of the *G10 countries and Switzerland agreed to improve the methods of assessment of country risk exposure. **1986** *Times* 4 Mar. 17/5 The Group of Ten industrialized countries are to meet on March 13- 14. The G10 'deputies' meet partly to prepare the ground for the meeting of the interim committee of the International Monetary Fund. **1956** *Rep. Properties War Gases* (*Edgewood Arsenal, Md.*) I (*title*) *G-agents. **1968** *New Scientist* 29 Feb. 465/1 The G-agents (nerve gases) .. are quick killers. **1955** *Times* 7 June 7/2 The 'guaranteed annual wage'—*G.A.W.—has for long been a major objective in the programmes of the American trade union movement. **1880** *News & Press* (Cimarron, N.M.) 23 Dec. 1/7 Well, I've got the *g.b... I've been fired! **1917** G. B. MCCUTCHEON *Green Fancy* 157 Guess I'm going to get the G.B. 'fore long. **1920** *Michelin Guide to Great Britain* (ed. 5) 807 To be carried in addition to the ordinary *GB plaque. **1926** *Automobile Assoc. Handbk.* iv. 157 An oval nationality plate bearing the letters G.B. .. must be carried at the rear of every car or motor cycle of British registration. **1937** M. SHARP *Nutmeg Tree* xii. 144 There were four cars standing outside, but only one with a G.B. plate. **1968–9** *A.A. Continental Handbk.* 29 A plate (GB for Great Britain) .. must be fixed .. next to the rear registration plate... GB. plates cost 2*s.* 6*d.* **1918** *Whitaker's Alm.* 143 *G.B.E., Knights Grand Cross or Dames Grand Cross [of the British Empire]. **1958** F. NORMAN *Bang to Rights* III. 166 Bottles was doing a lagging *G.B.H.! (Grievious Bodily Harm). **1966** L. SOUTHWORTH *Felon in Disguise* ii. 40 He did have a couple of arrests. One for malicious damage and the other for G.B.H. **1925** G. FRANKAU *Life—and Erica* xv. 189 It's no good making the *G.B.P. laugh *at* you. **1928** *Punch* 8 Feb. 150/3 The g.b.p. does like a wedding. **1941** H. G. WELLS *You can't be too Careful* 5 'You got the *G.C.,' said young Jewler. 'We're all proud of you.' **1951** *Times Educ. Suppl.* 27 July 597/4 The travel agency that can offer visitors to the Channel Islands duty-free scent and tobacco and also a *G.C.E. **1966** *Rep. Comm. Inquiry Univ. Oxf.* I. 64 The results of GCE examinations. **1945** *Electronic Engin.* XVII. 683 With the Battle of Britain by night must be associated .. the use of *G.C.I. or Ground Control Interception. **1947** CROWTHER & WHIDDINGTON *Science at War* Pl. vi (*caption*), The guiding of fighter aircraft to the enemy in the air by G.C.I. (Ground Controlled Interception). **1889** *Whitaker's Alm.* 108 The Most Eminent Order of the Indian Empire .. Knights Grand Commdrs. *G.C.I.E. **1871** *Ibid.* 70 Lord Lisgar, *G.C.M.G. **1978** *Daily Tel.* 24 Oct. 8/3 Children now aged nine are likely to be the first to take the new examination—provisionally to be called the General Certificate of Secondary Education (*GCSE). **1985** *Guardian* 10 Apr. 1/7 A boycott of development work for the new 16-plus General Certificate of Secondary Education (GCSE) will be announced today. **1962** *Economist* 20 Oct. 284/1 Investment might have had to .. constitute 24 per cent of *GDP by 1966. **1958** *Listener* 18 Dec. 1026/2 Herr Grotewohl ended by saying that the *G.D.R.'s main task was to demonstrate the 'superiority' of the socialist system. **1971** *Guardian* 8 Sept. 10/6 At least 100,000 dachas are now estimated to exist in the GDR. **1952** *Proc. Physical Soc.* B. LXV. 307 It was recommended that the use of the word 'billion' should be avoided in scientific literature. The use was recommended, for example, of either 10^9ev or *GEV (as agreed by IUPAP in 1948). **1954** *Nature* 12 June 1127/2 The bevatron has produced protons of energy 5 GeV. **1969** *Times* 5 Feb. 13/8 The new generation of even larger proton accelerators, like the proposed 300 GeV machine at Cern, will produce particles of sufficient energy to make it possible to observe some of the really short-lived resonances. **1888** C. M. YONGE *Our New Mistress* xvii. 161 She wanted me to help her in..her *G.F.S. Bible class. **1939** A. THIRKELL *Brandons* x. 264 She had been brought up..on mothers' meetings, G.F.S. meetings..and the hundred activities of the Vicarage. **1952** *Metabolism* July 356 The growth hormone used was Lot No. *GH-3. **1961** *Lancet* 29 July 235/2 The diabetogenic effect of G.H. in laboratory animals is..well established. **1856** F. NIGHTINGALE in C. Woodham-Smith *F. Nightingale* (1950) xii. 275 *G.H.Q. feeding their horses on the biscuits the men could not eat. **1914** *Isle of Man Weekly Times* 21 Nov. 7/4, I have been moved higher up, my address now being 'Adv. G.H.Q.' **1935** WODEHOUSE *Blandings Castle* ii. 37 The housekeeper's room at Blandings Castle, G.H.Q. of the domestic staff. **1962** *Times* 23 Nov. 5/2 The inner London education authority will consist of members of the *G.L.C. **1901** 'LINESMAN' *Words by Eyewitness* (1902) 246 Merely referring to it as such and such an hour *G.M. **1929** S. LEWIS *Dodsworth* xxxii, I bet I never went to bed before three g.m. once, the whole way over! **1928** W. M. SMART *Sun, Stars & Universe* iv. 49 The true Greenwich Mean Time (*G.M.T.). **1961** *Listener* 26 Oct. 657/1 The limited size of a British market with a *G.N.P. of some £25 billion. **1969** *Guardian* 25 July 10/4 The Apollo project..uses only 1 per cent of the American GNP. **1883** *Army Regulations* II. 45 Office of *G.O.C. Camp, Colchester. **1968** *Listener* 8 Feb. 167/1 There was a massive press conference held by the British GOC, General Keightley. **1884** *Punch* 23 Feb. 95/2 *G.O.M. been looking worn and irritable since Session opened. **1903** A. H. BEAVAN *Tube, Train*, etc. i. 2 This is by no means the oldest steam-engine at work in the kingdom, the doyen being one built as far back as 1767... It is said that this G.O.M. is more economical than many of the modern engines. **1944** *Gramophone* July 27/1 (*heading*) Coward of Sheffield England's G.O.M. of music. **1968** *Listener* 5 Sept. 316/3 The stonemason's son..who was eventually elevated to the position of GOM of letters. **1887** *Graphic* 30 Apr. 447/2 The ordinary general practitioner—the '*G.P.', as he is familiarly called. **1942** R. A. KNOX *In Soft Garments* viii. 60 Some ass of a French G.P. didn't know his own business. **1960** *Times* 17 Mar. 13/6 Rural G.P.'s evidently like the prospect more than others. **1935** D. L. SAYERS *Gaudy Night* ii. 30 She wormed round rather. Had a sort of *G.P. for Miss Shaw. **1922** JOYCE *Ulysses* 8 That fellow..says you have *g.p.i...General paralysis of the insane. **1930** *Daily Express* 8 Sept. 1/1 Pathological experiments..have enabled 'G.P.I.' to be diagnosed in its incipient stages. **1969** KING & NICOL *Venereal Dis.* (ed. 2) v. 62 The clinical manifestations of GPI do not usually appear until 10 years or more after infection. **1957** *Times* 4 Nov. 13/2 Some of the mass-production *G-plan designs are good, but have a sameness. **1967** E. WYMARK *As Good as Gold* ii. 33 The flat was strictly modern inside. The hall tended to G-plan. **1869** *All Year Round* 23 Jan. 180/1 The hard-worked servant of the *G.P.O. who handed in the 'comic' missive. **1955** *Times* 7 May 9/6 Could the G.P.O. be persuaded to undertake an operational research into the use of Post Offices? **1925** G. POPOFF *Tcheka* 238 The third period of the Tcheka dates from February 6, 1922. On this date the Tcheka was 'dissolved'; the '*G.P.U.', however, was immediately set up in its place. **1941** KOESTLER *Scum of Earth* 122 The dark silhouette of the..G.P.U. agent had replaced the..symbols of the struggle for a happier world. **1918** F. M. FORD *Let.* 13 Jan. (1965) 86 The doctors won't pass me *G.S., confound them. **1954** J. MASTERS *Bhowani Junction* vii. 62 She got on the push bike. It was a heavy ugly thing..what the Army calls a G.S. bicycle. **1927** *Jrnl. Exper. Psychol.* X. 206 The mucous surfaces manifest no electrical charges corresponding to the *G.S.R. **1964** *Philos. Rev.* LXXIII. 204 He exhibits no change in GSR, perspiration, and so forth. **1966** *Publ. Amer. Dial. Soc. 1964* XLII. 5 *Gran turismo* .. Also *GT. **1968** W. GARNER *Deep, Deep Freeze* xx. 192 He saw the red Ferrari 330 GT coupé in his rear mirror. **1839** *Daily Eastern Argus* (Portland, Maine) 17 May 2/2 *G.T.—This is said to be a common mode of making Sheriff's returns in the South West. It means, ' Gone to Texas'. **1839** *Georgia Messenger* (Macon, Ga.) 1 Aug. 2/6 G.T.T.—General Nathaniel Smith..has fled to Texas, with from $70,000 to $100,000 of Uncle Sam's money in his pocket. **1884** (*title*) G.T.T. Gone to Texas. Letters from our boys, ed. by Thomas Hughes. **1949** *Sat. Even. Post* 4 June 30/2 That famous old initialed forwarding address: 'G.T.T.' **1979**, **1983** *GUT [see UNIFIED *ppl. a.* 2]. **1984** *Nature* 11 Oct. 508/1 Many GUTs exist, and some have a property of profound cosmological importance. **1905** H. G. WELLS *Kipps* v. 106 'I suppose the G.V.—' began Kipps. 'He knows,' said the housekeeper. **1879** C. L. DODGSON *Let.* 24 Oct. in S. D. Collingwood *Life & Lett. L. Carroll* (1898) xi. 413 The young lady, who was travelling on the G.W. Railway. **1889** E. DOWSON *Let.* 18 Oct. (1967) 109, I bought it at Truro coming up the G.W.R. **1934** *Discovery* Nov. 314/2 Many expresses on the L.M.S. and G.W.R. now load up to 500 tons or over. **1970** R. B. WILSON (*title*) Go Great Western. A history of GWR publicity.

Ga (gɑː). Pl. **Ga, Gas.** [Native name.] The name of a Negro people of Ghana and their language. Also *attrib.* or as *adj.*

1858 J. ZIMMERMAN (*title*) A grammatical sketch of the Akra—or Gā—language. **1879** *Encycl. Brit.* X. 756/1 The south-eastern corner of the Gold Coast is occupied by another language known as the Ga or Acra, which comprises the Ga proper and the Adangme and Crobo dialects. **1884** *Ibid.* XVII. 318/1 *Ewe Group*: Acra (Ga), Fantee, [etc.]. **1955** P. STREVENS *Papers in Lang.* (1965) ix. 114 The languages spoken in this area are almost entirely confined to members of the Kwa Larger Unit, comprising such languages as Twi, Ga, Fante, [etc.]. **1962** [see ASHANTI]. **1963** *Listener* 7 Feb. 231/2 African languages are being studied as the modern languages of Europe are studied in European universities. A Ga student learns Akan. **1969** *Times* 22 Oct. (Ghana Suppl.) p. i/3 Not one Ewe among them, and only one Ga, the Minister for Housing. *Ibid.* p. ii/2 The Ga carved out a kingdom for themselves.

ga, obs. and north. form of GO *v.*

ga, obs. form of *gave*: see GIVE.

gab (gæb), *sb.*[1] Also 3–4 **gabbe.** [a. OF. *gab* (also *gap*; inflected *ga-s*) masc., *gabe* fem., mockery, derision; cf. It. *gabbo* jest, and ON. *gabb* neut., mockery. See GAB *v.*[1]]

†**1.** Mockery, derisive deception; a lie, deceit. ***without gab*** [OF. *sanz gas*]: without deception, of a surety. *Obs.*

a **1300** *Floriz & Bl.* 489 For ihc wene bithute gabbe þat þe Admiral me wule habbe. *a* **1310** in Wright *Lyric P.* xv. 49 Syker hit siweth me ful sore, Gabbes les ant luthere lore, sunnes bueth un-sete. *c* **1320** *Cast. Love* 507 Hose Pees loueþ, wiþ-outen gabbe, Pees wiþ-outen ende he schal habbe. **13..** *Guy Warw.* (A.) 2888 Þou schalt habbe..half mi lond wiþ-outen gabbe.

†**b.** A taunt. *Obs.*

a **1225** *Leg. Kath.* 2269 Porphire and alle hise..wið se soðe gabbes gremeden him se sare þæt [etc.].

2. An idle vaunt, a piece of brag or bravado. Also *Hist.* of the 'gabs' of Charlemagne and his knights (see quot. 1846). (The corresponding word in German chivalric romance was *gelpf* = OE. *ȝielp*.)

1737 OZELL *Rabelais* II. 226 *note*, Upon his saying, only by way of Gab..that [etc.]. **1846** WRIGHT *Ess. Mid. Ages* II. ii. 39 Charlemagne and his twelve peers..began each to make his 'gab', or joke, which consisted in an extravagant gasconade. **1889** C. T. MARTIN *Gaimar's Lestorie des Engles* II. p. xxxviii, The first is the *Gab* of Walter Tirel and the King..The King replies at once by more *Gab*.

gab (gæb), *sb.*[2] Not in dignified use. [See GAB *v.*[2] In Sc. often associated with GAB *sb.*[3]]

1. The action of gabbing or talking; conversation, prattle, talk, twaddle. Also *jocular nonce-use*: A language.

1790 A. WILSON *3rd Ep. to W. Mitchell*, Perhaps Rob G——y's auld grey pate..May join the social gab. **1811** J. POOLE *Hamlet Travestie* I. iii. 10 Then hold your gab, and hear what I've to tell. *a* **1839** PRAED *Poems* (1864) II. 58 The captain hates 'a woman's gab'. *a* **1845** HOOD *Sir J. Bowring* 5 All kinds of gabs he talks, I wis, From Latin down to Scottish. **1863** READE *Hard Cash* II. xv. 240 'Come, stash your gab, my lad', said Green. **1874** GREVILLE *Mem. Geo. IV* (1875) III. xxiii. 72 They certainly can't get the best of him at the gab. **1887** *Punch* 10 Sept. 111/1 Gladstone's gab about 'masses and classes' is all tommy rot. **1893** STEVENSON *Catriona* 19 There's no fair way to stop your gab.

b. ***the gift of the gab***: a talent for speaking, fluency of speech. (*Sc.* also *gift of the* GOB.)

[**1681** see GOB.] **1785** in GROSE *Dict. Vulg. Tongue.* **1794** GODWIN *Caleb Williams* 29 We knew well enough that he had the gift of the gab. **1820** J. W. CROKER in *Croker Papers* (1884) 20 Dec., A government cannot go on without the gift of the gab. **1850** T. A. TROLLOPE *Impress. Wand.* vii. 100 Our good gentle Florentines have a very inordinate gift of the gab.

2. *slang.* In phrases ***to blow the gab***: to blab, give information, 'peach'. (Cf. GAFF *sb.*[2] 2.) ***to flash the gab***: to show off in talk, to hold forth.

1785 GROSE *Dict. Vulg. Tongue* s.v., To blow the gab, to confess, or peach. **1819** MOORE *Tom Crib's Mem.* (1821) 12 While his Lordship..that very great dab At the flowers of rhet'ric is flashing his gab. **1834** H. AINSWORTH *Rookwood* III. v, Never blow the gab, or squeak.

3. *attrib.* and *Comb.* (jocular), as in ***gab-machine, -shop***; **gab-trees**, the jaws.

1728 W. STARRAT *Ep. to Ramsay* 38 Sae gash thy gab-trees gang. **1797** MARY ROBINSON *Walsingham* IV. 13, 'I always dose at the gab-shop' [i.e. the House of Commons], replied he. **1866** LOWELL *Biglow P.* Poet. Wks. 1890 II. 379 Nut while the twolegged gab-machine's so plenty, 'nablin' one man to du the talk o' twenty.

gab (gæb), *sb.*[3] *Sc.* [var. of GOB.] The mouth. ***to steek one's gab***: to be silent, make one silent.

1724 RAMSAY *Tea-t. Misc.* (1733) I. 8 He dighted his gab and pri'd her mou'. **1725** —— *Gent. Sheph.* I. i, Bannocks and a shave of cheese Will make a breakfast that..Might please the daintiest gabs. **1785** GROSE *Dict. Vulg. Tongue*, *Gab*, or *Gob*, the mouth. **1786** BURNS *Ordination* ix, Now Robinson harangue nae mair, But steek your gab for ever. *a* **1810** TANNAHILL *Poems* (1846) 105 Her mou's like the gab o' the fleuk. **1810** COCK *Simple Strains* 136 (Jam.) His menseless gab was fairly steeket. **1820** SCOTT *Abbot* xiv, 'Now, my mates'..'once again dight your gabs and be hushed.' **1861** RAMSAY *Remin.* Ser. II. 55 'I'm unco yuckie to hear a blaud o' yer gab.'

b. *Comb.*: **gab string** *slang* (see quot.).

1785 GROSE *Dict. Vulg. Tongue*, *Gab or gob string*, a bridle.

gab (gæb), *sb.*[4] [Of obscure origin: cf. Flem. *gabbe* notch, gash (in Kilian, glossed 'incisura').] (See quot. 1888.)

1792 *Specif. Kelly's Patent* No. 1879. 8 Clear of the notch or gabb of the catch lever. **1839** R. S. ROBINSON *Naut. Steam Eng.* 95 In the end of the rod is a notch, called a gab. **1846** YOUNG *Naut. Dict.* s.v. *Steam-engine* §32 The eccentric has a notch, or gab as it is called, fitting a pin in the gab-lever. **1888** *Lockwood's Dict. Mech. Engin.*, *Gab*, a hook, or open notch, in a rod or lever, which drops over a spindle, and forms a temporary connection between valve or other motions.

b. *Comb.*: **gab-lever** (see quot. 1888).

1839 R. S. ROBINSON *Naut. Steam Eng.* 97 When the notch in the rod is engaged with the stud on the gab lever, the engine works itself. **1888** *Lockwood's Dict. Mech. Engin.*, *Gab Lever*, generally any lever which is connected up by means of a gab; specifically the lever which forms the connection between the slide valve spindle and the eccentric rod in some forms of marine engine valve.

gab (gæb), *v.*[1] Forms: 2–4 **gabbe-n**, 4–6 **gabb(e**, (5 **gabe**), 3– **gab.** [app. a. OF. *gab(b)er* (also written *gauber*, *gaiber*, once, perh. erroneously, *jaber*), to mock, deride, jest; the word is found (perh. as an adoption from OFr.) as Pr. and OSp. *gabar*, It. *gabbare*, to mock, jest, Pg. *gabar* to praise, refl. to boast. Cf. the related GAB *sb.*[1]

Most etymologists regard the Rom. vb. and sb. as adoptions of the Teut. words which appear as ON. *gabba* to mock, *gabb* mockery (GAB *sb.*[1]), OFris. *gabbia* to accuse, prosecute (cf. sense 1 below), MDu. and MLG. *gabben* to mock, deceive. But in words of early adoption, Teut. *ga-* normally became *ja-* in Central French; further, the occurrence of *bb* in Teut. words (apart from hypocoristic and onomatopœic formations and WGer. *bb* from *bj*) is rare and etymologically obscure; and the chronology of the various Teut. forms would not forbid the supposition that they were all adopted from OFr. If the words be either Teut. or Rom. formations from a Teutonic root, they may perhaps be connected ultimately with GAPE *v.*; cf. the Icel. use of *gap* in the sense of clamour, jeers; on the other hand they may be onomatopœic formations expressing the notion of loud outcry, chatter; cf. GAB *v.*[2], GABBLE, GAGGLE *v.*]

†**1.** *trans.* To reproach, accuse. *Obs.*

c **1200** *Trin. Coll. Hom.* 65 We aȝen to gabben us seluen forþat we syneȝeden, alse þe holie man iob seið, Reprehendo me..Ich haue syneȝed and gabbe me suluen þeroffe.

†**2.** *intr.* To speak mockingly, to scoff. Const. *on, upon. Obs.*

a **1225** *Ancr. R.* 200 Lauhwen oðer gabben, ȝif him misbiueolle. *c* **1320** *Sir Tristr.* 2115 Þou gabbest on me so, Mi nem nil me nouȝt se. *c* **1380** WYCLIF *Sel. Wks.* III. 347 Þis blaspheme gabbiþ upon God, and seiþ þat al þ is is Goddis werk. *c* **1550** *Hye waye to Spyttel Ho.* 338 in Hazl. *E.P.P.* IV. 42 Where they lyst, for to gabbe and rayle. **1573** G. HARVEY *Letter-bk.* (Camden) 106 Doth sea ingender flame? You gabb fonde poetts, or in bowrde, You blason Neptune's name.

†**b.** *trans.* To mock. *Obs.*

c **1489** CAXTON *Sonnes of Aymon* xiv. 338 Ye wynne not moche by, for to gabbe me of this facyon.

†**3.** *intr.* To lie, tell lies. *Obs.*

a **1300** *Sarmun* 47 in *E.E.P.* (1862) 6 Soþ to sigge and noȝt to gab. *a* **1300** *Cursor M.* 5173 Yee gab and, certes, yee ha sin. **13..** *Guy Warw.* (A.) 2470 Y no gabbe nouȝt, for sothe to say. **1375** BARBOUR *Bruce* IV. 290 [Scho] askit quhy he gabbit had Of the Ansuer that he hir mad. *c* **1400** *Destr. Troy* 4303 As the gospell of God, þat gabbis not, says. *c* **1450** *Merlin* 31, I pray yow that ye sey the trouthe..and wite ye well yef ye gabbe enythynge, I know it wele i-nough. *c* **1475** *Partenay* 2410 A king ne shold lye ne be gabbyng.

†**b.** *trans.* To tell lies to, to deceive. *Obs.*

c **1275** *Sermun* 36 in *O.E. Misc.* 188 Bachares and brueres for alle men heo gabbe. *c* **1325** *Metr. Hom.* 7 That wiht lesinge Gabbid Adam and his ofspringe. *c* **1440** *York Myst.* xiii. 141 We! why gab ye me swa. *c* **1460** *Towneley Myst.* xxviii. 243 Might I se ihesu gost and flesh gropyng shuld not gab me.

4. *intr.* To boast, brag. quasi-*arch.* and *Hist.* (A modern adoption of the OF. word as occurring in the Charlemagne romances.)

1825 SCOTT *Talism.* ii, Their fashion..is..to gab of that which they dare not undertake. **1846** WRIGHT *Ess. Mid. Ages* I. ii. 39 Even Turpin, the archbishop, gabbed; and his boast was [etc.]. **1865** KINGSLEY *Herew.* xii, He would chant his own doughty deeds; and gab (as the Norman word was) in painful earnest.

gab (gæb), *v.*[2] [app. onomatopœic; cf. GABBLE *v.*] *intr.* To talk much or glibly; to chatter, prate.

1786 BURNS *Earnest Cry* x, Could I like Montgomeries fight, Or gab like Boswell. ?*a* **1800** *Earl Richard* xvii. in Child *Ballads* III. lxviii. (1885) 149/1, 'I wad shoot this wee pyet Sits gabbing on the tree.' **1844** MRS. CARLYLE *Lett.* I. 293 [He] came in to tea and sat there gabbing till ten o'clock. **1883** BLACK *Yolande* xx, 'Bout him the carles were gabbin'.

Hence 'gabbing *vbl. sb.*, chatter, idle talk; 'gabbing *ppl. a.*, that gabs; chattering, glib-tongued.

1794 *Flowers of Forest* in *Ritson's Sc. Songs* II. 3 Nae daffin, nae gabbin, but sighing and sabbing. **1830** GALT *Lawrie T.* II. v. (1849) 56 Giving such gabbing the go by. **1837** R. NICOLL *Poems* (1842) 79 He's a gash, gabbin' birkie, the Auld Beggar Man.

†**gab**, *v.*[3] *Obs.* [Cf. dial. *gobber-tooth*, *gubber-tush*, a projecting tooth; also GAG *v.*[2] 2, GAG-TOOTH.] *intr.* Of teeth: To project.

1601 HOLLAND *Pliny* XI. xxxvii. I. 337 They [teeth] stand gabbing out of the mouth.

Hence †**gabbed** *ppl. a.*, projecting.

1601 HOLLAND *Pliny* XI. xxxvii. I. 337 Goats haue none aboue but the 2 foreteeth. None haue gabbed tusks standing forth of the mouth.

†**gabarage.** *Obs.*$^{-0}$ (See quot.)

1706 PHILLIPS (ed. Kersey), *Gabarage*, that which Irish Goods are wrapped in. **1721** in BAILEY; and in mod. Dicts.

gabard, obs. form of GABBART.

gabarden, obs. form of GABERDINE.

gabardine: var. of GABERDINE (esp. in sense 1 e).

gabarre, gabart, gabbard, var. GABBART.

gabb, gabback, obs. ff. GAB, GABBOCK.

gabbardin(e, obs. form of GABERDINE.

gabbart ('gæbət). In recent use chiefly *Sc.* Forms: 6 **gabard, gaber,** 7 **gabart, gaboard, gabbord,** 7– **gabbard,** 9 **gabarre, gab(b)ert,** 8– **gabbart.** [ad. F. *gabarre* (now spelt *gabare*), ad. Pr. (also It. and Sp.) *gabarra* of unknown origin. Some of the forms may come from F. *gabarot, -otte,* dim. of *gabare.*] **1.** A sailing vessel for inland navigation; a sailing barge, lighter.

1580 R. HITCHCOCK *Politic Plat* in Arb. *Garner* II. 162 Thither cometh yearly three hundred lighters, called Gabers, with wines. **1666** *Lond. Gaz.* No. 24/1 Two Gaboards were sunck in this Harbour. **1775** T. CAMPBELL *Diary Visit Eng.* in Napier *Boswell* (1884) V. 222 Little gabbards, with coals, and groceries, &c., come up here from Bristol. **1818** SCOTT *Rob Roy* xxxvi, Coal-barges and gabbards. [The spelling *gabbart* occurs in ch. xxxi.] **1828** —— *F.M. Perth* xvi, She sailed in a gabbart for Dundee. **1877** in *Law Rep.* App. Cases II. 844, I owned gabbarts [*foot-note* scows] on the Leven for about twenty years.

attrib. **1776** G. SEMPLE *Building in Water* 112 A few Gabbard-men and Labourers.

2. (Freq. **gabbard.**) A support used in erecting a scaffold.

1897 *Ardrossan & Saltcoats Herald* 31 Dec. 3 The position of one of the gabbard legs. *Ibid.*, The second gabbard from the north wall, not far from the centre of the scaffold. **1962** *Engineering* 13 Apr. 489/1 Peine tower cranes ..are being used, as well as two 10-ton derricks on gabbards.

gabbe, obs. form of GAB.

gabber ('gæbə(r)), *sb.*[1] Also 4–5 **gabbere,** 5 **gabbar.** [f. GAB *v.*[1] + -ER[1].] One who gabs.

†**1.** A mocker; a deceiver; a liar. *Obs.*

c **1386** CHAUCER *Pars. T.* ¶15 He is a Iaper and a gabber, and no verray repentant, that eftsoone dooth thyng, for which hym oghte repente. *c* **1400** MAUNDEV. (1839) xiv. 160, I schal speke a litille more of the Dyamandes..to the ende that thei that knowen hem not, be not disceyved be Gabberes [F. *barratours*], that gon be the Contree, that sellen hem. **1450** *Pol. Poems* (Rolls) II. 237 Gabberys gloson eny whare.

2. One who utters 'gabs' (see GAB *sb.*[1] 2).

1869 T. WRIGHT in *Student* II. 449 Sir Ken was celebrated as the most accomplished gabber in King Arthur's court.

gabber ('gæbə(r)), *sb.*[2] [f. GAB *v.*[2] + -ER[1].] A chatterer, prater.

1793 *Char.* in *Ann. Reg.* 250 My reputation of being a good gabber, that is to say, possessing a considerable share of low quaint language. **1854** H. MILLER *Sch. & Schm.* xv. (1857) 339 The direction will be apparently in the hands of a few fluent gabbers.

†'**gabber,** *v. Obs.*[−1] [onomatopœic; cf. JABBER, GIBBER, also GAB *sb.*[2] and *v.*[2], GABBLE. Du. *gabberen* has the same sense.] *trans.* To talk volubly, to jabber.

1706–7 FARQUHAR *Beaux Strat.* III. i, He and the count's footman were gabbering French. **1808** JAMIESON, *Gabber,* to jabber, to gibber, to talk incoherently.

Hence '**gabbering** *vbl. sb.* Also '**gabber** *sb.*, jabber.

1796 COLERIDGE in Mrs. Sandford *T. Poole & Friends* (1888) I. 155 Their unmeaning gabber of flattery. **1822** BEWICK *Mem.* 4 The gabbering and noise they made, was enough to stun any one.

gabbert, var. GABBART.

†**gabbery.** *Obs. rare.* [f. GAB *v.*[1] + -ERY; cf. OF. *gaberie.*] (See quot.)

1627 MINSHEU *Ductor,* Gabberies, gabbings, wilie deceits, gullings or cheatings. **1676** in COLES. **1721** in BAILEY.

gabbiness ('gæbɪnɪs). [f. GABBY *a.* + -NESS.] Garrulousness; talkativeness.

1952 S. KAUFFMANN *Philanderer* (1953) ii. 27 Perry Downing reduced that restraint to a minimum because of his gabbiness and vulgarity. **1961** *Guardian* 10 Oct. 7/3 The gabbiness of the Chicago musicians, who wrote prolifically about themselves.

gabbing ('gæbɪŋ), *vbl. sb.* [f. GAB *v.*[1] + -ING[1].] The action of the vb. GAB.

†**1.** Lying, falsehood, a lie. *Obs.*

a **1250** *Owl & Night.* 626 Thu me telst of other thinge, Of mine briddes seist gabbinge. *a* **1300** *Cursor M.* 5176 'Fader,' þai said, 'mis-tru vs noght, þat we þe now ha gabbing broght' **1377** LANGL. *P. Pl.* B. xx. 124 With glosynges and with gabbynges he gyled þe peple. *a* **1400** *Hymns Virg.* (E.E.T.S.) 108 Bakbyte þou no mon blod ny bon But ay let gabbynges glyde and gon. *c* **1440** *Partonope* 7097 Ye were neuer wont to use gabbyng. *c* **1450** *Merlin* 13, I shall well knowe yef ye haue made eny gabbynge. **1450–1530** *Myrr. our Ladye* 328 Here beware that ye make no gabbynge. **1513** DOUGLAS *Æneis* I. Pref. 203 Was it nocht eik als possible Eneas, As Hercules or Theseus to hell to pas? Quhilk is na gabbing suthlie, nor na lie.

2. The action of the vb. GAB (sense 4).

1869 T. WRIGHT in *Student* II. 449 This proceeding was called gabbing, and the boasts and jests were called gabs.

gabbion(e, obs. form of GABION.

gabble ('gæb(ə)l), *sb.* [f. the vb.]

1. Voluble, noisy, confused, unintelligible talk.

1602 MARSTON *Ant. & Mel.* II. Wks. 1856 I. 26 Taint not thy sweete eare With that sots gabble. **1667** MILTON *P.L.* XII. 56 Forthwith a hideous gabble rises loud Among the Builders. **1750** JOHNSON *Rambler* No. 74 ¶10 Where there are children, she hates the gabble of brats. **1806–7** J. BERESFORD *Miseries Hum. Life* (1826) v. iv, A crew of savages whose laughter and gabble are all that you are allowed to hear. **1830** J. JEKYLL *Corr.* 8 July (1894) 241 Holland House ..is..the very focus of political gabble. **1862** LOWELL *Biglow P.* Poems 1890 II. 346 Gabble's the short cut to ruin. **1874** GREEN *Short Hist.* viii. §3. 480 The stately reserve [of Charles]..contrasted favourably with the gabble and indecorum of his father.

2. The inarticulate noises made by animals.

1601 SHAKS. *All's Well* IV. i. 22 Choughs language, gabble enough, and good enough. **1638** SHIRLEY *Mart. Souldier* III. i. in Bullen *O. Pl.* I. 203 If they do but once open and spend there gabble, gabble, gabble, it will make the Forest ecchoe. **1644** MILTON *Areop.* (Arb.) 72 In their envious gabble [the birds] would prognosticat a year of sects and schisms. **1847** L. HUNT *Jar Honey* iv. (1848) 48 The turtles stun one with their yawning gabble.

gabble ('gæb(ə)l), *v.* Also 7 **gable.** [onomatopœic; cf. GABBER and the words there cited; also MDu. *gabbeln* of similar meaning; and GAGGLE *v.*]

1. *intr.* To talk volubly, inarticulately and incoherently; to chatter, jabber, prattle. Also, to read so fast as to be unintelligible.

1577 STANYHURST *Descr. Irel.* i. 4 in Holinshed *Chron.* I, He that dooth not perceyue, what is fitting or decent for euerye season, or gabbleth more then he hath commission to doe. **1601** SHAKS. *Twel. N.* II. iii. 95 Haue you no wit, manners, nor honestie, but to gabble like Tinkers at this time of night? **1628** FORD *Lover's Mel.* II. i, I'll keep the old man in chat, whilst thou gabblest to the girl. **1663** BUTLER *Hud.* I. i. 101 Which made some think when he did gabble Th' had heard three Labourers of Babel. **1768–74** TUCKER *Lt. Nat.* (1852) I. 36 A careless nurse..gabbling among her gossips, without attention to her charge. **1810** CRABBE *Borough* vi. Wks. 1834 III. 122 And lisps and gabbles if he tries to talk. **1829** LYTTON *Disowned* 7 Are you still gabbling at the foot of the table. **1860–1** FLO. NIGHTINGALE *Nursing* 402 If there is some matter which must be read to a sick person, do it slowly. People often think that the way to get it over with least fatigue to him is to get it over in least time. They gabble. **1868** HAWTHORNE *Amer. Note-Bks.* (1879) I. 48 We could hear them within the hut, gabbling merrily.

quasi-*trans.* **1849** C. BRONTE *Shirley* i, The confusion of tongues which has gabbled me deaf as a post.

2. *trans.* To utter rapidly and unintelligibly. Also with *over.*

1758 *Monthly Rev.* 308 Gabbling infidelity and laughing at the religion of his country. **1794** MATHIAS *Purs. Lit.* (1798) 382 He..like Macpherson, glibly gabbles Erse. **1798** COLERIDGE *Fears in Solit.* 72 We gabble o'er the oaths we mean to break. **1829** SCOTT *Jrnl.* 13 July, Gabbling eternally much that I did, and more that I did not, understand. **1851** D. JERROLD *St. Giles* xxii. 222 Tangle rolled upon his side, gabbling something in his sleep. **1870** R. B. BROUGH *Marston Lynch* xxxi. 342 The contemptuous haste of an actor gabbling a part.

3. Of geese, etc.: To utter with rapidity inarticulate sounds. More commonly GAGGLE.

1697 DRYDEN *Virg. Past.* IX. 48, I..gabble like a Goose, amidst the Swan-like Quire. **1770** GOLDSM. *Des. Vill.* 112 The noisy geese that gabbled o'er the pool. **1820** BYRON *Mar. Fal.* IV. ii. 299 The geese in the Capitol..gabbled till Rome awoke. **1865** S. EVANS *Bro. Fabian's MS.* 23 Gabbling and plashing half across the pool..Wrestles the gander.

gabblement ('gæb(ə)lmənt). [f. GABBLE *v.* + -MENT.] Gabbling, rapid unintelligible noise.

1833 M. SCOTT *Tom Cringle* xviii. (1859) 515 The old Gander again set up his gabblement. **1837** CARLYLE *Fr. Rev.* II. v. iv, Caperings, shoutings and vociferation,—which.. dwindle into staggerings, into quick gabblement.

gabbler ('gæb(ə)lə(r)). Also 7–8 **gabler.** [f. GABBLE *v.* + -ER[1].] One that gabbles.

1625 JACKSON *Orig. Unbeliefe* xxiv. 238 Such sharers in the office of intercession, as the Creeple and the Gabler are in mens benevolences at Faires or Markets. **1708** MOTTEUX *Rabelais* (1737) V. 215 Wheadling Gablers..Spoilers of Paper. **1780** JOHNSON *Lett. to Mrs. Thrale* 27 July, We are none of the giddy gabblers, we think before we speak. **1879** SALA *Paris herself again* (1880) I. xvii. 269 The few French gentlemen whom the guttural gabblers have not driven away sit silent in corners.

Gabble-ratch: see GABRIEL.

gabbling ('gæb(ə)lɪŋ), *vbl. sb.* [f. GABBLE *v.* + -ING[1].] The action of the vb. GABBLE.

1599 NASHE *Lenten Stuffe* Wks. (Grosart) V. 251 Their clacke or gabbling to this purport. **1633** FORD *Love's Sacr.* III. i, Foh! do not trick me off; I overheard your gabbling. **1685** STAFFORD in *Dryden's Misc.* II. (1685) 440 Time and patience..To tell the Gabblings of each Hag and Ghost. **1712** BUDGELL *Spect.* No. 389 ¶9 Having no language..but a confused gabbling which is neither well understood by themselves or other. **1769** GOLDSM. *Roman Hist.* (1786) I. 181 The garrison were awaked by the gabbling of some sacred geese. **1833** HT. MARTINEAU *Cinnamon & Pearls* ii. 26 Mixed with their chaunt came the mutterings and gabblings of the charmers. **1876** BLACK *Madcap V.* xl. 352 A people..prone to gabbling after dinner.

gabbling ('gæb(ə)lɪŋ), *ppl. a.* [f. GABBLE *v.* + -ING[2].] That gabbles. ***gabbling crow*** (see quot. 1756).

1625 HART *Anat. Ur.* I. i. 8 Her gabling gossips were officiously attending a better euent then they found. [Cf. quot. *c* 1624 s.v. GADLING 4.] **1756** P. BROWNE *Jamaica* 472 The gabbling Crow. This bird..is very noisy and seems to imitate the sounds of most syllables in every language, in its gabblings. *a* **1771** SMOLLETT *Burlesque Ode* 27 Nor to the waddling duck or gabbling goose Did she glad sustenance refuse. **1821** CLARE *Vill. Minstr.* I. 24 Their gabbling talk did Lubin's cares beguile. **1873** BLACK *Pr. Thule* xvii, Don't you know the mischief your gabbling tongue might make? **1877** M. GRANT *Sun-Maid* iv, I am a gabbling silly old thing. **1883** *Longm. Mag.* July 293, I remember a gabbling sound of words.

gabbock ('gæbək). *Sc.* and *Anglo-Irish.* Also 8 **gabback,** 9 **gabbok, -buck, gobbock.** [a. Ir. *gobóg* a dog-fish, a sand-eel; Sc. Gael. *gobag.*] A dog-fish.

Quot. 1719 is doubtful. Jamieson, after Sibbald, interprets *gappocks* as = 'gobbets, morsels, pieces'.

1719 D'URFEY *Pills* VI. 352 There'll be..Fish of geud Gabback and Skate. [Herd *Scot. Songs* (1776) II. 25 With fouth of good gabbock of skate. Ritson *Scot. Songs* (1794) I. 211 And fouth of good gappoks of skate.] **1867** SMYTH *Sailor's Work-bk.*, *Gabbok,* a voracious dog-fish which infests the herring fisheries in St. George's Channel. **1880** *Antrim & Down Gloss.*, *Gabbuck* or *Gobbock,* the piked dog-fish.

gabbord, obs. form of GABBART.

gabbro ('gæbrəʊ). *Geol.* [a. It. *gabbro.*] (See quot. 1864–72.)

1837 DANA *Syst. Min.* 288 Saussurite occurs in primitive regions, and with hornblende and augite constitutes the rocks called gabbro and euphotide. **1864–72** WATTS *Dict. Chem.* II. 756 *Gabbro,* the name given by the Italian artists ..to a rock essentially composed of felspar and diallage, called by the French geologists euphotide. **1879** RUTLEY *Study Rocks* x. 120 Enstatite occurs in Iherzolite and certain gabbros.

Hence **ga'bbroic, gabbro'itic** *adjs.*, of or pertaining to gabbro; having the nature of gabbro.

1884 *Science* July IV. 71 Gabbroic and granitic rocks. **1893** *Jrnl. Geol.* I. 595 Diabases from dykes..in which the gabbroitic as well as the diabasic structures are well exhibited. **1895** *Ibid.* III. 1 The rarity of olivine in the granulitic rocks is in marked contrast with its abundance in the gabbroitic variety.

gabbroid ('gæbrɔɪd), *a. Petrol.* [f. GABBR(O + -OID.] Resembling gabbro; *spec.* belonging to the petrographic clan containing the gabbro and dolerite families, the rocks of which contain a high proportion of ferromagnesian minerals. Also as *sb.* Hence **ga'bbroidal** *a.*

1900 *Amer. Geologist* XXVI. 151 (*heading*) Mineralogical and petrographic study of the gabbroid rocks of Minnesota, and more particularly of the plagioclasytes. **1904** CHAMBERLIN & SALISBURY *Geol.* (1905) I. 432 The term *gabbroids* may be used to include the dark crystalline rocks in which the ferromagnesian minerals predominate, as the diorites, gabbros, dolerites, peridotites, etc. *Ibid.*, The granitoids are usually acidic and the gabbroids usually basic. **1931** *Mineral. Abstr.* IV. 401 Chemical analyses of the differentiation products of a gabbroidal magma, viz. diorite-pegmatite, diorite-aplite [etc.]. **1940** *Geogr. Jrnl.* XCV. 394 The association of gabbroid and granophyric rocks. **1965** G. J. WILLIAMS *Econ. Geol. N.Z.* x. 160/2 These lenses..were invaded by gabbroidal and peridotitic dykes conformably with the bedding planes.

gabbronite, gabronite ('gæbrənaɪt). *Min.* [f. GABBRO + -(N)ITE; so called by Schumacher in 1801.] A compact variety of scapolite, somewhat resembling gabbro.

1808 T. ALLAN *Names Min.* 33 Gabbronite..from Arendal. **1852** BRANDE *Dict. Sci. Lit. & Art* Supp., *Gabronite,* a mineral found in a vein of titaniferous iron near Arendal in Norway.

gabbuck: see GABBOCK.

gabby ('gæbɪ), *a.* orig. *Sc.* [f. GAB *sb.*[2] + -Y[1].] Abounding in gab; garrulous, talkative.

1719 HAMILTON *Ep. A. Ramsay* in *Ramsay's Poems* (1721) I. 197 On condition I were as gabby As either thee or honest Habby. **1785** R. FORBES *Poems Buchan Dial.* 7 Altho' mair gabby he may be Than Nestor wise and true. **1790** A. WILSON *Callamphitre's Elegy* Poet. Wks. (1846) 106 But now nae mair he'll bless their bield, Wi' gabby cracks and stories. **1832–53** *Whistle-Binkie* (Sc. Songs) Ser. I. 91 Ae mornin', wee Rabie, fu' canty and gabbie, Gat up frae his nestie an' buskit him braw. **1858** M. PORTEOUS *Souter Johnny* 11 Had gabby skill To crack a joke. **1899** ADE *Fables in Slang* 124 He was a Gabby Young Man, and he could Articulate at all Times, whether he had anything to Say or not. *a* **1911** D. G. PHILLIPS *Susan Lenox* (1917) II. viii. 214, I was awful gabby downstairs. Yes—I told him. **1949** 'J. TEY' *Brat Farrar* xix. 176 Never very 'gabby' at any time. A quiet boy? Yes, a nice quiet boy. **1958** M. ALLINGHAM *Hide my Eyes* 125 As for the public, they're interfering, gabby, can't keep their traps shut. **1965** *Spectator* 22 Jan. 108/2 Hubert Humphrey shows himself a gabby and literate and battling soul. **1970** *New Yorker* 28 Nov. 116/2 The women ..were mostly political and gabby.

†'**gabel,** *v. Obs.*[−1] *trans.* To mark (sheep) on the ear in some particular way.

1715 [see FARTHING 1 b].

gabel(l, obs. form of GABLE.

gabelkind, obs. form of GAVELKIND.

gabelle (ga'bɛl). Also 5–8 **gabel(l,** 6 **gable.** [a. F. *gabelle,* ad. med.L. *gabella,* a deriv. from *gablum, gabulum,* a tax, impost, a word of Teut. origin; see GAVEL. Cf. Pr. and Sp. *gabela,* It. *gabella.* From the 16th cent. it is rarely used by English writers except as a foreign word, referring esp.

to France and Italy.] A tax; *spec.* the salt-tax imposed in France before the Revolution.

1413 *Pilgr. Sowle* (Caxton 1483) IV. xxxiii. 81 Other counceylours of the kynge..haue for to sene in special to gouernaunce of his propre goodes..gabelles and customes. *c* **1460** FORTESCUE *Abs. & Lim. Mon.* x. (1885) 131 For wych cause the gabell off the salt, and the quaterimes of the wynes were graunted to the kynge by the iij estates off Fraunce. **1523** LD. BERNERS *Froiss.* I. clv. 187 The thre estates ordenid ..that the gabell of salt shulde ron through the realme. **1631** MASSINGER *Emperor East* I. ii, No man should dare To bring a salad from his country garden Without the paying gabel. *c* **1645** HOWELL *Lett.* II. lxiv. (1650) II. 100 England.. having neither the Gabells of Italy, the Tallies of France, or the Accise of Holland laid upon them. **1681** COLVIL *Whigs Supplic.* (1751) 83 Like Massanello freeing Naples From Gabells put on roots and apples. **1721** STRYPE *Eccl. Mem.* II. II. xx. 404 There being already many new imposts and gabels, beside the ordinary excise. **1756** C. LUCAS *Ess. Waters* II. 34 In France..on account of the heavy gabel or excise..no man dares to purify salt for his own table. **1794** J. GIFFORD *Louis XVI*, 185 This was no less than the total abolition of the Gabelles throughout France. **1835** LYTTON *Rienzi* x. vii, A gabelle was put upon wine and salt. **1866** ROGERS *Agric. & Prices* I. ix. 156 With Cambridge the levy of this gabelle is regular.

fig. **1649** JER. TAYLOR *Gt. Exemp.* III. Ad §15. 137 The tribute which he demands are..Faith, Hope, and Charity; no other gabels but the duties of a holy spirit.

b. *attrib.* as ***gabelle-house, -man, -pence.***

1650 HOWELL *Giraffi's Rev. Naples* I. 15 Quarters of the City, where all the *Gabell houses were. **1837** CARLYLE *Misc.* (1857) IV. 76 He flung *gabellemen and excisemen into the river Durance..when their claims were not clear. **1884** *Athenæum* 16 Aug. 209/2 Simon de Montfort's charter for the remission of *gable-pence and bridge-silver to the burgesses of Leicester.

Hence **'gabelled** *ppl. a.*, liable to a gabelle or tax.

1650 HOWELL *Giraffi's Rev. Naples* I. 10 They wold buy no gabell'd fruit.

†**ga'beller.** *Obs.* Also in Fr. form **gabellier.** [f. GABELLE + -ER¹.] A collector of the gabelle, a tax-gatherer.

1599 SANDYS *Europæ Spec.* (1632) 159 To bee thus dayly racked, fleyed and devoured, by so many pety tyrants as it were with their prolling Gabelliers. **1670** COTTON *Espernon* III. XI. 539 They drew up a List of above four hundred of the best Families of the City, under the Title of Gabellers. **1685** J. WRIGHT *View Late Troub.* Pref., To their tumultuous burning the gabeller's goods I think I may, not unaptly, compare our burning the pope. **1698** LASSELS *Voy. Italy* II. 182 He [Masaniello] commanded them to cast into the fire all the goods, papers, plate, beds, hangings, &c., of the Gabelliers.

gaber, obs. form of GABBART.

gaberdine ('gæbədi:n, -'di:n). Forms: 6 **gawbardyne, -berdyne, gabarden, -berdin,** 6-7 **gabberdine,** 6-9 **gab(b)ardin(e,** 6- **gaberdine.** [The earliest forms appear to be directly a. OF. *gauvardine, galvardine, gallevardine*, perh. a derivative of MHG. *wallevart* pilgrimage (for the sense cf. *pelerine*); the word passed into other Rom. langs. as It. *gavardina*, Sp. *gabardina*, the latter of which has influenced the form of the Eng. word.]

1. A loose upper garment of coarse material; a smock frock.

1520 *Lanc. Wills* (Chetham Soc.) I. 39, I bequeth unto litill Tom^s Beke my gawbardyne to make hym a gowne. **1567** DRANT *Horace's Ep. to Mæcenas* in *Art Poet.* C iij a, My cote is bare, my gawberdyne amis. **1610** SHAKS. *Temp.* II. ii. 40 My best way is to creepe vnder his Gaberdine. **1663** BUTLER *Hud.* I. iii. 917 He disrob'd his Gaberdine. **1791** COWPER *Odyss.* XIX. 397 Spread his couch..with fleecy gaberdines And rugs of splendid hue. **1859** LANG *Wand. India* 158 A huge pocket at the back of his chogah (a sort of gaberdine).

b. As a garment worn by Jews, perh. orig. a reminiscence of Shakspere's phrase.

1596 SHAKS. *Merch. V.* I. iii. 113 You..spet vpon my Iewish gaberdine. **1817** MAR. EDGEWORTH *Harrington* iii. (1832) 28 Before his eyes we paraded the effigy of a Jew, dressed in a gabardine of rags and paper. **1820** SCOTT *Ivanhoe* v, The very gaberdine I wear is borrowed from Reuben of Tadcaster.

c. As worn by almsmen or beggars.

1839 CARLYLE *Chartism* iii. 121 Scramble along..with thy pope's tiaras..and beggar's gabardine. **1866** ROGERS *Agric. & Prices* I. v. 120 The garb of the fourteenth century is still seen in the almsman's gaberdine. **1890** F. W. ROBINSON *Very Strange Family* 17 His long blue gaberdine fluttering in the breeze.

d. In local use, a child's loose frock or pinafore.

Mod. (*Kent*), 'If you put a good gaberdine on a child it covers everything else, and makes him look tidy.'

e. Freq. **gabardine.** *spec.* a variety of twill-woven cloth, usu. of fine worsted.

1904 *Ladies' Field* 14 May 426/1 Gabardine, a material of flax and cotton, with a wool lining, both gabardine and lining being waterproofed. **1908** *Times* (weekly ed.) 14 Aug. p. iii/2 Gabardine is a material which has many qualities not to be overlooked when it is a question of sporting dresses. **1923** G. C. DENNY *Fabrics* 46 Gabardine or gaberdine (wool). A firm material similar to whip cord. **1938** 'E. QUEEN' *Four of Hearts.* (1939) xi. 153 She looked lovely..in a tailored gabardine suit.

2. *transf.* and *fig.* Dress, covering; also (with allusion to Shaks. *Temp.* II. ii. 40), protection.

1594 CAREW *Huarte's Exam. Wits* Ded. of Transl., Your Booke returneth vnto you clad in a Cornish Gabardine. **1645** MILTON *Tetrach.* Wks. (1847) 206/1 If his canonical gabardine of text and letter do not now sit too close about him. **1847** LD. G. BENTINCK in *Croker Papers* 8 Sept. (1884), They have crawled into the House of Commons under the gabardine of the Whigs. **1879** LOWELL *Let.* 15 Jan., Lett. (1894) II. 266 There are great patches of green on the brown gaberdine of the Campiña.

Hence **'gaberdined** *ppl. a.*, clothed in a gaberdine.

1863 W. B. JERROLD *Sign. Distr.* 263 The gaberdined Jews chattered incessantly.

gaberlunzie (ˌgæbə'lʌnzɪ, -jɪ). *Sc.* Also 6 pl. (? or genitive) **gabirlenzeis,** 9 **gaberloony.** [Of unknown origin; *-lunzie* is traditional Sc. spelling for *-lunyie* (see G), which would be pronounced (-'lʏnjɪ).]

1. A strolling beggar or mendicant. Also, a beadsman (see BEADSMAN 2 b).

1508 in Pitcairn *Crim. Trials Scotl.* I. I. 61 Nov. 19— Andrew Crossar, Convicted..of art and part of the Slaughter of Adam Turnbull of Chalmerlane-Newtoune, and Adam Turnbule, called Gabirlenzeis. **1794** PICKERING *'Keen blaws the Wind'* in *Burns' Wks.* (1856) IV. 91 The Gaber-lunzie tirls my sneck, And shivering tells his waefu' tale. **1816** SCOTT *Antiq.* xii, It just does its office in barking at a gaberlunzie like me. **1826** J. WILSON *Noct. Ambr.* Wks. 1855 I. 64 The political Economy creatures are a cruel set —greedier themselves than gaberlunzies. **1875** *Gd. Words* 280 Gaberlunzies, with blue coat and tin badge, still wandered from door to door begging. **1880** *Blackw. Mag.* Apr. 476 Crowds of sturdy beggars and gaberlunzies in the highest degree picturesque, assail him.

fig. **1856** R. A. VAUGHAN *Mystics* (1860) II. 265 That gaberlunzie, Memory (whose wallet has so many holes), would step in oftener.

appositively. ?*a* **1700** *Song* in Ramsay *Tea-t. Misc.*, The Gaberlunzie-man. **1816** SCOTT *Antiq.* xxvii, There was never sic a braw propine as this sent..through the hands of a gaberlunzie beggar. **1824** —— *Redgauntlet* Let. xi, An auld gaberlunzie fiddler. **18..** WHITTIER *Prose Wks.* (1889) I. 337 We used to see one or more 'gaberlunzie men', pack on shoulder and staff in hand.

transf. **1830** GALT *Lawrie T.* I. ii, The gaberloony winter arose from the chumly-lug.

2. App. the trade or calling of gaberlunzie.

It is perhaps from this instance that the sense of 'wallet' has been derived by editors.

?*a* **1700** *Song* in Ramsay *Tea-t. Misc.* (1733) I. 86 To follow me frae town to town And carry the Gaberlunzie on.

gabert, obs. form of GABBART.

gabfest ('gæbfɛst). *slang* (chiefly *U.S.*). [f. GAB *sb.*² + FEST.] A gathering for talk; a spell of talking; a prolonged conference or conversation.

1897 *Boston Transcript* 7 Jan. 15/7 A Chicago paper speaks of the speechmaking on Andrew Jackson's day as 'the Democratic gabfest'. **1910** W. M. RAINE *B. O'Connor* 101 I'll leave you and your jelly fish Scotty to your gabfest. **1942** J. D. CARR *Seat of Scornful* xi. 147 When can I come and see you for a bit of gabfest about this business? **1960** *Spectator* 30 Sept. 470 A shambles as big as the Labour gabfest. **1971** 'D. CORY' *Sunburst* v. 78 A watching brief on the Common Market gabfest.

Gabian ('geɪbɪən). [f. the name of the locality where it is found.] ***Gabian oil*** (see quot.).

1852 BRANDE *Dict. Sci. Lit. & Art* Supp., *Gabian oil*, a petroleum or mineral naphtha exuding from the strata at Gabian, a village in Languedoc.

gabion ('geɪbɪən). Forms: 6-7 **gabbion(e,** 7 **gab(b)yon,** 6- **gabion.** [a. F. *gabion*, ad. It. *gabbione* augmentative of *gabbia* cage:—L. *cavea*. Cf. It. *gaggia* = F. *cage*:—*cavea*: see CAGE.]

1. A wicker basket, of cylindrical form, usually open at both ends, intended to be filled with earth, for use in fortification and engineering.

1579 DIGGES *Stratiot.* 113 Graund Maunds, or Gabbions. **1598** BARRET *Theor. Warres* v. iv. 137 To place and fill the gabbions; to digge earth for the same. **1625** MASSINGER *New Way* v. i, With these gabions guarded, Unload my great artillery. **1656** DAVENANT *Siege Rhodes* I. Dram. Wks. 1873 III. 289 More gabions, and renew the blinds. **1747** *Gentl. Mag.* 437 The sapper..putting the earth which he diggs up into the gabion. **1828** J. M. SPEARMAN *Brit. Gunner* (ed. 2) 229 There is also a smaller description of gabions, in the form of a frustum of a cone. **1874** KNIGHT *Dict. Mech.* I. 932 Gabions filled with stones are used in civil engineering as defences for starlings of bridges. **1876** BANCROFT *Hist. U.S.* V. lvii. 131 The gabions and the interstices of the fascines were filled with snow.

¶ **2.** Used *fig.* (with allusion to quots. 1638) by Scott.

1638 ADAMSON *Muses Threnodie* (*note*), The ornaments of his Cabin, which by a Catachrestic name, he usually calleth *Gabions*. *Ibid.* (*title of piece*), Inventarie of the *Gabions*, in M. George his Cabinet. *a* **1832** SCOTT in *Harper's Mag.* LXXVIII. (1889) 779 [Gabions are] curiosities of small intrinsic value, whether rare books, antiquities, or small articles of the fine or of the useful arts. **1837** LOCKHART *Scott* (1838) VII. 218 Sir Walter..began..to dictate of Laidlaw what he designed to publish in the usual novel shape, under the title of 'Reliquiæ Trottcosienses, or the Gabions of Jonathan Oldbuck'.

3. *attrib.* as ***gabion-battery, stuff***; **gabion-knife,** a knife for cutting the osier twigs in making gabions.

1633 T. STAFFORD *Pac. Hib.* III. ii. (1810) 525 Nor wood for necessary use, or gabion stuffe within three miles of it.

gabionade (geɪbɪə'neɪd). Also 8-9 **gabionnade.** [ad. F. *gabionnade*: see GABION and -ADE.] A work formed of gabions, whether in fortification or engineering.

1706 in PHILLIPS (ed. Kersey), *Gabionnado*. **1721** in BAILEY, *Gabionnade*. **1828** J. M. SPEARMAN *Brit. Gunner* (ed. 2) 231 Gabionnade, a term employed to denote a work thrown up in haste. **1880** KINGLAKE *Crimea* VI. vi. 375 The construction of a thick gabionade. **1893** *Times* 29 May 11/1 Engineers put together Jones's gabions, and with them and sandbags constructed a gabionade.

gabionage ('geɪbɪənɪdʒ). [ad. F. *gabionnage*: see GABION and -AGE.] *collect.* Gabions as a whole; the supply of gabions (Webster 1864).

gabionate ('geɪbɪəneɪt), *v.* [f. GABION + -ATE³.] *trans.* To protect with or as with gabions.

a **1693** URQUHART *Rabelais* III. viii. 72 His Lady..advised him to shield, fence, and gabionate it with a..Helmet.

gabioned ('geɪbɪənd), *ppl. a.* [f. GABION + -ED².] Having gabions or something resembling gabions; protected with or as with gabions.

1589 *Late Voy. Sp. & Port.* (1881) 59 The 4 day were planted..two demie Canons and two Culverings against the towne, defended or gabbioned with a crosse wall. **1619** LUSHINGTON *Repet. Serm.* in *Phenix* (1708) II. 484 A firm Rock spread out of the Roots of Golgotha, gabion'd and rough-cast with Flint. **1633** T. STAFFORD *Pac. Hib.* III. vi. (1810) 547 The place will be so trenched and gabioned, as you must runne upon assured death. **1860** RUSSELL *Diary India* I. 378 Floating batteries, strongly parapetted and gabioned.

†**gabionized,** *pa. pple. Obs.*⁻⁰ [See -IZE.] = GABIONED.

1611 FLORIO, *Gabbionato*, Gabbionized.

gable ('geɪb(ə)l), *sb.*¹ Forms: α. *Sc.* and *north.* 4-9 **gavel(l,** 4-6 **gavyll,** 5 **gavul, gawill,** 4, 7 **gavil(l.** β. 5 **gabyl, gabul,** 7-8 **gabel(l,** 4- **gable.** [The northern form *gavel* (still in Scotland pron. 'gev(ə)l) is perh. directly a. ON. *gafl* masc., of the same meaning (Sw. *gafvel*, Da. *gavl*). The southern form *gable* might be a dial. variant of this (cf. *nable* for *navel*), but is more prob. a. OF. *gable, jable* masc., which is not found in other Rom. langs., and is prob. a. ON. *gafl*.

The corresponding words in the other Teut. langs. (OTeut. types **gablâ, -ljâ*) have the sense of 'fork': so OE. *ȝ(e)afol*, OS. *gaflia* (Gallée *OS. Texts* 157), MDu. *gaffel(e* (Du. *gaffel*), OHG. *gabala* (MHG., mod.G. *gabel*) fem.; app. cognate are OIr. *gabul, gobul*, Welsh *gafl*, fork (of the body, of a branch); the L. *gabalus*, app. meaning some kind of gallows or cross, is by some supposed to be lit. 'fork', and to have been adopted from Teut. or Celtic. In Goth. and WGer. the sense 'gable' is expressed by words that appear to be related by ablaut to the word for 'fork'; Goth. *gibla* wk. masc. πτερύγιον, 'pinnacle' of the temple, MDu. *ghevel* (Du. *gevel*), OHG. *gibil* (mod.G. *giebel*) masc. With different sense, but agreeing in root, grade, and suffix, are OHG. *gebal* head, *gibilla* crown of the head, app. cognate with Gr. κεφαλή head (OAr. root **ghebh*). Possibly the primitive meaning of the words may have been 'top', 'vertex'; this may have given rise to the sense of 'gable', and this latter to the sense of 'fork', a gable being originally formed by two pieces of timber crossed at the top supporting the end of the roof-tree (see FORK *sb.* 7).]

1. a. The vertical triangular piece of wall at the end of a ridged roof, from the level of the eaves to the summit.

α. **1374** in *Hist. Dunelm. Scrip. tres* App. p. cxli, Unum gavel capellæ super portam. **1379** *Mem. Ripon* (Surtees) III. 101 Emendand. in le Westgavell, 15*s.* 3*d.* *c* **1425** WYNTOUN *Cron.* VII. x. 275 That west gawill alsua In till hys tyme all gert he ma. **1531-2** *Durham Househ. Bk.* (Surtees) 176 Ac in fine aulæ super le gavylls. **1680** A. HAIG in J. Russell *Haigs* xi. (1881) 309 Putting up in the waster gavills, to the heads, 3 chimlies. **1703** T. N. *City & C. Purchaser* 148 Gavel, a word used by some, by which they mean the same as Gable. **1753** *Scots Mag.* Apr. 164/1 The gavel of..Reid's land..to be taken down and rebuilt. **1894** CROCKETT *Lilac Sunbonnet* 77 Sitting by the gable end (the 'gavel' as it was locally expressed).

β. *c* **1386** CHAUCER *Miller's T.* 385 And whan thou..hast ..broke an hole on heigh upon the gable Unto the gardinward, over the stable. *c* **1430** LYDG. *Min. Poems* 204 Wyde as a chirche that hath a gabyl. **1703** MOXON *Mech. Exerc.* 141 The principal Rafters, Purlins, Gables, &c. are also fram'd and set up. **1828** SCOTT *F.M. Perth* iii, Be at the lattice window on our east gable by the very peep of dawn. **1839** MISS MITFORD in L'Estrange *Life* (1870) III. vii. 97 A porch and great gables with spread-eagles distinguish it. **1876** MISS BRADDON *J. Haggard's Dau.* I. 5 With steep gables and curious abutments.

transf. **1896** SIR R. TEMPLE *Story of my Life* I. x. 212 The icy and snowy gables, towers, pinnacles of the mid-Himalayan range.

b. Any architectural member having the form of a gable, as a triangular canopy over a window or a doorway. See GABLE-END 2.

1850 PARKER *Gloss. Archit.* (ed. 5) 225 *Gablets*, small ornamented gables formed over tabernacles, niches, buttresses, etc.

2. The triangular-topped end wall of a building; a gable-end.

1362 LANGL. *P. Pl.* A. III. 50 Woldustow Glase þe Gable and graue þerinne þi nome. *c* **1440** *Promp. Parv.* 183/2 Gabyl, or gable, pykd walle. *a* **1661** FULLER *Worthies*, *Exeter* I. (1662) 273 The Houses stand sidewaies backward into their Yards, and onely endwaies with their Gables towards the Street. **1806** *Gazetteer Scotl.* (ed. 2) 318 Towards the street, the ends or gables of the houses are placed. **1874** in PARKER *Goth. Archit.* Gloss. 324.

3. *Mech.* (See quot.)

1888 *Lockwood's Dict. Mech. Engin.*, *Gable*, the outer ends of the cranked portion of a crank shaft. Dressing this down square is termed cutting the gable.

4. *attrib.* and *Comb.*, as ***gable-belfry***, ***-coping***, ***-perch***, ***-roof*** (hence ***gable-roofed*** adj.), ***-wall***; ***gable-shaped*** adj.; ***gable-wise*** adv.; **gable-cresting** = *gable-coping*; †**gable-fork** = FORK *sb.* 7; **gable-topped** *a.*, topped by a gable, having a gable-shaped top; **gable-window**, a window in the gable or gable-end of a building.

1894 E. H. Barker *Summ. in Guyenne* 67 A little old Gothic church with a *gable-belfry. **1860** G. E. Street in *Archæol. Cantiana* III. 115 Surmounted by a high-pitched roof, finished with *gable-copings and crosses. **1886** Willis & Clark *Cambridge* III. 553 Elaborate *gable-cresting of the time of James I. **1371** *Durh. Halm. Rolls* (Surtees) 111 Reparabit unam grangiam de uno pare de siles et duobus *gauilforks. **1855** M. Arnold *Balder* Poems 1877 I. 151 And in Valhalla from his *gable-perch The golden crested cock began to crow. **1850** Parker *Gloss. Archit.* (ed. 5) 254 *note*, A hipped-roof is quite distinct from a *gable-roof. **1742** Browne Willis *Survey Cath.* II. [III.] 334 The great Cross Isle or Tansept is *Gabell roof'd in a sloping Fashion. **1850** Leitch *Müller's Anc. Art* §46 In the walls of Mycenæ and Larissa..are to be found *gable-shaped passages formed of blocks resting against each other. **1842** *Civil Engin. & Arch. Jrnl.* V. 81/1 Some..architects..give us a gable-topped and an elliptic bed-topped window alternately. **1903** Ld. R. Gower *Rec. & Remin.* 214 A small gable-topped building. **1923** R. G. Collingwood *Roman Brit.* 86 A gable-topped canopy. **1442** *Building Accts. Thame Ch.* in *Oxf. Archit. & Hist. Soc. Proc.* (1860–4) N.S.I. 274 John Walschef 5 dayys for to take a down y *gabul wall. **1886** Willis & Clark *Cambridge* II. 162 The space between the screen and the gable wall of the Hall. **1447–8** Hen. VI in Lyte *Eton Coll.* (1875) 501 A grete *gable wyndowe of ix dayes. **1872** Ruskin *Fors Clav.* xxi. 12 A branch or two of larch, set *gable-wise across them.

†'**gable**, *sb.*[2] *Obs.* Also 5–6 **gabul(le**, 6 **gabel(l**. A variant of CABLE *sb.*, frequent in the 15–16th c. Also *attrib.* and *Comb.*, as ***gable-rope***; ***gable-like***, ***-long*** adjs.

1420 [see CABLE]. *a* **1440** *Sir Eglam.* 1193 Hys gabulle and hys ropys everechone Was portrayed verely. *c* **1440** *Bone Flor.* 1864 They stroke the sayle, the gabuls braste, They hyed them a bettur spede. *c* **1500** *Debate Carpenter's Tools* in Halliw. *Nugæ Poet.* 18 'Softe, ser,' seyd the gabulle-rope, 'Methinke gode ale is in ȝour tope.' **1535** *Act 27 Hen. VIII*, c. 4 §4 Any person..taking any vitailes, gabels, ropes, ankers, or sayles. **1542** *Lam. & Piteous Treat.* in *Harl. Misc.* (Malh.) I. 239 Our shyppes, losyng theyr ancres and gables, were broken and beaten in peces. **1582** N. Lichefield tr. *Castanheda's Conq. E. Ind.* ix. 25 b, Those which watched in the shippe Berrio, felt the gabell of the same wagging. **1607** Topsell *Four-f. Beasts* (1658) 156 Revenge of malice is too little to satisfie a serpent, she twineth her gable-like body about the throat of the amazed elephant. **1608** —— *Serpents* (1658) 612 She twineth her gable-long body about his neck. **1615** Chapman *Odyss.* v. 333 Which, with dispatch, he wrought, Gables, and halsters, tacklings.

b. *fig.* Bonds, chains.

1602 *Content. betw. Lib. & Prod.* II. iv. in Hazl. *Dodsley* VIII. 350 Sweet Money, that gables of bondage unbinds.

Hence †'**gable** *v.*, ? to stretch ropes across.

1649 *Thomason Tracts* (Brit. Mus.) CCCCXLII. vi. 52 They had gabled all their streets.

gable ('geɪb(ə)l), *v.* [f. GABLE *sb.*[1]] **a.** *trans.* To make (a roof) end in a gable. **b.** *intr.* To form gables.

1848 H. Webb *Sk. Cont. Eccles.* 14 The roofs of all four arms of the great cross are extremely high; but though gabling nobly in the nave and transept fronts, and ending apsidally in the choir, they are all four hipped in the most ugly way, instead of gabling on the central lantern. **1874** Micklethwaite *Mod. Par. Churches* 23 Its roof must be gabled.

gable, obs. form of GABBLE, GABELLE.

gabled ('geɪb(ə)ld), *ppl. a.* [f. GABLE *sb.*[1] or *v.* + -ED.] Furnished with a gable or gables.

1849 Freeman *Archit.* 189 Covered with a cupola, which again is sometimes gabled. **1862** H. Marryat *Year in Sweden* II. 235 Before you stands an old gabled mansion. **1877** Mrs. Forrester *Mignon* I. 48 A low long house with gabled roof. **1886** Mary Linskill in *Gd. Words* 5 Some of the houses stood with their gabled ends towards the street.

'**gable-,end.** An end-wall that is surmounted by a gable.

α. **1464** *Nottingham Rec.* II. 374 A lode cley to dawbe þe gavulende with. **1597** *Wills & Inv. N.C.* (Surtees 1860) 344 Aboute one yeard above the floore, on the south gavell end. **1795** Macneill *Will & Jean* I. xxii, Up the gavel end thick spreading, Crap the clasping ivy green.

β. *a* **1380** *St. Bernard* 299 in Horstm. *Altengl. Leg.* (1878) 46 In þe gable end of þe churche Ben þreo wyndouwus. **1427** in Heath *Grocers' Comp.* (1869) 5 The West Gabylende of the Halle. **1562** J. Heywood *Prov. & Epigr.* (1867) 179 Gable endes, cambers, parlers. **1601** B. Jonson *Poetaster* III. i, I affect not these high gable-ends, these Tuscan tops, nor your coronets, nor your arches, nor your pyramids. **1708** S. Molyneux in *Phil. Trans.* XXVI. 38, I found all was done on or near the Gabel-end of the House. **1838** Lytton *Alice* 61 Do tell me to whom that old house belongs—with the picturesque gable-end, and Gothic turrets. **1840** Barham *Ingol. Leg.*, *Leg. Folkestone*, The numerous gable-ends and bayed windows. **1878** Sir G. Scott *Lect. Archit.* I. 296 Perhaps..now only some one gable-end..shows the noble scale of the ancient church.

†**2.** Used for GABLE *sb.*[1] 1, 1 b. *Obs.*

1632–33 *Contract* in Willis & Clark *Cambridge* (1886) II. 697 The Gable-ends ouer the Windowes in yᵉ Roofe to be of Bricke. **1703** Moxon *Mech. Exerc.* 163 The Angle a Gable-end is set to, is called the Pitch of the Gable-end.

3. *transf.* and *fig.*

1794 Mathias *Purs. Lit.* (1798) 329 Lord Monboddo believed..that men had once tails depending from the gable end of their bodies. **1834** *Oxf. Univ. Mag.* I. 16 They have ..satisfied themselves with narrow, contracted, and, as it were, gable end views of the monetary edifice.

Hence '**gable-,ended** *a.*, having a gable-end.

1823 P. Nicholson *Pract. Build.* 129 Gable-ended roofs, unless properly supported by ties, are liable to thrust out the walls. **1851** H. Melville *Whale* ii. 10 A gable-ended old house, one side palsied as it were and leaning over sadly.

gablet ('geɪblɪt). [a. AF. *gablet*: see GABLE *sb.*[1] and -ET[1].] A little gable, esp. one constructed as an ornament over a tabernacle, niche, buttress, etc.

[**1395** *Contracts for tomb of Rich. II & Anne* in Rymer *Fœdera* (1709) VII. 798/1 Et auxi ferrount Tabernacles, appelles Hovels, ove Gabletz, de dit Metall Endorrez, as Testes.] *a* **1440** *Sir Degrev.* 1462 Alle the wallus of geete, With gaye gablettus and grete. **1512–3** *Contract* 4 Jan. in Willis & Clark *Cambridge* (1886) I. 610 With Fynyalles, ryfant gablettes, Batelmentes..and euery other thyng belongyng to the same. **1846** *Ecclesiol.* V. 17 These are generally worked in the three faces into gablets. **1861** *Times* 12 Oct., A dim perspective of gables, gablets, dormers, and pointed roofs. **1866** G. Macdonald *Ann. Q. Neighb.* ii. (1878) 20 It lifted its gablet carved to look like a canopy.

Hence '**gableted** *ppl. a.*, furnished with a gablet or gablets.

1865 *Athenæum* No. 1959. 658/3 A column..surmounted by a gableted head. **1887** *Stratford-on-Avon Her.* 21 Oct. 8/3 The central spire has on four opposite sides gableted spire lights.

gablett, obs. form of GOBLET.

gabling, obs. form of GABBLING.

gablock ('gæblək). *Obs.* exc. *dial.* Also 9 **gablack, gaflock.** [var. of GAVELOCK.]

†**1.** An artificial metallic spur for a fighting cock. *Obs.*

1688 R. Holme *Armoury* II. 252/2 Gablocks are Spurs made of Iron, or Brass, or Silver and are fixed on the Legs of such Cocks as want their natural Spurs, some call them Gaffs. **1706** in Phillips (ed. Kersey). **1848** in Craig, and in mod. Dicts.

2. *dial.* An iron crowbar.

c **1746** J. Collier (Tim Bobbin) *View Lanc. Dial.* Wks. (1862) 62 Truth on honesty..ston os stiff os o gablock. **1747** Hooson *Miner's Dict.* s.v. *Gablock*..we are seldome without one in the Works, which is straight and about a Yard long, and of very good Use to wrest a Stone, or a Spark of Ore that is large. **1855** Morton *Cycl. Agric.* II. 723 *Gablock, Gavelock*, an iron bar for putting up hurdles with.

gaboard, obs. form of GABBART.

Gaboon, gaboon (gə'bu:n). Also **Gabun.** [The name of a province and river in West Africa.]

1. A hardwood from the tree *Aucoumea klaineana*. Also *attrib.*

1910 *Encycl. Brit.* VIII. 843/2 The heart-wood is very black and hard and is known as black ebony,..and Gabun, Lagos, Calabar or Niger ebony. **1913** *Chambers's Jrnl.* Aug. 621/1 Gaboon mahogany is another timber which the wood-worker regards with disdain, owing to its softness. **1920** A. L. Howard *Man. Timbers of World* 140 Gaboon. *Boswellia Klaineana*... This..useful wood..fills a place of importance which justifies a title which would give it individuality, though it should not be called mahogany. *Ibid.*, Gaboon has been tried for the purpose of making aeroplane propellers. **1960** *Guardian* 29 Sept. 9/1 Another very pleasant thing about the classrooms is the row of gaboon-faced sliding doors.

2. Comb., as **Gaboon adder** or **viper** [tr. F. *échidnée du Gabon* (Duméril & Bibron, in *Erpétologie générale* (1854) VII. 1428)], a snake, *Bitis gabonica*.

1928 *Daily Tel.* 29 May 6 Specimens of the green mamba and gaboon viper from West Africa. **1954** J. A. Pringle *Common Snakes* 26 Gaboon Adder... This snake is widely distributed in the Western forest of tropical Africa..but its occurrence in the Union is restricted to the northern tips of Zululand and South West Africa. **1965** R. & D. Morris *Men & Snakes* i. 16 The Gaboon viper has a pair of enlarged scales between its nostrils which stick out like two little horns.

Gabriel ('geɪbrɪəl). [Heb. *Gabhrīēl* (LXX and N.T. Γαβριήλ).] The name of one of the archangels: see Dan. ix. 21; Luke i. 19, 26. Used in certain phrases, as **Gabriel-bell** (see quot.); **Gabriel('s)-hound** (see quots.); **Gabriel-rache, -rachet** (in some dialects corruptly *Gabble-ratch, -ratchet*) = *Gabriel-hound*.

1849–53 Rock *Ch. of Fathers* III. ix. 338 There yet hangs the *Gabriel-bell..which the sexton had to ring at morn and evening every day as a bidding to the people..that they should greet our Lady with these five 'Hail Marys'. ?**16..** Kennett in *MS. Lansd.* 1033 in *Cath. Angl.* 147 *note*, At Wednesbury in Staffordshire, the colliers going to their pits early in the morning hear the noise of a pack of hounds in the air, to which they give the name of *Gabriel's Hounds, though the more sober and judicious take them only to be wild geese, making this noise in their flight. **1876** *Whitby Gloss.*, *Gabriel hounds*, the flocks of yelping wild geese high in the air, migrating southward in the twilight evenings of autumn, their cry being more audible than the assemblage is visible. As the foreboders of evil, people close their ears and cover their eyes until the phalanx has passed over. **1483** *Cath. Angl.* 147/2 *Gabrielle rache, *camalion.* [**1808–25** Jamieson, *Gaubertie-shells*..a hobgoblin who..has been heard to make a loud roaring, accompanied with a barking similar to that of little dogs..and a clattering resembling that of shells striking against each other. *Lanarks.*] **1891** Atkinson *Last of Giantkillers* 196 He also told me a very great deal about the Gabriel-rachet..and all that it could ever foreshow. **1893** J. H. Turner *Hist. Brighouse* 240 No wonder that hobgoblins..gabble-ratches and headless-horses scoured the country.

†**Gabrill**, ? punning alteration of GABBLE *sb.*

1596 Nashe *Saffron Walden* Wks. (Grosart) III. 78 Now where be our honorable Caualiers, that keepe such a prating and a gabrill about our Gabriell and his admirable stile.

gabronite: see GABBRONITE.

gaby ('geɪbɪ; *dial.* 'gɔ:bɪ). *colloq.* and *dial.* Also **gab(b)ey, gawby, gauvey.** [orig. in north. and midland dialects; of unknown etymology; some have suggested a connexion with GAPE (cf. Icel. *gapi* 'rash, reckless person'); but the dial. forms hardly favour this.] A simpleton.

1796 Grose *Dict. Vulg. Tongue* (ed. 3) *Gabey*, a foolish fellow. **1833** Marryat *P. Simple* xxxiv, The marine officer is a bit of a gaby, and takes offence where none was meant. **1848** Thackeray *Van. Fair* lxvii, She is still whimpering after that gaby of a husband. **1863** Mrs. Toogood *Yorksh. Dial.*, He's such a gauvey it's now use to tell him how to do it. **1875** Ouida *Signa* I. iv. 47 What a gaby a man is without a wife! **1885** Stevenson *Child's Gard.* 78 While we stand watching her, Staring like gabies.

Hence '**gabyhood** [-HOOD], the state or condition of a gaby; a state resembling that of a gaby.

1836 *Fraser's Mag.* XIV. 736 The narrative opens with a very lively description of the gabyhood of Paris in 1579.

gad (gæd), *sb.*[1] Forms: 4–7 **gadd**, 5–6 **gadde**, 8–9 *Sc.* **gaud, gawd**, 4– **gad**. [a. ON. *gadd-r* spike, nail = OHG. and MHG. *gart*, Goth. *gazd-s*:—OTeut. **gazdo-z* (cf. L. *hasta*). From the OTeut. deriv. **gazdjâ* comes OHG. *gerta* (G. *gerte*), OE. *ȝerd, ȝierd, ȝyrd*: see YARD. The original sense is probably that of 'spike' (as in Goth. and ON.), but the name is also given to the handle or shaft to which this is fixed (as in L. *hasta*); hence the meaning 'rod'. The development of the word in Eng. has also been influenced by its similarity, both in form and in meaning, to OE. *gád* GOAD, with which it is not originally connected. The forms are not always easy to separate.]

1. A sharp spike of metal. *Obs.* exc. *Hist.*

a **1225** *Leg. Kath.* 1945 Let þurhdriuen þrefter þe spaken & te felien mid irnene gadien. ? *a* **1400** *Morte Arth.* 3621 Gryme gaddes of stele, ghywes of iryne. **1563** Golding *Cæsar* VII. 225 b, Stakes of a fote long stickt full of Iron hokes, and theis thei called gaddes [L. *stimulos*]. **1600** F. Walker *Sp. Mandeville* 145 b, A light Armour..full of short sharpe gaddes or Bodkins. **1834** [see GADLING.[1]]. **1868** Cussans *Her.* vii. 104 It [the caltrap] was formed of four short but strong spikes, or Gads.

†**b.** Applied to a stylus. *Obs.*

1570 Foxe tr. *Prudentius' Death Cassianus* in *A. & M.* (ed. 2) 129/1 These gads were but their pens wherewyth Theyr tables wrytten were. **1588** Shaks. *Tit. A.* IV. i. 103, I will goe get a leafe of brasse, And with a Gad of steele will write these words.

c. = GADLING[1]. (Cf. GAD *v.*[1] a.)

1830 Meyrick *Illustr. Anct. Arms & Armour* Plate lxxix, *Fig.* 2 A long gauntlet of the time of Elizabeth. In this specimen the gads lap over upwards.

2. A bar of metal, esp. of iron or steel; also, an ingot. ? *Obs.* In *Her.*, 'a rectangular plate of steel, borne in the Arms of the Ironmongers' Company' (Cussans).

c **1250** *Gen. & Ex.* 3185 On an gold gad ðe name god Is grauen. **1387** Trevisa *Higden* (Rolls) VI. 199 Slegges and hameres, wiþ þe whiche smythes smyteþ and tempreþ grete gaddes of iren. **1430–40** Lydg. *Bochas* IX. xxxi. (1554) 210 b, Theodorus..On his body layde gaddes read brenning. **1513** Douglas *Æneis* VIII. xii. 50 Slang gaddis of irne, and stane kast gret plente. **1581** W. Stafford *Exam. Compl.* ii. (1876) 60 Then I had as liefe haue smal gadds or plats of Siluer and Gold, without any coyne at al. **1587** *Mirr. Mag.*, *Wolsey* lvii, To fawning doggs some times I gaue a bone, And flong some scrapps to such as nothing had; But in my hands, still kept the golden gad, That seru'd my turne. **1686** Plot *Staffordsh.* 374 They cut it [steel] into narrower barrs about half an inch over, and then break it into short pieces of an inch, or two inches long, call'd Gadds. **1703** Moxon *Mech. Exerc.* 58 Flemish-steel is made..some in Bars and some in Gads. **1741** *Compl. Fam.-Piece* I. i. 69 Quenching..in this Liquor a Gad of Steel, about eight or ten Inches long. **1814** Scott *Wav.* xxx, 'Deil be in me but I put this het gad down her throat.' **1826** *Ann. Reg.* Chron. 29/2 The gaud or iron bar and the ring to which he was fastened. [Cf. GAID.] **1895** Crockett *Men of Mosshags* 377 After levelling a file [of soldiers] with his gaud of iron.

b. *Mining.* A pointed tool of iron or steel (see quot. 1881).

1671 *Phil. Trans.* VI. 2104 The Instruments commonly used in Mines..are..Gadds, or Wedges of 2*l.* weight, 4 square, well steeled at the point. **1753** Chambers *Cycl. Supp.*, *Gad*, in mining..is a small punch of iron with a long handle of wood. **1800** Mar. Edgeworth *Lame Jervas* i. (1832) 6 A pickaxe and a gad were put into my hands. **1881** Raymond *Mining Gloss.*, *Gad*, 1. a steel wedge, 2. a small iron punch with a wooden handle used to break up ore.

3. A spear. *Obs.* exc. *Hist.*

1548 W. Patten *Exped. Scotl.* in Arb. *Garner* III. 85 Four or five of this Captain's prickers with their gads ready charged. *Ibid.* 133 The Scottish prickers, within less than their gad's length asunder. *a* **1555** Ridley in *Cert. godly Conf.* (1556) 33 b, I haue knowen my contreiemen watche nighte and daie in their harnesse..and their speares in their hands (you call them northen gads). **1820** SCOTT *Monast.* xiv, I took a young Southern fellow out of saddle with my lance, and cast him, it might be, a gad's length from his nag.

4. A pointed rod or stick used for driving oxen; a goad; also *dial.* (see quots. 1796 and 1855).

c **1300** *Havelok* 279 Al Engelond was of him adrad So his þe beste fro þe gad. **1398** TREVISA *Barth. De P.R.* XVIII. xiv. (1495) 774 An oxe herde yockyth the oxen..and pricketh the slowe with a gad and makyth them drawe euen. **1514** BARCLAY *Cyt. & Uplondyshm.* (Percy Soc.) 15 Than brought our Lorde to them the carte & harowe, The gad & the whyp. **1535** COVERDALE *Judg.* iii. 31 Samgar..which slewe sixe hundreth Philistynes with an oxes gadd. **1607** *N. Riding Rec.* (1883) I. 78 Tho. Hildreth presented for that armed with gaddes he had assaulted John Pearson. **1796** W. MARSHALL *Yorksh.* (ed. 2) II. 321 *Gad*, a supple, tapering rod, six or seven feet long, with a leathern thong, about three feet long, fastened to the weaker end. **1855** ROBINSON *Whitby Gloss.*, *Gad*, a tapering rod ended with a leather thong as a whip for driving a team of horses or oxen. **1863** J. L. W. *By-gone Days* 10 The long gad or goad with which he impelled the horses or oxen.

†**b.** Phrase. ***upon the gad***: as if pricked with a gad; suddenly. (Cf. *upon the spur of the moment.*) *Obs.*

1605 SHAKS. *Lear* I. ii. 26 All this done Vpon the gad?

5. *dial.* A rod or wand, esp. a fishing-rod. Also, a stake or stout stick.

1535 FISHER *Wks.* (1876) 395 And hys blessed heade so Crowned, they dyd beate it downe with a gadde, or a harde Reede. **1552** HULOET, Angling gad, or rodde, *pertica.* **1796** W. MARSHALL *Yorksh.* (ed. 2) Gloss. s.v. (E.D.S.), A fishing-rod is in like manner called a 'fishing-gad'. **1829** T. DOUBLEDAY *Fisher's Call* in *Anniversary* 64 Then up an' rig your gads, And to it, fishers, to it! **1847** FOSTER in *Whistle-Binkie* (Scot. Songs) Ser. II. (1890) 230 The lang sma' taper gad is swung Around wi easy slight. **1863** BARNES *Dorset Gloss.*, *Gad*, a hedge stake, or stout stick. **1887** T. HARDY *Woodlanders* iii, An armful of gads thrown on the still hot embers caused them to blaze up cheerfully.

6. A measuring rod for land; hence, a measure of length differing in various districts. Cf. GOAD *sb.*

c **1440** *Promp. Parv.* 184/1 *Gad*, to mete wythe londe (*P.* gadde, or rodde), *decempeda.* **1502** ARNOLDE *Chron.* (1811) 173 In dyuers odur placis in this lande they mete ground by pollis gaddis and roddis some be of xviij. foote some of xx fote and som xvi fote in length. **1599** SKENE *De Verb. Sign.* s.v. *Particata*, Ane rod is ane staffe, or gade of tymmer, quhairwith land is measured. **1706** PHILLIPS (ed. Kersey), *Gad*, or Geometrical Pearch, a Measure of Ten Foot, and in some places but Nine Foot.

b. A division of an open pasture, in Lincolnshire usually $6\frac{1}{2}$ feet wide; = SWATH.

1593 *Kirton-in-Lindsey Court Roll* (*N.W. Linc. Gloss.*). **1717** *N. Riding Rec.* VII. 285, I am seized of..four gads in the Bishop Ings. **1794** *Act Inclos. S. Kelsey* 19 Owners and Proprietors of Gads in a certain Piece of Ground..each Gad being Two Roods, Two Perches and a Half.

7. Comb.: **gad-bit** (see quot.); **gad-cracking** (see *gad-whip* 1889); **gad-crook, -hook, -meadow** (see quots.); **gad-nail** (see quot. 1841); **gad-sledge** *Mining*, a sledge hammer for driving gads; †**gad-staff** = GAD *sb.*¹ 4; †**gad-steel** (see quot. 1703); **gad-stick** = GAD *sb.*¹ 4; †**gad-wand** = GAD *sb.*¹ 4, 6; **gad-whip**, a heavy cart-whip. Also GAD-BEE, GAD-BREEZE, GAD-FLY, GAD-MAN.

1847–78 HALLIWELL, *Gad-bit, a nail-passer. **1841** HAMPSON *Medii Ævi Kalend.* I. 182 At Hundon, in Lincolnshire, there is still annually practised on this day [Palm Sunday] a remarkable custom, called *Gad Cracking. **1886** ELWORTHY *W. Somerset Word-bk.*, *Gad-crook, a long pole with an iron hook or claw. **1847–78** HALLIWELL, *Gad-hook, a long pole with an iron hook attached to it. *Somerset.* **1787** *Surv. Manor Kirton-in-Lindsey* in *N.W. Linc. Gloss.* s.v., All the lands in the Ings are laid out in gads or swaths; they are called *gad-meadows. **1375–6** *Abingdon Acc.* (Camden) 28 Item in clauis, *gadnayl et bordnayl..ij *s.* ij *d.* **1841** HARTSHORNE *Salop. Antiqua* Gloss., *Gadnail*, a long and stout nail used chiefly in fastening posts and rails. **1874** J. H. COLLINS *Metal Mining* 61 These boring sledges are sometimes used for driving wedges or 'gads'..Sometimes a special '*gad-sledge' is provided for the purpose. **15..** *Wyf of Auchtirmuchty* 46 (Laing), Scho lowsit oxin aucht or nyne, And hynt ane *gad-staff in hir hand. *a* **1618** *Rates Merchandize* L ij a, *Steele*, vocat. *Gad-steele the halfe barrell. **1622** MALYNES *Anc. Law-Merch.* 270 Good Steele in barres, and also Gad Steele. **1703** MOXON *Mech. Exerc.* 58 Flemish-steel is made..some in Bars and some in Gads, and is therefore by us call'd Flemish-steel, and sometimes Gad-steel. **1375** BARBOUR *Bruce* x. 232 He than lete the *gad wand fall. **1513** DOUGLAS *Æneis* IX. x. 47 And passand by the plewis, for gad wandis, Broddis the oxin wyth speris in our handis. **1570** LEVINS *Manip.* 23/7 A Gadwande, *partica.* **1827** G. P. J. in Hone *Every-day Bk.* II. 394 A very large ox-whip, called here a *gad-whip. [Speaking of the Broughton tenure: see next quot.] **1842** WHITE *Hist. Lincolnsh.* 570 On Palm Sunday, a person from Broughton brings [into Caistor Church porch] a large whip, called a gad whip, the stock of which is made of wood, tapered towards the top; the thong is large, and made of white leather. [He cracked the whip three times, this being the service by which the land at Broughton was held.]

gad (gæd), *sb.*² Short for 'gad-fly' (Halliwell 1847–78); also in comb. ***gad-stricken*** adj.

1658 ROWLAND *Moufet's Theat. Ins.* 937 Those famous Poets of old were said to be *Oestro perciti*, stung with this furious Fly called *Oestrum*. Plutarch cals them Gad-stricken.

gad (gæd), *sb.*³ [f. GAD *v.*²] The action of gadding or rambling about. Only in phrase ***on, upon the gad***: on the move, going about.

c **1815** JANE AUSTEN *Persuas.* (1833) I. vi. 252 Mrs. Charles's nursery-maid..is always upon the gad. **1863** MRS. GASKELL *Sylvia's L.* II. 204 Thou might have a bit o' news to tell one after being on the gad all the afternoon.

gad (gæd), *sb.*⁴ *Anglo-Irish* and *Mil.* [a. Ir. and Gael. *gad.*] A band or rope made of twisted fibres of tough twigs.

1728 *Songs Costume* (Percy Soc.) 216 Or if you'd be reckon'd tight Irish lads, Throw off your cravats and bands, and tie on your gads, And then you'll resemble your primitive dads. **1834** *Brit. Husb.* I. 175 They are generally harnessed with ropes, and collars of straw, or gads. **1841** S. C. HALL *Ireland* II. 22 [They] at once twisted a gad round his neck and hung him from the next tree. **1859** F. A. GRIFFITHS *Artil. Man.* (1862) 254 The gads are made of rods 5 feet long, first twisted until the fibres separate.

Gad (gæd), *sb.*⁵ Now *rare* exc. *arch.* [Minced pronunciation of GOD. Cf. AGAD, EGAD.]

1. Substituted for *God*, in various phrases, chiefly asseverative or exclamatory; esp. in ***by Gad!***

1611 BEAUM. & FL. *Knt. Burn. Pestle* Induct., By gad, if any of them all blow wind in the tail on him, I'll be hanged. **1663** DRYDEN *Wild Gallant* I. i, He's a bold fellow, I vow to gad. **1741** RICHARDSON *Pamela* II. 230 A Challenge, A Challenge, by Gad! **1771** FOOTE *Maid of B.* III. Wks. 1799 II. 237 Mercy a Gad! **1777** SHERIDAN *Trip to Scarborough* v. ii, Gad take me, but they are all in a story! **1840** THACKERAY *Bedford-Row Conspir.* ii, By gad, sir..I never will give you a shilling. **1875** W. S. HAYWARD *Love agst. World* 44 If either of the young dogs wants to quarrel, by gad, sir, he shall quarrel with me.

b. Elliptically = 'God give'. (Cf. 'God ye good den,' Shaks. *Rom. & Jul.* II. iv. 116.) quasi-*arch.*

1849 JAMES *Woodman* xv, Gad ye good night, lords and ladies.

c. ***Gads me, Gads my life***: ? God save me, my life.

1632 MASSINGER & FIELD *Fatal Dowry* III. i, Gads me! he's angry. **1694** CONGREVE *Double Dealer* II. iv, Gad's my life, the man's distracted! **1764** FOOTE *Mayor of G.* I. Wks. 1799 I. 174 Gad's my life, sure as a gun that's her voice.

2. quasi-*int.* perhaps by omission of 'by'.

1608 ARMIN *Nest Ninn.* (1842) 5 And, gad, she will. **1679** DRYDEN *Tr. & Cr.* III. i, Gad, that's exceeding foolish. **1831** LYTTON *Godolphin* 12 Gad, if I were some years younger, I would join them myself. **1881** BESANT & RICE *Chapl. of Fleet* I. 41 Gad! there will be a pretty storm with my lady when she hears it.

3. In various phraseological combinations, as ***Gadsbobs, Gadsbodikins, Gadsbud, Gadsbudlikins, Gadslid, Gadsniggers, Gadsnigs, Gadsnouns, Gadsokers, Gadsookers, Gadsprecious, Gadswookers, Gadswoons, Gadzookers, Gadzooks***, for the explanation of which see the corresponding forms under GOD 14.

1695 CONGREVE *Love for L.* IV. vi, *Gads bobs, does he not know me? **1676** WYCHERLEY *Pl. Dealer* III. i, *Gads-bodikins, you puny upstart in the law, to use me so! **1696** SOUTHERNE *Oroonoko* I. ii, If my husband were alive, Gads-bodykins, you wou'd not use me so. **1694** CONGREVE *Double Dealer* I. iii, *Gadsbud, much better as it is. **1792** WOLCOTT (P. Pindar) *To a Fly* Wks. 1812 III. 167 Gadsbud..thou are not dead. **1698** VANBRUGH *Æsop* II. Wks. (Rtldg.) 374/2 Your friend was a witty person, *gadsbudlikins! **1598** B. JONSON *Ev. Man in Hum.* I. i, And by *gads-lid I scorn it. **1657** *Lust's Domin.* IV. v. in Hazl. *Dodsley* XIV. 164 By Gad's-lid, if I run not After them like a tiger, hough me. **1715** tr. *C'tess D'Aunoy's Wks.* 438 By *Gads-niggers I will have this Pasty. **1651** RANDOLPH, etc. *Hey for Honesty* III. i, Her will tug out her sword, and, *gads nigs! let her take very many heed, her will carbonado very much legs and arms. **1676** WYCHERLEY *Pl. Dealer* III. i, *Gads-nouns! I love thee more and more. **1687** MONTAGUE & PRIOR *Hind & P. Transv.* 6 *Gadsokers! Mr. Johnson, does your Friend think I mean nothing but a Mouse, by all this? **1672** VILLIERS (Dk. Buckhm.) *Rehearsal* II. v. (Arb.) 65 Ah, gadsookers, I have broke my Nose. **1708** *Trip to Dunkirk* in *Harl. Misc.* I. 210 The French, as they say..Are coming, gadsookers! to pay us a visit. **1676** WYCHERLEY *Pl. Dealer* III. i, *Gads-precious! you hectoring person, you, are you wild? **1698** VANBRUGH *Æsop* II. Wks. (Rtldg.) 373/2 *Gadswookers! do people use to ask for folks when they have nothing to say to 'em? **1826** SCOTT *Woodst.* x, *Gadswoons, I would have a peep. **1694** ECHARD *Plautus* 197 Tra. You Dog, there's no such Fish. *Gripus.* *Gad-zooks, but there is tho'. **1751** SMOLLETT *Per. Pic.* (1779) II. xxxvii. 25 'Gadszooks!' said he, 'what business had you with that?' **1838** DICKENS *Nich. Nick.* xxiv, Gadzooks, who can help seeing the way to do it?

gad (gæd), *v.*¹ [f. GAD *sb.*¹] **a.** *trans.* To furnish with gads or a gad. **b.** *intr.*, *Mining*, To use a gad; *trans.* to break up (rock) by means of a gad. (Cf. GADDER¹, GADDING *vbl. sb.*¹) **c.** *trans.* To fasten with a gad-nail. Hence '**gadded** *ppl. a.*

18.. PLANCHÉ (Cent.), The gauntlets..are richly ornamented on the knuckles, but not gadded. **1841** HARTSHORNE *Salop. Antiqua* Gloss., *Gad*, to affix, fasten. Ex. 'Gad it to', chiefly with reference to iron-work.

gad (gæd), *v.*² [Of obscure origin. The common view, that it is f. GAD *sb.*² (the supposed primary sense being 'to rush about like an animal stung by gad-flies') is possible, but does not appear to be favoured by our quots.; the few passages which in any degree countenance it are collected under 1 b. Possibly it was a back-formation from GADLING in its later sense of 'vagabond'.]

1. *intr.* To go from one place to another, to wander; *esp.* to wander about with no serious object, stopping here and there, to rove idly. Also ***to gad about, abroad, out.***

c **1460** *Towneley Myst.* (E.E.T.S.) ii. 149, I hold the mad! wenys thou now that I list gad To gif away my warldis aght? **1529** MORE *Comf. agst. Trib.* III. Wks. 1241/2 To..hold hymself content with that place, & longe not to be gadding out any where elles. **1554** MARTIN *Marr. Priests* xii. Dd iiij b, Whyle the virgins..will nedes..gooe raunginge and gaddinge abrode. **1570–6** LAMBARDE *Peramb. Kent* (1826) 264 Such, as..gadded to Sainct Thomas for helpe and devotion. **1605** CAMDEN *Rem.* (1637) 373 He was alwayes gadding up and downe the world, and had little rest. **1710** PHILIPS *Pastorals* i. 52 She gads where-e'er her roving Fancy leads. *a* **1732** T. BOSTON *Crook in Lot* (1805) 15 Gadding abroad to satisfy her youthful curiosity. *c* **1815** JANE AUSTEN *Persuas.* (1833) I. i. 252 Her upper house-maid and laundry maid are gadding about the village all day long. **1862** MRS. H. WOOD *Mrs. Hallib.* I. xxi. 114 There's Betsy ..gadding out somewhere ever since she came home. **1880** WEBB *Goethe's Faust* II. vi. 157 'Twould injure me with folks, where'er I gadded.

†**b.** Rarely used for: To rush madly about. (In Dryden said of cattle, with distinct etymological reference to GAD *sb.*²) *Obs.*

1552 ELYOT, *Bacchor*..to renne, gadde, and rage as it were a mad man. **1561** STOW *Eng. Chron.* (1580) 39 Women gadding vp & down franticklу in mourning weedes, their haire hanging about their eares, & shaking firebrands. **1678** DRYDEN & LEE *Œdipus* I. Wks. 1883 VI. 141 You shall see them toss their tails, and gad, As if the breeze had stung them. **1688** J. CLAYTON in *Phil. Trans.* XVII. 793 The most of the Cattle will set on gadding, and run..to the River to drink the Salt Water. **1697** DRYDEN *Virg. Georg.* III. 240 Their Stings draw Blood; And drive the Cattle gadding thro' the Wood.

2. *fig.* To go wandering, in desire or thought; to leave the true path. Now *rare.*

1579 TOMSON *Calvin's Serm. Tim.* 4/2 When she gaddeth not astray from the simplicitie of the Gospel. **1600** HEYWOOD *1st Pt. Edw. IV* Wks. 1874 I. 61 Yet, idle eye, wilt thou be gadding still? **1641** MILTON *Prel. Episc.* 6 While we leave the Bible to gadde after these traditions. *a* **1688** CUDWORTH *Immut. Mor.* (1731) 98 Sense wholly gazes and gads abroad. **1692** LOCKE *Educ.* § 167 'Tis no wonder their Thoughts should..seek better Entertainment in more pleasing Objects, after which they will unavoidably be gadding. **1871** B. TAYLOR *Faust* (1875) II. I. iii. 32 If I once regardless gadded For the world my hopes are vain.

†**3.** Of inanimate objects: To move about. *Obs.*

1583 STANYHURST *Æneis* III. (Arb.) 72 Thee roads, thee countrey, thee towns fro oure nauye be gadding. **1600** FAIRFAX *Tasso* XVII. xxi, Th' Arabians next that haue no certaine stay, No house, no home..But euer..From place to place their wandring cities gad. **1618** BOLTON *Florus* IV. i. 260 The frenzie had gadded over the Alpes.

4. Of a plant, tree, etc.: To spread hither and thither, to straggle in growth. *arch.*

1637 [see GADDING *ppl. a.*]. **1675** EVELYN *Terra* (1729) 35 Keep the roots from gadding too far from the Stem. **1752** MASON *Elfrida* 212 The ivy gadding from th' untwisted stem, Curtains each verdant side. **1820** WORDSW. *Fort Fuentes*, Now gads the wild vine o'er the pathless ascent.

†**5.** quasi-*trans.* with cognate object. *Obs.*

1581 J. BELL *Haddon's Answ. Osor.* 38 They gadde many a weerysome journey on pilgrimage unto them.

b. *slang.* (See quot.)

1846 R. L. SNOWDEN *Mag. Assist.* 346 Going without shoes, gadding the hoof. **1865** in HOTTEN *Slang Dict.* (1874).

gadabout ('gædəbaʊt), *a.* and *sb.* [f. GAD *v.*² + ABOUT.]

A. *adj.* Given to gadding or roving, wandering.

1817 SCOTT *Let. to Mrs. Clephane* 23 Mar. in *Lockhart*, The frivolous..gad-about manners of many of our modern belles. **1851** HELPS *Comp. Solit.* iii. (1874) 25 Foolish gad-about, dinner-eating, dancing people. **1857** HUGHES *Tom Brown* I. i, The gadabout propensities of my countrymen.

B. *sb.* One who gads about, esp. from motives of curiosity or gossip.

1837 PALMER *Devonsh. Dialogue* Gloss., *Gad-a-bout*, a gossiping rambling sort of person. **1849** LYTTON *Caxtons* 140 Your shrew-mice are sad gad-abouts. **1859** SMILES *Self-Help* iii. (1860) 66 He even ran some risk of becoming a gadabout and busy-body. **1883** *Harper's Mag.* July 295/1 It is incapacity in this direction which makes gad-abouts of some women.

†**gad-abroad** = GADABOUT *sb.*

1810 W. TAYLOR in Robberds *Mem.* II. 295, I am become quite a gad-abroad.

Gadarene ('gædəri:n), *a.* Also † **Gadarean.** [ad. late L. *Gadarenus*, f. Gr. Γαδαρηνός inhabitant of Gadara, a town of ancient Palestine near the Sea of Galilee.] Of or pertaining to Gadara; used allusively, esp. of a headlong rush or flight, with reference to the story in Matt. viii. 28 of the swine that rushed down a steep cliff into the sea and drowned.

1820 Gadarean [see PIG *sb.*¹ 2 a]. **1899** KIPLING *Stalky & Co.* 210 'This man,' said M'Turk, with conviction, 'is *the* Gadarene Swine.' **1919** *Brit. Manufacturer* Nov. 30/2 In such case we are a debtor nation, and our path is likely to lead us downhill like the Gadarene swine. *a* **1930** D. H. LAWRENCE *Phoenix* (1936) v. 600 A vast mob which may at any moment start to bolt down to the precipice Gadarene-wise. **1952** [see BOUZOUKI].

ˈgad-ˌbee. [f. GAD *sb.*[1]] = GAD-FLY I.
1530 PALSGR. 223/2 Gadde be a flye, *bourdon.* **1601** HOLLAND *Pliny* I. 318 The bigger kind of bees..and this vermin is called Oestrus (*i.* the gad-bee or horse flie). **1639** HORN & ROB. *Gate Lang. Unl.* xix. §221 Cattell stricken with a gad-bee, skip up and down, and run about. **1731** *Rape Helen* ii, Like an heifer, when her back sustains Of biting gadbees the deep piercing pains. **1829** GLOVER *Hist. Derby* I. 177 *Oestrus Curvicauda,* Gadbee or Dun Fly. **1842** BROWNING *Artemis Prologizes* 21 A noisome lust that, as the gadbee stings, Possessed his stepdame.

†**b.** *fig.* in phrase ***to have a gad-bee in one's brains***: to be crazy. Cf. BEE[1] 5. *Obs.*
1682 MRS. BEHN *False Count* II. ii, What means he? sure he has a gad-bee in his brains.

†**gad-breeze.** *Obs. rare*$^{-1}$. [f. GAD *sb.*[1] + BREEZE *sb.*[1]] = GAD-FLY I.
1703 *Country Farm. Catech.,* I can liken him to nothing but my bald heffer when she's got the gad-breeze in her tail.

gadbush, var. GODBUSH.

gaddel, obs. form of GADWALL.

gadder[1] (ˈgædə(r)). [f. GAD *v.*[1] + -ER[1].] An instrument for splitting rock.
1887 *Sci. Amer.* LVI. 21 It is claimed for the diamond gadder that it will do its work at the rate of 180 feet a day.

gadder[2] (ˈgædə(r)). [f. GAD *v.*[2] + -ER[1].] One who gads. †Also ***gadder-about, -abroad.***
1550 BALE *Apol.* 98 Gadders, pylgrymes and ydoll sekers. **1550** —— *Image Both Ch.* xxii. Kk vij b, Gadders to Compostel, Rome, Trier, and Tholose. **1568** GRAFTON *Chron.* II. 106 An idle gadder about. **1577** B. GOOGE *Heresbach's Husb.* III. (1586) 154 The Mastie..no gadder abroade, nor lavish of his mouth. **1625** GILL *Sacr. Philos.* Concl. 207 Hauing brought my houshold to a few, and them no gadders abroad, but such as were easily commanded to stay within. **1678** DRYDEN *Kind Keeper* Epil., When these grow up, Lord, with what rampant Gadders Our Counters will be throng'd. **1725** BRADLEY *Fam. Dict., Bandog,* a Dog ..not..too gentle of Disposition, nor lavish of his Barking, no Gadder. **1777** JOHNSON *Let. to Mrs. Thrale* 19 May, You will become such a gadder. **1863** *Chambers' Bk. of Days* I. 682 A gadder after amusements.

gaddi: see GADI.

gadding (ˈgædɪŋ), *vbl. sb.*[1] [f. GAD *v.*[1] + -ING[1].] The action or process of splitting rock with gads.
1753 CHAMBERS *Cycl. Supp., Gad,* in mining..the working by this instrument is there called gading. **1884** KNIGHT *Dict. Mech.* IV. 364/2 Fig. 1123 shows the drill mounted on car for gadding.

b. *Comb.*: **gadding-car, -machine** (see quots.).
1884 KNIGHT *Dict. Mech.* IV. 364/2 *Gadding Car* (Quarrying), one arranged to carry a drilling machine so as to present it to drill a series of holes in line. **1887** *Sci. Amer.* LVI. 21 The gadding machines..drill or bore circular holes along the bottom and sides of the blocks, into which wedges are introduced and the stone split from its bed.

gadding (ˈgædɪŋ), *vbl. sb.*[2] [f. GAD *v.*[2] + -ING[1].] The action of the vb. GAD. Also ***gadding-about.***
1545 BRINKLOW *Lament.* 4 b, What is their gaddinge with 'ora pro nobis' vnto creatures..? Is it ought elles but abhominacion? **1550** BALE *Apol.* 108 b, Gapynges, gaddynges, ydoll sensynges. **1589** R. ROBINSON *Gold. Mirr.* (1851) 57 No wandring vnto waks, those dayes did women vse, Nor gadding vnto greens, their life for to abuse. **1649** G. DANIEL *Trinarch., Hen. IV,* cccxxviii, Hee charmes the gaddings of opinion, With the loud Cimball of their Liberties. **1662–3** PEPYS *Diary* 1 Jan., Willing to make an end of my gaddings and to set to my business. **1760** GOLDSM. *Cit. W.* xlv, Neither pride, nor debauchery, nor a love of gadding. **1786** COWPER *Lett.* Wks. (1835–7) VI. 9 Unaccountable gaddings and caprices of the human mind. **1820** W. IRVING *Sketch Bk.* II. 155 There is nothing going on but gossiping and gadding about. **1865** MISS BRADDON *Sir Jasper* I. vii. 164 'No gadding after dark, Doll,' he said in a warning voice.
attrib. **1840** R. BREMNER *Excurs. Denmark, Norway,* etc. II. 375 During this gadding season. **1862** SALA *Seven Sons* I. viii. 183 A gadding-about mania seized on all ranks and conditions of men.

gadding (ˈgædɪŋ), *ppl. a.* [f. GAD *v.*[2] + -ING[2].] That gads or gads about, wandering, straggling.
1598 FLORIO, *Mattana,*..a madding or gadding humour. **1602** WARNER *Alb. Eng.* IX. lii. 234 Our gadding Thoughts conceite the Cloudes. **1625** BACON *Ess., Envy* (Arb.) 512 Envy is a Gadding Passion, and walketh the Streets and doth not keepe home. **1637** MILTON *Lycidas* 37 With wild thyme and the gadding vine o'ergrown. **1727** FIELDING *Love in sev. Masq.* Wks. 1775 I. 41 The Traps are no gadding family, our women stay at home and do business. **1777** WARTON *Inscript. Hermitage* iii. 24 Fantastic ivy's gadding spray. **1819** S. ROGERS *Human Life* 545 Soon through the gadding vine the sun looks in. **1829** CARLYLE *Misc.* (1857) II. 26 A gadding, feather-brained set of wantons. **1859** TENNYSON *Guinevere* 310 The good nuns would check her gadding tongue Full often. **1873** SYMONDS *Grk. Poets* x. 312 The stone walls..are..fragrant with gadding violets that ripple down their sides.

Hence ˈ**gaddingly** *adv.*
1552 HULOET, Gaddingly, as they that went on pilgrimage, *peregre.* **1567** DRANT *Horace's De Arte Poet.* B vij, He that dothe belch out puffinge rymes And gaddingly doth straye. **1755** in JOHNSON, whence in later Dicts.

gaddre, obs. f. GATHER *sb.*, pluck (of an animal).

†ˈ**gaddy,** *a. Obs. rare*$^{-1}$. [f. GAD *v.*[2] + -Y[1].] Given to gadding or roving about.
1637 RUTHERFORD *Let. to Lady Busbie* (1894) 525, I would my sufferings..might buy an agreement betwixt His fairest and sweetest love, and His gaddy (Jer. ii. 36) lewd wife.

gade (geɪd). [ad. mod.L. *gadus,* ad. Gr. γάδος codfish; cf. F. *gade.*] A fish belonging to the genus *Gadus*; a codfish.
1836 YARRELL *Brit. Fishes* II. 195 The Silvery Gade ..*Gadus argenteolus*..Montagu. **1876** SMILES *Sc. Natur.* xvi. (ed. 4) 339 It was a long-lost fish—Montague's Midge, or the Silvery Gade.

gade: see GAID.

gade, var. *gaed,* Sc. pa. t. of GO.

gadean (ˈgeɪdɪən). [f. mod.L. *gad-us* (see GADE) + -(E)AN.] A fish belonging to the family *Gadidæ,* of which the typical genus is *Gadus* (cod).
1854 BADHAM *Halieut.* 352 Having found, on the Cretan coast, a gadean which..accords with the ass-fish of the ancients. **1887** *N. & Q.* 7th Ser. IV. 278 The only marine gadean common in Italy, the hake.

gader, obs. form of GATHER.

ˈ**gad-ˌfly.** [f. GAD *sb.*[1]]
1. The popular name of a fly which bites and goads cattle, esp. a fly of the genus *Tabanus* or of the genus *Œstrus*; a bot-fly, breeze.
1626 T. H. *Caussin's Holy Crt.* 120 It was like..as a bull stung with a Gad-fly. **1727–46** THOMSON *Summer* 499 Light fly his slumbers, if perchance a flight Of angry gadflies fasten on the herd. **1831** YOUATT *Horse* xiii. (1843) 289 A species of gad-fly, the œstrus equi, is in the latter part of the summer exceedingly busy about horses. **1841–4** EMERSON *Ess.* Ser. I. i. (1876) 25 The nomads of Africa were constrained to wander by the attacks of the gadfly, which drives the cattle mad.

2. *fig.* One who irritates, torments, or worries another. Also (after L. *œstrus*), an irresistible impulse to some course of action.
1649 G. DANIEL *Trinarch., Hen. IV,* cccxlvii, Rather then have the Gad-flyes of an ill-Disposed Army on their shoulders feed. **1807–8** W. IRVING *Salmag.* (1824) 243 It is our misfortune to be frequently pestered..by certain critical gad-flies. **1864** LOWELL *Fireside Trav.* 314 Bitten with the Anglo-Saxon gadfly that drives us all to disenchant artifice.

†**3.** With allusion to GAD *v.* **a.** In phrase ***to have a gad-fly***: to be fond of 'gadding about'.
1591 LYLY *Sappho* II. iii, My mistresse, I thinke, hath got a gadfly, never at home, and yet none can tell where abroade. **1754** RICHARDSON *Grandison* I. viii, You have neither wings to your shoulder, nor gad-fly in your cap: you love home.

†**b.** A person who is constantly 'gadding about'.
1614 BEAUM. & FL. *Wit. at Sev. Weapons* IV. ii, Where are those gad-flies going? to some junket now. **1754** RICHARDSON *Grandison* I. xviii. 125 Your Harriet may turn gad-fly, and never be easy but when she is forming parties.

4. *attrib.,* as ***gad-fly time***; ***gad-fly haunted*** adj.
1846 C. G. PROWETT *Prometh. Bound* 28 The gadfly-haunted maid, whose charms have power To smite Jove's heart with love. **1893** D. JORDAN ('Son of the Marshes') *Forest Tithes, etc.* 197 In gadfly time it was a fine sight to see a herd of cattle charging along.

gadge, *sb.* ? *pseudo-arch.* Used by Browning as the name of some instrument of torture.
Perh. a mistaken phonetic apprehension of *gagge,* old spelling of GAG *sb.*[1]
1845 BROWNING *Soul's Trag.* I. 332 The dead back-weight of the beheading axe! The glowing trip-hook, thumb-screws and the gadge!

gadge (gadʒ), *v. Sc. intr.* (See quot.)
1719 RAMSAY *2nd Answ. Hamilton* iii, It sets ye well indeed to gadge! *Ibid.* Gloss., *Gadge,* to dictate impertinently, talk idly with a stupid gravity.

gadge, obs. f. GAGE *sb.*[1] and Sc. f. GAUGE.

gadget (ˈgædʒɪt). Also formerly **gadjet.** [Origin obscure. First known in use among seafaring men, and said by several correspondents to have been current *c* 1870, and by a few as far back as the fifties of the nineteenth century, but not found in print before 1886.
One of the most plausible etymological suggestions is F. *gâchette,* which is or has been applied to various pieces of mechanism, e.g. in a lock and in a gun; it is a dim. of *gâche* staple (of a lock), wall-staple or hook. The possibility of connexion with F. *engager* to engage (one thing with another) has also been suggested; cf. dial. F. *gagée* tool, instrument. Derivation from GAUGE is improbable.]

Used as an indefinite or general name for: a comparatively small fitting, contrivance, or piece of mechanism.
1886 R. BROWN *Spunyarn & Spindrift* xxxi. 378 Then the names of all the other things on board a ship! I don't know half of them yet; even the sailors forget at times, and if the exact name of anything they want happens to slip from their memory, they call it a chicken-fixing, or a gadjet, or a gill-guy, or a timmey-noggy, or a wim-wom—just *pro tem.,* you know. **1902** KIPLING *Traffics & Discov.* (1904) 179 Steam gadgets always take him that way. *Ibid.* 190 You've certainly got the hang of her steamin' gadgets in quick time. **1907** *Motor Boat* 4 July 439/1 There will be no harm in pointing out a few of the requirements of a Whitehead torpedo, which will enable the reader to appreciate the number of 'gadgets' which are involved. **1911** C. E. W. BEAN *'Dreadnought' of Darling* ii. 30 He had known every stick in their sides and every gadget on their decks. **1914** KIPLING *New Army* (1915) 39 They have installed decent cooking ranges and gas, and the men have already made themselves all sorts of handy little labour-saving gadgets. **1918** *Glasgow Even. News* 14 Sept. 6 There are a variety of gadjets connected with a motor-car; an aeroplane is replete with them—thermometer, barometer, altimeter, and the pilot only knows what besides. **1923** 'B. M. BOWER' *Parowan Bonanza* i. 12 Solid ledge of gold... Knock it off in chunks with a single-jack and gadget. **1927** *Glasgow Herald* 18 Aug. 9 Innumerable motor car and wireless gadgets. **1951** *Good Housek. Home Encycl.* 46/1 Too many kitchen gadgets are discarded because so much time is required for their cleaning.

b. *spec.* in local use. A winch or similar mechanical gear for discharging vessels; also, a craft equipped with such gear.
1899 *Bristol Times & Mirror* 10 June 3/8 The gadget which was used in the discharge of vessels was being towed down the Harbour... The man who was steering the gadget rather lost his head... There was ample room for the gadget to have passed through if it had been steered properly. **1931** *Ibid.* 16 May, Pulley gear was rigged to the stays or spars of the sailing ship over the hold, and the heaving rope passed to the winch drum of the gadget lying alongside.

c. *transf.* and *gen.* An accessory or adjunct; a knick-knack or gewgaw.
1915 'BARTIMEUS' *Naval Occas.* 142 Look here, old lady, here's a gadget I got for you—he fumbled with the tissue paper enclosing a little leather case. **1922** *Blackw. Mag.* Apr. 421/1, I had to work with concordances, glossaries, all sorts of gadgets. **1925** *Ibid.* Sept. 423 Another waiter offered a selection of 'gadgets', —the appetising morsels of anchovy, stuffed-olive, or pâté.

d. *Glass-making.* A spring-clip used for gripping the foot of a wine or other footed glass when it is being shaped.
1918 P. MARSON *Glass & Glass Man.* 83 The servitor has now done his part of the work, and the glass is handed to the workman. It is then cracked off, and the foot caught by a spring clip arrangement attached to a pontil, called a 'gadget'. **1923** H. J. POWELL *Glassmaking in England* 43 *Gadget,* a spring-clip, attached to a puntee, to hold foot of wine glass, while the bowl is being finished, in order to prevent puntee-mark.

2. *attrib.* and *Comb.*
1924 *Illustr. London News* 24 May 931/2 A paradise for the 'gadget-loving' boy. **1941** *Amer. Speech* XVI. 316/2 *Gadget bag,* a case for camera accessories. **1945** Gadget-ridden [see *chromium-plated* s.v. CHROMIUM 2]. **1946** *Consumers' Guide* (U.S.) May 16/1 Job-hungry GI's and gadget happy housewives make shining targets for swindlers. **1949** 'J. TEY' *Brat Farrar* i. 8 Ulysses..was 'without doubt..a gadget-contriver'. **1964** E. A. NIDA *Toward Sci. Transl.* xii. 252 Of course, MT does capture the imagination, especially of the gadget-minded public.

Hence **gadgeˈteer,** a person given to the use or invention of gadgets; ˈ**gadgetry,** gadgets collectively; the use of gadgets; ˈ**gadgety** *a.* having the qualities or characteristics of a gadget; fitted with a gadget or gadgets.
1920 *Christian World* 19 Aug. 4/1 The door of my bedroom in one great American hotel was a blazing triumph of sheer gadgetry. **1937** *Night & Day* 26 Aug. 24/1 The Tanova self-supporting sock looked pathetically gadgety on the plaster legs in the window. **1938** *Reader's Digest* Mar. 93/1 Such Yankee ingenuity usually brings the gadgeteer to grief. **1957** *London Mag.* Aug. 52 It is a scarcely individualized appetite that desires gadgetry and goods, and calls them Utopia. **1958** *Times* 22 July 9/7 The temple of gadgetry known as the underground control room. **1962** *Punch* 19 Sept. 397/1 A good gadgety camera. **1964** M. GOWING *Britain & Atomic Energy* ii. 82 They did not even commit the error ascribed to 'gadgeteers', of believing they had a monopoly of their invention. **1967** *Daily Tel.* 29 Mar. 12/7 Despite the latest gadgetry—echo-sounders, freezer trawlers, automatic gear—the commercial sea fisherman remains basically a hunter.

Gadhelic (gəˈdɛlɪk), *a.* and *sb.* Also 8 **Gaedhlic,** 9 **Gaedhlic**: cf. GOIDELIC. [Literary formations from Ir. *Gaedheal,* pl. *Gaedhil,* OIr. *Gáidel, Góidel,* pl. *Gáidil, Góidil,* the original form of GAEL.] = GAELIC, in uses other than the customary application to the Gaels of Scotland.
The forms *Gadhelic* and *Goidelic* are used by modern philologists for 'pertaining to the Gaels (in the widest sense)'; the earlier forms, now obsolete, are in our quots. used for 'Irish Gaelic'.
1796 MORSE *Amer. Geog.* II. 183 The Gaedhlic, or Scottic, the purest and most ancient of all the Celtic dialects. **1861** O'CURRY *Lect. MS. Mat.* 3 Ample materials still remain in the Gaedhlic or Irish language. **1865** *Athenæum* No. 960. 687/2 The Gadhelic and the Cymric were used in Gaul. **1875** WHITNEY *Life Lang.* x. 183 The Gadhelic group includes the Irish.

‖**gadi** (ˈgɑːdɪ), **gaddi** (ˈgʌdɪ). Also gadhi, gâdi, guddy, -ee. [Marathi *gādī,* Bengali *gādi,* Hind. *gaddī,* lit. cushion.] The cushioned throne of an Indian ruler; *transf.* = THRONE *sb.* 5 a.
1855 H. H. WILSON *Gloss. Judicial & Revenue Terms.* **1879** E. ARNOLD *Light of Asia* II. 333 The marriage feast was kept, as Sâkyas use, The golden gadi set, the carpet spread. **1886** YULE & BURNELL *Hobson-Jobson* s.v. *Guddy, Guddee,* 'To be placed on the *guddee*' is to succeed to the Kingdom. **1906** *Westm. Gaz.* 6 Sept. 4/3 The Jâm died in 1895, whereupon this child was installed on the gâdi of Jamnagar by Colonel Hancock, then 'Agent to the Governor' in Kathiawar. **1923** *Blackw. Mag.* Jan. 10/1 He had had a very narrow escape of being deposed from the *gadi.* **1927** *Times* (weekly ed.) 29 Sept. 346/2 The Nawab of Bhopal succeeded to *gadi* on the death of the Begum his mother. **1960** J. MASTERS *Venus of Konpara* 18 He succeeded to the gaddi, the cushion which was the Indian symbol of rule. **1961**

Times 23 Jan. (India Suppl.) p. viii/1 The welfare state has succeeded to the *gaddi* of Raja Sansar Chand.

gadid (ˈgeɪdɪd). *Ichth.* [f. mod.L. *gad-us* cod + -ID.] = GADOID *sb.*

1889 in *Century Dict.* (citing T. GILL).

gadine (ˈgeɪdaɪn). *Ichth.* [f. as prec. + -INE.] = GADOID *sb.*

1888 *Riverside Nat. Hist.* III. 268 The common cod-fish (*Gadus morrhua*).. may be briefly defined as a gadine with the lower jaw shutting within the upper.

gadinic (gəˈdɪnɪk), *a. Chem.* [f. as prec. + -IC.] In *gadinic acid* (see quot.).

1864 WATTS *Dict. Chem.*, *Gadinic acid*, a crystalline fatty acid, obtained from cod-liver oil.

Gaditan (ˈgædɪtən), *a.* and *sb.* Also **Gaditane** (-teɪn). [ad. L. *Gādītānus*, f. *Gādēs* Cadiz.] **A.** *adj.* Of or belonging to Cadiz. **B.** *sb. pl.* The inhabitants of that city.

1607 TOPSELL *Four-f. Beasts* 315 The Gaditan wer most honored herewith, for at one time and for one battel they created 400 [Equites]. **1626** MASSINGER *Rom. Actor* III. ii, Like a Gaditane strumpet I shall look to see you tumble. **1967** 'LA MERI' *Sp. Dancing* (ed. 2) x. 123 The gaditanes used them when they conquered fashionable Rome.

Gaditanian (gædɪˈteɪnɪən), *a.* and *sb.* [f. as prec. + -IAN.] **A.** *adj.* Of or belonging to Cadiz in Spain, or its inhabitants. **B.** *sb.* An inhabitant or native of Cadiz.

1845 R. FORD *Hand-bk. Trav. Spain* II. ii. 18 Gaditanian dances.. are more marked by energy than by grace. **1882** in OGILVIE. **1967** 'LA MERI' *Sp. Dancing* (ed. 2) v. 66 Some say the dances of Cadiz in Gaditanian days come under this style.

Gadite (ˈgeɪdaɪt), *a. rare*⁻¹. [f. L. *Gād-ēs* + -ITE.] Belonging to Gades or Cadiz.

1808 SCOTT *Marm.* I. Introd. 72 Lo here his grave Who victor died on Gadite wave.

gadling[1] (ˈgædlɪŋ). [f. GAD *sb.*[1] + -LING.] One of the small spikes of metal affixed to the knuckles of a gauntlet.

[*a* **1360** *Chronicon Galfridi le Baker* (1889) 113 Thomas quibusdam stimulis curtis et acutis quos manum dextram comprimendo digitorum nodi radicales e cirotecis laminatis expresserunt, et eos moderni vocant gadelinges, nudam Johannis faciem wlneravit.] **1592** STOW *Ann.* 386 Certayne prickes both short and sharpe, then [1351: see above] called Gadlings, beeing closed in the ioyntes of his right gauntlet. **1834** PLANCHÉ *Brit. Costume* x. 138 The backs of the leathern gauntlets were also furnished with overlapping plates, and the knuckles armed with knobs or spikes of iron, called gads or gadlings. **1877** *Athenæum* 3 Nov. 571/3 Earl Ralph wears.. gadlings on his gauntlets.

†**gadling**[2]. *Obs.* Forms: 1 **gædeling**, 3–5 **gad-, gedeling, -(e)lyng** (in late MSS. corruptly, **godlinge, geldinge**), 4–7 **gadling**. [OE. *gædeling* = OS. *gaduling*, OHG. *gateling* (MHG. *getelinc*), Goth. *gadiligg-s* :—OTeut. **gaduliŋgo-z* f. root **gad-* (in OE. *gæd* fellowship, *ȝegada* companion, GATHER *v.*) + -LING.]

1. Originally, a companion or fellow, in good sense; esp. a companion in arms.

Beowulf 2617 His gædelinges guðgewædu. *c* **1000** *Daniel* 422 Hwa þa ȝyfe sealde ȝingum gædelingum. *c* **1205** LAY. 12335 Alle þa gadelinges Alse heo weoren sunen kinges. *a* **1250** *Prov. Ælfred* 312 in *O.E. Misc.* 120 So is mony gedelyng godlyche on horse. **13..** *K. Alis.* 1192 Fiftene thousand of fot laddes.. And alle stalworthe gadelynges.

2. In bad sense, as a term of reproach: A base, low-born person, a 'fellow'.

1297 R. GLOUC. (1724) 310 þe beste body & noblest.. yslawe was þoru a gadelyng, so vyllyche, alas! *c* **1400** *Gamelyn* 107, I am no worse gadelyng.. But born of a lady, and geten of a knight. *c* **1475** *Rauf Coiȝear* 612 Quhair gangis thow, Gedling, thir gaitis sa gane? ? *a* **1500** *Chester Pl.* (E.E.T.S.) x. 237 That false gedlinge [*v.r.* gelding]. **15..** *Robd. Cysille* in Hazl. *E.P.P.* I. 273 Fals thefe, and fowle gadlyng, Thou lyest falsely.

3. A wanderer, wayfarer, vagabond.

a **1542** WYATT in *Tottel's Misc.* (Arb.) 41 The wandring gadling, in the sommer tyde, That findes the Adder with his rechlesse foote. **1565** *Maister Randolphes Phantasey* 539 The amased lewsarde.. from the wandringe gadlinge hasteth amayne.

4. Hence *attrib.* (in sense of 'wandering', as if formed from a verb *gaddle*); also as *vbl. sb.*

1594 CAREW *Tasso* (1881) 98 Nor on the promisde ten alone relyes, But trusts he stealth should more a gaddling lead. *c* **1624** LUSHINGTON *Resur. Serm.* (1659) 15 Three way-going women, gadling gossips that came from Galilee. **1676** COLES, *Gadling*, stradling. **1706** PHILLIPS (ed. Kersey), *Gadling* (old word), straggling.

†**gadman.** *Chiefly Sc. Obs.* Also 8–9 *Sc.* **gaudsman**, 9 **gadsman**. [f. GAD *sb.*[1]] The man or boy who directed or guided a team by means of a gad or goad, esp. in ploughing; a goadsman.

c **1450** HENRYSON *Mor. Fab.* 73 His Gadman and hee, His stots hee straught with Benedicite. **1515** *Ld. Treas. Acc. Scotl.* in Pitcairn *Crim. Trials* I. 260*, xij cartaris ane hundrethe and xx pynouris and ix gadmen, being careand the Artalzery fra Edinburghe to Streueling. **1786** BURNS *Inventory*, A gaudsman ane, a thrasher t'other. **1827** HONE *Every-Day Bk.* II. 1656 Pig drivers and gadsmen. **1863** J. L. W. *By-gone Days* 10 With every plough two persons were engaged, one the ploughman.. the other the gadman, from the long gad or goad with which he impelled the horses or oxen.

gadoid (ˈgeɪdɔɪd), *sb.* and *a.* [f. mod.L. *gad-us* (ad. Gr. γάδος) cod + -OID.] **A.** *sb.* A fish of the family *Gadidæ*, of which the cod is the type. **B.** *adj.* Of, belonging to, or resembling the *Gadidæ*, or cod-fishes.

1842 BRANDE *Dict. Sci. Lit. & Art*, *Gadoids*, a family of soft-finned fishes.. of which the cod-fish.. may be regarded as the type.. The general character of the gadoid family is [etc.]. **1861** HULME tr. *Moquin Tandon* II. III. i. 102 The following are the other Gadoids [besides the Cod] which principally furnish the Cod-liver oil. **1865** *Reader* No. 110. 143/2 Fishes which resemble at first Gadoïds or Blennioïds. **1880** *Nature* XXI. 202 This rare and remarkable gadoid fish of the Mediterranean.

gadoˈlinic, *a.* [f. as next + -IC.] Derived from gadolinite.

1820 *Edin. Rev.* XXXIV. 57 A breccia composed of.. gadolinic yttria.

gadolinite (ˈgædəlɪnaɪt). *Min.* [Named in 1802 after the mineralogist *Gadolin*: see -ITE.] Silicate of yttrium, found in black crystals.

1802 *Nicholson's Jrnl.* III. 251 The earth last discovered in gadolinite. **1807** T. THOMSON *Chem.* (ed. 3) II. 70 Hitherto yttria has been found only in the black mineral first analysed by Gadolin, and hence called Gadolinite.

attrib. **1883** *Athenæum* 14 Apr. 480/3 The principal gadolinite earths—yttria, terbia, erbia, etc.

gadolinium (gædəʊˈlɪnɪəm). *Chem.* [mod.L. (J. C. G. de Marignac 1886, in *Compt. Rend.* CII. 902), f. GADOLIN(ITE + -IUM.] A metallic element of the lanthanide series which is present in monazite, gadolinite, and other rare earth minerals and forms a series of mostly colourless salts in which it is trivalent; it resembles steel in appearance and is strongly magnetic below room temperature. Symbol Gd, atomic number 64.

1886 *Jrnl. Chem. Soc.* L. 667 Marignac gives the name *Gadolinium* (Gd) to the substance which has hitherto been provisionally distinguished as Yα. **1920** *Ibid.* CXVIII. II. 317 The fractional crystallisation of the acetates effects a rapid separation of gadolinium from samarium and didymium. **1924** J. W. MELLOR *Comprehensive Treat. Inorg. & Theor. Chem.* V. xxxviii. 686 The terbium family of rare earths is arbitrarily taken to include the three elements, europium, Eu; gadolinium, Gd; and terbium, Tb. **1938** R. W. LAWSON tr. *Hevesy & Paneth's Man. Radioactivity* (ed. 2) x. 119 Gadolinium.. absorbs slow neutrons very strongly. **1959** *Electronic Engin.* XXXI. 589/2 New kinds of ferromagnetic ferrites are continually being discovered: gadolinium ferrite types have been investigated. **1961** WOYSKI & SILVERNAIL in Spedding & Daane *Rare Earths* xxi. 517 Gadolinium.. has been used to obtain extremely low temperatures, the classic example being Giauque's experiments.., in which a temperature of 0·29 K was obtained by the adiabatic demagnetization of gadolinium sulfate octahydrate.

gadroon (gəˈdruːn). Also 8 **gaudron**, in mod. Dicts. **godroon**. [ad. F. *godron* (OF. *goderon*, *gauderon*), of uncertain origin.]

One of a set of convex curves or arcs joined at their extremities to form a decorative pattern (which may be described as the reverse of 'fluting') used in the ornamentation of gold and silver plate, in architecture, costume, etc. Chiefly in *pl.* Also *attrib.* as ***gadroon ornament, pattern***.

1723–24 CHAMBERS tr. *S. le Clerc's Archit.* I. 125 Gaudrons of the Ball. **1855** tr. *Labarte's Arts Mid. Ages* xxv, Ornamented with gadroon sculptures. *Ibid.* xxvii, Cut in gadroons. **1878** MISS BRADDON *Open Verd.* xxxviii. 261 A monster salver.. with massive gadroon edges. **1882** CAULFEILD & SAWARD *Dict. Needlework*, *Gadroon*, a term employed in dressmaking and millinery, borrowed from architecture, denoting a kind of inverted fluting or beading. Plaits of a similar form are made on caps and cuffs, as composing a decorative style of trimming. **1883** KERRY *Hist. Ch. St. Lawrence, Reading* 121 This dish has a double ogee-shaped edge with gadroon bordering. **1893** *Athenæum* 14 Jan. 60/1 The central ornaments, external to the space for the enamelled shield of the owner's arms, are whirling gadroons.

gadrooned (gəˈdruːnd), *ppl. a.* In mod. Dicts. **godrooned**. [ad. F. *godronné*, f. *godron* GADROON.] Ornamented with gadroons.

1748–9 *Gen. Advertiser* No. 4440, 3 Dozen of gadroon'd shap'd Plates. **1753** *Pub. Advertiser* 3 Oct. 3/2 Two high gadrooned Candlesticks. **1876** *Whitby Gloss.*, *Gadrooned*, embossed as the edge of a silver salver. Old local note. **1881** *Jrnl. R. Archæol. Inst.* XXXVIII. 461 This vessel had a deep gadrooned silver edge at the top. **1894** *Daily News* 8 Mar. 3/7 A Queen Anne porringer and cover (date 1706), on gadrooned foot.

gadrooning (gəˈdruːnɪŋ), *vbl. sb.* [f. GADROON + -ING[1].] The process of ornamenting with gadroons; ornamentation consisting of gadroons.

1882 *Mag. Art* May 278 Plain gadrooning, or chased strap-work being the principal.. ornament in vogue.

gadso (ˈgædsəʊ), *int.* Also 7 **gads so**. [A var. of CATSO, through false connexion with other oaths beginning with GAD.]

1687 CONGREVE *Old Bach.* IV i, Gads so, there he is, he must not see me. **1764** FOOTE *Mayor Garrat* II. Wks. 1799 I. 179 Gad-so! the candidates are coming. **1816** SCOTT *Antiq.* xxxvi, 'Gadso!' ejaculated Oldbuck, 'these great men use one's house and time as if they were their own property.' **1838** DICKENS *O. Twist* iv, Gadso!.. that's just the very thing I wanted to speak to you about.

gaduin (ˈgædjuːɪn). [irreg. f. mod.L. *gadu-s* cod + -IN.] A fatty substance found in cod-liver oil.

1861 HULME tr. *Moquin-Tandon* II. III. i. 105 Cod-liver oil is a compound of oleine [etc.].. there is also found a.. particular principle called Gaduine. **1864** WATTS *Dict. Chem.*, *Gaduin*, a peculiar brown substance contained in cod liver oil (De Jongh).

gadwall (ˈgædwɔːl). Also 7 **gaddel**, 9 **gadwell**. A freshwater duck, *Anas strepera* or *Chaulelasmus streperus*, of the north of Europe and America; the grey duck or grey.

1666 MERRETT *Pinax Rerum Nat. Brit.* 180 A Gaddel. **1674** RAY *Collect. Words, Water Fowl* 93 The Gadwall or Gray. **1709** DERHAM in *Phil. Trans.* XXVI. 466 The Gadwall. **1777** G. FORSTER *Voy. round World* I. 157 A small brown duck, which is nearly the same as the English gadwall. **1848** C. A. JOHNS *Week at Lizard* 333 Gadwall (*Anas strepera*).—Rare. **1884** LD. MALMESBURY *Mem. Ex-minister* I. 26 We also killed a great many wild duck, gadwells, and snipe, by walking through the marshes.

†ˈ**gadza.** *Obs.* Some textile fabric.

a **1618** *Rates Merchandize* G iv, Gadza of all sorts without gold or siluer, the yard xvjd. Gadza stript with gold or siluer, the yard ijs. vjd.

ga'e, gae, var. *gi'e*, Sc. pa. t. of GIVE.

gae, Sc. and north. var. GO; obs. Sc. f. JAY.

†**Gaedelian**, *a. Obs. rare.* [f. OIr. *Gaedel* a Gael + -IAN: see GADHELIC and GAELIC.]

Belonging to the Gaelic branch of the Celtic race.

1796 MORSE *Amer. Geog.* II. 183 The Gaedelian or Scottish colony.

Gaekwar (ˈgaɪkwɑː(r)). Also **Guickwar, Guicowar**. [ad. Marathi *gāekwāḍ*, lit. cowherd.] The title of the native ruler of Baroda in India.

1813 J. FORBES *Oriental Mem.* II. xviii. 84 These princes were all styled Guickwar, in addition to their family name. .. The word literally means a cow-keeper, which, although a low employment in general, has, in this noble family among the Hindoos, who venerate that animal, become a title of great importance. **1854** E. THORNTON *Gazetteer India* I. 266 Baroda,.. the capital of the territory of the prince called the Guicowar. **1881** W. W. HUNTER *Imp. Gazetteer India* I. 451 The Gáekwár of Baroda is entitled to a salute of 21 guns. **1921** *Glasgow Herald* 26 Nov. 7 The Maharaja—better known here [*sc.* Baroda] and in England as the Gaekwar. **1953** B. SUBBARAO *Baroda through Ages* III. 129 The capture of Baroda in 1734.. inaugurates a new era in the history of Baroda under the Gaekwars.

Gael (geɪl). [a. Sc. Gael. *Gaidheal* a member of the Gaelic race = OIr. *Gaidel, Goidel*.

The Irish Celts call themselves by the same name, but the word first became familiar to English readers as denoting the Scottish Highlanders, and only in more recent times has it been applied to the Irish branch.]

A Scottish Highlander or Celt; also, an Irish Celt.

[**1596** DALRYMPLE tr. *Leslie's Hist. Scot.* I. 73 Calling thame al Scottis.. albeit is plane and euident that mony hundir ȝeiris eftir, thay war called Gathelis fra Gathel.] **1810** SCOTT *Lady of L.* v. ii, The Gael around him threw His graceful plaid of varied hue. **1895** J. H. STAPLES in *Trans. Phil. Soc.* 202 The old Gaels possessed the voiceless 'qu'.

Hence **ˈGaeldom** [-DOM], the land of the Gaels; Gaelic culture or civilization; the Gaelic people.

Perhaps modelled on Sc. Gael. *Gaidhealachd* the country inhabited by the Gaelic-speaking race.

1860 J. F. CAMPBELL *Tales W. Highlands* (1890) I. Introd. 15 What part of the Gaeldom are you from? **1890** D. HYDE *Beside Fire* p. xxx, This story.. was carried by some Irish bard.. to the Gaeldom of Scotland. **1891** *Sat. Rev.* 5 Sept. 277/1 Mr. Blackie's invasions of Gaeldom did not do very much.. for Celtic philology. **1898** *Folk-Lore* IX. I. 46 Until 300 years ago there was practical identity between the mythical and heroic literature of the two main divisions of Gaeldom—Ireland and Scotland. **1925** D. CORKERY *Hidden Ireland* x. 300 It was a Gael who wrote this poem, a Gael whose mind was nurtured in Gaeldom. **1930** W. B. YEATS *Diary* 20 Oct. (1944) 56 The devout Catholicism and enthusiastic Gaeldom. **1959** *Listener* 20 Aug. 292/2 A reader .. might well wonder whether Gaeldom, having 'declined', is now dead. **1963** *Economist* 19 Oct. 252/1 Scottish Gaeldom's great annual festival.

Gaelic (ˈgeɪlɪk), *a.* and *sb.* Forms: 8 **Gaelick, Galic**, 9 **Gaelic**. Cf. GADHELIC. [f. GAEL + -IC. The form *Galic* perhaps represents Sc. Gael. *Gaidhlig* (ˈgaːlɪk), while *Gaelic* is a fresh formation from GAEL = *Gaidheal* (ˈgaɪəl). The word is first used to denote the language, etc., of the Scottish Gael, in more recent times that of the Irish branch also.]

A. *adj.* **1.** Of or pertaining to the Gaels or Celtic inhabitants of the highlands of Scotland; occas. in wider sense, pertaining to that branch of the Celts which includes the Scottish Gaels with the Irish and Manx.

[**1596** DALRYMPLE tr. *Leslie's Hist. Scot.* I. 73 Quhilke commounlie is callit.. the Gathelik toung, albeit corruptetlie.] **1774** PENNANT *Tour Scotl. in 1772*, 249 Stones .. with Galic inscriptions. **1787** BURNS *Let. to Miss M.*

Chalmers Wks. (Globe) 352 It was the tune of a Gaelic song. **1828** SCOTT *F.M. Perth* xxvii, We have not a Gaelic word by which we can even name a maker of gloves. **1831** in *Sir J. Sinclair's Corr.* II. 408 The history and origin of the Gaelic people. **1846** MCCULLOCH *Acc. Brit. Empire* (1854) I. 299 The Gaelic language prevails throughout almost all Inverness-shire. **1895** J. H. STAPLES in *Trans. Phil. Soc.* 210 These Gaelic changes are of a special and only temporary nature.

2. *Gaelic coffee*, coffee with cream and Irish whisky.

1952 *Coffee Trade News* May 8 As one of the Scots Quartette who were introduced to Gaelic coffee in Dublin last week, I share their curiosity as to whether it would prove as popular in Scotland as in the land of its invention. **1967** J. B. PRIESTLEY *It's Old Country* iii. 29 She invited him to take Gaelic coffee in her sitting room.

B. *sb.* The Gaelic language.

1775 BOSWELL *Let. Johnson* 18 Feb. in *Life Johnson*, It is affirmed that the Gaelick (call it Erse or call it Irish) has been written in the Highlands and Hebrides for many centuries. **1806** *Gazetteer Scotl.* (ed. 2) 267 The Gaelic is the language of the people. **1876** GRANT *Burgh Sch. Scotl.* II. xiii. 372 *note*, Children who can only speak Gaelic. **1895** J. STRACHAN in *Trans. Phil. Soc.* 192 *note*, There is no evidence that the Irish rule ever held good in pure Scotch Gaelic. **1897** *Gaelic Jrnl.* VIII. 96/1 The influence exerted on the minds of the Irish-speakers..when they found people coming long distances..in order to learn Gaelic.

Comb. **1897** *Daily News* 8 Mar. 2/4 There were 254,000 Gaelic-speaking persons in Scotland.

Gaelicism (ˈgeɪlɪsɪz(ə)m). [f. GAELIC + -ISM.] The quality or state of being Gaelic.

1895 *Cath. News* 14 Sept. 6 Those two events made an end of the Gaelicism of the Gaelic race.

Gaelicize (ˈgeɪlɪsaɪz), *v.* [f. GAELIC + -IZE.] *trans.* To make Gaelic, treat as Gaelic.

1807 W. TAYLOR in *Ann. Rev.* V. 587 So Oakhampton, which is naturally expounded in Saxon, the town of the home of the oaks, is here Gaelicized into water-border-town.

gaelly, obs. form of GILLIE.

Gaeltacht (ˈgeɪltəxt). [Ir.] A region in Ireland in which Irish is the vernacular; also, these regions collectively. Also *attrib.*

1929 A. DE BLÁCAM *Gaelic Lit. Surveyed* i. 7 He who dwells in the Gaeltacht learns to relish the neat turn of phrase, the proverbial allusion, and the apt retort. **1956** B. INGLIS *Story of Ireland* iv. 232 The number of Irish speakers in the country had continued to shrink, and the 'Gaeltacht' areas—where Irish was the vernacular—were losing their Irish speakers fast. **1969** *Guardian* 16 July 7/1 She would like..to move back to the West, to the Gaeltacht where Irish is spoken as the native language.

gaer, var. GARE *sb.*[2]

gaerish, obs. form of GARISH.

Gaertner[1] (ˈgɛətnə(r)). Also **Gärtner**. The name of August *Gaertner*, German bacteriologist (1848–1934), used attrib. or in the possessive to designate *Salmonella enteritidis*.

1899 MUIR & RITCHIE *Man. Bacteriol.* (ed. 2) 331 During the last few years, in some epidemics of meat- poisoning, similar bacilli differing slightly from Gaertner's bacillus have been isolated. **1928** *Jordan & Falk's Bacteriol. & Immunol.* 444 The term 'Gärtner bacillus' came to be used by some writers..as a general term synonymous with 'paratyphoid bacillus'. **1928** *Daily Express* 11 Aug. 7/1 Death was due to heart failure following infection by the bacillus gaertner from ham purchased in the police canteen. **1930** *Brit. Med. Jrnl.* 22 Mar. 546/1 The patient's serum after operation contained no agglutinins for the organism, isolated, a feature not unusual in Gaertner infections.

Gaertner[2]. *Med.* Also **Gärtner**. [The name of G. *Gaertner*, Austrian physician (1855–1937).] ***Gaertner's phenomenon***, the degree of fullness of the veins of the arm as it is raised to varying heights as indicating the degree of pressure in the right auricle. ***Gaertner('s) tonometer***, an instrument for measuring blood-pressure by means of a compressing ring applied to the finger.

1901 *Boston Med. & Surg. Jrnl.* 8 Aug. 150/1 The blood pressure taken in the finger by the Gärtner tonometer might approximate the mean pressure..but such an approximation would be accidental and uncertain. **1903** G. W. CRILE *Blood-Pressure* 310 Gaertner's tonometer.. consists of a pneumatic ring about 1 cm. in height and 2½ cm. in diameter. *Ibid.* 354 With the Gaertner tonometer he noted that..the pressure fell once from 120 to 90. **1915** STEDMAN *Med. Dict.* (ed. 3) *G [aertner]'s vein phenomenon*, varying fulness of the veins of the arm as the limb is raised to different heights, affording an index to the amount of pressure in the right auricle. **1928** G. W. NORRIS et al. *Blood-Pressure* (ed. 4) iv. 380 Gärtner's phenomenon. **1934** J. F. H. DALLY *High Blood Press.* (ed. 3) xv. 245 Gärtner's tonometer (1899) afforded another index of systolic pressure by the point at which colour returned to the skin of the blanched finger after removal of compression.

Gaertner, erron. var. GARTNER.

Gætulian, var. GETULIAN *a.* and *sb.*

gaff (gæf), *sb.*[1] Also 3, 7–9 **gaffe**. [a. F. *gaffe* = Sp., Pg. *gafa* fem., Pr. *gaf* masc., boat-hook.]

1. a. An iron hook; a staff or stick armed with this. Now only *dial.*

a **1300** *Sat. People Kildare* iv. in *E.E.P.* (1862) 153 Hail, seint dominik with þi lang staffe hit is at þe ouir end crokid as a gaffe. **1867** W. F. ROCK *Jim an' Nell* lxxiv. (E.D.S. No. 76), A guidestrap, hayvor-seed, A gaff, dree picks vrom Varmer Reed. *Ibid.* Gloss., *Gaff*, an instrument with long handle, used to pull furze out of the furze-rick.

b. *spec.* A barbed fishing spear; also, a stick armed with an iron hook for landing large fish, *esp.* salmon. Phrase, ***to bring*** (a hooked fish) ***to gaff***.

1656 BLOUNT *Glossogr.*, *Gaffe*, an iron hook where-with Seamen pull great Fishes into their ships. **1706** in PHILLIPS (ed. Kersey). **1774** GOLDSM. *Nat. Hist.* VI. IV. iii. 394 They begin to knock it [a turtle] on the head with their gaffs. **1844** W. H. MAXWELL *Sports & Adv. Scotl.* (1855) 338 The poacher, with a gaff and torch, selects some gravelly ford. **1885** BLACK *White Heather* iii, Ronald had got him transfixed on the gaff and landed. **1886** *Q. Rev.* Oct. CLXIII. 351 When a fish is beat and is being brought to gaff, much caution is necessary.

2. *Naut.* 'A spar used in ships to extend the heads of fore-and-aft sails which are not set on stays' (Adm. Smyth).

1769 FALCONER *Dict. Marine* (1789) Rrijb, In the schooner both the mainsail and foresail are extended by a boom and gaff. **1796** HUDDART in *Phil. Trans.* LXXXVII. 32 The angle made by the gaff and mast. **1840** R. H. DANA *Bef. Mast* ix. 22 We..pulled for a light, which, as we came up, we found had been run up to our trysail gaff. **1893** H. M. DOUGHTY *Wherry in Wendish Lands* Introd. 15 One sail with very high peak and an enormous gaff.

3. a. A steel spur for a fighting cock: = GABLOCK 1 and GAFFLE 3. **b.** The spike of a spur.

a. 1688 [see GABLOCK 1]. **1706** PHILLIPS (ed. Kersey), *Gaff*, an artificial Spur for a Cock. **1893** in FARMER *Slang Dict.*

b. 1808 PIKE *Sources Mississ.* III. iv. (1895) 788 The dragoons wear..a sort of jack-boot.. to which are fastened, by a rivet, the spurs, the gaffs of which are sometimes near an inch in length.

†**4.** *Card-sharping.* 'A ring worn by the dealer' (Farmer). *Obs.*

5. *attrib.* and *Comb.*, as (sense 1) ***gaff(s)-man***, ***-net***, ***-point***; (sense 2) ***gaff-end***, ***-jaw***, ***-sail*** (also *attrib.*); ***gaff-rigged*** adj.; **gaff-hook** = sense 1; **gaff-setter**, a boat-hook; **gaff-string** (see quot.). Also GAFF-TOPSAIL.

1851 *Voy. Mauritius* i. 10 Up ran certain bits of red and blue and yellow bunting to her *gaff-end. **1844** J. T. HEWLETT *Parsons & W.* xi, Boots seized the *gaff-hook.. and was going to plunge it deep into the pike's jaws. **1854** BADHAM *Halieut.* 17 They had neither..gaff-hook, nor landing-net. **1894** *Westm. Gaz.* 25 July 7/2 *Vigilant's* *gaff-jaws broke, and just as *Britannia* was catching up, her spinnaker went wrong. **1875** F. FRANCIS in *Encycl. Brit.* II. 39/2 The *gaffsman..drags it out of the water to the land. **1885** *Athenæum* 14 Mar. 337/3 A Norwegian gaff-man's feelings are not very acute. **1867** SMYTH *Sailor's Word-bk.*, *Gaff-net*, a peculiar net for fishing. **1845** *Blackw. Mag.* Aug. 288 His armour of scales defied the *gaff-point. **1933** 'L. LUARD' *All Hands* 256 A gaff-rigged ketch. **1961** *Times* 5 Aug. 7/7 They made the crossing in a gaff-rigged yawl. **1886** J. M. CAULFEILD *Seamanship Notes* 2 In setting a *gaff-sail..keep the throat ahead of peak. **1891** *Daily News* 9 Sept. 3/3 The veteran..won the match for sprit and gaff sail boats by a long way ahead. **1861** MAYHEW *Lond. Labour* III. 270 The staffsman then fastens the staff to the lighter by means of the *gaffstring or rope attached to the side of the vessel.

gaff (gæf), *sb.*[2] *slang.* [Of obscure origin; cf. GAB *sb.*[1], OE. (*ȝe*)*gaf-spræc*, blasphemous or ribald speech, Sc. local '*gaff*, loud, rude talk', '*to gaff*, to talk loudly and merrily' (Jam.), and mod.F. (colloq.) *une gaffe*, a remark by which one 'puts one's foot into it'.]

1. a. ? Vociferation, outcry. **b.** Humbug, 'stuff and nonsense'.

1825 C. M. WESTMACOTT *Eng. Spy* I. 267 Stifle e'en a bull-dog's gaff. **1877** *Five Yrs.' Penal Serv.* iv. 151, I also saw that Jemmy's blowing up of me was all 'gaff'.

2. Phrase. ***to blow the gaff***: (*fig.*) to let out a secret; to reveal a plot, or give convicting evidence.

1812 J. H. VAUX *Flash Dict.*, Blow the gaff. **1833** MARRYAT *P. Simple* xliii, I wasn't going to blow the gaff, so I told him, as a great secret, that we got it [the gun] up with a kite. **1877** *Five Yrs.' Penal Serv.* ii. 122 The prisoner..quietly bides his time till the chief warder comes round, then asks to speak to him, and 'blows the gaff'.

3. ***to stand the gaff***, to receive severe treatment, criticism, etc. Similarly ***to give, take,*** etc., ***the gaff***. *U.S.*

1896 ADE *Artie* xii. 111 If he gets the gaff he'll be flat on his back. **1899** A. THOMAS *Arizona* 124 Will they stand the gaff? Will they set sixty hours in the saddle..? **1903** *McClure's Mag.* Oct. 563 'Good,' they cheer, when you find fault; 'give us the gaff. We deserve it and it does us good.' **1910** W. M. RAINE *B. O'Conner* 244 Neil has got to stand the gaff for what he's done. **1924** —— *Troubled Waters* xviii. 194 Just because he shuts his mouth and stands the gaff.

gaff (gæf), *sb.*[3] *Obs.* exc. *dial.* Also 6 **gaffe**. [short for GAFFER.] = GAFFER 1.

1573 TUSSER *Husb.* xxii. (1878) 60 Mixe well (old gaffe) horse corne with chaffe. **1877** in *N.W. Linc. Gloss.*, *Gaff*.

gaff (gæf), *sb.*[4] *slang.* [Of unknown origin.]

1. A fair.

1753 J. POULTER *Discov.* 31 The first Thing they do at a Gaff is to look for a Room clear of Company. **1811** *Lex. Balatron.* s.v., The drop coves maced the joskins at the Gaff; the ring-droppers cheated the countryman at the fair. **1821** HAGGART *Life* 22 We stopped at this place two days, waiting to attend the Gaff.

2. Any public place of amusement. Hence the term has passed into the literary vocabulary as the name for the low class of theatre or music-hall to which it is most frequently applied by slang speakers. Also ***penny-gaff***.

1812 J. H. VAUX *Flash Dict.* s.v., Any public place of amusement is liable to be called the gaff, when spoken of in flash company. **1856** *Chamb. Jrnl.* 11 Oct. 228/1 Would you root out the Penny Gaff, and compel the penny-paying public..to find amusement elsewhere? **1861** MAYHEW *Lond. Labour* III. 144 When a professional goes to a gaff to get an engagement, they in general inquire whether he is a good ballet performer. **1863** *Q. Rev.* July CXIV. 264 He knows them all..from the chief opera-house..to the humblest gaffs (as we believe they would be called in London). **1864** *Sat. Rev.* 30 Apr. 516 A piece of histrionics rather below the mark of a penny gaff. **1887** *Contemp. Rev.* Mar. 400, I had always wanted to see a Penny Gaff since I first read my Dickens.

3. a. A house, shop, or other building.

1932 G. S. MONCRIEFF *Café Bar* viii. 73 He went back to his gaff and broke into the gas meter. **1936** J. CURTIS *Gilt Kid* ii. 20, I had it off last week.., not a big job, just a little snout gaff. **1938** G. GREENE *Brighton Rock* III. iii. 125 The barred and battlemented Salvation Army gaff. *Ibid.* v. i. 188 It's the best road-house this side of London... You can't pick 'em [*sc.* girls] up in this gaff. **1961** J. MACLAREN-ROSS *Doomsday Book* I. viii. 86, I was keeping an eye on the gaff —seen you going in. **1971** *Fremdsprachen* XV. 63 Two new words..for a flat or dwelling are 'pad' and 'gaff'.

b. *spec.* A brothel; a prostitute's room.

1947 *New Statesman* 10 May 330/3 In most cases the girls do not live where they work (they call this their 'gaff'). **1959** *Streetwalker* i. 14 Take a cab for the five minutes drive back to your gaff, or flat.

gaff (gæf), *v.*[1] [f. GAFF *sb.*[1]] *trans.* To seize or strike (a fish) with a gaff; also, to draw *out* with a gaff.

1844 J. T. HEWLETT *Parsons & W.* xi, I bid him..slack his hand the moment I had gaffed him [the pike]. **1851** NEWLAND *Erne* 352, I..gaffed him out of the great boiling turnhole below. **1867** B. OSBORNE *Sp. in Ho. Com.* 8 Apr., The hon. member for Lincolnshire, though a solitary fish, rose to the occasion, and he was safely gaffed and landed. **1882** *Garden* 11 Feb. 101/1 The Japanese were gaffing salmon.

Hence **ˈgaffing** *vbl. sb.*; also *attrib.* Also **ˈgaffer**, one who gaffs fish. (In some mod. Dicts.)

1837 M. DONOVAN *Dom. Econ.* II. 171 Spearing, gaffing, and harpooning, are amongst the most obvious methods. **1886** *Fishing* 18 Sept. 417 He hooked a large grilse, but lost him in gaffing. **1895** *Blackw. Mag.* Aug. 288 Harry brought him within gaffing distance.

gaff (gæf), *v.*[2] **1.** *intr.* To gamble, *esp.* to 'toss up'. *slang* and *colonial.*

1812 J. H. VAUX *Flash Dict.*, *Gaff*, to gamble with cards, dice, &c., or to toss up. **1828** 'JON BEE' *Living Pict. Lond.* 243 Though any gentleman would gaff for a pound, there or any where else. **1889** BOLDREWOOD *Robbery under Arms* (1890) 17 Catch him gaffing! no, not for a sixpence.

2. *trans.* To deceive or trick; to make (a game or device) crooked or dishonest. *orig. U.S.*

1934 J. PROSKAUER *Suckers All* 15 He was..putting in slot machines for a racketeer, and 'gaffing' them..to increase the house percentage. *Ibid.* v. 77 There *was* a way of gaffing every game. **1935** N. ERSINE *Underworld & Prison Slang* 39 *Gaff*, to cheat. **1963** *New Scientist* 6 June 553 Roulette wheels can of course be crookedly fixed ('gaffed' is the trade term). **1965** H. GOLD *Man who was not with It* xv. 135, I want to play you straight fifty-fifty, not gaff you for fifty-fifty.

Hence **ˈgaffing** *vbl. sb.* Also **ˈgaffer**, one who 'gaffs' or 'tosses up'.

1828 'JON BEE' *Living Pict. Lond.* 241, I know of but one such public-house where gaffing is carried on to any amount... If the person calling for 'man' or 'woman', is not right or wrong at five pieces, neither of the gaffers win or lose, but go again.

gaff (gæf), *v.*[3] *Theat.* [f. GAFF *sb.*[4]] *intr.* 'To play in a gaff' (Farmer).

gaff, var. of or error for *goff*, GOLF.

1688 R. HOLME *Armoury* III. 154/1 Pythus, the first inventer of many Games at Ball: I do not say of Gaff, Tennis, or Paille-Maille.

gaffe (gæf). Also **gaff**. [Fr. (see GAFF *sb.*[2]).] A blunder, an instance of clumsy stupidity, a 'faux pas'.

1909 *Pall Mall Gaz.* 12 Apr. 1/1 These two gentlemen, whose weather predictions are still listened to with some deference, have made a bad 'gaffe', to use a popular slang expression. **1922** *Blackw. Mag.* Mar. 303/1, I had obviously said the wrong thing, committed a gaffe. **1924** GALSWORTHY *White Monkey* I. ii, 'He's a bit romantic, of course.' 'Oh! Have I made a gaff?' 'Not a bit; jolly good shot.' **1928** C. MACKENZIE *Extremes Meet* 207 Knowing nothing, you might easily make a bad gaffe. **1959** *Economist* 6 June 922/2 It would be too silly if this newspaper *gaffe* induced..any future prime minister to relapse yet further into the grave political vice of showing immutable loyalty to his friends.

gaffel(l, var. of GAFFLE, *Obs.*

gaffelage, var. f. GAVELAGE, *Obs.*

gaffer (ˈgæfə(r)). Also 6, 8 **gaffar**. [The analogy of the continental synonyms, F. *compère*, *commère*, Ger. *gevatter*, would suggest that *gaffer*, *gammer* are contractions of *godfather*, *godmother* rather than of *grandfather*, *-mother*;

but the change of vowel may be due to association with these words.]

1. A term applied originally by country people to an elderly man or one whose position entitled him to respect.

a. Prefixed by way of respect (sometimes with an affectation of rusticity) to a proper name, the designation of a calling, office, etc. In 17–18th c. the usual prefix, in rustic speech, to the name of a man below the rank of those addressed as 'Master' (cf. GOODMAN).

1575 J. STILL *Gamm. Gurton* v. ii, Then chad ben drest be-like, as ill by the masse, as gaffar vicar. **1635** PAGITT *Christianogr.* 200 Were they called Gaffer Bishops, or had they not more honorable Titles? **1651** RANDOLPH, etc. *Hey for Honesty* I. i. Wks. (1875) 386 This same gaffer Phoebus is a good mounte-bank and an excellent musician. **1693** G. FIRMIN *Rev. Mr. Davis's Vind.* iv. 31 For a Man, who before was but a Gaffer, to be now called Master, to have the people follow him, and he to frequent their Tables, is a better Trade, then to be Threshing, or such like work. **1714** GAY *Sheph. Week* v. 151 For Gaffer Tread-well told us, by the by, Excessive Sorrow is exceeding dry. **1742** FIELDING *J. Andrews* I. ii, Mr. Joseph Andrews..was esteemed to be the only Son of Gaffar and Gammer Andrews. **1806** FESSENDEN *Democr.* I. 89 Made them shake hands both wig and tory As Gaffer Homer tells the story. **1828** SCOTT *F.M. Perth* xvi, You have marred my ramble, Gaffer Glover.

b. Used simply as a title of address, often with no intimation of respect = *my good fellow.*

1590 R. W. *Three Lds. & Ladies Lond.* in Hazl. *Dodsley* VI. 395 You speak too late, gaffer, having challenged preheminence. **1628** FORD *Lover's Mel.* III. iii, I pray your blessing, gaffer. *a* **1659** CLEVELAND *Answ. to Pamph.* Poems, etc. (1677) 132 But, hark you, Gaffer; you that will tear the Speech and blow away the Sand. **1755** SMOLLETT *Quix.* (1803) IV. 58 'Gaffer,' said he, 'is there stuff enough here to make me a cap?' **1796** G. M. WOODWARD *Eccent. Excurs.* 89 The [Bucks] women, resolving not to drop a good old custom, call their husbands Gaffer. **1856** J. H. NEWMAN *Callista* 67 My good old gaffer, you're one of the old world. **1884** J. PAYNE *Tales fr. Arabic* II. 42 Harkye, gaffer! Thou hast no knowledge of this ass's case.

2. An elderly rustic; an old fellow. Also simply, a fellow.

1589 *Pappe w. Hatchet* 7 Now haue at you all my gaffers of the rayling religion. **1653** URQUHART *Rabelais* II. xxxi, The best little gaffer that was to be seen between this and the end of a staffe. **1710** *Dame Huddle's Let.* (N.) My gaffer only said, he would inform himself as well as he could against next election and keep a good conscience. **17..** *Country Vicar* in Fawkes *Poems* (Chalmers) 278 And through the parish, with their how d'ye, Go to each gaffer and each goody. **1862** T. A. TROLLOPE *Marietta* I. iii. 41 The gaffers and gammers of the quarter..gossiped Tuscan-wise on their doorsteps. **1882** MISS BRADDON *Mt. Royal* II. iii. 27 The old gaffers and goodies had known her all their lives.

3. A master, a 'governor'. *Obs.* exc. *dial.*

a **1659** CLEVELAND *Gen. Poems, etc.* (1677) 88 Every twice a day the Teaching Gaffer Brings up his Easter-book to Chaffer. **1735** DYCHE & PARDON, *Gaffer*, a familiar Word mostly used in the Country for Master. **1876** *Surrey Gloss.* s.v., 'Look out! here comes the gaffer.' **1881** *Leicestersh. Gloss.*, *Gaffer*, the master of the house, farm, etc.

b. The foreman or overman of a gang of workmen; a headman.

1841 HARTSHORNE *Salop. Antiqua* Gloss., *Gaffer*, a superintendant, overlooker, head workman, leader of a band of reapers. **1856** *Househ. Words* XIII. 545/2 Their own arrangement was made..entirely by the men and their gaffers (sub-contractors). **1862** *Chamb. Jrnl.* 215/2 The overman, or 't' gaffer', as the banksman called him, at once volunteered to shew me over the mine. **1897** *Daily Chron.* 28 Oct. 4/7 Some of the employers and gaffers keep public-houses and provision shops.

Hence **'gaffership**, the position of gaffer.

1895 *Cornh. Mag.* July 20 This 'gaffership' suited Cleg so well that [etc.]

†**'gaffle.** *Obs.* Also 5 gaffolle, 6–7 **gaffel**(l, 7 **gafel**, 8 gafle. [prob. a. Du. *gaffel* = OE. *ȝeafol*, Ger. *gabel* fork: see GABLE.]

1. A steel lever for bending the cross-bow.

1497 *Naval Acc. Hen. VII* (1896) 110 Bowes v, Arowes v ..Shot of ston for demy curtowes..clij, Gaffolles of iren.. ij. **1598** FLORIO, *Martinello*, a gaffell, a racke or bender of a bow. **1630** DRAYTON *Muses' Elys.* vi, My cross-bow in my hand, my gaffle on my rack To bend it when I please. **1672** *Compl. Gunner* III. xv. 12 Certain strong Cross-bows to bend with Racks or Gaffels. **1706** in PHILLIPS (ed. Kersey). **1721–92** in BAILEY. And in mod. Dicts.

2. A rest for a musket: = FORK 6 b, FORCAT.

In *Cent. Dict.* The Du. word had this sense among others, but Eng. examples are wanting.

3. A steel spur for fighting cocks. (Cf. GAFF *sb.*[1] 3 a and GABLOCK 1.)

1755 in BAILEY (ed. Scott). **1776** BRAND *Pop. Antiq.* (1777) 379 *note*, The Gafle is a mere modern Invention.

Hence **'gaffled** *ppl. a.*, armed with 'gaffles' or spurs.

1790 J. WILLIAMS *Shrove Tuesday* (1794) 8 We [cocks] assume the spatterdash and spur Gaffled and clad in brightly burnish'd steel.

†**'gafflet.** *Obs.* [f. GAFFLE + -ET[1].] = GAFFLE 3.

1714 [MACKY] *Journey through Eng.* (1723) I. 130 [Cocks] wear Steel-Spurs (call'd, I think, Gafflets) for their surer Execution. **1757** *Lond. Chron.* 22 Mar. 279 In setting two Cocks to at the Pit, one of them struck one of his Gafflets into the Back of his Right Hand.

†**'gafflin.** *Obs. rare*[−1]. [? a. OF. *gaveline*, var. *javeline* JAVELIN.]

1540 *Lanc. Wills* II. 139 A gafflyn hedde.

gaff-topsail.

1. 'A light triangular or quadrilateral sail, the head being extended on a small gaff which hoists on the topmast, and the foot on the lower gaff' (Adm. Smyth). Also *attrib.*, as ***gaff-topsail-hook.***

1794 *Rigging & Seamanship* I. 83 Over the head of the mainsail a gaff topsail. **1833** M. SCOTT *Tom Cringle* viii, What a gaff-top sail she has got—my eye! **1835** SIR J. ROSS *Narr. 2nd Voy.* iv. 44 Taking in the Mainsail, gaff topsail. **1875** BEDFORD *Sailor's Pocket Bk.* x. 349 Gaff top sail *Voile à corne.* **1884** KNIGHT *Dict. Mech.* IV. 365/1 *Gaff-topsail Hook*, a mousing hook for a gaff topsail with rope sheet. *fig.* **1840** MARRYAT *Poor Jack* ii, Your mother..with.. such a rakish gaff topsail bonnet, with pink pennants.

2. *U.S.* 'A kind of sea-catfish, *Ælurichthys marinus*' (Cent. Dict.).

gafol, gafol-, OE. ff. (used *Hist.*) of GAVEL, GAVEL-.

gag (gæg), *sb.*[1] Also 6–7 gagg(e. [app. f. GAG *v.*[1]]

1. a. Something thrust into the mouth to keep it open and prevent speech or outcry; in *Surg.*, an apparatus for distending the jaws during an operation.

1553 T. WILSON *Rhet.* 117b, Musicians in England have vsed to put gagges in childrens mouthes that they might pronounce distinctely. **1580** SIDNEY *Arcadia* III. (1590) 236 They left Miso with a gagge in her mouth and bound hand and foot. **1625** FLETCHER & SHIRLEY *Nt. Walker* III. v, Untye his feet; pull out his gag, He will choak else! **1697** DRYDEN *Virg. Georg.* III. 611 Some..With Gags and Muzzles their soft Mouths restrain. **1796** H. HUNTER tr. *St.-Pierre's Stud. Nat.* (1799) III. 359 He put a gag in my mouth, and..fastened my hands behind my back. **1818** JAS. MILL *Brit. India* II. IV. iv. 158 Lest he should address the people, a gag was stuffed into his mouth. **1857** W. COLLINS *Dead Secret* v. ii, If I only knew where to lay my hand on a gag, I'd cram it into your..mouth! **1885** DU CANE *Punishm. & Prev. Crime* 14 For women scolds the branks or gag.. were authorised punishments.

b. *fig.* (Now often applied opprobriously to the action of a parliamentary majority in 'closuring' a debate.) Also *attrib.*

1623 M. KELLISON (*title*), The Gagge of the Reformed Gospell. **1629** T. ADAMS *Serm.* Wks. 890 The Eye-lidde is set open with the gagges of Lust and Enuie. **1641** MILTON *Animadv.* (1851) 190 Your Monkish prohibitions, and expurgatorious indexes, your gags and snaffles. **1707** J. STEVENS tr. *Quevedo's Com. Wks.* (1709) 249 It was convenient to stop his Mouth with a Silver Gag. **1798** *Aurora* (Phila.) 1 Aug. (Th.), Query have the Cherokees any gag-bill? **1840** J. Q. ADAMS *Mem.* X. 273 Then came Atherton, of New Hampshire, the man of the mongrel gag. **1861** *Congress. Globe* App. 49/1 The Pacific railroad bill, just passed through this House under the 'gag', and in violation of the constitution. **1863** W. PHILLIPS *Speeches* xix. 427 The nineteenth century requires sterner gags than the eighteenth. **1890** *Spectator* 6 Sept., The American Senate has adopted the principle of fixing a time at which the vote on a Bill resisted by obstruction must be taken..The House of Representatives has already adopted this peremptory 'gag'.

c. *School slang.* (See quot.) Cf. GAG *v.*[1] 1.

1820 LAMB *Elia* Ser. I. *Christ's Hosp. 35 Yrs. Ago*, L. has recorded the repugnance of the school to gags, or the fat of fresh beef boiled.

2. *Coal-mining.* (See quots.)

1747 HOOSON *Miner's Dict.*, *Gag*, a slight bit of Timber that is soon made for the present purpose, to clap in..to keep some one Pair or more from settling, which is already begun, and so to stay it for some little time, till better may be had. **1883** GRESLEY *Gloss. Coal Mining*, *Gags*, chips of wood in a sinking pit bottom, or sump. **1888** GREENWELL *Gloss. Coal Trade Terms* (ed. 3), *Gag*, an obstruction in the falls or lids of a bucket or clack which prevents them from working.

3. *Theat.* **a.** Expressions, remarks, etc. not occurring in the written piece but interpolated or substituted by the actor.

Perh. developed from the sense explained in quot. 1747 under 2, which possibly may have been current in other than mining applications. But cf. GAG *sb.*[2], *v.*[3]

1847 *Illustr. Lond. News* 10 July 27/1 Actors who are too much given to 'gag' at the present day. **1861** MAYHEW *Lond. Labour* III. 126 The performance consisted of all gag. I don't suppose anybody knows what the words are in the piece. **1884** SYMONDS *Shaks. Predecess.* viii. 288 Jigs were written in rhyme, plentifully interspersed with gag and extempore action. **1887** FRITH *Autobiog.* I. xxv. 383 If he [the actor] found his gag tell upon the audience he repeated it.

b. ? The 'mounting' of a piece. *rare.*

1841 *Punch* I. 106/1, I shall do the liberal in the way of terms, and get up the gag properly, with laurels and other greens, of which I have a large stock on hand.

c. A joke; a humorous remark, situation, action, etc. Cf. GAG *sb.*[2], esp. quots. 1819 and 1880.

1863 H. MORFORD *Sprees & Splashes* i. 12 All play-goers will remember..a piece of pure nonsense by Brougham, in which an old hunks is intruded upon by his daughter's lover in disguise, the whole farce crowded full of gags. **1923** WODEHOUSE *Inimitable Jeeves* xv. 195 That..curate wanted to give the public some rotten little fairy play..without one good laugh or the semblance of a gag in it. **1929** M. LIEF *Hangover* 235 Maybe I can tell you about the gag one of our better-known critics pulled in his review of Dillingham's new musical comedy..he wrote: 'Eulalia Duncan sang so off-key last night that she had great difficulty moving her vowels.' **1965** *New Statesman* 16 Apr. 607/1 Braid Scots is spoken only by comedians, as a gag. *Ibid.* 621/1 Chekhov, still a one-word gag about gloom to P. G. Wodehouse and Noel Coward.

4. *attrib.* and *Comb.*: **gag-bill**, a theatrical bill summarizing the sensational episodes of a play; **gag-bit** (see quot.); **gag-book**, a book containing gags; a joke-book; **gag-eater** *School slang* (see 1 c); **gag-law** *U.S.*, 'a law or regulation made and enforced for the purpose of preventing or restricting discussion' (*Cent. Dict.*); **gag-man** (orig. *U.S.*), a deviser or writer of gags; also, a comedian; so ***gag-writer***; ***-writing***; **gag-piece** *Theat.*, a 'piece' or play in which 'gag' is freely used; **gag-rein, -runner** (see quots.); **gag-snaffle**, a powerful snaffle (see quot.).

1885 J. K. JEROME *On Stage* 147 The old man has got the knack of making out good *gag bills. **1868** ATKINSON *Cleveland Gloss.*, *Gag-bit*, a bit of very powerful description, used for breaking horses, &c. **1909** B. WILLIAMS *Actor's Story* xix. 259 Not having a '*gag' book I had to think how to adapt a scene suitable for my particular line of business. **1961** *Guardian* 23 June 7/5 Peter de Vries's latest novel..reads like a gag-book. **1820** LAMB *Elia* Ser. I. *Christ's Hosp. 35 Yrs. Ago*, A *gag-eater in our time was equivalent to a goul..and held in equal estimation. **1808** J. Q. ADAMS *Wks.* (1854) IX. 604, I would not repeal it, though it should raise a clamor as loud as my *gag-law. **1870** EMERSON *Soc. & Solit.* ix. 192 No exclusions, no gag-laws can be contrived. **1882** *Times* 28 Mar. 9/4 The strange instrument [the Cloture]..which a few years ago he called the 'gag-law'. **1928** *Sunday Express* 15 Jan. 4 'Gag men' have long flourished in America. One of them thought of making the villain sit on a red-hot stove. **1928** *Collier's* 29 Dec. 28/3 'What you need is a smart gag man,' I say. **1951** DYLAN THOMAS *Let.* 12 Apr. (1966) 357, I am about to take on a new job; co-writing, with the best gagman in England ..a new comic series for the radio. **1957** *Observer* 29 Sept. 12/3 A quiet, mike-clutching gagman, in a discreetly elegant grey suit. **1865** in HOTTEN *Slang Dict.* (1874) s.v., In certain pieces this [gagging] is allowed by custom, and these are called *gag-pieces. *The Critic, or a Tragedy Rehearsed* is one of these. **1874** KNIGHT *Dict. Mech.* I. 934/2 **Gag-rein* (Saddlery), a rein which passes over runners attached to the throat-latch, so as to draw the bit up into the corners of the horse's mouth when pulled upon. *Ibid.* 935/1 **Gag-runner* (Harness), a loop depending from the throat-latch; through it the gag-rein passes to the bit. **1856** 'STONEHENGE' *Brit. Sports* II. III. i. §3. 395 The *Gag Snaffle is also a useful adjunct with pullers that get their heads down... If the horse does not pull, it is not more severe than a common snaffle; but if he does, it acts with double power, owing to the pulley-like attachment of the rein, and to its drawing against the angle of the mouth. **1959** *Listener* 23 July 124/1 A team of *gag-writers. **1928** H. CRANE *Let.* 27 Mar. (1965) 321 Meanwhile there are mechanical jobs such as title-writing, *gag-writing, 'continuity' writing, etc. **1959** *Spectator* 11 Sept. 342/2 A young undertaker's clerk given to gag-writing.

gag (gæg), *sb.*[2] *slang.* [This and the related GAG *v.*[3], which occurs earlier, may be fig. uses of GAG *sb.*[1] and *v.*[1], with the notion of thrusting something down the throat of a credulous person, or testing his powers of 'swallowing'. On the other hand, the words may be of onomatopœic origin (cf. GAGGLE) with the original sense of 'unmeaning chatter'. In the context of the quots, from Lockhart 1819, the sb. and vb. are said to be expressions current in Glasgow; but the form actually used there appears to be GEGG.]

A 'made-up' story; a piece of deception, an imposture, a lie. ***broad gag*** (see quot.).

1805 *Townsman* (Manchester) in *Spirit Publ. Jrnls.* (1806) IX. 364, I hate to hear such gag about a Goliath of thirteen. **1819** [LOCKHART] *Peter's Lett. to Kinsfolk* III. 241 Whether the Gag come in the shape of a compliment to the Gaggee, or some wonderful story, gravely delivered with every circumstance of apparent seriousness. **1823** 'JON BEE' *Dict. Turf*, *Gag*, a grand imposition upon the public; as a mountebank's professions, his cures, and his lottery-bags, are so many broad gags. **1871** *All Year Round* 18 Feb. 288 You won't bear malice now, will you? All gag of mine, you know, about old Miss Ponsonby. **1874** HOTTEN *Slang Dict.*, *Gag*, a lie; 'a gag he told to the beak'. **1880** *Antrim & Down Gloss.*, *Gag*, a joke; a deception. **1885** *Daily News* 16 May 5/2 We need not gratify the Mahdi by believing any bazaar 'gag' he may circulate.

b. *U.S.* A laughing-stock.

1840 HALIBURTON *Clockm.* III. ii. 27 'Sam,' says he, 'they tell me you broke down the other day in the house of representatives, and made a proper gag of yourself.'

gag (gæg), *sb.*[3] *U.S.* [Local name.] A large serranoid fish, *Mycteroperca microlepis*, found off the coasts of the southern United States.

1884 G. B. GOODE *Fisheries U.S.* I. 413 There appear to be..at Key West, as well as in Bermuda, various local forms closely related to this [*sc.* the rock-fish], one of which is known by the name 'Gag'. **1896** JORDAN & EVERMANN *Fishes Amer.* 1177 *Mycteroperca Microlepis* (Gag). **1950** R. A. DAHNE *Salt-Water Fishing* viii. 155 The gags seems to be increasing in popularity with many salt-water anglers.

gag (gæg), *v.*[1] Also 5 **gaggyn**, 6 **gagge**, 7 **gagg**. [app. imitative of the sound made in choking.]

1. †**a.** *trans.* To strangle, suffocate. *Obs.*

c **1440** *Promp. Parv.* 184/2 Gaggyn, or streyne be the þrote, *suffoco*.

b. *intr.* To choke, *lit.* and *fig.* Also, to retch. Also *trans.* (causatively).

1707 HICKERINGILL *Priest-cr.* II. v. 49, I do not, in the least, wonder, that he (that swallows Transubstantiation) should Gagg at believing, that [etc.]. *a* **1825** FORBY *Voc. E. Anglia*, *Gag*, to nauseate; to reject with loathing, as if the throat were closed against the admission of what is offered; to make an unsuccessful effort to vomit. **1883** *Hampsh. Gloss.*, *Gag*, to choke; like a dog or cat in eating greedily. **1908** *Practitioner* Sept. 367 The operation causes a little gagging and retching at first, but the patient soon becomes accustomed to the feeling of the cords in the throat. **1939** H. HODGE *Cab, Sir?* 49 The stench of stale beer and cheap scent makes me gag. **1945** J. STEINBECK *Cannery Row* xvii. 70 The idea gagged him, but he couldn't let it alone. **1963** M. DUGGAN in C. K. Stead *N.Z. Stories* (1966) 97 Suppose you gag a little at the sugar coating, its the same old fundamental toffee, underneath.

2. a. *trans.* To stop up the mouth of (a person) with a gag in order to prevent speech or outcry; to put a gag into (the mouth) in order to keep the jaws distended.

1509 HAWES *Past. Pleas.* XXXII. (Percy) 159 We saw men in great tormenting, With many ladies, that their mouthes gagged. **1530** PALSGR. 559/2, I gagge one, I putte a gagge in his mouthe that he shulde nat speke nor krye, *je embaillonne.* **1601** B. JONSON *Poetaster* v. iii, Gag him, we may haue his silence. **1712** ARBUTHNOT *John Bull* IV. i, He could have John gagged and bound whenever he pleased. **1794** MRS. RADCLIFFE *Myst. Udolpho* lii, They fastened my arms, and gagged my mouth. **1828** SCOTT *F.M. Perth* xxiii, 'Let him be gagged instantly', said Albany. **1886** W. J. TUCKER *E. Europe* 195 He bound me, and then gagged my mouth. **1895** ERICHSEN *Surgery* (ed. 10) II. 691 If the patient be efficiently gagged.

b. To stop the mouth of (an animal) with or as with a gag.

1591 HARINGTON *Orl. Fur.* XI. xlviii. (1607) 85 That one alone the monster should assaile, And gag him with an anker in such sort To make his strength, and life, and all to faile. **1625** BACON *Ess.*, *Goodness* (Arb.) 201 A Christian Boy in Constantinople, had liked to haue been stoned, for gagging, in a waggishnesse, a longe Billed Fowle.

c. *transf.* and *fig.*, esp. to deprive of power or freedom of speech; to stop the mouth of.

1601 SHAKS. *Twel. N.* I. v. 94 Vnles you laugh and minister occasion to him, he is gag'd. **1640** LD. FAULKLAND *Sp.* in Rushw. *Hist. Coll.* III. (1692) I. 139 He had as it were gagg'd the Commonwealth, taking away (to his power) all Power of Speech from that body. **1647** TRAPP *Comm. Matt.* ix. 32 Satan still gags many to this day, that they cannot pray to God. **1792** BURNS *Let. to Mrs. Dunlop* 6 Dec. 77, I am a placeman, you know; a very humble one, indeed, Heaven knows, but still so much as to gag me. **1827** MACAULAY *Ess.*, *Machiav.* (1887) 48 The time was not yet come when eloquence was to be gagged, and reason to be hoodwinked. **1859** HELPS *Friends in C.* Ser. II. II x. 267 Without gagging our press. **1871** L. STEPHEN *Playgr. Europe* xii. (1894) 294 The continuous snow-fields.. have gagged the torrent. **1874** GREEN *Short Hist.* vi. §6. 331 The Church was gagged and its pulpits turned into mere echoes of Henry's will.

†**3.** To prop *open* (a window). *Obs.*

1604 *Meeting of Gallants* 18 He gagged open the Windowes.

4. a. To confine unduly the mouth of, or apply a gag-bit to (a horse). **b.** To obstruct the working of (a valve), to stop up the valves of (an engine).

1833 *Regul. Instr. Cavalry* I. 75 The reins.. are to be shortened by degrees, and with great care not to gag, or confine the horse too much. **1839** [see GAGGED]. **1857** WRIGHT *Provinc. Dict.*, *Gag*, to hinder motion by tightness. *Northampt.* **1868** ATKINSON *Cleveland Gloss.*, *Gag*, To apply a very powerful bit, such as is used in breaking young horses or governing restive ones. **1888** *Engineer* June LXV. 468 The men who gagged the valve knew quite well what they were about.

5. *Theat.* **a.** *intr.* To introduce 'gag' into a piece. (See GAG *sb.*[1] 3.)

1852 DICKENS *Bleak Ho.* xxxix, The same vocalist 'gags' in the regular business like a man inspired. **1876** *Tinsley's Mag.* XVIII. 180 They 'gag' to such an extent that the author oftentimes does not recognise his own dialogue.

b. *trans.* To fill *up* (a piece) with 'gag'.

1861 MAYHEW *Lond. Labour* III. 141 We only do the outline of the story and gag it up. **1889** L. WALLACK *Mem.* 162, I have read the part very carefully, and if you will let me gag it and do what I please with it, I will undertake it.

c. *intr.* To tell a joke or jokes. Also *trans.*, with the joke as object.

1942 in BERREY & VAN DEN BARK *Amer. Thes. Slang* §281/11. **1959** I. & P. OPIE *Lore & Lang. Schoolch.* iii. 53 'Do you know where Smudger takes his girl?' gags the would-be comic.

Hence **'gagging** *vbl. sb.* and *ppl. a.*

1817 COLERIDGE *Biog. Lit.* (1870) 85 Whatever the motives of ministers might have been for the sedition, or as it was then the fashion to call them, the *gagging* bills. **1861** MAYHEW *Lond. Labour* III. 126 And after a little business between them, all gagging, he says 'Slave! get back to the castle.' **1892** *Athenæum* 6 Feb. 173/2 But for his [Canning's] gagging of the European press.. some dismal or unseemly things would not have happened. **1893** *Times* 14 July 9/5 The gagging resolution excluded all debate on the remaining clauses. **1895** ERICHSEN *Surgery* (ed. 10) II. 690 Efficient gagging is one of the most essential parts of all operations on the tongue.

†**gag,** *v.*[2] *Obs.* Also 6 (? *misspelling*) gage, 7 gagg. [? onomatopœic; cf. JAG *v.*]

1. *trans.* To jerk; to strike with a sharp blow. Also, to toss *up* (the head); cf. Sc. GECK *v.*

It is uncertain whether quot. 1587 belongs to this word. **1587** FLEMING *Contn. Holinshed* III. 1019/2 Minding to haue striken the man to whom he leuelled the shot: but gaging his hand, and missing his marke, he stroke his owne and best freend John Peter. **1610** HEALEY *St. Aug. Citie of God* XIV. xv. 518 A man sometimes.. will be angry at sencelesse things, as to gag his pen [L. *ut stilum collidat*] in anger when it writes badly. **1617** MARKHAM *Caval.* v. 56 Whence hee first learnes to gagg vp his head to loose his reyne.

2. a. *trans.* ? To wound or prick. **b.** *intr.* To make thrusts or pricks (*at*).

1570 FOXE tr. *Prudentius' Death Cassianus* in *A. & M.* (ed. 2) 129/2 Some other gage hys flesh and ioyntes as with a poynted nall. **1622** MABBE tr. *Aleman's Guzman d'Alf.* II. 180, I was ever so mightily pricked on to revenge, as if (like a beast) the spurres thereof lay still gagging at my sides.

3. *intr.* To project, stick out. [Cf. GAG-TOOTH.]

1599 MINSHEU, *Púa*, any naile or such like sticking or gagging out. **1886** *Cheshire Gloss.*, *Gagging out*, sticking out, projecting.

gag (gæg), *v.*[3] *slang.* [See GAG *sb.*[2]] **a.** *trans.* To deceive, take in or impose upon (a person), to ply with talk, to 'stuff'. **b.** *intr.* To practise imposture. *to gag on*: to 'round' on, inform against.

1777 MAD. D'ARBLAY *Early Diary* 7 Apr., In the most capital scene.. I endeavoured, what I could, to soften off the affectation of her sudden change of disposition, and I gagged the gentleman with as much ease as my very little ease would allow me to assume. **1781** G. PARKER *View Soc.* II. 154 Having discovered the weak side of him he means to gag. *Ibid.* II. 155 An old Soldier had gagg'd about London many years. His mode for provoking compassion was to [etc.]. **1819** [LOCKHART] *Peter's Lett. to Kinsfolk* III. 241 Gagging .. signifies, as its name may lead you to suspect, nothing more than the thrusting of absurdities, wholesale and retail, down the throat of some too credulous gaper. **1823** 'JON BEE' *Dict. Turf* s.v., He, in excuse, swears he said 'they were' and not 'are alive'. He thus gags the public. **1825–80** JAMIESON, *Gag*, to play on one's credulity, a cant term used in Glasgow. **1828** G. SMEATON *Doings in Lond.* 28 Gagging has been practised of late to a considerable extent on simple countrymen. **1874** HOTTEN *Slang Dict.*, *Gag*, to hoax, 'take a rise' out of one; to 'cod'. **1891** *Tramps* in *Gentl. Mag.* Apr. CCLXX. 390 She.. besought them with (crocodile) tears not to 'gag' on them, in other words not to give information to the police.

gaga ('gɑːgɑː, 'gægə), *a.*, (*adv.*), and *sb. slang.* Also ga-ga. [a. F. *gaga* a senile person; senile.]

A. *adj.* Doting, exhibiting senile decay; mad, 'dotty'; fatuous. Also as *adv.*

[**1905** *Daily Chron.* 18 Mar. 8/6 'Ah, you English,' quoth Mr. De Vries not so long ago, after a round of the London theatres, 'you like to laugh—ga-ga!'.. Is not that the pathetic cry of our present drama, 'Ga-ga!'] **1920** F. M. FORD *Let.* 26 July (1965) 116 The V.G.F. [*sc.* Victorian Great Figure] must be gaga! **1921** M. BARING *Passing By* 210 Sir Arthur is quite gaga and took me for George the whole evening. **1926** E. FERBER *Show Boat* xix. 385 Nola darling, you've just gone gaga, that's all. What do you mean by staying down there in that wretched malarial heat! **1927** *Sunday Express* 13 Mar. 4 The conventional pictures of a young man and a young woman looking 'ga-ga' at each other. **1929** W. J. LOCKE *Ancestor Jorico* xviii, 'But why did he leave the half-million to his son, in his will?' '*Gaga*, my dear Binkie. Just *gaga*. Senile, if you'd like it better.' **1956** C. P. SNOW *Homecomings* xvii. 116 Hiding behind his smoke-screen of platitudes like an amiable old man already a bit ga-ga. **1961** A. WILSON *Old Men at Zoo* iii. 158 If Godmanchester was so gaga that he blabbed like this, then our prospects were alarming.

B. *sb.* A doting or senile person; a madman.

1938 S. BECKETT *Murphy* xi. 240 Mr. Endon.. the most biddable little gaga in the entire institution. **1941** KOESTLER *Scum of Earth* 180 Couldn't understand what he said... Disastrous old gaga.

‖**gagaku** ('gagakuː). [Jap., f. *ga* authentic, graceful, noble + *gaku* music.] A type of Japanese instrumental music performed chiefly on ceremonial occasions at the Imperial court and closely resembling the secular music of ancient China during the Tang period.

[**1893** F. T. PIGGOTT *Mus. Japan* I. 14 The new Musical Bureau was christened '*Gagaku Rio*': *Ga* meaning 'tasteful', and therefore, in old days as in new, an equivalent to something but lately introduced from foreign parts.] **1936** K. SUNAGA *Jap. Mus.* ii. 24 *Gagaku* is the special form of music performed in the ceremonies of the Imperial Court, as well as music and dancing performed on such other occasions as banquets and entertainments. **1968** *Daily Tel.* 15 Nov. 19/8 During the 30-minute acceptance ceremony in Tokyo this morning, court musicians, wearing resplendent period costumes, played age-old instruments to produce ancient music known in Japan as 'gagaku'.

†**gagate.** *Obs.* Also 1, 6–7 gagates, 4 gogathes. [ad. L. *gagātes*, Gr. γαγάτης, said by Pliny to be derived from the name of the town *Gagæ* and river *Gages* in Lycia. An OF. form of the word has passed into Eng. as JET.]

1. Jet.

c **900** tr. *Bæda's Hist.* I. i. (1890) 26 Her biþ eac ȝemeted gagates: se stan biþ blæc gym. **1387** TREVISA *Higden* (Rolls) I. 337 þere is i-founde a stoon þat hatte gogathes [*v.r.* gagates]. **14..** *Med. Receipts* in *Rel. Ant.* I. 53 Tak a stane that es called a gagate. **1559** MORWYNG *Evonymus* 290 Tilestones, Gagate, Aumber. **1567** MAPLET *Gr. Forest* 8 Gagates is of the precious sort also, which was first found in Sicilie in a certain floud called Gagatus. **1688** R. HOLME *Armoury* II. 40/2 The Gagate.. of which there are two kinds, the one russet colour and the other black. **1708** *Brit. Apollo* No. 101. 2/1 Gagates kindle in Water.

2. Sometimes confused with AGATE (*achates*).

a **1661** FULLER *Worthies*, *Yorksh.* III. (1662) 185 The Agate, vastly distinct from Geat, is also named Gagates.

3. *attrib.*, in *gagate stone*.

1602 WARNER *Alb. Eng.* IX. xlvii. (1612) 220 Tush, in those times weare no such toyes as Gagate stones to trie, By foysting them in Potions, if a Maide had trode awrie.

gage (geɪdʒ), *sb.*[1] Also 6 gauge, gayge, guage, 6–7 gadge. [a. OF. *g(u)age* (F. *gage*) masc. = Pr. *gage-s*, Sp., Pg. *gage*, It. *gaggio*:—Rom. **gwadjo*, a. OTeut. **wadjo*[m]: see WED. The OF. variant *wa(i)ge* was adopted in the form WAGE.]

1. Something of value deposited to ensure the performance of some action, and liable to forfeiture in case of non-performance; a pawn, pledge, security.

1457 *Lichfield Gild Ord.* (1890) 19 Poore men dwelling within the citie aboueseid.. may be releeved by a sufficient gage or pledge leyd in-to the seyd cofre for borowing mony of the same. **1513–4** *Act 5 Hen. VIII*, c. 1 He shal.. bring in sufficient gage and plegge.. into the Kynges Court of Chauncerie or els to remayn in warde. **1614** RALEIGH *Hist. World* IV. i. §1. 160 He also left Philip.. for the gage of his promises to Pelopidas. **1690** LOCKE *Hum. Und.* IV. xix. Wks. 1714 I. 330 The Arguments that gain it Assent are the Vouchers and Gage of its Probability to us. **1765** H. WALPOLE *Otranto* iii. (1798) 52 'Here take my gage' [a ring]. **1768** BLACKSTONE *Comm.* III. xix, The sheriff is commanded to attach him, by taking gage, that is certain of his goods which he shall forfeit if he doth not appear. **1867** OUIDA *C. Castlemaine* (1879) 15 This shall be my gage, that I may speak.

b. In phrases, *at gage*, (*to deliver, give, leave*) *in gage*, (*to lay, lie, sweep*) *to gage*, (*to give*) *under gage*, *upon gage*; also *in gage of*.

1523 LD. BERNERS *Froiss.* I. ccliii. 375 The towne of Doway and Lisle delyuered in gage for money, y[t] [etc.]. **1534** —— *Gold. Bk. M. Aurelius* (1546) Z iv b, We put our lyfe in daunger, and lay our honour to gauge. **1560** RANDOLPH in Froude *Hist. Eng.* (1881) VI. 409 Was fain to leave his saffron shirt in gage. **1563–87** FOXE *A. & M.* (1596) 1661/1, I will lay my gowne to gage. **1565–73** COOPER *Thesaurus*, *Bona praedia*, gages: goodes lying to gage. **1573** TUSSER *Husb.* xciv. (1878) 185 Ill huswiferie sweepeth her linnen to gage. **1579** FENTON *Guicciard.* II. (1599) 92 Thirty thousand duckats.. giuen vnder gage of the kings iewels. **1579–80** NORTH *Plutarch* (1676) 71 The common people.. borrowed Money.. upon gage of their bodies to serve it out. **1593** DRAYTON *Sheph. Garl.* III. iv, Learned Collin laies his pipe to gage. **1638** SIR R. COTTON *Abstr. Rec. Tower* 9 When his owne were at gage, he [etc.]. **1853** MERIVALE *Rom. Rep.* viii. (1867) 234 Appealing to his birth, rank, and aristocratic sentiments, in gage of his loyalty.

2. *spec.* A pledge (usually a glove thrown on the ground) of a person's appearance to do battle in support of his assertions. Hence, a challenge. Also *gage of battle*.

13.. *K. Alis.* 7236 He with-seith alle homage; And sendeth you, by sonde, gage. *c* **1450** LONELICH *Grail* lii. 865 Thanne Sire Piers, that was so dowhty A knyht.. Aȝens kyng Marahaus put his Gage. **1483** CAXTON *G. de la Tour* H iv, He accused one of treason the whiche anone casted his gage of bataylle unto hym. **1523** LD. BERNERS *Froiss.* I. ccci. 445 Caste downe your gage in that quarell, and ye shall fynde him that shall take it vp. **1590** GREENE *Orl. Fur.* Wks. (Rtldg.) 91/2, I will pawn my honour to his gage, He shall ere night be met and combated. **1600** FAIRFAX *Tasso* v. lviii, There take my gage, behold I offer it To him that first accus'd him in this cause. **1828** SCOTT *F.M. Perth* vi, A gauntlet flung down is a gage of knightly battle. **1857** KINGSLEY *Two Y. Ago* (1877) 55 He was going to throw down a very ugly gage of battle.

fig. **1890** BOLDREWOOD *Col. Reformer* (1891) 315 He was very loath to retreat from any gage of battle thus produced.

†**3.** *pl.* *Sc.* [prob. a late adoption of F. *gages* in the same sense.] Wages. *on the gages of*: in the pay of. *Obs. rare.*

1562 *Acts Sederunt* 2 Mar. (1790) 5 To haife the said College [of Justice] eiked the nowmer of six, and in the meyn tyme, the gauges to be eiked and augmentit. **1563–7** BUCHANAN *Reform. St. Andros* Wks. (1892) 14 The principal sal deduce sa mekle of hys gagis to be vsit to the common profet of the college. *Ibid.* 16 That na idle person be haldin on the gagis or expensis of the vniuersite.

4. *attrib.* and *Comb.*, as *gage-place*, *-selling*, *-thrower*; *gage-like* adj.

1847 TENNYSON *Princ.* v. 170 She.. flung defiance down *Gagelike to man. **1611** SPEED *Hist. Gt. Brit.* IX. vii. §13 The Castles of Rockesbrough and Berwicke, cautionarie Castles, or *gage places (for part of his ransome) should be restored. *c* **1530** LD. BERNERS *Arth. Lyt. Bryt.* (1814) 87 Marye, madame, this lady payeth wythout anye *gage sellyng [F *sans gage vendre*]. **1893** *Westm. Gaz.* 20 Dec. 3/1 Here was the opener, the *gage thrower in the lists, declaring that he was no party champion.

gage (geɪdʒ), *sb.*[2] *slang.* [perh. f. GAGE *sb.*[1], the sense being 'enough to pledge any one with', or var. GAUGE, a measure.]

1. A quart pot; a quart pot full.

c **1440** *Promp. Parv.* 186 Gage, lytylle belle (*S.* lytyll bolle). **1567** HARMAN *Caveat* (1879) 34 A gage of bowse, whiche is a quarte pot of drinke. **1622** FLETCHER *Beggar's Bush* III. iii, I crown thy nab with a gage of benebowse. **1652** BROOME *Jov. Crew* II. F iv b, I bowse no Lage but a whole Gage Of this I'll bowse to you. **1708** J. HALL *Mem.* 20 *Gage*, a pot. **1785** GROSE *Dict. Vulg. Tongue*, *Gage*, a quart pot, also a pint, (*cant*).

2. A pipe; a pipeful (of tobacco).

1676 in COLES. *a* **1700** B. E. *Dict. Cant. Crew*, *Gage*, a Pot or Pipe. Tip me a Gage, give me a Pot or Pipe. **1834** [see FOGUS].

gage (geɪdʒ), *sb.*[3] = GREENGAGE.

1888 *Daily News* 10 Sept. 7/1 Plums, with their congeners, damsons and gages, were but little thought of.

gage (geɪdʒ), *v.* Also 6 gagie, guage, gauge, gayge, 7 gaige. [ad. F. *gager* in same sense, or aphetic form of ENGAGE, to which it corresponds in several senses.]

†**1.** *trans.* To pledge or pawn; to mortgage the revenues of (a country). = ENGAGE *v.* 1. *Obs.*

1474 CAXTON *Chesse* III. v. (1481) G vij, They began..to axe and demande of her the besaunt that they had geuen to her. And she answerd That hit was holden and gaged vpon an ymage. **1555** EDEN *Decades* 243 The emperoure..gagied the Malucas & the spicerie to the kynge of Portugale. **1579–80** NORTH *Plutarch* (1676) 579 Hast thou not Plate, and Apparel to sell or gage or help him to some? **1592** STOW *Ann.* 1380. 443 Sir Iohn Philpot..released the armour which the souldiers had gaged for their victuals.

absol. **1555** W. WATREMAN *Fardle Facions* App. 337 If he that hath gauged be a manne of substaunce: lette the creditour keep the gauge vntill the restitucion of the lone be made.

†**b.** To give a pledge for; to undertake to make. *Obs.*$^{-1}$

1622 CALLIS *Stat. Sewers* (1824) 232 Neither would the Court order the defendant to gage deliverance.

†**c.** *to gage battle*: to pledge oneself to judicial combat. Cf. F. *gager bataille*. *Obs.* (Cf. WAGE *v.*)

1586 FERNE *Blazon Gentrie* 77 If one gentleman shall detract from the honor of another..let combate be guaged. **1600** TATE in Gutch *Coll. Cur.* I. 8 Battel personal gaged betwixt the subjects of one kingdom in criminal causes. **1620** J. WILKINSON *Coroners & Sherifes* 22 The defendant shall not gage battel in such appeales.

2. To stake, wager; to risk, bet. *Obs.* or *arch.*

1599 JAS. I *Βασιλ. Δωρον* (1603) III. 124 Only to gage so much of his owne money, as he pleaseth, vpon the hazarde of the running of the cardes. **1602** SHAKS. *Ham.* I. i. 91 Against the which, a Moity competent Was gaged by our King. **1603** KNOLLES *Hist. Turks* (1621) 67 Assailed by the Christians, with such furie, as if they had thereon purposed to gage their whole forces. **1750** HODGES *Chr. Plan* (1755) 51 Doing the same, as if he had staked or gaged his seventh, i.e. all his hopes of the divine vision. **1814** SCOTT *Ld. of Isles* II. vii, And 'gainst an oaken bough I'll gage my silver wand of state.

b. *fig.* To pledge, offer as a guarantee or forfeit (one's head, life, etc.). (Cf. ENGAGE *v.* 2.)

a **1529** SKELTON *Vox Populi* xiii. 11 My hed I hold and gage, There wylbe greate outrage. **1573** ESSEX in Ellis *Orig. Lett.* Ser. II. III. 32 To all which pointes I gage myne honour and faith. **1583** STUBBES *Anat. Abuses* I (1877) 112 That thei would paie hym, or els thei would guage their neckes. **1599** *Warn. Faire Wom.* I. 279, I will gage my hand, Few women can my mistress force withstand. **1603** KNOLLES *Hist. Turks* (1621) 10 The clergiemen that had before for his safetie gaged their faith. **1633** FORD *'Tis Pity* v. iii, This feast, I'll gage my life, Is but a plot to train you to your ruin. **1876** G. W. COX *Gen. Hist. Greece* IV. i. 510 A guide sent to them by the headman of this place gaged his life as a forfeit if he failed.

†**3.** To bind as by a formal promise. *Obs.* (Cf. ENGAGE *v.* 4.)

1489 *Plumpton Corr.* p. xcviii, You have ministered unto us cause, as gaged to remember you in time to come. **1606** SHAKS. *Tr. & Cr.* v. i. 46 Heere is a Letter from Queene Hecuba, A token from her daughter..Both taxing me, and gaging me to keepe An Oath that I haue sworne.

4. *intr.* for *refl.* To assert on one's own responsibility *that*. (Cf. ENGAGE *v.* 6.)

1811 W. R. SPENCER *Poems* 19, I gage, though long our way, and drear, We reach our nuptial bed to day. **1865** J. BALLANTINE *Poems* 24 The other wore the crown of age, But a brighter one she found, I gage.

†**5.** *trans.* To fix or fasten *in* or *upon*. *Obs.* (Cf. ENGAGE *v.* 11 b.)

1703 MOXON *Mech. Exerc.* 192 The further or open side of the Male-screw is gaged in, or pin'd on the Female-screw with a wooden Pin thrust through two opposite Holes. *Ibid.* 228 This Neck is..gaged in the Shackle.

†**6.** To bind or entangle *in*. Cf. ENGAGE *v.* 13.

1596 SHAKS. *Merch. V.* I. i. 130 The great debts Wherein my time something too prodigall Hath left me gag'd.

Hence **gaged** *ppl. a.*, **'gaging** *vbl. sb.*, in senses of the vb.

1555 EDEN *Decades* 244 *margin*, The gageing of the Ilands of malucas. **1586** FERNE *Blaz. Gentrie* 153 Gaging of single battaile. **1602** WARNER *Alb. Eng.* XII. lxxv. (1612) 312 Elenor ..did tell The circumstances of her Ring..And shewes the gaged Tablet.

gage, gager, obs. forms of GAUGE, GAUGER.

‖**gage d'amour** (gaʒ damur). [Fr.] A pledge of love; a love-token.

1768 STERNE *Sent. Journ.* II. 144 His faith-less mistress had given his *gage d'amour* to one of the Count's footmen. **1838** DICKENS *Let.* 27 July (1965) I. 422 It is many months since I sent you a slight gage d'amour. **1873** TROLLOPE *Eust. Diamonds* xxxi. 60 That gage d'amour which you carry on your finger. **1930** 'R. CROMPTON' *William's Happy Days* vii. 157 He'd picked up a glove that she'd left in church last Sunday, and was treasuring it as a kind of *gage d'amour*.

gager: see GAGGER².

gagg(e, obs. form of GAG *sb.*¹ and *v.*¹

gagged (gægd), *ppl. a.* [f. GAG *v.*¹ + -ED¹.] In senses of the vb.

1839 R. S. ROBINSON *Naut. Steam. Eng.* 145 The safety valve..may become gagged or rusted, and incapable of motion. **1888** *Century Mag.* July N.S. XIV. 431 A gagged engine working at the full stroke of the pistons. **1894** *Westm. Gaz.* 25 June 2/2 The gagged clauses were passed without any discussion at all.

gaggee (gæˈgiː). *rare*$^{-1}$. [f. GAG *v.*³ + -EE.] One who is gagged; the victim of a 'gag' or deception.

1819 [see GAG *sb.*³].

gagger¹. (ˈgægə(r)). [f. GAG *v.*¹ + -ER¹.] One who gags, in senses of the vb.

1624 BP. R. MOUNTAGU *Gagg* (*running title*), An Answer to the late Gagger of Protestants. **1848** *Tait's Mag.* XV. 524 The gagger of the press. **1871** *Daily News* 14 Jan., The most incorrigible 'gagger' of his time. He said what he liked and almost did what he liked when on the stage. **1885** *Pall Mall G.* 13 July 1/2 The rule..from which, if the gaggers [*sc.* of the press] will leave us alone, we have no intention to depart.

Hence **'gaggership** *nonce-wd.*, a mock title of address.

1624 BP. R. MOUNTAGU *Gagg* 287 Your Gaggership.

'gagger². Also gager. [? f. GAG *v.*² + -ER¹.] (See quots.)

1858 SIMMONDS *Dict. Trade*, *Gagger*, a lifter used by the founder, consisting of a light T-shaped piece of iron. **1888** *Lockwood's Dict. Mech. Engin.*, *Gaggers* or *Gagers*, short conical or pyramidal projections, cast upon core plates and the plates for loam moulds, to assist the adhesion of the loam. The term is sometimes applied also to lifters.

gagger³ (ˈgægə(r)). *slang.* [f. GAG *v.*³ + -ER¹.] One who 'gags', cheats, or hoaxes.

1781 G. PARKER *View Soc.* II. 154 The high gagger..The low gagger. **1819** [LOCKHART] *Peter's Lett. to Kinsfolk* III. 242 The solemn triumph of the Gagger, and the grim applause of the silent witnesses of his dexterity, are alike visible in their sparkling eyes. **1841** *Punch* 23 Oct. I. 169 Men with 'swallows' like Thames tunnels: in fact accomplished gaggers.

gaggery (ˈgægərɪ). [F. GAG *v.*³ + -ERY.] The practice of gagging.

1819 *Blackw. Mag.* IV. 620 A species of wit peculiar to this mercantile city [Glasgow], and known in it by the name of gaggery. **1838** *Ibid.* XLIII. 681 And toasts, and tricks, and gaggery, And many a song between.

gaggle (ˈgæg(ə)l), *sb.* Forms: 4–9 **gagle**, 5–6 **gagyll**, 6– **gaggle.** [f. the vb.]

1. a. A flock (of geese); also *derisively*, a company (of women).

One of the many artificial terms invented in the 15th c. as distinctive collectives referring to particular animals or classes of persons; but unlike most of the others, it seems to have been actually adopted in use.

c **1470** in *Hors, Shepe & G.* etc. (Caxton 1479, Roxb. repr.) 30 A gagyll of ghees A gagyll of women. **1584** R. SCOT *Discov. Witchcr.* XIII. xxx. 338 A shoale of goslings, or (as they saie) a gaggle of geese. **1676** COLES, *A Gagle of geys*, a flock of Geese. **1827** COL. HAWKER *Diary* (1893) I. 309 A gaggle of more than average chattering women. **1882** SIR R. PAYNE GALLWEY *Fowler in Irel.* v, That last tempting gaggle of Brent Geese.

b. Also *transf.*, a group of people or things, esp. a disorderly assemblage; *spec.* (*slang*) a group of aircraft.

1946 G. GIBSON *Enemy Coast Ahead* 206 We started off first in squadrons, then in wings and finally in a sort of formation known as a group gaggle, meaning a flock of geese. **1946** E. C. CHEESMAN *Brief Glory* vi. 73 Ferry pilots had to fly in 'gaggles' to make it easier for the Observer Corps. **1956** J. E. JOHNSON *Wing Leader* i. 13 We curved across Berlin, sparred cautiously with large gaggles of Russian fighters. **1966** *Listener* 8 Sept. 354/1 There is hardly a modern skyscraper in midtown that does not have its gaggle of sightseers. **1971** *Islander* (Victoria, B.C.) 21 Mar. 14/3 A gaggle of sparsely inhabited islands.

2. Chatter, gabble.

1668 R. L'ESTRANGE *Vis. Quev.* (1708) 29 A Consort of loud and tedious Talkers, that Tired and Deafn'd the Company with their shrill and restless Gaggle.

gaggle (ˈgæg(ə)l), *v.* Forms: 4 **gagul**, 5–7 **gagle**, (5 **gagelyn**, 6 **gagyll**), 6– **gaggle**. [Prob. an onomatopœic formation (with frequentative suffix) on the syllable *gag* (*gag-gag*) often used to imitate the cry of the goose. Cf. GABBLE, CACKLE.

A similar imitation of the same sound appears as the root of OCeltic **gegâ*, Irish *geadh*, Welsh *gwydd*, goose, and of ON. *gagl* goose. Cf. also mod.Icel. *gagga* to gaggle.]

1. *intr.* Of geese: To cackle; see CACKLE *v.* 1. Also with *forth*.

1399 LANGL. *Rich. Redeles* III. 101 þey gaglide fforth on the grene, ffor they greved were. *c* **1440** *Promp. Parv.* 184/2 Gagelyn, or cryyn as gees, *clingo*. *a* **1483** *Burlesque* in *Rel. Ant.* I. 86 The goos gagult ever more, the gam was better to here. **1529** MORE *Supplic. Soulys* Wks. 302/2 This goseling ..gagleth again vpon the same matter. **1614** T. ADAMS *Devil's Banquet* 58 These are..the Geese in the Capitall to gaggle at Statesmen in the Common-wealth. **1744** *J. Claridge's Sheph. Banbury's Rules* 40 If geese gaggle more than usual, these are all signs of rain. **1851** D. JERROLD *St. Giles* xxiv. 245 [He] gave no ear to his own geese gaggling near his barn. **1884** *Pall Mall G.* 8 Mar. 4/2 Every bird gaggling his loudest.

quasi-*trans.* **1645** *Sacred Decretal* 3 Geese and Ganders.. hisse and gaggle him out of his Five pestilent senses.

†**2.** *transf.* and *fig.* To make a noise like geese; to talk volubly, to chatter. *Obs.*

c **1553** CHANCELOUR *Bk. Emp. Russia* in *Hakluyt* (1886) III. 50 But when the Priest is at seruice no man sitteth, but gagle and ducke like so many Geese. **1630** J. TAYLOR (Water P.) *Taylor's Goose* Wks. I. 105/1 How grauely they from place to place will waggle And how (like Gossips) freely will they gaggle. **1706** *Refl. Ridicule* (1707) 325 They gaggle all at a time; as if it was for a Wager, who should make the greatest noise.

†**3.** *trans.* To utter like a goose; to express with gaggling or cackling; to babble, prattle. Also with *out*. *Obs.*

1577 STANYHURST *Descr. Irel.* i. 3 in Holinshed *Chron.* I, It is not expedient that the Irishe tongue should be so vniuersally gagled in the English pale. *c* **1645** HOWELL *Lett.* (1688) IV. 476 A Countryman..answer'd That he thought the Geese about Oxford did gaggle Greek. **1650** B. *Discolliminium* 2 We need not fear..that she will gaggle any Treason. *Ibid.* 25 Had my Goose gagled out such a.. doctrine [etc.].

Hence **'gaggler**, one who gaggles, a goose.

1624 BP. R. MOUNTAGU *Gagg* To Rdr. 7 As meere a gaggler as euer grased vpon a greene.

gaggling (ˈgæg(ə)lɪŋ), *vbl. sb.* [f. GAGGLE *v.* + -ING¹.] The action of the vb. GAGGLE.

c **1440** *Promp. Parv.* 184/2 Gagelynge of geese or of ganders, *drancitus*. **1532** MORE *Confut. Tindale* Wks. 822/1 Except these geese go from theyr olde flock and giue ouer all theyr olde gagelynge [etc.]. **1548** CRANMER *Catech.* 238 We ought therefore to receaue the Sacrament vnder both kyndes, as Christe commaunded vs. And regarde not the gageling of theim that speake againste the vse of the sacramentes. **1600** HOLLAND *Livy* v. xlvii. (1609) 210 With their gaggling [*clangore*] and fluttering of their wings, M. Manlius..was awaked. **1654** VILVAIN *Theorem Theol.* Supp. 222 Thred bare Arguments, which make Mens ears glow to hear their harsh gaglings. **1674** N. FAIRFAX *Bulk & Selv.* 15 Logick and Philosophy cannot be uttered by..the hissing and gagling of Geese. **1896** J. SKELTON *Summers & Winters at Balmawhapple* I. 168 When the geese pass Mount Taurus they stap their pipes fu' o' gravel to avoid gaggling, and so by silence escape the eagles.

attrib. **1689** *Def. Liberty agst. Tyrants* 130 Then must the Geese play the Sentinels, and with their gagling noise, give an Alarm. **1775** ADAIR *Amer. Ind.* 80 Strangers imagine they make only a gaggling noise, like what we are told of the Hottentots, without any articulate sound.

gaggling (ˈgæg(ə)lɪŋ), *ppl. a.* [f. GAGGLE *v.* + -ING².] That gaggles.

1. Of geese: Cackling, gabbling.

1547–64 BAULDWIN *Mor. Philos.* (Palfr.) 32 Canst thou not at home suffer the gagling geese? **1622** WITHER *Mistr. Philar.* Wks. (1633) 590 The gagling Wildgoose and the snow-white Swan. **1713** *Guardian* No. 132 ¶6 If I have Company they are a parcel of chattering Magpies; if Abroad, I am a gaggling Goose.

2. Of persons, their actions, and attributes: Garrulous, chattering.

1553 BALE *Vocacyon* in *Harl. Misc.* (Malh.) I. 338 Their gaddinge and gagglinge processions. **1565** GOLDING *Ovid's Met.* IV. (1593) 80 Is heard the noise Of gagling women's tatling tongues. **1622** ROWLANDS *Gd. Newes & Bad Newes* 30 A gossip of the gaggling crew Into a humour of contention grew. **1688** H. CARE *King's Right Indulg. Asserted* 12 [They] allowed freedom of dispute to the Hereticks, and permitted their Gagling Loquacity.

gagle, var. GAGGLE *sb.* and *v.*

gagliard, -ise, obs. forms of GALLIARD, -ISE.

†**gagrill.** *Obs.* [? Cf. GANGREL *dial.*, a toad.] Some insect or reptile.

14.. *Pict. Voc.* in Wr.-Wülcker 766 *Hec septipedia*, a gagrylle.

gagster (ˈgægstə(r)). *colloq.* [f. GAG *sb.*¹ + -STER.] One who makes 'gags' or jokes; a gag-writer or comedian.

1935 E. WEEKLEY *Something about Words* 65 The very modern gagster, at the theatre. **1959** *Listener* 5 Nov. 797/3 Music-hall gagsters. **1961** *Observer* 16 July 5/3 He writes his own material (another break with the Bob Hope generation and their teams of gagsters).

†**gag-tooth.** *Obs.* Also 7 **gagged-tooth.** [Cf. GAG *v.*² 3; also GAB *v.*³, *gam-tooth, gang-tooth, gap-tooth, gat-tooth.*] A projecting or prominent tooth.

1585 HIGINS tr. *Junius' Nomenclator* 29 *Dentes exerti*, Gag teeth or teeth standing out. **1593** G. HARVEY *Pierce's Super.* Wks. (Grosart) II. 225 Take heede of the man whom Nature hath marked with a gag-tooth; Art furnished with a gag-tongue; and Exercise armed with a gag-penne; as cruell and murdrous weapons, as euer drewe blood. **1602** *2nd Pt. Return fr. Parnass.* I. ii. 316 A fellow..whose muse was armed with a gagtooth. **1679** BURNET *Hist. Ref.* I. II. 41 She was ill-shaped and ugly; had Six Fingers, a Gag-tooth. **1680** *Lond. Gaz.* No. 1547/4 One Richard Taffin..[with] a gag'd Tooth on the upper Jaw.

gag-toothed, *a.* Having a projecting or prominent tooth.

1579 LYLY *Euphues* (Arb.) 116 If shee be gagge-toothed tell hir some merry iest to make hir laughe. **1592** NASHE *P. Penilesse* (ed. 2) 14a, A leane gagtoothd Beldam. **1606** CHAPMAN *Gentl. Usher* I. i. A iv b, The busky groues that gag-tooth'd boares do shrowd. **1868** J. RICHARDSON, etc. *Mus. Nat. Hist.* II. 150 Gag-toothed Galaxias (*Galaxias brocchus*).

gagul, gagyll, obs. forms of GAGGLE.

gah (gɑː), *int.* [Echoic.] An exclamation indicating impatience or exasperation.

1917 R. NICHOLS *Ardours & Endurances* I. 38 The German line Vanishes in confusion, smoke. Cries, and cry Of our men, '*Gah, yer swine!*' **1936** 'N. BLAKE' *Thou Shell of Death* iii. 50 Gah! Walks like a jaguar with the gripes. **1947** —— *Minute for Murder* x. 236 'Affair'—gah, what a word! **1953** A. MILLER *Crucible* (1956) I. 20 Gah! I'd almost forgot how strong you are, John Proctor! **1966** M. PROCTER *His Weight in Gold* viii. 66 'Gah!' he told himself. 'Ham Wayman, you're going daft.'

gahnite (ˈgɑːnaɪt). *Min.* [f. *Gahn*, the name of a Swedish mining engineer and chemist + -ITE.]

An oxide of zinc and alumina, or zinc aluminate occurring in octahedrons; called also *zinc-spinel*.

1808 T. ALLAN *Names Min.* 33 *Gahnite*.. a species of zinc ore. **1879** RUTLEY *Study Rocks* xiv. 298 The rock contains as accessories.. fahlunite, gahnite, chlorospinel, etc.

gai, obs. form of GO.

gaiassa (gaɪˈæsə). Also 9 **caiash**. [Arab. *ḳayyāsa*.] A high-stemmed vessel with lateen sails used on the Nile for carrying freight.

1818 H. LIGHT *Trav. Egypt* II. i. 123, I began to descend the Nile in a small caiash or barge. **1906** *Westm. Gaz.* 21 Mar. 3/2 One of the most heterodox of boats to European eyes is the 'Gaiassa' of the Nile. **1938** *Times Lit. Suppl.* 31 Dec. 829/1 The craft in question being, persumably, *gaiassas*.

gaid, gade. *Sc. Obs.* exc. *Hist.* [Phonetically equivalent to GOAD, OE. *gád*, but in sense 1 connected with GAD *sb.*[1] 2.] **1.** A bar of metal; esp. the iron bar which formerly crossed the condemned cell in a Scotch prison, upon which ran the iron ring which fastened the shackles.

? *a* **1500** *Rowlis Cursing* 263 Lyk to ane gaid of yrne or steill That doun war sinkand in ane weell. **1629** in Pitcairn *Crim. Trials Scot.* I. 68* *note*, They instantlie wardit him, and patt baith his feitt on the gade. **1647** in Cramond *Ann. Banff* (1891) I. 92 He is decerned to plenish the gaid Sufficientlie with seaven sufficient shakellis. [**1829** SCOTT *Guy M.* lvii *foot-note*, When a man received sentence of death he was put upon *the gad*, as it was called, that is, secured to the bar of iron in the manner mentioned in the text.]

2. = GOAD.

1682 PEDEN in *Biogr. Presbyt.* (1838) I. 51 Their Theats will burn, and their Swingletrees will fall to the Ground.. and the Gade-men will throw away their Gades.

gaie, gaiell, obs. forms of GAY, GAOL.

‖**gaieté de cœur** (gete də kœr). [Fr.] Light-heartedness; playfulness.

1728 VANBRUGH & CIBBER *Prov. Husb.* I. i. 4 Take a frolicksome Supper at an India House—perhaps, in her *Gayeté de Cœur* toast a pretty Fellow. **1747** H. WALPOLE *Let.* 24 Nov. (1903) II. 295, I did not mention returning to Florence out of *gaieté de cœur*. **1886** C. M. YONGE *Chantry House* I. xiii. 119 Emily.. in youthful *gaieté de cœur* had got a little tired of her. **1936** *Times Lit. Suppl.* 4 July 558/2 The latest ebullition of his [*sc.* the Regent's] *gaieté de coeur* is to make the French Ambassador's wife drunk at table.

gaiety (ˈgeɪɪtɪ). Forms: 7–8 **gaity, gayity**, 6–9 **gayety**, 7– **gaiety**. [ad. F. *gaieté, gaîté*, f. *gai* GAY.]

1. a. The quality or condition of being gay; cheerfulness, mirth. Esp. in phr. ***the gaiety of nations***, the cheerfulness or pleasure of a large number of people; general gaiety or amusement (freq. used hyperbolically or ironically).

1647 W. BROWNE tr. *Gomberville's Polexander* IV. v. 335 Carrying in her countenance a gaity, and extraordinarie calm. **1670** WALTON *Lives* IV. 273 George Herbert.. manag'd it with as becoming and grave a gaiety, as any had before, or since his time. **1710** ATTERBURY *Serm.* (1734) I. 328 Prophane Men.. who stick not, in the Gayety of their Hearts, to say that a strict Piety is good for nothing. **1724** RAMSAY *Tea-t. Misc.* (1733) I. p. v, Our Scots tunes.. have an agreeable gaiety and natural sweetness. **1779** JOHNSON *Life of Edmund Smith* in *Prefaces* IV. 61 That stroke of death [Garrick's], which has eclipsed the gaiety of nations, and impoverished the publick stock of harmless pleasure. **1784** COWPER *Task* I. 557 Such health and gayety of heart enjoy The houseless rovers of the sylvan world. **1807** G. CHALMERS *Caledonia* I. III. v. 363 We see little.. of rulers.. in the gaiety of their felicities. **1875** HAMERTON *Intell. Life* x. vi. (1876) 367 Gayety the best legacy of youth. **1967** *Guardian* 15 Dec. 7/4 Nowadays.. musical comedies all seem to hearken back to Old Vienna or Gay Paree, and they don't exactly contribute to the gaiety of nations. **1968** *Listener* 29 Aug. 264/2 Analysts have added substantially to the gaiety of nations, by the cheerful and ingenious inventiveness with which they have produced fantastic and highly risible analyses of all and sundry.

†**b.** Levity, thoughtlessness. [So often F. *gaîté de cœur*.] *Obs.*

1647 CLARENDON *Hist. Reb.* VII. §118 Here Sr William Waller, out of pure gayety, departed from an advantage he could not again recover.

2. Merrymaking, festivity, pleasure-seeking; a festive occasion, a lively entertainment; freq. in *pl.*

1634 HABINGTON *Castara* (Arb.) 143 The soule which doth with God unite, Those gayities how doth she slight Which ore opinion sway? **1654** H. L'ESTRANGE *Chas. I* (1655) 129 So braue a spectacle.. set the London Dames on longing to behold such gaiety within their City walls. **1681** GLANVILL *Sadducismus* (1682) Ded., The deceitful gayeties that steal us away from God. **1767** J. PENN *Sleepy Serm.* iii, The middling people.. have a taste for gaiety and extravagance. **1791** MRS. RADCLIFFE *Rom. Forest* i, He was allured by the gaieties of Paris. **1812** LADY GRANVILLE *Lett.* (1894) I. 33 My last gaiety was at Lady Essex's on Sunday. **1873** SYMONDS *Grk. Poets* x. 319 Among the mountains an Italian of the present day.. is always longing for town gaieties. **1887** *Daily News* 29 June 5/3 That funny piece.. in which a little girl is carried off to a garrison gaiety.

3. Bright appearance or ornamentation; showiness; showy dress; occas. *pl.*

a **1657** LOVELACE *Poems* (1659) 60 Have you not marked their Cœlestial play, And no more peek'd the gayeties of day. **1695** WOODWARD *Nat. Hist. Earth* III. i. 149 The Gayeities [*sic*] and Embelishments that we might seek for in it [the Earth]. **1695** LUTTRELL *Brief Rel.* (1857) III. 538 The Jacobites appear'd in their utmost gayety. **1739** J. TRAPP *Right. over-much* (1758) 17 No sort of gayety or expensiveness in dress is permitted. **1756** W. DODD *Fasting* (ed. 2) 9 Solicitous about the niceties and gayeties of dress. **1838** *Penny Cycl.* X. 326/1 A garden in which the objects desired.. are show, gaiety, and neatness. **1866** J. G. MURPHY *Comm. Exod.* xxxiii. 4–6 They begin to lay aside all gaiety in dress.

4. (With capital initial.) The name of a former London theatre famous, esp. in the 1890s, for its musical shows, used *attrib.* of features characteristic of these shows. **Gaiety girl**, a performer in such a show; also *transf.*

1890 G. B. SHAW *London Mus. 1888–89* (1937) 314 These can aspire to kicking through a Gaiety *pas de quatre*. **1898** *People* 27 Feb., One of the brightest and most graceful of 'Gaiety' girls. **1910** G. K. CHESTERTON *G. B. Shaw* 143 Shaw.. introduced the Gaiety Girl, but did not represent her life as all gaiety. **1946** BRAHMS & SIMON *Trottie True* ii. 20 There was nothing she could do to stop the man nipping off to a stage door and taking a Gaiety Girl out to supper. **1963** *Listener* 10 Jan. 58/1 The black stockings and swirling skirts of the Gaiety Girls. **1965** C. FREMLIN *Jealous One* xx. 156 This gaiety-girl business is all fairly new. It's not natural to her. She's one of Nature's frumps, really. **1970** *Guardian* 19 Dec. 6/2 There were Gaiety Girls on garlanded swings.

†**gaig**, *v.* *Obs.*[−1] [f. local Sc. *gaig* (? GAG *sb.*[2]) a cleft, chink (Jam., who gives also *geg* sb. and v. in the same senses).] *trans.* To chap, crack (earth). Only in *pass.*

1585 JAS. I *Ess. Poesie* (Arb.) 14 Let Readers think they fele the burning heat, And graithly see the earth, for lacke of weit, With withering drouth and Sunne so gaigged all.

gaige, obs. form of GAGE *v.*

†**gaigeour.** *Obs. Sc.* [ad. F. *gageure* wager, f. *gager* GAGE *v.*] A wager or bet.

1599 JAS. I *Βασιλ. Δωρον* (1603) III. 124 To gage so much of his owne money, as he pleaseth, vpon the hazarde of the running of the cardes or dice; as well as he would doe vpon the speede of a Horse or a Dog, or any such like gaigeour. And so, if they be vnlawfull, all gaigeours vpon vncertainties must likewayes be condemned.

gaignage, obs. form of GAINAGE.

gail: see GYLE.

gail(e, gailer, -or, obs. ff. GAOL, GAOLER.

gaill, Sc. form of GALE *v.*[1]

gaillard, gaillard-: see GALLI-.

‖**Gaillardia** (geɪˈlɑːdɪə). [mod.L.; named by Fougeroux, in memory of M. *Gaillard*, an amateur botanist.] A genus of composite plants, producing showy flowers, for the most part red with a border of yellow.

1888 *Daily News* 25 July 7/2 Messrs. Kelway and Son's gaillardias. **1897** *Ibid.* 30 June 2/3 Japanese iris and gailardias.

gailvat: see GYLE.

gaily, gayly (ˈgeɪlɪ), *adv.* [f. GAY *a.* + -LY[2].]

The spelling *gaily* is the more common, and is supported by the only existing analogy, that of *daily*.

In a gay manner.

1. With reference to dress, etc.: Brightly, showily, smartly, splendidly.

13.. *Gaw. & Gr. Knt.* 597 A sadel, þat glemed ful gayly with mony gold frenges. ? *a* **1400** *Morte Arth.* 912 His gloves gaylyche gilte, and gravene at þe hemmez. *c* **1440** *Gesta Rom.* lxxi. 388 (Add. MS.) This man.. noryshede hem wel, ande arayede hem gayle. **1646** CRASHAW *Steps to Temple* 83 Brother of fear! more gaily clad, The merrier fool o' th' two, yet quite as mad. **1709** POPE *Ess. Crit.* 744 Like some fair flow'r.. That gayly blooms, but ev'n in blooming dies. **1751** GRAY *Ode Spring* iii, Some show their gaily gilded trim Quick-glancing to the sun. **183.** TENNYSON *Coquette* ii, A nobler yearning never broke her rest Than but to dance and sing, be gaily drest. **1876** C. G. FINNEY *Mem.* ix. 115 A young woman.. who had two or three tall plumes in her bonnet, and was rather gayly dressed.

2. With reference to bearing and manner: Cheerfully, joyously, festively; airily, jauntily.

c **1420** *Anturs of Arth.* iii, And thus Dame Gaynour the gode, gayli ho glidus The gatys with Syr Gawan by a grene welle. **1514** BARCLAY *Cyt. & Uplondyshm.* (Percy Soc.) p. xlviii, Many fooles thinke it nothing so While they see courtiers outwarde so gayly go. **1588** A. KING tr. *Canisius' Catech.* 87 Ye kirk moued be knauledge and experience of theis fruicts vses gaylie to sing. **17..** ? SWIFT *Orpheus burlesqued* 42 Wights, who travel that way daily, Jog on by his example gaily. **1768** STERNE *Sent. Journ.* (1778) II. 21 (Hotel at Paris) The event I treated gaily came seriously to my door. **1778** MAD. D'ARBLAY *Diary* 23 Aug., At tea we all met again, and Dr. Johnson was gaily sociable. **1851** THACKERAY *Eng. Hum.* (1853) 97 Addison wrote his papers as gaily as if he was going out for a holiday. **1884** W. C. SMITH *Kildrostan* 63 And the grouse-cock gaily crowing Fears not either dog or gun.

3. Chiefly *Sc.* and *dial.* Fairly; tolerably; pretty well. In this sense also Sc. ***gaylies***; cf. the synonymous *gaylans* (Jam.), where the suffix = -LINGS; and see GEY *adv.*

1553 T. WILSON *Rhet.* 116 b, For this purpose.. they woulde haue serued gayly well. **1568** *Let.* in *Antiq. Rep.* (1808) II. 394 A new Devyce of Heade dressyng setteth forth a Woman gaylye well. **1721** KELLY *Scot. Proverbs* 400 How dee yee.. Bra'ly, finely, Geily at least. **1786** BURNS *Address of Beelzebub* 34 Your factors, grieves, trustees and bailies, I canna' say but they do gaylies. **1790** MRS. WHEELER *Westmld. Dial.* (1821) 113 Tom is gaylie weel. **1839–47** TODD *Cycl. Anat.* III. 51/2 He.. always replied that he was going on 'gaily'. **1840** DE QUINCEY *Style* II. Wks. 1862 X. 224 'It's gaily nigh like to four mile like.' **1855** ROBINSON *Whitby Gloss.*, *Gayly*, in good health. 'We're all gayly.'

4. *Comb.*, as ***gaily-bedizened, -breaking, -chequered, -dressed, -flowered, -jewelled, -throbbing, -warbling*** adjs.

1897 *Daily News* 17 June 6/4 The *gaily-bedizened arm of the breakwater showed the scene of the ceremony. **1890** BOLDREWOOD *Col. Reformer* (1891) 149 The rippling, *gaily-breaking billow. **1730–46** THOMSON *Autumn* 40 A *gaily-chequered heart-expanding view. **1835** WILLIS *Pencillings* I. xviii. 130 Their *gaily-dressed chasseurs are in waiting. **1897** *Daily News* 17 Feb. 9/4 Dainty summer dresses and *gaily-flowered hats. **18..** POE *City in the Sea* Poems (1859) 95 Not the *gaily-jeweled dead Tempt the waters from their bed. **1810** *Associate Minstrels* 23 Tell me what *gaily-throbbing heart.. Ere Summer gild another sky, Beneath the valley's clods shall lie? **1735** SOMERVILLE *Chase* IV. 462 Bid the loud Horns, in *gayly-warbling Strains, Proclaim the Felon's Fate.

†**gain**, *sb.*[1] *Obs.* Forms: α. 3 **gaȝhenn**, 5 *Sc.* **gawin**; β. 3 **gein**, 4 **geyn, gayne**. [The two main forms are app. adopted respectively from ON. *gagn* (Sw. *gagn*, Da. *gavn*) and *gegn*, parallel forms of a sb. developed from the absol. use of the neut. of the adj. *gegn* (see GAIN *a.*). The word became obsolete in the 15th century, about which time the F. *gain* came into the language, with a closely allied meaning. See GAIN *sb.*[2]] Advantage, use, avail, benefit; remedy, help.

α. *c* **1200** ORMIN 13923 All swa summ till Natanael full litell gaȝhenn wære. *c* **1475** *Rauf Coilȝear* 383 That I haue hecht I sall hald.. Quhidder sa it gang to greif or to gawin.

β. *a* **1225** *St. Marher.* 18 Ah hit were þi gein þet tu þe gest unblescet ant ti god baðe efter blescunge ga. **13..** *Gaw. & Gr. Knt.* 2349 Al þe gayne þow me gef, as god mon schulde. *c* **1374** CHAUCER *Anel. & Arc.* 206 But whan she saw that hir ne gat no geyn. **1430–40** LYDG. *Bochas* II. xii. (1554) 50 b, Her lord infect with sodain pestilence There was no geyn but he must nedes dye.

gain (geɪn), *sb.*[2] Forms: 5–6 **gayne**, 6–7 **gaine**, 7– **gain**. [a. OF. *gain, gaain* (mod.F. *gain*) masc., *gaigne, gaaigne* fem. (mod.F. *gagne*), f. *gaaigner* GAIN *v.*[2]

The OFr. sbs. had, in addition to the senses adopted in Eng., other senses related to those of the vb., e.g. 'cultivated land', 'crop', 'harvest'.]

†**1.** Booty, prey, spoil. *Obs.*

1473 WARKW. *Chron.* 2 The Scottesche hoost supposed it hade be doone for some gayne. **1481** CAXTON *Godfrey* clxxvii 261 One shippe.. whiche was goon for somme gayne vpon the see cam alle laden with grete gayne. **1490** —— *Eneydos* lii. 145 With the gayne of the knyghtes, & wyth the proye that they had goten. [**1548** HALL *Chron.*, *Hen. VI*, 119 b, Being content with their prey and gayne, [they] began to retraite.]

2. a. Increase of possessions, resources or advantages of any kind, consequent on some action or change of conditions; an instance of this; profit, emolument; opposed to *loss*. Also (in somewhat rhetorical use), acquisition of wealth viewed as an object of desire; 'lucre', 'pelf'.

1496–7 *Act 12 Hen. VII*, c. 13 §12 Implementis of Houshold.. wherby.. they take no gayne ner wynnyng. **1538** STARKEY *England* I. ii. 1043 Wythout regard of pryuate gayne and profyt. **1548** HALL *Chron.*, *Hen. VI*, 113 Where (after long fightyng) bothe parties departed without either greate gain or losse. **1640–1** *Kirkcudbr. War-Comm. Min. Bk.* (1855) 148 For the tanning of the best ox hyde, for materials, paines and gaine (*printed* ganie) fiftie shillings. **1745** *De Foe's Eng. Tradesm.* i. (1841) I. 6 He.. knows.. what gain is made of them, and what loss, if any. **1770** GOLDSM. *Des. Vill.* 424 Teach erring man to spurn the rage of gain. **1834** J. H. NEWMAN *Par. Serm.* (1837) I. x. 157 They make a gain of godliness. **1849** MACAULAY *Hist. Eng.* I. 303 Greedy as they were of gain, they seldom became rich. **1866** J. MARTINEAU *Ess.* I. 233 Disbelief.. will bring no logical gain. **1878** BROWNING *La Saisiaz* 26 This first life claims a second, else I count its gain no gain.

Proverb. *c* **1620** Z. BOYD *Zion's Flowers* (1855) 153 Men say right well, that gaine still easeth paine.

b. In *plur.* Sums acquired by trade or in other ways; emoluments, profits, winnings, etc. (†Formerly sometimes treated as *sing.*)

1546 J. HEYWOOD *Prov.* (1867) 30 Light gaynes make heauy purses. **1554** LATIMER in Strype *Eccl. Mem.* (1822) III. ii. 290 If their offering did not bringe gaynes withal, it shulde not be so often done. **1600** HOLLAND *Livy* XXXI. xlv. (1609) 800 The gaines would hardly quit the paines [L. *vix operæ pretium erat*]. **1622** MABBE tr. *Aleman's Guzman d'Alf.* II. 343 Out of that gaines.. I made me a suit after the fashion of an old Gally-slaue. **1697** DRYDEN *Virg. Georg.* I. 74 That Crop.. bursts the crowded Barnes, with more than promis'd Gains. **1735** BERKELEY *Querist* §52 Whether small gains be not the way to great profit? **1795** BURKE *Th. on Scarcity* Wks. 1842 II. 248 The labouring people did, either out of their direct gains, or from charity.. fare better than they did. **1855** MACAULAY *Hist. Eng.* IV. 120 The enormous gains, direct and indirect, of the servants of the public went on increasing, while the gains of every body else were diminishing. **1875** MAINE *Hist. Inst.* iv. 110 Where a joint-family claimed the gains of a dancing-girl. **1893** *Bookman* June 83/1 Having got into evil odour by their dubious gains.

c. In extended sense: An increase (whether beneficial or not) in amount, magnitude, or degree. Opposed to *loss*.

1851 CARPENTER *Man. Phys.* (ed. 2) 412 The gain in weight by the absorption of oxygen and nitrogen even exceeds the loss occasioned by the exhalation of carbon. **1863** LYELL *Antiq. Man* 29 A measure of the rate of the gain of land in seven centuries and a half. **1864** Mrs. Carlyle *Lett.* III. 206, I was weighed yesterday and found a gain of five pounds. **1869** Blackmore *Lorna D.* i, One with another, hard they go, to see the gain of the waters.

d. *Electronics.* An increase in power, voltage, or current, expressed as the ratio of the increased quantity to the original quantity or (more commonly) as the logarithm of this; **gain control** (see quot. 1930).

1922 Glazebrook *Dict. Appl. Physics* II. 862/2 The 'loss' in such a case will actually be a 'gain'. That is, in such a case greater current will flow into the receiving circuit when the apparatus is inserted than when it is omitted. **1929** K. Henney *Princ. Radio* xiii. 309 There is a voltage step-up in the transformer, therefore some voltage gain may be secured by its use. **1930** *Sel. Gloss. Motion Pict. Techn.* (*Acad. Motion Pict., Hollywood*), *Gain control*, device for varying the gain of an amplifier. **1936** R. S. Glasgow *Princ. Radio Engin.* vii. 171 Since the decibel is a logarithmic unit, the total gain of an amplifier can be conveniently found by adding together the gains of the individual stages. **1950** *Sci. News* XV. 19 The platinum electrode..is connected to a valve amplifier of high gain. **1959** K. Henney *Radio Engin. Handbk.* (ed. 5) v. 29 The effectiveness of the coupled circuit of Fig. 44 is determined by its gain and its selectivity. **1961** N. H. Crowhurst *High Fidelity Sound Engin.* iii. 79 The effect of a gain control is to alter volume or loudness. **1962** A. Nisbett *Technique Sound Studio* ii. 38 The speech may be at such a low level that considerable gain has to be used, and noise from the amplifier becomes apparent. **1970** D. F. Shaw *Introd. Electronics* (ed. 2) xii. 267 The current gain in a junction transistor is normally less than unity.

†**3.** A source of gain (= Gr. κέρδος). *Obs.*⁻¹

1655 Stanley *Hist. Philos.* I. (1701) 22/1 To examine by what gain every Man maintained himself.

4. The action of acquiring (a possession), winning (a battle), etc. *rare.* [Cf. F. *le gain d'une bataille.*]

1576 Gascoigne *Steele Gl.* (Arb.) 70 They stoode content, with gaine of glorious fame..To leade a life like true Philosophers. **1844** *Fraser's Mag.* XXX. 178/1 The gain of the battle has been ascribed to the aid of the Swedes.

5. *Comb.*: (sense 2), as ***gain-devoted***, ***-getting***, ***-greedy***, ***-spurred***, ***-thirsty*** adjs.; †***gain-sharing***, †***gains-taking*** vbl. sbs.

1784 Cowper *Task* I. 682 In proud, and gay, And *gain-devoted cities. **1894** *Church Building Quarterly* (N.Y.) July 143 [Church-spires] are eloquent reminders to a gain-saying and *gaingetting people that there are better things to think of than the whirling wheels of our manifold industries. **1591** Sylvester *Du Bartas* I. iii. 523 You..*Gain-greedy Chapmen. **1894** *Daily News* 23 Nov. 5/3 '*Gain-sharing' and other systems of remuneration akin to profit sharing. **1591** Sylvester *Du Bartas* I. iii. 282 Saving that our *gain-spurr'd Pilots finde, In our dayes, Waters of more wondrous kinde. **1549** Coverdale, etc. *Erasm. Par. 2 Cor.* 52 Neither with high lokes, nor with bandes of men, nor with *gaynes taking. *a* **1618** Sylvester *Arctophilos's Epist.* 62 Who forbids *gaine-thirsty Chapmen cheapen Another's ware.

gain (geɪn), *sb.*³ *techn.* [Of obscure origin; in sense 1 it might be a use of gain *sb.*² It is not certain that senses 1 and 2 belong to the same word.]

1. (See quots.; = tusk, horn.)

1679 Moxon *Mech. Exerc.* ix. 167, 168 *Gain*, the bevelling shoulder of a Joyst, or other Stuff..the thickness of the shoulder is cut into the Trimmer also Bevilling upwards, that it may just receive that Gain. **1842** Gwilt *Archit.* Gloss., *Gain*, in carpentry, the bevelled shoulder of a binding joist, for the purpose of giving additional resistance to the tenon below.

2. a. *Carpentry* and *Build.* (? *U.S.*) A notch, groove, niche (see quots.).

Knight *Dict. Mech.* 1874 gives also the sense 'a mortise.' **1848** Craig, *Gain*..a lapping of timbers, or the cut that is made for receiving a timber. **1865** E. Burritt *Walk Land's End* 358 Its four walls run up perfectly plain, with-out a break, except a gain cut in one for a small stone saint, called St. Nectan. **1874** Knight *Dict. Mech.* I. 935 s.v. *Gaining-machine*, Two circular saws are placed at a distance apart equal to that of the desired gain. **1884** *Ibid.* IV. 366 *Gain*, a notch, as made in the side or edge of a piece of timber to receive another bar of the frame.

b. *Coal-mining.* A transverse channel or cutting made in the sides of an underground roadway.

1883 in Gresley *Gloss. Coal Mining.*

gain, *a. Obs.* exc. *dial.* Forms: 1 *compar.* **ʒénra**, 4–5 **geyn, gayn**, 5 **gayne, gane**, 6– **gain**. [a. ON. *gegn* adj., straight, direct, favourable, helpful:—OTeut. **gagino-*, *gagano-*, whence OE. **ʒeʒn* (found once in the comparative: see below); otherwise the stem is not found as adj. outside Scand., but occurs both in Scand. and WGer. as a prefix (ON. *gagn-*, OHG. *gagan-*, *-en-*, *gegin-*, MHG. and mod.G. *gegen-*, OE. *ʒeʒn*: see gain-), and in prep. and advb. forms (ON. *gegn* against, right opposite, contrary to, *gegnum* through, OHG. *gagan*, *gegin*, MHG. and mod.G. *gegen* towards, opposite to, OE. *ʒeʒninga* directly, straightway, altogether, *ʒeʒnum* forward; and see gain *prep.*).

For the root of the Teut. **gagano-*, *-ino-*, which seems to express the sense of direct motion or direct opposition, no certain explanation is known. Some have supposed it formed by reduplication from the root of Go, and cognate with the (also reduplicated) Gr. κίχημι I attain, meet with.]

1. Of roads or directions: Near, straight; esp. in superl. form, as ***the gainest way***. [Cf. ON. *hinn gegnsta veg* acc.]

a **1000** *Epistola Alexandri*, Ðe ða ʒenran weʒas cuðan ðara siðfato [*qui brevitates itinerum noverant*]. *c* **1330** R. Brunne *Chron.* (1810) 319 Sir Jon tok the gayn stie. *c* **1350** *Will. Palerne* 4189 þei..went forþ on here way wiʒtli and fast euer þe geynest gatis to goo to þe soþe. *c* **1470** Henry *Wallace* IV. 771 To the south ʒett the gaynest way he drew. **1538** Leland *Itin.* I. 53 A vj Miles, by the gainest way. **1553** Grimalde *Cicero's Offices* II. (1558) 90 Socrates did saye: thys to bee the nerest and (as it wer) the gayne way to glory. **1647** H. More *Song of Soul* II. App. lxxxi, Which I conceive no gainer way is done Then by [etc.]. **1768** Ross *Helenore* I. 17 [She] to the glen the gainest gate can fare. **1892** Tennyson *Churchw. & Curate* iv, Fur I wur a Baptis wonst..Till I fun that it warn't not the gaäinist waäy to the narra Gaäte. *Midland Proverb* Roundabout is sometimes gainest.

b. In adverbial usage, ***the gainest*** [= ON. *et gegnsta* neut.]. Also ***at (the) gainest***: by the shortest way: *occas.* = at random.

13.. *Gaw. & Gr. Knt.* 1973 For to f[e]rk þurʒ þe fryth, & fare at þe gaynest. *c* **1400** *Destr. Troy* 2996 The lady..glod on full gayly þe gaynist to the bonke. **1494** Fabyan *Chron.* VII. 558 He drewe his swerde and layed about hym at yᵉ geynyst. **1549** Chaloner *Erasm. on Folly* Riva, Lyke a woman shotyng foorthe my bolte at the gainest. **1635** *Voy. Foxe & James to N. West* (Hakluyt Soc.) 437, I direct my course at gainest.

2. Of persons: Ready, well-disposed, kindly.

a **1310** in Wright *Lyric P.* vi. 29 Geynest under gore, herkne to my roune. *c* **1330** R. Brunne *Chron.* (1810) 134 þe ʒong kyng with gode man þat wer gayn Purueid his wendyng. **1441** *Pol. Poems* (Rolls) II. 207 Hys grace to me was evermore gayne, Thowgh I had don so gret offence. ? *a* **1500** *Chester Pl.* (E.E.T.S.) ix. 7 Thou sende vs grace, if thou be gaine, to come to thee to nighte. **1508** Dunbar *Tua mariit wemen* 78 When I gottin had ane grume, ganest of vther.

3. Of things: Available, handy, useful, convenient.

13.. *E.E. Allit. P.* B. 259 To wham god hade geuen alle þat gayn were. *c* **1320** *Sir Tristr.* 878 Wiþ þat was comen to toun Rohand wiþ help ful gode And gayn. **1840** *Evid. Hull Docks Comm.* 80 The dock would be so much gainer. **1868** Atkinson *Cleveland Gloss.*, *Gain*, near at hand, and so, handy, convenient.

†**gain**, *v.*¹ *Obs.* Forms: 3 *Orm.* **geʒʒnenn**, 4–6 **gayn(e**, 4, 6 **gaine**, 4–5 **geyn(e**, 6 **gane**, 4, 8 **gain**. Also 5 *north.* **gwane**. [a. ON. *gegna*, primarily, to meet, encounter, hence, to be meet, fit or suitable, from the adj. and adv. *gegn* against, opposite to (cf. gain *a.*). The form *gawne* may be due to the less common ON. *gagna*, a derivative of *gagn* = *gegn*, but was perhaps influenced by the vowel of *gawin*, the northern var. of gain *sb.*¹]

1. *intr.* To be suitable, useful, or advantageous; to avail, help; to serve, suffice (*for*). *Const.* dat. of person.

c **1200** Ormin 14480 þatt mikell maʒʒ þe geʒʒnenn her To winnenn heffness blisse. *c* **1230** *Hali Meid.* 45 Ne geineð þe nawt sweoke. **13..** *E.E. Alitt. P.* A. 343 For anger gaynez þe not a cresse. *c* **1386** Chaucer *Knt.'s T.* 318 Thou and I been dampned to prisoun Perpetuelly, us gayneth no raunsoun. **1412–20** Lydg. *Chron. Troy* III. xxiv, That hym ne geyneth plate, shelde nor targe. *c* **1460** *Towneley Myst.* (E.E.T.S.) xxx. 561 Youre pride and youre pransawte what wille it gawne? *c* **1500** *Lancelot* 121 It ganyth not..The seruand for to disput with ye lord. **1560** Rolland *Crt. Venus* II. 135 Thair was na thing absent Of gold, nor silk, that ganit sic cumpanie. **1603** *Philotus* xxi, Ane pair of Pleuaris..Ane cup of Sack..May for ane breckfast gaine. **1724** Ramsay *Tea-t. Misc.* (1733) I. 61 Ae pair [of shoon] may gain ye haff a year.

2. *trans.* **a.** To be an equipoise or balance *to*. **b.** *trans.* Of sleep: To come upon (a person). **c.** To meet, encounter, oppose.

c **1350** *Will. Palerne* 2473 So glad was he þanne þat na gref vnder god gayned to his ioye. *c* **1400** *Destr. Troy* 6046 This Agamynon, the grete, gaynit no slepe, Bise was the buerne all the bare night. ? *a* **1500** *Chester Pl.* viii. 157 There is none so great that me [Herod] dare gaine.

gain (geɪn), *v.*² Forms: 6–7 **gayne, gaine**, 7– **gain.** [App. first recorded in 16th c.; ad. F. *gagner* (earlier spelling *gaigner*):—OF. *gaaignier* = Pr. *gazanhar*, OSp. *guadañar* (to mow), It. *guadagnare*:—Com. Rom. **gwadaniare*, ad. OHG. **weidinjan* (recorded form *weidenen*), used in two main senses (1) to graze, pasture, (2) to go in quest of fodder or food, to forage, hunt or fish, f. *weida* str. fem., fodder or food, pasture, pursuit of fodder or food, hunting (mod.Ger. *weide* pasture, pasturage), corresp. to OE. *wáð*, ON. *veið-r* hunting:—OTeut. **waiþâ*, *-þjâ*. The twofold sense of the OHG. verb seems to be reflected in the Rom. form, which was used for 'to cultivate land' (so in OFr.; see gain *v.*³, gainage, gainor), as well as for 'to gain, win, earn'; the latter sense, which the word retains in mod.Fr. and It., may be in part developed from the OHG. sense 'to hunt'.]

1. a. *trans.* To obtain or secure (something which is desired or advantageous).

1570 Levins *Manip.* 200 To Gayne, *lucrari.* **1579** Lyly *Euphues* (Arb.) 93 If the Gods thought no scorne to become beastes to obteine their best beloued, shall Euphues be so nice in chaunging his coppie to gayne his Ladie? **1595** W. C[larke] in *Shaks. C. Praise* 15 To gaine pardon of the sinne to Rosemond. **1638** Rouse *Heav. Univ.* x. (1702) 152 Let therefore both the plenty and excellency of thy fruit gain glory and praise to the Heavenly Husband-man. **1736** Butler *Anal.* I. iii. Wks. 1874 I. 54 The pleasure or advantage in this case, is gained by the action itself. **1814** Scott *Wav.* x, Rose..ran with the speed of a fairy, that she might gain leisure..to put her own dress in order. **1816** J. Smith *Panorama Sc. & Art* II. 144 Part of the effect which would otherwise be gained is lost. **1828** D'Israeli *Chas. I*, I. ii. 22 Whatever art and practice could acquire, he gained. **1892** *Speaker* 3 Sept. 292/2 Christians have not gained their belief by the method on which he lays so unremitting a stress.

¶ In the following passage the word is a literal rendering of the Gr. κερδαίνειν. The sense of the original is disputed; most scholars, regarding the clause as qualified by the foregoing negative, take the verb as having, with or without a touch of irony, the extended sense 'to obtain whatever good or bad' (Johnson, s.v. *Gain*); so Liddell and Scott, also Revised Version ('gotten'). Others assign to the Gr. vb. the sense 'to spare oneself, avoid, save'; so De Wette, Alford, Blass, and others. Both uses of the vb. occur in Gr. writers; it is not at all clear which view was taken by the translators, or whether they deliberately adopted an ambiguous rendering.

1557 N. T. (Genev.) *Acts* xxvii. 21 Ye should have hearkened to me, and not haue lowsed from Candie, and to haue gayned this iniurie and losse. [Similarly in **1611**.]

b. Phrase. ***to gain time*** [= F. *gagner du temps*, *gagner temps*]: to obtain a delay by pretexts, by a slow or circuitous mode of procedure, etc. ***to gain the ear of***: to induce to listen favourably (see ear *sb.* 6). ***to gain the wind*** [= F. *gagner le vent*]: *Naut.* (see quot. 1867).

[**1611** Bible *Dan.* ii. 8, I know of certeinty that ye would gaine the time (a literal rendering of the Aramaic *zbn*).] **1724** De Foe *Mem. Cavalier* (1840) 49 Ambiguous answers..might serve to gain time. **1735** Pope *Prol. Sat.* 367 If on a pillory, or near a throne, He gain his prince's ear, or lose his own. **1792** Cowper *To Wilberforce* 7 Thou hast achieved a part; hast gained the ear of Britain's senate to thy glorious cause. *a* **1859** Macaulay *Hist. Eng.* V. 157 His eloquence had gained for him the ear of the legislature. **1867** Smyth *Sailor's Word-bk.* s.v., *To gain the wind*, to arrive on the weather-side of some other vessel in sight, when both are plying to windward. **1884** [see ear *sb.* 6]. **1885** J. Payn *Talk of Town* I. 89 Frank Dennis was of the party and could gain her ear at any moment.

c. With *infinitive* as object [= F. *gagner à être*, *à faire*]: To attain, get (to be or to do something). Now *rare.*

1648 *Eikon Bas.* xi. 78 Whose Propositions may soon proov violent oppositions, if once they gain to bee necessarie impositions upon the Regal Autoritie. **1833–40** J. H. Newman *Ch. of Fathers* (1842) 295 By fasting, Daniel gained to interpret the King's dream. **1873** Browning *Red Cott. Nt.-cap* 230 What if I gain thereby nor health of mind ..Nor gain to see my second baby-hope.

2. a. To obtain (a sum of money) as the profits of trade or speculation; to be benefited to the extent of (so much) by any transaction or event; to obtain, earn, 'make' (a livelihood).

1530 Palsgr. 559/2 Some men gayne more of a thyng of naught than many marchauntes do that venture over see. **1538** Elyot, *Quæstuariæ artes*, craftes, wherby men do gayne money. **1611** Bible *Matt.* xxv. 22 Lord, thou deliueredst vnto me two talents: behold I haue gained [**1535** Coverdale, wonne] two other talents besides them. —— *Luke* xix. 16 Lord, thy pound hath gained ten pounds. **1672** Petty *Pol. Anat.* (1691) 38 There are also..sworn Attornies, gaining about 170*l.* per ann. one with another. **1864** Tennyson *En. Ard.* 258 She..Gain'd for her own a scanty sustenance. *Mod.* He gains a hundred a year by his change of employment. He gained £1000 by the fall in consols.

b. In wider sense: To obtain (a quantity of anything, an amount of available space or time) by way of increment or addition.

1612 Brinsley *Lud. Lit.* 105 For parsing to do it of them-selues: as reading a lecture without any question asked.. which maner of parsing gaineth half the time which is spent therin commonly. **1730** Capt. W. Wriglesworth *MS. Log-bk. of the 'Lyell'* 2 Dec., New stowed the Lar-board side of the Lazaretto forward, and gained 2 Butts over the Scuttle, and small Cask over them.

3. a. *absol.* or *intr.* To make a gain or profit; to be benefited or advantaged, whether pecuniarily or otherwise.

c **1572** Gascoigne *Fruites Warre* lxix, Though he gaine & cram his purse with crounes,..He nought forseeth what treasons dwells in Townes. **1590** Shaks. *Com. Err.* III. ii. 51 He gaines by death, that hath such meanes to die. **1865** Kingsley *Herew.* Prel. (1877) 10 We have gained, doubtless, by that calamity. **1875** Jowett *Plato* (ed. 2) V. 489 When they [mankind] might gain in moderation they prefer gains without limit.

b. To improve *in* some specified respect. [= F. *gagner en.*]

1841 Emerson *Compensation* Wks. (Bohn) I. 40 Our popular theology has gained in decorum and not in principle. **1847** Tennyson *Princess* VII. 265 He [must] gain in sweetness and in moral height. **1890** *Chamb. Jrnl.* 17 May 309/2 The experience will gain in romance from our necessities.

c. To improve in effect, appear to greater advantage (by comparison or contrast).

1855 Macaulay *Hist. Eng.* III. 475 The English Liturgy indeed gains by being compared even with those fine ancient Liturgies from which it is to a great extent taken.

d. Of a clock, watch, etc.: to become fast (fast *a.* 8 c); to indicate a time ahead of the correct time. Also *trans.*, to run fast by the amount of (a specified period).

1861 *Horological Jrnl.* June 123/2 When the watch is in a horizontal position, the weight of the balance is supported on a single point, hence its greater freedom of motion and tendency to gain. *Ibid.* Nov. 36 Columns 3 to 7 show the mean daily rate for each of the five weeks, *gaining* when no sign is used, and *losing* when the – sign is used. **1863** *Ibid.* July 121/1 In the same temperature..it was gaining two seconds and one tenth. **1870** 'Mark Twain' in *Galaxy* X. 882/2 My beautiful new watch had run eighteen months without losing or gaining. **1917** H. E. Dudeney *Amusements in Math.* 10/1 Does that watch gain or lose, and how much per hour? *Ibid.* 153/2 It gains $\frac{5}{11}$ of a minute in 65 minutes. **1946** D. de Carle *Pract. Watch Repairing* 154 It is possible to make the watch gain by making the balance heavy at its lowest point. *Ibid.* 266 The watch may suddenly gain a few seconds due to the coils of the balance spring sticking together. **1970** *Encycl. Brit.* XXIII. 267/2 The watch would tend to gain.

4. *trans.* To acquire or reclaim (land) from the sea, etc. Const. *from, out of,* †*upon.*

1641 Evelyn *Mem.* (1857) I. 26 This part of Amsterdam is built and gained upon the main sea, supported by piles. **1691** T. H[ale] *Acc. New Invent.* p. lxxii, Wharfing, gain'd from the Thames, and..probably..all Thames-street..was gain'd out of the Thames. **1765** *Act 5 Geo. III.* c. 26 Preamb., Lands thentofore overflowed by and then gained from the sea and reduced to dry soil. **1774** Goldsm. *Nat. Hist.* (1776) I. 132 In proportion as land is gained at one part, it is lost by the overflowing of some other. **1845** Stephen *Comm. Laws Eng.* (1874) I. 452 Lands gained from the sea.

5. a. To obtain or win as the result of a contest; †to take or capture in fight.

1548 Hall *Chron., Hen. V,* 66 b, Perceivyng the walles skaled and the market place gained. *Ibid., Hen. VI,* 176 After the kynges navye gayned, and his capitayns..taken and destroied. *Ibid.* 177 The great victorie, gayned by hys parte, at the feld of Northampton. **1617** F. Moryson *Itin.* II. 83 When we had gained the trenches, the Vanguard made a stand. **1682** Wood *Life* 22 Nov., The Duke of York hath gained the point as to the penny post against Docuray the manager of it. **1782** Cowper *Truth* 16 A meaner than himself shall gain the prize. **1867** Freeman *Norm. Conq.* (1876) I. App. 701 He of course gains a complete victory. **1885** *Manch. Exam.* 29 June 5/1 In that case the worst tendencies of the party will gain the upper hand. **1892** *Times* (weekly ed.) 11 Nov. 5/2 A judgment gained against the railway company in the Law Courts.

b. To be victorious in.

1725 Watts *Logic* III. ii. §6 Either I shall gain the cause or lose it. **1852** Tennyson *Death Dk. Wellington* 96 He that gain'd a hundred fights.

†**c.** *absol.* ***to gain of***: to win an advantage over.

1548 Hall *Chron., Hen. VI,* 125 b, Leavyng bothe the nacions, daily studiyng how to greve, and gain of the other. **1605** Camden *Rem.* 8 That the most puissant Roman forces, when they were at the highest, could not gaine of them.

6. a. To bring over to one's own interest or views, to persuade (often in bad sense, to bribe); also ***to gain over.*** [So F. *gagner.*]

1582 N. T. (Rhem.) *Matt.* xviii. 15 If he shal heare thee, thou shalt gaine [Gr. ἐκέρδησας, Vulg. *lucratus eris*] thy brother. **1582** Stanyhurst *Æneis* II. (Arb.) 46 His malice hee fostred, tyl that priest Calchas he gayned. **1697** Dryden *Æneid* I. 953 To come with presents laden, from the port, To gratify the queen, and gain the court. **1790** *Bystander* 91 Gradually, since that time, have the theatres gained over the newspapers. **1813** Byron *Corsair* III. viii, I have gain'd the guard. **1834** J. H. Newman *Par. Serm.* (1837) I. xxiii. 348 He did not try to gain him over by smooth representations. **1878** R. W. Dale *Lect. Preach.* i. 17 It is much easier to lose friends than to gain opponents.

b. With following *inf.*: To persuade, prevail upon (now *rare* exc. with *over*). †Also, to persuade *into* a course of action.

1681 Dryden *Abs. & Achit.* 404 And gain'd our Elders to pronunce a Foe. **1683** —— *Vind. Dk. Guise* Wks. 1883 VII. 188 For Henry III. could never be gained to pass it, though it was proposed by the Three Estates at Blois. **1715** Jane Barker *Exilius* II. 85 Almon..begg'd of her to gain me, if possible, to come once more to him. **1741** Middleton *Cicero* II. ix. 251 [Antony] having thus gained Lepidus into his measures, he made use of his authority and his forces to harass and terrify the opposite party. **1818** Jas. Mill *Brit. India* II. iv. iv. 128 By a sum of money, Bussy gained the deputy Governor to admit him secretly with his troops into the fort.

7. a. To reach, arrive at (some point desired or aimed at).

1605 Shaks. *Macb.* III. iii. 7 Now spurres the lated traueller apace, To gayne the timely inne. **1667** Milton *P.L.* v. 174 Sun..sound his praise..both when thou climb'st, And when high Noon hast gaind. **1720** Ozell *Vertot's Rom. Rep.* II. xiv. 334 Antony press'd by Decimus Brutus, endeavoured to gain the Alps. **1784** Cowper *Task* I. 278 The summit gained, behold the proud Alcove That crowns it! **1826** Disraeli *Viv. Grey* II. xii, At last a sofa was gained, and the great lady was seated. **1855** Macaulay *Hist. Eng.* IV. 111 There were some who..sprang into the river and gained the opposite bank.

†**b.** *absol.* ***to gain in***: to get home, or to reach a place of refuge. *Obs.*

1828 Sir J. S. Sebright *Observ. Hawking* 41 They must be found in an open country; and the wood, which is their place of retreat, must be so situated as to oblige them to fly against the wind to gain in.

c. To succeed in traversing, accomplish (a certain distance of a journey). Now *rare.*

1733 Swift *Apol.* 133 You unus'd have scarcely strength To gain this walk's untoward length. **1847** Marryat *Childr. N. Forest* xiii, Edward had gained above eight miles of his journey.

†**d.** ***to gain one's way***: to advance, make progress. *Obs.*

1768 Sir W. Jones *Solima* Poems (1777) 4 Through the thick forest gains her easy way.

8. ***to gain ground*** [= F. *gagner du terrain, du pays*]: originally *Mil.* to conquer ground from an adversary: cf. equivalent phrases s.v. ground; hence in the following uses: **a.** To make progress, advance; to acquire ascendency.

1625 Bacon *Ess., Suspicion* (Arb.) 134 But in fearefull Natures, they [suspicions] gaine Ground too fast. **1736** Berkeley *Let. to S. Johnson* 12 Mar., Wks. 1871 IV. 245 Learning and good sense are gaining ground among them. **1764** Foote *Patron* I. Wks. 1799 I. 331 A glorious cargo of turtle..the captain assures me they greatly gain'd ground on the voyage. **1807** *Med. Jrnl.* XVII. 440 He recommended this particular practice to the world. Since then, it has been progressively gaining ground. **1838** Thirlwall *Greece* III. 319 The Chalcidians appear to have gained ground in the peninsula of Athos. **1862** H. Spencer *First Princ.* I. iv. §22 (1867) 68 The conviction, so reached, that human intelligence is incapable of absolute knowledge, is one that has been slowly gaining ground as civilization has advanced. **1888** Mrs. H. Ward *R. Elsmere* II. xxxvi, Nay, she had flattered herself that Mr. Flaxman, whom she liked, was gaining ground.

b. ***to gain ground on*** (†*of*): to make progress at the expense of, to encroach upon.

1644 Sir G. Markham in *Calend. St. Papers* Domestic Ser. (1888) 86, I hear that Essex loses credit with his party, and Waller gains ground of him. **1751** R. Paltock *P. Wilkins* (1884) II. xxv. 294 My melancholy for the death of my wife, which I hoped time would wear off, rather gained ground upon me. **1767** Blackstone *Comm.* II. 75 Villeins, by this and many other means, in process of time gained considerable ground on their lords. **1849** Macaulay *Hist. Eng.* I. 240 The Parliament was slowly, but constantly, gaining ground on the prerogative.

c. ***to gain ground upon***: to advance nearer to a person pursued.

1816 Scott *Antiq.* vii, Each minute did their enemy gain ground perceptibly upon them!

†**d.** ***to gain ground of***: to draw further away from (a pursuer), surpass in speed. *Obs.*

1719 De Foe *Crusoe* I. xiv, He outstript them..in running, and gained ground of them.

9. *intr.* or *absol.* with preps.

a. ***to gain from***: to get further away from (a pursuer). ? *Obs.* (Cf. 8 d.)

1805 Sir E. Berry in Nicolas *Nelson's Disp.* (1846) VII. 118 *note,* I had the satisfaction to perceive that we gained from the Three-decker.

b. ***to gain on*** or ***upon*** [= F. *gagner sur*]: to encroach upon (now only of the sea encroaching on the land). (Cf. 8 b.)

1647 N. Bacon *Disc. Govt. Eng.* I. lxix. (1739) 179 It was no time for him to gain upon the people's Liberties. **1697** Dryden *Virg. Georg.* I. 500 Herons..mounting upward..Gain on the Skies, and soar above the Sight. **1727** A. Hamilton *New Acc. E. Ind.* I. xxvi. 323 They built a fine City on the Rivers Side, about 3 Leagues from the Sea; but the Sea gaining on the Land yearly, it is not now above 100 Paces from it. **1842** Tennyson *Golden Year* 29 Oceans daily gaining on the land. **1849** Macaulay *Hist. Eng.* I. 345 The sea was gradually gaining on the buildings, which at length almost entirely disappeared.

c. ***to gain on*** or ***upon*** [= F. *gagner sur*]: to come closer to some object pursued. (Cf. 8 c.)

1719 De Foe *Crusoe* 19 Finding the Pirate gain'd upon us ..we prepared to fight. **1748** *Anson's Voy.* II. v. 177 We gained considerably on the chace. **1841** James *Brigand* iii, We are gaining on them quick. **1864** Tennyson *Voyage* viii, And still we follow'd where she led, In hope to gain upon her flight.

d. ***to gain on*** or ***upon***: to win favour with.

1640 tr. *Verdere's Romant of Romants* I. 41 The most agreeable services he is able to do her..have already so gained upon her, as she hath wholly given her self unto him. **1652** Sir E. Nicholas in *N. Papers* (Camden) 305, I never heard that Mr. Attorney was popular with the K.'s party, nor do I take his disposition to be such as is like to gain much on the affections of many men. *a* **1715** Burnet *Own Time* II. 16 Lady Bellasis gained so much on the duke, that he gave her a promise under his hand to marry her. **1848** Dickens *Dombey* v, She don't gain on her papa in the least. **1884** *Manch. Exam.* 12 May 5/3 Mr. Villiers Stanford's beautiful opera..gains more and more upon musicians at each successive hearing.

†**e.** ***to gain upon*** = 'to prevail upon'; cf. 6 b.

1790 A. M. Johnson *Monmouth* III. 107 The sweet idea that my entreaties may gain upon the King to spare his nephew, will supply this emaciated frame with strength, and my soul with fortitude.

†**f.** ***to gain into***: to grow into, to come to be.

1756 P. Browne *Jamaica* I. ii. §4 (1789) 23 They are observed to be remarkably fond of grandeur and distinction, which, doubtless, proceeds from the general obsequiousness of their numerous slaves and dependents, as well as from the necessity of keeping them at a distance; which in time gains into a habit.

†**gain**, *v.*[3] *Obs. pseudo-arch.* [ad. AF. *gaaignier* to cultivate (land).] (See quots.)

1641 *Termes de la Ley* 170 (tr. *Act 51 Hen. III*) That no man of religion or other shall be distreined by the beasts that gaine his land. **1708** *Ibid.* 383 Of old to Gain Land was as much as to Till and Manure it.

gain (geɪn), *v.*[4] ? *U.S.* [f. gain *sb.*[3]] *trans.* 'To mortise' (*Cent. Dict.*); 'to fasten with gains or notches, or cut gains in, as floor-timbers' (Funk).

1874 [implied in gaining *vbl. sb.*[2]].

gain, *adv.*[1] *Obs.* exc. *dial.* Also 4 **gayn, gayne.** [f. gain *a.*] Straight, direct; *full gayne*: quickly; also, very nearly.

In the passages quoted from the Fairfax MS. of the *Cursor M.* the other texts have differing readings; the Gött. MS. has 4142 *forgan,* 5171 *gan* (riming with *slan*) which may be the original.

c **1320** *Sir Tristr.* 1560 Þe quen..To a baþ gan him lede Ful gayn. [*c* **1340** *Cursor M.* 4142 (Fairf.) And wete our fader atte he be slayne his liue dayes ar past ful gayne. *Ibid.* 5171 (Fairf.), xxx. ȝere ys comyn fulle gayne syn he wiþ wild bestes was slayne.] *c* **1400** *Destr. Troy* 2813 Gayn vnto Grese on þe gray water, By the Regions of Rene rode þai ferre.

b. *dial.* Used to qualify adjectives and adverbs: Pretty, tolerably, fairly. [Cf. the Sc. *gey an'* under gey.]

1893 *Northumbld. Gloss.* s.v., 'She's gain fresh this mornin'. Aa've hed a gain thrang time on 't thi day.' **1895** *Gloss. E. Anglia* s.v., 'Gain quiet', pretty quiet.

†**gain**, *adv.*[2] *Obs.* Also 3 **ȝein.** [app. arising from separation of the prefix gain-.] Again, back again.

c **1275** Lay. 22136 Þat he to him come..to habbe ȝein his owe. *a* **1300** *Cursor M.* 12809 Mi breþer leif and mi frend, Yee sal gain to yur maisturs wend. *Ibid.* 22623 Þou yeild us gain vr ostel nu, þat us es reft, and we ne wat hu.

†**gain**, *prep. Obs.* Forms: 3 **ȝæn,** 4 **gain(e, gayn(e, gan,** 4–5 **geyn,** 5 **gayn,** 6 **geyne.** [app. a. ON. *gegn*: see gain *a.*

Not known in OE., the instances given in Dicts. being due to erroneous readings. Ormin's *ȝæn* seems to be short for *onnȝæn* again.]

1. Against, over against, contrary to.

c **1200** Ormin 2322 All all swa summ Elysabæþ Shall nu ȝæn kinde childenn. *a* **1300** *Cursor M.* 21825 Anoþer king gan þe sal rise. *Ibid.* 22631 Windes on ilk side sal rise, Sa fast gain oþer sal þai blau. **14..** *Pol. Rel. & L. Poems* (1866) 111 Gayn gostly enmys thynk on my passion. *a* **1529** Skelton *Knolege, aquayntance,* etc. 20 Geyne surfetous suspecte the emeraud comendable.

2. Towards, to meet with.

a **1300** *Cursor M.* 5244 Joseph of his fader herd, Wit his curt gain him he ferd. *Ibid.* 19920 Quen þai o petre vnderstod, His cuming son gain him þai yod.

3. Of time: Towards, near. Now in Sc. gin.

c **1475** *Partenay* 345 Where it were gayn night or at morne erlie.

gain-, *prefix*, in OE. *ȝeȝn-, ȝéan-* (see gain *a.*), was formerly employed to form various combinations, chiefly verbal, in the same way as again-, which was in more frequent use. Its senses are chiefly those of opposition, return, or reversal, answering to Lat. *re-*. These combs. are now obsolete, with the exception of gainsay, and the technical term gainshire. Compare also the forms given under again- and its compounds.

1. Against, in opposition to; **gain-race** [= L. *occursus*], a running against, meeting; **gain-saw**, contradiction; **gain-set** *v.*, to set over against, oppose; **gainspeaker**, a gainsayer, opponent; **gain-speaking**, opposition. Also gaincall *sb.*, -cope, -say, -stand, -strive, -turn.

a **1340** Hampole *Psalter* xviii. 7 His *gaynras til þe highest of him [L. *occursus ejus usque ad summum ejus*]. *Ibid.* lviii. 5 Rise in my gaynrase [L. *exurge in occursum meum*]. *a* **1300** *Cursor M.* 8382, I þat es þine hand-womman, For me *gainsagh þar sal be nan. *a* **1300** *E.E. Psalter* lxxix. 7 [lxxx. 6] Thou set us in gaine-sagh [L. *in contradictionem*] til our neghburs. **1435** Misyn *Fire of Love* 48 Sum for soth *gaynsettand, says: Actife lyfe is more fruytfull. **1594** Carew *Huarte's Exam. Wits* vi. 73 This humour aideth the vnderstanding with two qualities, and gainsetteth it selfe only with one. **1575** (*title*) A brief Rehearsal of the Belief of the goodwilling in England, which are named the Family of Love: with the Confession of their upright Christian Religion, against the false accusations of their *Gainspeakers. **1583** Golding *Calvin on Deut.* clxxv. 1087 Also it was his wil to cause this last song to be receiued without *gain speaking.

2. Reciprocal action; in return; **gainclap**, a blow in return, a counter stroke. Also gain-giving, -yield.

a **1225** *Leg. Kath.* 129 Ha ȝeald ham swuche ȝain-clappes, ..þæt al ha cneowen ham crauant & ouercumen.

3. Restoration or return to previous state; back again; **gain-buy** *v.*, to buy back, redeem; so **gain-buyer**, a redeemer, **gain-buying**, redemption; **gain-cover**, *v.*, to recover, regain; **gain-taking**, taking back again; **gain-turning**, returning. Also gaincall *v.*, -chare, -come.

1435 Misyn *Fire of Love* I. viii. 16 Þat he mankynd fro þe fendes power myȝt *gaynby. *c* **1440** *Promp. Parv.* 189/2 Geynebyyn, or byyn a-ȝene, *redimo.* **1435** Misyn *Fire of Love* I. ii. 5 No meruayl if þai plese noȝt our *gaynbyer. *Ibid.* I. xx. 44 Of cristis *gaynbyinge þa ar no partiners. *a* **1300** *Cursor M.* 29203 Thoru scrift..sal we *gain couer þe grace til heuen. **1538** *Aberd. Reg.* V. 16 (Jam.) Deforsing of the officiare in execucion of his office in the *gane taking of ane caldrown poundit be the said officiare. **1340** Hampole *Pr. Consc.* 1718 Of bodily ded es no *gayn-turnyng, For of erthly lyf it es endyng. **1435** Misyn *Fire of Love* II. vi. 80 Þat hys mynde bisily to crist with-out gayn-turnynge has nott.

4. Repetition; over again, anew; in the *nonce-wds.* **gain-birth** [= Gr. παλιγγενεσία], regeneration; **gain-rising** [= Gr. ἀνάστασις], resurrection.

c **1550** Cheke *Matt.* xix. 28 Je y[t] hav folowed me in y[e] gain birth. *Ibid.* xxii. 23 Y[e] Saddoucais..who sai yeer is no gainrising.

gainable ('geɪnəb(ə)l), *a.*[1] Also 7 **gaineable**. [f. GAIN *v.*[2] + -ABLE; cf. F. *gaignable, gagnable.*] Attainable, capable of being gained or won over.

1611 *Cotgr., Gaignable,* gettable, winnable, gaineable. **1670** G. H. *Hist. Cardinals* III. III. 327 With paper in hand, [they] reckon'd up as many gainable persons, as made up their number. **1837** CARLYLE *Fr. Rev.* II. III. iv, Summon the National Assembly to follow you, summon what of it is Royalist, Constitutional, gainable by money; dissolve the rest. **1856** RUSKIN *Mod. Paint.* III. IV. x. §22. 147 Greatness in art..is not a teachable nor gainable thing, but the expression of the mind of a God-made great man.

†**gainable**, *a.*[2] *Obs. rare.* Also 7–9 *Hist.* WAINABLE. [a. OF. *gaignable*, f. *gaignier* (see GAIN *v.*[1]) in the early sense to till, cultivate: see GAIN *v.*[3]] Of land: Cultivable.

1480 CAXTON *Ovid's Met.* XV. iv, Lenchayde was, of olde tyme, gaynable lond; now the see encloseth it. **1481** —— *Godfrey* xlv. (1893) 85 The londe is ful of..large mareyses in suche wyse that there is but lytil londe gaynable.

†**gainage**. *Obs.* Also 4 **gaignage, gaynage**, 6–9 *Hist.* WAINAGE. [ad. AF. *gaignage* (Anglo-L. *wainagium*), f. *gaigner*: see prec.]

1. The profit or produce derived from the tillage of land.

1390 GOWER *Conf.* I. 358 As the true man to the plough Only to the gaignage entendeth. *c* **1394** *P. Pl. Crede* 197, I trowe þe gaynage of þe ground, in a gret schire Nolde aparaile þat place, oo poynt til other ende.

2. Husbandry, agriculture.

1625 MARKHAM *Inrichm. Weald Kent* 4 We haue mention of Marle in bookes of gainage or husbandry.

3. In the Law Dicts. of the 17–18th c., the word is given with various conjectural explanations which relate to the use of *wainnagium* in the passage of Magna Carta quoted below. The interpretation 'implements of husbandry' is probably correct, though it led to an erroneous derivation from *wain*.

[**1215** *Magna Carta* c. 20 in Stubbs *Sel. Chart.* 299 Liber homo..pro magno delicto amercietur..salvo contenemento suo; et mercator..salva mercandisa sua; et villanus..salvo wainnagio suo.] **1607** COWELL *Interpr., Gainage, (Wainagium)*..signifieth..the land held by the baser kind of Sokemen or villeines. **1706** PHILLIPS (ed. Kersey), *Gainage*, or *Wainage*, a Word anciently us'd to signify all Plough-tackle, and necessary Implements of Husbandry.

†'**gainand**, *ppl. a. Sc.* and *north. dial. Obs.* Forms: 4 **gainand**, 4–6 **gaynand, ganand**, 6 **ganeand**. [northern pr. pple. of GAIN *v.*[1]: see -AND[1].] Appropriate, becoming, suitable.

a **1300** *Cursor M.* 16556 In tua þis tre þai scare, Als mikel als þai sagh to þaim gainand. *c* **1375** *Sc. Leg. Saints*, 7 *Sleperis* 210 A house to byge in-[to] þat hil, þat gaynand ware his hyrdis til. *c* **1475** *Rauf Coilȝear* 786, I will the ganandest gait to that gay glyde. **1513** DOUGLAS *Æneis* V. xi. 77 Now is the tyme ganand our werk to speid. **1556** LAUDER *Tractate* 299 Except ȝe vnderstude..Thame apt and ganand for the ȝok. **1583** *Leg. Bp. St. Androis* 610 in *Satir. Poems Reform.* xlv, A ganeand maister for sic a man.

†'**gaincall**, *sb. Obs. rare.* [f. GAIN- I + CALL *sb.*] A calling out against; a counter-prayer, opposition.

a **1300** *Cursor M.* 28783 Quat bot a prai for þi welle Ano er prai for þin vn-sele,..For if þai [? *read* he, *sc.* god] here þe tan mai fall, þe tother him lettes wit his gain call. **1535** STEWART *Cron. Scot.* II. 664 Without ony gane-call, In that counsall tha war maid erlis all.

†'**gaincall**, *v. Obs. rare.* [f. GAIN- 3 + CALL *v.*]

1. *trans.* To revoke, retract, withdraw.

1535 STEWART *Cron. Scot.* III. 196 He thocht he wald ganecall That he had said, and wirk ane vther way.

2. To bring back again, recall.

1611 SPEED *Hist. Gt. Brit.* IX. xvii. (1632) 894 Sith things past cannot be gaine-called.

3. To call to mind.

1434 MISYN *Mending of Life* 115 Fantasy of syn he gedyrs to-gidyr of old schrewdnes & likynge of luf past he gayn-cals. **1535** STEWART *Cron. Scot.* II. 542 The skayth pertenis to ws all, The quhilk this tyme that ȝe sould nocht ganecall.

Hence †'**gaincalling** *vbl. sb., Sc. Law*, withdrawing, revocation.

1489 *Acta Audit.* (1839) 142/1 þat þe forsaid partiis sall stand at þar deliuerance Irrevocabilly but ony ganecalling. **1549** *Sc. Acts Mary* (1814) II. 602 And ordains þe samyne to stand in strenth, force, and effect in all tyme cuming, w'out ony gancalling, reuocatioune or retractatioune.

†**gainchare**. *Obs.* Forms: 1 **ʒéancyr**, 4 **ȝeynchar**, 5 **gayne chare, geyn char**. [OE. *ʒéancyr*: see GAIN- *prefix* and CHARE *sb.*[1] The word seems to survive in the technical term GAINSHIRE.] A return, way of returning, means of escape.

c **1000** *Ags. Ps.* (Spelman) xviii. 7 [xix. 6] Fram hean heofone is utgang his, and ʒeancyr [L. *occursus*] his oþ to heahnesse his. *c* **1150** *Eadwine's Psalter* ibid., Edryne *vel* ʒencyr. *a* **1310** in Wright *Lyric P.* xiv. 46 Ah feyre levedis be on-war, To late cometh the ȝeyn-char, when love ou hath y-bounde. *c* **1340** *Cursor M.* 21922 (Trin.) þo þat bifore wol not be war þenne shul þei fynde no ȝeyn char. ? *a* **1500** *Chester Pl.* (E.E.T.S.) 435 Alas! ther is no gayne Chare, skape maye I not this chance.

So †**gain-charing**.

c **1275** *Sinners Beware* 58 in *O.E. Misc.* 74 þar nys no yeyn cherrynge ne..non endynge.

†**gaincome**. *Obs.* [f. GAIN- 3 + COME; OE. *ʒeáncyme* means meeting, *occursus*.] A coming again, return.

a **1225** *Ancr. R.* 234 þet tu his ȝeincume underuo þe gledluker. *c* **1300** *Cursor M.* 19043 (Laud) The appostils eche day To the temple went to pray; At hir yene come the mete they yaff To eche. *c* **1400** *Destr. Troy* 2026 Full glad of þat gest and his gayne come. *c* **1450** HENRYSON *Test. Cres.* 55 But quhen he sawe passit baith day and hour Of hir gaincome. **1567** TURBERV. *Ovid's Ep.* 28 b, And I (to further this my woe) thy gainecome did desyre.

So †**gaincoming**.

a **1340** HAMPOLE *Psalter* cxi. 9 He losis hope of gayn-cumynge. **1375** BARBOUR *Bruce* II. 450 Sa dred thai far the gayne-cummyng Off schir Robert, the douchty king. **1565** *Answ. Kirk* in Keith *Hist. Ch. Scot.* (1734) 550 To the gaynecomeing of our Lord Jesus Chryst.

†'**gaincope**, *v. Obs.* Forms: 5 **geynecowp**, 6–8 **gaincope**, 7 **gainecope**. [f. GAIN- *prefix* I + COPE *v.*[2]] *trans.* To catch up with, intercept or encounter another person by taking a short cut.

c **1440** *Promp. Parv.* 189/2 Geynecowpyn, or chasyn, or stoppyn in gate [*K., H.* geynstoppyn of gate, *S.* geyne cowpyn or charyn], *sisto.* **1565** GOLDING *Ovid's Met.* III. (1593) 62 These came forth later than the rest, but coasting thwart a hill, They did gain-cope him as he came, and hild their master still. **1674–91** RAY *S. & E.C. Words* 99 *To Gaincope*, to go cross a field the nearest way to meet with something. **1692** R. L'ESTRANGE *Josephus' Wars* II. ii. (1733) 614 As he was upon his Flight across a steep Bottom, Gratus gain-cop'd him.

fig. **1602** ROWLANDS *Greenes Ghost* 26 When they see a fellow leape from the subiect he is handling..they should skip it ouer, and..gainecope him at the next turning point to his text. **1643** ROBOTHAM *Gate Lang. Unl.* To Rdr. Ciiij a, Some indeed there have bin..who striving to gaincope these ambages..have..made their voyage in halfe the time.

Hence †**gaincoping** *ppl. a.*

1594 NASHE *Terrors Nt.* Ep. Ded., How to be gainfull and gain-coping nauigators.

gaine (geɪn). [Fr., = sheath.] A metal tube attached to a fuse (see quots.).

1918 *Nature* 14 Nov. 218/1 The gaine is a metal tube screwed to the fuse, which enters a cavity in the filling and makes good contact with it. **1932** LLOYD GEORGE *War Mem.* II. xix. 592 A gaine..is a tube filled with explosive, attached under the nose-cap of a high-explosive shell... Its purpose is to ensure that the detonation of the fuse in the nose-cap shall effectively detonate the contents of the shell.

gaine, gaine-, obs. forms of GAIN, GAIN-.

gained (geɪnd), *ppl. a.* [f. GAIN *v.*[2] + -ED[1].] Obtained, acquired. Of time: Saved.

1598 R. BARRET *Mod. Warres* 137 To vndermine walles and to raze those of any gained places downe. **1850** WHITTIER *Pr. Wks.* (1866) I. 344 He was told that this was his gained time, and that he was engaged for himself. **1875** BROWNING *Aristoph. Apol.* 10, I kept the gained advantage.

b. *Naut. gained day*: 'the twenty-four hours or day and night gained by circumnavigating the globe to the eastward.' (Adm. Smyth.)

gainer ('geɪnə(r)). Also 6 **geyner**, 6–7 **gayner**. [f. GAIN *v.*[2] + -ER[1].] One who gains, makes profits, or derives advantage.

1538 ELYOT, *Lucrio*, a couetous manne, an inordynate gayner. **1548** FORREST *Pleas. Poesye* in *Starkey's England* Pref. 88 If merchauntes..Shoulde bee enriched and made grete geyners. **1590** LAMBARDE *Office Alienation* in *Bacon's Wks.* 1730 III. 554 The client, besides..retaining a good conscience..is alway a gainer, and by no means can be at any loss. **1716** ADDISON *Freeholder* No. 42 ¶6 By extending a well-regulated Trade we are as great Gainers by the Commodities of many other Countries as of our own Nation. **1844** H. H. WILSON *Brit. India* III. 161 The interests of British India..will be gainers by the contest. **1884** *Truth* 13 Mar. 375/2 We should be losers rather than gainers.

†**gainery**. *Obs.* [ad. OF. *gaignerie, gaaignerie*, tillage of ground, etc. Cf. GAIN *v.*[3] and GAINAGE.]

a. A farm. **b.** (See quot. 1670.)

1424 *E.E. Wills* (1882) 57 All myn other howshold, saf suche as longeth to þe gamerye [? *read* gainerye]. **1670** BLOUNT *Law Dict., Gainery* (Fr. *gaignerie*), Tillage or Tilling, or the Profit raised of Tillage, or of the Beasts used therein.

gainesse, obs. form of GAYNESS.

gainful ('geɪnfʊl), *a.* [f. GAIN *sb.*[2] + -FUL.]

1. Productive of gain or profit; profitable, advantageous. Now *rare* exc. as in b.

1555 BALE in Strype *Eccl. Mem.* III. App. xxxix. 108 It promiseth ful remission of our sins thro Christ's gainful sufferings. **1600** HAKLUYT *Voy.* (1810) III. 144, I hope..that your skill in navigation shall be gaineful unto you. **1658** *Whole Duty Man* ii. §18. 19 We are to consider it, as the gainfullest, as the joyfullest day of the week. **1861** M. ARNOLD *Pop. Educ. France* Introd. 36 An intervention gainful and agreeable to friends, injurious and irritating to enemies. **1884** *Manch. Exam.* 14 Nov. 5/3 They have no objection to the expedition, which will be gainful to them in many ways.

b. *esp.* Leading to pecuniary gain; lucrative, remunerative.

1561 T. NORTON *Calvin's Inst.* IV. 86 By this pretence they make moste gainefull markets. **1610** HOLLAND *Camden's Brit.* I. 717 The Hollanders and Zelanders..make a very gaineful trade thereof [herrings]. **1692** SOUTH *Serm.* (1697) I. 540 He will dazle his Eyes..with the luscious Proposal of some gainfull Purchase. **1779–81** JOHNSON *L.P., Savage Wks.* III. 252 Savage..then attempted a more gainful kind of writing. **1791** NEWTE *Tour Eng. & Scotl.* 302 It is likely to turn out a very gainful undertaking. **1824** MISS MITFORD *Village* Ser. I. (1863) 104 She..speedily established a regular and gainful trade in milk. **1871** FREEMAN *Norm. Conq.* (1876) IV. xvii. 85 The gainful Crafts of the goldsmith and the moneyer.

¶ In the following quot. *gainful* is treated in some Dicts. (after Sympson) as a different word, f. GAIN *prep.*, and meaning 'untractable, fractious'; but the context seems to admit of the interpretation 'lucrative'.

1621 FLETCHER *Pilgrim* IV. iii. (1647) You will find him gainfull, but be sure ye curb him.

2. Of persons and their actions: Bent upon making gain; adapted to make gain. *rare.*

1870 MORRIS *Earthly Par.* III. IV. 26 Ah, for these gainful men—somewhat indeed Their sails are rent, their bark beat. **1871** SMILES *Charac.* xi. (1876) 308 Withdrawing the mind from thoughts that are wholly gainful, by taking it out of its daily rut. **1882** FARRAR *Early Chr.* II. 66 Men make gainful plans for the future without any reference to God.

Hence '**gainfully** *adv.*, '**gainfulness**.

1549 COVERDALE, etc. *Erasm. Par. 2 Cor.* ix. 8 God..is sufficiently able..to make your almesdedes gaynfully to returne vnto you. **1628** STRAFFORD in Browning *Life* (1891) 292, I am..gainfully, commodiously seated for the service both of king and people. **1646** JENKYN *Remora* 30 The toothsom gainfullnesse of a silver shrine. **1668** HOWE *Bless. Righteous* (1825) 163 If you would comprehend the gainfulness [of godliness] fully. **1868** MAINE *Vill. Commun.* (1876) 393 The Bar is getting to be more and more preferred to Government service..both on the score of its gainfulness and on the score of its independence. **1880** *Nat. Respons. Opium Trade* 27 Drawbacks to the gainfulness of the opium trade to India.

gain-giving, *vbl. sb.* [f. GAIN- *prefix* 2 + GIVING *vbl. sb.*]

†**1.** A giving in return, making return. *Obs.*

1375 BARBOUR *Bruce* I. 115 He ȝe..consideryt his vsage That gryppyt ay, but gayne-gevyng.

2. A misgiving. *Obs.* exc. *arch.*

1602 SHAKS. *Ham.* V. ii. 226 It is but foolery; but it is such a kinde of gain-giuing as would perhaps trouble a woman. **1887** S. COLERIDGE *Demetrius* 11 There crept over the mother's heart a gaingiving undefined but strong and deep.

gaining ('geɪnɪŋ), *vbl. sb.*[1] [f. GAIN *v.*[2] + -ING[1].]

1. The action of the vb. GAIN[2].

a **1553** UDALL *Royster D.* II. iii. (Arb.) 36 No man complainyng..For losse or for gainyng. **1633** P. FLETCHER *Purple Isl.* III. xix, His gaining is their losse, his treasure their distressing. **1652** MILTON in *Four C. Eng. Lett.* 99 The gaineing of those four languages. **1745** PICTON *L'pool Munic. Rec.* (1886) II. 109 For the gaining of more certain intelligence. **1879** *Cassell's Techn. Educ.* IV. 396/2 This movement is slightly in excess of the circumferential velocity of the front rollers..and the excess is called the 'gaining' of the carriage.

2. *concr.* esp. in plur.: That which is gained; profits, emoluments.

a **1631** DONNE in *Select.* (1840) 279 Tell me where thy purchase lies, and show What thy advantage is above below: But if thy gainings do surmount expression, Why doth [etc.]. **1824** MRS. SHERWOOD *Waste Not* II. 5 Such poor gainings too as you have. I should not wonder, if you had never touched a farthing of the old lady's money.

gaining ('geɪnɪŋ), *vbl. sb.*[2] [f. GAIN *v.*[4]] The cutting of gains (see GAIN *sb.*[3]) in wood. In *Comb.* **gaining-machine**, a machine for cutting gains in a beam.

1874 in KNIGHT *Dict. Mech.*

'**gaining**, *ppl. a.* [f. GAIN *v.*[2] + -ING[2].] That gains in various senses of the verb. †Of manner, etc.: Winning. ***gaining-twist***: in rifled fire-arms, a twist of the grooves that increases regularly toward the muzzle (Brande & Cox 1866).

1642 ROGERS *Naaman* 451 They keep all they haue, and still are on the gaining hand till they attain their desire. **1731** WODROW *Corr.* (1843) III. 481 Though I take it to be your duty to write to him, and perhaps in such soft and gaining terms, yet I fear he is so stiff and self-willed, some-what more of salt would have been as effectual. *c* **1685** HALIFAX *Char. Chas. II* (1750) 33 A plain, gaining, well-bred, recommending kind of Wit. **1755** MAGENS *Insurances* II. 141 Whenever the Goods come to a gaining Market..and when they come to a losing Market. **1880** *Antrim & Down Gloss., Gaining*, winsome, loving.

†'**gain-legged**, *a.*

1593 PEELE *Chron. Edw. I*, Ciij a, But if kinde Cambria deigne me good aspect, Ile short that gainlegd Longshanke by the top.

†'**gainless**, *a.*[1] *Obs. rare.* In 3 **gaȝhennlaes**. [f. GAIN *sb.*[1] + -LESS.] Of no avail.

c **1200** ORMIN 13946 Annd tanne waere uss gaȝhennlaes þatt Crist wass daed o rode.

gainless ('geɪnlɪs), *a.*[2] [f. GAIN *sb.*[2] + -LESS.]

1. Producing no gain; unprofitable; useless.

1640 O. SEDGWICKE *Christs Counsell* 39 For our communion with God, it will grow more strange, less confident, and more gainless. **1654** HAMMOND *Answ. Animadv. Ignat.* ii. §1. 24 The several gainlesse paines that his sharp Animadversion hath..cost each of us. **1658** *Whole Duty Man* vi. §14 (1687) 56 It is not only gainless, but painful and uneasie also. **1878** SWINBURNE *Poems & Ball.* Ser. II. 76 Some gainlesse glimpse of Proserpine's veiled head.

2. *nonce-use.* Indifferent to gain.

1876 J. MARTINEAU *Hours Th.* (1877) 24 The godless lover of gain and the gainless lover of God are fanatics both.

Hence **'gainlessness**, the state of being gainless.

1667 *Decay Chr. Piety* v. ¶23 And the parallel holds too, in the gainlesness as well as laboriousness of the work.

gainly ('geɪnlɪ), *a.* Forms: 4 gaynlych, gaynly, 9 (*Sc.* ganelie) gainly. [f. GAIN *a.* + -LY[1].]

1. Proper, suitable, becoming. *Obs.* exc. *Sc. dial.*

13.. *Sir Beues* (A.) 3103 Þe mesager spak a gainli word before þemperur is bord. **1825–80** JAMIESON, *Ganelie*, proper, becoming, decent. *Loth.*

†**2.** Ready to help, kindly, gracious. *Obs.*

13.. *E.E. Allit. P.* B. 728 Þat nas neuer þyn note.. þat art so gaynly a god & of goste mylde!

3. a. Of conduct: Graceful, tactful. **b.** Of bodily form, attitude, or movement: The reverse of ungainly; graceful, shapely.

1855 MAYHEW *Wond. Sc.* xiv. (1862) 317 The curls.. had now been displaced, and the hair twisted into the more womanly, but less gainly, protuberance at the back. **1871** HAMILTON in *Bp. Hall's Medit.* Life 24 By his prudent and gainly conduct he reclaimed all the refractory. **1886** C. GIBBON *Clare of Claresmede* II. i. 8 She remembered a tall, gainly youth, with dark hair and eyes.

Hence **'gainliness**.

1886 C. GIBBON *Clare of Claresmede* II. xii. 195 There was as little goodness in his spirit as there was gainliness in his appearance. **1894** DU MAURIER *Trilby* iii. 142 The symmetry and the gainliness of the athlete.

gainly ('geɪnlɪ), *adv. Obs.* exc. *dial.* Forms: 3 *Orm.* geʒʒnlike, 4 gayne(e-, gein-, geynliche, -ly, 7 gainely, 7, 9 gainly. [f. GAIN *a.* + -LY[2].]

1. Suitably, fitly, conveniently, readily.

c **1200** ORMIN 18084 Þatt wass inoh geʒʒnlike don & all wiþþ Godess wille. **13..** *Gaw. & Gr. Knt.* 476 He glent vpon syr Gawen, & gaynly he sayde. *c* **1350** *Will. Palerne* 744 Whan he geinliche was greiþed he gript his mantel. **1600** HOLLAND *Livy* I. xxxiv. (1609) 25 An eagle set it [his bonnet] gainly and handsomely on his head againe [L. *capiti apte reponit*]. **1601** —— *Pliny* II. 13 Conuenient allies betweene to giue.. passage for men to come and goe gainely. **1876** *Whitby Gloss., Gainly*, adv. eligibly situated. **1882** *W. Worc. Gloss., Gainly*, quickly, handily.

†**2.** Thoroughly, completely; very (with adjs.).

c **1350** *Will. Palerne* 636, I schal þurth craft þat ich kan keuer ȝou, I hope, Mow I geten a grece þat I gaynli knowe. *Ibid.* 3353 Þer-of þe king was geynli glad and graunted his wille. **1642** H. MORE *Song of Soul* II. App. xxxv, A while this Universe here we will feign Corporeall, till we have gainly tride, If ought that's bodily may infinite abide.

†**'gainor**[1]. *Law. Obs. rare.* Also 7 gainour, gainure. [ad. OF. *gaigneure, gaaigneure* tillage. See GAIN *v.*[3] and GAINAGE.] Tillage, cultivation; in phrase *in gainor*, designating land in the occupation of a socage tenant.

1607 COWELL *Interpr.* s.v. *Gainage*, The oxegang is alwaies of a thing that lyeth in gainor. **1610** W. FOLKINGHAM *Art of Survey* II. vii. 60 Bouata is properly vsed of Lands in Gainour, viz. vsually plowed.. It is not reputed in Demesne, but in Gainor. **1670** BLOUNT *Law Dict., Gainure*, tillage.

†**gainor**[2]. *Law. Obs. rare*[−1]. [ad. OF. *gaigneur, gaaignor* etc., a husbandman. See GAIN *v.*[3]] A cultivator, husbandman.

1607 COWELL *Interpr.* s.v. *Gainage*, Gainor.. is used of a sokeman that hath such land in his occupation.

†**'gainpain.** *Obs.* In ? 6 gaynepayne. [a. OF. *gaignepain* (in 13th c. *wagnepan*) a sort of gauntlet. Commonly identified with the F. *gagnepain*, lit. 'bread-winner' (f. stem of *gagner* GAIN *v.*[2] + *pain* bread), which is recorded from the 17th c. in the sense 'tool by which one gains one's bread', but is prob. of much older formation, as it appears *c* 1320 in Eng. as *weine pain* (*Sir Beues* 926: see WAYNPAIN), in the sense 'man who has to earn his bread'. This derivation does not seem to suit the sense 'gauntlet', and perh. two distinct words have been confounded by popular etymology; the sense of 'sword' is hardly authenticated even in Fr.; if genuine, it may well have been a casual application of the surviving word.]

1. A sort of gauntlet.

c **1430** *Pilgr. Lyf Manhode* I. cxxii. (1869) 64 Swich continence thus doubled is cleped of summe men gayn payn, For bi it is wunne the bred bi the whiche is fulfilled the herte of mankynde and that was figured heer bifore in the bred that Dauid askede For Achimelech wolde nevere graunte it him ne take it him bifore that he wiste he was gloued and armed with gayn paynes. ? *c* **1500** *Rom. Monk* (Sion Coll. MS.) (Halliwell), Affter I tooke the gaynepaynes and the swerd with which I gurde me, and sithe whane I was thus armed, I putte the targe to my side.

¶**2.** Explained in accordance with the Fr. dicts., as 'The ancient name of the sword used at tournaments'. But evidence of the Eng. use of the word in this sense is wanting.

1824 MEYRICK *Antient Armour* III. Gloss., *Gayne-payne*, an English name for a large sword without point, from the French gagne-pain. The appellation was transferred from the field of battle to the tilt-yard, having been the bread-earner of the soldier. **1847** in HALLIWELL; and in mod. Dicts.

†**gains**, *prep. Obs.* Forms: 3 yeynes, 4 gaynes, gaines, gains. [f. GAIN *prep.* + genitive ending -*es*; perh. to be regarded as short form of OE. *tóʒeʒnes*: see AGAINST.]

c **1275** *Serving Christ* 7 in *O.E. Misc.* 90 Yef we habbeþ werkes yeynes þi wille wrauht. *a* **1300** *Cursor M.* 16696 'Fader', he said, 'for-giue þou þaim þat þai do gains me'. *Ibid.* 24845 Þe wind ras gains þam vnride.

gainsay ('geɪnseɪ), *sb.* [f. next; cf. *gainsaw* (GAIN- *pref.* 1).] †**a.** A matter of dispute, a moot question (*obs.*). **b.** Contradiction.

1559 Cox in Strype *Ann. Ref.* I. App. xxii. 60 The matter of images hath always been a gainsay sith they entred first into the Church. **1601** W. WATSON *Decacordon* (1602) 317 To allow, admit, ratifie and confirme without all gainesay, controlment, or contradiction. **1820** W. IRVING *Sketch Bk., Sleepy Hollow* (ed. 2) II. 371 He.. was the umpire in all disputes, setting his hat on one side, and giving his decisions with an air and tone that admitted of no gainsay or appeal. **1889** F. HALL in *Nation* (N.Y.) XLIX. 334/2 He has, beyond gainsay, established his intrepidity, if nothing else.

gainsay ('geɪnseɪ, ˌgeɪn'seɪ), *v.* Inflected **-saying, -said** (rarely **-sayed**). [f. GAIN- *pref.* 1 + SAY *v.* Now a purely literary word, and slightly *arch.* The stress is even or variable; the vbl. sb. is commonly *'gainsaying*. In *gainsaid* the last syllable is usually (-seɪd), not (-sɛd).]

1. *trans.* To deny.

a **1300** *Cursor M.* 883 (Gött.) All þis may scho noght gain say. *c* **1330** R. BRUNNE *Chron.* (1810) 154 If he it geynsay, I wille proue it on him. **1489** CAXTON *Faytes of A.* I. i. 8 Yf it happene that ye said aduersarye delyuer deffences & wyll gaynsaye it. **1530** PALSGR. 560/1 If I have sayd it I wyll nat gayne saye it. *c* **1570** *Pride & Lowl.* (1841) 22 That this is true and may not be denyed, I wyll averre, and yf he it gayne say, I am content by verdict it be tryed. *a* **1619** FOTHERBY *Atheom.* I. viii. § 1. (1622) 55 He, which dare gain-say a thing so generally received. **1682** BUNYAN *Holy War* 113 He that gainsays the truth of this must lie against his Soul. **1728** T. SHERIDAN *Persius* vi. (1739) 91 Gainsay it if you dare. **1826** E. IRVING *Babylon* II. VII. 168 Whether he will in person appear.. we dare neither say nor gainsay. **1867** FREEMAN *Norm. Conq.* (1876) I. vi. 498 Facts which cannot be gainsayed. **1874** DASENT *Tales fr. Fjeld* 350 So when the Sheriff asked him Matt did not gainsay that he had slain the parson.

2. To speak against, contradict.

c **1340** *Cursor M.* 14817 (Fairf.) Nane man may him gaine-sagh. [The other texts have *sb.*] *c* **1450** *St. Cuthbert* (Surtees) 2086, Bot oft tymes schortely him gainsayed. **1581** J. BELL *Haddon's Answ. Osor.* 506 Not we onelye do gaynesay you, but the whole authority of Gods Testament doth determine agaynst you. **1689–92** LOCKE *Toleration* III. x. Wks. 1727 II. 463 And that certainly you may think safely, and without fear of being gain-said. **1742** R. BLAIR *Grave* 230 The Grave gainsays the smooth-complexion'd Flattery, And with blunt Truth acquaints us what we are. **1874** CARPENTER *Ment. Phys.* I. viii. (1879) 374 We have evidence that can scarcely be gainsaid.

3. To speak or act against, oppose, hinder.

c **1340** *Cursor M.* 5769 (Trin.) Þat þei not ȝein seye [*earlier texts* say again] my sonde wiþ my tokenes þou shalt hem fonde. *c* **1440** *York Myst.* x. 198 My lord god will I noght gayne-saye. *c* **1489** CAXTON *Blanchardyn* xxxviii. 143 That wold hem lete or gaynsey thentre therof. **1550** CROWLEY *Way to Wealth* B iv, No man durste gaine saye your doinges for feare of displeasure. **1601** R. JOHNSON *Kingd. & Commw.* (1603) 34 The waters.. gainsaid and put a period to their further progresses. **1667** MILTON *P.L.* IX. 1158 Too facil then thou didst not much gainsay, Nay didst permit, approve, and fair dismiss. **1768** BEATTIE *Minstr.* I. xlix, Or shall frail man heaven's dread decree gainsay. **1826** SCOTT *Woodst.* ii, 'Yet be ruled, dearest father, and submit to that which we cannot gainsay.' **1852** M. ARNOLD *Empedocles on Etna* I. ii, Why is it, that still Man.. believes Nature outraged if his will's gainsaid?

4. To refuse. *rare.*

c **1330** R. BRUNNE *Chron.* (1810) 9 Kynewolf.. toke þe feaute of þe kynges alle.. Bot of Kent and Lyndesay and Northumberland. Þise þre kynges geynsaid it hym. *c* **1532** DEWES *Introd. Fr.* in *Palsgr.* 923 To be gainsayeng and refusyng good counsayle. **1575** R. B. *Appius & Virg.* in Hazl. *Dodsley* IV. 126 Would I gainsay her tender skin to bathe, where I do wash? **1667** PEPYS *Diary* (1879) IV. 310 It is not in his nature to gainsay anything that relates to his pleasures.

gainsayer ('geɪnseɪə(r)). [f. prec. + -ER[1].] One who gainsays, speaks against or opposes.

1435 MISYN *Fire of Love* II. iii. 73 Þat gostly songe with bodily acordis not; & þe cause & þe errour of gaynsayars. **1549** LATIMER *3rd Serm. bef. Edw. VI* (Arb.) 76 Ther were gainsaiars that spurned.. that whympered agaynste him. **1597** HOOKER *Eccl. Pol.* v. ii. §2 Able to bring such proofe of their certaintie, as may satisfie gaine-sayers. **1651** N. BACON *Disc. Govt. Eng.* II. i. (1739) 7 The King may dissolve the Parliament at his pleasure, and all gainsayers are Traitors. **1725** SWIFT *Drapier's Lett.* Wks. 1755 V. II. 76 With the universal approbation of all people, without one single gainsayer. **1840** CARLYLE *Heroes* vi. (1858) 362 Military Dictators, each with his district, to coerce the Royalist and other gainsayers. **1841–4** EMERSON *Ess.* Ser. I. iv. (1876) 113 Then you put all gainsayers in the wrong.

gainsaying ('geɪnseɪɪŋ), *vbl. sb.* [f. as prec. + -ING[1].] The action of the vb. GAINSAY. ***without gainsaying***: without contradiction, unquestionably.

c **1330** R. BRUNNE *Chron.* (1810) 104 His broþer Henry is heyre.. Of alle Normundie, withouten geynsayng. **1375** BARBOUR *Bruce* I. 580 Than thocht he to have the leding Off all Scotland, but gane-saying. **1485** CAXTON *Paris & V.* 19 That was withoute ony gaynsayeng. **1549** *Act 3 & 4 Edw. VI*, c. 3. §2 Lords.. might approve themselves of their Wastes.. nothwithstanding the Gainsaying and Contradiction of their Tenants. **1611** BIBLE *Transl. Pref.* 1 The same endured many a storm of gaine-saying or opposition. **1719** DE FOE *Crusoe* II. iv, There was no gainsaying it. **1873** OUIDA *Pascarel* I. 53 In that gentle way of his which, as you know, there is no gainsaying.

'gainsaying, *ppl. a.* [f. as prec. + -ING[2].] Given to contradiction, contumacious. Hence †**'gainsayingness**.

1489 CAXTON *Faytes of A.* III. iv. 173 He ought to lese hys hed whiche is rebell and gainsainge in ordynaunce of a bataylle. **1611** BIBLE *Rom.* x. 21 A disobedient and gainesaying people. **1648** J. GOODWIN *Youngling Elder* 65 The grace of God.. takes away all actuall rebelliousnesse or gainsayingnesse of the will.

Gainsborough ('geɪnzbərə). [The name of Thomas *Gainsborough* (1727–88), English painter.] **1.** A portrait painted by Gainsborough.

1798 J. CONSTABLE *Let.* 2 Dec. (1964) II. 16 Consequently I have not taken advantage of your friendship or Mr. Strutt's good nature respecting the Gainsborough. **1894** W. ARMSTRONG *Gainsborough* 83 As refutations of Sir Joshua we could name many Gainsboroughs which beat the *Blue Boy*. **1903** A. B. CHAMBERLAIN *Gainsborough* 132 She [*sc.* Signora Grassi] called her house a 'painted Paradise' because of the Gainsboroughs hanging there. **1958** E. WATERHOUSE *Gainsborough* 13 An almost unknown painter some of whose works.. are curiously similar to early Gainsboroughs.

2. A large broad-brimmed hat of the type worn by women in Gainsborough's portraits. In full, ***Gainsborough hat***.

1878 *Cassell's Fam. Mag.* Aug. 569/2 The.. wearers of the Gainsborough, Rembrandt, and beef-eater hats. **1884** [see CART-WHEEL *sb.* 5]. **1904** *Westm. Gaz.* 12 Aug. 5/1 Extemporised Gainsboroughs. **1928** *Amer. Speech* IV. 92 One remembers the Gainsborough hat.

gainshire ('geɪnʃə(r)), *sb. dial.* [prob. a local survival of GAINCHARE.] **a.** (See quot. 1814.) **b.** *Sheffield Cutlery.* A barb on the tang of a knife, to prevent its being pulled out of the handle. So **'gainshire** *v.*, to barb (a tang).

1814 PEGGE *Suppl. to Grose, Gain-shire* or *Gain-shere*, the barb of a fishing-hook, Derb. **1820** *Specif. Brownill's Patent* No. 4474 As a further security for the keeping on of the cap I spread or beat out the end of the tang, if a round tang, or make what is called a gainshire. **1888** *Sheffield Gloss.* s.v., When the tang of a knife is notched in various places, like a barbed arrow, so that when driven into the handle it will not come out, it is said to be gainshired.

†**'gainsome**, *a.*[1] *Obs. rare.* [f. GAIN *sb.*[2] + -SOME.] Profitable, lucrative, advantageous.

1569 E. HAKE *Newes Powles Churchyarde* (1579) D ij, They stick not it to call A gainesome Occupation. **1646** *Tythe-Gatherers no Gospel Officers* 18 Free for every man to betake himselfe to which of them he pleases, and thinkes will prove most gainsome and beneficiall to him.

'gainsome, *a.*[2] *Obs.* exc. *dial.* [f. GAIN *a.* + -SOME.] Ready, prompt, ? †willing to assist.

1626 MASSINGER *Rom. Actor* IV. ii, To personate a gentleman, noble, wise, Faithful, and gainsome. **1889** *N.W. Linc. Gloss.* (ed. 2), *Gainsome*, expert, handy.

gainst, *prep.* Also **'gainst**. [Rather a poetic aphetizing of AGAINST than the direct descendant of GAIN, GAINS. For other examples see AGAINST.]

1590 SPENSER *F.Q.* II. xii. 38 Both firmely armd for every hard assay, With constancy and care, gainst daunger and dismay. **1590** MARLOWE *Edw. II*, III. ii, A bloody part, flatly gainst law of arms! **1601** WEEVER *Mirr. Mart.* D iv, That gainst the Pope I should in no wise stand. **1649** G. DANIEL *Trinarch., Hen. V*, cxxxi, A strange Doctrine Irrelative; but lately vrg'd 'Gainst Harrie's Title.

†**gainstand**, *sb. Obs. rare.* [f. GAIN- *pref.* 1 + STAND *sb.*] Opposition, resistance.

c **1470** HARDING *Chron.* CII. ix, Tharchbyshop Egbert.. the primacye and pall brought to Yorkes lande, graunted without gaynstand. **1535** STEWART *Cron. Scot.* II. 437 We.. At oure plesour agane ȝow ma proceid, Without gane-stand of ȝow or ony dreid.

gainstand (geɪn'stænd), *v. Obs.* or *arch.* [f. GAIN- *pref.* 1 + STAND *v.* Common down to *c* 1650, after which it falls out of use, except as an archaism.] *trans.* To withstand, oppose, resist.

c **1400** *Apol. Loll.* 25 Ilk crature wiþ God auȝt to ȝenstond falshed. *c* **1450** *St. Cuthbert* (Surtees) 4932 And he na power had To gayne stande þaim in batayle. **1552** LYNDESAY *Monarche* 5222 The kyng of Kyngis he sall ganestand. **1563–83** FOXE *A. & M.* (1583) II. 1255/2 Vnless theyr purpose be vtterly to impugne & gainstand the scripture. **1653** URQUHART *Rabelais* I. liii, They make a vassal to gain-stand his Lord. **1839** BAILEY *Festus* xxx. (1848) 342 And seek ye to gainstand the faith in God?

†**b.** In northern dialects the pr. pple. was used in 14–15th c. in the phr. ***not gainstanding*** = NOTWITHSTANDING.

c **1375** *Sc. Leg. Saints, Justin* 44 Hou Eraclius þe emperoure.. þe son of Cosdre slew in ficht nocht-gand-standine his gret mycht. *c* **1440** *York Myst.* x. 55 Noght gaynestanding our grete eelde A semely sone he has vs sente.

Hence **gain'standing** *vbl. sb.* and *ppl. a.* Also **gain'stander**, an opposer, opponent.

a **1340** HAMPOLE *Psalter* xvi[i]. 9 [8] Fra gayn standand [L. *a resistentibus*] til þi right hand; kepe me as þe appile of þe eghe. *c* **1450** *Lay Folks Mass Bk.* Bidding Prayer iii. 69 Gaynstanding and restrenyng of þare power. **1535** STEWART *Cron. Scot.* II. 414 Sen weill we wait na gane-standing to get. *c* **1575** BALFOUR *Practicks* (1754) 22 Nane sall be repute as loyall.. subjectis to our soverane Lord.. bot be puneisabill as rebellaris and ganestandaris of the samin. **1637** GILLESPIE *Eng. Pop. Cerem.* III. iii. 44 Their poore shifts are too weake for gainstanding it. **1674** N. FAIRFAX *Bulk & Selv.* 7 He is, at the same time the evil thing is done, as much the cause of the gainstanding good that is not done. **1825** SCOTT *Talism.* xi, The three lions passant of England . . must take precedence of beast, fish or fowl, or woe worth the gainstander.

†**gain'strive**, *v. Obs.* [f. GAIN- I + STRIVE *v.*]
1. *trans.* To strive against, oppose.
1549–62 STERNHOLD & H. *Ps.*, *Da pacem*, The Word to offer thou dost not slacke, Which we unkindly gaine-strive. **1557** GRIMALD *Cicero's Death* 47 in *Tottel's Misc.* (Arb.) 124 In case yet all the fates gaynstriue vs not. **1590** SPENSER *F.Q.* II. iv. 14 In his strong armes he stifly him embraste, Who him gain-striving nought at all prevaild.
2. *intr.* To make resistance.
1596 SPENSER *F.Q.* IV. vii. 12 Whenever in his powre He may them catch, unable to gainestrive.
Hence †**gain'striving** *vbl. sb.*
1583 GOLDING *Calvin on Deut.* lxix. 423 We must hold on in so doing, what hardnes and gainestriuing soeuer wee meete withal. **1601** DENT *Pathw. Heav.* 94 You which vse no meanes at all, nor any gainestriuing, but willingly giue place to the Diuell.

†**gainturn**. *Obs.* [f. GAIN- *pref.* 3 + TURN *sb.*] A turning back; an evasion.
a **1225** *Leg. Kath.* 2118 Bute ȝef þu þe timluker do þe i þe ȝeinturn. *c* **1350** *Will. Palerne* 3552 No 3 ain-torn schuld lette. **1566** KNOX *Hist. Reform.* Wks. 1846 I. 210 At lenth the Scottishmen gave back, and fled without gane turne.

gain-twist. *U.S.* [f. GAIN *v.*[2] + TWIST *sb.*]
A rifle with a *gaining-twist* (see GAINING *ppl. a.*).
1867 F. H. LUDLOW *Fleeing to Tarshish* 166, I done it once, when Judge Lynch sot on a bush whacker, and I'd rather give my best gain-twist than do it again.

†'**gainward**, *prep. Obs. rare*[−1]. [f. GAIN- *pref.* I + -WARD: see AGAINWARD.] Towards, facing, over against.
a **1541** WYATT *Poet. Wks.* (1861) 161 For I with spur and sail go seek the Thames, Gainward the sun.

†**gainy**, *a. Obs. rare.* In 6 geanie, 7 ganey. [f. GAIN *sb.*[2] (?and *sb.*[1]) + -Y[1].] **a.** Profitable, advantageous. **b.** Of the nature of gain.
1573 TUSSER *Husb.* (1878) 8 Loiterers I kept so meanie . . that, that waie nothing geanie, was thought to make me thriue. **1614** *Scourge of Venus* B vij b, And when you seeke to gaine the loue of such Let my experience thus much you assure They Fawlcon-like stoop to a ganey lure.

†**gainyield**, *sb. Obs. Sc.* Forms: 6 gayn-, genȝeild, ganȝeld, ganȝell, genȝell. [f. GAIN- *pref.* 2 + YIELD *sb.* (ON. had *gagngiald* as a law term). The normal stress was on the first syllable (whence the forms *gan-*, *genyell*), but in verse the stress varies.] Recompense, return, reward.
1513 DOUGLAS *Æneis* II. ix. 54 The goddis mocht condingly the forȝeld, Eftir thi desert rendring sic ganȝeld. *Ibid.* VII. viii. 43 Set the to ganestand Thir perellis, but all thankis or gaynȝeild. **1568** BALNEVIS in *Bannatyne MS.* (Hunter. Club) 392 Out of thair schynnis the substance rynnis, Thay gett no genyell ellis. **1570** *Satir. Poems Reform.* xx. 62 At thame rycht fane or els be slane: That ganȝell will thay ȝeild.

†**gain-'yield**, *v. Obs.* [f. GAIN- *pref.* 2 + YIELD *v.*] *trans.* To give in return, make return of.
1435 MISYN *Fire of Love* I. xxvi. 55 If þou þerfore desires be lufyd, lufe, for lufe gayn-ȝeldis þe self.

gaip, obs. form of GAPE.

gair (gɛr). *Sc.* and *north. dial.* Also **gare**. [a. ON. *geire* wk. masc., of the same meaning = OE. *gára* GORE *sb.*] An isolated strip of tender grass.
1807 A. DUNCAN *Dis. Sheep* in *Prize Ess. Highl. Soc. Scotl.* III. 524 Heath intermixed with gairs, that is, strips of very fine grass. **1818** HOGG *Brownie Bodsbeck* I. 37 They had amaist gane wi' a' the gairs i' our North Grain. **1880** EDWARDS *Mod. Scot. Poets* I. 34 The martyrs . . Forgathered on some green gair. **1882** J. HARDY in *Proc. Berw. Nat. Club* IX. No. 3. 452 These 'green gairs' and the patches of marshy ground broke up the continuity of the heather. **1893** *Northumbld. Gloss.* s.v., A *gair* is a bright, green, grassy spot, surrounded by bent or heather. Also an irregular strip of green turf running down the side of a moorland hill.

gair: see GARE.

gaird, gairdone, Sc. var. GUARD, GUERDON.

gairfish, obs. form of GARFISH.

gairfowl, gairish: see GAREFOWL, GARISH.

gairth, Sc. form of GARTH.

gais, obs. Sc. form of GAUZE *sb.*

gaisling, Sc. form of GOSLING.

gaison, var. GEASON, *Obs.*

gaiss, obs. Sc. form of GUESS.

gaist, Sc. form of GHOST; obs. form of GUEST.

gait (geɪt), *sb.*[1] Also 6–8 gate, 7 gaite. [A particular use of GATE *sb.*[2], q.v. for the other senses, now chiefly Sc. and dial., 'way', 'road', 'going', 'course', etc.
Until the 17th c. the spelling *gait* was rare exc. *Sc.*; before the middle of the 18th c. it became universal for this sense of the word, which was the only one that survived in general literary use.]
a. Manner of walking or stepping, bearing or carriage while moving, walk, step. Also *fig.*, esp in phr. ***to go one's (own) gait***, to go one's own way; to pursue one's own course. (For literal senses of this phr. see GANG *v.*[1] 1 b, GATE *sb.*[2])
1509 BARCLAY *Shyp of Folys* (1570) 19 Their gate and looke proude and abhominable. **1591** SPENSER *M. Hubberd* 600 Scarse thy legs uphold thy feeble gate. **1660** STANLEY *Hist. Philos.* IX. (1701) 372/1 He considered their presence and their gaite, and the whole motion of their body. **1663** BUTLER *Hud.* I. i. 427 He was well stay'd, and in his gate Preserv'd a Grave, Majestick State. **1726–7** SWIFT *Gulliver* I. iv, We can plainly discover one of his heels higher than the other; which gives him a hobble in his gait. **1752** FIELDING *Amelia* III. xi, With this face and in the most solemn gait she approached Amelia. **1774** GOLDSM. *Nat. Hist.* (1776) V. 192 Its restless gait and odd chuckling sound distinguish it sufficiently from all other birds. **1806–7** J. BERESFORD *Miseries Hum. Life* (1826) III. Introd., My limping gait. **1834** MCMURTRIE *Cuvier's Anim. Kingd.* 338 Their gait in general is very slow. **1865** KINGSLEY *Herew.* i, He was more fit from his gait to be a knight than a monk. **1865** 'MARK TWAIN' *Celebr. Jumping Frog* (1867) 37 Preachin' was his nateral gait. **1874** L. STEPHEN *Hours in Library* (1892) I. vii. 241 Our great writers generally settle down to a stately but monotonous gait, after the fashion of Johnson. **1922** J. B. PRIESTLEY *Papers from Lilliput* 31 Caring little whether he is still a shepherd or metamorphosed into a fisherman or cobbler, so long as he is still with us, going his own fantastic gait. **1940** H. READ *Annals of Innocence* II. ii. 82 These are qualities to be enjoyed by non-poetic people: the poet must go his own gait. **1958** *Times* 4 Oct. 9/5 Miss Watts, whose voice is of the right weight and gait for Bach.
b. *pl.*, *esp.* of a horse: Paces.
1684 *Lond. Gaz.* No. 1916/4 Lost . . a black Gelding . . the near Foot behind White, a small Star, and all his gates very well. **1709** *Ibid.* No. 4540/8 Stoln or strayed . . a Bay Gelding . . hath all his Gates. *a* **1717** PARNELL *Anacreontic* vii, Cupid mock'd his stammring Tongue With all his staggring Gaits. **1890** *Anthony's Photogr. Bull.* III. 195 In photographing the various gaits of a saddle horse, it is best to [etc.].
c. *Comb.*: †**gait-trip**, manner of walking.
1583 STANYHURST *Æneis* I. (Arb.) 40 Too moothers counsayl thee fyrye Cupido doth harcken Of puts he his feathers, fauoring with gatetrip Iulus.
Hence '**gaited** *ppl. a.*, having a (specified) gait or manner of walking or stepping.
1588 SHAKS. *L.L.L.* III. i. 56 You must send the Asse vpon the Horse for he is verie slow gated. **1593** —— *Rich. II*, III. ii. 15 Let thy Spiders, that suck vp thy Venome, And heauie-gated Toades lye in their way. **1593** NASHE *Christ's T.* (1613) 128 So many . . heauy-gated lumbereres into the Ministry are stumbled. **1712** *Lond. Gaz.* No. 5037/15 Lost . . a . . Gelding . . extraordinary well Gated.

gait (geɪt), *sb.*[2] *dial.* Also 8 **geate**. (See quots.)
1788 W. MARSHALL *Yorksh.* Gloss. II. 330 *Gait*, a single sheaf of corn, bound near the top, and set upon its butts. **1799** J. ROBERTSON *Agric. Perth* 158 When the geates are dry, or ready to be gathered in. **1825** LOUDON *Agric.* §2940 When the single sheaves (gaites) have remained in this position for a few days, if [etc.]. **1893** *Northumbld. Gloss.*, *Gait*, sheaves set up singly in a corn field.

gait (geɪt), *sb.*[3] *dial.* [app. a special use of GATE *sb.*[2], act of going; cf. GANG in the same sense.] (See quot. 1854.)
1827 CLARE *Sheph. Cal.* 162 Or gait of water from the pump to fetch. **1854** MISS BAKER *Northamptonsh. Gloss.* s.v., A *gait* of water is two buckets carried with a yoke; evidently from *gait* a going, as much as a man can walk with.

gait (geɪt), *v.*[1] *dial.* Also 8 **gate, geat**. [f. GAIT *sb.*[2]] *trans.* To set up (reaped corn) in single sheaves or 'gaits' to dry.
1797 BAILEY & CULLEY *View Agric. Northumbld.* 95 Wheat is set up in stooks of twelve sheaves each; oats and barley are ('gated') set up in single sheaves. **1805** R. W. DICKSON *Pract. Agric.* II. 794 Gaiting and hutting the corn. **1844** STEPHENS *Bk. of Farm* III. 1066, I would not hesitate to gait any sort of oats when wet with dew in the morning.
Hence '**gaiting** *vbl. sb.*, the action of the vb.; also *concr.* = GAIT *sb.*[2]
1799 J. ROBERTSON *Agric. Perth* 157 This practice is provincially called geating. **1825** BROCKETT *N. Country Wds.*, *Gaitings*, single sheaves of corn set up to dry.

gait (geɪt), *v.*[2] *dial.* or *techn.* [app. f. *gait* GATE *sb.*[2]; cf. 'to set AGATE'.] *trans.* To put in working order, fix up.
1846 *Brockett's N. Country Wds.* (ed. 3) s.v., To *gait* in Lancashire, is to prepare a loom for weaving. **1869** *Eng. Mech.* 12 Nov. 217/3 Will any of your numerous readers be kind enough to inform me of the best plan of gaiting a pair of cart wheels, so that they run with ease and freedom? *Ibid.* 26 Nov. 264/3 'Lancasterian' may gait his wheels by placing a straight edge to the back of the nave, parallel with the face of the spoke, then take the level [*read* bevel] along the inside of the buss [etc.]. **1895** *Bury Times* 6 Apr. 6/3 He had gaited a great many looms.

gait, northern form of GOAT.

gait, var. GET *sb.*, *Sc.*, offspring, child.

‖**gaita** ('gaita). [Sp.] A Spanish musical instrument resembling the bagpipes. So **gai'tero**, a piper.
1846 R. FORD *Gatherings from Spain* vii. 77 The tune of the *gaita*, or Moorish bagpipe. **1922** *Glasgow Herald* 14 Aug. 4 Within the deep, wide recess of the chimney the son of the house is singing to the accompaniment of the 'gaita'. **1927** *Chambers's Jrnl.* 29 Oct. 758/2 Their little *gaitas* (bagpipes) tasselled with the national colours of red and yellow. *Ibid.*, A famous band of *gaiteros*, or pipers. **1967** 'LA MERI' *Sp. Dancing* (ed. 2) ii. 32 The *gaita* . . is a bagpipe, green in color, which is the same as the better-known bagpipes of Scotland and Ireland.

gaiten, *sb. dial.* [? dial. pron. of *gaiting*, f. GAIT *v.*[1] + ING.[1]] = GAIT *sb.*[2] Hence (?) **gaiten** *v.* = GAIT *v.*[1]; **gaitning** *vbl. sb.*, **gaitner** (see quots.).
1831 LOUDON *Agric.* (ed. 2) §3176 *Gaiting*, or *gaitning*, as it is called in Northumberland. *Ibid.*, The gaitner follows immediately after about eight or nine sheaves have been cut and laid down. *Ibid.*, He . . brings the gaitning (sheaf) up to the left knee. *Ibid.*, Gaitned sheaves are not good to keep standing in stormy weather. **1893** *Northumbld. Gloss.*, *Gaten*, *Gaiteen*, or *Gaitin*, a single sheaf of corn set on its end in a harvest field to dry.

gaiter ('geɪtə(r)), *sb.*[1] [a. F. *guêtre* (in 15th c. *guietre*); of unknown origin; there are Rom. synonyms without *r*, as Walloon *guett*, Sardinian *ghetta*, mod.Pr. *gueto*: see Körting *Lat. Rom. Wb.* s.v.]
1. A covering of cloth, leather, etc. for the ankle, or ankle and lower leg.
1775 [cf. *half-gaiter*: see HALF II. 1]. **1802** C. JAMES *Milit. Dict.*, *Gaiters*, a sort of spatterdashes, usually made of cloth, and are either long, as reaching to the knee, or short as only reaching just above the ancle; the latter are termed half-gaiters. **1812** H. & J. SMITH *Rej. Addr.*, *Theatre* 71 Lax in their gaiters, laxer in their gait. **1837** DICKENS *Pickw.* xii, Mr. Weller was furnished with . . light breeches and gaiters. **1865** —— *Mut. Fr.* I. v, Thick leather gaiters. **1880** *Plain Knitting* 19 Gaiters (i.e. legs of stockings without feet) . . are very useful to those who are obliged to walk out in all weathers. **1886** HALL CAINE *Son of Hagar* II. xvi, Parson Christian stood near her in silk gaiters.
2. *U.S.* (See quots.)
1864 WEBSTER, *Gaiter*, a kind of shoe, consisting chiefly of cloth, and covering the ankle. **1889** *Century Dict.*, *Gaiter*, Now, also, a shoe of similar form, with or without cloth, generally with an insertion of elastic on each side.
3. *attrib.* and *Comb.*, as ***gaiter-maker***, ***-strap***; **gaiter-boot**, **-shoe** (orig. *U.S.*) = sense 2.
1840 *Picayune* (New Orleans) 30 July 2/4 Many of the ladies of Philadelphia . . now wear . . gaiter boots, with little straps of black leather. **1849** N. P. WILLIS *Rural Lett.* 230 Dandies strolling and stealing an occasional look at their loose *demi-saison* pantaloons and gaiter-shoes. **1862** CARLYLE *Fredk. Gt.* IX. x. (1865) III. 152 From big guns and wagon-horses down to gun-flints and gaiter-straps. **1875** MRS. STOWE *We & Neighbors* x. 106 Looking as if they never had heard of a French hat or a pair of gaiter-boots. **1894** *Daily News* 29 Dec. 3/6 Her husband was a gaiter maker. **1932** 'A. BRIDGE' *Peking Picnic* x. 111 Blue trousers tucked into high white gaiter boots.

'**gaiter**, *sb.*[2] *Obs.* exc. *dial.* Forms: 1 gáte tréow, 4–5 gaitrys, gattris, gaytre, 6 gadrise, gaten(-tree), gater, (8 garter), 6–9 gatten, 7–9 gatt(e)ridge, gatter, gaiter. [The OE. *gáte tréow* = goat's tree; but app. this has mixed with a synonym of which the OE. form, if it existed, would be **gáte hrís* (*hrís*, RISE, bush). The forms are partly northern, with (eː) for OE. *á*, and partly exhibit the vowel-shortening common in the first element of compounds.] A name properly belonging to the Dogwood (*Cornus sanguinea*), but in various districts applied to other similar shrubs, as the Spindle-tree (*Euonymus europæus*). Also *attrib.* in ***gaiter-berry***, ***-bush***, ***-tree***.
c **1000** *Saxon Leechd.* II. 86 Wiþ þære adl þe mon hæt circul adl, genim . . gatetreow . . wyl on wætre swiþe. *c* **1386** CHAUCER *Nun's Pr. T.* 145 Laxatyues . . Of catapuce, or of gaitrys [*vrr.* gaytres, gaytrys, gattris, gaytre] beryis. **1548** [see DOG-TREE 1]. **1578** LYTE *Dodoens* VI. li. 725 Dogge berie or Gatten tree. **1597** GERARDE *Herball* III. cv. (1633) 1467 In the North Country they call it Gaten tree or Gater-tree. **1660** RAY *Catalog. Plant. Cantab.* 39 *Cornus fœmina* . . Dogberry or Gatter tree. **1691** —— *S. & E. Country Wds.*, *Gatteridge-tree* is *Cornus fœmina*, or Prickwood, and yet Gatteridge-berries are the Fruit of *Euonymus Theofrasti*, i.e. Spindle-tree or Louse-berry. **1692** COLES, *Gaiter-berries*, of the Gaiter-tree, prickwood. **1796** WITHERING *Brit. Plants* (ed. 3) II. 200 *Cornus sanguinea* . . Gatten tree. *Ibid.* 259 *Evonymus europæus* . . Gatteridge Tree. **1819** CRABBE *T. of Hall* VII. 158 Dwarf trees and humbler shrubs . . Haw, gatter, holm, the service and the sloe.

gaiter ('geɪtə(r)), *v.* [f. GAITER *sb.*[1]] *trans.* To dress or furnish with gaiters. Hence '**gaitered** *ppl. a.*
1760 *Proceedings Crt.-martial Ld. G. Sackville* 11 The Cavalry must be saddled; the Artillery-Horses harnessed, and the Infantry gatered. **1848** CRAIG, *Gaiter*, to dress with gaiters. **1852** SMEDLEY *L. Arundel* xxviii. 230 A leather-gaitered and corduroyed Christian. **1892** *Pall Mall G.* 23 Sep. 6/2 The cocked-hatted and gaitered troops of the First Republic.

gaiterless ('geɪtəlɪs), *a.* [f. GAITER *sb.*[1] + -LESS.] Having no gaiters, without gaiters.
1839 *New Monthly Mag.* LVI. 485 The gaiterless calf of the angry gentleman's healthy leg.

gaitling, *Sc.* [dim. of *gait* GET *sb.* offspring, child.] A young child, an infant.

1831 SCOTT *Ct. Robt.* Introd. Addr., The least gaitling among them all.

gaitt, var. GET *sb. Sc.*, offspring, child.

gaity, obs. form of GAIETY.

‖**gaize** (geɪz). *Geol.* [Fr.] A fine-grained micaceous and calcareous sandstone found in Cretaceous beds in northern France and southern England.

1885 A. GEIKIE *Text-bk. Geol.* (ed. 2) VI. 832 A porous calcareous and argillaceous sandstone known as *Gaize*, containing a large percentage of silica soluble in alkali. **1949** KIRK & OTHMER *Encycl. Chem. Technol.* III. 430 Along the valleys of the Meuse and Ardennes in France is an extensive formation of.. gaize. This material.. is used as a pozzolanic admixture with portland cement. The mixture is known as *gaize cement*. **1955** G. G. WOODFORD tr. *Gignoux's Stratigr. Geol.* viii. 419 In the southern part of the Ardennes.. we already know that its base is composed of the top of the *gaize* with *Mortoniceras rostratum*.

gal, var. of CAL.

1808 POLWHELE *Cornish-Eng. Voc.*, *Gal*, rust. **1849** WEALE *Dict. Terms.*, *Gal*, in Cornish, rusty iron ore. **1875** [see CAL].

gal, obs. f. GALL; var. GOLE *Obs.*, luxurious.

gal[1] (gæl), vulgar or dial. pronunciation of GIRL.

1795 B. DEARBORN *Columbian Gram.* 135 Improprieties, commonly called Vulgarisms, [include].. Gal for girl. **1824** J. WIGHT *Mornings at Bow St.* 132 *Gal*—cockney for *girl.* **1837** DICKENS *Pickw.* iv. 39 My daughters, gentlemen—my gals these are. *Ibid.* xxxii. 343 You *are* a nice gal and nothin' but it. **1842** ORDERSON *Creol.* xv. 173 You should speak to the gal first. *a* **1845** HOOD *Love has not Eyes* v, He'll swear that in her dancing she cuts all others out, Though like a Gal that's galvanised, she throws her legs about.

gal[2] (gæl). [f. the name *Galileo*: see GALILEAN *a.*[2]] A unit used in expressing the value of the acceleration due to gravity and equal to one centimetre per second per second.

1914 O. KLOTZ in *Nature* 13 Aug. 611/2 So long ago as 1909 Wiechert used the term 'gal' in the report for the Göttingen earthquake station for that unit, being the first syllable of Galileo... Others, as well as myself, have used 'gal' or rather 'milligal' in analyses of earthquakes... Dyne is the unit of force, gal the unit of acceleration. **1935** *Nature* 23 Mar. 471/1 A particular case as example in which an error of 0.01 gal in '*g*' would lead to an error of 40 ft. in geoidal elevation. **1937** *Geogr. Jrnl.* LXXXIX. 92 Unfortunately the old Helmert (1901) is used instead of the international formula adopted at Stockholm in 1930, in which the equatorial value of '*g*' is greater by 0.019 gals (= cm. per sec. per sec.). **1955** *Sci. Amer.* Sept. 165/3 Painstaking pendulum measurements have established the value of gravity as 981.274 gal. **1971** *Geophysical Jrnl.* XXII. 449 With the general adoption of the International System of Units.. the c.g.s. unit of acceleration, the gal (or Gal), is doomed to obsolescence.

gala[1] ('gɑːlə, 'geɪlə). [a. F. *gala*, a. It. *gala*.]

1. Gala dress, festal attire. *Obs.* exc. in phr. ***in gala*** (= F. *en gala*).

1625 ASTON *Let.* in *Cabala* (1654) I. 53 Whereupon this King, and the whole Court put on Galas. **1757** CHESTERF. *Lett.* (1792) IV. 88, I love to see those, in whom I interest myself, in their undress rather than in gala. **1787** *Gentl. Mag.* LVII. II. 1186/1 His Majesty and the latter [grandees] being covered, and all in grand gala or uniforms. **1867** MACGREGOR *Voy. Alone* (1868) 59 The streets were dressed in gala. **1876** BANCROFT *Hist. U.S.* V. ii. 104 Apparelled on Sunday morning in gala, as if for the drawing-room, he constantly marched out all his house-hold to his parish church.

†**2.** Festivity, gaiety, rejoicing: esp. in ***days of gala***.

1716 LADY M. W. MONTAGU *Let. to C'tess X——* 1 Oct., The ladies.. declare that on such a day the assembly shall be at their house in honour of the feast of the Count or Countess—— such a one. These days are called days of Gala. **1788** *Gentl. Mag.* LVIII. I. 78/2 The anniversary of her Majesty's name-day was celebrated at the Russian court with great gala. **1789** MRS. PIOZZI *Journ. France* I. 85 Damask hangings and gold lace.. upon days of gala. **1799** SIR W. HAMILTON in *G. Rose's Diaries* (1860) I. 226 We have had.. three days' gala and illuminations. **1809** W. IRVING *Knickerb.* (1861) 99 The standard of our city, reserved like a choice handkerchief for days of gala, hung motionless on the flag-staff.

3. A festive occasion; a festival characterized by the display of finery and show.

[**1777** SHERIDAN *Sch. Scand.* I. ii, A girl.. who never knew.. dissipation above the annual gala of a race ball.] **1800** *Sporting Mag.* XV. 51 A certain Lord gave a grand gala to the members of the volunteer corps. **1851** D. JERROLD *St. Giles* xv. 153 Ladies had dressed themselves as for a gala. **1884** *York Herald* 27 Aug. 3/6 A meeting.. for the purpose of inaugurating a Volunteer gala.. the gala to be held in the park.. attached to Thirsk Hall. *Mod.* A Fête and Gala will be held in —— Park on Bank Holiday.

4. *attrib.* and *Comb.*, as ***gala dinner***, ***flag***, ***performance***, ***show***; **gala day**, a day of festivity, finery and show; so ***gala hour***, ***night***; **gala dress**, a dress suited for or worn at a gala; fine or showy dress; so ***gala attire***, ***clothes***, ***coat***, ***habit***, ***suit***, ***uniform***, and the like; **gala meet**, a (hunting) meet attended with festivities.

1762 STERNE *Tr. Shandy* VI. xxiv, The Corporal.. never put it [a Montero-cap] on but upon gala-days. **1766** S. SHARP *Lett. from Italy* xxi. 86 Some of these persons of quality.. order the undertaker of the opera to let out their boxes when they do not go themselves, and often stay at home purposely on *gala* nights. **1773** BRYDONE *Sicily* xxx. (1809) 288 The triumphal car was preceded by.. all the city officers in their gala uniforms. **1797** MRS. RADCLIFFE *Italian* xvii, The doors of the theatre were thronged with Roman Ladies in their gala habits. **1805** C. WILMOT *Let.* 29 Aug. in *Russ. Jrnls.* (1934) II. 177 There is hardly any of the Costume of Women, & what there is not in their *Gala dress.* **1824** W. IRVING *T. Trav.* I. 9 The old lady appeared in her gala suit of faced brocade. **1845** ALB. SMITH *Fort. Scatterg. Fam.* xxii. (1887) 72 [He] dragged him by sheer muscular strength to Rosherville every gala night. **1851** *Ord. & Regul. R. Engin.* xix. 104 The first and last to be supplied to the Superior Stations, as Gala, and Common or Storm Flags. **1852** MRS. STOWE *Uncle Tom's C.* xx. 211 A libation of dirty slop would unaccountably deluge them from above when in full gala dress. *a* **1876** J. H. NEWMAN *Hist. Sk.* II. I. x. 193 The day of entertainment was made quite a gala day. **1894** *Field* 1 Dec. 828/1 A gala meet was anticipated at Mullaboden. **1925** R. GRAVES *Welchman's Hose* 35 A Frenchman was struck dead by a meteorite, That was the sort of gala-show it was! **1932** E. SITWELL *Bath* 238 Lord Chesterfield.. speaks of one of these gala-performances. **1934** A. HUXLEY *Beyond Mexique Bay* 6 He.. decreed that our dinner, every third or fourth day should be called a Gala Dinner. **1966** *Illustr. London News* 30 July 22 Princess Muna went with the King, the Duke of Gloucester.. and the Duchess to the Royal Opera house, where they saw a gala performance of Giselle.

b. As *adj.*, festive, gay. Chiefly *N. Amer.*

1954 R. HAYDN *Jrnl. Edwin Carp* 242 Never.. has 35 Gubbion Avenue known a celebration more gala than our wedding breakfast. **1964** *McCall's Sewing* iii. 36/2 When you want to feel really dressed up and ready for a big night, try the real evening fabrics. You'll feel more gala. **1968** *Globe & Mail* (Toronto) 17 Feb. 25/7 The whole thing will be very gala and a lot of fun.

gala[2] ('gælə). [short f. *Galashiels*, a town where this fabric is made.] (See quots.)

1858 SIMMONDS *Dict. Trade*, *Gala*, a Scotch cotton fabric. **1882** CAULFEILD & SAWARD *Dict. Needlework* 219 *Gala*, a Scotch cotton fabric, employed for servants' dresses. Gala is said to be only a local name.

galabiya (ga'laːbija). Also **gal(l)abea**, **-beeah**, **-bia**, **-bieh**, **-biyah**, **-biyeh**, **-bya**. [= Arab. *jallābīya*, pop. equivalent of *jilbāb*.] A smock-like garment worn in Arabic-speaking Mediterranean countries.

1725 J. WINDUS *Journey to Mequinez* 29 A Gelebia.. is made of a course and thick wrought woollen Stuff, without Sleeves, but Holes to put their Arms thro', it reaches to their Knees, and hangs loose about their Bodies like a Sack. **1820** J. G. JACKSON *Account of Timbuctoo* 200 Their costume is a *jelabea*, and a belt, without shoes or head dress. **1839** J. DAVIDSON *Notes Trav. Afr.* 12 The *jelábiyah* are merely coarse sacks, with holes in them for the arms to pass through. **1892** D. A. CAMERON *Arabic-Engl. Vocab.* 45 'Galábiya'. **1900** A. CONAN DOYLE *Green Flag* 328 Tell them to undo the man's galabeeah. **1916** V. HORSLEY in S. Paget *Sir V. Horsley* (1919) 321 The small boys.. are given the head-dress and a few feet of stuff for a galabea. **1921** *Chambers's Jrnl.* 26 Mar. 265/1 A figure in a blue *galabieh* and a white-turbaned tarboosh. **1965** *Economist* 2 Jan. 25/1 The [Egyptian] working man in the towns.. rustles a few more notes in his trouser (no longer, let us note in passing, his galabiya) pocket.

†**galace, gallace.** *Obs.* [of uncertain origin; it is difficult to regard it as corruptly ad. F. *guilloche*.] ? = GUILLOCHE.

1663 GERBIER *Counsel* 71 The single gallace five inches and half broad, twelve pence per foot.. Flowers for the Crosse worke in the galace.. eight shillings per piece.

galache, obs. form of GALOSH.

galactan (gə'læktæn). *Chem.* [a. G. *galactan* (C. Scheibler 1882, in *Neue Zeitschr. f. Rübenzucker-Industrie* VIII. 277/1), adapted from *galactin* (f. Gr. γαλακτ-, γάλα milk) to conform with G. *dextran* DEXTRAN.] Any of a group of polysaccharides that yield galactose on hydrolysis and occur in many plants, esp. algæ, lichens, mosses, and conifers, and a few animals.

1886 *Jrnl. Chem. Soc.* L. 609 This carbohydrate [from the seed of *Lupinus luteus*] very closely resembles galactin (or adopting Scheibler's nomenclature galactan), obtained by Muntz from the seed of the lucerne. **1912** C. A. BROWNE *Handbk. Sugar Analysis* xix. 599 In the galactans d-galactose shows the same tendency to form combinations with other sugars..; there are arabogalactans, xylogalactans, mannogalactans, glucogalactans and other combinations. **1963** FLORKIN & STOTZ *Comprehensive Biochem.* V. vii. 222 Galactans of animal origin are rare. The snail *Helix pomatia* and a few other cold-blooded animals produce a highly branched levorotatory galactan containing D-galactose and a lesser amount of L-galactose.

galactase (gə'lækteɪz, -eɪs). *Biochem.* [f. GALACT(O- + -ASE.] A proteolytic enzyme present in the milk of many animals.

1898 *Proc. Amer. Assoc.* XLVII. 232 The authors [*sc.* S. M. Babcock and H. L. Russell].. discovered an inherent proteolytic ferment in milk, to which they have given the name galactase. **1901** C. A. MITCHELL tr. *Oppenheimer's Ferments* x. 118 Galactase.. is stated to work best in weakly alkaline media, and to resemble trypsin, though not to be identical with it. **1937** A. L. & K. G. B. WINTON *Struct. Foods* III. I. 185 The part played by enzymes in the ripening of cheese is complex. Some of these are derived from the milk or starter, others are formed by micro-organisms. Galactase.. belongs to the former class.

galactic (gə'læktɪk), *a.* [ad. Gr. γαλακτικός, f. γαλακτ-, γάλα, milk. Cf. F. *galactique*.]

1. Of or pertaining to milk. = LACTIC.

1844 HOBLYN *Dict. Med.*, *Galactic acid*, *Lactic acid*, the acid of milk. **1854** in MAYNE; and in mod. Dicts.

2. *Astron.* Of or pertaining to the Galaxy or Milky Way; of or pertaining to another galaxy or to galaxies in general; ***galactic belt***, the Milky Way; ***galactic circle*** (see quot. 1893); ***galactic concentration***, the increase in the number of stars from the galactic poles to the galactic equator; ***galactic co-ordinates***, spherical co-ordinates used in astronomy, comprising galactic latitude and longitude; ***galactic equator***, a great circle passing as nearly as possible through the middle of the Milky Way; ***galactic latitude***, latitude measured from the galactic equator; ***galactic longitude***, longitude measured from some reference point on the galactic equator, usu. defined either by the direction of the centre of the galaxy or by the intersection of the galactic and the celestial equators; ***galactic plane***, the plane defined by the galactic equator; ***galactic poles***: the two opposite points of the heavens, situated at 90° from the galactic circle; ***galactic system***, the galaxy containing the sun and most of the visible stars; ***galactic zone*** = *galactic belt*.

1839 BAILEY *Festus* xix. (1848) 224 Her brow [grew] Brighter with thought, as with galactic light Mid heaven when clearest. **1849** J. F. W. HERSCHEL *Outl. Astron.* xv. 534 The following table, expressing the densities of the stars at the respective distances, 1, 2, 3, &c., from the galactic plane. *Ibid.* 535 The law of the visible distribution of stars over the southern galactic hemisphere, or that half of the celestial surface which has the south galactic pole for its center. **1849** *Ibid.* (ed. 10) § 793 The density of star-light.. is least in the pole of the Galactic circle. **1856** *Chamb. Jrnl.* V. 397 The phalanx of star-hosts made galactic or milky by distance. **1878** S. NEWCOMB *Pop. Astron.* IV. 417 Telescopic stars.. are least numerous in the regions most distant from the galactic belt. **1888** C. A. YOUNG *Text-bk. Gen. Astron.* xxi. 510 The 'galactic plane' 'is to sidereal what the ecliptic is to planetary astronomy, a plane of ultimate reference, the ground plan of the sidereal system'. **1890** A. M. CLERKE *Syst. Stars* xxiii. 355 The bright spaces of the galactic zone are commonly surrounded and set off by dark winding channels. *Ibid.* 359 A regular progression of density from the galactic poles to the galactic equator. *Ibid.*, Two or three hundred 'beginning, or gathering clusters', might be pointed out in the galactic system. **1893** GORE *Astron. Gloss.*, *Galactic Circle*, a term applied to the mean or centre line of the Galaxy, or Milky Way zone. **1906** *Rep. Brit. Assoc.* 1905 260 Mean values were computed for different galactic latitudes by combining the results of regions at equal distances from the Milky Way. **1914** A. S. EDDINGTON *Stellar Movements* viii. 165 The stars with proper motions greater than 10″ per century show no galactic concentration; they are all comparatively near to us. *Ibid.* ix. 196 A systematic dependence on galactic longitude in some of the zones. **1926** *Encycl. Brit.* I. 252/1 In plan the system is elongated with its axis in galactic longitude 325°. **1930** R. H. BAKER *Astron.* xi. 442 The galactic equator is the great circle halfway between the galactic poles. **1931** W. M. SMART *Text-bk. Spherical Astron.* xi. 276 The galactic co-ordinates of *S*. **1936** E. HUBBLE *Realm Nebulæ* vi. 125 The galactic system is a member of a typical, small group of nebulæ which is isolated in the general field. **1965** J. B. SYKES tr. *Ogorodnikov's Dynamics Stellar Syst.* i. 25 The choice of any particular coordinate system is a matter of convenience. In stellar astronomy the most frequently used is that of galactic coordinates, defined by the galactic equator and the galactic poles. **1971** *Nature* 18 June 437/1 Results from sounding rocket experiments.. have revealed the existence of cosmic X-ray sources at high galactic latitude.

galactin (gə'læktɪn). [f. Gr. γαλακτ-, γάλα, milk + -IN.] **a.** (See quots. 1838–48.) **b.** 'The coagulating principle of milk' (Mayne *Expos. Lex.* 1854). **c.** (See quot. 1864.) **d.** = LACTIN (*Syd. Soc. Lex.* 1885).

1838 T. THOMSON *Chem. Org. Bodies* 449 When the milk of the cow-tree is evaporated.. and the dry residue digested in alcohol, a substance is dissolved, which.. constitutes galactin. **1848** CRAIG, *Galactin*, a vegetable substance, obtained from the sap of the *Galactodendron utile*, or Cow-tree of South America, and used as a substitute for cream. **1864** WATTS *Dict. Chem.*, *Galactin*, a gelatin-yielding substance said by Morin to exist in milk.

†**galactite.** *Obs.* [ad. L. *galactītēs*, a. Gr. γαλακτίτης, f. γαλακτ-, γάλα, milk.]

1. A precious stone of a white colour.

1591 PERCIVALL *Sp. Dict.*, *Lechera piedra*, a precious stone called Galactite. **1606** SYLVESTER *Du Bartas* II. iv. II. *Trophies* 51 Base morter serveth to unite Red, white, gray, marble, jasper, galactite. **1656** in BLOUNT *Glossogr.*

2. *Min.* An obsolete name for natrolite.

1832 C. U. SHEPARD *Min.* 244 Galaktite. **1864** WATTS *Dict. Chem.*, *Galactite*, a calcareous variety of natrolite, found at Kilpatrick and Bishoptown in Scotland.

galacto- (gəlæktəʊ), before a vowel *galact-*, combining form of Gr. γάλα, γαλακτ-, milk, occurring in various scientific compounds. **ga'lactagogue** *a.* [Gr. -αγωγός leading], inducing a flow of milk; also *sb.* anything that does this. **ga'lactocele** [ad. mod.L. *galactocēlē*: CELE *sb.*] (see quot.). **ga,lacto-ge'netic** *a.* [cf. GENETIC], adapted to produce milk; also *sb.* anything that does this. **galac'tometer** [Gr.

μέτρον measure] = LACTOMETER. **galac'tophagist** [f. Gr. γαλακτοφάγ-ος milk-fed + -IST], one who feeds or lives chiefly on milk; so **galac'tophagous** *a.* [cf. F. *galactophage*], feeding on milk. **ga'lactophore**, a galactophorous duct. **galac'tophorous** *a.* [f. Gr. γαλακτοφόρ-ος milk-bringing + -OUS; cf. F. *galactophore*], conveying milk; ***galactophorous ducts*** (see quot. 1819). **ga,lactopo'etic, -poi'etic** *a.* [Gr. ποιητικ-ός, f. ποιέ-ειν to make], that tends to produce milk; also *sb.* anything that does this. **ga,lactopoi'esis** [Gr. ποίησις production], the production of milk (see also quot. 1961). †**ga'lactopote** [ad. Gr. γαλακτοπότης], a drinker of milk; hence **galacto'potic** *a.* **galacto'rrhœa**, also badly *galactirrhœa* [Gr. ῥοία a flowing], an excessive flow of milk.

1854 MAYNE *Expos. Lex.*, *Galactagogus*, causing the flow of milk..*galactagogue. **1875** H. C. WOOD *Therap.* (1879) 456 A good deal has been written in regard to the use of the leaves of the castor-oil plant as a galactagogue. **1876** BARTHOLOW *Mat. Med.* (1879) 470 It is questionable whether castor-oil leaves have a special galactagogue property. **1854** MAYNE *Expos. Lex.*, *Galactocēle* [Lat.], a *galactocele. **1878** T. BRYANT *Pract. Surg.* (1879) II. 257 Galactocele is a milk tumour found in the breast during lactation. **1661** LOVELL *Hist. Anim. & Min.* 412 Aliments of good and much juyce, and easy concoction, *galactogeneticks. **1842** FRANCIS *Dict. Arts*, *Galactometer, an instrument for ascertaining the specific gravity of milk. **1730–6** BAILEY (folio), **Galactophagist*, a Milk-eater, a Milk-sop. **1853** SOYER *Pantroph.* 168 The Getes and Scythians were galactophagists, or drinkers of milk. **1885** *Syd. Soc. Lex.*, **Galactophagous*, milk eating. **1904** G. S. HALL *Adolescence* I. vi. 420 Both the *galactophores or glands and the supportive areolar tissue develop rapidly. **1961** *Lancet* 29 July 241/2 Saline solutions of the human pituitary fractions were injected, via the teat galactophore openings. **1730–6** BAILEY (folio), **Galactophorous*, carrying or conveying Milk. **1819** *Pantologia*, **Galactophorous ducts*, the excretory ducts of the glands of the breasts of women, which terminate in the papilla or nipple. **1842** DUNGLISON *Dict. Med. Sci.* (ed. 3) 319/1 **Galactopoiesis*, galactosis. **1948** *New Biol.* IV. 127 A distinction has..been drawn between lactogenesis—the power of initiating milk secretion—and galactopoiesis—the power of maintaining the flow of milk once it has been started. **1961** KON & COWIE *Milk* I. iv. 164 The term 'galactopoiesis', i.e., the enhancement of an established milk secretion, is used by some research workers in the more general sense of the maintenance of milk secretion. **1661** LOVELL *Hist. Anim. & Min.* 412 Debility of the *galacto-poietick faculty. **1684** tr. *Bonet's Merc. Compit.* XI. 371 Henbane, and such Narcoticks..extinguish the galacto-poietick faculty in the Breasts. **1864** WEBSTER, *Galactopoietic*, a substance which facilitates the production, or increases the flow of milk. **1626** MINSHEU *Ductor* (ed. 2) **Galactopote*, a drinker of milke. **1727** BAILEY vol. II, *Galactopote*, a Milk Drinker. **1623** COCKERAM II, One that still drinkes milke, *Galactopoticke*. **1848** CRAIG, **Galactirrhœa*. **1852** JAS. MILLER *Surgery* xxvi. (ed. 2) 321 *Galactirrhœa*. **1875** H. C. WOOD *Therap.* (1879) 550 Another employment of ergot for the purpose of restraining excessive secretion is in *galactorrhœa.

galactoid (gəˈlæktɔɪd), *a.* [f. Gr. γαλακτ-, γάλα, milk + -OID.] Milk-like, resembling milk.

1885 in *Syd. Soc. Lex.*

galactonic (gælæk'tɒnɪk), *a.* *Chem.* [tr. G. *galactonsäure* galactonic acid (H. Kiliani 1885, in *Ber. d. Deut. Chem. Ges.* XVIII. 1551), f. GALACT(OSE + -ONIC.] ***galactonic acid***: a monobasic sugar acid, $CH_2OH(CHOH)_4COOH$.

1885 *Jrnl. Chem. Soc.* XLVIII. 967 *Galactonic acid*, $C_6H_{12}O_7$, is best prepared by the action of bromine on an aqueous solution of lactose. **1956** *Biochem. Jrnl.* LXIV. 21/2 The enzymic reduction of derivatives of D-galacturonic acid to derivatives of L-galactonic acid has been demonstrated in peas. **1957** *Jrnl. Biol. Chem.* CCXXVII. 748 An initial oxidation of galactose to galactonic acid is followed by a conversion of galactonic acid..to yield pyruvic acid.

galactosæmia (gə,læktəʊˈsiːmɪə). *Med.* Also **galactosemia**. [f. GALACTOS(E + Gr. αἷμα blood: see -IA¹.] **a.** The presence of galactose in the blood. **b.** A metabolic disorder (of which galactose in the blood is a symptom) resulting from a hereditary inability to metabolize galactose.

1934 *Biol. Abstr.* VIII. 1431/1 [There is a] need in clinical studies of galactosemias and galactosurias, of regulating the proportions of glucose and galactose. **1945** BRUCK & RAPOPORT in *Amer. Jrnl. Dis. Child.* LXX. 267 (*heading*) Galactosemia in an Infant with Cataracts. *Ibid.* 272/1 The ability of the liver to convert and to store galactose seems to be impaired but not completely lost in galactosemia. **1958** *Observer* 5 Jan. 9/1 She has a condition called 'congenital galactosaemia', which is an inherited inability to break down another sugar found in milk, known as galactose. **1970** R. M. GOODMAN *Genetic Disorders Man* xvii. 872/2 The presence of galactose in the blood or urine is not a reliable indication of galactosemia.

galactosamine (,gælæk'təʊsəmiːn). *Chem.* [ad. G. *galaktosamin* (Schulz & Ditthorn 1900, in *Zeitschr. Phys. Chem.* XXIX. 373), f. GALACTOSE + AMINE.] Any amino derivative of galactose; *spec.* 2-amino-2-deoxy-D-galactose (chondrosamine), $C_6H_{13}NO_5$.

1900 *Jrnl. Chem. Soc.* LXXVIII. I. 478 (*heading*) Galactosamine, a new amino-sugar. **1956** *Nature* 28 Jan. 186/2 A substance reacting as a hexosamine but which is not glucosamine or galactosamine has been found. **1969** *New Scientist* 23 Jan. 187/2 Mucopolysaccharide contains two amino sugars in large amounts, glucosamine and galactosamine.

galactose (gəˈlæktəʊs). [f. Gr. γαλακτ-, γάλα, milk + -OSE². Cf. DEXTROSE.] (See quots.)

1869 ROSCOE *Elem. Chem.* 396 Dilute acids convert lactose into a peculiar glucose, called galactose. **1878** KINGZETT *Anim. Chem.* 404 Milk sugar is also first converted into galactose before it ferments.

galactoside (gəˈlæktəsaɪd). *Chem.* [a. F. *galactoside* (M. Berthelot *Chim. org. fondée sur la Synthèse* (1860) II. III. iii. 286), f. GALACTOSE + -IDE.] Any glycoside in which the sugar is galactose. Hence **ga,lacto'sidase**, any enzyme that hydrolyses a galactoside to galactose and an aglycone; **galacto'sidic** *a.*, of, pertaining to, or characterized by a galactoside.

1862 H. WATTS tr. *Gmelin's Hand-bk. Chem.* XV. 317 He [*sc.* Berthelot] then subdivides the saccharides into—glucosides..; levulosides..; galactosides. **1902** *Jrnl. Chem. Soc.* LXXXII. I. 263 *Tetra-acetyl-β-phenolgalactoside*, $C_{20}H_{24}O_{10}$, crystallises from dilute alcohol or from benzene in stout prisms... This galactoside is not hydrolysed by yeast extract. **1917** *Chem. Abstr.* XI. 2819 (*heading*) Detection of β-galactosidase in the vegetable kingdom. **1950** *Jrnl. Bacteriol.* LX. 390 Several of the problems of the enzyme chemistry of galactosidase..require the use of preparations more highly purified than can be readily accomplished with bacterial enzymes. **1952** *Biol. Abstr.* 2533/2 The formation of beta-galactosidase (I) by *E. coli* is induced exclusively by substances possessing an intact galactosidic radical. **1956** *Nature* 10 Mar. 478/2 Only enzymes capable of splitting α-glucoside and α-galactoside linkages were required to be present.

galacturonic (gə,læktjuːˈrɒnɪk), *a.* *Chem.* [ad. G. *galacturonsäure* galacturonic acid (F. Ehrlich 1917, in *Chemiker-Zeitung* 7 Mar. 197/2), f. GALACT(OSE + URONIC *a.*] ***galacturonic acid***: the uronic acid derived from galactose.

1917 *Chem. Abstr.* XI. 2583 E[hrlich] isolated from the decompn. products of pectin *d*-galacturonic acid, a new isomer of glucuronic acid of the animal kingdom, and the *d*-form of E. Fischer's racemic aldehyde mucic acid. **1930** *Jrnl. Biol. Chem.* LXXXVI. 491 Flax pectin..is made up of 61 per cent of galacturonic acid, and the pectic acid from orange peelings..is composed of 73.7 per cent of galacturonic acid. **1957** *Sci. News* XLV. 82 Hexuronic acids such as glucuronic acid and galacturonic acid with the molecular formula $C_6H_{10}O_7$.

galage, obs. form of GALOSH.

galago (gəˈleɪgəʊ). [a. mod.L. *galago*.] A genus of *Lemuridæ*, of nocturnal habits, found in Madagascar and parts of Africa.

1848 in CRAIG. **1861** *Proc. R. Soc.* No. 45. 376 Description of the Brain of a Galago. **1884** *American* VIII. 218 True monkeys are scarce, but galagos and certain other lemurids are common.

galah (gəˈlɑː). [native Australian *galah*.] **1.** Australian name for the Rose-breasted Cockatoo (*Cacatua roseicapilla*).

1890 LYTH *Golden South* xiv. 127 The galahs, with their delicate gray and rose-pink plumage, are the prettiest parrots. **1896** *Westm. Gaz.* 6 Oct. 2/1 The galahs, the rose-breasted parrots, would scream at him.

2. *Austral. slang.* A fool, simpleton.

1944 L. GLASSOP *We were Rats* xxv. 142 When will these galahs wake up? **1949** *Geogr. Mag.* Feb. 374 A foolish person is often called a *galah*, after the name of the garrulous bird. **1960** *Encounter* XIV. 28 Don't be a galah, Art and I are old drinking cobbers. **1965** E. BROWN *Big Man* vii. 56, I have to report for special duty because of this Pommie galah. **1971** *Guardian* 9 Sept. 9/5 He has visited the mineral belt and met the..larrikins, galahs and dills who gravitate to such a scene.

Galahad ('gæləhæd). [The name of the noblest knight of the Round Table in Arthurian legend.] A man having the qualities of the legendary Sir Galahad; one characterized by nobility, integrity, courteousness, etc. Also *attrib.*

1870 C. M. YONGE *Caged Lion* xv. 263 A Galahad would he strive to be. **1911** G. B. SHAW *Getting Married* Pref. 145 Our bachelors and widowers would no longer be Galahads. **1921** D. H. LAWRENCE *Sea & Sardinia* 76 We have set forth, politically, on such a high and Galahad quest of holy liberty. **1967** 'E. TREVOR' *Freebooters* xxi. 223 He'd thought he was just a tin Galahad trying to share Sgt Proctor's martyrdom by yapping about it.

galai, obs. form of GALLEY.

galainy, var. GALEENY.

Galalith ('gæləlɪθ). Also written with lower-case initial letter. [Gr. γάλα milk + λίθος stone.] A proprietary name for a product resembling celluloid made from the casein of milk with the addition of other substances, used as a substitute for horn, celluloid, ivory, etc.

1901 *Trade Marks Jrnl.* 20 Mar. 296 Galalith. Goods, included in Class 50.., made of Celluloid-like Material consisting of an Animal Substance (viz., Dried Curds) Hardened by means of Formaldehyde. Vereinigte Gummiwaaren-Fabriken Harburg-Wien..in the United Kingdom, c/o Haseltine, Lake, & Co.,..London. **1922** *Daily Mail* 13 Nov. 1 A number of curved galalith handles, in all white or antique colour. **1934** [see CONSTRUCTIVIST *a.* and *sb.*]. **1963** G. S. BRADY *Materials Handbk.* (ed. 9) 148 The first commercial casein plastic was called *Galalith*, meaning *milkstone*.

Galam butter. [f. *Galam*, a formerly French district on the Senegal.] (See quots.)

1855 OGILVIE, Supp., *Galane* [sic] *butter*, a solid oil or fat obtained from a plant of the genus Bassia, the *B. butyracea*. **1857** HENFREY *Bot.* 354 Another species [of *Bassia*] in Africa is said to yield the Shea or Galam butter mentioned by travellers. **1873** HOOKER *Gen. Syst. Bot.* 536 From the seeds of *Bassia butyracea*, in India, and of *B. Parkii*, in Senegal a fixed oil is expressed (Galam Butter), which quickly curdles, and is much used as food.

galamelle, var. CANAMELL, *Obs.*

†**ga'lancie.** *Obs.* [f. F. *galant* GALLANT: see -CY.] Delicacy, nicety.

1581 MULCASTER *Positions* xxxviii. (1887) 171 This is a point of such galancie, if my purpose were to praise them.

galand, -ine, obs. ff. GALLANT, GALANTINE.

galaney, var. GALEENY.

galanga (gəˈlæŋgə). Also 5 **galonga**, 5–7 GALINGA. [a. med.L. *galanga, galenga, galinga*: see GALINGALE.] = GALINGALE.

[**1309–10** *Durh. MS. Cell. Rolls*, j li. de Galanga.] *c* **1485** *Digby Myst.* (1882) III. 339 Dya, galonga, ambra, and also margaretton. **1538** TURNER *Libellus*, Galanga, Galangale, *Cyperus Babylonicus*. **1605** TIMME *Quersit.* III. 172 Take of the root of zedoary..of goatesbeard, galanga..of each three ounces. **1838** *Penny Cycl.* XI. 35/1 *Galanga*, or *Galangal*, is usually supposed to have been introduced by the Arabs, but it was previously mentioned by Ætius.

galangal(e: see GALINGALE.

†**galange.** *Obs.* [a. OF. *galange* (Cotgr.) galingale.] = GALINGALE.

1599 HAKLUYT *Voy.* II. I. 277 Galange, from China, Chaul, Goa, & Cochin.

galangin (gəˈlæŋgɪn, gəˈlændʒɪn). *Chem.* [a. G. *galangin* (E. Jahns 1881, in *Ber. d. Deut. Chem. Ges.* XIV. 2385), f. GALANG(A + -IN¹.] A derivative of flavone, 3,5,7-tri-hydroxyflavone, present in a species of galingale (*Alpinia officinarum*).

1882 *Jrnl. Chem. Soc.* XLII. 209 Galangin is deposited from a solution in absolute alcohol in six-sided plates. **1918** PERKIN & EVEREST *Nat. Organic Colouring Matters* vii. 177 Galangin, $C_{15}H_{10}O_5$, the second constituent of galanga root, crystallizes in yellowish-white needles, melting-point 214–215°, soluble in alkaline solutions with a yellow colour. **1961** *Encycl. Brit.* II. 27/1 Among the better known of the anthoxanthins..may be mentioned..galangin.

‖**galant** (galɑ̃, gəˈlɑːnt), *a.* and *sb.* *Mus.* [a. Fr. and G. *galant* (see GALLANT *a.* and *sb.*).]

A. *adj.* Designating or pertaining to a light and elegant style of eighteenth-century music, esp. that of harpsichord composers, contrasted with baroque music. **B.** *sb.* This style of music.

1949 *Scrutiny* XVI. 76 A coherently consistent style like classical baroque or Mozartian *galant*. **1953** *Times Lit. Suppl.* 20 Feb., The reinstatement of medieval, Baroque, or 'galant' conditions. **1959** D. COOKE *Lang. Mus.* v. 232 To their ears, nurtured on the normal 'tasteful' classical style of the *galant* and *rococo* periods, Mozart's exploitation of the expressive power of music..appeared to be wild and perverse experiments.

galant, obs. form of GALLANT.

†**galanta gaye**, *adv. Obs.*$^{-1}$ [app. a. Fr. phrase *galant et gai*.] Gallantly.

1558 PHAËR *Æneid.* v. M ivb, They went with garnisht heads, and bare theyr gifts galanta gaye.

‖**galanterie** (galɑ̃t(ə)ri). [Fr., see GALLANTRY.] †**1.** = GALLANTRY 2 a. *Obs.*

1616 T. ROE *Jrnl.* 1 Nov. (1899) II. 320, 10,000 horse, many in Cloth of Gould.., all in Galanterie.

2. *Mus.* (See quot. 1938). (Also with Ger. pl. **galanterien**.)

1911 *Encycl. Brit.* XXVI. 52/1 Then come the *galanteries*, from one to three in number. **1938** *Oxf. Compan. Music* 351/2 In the classical suite of the earlier eighteenth century the Galanterien are those movements which are not essential to the scheme and may perhaps be looked upon as interpolations of light relief.

3. Courtesy, politeness, esp. to women.

1920 D. H. LAWRENCE *Lost Girl* vii. 133 He had an amiable and truly chivalrous *galanterie*. **1959** *Times* 3 June 7/3 Eighteenth-century *galanterie*.

galantine ('gæləntɪn, -iːn). Forms: 4–6 **gala(u)ntyne**, 5–7 **galentine, -yn(e**, (5 **galyntyne**, 6 **galandyne, galendine**), 7–9 **gallantine**, (7 **galiantine**), 8– **galantine**. [a. F. *galantine*, altered from *galatine* a sauce for fish, being connected in popular etym. with the adj. *galant* (see GALLANT *a.*) in the sense of agreeable.]

†**1.** A kind of sauce for fish and fowl. *Obs.*

a **1400** CHAUCER *To Rosemounde* 17 Nas never pyk walwed in galauntyne As I in love am walwed and y-wounde. *c* **1420** *Liber Cocorum* (1862) 25 Take lampreyes..Serve with galentine, made in sale, With gyngere, canel and galingale. *a* **1440** *Sir Degrev.* 1399 Sche brouȝt fram the kychene.. Hasteletus in galantyne. **1513** *Bk. Keruynge* in *Babees Bk.* 281 Fresshe lampraye bake..with a spone take out galentyne, & lay it vpon the brede. **1598** FLORIO, *Prognata*,

..venison sauce or galandine for swans. **1658** SIR T. MAYERNE *Archimag. Anglo-Gall.* ix. 5 When it is baked make a galentine of Claret-wine and Cinnamond and sugar, and poure it on the Pye.

†**2.** A dish made of sopped bread and spices.

1530 PALSGR. 602/2 Laye some breed in soke, for I wyll have some galantyne made.

3. A dish of veal, chickens, or other white meat, freed from bones, tied up, boiled, and served cold with the jelly.

1725 BRADLEY *Fam. Dict.* s.v. *Sausages,* To make a galantine with the royal sausages. **1730–6** BAILEY (folio), *Galantine* [in Cookery], a particular way of dressing a Pig. **1849** THACKERAY *Pendennis* xlv, Soups, grapes, pâtés, galantines. **1870** *Pall Mall G.* 25 Nov. 12 He insists upon entertaining him hospitably with galantine, mayonnaise, and Marsala.

galanty show (gəˈlæntɪˌʃəʊ). Also 9 **gal(l)antee, -tée, -té, -ti, gallanty.** [perh. a. It. *galanti*, pl. of *galante*: see GALLANT.]

Where the word is really colloquially current the stress seems to be always *ga'lanty*, though our first quot. has *'gallantee*, which appears in some recent Dicts.

A shadow pantomime produced by throwing shadows of miniature figures on a wall or screen.

1821 T. HOOK in *John Bull* 22 Apr., Oh yes, I have been, ma'am, to visit the Queen, ma'am, With the rest of the gallantee-show. *a* **1845** HOOD *9th Nov.* v, The show is merely a gallanty-show, Without a lamp or any candle in. **1846** MRS. GORE *Eng. Char.* (1852) 147 If you send to order the dancing-dogs or galanté-show to amuse your nursery. **1861** MAYHEW *Lond. Labour* III. 73 'The galantee show don't answer, because magic lanterns are so cheap in the shops.' **1883** *Daily Tel.* 5 Sept. 5/1 Some enterprising theatrical manager regales them with a nocturnal gallanty show.

Hence **galanty showman.**

1843 *P. Parley's Ann.* IV. 366 They were received by 'artificial cock-crowing', by the galanti showman. **1852** D. JERROLD *Wks* (1864) II. 394 'Gentlemen', said the gallantee-showman, 'I hate suspicion'.

galany, var. GALEENY.

galapectite (ˌgæləˈpɛktaɪt). *Min.* [f. Gr. γάλα milk + πηκτ-ός congealed (f. πηγνύναι to fix) + -ITE. Named by Breithaupt in 1832] A milk-white variety of halloysite.

1837 *Amer. Jrnl. Sc.* XXXI. 269 Galapectite, from Silesia.

‖**gala'pee.** A West Indian tree, *Sciadophyllum Brownei.*

1756 P. BROWNE *Jamaica* 189 The Galapee or Angelica tree. This tree grows at the foot of the red hills near the Angels. **1889** in *Century Dict.*

galary(e, obs. forms of GALLERY.

galashoe, galatch, obs. forms of GALOSH.

galatea (gælәˈtiːә). [From H.M.S. *Galatea*, the vessel commanded by the Duke of Edinburgh in 1867; the material was used for children's 'sailor suits'.] (See quot. 1882.)

1882 CAULFEILD & SAWARD *Dict. Needlework., Galatea,* a cotton material striped in blue on a white ground. It is made for women's dresses, and washes well. **1894** *Athenæum* 17 Nov. 669/1 During the Revolutionary and Napoleonic war our seamen wore trousers of striped stuff resembling 'galatea'.

Galatian (gəˈleɪʃ(ɪ)ən), *sb.* and *a.* [f. *Galatia* + -AN.] **A.** *sb.* **a.** A native or inhabitant of Galatia, an ancient country of central Asia Minor. **b.** *pl.* St. Paul's Epistle to the Galatians. **B.** *adj.* Of or pertaining to Galatia or its people.

1587 J. PRIME *Exposition upon St. Paul to Galathians* 15 The Galathians were deeply plunged in the sea, the fault was most in the mariners. **1611** BIBLE *Galat.* iii. 1, O foolish Galatians [1388 Wyclif: Galathies; 1526 Tindale: Galathyans], who hath bewitched you? **1842** BROWNING *Bells & Pomegranates* III. 6/2 There's a great text in Galatians, Once you trip on it, entails Twenty-nine distinct damnations. **1853** J. BROWN *Exposition Epistle of Paul to Galatians* v. ii. 208 Some of the Galatian converts had yielded to the Judaising teachers. **1879** *Encycl. Brit.* X. 19/2 Unless the churches of Derbe, Lystra, &c., be regarded as Galatian, we are left in ignorance of the names..of the churches addressed. *Ibid.* 20/1 The Galatians..continued to make use of their ancient dialect. **1912** C. W. EMMET *St. Paul's Epistle to Galatians* p. xxi, Romans was in fact originally written as a circular letter addressed to mixed Churches..at the same time as Galatians. **1950** R. HEARD *Introd. N.T.* xviii. 182 Who were the Galatians? This is one of the classical controversies of New Testament criticism. Two answers are possible. The first..is that they were the inhabitants of North Galatia... The second answer, more generally accepted by recent critics, is that the 'Galatians' were not Galatians by race..but Christians of those towns in the southern part of the Roman province of Galatia which Paul and Barnabas had visited on their first missionary journey. **1957** *Oxf. Dict. Chr. Ch.* 535/1 St. Paul wrote this letter to his Galatian converts.

galaunt(e, obs. form of GALLANT.

galavant, var. GALLIVANT.

galawis, obs. form of GALLOWS *sb.*

galax (ˈgælæks). *Bot.* [mod.L. (Linnæus *Species Plantarum* (1753) I. 200); cf. Gr. γαλαξίας GALAXY.] An evergreen plant of the genus so called of the family Diapensiaceæ, native to the south-eastern United States, and having white flowers and shiny leaves.

1804 *Bot. Mag.* XX. 754 (*heading*) Galax Aphylla. Carolina Galax... Michaux found it on the high mountains of Carolina, flowering in May. **1894** W. FALCONER in W. Robinson *Wild Garden* (ed. 4) viii. 84 The sombre-hued Pyrola and Galax. **1898** B. TORREY in *Atlantic Monthly* Apr. 458/2, I could only conjecture the plant to be galax. **1922** M. B. HOUSTON *Witch Man* xi, The darkly polished galax leaves. **1959** C. DORMON *Flowers Native to Deep South* 88 Everyone has seen the shining, stiff leaves of Galax in florists' wreaths and bouquets.

galaxy (ˈgæləksɪ), *sb.* Forms: α. 4–7 (from med.L.) **galaxias,** 6–7 **galaxia;** β. 4, 7 **gal(l)axie, -ye,** 8– **galaxy.** [ad. OF. and F. *galaxie*, ad. L. *galaxias* (med. Lat. also *galaxia*), Gr. γαλαξίας, f. γαλακτ-, γάλα milk.]

1. a. A luminous band or track, encircling the heavens irregularly, and known to consist of innumerable stars, perceptible only by means of the telescope; the Milky Way.

α. **1398** TREVISA *Barth. De P.R.* VIII. viii. (1495) 305 Galaxias is a cercle of heuen more fayr and bryghte than other cercles. **1569** J. SANFORD tr. *Agrippa's Van. Artes* 43 b, The Astrologers be yet ignorant what Galaxias is, that is to saie, the Milkie circle. **1583** T. WATSON *Centurie of Loue* xxxi. Annot. Poems (Arb.) 67 Galaxia..is a white way or milky Circle in the heauens. **1613** HEYWOOD *Silver Age* II. Wks. 1874 III. 98 Let Iuno..With her quicke feet the galaxia weare. **1625** USSHER *Answ. Jesuit* 333 Pointing to the Galaxias or milky circle. *a* **1680** CHARNOCK *Attrib. God* (1834) II. 6 That combination of weaker stars, which they call the Galaxia.

β. *c* **1384** CHAUCER *H. Fame* II. 428 See yonder, lo, the Galaxyë Which men clepeth the Milky Wey, For hit is whyt. **1651** CLEVELAND *Poems* 1 A brown, for which, Heaven would disband The Gallaxye, and stars be tann'd. **1714** DERHAM *Astro-Theol.* Prel. Disc. p. xlvi, The Galaxy being well known to be the fertile place of New Stars. **1805** WORDSW. *Vaudracour & Julia* 97 Meanwhile the galaxy displayed Her fires. **1854** MOSELEY *Astron.* xci. (ed. 4) 234 The Galaxy, or Milky-way, passes through the heavens like an irregular zone. **1878** STEWART & TAIT *Unseen Univ.* ii §84 The life of whole systems, perhaps even of whole galaxies, would thus disappear.

b. Any of the numerous large groups of stars and other matter that exist in space as independent systems; *spec.* (often with capital initial) the group that contains the solar system and whose plane of maximum star density gives rise to the observed Milky Way.

1848 J. P. NICHOL *Stellar Universe* iii. 59 Superb groups or galaxies separated from each other by gulfs so awful, that they surpass the distances which divide star from star... Amid this system of clusters, floats the galaxy whose glories more nearly surround us. **1888** C. A. YOUNG *Gen. Astron.* xxi. 503 The belief that these star-clusters are *stellar universes,*—'galaxies', like the group of stars to which the writers supposed the sun to belong. **1930** R. H. BAKER *Astron.* xii. 480 The existence of galaxies beyond the Milky Way was finally demonstrated by Hubble in 1925. **1966** F. HOYLE *Galaxies, Nuclei & Quasars* i. 1 The best known galaxy is naturally the one we live in... In total mass and in size it seems to be much like the nearest of the large external galaxies, the nebula in Andromeda. **1968** D. S. EVANS *Observation Mod. Astron.* vii. 228 The spiral character of the Galaxy cannot be so marked as that in some external galaxies.

2. *transf.* and *fig.*; now chiefly applied to a brilliant assemblage or crowd of beautiful women or distinguished persons.

1590 GREENE *Never too late* Wks. (Rtldg.) 298 The milk-white galaxia of her brow. *a* **1631** DONNE *Poems* (1650) 51 Upon this Primrose hill, Where..Their form and their infinitie Make a terrestriall Galaxie. **1640** BP. HALL *Rem. Wks.* (1660) 45 Others [stars] small, and scarce visible in the Galaxy of the Church. **1649** G. DANIEL *Trinarch., Rich. II,* clxxxiii, My verse had trod The Galaxie of fame, to Crowne his merit. **1704** STEELE *Lying Lover* Prol., Where such bright Galaxies of Beauty sit. **1762** GOLDSM. *Cit. W.* lxiii, The brightness of a single genius seemed lost in a galaxy of contiguous glory. **1802** WELLINGTON in Gurw. *Desp.* I. 376 The Hon. Mount-Stuart Elphinstone, Mr. Wilks, and Major Munro..were also constellations in that galaxy. **1820** SCOTT *Monast.* xvi, The smiles of those beauties, who form a galaxy around the throne of England. **1838–9** HALLAM *Hist. Lit.* III. vii. III. §19. 361 The heiress of this family became the central star of so bright a galaxy. **1842** ORDERSON *Creol.* xix. 228 His countenance was a galaxy of joy. **1862** SALA *Seven Sons* I. vii. 164 A waiter was present solemnly lighting a galaxy of wax-candles. **1887** FRITH *Autobiog.* III. xxviii. 407 A galaxy of ability that is truly remarkable.

3. *U.S.* ***brandy-galaxy***, ? brandy and milk.

1845 *P. Parley's Ann.* VI. 176 Will was especially fond of mint julip, and brandy galaxy.

4. *attrib.*

1867–77 G. F. CHAMBERS *Astron.* VI. iv. 536 A splendid galaxy cluster. **1884** *Century Mag.* XXVII. 916 If the Kantian galaxy-theory were true.

†**galaxy** (ˈgæləksɪ), *v.* *Obs.*⁻¹ [f. prec. sb.] *trans.* To gather like a galaxy *into* (something).

1702 C. MATHER *Magn. Chr.* III. IV. i. (1852) 585 Let all their vertues then be galaxied into this one indistinct lustre.

†**galay**, *v.* *Obs.*⁻¹ [Of unknown origin. Hart's ed. has *stakker.*] *intr.* To reel; to stagger.

1375 BARBOUR *Bruce* II. 422 And to philip sic rout he raucht, That thocht he wes off mekill maucht, He gert him galay disyly.

galay, galays, obs. ff. GALLEY, GALLOWS *sb.*

†**'galbanated,** *ppl. a.* *Obs. rare*⁻¹. [f. mod.L. **galbanāt-us* (f. GALBANUM) + -ED¹.] Treated with an infusion of galbanum.

1693 SALMON *Bates' Dispens.* (1699) 188/1 This Galbanated Tincture..is a most admirable Opener.

†**galbane.** *Obs.* Also 1, 4 **galban.** [Anglicized form of GALBANUM.] = GALBANUM 1.

c **1000** *Sax. Leechd.* II. 174 Læcedom..alwan wiþ untrymnessum & galbanes wiþ nearwum breostum. **1388** WYCLIF *Exod.* xxx. 34 The Lord seide to Moises, Take to thee swete smellynge spyceries..galban of good odour, and pureste encense. *c* **1420** *Pallad. on Husb.* I. 905 Eek brymstoon and galbane oute chasith gnattis. **1555** EDEN *Decades* 250 They are these folowynge..Ammoniac, Galbane.

†**gal'banean,** *a.* *Obs.*⁻¹ [f. L. *galbane-us* (f. *galbanum*) + -AN.] Of or pertaining to galbanum.

1697 DRYDEN *Virg. Georg.* IV. 383 This when thou seest, Galbanean Odours use, And Honey in the sickly Hive infuse.

galbanum (ˈgælbənəm). [a. L. *galbanum* = Gr. χαλβανή; prob. repr. an Oriental word etymologically identical with Heb. *ḥelbᵉnāh* (? f. root *ḥālab* to be fat), which the LXX. and Vulg. render by these words.]

1. A gum resin obtained from certain Persian species of *Ferula*, esp. from *F. galbaniflua* and *F. rubricaulis.*

1382 WYCLIF *Exod.* xxx. 34 Stacten, and onycha, galbanum [*printed* galbantum] of good smel, and essence most liȝtynge. **1398** TREVISA *Barth. De P.R.* XVII. lxxvii. (1495) 651 Galbanus is an herbe and the juys therof hyghte Galbanum. *c* **1450** *M.E. Med. Bk.* (Heinrich) 82 Take..I quarter of gomme galbanum. *c* **1575** *Perf. Bk. Kepinge Sparhawkes* (Harting 1886) 31 To drawe ought any swellinge take a lytle galbanum. **1691** J. WILSON *Belphegor* v. ii, I'll have ye burnt in effigy, with brimstone, galbanum, aristolochia, hypericon, and rue. **1789** W. BUCHAN *Dom. Med.* (1790) 689 Gum ammoniac and galbanum, strained, of each half a pound. **1851–9** HOOKER in *Man. Sci. Enq.* 424 Galbanum is said to be imported into Russia in large quantities by way of Astrachan. **1855** SINGLETON *Virgil* I. 171 With the fume of galbanum To chase the fell chelydri.

2. *fig.* after French usage: Empty protestations or representations, bosh, humbug.

1764 CHESTERF. *Lett.* (1792) IV. 210 Give them a good deal of Galbanum in the first part of your letter. **1838** HALIBURTON *Clockm.* Ser. II. xii, How his weak eye would have sarved him a' utterin' of this galbanum, wouldn't it?

3. *attrib.* and *Comb.*, as ***galbanum-pill***; ***galbanum-yielding*** adj.

1803 *Med. Jrnl.* X. 50 Two compound galbanum pills were given every four hours. **1876** HARLEY *Mat. Med.* (ed. 6) 599 Galbanum-yielding Plants grow plentifully on the slopes of the Mountain ranges of Northern Persia.

†**galbart.** *Obs. Sc.* Also 6 **galbarte, ga(u)bart.** [? shortened from GABERDINE.] = GABERDINE.

1488 in *Ld. Treas. Acc. Scotl.* (1877) I. 135 Item..for thre elne of Fransche browne to be a galbart to the King vjli. ? *a* **1500** *Rowlis Cursing* 233 [No tailor could make] Ane gabart for a deill compleit. **1521** *Burgh Recds. Stirling* 4 Oct. (1887) 13 Item, ane gaubart of russat, xxs. **1530** LYNDESAY *Test. Papyngo* 1094 First, to the Howlet..I laif my gaye galbarte of grene.

galbe (gælb). Also **galb.** [Fr. (cf. GARB *sb.*² 1 b).] A contour, outline or profile (see quots.).

1899 *Cent. Dict., Galbe,*..in *art,* the general outline or form of any rounded object, as a head or vase; especially, in architecture, the curved form of a column, a Doric capital, or other similar feature. **1909** J. R. WARE *Passing Eng.* 138/2 *Galbe* (Thieves'), profile of a violent character, and even applied to any eccentricity of shape above the knees. **1926** R. FRY *Transformations* 71 Look..at the neck of the jar..the clear salience of the lip which is exactly enough..to give a perfect close to the curves of the galb that leads up to it. **1936** H. READ *Meaning of Art* (ed. 2) II. 101 On pottery..it is found in the *galbe* or outline which the pot makes.

Galbraithian (gælˈbreɪθɪən), *a.* and *sb.* [f. the name of J. K. *Galbraith* (born 1908), U.S. economist and diplomat + -IAN.]

A. *adj.* Of, pertaining to, or characteristic of J. K. Galbraith and his writings. **B.** *sb.* One who favours or is influenced by the writings of J. K. Galbraith.

1960 *Guardian* 15 June 2/4 The familiar Galbraithian indictment of 'private opulence and public squalor'. **1961** *Times Lit. Suppl.* 27 Jan. 51/2 The contemporary (Galbraithian or 'affluent') conception of the welfare state. **1966** *Economist* 23 Apr. 374/2 He is a Galbraithian in his belief that wealth..is outrunning welfare, social justice and the means of a good life.

galbulus (ˈgælbjʊləs). *Bot.* [a. L. *galbulus* the fruit of the cypress.] (See quots.)

1706 in PHILLIPS (ed. Kersey). **1844** HOBLYN *Dict. Med., Galbulus,* a kind of cone, differing from the strobile only in being round, and having the heads of the carpels much enlarged. The fruit of the Juniper is a galbulus. **1872** OLIVER *Elem. Bot.* II. 245 These scales become woody and peltate, constituting a modification of the cone, called a galbulus. **1880** GRAY *Struct. Bot.* vii. §2. 303 A cone when spherical, and of thickened scales with narrow base, as that of Cypresses, has been termed a Galbulus.

†**gald,** *v.* *Obs.* Also 6 **galde, gawld,** 7 **gauld.** [var. of GALL *v.* developed from the pa. pple.] = GALL *v.*

1555 EDEN *Decades* 358 Sum of theym are so galded that they are..made lame. **1576** TURBERV. *Venerie* 31 The keepers of houndes hauing a heauy hande in rubbing and trimming them, might galde of the skinne. *a* **1577** GASCOIGNE *Flowers* Wks. (1587) 83 As I gaze thus galded all with griefe. **1598** GRENEWEY *Tacitus' Ann.* XII. viii. 165 The one galding them with darts and Iauelins, and the others marching thicke and close togither. **1633** T. JAMES *Voy.* 23 Our Cable galded off..we lost our Anker.

Hence †**gald** *sb.*, †**galding** *vbl. sb.*, = GALL *sb.*[2]

1611 BOYS *Wks.* (1629) 512 They like busie flies are buzzing alwayes on the sores and gaulds of the church. **1684** *Lond. Gaz.* No. 1950/4 A bay Gelding thick grown, without any White except Galdings.

†'**galder.** *Obs.* [OE. *galdor, gealdor* (= ON. *galdr*), f. *galan* to sing.] A charm, or incantation.

Beowulf (Z.) 3052 Iu-monna gold galdre bewunden. *c* **1000** *Sax. Leechd.* II. 352 þas galdor mon mæg singan on wunde. *c* **1205** LAY. 19257 Heo bigolen þat child mid galdere swiðe stronge.

gale (geɪl), *sb.*[1] Forms: 1-3 **gaᵹel, gaȝel,** 4 **gayl,** 5-7 **gaul(e,** (5 **gawl, gawyl, gayle,** 6 **golle**), 6-9 **gall(e,** 5- **gale.** [OE. *gaᵹel, gaᵹol* str. ? masc. (also *gaᵹelle, -olle* wk. fem.) = MDu. *gaghel*, Du. and mod.G. *gagel*, and perh. ON. **gagl* in *gaglviðr*, which may denote this plant (f. **gagl* gale + *við-r* wood), though this is very doubtful. The phonology of the mod. form is somewhat obscure.] The bog-myrtle, *Myrica Gale* (the mod.L. specific name is adopted from Eng.); also called ***sweet gale.***

c **1000** *Sax. Leechd.* III. 6 Nim þre leaf gaᵹeles. *c* **1265** *Voc.* in Wr.-Wülcker 559/22 *Mirtus*, gaȝel. *a* **1387** *Sinon. Barthol.* (Anecd. Oxon.) 22 Gayl, *mirta. a* **1400-50** *Alexander* 4094 Full of gladen & of gale & of grete redis. *c* **1440** *Promp. Parv.* 189/1 Gawl..*mirtus.* **1483** *Cath. Angl.* 147/2 Gayle..*mirtus.* **1538** LELAND *Itin.* I. 40 The fenny part of Axholm berith much Galle, a low frutex, swete in burning. **1568** TURNER *Herbal* III. 47 Called..in Cambridge shyre Gall, in Summerset shyre Goul or Golle. **1751** J. BARTRAM *Observ. Trav. Pennsylv.*, etc. 36 On the banks I found the gale like the European. **1807** CRABBE *Birth Flattery* 310 Gale from the bog shall yield Arabian balm. **1842** TENNYSON *Edwin Morris* 110, I..heard with beating heart The Sweet-Gale rustle round the shelving keel. **1877** *N.W. Linc. Gloss.*, *Gale*, the fragrant bog-myrtle, often called 'sweet-gale'.

b. *attrib.* and *Comb.*, as ***gale-bush, -plant, -sheaves***; **gale-beer**, a drink made from twigs of sweet-gale; **gale-worts**, a book name for plants of the N.O. *Myricaceæ* (Lindley *Veg. K.* 1846, p. 256).

1597 GERARDE *Herbal* III. lxviii. 1228 This Gaule groweth plentifully..in the Ile of Elie, and in the Fennie countries thereabouts, whereof there is such store..that they make fagots of it and sheaues, which they cal Gaule sheaues, to burne and heate their ouens. **1805** FORSYTH *Beauties Scotl.* II. 258 The hazel, the dwarf willow, the gall plant. **1863** *N. & Q.* Ser. III. IV. 311 'Gale beer', brewed from a plant growing on the moor above Ampleforth, in Yorkshire, is made and sold by Mrs. Sigsworth of the 'Black Horse'. **1887** W. RYE *Norfolk Broads* 50 The myrtle-like leaved sweet gale bushes. **1893** K. SIMPSON *Jeanie o' Biggersdale* 111 She baked, she washed, she brewed gale-beer.

†**gale**, *sb.*[2] *Obs.* Also 3 **gal.** [Two words are perh. represented here: (1) ME. *gal* (f. *galen*, OE. *galan* to sing) = MHG. *gal*; (2) OF. *gale* gaiety = It. *gala*: see GALA.]

1. Singing, a song; merriment, mirth.

c **1200** *Trin. Coll. Hom.* 197 þat hie ne muge heren here remenge ne here gal. *c* **1275** *Luue Ron* 126 in *O.E. Misc.* 97 þar-inne is vich balewes bote, blisse, and Ioye, and gleo, and Gal. **13..** *K. Alis.* 2548 The nyghtyngale In wode, makith miry gale. *a* **1310** in Wright *Lyric P.* v. 26 He is faucoun in friht dernest in dale, Ant with everuch a gome gladest in gale. *c* **1315** SHOREHAM 107 þorȝ his oȝene gale.

b. said of the voice of an animal.

1460 *Lybeaus Disc.* (ed. Kaluza) 1059 Hornes herde þey blowe And houndes grete of gale.

2. Speech, talk.

13.. *K. Alis.* 2047 Listenith now, and letith gale, For now ariseth a noble tale. **13..** *Coer de L.* 3546 On knees we tolde hym our tale, But us ne gaynyd no gale. *c* **1380** *Sir Ferumb.* 1889 So grym a was in Gale.

gale (geɪl), *sb.*[3] Also 6-7 **gaile, gayle,** (? 7 **gall**). [Of obscure origin.

Possibly elliptical for *gale* (or *gall*) *wind* (see quot. 1619 in 3) where *gale* may have been originally an adj. Some scholars suppose that the word is in some way connected with Da. *gal*, Norw. *galen* (neut. *galet*), mad, furious, bad (often said of weather), ON. *galenn*, mad, frantic (? lit. enchanted, bewitched), pa. pple. of *gala*, to sing. The spelling and rimes in the earliest quot., however, seem to disprove this.]

1. a. A wind of considerable strength; in nautical language, the word chiefly 'implies what on shore is called a storm' (Adm Smyth), esp. in the phrases ***strong, hard gale*** (a ***stiff gale*** is less violent, a ***fresh gale*** still less so); in popular literary use, 'a wind not tempestuous, but stronger than a breeze' (J.). Also ***gale of wind.*** In restricted use, applied to a wind having a velocity within certain limits (see quots.). ***equinoctial gale*** (see EQUINOCTIAL 2 b).

a **1547** SURREY *Proem. to 73rd Psalm*, I..constrayned am to beare my sayles ful loo, And never could attayne some pleasaunt gaile [*rimes* saile, assaile, availe, faile]. **1558** PHAER *Æneid* v. 900 Frend Palynure, lo how the tydes them selues conueies the fleete, This gale by measure blowes. **1596** SHAKS. *Tam. Shr.* I. ii. 48 What happie gale Blowes you to Padua heere, from old Verona. **1600** HAKLUYT *Voy.* III. 424 At noone we had a fresh gale in the poupe. **1626** CAPT. SMITH *Accid. Yng. Seamen* 17 A calme, a brese, a fresh gaile, a pleasant gayle, a stiffe gayle. **1698** FROGER *Voy.* 38 We set sail again..with a favourable Gale of Wind. *a* **1700** DRYDEN *Ovid's Met.* xi. 668 At the Close Of Day a stiffer Gale at East arose. **1727** SWIFT *Gulliver* II. v, The ladies gave me a gale with their fans. **1772** J. ROBERTSON *Navig.* VI. 354 *note*, A common brisk gale is about 15 miles an hour. **1774** M. MACKENZIE *Maritime Surv.* 99 Hard Gales of Wind in any Place, especially if it blows in the Direction of the Flood, swells the Tide to an uncommon Height. **1801** [see STORM *sb.* 1 b]. **1808** *Med. Jrnl.* XIX. 470 We had some smart gales of wind. **1846** McCULLOCH *Acc. Brit. Empire* (1854) I. 261 High gales are generally from the west. **1859** REEVE *Brittany* 137 There was little promise of the gale abating. **1884** PAE *Eustace* 195 The wind still blew a stiff gale. **1899** *Westm. Gaz.* 24 Jan. 4/3 A gale is not a gale until it has reached Force 7 on the Beaufort scale, though many people lightly class all heavy winds as gales. **1923** N. SHAW *Forecasting Weather* (ed. 2) 456 As a result of the investigation of 1905 we now classify winds with velocity above 75 miles per hour as hurricane winds, those with velocity between 64 and 75 miles per hour as storm winds, and those between 39 and 63 as gales. **1963** *Meteorol. Gloss.* (*Met. Office*) 109 *Gale*, a wind of a speed between 34 and 40 knots (force 8 on the Beaufort scale of wind force, where it was originally described as 'fresh gale'), at a free exposure 10 metres (33 feet) above ground. *Ibid.*, Statistics of gales refer to the attainment of mean speeds of 34 knots or over.

b. *Poet.* and in rhetorical language often used for: A gentle breeze.

1728-46 THOMSON *Spring* 872 Can fierce passions vex his breast, While every gale is peace, and every grove Is melody? **1742** COLLINS *Eclogues* I. 15 Wanton gales along the valleys play. **1791** MRS. RADCLIFFE *Rom. Forest* v, The fresh gale came scented with the breath of flowers. *a* **1839** PRAED *Poems* (1864) I. 201 The breath of vernal gales. **1871** R. ELLIS *Catullus* lxiv. 282 The warm west-wind, in gales of foison alighting.

c. regarded as the vehicle of odours.

1711 ADDISON *Spect.* No. 56 ¶3 He felt a Gale of Perfumes breathing upon him. **1749** JOHNSON *Van. Hum. Wishes* 46 The tainted gales. **1797** *Monthly Mag.* III. 92 A new project of nutrition, by inhaling the gales of baker's, cheesemonger's, and cook's shops. **1808** J. BARLOW *Columb.* I. 132 And gales etherial breathe a glad perfume. *c* **1820** S. ROGERS *Italy* II. (1828) 11 An underwood of myrtle, that by fits Sent up a gale of fragrance.

d. *transf.* and *fig.* †***with a full gale***: ? without any interruption.

1623 MASSINGER *Dk. Milan* I. iii, One gale of your sweet breath will easily Disperse these clouds. **1647** CLARENDON *Hist. Reb.* II. §55 The Scots..brought all their mischievous Devices to pass, with ease, and a prosperous Gale in all they went about. **1663** H. POWER *Experim. Philos.* 39 It is far more ingenious to believe it to be a gale of Animal Spirits, that, moving from her head along her back to her tail..is the cause of her [the snail's] progressive motion. **1669** MARVELL *Corr.* cxvi. Wks. 1872-5 II. 276 Unless we should finde.. some unexpected gaile of opportunity that would be sure waft us quite over. **1675** PHILLIPS *Theatr. Poet.* 162 That which is chiefly pleasant in these Poems [Herrick's], is now and then a pretty Floury and Pastoral gale of Fancy. **1731** SWIFT *Corr.* Wks. 1841 II. 646 Passions..are the gales of life; let us not complain that they do not blow a storm. *a* **1734** NORTH *Lives* III. 98 On the fifth night he slept with a full gale till morning, without any waking at all. *c* **1800** K. WHITE *Lett.* Wks. (1837) 323 Contending gales of doubt and apprehension. **1827** POLLOK *Course T.* 111, Her sails.. nicely set, to catch the gale Of praise. **1842** TENNYSON *Vis. Sin* ii. 12 The music..Rose again from where it seem'd to fail, Storm'd in orbs of song, a growing gale.

2. *fig.* A state of excitement or hilarity. *U.S.*

18.. BROOKE *Eastford* (Bartlett), The ladies, laughing heartily, were fast going into what, in New England, is sometimes called a gale. **1885** HOWELLS *Silas Lapham* (1891) I. 238 When she gets into one of her gales there ain't any standing up against her. **1894** *Cassell's Mag.* Apr. 362/2 Going off into a gale of merriment at the recollection.

3. *attrib.* and *Comb.*: ***gale force, -warning; gale-bent, -lashed*** adjs.; also †**gale-wind**, a stormy wind, gale.

In quot. 1619 *gale, gall* may conceivably represent Sc. *gell* 'intense, keen, brisk' (Jam.).

1883 *Harper's Mag.* Jan. 209/2 The dwarf oaks grow scraggy and *gale-bent atop. **1902** *Daily Chron.* 4 Mar. 5/2 Southerly winds were blowing in all parts of the British Isles yesterday, reaching *gale force on the west coast of Ireland. **1967** C. B. CHRISTESEN in *Coast to Coast 1965-6* 32 The impact of gale-force winds was such that at first we thought the ship had struck a rock. **1896** *Westm. Gaz.* 19 June 3/1 Ushant and its neighbouring isles..rising from amidst the *gale-lashed waves. **1918** *Meteorol. Gloss.* (*Met. Office*) 128 *gale-warning. Notice of threatening atmospherical disturbances on or near the coasts of the British Islands are issued by telegraph from the Meteorological Office to a number of ports and fishery-stations. **1940** C. DAY LEWIS tr. *Georgics of Virgil* I. 26 Another gale-warning often is given by shooting stars. **1969** C. R. BURGESS *Suppl. Meteorol. for Seamen* 2 These forecasts include Gale warnings, General weather synopsis and expected changes within the next 24 hours. **1619** Z. BOYD *Last Battell* (1629) 544 This world is like a working sea, wherein sinne like a *gall winde or strong tyde carrieth many tribulations..from Countrie to Countrie. *Ibid.* 1256 Our life like smoke or chaffe is carried away as with a gale winde.

gale (geɪl), *sb.*[4] [? contracted from GAVEL.]

1. A periodical payment of rent, the amount paid periodically. ***hanging-gale***: the rent due at the previous gale-day; arrears of rent.

1672 PETTY *Pol. Anat. Irel.* (1691) 75, 300 M. would pay one half years Gale of all the land. **1809-12** MAR. EDGEWORTH *Absentee* Wks. 1832 IX. 196 The balance due of the hanging-gale. **1828** *Blackw. Mag.* XXIV. 224 A receipt for the last gale of the rent reserved in the lease under which they claim to vote. **1862** H. COULTER *West Irel.* 214 There is no such thing known in Erris as a hanging gale. **1882** *Standard* Aug. 2/4 The effect of sweeping away the hanging gale would be that the landlord would be unable to collect the rent due in May, 1882. **1888** *Times* (weekly ed.) 16 Nov. 20/4 They all paid a deposit of £1, and one lodged a gale's rent less 40 per cent.

b. A rent-audit.

1881 *Leeds Mercury* 4 Jan. 6 The half-yearly gales or audits are held on the second and third weeks of May and December.

2. An instalment (of money). *rare* exc. *local U.S.*

1845 LD. CAMPBELL *Chancellors* (1857) V. civ. 31 Calculating when another gale of salary would become due. **1854** *N. & Q.* 1st Ser. IX. 408/2 The word Gale is used in the West of Philadelphia in the sense of an instalment.

†**3.** A lordship or toll (on fish). *Obs. rare*[−1].

c **1640** J. SMYTH *Hundred of Berkeley* (1885) 321 The fisher-man sets the price of such his fish. The Lord chooseth whether hee will take the fish and pay halfe that price to the fisherman; or refuse the fish and require halfe the price.. The price or moity taken is called the Gale.

4. In the Forest of Dean: The royalty paid by a 'free-miner' for a plot of land, with the right to dig for coal, iron, or stone; a licence or grant of land for this purpose; the area of land granted.

1775 in Nicholls *Forest Dean* (1858) 285 Untill you have satisfied and paid me his Majesty's gale and dues for working and getting coal in such pits for two years last past. **1832** in *5th Rept. Dean Forest Comm.* (1835) 70 If we open gales in different parts of the Forest, we must pay the gale for each. **1838** *Act 1 & 2 Vict.* c. 43. §29 Such gales..so forfeited shall be subject to be again galed or leased. **1880** J. WILLIAMS *Rights of Common* 177 Gales or licences for making stone quarries in inclosed land. **1884** *Law Times* 31 May 78/2 In 1846 M. was in possession of two gales in the Forest of Dean.

5. *attrib.*, as (sense 1) ***gale-day***; (sense 4) ***gale-book, -fee.***

1832 in *5th Rept. Dean Forest Comm.* (1835) 70, I went to the galer, and had it transferred in the gale-book. Quarries have been sold to foreigners, but their names cannot be put in the gale-book. *Ibid.* 71 A gale-fee of 2s. for every 20 yards. **1862** H. COULTER *West Irel.* 215 A few days after the Gale day another bailiff..distrained for the Rent which had been paid. **1880** J. WILLIAMS *Rights of Common* 177 To exact gale-fees or rents in respect thereof [stone-quarries].

†**gale**, *v.*[1] *Obs.* Also 6-7 *Sc.* **gail(l.** [OE. *galan* str. vb. (pa. t. *gól*, pa. pple. *galen*) = OHG. *galan*, ON. *gala*; cognate with GALE *sb.*[2], *-gale* (singer) in NIGHTINGALE; another grade of the root appears in YELL. The strong inflexion appears not to have survived beyond OE.]

1. *intr.* and *trans.* To sing; also, to deliver an oracular response.

Beowulf 786 þara þe of wealle wop ȝehyrdon, gryreleoð galan godes andsacan. *a* **1000** *Boeth. Metr.* vii. 3 Se Wisdom. glio-wordum gol gyd. *a* **1400-50** *Alexander* 798* Right as my graceux gode hase galet me before. *Ibid.* 2257 þan gales þaire god a-gayn & þus spekis. *c* **1480** *Crt. of Love* 1356 '*Domine labia*' gan he crye and gale.

2. *intr.* Of a dog: To bark, yelp. Of a bird, esp. the cuckoo: To utter its peculiar note.

c **1205** LAY. 20858 Hunten þar talieð, hundes þer galieð. ? *a* **1400** *Morte Arth.* 927 Thare galede þe gowke one grevez fulle lowde. *c* **1440** *Promp. Parv.* 185/1 Galyn, as crowys, or rokys, *crocito.* **1530** LYNDESAY *Test. Papyngo* 96 Gaill lyke ane goik, and greit quhen scho wes wa. *c* **1560** A. SCOTT *Of May* 26 In May begynnis the golk to gaill.

3. *transf.* To make an outcry, exclaim against something.

c **1386** CHAUCER *Friar's T.* 1336 Now telleth forth, thogh that the Somnour gale. **1412-20** LYDG. *Chron. Troy* IV. xi, Though men on it galen aye and crye. *c* **1440** *York Myst.* xxxiii. 23 þat gome þat gyrnes or gales, I myself sall hym hurte full sore.

gale (geɪl), *v.*[2] *Naut.* [f. GALE *sb.*[3]] *intr.* To sail *away* as if before a gale. Now *rare.*

1692 *Smith's Seaman's Gram.* xvi. 78 In faire weather when there is but little Wind that Ship which hath most Wind and sails fastest is said, to gale away from the other. **1739** *Encour. Sea-f. People* 39 It being little Wind, and they galing away out of his Reach, he left pursuing them. **1867** SMYTH *Sailor's Word-bk.*, *To gale away*, to go free.

gale (geɪl), *v.*[3] [f. GALE *sb.*[4]] *trans.* To grant or take the gale of (i.e. the right of working) a mine, etc.

1832 in *5th Rept. Dean Forest Comm.* (1835) 70, I consider myself entitled to have a coal-pit galed to me, because I am born of free parents within the hundred. *Ibid.* 71, I have not galed any new works of late years. **1839** *Heref. Gloss.* s.v., In the Forest of Dean, to gale (*i.e.* to gavel) a mine is to acquire the right to work a mine from the officer called a gaveller, and to pay the share of the crown. **1890** *Gloucester Gloss.* s.v., Formerly stone quarries were galed, but they are now leased.

gale, obs. form of GALL *sb.*[1], GALLEY, GOAL.

galea ('geɪlɪə). [a. L. *galea* helmet.]

1. Applied in *Bot.*, *Zool.*, etc. to various structures resembling a helmet in shape, function, or position; e.g. the upper part of a labiate flower; the membrane covering the jaws of the Orthoptera and some other insects; a horny cap on the head of a bird; and the like.

1834 McMURTRIE *Curvier's Anim. Kingd.* 394 The maxillae are always terminated by a dentated and horny piece covered with a galea. **1836** *Penny Cycl.* V. 252/3 *Galea*, the upper lip of a labiate flower. **1877** HUXLEY *Anat. Inv. Anim.* vii. 402 Two processes terminate the stipes; of these the anterior and outer, the galea, is soft, rounded, and possibly sensory in function. **1880** [see GALEATE]. **1881** BENTHAM in *Jrnl. Linn. Soc.* XVIII. cx. 344 The petals are connivent in a galea over the column.

2. *Med.* **a.** 'A pain in the Head so call'd because it takes in the whole Head like a helmet' (Phillips 1706). **b.** 'A term for a bandage for the head, somewhat like the form of a helmet' (Mayne *Expos. Lex.* 1854).

†**galeable,** *a. Obs.*⁻¹ [f. GALE *sb.*⁴ + -ABLE.] Liable to a gale, i.e. a toll or lordship.

c **1640** J. SMYTH *Hundred of Berkeley* (1885) 321 Theis fore-said sorts only are called Galeable fishes or the gale fishinge.

ˈ**galeage.** Also **galiage.** [f. GALE *sb.*⁴ or *v.*³ + -AGE.] Royalty paid for a grant of land in the Forest of Dean: see GALE *sb.*⁴ 4.

1881 RAYMOND *Mining Gloss., Galiage,* royalty. **1890** *Gloucester Gloss.* s.v., Many gales both of iron and stone now fall in to the Crown, through the failure to pay the ground-rent or galeage.

galeas(s(e, obs. forms of GALLIASS.

galeate (ˈgælɪeɪt), *a. Nat. Hist.* [ad. L. *galeātus,* f. *galea* helmet.] = GALEATED 1 and 2.

a. 1706 PHILLIPS (ed. Kersey), *Cucullate Flowers* are such as resemble the Figure of a Helmet, or Monk's Hood; being otherwise termed Galeate and Galericulate Flowers. **1826** KIRBY & SP. *Entomol.* (1843) III. 26 The upper lobe somewhat resembles the galeate maxilla just named; but consists of two joints. **1861** BENTLEY *Bot.* 227 In the Monkshood, the superior sepal is prolonged upwards into a sort of hood or helmet-shaped process, in which case it is said to be hooded, helmet-shaped, or galeate. **1880** GRAY *Struct. Bot.* vi. §5. 247 Galeate is a term applied to a corolla the upper petal or part of which is arched into the shape of a casque or helmet, called the Galea: as in Aconite and Lamium.

galeated (ˈgælɪeɪtɪd), *ppl. a.* [f. as prec. + -ED¹.]

1. Shaped like a helmet.

1686 *Phil. Trans.* XVI. 286 The Flowers are Monopetalous, labiated for the most part or galeated. **1750** G. HUGHES *Barbadoes* 155 The flowers are of the galeated, monopetalous kind. **1859** R. F. BURTON *Centr. Afr.* in *Jrnl. Geog. Soc.* XXIX. 222 Patches and beauty-spots in the most eccentric shapes—buttons, crescents, and galeated lines.

2. *Zool.* Covered as with a helmet; furnished with a galea.

1728 WOODWARD *Fossils, Lett.* i. 10 An Echinites, and form'd in the shell of the galeated *Echinus Spatagus.* **1749** *Phil. Trans.* XLVI. 146, I have seen some Specimens of the common pileated and galeated Echinites.

3. Furnished with a helmet; wearing a helmet.

1760 SWINTON in *Phil. Trans.* LI. 855 The drapery likewise of the galeated figure..is something different. **1879** H. PHILLIPS *Notes Coins* 9 The galeated head of Minerva.

b. *fig.* ***galeated preface***: a rendering of L. *prologus galeatus,* the name given to Jerome's preface to his Latin version of Samuel and Kings.

1772 NUGENT tr. *Hist. Fr. Gerund* Pref. 9 A galeated preface would be too latinized a term for a work not professedly divine.

galeaze, galeche, obs. ff. CALASH, GALLIASS.

galee (geɪˈliː). [f. GALE *v.*³ + -EE.] One to whom a gale (GALE *sb.*⁴ 4) has been granted; the tenant of a gale.

1884 *Law Times* 19 July 211/2 There is no fixity of tenure in the gales so as to enable the galees to raise the necessary funds. **1888** *Ibid.* LXXXV. 150/2 The possession of such property conferred upon the galee a licence to work the mine.

galee, obs. form of GALLEY.

galeeny (gəˈliːnɪ). Also 8 **galina,** 9 **galan(e)y, -ainy, -eny, -iny, gallini.** [a. Sp. *gallina morisca* (Minsheu 1623) lit. 'Moorish hen', or its equivalent in Pg. or It.] A guinea fowl.

1796 STEDMAN *Surinam* II. xxv. 234 They had also here the tame galinas, or Guinea-hens, called tokay. **1801** JANE AUSTEN *Lett.* (1884) I. 263 Bantam cocks and Galinies. **1812** J. H. VAUX *Flash Dict., Galaney,* a fowl. **1869** BLACKMORE *Lorna D.* vi, 'Men is desaving, and so is galanies'. **1887** MRS. M. L. WOODS *Village Trag.* ii, 'Girls..as don't know a hen's egg from a galeeny's'. **1887** *S. Chesh. Gloss., Galainy,* a guinea fowl. **1888** *Berksh. Gloss., Gallini,* the Guinea fowl.

galega (gəˈliːgə). [mod.L.; of uncertain origin.] A genus of the N.O. *Leguminosæ,* Goat's rue.

1685 BOYLE *Salub. Air* 89 The juice of Goat's-rue, or as others call it Galega. **1882** *Garden* 12 Aug. 131/3 The Galegas..are just now grand border plants.

†**galegale.** *Obs.*⁻¹ [A ludicrous perversion of *nightingale,* f. *galen* GALE *v.*¹] A noisy fellow; a 'sing-song'.

a **1250** *Owl & Night.* 257 Thu hattest niȝtingale, Thu miȝtest bet hoten galegale, Vor thu havest to monie tale.

galege, galei, obs. ff. GALOSH, GALLEY.

Galego, var. GALLEGO.

galeid (ˈgeɪlɪɪd). [ad. mod.L. *Galeidæ,* f. *Galeus* = Gr. γαλεός, name of the typical genus.] A shark of the family *Galeidæ* (*Cent. Dict.*).

Hence **gaˈleidan** [see -AN] = GALEID.

1868 SIR J. RICHARDSON, etc. *Museum Nat. Hist.* II. 164 Order XII Galeods or Sharks..Family V.—Galeidans (*Galeidæ*).

galeie, obs. form of GALLEY.

Galen (ˈgeɪlən). Also 4-6 **Galien.** [ad. L. *Galēnus* (in med.L. also *Galienus*), Gr. Γαληνός.]

A celebrated physician of the 2nd century A.D., born at Pergamus in Asia Minor. Hence, jocularly: A physician.

[*c* **1369** CHAUCER *Bk. Duchesse* 572 Ne hele me may phisicien, Noght Ypocras ne Galien.] **1598** SHAKS. *Merry W.* II. iii. 29 What saies my Esculapius? my Galien? my heart of Elder? **1607** [see EMPIRICUTIC]. **1652** ASHMOLE *Theat. Chem.* Annot. 460 Every Galen hath his Plague. **1714** PEARCE *Spect.* No. 572 ¶2 Though Impudence and many Words are as necessary to these Itinerary Galens as a laced Hat or a Merry Andrew. **1833** M. SCOTT *Tom Cringle* xiv, Then followed the two Galens, and little Reefpoint. **1893** FARMER *Slang, Galen,* an apothecary.

Hence **Gaˈlenian** *a.* [see -IAN] = GALENIC *a.*¹, GALENICAL *a.*¹ ˈ**Galenism** [see -ISM], the medical principles or system of Galen. Also in combining form, as in † **Gaˈleno-chemist,** ? one who employs both Galenic and chemical remedies.

1665 G. THOMSON *Galeno-pale* iv. 19 They..of a sudden will all become Chymists; but Galeno-Chymists. **1727-51** CHAMBERS *Cycl.* s.v. *Galenic,* Paracelsus..exploded Galenism, and the whole Peripatetick doctrine. **1800** *Med. Jrnl.* III. 256 The doctrine of their functions still savoured of the old Galenian Theory. **1869** O. W. HOLMES *Med. Ess.* vi. (1883) 318 When we say 'cool as a cucumber', we are talking Galenism. **1896** F. RYLAND *Logic* 102 The fourth figure is still sometimes called the Galenian figure.

galena (gəˈliːnə). *Min.* Also 7-9 **galæna.** [a. L. *galēna,* a name applied by Pliny to lead at a certain stage in the process of smelting; commonly, but perh. erroneously, identified with Gr. γαλήνη a calm.] Native lead sulphide; the common lead ore. ***false*** or ***pseudo galena*** = BLACK JACK 2. Also called *lead-glance.*

[**1601** HOLLAND *Pliny* II. 517 The third part of the vein which remaineth behind in the furnace, it is Galæna, that is to say, the very mettal it selfe of lead.] **1671** J. WEBSTER *Metallogr.* xiii. 201 *Galena,* or the hardest of Lead ore. **1753** CHAMBERS *Cycl. Supp., Galena,* a name given by mineralists to a species of poor lead ore. **1796** KIRWAN *Elem. Min.* (ed. 2) II. 218 Lead in Galena is in its metallic state. **1812** BRACKENRIDGE *Views Louisiana* (1814) 148 The ore is what is called potter's ore, or galena, and has a broad shining grain. **1879** ATCHERLEY *Boërland* 186 Parkins showed me a reef of galena on his farm.

attrib. **1806** *Gazetteer Scotl.* 552 A specimen of galena lead ore was found in a small stream which runs into the Quair. **1872** R. B. SMYTH *Mining Statist.* 91 Traces of silver have been found by the lessees of a galena lease at Murindal Creek. **1872** RAYMOND *Statist. Mines & Mining* 24 The greater number of the veins located near the center of the district are so-called 'galena ledges'.

Galenic (gəˈlɛnɪk), *a.*¹ [f. GALEN + -IC.] Of or pertaining to Galen, to his followers, to his principles and practice; *esp.* pertaining to vegetable preparations, as distinguished from chemical remedies. Also playfully used for: Medical. ***Galenic figure***: in *Logic* (see GALENICAL *a.*¹).

1668 MAYNWARING *Compl. Phys.* 64 Galenick Physitians are of two sorts: the Rigid Galenist, and the Galeno-Chymist. **1707** FLOYER *Physic. Pulse-Watch* I Concerning the old Galenic Doctrine about the Pulses. **1710** SALMON (*title*), English Herbal, or the History of plants, names, species, descriptions..galenick and chymick virtues and uses. **1711** ADDISON *Spect.* No. 124 ¶2 The ordinary Writers of Morality prescribe to their Readers after the Galenick way; their Medicines are made up in large Quantities. An Essay-Writer must practise in the Chymical Method, and give the Virtue of a full Draught in a few Drops. **1771** *Muse in Miniat.* 50 Debar'd O Sun! thy great galenic skill, Earth shuts her pores, and Nature's pulse stands still. *a* **1856** SIR W. HAMILTON *Logic* (1860) I. 401 The first notice of this Galenic Figure is by the Spanish Arabian, Averroes. **1869** O. W. HOLMES *Med. Ess.* vi. (1883) 339 Remedies..both Galenic and chemical: that is, vegetable and mineral.

galenic (gəˈlɛnɪk), *a.*² [f. GALENA + -IC.] Pertaining to or containing galena.

1828 in WEBSTER; and in later Dicts.

Galenical (gəˈlɛnɪkəl), *a.*¹ and *sb.* Also 7 **-all, Gallenical.** [f. GALENIC *a.*¹ + -AL¹.] **A.** *adj.* = GALENIC *a.*¹ ***Galenical figure***: in *Logic* (see quot. 1774).

1652 ASHMOLE *Theat. Chem.* Annot. 461 Albeit I magnifie Chemicall Phisique, yet I do not lessen the due commendations that belong to Galenicall. **1671** GLANVILL *Disc. M. Stubbe* 12 Galenical Physicians. **1712** tr. *Pomet's Hist. Drugs* I. 133 They are much us'd in Physick among several galenical Compositions. **1741** WATTS *Improv. Mind* I. xvii. Wks. VIII. 125 Whether chemical or galenical preparations. **1741** CHAMBERS *Cycl.* s.v. *Figure,* It is called the fourth..and by others, the galenical Figure. **1768** W. DONALDSON *Sir Barth. Sapskull* I. 214 My face was disguised by a galenical mask. **1774** REID *Aristotle's Logics* iii. §2 It [the fourth figure of syllogism] was added by the famous Galen, and is often called the Galenical. **1854** MAYNE *Expos. Lex., Galenical medicine,* the medical principles taught by Galen, which consisted in an almost entire reliance on simples. **1880** *Daily Tel.* 20 Sept., Galenical Laboratory. [Wanted] In the above department of a wholesale druggist, a young man who thoroughly understands the manufacture of tinctures and galenical preparations on a large scale.

B. *sb.* A remedy such as Galen prescribed, a vegetable medicine, a simple.

1768 W. DONALDSON *Sir Barth. Sapskull* II. 139 He was occasionally supplied with chymicals and galenicals. **1840** BARHAM *Ingol. Leg.* Ser. I. *Leech Folkestone,* He swallowed, at the least, two pounds of chemicals and galenicals. **1884** *Times* 14 Aug. 3 Suggestions had recently been made for standardizing some of our galenicals.

Hence **Gaˈlenically** *adv.,* with galenical or vegetable remedies.

1681 SALMON (*title*), Compendium of Physick..showing the Signs and Judgments of curing all Diseases perform'd Astrologically, Gallenically, and Chemically. **1694** *Lond. Gaz.* No. 3020/4 The Cure of all sorts of Fevers; Galenically and Chymically performed.

galenical (gəˈlɛnɪkəl), *a.*² [f. GALENIC *a.*² + -AL¹.] = GALENIC *a.*²

1828 in WEBSTER; and in later Dicts.

galeˈniferous, *a.* [f. GALENA + -(I)FEROUS.] Containing or producing galena.

In recent Dicts.

Galenism: see after GALEN.

Galenist (ˈgeɪlənɪst). Also 7 **gallenist.** [f. GALEN + -IST.] One of those who followed the medical principles and practice of Galen.

1594 NASHE *Terrors Nt.* Wks. (Grosart) III. 249 This needie Gallaunt..rayleth on our Galenists, and calls them dull gardners and hay-makers in a mans belly. **1606** DEKKER *Sev. Sinnes* VII. (Arb.) 46 What Gallenist or Paracelsian in the world, by all his water-casting, and minerall extractions, would iudge [etc.]. **1692** TRYON *Good House-w.* xvi. 131, I had rather fall into the hands of an unskilful Gallenist, than of a rash and ignorant Chymist. **1727-51** CHAMBERS *Cycl.* s.v., The Galenists stand opposed to the chemists. **1869** O. W. HOLMES *Med. Ess.* vi. (1883) 319 These Galenists were what we should call 'herb-doctors' to-day. **1891** C. CREIGHTON *Hist. Epid. Brit.* 536 Sir Theodore Mayerne, the King's physician, who had been driven from Paris by the intolerance of the Galenists.

Hence †**Galeˈnistical** *a.* = GALENIC *a.*¹

1612 WOODALL *Surg. Mate* Wks. (1653) 236 They excel all Galenistical compositions for the eradicating inveterate maladies.

†ˈ**Galenite.**¹ *Obs.* [f. GALEN + -ITE.] = GALENIST.

1606 SYLVESTER *Du Bartas* II. iv. *Trophies* 793 A skilfull Galenite, Who (when the Crisis comes) dares even foretell Whether the Patient shall do ill or well. **1656** BLOUNT *Glossogr., Galenite,* one that studies or follows the Aphorisms of Galen, the ancient great Physitian.

galenite² (gəˈliːnaɪt). *Min.* [f. GALENA + -ITE.] = GALENA.

1868 DANA *Min.* 41 All galenite is more or less argentiferous.

galenobismutite (gəˌliːnəʊˈbɪzmjuːtaɪt). *Min.* Also **-muthite.** [ad. Sw. *galenobismutit* (H. Sjögren 1878, in *Geol. För. Stockh. Förh.* IV. 110), f. GALEN(A + -O + BISMUTH + -ITE¹.] A sulphide of lead and bismuth usu. occurring as light grey columnar or fibrous masses.

1880 *Jrnl. Chem. Soc.* XXXVIII. 14 Bismuth occurs in Wermland..as the new mineral galenobismuthite, $PbS.Bi_2S_3$. **1962** *Acta Crystallogr.* XV. 691 (*heading*) A redetermination of the crystal structure of galenobismutite, $PbBi_2S_4$.

galenoid (gəˈliːnɔɪd), *a.* and *sb.* [f. GALENA + -OID.] **A.** *adj.* Resembling galena.

1884 *Athenæum* 26 Apr. 541/1 Depositing..a lustrous galenoid coating by the decomposition of an alkaline solution of lead tartrate with sulphur urea.

B. *sb. Cryst.* (See quot.)

[The form occurs most freq. in galena, whence the name.] **1882** A. H. GREEN *Phys. Geol.* II. (ed. 3) 45 The complete form is bounded by 3 x 8 = 24 equal and similar isosceles triangles; it is called..the Trigonal Trisoctahedron, or the Galenoid.

galeny, var. GALEENY.

galeod (ˈgeɪlɪɒd). *Ichth.* [ad. Gr. γαλεώδης resembling a shark, f. γαλεός (see next).] A shark.

1868 [see GALEIDAN].

galeoid (ˈgeɪlɪɔɪd), *a.* [ad. Gr. γαλεοειδής, f. γαλεός a kind of shark: see -OID.] **a.** *Ichth.* Resembling a shark or dog-fish. **b.** *Ent.* Belonging to the arachnidans of the family *Galeodidæ.*

1847 JOHNSTON in *Proc. Berw. Nat. Club.* II. v. 217 The Ἀλώπηξ, Aristotle tells us, is a Shark or galeoid fish.

galeon, -oon, obs. forms of GALLEON.

galeopithecus (ˌgeɪlɪəʊpɪˈθiːkəs). [mod.L., f. Gr. γαλέη marten-cat + πίθηκος ape.] A flying lemur. See FLYING *ppl. a.* I b.

1835-6 TODD *Cycl. Anat.* I. 595/1 The remarkable genus Galeopithecus. **1848** CARPENTER *Anim. Phys.* xii. (1872) 504 The Galeopithecus or Flying Lemur.

galeot, obs. f. GALLIOT¹; var. GALLIOT².

gale pote, obs. form of GALLIPOT.

galer ('geɪlə(r)). Also 7 **galor**. [f. GALE *sb.*⁴ + -ER, -OR. Cf. GAVELLER.] In Gloucestershire: †**a.** The farmer or collector of the 'gale' or manorial duty on fish (*obs.*). **b.** The agent for the letting of 'gales' or mining licences.

c **1640** J. SMYTH *Hundred of Berkeley* (1885) 321 The Lords servant or farmer thereof, the Galor. **1832** in *5th Rep. Dean Forest Comm.* (1835) 70, I never sold a gale, but I have bought quarries. I went to the galer, and had it transferred in the gale-book.

‖**galère** (galɛr). [Fr., lit. galley; also *fig.* (cf. GALLEY *sb.* 1 b).] A coterie, circle; a (usu. undesirable) set of people; an unpleasant place or situation.

1756 CHESTERFIELD *Let.* 26 Nov. (1777) II. 435, I most frequently..congratulate..myself for having got out of that *galère.* **1842** MILL *Let.* 11 Mar. in *Wks.* (1963) XIII. 507 Everybody now condemns the folly of involving ourselves in that *galère.* **1895** S. WEYMAN *Mem. Minister of France* iii. 121 'Why, your excellency,' he cried, in a tone of boundless surprise, 'what are you doing in this *galère?*' **1961** D. G. JAMES *M. Arnold* i. 15 If it comes to 'ruling ideas' what was Newman doing in a *galère* which contained Goethe and Sainte-Beuve? **1963** *Times* 26 Sept. 17/5 The head of the Security Service gave this ruling on February 1:—'Until further notice no approach should be made to anyone in the Ward *galère.*'

galericulate (ˌgælɪə'rɪkjʊleɪt), *a. Bot.* [f. L. *galēricul-um* (dim. of *galērum* cap) + -ATE².] Capped, furnished with a cap; = GALEATE.

1706 [see GALEATE]. **1755** in JOHNSON; and in mod. Dicts.

†**galericulated,** *ppl. a. Obs.* [f. as prec. + -ED.] = prec.

1698 *Phil. Trans.* XX. 468 A broad, round, galerniculated [*sic*] Lip, the Center of which opens into the Hollow of the Flower. **1725** [see CUCULLATED 2].

galerite (gə'lɪəraɪt). [ad. mod.L. *galērītēs*, f. *galēr-um* cap: see -ITE.] A fossil sea-urchin of the genus *Galerites.*

1828 in WEBSTER; and in later Dicts.

†**galern.** *Obs.*⁻¹ [ad. F. *galerne* = Pr. *galerna*, Sp., Pg., *galerno*; of uncertain origin.] (See quot.)

[**14..** J. YONGE *Secreta Secretorum* 153 The lordshupp of solerne ther as the day dawyth, neyther of galerne the baillie, ther as the nyght nyghtyth.] **1693** EVELYN *De La Quint. Compl. Gard.* I. 145 The Galern, otherwise called the North, and North North-West Wind, which reigns commonly in the Month of April.

galette (gə'lɛt). [a. F. *galette.*] A broad thin cake of bread or pastry.

1775 J. JEKYLL *Corresp.* (1894) 51 He was crammed with the galette or cake of the vintage. **1840** T. A. TROLLOPE *Summer in Britt.* II. 61 He was, in short, a merry, careless fellow, eating the galette when he could get it [etc.]. **1865** MILTON & CHEADLE *North W. by Land* 53 Taking a couple of 'gallettes' [*sic*], or unleavened cakes, a-piece, [we] set out on a forced march to the Fort.

galewes, -is, -ys, obs. forms of GALLOWS *sb.*

galey(e, obs. forms of GALLEY.

†**galful,** *a. Obs.* [f. *gal* GALE *sb.*² + -FUL.] Of a deity: ? Ready to give oracular responses (cf. GALE *v.*¹ 1).

1340–70 *Alex. & Dind.* 389 Ne we for sake of our sinne no sacrifice maken To oure galfule god. *Ibid.* 668 For mercurie miche spak to mentaine iangle, ȝe holden him galful & god, & god of the tounge.

‖**Galgenhumor, galgenhumor** ('galgən huːˌmoːr). [G., f. *galgen* gallows + *humor* humour.] = *gallows-humour* (GALLOWS *sb.* 8).

1912 O. ONIONS *In Accordance with Evidence* 273 This *galgenhumor* almost mastered me as the paper again crept up to take another peep at him. **1948** MENCKEN *Amer. Lang.* Suppl. II. 727 Not a few of these terms show *Galgenhumor*, *e.g.*, *meat-wagon* for an ambulance. **1959** *Observer* 26 Apr. 25/4 Berliners, with their *Galgenhumor* and *Schnoddrigkeit.* **1963** AUDEN *Dyer's Hand* 523 The Gravedigger's song in Hamlet is..an expression of the *galgenhumor* which suits his particular mystery.

galghes, galhe(fork), galhouse, -hows, obs. forms of GALLOWS *sb.*

galiace, var. GALLIASS.

galiage, var. GALEAGE.

†**'Galianes,** *sb. pl. Obs.*⁻¹ [f. *Galien* GALEN.] 'Drinks named after Galen' (Skeat).

c **1386** CHAUCER *Pard. Pream.* 20 Thyn ypocras, and eek thy Galiones [*v.rr.* galyans, Galianes, Galiounes] And euery boyste ful of thy letuarie.

galiantine, galiard(e, galias(s(e, galiaudise, galic, obs. ff. GALANTINE, GALLIARD, GALLIASS, GALLIARDISE, GAELIC.

Galician (gə'lɪθɪən, gə'lɪʃ(ɪ)ən), *a.*¹ and *sb.*¹ [f. *Galicia* + -AN.] **A.** *adj.* Of or pertaining to Galicia, a province in north-west Spain, or its inhabitants. **B.** *sb.* An inhabitant of Galicia; also, the language of Galicia.

1749 U. RHYS *Account Spain & Portugal* 23 The *Galicians* make good Soldiers; and are pleased with the Profession. **1809** tr. *A. de Laborde's View Spain* II. 428 This road is frequented by..a great many Galician workmen. *Ibid.* 456 The Galician who serves either his master, or the public, or in the army, is contented to appear a slave. **1823** T. Ross tr. *Bouterwek's Hist. Span. Lit.* I. 13 The vulgar idiom spoken by the Galician water-carriers in Madrid. **1828** *Encycl. Metrop.* (1845) XIX. 438/1 The Galicians, or Galegos as the Spaniards call them, are a grave and sober people. **1927** *Chambers's Jrnl.* 29 Oct. 759/1 Her head is the Galician woman's carry-all. **1960** W. D. ELCOCK *Romance Lang.* v. 428 Galician, in the meantime, degenerated to a patois status; it is still widely spoken and practised as a literary cult by local enthusiasts. *Ibid.*, Probably the earliest specimen of Galician-Portuguese to have survived is an act of partition dated 1230. **1966** *Tablet* 29 Jan. 144/2 Other Spanish languages, such as Basque and Galician. **1969** *Daily Tel.* (Colour Suppl.) 10 Jan. 32/1 The Asturians and Galicians dance in strong colours, kicking with controlled but fierce abandon.

Galician (gə'lɪʃ(ɪ)ən), *a.*² and *sb.*² [f. *Galicia* + -AN.] **A.** *adj.* Of or pertaining to Galicia, a region of Poland and West Russia, or its inhabitants. **B.** *sb.* An inhabitant of Galicia. Also used loosely in Canada to denote a Central European immigrant.

1835 *Penny Cycl.* III. 131/2 The Galician soil is no where so productive as in the districts of Zloczoff and Stanislawoff. **1903** *Eye Opener* (High River, Alta.) 25 July 3/3 The lost tribes of Israel, in the dishevelled shapes of Galicians and Doukhobors. **1909** *Chambers's Jrnl.* Mar. 154/1 It is customary in the West to classify the various contingents which come from east-central Europe as Galicians. **1918** C. G. MONTEFIORE *Lib. Judaism & Hellenism* v. 246 It has been too rashly assumed that the Russian, Polish and Galician 'masses' must be for ever wedded to Orthodox Judaism. **1927** *Times* (weekly ed.) 16 June 664/4 He took charge of a Red-Cross unit on the Galician front. **1960** S. BECKER tr. *Schwarz-Bart's Last of Just* (1961) III. 93 The young Galician followed him with a constrained smile.

†**galiegross.** *Obs.* Also **galligross.** [ad. It. *galea grossa* great galley.] A great galley.

1628 SIR K. DIGBY *Voy. Medit.* (1868) 38, I had intelligence that there was great force of galliones and galligrosses in the roade that might happily oppose me. **1652** URQUHART *Jewel* Wks. (1834) 245 Whether they had galleys, galeons, galiegrosses, or huge war ships, it was all one to him.

galigal, obs. form of GALINGALE.

Galignani (gælɪ'njɑːnɪ). *Obs.* exc. *Hist.* [f. the name of its founder, Giovanni Antonio *Galignani* (1752–1821).] Colloquial appellation of the English-language newspaper *Galignani's Messenger*, founded in 1814 and published daily in Paris until 1884 (and continued until 1904 as the *Daily Messenger*).

1822 M. EDGEWORTH *Let.* 5 Jan. (1971) 309 In Florence.. there is..a sort of coffee-house, where many English newspapers are openly read daily—..Galignani and others. **1837** H. C. ROBINSON *Diary* 2 Aug. (1967) 180, I found opportunity today..to read some *Galignanis.* They contained an account of the borough elections. **1848** THACKERAY *Van. Fair* lxvi. 695 Jos was in his great chair dozing over Galignani. **1868** GEO. ELIOT *Let.* 24 July (1956) IV. 460 We have been chiefly in regions innocent even of Galignani. **1880** *Ibid.* 12 May VII. 277 We read in Galignani yesterday that Sir W. Harcourt is turned out of Oxford!

Galilean (gælɪ'liːən), *a.*¹ and *sb.*¹ Also **Galilæan.** [f. L. *Galilæ-a* (Gr. Γαλιλαία Galilee) + -AN.]

A. *adj.* Of or belonging to Galilee, the most northerly province of Palestine. Also, Christian.

1637 MILTON *Lycidas* 109 Last came, and last did go, The Pilot of the Galilæan lake. **1671** MILTON *P.R.* III. 233 Thy life hath yet been private, most part spent At home, scarce view'd the *Gallilean* Towns. **1821** SHELLEY *Hellas* (1822) l. 550 Every Islamite who made his dogs Fat with the flesh of Galilean slaves. **1927** W. B. YEATS *Resurrection* in *Adelphi* IV. 729 He walked that room and issued thence In Galilæan turbulence. **1958** A. TOYNBEE *East to West* 210 The southern face of the Galilaean highlands is blurred.

B. *sb.* A native or an inhabitant of Galilee; used by pagans as a contemptuous designation for Christ, and hence as a synonym for 'Christian'. Also, a member of a fanatical sect which arose in Galilee in the 1st century.

1611 BIBLE *Acts* ii. 7 Behold, are not all these which speake, Galileans? **1683** *Life Julian* 100 After he received that mortal blow, he..cryed out, Thou hast overcome, O Galilean. **1686** HORNECK *Crucif. Jesus* xxiii. 697 A Galilean was a nick-name; when the Jews called one a Galilean, they meant an inconsiderable person. **1776** GIBBON *Decl. & F.* I. xvi. 526 Under the appellation of Galilæans, two distinctions of men were confounded, the most opposite to each other in their manners and principles; the disciples who had embraced the faith of Jesus of Nazareth, and the zealots who had followed the standard of Judas the Gaulonite. **1811** SHELLEY *Let.* 24 Apr. (1964) I. 66 The Galilean is not a favorite of mine. **1866** SWINBURNE *Poems & Ballads* 78 Wilt thou yet take all, Galilean? *Ibid.* 79 Thou hast conquered, O pale Galilean; the world has grown grey from thy breath. **1957** *Encycl. Brit.* IX. 976/1 Deborah, Jonah, Elisha and perhaps Hosea were Galileans.

Galilean (gælɪ'liːən), *a.*² (and *sb.*²) Also **Galileian.** [f. *Galileo* the celebrated Italian astronomer + -AN.] **A.** *adj.* **a.** Distinctive epithet of the form of telescope invented by Galileo. Discovered by Galileo, as ***Galilean satellite***, any of the largest four moons of the planet Jupiter; also, pertaining to or arising out of the work of Galileo.

1727–51 CHAMBERS *Cycl.* s.v. *Telescope*, The Galilean or Dutch telescope. **1757** W. EMERSON *Doctrine of Fluxions* (ed. 2) p. viii, Let a heavy Body descend through a perpendicular Height of 16½ Feet in one Second of Time, according to the Gallilean Hypothesis of Gravity. **1769** FRANKLIN *Lett.* Wks. 1887 IV. 234, I have got from Mr. Ellicot the glasses, &c., of the long Galilean telescope. **1878** NEWCOMB *Pop. Astron.* II. i. 108 The Galilean telescope was ..of the simplest construction. **1903** J. J. FAHIE *Galileo* v. 94 From about 1637, Francesco Fontana of Naples also began to turn out good glasses [*sc.* lenses] of the Galilean pattern. **1911** *Encycl. Brit.* XV. 564/1 In apparent brightness each of the four Galilean satellites may be roughly classed as of the sixth magnitude. **1944** *Chambers's Techn. Dict.* Suppl. 961/1 *Galilean binoculars*, binoculars in which the objectives are of the usual doublet telescope objective type and the eyepieces are negative lenses. **1954** A. R. HALL *Scientific Revolution* vi. 168 By its attention to actual phenomena Galilean science was made real and experiential. **1970** *Nature* 25 Apr. 316/1 It should be possible by 1974 to obtain radar echoes from the Galilean satellites of Jupiter.

b. *Physics.* Pertaining to the properties of space and time assumed in classical physics; ***Galilean transformation***, a transformation of co-ordinates in which the classical laws of motion remain unchanged.

1910 *Sci. Abstr.* XIII. 261 Mathematically these principles are represented by an invariance or co-variance with respect to certain transformations. These transformations are (1) for Newtonian mechanics the 'Galilean transformation'..; (2) for Lorentz's electro-dynamics the 'Lorentz transformation'. **1918** A. S. EDDINGTON *Rep. Relativity Theory Gravitation* ii. 18 The laws of mechanics and electrodynamics are usually enunciated with respect to 'unaccelerated rectangular axes', or, as they are often called, 'Galilean axes'. *Ibid.* v. 48 The path of a particle in Galilean co-ordinates (*i.e.*, under no forces) is a straight line. **1920** R. W. LAWSON tr. *Einstein's Relativity* iv. 11 A system of co-ordinates of which the state of motion is such that the law of inertia holds relative to it is called a 'Galileian system of co-ordinates'. **1922** E. P. ADAMS tr. *Einstein's Meaning Relativity* III. 65 There are finite regions, where, with respect to a suitably chosen space of reference, material particles move freely without acceleration, and in which the laws of the special theory of relativity..hold with remarkable accuracy. Such regions we shall call 'Galilean regions'. **1960** R. M. PALTER *Whitehead's Philos. Sci.* viii. 166 Newton's laws of motion are covariant with respect to Galilean transformations (i.e., transformations which carry one inertial system into another).

B. *sb.* One who holds or supports Galileo's views.

1925 A. N. WHITEHEAD *Sci. & Mod. World* (1926) viii. 186 The difference is very analogous to that between the Galileans and the Aristotelians: Aristotle said 'rest' where Galileo added 'or uniform motion in a straight line'.

Galilee ('gælɪliː). Also 6 **Galleley.** [a. OF. *galilee*, a med.L. *galilæa* (Du Cange), a use of the proper name (see GALILEAN *a.* 1). Possibly the allusion is to Galilee as an outlying portion of the Holy Land, or to the phrase 'Galilee of the Gentiles' (*Matt.* iv. 15).] A porch or chapel at the entrance of a church.

According to some authorities, the L. word was also applied to the western extremity of the nave, as being a part regarded as less sacred than the rest.

[*a* **1186** *Charter* in Greenwell *Durh. Cath.* (1892) 48 *note*, Super altare Beatæ Mariæ in occidentali porte ejusdem ecclesiæ quæ Galilæ a vocatur.] **1593** *Rites of Durham* (Surtees) 36 A chappell maide and dedicated to the blessed Virgin Marie, now cauled the Galleley. **1814** SOUTHEY *Roderick* XXIV. 29 There was a church..and here within An oaken galilee, now black with age, His old Iberian ancestors were laid. **1848** RICKMAN *Archit.* 128 The most gorgeous porch of this style in existence is the Galilee at the west end of Ely cathedral. **1892** *Pall Mall G.* 31 Oct. 5/1 The extension of the chapel, by the addition of a galilee, was entrusted to [etc.].

b. *attrib.* as in ***Galilee-bell, -door, -porch, -steeple.***

1593 *Rites of Durham* (Surtees) 33 Over the Galleley dour ther, in a belfray called the Galleley steple, did hing iiij goodly great Bells. *Ibid.* 35 And dyd rynne streight waie to the Galleley Bell and tould it, to th' intent any man that hard it might knowe that there was som man that had taken Saunctuarie. **1839** LONGF. *Hyperion* IV. i, My arabesques.. and Holy-Roods and Galilee-steeples. **1868** *Less. Mid. Age* 354 There is a Galilee porch at the south-west corner of the great transept. **1879** SIR G. SCOTT *Lect. Archit.* I. 127 The Galilee porch at Ely..is one of the most magnificent specimens of the fully-developed style in the country.

galimatias (gælɪ'mætɪəs, gælɪ'meɪʃ(ɪ)əs). Also 7 **galimatia,** 8 **gallimatia(s, galimathias.** [a. F. *galimatias*, a word of unknown origin, first found in the 16th century; cf. *galimafrée* GALLIMAUFRY, and see conjectures in Littré.]

Confused language, meaningless talk, nonsense.

1653 URQUHART *Rabelais* I. ii, A Galimatia of extravagant conceits. **1712** ADDISON *Spect.* No. 275 ¶6 The great Cavity was filled with a kind of Spongy Substance, which the French Anatomists call Galimatias and the English, Nonsense. **1728** LD. HERVEY *Let. to Lady M. W. Montagu* 28 Oct. in *Lady M.'s Lett.*, If you do not dislike long letters, and an unstudied galimatias of tout ce qui se trouve au bout de la plume (comme dit Madame de Sévigné), let me know it. **1824** H. C. ROBINSON *Diary* 10 June (1869) II. x. 274 Now it seemed to me that Mr. C—— had no opinions, only words, for his assertions seemed a mere *galimatias.* **1860** FARRAR *Orig. Lang.* vi. 144 Simple thoughts overlaid with galimatias.

b. *transf.* A mixture, medley.

1762 H. WALPOLE *Lett. to Montagu* clxv, Her dress, like her language, is a galimatias of several countries.

gali'meta-wood. Also **galemeta**. The wood of a West Indian tree (*Dipholis salicifolia*).

1756 P. BROWNE *Jamaica* 201 The White Bullytree, or Galimeta-wood. This tree..is of a pale yellow colour, and reckoned a good timber-wood.

galina, var. GALEENY.

galinasso, var. of GALLINAZO.

†**galinga**. *Obs.* Also **galingay, galyngaye**, GALANGA. [a. med.L. *galinga*: see next.] = next.

1483 *Cath. Angl.* 149/1 Galynga, *galinga*. **a 1500** *Recipes* in *Babees Bk.* 53 When it is thyk, do þer-to gode spyces, gynger & galingay & canyll & clows, & serue it forthe. **1688** R. HOLME *Armoury* II. 57/2 Cyperus, or English Galinga, or the Bull-rush hath in the top of a few short leaves.

galingale ('gælɪŋgeɪl). Forms: (1 **gallengar**), 4-5 **galyngal(e**, 5 **ganyngale**, 6 **gallyngale, galigal**, 6-9 **galingal**, 7 **gallingale, galingame, galingall**, 6-9 **galangal(e**, 7 **galangall, calangall**, 6, 8 **galengal**, 8 **galengale**, 4- **galingale**. [ad. OF. *galingal* (*garingal*), a. Arab. *khalanjān* or *khaulinjān*, said to be a. (through Pers.) Chinese *Ko-liang-kiang*, lit. 'mild ginger from Ko,' a prefecture in the province of Canton. The word appears also as med.L. *galanga, galinga* (F. *galangue*), MDu. *galigaen* (Du. *galigaan, galgant*), MHG. *galgan* (mod.Ger. *galgant*). Several of these continental forms are, like the English word, applied to some kind of sedge and its dried roots, as well as to the oriental product.]

1. The aromatic root of certain East Indian plants of the genera *Alpinia* and *Kæmpferia*, formerly much used in medicine and cookery.

c **1000** *Sax. Leechd.* III. 12 þonne do ðu pipor, & sideware, & gallengar, & ʒingifre. *c* **1305** *Land Cokayne* 73 The note is gingeuir and galingale. *c* **1386** CHAUCER *Prol.* 381 A Cook they hadde with hem for the nones To boille the chiknes with the Marybones And poudre Marchant tart and galyngale. **1480** CAXTON *Ovid's Met.* x. vii, Ther groweth galyngal, cytoual, gynger canel & encens. **1553** EDEN *Treat. Newe Ind.* (Arb.) 23 In this Iland is greate plentie of pepper, Nuttemegges, Spikenarde, Galangale, and other spices. **1607** TOPSELL *Four-f. Beasts* 373 It were good..to put thereunto some Cinamon, Ginger, Galingale, & such hot pieces. **1697** DAMPIER *Voy.* II. I. 63 China root, Galingame, Rhubarb, Ginger, &c. **1736** BAILEY *Househ. Dict.* 49 Cardamums, Cloves, Cubebs, Galangal, Ginger, Mace and Nutmegs. **1830** LINDLEY *Nat. Syst. Bot.* 267 The warm and pungent roots of the greater and lesser Galangale are..used by the Indian doctors in cases of dyspepsia.

†**b.** A dish seasoned with galingale. *Obs.*

a **1616** BEAUM. & FL. *Bloody Bro.* II. ii, Put in some of this [*sc.* poison], the matter's ended; Dredge you a dish of plovers, there's the art on't; Or in a galingale, a little does it.

2. Applied to an English species of sedge, *Cyperus longus*, sometimes distinguished as 'English galingale', the root of which has similar properties to those of the true galingale.

1578 LYTE *Dodoens* III. xxiii. 346 The roote of Cyperus or English Galangal is hoote and dry in the third degree. **1589** COGAN *Haven Health* (1636) 84 Galingale, or rather Cipresse roots, though it bee rare, yet is it found in some Gardens. **1832** TENNYSON *Lotos-Eaters* 23 Many a winding vale And meadow, set with slender galingale.

3. *attrib.*, as ***galingale-root***.

c **1611** CHAPMAN *Iliad* XXI. 332 The lote trees, sea-grass reeds, And rushes, with the galingale roots..all were fir'd. **1743** *Lond. & Country Brew.* III. (ed. 2) 226 Add a Pound or two of Galingal-Roots to it.

galinipper, galinule: see GALL-.

galiny, var. GALEENY.

‖**galion**[1]. *Obs.* Also 6-7 **gallion**. [Gr. γάλιον.] The plant *Galium verum* or Lady's Bedstraw. See GALIUM.

1548 TURNER *Names of Herbes* (1881) 38 Galion or gallion is named in englishe in the North countrey Maydens heire. **1578** LYTE *Dodoens* IV. lxxv. 539 Gallion hath small, rounde, euen stemmes, with very small narrowe leaues. **1616** SURFL. & MARKH. *Country Farme* 497 Likewise the seed of Gallion or petty Mugguet.

†**galion**[2]. *Obs.* ? The fore part of a ship.

1604 E. GRIMSTONE *Hist. Siege Ostend* 149 The vice-admirall..brake halfe the Galion of his owne shippe, and cut of all the hinder part of her.

galion, obs. form of GALLEON.

galiongee (gæljən'dʒiː). [a. Turk. *qālyūnjī*, deriv. of *qālyūn*, a. It. *galeone* GALLEON.] A Turkish sailor.

1813 BYRON *Br. Abydos* II. ix, All that a careless eye could see In him was some young Galiongée. **1821** *Blackw. Mag.* IX. 136 The Pacha..call'd to him a Galiongee. **1823** C. B. SHERIDAN in *Joanna Baillie's Collect. Poems* 104 Our Galiongees were her life and her breath.

galiot: see GALLIOT.

galipine ('gælɪpiːn). *Chem.* Also **-in**, †**-eïne**. [ad. It. *galipeina* (Koerner & Böhringer 1883, in *Gazzetta Chim. Ital.* XIII. 365), f. mod.L. *Galipea*, a generic name of the tree producing Angustura bark.] An alkaloid, $C_{20}H_{21}NO_3$, obtained from Angustura bark. Similarly **galipoidine** (gælɪ'pɔɪdiːn) [ad. G. *galipoidin* (Tröger & Runne 1911, in *Arch. Pharm.* CCXLIX. 184)], an alkaloid, $C_{19}H_{15}NO_4$; **galipoline** (gæ'lɪpəliːn) [ad. G. *galipolin* (Späth & Papaioanou 1929, in *Monatsh. Chem.* LII. 129)], an alkaloid, $C_{19}H_{19}NO_3$.

1884 *Jrnl. Chem. Soc.* XLVI. 341 In the mother-liquors from which the cusparine was originally precipitated..another alkaloïd is found, to which the authors have given the name of *galipeïne*, $C_{20}H_{21}NO_3$. **1911** *Ibid.* C. I. 482 Angostura bark contains..a new alkaloid, now named galipoidine. **1912** *Ibid.* CII. I. 896 Galipine is colourless when pure, and yields colourless salts; the yellow colour usually ascribed to the salts is due to the presence of impurities. **1913** T. A. HENRY *Plant Alkaloids* 404 Galipine, $C_{20}H_{21}O_3N$, crystallises from alcohol or ether in prisms. *Ibid.*, Galipoidine, $C_{19}H_{15}O_4N$, m.p. 233°, is sparingly soluble in most organic solvents. **1929** *Chem. Abstr.* Oct. 4703 Extn. of angostura bark with EtOH for 8 days and working up the alkali-sol. portion given galipolin..which gives galipin on methylation. **1939** T. A. HENRY *Plant Alkaloids* (ed. 3) 393 Galipoline..contains two methoxyl groups, and on methylation by diazomethane yields galipine. **1968** I. L. FINAR *Org. Chem.* (ed. 4) II. xiv. 643 A number of alkaloids have been isolated from angostura bark, e.g., cusparine, galipine, galipoline, etc.

galipot ('gælɪpɒt). Also **gallipot**. [a. F. *galipot, galipo*, of unknown origin, perhaps connected with OF. *garipot*, a species of pine-tree. But cf. Littré *Suppl.*] The turpentine or resin which exudes from, and hardens upon, the stem of certain pines.

1791 W. NICHOLSON tr. *Chaptal's Elem. Chem.* (1800) III. 73 Galipot, a concrete resinous juice, of a yellowish white colour and strong smell..comes from Guienne, where it is afforded by two species of pine. **1804** TINGRY *Varnisher's Guide* (1816) 19 This turpentine, when it has acquired consistence by exposure to the air, forms what is called gallipot.

attrib. **1842** FRANCIS *Dict. Arts*, *Galipot varnish*.

galipot, obs. form of GALLIPOT.

galium ('geɪlɪəm). *Bot.* [a. mod.L. *galium*, ad. Gr. γάλιον BEDSTRAW 2.] A genus of plants (N.O. *Rubiaceæ*): = BEDSTRAW 2.

1548-1616 [see GALION[1]]. **1785-94** MARTYN *Rousseau's Bot.* xv. 164 Galium has a salver shaped corolla and two roundish seeds. **1880** C. R. MARKHAM *Peruv. Bark* 142 A little galium by the road-side.

†**galiwhistell**. *Obs.* [Cf. OF. 'ung sifflet de galer d'argent', in a list of jewels dated 1474. ?Connected with *galer* vb., to make merry, dance.]

1423 *Indenture* in *Rot. Parl.* IV. 219 Item 1 Galiwhistell d'or pois' dim. unc', pris x s. Item, 1 Muskball d'or.

galjoen (xa'ljuːn). *S. Afr.* [Afrikaans, = Du. *galjoen* galleon.] The sea-fish *Coracinus capensis* (family Coracinidæ); also any of several related fish of the family Coracinidæ.

[**1853** L. PAPPE *Edible Fishes Cape of Good Hope* 23 *Dipterodon Capensis*..(*Galjoenvisch, Galleon-fish.*)... This fish, more plentiful in the Western Division of the Colony, is highly esteemed as food.] **1900** *Trans. S. Afr. Philos. Soc.* XI. 221 The Galjoen also can readily be supposed to have derived its name from its resemblance in shape to the high built three-decker..called..by the Dutch 'Galjoen' or 'Galleon'. **1949** L. G. GREEN *In Land of Afternoon* (1950) xviii. 226 In fine weather many a galjoen is landed on those rocks. **1971** *Cape Times* 20 Aug. 22/3 One angler..took nine galjoen.

gall (gɔːl), *sb.*[1] Forms: 1 **ʒealla**, (**ealla**), *Anglian* **galla**, 3-4 **ȝalle**, 3-6 **galle**, 4 **gawle**, 4-5 **gal, gale**, 6-7 **gaule**, 7-8 **gaul**, 7 **gawl**, 6-9 *Sc.* **gaw**, 4- **gall**. [OE. *ʒealla* wk. masc., agrees in meaning with OS. *galla* fem., MDu. *galle* fem., (Du. *gal* fem.), OHG. *galla* fem., (MHG. and G. *galle* fem.), and ON. *gall* str. neut. (but Swed. *galle* masc., *galla* fem., Da. *galde* com.):—OTeut. types **gallo*[m], *gallon-, -ôn-*:—pre-Teut. **gholno-*.

The pre-Teut. root **ghol-*, **ghel-*, which is represented also in Gr. χολή, χόλος, and in L. *fel*, is perhaps the same as that of OE. *geolo* yellow (:—OTeut. **gel-wo-*), L. *helvus*, Gr. χλω-ρός, the gall being thus named from its colour.]

I. 1. a. The secretion of the liver, bile. Now applied only (exc. in *Comb.*) to that of the lower animals, esp. to *ox gall* (see OX) as used in the arts. (From the earliest period often used, like L. *fel*, F. *fiel*, etc., as the type of an intensely bitter substance.)

c **825** *Vesp. Psalter* lxviii. 7 Saldun in mete minne gallan. *c* **1000** ÆLFRIC *Gloss.* in Wr.-Wülcker 160/40 *Fel, uel bilis*, ʒealla. *c* **1000** *Ags. Gosp.* Matt. xxvii. 34 And hiȝ sealdon hym win drincan wið eallan [*MS. Bodl.* ʒeallan] ʒemenged. *c* **1200** *Vices & Virtues* (1888) 119 Aȝeanes þat underfeng godd ðe bit r)e ȝalle on his muðe. *a* **1225** *Ancr. R.* 106 He smeihte galle on his tunge. *a* **1300** *Cursor M.* 24046 þai gaf him gall to drinc. *c* **1374** CHAUCER *Troylus* IV. 1109 (1137) The woofull teres þat þei letyn fall As bitter wer..as is ligne Aloes or gall. **14..** *Metr. Voc.* in Wr.-Wülcker 627/8 *Fel*, gal. *a* **1547** SURREY *Ps.* lxxiii. 22 Lyke cupps myngled with gall, of bitter tast and sarver. **1615** CROOKE *Body of Man* 43 The bladder of Gaul purgeth away the Choller from that meate. **1732** ARBUTHNOT *Rules of Diet* 405 Gall is the greatest Resolvent of curdled Milk. **1795** WOLCOTT (P. Pindar) *Pindariana* Wks. 1812 IV. 218 Tis sweetness tempts the insects from the skies; Gall needeth not a flapper for the flies. **1860** C. SANGSTER *Sonn.* 176 The sweat oozed from me like great drops of gall.

b. *fig.* with reference to the bitterness of gall. ***to dip one's pen in gall***, to write with virulence and rancour. (Cf. quot. 1641 in sense 3 a.)

Probably derived from instances like those in quots. 1601, 1605, where there appears to be a pun on GALL *sb.*[3] (the oak-gall, which is used in the manufacture of ink).

c **1200** ORMIN 15419 To birrlenn firrst te swete win and siþþenn bitterr galle. *a* **1300** *Cursor M.* 25729 Hony þai bede and gif vs gall. *a* **1415** LYDG. *Temp. Glass* 192 Allas þat euer þat it shuld[e] fal, So soote sugre Icoupled be with gall! [**1601** SHAKS. *Twel. N.* III. ii. 52 Let there bee gaulle enough in thy inke, though thou write with a goose-pen, no matter: about it. **1605** *1st Pt. Ieronimo* II. iii. 14 *Ier.* What, is your pen foule? *Hor.* No, Father, cleaner then Lorenzoes soule; Thats dipt in inck made of an enuious gall; Elce had my pen no cause to write at all.] **1611** MIDDLETON & DEKKER *Roaring Girle* III. D.'s Wks. 1873 III. 181 Loues sweets tast best, when we haue drunk downe Gall. **1624** QUARLES *Div. Poems, Job* xii. 88 His Plenty..shall Be Hony, tasted, but digested, Gall. **1750** J. DOVE *Creed founded on Truth* 15, I shall omit the Consideration of the particular Reasons of these Differences, because I would not dip my pen in Gall. **1752** MASON *Elfrida* 56 Relentless Conscience Pours more of gall into the bitter cup Of their severe repentance. **1824** W. IRVING *T. Trav.* II. 53 And yet was free from the gall of disappointment. **1828** *Imperial Mag.* Apr. 362/1 In the same spirit of bitter enmity..the Doctor has dipped his pen in gall, to blast the memory of that good man. **1892** *Rev. Reviews* V. 376/1 In the *Contemporary Review* for April an anonymous writer dips his pen in gall in order to depict the German Emperor. **1946** W. S. MAUGHAM *Then & Now* 228 His pen had been dipped in gall and as he wrote he chuckled with malice.

c. in Biblical phrases.

1382 WYCLIF *Lam.* iii. 19 Recorde of porenesse and of myn ouergoing, and of wrmod and of galle. —— *Acts* viii. 23 Forsoth in galle of bittirnesse and bond of wickidnesse I se thee for to be. **1726-46** THOMSON *Winter* 1055 Why the good man's share In life was gall and bitterness of soul. **1893** *Times* 25 Apr. 10/1 A Bill the very idea of which is gall and wormwood to the Protestant artisans.

2. a. The gall-bladder and its contents.

c **1200** ORMIN 1259 Forr cullfre iss milde, and meoc, and swete and all wiþþutenn galle. *c* **1330** *Arth. & Merl.* 7176 þat schulder & arm & ribbes alle He doun kitt wiþ liuer & ȝalle. **1390** GOWER *Conf.* III. 100 The drie coler with his hete, By wey of kinde his propre sete Hath in the galle, where he dwelleth. *c* **1400** *Lanfranc's Cirurg.* 172 Of þe galle we makiþ noon anothamie, for al oure science makiþ noon mencioun of a wounde in þe galle. *c* **1430** LYDG. *Min. Poems* (Percy Soc.) 56 To have a galle, and be clepid a douffe..It may wele ryme, but it accordith nought. **1541** R. COPLAND *Guydon's Quest. Chirurg.* I ij a, What is ye galle?..It is a bag or bladder panyculous set in the holownes of the lyuer. **1590** SPENSER *F.Q.* I. ii. vi, He..did..wast his inward gall with deepe despight. **1635** HEYWOOD *Hierarch.* VII. 416 Her Gall being burst, she would be seene to swim. **1671** SALMON *Syn. Med.* III. xxii. 403 Ground-Ivy, it is a wound-herb, opens the Lungs and Gall, cleanses the Reins. **1743** *Lond. & Country Brew.* II. (ed. 2) 151 Two different Juices from the Gaul and Sweet-bread. **1820** *Blackw. Mag.* VII. 470 Only a gut, a gaw, and a gizzard. **1897** MARY KINGSLEY *W. Africa* 543 The gall-bladder is most carefully removed from the leopard and burnt *coram publico*..This burning of the gall, however..is done merely to destroy it.

†**b.** Short for 'sickness of the gall', a disease in cattle. *Obs.*

1577 B. GOOGE *Heresbach's Husb.* III. (1586) 135 b, *margin*, The Gal, or Yellows [*In the text*: The sickenesse of the Gall is knowen by the running eies (etc.)].

3. a. Bitterness of spirit, asperity, rancour (supposed to have its seat in the gall: see 1390 in sense 2).

c **1200** ORMIN 1253 And arrt te sellf aȝȝ milde and meoc annd all wiþþutenn galle. *a* **1340** HAMPOLE *Psalter, Song Hezekiah* 497 Wiþouten gall of yre and wickidnes. **1377** LANGL. *P. Pl.* B. XVI. 155 Falsenesse I fynde in þi faire speche, And gyle in þi gladde chere, and galle is in þi lawghynge. **1577-87** HOLINSHED *Chron.* II. 43/1 A pleasant conceited companion, full of mirth without gall. **1641** J. JACKSON *True Evang. T.* II. 152 Breaches of charity..by virulencie and gall of our pennes, and by the violence of our hands. **1781** GIBBON *Decl. & F.* III. xlviii. 29 Their votaries have exhausted the bitterness of religious gall. **1849** ROBERTSON *Serm.* Ser. I. xxi. (1866) 349 The bitterness which changes the milk of kindly feelings into gall. **1887** HALL CAINE *Deemster* xxxvi. 236 Fellows who had shown ruth for the first time, began to show gall for the hundredth.

†**b.** Spirit to resent injury or insult. *Obs.*

1390 GOWER *Conf.* I. 303 And if it fal..A man to lese so his galle Him aught..the name bere of pacient. *c* **1450** *Cokwolds Daunce* 96 in Hazl. *E.P.P.* I. 42 And ȝet for all hys grete honour, Cokwold was Kyng Arthour, Ne galle non he had. **1604** SHAKS. *Oth.* IV. iii. 93 We haue galles: and though we haue some Grace, Yet haue we some Reuenge. *c* **1680** BEVERIDGE *Serm.* (1729) I. 130 If there be any such thing as gall in us.

†**c.** Hence, ***to break one's gall***: in early use, to break the spirit, cow, subdue; in later *slang* (see quot. 1785). *Obs.*

c **1460** *Towneley Myst.* xxiii. 589, I warand you..That he shall soyn yelde the gast, ffor brestyn is his gall. **1508** DUNBAR *Flyting w. Kennedie* 183 Obey, theif baird, or I sal brek thy gaw. *c* **1530** *Remedie of Love* lxv, in *Chaucer's Wks.* (1532) 368 a/1 Whiche she perceyuyng brasteth his gal And anon his great wodenesse dothe fal. **1586** J. HOOKER *Girald. Irel.* in *Holinshed* II. 142/2 The deputie, when he had broken the galles of them, & had thus dispersed them..returned towards Dublin. **1625-6** PURCHAS *Pilgrims* II. 1638, I still defied them..which in a manner broke their very galls. **1785** GROSE *Dict. Vulg. Tongue* s.v., His gall is not yet broken, a saying used in prisons of a man just brought in, who appears melancholy and dejected.

4. Assurance, impudence. orig. *U.S. slang*.

1882 *Denver Republican* 23 Jan. 4/1 There is only one word which thoroughly expresses the quality of Dr. Anderson's communication. That word is the strong expression, 'gall'. **1890** *Cambridge* (Mass.) *Frozen Truth* 28 Nov. 2/3 And 'gall', of which Joe always had plenty, especially as a politician. **1891** *Voice* (N.Y.) 31 July, With infinite 'gall' he has opened an office for the sale of 'original packages' only a few feet away. **1936** 'I. HAY' *Housemaster* xvi. 210 And what do you think they had the gall to do then? **1948** WODEHOUSE *Spring Fever* xv. 153 He was a young man abundantly equipped with what he called *sang froid* and people who did not like him usually alluded to as gall.

II. In certain transferred uses.

†**5.** Poison, venom. *Obs.*

[Traces of a confusion between the notions of 'bitter' and 'poisonous' are found in many langs. (see, e.g., *Deut.* xxxii. 32–34); it was also anciently believed that the venom of serpents, etc. was produced from their gall (Plin. *N.H.* XI. cxciii). Cf. 'sagitta armata felle veneni', Virg. *Æn.* xii. 857.]

1340 HAMPOLE *Pr. Consc.* 6755 Galle of draguns þair wyne sal be, And wenym of snakes þar-with. **1382** WYCLIF *Deut.* xxxii. 33 Gal of dragouns the wyne of hem, and venym of eddres vncurable. *a* **1450** *Le Morte Arth.* 1654 How in an appelle he dede the galle.

6. ***gall of the earth*** [L. *fel terræ*, F. *fiel de terre*]: a name given to the Lesser Centaury, from its bitterness: cf. *earth-gall* (EARTH *sb.*[1] B. II). Also applied to other plants.

1567 MAPLET *Gr. Forest* 37 Centorie is called the bitter Herbe..some cal it the gal of the earth. **1605** TIMME *Quersit.* III. 148 Out of the lesser centaurie, which some call the gaule of the earth, much salt is extracted. **1848** CRAIG, *Gall of the earth*, a name given in North America to the plant *Sonchus floridanus*, a species of the Sow-thistle.

7. The scum of melted glass [F. *fiel de verre*]: see GLASS-GALL.

III. 8. *Comb.*, as ***gall-like*** adj. Also **gall-bag, -cyst**, the vessel containing the gall = GALL-BLADDER; **gall-drop**, a drop of gall or bitterness; **gall-duct, -passage, -pipe**, the tube through which the bile passes; **gall-sickness** [= Du. *galziekte*, Ger. *gallsucht*], (*a*) a form of intermittent fever, common in the Netherlands (*Syd. Soc. Lex.*); (*b*) the name [tr. Du. *galziekte*] given in South Africa to diseases of the liver in cattle, sheep, and goats; †**gall's purse** = *gall-bag*; †**gall-wet** *a.*, steeped in gall or bitterness. Also GALL-BLADDER, GALL-STONE.

1625 HART *Anat. Ur.* I. ii. 15 A yellow..colour of the skinne doth better declare any obstruction of the *gall-bagge ..then the vrine. **1794** COLERIDGE *Death Chatterton* 109 For oh! big *gall-drops..Have blackened the fair promise of thy spring. **1702** J. PURCELL *Cholick* (1714) 49 The Preternatural Position of Parts; as of the *Gall-duct inserted into the Stomach. **1876** *Clin. Soc. Trans.* IX. 85 The fissure was chiefly occupied superficially by a very dilated gall-duct, so large that the index finger entered it readily on opening it. **1605** TIMME *Quersit.* I. xvi. 85 They abounde with a certaine *gaulike bitternesse. **1676** COOKE *Marrow Chirurg.* 390 In it [the Duodenum] are inserted the *Gall-passage, *Ductus Choledochus & Ductus Wirtzungianus* or *Pancreaticus*. **1712** BLACKMORE *Creation* VI. 520 Which.. striving thro' the *Gall-pipe, here unload Their yellow Streams, more to refine the Flood. **1875** J. NOBLE *Descrip. Handbk. Cape Colony* 259 The 'gal zeickte' or *gall sickness is also a common disease. **1896** R. WALLACE *Farm. Industr. Cape Col.* 288 Deaths in Cape Colony from gall-sickness. **1953** *Official Yr. Bk. Union S. Afr. 1950* XXVI. I. xix. 914 *Anaplasma marginale*, the cause of gallsickness in cattle. **1528** PAYNEL *Salerne's Regim.* B iij b, The other necessite is in respecte of the *galles purse. **1597–8** BP. HALL *Virgid., Sat.* II. Prol., With *gall-weet words and speeches rude, Controls the maners of the multitude.

gall (gɔːl), *sb.*[2] Forms: 1 **ȝealla**, 4–6 **galle**, 4–7 **gaule**, 7 **gal**, 6–9 *Sc.* **gaw**, 6– **gall.** [OE. *ȝealla* wk. masc., a sore on a horse, corresponds in meaning to MSw. *galle* wk. masc., MLG., MHG., mod.G. *galle* fem., Du. *gal* fem.; in Ger. and Du. the word has or has had (see Grimm *Wb.* and the *Nederl. Woordenb.*) the senses 'pimple or blister generally, barren spot in a field, flaw or rotten place in a rock', etc. All these words are in the several langs. formally identical with those repr. GALL *sb.*[1], and it seems not unlikely that they may be actually identical; the notion of 'venom' (GALL *sb.*[1] 5) passes easily into that of 'envenomed sore' (cf. FELON *sb.*[2]); the other senses illustrated below may be explained as referring to the gall as a part of the carcass which has to be removed as useless and offensive. The ON. and MSw. *galle* wk. masc., 'fault, defect' (in phrases equivalent to 'without gall'), seems to admit of the same explanation.

It is, however, probable that words of different etymology have influenced the sense-development in the Eng. and other Teut. langs. In the Rom. langs. the word for GALL *sb.*[3] (F. *galle*, It. *gala*, Sp. *agalla*) was used for a swelling on the fetlock of a horse (= Ger. *floszgalle*, *windgalle*, Eng. WINDGALL), and Ger. writers of the 16th c. argue that the word ought, being a transferred use of *galle* gall-nut, to be limited to this specific meaning. In Eng. the word seems to have been influenced (through GALL *v.*) by OF. *galler*, *galer* to rub, scratch, gall: possibly also by F. *gale* fem., itch, scurf, scab (also, flaw in cloth, whence Du. *gaal*); the source of these words is unknown, one suggestion being that they are derived from L. *galla* GALL *sb.*[3]]

1. Originally, a painful swelling, pustule, or blister, esp. in a horse (cf. WINDGALL). In later use (? influenced by GALL *v.*), a sore or wound produced by rubbing or chafing.

c **1000** *Sax. Leechd.* II. 156 Wið horses ȝeallan. Lacna ðone ȝeallan mid [etc.]. *c* **1440** *Promp. Parv.* 185/1 Galle, soore yn mann or beeste, *strumus, marista* [? = *marisca*, hæmorrhoid ?]. **1514** BARCLAY *Cyt. & Uplondyshm.* (Percy Soc.) p. ix, See how my handes are with many a gall, And stiffe as a borde by worke continuall. **1571** *Satir. Poems Reform.* xxvi. 167 Tuiche anis the gaw and yan the hors wil fling, Fra tyme ye spur and hit him on the quik. **1600** HOLLAND *Livy* XXVIII. xxvii. (1609) 681 Full against my will I touch these points, as sores and gals [*vulnera*] that will not abide the rubbing. **1702** *Lond. Gaz.* No. 3807/4 Lost or Stolen..a brown Bay Horse..a Gall on the near side. **1855** KINGSLEY *Westw. Ho!* (1889) 329 He only got one shrewd gall in his thigh.

†**b.** In specific applications (see quots.). *Obs.*

1575 TURBERV. *Faulconrie* 345 Divers times there rise up knubbes upon ye feete of hawkes, as upon the feete of Capons, which some call Galles and some goutes. **1741** *Compl. Fam.-Piece* III. 504 Of the Gall in Swine..This Distemper shews itself by a Swelling that appears under the Jaw.

†**c.** ***to claw, rub, hit on the gall***: *fig.* to touch (a person) on a sore or tender point. Also *absol. Obs.*

c **1386** CHAUCER *Wife's T.* 84 Ther is noon of vs alle If any wight wol clawe vs on the galle That we nel kike for he seith vs sooth. **1523** SKELTON *Garl. Laurel* 97 Yet wrote he none ill Sauynge he rubbid sum vpon the gall. **1585** ABP. SANDYS *Serm.* xiv. 242 Herod heard John gladly while hee carped others, but hee could not abide to bee rubbed on the gall himselfe. **1640** SANDERSON *Serm.* II. 172 We shall scarce read a chapter, or hear a sermon, but we shall meet with something or other that seemeth to rub upon that gaul.

2. *fig.* Something galling or exasperating; a state of mental soreness or irritation.

1591 *Troub. Raigne K. John* II. (1611) 104 The other griefe, I that's a gall indeed, To thinke that Douer castle should hold out Gainst all assaults. **1596** SPENSER *State Irel.* (Globe) 612/2 They did great hurt unto his title, and have left a perpetuall gall in the myndes of that people. *a* **1626** BP. ANDREWES *Serm.* x. (1661) 462 The gals, that sin makes in the conscience, are the entering of the iron into our soul. **1832** LYTTON *Eugene A.* I. ix, In a few days he might be rid of the gall and the pang. **1880** MRS. PARR *Adam & Eve* xxxi. 421 This..was a gall which of late she had been frequently called upon to endure.

†**3.** A person or thing that harasses or distresses.

1537 *St. Papers Hen. VIII*, II. 411 Theise men, being inhabited in soch a gall of the countrie as thei be, been soche a staye and lett to the King that onles thei be subdued, His Grace shall never be in securitie. **1596** SPENSER *State Irel.* (Globe) 645/1 It is both a principall barre and impeachement unto theeves..and also a gall agaynst all rebells and outlawes. *Ibid.* 654/1 For if they [the Irish] might be suffred to remayne about the garrison..they would..be ever after such a gall and inconvenience unto them, as that [etc.].

†**b.** Galling or harassing effect. *Obs.*

1548 HALL *Chron., Hen. VI*, 112 b, The Frenchmen, not able to abide the smart, and gaules of the arrowes, fled a pace.

4. A place rubbed bare; an unsound spot, fault or flaw; in early use also a breach. Now only *techn.*

1545 ASCHAM *Toxoph.* (Arb.) 114 A bowe..not marred with knot, gaule, wyndeshake, wem, freate or pynche. **1603** KNOLLES *Hist. Turks* (1621) 1105 They..with great labour and industrie repairing the breaches and gaules made by the artillerie. **1617** MARKHAM *Caval.* II. 203 Being comd into some large and even hie-way, without either ruttes or gaules to occasion stumbling. **1618** W. LAWSON *New Orch. & Garden* (1623) 23 Young twigs are tender, if boughs or armes touch and rub, if they are strong, they make great galls. **1639** [see FRET *sb.*[2] 1]. **1721** KELLY *Sc. Prov.* 218 It is a good Tree that hath neither Knap nor Gaw. **1787** BEST *Angling* ii. (1822) 12 Angling line. To make this line..you are to take care that your hair be round and clear, and free from galls, scales or frets. **1881** GREENER *Gun* 268 In the cheaper grades a few small shakes, galls, and want of figure are not accounted faults.

b. *Sc.* A fault, dike.

1805 FORSYTH *Beauties Scotl.* II. 470 The coal-field from Saltcoats to Garnock is cut into three parts by two great dikes or natural walls of whinstone..here termed galls.

5. A bare spot in a field or coppice (see GALL *v.*[1] 3). In the southern U.S. a spot where the soil has been washed away or exhausted.

1573 TUSSER *Husb.* li. (1878) 114 Bare plots full of galles if ye plow ouerthwart, and compas it then, is a husbandlie part. **1710** HILMAN *Tusser Rediv.* Jan. 7 Gauls are void Spaces in Coppices which serve for nothing but to entice the Cattel into it, to its great Damage. **1790** W. MARSHALL *Midl. Counties* II. 437 Gloss., *Galls*, vacant or bald places in a crop. **1813** SIR J. CULLUM *Hist. Hawsted & Hardwick* iii, *Sand-galls*, spots of sand in a field where water oozes, or, as we say, 'spews up'; and lands where such spots are frequent, are called *galty* lands. **1879** MISS JACKSON *Shropsh. Word-bk.*, *Gall*..(3), a stiff, wet, 'unkind', place in plough-land. **1891** T. N. PAGE *Ole Virginia* 140 The log cabin, set in a gall in the middle of an old field all grown up in sassafras.

†**6.** Filth, impurity; *fig.* 'the offscourings', refuse. *Obs.* [With *galle oþer glet* in the first quot., cf. early mod.Ger. *voller galle und glesz* (Grimm), said of a rock full of unsound places. Cf. also GALL *sb.*[1] 7.]

13.. *E.E. Allit. P.* A. 1059 With-outen fylþe oþer galle oþer glet. *Ibid.* C. 285 Thaȝ I be gulty of gyle as gaule of prophetes.

7. *Comb.*, as †**gall-rubbed** *a.*, rubbed in such a way as to be chafed; **gall-spot**, a mark produced by chafing.

1725 BRADLEY *Fam. Dict.* s.v. *Bone Spavin*, Take the Root of Elecampane..wrap it in a Paper and roast it soft, and after it is *gall-rubb'd and chafed well, clap it on. **1713** *Lond. Gaz.* No. 5157/4 Some white *Gall-spots on her Withers.

gall (gɔːl), *sb.*[3] Forms: 4–6 **galle**, 6–7 **gaul(e, gawle, 8 gawl, 5– gall.** [a. F. *galle* = It. *galla*, Sp. *galla* (in Minsheu *galha*):—L. *galla* the oak-apple, gall-nut; Sp. has also *agalla*.]

1. An excrescence produced on trees, especially the oak, by the action of insects, chiefly of the genus *Cynips*. Oak-galls are largely used in the manufacture of ink and tannin, as well as in dyeing and in medicine.

1398 TREVISA *Barth. De P.R.* XVII. civ. (Tollem. MS.), The mall (Mandragora) haþ white leues..and apples groweþ on þe leues, as galles groweþ on oken leues. *c* **1440** *Promp. Parv.* 185/1 Galle of appulle, or oþer frute (*P.* galle, oke appyll, *galla*). **1481** CAXTON *Myrr.* I. xviii. 57 Neyther montayne ne valeye..taketh not away fro therthe his roundenesse no more than the galle leueth to be rounde for his prickis. **1562** TURNER *Herbal* II. 109 b, A gall is the fruite of an oke and specially of the lefe. **1616** SURFL. & MARKH. *Country Farme* 28 He shall know a fruitfull and fertile yeare, if he see in the Oke apples, commonly called Gals, a Flie engendred and bred. **1697** DRYDEN *Virg. Georg.* IV. 389 To these add pounded Galls, and Roses dry. **1776–96** WITHERING *Brit. Plants* (ed. 3) II. 388 The balls, or galls upon the leaves, are occasioned by a small insect with four wings. **1842** TENNYSON *Talking Oak* 70, I swear (and else may insects prick Each leaf into a gall). **1869** [see CASE *sb.*[2] 2 c]. **1882** *Garden* 14 Oct. 335/2 Another very interesting gall is the Artichoke gall..so called from its somewhat resembling in form a Globe Artichoke.

2. *attrib.* and *Comb.* **a.** simple attrib., as ***gall-knob***; also in the names of various insects producing galls, as ***gall-beetle, -gnat, -insect, -louse, -mite, -moth, -wasp***; **b.** objective, as ***gall-bearing, -making, -producing*** adjs. Also **gall-apple** = sense 1; **gall-berry, gallberry** *U.S.*, a holly (*Ilex glabra* or *I. coriacea*); also *attrib.*; **gall-bush** *U.S.*, the gall-berry bush; **gall-leaf**, a leaf upon which a gall is formed; **gall-oak**, †**-tree**, the oak (*Quercus infectoria*) upon which are produced the galls of commerce; **gall-steep**, 'a bath of nutgalls, for the process of galling in Turkey-red dyeing' (Cassell); **gall-wasp**, a gall-producing, hymenopterous insect of the family Cynipidæ. Also GALL-FLY, GALL-NUT.

1612 WOODALL *Surg. Mate* Wks. (1653) 203 *Gall-apples or Gals is thereto a good medicine. **1828** DE QUINCEY *Toilette Hebr. Lady* in *Blackw. Mag.* XXIII. 297 A preparation of vinegar and gall-apples. **1851** LAYARD *Pop. Acc. Discov. Nineveh* vi. 117 The valley of Berwari is well wooded with the *gall-bearing oak. **1709** J. LAWSON *New Voyage Carolina* 90 *Gall-Berry-Tree, bearing a black Berry, with which the Women dye their Cloathes and Yarn black. **1834** J. J. AUDUBON *Ornith. Biogr.* II. 191 The holly, ..the gall-berry, and the poke, are those which they first attack. **1901** C. MOHR *Plant Life Alabama* 816 With gallberry bushes for the undergrowth. **1938** M. K. RAWLINGS *Yearling* i. 7 Open gallberry flats spread without obstructions. *Ibid.* iv. 40 The gallberry bushes. **1962** KURZ & GODFREY *Trees of N. Florida* 205 The large or sweet gallberry (*Ilex coriacea*) is more often seen as a shrub than a tree. It is not uncommonly associated with the shrubby, bitter gallberry, *Ilex glabra* (L.) Gray. **1728** in *N. Caroline Col. Rec.* (1886) II. 802 They measured..16 chains and 70 links to a *Gall Bush. **1835** J. MARTIN *Gaz. Virginia* 41 An ever-green shrub, called the gall-bush,..bears a berry which dies a black color like the gall of an oak—and hence its name. **1759** B. STILLINGFL. *Econ. Nat.* in *Misc. Tracts* (1762) 86 When the *gall-insect called cynips, has fixed her eggs in the leaves of an oak, the wound of the leaf swells. **1892** L. F. DAY *Nat. in Ornam.* ii. 23 In the poplar too, the prominent *gall-knob at the base of the leaf-stalk is distinctly characteristic. **1865** E. PEACOCK in *Athenæum* 18 Mar. 388 When this happens, the *gall-leaves become prominent objects. **1868** WOOD *Homes without H.* xxvi. 505 There are also *gall-making insects among the Diptera. **1881** MISS ORMEROD *Man. Inj. Ins.* 179 The diseased growths formed of irregular masses of twigs..are caused by this *Gall-mite. **1597** GERARDE *Herbal* Table Eng. Names, *Gall tree, and *Gall oke with his kinds. **1835** BOOTH *Analyt. Dict.* 91 The *Quercus insectifera*, or Gall-oak, is a native of Asia. **1859** DARWIN *Orig. Spec.* i. (1872) 6 The complex and extraordinary out-growths which invariably follow from the insertion of a minute drop of poison by a *gall-producing insect. **1879** *Encycl. Brit.* X. 44/1 Among the Hymenoptera are the *gall-wasps. **1925** *Glasgow Herald* 28 June 4 The rose gall-wasp (Rhodites). **1965** L. H. NEWMAN *Man & Insects* I. 86 Many of the gall wasps have alternating generations.

gall (gɔːl), *v.*[1] Forms: 5–7 **galle**, 6 **guall**, 6–7 **gaule**, 6–9 **gaul**, 7–8 **gawl**, 6–9 *Sc.* **gaw**, 6– **gall.** [f. GALL *sb.*[2]; app. orig. a back-formation from GALLED *ppl. a.*[2]; the sense may have been influenced by association with OF. *galler* 'to gall, fret, itch; also, to rub, scrape, scrub, claw, scratch where it itcheth' (Cotgr.).]

1. *trans.* To make sore by chafing or rubbing.

c **1440** *Promp. Parv.* 185/1 Gallyn, or make gallyd, *strumo*. **1530** PALSGR. 560/1, I galle a horse backe with sadell or otherwyse, *je refoulle*. *Ibid.*, I gall, as one dothe his buttockes with rydyng, *je me escorche les fesses*. **1602** SHAKS. *Ham.* v. i. 153 The toe of the Pesant comes so neere the heeles of our Courtier, hee galls his Kibe. **1696** tr. *Du Mont's Voy. Levant* 34 My Horse, who was gall'd under the Saddle-Bow. **1703** MOXON *Mech. Exerc.* 201 The Pole.. may draw..your Thigh against the underside of the Cheek of the Lathe, and..Gawl, and also tire your Thigh. **1782** COWPER *Gilpin* 76 The snorting beast began to trot, Which gall'd him in his seat. **1821** JOANNA BAILLIE *Met. Leg.*,

Columbus xlii, Base irons his noble pris'ner gall. **1844** ALB. SMITH *Adv. Mr. Ledbury* lv. (1886) 168 [His] feet were somewhat galled with the hard walking of the previous days.

†**b.** *to gall off*: to rub off, remove by chafing.

1602 MARSTON *Ant. & Mel.* II. Wks. 1856 I. 21 Her wit stings, blisters, galles off the skinne. **1677** *Lond. Gaz.* No. 1220/4 A dapple gray Gelding.. the hair being gauled off of his breast, by drawing in a Coach. **1694** *Ibid.* No. 3027/4 The hair is galled off from the off Thigh and Ribs.

2. To fret or injure (inanimate objects) by rubbing or contact.

1600 HAKLUYT *Voy.* III. 66 The Gabriell.. had her Cable gauld asunder with a piece of driuing yce. **1618** W. LAWSON *New Orch. & Garden* (1623) 22 You shall see the tops of trees rubd off, their sides galled like a galled horses backe. **1693** EVELYN *De la Quint. Compl. Gard.* 19 Make several holes in the Earth with some Iron-Pin.. but withal so cautiously, as not to gall any of the Roots. **1793** *Trans. Soc. Arts* XI. 21 We.. cut out every branch that was decayed or galled. **1796** C. MARSHALL *Garden.* viii. (1813) 106 Take care to fix the stake firmly, and to tie the tree so with a firm hay band that it may not easily get galled.

†**3.** To break the surface of, produce furrows or cavities in (ground, soil), to fret or wash *away*. *Obs.*

1577–87 HOLINSHED *Chron.* III. 1223/2 Three men riding vpon the causeie, being then ouerflowne.. chanced to come into a place where the water had galled awaie the earth. **1603** KNOLLES *Hist. Turks* (1621) 537 The light sands in many places gauled deepe with the wind, wonderfully troubleth the wearie passengers. **1691** RAY *Creation* I. (1704) 103 It would gall the ground, wash away Plants by the Roots, overthrow Houses.

4. *fig.* To vex, harass, oppress. (Chiefly said of a metaphorical 'yoke', 'fetters', or 'harness'.)

1614 RALEIGH *Hist. World* II. i. §12. 232 The neckes of mortall men hauing been neuer before gawled with the yoke of forraine dominion. **1796** MORSE *Amer. Geog.* II. 484 Long and heavily did the Tartar yoke gall the neck of Russia. *a* **1839** PRAED *Poems* (1864) II. 129 And though its links be firmly set, I never found them gall me yet. **1863** GEO. ELIOT *Romola* I. xvi, Our old Florentine trick of choosing a new harness when the old one galls us.

5. To harass or annoy in warfare (esp. with arrows or shot).

1548 HALL *Chron., Hen. VI*, 124 b, The dastarde people.. galled and wounded with the shot of the arrowes. **1577–87** HOLINSHED *Chron.* III. 966/2 With shot of the English archers were so curried and galled that they were driuen to retire. **1603** KNOLLES *Hist. Turks* (1621) 535 As much as they could shunned to encounter their enemies with their horsemen, labouring only to gaule them with shot. **1697** DRYDEN *Virg. Georg.* IV. 446 Flights of Arrows from the Parthian Bows, When from afar they gaul embattel'd Foes. **1731** J. GRAY *Gunnery* Pref. 17 By these engines they gauled the enemy at a distance. **1814** SCOTT *Ld. of Isles* I. xxix, Where bowmen might in ambush wait,.. To gall an entering foe. **1865** M. ARNOLD *Ess. Crit.* vii. (1875) 270 The surrounding multitudes galled them from a distance with a cloud of arrows.

6. To harass or annoy mentally, render sore in spirit, irritate.

1573 G. HARVEY *Letter-bk.* (Camden) 18 So that I have not yit bene so courst and gald in our own Hous, as I am like hereafter to be pincht and nipt in the Regent Hous. **1597** MONTGOMERIE *Cherrie & Slae* 1205 Quhen Hope was gawd into the quick. **1621** BURTON *Anat. Mel.* I. ii. IV. iv. 196 Many men are as much gauled with a calumny, scurrile & bitter iest, a libel, a pasquill.. as with any misfortune whatsoeuer. **1703** ROWE *Fair Penit.* I. i. 129 Ere long I mean to meet 'em Face to Face And gaul 'em with my Triumph. **1791** BOSWELL *Johnson* May an. 1738, Cramped and galled by narrow circumstances. **1831** LYTTON *Godolphin* 4 You will delight to gall their vanities.

†**b.** *intr. to gall at*: to scoff at. *Obs.*

1599 SHAKS. *Hen. V*, V. i. 77, I haue seene you gleeking and galling at this Gentleman twice or thrice.

7. *intr.* To become sore or chafed. †Also *fig.*

1614 B. JONSON *Barth. Fair* II. i, Thou'lt gall between the tongue and the teeth, with fretting. **1721** RAMSAY *El. Patie Birnie* 88 He gaw'd fou sair. **1737** BRACKEN *Farriery Impr.* (1756) I. 332, I.. am very apt to gall and have the Skin fretted off. *Ibid.* II. 161 A young Horse's Back.. will fret, gall, and be full of Warbles, with even the least Journey.

†**b.** ? To crack. (Cf. GALL *sb.*[2] 4.) *Obs. rare*$^{-1}$.

1770–4 A. HUNTER *Georg. Ess.* (1803) I. 515 The wood looked well, and did not seem to gall or warp so much as Fir of the same age and seasoning would have done.

gall (gɔːl), *v.*[2] *Dyeing.* [f. GALL *sb.*[3]] *trans.* To impregnate with a decoction of galls.

1581 [cf. GALLED *ppl. a.*[2]]. **1822** IMISON *Sc. & Art* II. 194 Silk is dyed black as follows. After boiling it with soap, it is galled, and afterwards washed. **1853** URE *Dict. Arts* I. 180 For the dyeing of raw silk black, it is galled in the cold, with the bath of galls which has already served for the black of boiled silk.

gall-, see GALLO-[2].

Galla (ˈgælə). Pl. **Galla, Gallas.** A member of a group of Hamitic peoples inhabiting equatorial Africa, allied to the Ethiopians in language and origin; also, their language. Also *attrib.* or as *adj.*

1875 *Encycl. Brit.* I. 263/2 The next great branch of the Ethiopic race comprehends the Galla, who occupy an immense tract in Eastern Africa... Our knowledge of them is chiefly confined to those Gallas who conquered Abyssinia. **1878** K. JOHNSTON *Africa* xiv. 286 The Somâli and Galla people are as closely related as they are hostilely disposed towards each other. **1892** A. S. WHITE *Devel. Africa* (ed. 2) 101 As agriculturists and herdsmen, and in the industrial arts, the Galla bordering on Abyssinia and the Somâl of the Coast towns are the most advanced. **1895** A. H. KEANE *Africa* I. 489 The typical Gallas of Kaffa and surrounding regions are perhaps the finest people in all Africa. *Ibid.* II. 570 The Galla love of roaming. **1920** *Blackw. Mag.* May 678/2 The poor old Galla vendor clucking with rage. **1932** W. L. GRAFF *Lang.* 404 The most important [Cushitic] dialects are.. Somali, Galla, [etc.]. **1970** *Encycl. Brit.* IX. 1094/1 The Galla.. used to make a pilgrimage to the Abba Muda, 'father of anointing',.. the personification of Galla law and tradition.

gallace: see GALACE.

gallacetophenone (gəˌlæsɪtəʊfɪˈnəʊn, ˌgæl əsiːtəʊˈfiːnəʊn). *Chem.* [ad. G. *gallacetophenon* (Nencki & Sieber 1881, in *Jrnl. prakt. Chem.* XXIII. 537), f. GALL- + ACETOPHENONE.] A yellow crystalline compound, $C_6H_2(OH)_3COCH_3$, formerly used in ointments for skin-diseases and as a mordant dye-stuff.

1881 *Jrnl. Chem. Soc.* XL. 811 Gallacetophenone is obtained on heating pyrogallol with glacial acetic acid and zinc chloride at 145°. **1893** E. KNECHT et al. *Man. Dyeing* II VII. 628 Alizarin-yellow C or gallacetophenone is produced by the action of glacial acetic acid and chloride of zinc on pyrogallol. **1904** H. W. STELWAGON *Treat. Dis. Skin* (ed. 3) III. 238 Gallacetophenone is likewise employed in this disease [*sc.* psoriasis], in the form of an ointment. **1952** K. VENKATARAMAN *Chem. Synthetic Dyes* II. xxvi. 796 Alizarin Yellow C.., one of the earliest synthetic mordant dyes, was gallacetophenone.

gallage, gallaglass, gallande, obs. ff. GALOSH, GALLOGLASS, GALLON.

gallamine (ˈgæləmiːn, -ɪn). *Chem.* Also -in. [f. GALL- + AMINE.] **1.** ***gallamine blue*** (also with capital initial letters), a basic mordant dye of the oxazine series.

1889 *Jrnl. Soc. Dyers & Colourists* 25 Nov. 171/1 Gallamine blue produces on wool, mordanted with chrome and tartar, a blue which somewhat resembles in shade that obtained with gallocyanine, with which gallamine blue is indeed closely related. **1905** *Jrnl. Chem. Soc.* LXXXVIII. I. 831 The yield of gallamine-blue, $C_{15}H_{13}O_4N_3$,HCl, obtained by treating gallamide in alcoholic solution with nitrosodimethylaniline, is largely increased by using an excess of the latter. **1935** *Jrnl. Comparative Neurol.* LXI. 120 The gallamin blue method is thus of a great importance as a neurological stain. **1952** K. VENKATARAMAN *Chem. Synthetic Dyes* II. xxv. 783 The Gallocyanine derivative prepared from gallamide is marketed as the soluble bisulfite compound, Gallamine Blue.

2. In full ***gallamine triethiodide***. A whitish powder, $C_6H_3[O{\cdot}(CH_2)_2{\cdot}N(C_2H_5)_3]_3I_3$, having a slightly bitter taste and used as a neuromuscular blocking drug.

1951 *Proc. R. Soc. Med.* XLIV. 375 Flaxedil, or Gallamine triethiodide, as it is now named by the British Pharmacopœial Commission, is a British production of a synthetic curarizing agent.. which was first synthesized in France. **1961** *Lancet* 26 Aug. 486/2 The man was given a small dose of atropine by mouth and 1.5 ml. gallamine triethiodide ('Flaxedil') intravenously. **1963** A. H. DOUTHWAITE *Hale-White's Materia Medica* (ed. 32) 210 Gallamine is used chiefly to obtain adequate muscular relaxation for surgical operations carried out under general anæsthesia.

gallanilide (gæˈlænɪlaɪd). *Chem.* [f. GALL- + ANILIDE.] An anilide of gallic acid, $C_6H_2(OH)_3{\cdot}CONH{\cdot}C_6H_5$, used in the manufacture of some dyes.

1883 *Jrnl. Chem. Soc.* XLIV. 335 Gallanilide is deposited as a crystalline mass when digallic acid is dissolved in aniline. **1916** E. KNECHT et al. *Man. Dyeing* (ed. 3) II. VII. 620 Gallanilide blue is produced by the action of gallanilide on nitrosodimethylaniline and subsequent treatment with aniline. **1924** *Chem. Abstr.* XVIII. 2009 The ferric salt.. of gallanilide.. is a dark violet powder. **1952** K. VENKATARAMAN *Chem. Synthetic Dyes* II. xxv. 783 The Gallocyanine derivative prepared from gallamide is marketed as the soluble bisulfite compound, Gallamine Blue... The gallanilide analog is Gallanil Violet.

gallant (ˈgælənt, gəˈlænt), *a.* and *sb.* Forms: 4–6 **galaunt(e**, 5–8 **galant(e**, 5–6 *Sc.* **galland**, 6 **gallante, -aunt, -aunde**, 6– **gallant.** [a. F. *galant* (recorded from the 14th c.), pa. pple of OF. *galer* to make merry, make a show, (connected with *gale* merrymaking = It., Sp. *gala*; see GALE *sb.*[2] and GALA). The early senses of the adj. in Fr. are: 'dashing, spirited, bold' (obsolete in Fr., but the source of the prevailing sense in mod.Eng.); 'gay in appearance, handsome, gaily attired'; and 'fitted for the pleasures of society, attractive in manners, courteous, polished'. The last of these gave rise in mod.Fr. to the specialized senses 'politely attentive to women', and 'amorous, amatory', which were adopted into Eng. in the 17th c., and are usually distinguished by the accentuation *ga'llant*. The It. *galante*, courteous, honourable, and Sp. *galante*, gaily dressed, sprightly, *galan, galano* gaily dressed, seemed to have been adopted from French. The use as sb., which is recorded in Eng. somewhat earlier than the adjectival use, was adopted from Fr., in which language all the senses of the sb. had been developed.

The origin of the OFr. verb. *galer* is disputed. The view of Diez, that it was f. the OHG. *geil* = ME. GOLE, wanton, is now abandoned, as the normal Central French form on that supposition should begin with *j*; the form *galer* (for which *waler* occurs as a variant) points to an original initial *w*. Hence most recent scholars regard the vb. as ad. OHG. *wallôn* to wander, go on pilgrimage; but the transition of sense offers difficulties that are not fully cleared up.]

A. *adj.*

1. a. Gorgeous or showy in appearance, finely-dressed, smart. *arch.*

c **1420** LYDG. *Assemb. Gods* 296 Then was there set the god Cupido, All fresshe & galaunt & costlew in aray. **1508** FISHER 7 *Penit. Ps.* cxxx. Wks. (1876) 203 By wantonesse of wordes, by wanton lokes, galant apparayle of thy body, [etc.] **1551** ROBINSON tr. *More's Utop.* II. (1895) 132 The houses be curiously builded, after a gorgiouse and gallaunt sort. **1578** T. N. tr. *Conq. W. India* 139 The Mexican brought.. garments of Cotten exceeding gallant. **1589** R. ROBINSON *Gold. Mirr.* (Chetham Soc.) 2 And in a galland garden stood this famous Dame. **1597** GERARDE *Herbal* II. lxxi. 302 On the top of the stalke standeth a most gallant flower verie double. **1598** BARRET *Theor. Warres* II. i. 20 He shall alwaies go gallant and well armed. **1617** MARKHAM *Caval.* VI. 35 The brauelier will your horses maine or taile curle, and the gallanter it will appeare to the beholders. **1665–76** REA *Flora* 75 It beareth the biggest, doublest, and gallantest flower of all the double Daffodils. **1671** *Lond. Gaz.* No. 544/3 She appeared extraordinary rich and gallant, being adorned with great quantities of Pearls, and other precious stones. **1794** BURNS *Song, Young Jamie*, Young Jamie, pride of a' the plain, Sae gallant and sae gay a swain. **1809** W. IRVING *Knickerb.* III. iv. (1849) 164, I must confess these gallant garments were rather short. **1897** *Daily News* 30 Mar. 5/3 The Lord Mayor of Dublin, accompanied by the High Sheriff and the Town Clerk, gallant in scarlet robes, ermine trimmed.

†**b.** Of language: Full of showy expressions, ornate, specious. *Obs.*

1484 CAXTON *Chivalry* 77 The armes with whiche lecherye warreth chastyte ben yongthe beaulte queynt vestures and galaunt falshede. **1552** HULOET, Gaye or galaunt speach, *phaleratus sermo.*

c. *Mus.* = GALANT *a.*

1925 *Musical Q.* XI. 356 (*title*) The 'gallant' style of music. *Ibid.*, Gallant, the secular homophonous style of courtly, amatory and dramatic music whose evolution during the seventeenth and eighteenth centuries runs nearly parallel with that of rococo architecture.

†**2.** Of women: Fine-looking, handsome. *Obs.*

1552 HULOET, Galaunt wench, *bellula.* **1579** LYLY *Euphues* (Arb.) 51 This gallant girle, more faire then fortunate, and yet more fortunate then faithful. **1613** WITHERS *Abuses Stript & Whipt* II. ii, Some gallant Lasse along before him sweeps. ? **1650** *Don Bellianis* 173 The gallant Princess Persiana.

†**3.** Suited to fashionable society; indulging in social gaiety or display; attractive in manners, polished, courtier-like. *Obs.*

1500–20 DUNBAR *Poems* xix. 6 Gif I be galland, lusty and blyth. **1548** LATIMER *Ploughers* (Arb.) 25 Thei hauke, thei hunt, thei card, they dyce, they pastyme in theyr prelacies with galaunte gentlemen. **1583** STUBBES *Anat. Abus.* I. (1879) 98 He is but a beast that.. would abstaine from such gallant pastyme.

absol. **1645** WALLER *Of her Chamber* 15 The Gay, the wise, the gallant, and the grave.

4. a. *loosely*, as a general epithet of admiration or praise: Excellent, splendid, 'fine', 'grand'. Cf. BRAVE *a.* 3. Now *rare* exc. with mixture of sense 1 or 5.

1539 TAVERNER *Erasm. Prov.* (1552) 24 Nothynge is so galaunt, so excellent, that can longe content the mynde. **1623** BINGHAM *Xenophon* 84 It was a gallant sight, to behold the army standing so imbattelled in the field. **1641** FRENCH *Distill.* v. (1651) 124 A few drops.. put into any Wine giveth it a gallant relish. **1649** J. H. *Motion to Parl. Adv. Learn.* 16 Our Accademies.. teach.. the gallantest Theories of knowledge. **1662** R. MATHEW *Unl. Alch.* §33. 29 He presently fell asleep, and also into a gallant breathing sweat. **1676** J. COOKE *Marrow Chirurg.* 819 Camphore.. given in cooling Juleps.. is gallant to quench violent heat in Malign Fevers. **1724** DE FOE *Mem. Cavalier* (1840) 78 Here was also a stable of gallant horses. **1812** *Sporting Mag.* XXXIX. 185 A fox was run on Saturday.. in a very gallant style. **1851** THACKERAY *Eng. Hum.* iv. (1858) 174 They played for gallant stakes—the bold men of those days.

b. often used as an admiring epithet for a ship: 'Noble', stately; now usually with mixture of sense 5 and some notion of personification.

1583 STANYHURST *Æneis* I. (Arb.) 21 Three gallant vessels. **1610** SHAKS. *Temp.* V. i. 237 Our royall, good, and gallant Ship. **1757** GRAY *Bard* II. ii, In gallant trim the gilded vessel goes. **1790** COWPER *My Mother's Pict.* 88 A gallant bark from Albion's coast. **1838** PRESCOTT *Ferd. & Is.* II. II. iv. 450 A more gallant and beautiful armada never before quitted the shores of Spain. **1868** GLADSTONE *Juv. Mundi* ii. (1870) 55 We may consider the name of the ship Argo as meaning.. 'stout', able to do battle with the waves, as we now say a good or a gallant ship.

5. a. Chivalrously brave, full of noble daring.

1596 SHAKS. *1 Hen. IV*, IV. iv. 26 And there is my Lord of Worcester, And a Head of gallant Warriors, Noble Gentlemen. **1597** —— *2 Hen. IV*, III. ii. 68. **1611** CORYAT *Crudities* 236 Like a peerelesse Monarch garded with many legions of the gallantest Worthies. **1663** BUTLER *Hud.* I. ii. 249 The gallant Bruin march'd next him. **1713** STEELE *Guardian* No. 18 ¶6 Our galant countryman, Sir Philip Sydney. **1769** *Junius Lett.* xv. 64 These gallant, well-disciplined troops. **1781** GIBBON *Decl. & Fall* III. 172 The gallant answer which checked the arrogance of that ambitious prince. **1845** S. AUSTIN *Ranke's Hist. Ref.* III. 639 He.. had all the parts and qualities of a gallant soldier. **1859** SMILES *Self-Help* i. (1860) 10 The gallantest of British sea-men. **1868** MILMAN *St. Paul's* 426 Sherlock made a gallant defence.

quasi-*adv.* **1590** SHAKS. *Mids. N.* I. ii. 25 (Qo.) A louer that kils himselfe, most gallant [**1623** gallantly], for loue.

b. Used, esp. in parliamentary language, as the conventional epithet of a military or naval officer.

1875 LUCY *Diary Two Parl.* (1885) I. 49 The gallant captain always begins to address the House in a breathless, gasping manner. *Ibid.* 81 The hon. and gallant gentleman.

6. (Usually *ga'llant*). Markedly polite and attentive to the female sex.

a **1680** BUTLER *Rem.* (1759) I. 216 Th' antique Sage, that was gallant t'a Goose. **1728–46** THOMSON *Spring* 584 The gay troops begin In gallant thought to plume the painted wing. **1732** POPE *Ep. Bathurst* 307 Gallant and gay in Cliveden's proud alcove, The bow'r of wanton Shrewsbury and love. **1754** RICHARDSON *Grandison* (1781) VI. xxiv. 137 Sir Charles fell immediately into the easiest (shall I say the gallantest?) the most agreeable conversation. **1798** JANE AUSTEN *Northang. Abb.* xiii, The general attended her himself to the street-door, saying everything gallant as they went down stairs.

7. (Usually *ga'llant.*) Of or pertaining to (sexual) love, amorous, amatory. Now somewhat *rare*.

1673 DRYDEN *Marr. à la Mode* III. i, The *Billets doux*.. are so French, so *gallant*, and so *tendre.* **1724** SWIFT *Corinna* 29 Her common-place book all gallant is.. She pours it out in Atalantis. **1774** CHESTERF. *Lett.* (1792) I. lxvi. 185 A little gallant history, which must contain a great deal of love.. the subject must be a love affair. **1849** TICKNOR *Span. Lit.* II. xxix. 529 *note*, Some of the contents of which are too gallant to be very nun-like.

8. *Comb.*, as ***gallant-hearted***, ***-minded*** adjs.; †***gallant-springing*** *a.*, 'growing up in beauty' (Schmidt).

1594 SHAKS. *Rich. III*, I. iv. 227 When gallant springing braue Plantagenet.. was strucke dead by thee. **1598** BARRET *Theor. Warres* Pref. 5 All gallant minded gentlemen. **1848** DICKENS *Dombey* xxxii, His hopes of the generous, handsome, gallant-hearted youth.. began to fade.

B. *sb.*

1. a. A man of fashion and pleasure; a fine gentleman. (Sometimes with added notion of A. 5.) *arch.*

1388 *Pol. Poems* (Rolls) I. 274 Galauntes [are] purs penyles. **1430–40** LYDG. *Bochas* V. xxv. (1554) 138 b, Thei toke a galaunt, borne of lowe linage, Called Prompalus.. And affirmed.. how he was sonne and iust heire in substance To Epiphanes. **1513** DOUGLAS *Æneis* IX. iii. 200 Ilkane ane hundreth fallowys reddy boun Of ȝoung gallandis. **1598** BARCKLEY *Felic. Man* (1631) 662 Though the gallants think thee rude, because in all things thou doest not imitate them. **1627** DRAYTON *Agincrt.* ccxciv, That braue French Gallant, when the fight began, Whose lease of Lackies ambled by his side, Himselfe a Lacky now most basely ran. **1633** BP. HALL *Hard Texts* 608 All the stout gallants of Judæa do roare and lament. **1645** EVELYN *Mem.* (1857) I. 168 The streets are full of gallants. **1684** BUNYAN *Pilgr.* II. Introd. 89 Brave Galants do my Pilgrim hug and love. **1719** D'URFEY *Pills* V. 349 Ye Side-Box Gallants, whom the vulgar call Beaus. **1789** BURNS *Song* Poet Wks. (Globe) 251 My Harry was a gallant gay. **1810** SCOTT *Lady of L.* I. iv, And many a gallant, stayed per-force, Was fain to breath his faltering horse. **1828** —— *F.M. Perth* ii, The young gallants of the Royal Court. **1874** GREEN *Short Hist.* vii. §5. 389 Gallants gambled away a fortune at a sitting.

†**b.** Of a woman: A fashionably attired beauty. *Obs.*

c **1550** *Lusty Juventus* C iv b, Now by the masse I perceyue that she is a gallaunde. **1606** DEKKER *Sev. Sinnes* Induct. (Arb.) 8 Thou [London] that wert before the only Gallant and Minion of the world. **1662** PEPYS *Diary* 4 Sept., She would fain be a gallant.

†**2. a.** Used in the vocative as a courteous mode of address, *esp.* in plural; = 'Gentlemen'. Also with playful or semi-ironical tone, as in ***this gallant*** = 'this fine fellow'. *Obs.*

c **1470** HENRY *Wallace* VIII. 1022 Had we ȝon gallandis doun, On the playn ground, thai wald mor sobyr be. *c* **1489** CAXTON *Sonnes of Aymon* xxii. 477 Reynawde called ten of his folke and sayd to theym, 'Galantes [Fr. *Barons*], goo fet me the duke rychard'. **1501** DOUGLAS *Pal. Hon.* III. 21 Then suddanelie my keipar to me said, Ascend galland. **1591** SHAKS. *1 Hen. VI*, III. ii. 41 God morrow Gallants, want ye Corn for Bread? **1633** T. STAFFORD *Pac. Hib.* II. vi. 162 Whereby the indifferent Reader may perceiue with what prepared hatred, and prepensed malice this Gallant was affected. **1669** DRYDEN *Tyrannic Love* Epil. 11 Gallants, look to 't. **1714** POPE *Epil. to 'Jane Shore'* 24 Faith, gallants, board with saints, and bed with sinners. **1810** SCOTT *Lady of L.* V. xvii, Exclaim not, gallants! question not.

†**b.** *pl.* One's (military) followers. *Obs.*

1526 SKELTON *Magnyf.* 1526 Galba, whom his galantys garde for agaspe. **1555** J. PROCTOR *Hist. Wyat's Rebell.* in Arb. *Garner* VIII. 49 Being roughly charged therewith by Wyat and others his gallants.

3. (Sometimes *ga'llant.*) One who pays court to ladies, a ladies' man. Now somewhat *rare*. Also, a lover; in a bad sense, a paramour.

a **1450** *Knt. de la Tour* (1868) 65 He toke alle her iuellys and rynges that was geuen her by galauntys forto haue had her to do foly. **1598** SHAKS. *Merry W.* II. i. 22 One that is well-nye worne to peeces with age To show himselfe a yong Gallant. **1664** CHAS. II in Julia Cartwright *Henrietta of Orleans* (1894) 153 A handsome face without mony has but few galants, upon the score of marriage. **1691** DRYDEN *K. Arthur* Epil. 41 And he that likes the music and the play Shall be my favourite gallant today. **1708** *Brit. Apollo* No. 31. 3/2 And loose a Gallant by resenting a kiss. **1733** H. WALPOLE *Lett. to Mann* (1857) VI. 20 Pride was their mother, and whoever she laid them to, Hypocrisy was her galant. **1774** GOLDSM. *Retal.* 65 His gallants are all faultless, his women divine. —— *Nat. Hist.* (1776) V. 290 When the female [pigeon] admits the addresses of a new gallant. **1875** FORTNUM *Majolica* vii. 63 Small plates.. which it was then the fashion for gallants to present, filled with preserves or confetti, to ladies. **1886** A. ARNOLD in *Academy* 18 Dec. 404 How few nowadays use the word 'gallant' to describe a lady's man.

¶**4.** Given by Gerarde as the name of a kind of Anemone.

1597 GERARDE *Herbal* Table Eng. Names, Gallant, that is Anemone, Windflower. *a* **1667** SKINNER *Etymol. Bot.*, *Gallant*, Anemone, sic dicta ob eximiam florum pulchritudinem.

†**5.** *Naut.* A name formerly applied to 'all flags borne on the mizen-mast' (Adm. Smyth). *Obs.*

gallant (gə'lænt, 'gælənt), *v.* [f. the adj.]

I. (? stressed *'gallant.*)

1. *intr.* To play the gallant or dandy, to 'cut a dash'. Also ***to gallant it.*** *rare.*

1608 MACHIN *Dumb. Knt.* I. B 3 b, Be patient wench, and thou shalt shortly see me gallant it with the best. **1888** LIGHTHALL *Yng. Seigneur* 74 As Papal Zouave, he embarked for Rome to gallant in voluminous trousers on four sous a day.

†**2.** *trans.* To make gallant or fine, to deck out in a showy manner. *Obs.*

1614 J. COOKE *Tu Quoque* I 3 b, Enter Bubble gallanted. *Bub.* How Apparell makes a man respected; the very children in the streete do adore mee.

II. (Usually stressed *ga'llant.*)

3. *intr.* To play the gallant, flirt, dally *with*. Also ***to gallant it.***

1744 E. HEYWOOD *Female Spectator* (1748) I. 97 She.. gallants it with every pretty fellow she comes in company with. **1749** GARRICK *Lethe* I. Wks. 1798 I. 17 I'll lay six to four that he has been gallanting with some of the beauties of antiquity. **1809** MAR. EDGEWORTH *Manœuvring* x, Captain Jemmison went on shore to.. spend his time in great dissipation.. eating, dressing, dancing, gallanting. **1859** SALA *Tw. round Clock* (1861) 71 Now we are in Horace Walpole's time, and the macaroni-cynic of Strawberry Hill is gallanting in the Mall with Lady Caroline Petersham. **1888** SNODGRASS *Heine's Wit*, etc. (ed. 2) 208 Nor.. did he gallant with the crowned relatives of the Cæsars.

transf. **1762** STEVENSON *Crazy Tales* 27 A Horse gallanting with a Mare. **1847** *Blackw. Mag.* LXII. 666 Small must have been the population, when these.. great inexpressibles, gallanted with the ladies' large hoop farthingales.

b. To gad about idly, 'gallivant'. *Sc.*

1804 TARRAS *Poems* 143 In kirk-yard drear they may gallant, An' mak his turf their fav'rite haunt. **1822** GALT *Steam-boat* vii. 141 It is.. believed.. that the witches are in the practice of gallanting over field and flood.. in the shape of cats and mawkins. **1825–80** JAMIESON s.v., Women who gad about idly, and with the appearance of lightness, in the company of men, are said to gallant with them.

4. *trans.* To play the gallant to (a woman), pay court or lover-like attentions to, flirt with.

1672 J. LACY *Dumb Lady* III. 37, I find the Doctor has a mind to gallant me. **1769** *Misc.* in *Ann. Reg.* 168/1 Abbes are always gallanting the ladies. **1817** MAR. EDGEWORTH *Harrington* (1832) 151 He was gallanting the Polish lady. **1865** CARLYLE *Fredk. Gt.* XVI. iii. VI. 165 That young Durchlaucht.. whom we saw gallanting the little girl.. some years ago. **1883** A. DOBSON *Fielding* vii. 181 When he visits a friend or gallants the ladies.

transf. **1717** CIBBER *Non-Juror* II, He us'd to make the Maids lock up the Turky-cocks every Saturday Night, for fear they should gallant the Hens on a Sunday. *c* **1850** *Arab. Nts.* (Rtldg.) 11 The cock.. was gallanting one of his hens.

†**b.** To caress (a hand) gallantly. *Obs.*

1672 DRYDEN *Assignation* III. i, I have tried every bar [of the grate] many a fair time over; and at last have found out one, where a hand may get through, and be gallanted.

5. *esp.* To act as cavalier or escort to (a lady), to attend or conduct (her) to some place.

1690 CROWNE *Eng. Friar* I. 4 Young Ranter talks to her, gallants to her coach, follows her home. **1728** VANBR. & CIB. *Prov. Husb.* III. i, The ladies.. wanted you to help gallant them. **1814** MISS MITFORD in L'Estrange *Life* (1870) I. 280 The.. House of Commons, where we were gallanted by half a dozen members. **1872** GEO. ELIOT *Middlem.* I, Ladislaw gallants her about sometimes.

b. In a wider sense: To conduct, escort, convey.

1806 W. IRVING in *Life & Lett.* (1864) I. 170 Show this scrawl to nobody, but gallant it, as quick as possible, to the fire. **1807–8** —— *Salmag.* (1824) 196 His first care, on making a new acquaintance, is to gallant him to old Cockloft's. **1817** LADY GRANVILLE *Lett.* (1894) I. 119 Mr. Agar Ellis, whom I invited, carried there, and gallanted about. **1841** CATLIN *N. Amer. Ind.* (1844) II. xxxvii. 46 The one [buffalo] which I saw fit to gallant over the plain alone ..led me a hard chase. **1854** HAWTHORNE *Eng. Note-bks.* (1883) I. 441 The little black steamer.. sometimes gallanting a tall ship in and out.

†**6.** ***to gallant a fan.*** **a.** (See quot. *a* 1700). **b.** (? a misapprehension.) To handle or manipulate a fan. *Obs.*

a **1700** B. E. *Dict. Cant. Crew*, *Gallant a Fan*, to break it with Design, on Purpose to have the.. Favour to Present a better. **1711** ADDISON *Spect.* No. 102 ¶ 10, I teach young Gentlemen the whole Art of Gallanting a Fan. *N.B.* I have several little plain Fans made for this Use, to avoid Expence. **1748** RICHARDSON *Clarissa* (1811) V. 303 Charlotte galanting her fan, and swimming over the floor without touching it. **1754** —— *Grandison* (1811) III. iv. 24 Galanting her fan.

Hence **gallanting** *vbl. sb.* and *ppl. a.*

1664 BUTLER *Hud.* II. i. 644, I rather hop'd I should no more Hear from you o' th' gallanting score. **1707** *Reflex. upon Ridicule* 133 Amours, Adventures, gallanting Stories. **1715** M. DAVIES *Athen. Brit.* I. 21 The Gallanting Pamphlet stiled The Pastime of Pleasure. **1797** *Monthly Mag.* III. 537 He was of a gallanting turn, although he only made love to old ladies. **1819** J. H. VAUX *Mem.* II. 30 She would, by artful gallanting with a gentleman, facilitate my design upon his pockets. **1830** GALT *Lawrie T.* II. xi. (1849) 77 To spend money in such gallanting was a thing I had never thought of. **1869** *Latest News* 10 Oct. 6 Young men who do their gallanting away from the city.

gallantee, var. GALANTY.

'gallanthood. *rare*⁻¹. [f. GALLANT *sb.* + -HOOD.] 'Gallants' collectively, chivalry.

1881 PALGRAVE *Vis. Eng.* 134 Half our best treasures of gallanthood there, with axe and with glaive.

†**gallantify**, *v. Obs. rare.* [f. GALLANT + -(I)FY.] *trans.* (See quot.)

1672 J. LACY *Dumb Lady* I. 6 *Isa.* Sirrah, talk of poisoning my children, and I'l have thee so gallantified. *Dr.* Gallantified? prethee what's that, Wife? *Isa.* To be gallantified, is to be soundly cudgel'd, sirrah.

gallantine, var. GALANTINE.

†**'gallantise.** *Obs.* [a. OF. *galantise*, f. *galant* GALLANT *a.*: see -ICE[1].] Gallantry, gallant bearing, courtliness.

c **1520** *Treat. Galaunt* (1860) 12 Our gentylnes for galauntyse haue we lefte there. **1566** PAINTER *Pal. Pleas.* 152 The thousand slippery sleightes of Loves gallantise. **1591** SYLVESTER *Du Bartas* I. vi. 906 Whom all the Showes of State.. Gray-headed Senate and Youth's gallantise Grac't not so much, as onely this Device. **1596** *Life Scanderbeg* 10 The gallantise and bravery of thy youth.

†**gallantish**, *a. Sc. Obs.* [f. GALLANT *sb.* or *a.* + -ISH.] ? Fond of display.

1802 BRUCE *Diss. Suprem.* in *Life Knox* (1813) I. 421 A weak, fickle, freakish, bigotted gallantish or imperious woman.

†**gallan'tissimo.** *Obs. rare.* [a. It. *galantissimo*, superl. of *galante* GALLANT *a.*] As a mode of address = Most gallant sir!

1684 J. LACY *Sir H. Buffoon* II. ii, But why, my Gallantissimo's, do you not address to the rich Heiresses?

gallantize ('gæləntaɪz), *v.* Now *rare.* [f. GALLANT + -IZE. Cf. F. *galantiser* to treat with gallantry.]

1. *intr.* To play the gallant; esp. in ***to gallantize it.***

1603 FLORIO *Montaigne* III. v. (1632) 490 So they may gallantize and flush it in noveltie. **1611** COTGR., *se Gorgiaser*, to flaunt, braue, or gallantize it. **1706** PHILLIPS (ed. Kersey), To *Gallantize*, to play the Gallant. **1807–8** W. IRVING *Salmag.* (1824) 325 They do ponder on noughte but how to gallantize it at balls, routs, and fandangoes.

2. *trans.* To play the gallant to (a woman); to court.

1728 MORGAN *Algiers* II. iii. 239 The meanest.. never furnish their Visitors with such opportunities of gallantizing their wives, as the French and other Novelists.. would insinuate. **1736** ELIZA STANLEY tr. *Hist. Prince Titi* 22 A certain Privy Counsellor, who.. gallantised all the young Girls he came near. **1872** LYTTON *Parisians* IX. iii, There was a gal.. whom I gallantised.

gallantly ('gæləntlɪ, gə'læntlɪ), *adv.* [f. GALLANT *a.* + -LY[2].] In a gallant manner.

1. In gorgeous style, showily.

1552 LATIMER *Fruitf. Serm.* (1575) II. 148 Our Clergymen whiche go so gallauntly now a dayes. I heare say that some of them weare Veluet shoes and Veluet slyppers. **1582** BRETON *Flourish on Fancy* (Grosart) 17/1 Thus shall you see her Bed and Chamber, brauely deckte: And every roome.. set out in each respect, so gallantlie. **1603** KNOLLES *Hist. Turks* (1621) 1260 A gard of an hundred tall souldiours, gallantly apparelled all in blew. **1650** FULLER *Pisgah* IV. vi. 110 On her wedding-day, how gallantly does she come forth as a Bride adorned for her husband? **1753** HANWAY *Trav.* (1762) I. iii. xxxii. 139 A party of fifty persons, gallantly dressed, well mounted and armed. **1851** LONGF. *Gold. Leg.* III. *In front of Cathedral* 23 A crowd.. Gaily and gallantly arrayed!

2. In an excellent manner, splendidly, finely.

1552 HULOET, Galauntly, *belle, pollite, pollucibiliter.* **1588** GREENE *Pandosto* (1607) 23 Which attire became her so gallantly, as shee seemed to be the Goddesse Flora her selfe. **1719** DE FOE *Crusoe* II. ix, They were gallantly armed. **1838** L. E. LANDON *Leg. Teignmouth* ii, And gallantly the white sails swept On, on before the wind.

3. In a brave or spirited manner, courageously, heroically.

1590 SHAKS. *Mids. N.* I. ii. 25 (Fo.) A Louer that kills himselfe most gallantly for loue. **1653** SIR E. NICHOLAS in *N. Papers* (Camden) II. 37 Lo. Taff answeared gallantly that he appeared not there as a tale-carrier. *a* **1674** CLARENDON *Hist. Reb.* VIII. §14 The foot behaved themselves very gallantly. **1774** FLETCHER *Doctr. Grace & Justice* Wks. 1795 IV. 195 They fought gallantly for many glorious truths. **1839** JAMES *Louis XIV*, I. 157 The place was gallantly defended.. by the garrison. **1856** FROUDE *Hist. Eng.* I. 357 'Threaten such things to rich and dainty folk, which have their hope in this world', answered Elston, gallantly, ' we fear them not'.

4. With courtesy or politeness, esp. in the exaggerated style of a gallant or courtier; in recent use, only of behaviour towards women.

1611 COTGR., *Gaillardement*.. gallantly, like a gallant. **1692** DRYDEN *St. Evremont's Ess.* 343 One may say seriously of it, what has been gallantly said of Love, 'All other Pleasures are not worth its Pains'. **1765** H. WALPOLE *Otranto* v. (1798) 83 The latter retired.. gallantly telling the prince, that his daughter should amuse his highness, until himself could attend him. **1800** MRS. HERVEY *Mourtray Fam.* I. 253 Lord Wilmington, snatching her hand, gallantly pressed it to his lips. **1814** SCOTT *Wav.* xv, Mac-Ivor said, very gallantly, he would never raise his hand against a grey head that was so much respected as my father's. **1865** MISS CLAYTON *Cruel Fort.* II. 268 The Colonel.. gallantly conducted her to the door.

gallantness ('gælәntnɪs). Now *rare*. [f. GALLANT *a.* + -NESS.] The quality or state of being gallant, in various senses.

c **1450** in *Rel. Ant.* I. 75 Sum pepyl that levyn now on dayes, Ar mekyl set on galantnesse. **1555** EDEN *Decades* 209 *margin*, Their galantnes in the warres. **1575** TURBERV. *Faulconrie* 151 His gadding moode and gallantnesse of minde. **1608–11** BP. HALL *Epist.* VI. vi, In gallantnesse of spirit without haughtinesse. *a* **1639** W. WHATELEY *Prototypes* I. xix. (1640) 192 Any gallantnesse of attire or houseroome. *a* **1652** J. SMITH *Sel. Disc.* ix. 432 That bravery and gallantness..is nothing else but the swelling of their own unbounded pride and vain-glory. **1706** PHILLIPS (ed. Kersey), *Gallantry*, or *Gallantness*, courteous Behaviour, Genteelness..; Courtship; also Bravery, remarkable courage. **1721–92** BAILEY, *Gallantness*, Intrigue or Amour.

†**gallantrize**, *v. Obs. rare.* [f. GALLANTRY + -IZE.] Only in *to gallantrize it*: to indulge one's propensity for gallantry. = GALLANTIZE.

a **1693** URQUHART *Rabelais* III. viii. 71 The more flauntingly to gallantrize it [orig. *pour plus gorgias estre*].

gallantry ('gælәntrɪ). [ad. F. *galanterie*, f. *galant* GALLANT *a.* and *sb.*: see -ERY.]

†**1.** Gallants collectively; gentry, fashionable people. *Obs.*

1606 SHAKS. *Tr. & Cr.* III. i. 149 Hector..and all the gallantry of Troy. *a* **1635** NAUNTON *Fragm. Reg.* (Arb.) 33 So were likewise the Civill wars of France..the Fence-schools that inured the youth and Gallantry of the Kingdom. **1660** EVELYN *Mem.* (1857) I. 357, I went to Hyde Park, where was His Majesty, and abundance of gallantry. **1688** R. HOLME *Armoury* III. 209 I, I shall next proceed to give you some examples of Countrey fashions..not of the Gallantry of those Countreys..but of the commonalty.

†**2.** Fine or gay appearance or show, splendour, magnificence. *Obs.*

1613 PURCHAS *Pilgrimage* VII. viii. 693 They liued miserably, yet for gallantry ware bones and peeces of dried flesh about their neckes. **1650** FULLER *Pisgah* III. i. 411 The old men..who could call to minde the greatness and gallantry of the former [Temple]. **1662** STILLINGFL. *Orig. Sacr.* Ep. Ded. A ij, They seem to envy the gallantry of Peacocks, and strive to outvy them in the gayety of their Plumes. **1724** R. WELTON *Substance Chr. Faith* 19 In whatever gallantry a man appears upon the stage, he must retire, and be undress'd. **1801** STRUTT *Sports & Past.* Introd. 5 The pomp and gallantry that we find recorded with poetical exaggeration in the legends of knight-errantry.

†**b.** A form of display or adornment; an elegant practice or habit. *Obs.*

1633 A. H. *Parthen. Sacra* xvii. 191 The greatest gallantrie of Ladies, is to haue them [pearls] dangling at their eares by half dozens. **1650** BULWER *Anthropomet.* ix. 103 [They] bore holes in their Cheeks for a Gallantry. **1720** MRS. MANLEY *Power of Love* (1741) 16 Justs and Tournaments were then the greatest gallantry of the Age.

†**c.** *concr.* in *pl.* Pretty things, knick-knacks. Cf. F. *galanterie*. *Obs.*

1687 *Lond. Gaz.* No. 2221/7 Great quantities of Sweet-Meats, Aqua-Frescas, and other Galantries. **1716** LADY M. W. MONTAGU *Let. to C'tess Mar* 14 Sept., Besides these a set of fine china for the tea-table, enchased in gold, japan trunks, fans, and many gallantries of the same nature. *c* **1720** —— *Lett.* (1837) II. 47 Every matron..saluted her with a compliment and a present, some of jewels, others of pieces of stuff, handkerchiefs, or little gallantries of that nature.

3. Bravery, dashing courage, heroic bearing.

1647 CLARENDON *Hist. Reb.* VI. §250 Sir John Berkly..with great diligence, and galantry, visiting all places in Devon..took many Prisoners of name. **1688** in Gutch *Coll. Cur.* I. 379 The Bishops Council behav'd themselves in this weighty matter with a great deal of gallantry and plainness. **1769** *Junius Lett.* xxv. 116 With the unpremeditated gallantry of a soldier. **1841** ELPHINSTONE *Hist. Ind.* II. 307 He defended himself with great gallantry. **1856** EMERSON *Eng. Traits, Times* Wks. (Bohn) II. 119 Hence, too, the heat and gallantry of its onset.

†**b.** A brave or gallant deed. *Obs.*

1652 F. KIRKMAN *Clerio & Lozia* 190 He took the Bassa, and with this handful of men performed a world of gallantries. **1691** TATE in *Petty's Pol. Anat.* Ep. Ded. A iij b, But a single Gallantry appear'd not sufficient for the Heir of Ormond. **1711** SHAFTESB. *Charac.* (1737) I. 20 The crusades, the rescuing of holy lands, and such devout gallantrys are in less request than formerly.

†**4.** Excellence. *Obs.*

1650 FULLER *Pisgah* II. xi. 228 The gallantry of his strength. **1657** R. LIGON *Barbadoes* 87 It was a strong and lofty Plant, and so vigorous, as..to forbid all Weeds to grow very neer it; so thirstily it suck't the earth for nourishment, to maintain its own health and gallantry.

5. Courtliness or devotion to the female sex, polite or courteous bearing or attention to ladies.

1675 OTWAY *Alcibiades* III. i, I may believe it Gallantry, not Love. **1746** W. HARRIS in *Priv. Lett. Ld. Malmesbury* I. 46 His Grace shows as much gallantry as ever to a certain maid of honour. **1825** LYTTON *Zicci* 11 Glyndon accosted Isabel with impassioned gallantry. **1841–4** EMERSON *Ess., Love* Wks. (Bohn) I. 78 From exchanging glances, they advance to acts of courtesy, [and] of gallantry.

†**b.** Loyalty, devotion (to a monarch). *Obs.*

1648 *Hamilton Papers* (Camden) 190, I hope your Lop[s] greate goodnesse and galantry to the King will defend him from so high a miserie.

6. A polite or gallant action or speech, a courtesy.

1673 DRYDEN *Marr. à la Mode* II. i, The prince..said a thousand gallantries. **1702** STEELE *Funeral* II. (1734) 37 Here's the Lute..hold the Song upon your Hat..'Tis a pretty Gallantry to a Relation. **1737** POPE *Hor. Epist.* II. i. 145 The Soldier breath'd the Gallantries of France. **1838** DICKENS *O. Twist* xviii, To exchange a few gallantries with the lady. **1896** *Daily News* 16 Oct. 5/2 Men are polite because they think women inferior to them. If they looked upon us as their equals, these stupid gallantries would cease.

7. The occupation or behaviour of a gallant.

1632 MASSINGER & FIELD *Fatal Dowry* V. i, I'm of your sect, and my gallantry but a dream. **1665** BOYLE *Occas. Refl.* V. ix. (1845) 331 Those Excesses, that are misnam'd Gallantry. **1711** POPE *Temp. Fame* 381 The men of pleasure, dress, and gallantry. **1714** ADDISON *Spect.* No. 576 ¶1 A range of broken Windows, and other the like Monuments of Wit and Galantry. **1880** L. STEPHEN *Pope* iv. 101 His [Pope's] frame was not adapted for the robust gallantry of the time.

8. Amorous intercourse or intrigue.

1678 D'CHESS CLEVELAND *Let. to Chas. II* in Miss Berry *Soc. Life Eng. & Fr.* (1831) 91 All the world knew that all things of gallantry were at an end with you and I. **1704** SWIFT *Mech. Operat. Spirit* in *T. Tub*, etc. 317 All Companions of great Skill and Practice in Affairs of Gallantry. **1774** *Chesterfield's Lett.* (1792) I. Advt. 14 Gallantry with married women. **1774** T. HUTCHINSON *Diary* 15 Sept. I. 242 She was not without a charge of gallantry. **1819** BYRON *Juan* I. lxiii, What men call gallantry, and gods adultery. **1874** PUSEY *Lent. Serm.* 28 Persons..notorious for their immorality (gallantry, the world calls it).

†**b.** An intrigue with one of the opposite sex.

1706–7 FARQUHAR *Beaux Strat.* II. i, The French are a People that can't live without their Gallantries. **1727** SWIFT, etc. *Mem. P.P.* Misc. II. 272, I layed aside the powder'd Gallantries of my Youth. **1750** CHESTERF. *Lett.* (1774) III. 28 Every French woman of condition is more than suspected of having a gallantry.

†**gallantship.** *Obs. rare.* [f. GALLANT *sb.* + -SHIP.] The condition or dignity of a gallant; in quot. a mock title.

1579 G. HARVEY *Letter-bk.* (Camden) 65 Your gallantshipp would peradventure terme it zeale and devotion.

†**gallanture.** *Obs. rare*[−1]. [irregularly f. GALLANT *sb.* + -URE.] = GALLANTRY 7.

a **1683** OLDHAM *On Morwent* xxvii. Remains (1684) 74 Gallants, who their high Breeding prize Known only by their Gallanture and Vice.

gallary, obs. form of GALLERY.

gallate ('gælәt). *Chem.* Also 8–9 **gallat**. [f. GALL-IC *a.*[2] + -ATE.] A salt of gallic acid.

1794 G. ADAMS *Nat. & Exp. Philos.* I. App. 547, 14 Gallats, the alkaline, of a green colour. **1807** T. THOMSON *Chem.* (ed. 3) II. 348 It [gallic acid] combines with alkaline bodies..The compounds formed have received the name of gallates. **1876** HARLEY *Mat. Med.* (ed. 6) 422 The gallates of the heavy metals are insoluble.

†'**gallature.** *Obs.* [ad. It. *gallatura*, f. *gallare* to fecundate (an egg), f. *gallo* cock; the word may have been also mod.Lat.] The germ in an egg.

1650 SIR T. BROWNE *Pseud. Ep.* III. xxvii. 151 Whether it [the chicken] be not made out of the grando, gallature, germe or tredde of the egge..doth seem of lesser doubt. **1658** —— *Gard. Cyrus* iii. 52 Whether it be not more rational Epicurisme to contrive whole dishes out of the nebbes..then from the Gallatures and treddles of Egges.

gallaunde, -aunt, obs. ff. GALLON, GALLANT.

Gallaway, -axye, obs. ff. GALLOWAY, GALAXY.

†'**gall-bitten**, *a. Obs.* In 5 **galbeton**. [f. GALL *sb.*[2]] ? Bitten so as to have galls on the flesh.

1482 *Rot. Parl. 22 Edw. IV*, VI. 222 Nor that any suche Merchaunt nor Palyngman, medell any Galbeton, storven or pilled Elys, with good Elys.

gall-bladder ('gɔːl,blædә(r)). [f. GALL *sb.*[1] + BLADDER *sb.*] The vessel in the animal system which contains the gall or bile.

1676 J. COOKE *Marrow Chirurg.* 394 The Gall-Bladder is Pear-like. **1767** GOOCH *Treat. Wounds* I. 410 An Officer received a wound in the inferior part of the Gall-Bladder. **1797** M. BAILLIE *Morb. Anat.* (1807) 253 It frequently happens that gall-stones are found in the gall-bladder after death. **1872** HUXLEY *Phys.* v. 118 Opening into the hepatic duct is seen the duct of a large oval sac, the gall-bladder.

gall-darned, var. GOLDARNED *ppl. a.*

galle, obs. form of GALL *sb.*

galleass: see GALLIASS.

galled, *ppl. a.*[1] *nonce-wd.* [f. GALL *sb.*[1] + -ED[2].] Mixed with gall, made bitter.

1604 F. HERING *Mod. Defence* 24 Hee that should taste your sweetned Gall, would call it sugar, and not sugred gall.

galled (gɔːld), *ppl. a.*[2] [orig. f. GALL *sb.*[2] + -ED[2], but afterwards taken as f. GALL *v.*[1] + -ED[1].]

1. a. Affected with *galls* or painful swellings. **b.** Sore from chafing. Often preceded by some defining word, as ***harness-galled, saddle-galled, spur-galled, trace-galled.***

c **1000** *Sax. Leechd.* II. 156 Gif hors geallede sie. **1390** GOWER *Conf.* II. 46 The hors, on which she rode, was black, All lene and galled upon the back. **1430–40** LYDG. *Bochas* I. xx. (1554) 37 b, A galled horse, the sooth if ye list se, who trucketh him boweth his back for dred. *c* **1440** *Promp. Parv.* 185/1 Gallyd (*S.* gally), *strumosus*. **1546** J. HEYWOOD *Prov.* (1867) 69, I rub the gald hors backe till he winche. **1602** SHAKS. *Ham.* III. ii. 253 Let the galld iade winch: our withers are vnrung. **1660** W. SECKER *Nonsuch Prof.* 151 Most persons are like gauld horses that cannot indure the rubbing of their sores. **1818** *Art Preserv. Feet* 124 Trusting to the apparently insignificant name of a galled toe. **1849** MACAULAY *Hist. Eng.* (1871) I. iii. 207 Less sympathy than is now felt for a galled horse or an overdriven ox. **1866** LIVINGSTONE *Last Jrnls.* (1873) I. 146, I had a galled heel.

2. *fig.* Irritated, vexed, unquiet, distressed.

1601 DENT *Pathw. Heaven* 328, I will leaue you to God, and to your galled conscience. **1621** BP. HALL *Heaven upon Earth* §4 The galled soule doth after the wont of sicke Patients seeke refreshing in variety. **1821** CLARE *Vill. Minstr.* I. 161 Gall'd jealousy, like as the tide, ebbs to rest. **1837** LYTTON *E. Maltrav.* 243 His galled and indignant spirit demanded solitude.

3. Of land: Bare through exhaustion or removal of soil.

1881 *Leicester Gloss.*, *Galled*..also applied to land having patches on which the crop has not grown or has been withered. **1883** C. F. SMITH in *Trans. Amer. Philos. Soc.* 49 Galled spots in a field are places where the soil has been washed away, or has been so exhausted that nothing will grow.

4. *Comb.*, as ***galled-back, -backed*** adjs.

1612 DRAYTON *Poly-olb.* VII. 309 Thereby now doth only graze The gall'd-backe carrion Iade. **1690** *Lond. Gaz.* No. 2604/4 A Dark bay stray Nag..blind of the near eye, gall'd backt.

Hence '**galledness**.

1569 R. ANDROSE tr. *Alexis' Secr.* IV. II. 15 Against the galdnesse of the feete.

galled (gɔːld), *ppl. a.*[3] *Dyeing.* [f. GALL *v.*[2] + -ED[1].] Treated with a decoction of gall-nuts.

1581 *Act 23 Eliz.* c. 9 §3 Hosen, have been dyed with..a galled and mathered Black.

Gallegan (gæl'eɪgәn), *a.* and *sb.* [f. next + -AN.]

= GALICIAN *a.*[1] and *sb.*[1]

1845 R. FORD *Hand-bk. Trav. Spain* I. I. xv. 59 A Gallegan or Asturian makes the best groom. **1922** *Glasgow Herald* 14 Aug. 4 The 'arrival'..of the Gallegans. **1927** *Chambers's Jrnl.* 759/2 The pipers..break off their meal to chant an impromptu couplet in the Gallegan dialect.

Gallego, gallego (gæl'eɪgәʊ). Also **Galego, Gallejo** [Sp.] = GALICIAN *sb.*[1] (In quots. 1600, a Galician ship.)

1600 HAKLUYT *Voy.* III. 631 We had before lost sight of a smal Galego on the coast of Spaine. *Ibid.* 633 An old Galego which I caused to be fashioned like a galley. **1656** BLOUNT *Glossogr.*, *Gallego* (Spa.), a man of Galitia. **1811** J. CARR *Descr. Trav. Spain* 50 The Gallejos (pronounced Gallegos) or Galicians are a remarkably fine athletic race of men. **1828** [see GALICIAN *a.*[1] and *sb.*[1]]. **1846** THACKERAY *Cornhill to Cairo* i. 6 A little..boat, rowed by three ragged gallegos. **1925** *Chambers's Jrnl.* 10 Oct. 705/1 The Gallegos are for the most part miserably poor. **1957** P. KEMP *Mine were of Trouble* v. 85 General Franco is a gallego (Galician), with all the obstinacy and subtlety of that race.

gallein ('gælɪɪn). [f. GALL-IC *a.*[2] + (-E)IN.] A brown-red powder, or small green crystals, obtained by heating pyrogallol and phthalic anhydride. Used as a dye.

1871 *Jrnl. Chem. Soc.* IX. 700 Gallein is decomposed by heat like hæmatein, carbonisation taking place. **1885** in *Syd. Soc. Lex.* **1953** H. W. GRIMMEL in H. Gilman *Org. Chem.* III. iv. 317 This dye [*sc.* Coerulein] is obtained from Gallein by treatment with concentrated sulfuric acid at 200°.

Gallenical, gallenist: see GALENICAL, -IST.

galleon ('gælɪәn). Forms: 6–7 **galion, gallion,** (*Sc.* **galȝeon, gailȝeown**), 7 **galeoon, gallioon, -oun,** 6–9 **galeon,** 8–9 **galloon,** 7– **galleon.** [a. F. *galion*, and Sp. *galeon*, It. *galeone* (= Pg. *galeão*), med.L. *galiōn-em, galeōn-em*, deriv. of *galea* a galley. The form *galloon* is probably colloq. from nautical usage.] A kind of vessel, shorter but higher than the galley; a ship of war, esp. Spanish; also, the large vessels used by the Spaniards in carrying on trade with their American possessions (in modern usage chiefly in this connexion).

1529 LYNDESAY *Complaynt* 406 Idyll lownis Sall fetterit be in the gailȝeownis. *a* **1608** SIR F. VERE *Comm.* 27 Fortie or fiftie tall ships, whereof were four of the kings greatest and warlikest Gallions. **1665** MANLEY *Grotius' Low C. Warres* 449 There were four Galeoons..every one of them carrying fifty Guns, or more, and near 700 men. **1761–2** HUME *Hist. Eng.* (1806) III. xlii. 491 A hundred were galleons..of greater size than any ever before used in Europe. **1805** DIBDIN in *Naval Chron.* XIII. 394 We took A Galloon, And the Crew touch'd the Agent for cash to some tune. **1872** YEATS *Growth Comm.* 213 In a few years they had compelled eleven Spanish galleons to strike their flags.

b. *fig.* A great prize or catch, referring to the capture of Spanish galleons by English privateers.

1706–7 FARQUHAR *Beaux Strat.* IV. ii, This Prize will be a Galleon, a *Vigo* Business. I warrant you we shall bring off three or four thousand Pound.

gallepyn, var. GALOPIN, *Obs.*

'**galler.** *rare*[−1]. [f. GALL *v.*[1] + -ER[1].] One who galls or irritates.

1674 N. FAIRFAX *Bulk & Selv.* 114 A willingness to be rid of those gallers that twinge the brain of the stiff maintainer of this.

gallerian (gә'lɪәrɪәn). Also 7–8 **gallerien.** [ad. F. *galérien*, f. *galère* slave-galley.] A galley-slave.

1631 MASSINGER *Believe as You List* V. i, This Gallerien Was not Antiochus. **1713** DARRELL *Gentl. Instr.* (ed. 5) Supp. viii. §5. 89 The Prerogative of a private Centinel above a Slave lies only in the Name, and the Advantage, if any, stands for the Gallerien. **1836** MARRYAT *Midsh. Easy* (1863) 218 Don Silvio with one hundred and fifty gallerians, let loose on the coast yesterday afternoon!

galleried (ˈgælərɪd), *ppl. a.* Also 6–7 **gallered.** [f. GALLERY + -ED.] Furnished with a gallery.

1538 LELAND *Itin.* IV. 103 On each syde this Street the House be gallered; soe that men may passe drye by them if it raine. **1848** B. WEBB *Continental Ecclesiol.* 24 The west window is noble, with a transome which is galleried. **1849** ALB. SMITH *Pottleton Leg.* 421 The entrance to an old galleried inn in the Borough. **1896** *Century Mag.* Apr. 931 It is radically unlike those columned and galleried.. churches.

gallery (ˈgælərɪ), *sb.* Forms: 6 **galary(e,** 6–7 **gallerie,** 7 **gallary,** 6, 8 **galery,** 6– **gallery.** [ad. F. *galerie* = Sp. *galeria*, Pg. *galaria*, It. *galleria* = med.L. *galeria*, of unknown origin.]

1. A covered space for walking in, partly open at the side, or having the roof supported by pillars; a piazza, portico, colonnade.

a **1500** *Assembly Ladies* 165 The galeryes right wonder wel y-wrought. **1533** BELLENDEN *Livy* I. (1822) 67 To be edifyit ..with tavernis and galaris [L. *porticus*], to sauf thaim fra somer schouris, or fra fervant hetis of the sone. **1594** J. KING *Jonas* xxvii. 358 Chrysippus, who was saide to proppe vp the gallery of the Stoickes. **1601** HOLLAND *Pliny* II. 496 This image of hers was set vp in the great gallery or publick walking-place of Metellus. **1648** in Willis & Clark *Cambridge* (1886) I. 260 The rebuilding of yᵉ Gallery in yᵉ fellowes orchard. **1760** tr. *Keysler's Trav.* II. 195 The vestry leads to the gallery or cloisters of the convent. **1796** H. HUNTER tr. *St. Pierre's Stud. Nat.* 1799 III. 729 There is in the gallery of the Tuilleries, on the right as you enter the gardens, an Ionic column.

2. a. A long, narrow platform or balcony, constructed on the outside of a building, at some elevation from the ground, and open in front except as having a balustrade or railing.

1509 FISHER *Serm. Hen. VII*, Wks. (1876) 278 His walles and galaryes of grete pleasure. **1513** MORE *Rich. III*, Wks. 65/1 Hee came foorth of his chamber, and yet not down vnto them, but stode aboue in a galarye ouer them. **1598** YONG *Diana* 57 The Lady is in the gallerie ouer her garden, taking the fresh aire of the coole night. **1611** BIBLE *Ezek.* xlii. 3 Ouer against the pauement which was for the vtter court, was gallerie against gallery in three stories. **1717** LADY M. W. MONTAGU *Let. to Mrs. Thistlethwayte* 1 Apr., The first house has a large court before it, and open galleries all round it.. This gallery leads to all the chambers. **1793** SMEATON *Edystone L.* §24 The lantern for the lights, surrounded by a gallery or balcony. **1842** DICKENS *Lett.* (1880) I. 69 A wide handsome gallery outside every story. **1871** L. STEPHEN *Playgr. Europe* iv. (1894) 94 We lounged lazily in the wooden gallery, smoking our pipes. **1894** *Daily News* 26 Mar. 5/4 Our old coaching inns, with their roomy yards and railed galleries.

b. A similar passage on the roof of a house.

1535 COVERDALE *1 Kings* vi. 10 He buylded a galery also aboue vpon the whole house fyue cubytes hye. **1832** TENNYSON *Pal. Art* 29 Round the roofs [ran] a gilded gallery That lent broad verge to distant lands.

c. *Arch.* A long narrow passage either made in the thickness of a wall, or supported on corbels, having its open side towards the interior of a building, and serving both for ornament and as a means of communication.

1756–7 tr. *Keysler's Trav.* (1760) I. 391 A gallery which leads round the inside near the roof, from whence the church makes a beautiful appearance.

d. *Naut.* A balcony built outside the body of a ship, at the stern (***stern-gallery***), or at the quarters (***quarter-gallery***).

1627 CAPT. SMITH *Seaman's Gram.* ii. 11 The Brackets are little carued knees to support the Galleries. **1679** *Lond. Gaz.* No. 1393/1 During which time, our Quarter took fire, and burnt the Gallery, but we happily quencht it. **1720** DE FOE *Capt. Singleton* xviii. (1840) 315 As to her quarter, the carpenters made her a neat little gallery on either side. **1797** NELSON in A. Duncan *Life* (1806) 41 A soldier.. having broken the upper quarter-gallery window, I jumped in. **1806** A. DUNCAN *Nelson* 37 From her poop and galleries, the enemy sorely annoyed.. the British. **1872** [EARL PEMBROKE & G. H. KINGSLEY] *South Sea Bubbles* i. 14 They lay under the stern gallery of the frigate.

†**e.** *Aeronaut.* An enclosed platform attached to a balloon to carry passengers. *Obs.*

1784 *London Chron.* LVI. 1/3 Yesterday.. an air balloon ..was let off at Versailles... There was a large gallery fixed to it, in which were M. Charles, M. James, M. Montgolfier, and an Officer of the army. **1905** G. BACON *Balloons* ii. 28 Instead of a gallery to carry the passengers, as in the 'Montgolfier', a car shaped like a boat was suspended from the net.

3. A platform, supported by columns or brackets, projecting from the interior wall of a building, and serving e.g. to provide additional room for an audience. **a.** *gen.*

1715 S. SEWALL *Diary* 4 Feb. (1882) III. 38 Mr. Hiller read it, out of the Council-Chamber Gallery. **1814** SCOTT *Wav.* iii, The library.. a large Gothic room, with double arches and a gallery. **1854** WILLIS in Willis & Clark *Cambridge* (1886) III. 168 The proposed Museum.. has a gallery running round.

b. In churches.

1630 J. TAYLOR (Water P.) *Wks.* III. 56/2 And twenty pound he gaue to build a Gallerie in the same Church. **1642** FULLER *Holy & Prof. St.* II. xiv. 103 As for out-lodgings (like galleries, necessary evils in populous Churches) he rather tolerates then approves them. **1690** S. SEWALL *Diary* 11 Sept. (1878) I. 330 Having also found that sitting so near the out-side of the House [*sc.* the meeting-house] causeth me in Winter-time to take cold in my head, I removed into the Gallery. **1712** PRIDEAUX *Direct. Ch.-wardens* (ed. 4) 38 If the Church-wardens would.. make a new Gallery, or add anything else to the Church. **1868** MILMAN *St. Paul's* xix. 494 My voice was heard distinctly in every part of the building, up to the western gallery. **1879** SIR G. SCOTT *Lect. Archit.* I. 54 In churches of the same kind, however, we find the groined vault used to carry a gallery in the aisles.

c. In a theatre. Now *spec.* the highest of such projecting platforms, containing the cheapest seats.

1690 CROWNE *Eng. Friar* IV. Dram. Wks. 1874 IV. 84, I am.. Governor o' the eighteen-penny gallery i' the play house. *a* **1704** T. BROWN *Prol. Persius* Wks. 1730 I. 51, I, who never pass'd, as yet, The test of the misjudging pit; Nor i' th' galleries tickled Crowd. **1816** *Times* 25 Jan. In what part of the theatre was the one-shilling gallery? **1838** DICKENS *Nich. Nick.* xxiv, The people were cracking nuts in the gallery.

d. In a senatorial chamber. Also ***ladies'-, members'-, press-, strangers'-gallery.***

1753 *Scots Mag.* XV. 28/2 There are.. strangers in our gallery. **1847** EMERSON *Repr. Men, Napoleon* Wks. (Bohn) I. 367 Dumont relates that he sat in the gallery of the Convention, and heard Mirabeau make a speech. **1897** LUCY in *Daily News* 9 Apr. 7/2 News reached the Press Gallery to-night of the death of Mr. Doyle, one of the oldest members of the Press Gallery.

e. The part of a Friends' meeting-house occupied by the ministers or elders; ***gallery Friend***, a Quaker minister or elder.

1802 W. MATTHEWS *Recorder* I. 121 The galleries of London. **1913** *Jrnl. Friends' Hist. Soc.* Jan. 2 Jane Wigham .., the second wife of John Wigham, Tertius, was also a gallery Friend. **1921** R. M. JONES *Later Per. Quakerism* I. 58 The phrases so characteristic of Molinos, Guyon, Fénelon.. were heard everywhere in Quaker 'galleries'.

4. *transf.* **a.** The assemblage of persons who occupy the gallery portion of a theatre, the 'gods'; formerly often in *pl.* Hence *fig.* the less refined or instructed portion of the public. ***to play the gallery***: to act the part of gallery-spectators. ***to play to*** (or ***for***) ***the gallery***: to address oneself to those in the gallery (also *fig.*).

1649 LOVELACE *Poems* 77 He should have wove in one, two Comedies; The first for th' Gallery.. Th' other for the Gentlemen oth' Pit. **1704** J. TRAPP *Abra-Mulé* Prol. 16 Nor bless the Gall'ries with the Sweets of Rhime. **1809** BYRON *Bards & Rev.* xxviii, Kenney's 'World'.. Tires the sad gallery, lulls the listless pit. **1870** *Echo* 23 July 5/4 We were ..constantly called in to 'play the gallery' to his witty remarks. **1872** *Standard* 23 Oct. 5/4 His dispatches were, indeed, too long and too swelling in phrase; for herein he was always 'playing to the galleries'. **1878** IRVING *Stage* 28 That same gallery which at first roared itself hoarse, while the play went on in dumb-show, became hushed in rapt admiration. **1890** *Scotsman* 18 Aug., He [Mr. Blaine] was playing for his Irish gallery. **1892** *Law Times* XCII. 156/1 We hope that.. advocates will be courteous to judges, to opposing counsel, and to witnesses, and not play to the gallery. **1896** *Westm. Gaz.* 10 June 4/2 The 'gallery' will be most interested in the three couples [of golf players].

b. The body of persons who occupy a public gallery in a senatorial chamber.

1817 *Parl. Deb.* 568 He addressed himself principally to his friends on his right and left, and in so inaudible a voice that his remarks did not reach the gallery. **1844** LD. BROUGHAM *Brit. Const.* ix. §2 (1862) 119 The mischief arose from suffering the galleries [of the French National Convention] to interfere with their plaudits or their hisses. **1849** MACAULAY *Hist. Eng.* II. 383 The Solicitor spoke at great length and with great acrimony, and was often interrupted by the clamours and hisses of the audience.. The galleries were furious.

c. At écarté, the spectators who are betting on either player and are allowed to offer suggestions.

1890 'BERKELEY' *Écarté & Euchre 28* French Écarté. When several persons desire to join in a game of Écarté, it is generally arranged in the following manner. Two of the number sit down to play a game in the usual way, .. and the remainder, called 'The Gallery', are allowed to take part in the game to the extent of betting on the player of their choice, and advising him, if necessary. **1897** R. F. FOSTER *Complete Hoyle* 255 Any person in the gallery is allowed to draw attention to errors in the score, and may advise the player he is backing, or even play out the game for him.

d. A group of spectators at a golf match or other game or sport. Also *transf.*

1891 H. G. HUTCHINSON *Hints on Golf* (ed. 6) 71 If you rise to such heights of golfing powers as to attract a gallery. **1894** *Strand Mag.* VIII. 661/2 One can do very well without a gallery when one is trying a new experiment on 'ski'. **1899** *Captain* II. 65/2 The gallery of white-robed spectators. **1906** *Westm. Gaz.* 21 Sept. 4/2 It is virtually impossible for a player attended by a big 'gallery' to lose his ball. **1925** J. BUCHAN *John Macnab* iii. 59 Sir Archie was aware that his style of jumping was not graceful and he was discomposed by this sudden gallery. **1970** *New Yorker* 10 Oct. 183/1 The gallery had virtually won him the fourth set with a huge surge of support.

5. a. A long narrow apartment, sometimes serving as a means of access to other parts of a house; a corridor.

1541 BARNES *Wks.* (1573) 210/1, I was brought afore my Lorde Cardinall into his galary, and there hee reade all myne articles. **1669** in Willis & Clark *Cambridge* (1886) III. 326 The roofe of the said building to conteine and be devided into five roomes or gallaryes. **1711** STEELE *Spect.* No. 109 ¶1 We were now arrived at the Upper-end of the Gallery, when the Knight faced towards one of the Pictures. **1828** SCOTT *F.M. Perth* xii, Brother Cyprian, at the end of a long gallery, opened the door of a small apartment. **1868** J. H. BLUNT *Ref. Ch. Eng.* I. 95 A gallery communicating between his residence and the monastery.

b. A shooting-gallery (see SHOOTING *vbl. sb.* 8 b.).

1848 MRS. GASKELL *M. Barton* II. ii. 33 Some workman with whom her son had made some arrangement about shooting at the gallery. **1897** *Sears, Roebuck Catal.* 779/3 Gallery Targets.

6. An apartment or building devoted to the exhibition of works of art. (See also quot. 1950.)

1591 SHAKS. *1 Hen. VI*, II. iii. 37, Long time thy shadow hath been thrall to me, For in my Gallery thy Picture hangs. **1625** BACON *Ess. Friendship* (Arb.) 165 For a Crowd is not Company; And Faces are but a Gallery of Pictures.. where there is no Loue. **1638** JUNIUS *Paint. Ancients* 339 A Gallery in the suburbs of Naples, looking toward the West, which was richly furnished with many good pieces. **1782** SIR J. REYNOLDS *Disc.* xi. (1842) 198 In going through a gallery where there were many portraits of the last ages. **1818** BYRON *Ch. Har.* IV. lxi, For I have been accustom'd to entwine My thoughts with nature rather in the fields Than Art in galleries. **1847** EMERSON *Poems, Day's Ration*, Why need I galleries, when a pupil's draught After the master's sketch fills and o'erfills My apprehension? **1883** LD. CAIRNS in *Standard* 9 May 2/5 The galleries would not be kept open after six o'clock. **1950** *Manch. Guardian Weekly* 12 Oct. 15/1 In general in the United States a 'gallery' is a place that shows paintings and sells them, a 'museum' is one that simply shows them.

7. a. *Mil.* and *Mining.* An underground passage, horizontal or nearly so; a level or drift.

1631 PREMPART *Siege Busse* 7 Counte Ernst.. was advised by his Ingener.. to make a great Gallerie directly vpon the Citie from the letter N. **1659** HAMMOND *On Ps.* cxxxix. 1–5 Paraphr. 673 A man can no more escape or march undiscovered out of a city the most closely besieged, when the galleries are prepared. **1711** *Mil. & Sea Dict.* (ed. 4), *Galery*,.. also us'd for the Branch of a Mine, that is, a narrow Passage under Ground, leading to the Mine that is carry'd on under any Work design'd to be blown up. **1799** KIRWAN *Geol. Ess.* 249 The basalt reposed on clay, into which a gallery was worked without meeting the basalt. **1838** LYTTON *Leila* I. v, Till he came at length into a narrow, dark, and damp gallery, that seemed cut from the living rock. **1853** URE *Dict. Arts* II. 175 The most ordinary dimensions of galleries [in mines] are a yard wide and two yards high. **1884** *Manch. Exam.* 22 Feb. 5/2 The air is carried along to the extremities of the workings in galleries constructed of canvas, technically known as brattice cloth.

b. *Mil.* (See quot. 1704.) ? *Obs.*

1704 HARRIS *Lex. Techn.*, *Gallery*, in Fortification, is a covered Walk, the Sides whereof are Musket-proof, consisting of a double Row of Planks lined with Plates of Iron.. These Galleries are frequently made use of in the Moat already filled with Faggots and Bavins, to the end that the Miner may approach safe to the face of the Bastion, when the Artillery of the opposite Flank is dismounted. **1711** *Mil. & Sea Dict.* (ed. 4), *Galery*, a Passage made across the Ditch of a Town besieg'd, with Timbers fastened on the Ground and plank'd over. **1716** *Lond. Gaz.* No. 5476/1 The Heads of the Bridges, or Galleries, over the Ditch of the Palank, had been damaged.

†**c.** *Mil.* A 'lane' or open space between ranks or bodies of men.

1591 GARRARD *Art Warre* 212 The spaces, intervalles, galeries and passages, which are amongst the ranks.. do serue [etc.].

8. †**a.** A passage made by a deer, etc. through brushwood (*obs.*; cf. ENTRY 7 c). **b.** A passage made by an animal underground, or through a rock.

1674 N. COX *Gentl. Recreat.* (1677) 68 If you would know the height and thickness of the Hart, observe his Entries and Galleries into the Thickets, and what Boughs he hath over-stridden. **1849** MURCHISON *Siluria* iii. 40 The.. galleries made by Crustaceans.

9. *Real Tennis.* (See quot. 1878.) ***winning-gallery***, the opening most remote from the dedans or service-side.

1699 BOYER *Compl. Fr. Master* IV. Fam. Dial., *J'ay mis sa Balle dans le petit trou, ou dans la Galerie.* I put his Ball into the Hazard, or the Gallery. **1829** *Lond. Encycl.* in *Blaine's Rur. Sports* (1840) 133 Upon the entrance of a tennis court there is a long gallery which goes to the dedans, that is, a kind of front gallery, into which, whenever a ball is struck, it tells for a certain stroke. This long gallery is divided into different compartments or galleries, each of which has its particular name. **1878** J. MARSHALL *Ann. Tennis* 157 *Galleries*, the openings beneath the side-pent-house, including the first, second, and last galleries, the door, and the line-opening, on each side of the net. *Ibid.* 183 Every ball which either falls short or enters a gallery (except always the winning-gallery) counts for nothing.

10. An ornamental parapet or railing running along the edge of a table, shelf, or the like.

1853 *Cabinet-maker's Assistant* II. 35 Writing Tables.. The centre shelf should be hinged at the back.. The gallery may either be of fret-work or of bronze.

11. In a lamp: A bevelled ring for supporting a globe or shade.

12. *attrib.* and *Comb.* **a.** simple attrib., as (sense 1) ***gallery-walks***; (sense 2, 3) ***gallery-stairs***; (sense 3 b) ***gallery-critic, -door, -keeper***; (sense 3 c, d) ***gallery boy, girl, god, goddess,*** (***twopenny***) ***gallery-man, queue, ticket***; (sense 6) ***gallery-attendant, -exhibition, -goer, -picture, -trotter***; (sense 7) ***gallery-case, -frame***; also ***gallery-like*** adj. **b.** Special comb., as **gallery camera** (see quot. 1968); **gallery forest** = *fringing forest*; **gallery-furnace** (see quot.); **gallery grave**, a tunnel-shaped megalithic tomb; **gallery-hit**, a piece of showy play (primarily by a batsman in cricket) intended to gain applause from uncritical spectators; so ***gallery-hitting***; **gallery-ladder** (see quot.); **gallery-play**, playing to the gallery (see sense 4 a above); showy play designed to gain applause; also *fig.*; **gallery-post** *Real Tennis* (see quot.); **gallery-practice**, indoor photography; **gallery-road**, 'an artificial roadway constructed on piles' (*Cent. Dict.*); **gallery-shot, -stroke** (cf. *gallery-hit*).

1895 M. H. JUDGE in *M.H.J. & Lord's Day Act* (1897) 30 So far as the actual *gallery attendants are concerned. **1887** *Courier-Journal* (Louisville, Ky.) 3 Feb. 1/4 The *gallery boys stood up and again and again clapped their hands. **1911** BEERBOHM *Zuleika D.* ii. 15 All the gallery-boys..were scornful of the sweethearts wedged between them. **1964** E. CHAMBERS *Camera & Process Work* iv. 26 (*caption*) Elevation and plan of a *gallery camera. **1968** *Gloss. Terms Offset Lithogr. Printing* (*B.S.I.*) 13 *Gallery camera*, a camera in which the photographic material is transported from the darkroom to the camera in a dark slide. **1851** J. S. MACAULAY *Field Fortif.* 229 Making gabions, fascines, blind-frames, and *gallery cases. **1784** COWPER *Task* II. 365 Transforms old print To zigzag manuscript, and cheats the eyes Of *gallery critics by a thousand arts. **1480** *Wardrobe Accts. Edw. IV* (Nicolas 1830) 127 For a holowe key for the *galary dore of the same Wardrobe viij *d.* **1857** RUSKIN *Pol. Econ. Art* ii. (1868) 129 There is one disadvantage attached necessarily to *gallery exhibition, namely, the extent of mischief which may be done by one foolish curator. **1920** A. H. UNWIN *W. Afr. Forests* vii. 130 *Hexalobus morepetalus*... Grows to large tree in *Gallery Forests—small in Savannah. **1937** *Discovery* Apr. 100/2 The savannah country, into which the gallery forests, with their accompanying forest-frequenting birds, shoot out long tongues—remnants of a once continuous forested area. **1927** E. WALLACE *Feathered Serpent* xiii. 169 You'll probably be pulled up by *gallery girls who want autographs. **1851** J. S. MACAULAY *Field Fortif.* 190 The false frame..is a little shorter and wider than the *gallery-frames. **1881** RAYMOND *Mining Gloss.*, **Gallery-furnace*, a retort-furnace used in the distillation of mercury. **1851** *Gallery god [see GOD *sb.* 4]. **1812** *Gallery Goddess [see GOD *sb.* 4]. **1888** *Pall Mall G.* 22 May 5/2 There are several minor collections on show at the present time worth the attention of the *gallery goer. **1937** *Proc. Prehist. Soc.* III. 86 The brilliance of the Breton passage grave culture has long obscured the existence of *gallery graves in Brittany. **1963** G. DANIEL in Foster & Alcock *Culture & Environment* ii. 14 Suggesting that it was in the area from south Finistère to the Vendée were found the tombs most likely to be the prototypes of the Gallery Graves and Transepted Gallery Graves and Rectangular Chambers of south Wales. **1882** CASSELL, **Gallery-hit*. **1888** W. G. GRACE in Steel & Lyttleton *Cricket* ix. (Badm.) 307 On such a wicket as this do not go in for lofty and '*gallery' hitting. **1682** WHITELOCKE *Mem. Chas. I*, 16 Dec. an. 1645 Thirty Pounds given to the *Gallery-keepers at St. Margaret's Church. **1706** PHILLIPS (ed Kersey) s.v. *Ladders*, The *Gallery-Ladder, made of Ropes, and hung over the Galleries and Stern, for ent'ring by the Ship's Stern out of the Boat, when the Weather is foul. **1796** C. SMITH *Marchmont* I. 259 The *gallery-like passage that led to the stairs. **1607** BEAUM. & FL. *Woman-Hater* Prol., I do pronounce this, to the utter discomfort of all two-penny *Gallery men. **1897** LUCY in *Daily News* 9 Apr. 7/2 He was familiarly known to more than one generation of Gallery-men. **1871** F. GALE *Echoes Cricket Fields* v. 23 Frequent useless appeals to the umpire, a practice which Nyren condemned as being what we now call '*gallery play'. **1899** *Westm. Gaz.* 31 Jan. 7/2 A weak opposition, evidently disposed to indulge in 'gallery' play. *a* **1914** J. E. RAPHAEL *Mod. Rugby Football* (1918) vi. 107 'Gallery play' should only be resorted to as a last desperate resource. **1916** 'BOYD CABLE' *Action Front* 121 You've..done good work for your first show; don't spoil it with rank gallery play. **1923** KIPLING *Land & Sea T.* 21 In the Great War there was very little suspicion, or chance, of gallery play for the V.C. **1878** J. MARSHALL *Ann. Tennis* 157 **Gallery-post*, the post which separates a gallery from the gallery next beyond it. **1891** *Anthony's Photogr. Bull.* IV. 168 The so-called professional, who has been trained in the routine of *gallery practice. **1934** A. P. HERBERT *Holy Deadlock* 143 Nobody in the *gallery queue would have recognised their Mary Moon. **1894** FARMER *Slang*, **Gallery shot*. **1897** *Pall Mall Mag.* Nov. 401 It is a gallery shot in a sense..for the bird is flying level. **1616** in *Crt. & Times Jas. I* (1849) I. 435 The king..stood on the *gallery stairs at Whitehall to see the prince come along from Richmond. **1856** *Chamb. Jrnl.* 11 Oct. 226/2 The gallery-stairs of a theatre. **1789** *Loiterer* 18 Apr. 5 A woman who pawned her prayer book for a *gallery ticket. **1833** R. DYER 9 *Yrs. of Actor's Life* 137 His actors being..the companions of any who are likely to take a gallery ticket. **1883** *Pall Mall G.* 1 Sept. 5/1 A reminder to bewildered '*gallery-trotters' of the pictures they have seen in the various exhibitions of the season. **1553** GRIMALDE *Cicero's Offices* II. (1558) 98 b, Sightcourtes, *galerywalkes, and new churches, the more reuerently I finde fault with, for Pompeyus sake.

Hence **'galleryful**, as much as a gallery will hold; **'galleryite**, one who occupies a seat in a gallery.

1885 *Art Jrnl.* 126/1 Where a work contains as much teaching as a whole galleryful its rightful place is by itself. **1894** DU MAURIER *Trilby* ii. 93 A whole galleryful of fiddles. **1895** *Westm. Gaz.* 18 Sept. 8/2 Surely, the galleryites, or, rather, playgoers generally, are not infallible in their judgment?

gallery ('gælərı), *v.* [f. GALLERY *sb.*]

1. *trans.* To furnish with a balcony or gallery.

1616 SIR R. BOYLE *Diary* in *Lismore Papers* (1886) I. 138 Which [sum] I bestowd to have the Church of Tallagh galleried round about. *Ibid.* 139 Thomas Carter..delivered Mr. Langredg of my money v^{li} ster. to begyn the gallerying of the church at Tallagh. **1888** *Pall Mall G.* 12 Sept. 8/2 The Place Victor Emmanuel was galleried round with seats for 20,000 people. **1894** *Speaker* 12 May 524/2 The..benchers plastered it and pewed it and galleried it.

b. *Mil.* To make an underground passage.

1808 J. BARLOW *Columb.* VII. 627 Their mining arts the staunch besiegers ply, Delve from the bank of York and gallery far, Deep subterranean, to the mount of war.

2. *intr. nonce-use.* To 'take' with, or appeal to, the audience in a theatre-gallery.

1672, 1831 [see BOX *v.*[1] 11].

gallesh, obs. form of CALASH.

gallet ('gælıt). [ad. F. *galet* rounded pebble on the beach; also, a chip, f. OF. *gal*, of uncertain origin.] A chip or splinter of stone.

1712 J. JAMES tr. *Le Blond's Gardening* 45 The coarser Stone or Gallets.

gallet ('gælıt), *v.* [f. prec. sb.] = GARRET *v.*

1851 W. LAXTON *Builder's Price Book* (ed. 28) 127 Kentish rag stone..Galleting the joints externally, extra per foot super 1½*d.*

gallewasp: see GALLIWASP.

galley ('gælı), *sb.* Forms: 4–6 **galai, -ay(e**, (4 **gaylay**, 6 **ghallai**, 7 **gallay**), **gale(e, -ei(e, -ey(e**, 5–6 **galy(e**, (5 **gaili**), 6–8 **gally(e**, (6 **gallie**), 4– **galley**. [ad. OF. *galie, galee*, med.L. *galea, galeia*, late Gr. γαλαία, γαλέα = Pr. *galeya, galea*, Sp. *galea* (obs.), Pg. *galé*, It. *galea, galia*.

The ultimate etymology is unknown. Cf. the synonymous F. *galère*, Pr., Sp., Pg. *galera*, It. *galeara*; also med.L. *galeida* (Du Cange), MHG. *galîde, galeide*, MDu. *galeide*, Icel. *galeið*.]

1. a. A low flat-built sea-going vessel with one deck, propelled by sails and oars, formerly in common use in the Mediterranean. Cf. GALLIASS. The rowers were mostly slaves or condemned criminals. Hence phr. ***to condemn***, or ***send, to the galleys***, and simply ***the galleys***, to indicate the punishment of a galley-slave. ***half, quarter galley*** (see quot. 1794).

a **1300** *K. Horn* 185 Us he dude lede Into a galeie, Wiþ þe se to pleie.. Wiþute sail and roþer. *c* **1330** R. BRUNNE *Chron.* (1810) 54 þe erle..did mak a riche galeie With fourscore armed knyghtes. *c* **1440** *Generydes* 4105 He saw a galy fayre and strong lay atte rode. **1480** CAXTON *Chron. Eng.* ccxliii. (1483) 293 He lete make galeys of werre. *a* **1533** LD. BERNERS *Huon* xx. 55 He shall..delyuer you shype or galee suche as shall be nessessary for you. **1560** DAUS tr. *Sleidane's Comm.* 328 Besides those that were put to death..very many were also condempned to the Galees. **1642** FULLER *Holy & Prof. St.* IV. xii. 297 This course hath emptied more full, then filled empty purses, and many thereby have brought a Galeon to a Gally. **1653** H. COGAN tr. *Pinto's Trav.* xlix. 193 His Fleet..was composed of five Foists, four Galliots, and one Gally Royal. **1682** *News fr. France* 10 No Sea-man nor Trades-man shall offer to go out of the Kingdom without leave, under the pain of being sent to the Gallies. **1699** ROBERTS *Voy. Levant* 15 At length we saw the half Galleys go their way. **1721** *Lond. Gaz.* No. 5982/2 Above London-Bridge [they] met with two Gallies, one rowing with Fourteen Oars, and the other with Eleven, loaden with Goods. **1794** *Rigging & Seamanship* I. 238 Half and Quarter Galleys are rigged and navigated the same as galleys; and take this denomination from their being much shorter. Bombay-galleys are like the former, but smaller, and mostly used by corsairs on the coast of Barbary. **1829** MACKINTOSH *Revol. of 1688* Wks. 1846 II. 100 The ministers of the Reformed faith were banished from France in fifteen days, under pain of the galleys. **1838** PRESCOTT *Ferd. & Is.* II. xx. (1845) III. 278 King Ferdinand's galleys were spread with rich carpets and awnings of yellow and scarlet. **1871** PALGRAVE *Lyr. Poems* 138 High on deck of their gilded galleys Our light sailors they scorn below.

transf. and *fig.* **1649** DRUMM. OF HAWTH. *Cypress Grove* Wks. (1711) 120 Who would not, rather than abide chained in this loathsome galley of the world, sleep ever. **1802** GOUV. MORRIS in Sparks *Life & Writ.* III. (1832) 166, I wish to get out of this galley, and live for myself. **1890** *Spectator* 2 Aug. 145/2 They and their daughters chain themselves down in the galley of fashion.

b. Used with allusion to Molière *Scapin* II. xi, *Que diable allait-il faire dans cette galère?* Cf. GALÈRE.

1859 DICKENS *T. Two Cities* v. 21 What the devil do *you* do in that galley there! **1874** LISLE CARR *Jud. Gwynne* I. ii. 47 After hunting for you everywhere..here I tumble on you amidst the howling wilderness of Furrowshire. But what on earth are you doing in this galley? **1909** G. B. SHAW in *Nation* 16 Jan. 601/1 Asking incredulously what the devil he is doing in *that* galley. **1948** R. SCOTT-JAMES in F. M. Ford *Man could stand Up* Pref. 5 Was he not that dextrous, fanciful, almost dilettante writer..? What was he doing in this galley?

2. Applied to the Greek or Roman war-ships, large vessels with one or more banks of oars.

1513 DOUGLAS *Æneis* VIII. ii. 29 Tua galeis did he cheis the ilk tyde. **1614** RALEIGH *Hist. World* III. (1634) 50 The one was a passage for Gallies to be cut behinde Mount Athos. **1788** GIBBON *Decl. & F.* V. liii. 497 The Dromones, or light gallies of the Byzantine empire, were content with two tier of oars. **1840** THIRLWALL *Greece* VII. lix. 335 Ptolemy himself escaped, it is said, with only eight galleys. **1882** OUIDA *Maremma* I. 150 Over that blue sea, where..the Etruscan pirates hunted the Latin galleys.

3. A large open row-boat, e.g. one appropriated to the captain of a man-of-war, one formerly used on the Thames by custom-house officers, and by the press-gang (Adm. Smyth); also, a large pleasure-boat.

1570 LEVINS *Manip.* 99/24 A Gallye, *phacellus.* **1718** LADY M. W. MONTAGU *Let. to Abbé Conti* 19 May, I..went across the canal in my galley. **1813** *Examiner* 5 Apr. 218/2 Lieut. Devon had only the brig's galley..with him. **1834** LYTTON *Pompeii* I. ii. 12 Crowded in the glassy bay were the vessels of commerce and the gilded galleys for the pleasures of the rich citizens. **1861** DICKENS *Gt. Expect.* liv, The Jack..asked me if we had seen a four-oared galley going up with the tide?

4. The cooking-room or kitchen on a ship. Cf. CABOOSE. Also, a ship's cooking-range.

1750 BLANCKLEY *Nav. Expositor*, *Gally* is a Place in the Cook-Room, where the Grates are set up, and in which they make Fires, for boyling or roasting the Victuals. **1830** SCOTT *Demonol.* i. 9 The sleeper started up with a ghastly and disturbed countenance, and..proceeded to the galley, or cook-room of the vessel. **1840** R. DANA *Bef. Mast* vi. 14 When I went to the galley to get a light, I found the cook inclined to be talkative. **1853** KANE *Grinnell Exp.* xxxiv. (1856) 301 Three stoves and a cooking galley, four Argand and three bear-fat lamps. **1866** NORDHOFF *Young Man-of-War's Man* i. 12, I got my pot..and proceeded to the 'galley' or cooking range.

5. *Printing.* **a.** [F. *galée.*] An oblong tray of brass, wood, or zinc, to which the type is transferred from the composing-stick.

1652 URQUHART *Jewel* Wks. (1834) 182 His [the setter's] plenishing of the gally, and imposing of the form. **1683** MOXON *Mech. Exerc.* II. 25 Our Master Printer is also to provide Galleys of different sizes. **1777** HOOLE *Comenius' Vis. World* (ed. 12) 118 He putteth these in a gally till a page be made. **1864** *Daily Tel.* 28 June, Three or four compositors..bring up their various contribution of type to the long 'galley' in which the article is put together.

b. A galley-proof; = SLIP *sb.*[2] 10 d.

1890 in WEBSTER. **1934** T. R. COWARD in G. Gross *Publishers on Publishing* (1961) 149 When the corrections are made, the galleys go back to the printer and are made into page proofs. **1951** S. JENNETT *Making of Books* I. vi. 88 The page proofs come to the reader, and must be checked against the corrected galleys, to see that all the corrections have been carried out. **1971** *Times Lit. Suppl.* 20 Aug. 999/1, I *have* had galleys from Penguin Books, but more usually the finished product, fresh misprints and all.

6. (See quot.) [= F. *galère.*]

1789 J. KEIR *Dict. Chem.* 96/2 Distillers of aqua fortis do not use retorts, but stone-ware bottles, with short crooked necks..Two rows of these vessels are disposed opposite to each other, in an oblong furnace called a galley; and a wood fire is used for the distillation.

7. *attrib.* and *Comb.*, as (sense 1) ***galley-fashion, -fight, -fleet, -kind, -oar***; also ***galley-like*** adj.; (sense 4) ***galley-fire***.

1691 LUTTRELL *Brief Rel.* (1857) II. 294 Several persons are going to build privateers..after the *gally fashion with oares. **1695** *Ibid.* III. 508 Some tenders built galley fashion. **1599** HAKLUYT *Voy.* II. II. 122 We now haue had experience of *Gally-fight. **1836** MARRYAT *Midsh. Easy* xxvii, 'What a bore to have no *galley fire lighted,' said one of the youngsters. **1791** *Hist. Europe* in *Ann. Reg.* 186/2 The number of land forces which he had on board the *galley-fleet. **1711** SHAFTESB. *Charac.* (1737) III. 97 We, essay-writers, are of the small-craft or *galley-kind. **1627** CAPT. SMITH *Seaman's Gram.* xii. 55 Her Bow and chase so *Gally-like contriued, should beare as many Ordnances as with conueniency she could. **1838** LYTTON *Alice* I. x, My own unceasing avocations which chain me like a slave to the *galley-oar of politics.

8. Special comb.: **galley-arch** (see quot.); †**galley-bird**, a galley-slave; **galley-brand**, a mark or brand on a galley-slave; **galley-built** *a.* (see quot.); †**galley-cassock**, a garment worn by galley-slaves; **galley-dungeon**, ? a dungeon in which galley-slaves are confined; †**galley-fish**, ? a 'Portuguese man-of-war' (*Physalia*); †**galley-frigate**, ? a frigate built like a galley; **galley-growler** (see quot.); **galley-house** = *galley-arch*; †**galley-matter**, an offence to be punished by condemnation to the galleys; **galley-nose** (see quot.); **galley-packet**, a made-up story, lie, 'yarn'; **galley-pepper** (see quot.); **galley-press**, 'a small hand-press for pulling proofs in slip form' (Jacobi); **galley-proof**, a proof in slip form taken from type on a galley; **galley-punt, -rack, -slang** (see quots.); **galley-slip** = *galley-proof*; **galley-stick, -stoker** (see quots.); **galley-yarn** = *galley-packet*. Also GALLEY-FOIST, GALLEY-HALFPENNY, GALLEY-MAN, GALLEY-SLAVE, etc.

1867 SMYTH *Sailor's Word-bk.*, **Galley-arches*, spacious and well-built structures in many of the Mediterranean ports for the reception and security of galleys. **1655** T. WHITE *Obedience Govt.* 124 A knot of slaves and *Galley-birds. **1856** W. E. AYTOUN *Bothwell* (1857) 80 More like a hideous *galley-brand Than any wound from peace or war. **1769** FALCONER *Dict. Marine* (1789) R r iij b, When the waist of a merchant ship is only one or two steps of descent from the quarter-deck, and fore-castle, she is said to be *galley-built. **1583** T. STOCKER tr. *Hist. Civ. Wars Low C.* I. 47 b, The officers of the Inquisition bryng vnto them Saint Bennets furniture of apparrel, which is a *gally cassocke [orig. *habillement de galere*] without sleeues. **1723** *Pres. State Russia* II. 337 The insupportable Slavery on the Gallies and in the *Gally-Dungeons. **1591** SYLVESTER *Du Bartas* I. v. 381 But O! what stile can worthily declare (O! *Galley-Fish, and thou Fish-Mariner..) your dexterity In Sailer's Art! **1774** GOLDSM. *Nat. Hist.* VI. 293 The animal I mean is the Galley Fish, which Linnaeus degrades into the insect tribe, under the title of the Medusa. **1600** HAKLUYT *Voy.* III. 709 The choice being made for the place to build the *gally-frigat, ashore it was brought. **1867** SMYTH *Sailor's Word-bk.*, **Galley-growlers*, idle grumblers and skulkers, from whom discontent and mutiny generally derive their origin. **1699** DAMPIER *Voy.* II. I. iv. 77 These *Galley-Houses are 50 or 60 paces from the River side. **1644** EVELYN *Diary* (1827) I. 129 It is made a *gally matter to carry a knife whose point is not broken off. *a* **1734** NORTH *Lives* (1826) II. 324 It is no less than galley-matter for any man to kill deer or hog, except at this general hunt. **1867** SMYTH *Sailor's Word-bk.*, **Galley-nose*, the figure-head. **1785** MRS. A. M. BENNETT *Juvenile Indiscretions* (1786) V. 147 Why, sure, Miss, that must be a *galley-packet somebody or other has told you. **1867** Smyth *Sailor's Word-bk.*, *Galley-packet*, an unfounded rumour. *Ibid.*, **Galley-pepper*, the soot or ashes which accidentally drop into victuals in cooking. **1891** Jacobi *Printing* ii. 48 In establishments where..a class of work is executed which necessitates slip proofs, a *galley-press is a requisite article. **1892** —— *Notes on Bks. & Printing* 42 **Galley proofs*, these proofs supplied in slip form—not made up into pages. **1883** W. C. Russell *Sailors' Lang.*, **Galley-punt*, an open sailing-boat used by pilots in the Channel off the Forelands. **1888** Jacobi *Printer's Voc.* **Galley-racks*, receptacles for galleys. **1867** Smyth *Sailor's Word-bk.*, **Galley-slang*, the neological barbarisms foisted into sea-language. **1889** H. B. Wheatley *How to Catalogue* iii. 58 These additions [to a catalogue]..may be printed from time to time at short intervals on *galley slips. **1894** Hall Caine in *My First Bk.* 72, I asked Mr. Theodore Watts..to read some 'galley' slips of it. **1888** Jacobi *Printer's Voc.*, **Galley sticks*, long side-sticks used for quoining up galleys. **1867** Smyth *Sailor's Word-bk.*, **Galley-stoker*, a lazy skulker. **1874** Hotten *Slang Dict.* 172 **Gally-yarn*, a sailor's term for a hoaxing story. **1884** Henley & Stevenson *Admiral Guinea* III. iv, You the one overtaken and denounced; and you spin me a galley yarn like that? **1905** *Daily Chron.* 11 July 3/4 Mr. Baring-Gould has gathered up all the old galley-yarns.

†9. Used in *Comb.* to designate various vessels or utensils, as *galley-cup*, *-dish*, *-glass*, *-grewse* (? = cruse). Also galley-tile, gallipot, q.v. for the explanation.

1481–90 *Howard Househ. Bks.* (Roxb.) 389 Item, paid for v. galeygrewsis xvd. **1576** Baker *Jewell of Health* 150a, Straw a part in the bottome of a broade or gallie glasse. **1642** *Rates Merchandize* 28 Gally dishes, the dozen..00.01.06.

galley ('gælı), *v. nonce-wd.* [f. the sb.] *trans.* To transport in a galley.

1864 Burton *Scot Abr.* 118 The cost and peril of galleying an invading army across the Straits.

galley-foist. *Obs.* exc. *Hist.* [f. galley *sb.* + foist *sb.*[1]] A state barge, esp. that of the Lord Mayor of London.

1589 Fleming *Virg. Georg.* IV. 66 Carried..about his grounds in painted gallefoistes. **1609** B. Jonson *Sil. Wom.* IV. ii, When the Gally-foist is a-floate to Westminster! **1616** Beaum. & Fl. *Scornf. Lady* I. ii, Captains of Gally-foists, such as in a clear day have seen Callis. *c* **1640** [Shirley] *Capt. Underwit* I. in Bullen *O. Pl.* II. 324 No Lord Maiors day, no gulls nor gallifoists. **1691** T. H[ale] *Acc. New Invent.* p. xvi, Such *Epistolæ obscurorum Virorum* should meddle with the Gally-foists of my Lord Mayor's Show, and not first Rate Ships. **1785** in Grose *Dict. Vulg. Tongue.* **1867** in Smyth *Sailor's Word-bk.*

fig. **1624** Heywood *Captives* I. in Bullen *O. Pl.* IV, Sayle this way thoue galley foyst of galls and garbadge!

attrib. **1612** Dekker *Lond. Triumph.* Wks. 1873 III. 257 Their thunder (according to the old gally-foyst fashion), was too lowd for any of the Nine Muses to be bidden to it.

galleyglass, obs. form of galloglass.

†**galley-halfpenny.** *Obs.* Forms: see galley and halfpenny. [f. galley *sb.* + halfpenny.] A silver coin, said to have been introduced into England by the sailors of the Genoese and other galleys that traded to London. Its use was prohibited by law early in the 15th cent.

1409–10 *Act 11 Hen. IV*, c. 5 Ordeinez est & establiz que les ditz galihalpenyes jãmes ne courgent en paiement..deinz le roiaulme Dengleterre. **1460** Capgrave *Chron.* (Rolls) 313 In this tyme [4 Henry V] was it defendid that galey halfpenies schuld not be used. **1521–2** *Churchw. Acct.-bk.* in *N. & Q.* 4th Ser. II. 344 Resaved for ij vnces of galy halfepenys sold this yere vis. iiijd. **1542** Becon *Policy War* Pref, Wks. (1564) 125b, My riches are not worth a Gally halfe peny. **1619** Dalton *Countr. Just.* cvii. (1630) 277 Money called Galley halfepence..to bring and put in payment any such was made felonie by the Statute. **1710** Hearne *Collect.* (O.H.S.) II. 338 The half-pence of Janua (commonly call'd Gally-half-pence).

'galley-man. [f. galley *sb.* + man *sb.*]

1. One who rows in a galley.

1352 Minot *Poems* (Hall) III. 57 þe galay men held vp þaire handes. *a* **1572** Knox *Hist. Ref.* Wks. 1846 I. 220 The galayis and the galay-men did boyth eschape. **1589** Cogan *Haven Health* ii. (1636) 22 The Gally-man..the Carier, ease the tediousnesse of their labour..with singing and whistling. **1672** Leycester *Antiq. Chesh.* II. ii. 115 There were fifty skilful Oars or Galleymen. **1836–48** B. D. Walsh *Aristoph.* 259 *note*, The Athenian Galley-men taking cushions to sit upon. *a* **1845** Hood *She is far from Land* 20 Pirates, and Sallee-men, Algerine galleymen.

†2. (See quots.) *Obs.*

c **1550** *Disc. Common Weal Eng.* (1893) 127 These gally men, mercers, fustian sellers, grocers, poticaries, that selles vs anie ware made beyond the sea. **1706** Phillips (ed. Kersey), *Galley-men*, certain Genoese Merchants formerly so call'd, because they usually arriv'd in Galleys, landed their Goods at a Place in Thames-street, nam'd Galley-key, and traded with their own small Silver Coin call'd Galley-half-pence.

galley-nipper, var. gallinipper.

galleypot, obs. form of gallipot.

'galley-slave. [f. galley *sb.* + slave *sb.*]

1. One who is condemned to work at the oar in a galley. Often *fig.* as a type of painful slavery.

1567 Turberv. *All Things haue release*, etc. 21 A gally-slave I seeme vnto my selfe to bee. **1626** Bacon *Sylva* §733 Gally Slaues, notwithstanding their Misery otherwise, are commonly Fat and Fleshy. **1683** Kennett tr. *Erasm. on Folly* 38 He is worse than a Gally-slave to his own lusts. **1701** *Lond Gaz.* No. 3715/1 The Galley-Slaves..had agreed together to throw their Officers and the Soldiers over-board. **1780** Cowper *Table T.* 327 Worse than the deeds of galley-slaves broke loose. **1836** Marryat *Midsh. Easy* xxxii, They ..perceived the house surrounded by the galley-slaves. **1875** Helps *Ess.*, *Domestic Rule* 39 We should not attempt to tie them up to their duties, like galley-slaves to their labour.

†2. *Printing.* (See quot.) *Obs.*

1683 Moxon *Mech. Exerc.* II. 362 The Compositers are Jocosely call'd Galley Slaves; Because allusively they are as it were bound to their Gallies.

†**galley-tile.** *Obs.* Forms: 7 galletyle, gallietile, 8 gall(e)ytile. [f. galley *sb.* + tile *sb.*: see gallipot.] A glazed tile used for wall-decoration. Also *collect.*, the material of which these are made.

1610 W. Folkingham *Art of Survey* 4 Gallie and Thacke Tiles. *a* **1626** Bacon *Wks.* (1857) III. 804 It is to be known of what stuff galletyle is made, and how the colours in it are varied. **1719** De Foe *Crusoe* II. xiv, The little square Tiles we call Galley-Tiles in England, all made of the finest China. **1720** Strype *Stow's Surv.* II. v. xv. 240 Making Gally paving Tiles and Vessels for Apothecaries. **1768** Cook *First Voy.* I. i. in Hawksworth *Voy.* 1773 II. 8 The other side is divided into wards, each of which is..neatly lined with gally-tiles.

'galleytrough. *Sc.* Also 8 gallytrough, 8–9 gerletroch. [Of unknown origin.] A local name (Lochleven) for the char.

a **1722** Sir R. Sibbald (Jam.), Piscis in lacu Levino—Gerletroch. **1793** *Statist. Acc. Scotl.* VI. 167 The gallytrough or char abounds in the Loch. **1806** Forsyth *Beauties Scotl.* IV. 26 The species [of trout] called the galley trough or char is that chiefly admired. **1810** P. Neill *List Fishes Frith of Forth* 16 (Jam.) The *S. Alpinus*, Red Char, or Gerletroch.

galley-wat, obs. form of gallivat.

galley-west ('gælıwɛst), *adv. colloq.* (orig. and chiefly *U.S.*). Also galleywest, gallywest. [An alteration of Eng. dial. *colly-west*, *weston*: see E.D.D. and Collyweston 2.] Phr. *to knock galley-west*, to knock sideways or askew; to bring to confusion; to knock out or dispose of completely.

1875 'Mark Twain' *Lett.* (1917) I. 250 Your verdict has knocked what little [critical penetration] I did have gally-west! **1884** —— *Huck. Finn* xxxvii. 382 Then she grabbed up the basket and slammed it across the house, and knocked the cat galleywest. **1891** M. E. Ryan *Pagan of Alleghanies* xiv. 184 Here you come with your theories of hue and knock my serenity galley-west. **1892** Kipling *Lett. of Travel* (1920) 66 It knocks pleasant domestic arrangements galleywest. **1936** J. Dos Passos *Big Money* 77 A wave had knocked him galleywest. **1938** S. Chase *Tyranny of Words* viii. 87 Einstein shattered a whole cosmology of concepts. Let us not be knocked galley-west again, says Bridgman.

galleyworm, gallyworm ('gælıwɜːm). [f. galley *sb.* + worm *sb.*, from the resemblance to a galley propelled by numerous oars.] An insect of the class *Myriapoda*; an iulus.

1658 Rowland *Moufet's Theat. Ins.* 1047 All these Gally-worms, if they be touched roll themselves up, and become round. **1752** Sir J. Hill *Hist. Anim.* 17 *Gally-worm*, the brown Iulus, with a hundred legs on each side. **1774** Goldsm. *Nat. Hist.* VII. 303 The Gally worm differs from the scolopendra, in having double the number of feet. **1835** Kirby *Hab. & Inst. Anim.* II. xvi. 66 De Geer..thinks that the common *Julus* [foot-note *J. terrestris*], or Gallyworm feeds upon earth. **1873** Dawson *Earth & Man* vi. 136 Galley-worms or millipedes; wingless, many-jointed, and many-footed crawlers, resembling worms, but more allied to insects.

gall-fly ('gɔːlflaı). [f. gall *sb.*[3]] An insect (of the genus *Cynips*) which produces galls on trees.

1822–34 *Good's Study Med.* (ed. 4) I. 316 The larvæ of the *cynips querci*, or gall-fly. **1868** Wood *Homes without H.* xxv. 482 Cynipidae..are popularly known as Gall Flies.

†**'gall-ful**, *a. Obs. rare.* [f. gall *sb.*[1] + -ful.] Full of gall; bitter, malignant.

1596 R. L[inche] *Diella* xii. in Arb. *Garner* VII. 195 Convert to sugared pleasure, gall-ful pain! **1608** T. Morton *Preamb. Encounter* Pref. 3 Casting vpon me all the cankred and galfull termes it could vtter.

gallgaskin, gall-house, galliace, obs. ff. galligaskin, gallows, galliass.

†**galliac(k**, *a. Obs.* (See quot. 1706.)

1530 *Privy Purse Exp. Hen. VIII* (1827) 24 For iij tonne of white wyne of galiake. **1703** *Art & Myst. Vintners* 69 Then have you Galliack Wines in Pipes and Hogsheads. **1706** Phillips (ed. Kersey), *Gaillac*, or *Galliac* Wine, a sort of French Wine, so call'd from *Gaillac*, a Town of Languedoc, where it is made.

galliambic (gælı'æmbık), *a.* and *sb.* [f. L. *galliamb-us* a song of the *Galli* or priests of Cybele (f. *Gallus* + iambus) + -ic.]

A. *adj.* Epithet of a lyric metre (founded on the Ionic a minore tetrameter catalectic, with anaclasis), supposed to have been used by the priests of the Phrygian Cybele in their songs.

a **1876** M. Collins *Pen Sketches* (1879) I. 215 Catullus relates the madness of Atys in a wonderful wild measure, intended to represent the ravings of that mystic priesthood, and thence called galliambic. **1893** *19th Cent.* Mar. 448 The galliambic rhythm of *Boadicea* is borrowed from..the celebrated *Attis*.

B. *sb.* The galliambic metre; a verse written in this metre.

a **1846** Landor *Wks.* (1876) II. 175 *note*, The Galliambic of Catullus may be a relic (the only one) of Phrygian poetry. *a* **1876** M. Collins *Pen Sketches* (1879) I. 215 There were at that time no English galliambics; but Mr. Tennyson has since written them [in *Boadicea*] with great power. **1887** *Athenæum* 11 June 759/3 [George Meredith's] 'Phaéthôn', an achievement in the galliambic measure, which..should be read, not as galliambics, but as poetry pure and simple, while English poetry endures.

†**gallian** ('gælıən), *a. Obs.* [f. L. *Galli-a* Gaul + -an.] Gallic, French. Also as *sb. pl.*

1591 Shaks. *1 Hen. VI*, v. iv. 139, I am possest With more then halfe the Gallian Territories. **1611** —— *Cymb.* I. vi. 66. **1630** J. Taylor (Water P.) *Wks.* II. 18/2 The Spanish Pip, or else the Gallian Morbus. *Ibid.* III. 63/1 The Britaines, Gallians, and Hibernians.

galliard ('gælıəd), *a.* and *sb.*[1] Forms: 4–9 gaillard(e, gal(l)yard(e, 5–9 galiard(e, 5–6 galȝart, 6 galyeard (galȝard, galȝeard, gagliard), 6– galliard. [ad. OF. and F. *gaillard*, *-art* (mod.F. *gaillard*) = Pr. *galhart*, Sp., *gallardo*, Pg. *galhardo*, It. *gagliardo* adj., of unknown origin: for the suffix see -ard. The sb. B 2, 3, is a. F. *gaillarde*, properly the fem. of the adj.]

A. *adj.*

1. Valiant, hardy, 'stout', sturdy. *Obs.* exc. *arch.*

?*a* **1400** *Morte Arth.* 1265 Sir Gawayne and syr Gryme, these galyarde knyghtez. *c* **1450** Holland *Howlat* 540 Mony galiard gome was on the ground levit. **1535** *Let.* in Froude *Hist. Eng.* II. 299 There was a galiard assault given before five o'clock in the morning. **1536** *Rem. Sedition* 2a, He [Sertorius] had also two horses, thone galyarde, lusty, and of a thycke tayle. **1598** Barret *Theor. Warres* III. ii. 46 It doth much import that the front be gaillard and strong. **1650** Howell *Giraffi's Rev. Naples* 130 And it was held convenient by all to com to som gaillard resolution. **1862** H. Marryat *Year in Sweden* II. 241 We pass by gutted towers, four stories high, with machicolations fresh as yesterday—gaillard and daring.

2. Lively, brisk, gay, full of high spirits. *arch.*

c **1386** Chaucer *Cook's T.* 3 Gaillard he was as Goldfinch in the shawe. *c* **1475** *Rauf Coilȝear* 785 Amang their Galȝart Gromis I am bot ane Gest. **1513** Douglas *Æneis* VIII. Prol. 31 The galiart grum grunschis at grammis hym greuis. **1652** Evelyn *State France* Misc. Writ. (1805) 92 There lives not ..a more frank, galiard, and supine people. **1671** Shadwell *Humorist* II. Wks. 1720 I. 172 Come, Madam, let's be frolick, galliard, and extraordinary brisk. **1819** W. Tennant *Papistry Storm'd* (1827) 176 The faemen grew galyard now, and crouse ilk ane. **1820** Byron *Mar. Fal.* I. i. 21 Steno's a patrician, Young, galliard, gay, and haughty. **1835** W. Irving *Crayon Misc.* (1849) 20 A young Swiss Count..galliard in the extreme, and prone to every kind of wild adventure. **1868** Browning *Ring & Bk.* II. 194 These wretched Comparini were once gay And galliard, of the modest middle class.

†3. Having a gay appearance, spruce. *Obs.*

1513 Douglas *Æneis* XII. Prol. 150 Ane paradice it semyt to draw neyr Thyr galȝart gardyngis and ilke greyn herbere. **1599** Jas. I *Βασιλ. Δωρον* (1603) 112 Faile neuer in time of warres to be galliardest and brauest, both in cloathes and countenance. *a* **1605** Montgomerie *Misc. Poems* xiii. 25 Love maks men galȝard in their geir.

Hence †**'galliardly** *adv.*, †**'galliardness.**

1542 *St. Papers Hen. VIII* (1830) I. 736 He..went galyardly to the matyer. **1550** Nicolls *Thucyd.* 222b, They saylled and gouernedde their shyppes more galliardly than the othere. **1653** Bogan *Mirth Chr. Life* 30 How galliardly does the prophet cry out. **1654** Gayton *Pleas. Notes* IV. vi. & vii. 206 His sprightfull pleasance and galliardnesse abated.

B. *sb.*

1. †a. A man of courage and spirit (*obs.*). b. A gay fellow; a man of fashion (*arch.*).

1532 More *Confut. Tindale* Wks. 552/2 When the rage is ones passed, then rise up like lusty galiardes agayn, and fight a freshe. *a* **1658** Cleveland *Mixt Assembly* 87 Selden hee's a Galliard by himself. **1768** W. Donaldson *Sir Barth. Sapskull* II. 218 My fame..made my name famous among the gaillards of the town. **1828** [see galliardise]. **1854** Mrs. Oliphant *Magd. Hepburn* I. 296 God and the truth dwell not among galliards and gay companie.

2. A quick and lively dance in triple time. *Hist.*

1533 Elyot *Cast. Helthe* (1539) 50b, Vehement exercise is compounde of violent exercise and swifte whan they ar ioyned togither at one tyme, as dansyng of galyardes. **1549** *Compl. Scot.* vi. 66 Dansand base dansis, pauans, galȝardis, turdions, braulis, and branglis. **1601** Shaks. *Twel. N.* I. iii. 137 Why dost thou not goe to Church in a Galliard, and come home in a Carranto? **1656** Heylin *Surv. France* 2 Nothing but a nimble galliard filled with capers. **1746** W. Thompson *Hymn to May* xlvi. 3 In the nimble-footed galliard, all, Shepherds and shepherdesses, lively, join. **1808** Scott *Marm.* v. xii, Never a hall such a galliard did grace. **1849** Sir J. Stephen *Eccl. Biog.* (1850) I. 157 Whether the lute should breathe a summons to the gaillard, or the trumpet ring out an alarm to the battle [etc.].

†3. The air to which the galliard was danced. *Obs.*

1545 Ascham *Toxoph.* (Arb.) 39 Whether these..galiardes..be lyker the musike of the Lydians or the Dorians, you that be learned iudge. **1597** Morley *Introd. Mus.* 181 How manie foures of semibreues you put in the straine of your pauan, so many times sixe minimes must you put in the straine of your galliard. *a* **1613** Overbury *A Wife* (1638) 89 He whistles his owne Galliard. **1789** Burney *Hist. Mus.* III. i. 87 This strain was usually followed by the Galliard.

attrib. **1626** Bacon *Sylva* §113 As when Galliard Time, and Measure Time, are in the Medly of one Dance. **1674** Playford *Skill Mus.* I. x. 33 The Imperfect of the More..is much used in Airy Songs and Galiards, and is usually called Galiard or Triple Time.

galliard ('gælɪəd), *sb.*² *Geol.* [Of unknown origin.] (See quots.)

1875 *Ure's Dict. Arts* (ed. 7) II. 531 *Galliard*, a North of England term for a hard, smooth, flinty grit. **1877** A. H. GREEN *Phys. Geol.* ii. §6. 68 Very siliceous Sandstones with an even close grain are called Cank, Cankstone, or Galliard.

galliardise ('gælɪəˌdaɪz). *arch.* Also 6 ?galiardise, 7 galliardize, gagliardise, 9 gaillardise. [ad. F. *gaillardise*, f. *gaillard* GALLIARD *sb.*] Gaiety, mirth, revelry. Also, a merry trick.

c **1570** *Pride & Lowl.* (1841) 58 A man..Whose trade is galiaudise [? *read* galiardise], drinke, and disport. **1619** T. MILLES tr. *Mexia's Treas. Anc. & Mod. Times* II. x. xiii. 962/1 Landgartha..obseruing some rare galliardise, euen in the gracefull lookes of her female followers. **1643** SIR T. BROWNE *Relig. Med.* II. §11, I am no way facetious, nor disposed for the mirth and galliardize of company. **1828** SCOTT *F.M. Perth* xxx, 'How stands it with the bona robas and the galliards?' 'Little galliardise stirring, my lord.' **1842** L. HUNT *Palfrey* v. 129 This were a crowning galliardise For king himself to tell in hall. **1893** *Harper's Mag.* Feb. 394 Your life is one long gaillardise.

Hence †'**galliarˌdizing** *ppl. a.*, tending to revelry; enlivening, exciting to levity.

1697 COLLIER *Immor. Stage* vi. (1730) 182 The Tunes are generally airy and gailliardizing. **1703** —— *Ess. Mor. Subj.* II. 25 One word of Church Musick..There must be..no light and galliardizing notes.

'**galliardism.** *rare*⁻¹. [f. GALLIARD *a.* + -ISM.] = GALLIARDISE.

1745 ELIZA HEYWOOD *Female Spect.* (1748) III. 285 The phlegmatic disposition of the English can ill endure any galliardisms in the females belonging to them.

galliass, galleass ('gælɪæs). *Obs.* exc. *Hist.* Forms: 6–9 gal(l)eass(e, -ias(s(e, 6 galeaze, 7 gal(l)iace, galleace, galeas, 6– galliass. [ad. OF. *galeace*, *galeasse*, *galiasse*, also *gall-*, ad. It. *galeaza*, augmentative of *galea* GALLEY *sb.*] A heavy, low-built vessel, larger than a galley, impelled both by sail and oars, chiefly employed in war.

1544 *St. Papers Hen. VIII* (1834) III. 504 Foure hundred galleys, foystes, and galyasses. **1549** *Compl. Scot.* vi. 42 This gaye galliasse, beand in gude ordour. **1596** SHAKS. *Tam. Shr.* II. i. 380. *a* **1642** SIR W. MONSON *Naval Tracts* III. (1704) 360/1 A Galleass is built..low and snug..and carries the Force of a Ship..the thing that gives her Advantage in Fight, is her Oars. **1677** F. SANDFORD *Genealog. Hist. Eng.* 79 The sinking the great Galeas of the Saracens. **1721** *Phil. Trans.* XXXI. 246 The Crew should be under some Covert, as they are in a Galeass. **1769** FALCONER *Dict. Marine* (1789) Gg, The quarter of a first-rate galley, otherwise called a galleasse. **1777** WATSON *Philip II*, (1839) 447 The principal galeass, commanded by Moncada..was driven ashore near Calais. **1858** FROUDE *Hist. Eng.* III. 248 A French galliass and galleon..attempted to cut out two merchantmen. **1888** *Cassell's Mag.* Aug. XIV. 559 Galleon and caracke and galleasse Crashed down the stream of flight.

transf. and *fig.* **1592** G. HARVEY *Pierce's Super.* 140 Whom ..I officiously recommende to the Ship of Fooles and the galeasse of Knaues. **1602** MARSTON *Ant. & Mel.* v. Wks. 1856 I. 63 Here's such a companie of flibotes, hulling about this galleasse of greatnesse, that there's no boarding him.

†**b.** *attrib.* in †**galliass-breeches**, a jocular augmentative of *gally-breeches*.

1596 NASHE *Have with you* Wks. (Grosart) III. 51 Farre more boystrous and cumbersome than a pair of Swissers omnipotent galeaze breeches.

Gallic ('gælɪk), *a.*¹ and *sb.* [ad. L. *Gallic-us* Gaulish (in mod.L. 'French'), f. *Gallus* GAUL.]

A. *adj.* **a.** Of or pertaining to, or characteristic of, the Gauls or Gaul; Gaulish.

1796 H. HUNTER tr. *St.-Pierre's Stud. Nat.* (1799) III. 353 Venus had descended on this part of the Gallic shore. **1881** F. E. WARREN *Celtic Liturgy* 59 Gallic sailors with their ship came to Iona.

b. Often used as a rhetorical or (now chiefly) semi-humorous synonym for 'French'; sometimes with allusion to characteristics which the French are supposed to have inherited from their Gaulish ancestors. †*His Gallic Majesty*: the king of France.

1672 CROWNE *Chas. VIII*, II. Dram. Wks. 1873 I 152 I' th' glories of the Gallic Court. **1712** ADDISON *Spect.* No. 481 ¶6 A little warm fellow..fell most unmercifully upon his Gallic majesty. **1756** JOHNSON *Let. to Dr. Hawksworth* Mar., It is too Gallick. **1778** ABIGAIL ADAMS in *J. Adams' Fam. Lett.* (1876) 331 My imagination sets you down upon the Gallic shore. **1879** GEO. ELIOT *Theo. Such* xi. 190 It is his habit to talk with a Gallic largeness and refer to the universe. **1888** F. HUME *Mad. Midas* I. Prol., We will Match our Gallic wit against these English fools.

c. In combining form, as ˌ**Gallico-'Anglian**, an Englishman who favours the French.

1804 J. LARWOOD *No Gun Boat* 8 Is there a Gallico-Anglian who has the perverseness to say that [etc.].

B. *sb.* A Frenchman. *rare*⁻¹.

1755 J. ADAMS *Let.* 12 Oct. in Webster *Adams & Jefferson* 17 If we can remove the turbulent Gallicks, our people.. will in another century, become more numerous than England itself.

gallic ('gælɪk), *a.*² *Chem.* [ad. F. *gallique*, f. L. *galla* (= F. *galle* GALL *sb.*³): see -IC.] Only in ***gallic acid***: a crystalline acid prepared from the oak-gall and other vegetable products.

1791 HAMILTON tr. *Berthollet's Dyeing* I. I. I. v. 74 To which the name of gallic acid has been given from galls. **1800** tr. *Lagrange's Chem.* II. 86 Red sulphate of iron..is precipitated black by the gallic acid. **1883** *Hardwich's Photogr. Chem.* (ed. Taylor) iv. 117 On..brushing with a solution of Gallic Acid, a manifest difference will be observed.

gallica ('gælɪkə). [f. L. *Gallicus* GALLIC *a.*¹] A species of rose, *Rosa gallica*; a plant or flower of a variety of this species.

1848 W. PAUL *Rose Garden* I. iv. 51 Summer Roses: Provence, 8. Moss, 10. Damask, 6. Alba, 6. Gallica, 75. **1869** S. R. HOLE *Bk. about Roses* xi. 160 These variegated Roses..are affiliated in the catalogues to the family of Gallicas. *Ibid.* 161 Let us suppose that they could distinguish at any distance the Gallica from the Provence Rose. **1912** E. WILLMOTT *Genus Rosa* II. 329 The *gallica* Rose having been common in gardens throughout Europe from very early times. **1962** I. MURDOCH *Unofficial Rose* xvi. 154 Despatched to the rose slopes to cut a bunch of gallicas.

Gallican ('gælɪkən), *a.* and *sb.* Also 7 gallicane. [ad. L. *Gallicānus*, f. *Gallic-us* GALLIC *a.*¹ Cf. F. *gallican* (not *-ain*) in ecclesiastical sense.]

A. *adj.*

1. a. *gen.* = GALLIC *a.*¹ *Obs.* exc. in palæographical use.

1598 GRENEWEY *Tacitus Descr. Germanie* VI. 270 The Gallican toong doth conuince the Gothinos..not to be Germans. **1628** LE GRYS tr. *Barclay's Argenis* 215 He therefore (a wickednesse not familiar with our Gallicane spirits) attempted vs both with poyson. **1708** *Lond. Gaz.* No. 4426/8 The Popish Pretender and Pupil of the Gallican Tyrant. **1805** T. HARRAL *Scenes of Life* I. 100 The culprit pleaded the restraint of marriage upon the will, and upon the affections, with every other common-place sophism of Gallican philosophy. **1883** I. TAYLOR *Alphabet* II. 176 *note*, A copy of the Sermons of St Severianus..must also represent the Gallican script, which was the parent of the Irish uncial.

b. *Eccl.* (= med.L. *Gallicanus*), the distinctive epithet of the ancient Church of Gaul or France, and of its characteristic usages, liturgies, etc. as compared with those of other national Churches of the Roman communion. Hence applied to that school of French Roman Catholics of which Bossuet was the leader, which maintains the right of the French Church to be in certain important respects self-governing, and free from papal control; opposed to *Ultramontane*.

[**1169** BECKET *Let. to Pope Alexander* in *Mat. Hist. Thos. Becket* (1885) VII. dlxxxiii. 121 Forma fidelitatis exigit in ecclesia Gallicana et Anglicana [etc.].] **1633** BP. MORTON *Disch.* 5 *Imputations* 263 For the defence and preservation of the Gallicane Regalities and Liberties. **1670** G. H. *Hist. Cardinals* I. I. 2 The Vigilance of France in maintaining the Gallicane Rites. *Ibid.* 16 The French keep close to their Gallican Church. **1724** WATERLAND *Athan. Creed* iv. 61 This more correct Psalter..obtain'd first in Gaul about 580 ..From which circumstance it came to have the name of Gallican, in contradistinction to the Roman. **1850** NEALE *East. Ch.* I. I. 15 The Gallican theory [of church government] views the Church as a constitutional monarchy.

†**2.** = *French-sick*: see FRENCH 7. *Obs.*

1694 WESTMACOTT *Script. Herb.* 3 Sweet Almonds..are commonly allowed by Physicians, to be eaten with a few Raisins..for a Supper, by their Gallican Patients. *Ibid.* 25.

B. *sb.* **a.** One who favours friendly relations with France. *rare.* **b.** A member of the Gallican party in the French Church.

1876 BANCROFT *Hist U.S.* VI. xlvi. 302 In regard to the foreign relations of the country [United States], Congress was divided between what the French envoy named 'Gallicans' and 'anti-Gallicans'. **1882** *Athenæum* 8 July 41/3 He is no Papist or Ultramontane, but a Gallican..a genuine Gallican of the school of Bossuet.

Hence '**Gallicanist**, one who favours the independence of the Gallican Church.

1715 M. DAVIES *Athen. Brit.* I. 64 Gallicanists, Italicanists, Secular Priests. **1882–3** SCHAFF *Encycl. Relig. Knowl.* III. 1986 As the former proved him to be a Jansenist, and the latter a Gallicanist, a conflict with the Jesuits was unavoidable.

Gallicanism ('gælɪkənɪz(ə)m). [f. GALLICAN + -ISM.] The principles and practice of the Gallican party (see GALLICAN *a.* 1 b).

1858 *Westm. Rev.* Oct. 330 Gallicanism..has died under ..the irruption of liberal opinion. **1869** *Pall Mall G.* 15 Nov. 2 It would surely shock Archbishop Manning to learn that such rank 'Gallicanism'..is being taught under authority.

¶ Used erroneously for GALLICISM. *rare.*

1885 *Law Times* 28 Mar. 385/1 What may be conveniently described, to use a Gallicanism, as a 'contradictory' judgment.

‖**Gallice, gallice** ('gælɪsiː), *adv.* [L., 'in Gaulish'.] In French.

1889 in *Cent. Dict.* **1897** G. DU MAURIER *Martian* i. 44 He had received from Barty a sore eye too—*gallicè*, 'un pochon'.

gallicide ('gælɪsaɪd). *nonce-wd.* [f. L. *gall-us* cock + -CIDE I.] A killer of fowls (in quot. = a fox).

1897 BOLDREWOOD *My Run Home* xxvi. 248 Resolute cast himself, all teeth and bristles, upon the reeling gallicide.

gallicinite, var. GALLIZINITE *Obs.*

Gallicism ('gælɪsɪz(ə)m). [a. F. *gallicisme*, f. L. *gallic-us* GALLIC *a.*¹: see -ISM.]

1. An idiom or mode of expression belonging to the French language, esp. one used by a speaker or writer in some other language; also, in generalized sense, free use of French idiom, 'Frenchy' kind of diction.

1656 BLOUNT *Glossogr.*, *Gallicism*, the form of speech, or custom of the French. **1683** *Apol. Prot. France* ii. 19, I can scarce believe..that it was written in French; how-ever, some Gallicisms are put in to make you believe it. **1759** LADY M. W. MONTAGU *Let. to Sir J. Steuart* 19 July, I hope you won't think this dab of Italian..an affectation like his Gallicisms. **1821** *New Monthly Mag.* II. 310 It is useless investigating the crowd of gallicisms that might be presented. **1833** MACAULAY *Ess.*, *Walpole* (1843) II. 107 His style is more deeply tainted with Gallicism [*Edinb. Rev.* Oct. (1833) 233 Gallicisms] than that of any other English writer with whom we are acquainted. **1861** MAINE *Anc. Law* (1874) 37 Each group of circumstances..receives, to employ a gallicism, a sort of consecration. **1867** MACFARREN *Harmony* iii. (1876) 115 Its use has come to be regarded as a musical Gallicism.

2. A French characteristic, custom, mode of thought, or the like.

1715 M. DAVIES *Athen. Brit.* I. 295 A higher pitch of Gothisms and Gallicisms in Religion, as well as in Words.

Gallicize ('gælɪsaɪz), *v.* [f. L. *Gallic-us* GALLIC *a.*¹ + -IZE.]

1. *intr.* To become Gallic or French; to adapt oneself to French habits, speech, etc.

1775 J. JEKYLL *Corr.* 29 Mar. (1894) 2 We have Gallicised in some measure already. *a* **1843** SOUTHEY *Comm.-pl. Bk.* Ser. II. (1849) 373 When France upon the decline of Spain, succeeded to its places of dominion, the Company [Jesuits] gallicized.

2. *trans.* To render French-like; to Frenchify.

1773 KENRICK *Rhet. Gram.* §3 The French..having not only gallicised terms of art and appellatives; but even given Christian names to Pagans. **1804** W. TAYLOR in *Ann. Rev.* II. 635 Conspiring to Gallicize the manners of the British. **1835** SYD. SMITH *Let.* 11 Dec., Being, since my travels, very much gallicized in my character, I ordered a pint of claret. **1863** KIRK *Chas. Bold* II. 158 France seeks..to Gallicize whatever comes to her from abroad.

Hence '**Gallicized** *ppl. a.*, '**Gallicizing** *vbl. sb.* (also *attrib.*) and *ppl. a.*

1804 W. TAYLOR in *Ann. Rev.* II. 233 The dissenting teachers gradually abandoned the propagation of opinions to the gallicizing philosophers. **1849** THACKERAY *Pendennis* lix, The daughter..with her Gallicised graces and.. affectations. **1867** FREEMAN *Norm. Conq.* (1877) I. iv. 252 The Christianizing, the Gallicizing, and the feudalizing process, all went on. **1892** *Athenæum* 3 Dec. 773/1 It is difficult to see..that there is any such general gallicizing of our contemporary poetry. **1893** *Nation* (N.Y.) 5 Jan. 14/3 Was the English author..given to Latinizing or to Gallicizing?

Gallicizer ('gælɪsaɪzə(r)). [f. GALLICIZE + -ER¹.] One who Gallicizes: in quot., a French partisan.

1859 *Sat. Rev.* VIII. 61/2 It was admitted even by the loudest Gallicizers that the possession of Lombardy by Austria could by no possibility furnish a cause of war to France.

gallie, obs. form of GALLEY, GALLOWS *sb.*

galliet(te, obs. form of GALLIOT.

galliform ('gælɪfɔːm), *a. Ornith.* [ad. mod.L. *galliform-is*, f. L. *gall-us* cock + *forma* form.] Belonging to the *Galliformes*, an order of birds, including ostriches, gallinaceous birds, rails, cuckoos, and parrots. (In recent Dicts.)

galligaskin (ˌgælɪ'gæskɪn). Now chiefly in *pl.* Forms: 6 garragascoyne, 6–7 galli-, gally gascoi(g)n(e, -gascoyn(e, (6 galigascon, gallie gascoine, gallo-gascaine, 7 gallgaskin), 7–9 gally-gaskin, (9 galigaskin), 7– galligaskin. [app. an interpretative corruption of the 16th c. F. *garguesque*, a metathetic var. of *greguesque*, ad. It. *grechesca* sb., originally fem. of *grechesco* Greek (this kind of hose being in 16th c. described as *alla grechesca* = F. *à la grecque* in the Greek fashion). The surviving Fr. word in this sense is *grègue*, ad. Pr. *grega* or Sp. *griega*, orig. the fem. of the adj., Pr. *grego*, Sp. *griego*, Greek.

The form *garragascoynes* seems to prove that the Fr. word is really the source. The synonymous *gally-breeches*, *gally-slops* (see GALLY *a.*¹ or *sb.*) occur earlier than, and *gasco(y)n*, GASKIN¹, about the same time with, the present word. If they are really older, the perversion of *garguesque* into *galligaskin* is fully accounted for. They may, however, have originated in a false analysis of *galligaskin*, which in that case must have been corrupted from *garguesque* by the influence of GASCON and GALLEY *sb.* (less probably L. *Galli-*, *Gallus*, GAUL, or *gally* GALLOWS *sb.* in the sense 'braces'). The early examples associate galligaskins with 'shipmen's hose', and imply that the fashion belonged to the south of Europe, so that it would be very natural for popular etymology to connect the word with *galley*.]

1. A kind of wide hose or breeches worn in the 16th and 17th c.; later, a more or less ludicrous term for loose breeches in general.

a. *sing.* Also *attrib.* in ***galligaskin breeches***.

1577 HOLINSHED *Chron.* II. 1859/1 Galeygascoyne breeches all of Crimosyn satyn. **1592** *Def. Conny Catching* (1859) 57 The venetian and the galligascaine is stale, and trunke slop out of use. **1610** ROWLANDS *Martin Mark-all* 27 Their hose sometimes Spanish, like to Shipmens hose, and sometimes close to the buttocke like the Venetian galligascoigne.

b. *pl.*

1577 HARRISON *England* II. xxii. (1877) I. 343 A well-burnished gentleman..hath borne threescore at once in one paire of galigascons. **1581** B. RICHE *Farewell Mil. Prof.* Conclusion D d iij, In their Hoose so many fashions as I can not describe, sometymes Garragascoynes, breached like a Beare. **1620** SHELTON *Quix.* IV. xix. 149 He began to untruss his Points: the Opinion is that he had but one before, which held up his Gally-Gascoins. **1703** J. PHILIPS *Splendid Shilling* 121 My Galligaskins, that have long withstood The Winter's Fury. **1761** STERNE *Tr. Shandy* IV. xxvii, His whole thoughts..were taken up with a transaction which was going forwards..within the precincts of his own Galligaskins. **1794** in *Poet. Reg.* (1807) 401 While in Rhyme's Galligaskins I enclose The broad posteriors of thy brawny prose. **1801** *Sporting Mag.* XVII. 19 His galligaskins have been made by the same needle-jerker. **1832** CARLYLE *Misc.* (1857) III. 72 What jackets and galligaskins had they.

2. Leggings, gaiters. *dial.*

1859 TROLLOPE *West Ind.* x. 150 He wears a huge pair..of galligaskins..made of thick stiff leather but so as to fit the leg exactly. **1868** BROWNING *Ring & Bk.* VIII. 43 Gossips too..put galligaskin off At entry of a decent domicile. **1877** *N.W. Linc. Gloss.*, Gallygaskins, gaiters. **1886** ELWORTHY *W. Somerset Word-bk.*, *Galligaskins*, rough leather over-alls, worn by thatchers, hedgers and labourers.

3. A variety of the cowslip (*Primula veris*).

1629 PARKINSON *Paradisi* xxxv. 245 There is another kinde [of cowslips] which doe somewhat resemble mens hose that they did weare and took the name of Galligaskins from thence.

appositive. **1882** *Garden* 28 Jan. 56/3 Can any information be obtained as to the origin of the Galigaskins Primrose?

Hence **galli'gaskined** *ppl. a.*, wearing galligaskins.

1854 WALTER *Last of Old Squires* xiii. 137 The good old man..with gun in hand from the paper-mill-cover, or galigaskined from the farm!

galligross, var. GALIEGROSS, *Obs.*

Gallimania, bad form of GALLOMANIA: see GALLO-[1].

c **1793** *Spirit Publ. Jrnls.* I. 125 That febrile disposition and hectic heat commonly called *Gallimania*.

gallimatia(s, obs. form of GALIMATIAS.

gallimaufry (gælɪˈmɔːfrɪ), *sb.* Forms: 6–7 gallie-, gally-, gal(l)imafry, -ay, -ey, -ie, -ee, 7 gal(l)amafrie; 6–7 galli-, gallymalfreye, -maulfry, -malfrie; 6–7 gallimaufray, -maufrie, 7 galley-, gallymaufr(e)y, -mawfrey, (galymaufry, gallemaufry, gallomawfry, gallimof(f)ry, -mophory, gallerie-maufry), 7–8 gallamaufr(e)y, 6–9 gallimaufrey, -mawfry, 6– gallimaufry. [ad. F. *galimafrée*, of unknown origin.]

1. A dish made by hashing up odds and ends of food; a hodge-podge, a ragout. *rare* exc. *dial.*

1591 PERCIVALL *Sp. Dict.*, *Nogada salsa*, a gallimaufry of nuts. **1607** DEKKER *Westw. Hoe* II. Wks. 1873 II. 294 Lattin whole-meats are nowe minc'd, and serude in for English Gallimafries. **1623** T. SCOTT *God & King* (1633) 2 That I may neither slovenly chop it into gobbits, nor curiously mince it to a gallamafrie. *a* **1693** URQUHART *Rabelais* III. xvii, The Devil mince me into a Galli-mafry, if I do not tremble for fear. **1721–1800** in BAILEY. **1859** HALIBURTON *Season Ticket* vii, The Gallimaufry at once tempts and satisfies. **1883** *Almondbury Gloss.*, *Gallimawfry*, and by corruption Gallimawverty, a mixture of several sorts of meat.

2. *transf.* and *fig.* A heterogeneous mixture, a confused jumble, a ridiculous medley.

1551–6 ROBINSON tr. *More's Utopia* (Arb.) 64 Suche a tragy-call comedye or gallymalfreye. **1579** E. K. *Ded. to Spenser's Sheph. Cal.*, So now they haue made our English tongue a gallimaufray, or hodgepodge of all other speches. **1592** CHETTLE *Kinde-harts Dr.* (1841) 29 Hee put me downe with such a galliemafrey of Latine ends that I was glad to make an end. **1613** PURCHAS *Pilgrimage* II. viii. 128 And after by marriages with some false Christians, made such a galli-maufrey as [etc.]. **1653** URQUHART *Rabelais* II. vii. 42 The hotchpotch or gallimafree of the perpetually begging Friars. **1668** R. L'ESTRANGE *Vis. Quev.* (1708) 57 Are you the Author then (quoth I) of that Gallimaufry of Prophesies, that's Publish'd in your Name? **1678** SALMON *Pharm. Londin.* 670 This is one of the greatest Gally-maufries that ever I saw: but it was intended as an Antidote against Plague. **1872** PLANCHÉ *Recoll.* II. xviii. 245 To me, the glittering gallimaufry in which all the ingenuity and beauty of the original fairy tale was lost and destroyed. **1892** A. BIRRELL *Res Judic.* xi. 260 At present it [the history of the Reformation] is but a hotch-potch, a gallimaufry, a confused mingle-mangle of divers things jumbled or put together.

3. A promiscuous assemblage (of persons).

1598 SHAKS. *Merry W.* II. i. 119 He wooes both high and low..he loues the Gally-mawfry (Ford) perpend. **1877** *Holderness Gloss.*, *Gallimawfry*, a gathering, or set of persons or things. Generally used in an unfavourable sense.

4. Said somewhat contemptuously of a person: A man of many accomplishments; a composite character. Now *rare*.

1600 DEKKER *Gentle Craft* Wks. 1873 I. 21 Peace pudding broth..peace you gallimafrey. **1632** MASSINGER & FIELD *Fatal Dowry* II. ii, A good, foolish, knavish, sociable gallimaufry of a man. **1663** COWLEY *Cutter Coleman St.* II. v, Why how now my little Gallimaufry, my little Oleopodrido of Arts and Arms! **1781** G. PARKER *View Soc.* I. 207 A compound of Player, Soldier, Stroller, Sailor, and Tinker! An odd gallimaufry! **1844** DISRAELI *Coningsby* I. v. Perhaps the most ludicrous characteristic of these factious gallimaufreys was an occasional assumption of the high moral and admonitory tone.

5. *attrib.*

1630 J. TAYLOR (Water P.) *Wks.* I. 110 These Galley-maufry humours. *a* **1734** NORTH *Exam.* II. iv. (1740) 242 Such a Gallimaufry Piece of Nonsense it was. **1769** S. PATERSON *Another Traveller!* II. 204 The gallimaufry list of pill-and-drop-mongers.

Hence **galli'maufrical** *a*, miscellaneous.

1836 *New Monthly Mag.* XLVII. 227 It has been the custom..to get up a gallimaufrical performance that is not deemed dramatic.

gallimaufry (gælɪˈmɔːfrɪ), *v. rare*⁻¹. [f. the sb.] *trans.* To cut up into a hodge-podge; to make mince-meat of. In quot. *fig.*

1831 *Fraser's Mag.* III. 197 In chapter the third, the satire rolls only against Long's hotel, which is thus wickedly gallimawfred.

Hence †**galli'maufrier**, one who makes a gallimaufry or medley (of something).

1592 NASHE *4 Lett. Confut.* K b, The gallimafrier of all stiles in one standish.

gallinacean (ˌgælɪˈneɪʃ(ɪ)ən), *a.* and *sb.* Also 9 -acian. [f. as next + -AN.] **A.** *adj.* = GALLINACEOUS; in quot. = concerned with domestic fowls. **B.** *sb.* A bird of the order *Gallinaceæ* or *Gallinæ*.

1842 BRANDE *Dict. Sci.* etc., *Gallinaceans*. See *Rasores*. **1851** *Q. Rev.* LXXXVIII. 326 The gallinacian leech, like the mountebank of former days, has to exercise his wits for pure benevolence.

gallinaceous (ˌgælɪˈneɪʃəs), *a.* [f. L. *gallīnāce-us* (f. *gallīna* a hen) + -OUS.]

1. Of or belonging to the order *Gallinæ*, which comprises all the ordinary domestic poultry, and many other birds, such as pheasants, partridges, etc.

1783 LATHAM *Synopsis Birds* II. II. 668 Order V. Gallinaceous. **1802** PALEY *Nat. Theol.* xv. 185 Spallanzani has remarked a circumstantial resemblance between the stomachs of gallinaceous fowls and the structure of corn-mills. **1861** WHYTE MELVILLE *Good for Nothing* II. 77 An example of the want of wisdom in the gallinaceous tribe.

2. *humorously.* **a.** Resembling that of a cock; 'cocky'. **b.** Consisting of fowls.

1879 G. MACDONALD *Sir Gibbie* I. xix. 255 With all the gathered wisdom of Edinburgh in his gallinaceous cranium. **1885** LADY BRASSEY *The Trades* 493 We returned to the hotel, where another meal, as gallinaceous as that of yesterday, awaited us.

gallinaginous (ˌgælɪˈnædʒɪnəs), *a.* [f. mod.L. *gallīnāgin-em*, *gallīnāgo* woodcock (f. *gallīna* hen) + -OUS.] Of or pertaining to a woodcock. *gallinaginous crest*, transl. L. *caput gallinaginis*, lit. 'woodcock's head'; the prominent fold of the lining membrane in the prostatic portion of the urethra.

1876 GROSS *Dis. Bladder* 563 Acute inflammation of the gallinaginous crest is most commonly induced by an extension of gonorrhoeal inflammation.

gallinazo (ˌgælɪˈnɑːzəʊ). Also 8 galinasso, 9 gallinaso. [corruptly a. Sp. *gallinaza* a vulture, f. *gallina* hen + augmentative suffix *-aza*.] An American vulture (*Cathartes aura* or *Catharista atrata*).

1760–72 tr. *Juan & Ulloa's Voy.* (ed. 3) I. 58 These are equally fierce and carnivorous with the former; and called the kings of the gallinazos. **1774** GOLDSM. *Anim. Nat.* V. 113 Vultures, or galinassos, as the Spaniards call them. **1833** M. SCOTT *Tom Cringle* iii, I looked up and saw a gallinaso, the large carrion-crow of the tropics, sailing seaward. **1845** DARWIN *Voy. Nat.* ix. (1873) 183 From these facts the condor, like the gallinazo, must be considered as a gregarious bird.

galline (ˈgælaɪn, -ɪn), *a. rare.* [f. L. *gall-us* cock + -INE.] = GALLINACEOUS.

1883 A. NEWTON in *Encycl. Brit.* XV. 827/2 The Brush-Turkey..was originally described by Latham in 1821 under the name of the New Holland Vulture, a misleading designation which he subsequently tried to correct on perceiving its Galline character. **1895** *Pop. Sci. Monthly* Apr. 763 Other birds possessing galline affinities are the well-known curassows.

galling (ˈgɔːlɪŋ), *vbl. sb.*[1] [f. GALL *v.*[1] + -ING[1].]

1. The action of the verb GALL in various senses; the condition of being galled.

1546 PHAER *Bk. Childr.* (1553) U v a, [It] is..good for the galling or chaffing of yᵉ fete. **1573** TUSSER *Husb.* lvii. (1878) 133 Er winter preuenteth, while weather is good, for galling of pasture get home with thy wood. **1598** R. BARRET *Mod. Warres* 96 Their vollie in their face would bee no small galling vnto them. **1646** SIR T. BROWNE *Pseud. Ep.* I. viii. 31 Vitex or Agnus Castus held only in the hand, preserveth the rider from galling. **1678** MARVELL *Def. John Howe* Wks. 1875 IV. 196 It is a certain remedy against all gauling, at least by this argumentation. **1754** *Dict. Arts & Sc.* I. 633 Pieces of brass, with holes in them, put into wooden shivers, to keep them from splitting and galling by the pin of the block. **1799** H. T. COLEBROOKE *Life* (1873) 440 Four [elephants] were disabled, by the galling of their backs, from carrying their usual burdens.

†**2.** The result of galling; in *pl.*, galls, galled spots. *Obs.*

c **1440** *Promp. Parv.* 185/1 Gallynge, *strumositas*. **1607** TOPSELL *Four-f. Beasts* (1658) 320 Honey and Verdigrease boyled together..is a good Ointment for all gallings on the withers. **1725** BRADLEY *Fam. Dict.* s.v. *Transplanting*, A good Piece of Rope tyed about the neck of the Trees upon a whisp of Straw, preserves them from gallings.

3. *Comb.*, as **galling-leather**, a piece of leather to prevent galling or chafing.

1794 W. FELTON *Carriages* (1801) I. 130 The Coachman's Seat is covered with cloth..lined at the bottom ends with pieces of leather, called galling-leathers. *Ibid.* II. 188 The galling-leather is sewed under that part of the harness where there is a buckle, to prevent it from galling the horse.

galling (ˈgɔːlɪŋ), *vbl. sb.*[2] [f. GALL *v.*[2] + -ING[1].] The treatment of material with galls, as a preliminary of the actual process of dyeing it.

1791 HAMILTON tr. *Berthollet's Dyeing* I. I. I. v. 105 Silk acquires by galling a [permanent] weight. **1800** tr. *Lagrange's Chem.* II. 275 Galling consists in macerating any piece of stuff in a decoction of gall-nuts. **1816** J. SMITH *Panorama Sc. & Art* II. 543 After the galling, the silk is put into a solution of sulphate of iron.

galling (ˈgɔːlɪŋ), *ppl. a.* [f. GALL *v.*[1] + -ING[2].] That galls.

1. Chafing, irritating or harassing physically.

1647 H. MORE *Song of Soul* II. ii. II. xxxiii, What tells the hand or head the toes great grief, When it alone is pinch'd with galling shooes? **1670** MILTON *Hist. Eng.* II. Wks. (1851) 53 What with gauling Darts and heavie strokes the Britans who wore neither Helmet nor Cuirass to defend them, were at last overcome. **1703** POPE *Thebais* 185 As stubborn steers..joined reluctant to the galling yoke. *a* **1839** PRAED *Poems* (1864) II. 283 And looks with marvel on his galling chain. **1879** MᶜCARTHY *Own Times* II. xx. 89 They [the Ministry] were placed between two galling fires.

2. *fig.* Irritating, offensive to the mind or spirit.

1583 BABINGTON *Commandm.* vi. (1590) 253 The occasions of anger in many men are..nipping words, and gawling speeches. *a* **1653** GOUGE *Comm. Heb.* xiii. 5 Covetousnesse is a gawling sinne. It works a continual vexation. **1790** BURKE *Fr. Rev.* 105 The anodyne draught of oblivion..is well calculated to preserve a galling wakefulness. **1820** W. IRVING *Sketch Bk.* I. 46 Ruin in fashionable life is accompanied by so many galling mortifications. **1876** GREEN *Stray Stud.* 221 The more galling and oppressive instances of serfdom seem to have slipped unconsciously away.

Hence **'gallingly** *adv.*, **'gallingness**.

1647 BOYLE *Let.* Wks. I. p. xxxix, I never found that people discontented with their own church-government (the gallingness of whose yoke is the grand scare-crow that frights us here). **1802** JOANNA BAILLIE *Ethwald* II. iv. ii, One who, new to greatness, Feels its unwieldy robe sit on his shoulders Constrain'd and gallingly. **1852** ROBERTSON *Serm.* Ser. III. xvii. 220 Law bears gallingly on those who want to break it.

gallingale, obs. form of GALINGALE.

gallini, dial. form of GALEENY.

gallinicide (gəˈlɪnɪsaɪd). *nonce-wd.* [f. L. *gallīni-* comb. form of *gallīna* hen + -CIDE (2).] The killing of hens or poultry.

1883 *Pall Mall G.* 17 Mar. 4/1 He sends in his claim for damages sustained by gallinicide to the 'poultry fund' of the neighbouring hunt.

gallinipper (ˈgælɪˌnɪpə(r)). Chiefly *U.S.* Also gali-, gall(e)ynipper. [Of uncertain origin.] A large mosquito.

1818 *Sporting Mag.* I. 261 Smaller flies from the gallinipper to the moschetto, began to muster in all directions. **1838** HALIBURTON *Clockm.* Ser. II. iii, He jump'd up..a snappin' of his fingers, as if he wor bit by a galley-nipper. **1867** A. L. ADAMS *Wand. Nat. India* 59 That prince of gallynippers, the sandfly, whose bite produces a painful..swelling.

gallinivorous (gælɪˈnɪvərəs), *a. nonce-wd.* [f. L. *gallīni-* comb. form of *gallīna* hen + *-vor-us* devouring + -OUS.] Feeding on fowls or poultry.

1862 *Fraser's Mag.* July 85 Man is not strictly a 'gallinivorous' animal, and has a tendency to tire of perpetual poultry.

gallinule (ˈgælɪnjuːl). [ad. mod.L. *gallīnula*, the scientific name of the genus (in late L. the word occurs for a chicken), dim. of L. *gallīna* hen.] Book-name for a genus of birds, typified by the moor-hen (*Gallinula chloropus*). Also extended to other birds of allied genera.

1776 PENNANT *Zool.* II. 409–11 Gallinule..215. Spotted..217. Common. **1785** LATHAM *Synopsis Birds* III. I. 258 Common Gallinule..Common Water-Hen or More-Hen. **1833** C. STURT *2 Exped. S. Australia* I. i. 39 Various tribes of the galinule [*sic*]..made incessant noises around us. **1872** A. DOMETT *Ranolf* XVII. §3. 274 That rich gallinule of velvet violet plumage proud. **1888** *Riverside Nat. Hist.* IV. 131 The purple-gallinules..typified by the European species (*Porphyrio porphyrio*) and the American *Ionornis martinica*.

So **gallinuline** *a.*, pertaining to the gallinule.

1895 *Pop. Sci. Monthly* Apr. 764 It falls into line with another gallinuline character.

Gallio (ˈgælɪəʊ). The name of a Roman proconsul of Achaia, whose refusal to take action is recorded in Acts xviii. 17 ('And Gallio cared for none of those things'), applied *gen.* to one who is indifferent. Hence **'Gallio-like** *a.*

and *adv.*; **Gallionic** (gælɪ'ɒnɪk) *a.*, characteristic of a Gallio, indifferent.

1850 [see CARER]. 1855 MACAULAY *Hist. Eng.* III. xiii. 293 Unhappily, Scotland was ruled, not by pious Josiahs, but by careless Gallios. 1865 L. STEPHEN *Sk. from Cambridge* xii. 137 Our prevailing tone is what I should venture to describe as one of quiet good sense, and what fanatics would consider to be only fit for careless Gallios. *Ibid.* 140 A Gallio is generally a pleasant companion. 1884 S. J. REID *Sydney Smith* x. 240 Gallio-like, he cared for none of these things. 1909 *Westm. Gaz.* 8 Mar. 4/3 Gallio-like bargain. 1920 *Q. Rev.* Oct. 403 Japan seemed Gallionic all the time. 1926 *Glasgow Herald* 20 Mar. 8 The Gallionic attitude of the soldiers along the various lines of the route.

gallion, var. form of GALION, GALLEON.

galliot[1] ('gælɪət). Forms: 4, 7 galiote, 5 galyet, 6 galyote, galyott, galliet(te, 7 galliote, galliott, 7–8 galeot, 8–9 galiot, (in Dicts.) galleot, 6– galliot. See also GALLIVAT. [a. F. *galiote* fem. (OF. also *galiot* masc.) = Sp. and Pg. *galeota*, It. *galeotta*, dim. of the Com. Rom. *galea* GALLEY *sb.*[1]]

1. A small galley or boat, propelled by sails and oars, used for swift navigation; in English applied esp. to Spanish and Mediterranean vessels.

1352 *Pol. Poems* (Rolls) I. 65, Viij. and xl. galays and mo ..And other many of galiotes, With grete noumber of smale botes. 1480 CAXTON *Descr. Brit.* VIII. xiv, Seven carryks of Gene, and fyfty other vessels, as hulkes, barges, galeys and galyetis. *c*1500 in *Arnolde's Chron.* (1811) p. xxviii, Galyottis of Spayne with odir smale shippis of warre, come a londe at Grauesende. 1579 FENTON *Guicciard.* II. (1599) 88 The hauen..conteined fiue ships, foure light galleis, a galliot, and a gallion. 1650 FULLER *Pisgah* V. xxi. 184 Those seventy lesser ships, and Galliots, brought..out of the Bosphorus. 1728 MORGAN *Algiers* II. ii. 221 Some Turkish Merchants..built and armed out a Galeot, or Light-Gally. 1799 NELSON 11 Feb. in Nicolas *Disp.* (1846) III. 262 The Officer who is to command the Galliots and Gun-boats. 1876 BANCROFT *Hist. U.S.* I. i. 15 Cartier moved his two large vessels safely into the deep water of the river..and in his galiot sailed up the majestic stream.

2. [In Du. *galjoot.*] A Dutch cargo-boat or fishing-vessel.

1794 *Rigging & Seamanship* I. 239 *Galliot.* Is a large Dutch vessel, of burthen, with one mast and a bowsprit. 1861 THORNBURY *Turner* (1862) I. 263 The ships are the heavy one-masted Dutch galliots once common on the Thames. 1884 *Mag. of Art* Apr. 253/2 Now..almost any day, are to be seen..a little fleet of Dutch galliots.

3. Used of ancient Roman vessels or galleys. ?*Obs.*

1718 ROWE tr. *Lucan* III. 797 On either Wing the larger Vessels ply, While in the Center safe the lesser Galiots lie. *c*1800 K. WHITE *Childhood* II. 165 The blood-fraught galliots of Rome.

4. = BOMB-KETCH. [= F. *galiote à bombes.*]

1867 SMYTH *Sailor's Word-bk.* s.v. *Galleot*, Some also call the bomb-ketches galliots.

5. *Comb.*, as †**galliot-hoy**, †**pink**, **yacht**, small vessels resembling a Dutch galliot in build.

1665 *Lond. Gaz.* No. 12/1 Captain Robinson hath sent into Falmouth a *Galliot-Hoy, bound for Bordeaux. 1689 *Ibid.* No. 2496/4 A Galliot-Hoy..being seven Foot and a half under the Beam, 56 Foot in length. *Ibid.* No. 2517/4 There will be exposed to Sale..a *Galliot Pink called the *Mermaid of Amsterdam.* 1709 *Ibid.* No. 4543/3 A Galliot Pink..burthen about 90 Tuns, Holland built. *a*1895 LD. CLARENCE PAGET *Autobiog.* i. (1896) 5 He had a Dutch *galliot yacht..which used to cruise with the royal squadron.

†**galliot**[2]. *Obs.* Forms: 5 galyot, 6 galyott, galliot, 7 galeyot, galeot. [a. OF. *galiot* sailor in a galley, galley-slave, pirate = It. *galeotto*, med.L. *galiotus*, *galeota*, deriv. of *galea* GALLEY.]

1. A pirate. *rare.*

*c*1425 *Eng. Conq. Irel.* (E.E.T.S.) 22 We come nat ynto thys land as hyryng men, ne for no couetyse of gold, ne of syluyr, ne galyotz ne robbers.

2. A sailor or rower on board a galley, whether slave or free.

1506 GUYLFORDE *Pilgr.* (Camden) 15 In the whyche tyme the patrone, Galyottis, and pylgrimes, took in woode, water, &c. 1593 MUNDAY *Def. Contraries* 84 See we not in the Gallies that they giue the Oare to the strongest and most mighty Galliots? 1612 *Benvenuto's Passenger* I. 73 Oh, now all begins to passe betweene the Galeot, and the Marriner. 1654 COKAINE *Dianea* IV. 350 Being informed of the fire..he ..commanded it should be quenched, supposing it kindled by accident through the carelessnesse of the Galeyots, or Marriners.

Gallipoli (gæ'lɪpəlɪ). The name of a town in Apulia, Italy, used to designate the olive-oil exported from there. ***Gallipoli soap***, soap made from this oil.

1822 C. LILLIE *Brit. Perfumer* xl. 223 Gallipoly Soap. This, like the French soap, above described, comes in large cakes, which generally smell so strong of bad oil, as hardly to be borne. 1839 URE *Dict. Arts* 541 *Gallipoli oil*, is a coarse olive oil, containing more or less mucilage. 1868 F. H. JOYNSON *Metals* 120 Common rosin, melted with a little gallipoli oil and spirits of turpentine. 1884 W. S. B. MCLAREN *Spinning* (ed. 2) 45 If..oil is used..it should be the best quality of olive. Gallipoli is the name for the very best.

gallipot ('gælɪpɒt). Forms: 5 galy pott, gale pote, 6 galey potte, galeye pot, gallie potte, 6–8 gally pot (gally-pot), 7 gollee-, galley-pot, 8 galipot, 7– gallipot. [The first element in this word (occurring also in GALLEY-DISH, GALLEY-TILE) is of uncertain origin, but possibly identical with GALLEY *sb.*[1], in which case the words etymologically denote pottery such as was brought in *galleys*, i.e. imported from the Mediterranean. Cf. GALLEY-HALFPENNY.

The Du. synonym *gleipot* is not recorded till a century later than the date of our earliest examples of the English word, and the editors of the great Dutch dictionary think that its first element may possibly be identical with *glei* (frequent in the 17th c.), a variant of *galei* GALLEY *sb.*[1] In support of this view, it is pointed out that the Du. *kraakgoed*, *kraakporselein* mean literally 'porcelain imported in *carracks*', and a passage is quoted from the *Inv. v. Brussel* II. 206 which mentions 'glass-wares brought in galleys and carracks' (*que les galees et les caraques amenent*). Farther, *gleyers-werk* is explained by Kilian as meaning Balearic or Majorcan pottery (cf. MAJOLICA). On the other hand, the word *glei* is given in Kilian and Du. dicts. of the 17th c. as a name for porcelain clay; but it has not been found in any text, except in the compound *gleybacker*, *geley backer* 'porcelain baker'; and it may have been merely formed by misinterpretation of the compounds *gleipot* and *gleiwerk*, *gleigoed* (glazed pottery).]

1. A small earthen glazed pot, *esp.* one used by apothecaries for ointments and medicines.

1465 *Mann. & Househ. Exp.* 285 Item, the same day my mastyr paid for a galy pott, iij. d. 1552 HULOET, Galey potte, *culullus.* 1605 BACON *Adv. Learn.* I. 16 That, which Plato sayd of his Maister Socrates, whom he compared to the Gallypots of Apothecaries, which on the out side had Apes and Owles and Antiques, but contained with in soueraigne and precious liquors and confections. 1678 R. L'ESTRANGE *Seneca's Mor.* To Rdr. p. xxii, They make me think of Gally-Pots in an Apothecaries Shop. 1739 CLAYTON in *Phil. Trans.* XLI. 62, I Took a small Gally-pot, such as the Apothecaries in the North of England make use of. 1796 MRS. GLASSE *Cookery* xxi. 322 Pour it into small high Gallipots, like a sugar-loaf at top. 1855 DICKENS *Dorrit* I. vi, Traps [for flies] of vinegar and sugar in gallipots. 1870 LUBBOCK *Orig. Civiliz.* vi. (1875) 290 A great number of blacks assembled about a pond, bringing with them a sheep and some gallipots. 1880 *Antrim & Down Gloss.*, *Gaily pot*, a jam pot.

b. *transf.* and *fig.*

1630 DEKKER *2nd Pt. Honest Wh.* Wks. 1873 II. 106 She is the Gally-pot to which these Drones flye. 1883 STEVENSON *Treas. Isl.* IV. xvii, The little gallipot of a boat that we were in was gravely overloaded.

†c. applied to a silver vessel. *Obs.*⁻¹

1515 *Will of W. Willer* (Somerset Ho.), A Galey potte of silver double gilt.

2. *transf.* (in jest or contempt). One who handles gallipots; an apothecary.

1785 GROSE *Dict. Vulg. Tongue*, *Gallipot*, nick name for an apothecary. 1828 SCOTT *F.M. Perth* vii, Turning a stern look on the alarmed Pottingar, broke out..'Thou walking skeleton! thou asthmatic gallipot!' 1842 S. LOVER *Handy Andy* iii. 29 The widow in the meantime had been left to the care of the apothecary's boy..and truly her sobs..amazed young gallipot. 1848 THACKERAY *Bk. Snobs* xxvii, 'One may ask one's medical man to one's table certainly; but his family, my dear Mr. Snob!' 'Half a dozen little gallipots', interposed Miss Wirt.

†'**gallish**, *a.*[1] *Obs. rare.* Forms: 6 gaulish, gallishe, 7–8 gallish. [f. GALL *sb.*[1] + -ISH.]

1. Belonging to the gall, bilious.

1551 TURNER *Herbal* I. A v b, Wormwode..dryueth furth ..cholerike and gallishe humoures out of the stomack.

2. Tasting like gall, bitter.

1648 HEXHAM *Dutch Dict.* (1660), *Galachtigh*, gallish, or as bitter as Gall.

b. *fig.*

1595 SOUTHWELL *St. Peter's Compl.* 69 The pleasing rellish of his former loue, In gaulish thoughts to bitter taste doth proue. 1769 BLACKSTONE *Comm.* IV. 95 *Crimen animo felleo pe petratum*, with a bitter or gallish inclination.

†**gallish**, *a.*[2] *Obs. rare*⁻¹. [f. GALL *sb.*[3] + -ISH[1].] Of the nature of galls.

1677 PLOT *Oxfordsh.* 161 Neither the nuts nor the horn having any thing gallish, the Vitriol of the Earth could have no power on them.

gallisin ('gælɪsɪn). *Chem.* Also -ine. [a. G. *gallisin* (Schmitt & Cobenzl 1884, in *Ber. d. Deut. Chem. Ges.* XVII. 1003), f. *gallisieren*: see GALLIZE *v.* and -IN[1].] An amorphous unfermentable substance obtained from commercial glucose, now regarded as a mixture.

1884 *Jrnl. Chem. Soc.* XLVI. 981 The authors [*sc.* C. Schmitt and A. Cobenzl]..have succeeded in separating from fermented glucose (prepared from potato-starch) an intensely hygroscopic substance which they have named gallisin. 1890 *Chem. News* 14 Mar. 132/2 In the analysis of eleven samples of commercial starch-sugar the quantities of gallisine found were from 22.49 to 6.82 per cent. 1938 *Thorpe's Dict. Appl. Chem.* (ed. 4) II. 299/1 The product variously known as isomaltose, gallisin, revertose is now regarded as a mixture of maltose with other substances. 1965 K. MAYER tr. *Staněk's Oligo-saccharides* vi. 108 The substances so obtained and designated by various names (such as gallisin, revertose, δ-dextrose, and dextrinose) were undoubtedly not chemical individuals.

gallisize: see GALLIZE.

†**gallitzinite** (gæ'lɪtsɪnaɪt). *Min. Obs.* Also Gallizinite. [Named in 1801 after the name of Prince *Gallitzin* (who discovered the mineral): see -ITE.] A variety of rutile, now called NIGRINE.

1814 ALLAN *Min. Nomenclature* 50 Gallizinite. 1820 R. JAMESON *Syst. Min.* III. 132 Gallitzinite.

gallitzinite, var. GALLIZINITE. *Obs.*

gallium ('gælɪəm). [mod.L.; said to be f. L. *gallus* cock, a translation of *Lecoq.*] A soft, tough, bluish-white metal, easily melted, discovered by M. Lecoq de Boisbaudran (1875) in a zinc-blende from the Pyrenees.

1875 *Fam. Herald* 6 Nov. 14/2 The new metal, which is called gallium, was found by the spectroscope in zinc ores. 1885 *Athenæum* 17 July 84/2 This metal appears..to be probably gallium.

gallivant (gælɪ'vænt, 'gæ-), *v.* Also **galavant**, **galivant**. [Perhaps a humorous perversion of GALLANT *v.* Usually in the pres. part. *gallivanting.*] *intr.* To gad about in a showy fashion, esp. with persons of the other sex. Also merely = FLIRT.

1823 W. H. PYNE *Wine & Walnuts* (1824) II. xxi. 300 Sitting at his ease, galavanting with a publican's daughter. 1835 LADY GRANVILLE *Lett.* 12 Feb. (1894) II. 184, I foresee she will be always galivanting with Lady Wharncliffe. 1838 DICKENS *Nich. Nick.* xxxviii, Else I shall have my maid gallivanting with somebody who may rob the house. 1851 DE QUINCEY *Ld. Carlisle on Pope* Wks. XIII. 25 If she chose to go galavanting amongst the clouds, Pope, for his part, was the last person to follow her. 1875 W. S. HAYWARD *Love agst. World* 32, I did not consider it right or proper that a lady..should be gallivanting about the country with those three fellows. 1894 *Q. Rev.* Oct. 503 The language came natural to him [Lope de Vega] when gallivanting with Filis.

gallivanting (ˌgælɪ'væntɪŋ, 'gælɪvætɪŋ), *vbl. sb.* [f. GALLIVANT *v.* + -ING[1].] The action of the verb.

1826 SCOTT *Jrnl.* 9 Feb., If we had been so [in retreat] last year, instead of gallivanting to Ireland, this affair might not have befallen. 1839 THACKERAY *Fatal Boots* (1869) 354, I have given up gallivanting, as I call it. 1869 TROLLOPE *He Knew* xv. (1878) 83 It don't mean much, only just idle talking and gallivanting. 1884 *Punch* 16 Feb. 76/1 This comes of gallivanting round with Emperors, Kings, Prime Ministers, and Poet-Laureates.

galli'vanting, *ppl. a.* [f. as prec. + -ING[2].] That gads about, or flirts.

1819 'R. RABELAIS' *Abeillard & Heloisa* 18 But does that gallivanting god Deign to give Taylor answering nod? 1865 DICKENS *Mut. Fr.* III. i, You can't be a gallivanting dodger. 1884 *Harper's Mag.* Aug. 327/1 A lone lorn wife of many a galivanting husband.

†**gallivat.** *Obs.* Forms: 7 gellywat(te, 8 galleywat(t, gallevat, 8–9 gallivat. [ad. Pg. *galeota* through East Indian channels: cf. GALLIOT[1].] A large boat used in the Eastern seas, having a triangular sail as well as oars.

1613 DOWNTON in Purchas *Pilgrims* (1625) I. 501 As soone as I anchored, I sent..Master Spooner, and Samuell Squire in my Gellywatte to sound the depths within the sands. 1756 *Gentl. Mag.* XXVI. 620 A number of vessels called galley-wats, about the size of our Gravesend tilt-boat, carrying six swivel guns, and 60 men. 1790 BEATSON *Nav. & Mil. Mem.* II. 41 The gallivats are large row-boats, built like grabs, but of smaller dimensions, the largest seldom exceeding seventy tons. 1862 BEVERIDGE *Hist. India* I. III. vii. 510 The gallivats..combined the double advantage of sailing and row boats.

galliwasp ('gælɪwɒsp). Also 8 gallewasp. [Of unknown origin.] A small lizard (*Celestus occiduus*), found in the West Indies.

1725 SLOANE *Jamaica* II. 334 A Galliwasp. This appear'd in all things to be a great Scinc. 1796 MORSE *Amer. Geog.* I. 765 The fens and marshes do [breed] the guana and gallewasp; but these last are not venomous. 1834 M. G. LEWIS *Jrnl. W. Ind.* 113 A Galli-wasp..This is the Alligator in miniature. 1855 KINGSLEY *Westw. Ho!* II. ix. 253 Sitting on the sandy turf, defiant of galliwasps and jack-spaniards.

gallize ('gælaɪz), *v.* Also **gallisize.** [From Dr. L. *Gall* of Treves, the inventor of the process. In Ger. *gallisiren*, of which the form *gallisize* seems to be a blundered adaptation.] *trans.* To treat (unfermented grape-juice) with water and sugar, so as to increase the quantity of wine produced.

Hence '**gallisized** *ppl. a.*, '**gallisizing** *vbl. sb.* Also **galli'zation**, the process of gallizing.

1888 PROF. DITTMAR in *Encycl. Brit.* XXIV. 603/1 Science affords a means of distinguishing a gallisized from a natural wine. *Ibid.*, One mode of assisting nature in wine-making is the process of 'gallisizing', so called from its inventor (Gall), which is largely practised on the Rhine. 1891 *Cycl. Temp. & Prohib.* (U.S.) 647/1 Gallization, a method of increasing the quantity [of wine] by the infusion of sugar, acid and water.

†**ga'llizinite.** *Min. Obs.* Also **gallitzinite**, **gallicinite.** [First used by Beudant in 1824; f. the Ger. name *gallitzenstein*, lit. 'stone from Galicia': see -ITE.] Native sulphate of zinc, goslarite.

1837 ALLAN *W. Phillips' Min.* 376 Gallizinite. 1843 E. J. CHAPMAN *Min.* 14 Gallitzinite. 1861 H. W. BRISTOW *Gloss. Min.* 148 Gallicinite.

gallizinite, var. GALLITZINITE. *Obs.*

gall-less ('gɔːllɪs), *a.* [f. GALL *sb.*[1] + -LESS.] Possessing no gall. Hence, free from bitterness or malice; incapable of being roused to anger.

1398 TREVISA *Barth. De P.R.* XVIII. xix. (1495) 779 Camelles ben beestys of long lyfe for they ben gallelesse. **1658** *Whole Duty Man* xvii. §19. 147 A Dove, a meek and gall-less creature. **1663** COWLEY *Verses & Ess.* (1669) 17 Ah! mild and gaulless Dove. **1726** SAVAGE *Sir T. Overbury* III. i, Tho' the soft Dove brood gall-less o'er your Breast, Yet let the wary Serpent arm your Mind. **1831** SCOTT *Ct. Robt.* xxviii, When I consider from what prison he was brought, and in what guise he inhabited it, I cannot believe in this gall-less disposition. **1843** LYTTON *Last Bar.* I. vii, And the poor student, usually so mild and gall-less, stamped his foot in impotent rage. **1884** *Pall Mall G.* 10 Sept. 5/1 The idyllic, guileless and gall-less life.

gall-nut ('gɔːlnʌt). [f. GALL *sb.*[3]] = GALL *sb.*[3] 1.

1572 HULOET, Galle nutte, suche as is put into inke, *galla.* **1601** HOLLAND *Pliny* II. 177 Gal-nuts. **1712** tr. *Pomet's Hist. Drugs* I. 75 Round Fruit, of the Size of Gall-Nuts. **1838** *Penny Cycl.* s.v. *Gallic acid*, A large portion of the acid exists ready formed in the gall-nut.

Gallo-[1] ('gæləʊ), combining form (after Gr. analogies) of L. *Gallus* a Gaul.

1. In classical Latin it occurs only in *Gallo-græci*, Gauls who went east and settled in Asia Minor; also *Gallo-græcia*, the country inhabited by these Gauls, Galatia. Hence †**Gallo-græcians**, †**Gallo-greeks** *pl.*, Galatians.

1601 HOLLAND *Pliny* I. 221 King Antiochus hauing in battaile slaine..a brave horsman of the Gallogreeks or Galatians, became maister of his horse. **1618** BOLTON *Florus* II. xi. (1636) 124 Those Gallo-Græcians, as their compound name sheweth, were a mixt and mongrell people. [**1625** BACON *Ess.*, *Vicissitude* (Arb.) 573 It is true, the Gaules were Westerne; But we reade but of two Incursions of theirs; the one to Gallo-Grecia, the other to Rome.]

2. Used with the sense of 'Gallic' (i.e. French) in various mod.Eng. formations. **a.** Prefixed (with hyphen) to certain designations of nationality, as ˌ**Gallo-A'merican** *a.*, of combined French and American character; ˌ**Gallo-'Briton**, one partly French and partly British (either in birth or sympathies); ˌ**Gallo-'Celtic** *a.*, belonging to the Celts of France; ˌ**Gallo-'German** *a.*, belonging to both French and Germans. **b.** In objective formations on assumed Gr. types (in most instances adopted from Fr.), as '**Galloman** [ad. F. *Gallomane* (Gr. -μανής mad after)] = *Gallomaniac*; **Gallo'mania** [ad. F. *Gallomanie* (Gr. -μανία: see MANIA)], an unreasoning attachment to France or French customs; **Gallo'maniac**, one who is affected with Gallomania; also as *adj.*; '**Gallophil** [Gr. -φίλος loving, friendly to], a friend of France and its interests; **Ga'llophilism**, fondness for France, friendliness towards it; '**Gallophobe** [Gr. -φόβος fearing], one who is affected with Gallophobia; also as *adj.*; **Gallo'phobia** [ad. F. *Gallophobie*, Gr. -φοβία dread of], morbid dread of the French, or abhorrence of what is French.

1797 T. JEFFERSON *Writ.* (1859) IV. 186 If Louisiana becomes a *Gallo-American colony. **1828** SYDNEY SMITH in *Mem.* (1885) II. 293 The travels of the Gallo-American gentleman..are, I suppose, those of M. Simond. **1819** *Hermit in Lond.* III. 116 A kind of Amphibious animal, a *Gallo-Briton. *a* **1711** KEN *Blandina* Poet. Wks. 1721 IV. 516 Death and Infernal Pow'rs decreed The *Gallo-Celtick Saints should bleed. **1861** J. G. SHEPPARD *Fall Rome* viii. 441 The great *Gallo-German river. **1787** T. JEFFERSON *Writ.* (1859) II. 317 It will be of great consequence to France and England, to have America governed by a *Galloman or Angloman. **1802** *Ibid.* VIII. 163 To suppose we are Gallomen or Anglomen [*sic*!]. **1819** *Metropolis* (ed. 2) III. viii. 180 This Galloman appeared a little put down. **1877** D. M. WALLACE *Russia* xxv. 388 In a word, *Gallomania had become the prevailing social epidemic of the time. **1819** *Hermit in Lond.* III. 117 The British *Gallomaniac ought to know better. **1840** DISRAELI *Corr. w. Sister* 15 Oct. (1886) 163 *On dit* that even Lord Holland, that old Gallomaniac, ratted to Palmerston. **1897** *Daily News* 28 Aug. 4/6 In the years which immediately preceded the French Revolution the British aristocracy was notoriously Gallomaniac. **1889** *Times* 26 Jan. 7/3 The appointment of Señor Albareda to the Quirinal would not be looked on favourably at Rome, because he is a very pronounced *Gallophil. **1894** *Westm. Gaz.* 16 Feb. 7/2 The ardent *Gallophilism which characterized many Russian gatherings at the time of the Toulon and Paris *fêtes.* **1883** *Pall Mall G.* 31 July 8/2 The *Opinion* says 'the *Gallophobes on the other side of the Channel will gain nothing by their agitation against us'. **1886** *Athenæum* 6 Mar. 324/2 Mr. Gallenga is too pronounced a Gallophobe to be able to make his French *attachés* true to life. **1897** *Pall Mall G.* 2 June 7/3 Gallophobe Englishmen grew alarmed, but they have got their sop. **1803** in *Spirit Publ. Jrnls.* (1804) VII. 246 Strong renewed symptoms of Anglo and *Gallo-phobia. **1881** *Athenæum* 6 Aug. 165/3 His [Landor's] Gallophobia evidently strikes Prof. Colvin with astonishment.

gallo-[2] ('gæləʊ), also before a vowel **gall-**, combining form of GALLIC *a.*[2] in the names of compounds derived from gallic acid or related substances, as *gallanilide*, *gallein*, *gallocyanine*, *gallo-nitrate*, *gallo-tannate*, etc.

†'**galloc.** *Obs.* Also 1 gallac, galluc. [perh. corruptly ad. late L. *anagallicum* (also *anagalla*; cf. class. L. *anagallis*, supposed to mean 'pimpernel'); see quot. *c* 1450 s.v. COMFREY.] The plant comfrey (*Symphytum officinale*).

In OE. vocabularies the word renders not only *sinfitum* and *confirma* (comfrey) but also *galla* (in class. L. = gall-nut), *adriatica*, *adriaca* (of unknown meaning), and *mālum terræ* (in class. L. = birthwort). It is not clear whether the L. words were in late L. applied to the comfrey, or whether *galluc* denoted several different plants, or, finally, whether the glosses are mere mistranslations.

[*c* **725** *Corpus Gloss.* 949 Galla, galluc.] *c* **1000** *Sax. Leechd.* I. 162 Ðeos wyrt þe man confirman & oðrum naman galluc nemneð. *a* **1100** *Voc.* in Wr.-Wülcker 299/20 *Sinfitum*, gallac. *c* **1265** *Plant Voc.* Ibid. 555/4 *Cumfiria*, cumfirie, galloc.

galloch, obs. form of GALOSH.

gallocyanine (ˌgæləʊ'saɪəniːn, -ɪn). *Chem.* Also -in. [a. F. *gallocyanine* (H. Kœchlin 1882, in *Bull. Soc. Chim.* XXXVIII. 97, 162), f. GALLO-[2] + CYANINE.] A green crystalline substance, $C_{15}H_{12}N_2O_5$, obtained from gallic acid and used as a bluish-violet mordant dye for wool and cotton and in calico-printing; also, any of a group of structurally similar dyes of the oxazine series that are derived from gallic acid.

1883 H. KŒCHLIN in *Chem. News* 13 Apr. 170/1 By allowing an alcoholic solution of nitroso-dimethylaniline hydrochlorate to react in heat upon the tannins, as upon gallic acid, there are obtained violet colouring-matters, verging more or less upon a blue according to the nature of the tannin employed. These colouring-matters..the author names gallo-cyanines. **1893** E. KNECHT et al. *Man. Dyeing* II. VII. 624 Gallocyanin yields a bright blue-violet shade, which resists light, soap, and acids very well, but is not fast to soda. **1956** HICKINBOTTOM & GARWOOD in E. H. Rodd *Chem. Carbon Compounds* IIIB. xii. 781 The so-called gallocyanine dyes, mordant dyes of the oxazine series, largely used in calico printing. **1958** J. R. BAKER *Princ. Biol. Microtechnique* xii. 242 A basic dye may be used..to obtain an approximation to the amount of DNA in a nucleus or of RNA in a nucleolus or in the cytoplasm. A mordant-dye, chrome alum/gallocyanine..is particularly recommended for this purpose. **1960** HOWARD & RAMAGE in E. H. Rodd *Chem. Carbon Compounds* IVC. xvii. 1546 The gallocyanines ..are important for application in calico printing, with chromium salts and tannin mordant.

galloglass ('gæləglɑːs, -glæs). *Obs.* exc. *Hist.* Forms: α. 6 galloglas(se, galoglas, galloweglass, gallyglasse, 7 galli(n)glass(e, (gallowgross), 9 gallaglass, 6–7, 9 galloglass, gallowglass. β. 6 galloglogh, 7 gallegalagh, 7, 9 galloglagh, 8–9 galloglach. [a. Ir. and Gael. *gall-óglách*, f. *gall* foreigner, stranger + *óglách* youth, servant, warrior. The etymologically correct form *galloglagh* appears later than the erroneous *galloglass*, which was prob. the result of the pl. *gallogla(gh)s*; in some early instances *galloglas* seems to be used as a pl., but *galloglasses* is found already in our earliest quot.

The statement, made on etymological grounds by Spenser (*State of Irel.* 640/1, Globe ed.), that the 'galloglasses' were originally English mercenaries, seems doubtful; *gall* is used of foreigners or strangers generally, and, although mainly applied to the English in Spenser's day, may not have been so restricted at the time when the compound was formed.]

1. One of a particular class of soldiers or retainers formerly maintained by Irish chiefs.

α. *c* **1515** *St. Papers Hen. VIII* (1834) II. 5, 500 sperys 500 galloglasseis, and 1000 kerne. **1520** *Ibid.* 46, 18 baners of galoglas. *c* **1538** R. COWLEY in Ellis *Orig. Lett.* Ser. II. II. 96 Which bere all the burdon of the chargis of holding horsemen, galloglas and kerne. **1540** *St. Papers Hen. VIII* (1834) III. 169 The saide Cahir shall pay yerely..the tributes and summes of mony, with refeccions and sustencions of all the galloglasses, as was accustumed to be payed by his auncetours. **1577** STANYHURST *Descr. Irel.* in *Holinshed* II. 45/1 The fourth degree is a galloglasse, vsing a kind of pollax for his weapon. **1600** DYMMOK *Ireland* (1843) 7 The Galloglass are pycked and scelected men of great and mightie bodies, crewell without compassion. **1610** HOLLAND *Camden's Brit.* II. 147 Souldiours set in the rere gard, whom they terme Galloglasses, who fight with most keene hatchets. **1814** SCOTT *Ld. of Isles* I. viii, Loud shouts each hardy galla-glass. **1875** LOWELL *Spenser* Pr. Wks. 1890 IV. 296 In October the wild kerns and gallowglasses rose in no mood for sparing the house of Pindarus.

β. **1534** *St. Papers Hen. VIII* (1834) II. 185, 10 scor spearys, callid galloglogh is. **1610** HOLLAND *Camden's Brit.* II. 172 Fennyngher O-Conghir slew Cale-Rothe and with him of Galloglahes and others about three hundred. **1848–51** J. O'DONOVAN *Ann. 4 Masters* (1856) I. 119 *note*, The bands of kernes and galloglaghs or gallowglasses, supported by the Irish chieftains of the later ages.

2. In the Highlands: = HENCHMAN 2.

1703 M. MARTIN *Descr. W. Isl. Scotl.* 104 Every Chieftain had a bold Armour-Bearer, whose business was always to attend the Person of his Master night and day to prevent any surprize, and this man was called Galloglach.

3. *attrib.* in *galloglass-axe.*

1580 HOOKER *Life Sir P. Carew* in *Archæol.* XXVIII. 139 Everye man toke a galloweglasse axe of theires who were slayne. **1596** *Lanc. Wills* III. 4 A gally glasse axe.

gallon ('gælən). Forms: 3–4 galun, 4–5 galoun, 5 galown, 5–7 galon, 6 galne (gal(l)ond(e, galla(u)nde, 7 gallante), 6– gallon. [a. ONF. *galun*, *galon*, Central OF. *jalon*, etc. (= med.L. *galōn-em*), app. cogn. with F. *jale* bowl. Cf. the diminutive form OF. *galet*, *jalet* masc., med.L. *galleta* fem., a measure for wine, OE. *ȝellet* bowl (? from Rom. or popular L.), Pg. *galheta* mug; also OF. *galaie*, *galeie*, *jalaie*, etc., fem. a measure for liquids, grain, etc. The ultimate origin is unknown.]

1. An English measure of capacity. The imperial gallon contains 277¼ cubic inches: the winegallon of 231 cubic inches is the standard in the United States.

c **1300** in Wright *Relig. Songs* vii. 37 Bachares and brueres ..Loȝe heo holdet hore galun, mid berme heo hine fulleth. **1362** LANGL. *P. Pl.* A. v. 187 He that repenteth rathest schulde arysen aftur And greten sir Gloten with a galun of ale [B. a galoun ale]. *c* **1386** CHAUCER *Manciple's Prol.* 24 Ther is falle on me swich heuinesse..þat me were leuere slepe, Than the beste galon wyn in Chepe. *c* **1420** *Liber Cocorum* (1862) 26 To a pot of oyle of on galon, And of hony a qwharte thou take. **1509** BARCLAY *Shyp of Folys* (1570) 230 Some voyde mo cups then man would thinke possible, And other some galons, so that theyr ioynts are feble. **1542** RECORDE *Gr. Artes* (1575) 204, 8 pounde (or 8 pyntes) doe make a Gallon. *a* **1656** USSHER *Ann.* an. 3679 (1658) 275 He that drank most, was one Promachus, who drank off fower gallons and one pottle. **1725** BRADLEY *Fam. Dict.* s.v., In Liquids two Pottles, or four Quarts, or eight Pints, make one Gallon..But in dry Measure, two Gallons, which is six Pottles, make one Peck. **1827** LYTTON *Pelham* I. ii. 12 The men drank ale by the gallon. **1862** ANSTED *Channel Isl.* IV. App. A. (ed. 2) 566 The Jersey wine gallon, as commonly estimated, contains rather more than two hundred and forty seven cubic inches English.

b. As a dry measure for corn, bread, etc.

1684 R. H. *School Recreat.* 132 Take a Gallon of Wheat, and Oat-meal-flower. **1725** [see 1]. **1883** *Harper's Mag.* Apr. 657/2, I ask questions in order to discover what a gallon of bread is. **1887** *Kent Gloss.* s.v., 'I'd far rather pay a shilling for a gallon of bread than have it so very cheap.'

c. *fig.* A large amount.

1575 G. HARVEY *Letter-bk.* (Camden) 90 To requite your gallonde of godbwyes.

†**2.** A vessel for holding liquids (tr. L. *lagena*).

1382 WYCLIF *Isa.* xxx. 14 And shal be to-mynusht, as is to-brosid the galoun of the crockere. —— *Mark* xiv. 13 A man beringe a galoun of watir. **1459** in *Paston Lett.* I. 472, ij. galons, with gilt verges.

3. *attrib.*, as *gallon-bottle*, *-measure*, *-pot.*

1459 in *Paston Lett.* I. 469 ij. galon pottes, all gilt. *Ibid.* 488, j. payre galon bottels of one sorte. **1465** in Heath *Grocers' Comp.* (1869) 424, ii Galon Pottis chased and half gylte. **1481** *Durham MS. Cell. Roll*, j galon mesour.

gallonage ('gælənɪdʒ). [f. GALLON + -AGE; after TONNAGE *sb.*] An amount in gallons; a quantity of liquid produced or sold.

1909 in *Cent. Dict.* Suppl. **1930** *Economist* 11 Oct. 662/1 Stocks of both crude and gasoline in the hands of the producers, the refiners and the distributors are so huge that the struggle for 'gallonage' is growing hotter daily. **1936** A. G. STREET *Gentleman of Party* iv. 80 The figures on the churn tickets..showed the daily gallonage. **1967** *Times Rev. Industry* Mar. 59/3 Shell obviously does not reveal the extra gallonage achieved. **1970** *Country Life* 1 Oct. 855/1 In terms of gallonage on which duty has been paid..the total of 13 million gallons up to June is only about 7 per cent down.

gallo-nitrate (ˌgæləʊ'naɪtreɪt). [f. *gallo-* = GALLIC *a.*[2] + NITRATE.] A combination of gallic and nitric acids with a base.

1841 FOX-TALBOT *Patent Specification* No. 8842 Take a sheet of iodized paper and wash it over with this gallo-nitrate of silver. **1854** J. SCOFFERN in *Orr's Circ. Sc.* Chem. 89 Gallo-nitrate of silver.

galloon (gə'luːn). Forms: 7 galloune, galoone, galloom(e, galoom(e, 7–8 galloone, 7– galoon, galloon. Also in Fr. form 9- galon. [ad. F. *galon*, vbl. sb., from the verb *galonner*. The sb. first appears in the 17th c., the verb is as old as the 12th c., and originally means to dress the hair with gold bands or other ribbons. Its origin is uncertain; a connexion with the root of GALLANT seems possible; the Sp. *galon* and It. *gallone* are prob. adopted from Fr.] A kind of narrow, close-woven ribbon or braid, of gold, silver, or silk thread, used for trimming articles of apparel; a trimming of this material. (See quot. 1882.)

1604 in *Lismore Papers* Ser. II. (1887) I. 106 Neaples galloune to yᵉ same Dublett. ? **1648** DAVENANT *Vacat. in Lond.* Wks. (1673) 290 In Liv'ry Short, Galloome on Cape, With Cloak-bag Mounting high as Nape. **1681** *Lond. Gaz.* No. 1651/4 A Negro Boy about 18 years old, with a broad brimm'd white Hat, edged with Silver Galoom. **1727** in *Mrs. Delany's Life & Corr.* (1861) I. 144 Gold chains..were tacked on the robing of her gown in loose scollops in the manner of a galloon. **1753** HANWAY *Trav.* (1762) I. VII. xcvii. 453 His livery is yellow, laced with a galloon of blue silk and silver. **1864** CARLYLE *Fredk. Gt.* XII. iv. (1865) IV. 154 Footmen, grand as galoon and silver fringe could make them. **1877** in A. Adburgham *Shops & Shopping* (1964) xvi. 178 A light blue cashmere, trimmed with diagonal bands of oriental galon and cream lace. **1882** CAULFEILD & SAWARD *Dict. Needlework*, *Galloon.* There are two descriptions of this article. One is a strong, thick gold lace..It is woven with a pattern in threads of gold or silver, on silk or worsted ..and is employed in uniforms and on servants' livery hats. The other is of wool, silk or cotton combined with silk or worsted, and is used for trimming and binding articles of dress, hats, shoes, and furniture. This sort is only a narrow ribbon. **1890** *Daily News* 21 Oct. 2/1 Gold, silver, and steel are to be more used than ever in embroideries and on galons for trimmings. **1896** *Ibid.* 30 May 9/2 A white damask silk was edged all round the hem with marabout feathers, on each side of them being embroidered a thick galloon of pearls, diamonds, and emeralds. **1923** *Daily Mail* 1 Mar. 15

A practical day gown..girdled with wool galon. **1939–40** *Army & Navy Stores Catal.* 1077/3 Galon for trimming.

b. *attrib.*, as †*galloon-lace* = galloon; †*galloon-gallant*, ? one who is gaily dressed.

1611 COTGR. s.v. *Galonné, Tresses gallonées*, lockes plaited, or tyed vp with gallone lace. *a* **1611** BEAUM. & FL. *Philaster* v. iv, Oh, for a whip to make him galloon-laces! **1622** FLETCHER *Sea-Voy.* I. iii, Thou Galloon gallant, and Mammon you That build on golden mountains! **1759** *Char.* in *Ann. Reg.* 281/1 Sixteen men..all in rose colour with galloon lace.

Hence **ga'llooned** *a.* [cf. F. *galonné*], trimmed with galloon; also *fig.*

1831 CARLYLE *Sart. Res.* I. vii, Enormous habiliments, that were not only slashed and gallooned, but artificially swollen-out. **1862** H. MARRYAT *Year in Sweden* I. 237 The morning dawns—the sky gallooned in stripes, and spangled o'er with gold. **1863** THORNBURY *True as Steel* II. 120 His outer robe..had tight sleeves gallooned with lace.

galloon, galloot, obs. ff. GALLEON, GALOOT.

gallop ('gæləp), *sb.* Also 6 **galop(pe**; and see WALLOP *sb.* and GALOP. [a. OF. *galop* (app. f. *galoper* to GALLOP), which is found from the 11th c. onwards, in early instances generally in the plural as acc. with verbs of motion (*vint les galops*, Chan. de Rol. 731). The word first appears in English in the 16th c.; but the ONF. form **walop* had been adopted in ME., and was used in the sense of 'gallop' as late as *c* 1480.]

1. a. The most rapid movement of a horse (occas. of other quadrupeds), in which in the course of each stride the animal is entirely off the ground, with the legs flexed under the body. In early use chiefly as descriptive addition to a verb. Phr. †*to ride (a) gallop*: now *at* (formerly also *on, upon, in, with*) *a gallop.*

1523 LD. BERNERS *Froiss.* I. lxi. 83 The frenchmen euer rode a great Galoppe towarde the bridge. **1553** BRENDE *Q. Curtius* N vij, He caused them put spores to their horses, and passed forwardes a gallop. **1570** LEVINS *Manip.* 169/27 A Gallop, *extensus cursus.* **1600** J. LANE *Tom Telltroth* (1876) 126 The first rides gallop into miserie. **1645** SLINGSBY *Diary* (1836) 176 Our horse, upon a Gallop wth out once drawing up, advanceth toward ym. **1723** *Lond. Gaz.* No. 6228/3 He goes in a little Gallop very easy. **1782** COWPER *Gilpin* 87 That trot became a gallop soon In spite of curb and rein. **1814** S. ROGERS in *Mem. T. Moore* (1856) VIII. 186 Our horses were almost always in a gallop. **1832** *Regul. Instr. Cavalry* II. 16 The gallop to be eleven miles an hour. **1840** DICKENS *Barn. Rudge* ii, He was hurrying on at the same furious gallop which had been his pace when the locksmith first encountered him. **1859** *Musketry Instr.* 29 If an object fired at be moving, whether it be a man walking or a horse at a gallop. **1873** MUYBRIDGE *Descr. Zoopraxography* 37 The gallop is the most rapid method of quadrupedal motion; in its action the feet are independently brought to the ground; the spring into the air as in the canter is effected from a fore foot, and the landing upon the diagonal hind-foot.

b. A ride at this pace.

1602 WARNER *Alb. Eng.* IX. xlvii. (1612) 220 Swift gallops tier both man and horse. **1678** BUTLER *Hud.* III. iii. 365 Led his troops with furious gallops, To charge whole regiments of scallops. **1826** DISRAELI *Viv. Grey* II. xi, Vivian rode out alone..to cure his melancholy by a gallop. **1891** E. PEACOCK *N. Brendon* I. 242 The long gallop had done Narcissa good.

c. A track designed or suited for the galloping or exercising of horses.

1848 TROLLOPE *Kellys & O'Kelleys* II. ii. 45 They've proper gallops there, which we haven't. **1923** in F. Siltzer *Newmarket* App. 269 Horses not completing the full length of a gallop..must at once walk off the gallop to the nearest Walking Ground. **1927** *Times* 6 July 10/5 Scotland Lodge Estate, 1,009 acres,..including the residence, stud farm, and gallops. **1935** *Proc. Prehist. Soc.* I. 16 Along the main ridge of the spur..is a broad gallop. **1971** *Country Life* 18 Feb. 381/4 Had anyone been out on the Newmarket gallops earlier..they would have seen him at work tirelessly.

2. *transf.* and *fig.*

1651 N. BACON *Disc. Govt.* II. xvi. (1739) 85 The Duke of York, and other Lords, not liking this Gallop, endeavour to stop her pace. **1693** DRYDEN *Juvenal* (1697) p. lxiii, Horace is always on the amble, Juvenal on the gallop..He goes with more impetuosity than Horace. **1705** VANBRUGH *Confed.* I. i, Heav'n shield, I say; but Dick's upon the Gallop. **1768–74** TUCKER *Lt. Nat.* (1852) I. 428 Writing off a gallop and furnishing sheets for the press faster than they could be printed off. **1878** STEVENSON *Inland Voy.* 162 In wide sweeps, and with a swift and equable gallop, the ceaseless stream of water visits and makes green the fields. **1894** R. C. LESLIE *Waterbiog.* xiii. 237 A fast powerful boat becomes as necessary to a man..as a good horse. In her, with a fresh breeze, he can always enjoy..a few hours' gallop over the nearest stretch of broad salt water.

3. With defining word. **a.** *false gallop*: orig. a canter; now only *fig.* **b.** *full gallop*: the extreme pace of which a horse is capable; also used *adv.* = 'at full gallop'; also *fig.* **c.** *snail's gallop*: jocularly used for an extremely slow pace. †**d.** *gallop galliard* [F. *galop gaillard*] (see quot.).

See also HAND-GALLOP, and *Canterbury gallop* under CANTERBURY A 2.

a. *a* **1533** LD. BERNERS *Huon* ci. 335 By the counsell of Huon they returnyd a fause galop [orig. *les petis galoys*] towardes theyr cyte. **1587** SADLER *De procreandis*, etc. *equis* v. C ij a, Nouerit plene equus a succussatura, ad celeriorem paulo progressum, a celeriore ad citatiorem cursum ascendere [etc.]..At, vt clare anglice dicam: my meaning is that your horse know thorowly from his trot, to rise to his false gallope, from his false gallope yet to a swifter, and then from this swifter to descend to his false gallope, and trot againe, by turnes. **1593** NASHE *Apol. P. Pennilesse* D i b, I would trot a false gallop through the rest of his ragged Verses, but that if I should retort the rime dogrell aright, I must make my verses (as he doth his) run hobling [etc.]. **1599** SHAKS. *Much Ado* III. iv. 94 What pace is this that thy tongue keepes? Not a false gallop. **1600** —— *A.Y.L.* III. ii. 119 This is the verie false gallop of verses. **1617** MORYSON *Itin.* III. II. i. 60 Hee may not ride these a false gallop, as they vse to ride post-horses, for if he that receiues the horse, can find..that hee hath ridden an extraordinarye pace, hee shall pay ten soulz. **1635** QUARLES *Embl.* I. v. (1718) 23 Lust is a sharp spur to vice, which always putteth the affections into a false gallop.

b. **1569** UNDERDOWN *Ovid agst. Ibis* I iv b, Curtius, to deliuer the city, all armed vppon a goodly courser, with a full galloppe rode into the same. **1709** MRS. D. MANLEY *Secret Mem.* (1736) II. 135 He saw the Duke..riding upon a full Gallop. **1733** SWIFT *Answ. Sheridan's Simile* 118 When Jove would some fair nymph inveigle, He comes full gallop on his eagle. **1791** MRS. RADCLIFFE *Rom. Forest* xi, Coming now to a more open part of the forest, he set on a full gallop. **1797** M. ROBINSON *Walsingham* II. 50, I was awakened..by the sound of a horse's hoofs, which advanced on full gallop. **1810** WELLINGTON *Let.* 11 Nov. in Gurw. *Desp.* (1838) VI. 613 To remind your friends in the Cortes that they should not always go full gallop. **1828** SCOTT *F.M. Perth* xxxii, A body of horsemen advancing at full gallop. **1896** *Daily News* 16 Oct. 6/4 These letters of Magee's, written off, as it were, at full gallop..are among the very best in the English language.

attrib. **1803** M. CHARLTON *Wife & Mistress* I. 11 She declined this kind of full-gallop charge, for gentler and more promising manœuvre.

c. **1707** J. STEVENS tr. *Quevedo's Com. Wks.* (1709) 398 A Physician riding along on his Mule, a Snails Gallop. **1791** 'G. GAMBADO' *Ann. Horsem.* iv. (1809) 84 Neither whip nor spur can get him out of a snail's gallop.

d. **1611** COTGR., *Galop gaillard*, the Gallop Galliard; or..one pace, and a leape. **1614** MARKHAM *Cheap Husb.* I. ii. (1668) 28 At the end of every third or fourth advancing..make him bound aloft; then put him to his corvet again..and then make him bound again; and thus at the end of every third advancing make him bound for the length of a tilt bar ..this is called the *gallop galliard*. **1617** —— *Caval.* II. 241 The next lesson to this, is the galloppe galliard.

4. *Comb.*: †**gallop-rake** = sense 1.

1653 URQUHART *Rabelais* II. xiv. 100, I ran away a faire gallop-rake [F. *m'enfuis le beau galot*], and God he knows how I did smell my shoulder of mutton.

gallop ('gæləp), *v.* Forms: 6 **galop(e**, 6– **gallop**. See also WALLOP *v.* [a. F. *galoper*, = Pr. *galaupar*, Sp. Pg. *galopar*, It. *galoppare*. No satisfactory origin has yet been suggested for these forms; the Pr. form suggests that the word may be a compound of the Teut. **hlaup-an* to LEAP, run, with some prefixed word. The initial must originally have been *w*; the OF. **waloper* vb., **walop* sb., have not been found, but their existence is proved by the adopted forms, Flem., MHG. *walop* sb., MHG. *walopiren* vb., ME. *walop* sb., *walope* vb. The Eng. verb *walope*, WALLOP, survived into the 16th c., when it was superseded by the present verb, app. a new adoption from F. *galoper*.

In *K. Alis.* 461, Weber's ed. reads 'The deor *galopith* by wodis side', following the Lincoln's Inn MS. The earlier Bodl. MS., however, has *galpep*. The passage is not in the AF. original by Thomas or Eustace of Kent. The reading of the Bodl. MS. is prob. correct, but perh. the reading of the later MS. may prove that the vb. *galope* existed in 14–15th c.]

1. *intr.* Of a horse (occas. of other quadrupeds): to go at a gallop (see GALLOP *sb.* 1).

a **1533** LD. BERNERS *Huon* lv. 185 The horse wold nother trot nor galop. **1570** LEVINS *Manip.* 169 To Gallop, *fundere gradus.* To Wallop, *idem, cursitare.* *a* **1631** DONNE *Poems* (1633) 137 His steeds will bee restrain'd But gallop lively downe the Westerne hill. **1697** DRYDEN *Virg. Georg.* III. 148 Fearing to be seen, The Leacher gallop'd from his Jealous Queen. **1707** *Lond. Gaz.* No. 4282/4 Stolen or strayed..a bright bay Gelding..4 Years old past, walks, trots, gallops, and leaps. **1835** W. IRVING *Tour Prairies* 159 They had also seen a fine wild horse, which, however, had galloped off with a speed that defied pursuit.

†**b.** *trans.* To pursue or chase at a gallop. *Obs.* [So F. *galoper*.]

1580 BLUNDEVIL *Horsemanship* I. (1609) 7 To gallop the bucke, or followe a long winged Hawke.

fig. **1626** T. H. *Caussin's Holy Crt.* 112 A thousand Princes, and phantastique great Ladies, haue galloped Honour vpon the full speed.

c. *Racing.* *to gallop to a standstill*: to tire out.

1892 *Daily News* 2 Mar. 3/6 Silvercrown..a celebrated racehorse..having galloped eighteen horses to a standstill for the Crawford Plate at Newmarket in 1886.

2. *intr.* Of a horseman: To ride at full speed. Also with advs., as *forth, in, off.*

1523 LD. BERNERS *Froiss.* I. cxl. 69 b, He dasshed his spurres to his horse, and galoped forth in suche wyse that his kepars loste him. **1568** GRAFTON *Chron.* I. vii 186 She and her Gentlewoman..galoped thorough the Towne. **1599** SHAKS. *Hen. V*, IV. vii. 89 Yet a many of your horsemen peere And gallop ore the field. **1724** DE FOE *Mem. Cavalier* (1840) 140 The scouts came galloping in. **1791** MRS. RADCLIFFE *Rom. Forest* i, They..then placed them on two horses, a man mounted behind each, and they immediately galloped off. **1807–8** W. IRVING *Salmag.* (1824) 72 A squadron of hardy veterans..who..trot and amble, and gallop..through every street. **1885** TENNYSON *Charge Heavy Brigade* ii, Up the hill Gallopt the gallant three hundred.

3. *trans.* To make (a horse, etc.) go at full speed.

a **1533** LD. BERNERS *Huon* liii. 178, I can ryght wel..rynne & galop a hors. **1617** MARKHAM *Caval.* II. 145 And when you doe gallop him, you shal not at the first gallop him aboue fiue or sixe times vpon one hand. **1737** POPE *Hor. Epist.* II. i. 14 Let your Muse take breath, And never gallop Pegasus to death. **1838** *Penny Cycl.* XII. 309/2 If, immediately after drinking his fill, he were galloped hard. **1884** J. COLBORNE *Hicks Pasha* 68 Then the bridegroom and his men went through a fantasia, galloping their dromedaries at full speed.

†**4.** To traverse (a space) rapidly on horseback or by means of horses. *Obs.*

1588 SHAKS. *Tit. A* II. i. 7 The golden Sunne..Gallops the Zodiacke in his glistering Coach.

fig. **1590** NASHE (*title*), First Parte of Pasquils Apologie wherein he renders a Reason of his long Silence and gallops the Fielde with the Treatise of Reformation written by John Penrie. *Ibid.* I. D iv b, I haue..galloped the fielde to make choyse of the ground where my battaile shall be planted.

5. *transf.* and *fig.* (from senses 1 and 2).

1583 STANYHURST *Æneis* iv. (Arb.) 101 Furth she [Fame] quicklye galops, with wingflight swallolyke hastning. **1593** SHAKS. *2 Hen. VI*, I. iii 154 Shee's tickled now, her Furie needs no spurres, Shee'le gallop farre enough to her destruction. **1600** —— *A.Y.L.* III. ii. 329. **1626** L. OWEN *Spec. Jesuit.* (1629) 31 They [the Iesuites] came galloping so fast into hell, and grew to be so many, that Lucifer was afraid. **1630** J. TAYLOR (Water P.) *Wks.* II. 130/1 His Tongue much like a Hackney goes all paces..It gallops and false gallops, trots and ambles. **1681** *Trial S. Colledge* 44 Pray Sir, you go too fast already, as you are still gallopping. **1725** RAMSAY *Gent. Sheph.* II. ii, They gallop fast that deils and lasses drive. **1841** S. C. HALL *Ireland* I. 151 The mountain torrents crawl or gallop to mingle with the broad Atlantic.

b. *to gallop away*: to talk fast, to 'rattle on'.

1711 SWIFT *Lett.* (1767) III. 183 How you gallop away in your spleen and your rage about repenting my journey. **1875** JOWETT *Plato* (ed. 2) II. 237 Pray observe how I gallop away when I get on smooth ground.

c. *to gallop over* or *through*: to hurry over (in reading or reciting), to read cursorily.

1782 MAD. D'ARBLAY *Let. to S. Crisp* 25 Feb., The unreasonable hurry with which I was obliged to gallop over such a book. **1826** J. W. CROKER in *C. Papers* 13 Nov. (1884), Do not gallop through my letter..but read it over and over again. **1859** H. C. WATSON in *Darwin's Life & Lett.* (1887) II. 226, I could not rest till I had galloped through the whole. **1875** JOWETT *Plato* (ed. 2) II. 113, I will gallop through the discourse as fast as I can.

†**6.** To dance rapidly; to dance a GALOP. *Obs.*

1806–7 J. BERESFORD *Miseries Hum. Life* (1826) III. xxi, You instantly tear down the dance..incessantly vociferating as you ramp and gallop along. **1826** *Lover's Quarrel* in *Lit. Souvenir* 6 When I dance with Sir Dunce, or gallop with Sir Gosling?

7. *trans.* To convey rapidly by means of galloping horses.

1882 *Let. of Officer* in *R. Acad. Catal.* (1883) 95 We galloped the left gun at it and it went into the ditch with a bump. **1897** *Daily News* 2 Feb. 7/4 Commander Wells was galloped over from headquarters in a hose van.

'gallop, *v.*[2] *Obs.* exc. *dial.* [Prob. onomatopœic; cf. WALLOP.] *intr.* and *trans.* To boil.

?*a* **1605** MIDDLETON *Witch* I. ii, *Hecate.* Boil it well. *Hoppo.* It gallops now. **1888** *Sheffield Gloss.*, *Gallop*, to boil quickly. 'The pot gallops'.

Hence **galloped beer** (see quot.).

a **1825** FORBY *Voc. E. Anglia*, *Gallopped-beer*, small beer for present drinking, made by simple boiling, or, as it is called, gallopping, small quantities of malt and hops together in a kettle.

gallopade (gælə'peɪd), *sb.* Also **galopade, galloppade.** [a. F. *galopade*, f. *galoper* to gallop: cf. GALOP.]

1. A lively kind of dance, of Hungarian origin.

1831 LD. HOUGHTON in Wemyss Reid *Life* (1891) I. 104 The Germans put my waltzing to shame..and actually scoff at my gallopade. **1835** L. HUNT *Capt. Sword* iii. 13 The galopade, strange agreeable tramp, Made of a scrape, a hobble, and stamp. **1879** G. MEREDITH *Egoist* III. xii. 249 He thought her a delightful partner for a dance, and found her rather tiresome at the end of the gallopade.

transf. **1831** *Westm. Rev.* XIV. 181 In an early number we printed an account of this gentleman's 'gallopades' across the thistly plains of South America.

2. In the *manège*: A sidelong or curveting kind of gallop.

1753 CHAMBERS *Cycl. Supp.*, *Gallopade.*

Hence **gallo'pade** *v. rare*, to dance a gallopade; **gallo'pading** *vbl. sb.*

1831 *Westm. Rev.* XIV. 424 She waltzes, gallopades, sings, plays, draws. **1833** M. SCOTT *Tom Cringle* xi, Then a tremendous gallopading, in which Tailtackle was nearly capsized over the wharf. **1842** TENNYSON *Amphion* 40 The shock-head willows two and two By rivers gallopaded.

galloper ('gæləpə(r)). Also 6–9 **gallopper.** [f. GALLOP *v.*[1] + -ER[1].]

1. a. A horse which has special powers of galloping.

1650 R. STAPYLTON *Strada's Low C. Warres* VII. 60 He loved her above all the Horse in his Stables, she being an excellent galloper. **1769** *De Foe's Tour Gt. Brit.* III. 156, I believe that some of the Gallopers of this county..will outdo..the swiftest Horse that was ever bred in Turky or Barbary. **1845** BROWNING *How they brought the good News*, I saw my stout galloper Roland. **1886** *St. Stephen's Rev.* 13 Mar. 11/2 She [a mare]..is a slovenly fencer, but is a fairly good galloper.

b. A wooden horse on a merry-go-round; a roundabout with such horses on it.

1945 *Archit. Rev.* XCVII. 50/2 These gallopers continued without competitors for more than thirty years. *Ibid.*, The real thrill of the galloper had to await the successful results of the patient toil of the steam engineers before it could be realized. **1968** D. BRAITHWAITE *Fairground Archit.* iii. 55 Initially rating second in popularity to the 'Gallopers', the 'Scenic Railway' attained a higher point in terms of fairground architecture. *Ibid.* vii. 122 Both 'Galloper' and switchback had a fixed centre.

2. One who gallops on horseback, esp. of hunters.

1576 TURBERV. *Venerie* 35 The gallopers, prickers, and huntsmen on horsebacke seying their houndes strong enough..shall then beginne to enter and to teach them. **1583** STANYHURST *Æneis* IV. (Arb.) 99 With the hounds quick-senting, with pricking galloper horsman. **1696** tr. *Du Mont's Voy. Levant* 33 We..cou'd neither see nor hear the least News of our Gallopers. **1820** SCOTT *Monast.* ix, The Sub-Prior..without having any farther interview with Christie the galloper, answered by giving the promise. **1871** *Daily News* 22 Sept., One galloper found himself in the bottom of a muddy ditch, with his horse directly on top of him.

3. *Mil.* An aide-de-camp, or orderly officer.

1871 *Daily News* 18 Sept., The group of generals, field officers, and dashing gallopers. **1896** *Ibid.* 5 Feb. 5/4 Sir John Willoughby..appointed me 'galloper', or volunteer orderly officer to him.

4. *fig.* One who proceeds at great speed. Also one who gads about.

1671 M. BRUCE *Good News Evil T.* (1708) 31 Thou art.. now a Galloper in the ways of God. **1695** CONGREVE *Love for L.* I. ii, Well, lady galloper, how does Angelica? **1713** STEELE *Guardian* No. 132 ¶6 If abroad, I am a gaggling Goose; when I return, You are a fine Galloper; Women, like Cats, should keep the House. **1765** STERNE *Tr. Shandy* VII. iv, There is not a gallopper of us all, who might not have gone on ambling quietly on his own ground.

5. A light field-gun, formerly attached to regiments; also *attrib.* in ***galloper carriage, -gun.***

1746 *Rep. Cond. Sir J. Cope* 45 Assembled at Sterling with four Cohorns, four 'Gallopers', Provisions, &c. **1802** WELLINGTON *Jrnl.* in Gurw. *Desp.* I. 378, I received from General Stuart..information regarding the galloper carriages..I reported to the General..the state of the galloper guns of the regiments. **1803** LAKE in Owen *Wellesley's Desp.* 405 As many of the field pieces as could be brought up, with the gallopers attached to the cavalry, formed four different batteries. **1847** MRS. SHERWOOD *Life* xxvi. 438 He was now engaged in drawing up six-pound gallopers, and forming a battery. **1876** JAS. GRANT *Hist. Ind.* I. lv. 280/2 When Tippoo opened a..cannonade from fifteen of his light galloper guns.

galloping ('gæləpɪŋ), *vbl. sb.* Also 7-9 gallopping. [f. GALLOP *v.* + -ING[1].]

1. The action of the verb GALLOP.

1605 SHAKS. *Macb.* IV. i. 140, I did heare The galloping of Horse. Who was't came by? *a* **1687** COTTON *Poems* (1689) 93 His [Pegasus'] days of galloping are ended, Unless I with the spur do prick him. **1820** W. IRVING *Sketch Bk.* II. 251 Others fancied that they heard the galloping of horses over their heads. **1890** BOLDREWOOD *Col. Reformer* (1891) 101 Galloping about there was..but often the rides were long, weary, and unexciting.

2. *attrib.* as ***galloping country, sound***; **galloping sketch**, a sketch of a locality made after a rapid ride through it.

1812 SIR R. WILSON *Priv. Diary* (1861) I. 110 For the first twelve miles we proceeded slowly, although over very fine galloping country. **1826** SCOTT *Woodst.* iv, There was a distant rustling among the withered leaves, a bouncing or galloping sound on the path. **1851** J. S. MACAULAY *Field Fortif.* 248 Even galloping sketches have their uses.

galloping ('gæləpɪŋ), *ppl. a.* [f. as prec. + -ING[2].]

1. That gallops, in senses of the vb. ***galloping consumption***: a consumptive disease which makes rapid progress.

1642 HOWELL *For. Trav.* (Arb.) 69 For the Italians have a Proverb, that a galloping horse is an open sepulcher. **1646** BUCK *Rich. III*, I. 37 The King..pursued the Duke, not only with a galloping Army, but with Edicts and Prescriptions. **1674** R. GODFREY *Inj. & Ab. Physic* 130 Having for many months laboured under a Galloping Consumption and made use of diverse Physicians in vain. **1697** *Lond. Gaz.* No. 3336/4 Stole..a bright bay Mare..a true Yorkshire galloping Breed. **1802-12** BENTHAM *Rationale Jud. Evid.* (1827) v. 64 The father in full vigour, the son in a galloping consumption.

fig. **1755** J. AMORY *Mem.* (1769) II. 167 No galloping eyes, or the least inattention in their devotion. **1770** N. NICHOLLS in *Corr. w. Gray* (1843) 115 What a blessing it is to have a galloping imagination. **1897** A. MORRISON *Child Jago* xxxiv, Ever since they had taken him he had been oppressed by this plague of galloping thought.

b. ***galloping nun***: (see quot. 1715; Milton's allusion is obscure).

1641 MILTON *Animadv.* (1851) 199 Our Liturgie hath run up and down the world like an English gallopping Nun, proffering her selfe, but we heare of none yet that bids money for her. **1715** M. DAVIES *Athen. Brit.* I. 152 Having espous'd one of the Countesses of Mansfield, who had been a Chanoness or Dame of the Monastery of Girrisheim, a Temporal Religious Pensioner, or what is vulgarly call'd a Galloping-Nun, without any Votes [i.e. vows].

c. *Mil.* ***galloping carriage*** = 'galloper carriage'; see GALLOPER 5.

1883 *Daily News* 27 July 2/1 A 'galloping carriage' designed by Lord C. Beresford to carry a Nordenfeldt gun.

2. *Comb.*: †**galloping-like** *a.*, having the appearance of a good galloper.

1711 *Lond. Gaz.* No. 4839/4 Lost, or Stole..a strait, young, gallopping-like bay Mare.

gallore, obs. form of GALORE.

ˌ**Gallo-'Roman**, *a.* and *sb.* [GALLO-[1].] **A.** *adj.* Belonging to Gaul when it formed part of the Roman Empire. **B.** *sb.* An inhabitant of Gaul under Roman rule; also, the language of these people.

1841 T. ARNOLD *Lect. Mod. Hist.* 33 Throughout the south of France the population is predominantly..of Gallo-Roman origin. **1861** W. H. ANDERTON tr. *Dupanloup's Sermon Cath. Ireland* 8 Saint Patrick, that young Gallo-Roman whom we had sent to her [*sc.* Ireland]. **1879** *Encycl. Brit.* IX. 528/1 These were also the days of what is called 'the Gallo-Roman empire'. *Ibid.* 528/2 The Visigoths and Gallo-Romans defeated the terrible hordes of Attila. **1933** [see CATALAN]. **1934** M. K. POPE *From Lat. to Mod. Fr.* I. ii. 11 Thus the Romance languages in their early stage, Gallo-Roman, Hispano-Roman, Italo-Roman, etc, slowly took shape. The Gallo-Roman styled himself *romanus*. **1962** H. R. LOYN *Anglo-Saxon England* i. 16 Name of townships that trace unbroken descent from the name of their eponymous Gallo-Roman estate-owners.

gallosh, galloshoes, -shoos, obs. ff. GALOSH.

gallo-tannate (ˌgæləʊ'tænət). [f. GALLO-TANN(-IC) + -ATE.] A compound of gallo-tannic acid with a base.

1864 WATTS *Dict. Chem.* II. 767 Gallotannates or Tannates. **1876** HARLEY *Mat. Med.* (ed. 6) 248 Astringent vegetable infusions, which precipitate the lead as insoluble gallo-tannate.

gallo-tannic (ˌgæləʊ'tænɪk), *a.* [f. *gallo-*, taken as comb. form of L. *galla* GALL *sb.*[3] + TANNIC.] In ***gallo-tannic acid***, tannic acid prepared from nut-galls.

1858 in SIMMONDS *Dict. Trade.* **1873** *Fownes' Chem.* (ed. 11) 640 Gallotannic acid $C_{27}H_{22}O_{17}$, the acid contained in the gall-nuts of *Quercus infectoria* and other species of oak.

gallo-tannin (gæləʊ'tænɪn). [f. as prec. + TANNIN.] Tannin prepared from nut-galls.

1891 *Anthony's Photogr. Bull.* IV. 128 Gallo-tannin (the ordinary tannin) produces a similar blue black coloration.

gallote, galloune, galloure, gallous, obs. ff. GALLIOT, GALLOON, GALORE, GALLOWS *sb.*

Gallovidian (gælə'vɪdɪən), *a.* and *sb.* In 7 Gallowedian. [f. med.L. *Gallovidia* + -AN. *Gallovidia* (also *Galloweithia*, *Galweia*, etc.) is a Lat. form of Welsh *Gallwyddel* = Irish *Gall-gaidhil*, lit. 'foreign Gaels', now Galloway, a district in the SW. of Scotland (the shires of Wigton and Kircudbright).]

A. *adj.* Belonging to Galloway. **B.** *sb.* A native of that district.

1632 LITHGOW *Trav.* 495 Gallowedian Nagges. **1824** MACTAGGART (*title*) The Scottish Gallovidian Encyclopedia. **1863** W. ANDERSON *Geneal. & Surn.* in *Herald & Genealogist* (1865) July 254 The name, however, has neither a Scotch, nor an English derivation, being purely Celtic and Gallovidian. **1875** W. MCILWRAITH *Guide Wigtownshire* 52 The Romans were no peaceable visitants of the pagan Gallovidians.

†**gallow**, *v.*[1] *Obs.*[−1] In 4 galwe. [f. *galwe* GALLOWS *sb.*] *trans.* To hang on a gallows or cross.

a **1400** *Leg. Rood* (1871) 132 Wiþ grete lewes he is galwed, And dyeþ for Monnes gelte.

gallow ('gæləʊ), *v.*[2] *rare*[−1]. *intr.* Of a bird: To cluck, to scream. Hence '**gallowing** *ppl. a.*

1825 HOGG *Q. Hynde* 80 The capperkailzie scorn'd to flee But gallow'd on the forest tree. **1830** AIRD in *Blackw. Mag.* XXVIII. 817 Choked shrieks..And gallowing cries.. thicken'd the midnight air.

gallow, obs. form of GALLY *v.*, to frighten.

Galloway ('gæləweɪ). Also 6-8 **Gallaway** and also with small initial. [The name of a district in the SW. of Scotland, used *attrib.* and hence as a common noun.]

1. a. One of a small but strong breed of horses peculiar to Galloway; hence a small-sized horse, esp. for riding. Also ***Galloway-mare, -nag.***

1597 SHAKS. *2 Hen. IV*, II. iv. 205 Know we not Galloway Nagges? **1597-8** BP. HALL *Sat.* IV. iii. 56 Because his dame was swiftest Trunchefice, Or Runcevall his syre; himself a Gallaway. **1612** DRAYTON *Poly-olb.* iii. 40 The rank-riding Scots upon their gallowayes. **1641** MILTON *Animadv.* (1851) 240 Spare your selfe, lest you bejade the good galloway. **1676** *Lond. Gaz.* No. 1071/4 Another small Plate to be Run for by Gallawayes. **1713** *Guardian* No. 91 ¶13 That Horse shall forthwith be Sold, a Scotch Galloway bought in its stead for him. **1796** STEDMAN *Surinam* I. ix. 210 His galloway sprung, rider and all, through a hedge of thick limes. **1825** SCOTT *Talism.* xv, My Ralph, whom I left training his galloway nag, on the banks of the Irthing. **1831** YOUATT *Horse* (1866) 103 A horse between thirteen and fourteen hands in height is called a Galloway, from a beautiful breed of little horses once found in the south of Scotland..The pure galloway was said to be nearly fourteen hands high, and sometimes more; of a bright bay, or brown, with black legs, small head and neck, and peculiarly deep and clean legs. **1894** *Times* 16 Apr. 3/3 This was a claim for £22 10s. for hire of a racing galloway mare.

b. *attrib.* and *Comb.* as ***Galloway-race***; ***Galloway-sized*** adj. Also **Galloway-plate**, a racing prize, run for by Galloways.

1707 *Lond. Gaz.* No. 4343/7 On Thursday the *Galloway-Plate of 10l. Value will be run for, 9 Stone, 3 Heats. **1894** *Times* 16 Apr. 3/3 She was entered for a *galloway race at North Walsham. **1794** W. FELTON *Carriages* (1801) II. 76 The appearance of both ought to be conformable to each other, therefore a middling-sized phaeton, to the middling, or *galloway sized horses, suits best.

2. One of a breed of cattle peculiar to Galloway. Also *attrib.*

1805 FORSYTH *Beauties Scotl.* II. 373 That famous breed of cattle known by the name of galloways. **1849** W. & J. DEANS in J. Deans *Pioneers of Canterbury* (1937) app. 284 We would strongly advise that a few bulls of the Galloway breed should be sent out. **1862** [see ABERDEEN 1]. **1867** MCDOWELL *Hist. Dumfries* (1873) 707 The dusky Galloways composed the bulk of the cattle at the Dumfries market. **1960** *Times* 25 Jan. 19/1 When choosing our Galloway calves in 1948 we had this point in view.

Galloway dike. *Sc.* [from the district name: see prec.] 'A wall built firmly at the bottom, but no thicker at the top than the length of the single stones, loosely piled the one above the other' (Jam.).

1791 *Statist. Acc. Scotl.* I. 451 The..most general fence is the Galloway dike. **1814** SCOTT *Diary* 4 Aug. in *Lockhart*, It would be easy to form a good farm by enclosing the ground with Galloway dykes.

gallow-balk, -clapper, -tree: see GALLOWS-.

†'**gallow-**ˌ**grass.** *Obs.* [f. GALLOW(S + GRASS.] A slang name for hemp, from its use for ropes and halters.

1562 BULLEYN *Bk. Simples* 27 b, An herbe whiche light fellowes merily will call Gallowgrasse, Neckeweede, or the Tristrams knot. **1630** J. TAYLOR (Water P.) *Praise Hempseed* Wks. III. 66 a/2 Wherefore in Sparta it ycleped was, Snickup, which is in English Gallow-grasse.

gallows ('gæləʊz), *sb.* Forms: α. *sing.* 1 **galʒa, ʒealʒa**, (3 *Comb.* **galhe-**), 3-4 **gal(e)we**, (5 *Comb.* **galle-**), 5-6 **galow(e**, 6-7 **gallow**, 7-9 **gall(e)y.** β. *pl.* in *sing.* sense, later construed as *sing.* 3-5 **galwes**, (4 **galewis, -ewys, -uus**), 4-5 **galus**, (5 **galhouse, -hows, galohous**), 5-6 **gallous, galowes**, (5 **galawis, -ays, -ewes, galghes, galos, -ouys, -owys**), 6-7 **gallowes**, (6 **galoss, gallhouse, gallies, -oes, -owes, -us**), 9 **gallos, -us**, 6- **gallows**. γ. with additional *pl.* suffix, 6 **gal(l)osses**, 7-9 **gallowses**, (9 **gallaces, -usses**). [OE. *galʒa*, *ʒealʒa* wk. masc. = OFris. *galga*, OS. and OHG. *galgo* (Ger. *galgen*), ON. *galge* (Da. and Sw. *galge*), Goth. *galga*:—OTeut. **galgon-*; perh. cogn. with Lith. *žalga*, Armen. *dzaλk* pole.]

1. An apparatus for inflicting the punishment of death by hanging, usually consisting of two uprights and a cross-piece, from which the criminal is suspended by the neck. Sometimes used as equivalent to CROSS. See CROSS *sb.* 1.

In OE. the sing. *galʒa* and the pl. *galʒan* are both used for 'a gallows', the pl. having reference presumably to the two posts of which the apparatus mainly consisted. Occasional examples of the sing. form occur in ME., and even down to the 17th c.; but from the 13th c. onwards the plural *galwes* and its later phonetic representatives have been the prevailing forms. So far as our material shows, Caxton is the first writer to speak of 'a gallows', though he also uses the older expression 'a pair of gallows'; but it is, of course, possible that the pl. form was sometimes treated as a sing. much earlier. From the 16th c. *gallows* has been (exc. *arch.* in 'pair of gallows') used as a sing., with a new plural *gallowses*; the latter, though perh. not strictly obsolete, is now seldom used; the formation is felt to be somewhat uncouth, so that the use of the word in the plural is commonly evaded.

α. *Beowulf* (Z.) 2446 Swa biđ ʒeomor-lic gomelum ceorle to ʒebidanne, þæt his byre ride ʒiong on galʒan. *a* **1000** *Juliana* 482 Sume ic rode befealh þæt hi..on hean galʒan lif aletan. *c* **1000** ÆLFRIC *Gloss.* in Wr.-Wülcker 116/19 *Patibulum*, galʒa. **1483** *Cath. Angl.* 149/1 A Galowe, *furca*. **1535** COVERDALE *Esther* v. 14 Let them make a galowe of fiftye cubites hie. **1561** T. NORTON *Calvin's Inst.* Calvin's Pref., Worthy of a thousand fires and gallowes. **1567** DRANT *Horace, Ep.* xvi. F j, With gyues, and fetters Ile tame the vnder a galow dyre. **1681** W. ROBERTSON *Phraseol. Gen.* (1693) 1014 Do you look I should..praise you, who deserved the Gallow so lately?

β. *c* **1300** *Havelok* 1161 Thou shal to the galwes renne. *c* **1330** R. BRUNNE *Chron.* (1810) 172 Galwes do ȝe reise, and hyng þis cheitefe. *a* **1400-50** *Alexander* 1813 And for þaire souerayne sake þam send to þe galawis. **1480** CAXTON *Chron. Eng.* ccxliv. (1482) 305 There was made a newe payre of galewes and a strong cheyne and a coler of yren for hym. *c* **1489** —— *Blanchardyn* xlviii. 187 He shold doo make and to be sette vp a galhouse. **1549** *Compl. Scotl.* xii. 102 Tua speyris..stude vp fra the eyrd lyik ane gallus. **1589** *Marprel. Epit.* C iv, The theefe on the gallowes was saued without them. **1600** SHAKS. *A.Y.L.* III. ii. 345 Who doth he [Time] gallop withal?.. With a theefe to the gallowes. *a* **1627** HAYWARD *Edw. VI* (1630) 64 He took the maior aside and.. required of him that a paire of gallowes should be framed and erected. **1689** WOOD *Life* 19 Dec. (O.H.S.) III. 318 A gallowes being erected before Temple gate. **1756-7** tr. *Keysler's Trav.* (1760) I. 409 Two ladders are placed against the gallows. **1818** SCOTT *Hrt. Midl.* vii, 'Why do you trifle away time in making a gallows?—that dyester's pole is good enough for the homicide.' **1855** MILMAN *Lat. Chr.* XIV. vii. (1864) IX. 222 In the older versions the now ignoble words 'hanging and the gallows' were used instead of the Crucifixion and the Cross.

γ. **1562** TURNER *Herbal* II. 46 a, Mandrag..groweth not vnder gallosses. **1673** [R. LEIGH] *Transp. Reh.* 108 Make bonfires of the gallowses, set open all the prisons. **1775** J. SULLIVAN in Sparks *Corr. Amer. Rev.* (1853) I. 72 That all our liberty-poles will soon be converted into gallowses. **1801** HELEN M. WILLIAMS *Sk. Fr. Rep.* I. xvii. 209 Previous to this epocha, gallowses had been erected at Naples.

2. a. The punishment itself.

1483 CAXTON *Cato* A vij, His fader.. bought him ageyn fro the galowes and fro dyshonest dethe. **1522** MORE *De quat. Noviss.* Wks. (1557) 82 His galowes & death standeth within .x. mile at yᵉ farthest, & yours within .lxxx. *a* **1533** FRITH *Disput. Purg.* (1533) G v b, When we say that such a man hath delyuered his freende from the gallowes, we mean not that he was all ready hanged. **1603** SHAKS. *Meas. for M.* I. ii. 84 What with the sweat, what with the gallowes, and what with pouerty, I am Custom-shrunke. **1730** in *Swift's Lett.* (1768) IV. 251 Into their secular hands the poor authors must be delivered to.. pillories, whippings, and the gallows. **1836** HOR. SMITH *Tin Trump.* (1876) 174 Gallows—a cure without being a prevention of crime. **1881** BESANT & RICE *Chapl. of Fleet* I. 48 The gallows did not terrify these evil-doers.

b. ***to have the gallows in one's face***: to have the look of one predestined to or deserving the gallows.

1610 SHAKS. *Temp.* I. i. 32 This fellow.. hath no drowning marke vpon him; his complexion is perfect Gallowes. **1710** PALMER *Proverbs* 114 The gallows is almost as visible in their face as their nose: as is often to be seen in a thoro'pac'd villain. **1768** GOLDSM. *Good-n. Man* v. (Globe) 637/1 Hold him fast, the dog; he has the gallows in his face. **1835** MARRYAT *Jac. Faithf.* viii, 'There's gallows marked in his face', observed another.

c. *Proverbs.*

13.. *Sir Beues* (A.) 1217 Deliure a þef fro þe galwe, He þe hateþ after be alle halwe! **1484** CAXTON *Fables of Æsop* I. x, Yf ye kepe a man fro the galhows he shalle neuer loue yow after. **1583** GOLDING *Calvin on Deut.* li. 307 Saue a theefe from the gallowes and hee will helpe to hang thee. **1592** GREENE *Disput.* 3 He that feares the Gallowes shal neuer be good theefe. **1593** NASHE *Christ's T.* Pref. Ep., Saue a thief from the gallows, and hee'le be the first to shew the way to Saint Gilesesse.

3. One deserving the gallows; a gallows-bird.

1588 SHAKS. *L.L.L.* v. ii. 12 He hath beene fiue thousand yeeres a Boy. I, and a shrewd vnhappy gallowes too. **1611** BEAUM. & FL. *Knt. Burn Pestle* I. iii, Though he be a notable gallows, yet I'll assure you his master did turn him away. **1749** B. MARTIN *Eng. Dict.*, *Gallows*, a wicked rascal. **1838** DICKENS *O. Twist* xi, 'Now, young gallows!' This was an invitation for Oliver to enter through a door.. which led into a stone cell.

†**4.** Used to render L. *furcæ*. **a.** = FORK 5 b. **b.** ***Gallows of Caudium*** = *Caudine Forks*: see FORK 14. *Obs.*

1565–73 COOPER *Thesaurus*, *Abire sub iugum*.. to passe or go vnder the gallies. **1618** [see FORK 5 b (*a*)].

5. Applied to various objects consisting of two or more supports and a cross-piece. †**a.** An iron support for a pot over a kitchen fire. Cf. GALLOWSBALK. *Obs.*

1512 *Will* in *Southwell Visit.* (1891) 116, I bequeth to the chauntrye priest.. oon paire of galoes of yrne. **1576** *Inv.* in *Ripon Ch. Acts* (Surtees) 378 A paire of iron gallows.

b. *Naut.* (See quot. 1867.)

1769 FALCONER *Dict. Marine* (1789) D d iij b, Their [booms'] after-ends are usually sustained by a frame called the gallows. **1867** SMYTH *Sailor's Word-bk.*, *Gallows*, the cross-pieces on the small bits at the main and fore hatch-ways in flush-decked vessels, for stowing away the booms and spars over the boats.

†**c.** *Printing.* 'A frame used for supporting the tympans of the old wooden presses when turned up' (Jacobi). *Obs.*

1683 MOXON *Mech. Exerc.* II. 328 One Press-man.. will Beat so soon as he has laid the Tympan on the Gallows after Pulling. **1808** C. STOWER *Printer's Gram.* 506* Fig. 8 is the gallows, in which the frame A, B, B is screwed to the front of the carriage, between the joints of the tympan. **1833** J. HOLLAND *Manuf. Metal* II. 210 The gallows for the tympans is also removed.

d. A gymnastic apparatus.

1817 SOUTHEY *Jrnl.* in C. C. Southey *Life & Corr.* IV. 268 Others were swinging in such attitudes as they liked from a gallows. **1827** ARNOLD *Let.* in Stanley *Life & Corr.* (1844) I. 72 When.. I could no more.. hang on a gallows, nor climb a pole.

e. A part of a plough (see quot. 1842).

1840 *Jrnl. R. Agric. Soc.* I. III. 219 An old Berkshire plough (with a high gallows in front). **1842** JOHNSON *Farmer's Encycl.*, *Gallows of a plough*, a part of the plough-head, so named by farmers, from its resemblance to the common gallows. It consists of three pieces of timber, of which one is placed transversely over the heads of the other two.

f. (See quots.)

1866 LADY BARKER *Station Life in New Zeal.* x. 64 The 'gallows', a high wooden frame from which the carcases of the butchered sheep dangle. **1883** GRESLEY *Gloss. Coal Mining*, *Gallows*, a crown-tree with a prop placed underneath each end of it. **1883** *Hampshire Gloss.*, *Gallows*, a frame formed by fixing four poles, two and two, in the ground, crossed X wise, and laying another pole across, against which planks or boards are set when sawn out, to dry. **1883** *Standard* 7 Sept. 5/3 They attacked.. the carcases on the 'meat gallows'. **1890** BOLDREWOOD *Col. Reformer* (1891) 350 The 'gallows' of the colonists, a rough, rude contrivance consisting of two uprights and a crosspiece for elevating slaughtered cattle.

6. 'Suspenders' for trousers; braces. Now *dial.*, *Sc.* and *U.S.*, in the form *gallowses*, whence occas. *gallows* for a single brace. Freq. in the form *gallus* in the U.S.

So *galgen* in Swiss German; also Du. (vulgar).

1730–6 BAILEY (fol.), *Gallowses*, contrivances made of cloth, and hooks and eyes, worn over the shoulders by men to keep their breeches up. **1813** SOUTHEY *Lett.* (1856) LV. 530 *note*, He.. used to have books, pen, ink and paper, breeches, gallowses, neck cloth, and rolls and butter, all upon the breakfast table at the same time. **1827** SIR J. BARRINGTON *Pers. Sk.* II. 50 The ball appeared to have hit the buckle of his gallows (yclept suspenders) by which it had been impeded. **1830** R. WARNER *Lit. Recoll.* I. 100 His under-clothes unsupported by those indispensable articles of decent attire denominated gallows. **1837** HALIBURTON *Clockm.* Ser. I. xv. 141 Chock full of spring like the wire eend of a bran new pair of trowser gallusses. **1868** WAUGH *Sneck-Bant* ii. 38 His breeches wur nobbut fastened wi' one gallace. **1884** J. RENTON in *Mod. Scott. Poets* Ser. VII. 51 My gallowses baith strang and guid. **1888** *Sheffield Gloss.*, *Gallaces*, braces for the trousers. **1896** CROCKETT *Cleg Kelly* xiv. 104 The tattered trousers with one 'gallus' displayed across the blue shirt. **1932** W. FAULKNER *Light in August* xviii. 404 Even if I dont wear no tin star on my galluses. **1932** E. CALDWELL *Tobacco Road* xiv. 166 He stepped into his overalls, put one arm through a gallus. **1942** O. NASH *Good Intentions* 145 To supply each of my pairs of pants with its own set of galluses. **1957** R. A. HEINLEIN *Door into Summer* (1967) iii. 51 Oh, I'm a gallus-snapper when I get started; you should see me wear women's hats at parties.

7. *attrib.* and *Comb.*, as (sense 1) ***gallows*** †***-knowe*** (= knoll), ***-maker***, ***-pin***, ***-rope***; ***gallows-ward*** adv.; (sense 2) ***gallows-free*** adj., ***gallows-worthy*** adj. and sb.; (sense 2 b) ***gallows-mark***; (sense 5) ***gallows-frame***, ***-timber***; (sense 6) ***gallows-buttons***.

1836–54 BYWATER *Sheffield Dial.* 162 'Thah mah breik all the *gallos buttons off.' **1881** RAYMOND *Mining Gloss.*, **Gallows-frame*, a frame over a shaft, carrying the pulleys for the hoisting cables. **1681** DRYDEN *Abs. & Achit.* II. 431 Let him be *gallows-free by my consent. **1864** A. MCKAY *Hist. Kilmarnock* (1880) 342 They were led from the town to suffer punishment at the *gallows-knowe. **1602** SHAKS. *Ham.* v. i. 49 *Clo.* What is he that builds stronger than either the mason, the shipwright, or the carpenter? *Other.* The *Gallowesmaker; for that Frame outliues a thousand Tenants. **1767** BUSH *Hibernia Cur.* (1769) 7 A fellow.. with a *gallows-mark upon his face. *c* **1750** *Mary Hamilton* in Child *Ballads* (1889) III. 125 To see the face of his Molly fair Hanging on the *gallows pin. **1839** CARLYLE *Chartism* iii. 121 Scramble along.. with thy.. plebeian *gallows-ropes. **1859** DICKENS *T. Two Cities* I. v, Foreheads knitted into the likeness of the gallows-rope. **1851** GREENWELL *Coal-trade Terms Northumb. & Durh.* 28 **Gallows Timber*, a crown-tree, with a prop placed under each end. *a* **1895** STEVENSON *Weir of Hermiston* iii. (1896) 49 The man.. was hunted *gallowsward with jeers. **1819** *Sporting Mag.* III. 214 Many respectable.. sinners, deliberately.. commit *gallows-worthy crimes. **1828** *Ibid.* XXI. 226 The master.. attended by one of those gallows-worthies.

8. Special comb.: **gallows-apple** *slang* (*to make gallows-apples of* = to hang); **gallows-bitts** = 5 b; †**gallow-breed** *Sc.* = GALLOWS-BIRD; **gallows-brood**, a number of young gallows-birds: see GALLOWS-BIRD; **gallows-climber**, one doomed to climb the ladder at the gallows, i.e. to be hanged; **gallows-face**, one who bears the mark of the gallows in his face (cf. 2 b); hence **gallows-faced** *adj.*; **gallows-foot**, the space immediately in front of the gallows; †**gallow-fork** = GALLOWS-TREE; **gallows-gate** *dial.* (see quot.); **gallow-lea**, a level place on which the gallows was erected; **gallows-humour**, grim, ironical humour; 'sick' humour; cf. GALGENHUMOR; **gallows-locks**, hair that hangs like gallows ropes; **gallows-ripe** *a.*, ready to be hanged; **gallows-rounded** *a.*, (of hair) cut round like that of a condemned criminal; **gallows-sockets**, *Printing* (see quot.); **gallows-stanchions** = 5 b; †**gallows-strings**, a term of reproach (cf. *hang-string*); **gallows-tool** (see quot. and cf. sense 5); **gallows-top** = 5 b.

1830 LYTTON *P. Clifford* vii. 126 They're resolved to make *gallows apples of all such Numprels (*Nonpareils*) as you. **1815** *Falconer's Dict. Marine* (ed. Burney), **Gallows-bits*, on flush-decks, a strong frame of oak about eight inches square, made in the form of a gallows, and fixed at the fore and main hatchway, to support the spare top-masts, yards, booms, boats, etc. **1508** DUNBAR *Flyting w. Kennedie* 141 Lyk to ane *gallow breid, Ramand, and rolpand, beggand koy and ox. **1831** SCOTT *Diary* 8 Jan. in *Lockhart*, A little *gallows-brood they were and their fate will catch it. **1668** DAVENANT *Man's the Master* III. i, Pattern of rogues! thou *gallows climber! **1724** RAMSAY *Gent. Sheph.* IV. i, I crave your pardon, *gallows-face!' **1769** H. BROOKE *Fool of Qual.* IV. xvii. 67 Art thou there, thou rogue, thou hang-dog, thou *gallows-faced vagabond? **1818** SCOTT *Hrt. Midl.* iv, And had just cruppen to the *gallows-foot to see the hanging. *a* **1225** *Ancr. R.* 174 Touward þe waritreo [*v.r.* *galheforke] of helle. **1893** *Wiltsh. Gloss.*, **Gallows-gate*, a light gate, consisting only of a hinged style, top-rail and one strut. **1901** W. D. HOWELLS in *North Amer. Rev.* Nov. 710 The honors are not quite so easy in the matter of *gallows-humor. **1935** *Archit. Rev.* LXXVII. 31/1 These may not be altogether unintentional touches of what the Germans call 'gallows-humour'. **1958** *Times* 17 July 4/3 The explosive vitality, full-blooded sentiment, and gallows humour that pervade the play. **1582–8** *Hist. Jas. VI* (1804) 135 Thair was interchange of thir twa maid with consent of all pairties at the *gallowlee betuix Edinburghe and Leith. **1828** SCOTT *F.M. Perth* iii, Thou must be bold, Henry; and bear thyself not as if thou wert going to the gallow-lee. **1809** W. IRVING *Knickerb.* (1812) II. 79 His hair hung in straight *gallows locks about his ears. **1837** CARLYLE *Fr. Rev.* II. v. iii. 270 Jourdan himself remains unhanged; gets loose again as one not yet *gallows-ripe. **1567** DRANT *Horace, Ep.* xix. F vij, What though one.. Should Cato counterfeate.. in his *gallowes rounded hayre. **1841** W. SAVAGE *Art Print.* 249 **Gallows Sockets.* Two pieces of wood with square mortises in them, to receive the ends of the gallows; they are nailed or screwed upon the plank behind the tympans. **1675** COTTON *Scoffer Scoft* 86, I, hang him, little *Gallow-strings, He does a thousand of these things. **1884** F. J. BRITTEN *Watch & Clockm.* 110 **Gallows Tool*, a tool in which a pinion is placed by clockmakers when the leaves on bottoms are to be filed.

gallows (ˈgæləʊz, ˈgæləs), *a.* [Developed from the *attrib.* use of the sb. In the first quot. perh. intended as a derivative (f. *gallow* + *-ous*).]

1. Fit for the gallows; deserving to be hanged; villainous, wicked. Now only *dial.* in weaker sense, esp. of children: Impish, wild, mischievous. ***gallows air*** = *hangdog air*: see HANGDOG *a.*

c **1425** *Found. St. Bartholomew's* (E.E.T.S.) 37 This gallowus man toke hym by the skyrtis of his palle or mantyl. **1551** ROBINSON tr. *More's Utopia* I. (1805) 76 No gallous wretche, I am not angry. *c* **1708** [? E. WARD] *Welsh Monster* 33 For ev'ry Line did in it bear Such a rebellious Gallows Air, That [etc.]. **1785** BURNS *Earnest Cry* 54 An' plunder'd o' her hindmost groat By gallows knaves. **1820** W. IRVING *Sketch Bk.* (1859) 23 Wolf.. sneaked about with a gallows air. **1882** *Lanc. Gloss.*, *Gallows*, cunning, designing full of duplicity. **1884** *Upton Gloss.* s.v., ''Taint as the lad's wicked, nor yet spiteful, but 'e's desp'rut gallus.' **1892** G. HAKE *Mem. 80 Yrs.* 44 They [King's Ward boys at Christ's Hospital circa 1820] were always considered a very gallous [*sic*] set, which in the school vocabulary signified 'daring'.

2. *dial.* and *slang.* [Prob. from the adv. Cf. BLOODY *a.* 10.] As an intensive: Very great, excellent, 'fine', etc.

1789 G. PARKER *Life's Painter* 132 While some their patter flash'd in gallows fun and joking. **1830** LYTTON *P. Clifford* III. x. 232 If so be as ow little Paul vas a vith you, it vould be a gallows comfort to you. **1888** *Berksh. Gloss.*, s.v., A gallus lot on 'um (a large number of them).

3. *Comb.*: **gallows-looking** *a.*, looking fit for the gallows, having a hang-dog look.

1809 W. IRVING *Knickerb.* (1812) II. 72 Their gallows-looking myrmidons. **1842** BARHAM *Ingol. Leg.*, *Misadv. Margate*, A little gallows-looking chap.

Hence **ˈgallowsness** *dial.*, mischief, perversity.

1859 GEO. ELIOT *A. Bede* 62, I never knew your equals for gallowsness.

gallows (ˈgæləʊz, ˈgæləs), *adv. dial.* and *slang.* [f. the sb.] With intensive force: Extremely, very, 'jolly'.

a **1823** *Song* in *Byron's Juan* XI. xix. *note*, Then your Blowing will wax gallows haughty, When she hears of your scaly mistake. *a* **1845** HOOD *Forl. Sheph. Compl.* ix, I've been so gallows honest in this Place. **1862** H. KINGSLEY *Ravenshoe* II. xv. 163 The pleece come in, and got gallus well kicked about the head. **1892** MRS. S. BATSON *Dark* II. v. 100 'A gallus bad wench her be!'

ˈgallow(s)-balk. *Obs.* exc. *dial.* Forms: 7–9 gally-bauk, 9 galley-baak, -bawk, gallibauk, gally-balk, 6– gallow(s-balk. [f. GALLOWS *sb.* + BALK.] The iron bar in the chimney from which the pot-hooks hang.

1583 *Inv.* in *Ripon Ch. Acts* (Surtees) 380 Gallow balk, ij reckens withe gallow crokes, tonges, and fyre sholl, 12*s.* **1668** in *Best's Farm. Bks.* (Surtees) 175 One still, one iron range, gallow-balk, and crooks. **1691** RAY *N.C. Words* 29 A Gally-bauk. **1855** in ROBINSON *Whitby Gloss.* **1881** *Leicester Gloss.*, *Gallow-balk* or *Gallows-balk*.

gallows-bird (ˈgæləzbɜːd). [f. GALLOWS *sb.* + BIRD *sb.*] One who deserves to be hanged. Also *occas.*, one who has been hanged.

1785 GROSE *Dict. Vulg. Tongue*, *Gallows bird*, one that deserves hanging. **1796** *Ibid.* (ed. 3), *Gallows bird*, a thief or pick-pocket; also one that associates with them. **1828** SCOTT *F.M. Perth* ii, Had this been in another place, young gallow's bird, I had stowed the lugs out of thy head. **1860** READE *Cloister & H.* II. i. 11 'It is ill to check sleep or sweat in a sick man', said he. 'I know that far, though I ne'er minced ape nor gallows-bird'. **1888** *Harper's Mag.* LXXVI. 415 The famous converted 'gallows bird'.. proclaims the good word in lamentable accents.

†**gallow(s)-clapper.** *Obs.* [f. GALLOWS *sb.* + CLAPPER. ? From the swinging of the body to and fro like the clapper of a bell or of a scarecrow.] = GALLOWS-BIRD.

1570 LEVINS *Manip.* 81/4 A Gallowclapper, *furcifer*. **1583** GOLDING *Calvin on Deut.* li. 305 It is not only the gallowes-clappers that say so I meane those whose faultes and crymes are manifest. **1640** BROME *Antip.* II. ix. Wks. 1873 III. 271 Come, come, ye Gallows-clappers. **1708** MOTTEUX *Rabelais* v. vii, Their Worships as he call'd them were about a score of fusty Crackropes and Gallowclappers.

ˈgallows-tree. Before 19th c. gallow-; see forms of GALLOWS *sb.* [OE. *galʒ-tréow*, Northumb. *galʒa-tre* (= ON. *gálga-tré*), f. *galʒa* gallows + *tréow* tree.]

1. = GALLOWS *sb.* 1.

Beowulf 2940 Cwæð he on merʒenne meces ecgum ʒetan wolde, sum[e] on galʒ treowu[m fuʒlum] to gamene. *a* **1000** *Durham Ritual* (Surtees) 23 Ðin rodes galga tre. *c* **1290** *S. Eng. Leg.* I. 43/300 Heng up-on þe galu-treo. **13..** *Guy Warw.* (A.) 4764 Ȝe schul.. heye hong on galwe tre. *c* **1422** HOCCLEVE *Jereslaus' Wife* 436 Shee espyde A galwe tree to which men a theef ledde. **1500–20** DUNBAR *Poems* xlix. 23 In his suppleis On gallow treis ȝitt dois he glowir. **1600** HOLLAND *Livy* I. xxvi. (1609) 19 Let them.. hang him upon a cursed gallow tree [L. *infelici arbori*] by a rope. *a* **1716** SOUTH *Serm.* (1744) X. vii. 231 He that mistakes.. the gallow-tree for a triumphal arch. **1748** THOMSON *Castle Indol.* II. 446 Most like to carcase parched on gallow-tree. **1818** SCOTT *Hrt. Midl.* ii, The fatal day was announced to the public, by the appearance of a huge black gallows-tree. **1878** *Masque Poets* 97 The gallows-tree was never built for handsome lads like you.

†**2.** = GALLOWS *sb.* 5 a. Cf. GALLOW(S)-BALK.

1590 *Inv.* in *Midl. Co. Hist. Coll.* II. 31 Item j galowe tree ij Rekyrons.

galls (gɔːlz), *pl. dial.* Also **sea galls**. [= Du. *gallen*, of obscure origin, for which *kwallen* (also *zeekwallen*) is more common.] The jelly-fish, or sea-nettle (*Medusa*).

1817 J. Evans *Excurs. Windsor*, etc. 458 A quantity of sea galls (a white sort of glutinous substance)..It is a kind of zoophite, I presume. **1887** *Kent Gloss.*, *Galls*, jelly fish.

†**gallsome**, *a. Obs. rare*⁻¹. In 7 galsome. [f. GALL *sb.*¹ + -SOME.] Having the nature of gall.

1633 T. Morton *Disch. Imput.* 210 Such Accusations.. any vulgar man..may cry out upon, and condemne, both of galsome bitternesse, and of wilfull fraud and falsehood.

gall-stone ('gɔːlstəʊn). [f. GALL *sb.*¹ + STONE *sb.*] A morbid calculous formation in the gall-bladder.

1758 *Phil. Trans.* L. 543 An Account of Two extraordinary Cases of Gall-Stones. **1787** Sir J. Hawkins *Life Johnson* Wks. I. 553 He had frequent fits of pain which indicated the passage of a gall-stone. **1876** tr. *Wagner's Gen. Pathol.* 321 Gall-stones occur especially in the gall-bladder.

b. *attrib.*

1846 *Proc. Berw. Nat. Club* II. No. 14. 174 *Pileus* convex, ..of a uniform gall-stone yellow. **1883** G. Harley *Dis. Liver* xi. 607 The pathology of gall-stone pain.

gallthrop, -trap(pe, obs. forms of CALTROP.

Gallup ('gæləp). The name of the American statistician George Horace *Gallup* (born 1901), used *attrib.* (chiefly in ***Gallup poll***) to denote an assessment of public opinion made by ascertaining the opinions of a representative cross-section of the people; a public-opinion poll. Hence occas. **Gallup-poll** *v. intr.*, to take a Gallup poll; also *trans.*, to receive (a certain number of votes) in a Gallup poll.

1940 *Illustr. London News* CXCVII. 565 According to the latest U.S. Gallup poll as we go to press, President Roosevelt is assured of a total of 410 electoral votes. **1941** *Electronic Engin.* XIV. 383 It would be interesting to have a Gallup Survey..of reasons why manufacturers have not adopted electronic aids. **1948** A. Toynbee *Civilization on Trial* ii. 16 If it were made the subject of a world-wide Gallup Poll, there would be no unanimity in the answer. **1951** *Listener* 23 Aug. 297/1 A kind of gallup-poll mentality. **1951** Koestler *Age of Longing* I. x. 181 You don't have to go around gallup-polling to see that the people of France have only one wish. **1963** C. Irving et al. *Scandal '63* xx. 222 Neville Chamberlain..Gallup-polled 32 per cent in 1940. **1966** *Observer* 30 Oct. 27/1 The age of Gallup Polls and TV documentaries.

gallus, var. of GALLOWS *sb.*

†**gall-wort**. *Obs.* [f. GALL *sb.*¹ + WORT.] A name for Toad-flax (*Linaria vulgaris*), and perh. for the Lesser Centaury (*Erythræa Centaurium*).

1577 B. Googe *Heresbach's Husb.* III. 135 b, Take..Gallwort, beastes Loongwort, Planten leaues [to cure the 'sicknesse of the Gall' in cattle]. **1587** Mascall *Govt. Cattle* (1600) 277 For the staggars in a hog, giue him of the hearbe called starewort or gallwort in milke, and he shall amend. **1657** W. Coles *Adam in Eden* 313 It is called also Toad-Flax ..and Flax-weed; in Sussex, Gallwort.

†'**gally**, *a.*¹ or *sb.* used *attrib. Obs.* [Of uncertain origin; possibly attrib. use of GALLEY *sb.*, denoting garments worn by sailors or by galley-slaves (cf. *galley cassock* in GALLEY *sb.* 8); possibly evolved from a supposed analysis of GALLIGASKIN, though in our quots. appearing earlier than that word.] In ***gally breeches, hose, slops***, app. synonymous or nearly so with GALLIGASKINS.

1567 Harman *Caveat* 35 They commenly go in frese ierkynes and gally slopes. **1570** Drout *Gaulfrido & Barnardo* 182 They pull in peeces fast Their gally breeches all a rowe. **1583** Stubbes *Anat. Abus.* I. (1877) 56 Some be called french-hose, some gally-hose..The Gally-hosen are made very large and wide. **1622** Mabbe tr. *Aleman's Guzman d'Alf.* II. 334, I nimbly tooke out two little bundles, but somwhat weighty withall, which I presently convay'd very handsomely into my Gally-sloppes.

gally ('gɔːlɪ), *a.*² ? *Obs.* Also 6 gallie, -ye, -ey, gawlie, -ye. [f. GALL *sb.*¹ + -Y¹.] Gall-like, resembling gall in taste, bitter. Chiefly *fig.*

c **1530** *Remedie of Love* lxv, in *Chaucer's Wks.* (1532) 368 a/1 Ful of melancoly and gally yre. **1550** Cranmer *Defence* 92 a, He abhorreth all gally and bytter drynkes of synne. **1566** Drant *Horace, Sat.* I. iii. B v b, Then, gawlye wordes..He doth put vp..at those which from him fled. **1658** *Torments of Hell* in *Phenix* (1708) II. 444 Their Ears are afflicted with horrible and hideous Outcries..their Tongues with gally Bitterness, the whole Body with intolerable Fire. **1665** R. Hooke *Microgr.* 143 And then by the anger of the Fly is his gally poisonous liquor injected.

gally ('gɔːlɪ), *a.*³ *Obs.* exc. *dial.* Also 7, 9 gaully, 9 *dial.* galey, goiley. [f. GALL *sb.*² + -Y¹.]

†**1.** Having galls or sores. *Obs.*⁻¹

c **1440** *Promp. Parv.* (Winchester MS.) [See GALLED *ppl. a.*²]

2. Full of galls, i.e. bare or wet places.

1602 Carew *Surv. Cornwall* I. 19 a, Some of the gaully grounds doe also yeeld plenty of *Rosa solis*. **1607** Norden *Surv. Dial.* v. 201, I see in some meddowes gaully places, where litle or no grasse at al groweth, by reason (as I take it) of the too long standing of the water. *a* **1722** Lisle *Husb.* (1757) 187, I was mowing broad-clover, where some of it in gully-places [? *read* gally places] was short. **1790** W. Marshall *Midl. Counties* II. 437 Gloss., *Gally*, scattered with galls. **1867** W. F. Rock *Jim an' Nell* Gloss. (E.D.S. No. 76), *Galey* or *Goiley*, damp, as ground where springs rise. **1881** *I. of Wight Gloss.*, *Gaully*, thin and bad: applied to defective spots in crops of turnips or corn.

gally ('gælɪ), *v.* Also 7 **gallow**. [OE. *a-gælwan* to alarm.] **a.** *trans.* To frighten, daze, scare, startle. Now only *dial.* and in the whale fishery. Also *dial.* to scare away.

1605 Shaks. *Lear* III. ii. 44 The wrathfull Skies Gallow the very wanderers of the darke And make them keep their Caues. *a* **1704** T. Brown *Wks.* (1708) III. 102 The People look'd as if they were gallied. **1823** *New Monthly Mag.* VII. 231 We were one and all mortally gallied at the sight. **1840** Marryat *Poor Jack* vi, They [bull whales] are..easily 'gallied', that is, frightened. **1874** C. M. Scammon *Marine Mammals* III. iii. 227 The whale is approached in the most cautious manner, to avoid 'gallying' it. **1883** *Hampshire Gloss.*, 'Galley them pigs out o' the peasen.' **1886** *W. Somerset Word-bk.*, *Gally*, to frighten. (Very common.)

¶ ? Used for 'to infuriate'.

1660 *Mrs. Rump* 1 It's enough to gally a Gentlewoman of her quality to be despised by every idle boy.

b. *Comb.*: **gally-baggar, -beggar, -crow** (also written **galli-**), dial. names for a scarecrow.

1825 Britton *Beauties Wilts.* Gloss. (E.D.S.) *Gally-crow*, a scare-crow in a garden, called in the Isle of Wight a *gally-baggar*. **1829** in Col. Hawker *Diary* (1893) I. 355 'Gallibaggers', a term used by the clods for anything to frighten away birds. **1879** T. Hardy *Ret. Native* I. iii, What ghastly gallicrow might the poor fellow have been like? **1886** Elworthy *W. Somerset Word-bk.*, *Gally Beggar*, any object which may inspire a superstitious dread, as a ghost, or any frightening object dimly seen.

Hence '**gallied** *ppl. a.*

1787 Grose *Prov. Gloss.*, *Gallied*, frightened. Exm. **1851** H. Melville *Moby Dick* III. i. 9 That strange perplexity of inert irresolution, which, when the fishermen perceive it in the whale, they say he is *gallied*. **1857** *Fraser's Mag.* LVI. 73 Crack! goes the rifle from the hidden nook among the 'gallied' herd. **1888** 'R. Boldrewood' *Robbery under Arms* II. iii. 48 They seemed awfully gallied about being stuck up and robbed of it [*sc.* gold]. **1903** Kipling *Five Nations* 14 Our gallied whales are blind! **1946** K. Tennant *Lost Haven* (1947) xix. 318 Look here, Alec. I was wondering if you could come and have a look at a little job I've got that I'm a bit gallied about.

gallyard, gally(e, obs. ff. GALLIARD, GALLEY.

gally(e)pot, obs. form of GALLIPOT.

gallyglass, obs. form of GALLOGLASS.

gallyngale, obs. form of GALINGALE.

gallynipper, var. GALLINIPPER.

gallypatch, var. CALIPASH.

1674 Josselyn *Voy. New Eng.* 38 Having taken off their shells (that on their back being fairest, is called a Gally patch).

gally-tile, obs. form of GALLEY-TILE.

gallywatte, obs. form of GALLIVAT.

galmound, galmounding: see GAMOND.

galne, galness, obs. ff. GALLON, GOLENESS.

†'**galnes**. *Sc. Law. Obs.* [a. Welsh *galanas* murder; also (in old laws) a fine for murder. The appearance of the Welsh term beside the Gaelic CRO of the same meaning is remarkable.] A fine for homicide. Only in ***cro and galnes***: see CRO.

1609 Skene *Reg. Maj.* 74 Gif the wife of ane frie man is slane..her friend sall haue the Cro and Galnes.

galoch(e, obs. form of GALOSH.

Galois (galwa). The name of É. *Galois* (1811–32), French mathematician, used *attrib.* to designate various concepts in algebra arising out of his work, as ***Galois field***, a field with a finite number of elements; ***Galois function, group, resolvent, theory***. So **Ga'loisian** *a.*

1893 E. H. Moore in *Bull. N.Y. Math. Soc.* III. 75 The Galois-field of order s = qⁿ, GF[qⁿ], consists of the system of qⁿ incongruous classes (modulis q, $F_n(\xi)$) of rational integral functions of ξ with integral coefficients. *Ibid.*, Galois theory. **1898** *Bull. Amer. Math. Soc.* IV. 335 This is precisely the Galoisian scheme of solution. **1899** *Ibid.* V. 237 Galois group. **1900** J. Pierpont in *Ann. Math.* 2nd Ser. I. 124 Any one of the equations $G_k(t) = 0$ is called a Galoisian Resolvent of (A) for R. *Ibid.* 125 We shall for convenience of notation take $G_1 = 0$. We shall call this *the* Galoisian Resolvent. **1901** Burnside & Panton *Theory of Equations* (ed. 4) II. xx. 246 This function, ψ_1, is called the Galois Function. *Ibid.* 257 The equation of the Nᵗʰ degree whose roots are these N values, viz., $\Psi(z) \equiv (z - \psi_1)(z - \psi_2)..(z - \psi n) = 0$, is called the Galois resolvent. **1937** R. D. Carmichael *Introd. Groups of Finite Order* ix. 255 A particular Galois field, so far as its abstract properties are concerned, is completely determined by its order. **1963** G. D. Mostow et al. *Fund. Struct. Algebra* x. 297 Galois theory shows that the roots of the polynomial can be obtained from the coefficients a_i by ordinary field operations (+, −, ×, ÷) and root extractions if and only if the Galois group is solvable. **1965** Patterson & Rutherford *Elem. Abstract Algebra* iii. 97 It can be shown that for each prime number *p* and each positive integer *n*, there is essentially only one field consisting of p^n elements; this..is called a *Galois field*.

galon, var. GALLOON.

galoot (gə'luːt). *slang.* Also **galloot, geeloot.**

1. *Naut.* (See quot. 1867.)

1812 J. H. Vaux *Flash Dict.*, *Galloot*, a soldier. **1835** Marryat *Jac. Faithf.* xxxiv, Four greater galloots were never picked up. **1865** *Slang Dict.*, *Geeloot*. **1867** Smyth *Sailor's Word-bk.*, *Galoot*, an awkward soldier..A soubriquet for the young or 'green' marine.

2. 'An awkward or uncouth fellow: often used as a term of good-natured depreciation' (*Standard Dict.*). orig. *U.S.*

1866 'Artemus Ward' *Among the Fenians* (Hotten) 30 Wake, Bessy, wake, My sweet galoot! **1869** 'Mark Twain' *Innoc. at Home* 22 He could lam any galoot of his inches in America. **1876** Besant & Rice *Gold. Butterfly* xxvi. 199 Until the Golden Butterfly brought him to Limerick City.. he was but a poor galoot. **1892** Stevenson & L. Osbourne *Wrecker* (ed. 2) 137 'My dear boy, I may be a galoot about literature, but you'll always be an outsider in business.' **1898** *Bulletin* (Sydney) 6 Aug. 32/4 'Who's that galoot 'as lost his 'orse, Sis?' Bendigo was asking. **1944** A. Clarke *Coll. Plays* (1963) 223 Big galoots in hobnailed boots! **1946** I. L. Idriess *In Crocodile Land* xxx. 209 We'll lock this silly galoot up. **1966** *New Statesman* 8 Apr. 497/3 The galoots who blew up Nelson's Pillar.

galop ('gæləp). Formerly also **galope, -oppe.** [a. F. *galop*: see GALLOP *sb.* (Earlier in the present century, Fr. had *galope* fem. in this sense.)] 'A lively dance in 2–4 time, originally a separate and independent dance, but now also forming a portion of a set of quadrilles' (Stainer & Barrett).

1837 *Hamilton's Dict. Mus. Terms* (ed. 4), *Galop* (German). *Galoppe* (French), a quick species of dance, generally in 2/4 time. **1840** Hood *Up Rhine* 17, I could not help associating its regular tramp, tramp, tramp, with the tune of a galoppe I had recently performed. **1864** in Webster (*galop*), and in later Dicts.

Hence '**galop**, *v.*, to dance a galop.

1840 T. Hook in *New Monthly Mag.* LVIII. 155 They dance quadrilles fatiguingly, and galope as if they were going to fly out of the windows.

†**galopin**. *Obs.* Also 6–7 gal(l)apine, gallepyn, gallopin. [a. F. *galopin*, f. *galoper* to gallop.] A turnspit; an errand-boy; a page.

1567 in G. Chalmers *Life Mary Q. Scots* (1818) I. 177 Christell Lamb, gallepyn, in the kitching. **1578** *Househ. Ord.* (1790) 252 Gallapines; apparell for them of the hall, kytchen, and pryvy kytchin. *a* **1610** *Diet*, etc. *Dk. York* in *Archæologia* (1806) XV. 7 For the Kytchen and Gallopins. **1824** Scott *St. Ronan's W.* xxxiv, So saying, he gave the little galopin his donative, and a slight rap on the pate.

†'**galor**. *Obs.* [f. GALE *sb.*⁴ + -OR.] One who holds a 'gale' (see GALE *sb.*⁴ 4).

galore (gə'lɔə(r)), *adv.* and *sb.* Also 7–8 gil(l)ore, gallo(u)re, 9 *Sc.* gelore, *dial.* golore, galoor. [ad. Irish *go leór* (= Gaelic *gu leòr, leòir*) to sufficiency, sufficiently, enough, f. *go, gu* to + *leór* sufficiency, sufficient. Now commonly viewed as Irish; in some earlier examples the proximate source seems to have been Sc. Gaelic.] **A.** *adv.* In abundance or plenty. **B.** *sb.* Abundance or plenty (*of* something); also ***in galore***.

1675 Teonge *Diary* (1825) 25 Provinder good store, beife ..chickens, henns, gallore. **1711** E. Ward *Quix.* I. 292 Having stufft..His Guts with Food and Wine Galloure. **1768** Ross *Fort. Sheph.* I. 47 This day she fuish the best of cheer gilore. **1826** Scott *Jrnl.* 10 Apr., Sent off proofs and copy galore before breakfast. **1849** Ruxton *Life in Far West* i. 21 Galore of alcohol to ratify the trade. **1855** Reade *Clouds & Sunsh.* 8 They were set in a corner with beef and ale galore. **1863** *Tyneside Songs* 93 Aw dreamt aw..fand greet big lumps in galore.

galosh, golosh (gə'lɒʃ), *sb.* Forms: 4–9 galoche, 5–8 galloche, 5 galoch, galoge, galache, 5–7 gal(l)age, galeg(g)e, 7 galatch, galeach, galoach, golosse (? golossian), *pl.* galloshios, gala-, gal(l)oshoes, -shoos, (goloschoose, colloshoo's), 7–8 *pl.* goloshoes (rarely *sing.* goloshoe), 9 goloe-shoes, 7–8 gallosh, 7– galosh, 9 golosh, (calash, colosh). [a. F. *galoche* fem.:—(according to Hatz.-Darm.) popular L. **galopia* f. **galopus*, a. Gr. καλόπους (stem -ποδ-) shoemaker's last (whence dim. καλοπόδιον), f. κᾶλον wood (only pl. logs) + πούς foot. In med.L. *galopedium* occurs for 'wooden shoe'; see also *calopedes* in Du Cange. The Sp. *galocha*, It. *galoscia*, are prob. adopted from Fr. Some forms of the Eng. word show assimilation to *shoe*.]

1. a. In early use: A wooden shoe or sandal fastened to the foot with thongs of leather; a rustic patten or clog; a shoe with a wooden sole and an upper of leather or other soft material. The name seems to have been variously applied, and in the earliest quots. may be a general term for a boot or shoe. **b.** In later use: An over-shoe (now usually made of india-rubber) worn to protect the ordinary shoe from wet or dirt. 'Rare in U.S.' (*Cent. Dict.*).

1377 Langl. *P. Pl.* B. xviii. 14 As is þe kynde of a knyȝte þat cometh to be dubbed, To geten hem gylte spores or galoches ycouped. *c* **1386** Chaucer *Sqr.'s T.* 10868 Ne were worthy to unbokel his galoche. *c* **1440** *Promp. Parv.* 184/2

Galache, or galoche, vndyr solynge of mannys fote ..*crepitum*. **1496** *Dives & Pauper* (W. de W.) 38/1 They wente not alwaye fully barefote, but somtyme with galoches, a sole byneth and a fastnynge aboue the fote. **1523** *Act 14 & 15 Hen. VIII*, c. 9 Any showes, bootes, or galeges. **1572** BOSSEWELL *Armorie* III. 17 A Shooe called a Gallage or Patten, whiche hath nothing on the feete but onely Latchettes. **1579** SPENSER *Sheph. Cal.* Feb. 244 My galage [is] growne fast to my heele. *Gloss., Galage*, a start-uppe or clownish shoe. **1606** HEYWOOD *Challenge* I. i. (1636) 10 Some slovenly Boote, to be dabled in the durt without a Galoach. **1607-8** *Wardr. Bk. Pr. Henry* in *Archæol.* XI. 93 Sixteen gold buckles..to buckle a pair of golosses with gold, ls. **1646** in *Archæol. Cantiana* (1883) XV. 162 For a pa. of boots with goloschooes oo . 16 . oo. **1649** W. M. *Wandering Jew* (1857) 16 By his slash'd doublet, high galloshes, and Italian purld band [hee should be] a Frenchman. **1652** KIRKMAN *Clerio & Lozia* 16 He had Gloves perfum'd, his Colloshoo's of Velvet. **1665** PEPYS *Diary* 15 Nov., My Lady Batten walking through the dirty lane with new spick and span white shoes, she dropped one of her galoshes in the dirt. **1676** ETHEREDGE *Man of Mode* I. i. 15 'Tis but despising a Coach, humbling yourself To a pair of Goloshoes. **1688** R. HOLME *Armoury* III. 14/2 Galloshios are false shooes, or covers for shooes. **1713** KENNETT *Romæ Antiq. Notit.* (ed. 5) 325 The sole was of wood like our old galoches, or the sabots of the French peasants. **1737** OZELL *Rabelais* II. 219 *Galloches*, high wooden Pattins or Clogs... It also means a Sort of Slipper worn over the Shoes. **1779** JOS. BURTON *Patent Specif.* No. 1210 Improvements in women's clogs by a goloshoe or clog of an entire new make. **1823** CARLYLE *Early Lett.* (1886) II. 251, I walk to and fro with a great-coat, galoches, and a huge hairy cap. **1850** *Mechanics' Mag.* LII. 69, I have found the india-rubber goloshes invaluable. **1856** R. GARDINER *Handbk. of Foot* 54 The india-rubber and gutta-percha colosh. *a* **1863** THACKERAY *Sketches, Lady in Opera-Box*, Can I come in goloshes, and take them off in the ante-chamber? **1870** BROUGH *Marston Lynch* ii. 11 She had trudged down the road through the snow..in a hood and goloshes. **1872-6** VOYLE & STEVENSON *Milit. Dict.* (ed. 3) 167 Leather goloshes are large, loose, untanned leather boots..intended to be worn in magazines, powder-houses [etc.]..and are made..to cover the ordinary shoe or boot. **1893** EARL DUNMORE *Pamirs* II. 332 Being either obliged to remove my boots, or being supplied with large slippers to put over them like galoshes.

†**c.** ***Dutch galoshes***: skates. ? *nonce-use*.

a **1687** COTTON *Gt. Frost, Poems* (1689) 104 And had [I] but Dutch goloshoes on, At one run I would slide to Lon——.

2. A piece of leather or other material running round the lower part of a boot or shoe above the sole (sometimes as an additional covering or edging).

1853 *Boot & Shoe-maker's Assist.* 22 To cut a calash for a side-laced..boot. **1856** R. GARDINER *Handbk. of Foot* 49 The best position for this seam, whether it pertains to an Adelaide-front or a colosh. **1893** *Times* 8 July 12/2 Kid and patent leather Balmorals, and kid with calf galosh.

ga'losh, go'losh, *v.* Also 9 **calash, colosh.** [f. prec. sb.] *trans.* To furnish (a boot or shoe) with a galosh. Hence **ga'loshed** *ppl. a.*

1804 JANE AUSTEN *The Watsons* (1879) 340 Nankeen galoshed with black looks very well. **1827** HONE *Every-day Bk.* II. 1635 The shoe is of white kid leather, calashed with black velvet. **1840** BARHAM *Ingol. Leg., Grey Dolphin*, His boots..had been 'soled' and 'heeled' more than once; had they been 'goloshed', their owner might have defied Fate! **1856** R. GARDINER *Handbk. of Foot* 49 Walking or Winter Boots..coloshed with..calf leather. **1883** *London Advt.*, Calf Galoshed Clump Sole 10-Button Boots.

galoun, -own, obs. forms of GALLON.

†**galp**, *v. Obs.* (exc. as surviving in GAWP *dial.*). [Not found in OE.; the form agrees with OS. *galpôn* to boast; MDu., Du. *galpen* to yelp, bark, howl; Middle Ger. *galpen* to bark; cognate with YELP (OE. *ȝielpan* str., to boast, ON. *gialpa* to yelp).

The Eng. sense is not found in the other Teut. langs. and the etymological identity of the word is not quite certain; the Eng. vb. may be an onomatopoeic alteration of GAPE.]

1. *intr.* To gape, yawn. Of a deer: ? to pant (or perhaps to 'bell': cf. sense 3).

13.. *K. Alis.* 461 (Bodl. MS.) Þe dere galpeþ [*Lincoln's Inn MS.* galopith] by wode syde. **1377** LANGL. *P. Pl.* B. XIII. 88 And thanne shullen his guttis godele and he shal galpen after. **1401** *Pol. Poems* (Rolls) II. 100 ȝour capped maistres ..galpen after grace bi symonye ȝour sister. **1519** HORMAN *Vulg.* 46 He that galpeth, or claweth his heed, or panteth. **1532** MORE *Confut. Tindale* Wks. 709/2 The good godlye man..galpeth, and getteth hym downe of the pulpet.

b. *transf.* of a chasm. Also *fig.* to gape *after*, to be eagerly desirous of something.

1546 *Supplic. Poore Comm.* (E.E.T.S.) 81 Them that galp, and loke after the crowne of this realme after your daies. **1577** KENDALL *Flowers & Epigr.* 90b, Thy graue, which galpes, thee to deuour. **1583** STANYHURST *Æneis* III. (Arb.) 83 Charybdis..with broad iaws greedelye galping.

2. *trans.* To vomit *forth*; also *fig.*, to give *up* (the ghost).

1529 MORE *Comf. agst. Trib.* I. Wks. 1162/2 Long was it not ere they galped up the ghoste. **1558** PHAER *Æneid* III. H iv, And lompes of fleshe with wine he galpyd fourth.

¶**3.** Of an animal: To yelp.

[One of Caxton's borrowings from Du.]

1481 CAXTON *Reynard* (Arb.) 22 He mawede and galped so lowde that martynet sprang vp. *Ibid.* 95 She galped and cryde so lowde for the smarte that she had..that the men of the village cam out with stauys.

Hence †**'galping** *vbl. sb.* and *ppl. a.* Also †**'galper**, one who gapes; †**galp** *sb.*, the action of gaping.

c **1386** CHAUCER *Sqr.'s T.* 342 With a galpyng mouth hem alle he keste. **1387** TREVISA *Higden* (Rolls) V. 389 Þat pestilence..ofte slow men wiþ galpynge and snesinge. ? *a* **1500** in *Audelay's Poems* (Percy Soc.) Notes 85 Jangler cum jasper, lepar, galper quoque, draggar. **1545** RAYNOLD *Byrth Mankynde* (1564) 84b, Ouermuch galpyng and reachyng vpwardes. **1577-87** HOLINSHED *Chron.* II. 28/2 With gastlie galpe of grislie bug. **1583** STANYHURST *Æneis* III. (Arb.) 91 In belche galp vometing with dead sleape snortye the collops.

galpon (gæl'pəʊn). [Local name.] In South America, a building given to the use of labourers on a farm.

1894 *Proc. Zool. Soc.* 305 Behind some wood piled up at the side of the big galpon. **1918** W. H. HUDSON *Far Away & Long Ago* xiv. 193 My father went to the *galpon*, the big barnlike building used for storing wood, hides, and horsehair. **1961** G. DURRELL *Whispering Land* (1965) iii. 67 A small white *estancia*..and to left of it a large Dutch barn or *galpón*.

galravage, -itch, etc.: see GILRAVAGE, *Sc.*

†**galstre**, *v. Obs. rare*$^{-1}$. Also gelstre. [perh. some kind of derivative of OE. *galan* GALE *v.* to sing, cry out (? through a fem. agent-n. in *-stre*); Ger. dialects have *galstern, gelstern* to scream, make a noise, associated with *galster* (? repr. OHG. *âgalstria*) magpie. The word survives in GAUSTER *dial.* to boast, to laugh uproariously.]

intr. To make a noise or outcry.

a **1225** *Ancr. R.* 128 Gelstreð [*v.r.* galstres], ase þe uox deð, & ȝelpeð of hore god.

Galsworthian (gɔːlz'wɜːðɪən), *a.* [f. the name of John *Galsworthy* (1867-1933), English novelist and playwright.] Of, pertaining to, or characteristic of John Galsworthy or his work.

1912 *Eng. Rev.* June 494 A grim, almost Galsworthian, unpleasantness. **1928** *Daily Express* 24 May 10/6 A tight-lipped Galsworthian pessimist like the Duke of Wellington or Lord Kitchener. **1936** *Times Lit. Suppl.* 3 Oct. 789/1 For her fellow-mortals..she has an almost Galsworthian compassion.

galt. *Obs.* exc. *dial.* Also 5 **galte**, 7 **gawt, gaute, gault.** [a. ON. *gǫlt-r* str., *galte* wk. masc., boar; cf. OHG. *galza, gelza* sow (MHG. *galze, gelze*, mod.G. *gelze*; related to GILT *sb.*).] A boar or hog.

? *a* **1400** *Morte Arth.* 1101 Greesse growene as a galte, fulle grylych he lukez! *a* **1400-50** *Alexander* 4743 Vmquile he groned as a galt with gryzely latis. *a* **1500** *Colkelbie Sow* I. 160 Mony long tuthit bore, And mony galt, come befoir. **1552** HULOET, Galt, or yonge hogge..*porcetra*. **1641** BEST *Farm. Bks.* (Surtees) 142 Libbers have..nothinge for the gautes, for they will geld them as fast as they can take them upp. **1673** *Yorksh. Dial.* 8 (E.D.S. No. 76) Me draugh's for th' Gilts and Gaults i' th' Sty. **1684** *Ibid.* 83 Than thou may sarra Gawts and Gilts with Draffe. **1895** *Lakeland & Iceland Gloss., Galt*, a male pig.

galt: see GAULT, *Geol.*

galt(h)rop(e, -trap, -troppe, obs. ff. CALTROP.

Galton ('gɔːltən). The name of Sir Francis *Galton* (1822-1911), English scientist and anthropologist, used in: ***Galton's law***, the formula proposed by him to account for ancestral heredity, by which the parents each contribute a quarter of the characters to their offspring, the grandparents each contribute an eighth of the characters, and so on; also, the tendency of offspring of outstanding parentage to regress to, or below, the average for the species; so ***Galton's curve***, etc.; ***Galton('s) whistle*** (see quots). Hence **Gal'tonian** *a.*

1889 A. R. WALLACE *Darwinism* xiv. 414 'Panmixia', or free intercrossing, will co-operate with Galton's law of 'regression towards mediocrity', and the result will be that ..the organ in question will rapidly decrease till it reaches a mean value considerably below the mean of the progeny that has usually been produced each year. **1890** W. JAMES *Princ. Psychol.* I. x. 298 One may, I think, without fear of being upset by any further Galtonian circulars, believe that all men must single out from the rest of what they call themselves some central principle. **1903** *Daily Chron.* 31 July 5/2 'Galton's law',..now one of the cardinal principles of biology. **1904** J. A. & M. R. THOMSON tr. *Weismann's Evol. Theory* II. 206 Galton's curve of frequency of variations. **1904** GOODCHILD & TWENEY *Technol. & Sci. Dict.* 245/1 *Galton's whistle*, a sounding pipe, resembling in principle a very small closed organ pipe, producing a note of very high frequency. Used in experiments on the limit of audition. **1907** V. L. KELLOGG *Darwinism To-day* 71 Variation..is subject to Galton's law of regression. **1908** J. A. THOMSON *Heredity* ix. 335 Mendelian formulæ apply to the progeny of known crosses or hybrids, while Galtonian formulæ apply to intra-racial heredity. **1931** *Discovery* Apr. 106/2 It might be a Galton whistle, which is too high-pitched to be audible to man. **1953** A. HUXLEY *Let.* 21 June (1969) 676 Do Galtonian visualizers react in a different way from non-visualizers.

galumph (gə'lʌmf), *v.* [Invented by 'L. Carroll' (perh. with some reminiscence of *gallop, triumphant*). The sense in current use may vary according to different notions of what the sound expresses. Cf. CHORTLE *v.*] *intr.* Orig., to march on exultingly with irregular bounding movements. Now usu., to gallop heavily; to bound or move clumsily or noisily. Hence **ga'lumphing** *ppl. a.* and *vbl. sb.*, *lit.* and *fig.*

1872 'L. CARROLL' *Through Looking-Glass* i. 22 He left it dead, and with its head He went galumphing back. **1881** *Punch* 27 Aug. 94/2 The [H.M.S.] *Hercules* got up steam and went on her way westward galumphing. **1888** *N. York World* 13 May (Farmer), A green bobtail car that galumphed through Lewis Street at a high rate of speed. **1891** *Harper's Mag.* Aug. 378/2 He [a dog] became a.. playful, gracefully galumphing, and most affectionate monster. **1893** *Nation* (N.Y.) 29 June 476/2 It is his humor, his 'galumphing' humor, which strikes a chill to the heart. **1901** *Westm. Gaz.* 15 Aug. 2/2 A postman in uniform galumphed about on a farm-horse. **1903** *Daily Chron.* 31 Oct. 8/1 There would be such a galumphing up their stairs that peace and security would forsake them. **1930** C. MACKENZIE *April Fools* xii. 271 Viola..had slept through the stifled cries of her parents beneath the bedclothes when Beyle [*sc.* a bull-dog] was galumphing round their room. **1965** S. RAVEN *Friends in Low Places* vi. 129 In the hall was a galumphing lass with a lot of jerseys and a po face.

galumptious: see GOLUPTIOUS *a.*

galun, obs. form of GALLON.

galvanic (gæl'vænɪk), *a.* [f. GALVAN-ISM + -IC. Cf. F. *galvanique*.] **a.** Of, pertaining to, or produced by galvinism. ***galvanic battery***, an apparatus constructed for the production of galvanic electricity. ***galvanic belt***, a belt containing a galvanic apparatus to be worn round the body for therapeutic purposes. ***galvanic electricity*** = GALVANISM. ***galvanic pile***, a 'pile' (see quot. 1802) for the production of galvanic electricity. ***galvanic skin response*** (or ***reflex***), the rapid variation in the electrical conductivity of the skin as a measure of the effect of an emotional stimulus on autonomic activity.

1797 *Monthly Mag.* III. 348 The acrid humour which the Galvanic irritation would produce. **1801** *Phil. Mag.* X. 93 He [*sc.* Cruickshank] employs a galvanic battery of his own invention. **1802** *Med. Jrnl.* VIII. 524 The Galvanic pile of Volta..consisted of thirty pieces of silver, and as many of zinc..with pieces of cloth that were dipped in a saturated solution of common salt. *Ibid.* 553 The Galvanic belt is an electrical apparatus, constantly in action as long as it is worn. **1803** LAMB *Lett.* (1888) I. 206 'Tis a gentle ghost, and in this Galvanic age it may have a chance. **1856** EMERSON *Eng. Traits, Race* Wks. (Bohn) II. 23 Perhaps the Ocean serves as a galvanic battery to distribute acids at one pole, and alkalies at the other. **1869** W. P. MACKAY *Grace & Truth* (1875) 238 The movements in Christian service of an unconverted man are the galvanic movements of a corpse. **1927** C. W. DARROW in *Jrnl. Exper. Psychol.* X. 197 Employing the term *galvanic skin reflex* (galvanische Hautreflex) because it is less misleading than the term psychogalvanic reflex. **1962** *Listener* 19 Apr. 691/2 With special instruments you can measure electrical changes in the skin when a person is emotionally upset or aroused, changes which we call the galvanic skin response, and which are made use of in the so-called 'lie detector'.

b. *fig.* with allusion to the effects of the application of galvanism.

1807 OPIE in *Lect. Paint.* iii. (1848) 292 This is mere galvanic encouragement; it may excite a few convulsive twitches, but will never inspire the arts with life and efficient activity. **1831** [see GALVANIZE *v.* 1]. **1852** HAWTHORNE *Mosses, Feathertop*, Purposing a smile of courtesy, he had deformed his face with a sort of galvanic grin. **1865** DICKENS *Mut. Fr.* I. x, Drops asleep, and has galvanic starts all over him.

Hence **gal'vanical** *a.*, **gal'vanically** *adv.*

1840 WHEWELL *Philos. Induct. Sc.* I. 263 The phenomena of magnets, of electrical bodies, of galvanical apparatus, seem to form obvious material for such sciences. **1848** LYTTON *Caxtons* II. VII. xxxiii, Galvanically I brace up energies half palsied by disuse. **1869** *Eng. Mech.* 19 Nov. 229/3 Copper..tinned (galvanically). **1890** BOLDREWOOD *Col. Reformer* (1891) 103 The..animal bounded galvanically upward.

galvanism ('gælvənɪz(ə)m). [a. F. *galvanisme*, f. the name of Luigi Galvani who first described the phenomena in 1792: see -ISM.] Electricity developed by chemical action. Also, the application of this for therapeutic purposes.

1797 *Monthly Mag.* III. 224 Volta..is employed..on an extensive work relative to Metallic Influence, or Galvanism. **1806** SURR *Winter in Lond.* (ed. 3) II. 179 He expects, by learning Galvanism, to be able to bring his dead horses to life again. **1862** GOULBURN *Pers. Relig.* ii. (1873) 12 But Galvanism is not the life; it only rouses the dormant powers of life. **1870** EMERSON *Soc. & Solit., Civiliz.* Wks. (Bohn) III. 11 The forces of steam, gravity, galvanism..serve us day by day.

galvanist ('gælvənɪst). [f. GALVAN-ISM + -IST.] One who is versed in galvanism.

1805 R. CHENEVIX in *Phil. Trans.* XCV. 113 M. Ritter, the celebrated Galvanist of Jena. **1866** M. MACKENZIE *Laryngoscope* vi. (ed. 2) 100 External faradization was vigorously employed by an experienced galvanist.

galvanistical (ˌgælvə'nɪstɪkəl), *a.* [f. prec. + -IC + -AL[1].] Of, pertaining to, or versed in galvanism.

1816 T. L. PEACOCK *Headlong Hall* iii, Mr. Panscope the chemical, botanical, galvanistical..philosopher.

galvanization (gælvənaɪ'zeɪʃən). [f. GALVANIZE *v.* + -ATION.]

1. The process of subjecting (a person, nerve, etc.) to the action of galvanism.

1860 in FOWLER *Med. Voc.* **1874** CARPENTER *Ment. Phys.* App. (1879) 712 In the galvanization of an ordinary nerve. **1876** DUHRING *Dis. Skin* 227 Central galvanization is also recommended.

2. The state of being galvanized. In quot. *fig.*

1875 *Contemp. Rev.* XXVI. 435 A kind of galvanization produced by fear.

galvanize ('gælvənaɪz), *v.* Also -ise. [ad. F. *galvaniser*: see GALVANISM and -IZE.]

1. *trans.* To apply galvanism to; to stimulate by means of a galvanic current. Also *absol.*

1802 *Med. Jrnl.* VIII. 259 The heat is likewise increased in the part which is galvanised. **1825** SYD. SMITH *Wks.* (1867) II. 203 Galvanise a frog, don't galvanise a tiger. **1831** CARLYLE *Sart. Res.* (1858) 142 Those spasmodic, galvanic sprawlings are not life; neither indeed will they endure, galvanise as you may, beyond two days. **1839–47** TODD *Cycl. Anat.* III. 41/2, I galvanized a little boy with paralysis of the left leg. **1850** ROBERTSON *Serm.* Ser. III. ix. 117 You may galvanize the nerve of a corpse till the action of a limb startles the spectator with the appearance of life.

b. *fig. esp.* in phrase ***to galvanize to*** or ***into life*** (also ***to galvanize life into***).

1853 C. BRONTË *Villette* iii, Her approach always galvanized him to new and spasmodic life. **1869** GOULBURN *Purs. Holiness* xxi. 203 She would fain galvanize the soul into life by a sudden shock. **1880** *Daily News* 9 Jan. 3/1 To galvanise a little more life into the market. **1883** *Harper's Mag.* Mar. 537/1 A very old inn, that seemed suffering the first pangs of being galvanized back to life and modernity.

2. To cover with a coating of metal by means of galvanic electricity. Commonly but incorrectly applied to the coating of iron with zinc to protect it from rusting, though no galvanic process is ordinarily employed.

1839 [see GALVANIZED *ppl. a.* 2]. **1864** WEBSTER, *Galvanize*, to plate, as with gold, silver, &c., by means of galvanism. **1869** ROSCOE *Elem. Chem.* 230 Zinc..is employed as a protecting covering for iron, which when thus coated is said to be galvanized. **1879** *Cassell's Techn. Educ.* I. 61/2 The wire is 'galvanised' or coated with metallic zinc.

absol. **1892** *Workshop Receipts* 287 It is an advantage, with all sheets thicker than 20 gauge, to galvanize after corrugation.

galvanized ('gælvənaɪzd), *ppl. a.* [f. GALVANIZE *v.* + -ED[1].]

1. Subjected to, or stimulated by, galvanism.

1820 *Med. & Phys. Jrnl.* XLIII. 387 The lungs of the galvanized rabbit had some blotches on their surface.

b. *fig.*

1843 CARLYLE *Past & Pr.* II. xv, Dead or galvanised Dilettantism. **1873** MISS BROUGHTON *Nancy* III. 99, I practise a galvanised smile, and say out loud..'Yes, delightful!' **1873** F. HALL in *Scribner's Monthly* VI. 466/1 Within a few years a galvanized sort of life has been seen breathed into the investigation, by Hindus, of their ancient scriptures.

2. Coated with metal by galvanism. Also, incorrectly, in ***galvanized iron***, the trade name of iron coated with zinc.

1839 URE *Dict. Arts*, *Galvanized iron*, is the somewhat fantastic name newly given in France to iron tinned by a peculiar patent process. **1860** *Merc. Marine Mag.* VII. 114 The galvanized rings..run..along the..rod. **1887** RIDER HAGGARD *Jess* xxviii, The stables and outhouses..were roofed with galvanised iron.

galvanizer ('gælvənaɪzə(r)). [f. GALVANIZE *v.* + -ER[1].] One who or that which galvanizes.

1864 in WEBSTER. **1883** *West Chester* (Pennsylv.) *Local News* XII. No. 28. 1 The galvanizers in Oliver and Roberts' wire mill..struck on Wednesday. **1887** *Daily News* 24 Oct. 2/5 Tin plate makers and galvanisers are tolerably well engaged.

galvanizing ('gælvənaɪzɪŋ), *vbl. sb.* [f. as prec. + -ING[1].] The action of the verb GALVANIZE; the process of galvanizing (iron).

1860 PIESSE *Lab. Chem. Wonders* 12 This operation, which is called galvanising, entirely prevents the iron from rusting. **1883** *Pall Mall G.* 14 Nov. 12/2 Industries in which women are largely employed—that is to say, chain-making, brick-making, and the galvanizing of iron. **1891** *Engineer* 4 Sept. 199 The zinc is electropositive to the iron, and its corrosion takes place while the iron is protected; this circumstance gave rise to the use of the word 'galvanising'.

attrib. **1854** DICKENS *Hard T.* (1868) 2 He seemed a galvanizing apparatus, too.

galvano- ('gælvənəʊ), used as combining form of GALVANIC or GALVANISM, in various hyphened compounds, as **galvano-caustic** *a.*, relating to the use of galvanic heat as a caustic; **galvano-caustics**, 'the science of the galvano-cautery' (*Syd. Soc. Lex.* 1885); **galvano-cauterization**, cauterization by means of the galvano-cautery; **galvano-cautery**, a cautery heated by galvanism; **galvano-ceramics**, ? pottery coated with metal by electro-deposition; **galvano-magnetic** *a.*, pertaining to galvano-magnetism; **galvano-magnetism**, magnetism produced by galvanic electricity; **galvano-motive** *a.*, ? moved by galvanism; **galvano-puncture**, the introduction into the tissues of fine needles, connected with the poles of a galvanic battery; **galvano-therapeutics**, 'the use of galvanism for the cure or relief of disease' (*Syd. Soc. Lex.* 1885); **galvano-thermometer**, 'an instrument for measuring the heating effect of a galvanic current' (Cassell).

1862 *New Syd. Soc. Year-bk.* 238 The *Galvano-caustic Apparatus. **1872** COHEN *Dis. Throat* 91 Severing the parts with the *galvano-cautery instead of the knife. **1874** VAN BUREN *Dis. Genit. Org.* 9 Galvano-cautery may be employed in amputation. **1844** *Art Union Jrnl.* July 229 The new productions of this novel art have received the affected name of *galvano-ceramics. **1838** *Proc. Amer. Phil. Soc.* I. 65 Rotary Multiplier or *Galvano-motive needle. **1872** J. H. BENNETT *Physiol.* 155 The operation of *galvano-puncture, first proposed by M. Prevaz in 1833.

galvanograph ('gælvənəʊgrɑːf, -græf). [f. GALVANO- + -GRAPH.] 'A plate formed by the galvanographic process; an impression taken from such a plate' (Ogilvie). Hence **ˌgalvano'graphic** *a.*, pertaining to galvanography.

galvanography (gælvə'nɒgrəfɪ). [f. as prec. + Gr. -γραφία writing.] **a.** 'A method of producing plates for copperplate engraving by the galvanoplastic process without etching' (Ogilvie). **b.** (See quot.)

1854 FAIRHOLT *Dict. Art*, *Galvanography*..is one of the most beautiful and successful inventions of modern times, as by its means plastic objects..may be exactly copied in copper, and bronzed or gilt.

galvanology (gælvə'nɒlədʒɪ). [f. GALVANO- + -LOGY.] 'A treatise on galvanism, or a description of its phenomena' (Craig 1848). So **galva'nologist**, 'one who describes the phenomena of galvanism' (Craig 1848).

galvanometer (gælvə'nɒmɪtə(r)). [f. GALVANO- + METER.] An apparatus for detecting the existence and determining the direction and intensity of a galvanic current.

1802 *Med. Jrnl.* VIII. 253 The piles..showed no remarkable difference in their effects; however, I do not deny that some difference may be perceived by means of the Galvano-meters. **1830** HERSCHEL *Stud. Nat. Phil.* 356 The galvanometer..an instrument whose range of utility lies among electric forces which we have no other means of rendering sensible. **1832** *Nat. Philos.*, *Electro-Magnet.* viii. §125. 44 (U.K.S.) For the purpose of comparing the intensities of two electrical currents, an instrument has been contrived, which has been termed the Differential Galvanometer. **1862** LYTTON *Str. Story* I. 165 If you clutch the cylinder firmly with the right hand, leaving the left perfectly passive, the needle in the galvanometer will move from west to south. **1877** ROSENTHAL *Muscle & Nerves* 162 Another form of apparatus, called the tangent galvanometer. **1879** G. PRESCOTT *Sp. Telephone* p. iii, Sir William Thomson..has given us the beautifully sensitive mirror galvanometer.

Hence **ˌgalvano'metric**, **ˌgalvano'metrical** *adjs.*, pertaining to the galvanometer or to galvanometry. **galva'nometry**, the measurement of galvanic currents.

1845 GROVE *Contrib. Sc.* in *Corr. Phys. Forces* (1874) 290 The second gave not the slightest galvanometric deflection. **1875** GAMGEE tr. *Hermann's Hum. Phys.* (1878) 287 The muscular current may be demonstrated by methods other than the galvanometric. **18..** *Engineer* LXV. 510 (Cent.) The parts of the stand include..the necessary clamping screws for electrical and galvanometrical connections.

galvanoplastic (ˌgælvənəʊ'plæstɪk), *a.* [f. as next + -IC.] Of or pertaining to galvanoplasty.

1848 *Art Union Jrnl.* Feb. 49 It is placed in a galvano-plastic apparatus, in which it remains till it is galvano-plastically covered. **1851** R. HUNT in *Art Jrnl. Illust. Catal.* I. p. iv*/2 The applicability of the galvano-plastic Art, as our Continental friends delight to call it, to the production of large works. **1867** *Philatelist* I. 165 The galvanoplastic multiplication of the types.

Hence **ˌgalvano'plastically** *adv.*

1848 [see prec.]. **1882** *Nature* XXVI. 144 A series of organic bodies coated galvanoplastically.

galvanoplasty (ˌgælvənəʊ'plæstɪ). [f. GALVANO- + Gr. -πλαστ-ός moulded + -Y[3]. In F. *galvanoplastie*.] The process of coating any substance with metal by galvanism.

1870 *Eng. Mech.* 18 Mar. 651/2 Galvanoplasty can be applied to coat this silver with a surface of copper. **1887** *Pall Mall G.* 29 Sept. 2/3 The necessary deposit on the plate is produced (which renders it capable of printing impressions like a mezzotint plate) by means of the electric pile—the process of galvanoplastie, that is to say.

galvanoscope ('gælvənəʊˌskəʊp). [f. GALVANO- + Gr. -σκόπος looker.] An instrument for ascertaining the presence of galvanic electricity.

1832 *Nat. Philos.*, *Electro-Magnet.* viii. §111. 39 (U.K.S.) An instrument for detecting small quantities of galvanic electricity, or Galvanoscope. **1866** R. M. FERGUSON *Electr.* 141 The Astatic Galvanometer..is used either simply as a galvanoscope, to discover the existence of a current, or as a measurer of the strengths of weak currents.

Hence **ˌgalvano'scopic** *a.*, pertaining to, or of the nature of, a galvanoscope; ***galvanoscopic frog***, a frog used as a galvanoscope. **galva'noscopy**, 'the employment of galvanism in physiological experiment or for diagnostic purposes; also, the use of the galvanoscope' (*Syd. Soc. Lex.* 1885).

1839–47 TODD *Cycl. Anat.* III. 720/2 This preparation is the galvanoscopic frog. **1843** GROVE *Contrib. Sc.* in *Corr. Phys. Forces* (1874) 266 Here we have no slight galvanoscopic effects. **1870** *Eng. Mech.* 11 Mar. 626/1 Galvanoscopic Lantern. **1873** A. FLINT *Nerv. Syst.* iii. 113 If the nerve of a galvanoscopic frog's leg be placed in contact with the muscles of another leg prepared in the same way.

galvanotaxis (ˌgælvənəʊ'tæksɪs). *Biol.* [mod.L., f. GALVANO- + Gr. τάξις arrangement.] The disposition exhibited by certain organisms of movement in relation to the direction of an electric current or field. Hence **ˌgalvano'tactic** *a.*

1899 F. S. LEE tr. *Verworn's Gen. Physiol.* v. 455 Galvanotaxis. It is characteristic of the galvanic current that it always calls out phenomena of polar excitation. **1905** Galvanotactic [see ANODIC *a.* 3]. **1961** *New Scientist* 3 Aug. 278 The voltage gradient across the width of the fish is sufficient to induce galvanotaxis and turn it in the direction of the positive electrode. **1965** *Ibid.* 29 Apr. 303/1 The orientation of the whole organism during exposure to direct current—the phenomenon known as 'galvanotactic' or 'electrotactic' response.

galva'notropism [f. GALVANO- + Gr. τρόπ-ος turning + -ISM.] The phenomenon of curvature produced in growing plant-organs by the passage of electric currents through them; movement produced in plants or animals by the stimulus of an electric current. Hence **ˌgalvano'tropic** *a.*

1885 VINES in *Encycl. Brit.* XIX. 60 These phenomena are spoken of as 'galvanotropism'. **1895** *Science Progress* IV. 100 The essential fact upon which the galvanotropic effect turns is that current down the animal has a quieting action, current up the animal an exciting action. *Ibid.* 101 Fertilised frog's eggs..exhibit remarkable galvanotropic effects. *Ibid.*, There is in many cases a remarkable orientation in relation to the current—'galvanotropism'. **1918** J. LOEB *Forced Movements* iv. 41 Galvanotropic reactions are found throughout the whole animal kingdom. *Ibid.* 42 Phenomena of galvanotropism can be observed also in infusorians. **1936** *Discovery* June 198/1 The planarian *Leptoplana variabilis* is negatively phototropic and kathodically galvanotropic. **1959** T. H. SAVORY *Instinctive Living* iii. 28 Some of them are synonyms—e.g. electrotropism and galvanotropism.

Galvayne ('gælveɪn). The name of Sidney *Galvayne*, a writer on horses, used *attrib.* to designate a method or devices for breaking in a horse; so as *v. trans.*, to break in (a horse) by Galvayne's method; so **Gal'vayning** *vbl. sb.* Also ***Galvayne's mark*** (see quot. 1908).

1905 S. GALVAYNE *20th Cent. Bk. Horse* 23 'Galvayning' is really a scientific utilization of the animal's strength against itself... The 'Galvayne' position is attained by tying the animal's head round with the halter-shank, or the 'Galvayne' strap, to its tail. *Ibid.* 29 Once you have got the horse properly 'Galvayned', watch it carefully for a little while before proceeding further. *Ibid.* 32 If the animal be 'Galvayned' on the 'near' side, the trainer must work on the 'off'. **1908** *Animal Managem.* 43 At ten years 'Galvayne's mark', a depression on the outer side of the upper corner incisor, appears. **1911** *Encycl. Brit.* XIII. 725/1 Galvayning is accomplished by bending the horse's neck round at an angle of thirty-five to forty degrees and tieing the halter to the tail. **1942** 'M. INNES' *Daffodil Affair* I. v. 31 Well I always suspected rareying with Daffodil—though, mind you, it may have been galvayning all the same.

[**galverly**, *adv.* Explained as: Cleverly, actively. Error for *galierdly*, GALLIARDLY.

1836 in RICHARDSON [quoting Wriothesley *To Sir T. Wyatt* Oct. 1537, A light gennet that is young and trotteth galverly; but the orig. MS. reads *galierdly*]. Hence in some later Dicts.]

Galwegian (gæl'wiːdʒɪən), *a.* and *sb.* Also **Gallowegian**. [f. *Galloway*, on the analogy of *Norroway*, *Norway*, *Norwegian*. See GALLOVIDIAN.] **A.** *adj.* Belonging to Galloway. **B.** *sb.* An inhabitant or native of Galloway.

1774 COLLYER *Hist. Eng.* II. 72 The Galwegians..charged with..fury. **1828** SCOTT *F.M. Perth* xi, The barbarous Galwegians, and licentious followers of the Douglas. **1870** RAMSAY *Remin.* iii. (ed. 18) 64 An old Gallowegian lady. **1883** *Athenæum* 22 Dec. 814/1 Is Kelly a Bristol name? It has to modern ears an Irish or Galwegian ring.

galyet, obs. form of GALLIOT[1].

†**galyor**. *Obs.*[−1] A trade designation of some kind; possibly = Du. *gleyer* (dealer in earthenware brought in galleys: see GALLIPOT), or GALLEYMAN 2.

c **1515** *Cocke Lorell's B.* (Percy Soc.) 9 Whyte tanners, galyors, and shethers.

galziekte (gaːl'ziːktə, ||'xalziktə). Also **gallziekte**. [Du.] = *gall-sickness* (GALL *sb.*[1] 8). Also *attrib.*

1871 J. MACKENZIE *10 Yrs. N. Orange River* xiii. 261 Examination of the horse after death throws little light upon the subject. The Dutch call it 'gall-ziekte'; the English, inflammation. **1875** [see *gall-sickness* s.v. GALL *sb.*[1] 8]. **1912** *Agric. Jrnl. Union S. Afr.* Aug. 177 A strong smelling weed, often sent to us under the name of *galziekte bosch*, and considered by many farmers to be a cure for galziekte.

gam (gam), *sb.*[1] *Sc.* [Perh. onomatopœic. Cf. GAMP *v.*

The formation may have been partly suggested by some of the many words with initial *ga-* that refer to prominent or ugly teeth; cf. *gabbed, gag-tooth, gang-tooth, gap-tooth, gat-tooth*, etc. An adj. '*gam*, overlapping and twisted, applied only to the teeth' cited from a Banff Glossary (Jam. 1880), may perh. have arisen from the attrib. use of the sb. Etymological connexion with *gum* (Sc. obs. *gume*, OE. *góma*) seems to be phonologically impossible.]

1. In *pl.* Large teeth, tusks.

? *a* **1500** *Rowlis Cursing* 18 He that saulis saifis and dammis Beteich the devill thair guttis and gammis. **1508** KENNEDIE *Flyting w. Dunbar* 363 Thou wald be fayn to gnaw, lad, with thy gammis..banis behynd doggis bakkis. **1513** DOUGLAS *Æneis* v. viii. 98 Scheddis of bluid furth spittand throw his lippis, With bludy gammis [L. *dentes*]. **1535** STEWART *Cron. Scot.* I. 415 With glowrand ene and girnand gammis greit. **1825–80** JAMIESON *s.v.*, In Ang[us]..they say *greit gams*, large teeth; sometimes, *gams o' teeth*.

2. (Perh. only *arch.* and confounded with GUM.) The mouth.

1724 RAMSAY *Evergreen* II. 20 (altered from Dunbar) Quod scho, my Clip, my unspaynd Lam [*Dunb.* gyane], With Mither's Milk ȝit in your Gam [*Dunb.* mychane]. **1840** *Bauld Braxy Tam* in *Whistle-Binkie* (Scot. Songs) (1890) I. 239 Wi' a black bushy beard and a liquory gam.

gam (gæm), *sb.*[2] *Naut.* [Perh. a dial. var. of GAME *sb.*, or adopted from some Scandinavian equivalent; cf. Da. *gammen*, Sw. *gamman*, Icel. *gaman*, sport, amusement, pleasure; but the Da. and Sw. dicts. do not record any technical sense as current among whalers.] **a.** A herd or school of whales. **b.** A social meeting of whalers at sea.

1850 SCORESBY *Whaleman's Adv.* xiii. (1859) 184 Gam is the word by which they designate the meeting, exchanging visits, and keeping company of two or more whale ships, or a sociable family of whales. **1851** H. MELVILLE *Whale* II. xi. 75 What does the whaler do when she meets another whaler in any sort of decent weather? She has a gam.

gam (gæm), *sb.*[3] *slang.* [Prob. the same as GAMB.] A leg.

1781 G. PARKER *Life's Painter* 143 If a man has bow legs, he has queer gams, gams being cant for legs. **1790** *Bystander* 391 It was not a fortnight before my gam came round again as well as ever. **1823** *New Monthly Mag.* VIII. 497, I was 'ware of him, and whipping out my gam, clutched him by shoulder and brisket. **1887** HENLEY *Villon's Gd. Nt.* iii, At you I merely lift my gam.

Comb. **1781** G. PARKER *Life's Painter* 173 Stockings—Gam-cases.

gam (gæm), *v.* [Cf. GAM *sb.*[2]]

1. *intr.* Of whales: To gather together and form a 'gam' or school.

1889 in *Century Dict.*

2. *trans.* Of whalers: To meet and hold intercourse with (the crew of another ship). Also *intr.*

1890 *Century Mag., Aug.* XL. 510/2 To 'gam' means to gossip. The word occurs again and again in the log-books of the old whalers. **1892** *N. York Sun* 1 May 1/2 (Funk), On Sept. 20 we met the bark Atlantic..and 'gammed' her.

3. *U.S. slang.* 'To engage in social intercourse; to make a call; to have a chat' (Farmer).

Hence **'gamming** *vbl. sb.*

1851 H. MELVILLE *Whale* liii. 268 There is another little item about Gamming which must not be forgotten here. **1890** *Century Mag., Aug.* XL. 511/1 Gamming is indeed a relic of one of the most romantic, and perhaps pathetic, phases of the whaler's life.

gam, obs. and dial. f. GAME; var. GAMME.

gamache, gamachio, obs. ff. GAMASH.

gama grass ('gæmə ˌgrɑːs, ˌgræs). Also **gamma grass.** [?Altered form of GRAMA[1].] (See quot. 1858.)

1858 SIMMONDS *Dict. Trade, Gama Grass*, a tall and esteemed fodder grass, the *Tripsacum dactyloides* of Linnæus, native of the south-eastern coasts of North America. **1883** *Times* 19 May 5 Eastward are..acres..well clothed with good strong closely-set Gamma Grasses.

† **gamahe, gamaieu.** *Obs.* See also CAMAIEU. [a. OF. *gamahe, gamahieu* (F. *camaieu*) = med.L. *gamahei* pl., Sp. *gamaeo*, MHG. *gamahee, gamahoe* CAMEO.] A cameo; also, a stone bearing natural markings resembling pictorial or ornamental figures, formerly valued as a talisman.

1638 JUNIUS *Paint. Ancients* 95 Lovers of..rarities use to call such a casuall painting of Nature, as commeth neere unto Art by the name *Gamahè*. **1656** BLOUNT *Glossogr.*, *Gamahez* (Arab.), are Talismans are Images, or Figures made by art, under certain Constellations; so Gamahez are such figures found so wrought by nature, held to be of greater vertue, being therefore worn by some persons. **1664** EVELYN *Sylva* (1776) 156 This wood [Ash] is nothing inferior to that of the Maple..being altogether as exquisitely diapered and waved like the Gamahes of Achates. **1678** CUDWORTH *Intell. Syst.* 856 Such beings as have fancy in them, commonly called animals—which are but some of sportful or wanton natures, more trimly artificial and finer gamaieus, or pretty toys.

gamahuche ('gæməhuːʃ), *v.* *slang.* Also **gamaruche.** [ad. Fr. *gamahucher.*] *trans.* To practise fellatio or cunnilingus (with); also *intr.* Also as *sb.* Hence **gamahucher.**

1865 E. SELLON *New Epicurean* (1875) 13 'Quick, quick, Blanche!' cried Cerise, 'come and gamahuche the gentleman.' **1867** —— *Ups & Downs of Life* 91 in H. S. Ashbee *Index Librorum Prohibitorum* (1877) 389 Augusta would strip naked, place herself in any attitude, let me gamahuche her, would gamahuche in her turn. **1868** *Index Expurgatorius of Martial* 15 Lesbia was a gamahucher. *Ibid.* 33 They agreed wonderfully well in both being gamahuchers. *Ibid.* 47 So I think no objection he'll raise, To a gamahuche even from you. **1879–80** *Pearl* (1970) 271 You may frig and gamahuche and try every plan, But fair fucking's the pride of an Englishman. **1888** P. PERRET *Tableaux Vivants* ix. 73 My dear, do you know, this is my only ambition! To gamahuche a lady of fashion! *c* **1888–94** *My Secret Life* X. 5 She gave me a gamahuche for a few minutes. **1893** FARMER & HENLEY *Slang* III. 107 Gamaruche. **1968** PARTRIDGE *Dict. Underworld* (ed. 3) 854 *French, go down, nosh*, are prostitutes'..verbs..for 'to gamaruche' a man.

gamald, obs. form of GAMBOL.

gamalian, obs. form of CHAMELEON.

c **1440** *Jacob's Well* (E.E.T.S.) 151 A lyere is lykenyd to a bryd, clepyd gamaltan [*read* gamalian]. þis bryd..wyl chaungyn hym to alle colourys, þat he seeth.

gamarstangue, var. GAMMERSTANG.

gamash (gə'mæʃ), *arch.* and *dial.* Chiefly in *pl.* Forms: 6 *sing.* **gamash,** 6–7 *pl.* **gamoshes,** 7 **gamaches, -chios, -shees, gammases, gama-, gammashoes,** 8–9 **gamashers,** 8 **gamogins,** 9 **gamashins (-ons),** 6– **gamashes.** [a. F. *gamache* (now only dial.) = It. *gamascia*, Pr. *garamacha, galamacha*; identified by Dozy with Sp. *guadamaci*, Pg. *guadamecim* (now obsolete), a kind of leather, believed to be a. Arab. *ghadāmasī*, f. the name of Ghadāmas in Tripoli, where a highly esteemed kind of leather was made.

In some of the forms the ending has evidently been assimilated to *shoes*.]

A kind of leggings or gaiters, worn to protect the legs from mud and wet.

1596 NASHE *Saffron Walden* 48 No French gowtie-leg with a gamash vpon it, is so gotchie and boystrous. **1607** MARSTON *What You Will* I. ii, My velvet slippers, cloth-of-gold gamashes: where are my cloth of silver hose? **1688** R. HOLME *Armoury* III. 13/1 He beareth Argent, a Roman Hose of Stockin, Sable..of us they are called Buskins and Gamashes. **1781** HUTTON *Tour to Caves* Gloss., *Gamashes*, Gamogins, a sort of spatterdashes. **1826** SCOTT *Woodst.* xxi, The leathern gamashes which defended his legs. **1855** ROBINSON *Whitby Gloss.*, *Gamashes*, gaiters or leggings of cloth or leather; called also spatterdashes.

gamasid ('gæməsɪd). [f. mod.L. *Gamas-us* (name of the typical genus introduced by Latreille in 1802) + -ID.] A parasitic mite of the family *Gamasidæ* of the order *Acarida*, the beetle-mite or spider-mite.

1891 A. D. MICHAEL in *Proc. Zool. Soc. Lond.* 638 (*title*) On the Association of Gamasids with Ants. *Ibid.* 643 Such a Gamasid as *L[ælaps] cuneifer*.

gamb, gambe (gæmb). *Her.* [a. OF. *gambe*, northern form of *jambe* leg: see JAMB.] The leg of an animal represented on a coat of arms.

1727 in BAILEY vol. II. **1765** PORNY *Heraldry* Gloss., *Gamb* or *Gambe*, an obsolete French word, signifying a Leg and used as such by Heralds for the leg of a Lion, or other Creature, born in Coats-of-arms. **1800** *Naval Chron.* III. 38 On a wreath a lion's gamb erect. **1821** SOUTHEY in *Q. Rev.* XXV. 280 [He] bade him take it [a ring] and ever after bear such a one in the fore gamb of the demy lion in his crest. **1882** CUSSANS *Her.* vi. (ed. 3) 87 A Leg, styled heraldically a Jambe, or Gambe, which is usually represented as *erased*, or torn from the body.

Hence † **gambed** *ppl. a.*, having legs. *Obs. rare*[−1].

a **1661** FULLER *Worthies, Cornwall* I. (1662) 203 Gamb'd like a goat [L. *est tibi gamba capri*], sparrow-thigh'd.

‖ **gamba**[1] ('gæmbə). [L. *gamba*: see JAMB.]

† **1.** The leg of a horse. *Obs. rare*[−1].

1607 TOPSELL *Four-f. Beasts* 284 Two little ribbes from the vpper part of the thigh to the *Gamba*..There are two vaines out of the Gambaes. *Ibid.* 285 The legges are called Gambæ of Campo, signifying treading.

2. *Anat.* (See quot.)

1842 BRANDE *Dict. Sci.*, etc., *Gamba*, a technical term in Mammalogy, applied by Illiger to the elongated metacarpus or metatarsus of the Ruminants and Solipeds.

gamba[2] ('gæmbə). Also 6–8 **gambo.** [Short for VIOL DA GAMBA.]

1. = VIOL DA GAMBA. Also *gamba viol.*

1598 MARSTON *Pygmal.* Sat. i. 138 I'le not endure that with thine instrument (Thy Gambo violl plac'd betwixt thy thighes)..Thou entertaine the time. **1612** DRAYTON *Poly-olb.* iv. 358 Some likewise there affect the Gamba with the voice, To shew that England could varietie afford. **1710** in E. D. Dunbar *Soc. Life Moray* (1865) 15, I can..play on the Treble and Gambo, Viol, Virginelles and Manicords.

fig. **1638** FORD *Fancies* I. ii, Fumble one with another on the gambos of imagination between their legs.

2. An organ-stop, resembling a violin or violoncello in tone. Also *gamba stop.*

1869 *Eng. Mech.* 31 Dec. 385/2 A gamba is a reedy toned stop. **1881** C. A. EDWARDS *Organs* 157 *Viol-di-Gamba.* This stop is not to be confounded with the German Gamba..The German Gamba, or Gamba proper, is a stop of louder intonation and somewhat larger scale. **1895** *Rec. Bucks.* VII. 331 The organ, which fills the western tower, has been enriched with a gamba stop.

gambad, obs. form of GAMBOL.

gambada, var. GAMBADO[2].

gambade (gæm'beɪd). [A readoption (by Sir W. Scott) of F. *gambade*: see GAMBOL.]

1. A leap or bound of a horse. (Cf. GAMBADO[2] 1.)

1823 SCOTT *Quentin D.* ix, Each fresh gambade of his unmanageable horse placed him in a new and more precarious attitude. **1834** *Tait's Mag.* I. 850 [He] gallops his Pegasus at such a fiery-footed pace, and makes so many strange gambades, curvets, and caracoles.

2. *fig.* A prank, freak, frolic.

1821 SCOTT *Fam. Lett.* 15 Feb., You must lay aside your frolics and gambades and take a manful journey-pace for a little while at least. **1825** —— *Jrnl.* (1890) I. 21 To Southey I wrote..touching on..his innocence as to those gambades which may have given offence. **1826** *Mem. Margravine of Anspach* I. viii. 304 A surprising pantomimic spectacle which would decide the fate of the universe in gambades.

gambado[1] (gæm'beɪdəʊ). Chiefly in *pl.* **gambadoes, -ados.** Also 7 **gambada's,** 8 **gambades** (?), 9 *dial.* **gambaders.** See also GAMBAGE. [f. It. *gamba* leg + -ADO.] A kind of large boot or gaiter, attached to a saddle, to protect the rider's legs and feet from the wet or cold. In later use sometimes applied to leather leggings or overalls fastened with clasps.

1656 BLOUNT *Glossogr.*, *Gambado*, a kind of leather instrument affixed to the Saddle in the place of Stirrops. *a* **1661** FULLER *Worthies* (1840) I. 318 Gambadoes, much worn in the west, whereby, whilst one rides on horseback, his legs are in a coach, clean and warm. **1661** F. HAWKINS *Youths Behav.* G 1, *Gambada's* [ed. **1663** gambagas], large leather cases or stirrups to keep the legs clean in riding. **1732** SWIFT *Corr.* Wks. 1841 II. 682, I make a shift to ride about ten miles a-day by virtue of certain implements called gambadoes, where my feet stand firm as on a floor. **1781** *Gentl. Mag.* Apr. 186 'Who made you those shoes? Mine are clumsy and thick as a pair of gambadoes.' **1814** SCOTT *Wav.* xxix, His thin legs tenanted a pair of gambadoes, fastened at the sides with rusty clasps. Thus accoutred, he stalked into the midst of the apartment. **1823** *Ann. Reg.* 316* Improvements in constructing gambadoes, or mud boots. **1865** LESLIE & TAYLOR *Sir J. Reynolds* I. 3 So absent, that riding on horseback in a pair of gambados, he dropped one by the way without missing it. **1886** ELWORTHY *W. Somerset Word-bk.*, *Gambaders*, a kind of leather shield or case for the legs of a horseman. They are attached to the stirrup-leathers ..They were very common within the writer's recollection.

gambado[2] (gæm'beɪdəʊ). Chiefly in *pl.* **gambados, -oes.** Also more correctly **gambadas.** [a. Sp. *gambada* = F. *gambade*: see GAMBOL *sb.*]

1. A bound or spring (of a horse): = GAMBADE 1.

1820 SCOTT *Monast.* xix, The discretion of the animal's pace would be no longer disturbed by the gambadoes of Sir Piercie and his prancing war-horse. **1843** LYTTON *Last Bar.* IV. vii, Anthony..made his horse back to the end of the lists, in a series of graceful gambadas and caracols.

2. A fantastic movement, as in dancing or leaping about; a caper.

1859 SALA *Gas-light & D.* xxiii, A fantastic imp..on whose brow is written 'Analysis'..executes maniacal gambadoes on the quartern loaves..uttering yells about chalk, alum, and dead men's bones. **1881** *Daily Tel.* 27 Dec., Whose contortions and gambados during his struggles with his captors..are as comic as they are nimble and graceful.

3. *fig.* Any sudden or fantastic action.

1857 C. BRONTE *Professor* xiii, Sending him a challenge or performing other gambadoes of the sort. **1865** *Daily Tel.* 7 Dec. 7/1 Before fighting a battle of this sort in a Scotch court, there are, of course, all kinds of preliminary judicial flourishes and gambadoes. **1891** STEVENSON in *Pall Mall G.* 17 Nov. 6/2 The correspondence was still passing when the president surprised Apia with a fresh gambado.

Hence **gam'bado** *v. intr.*, to prance, caper.

1829 [J. R. BEST] *Pers. & Lit. Mem.* 181 Seeing him gambadoing on the race-course, I turned my horse's head another way. **1847** THACKERAY *Christm. Bks.* (1872) 30 He sticks his thumbs into the armholes of his waistcoat, and advances, retreats, pirouettes and otherwise gambadoes. **1872** [EARL PEMBROKE & G. H. KINGSLEY] *S. Sea Bubbles* viii. 228 There was my princess with five others..frisking and gambadoing in the most fearful manner.

† **'gambage.** *Obs.* = GAMBADO[1].

1663 [see GAMBADO[1]]. **1725** *Brice's Weekly Jrnl.* 5 Nov. 4 A Bay Mare..with Briddle, Sadle, and Gambages. **1730–6** BAILEY (folio), *Gambages*, gambadoes, splatterdashes.

gambald(e, gambal(l, obs. ff. GAMBOL.

† **gambalocke.** *Obs. rare.* An Eastern riding-coat.

1615 G. SANDYS *Trav.* 153 A man of tall stature, clothed in a Gambalocke of scarlet, buttoned vnder the chin. **1674** BLOUNT *Glossogr.* (ed. 4), *Gambalock*, a kind of Riding-gown, button'd under the chin, used in the Eastern Countreys about Damascus, etc. **1708** KERSEY, *Gambalook.*

gambassoune, obs. form of GAMBESON.

gambaud(e, gambawd(e, obs. ff. GAMBOL.

gambeer (gæm'bɪə(r)), *v.* *U.S.* [? f. F. *gambier* a kind of iron hook used in certain trades.] *trans.*

'To gaff (mackerel) when they are swimming in a school beside a vessel' (*Standard Dict.*).

Hence **gam'beering** *vbl. sb.*; in quot. *attrib.*

1883 *Fisheries Exhib. Catal.* 195 Mackerel gaff or gambeering iron..used by New England fishermen.

gambeer, var. GAMBIER.

gamber ('gæmbə(r)). [var. CAMBER.] The concave curve of a boat's keel.

1857 P. COLQUHOUN *Comp. Oarsman's Guide* 31 *Shear* is the rising of the gunwale of a boat towards head and stern; *gamber* is the same on the keel; otherwise called *tripping up*.

gamberel, obs. form of GAMBREL.

gambeson ('gæmbɪsən). *Obs.* exc. *Hist.* Forms: 4 gaumbisoun, (campeson), 4-5 gambisoun(e, 5 gambesoun, gambassoune, gamesun, (-son), 7 gambesone, 9 gambeson, (-soon). [a. OF. *gambison*, *gambeison*, *wambizon*, etc. = Pr. *gambaiso*, med.L. *gambesōn-em*. A shorter form appears in OF. *gambais*, *wambais*, Pr. *gambais*, OSp. *gambax* = med.L. *gambesum*, *wambas-ium*.

The forms seem to descend from a Rom. type *wambésio* (subj.), *wambesióne* (obj.), commonly taken to be an adoption of some compound or derivative of OTeut. *wambâ* belly (see WOMB). The MHG. *wambeis*, *wambes* (mod. Ger. *wamms*), Du. *wambuis*, *wammes*, were adopted from OF.]

A military tunic, worn especially in the 14th c., made of leather or thick cloth, sometimes padded; it covered the trunk and thighs, and was originally worn under the habergeon, to prevent chafing or bruises, but was sometimes used as a defence without other body-armour.

13.. *K. Alis.* 5151 Armen hem in breny of yse, Withouten..aketoun, Oither plate, oither gaumbisoun. *c* **1420** *Anturs of Arth.* xxxi, His gloues and his gamesuns [*v.r.* gambesoun] gloet as the gledes. *a* **1440** *Sir Degrev.* 302 Gomes wyth gambisoune Lyes opone bent broune, And sterff undere stede. **1736** BAILEY (folio), *Gambezon.* **1835** LONGF. *Outre-mer* Prose Wks. 1886 I. 166 A band of Moorish knights gayly arrayed in gambesons of crimson silk. **1843** JAMES *Forest Days* II. xi, I will pink him to the quick, if his skin be as thick and hard as a German gambesoon. **1876** ROCK *Text. Fabr.* iv. 30 Many a rich gambeson garnished with silk, cadas, and cotton.

gambet ('gæmbɪt). Anglicized f. GAMBETTA.

1776 PENNANT *Zool.* (ed. 4) II. 391 *Gambet*: this species has been shot on the coast of Lincolnshire. **1847** GOSSE *Birds Jamaica* 350 About the..fresh-water morasses, this Sandpiper or Gambet is frequently seen.

gambett, obs. form of GAMBIT, GAMBOL.

‖**gambetta** (gæm'bɛtə). *Ornith.* [mod. Lat., a. It. *gambetta* (said now to be used for the Ruff), f. *gamba* leg.] (See quots.; some ornithologists have used the word as the name of a genus of which the Redshank (usually called *Totanus caladris*) was the typical species.)

1678 RAY *Willughby's Ornith.* 300 The Gambetta of Aldrovand is also near of kin to the Redshank..This Bird we saw at Milan in Italy..It is something less than a Lapwing..Its Bill is shorter than the Redshanks, longer than the Lapwings. **1753** CHAMBERS *Cycl. Supp.*, *Gambetta*, the name of a bird somewhat resembling the common redshank.

Gambia ('gæmbɪə). The name of a state of western Africa, used *attrib.* to designate a form of trypanosomiasis prevalent there.

1905 *Proc. R. Soc.* LXXIV. 389 These experiments go to show that the two diseases—Gambia Fever and Sleeping Sickness—..are distinct. **1908** *Practitioner* Feb. 224 The trypanosomata of Gambia fever (trypanosomiasis).

Gambian ('gæmbɪən), *a.* and *sb.* [f. *Gambia* (see prec.) + -AN.] **A.** *adj.* Of or pertaining to Gambia. **B.** *sb.* A native or inhabitant of Gambia.

1906 F. B. ARCHER *Gambia Colony* i. 23 It certainly merits more than a passing mention in any record..of Gambian history. **1913** DORLAND *Med. Dict.* (ed. 7), Gambian horse sickness. **1943** K. W. BLACKBURNE *Devel. & Welfare Gambia* i. 6 It is a question whether, in the case of Gambians, this [consent to international transfer of territory] would be forthcoming. **1957** C. MACINNES *City of Spades* I. v. 30 They talked in their barbarian Gambian language. *Ibid.* II. xi. 172, I..waited..in case those two Gambians might start some fight again. **1966** *Transition* (Uganda) XXVI. 20/1 In the work of his contemporary, the Gambian poet Lenrie Peters, the emphasis is slightly different.

gambier ('gæmbɪə(r)). Also **gambeer**, **gambir**. [Malay *gambīr*, the plant from which the substance is obtained, the decoction itself being called *getah gambīr*, gum of gambier.] An astringent extract prepared from an Eastern plant (*Uncaria Gambir*), and largely used for tanning and other purposes.

1830 LINDLEY *Nat. Syst. Bot.* 205 A lightish brown, bitter, and powerfully astringent extract, called Gambeer, is obtained at Malacca by boiling the leaves of Nauclea Gambeer. **1853** C. MORFIT *Tanning*, etc. 68 Gambir,—This is an astringent extract, imported from the East Indies under the name of *terra japonica*. **1883** RAJAH BROOKE in *Pall Mall G.* 19 Nov. 2/1 Our crops of pepper and gambir are steadily increasing. **1887** L. OLIPHANT *Episodes* 163 Chinamen engaged in the cultivation of gambier.

gambist ('gæmbɪst). *Music.* [f. GAMBA[2] + -IST.] A performer on the viola da gamba.

1823 in CRABB *Technol. Dict.* **1879** P. DAVID in Grove *Dict. Mus.* I. 580 [They] speak of the elector as an accomplished gambist.

gambit ('gæmbɪt). *Chess.* Also 7-8 **gambet(t.** [Ultimately ad. It. *gambetto* (= *gambet*, *jambet*) tripping up the heels (in wrestling), f. *gamba* leg.

The history of the word appears to be somewhat involved. The earliest application to chess-playing seems to have been made in Sp., in the adapted form *gambito* (Ruy Lopez *Libro del juego del axedres* 1561, cap. vii, where the Italian etymology is given). The Italians seem at first to have readopted the word as *gambitto* (Polerio *a* 1575 in *MS. Ital.* 955, *Bibl. Nat. Paris*, who opposes *giuochi piani* to *giuochi gambitti*); later they employed the native form *gambetto*, whence the earliest Eng. form *gambet(t*. The Fr. and later Eng. *gambit* are from Sp.]

1. A method of opening the game, in which by the sacrifice of a pawn or piece the player seeks to obtain some advantage over his opponent. The original gambit is that by which a bishop's pawn is offered (King's or Queen's gambit), but the name is also given to other openings, many of which are distinguished by special names (see quots. 1871-3).

1656 BUDDEN tr. *Biochimo's Chesse-play* title-p., Illustrated with almost an hundred Gambetts. **1735** BERTIN *Chess* Rules p. vii, The gambet is, when he that first [?*read* that plays first] gives the pawn of the king's bishop, in the second move for nothing, the other keeps it, or takes another for it, if he is obliged to lose. **1745** STAMMA *Chess* Pref. 17 There is another Gambett, where three Pawns are given away; and therefore it is called the three Pawns, or Cunningham's Gambett, from the supposed Inventor. **1847** C. KENNY *Man. Chess* 34 Gambit—an opening in which the Bishop's Pawn is given up for an attacking position. **1871** M. COLLINS *Mrq. & Merch.* II. x. 294 Who..taught her the Mortimer attack in the Evans gambit. **1873** —— *Squire Silchester* II. iv. 40 The Squire and Simonet were already at chess, deep in the Cochrane gambit.

b. *fig.*

1855 DK. BUCKHM. *Crt. & Cabinets Geo. III*, III. 115 The dashing gambit which his opponent directed, was neither evaded with caution nor defended with skill. **1860** HOLMES *Elsie V.* xxii. (1891) 328 The Widow's gambit was played, and she had not won the game. **1863** LD. W. P. LENNOX *Biogr. Remin.* I. 237 The Emperor's genius in the art of war had devised a brilliant gambit in this military game of chess. **1884** G. ALLEN *Philistia* I. 19 Each of us has his own game to play, and..he must play it on his own gambit to a great extent.

2. *Comb.*, as ***gambit-pawn***.

1869 *Boy's Own Bk.* (1880) 588 The pawn sacrificed in opening a gambit, as well as the pawn which captures the offered pawn, are called gambit pawns. **1886** *Daily News* 20 July 3/1 Zukertort took the gambit pawn, whereupon white played B K 2, and the result was the king's bishop's gambit limited.

gamble ('gæmb(ə)l), *sb.*[1] Chiefly *colloq.* [f. GAMBLE *v.*]

1. An act of gambling; a gambling transaction. Also in phr. ***on the gamble***: engaged in a spell of gambling.

1879 E. S. BRIDGES *Round World in 6 Months* 138 Many English come here..to get fresh air and indulge in a gamble. **1887** RIDER HAGGARD *Jess* ii, Her brute of a husband was always on the drink and gamble. **1890** SAINTSBURY in *New Rev.* Feb. 141 The real point is the chance, the uncertainty, the gamble.

2. *transf.* Any transaction or pursuit involving risk and uncertainty.

1823 in Cobbett *Rur. Rides* (1885) I. 289 This hop growing and dealing have always been a gamble. **1881** *Sat. Rev.* 9 July 40/2 Politics, in fact, are 'a big gamble'. **1897** *Westm. Gaz.* 29 Apr. 4/2 Gold mines are necessarily a gamble.

'gamble, *sb.*[2] *Obs.* exc. *dial.* [var. of GAMBREL.]

1. = GAMBREL 2. Also *attrib.*

1703 *Lond. Gaz.* No. 3970/4 Has had the Farcy on the near Leg behind..and has had a great Sore on that gamble Joynt. **1720** *Ibid.* No. 5883/3 White Legs behind almost up to his Gambles. **1886** ELWORTHY *W. Somerset Word-bk.*, *Gamble*, the hock or elbow-joint of a hind-leg. Never applied to the entire leg, nor confined to horses. Properly the word applies to the strong tendon just above the joint.

2. = GAMBREL 1; also ***gamble-stick***.

1876 *Surrey Gloss.*, *Gamble-stick*, the crooked piece of wood used to hang up a pig or other slaughtered animal.

gamble ('gæmb(ə)l), *v.* [The vb. has not been found till about 1775-86; the apparent derivatives GAMBLER, GAMBLING *ppl. a.*, occur earlier, and in the 18th c. were regarded as slang. The word is prob. a dialectal survival of an altered form of ME. *gamene-n*, OE. *gamenian* to sport, play, f. *gamen* GAME *sb.*; cf. '*gamel*, to gamble, to gambol; *gamler*, a gambler' (*Northumb. Gloss.*); cf. also the rare 16-17th c. *gameling* ppl. a. and vbl. sb., which seem to imply a vb. *GAMEL. Continental Teut. words of similar meaning and form are MHG. *gämeln* to jest, sport, play (still in various Ger. dialects), Swiss Ger. *gammeln* to make merry, whence *gammler* buffoon, jester.]

1. a. *intr.* To play games of chance for money, *esp.* for unduly high stakes; to stake money (*esp.* to an extravagant amount) on some fortuitous event.

As the word is (at least in serious use) essentially a term of reproach, it would not ordinarily be applied to the action of playing for stakes of trifling amount, except by those who condemn playing for money altogether.

1775 ASH, *Gamble* [printed *Gamblet*], to game, to cheat; to make a practice of gaming. **1786** BURNS *Twa Dogs* 154 At operas an' plays parading, Mortgaging, gambling, masquerading. **1818** TODD, *To Gamble*, to play extravagantly for money. A word of contempt. **1838** DE MORGAN *Ess. Probab.* 101 It should seem as if we were thus told either not to gamble at all, or else to play incessantly. **1873** OUIDA *Pascarel* I. 45, I saw everybody gamble. **1884** W. C. SMITH *Kildrostan* 78 When he won my hand, which brought much wealth, He promised ne'er to gamble while he lived.

fig. **1850** CARLYLE *Latter-d. Pamph.* vi. (1872) 196 Gambling against the world for life or for death. **1876** GEO. ELIOT *Dan. Der.* III. xxv, He was almost in danger of forgetting that he was merely gambling in argument.

b. *slang* in phr. ***you may gamble on that***.

1886 'ARTEMUS WARD' *In Washington*, You ain't goin' to fool female Young America much. You may gamble on that. **1896** *Pall Mall Mag.* 14 Sept., There will be trouble for some one. You can gamble on that.

2. a. *trans.* To stake, risk in gaming.

1885 O. W. HOLMES Jr. in *Law. Q. Rev.* Apr. 172 Tacitus says that the Germans would gamble their personal liberty and pay with their persons if they lost. **1922** JOYCE *Ulysses* 763 When do you ever see women rolling around drunk like they do or gambling every penny they have and losing it on horses. **1930** *Publishers' Weekly* 8 Feb. 706 He would not have gambled his money upon them by adding them to his list.

b. To lose by gambling. Usu. with *away* or *off*.

a **1808** F. AMES *Infl. Democr.* iii. (1835) 108 Bankrupts and sots, who have gambled or slept away their estates. **1836** W. IRVING *Astoria* II. 290 They gamble away every thing they possess, even to their wives and children. **1848** THACKERAY *Van. Fair* lxiv, When she got her money she gambled; when she had gambled it she was put to shifts to live. **1865** LECKY *Ration.* (1878) II. 236 Men who had gambled away their liberty. **1874** 'H. CHURTON' *Toinette* xii, Loyd probably traded her off, perhaps gambled her off, in some drunken spree. **1888** F. HUME *Mad. Midas* I. i, He gambled away large sums at his club.

gambler ('gæmblə(r)). [See GAMBLE *v.*]

†**a.** In early use: A fraudulent gamester, a sharper, 'rook.' **b.** One who habitually plays for money, *esp.* for extravagantly high stakes (see the vb.).

1747 *Gentl. Mag.* 35 Composed of gamesters, commonly call'd gamblers, players, women of the town. **1755** JOHNSON, *Gambler* (a cant word, I suppose, for *game* or *gamester*), a knave whose practice it is to invite the unwary to game and cheat them. **1784** *Cook's 3rd Voy.* III. v. vii. 144 It is very remarkable that the people of these islands are great gamblers. They have a game very much like our draughts. **1827** LYTTON *Pelham* xxv, You suppose him to be more a gambler than a gamester, viz., more acute than unlucky. **1838** DE MORGAN *Ess. Probab.* 102 A gambler (meaning a bold venturer, which the term commonly implies) ceases to be such when he makes his stakes bear a proper proportion to his capital. **1891** *Daily News* 12 May 4/7 These ingenious speculators, 'these gamblers miscalled statesmen', to quote Professor Tyndall's phrase.

gamblesome ('gæmb(ə)lsəm), *a.* [f. GAMBLE *v.* + -SOME.] Addicted to gaming.

1884 *Sat. Rev.* 16 Feb. 201 The whole world seems in a gamblesome humour. **1884** *Daily News* 24 July 5/1 The whole country was then a very gamblesome country, and a match at cricket for love..would have been derided.

Hence **'gamblesomeness**, fondness for gaming.

1881 *Sat. Rev.* 1 Jan. 14 Relying perhaps..on the natural gamblesomeness of the French.

gambling ('gæmblɪŋ), *vbl. sb.* [f. GAMBLE *v.* + -ING[1].] **a.** The action of the vb. GAMBLE.

1784 [see b]. **1792** *Looker-on* No. 21 ¶6 She had an inbred abhorrence of gambling. **1812** L. HUNT in *Examiner* 14 Sept. 578/1 Their gamblings, dissipations. **1845** DARWIN *Voy. Nat.* viii. (1879) 156 Robberies are a natural consequence of universal gambling. **1897** WESTCOTT *Chr. Aspects of Life* 231 The State..must deal in some way with gambling.

b. *attrib.*, as ***gambling-booth***, ***-club***, ***-debts***, ***-den***, ***-game***, ***-hall***, ***-hell***, ***-house***, ***-instinct***, ***-joint***, ***-machine***, ***-practice***, ***-school***, ***-spirit***, ***-table***.

1850 MERIVALE *Rom. Emp.* (1865) I. ii. 71 Public and private life had become one great *gambling-booth. **1966** *Listener* 10 Mar. 361/1 A picture of *gambling clubs in Manchester. **1852** MRS. STOWE *Uncle Tom's C.* xxxiv, The wretch offered to buy me..of Henry, to clear off his *gambling debts. **1837** W. IRVING *Capt. Bonneville* III. 168 These *gambling games were kept up throughout the night. **1812** SIR R. WILSON *Diary* I. 38 After dinner went..to the conversazione, which is a great *gambling hall, or 'hell' in classical terms. **1877** BLACK *Green Past.* xiii, A convenient little *gambling-hell for those who had grown reckless. **1839** W. CHAMBERS *Tour Belgium* 71/1 The town authorities relaxed, and the present elegant *gambling-houses have been erected. **1880** MCCARTHY *Own Times* IV. liv. 161 A man who keeps a gambling-house is the proprietor of an unlawful establishment. **1890** SAINTSBURY in *New Rev.* Feb. 141 The Republic appeals..to the *gambling instinct in human nature. **1901** S. E. WHITE *Westerners* xiii. 94 Bunco men can clean him out in a *gambling joint. **1925** B. TRAVERS *Mischief* v, Who does Captain Dumfoil expect to find running a gambling joint? The Archbishop of Canterbury? **1935** AUDEN & ISHERWOOD *Dog beneath Skin* II. iii. 101 *Gambling-machines and switch-backs. **1784** COWPER *Tiroc.* 246 Some sneaking virtue lurks in him, no doubt, Where neither strumpets' charms, nor drinking-bout, Nor *gambling practices, can find it out. **1935** A. J. CRONIN *Stars look Down* I. ii. 17 Some colliers..that made up the *gambling school in ordinary times—squatted upon their hunkers against the wall. **1850** ROBERTSON *Serm.* Ser. III. ii. 17 There is a *gambling spirit in human nature. **1852** M. EASTMAN *Aunt Phillis's Cabin* 210 He fancied he would find happiness..at the *gambling table. **1857** C. KINGSLEY *Two Y. Ago* I. i. 26 He's..croupier at a gambling-table. **1891** H. CAMPBELL *Darkness & Daylight* (1895) xxxiii. 639 Whenever they have money, no matter how obtained, they generally drop the most of it at the gambling-tables.

'gambling, *ppl. a.* [See GAMBLE *v.*] That gambles or plays for high stakes; *orig.* that plays unfairly, that cheats at play.

1726 *Whole Art & Myst. Mod. Gaming* 111 The very Heads of such Families may not improperly be call'd the Game of (what they with a just Derision of their own Vileness term) the Gambling Fraternity. **1775** ASH, *Gambling* (p.a. from gamble), gaming, cheating by unfair methods of play.

gambo ('gæmbəʊ). *Welsh* and *W. Midlands dial.* Also **gamboo**. A kind of sledge; a simple kind of cart or trolley. Also *attrib.* and *Comb.*

1836 J. DOWNES *Mt. Decam.* I. 50 Gamboo, a sledge without wheels for bringing in the hay harvest. **1878** *N. & Q.* 5th Ser. X. 105/1 Some Radnorshire Words... *Gambo*, a cart of the very simplest construction. **1887** F. T. HAVERGAL *Herefordshire Words* 16/1 *Gambo*, *Gamber*, or *Gambrel*, a cart with sides only; no front or back. **1894** *Hereford Times* 28 July 5/6 Wanted, Timber Haulier, with four horses, waggons, and gamboes. **1945** DYLAN THOMAS *Let.* 30 July (1966) 278 There's his brown hen cluck in the gambo-swished mud. **1950** —— in *Botteghe Oscure* VI. 336 Butter fat goosegirls, bounced in a gambo bed. **1951** —— *Let.* 28 May 360 The word *gambo* means a farm-cart. **1963** W. H. BOORE *Valley & Shadow* v. 21 Ten coaches, apart from the hearse, and a gambo from the farm to carry the overflowering of tribute. **1967** *Listener* 16 Feb. 229/2, I unearthed a two-wheeled hay-wagon, locally known as a gambo.

gambo, obs. form of GAMBA[2].

gambodiate, -dic: see GAMBOGIATE, -GIC.

gamboge (gæm'bəʊʒ, -buːʒ, -dʒ). Forms: (7 **cambugium, gambaugium, -bugia, cambodia**, 7–8 **cambogium**, 8 **gambogia, -bozia, -boidea, -bogium**), 8 **gumboge**, 9 **camboge**, 8– **gambouge, gamboge**, (*Dict.* **gambooge**). [ad. mod.L. *gambogium* etc. (now in pharmacy *cambogia*), f. various forms of the name of *Cambodia*, the country from which the substance is obtained. The deriv. is given by Dampier in 1699 (Suppl. to *Voy. round World*, vi. 105).]

1. A gum-resin obtained from various trees of the genus *Garcinia*, natives of Cambodia, Siam, etc. It is largely used as a pigment, giving a bright yellow colour, and also as a drastic purgative in medicine.

[**1634** J. BATE *Myst. Nat.* 126 Take saffron or Cambugium. **1635** —— *Bk. Extrav.* 210 Orpiment and gambaugium are both very good yellows. **1688** R. HOLME *Armoury* II. 85/2 Cambugia, whither Gum, or Juice dried, is not certain.] **1712** tr. *Pomet's Hist. Drugs* I. 178 Gamboge ought to be chosen of a bright yellow Colour a little inclining to Red. **1772–84** COOK *Voy.* (1790) I. 224 It yields a bright yellow resin, that resembles gumbouge. **1821** CRAIG *Lect. Drawing* v. 310 The whole picture or drawing must be washed over with a mixture of Venetian red and gambouge. **1863** BARING-GOULD *Iceland* 208 The guest room walls are painted gamboge to a height of three feet. **1876** BARTHOLOW *Mat. Med.* (1879) 485 Gamboge is rarely prescribed alone as a cathartic.

b. The plant from which gamboge is obtained.

1876 HARLEY *Mat. Med.* (ed. 6) 698 The Gamboge is native of Siam and Cochin-China.

2. *attrib.*, as ***gamboge-plant***, ***-resin***, ***-tree***, ***-yellow***.

1837 *Penny Cycl.* VII. 367/2 The chin and throat gamboge-yellow. **1838** *Ibid.* XI. 68/1 The true gamboge-tree of Ceylon has been determined to belong to a new genus named Hebradendron. *Ibid.* XII. 90/2 A plant..which he thought might be the gamboge plant, as it contained a yellow purgative juice in the rind of its fruit. **1885** G. S. FORBES *Wild Life in Canara* 42 The same gamboge resin distils from both [wild and cultivated mangosteen] trees.

gambogian (gæm'bəʊdʒɪən), *a.* [f. GAMBOGE + -IAN.] Gamboge-coloured.

1797 LAMB *Lett.* (1837) I. iii. 58 Of a dirty drab-coloured yellow—a dull gambogian.

gambogiate (gæm'bəʊdʒɪət). Also **gambodiate**. [f. GAMBOGE + -(I)ATE[1].] A combination of gambogic acid with a metallic base.

1839 JOHNSTON in *Phil. Trans.* CXXIX. 284 Gambodiates of Potash and Soda. **1880** *Chambers' Encycl.* (U.S.) s.v. *Gamboge*, Yellow precipitate of gambogiate of lead.. Gambogiates of copper and iron.

gambogic (gæm'bəʊdʒɪk), *a.* Also **gambodic, cambogic**. [f. GAMBOGE + -IC; cf. F. *gambodique*.] Only in ***gambogic acid***, a resin which is the chief constituent of gamboge.

1839 JOHNSTON in *Phil. Trans.* CXXIX. 284 Salts of Gambodic Acid. **1848** CRAIG, *Gambogic*. **1875** WOOD *Therap.* (1879) 474 In order for gambogic acid to act as a purgative the presence of bile in the intestine is necessary.

gambo-goose ('gæmbəʊ,guːs). The spur-winged goose (*Plectropterus gambensis*).

1678 RAY *Willughby's Ornith.* 361 The Gambo-Goose, or Spur-wing'd Goose.

gamboile, obs. form of GAMBOL.

gamboised ('gæmbɔɪzd), *ppl. a. Antiq.* [ad. OF. *gamboisé, gambesié* etc., quilted or padded; cf. GAMBESON.] Quilted, padded.

1834 PLANCHÉ *Brit. Costume* 86 The word gamboisé or gamboised..was afterwards applied to saddles and other padded, stitched, or quilted articles. **1839** STONEHOUSE *Axholme* 234 The thighs appear to be covered with a gamboised or quilted defence, which reaches to the knees. **1855** tr. *Labarte's Arts Mid. Ages* xxxii, Gamboised or padded with cotton.

gambol ('gæmbəl), *sb.* Forms: α. 6 **gambad, -baud(e, -bawd**, 6 *Sc.*, *pl.* **gambatis, -bettis**. (See also GAMOND.) β. 6 **gambald(e, -bauld(e, gam(m)ald, gambold(e**. γ. 6 **gambal, -boile**, 7 **gambole**, 7– **gambol**. [a. F. *gambade* leap or spring. ad. It. *gambata* f. *gamba* leg (F. *jambe*).

The word appears first at the beginning of the 16th c. The ending *-ade* seems almost from the first to have been confused with the then more common *-aud, -auld*. Subsequently the *d* was dropped in *gambald*; cf. *curtal* from earlier *curtald*.]

†**1.** The bound or curvet of a horse. *Obs. rare.* (Cf. GAMBADE.)

α. **1503** in Leland *Collect.* (1770) IV. 281 The said Lord.. maid his Devor at the Departynge, of Gambads and Lepps. *a* **1533** LD. BERNERS *Huon* lv. 187 Then he cam to kyng yuoryn with .xx. gambaudes.

2. A leap or spring in dancing or sporting, a caper, frisk. Now chiefly *pl.*, of the sportive movements of children and animals.

α. **1513** DOUGLAS *Æneis* XIII. ix. 107 And gan do dowbill brangillis and gambatis (*v.r.* gambettis)..Athir throu other reland, on thair gys. *c* **1530** LD. BERNERS *Arth. Lyt. Bryt.* (1814) 248 Than came forth juglers with theyr fals castes.. and damoyselles wyth theyr gambawdes. **1575** LANEHAM *Let.* 24 Such feats of agilitiee, in..leaps, skips, springs, gambauds, soomersauts, caprettez & flyghts.

arch. **1831** SCOTT *Ct. Robt.* xvi, In this last gambaud the torch which he bore was extinguished.

β. **1530** PALSGR. 548/2, I fetche a gambolde or a fryske in daunsyng, *je fays vne gambade* or *vne frisque*. Holde me a cappe, I wyll fetche a gambalde as hye as I may reache. **1580** SIDNEY *Arcadia* I. (1590) 72 Were full of such leaps and gambolds. **1583** STANYHURST *Æneis* III. (Arb.) 79 Soom feloes naked With wrastling gambalds..for maystrye doe struggle. **1590** L. LLOYD *Diall Daies* I. 181 Such madde frisking, skipping and strange gamalds of daunsing.

fig. **1592** G. HARVEY *Pierce's Super.* 15 To teach his mother-tongue such lusty gambolds.

γ. *c* **1600** DAY *Begg. Bednall Gr.* IV. i. (1881) 72 What Gamballs have ye here now? ha! **1611** SHAKS. *Wint. T.* IV. iv. 335 A Dance, which the Wenches say is a gally-maufrey of Gambols. **1641** BROME *Jovial Crew* II. Wks. 1873 III. 390 Let us hear and see something of your merry Grigs, that can sing, play Gambals, and do Feats. **1653** URQUHART *Rabelais* I. xxxv, He fetched a gambole upon one foot. **1782** COWPER *Gilpin* xxxiv, Thus all through merry Islington These gambols he did play. **1865** DICKENS *Mut. Fr.* III. vii, After a variety of awkward gambols.

b. (See quot. 1706.)

1706 PHILLIPS (ed. Kersey), *Gambols*, certain Sports or Tumbling Tricks in use about Christmas-time. **1712** ADDISON *Spect.* No. 269 ⁋8 If they had not good Cheer, warm Fires, and Christmas Gambols to support them.

c. *transf.* and *fig.* in *pl.* Frolicsome movements or proceedings. Rarely *sing.*, a frolic, merrymaking.

1596 SHAKS. *Merch. V.* III. i. 93 Those crisped snakie golden locks Which makes such wanton gambols with the winde. **1741** RICHARDSON *Pamela* (1824) I. 59, I am but a silly poor girl, set up by the gambol of fortune for a May-game. **1768–74** TUCKER *Lt. Nat.* (1852) I. 592 The flighty gambols of chance are objects of no science, nor grounds of any dependence whatever. **1807–8** W. IRVING *Salmag.* (1824) 89 The eccentric gambols of the famous comet. **1824** —— *T. Trav.* I. 65 There was a gambol carrying on within, enough to have astonished St. Anthony himself. **1878** M. A. BROWN *Nadeschda* 14 From wanton gambols taking rest In a bed of flowers lay the brook.

†**3.** A toy, plaything. *Obs.*

1581 J. BELL *Haddon's Answ. Osor.* 309 b, To hang pelting gamboldes upon them [Saints' Images], made of waxe, wood, leid, or other metall. **1630** J. TAYLOR (Water P.) *Vertue Tayle* Wks. II. 133/1 A pretty gamball, cal'd a Swing.

†**4.** *attrib.* (quasi-*adj.*) Sportive, playful. *Obs.*

1597 SHAKS. *2 Hen. IV*, II. iv. 273 Such other Gamboll faculties hee hath, that shew a weake minde, and an able Body. **1622** MABBE tr. *Aleman's Guzman d'Alf.* I. 132 Other were full of their gamboll-tricks, each man having his severall Posture. **1664** H. MORE *Myst. Iniq.* 447 It look'd alwaies to me so like a gambal trick, that I could not but place it among the earlier Legends or pious Fictions of the Church.

gambol ('gæmbəl), *v.* Inflected **gambolled** (-bəld), **gambolling** (U.S. often with single *l*). Forms: α. 6 **gambade, gambaud, gambawd**. β. 6 **gambaulde**. γ. 6 **gambole**, 7– **gamboll, gambol**. [ad. F. *gambader*; cf. the sb.]

†**1.** *intr.* Of a horse: To bound or curvet. *rare.*

1507 *Justes May & June* 113 in Hazl. *E.P.P.* II. 117 On horses gambawdynge wonderously That it semed..That they wolde have hanged styll in the skye. *a* **1533** LD. BERNERS *Huon* lv. 187 When the horse felte the sporres he began to lepe & gambaud & galop as it had ben the thonder.

2. To leap or spring, in dancing or sporting; now chiefly of animals or children.

1508 FISHER 7 *Penit. Ps.* cii. Wks. (1876) 156 Redy at all tymes..to daunce, to gambade, to lepe and to synge. **1590** SHAKS. *Mids. N.* III. i. 168 Be kinde and curteous to this Gentleman, Hop in his walkes, and gambole in his eies. **1667** MILTON *P.L.* IV. 345 Bears, Tygers, Ounces, Pards Gambold before them. *c* **1705** POPE *Jan. & May* 462 Their pigmy king, and little fairy queen, In circling dances gamboll'd on the green. **1792** *Munchausen's Trav.* xxiv. 104 The noble sphinx gamboling like a huge leviathan. **1841** LYTTON *Nt. & Morn.* I. i, The urchins gambolled round the grave-stones on the Sabbath. **1850** TENNYSON *In Mem.* xxx, At our old pastimes in the hall We gambol'd, making vain pretence Of gladness.

3. *transf.* and *fig.*

1602 SHAKS. *Ham.* III. iv. 144, I the matter will re-word; which madnesse Would gamboll from. **1796** BURKE *Regic. Peace* iii. Wks. VIII. 418 A nation, gamboling in an ocean of superfluity. **1824** SCOTT *Fam. Lett.* 4 Apr. (1894) II. 199, I have gambolled a little in the entrance hall, which I knew was not in very good taste when I did it. **1856** R. A. VAUGHAN *Mystics* (1860) I. 248 Our little world has been gambolling like children let loose from school. **1890** TALMAGE *From Manger to Throne* 107 The current is greatly accelerated and then goes gamboling into Lake Gennesaret.

quasi-*trans.* **1649** G. DANIEL *Trinarch.*, *Rich. II*, cccxliv, The Pye but chatters to a Country Cure, And gambolls wth the Sparrowes in a Bush, Rude Rhetoricke.

†**'gamboller**. *Obs. rare*$^{-1}$. [f. GAMBOL *v.* + -ER[1].] One who performs antics.

1587 GOLDING *De Mornay* xxiii. 349 Some Dauncer or Gambolder had displeased them at the Gamings and Shewes.

gambolling ('gæmbəlɪŋ), *vbl. sb.* [f. GAMBOL *v.* + -ING[1]. Some dial. glossaries give the accent as *gam'bowling*.] The action of the verb GAMBOL.

1522 SKELTON *Why nat to Court* 70 With gambaudynge thryftlesse, With spende and waste witlesse. **1525** LD. BERNERS *Froiss.* II. cv. [ci.] 307 He..spurred his horse, so that by gambaldyng of the horse the impostume brake in his body. **1583** GOLDING *Calvin on Deut.* ix. 53 Not to fall to Gambolding at our owne pleasure and fansie, but to followe the way quietly which he sheweth vs. *c* **1746** *Exmoor Courtship* 568 (E.D.S.) Gamboyling. **1827** HARE *Guesses* Ser. II. (1873) 554 How great is the interval between gamboling and gambling. **1884** *St. James's Gaz.* 26 Sept. 6/1 The brutal gambolling and the obscene language of young roughs.

gambolling ('gæmbəlɪŋ), *ppl. a.* [f. GAMBOL *v.* + -ING[2].] That gambols.

1552 HULOET, Gambaldynge horses, beyinge ful of gambaldinge and praunsynges. **1567** *Triall Treas.* (1850) 21 Oyes! is there any man or woman that hath lost A gambolling gelding with a graye tayle. **1830** TENNYSON *Sea-Fairies* 11 Down shower the gambolling waterfalls From wandering over the lea.

gambon(e, obs. form of GAMMON *sb.*

gamboo, var. GAMBO.

gambooge, gambouge, var. GAMBOGE.

'gambrel. *Obs.* exc. *dial.* Forms: 6–7 **gambrell**, 7 **gamberel, gambril(l, gamrell**, (8–9 *dial.* **gammerel**), 7– **gambrel**. See also CAMBREL, CHAMBREL, GAMBLE *sb.*[2] [Perh. a. OF. (Norman) **gamberel*, the pl. of which occurs in a document of 1452 (Godefroy); 'Les bouchiers d'Evreux, quant ilz passent parmi le bois dudit seigneur, peulent prendre...des *gambereaulx* et des verges pour prendre leurs bestes.' This seems to agree with sense 1 of the English word, and *gambier* is still found in Normandy with this meaning (Littré *Suppl.*).

As F. *gambier* means also a hooked stick (see GAMBEER), and the Eng. CAMBREL is synonymous with *gambrel* in both its applications, a derivation from the Celtic **cambo-* crooked (see CAM *a.*) seems not unlikely; for sense 2 cf. HAM *sb.*[1], which appears to be from the same root.]

1. a. (See quot. 1887); = CAMBREL 1.

1547 SALESBURY *Welsh Dict.*, *Kambren kic*, a gambrell. **1606** CHAPMAN *Mons. D'Olive* Plays 1873 I. 228 My selfe indeed..spide two of them hang out at a stall with a gambrell thrust from shoulder to shoulder, like a Sheepe that were new flead. **1618** W. LAWSON *New Orch. & Garden* (1626) 37 The common homely Proverbe: Soone crookes the tree that good Gamrell must bee. *a* **1640** DAY *Peregr. Schol.* (1881) 44 And first a Butcher..stands up and sweares..he wold cutte his throate and hang him up by the heles of a gambrill. **1887** *Kent Gloss.*, *Gambrel* or *Gamblestick*, a stick used to spread open and hang up a pig or other slaughtered animal.

b. A similar piece of wood for hanging clothes upon.

a **1652** BROME *City Wit* IV. i. Wks. 1873 I. 335 When she reads my poverty agen, And that these Garments must return to th' Gambrels, Her scorn will be impetuous.

2. a. The joint in the upper part of a horse's hind leg: the hock: = CAMBREL 2.

1601 HOLLAND *Pliny* I. 225 Calues..whose taile reacheth to the joint of the haugh or gambrill. **1687** *Lond. Gaz.* No. 2278/4 A Coach-Horse..a Scar upon his near Gamberel. **1725** BRADLEY *Fam. Dict.* s.v. *Horse-feeder*, Bathe his Legs well from the Knee and Gambrels downwards. *c* **1788** HOWARD *Encycl.* II. 1157/2 His hocks or gambrels neither standing too wide, nor too near together. **1880** *E. Cornw. Gloss.*, *Gambrel*, the hock of the animal.

b. *dial.* In human beings: The under side of the thigh just above the knee.

c **1746** *Exmoor Scolding* 153 (E.D.S.) Gammerels. **1886** ELWORTHY *W. Somerset Word-bk.* s.v., Shockin pain in my gammerel.

3. *U.S.* Short for *gambrel roof*.

1859 in BARTLETT *Dict. Amer.* 1873 T. W. HIGGINSON *Oldport Days* 45 Sometimes with the long, sloping roof of Massachusetts, oftener with the quaint 'gambrel' of Rhode Island.

4. *attrib.* and *Comb.*, as ***gambrel-joint, sinew.*** Also **gambrel-roof** orig. *U.S.*, a curved or hipped roof, so called from its resemblance to the shape of a horse's hind-leg; hence ***gambrel-roofed*** adj.

1876 J. BURROUGHS *Winter-Sunshine* iv. 104 A fox struggling with a trap which held him by the hind leg, above the *gambrel-joint! [1737 in *Old-Time New Eng.* (1926) July 21 One Tenement two Stories upright, with a Gambering Roof.] 1765 *Massachusetts Gaz.* 19 Dec. (Th.), A large building with two upright Stories and a *Gambrel Roof. 1851 S. JUDD *Margaret* vi. 30 Here and there was a house in the then new style, three-storied, with gambrel roof and dormer windows. 1861 MRS. STOWE *Pearl Orr's Isl.* 31 The afternoon sunbeams.. are painting the gambrel-roof with a golden brown. 1779 in *Mass. Hist. Soc.* 2nd Ser. II. 466 The [Indian] Queens Pallace was a *gambril ruft house. 1824 *Microscope* 21 Feb. (Th.), In a gambrel-roof'd house,.. She dwelt with a heart void of care. 1858 MRS. STOWE *Minister's Wooing* i, A small farm, with a modest, 'gambrel-roofed,' one-story cottage. 1715 *Lond. Gaz.* No. 5341/4 A white spot on the *gambrel Sinew on the near Leg behind.

Hence **'gambrelled** *pa. pple.*, stuck on a gambrel.

a 1625 FLETCHER *Nice Valour* IV. i, Ile box you.. And carrie you gambril'd thither like a mutton.

gambroon (gæm'bru:n). [Presumably named from *Gambroon*, a town on the Persian Gulf (otherwise called Bender Abbasi).] (See quots.)

1831 *Lincoln Herald* 9 Sept. 3/6 A shooting jacket of green gambroon. 1847 LYTTON *Lucretia* (1853) 141 No amateur in neat gambroon, manufactured by Inkson. 1858 SIMMONDS *Dict. Trade, Gambroon*, a kind of twilled cloth for linings. 1892 *Ibid.* Suppl., *Gambroons*, an all-wool fabric for men's wear. 1894 HARRIS *Techn. Fire Insur. Comment., Gambroon*, twilled linen-cloth for linings of dresses.

attrib. 1845 STOCQUELER *Handbk. Brit. Ind.* (1854) 84 A couple of pair of merino or gambroon trousers.

game (geɪm), *sb.* Forms: α. 1–5 **gamen**, 1 **gomen**, 3–5 **gamin, -yn**, ? 5 **gamon**, (4, 6 *pl.* **gamnes**), 4–5 **gammen, -in, -yn**, ? 5 **gammon**, 3–5 **gomen**, (4 *pl.* **gomnes**), 4 *Kent.* **gemen**; β. 3–6 **gamme**, 4–5 (9 *dial.*) **gam**, 3–4 **gome**, 4 *Kent.* **geme**, 6 *Sc.* **gemm**, 3– **game**. [Com. Teut.: OE. *gamen, gomen* str. neut. = OFris. *game, gome*, OS., OHG. *gaman* (MHG. *gamen*) joy, glee, ON. *gaman* (Sw. *gamman*, Da. *gammen*) game, sport, merriment; regarded by most Germanists as etymologically identical with Goth. *gaman* neut., participation, communion, f. *ga-* prefix, together, 'com-' (see Y- *prefix*) + root of MAN. If this explanation be correct, the OTeut. accentuation (as in a few other nouns formed with *ga-*) has been preserved because the word had already in the prehistoric period ceased to be apprehended as a compound.]

I. 1. Amusement, delight, fun, mirth, sport. Often in ***game and glee, game and play, joy and game***; also ***game and solace***. ***upon her game***: in fun. ***no game*** = 'no fun'. *Obs.* exc. *dial.*

Beowulf 1160 Gamen eft astah, beorhtode benc-sweʒ. a 1000 *Boeth. Metr.* ix. 17 He het him to gamene ʒeara forbærnan Romana buriʒ. a 1200 *Moral Ode* 288 Nis it bute gamen and gleo al þat man mai here dreoʒen. c 1250 *Hymn Virg.* 21 in *Trin. Coll. Hom.* 258 þer nis nouþer gome ne gleo auȝ þer is pine wiðute fin. 1297 R. GLOUC. (Rolls) 370 To honti and to winne is mete & to abbe solas & game. a 1300 *Cursor M.* 12554 (Cott.) Quen þis meigne was gadird samen þam wanted ai þeir gasteli gamen Til þat iesus was cummen in place. c 1320 *Sir Tristr.* 1918 A loghe þai founden made, Was ful of gamen and play. c 1340 *Cursor M.* 3445 (Fairf.) Rebecca.. now.. bredis twa for ane of twynlynges þat hir þuȝt na gam [*other texts* gamen]. 13.. *Guy Warw.* (A.) 3116 þan answerd þe riche soudan þat hadde no gamen of than. 1375 BARBOUR *Bruce* III. 465 [Bruce] maid thaim gamyn and solace. c 1386 CHAUCER *Sir Thopas* 129 His murie men comanded he To make hym bothe game and glee. c 1400 *Sowdone Bab.* 3199 So thay livede in ioye and game. c 1425 *Seven Sag.* (P.) 1454 My wyf hase put in the pyne In the dore oppon hyre game. c 1430 *Pilgr. Lyf Manhode* II. cli. (1862) 136 If j ete it, grace dieu wolde holde it no game [F. *nen seroit pas contente*]. c 1440 *York Myst.* xxxi. 164 We schall haue goode game with þis boy. c 1450 *St. Cuthbert* (Surtees) 1188 Com þe batemen with gamen and gle. c 1485 *Digby Myst.* (1882) v. 605 To be false, men reportith it game. 1523 FITZHERB. *Husb.* §153 It is conuenient for euery man.. to haue playe and game accordynge to his degre. 1549–62 STERNHOLD & H. *Ps.* xxxiii. 21 Our soule in God hath ioy and game. 1560 ROLLAND *Crt. Venus* IV. 400 All game and gle fra me euer adew. 1580 SIDNEY *Ps.* XL. vi, A, ha! this is good game. 1588 SHAKS. *L.L.L.* v. ii. 360 We haue had pastimes heere, and pleasant game. 1879 WAUGH *Chimney Corner* 41 It's rare gam, too [snowballing]—as lung as a body doesn't get hit theirsel'.

2. †a. Jest, as opposed to *earnest*. Also (with *a*), a joke or jest. *Obs.* exc. as in b.

c 1250 *Gen. & Ex.* 3498 Tac ðu nogt in idel min name, Ne swer it les to fele in gamen. a 1340 HAMPOLE *Psalter* v. 6 Til perfite men it fallis not to leghe, nouþer in ernest ne in gamen. c 1386 CHAUCER *Clerk's T.* 677 But nathelees, for ernest ne for game He of his crueel purpos nolde stente. 1387 TREVISA *Higden* (Rolls) VII. 111 A preost Edmond.. seide in game, 'Why chese ȝe nouȝt me myself'. 1390 GOWER *Conf.* I. 19 But yet betwene ernest and game Ful oft it torneth other wise. 1447 BOKENHAM *Seyntys* (Roxb.) 261 Here aftyr neythir in ernyst nere game No mortal husbonde to me do name. 1590 SPENSER *F.Q.* I. xii. 8 They.. crowned her twixt earnest and twixt game. 1590 SHAKS. *Mids. N.* I. i. 240 As waggish boyes in game themselues forsweare. 1626 in *Crt. & Times Chas. I* (1848) I. 173 What think you? for I know not. Is it a game or a verity?

b. Phr. ***to make (†a) game of*** (also †***on***): to make fun of, jest at, turn into ridicule. ***to make game (to be)***: to pretend for fun (*rare*).

c 1460 ROS *Belle Dame sans Mercy* 226 Whanne I speke aftir my beste avise Ye sett it nought, but make ther-of a game. a 1541 WYATT *Poems, To my Lute* 23 Vengeance shall fall on thy disdaine, That makest but game on earnest paine. 1580 SIDNEY *Ps.* XXXIX. v, That fooles of me maie make their game. 1671 MILTON *Samson* 1329 Do they not seek occasion of new quarrels, On my refusal, to distress me more, Or make a game of my calamities? 1745 *Hist. Coldstream Guards* 25 Oct. (Farmer), If the militia are reviewed to-morrow by his Majesty, the soldiers of the third regiment of Guards are to behave civilly and not to laugh or to make any game of them. a 1810 MRS. TRIMMER *Two Farmers* (1829) 26 Mrs. Mills.. made great game of her and her husband. 1849 MACAULAY *Hist. Eng.* vi. (1858) II. 72 She had all the talents which qualified her.. to make game of his scruples. 1870 DICKENS *E. Drood* iii, Some of the girls made game to be their brothers. 1875 JOWETT *Plato* (ed. 2) I. 220 They fancied that Ctesippus was making game of them.

†c. An object of ridicule, laughing-stock. Also ***laughing game***. *Obs.*

1562 JEWEL *Apol. Ch. Eng.* I. 9 [They] did count them no better then.. the of-scourings and laughing games of the whole worlde. 1591 SPENSER *Tears Muses* 204 Those sweete wits.. Are now despizd, and made a laughing game. 1694 SOUTHERNE *Fatal Marr.* II, Am I then the sport, The Game of Fortune, and her laughing Fools?

3. a. An amusement, diversion, pastime. †Also *collect.*, play, diversion. †***at game***: at play.

a 1225 *Ancr. R.* 318 Ich.. biheold hit, & oðe wrastlinge & oðer fol gomenes. a 1300 *Cursor M.* 25501 Ken us lauerd.. of vr sinnes son to rise.. and leue vr gamens grill. 13.. *Gaw. & Gr. Knt.* 1319 þe lorde of þe londe is lent on his gamnez. a 1340 HAMPOLE *Psalter* xvi. 12 As foles þat gedirs til a somere gamen. 1362 LANGL. *P. Pl.* A. XI. 37 Lecherie and losengrie.. beoth gamus nou a dayes. c 1380 WYCLIF *Wks.* (1880) 246 A wilde pleiere of someres gamenes. c 1450 *St. Cuthbert* (Surtees) 1047 He suld noght childres gammys su. 1549 *Compl. Scotl.* 13 To pas til hunting and til other gammis, conuenient for ther nobilitie. 1567 *Satir. Poems Reform.* iii. 40 Not hir fyrst spous.. In portratour and game mycht be his peir. 1577–87 HOLINSHED *Chron.* II. 53/2 Refusing an excellent clearke, because he saw him somewhat lightlie demeaning himselfe at game. 1660 JER. TAYLOR *Duct. Dubit.* IV. i. ii. §30 Johannes Sarisburiensis allows of every game;.. if it can ease our griefs. 1685 BAXTER *Paraphr. N.T.* Matt. xi. 16–17 The unbelievers of this generation, do as children in their games, complain of one another.. you are cross to us whatever game we play. 1875 JOWETT *Plato* (ed. 2) V. 12 The discourse of the three old men is described by themselves as an old man's game of play. 1884 J. SULLY *Outl. Psychol.* xii. (1886) 548 In their games children are actors, architects, and poets, and sometimes musical composers as well.

b. *spec.* Amorous sport or play, now esp. signifying sexual intercourse.

c 1230 *Hali Meid.* 31 Alle hise fulitoheschipes, and hise unhende gamenes.. ha schal.. þolien ham alle. c 1275 *Lutel Soth Sermun* 78 in *O.E. Misc.* 190 He mai quiten hire ale and soþen do þat gome. 1297 R. GLOUC. (Rolls) 604 So longe hii dude such sacrefise & pleide such game. þat hii adde an doȝter averne was hire name. c 1400 *Destr. Troy* 1506 Thretty sonnes besydes, als other wemen, þat he [Priam] gate on his gamen. 1522 *World & Child* in Hazl. *Dodsley* I. 244, I am a child.. Gotten in game and in great sin. 1606 SHAKS. *Tr. & Cr.* IV. v. 63 Set them downe For sluttish spoyles of opportunitie; and daughters of the game. 1938 G. GREENE *Brighton Rock* VI. ii. 259 What mattered was the game. The two main characters made their stately progress towards the bed sheets. 1964 *Mademoiselle* Sept. 164 There's a new dance, the Ska—like The Game set to music.

c. *colloq.* An amusing incident; a piece of fun; a 'lark'.

1838 DICKENS *Oliver Twist* xvi, 'I can't bear it; it is such a jolly game.. Oh, my eye, what a game!' 1857 HUGHES *Tom Brown* II. iii, 'Oh, here's a game', whispered the rest of us, and we all cut upstairs after the Doctor. *Ibid.*, We had such a game with him one day last half.

4. a. A diversion of the nature of a contest, played according to rules, and displaying in the result the superiority either in skill, strength, or good fortune of the winner or winners. For ***round, square game***, see ROUND, SQUARE. †***at game***: at play.

a 1300 *Cursor M.* 28338 Til idel gammes, chess and tablis. 1340 *Ayenb.* 45 Kueade gemenes ase byeþ þe gemenes of des and of tables. a 1400–50 *Alexander* 2272 What gome sall þis gamen begyn vpon first? 1515 *Nottingham Rec.* III. 344 Caredys and odar gammys for money. 1530 *Privy Purse Exp. Hen. VIII* (1827) 17 Item.. paide.. to Domyngo for soo moche money As his grace loste to him at game, iiij C *li.* 1530 in W. H. Turner *Select. Rec. Oxford* 86 [They] do mayntayne.. unlawfull gamys of the tenys. 1715 tr. *C'tess D'Aunoy's Wks.* 208 There was a numerous Assembly of Persons of Distinction, several Tables where they were at Game. 1716 LADY M. W. MONTAGU *Let. to C'tess Mar* 14 Sept., I could not play at a game I had never seen before. 1815 *Encycl. Brit.* III. 487 *Beast*, among gamesters, a game at cards. 1863 GEO. ELIOT *Romola* II. iii, A game in which there was an agreeable mingling of skill and chance.

b. *Gr.* and *Rom. Antiq.* Usually *pl.* (= L. *ludi*): Athletic, dramatic, and musical contests; gladiatorial and other shows.

c 1400 *Destr. Troy* 1620 In þat Cite.. Mony gaumes [?*read* gammes] were begonnen þe grete for to solas. 1567 DRANT *Horace's Ep.* I. xiv, A farmer, thou the townish games doste burne for. 1579–80 NORTH *Plutarch* (1676) 765 Many Games of price were played at Athens. 1593 SHAKS. *3 Hen. VI*, II. iii. 53 Promise them such rewards As Victors weare at the Olympian Games. 1601 HOLLAND *Pliny* I. 189 Lycaon hath the report of setting out the firste publicke games.. in Arcadia. 1602 SHAKS. *Jul. C.* I. ii. 178 The Games are done, And Cæsar is returning. 1662 STILLINGFL. *Orig. Sacr.* I. vi. §3 After the institution of the Olympick game [*sic*, here and elsewhere] by Pelops. 1734 tr. *Rollin's Anc. Hist.* VII. x. (1827) III. 346 Musical games were always exhibited in the theatre. 1833 *Philol. Mus.* II. 74 One Cleomedes of Astypalæa killed a man at the Olympic games, boxing with him. 1880 L. WALLACE *Ben-Hur* vii. 35 Herod, more Greek than Jew.. with all a Roman's love of games and bloody spectacles.

c. ***the game***: the proper method of playing; correct play. *lit.* and *fig.* (See also PLAY *v.* 16 b.)

1854 WHYTE MELVILLE *Gen. Bounce* I. ix. 198 If honesty's the game, you've a right to your share, what Mrs. Kettering intended you should have. 1889 G. DRAGE *Cyril* I. vii. 60, I really think he is.. not playing the game. a 1898 *Mod.* That's not the game.

d. *pl.* In Scotland, a number of contests in athletics, piping, and dancing held esp. in various Highland centres; a meeting for the purpose of holding such contests; freq. in ***Highland games***.

1822 *Inverness Jrnl.* 4 Oct., One of the spectators of the Highland games, yesterday, was plundered of a gold watch. 1831 *Aberdeen Jrnl.* 31 Aug., The Games were contested with a spirit which would have pleased our friend the Ettrick Shepherd himself. 1905 *Westm. Gaz.* 15 Oct. 7/2 The competitors have.. piped their way up to the games ground. 1948 A. RAEBURN *This is Scotland* 54 There are balls and Highland Games, where tossing the caber, throwing the hammer, Highland dancing and other professional spectacles are arranged.

e. *pl.* Athletics or sports as organized in a school, college, etc. Freq. *attrib.* (see sense 16 c).

1895 KIPLING *Day's Work* (1898) 343 He blossomed into full glory as head of the school, ex-officio captain of the games. 1899 —— *Stalky & Co.* 66 King and Macrea, fellow house-masters, had borne it in upon him that by games, and games alone, was salvation wrought. 1934 LD. BERNERS *First Childhood* xi. 105 At my preparatory school, it [*sc.* Latin grammar] ceased to be a game (as did also games themselves). 1960 J. BETJEMAN *Summoned by Bells* vii. 67 Greatest dread of all, the dread of games!

f. ***The Game***: a form of charades.

1940 S. LEWIS *Bethel Merriday* xiv. 119 That monstrous form of charades called 'The Game'. 1960 S. FOOT *Emergency Exit* vii. 51 They played 'The Game' after dinner. 1962 E. ROOSEVELT *Autobiogr.* xxx. 230 We played The Game—a form of charades. Queen Elizabeth.. chose the words that the rest of us were called upon to act out.

5. *fig.* a. A proceeding, scheme, intrigue, undertaking, followed up like a game. So often, ***to play a losing, a waiting game***. †***to make a saving game of it***: to retrieve one's losses in the end. Colloq. phr. ***two can play at that game***: others can act in a similar way (usu. said as a threat of retaliation for unfair dealing).

c 1250 *Gen. & Ex.* 1214 Ysmael pleide hard gamen. c 1300 *Seyn Julian* 184 Heo ne schal me wraþþi þus nammore: Ichulle pleie anoþer game. 13.. *Poem in Vernon MS.* 407 b (Anglia VII. 292) Charite I rede þat we beginne As bifore alle oþer games. 1430–40 LYDG. *Bochas* I. i. (1544) 2 b, Unto Adam this was an uncouth game To be constrained from rich apparayle In barraine earth to seken his vitayle. ? a 1500 *Chester Pl.* (E.E.T.S.) vi. 260 In mydds the world by any waie this gamon shall begin. *Ibid.* xii. 4 A gammon I will assay. 1614 RALEIGH *Hist. World* III. viii. §6. 98 The grauitie.. vsually found in the Lacedæmonians hindred them from playing their game handsomely against so nimble a wit. 1650 R. STAPYLTON *Strada's Low C. Warres* VI. 63 Alva.. resolved to play his game warily. 1654 H. L'ESTRANGE *Chas. I* (1655) 53 The Commons.. thought themselves worsted, should he now at last make a saving game of it. 1670 COTTON *Espernon* III. IX. 470 Perhaps in his life he never had so hard a Game to play. 1719 DE FOE *Crusoe* II. v, The savages would go.. thither to play the old game over again. 1795 WINDHAM *Sp.* 27 May (1812) I. 279 He was playing a deep game. 1795–1814 WORDSW. *Excurs.* III. 285 An intellectual game pursued With curious subtilty. 1821 J. W. CROKER in *Diary* 7 June (1884), Lord L. was playing a game, and.. not quite a fair one. 1826 DISRAELI *Viv. Grey* V. xiii, Now, gentlemen, I have another game to play. 1826 SCOTT *Woodst.* II. iii. 79 I'll show you that two can play at the game of wrestling. 1838 PRESCOTT *Ferd. & Is.* (1846) II. xviii. 161 While this game of diplomacy was going on. 1842 *Knickerbocker* Apr. 355 I'll show him that *two* can play at that game. 1844 THIRLWALL *Greece* VIII. lxii. 188 He was negotiating with the Achæans, and playing a double game. 1851 MAYHEW *Lond. Labour* I. 245 The game got stale, or Peter became honest. 1889 JESSOPP *Coming of Friars* ii. 108 He had a very difficult game to play during the eleven years he was Bishop. 1894 WOLSELEY *Marlborough* II. xlix. 44 James.. could not play a losing game. *Ibid.* xci. 434 No man ever knew better how to play a waiting game. 1911 BEERBOHM *Zuleika D.* xv. 230 The Socratic manner is not a game at which two can play. 1955 G. GREENE *Quiet American* I. iv. 60 They must have been caught in a cross-fire, trying to get back, and I suppose every man of us along the bank was thinking, 'Two can play at that game.'

b. A person's policy or plan of action; esp. in such jocular phrases as ***that's your little game! the same old game!*** Also, the course best suited to one's interests.

a 1698 TEMPLE *Wks.* (1757) II. 226 Which seems to be the present game of that crown. 1728 VANBR. & CIB. *Prov. Husb.* II. i, And now pray let's see your Game. 1808 SIR J. MOORE *Let. to Castlereagh* 28 Dec. in J. Moore *Narr. Campaign* (1809) 301 In the present state of things, it [a battle] is more Buonaparte's game than mine. 1840 E. E. NAPIER *Scenes & Sports For. Lands* I. i. 16 My game was now quite the reverse from what it had been at starting. 1857 READE *Course True Love* 21 Mrs. Trimmer's game was not to see her. 1870 R. B. BROUGH *Marston Lynch* xvii. 164 Your game is to identify yourselves with the imperial families. 1885 RUSKIN *Pleas. Eng.* 108 These three thousand men

..[design to] overthrow the Greek empire! That was their little game!—a Christmas mumming to purpose. **1887** SIMS *Mary Jane's Mem.* 300 Missus saw what her game was. **1893** WAWN *S. Sea Islanders* 94 They determined to spoil my little game.

c. ***to play the game of***: to act so as to secure the advantage or interest of.

1657 BAXTER *Min. agst. Malign.* §7. 4 It is apparent that these enemies of the Ministers, are playing the Papists game. **1808** SIR J. MOORE *Let. to Marq. Romana* 23 Dec. in J. Moore *Narr. Campaign* (1809) 164 It is playing the Enemy's game to draw him to attack our armies in rotation. **1847** GROTE *Greece* II. l. (1862) IV. 385 A selfish oligarchical party, playing the game of a foreign enemy. **1893** *Leeds Mercury* 11 May 4/8 The English Radicals did not see why they should play the Unionist game by voting for Mr. Russell's amendment.

d. *pl.* 'Dodges', tricks.

1660 *Trial Regic.* 49 His Hand is in at all Games. *a* **1845** HOOD *Tale Trumpet* xxviii, The lower orders are up to such games. **1894** FENN *In Alpine Valley* I. 55 If you are going to carry on these games, let's..shake hands and separate. **1897** *Daily News* 24 Apr. 2/1 But none of your games with Mary Roxbury. She knows her rights.

e. ***the game***: thieving, housebreaking; freq. in phr. ***on the game.*** *Thieves' slang.*

1739 W. UDALL in *Ordinary of Newgate's Account* II. 14/1, I, and others went out again upon the Old Game, till I was taken up for Clacking the Doctor. **1811** *Lex. Balatron.* sig. G2, *Game*, any mode of robbing. **1839** H. BRANDON *Poverty, Mendicity & Crime* Gloss., *On the game*, thieving. **1905** *Daily Chron.* 14 Apr. 6/6 Paolillo pressed me to go out 'on the game'.

f. ***the game*** : prostitution; usu. in phr. ***on the game.*** (Cf. quot. 1606 for sense 3 b above.) *slang.*

1898 *Daily News* 21 July 8/6 The prosecutrix pestered her to 'go on the game', i.e. the streets. **1911** F. HARRIS *Women of Shakespeare* 194 The phrase of the prostitute to-day on the streets of London is: 'I'm on the game.' **1958** [see BRASS *sb.* 2 g]. **1963** T. & P. MORRIS *Pentonville* viii. 191 This is almost certainly an underestimate of the number who are either married to prostitutes or have women 'on the game' as an additional source of income. **1969** T. PARKER *Twisting Lane* 201 Betty's on the game, isn't she? Has she got you at it too?

6. a. A definite portion of play in any 'game' (sense 4), terminated by the victory of one side, or the recognition that no victory can be gained; 'a match at play' (J.).

In mod. use the exact meaning of the term is often determined somewhat arbitrarily by the rules of the particular 'game' concerned. In card-playing, a 'game' ends when every player has played all his cards, though usually the contest is not considered as ended until a definite number of 'games' (in Whist, a 'rubber') have been played. In some sports a 'game' ends after a prescribed number of acts have been performed, or a prescribed number of partial victories gained.

a **1250** *Owl & Night.* 1666 Riȝt swa me gred þe manne a schame þat taveleth and forleost þat game. **1532** *Privy Purse Exp. Hen. VIII* (1827) 186 Item..paied to Rogers for xv games the whiche the kinges grace loste to him at tenes at xls. a game, xxx *li.* **1611** SHAKS. *Wint. T.* I. ii. 248 A Foole, That seest a Game play'd home, the rich Stake drawne, And tak'st it all for ieast. **1838** DICKENS *Nich. Nick.* i, Thus two people who cannot afford to play cards for money, sometimes sit down to a quiet game for love. **1862** PARDON *Whist* 20 A Rubber is two games won out of three. **1875** W. S. HAYWARD *Love agst. World* 78, I will play you three games for £500 each. **1890** J. M. HEATHCOTE *Tennis* (Badm.) vi. 105 The scoring of the game was as follows: 6 games to 3, 6 games to 5, 5 games to 6, 6 games to 5.

fig. **1826** DISRAELI *Viv. Grey* IV. vi, At your age life cannot be the lost game you think it. **1895** *United Service Mag.* July 429 He [Arabi] gave up the game and began..to withdraw his reserves.

b. Phrases (often used *fig.*). ***the game is up, is over*** = is lost. ***to force the game*** (see FORCE *v.*[1] 3 c and 5). †***to play the whole game*** (see quot. 1732). †***out of one's game***: not playing. ***to have the game out***: to play it to the end. ***game and game***: one game scored to each side. ***game, set, and match***, a complete and decisive victory (from the use in Lawn Tennis).

1711 SHAFTESB. *Charact.* (1737) III. IV. ii. 218 If they lay resty and out of their Game, chamber'd and idle. **1732** BERKELEY *Alciphr.* II. §3 In our Dialect..a Sharper is one that plays the whole game. **1808** SIR J. MOORE *Let. to Ld. Castlereagh* 26 Nov. in J. Moore *Narr. Campaign* (1809) 267 Unless I plainly see that the game is up, and resistance on the part of Spain vain. **1848** THACKERAY *Van. Fair* lv, The Game, in her opinion, was over in that little establishment. **1867** FREEMAN *Norm. Conq.* (1876) I. vi. 500 Godwine might well think the game was up. **1872** [EARL PEMBROKE & G. H. KINGSLEY] *S. Sea Bubbles* ix. 235 'You may say your prayers now', replied I, with a ghastly grin, 'for the game's up with us'. **1873** DIXON *Two Queens* I. I. vi. 44 She was..the only human being who could force his game. **1875** JOWETT *Plato* (ed. 2) II. 274 He is very eager that Callicles and Socrates should have the game out. **1888** J. PAYN *Myst. Mirbridge* (Tauchn.) I. xv. 175 All lawn-tennis..is over for to-day..just as we were game-and-game, too. **1968** *Listener* 15 Aug. 210/2 This seemed to be game, set and match to the garage. **1969** *Sunday Express* 6 Apr. 4 It was game, set, and match to the passenger.

c. with qualifying adj. (***to play***) ***a good, a poor,*** etc. ***game***: to be a skilful player (or the contrary). †***a great, small, high,*** or ***low game***: indicating the magnitude of the stakes played for.

1523 FITZHERB. *Husb.* §153 A pore man..wyll playe as great game..as gentylmen were wont to do. **1641** VICARS *Jehovah-Jireh* (1644) 179 The Divill, who..is willing to play at small games, rather than sit out and bee idle. **1674** HICKMAN *Quinquart. Hist.* (ed. 2) 191 In all the third Part, our Historian is put to horrible shifts, and plays a very low game indeed. **1708** *Brit. Apollo* I. Supernum. No. 4. 1/2 'Tis somewhat like the High Game at Putt. **1885** *Harper's Mag.* Mar. 628/1, I play a wretched game.

d. Position or advantage in play.

1677 DRYDEN *To Mr. Lee* 6 Mutual Vouchers for our Fame we stand, And play the Game into each other's hand. **1774** BURKE *Corr.* (1844) I. 505 We may play into the adversary's hand the advantageous game which we have obtained. **1917** J. DU MONT tr. *Lasker's Chess Strategy* iv. 24 The mobility of the White Queen..begins to have a threatening effect on Black's game. **1952** E. LASKER *Chess Secrets* 271 Had I kept my Bishop back at QB1, and castled instead, this advance would have given me a satisfactory game.

e. The course or event of a game. Also *fig.*

1827 HALLAM *Const. Hist.* (1876) II. xii. 409 France..held the game in her hands. **1878** C. D. YONGE *3 Cent. Mod. Hist.* xxiv. 570 Napoleon has himself said that in war the game is with him who commits the fewest faults. **1888** F. HUME *Mad. Midas* I. ii, You'll have the game in your own hands.

f. A person's performance in a particular game; the normal standard of one's play; ***to be on*** (or ***off***) ***one's game***, to be playing well (or badly); to be in (or out of) form. Cf. quot. 1885 under sense 6 c above.

1851 J. PYCROFT *Cricket Field* ii. 30 What can surpass a hardly-contested match when you have been manfully playing an up-hill game. **1873** J. BLACKWOOD *Let.* 7 June in *Geo. Eliot's Lett.* (1955) V. 421, I..backed Tommy when most folk thought he was off his game! **1887** F. GALE *Game of Cricket* 59 We had played..together, and knew each other's game. **1891** H. G. HUTCHINSON *Hints on Golf* 16 What am I doing wrong, Tom? I'm quite off my game. *Ibid* 52 If you are one of the many golfers who overrate their game. **1904** S. A. MUSSABINI *Mannock's Billiards* i. 23 It is wonderful how strength of nerve improves with the strength of one's game. **1920** *Westm. Gaz.* 16 Oct. 2/2 Their disregard of the recognized rules was accentuated by the fact that neither man was on his game.

†**7.** The winning position, the victory in a contest, the mastery (in early use ***the best game***). Also, the prize contended for. *Obs.*

(For expressions like *to win, lose the game*, from which this sense may have originated, see 6.)

c **1380** WYCLIF *Sel. Wks.* II. 258 Two men..rennen a space for a priis, and he þat comeþ first to his ende shal have þe gamen þat is sett, wheþer it be spere..or oþir þing þat is putt. *c* **1510** *Lytell Geste Robin Hode* v, That all the best archers shold come..And that shoteth all ther best The game shall bere a way. **1526** *Pilgr. Perf.* (W. de W. 1531) 62 b, But all that can loue God moost..feruently, be moost ..lyke in this course to gete the best game (as saynt Paule sayth). **1548** HALL *Chron., Hen. VI*, 167 Kyng Henry..and Richard duke of Yorke..wresteled for the game, and strove for the wager. **1549** COVERDALE, etc. *Erasm. Par. Phil.* 8 Let vs make spedye haste..to atteine the game [= L. *bravium*] of immortalitie. **1572** R. H. tr. *Lauaterus' Ghostes* To Rdr. (1596) A ij b, This Authour may..be..adiudged to the best game. **1589** PUTTENHAM *Eng. Poesie* I. xviii. (Arb.) 53 The shepheards..sang and played on their pipes for wagers, striuing who should get the best game. **1621** BP. ANDREWES *Serm. Fasting* v. (1856) I. 392 To win but a prize, at a running or a wrestling..and all is but for a poor silver game.

8. In various applications. **a.** A 'set' of players. †**b.** A HAND at cards. **c.** *pl.* In trade use: The apparatus for playing particular games. **d.** The number of points required for winning a game. **e.** The state of the game. **f.** In certain card games: The possession, at the end of a game, of the largest number of pips, for which the player scores one or more points. **g.** ***within, out of*** (***one's***) ***game***: within, out of one's range of play (in Croquet, etc.).

a. 1741 RICHARDSON *Pamela* (1824) I. xxiii. 35 Why can't they make their game without me?

b. 1746 HOYLE *Whist* (ed. 6) 22 Your Game consists of King, Queen [etc.].

c. 1895 *Strand Mag.* June 607 How Games are Made.

d. 1830 'EIDRAH TREBOR' *Hoyle made familiar* 6 Ten is game. *Ibid.* 8, *Points* are gained by honours and tricks, and ten constitute the game.

e. *Mod.* The game is four all, love three, etc.

f. 1830 'EIDRAH TREBOR' *Hoyle made familiar* 63 *All Four* ..Four chances..for each of which a point is scored, namely, *High*..*Low*..*Jack*..*Game*, the majority of pips, collected from the tricks taken by the respective players.

g. 1874 J. D. HEATH *Croquet Player* 52 Unless your partner lie at the boundary, far out of the adversary's game.

h. *Chess.* (i) A method of play, esp. a series of initial moves; cf. *close game* (CLOSE *a.* and *adv.* A. 2 c), *open game.*

1750, etc. [see CLOSE *a.* and *adv.* A. 2 c]. **1845** *Souvenir Bristol Chess Club* 59 This move produces the opening known by the name of 'The two Knights' game'. **1894** J. MASON *Princ. Chess* iv. 188 The *Scotch Game* may or may not be a Gambit. **1952** E. LASKER *Chess Secrets* 414 To steer into his favorite game, the Vienna variation of the King's Gambit. **1968** BOTT & MORRISON *More Chess for Children* 158 (*heading*) Four knights' game.

(ii) A sequence of moves forming a recognized stage in the play, esp. in *end-game* (END *sb.* 25), *middle game.*

1884, etc. [see END *sb.* 25]. **1894**, etc. [see MIDDLE *a.* 6]. **1949** H. GOLOMBEK *World Chess Championship 1948* 219 He was quite outplayed in the early middle game. **1952** E. LASKER *Chess Secrets* 273 The clearest understanding of opening and endgame strategy was not sufficient..unless it was matched by masterly middle game tactics.

†**9.** Sport derived from the chase. ***dog of game***: one used in hunting or sporting. ***to be in game***: to be engaged in the chase. *Obs.*

1297 R. GLOUC. (Rolls) 8649 He..nolde no leng abide þat he nolde to is game..He wende him vorþ an honteþ. *c* **1330** R. BRUNNE *Chron.* (1810) 94 þe Kyng herd his messe, to gamen þan wild he go. **1375** BARBOUR *Bruce* VII. 402 He vent till hwnt, for till assay Quhat gammyn wes in that cuntre. *c* **1400** *Melayne* 853 Sixty grewhondes vn to þ[e] gamen. **1523** *Act 14 & 15 Hen. VIII*, c. 10 Noble men..used and exercised the game of huntynge of the Hare. **1576** FLEMING *Caius' Eng. Dogs* in Arb. *Garner* III. 236 These hounds..use not that liberty to range at will, which they have otherwise when they are in game. **1591** *Troub. Raigne K. John* (1611) 49 Tis best we follow now the game is faire. **1592** WARNER *Alb. Eng.* VII. xxxvii. (1597) 180 Fatly do they feede Mongst Beasts of chace and birds of game. **1593** SHAKS. *3 Hen. VI*, IV. v. 11 If about this houre he make this way, Vnder the colour of his vsuall game, He shall [etc.]. **1629** H. BURTON *Babel no Bethel* 78, I am neither of the hound nor Spaniel kinde, dogges of game. **1650** FULLER *Pisgah* I. II. iv. 111 The neighbouring Desert affording the pleasure of the Game. **1671** MILTON *P.R.* II. 342 Beasts of chase, or fowl of game. **1719** DE FOE *Crusoe* I. ii, This [lion] was Game indeed to us, but this was no Food.

10. a. The object of the chase; the animal or animals hunted.

14.. *Piers of Fullham* in Hartshorne *Metr. Tales* 122 And steleth away his ffelowes game, And that the ffayrest and fattest of the ffocke. **1486** *Bk. St. Albans* B iv b, Many howndys will benymme theym theyre gamme from ther fote. **1526** *Pilgr. Perf.* (W. de W. 1531) 49 The other houndes that seeth y[e] game foloweth y[e] same through thycke & thynne. **1555** W. WATREMAN *Fardle Facions* II. viii. 169 He is carried vppon an Elephantt: and euen so..throweth the darte at his game. **1611** SHAKS. *Cymb.* III. iii. 98, 107 Hearke, the Game is rows'd..The Game is vp. **1731** ARBUTHNOT *Aliments* iv. (1735) 78 All Hounds [will follow] the particular Game they have in Chase. **1808** SCOTT *Marm.* II. Introd. 24 The wolf I've seen, a fiercer game. *Mod. Ballad*, Hark forward! Our game's in view, which we pursue With deep-toned horn.

fig. **1697** DRYDEN *Virg. Past.* x. 90 No Game but hopeless Love my thoughts pursue. *a* **1721** PRIOR *Cloe Hunting* 20 At human hearts we fling, nor ever miss the game.

b. *transf.* and *fig.* An object of pursuit; also, an object in view. ***fair game***: a legitimate object of pursuit, attack, etc.; also ***forbidden game.***

1573 G. HARVEY *Letter-bk.* (Camden) 9 To take occasion of nu matter and fresh game. **1600** *Chester Pl.* Proem 44 Then our desier is to satisfie—for that is all our game. **1680–90** TEMPLE *Ess., Gardening* Wks. 1731 I. 172 The Knowledge of such Things is not our Game. **1712** ADDISON *Spect.* No. 311 ¶6 Widows are indeed the great Game of your Fortune-hunters. **1720** DE FOE *Capt. Singleton* x. (1840) 182 We saw our game standing in for the bay. **1780** COWPER *Table T.* 114 A monarch's errors are forbidden game. **1816** J. WILSON *City of Plague* II. v, The Plague..passes to such game, As thou, and smooth-faced maidens like to thee. **1825** MACAULAY *Ess., Milton* (1854) 23 They were indeed fair game for the laughers. **1847** MARRYAT *Childr. N. Forest* vii, Deerstalking is all very well, but I fly at higher game. **1852** MISS YONGE *Cameos* I. xxx. 257 As to the unfortunate Jews, each party considered them fair game. **1872** C. GIBBON *For the King* xvi, At any rate she is game much too high for him.

11. *collect.* **a.** Wild animals or birds such as are pursued, caught or killed in the chase.

c **1290** *S. Eng. Leg.* I. 393/13 Among opur game huy founden ane heort. *a* **1300** *Cursor M.* 3522 (Gött.) þat day gamen [*Cott.* wayth] fand he noght. *c* **1350** *Will. Palerne* 387 þemperour..fond al his fre ferd, þat hadde take þat time moche trye game. **1488–9** *Act 4 Hen. VII*, c. 6 The dere and game in the same [forest] is destroied and goon. **1672** MARVELL *Reh. Transp.* I. 58 One may beat the Bush a whole day, but..for all game, onely spring a Butterfly. **1712** E. COOKE *Voy. to S. Sea* 324 There was Water, Tortoise and Game enough at the middle Island. **1762–71** H. WALPOLE *Vertue's Anecd. Paint.* (1786) III. 257 He was particularly famous for representations of partridges and dead game. **1774** GOLDSM. *Nat. Hist.* (1776) III. 110 Sanguinary laws were enacted to preserve the game. **1807** PIKE *Sources Mississ.* II. App. 26 It appeared as if we had just gotten into the region of game. **1833** HT. MARTINEAU *Charmed Sea* iii. 31 She..began..to distinguish the traces of game and wild animals. **1860** BURTON *Centr. Afr.* I. viii. 251 The country round is full of large game, especially elephants, giraffe, and zebras. **1862** *Act 25 & 26 Vic.* c. 114 §1 The Word 'Game' in this Act shall..be deemed to include any One or more Hares, Pheasants, Partridges, Eggs of Pheasants and Partridges, Woodcocks, Snipes, Rabbits, Grouse, Black or Moor Game, and Eggs of Grouse, Black or Moor Game.

b. The flesh of such animals used for food.

1848 THACKERAY *Van.Fair* ix, What good dinners you have—game every day..and no end of fish from London. **1853** SOYER *Pantroph.* 194 These same men..did not touch young game; they thought it indigestible. **1885** FOTHERGILL *Dis. Sedent. Life* xxxii. 280 Such meat as is taken should consist of white meat, fish or fowl, and game.

c. jocularly, of vermin.

1748 G. WASHINGTON *Jrnl.* 16 Mar., Writ. 1889 I. 2 We cleaned ourselves (to get Rid of ye Game we had catched ye night before).

d. *slang.* (See quot.)

1676 *Song* in *Warn. Housekprs.* 5 When that we have bit the bloe, we carry away the game. *a* **1700** B. E. *Dict. Cant. Crew*, *Game*, Bubbles drawn in to be cheated. **1785** GROSE *Dict. Vulg. Tongue* s.v. *Game.*

12. A flock or herd of animals kept for pleasure. *Obs.* exc. in ***a game of swans.***

1482 *Rot. Parl. 22 Edw. IV*, VI. 224 Forsomoche that as well the Kyng oure Soverayn Lord, as other Lordes..have ben gretely replenysshed of Markes and Games of Swannes, in divers Countres. **1488** *Will of Develyn* (Somerset Ho.), My game of swannys. **1560** in W. H. Turner *Select. Rec. Oxford* 285 For upping of half game [swans] in cowe meade. **1570** *Order for Swannes* in Hone *Every-day Bk.* (1827) II. 960 No person..shall go on marking without the Master of the Game, or his Deputie be present. **1576** TURBERV. *Venerie* 235 If they be many feeding out togethers, we say it is a fayre game of conies. **1577** in W. H. Turner *Select. Rec. Oxford* 393 The Quenes ma[ties] servaunte that kepeth her game of beres. **1577** Harrison *England* II. xix. (1878) I. 307 How manie families these great and small games (for so most keepers call them) haue eaten up. **1683** *Lond. Gaz.* No. 1871/4 The Office and Place of Master of His Majesties Game of Swans within the River of Thames. **1788** Nichols *Progr. Q. Eliz.* (1823) I. 321 Lord Berkeley had a stately game of red deer in the park adjoining. **1889** *Times* 12 Aug. 3/2 There has also been time out of mind..a game of swans building, nesting and breeding there.

13. ***cock of the game*** (see cock *sb.*[1] 2 b).

1575, etc. [see cock *sb.*[1] 2 b]. **1684** R. H. *School Recreat.* 134 Distempers incident to the Cock or Chick of the Game. **1719** D'Urfey *Pills* III. 329 You have the Name, And would accounted be Cocks of the Game. **1822** Scott *Nigel* xiv, It will be long ere his lordship ruffles a feather with a cock of the game.

14. The characteristics of a game-fowl; spirit for fighting, pluck, endurance. Also predicatively, ***thorough game, all game***, said of a person possessed of these qualities. Cf. game *a.*

1747 J. Godfrey *Sc. Defence* 64 Smallwood (a boxer) is thorough game. *c* **1783** *Roxb. Ball.* (1890) VII. 93 Such horses of mettle and game As are worthy to be recorded in fame. **1812** *Sporting Mag.* XXXIX. 18 The champion's tried game made him yet a favourite. **1813** *Ibid.* XLII. 243 A young bull of great game, made play for no less than nine-and-twenty dogs. **1823** Byron *Juan* VIII. cx, The fifth ..died all game and bottom. **1829** Marryat *F. Mildmay* v, He never showed more game. **1845** Dickens *Lett.* (ed. 2) I. 139 They were thorough game and didn't make the least complaint. **1867** *Criminal Chronol. York Castle* 135 This man made a stout resistance, being a very powerful fellow and good game.

15. Short for *game-fowl*. In quots. *collect.* with plural concord.

1867 Tegetmeier *Poultry Bk.* xii. 123 Game are preeminently the English fowl; in no other country but our own is the true-bred Game cock indigenous. *Ibid.* 124 The varieties of Game are very numerous.

II. *attrib.* and *Comb.*

16. a. simple attrib. (chiefly in sense 11; cf. also game *a.*[1]), as ***game-beast, -bird, -country, -craft,*** †***-dog*** (cf. *dog of game* in sense 9), ***-drive, -land, -larder, -list, -park, -path, -pie, -pit, -pouch, -preserve, reserve, -season, -shot.***

1895 *Westm. Gaz.* 21 Sept. 2/2 The largest *game beast of the Polar regions. **1878** R. Jefferies *Gamekeeper at home* vii. 161 The less respectable breeders who rear *game birds like poultry for sale. **1855** W. Irving *Tour Prairies* xviii, We were getting more and more into the *game country. **1883** *Century Mag.* Aug. 485/2 The *gamecraft and markmanship of future generations. **1702** W. J. *Bruyn's Voy. Levant* xiv. 79, I found it harder in my Travels in Turkey to keep a *Game Dog, which I always had with me, than to keep my Self. **1895** W. C. Scully *Kafir Stories* 98 These *game-drives were fraught with considerable danger. **1931** J. Mockford *Khama* vii. 60 The rich tribute in hides, ivory, and ostrich-feathers which the Masarwa bushmen and other vassals occupying the *game-land..brought annually to Shoshong. **1958** *Listener* 16 Jan. 102/1 But unspoilt gamelands, such as those in the Congo, afford unrivalled opportunities for a study of natural balances. **1812** *Sporting Mag.* XXXIX. 135 Produced to the *game larder..the following enormous list of slaughter. **1856** Kane *Arct. Expl.* II. vii. 79 The tide-holes of the spring, where we can add waterfowl to our *game-list. **1897** J. L. Allen *Choir Invisible* xiii, The great neutral *game-park of the Northern and the Southern Indians. **1963** A. Smith *Throw out Two Hands* x. 111 Even the Serengeti, the main game park, had closed its gates. **1856** C. J. Andersson *Lake Ngami* xxxi. 404, I struck into a large '*game path'. **1935** L. G. Green *Great Afr. Mysteries* xiv. 181, I saw the first crocodile, waiting at a gamepath to grip its victim by the nose. **1827** H. G. Lewis *Let.* 13 Oct. in J. Constable *Corr.* (1966) IV. 70 This accompanys a French *game pye, made by my Cook. **1888** Lowell in *Daily News* 26 July 6/3 Longfellow, my friend and neighbour, asked me to come and eat a game pie with him. **1893** Selous *Trav. S.E. Africa* 409 Many oxen were killed by falling into old *game pits. **1808** Scott *Marm.* v. Introd. 10 The *game-pouch, fishing-rod, and spear. **1863** Kingsley *Water Bab.* 8, Miles of *game-preserves in which..the collier-lads poached at times. **1921** *Daily Colonist* (Victoria, B.C.) 27 Mar. 27/2 These [Queen Charlotte] islands would make the greatest *game reserve in the world. **1962** J. G. Bennett *Witness* xix. 231 My visit to the game reserves in Kenya and other parts of Africa. **1800** Windham *Sp. Parl.* 18 Apr. (1812) I. 340 Those very Gentlemen who in the *game-season, as it has been justly said, become their own butchers and poulterers. **1901** Kipling *Kim* xiii. 336 Hurree was no *game-shot,—the snick of a trigger made him change colour. **1927** A. Conan Doyle *Case Bk. S. Holmes* 82 The famous game-shot, sportsman, and man-about-town was a big, swarthy fellow.

b. objective, as (senses 3 and 4) ***game-playing*** sb. and adj.; ***game-shy*** adj.; (senses 10, 11) †***game-finder, -hunting, -preserver, -preserving, -shooting, -stealer; game-destroying*** adj.; (sense 11) ***game-dealer, -finding*** sb. and adj.; ***game-proof*** adj.

1876 J. S. Ingram *Centenn. Exposition* 691 One of the oldest *game-dealers in the West. **1860** G. H. K. *Vac. Tour* 127 Of all snarling, ill-conditioned, *game-destroying brutes in the world, the wild-cat is the worst. **1664** H. More *Myst. Iniq.* xxi. 81 Officious Intelligencers or *Game-finders for such as pursue the pleasures of Venus. **1922** R. Leighton *Compl. Bk. Dog* xi. 159 A better dog for *game-finding than could have been found in any other part of the world. **1960** *Times* 24 Sept. 9/4 A game-finding dog. **1886** *Pall Mall G.* 9 Dec. 2/2 There is still much large *game-hunting for riflemen who go west. **1908** *Westm. Gaz.* 18 Apr. 3/1 Centralisation will mean larger public-houses and greater attractions owing to the crowds, *game-playing,.. and late hours. **1909** *Ibid.* 8 Nov. 4/3 They were at 'famous' game-playing schools. **1947** Auden *Age of Anxiety* (1948) v. 111 Barns and shrubberies For game-playing gangs. **1970** *Guardian* 29 Apr. 9/6 The long-term objective of Women's Liberation..is an end of 'game-playing' between men and women. **1800** Windham *Sp. Parl.* 18 Apr. (1812) I. 339 Quarrels between the game-invaders and the *game-preservers. **1848** Thackeray *Van. Fair* xlv, He talked about crops..entered into poaching and *game preserving with ardour. **1908** *Daily Chron.* 21 Aug. 7/3 A nine-foot *game-proof fence of woven buffalo wire. **1963** *Times* 10 May 10/7 A game-proof ditch between the forest boundaries and the settlement schemes. **1894** Astley *50 Years Life* I. 251 At no other *game-shooting have I laughed so much. **1932** Auden *Orators* III. 92 To work-shy and *game-shy kind. **1825** *Sporting Mag.* XVI. 336 Should we not also have *game-stealers?

c. *attrib.* and *Comb.* uses of the plural, esp. in sense 4 e, as ***games-mad*** adj., ***games-mania, -master, -mistress, -room, -worship.***

1960 C. Day Lewis *Buried Day* vi. 108 A *games-mad school. *Ibid.* 128 The Sherborne *games-mania. **1902** *Daily Chron.* 16 July 7/1 Special *games-masters and mistresses. **1965** G. McInnes *Road to Gundagai* x. 159 Our combined sergeant, wet-nurse, games-master, school-teacher and doctor. **1907** *Westm. Gaz.* 18 July 10/2 The home supplies also a temperance bar..and *games rooms. **1959** *House & Garden* June 44 The house is on three floors. At garden level is a large gamesroom. **1960** C. Day Lewis *Buried Day* iv. 68 Though we were encouraged to enjoy our games, there was no *games-worship.

17. Special comb.: **game-act**, an Act of Parliament regulating the killing of game; **game-bag**, a bag for holding the game killed by a sportsman; **game ball** (*Tennis*), the position in which one side requires a single point in order to win; *pred. a.* (*Anglo-Irish slang*), excellent, fine; **game bantam**, a bantam of a fighting breed (cf. game-cock); **game-battle** (*nonce-wd.*), an affray with poachers; †**game-bear**, a bear chained up for baiting; **game-board** = board *sb.* 2 c; **game-book** (see quot. 1807); **game-cast** (*Bowls*), a ball placed so as to make sure of the game; **game-certificate** = *game-licence*; **game-chick**, a game-chicken; **game-chicken**, a young game-fowl; **game chips**, very thin fried chipped potatoes served with game (sense 11 b); **game debt**, a debt incurred by play or gaming; **game-egg**, an egg laid by a game-fowl; **game-fish**, a fish which affords sport to the angler in its capture; **game-forcing** *a.*, in *Bridge*, denoting a bid intended to instruct one's partner to continue the bidding until a contract is reached that will win a game; †**game-goblin**, a sprite that plays pranks at night; **game-goer**, in *Bridge*, a bid that undertakes to win a game; so **game-going** *a.*; **game-hen** (see game-fowl); **game-hole**, the last hole in a cribbage-board; †**game-house** = gaming-house; **game-licence**, a licence to kill or deal in game; **gamelike** *adv.* [after *warlike*], for purposes of sport; †**game-man**, ? a jester, joker; †**game-mistress** (cf. sense 3 b); **game-piece**, (*a*) = piece *sb.* 12; (*b*) a painting of game (sense 11); †**game-place**, a place where games are played, an arena for contests; †**game-play**, a stage-play; †**game-player**, an athlete or actor; **game-rhyme**, a rhyme used in a game; **game show** orig. *U.S.*, a television light-entertainment programme in which celebrities or members of the public compete in a game or quiz, often for prizes; **game-tenant**, one who rents the shooting or fishing on an estate; **game(s) theory**, the mathematical theory of situations of conflict (such as occur in games of skill, in economics, and in war), esp. as used to determine the most advantageous strategy for any of the participants; hence **game-theoretic, -theoretical** *adjs.*; **game-theorist**; **game-trespass**, trespassing in pursuit of game; **game-warden** (see warden *sb.*[1] 7 b). Also game-cock, game-fowl, game-keeper, game-law.

1711 Addison *Spect.* No. 122 ¶3 He is just within the *Game-Act, and qualified to kill an Hare or a Pheasant. **1826** Miss Mitford *Village* Ser. II. (1863) 349 Powder-horns, shot-belts, and *game-bags scattered about. **1893** *Westm. Gaz.* 26 Apr. 5/3 Here he was unfortunate, losing by a 'let' when the game stood at *gameball—10. **1916** Joyce *Portrait of Artist* iii. 119 That's game ball. We can scut the whole hour. **1922** —— *Ulysses* 224 That'll do, game ball, Blazes Boylan said. **1867** Tegetmeier *Poultry Bk.* xxiii. 248 *Game Bantams, both cocks and hens, should be exact and perfect diminutives of the ordinary Game fowl. **1826** in Cobbett *Rur. Rides* (1885) II. 200 There was another young man..on account of another *game-battle, hanged on the same gallows! *a* **1625** Beaum. & Fl. *Custom Country* IV. iv, Do not make a *game-bear of me, to play me hourly, And fling on all your whelps. **1934** *Discovery* Oct. 287/2 Though found in Central Ireland, this *game-board betrays Celto-Norse influences in the border pattern. **1807** Southey *Lett. from England* I. xxv. 293 A *game book, as it is called, is one of the regular publications, wherein the sportsman may keep an account of all the game he kills, the time when, the place where. **1964** R. Perry *World of Tiger* i. 10 On a first examination of the game-books it seems a miracle that there could have been any tigers left alive in India by the end of that [*sc.* the nineteenth] century. **1724** Bp. Downes in Nicolson *Epist. Corr.* 584 A *Game-cast lay so near the Jack, that there was no drawing it, or possibility of saving the game without driving the Jack out of the green. **1812** *Act 52 Geo. III*, c. 93 §5 *marg.*, Additional Duties assessed for Current Year, except on *Game Certificates, which commence from 5th April 1813. **1937** *Brit. Birds* XXXI. 166 A special *game-chick and poultry investigation. **1748** Richardson *Clarissa* (1811) III. 236 A *game chicken that was continually pecking at another. **1844** Thirlwall *Greece* VIII. 155 Democrates only warned him, 'if he had any designs upon Sparta, to hasten them before this game-chicken's spurs were grown'. **1951** *Good Housek. Home Encycl.* 478/2 Accompaniments vary slightly for different birds, but thin gravy, *game chips and fried crumbs are usual. **1961** G. Smith *Business of Loving* xi. 222 Some pheasant with game chips. **1824** Miss Ferrier *Inher.* xxxii, Owing E. L. seven thousand pounds for his *game debts. **1699** Garth *Dispens.* IV. 105 Thus Boys hatch *Game Eggs under Birds o'prey, To make the Fowl more furious for the Fray. **1897** *Westm. Gaz.* 20 May 10/1 The attention of rural police and magistrates is almost monopolised by game egg charges. **1883** *Fisheries Exhib. Catal.* 277 Our freshwater fish-fauna is certainly poor in *game-fish. **1945** Phillips & Reese *How to play Bridge* v. 28 *Game-forcing bids of unlimited strength. A jump bid in a new suit, such as Two Spades over One Heart, or Three Clubs over One Diamond. **14..** *Voc.* in Wr.-Wülcker 597/31 *Negocius..hic dicitur demon nocturnus qui illudit homines, vel qui ludit cum hominibus*, the *game gobelyn. **1929** M. C. Work *Compl. Contract Bridge* 7 Dealer having made a bid that is not a *game-goer. **1929** M. C. Work *Compl. Contract Bridge* i. 6 The dealer's first concern when he picks up his hand is to get his side into a *game-going contract if game is in their cards. **1867** L. Wright *Pract. Poultry Keeper* ii. (1885) 15 When there is a good wide range of any kind, a few *Game hens may be found profitable. **1870** Hardy & Ware *Mod. Hoyle, Cribbage* 89 Sixty one holes each including the 'home' or the *game-hole. **1579** Northbrooke *Treatise* 48 Common *game-houses and tabling houses. **1861** *Act 24 & 25 Vic.* Index, *Game Licences. **1581** Mulcaster *Positions* xviii. (1887) 78 Who used it [fencing] warlike for valiauntnesse in armes..*game-like to winne garlandes and prices. **1340** *Ayenb.* 63 þe hyeȝinges of þe lozeniour and of þe *gememan and of þe scorneres. **1676** Etheredge *Man of Mode* II. ii, Go on, be the *game-mistress o' the town, and enter all our young fops as fast as they come from travel. **1929** *Daily Express* 3 Jan. 15/5 How these *game-pieces..were played in olden days. **1956** Hedström & Taylor tr. *Bergström's Dutch Still-Life Painting* vii. 247 The Dutch game-piece, with which we shall..include pictures of dead domestic birds, is a late branch of still-life painting. **1547–64** Bauldwin *Mor. Philos.* (Palfr.) 90 He, which in the *game place runneth swiftest, and continueth still his pace, obtaineth the crowne for his labour. **1606** Day *Ile of Guls* II. ii. (1881) 39 The Ladies reskewed and the Princes, like crauens, beate out of the game-place! **1564** tr. *Jewel's Apol.* E iiij b, They were laughed and iested at openly of the people in the common *game-playes. **1552** Huloet, *Game players, *ludii*. **1564** Becon *Humble Supplic.* Wks. III. 18 b, The papistes decke themselues lyke Hycke scorner in game players garmentes. **1587** Golding *De Mornay* i. 10 Caligula, who threatned the Ayre if it rained upon his Gameplaiers. **1927** W. E. Collinson *Contemp. Eng.* 13 Old *game-rhymes from the district. **1959** I. & P. Opie *Lore & Lang. Schoolch.* vii. 112 Shirley Temple and Deanna Durbin are two of the stars most often mentioned in game rhymes. **1961** *Sat. Even. Post* 21 Oct. 19/1 The set announced, 'It's Time to *Say When!*' and after a commercial, the first of the day's '*game shows' began. **1975** *Business Week* 24 Feb. 78/2 With much..time filled by adult game shows, McGannon is asking that stations be obliged to set aside a time..when only children's programs would be allowed on the air. **1984** *Broadcast* 7 Dec. 22/1 The year has seen the successful development of a new game show for Channel Four. **1891** *Pall Mall G.* 10 Nov. 5/2 Mr. A. Williamson, *game tenant, for the past two seasons has made a great pet of this animal. **1962** *Antioch Rev.* XXII. 8 What are we to think of a civilization which has not been able to talk about killing almost everybody except in prudential and *game-theoretic terms? **1962** *Listener* 19 Apr. 693/2 Weapons systems and *game-theoretical studies. **1964** K. Winetrout in I. L. Horowitz *New Sociol.* 156 As a mathematician, he may become a *game-theorist with Herman Kahn and others. [**1928** J. von Neumann in *Math. Ann.* C. 295 (*heading*) Zur Theorie der Gesellschaftsspiele.] **1954** J. D. Williams *Compleat Strategyst* i. 13 One-person games are uninteresting, from the *Game Theory point of view... Most of the work done to date in Game Theory deals with the two-person game. **1957** Luce & Raiffa *Games & Decisions* i. 10 Game Theory is a model for situations of conflict among several people, in which two principal modes of resolution are collusion and conciliation. **1959** I. Jefferies *13 Days* iii. 38, I don't like cards, but I did some games-theory once and I could handle the well-known ones. **1961** *Listener* 12 Oct. 558/1 The 'game theory', as it is now being called, is being used to construct quite sophisticated theoretical frameworks to a variety of natural phenomena... Its mathematics can..be used to deal with matters not always thought of as games, such as military situations, labour-management relationships and foreign trade. **1969** B. Sutton-Smith in R. D. Abrahams *Jump-Rope Rhymes* p. ix, Much of the work of the world is carried on through mathematical games theory. **1971** G. K. Roberts *Dict. Political Anal.* 86 Game theory is a useful analytical technique, and has been employed in the study of ..campaign tactics in an election, coalition formation,..etc. **1896** *Westm. Gaz.* 5 Dec. 7/2 If..they lost the first hare on the prosecutor's land, and started another on the same land, they were guilty of *game-trespass.

game (geɪm), *a.*[1] [f. the sb. (sense 15).]

a. Having the spirit of a game-cock; full of pluck, showing 'fight'; plucky, spirited. (Said of animals, and of persons, their actions and attributes.) Esp. in Australia in colloq. phr. (*as*) ***game as Ned Kelly***: very spirited or brave.

1727 [see c]. **1765** *Meretriciad* 20 You're game egad—too much for such a cur. **1809** *Sporting Mag.* XXXIV. 3 What they term a game fellow. **1815** L. Simond *Tour. Gt. Brit.* (ed. 2) I. 127 *note*, A tried cock, dog, or man, is game. **1827–39** De Quincey *Murder* Wks. 1862 IV. 16 If these Friesland hounds had been game we should have no Cartesian philosophy. **1836** W. Irving *Astoria* I. 230 American hunters..possessed of the true game spirit of the west. **1851** MAYNE REID *Scalp Hunt.* xxiii, She [the mare] was evidently game to the backbone. **1852** R. S. SURTEES *Sponge's Sp. Tour* lxviii. 379 The burning scent of a game four-legged fox. **1867** F. FRANCIS *Angling* ix. (1880) 335 The white-trout is one of the gamest fish that swims. **1888** ANNIE S. SWAN *Doris Cheyne* iii. 54 You're game, Miss Doris; you have a spirit equal to the occasion. **1897** MARY KINGSLEY *W. Africa* 399 They brought with them no experience in dealing with a great rapid river; but they tackle it in a game way. **1941** BAKER *Dict. Austral. Slang* 30 *Game as Ned Kelly*, highly courageous; willing to tackle big odds. **1956** S. HOPE *Diggers' Paradise* 89 A common expression on the lips of Aussies of both sexes to describe someone engaged in a risky enterprise is 'he's as game as Ned Kelly'. **1969** *Sun-Herald* (Sydney) 13 July 13/3, I asked him [*sc.* Mick Jagger] if he had heard the expression 'as game as Ned Kelly'. He said he had.

Comb. **1886** *Pall Mall G.* 2 Aug. 5/2 Some rather game-looking, but attenuated, salmon-shaped fish were denominated herring hake.

b. Having the spirit or will *for* or *to do* (something adventurous).

1856 READE *Never too late* I. xxi. 216, I am game to try. **1859** H. KINGSLEY *G. Hamlyn* II. ix. 164 That's a little more than you're game for, I'm thinking. **1874** DASENT *Tales fr. Fjeld* 14 He was quite game to do that.

c. ***to die game***: to meet death resolutely; *fig.* to maintain one's spirit and endurance to the last.

1727 GAY *Beggar's Opera*, Good bye, captain..die game, captain. **1815** SCOTT *Guy M.* liv, The ruffian lay perfectly still and silent. 'He's gaun to die game ony how', said Dinmont. **1840** MARRYAT *Poor Jack* xliii, I shall die game. **1873** H. SPENCER *Stud. Sociol.* viii. (1874) 186 The mob of roughs who witness the hanging of a murderer..half condone his crime if he 'dies game'. **1886** SIR F. H. DOYLE *Remin.* 167 Undisguisedly exulting that he and his borough had died game.

game (geɪm), *a.*[2] [Etymology uncertain.

App. adapted from north midland dialects, where it has the form *gam*, homophonous with the local pron. of GAME *sb.*[1]; perh. shortened from the synonymous GAMMY. The suggestion that it is adopted from Welsh *cam* (fem. *gam*) crooked, is unlikely, as the alleged primary sense of 'crooked' which is given in Dicts. seems to be an etymological figment.]

Of a leg or arm: Lame. Also *transf.*

1787 GROSE *Provinc. Gloss.*, *Game-leg*, a lame leg. **1818** SCOTT *Hrt. Midl.* xxviii, A queer, knowing, shambling animal, with a hatchet-face, a squint, a game-arm, and a limp. **1849** THACKERAY *Pendennis* II. iii, Warrington..said that Bacon had got the game chair, and bawled out to Pen to fetch a sound one from his bedroom. **1854** W. GASKELL *Lect. Lanc. Dial.* i. 4 A poor schoolfellow of mine who had a bent leg..was commonly said to have a 'gam' leg. **1875** J. PAYN *Walter's Word* I. i. 4 You see..with a game-arm..and a game-leg..one feels a little helpless.

game (geɪm), *v.* Forms: α. 1 gam(e)nian, 3–5 gam-, gomen-en, 4 gamne-n, 4, 6 gamen. β. 3 gome-n, 4–5 gam(m)e-n, -yn, 4 gayme, (7–9 *dial.* gam), 3– game. [The α. forms represent OE. *gam(e)nian* (= ON. *gamna*), f. *gamen*, GAME *sb.*[1] The β. forms, which appear first in the 13th c., are strictly another word, independently f. the later shortened form of the sb.]

1. *intr.* To play, sport, jest; to amuse oneself; *occas.* to indulge in amorous play. *Obs.* exc. *dial.*

α. *c* **1000** ÆLFRIC *Gen.* xix. 14 Þa wæs him ȝeþuht, swilce he gamniȝende spræce. *a* **1050** *Liber Scintill.* lv. (1889) 172 Gamenian [L. *jocari*] mid cnafan. *a* **1300** *Floriz & Bl.* 31 Hi ..pleide and gamenede ehc wiþ oþer. *a* **1400–50** *Alexander* 4370 Quen we gamen suld & glade we grete & we pleyn. **1583** STANYHURST *Æneis*, etc. (Arb.) 153 Thee owtragious oathes hee vsed too thunder owt in gamening.

β. *a* **1225** *Ancr. R.* 368 Þet heo gleowede and gomede and wedde mid oðer men. *c* **1485** *Digby Myst.* (1882) I. 329 If ye abide, watkyn, you and I shall game with my distaff that is so Rounde. **1561** *Schole-ho. Wom.* 264 in Hazl. *E.P.P.* IV. 115 Bid him go, when he would game, Unto his customers. **1594** DANIEL *Compl. Rosamond* (ed. 2) xlix, We see the fair condemned that never gamed. *a* **1652** BROME *Mad Couple* III. Wks. 1873 I. 55 My Lord Lovelies Gammed with her. **1886** *S.W. Linc. Gloss.* s.v., 'They were gamming', that is, playing in fun.

†**b.** ***to game at***: to make fun of, deride. *Obs.*

1621 W. SCLATER *Tythes* (1623) 54 When I..affirme first fruits mysticall resemblances of Christ..how merily game you at mee!

†**2.** *trans.* To amuse, please, give pleasure to.

α. *a* **1300** *Cursor M.* 7409 Quen [dauid] wit gleu wald him gammen, His scepe þam-self war sembel samen. **13..** *Sir Beues* (A.) 3192 Ne gamnede hire þat gle riȝt nouȝt. *c* **1330** R. BRUNNE *Chron.* (1810) 18 Sone with þe Danes gamned þam no glewe.

β. *c* **1430** *Sir Tryam.* 462 Moche myrthe was them amonge, But ther gamyd hur no glewe.

†**b.** *impers.* with dat. of pronoun: I (he, etc.) am (is, etc.) pleased or delighted. *Obs.*

α. *a* **1225** *St. Marher.* 11 Me gomeneð ant gledeð al of gastelich murðe.

β. *c* **1205** LAY. 4588 Godlac hauede a god scip: ne gomede him no wiht.

†**c.** *slang.* To make fun of. *Obs.*

a **1700** B. E. *Dict. Cant. Crew* s.v., What you game me?

3. *intr.* To play at games of chance for a prize, stake, or wager; to gamble. Also quasi-*trans.* with cognate obj.

α. **1510–61** [see GAMING *vbl. sb.*].

β. **1529** *Privy Purse Exp. Hen. VIII* (1827) 14 Item delivered to the kinges grace owne handes for to game therew' now at this tyme of Cristemas, C *li.* **1555** W. WATREMAN *Fardle Facions* II. xi. 249 Thei [Turkes] game not for money, or any valewe elles. **1610** B. JONSON *Alch.* III. ii, Why would you be a gallant, and not game? **1648** JENKYN *Blind Guide* iii. 49 A fit cock for such a cock-pit as you game in. **1706** ESTCOURT *Fair Examp.* II. ii, But for the future, if she must game, if she must play, it shall be like Children, for crooked Pins and Counters. **1762** GOLDSM. *Nash* 28 Tho' he gamed high, he always played very fairly. **1777** SHERIDAN *Sch. Scand.* IV. ii, 'Tis a great pity he..loves wine and women so much..And games so deep. **1823** BYRON *Juan* XIV. xviii, When we have..gamed our gaming. **1834** HT. MARTINEAU *Farrers* iv. 58 The same power may tempt the people to game in lotteries. **1863** GEO. ELIOT *Romola* I. xiv, Certain ragged men..were inviting country people to game with them.

b. quasi-*trans.* with advb. compl.: To throw *away* (money), wile *away* (time) by gambling.

1634 HEYWOOD & BROME *Lanc. Witches* I. H.'s Wks. 1874 IV. 182 No longer agoe than last holiday evening he gam'd away eight double ring'd tokens. **1709** MRS. CENTLIVRE *Gamester* v. (1723) 191 He gam'd it away, brother. **1760** C. JOHNSTON *Chrysal* (1822) I. 222 The profusion with which she gamed away her money. **1782** BURKE *Ref. Repr.* Wks. 1812 V. 398 It is for fear of losing the inestimable treasure we have, that I do not venture to game it out of my hands for the vain hope of improving it. **1837** MRS. CAULFEILD *Deluge* 116 Here are dice—Let's..game away these dismal hours.

'game-cock. [f. GAME *sb.* + COCK *sb.*[1]] A cock bred and trained for fighting, or of the breed suitable for the sport of cock-fighting.

1677 WYCHERLEY *Plain Dealer* IV. ii, Young lovers, like game-cocks, are made bolder by being kept without light. **1693** LOCKE *Educ.* §145 They..managed the Dispute as fiercely as two Game-Cocks in the Pit. **1814** W. SKETCHLEY (*title*), The Cocker: containing every information to the breeders and amateurs of that noble bird, the Game Cock. **1837** W. IRVING *Capt. Bonneville* (1849) 27 He is like a game-cock among the common roosters of the poultry-yard.

fig. **1727** GAY *Fables* I. *Eleph. & Bookseller* 76 No author ever spar'd a brother, Wits are game-cocks to one another. *a* **1895** LD. CLARENCE PAGET *Autobiog.* iv. (1896) 80, I consoled myself with the feeling that, at all events, he was an old gamecock, and would do his country credit if he went into action.

'game-fowl. [f. GAME *sb.* + FOWL *sb.*] **a.** A fowl of some species regarded as game: see GAME *sb.* 11. **b.** A domestic fowl of the species used in cock-fighting.

1784 COWPER *Task* III. 312 Should never game-fowl hatch her eggs again, Nor baited hook deceive the fish's eye. **1867** TEGETMEIER *Poultry Bk.* xii. 123 The..superiority of the Game fowls bred in England has been entirely due to the practice of cock-fighting.

†**'gameful,** *a. Obs.* Also 3 gome(n)ful(le, 4–7 gam(e)full. [f. GAME *sb.* + -FUL.]

1. Joyful, playful, sportive, jesting.

c **1205** LAY. 21430 Þa loh Arður..and þus ȝeddien agon mid gomenfulle worden. *a* **1225** *St. Marher.* 10 Icham gomeful ant gled lauerd of thi godlec. **1398** TREVISA *Barth. De P.R.* XVIII. lxxix. (1495) 831 Wyse and wytty kynde makyth to vs gamefull thynges and wonderfull to shewe his myght. *a* **1627** MIDDLETON *Chaste Maid* III. iii, Which will make tedious years seem gameful to me. **1725** POPE *Odyss.* XIX. 667 But my remnant life Heaven shall determine in a gameful strife.

2. Fond of field sports.

1704 D'URFEY *Heir Adopted* 272 The gameful Prince to sports inclin'd..Did Hawking most prefer.

3. Abounding in game.

1610 HOLLAND *Camden's Brit.* I. 290 Of gamefull parks, of meadows fresh. **1695** BLACKMORE *Pr. Arth.* IV. 574 For warlike Toil he leaves the gameful Wood. **1704** POPE *Windsor For.* 95 Now range the hills, the gameful woods beset.

Hence **'gamefully** *adv.*, playfully, jestingly.

1387 TREVISA *Higden* (Rolls) VII. 111 A preost..seide in game 'Why chese ȝe nouȝt me myself?' Whos gaume oþere nouȝt takynge gamfully [etc.].

†**'gamegall.** *Obs.*[−1] [f. GAME *sb.* + GALL *sb.*[2] (? Or mispr. for *gainegall, f. GAIN- *pref.*)] A satirical retort.

1577 STANYHURST *Hist. Irel.* III. 90 in Holinshed *Chron.* I, Shortly after this quippyng gamegall..the Counsaile road to Drogheda.

'game,keeper. [f. GAME *sb.* + KEEPER *sb.*] A servant employed in taking care of game, to prevent poaching, etc.

1670–1 *Act 22 & 23 Car. II*, c. 25 § 1 Bee it enacted..That all Lords of Mannours..may..authorize one or more.. Game-keepers..who..may take and seize all such Gunns, Bowes [etc.]. **1679–88** *Secr. Serv. Money Chas. & Jas.* (Camden) 97 To be..paid over to the ten keepers and one game keeper in Windsor Forrest. **1772** BARRINGTON in *Phil. Trans.* LXII. 305 A greyheaded game-keeper always saw the partridge on the ground before they rose. **1860** *All Year Round* No. 71. 485 It is the gamekeeper's business to repress poachers.

Hence **'gamekeepery** *a.*, *nonce-wd.*, of or befitting a gamekeeper. So also **'gamekeeping** *vbl. sb.*

1858 R. S. SURTEES *Ask Mamma* i. 2 The vulgar groomy gamekeepery styles of dress. **1878** R. JEFFERIES *Gamekeeper at Home* ii. 44 The profession of gamekeeping is in no danger of falling into decay from lack of demand for the skill in woodcraft it implies.

†**'gamel,** *v. Obs.*[−0] [frequentative f. GAME *v.*, or altered form of *gamen*; see GAMBLE *v.*] *intr.* To play games. Only in †**'gameling** *vbl. sb.* and *ppl. a.*

1594 WILLOBIE *Avisa* xxiii, I am no common gameling mate, That list to bowle in euery plaine. **1598** T. BASTARD *Chrestoleros* v. xxxvi, This gameling and this wanton luxurie ..will vndoe him.

gamelan ('gæməlæn). Also **gamelang.** [Javanese, f. *gamel* to handle.] A type of orchestra common in the East Indies, esp. in Java, consisting mainly of percussion instruments with some woodwind and string ones. Also *transf.* and *attrib.*

1817 T. S. RAFFLES *Hist. Java* I. viii. 469 The musical instruments of the Javans are peculiar. Several of them are necessary to compose a *gámelan*, set, or band. **1869** A. R. WALLACE *Malay Archip.* I. vii. 161 A native band or Gamelang, was playing almost all the evening. **1949** C. MCPHEE in *Musical Q.* XXXV. 250 Just at what point the gamelan emerged from a small ensemble of gongs into the elaborately organized orchestra it is today is not known. **1965** *New Statesman* 10 Sept. 370/2 The wild music that Boulez scores for his gamelan orchestra of xylophones, harps, celesta, vibraphone, piano and multitudinous bells. **1967** J. CLEARY *Long Pursuit* viii. 180 Behind him half a dozen musicians had begun to play, two of them on percussion instruments like a xylophone, the others with gongs, cymbals and a drum. 'The gamelan, that is the orchestra, plays what the Darlan tells it.'

b. A percussion instrument resembling a xylophone, used in the East Indies.

1934 in WEBSTER. **1967** *Listener* 10 Aug. 170/1 A woman singer and a gamelan-player moved through the Pullman coaches.

'game-law. [f. GAME *sb.* + LAW.] Usually *pl.* Laws enacted for the preservation of game.

1714 (*title*), The Game Law..5th ed. **1769** BLACKSTONE *Comm.* IV. xxxiii, Though the forest-laws are now mitigated ..yet from this root has sprung up a bastard slip known by the name of the game-law. **1823** SYD. SMITH *Wks.* (1867) II. 32 The game laws have been carried to a pitch of oppression which is a disgrace to the country. **1856** EMERSON *Eng. Traits, Race* Wks. (Bohn) II. 32 The severity of the game-laws certainly indicates an extravagant sympathy of the nation with horses and hunters. **1875** STUBBS *Const. Hist.* §472 This early game-law was primarily intended to stop the meetings of labourers and artificers.

fig. **1820** W. IRVING *Sketch Bk.* (1849) 103 The library was a kind of literary 'preserve', subject to game-laws.

gameless ('geɪmlɪs), *a.* [f. GAME *sb.* + -LESS.] Of a country, district, etc.: Containing or producing no game.

1848 in CRAIG. **1864** *N. Brit. Rev.* Dec. 420 A more gameless forest does not exist. **1891** MISS DOWIE *Girl in Karp.* 104 A fine Scotch contempt for this gameless region.

gamelos, obs. form of CHAMELEON.

†**'gamely,** *a. Obs.* [OE. *gamelic*, **gamenlic*, f. *gamen* GAME + *-lic* -LIKE.] **a.** (OE. only): Theatrical. **b.** Sportive, merry.

1... *Gloss.* in *Haupt's Zeitschrift* IX. 459 *Ridiculosum*, gamelic *vel* bismerlic. *Ibid.* 508 *Theatrales*, gamelicum. *c* **1425** *Fortune* in *Rel. Ant.* II. 8 A lok of that leuedy..Mi gode gameliche game gurte to grounde.

†**'gamely,** *adv.*[1] *Obs.* Forms: 1 gamenlíce, 3 gamli, 4 gamelich(e, gomenly, gamely. [OE. *gamenlíce*, f. *gamen* GAME *sb.* + *-líce* -LY[2]. Cf. prec.] Sportively. **a.** (OE. only): Artfully, deceitfully. **b.** Blithely, joyfully, playfully, excellently.

c **1000** ÆLFRIC *Josh.* ix. 3 Hwæt þa þa Gabaniscean gamenlíce ræddon. *a* **1300** *Cursor M.* 25717 King þat all craftes can, Sua gamli [*but perh. we should read* gainli] has þou graithid for man, þat [etc.]. **13..** *Gaw. & Gr. Knt.* 1079 Þenne watȝ Gawan ful glad, & gomenly he laȝed. *c* **1350** *Will. Palerne* 427 To grete wel his gode wiif & gamely þerafter alle his freliche felawes.

gamely ('geɪmlɪ), *adv.*[2] [f. GAME *a.*[1] + -LY[2].] With spirit, pluckily, courageously.

1861 WHYTE MELVILLE *Mkt. Harb.* 131 Hotspur.. struggled gamely to the top. **1879** BEERBOHM *Patagonia* viii. 127 They [horses] will..dash away..as gamely as if they had just been saddled. **1889** *Pall Mall G.* 8 Aug. 7 One of the dogs gamely gripped him [the otter].

†**'gamelyn.** [ad. F. *camelin*, *sauce cameline* (Cotgr.).] 'A dainty Italian sauce' (Cotgr.). Also *sauce gamelyn.* Cf. CAMELINE *sb.*[2] 2.

c **1460** J. RUSSELL *Bk. Nurture* 539 Sawce gamelyn to heyron-sewe. *Ibid.* 541 Also for bustard, betowre, & shovelere, gamelyn is in sesoun.

gamen(e, obs. form of GAME.

gamene (gə'miːn). *Comm.* Also 8 gemean, 9 game(e)n. [Anglicized pronunc. of Du. *gemeen* common.] (See quot. 1858.)

1703 THORESBY *Let. to Ray* (E.D.S.), *Gemean mather*, the common sort. **1858** HOMANS *Cycl. Comm.* 1297 Dutch or Zealand madder..is divided..into four qualities, distinguished by the terms mull, gamen, ombro, and crops ..The first species..consists of a powder formed by pounding the very small roots..It is comparatively low priced..A second pounding separates about a third part of the larger roots; and this..is sold here under the name of gamene, or gameens.

gamener: see GAMNER, *Obs.*

gameness ('geɪmnɪs). [f. GAME *a.*[1] + -NESS.] The quality of being game; spirit displayed in endurance; courage, pluck.

1810 *Sporting Mag.* XXXVI. 80 This sort of gameness always gets a man the worst of the battle. **1861** HUGHES *Tom Brown at Oxf.* xxiv, Whatever else you might think of Blake, there was no doubt about his gameness. **1882** *Nature* XXV.

216 Both species..exhibit gameness and endurance second to no other fish.

gamening, obs. form of GAMING.

game plan. orig. *U.S.* Also **game-plan, gameplan.** [f. GAME *sb.* + PLAN *sb.*] **a.** *Sport.* (orig. *Amer. Football*). A detailed strategy worked out in advance for winning a particular match.

1949 H. O. CRISLER *Mod. Football* xix. 251 If the defensive line is weak, thrusts at the middle become part of the game plan. **1960** P. W. BRYANT *Building Championship Football Team* x. 212 The defensive and offensive coaches will meet..and review our final game plans. **1967** HOLLANDER & ZIMMERMAN *Football Lingo* 53 A resourceful coach will alter his game plan if his opponent comes up with something unexpected. **1977** *Washington Post* 6 Jan. E11/2 Sammie White, Ahmad Rashad and Stu Voigt are fine receivers, although White obviously wasn't in Grant's game plan against Los Angeles. **1986** *Jrnl.* (Fairfax Co., Va.) 28 May A14/6 The Renegades kept to their game plan of a balanced attack.

b. *fig.* A plan of campaign, esp. in politics; a strategy for achieving a desired result or realizing an ambition.

1941 NEVILLE & CHAPLIN *Never give Sucker Even Break* (1973) 47 Now she puts her hands over her head and follows his game plan. **1970** *Time* 1 June 39/1 The nation's No. 1 football fan [*sc.* President Nixon] had a 'game plan' that his advisors said would stop inflation. **1977** C. MCFADDEN *Serial* (1978) xxi. 48/1 Harvey decided the best game plan was to stay loose. **1977** *Kuwait Times* 1 Nov. 6/4 The Politics of Defeat is a broadside against the entire Carter administration game-plan in the Middle East. **1984** *Times* 5 Nov. 13/2 There was no grandiose career 'gameplan'.

gamer ('geɪmə(r)). See also GAMNER. [f. GAME *v.* + -ER[1].] †**a.** A gamester, an athlete (*obs.*). **b.** One who hunts game, a sportsman (*nonce-use*).

c **1620–30** [see GAMNER 2]. **1887** *Sci. Amer.* 15 Jan. 37 [Labrador] certainly deserves the attention of gamers, fishers [etc.].

gamesman ('geɪmzmən). [f. GAME *sb.* + MAN *sb.*[1]; cf. next.] **1.** = MAN *sb.*[1] 15.

1931 *Antiquity* V. 464 Gamesmen of the same form and material have been unearthed by Watelin at Kish.

2. One who engages in games or sports; *spec.* one who is skilled in gamesmanship.

1947 S. POTTER *Gamesmanship* ii. 21 Psychological tendency, if not temporal necessity, will cause him to drive faster, and—behold! now the gamesman can widen his field and bring in carmanship. **1959** *Punch* 19 Aug. 37/1 If Henry V sending those tennis balls to the King of France wasn't a gamesman I don't know one. **1961** *Times* 8 Mar. 17/7 C. W. Brasher, a member of Achilles, which has had more than its fair share of gamesmen, has admitted that he could bring a mile time of 4 mins. 15 sec. down by 10 sec. with a series of excuses..about track, spikes, and wind. **1963** *Punch* 21 Aug. 264/3 One..wonders how the modern gamesman ever has time to play any games. **1969** *Observer* 21 Dec. 6/1 Academics..can't even think like..Nasser because he's a leader and the gamesmen are just pretending to be.

gamesmanship ('geɪmzmənʃɪp). [f. GAME *sb.* + -MANSHIP.] Skill in winning games, esp. by means that barely qualify as legitimate. Also *transf.*

1947 S. POTTER (*title*) The theory & practice of gamesmanship or the art of winning games without actually cheating. **1952** E. GRIERSON *Reputation for Song* ii. 11 This was so like Laura, with whom a hand she could not play was a hand wasted, but Mr. Clarke, a practitioner of 'gamesmanship' himself, would not be rushed. **1960** *Guardian* 23 Mar. 9/3 Mr. Smirnov..assumed a more confidential manner towards the end of his essay in gamesmanship. **1967** *Times* 8 Apr. 13/6 Sportsmanship..is a switched-off word that has lost ground to gamesmanship.

gamesome ('geɪmsəm), *a.* Also 4 **gamsum**, 5–6 **gamsome.** [f. GAME *sb.* + -SOME.] Full of game or play; frolicsome, merry, playful, sportive.

c **1350** *Will. Palerne* 4193 Sche gamsum & glad goþ hem a-ȝens. **1483** *Cath. Angl.* 149/1 Gameson (*A.* Gamsome), *ludibundus.* **1580** LYLY *Euphues* (Arb.) 274, I now taking heart at grasse, to see hir so gamesome. **1610** HOLLAND *Camden's Brit.* I. 363 Whether they have beene..living creatures, or the gamesome Sports of Nature. *a* **1659** CLEVELAND *Wks.* (1687) 261 The looser pastime of her gamesome Hair. **1735** THOMSON *Liberty* III. 321 The Shepherd..Sits piping to his Flocks and gamesome Kids. **1794** COLERIDGE *To a young Ass*, How thou wouldst toss thy heels in gamesome play! **1841** BROWNING *Pippa* Introd. 24 As if earth turned from work in gamesome mood. **1863** HAWTHORNE *Our Old Home, Near Oxford* (1879) 189 The stags..bounded away, not affrighted, but only shy and gamesome.

Hence **'gamesomely** *adv.*, in a gamesome manner; playfully, sportively; **'gamesomeness**, the quality of being gamesome.

1601 WEEVER *Mirr. Mart.* Bij b, To catch the baulme-sweete breathing of the aire, Which gamesomlie into their bosomes got. **1684** BUNYAN *Pilgr.* II. 45 The fatter the Ox is, the more gamesomly he goes to the Slaughter. **1727** BAILEY vol. II, Gamesomeness. **1813** MOORE *Post-bag* I. 52 A pretty contrivance..Which, however high-mettled, their gamesomeness checks. **1847** HELPS *Friends in C.* (1861) I. ii. 23 The monkey imitates from imitative skill and gamesomeness. **1884** *Graphic* 29 Nov. 566/3 In strength a man, in gamesomeness a child. **1890** *Blackw. Mag.* CXLVIII. 58/2 The smoke puffs gamesomely down the chimney.

gamester ('geɪmstə(r)). Also 6 *Sc.* **gemster**, 6–7 **gamster.** [f. GAME *sb.* + -STER.]

1. a. A player at any game; also, an athlete.

1581 MULCASTER *Positions* xx. (1887) 82 Is it euer red that the athlets or gamesters vsed walking for an exercise? **1601** HOLLAND *Pliny* II. 304 Professed wrestlers, runners and such gamesters at feats of actiuity. **1624** QUARLES *Div. Poems, Job.* xvi. 10 Young Standers-by doe oftentimes see more, Then elder Gamesters. **1662** BLOUNT *Boscobel* II. 9 His Majestie was askt by one of the Gamesters, if he could play a game of Ball call'd *Fives.* **1699** BENTLEY *Phal.* 53 The Gamesters at those Exercises were very stupid and thick-skull'd Fellows. **1775** ADAIR *Amer. Ind.* 400 The gamesters are equal in number on each side. **1832** P. EGAN *Bk. Sports* 340/2 The great interest attached to cricket-matches..will warrant something more than the mere comparison of numbers and names of the gamesters. **1942** BERREY & VAN DEN BARK *Amer. Thes. Slang* §636/1 Athelete; player, ..*gamester.* **1965** *Eng. Studies* XLVI. 464 Gamesters are cheered by *pepsters* and *rallisters.*

b. *dial.* (Berks.) A player at backsword and wrestling.

1857 HUGHES *Tom Brown* I. ii, A pair of heavy single-sticks, with which Benjy himself had won renown long ago as an old gamester. **1859** —— *Scour. White Horse* v. 92 That prizes be awarded for..Backsword Play, Old gamesters, 8*l.*, Young gamesters, 4*l.*, Wrestling, Old Gamesters, 5*l.*, Young Gamesters, 4*l.* *Ibid.* vi. 119 'Who are the old gamesters?' I asked of the man next me. 'Them as has won or shared a first prize at any revel', answered he. **1888** *Berksh. Gloss.*, *Ge-amster*, or *Gaaymester*, one who is skilled at single stick.

†**2.** An actor. *Obs. rare*$^{-1}$.

1596 DALRYMPLE tr. *Leslie's Hist. Scot.* I. 235 Kardes and Bardis, Gemsteris [L. *histriones*] Glouttounis and syk kynd of men.

3. One who habitually plays at games of chance for money or other stake; a gambler.

1553 T. WILSON *Rhet.* 51 No greater gamester in a whole countrey. **1607–8** *N. Riding Rec.* (1884) I. 106 He is a gamester at cardes and dish would waist his estate therby. **1676** DRYDEN *Aurenz.* Prol. 23 A loosing Gamester let him sneak away. **1773** GOLDSM. *Epil. Intended for Mrs. Bulkley*, The Gamester..Oft risks his fortune on one desperate throw. **1880** BROWNING *Clive* 93 Your high-flown gamesters hardly take Umbrage at a factor's elbow if the factor plays his stake.

fig. **1645** BP. HALL *Remedy Discontents* 33 The World is a cheating gamester, suffering us to win at the first. **1647** CLARENDON *Hist. Reb.* II. §93 The Scots needed not now advance their Progress, their Game was in the hands..of better Gamesters. **1851** GALLENGA *Italy* 344 Had he reckoned the odds like other political gamesters, he would [etc.].

†**4.** A merry, frolicsome person. *Obs.*

1598 B. JONSON *Ev. Man in Hum.* I. i, T' have ta'en on trust Such petulant, jeering gamesters, that can spare No argument or subject from their jest. **1613** SHAKS. *Hen. VIII*, I. iv. 45 You are a merry Gamster My Lord Sands.

†**5.** One addicted to amorous sport (see GAME *sb.* 3 b); a lewd person, whether male or female.

1601 SHAKS. *All's Well* v. iii. 188 She's impudent my Lord, And was a common gamester to the Campe. **1621** FLETCHER *Wild Goose Chase* II. iii, Good women scorn such gamesters. **1629** MASSINGER *Picture* I. ii, Thou wast at twelve a gamester, and since that, Studied all kinds of females. *a* **1668** DAVENANT *News fr. Plymouth* III. Dram. Wks. 1873 IV. 145 This I assure you Your satin gamesters practise.

transf. *c* **1640** J. SMYTH *Lives Berkeleys* (1883) I. 156 The Rams..were not admitted all at one tyme..but some reserved..vntill the former gamsters had wasted their strength.

6. (See quot. and cf. GAME *sb.* 12.) *Obs.* exc. *Hist.*

1880 CLARK in *Encycl. Brit.* XI. 701/1 The keeper who looked after them [a 'game' of swans] was the 'gamester'. **1957** N. F. TICEHURST *Mute Swan in Eng.* 121 *Gamester, gamster*, an owner of a game of swan.

gamestress ('geɪmstrɪs). ? *Obs.* [f. prec. + -ESS.] A female gamester.

1651 HOWELL *Venice* 4 She hath allwayes bin..chosen rather to be a Spectatrix or Umpresse, than a Gamestresse. **1665** FLECKNOE *Enigm. Char.* (ed. 2) 10 Of a Gamestress. **1796** MAD. D'ARBLAY *Camilla* V. x. v. 351 To two characters..she unites yet a third..that of a gamestress.

†**'gamestry.** *Obs.*$^{-1}$ [f. GAMESTER + -Y[1].] The practice of gaming.

1599 SANDYS *Europæ Spec.* (1632) 59 If there were any which should still..persist in that wicked gamestrie.

gamesun, obs. form of GAMBESON.

gametal ('gæmɪtəl), *a.* [f. GAMETE + -AL[1].] Having the character of a gamete; conjugating, reproductive, generative.

1888 J. NELSON in *Amer. Jrnl. Psychol.* I. 390 The presence of the reproductive elements exerts a constant stimulus upon the brain cells, which causes them to generate characteristic dreams, that in turn react to produce expulsion of the gametal cells. **1891** M. HARTOG in *Nature* 17 Sept. 484/2 Gametal or gametal nuclei.

gametangium (gæmɪ'tændʒɪəm). Pl. **gametangia.** Also **gametange.** [mod.L., f. *gameta* GAMETE + Gr. ἀγγεῖον vessel.] The cell or organ in which gametes are produced.

1886 VINES in *Encycl. Brit.* XX. 427/2 In Acetabularia the whole of the protoplasm of the gametangium is not used up in the formation of the gametes. **1889** BENNETT & MURRAY *Cryptog. Bot.* 272 The conjugating bodies..are motile ciliated swarm-spores or *zoogametes*, produced by free-cell formation in ordinary or in slightly differentiated cells of the filament, hence termed *gametanges*, their conjugation resulting in the production of a *zygosperm.* **1952** *New Biol.* XIII. 103 A transverse wall is formed a short distance behind each tip, so dividing each swollen branch into two portions, the distal portion being known as a gametangium. **1964** *Oceanogr. & Marine Biol.* II. 198 Gametangia have hitherto been unknown in the genus *Udotea.*

gamete (gæ'miːt, 'gæmiːt). *Biol.* [ad. mod.L. *gameta* ad. Gr. γαμετή a wife, γαμέτης a husband, f. γαμεῖν to marry, f. γάμος marriage.] (See quot. 1887.) Also *Comb.*

1886 S. H. VINES in *Encycl. Brit.* XX. 425/1 This fusion of two similar reproductive cells—this conjugation, as it is termed—is one of the simplest forms of the sexual process; the zygospore is then a sexually produced spore, and the two cells which conjugate to form it are spoken of as *gametes*, —*planogametes* when they possess cilia, *aplanogametes* when they do not. **1887** tr. *De Bary's Fungi* 495, *Gamete*, sexual protoplasmic body..which on conjugation with another gamete of like or unlike outward form gives rise to a body termed zygote. Same as *conjugation-cell.* **1891** M. HARTOG in *Nature* 17 Sept. 484/1 *Anisogamy.* The union of two gametes differing chiefly in size. **1914** GEDDES & THOMSON *Sex* ii. 45 These foci of gamete-making began to be enclosed ..and nourished by adjacent tissue. **1927** HALDANE & HUXLEY *Animal Biol.* ii. 63 Before gamete-formation, the two members of such a pair segregate. **1963** R. P. DALES *Annelids* viii. 164 The posterior gamete-producing segments.

gametic (gæ'metɪk, -'iːtɪk), *a.* *Biol.* [f. GAMETE + -IC.] Of or pertaining to gametes.

1905 R. C. PUNNETT *Mendelism* 25 The theory of gametic purity can be further tested by deducing from it the results which should follow from crossing the heterozygote with either of the homozygotes. *Ibid.* 64 Gametic coupling. **1955** *Sci. News Let.* 2 Apr. 210/1 The third system is 'gametic selection'. This means that the germ cell carrying the disease is more likely to result in offspring than other cells. **1962** *Lancet* 29 Dec. 1383/2 It is difficult to see how selection against a given gametic genotype could occur at all on the female side.

gameto-, combining form of GAMETE, as **ga'metocyst**, a cyst containing two associated gametocytes; **ga'metocyte**, a cell that gives rise to gametes; **gameto'genesis**, the formation of gametes; **gameto'genic, -'ogenous** *adjs.*, giving rise to gametes or to reproductive cells; **game'togeny, -'togony** = *gametogenesis*; **gameto-nucleus** (see quot.); **ga'metophore** *Bot.*, a modified branch or filament bearing sexual organs; so **gameto'phoric** *a.*; **gametophyte**, the sexual form of a thallophyte, as distinguished from the sporophyte, or asexual form; **gameto'phytic** *a.*, pertaining to or occurring on a gametophyte.

1926 C. M. WENYON *Protozool.* I. I. 134 A cyst may be formed around two gametocytes, as in the case of gregarines. It is then distinguished as a *gametocyst. **1955** HUNTER & LWOFF *Biochem. & Physiol. Protozoa* II. 190 The gametes escape from the gametocyst of *Trichonympha* after it is ingested by the roach. **1899** *Nature* 3 Aug. 322/2 The parasites [of malaria] reach their highest development within the vertebrate host, and become either (*a*) sporocytes or (*b*) *gametocytes. **1925** E. B. WILSON *Cell* (ed. 3) vii. 594 The nucleus of each gametocyte now divides successively to form a number..of gamete-nuclei which pass to the periphery and here are budded off..to form minute true gametes. **1966** *New Scientist* 1 Sept. 482/1 The original, parent parasite in the red cell may produce..a merozoite ..[or] a gametocyte. **1900** B. D. JACKSON *Gloss. Bot. Terms* 108/1 **Gametogenesis*, the production of gametes. **1946** *Nature* 14 Dec. 879/1 In the adult *Drosophila*..mustard gas produces a selective action on gametogenesis. **1966** F. A. E. CREW *Found. Genetics* viii. 154 The essential features of gametogenesis are the pairing or conjugation of the two members of each of homologous chromosomes, their separation without any longitudinal splitting and their passage into the nuclei of the two daughter cells. **1900** B. D. JACKSON *Gloss. Bot. Terms* 108/1 **Gametogenic*, giving rise to gametes. **1903** J. B. FARMER et al. in *Proc. R. Soc.* LXXII. 500 The gametogenic tissues which are destined to become the reproductive elements. *Ibid.*, The term *gametogenic*, as here proposed, is also intended to include the primary sporogenous tissue of plants. **1971** *Nature* 2 July 65/1 The gametogenic events of the living testis. **1903** E. A. MINCHIN in E. R. Lankester *Treat. Zool.* I. II. 210 The gametocytes are termed *gametogenous monoonts, the formation of gametes being regarded as a special case of monogony. **1900** B. D. JACKSON *Gloss. Bot. Terms* 108/1 **Gametogeny*, the production of gametes. **1971** *Nature* 9 Apr. 408 By the fourth week gametogeny has been completed and mating has begun. **1910** H. B. FANTHAM in *Proc. Zool. Soc.* II. 678 The processes leading to the formation of the gametes may be termed *gametogony. **1969** *New Scientist* 8 May 306/1 A tiny protozoan that divides its time between a sexual cycle (gametogony)..and two asexual cycles. **1891** M. HARTOG in *Nature* 17 Sept. 484/1 The *gameto-nucleus is formed by the union of several nuclei. **1895** D. H. CAMPBELL *Struct. & Devel. Mosses & Ferns* i. 2 The gametophyte itself may show two well-marked phases, the protonema and the *gametophore. **1957** H. C. BOLD *Morphol. Plants* xvi. 290 The leafy *Sphagnum* plant sometimes is called the leafy gametophore.., inasmuch as it bears the sex organs when mature. **1895** D. H. CAMPBELL *Struct. & Devel. Mosses & Ferns* vi. 155 The sexual organs are borne either separately or together at the summit of the *gametophoric branches. **1895** *Gametophyte [see gametophore above]. **1897** WILLIS *Flower. Pl.* I. 16 These are often termed gametes, and the plant bearing them the gametophyte. **1905** D. H. CAMPBELL *Struct. & Devel. Mosses & Ferns* (ed. 2) 640/2 *Gametophytic buds. **1919** F. O. BOWER *Bot. Living Plant* III. xxi. 341 This gametophytic budding is less common here [*sc.* in ferns] than in the Bryophytes. **1959** FOSTER & GIFFORD *Compar. Morphol. Vascular Plants* ii. 20 The alternation of sporophytic and gametophytic generations in the life cycle.

gametoid ('gæmɪtɔɪd), *sb.* and *a. Biol.* [f. GAMET(E + -OID.] **A.** *sb.* (See quot. 1953.) **B.** *adj.* Having the form or function of a gamete; gamete-like.

1891 [see ZYGOTOID]. **1903** *Proc. R. Soc.* LXXII. 503 The evidence justifies us in.. correlating the appearance of these 'gametoid' neoplasms with the result of a stimulus which has changed the normal somatic course of cell development into that characteristic of reproductive (not embryonic) tissue. **1908** *Practitioner* Feb. 226 Neither gametoid cells, nor flagellated forms of this parasite, have been observed. **1953** I. F. & W. D. HENDERSON *Dict. Sci. Terms* (ed. 5) 165/2 *Gametoid*, a structure behaving like a gamete, as apocytes uniting to form a zygotoid.

gamey: see GAMY.

gamgaron, obs. form of KANGAROO.

Gamgee, gamgee ('gæmdʒiː). The name of Joseph Sampson *Gamgee* (1828–1886), English surgeon, used attrib. (usu. in ***Gamgee tissue***) or absol. to designate a wound-dressing invented by him, consisting of a thickness of cotton-wool between two thin layers of gauze.

1895 *Army & Navy Co-op. Soc. Price List* 699/2 Gamgee Tissue.. per lb 2/6. **1906** *Practitioner* Nov. 674 The application of a baked or scorched pad of Gamgee tissue. **1924** *Glasgow Herald* 8 Apr. 10 Strips of emergency field-dressing gamgee. **1937** 'A. BRIDGE' *Enchanter's Nightshade* xxvi. 347 The complicated apparatus of poultices and gamgee jackets.

gamic ('gæmɪk), *a.* [ad. Gr. γαμικός, relating to marriage, f. γάμος marriage.]

1. *Biol.* Having a sexual character; sexual.

1864 H. SPENCER *Princ. Biol.* I. 229 In each ovarium along with the rudiments of agamic eggs.. there usually.. exists the rudiment of an ephippial egg; which, from sundry evidences, is inferred to be a sexual or gamic egg. *Ibid.* 230 Four times.. as great as that contained in a gamic brood.

2. *Geom.* ***gamic edges***, corresponding edges of an autopolar polyhedron. Also as *sb.*

1856 KIRKMAN in *Phil. Trans.* CXLVII. 184 Two such edges I call a gamic pair, or a pair of gamics, either being the gamic of the other.

† **'gamical**, *a. Obs.*$^{-1}$ In 7 gamacal. [f. Gr. γαμικ-ός (f. γάμος marriage) + -AL[1].] Of or pertaining to marriage or to a husband; marital.

1660 R. COKE *Power & Subj.* 12 Humane Laws are three-fold, viz. Secular, Temporal, or Civil.. or Gamacal, viz. the Laws of the Husband; or Paternal.

gamin (gamɛ̃). [a. F. *gamin.*] A neglected boy, left to run about the streets; a street Arab.

1840 THACKERAY *Paris Sk.-bk.* (1872) 6 There are the little gamins mocking him. **1864** F. W. ROBINSON *Mattie, a Stray* x, One Kent Street gamin out of business and dodging the policeman behind a Patent Safety. **1873** MISS YONGE *Pillars of Ho.* I. vi. (1880) 134 'Our little gamin has the most of the Good Samaritan in him', said Mr. Audley.

gamine (ga'min). [Fr.] A female gamin; an attractively pert, mischievous or elfish girl or young woman, usually small and slim. Also *attrib.* or quasi-*adj.*

1899 C. SCOTT *Drama of Yesterday* II. 243 A veritable *gamine*, there is no other word which so thoroughly expresses her. **1921** *Glasgow Herald* 23 Apr. 4 The 'Coquette' is an unscrupulous milliner's assistant, a regular 'gamine', who plays off a lover against a husband. **1925** D. H. LAWRENCE *St. Mawr* 8 He was fascinated by Lou's quaint aplomb.. her *gamine* knowingness. **1957** 'D. RUTHERFORD' *Long Echo* vii. 131 The actress.. who had lately adopted the gamine style of hair-cut. **1962** I. MURDOCH *Unofficial Rose* xxvi. 250 The puckish *gamine* who, alas, sometimes enjoyed teasing and tormenting him.

‖ **gaminerie** (gaminri, gə'miːnərɪ). [Fr.] The behaviour or characteristics of a gamin or gamine.

1917 J. AGATE *Buzz, Buzz!* 221 With the interment of his little friend [*sc.* a monkey] Anatole buried for ever his own *gaminerie*. **1930** *Observer* 1 June 15 Amused by the rich *gaminerie* of Miss H. **1960** A. POWELL *Casanova's Chinese Restaurant* 51 Determination not to be jockeyed out of either his *gaminerie* or accustomed manner of ordering his own life.

So **gami'nesque** *a.*, resembling or characteristic of a gamin or gamine.

1928 *Manch. Guardian Weekly* 17 Aug. 135/2 She lets fly a full handful of her best gaminesque tricks. **1940** H. G. WELLS *Babes in Darkling Wood* I. i. 26 Our young people cast off the cares of the world abruptly and became gaminesque.

gaming ('geɪmɪŋ), *vbl. sb.* Also 6 **gam(e)ning.** [f. GAME *v.* + -ING[1].]

1. The action or habit of playing at games of chance for stakes; gambling.

a. c **1510** BARCLAY *Mirr. Gd. Manners* (1570) E iv, An olde man can play, and keepe his grauitie Of death the remembrance his gamning ought to be. **1545** ASCHAM *Toxoph.* (Arb.) 51 To him that compared gamning with shoting wyll I answere. **1561** DAUS tr. *Bullinger on Apoc.* (1573) 14 b, To abuse the Sonday, in gamenyng, drinkyng, dauncyng, and worldly businesse.

β. **1501** *Bury Wills* (Camden) 90 Suche mony as I haue wanne or loste in gamyng. **1571** GOLDING *Calvin on Ps.* xviii. 21 The master of a gaming by whose assurance and leading he is brought foorth to thencounter. a **1602** W. PERKINS *Cases Consc.* (1619) 327 Wee may not liue idlely, and giue our selues to riot and gaming. **1668** EVELYN *Mem.* (1857) II. 35, I saw deep and prodigious gaming at the Groom-Porter's. a **1715** BURNET *Own Time* (1766) II. 113 He loved gaming the most of any man of business I ever knew. a **1797** BURKE *Fragm. Tract Popery Laws* Wks. IX. 364 Such deep gaming for stakes so valuable ought not to be admitted. **1856** EMERSON *Eng. Traits, Aristocracy* Wks. (Bohn) II. 86 Gaming, racing, drinking, and mistresses bring them down.

†**2.** *Gr.* and *Rom. Antiq.* The celebration of games; an athletic or musical contest. *Obs.*

1587 GOLDING *De Mornay* i. 10 Greate Personages, whose Images.. were turned into Idolles, their woorthie doings into yeerely Gamings. **1600** HOLLAND *Livy* XLV. xxxii. (1609) 1223 At the great and solemne gamings [L. *magnis ludis*] in Greece. **1606** —— *Sueton.* 188 Those Cities and states where solemne gamings of musicke are usually held.

3. *attrib.* and *Comb.*, as ***gaming board, -humour, -ordinary, -place***; **gaming-proof** *a.*, proof against temptations to gaming. Also GAMING-HOUSE, -TABLE.

1932 *Discovery* Nov. 341/2 A magnificent *gaming board is unique among Irish examples of Norse culture. **1938** *Burlington Mag.* July 40/1 Inlaid gaming boards. **1589** *Pappe w. Hatchet* C iv a, You would make the Church like *Primero*, four religions in it, and nere one like another. I cannot out of his *gaming humour. ? c **1600** *Distracted Emp.* I. i. in *Bullen O. Pl.* III. 166 Thy gameing humor hath been like a fyer. **1712** SWIFT *Let. Eng. Tongue* Wks. 1755 II. I. 189 All the odd words they have picked up in a coffee-house, or a *gaming ordinary, are produced as flowers of style. **1864** BURTON *Scot Abr.* I. v. 254 That.. a censor be appointed.. to go now and then to the billiard-tables, and to the other *gaming-places. **1810** *Sporting Mag.* XXXVI 122 Half a dozen officers all *gaming-proof, with empty purses.

'gaming, *ppl. a.* [f. GAME *v.* + -ING[2].] That games; †sportive, jocular.

1552 HULOET, Gaminge or full of game, *iocosus.* **1617** R. CLAYTON in *Lismore Papers* Ser. II. (1887) II. 112 Gibson the gamming mynistir delivered mee this letter. **1700** T. BROWN tr. *Fresny's Amusem. Ser. & Com.* 104 If he had seen any of our Gaming Ladies there.

'gaming-house. [f. GAMING *vbl. sb.* + HOUSE.] A house where gaming is practised.

1624 SANDERSON *Serm.* I. 251 A prodigal gallant.. will set.. hundreds of them [pounds] flying at one afternoons sitting in a gaming-house. **1709** *Lond. Gaz.* No. 4525/3 The Groom-Porter doth hereby declare, that he neither Licenses or Tolerates any Person to Game, or keep Gaming-Houses. **1755** SMOLLETT *Quix.* (1803) IV. 92 This gentleman has been at play at that there gaming-house over the way. **1836** MARRYAT *Japhet* lv, I passed the gaming-house—I did pass it; but I returned, and lost every shilling.

'gaming-ˌtable. [f. GAMING *vbl. sb.* + TABLE.] A table used for the purpose of gaming.

1598 BARRET *Theor. Warres* IV. iv. 113 He ought not to suffer them anie gaming Tables. **1709** *Lond. Gaz.* No. 4525/3 Whereas several People keep Gaming-Houses, Gaming-Tables, Raffling-Shops. **1777** ROBERTSON *Hist. Amer.* (1783) II. 187 Their furs.. their clothes, their arms, are staked at the gaming-table.. upon a single cast. **1818** COBBETT *Pol. Reg.* XXXIII. 176 Money lost by him at the gaming-table or on the highway. **1884** J. HALL *Chr. Home* 130 Money flowed freely around the gaming-table.

gamma ('gæmə). [Gr. γάμμα.]

1. a. The third letter of the Greek alphabet, Γ, γ.

c **1400** MAUNDEV. (1839) iii. 20 Here ȝee may seen hem [Lettres], with the Names.. α Alpha, β Betha, γ Gamma [etc.]. **1775** in ASH. **1885** *Athenæum* 11 July 48/2 Whenever it occurs this intrusive gamma is hard.

b. An examiner's third-class mark. Also *transf.* and *attrib.*

1932 A. HUXLEY *Brave New World* xi. 188 The fifty-six.. machines were being manipulated by fifty-six aquiline and ginger Gammas. *Ibid.* xii. 204 A creature with a Gamma-Minus physique. **1956** L. E. JONES *Edwardian Youth* iv. 98 A Second Class in Greats, thanks to 'Gammas' for Greek and Latin composition. **1958** [see BETA 3]. **1959** E. WAUGH *R. Knox* iv. 94 To qualify for a first it was necessary to get alphas in seven papers... A gamma cancelled an alpha. Betas were neutral. **1961** M. BEADLE *These Ruins are Inhabited* (1963) vi. 85 He's my gamma card... That's what the fellows call it. Because the lowest grade is gamma.

c. Used as a symbol for various quantities, etc., in science, etc.:

(i) *Metallurgy.* (*a*) Applied to one of a series of allotropic forms of a metal, as ***gamma iron***, the allotrope of iron stable between 910°C and 1,403°C, characterized by a face-centred cubic crystal structure. (*b*) Applied to a solid solution in a range of alloys, as ***gamma brass***, the third of a series of alloys of copper and zinc.

1896 F. OSMOND in *Jrnl. Iron & Steel Inst.* XLIX. 180 It was necessary to distinguish at least three molecular states of iron, which were respectively stable within certain limits of temperature: α below 700°, β between a range of 750° to 860°, γ above 860°. *Ibid.* 187 The distinction established between γ and β iron.. is not an arbitrary, but an experimental one. **1902**, etc. [see ALPHA 3 d]. **1904** E. S. SHEPHERD in *Jrnl. Physical Chem.* VIII. 435 Copper and zinc unite to form six series of solid solutions, which have been distinguished [in this paper] as α, β, γ, δ, ε, and η. **1925** *Phil. Mag.* L. 311 Some authors have supposed γ-brass to be $CuZn_2$, while others believe that it is a solid solution of zinc in Cu_2Zn_3. **1956** G. S. BRADY *Materials Handbk.* (ed. 8) 116 Gamma brass, with the zinc above 45%,.. is not easily worked either hot or cold. **1963** W. H. DENNIS *Metallurgy Ferrous Metals* i. 4 From 1,403°C to its melting point it again changes from the f.c.c. gamma iron to b.c.c. delta iron.

(ii) *Physics.* ***gamma rays*** or ***radiation***, electromagnetic radiation of very short wavelength emitted by radioactive substances, orig. regarded as the third and most penetrating kind of radiation emitted by radium but now known to be identical with very short X-rays. So ***gamma ray*** or ***particle***, a single photon of gamma radiation.

1903 RUTHERFORD in *Phil. Mag.* Feb. 177 The γ rays, which are non-deviable by a magnetic field, and which are of a very penetrating character. **1904** R. J. STRUTT *Becquerel Rays* iii. 83, I have succeeded in observing the γ-radiation from 10 milligrammes of radium bromide. **1926** R. W. LAWSON tr. *Hevesy & Paneth's Man. Radioactivity* iv. 49 A γ-'particle' produces 1·5 pairs of ions per unit of length. **1930** J. BUCKINGHAM *Matter & Radiation* 31 The longest X-rays have the properties of the shortest ultra-violet rays and the longest Gamma-rays merge into the shortest X-rays. **1942** S. TOLANSKY *Introd. Atomic Physics* xvi. 272 The nucleus, being usually left in an unstable condition after the departure of the β-particle, reverts back to a more stable state, the surplus energy being radiated as a γ-ray. **1957** [see BETA 2 f]. **1958** *Listener* 30 Oct. 704/1 Food-preservation by gamma radiation. **1961** *Aeroplane* C. 391/1 This will be the first attempt at 'gamma ray astronomy' from a satellite. Scientists are now limited in their study of extra-terrestrial gamma radiation because their measurements are affected by existing radiation in the Earth's atmosphere. **1969** *Times* 29 Sept. 12/6 What is almost certainly the discovery of the first gamma ray star has now been reported.

Hence ellipt. for *gamma rays* in ***gamma counter, emitter, irradiation***, etc.; so ***gamma emitting*** adj.

1929 *Brit. Med. Jrnl.* 14 Sept. 508/1 (*heading*) The effect of gamma irradiation on cell division. **1949** W. S. EASTWOOD *Surv. Pile Made Isotopes* 1 Sources of this kind have previously been confined to the natural gamma emitting elements. **1949** *Non-Destructive Testing* VIII. II. 23/1 It is standard practice in gamma radiography to place the film between sheets of lead when making an exposure. **1951** *Nucleonics* IX. I. 50 British industry has never made wide use of the natural gamma emitters radium and radon for radiography. **1953** *Ann. Reg. 1952* 403 Gamma radiography (the method of photographing through solid objects such as metals). **1955** *Gloss. Terms Radiology* (*B.S.I.*) 6 *Gamma emitter*, an atom whose radioactive decay process is associated with the emission of gamma rays. **1961** *Lancet* 16 Sept. 633/2 Rb is a hard gamma emitter. **1971** *Nature* 4 June 324/1 Radioactivity was measured in a well-type gamma counter.

(iii) *Photogr.* The gradient of the straight-line portion of the characteristic curve of a photographic emulsion, taken as measuring the contrast of the developed image compared with that of the scene photographed; hence *loosely*, contrast. Similarly in *Television*, a measure of the contrast of the transmitted picture compared with that of the scene televised.

1903 *Photogr. Jrnl.* XLIII. 48 The relation between the development factor (afterwards called γ) and the time of development (*t*). **1935** *Discovery* Mar. 85/1 When the plate is removed from the [compound] developer it generally has a lower contrast (gamma) than if it had been normally developed. **1937** A. T. WITTS *Telev. Cycl.* 65 *Intensity contrast*, the contrast in detail in a picture, sometimes referred to as the gamma of the picture. **1961** G. MILLERSON *Technique Telev. Production* iii. 48 From the angle of the slope, the curve's gamma can be deduced (tan α)... A low gamma device accepts a wide contrast range, but compresses it to fit reproduction limits. **1962** *Unesco Bull. Libr.* XVI. 16 A high value of gamma is desirable in photographic reproduction of lines, as in the pages of a printed book.

(iv) A unit of magnetic field strength, 10^{-5} oersted.

1903 *Nature* 5 Nov. 6/1 There was a movement of the declination needle to the west through about 34′, and a diminution of 240 γ in the horizontal force. **1967** *New Scientist* 7 Dec. 617/2 The lunar magnetic field is no bigger than two gammas.

(v) A unit of mass, one millionth part of a gramme.

1931 *Industrial & Engin. Chem.* (*Analytical Ed.*) 15 July 314/2 The value obtained was 4·0 γ copper per gram (1 γ = 0·001 mg.) for the combined filtrates. **1940** *Ibid.* 15 June 359/2 The Committee on Nomenclature, Spelling, and Pronunciation of the American Chemical Society has approved the following recommendation of the Division of Microchemistry: For 0·001 milligram the term 'microgram', designated by the symbol γ (the word 'gamma' should not be used as a substitute for 'microgram'). **1956** A. HUXLEY *Let.* 23 Sept. (1969) 807 Fifty gamma of LSD were sufficient to produce in me virtually the full effect of the standard dose. **1963** JERRARD & MCNEILL *Dict. Sci. Units* 55 In 1937 it was claimed that the gamma was being superseded by the microgramme in the United Kingdom whereas the gamma reigned supreme in the U.S.A. and continental Europe.

(vi) ***gamma globulin*** (see quot. 1957).

1937 A. TISELIUS in *Biochem. Jrnl.* XXXI. 1466 The fastest of these components could be identified with serum albumin. The other three.. are more or less completely precipitated by half saturation with ammonium sulphate. They will therefore be named α, β, and γ serum-globulin. *Ibid.* 1473 The β- and γ- globulins gave rather diffuse boundaries. **1957** *Dorland's Med. Dict.* (ed. 23) 563/2 *Gamma g[lobulin]s*, globulins of plasma which in neutral or alkaline solutions have the slowest electrophoretic mobility... Most antibodies are gamma globulins. **1960** M. E. FLOREY *Clin. Appl. Antibiotics* II. vii. 202 Gamma globulin has been considered to play a part in enhancing the effect of antibiotic therapy. **1970** *Nature* 7 Nov. 509/2 'Immunoglobulin' thus superseded 'γ-globulin'.

†**2.** = GAMUT. [See GAMME.] *Obs.*

1622 PEACHAM *Compl. Gent.* xi. (1634) 104 Two Lutes of equall size being.. tuned Vnison, or alike in the Gamma, G sol re vt. **1724** *Explic. For. Words Mus.*, *Gama* or *Gamma*, is what we call the Gamut. **1825** DANNELEY *Encycl. Mus.*, *Gamme.. Gamma, Gamut* or *Gammut.*

†**3.** *Surg.* (See quot.) *Obs.* Cf. GAMMOT.

1848 CRAIG, *Gamma*..a surgical instrument used for cauterising a hernia—so called from its shape resembling that letter. **1854** in MAYNE *Expos. Lex.*

4. A common moth, *Plusia gamma*. In full ***gamma moth***.

1869 *Eng. Mech.* 24 Dec. 345/2 The..caterpillar of the Gamma moth is an instance. **1882** *Cassell's Nat. Hist.* VI. 65 Several of the *Plusidæ* are also day-flying Moths. The well-known Gamma Moth or Silver Y (*Plusia gamma*) is one of these.

5. *Comb.*, as ***gamma-shaped*** adj.; **gamma-function** *Math.* (see quot. 1865).

1865 B. PRICE *Infinit. Calc.* (ed. 2) II. 155 The symbol $\Gamma(n)$, devised by Legendre, has been of late ordinarily employed to denote it; so that we have

$$\Gamma(n) = \int_0^\infty e^{-x}x^{n-1}dx.$$

For this reason and for the sake of a distinctive name, the definite integral has been called the Gamma-function. **1875** B. WILLIAMSON *Integral Calc.* 150 All definite integrals which are reducible to Gamma-functions. **1893** W. M. RAMSAY *Ch. in Rom. Emp.* xii. 262 A gamma-shaped crypt, attached to a small chapel.

‖**gammadion** (gæˈmeɪdɪɒn). Also **gammation.** [a. late Gr. γαμμάτιον, γαμμάδιον, f. γάμμα.] A decorative pattern formed of repetitions or combinations of the shape of the Greek letter gamma (Γ); by antiquaries applied chiefly to the particular device called otherwise FYLFOT; also to a figure composed of four gammas placed back to back in such a way as to form a voided Greek cross.

1848 B. WEBB *Cont. Ecclesiol.* 432 Apostles with gammadæ [*sic*] on their robes. **1872** *Gloss. Eccl. Terms* (ed. Shipley), *Gammadion*, the same as *Gammadium* or *Fylfot*. **1876** ROCK *Text. Fabr.* v. 36 This word Gammadion was a word applied as often to the patterns on silks as to the figures wrought on gold and silver. **1877** LEE *Gloss. Liturg. & Eccl. Terms, Fylfot*..was also called Gammation..the Greek term for this mystical device. **1889** ELVIN *Dict. Heraldry, Gammadion*, a Cross potent rebated.

attrib. **1869** MRS. PALLISER *Lace* ii. 19 Two specimens of ..network..the one ornamented with..shields and crosses, the other with the mediæval gammadion pattern.

gamma grass, var. GAMA GRASS.

gammald, obs. Sc. form of GAMBOL.

gammarid (ˈgæmərɪd). [ad. mod.L. *Gammarid-æ*, f. L. *gammar-us* (*cammarus*), a. Gr. κάμμαρος a sea-crab or lobster: see -ID.] An individual of the family *Gammaridæ* of amphipodous crustacea, of which the typical genus is *Gammarus*.

1852 DANA *Crust.* II. 825 The family of gressorial Gammarids.

gammarine (ˈgæmərɪn). *Zool.* [f. L. *gammarus* (see prec.) + -INE.] (See quot.)

1842 BRANDE *Dict. Sci.*, etc., *Gammarines, Gammarina*, the name of a family of Amphipodous Crustaceans, having the genus *Gammarus*, or the sand-hopper, as the type.

gammarolite (gəˈmærəlaɪt). [f. L. *gammarus* crab + -LITE.] A fossil crustacean of the genus *Gammarus* or some allied genus.

1846 SMART, *Gammarolite*, a fossil crab.

gammaut, obs. form of GAMUT.

†**gamme.** *Mus. Obs.* Also 5–7 gam. [a. F. *gamme*, ad. It. and med.L. *gamma*, a. Gr. GAMMA, the letter Γ, used as the symbol of the lowest note in the mediæval scale.] = GAMUT.

1390 GOWER *Conf.* III. 90 Now highe notis and now lowe, As by the gamme a man may knowe. *c* **1440** *Promp. Parv.* 185/2 Gamme of song, *gamma*. *c* **1470** *Burlesque* in *Rel. Ant.* I. 86 The goos gagult ever more, the gam was better to here. **1597** MORLEY *Introd. Mus.* 2 Here is the Scale of Musicke, which wee terme the Gam. **1669** COKAINE *Poems, Elegie T. Pilkington* 78 Yet he at Gamut frequent was, and taught Many to play, till Death set his Gam out. **1727–41** CHAMBERS *Cycl., Gammut*, or *Gamm*. **1730–6** BAILEY (folio), *Gam*, the first or gravest note in the modern scale of musick.

gammen, obs. form of GAME.

gammer (ˈgæmə(r)), *sb.* Also 6–8 **gammar**, 5 (once) **gandmer.** [See GAFFER. The spelling *gandmer* in 1589 shows that the word was then regarded as a corruption of *grandmother*.] A rustic title for an old woman, corresponding to GAFFER for a man.

1575 J. STILL (*title*), A Ryght Pithy, Pleasaunt and merie Comedie: Intytuled Gammer Gurtons Nedle. *Ibid.* I. iii, My Gammer is so out of course, and frantyke all at ones. **1589** R. HARVEY *Pl. Perc.* 1 Now gandmer are not these your examples moralized? **1614** B. JONSON *Barth. Fair* v. vi, Hee has stolne gammar Vrsla's panne. **1634** HEYWOOD & BROME *Lanc. Witches* II. H.'s Wks. 1874 IV. 199 But gammer are not you a Witch? **1719** D'URFEY *Pills* (1872) III. 18 Our honest old Gammer is laid in the Clay. **1742** FIELDING *J. Andrews* IV. xv, The pedlar..listened with the utmost attention to gammer Andrews's story. *c* **1815** *Houlston's Juvenile Tracts, Cork Jacket* 1, 'I will tell you a tale' said old Gammer Green. **1833** TENNYSON *Goose* ix, Then yelp'd the cur, and yawl'd the cat; Ran Gaffer, stumbled Gammer. *a* **1845** HOOD *Tale Trumpet* viii, There never was such a deaf old Gammer! **1866** BLACKMORE *Cradock Nowell* xv, The rector having learned every gammer's alloverishness and every gaffer's rheumatics.

gammer (ˈgæmə(r)), *v. dial.* [Perh. f. prec. sb.; cf. *gossip*, F. *commérage*, etc.] *intr.* To idle.

1788 W. MARSHALL *Yorksh.* II. 331 To *Gammer*, to idle. **1876** *Whitby Gloss.* s.v., 'Gying gammering about', sauntering and tattling all over.

gammerel, dial. form of GAMBREL.

gammerstang (ˈgæməstæŋ). *dial.* Also 6 **gamarstangue**, 8–9 **gammerstags**, 9 *Sc.* **-stel**, **gomerstang.** [? f. GAMMER *sb.* (but cf. GOMEREL) + STANG pole.]

1. A tall, awkward person, usually a woman.

1570 LEVINS *Manip.* 23 A Gamarstangue, *oblongula*. **1684** *Yorksh. Dial.* 348 (E.D.S. No. 76) Wad ta saw thy-sell, thou great Gammerstang! For sham, Woman! **1802** R. ANDERSON *Cumbld. Ball.* 25 Souple gammerstang! **1876** *Whitby Gloss., Gammerstags*, a large awkward female. **1882** *Lanc. Gloss., Gammerstang* (N. Lanc.), an awkward, tall, slender person, male or female. **1890** HALL CAINE *Bondman* xxiv, 'The sweep!' 'the thief!' 'the wastrel!' 'the gomer-stang!' they called him.

2. A rude, wanton girl.

1788 W. MARSHALL *Yorksh.* II. 331, *Gammerstags*, an idle, loose girl. **1825–80** JAMIESON, *Gammerstel*, a foolish girl. **1868** ATKINSON *Cleveland Gloss., Gammer-stags, gammer-stang*, an idle or rude and wanton wench.

†ˈ**gammet.** ? = GRUMMET[2].

1778 FOORD in *Trans. Soc. Arts* (1784) II. 215, I still fix the line to the Harpoon..with the addition of what I call a Snap Gammet, which Gammet is made of rattlin line, traverses in the Harpoon, next the breech, and is sized to the line about two feet from the end or noose, with about eight turns of Whale line yarn; which Gammet or sizeing, puts the line in motion, and breaks, but does not hurt the line.

Gammexane (gæˈmɛkseɪn, ˈgæməkseɪn). Also **gammexane.** [f. *gamma*-hexachlorocyclo*hexane*, the systematic chemical name.] The proprietary name of an isomer of benzene hexachloride used as an insecticide.

The proprietary term was re-registered as *Gammexan* in 1951 (*Trade Marks Jrnl.* 3 Oct., p. 920).

1945 *Trade Marks Jrnl.* 7 Nov. 541/1 *Gammexane*, pharmaceutical substances for human use and for veterinary use; sanitary substances, insecticides, preparations for destroying vermin. Imperial Chemical Industries Limited. **1945** [see BENZENE 3]. **1961** C. H. DOUGLAS-TODD *Pop. Whippet* 148 Gammexane powder..will kill all living insects on a dog.

gammin, obs. form of GAME.

†ˈ**gammock**, *sb.*[1] *Obs.* [var. CAMMOCK.] The plant *Ononis spinosa* or Rest-harrow.

1578 LYTE *Dodoens* VI. x. 669 Gammocke or ground Furze. **1605** TIMME *Quersit.* I. xiii. 65 The salt of gammock, other-wise called rest-harrow, petty whynne, or ground furze.

gammock (ˈgæmək), *sb.*[2] *dial.* [? f. GAME *sb.*[1] + -OCK.] A game, jest, piece of fun; also (without *a* or plural) fun, frolic, foolish sport.

1819 'R. RABELAIS' *Abeillard & Heloisa* 176 'Tis but a fash'nable gammock. **1823** 'JON BEE' *Dict. Turf, Gammocks*, running up and down, as in a fair, rolling among the hay, or flaunting at Vauxhall. **1827** *Examiner* 517/2 The gammocks of a set of indiscriminating monument-destroyers. **1841** HARTSHORNE *Salop. Antiqua* Gloss., *Gamock*, foolish sport, practical jokes. **1891** *Sheffield Gloss.* Supp. *s.v.*, 'She's too much gammock about her.'

gammock (ˈgæmək), *v.* [f. prec.] *intr.* To 'lark about', frolic or romp.

1854 MISS BAKER *Northants. Gloss.* s.v., 'Our John's always going gammocking about.' **1863** SALA *Capt. Dangerous* I. viii. 225, I was gammocking in a hayfield with another lass. **1886** *Chester Gloss., Gammock*, to play pranks. **1891** in *Wiltsh. Gloss.*

gammon (ˈgæmən), *sb.*[1] Forms: 5–6 **gambon(e**, 6 **gammound, gamond(e**, (*Sc.* **gawmond**), 6–7 **gammond, gamon**, 9 *Sc.* **gammont**, 6– **gammon.** [a. ONF. *gambon* (mod.F. *jambon*) ham, f. *gambe* (mod.F. *jambe*) leg.]

†**1.** The ham or haunch of a swine. Also *transf.*

1486 *Bk. St. Albans*, F iij b, The peestellis and the gambons deperte theym .ij. **1601** HOLLAND *Pliny* II. 332 In the pestle and gammond both of a swine, there be certain ioint whirlbones. **1611** COTGR. s.v. *Accule*, The wild Bore.. brought vnto a bay sets him on his Gammons. **1613** BEAUM. & FL. *Captain* II. ii, I would have him [Captain Jacomo] buried Even as he lyes, crosse legg'd, like one o' th' Templers, (If his west-phaly gammons will hold crossing).

2. The bottom piece of a flitch of bacon, including the hind leg; also, a smoked or cured ham.

a **1529** SKELTON *El. Rumming* Wks. (1736) 132 Than came haltynge Jone And broughte a gambone Of bakon that was reastye. **1555** EDEN *Decades* 3 The other moste fleshy partes they pouder for store as we do..gammondes of bakon. **1658** R. WHITE tr. *Digby's Powd. Symp.* (1660) 40 If one put gammons of bacon, or beef, or any other flesh within the chimney. **1719** D'URFEY *Pills* (1872) I. 268 A good Westphalia Gammon Is counted dainty Fare. **1771** GOLDSM. *Haunch Venison* 10 In some Irish houses, where things are so-so, One gammon of bacon hangs up for a show. **1808** SCOTT *Marm.* III. iii, Gammons of the tusky boar. **1851** D. JERROLD *St. Giles* xviii, Here's the bread and cheese, and all that's left o' the gammon o' bacon.

3. *Sc. dial.* (See quot.)

1825–80 JAMIESON, *Gammonts, gammons*, the feet of an animal; often those of pigs, sometimes called petit-toes.

4. *Comb.*, as ***gammon-faced***, ***-visaged*** adjs.; **gammon-essence** (see quot.).

1604 MARSTON *Malcontent* IV. iii, The sallow Westphalian, gamon-faced zaza, Cries, Stand out. **1630** J. TAYLOR (Water P.) *Wks.* II. 17 Thou kildst the gammon visag'd poore Westphalians. **1706** PHILLIPS (ed. Kersey), *Gammon-Essence* (in Cookery) is made of thin Slices of Gammon of Bacon dress'd in a Stew-pan with a Ragoo.

gammon (ˈgæmən), *sb.*[2] *Naut.* [Of unknown origin: some have conjectured that it is f. GAMMON *v.*[3], and that the latter contains an allusion to the tying up of a *gammon* or ham.]

1. The lashing of the bowsprit. Now usually called GAMMONING.

1689 S. SEWALL *Diary* 12 Nov. (1882) I. 281 Strengthen the Bolt-sprit, the Gammon of which was loosed. **1748** *Anson's Voy.* I. viii. 82 They had broke their fore-stay and the gammon of the bowsprit.

2. *Comb.*, as **gammon-knee, -plate, -shackle** (see quots.).

1846 YOUNG *Naut. Dict.* s.v. *Gammoning*, It is generally made fast to a ring, called the Gammon-shackle, formed on the end of the Gammon-plate, which is an iron plate bolted to the stem. **1867** SMYTH *Sailor's Word-bk., Gammon-knee*, a knee-timber fayed and bolted to the stem a little below the bowsprit.

gammon (ˈgæmən), *sb.*[3] [app. a survival of the ME. *gamen* GAME *sb.*[1], or a noun of action f. *gamne* vb. (see GAME *v.*[1]). Possibly *gammon* and *backgammon* may have been used to denote different degrees of victory in the game of 'tables', before they came to be used as names for the game itself; on this view sense 2 below and sense 2 of BACKGAMMON would come before sense 1, but in each case the application to the game itself is recorded earlier.]

1. The game of backgammon. Now *rare.*

1730–46 THOMSON *Autumn* 528 Or the quick dice, In thunder leaping from the box, awake The sounding gammon. *a* **1734** NORTH *Lives* (1826) I. 17 Whatever games were stirring, at places where he retired, as gammon, gleek, piquet, or even the merry main, he made one. **1800** MRS. HERVEY *Mourtray Fam.* III. 81 Mr. Chowles was above, playing at gammon with mistress. **1826** J. WILSON *Noct. Ambr.* Wks. 1855 I. 124 The tailor at Yarrow ford dang ye all to bits baith at gammon and the dambrod.

2. A term at backgammon, denoting a degree of victory which scores equal to two 'hits' or 'games' (see quots. 1844, 1868).

1735 DYCHE & PARDON, *Gammon*..a Term in a Play called Back Gammon. **1778** C. JONES *Hoyle's Games Impr.* 165 Six and Five, a Man to be carried from your Adversary's Ace Point, as far as he can go, for a Gammon or for a Hit. **1800** *Gentl. Mag.* I. 163 And by quick taking off, a gammon win. **1844** *Backgammon* 47 If one combatant have not removed his first man before the other has removed his last, 'a gammon' is lost and won, which is equivalent to two games. **1868** *Boy's Own Bk.* 590 If you can bear all your men away before your adversary has borne off one man, you win the gammon..But if your adversary is able to bear one of his men, before you have borne all yours, then your victory is reduced to a hit.

3. *Comb.*, as ***gammon-board***, ***-player***.

1814 *Monthly Mag.* XXXVII. 47 It may be inferred that he too was a gammon-player. **1851** 'NIMROD' *The Road* 17 You'll have the gammon-board all to yourself.

gammon (ˈgæmən), *sb.*[4] *slang* or *colloq.* Also 8 **gamon.** [app. originally thieves' slang. Commonly identified with ME. *gamen* GAME *sb.*[1]; but the chronological gap is very great, and the meaning in which the mod. word first appears does not favour this etymology. Perh. there may be some untraceable jocular allusion to GAMMON *sb.*[3] (cf. next vb., sense 2), or even *sb.*[2]]

1. *Thieves' slang.* In phrases ***to give gammon*** (see quot. 1720). ***to keep in gammon***: to engage (a person's) attention while a confederate is robbing him.

1720 A. SMITH *Hist. Highwaymen* III. 358 *Give me Gammon.* That is, to side, shoulder, or stand close to a Man, or a Woman, whilst another picks his, or her Pocket. **1821** HAGGART *Life* 51 Going out at the door, Bagrie called the woman of the house, kept her in gammon in the back-room, while I returned and brought off the till. *Ibid.* 68, I whidded to the Doctor, and he gave me gammon.

2. Talk, chatter. Usually ***gammon and patter***.

1781 G. PARKER *View Soc.* I. 208, I thought myself pretty much a master of *Gammon*, but the Billingsgate eloquence of Mrs. P—— not only exceeded me, but outdid all that I had ever known eloquent in that way. **1789** —— *Life's Painter* (ed. 2) 186 *Gammon and Patter*, Jaw talk, etc. **1796** *Grose's Dict. Vulgar Tongue, Gamon and Patter*, commonplace talk of any profession; as the gamon and patter of a horse-dealer, sailor, etc.

3. Ridiculous nonsense suited to deceive simple persons only; 'humbug', 'rubbish'.

1805 T. HARRAL *Scenes of Life* III. 105 'Come, come, none of your gammon!' cried one, 'tell us where the other black sheep is'. **1811** *Lex. Balatron.* s.v., What rum gamon the old file pitched to the flat. **1811** J. POOLE *Ham. Travestie* 30 Come, that won't do, my lord;—now that's all gammon. **1837** DICKENS *Pickw.* xxiv, Some people maintains that an Englishman's house is his castle. That's gammon. **1845** DISRAELI *Sybil* (Rtldg.) 285 Morley has got round them, preaching moral force, and all that sort of gammon. **1870** H. SMART *Race for Wife* x, Come, old fellow, no gammon.

b. quasi-*int.* Humbug! Fudge!

1827 R. B. PEAKE *Comfort. Lodg.* I. iii, *Sir H.* (Aside) Gammon! **1855** THACKERAY *Rose & Ring* xv, 'Gammon!' exclaimed his Lordship. **1885** F. A. GUTHRIE *Tinted Venus* 4 'Gammon!' said Jauncey, 'that isn't it'.

gammon ('gæmən), *v.*[1] [f. GAMMON *sb.*[3]]

1. *trans.* To beat at backgammon by a 'gammon'.

1735 SAVAGE *Progr. Divine* 75 At tables now! But oh, if gammon'd there, The startling echoes learn, like him to swear! **1823** 'JON BEE' *Dict. Turf* s.v., In back-gammon playing, the loser of two games following is said to be gammoned. **1867** *Gd. Words* 422/1 'More fool you', remarked his father, without looking up from the backgammon board. 'There, madam, you are gammoned.' **1870** HARDY & WARE *Mod. Hoyle, Backgammon* 142 Having gained these points, you have a fair chance to gammon your adversary.

fig. **1694** ECHARD *Plautus' Rudens* II. iv. 168 Ne'r a Gamester of 'm all has half the Cunning. Faith, 'twas an excellent Cast; 'thas quite gammon'd the Rascal.

†**2.** *intr.* To cheat at play in some particular way. *Obs.*

1700 *Step to Bath* (ed. 2) 14 There was Palming, Lodging, Loaded Dice, Levant, and Gammoning.

gammon ('gæmən), *v.*[2] [f. GAMMON *sb.*[1]] *trans.* To cure (bacon) by salting and smoking.

1836 SMART, *Gammon*, to salt and dry. **1848** CRAIG, *Gammon*..to make bacon, to pickle and dry in smoke.

gammon ('gæmən), *v.*[3] *Naut.* [See GAMMON *sb.*[2]] *trans.* To lash (the bowsprit) with ropes to the stem of a ship. Said also of the rope.

1711 W. SUTHERLAND *Shipbuild. Assist.* 62 To gammon the Bowsprit. **1729** CAPT. W. WRIGLESWORTH *MS. Log-bk. of the 'Lyell'* 5 Sept., Gammon'd the Bowsprit, Rigg'd the Mizon-topmast. *c* **1850** *Rudim. Navig.* (Weale) 120 The rope..that gammons the bowsprit. **1867** SMYTH *Sailor's Word-bk.*, *Gammon*, to pass the lashings of the bowsprit.

gammon ('gæmən), *v.*[4] *slang* or *colloq.* [f. GAMMON *sb.*[4]]

1. *intr.* To talk (plausibly or persuasively).

1789 G. PARKER *Life's Painter* (ed. 2) 186 A fellow that speaks well, they say he gammons well, or he has a great deal of rum patter. **1833** M. SCOTT *Tom Cringle* ii, You gammons so about the rhino that we must prove you a bit.

2. To feign, pretend.

1812 J. H. VAUX *Flash Dict.* s.v., *To gammon lushy* or *queer* is to pretend drunkenness or sickness. **1821** P. EGAN *Life Lond.* vi. 346 Logic gammoned to be the cadger in fine style, with his crutch and specs. **1864** ELIZ. A. MURRAY *E. Norman* II. 11, I got up in a temper, and told him to leave me. He laughed, and said I was gammoning. **1868** H. C. R. JOHNSON *Argent. Alps* 111 Keeping his eyes on the document, and 'gammoning' to read it.

3. *trans.* To stuff with ridiculous nonsense, to humbug, deceive, hoax. Const. *into*, *out of*.

1812 J. H. VAUX *Flash Dict.* s.v., A man who..by a plausible defence has induced the jury to acquit him..is said by his associates to have gammoned the twelve in prime twig. **1821** EGAN *Life in London* V. 289 Flashy Nance (who had gammoned more seamen out of their vills and power than the ingenuity or palaver of twenty of the most knowing of the frail sisterhood could effect). **1825** BUCKSTONE *Bear Hunters* I. i, There! that's just the way she gammons me at home. **1836** DICKENS *Sk. Boz.* v, I..waited at table, and gammoned the servants, and nobody had the least idea I was in possession. **1837** —— *Pickw.* xiii, So then they pours him out a glass o' wine, and gammons him about his driving, and gets him into a reg'lar good humour. **1873** BLACK *Pr. Thule* ix, To go and gammon old Mackenzie into the belief that he can read poetry.

Hence **'gammoning** *vbl. sb.* and *ppl. a.* Also **'gammoner**, one who gammons; one who 'gives gammon' (see GAMMON *sb.*[4] 1) to an accomplice.

1812 J. H. VAUX *Flash Dict.* s.v. *Gammon*, A thief detected in a house which he has entered upon the sneak..will endeavour by some gammoning story to account for his intrusion. **1821** HAGGART *Life* 66 The Doctor came from the kitchen, and played the part of the gammoner so well, that I made my escape without being observed. **1823** MONCRIEFF *Tom & Jerry* I. i, Fly to the gammoners, and awake to everything that's going on. **1838** DICKENS *Nich. Nick.* xvi, The same gentleman who had expressed an opinion relative to the gammoning nature of the introductory speech. **1881** *Argonaut* (S. Francisco) 2 Apr., Mr. M——, one of the oiliest of oily gammoners.

gammoning ('gæmənɪŋ), *vbl. sb. Naut.* [f. GAMMON *v.*[3] + -ING[1].] The lashing of ropes by which the bowsprit is made fast to the stem or cutwater.

1833 M. SCOTT *Tom Cringle* iii, The Negro threw himself on the Gammoning of the bowsprit. **1853** KANE *Grinnell Exp.* xxxii. (1856) 280 Her bowsprit..is now completely forced up, broken short off at the gammoning. **1867** SMYTH *Sailor's Word-bk.*, *Gammoning*, seven or eight turns of a rope-lashing passed alternately over the bowsprit and through a large hole in the cut-water, the better to support the stays of the foremast.

gammoothe, obs. form of GAMUT.

†**'gammot.** *Obs. rare.* [var. GAMUT (cf. It. '*gamaut*, a note in Musike, also the name of a Barbers toole' (Florio).

The instrument, also called GAMMA, received its name from its resemblance in shape to the letter *Γ*, the symbol of the musical note *gamma ut*.]

(See quot.)

1585 HIGINS tr. *Junius' Nomenclator* 263 *Scolopomachærium*..an instrument seruing to cut out the rootes of vlcers or sores: it is called the incision knife, or gammot. **1656** in BLOUNT *Glossogr.* **1721–92** in BAILEY.

gammut(h, obs. form of GAMUT.

gammy ('gæmɪ), *a. dial.* and *slang.* [dial. equivalent of GAMY.]

1. *Tramps' slang.* Bad, not good.

1839 in 'DUCANGE ANGLICUS' *Vulg. Tongue, Gammy*, bad. *Gammy stuff*, spurious soap or medicine. **1846** R. L. SNOWDEN *Magistr. Assist.* 344 Bad coin, Gammy lowr. **1851** MAYHEW *Lond. Labour* I. 364 A mark being placed on the door post of such as are bone or gammy in order to inform the rest of the school where to call and what houses to avoid.

2. *Theatr.* (See quot.)

1889 BARRÈRE & LELAND *Slang*, *Gammy*..old, ugly, *passée*.

3. Lame; disabled through injury or pain. Cf. GAME *a.*[2] Also as *sb.* a lame person.

1879 MISS JACKSON *Shropsh. Word-bk.* s.v., 'A gammy fut.' **1893** in FARMER *Slang*. **1913** *Punch* 23 Apr. 331 Gammy thumb! The rest o' the squad ain't got gammy thumbs, has they? **1947** D. M. DAVIN *Gorse blooms Pale* 80 That gammy foot of mine.

gammy ('gæmɪ), *sb. slang.* [? f. prec.] Cant, the canting language.

1893 FARMER *Slang* s.v., citing (in error) Grose *Dict. Vulg. Tongue* (1785), Do you stoll the gammy? Do you understand cant?

†**'gamner, 'gamener.** *Obs.* [f. *gamen* vb. (see GAME *v.*[1]) + -ER[1].]

1. A gamester, a player, a gambler.

1509 BARCLAY *Shyp of Folys* (1570) 148 Such are great gamners hauing small substance. **1529** MORE *Comf. agst. Trib.* I. Wks. 1162/2 Then left them their gameners and slily slonke awaye. **1563** ABP. PARKER *Articles*, Whether your Persons, Vicars, and Curates be common gameners. **1565** J. HALLE *Hist. Expost.* p. xvii, If thou have not as great desyre to thy boke, as the greatest gamner hath to his game, thou shalte never worthily be called cunnyng in this art.

2. An athlete.

1567 *Bauldwin's Mor. Philos.* II. v. 77b, The gamner breaketh his leg in dauncing..his arme, his shoulder, or his necke in wrastling. [So in later eds. until **1600**; eds. **1610** gammer, *c* **1620–30** gamer.]

gamning, obs. form of GAMING.

gamo- (ˌgæmə-, 'gæməʊ-), combining form of Gr. γάμος marriage, used in various mod. scientific terms, as **gamo'mania** [MANIA] (see quot.); **gamo'morphism** [Gr. μορφ-ή form] (see quot.). Chiefly in adjs. used in Botany, describing plants or organs in which certain specified parts are united together, as **gamo'gastrous** [Gr. γαστήρ stomach] (see quot.); **gamo'petalous** [PETAL], having the petals united; **gamo'phyllous** [Gr. φύλλον leaf], having the leaves united; **'gamophyte** (see quot.); **gamo'sepalous** [SEPAL], having the sepals united.

1876 BALFOUR in *Encycl. Brit.* IV. 142/1 The union..may take place by the ovaries alone, while the styles and stigmata remain free, the pistil being then *gamogastrous. **1885** *Syd. Soc. Lex.*, *Gamogastrous*, a term applied to a pistil in which the ovaries are more or less completely united and the respective styles and stigmata remain free. *Ibid.*, **Gamomania*, a form of insanity characterised by strange and extravagant proposals for marriage. **1866** BRANDE & COX *Dict. Sci.* etc. II. 10 **Gamomorphism*, that stage of developement of organised beings in which the spermatic and germinal elements are formed, matured, and generated, in preparation for another act of fecundation, as the commencement of a new genetic cycle. **1830** LINDLEY *Nat. Syst. Bot.* 161 Their petals cohere in a long tube of the same nature as that of *gamopetalous *Crassulaceae.* **1872** OLIVER *Elem. Bot.* I. iv. 36 The corolla is gamopetalous and irregular. *Ibid.* I. v. 50 In this instance the perianth is *gamophyllous. **1880** BAKER in *Jrnl. Linn. Soc.* XVIII. 14 The Aloes..are characterized by their gamophyllous perianth. **1889** GIBSON *Elem. Biol.* 132 The term *gamophyte will be employed throughout in preference to oophyte, as taking into account both the male and the female sexual organs. **1835** LINDLEY *Introd. Bot.* (1848) I. 329 The word *gamosepalous has been proposed, but it is not much employed. **1860** OLIVER *Less. Bot.* (1873) 29 The calyx is gamosepalous; that is, composed of coherent sepals.

gamogenesis (gæmə'dʒɛnɪsɪs). *Biol.* [See GAMO- and -GENESIS.] (See quot. 1885.)

1861 J. R. GREENE *Man. Anim. Kingd.*, *Cœlent.* 75 'Gamogenesis', in which the ovum to be developed, must first be brought into contact with spermatozoa. **1864** H. SPENCER *Illustr. Univ. Progr.* 370 Multiplying only by gamogenesis. **1885** *Syd. Soc. Lex.*, *Gamogenesis*, generation by the conjunction of structures from different individuals, being sexual reproduction.

Hence **gamoge'netic** *a.* [see GENETIC], of or pertaining to gamogenesis, producing or produced by gamogenesis; **gamoge'netically** *adv.*, in a gamogenetic manner (*Cent. Dict.*).

1864 H. SPENCER *Princ. Biol.* I. 226 Gamogenetic structure. **1877** HUXLEY *Anat. Inv. Anim.* Introd. 28 Agamogenetic and gamogenetic reproduction. **1888** J. T. GULICK in *Jrnl. Linn. Soc.* XX. 216 Every gamogenetic species.

gamogins, var. GAMASHES.

†**'gamond.** *Sc. Obs.* Forms: 6 **gamount, galmound, -mand, gawmound.** [from earlier *gambat* = F. *gambade*; see the forms under GAMBOL *sb.* The form may be due to some association with *gamount* = GAMMON *sb.*[1]] A gambol, or leaping movement in dancing.

1500–20 DUNBAR *Poems* xxvi. 11 He bad gallandis ga graith a gyiss, And kast vp gamountis [*M.* gambauldis, *R.* galmandis] in the skyis, That last came out of France. **1535** LYNDESAY *Satyre* 452 Now hay! for ioy and mirth I dance. Tak thair ane gay gamond of France. *a* **1572** KNOX *Hist. Ref.* Wks. 1846 I. 43 He lapp up mearely upoun the scaffold, and, casting a gawmound, said, 'Whair ar the rest of the playaris?' *a* **1591** ADAMSON in R. Ford *Harp Perthsh.* (1893) 4 Ay when I hit the mark I cast a gamound.

Hence †**'gamonding** *vbl. sb.*

1549 *Compl. Scot.* vi. 66 It vas ane celest recreation to beheld ther lycht lopene, galmonding [*orig. ed.* galmouding], stendling bakuart and forduart.

gamont ('gæmɒnt). *Biol.* [a. G. *gamont* (M. Hartmann 1904, in *Biol. Centralbl.* XXIV. 25), f. GAM(ETE + Gr. ὀντ-, ὤν, pres. pple of εἶναι to be, exist.] In Protozoa, a cell that produces gametes.

1912 E. A. MINCHIN *Introd. Stud. Protozoa* ix. 181 It would perhaps be better to replace the terms 'schizont' and 'sporont' by 'agamont' and 'gamont' respectively. **1957** *New Biol.* XXIV. 27 Typically there are two distinct generations [in foraminifera], namely a sexual one (the gamont) which alternates with an asexual one (or schizont). **1965** V. A. DOGIEL *Gen. Protozool.* (ed. 2) vii. 349 In *Adelina* a male and female gamont are invested in a thin membrane, under which the female gamont is transformed into a female gamete, while the male gives rise to 4 gametes.

gamosh, var. GAMASH.

Gamp (gæmp), *sb.* [after *Mrs. Sarah Gamp*, a monthly nurse in Dickens' *Martin Chuzzlewit*, who carried a large cotton umbrella.]

1. A woman resembling Mrs. Gamp; a monthly nurse or sick nurse of a disreputable class.

1864 *Sun* 28 Dec. 2/6 'A regular Gamp', meaning thereby ..a fat old dowdy of a monthly nurse, or a very large, bulgy, loosely tied cotton umbrella. **1889** A. R. HOPE in *Boy's Own Paper* 3 Aug. 697/2 She was a trained hospital nurse of the class that is fast driving last generation's Sally Gamps out of the field.

2. An umbrella, esp. one tied up in a loose, untidy fashion.

1864 [See 1]. **1883** G. R. SIMS *Lifeboat*, etc., *Midsummer Day*, He donned his goloshes, and shouldered his gamp. **1887** J. A. STERRY *Lazy Minstrel* (1892) 134, I trust your Gamp is water-tight!

attrib. **1881** *Macm. Mag.* XLV. 62 Grasping his gamp umbrella at the middle.

gamp (gæmp), *a. Sc.* ? Playful, sportive.

1776 in Herd *Collect. Sc. Songs* II. 23 She is sae jimp, sae gamp, sae gay.

gamp (gæmp), *v. Sc.* [echoic; cf. *champ.*] *trans.* 'To eat greedily, devour, gulp' (Jam.).

1805 A. SCOTT *Poems* 154 (Jam.) A wally dish o' them weel champit,—How glibly up we'll see them gampit, As clean's a bead.

gamphrel ('gæmfrəl). *Sc.* [Cf. GOMEREL.] A fool, a stupid or senseless fellow, a blockhead.

1728 RAMSAY *Fables, Horse's Compl.*, To gallop with some gamphrel idle.

gampish ('gæmpɪʃ), *a.* [f. GAMP *sb.* + -ISH.] Of an umbrella: Like Mrs. Gamp's, loosely tied up, bulging. Hence **'gampishness.**

1863 W. CORY *Lett. & Jrnls.* (1897) 90 His master was making up my Bond-Street umbrella into a double bulge of gampishness. **1864** *Derby Day* ii. 18 As if you had been mortifying the flesh by carrying a gampish umbrella up Piccadilly, and back again. **1883** FENN *Middy & Ensign* xxviii. 174 An unmistakeable gingham, with a decidedly Gampish look.

gampless ('gæmplɪs), *a.* [f. GAMP *sb.* 2.] = UMBRELLALESS *a.*

1893 M. E. MANN *In Summer Shade* I. ix. 208 Any old gampless woman of the congregation. **1899** *Westm. Gaz.* 2 Oct. 6/2 To provide 'gampless' seatholders with umbrellas.

gamsigradite ('gæmsɪˌgrædaɪt). *Min.* [f. *Gamsigrad* in Serbia, where it is found + -ITE.] A velvet-black variety of amphibole.

1862 *Amer. Jrnl. Sc.* Ser. II. XXXIV. 213 Breithaupt has given the name gamsigradite to a black hornblende, from Gamsigrad, in Servia. **1864** in WATTS *Dict. Chem.* II. 771.

gamut ('gæmət). Forms: 6 **gamo(u)th,** (**gammouthe,** 7 **-oothe,** 7 **gam(m)uth,** 6–7 **gamma ut** (7 **gammaut**), **gam-ut,** 8 **gammut,** 6– **gamut.** [Contraction of med.L. *gamma ut*; f. GAMMA the name of the symbol *Γ* (introduced in the Middle Ages to represent a note one tone lower than the *A* which began the scale inherited from classical times) + *ut*, the first of a series of six syllables used as the names of the six notes forming a hexachord.

The names of the six notes are from certain initial syllables in the following sapphic stanza (Hymn for St. John Baptist's day): *Ut* queant laxis *re*sonare fibris *Mi*ra gestorum *fa*muli tuorum, *Sol*ve polluti *la*bii reatum, Sancte Iohannes.]

1. The first or lowest note in the mediæval scale of music, answering to the modern G on the lowest line of the bass stave. *Obs.* exc. *Hist.*

1530 PALSGR. 224/1 Gammouthe, *gamme*. **1596** SHAKS. *Tam. Shr.* III. i. 73 *Gamouth* I am, the ground of all accord:

A re to plead Hortensio's passion. **1597** MORLEY *Introd. Mus.* 4 The first note standeth in *Gam-vt*. **1630** J. TAYLOR (Water P.) *Bawd* Wks. I. 96/1 There is not any note aboue *Ela*, or below *Gammoth*, but she knows the *Diapason*. *a* **1653** G. DANIEL *Idyll* v. 147 From Gamut Earth, notes above Ela Ayre. **1674** PLAYFORD *Skill Mus.* I. i. 2 According to these three Septenaries, Gam-ut is the lowest Note. **1677** PLOT *Oxfordsh.* 12 [An Echo]..which answers to no Note so clearly as to Gamut.

2. The 'Great Scale' (of which the invention is ascribed to Guido d'Arezzo), comprising the seven hexachords or partial scales, and consisting of all the recognized notes used in mediæval music. It extended from *Γ ut* (= G on the lowest line of the bass stave) to *E-la* (= E in the highest space of the treble). *Obs.* exc. *Hist.*

a **1529** SKELTON *Agst. comely coystrowne* 13 Wks. 1843 I. 15 But for in his gamut carp that he can, Lo, Jak wold be a jentylman! **1596** *Pathw. to Mus.* A ij a, It is needfull for him that will learne to sing truely, to vnderstand his Scale, or (as they commonly call it) the *Gamma vt.* **1596** SHAKS. *Tam. Shr.* III. i. 71, I am past my gamouth long agoe. **1622** MABBE tr. *Aleman's Guzman d'Alf.* II. 94 Many of them could say their Gammoothe..but knew not how to proue a note. **1674** PLAYFORD *Skill Mus.* I. i. 3 The Gam-ut is drawn upon fourteen Rules and their spaces, and doth comprehend all Notes or Sounds usual in Musick. **1782** BURNEY *Hist. Mus.* (1789) II. ii. 85 The whole scale was called gammut. **1825** DANNELEY *Encycl. Mus.* s.v. *Gamme*, This gamut comprised in all, twenty notes, viz. from G, first line bass clef, to the sixth of its double octave, or to the fourth space E, treble clef.

3. Hence in later use: The whole series of notes that are recognized by musicians. Sometimes also used for: The major diatonic scale, or the 'scale' recognized by any particular people, or at any period.

1709 ADDISON *Tatler* No. 157 ¶13 They make a greater Sound than those who are possessed of the whole Gammut. **1774** 'JOEL COLLIER' *Mus. Trav.* 10 She..screamed..most harmoniously through the whole gamut from *a* to *g* inclusively. **1791** MRS. RADCLIFFE *Rom. Forest* v, There was more of the bass than of any other part of the gamut in his performance. **1827** CARLYLE *Misc., Goethe* (1869) 183 It was chanted through all the notes of the gamut. **1860** TYNDALL *Glac.* II. i. 227 This spectrum is to the eye what the gamut is to the ear. **1864** TENNYSON *Sea-dreams* 227 And ever as their shrieks Ran highest up the gamut.

b. The compass or full range of notes which a voice or instrument is capable of producing.

1639 J. CRUSO *Art of Warre* Ded., A souldiers Gammaut goes farre beyond E-la. **1644** MILTON *Areop.* (Arb.) 50 The gammuth of every municipal fidler. **1825** DANNELEY *Encycl. Mus.* s.v. *Gamme*, At the present day the word gamut denotes the compass of sounds for each instrument, viz. from the highest to the lowest note.

4. *transf.* and *fig.* The whole scale, range, or compass of a thing.

1626 T. H. *Caussin's Holy Crt.* 14 Chaunge the Gamuth, and say, He is noble, he hath therfore the more obligation to be perfect. **1753** HOGARTH *Anal. Beauty* xii. 97 The painter's gamut. **1824** F. JEFFREY *Ess. Beauty, Encycl. Brit.* Suppl. II. 193/1 Various learned treatises upon the natural gamut of colours. **1859** DICKENS *T. Two Cities* II. i, The sounders of three-fourths of the notes in the whole gamut of Crime. **1864** BURTON *Scot. Abr.* III. i. 122 He ran over the gamut of Latin metre. **1883** *Harper's Mag.* 822/2 The.. stocks were running..up and down the gamut from $1 to $700 a share.

5. *Comb.*, as †**gamut-string** (see quot.).

1674 PLAYFORD *Skill Mus.* II. 92 The Bass-Viol..is usually strung with six strings..the fifth, the Tenor, or Gam-ut String.

gamy ('geɪmɪ), *a.* Also 9 **gamey**. [f. GAME *sb.* + -Y[1].]

1. Abounding in game. Of a sportsman: Bent upon game.

1848 *Blackw. Mag.* LXIV. 170 The keen sportsman..will find abundant pastime and recreation in so gamy a land as this. **1863** *Pilgr. over Prairies* I. 14 An individual..whose.. weather-stained red coat, and gamy cast of eye, seemed to bespeak a huntsman. **1892** *Field* 10 Dec. 883/3 Any gamey or rabbity district.

2. Spirited, plucky: showing fight to the last.

1844 DICKENS *Mart. Chuz.* xi, 'Well..wot if I am [shot]; there's something gamey in it, young ladies, ain't there?' **1867** F. H. LUDLOW *Fleeing to Tarshish* 142 Mounted on a gamy thoroughbred. **1881** *Century Mag.* XXIII. 45/1, I crept out of the fortress with half a dozen stalwart and gamy U.S. regulars at my heels. **1883** *Ibid.* XXVI. 383/2 The artificial fly alone should be used to lure the gamy bass.

3. Having the flavour of game that has been kept till it is 'high'.

1863 W. C. BALDWIN *Afr. Hunting* 267 Nothing approaches the parts most relished by the natives in richness of flavour and racy, gamey taste. **1865** DICKENS *Mut. Fr.* I. xi, The haunch of mutton vapour-bath having received a gamey infusion. **1884** R. WALKER *Five Threes* 59 The latter [a kangaroo] being rather gamey, the effects were counteracted by having a pocket full of orange blossom.

fig. **18..** LOWELL *FitzAdam's Story* Poet. Wks. 1890 IV. 225 His language, wherethrough ran The gamy flavor of the bookless man.

-gamy, *suffix*, f. Gr. γάμος marriage + -Y[3], appended to Gr. stems to form sbs. with the senses: (*a*) 'marriage (of the type specified)', as in ENDOGAMY, EXOGAMY, HYPERGAMY; (*b*) '(such a) means of fertilization or reproduction', as in ALLOGAMY, CLEISTOGAMY, POROGAMY. Cf. BIGAMY, MONOGAMY, POLYGAMY.

Gamza ('gæmzə, 'gʌmzə). Also **Gumza**. [Bulgarian.] A dark red grape of Bulgaria, or the red wine made from it. Also *attrib.*

1959 *World Crops* XI. 111/1 The most universally grown is the *Gumza red grape*. The typical Gumza red wines are made mainly in northern Bulgaria. Gumza grapes are grown in some neighbouring countries. **1959** *Wine & Spirit Trade Rev.* 13 Feb. 32/2 *Mavroude* and *Gamza* [are] dark reds. **1961** *Spectator* 7 Apr. 495 The red Gamza, which is fresh and flavoury, rather like a Beaujolais.

gan (gæn). *slang.* [Perh. connected with GANE *v.*; or possibly a. Welsh *geneu*, Cornish *ganau*, mouth.] The mouth.

1567 HARMAN *Caveat* (1869) 82 *Gan*, a mouth. **1609** DEKKER *Lanthorne & Candle-lt.* C j b, Thou shalt pek my Iere In thy Gan. **1641** BROME *Joviall Crew* II. Wks. 1873 III. 391 This Bowse is better then Rum-bowse, It sets the Gan a gigling. *a* **1700** B. E. *Dict. Cant. Crew*, *Gan*, a Mouth, *Ganns*, the Lipps. **1725** in *New Cant. Dict.* **1785** in GROSE *Dict. Vulg. Tongue*, s.v.

gan, erron. form of *can* in *to can thanks* (see CAN *v.*[1] 10).

gan, pa. t. of GIN; obs. infin. of GO.

ganaderia (gænədɪ'rɪə). [Sp., f. *ganado* livestock, cattle.] A cattle-ranch or stock farm.

1860 MAYNE REID *Odd People* 62 A 'ganaderia' of cattle, or a plantation of cocoa trees [in S. America]. **1960** *Guardian* 16 Sept. 16/6 At Méjanes, he has turned his ganaderia into a luxury holiday centre.

ganand, var. GAINAND, and *gangand* GANGING.

ganat(te, obs. form of GNAT.

ganate, obs. form of GANNET.

†**ganch**, *sb. Obs.* In 7-9 **gaunch**. [related to GANCH *v.* (F. *ganche* in the original of quot. 1718.)]

1. The apparatus employed in the execution of criminals by ganching; the punishment itself.

1625-6 PURCHAS *Pilgrims* II. 1623 By reason of that torment hee died presently upon the Gaunch. **1686** J. SCOTT *Chr. Life* (1747) III. 91 Scorch their tender Parts with Fires, and rake their Bowels with Spikes and Gaunches. **1718** OZELL tr. *Tournefort's Voy.* I. 72 The Gaunch is a sort of Estrapade, usually set up at the City-gates. The Executioner lifts up the Criminal by means of a pully, and then letting go the rope, down falls the wretch among a parcel of great iron flesh-hooks. *a* **1783** H. BROOKE *Fool of Qual.* (1792) V. 254, I would rather suffer the gaunch than [etc.].

2. A gash or wound made by a boar's tusk. (Cf. GANCH *v.* 2.) *arch.*

1818 SCOTT *Br. Lamm.* ix, I have heard my father say.. that a wild boar's gaunch is more easily healed than a hurt from the deer's horn.

†**ganch**, *v. Obs.* Also 7-8 **gaunch**, 7 **gansh**. [ad. F. ***gancher** (in pa. pple. *ganché* 'Let fall (as in a strappado) on sharp stakes pointed with yron, and thereon languishing vntill he dye,' Cotgr.) ad. It. **ganciare*, f. *gancio* hook = Sp. *gancho*.]

1. *trans.* To impale (a person) upon sharp hooks or stakes as a mode of execution.

1615 G. SANDYS *Trav.* I. 66 The offending woman they drowne, and the man they gansh. **1655** *Massacres in Piedmont* 35 They gaunched many..after the Turkish manner. **1690** DRYDEN *Don Sebast.* III. ii, Take him away; ganch him, impale him, rid the world of such a monster. **1718** OZELL tr. *Tournefort's Voy.* I. 72 If a Cain happens to be taken they give him no quarter, he is either impal'd or gaunch'd. *a* **1783** H. BROOKE *Fool of Qual.* (1792) IV. 86 In about five days after, a convict was to be ganched.

2. Of a boar: To tear or gash with the tusk (in pa. pple. *ganched*).

1621 G. SANDYS *Ovid's Met.* III. (1626) 50 Fierce Saluage, [a dog] lately ganched by a Bore. **1649** G. DANIEL *Trinarch., Hen. V*, ccv, One, ganch't i' th' flanke, breakes with a Restive Scorne; And claps his Crest through. **1783** *Ainsworth's Lat. Dict.* (Morell) IV, s.v. *Adonis*, Being gaunched by a boar's tusks, he died in the bloom of his youth.

Hence †'**ganching** *vbl. sb.* and *ppl. a.*

1614 W. DAVIES *Trav.* etc. B iij b, Their ganshing is after this manner: He sitteth vpon a wall, being five fadomes high ..right vnder the place where he sits, is a strong Iron hooke fastned, being very sharpe; then is he thrust off the wall vpon this hooke with some part of his body, and there he hangeth sometimes two or three daies before he dieth. **1621** G. SANDYS *Ovid's Met.* VIII. (1626) 158 The dogs he [a boar] wounds with ganching blowes. **1683** in *Phil. Trans.* XIV. 443 For any hainous crime against the Government either Gaunching or excoriation, or cutting off the legs and arms.

gander ('gændə(r)), *sb.* Forms: 1 **gan(d)ra**, 3-4 **gandre**, 5 **gandere**, (**-dir**, **-dur**), **gonder**, 6 **gaundre**, *Sc.* **ganar**, **gan(n)er**, 9 *dial.* **ganner**, **gonder**, 4- **gander**. [The orig. stem is perhaps ***ganron-**, the *d* being a euphonic insertion between *n* and *r* as in *thunder*:—OE. *þunor*. Outside of English the word is found only in Du., LG. and South Ger. *gander*, MLG. *ganre*; the other Teut. languages show different formations, as G. *gänserich* (earlier *ganser*), ON. *gasse*, Sw. *gåse*.

Although used as the masc. of GOOSE (OE. *gós*:—OTeut. **gans-*) there is some doubt whether it is etymologically cognate with that word. While *goose* represents an OAryan **ghans-* with palatal *gh-*, it is possible that OE. *gan(d)ra* may be cognate with Lith. *gàndras* stork; this would imply a root beginning with velar *gh-*, to which may also be referred OE. *ganot* GANNET, OHG. *ganazzo*, *ganzo* (MHG. *ganze*, also *genz*), Du. *gent*, all meaning 'gander'. Cf. *ganta*, said by Pliny *N.H.* x. xxii. 27 to be the Ger. name of a small white goose, OF. *gante*, *jante*, *gente*, wild goose, Pr. *ganta* wild goose (in the mod. dialects variously used for 'wild goose', 'black stork', and 'heron'). It has been conjectured that *gander* may have been originally the special name of some kind of water-bird, and that its association with *goose* is accidental, perh. arising from the alliterative phrase 'goose and gander'.]

1. a. The male of the goose.

c **1000** ÆLFRIC *Gram.* (Z.) 307 *Anser*, gandra [*v.r.* ganra]. *c* **1220** *Bestiary* 392 Ðe coc and te capun ȝe [the fox] fecceð ofte in ðe tun, And te gandre and te gos, bi ðe necke and by ðe nos, haleð is to hire hole. *c* **1400** MAUNDEV. (1839) xx. 216 In theise vyneres ben so many Wylde Gees and Gandres. *c* **1400** *Lanfranc's Cirurg.* 197 Her [leper's] skyn..wole bicome as it were þe skyn of a gandir þat hise feþeris weren pilid awey. *c* **1430** LYDG. *Hors, Shepe, & G.* (Roxb.) 8 Ghoos ne gander ne grene gosselyng. **1513** DOUGLAS *Æneis* VIII. xi. 33 The syluer ganer, flyghterand wyth lowd skry. **1548** CRANMER *Catech.* 24 b, These papistes..say that thys verse..is verefied of the gose and the gaundre. **1630** J. TAYLOR (Water P.) *Vertue of Tayle* Wks. II. 126/1 Grand Gouernour of Guls, of Geese and Ganders. **1766** [ANSTEY] *Bath Guide* ad fin., Fat be the gander that feeds on thy grave. **1774** GOLDSM. *Nat. Hist.* VI. xi. 123 The female hatches her eggs with great assiduity; while the Gander visits her twice or thrice a day. **1887** BOWEN *Virg. Eclog.* IX. 36 A cackling gander among sweet swans of the stream.

b. *Phrases* and *proverbs.*

1509 BARCLAY *Shyp of Folys* (1570) 68 That goose that still about will wander..Shall home come agayne as wise as a gander. *a* **1529** SKELTON *Image Hypocr.* III Doctour Pomaunder As wise as a gander Wotes not wher to wander. **1579** LYLY *Euphues* (Arb.) 275, I..haue heard, that as deepe drinketh the Goose as the Gander. *a* **1704** T. BROWN *New Maxims* Wks. 1720 IV. 123 What is Sawce for a Goose is Sawce for a Gander. **1881** SAINTSBURY *Dryden* v. 102 But what is sauce for the nineteenth-century goose is surely sauce for the seventeenth-century gander.

2. *fig.* **a.** A dull or stupid person; a fool, simpleton.

1553 T. WILSON *Rhet.* 20 b, Another for a Gose, that graseth upon his ground, tries the lawe so hard, that he proves himself a Gander. **1589** *Pappe w. Hatchet* C ij b, Finding nothing but dung, the gander wisht his goose alive. **1630** J. TAYLOR (Water P.) *Wks.* II. 161 But prethee hold thy prating, witlesse Gander, Shalt ne'r haue honor to become my Pander. **1709** *Brit. Apollo* II. No. 49. 2/2 Many Women wou'd make meer Ganders of such wise Querists. **1816** J. GILCHRIST *Philos. Etym.* 216 Perhaps some great critical gander will come flapping and flourishing out of the flock.

b. *slang.* 'A married man; in America one not living with his wife; a grass-widower' (Farmer).

c. A look or glance (see quot. 1914). *slang* (orig. *U.S.*). Cf. GANDER *v.* 1 b.

1914 JACKSON & HELLYER *Vocab. Criminal Slang* 36 *Gander*, an inquisitorial glance; a searching look; an impertinent gazing or staring. Also the simple act of looking or seeing... 'Take a gander at this dump as we pass...' **1937** D. RUNYON *More than Somewhat* i. 16 Now I am taking many a gander around the bedroom to see if I can case the box of letters. **1943** [see GANDER *v.* 1 b]. **1959** A. LEJEUNE *Crowded & Dangerous* viii. 91, I was sitting..taking a gander at what's running at 'urst Park. **1971** *Sci. Amer.* Oct. 74 (Advt.), Take a gander at the see-through door below. See that corrugated piece of steel?

3. *attrib.* and *Comb.*, as *gander-feast*, *-goose*, *-neck*; *gander-gutted* adj.

1586 WARNER *Alb Eng.* III. xvi. (1589) 66 Their *Gander Feast, what Manlius and Camillus did therein..I pretermit. **1631** BRATHWAIT *Whimzies, Decoy* 28 As one borne to more meanes than braines, hee behaves himselfe like a very *gander-goose. **1837** HALIBURTON *Clockm.* Ser. I. xviii, A real *gander-gutted lookin critter, as holler as a bamboo walkin cane. **1602** MARSTON *Ant. & Mel.* I. Wks. 1856 I. 14 A *gander neck, A thinne lippe, and a little monkish eye.

4. Special comb. (mainly *slang*): **gander-month, -moon**, the month after a wife's confinement (? allusion to the gander's aimless wandering while the goose is sitting); **gander-mooner**, a husband during this period; **gander-party** *U.S.* (see quot.); **gander-pull, -pulling** *U.S.*, a sport in which a horseman riding at full speed tries to clutch the greased neck of a live gander suspended by the feet and to pull its head off (cf. *goose-riding*); **gander's wool**, feathers. Also, in the name of a plant, **gander-scurvy-grass**.

1636 DEKKER *Wond. Kingdome* II. C iij, Is't *Gander moneth with him? *a* **1652** BROME *Eng. Moor* III. i. Wks. 1873 II. 40 I'le keep her at the least this Gander moneth, While my fair wife lies in. **1796** *Grose's Dict. Vulg. Tongue* (ed. 3), *Gander Month*, that month in which a man's wife lies in: wherefore, during that time, husbands plead a sort of indulgence in matters of gallantry. **1886** *Chesh. Gloss.* s.v. *Gonder-moon*, Oh, it's *gonder moon wi' 'im; he's lost and dusna know what he's doin'. **1617** MIDDLETON & ROWLEY *Faire Quarr.* IV. iv. 139 Wandering *gander-mooners, Or muffled late night-walkers. **1866** LOWELL *Biglow P.* Introd., Poems 1890 II. 196 **Gander-party*, a social gathering of men only. **1843** HALIBURTON *Attaché* II. iv. 58 It puts me in mind of '*Gander Pulling'. [A description follows.] **1885** MISS MURFREE *Proph. Gt. Smoky Mount.* v. 103 They were making ready for the gander-pulling. **1691** ABP. SANCROFT *Let.* in D'Oyly *Life* II. 12 *Gander-scurvey-grass. **1600** BRETON *Pasquil's Fool's-cappe* (Grosart) 23 Such braines belined with *Gander's wooll.

Hence '**ganderism**, conduct of or befitting a gander; '**ganderous** *a.*, pertaining to a gander. *nonce-wds.*

1630 J. TAYLOR (Water P.) *Taylor's-Goose* Wks. I. 111/2 The Gander in my face with fury flew..My Horse he started, to the ground I went, Dismounted in that (Ganderous) tournament. I should say Dangerous, but sure I am That Ganderous is a Dangerous Anagram. **1888** *Blackw. Mag.* Sept. 415 This little piece of ganderism put my gay visitant into excellent good-humour.

gander ('gændə(r)), *v.* Also gonder, *Sc.* gainder. [f. prec.]

1. *intr.* †**a.** (See quot. 1687.) *dial.* **b.** To wander aimlessly, or with a foolish air like that of a gander. Also, to look or glance (see later quots.) *dial.* or *colloq.* (now chiefly *U.S.*).

1687 MIEGE *Gt. Fr. Dict.* II. s.v., To go a gandering, whilst his Wife lies in, *chercher à se divertir ailleurs* [etc.]. **1822** HOGG *Perils of Man* III. vii. 202 What are ye gaun gaindering about that gate for, as ye didna ken whilk end o' ye were uppermost. **1865** H. KINGSLEY in *Macm. Mag.* June 131 The deerhounds get between every body's legs..and gander about idiotically. **1886** *Chesh. Gloss.*, s.v., Wheer art gonderin to? **1887** T. DARLINGTON *Folk-Speech S. Cheshire* 206 *Gonder*, to stretch the neck like a *gander*, to stand at gaze. 'What a't gonderin' theer fur?' **1903** *Cincinnati Enquirer* 9 May 13/1 *Gander*, to stretch or rubber your neck. **1935** *Amer. Speech* X. 17/2 To wander about looking for someone or something. Modern *to gander*. **1939** *Ibid.* XIV. 239/2 *To gander*, to examine. **1943** HUNT & PRINGLE *Service Slang* 33 *Gander*, a look through the mail, a glance over another's shoulder at a letter or paper. To perpetrate this long-necked nuisance.

2. *transf.* To ramble in talk. *dial.*

1858 HUGHES *Scouring White Horse* v. 95 'But about the sports, William?' 'Ees, Sir, I wur gandering sure enough', said the old man. **1867** H. KINGSLEY *Silcote of S.* xlix. (1876) 360 You sit gandering in that chair. **1886** *Chesh. Gloss.*, *Gonder*, to ramble in conversation, to become childish.

'gandergoose. *Obs.* exc. *dial.* Forms: 6 **gandergose, -gosses,** 7 **-glass (-grass),** 6–9 **-goose** (9 **gandigoslings**). Also 6 **kandlegostes,** 9 **dandy goshen, -goslings.** [Of uncertain origin. Skinner (1671) suggests GANDER and *goss* = GORSE, but the proper form of the word is doubtful.] The plant *Orchis mascula.*

c **1550** LLOYD *Treas. Health* (Copland) E ij a, Anoint the eyes that are bleraid wt the ioyce of gandergose or lady traces. **1552** ELYOT, *Orchis*..some call it in English gandergoose some raggewoorte. **1613** DENNYS *Secr. Angling* in Arb. *Garner* I. 157 Purple narcissus like the morning rays, Pale Gander-glass and azure culverkeys. **1783** *Ainsworth's Lat. Dict.* (Morell) 1 I, **Cynosorchis*..also gander-goose, or rag-wort. **1893** *Wiltsh. Words, Gandigoslings*, early Purple Orchis. Also Dandy-goslings.

Gandharva (gæn'dɑːvə). *Hindu Mythol.* Also **Gandharba, -arwa.** [Skr., cf. Gr. κένταυρος: see CENTAUR.] (See quot. 1876).

1846 H. H. WILSON *Sk. Relig. Sects Hindus* ii. 17 A few of the *Tántrikas* worship the *Siddhas*, or Genii,..the same class furnishes occasional votaries of the..*Gandharbas*, and even of the..goblins and ghosts. **1856** M. MÜLLER *Chips* (1867) II. xvi. 102 Then the Gandharvas sent a flash of lightning. **1876** *Encycl. Brit.* IV. 208/2 The retinue of Indra consists chiefly of the *Gandharvas*..a class of genii, considered in the epics as celestial musicians. **1934** *Burlington Mag.* Sept. 169/1 Their decoration..may show Gandharwas flying or playing musical instruments. **1956** K. CLARK *Nude* vii. 276 In India..they appear in the 6th century..as flying gandharvas. **1968** *Indian Mus. Jrnl.* V. 8 The human Gandharva-s (genii).

Gandhi ('gændɪ). The name of M. K. *Gandhi* (1869–1948), Indian political leader and social reformer, applied *attrib.* to a close-fitting white cap with a wide band encircling the head.

1921 E. M. FORSTER *Let.* 19 Sept. in *Hill of Devi* (1953) 125 Crowds of the Nagpur people..wearing the white Gandhi cap. **1963** M. MALIM *Pagoda Tree* xv. 94 A portentous Hindu in a snowy *dhoti*, a fawn cotton jacket and a 'Gandhi cap'. **1967** H. R. F. KEATING *Inspector Ghote caught in Meshes* x. 142 Here and there a turban or a Gandhi cap or the vivid splash of a sari.

Gandhian ('gændɪən), *a.* [f. prec. + -IAN.] Of, pertaining to, or characteristic of Gandhi. So **Gandhi-'esque** *a.*, resembling or characteristic of Gandhi and his principles; **'Gandhism, 'Gandhi-ism,** Gandhian principles or actions; **'Gandhist,** a follower of Gandhi; also *attrib.*

1921 *Daily Tel.* 7 Mar. 7/1 Some..have resolutely opposed the Gandhian policy. **1921** *Public Opinion* 2 Dec. 554/3 The inherent selfishness of Ghandi-ism. **1921** *Glasgow Herald* 2 Dec. 8 It is..undesirable..to mention 'Ghandhism' just now in this picturesque Rajput city. *Ibid.* 12 Dec. 9 Protests from some few Gandhists. **1928** *Observer* 15 Jan. 4 The general Gandhist idea. **1954** M. LOWRY *Let.* 10 May (1967) 367 Endeavouring to remedy this in the approved Gandhi-esque manner. **1954** *Encounter* Dec. 11/2 Gandhism..visualises ultimately a stateless society. **1958** J. V. BONDURANT *Conquest of Violence* i. 6 Prominent among Gandhian *principles* are non-violence, adherence to truth, and dignity of labor. **1963** *Guardian* 23 Feb. 4/7 Simple, authoritative and very Gandhi-esque. **1966** *Listener* 6 Jan. 14/2, I detected a desire to return to Gandhi-ism: 'Let us do without aid, without American wheat; let us starve if necessary, but regain our economic independence and self-respect.' **1971** *Hindustan Times Weekly* (New Delhi) 4 Apr. 3/6 The oldest survivors of the freedom struggle and Gandhian methods.

gandir, gandre, obs. forms of GANDER.

gandmer, obs. form of GAMMER.

gandoura (gæn'duərə). Also **gandourah, gandura(h).** [ad. Algerian Arab. *gandūra*, classical Arab. *ḳandūra*.] A long, loose gown worn mainly in the Near East and North Africa.

1851 *Illustr. Catal. Gt. Exhib.* IV. I. 1262/2 Gandoura, made of wool and silk. **1902** *Daily Chron.* 12 June 7/5 Wearing only his rich white gandurah. **1927** *Glasgow Herald* 17 Sept. 4 The Cadi in spotless burnous and fine white linen gandoura. **1951** R. SENHOUSE tr. *Colette's Chéri* (1963) 131 The coloured lining of the white gandoura she put on was suffused with a vague pink.

gandrees, var. GANTREES.

gandy dancer ('gændɪ 'dɑːnsə(r), 'dæns-). *slang* (orig. *U.S.*). [Orig. uncertain.] A railroad maintenance-worker or section-hand. Hence **gandy dancing.**

1923 N. ANDERSON *Hobo* vi. 93 A 'gandy dancer' is a man who works on the railroad track tamping ties. **1929** *Amer. Speech* V. 172 Gandy dancing is not considered a very honorable profession. **1933** *Ibid.* VIII. 26/2 *Gandy dancer*, section hand. (From the rhythmic up-and-down motion of workers pumping a handcar.) **1957** J. KEROUAC *On Road* (1958) III. vi. 215 Working in a railroad gandy-dancing cookshack. **1959** J. THURBER *Years with Ross* iv. 63 They discussed the parlance of railroading—deadhead, highball, whistle stop, gandy dancer. **1970** F. MCKENNA *Gloss. Railwaymen's Talk* 35 Footplatemen have a great regard for gandy dancers, the men who keep the rail safe for the train to run over.

†**gane,** *sb. Sc. Obs.* Also 6 **gan.** [Perh. related to GANE *v.*] ? An ugly countenance.

15.. ? DUNBAR *Interl. Droichis* 164 Vale to me a mekle wyf, A gret ungracious gane. **1500–20** DUNBAR *Poems* lxxv. 56, I luif rycht weill 3our graceles gane. **1508** —— *Flyting* 167 Thy gane it garris us think that we mon de. *Ibid.* 199. **1513** DOUGLAS *Æneis* VIII. iv. 180 As to behald his vgly ene tuane, His terrible vissage, and his grysly gane.

†**gane,** *v. Obs.* Forms: α. 1 **gánian,** 4–6 **gane,** 5 **gayne.** β. 3 **gonien,** 4–5 **gone,** 5 **goon** (? **gwone**). [OE. *gánian* = OHG. *geinôn*:—OTeut. **gainôjan*; related to the synonymous OE. *ʒínan* str. vb. = ON. *gína*, and OE. *ʒinian*, *ʒeonian* wk. vb. = OHG. *ginôn*, *ginên* (MHG. *ginen*, *genen*, mod.Ger. *gähnen*), MDu. *genen* (in Kilian *ghienen*), and OSl. *zinati*, Lith. *žinąti*. The same root (OAryan **ghei-*) without the *n* suffix, has given rise to vbs. of similar meaning in most of the European branches of the Aryan family: cf. OSl. *zijati*, Lith. *zioti*, L. *hiāre*, *hi-scĕre*, OHG. *gîjên*, *gîen*, also (with *w* suffix) *giwên* (MHG. *giwen*, *gewen*), Du. *geeuwen*; the ONorthumbrian *giwiʒa* to ask, demand, may correspond to this.

The normal ME. form of OE. *gánian* would be *gane-n* in Northern dialects and *gone-n* in other dialects. This agrees generally with the recorded distribution of the forms, but *gane* occurs in Chaucer. The relation of this word to the synonymous ME. *ȝane*, *ȝone* (see YAWN *v.*) is obscure.]

intr. To open the mouth wide, to gape or yawn.

α. *c* **1000** *Ags. Ps.* (Th.) cviii. 1 [cix. 2] þeah þe me synfulra, inwitfulra, muðas on ganian [L. *os apertum est*]. *a* **1100** *Gloss.* in Wr.-Wülcker 462/26 *Oscitantes*, ganiende. *c* **1386** CHAUCER *Manciple's Prol.* 35 See how he ganeth lo this dronken wight As though he wolde swolwe vs anonright. *c* **1460** J. RUSSELL *Bk. Nurture* 294 Be not gapynge nor ganynge, ne with þy mouth to powt. **1483** *Cath. Angl.* 149/2 To Gane (*A.* Gayne), *fatiscere, hiare.* **1530** PALSGR. 560/1 He ganeth as he had nat slepte ynoughe. **1570** LEVINS *Manip.* 19/7 To Gane, yane, *oscitare.*

β. *c* **1250** *Meid Maregrete* xliii, Ho sei a foul dragun ine þe hurne glide Berninde ase fur, ant goninde ful wide. **1390** GOWER *Conf.* II. 263 And tho she gan to gaspe and gone, And made signes many one. *c* **1420** *Avow. Arth.* xii, He [the boar] began to romy and rowte And gapes and gones. **14..** *Tundale's Vis.* 1250 To Satanas cast we hym that grymly gwonis [*v.r.* gronis] He schalle hym swolow all attoonis. *c* **1460** *Towneley Myst.* xvii. 47 And all nyght after grankys and goonys On slepe tyll I be broght.

Hence †**'ganing** *vbl. sb.*, gaping or yawning.

c **1000** ÆLFRIC *Gloss.* in Wr.-Wülcker 162/37 *Oscitatio*, ganung. *c* **1440** *Promp. Parv.* 185/2 Ganynge or ȝanynge, *oscitatus.* **1483** *Cath. Angl.* 149/2 A Ganynge, *hiatus.*

gane, var. *gone* pa. pple. of GO.

gane-, obs. form of GAIN-.

†**ganefish.** *Obs.* [Of obscure origin: conceivably a mistake for *garrefish.*] = GARFISH.

1611 COTGR., *Aiguille*..a Horne-backe, Piper-fish, Gane-fish. *Arfie*, a Hornefish, Hornebeake, Snacotfish, Ganefish, Piperfish. **1847–78** HALLIWELL, *Gane-fish*, a hornbeak. *Somerset.* [Not in any Somersetshire glossary.]

ganer, ganet(te, obs. ff. GANDER, GANNET.

gang (gæŋ), *sb.*[1] Also (in senses 1–4 only) 1 **gong;** (in sense 8) **ganne.** See also GONG, and for ff. with ʒ-, *i-*, ȝ-, YONG *sb.* [O.E. *gang*, *gong* str. masc. = OFris. *gong*, *gung*, OS. *gang* (Du. *gang*), OHG. *gang* (MHG., mod.G. *gang*), ON. *gang-r* (Da. *gang*, Sw. *gång*), Goth. *gagg-s*:—OTeut. **gaŋgo-z*, noun of action related to **gaŋgan* GANG *v.*[1], to go. Cf. the cognate ON. *ganga* wk. fem., walking, course, *gǫng* neut. pl., a passage, lobby (from which some of the Eng. senses may possibly be derived).]

I. Action or mode of going; way, passage.

†**1.** *pl.* Steps, goings, journeyings. (OE. only.)

c **825** *Vesp. Psalter* xvi[i]. 5 Gefreme gongas [L. *gressus*] mine in stiʒum ðinum. *c* **1000** *Sax. Leechd.* I. 76 Gif mon on mycelre rade, oþþe on miclum gangum weorðe ʒeteorad.

†**2. a.** The power of going, ability to walk about.

Beowulf 968 Ic hine ne mihte, þa metod nolde, ganges ʒetwæman. *a* **1175** *Cott. Hom.* 229 He forȝiaf blinde manne ȝeseohðe, and halten and lamen richte gang. *a* **1225** *Leg. Kath.* 500 Earen buten herunge, honden buten felunge, fet buten a ȝonge. *a* **1300** *Cursor M.* 24000 O wijttes all me wantid might, Gang, and steyuen, and tung, and sight, All failled me þat tide.

†**b.** Manner of going, gait or carriage. *Obs.*

a **1300** *Cursor M.* 28516 Lucheri has don me scrud Me-self, and bere my bodi prud In gang, in chere, in contenance. *a* **1327** in *Rel. Ant.* I. 124 Nou nabbe y nout that ȝong That speche ne that song. **1606** HOLLAND *Sueton.* 155 Some special one, whose gesture habitt and gang [L. *incessum*] hee might..imitate. **1626** W. SCLATER *Expos. 2 Thess.* (1629) iii. 9 Casually..may..children sometimes [fall] on fathers gestures, or gange of body.

†**c.** The act of walking. *Obs.*

1500–20 DUNBAR *Poems* li. 23 His gang garris all ȝour chalmeris schog.

†**d.** *fig.* Currency (of money; cf. ON. *gang-silfr*, current coin). *Obs.*

1488 *Sc. Acts Jas. IV* (1814) II. 208/2 þe said penny of gold to haue course & gang for xxx. þe saidis grotis.

†**3. a.** A journey; sometimes with definition of extent, as *a day's gang.* *Obs.*

c **950** *Lindisf. Gosp.* Luke ii. 44 Cuomon ʒeong dæʒes [L. *iter diei*; *c* **975** *Rushw.* gonga dæʒes]. *c* **1020** *Rule St. Benet* (Logeman) 86 þa þa on gange synd asende [L. *qui in itinere sunt directi*]. *c* **1200** ORMIN 8909 Ferrdenn towarrd Nazaræþ An daȝȝess gang till efenn. *c* **1205** LAY. 1298 þeonne he ferden forð wel feole dawen ȝong. *a* **1225** *Leg. Kath.* 2502 From þeonne as ha deide, twenti dahene ȝong. *a* **1300** *Cursor M.* 5983 Thre dais gang, na mare ne less, We must weind in to wildirness.

†**b.** A travelling or resorting. *Obs.*

1645 PAGITT *Heresiogr.* (1647) 84 By reason of a gang of silly women with child to the Image of our Lady of Steining ..to which they did trot with many rich offerings.

4. a. A way, road, or passage. Now *dial.*

(With quot. 1882 cf. ON. *gǫng* neut.-pl. a passage, lobby.)

c **950** *Lindisf. Gosp.* Mark i. 3 Rehta doeð stiʒa *vel* ʒeongas his [*c* **975** *Rushw.* gongas]. **971** *Blickl. Hom.* 109 þa men þe bearn habban..him tæcean lifes weʒ & rihtne gang to heofonum. **1855** ROBINSON *Whitby Gloss.*, *Gang*, a term synonymous with road, often used with a specific or descriptive prefix, as *Bygang*, *Crossgang*, *Downgang*, *Outgang*, *Upgang*. **1876** *Mid. Yorksh. Gloss.*, *Gang*, division of a mine..a continuous succession of galleries or gangs. *Ibid.*, *Gang*, a path; also, a narrow way of any kind. **1882** *Lanc. Gloss.*, *Gang*, a lobby in a farm-house.

†**b.** The course of a stream. *Obs.*

c **893** K. ÆLFRED *Oros.* II. iv. §6 On þære ea gong. **1467** *Acta Audit.* (1839) 8/1 þe actioune..anent þe abstractioune of þe water of Northesk fra þe ald gang. Similarly in **1493** *Acta Dom. Conc.* (1839) 307.

c. A walk or pasture for cattle; also, the right of pasturing. *Sc.* and *north. dial.*

1808–80 JAMIESON, *The haill gang*, the whole extent of pasture. '*A fine gang*, an excellent pasture. **1820** SCOTT *Monast.* xviii, 'The gang of two cows and a palfrey on our Lady's meadow', answered his brother officer.

†**5.** A step or rung of a ladder. *Obs.*

1688 R. HOLME *Armoury* III. 327/1 The Roofe Ladder.. is usually made with broad Ganges to go into the higher storyes.

6. *dial.* A turn or spell at any work or exercise; see GO *sb.*[1] [Cf. Du. *gang* (obs.), Da. *gang*, Sw. *gång*, a time, occasion.]

1879 *Cumbld. Gloss.*, *Gang*, turn to play. 'It's thy gang noo.'

7. *Sc.* The quantity or amount usually carried at one time (cf. GAIT *sb.*[3] and Du. *een gang water*, Ger. *ein gang wasser*, two pailfuls).

1590 in R. Chambers *Domestic Ann.* (1858) I. 201 *note*, John Borthwick, baxter, to get four boins of beer, with four gang of ale, and to furnish bread. **1808–25** JAMIESON s.v., *A gang of peats*, the quantity brought by a number of ponies at each trip (Shetland). **1827** POLLOK *Let.* in *Life* (1841) 357 The said servant shall, at each returning gang of milk, churn one of the churns. **1858** RAMSAY *Remin.* Ser. I. (1860) 50 They've drucken sax gang o' watter.

¶ The OE. *gang*, *gǫng*, privy, appears in later Eng. only as GONG, q.v.

II. A set of things or persons.

8. a. A set of articles such as are usually taken together.

So Ger. *gang*; applied, e.g. to a set of cart-wheels, of horseshoes, etc.

c **1340** *Durh. MS. Alm. Roll*, v ganges de feleis. **1395–6** *Ibid.*, j gange del spaks. **1453–4** *MS. Hostill. Roll, Durham*, iij gang et di..de felys pro rotis inde fiendis, iij gang del spekys. **1558** *Wills & Inv. N.C.* (Surtees 1835) 162 Twoo gang of wayne fellowes wth heades and moldeburdes. **1580** *Extracts Aberdeen Reg.* (1848) II. 38 The gang of..horss schone. **1670** NARBOROUGH *Jrnl.* in *Acc. Sev. Late Voy.* I. (1694) 28 The main Mast must be unrig'd, and a new gang of shrouds fitted. **1674–91** RAY *N.C. Words* 29 *Gang*, a row or set, v.g. of teeth or the like. It is in this sense a general word all over England. **1726** SHELVOCKE *Voy. round World* 163, I had fitted her with a gang of oars, and upon trial they gave way after the rate of 3 knots. **1796** MRS. GLASSE *Cookery* vi. 101 Boil a gang of calf's-feet to a strong jelly. **1829** MARRYAT *F. Mildmay* iii, Didn't we make a gang of white hammock-cloths fore and aft. **1886** *Ripon Chron.* 4 Sept. 8/3 Beast feet from 10*d.* to 1*s.* per gang of four.

b. *esp.* A set of tools or implements so arranged as to work simultaneously.

1806 A. Young *Agric. Essex* (1813) I. 147 Mr. Rogers.. uses a gang of extremely light harrows. 1874 Knight *Dict. Mech.* I. 940/2 Gangs of plows have been arranged for work by attaching a number of plows to a bar at proper distances. 1883 *Harper's Mag.* Nov. 824/2 A 'gang', as a set of saws is called..arranged at different intervals.

9. a. A company of workmen.

This and the following senses appear to be peculiar to Eng.; the ON. *drauga-gangr*, etc., have often been compared, but *-gang-r* in these compounds means not 'gang', but the act of going about. It would appear that in nautical use the word meaning 'set of things' (sense 8) was extended to the sense 'set of persons', 'crew', which had earlier been expressed by the cognate and like-sounding GING.

1627 Capt. Smith *Seaman's Gram.* vi. 27 Man the Boat is to put a Gang of men, which is company into her, they are commonly called the Coxswaine Gang. 1668 Pepys *Diary* (1877) V. 159 Home to dinner with my gang of clerks. *a* 1700 B. E. *Dict. Cant. Crew, Gang*..a Society of Porters under a Regulation. 1706 Phillips (ed. Kersey) s.v., In Sea-Affairs, *Gangs* are the several Companies of Mariners belonging to a Ship [etc.]. 1775 Romans *Florida* 182 Hogshead staves of white oak are made by what are called gangs of people; a stave making gang consists of five persons. 1812–16 J. Smith *Panorama Sc. & Art* I. 185 A gang, consisting of 6 persons, will make 20,000 bricks in the course of a week. 1863 Fr. A. Kemble *Resid. in Georgia* 25 There are here a gang of coopers. 1891 *Law Times Rep.* LXV. 577/1 He was unloading four ships, each with a gang of four men.

b. A company of slaves or prisoners.

1790 Burke *Fr. Rev.* Wks. 1808 V. 83 A gang of Maroon slaves, suddenly broke loose from the house of bondage. 1832 Ht. Martineau *Demerara* i. 7 The second gang consisted of young boys and girls. 1883 Ouida *Wanda* I. 13 Now and then a gang of such captives would go by on foot and chained.

10. a. Any band or company of persons who go about together or act in concert (chiefly in a bad or depreciatory sense, or associated with criminal societies). *transf.* a social set. *colloq.*

1632 in *Crt. & Times Chas. I* (1848) II. 197 Nutt the pirate..with all his gang of varlets. 1677 R. Cary *Palæol. Chron.* II. I. xiii. 126, I have a question to move on the behalf of the Gang of Chronographers. 1701 *Lond. Gaz.* No. 3755/8 Supposed to be concerned with a Gang of House-breakers. 1782 Wolcot (P. Pindar) *Odes to R.A.'s* xi. Wks. 1812 I. 38 And as a gang of thieves a bustle make With greater ease, your purse to take. 1849 Macaulay *Hist. Eng.* iv. I. 505 Disgusted his friends by joining what was then generally considered as a gang of crazy heretics. 1883 *Law Times* LXXV. 130/2 The breaking up of gangs of criminals through the operation of long terms of penal servitude. 1945 A. Kober *Parm Me* 28 The bunch is waiting at my house. I thought I'd call fa you and take you over, so that we'd meet the gang. 1955 G. Freeman *Liberty Man* I. i. 15 All the gang would be there, and she'd be ever so proud of him.

b. *to be of a gang*: to belong to the same society, to have the same interests.

The resemblance between this and OF. *estre a une gaaigne*, to be member of a company, is probably accidental.

1669 Pepys *Diary* 4 Mar., This company, both the ladies and all, are of a gang. 1681 *Trial S. Colledge* 24 Here are several of them my Lord, they are all of a gang. *Mr. Serj. Jefferies.* Not of your gang, Mr. Colledge.

c. *Gang of Four* [tr. Chinese *sìrénbāng*, f. *sì* four + *rén* human being, person + *bāng* gang, clique], a nickname for four leading members of the Cultural Revolutionary Left accused after the death of Mao Tse-tung of counter-revolutionary conspiracy and Marxist revisionism, and discredited in October 1976 by the Communist Party Central Committee of the People's Republic of China.

1976 *Peking Rev.* 29 Oct. 7/2 The Party Central Committee headed by Chairman Hua Kuo-feng smashed the scheme of the 'gang of four' to usurp Party and state power. 1977 'S. Leys' *Chinese Shadows* (1978) ii. 88 The downfall of the 'Gang of Four'..in late 1976 marked the end of Shanghai as a citadel of radical Maoism. 1978 *Times* 29 Sept. (China Suppl.) p. iii/1 The country's agricultural performance since the fall of the Gang of Four has been disappointing. 1978 *Chinese Lit.* XII. 117 This so-called evidence was fabricated by Chu Lan, a group of 'gang of four' writers. 1983 *Atlantic Monthly* July 28/2 The postmortem on China's intermittent troubles..has moved its target from Mao's widow and her three Shanghai associates (Gang of Four) to the role of Mao in the Gang's ultra-leftism.

d. *Gang of Three* (*Four, Five*, etc.), a term applied to any group of people who are outspoken in their advocacy of a particular policy or who take a minority view on an issue; used *esp.* of a group of British Labour front-bench MPs who were openly critical of their Party, and left it to form the Social Democratic Party in 1981.

1977 *Economist* 9 Apr. 51 The unhappy Congressmen have directed their wrath at her kitchen cabinet—the so-called gang of four, headed by Sanjay Gandhi. 1980 *Washington Post* 12 Mar. A17 He added Assistant Secretary of State Harold Saunders, calling the officials a 'Gang of Five' against Israel. 1980 *Daily Tel.* 9 Aug. 7 Mr. William Rodgers..brushed aside Mr. David Steel's appeal for Labour's so-called 'Gang of Three' to give up their fight against the Left of their party. 1981 *Nature* 12 Nov. 105/1 Hoyle..[,] W. A. Fowler and the two Burbidges.., now known as the gang of four. 1983 *New Republic* 8 Aug. 16/1 David Owen, Shirley Williams, William Rodgers, and Roy Jenkins—The Gang of Four—eventually took two dozen Labour M.P.s with them. 1983 *National Rev.* (U.S.) 25 Nov. 1488 'No first use'..owes its prominence to its advocacy by 'the gang of four' (Bundy, Kennan, McNamara, and Gerard Smith). 1985 *Guardian* 21 May (London ed.) 32/7 He did not reserve his characteristic gentleness for Mr Bill Rodgers, one of Mrs Williams's co-defectors in the Gang of Four. 1985 *Coal Outlook* 23 Dec. 4/1 Gradison and two other commissioners became known as the 'Gang of Three' for their strong emphasis on railroad freedoms.

11. *U.S.* A collection or herd of animals of the same species, esp. of elk or buffalo. †Also, a pack of dogs.

1740 *Hist. Jamaica* vii. 183 None shall hunt any Gang of Dogs within four miles of any crawl or Settlement. 1807 P. Gass *Jrnl.* 37 This day we saw several gangs, or herds, of buffaloe on the sides of the hills. 1882 *Standard* 10 Feb. 5/3 It might puzzle..to..tell what is the precise difference in the vocabulary of the hunter between a 'herd' and a 'gang' of elk.

III. 12. *attrib.* and *Comb.*, as (sense 8 b, denoting implements worked in sets) ***gang-cultivator, -drill, -edger, -loom, -plough, -press, -punch, -saw***; (senses 9, 10) ***gang-boss, -driver, -fight, -leader, -life, -man, -master, -robber, -robbery, -system, -war, -warfare, -work***. Also **gang-bang** *slang* (orig. *U.S.*), an occasion on which several men have sexual intercourse one after another with one woman; hence as *v. trans.* and *intr.*; **gang-boose** (see quot.); **gang-mill**, a saw-mill in which gang-saws are used; **gang-rape** *v. trans.*, to force (a woman) to have sexual intercourse with a succession of men at one time (see also quot. 1975); also as *sb.*, (an instance of) rape committed in this manner; cf. *gang-bang*; **gang-rider** (see quot.); **gang-road** (*local*), a road between a harbour and the buildings; **gang-shag** *slang* (orig. *U.S.*) = *gang-bang* above. See also GANGLAND.

1953 *San Francisco News* 14 Oct. 23/3 'Wonder gear', it developed, is an attractive girl, in Navy lingo, and '*gang-bang' is a juicy party involving wine, women and song. 1957 *Nation* 23 Feb. 161/1 Sometimes he lapses into pages of terrifying gibberish that sound like a tape recording of a gang bang with everybody full of pod, juice and bennies all at once. 1967 G. Legman *Fake Revolt* 30 The gang-bang ethic. 1968 B. Turner *Sex Trap* xxi. 193 What's the next arrangement to be? A gang-bang for the whole Vice Squad? 1969 *Guardian* 16 Aug. 7/3 A pretty 18-year-old girl..used to 'stuff' herself with heroin and let herself be 'gang-banged' all the time. 1967 G. Legman *Fake Revolt* 28 Wife-swapping, husband-ditching, *gang-banging, and the rest. 1847 Halliwell, **Gang-boose*, the narrow passage from a cow-house to the barn. *North.* 1882 *Lanc. Gloss.*, *Gang-boose.* 1887 C. B. George *40 Yrs. on Rail* ix. 193, I was in charge of a construction train, being engineer, conductor and *gang-boss combined. 1923 'R. Daly' *Enchanted Isl.* xii. 109 Tulagi, the chief gang-boss, will keep the other boys up to their work [on the copra plantation]. 1931 *Times Lit. Suppl.* 18 June 485/1 The modern 'gang-boss' and his henchmen in the boot-legging and hijacking world in America. 1874 Knight *Dict. Mech.* I. 940/2 *Gang-cultivator. 1884 *Ibid.* IV. 374 *Gang-drill. 1864 Kingsley *Rom. & Teut.* ii. (1875) 19 Left their slaves to the tender mercy of..stewards and *gang-drivers. 1879 *Lumberman's Gaz.* 15 Oct., The roller edger, now almost wholly superseded by the *gang or parallel edger. 1880 *Northwest. Lumberman* 24 Jan., The mill will be equipped throughout with..gang edgers. 1932 H. Simpson *Boomerang* x. 271 A man left lying insensible in the wake of a *gang-fight. 1958 *New Statesman* 20 Dec. 880/3 The films have conditioned us to demanding a high degree of realism in this kind of gang-fight. 1865 *Spectator* 21 Jan. 64 It is not open to him to make an outsider or new comer *gangleader out of his turn. 1949 M. Mead *Male & Female* xv. 309 This asocial *gang-life of boys provides a basis for the adult criminal world in America. 1876 L. P. Brockett *Silk-Industry* xvii. 99 Ribbons are usually woven on *gang-looms. 1867 J. E. White in E. R. Pike *Human Doc. Vict. Golden Age* (1967) 218 The *gangman acts as foreman or overlooker. 1896 *Current Hist.* (Buffalo, N.Y.) VI. 937 The following day four gang-men were killed near Dalijal. 1928 *Daily Express* 10 Oct. 6 We can hide you away where all the gangmen in London won't find you. 1955 E. Waugh *Officers & Gentlemen* 153 The gangmen of the departments closed in for the kill. 1964 A. Swinson *Six Minutes to Sunset* ii. 42 At midnight the railway between Chheharta and Khasa was torn up, the job being done expertly with gangmen's tools. 1884 Rogers *6 Cent. Work & Wages* II. 511 His young children..taken from him and put under the care of a *gangmaster. 1893 *Westm. Gaz.* 1 Feb. 2/1 His place is.. between the official leaders of his party and the mass of those whose appointed generals they are, and not their gang-masters. 1879 *Lumberman's Gaz.* 15 Oct., David Fox of Bay City..put in the first *gang-mill upon the Saginaw river. 1856 Olmsted *Slave States* 9, I sow wheat and guano together, and plow them in with a *gang-plow. 1894 *Times* (weekly ed.) 2 Feb. 89/3 A man with two yoke of oxen and a gang-plough breaks up a quarter section (160 acres) during five spring and summer months. 1884 Knight *Dict. Mech.* IV. 375 **Gang-press.* 1874 *Ibid.* I. 941/2 **Gang-punch.* 1969 H. Waugh *Young Prey* iv. 67 She's the kind of DOA I'd expect to find down in Homicide South—some runaway, some would-be hippie who got herself *gang-raped. 1975 *Business Week* 17 Mar. 10/1 Who else could fit embezzlement, stock fraud,..and homosexual gang rape into a book on commercial banking? 1977 *Daily Mirror* 16 Mar. 11/6 Six soldiers who plotted a gang rape chose a 17-year-old village girl as their victim. 1983 P. Kurth *Anastasia* (1985) I. 14 Stories later spread in monarchist circles of their being tied naked to chairs and gang-raped by crazed Bolsheviks. 1984 *Times Lit. Suppl.* 19 Oct. 1183/4 She had just suffered..'gang-rape' at the hands of a quartet of avant-garde musicians. 1889 *Century Dict.*, **Gang-rider*, one who rides on mine-cars or trams. 1840 *Evid. Hull Docks Comm.* 52 There is no quay room except the *gang road along there. 1895 Sir W. Hunter *Old Missionary* iv. 107 Two fraternities of *gang-robbers. 1831 *Edin. Rev.* LIII. 450 Those who have merely heard or read what *gang-robbery is. 1887 *Spectator* 19 Mar. 383/2 That earliest, safest, and most profitable of all forms of crime,—violent gang-robbery. 1873 J. Richards *Wood-working Factories* 127 To manufacture thin boards cheaply, the *gang saw must be used. 1877 *Lumberman's Gaz.* 8 Dec. 362 The 'gang-saw', a congregation of saws hung together in a frame or sash. 1927 F. M. Thrasher *Gang* xiii. 237 The *gang shag includes boys from sixteen to twenty-two years of age. It is a party carried on with one woman by from fifteen to thirty boys from one gang or club. A mattress in the alley usually suffices for this purpose. 1891 *Pall Mall G.* 12 Dec. 7/1 They are the outcome of division of labour; they are largely the result of the '*gang system'. 1932 *Amer. Speech* VII. 253 A cycle of *gang war pictures. 1959 Wyndham Lewis *Let.* 12 Dec. (1963) 514 The people were no more troubled than Chicagoans are by gang-wars. 1934 Webster, *Gang warfare. 1962 *John o'London's* 8 Mar. 235/1 Gang-warfare and teenage problems. 1896 *Westm. Gaz.* 30 Sept. 5/1 Almost more important than the question of wages is the question of the organisation of *gang work.

gang (gæŋ), *sb.*[2] *Fishing.* ? = GANGING *vbl. sb.*[3]

1883 [see GANGING *vbl. sb.*[3]].

gang, *v.*[1] *Obs.* exc. *Sc.* and *dial.* Forms: α. 1 **gongan**, *Northumb.* **ȝeonga**, 3 **ȝeonge, ȝonge, gonge**, 4 **gong**. β. 1 **gangan**, 3 **gangen** (*Orm.* **ganngenn**), 4 **gange** (*Sc. pple.* **ganand**), 3– **gang** (9 *Sc.* and *dial.* **gan, geyng**). [Common Teutonic: OE. *gangan, gǫngan* = OFris. *gunga*, OS. *gangan* (MDu. *gangen*), OHG. *gangan* (MHG. *gangen*), ON. *ganga* (Sw. *gånga*, Da. *gange* obs.), Goth. *gaggan*:—OTeut. **gaŋgan*. In ME. no traces remain of the pa. t. (OE. *ȝeong, ȝieng, gang*, OFris. *geng, ging*, OS. *geng*, OHG. *giang, gieng*, ON. *gekk*:—OTeut. **gegaŋg-*) or of the pa. pple. (OE. *ȝegangen*, etc.). The use of the verb is also greatly restricted in favour of GO, OE. *gán*, which finally supplanted *gang* exc. in the northern dialects. The same tendency appears in most of the cognate languages; thus Du. *gaan* (pa. t. *ging*, pa. pple. *gegaan*), G. *gehen* (*ging, gegangen*), Sw. *gå* (*gick, gått*), Da. *gaa* (*gik, gaaet*), but Icel. *ganga* (rarely *gá* from Da.). *Gang*, however, survives to some extent in various G. dialects and in Fris. The OTeut. *gaŋgan* is prob. related to Lith. *žengiù* I stride, go, Skr. *jáṅghā* the lower part of the leg, from the root **ghoŋgh-*, **gheŋgh-*. For the relation between this and GO, see the latter.

In Sc. *gang* is now used chiefly in the inf. and pres. tense, while *go* furnishes the pa. t. (*gaed*) and the pa. pple.]

1. *intr.* To walk, go. (Chiefly *lit.*)

α. *Beowulf* 711 Þa com of more..Grendel gongan. *c* 950 *Lindisf. Gosp.* Mark xiv. 42 Arisað gæ we *vel* wutun ȝeonga. *c* 1205 Lay. 27764 Walwain gon ȝeonge ȝeond þat wæl muchele. *c* 1300 *Havelok* 843 Betere is þat þu henne gonge, Þan þu here dwelle longe. *c* 1340 *Cursor M.* 13267 (Trin.) Ihesu þouȝt hit was ful longe Wiþouten felowshipe to gonge.

β. *Beowulf* 314 Þæt hie him to mihton ȝegnum gangan. 971 *Blickl. Hom.* 123 Þu scealt on eorþan gangan. *c* 1200 Ormin 12855 He þær þe Laferrd Crist Sahh ganngenn & nohht stanndenn. *c* 1300 *Havelok* 370 Til þat he kouþen speken wit tunge, Speken and gangen, on horse riden. 1340 Hampole *Pr. Cons.* 1396 By þis way byhoves us al gang, Bot be we war we ga noght wrang. 1377 Langl. *P. Pl.* B. XIV. 161 And ȝit is wynter for hem worse..for wete-shodde thei gange. *c* 1460 *Towneley Myst.* vi. 87 *Deus.* The day spryngis; now lett me go. *Iacob.* Nay, nay, I will not so, Bot thou blys me or thou gang. 1549 *Compl. Scotl.* v. 34 Quhen ve ar tirit to gang on oure feit, ve ar solist to seik horse to ryde. 1638 *Penit. Conf.* v. (1657) 77 But you whose sins are of a deeper grain..gang ye on pilgrimage to Rome. 1712 Arbuthnot *John Bull* III. iii, 'I do not care for your flaunting beaus, that gang with their breasts open.' 1786 Burns *Twa Dogs* 12 Some place far abroad, Where sailors gang to fish for Cod. 1866 G. Chatt *Poems* 87 The bairns was put to wark as seun as they could gan. 1886 Hall Caine *Son of Hagar* I. iv, I must gang away at once.

b. quasi-*trans.* (Cf. GO.)

c 1375 *Sc. Leg. Saints, Jacobus minor* 803 Þane tytus bad hyme gange his way. *c* 1470 Henry *Wallace* I. 250 Thai left him swa, and furth thar gait can gang. 1508 Dunbar *Poems* v. 29 Out of hevin the hie gait cought (*B.* cowth) the wif gang. 1637 B. Jonson *Sad Sheph.* II. i, False gelden, gang thy gait. 1822 Scott *Pirate* v, Put up your pipes, and gang your gait. 1893 *Northumbld. Gloss.* s.v., 'Gan yor aan gait', go your own way.

c. = GO in transferred or fig. senses. *rare.*

1595 *Extracts Aberdeen Reg.* (1848) II. 120 To reull the saidis tua knockis, and to cause thame gang and strik the houris richtlie bayth nicht and day. 1603 Owen *Pembrokesh.* (1891) 269 Fowlinge also claimeth a place with the pleasures of this Countrey..yt shall gang amonge them and truelye not vnworthylye. 1826 J. Wilson *Noct. Ambr.* Wks. 1855 I. 282 Ane o' the bawbees o' an obsolete sort, that wadna gang nowadays.

2. In Phrases. (Cf. GO.)

a 1300 *Cursor M.* 10898 Sco had conceiued of hir husband, Sex monet nu wit child gangand. 1603 *Philotus* xxvii, Ȝe sall weir..Ȝour Myssell quhen ȝe gang to gait. 1768 Ross *Helenore* II. 74 She says, my heart is like to gang awa', An' I maun e'en sit down, or else I'll fa'. *Ibid.* 85 For it ungangs me fair, gin at the last To gang together binna found the best. 1785 Burns *To a Mouse*, The best laid schemes o' mice an' men Gang aft a-gley. 1893 *Northumbld. Gloss.* s.v., 'To gan wi'' is to make away with.

3. In phraseological *Combs.* employed substantively or attributively, as ***the gang-bye***, the go-by, the action of passing one without notice; ***gang-there-out***, homeless, vagabond (cf. *run-there-out*).

1815 SCOTT *Guy M.* i, I darena for my life open the door to ony of your gang-there-out sort o' bodies. **1818** —— *Rob Roy* xxiii, We gang-there-out Hieland bodies are an unchancy generation. —— *Br. Lamm.* xxv, Mercy on me that I suld live in my auld days to gie the gang-bye to the very writer.

gang (gæŋ), *v.*[2] [f. GANG *sb.*[1] 9.]

1. a. *trans.* To arrange in a gang; also *to gang out*: to arrange in companies.

1856 OLMSTED *Slave States* 234 They were worked, white and black slaves, criminal and bonded servants, all ganged together. **1885** *St. James's Gaz.* 18 July 8/1 After the Penjdeh incident about two thousand men were ganged out to strengthen the works.

b. To arrange (implements or instruments) in gangs (GANG *sb.*[1] 8 b). Hence **ganged** *ppl. a.*

1900 *Yearbk. U.S. Dept. Agric.* 540 The plows are usually ganged, two to one frame. **1938** *Nature* 3 Sept. 446/1 The use of a motor driving the main ganged variable condenser. **1942** *Electronic Engin.* XV. 9 The tuning.. is carried out by ..variometers ganged together and controlled by a single knob. **1964** *Economist* 6 June 1149/2 Adaptation..made it feasible for disc-plows to be 'ganged' so that several could be pulled at once. **1971** *Hi-Fi Sound* Feb. 41/2 (Advt.), Rotary knob ganged controls for tone, balance and volume.

2. a. *intr. to gang in*: to come in a gang. Also, to go in company *with*.

1891 MISS WILLARD in *Voice* (N.Y.) 12 Nov., The dozen or fifteen barefooted urchins who in the later summer season ganged in from the river side and prairie. **1928** W. A. WHITE *Masks in Pageant* 348 He was frail [in his boyhood] and never ganged with his fellows.

b. *to gang up* (*with, on*): to form a gang or combine (with, against). *colloq.* (orig. *U.S.*).

1925 T. A. BOYD *Points of Honor* 50 Then I set out to kick hell out of 'im. I'd a done it too if they hadn't a ganged up on me. **1940** *Nature* 6 July 36/2 The old folks..and the youngsters..are 'ganging up' on the half of the population that does the work. **1942** BERREY & VAN DEN BARK *Amer. Thes. Slang* §343/6 Affiliate or associate with,..*gang up with*. **1942** D. POWELL *Time to be Born* (1943) xiv. 332 Things must have gone wrong with her!.. Maybe he's got people to gang up against her. **1944** *Hutchinson's Pict. Hist. War* 27 Oct. 1943–11 Apr. 1944 365 A change in U-boat tactics was essential if they were to gang-up on and strike at our convoys. **1946** 'P. QUENTIN' *Puzzle for Fiends* viii. 64 Thought he was Jesus Christ..with a lot of Satans ganging up on him. **1951** *Ann. Reg. 1950* 47 A fear that Germany and France might 'gang-up' in Europe without Britain. **1959** 'J. BYROM' *Take Only as Directed* i. 16 He'll get David to gang up with him and stop me sailing.

ganga, var. GANJA.

gangan ('gæŋ,gæn). Also gang-gang. [Native word.] An Australian cockatoo (see quot. 1898).

1833 STURT 2 *Exped. S. Australia* I. Introd. 38 Upon the branches..the gangan, and various kinds of pigeons were feeding. **1891** E. KINGLAKE *Australian at Home* 124 You hear the sweet note of the wonga pigeon or the hoarse scream of the ganggang. **1898** MORRIS *Austral Eng.*, *Gang-gang*, or *Gan-gan*, the aboriginal word for the bird *Callocephalon galeatum*..so called from its note; a kind of cockatoo, grey with a red head, called also *Gang-gang Cockatoo*. **1965** *Austral. Encycl.* II. 440/1 The smallest cockatoo is the gang-gang..of south-eastern Australia and Tasmania.

gangand, obs. form of GANGING *ppl. a.*

gangar, obs. form of GANGER.

‖**'gangart.** *Min. rare.* [a. G. *gangart*, f. *gang* vein, lode + *art* kind.] = GANGUE.

1811 PINKERTON *Petral.* I. Introd. 33 He who cannot distinguish gems without being informed of their countries, sites, and gangarts. *Ibid.* I. 560 The usual gangart of diamonds..is a ferruginous pudding-stone.

'gang-board. Chiefly *Naut.* [f. GANG *sb.*[1]]

1. (See quot. 1850, and cf. GANGWAY 3.)

1748 SMOLLETT *Rod. Rand.* xxiv. (1804) 164 Some of the company..stood upon the gang-boards to see us enter. **1809** *Naval Chron.* XXI. 299 There were also some empty casks placed under the gang-board. *c* **1850** *Rudim. Navig.* (Weale) 120 *Gangboards*, narrow platforms within the sides, next the gunwales, which connect the quarter-deck to the forecastle. Each is composed of three or four deals fayed and bolted together edgewise. **1867** in SMYTH *Sailor's Word-bk.*

2. A plank, usually with cleats or steps nailed on it, for walking upon, esp. into or out of a boat.

1777 *Cook's 2nd. Voy.* II. III. iv. 47 As we were putting off the boat, they laid hold of the gang-board, and unhooked it off the boat's stern. **1803** WELLINGTON in Gurw. *Desp.* (1837) I. 488 The gang boards are then laid across the ends of the chesses on each edge of the bridge. **1840** MARRYAT *Poor Jack* xiv, They threw out their gang-board. **1887** *Poor Nellie* (1888) 34 You must climb up from the punt or walk along the gangboard by yourself.

3. A plank along the bottom of a racing-boat.

1857 P. COLQUHOUN *Comp. Oarsman's Guide* 29 A backbone is the modern substitute for the gang board which 20 years ago ran down an eight from the after to the forward thwart, to stiffen the boat and for the crew to walk along.

4. 'The boards ending the hammock-nettings at either side of the entrance from the accommodation-ladder to the deck' (*Cent. Dict.*).

'gang-cask. *Naut.* [f. GANG *sb.*[1] + CASK.] A water-cask used on board ships (see quots.).

1779 FORREST *Voy. N. Guinea* 169 On the edges of the canoe..I put a gang cask, with which the owner paddled into a fresh water river. **1867** SMYTH *Sailor's Word-bk.*, *Gang-casks*, small barrels used for bringing water on board in boats..usually containing 32 gallons. **1882** CASSELL s.v. *Breaker*, The gang cask..contains the drinking water for the ship's company.

'gang-days. *Obs.* exc. *Hist.* [f. GANG *sb.*[1] + DAY; so called from the processions held on these days. ON. *gangdagar*, OSw. *gangdaghar* are perh. from OE.] The three days preceding Ascension-day or Holy Thursday; also called Rogation-days.

891 *O.E. Chron.* (Earle) 88 þy ilcan ȝeare ofer Eastron ymbe gang daȝas oþþe ær. *a* **1225** *Ancr. R.* 412 Uridawes and umbridawes and ȝoing dawes [so *MS. Nero*; *Titus* ȝong dahes; *Cleop.* ȝeoncdaȝes; *Corpus omits*] and uigiles. *c* **1290** *S. Eng. Leg.* I. 441/359 In a time atþe gangdawes [*v.r.* roueisouns]: þis holie man al-so prechede a day at Oxenford. **1469** *Househ. Ord.* (1790) 101 Item, Beves..by the yere, vii weekes rebated for Lent and gang daies, 410. **1571** GRINDAL *Articles* B ij b, Whether..the parson, vicar [etc.]..in the dayes of the Rogations, commonly called the gang dayes, walke the accustomed bounds of your Parish. **1634** CANNE *Necess. Separ.* (1849) 123 The observation of Gangdays, or rogation week, is wholly popish. **1895** J. BROWN *Pilgr. Fathers* I. 38 The perambulation of the parish bounds in cross-week or gang-days.

gangdom ('gæŋdəm). [f. GANG *sb.*[1] + -DOM.] = GANGLAND.

1926 *Springfield* (Mass.) *Union* 20 Apr. 7 A definite inquiry into gangdom's manipulations. **1930** *Observer* 19 Oct. 17 A mere commonplace of New York gangdom. **1935** J. T. FARRELL *Judgment Day* (1936) iii. 515 Lonigan and.. Gallagher together leaped up the career of gangdom's adventurous ladder to fame. **1935** *Amer. Speech* X. 10/1 An age when highly organized gangdom had no voice in the government.

gange (gændʒ), *v.* [Of obscure origin; derivation from F. *ganse* braid, has been conjectured.]

1. *trans.* To protect (a fish-hook, part of a fishing-line) with fine wire.

1861 COUCH *Brit. Fishes* I. 38 The line..was armed or as a fisherman..would say was ganged with flexible brass wire twisted regularly and firmly round it. **1880** *W. Cornwall Gloss.* s.v., To gange a hook is to cover it with fine brass or copper wire, to prevent its being bitten off by the fish.

2. 'To fasten (a fish-hook) to the end of a section of line called the *ganging*' (*Cent. Dict.*).

gange, obs. form of GANG *sb.* and *v.*[1]

†**gangean**, *a. Obs. rare*–°. [? f. Sp. *ganga* the pin-tailed grouse + -EAN.] (See quot. 1623.)

1623 COCKERAM, *Gangean colour*, diuers colours in one together, as in a Mallard or Pigeon's necke. **1661** in Peacham *Compl. Gent.* (ed. 3) 155 [*printed* gangran].

ganger ('gæŋə(r)), *sb.*[1] *Obs.* exc. *dial.* and *arch.* Also 5 **gangar**, 9 **ganner**. [f. GANG *v.*[1] + -ER[1]. Cf. Du. *ganger*, G. *gänger*.

OE. **gangere* (Somner) is not authenticated.]

1. One who goes or travels on foot.

Rolf the Ganger, a modern rendering of ON. *Gǫngu-Hrólfr* (where *gǫngu* is the genit. of *ganga*: see GANG), the designation of a Norseman who has been from a very early period conjecturally identified (but erroneously) with the 'Rollo' or 'Rou' of Norman history.

1424 *Sc. Acts Jas. I* (1814) II. 6/2 That thar be ordanyt hostilaris and resettis haifande stabillis and chawmeris to ridaris and gangaris. **1852** MISS YONGE *Cameos* (1877) I. i. 5 Rolf, called the ganger or walker, as tradition relates, because his stature was so gigantic..he always fought on foot. **18..** FROUDE in Skelton *Summ. & Wint. Balmawhapple* (1897) II. 215 Long ages now beneath the soil The ganger has been lying.

b. Phr. ***comers and gangers*** (see quot.).

c **1400** MAUNDEV. (Roxb.) xxx. 136 Prestre Iohn hase ilk a day in his courte etand ma þan xxxm of folke, withouten commers and gangers. **1876** *Whitby Gloss.* s.v., 'Gangers and comers', people in and out; visitors.

2. A fast-going horse.

ON. *gangari*, Da. *ganger* steed, palfrey, common in mediæval romances and ballads, were prob. suggested by med.L. *gradarius* or *ambulator* (cf. OF. *cheval ambleur*) and thus different in origin and meaning.

1818 SCOTT *Rob Roy* xxvii, It's a weel-kend ganger; they ca' it Souple Tam. *a* **1825** FORBY *Voc. E. Anglia*, *Ganger*, a goer, a speedy horse. **1868** ATKINSON *Cleveland Gloss.*, *Ganger*, a goer, usually, if not exclusively, applied to a horse.

3. *Comb.*, as ***ganger-before***, ***-between***.

1483 *Cath. Angl.* 149/2 A Ganger be-twene, *mediator*, *-trix*. **1595** DUNCAN *App. Etymol.* (E.D.S.) *Anteambulo*, a ganger before, a convoyer.

ganger ('gæŋə(r)), *sb.*[2] [f. GANG *sb.* or *v.*[2] + -ER[1].] An overseer in charge of a gang of workmen.

1849 ALB. SMITH *Pottleton Leg.* 15 His companion..was known in the village as 'The Ganger'..a sort of sub-contractor for the works..collecting his own men and paying them. **1860** *Artist & Craftsman* 278 The man was a ganger, as it is termed in the technical phraseology, a sort of serjeant of the working army. **1860** W. H. RUSSELL *Diary in India* II. xxi. 409 A ganger, or head navvy..is placed over hundreds of men. **1894** *Times* 5 Feb. 3/2 A man named Eames acted as foreman or ganger, on board the Crowaiti, in the interests of the stevedores.

appositive. **1886** *Daily News* 28 Dec. 7/2 J. K., a ganger platelayer, deposed to finding the deceased's body.

ganger ('gæŋə(r)), *sb.*[3] *Naut.* [? Short form of FOREGANGER.] (See quot. 1882.)

c **1860** H. STUART *Seaman's Catech.* 55 The upper ends are then ready for shackling to the ganger. **1882** NARES *Seamanship* (ed. 6) 162 *A ganger*, two or more lengths of chain cable shackled to the sheet anchor. It enables part of the sheet cable always to remain bent.

†**'ganger**, *v. Obs.* [back-formation from GANGRENE, influenced by CANKER: cf. It. *gangrire* to gangrene (Florio); also '*Ganger*, a canker, fester, venom' (*Surrey Provincialisms*, E.D.S.).]

intr. To gangrene, mortify.

1685 M'ALPIE in *Harp of Renfrew.* Ser. II. (1873) 31 They ..Most be cutt off like corrupt member, Least yt the body all should ganger. **1696** A. DE LA PRYME *Diary* (Surtees) 102 An ape..bit his hand, which bite he slighting, it gangered and killed him. **1725** BRADLEY *Fam. Dict.* s.v. *Wound*, When the Parts Ganger, you must make use of the Spirit of Motherwort.

gangerell, -ill, var. GANGREL.

Gangetic (gæn'dʒɛtɪk), *a.* [ad. L. *Gangēticus*, f. *Ganges*, a. Gr. *Γάγγης*.] Belonging to the river Ganges. †Also *sb. pl.*, those who live on the banks of the Ganges (*obs.*).

1677 SIR T. HERBERT *Trav.* 57 The Romans embalm; the Gangetiques drown. **1830** LYELL *Princ. Geol.* I. 244 The Gangetic delta. **1841** ELPHINSTONE *Hist. Ind.* I. iii. 265 Three other columns in Gangetic India. **1886** *American* XI. 168 Gavials, or Gangetic crocodiles.

†**'gang-flower.** *Obs.* [f. GANG *sb.*[1] (see quot.).] The milkwort (*Polygala vulgaris*).

1597 GERARDE *Herbal* II. clx. §6. 450 Milkewoort is called *Ambarualis flos*..bicause it doth specially flourishe in the Crosse or Gang weeke, or Rogation weeke..in English we may cal it Crosse flower or Gang flower. **1706** in PHILLIPS (ed. Kersey); and in mod. Dicts.

gang-gang, var. GANGAN.

ganȝeld, -ȝell: see GAINYIELD.

†**'Gangic**, *a. Obs. rare.* [f. L. *Gang-es* + -IC.] Belonging to the river Ganges.

1605 SYLVESTER *Du Bartas* II. iii. III. *Law* 1250, I undertake a thing As hard almost, as in the Gangic Seas To count the waves. **1656** BLOUNT *Glossogr.*, *Gangick*, of or pertaining to Ganges a great River in India Oriental.

'ganging ('gæŋɪŋ), *vbl. sb.*[1] *Obs.* exc. *Sc.* and *dial.* Also 9 **gannin.** [f. GANG *v.*[1] + -ING[1].]

1. The action of the verb GANG in various senses.

1489 *Barbour's Bruce* XIV. 400 (MS. E.) Quhen the Erle Thomas persawing Had off thair cummyng and thair ganging [*C.* gaderyng]. **1548** *Aberdeen Reg.* V. 20 (Jam.) The bailye continevit the ganging of the actioun. **1583** *Leg. Bp. St. Androis* 101 in *Satir. Poems Reform.* xlv, What fruite come of his ganging thair? **1768** ROSS *Helenore* (1778) 39 Gin ganging winna do't, though I sud creep.

b. The power of walking.

a **1300** *Cursor M.* 12260 A commament nu mak i here..at þai sight haf þat ar blind..And ganging þat ar lame o fote.

c. *ganging to*: going down, setting (of the sun).

1533 BELLENDEN *Livy* III. (1822) 245 He commandit all the young and lusty men..to mete him in Campus Martius afore the son ganging to. **1546** *Extracts Aberdeen Reg.* (1844) 230 And finaly to gif furth thair decreit and ordinance thairin till that same day or the sone ganging to.

d. *ganging on*: a going on, proceeding.

1847–78 in HALLIWELL. **1855** ROBINSON *Whitby Gloss.* s.v., 'What kin o' gangings on has there been?' what kind of doings. 'A bonny ganging on', fine to do.

2. Walking in procession (on GANGDAYS).

1555 W. WATREMAN *Fardle Facions* II. xii. 293 At the whiche time [Ascensiontide] there be made ganginges with the lesse Letanies from one Churche to another, all Christendome ouer. **1849–53** ROCK *Ch. of Fathers* III. ix. 222 Monday, Tuesday and Wednesday in Ascension-week were called gang-days, from the custom of ganging, or walking in religious procession. **1895** *E. Anglian Gloss.* s.v., 'To go ganging', to beat the parish bounds.

3. *Comb.*, as **ganging-gown**, a travelling cloak; **ganging-staff**, a walking-stick.

1583 *Leg. Bp. St. Androis* 569 in *Satir. Poems Reform.* xlv, His sarkis, his schone, his ganging gowne. **1595** DUNCAN *App. Etymol.* (E.D.S.) *Scipio*, a ganging-staff.

ganging ('gæŋɪŋ), *vbl. sb.*[2] [f. GANG *v.*[2] + -ING[1].] The combining of work-people into gangs or companies.

1865 *Pall Mall G.* 13 May 2 The corrupting influences of 'ganging' are naturally worse where boys and girls are employed together. **1886** *Gd. Words* 42 If some other system could be devised, which should supersede ganging.

ganging ('gændʒɪŋ), *vbl. sb.*[3] [f. GANGE *v.* + -ING[1].] **a.** 'The act of fastening a fish-hook to the line'. **b.** 'A section or part of a fishing-line to the free end of which a hook is ganged' (*Cent. Dict.*). Also *Comb.* **ganging-line**, 'the ganging of a fishing-line, especially when different from the rest of the line' (*Cent. Dict.*).

1883 *Fisheries Exhib. Catal.* 195 Spanish gut as imported for the manufacture of leaders; single, double, and twisted gut leaders, minnow gangs, brails, gangings, used in various sea fisheries.

ganging ('gæŋɪŋ), *ppl. a. Obs.* exc. *Sc.* and *dial.* [f. GANG *v.*[1] + -ING[2].]

1. That goes or walks.

a **1100** *O.E. Chron.* an. 1085 He ferde into Engla lande mid swa myclan here ridendra manna and gangendra. *a* **1300** *Cursor M.* 401 Al gangand best þe sext day, And adam bath he wroght on clai.

Proverb. c **1300** [see FOOT *sb.* 2]. ? **1785** *Ferguson's Scot. Prov.* in Ramsay *Remin.* v. (1870) 139 A gangang fit is aye gettin (gin it were but a thorn).

2. That is in operation or in working order.

[*a* **1154** *O.E. Chron.* an. 1131 Swa þæt on þa tun þa wæs tenn ploȝes oðer twelfe gangende ne belæf þær noht an.] **1574** *Sc. Acts Jas. VI* (1814) III. 93/1 Of euery gangand [salt-]pan thre bollis to be delieuerit oulk[l]ie. *a* **1724** *Johnie Armstrang* in Ramsay *Ever-Green* (1824) II. 192 Gude Four and twenty ganging Mills That gang throw a the Zeir.

b. ***ganging-gear, -graith*** (see quots.); ***ganging plea***, a lawsuit continuing indefinitely.

1808-18 JAMIESON, *Gangin graith*, the furniture of a mill which a tenant is bound to uphold. **1816** SCOTT *Antiq.* ii, A ganging plea that my father left me, and his father afore left to him. **1847-78** HALLIWELL, *Ganging gear*, the machinery of a mill.

gangland (ˈgæŋlænd). orig. *U.S.* [f. GANG *sb.*[1] + LAND *sb.*] The domain of gangsters; the underworld; gangs or gangsters collectively. Also *attrib.*

1912 A. H. LEWIS *Apaches N.Y.* 15 The first lesson of Gangland is never to inform nor give evidence. **1928** *Daily Tel.* 28 Aug. 7/5 A bomb, known in gangland parlance as a 'pineapple'. **1932** E. WALLACE *When Gangs came to London* viii. 64 Gangland does not talk scandal even of its worst enemies. **1966** *Observer* 25 Sept. 1/5 (*headline*) Police stop gangland carve-up. **1971** *Daily Tel.* 15 Sept. 1/1 Police believe a gangland killing may be connected with the discovery early yesterday of a bloodstained car at Chigwell, Essex.

† ˈ**gangle**, *v. Obs.* [a. ONF. *gangler* = Central OF. *jangler, gengler* to JANGLE.] = JANGLE *v.*

13.. *K. Alis.* 7413 While they weore so in mangle, Theo Yndiens gan gangle [*MS. Laud* 622 bigonnon Jangle]. **1340** *Ayenb.* 226 Huerof zaynte Pauel wyþ-nimþ þe yonge wyfmen wodewen þet were ydele and bysye to guonne an to comene ganglinde and to moche spekinde. *a* **1350** *Life Jesu* (Horstm.) 862 Ȝwane he was so wroth for Marchaundise þat he In þe temple i saiȝ Hov wroth wole he beo with cristine Men þat gangliez In churche al dai!

gangliac (ˈgæŋglɪæk), *a.* [f. GANGLI-ON + -AC.] Relating to a ganglion. So ˈ**ganglial** *a.* [-AL], ˈ**gangliar** *a.* [-AR], pertaining to, or resembling a ganglion.

1848 CRAIG, *Gangliac.* **1860** WORCESTER *Ganglial* (citing COPELAND). **1881** G. S. HALL *Germ. Cult.* 215 The course of these fibres is often marked by very peculiar round or biscuit-formed bodies, probably not gangliar in their nature. **1885** *Syd. Soc. Lex.* (all three words).

gangliated (ˈgæŋglɪeɪtɪd), *ppl. a.* [f. GANGLI-ON + -ATE[3] + -ED[1].] Furnished with ganglia.

1804 CARLISLE in *Phil. Trans.* XCV. 29 The sensorial power, derived by those muscles from the gangliated nerves. **1835-6** TODD *Cycl. Anat.* I. 206/2 The nervous system is gangliated, as in all the articulate animals. **1889** MIVART *Truth* 168 A system of gangliated nerves in the substance of the heart.

gangliectomy (gæŋglɪˈɛktəmɪ). *Surg.* [f. GANGLI(ON + -ECTOMY.] = GANGLIONECTOMY.

1903 *Alienist & Neurol.* Feb. 20 That great operation on the nervous system, trigeminal gangliectomy. **1970** *Excerpta Med. Ser. IX* XXIV. 642/1 Lumbar gangliectomy for obliterative diseases in a stage of destruction was performed on 92 patients.

gangliform (ˈgæŋglɪfɔːm), *a.* Also **ganglioform**. [f. GANGLI(ON + -FORM.] Having the form of a ganglion.

1681 tr. *Willis' Rem. Med. Wks.* Vocab., *Ganglioform*, of the shape of ganglias, or the heads of mushrumps. **1831** R. KNOX *Cloquet's Anat.* 457 Its filaments..all terminate in a depressed, semilunar gangliform plexus. **1845** TODD & BOWMAN *Phys. Anat.* I. 246 The former is evidently an aggregate of gangliform swellings, each possessing the characters of a nervous centre.

gangling (ˈgæŋglɪŋ), *ppl. a.* [f. as if **gangle* to go about, straggle, frequentative f. GANG *v.*[1]: cf. GANGREL.] Of straggling growth; loosely built.

1808-25 JAMIESON, *Gangling*, straggling. *Roxb.* **1843** ALB. SMITH *Phys. Evening Parties*, She sends her two brothers, tall, gangling, awkward young men. **1847-78** HALLIWELL, *Gangling*, tall, slender, delicate, generally applied to plants. *Warw.* **1881** *Leicestersh. Gloss.*, *Gangling*, awkwardly long in stature; ill-made and uncouth. **1893** *Harper's Mag.* LXXXVII. 155/1 The long-legged, gangling sheriff retired. **1935** A. SQUIRE *Sing Sing Doctor* v. 63 Tall and gangling, Fay had a long-jawed horse face. **1943** C. S. FORESTER *Ship* 176 Tall and gangling and clean-shaven. **1953** 'N. SHUTE' *In Wet* x. 350 A black haired, lean, gangling lad of twenty. **1955** *Times* 18 Dec. 3/2 The massive gangling figure of Mr —— hurtled out of his room.

ganglioform: see GANGLIFORM.

ˈ**ganglioid**, *a.* [f. GANGLI-ON + -OID.] 'Resembling a ganglion' (*Syd. Soc. Lex.* 1885).

ganglion (ˈgæŋglɪən). Pl. **ganglia.** Also 7 **ganglias**, 8-9 **ganglions.** [a. Gr. γάγγλιον a tumour under the skin, on or near tendons or sinews; used by Galen to denote the complex nerve-centres, and now chiefly employed in that sense.]

1. *Path.* A tumour or swelling of the sheath of a tendon. 'Also, applied to an enlarged bursa mucosa' (*Syd. Soc. Lex.* 1885).

[**1671** SALMON *Syn. Med.* I. xlviii. 114 Γάγγλιον, Ganglion Lupia, a Wen.] **1681** tr. *Willis' Rem. Med. Wks.* Vocab., *Ganglia*, things like the heads of mushrumps in the body. **1704** F. FULLER *Med. Gymn.* (1711) 202 Let us but consider ..the Cure of a Ganglion, a Tumour in a Tendon. **1791** *Nat. Hist.* in *Ann. Reg.* 45/2 A German woman..had several swellings or ganglions upon different parts of her head from one of which a horn grew. **1807-26** S. COOPER *First Lines Surg.* (ed. 5) 184 A ganglion is a small hard tumour.. composed of a cyst..connected with a subjacent tendon, and filled with a fluid resembling the white of an egg.

2. a. *Phys.* An enlargement or knot on a nerve, forming a centre from which nerve-fibres radiate.

1732 ARBUTHNOT *Rules of Diet* 369 In the Ganglia where they [the Nerves] are tied together. **1797** *Monthly Mag.* III. 209 The ganglions are connected to each other, by a very slender medullary cord. **1805** *Med. Jrnl.* XIV. 328 All nerves rising from the spinal marrow..pass on their way through nervous knots, ganglia. **1851** WOODWARD *Mollusca* 21 The points from which the nerves radiate, are enlargements, termed centres (*ganglia*). **1875** *Encycl. Brit.* II. 273/1 Nervous System [of Arachnida]. This consists of ganglia or nerve-knots, formed by enlargements of longitudinal nervous cords.

b. *Phys.* A collection of grey matter (neurine) in the central (cerebro-spinal) nervous system, forming a nerve-nucleus.

1855 H. SPENCER *Princ. Psychol.* (1872) I. I. ii. 27 A mass of grey matter with imbedded vesicles— a nerve-centre or ganglion. **1879** CALDERWOOD *Mind & Br.* ii. 31 These represent the largest nerve ganglions of grey and white matter at the base of each hemisphere.

c. *fig.* (*a*) *nonce-use.* A point from which many lines diverge. (*b*) A centre of force, activity, or interest.

(*a*) **1852** MISS FOX *Jrnls.* (1882) II. 196 Meanwhile, what we each have to do is to endeavour to walk steadily in the path which we clearly see straight before us; and when we come upon a perplexing ganglion of paths, wait patiently and take our bearings.

(*b*) **1828** SIR W. NAPIER *Penins. War* (1878) I. 25 Thus linking his operations together, Napoleon hoped, by grasping as it were the *ganglia* of the insurrection, to paralyze its force. **1831** CARLYLE *Sart. Res.* I. xi, A little ganglion, or nervous centre, in the great vital system of immensity. **1850** —— *Latter-d. Pamph.* vii. (1872) 226, I see new ganglions of human population establishing themselves. **1882** STEVENSON *Mem. & Portraits* xv. (1887) 258 If Rawdon Crawley's blow were not delivered, Vanity Fair would cease to be a work of art. That scene is the chief ganglion of the tale.

3. *Phys.* A lymphatic gland.

1831 R. KNOX *Cloquet's Anat.* 759 The lymphatic ganglia of the inferior extremities.

4. 'Applied to the class of organs to which the spleen, the thymus gland, the thyroid body, and the adrenals belong' (*Syd. Soc. Lex.* 1885).

5. *Bot.* A swelling on the mycelium of certain fungi.

1866 *Treas. Bot.* 518 *Ganglia*, the mycelium of certain fungals. **1885** in *Syd. Soc. Lex.*

6. *Comb.*: **ganglion-blocking** *a.*, preventing the transmission of nerve impulses across the synapse in a ganglion; **ganglion-cell, -corpuscle, -globule**, a nerve-cell in the grey matter of the central nervous system. Cf. GANGLIONIC *a.*

1848 CARPENTER *Anim. Phys.* i. (1872) 77 These nerve-vesicles, sometimes known as ganglion-globules, may be regarded as originally spherical or nearly so in form. **1856-8** W. CLARK *Van der Hoeven's Zool.* I. 11 These ganglion-corpuscles are very dissimilar in form and size. **1865** *Pub. Opin.* 21 Jan. 79 A current, originating in a ganglion cell, would possibly give rise to many induced currents as it traversed a caudate nerve cell. **1877** ROSENTHAL *Muscles & Nerves* 105 Certain cell-like structures called nerve-cells, or ganglion-cells. **1951** *Brit. Med. Jrnl.* 14 Apr. 775/2 When using ganglion-blocking agents..it is necessary to remember that the response to drugs and procedures affecting the blood pressure will necessarily be exaggerated, as the mechanisms maintaining a normal blood pressure are weakened. **1962** H. BURN *Drugs, Med. & Man* vi. 65 In the presence of one of these substances, which are called ganglion-blocking drugs, the acetylcholine when liberated is unable to stimulate the next fibre.

ganglionary (ˈgæŋglɪənərɪ), *a.* [f. prec. + -ARY. Cf. F. *ganglionnaire.*] Furnished with ganglia.

1830 R. KNOX *Béclard's Anat.* 361 The Sympathetic Nerve..is a nervous and ganglionary cord.

ganglionated (ˈgæŋglɪəˌneɪtɪd), *ppl. a.* [f. GANGLION + -ATE[2] + -ED[1].] = GANGLIATED.

1836-9 TODD *Cycl. Anat.* II. 946/1 The nerves for the future wings are..derived..from the ganglionated portion alone. **1880** BASTIAN *Brain* vi. 106 A chain of minute ganglia lying upon the great ventral ganglionated cord.

ganglionectomy (ˌgæŋglɪəˈnɛktəmɪ). *Surg.* [f. GANGLION + -ECTOMY.] Excision of a ganglion.

1925 *Jrnl. Amer. Med. Assoc.* 20 June 1908/2 (*title*) Treatment of Raynaud's disease by lumbar ramisection and ganglionectomy. **1937** *Brit. Jrnl. Surg.* XXXIV. 788 Sympathetic ganglionectomy is the usual surgical treatment of Raynaud's syndrome and other vasospastic states of the extremities. **1970** GURDJIAN & THOMAS *Operative Neurosurg.* (ed. 3) 463 Leriche used cervical and stellate ganglionectomy with some favorable results.

ganglionic (gæŋglɪˈɒnɪk), *a.* [f. GANGLION + -IC.] **a.** Relating to, composed of, or furnished with, ganglia.

1826 KIRBY & SP. *Entomol.* IV. 3 The ganglionic [type] is where the nervous system consists of a series of ganglions connected by nervous threads or a medullary chord. **1860** H. SPENCER in *Macm. Mag.* I. 395 An impression on the end of an afferent nerve is conveyed to some ganglionic centre. **1880** BASTIAN *Brain* 28 The grey matter of the nervous system is, for the most part, ganglionic tissue.

b. ***ganglionic blocking*** = ***ganglion-blocking*** adj.

1946 ACHESON & MOE in *Jrnl. Pharmacol. & Exper. Therap.* LXXXVII. 236 We therefore propose that the predominant action of tetraethylammonium ion, which accounts for its vasodepressor and cardiodecelerator effects, be called simply a ganglionic blocking effect. **1961** A. GOTH *Med. Pharmacol.* vii. 99 The majority of the ganglionic blocking drugs are quaternary ammonium compounds.

ganglionized (ˈgæŋglɪənaɪzd), *ppl. a.* [f. as prec. + -IZE + -ED[1].] Knotted like a ganglion.

1875 BLAKE *Zool.* 296 Arachnida.—The trachea for respiration branched, but not ganglionized.

ganglionless (ˈgæŋglɪənlɪs), *a.* [f. as prec. + -LESS.] Free from, or destitute of, ganglia.

1834 *Good's Study Med.* (ed. 4) III. 5 *note*, The ganglionless portion of the fifth, and the hard portion of the seventh nerve. **1836-9** TODD *Cycl. Anat.* II. 943/1 The ganglionless upper or internal column of fibres.

gangliopathy (gæŋglɪˈɒpəθɪ). [f. GANGLIO-N + -PATHY.] A diseased condition of the central ganglia of the sympathetic system.

1885 in *Syd. Soc. Lex.*

Hence **ganglioˈpathic** *a.*, belonging to gangliopathy.

1889 in *Century Dict.*

ganglioside (ˈgæŋglɪəʊsaɪd). *Biochem.* [a. G. *gangliosid* (E. Klenk 1942, in *Zeitschr. f. physiol. Chem.* CCLXXIII. 76), f. GANGLI(ON + -OSIDE.] Any of a group of glycolipids present chiefly in the grey matter of man and some animals and distinguished from cerebrosides by the presence of neuraminic acid among the products of their hydrolysis.

1943 *Chem. Abstr.* XXXVII. 5743 (*heading*) The gangliosides and cerebrosides of cattle spleen. **1955** R. J. ROSSITER In K. A. C. Elliott et al. *Neurochem.* ii. 20 In the brains of patients suffering from Tay-Sach's disease the cerebrosides are largely replaced by gangliosides. **1969** *New Scientist* 2 Jan. 32/2 Tetanus toxin is adsorbed by nerves, in particular by the chemical components known as gangliosides.

gangly (ˈgæŋglɪ), *a.* orig. *U.S.* [Alteration of GANGLING *ppl. a.*: cf. -Y[1].] = GANGLING *ppl. a.*

1872 'MARK TWAIN' *Roughing It* vii. 34, I should have shot that long gangly lubber they called Hank, if I could have done it without crippling six or seven other people. **1950** G. GREENE *Third Man* i. 7 His long gangly legs. **1965** *Punch* 11 Aug. 215/2 How..does his gangly stature and personality still impose itself?

† **Gang-Monday.** *Obs. rare*⁻¹. [see GANG-DAYS.] Monday in Rogation-week.

1579 FULKE *Heskins' Parl.* 317 There would not one learned Papist be left aliue on gang Monday.

ˈ**gang-plank.** orig. *U.S.* Also **gangplank.** [f. GANG *sb.*[1] + PLANK.] A landing-plank; a gang-board.

1846 *Knickerbocker* XXVII. 469 The last bell rang; the gangplank was drawn in-board; the hawsers were cast off. **1861** OLMSTED *Journ. Cotton Kingd.* I. 142 A fat mulatto woman..shouted, as she caught him off the gang-plank, 'Oh Massa George, is you come back!' **1887** *Times* 29 Aug. 4/5 The moment the gang-planks are fixed a crowd of stevedores rush aboard. **1961** F. M. BURGESS *Dict. Sailing* 100 *Gang-plank*, a long narrow plank, fitted with treads, to enable people to walk over the bow of a beached boat.

gangræna, -græne, -green: see GANGRENE.

gangrel (ˈgæŋgrəl). *dial.* and *arch.* Forms: 6 gangarall (*pl.* gangralis), 6-7 gangrill, 7 gang(e)rell, 8 gangril, 9 gangerill, 7- **gangrel.** [app. f. GANG *sb.*[1] or *v.*[1], on some obscure analogy; cf. *poveral* (with which this word is associated in quot. 1538); the ending occurs, though perh. from diverse sources, in several depreciative terms, as *haverel, mongrel, gomeril, doggrel, wastrel.* A derivative of the same root with similar meaning is MHG. *gengelære*, G. *gängler* (in 18th c. said of a packman or pedlar), f. *gängeln* to walk about.

There is no connexion (beyond identity of root-syllable) with ON. *Gangleri* (mythical name), which has often been compared: the endings have only a chance resemblance.]

1. A vagabond: a wandering beggar.

c **1340** HAMPOLE *Perfect Living* viii. in Wks. 1895 I. 33 Gangrels, and Iangelers, & kepers of comers and gangars arely & late. **1530** *Extracts Aberdeen Reg.* (1844) 130 That na strangearis nor gangerallis cum within the samyn. *a* **1605** POLWART *Flyting* 772 Gleyd gangrell, auld mangrell. **1625** GILL *Sacr. Philos.* VII. 92 When all charity is put only in the maintenance of idlenesse and begging Gangrels. **1855** ROBINSON *Whitby Gloss.*, *Gangerill*, a pedlar, a beggar. **1895** CROCKETT *Men of Mosshags* 329 Out on you, gangrel.

b. *attrib.* or *adj.* Vagabond, vagrant.

1538 *Aberdeen Reg.* V. 15 (Jam.) That na strangearis nor gangralis puirralis be ressate nor haldyn in this tovnne. **1637-50** ROW *Hist. Kirk* (1842) 457 His wife for povertie turned ane gangrell poore woman, selling some small wares. **1776** C. KEITH *Farmer's Ha'* 33 There's mony a sturdy gangrel chiel That might be winnin' meat fu' weel. **1785** BURNS *Jolly Beggars* 8 A merry core O' randie, gangrel bodies. **1815** SCOTT *Guy M.* iii, He's nae gentleman..wad grudge twa gangrel puir bodies the shelter o' a waste house. **1870** MORRIS *Earthly Par.* II. III. 40 This gangrel thief thought fit to tread The grass to mammocks by my head. **1895** CROCKETT *Sweeth. Trav.* 93 Without troubling about suspicious gangrel bodies.

2. A lanky, loose-jointed person. (Cf. GANGLING.)

1585 HIGINS tr. *Junius' Nomenclator* 449/1 A long gangrell: a slim: a long tall fellow that hath no making to his height. **1606** HOLLAND *Sueton. Annot.* 36 b, Ajax..unto whom or to whose long pike rather, he likeneth this gangrell. **1611** COTGR., *Trente-costes*, a gangerell, slimme, long luske, lanke loobie. **1721** BAILEY, *Gangrel*..a tall ill-shaped Fellow. **1873** *Swaledale Gloss.*, *Gangrel*, an awkward fellow. **1884** *Upton-on-Severn Gloss.*, *Gangril*, a lanky, ungainly creature, whether man or beast.

b. *attrib.* as adj.

1650 BULWER *Anthropomet.* 10 A long gangrel neck, which would have made the head look as set upon a pole.

3. *Sc.* A child just beginning to walk. *rare.*

1768 ROSS *Helenore* 6 Helenore, a gangrel now was grown, And had begun to toddle about the town.

4. *north. dial.* A toad. Cf. GAGRILL.

1500-20 DUNBAR *Poems* liv. 7 Scho is tute mowitt lyk an aip, And lyk a gangarall [*v.r.* gangarull] unto graip. **1847-78** in HALLIWELL. **1855-76** in *Whitby Glossaries.*

gangren, -ena, obs. forms of GANGRENE.

† **'gangrenate,** *ppl. a. Obs. rare.* [f. GANGRENE *sb.* + -ATE[2].] In a state of gangrene.

1634 T. JOHNSON *Parey's Chirurg.* x. xi. (1678) 238 A putrid..vapour, exhaling from the hurt and gangrenate part of the Brain.

† **'gangrenate,** *v. Obs.* Also 6 **cancrenate,** 7 **gangrinate, gangreenate.** [f. as prec. + -ATE[3].]

1. *intr.* To become gangrenous.

1753 N. TORRIANO *Gangr. Sore Throat* 45 The Lungs, being over-heated, ulcerate and gangrenate.

2. *trans.* To make gangrenous. In quot. *fig.*

1660 *Speech to Gen. Monk* 1 Ambition that did Gangrinate the State.

Hence † **'gangrenated** *ppl. a.*, gangrened.

1582 [see CANCRENATED]. **1612** WOODALL *Surg. Mate* Wks. (1653) 163 Like the colour of a gangrenated or mortified member. **1693** SALMON *Bate's Disp.* iii. (1713) 121/2 Outwardly, it is anointed upon gangreenated Parts. **1758** J. S. *Le Dran's Observ. Surg.* (1771) 185, I..found..a black gangrenated Spot.

† **gangre'nation.** *Obs. rare.* [f. as prec. + -ATION.] A condition of gangrene or mortification.

1597 A. M. tr. *Guillemeau's Fr. Chirurg.* 38/2 Some mortificatione or Gangrænatione. **1599** —— tr. *Gabelhouer's Bk. Physicke* 311/1 Otherwise we might easilye bringe therin a Gangrænation.

gangrene ('gæŋgriːn), *sb.* Forms: α. 6 **cancrena,** 6–7 **gangrena,** 7 **gangræna;** β. 6 **gangræne,** 7 **gangren, gangriene,** 7–9 **gangreen,** 7– **gangrene.** [ad. L. *gangræna* (-*grēna*), a. Gr. γάγγραινα: cf. F. *gangrène*; also It. and med.L. *cancrena* (whence the earliest Eng. form).]

1. A necrosis or mortification of part of the body, extending over some considerable area in a visible mass. Sometimes used to denote the first stage of mortification.

1543 TRAHERON tr. *Vigo's Chirurg.* II. xvi. 26/1 Cancrena is not taken for fleshe deade altogether, but for that whyche begynneth to putrifye by lyttle and lyttle. **1563** T. GALE *Chirurg.* I. 44 a, A fracture hauinge wyth hym ioyned gangrena. **1573** *Ann. Barber-Surg. Lond.* (1890) 317 Mr. Watson of the Towre which dyed of Gangrena in his fote. **1597** A. M. tr. *Guillemeau's Fr. Chirurg.* 2/4 Out of the which proceedeth a Gangræne or mortificatione. **1626** BACON *Sylva* §333 It appeareth also in the Gangreen or Mortification of Flesh, either by Opiates, or by Intense Cold. *c* **1720** W. GIBSON *Farrier's Guide* II. liii. (1738) 206 A Gangrene is a sudden, violent, and excessive inflammation ..and is no other than a beginning Mortification. **1789** W. BUCHAN *Dom. Med.* (1790) 577 Straining it too much might occasion an inflammation of the parts, and endanger a gangrene. **1838** THIRLWALL *Greece* II. XIV. 245 A gangrene had begun in his injured limb. **1866** A. FLINT *Princ. Med.* (1880) 52 Necrosis with decomposition..is usually called gangrene, although this term is also often applied to forms of simple necrosis.

2. *fig.*

1602 W. WATSON *Quodlibets of Relig. & State* 41 These.. men haue bespattered with a most dangerous Gangrene, the whole bodie misticall of Christ. **1607** MIDDLETON *Five Gallants* II. iii. D 4 b, It may growe to a gangrene in our credits and bee incurable. **1612** T. JAMES *Jesuits Downef.* 47 Jesuitisme from a Serpigo, is become a Gangræna, it must therefore be cut of. **1655** FULLER *Ch. Hist.* I. iv. §21 But now (alas!) the Gangrene of that Heresy began to spread it self into this Island. **1758** JOHNSON *Idler* No. 22 ¶3 To the community..corruption is a gangrene. **1834** HT. MARTINEAU *Moral* II. 66 Our pauper system..the great political gangrene of England. **1896** GLADSTONE in *Daily News* 1 June 7/5 If they [religious controversies] do not proceed to gangrene and to mortification, at least they tend to harden into fixed facts.

3. *attrib.* †Also quasi-*adj.* Gangrenous.

1715 tr. *C'tess Daunoy's Wks.* 57 False Zealots, who cry'd out, that I was a Gangreen Member that was to be cut off from the rest of the Body. **1835** BROWNING *Paracelsus* IV. Poet. Wks. 1896 I. 53 Were your nature fit To be defiled, your eyes the eyes to ache At gangrene-blotches.

gangrene ('gæŋgriːn), *v.* [f. prec. sb. Cf. F. *gangrener.*]

1. *intr.* To become mortified.

1614 in *Crt. & Times Jas. I* (1849) I. 327 He had a swelling in the thigh, which..grew so angry, that it gangrened and made an end of him. *a* **1654** SELDEN *Table-T.* (Arb.) 42 Your Leg will Gangreen within three days. **1671** MILTON *Samson* 621. **1707** *Curios. in Husb. & Gard.* 109 It prevents a Wound from gangrening. **1788** BURKE *Sp. agst. W. Hastings* Wks. XIII. 323 They made rods of a plant highly caustick and poisonous..every wound of which festers and gangrenes. **1870** *Daily News* 22 Sept., Such was the predisposition to disease that the slightest wound gangrened and became incurable.

fig. **1618** NAUNTON in *Fortesc. Papers* (Camden) 74 The divisions and rentes which they plotted betwene the protestantes doe now begin to gangren amonge themselves.

2. *trans.* To bring into a state of mortification.

The first two quots. possibly belong to sense 1 or to GANGRENED *ppl. a.*

1607 SHAKS. *Cor.* III. i. 307 The seruice of the foote Being once gangren'd, is not then respected For what before it was. **1626** BACON *Sylva* §788 In the cold Countries, when Mens Noses and Ears are mortified, and (as it were) Gangrened with cold. *a* **1673** G. SWINNOCK in Spurgeon *Treas. Dav.* cxli. 5 When he had by sin, and continuance in it, so gangrened his flesh, and corrupted himself. **1683** A. SNAPE *Anat. Horse* III. v. 112 The Matter by that means is there stayed, and..ulcerates and gangrenes all the passages of the Nostrils. **1819** SHELLEY *Cenci* II. i, When the rust Of heavy chains has gangrened his sweet limbs. **1868** DUNCAN tr. *Figuier's Ins. World* ii. 72 They have been known to reach the ball of the eye, and to gangrene the eyelids.

fig. **1803** tr. *d'Arnaud's Lorimon* II. 120, I have..sworn that avarice had not gangreened your soul to the degree report had spread abroad. **1886** *Pall Mall G.* 2 June 1/1 He is said to be free from that intense personal feeling which gangrenes our politics.

gangrened ('gæŋgriːnd), *ppl. a.* Also 7 **gangreen'd.** [f. GANGRENE *v.*: cf. F. *gangrené.*]

1. Affected with gangrene.

1611 COTGR. s.v. *Dieu, Vne Iambe de Dieu*, soe doe the canting, and blasphemous rogues of France tearme a cankered, gangrened, or desperately-sore leg. **1682** DRYDEN & LEE *Dk. of Guise* v. i, In which, indeed, they assert the public good, And, like sworn surgeons, lop the gangrened limb. **1813** J. THOMSON *Lect. Inflam.* 553 When a gangrened limb..is cut off in the dead part, no hemorrhage occurs. **1866** ALGER *Solit. Nat. & Man* IV. 254 The disease which the surgeons laid bare in his gangrened vitals and brain.

fig. **1653** JER. TAYLOR *Serm.* I. (1655) 272 These inclinations and evill forwardnesses, this dyscrasie and gangren'd disposition. **1799** J. ROBERTSON *Agric. Perth* 554 These individuals..are the gangrened members of society. **1830** *Edin. Rev.* L. 467 The Sultan has lopped the gangrened limb.

2. Belonging to gangrene.

1762 FALCONER *Shipwr.* II. 434 Thus when some limb is seized with gangren'd pains.

gangrenescent (gæŋgriː'nɛsənt), *a.* [f. as prec. + -ESCENT.] Becoming gangrenous.

1828-32 in WEBSTER; and in subsequent Dicts.

† **'gangrenize,** *v. Obs. rare*[−1]. [f. GANGRENE *sb.* + -IZE.] *intr.* = GANGRENE *v.* 1.

1597 A. M. tr. *Guillemeau's Fr. Chirurg.* 50/3 The wounds doe putrifye and gangrænize.

gangrenous ('gæŋgrɪnəs) *a.* [f. GANGRENE *sb.* + -OUS. Cf. F. *gangréneux* (16th c.).]

1. Having the nature of gangrene, or affected with it.

1612 WOODALL *Surg. Mate* Wks. (1653) 405 Such Pestilential Gangrenous spots after separate of themselves. **1732** ARBUTHNOT *Rules of Diet* 291 Eruptions on the Skin, dark, livid, lead-colored and gangrenous. **1809** *Med. Jrnl.* XXI. 455 The lungs were livid, with a gangrenous inflammation on their posterior part. **1865** RUSKIN *Sesame* 7 We call it 'mortification', using the same term which we should apply to a gangrenous and incurable wound.

fig. **1855** *Tait's Mag.* XXII. 247 Lombardy is a gangrenous limb of Austria. **1880** BURTON *Reign Q. Anne* III. xx. 279 As there is a gangrene of the body..so is the intellect often tainted by gangrenous spots, that [etc.].

2. Resembling a gangrened spot (in colour).

1824 GALT *Rothelan* I. i. iii. 25 His complexion became of a gangrenous yellow.

gangriene, obs. form of GANGRENE *sb.*

gangril(l, var. GANGREL.

gangrinate, var. GANGRENATE *v. Obs.*

gangsman ('gæŋzmən). [f. GANG *sb.*[1] + MAN: for the *s* cf. *craftsman* etc.]

1. A dock-porter.

1793 *Wet Docks of Lond.* 16 *Gangsmen*, these are porters stationed under the wharfingers.

2. One who has charge of a gang of workmen.

1863 RUSSELL *Diary North & South* I. 192 One big slouching negro, who seemed to be a gangsman or something of the kind, followed us. **1897** *Westm. Gaz.* 3 Feb. 2/1 The post of gangsman or 'mate' is thus a good one.

3. = GANGSTER 1.

1923 *Glasgow Herald* 30 Aug. 7 The complete story of the gangsmen and their crimes.

gangster ('gæŋstə(r)). orig. *U.S.* [f. GANG *sb.*[1] + -STER.] **1.** A member of a gang of criminals. Also *attrib.* and *Comb.*

1896 *Columbus* (Ohio) *Even. Dispatch* 10 Apr. 4/2 The gangster may play all sorts of pranks with the ballot box, but in its own good time the latter will get even by kicking the gangster into the gutter. **1911** *N.Y. Even. Post* 17 June 6 A musician, returning to his home, was knocked down and killed by a group of gangsters. **1928** *Daily Express* 31 July 8/2 Finding the three Brighton gangsters guilty of murder. **1935** WODEHOUSE *Blandings Castle* x. 253 Kind of tough and ugly he looks, like something out of a gangster film. **1938** F. D. SHARPE *Sharpe of Flying Squad* xv. 164 London at that time was in some danger of becoming a gangster-ridden city like Chicago. **1948** F. R. LEAVIS *Great Tradition* i. 4 One applauds the determination to explode the gangster-hero.

2. A member of a gang of workmen. *rare.*

1927 *Daily Express* 20 June 1/5 Gangsters followed with new ballast and new track.

Hence **'gangsterdom** = GANGLAND; **'gangsterish** *a.*, resembling or characteristic of a gangster or gangsters; **'gangsterism,** the actions or methods of gangsters.

1923 *Nation* 26 Dec. 743/1 The autobiography of one who has come up in the world from sneak-thiefery and gangsterdom. **1927** *New Masses* Mar. 19/4 Gangsterism reigned supreme, both in and out of the convention hall. **1932** *New Statesman* 7 May 581/1 The alternative is a steady growth of gangsterdom. **1934** *Times* 31 July 10/2 Political 'gangsterism'..is only an extreme manifestation of the temper which is being allowed to dominate the whole political outlook. **1945** G. MILLAR *Maquis* viii. 165 The Resistance in the Haute-Saône followed more gangsterish lines than that of..the Doubs. **1947** *Penguin New Writing* XXXI. 68 He walked with a manly, indifferent saunter, eyes half-closed in gangsterish confidence. **1958** *Times Lit. Suppl.* 31 Jan. 67/2 More tales of American night-life and gangsterdom between the wars. **1962** *Daily Tel.* 19 Mar. 13/4 The economic gangsterism of capitalism.

† **'Gang-tide.** *Obs. rare.* = GANG-DAYS.

1530 PALSGR. 804 At gangetyde, *aux rouuaisons.* **1630** in *Descr. Thames* (1758) 76 One Week before Gang-tide yearly.

b. *attrib.*, as *Gang-tide gate.*

1589 WARNER *Alb. Eng.* v. xxiv. 108 At Ewle we wonten.. To haue gud spiced Sewe, and Roste..At Fasts-eue pan-puffes: Gang-tide gaites did alie Masses bring.

† **'gang-tooth.** *Obs.* [Perh. a corrupt form of GAG-TOOTH.] A large projecting tooth.

1603 HARSNET *Pop. Impost.* xiv. 71 Hell mouth in the old plaies painted with great gang teeth. **1607** TOPSELL *Four-f. Beasts* (1658) 153 Teeth which are called *Fannæ* or Gang-teeth, standing out of the mouth..are given for weapon and defence to beasts, and such are an Elephants. **1673** A. MARVELL *Stoo him Bayes* 34 In sign that this is Sooth, I bite it with my Gang tooth.

gangue (gæŋ). Also **gang.** [a. F. *gangue*, ad. Ger. *gang* a vein or lode of metal, of the same origin as GANG *sb.*[1]: see also GANGART.] The earthy or stony matter in a mineral deposit; the matrix in which an ore is found.

1809 GREGOR in *Phil. Trans.* XCIX. 196 The gangue is a white quartz. **1815** W. PHILLIPS *Outl. Min. & Geol.* (1818) 60 An earthy or stony substance which..is termed the gangue or matrix of the metal or ore. **1871** *Trans. Amer. Inst. Mining Eng.* I. 95 Their earthy portions we designate as their 'matrix' or 'gangue'.

attrib. **1872** RAYMOND *Statist. Mines & Mining* 22 Those ores bearing much gangue matter..can easily be assorted.

gang-up ('gæŋʌp). *colloq.* [f. GANG *v.*[2] 2 b.] An act of 'ganging up'; a meeting of a gang; *spec.* = *gang-bang.* (See also quot. 1936.)

1936 *Metronome* Feb. 21/3 *Gang up*, medley. **1949** *Time* 27 June 29 Congress was..harassed by a Communist gang-up with Bose. **1951** E. WATERS *Eye on Sparrow* vi, This is the gang-up. Men like that put you to sleep with their drops. Then one man after another goes in and takes you. **1957** *Economist* 7 Dec. 876/2 Trying to bring about the closest possible pre-conference accord between the British and German governments without giving other Nato partners the impression of an Anglo-German 'gang-up'. **1967** G. STEINER *Lang. & Silence* 137 The narrative of an S.A. gang-up in a beer hall is unforgettable.

gangway ('gæŋweɪ). [OE. *gangweȝ*, f. GANG *sb.*[1] + *weȝ* WAY; cf. G. (dial.) *gangweg*, ON. *gangvegr*, Sw. *gångväg.*]

1. A road, thoroughfare, or passage of any kind; *rarely*, a 'lane' opened through a crowd. *Obs.* exc. *dial.*

c **1000** ÆLFRIC *Gloss.* in Wr.-Wülcker 146/31 *Actus*, anes wænes gangweȝ. *Uia*, tweȝra wæna gangweȝ. **1736** LEWIS *Hist. Thanet* Gloss., *Gang-way*, a thorowfare, entry, passage. **1788** J. MAY *Jrnl. & Lett.* (1873) 99 Near this place was cut..a vista through the forests..forty feet wide.. making a magnificent gangway. **1802** SPENCER in *Naval Chron.* VII. 81 We got a gangway made among the ship's company for the Admiral to walk forward. **1880** *Antrim & Down Gloss.*, *Gang-way*, a frequented thoroughfare.

2. a. A passage in a house or other building; *esp.* a passage between rows of seats in a public edifice.

1702 *Burlesque L'Estrange's Quevedo* 102 To thrust thro' Doors, or some Gang-way. **1834** *Brit. Husb.* I. 100 The beast-house contains standing for sixteen head of cattle, eight on each side of the gang-way. **1877** J. C. COX *Ch. Derbysh.* III. 239 The monument..used to be in the gang-way of the nave. **1891** *Times* 10 Oct. 11/2 The plan of filling up the gangways with stools cannot be commended.

b. In the House of Commons, the cross-passage about half-way down the house, giving access to the rear-benches. Rarely *pl.*

The members sitting *above the gangway* are the ministers and ex-ministers with such private members as profess more or less close agreement with the policy of the official leaders of their respective parties.

1875 F. I. SCUDAMORE *Day Dreams* 3 Counting the members as they passed the gangway. **1876** *World* V. No. 107. 4 The applause..was almost wholly confined to a handful of English Radicals below the gangway. **1886** *Manch. Exam.* 14 Jan. 5/6 Members unable to obtain places were inconveniently crowded about the gangways.

c. *Build.* (See quot.)

1823 P. NICHOLSON *Pract. Build.* 585 *Gangway*; in building, the temporary rough stair, set up for ascending or descending, before the regular stair is built.

3. *Naut.* **a.** A narrow platform on deep-waisted ships, leading from the quarter-deck to the forecastle, for convenience in walking from one to the other: = GANGBOARD 1.

1688 *Lond. Gaz.* No. 2317/1 Our Commander, being.. forward by the Gang-Way giving his Orders, the Gun split and struck him down. **1748** *Anson's Voy.* I. iii. (ed. 4) 42 Some endeavoured to escape along the gangways into the forecastle. **1797** NELSON in A. Duncan *Life* (1806) 42, I passed..on the larboard gang-way, to the forecastle. **1865** KINGSLEY *Herew.* v, A fighting gangway along the sides.

b. A narrow passage left in the hold of a laden ship.

1780 in FALCONER *Dict. Marine.*

c. The opening in the bulwarks by which persons enter or leave a vessel; now more commonly the means of communication laid between this and the shore or another vessel. (Cf. GANG-BOARD 2 and GANG-PLANK.)

1780 FALCONER *Dict. Marine, Gangway* is also that part of a ship's side, both within and without, by which the passengers enter and depart. It is for this purpose provided with a sufficient number of steps, or *cleats*, nailed upon the ship's side, nearly as low as the surface of the water; and sometimes furnished with a railed accommodation-ladder. **1799** NELSON in Nicolas *Disp. & Lett.* (1845) I. 5 The Master ran to the gangway to get into the boat. **1810** *Sporting Mag.* XXXV. 285 Captain Lake came on deck, and came to the gangway. **1833** MARRYAT *P. Simple* ix, The whole ship's company..had assembled at the gangways. **1848** ALB. SMITH *Chr. Tadpole* xi. (1879) 105 The carts.. would have done for gangways at steamboat piers. **1870** MORRIS *Earthly Par.* II. III. 330 They came full soon To where the gangway ran out from the ship On to the black pier. **1877** BLACK *Green Past.* xxvii, Then we climbed up the gangway and reached the deck of the noble and stately ship.

d. A plank along the bottom of a rowing-boat. (= GANG-BOARD 3.)

1871 L. STEPHEN *Playgr. Eur.* xiii. (1894) 304 The corpulent elder, who rowed when boats had gangways down their middle.

e. ***to bring to the gangway***: 'to punish a seaman by seizing him up to a grating, there to undergo flogging' (Smyth *Sailor's Word-bk.* 1867).

1815 in *Falconer's Dict. Marine* (ed. Burney).

f. Used interjectionally, as a demand to clear the way.

1925 FRASER & GIBBONS *Soldier & Sailor Words* 101 *Gangway, make way for a naval officer!* An expression, heard sometimes among New Army men in the War,..meaning 'Get out of the way', 'Stand back', 'Clear a passage'. 'Gangway!' is ordinarily a common warning call on board ship, meaning as above. **1942** O. NASH *Good Intentions* 56 Gangway, you motoring proletariat. **1946** E. O'NEILL *Iceman Cometh* (1947) IV. 219 Gangway for two good whores!

4. *Mining.* (See quots.)

1776 PRYCE *Min. Cornub.* 321 *Gangway.* When a Fissure or Lode is excavated in the backs or former upper workings of the Mine, it is sallered with boards, and the deads are thrown there..: however, if they leave room sufficient for the workmen to roll stuff, or walk upon them from one Shaft to another, they call it a Gangway. **1824** MANDER *Derbysh. Miner's Gloss., Gangway* is the horizontal passage made in the Mine, along which the Bouse is conveyed to the tail end of the shaft. **1881** RAYMOND *Mining Gloss., Gangway*, a main level, applied chiefly to coal mines.

5. *attrib.* and *Comb.*, as (sense 2 a) ***gangway seat***; **gangway-bridge, -ladder** (see quots.); **gangwayman**, one in charge at a ship's gangway (in loading); **gangway netting**, in war-ships, the netting with which the gangway between quarter-deck and forecastle is fenced, and in which some of the hammocks are stowed.

1791 R. MYLNE *Rep. Thames & Isis* 53 Upon this weir, a sloping *gangway bridge, with double railing, should be constructed so as to go across the Bridge. **1883** W. C. RUSSELL *Sailors' Lang.*, **Gangway-ladder*, a ladder over the side by which a ship is entered. **1882** *Standard* 26 Aug. 3/7 A man should have watched the case and given orders to the *gangwayman. **1805** in Nicolas *Disp. Nelson* (1846) VII. 194 *note*, The *gangway netting and hammocks completely shot to pieces. **1924** GALSWORTHY *White Monkey* I. iii. 19 They occupied those *gangway seats in the front row of the dress circle of which Fleur had a sort of natural monopoly. **1939** G. GREENE *19 Stories* (1947) 155 He sat down in a gangway seat. **1971** E. PAUL *Reluctant Cloak & Dagger Man* x. 123, I walked up the plane and saw that Tanya had a window seat. The gangway seat next to her was empty.

† **'Gang-week.** *Obs.* [OE. *gangwuce*, f. GANG *sb.*[1] + *wuce* WEEK; cf. G. *gangwoche*, Sw. *gång-vecka*, ON. *gangdaga-vika.*] Rogation week, in which the GANG-DAYS fell.

c **1000** *Ags. Gosp.* Mark xvi. 14 *margin*, Ðis sceal on þunres dæg innan þære gang-wucan. **1530** PALSGR. 809 In the gange weke, *la sepmaine des rouuaysons.* **1553** tr. *Beza's Admon. Parlt.* (1566) D b, In the gang weke, when banners and belles..rangeth aboute in many places. *a* **1571** JEWEL *On 2 Thess.* (1611) 129 They haue vsed in Rome, in their generall processions in gang week to goe to these seuen hils. **1607** *Schol. Disc. agst. Antichr.* II. vi. 76 What meaneth else their decking of crosses in gang-weeke? **1656** BLOUNT *Glossogr.* s.v. *Rogation week*, In the North of England it is called Gang week from the Ganging, or going on procession [etc.]. **1730–6** in BAILEY (folio); and in later Dicts.

Ganimede, -medean: see GANY-.

ganister ('gænɪstə(r)). Also 9 gannister, -ester. [A local word of unknown origin.] A close-grained siliceous stone from the lower coal-measures in Yorkshire, ground down to form furnace-hearths, etc. (See also quot. 1881.) Also *attrib.* and *Comb.*

1811 [see CROWSTONE 2]. **1829** GLOVER *Hist. Derby* I. 53 Crowstone or ganister. *a* **1835** PHILLIPS & DAUBENY in *Encycl. Metrop.* (1845) VI. 587/2 The ganister or calliard rocks of the coal strata. **1855** J. PHILLIPS *Man. Geol.* 191 Ganister measures. **1881** RAYMOND *Mining Gloss., Ganister*, a mixture of ground quartz and fire-clay, used in lining Bessemer converters. **1883** *Yorksh. Archæol. Jrnl.* VIII. 158 Alderman Clark noticed..among broken gannester, what seemed a curious stone. **1889** *Q. Rev.* July 142 The lining used was Sheffield ganister. **1890** W. J. GORDON *Foundry* 107 The ganister lining of the converter is replaced by bricks of magnesian limestone. **1902** *Daily Chron.* 12 May 3/1 Ganister crushing. **1956** W. EDWARDS in D. L. Linton *Sheffield* 13 Only the Soft Bed and Ganister Coal are locally fit to work.

‖ **ganja** ('gændʒə). Also 9, **ganjah, gunja; ganga.** [Hindi *gāṅjhā.*] A preparation of Indian hemp (*Cannabis sativa*, variety *indica*), strongly intoxicating and narcotic.

1800 WELLINGTON *Suppl. Desp.* (1858) II. 162 No manner of duties or customs was allowed to be exacted from any article brought into camp, excepting country-arrack, opium, ganja, or bhang, and toddy. **1826** HOCKLEY *Pandurang Hari* III. xii. 345 They produced their ganga and opium, and began to smoke. **1845** STOCQUELER *Handbk. Brit. India* (1854) 345 They smoke tobacco, as also ganjah (*Cannabis Indica*), to a great extent. **1886** in YULE *Hobson-Jobson*, Gunja. **1892** *Times* 18 Nov. 3/6 Ganja is an excitant of the most powerful description leading to violent crime. **1957** C. MACINNES *City of Spades* I. xii. 98 Many good men..have lived inside penitentiaries on account of that goddamned ganga. **1959** A. SALKEY *Quality of Violence* viii. 117 He.. poured out some *ganga powder* and started to fix the powder ..along a section of a dry banana leaf. *Ibid.* 118 If you want to smoke the *ganga*, at least you could offer me some, too.

† **gank.** *Min. Obs.*[−1] (See quot.) Hence **'ganky** *a.*, containing or resembling 'gank'.

1747 HOOSON *Miner's Dict.* I iv b, *Gank*, a Soil lying in some Veins of a very Red or Yellow colour, sometimes Branching and Spreading itself in small Strings or Joynts to the Rachill, by which Signs it is very probable a Vein may be discovered; some Veins are naturally much inclined to it, such we call Gankey Veins. *Ibid.* S ij b, The Joynts in it are of a red Colour, or gankey.

gann, obs. pa. t. of GIN *v.*, to begin.

gannard, obs. form of GANNET.

† **ganne,** *v. Obs.*[−1] [ad. L. *gannīre* to bark.] *intr.* To bark as a fox. Hence † **'ganning** *vbl. sb.*

1607 TOPSELL *Four-f. Beasts* (1658) 100 The Harts fear the ganning of Foxes. *Ibid.* 175 The Latins have a proper word for the voice of a Fox, which is, *Gannio Gannire*, to Ganne.

† **'ganneker.** *Obs.* An alehouse-keeper.

c **1380** *R. Brunne's Handl. Synne* 2453 (Dulwich MS.) Gannokerys [F. *cauersin*; R. Brunne erron. *tauuarsyns*, which this scribe app. associated with *taverne*] and vsureris: þese arn lucyferys perys. **1424** *Proclam. Mayor of Norwich* in *Promp. Parv.* 186 *note*, That all Brewsters and Gannokers selle a gallon ale of the best..for 1*d.* *ob.* *c* **1440** *Promp. Parv.* 185/2 Ganneker (*S.* ganokyr).

gannen ('gænɪn). *Mining.* [? dial. pron. of GANGING *vbl. sb.*] (See quot.)

1883 GRESLEY *Gloss. Coal Mining, Gannen*, a *board* down which coals are conveyed in *tubs* running upon rails.

ganner, gannester, var. GANGER, GANISTER.

gannet ('gænɪt). Forms: α. 1 **ganot,** 5 **ganate, -ette,** 6 **gannett, (gannard),** 8 **ganet,** 6– **gannet.** β. 5–6 **gante,** 6–9 **gaunt(e,** 6, 8 **gant.** [OE. *ganot* str. masc., is cogn. with Du. *gent*, MHG. *ganiz, genz* str. masc., OHG. *ganazzo* (MHG. *ganze*) wk. masc., all meaning 'gander':—OTeut. types **ganito, ganoto(n*, f. the same root as GANDER. The Teut. word was early adopted in Rom.; the OF. form *gante* may be the source of the β forms in Eng.] **1.** The Solan goose (*Sula bassana*).

α. *Beowulf* 1862 Ofer ganotes bæð. *a* **1000** *O.E. Chron.* an. 975 þa wearð eac adræfed..Oslac of earde..ofer ganotes bæð. *c* **1450** *M.E. Med. Bk.* (Heinrich) 202 Ganates grece. *a* **1490** BOTONER *Itin.* (Nasmith 1778) 111 Ibi nidificant aves vocatæ ganettys. **1556** W. TOWRSON in Hakluyt *Voy.* (1589) 123 We got certaine foules like vnto Gannards. **1570** LEVINS *Manip.* 88/4 A gannet, bird, *penelops.* **1602** CAREW *Cornwall* 34 a, Certaine birds called Gannets soare ouer and stoup to prey vpon them. **1688** R. HOLME *Armoury* II. 263/1 The Cornish Gannet, called also a Skua. **1766** PENNANT *Zool.* (1768) II. 482 The Gannets are birds of passage. **1802** BINGLEY *Anim. Biog.* (1813) II. 358 The Gannet, or Solan Goose. **1845** DARWIN *Voy. Nat.* (1852) 457 The gannets sitting on their rude nests gaze at one with a stupid yet angry air.

β. *c* **1440** *Promp. Parv.* 186/1 Gante, byrde, *bistarda.* *a* **1529** SKELTON *P. Sparowe* 447 The gaglynge gaunte, and the churlysshe chowgh. **1546** BALE *Eng. Votaries* I. (1550) 32 b, Yet droue she out all the gantes or bystardes there, yf their churche legende be true. **1600** HAKLUYT *Voy.* (1810) III. 195 A great white foule, called of some a Gaunt. **1780** A. YOUNG *Tour Irel.* I. 348 They judge of the shoal being there by the Gant, a bird that pursues the fish.

2. A greedy person, esp. a greedy seaman. *slang.*

1929 F. C. BOWEN *Sea Slang* 56 *Gannet*, a greedy seaman. **1950** P. TEMPEST *Lag's Lexicon* 91 The bet may be on how many plates of porridge one 'gannet' can put away at a sitting. **1969** *Gandalf's Garden* IV. 34/3 (Advt.), Welcome to our humble guest house all holiday-makers, meditators, yogis or vegetarian gannets.

gannetry ('gænɪtrɪ). [f. GANNET + -RY.] A breeding-place for gannets.

1913 J. H. GURNEY *Gannet* xi. 324 Let us..fix a date and suppose a census taken at every Gannetry on the 1st May, 1910. **1960** WILLIAMSON & BOYD *St. Kilda Summer* 113 St. Kilda has much the biggest gannetry in the northern hemisphere, and..more than one-fifth of the North Atlantic gannets nest there. **1971** *Stornoway Gaz.* 10 July 4/8 The world's greatest gannetry, in which is estimated 44,000 pairs of gannets breed.

gannister var. GANISTER.

[**gannok,** spurious word due to misreading of the proper name Talbot in Henry of Huntingdon.

The best text of Langtoft's AF. chronicle has the name as *Galbot*; later texts corrupted it into *gannoc, gannok*; R. Brunne took it for an appellative, prob. supposing it to mean 'standard', as it is explained by Hearne and Mätzner.

c **1330** R. BRUNNE *Chron.* (1810) 113 Steuen..In Herford fulle stoutely his gannok has vp set.]

ganocephalan (,gænəʊ'sɛfələn). [f. mod.L. *ganocephal-us* (f. Gr. γάνος brightness + κεφαλή head) + -AN.] A fish of the extinct order *Ganocephala* (so called because their heads were covered with shining bony plates). So **gano'cephalous** *a.*, belonging to this order.

1865 OWEN in *Geolog. Mag.* II. 6 Ganocephalous and Labyrinthodont cranial bones. *Ibid*, The ribs..were better developed than they are in Ganocephalans or in modern Batrachians.

ganodont ('gænəʊdɒnt). *Palæont.* [f. mod.L. *Ganodonta* (J. L. Wortman 1896, in *Bull. Amer. Mus. Nat. Hist.* VIII. 259), f. Gr. γάνος brightness + ὀδόντ-, ὀδούς tooth.]

= TÆNIODONT.

1897 *Natural Sci.* Sept. 153 The Eocene Ganodonts of the northern hemisphere.

ganoid ('gænɔɪd), *a.* and *sb.* [a. F. *ganoïde* (Agassiz), f. Gr. γάνος brightness + -ειδής: see -OID.]

A. *adj.*

1. Of a fish-scale: Having a smooth shining surface, from being covered with a layer of enamel.

1854 OWEN in *Circ. Sc., Organ. Nat.* I. 46/2 The ganoid plates..are..more close set. **1872** NICHOLSON *Palæont.* 307 Ganoid scales..occur also in some of the Bony Fishes.

2. Of a fish: Covered with polished bony plates or scales; distinctive epithet of an order of fishes (mod.L. *Ganoidei*).

1847 ANSTED *Anc. World* iv. 62 The first of the two groups, that of which the sturgeon and the bony pike are characteristic, is called Ganoid. **1859** DARWIN *Orig. Spec.* iv. (1878) 83 It is in the fresh water basins that we find seven genera of ganoid fishes. **1876** PAGE *Adv. Text-bk. Geol.* xviii. 343 Of the fishes the majority are still placoid and ganoid.

B. *sb.* A ganoid fish.

1839 G. ROBERTS *Dict. Geol., Ganoïds* or *Ganoïdians*, Dr. Agassiz's second order of fishes. **1859** DARWIN *Orig. Spec.* xi. (1878) 308 The ganoids stand intermediate between the selaceans and teleosteans. **1878** A. H. GREEN, etc. *Coal* ii. 52 All the modern Ganoids, with the exception of the sturgeon, are fresh-water fish.

Hence **ga'noidal** *a.* = GANOID A. 2. **ga'noidean** *a.* and *sb.*, **ga'noidian** *a.* and *sb.* = GANOID A. 2 and B.

1839 Ganoïdians [see GANOID B]. **1841** H. MILLER *O.R. Sandst.* iv. 73 A fourth order, the Ganoidean or shining-scaled order. **1854** —— *Sch. & Schm.* xxiv. (1857) 527, I formed my first imperfect acquaintance with the recent ganoidal fishes in 1836. **1861** GEIKIE in *Gd. Words* Feb. 75 There are still some representatives of the ganoidal type of fish.

ganoin ('gænəʊɪn). Also **-ine.** [f. Gr. γάνο-ς brightness + -IN.] (See quot. 1872.) Also *attrib.*

1859 TODD *Cycl. Anat.* V. 481/2 The edges of its 'Lepidine' layer do not remain in contact with the ganoin layer. **1872** NICHOLSON *Palæont.* 307 Ganoid scales, composed of an inferior layer consisting of bone covered by a superficial layer of hard polished enamel (the so-called 'ganoine').

ganomalite (gə'nɒməlaɪt). *Min.* [f. Gr. γάνωμα brightness + -LITE. (Named by Nordenskiöld 1876.)] A silicate of lead and manganese, resembling tephroite, but with high lustre.

1878 *Min. Mag.* II. 149 New minerals from Longban.. Atopite..ganomalite, jacobsite.

ganophyllite (gænəʊ'fɪlaɪt). *Min.* [ad. G. *ganophyllit* (A. Hamberg 1890, in *Geol. Fören. Stockholm Förh.* XII. 586), f. Gr. γάνος brightness + φύλλον leaf: see -ITE[1].] A brown hydrous silicate of manganese and aluminium.

1892 *Jrnl. Chem. Soc.* LXII. II. 1412 *Ganophyllite*.. occurs in fairly large, monosymmetric crystals. **1948** *Mineral. Mag.* June 347 Ganophyllite..readily lost water when heated.

ganosis (gə'nəʊsɪs). [a. Gr. γάνωσις, f. γάνος brightness, f. γάνουν to polish.] (See quots.)

[**1896** E. SELLERS in K. Jex-Blake tr. *Pliny's Hist. Art* 157/2 The process [sc. *circumlitio*, a kind of painting] must be kept distinct from the γάνωσις or toning down of the whole statue.] **1911** *Encycl. Brit.* XX. 485/2 When the plaster wall surface has been carefully smoothed it must be anointed with a mixture of wax, resin and oil, which is to be driven in by heat, and then polished till the surface shines like a mirror. This is a classical process referred to by Vitruvius under the name 'ganosis', as applied to the nude parts of marble statues, possibly to tone down the cold whiteness of the material. **1962** R. C. HAGGAR *Dict. Art Terms* 147/2 *Ganosis*, the removal of the dead-white surface of Greek sculpture by applying beeswax and polishing with a cloth, which gives a warm, buttery complexion to the marble.

gansa, gansaw, obs. forms of GANZA.

†**gansel.** *Obs.* Forms: 5 **gauncely(e, gawncel(y, gaunsell(e,** 5, 8–9 *Sc.* **gansell.** [ad. OF. *ganse aillie* garlic-sauce, f. *ganse, janse*, app. meaning some kind of sauce (*jause* also occurs, riming with *sauce*) + *aillie* some kind of derivative from *ail* garlic. In later Fr. *jance d'aulx* is used in the same sense.] A garlic sauce, used esp. for goose.

c **1420** *Liber Cocorum* (1862) 29 Gawncel for þe gose. Take garlek and grynde hit wele forþy [etc.]. *c* **1430** *Two Cookery-bks.* 23 Hennys in Gauncelye.—Take hennys an roste hem, take mylke an Garleke an grynd it. **1483** *Cath. Angl.* 152/1 Gavnselle, *applauda*.

b. *fig.* in proverbial use.

c **1450** HENRYSON *Mor. Fab.* 14 Thy goose is good, thy gansell sowre as gall. **1721** KELLY *Scot. Prov.* 30 A good Goose, but she has an ill gansel.

gansey ('gænzɪ). Also **gansy, ganzee, ganzey, ganzie, ganzy.** Dial. var. GUERNSEY 2 a; a jersey.

1886 J. J. H. BURGESS *Shetland Sketches* 68 He rubbit aff da shute wi' da sleeve o' his gansey. **1922** JOYCE *Ulysses* 469 In workman's corduroy overalls, black gansy with red floating tie and apache cap. **1935** S. BECKETT *Echo's Bones*, Scarlet and blue ganzies. **1961** *Guardian* 13 Dec. 7/3 He had on an old cap, no muffler, and a faded red ganzey under a fraying jacket. **1969** J. WOOD *Three Blind Mice* vi. 82 Who ever went tae sea in those latitudes without his sea-boots and a decent ganzie on his back?

gansh, var. GANCH *v. Obs.*

gant, gaunt (gɑːnt, gɔːnt), *sb. Sc.* [f. next.] A yawn, a gape; gaping.

1513 DOUGLAS *Æneis* VI. viii. 36 The soundis brak with gasping, or a gant. **17..** *The Ghaist* 4 When the lang drawlin' gaunt, an' drowsy ee, Shaw't bed-time come. **1826** J. WILSON *Noct. Ambr.* Wks. 1855 I. 160 They..put up their hands to their chafts to conceal a bit gaunt.

gant, gaunt (gɑːnt, gɔːnt), *v. Sc.* Forms: 6, 9 **gant,** 8–9 **gaunt.** [? repr. an OE. **gánettan*, freq. f. *gánian* to yawn: see GANE *v.*] *intr.* To yawn, gape.

1513 DOUGLAS *Æneis* III. viii. 144 Quhen he list gant or blaw, the fire is bett. **1715** RAMSAY *Christ's Kirke Gr.* II. xviii, Ilk weary wight Was gaunting for his rest. **1790** BURNS *'Kind Sir, I've read your paper through'* 4 This mony a day I've grain'd and gaunted, To ken [etc.]. **1818** SCOTT *Hrt. Midl.* x, I never ask what brings the Laird of Dumbiedikes glowering here..day after day, till we are a' like to gaunt our chafts aff. **1886** STEVENSON *Kidnapped* xxvi. 272 When he gants his last on a rickle of cauld stanes.

Hence **'ganting, 'gaunting,** *vbl. sb.*

1568 SKEYNE *The Pest* (1860) 12 Ganting of mowthe. **1597** LOWE *Chirurg.* (1634) 53 Of the which commeth ganting, rifting, winds. *a* **1605** MONTGOMERIE *Flyting w. Polwart* 346 All groomes, when thou greits, at thy ganting bee agast. **1850** *Whistle-Binkie* (Scot. Songs) (1890) II. II. 54 Awa' wi' your gaunting!

gant(e, obs. form of GANNET.

ganted, U.S. var. GAUNTED *a.*

gantelet, obs. form of GAUNTLET.

†**'gantellage.** *Obs.*⁻¹ In 7 **gauntellage.** [app. related to OF. *gantier* GANTRY, as OF. *chantellage* to the parallel form *chantier*.] (See quot.)

1611 COTGR., *Droict de Chantellage*, gauntellage; or a certaine fee due vnto some Lords for the Gauntries whereon wine, thats any way to be sold, doth stand.

gantlet, obs. form of GAUNTLET.

'gant,line. *Naut.* = GIRTLINE.

1840 [see GIRT-LINE]. **1882** NARES *Seamanship* (ed. 6) 61 Put one gantline on each sheer head. **1938** J. MASEFIELD *Dead Ned* 45 They'd have laid me out and stripped me to a bare gantline, but for him.

gantlope ('gæntləʊp). Now *rare* exc. in the more corrupt form GAUNTLET². Forms: 7–8 **gant(e)lop,** 7 **gantloop,** 8 **gauntlope,** 7– **gant(e)lope.** [corruptly a. Sw. *gatlopp*, MSw. *gatu-lop* (f. *gata* lane, GATE *sb.*² + *lopp* course).

ON. had *gǫtupíófr*, explained as a thief punished by running the 'gantlope'. The Sw. word prob. became known in England through the Thirty Years' War; the equivalent *gassenlaufen* is found in Ger.]

A military (occas. also naval) punishment in which the culprit had to run stripped to the waist between two rows of men who struck at him with a stick or a knotted cord. *rare* exc. in *to* †*pass, run the gantelope.*

1646 SHAFTESBURY *Diary* 11 Apr. in W. D. Christie *Life* (1871) I. 34 Three were condemned to die, two to run the gantelope. **1656** BLOUNT *Glossogr.*, *Gantlope* (*Ghent Lope*), a punishment of Souldiers, first invented at Ghent..and therefore so called. **1706** LUTTRELL *Brief Rel.* (1857) VI. 90 The regency of Saxony..caused..400 to run the gantlope, for not doing their duty. **1749** FIELDING *Tom Jones* VII. xi, Others [said] that he deserved to run the gantlope. **1756–7** tr. *Keysler's Trav.* (1760) I. 175 In the Piedmontese service, every offence of this nature is punished with the gantlope. **1807** J. MILNER *Martyrs* I. ii. 51 They were ordered to run the gantelope between the hunters..and were severely lashed.

transf. and *fig.* **1649** T. FORD *Lus. Fort.* *2 Being now exposed to run the Gantelope of the Worlds censure. **1655** FULLER *Ch. Hist.* x. i. §25 This Petition ran the Gantlop throughout all the Prelaticall party. **1662** PETTY *Taxes* 55 When a new Invention is first propounded..the poor Inventor runs the Gantloop of all petulent wits. *a* **1694** TILLOTSON *Serm.* (1742) III. 140 We cannot but wonder..that in running the gantlope of a long life..we have escaped so free. **1747** *Gentl. Mag.* 233, I ran the gantlop thro' a number of soldiers to an obliging landlord. **1754** RICHARDSON *Grandison* VI. xxv, To run the female gauntlope. **1785** DRINKWATER *Hist. Siege Gibraltar* (1786) 329 They were in this manner obliged to pass the gantlope of our fire. **1804** J. LARWOOD *No Gun Boats* 8 We must re-run the gantelope of our Bounties and Recruitings. **1836** *Edin. Rev.* LXIV. 71 No doubt he ran the usual gantelope of jokes.

gantry, gauntry ('gæntrɪ, 'gɔːntrɪ). Forms: α. 6–9 **gantree,** 7 **gauntrie,** 8–9 **gaun-, gawntree, gauntry,** 7– **gantry.** β. (*pl.* used as *sing.*) 8–9 **gauntress, -trice.** [Of doubtful origin; app. f. GAWN + TREE; but this may be an etymologizing perversion of OF. *gantier* (14th c. in Du Cange s.v. *cantarium*), var. of *chantier* (:—med.L. *cantārium*) gantry.]

1. A four-footed wooden stand for barrels.

α. **1574** *Richmond Wills* (Surtees) 251, ix hogesheads in the buttrie with the gantrees and traves there. **1611** COTGR., *Ponton*,..a Stilling, or Gauntrie for Caske to stand on. **1674–91** RAY *N.C. Words* 30 A Gauntry. **1724** RAMSAY *Tea-t. Misc.* (1733) I. 105, I..paid him upon a gantree As hostler wives should do. *a* **1774** FERGUSSON *Hallowfair* Poems (1845) 13 At Hallowfair where brousters rare Keep guid ale on the Gantrees. **1816** SCOTT *Old Mort.* viii, The housekeeper..is neither so young nor so handsome as to tempt a man to follow her to the gauntrees. **18..** MATHER *Songs* 17 (Sheffield Gloss.) Our brewing tubs and gantries are over turn'd all. **1893** PEEL *Spen Valley* 282 Great gauntries where were..once stored multitudes of barrels of the strong ale.

β. **1807** J. HALL *Trav. Scotl.* I. 226 Gauntrice (so they call the wooden frame or stand on which they place their barrels, when they are to be tapped). *a* **1811** GRAHAME in Hone *Every-day Bk.* (1827) II. 1179 The frothing bickers..Are drained, and to the gauntress oft return.

2. a. A frame or platform for carrying a travelling-crane or similar structure.

1810 *Hull Improv. Act* 54 Any..frame gantry or other article. **1861** *Times* 7 Oct., There were two travelling-cranes on the gantry over the bridge. **1882** *Engineer* 24 Feb. 133/2 Alongside these docks is a gantry, on which work steam cranes. **1896** *Nature* 24 Sept. 515 The scheme adopted was to erect a high gantry supported by towers on either bank.

attrib. **1888** *Lockwood's Dict. Mech. Engin.* 157 *Gantry crane*, an overhead travelling crane carried on a gantry. **1943** J. S. HUXLEY *TVA* 23 Gantry cranes swung the concrete from the mixing barges to the forms. **1958** *Engineering* 7 Mar. 298/3 The gantry tower, which is used in preparing the vehicle for flight, is being moved away from the launching area.

b. A structure crossing several railway-tracks to accommodate signals.

1889 G. FINDLAY *Eng. Railway* 79 The fitting shop at Crewe turns out about nine signals per week, including composite or bracket and gantry posts. **1902** *Encycl. Brit.* XXXII. 144/1 In cases where room must be economized, signals are usually placed on narrow overhead bridges or 'gantries' spanning a number of tracks. **1939** R. S. LYONS *Wonders Mod. Industry* iii. 35 Ten rail-joints, then Exe Station; ten more rail-joints, then signal gantry, bridge. **1958** DAY & COOPER *Railway Signalling Systems* viii. 124 The train stops must always be beside the line to which they refer, but the signals, with which they must be connected may be on a gantry or bracket some distance from that line.

Hence (from the β form) **'gauntress** *v. trans.*, to mount on a beer-stand.

1812 W. TENNANT *Anster F.* VI. xxiv, Gawntress'd round each ruddy fire about, Hogheads of porter..spout Their genial streams.

Gantt (gænt). The name of Henry Laurence *Gantt* (1861–1919), American management consultant, used *attrib.* to designate a chart in which a series of horizontal lines shows the amount of work done or production completed in certain periods of time in relation to the amount planned for those periods.

1918 L. P. ALFORD in *Industrial Management* Feb. 100/2 The supply division of the Ordnance Bureau of the Army..has its information in regard to requirements and progress in graphical form on the Gantt charts. **1923** W. CLARK *Gantt Chart* i. 5 In the Gantt chart a division of space represents both an amount of time and an amount of work to be done in that time. **1958** J. F. MAGEE *Production Planning & Inventory Control* ix. 223 Gantt charts make use of a horizontal scale marked in time units. A series of horizontal lines..is used to display data.

†**ganyie.** *Sc. Obs.* Forms: 5 **ganȝe, gaynyhe,** 6 **ganye, gan-, genȝie,** 6–7 **gainyie, -ȝe.** [Of obscure origin; there was an Irish *gainne* of similar meaning. Du Cange s.v. *Ganeo* quotes an undated gloss '*ganeo*..hasta vel jaculum, lingua Gallica', but the word is not known in OFr.

A supposed 14th c. example often cited (from *Alisaunder* 292) is prob. a mistake; the *gamus* of the MS. should prob. be corrected into *gairus*, not into *gainus*.]

An arrow, or similar missile, esp. a crossbow-bolt. In late use chiefly in the alliterative phrase *gun and ganyie.*

c **1425** WYNTOUN *Cron.* VIII. xxxvii. 59 Willame off Dowglas thare wes syne Wyth a spryngald gaynyhé throw the thé. *c* **1470** HENRY *Wallace* x. 816 Weyll stuft thai ar with gwn [and] ganȝe off steill. **1500–20** DUNBAR *Poems* lxxviii. 4 So sair the magryme dois me menȝie, Perseing my brow as ony ganȝie. **1535** STEWART *Cron. Scotl.* II. 19 The citie..he did assaill, With gun and ganȝie. *a* **1598** ROLLOCK *On 2 Thess.* ii. 5–8 (1606) 76 Commes he on with this worldly armour, gunnes and gainyies, I aske of thee?

Ganymede ('gænɪmiːd). Also 6 **ganymedes,** 6–7 **ganimed(e,** (7 **genymade**). [ad. L. *Ganymēdēs*, a. Gr. Γανυμήδης a Trojan youth, whom Zeus made his cupbearer.]

1. A cupbearer, a youth who serves out liquor; humorously, a pot-boy.

1608 MIDDLETON *Mad World* II. i, Shall I be bold with your honour, to prefer this aforesaid Ganymede to hold a plate under your lordship's cup? **1656** COWLEY *Misc.*, *Grasshopper* 8 Nature selfe's thy Ganimed. **1693** CONGREVE in *Dryden's Juvenal* Sat. xi. (1697) 291 A raw unskilful Lad ..At once my Carver and my Ganymede. **1826** SCOTT *Woodst.* ix, The cavalier..arrested the progress of the retiring Ganymede. **1841** *Punch* I. 101/2 Lo! Ganymede appears with a foaming tankard of ale. **1878** H. M. STANLEY *Dark Cont.* I. vii. 153 The foaming jar is ready, and the dusky Ganymede attentive.

2. A catamite.

1591 PERCIVALL *Sp. Dict.*, *Puto*, a ganymedes, *Cynaedus*. **1603** HOLLAND *Plutarch's Mor.* 568 A yoong beardlesse Genymade whom he loved. *a* **1649** DRUMM. OF HAWTH. *Poems* Wks. (1711) 55, I crave Thou wilt be pleas'd, great God, to save My sov'reign from a Ganymede. **1708** MOTTEUX *Rabelais* V. (1737) 217 Ganymedes, Bardachoes, Hufflers.

3. The name given to the largest satellite of the planet Jupiter.

1868 LOCKYER *Guillemin's Heavens* (ed. 3) 232.

†**Ganymedean.** *Obs.*⁻¹ [f. L. *Ganymēdē-us* pertaining to Ganymede + -AN.] One who follows the practices of a Ganymede (see GANYMEDE 2).

1603 HARSNET *Pop. Impost.* 160 Pandars, Ganimedeans, Enhausers of Lust.

ganyngale, obs. form of GALINGALE.

ganza ('gænzə). Also 7 **gansa, gansaw.** [app. Godwin took the word from the reading of the old edd. of Pliny *N.H.* x. xxii; see quot. 1601.] One of the birds (called elsewhere 'wild swans') which drew Domingo Gonsales to the moon in the romance by Bp. F. Godwin (see quot. *a* 1633).

[**1601** HOLLAND *Pliny* I. 281 The Geese there, be all white; but lesse of bodie than from other parts: and there they be called Ganzæ.] *a* **1633** [GODWIN] *Man in the Moone* (1638) 27 All my Gansa's were not of sufficient strength to carry him. *Ibid.* 41 My Ganza's. **1648** WILKINS *Math. Magick* II. *Dædalus* vii. 202 Others..have conjectured a possibility of being conveyed through the air by the help of fowls; to which purpose the fiction of the Ganzas, is the most pleasant and probable. **1652** BP. HALL *Invis. World* I. §7. 146 Men, who, as if upon Domingo Gonsales his engine, they had been mounted by his Ganzaes from the Moon to the Empyreall heaven. **1664** BUTLER *Hud.* II. iii. 782 They are but idle Dreams and Fancies, And savour strongly of the Ganzas. **1668** H. MORE *Div. Dial.* I. 531 O that the invention of the Gansaws were once perfected, that I might make my first Visit to our Neighbours in the Moon! **1813** [see CUNEAL *a.*].

gaol (dʒeɪl), **gaoler** ('dʒeɪlə(r)), variant spellings of JAIL, JAILER. In British official use the forms with G are still current; in literary and journalistic use both the G and the J forms are now admitted as correct; in the U.S. the J forms are standard.

gaon ('gɑːəʊn). Pl. **gaonim, gaons, geonim.** [Heb. *gā'ôn* (pl. *gᵉônîm*) excellence (Ps. xlvii. 4), pride (Prov. xvi. 18).] Used as an honorific for the heads of Jewish academies in Babylonia, Palestine, Syria, and Egypt from the 6th to the 11th centuries; later in Spain, Italy and in the eighteenth century in Vilna applied to any person outstandingly gifted in language and art; (after 19th- and 20th-century Yiddish usage) a genius, prodigy. Hence **ga'onic** *a.*

1780 *Encycl. Brit.* V. 3178/2 *Gaons*, a certain order of Jewish doctors, who appeared in the East, after the closing of the talmud. **1892** ZANGWILL *Childr. Ghetto* (1893) I. vii. 71 The light of his generation, the great Gaon..Rav Shemuel. *Ibid.* 72 It was like the Wilna Gaon come again. **1934** WEBSTER, Gaonic. **1935** S. LEWIS *It can't happen Here* xviii. 191 You Geonim never lap up anything but snow cooled nectar. **1941** G. G. SCHOLEM *Major Trends in Jewish Mysticism* ix. 341 The 'Gaon' Elijah of Vilna, the outstanding leader of Lithuanian Jewry. *Ibid.* 352 Assuming that these passages are subsequent Gaonic interpolations. **1964** H. KEMELMAN *Friday the Rabbi slept Late* (1965) i. 23 'What do you think of the Rabbi now?'..'A gaon,..a regular gaon.' **1968** *New Scientist* 23 May 385/3 The responsa written by Jewish legal experts in Medieval Spain since the period of the *gaonim* (spiritual heads of communities).

gap (gæp), *sb.*[1] Also 4–6 **gappe**, 6–7 **gapp**. [a. ON. *gap* chasm (only in the mythological name *Ginnunga-gap*), wide-mouthed outcry (Sw. *gap*, Da. *gab* open mouth, also opening, chasm); sb. related to ON. and Sw. *gapa*, Da. *gabe* to GAPE.] Any opening or breach in an otherwise continuous object; a chasm or hiatus.

1. a. A breach in a wall or hedge, as the result of violence or natural decay.

c **1380** *Sir Ferumb.* 4989 So harde þay þrewe a3en þe wal.. And succh a gappe þay made þer-on. *Ibid.* 5164 To þe gappes [*orig.* holes] buþ þay come. *c* **1400** *Rom. Rose* 4023 Rise up.. And stoppe sone and delyverly Alle the gappis of the hay. *c* **1440** *Promp. Parv.* 186/1 Gap of a walle, *intervallum.* **1523** FITZHERB. *Husb.* §141 Or to fynde a gap or a sherde in his hedge. **1584** *Vestry Bks.* (Surtees) 16 For mendinge a gappe in the churchyard wall.. ij d. **1604** *Eng. Gilds* (1870) 434 No man shall make yates or gapes in the common feild. **1666** BUNYAN *Grace Ab.* ¶54, I saw as it were a narrow gap like a little doorway in the wall. **1712** ADDISON *Spect.* No. 315 ¶14 Satan, after having long wandered upon the surface, or outmost Wall of the Universe, discovers at last a wide Gap in it. **1821** SHELLEY *Boat on Serchio* 82 Those green harbours Farmers called gaps, and we schoolboys called arbours. **1843** LEVER *J. Hinton* xxii, We came to a low stone wall, through a gap of which we passed. *fig.* **1595** SHAKS. *John* III. iv. 32, I will.. stop this gap of breath with fulsome dust.

†**b.** Phrase. ***to stop two gaps with one bush***: 'to kill two birds with one stone', to accomplish two ends at once. *Obs.*

1546 J. HEYWOOD *Prov.* (1867) 78, I will learne, to stop two gaps with one bushe. **1638** SANDERSON *Serm.* II. 97 This common usage of the phrase, as it well preserveth the sence, so doth it also (that I may stop two gaps with one bush) justifie the truth of this charge in my text.

†**2.** *fig.* **a.** An opening or breach by which entry may be effected or attack made; more rarely of a way of escape. *Obs.*

1548 in Strype *Eccl. Mem.* II. II. App. Q. 56 Many good men.. study to devise good laws.. so.. a great many.. labour to defeat them: and as the common saying is to find gapps and starting holes. **1577** HANMER *Anc. Eccl. Hist.* (1619) 60 Lest that thereby men be troubled and a Gappe left open to the malice of Sycophants. **1624** SIR R. KNIGHTLEY in *Fortesc. Papers* (Camden) 196 Which is interpreted a gapp for an escape if any can be made either by mischeife or money. *a* **1628** PRESTON *Breastpl. Love* (1631) 215 The standing still and not hastening to the gappe. **1722** DE FOE *Col. Jack* (1840) 286 No gap open where we could have the least apprehensions of any evil breaking in upon us. **1756** in Temple & Sheldon *Hist. Northfield, Mass.* (1875) 294 We humbly beg of you.. to guard us in our husbandry .. and that we may not be a gap open as in times past.

†**b.** *esp.* in phrases. ***to stand in the gap***: to act as defender. ***to open a gap***: to give access, afford passage or opportunity. ***to stop a gap***: to close a breach, secure a weak point, prevent attack. *Obs.*

1535 COVERDALE *Ezek.* xiii. 5 They stonde not in the gappes, nether make they an hedge for the house of Israel. *Ibid.* xxii. 30. *c* **1555** HARPSFIELD *Divorce Hen. VIII* (Camden) 273 So dangerous a matter it is to open once the gap to errors and heresies. **1596** SPENSER *State Irel.* Wks. (Globe) 621/2 Such a gapp of mischeif lyeth open therby, that I could wish it were well stopped. **1599** THYNNE *Animadv.* (1875) 51 To stoppe that gappe, I will answere, that Chaucers woorkes haue byn sithens printed twyce. **1631** GOUGE *God's Arrows* I. §45. 77 When there is none to stand in the gap, how should his wrath be stayed? **1664** J. KEYMOR *Dutch Fishing* in *Phenix* II. 225 To open the Gap of Traffick, and to make fulness of Trade. *c* **1680** BEVERIDGE *Serm.* (1729) II. 116 As if it opened a gap to all manner of licentiousness. **1757** G. WASHINGTON *Lett.* Writ. 1889 I. 508 The inhabitants see, and are convinced of this, which makes each family afraid of standing in the gap of danger.

†**3.** A gash or wound in the body. *Obs.*

? *a* **1500** *Lament. Virgin Mary* in *Chester Pl.* (Shaks. Soc.) II. 208 To see my sone y have grete peyne, In hys breste so grete a gappe ys. **1541** R. COPLAND *Guydon's Quest. Chirurg.* N iij b, The .ix. place is vpon the eares & gappes of depe woundes. **1600** FAIRFAX *Tasso* XI. xlv, Through his right eie Clorindaes seu'nth shaft went And in his necke broke forth a bloodie gap.

4. a. A notch; a small break or opening in an edge or surface. Now *rare.*

1530 PALSGR. 224/1 Gappe in a knyfe, *hoche.* **1591** [see HARD *a.* 21]. *c* **1645** HOWELL *Lett.* (1892) I. 316 The Jews.. when they kill any Creature.. cut the Throat with a Knife without a Gap. **1668** CULPEPPER & COLE *Barthol. Anat.* Man. IV. vi. 342 There is observed in that place a Gap or Chink. **1833** J. HOLLAND *Manuf. Metal* II. 257 The pinion of the axle.. coming to the gap at D.. sinks or rises in the slit. **1884** BOWER & SCOTT *De Bary's Phaner.* 443 The passages are.. short, and relatively broad, and may more properly be termed gaps or cavities.

†**b.** A notch or slit made in a swan's beak, as a private mark. *Obs.*

1558–9 *Will of W. Yatles* (Somerset Ho.), My swane mark of the twoo gappes and the Staple. **1656** in *Linc. N. & Q.* (1897) V. 92 One Swanne mark of the Gapp with the Penney cross in alt on the nere side.

5. a. A break or opening in a range of mountains; a pass or gorge (very common in U.S.).

1555 EDEN *Decades* 350 Ouer the sayde byght you shall se a great gappe in the mountayne. **1709** ADDISON *Tatler* No. 161 ¶8 Two great Gaps that led thro' this Circuit of Mountains. **1788** M. CUTLER in *Life, Jrnls. & Corr.* (1888) I. 403 We passed the narrows or gaps of two ranges of high mountains. **1816** J. BIGELOW in *New-Eng. Jrnl. Med. & Surg.* V. 323 From this town a road has been cut, passing through a gap of the mountains to Portland. **1847** PARKMAN *Oregon Tr.* (1872) 180 We reached the gap, which was like a deep notch cut into the mountain-ridge. **1890** BOLDREWOOD *Miner's Right* xv. 153 An ugly lot to meet in one of those narrow rocky gaps, as they call them, over the line of ranges.

b. With defining word: ***water-gap***, one which is deep enough to serve as the course of a stream (*Cent. Dict.*); ***wind-gap*** (see quot. 1889).

1779 D. LIVERMORE in *Coll. New Hampsh. Hist. Soc.* (1850) VI. 314 This morning the troops.. pass the Windgap, so called, for its being the only pass for a number of miles through a long chain of mountains. **1877** A. B. SYLVESTER *Sk. North. N.Y.* 60 A water-gap, forming a natural gateway through the mountains. **1889** J. D. WHITNEY *United States* 223 Gaps.. in which the depression in the ridge is not sufficiently deep to give passage to a watercourse are known as 'wind-gaps'.

c. *local.* (See quots.)

1825 *Brighton Commissioners' Act* §62 *Gap*, a road or descent from cliffs to sea-shore. **1868** ATKINSON *Cleveland Gloss.*, *Gap*, an opening at the Bank-top through which a path or track winding up the steep Bank-side finds its way on to the open moor.

d. A hole or chasm in the ground.

1696 WHISTON *Th. Earth* IV. (1722) 381 Its old Fissures were open'd.. and sufficient Gaps made. **1840** DICKENS *Barn. Rudge* ii, Great holes and gaps had worn into the soil, being now filled with water from the late rains.

6. a. An unfilled space or interval; a blank or deficiency; a break in continuity. Also, a disparity, inequality or imbalance; a break in deductive continuity; a (usu. undesirable) difference in development, condition, understanding, etc.; in modern use freq. qualified by a preceding sb., as in ***credibility gap, dollar gap, generation gap, missile gap*** (see under the first elements). Cf. senses 6 b and 7.

1605 SHAKS. *Macb.* III. i. 12 If he had beene forgotten, It had bene as a gap in our great Feast. **1670** MILTON *Hist. Eng.* II. Wks. (1847) 483/2 Were it not for leaving an unsightly gap so near to the beginning, I should have judg'd this Labour.. almost superfluous. **1675** J. PYNCHON in I. Mather *K. Philip's War* (1862) 237, I could be heartily glad if we were able to spare some men, but.. nine men out of this Towne.. makes a great gap. **1690** LOCKE *Hum. Und.* III. vi. (1695) 250 In all the visible corporeal World, we see no Chasms or Gaps.. the descent is by easie Steps, and a continued series of Things. **1754** RICHARDSON *Grandison* I. ix. 51 In that long gap of time as he called it. **1771** N. NICHOLLS *Corr. w. Gray* (1843) 126, I found the gap between Froissart and Comines, and longed for Monstrelet. **1853** SIR H. DOUGLAS *Milit. Bridges* (ed. 3) 85 A part of the bridge projecting from each bank, and a gap in the middle. **1865** KINGSLEY *Lett.* (1878) II. 214 His death is to me a great sorrow—a gap in my life which I feel and cannot fill. **1874** SAYCE *Compar. Philol.* vi. 236 There is no break, no sudden gap in nature; all follows in a regular unbroken order. **1892** *Law Times* XCII. 145/2 The gap on the walls caused by the removal of the portraits. **1930** *Economist* 13 Sept. 477/1 The widening gap between income and expenditure disclosed by the latest revenue return. **1940** *Ibid.* 30 Nov. 662/1 The 'gap' in the Budget is of the order of £2,000 millions a year. **1952** *Sat. Rev.* 20 Sept. 9/3 *Gap* ought to be removed from public speech, as in the dollar *gap*, the export *gap*, inflationary and deflationary gap. **1956** A. J. AYER *Probl. Knowl.* ii. 80 They accept the existence of the gap between evidence and conclusion, but they hold that it can be bridged by a legitimate process of inductive reasoning. **1959** *Times Lit. Suppl.* 22 May 305/1 The Gap that has come to enjoy the dignity of capital letters, namely, the gap that has opened up in the past hundred years between men of science and students of the humanities. **1964** *Philos. Rev.* LXXIII. 165 (*title*) The Gap between 'Is' and 'Should'. **1967** *Nature* 4 Mar. 851/1 The phenomenon which has become known as the technology gap is more a matter of management than of technology. **1968** *Listener* 29 Aug. 273/3 It's this imbalance which gives the Soviet Union such an advantage in its dealings with the West, and it's far more important than any 'gap' in technology or arms. **1969** *Mind* LXXVIII. 27 He deals with the logical gap by jumping it. **1971** *Nature* 25 June 481/1 The 'technology gap'—the supposed disparity between the United States and the rest of the industrialized world in the capacity to exploit advanced technology.

b. Phrases. ***to stop, to fill*** (***in*** or ***up***), ***to supply a gap***: to make up a deficiency, supply a want, fill a vacant space. Also, ***to bridge*** or ***close a gap***.

1523 FITZHERB. *Husb.* §146 A woman can nat get her lyuynge honestly wt spynnynge on the dystaffe, but it stoppeth a gappe. **1548** HALL *Chron.*, *K. Hen. VI*, 175 All though thei daily lost people.. yet their numbre was restored, and the gappe euer filled. **1655** SIR E. NICHOLAS in *N. Papers* (Camden) II. 222 He has already hindred 500li.. which would stop many a gapp now, it may be more then 2000li will at another time. **1711** SWIFT *Lett.* (1767) III. 217, I make a present of it [money] to stop some gaps. **1776** F. BULL *Let.* 28 Oct. in *Wilkes' Corr.* (1805) V. 85, I only mean to stop the gap for the present. **1835** THIRLWALL *Greece* I. v. 131 Invented merely to fill up a gap in chronology. **1845** MAURICE *Mor. & Met. Philos.* in *Encycl. Metrop.* II. 653/1 Theology would be.. brought in to supply gaps in the system which philosophy had tried to construct. **1879** FROUDE *Cæsar* xix. 311 He had a few levies with him to fill the gaps in the old legions. **1879** [see BRIDGE *v.*[1] 1 d]. **1927** *Cherwell* 25 June 238/1 A few days ago a London journalist was commenting.. on the cleavage between.. the Oxford Set and the young officers of the Guards... However, Mr. Drury Lowe is the one person.. who has successfully bridged this gap, if gap there be. **1944** *Ann. Reg. 1943* 50 The production of coal.. had fully kept pace with consumption and in fact somewhat exceeded it, so closing the previous 'gap' of eleven million tons annually. **1950** S. E. TOULMIN *Exam. Place of Reason* xv. 223 All his experience and wisdom are needed to bridge the gap between facts and values. **1957** *BBC Handbk.* 84 'Forces' Requests'.. is an attempt to close the gap between National Servicemen all over the world and their families at home in Britain. **1961** *Ann. Reg. 1960* 500 Efforts to 'bridge the gap' between the Common Market and the European Free Trade Association continued.

†**c.** Used to render L. *hiatus. Obs.*

1706 POPE *Let. to Walsh* 22 Oct., To come to the Hiatus, or Gap between two words.

d. *Aeronaut.* The vertical distance between the upper and lower wings of a biplane.

1909 *Hazell's Annual 1910* 487/2 Another tailless biplane is the Cody, the main planes of which have.. a gap of 9 ft. in the centre. **1915** W. E. DOMMETT *Aeroplanes & Airships* 33 The gap between the planes, which are staggered, is 4 ft. 9 in. **1916** H. BARBER *Aeroplane Speaks* 63 There will be.. loss of efficiency unless the gap between the top and bottom surfaces is equal to not less than $1\frac{1}{2}$ times the chord. **1936** B. JONES *Elem. Pract. Aerodynam.* vi. 99 Struts act as columns, and, if the gap is unduly big, the struts are excessively long and the structure is weak. **1949** J. W. VALE *Aviation Mechanic's Aircraft Man.* i. 25 The greater the gap, the smaller the interference of air flow between the upper and lower wing.

7. A breach or wide divergence in character or sympathies.

1857 BUCKLE *Civiliz.* I. vii. 458 Such is the great gap which separates the public men of our time from those who flourished under that bad system. **1876** FREEMAN *Norm. Conq.* V. xxiv. 495 There was.. a gap between him and the mass of his flock and Clergy.

8. *techn.* (See quot. and cf. *gap-bed lathe.*)

1873 C. P. B. SHELLEY *Workshop Appliances* vi. 190 A gap is an expedient for.. enabling a lathe to take in articles of much greater diameter.. without materially increasing its weight or general dimensions.

9. *attrib.* and *Comb.*, as ***gap-way***; (objective), ***gap-stopper***; ***gap-filling*** sb. and adj.; **gap-bed**, the bed of a gap-bed lathe; a gap-bed lathe; **gap-bed lathe** (see quot.); **gap-bridge**, a bridge or piece of casting which closes the gap in a gap-bed lathe when not in use; **gap-hunter**, one who in riding to hounds makes for the gaps, instead of riding straight; **gap-lathe** = *gap-bed lathe*; **gap-net** (? *obs.*), a net placed across a gap (cf. *gate-net*); **gap-rope** (see quot.); †**gap-wide** *a.*, gaping wide open; **gap-window** (see quot.).

1888 *Lockwood's Dict. Mech. Engin.* 157 **Gap bed*, a lathe bed having a portion recessed out in front of and below the headstock, to receive work larger in diameter than the height of the lathe centres, under ordinary conditions, will allow of. **1905** *Daily Chron.* 12 Sept. 1/3 (Advt.), Lathe, 7 in. centres, 12 ft. gap bed. **1955** C. T. BOWER *Bk. of Lathe* ii. 44 The gap bed is very popular with British lathe manufacturers, but it has never been thought desirable by American makers. *Ibid.* 45 General purpose lathes.. can have gap beds so that they can swing the unexpected big jobs. **1884** KNIGHT *Dict. Mech.* IV. 375 **Gap-bed lathe*, one with an opening in the bed or shears to allow a larger object to be turned. **1888** *Lockwood's Dict. Mech. Engin.*, *Gap bridge. **1890** W. JAMES *Princ. Psychol.* I. ix. 265 All the rest.. is *internodal* consciousness, giving us the sense of continuity, but having no significance apart from its mere *gap-filling function. **1958** *Times Lit. Suppl.* 14 Mar. 142/1 Thinking appears in an obvious sense as an exercise in gap-filling. **1964** C. DENT *Quantity Surveying by Computer* vi. 81 The whole of the vocabulary for that trade in which the heading occurs is now read on to the drum, in readiness for the gap-filling subroutine which is to follow. **1872** *Daily News* 26 Mar., Though a man.. should hunt properly, a woman need not be ashamed of being a '*gap-hunter'. **1879** *Cassell's Techn. Educ.* IV. 280/3 *Gap-lathes find employment chiefly in small work-shops. **1884** *Health Exhib. Catal.* 118/2 Powerful Double-geared Gap Lathe, self-acting and screw-cutting. **1727** *Philip Quarll* (1816) 28 An animal.. which he had found taken in one of the *gap-nets. **1883** *Man. Seamanship for Boys* 60 Foot-Line or *Gap Rope is a rope's end rove through a block at the bowsprit cap, and bent to an eyelet-hole in the foot of the jib, or to the clew of the jib. **1758** J. RUTTY *Spir. Diary* (ed. 2) 115 The Lord honoured me with a post of being one of the three *gap-stoppers on this occasion. **1857** S. OSBORN *Quedah* xix. 267 We swept through another *gapway in the hills. **1583** STANYHURST *Æneis* II. (Arb.) 51 Downe we beat oure rampiers, our towne wals *gapwyd ar opned. **1874** KNIGHT *Dict. Mech.* I. 942/1 **Gap-window*, a long and narrow window.

gap (gæp), *sb.*[2] [Cf. GAFF *sb.*[3]] ***blowing the gap***: blowing the gaff, giving information.

1821 P. EGAN *Real Life*, etc. I. xxiv. 557 He should like to smack the bit without blowing the gap.

gap (gæp), *v.* [f. GAP *sb.*[1]] **a.** *intr.* To break at the edge; to become jagged or notched. *rare.* **b.** *trans.* To make notches in. *dial. rare.* See also GAPPED.

1847–78 HALLIWELL, *Gap*, to notch, to jag. *South.* **1864** *Reader* 28 May 688 Iron was preferable to steel. Steel gapped and lost its edge. **1881** in *Isle of Wight Gloss.*

c. To make a gap or breach in or between; to open (a gap or passage). Cf. last quot. for GAPPED *ppl. a.* 2.

1893 *Funk's Stand. Dict.*, *Gap*,.. to make an opening or cause a hiatus or breach in. **1916** 'BOYD CABLE' *Action Front* 95 Eager hands tore down the sandbags to gap a passage for them. **1925** *Brit. Weekly* 5 Mar. 545/3 Demolishing two-thirds of the houses, and 'gapping' and 'loop-holing' the remainder. **1927** *Daily Express* 29 July 1/2 The sowing, 'gapping', 'singling', hoeing, and other processes. **1959** *Motor* 2 Sept. 76/1 Distributor points properly gapped.

d. *intr.* To be broken through at intervals; to have gaps; to gape open.

1948 D. BALLANTYNE *Cunninghams* 22 The cottage veranda gapped in places. **1951** in M. McLuhan *Mech. Bride* 74 Because it fits so well, the sides don't gap.

Hence **'gapping** *vbl. sb.*, a breaking into notches.

1683 EVELYN *Diary* 13 July, The gapping too of the razor, and cutting his own fingers, was a little strange.

gapare, obs. Sc. form of GAPER.

gape (geɪp), *sb.* Also 6 *Sc.* gaip, 8 gap(s). [f. GAPE *v.*]

1. The act of opening the mouth; a yawn.

1535 STEWART *Cron. Scot.* III. 466 The fox..with mony girne and gaip..makis debait als lang as that he ma. **1745** R. GRAVES *Euphrosyne* (1776) I. 70 Now a gen'ral gape goes round, And vapours cloud each sleepy head. **1806–7** J. BERESFORD *Mis. Hum. Life* (1826) VII. xviii, Balking a good gape, by forcing your lips close together.

2. a. An open-mouthed stare; a gaze of wonder or curiosity.

1660 FISHER *Rusticks Alarm* Wks. (1679) 306 Thou hast hung thy Reader up in the Air, and there left him among Gapes and Stares. **1768** *Woman of Honor* II. 83 Paintings, statues, monuments..that so vulgarly satisfy the silly superficial gape of travelling sight-mongers. **1863** MRS. C. CLARKE *Shaks. Char.* v. 118 A sea-port town—the inhabitants of which appear to have more leisure for gape and gossip than any others. **1870** *Daily News* 4 Oct., Numerous English tourists, bound for a gape at the battle-field of Sedan.

b. *fig.* A state of eagerness or wonder: also in phrase ***upon the gape***. ? *Obs.*

1712 ADDISON *Spect.* No. 452 ¶3 The Mind is not here kept in a perpetual Gape after Knowledge. **1713** STEELE *Englishm.* No. 24. 158 The chief skill is to keep them still upon the Gape. **1792** A. YOUNG *Trav. France* (1794) I. 8, I have been upon the full silly gape to find out things that I had not found before.

3. ***the gapes***: **a.** A disease in poultry, etc., of which frequent gaping is the symptom.

1799 *Med. Jrnl.* II. 204 There is a disease prevalent among the gallinaceous poultry in this country, called the gaps. **1864** *Intell. Observ.* No. 33. 197 Every keeper of poultry is acquainted with the 'gapes'. **1886** LD. WALSINGHAM & PAYNE-GALLWEY *Shooting* I. 158 The most destructive disease prevalent among partridges is that which is commonly known by the name of the 'gapes'.

b. *humorously.* A fit of yawning or staring.

c 1815 JANE AUSTEN *Persuas.* xx, Another hour of music was to give delight or the gapes, as real or affected taste for it prevailed. **1840** HALIBURTON *Clockm.* Ser. III. iii, What gave me the gapes was the scenes [at the theatre].

4. a. The expanse of an open mouth or beak.

1766 PENNANT *Zool.* (1768) II. 246 The gape of the bill, when opened, is near two inches from tip to tip. **1774** GOLDSM. *Nat. Hist.* (1776) VI. 214 The narwhal, however, has a much narrower gape than the great whale. **1829** GLOVER *Hist. Derby* I. 169 Pike..The gape of the jaw is wide. **1864** R. F. BURTON *Dahome* I. 38 He opens his gape like a fledgling to its parent. **1884** *Pall Mall G.* 18 Sept. 12/1 Hawks..remarkable for the size of their gape and the shortness of their beaks.

b. The part of the beak which can be opened; the line of commissure of the mandibles.

1833 R. MUDIE *Feath. Tribes Brit. Isles* (1841) I. 28 From the gape of the bill to the eyes a black streak extends. **1883** MARTIN & MOOLE *Verteb. Diss.* 93 Each so-called mandible is hard and horny at its tip, but becomes softer near the angle of the gape. **1886** W. W. FOWLER *Year w. the Birds* 83 The gape of the mouth furnished with strong hairs.

c. (See quot. 1848.)

1848 CRAIG, *Gape*, in Conchology, an opening in multivalves and bivalves when the valves are shut. **1875** HUXLEY & MARTIN *Elem. Biol.* xi. 104 At the edges of this 'gape' of the shell [of the fresh water mussel] the thickened margins of a part of the..mantle become visible. *Ibid.* 105.

5. a. A rent or opening of any kind.

1658 A. FOX *Wurtz' Surg.* I. iii. 7 Thereby the wound comes to its old gape and shape. **1853** G. JOHNSTON *Nat. Hist. E. Bord.* I. 251 This hurries along as the gape deepens, and becomes, at every step, more declivous. **1897** *Westm. Gaz.* 22 Apr. 3/2 She breaks off her thread with an energetic pull, and thus overstraining her last stitch causes in time an unseemly gape in that seam.

b. *Naut.* The principal crevice or crack in shaken timber.

1867 in SMYTH *Sailor's Word-bk.*

6. *Comb.*: **gape-worm**, the worm that causes the gapes (see 3 a).

1873 L. WRIGHT *Bk. Poultry* 196 The egg of the gape-worm. **1895** *Montgomery Ward Catal.* 217/3 Gape Worm Extractor..quickly removes, without injury to the chick, the worms..from the windpipe. **1935** *Discovery* Sept. 266 *Syngamus trachea*, the Gape Worm of poultry and other birds.

gape (geɪp), *v.* Forms: 3–4 **gapen**, 5 **gapyn**, 6 *Sc.* **gaip**, 9 *dial.* **ge(e)ap**, 5– **gape**. Also 3 (once) pa. t. **geapede**. [a. ON. *gapa* to open the mouth, gape, Sw. *gapa*, Da. *gabe* = MDu. and mod.Du. *gapen*, MLG. *gapen*, MHG. and G. *gaffen* to gape, stare. The word is not found in Gothic, and its further relations are uncertain; Skr. *jabh-*, Zend. *jab-* to yawn, gape, have been compared. In Eng. dialects there is some confusion with GALP *v.*

An OE. **gapian* may have existed (cf. early ME. *geapede* in quot. *a* 1225, which may represent a Mercian form with *o*-umlaut), but is not recorded; in the gloss '*Pando*, ȝeape' (Wr.-Wülcker 471/14), which is given in some Dicts. as an example of this verb, *pando* is abl. of *pandus* adj. In three passages of Chaucer (*Miller's T.* 258, 655; *Troil.* v. 1133) three of the best MSS. give *cape* instead of *gape*. This is prob. to be referred to LG. *kapen*, MHG. *kapfen*, *kaffen*, OHG. *kapfēn* to keep watch or outlook, a word not related to G. *gaffen*, but early confused with it.]

1. *intr.* To open the mouth wide, esp. in order to bite or swallow anything. Said also of the mouth.

c **1220** *Bestiary* 506 Ðis fis..ðanne him hungreð he gapeð wide. *a* **1225** *St. Marher.* 9 He..ȝeonede [*MS. Bodl.* geapede, *misprinted* ȝeapede] mid his wide geneow uppon hire. **13..** *Sir Beues* (A.) 2763 Ȝenande & gapande on him so, Ase he wolde him swolwe þo. *c* **1350** *Will. Palerne* 2372 þe werwolf..as a wod best went hem a-ȝens, Gapand ful grimli. **14..** *Tundale's Vis.* 149 Her mowthes wer wyde, þai gapud fast. **1530** PALSGR. 560/2, I gape, as a beest dothe that entendeth to byte, whiche holdeth his mouthe open afore. **1688** R. HOLME *Armoury* III. 294/1 Such Fellows..are fed with Roasted Pigs and good Ale as long as they can gape. **1710** STEELE & ADDISON *Tatler* No. 257 ¶11 Opening their Mouths as wide as they could gape. **1821** LAMB *Elia* Ser. I. *My First Play*, Heads that gape, and grin, in stone around the inside of the old Round Church of the Templars.

Proverbial phrases.

1546 J. HEYWOOD *Prov.* (1867) 17 He that gapeth till he be fed, Maie fortune to fast and famishe for hunger. **1577–87** HOLINSHED *Chron.* (1807–8) II. 389 A man ought not to chide with a foole, nor gape over an oven. **1709** *Brit. Apollo* II. No. 62. 2/2 She will gape like a Pig on a Spit.

b. *transf.* of earth, hell, etc.

c **1375** *Sc. Leg. Saints, Egipciane* 541 þar-for me wonderis..þat þe erd gapand wyd, me swelyt nocht. *c* **1460** *Towneley Myst.* vii. 205 Then shall hell gape and gryn. **1535** COVERDALE *Isa.* v. 14 Therfore gapeth hel, and openeth hyr mouth marvelous wyde. **1693** DRYDEN *Ovid's Met.* I. 739 Gape, Earth, and this unhappy wretch intomb. **1705** BERKELEY *Cave of Dunmore* Wks. 1871 IV. 507 This..water runs but a little way ere the rock gapes to swallow it. **1850** TENNYSON *In Mem.* lxx. 6 A gulf that ever shuts and gapes.

c. Of a bivalve: To open the shell.

1577 NORTHBROOKE *Dicing* (1843) 61 The crab presently putteth a little stone into the oyster as he gapeth. **1712** ADDISON *Spect.* No. 293 ¶9 An Oyster, which lay in the Neighbourhood of this Drop, chanced to gape and swallow it up.

d. Used jocularly for 'to open'.

1607 MIDDLETON *Michaelmas Term* I. i, He was here three days before the Exchequer gaped.

e. *trans.* To open (the mouth) wide. † ***to gape out***: to emit with open mouth. *rare.*

1608 ARMIN *Nest Ninn.* (1842) 32 So shee, forgetting modesty, gapte out a laughter. **1665** HOOKE *Microgr.* 204 Beyond these were two indented jaws DD, which he opened side-wayes, and was able to gape them asunder very wide. **1892** H. HUTCHINSON *Fairway Isl.* 11 A man's head gaped its mouth to ask..what young Quarrell wanted there.

2. *intr.* Of material objects, wounds, etc.: To open as a mouth; to split, crack, part asunder.

1577 B. GOOGE *Heresbach's Husb.* (1586) II. 87 After the tenth of June, when the ground gapes with the heate of the Sunne. **1601** HOLLAND *Pliny* II. 593 The Tyburtine stones ..if the heat of summer take them, they will gape and be ready to cleaue in sunder. **1688** R. HOLME *Armoury* III. 398/1 A Stitching Quill..is an instrument by means whereof a wound that gapeth is drawn together, or stitched up. **1828** SCOTT *F.M. Perth* xxii, Think'st thou..that..the wounds of the slaughtered corpse will gape? **1867** SMYTH *Sailor's Word-bk.* s.v., The seams gape, or let in water. **1882** VINES tr. *Sachs' Bot.* 799 If this portion [of the root] is split, the parts generally gape concavely outwards.

3. ***to gape on*** or ***upon***, now more commonly ***to gape at***: to stare at with open mouth, to gaze upon in curiosity or wonder.

c **1290** *S. Eng. Leg.* I. 108/66 On hire gapede alday swyþe muche folc þere..for hire continaunce was wonderful. **1514** BARCLAY *Cyt. & Uplondyshm.* (Percy Soc.) p. xliv, Upon the sewer well mayst thou gase and gape. **1581** SIDNEY *Apol. Poetrie* (Arb.) 67 What is it to make folkes gape at a wretched Begger, or a beggerly Clowne? **1621** BURTON *Anat. Mel.* II. ii. VI. iii. (1651) 299 The dog and hare, wolf and lamb.. stood all gaping upon Orpheus. **1755** SMOLLETT *Quix.* (1803) II. 6 Like a country villager gaping at rarities which he had never seen before. **1859** TENNYSON *Elaine* 451 Levaine gaped upon him As on a thing miraculous. **1885** *Manch. Exam.* 12 May 5/3 The larger the town the more ready are people to gape at new sights.

b. *absol.* To stare in wonder or admiration.

1377 LANGL. *P. Pl.* B. x. 41 Tho that feynen hem folis.. And do men for to gape. *c* **1386** CHAUCER *Miller's T.* 287 This Nicholas sat ay as stille as ston, And ever he gaped upward into the eire. *c* **1394** *P. Pl. Crede* 156 And whan y cam to þat court y gaped aboute. **1530** PALSGR. 560/2, I gape ..I loke stedfastly upon a thyng. **1646** SIR T. BROWNE *Pseud. Ep.* IV. i. 181 Man..was not meant to gape or looke upward with the eye. ? *a* **1700** *Song* in Ramsay *Tea-t. Misc.* (1733) I. 88 There's braw lads in Earnslaw..Wha gape and glowr with their eye, At kirk when they see my Marion. **1751** ELIZ. CARTER *Rambler* No. 100 ¶2 They may not gape, and wonder, and stare. **1830** CUNNINGHAM *Brit. Paint.* II. 195 When the wonder of the town began to abate, the country came gaping in.

4. ***to gape after*** or ***for*** (also † ***at***, † ***upon***): to be eager to obtain, to have a longing for (something).

c **1340** HAMPOLE *Prose Tr.* (1866) 41 As if þou ware abydande or gapand after sum qwent stirringe. *a* **1420** HOCCLEVE *De Reg. Princ.* 1408 Fulle many men knowe I that yane and gape After some fatte and riche benefice. *c* **1460** FORTESCUE *Abs. & Lim. Mon.* xx. (1885) 156 Importune suters wil gape vpon suche reuersiouns. *a* **1533** LD. BERNERS *Gold. Bk. M. Aurel.* (1546) C ij b, It is no newe thyng that men gape for hygh and frayle thynges. **1600** HOLLAND *Livy* XXX. xl. (1609) 768 He gaped at [L. *petens*] the honour of finishing the same [war]. **1638** F. JUNIUS *Paint. Ancients* 190 The basenesse of a minde that gapeth for nothing but money. **1672** MARVELL *Corr.* cc. Wks. 1872–5 II. 397 The greedy appetites of those who have been so many years gaping after this profit. **1758** JOHNSON *Idler* No. 3 ¶7 Multitudes..who awake in the morning, vacant of thought, with minds gaping for the intellectual food, which some kind Essayist has been accustomed to supply. **1827–48** HARE *Guesses* Ser. II. (1873) 540 It is not solely in the Gospel that people go out into the desert to gape after new spiritual incarnations.

b. with *inf.*: to desire eagerly *to do* (something).

a **1340** HAMPOLE *Psalter* xiii. 5 Glottery, þat..is ay gapand to take. *c* **1440** *Jacob's Well* (E.E.T.S.) 290 Whan oure lady com to þis munke..he gapid for to haue of here lycoure. **1561** T. NORTON *Calvin's Inst.* II. 98 If they finde the spring hed of the euell within themselues, why gape they to finde out foreine causes. **1635** PAGITT *Christianogr.* 222 Some others who gape to swallow up and make a prey of that little which remaineth. *a* **1748** PITT *Ep. to Spence* 22 Studying his looks, and watching at the board, He gapes to catch the droppings of my lord. **1815** *Sporting Mag.* XLVI. 122 Lincolnshire friends..are gaping with mouths wide open to have their curiosity satisfied.

†**c.** *absol.*; also *trans.* = ***gape after***. *Obs.*

1552 LATIMER *Fruitf. Serm.* (1575) 124, I pray God geue vnto us such hartes, that we may be content to liue in our calling, and not to gape farther. **1557** *Tottel's Misc.* (Arb.) 258 For whiles you knew I was your own, So long in vaine you made me gape. **1588** T. L. *To Ch. Rome* (1651) 13 Your ..brethren, which walke..gaping the comming of a second Messias.

†**5.** To gasp from pain, heat, etc. Also, of the dead, to have the mouth open. *Obs.*

1352 MINOT *Poems* vii. 135 Was þou noght, Franceis, with þi wapin Bitwixen Cressy and Abuyle? Whare þi felaws lien and gapin. **1398** TREVISA *Barth. De P.R.* XVIII. xlviii. (1495) 809 They byshadow themself with the fote whan they lye gapyng on the grounde in stronge hete of the sonne. ? *a* **1400** *Morte Arth.* 1076 He gapede, he groned faste, with grucchande latez, ffor grefe of þe gude kyng. *c* **1500** *Lancelot* 1090 One to the hart the spere goith throw the scheld, The knychtis gaping lyith in the feld. **1535** STEWART *Cron. Scot.* II. 185 Richt scharpe schutting on ilk syde mycht be sene, Quhen mony grume la gaippand on the grene. *a* **1572** KNOX *Hist. Ref.* Wks. 1846 I. 260 The Gray Freiris gapped, the Blak Frearis blew, the Preastis panted, and fled.

6. To yawn, esp. from weariness.

Now *rare* in southern Eng. and in literature; common *colloq.* in midland and northern districts.

c **1440** *Promp. Parv.* 186/1 Gapyn, *hio, oscito.* **1530** PALSGR. 560/1 There is never no man that gapeth but other he is wery or he lacketh somwhat. **1619** R. WESTE *Bk. Demeanor* 77 in *Babees Bk.* 293 To gape in such unseemely sort, with ugly gaping mouth, Is like an image pictured a blowing from the south. **1647** R. STAPYLTON *Juvenal* 186 He, at the sight of supper, wont to fall A yawning, gapes and gapes, and that is all. **1707** *Reflex. upon Ridicule* 134 He gapes in the Theatre. **1729** SWIFT *Lady's Jrnl.* 42 She stretches, gapes, unglues her eyes, And asks if it be time to rise.

b. ***to gape away***: to pass (the time) in yawning.

1883 *Harper's Mag.* Apr. 699/2 We scarcely saw a soul except a few..loafers gaping away the weary hours.

7. To bawl or shout. *Obs.* exc. *dial.*

1579 FULKE *Heskins' Parl.* 356 He gapeth and cryeth out vppon Oecolampadius. **1608** MIDDLETON *Fam. Love* I. ii, Peace, good Gudgeon, gape not so loud. **1687** MIEGE *Fr. Dict.* 11, He ever gapes, when he speaks, *il crie toujours, quand il parle.* **1876** *Whitby Gloss.*, *Geeap*, to gape. Also to bawl or talk loudly.

8. The vb.-stem in *Comb.*, as ***gape-jaw***; also **gape-eyed** *a.* (see quot.); **gape-gaze** *v. dial. intr.*, to gaze with open mouth, or with eagerness; **gape-scene**, ? *nonce-wd.* (see quot.).

1855 CHAMIER *My Travels* II. x. 164 There is not a window which has not one of these gape-scenes [Balconies]. **1863** MRS. GASKELL *Sylvia's L.* (ed. 2) I. 249 T' most part o' girls as has looks like hers are always gape-gazing to catch other folks' eyes. **1876** BROWNING *Shop* 7 What gimcracks, genuine Japanese; Gape-jaw and goggle-eye, the frog. **1889** *Century Dict.*, *Gape-eyed*, in *herpet*[*ology*], naked-eyed; having apparently no eyelids: as, the *gape-eyed* skinks.

gaper ('geɪpə(r)). Also 6 *Sc.* -are. [f. prec. + -ER[1].]

1. a. One that gapes; one that stares or gazes in wonder or curiosity.

a **1637** B. JONSON *Discov.* Wks. (Rtldg.) 748/1 The Taberlanes..of the late age, which had nothing in them but the scenicall strutting, and furious vociferation, to warrant them to the ignorant gapers. **1711** ADDISON *Spect.* No. 47 ¶3 The Dutch..hang up..what they call the Sign of the Gaper, that is, the Head of an Idiot dressed in a Cap and Bells, and gaping in a most immoderate manner. **1835** LYTTON *Rienzi* I. ix, The pope's notary hath set up a great picture in the Market-place, and the gapers say it relates to Rome. **1864–5** KNIGHT *Passages Work. Life* II. i. 5 Gapers from the country stood wonderingly upon the Parade.

†**b.** One who gapes or longs for a thing. *Obs.*

1559 *Mirr. Mag.*, *Worcester* xiv, And for my goodes and liuinges wer not small The gapers for them bare the world in hand [etc.]. *a* **1572** KNOX *Hist. Ref.* Wks. 1846 I. 351 Maister Gavine Hammiltoun, gapare for the Bischoprik of Sanctandrois. **1593** Q. ELIZ. tr. *Boeth.* (E.E.T.S.) 9 Paulin the consul..from the gapers [L. *hiantium*] Jawes I drew. **1628** WITHER *Brit. Rememb.* IV. 727 More gapers for the wealth Of such as dy'd.

2. *Ornith.* **a.** The open-bill (see quot. 1871). *rare.* **b.** One of the *Eurylæmidæ*; a broad-bill.

1871 DARWIN *Descent of Man* II. 217 The Gaper (*Anastomus oscitans*) of India. **1884–5** *Riverside Nat. Hist.* (1888) IV. 463 The blue-billed gaper (*Cymbirhynchus macrorhynchus*)..is found in Sumatra and Borneo.

3. (See quots.)

1828–32 WEBSTER (citing *Pennant*, but it is not in P.'s *Brit. Zool.*), *Gaper*, a fish with six or seven bands and tail undivided. [**1861** COUCH *Brit. Fishes* I. 195 From this peculiarity it was that among the Greeks it [*Serranus Cabrilla*] obtained the name of..Channos, or the Gaper.] **1889** *Cent. Dict.*, *Comber*, the *Serranus cabrilla*, also called ..*gaper*.

4. A bivalve mollusc of the family *Myidae*, the shell of which is open at one end: also ***gaper-shell***.

1853 FORBES & HANLEY *Brit. Mollusca* I. 160 *Myadæ.* The Gaper Tribe... The popular appellations of 'Gapers' may be applied to the whole tribe. **1868** WOOD *Homes without H.* v. 98 The common Gaper Shell (*Mya arenaria*), so called because one end of the shell gapes widely.

5. An easy catch in Cricket. *colloq.*

1903 WODEHOUSE *Prefect's Uncle* viii. 117 Seeing you miss a gaper like that right into your hands made me think I was playing stump-cricket with the juniors. **1963** *Times* 7 Feb. 3/3 Certain of the younger members of the side were dropping some regular 'gapers'.

Hence † **'gaperess**, a female gaper.

1660 HEXHAM *Nether-Dutch Dict.*, A woman Gaper or a gapresse.

gape-seed ('geɪpˌsiːd). Also 6–7 **gaping seed**, 7 **gapes-seed**. [f. GAPE *sb.* or *v.* + SEED *sb.*]

1. In sarcastic phrases ***to seek, buy,*** or ***sow gape-seed***: to stare gapingly at a fair or market, instead of transacting useful business.

1598 FLORIO, *Anfanare*.. to go idly loytring vp and downe as we say, to go seeking for a halfepenie worth of gaping seede. **1600** NASHE *Summers Last Will* Wks. (Grosart) VI. 144 If a fellow.. Should all his life time go from faire to faire, And buy gape-seede, hauing no businesse else. **1673** O. WALKER *Educ.* 195 They sow but gape seed which being harvested yields them a goodly crop of wonders. **1694** *Poor Robin* Aug., And by that means.. They for their Gapes-seed do pay dear. **1779** *Koran* I. xl. in *Sterne's Wks.* (Dublin) VI. 81 The nine days wonder had sown its gape-seed long before. The novelty grew stale. **1856** *N. & Q.* 2nd Ser. I. 362 Plenty of persons were 'sowing gape seed' at them. **1877** *N.W. Linc. Gloss.* s.v., 'She's gone to Brigg Stattus to saw gape-seed.'

2. Something stared at by a gaping crowd; also, the act of staring with open mouth.

a **1700** B. E. *Dict. Cant. Crew, Gape-seed*, whatever the gazing Crowd idly stares and gapes after; as Puppet-shows, [etc.] any thing to feed the eye. **1725** in *New Cant. Dict.* **1852** *Q. Rev.* Mar. 431 When was gapeseed ever too gross for gulping asinine cockney curiosity? **1876** MISS YONGE *Womank.* vii. 55 The National Gallery well gone through, and *not* treated as gape-seed, is a key to volumes of art. **1879** *Times* 29 May, Of the French team, Rayon d'Or came in for the most gapeseed.

b. One who stares with open mouth.

1885 *Sportsman* 23 June 2/4 (Farmer) The ring was surrounded by a fairly strong crowd of gapeseeds.

gaping ('geɪpɪŋ), *vbl. sb.* [f. GAPE *v.* + -ING¹.]

1. The action of the verb GAPE in various senses.

c **1374** CHAUCER *Boeth.* II. metr. ii. 24 (Camb. MS.) Crewel rauyne deuowrynge al that thei han getyn sheweth oother gapynges. *c* **1440** *Promp. Parv.* 186/1 Gapynge, *hiatus, hiacio.* **1581** MULCASTER *Positions* xv. (1887) 70 Those.. that be cumbred with much gaping and yawning. **1619** M. BOYLE in *Lismore Papers* Ser. II. (1887) II. 237 In Dublin there is much gapeing at Cashelles death. **1722** DE FOE *Moll Flanders* (1840) 279 The lady-milliner paid dear enough for her gaping after the queen. **1822–34** *Good's Study Med.* (ed. 4) III. 332 The particular kind of pandiculation, to which the first of these movements gives rise being called Oscitancy, Yawning or Gaping. **1870** MORRIS *Earthly Par.* II. III. 287 The painted dragon head that ye note now Grin at Jove's temple door with gapings vain.

2. A deep opening or chasm in the earth. ? *Obs.*

1539 TONSTALL *Serm. Palm Sund.* (1823) 70 Curtius.. was contente for sauyng of the citie of Rome.. to leape into a gapyng of the erth. **1603** KNOLLES *Hist. Turks* (1638) 281 They found such a deep and wide gaping of the rocke betwixt them and the enemy. **1684** T. BURNET *Th. Earth* I. 148 As we shewed before in explaining the chanel of the ocean, it left a gaping in the middle, or an abyss-chanel, as I should call it. *a* **1722** LISLE *Husb.* (1752) 27 There was not a piece of earth to be seen.. but it had large gapings in it.

3. *attrib.*, as † **gaping-seed** (see GAPE-SEED); **gaping-stock**, an object of open-mouthed wonder (cf. *gazing-, laughing-stock*).

1817 GODWIN *Mandeville* II. ii. 40, I was to be a gaping stock and a scorn to all the young volunteers.

gaping ('geɪpɪŋ), *ppl. a.* [f. as prec. + -ING².] That gapes, in various senses of the verb.

1588 SHAKS. *Tit. A.* II. iii. 249 Who art thou that lately did'st descend, Into this gaping hollow of the earth? **1607** TOPSELL *Four-f. Beasts* (1658) 365 He met with a gaping Lion. **1683** KENNETT tr. *Erasm. on Folly* 81 To be deafened with the noise of gaping boys. **1697** DRYDEN *Virg. Georg.* III. 439 Hov'ring there, With gaping Mouths, they draw prolific Air. **1730** SWIFT *Corr.* Wks. 1841 II. 636 We see Cato, and Brutus.. as they really were, and not such as the gaping multitude of their own age took them to be. **1749** JOHNSON *Van. Hum. Wishes* 48 Few know the toiling statesman's fear or care, The insidious rival and the gaping heir. **1854** WOODWARD *Mollusca* II. 246 Bivalves are said to be 'close' when the valves fit accurately, and 'gaping' when they cannot be completely shut. **1872** DARWIN *Emotions* ix. 236 No determined man probably ever had an habitually gaping mouth. **1884** *Public Opinion* 11 July 30/1 The people's representatives are made to stand like gaping fools before the universe.

Comb. **1670** BROOKS *Wks.* (1867) VI. 303 Gaping-mouthed men are noted for fools by Lucian.

Hence **'gapingly** *adv.*, with open mouth; eagerly; amazedly. †Also, with hiatus.

1572 BUCHANAN *Detect. Marie Q. Scottes* G ij, Sche that quhilere gapingly sought for euery small breath of suspicioun against her husband.. of her awne accorde offreth him a louer. **1573–80** BARET *Alv.* B 1341 To coine wordes so in his style that vowels meete together gapingly. **1812** L. HUNT in *Exam.* 14 Dec. 785/1 He has not been accustomed to be.. so gapingly at a loss. **1883** STEVENSON *Silverado Sq.* (1886) 43, I hearkened to it by the hour, gapingly hearkened, and let my cigarette go out.

gapish ('geɪpɪʃ), *a. rare*⁻¹. [f. GAPE *sb.* + -ISH¹.] Having a tendency to gape.

1850 J. STRUTHERS *Autobiog.* vi. Poet. Wks. I. 79 Others, with mouths rather gapish, May be standing stock still.

gapped (gæpt), *ppl. a.* Also 7 **gapt**. [f. GAP *sb.*¹ or *v.* + -ED.]

1. Having the edge notched or serrated.

1562 TURNER *Herbal* II. 110 Cinkfoly.. hath leues lyke minte.. diuided or gapped lyke a saw. **1607** ROWLANDS *Guy, Earl Warw.* 5 His broken Launce, gapt Faulchion, batter'd Shield. **1655** GURNALL *Chr. in Arm.* III. vi–xviii. IX. ii. (1662) 294 If the Workmans Tools be blunt or gapt, no work can be well done, till a new edge be set on them. **1765** STERNE *Tr. Shandy* VIII. xxvii, If Mrs. Wadman had given him a cut with a gap'd knife across his finger. **18..** LOWELL *Kossuth* Poet. Wks. (1879) 101 When gapped and dulled her cheaper tools, Then she a saint or prophet sends.

fig. **1754** RICHARDSON *Grandison* (1781) I. xvii. 111, I will never meet at hard-edge with her; if I did.. I should be confoundedly gapped.

2. Broken through at intervals; full of holes or breaches.

1854 H. MILLER *Sch. & Schm.* (1858) 238 Its bulging walls and gapped roof, that showed the bare ribs through the breaches. **1864** CARLYLE *Fredk. Gt.* IV. 121 Closing its gapped ranks. **18..** TENNYSON *Def. Lucknow* 42 Take aim at their leaders—their masses are gapp'd with our grape.

3. *Mus.* Designating a scale or mode with less than seven notes, esp. the pentatonic scale.

1910 D. MACDONALD *Irish Music* 3 The Ancient Irish used the gapped scale in many of their airs. **1933** *Times Lit. Suppl.* 2 Mar. 139/1 The gaps in the gapped modes are what gives such modal tunes their decisive character. **1962** *Listener* 5 July 37/2 The suggestion of gapped scales.

gappy ('gæpɪ), *a.* [f. GAP *sb.*¹ + -Y¹.] Full of gaps or deficiencies.

1846 *Jrnl. R. Agric. Soc.* VII. II. 377 They will have a weak and gappy crop. **1848** *Ibid.* IX. I. 26 Exceedingly thin or gappy [hedges]. **1885** *Academy* 20 June 433 The text is uncomfortably gappy. **1891** *Sat. Rev.* 25 July 115/1 In a certain limited and gappy sense we should imagine him to be tolerably well read in the most modern literature.

gaps, obs. form of *gapes* pl.: see GAPE *sb.* 3 a.

'gap-stead. *Obs.* exc. *dial.* [f. GAP *sb.*¹ + STEAD *sb.*] An opening in a wall or hedge, left for convenience of passage.

1644 SLINGSBY *Diary* (1836) 132 Making good our ground we became at last masters of theirs, but fain to seek it thro Gapsteads and places of disadvantage. **1651** in *N.W. Linc. Gloss.* (1889) *s.v.*, That the said Lorence make a sufficient yate into the little field and that he raise his gapstead [etc.]. **1876** *Mid. Yorksh. Gloss.* s.v. *Gap*, A gateway is often called a *gapstead*. **1883** *Almondbury Gloss.*, *Gapstead*, an interval in a field wall intended for a gate, or merely used for the passage of cattle.

gap-toothed ('gæpˌtuːθt), *a.* [f. GAP *sb.*¹ + TOOTHED.] Having the teeth set wide apart.

In quot. 1700 substituted for Chaucer's *gat-tothed*.

1567 GOLDING *Ovid's Met.* VIII. 108 b, Where seeking long for Famine she the gaptoothd [**1584–7** gagtoothd] elf did spie. **1577** HELLOWES *Gueuara's Chron.* 121 Antoninus Pius was of an high stature, thicke bearde, white, rare and gap-tothed. **1700** DRYDEN *Fables* Pref., Wks. (Globe) 501 The broad-speaking gap-toothed wife of Bath. **1802** LAMB *Lett.* (1888) I. 193 Those rotten-jawed, gap-toothed, old worn-out chaps of hell. **1842** TENNYSON *Vis. of Sin* 60 A gray and gap-tooth'd man as lean as death. **1886** D. C. MURRAY *1st Pers. Sing.* xviii. 138 Grinning at him with a horrible gap-toothed laugh.

gapy ('geɪpɪ), *a. rare.* Also **gapey**. [f. GAPE *sb.* or *v.* + -Y¹.] **a.** Disposed to yawn. **b.** Of chickens: Affected with the gapes.

1830 MISS MITFORD *Village* Ser. IV. (1863) 249 He was gapy and fidgetty. **1890** *Londsburg Californian* 4 Sept. 6/1 See that every gapey chick eats.

gar (gɑː(r)), *sb.* Also **garr, guard**. [Short f. GARFISH.]

a. A fish of the Pike or Esox family of the genus *Belone*, having long bill-like jaws; the gar-fish or gar-pike.

1765 J. BARTRAM *Jrnl.* 27 Dec. in Stork *Acc. E. Florida* (1766) 10 'Tis full of large fish, as cats, garr, mullets. **1791** W. BARTRAM *Carolina* 145 Alligators and gar were numerous in the bason. **1849** *N.S. Wales*, etc. xi. 99 The best kind of fish are guard, mullet, and schnapper. **1857** R. TOMES *Amer. in Japan* vi. 136 The varieties of fish are not numerous. Among those taken in the seine belonging to the 'Susquehanna', there were.. two varieties of perch, the gar, and the common ray. **1893** *Critic* (U.S.) 7 Jan. 9/1 Thus charming days were passed.. watching gars playing leap-frog with Brer Turtle [etc.].

b. A ganoid fish of the genus *Lepidosteus*, having a similar general form but with rhombic scales. ***alligator-gar***, a gar (*L. tristœchus*) with a head somewhat resembling that of an alligator.

1843 MARRYAT *Mons. Violet* xliv, The alligator gar is sometimes ten feet long. **1885** C. F. HOLDER *Marvels Anim. Life* 32, I have seen the great armoured gar rise again and again for the air.

gar (gɑː(r)), *v.* Chiefly *Sc.* and *north. dial.* Forms: 3–4 **ger**, 4–5 **gere**, 5 **gerre**, 4–7 **gare**, 6–8 **garr(e**, 3– **gar**. [a. ON. *ger(v)a, gør(v)a, gjǫr(v)a, geyra* (Sw. *göra*, Da. *gjöre*) to make, do, etc. = OE. *ʒierwan* (also *ʒearwian*) to prepare (see YARE *v.*), OS. *garuwian, gerwian*, OHG. **garwjan* (recorded form *gar(a)wan*; MHG. *gärwen, gerwen*, mod.G. *gärben, gerben*):—OTeut. **garwjan*, f. the adj. **garwu-* ready = OE. *ʒearo* YARE (cf. GARE *a.*). The orig. sense of the Scand. verb 'to do', 'to make' (something), is rare in Eng. which chiefly employs 'gar' with the meaning 'to cause' (to do or to be done) agreeing with one of the uses of the vb. *make.*]

†**1.** *trans.* To do, perform; to make. *Obs. rare.*

a **1300** *Cursor M.* 13835 Vr halidai noght he for-beres, Bot mani dedes o þaim he geres. **1428** *Surtees Misc.* (1888) 3 And so he gart yarof, als he graunted, ixˣˣ peces & xij. **1457** *Nottingham Rec.* II. 366 For garyng of iij. mals and nels. *c* **1460** *Towneley Myst.* (E.E.T.S.) iv. 104 Thi lufly chere makis my hert glad, And many a tyme so has it gart. **1662** *Kinross Witch Trial* in *Proc. Soc. Antiq. Scot.* (1888) 231 He, being leading his father's peats.. throo a heap of the said Janet Paton's muck, the said Janet said she should gar him alse good.

2. To make, to cause, in various constructions. **a.** with simple *object*: To cause, to occasion. *rare.*

c **1460** *Towneley Myst.* (E.E.T.S.) ii. 44 Gog gif the sorow, boy; want of mete it gars. **1590** LODGE *Euphues' Gold. Leg.* in Halliw. *Shaks.* VI. 67 Alas, said he, what garres thy grief? *a* **1592** GREENE *Jas. IV*, I. Wks. (Rtldg.) 195/2 What gars this din of mirk and baleful harm. **1855** ROBINSON *Whitby Gloss.*, *Gar*, to cause, to compel. 'It gars me great pain.'

b. with *object* and *active inf.* (*to* usually omitted): To make or cause *one* to *do* something, etc.

a **1300** *Cursor M.* 17160 (Gött.) Oft þu geris mi wondis blede. *a* **1340** HAMPOLE *Psalter* xix. 8 [xx. 7] Proude horsis þat will stumbill & gere vs breke oure neke. **1377** LANGL. *P. Pl.* B. xx. 56 He cutte awey treuthe, And gert gyle growe þere. *c* **1420** *Lay Folks Mass Bk.*, *York Hours* 43 þai.. gerte hym bere on his bak þe cros. **15..** *Chevy Chase* ii. 15 in *Percy's Rel.*, Many a doughete the garde to dy. **1535** STEWART *Cron. Scot.* II. 310 Fals Fortoun.. makis him to fall Doun fra the hicht, garrand him licht so law. **1589** PEELE *Eclog.* I. Wks. (Rtldg.) 561/1 Herdgroom, what gars thy pipe to go so loud? *a* **1670** SPALDING *Troub. Chas. I* (1829) 9 The earl.. resolves to gar one devil ding another. **1724** RAMSAY *Tea-t. Misc.* (1733) I. 101 My dady was harsh, My minny was warse, That gart him gae yont the sea. **1790** BURNS *Tam O'Shanter* 123 He screw'd the pipes and gart them skirl. **1816** SCOTT *Antiq.* ix, But ye like to gar folk look like fools. **1878** *Cumbld. Gloss*, *Gar*, to compel. 'A'll gar tha gang.' **1894** CROCKETT *Lilac Sunbonnet* 68 A dinnle in the elbuck that garred ye loup like a troot.

†**c.** with *object* and *inf. pass.*: To cause something to be done; to have something done. *Obs.*

a **1300** *Cursor M.* 4870 Pharaon, þat all his chaf can gar be don. *c* **1350** *Will. Palerne* 2793 Greue þe nouȝt for goddes loue þat gart þe be fourmed. *c* **1400** MAUNDEV. (Roxb.) iii. 8 Saynt Anne.. wham saynt Helene gert be broght fra Ierusalem. **1469** *Plumpton Corr.* 21 Also that you gar the malt be windowd. *c* **1489** CAXTON *Sonnes of Aymon* xxvi. 567, I shall gare theym bothe to be hanged. **1549** *Compl. Scot.* 2 The actis that ȝour prudens garris daly be execut. **1585** JAS. I *Ess. Poesie* (Arb.) 50 Mount heigh vp through the air, To gar thy heat and beames be law and neir.

†**d.** with *inf.* (rarely preceded by *to*) simply: ***to gar do, make***, etc.: To cause to be done, made, etc. *Obs.*

c **1330** R. BRUNNE *Chron.* (1810) 64 Ageyn þe erle Godwyn he gert sette assise. **1393** LANGL. *P. Pl.* C. VI. 147 Gregorie þe grete clerk gart write in bokes The ruele of alle religious. **1429** *Test. Ebor.* (Surtees) 420 Labour that he sall do and gar do for me. **1470–85** MALORY *Arthur* II. vi, He garte to vnarme hym and bete hym with thornys. *Ibid.* XX. xvi, I wylle founde & gar make an hows of relygyon. *c* **1500** *Lancelot* 2416 Euery thyng that In yhour myster lyis, I sall gar ordan at yhour awn dewys. **1570** BUCHANAN *Chamæleon* Wks. (1892) 47 He sollicitat some previe men gar hang hir. *a* **1615** *Cron. Erlis of Ross* (1850) 20 He gart bigg two stone barns.

†**3.** To cause to go, to drive. *Obs. rare.*

1586 J. HOOKER *Chron. Irel.* in Holinshed II. 179/1 The erle.. had not beene heard of since he was garred out of Harlo wood. **1611** L. BARRY *Ram Alley* v. in Hazl. *Dodsley* X. 363 By heaven I'll gar my whinyard through your womb!

4. Wrongly used for: To be amiss with, to ail.

1614 J. DAVIES *Eglog. Willie & Wernocke* 8 What gars my Willy that he so doth wane? **1640** *King & Poor North. Man* 209 in Hazl. *E.P.P.* IV. 301 What gares these babes and babies all? Some ill have they done that they hang by the walls?

gar (gɑː(r)), *int.* = GAD.

1598 [see BEGAR]. **1877** BESANT & RICE *Harp & Cr.* iv. 29 Gar! If I could crush him to powder beneath my feet.

†**garabee.** *Obs. rare.* ? = GAD-BEE.

1692 HICKERINGILL *Good Old Cause* 28 Like Beasts stung with a Garabee or Hornet. *Ibid.* 29. **1702** C. MATHER *Magn. Chr.* VII. vi. §12. 52/1 They were just like Beasts that are stung with a Garabee, or Hornet; they ran they knew not whither.

Garagantua, -an: see GARGANTUA, -AN.

garage ('gærɑːʒ, 'gærɪdʒ), *sb.* [F. *garage*, f. *garer* to shelter.] **1. a.** A building, either private or public, intended for the storage and shelter of motor vehicles while not in use. **b.** A commercial establishment that sells petrol, oil, and similar products and freq. also undertakes the repair and servicing of motor vehicles. Also *attrib.* and *Comb.*

1902 *Daily Mail* 11 Jan. 6/7 The new 'garage' founded by Mr. Harrington Moore, hon. secretary of the Automobile Club... The 'garage', which is situated at the City end of Queen Victoria-street,.. has accommodation for eighty cars.

1902 *Times* 1 Mar. 4/3 Motor Garage. **1902** A. C. Harmsworth et al. *Motors* 65 The simplification of the motor engine and the establishment of *garages*. *Ibid.* 306 In stations or 'garages' where a number of cars are kept. **1909** *Westm. Gaz.* 13 Apr. 4/2 A Midland firm of garage proprietors. *Ibid.* 18 Nov. 5/3 Customers who need garage room for business and private vehicles. **1934** P. A. Reynolds *Garage Organiz. & Managem.* i. 4 The third type of garage is..the Full Service business, which caters, in addition to the services already mentioned, for repairs of every description. **1940** C. S. Lewis *Let.* 1 Jan. (1966) 174 Garage-hands and motor touts. **1958** [see forecourt]. **1965** *New Society* 11 Nov. 8/3 Whether it is garage or street parking or car ports..most people want their cars conveniently near their homes... The garage court is sometimes advanced as a compromise. **1971** 'H. Calvin' *Poison Chasers* i. 9 The garage man..had come into the public bar. **1971** *Oxford Times* 3 Dec. 24 (Advt.), Excellently maintained detached freehold House... Separate access to brick garage.

2. A hangar for the storage of aircraft. (Disused.)

1909 A. Berget *Conquest of Air* II. vii. 280 The construction of *garages*, landing stations and shelters.

3. Special Comb. **garage sale** *U.S.*, a sale of unwanted used goods and possessions, usu. held (in the garage of) a private house; cf. *yard sale* s.v. yard *sb.*[1] 6 (*c*).

1966 *Daily Union* (Sacramento) *Family Weekly Mag.* 17 July 12/2 A couple..held a *garage sale on three consecutive weekends and..sold out..countless items. **1982** *Chicago Sun-Times* 21 Sept. 16/1 You can sell just about anything at a garage sale—including bowling trophies or a single boxing glove—if you know how.

garage ('gærɑːʒ, 'gærɪdʒ), *v.* [f. prec.] *trans.* To place (a motor vehicle) in a garage for storage or repairs; to accommodate (a motor vehicle) at a garage. Also *absol.*

1906 *Daily Chron.* 26 May 3/7 They will garage your car .., wash it, clean it, adjust it, repair it, keep it always at 'concert pitch'. **1907** (*title*) Where to garage. **1928** Galsworthy *Swan Song* vii. 55 Having garaged his car, he remembered that he had not lunched. **1972** *Daily Tel.* 3 Feb. 15/3 We hope it will not be too long before Mr Hayward can..garage his car.

Hence **'garaging** *vbl. sb.*, garage accommodation.

1926 *Glasgow Herald* 23 Mar. 9 One or two of the great London stores which had provided garaging for the use of their customers. **1936** *Evening Standard* 30 May 14/1 To save himself 7s. 6d. a week garaging. **1968–9** *A.A. Continental Handbk.* 375/2 There are facilities for garaging, minor repairs, and refuelling.

garagist ('gærɑːʒɪst). Also ‖**garagiste.** [Fr. *garagiste.*] The owner or proprietor of a commercial garage; an employee of a garage.

1928 *Observer* 11 Mar. 12/2 The wayside garagist who sold the tins of petrol. **1958** *Spectator* 22 Aug. 247/3 The can was filled up by an Old Etonian *garagiste.* **1961** P. Ustinov *Loser* iv. 71 The local mechanic and only garagist for kilometers round. **1967** *Punch* 20 Sept. 426/1, I had not expected to meet with so much opposition and dismay when I casually mentioned my intention to the garagists. **1967** *Observer* (Colour Suppl.) 22 Oct. 33/3, I arrived at a French garage..one night and announced that the engine was falling out. The *garagiste* greeted the news with the tired smile of those accustomed to dealing with the ignorant.

garamity, var. gor-amity.

Garamond ('gærəmɒnd). *Typogr.* [f. the name of Claude *Garamond* (died 1561), a French typefounder.] Any of a class of typefaces cut by Garamond or based on his design or that of Jean Jannon. Also *attrib.*

[**1780** *Encycl. Brit.* V. 3178/2 The small Roman was, by way of excellence, known among the printers of these nations by the name of *Garamond's small Roman.*] **1868** H. N. Humphreys *Hist. Art Printing* ix. 144 The small Roman letters of this skilful engraver became technically known, not only in France, but in other countries, as Garamond type. **1926** 'P. Beaujon' in *Fleuron* V. 160 The seventeenth century..produced..[a] roman and italic *derived* from Garamont's designs..which..survives as the 'original Garamond'... There can be little doubt that this is the design of Jean Jannon, dating from 1615. **1928** *Scholartis Press Catal.* June, Printed by the Westminster Press in 14 point Garamond. **1929** *Encycl. Brit.* XVIII. 509/2 The 'Garamond' type steadily acquired influence. **1931** *Times Lit. Suppl.* 25 June, Suppl. p. i/3, The brilliant Garamond setting for Louys' 'Roi Pausole'. *Ibid.* p. i/4 Jules Meynial shows..a catalogue well printed in handset Garamond. **1962** D. B. Updike *Printing Types* (ed. 3) II. xxiii. 234 While the Cloister or the Garamond—both brought out by the American Type Founders Company—may not be absolutely necessary to an office, a type of this historic class should be selected. **1966** H. Williamson *Methods Bk. Design* (ed. 2) viii. 85 The Garamond series was the first in the ambitious programme of matrix production undertaken by Monotype in 1922. *Ibid.*, Jannon, at the outset of his career, used Garamond types, and although he based his design on them it was new in several ways.

‖**garance** (garɑ̃s). [Fr., see garancin.] = garancin.

1896 [see free-board 2]. **1931** *Times Lit. Suppl.* 22 Jan. 56/3 Names of the dyes and juices..garance and arzica.

garancin ('gærənsɪn). *Chem.* Also -ine. [a. F. *garancine*, f. *garance* madder: see -in.] A dyeing substance obtained from madder.

1843 F. Steiner *Patent* in Ure *Dict. Arts* (1853) I. 841 Garancine. **1872** Oliver *Elem. Bot.* II. 190 Garancine.. prepared from Madder by the action of sulphuric acid.

garand, -ante, -end, var. guarand, *Obs.*, guarantee.

†**garant, geraud.** *Obs. rare*—[1]. Blundered readings in the Eng. versions of Mandeville for OF. *geracites*, ad. L. *hierācītēs* (Pliny) 'a stone of the colour of a hawk's neck'.

c **1400** Maundev. (1839) xx. 220 Many Clustres of Grapes ..alle of precious Stones..the blake ben of Onichez and Garantez. *Ibid.* (Roxb.) xxiii. 107 geraudes [F. *geracites*].

garaus, -ausse, obs. ff. carouse.

garavanca, -ance, -anza, obs. ff. calavance.

1628 Digby *Voy. Medit.* (1868) 75 All six were laden with wheate, garauanzas and cheese. **1699** in *Misc. Cur.* (1708) III. 391 They eat parched Garavancas, parched Almonds, and Beans. **1770** Franklin *Let. to J. Bartram* 11 Jan. in Darlington *Mem. Bartram* (1849) 404, I send..also some Chinese Garavances.

garb (gɑːb), *sb.*[1] Also 6–7 **garbe.** [a. ONF. *garbe* (Central OF. *jarbe*, mod.F. *gerbe*) = Cat. and Sp. *garba*; of Teut. origin; cf. the synonymous OHG. *garba* (mod.G. *garbe*), OS. *garba, garva* (Du. *garve, garf*).

On the assumption that the primary sense of OTeut. **garbâ-*, as of the equivalent L. *manipulus*, was 'handful', it is usually referred to the Aryan root **ghrebh-* (Skr. *grbh*, to grasp, OSl. *grabiti* to seize, Lettish *grâb-t* to grasp).]

1. A wheat-sheaf. *Obs.* exc. *Her.* (see quot. 1882).

1502 Arnolde *Chron.* (1811) 210 Noo forestir fro henceforth or bayli make scotal or gadir garbe or otes or any corne..but be the sight and othe of xij. regarders. **1572** Bossewell *Armorie* II. 108 The Garbe is of the Sonne royally supported with two Lyons. **1610** Guillim *Heraldry* III. ix. (1611) 112 There is a kind of wretched cormorants whose Garbs are so fast bound that the poor curseth their mercilesse hearts. *a* **1661** Fuller *Worthies, Cheshire* I. (1662) 171 The Cheshire Gentry were good house-keepers, because they gave so many wheat-sheaves..in their Coats of Armes. Indeed I have told no fewer then six and twenty, called *Garbs* in Herauldry, which are born in the several Coat-Armours of the Gentry of this County. **1763** *Brit. Mag.* IV. 189 A garb, or, supported by two lions. **1844** A. Page *Suppl. Kirby's Suffolk Trav.* 901 Vernon: or; on a fess, azure, three garbs of the first. **1882** Cussans *Her.* vi. (ed. 3) 106 A more frequent Charge is a Sheaf of Wheat, called a Garb..When a Garb is of any grain other than wheat, it must be mentioned; as, a *Garb of Oats*, &c. Sometimes the straw is of a different tincture from the ears, as *a Garb vert, eared or.* Garbs are usually *or.*

2. *Comb.*: **garb-tithe.**

c **1630** Risdon *Surv. Devon* §42 (1810) 45 The garb tythes and spiritual profits of the manor.

garb (gɑːb), *sb.*[2] Also 6–7 **garbe.** [ad. (directly or through the 16th c. F. *garbe*, now *galbe*) It. *garbo* (= Sp., Pg. *garbo*) grace, elegance; of Teut. origin: cf. OHG. *garawî* preparation, adornment (and the cognates cited s.v. gear).]

†**1.** Grace, elegance, stylishness of manners or appearance. [= F. *galbe*, It. *garbo.*] *Obs.*

1591 Lyly *Endym.* II. ii. 24 *Dares.* If you be good wenches make as though you loue him, and wonder at him. *Fauil.* We will doe our parts. *Dares.* But first let vs stand aside, and let him vse his garbe, for all consisteth in his gracing. **1603** Florio *Montaigne* III. v. 537 Surely it's [love's] course hath more garbe [F. *galbe*], when it is commixt with vnaduisednesse and trouble. **1656** Blount *Glossogr.*, *Garbo*, a garbe, comeliness, gracefulness or good fashion. **1670** Lassels *Voy. Italy* I. 211 Find the house open to all comers and goers both Ladyes and gentlemen, that are of any garbe [cf. p. 152 Coaches double lined with Ladyes and Gentlemen of Garbo].

†**b.** Grace of outline; elegant curvature. [So It. *garbo*, F. *galbe.*] *Obs.*

1613–39 I. Jones in Leoni *Palladio's Archit.* (1742) II. 43 The putting of the under Boultel and Casement with their several Centers as this here is, hath only the Measure-case but not the Garb.

†**2.** A person's outward bearing, behaviour, carriage, or demeanour. *Obs.*

1605 B. Jonson *Volpone* IV. i, First, for your garb, it must be grave and serious, Very reserv'd and lock'd; not tell a secret On any terms, not to your father. *a* **1661** Fuller *Worthies, Surrey* III. (1662) 82 So graceful is their Garbe, that they make any kind of Cloathes become themselves. **1703** Rowe *Ulyss.* I. i. 299 This sullen Garb, this moody Discontent.

†**3.** Style, manner, fashion; manner of doing anything, style of living, form of behaviour. Also, a prevailing 'mode' or custom, 'the fashion'. *Obs.*

1599 Shaks. *Hen. V*, v. i. 80 You thought, because he could not speake English in the natiue garb, he could not therefore handle an English Cudgell. **1599** B. Jonson *Ev. Man out of Hum.* IV. iv, His seniors give him good slight looks, After their garbe. **1618** Bolton *Florus* (1636) 71 Carrying himselfe..overloftily, and above the garbe of a fellow-citizen. **1642** Fuller *Holy & Prof. St.* II. vi. 72 Others..use some obsolete garb in their garments, gestures, or discourse. **1647** W. Browne tr. *Gomberville's Polexander* II. 48 In a very ill garbe she returned my complements. **1668** *Leather-more or Advice conc. Gaming* (ed. 2) 8 A young fellow..had by strange Fortune runne up a very small summe to fifteen hundred pounds, and put himself into a Garb accordingly, could not give over, plaid on..lost it all, run mad, and so dyed. **1694** Evelyn *Diary* 22 Apr., The younger son..lived in the garb and equipage of the richest nobleman.

†**b.** Fashion, make, sort (in quot. 1599 with allusion to garb *sb.*[1]; cf. L. *ejusdem farinæ*).

1599 B. Jonson *Ev. Man out of Hum.* II. i, I am so haunted at the court, and at my lodging with your refined choice spirits, that it makes me clean of another garb, another sheaf, I know not how! **1605** Carew in *Lett. Lit. Men* (Camden) 99 Wee may still enrich our language with others [words] of the like garbe.

4. Fashion of dress, esp. official or other distinctive dress; hence *concr.* dress, costume.

1622 Peacham *Compl. Gent.* xv. 191 Be thriftie also in your apparrell and clothing..vsing that moderate and middle garbe, which shall rather lessen then make you bigger then you are. *a* **1625** Fletcher *Love's Pilgr.* I. i, In hose and doublet, The horse-boy's garb. **1727** A. Hamilton *New Acc. E. Ind.* II. xxxvi. 50 Their bodily Garb is a Frock of Cotton Cloth. **1756** C. Lucas *Ess. Waters* III. 260 He is stripped of his wet garb. **1771** Mackenzie *Man Feel.* xxviii. (1803) 48 A man entered, in the garb of an officer. **1789** Mrs. Piozzi *Journ. France* I. 409 Many gentlemen wear black as the court garb. **1835** Thirlwall *Greece* I. vii. 275 He went out at the gate, disguised in a woodman's garb. **1843** Lever *J. Hinton* xviii, I wished to be a soldier in more than the mere garb.

b. *transf.* and *fig.*

1667 Milton *P.L.* II. 226 Words cloath'd in reasons garb. *a* **1745** Swift *Wks.* (1841) II. 137 This [weeping] may prove to be no more than the very garb and outward dress of a contrite heart. **1758** *Monthly Rev.* 618 These books were.. precious..notwithstanding their torn and mouldy garb. **1833** N. Arnott *Physics* (ed. 5) II. 126 The earth..soon becomes covered..with its thick garb of green. **1859** Masson *Brit. Novelists* i. 9 Heroic themes..invested with the garb of verse. **1877** Black *Green Past.* vii. He had for the moment thrown off his customary garb of indifference or cynicism.

5. *Comb.*: †**garb-master,** one who professes the art of polite behaviour.

1599 B. Jonson *Cynthia's Rev.* v. ii, You see he has played down your grand garb-master, here.

Hence **'garbless** *a.*, without clothing.

1838 *New Monthly Mag.* LII. 117 He..bade thee ride at noon our city through, Garbless and guardless.

garb (gɑːb), *v.* [f. prec. sb.] *trans.* To cover with a garb, to clothe, dress.

1846 Hawthorne *Mosses* II. i. 11 Thus garbed they go in search of new discoveries. *a* **1851** Moir *Poems, Shadow Truth* ii, Garb'd in white Religion's robes. **1875** Tennyson *Q. Mary* III. i, These black dog-Dons Garb themselves bravely. **1888** L. Hearn in *Harper's Mag.* LXXVII. 215/2 Women..very simply, almost savagely, garbed.

b. *dial.* Also with *out.* (See quots.)

1868 Atkinson *Cleveland Gloss.*, *Garb*, to bedeck, array in a gaudy fashion; almost invariably implying tasteless or vulgar finery. **1876** *Whitby Gloss.*, *Garb out*, to dress for display. 'Desperately garb'd out' outrageously fine.

c. *fig.*

1836 J. H. Newman in *Lyra Apost.* (1849) 51 The rich earth, garbed in its daintiest dress Of light and joy. **1848** Lytton *Harold* VIII. vi, The boughs the leaves had garbed. **1856** Dobell *Eng. in Time of War*, '*The Rain is on the Roof*,' To garb with joy The naked soul of Grief.

Hence **garbed** *ppl. a.*, dressed (in a specified fashion); **'garbing** *vbl. sb.*

1599 Nashe *Lenten Stuffe* 25 A treatise as bigge garb'd as the french Academy. **1673** R. Head *Canting Acad.* 100 He being always well garbed. **1887** *Daily Tel.* 3 May 5/7 The Academy galleries held a variously garbed crowd. **1889** *Cornhill Mag.* 219, I complete my hasty garbing under his eyes.

garbage ('gɑːbɪdʒ), *sb.* Forms: 6–8 **garbidge, -ish(e,** (6 **garbadge, -edge, garvage**), 5– **garbage.** [Of obscure origin; prob. adopted from AF., like many other words found in early cookery books. Derivation from OF. *garbe* sheaf is probable for sense 4, and possible for the other senses.]

1. The offal of an animal used for food; esp. the entrails. Rarely, the entrails of a man.

c **1430** *Two Cookery bks.* I. 9 Take fayre garbagys of chykonys, as þe hed, þe fete, þe lyuerys, an þe gysowrys. **1530** Palsgr. 224/1 Garbage of a foule, *petitoye.* **1573–80** Baret *Alv.* B. 1071 To pulle out the garbishe or guttes of a thing. **1638** Ford *Fancies* IV. i, Rotten in thy maw, thy guts and garbage! **1664** Butler *Hud.* II. iii. 31 Augury, That out of Garbages of Cattel Presag'd th' events of Truce or Battel. **1682** *Weekly Mem.* 255 The blood, bowels, and the other garbish are taken out. **1707** Mortimer *Husb.* 86 In New-found-land they improve their Ground with the Garbish of Fish. **1728** R. North *Mem. Musick* (1846) 60 These people made no scruple of handling gutts and garbages. **1843** Borrow *Bible in Spain* 322 The carrion vulture..disputing with the brutes the garbage.

2. Refuse in general; filth. †Also used for garble *sb.*[1]

1583 Stanyhurst *Æneis* III. (Arb.) 77 With ramd cramd garbadge, theire gorges draftye be gulled. **1615** G. Sandys *Trav.* 240 This fountaine was said to grow thicke, and sauour of garbidge, at such time as they celebrated the Olympiads. **1625** Purchas *Pilgrims* II. 1783 Cloues.. whensoeuer they are made cleane, and seperated from their garbish. **1776** Adam Smith *W. N.* I. viii. (1869) I. 75 They [the Chinese] are eager to fish up the nastiest garbage thrown overboard. **1887** *Spectator* 9 July 621/1 The river was the receptacle of the garbage and sewage of these domiciles.

3. *fig.* Chiefly in the sense of worthless or foul literary matter.

1592 Nashe *P. Penilesse* (ed. 2) 39 a, Let not your shops be infected with anie such..stinking garbadge. **1606** Day *Ile of Guls* I. i. (1881) 11 Almes-basket-scraps, the very fall and garbidge of gentry. **1759** Grainger tr. *Sulpicia's Poems* ix. 6 Rare Taste, and worthy of a Poet's Brain, To prey on Garbage. **1803** Jane Porter *Thaddeus* xxii. (1831) 194 She flew with voracious appetite to sate herself on the garbage of any circulating library. **1812** D'Israeli *Calam. Auth.* (1867)

135 The public appetite..afterwards indignantly rejected the palatable garbage. **1882** Miss Braddon *Mt. Royal* III. vi. 124 Any garbage is food for a woman's vanity.

†**4.** (See quots.) *Obs.* [cf. dial. F. *gerbée, garbée* used in a similar sense (see Godefroy *s.v.*).]

1526 *Househ. Ord.* (1790) 206 All such horses..to be substantially served according to their allowance..in Hay, Garbage, and Litter. **1617** Markham *Caval.* I. 6 That which Horsemen call garbadge, which is wheate strawe and the eares, chopt small together. **1887** *Kent Gloss., Garbage*, a sheaf of corn, Latin *garba*; a cock of hay; a fagot of wood, or any other bundle of the..fruits of the earth.

5. *attrib.* and *Comb.*, as ***garbage-barrel, -box, can, collection, collector, disposal, -inspector*** (all chiefly N. Amer.); **garbage disposal unit** (or **disposer**), a device, usually fitted to the waste-pipe of a kitchen-sink, which grinds up and disposes of small amounts of kitchen waste, esp. the remains of food.

1889 *Century Mag.* Sept. 750/1 Judges, lawyers, and notaries out of whose professional *garbage barrel he enjoyed a..privilege of feeding! **1882** Sala *Amer. Revis.* (1885) 175 The *garbage-boxes or ash-barrels..are still the same unsightly..nuisances. **1906** *N.Y. Even. Post* 23 Aug. 2 The landlords are not providing the tenants with *garbage and ash cans. **1914** Kipling *Lett. of Travel* (1920) 231 Every conceivable subject from the disposal of a garbage-can to that of a corpse. **1967** E. M. Noblet in *Coast to Coast 1965–6* 164 A pitiless tipping into the street of the.. garbage-can contents of human lives. **1911** *Daily Colonist* (Victoria, B.C.) 20 Apr. 6/3 The new system of *garbage collection will be inaugurated as soon as a sufficient number of garbage cans are secured. **1968** *Globe & Mail* (Toronto) 3 Feb. 10/6 Other services such as mail, transportation and garbage collection have come to a halt. **1924** *Collier's* 19 Jan. 19/3 They determine whether the *garbage collector or the street cleaner is responsible for the removal of dead cats from blind alleys. **1953** *Manch. Guardian Weekly* 8 Oct. 5 City garbage collectors had been especially indolent. **1900** *Engineering Mag.* XIX. 732 *Garbage disposal and water supply. **1949** *Official Gaz.* (U.S. Pat. Off.) 6 Sept. 73/1 Electrically-driven, *Garbage Disposal Unit. **1954** *Good Housek. Home Encycl.* 113/1 An electric garbage disposal unit can be fitted into the waste-pipe of some sinks. **1958** *Times* 13 Jan. 11/2 There is a garbage disposal unit for attachment to the sink which will eliminate all food waste such as small bones, vegetable scraps and peelings, fibrous material. **1940** S. Lewis *Bethel Merriday* xxiv. 245 We're paying for..the new electric *garbage disposer. **1896** *Daily News* 3 June 4/1 The responsible, if not dignified post, of *garbage inspector.

†**garbage** (ˈgɑːbɪdʒ), *v. Obs.* Forms: see the sb.; also 6 **garbaige**. [f. prec. sb.]

1. *trans.* To disembowel; to remove the offal from; to gut (fish).

1542 Udall *Erasm. Apoph.* II. 161 His cooke found the same ryng in the bealy of a fishe which he garbaiged to dresse for his Lordes dyner. **1601** Weever *Mirr. Mart.* C iij, Men departed, Bowel'd, puld out, and garbisht euery day. **1610** Holland *Camden's Brit.* I. 186 Pilchards..are there taken, garbaged, salted, hanged in the smoke. **1672** Josselyn *New Eng. Rarities* 8 A Turkie Cock, that when he was pull'd and garbidg'd, weighed thirty pound.

2. *intr.* To feed on offal. In quot. *fig.*

1650 A. Niccholes *Disc. Marr. & Wiving* vii. in *Harl. Misc.* (1744) II. 152 Lust..will garbadge without all Respect, or Controul, upon Adultery, Fornication [etc.].

†**ˈgarbager.** *Obs.* [perh. AF.; f. garbage *sb.* + -er[2].] In ***serjeant garbager***: an officer of the royal kitchen, who had charge of the poultry.

1601 F. Tate *Househ. Ord. Edw. II*, §52 (1876) 36 A serjant garbager of the kitchin..shal receve the pullaine.. and scald them.

garbanzo (gɑːˈbænzəʊ). Also 8 **garvanzo**. [Sp.: see calavance.] The chick-pea, *Cicer arietinum*.

1759 tr. *Venegas's Nat. & Civ. Hist. Calif.* I. 45 The same success attended the experiments made with..garvanzo, or a kind of pease. **1841** G. Borrow *Zincali* I. vi. 104 A puchéra, the ingredients of which were beef, bacon, garbanzos, and berdolaga. **1918** *Chambers's Jrnl.* Jan. 33 The fat Castilian garbanzos. **1925** *Glasgow Herald* 31 July 6 These garbanzos or chichis give the peculiar flavour to soups. **1933** H. Allen *Anthony Adverse* VIII. lxi. 998 The ever-present garbanzo or chick-pea. **1950** C. S. Forester *Mr. Midshipman Hornblower* 275 To taste salt beef and biscuit again, and never again to taste beans and garbanzos.

garbe, garbedge, obs. ff. garb, garbage.

garbel-: see garble-.

garbell, obs. form of garboard.

[**garb-feathers.** Error for *barb feathers* (see barb *sb.*[1] 2).

[**1486** *Bk. St. Albans* bj, The federis vnder the beke be calde the barbe federis.] **1676–1732** Coles *Garbe feders*, the Feathers under a Hawk's beak. **1721–92** Bailey, Garbe feeders [*sic*.]. **1848** Halliwell, *Garb feathers*, the feathers under the bill of a hawk (citing *Berners*, i.e. quot. 1486).]

garbidge, garbish, obs. forms of garbage.

†**garbist.** *Obs. rare.* [f. garb *sb.*[2] + -ist.] One who is skilled in polite behaviour.

1640 Brome *Sparagus Garden* iv. x, Yes, this is backsword Complement: this wipes off the false praise which the first thrust on: you must bee seene in both, or you are no true garbist else.

garblable, obs. form of garbleable.

garblage (ˈgɑːb(ə)lɪdʒ). In 8 **garblage**, 9 *Hist.* **garbellage**. [f. garble *v.* + -age.] **a.** The duty or province of a garbler. †**b.** The refuse that has to be garbled or taken out of any commodity. *Obs.*

1727 A. Hamilton *New Acc. E. Ind.* II. xliii. 120 We seldom find less than 10 or 12 per cent. Garblage. **1829** Heath *Grocers' Comp.* (1869) 60 Any merchant who should ..sell spices, or other merchandize belonging to garbellage.

garble (ˈgɑːb(ə)l), *sb.* Also 6–7 **garbell, -byll.** [prob. ad. It. *garbello* (whence F. *grabeau*, which has had all the Eng. senses), f. *garbellare* to garble.]

†**1.** Refuse (of spices); extraneous matter. *Obs.*

1502 Arnolde *Chron.* (1811) 234 The garbyll of macis. **1603–4** *Act 1 Jas. I*, c. 19 §2 If any the said Spices..shall be mixed with any Garbles..after..the same shalbe first garbled..by the Garbler thereunto appointed. **1640** in Entick *London* II. 175 Garble of cloves, of Almonds. **1721** Bailey, *Garbles*, the Dust, Soil or Filth, separated by garbling. **1809** R. Langford *Introd. Trade* 132 *Garble*, the refuse from spices, drugs, &c.

†**2.** Merchandise containing an admixture of refuse or waste. *Obs.*

1618 Dalton *Country Just.* 116 Euery thing which beareth the name of Garbell, and whereof issueth a refuse, or waste. **1638** Penkethman *Artach.* D 8 Pitch, tarre, hempe ..allome, wooll, silke and all other things that beare the name of Garbell and doe yeeld a refuse or waste.

b. A mixture of base and precious metal; = alloy 5.

1839 Ure *Dict. Arts* etc. 1058 The acid must be boiled on the granulated garble, or alloy, to effect the solution of the silver. **1868** in E. Seyd *Bullion & For. Exch.* 190.

3. The process of garbling, in various senses.

1808 Wolcott (P. Pindar) *To Nollekens* Wks. 1816 IV. 410 Did not the lady smile upon the garble [*i.e.* the mutilation of a statue]. **1829** Heath *Grocers' Comp.* (1854) 60 The officer..was sworn..to observe that the garble of merchants goods should be impartial.

garble (ˈgɑːb(ə)l), *v.* Also 6–7 **garbel.** [App. originally a term of Mediterranean commerce, ad. It. *garbellare*, ad. Arab. *gharbala* (also *karbala*) to sift, select, related to *ghirbāl, kirbāl*, sieve; cf. Sp. *garbillare* to sift corn, *garbillo* corn-sieve. The It. word was adopted also in Fr.; the pa. pple. *garbellé* occurs in a quot. given by Godefr. erroneously s.v. *gerbele*; from 16th c. the vb. appears as *grabeler*.

The twofold form of the Arab. words shows that they are not of native formation; a probable source has been found in the late L. *crībellare*, f. *crībellum* dim. of *crībrum* sieve.]

†**1.** *trans.* To remove the garble or refuse from (spice, etc.); to sift, cleanse (const. *of*); also, to sift *out*. *Obs.*

1599 Hakluyt *Voy.* II. 177 [At Alexandria] all sortes of spices be garbled after the bargaine is made. **1619** in *Crt. & Times Jas. I* (1849) II. 172 He hath granted..four-pence halfpenny upon every chaldron of sea coal, to see they may be better garbled or cleansed. **1657** R. Ligon *Barbadoes* (1673) 79 We fall all a Coughing, which lasts..as long as we are garbling it [red pepper]. **1687** *Phil. Trans.* XVI. 503 They..will crumble into Grains, and the Wings separate from them, which must be garbled out. **1722** De Foe *Moll Flanders* (1840) Pref. 12 The whole relation is carefully garbled of all its levity and looseness. **1789** Saunders in *Phil. Trans.* LXXIX. 107 Seed lac is only the stick lac broke into small pieces, garbled, and appearing in a granulated form. **1812** J. Smyth *Pract. Customs* (1821) 65 Cochineal may be screened and garbled in the presence of the proper officers.

2. To select or sort out the best in (any thing or set of things); to take the pick of. Now *rare* exc. in ***to garble the coinage***. Also with *out*.

1483 [see garbling *vbl. sb.*]. **1630** J. Taylor (Water P.) *Wit & Mirth* Wks. II. 176 Wit and Mirth.. Apothegmatically bundled vp and garbled at the request of old John Garret's Ghost. **1660** tr. *Amyraldus' Treat. conc. Relig.* II. 177 Why did not Cicero garble [Fr. orig. *esplucher*] all those different Opinions..to frame a good one if possible? *a* **1661** Fuller *Worthies* (1840) II. 344 A privilege ..to garble the live pigs in the markets of the city. **1708** Ozell tr. *Boileau's Lutrin* v. 90 Each Glutton hunts, and garbles out Nice Bits. **1720** *Stow's Surv. Lond.* (ed. Strype) II. 239/2 To prevent this Office of garbling Wools, the Haberdashers interposed. **1814** W. Taylor in *Monthly Rev.* LXXIV. 308 It has been found necessary to garble his parterre, to throw away the flowerets that are off show [etc.]. **1859** R. F. Burton *Cent. Afr.* in *Jrnl. Geog. Soc.* XXIX. 438 The gum..is then carefully garbled with due regard to colour and size. **1875** Jevons *Money* viii. 81 Hence arises the practice, extensively carried on in the present day in England, of *picking* and *culling*, or, as another technical expression is, *garbling* the coinage, devoting the good new coins to the melting-pot, and passing the old worn coins into circulation again.

†**b.** *esp.* To 'sift' or 'weed' (an army, corporation, etc.) so as to exclude unfit or uncompliant members. Also ***to garble out***: to remove (objectionable persons) after selection. *Obs.*

1650 Fuller *Pisgah* II. viii. 174 But his army must be garbled, as too great for God to give victory thereby. **1658** Osborn *Adv. Son* (ed. 6) 2 By garbling out of them all Boys of an incapacity. **1661** in Cobbett *Parl. Hist.* (1808) IV. 219 The house of commons was first garbled, and then turned out of doors. **1690** *Plain English* 7 Who garbled Corporations, and deprived Men of their greatest Civil Rights. **1736** Lediard *Life Marlborough* I. 64 Colleges were attempted to be garbled, and immemorial Foundations broken in upon..to make Room even for Profligates, if new Converts. **1770** *Junius Lett.* xl. 207 The army..will not submit to be garbled. **1809** *Ann. Reg.* 230 The government ..set itself to garble the army to its mind.

3. To make selections from with a (usually unfair or mischievous) purpose; to mutilate (a statement, writing, etc.) with a view to misrepresentation.

1689–92 Locke *Toleration* III. vii. Wks. 1727 II. 376 To garble thus the Truths of Religion, and by their own Authority take some not necessary to Salvation. **1736** Bolingbroke *Patriot.* Advt. (1749) 9 More properly the writings of others than his, considering how they had been garbled. **1794** Burke *Rep. Lords' Jrnls.* Wks. 1842 II. 623 To break to pieces and to garble those facts. **1818** Jas. Mill *Brit. India* III. vi. i. 42 The late Governor-General..had withheld, mutilated, or garbled the correspondence. **1833** Peel in *Croker Papers* 29 Sept. (1884), The evidence has been since garbled in publication. **1877** C. Geikie *Christ* lxi. (1879) 750 Those who came forward garbled, or misunderstood the words of Jesus. **1888** Frith *Autobiog.* III. viii. 175 He had..garbled the title of her picture in the Catalogue. **1895** F. Hall *Two Trifles* 8 By garbling me he indulges in uncandid suppression of the truth.

¶**4.** Confused with garbage *v.* = garbage *v.* 1.

1661 Lovell *Hist. Anim. & Min.* Introd. d 2, Birds.. rightly killed, garbelled, and pulled.

garble, obs. form of garboard.

garbleable (ˈgɑːb(ə)ləb(ə)l), *a. Obs.* exc. *Hist.* Also 7 **garblable.** [f. garble *v.* + -able.] Liable to be garbled: see garble *v.* 1.

1603–4 *Act 1 Jas. I*, c. 19 §1 All Spices, Wares, Drugges, and other Merchandizes garbleable. **1690** Leybourn *Curs. Math.* 8 All sorts of Wares or Merchandise, garblable, as Sugar, Pepper, Cloves, &c. **1707** *Act 6 Anne* c. 68 §3 Owners of any spices..or merchandizes garbleable. **1800** [see garbler 1].

garbled (ˈgɑːb(ə)ld), *ppl. a.* [f. garble *v.* + -ed[1].] In senses of the vb.

1623 *St. Papers* Col. 144 Cloves..the price set at 6*s.* 6*d.* garbled and 5*s.* 8*d.* ungarbled. **1774** Burke *Sp. Amer. Tax.* Wks. 1842 I. 167 The fullest, most impartial, and least-garbled body of evidence that ever was produced to this house. **1814** R. Bland *Prov.* I. Pref. 10 This garbled edition was printed at Florence. **1855** Macaulay *Hist. Eng.* IV. xix. 354 The Just Vindication consists chiefly of garbled extracts from the Areopagitica of Milton. **1871** Blackie *Four Phases* i. 54 A garbled statement constructed upon the principle of pushing into prominence everything that is bad.

garbler (ˈgɑːblə(r)). [f. garble *v.* + -er[1].]

1. An official who garbled spices, etc. (i.e. removed the refuse from them); a sifter. *Obs.* exc. *Hist.*

1592 Greene *Upst. Courtier* F ij a, You buy of the Garbellers of spices, the refuse that they sift from yͤ Marchant. **1707** *Act 6 Anne* c. 68 §3 A fit and able person to execute the office of garbler within the city of London. **1800** Colquhoun *Comm. Thames* xi. 332 A Garbler who, at the request of the Owner of any Spices or Drugs garbleable.. shall garble the same. **1829** Heath *Grocers' Comp.* (1854) 61 Thomas Halfmark was chosen and sworn garbeller of spices and of sotill ware.

2. †**a.** A censor of the press (*obs.*). **b.** One who garbles or mutilates (literary works, statements, etc.).

a. **1656** Earl Monm. *Advt. fr. Parnass.* 170 The publick garblers of Poetry..brought these two Latin verses to the test. **1693** in Wood *Life* (O.H.S.) III. 430 If thus th' Athenian garblers should proceed Their great Bodleian library to weed.

b. *a* **1693** Urquhart *Rabelais* III. Prol. 16 You Pettifoggers, Garbellers, and Masters of Chicanery. **1710** Swift *Examiner* No. 19 ¶8 There was a farther Secret in this Clause, which may best be discovered by the first Projectors, or at least the Garblers of it.

Hence †**ˈgarblership**, the office or function of a garbler.

1569 *Proc. Crt. Com. Counc. Lond.* Repert. 16 lf. 494 The office of the garbelershippe of spices. **1720** *Stow's Surv. Lond.* (ed. Strype) II. 239/2 Suit was made by some light Persons for an Office of Garblership of foreign wools.

garbling (ˈgɑːblɪŋ), *vbl. sb.* [f. garble *v.* + -ing[1].] The action of the verb garble.

†**1.** The action or process of picking or selecting (spices, etc.), or of removing the refuse or the inferior specimens from merchandise, etc. *Obs.*

1483 *Act 1 Rich. III*, c. 11 §1 They wil not suffre any garbelyng of theym to be made but selle good and bad at so excessyf price togedyr ungarbeled. **1518** *Acc.* in *Archæol.* XLVII. 310 For..letheryng, bokelyng, and garbelyng of m[l]m[l]xlvij complete harnes. **1591** (*title*), A profitable.. Discourse for the Meeting with the bad Garbelling of Spices used in these Daies. **1621** Elsing *Debates Ho. Lords* (Camden) 89 The Prince's mocion..touchinge the garblinge of Tobacco. **1662** H. Stubbe *Ind. Nectar* iv. 70 There ought to be a great care in the Picking, Garbling, and preparing the [Cacao] Nuts. **1687** in Heath *Grocers' Comp.* (1869) 61 The Company's right in the garbling of spices. **1800** Colquhoun *Comm. Thames* xi. 327 Certain other privileges also attach to the Garbling of Merchandise Imported. **1809** R. Langford *Introd. Trade* 132 *Garbling*, the clearing the refuse from any commodity.

†**b.** *transf.* The action or process of 'sifting' (a corporation, etc.) so as to exclude unfit or uncompliant members. *Obs.*

a **1661** Fuller *Worthies* (1840) II. 449 The general purging and garbling of the Judges. **1663** *Flagellum, or O. Cromwell* (1672) 61 Their Propositions being more rigid since the last garbling by the Army. **1690** *Andros Tracts* II. 43 Jobbs..which sometimes Required shaking off a Testimony or Garbling of a Jury.

2. The action or process of making selections with a view to misrepresentation.

1861 BRIGHT *Sp. on India* 19 Mar., He knows there have been garbling and mutilation..in those despatches. **1885** *Ch. Times* 12 June 456 All kinds of quibbles, equivocations, garblings, and direct falsehoods.

3. (See quot.)

1867 SMYTH *Sailor's Word-bk.*, *Garbling*, the mixing of rubbish with a cargo stowed in bulk.

4. *concr. pl.* The refuse or remainder of a staple commodity after selection of the best.

1881 *Daily News* 21 Jan. 6/8 Gums..olibanum..sold at 58*s.*; garblings, 27*s.* 6*d.*; siftings, 25*s.* 6*d.* **1886** HARRIS *Techn. Dict. Fire Insur.*, *Garblings*, pickings of wool, cotton, and like material.

Garbo[1] ('gɑːbəʊ). The name of the film actress Greta *Garbo* (real name Greta Gustafsson; born 1905), used in various locutions (chiefly *colloq.*) as: *to do a Garbo*, to behave like Greta Garbo; to be aloof or retiring; to seek seclusion; **Garboesque, Garboic, Garboish, Garbo-like** *adjs.*, resembling or characteristic of Greta Garbo; **Garbo hat**, a felt hat with a wide floppy brim.

1934 [see DO *v.* 11 d]. **1934** *Tit-Bits* 31 Mar. 12/2 'To do a Garbo'..means to be proud, aloof and unbending. **1937** *Times* 18 Oct. 15/4 We all fully understand the necessity for these Garboic tactics. **1942** JESPERSEN *Mod. Eng. Gram.* VI. xix. 326 Thus we have *Casanovesque*.., *Garboesque* (NP [= in a newspaper] 1936). **1955** A. WEST *Heritage* vi. 255 She was wearing a Garboish hat that framed her entirely unmade-up face. **1958** *Vogue* Apr. 134 (*caption*) A grey flannel Garbo pull-on hat. **1958** J. COURAGE in C. K. Stead *N.Z. Short Stories* (1966) 32 The night-sister and her Garbo-like face. **1962** N. FREELING *Love in Amsterdam* II. 74 Her features..had, indeed, the Garboesque cast that is exceedingly attractive. **1963** —— *Because of Cats* vii. 105 Housewives..in playsuits and sunglasses and Garbo hats, languidly pushing energetic toddlers—also in Garbo hats—in go-carts. **1967** N. MARSH *Death at Dolphin* ii. 38 He loathes publicity and does a Garbo. **1970** R. JOHNSTON *Black Camels* ii. 27 You really are in your Garbo mood, Ben.

garbo[2] ('gɑːbəʊ). *Austral. slang.* [f. GARBAGE *sb.* + Austral. dim. suff. -o[2].] A dustman, a collector of rubbish.

1953 BAKER *Australia Speaks* iv. 105 *Garbo*, a garbage man. **1967** *Sunday Truth* (Brisbane) 19 Mar. 13/1 The wage of the 'garbo' is in excess of $40 a week. **1969** *Sunday Mirror* (Brisbane) 33 The garbos of Shrewsbury..are tired of wearing tattered jackets and trousers while emptying loads of old rubbish. **1971** *Guardian* 27 May 13/6 Australian garbos probably could not compete with English dustmen in the length and scale of their strikes.

garboard ('gɑːbɔəd). Also 7 garbell, -ble. [app. a. Du. *gaarboord* (obs.), explained by Winschooten (1681) as f. *gar-en* short for *gaderen* to GATHER + *boord* BOARD *sb.* Cf. F. *gabord* (1538 in Hatz.-Darm.).] The first range of planks laid upon a ship's bottom, next the keel; the corresponding range of plates in an iron vessel. Also *attrib.* as in ***garboard-plank, -plate, -seam***; **garboard-strake** = garboard.

1626 CAPT. SMITH *Accid. Yng. Seamen* 8 The Garbell strake is the outside plancke next the keele. **1627** —— *Seaman's Gram.* ii. 3 The Garbord is the first planke next the keele on the outside. **1691** T. H[ALE] *Acc. New Invent.* 40 Putting him upon thoughts (had it been practicable) of shifting her Garble-strake there. **1789** G. KEATE *Pelew Isl.* 157 The carpenter got one of the planks of the garboard strake on. **1834** M. SCOTT *Cruise Midge* (1859) 249 The shot..had only damaged two planks of the garboard streak. **1865** MRS. WHITNEY *Gayworthys* I. 172 The starboard garboard seam close by the stern, had opened. **1869** SIR E. REED *Shipbuild.* i. 7 An external iron keel..was applied, and connected to the original flat keel by garboard-plates. *Ibid.* 8 Intercostal plates were..secured below to the inner garboards. **1893** *Daily News* 26 June 5/8 The garboards, and bottom parts of the transverse frames.

garboil ('gɑːbɔɪl), *sb. Obs.* exc. *arch.* Forms: 6–7 garboyl, -boile, (6 -broyl, *Sc.* -bulle), 6–9 -boyle, 6– garboil. [ad. OF. *garbouil, garbouille* (= Sp. *garbullo*), ad. It. *garbuglio*, connected with L. *bullīre* to BOIL; the origin of the prefixed element is disputed.] Confusion, disturbance, tumult; an instance of this, a brawl, hubbub, hurlyburly.

1548 UDALL *Erasm. Par. Luke* xxi. 165 When ye shal heare all the worlde to bee in a garboile of sedicions. **1562** RANDOLPH in G. Chalmers *Mary Q. Scot.* (1818) I. 86 In all those garbulles, I assure your honour, I never saw the Queen merrier. **1600** E. BLOUNT tr. *Conestaggio* 55 The Citie of Lisbon, as also all the rest, were in great garboile. **1610** HOLLAND *Camden's Brit.* I. 66 Whiles Commodus was Emperour, Britannie was all of a Garboile. *a* **1655** VINES *Lord's Supp.* (1677) 112 To cut that intricate knot, that makes such a garboyle in the text. **1691** WOOD *Ath. Oxon.* I. 426 He journied to Rome..but..raising great garboyles among the Scholars of that place, Cardinal Boncompagno..expelled him thence. **1755** JOHNSON, *Garboil.* **1864** BURTON *Scot. Abr.* III. ii. 148 Before the intestine garboyles of this island. **1891** *Nat. Rev.* July 669 Far from the moiling crowd and garboyle of the world.

†'**garboil,** *v. Obs.* Also 6 garboyle. [f. prec. sb.] *trans.* To confuse, agitate, disturb.

1572 H. MIDDLEMORE in Ellis *Orig. Lett.* Ser. II. III. 5 The occasion presently profferyd, of the Lowe Contreys so greatly garboyled. **1594** CAREW *Huarte's Exam. Wits* vii. (1596) 101 Amongst the first qualities, there is none which so much garboileth this power as excessiue heat.

¶ Erroneously for GARBLE *v.* in various senses.

1555 EDEN *Decades* 332 Meltynge, fynynge, dryinge, garboylyng, and such other broylynges. **1574** HELLOWES *Gueuara's Fam. Ep.* (1577) 382 By their authority they thrust in themselues, to glosse the Bible, and garboile the scripture. **1599** A. M. tr. *Gabelhouer's Bk. Physicke* 201/2 Take a wilde Ducke, plucke him, and garboyle him. *a* **1715** BURNET *Own Time* (1766) II. 3 To tip down so many Lords at a time and to garboil the House, as often as any party should have a great majority. **1720** *Stow's Surv. Lond.* (ed. Strype) II. v. xiv. 229/1 They did garboil out of every hundred the Half of such Baggage and Refuse Stuff.

garbologist (gɑː'bɒlədʒɪst). Also **garbiologist**. [f. GARB(AGE *sb.* + -OLOGIST.] A dustman.

1965 *N.Z. Woman's Weekly* 4 Oct. 103/1 RCA tells us of their local 'garbiologists'. **1966** *New Scientist* 13 Jan. 97/3 One dustman in court last week called himself a garbologist. **1968** *Radio Times* 26 Sept. 23/4 Waste is now big technicological business. No wonder British dustmen are campaigning to have themselves officially renamed 'garbologists'.

garbology (gɑː'bɒlədʒɪ). orig. *U.S.* Also **garbageology**. [f. GARB(AGE *sb.* + -OLOGY; cf. GARBOLOGIST.] W. Rathje's term for the scientific study of the refuse of a modern society; the investigation of material discarded by a society considered as an aspect of social science.

1976 *National Rev.* (U.S.) 6 Feb. 70/2 The..theory behind this garbageology is that if we can learn about ancient peoples by studying their garbage, we can learn even more about present society the same way. **1976** *Telegraph* (Brisbane) 14 July 30/2 Garbology..is, he [*sc.* Dr. Rathje] believes, a social science. **1979** *Truck & Bus Transportation* Jan. 22 (*heading*) A quick course in advanced garbology. **1982** *Times* 12 Feb. 17/1 I'm always looking for truth about mankind and its creations, says William Rathje, a professor of garbology, with a Ph.D in anthropology. Rathje and his team search the garbage dumps of the United States... Rathje, who works at a 'garbage pavilion' in Tucson, hopes to start a museum of garbology.

†**garbred.** *Obs. rare*$^{-1}$. [app. f. *gare* = GORE (? or GARTH) + BREDE.]

1621 *N. Riding Rec.* (1894) I. 51 One parcell of meadowe called a garbred of meadow.

garce (gɑːs). Also **garse**. [a. Telugu *gārisa* (Yule).] 'A cubic measure for rice, etc. in use on the Madras coast, as usual varying much in value. Buchanan (infra) treats it as a weight' (Yule).

1752 T. BROOKS *Weights & Meas. E. Ind.* 6 Grain Measures..1 Garse, 8400 lbs. 0 oz. Avoirdupoise. **1759** in A. Dalrymple *Orient. Repert.* (1793) I. 120 Rice may be bought for about 12 Pagodas a Garce. **1807** F. BUCHANAN *Journ. Mysore* etc. I. 6 The proper native weights..are..20 Baruays (Candies) 1 Gursay, called by the English Garse.. The Garse [is] nearly 1205 lbs. **1811** P. KELLY *Univ. Cambist* I. 121 Madras..The Garce, corn measure, contains 80 Parahs or 400 Marcals. *Ibid.*, Madras..The Gursay (called by the English Garce) contains 20 Baruays.

garce, var. GARSE *sb. Obs.*

garcinia (gɑː'sɪnɪə). *Bot.* [mod.L. (Linnæus *Genera Plantarum* (1737) 343), f. the name of Laurent *Garcin* (1683–1751), French botanist and traveller, + -IA.] A member of the genus so named of tropical, evergreen trees, belonging to the family Guttiferæ and found in Asia, Africa, and Polynesia; some species produce gamboge, and another is the mangosteen.

1760 J. LEE *Introd. Bot.* xi. 25 In respect to its *Apex* or *Top*, it [*sc.* the calyx] is either *Acute, sharp*, as in *Primula*.. *Obtuse, blunt*, as in *Nymphæa* and *Garcinia*; or with one of its Indents *lopped off*, as in *Verbena*. **1886** G. NICHOLSON *Illustr. Dict. Gardening* II. 43/2 Garcinias thrive in a peat and loam compost. **1890** W. J. GORDON *Foundry* 126 The garcinia that yields the gamboge. **1951** *Dict. Gardening* (R. Hort. Soc.) II. 858/1 Garcinias need stove conditions and a compost of loam and peat.

†**garcion, garson.** *Obs.* (after 16th c. chiefly *Hist.*). Also 4 **garsoun, garesowne**, 7 **gartion, garsoon**. [a. OF. *garçun* (11th c.), *garcion, garzon, garchon*, etc. (mod.F. *garçon*) = Pr. *garso, guarzon*, Sp. *garzon*, Pg. *garção*, It. *garzone*, med.L. (12th c.) *garciōn-em*, for which *garciferum* (f. the analogy of *scutiferum*) occurs. The nom. form (med.L. *garcio*) is represented by OF. *gars* (mod.F. *gars* in jocular use, 'lad'), and perh. by Pr. *gart-z* adj. 'bad'. The primary sense is 'servant, attendant' (often used contemptuously, like 'knave', 'varlet'); the mod.Fr. senses 'boy', 'bachelor', are of later development.] A serving-man, groom; esp. a young man or boy servant.

13.. *K. Alis.* 2505 And damoselis to garsounes, Ther was mad al comunes. **13..** *Sir Beues* (A.) 2993 His sone þat was a proud garsoun. Men him clepede Beuoun. **13..** *Seuyn Sag.* (W.) 1428 Whether lord or garsoun. *c* **1450** *Merlin* 103 It ys grevouse thinge to vs to haue a garcion to be lorde ouer vs alle. **1562** J. HEYWOOD *Prov. & Epigr.* (1867) 170 Long wayghtyng and small wages makth poore garsons. **1598** HAKLUYT *Voy.* I. 19 Hasting shall finde 21. ships, in euery ship 21. men, and a Garcion, or Boy, which is called a Gromet. **1602** MIDDLETON *Blurt* III. i. E j b, She meanes her French garsoon. *c* **1640** J. SMYTH *Lives Berkeleys* (1883) I. 166 For a gartion or boy to attend him j[d] ob. the day. **1671** F. PHILLIPS *Reg. Necess.* 377 That no more but one Garson be allowed.

‖**garçon** (garsɔ̃). [Fr.: see prec.] **a.** A boy, serving-man, waiter; in Eng. use chiefly a waiter in a French hotel or restaurant.

1788 A. YOUNG *Jrnl.* 15 Sept. in *Travels* (1792) I. 87, I thought only of my poor mare being squeezed a night amongst the Bretagne garrans; sixpence, however, to the garçon, had effects marvelously to her ease. **1829** H. FOOTE *Compan. to Theatres* 142 Each spectator is expected to take refreshment, for which purpose marble tables, etc are in all parts of the theatre, and *garçons* are at hand to anticipate the wishes of the company. **1839** A. GRAY *Lett.* (1893) 156 Here we dined, and were charged four francs for dinner, besides sous to the garçon. **1850** E. RUSKIN *Let.* 9 Mar. in M. Lutyens *Effie in Venice* (1965) I. 153 Such a parting..with all the garçons, chambermaids, gondoliers. **1942** E. PAUL *Narrow St.* iii. 20 Georges, the *garçon*, was serving drinks to a couple of officials and an oyster vendor.

b. Also used *attrib.* or *Comb.* to designate a type of short hair-style for women, the Eton crop.

1956 A. WILSON *Anglo-Saxon Att.* I. iii. 87 A young woman with black garçon-cut hair.

‖**garçonnière** (garsɔ̃njɛr). [Fr.] A bachelor's rooms or flat.

1927 *New Statesman* 15 Oct. 17 A young rake who..turns his capercailzie hut into a *garçonnière*. **1938** H. G. WELLS *Apropos of Dolores* iii. 124 In Paris, in her world, there is no such thing as an innocent garconnière. **1945** E. WAUGH *Brideshead Revisited* viii. 178 Two emancipated American girls who shared a garconnière.

†'**garcopper.** *Obs.*$^{-1}$ [ad. Ger. *garkupfer*, f. *gar* ready, refined + *kupfer* copper.] Refined copper.

1799 W. TOOKE *View Russian Emp.* I. 105 Hermann reckons only from 1 to 5 per cent. garcopper.

garcrow, obs. form of GORCROW.

†**gard**[1]. *Obs.* [ad. F. *garde* (in *prendre garde à*): see GUARD *sb.*] Attention, watchfulness. Also, the object of one's attention.

a **1529** KINGESMYLL *Man's Est.* x. (1580) 62 This was his gard, he was still busie aboute these, the blinde, the leaper, the lame, the deafe, and the dedde. **1600** HOLLAND *Livy* XXIII. ix. (1609) 478 All their gard and regard, all their eyes upon him alone, what serve they for?

†**gard**[2]. *Obs.* Also **garde**. [ad. F. *garde* (Cotgr.).] The dew-claw of a deer or boar.

1576 TURBERV. *Venerie* 154 The gardes (which are his hinder clawes or dew clawes) should be great and open one from another. **1616** SURFL. & MARKH. *Country Farme* 691 The..wrinkles which are betwixt his gards and the heele.

gard[3] (gɑːd). *dial.* (Cornwall). (See quots.)

1602 CAREW *Cornwall* 30 b, A thick strong net..drawne at the boates sterne, gathering whatsoever it meeteth lying in the bottome of the water, out of which when it is taken vp they cull the oysters and cast away the residue, which they terme gard. **1865** R. HUNT *Pop. Rom. W. Eng.* Ser. I. 124 Clean all the platters..with water and gard (gravel sand).

gard, gard-: see GUARD, GUARD-.

Garda ('gɑːdə). Also with lower-case initial. Pl. (sense b) **Gardai, Gardaí** (gɑː'diː); **Gardas**. [Ir., guard.] **a.** The state police force of the Republic of Ireland, established in 1922, and known as the ***Garda Síochána*** [= 'Civic Guard'] since 1923. Also *attrib.*

1923 *Dáil Eireann Official Rep.* 31 July 1709 'An Act to establish in Saorstát Eireann, and regulate a Police Force to be called the Civic Guard.' *Cathal O'Shannon*: I move to substitute Garda Síochána for the words 'Civic Guard'. **1934** *Ibid.* 2 Mar. 2701, I am to take it from the Minister that there were no members of any force, except what we recognise as the old Gárda force, on these premises..until a week ago. **1943** *Ibid.* 13 May XC. 149 (*heading*) Gárda and the Franchise. **1959** *Chambers's Encycl.* XI. 25/1 In 1922 Eire formed the *Garda Siochána* under the general direction and control of a government commissioner. **1960** A. CLARKE *Later Poems* (1961) 76 How could the Garda Síochana Defend authority in pairs. **1973** J. BIGGS-DAVISON *Hand is Red* x. 135 Costello..reinforced the *Garda Síochaná* on the Border. **1970** *Times* 29 May 11/5 This [*sc.* gun-running] alerted the Garda (police) and the Government through the Ministry of Justice. **1975** *Evening Herald* (Dublin) 8 May 2/7 In Drogheda Garda station alone, where there are almost 70 men, only four have been paid. **1977** *Irish Times* 8 June 4/1 The girl had been seriously assaulted in the North Circular Road area a short time previously, the Garda statement added. **1986** *Evening Press* (Dublin) 21 May 1/1 Garda Intelligence had feared another major effort by the IRA to purchase arms in the United States.

b. A member of the Garda Síochána; an Irish policeman. Used in *pl.* for the police generally.

1943 *Dáil Eireann Parl. Deb. Official Rep.* 16 Nov. 2090 Mr. Byrne asked the Minister for Justice if he will state if he proposes to increase the number of uniformed Gárdái in the City and County of Dublin. **1958** [see DIAL *sb.*[1] 6 c]. *a* **1966** 'M. NA GOPALEEN' *Best of Myles* (1977) 149 Defendant.. refused to remove his cap. It was removed by a Gárda. **1970** *New Yorker* 31 Oct. 128/2 The *gardái* would block the roads after he'd passed by. **1975** *Evening Herald* (Dublin) 8 May 2/7 Efforts to speed up the paying out process have been made..but so far the Gardai have met with little success. **1977** *Belfast Tel.* 17 Jan. 4/6 Mr. Cooney said he would expect churchmen and politicians to give the same response as any other citizen in aiding the army and the gardai. **1986** *Munster Express* 6 June 2/4 The defendant was stopped by Garda Terry Butler at 11.30 p.m. on the date in question.

gardain(e, obs. form of GARDEN, GUARDIAN.

gardant, obs. form of GUARDANT.

† ˈ**gardantly**, *adv. Obs.*⁻¹ [f. F. *gardant* pres. pple. of *garder* to look + -LY².] Attentively.

1574 J. JONES *Nat. Beginning Grow. Things* 37 How Gardantly therfore these are to be Regarded, wise men easely seeth.

‖**garde-bras** (gardəbra). Also 5 (in anglicized forms) **gardbrace**, **garbrasse**, 7 **gardebrace**, 9 *erron.* garde-de-bras. [F. *garde-bras*, f. *garde-r* to guard + *bras* arm.] 'An additional piece of armour placed on the upper part of the gauntlet, or fastened to the elbow-plates' (Fairholt).

1459 in *Paston Lett.* I. 487 Item, j. garbrasse. *c* **1489** CAXTON *Blanchardyn* xxiv. 83 The sleue of cloth of gold.. whiche he couched along his shoulder in stede of gardebras. *a* **1500** *Chaucer's Dreme* 1556 Without was left not one, Horse, male, trusse, ne bagage, Salad, speare, gardbrace ne page But was lodged and roome ynough. **1679** BLOUNT *Anc. Tenures* 104 This Gardebrace is otherwise called vambrace, and signifies Armor for the Arme. **1874** BOUTELL *Arms & Arm.* x. 204 The plates that were fixed to the elbow-pieces were entitled *gardes-de-bras*.

† **gardecaut**. *Obs.* [corruption of F. *gardecorde*, f. *garder* to GUARD + *corde* CORD.] (See quot.)

1706 PHILLIPS (ed. Kersey), *Gardecaut*, or *Gard-du-cord*, is that which stops the Fusee of a Watch when wound up. **1721** in BAILEY.

‖**garde champêtre** (gard ʃɑ̃pɛtr). [Fr., lit. 'rural guard'.] A rural policeman; a gamekeeper.

1814 M. BIRKBECK *Journey through France* 97 In the country, the Garde champetres, a revolutionary institution, are the great means.. of crushing them [*sc.* crimes] in the egg. **1831** *Edin. Rev.* LIV. 309 The village poacher will find him [*sc.* the farmer] a more active *garde champêtre* than any keeper. **1957** G. BELLAIRS *Death in High Provence* iii. 29 The *garde champêtre*, the mayor's run-about, mainly concerned with duties as game and forest warden.

‖**garde-du-corps** (gardədykɔr). [Fr.; lit. 'guard of the body'.] A body-guard; a member of a body-guard.

1651 EVELYN *Diary* 7 Sept., Then came.. the *garde du corps* and other officers. **1701** FARQUHAR *Sir H. Wildair* III. i, For not one of these fellows stirs about without his *garde-du-corps*. **1703** DE FOE *On Standing Army* Misc. 206 Queen Elizabeth, tho' she had no *Guard du Corps*, yet she had her *Guards du Terres*[!] **1710** *Examiner* No. 11 ¶5 I have heard of a certain Illustrious Person, who having a *Guard du Corps*, that forc'd their Attendance on him, put them into a Livery, and maintain'd them as his Servants. **1849** THACKERAY *Pendennis* xxviii, Mirobolant.. killed four *gardes-du-corps* with his own point in the barricades of July.

gardein, obs. form of GUARDIAN.

‖**Garde Mobile** (gard mɔbil). [Fr.] A French military force, now chiefly engaged in police activity; also (usu. with lower-case initials), a member of this force.

1848 *Illustr. London News* 1 July 428/3 The great barricade was stormed by National Guards, Cuirassiers, Republican Guards, and Gardes Mobiles. **1848** *Observer* 2 July 3/1 The combat was altogether fought by the army, the Garde Mobile, and by the shopkeepers and middle classes of Paris. **1857** C. M. YONGE *Dynevor Terr.* I. xx. 334 The brave boy *gardes mobiles* came crowding round him, all black with powder. **1935** G. GREENE *Basement Room* 87 Praying secretly to the Virgin to send an angel, to send the police, to send the Gardes Mobiles.

garden (ˈgɑːd(ə)n), *sb.* Forms: 4 **garthen**, (6 **-yne**, **-ynge**), 4-7 **gardin(e**, **-yn(e**, (5-6 *Sc.* **-ing**, **-yng**), 4-6 **gardain**, **-ayn(e**, **-ein(e**, **-eyn(e**, (6 **gardene**, *Sc.* **gairden**, **-ing**), 6- **garden**. [a. ONF. *gardin* (Central F. *jardin*):—pop. L. **gardīn-um*, f. **gard-um* (OF. *gard*, *gart*, *jart*, garden) a. Teut. **gardo-z* (Goth. *gard-s*, OHG. *gart*, OS. *gard*, OE. *ȝeard*, ON. *garð-r*, enclosure: see GARTH and YARD). The Teut. langs. have also a wk. form, with the special sense 'garden': OFris. *garda*, OS. *gardo* (Du. *gaarde*), OHG. *garto* (MHG. *garte*, mod.G. *garten*). Cf. Pr. *gardi*, *jardi*, *jerzi*, and *jardina* fem. (also Sp. *jardin*, Pg. *jardim*, It. *giardino*, which appear to be adoptions from Fr. or Pr.).]

I. 1. a. An enclosed piece of ground devoted to the cultivation of flowers, fruit, or vegetables; often preceded by some defining word, as ***flower-***, ***fruit-***, ***kitchen-***, ***market-***, ***strawberry-garden***, etc.

13.. *K. Alis.* 1028 With samytes, and baudekyns Weore cortined the gardynes. **13..** *E.E. Allit. P.* A. 260 Your perle is.. in þis gardyn gracios gaye, Here-inne to lenge for euer & play. *c* **1386** CHAUCER *Wife's Prol.* 765 Yif me a plante of thilke blissed tre And in my gardyn planted it shal bee. *c* **1440** *Gesta Rom.* xxxi. 118 (Harl. MS.) The knight.. yede abowte in the gardin, and soute the clewe, & fonde it. **1513** MORE *Rich. III* Wks. 53/2 My lord you haue very good strawberies at your gardayne in Holberne. **1522** *Wills & Inv. N.C.* (Surtees 1835) 106 The garthynges and Orchard perteyning thereto. **1577** HARRISON *England* II. xx. (1878) I. 323, I comprehend therefore vnder the word 'garden', all such grounds as are wrought with the spade by mans hand. **1611** SHAKS. *Cymb.* I. i. 81 Ile fetch a turne about the Garden. **1680-90** TEMPLE *Ess. Gardening* Wks. 1731 I. 174 The Use of Gardens seems to have been the most ancient and most general of any sorts of Possession among Mankind. **1756-7** tr. *Keysler's Trav.* (1760) IV. 356 The garden is on a slope, or gentle declivity; and very much resembles prince Eugene's garden. **1820** SHELLEY *Sensit. Pl.* II. 29, I doubt not the flowers of that garden sweet Rejoiced in the sound of her gentle feet. **1856** STANLEY *Sinai & Pal.* iii. (1858) 191 Eastern gardens.. are not flower gardens, nor private gardens, but the orchards, vineyards or fig enclosures round a town. **1872** YEATS *Techn. Hist. Comm.* 36 A wall picture of an ancient Egyptian garden has been preserved.

fig. *a* **1340** HAMPOLE *Psalter* Prol., Þis boke is cald garthen closed, wel enseled. **1435** MISYN *Fire of Love* I. xxx. 65 Þe saule truly þat boyth is sweyt be schynynge of consciens, & fayr be charite of endles lufe, cristis gardyn may be cald.

b. *pl.* Ornamental grounds, used as a place of public resort, usually with some defining word, as ***Botanic(al***, ***Zoological Gardens***, etc.

1838 *Penny Cycl.* XI. 73/2 Rivalling these imperial structures are the gardens of St. Petersburg. **1884** *Scotsman* 29 Jan. 2, I have just returned from my usual stroll in the Botanical Gardens.

c. *transf.* Applied to a region of remarkable fertility. ***the Garden of England***: a name given to various counties, esp. Kent and Worcestershire.

1596 SHAKS. *Tam. Shr.* I. i. 4, I am arriu'd for fruitful Lombardie, The pleasant garden of great Italy. **1716** LADY M. W. MONTAGU *Let. to Mrs. Smith* 5 Aug., The whole country appears a large garden. **1885** FARJEON *Sacred Nugget* I. vii, 'Yes, sir, Kent's my county, but even in the garden of England they can't grow finer roses than them'.

d. ***to cultivate one's garden*** [after Voltaire *Candide* (1759) xxx, 'Il faut cultiver notre jardin'], to attend to one's own affairs.

[**1759** tr. *Voltaire's Candid* xxx. 132 All that is very well, answered Candid, but let us take care of our garden.] **1931** O. W. HOLMES *Let.* 7 May (1964) 324 It would be a bore to be ill abroad and I suppose there would be a good chance of being so. I will cultivate my garden. **1933** L. STRACHEY *Characters & Comm.* I. ii. 13 The precept 'Il faut cultiver notre jardin' has come down to the degenerate descendants of Candide in the form of 'Have an eye to the main chance'—a very different exhortation. The twentieth century has learned to cultivate its garden so well that it makes a profit of ten per cent. **1955** R. M. MACIVER *Pursuit of Happiness* iv. 35 We must cultivate our own garden and find the joy of doing it in our own hearts.

e. Colloq. phr. ***everything in the garden is lovely***, the situation is perfectly satisfactory; all is well.

[**1909** J. R. WARE *Passing Eng.* 125/1 *Everything is nice in your garden*, a gentle protest against self-laudation... This is said to be derived from one of the young princesses (probably a daughter of the Princess Beatrice) who made this reply when something in her garden at Osborne was praised by Her Majesty.] **1910** 'G. B. LANCASTER' *Jim of Ranges* v. 110 You're all right, 'n I'm aw right..'n ev'y thing'n the garden's lovely. **1924** C. MACKENZIE *Old Men of Sea* v. 71 The financial outlook's lovely. It's lovely, Mr. Marsham. Yes, everything in the garden's lovely, as Marie Lloyd used to sing. **1939** O. LANCASTER *Homes Sweet Homes* 56 Everything in the garden, to use a contemporary phrase, was lovely. And then.. the prevailing optimism received a shock. **1941** A. CHRISTIE *Evil under Sun* ii. 30 Then everything in the garden—or shall we say at the seaside?—is lovely, Mademoiselle. **1969** *Guardian* 13 Feb. 4/3 But not everything in the garden was lovely and the public, in particular, was not sure what higher education was for.

f. ***to lead*** (someone) ***up the garden (-path)***, to lead on, entice; mislead, deceive. *colloq.*

1925 E. MANNIN *Sounding Brass* I. viii, They're cheats, that's wot women are! Lead you up the garden and then go snivellin' around 'cos wot's natcheral 'as 'appened to 'em. **1927** G. D. H. & M. COLE *Murder at Crome House* ix. 94 To lead Flint up the garden-path and relieve him of his cash. **1957** I. MURDOCH *Sandcastle* ii. 29 I'm going to lead her up the garden. I've got her thoroughly foxed so far. **1963** *Times* 29 Jan. 12/6, I made these confessions to lead the police up the garden path.

2. a. Short for *Covent-garden*, *Hatton-garden* (quot. 1890), localities in London.

1763 *Brit. Mag.* IV. 415 A fashionable coffee-house in the neighbourhood of the Garden. **1851** MAYHEW *Lond. Labour* I. 81 Not only is the 'Garden' itself all bustle and activity, but [etc.]. **1884** J. PAYN *Some Lit. Recollect.* iv. in *Cornh. Mag.* Mar. 257 She [Miss O'Neill] talked of 'the Garden' and 'the Lane' and was very fond of recitation. **1890** *Tit Bits* 29 Mar. 389/2 The cut stones are chiefly sold to the large dealers in the 'Garden'.

b. *pl.* Often used with some local prefix as the name of a square or street, in the suburbs of London, and (by imitation) in many other towns.

1848 THACKERAY *Van. Fair* lx, 'Gardens' was a felicitous word not applied to stucco houses with asphalte terraces in front, so early as 1827.

3. As a name for the school of Epicurus (who taught in a garden).

Diog. Laert. uses οἱ ἀπὸ τῶν κήπων as a name for the sect; cf. also Cicero, *horti Epicuri*.

1867 M. PATTISON *Serm.* (1885) 164 [Neither] the Porch, the Garden, nor the Academy.

II. *attrib.* and *Comb.*

4. a. simple attrib. (= of or belonging to a garden, for use in a garden), as ***garden-alley***, ***-bed***, ***-bench***, ***-book***, ***-bower***, ***-boy***, ***-close***, ***-court***, ***-croft***, ***-door***, ***-earth***, ***-fence***, ***-field***, ***-hat***, ***-hedge***, ***-island***, ***-islet***, †***-knot***, ***-lawn***, ***-matter***, ***-mould***, ***-order***, ***-pale***, ***-rake***, ***-refuse***, ***-scissors***, ***-seed***, ***-shade***, ***-shears***, ***soil***, ***-tillage***, ***-tool***, ***umbrella***, ***-walk***, ***-wall***, ***-wicket***; **b.** objective, as ***garden-watering*** vbl. sb.; ***garden-loving*** adj.; **c.** instrumental, as ***garden-girdled***, ***-surrounded*** adjs. Also ***garden-like*** adj.; ***garden-ward(s***, ***-wise*** advs.

1622 DRAYTON *Poly-olb.* XXVI. 120 The Flowry Vallies.. lying sleeke and smooth, as any *Garden-Allies. **1633** G. HERBERT *Temple, Church Milit.* 127 Here Sinne took heart, and for a *garden-bed Rich shrines and oracles he purchased. **1881** ROSSETTI *Ball. & Sonn., King's Trag.* (1882) 128 Couched on the happy garden-bed. **1863** LANDOR *Heroic Idylls, Meliton & Lily* 5 Sit on this *garden-bench and hear a song. **1903** *Bookman* XXV. 61/1 The volume now before us comes opportunely as a justification of what has grown to be called a '*garden book'. **1906** A. BENNETT *Let.* 6 Mar. (1966) I. 70, I expect another is his garden-book. **1937** A. LAMPLUGH (*title*) The garden book. **1798** COLERIDGE *Anc. Mar.* VII. xviii, In the *Garden-bower the Bride And Bride-maids singing are. **1936** *Discovery* Aug. 243/1 The common Kenya *garden-boy—whom I have known to plant a cherished seedling upside down, and then thoughtfully water it. **1951** D. LESSING *This was Old Chief's Country* i. 12 Working in our house as servants were always three natives: cook, houseboy, garden boy. **1850** MRS. BROWNING *Poems* II. 277 Who will fetch from *garden-closes Some new garlands while I speak? **1800** *Misc. Tracts* in *Asiatic Ann. Reg.* 98/1 To the north of the Sungee Dalaun is another *garden court, containing public offices. **1871** R. ELLIS *Catullus* lxii. 48 Look in a *garden-croft when a flower privily growing [etc.]. **1502-3** *Privy Purse Exp. Eliz. York* (1830) 20 *Gardeyn dore. **1601** SHAKS. *Twel. N.* III. i. 103. **1695** WOODWARD *Nat. Hist. Earth* (1723) 13 That blackish Layer of Earth or Mould which is called by some *Garden-Earth. **1856** EMERSON *Eng. Traits, Char.* Wks. (Bohn) II. 57, I suppose never nation built their party-walls so thick, or their *garden-fences so high. **1837** J. E. MURRAY *Summer Pyrenees* II. 85 His own particular moulin, in which he grinds the produce of his *garden-field. **1882** OUIDA *Maremma* I. 1 The cathedral square of *garden-girdled Grosseto. **1857** DICKENS *Dorrit* I. xxviii. 246 In her simple *garden-hat. **1967** E. TAYLOR *Second Thursday* iii. 39 Anna's garden hat.. lay at the bottom of the steps. *c* **1420** *Pallad. on Husb.* III. 569 To make a *gardyn hegge. *a* **1746** HOLDSWORTH *On Virgil* (1768) 89 Our old willows.. particularly some in the *Garden-Island in St. James' Park. **1821** SHELLEY *Prometh. Unb.* II. v, Till through elysian *garden-islets.. The boat of my desire is guided. **1626** BACON *Sylva* §111 In *Garden-knots, and the Frets of Houses, and all equall and well answering Figures. **1845** *Zoologist* III. 1056 Those pests, that raise such unsightly balls of earth upon *garden-lawns. **1829** LYTTON *Devereux* III. iv, I had entered into a more wooded and *garden-like description of country. **1838-42** ARNOLD *Hist. Rome* (1846) I. ii. 35 Its garden-like farms. **1851** *Beck's Florist* 243 In this condition they are purchased by persons having *garden-loving friends at home. **1577** B. GOOGE *Heresbach's Husb.* II. (1586) 49 To shew me some part of your great knowledge in *Garden matters. **1707** MORTIMER *Husb.* 131 They [Hops] delight most in the rich black *Garden-mold, that is deep and light, and that is mixed rather with Sand than Clay. **1782** MARSHALL in *Phil. Trans.* LXXIII. 221 One I find laid up in the fold of a.. turnip leaf was.. formed by putting.. garden mould to them. **1792** A. YOUNG *Trav. France* 5 Nothing can be more beautiful, or kept in more *garden order, if I may use the expression. **1828-40** BERRY *Encycl. Her.* I, **Garden-pales* are sometimes borne in coat-armour, generally issuing from the base and fitchée, or pointed at the top, and conjoined. **1844** J. T. HEWLETT *Parsons & W.* vi, Our garden-pales ran parallel with the high road. **1743** W. ELLIS *Mod. Husb.* (1744) Aug. xvi. 83 A man with a *Garden-rake raked in Cole-seed all over it. **1858** J. A. WARDER *Hedges & Evergreens* 60 A light garden-rake. **1868** PEARD *Water-farm.* xv. 159 Chopped *garden-refuse.. will answer admirably. **1832** MISS MITFORD *Village* Ser. v. (1863) 433 It turned out to be only the clinking of a pair of *garden-scissars. **1605** J. ROSIER *Voy. G. Waymouth* (1887) 105 We.. digged a plot of ground, wherein, amongst some *garden seeds, we sowed peaze and barley. **1719** DE FOE *Crusoe* I. xviii, Some garden-seed. *a* **1711** KEN *Preparatives* Poet. Wks. 1721 IV. 92, I to a *Garden-Shade withdrew. **1629** J. PARKINSON *Paradisi* iii. 5 Thrift.. may be kept, being cut with a pair of *Garden sheeres. **1708** MOTTEUX *Rabelais* V. ix. (1737) 36 A Pair of Garden-shears. **1848** *Cultivator* V. 213, I.. potted it in common *garden soil. **1875** MRS. STOWE *We & Neighbors* ii. 20 Catnip.. which grew in a bit of garden soil back of the house. **1939-40** *Army & Navy Stores Catal.* 63/2 Loams, garden soils. **1874** LISLE CARR *Jud. Gwynne* II. vii. 170 The secluded *garden-surrounded villa, in Old Kensington. **1707** MORTIMER *Husb.* ii. 106 Peas and Beans are what belong to *Garden Tillage as well as that of the Field. **1664** EVELYN *Kal. Hort.* (1729) 190 Cleanse, mend, sharpen.. *Garden Tools. **1832** TENNYSON *New-Year's Eve* xii, She'll find my garden-tools upon the granary floor. **1907** *Army & Navy Stores Catal.* 238/3 *Garden Umbrella.. with brass jointed stem, 6 ft. long.. with spike to screw into the ground. **1970** *Times* 28 May 8/1 In Sweden.. one household in 15 owns.. a garden umbrella. **1971** *E. Afr. Standard* (Nairobi) 10 Apr. 2/1 (Advt.), Garden umbrellas —picnic sets—safari mattresses. **1757** DYER *Fleece* III. 132 And now he strains the warp Along the *garden-walk, or highway side. **1850** MRS. BROWNING *Poems* II. 17 She looks down the garden-walk caverned with trees. *c* **1386** CHAUCER *Knt.'s T.* 202 The grete tour.. Was evene ioynant to the *gardin-wal. **1582** BRETON *Flourish Fancie* (Grosart) 54/1 Let, Lord, this tree be set within thy Garden-wall Of Paradise. **1870** MISS BRIDGMAN *R. Lynne* I. i. 9 The garden-wall of the.. house. *c* **1386** CHAUCER *Miller's T.* 386 Unto the *gardin-ward. **1895** CROCKETT in *Cornh. Mag.* Oct. 348 He.. showed signs of moving *gardenwards. **1896** *Daily News* 27 July 4/3 The period of supply could be extended if the consumers would only be careful.. to abstain from *garden-watering and other.. wasteful habits. **1826** in Cobbett *Rur. Rides* (1885) II. 50, I rode up to the *garden-wicket of a cottage. **1885** BURTON *Arab. Nts.* (1887) III. 134 Its courtyard is laid out *garden-wise.

5. a. Applied to vegetables, with the sense 'cultivated or growing in a garden', often distinctively opposed to 'wild'; as ***garden-creeper***, ***-flower***, ***-fruit***, ***-herb***, ***-plant***, ***-tree***, ***-vegetable***, ***-weed***; also in plant-names, indicating cultivated kinds, as †***garden-basil***, ***-gilliflower***, ***-honesty***, ***-madder***, ***-mint***, ***-nightshade***, ***-pea***, ***-pine***, ***-poppy***, ***-rocket***, ***-succory***; † **garden-balsam** (see quot.); **garden-clover**, *Melilotus cærulea* (see CLOVER *sb.* 2);

garden-cress, -cresses, *Lepidium sativum* (see CRESS 1 a); **garden-ginger**, cayenne pepper; †**garden-globe**, a sort of apple; †**garden-rod**, ? = GOLDEN-ROD; †**garden-sperage**, asparagus; **garden-trefoil** (see CLOVER *sb.* 2 and quot. 1548 there).

1633 JOHNSON *Gerarde's Herbal* II. 1195 The gardiners and herbe women in Cheapside commonly call it [*Trifolium odoratum*] and know it by the name of Balsam, or *garden Balsam. **1674** HICKMAN *Quinquart. Hist.* Ep. (ed. 2) A iv, Some in old times..thought *Garden-Basil..would grow the sooner and better, if it were sown..with reproaches and evil speaking. **1548, 1626** *Garden Claver [see CLOVER *sb.* 2]. **1844** MRS. BROWNING *Lost Bower* liii, Never *garden-creeper crossed it With so deft and brave an air. **1577** B. GOOGE *Heresbach's Husb.* (1586) 58 *Garden cresses..are sowed in the Spring. **1713** J. PETIVER in *Phil. Trans.* XXVIII. 202 This is a very elegant Plant, its lower Leaves being deeply cut, finer than the common Garden Cress. **1832** *Veg. Subst. Food* 304 Garden Cress..mixed with the young leaves of mustard..is the most esteemed of all..salads. **1770** GOLDSM. *Des. Vill.* 138 Near yonder copse, where once the garden smiled, And still where many a *garden-flower grows wild. **1838** DICKENS *O. Twist* xxxii, The garden-flowers perfumed the air with delicious odours. *c* **1511** *1st Eng. Bk. Amer.* (Arb.) Introd. 29/1 *Gardeynes frutes is there muche gretter than in our landes of Europa. **1551** TURNER *Herbal* 83 The roote of the *gardyn Gelouer is good agaynst the plage. **1597** GERARDE *Herbal* Supp., *Garden Ginger is *Piperitis*. **1600** SURFLET *Country Farme* III. xlix. 528 The shortstart..hony-meale and *garden globe..rare and singular apples. **1563** HYLL *Garden.* (1593) 164 The wilde hearbs are stronger in vertue then the *garden hearbs. **1567** MAPLET *Gr. Forest* 33 Beete is a Gardain Herbe, and in good plentie with vs. **1715** J. PETIVER in *Phil. Trans.* XXIX. 243 Its Root or lower Leaves, in Shape, resemble *Garden Honesty. **1578** LYTE *Dodoens* IV. lxxiii. 537 The husbanded or *garden Madder. **1530** PALSGR. 224/1 *Gardyne meynte, *meynte*. **1831** J. DAVIES *Man Mat. Med.* 433 Garden mint, *Mentha gentilis*, Lin. **1657** *Garden Night-shade [see 5 c]. **1882** *Garden* 16 Dec. 532/3 The Garden Nightshade..is a common annual weed. **1681** WOOD *Life* (O.H.S.) II. 558 In the ..months of Dec. and Jan. were *garden pees in blossom. **1832** *Veg. Subst. Food* 215 Garden peas..are raised by more careful and expensive culture for the purpose of being eaten green. *a* **1746** HOLDSWORTH *On Virgil* (1768) 533 He mentions the Pinus, which he calls Culta, meaning thereby the *Garden pine, to distinguish it from the Sylvestris. **1727** S. SWITZER *Pract. Gardiner* V. xlv. 237 Of this *phaseolus*..more species, than of any other *garden plant we have transmitted to us from foreign parts. **1671** SALMON *Syn. Med.* III. xxii. 416 *Garden Poppy, is narcoticke, provokes sleep, outwardly it easeth pain. **1832** *Veg. Subst. Food* 306 *Garden Rocket..cultivated by our ancestors..still..found in gardens on..the Continent. **1741** *Compl. Fam.-Piece* II. iii. 361 All sorts of fibrous rooted Plants..such as Holyoaks, *Garden-rods..and Hieraciums. **1577** B. GOOGE *Heresbach's Husb.* II. (1586) 54 The *Garden Sperage they were not acquainted with. **1601** HOLLAND *Pliny* II. 53 If a man be annointed with Asparagus or garden-Sperage..there will not (by report) a Bee come neere for to sting him. **1548** TURNER *Names of Herbes* (1881) 44 Intybus hortensis is of two sortes, the one is called Endyue, or whyte Endyue, and the other is called *gardine Succory. **1626** BACON *Sylva* §517 Whatsoeuer will make a Wild Tree a *Garden-Tree, will make a Garden-Tree to haue lesse Core, or Stone. **1775** SHERIDAN *Rivals* III. iii, Like garden-trees, they seldom shew fruit. **1818** T. G. FESSENDEN *Ladies Monitor* 171 Provincial words [include]: ..*bete* for beet, a *garden vegetable. **1841** *N.Y. Hist. Soc. Coll.* 2nd Ser. I. 152 The Netherlanders..have introduced every kind of garden vegetables. **1664** EVELYN *Kal Hort.* (1729) 189 Knot-grass, the very worst of *Garden-weeds.

b. Prefixed to the names of animals, birds, and insects to indicate that their habitat is the garden; as ***garden-ant, -ousel, -snail, -worm***; **garden-mouse**, ? = *field-mouse*; **garden-spider** = *cross-spider* (see CROSS- B); **garden-warbler**, the bird *Sylvia hortensis*; **garden-white**, a white cabbage butterfly, of the genus *Pieris*.

1879 LUBBOCK *Sci. Lect.* iv. 134 The brown *garden-ant habitually makes use of the out-of-doors aphides. **1712** J. JAMES tr. *Le Blond's Gardening* 173 The *Garden-Mouse is an Animal that digs the Earth like a Mole. *a* **1691** BOYLE *Hist. Air* (1692) 231 For I have observed these two last dry springs, that there has been no soft *garden snails to be found abroad. **1774** GOLDSM. *Nat. Hist.* (1784) VII. i. 3 This is the garden-snail, that carries its box upon its back. **1802** BINGLEY *Anim. Biog.* (1813) III. 359 The labour of the *Garden Spider is very different from that of the former species. **1843** *Zoologist* I. 13 In the spring of 1841 the redstart..and *garden warbler were very numerous. **1892** *Daily News* 6 Oct. 5/1 The caterpillars of the *Garden White—the green grubs that do so much damage among the cabbages—are crawling up the walls. **1651–7** T. BARKER *Art of Angling* (1820) 37 Gather great *garden-worms. **1669** WORLIDGE *Syst. Agric.* (1681) 258 The Garden-worm is an excellent bait for a Salmon.

c. passing into adj., in the slang phr. ***common or garden***, a jocular substitute for 'common', 'ordinary'.

[**1657** W. COLES *Adam in Eden* xxix. 59 But the Common or Garden Nightshade is not dangerous.] **1892** *Autobiog. Eng. Gamekeeper* (J. Wilkins) 67 It was as large as a common—or garden—hen. **1896** *Daily News* 16 Oct. 3/4 Such common or garden proceedings not being to the taste of Noa. **1897** *Westm. Gaz.* 4 Aug. 8/2, I have—to make use of a common or garden expression—been 'rushed' in this matter.

6. Special comb.: **garden-butt**, a target set up in a garden for archery practice; **garden carpet**, (*a*) a species of Geometer moth (cf. *carpet-moth*); (*b*) (see quots. 1960 and 1963); **garden centre**, a place where gardening requirements are sold; **garden-chair**, †(*a*) a wheel or bath chair; (*b*) a chair intended for use in a garden; **garden city**, (*a*) a name given to Chicago and certain other cities (freq. with capital initials); (*b*) a town of limited size, surrounded by a wide rural or agricultural belt, and planned so as to combine the advantages of town and country; **Garden Colony**, a name given to Natal, on account of the wealth and beauty of its flora; **garden county** *U.S.*, the county (of a state) most resembling a garden; the most fertile and beautiful part; **garden-craft**, the management of gardens; gardening; **garden egg**, a Jamaican name for the egg-plant or its fruit; **garden-engine**, a portable force-pump used for watering gardens; **garden-frame** = FRAME *sb.* 13 c; **garden-glass**, (*a*) a bell glass used for covering plants in a garden; (*b*) (see quot. 1882); **garden gnome**, a figure of a gnome used as a garden ornament; **garden-ground**, (*a*) ground suitable for a garden; (*b*) a plot of ground appropriated to a garden; **garden magic**, magic practised by certain primitive tribes as an aid in the cultivation of their gardens; **garden-patch** *U.S.* = *garden-ground* (b); **garden-path**, a path in a garden (see also sense 1 f above); **garden-pea** (see sense 5 a above); *spec.* (see quot. 1960); †**garden-penny**, ? a tithe or payment levied upon garden-produce; **garden-plot**, a plot of land used as a garden; †**garden-roll** (*obs.*), **garden-roller**, a heavy cylinder fitted with a handle or shafts, for smoothing a lawn or path; **garden-room**, (*a*) space in a garden; (*b*) a room with a door or window opening out on to a garden; †**garden satin**, ? flowered satin; **garden sauce (sars, sarse, sass)** *U.S.*, garden vegetables (see SAUCE *sb.* 4 a); **garden seat**, a seat (of wood or metal) for use in a garden; a similar seat, holding one or two persons, fixed on the roof of an omnibus, etc.; hence **garden-seated** *a.*; †**garden-sin** (*nonce-wd.*), a weed; **garden spot** *U.S.*, (*a*) a garden or a place suitable for a garden; (*b*) a region notable for its fertility, climate, etc; **Garden State** *U.S.*, a name given to various American states, esp. New Jersey; †**garden-stead** = *garden-plot*; **garden suburb**, a suburb organized on the same lines as, or having some of the characteristics of, a garden city; †**garden-things**, produce of a garden; **garden town** = *garden city* (b); **garden-truck** *U.S.*, garden vegetables; **garden village**, a village organized on the same lines as, or having some of the characteristics of, a garden city; **garden-wall-bond** *Bricklaying* (see quot.); †**garden-ware** = *garden-things*. Also GARDEN-GATE, -HOUSE, -PARTY, -POT, -STUFF.

1599 PORTER *Angry Wom. Abingt.* E iij, When I had..carried my buckler before me like a *garden But. **1908** R. SOUTH *Moths Brit. Is.* II. 195 (*caption*) *Garden Carpet at rest. **1928** *Sunday Express* 8 July 10/4 A fine 'firdausi', or garden carpet. **1960** H. HAYWARD *Antique Coll.* 127/1 *Garden carpets*, Persian carpets, showing formal designs with figures and animals. **1963** *Times* 8 June 1/7 There is reason to believe that the first important carpet was known as the Garden Carpet. When the sons of the Prophet took Ctesiphon in A.D. 637 they discovered a vast woven fabric of over one thousand square yards in area,..in which the motive was a garden in the full beauty of spring... The garden carpet is a symbol—the emblems of life and death passing to eternity in an endless chain. **1965** C. KELWAY *Gardening on Sand* ix. 117 Look out for them [*sc.* dwarf trees] at the now-popular *garden centres where many may be seen growing in containers ready for taking home. **1971** *Guardian* 25 Sept. 7/1 Plant container-grown Roses, Flowering Shrubs, Conifers..Lymm Garden Centre—on A56. **1827** *Gentl. Mag.* XCVII. I. 546 This pole, like the handle of a *garden-chair, enables the guide to drive to the eighth of an inch, to avoid all obstacles, to turn corners. **1831** *Society* I. 122 Seated in the garden-chair appropriated to Miss Herford's use, and drawn by her favourite donkey, away went the cousins. **1851** H. MELVILLE *Whale* xxi. 111 Garden-chairs which are convertible into walking-sticks. **1853** KINGSLEY *Hypatia* xiii, The garden-chairs standing among the flower-beds. **1848** *Gem of Prairie* (Chicago) 25 Nov. 3/3 My rambles round the *Garden city. **1872** SCHELE DE VERE *Americanisms* 665 Savannah, in Georgia,..claiming the name of Garden City. **1898** E. HOWARD *To-morrow* i. 13 Garden City, the Town-country magnet, which it is intended to build. **1902** —— (*title*) Garden cities of tomorrow. **1903** *Times* 29 Aug. 4/5 The Garden City Pioneer Company (Limited) has acquired about 4,000 acres of land near Hitchin on which to build the first garden city. **1914** *Scotsman* 6 Oct. 7/2 There are at present in existence a number of schemes such as the First Garden City at Letchworth, and the various garden suburbs which have been successfully started in various parts of the country. **1927** *Daily Tel.* 1 May 9/4 The Federal Capital City of Australia..its splendid design on 'garden city' lines. **1966** W. L. CREESE (*title*) The search for environment. The garden city: before and after. **1896** 'S. CUMBERLAND' *What I think of S. Afr.* xv. 175 Natal is called the '*Garden Colony'. **1902** *Westm. Gaz.* 28 July 10/1 It is the Garden Colony of South Africa. **1872** *Newton Kansan* 21 Nov. 2/3 This bids fair to be the favored spot in the *garden county. **1891** J. D. SEDDING (*title*) *Garden craft, old and new. **1904** E. WHARTON *Italian Villas* 5 To enjoy and appreciate the Italian garden-craft one must always bear in mind that it is independent of floriculture. **1927** E. S. ROHDE (*title*) Garden-craft in the Bible, and other essays. **1811** W. J. TITFORD *Sks. Hortus Bot. Amer.* p. xiii, *Garden Egg. (*Solanum Melongena.*) Cut in slices, parboiled and fried, resembles fried eggs. **1964** E. HUXLEY *Back Street New Worlds* xiv. 141 The Shepherd's Bush market has a shop devoted wholly to West African foods..like..garden eggs and fou-fou. **1969** *Daily Tel.* 11 Jan. 14/1 Melongene is our own familiar aubergine known in Jamaica as 'garden egg'. **1815** *Specif. Edridge's Patent* No. 3948 Solder may in such instances be employed..to render the pump a fire or *garden engine. **1892** *Garden* 27 Aug. 179 The bushes were so bad, that I had them well sprayed with the garden engine. **1838** *Penny Cycl.* XI. 72/1 They were essentially greenhouses, although perhaps more like our *garden-frames. **1842** TENNYSON *Gardener's Dau.* 116 The *garden-glasses glanced, and momently The twinkling laurel scatter'd silver lights. **1882** OGILVIE, *Garden-glass*, 1. a round globe of dark-coloured glass, generally about 1½ foot in diameter, placed on a pedestal, in which the surrounding objects are reflected: much used as an ornament of gardens in Germany. **1946** *Woman & Beauty* Dec. 31 *Garden gnomes—*some* people like them. **1966** M. KELLY *Dead Corse* vii. 100 The owners of plastic flowers and garden gnomes, and plaster teal taking wing across the wall of the lounge-diner. **1711** *Lond. Gaz.* No. 4938/3 A Piece of *Garden-ground, and a Tenement thereupon. **1766** SMOLLETT *Trav.* I. xvi. 268 All the vineyards and garden-grounds for a considerable extent are vaulted underneath. **1808** TOLLER *Tithes* iv. 124 It is very usual..to agree with the occupiers of garden-ground for a stated composition by the acre. **1870** LONGF. *Wayside Inn* II. *Bell of Atri* 38 Rented his vineyards and his garden-grounds. **1929** B. MALINOWSKI *Sexual Life Savages* ii. 36 In *garden magic, the officiator plays an economically and socially important role and is the organizer and director of the work. **1957** P. WORSLEY *Trumpet shall Sound* iii. 71 The cult has come a long way from simple garden-magic. **1832** J. P. KENNEDY *Swallow Barn* II. 224 Little *garden-patches..where cymblings, cucumbers..flourished. **1924** R. CUMMINS *Sky-High Corral* 17 The fat cook puffed in from the garden patch. **1870** 'F. FERN' *Ginger-Snaps* 162 The irresolute hand..could only lead them up and down that narrow *garden path. **1932** B. NICHOLS (*title*) Down the garden path. **1629** J. PARKINSON *Paradisi* II. lii. 522 *Garden Pease are for the most part the greatest and sweetest kinds. **1681, 1832** Garden pea [see sense 5 a above]. **1951** E. DAVID *French Country Cooking* 231 Put the contents of a large tin of garden peas through a sieve. **1960** *Which?* June 120/1 Canned peas come in two forms, 'garden' and 'processed'. 'Garden' peas are canned when they are fresh... 'Processed' peas are dried peas which are soaked to bring them back to their ordinary size before they go through much the same canning procedure as garden peas. **1969** V. C. CLINTON-BADDELEY *Only Matter of Time* 37 Alice, bearing potatoes..and 'garden' peas which had not long been emancipated from the deep freeze. *a* **1641** BP. R. MOUNTAGU *Acts & Mon.* (1642) 400 Paying Tythes duly and truly, even to a *garden-penny, as wee call it, or of very flowers and pot-herbs that grow in our garden. **1647** *Husbandman's Plea agst. Tithes* 59 They pay never a peny to the Minister, except it be a garden peny, or a peck of Apples, or such like tithes. **1587** HARMAR tr. *Beza's Serm.* xxvi. 351 Their *garden-plots and orchards. **1610** GUILLIM *Heraldry* III. vii. (1611) 116 Knights and men of valour, whose worth must be tried in the field, not vnder a rose-bed or in a Garden-plot. **1845** *Florist's Jrnl.* 221 Affording even the suburban tyro a chance of ornamenting his garden-plot. **1794** G. ADAMS *Nat. & Exp. Philos.* III. xxxii. 302 Drawing a heavy *garden-roll. **1792** C. SMITH *Desmond* I. 59 A figure who gave me the idea of a *garden roller set on its end. **1852** MISS MITFORD *Recollect.* II. 169 Mr. Landor..seated on a garden-roller in the court. **1750** R. ROE *Let. to A. Johnson* 19 Where *garden-room enough is to be had. **1892** STEVENSON & OSBOURNE *Wrecker* xx. 317 The garden-room, whither Lady Ann had now retired. **1961** *Times* 6 May 11/3 This exquisite garden-room is the most perfect of its kind in Italy. **1971** *Country Life* 24 June 1593/1 At the end of this wall Captain Radcliffe built a terrace and portico or garden room of stone in the Grecian style. **1722** *Lond. Gaz.* No. 6068/8 A *Garden Sattin Night Gown lined with Cherry Silk, one Chince Gown. **1791** *Amer. Museum* X. 179 For want of *garden sauce, they..eat more flesh than is consistent with their health. **1833** J. NEAL *Down-Easters* I. 91, I wanted cabbage or potaters, or most any sort o' garden sarse. **1869** S. BOWLES *Our New West* xi. 231 A load of grain, pork, or 'garden sass'. **1873** J. H. BEADLE *Undevel. West* xxix. 504 The country West does not contain arable land enough to supply garden-sauce to an average population. **1921** C. GREER-PETRIE *Angeline at Seelbach* 11 The next thing he fotch us was some gyarden sass and some biled beef. **1837** DICKENS *Pickw.* xxxix, A *garden seat which happened..to be near at hand. **1879** F. W. ROBINSON *Coward Consc.* I. vii, There was a garden seat..upon the lawn. **1891** *Daily News* 13 Jan. 2/4 On the garden seats the passengers sat two abreast. **1895** *Westm. Gaz.* 29 Mar. 2/1 Many people..dislike getting on the top of a *garden-seated 'bus. **1664** EVELYN *Kal. Hort.* (1729) 210 Neglecting it till they [the weeds] are ready to sow themselves, you do but stir and prepare for a more numerous Crop of these *Garden-sins. **1687** T. FAUNCE in *Rec. Town Plymouth* (1889) I. 190 We are bounded by goodman Watsons *garden spot. **1813** *Niles' Reg.* IV. 317/2 The Rapids of the Miami may justly be termed the 'garden spot' of the territory. **1884** 'C. E. CRADDOCK' *In Tenn. Mts.* I. 53 She was welcomed to a chair and a view of the weed-grown 'garden-spot'. **1898** T. N. PAGE *Red Rock* 298 It's the garden spot of the world—the money's jest layin' round to waste on the ground. **1865** *Daily Morning Chron.* (Washington, D.C.) 29 Sept. 2/3 Verily, Illinois is justly called 'The *Garden State'. **1871** SCHELE DE VERE *Americanisms* 659 Kansas is often called the Garden State, from the beautiful appearance of rolling prairies and vast cultivated fields. **1948** *Sat. Even. Post* 20 Nov. 57/2 When the first nip of frost chills the New Jersey air, cooks in the Garden State revive this recipe. **1967** MRS. L. B. JOHNSON *White House Diary* 25 June (1970) 537 Betty Hughes was the tour guide... Her state [*sc.* New Jersey] is called the 'Garden State', and they have many truck farmers. **1609** *Manch. Court Leet Rec.* (1885) II. 249 The place..is Conuerted..into Certaine *gardensteeds. **1905** S. A. BARNETT *Let.* 28 Jan. in H. Barnett *Canon Barnett* (1918) II. 191 My wife has had a very busy week, interviewing people *re* the *Garden Suburb. **1914** Garden suburb [see *garden city*, above]. **1953** C. DAY LEWIS *Italian Visit* iii. 42 Here is one corner of a foreign field That is for ever garden suburb. **1772** BARKER in *Phil. Trans.* LXII. 44 *Garden-things, turnips, &c. were very much destroyed. **1915** P. GEDDES *Cities in Evolution* iii. 54 The conditions for labour and its real wages, in the innumerable *garden-towns and villages which are springing up. **1807** P. GASS *Jrnl.* 51 The Rees..had left..some *garden truck, such as squashes. **1923** M. WATTS *L. Nichols* 292 A wagon-load of garden-truck. **1915** *Garden village [see *garden town* above]. **1933** *Archit. Rev.* LXXIV. 120 He may preserve as much as he can and create a garden village which will be an addition to the neighbourhood. **1836** *Penny Cycl.* V. 410 *Garden-wall bond consists of three stretchers and one header in nine inch walls, but when fourteen inches thick, the Flemish bond is used. **1707** MORTIMER *Husb.* 432 A clay bottom is a much more pernicious Soil for Trees and *Garden-ware than Gravel.

garden ('gɑːd(ə)n), *v.* [f. the sb.; cf. F. *jardiner* (from 15th c.).]

1. a. *intr.* To cultivate a garden; to work in a garden as a gardener. †Also, to lay out a garden. **1577** B. GOOGE *Heresbach's Husb.* II. (1586) 53 b, I know in hot countries they garden all the winter long. **1625** BACON *Ess., Gardens* (Arb.) 555 When Ages grow to Ciuility..Men come to Build Stately, sooner then to Garden Finely. **1765** FRANKLIN *Let.* Wks. 1887 III. 391 You should have gardened long before the date of your last. **1832** TENNYSON *New-Year's Eve* xii, I shall never garden more. **1844** E. FITZ GERALD *Lett.* (1889) I. 137, I..read scraps of books, garden a little, and am on good terms with my neighbours.

b. *Cricket.* Of a batsman: to remedy any unevenness in the pitch by clearing away loose fragments, patting the ground flat, etc. *colloq.* **1897** *Encycl. Sport* I. 226/2 Fragments of grass and turf should be removed... The process of clearing the ground of *débris* is known to cricketers as 'gardening'. **1956** N. CARDUS *Close of Play* 15 They both attended to the turf every ball, 'gardening' assiduously, and how thoroughly Sutcliffe would pat the earth.

2. *trans.* To cultivate as a garden; to bring or form by cultivation *into* (a specified state). **1862** B. TAYLOR *Home & Abr.* Ser. II. I. 322 The trees have been judiciously spared..the long landscape..gardened into more perfect beauty. **1895** *Westm. Gaz.* 6 Feb. 3/3 The gallery of well-dressed women..suggests the simile of some gorgeous flower-bed, carefully gardened.

3. To supply with a garden or gardens. *rare.* **1865** *Athenæum* No. 1945. 154/3 They were there superbly housed and luxuriously gardened.

†**4.** (See quot.) *Obs.* [So F. *jardiner.*] **1706** PHILLIPS (ed. Kersey), *To Garden a Hawk*, ..is to put her on a Turf of Grass to chear her.

Hence **'gardenable** *a.*, capable of being gardened. **1804** COLERIDGE *Let.* 21 Apr. (1895) II. 476 Above the town, little gardens..are scattered here and there, wherever they can force a bit of gardenable ground.

garden, obs. form of GUARDIAN.

†**'gardenage.** *Obs.* Also 7 gardinage. [f. GARDEN *sb.* + -AGE. Cf. F. *jardinage.*]

1. The practice or employment of cultivating a garden; horticulture. **1601** HOLLAND *Pliny* II. 12 There was no one thing..lesse subiect to the will and pleasure of Fortune and Casualtie, than gardenage. *Ibid.* II. 28, I must not overpasse the gardinage to them belonging. **1693** EVELYN *De la Quint. Compl. Gard.* I. 89 Persons of Quality that divertise themselves there in Gardenage.

2. The produce of a garden; garden-stuff. **1733** J. TULL *Horse-hoing Husb.* v. 19 The eating unwholesom Gardenage. **1816** J. MAN *Hist. Reading* 147 This street was appropriated to the sale of fish and gardenage.

gardened ('gɑːd(ə)nd), *ppl. a.* [f. GARDEN *sb.* and *v.* + -ED.]

1. Cultivated like a garden. **1611** COTGR., *Iardiné*, gardened; made into, or wrought as, a Garden. **1808** J. BARLOW *Columb.* x. 239 Earth, garden'd all, a tenfold burden brings. **1867** HOWELLS *Ital. Journ.* 307 Around Verona stretch those gardened plains of Lombardy. **1883** *Atlantic Monthly* LII. 363 A gay gardened meadow.

2. Furnished or covered with gardens. **1829** J. WILSON in *Blackw. Mag.* XXVI. 543 The broomy burn That wimpled on round garden'd villages. **1844** MRS. BROWNING *Flower in Let.* x, No flowers our gardened England hath To match with these. **1862** H. MARRYAT *Year in Sweden* II. 404 A long line of gardened houses.

gardener ('gɑːd(ə)nə(r)). Forms: 4-5 gardenere, 4-6 gardyner(e, 4-8 gardiner, 5 garthyner(e, 6-8 gardner, 4- gardener. [a. ONF. *gardinier = OF. and mod.F. *jardinier* (12th c.), f. *gardin, jardin*: see GARDEN *sb.* and -ER². Cf. OHG. *gartinâri* (mod.G. *gärtner*).]

1. One who tends, lays out or cultivates a garden; *spec.* a servant employed to tend and cultivate a garden. *a* **1300** *Cursor M.* 17270 + 227 Scho [marie] wend not it had bene he, bot a gardiner. **1340** HAMPOLE *Pr. Consc.* 661 An ille tre may na gude fruyt bere, And þat knawes ilk gude gardynere. *c* **1460** *Towneley Myst.* xxvi. 563 Say me, garthynere, I the pray, If thou bare oght my lord away. **1601** HOLLAND *Pliny* XX. v. II. 41 The Syrians are great Gardiners, they..bee most curious in gardening. **1662** WOOD *Life* (O.H.S.) I. 462 [He] lived as a gardiner with a certaine gentleman. **1771** SMOLLETT *Humph. Cl.* (1815) 282, I was told..that almost all the gardeners of South Britain were natives of Scotland. **1865** RUSKIN *Arrows of Chace* (1880) II. 140, I have a gardener who..sees me gather a bunch of my own grapes without making a wry face. *fig.* **1604** SHAKS. *Oth.* I. iii. 324 Our Bodies are our Gardens, to the which, our Wills are Gardiners. **16..** HOWEL (J.), The gardener may lop religion as he please.

2. In names of plants: **gardener's delight**, **eye**, *Lychnis coronaria*; **gardener's garters** (see quot. 1880). **1597** GERARDE *Herbal* II. cxx. §2. 381 [The flowers of Rosecampion] were called the Gardners delight, or the Gardners eie. **1823** CORBETT *Petticoat T.* I. 240 Would you like some slips of apple ringy..or gardener's garters, or bachelor's buttons? **1880** BRITTEN & HOLLAND *Plant-n.*, *Gardener's garters*, the striped garden variety of *Phalaris arundinacea*.

Hence **'gardeneress**, a female gardener; also, a gardener's wife. **1647** W. BROWNE tr. *Gomberville's Polexander* I. 182 The fair Gardneresse, this while, held my arme. **1827** CARLYLE *German Rom.* III. 253, 270. **1893** *Star* 24 June 4/3 Good situations are always ready for good gardeneresses. **1896** *Daily Tel.* 23 Jan. 5/3 The first gardeneress Eve.

gardenership ('gɑːd(ə)nəʃɪp). [f. GARDENER + -SHIP.] †**a.** The art and practice of gardening (*obs.*). **b.** The office of a gardener. **1711** SHAFTESB. *Charac.* I. III. i. 286 'Tis no wonder if we slight the Gardenership, and think the manner of Culture a very contemptible Mystery. **1864** BURTON *Scot Abr.* I. ii. 99 People spoke of the succession to the hereditary gardenership of the lordship of Monteith.

gardenery ('gɑːd(ə)nərɪ). *rare*$^{-1}$. [f. GARDENER + -Y³.] The office or department of a gardener. **1892** KIRK *Abingdon Acc.* p. xxxvi, 79*s.* 7*d.* was transferred from the Pittancery to the Gardenery.

gardenesque ('gɑːd(ə)nɛsk), *a.* [f. GARDEN *sb.* + -ESQUE; after *picturesque.*] Partaking of the character of a garden; somewhat resembling a garden or what belongs to a garden. **1838** LOUDON *Arboretum Brit.*, The expression of gardenesque beauty, in individual trees differs from the picturesque, in being..at all times, regular or symmetrical. **1839** —— *Repton's Landsc. Garden* (1840) Introd. 8 This change has given rise to a school which we call the Gardenesque; the characteristic feature of which is the display of the beauty of trees, and other plants, individually. **1880-1** *Libr. Univ. Knowl.* (N.Y.) XI. 306 [Boston Common 'public garden'] is kept in gardenesque style as an arboretum and botanical garden. **1881** *Gard. Chron.* No. 417. 816 An attempt to give a sort of gardenesque character to a slope within view of the Castle by planting dwarf hardy shrubs in a formal arrangement of beds. *absol.* **1896** *Punch* 29 Aug. 102/2 No, by heavens, let the gardenesque perish Ere ever I axe that familiar old thorn!

gardenful ('gɑːd(ə)nfʊl). [f. GARDEN *sb.* + -FUL.] As many as a garden will contain. **1859** DICKENS *T. Two Cities* II. v, Like a great sunflower pushing its way at the sun from among a rank gardenfull of flaring companions.

,garden-'gate. [f. GARDEN *sb.* + GATE *sb.*¹]

1. A gate leading into a garden. *c* **1400** MAUNDEV. (1839) xix. 210 He smytethe on the Gardyn ȝate with a Clyket of Sylver. **1463** *Bury Wills* (Camden) 22 The grete gardeyn gate. **1731** POPE *Ep. Burlington* 30 Turn Arcs of triumph to a Garden-gate. **1838** DICKENS *O. Twist* xxix, A gig drove up to the garden-gate.

2. *dial.* Used as a name for various plants: Herb Robert (*Geranium Robertianum*), the Pansy (*Viola tricolor*), and London Pride (*Saxifraga umbrosa*). The fuller form is 'Kiss-me-behind-the-garden-gate' (Britten & Holland).

'gardenhood. *nonce-wd.* [f. GARDEN *sb.* + -HOOD.] Garden-like character. **1769** H. WALPOLE *Let. to Montagu* 11 May (1857) V. 161 A covered passage all round the garden..took off from the gardenhood.

'garden-house. [f. GARDEN *sb.* + HOUSE.]

1. Any small building in a garden; a summer-house. **1603** SHAKS. *Meas. for M.* v. i. 212 This is the body That ..did supply thee at thy garden-house In her Imagin'd person. **1678** DRYDEN *Limberham* I. i, I was just coming down to the garden-house. **1727** DE FOE *Secrets Invis. W.* (1735) 251 As he was sitting alone in a Summer-House as we call it, or Garden-House, as they more properly call it there [Leipsick]. **1821** SCOTT *Kenilw.* xx, Pointing to an old ruinous garden-house.

b. *dial.* and *U.S.* A privy. **1886** ELWORTHY *W. Somerset Word-bk.*, *Garden-house*, a privy; an out-door closet.

2. A dwelling-house situated in a garden; a suburban residence. **1607** DEKKER & WEBSTER *Northward Ho* II. ii, Because.. to be pent up in a narrow lodging here i' the city may offend her health, she shall lodge at a garden-house of mine in Moorfields. **1627** in *Crt. & Times Chas. I* (1848) I. 243 Sir Francis Barrington..is gone out of the Marshalsea to a garden-house in Southwark. **1673** R. HEAD *Canting Acad.* 74 Having an occasion to go over to the bank-side, in a Garden house. **1738** BIRCH *Life Milton* in *M.'s Wks.* I. 20 He..took an handsome Garden House in Aldersgate-street. **1845** STOCQUELER *Handbk. Brit. India* (1854) 133 Interspersed with the garden-houses, or suburban retreats of the wealthy merchants.

†**b.** In the early 17th c. often used for a house kept for immoral purposes. *Obs.* **1607** BEAUM. & FL. *Woman Hater* II. i, This is no garden house, in my conscience, shee went forth with no dishonest intent. *a* **1625** FLETCHER *Love's Cure* III. i, Thou shalt be my Bawd..Thy old wife [shall]..weare a hood, Nay keepe my garden-house.

gardenia (gɑːˈdiːnɪə). [mod.Lat., f. the name of Dr. Alex. *Garden* (died 1791), Vice-President of the Royal Society.] A genus of trees and shrubs, often spiny (N.O. *Rubiaceæ*), natives of the Cape of Good Hope and of tropical Asia and Africa. **1760** *Phil. Trans.* LI. 934 The professor has agreed to adopt this new genus by the name of Gardenia. **1863** ALCOCK *Capit. Tycoon* I. 76 But the gardinia [*sic*] and the camellia flourish also. **1881** MRS. C. PRAED *Policy & P.* III. 38 The strong scent of gardenias..floated towards him.

gardening ('gɑːd(ə)nɪŋ), *vbl. sb.* [f. GARDEN *v.* + -ING¹.]

1. The action or occupation of laying out or cultivating a garden; horticulture. **1577** B. GOOGE *Heresbach's Husb.* (1586) 53 b, In these parts they commonly begin their gardening..in the end of Februarie. **1665** BOYLE *Occas. Refl.* (1845) 57-8 A Stranger to the Art of Gardening. **1762-71** H. WALPOLE *Vertue's Anecd. Paint.* (1786) IV. 247 Gardening was probably one of the first arts that succeeded to that of building houses. **1877** MRS. FORRESTER *Mignon* I. 64 My nephew has done the gardening single-handed the last five years. *fig.* *a* **1577** GASCOIGNE *Hearbes, Weedes*, etc. Wks. (1587) 160 Gascoigns gardenings wherof were written in one end of a close walke which he hath in his garden this discourse following.

†**2.** *concr.* Grounds laid out as gardens. *Obs.*$^{-1}$ **1687** *Lond. Gaz.* No. 2284/4 At Worksop..is a large New House to be Lett, with good Cellaridge, Stabling, Gardning, and Land belonging to it.

3. *attrib.* **1577** B. GOOGE *Heresbach's Husb.* (1586) 53 b, Some devide their Gardening time by the Moneths. **1587** *Wills & Inv. N.C.* (Surtees 1860) 157 Twelve gardining shoviles 12/-. **1661** OGILBY *His Majesty's Entertainm.* 30 All Sorts of Graffing, and Gardening Tools. **1716** H. STEVENSON *Young Gard'ner's Director* p. iii, In all the Gard'ning Books. **1825** COBBETT *Rur. Rides* 41 The country presents a sort of gardening scene. **1830** MISS MITFORD *Village* Ser. IV. (1863) 312, I may consider myself in great luck to see what is called, in gardening language, 'so grand a show'. **1843** *Ainsworth's Mag.* IV. 473 She seemed ashamed neither of her gardening gloves..nor her quizzical companion. **1850** *Beck's Florist* 54 Gardening newspapers..find their way into every circle where a flower is loved. **1861** DELAMER *Fl. Gard.* 2 The gardening artist who, under such circumstances..fails to produce a pleasing..effect, is almost left without excuse. **1891** H. HERMAN *His Angel* 217, I had on my gardening suit. **1894** *Westm. Gaz.* 17 Sept. 3/3, I should like also to draw the distinction between gardening classes and a gardening club. **1932** D. C. MINTER *Mod. Needlecraft* 220/2 Remnants of cretonne..made up into a sewing or gardening apron. **1934** A. THIRKELL *Wild Strawberries* xiii. 277 The schoolroom, where Lady Emily kept some of her valuable old gardening books. **1964** E. BOWEN *Little Girls* III. v. 206 Gardening gloves crammed bulkily into a pocket.

gardening ('gɑːd(ə)nɪŋ), *ppl. a.* [f. GARDEN *v.* + -ING².] That gardens. **1647** W. BROWNE tr. *Gomberville's Polexander* I. 183 In an instant we saw a Gardning maiden become a Princess. **1822** LAMB *Elia* Ser. I. *Dream Children*, Now and then a solitary gardening man would cross me. **1850** *Beck's Florist* 287 All the gardening world used to talk of the 2000 varieties of Roses grown by the Messrs. Loddiges.

'gardenist. *nonce-wd.* [f. GARDEN *sb.* + -IST.] **1762-71** H. WALPOLE *Vertue's Anecd. Paint.* (1786) IV. 106 The domestic called a Gardiner..will remain the Gardiner, the projector I should propose to denominate a Gardenist.

gardenize ('gɑːd(ə)naɪz), *v. rare.* [f. GARDEN *sb.* + -IZE.] **a.** *intr.* To act as a gardener. **b.** *trans.* To render like a garden. Also *fig.* **1830** C. MATHEWS *Mem.* IV. iii. 61 A boor, who gardenizes and milks. **1887** *Voice* (N.Y.) (1888) 5 Jan. 2 [God] has promised that this world shall be gardenized and all evil extirpated. **1891** *Graphic* 24 Oct. 491/3 It is to be wished something could be done in the way of 'gardenising' ..Trafalgar Square.

gardenless ('gɑːd(ə)nlɪs), *a.* [f. GARDEN *sb.* + -LESS.] Destitute of gardens or of a garden. **1834** R. H. FROUDE *Remains* (1838) I. 367 Treeless fields and gardenless houses. **1882** *Harper's Mag.* LXIV. 102 The town itself is made up of a scattering, gardenless collection of log-cabins.

gardenly ('gɑːd(ə)nlɪ), *a. rare*$^{-1}$. [f. GARDEN *sb.* + -LY¹.] Appropriate to, or befitting, a garden. *a* **1819** W. MARSHALL *Rur. Econ.* (L.), The crop throughout being managed in a gardenly manner.

'garden-,party. [f. GARDEN *sb.* + PARTY.] A party held on a lawn, or in a garden. **1869** TROLLOPE *Phineas Finn* II. lxiv. 228 The Duke's garden party was becoming a mere ball, with privilege for the dancers to stroll about the lawn between the dances. *attrib.* **1874** J. D. HEATH *Croquet Player* 9 There is really no comparison between it and what may appropriately be called 'Garden-party Croquet'. **1896** *Westm. Gaz.* 25 June 2/3 The garden party season is now beginning.

'garden-pot. [f. GARDEN *sb.* + POT.]

†**1.** A watering-pot. *Obs.* **1580** HOLLYBAND *Treas. Fr. Tong*, *Vne Chantepleure*, a garden pot, a watering pot, the toppe of a Cesterne. **1591** SYLVESTER *Du Bartas* I. i. 368 Thence is't that Garden-pots, the mouth kept close, Let fall no liquor at their sive-like nose. **1614** T. ADAMS *Devil's Banquet* 32 The Garden-pot, that holds water but whiles the thumbe is vpon it.

2. A pot containing a plant; a flower-pot.
1808 *Phil. Trans.* XCIX. 175 When..the fibrous roots of trees are crowded together in a garden-pot, they are often found lifeless in the succeeding spring. *a* **1845** HOOD *Sniffing a Birthday* xvi, My freehold's in the garden-pot.

gardenship, obs. form of GUARDIANSHIP.

'garden-stuff. [f. GARDEN *sb.* + STUFF.] Plants grown in a garden; vegetables for the table.
a **1687** PETTY *Pol. Arith.* vi. (1691) 96 The..meliorating, and multiplying several sorts of Fruits, and Garden-Stuff. **1755** *Gentl. Mag.* XXV. 350 Cherries, peaches, pears, grain, and garden-stuff of all kinds. **1828** MISS MITFORD *Village* Ser. III. (1863) 64 She sold bread, butcher's meat, and garden-stuff, on commission.
attrib. **1849** CLOUGH *Amours de Voy.* III. 163, I am the ox in the dray, the ass with the garden-stuff panniers.

garderobe ('gɑːdrəʊb). Now only *Hist.* Also 4, 7 garderob, 6 gardrop, 6, 9 gardrobe. [a. F. *garderobe* (= It. *guarda-robba*: in ONF. *warderobe*: see WARDROBE), f. *garde-r* to keep, GUARD + *robe* ROBE.] Properly, a locked-up chamber in which articles of dress, stores, etc. are kept, a store-room, armoury, wardrobe (occas. also the contents of this); by extension, a private room, a bed-chamber; also a privy.
1333-4 *Durham MS. Cell. Roll*, In ij lib. de Maces de garderob. *a* **1450** *Knt. de la Tour* (1868) 111 The kingges doughter..made hym to be norisshed in her garderobe. **1470-85** MALORY *Arthur* v. x, I haue ben brought vp in the garderobe with the noble kynge Arthur many yeres for to take hede to his armour. **15..** *Inv. R. Wardrobe* (1815) 145 *margin*, In Feb. 1567 six of thir peces was tint in the K[ing's] gardrop at his death. **1606** *Table Unprinted Acts 18 Jas. VI*, An acquitance and discharge to the earle of Dumbar of the Kings Jewels and garderob. **1837** SIR F. PALGRAVE *Merch. & Friar* i. (1844) 24 'We have one of their eggs, set in silver, in our garderobe': exclaimed John Vinesauff, the cellarer. **1848** LYTTON *Harold* II. iii, 'Verily yes; vault, coffer, and garde-robe—stall and meuse—are well nigh drained', answered the monk. **1851** TURNER *Dom. Archit.* I. iv. 150 He built a new chapel, with a garderobe. **1856** WALBRAN *Ripon*, etc. 73 The walls of two spacious gard-robes, communicating with the dormitory.
attrib. **1867** *Murray's Guide Yorkshire* 282 A chamber with fireplace and garderobe seat.

†**garde-tramell.** *Obs.* Also gard-tramell. [f. F. *garde-r* to keep + *tramail* drag-net.] Some kind of fishing apparatus. Also *attrib.*
1497 *Naval Acc. Hen. VII* (1896) 83 Bowstrynges casting caltraps tallowe nettes for gard tramelles. *Ibid.* 87 Dise of Iren—ij baskettes, Gardtramell Netts—ij drifattes. *Ibid.* 89 Levers—[ij] xij, Gardetramell Stakes—c, Paving rammers of tymbre—iiij.

†**gardeviance.** *Obs.* Forms: 5 gardevian(s, -viant, -vyaunt, -vyan, -vya(u)ndes, -vyence, gardiviance, gardyvyans, 5-6 gardevya(u)nce, 6 gardefiance, -vianch, -viands, -viaunce, -wiat, gardyvyaunce, guarde-viandes, 6-7 gardeviance. [f. F. *garde-r* to keep + *viande(s* meat(s.]
1. Originally, a safe for meat; also, a chest for holding valuables; hence, usually, a travelling trunk or wallet.
1459 in *Paston Lett.* I. 484 Item, j gardevyaunt. *c* **1460** J. RUSSELL *Bk. Nurture* 1202 Closynge cloos howse chest & gardevyan, for drede of congettynge. **1463** *Mann. & Househ. Exp.* (Roxb.) 152 To brynge home my lordys gardevyence ffro London. **1481-90** *Howard Househ. Bks.* (Roxb.) 274 In a gardviande [my Lord has] a peir brigandines, a plakart, ij. bavieres, [and] iij. peire ganteletz. **1500-20** DUNBAR *Poems* xxxiii. 40 Full mony instrument for slawchtir Was in his gardevyance. **1552** HULOET, Bagge or gardeuiaunce to put meat in, *reticulum*. **1579** TWYNE *Phisicke agst. Fort.* I. xxxvii. 51 a, There was a great Guardeuiandes or Chest, wherein was great store of treasures. **1628** SIR R. BOYLE *Diary* in *Lismore Papers* (1886) II. 290 This day I receaved..a gardeviance..of usquabagh. **1706** PHILLIPS (ed. Kersey), *Garde-viant*, a Wallet for a Soldier to put his Victuals in.
¶**2.** Used contemptuously: 'Baggage', 'outfit'.
1563-83 FOXE *A. & M.* 1070/1 Then [folowed]..the monkes..with their glorious gardeuiance of Crosses, Candlestickes, and Vergers before them. *Ibid.* 1418/1 The people..began..to set vp the pageants of S. Katherine, and of S. Nicholas..with their gaye gardeuiance and gray amices.

gardevin, -vine ('gɑːdəvɪn, -vaɪn). *Sc.* Also gardyveen. [f. F. *garde-r* to keep + *vin* wine.]
a. A big-bellied wine-bottle. Also *attrib.* **b.** A case or closet for wine-bottles.
1805 *Chron.* in *Ann. Reg.* 375/2 Gardevin bottles..left behind by the besiegers. **1808** J. MAYNE *Siller Gun* IV. 145 The Town-clerk..Gar'd bring the great big gardevine, And fill the glasses. **1827** *Blackw. Mag.* XXII. 607 Your purse, your gardevin, and your tea-caddy, are continually exposed to depredation. **1870** RAMSAY *Remin.* vi. (ed. 18) 246 *Gardyveen*, Case for holding wine.

†**gardevisure.** *Her. Obs.* [? f. F. *garde-r* to keep, protect + *vis* sight + -URE.] The visor of a helmet.
1610 GUILLIM *Heraldry* VI. v. 265 This fashion of sidelong Helmet and openfaced with gardeuisure [*printed* gardenisure] over the sight, is common to all persons of Nobility vnder the degree of a Duke. **1739** in COATS *Dict. Her.* **1828-40** in BERRY *Encycl. Her.* I.

gardeyn(e, obs. form of GARDEN, GUARDIAN.

gardfish, obs. form of GARFISH.

gardian, -en, etc.: see GUARD-.

gardin(e, gardin-: see GARDEN, GARDEN-.

†**'gardnap.** *Obs.* Forms: 5 ?gardenat, 6 ?gardnett, gardnap, garnap(pe, -nep, -nop [a. OF. *gardenape, -nappe*, f. *garder* to protect + *nappe* cloth; cf. SANAP. (The forms *gardenat, gardnett*, may be due to an erroneous substitution of *natte* mat for *nappe* cloth.)] A round piece of wood or metal, a mat, or the like, placed under dishes at table in order to protect the table-cloth.
1489 *Acta Dom. Conc.* (1839) 131/1 A butter plait, a gardenat, a met almery. **1538** *Aberdeen Reg.* V. 16 (Jam.) Chargeour, plate, deiche, gardnap, trunscour of tyne. **1556** WITHALS *Dict.* (1568) 43 b/1 A garnappe [*ed.* **1602** garnap, **1608** garnep] to be layed vnder the potte vpon the table, to saue the table cloth cleane, *basis*. **1561** *Extracts Aberdeen Reg.* (1844) I. 336 Ane gardnett of tun. **1570** LEVINS *Manip.* 169/28 A garnop, *basis poculi*. **1573** *Extracts Aberdeen Reg.* (1848) II. 10 A garnett of brass.

Gardner ('gɑːdnə(r)). The name of Captain M. W. *Gardner*, used attrib. and absol. to designate a type of machine gun invented by him, which has two to five barrels side by side.
1884 *Illustr. London News* LXXXIV. 222/1 The force was drawn up..with three Gardners on the left and three Gatlings on the right. **1899** *Daily News* 30 Jan. 5/1 The workshops were turning out two Gardiners [*sic*] and two Maxims every month. **1903** A. CONAN DOYLE *Green Flag* 11 Caught in the blast of lead from a Gardner.

gardner, gardning: see GARDENER, -ING.

†**gardon.** *Obs.* [a. F. *gardon.*] A kind of roach (*Leuciscus idus*).
1611 COTGR., *Siege*, a seat..also the fish Gardon.

gardon, -oun, obs. forms of GUERDON.

†**'gardy.** *Sc. Obs.* Also 7-9 ga(i)rdie. An arm.
1513 DOUGLAS *Æneis* XI. xi. 64 He..Hys gardy vp has bendyt far abak, And threw the speir wyth all his fors and mycht. **1631** RUTHERFORD *Lett.* (1862) I. 77 The Lord will ..send one with a well-toothed, sharp hook, and strong gardies, to reap His harvest. *a* **1670** SPALDING *Troub. Chas. I* (1829) 27 He..had still a strong man upon ilk gardie, whether sleeping or waking. *a* **1774** FERGUSSON *Poems* (1807) 287 'Twas this that braced the gardies stiff and strang ..in ancient days. **1787** in *Burns' Wks.* II. 105 Tak him by the gardie.

gardyloo (gɑːdɪ'luː). Also 9 garde loo, jordeloo. [app. f. a pseudo-Fr. phrase *gare de l'eau* 'beware of the water'; in correct Fr. it would be *gare l'eau.*] A warning cry uttered (in old Edinburgh) before throwing dirty water from the window into the street. ***to make the gardyloo***: to throw the dirty water out.
[**1768** STERNE *Sent. Journ.* (1782) 48/2 It comes against you without crying '*garde d'eau!*'] **1771** SMOLLETT *Humph. Cl.* II. 227 The whole cargo is flung out of a back window.. and the maid calls *gardy loo* to the passengers. **1808** JAMIESON, *Jordeloo*. **1818** SCOTT *Hrt. Midl.* xxvii, She had made the gardyloo out of the wrang window. *Ibid.* xxxviii, The overwhelming cataract of her questions, which burst forth with the sublimity of a grand gardyloo. **1858** RAMSAY *Remin.* Ser. I. (1860) 260 The wellknown cry which preceded the missile and warned the passenger was *Garde loo!*

gardyn(e, -er(e: see GARDEN, ER.

gardyng, obs. form of CARDING, GARDEN.

†**gare**, *sb.*[1] *Obs.* Forms: 1 gár, 3 gore, 3-4 gare, (3 *Lay.* gære). [OE. *gár* str. masc. = OS., OHG. (MHG.) *gêr* (mod.Ger. revived in archaistic use as *gehr, ger*), ON. *geir-r*, Goth. **gais* (only found in proper names, as *Hario-gaisus*):—OTeut. **gaizo-z*. (The Goth. *gairu* σκόλοψ is unconnected.) The word was also in use among the Celtic peoples (hence OIrish *gāi, gae, ga* masc., from **gaiso*), and was known to the Greeks and Romans (Gr. γαῖσον, γαῖσος, also Γαισάται Celtic mercenaries armed with this weapon; L. *gæsum*). To the stem **ghaiso-* belongs also Gr. χαῖος, χαῖον shepherd's staff. The root **ghai-* perh. appears also in OE. *gād* GOAD:—**ghai-tá.*] A spear or javelin.
Beowulf (Z.) 1847 ȝif þæt ȝegangeð þæt ðe gar nimeð. *c* **1000** *Ags. Ps.* (Th.) liv. [lv.] 21 Hi word hira wel ȝesmyredon..eft ȝewurdon..scearpe garas [L. *jacula*]. *c* **1205** LAY. 27549 He heold on his honde ænne gare [*c* **1275** one spere] swiðe stronge. *c* **1250** *Gen. & Ex.* 3458 Dead ðolen, wið stones slaȝen Or to dead wið goren draȝen [L. *confodietur jaculis*. Exod. xix. 13].
b. wrongly used for 'sword'.
c **1330** *Amis. & Amil.* 1353 Thai fight gan, With brondes bright and bare..The steward smot to him that stounde.. With his grimly gare. *a* **1400** *Isumbras* 452 He sprange als any sparke one glede With grymly growndyne gare.

†**gare**, *sb.*[2] *Obs. rare.* Also 7 gaer. [An altered form of GERE.] A sudden and transient fit of passion. ? Also in *Comb.* **gare-brained** *a. dial.* (see quot. 1674-91). Hence (?) **'garish** *a. dial.* (see quot. 1674-91).
1606 WARNER *Alb. Eng.* XVI. cii. (1612) 404 But if shall one, els honest, erre through choler, vrg'd abuse, Or casually, their grudge or gaer admit no termes of truse. **1609** HOLLAND *Amm. Marcell.* XXXI. viii. 412 The whole multitude..set upon a furious and mad mood, hastened in a fell and cruell gare [L. *animisque concita truculentis*] to trie the utmost hazard of battaile. *Ibid.* XXXI. xii. 421 The Emperour in a certain gare [*other copies of the same ed. have* geare] and violent heat made hast to encounter them. **1642** ROGERS *Naaman* 390 In a gare and heat, they will runne, ride and take any paines; but only so long as the pang holds. **1674-91** RAY *S. & E.C. Words* 99 *Gare-brain'd*; very heedless..*Garish* is the same, signifying one that is as 'twere in a fright, and so heeds nothing.

†**gare**, *sb.*[3] *Obs.* [a. AF. *gare* = OF. *gard, jart.*] (See quot.)
1542 *Gt. Abridgem. Stat.* s.v. *Wolles*, That no denyzen or foren make any refuse of wolles but cot gare & vyllayn [**1358** *Act. 1 Edw. III*, c. 8 Sinoun cot, gare, & vileine tuson]. **1607** COWELL *Interpr.*, Gare is a course wooll full of staring haires, as..groweth about the..shankes of the sheepe. **1721** in BAILEY; and in later Dicts.

†**gare**, *sb.*[4] *Obs. rare*[−1]. [? ad. L. *garum* pickle.]
1562 TURNER *Herbal* II. 66 The most part vse Basil and eate it with oyl & gare sauce for a sowle or kitchen.

‖**gare** (gar), *sb.*[5] [Fr.] **a.** A dock-basin on a river or canal. **b.** A railway station. **c.** A pier, wharf, or the like.
1869 S. NORTHCOTE *Diary* 17 Nov. in A. Lang *Life* (1890) I. xi. 360 Two or three *gares* have been hollowed out, where vessels may lie. **1870** E. G. E. WARD *Jrnl.* 15 July in *Outside Paris* (1871) 2, I ran to the Gare of the Railway, and bought a paper just come from Paris. **1885** H. JAMES *Little Tour in France* (1900) xxxviii. 250 The whole despotic *gare*: the deadly *salle d'attente*, the insufferable delays over one's luggage, the porterless platform. **1902** *Encycl. Brit.* XXVII. 708/2 Commander Edwards, R.N., proceeded down the Canal, taking possession of the *gares* and dredgers. **1906** *Daily Chron.* 10 Sept. 5/6 When seen at the gare he was wearing a bowler hat and had a grey beard. **1912** *Q. Rev.* Oct. 315 Gares, or mooring stations, are now provided.

gare (gɛr), *a. Sc.* Also gair. [a. ON. *gǫrr, gørr, gerr, gærr* (:—**garwu-*), also written *geyrr*, ready, prone to (with gen.) = OE. *ȝearo, ȝearu* (ME. *ȝare* YARE), OS. *garu*, OHG. *garo* (MHG. *gare, gar*) ready. The change of meaning from 'ready' to 'eager', 'sharp', 'covetous' is also found with YARE in northern dialects.]
†**1.** Ready; sharp, keen. *Obs.*
1513 DOUGLAS *Æneis* VI. xiv. 30 With heding swerd, baith felloun, scherp, and gair.
2. *transf.* Eager, covetous, desirous of wealth; miserly.
1719 RAMSAY *Ep. to Hamilton* iii. 75 Thy raffan rural rhyme sae rare..gars fowk gae gare To ha'e them by them. **1788** PICKEN *Poems* 114 Gair bodies a', now mak yer mane, Auld honest Harry's dead and gane. *a* **1810** TANNAHILL *Poems* (1846) 13 Thy Mither's gair and set upon the warl. **1822** GALT *Sir A. Wylie* I. xxv. 227 He's a wee gair, I alloo.

‖**gare** (gɑː(r)), *v. imp.* Also 8 gar. [a. F. *gare* imperative of *garer* = OF. *garir, guarir*, ad. Teut. **warjan* (Goth. *warjan*, OHG., OS., OE. *werian*) to defend.] A cry of warning: Look out! beware! Also as simple imperative: Take care.
1653 URQUHART *Rabelais* I. xxvii, He hurried therefore upon them so rudely, without crying gare or beware, that he overthrew them like hogs. **1705** VANBRUGH *Confed.* IV. i, Hark! some body comes. Gar [ed. **1893** Gare] there, the enemy. **1896** C. DICK *Ways World* 35 She will e'en undertake 'interviewing', But *gare* how your secrets she gleans.

gare, var. GAIR *Sc.*; obs. form of GAR *v.*

gare, *Sc.* and *north*, form of GORE *sb.*

garefish, obs. form of GARFISH.

gare-fowl ('gɛəfaʊl). Also 7, 9 gairfowl. [ad. ON. *geir-fugl* = Faroese *gorfuglur*, Sw. *garfogel*, Da. (from Icel.) *geirfugl*. Hence also Gael. *gearbhul* garefowl, and F. *gorfou* a sort of penguin. The meaning of the first part of the compound is uncertain.] The great auk (*Alca impennis*).
[*c* **1549** ? MUNRO in Sibbald *De Animalibus Scotiæ* 22 Avis *Gare* dicta, Corvo Marino Similis, ovo maximo.] **1698** M. MARTIN *Voy. Kilda* (1749) 25 Gair-fowl..above the Size of a Solan Goose, of a black Colour. **1802** G. MONTAGU *Ornith. Dict.* (1833) 188 Gairfowl. A name for the Awk. **1863** KINGSLEY *Water Bab.* 264 Then we shall not be sorry because we cannot get a gairfowl to stuff. **1894** NEWTON in *Athenæum* 3 Mar. 281/3 Imagination has long had a large share in the accounts given of the garefowl or great auk.

gareisoun, obs. form of GARRISON.

gareland, obs. form of GARLAND.

†**garence**, ? var. GARAVANCE, CALAVANCE. *Obs.*
1610 W. FOLKINGHAM *Art of Survey* I. vii. 14 Panick, Amilcorne, Spelt-corn, Garences, Dewgrasse, Jobs-teares, Comin-seede, Annise-seede.

garesone, -oun, obs. forms of GARRISON.

garet(te, -teer, obs. ff. GARRET, GARRETEER.

†**garfangle.** *Obs. rare.* Also 5 garfangyl. [app. f. GARE *sb.*[1] + **fangle*, deriv. of FANG; cf. MDu. *gaerfang*, OFris. *gêrfong* (East Fris. *gerfonk*),

MLG. *gârfank*.] A fish-spear; also *Comb.*, as ***garfangle-hook***.

c **1440** *Promp. Parv.* 186/2 Garfangyl, or elger, *anguillaria, anguillare*. **1615** E. S. *Britain's Buss* in Arb. *Garner* III. 642 This Garfangle-hook is an ashen plant six or eight feet long; with an iron hook, like a boat hook, at the end of it.

garfish (ˈgɑːfɪʃ). Forms: 5 **garfysshe**, 6 **garefish**, 7 **garre-**, 8 **gair-**, 9 **gur(d)-**, **guard-**, 7- **garfish**. See also GAR *sb.* [app. f. GARE *sb.*[1] + FISH, in allusion to its long sharp nose.] A fish (*Belone vulgaris*) with a long spear-like snout, called also green-bone, horn-fish, sea-pike, etc. In America and Australia the name is given to other fishes of similar form, e.g. to various species of *Lepidosteus* and *Hemirhamphus*.

c **1440** *Promp. Parv.* 247/1 Horn keke, fysche (*S.* horne stoke; *P.* hornkek, or garfysshe). **1577** HARRISON *England* III. iii. (1878) II. 21 Of the long sort are congers, eeles, garefish, and such other of that forme. **1611** COTGR., *Orphie*, the Hornebeake, Hornekecke, Piper-fish, Garre-fish. **1699** L. WAFER *Voy.* 126 There is another sort of Fish on the North-Sea Coast, Which our Sea-men call Gar-fish.. They have a long Bone on the Snout..and 'tis very sharp at the end. **1756** P. BROWNE *Jamaica* (1789) 443 The Gar-Fish. Both the jaws of this fish are long and slender, and furnished with sharp conic teeth. **1810** P. NEILL *List of Fishes* 16 (Jam.) *Esox Lucius*, Sea-pike; Gar-pike; Guard-fish. **1850** CLUTTERBUCK *Port Phillip* iii. 44 In the bay are large quantities of..guard-fish. **1854** BADHAM *Halieut.* 304 Those singular green bones of the spine which are peculiar to the gar-fish. **1890** BOLDREWOOD *Miner's Right* xxxviii. 336, I wonder if they have got any of those delicious garfish for us.

attrib. **1775** ROMANS *Florida* 96 They make them frequently undergo scratching from head to foot through the skin with broken glass or gar fish teeth.

† **ˈgargalize**, *v. Obs. rare.* [var. GARGARIZE, prob. due to confusion with GARGLE.] To gargle.

1605 MARSTON *Dutch Courtezan* III. i. E ij a, Ile gargalize my throate with this Vintner, and when I have don with him, spit him out. **1611** COTGR., *Gargarizer*, to gargle, to gargalize [*sic*: but under all the related words (5 instances) Cotgr. uses the form *gargarize*].

garganet, obs. form of CARCANET. *rare*⁻¹.

1583 STANYHURST *Æneis* I. (Arb.) 39 Thee pearle and gould crowns too bring With garganet heauye.

garganey (ˈgɑːgənɪ). Forms: 7 **gargane**, (8-9 **gargany**), 7- **garganey**. [Taken from Gesner *Hist. Anim.* (1555) III. 127, who gives *garganey* (sic) as the It. name used about Bellinzona; the dim. *garganello*, he says, was in Italy applied to various other birds of similar appearance.] A species of teal (*Anas querquedula*).

1668 WILKINS *Real Char.* II. v. §4. 156 To the Teal-kind should be reduced that other fowl, of the like shape and bigness..called Gargane. **1678** RAY *Willughby's Ornith.* 377 The Garganey..In bigness it something exceeds the common Teal. **1766** PENNANT *Zool.* (1776) II. 512 Garganey ..in many places these birds are called the Summer Teal. **1863** KINGSLEY *Water Bab.* 269 The birds began to gather at Allfowlsness..harelds and garganeys, smews and gooseanders. **1876** SMILES *Sc. Natur.* xiii. (ed. 4) 259 The Teal, the Garganey..and the Eider Duck visit the loch occasionally in Winter.

† **Garˈgantua**. *Obs.* Also 6-7 **Garagantua**. [The name of the large-mouthed voracious giant in Rabelais.] A giant. Also *attrib.*

1571 GOLDING *Calvin on Ps.* lxxiii. 8 Gyantes, or one-eyed Gargantuas. **1579** FULKE *Heskins' Parl.* 164 Now riseth vp this Gargantua, and will proue..that one bodie may be in another. **1598** B. JONSON *Ev. Man in Hum.* II. i, I'll go near to fill that huge tumbrel-slop of yours with somewhat, an I have good luck: your Garagantua breech cannot carry it away so. [**1600** SHAKS. *A. Y. L.* III. ii. 238 You must borrow me Gargantuas mouth first.] **1651** RANDOLPH, etc. *Hey for Honesty* II. v, Mine are all diminutives, Tom Thumbs; not one Colossus, not one Gargantua among them.

Hence **garˈgantuan** *a.*, enormous, monstrous; also *Comb.*, as ***gargantuan-bellied*** adj.; **Garˈgantuism**, ? an extravagant idea; **Garˈgantuist**, one who resembles Gargantua.

1593 HARVEY *Pierce's Supererog.* Wks. (Grosart) II. 224 Pore I..that am matched with such a Gargantuist, as can deuoure me quicke in a sallat. **1596** NASHE *Haue with you* Wks. (Grosart) III. 49 This Gargantuan bag-pudding. **1619** PURCHAS *Microcosmus* xxvii. 267 His Gargantuan bellyed-Doublet with huge huge sleeves. **1630** RANDOLPH *Panegyr. to Shirley's Gratef. Serv.* A iij, My ninth lasse affords No lycophronian buskins nor can straine Garagantuan lines to Gigantize thy veine. **1866** CARLYLE *Remin.* (1881) I. 146 While his wild home-grown Gargantuisms went on. **1893** CURWEN *Hist. Booksellers* 276 Bogue's small venture stood a poor chance against enterprise of this gargantuan scale.

‖ **gargareon**. *Anat. Obs. rare.* [med.L., a. Gr. γαργαρεών.] The uvula.

1653 URQUHART *Rabelais* I. xlii, The fore-part of the throat called the gargareon. **1671** BLAGRAVE *Astrol. Pract.* 145 The defect lay wholly in the Uvula or Gargarean [*sic*].

† **gargarise**. *Obs.* Also 6 **gargarice**, **-yce**, **gargrise**. [f. GARGARIZE *v.*] A gargle.

1533 ELYOT *Cast. Helthe* (1541) 82 a, Taken very hote in a gargarise is right convenient. **1547** BOORDE *Brev. Health* cxix, Vse diuers tymes sternutacions with gargarices. **1606** BRETON *Ourania* D, To giue a vomit clister or Gargarise: Marking the Signe wherein faire Phœbe lyes. **1610** BARROUGH *Meth. Physick* I. xvii. (1639) 28 After you may particularly purge the head with gargarises and sternutations.

gargarism (ˈgɑːgərɪz(ə)m). ? *Obs.* Forms: 5-7 **gargarisme**, 6 **-izme**, **-ysme**, **-ysyne**, 7 **gargerisme**, 6-8 **gargarism**. [ad. L. *gargarisma*, a. Gr. *γαργάρισμα, f. γαργαρίζειν to gargle, of onomatopœic formation. Cf. F. *gargarisme*, Sp. and It. *gargarismo*. In mod. usage replaced by GARGLE *sb.*]

1. A gargle.

1398 TREVISA *Barth. De P.R.* VII. xxv. (1495) 242 Teeth that wagge ben fastnyd wyth Ensence and Mastyk and therto helpyth Gargarismis. *c* **1400** *Lanfranc's Cirurg.* 209 If þe enpostym be in a mannes mouþ, þan þou schalt make him no gargarisme. **1562** BULLEYN *Def. agst. Sickness, Compounds* (1579) 35 b, How prepare you a Gargarizme or washing Gurgle, for the Mouth and Throate? **1621** BURTON *Anat. Mel.* II. iv. II. iii. (1651) 382 Such as are not swallowed, but only kept in the mouth, are Gargarisms used commonly after a purge. **1783** C. BRYANT *Flora Diæt.* 296 An excellent gargarism for sore mouths.

fig. **1592** G. HARVEY *Pierce's Super.* 138 What honest mynde or Civill disposition is not accloied with these noisome and nasty gargarismes. **1612** WEBSTER *White Devil* II. i, Let me embrace thee, toad, and love thee, O thou abominable loathsome gargarism. **1639** DAVENANT *Salmac. Spolia* Dram. Wks. 1872 II. 316 A Gargarism of Florio's first-fruits, Diana de monte Major..to make a sufficient linguist without travelling. **1641** MILTON *Ch. Govt.* II. (1851) 178 Such a scholastical burre in their throats, as hath ..crackt their voices for ever with metaphysical gargarisms.

2. A disease of the throat, which attacks swine.

Prob. a learned substitution for GARGET[2] or GARGIL[2].

1607 TOPSELL *Four-f. Beasts* (1658) 530 Of the Gargarisme. This disease is called by the Latines, *Raucedo*, and by the Grecians, *Branchos*, which is a swelling about their chaps, joyned with Feaver and Head-ache. **1688** R. HOLME *Armoury* II. 182/1 Gargarism.

gargarize (ˈgɑːgəraɪz), *v.* ? *Obs.* Also 6-8 **gargarise**, 6 **gargrise**. [ad. L. *gargarizāre*, ad. Gr. γαργαρίζειν to gargle; also adopted in F. *gargariser*, Sp. *gargarizar*, It. *gargarizzare*. The modern word is GARGLE.]

1. *trans.* To wash or cleanse (the mouth or throat) with a gargle.

1533 ELYOT *Cast. Helthe* (1539) 86 a, It is..very holsome to gargarise the mouthe and brest with hony water. **1600** W. VAUGHAN *Direct. Health* (1633) 49 In this sort it may be taken..to gargarize the mouth of the reume. **1725** BRADLEY *Fam. Dict.* s.v. *Mouth*, Drink of it and gargarise your Mouth every Morning and after Meals therewith.

transf. **1719** HAMILTON *Ep. to Ramsay* I. 55 Wi' wine we'll gargarize our craig.

2. To gargle, or use (a liquid) as a gargle for cleansing the mouth and throat.

1578 LYTE *Dodoens* I. xx. 32 The decoction of this herbe in wine gargarised, doth purge the head from naughtie fleume. **1634** R. H. *Salernes Regim.* 144 If the patient receive the smoke..at the mouth, and after gargarise Wine into the throate.

3. *intr.* To perform the action of gargling.

1569 R. ANDROSE tr. *Alexis' Secr.* IV. I. 43 With the sayde water..cause the sicke person to gargarise, and he shall be hole. **1589** COGAN *Haven Health* i. (1612) 6 With the same ..you may gargarize or guddle in your throate. **1658** A. FOX *Wurtz' Surg.* II. ix. 79 Let the patient gargarize twice or thrice a day as occasion serveth.

Hence **ˈgargarizing** *vbl. sb.*, the action of gargling.

1533 ELYOT *Cast. Helthe* IV. ii. (1541) 82 Gargarising if it be not discretly used, may do more harme than good. **1610** BARROUGH *Meth. Physick* I. v. (1639) 8 Gargarising and sneesing may be used in time convenient.

gargel(l, obs. form of GARGOYLE.

† **garget**[1]. *Obs. rare.* Also 4 **gargaz**, **gargat**. [a. OF. *gargate*, *garguette* (both forms are found in mod. dialects) = It. *gargatta*, Sp. and Pg. *garganta*. It is doubtful whether these can be connected with F. *gorge*: see GARGIL[1], GARGOYLE.] The throat.

13.. *K. Alis.* 3636 Of Grece he smot a baroun..Thorugh the gargaz [*MS. Laud* garget] and the gorger. *c* **1386** CHAUCER *Nun's Pr. T.* 515 The fox stert up at oones, And by the garget [*v.r.* gargat] hente Chaunteclere.

garget[2] (ˈgɑːgɪt). Also 8-9 **gargut**. [perh. a special use of prec., originally denoting a disease of the throat, the other senses being derived from this. Cf. GARGIL[2].]

1. An inflamed condition of the head or throat in cattle and pigs.

1587 MASCALL *Govt. Cattle* (1627) 267 The garget is..a swelling and inflamation in the throat, behinde the iawes of the hogge. **1639** T. DE GREY *Compl. Horsem.* 61 It..causeth oft times fleshy stuffe like to the garget to grow in his throat. **1725** BRADLEY *Fam. Dict.* s.v., As for the Garget in the Head and Throat..it's a Cousin German to the Murrain, for the Cattle will swell and be puck'd under their Jaws like rotten Sheep. **1736** BAILEY *Househ. Dict.* 297 The Gargut or blood in Swine..It shews itself almost like a fever in swine, by their staggering in their gate, and their loathing their meat. **1797** W. GREEN in A. Young *Agric. Suffolk* 95 Turnips are apt to give them [calves] the garget, by which they very commonly die. **1808** CURWEN *Econ. Feeding Stock* 188, I had the mortification to find the greater part of them [cattle] attacked by the garget.

b. A similar disease in poultry.

1817 *Sporting Mag.* L. 261 The *roup*, the *gargut* and the *murrain*, are terms often applied indiscriminately to the diseases of fowls.

2. Inflammation in a cow's or ewe's udder.

1725 BRADLEY *Fam. Dict.* s.v. *Adder's tongue ointment*, It's..a most sovereign and excellent Remedy..for any hard Swellings..and particularly very good for a Garget in a Cow's Bag. **1849** STEPHENS *Book of Farm* (ed. 2) I. 607/1 The only complaint the ewe..is subject to is inflammation in the udder, or udder-clap, or garget. **1880** *New Virginians* I. 53 An infusion..is used as a fomentation for cows afflicted with garget.

3. *transf.* and *fig.* A distemper, plague. ***to run of*** (or ***on***) ***a garget***: to become diseased.

1615 T. ADAMS *Sacrif. Thankfuln.* 18 The Drunkard is without a head, the Swearer hath a Garget in his throat. —— *Mystical Bedl.* II. 56 If it were granted, that the Couetous were madde, the world it selfe would runne of a garget: for who is not bitten with this madde dogge? **1616** —— *Dis. Soule* viii. 31.

4. Short for ***garget-plant***.

1788 M. CUTLER in *Life, Jrnls. & Corr.* (1888) I. ix. 422 Garget, sow-thistle, etc. **1792** BELKNAP *Hist. New Hampsh.* III. 125 The Garget is a valuable plant.

5. *Comb.*: **garget-plant** *U.S.*, the Virginian poke-weed (*Phytolacca decandra*); **garget-root** *dial.*, the root of *Helleborus fœtidus*, or bear's foot.

1787 W. MARSHALL *Norfolk* Gloss. (E.D.S.) *Gargut-root*. **1882** *Garden* 13 May 326/3 The Poke Weed..the farmers around here call..Garget plant.

† **gargil**[1]. *Obs. rare.* Also 6 **gargill**, 7-8 **gargle**. [ad. OF. *gargouille* 'the weesle, or weason of the throat' (Cotgr.), perh. connected with L. *gurgulio*; see GARGLE and GARGOYLE.] The gullet.

1558-68 WARDE tr. *Alexis' Secr.* 29 b, A verie exquisite remedie against the disease called in Latine *angina*..which is an inflammation of the Muscle of the inner Gargill. **1559** MORWYNG *Evonym.* 146 Evyll distillacions, whiche, onles a man finde remeadye for, oftentimes the gargil is wasted. **1609** C. BUTLER *Fem. Mon.* (1634) 168. **1632** SHERWOOD, The gargle of the throte, *gargouïlle*. **1706** PHILLIPS (ed. Kersey), *Gargle*, the Gullet of the Throat.

gargil[2]. *Obs.* exc. *dial.* Forms: 7 **gargell**, **-gill**, **-gyll**, 7-8 **gargil**, 8 **gargol**, 7-9 **gargle**. [f. prec.: cf. GARGET[1].]

1. A disease in cattle and pigs, attacking the head and throat; a distemper, murrain.

1601 HOLLAND *Pliny* II. 216 The same is holden to be good for to heale the Squinancy or Gargle in swine. **1639** T. DE GREY *Compl. Horsem.* 277 The pestilence or plague.. some doe call it the murraine, others the garget, others the gargill. **1707** MORTIMER *Husb.* 187 For the Gargol in Hogs. The signs of which are, hanging down of the Head..moist Eyes, staggering, and loss of Appetite.

b. A similar disease in geese.

1614 MARKHAM *Cheap Husb.* VII. xvi. (1668) 121 For the ..infirmities in Geese, the most and worst they are subject unto is the Gargil. **1741** *Compl. Fam.-Piece* III. 510 The Gargil is a great Stopping of the Head in Geese.

2. An inflamed condition of the udder in cows.

c **1760** PEGGE *Derbicisms* (E.D.S. 78), *Gargle*, a distemper incident to cows, when they give bad milk, and have knots in the paps. **1886** *Chester Gloss.*, *Gargle*, an inflammation in a cow's udder, known to veterinary surgeons as *Mammitis*.

gargil(le, obs. forms of GARGOYLE.

† **gargilon**. *Obs. rare.* Forms: 4 **gargiloun**, **gargulun**, 5 **gargilon**. [a. OF. *garguillon* 'the pipe or throat-pipe, whereby meat passeth into the stomach or craw of birds' (Cotgr.), app. not recorded in the technical sense to which it is confined in English; f. *gargouille* throat. Cf. med.L. *gargaliōn-em*.] The gullet or œsophagus of a deer.

The explanation in quot. 1696 is evidently a mere guess.

c **1320** *Sir Tristr.* 508 He tiȝt þe mawe on tinde And eke þe gargulun. **13..** *Gaw. & Gr. Knt.* 1335 þay gryped to þe gargiloun, & grayþely departed þe wesaunt fro þe wynt-hole, & walt out þe guttez. **1486** *Bk. St. Albans* E vij b, Off the nomblys of the hert..How mony endys ther shall be hem with inne..but oon thyk nor thynne And that is bot the Gargilon. And all theys oder crokes and Roundulis bene. [**1696** PHILLIPS (ed. 5), *Gargilon*, an old Term in Hunting for the chief Part of the Heart in a Deer. **1721-1800** in BAILEY.]

gargle (ˈgɑːg(ə)l), *sb.* [f. GARGLE *v.*]

1. Any liquid used for gargling (see GARGLE *v.* 1, 2).

1657 W. COLES *Adam in Eden* vii. 16 Gargles likewise are made with Sage, Rosemary [etc.]. **1709** STEELE *Tatler* No. 94 ¶ 5 When it is used as a Gargle, it gives Volubility to the Tongue. **1789** W. BUCHAN *Dom. Med.* (1790) 675 Gargles have the best effect when injected with a syringe. **1826** SYD. SMITH *Wks.* (1859) II. 81 Our apothecaries rushing about with gargles and tinctures. **1877** ROBERTS *Handbk. Med.* (ed. 3) I. 157 Sore throat is best relieved by the use of some mild gargle.

fig. **1842** S. C. HALL *Ireland* II. 451 Such a Pierian gargle as 'strange straggling steers struggled in strenuous strife'.

2. *slang.* **a.** (See quot. 1860.) **b.** A drink, or draught of liquor.

1860 *Slang Dict.*, *Gargle*, medical student Slang for physic. **1889** *Sporting Times* 3 Aug. 3/1 (Farmer) We're just going to have a gargle—will you join us?

gargle (ˈgɑːg(ə)l), *v.* Forms: 6 **gargil(l**, 6- **gargle**; *Pa. t.* and *pa. pple.* 6 **gargalled**, **-geld**, **-goled**, **-guled**, 7 **gargl'd**, 7- **gargled**. [ad. F. *gargouiller* 'to gargle or gargarize; also, to rattle in the throat' (Cotgr.), f. *gargouille* throat: cf. GARGIL[1]. See also GURGLE *v.*

In It. both *gargagliare* and *gorgogliare* are found, and the Rom. and Teut. languages present a series of words in *garg-*, *gorg-*, *gurg-*, which refer to the throat or to gurgling noises produced in it. Diez supposes the vowel of F. *gargouille*, *gargatte*, etc. to be due to the influence of L. *gargarizare* upon words with original *o*, as F. *gorge*, It. *gorgia*, It. & Sp. *gorga*, but less definite causes were prob. at work in the whole range of these forms. In modern Eng. *gargle* has supplanted the older GARGARIZE, perhaps because it was more native in form, and was felt to be more expressive of the sound produced by the action.]

1. *trans.* To hold (a liquid) suspended and rattling in the throat, esp. for therapeutic purposes. ? *Obs.*

1527 ANDREW *Brunswyke's Distyll. Waters* A iij b, The same water luke warme dronke and gargoled in the throte in the mornynge, withdryveth the payne of the throte. **1578** LYTE *Dodoens* I. xlviii. 70 The iuyce of this herbe gargeld, or gargarised, healeth all inflammations. **1657** W. COLES *Adam in Eden* xliii. 75 The decoction of mint gargled in the mouth, cureth the Gums and Mouth that is sore. **1741** *Compl. Fam.-Piece* II. i. 55 Let the Patient gargle this as often as need requires.

transf. **1804** C. B. BROWN tr. *Volney's View Soil U.S.* 354 They will.. gargle their beloved cup, to enjoy the taste of it longer.

2. To wash (the throat or mouth) with a liquid held suspended in the throat.

1616 SURFL. & MARKH. *Country Farme* 45 Wash and gargle your teeth with the decoction of ground Yuie made in Wine. **1693** SALMON *Bates' Disp.* (1713) 674/1 You are to wash the Teeth, and gargle the Mouth and Throat therewith. **1763** J. BROWN *Poetry & Mus.* xi. 192 They [the Roman Actors] gargled the Throat with a Composition proper for the Purpose. **1803** *Med. Jrnl.* X. 381 He gargled his mouth with concentrated sulphuric and nitric acids. **1884** *Pall Mall G.* 16 Feb. 4 Each bather gargles mouth and throat with cold aromatized water.

3. *fig.* **a.** To utter with a sound as of gargling.

1635 WALLER *To Henry Lawes* 26 Those which only warble long, And gargle in their throats a song. **1719** FENTON *Prol. to Southerne's Spartan Dame*, So charm'd you were, you ceas'd awhile to doat On Nonsense, gargl'd in an Eunuch's Throat. **1779** SHERIDAN *Critic* I. i, The signors and signoras.. sliding their smooth semibreves, and gargling glib divisions in their outlandish throats. **1817** J. SCOTT *Paris Revisit.* (ed. 4) 267 A military man would gargle a *sacre* out of his throat.

†**b.** To read (a book) superficially, without digesting its contents. *Obs.*

1658 OSBORN *Adv. Son* (1673) 8 A few books well studied, and throughly digested, nourish the understanding more, than hundreds but gargled in the mouth. **1670** EACHARD *Cont. Clergy* 10 Having gargl'd only those elegant books at school, this serves them instead of reading them afterward.

4. *intr.* To perform the act of gargling.

1601 HOLLAND *Pliny* II. 122 If one gargle with it, it staies the Vvula from falling. **1693** SALMON *Bates' Disp.* (1713) 688/1 Dissolve a little of it in Red or Claret Wine, and gargle therewith. **1891** *Chambers' Encycl.* VIII. 536 In more severe cases the patient may gargle frequently with hot water.

b. *transf.* To make a noise in the throat, as in gargling.

1861 N. DAVIS *Carthage* 33 A camel.. gargling as it were with rage at their extreme laziness.

†**c.** To make a gurgling sound. *Obs.*

1681 COTTON *Wond. Peak* (ed. 4) 28 The Spring.. forc'd on still to more precipitous hast, By the succeeding streams, lyes Gargling there. **1727** BOYER *Dict. Angl.-Fr.*, To Gargle (as a purling stream does), *gazouiller*.

d. *slang.* To drink, 'liquor up'. (Cf. GARGLE *sb.*)

1889 *Sporting Times* 3 Aug. 5/5 (Farmer) We gargled. **1891** *Morn. Advert.* 2 Mar. (Farmer), It's my birthday; let's gargle.

Hence **'gargling** *vbl. sb.* and *ppl. a.*

1563 HYLL *Art Garden.* (1593) 68 The gargling of the same in the throte, doth help the disease called the squince. **1580** HOLLYBAND *Treas. Fr. Tong*, *Gargouillement*, a gargling. **1727** BOYER *Dict. Angl.-Fr.* s.v., The Gargling (*or* Purling) of a Stream. *Ibid.*, A gargling (*or* warbling) Brook. **1753** N. TORRIANO *Gangr. Sore Throat* 10 A kind of rattling in the Breast, like that made in the Throat by gargling.

gargle, var. GARGIL[2]; obs. f. GARGOYLE.

gargoill, obs. form of GARGOYLE.

gargol, obs. form of GARGIL[2], GARGLE.

‖**gargolette.** *rare*$^{-1}$. [a. F. *gargoulette*, perh. dim. of *gargoule*, *gargouille* a gargoyle.] An earthen vessel, used to cool water by evaporation.

1650 BULWER *Anthropomet.* 113 Thin Vessels made of black earth, the which are pierced in the neck; they call them Gargolettes.

‖**gargouillade** (gargujad). *Ballet.* [Fr., f. *gargouiller* to gurgle, bubble.] (See quots. 1957 and 1961.)

1930 CRASKE & BEAUMONT *Theory & Pract. Allegro Class. Ballet* 33 (*heading*) Gargouillade dehors. *Ibid.* 34 (*heading*) Gargouillade volé. *Ibid.* 76 Execute a *Gargouillade en dehors.* **1957** G. B. L. WILSON *Dict. Ballet* 132 *Gargouillade*, a brilliant series of steps in which the left leg describes two small circular movements in the air.. before the point of the left foot is drawn up to the knee of the supporting leg. **1959** *Times* 9 Jan. 6/2 He threw off the turns and leaps and *gargouillades*.. with marvellous *éclat*. **1961** WEBSTER, *Gargouillade*, a pas de chat with a double rond de jambe.

gargo(u)n, obs. form of JARGON.

gargoyle ('gɑːgɔɪl). Forms: 5 **gargulye, -gulle, -goill, -goyl, -gayle**, *pl.* **gargouys**, 5–6 **gargyle**, 6 **-gylle, -gille, -gell(e, gargle, (gargyne)**, 6–7 **gargel, -gil**, 7 **gargile**, 5, 9 **gargoyle**, 9 **gurgoyl(e, (gurgayle)**. [a. OF. *gargouille* (also *gargoule*, *gargole*, recorded in 13th c.) = Sp. *gargola*; app. a special sense of *gargouille* throat (cf. GARGIL[1], GARGLE *v.*), from the water passing through the mouths of the figures. The form *gurgoyle* is perhaps due to the influence of med.L. *gurgulio*.]

1. A grotesque spout, representing some animal or human figure, projecting from the gutter of a building (esp. in Gothic architecture), in order to carry the rain-water clear of the walls.

13.. *S. Erkenwald* 48 in Horstm. *Altengl. Leg.* (1881) 267 Hit was a throghe of thykke stone.. With gargeles garnysht aboute, all of gray marbre. **1412–20** LYDG. *Chron. Troy.* II. xi, And euery hous keuered was with lede And many gargoyl, and many hidous hede. *c* **1440** *Promp. Parv.* 186/2 Gargulye, yn a walle, *gorgona*, *gurgulio*. **1548** HALL *Chron.* (1809) 511 Out of the Mouthes of certain beastes or gargels did runne red, white, and claret wine. **1601** HOLLAND *Pliny* II. 552 His inuention it was to set vp Gargils or Antiques at the top of a Gauill end, as a finiall to the crest tiles. **1677** PLOT *Oxfordsh.* 66 It is also of excellent use to Statuaries, for making Moddels, Gargills, or Anticks. **1847** *Handbk. Engl. Ecclesiology* 185 Gurgoyles. **1851** LONGF. *Gold. Leg.* i, The spouts and gargoyles of these towers. **1883** STEVENSON *Silverado Sq.* 81 A rusty iron chute on wooden legs came flying, like a monstrous gargoyle, across the parapet.

fig. **1864** MISS YONGE *Trial* II. 233 Ethel here has too much sense; and that's what makes her such a dear old gurgoyle. **1875** TENNYSON *Q. Mary* I. iii, This old gaping gurgoyle [said of a priest]. **1889** *Spectator* 14 Dec. 841 Browning.. habitually uses it for this purpose—to carve verbal gurgoyles, grotesque figures of speech.

b. *transf.* A projection resembling a gargoyle.

1887 HALL CAINE *Deemster* ii. (1888) 9 A tall brass candlestick with gruesome gargoyles carved on the base.

2. *attrib.*, as ***gargoyle-face, -head; -faced*** adj.

1528 ROY *Rede Me* (Arb.) 54 What is it to se dogges and cattes Gargell heddes and Cardinall hattes Paynted on walles with moche cost. **1532** MORE *Confut. Tindale* Wks. 354/2 The bare vgly gargyle faces of their abhominable heresie. **1581** STUDLEY tr. *Seneca's Hippolitus* 60 b, Of ougly gargle-faced bigger Beare. **1848** *Archæol. Cambrensis* Ser. I. III. 220 Above the window runs a string course, with gurgoyl heads. **1886** H. F. LESTER *Under two Fig Trees* 138, I felt disposed to pity her.. despite her gurgoyle face.

Hence **'gargoyled** *a.*, ornamented with gargoyles.

1509 HAWES *Past. Pleas.* 15 [A tower] Gargeyld with grayhoundes and with many lyons. **1864** LONGF. *Divina Comm.* Sonnet ii, Fiends and dragons on the gargoyled eaves Watch the dead Christ between the living thieves.

gargoylism ('gɑːgɔɪlɪz(ə)m). [f. GARGOYLE + -ISM.] **1.** Grotesqueness. *rare.*$^{-1}$

1902 *Athenæum* 14 June 747/2 He is an artist in sensible nonsense, a master of gargoylism, a priest of the grotesque.

2. *Med.* A syndrome characterized by mental deficiency and skeletal deformities, including an abnormally large head, short limbs, and a protruding abdomen; Hurler's syndrome.

1936 ELLIS et al. in *Q. Jrnl. Med.* New Ser. V. 119 The association of a peculiar type of osseous dystrophy, with congenital clouding of the cornea,.. [etc.] has been noted sufficiently often to justify its being regarded as a definite syndrome... We have chosen the name 'Gargoylism' to describe it. **1965** R. H. DURHAM *Encycl. Med. Syndromes* 262 The term 'gargoylism' has been applied to this syndrome because the gross disfiguration resembles the gargoyles of Gothic architecture. **1970** C. G. TEDESCHI *Neuropath.* iii. 67/2 In contrast, the skull deformity of gargoylism belongs to the dolichocephalic variety.

gargrise: see GARGARISE, -IZE.

†**garguill.** *Obs. rare*$^{-1}$. [Of unknown origin; perh. some error. Cf. GARD *sb.*[2]] (See quot.)

1611 COTGR., *Os*, the Garguill or Dew-claw of a Stag, Bucke, Roe, etc.

gargulle, -gulye, etc., obs. ff. GARGOYLE.

gargulun, var. GARGILON. *Obs.*

gargut, gargyll, var. ff. GARGET[2], GARGIL[2].

†**gargyse.** *Obs. rare.* [Cf. GARGET, GARGIL.] A disease in cattle (see quot.).

1577 B. GOOGE *Heresbach's Husb.* 136 b, The Gargyse is a swelling beside the eye vppon the bone, like a botch, or a byle: yf your Bullocke haue it [etc.]. So **1741** *Compl. Fam.-Piece* III. 477.

gari, garial, vars. GHARRY, GAVIAL.

Garibaldi (gærɪ'bɔːldɪ, -'bældɪ). [The name of an Italian general (1807–82).]

1. a. A kind of blouse worn by women, originally made of a bright red stuff, in imitation of the shirt worn by Garibaldi and his followers, but later also of other colours. At first used *attrib.* as ***Garibaldi jacket.***

1862 *Illust. Lond. News* 27 Sept. 339/4 Ladies' Garibaldi Jackets. **1865** *Cornh. Mag.* Feb. 173 The furious, overgrown child's breast began to heave, and the heart within to melt behind the muslin Garibaldi. **1868** *Daily Tel.* 19 Aug., Dressed in a black skirt and the very reddest garibaldi that ever drove a bull to distraction. **1882** MRS. RIDDELL *Struggle for Fame* xxvi, Mrs. Felton.. was coming out.. arrayed in a black skirt and a white garibaldi.

b. A kind of hat.

1882 in OGILVIE; and in later Dicts.

2. A red pomacentrid fish of the Californian coast.

1885 *Riverside Nat. Hist.* (1888) III. 237 A species occurring along the southern Californian coast, and known as the goldfish, red perch, and Garibaldi—the *Hypsypops rubicundus.*

3. In full ***Garibaldi biscuit.*** A sandwich biscuit containing a paste of currants.

1896 J. T. LAW *Grocer's Man.* 87 *Garibaldi*.. with currants inside. **1909** H. G. WELLS *Tono-Bungay* III. iii. 276 Instead of offering me a Garibaldi biscuit, she asked me with that faint lisp of hers, to 'have some squashed flies, George'. **1951** C. V. WEDGWOOD *Last of Radicals* i. 30 A cup of tea, with 'Garibaldi' biscuits ('squashed flies' we called them).

Garibaldian (gærɪ'bɔːldɪən, -'bæl-), *a.* and *sb.* [f. GARIBALDI + -AN.] **A.** *adj.* Of, pertaining to, or supporting Garibaldi. **B.** *sb.* An adherent of Garibaldi. Also **Garibal'dino** *a.* and *sb.*, **Gari'baldist** *sb.*

1860 *Universe* 8 Dec. 1/2 The Garibaldian General Türr. **1861** E. DICEY *Cavour* xxiv, The Garibaldian Dictatorship. **1863** *All Year Round* 2 May 222/1 The Garibaldists are coming! **1864** *Dublin Rev.* July 144 Mr. Shaen, a zealous Garibaldian.. openly maintained that there had been 'a plot'. **1892** O'CLERY *Making of Italy* 121 The numerous expeditions which followed for the purpose of reinforcing.. the Garibaldian army. **1904** CONRAD *Nostromo* iv. 20 There were three doors in the front of the house, and each afternoon the Garibaldino could be seen at one or another of them. **1965** 'C. HIBBERT' *Garibaldi & his Enemies* I. iv. 67 The fear of the Garibaldians.. led the inhabitants to desert the town. *Ibid.* viii. 112 Anita had abandoned her Garibaldino uniform some days before.

†**garible.** *Obs. rare*$^{-1}$. [A sb. form related to the OF. verb *guerbloier*, *guebloier*, to play or sing in some special fashion, prob. the same word as *werbler* to quaver with the voice: see WARBLE.] ? A flourish in music.

13.. *Sir Beues* (A.) 3908 ȝhe hadde lerned of minstralcie, Vpon a fiþele for to play Staumpes, notes, garibles gay.

‖**garigue, garrigue** (garig). [Fr.] In the south of France, uncultivated land of a calcareous soil overgrown with low scrub; also, the vegetation found on such land.

1896 *Smithsonian Rep.* 414 Uncultivated lands, there called the garrigues. **1903** W. R. FISHER tr. *Schimper's Plant-Geogr.* III. v. 516 Such waste tracts, in South France termed '*garigues*', usually occur only on calcareous soil. **1914** A. G. TANSLEY in H. S. Thompson *Flowering Plants of Riviera* 6 In rocky places where the pines are not well developed or are absent altogether the limestone scrub is very open, and there is much bare rock between the shrubs. This type of vegetation is called *garigue.* **1963** G. BELLAIRS *Death in Wasteland* iv. 46 Part of it is *garrigue*, rocky uncultivated wasteland covered in prickly oaks. **1965** POLUNIN & HUXLEY *Flowers of Mediterranean* 11 Extensive areas of the hottest and driest terrain are covered with garigue.

†**gariofle.** *Obs. rare.* Also 6 **garyophyll.** [a. OF. *gariofile*, ad. med.L. *gariofilum* = L. *caryophyllum.* The popular Fr. form is *girofle*: see GILLYFLOWER.] A clove.

c **1400** MAUNDEV. (Roxb.) vii. 26 Gariofles, spikenarde, and oþer spiceries. *Ibid.* xxix. 131 Treesse berand garioflez and nute mugez. **1568** SKEYNE *The Pest* (1860) 25 Vsand thairwith Garyophyllis, and Cannell pulderit.

garish ('gɛərɪʃ), *a.*[1] Forms: 6 **gaurish, gawrish, gaerishe**, 6–7 **garishe**, 7 **garrishe**, 6– **garish**, (9 **gairish**). [The early spellings *gaurish*, *gawrish*, suggest derivation from GAURE *v.* to stare (cf. *garing-stocke*, var. *gawring-stock* = gazing-stock).

The suffix -ISH, however, is rarely appended to vb.-stems, and it is doubtful whether any certain instance occurs so early as the 16th c.]

1. Of dress, ornament, ceremonial, etc.: Obtrusively or vulgarly bright in colour, showy, gaudy.

1545 RAYNOLD *Byrth Mankynde* (1552) Prol. C ij b, Soch as.. seeke.. the abhominable and.. garishe setting forth of theyr mortal carcases. **1595** GOSSON *Quips Upst. Gentlew.* 260 in Hazl. *E.P.P.* IV. 261 The better sort, that modest are, Whom garish pompe doth not infect. **1618** E. ELTON *Compl. Sanct. Sinner* (1622) 27 That apparell, haply.. too garish for the fashion. **1631** SANDERSON *Serm. ad Aulam* (1681) II. 3 She will never be light or garish in her Attire. **1636** FEATLY *Clavis Myst.* xv. 205 The garish service of the Masse. **1675** TRAHERNE *Chr. Ethics* xxvi. 410 By this vertue [humility] we are inclined to despise our selves, and to leave all the garish ornaments of earthly bliss. **1756** *Demi-Rep.* 21 Nor garish dress corrupt the female mind. **1820** W. IRVING *Sketch Bk.* (1859) 51 Looking about.. with a vacant air, that showed her insensibility to the garish scene. **1827** KEBLE *Chr. Y.* 2nd Sund. Epiph. iv, The world's gay garish feast. **1837** W. IRVING *Capt. Bonneville* II. 44 Garish beads, and glittering trinkets, were bought at any price. **1855** THACKERAY *Newcomes* II. 161 Hymen.. exchanged his garish saffron coloured robe for decent temporary mourning.

fig. **1643** MILTON *Divorce* II. xxii. (1851) 128 The ceremoniall part, which led the Jews as children through corporal and garish rudiments. **1885** EDW. GARRETT *At Any Cost* xvii. 300 What a discord her appearance would have struck in his garish, rapid life.

2. Of colour: Excessively bright, glaring.

a **1568** ASCHAM *Scholem.* I. (Arb.) 54 Som new disguised garment..fond in facion, or gaurish in colour. **1611** CORYAT *Crudities* 260 All the most light, garish, and vnseemely colours. **1797** MRS. RADCLIFFE *Italian* xxxvi. (1824) 697 The colours were all too fresh and garish for the meek dejection of her woe. **1860** W. COLLINS *Wom. White* II. ii. 170 All of light garish colours.

b. of light (day, the sun, etc.).

1592 SHAKS. *Rom. & Jul.* III. ii. 25 That all the world will be in Loue with night, And pay no worship to the Garish Sun. **1632** MILTON *Penseroso* 141 Hide me from day's garish eye. **1788** V. KNOX *Winter Even.* I. i. 3 There seems to be something in the garish splendour of a bright sunshine. **1833** J. H. NEWMAN *Hymn, 'Lead Kindly Light'*, I loved the garish day. **1879** EDW. GARRETT *House by Wks.* II. 16 Lydia shrank from the morning hours and the garish sunshine.

3. Adorned to excess; too highly coloured or decorated.

1587 TURBERV. *Trag. T.* (1837) 47 Not forcing stately builded bowres, nor gallant garish tentes. **1604** DEKKER *1st Pt. Honest Wh.* x. Wks. 1873 II. 56 What fooles are men to build a garish tombe, Onely to saue the carcase whilst it rots. **1604** DRAYTON *Owl* 178 Wisdome not all, in every garish Bird, Shrewdly suspect. **1850** W. IRVING *Goldsmith* xi. 140 His essays..did not produce equal effect at first with more garish writings of..less value. **1858** DICKENS *Lett.* (1880) II. 73 All sorts of garish triumphal arches were put up. **1887** *Times* 27 Aug. 10/2 They are spoiling..the banks of the Grand Canal with enormous and countless garish signboards.

†**4.** Wanting in self-restraint, flighty. *Obs.*

1650 JER. TAYLOR *Holy Living* ii. §2. 70 Temperance is accompanied with gravity of deportment: greedinesse is garish, and rejoyces loosely at the sight of dainties. **1662–87** HY. MORE *Enthus. Triumph* (1712) 35 Blurting out any garish foolery that comes into their mind. **1678** SOUTH *Serm.* (1823) II. 160 Fame and glory makes the mind loose and garish.

†**5.** *adv.* = GARISHLY. *Obs.*

1589 R. HARVEY *Pl. Perc.* (1860) 34 If any aske why thou art clad so garish, Say thou art dubd the forehorse of the parish.

garish, *a.*[2]: see under GARE *sb.*[2]

garish, var. GUARISH *v.*, to cure.

garishly (ˈgɛərɪʃlɪ), *adv.* [f. GARISH *a.*[1] + -LY[2].]

1. In a garish manner; gaudily, glaringly; †proudly, wantonly.

1593 NASHE *Christ's T.* (1613) 149 Englishmen put all their felicitie in going pompously and garishly. **1635** R. BOLTON *Comf. Affl. Consc.* iv. 113 And guilded over garishly in His personated Angelicall glory. **1880** L. WALLACE *Ben-Hur* I. viii. 42 The sun streamed garishly over the stony face of the famous locality.

†**2.** With lack of self-restraint; flightily. *Obs.*

1606 HINDE *Eliosto Libidinoso* 56 Weakely starting vp and garishly staring about, especially on the face of Eliosto. *a* **1680** CHARNOCK *Attrib. God* (1834) II. 251 Who would venture rashly and garishly into the presence of..a king upon his throne?

3. *Comb.*, as ***garishly-adorned***, ***-furnished*** adjs.

1660 H. MORE *Myst. Godl.* v. xvi. 199 There is nothing in this new Jerusalem but what is pure and Apostolical; which is not so in the garishly-adorned Church that Grotius looks at. **1877** BLACK *Green Past.* xli, We began to revel in the sumptuousness of the vast and garishly-furnished hotels.

garishness (ˈgɛərɪʃnɪs). [f. as prec. + -NESS.]

1. Excessive display or brilliancy in dress, colour, etc.

1598 J. DICKENSON *Greene in Conc.* (1878) 156 Marshalling your bodies pride, thereby to attract more gazers on your garishnesse. **1664** H. MORE *Myst. Iniq.* 257 The Garishness of whores and the pranking up themselves to allure. **1814** W. TAYLOR in *Monthly Mag.* XXXVIII. 213 Time, and smoke..will eventually sift a vaporous powder over the picture, and then subdue its garishness of hue.

fig. **1813** COLERIDGE *Remorse* I. ii, There are woes Ill bartered for the garishness of joy! **1877** MORLEY *Crit. Misc.* Ser. II. 396 Bolingbroke, whose fine manners and polished gaiety give us a keen sense of the grievous garishness of Macaulay.

†**2.** Want of self-restraint, flightiness. *Obs.*

1649 JER. TAYLOR *Gt. Exemp.* II. Ad §12. 57 Lest the lavishnesse of his spirit should transport him to intemperance..to vanity, and garishnesse. **1651** —— *Serm. for Year* I. xii. 154 By a prosperous accident [we] are melted into joy and garishnesse, and drawn off from the sobriety of recollection. *a* **1684** LEIGHTON *Comm.* 1 Pet. iii. 13 And, possibly, gray hairs may have nothing under them but garishness and folly many years old. *a* **1716** SOUTH *Serm.* (1744) IX. v. 157 That pride and garishness of temper, that renders it impatient of the sobrieties of virtue.

garison, -oun, obs. forms of GARRISON.

garit(e, obs. form of GARRET.

garitour, var. GARRITOUR. *Obs.*

garland (ˈgɑːlənd), *sb.* Forms: 4 ger(e)lande, -lond, 4–6 garlande, (4 -launde), -lond(e, (5 -long), 5–6 -lant(e, (6 -lent), 6 gare-, guarland, 6–7 girlond, (6 ger-, girland), 7 ghirland, -lond, ghyrlond, guirlande, 4– garland. [a. OF. *garlande, gerlande, gallande* (also *guarlander* vb.) = Pr. *g(u)arlanda*, OSp. *guarlanda*, Cat. *garlanda*, med.L. *garlanda, gallanda.* The word is also found with a different vowel in the first syllable, as F. *guirlande*, Pr. *guirlanda*, It. *ghirlanda*, Sp., Pg. *guirnalda*; and no satisfactory origin has yet been suggested for it. In the 16th and 17th c. the spellings *ghir-, gir-, guirland* are freq. used by English wirters, in imitation of the Fr. and It. forms.]

1. a. A wreath made of flowers, leaves, etc., worn on the head like a crown, or hung about an object for decoration.

1303 R. BRUNNE *Handl. Synne* 997 Ȝyf þou euer yn felde, eyþer in toune, Dedyst floure gerlande or coroune. *c* **1385** CHAUCER *L.G.W.* Prol. 160 A garlond on his hed of rose levys. *a* **1400–50** *Alexander* 4599 Ȝour women has na.. Garlands ne no gay gere to glyffe in ȝour eȝen. **1526** TINDALE *Acts* xiv. 13 Brought oxen and garlondes vnto the churche porche. **1563** GOLDING *Cæsar* (1565) 75 b, Putting al their Senate to death..he sold the rest under a garlond [L. *sub corona*] for bondmen. *a* **1652** BROME *Love-sick Court* v. Wks. 1873 II. 170 Let his Priests lead..The horned Sacrifice, mantled with Ghirlonds. **1716** LADY M. W. MONTAGU *Let. to C'tess Mar* 14 Sept., It certainly requires ..much art and experience to dance upon May-day with the garland. **1756–7** tr. *Keysler's Trav.* (1760) II. 343 A fine painting, representing Diana crowning a sleeping Endymion with a garland of flowers. **1817** BYRON *Manfred* II. i, A quiet grave, With cross and garland over its green turf. **1830** D'ISRAELI *Chas. I*, III. xvii. 369 To strew rushes ..and to hang fresh garlands in the church were offices pleasing to the maidens. **1870** MORRIS *Earthly Par.* III. IV. 57 Round about her shapely head A garland of dog-violet.. meetly had she set.

fig. **1570** DEE *Math. Pref.* 10 Whose fayrest floure of their garland..was Arithmetike. **1594** in *Shaks. C. Praise* 6 Though Rome lament that she have lost The Gareland of her rarest Fame. **1596** SHAKS. *1 Hen. IV*, v. iv. 73 All the budding Honors on thy Crest, Ile crop, to make a Garland for my head. **1727–46** THOMSON *Summer* 1731 With thee, serene Philosophy! with thee, And thy bright garland, let me crown my song. **1781** COWPER *Convers.* 638 Virtue.. Crowned with the garland of life's blooming years. **1832** TENNYSON *Miller's Dau.* 208 Where Past and Present, wound in one, Do make a garland for the heart.

†**b.** Christ's crown of thorns. *Obs. rare.*

1377 LANGL. *P. Pl.* B. XVIII. 48 An other..bigan of kene thorne a gerelande to make. *c* **1460** *Christm. Carols* (Percy Soc.) 9 How xalt thou sufferin the scharp garlong of thorn?

c. A natural 'garland' or festoon.

1841 EMERSON *Addr., Method Nature* Wks. (Bohn) II. 224 Vegetable life, which..festoons the globe with a garland of grasses and vines. **1863** FR. A. KEMBLE *Resid. in Georgia* 19 An ivy..growing in profuse garlands from branch to branch.

d. A wreath of ribbons; chiefly *Naut.*

1846 YOUNG *Naut. Dict., Garland*, an ornament decked with ribbons hoisted up between the masts of a North Sea whaler on the first of May, &c., or in a vessel of war on the occasion of a marriage. **1868** ATKINSON *Cleveland Gloss., Garlands*, wreaths of ribbons enclosing a white glove, formerly borne at the funerals of young unmarried women. 2, Hoops bedecked with ribbons hung at the mast-head of whale-ships returning to port after a successful voyage. **1888** *Malta Chron.* 13 Mar. in *N. & Q.* 7th Ser. V. 284 At the mainmast head of the Alexandra was displayed..the garland consecrated to weddings by naval custom.

2. A wreath, chaplet, or coronet of some costly material, esp. of gold or silver work. *Obs.* exc. *Hist.*

13.. *Seuyn Sag.* (W.) 3234 Hir hed was gayly dubed and dyght With gerlandes al of gold ful bright. ? *a* **1366** CHAUCER *Rom. Rose* 869 Of orfrayes fresh was hir gerland, I..Saugh never, ywys, no gerlond yitt, So wel wrought of silk as it. **1536** in *Antiq. Sarisb.* (1771) 199 A garland of silver and gilt, set about with stones of divers colours. **1555** EDEN *Decades* 105 Garlandes of glasse and counterfecte stoones. **1585** T. WASHINGTON tr. *Nicholay's Voy.* II. iii. 73 b, A garlande of fine drawen gold. **1628–9** *Ann. Barber-Surg. Lond.* (1890) 397 Paid Mr Greene the Gouldsmith for the silver and making of 4 new Garlands..xxli. **1890** YOUNG *Ibid.* 506 Four very handsomely chased and wrought silver garlands or wreaths for crowning the Master and Wardens on Election Day.

3. A wreath, crown, etc. worn as a mark of distinction.

†**a.** A royal crown or diadem. *Obs.*

[**1247** MATTHEW PARIS (Du Cange), Rex veste deaurata, et coronula aurea, quæ vulgariter garlanda dicitur, redimitus] *c* **1330** R. BRUNNE *Chron.* (1810) 331 Þe garland Roberd tok, þat whilom was þe right, þe lond forto loke, in signe of kynge's myght. *a* **1400–50** *Alexander* 818 Þis renke & his rounsy þai reche vp a croune, As gome at has þe garland & all þe gre wonne. **1543** GRAFTON *Contn. Harding* (1812) 509 What about ye getting of the garland, keping it, lesing and winning again, it hath coste more English blood then hath the twise winning of Fraunce. **1548** HALL *Chron., Hen. IV*, 32 b, Wel qh the prince if you are kynge I wil haue the garland and trust to kepe it with the swerd..as you haue done. **1594** SHAKS. *Rich. III*, III. ii. 40, 41 *Cates.* Till Richard weare the Garland of the Realme. *Hast.* How weare the Garland? Doest thou meane the Crowne? *Cates.* I, my good Lord. **1615** CHAPMAN *Odyss.* I. 619 The girlond of this kingdom let the knees Of Deity run for.

b. The priest's fillet or band of wool worn in token of consecration to the service of a god. Cf. FILLET *sb.* 1.

1791 COWPER *Iliad* I. 34 Lest the garland of thy god And his bright sceptre should avail thee nought.

c. The wreath or crown conferred upon the victor in the Greek and Roman games, or upon the hero of any great exploit. Hence in phrases (chiefly *fig.*), ***to carry (away), gain, get, win, go away with*** (etc.) ***the garland*** = to be the victor in a contest, to gain the victory.

1500–20 DUNBAR *Poems* l. 20 At feistis and brydallis wpaland, He wan the gre, and the garland. **1587** GOLDING *De Mornay* xii. 166 The Garlond of Oke, he giueth..to such as..first..enter the breach, or get vp vpon the wall of a Towne..assaulted. **1593** Q. ELIZ. tr. *Boeth.* (E.E.T.S.) 81 As a Runner in a race has a guarland for which he ran, in rewarde. **1596** DANETT tr. *Comines* VI. 206 When war beginneth in England, in ten daies or lesse the one or the other getteth the garland. **1606** HOLLAND *Sueton.* 2 At the winning of Mitylenæ, Thermvs honored him with a Civike guirland. **1615** CROOKE *Body of Man* 25 Galen hath wonne the Girlond from them all. **1642** FULLER *Holy & Prof. St.* v. xv. 420 Where one gaineth a garland of bayes, hundreds have had a wreath of hemp. **1658** ROWLAND *Moufet's Theat. Ins.* 910 That [honey] which carries away the garland and is esteemed above the rest, is yellow. **1704** HEARNE *Duct. Hist.* (1714) I. 130 Yet perhaps he [Thucydides] has won the Garland from all those who have represented many and great affairs. **1725** COATS *Dict. Her.* (1739) s.v. *Crown*, There were also among the Romans several sorts of Crowns, or Garlands, given to those who had perform'd some signal Services in War, and were known by the Names of Triumphal, Civick, Vallar, Mural, Naval, and Obsidional. **1865** CARLYLE *Fredk. Gt.* XIII. xiii. V. 130 Nor is Prince Karl's left wing gaining garlands just at this moment.

†**d.** as worn by a 'May Queen', or by girls as the prize of some kind of competition. Hence, the girl who wears a garland. *Obs.*

1691 DRYDEN *Beautiful Lady of May* 4 The garland was given, and Phillis was queen. **1698** *Mem. St. Giles's* (Surtees) 93 Given the Lasses with the Garling, 1s. **1701** *Ibid.* Given to the Girle that had the Garland, 1s. 6d. **1704** *Ibid.* 99 Given the Two Garlings, 2s. **1706** *Ibid.* 101 Pd. the Garlands, 1s. 6d.

†**e.** *fig.* The principal ornament, the thing most prized, 'glory'. *Obs.*

1591 SPENSER *Ruins Rome* L'Envoy, Bellay, first garland of free Poësie That France brought forth. —— *M. Hubberd* 1185 The Realmes chiefe strength & girlond of the Crowne. **1607** SHAKS. *Cor.* I. i. 188 You..call him Noble, that was now your Hate: Him vilde, that was your Garland. **1637** B. JONSON *Sad Sheph.* III. ii, Marian, and the gentle Robin Hood, Who are the crown and ghirland of the wood.

4. *fig.* A collection of short literary pieces, usually poems and ballads; an anthology, a miscellany.

[**1526** *Pilgr. Perf.* (W. de W. 1531) 24 To cast suche floures & sentences as we haue gathered of ho y fathers sayntes & doctours togyder, as in one fardell, or in maner of a garlande.] **1612** R. JOHNSON (*title*), A Crowne-garland of Govlden Roses Gathered out of Englands royall garden. **1631** T. D. (*title*), The Garland of Good Will..Containing many pleasant Songs, and prety poems, to sundry new Notes. **1633** ROWLEY *Match Midnt.* II. D iij a, These are out of ballads, She has all the Garland of good will by heart. **1663** (*title*), Robin Hoods Garland; or delightfvl Songs. **1710** ADDISON *Whig Exam.* No. 1 ¶3 The new garland of riddles. **1765** PERCY *Ess. Anc. Minstr., Reliques* I. p. xxiii, In the reign of James I. they [Ballads] began to be collected into little Miscellanies, under the name of Garlands. **1864** A. BISSET *Omit. Chapt. Hist. Eng.* 304 Besides their circulation in garlands, broadsheets, and miscellanies.

5. a. The representation of a garland in metal, stone, etc.

c **1524** *Churchw. Acc. St. Mary Hill, London* (Nichols 1797) 127 Playne with a cover gilt, with a rose and a garlent in the bodom. **1838** BRITTON *Dict. Archit., Garland*..a wreath, or chaplet of branches, of foliage, or of flowers: also a sculptured representation of them on a frieze [etc.]. **1879** H. PHILLIPS *Addit. Notes Coins* 3 On the reverse a garland of olives encloses the words, *Godt heeft ons bewaert.*

b. *Her.* (See quot. 1882.)

1828–40 BERRY *Encycl. Her.* I, *Garland*, or *Chaplet*, is formed of a laurel, flowers, &c. **1864** BOUTELL *Her. Hist. & Pop.* ix. 44 Garlands are quartered upon the..monument of Lord Bourchier. **1882** CUSSANS *Her.* (ed. 3) 113 *Chaplet* or *Garland.* These terms are frequently, but erroneously, used to signify the same object. A Chaplet should be composed of four Roses, arranged at equal distances in a circle, the intervening spaces being filled up with leaves; and a Garland should be formed of laurel or oak leaves, interspersed with acorns.

6. Something that resembles a garland in circular form, or in the fact of surrounding another object.

a. *Arch.* (See quot. 1823.)

a **1490** BOTONER *Itin.* (Nasmith 1778) 221 Latitudo de le garlond continet xi pedes. **1823** WILLSON *Gloss. Pugin's Spec. Goth. Archit., Garland*, a band of ornamental work surrounding the top of a spire, tower, &c. **1849** WEALE *Dict. Archit., Garland*, an ornamental band used in Gothic work.

†**b.** *Med.* = CIRCLE *sb.* 8. *Obs.*

1548 RECORDE *Urin. Physick* x. (1651) 81 Round about the edge of the urine there appeareth a garland, circle, or ring. **1625** HART *Anat. Ur.* II. i. 51 The garland or vpper-most part of the vrine.

†**c.** A ring-like marking or band. *Obs.*

1578 LYTE *Dodoens* II. l. 210 There be other sortes of Narcissus founde, whose garland or circle in the middle of the flowers is white. **1673** *Lond. Gaz.* No. 791/4 A Brown and White Spanniel..a White streak in the Forehead..with a Garland about the Neck.

d. Of a target (see quot.).

1847–78 HALLIWELL, *Garland*, the ring in a target in which the prick or mark was set. **1867** in SMYTH *Sailor's Word-bk.*

7. *Mining.* (See quots.)

1819 REES *Cycl., Garland*..a spiral groove, made behind and in the stoning or ginging of a shaft, for collecting the water which oozes out of different strata. *Ibid.*, Garland also signifies a broad hoop of iron, or a square frame of wood, which is used in coal-pits, to hold on the coals which are last heaped on the corves or gang-waggons. **1883** GRESLEY *Gloss. Coal Mining, Garland.* [To the same effect as in Rees.]

8. *Naut.* **a.** A band or collar of rope (or iron) used for various purposes; **b.** (also *Mil.*) A receptacle for shot: see also SHOT-GARLAND; **c.** A kind of net (see quot. 1769).

a. **1495** *Naval Acc. Hen. VII* (1896) 189 Aparell for the.. maste ffeble..Garlandes of yron abought the mast hede. **1704** J. HARRIS *Lex. Techn., Garland* in a Ship is that Collar of Rope which is wound about the Head of the Mainmast to keep the Shrowds from galling. **1841** R. H. DANA *Seaman's*

Man. 107 *Garland*, a large rope, strap or grommet, lashed to a spar when hoisting it on board. **1883** W. C. Russell *Sailors' Lang.*, *Garlands*, fastenings formed of small stuff, used in taking in and out a mast.

b. 1697 Dampier *Voy.* (1729) I. 543 The Shot tumbled out the Lockers and Garlands. *c* **1850** *Rudim. Navig.* (Weale) 147 *Shot-lockers* or *garlands*. Apartments built up in the hold to contain the shot. Also pieces of oak plank, fixed against the head-ledges and coamings of the hatch and ladder-ways, or against the side between the ports, to contain the shot. **1859** F. A. Griffiths *Artil. Man.* (1862) 114 The round shot enclosed in a large grummet or garland. **1867** Smyth *Sailor's Word-bk.*, *Garland*..in shore-batteries, a band, whether of iron or stone, to retain shot together in their appointed place.

c. 1769 Falconer *Dict. Marine* (1776), *Garland*, a sort of net..used by the sailors as a locker or cupboard to contain their provisions. **1867** in Smyth *Sailor's Word-bk.*

9. *attrib.* and *Comb.*, as ***garland-forest***, ***-maker***, ***-weaver***, ***-wreath***; ***garland-like*** adj. and adv.; ***garland-wise*** adv.; **Garland Day**, (see quots.); **garland-flower**, (*a*) a flower suited for making garlands, (*b*) (see quot. 1866); **Garland Friday** (see quots.); †**garland-rose** (see quot.); †**garland-seam** *Anat.*, the coronal suture; **Garland Sunday** (see quots.); †**garland-thorn**, a name given by Gerarde to *Paliurus aculeatus* (Christ's Thorn), of which Christ's crown of thorns is supposed to have been made; **garland-well**, a well at which garlands were suspended as offerings.

1836 A. E. Bray *Descr. Tamar & Tavy* II. xxx. 289 Amongst the little boys, this day [*i.e.* 29th May, date of the Restoration 1660] goes by the name of **garland day*. **1959** I. & P. Opie *Lore & Lang. Schoolch.* xii. 262 At Abbotsbury in Dorset 13 May has long been 'Garland Day'. The children customarily carry round a large flower garland on a pole, and show it at front doors. **1563** Hyll *Art Garden.* (1593) 158 Sundry posie and *Garland floures. **1866** *Treas. Bot.* 520/1 *Garland flower*, a common name for *Hedychium*; also applied to *Daphne Cneorum*, *Pleurandra Cneorum*, and *Erica persoluta*. **1870** Morris *Earthly Par.* III. iv. 296 A close of pot-herbs and of garland flowers Goes up the hill-side. **1818** Byron *Ch. Har.* iv. cxliv, The *garland-forest, which the grey walls wear, Like laurels on the bald first Cæsar's head. **1960** *Cath. Herald* 22 July 8/1 Hawkers will not be allowed ..near Croagh Patrick from *Garland Friday [*i.e.* the Friday before Garland Sunday] until Reek Sunday. **1567** Maplet *Gr. Forest* 43 It..groweth round about and *garland like. **1824** Miss Mitford *Village* Ser. i. (1863) 11 With..a crisp and garland-like richness. **1552** Huloet, *Garland maker, *stephanoplocus*. **1580** Hollyband *Treas. Fr. Tong*, *Chapelier, on chapeliére*, a garland maker, a hatmaker, a stiller. **1635** Swan *Spec. M.* (1644) 244 Rosemarie, which some call the *garland rose, or in Latine Rosmarinus coronaria. **1576** Baker *Jewell of Health* 98 b, Anointed about the *garland seame, it taketh away all maner of payne and ache of the head. **1933** *Irish Press* 31 July 1/7 For fourteen centuries pilgrims have come to Croagh Patrick on *Garland Sunday. **1955** D. D. C. P. Mould *Irish Pilgrimage* ix. 134 Croagh Patrick attracts enormous crowds ..the pilgrimage goes..on the last Sunday of July, the so-called Garland or Garlic Sunday. **1597** Gerarde *Herbal* Table Eng. Names, *Garland Thorne, see Christes thorne. **1849** E. C. Otté tr. *Humboldt's Cosmos* II. 465 *note*, The celebrated *Garland-weavers of Athens. **1897** *Daily News* 20 Sept. 6/2 But besides curing and maleficent wells there were pin wells, *garland wells, and wishing wells. **1600** Fairfax *Tasso* xx. xx. 5 From the bosome of the burning sonne Proceeded this, and *garland wise the same. **1634** Milton *Comus* 850 For which the shepherds..throw sweet *garland wreaths into her stream.

garland ('gɑːlənd), *v.* [f. Garland *sb.*]

1. *trans.* To form (flowers) into a garland. *rare.*

c **1420** *Pallad. on Husb.* viii. 120 Other garlande hem [leves] and so depende, Into the wyn so they go not to depe. **1813** Shelley *Q. Mab* Ded. iii, Thine are these early wilding flowers Though garlanded by me.

2. To crown with a garland, to deck with garlands.

1593 Drayton *Sheph. Garl.* iv. xxix, Thy Poesie is garlanded with Baye. **1605** B. Jonson *Masque Blackness* Wks. (Rtldg.) 545/1 Their hair loose, and flowing, gyrlanded with sea grass. **1785** Burns *To Jas. Smith* ix, Then fareweel hopes o' laurel-boughs, To garland my poetic brows! **1804** J. Grahame *Sabbath* (1808) 84 When garlanding with flowers His helm. **1818** Keats *Endym.* i. 110 A troop of little children garlanded. **1824** Landor *Imag. Conv.* Wks. (1846) I. 23 Pat his hide forsooth! hug his neck, garland his horns! **1846** Ruskin *Mod. Paint.* I. i. i. i. §5 They..have thought it enough to garland the tombstone when they had not crowned the brow.

b. said of the material which forms the garland.

1602 Marston *Ant. & Mel.* v. Wks. 1856 I. 58 Let choyce delight Garland the browe of this tryumphant night. **1816** L. Hunt *Rimini* ii. 33 Still from tree to tree the early vines Hung garlanding the way in amber lines. **1832** Tennyson *Œnone* 99 The wandering ivy and vine..Ran riot, garlanding the gnarled boughs With bunch and berry and flower thro' and thro'. **1849** James *Woodman* viii, A bough of Christmas holly, garlanding a boar's head on a high festival.

c. *transf.* in *nonce-uses*. To surround or deck as with a garland.

1818 Scott *Hrt. Midl.* xxxvi, The Thames, here turreted with villas, and there garlanded with forests. **1820** Keats *Eve St. Agnes* xxiv, A casement high and triple-arched there was, All garlanded with carven imageries. *a* **1874** Longf. *Hanging of Crane* vi, I see the table..Garlanded with guests. **1881** J. Grant *Cameron*. I. iv. 58 A thatched edifice, garlanded round with dead wild-cats.

Hence '**garlanded** *ppl. a.*

1862 M. Hopkins *Hawaii* 91 When the priests..were preparing to sacrifice to them the garlanded ox. **1871** *Daily Tel.* 6 Nov., The May-pole is wholly defunct. No milkmaids dance with garlanded pails on their heads. **1880** Ouida *Moths* II. 33 Her bed of white satin, embroidered with garlanded roses.

garlandage ('gɑːləndɪdʒ). *rare*$^{-1}$. [f. Garland *sb.* + -age[1].] Display of garlands.

1885 Tennyson *Balin & Balan* 80 Woodland wealth Of leaf, and gayest garlandage of flowers, Along the walls and down the board.

garlander ('gɑːləndə(r)). *rare.* [f. Garland *sb.* + -er[1].] One who carries a garland on Garland Day.

1939 F. Thompson *Lark Rise* xiii. 234 One of the most dependable of the older girls, who was made responsible for the behaviour of the garlanders. *Ibid.* 237 Sometimes the garlanders would forsake the road for stiles and foot-paths.

garlanding ('gɑːləndɪŋ), *vbl. sb.* [f. Garland *v.* + -ing[1].] The action of the vb. garland; hence *concr.* that which forms a garland.

1831 *Blackw. Mag.* XXIX. 224 Many a green parasite trailed its fantastic garlanding of verdure. **1873** Mrs. Whitney *Other Girls* xxix. (1876) 379 These flung a grace of lightness over the closer garlanding. **1890** *Pall Mall G.* 5 Mar. 4/3 The portraits are in a dark tint, and the garlanding and the letterpress in gold.

garlandless ('gɑːləndlɪs), *a.* [f. Garland *sb.* + -less.] Without a garland.

1821 Shelley *Prometh. Unb.* iii. iv. 186 Dragged to his altars soiled and garlandless. **1848** in Craig.

garlandry ('gɑːləndrɪ). *rare.* [f. Garland *sb.* + -ry.] Garlands collectively, decoration composed of or resembling garlands.

1853 C. Bronte *Villette* I. xiv. 255 The lavished garlandry of woven brown hair amazed me. **1889** *Century Mag.* Aug. 590/2 Ceilings..beautiful with raised garlandry.

garlandy ('gɑːləndɪ), *a. nonce-wd.* [f. Garland *sb.* + -y[1].] Resembling garlands.

1830 Miss Mitford *Village* Ser. iv. (1863) 250 Art and literature..adorning with a wreathy and garlandy splendour all that is noblest in mind and purest in heart.

†**garle**, *sb. Obs. rare*$^{-1}$. [? Short f. garland.] A band or streak. (Cf. quot. 1673 in garland *sb.* 6 c.)

1677 *Lond. Gaz.* No. 1239/4 A middle sized Fox Beagle.. a white garle about her neck.

garle (gɑːl), *v. dial.* [f. *garle* adj.: see garled.] (See quots.)

a **1825** Forby *Voc. E. Anglia*, *Garle*, to mar butter in the making, by handling in summer with hot hands. This turns it to a curd-like substance with spots and streaks of paler colour, instead of the uniformly smooth consistency and golden hue, which it ought to have. *Mod.*, When woollen clothes, on being washed, take a mottled appearance, they are said by housewives to be garled, or to have garled.

garle, obs. form of girl.

garled ('gɑːld), *a. Obs.* exc. *dial.* Also 6 **garle**. [app. some kind of derivative of OF. *garre*, *garré* of similar meaning.] Spotted, speckled (chiefly of cattle); also *red-garled*.

1501 *Will of Pusey* (Somerset Ho.), One cowe garled. **1507** *Will of Crisall* (Ibid.), Ij kyne garle & schell and the garle bullok. **1558** *Will of J. Pysle* (Ibid.), A Redgarlde Cow. **1577–86** Holinshed *Chron.* I. 226 Red and fallow deer, whose colours are oft garled white and blacke. **1587** Harrison *England* iii. xii. (1878) ii. 78 The writers also diuide this stone into fiue kinds..the fourth is garled with diuerse colours, among which some are like drops of bloud. **1809** Batchelor *Orthoep. Anal. Eng. Lang.* 133 Garld, white thickly spotted with red, the outside spots small; applied to cows.

†**garlement.** *Obs. rare.* ? Corrupt form of *garnement*, garment.

c **1485** *Digby Myst.* (1882) ii. 16 Goodly besene with many a riche garlement.

garlic ('gɑːlɪk), *sb.* Forms: 1 gárléac, 3, 5 garlec, 4–5, 7 garleek, 4–6 -lek(e, (5 -lekke), 4, 6–7 -lik(e, 4–6 -lyk(e, 6–7 -licke, 6–9 garlick, 8– garlic. Also 5 garly, garle. [OE. *gárléac* (f. *gár* gare *sb.*[1] + *léac* leek); the corresponding ON. *geirlauk-r* is possibly from OE.]

1. a. A plant of the genus *Allium* (usually *A. sativum*) having a bulbous root, a very strong smell, and an acrid, pungent taste.

clove of garlic (see clove *sb.*[1] 1). *oil of garlic*, an essential oil obtained from the bulb and stem of the garlic.

c **1000** *Sax. Leechd.* II. 34 Genim cropleac & garleac ..gecnuwa wel tosomne. *c* **1265** *Voc. Plants* in Wr.-Wülcker 558/17 *Alleum*..garlec. *c* **1305** *Land Cokayne* 105 in *E.E.P.* (1862) 159 Hi bringeþ garlek gret plente. **1382** Wyclif *Num.* xi. 5 The leke, and the vniowns, and the garlekes [L. *allia*]. *c* **1425** *Voc.* in Wr.-Wülcker 644/28 *Hoc alleum*, garle. *Ibid.* 662/12 *Hoc alleum*, garly. *c* **1460** J. Russell *Bk. Nurture* 536 Roost beeff & goos with garlek, vinegre, or pepur. **1522** Skelton *Why not to Court* 106 They may garlycke pyll..Or pescoddes they may shyll. **1577** B. Googe *Heresbach's Husb.* ii. (1586) 60 b, Garlicke..groweth with a blade like the Onyon, but not hollow, the stalke round, and the flowres in the toppe in a round tuft. *a* **1627** Middleton *More Dissemblers* iv. i, *Cap.* Lov'st thou the common food of Egypt, Onions? *Dond.* I, and Garlick too. **1725** De Foe *Voy. round World* (1840) 291 Putting no garlick or onions into the sauce. **1796** C. Marshall *Garden.* xv. (1813) 235 Garlic is used for both culinary and medicinal purposes. **1838** T. Thomson *Chem. Org. Bodies* 485 Oil of Garlic is extracted from the bulbs and stem of the garlic. **1865** Kingsley *Herew.* i. 61 If he have not garlic to his roast goose every time he chooses.

fig. **1691** *New Discov. Old Intreague* xxiii, Give them their ancient Priviledges agen..The luscious Garlick of the former Reigns. [Allusion to *Numbers* xi. 5.] **1843** Lytton *Last Bar.* ii. ii, Is it for them to breathe garlic on the alliances of Bourbons and Plantagenets?

b. With qualifying words indicating different species; esp. **bear's garlic**, see bear *sb.*[1] 10; **hog's garlic** = prec.; **wild garlic** = crow-garlic.

1538 Leland *Itin.* III. 19 Diverse of [these] Islettes berith wyld Garlyk. **1597** Gerarde *Herbal* i. lxxxix. 142 Snakes Garlick. Harts Garlick or Stags Garlick. *Ibid.* 143 The great mountain Garlick groweth about Constantinople. **1626** Bacon *Sylva* §499 Where Kine feed upon Wilde Garlicke, their Milke tasteth plainely of the Garlicke. **1750** W. Ellis *Mod. Husbandm.* III. i. 42 (E.D.S.) Crow, or Wild, Garlic. **1818** *Withering's Brit. Plants* (ed. 6) II. 445 *Allium ampeloprasum*..Round-headed Garlic. **1861** Miss Pratt *Flower. Pl.* V. 266 Flowering Great Round-headed Garlic.

†**2.** The name of a popular jig or farce of the early part of the seventeenth century. *Obs.*

1614 R. Tailor *Hog hath lost Pearle* i. Bij b, *Ha.* Youle finde it worth Megge of Westminster, althouh it be but a bare Iigge. *Pla.* O lord sir, I would it had but halfe the taste of garlicke. *Ha.* Garlicke stinkes to this. **1630** J. Taylor (Water P.) *Wks.* ii. 159 And for his action he eclipseth quite, The Iigge of Garlick, or the Punks delight.

3. *attrib.* and *Comb.*, as ***garlic-bed***, ***bread***, ***-breath***, ***butter***, ***-eater***, ***-god*** (with allusion to Juvenal *Sat.* xv. 9), ***-head***, ***-monger***, ***-mortar***, ***-odour***, ***-pickle***, ***press***, ***salt***, ***-sauce***, ***sausage***, ***-seed***, ***-seller***, ***-smell***, ***-vinegar***; ***garlic-eating***, ***-like*** adjs. Also **garlic-snail**, a mollusc so called from its emitting a garlic-like odour.

1552 Huloet, *Garlicke bedde, *allectum*. **1951** E. J. Marvel *Cook it Ahead* 3 (*heading*) *Garlic Bread. **1960** 'I. T. Ross' *Murder out of School* xiv. 181 She brought a basketful of garlic bread from the oven. **1606** *Choice, Chance*, etc. (1881) 19 With such a *garlicke breath, as would haue poisoned a dog. **1663** Dryden *Wild Gallant* iv. i, What a garlick Breath my Lady Springwell had! **1942** C. Spry *Come into Garden, Cook* (1943) xv. 223 Take a whole loaf... Cut in thick slices... Spread the *garlic margarine or butter. **1950** E. David *Bk. Mediterranean Food* 40 *Garlic butter for snails*... Pound the garlic... Put the butter into the mortar and work it so that the garlic impregnates it..add the parsley..a very little salt, pepper and nutmeg. **1970** 'D. Craig' *Young Men may Die* viii. 60 We had to eat the specialities, snails in a slime of garlic butter. **1986** W. J. Burley *Wycliffe & Quiet Virgin* ix. 152 They ordered bowls of soup and bread rolls with garlic butter. **1607** Shaks. *Cor.* iv. vi. 98 The breath of *Garlicke-eaters. **1884** E. Barker *Through Auvergne* 80 When you live among an onion-eating or *garlick-eating people. **1679** *Confinement* 24 Their *Garlick-Gods, they might indeed adore; And to their Onyons, invocations poure. **1482** *Paston Lett.* III. 285 A standing pece white covered, with a white *garleek heed upon the knoppe. **1521** *Test. Ebor.* (Surtees) V. 202 Sex cocliaria argentea cum knoppes vocatis garlekhed. **1616–61** Holyday *Persius* 330 To taste each morn three times a garlick-head. **1836–48** B. D. Walsh *Aristoph., Acharn.* ii. v, If they saw a cucumber..or garlic-head. **1816** Accum *Chem. Tests* (1818) 221 The peculiar *garlic-like odour. **1393** Langl. *P. Pl.* C. vii. 373 Godefray þe *garlek-mongere. **1602** *Withals' Dict.* 187/2 A *garlike morter, *mortarium alliarium*. **1849** D. Campbell *Inorg. Chem.* 22 It has..a *garlic odour and taste. **1853** Hickie tr. *Aristoph.* (1872) II. 631 Content with *garlic-pickle. **1958** *Catal. County Stores Taunton* June 12 *Garlic Press. **1968** *House & Garden* May 15/2 Garlic press..useful all-metal kitchen utensil for pressing garlic..11/6. *c* **1938** *Fortnum & Mason Catal.* 52/2 Salt..*Garlic—per bot. 1/6. **1958** *Catal. County Stores Taunton* June 12 Garlic or Onion Salt. **1552** Huloet, *Garlicke sauce, *alliatum*. **1892** Garrett *Encycl. Cookery* I. 668 Garlick Sauce. **1905** *Daily Chron.* 5 Jan. 4/5 The remnants of [horse] flesh—which even the *garlic-sausage manufacturers cannot use. **1930** E. Waugh *Labels* 44 In the haversack on his back he carries a map and garlic sausage. **1968** P. Dickinson *Weathermonger* vi. 69 They..ate garlic sausage, processed cheese, bread and tomatoes. **1657** S. Purchas *Pol. Flying-Ins.* i. xv. 94 Bees gather..*Garlick-seeds. **1483** *Cath. Angl.* 150/2 A *Garleke seller, *allearius*. **1805** *Med. Jrnl.* XIV. 428 It may be distinguished by its *garlic smell. **1854** Woodward *Mollusca* (1856) 30 A few exhale peculiar odours, like the *garlic-snail (*helix alliaria*). **1892** Garrett *Encycl. Cookery* I. 668 *Garlic Vinegar.

b. *esp.* in popular names of plants, as **garlic-germander**, the water germander, *Teucrium Scordium*; **garlic-pear(tree**, the American plant *Cratæva gynandra*; **garlic-sage**, the wood sage or germander, *Teucrium Scorodonia*; **garlic-shrub** (see quot.); **garlic (treacle) -mustard**, †**garlic treaclewort**, *Sisymbrium Alliaria* (*Alliaria officinalis*); **garlic-tree** (see quot.); **garlic-wort** = *garlic-mustard*.

1548 Turner *Names of Herbes*, *Scordium*..may be called in englishe water Germander or *Garleke Germander. **1725** Sloane *Jamaica* II. 169 *Garlick Pear-Tree..The fruit has ..a mealy pulp..smelling like garlick, whence the name. **1756** P. Browne *Jamaica* (1789) 246 The thin-leafed Crateva or Garlick Pear. **1895** *Oracle Encycl.* II. 208/1 The garlic pear..blisters the skin. **1597** Gerarde *Herbal* ii. ccv. 535 Of Wood Sage, or *Garlicke Sage. **1861** Miss Pratt *Flower. Pl.* IV. 174 Wood Germander or Wood Sage..often called Garlic Sage, because when bruised, it has a slight odour of garlic. **1866** *Treas. Bot.* 520/1 *Garlic shrub, *Bignonia alliacea*; also *Petiveria alliacea*. **1861** Miss Pratt *Flower. Pl.* I. 129 *Garlic Treacle-mustard, Jack-by-the-Hedge, or Sauce-alone. **1597** Gerarde *Herbal* Table Eng. Names, *Garlicke Treaclewoort or Garlicke Mustard, and his kinds. **1882** J. Smith *Dict. Pop. Names Plants*, **Garlic*

Tree, a name in Jamaica for *Cratæva tapia*.. The fruit has a strong smell of Garlic. **1863** PRIOR *Plant-n.* 89 *Garlick-wort.. *Erysimum Alliaria*, L.

Hence **'garlic** *v. nonce-wd.*, to dose with garlic.

1830 tr. *Aristoph., Knights* 72 *Chorus.* Take this garlic, and swallow it down without chewing. *Sausage-seller.* Why? *Cho.* That, when garlicked, my friend, you may fight the better.

garlicky ('gɑːlɪkɪ), *a.* [f. GARLIC *sb.* + -Y[1].] Savouring or smelling of garlic.

1775 ASH (citing HOLLINGSWORTH), *Garlicky*, overgrown with garlick. **1786** *Francis, the Philanthropist* III. 22 This eternal succession of greasy stews and garlicky *ragouts.* **1858** *Sat. Rev.* 27 Nov. 536/2 A Neapolitan beggar.. bawls his garlicky breath into the face of his casual victim. **1861** *Court Life at Naples* 169 There was such a garlicky atmosphere about the lady. **1875** H. C. WOOD *Therap.* (1879) 198 A strong garlicky odor.

garlits ('gɑːlɪts). ? *Obs.* Also 8–9 **garliz.** [From *Görlitz* in Prussian Silesia, where there are linen manufactures.] (See quot. 1795.)

1696 J. F. *Merchants Ware-ho.* 21 The next is Garlits, whereof there are several sorts.. the first is a blew whiting.. There is another sort of Ell-wide Garlits, which is of a browner whiting. *Ibid.* 22 Several sorts of brown Garlits. **1795** ASH Suppl., *Garliz* (in commerce), a kind of linen cloth imported from Germany. **1812** J. SMYTH *Pract. of Customs* (1821) 124 Linen.. imported from Russia, Dantzic, Germany, [etc.], such as Dowlas, Lockrams, Garlix [*sic*], &c.

garment ('gɑːmənt), *sb.* Forms: α. 4 **garnyment** (*pl.* **garnemens**), 4–5 **garnement**, 5 **garneament.** β. 4– **garment**, (6 *Sc.* **garmont, -mond, germo(u)nt**). [a. OF. *garniment, garnement* (pl. *garnemens*) equipment, armour, vestments (in mod.F. only *mauvais garnement* rascal, or ellipt. for this) = OSp. *guarnimiento*, It. *guarnimento*, f. Rom. **gwarnire*, OF. and mod.F. *garnir* to furnish, fit out, equip; see GARNISH. The α-forms were the commoner down to *c* 1500; the β-form seems to have originated in the north.]

1. Any article of dress: in *sing.* esp. an outer vestment, a gown or cloak; in *pl.* = clothes. Now somewhat *rhetorical.*

α. **13..** *Seuyn Sag.* (W.) 2775 He let him make a garnement, Ase blak as ani arnement. *c* **1380** *Sir Ferumb.* 1395 Ryche garnymentz forþ sche drow, & by-tok hymen for to were. **1413** *Pilgr. Sowle* (Caxton 1483) IV. xxxvi. 84 A thycke chosen garnement a trayling gowne of twelue yerdes wyde. **1483** CAXTON *G. de la Tour* B vij b, For her pourfyls of her garnements ne of her hodes ben not grete ynough after the gyse that now is used.

β. **1340** HAMPOLE *Pr. Consc.* 521 A rym þat es ful wlatsome, Es his garment when he forth sal come. *c* **1400** *Destr. Troy* 1366 Pepull.. no hede toke Of golde ne of garmenttes, ne of goode stonys. *c* **1440** *Promp. Parv.* 187/2 Garment of clothe, made of dyuers clothys (*P.* colours), *panucia.* **1535** COVERDALE *Ecclus.* xxvii. 9 Yf thou folowest righteousnes, thou shalt get her, and put her vpon yᵉ as a fayre garment. **1605** SHAKS. *Lear* III. vi. 84 You sir, I entertaine for one of my hundred; only, I do not like the fashion of your garments. **1651** HOBBES *Leviath.* III. xxxiv. 209 Where extraordinary Understanding, though but in making [Aaron's] Garments.. is called the Spirit of God. **1732** LEDIARD *Sethos* II. VIII. 739 He got a sort of garment made for each of them. **1822** W. IRVING *Braceb. Hall* iii. 22, I have a reverence for these old garments. **1886** M. F. SHELDON tr. *Flaubert's Salammbo* 18 This garment.. swung down over his shoulders in such a manner as to effectually hide his face in shadow.

b. *fig.* The outward dress or covering in which anything is seen or manifested.

1585 ABP. SANDYS *Serm.* iv. 77 If thou be cloathed with the sweete garment of the sonne of God. *a* **1631** DONNE *Serm.* lxxvi. 768 Gods garments, those Scriptures in which God hath apparelled and exhibited his will. **1829** CARLYLE *Misc.* (1857) II. 78 The veil and mysterious garment of the Unseen. **1866** G. MACDONALD *Ann. Q. Neighb.* xiii. (1878) 247 To put these forms into the garments of words. **1876** MOZLEY *Univ. Serm.* vi. 134 The.. garment of the flesh.. encircles the human soul, and is the instrument of expression to it.

2. *Comb.*, as ***garment-dyer, -maker, -making, -trade, -worker.***

1596 J. NORDEN *Progr. Pietie* (1847) 173 Be not beholden to any nation for such trumpery, neither to the garmentmaker. **1876** ROCK *Text. Fabr.* i. 1 Other appliances for garment-making. **1885** *Instr. Census Clerks* 72 [Subdivisions of the Dyer's trade] Clothes, Garment Dyer. **1891** *Pall Mall G.* 19 Nov. 6/3 At a meeting of the National Convention of Garment Workers.. it was charged that the Hirsch Fund would be a certain cause of sweating in the garment trade.

garment ('gɑːmənt), *v.* [f. prec. sb.] *trans.* To dress or clothe; chiefly in pa. pple. *garmented.*

1614 CAMDEN *Rem.* 233 And thus were they garmented. **1623** tr. *Favine's Theat. Hon.* IX. xii. 417 Neither might garment themselves but with course Hempen and Hurden cloth. **1861** J. THOMSON *Ladies of Death* vii, Thou standest garmented in purest white.

b. *transf.* and *fig.*

a **1547** SURREY *Poems, Compl. Lover that defied Love* 4 He clothed fair the earth about with green, and every tree new garmented. **1801** SOUTHEY *Thalaba* VIII. x, Garmented with glory, in their sight Oneiza's Spirit stood. *a* **1851** MOIR *Poems, Dying Spaniel* v, When the snow-mantle garments the land. **1862** LONGF. *Wayside Inn* Prel. 129 Great volumes garmented in white, Recalling Florence, Pisa, Rome.

Hence **'garmenting** *vbl. sb.*

1614 CAMDEN *Rem.* 237 There will be.. strange garmenting of the body, not without deformitie of the minde.

garmentless ('gɑːməntlɪs), *a.* [f. as prec. + -LESS.] Without a garment.

1866 F. HALL in H. H. Wilson tr. *Vishṇu Purána* III. 310 *note*, Surrounded and guarded by garmentless women. **1884** J. PARKER *Apost. Life* III. 250 The poor, penniless, garmentless Apostle. **1890** *Sat. Rev.* 22 Nov. 575/2 A Joseph who had fled garmentless.

garmenture ('gɑːrməntjʊə(r)). [f. as prec. + -URE.] Clothing, array, attire.

1832 JAMES *Henry Masterton* xxxvii. 420 All the green garmenture of summer was gone. **1880** *Girl's Own Paper* Oct. 590 Cinderella.. Clothed in coarsest garmenture.

garmercye, var. GRAMERCY.

garmond, -mont, -mount, obs. ff. GARMENT.

garn ('gɑːn), *sb. north. dial.* Also 5 **garne**, 9 **gairn, gain.** [a. ON. *garn* = OE. *ȝearn*, YARN. See also GARNWIN, -WINDLE.] Yarn or worsted (see quot. 1876).

1483 *Cath. Angl.* 150/2 Garne (*A.* Garne *siue* ȝarn), *pensum.* To wynd Garne, *jurgillare.* **1695** KENNETT *Par. Antiq.* Gloss. s.v. *Draw-gere*, Yarn, still in the North call'd Garn; wooll workt into a thread. **1876** *Whitby Gloss.*, *Gain* or *Garn*, woollen yarn or worsted; though gain is made of short wool and is coarser [than worsted].

Phrase. c **1460** *Towneley Myst.* iii. 298 Ther is garne on the reyll other, my dame.

garn (gɑːn), *int.* Colloq. (chiefly Cockney) pronunciation of *go on* (see GO *v.* 86 j), often used to express disbelief or ridicule of a statement.

1886 in H. BAUMANN *Londinismen* 62/1. **1888** J. RUNCIMAN *Chequers* 80 Garn, you farthin' face! **1914** G. B. SHAW *Pygmalion* I, in *Nash's Mag.* Nov. 152/2 The Note Taker (*whipping out his book*). Heavens! what a sound!.. Ah —ah—ah—ow—ow—ow—oo! The Flower Girl (*tickled by the performance, and laughing in spite of herself*). Garn! **1922** 'R. CROMPTON' *Just—William* viii. 166 Garn! S'ours! We found it. **1925** *Glasgow Herald* 9 Jan. 8 He complained that if he used such words as 'garn' or 'struth' he was accused of vulgarity, whereas were he capable of imitating the peculiar sounds such as were heard from those north of the Tweed he would be able to move in any society. **1968** A. HOLDEN *Death after School* iii. 22 'Garn,' called out someone, 'tell us somefing we don't know!'

garn, var. GERN, *adv.*

†**garnade**[1]. *Obs.* [a. OF. (*pome*) *garnade* (var. of *grenate*) = POMEGRANATE; cf. GARNET.]

1. In Comb. ***apple-garnade*** = POMEGRANATE.

13.. *E.E. Allit. P.* B. 1044 Þe fayrest fryt þat may on folde growe, As orenge & oþer fryt & apple garnade.

2. ? A dish in ancient cookery, so called from being compounded with pomegranates.

c **1440** *Anc. Cookery* in *Househ. Ord.* (1790) 465 Garnade for X mees.. alay the rys with joyse of pomegarnetes.

†**garnade**[2]. *Obs. rare.* Also 5 **garnarde.** [a. OF. (Picard) *garnate*, whence MDu. *garnate*; Verwijs and Verdam conjecture that it may have meant wine flavoured with pomegranates, or perhaps wine from Grenada.] A kind of wine.

?*c* **1475** *Sqr. lowe Degre* 758 Wyne of Greke.. Antioche, and bastarde, Pyment, also, and garnarde. *c* **1481** CAXTON *Dialogues* (E.E.T.S.) 14/6 Vin dosoye et de garnate.. Wyn of oseye and of garnade.

garnap(pe, var. GARDNAP. *Obs.*

garnard(e, obs. forms of GARNER, GURNARD.

garnarde, var. GARNADE[2]. *Obs.*

garnary, var. GARNERY. *Obs.*

garneament, obs. form of GARMENT.

†**garnel**[1]. *Sc. Obs.* [A form of GARNER, perhaps influenced by F. *grenaille* refuse corn: see also GIRNEL.] A granary or barn.

1567 *Gen. Assembly* in Keith *Hist. Affairs Scot.* (1734) 589 He shall take no higher Prices than is appointed, nor put up in the Garnell. **1596** DALRYMPLE tr. *Leslie's Hist. Scot.* I. 48 Thay cal it, the Commoune Barn or garnel of Abirdine. **1821** GALT *Ann. Parish* xxxix. 313 He brought in two cargoes to Irville.. making for the occasion a garnel of one of the warehouses of the cotton-mill.

b. *attrib.*, as ***garnel-house.***

1663 *Inv. Ld. J. Gordon's Furniture*, Item, in the garnell house, twelff great Inglisch pewder plaites.

†**garnel**[2]. *Obs. rare*⁻¹. [? corruption of F. *grenaille* refuse corn.] An inferior kind of flour.

a **1752** DOUGLASS *Brit. Settlem. N. Amer.* (1753) 331 Five bushels Wheat yeilds (*sic*) about one hundred and three quarters merchantable Flower: the Garnel, or second Flower, pays for Cask and all other Charges.

†**garnel**[3], **gernel.** *Obs.* [a. Du. *garnaal*, dial. *garneel* = Ger. *garneele* shrimp; related and synonymous forms are Du. dial. *garnaat*, Flem. *geernaar(t*, High German dial. *garnat, granat, garner*, Belgian and North Eastern F. *grenat*, OF. *guernette*; of obscure origin: see *Wb. der Nederl. Taal.*] A species of shrimp.

1694 *Acc. Sev. Late Voy.* (1711) I. p. xxiv, Lobsters, Gernels, Star-fish, Mackrel. *Ibid.* II. 122 Of the Garnels or Prawns. *Ibid.* II. 124 Of the lesser Garnel or Shrimp.

garnement, obs. form of GARMENT.

garnep, var. GARDNAP. *Obs.*

garner ('gɑːnə(r)), *sb.* Forms: 2–4 **gerner(e**, 4 **gerniere**, 5 **garnar**, 6 **garnard(e, -erde, -yer**, 3– **garner.** [a. OF. *gerner, gernier, grenier* storehouse, garret:—L. *grānārium* (usually *grānāria* pl), GRANARY, f. *grānum* grain. Now less common than *granary*, except in rhetorical language. See also GARNEL[1], GARNERY, GIRNEL.] A storehouse for corn, granary.

c **1175** *Lamb. Hom.* 85 Þet corn me deð in to gerner, þet bitakeneð þe gode men þe scule bon idon in to heuene. *a* **1300** *Cursor M.* 4689 Garners [*Gött.* gerneris] and granges fild [he] wit sede, Maa þan i wit tung can rede. **1398** TREVISA *Barth. De P.R.* XVII. clxviii. (1495) 711 Whete is throsshen other trode to haue the moost pure to in to bernes other garners. **1496–7** *Act 12 Hen. VII*, c. 13 §12 The same Corne.. remayneth in the Berne Garner or in Stackis. **1577** B. GOOGE *Heresbach's Husb.* I. (1586) 42 b, The Garners, or corne loftes, wherein your Corne thus threasshed and cleansed shalbe layde, must stande hye. **1638** RAWLEY tr. *Bacon's Life & Death* 31 Garners, in Vaults under Ground, wherein they keepe Wheat and other Graines. *a* **1764** LLOYD *Henriade* Poet. Wks. 1774 II. 238 Their garners bursting with their golden grain. **1824** LANDOR *Imag. Conv.* (1826) I. 44 Your horse will not gallop far without them, though you empty into his manger all the garners of Surrey. **1889** *Pall Mall G.* 13 Oct. 7/2 A trapdoor leading to a garner above [a carriage-house].

fig. **1531** ELYOT *Gov.* I. xiv, A garnerde heaped with all maner sciences. *c* **1586** C'TESS PEMBROKE *Ps.* LXXVIII. x, He unclos'd the garners of the skies, And bade the cloudes ambrosian manna rain. **1816** SCOTT *Old Mort.* i, Yet you may be gathered into the garner of mortality before me, for the sickle of death cuts down the green as oft as the ripe. **1877** E. ARBER (*title*) An English Garner: Ingatherings from our History and Literature.

†**b.** A store-house for salt. (F. *grenier à sel.*)

1493 *Newminster Cartul.* (Surtees) 195, iiij Salt pannes.. wᵗ all yᵉ appᵗenance.. ij garners wᵗ all yᵉ grownde belongyng to ȝem. **1611** COTGR., *Gerbier*, a great Garner to keepe salt in.

c. *attrib.*, as ***garner-house.***

1815 SCOTT *Field of Waterloo* 6 The pestilential fumes declare That Carnage has replenish'd there Her garner-house profound.

garner ('gɑːnə(r)), *v.* [f. prec. sb.]

1. *trans.* To store (corn or other products of the earth) in a garner. Now chiefly *rhetorical.*

c **1375** *Sc. Leg. Saints, Nycholas* 224 We dare nocht þis quhet sel.. for.. to the emperoure garner mon we. **1474** *Househ. Ord.* (1790) 32 Wheate is never garnered there. **1837** CARLYLE *Fr. Rev.* I. VI. iii, The harvest is reaped and garnered; Yet still we have no bread. **1885** BIBLE (R.V.) *Isa.* lxii. 9 They that have garnered [**1611** gathered] it shall eat it. **1893** *Advance* (Chicago) 10 Aug., The wheat was being rapidly garnered into large, upright, clay receptacles, holding 20 bushels each.

2. *fig.* To collect or deposit as in a garner, to make a store of. ***to garner up, away***: to store or lay up, to put away.

1604 SHAKS. *Oth.* IV. ii. 57 But there where I haue garnerd vp my heart.. to be discarded thence. **1845–6** TRENCH *Huls. Lect.* Ser. II. ii. 171 The difficulty with which the world has ever persuaded itself of the death of any.. with whom it has garnered up its dearest hopes. **1857** HUGHES *Tom Brown* I. i, Until the old man with the scythe reaps and garners them away. **1866** NEALE *Sequences & Hymns* 82 Where the dust of Saints is garnered.

3. *intr.* To accumulate, to be stored up. *rare.*

1850 TENNYSON *In Mem.* lxxxii, For this alone on Death I wreak The wrath that garners in my heart.

Hence **'garnered** *ppl. a.*, **'garnering** *vbl. sb.*

1842 LONGF. *Slave in Dismal Swamp* vi, Fell, like a flail on the garnered grain. **1859** TENNYSON *Vivien* (Song), The.. little pitted speck in garner'd fruit. **1872** MORRIS *Love is enough* (1873) 27 But this is the harvest and the garnering season. **1876** —— *Sigurd* (1877) 2 His eve of the battle-reaping, and the garnering of his fame. **1892** *Athenæum* 19 Nov. 697/1 The education of life is but the garnering of the pictures cast by the few fragments of an infinite universe.

garnerage ('gɑːnərɪdʒ). *rare*⁻¹. [f. GARNER *sb.* + -AGE.] A garner, store-house.

1880 A. RALEIGH *Way to City* 56 Earth is worshipping heaven; yielding up her best fruits to that high garnerage.

†**'garnery.** *Obs. rare.* Also 6–7 **garnary(e.** [App. a mixed form from GARNER and GRANARY.] A granary.

1552 HULOET, Garnarye or garner, *cella penuaria.* **1598** STOW *Surv.* iii. (1603) 17 For the building of Conduits of a common Garnery. **1603** KNOLLES *Hist. Turks* (1621) 654 Sicilia, the garnerie and storehouse of Italie. **1607** TOPSELL *Four-f. Beasts* (1658) 398 Plaister the walls of your garnery therewith.

garnesch(e, -esh, -essh(e, obs. ff. GARNISH.

Garnesie (*violet*), var GUERNSEY.

garnesoin, var. GARNISON. *Obs.*

garnet[1] ('gɑːnɪt). Forms: 4 **gernet**, (4–5 *pl.* **grenaz**), 5 **garnette(s)**, 7 **garnat**, 6– **garnet.** [a. OF. **gernat, grenat* (whence also MDu. *garnate, gernate*), ad. med.L. *grānātum*, according to some a transferred use of L. *grānātum* POMEGRANATE (cf. next), the stone having probably been so called from its resemblance in colour to the pulp of the fruit; others consider it a derivative of med.L. *grānum*, *grāna* GRAIN, cochineal, red dye. See also GRANATE².]

1. A vitreous mineral, most commonly found as a distinct crystal, and in the form of a rhomboidal dodecahedron, but also occurring in other shapes. The precious garnet is of a deep transparent red colour, and is used as a gem.

a **1310** in Wright *Lyric P.* v. 25 Ase beryl so bryht, Ase gernet in golde, ant ruby wel ryht. *c* **1400** MAUNDEV. (1839) xx. 219 The rede ben of Rubies, and of Grenaz and of Alabraundynes. *c* **1460** *Emare* 156 Deamondes and koralle, Perydotes and crystall, And gode garnettes bytwene. **1555** EDEN *Decades* 234 But [these] haue sumwhat the colour of a granate which we commonly caule a garnet. **1688** R. HOLME *Armoury* II. 39/2 The Garnet, the Cornelian, are both red, some call them the Sardy stone. **1773** GOLDSM. *Stoops to Conq.* III. i, You shall make use of my garnets, till your jewels be found. **1813** BAKEWELL *Introd. Geol.* (1815) 81 Crystals called garnets are frequently interspersed in gneiss. **1876** PAGE *Adv. Text-bk. Geol.* iii. 53 Garnets were left projecting from pedicles of felspar.

2. *attrib.*, as *garnet-colour*, *-doublet*; *garnet-breasted*, *-coloured*, *-like*, *-red* adjs.; also **garnet-berry** (see quot.); **garnet-blende**, a sulphide of zinc; † **garnet-limpet** (see quot.); **garnet-rock**, a rock consisting mainly of garnet; **garnet-work**, ornamentation composed of masses of garnets.

1863 PRIOR *Plant-n.* 89 *Garnet-berry, the red currant, *Ribes rubrum*. **1837** DANA *Syst. Min.* 429 Dodecahedral *Garnet Blende..Sulphuret of Zinc. **1893** H. B. BAILDON *Rescue*, etc. 81 Golden-eyed and *garnet-breasted. **1783** HERSCHEL in *Phil. Trans.* LXXIII. 257 It is of a very fine deep *garnet colour. **1882** MISS BRADDON *Mt. Royal* II. iii. 25 Those deep *garnet-coloured patches which show where the red sea-weed lurks below. **1895** *Daily News* 20 Mar. 7/1 Sleeves and underskirt of garnet-coloured velvet. **1649** LOVELACE *Lucasta* Ded., So among the Orient Prize (Saphyr-Onyx Eulogies) Offer'd up unto your Fame: Take my *Garnet-Dublet Name. **1776** DA COSTA *Elem. Conchol.* i. 21 The *garnet-limpet has..many different appearances; nevertheless its elegant *garnet-like semi-transparent eye or top always characterizes it. **1838** T. THOMSON *Chem. Org. Bodies* 415 When mixed with sulphated peroxide of iron, it becomes *garnet-red. **1796** KIRWAN *Elem. Min.* (ed. 2) I. 368 *Garnet rock..consists of amorphous garnet, in which trap quartz, calcareous spar, and a very small quantity of blackish brown mica are found. **1883** A. H. CHURCH *Precious Stones* iv. 37 Can the same praise be honestly given to modern *garnet-work?

† **'garnet²**. *Obs.* Also 4-5 **gernet(t**. [a. OF. (*pome*) *garnette*, *gernate* POMEGRANATE; cf. GARNADE.] The pomegranate; also *garnet-apple*.

a **1400** *Pistill of Susan* 95 Grapus and garnettes gayliche þei grewe. *a* **1400-50** *Alexander* 4724 þai ware fedd all of frute..Of grapis & of gernets. *Ibid.* 5238 Lange lindis.. Growand full of gernetts & gracious frutes. *c* **1410** LYDG. *Life Our Lady* xlvii. (Caxton) G iv, The garnet appyl of colour golden hewed. [**1673** WEDDERBURN *Voc.* 17 (Jam.) *Mala granata*, apple-garnets.]

† **'garnet³**. Also 5 **garnette(s)**. [Of obscure origin; it has been conjectured to be a corrupted dim. of ONF. *carne* (:—L. *cardinem*) hinge.] *Obs.* exc. in CROSS-GARNET. A hinge of this form ⊢, the upright part being nailed to the support, and the horizontal to the door, shutter, etc.

1459 *Churchw. Acc., St. Mich. Cornhill*, For amendyng of the garnettes of ij pewes. **1483** *Act 1 Rich. III*, c. 12 §1 No merchaunt Straungier..brynge into this Realme..keys hynges and garnettes. **1657** HOWELL *Londinop.* 393 To hang by Jewmews or Garnets, so that they may be taken up and let down.

b. *attrib.*, as in *garnet-hinge*.

1882 in OGILVIE; and in later Dicts.

garnet⁴ ('gɑːnɪt). *Naut.* Also 5 **garnett(e**. [Of obscure origin; cf. Du. *garnaat*, *karnaat*, of similar meaning.]

1. (See quot. 1706.)

1485 *Naval Acc. Hen. VII* (1896) 68 Hoke ropes..ij. Garnetts..ij. yerd ropes for the top..ij. **1496** *Ibid.* 152 A payer of Garnettes with nayles weyng xij^lb^—xv^d^. **1627** CAPT. SMITH *Seaman's Gram.* v. 25 Any tackell, Pendant, Garnet. **1692** *Ibid.* I. xiv. 64 The main Tye and fall of the Garnet. **1706** PHILLIPS (ed. Kersey), *Garnet* (Sea-term), a Tackle with a Pendant-rope coming from the Head of the Main-mast, and a Block or Pulley strongly fasten'd to the Mainstay, to hoist all the Casks into a Ship, and such Goods as are not over-weighty. **1867** in SMYTH *Sailor's Word-bk.*

2. *Comb.*, as *garnet-block*, *-fall*.

1711 W. SUTHERLAND *Shipbuild. Assist.* 113 The Garnet-fall, a Tackle much used to hoist in all the Stores and Provisions. **1867** SMYTH *Sailor's Word-bk.*, *Clue-garnets*, a sort of tackle wove through a garnet-block.

Garnet⁵ ('gɑːnɪt). *slang*. [f. the name of Sir *Garnet* Wolseley (1833–1913), leader of several successful military expeditions.] Phr. *(all) Sir Garnet*, highly satisfactory; all right.

1894 *Sporting Times* 1 Sept. 1/4 The start was all 'Sir Garnet'. **1913** C. MACKENZIE *Sinister St.* I. I. iv. 61 That's All Sir Garnet, and don't you make no mistake. **1941** H. G. WELLS *You can't be too Careful* I. i. 17 'All's well with the Missus, Tewler?' he asked. 'All Sir Garnet, Sir,' said Mr. Richard Tewler. **1958** 'A. GILBERT' *Death against Clock* 111 She'd been knocked out..and her heart not being quite Sir Garnet did the rest.

† **garneter**. *Obs. rare.* Also 5 **garnetour**, 6 **garnettyer**, **garniter**. [a. OF. *garnetier*, *grenetier* the overseer of a granary or of a salt-store (*grenier à sel*), f. *grenier*, GARNER, GRANARY.] The superintendent of a granary.

a **1483** *Liber Niger* in *Househ. Ord.* (1790) 70 One groome garnetour to receive, to kepe, and to delyver the wheete comyng from the Countries. **1543** PAGET in *St. Papers Hen. VIII*, IX. 260 And the saliners do gyve out of hande 15000 muys of salt to be delivred to his garnettyers in Rowen. **1576** in Nichols *Progr. Q. Eliz.* II. 47 Edward Jakes Yeoman Garneter. **1598** *Fitzherbert's Husb.* IV. i. 135 At euery weekes end he shall commaund the Garniter to bring in his accounts.

garnetiferous (gɑːnɪ'tɪfərəs), *a.* [f. GARNET + *-fer* bearing + -OUS.] Producing garnets.

1852 TH. ROSS *Humboldt's Trav.* II. xvii. 80 *note*, The great mass of garnetiferous serpentines..form little distinct mounts. **1895** *Naturalist* 345 A block of garnetiferous schist was noted at base of cliff near Cowden.

garnett(e, obs. form of GARNET.

Garnett ('gɑːnɪt), *sb.* [f. the surname *Garnett*.] A 'Garnett's machine' (see GARNETT *v.*); **Garnett tooth**, a form of saw-tooth used in these machines.

1884 W. S. B. MCLAREN *Spinning* ix. 189 The machines by which the first three of these materials are made are various. The one for opening the looser waste is called a Garnett. **1892** J. NASMITH *Students' Cotton Spinning* 132 It is customary to cover the licker-in with a set of teeth... These are called 'Garnett' teeth.

garnett ('gɑːnɪt) *v.* [f. as the sb.] *trans.* To prepare (woollen waste) by means of a 'Garnett's machine' (see quot. 1886). Hence **'garnetted** *ppl. a.*

1886 HARRIS *Tech. Dict. Fire Insurance*, *Garnetting*, Garnett's machines are employed in woollen-mills for 'pulling' or dressing and preparing oiled worsted waste, for use (either alone or mixed with woollen yarn) in the manufacture of heavy woollen cloths. **1894** *Times* 17 Aug. 9/3 Mungo, shoddy, garnetted waste, and carded waste.

garnety ('gɑːnɪtɪ), *a. rare*⁻¹. [f. GARNET *sb.*¹ + -Y¹.] Having the appearance of garnet.

1875 H. C. WOOD *Therap.* (1879) 96 There are two officinal Tartrates of Iron, both occurring in garnety scales.

garnewyne, var. GARNWIN. *Obs.*

garney ('gɑːnɪ). (See quot.)

1867 SMYTH *Sailor's Word-bk.*, *Garney*, a term in the fisheries for the fins, sounds, and tongues of the cod-fish.

garnierite ('gɑːnɪəˌraɪt). [Named (by Clarke 1875) after Jules *Garnier*, a French geologist, the discoverer of the substance: see -ITE.] A green mineral found in New Caledonia, a hydrous silicate of nickel and magnesium.

1875 *Dana's Min.* App. ii. 23 The mineral..should properly receive the name garnierite. **1881** *Metal World* No. 21. 323 It is of an apple or pear green colour, and has been called garnierite (or naumeite).

garnish ('gɑːnɪʃ), *sb.* Forms: 5 **garnyssh**, **-niche**, **-nes**, 5-6 **garnysche** (**-nysshe**), **-nesh**, 6 **garnesshe**, **-nyshe**, **-nishe**, 5- **garnish**. [f. GARNISH *v.*¹]

† **1.** A set of vessels for table use, *esp.* of pewter (see quot. 1587). *Obs.*

1418 *Bury Wills* (Camden) 3 Item assigno eidem Ricardo ..dimidium garnyssh de vas' peutr'. *c* **1440** *Promp. Parv.* 187/2 Garnysche of vesselle (*K.* garniche), *garnitum*. **1464** *Mann. & Househ. Exp.* (Roxb.) 273 Item, the same day payd for a di. a garnyshe of vessellys, viij.s. iiij.d. *c* **1530** in Gutch *Coll. Cur.* II. 287 Item deliveryd oone garnysshe of silvar vessell. **1587** HARRISON *England* III. xi. (1878) II. 72 Such furniture of houshold of this mettall [pewter], as we commonlie call by the name of vessell, is sold vsuallie by the garnish, which doeth conteine twelue platters, twelue dishes, twelue saucers. **1674** JOSSELYN *Voy. New Eng.* 17 For one garnish of peuter 3*l.* *os.* *od.*

† **2.** Outfit, dress. *Obs. rare.*

1596 SHAKS. *Merch. V.* II. vi. 45, I should be obscur'd. *Lor.* So you are, sweet, Euen in the louely garnish of a boy.

3. Embellishment or decoration in general. Also *concr.* an ornament, ornamental appendage. *lit.* and *fig.* ? *Obs.*

1615 MARKHAM *Eng. Housew.* II. i. (1668) 3 Adorn the person altogether without toyish garnishes, or the gloss of light colours. **1647** CLARENDON *Contempl. Ps.* Tracts (1727) 383 No man being so presumptuously wicked, as not to put on some garnish and dress of virtue to impose on the world. **1683** KENNETT *Erasm. on Folly* 48 Unsullied from all artificial garnish. *a* **1708** BEVERIDGE *Priv. Th.* I. (1730) 89, I am so much taken with the Garnish and seeming Beauty of this world's vanities. **1727** BOYER *Dict. Angl.-Fr.*, Garnishes of Doors, Gates, *or* Porches, *les Ornemens, les embellissemens, les Fleurons, d'une Porte.*

† **b.** Trimming for articles of dress; some particular material used for this purpose. *Obs.*

1527 *Lanc. Wills* (1857) 17, I beqweth..to the parson of Sanct Michaells my garnech sarsnet typett. *c* **1540** *Churchw. Acc. St. Dunstan's, Canterbury*, Item v yardys and di of garnysshe xiij d ob.

4. Things placed round or added to a dish to improve its appearance at table; also *fig.* of literary 'dishes'.

1673 [R. LEIGH] *Transp. Reh.* 30 Your Text is all Margent, and not only all your Dishes, but your Garnish too is Pork. **1734** WATTS *Reliq. Juv.* (1789) 217 While the garnish of some [dishes] was profusely rich and gay, that of others was very coarse and poor. **1764** HARMER *Observ.* VII. iv. 147 The parched Cicers..are strewed singly, as a garnish, over other dishes. **1825** COLERIDGE *Aids Refl.* (1848) I. 180 In a book like this..the sauce and the garnish are to occupy the greater part of the dish. **1846** J. BAXTER *Libr. Pract. Agric.* (ed. 4) I. 100 The roots [of beet]..form a beautiful garnish, and are very much used as a pickle. **1883** *Chr. World* 28 Dec. 909/4 His highly-seasoned polemics, set out with such a garnish of misrepresentation.

† **b.** ? Side-dishes; also *attrib.* *Obs.*

16.. FLETCHER *Love's Pilgr.* II. iv, Portly meat, Bearing, substantial stuff, and fit for hunger, I do beseech you, hostess, first; then some light garnish, Two pheasants in a dish. **1641** *Ovatio Carolina* 18 At the South end whereof (two yards distance from the Table), was a Table of Garnish, of three yards square. *Ibid.* 19 Brawne, fishe, and cold baked meats, planted upon the Garnish or Side Table.

5. *slang.* Money extorted from a new prisoner, either as a jailer's fee, or as drink-money for the other prisoners (abolished by 4 Geo. IV. c. 43, §12). *Obs.* exc. *Hist.*

1592 GREENE *Upst. Courtier* D ij a, Let a poore man be arrested..he shal be almost at an angels charge, what with garnish, crossing and wiping out of the book..extortions.. not allowed by any such statute. *a* **1661** FULLER *Worthies* (1840) II. 447 When such prisoners have paid the bailiff's fees and garnish. **1704** SWIFT *T. Tub* Wks. 1768 I. 111 Like a fresh tenant of Newgate, when he has refused the payment of garnish. **1727** GAY *Beggars' Opera* II. vii. (1728) 27 [Gaoler, to a prisoner] You know the custom, Sir. Garnish, Captain, Garnish. **1752** *Gentl. Mag.* XXII. 239/2 The Sheriffs..have ordered that no debtor in going into any of the goals of London and Middlesex, shall for the future, pay any garnish. **1823** SCOTT *Peveril* xxxiii, Then the Master's side —the garnish came to one piece.

b. A similar payment among workmen; also *maiden-garnish*.

1759 GOLDSM. *Bee* No. 5 ¶ 20 There are numberless faulty expenses among the workmen—clubs, garnishes, freedoms, and such like impositions. **1859** *Autobiog. Beggar boy* 144 The gold old fuddling times of short turns, maiden garnishes, and a hundred other little imposts. **1865** *Slang Dict.*, *Garnish*, footing-money. *Yorkshire.* **1896** *Daily News* 28 Feb. 5/4 A fine of four gallons [of beer] is called a 'garnish', and when a man finds his first lot of work..he pays his 'maiden garnish'.

¶ **6.** *Prison slang.* Fetters.

[Perh. a misapprehension. The passage quoted above (sense 5) from Gay *Beggars' Opera* is followed by the words 'Hand down those fetters'. This may have led Johnson to assign a wrong meaning to the word.]

1755 in JOHNSON. **1893** in FARMER *Slang*.

7. *Comb.*, as *garnish-tinselled* adj.; also **garnish-bolt** (see quot.); **garnish-money** (= sense 5); **garnish-nail**, **-plate** (see quots.).

1874 KNIGHT *Dict. Mech.* I. 943/1 *Garnish-bolt (*Building*), a bolt having a chamfered or faceted head. **1632** B. JONSON *Magn. Lady* v. v, You are content with the ten thousand pound, Defalking the four hundred *garnish-money. *c* **1660** in J. Brown *Bunyan* viii. 182 Five shillings for sheets, five shillings for garnish money. *a* **1700** B. E. *Dict. Cant. Crew*, *Garnish-money*, what is customarily spent amongst the Prisoners at first coming in. **1725** in *New Cant. Dict.* **1802** C. JAMES *Milit. Dict.*, *Garnish-nails, diamond headed nails, formerly used to ornament artillery carriages. **1872-6** VOYLE & STEVENSON *Milit. Dict.*, *Garnish-plate, that part of the iron work of the O. P. gun carriage which covers the upper surface of the brackets. **1801** MAR. EDGEWORTH *Angelina* i, The *garnish-tinselled wand of Fashion has waved in vain.

garnish ('gɑːnɪʃ), *v.* Pa. t. and pa. pple. **garnished** (-nɪʃt). Forms: 4 **garnesche**, 5 **garnesshe**, **-ysche**, 5-6 **garnisshe**, **-ysshe**, 6 **garnysh(e**, **-ishe**, 6- **garnish**. In *pa. t.* and *pa. pple.* also 4-5 **garnyst**, 5 **garnest**, **-isett**, **-ized**, **-yssed**, 5-6 *Sc.* **garnist**, **-isit**, **-issed**. [ad. OF. *garniss-* lengthened stem of *garnir*, *guarnir*, *warnir* to fortify, defend (oneself), provide, prepare (mod.F. *garnir* to furnish) = Pr. *garnir*, OSp. *guarnir* (mod.Sp. *guarnecer*), It. *guarnire*, *guernire*, med.L. *g(u)arnire*. The OF. *garnir* had also the sense 'to warn'.

The form of the Rom. vb. points to adoption from a Teut. **warnjan*, prob. not identical with the vb. of this type meaning 'to ward off, prevent, refuse' (see WARN *v.*²), but related to the OTeut. vbs. **warnējan*, **warnōjan* (? originally intr. with the sense 'to become aware'), represented by OHG. *warnên*, *warnôn*, refl. to guard oneself, provide oneself (MHG. *warnen*, trans., to protect, guard, mod.G. *warnen* to warn), OE. *warnian* refl., to take warning, beware (ME. *wernen* trans. = WARN *v.*¹); the causative sense 'to make aware, warn', appears in late MHG. and ME. (also in MDu. *waernen*). These vbs. are cognate with OHG. (*fure*) *warna* precaution, preparation (MHG. *warne* provision), of which the vb. adopted in Rom. may be a derivative.]

I. To furnish, equip.

† **1.** *trans.* To furnish (a place) with means of defence; to garrison; to supply with men, arms, and provisions. *Obs.*

? *a* **1400** *Morte Arth.* 563 There salle appone Godarde a garette be rerede, That schalle be garneschte and kepyde with gude mene of armes. **1485** CAXTON *Chas. Gt.* 203 Panpylonne, whyche was ryght stronge of murayl and towres, & garnysshed wyth sarasyns. **1536** BELLENDEN *Cron. Scot.* (1821) I. 248 Sic thingis done, he garnist al the strenthis of Britane with men, munitionis, and vittalis. **1577** HOLINSHED *Hist. Scott.* 474/1 The Earl of Derby..should repayre to the West borders to garnishe the same for defence agaynst the enimies. **1786** *European Mag.* IX. 184 If on the right he garnishes his force, His left is threatened by the Prussian horse. [**1845** JAMES *Smuggler* III. 280 Go into the church; and garnish the windows with marksmen.]

† **2.** To equip or arm (oneself); in *pa. pple.*, equipped, armed. *Obs.*

? *a* **1400** *Morte Arth.* 722 Galyarde knyghtes Garneschit one the grene felde and graythelyche arayede. **1481** CAXTON *Godfrey* lv. 96 Solyman had sente them in to the cyte ffor to garnysshe them & make them redy. **1535** STEWART *Cron. Scot.* II. 13 The Romanis than sic prattik had in weir, And als tha war so garnist in thair geir. **1552** LATIMER *Fruitf. Serm.* (1584) 318 b, When the Deuill commeth, and findeth the heart of man not weaponed nor garnished with the word of God. *c* **1750** SHENSTONE *Elegies* xxiii. 21 See, garnish'd for the chase, the fraudful maid.

† **b.** *pass.* To be furnished *with* a retinue; to be attended or accompanied. *Obs.*

c **1477** CAXTON *Jason* 31 b, The fayr Myrro cam than to mete with Jason garnisshed with a gracious maintene. **1494** FABYAN *Chron.* v. cxvii. 92 He doubted how he was garnysshed of his meyneyall seruantis. **1602** PATERICKE tr. *Gentillet* 33 Whence commeth it that yet Princes are well attended on and garnished with flatterers.

† **3.** To dress, clothe, esp. in an elegant fashion.

1529 MORE *Comf. agst. Trib.* III. Wks. 1220/1 It maketh vs gooe much more gay and glorious in sight, garnyshed in sylke. **1566** PAINTER *Pal. Pleas.* I. 55 Ephestion..repaired vnto him with garments to garnishe him like a king.

4. To fit out with anything that adorns or beautifies; to decorate, ornament, or embellish (*with*, rarely †*of*). †Also *to garnish out*. Now somewhat *rhetorical*; sometimes with allusion to *Matt.* xii. 44.

13.. *E.E. Allit. P.* B. 1277 Þe gredirne & Þe goblotes garnyst of syluer. *a* **1400–50** *Alexander* 1533 An abite..Þat was garnest full gay with golden skirtis. **1490** CAXTON *Eneydos* xxi. 76 The nauye..whiche they haue garnyshed wyth floures, and garlandes. **1494** FABYAN *Chron.* I. iv. 10 Brute..founde it [the land]..garnysshed with many fayre Ryuers and Stremes. **1526** TINDALE *Matt.* xii. 44 When he is come, he fyndeth the housse empty and swepte and garnisshed [Gr. κεκοσμημένον]. **1577** HARRISON *England* II. xiii. (1877) I. 252 Curious peeces of work, wherewith to garnish his building. **1635** SWAN *Spec. M.* iii. §2 (1643) 48 As the outward heavens were garnished with Starres. *a* **1704** T. BROWN *Persius' Sat.* i. Prol., Wks. 1760 I. 51, I, who never..with Sir Courtly, roundelays Have made to garnish out new plays. **1820** SCOTT *Ivanhoe* iv, An under tunic of dark purple silk, garnished with furs. **1860** MAURY *Phys. Geog. Sea* x. §464 The coral islands, reefs, beds, and atolls with which the Pacific Ocean is studded and garnished. **1876** MISS BRADDON *J. Haggard's Dau.* II. 15 The kitchen was newly swept and garnished.

b. The pa. pple. sometimes occurs for: Furnished or fitted *with* (accessories).

[Partly a Gallicism, *garnir* being used in the wider sense of FURNISH *v.*; but in Eng. there is now almost always a reference to appearance rather than to utility.]

1663 GERBIER *Counsel* 94 Shutters..garnished without with battens. **1773** *Cook's 2nd Voy.* (1774) I. xiii. 175 The table was garnished round with hot bread-fruit, and plantains, and a quantity of cocoa-nuts brought for drink. **1837** DISRAELI *Venetia* I. ii, Several small rooms, scantily garnished with ancient furniture. **1863** GEO. ELIOT *Romola* I. i, A pedlar's basket, garnished..with small woman's-ware, such as thread and pins.

5. To decorate (a dish) for the table.

1693 DRYDEN *Juvenal's Sat.* v. 118 With what Expense and Art, how richly drest! Garnish'd with 'Sparagus, himself a Feast. **1741** *Compl. Fam.-Piece* i. ii. 111 Garnish with slic'd Orange and curl'd Bacon or Ham fry'd. **1796** MRS. GLASSE *Cookery* v. 52 Garnish the dish with lemon, and send it to table. **1886** M. F. SHELDON tr. *Flaubert's Salammbo* 4 Roasted antelopes, garnished with their horns.

† **6.** To adorn with any property or quality (chiefly *refl.* or *pass.*). *Obs.*

c **1450** *Mirour Saluacioun* 883 Werkes vertuouse Be whilk garnyst hire lif this virgine gloriouse. *c* **1489** CAXTON *Blanchardyn* xiv. 48 By the right grete vertue wherof he was garnysshed. **1531** ELYOT *Gov.* II. xxix, Consailours garnisshed with lernyng and also experience. **1577–87** HOLINSHED *Chron.* III. 1126/1 Let him finallie be garnished with the comelinesse of all vertuous conditions.

† **7.** *trans.* Of trees: To cover (a wall, etc.). Also *absol.* *Obs.*

1693 EVELYN *De la Quint. Compl. Gard.* I. 7 The Walls being Twelve Foot high or more, you must always let one Tree shoot up to garnish the Top, between two that shall garnish the Bottom. [Orig. *pour garnir le haut, entre deux qui garniront le bas.*] *Ibid.* Gloss., To Garnish well, is said of Wall, or any pallisaded Trees, when they spread well, and cover the Wall or Trelliss on all sides. **1712** J. JAMES tr. *Le Blond's Gardening* 43 The Palisades, or Trees on the Sides, coming to garnish and grow thicker, will in Time possess two Foot of a Side.

8. *slang.* To fit with fetters.

1755 in JOHNSON. **1893** in FARMER *Slang.*

II. *Law.* To warn. (Cf. Sc. *warnis* = warn.)

9. *trans.* **a.** To serve notice on (a person), for the purpose of attaching money belonging to a debtor.

a **1577** SIR T. SMITH *Commw. Eng.* (1633) 136 The Sheriffes order in serving this writ is to goe..to the land and there to garnish the partie by sticking up a sticke on his land. **1886** *Pall Mall G.* 13 Nov. 5 It will be a miracle if no one finds out who the trustee is; and as soon as his name is known he will be garnished to a certainty.

b. To serve (a person) with notice of certain payments to be made before he can be legally returned as an heir (abolished by 6 Geo. IV, c. 105).

1585 *Act 27 Eliz.* c. 3 §3 *Scire facias* shall be awarded..to garnish the same Heir. **1706** PHILLIPS (ed. Kersey), To *Garnish the Heir* is to warn the Heir; a Law-term.

c. To summon (a person) as party to a litigation already in process between others. Cf. GARNISHMENT 2.

garnished (ˈgɑːnɪʃt), *ppl. a.* [f. GARNISH *v.* + -ED[1].] In senses of the vb.: †Prepared for defence (*obs*); adorned, decked, furnished.

c **1440** *Promp. Parv.* 188/1 Garnyschyd, *garnitus.* **1526** *Pilgr. Perf.* (W. de W. 1531) 299 Those two blessed refeccyons..whiche neyther was in delycate dysshes, nor vpon ony table garnysshed, but on the grounde. **1533** BELLENDEN *Livy* (1822) 265 [The Romans] campit thame, with garnist oistis, on ane high montane. **1549** COVERDALE, etc. *Erasm. Par. 1 Pet.* 8 That theyr husbandes may be enticed by their goodly garnyshed maners. **1597** MORLEY *Introd. Mus.* 162 A wel garnished garden of most sweete flowers.

b. *Her.* Provided with appendages of different (specified) tincture.

1705 HEARNE *Collect.* 12 Dec. (O.H.S.) I. 126 The Arms of the University of Oxon are A field Jupiter, a Book Expansed in Fesse, Luna, garnished, having seven Labels with Seales, Sol, & this Inscription. **1864** BOUTELL *Her. Hist. & Pop.* xxi. §5 (ed. 3) 360 A book open ppr., garnished or. **1874** *Papworth's Coats of Arms* 948 Arg. a buglehorn garnished and stringed sa.

garnishee (gɑːnɪˈʃiː). *Law.* [f. GARNISH *v.* II + -EE.] One in whose hands money belonging to a debtor or defendant is attached at the suit of the creditor or plaintiff.

1627 SIR H. FINCH *Law* (1636) 373 If they were deliuered vpon other condition then the defendant alledgeth, the garnishee is at no mischiefe but the defendant. **1674** BLOUNT *Glossogr.* (ed. 4), *Garnishee.* **1853** T. I. WHARTON *Pa. Digest* 171 *Quære*, how is the law when the jury find specific articles in the hands of the garnishee. **1890** *Essex Chron.* 17 Jan., His Honour found for..the garnishee.

b. *attrib.*, as ***garnishee issue, order, proceedings, summons.***

1882 *Standard* 4 Feb. 2/4 The case came before Mr. Justice Watkin Williams..on a *garnishee issue. **1881** *Daily News* 17 Jan. 3/6 The plaintiff..had priority over the holders of the *garnishee orders. **1894** *Times* 13 Nov. 13/8 This was an appeal from an order made..in certain *garnishee proceedings. **1888** *West Briton & Cornw. Advert.* 22 Mar. 7/2 A Garnishee Case..A. J., grocer, was sued on a *garnishee summons..to show cause why he should not pay..£15.

Hence **garniˈshee** *v.*, to attach or arrest a debtor's money in this way; **garniˈsheement**, the process of attaching or arresting (cf. GARNISHMENT).

1892 *Daily News* 22 July 7/1 Their salary was recently garnisheed by a person to whom they owed commission. **1896** *Columbus* (Ohio) *Disp.* 15 Dec. 9 Employes who may have their wages garnisheed for debt have..to show..that they are being unjustly dealt with in the garnisheement.

garnisher (ˈgɑːnɪʃə(r)). [f. GARNISH *v.* + -ER[1].]

1. One who adorns or decorates.

c **1515** *Cocke Lorell's B.* (Percy Soc.) 10 Sylke women, pursers, and garnysshers. **1598** STOW *Surv.* xxviii. (1603) 247 Makers of haftes, and otherwise garnishers of Blades. **1727** BAILEY vol. II, *Garnisher*, he that adorns, sets off, &c.

2. *Law.* One who attaches the money of a debtor in the hands of another person.

1889 *Times* 29 Oct. 3/1 It was equally plain that the garnishee order did not make the garnisher a creditor of the garnishee.

garnishing (ˈgɑːnɪʃɪŋ), *vbl. sb.* [f. GARNISH *v.* + -ING[1].]

1. The action of the verb, in various senses.

1463 *Mann. & Househ. Exp.* (Roxb.) 223 Item, ffor my masteris spere gyldynge and garneshinge .xx.d. **1497** *Naval Acc. Hen. VII* (1896) 306 Bolte ropes for Garnyshying of the Ships sayles—xx. **1551** ROBINSON *More's Utop.* II. (Arb.) 79 But the gallant garnishinge and the beautifull settinge furth of it..that he left to his posteritie. **1638** F. JUNIUS *Paint. of Ancients* 332 Leaving the simplicitie of the ancients, beganne to spend themselves in garnishing of their works. **1691** RAY *Creation* (1714) 105 Architects..taking in Leaves and Flowers and Fruitage for the garnishing of their Work.

2. That which serves to decorate or furnish; also *pl.*

a **1470** TIPTOFT *Cæsar* iv. (1530) 6 Garnyshynge and other taklyngs belongyng to the shyppis. **1547–64** BAULDWIN *Mor. Philos.* (Palfr.) 47 Wisdome, vertue, and vnderstanding, are the garnishings of the soule. **1603** *Philotus* xxvii, With doubill Garnischings of gould And Craip aboue ȝour hair. **1669** BUNYAN *Holy Citie* 160 As for the garnishing of these Foundations, it is..twofold. **1796** MRS. GLASSE *Cookery* viii. 145 They make a fine garnishing, and give a dish a fine look. **1845** MRS. S. C. HALL *Whiteboy* vi. 52 Tattered carpets and broken chairs;—Such were the chief 'garnishings'. **1887** STEVENSON *Mem. & Portraits* v. 82 He scorned all flowers together. They were but garnishings for ladies' chimney-shelves.

b. *attrib.*

1559 MORWYNG *Evonym.* title-p., Balmes, Oyles, Perfumes, Garnyshing Waters. **1625** in Rymer *Fœdera* XVIII. 238 Thirtie seaven course Rubies, fortie twoe small garnishing Perles. **1688** R. HOLME *Armoury* III. 396/2 A Pricking or Garnishing Aul, this is for to make holes to adorn and to garnish Sadle Skirts with Silk, Silver, or Gold thrid.

garnishment (ˈgɑːnɪʃmənt). [f. GARNISH *v.* + -MENT. Cf. MDu. *garnissement*, perh. from an unrecorded OFr. word.]

1. Adornment, decoration.

1550 in Strype *Eccl. Mem.* (1721) II. xxix. 238 All manner of garnishments and apparel of silver and gold, such as altar-cloths, copes, &c. **1581** J. BELL *Haddon's Answ. Osor.* A ij b, Surely for the garnishment of phrase and style thereof I have no great regard. **1632** EARL OF CORK *Diary* in *Lismore Papers* Ser. I. (1886) III. 132 A garnishment of silver of gouldsmythes worck. **1721** STRYPE *Eccl. Mem.* I. ix. 91 Third persons, riff-raff and others, standing in the chambers for a garnishment. **1824** SCOTT *St. Ronan's* x, The art of making the worse appear the better garnishment.

2. *Law.* A legal notice or warning, either general, or for the special purposes of (*a*) summoning a third party to appear in a suit, (*b*) attaching money in the hands of an heir or other person.

1585 *Act 27 Eliz.* c. 3 §3 If the Heir do not..upon a Garnishment..shew..that the Executors have sufficient..to answer..the same Debt. **1621** BOLTON *Stat. Irel.* 41 (*Act 7 Edw. IV*) The Lieutenant of this land..shall have power to remove the Exchequer..by the garnishment of twentie and eight dayes. **1668** HALE *Pref. to Rolle's Abridgm.* 5 Garnishment and Interpleder were large titles at Common Law, but now much out of use. **1706** PHILLIPS (ed. Kersey), *Garnishment*, a Warning given to any for his Appearance, for the better clearing of the Cause, and informing of the Court. **1873** *Kent's Comm.* II. xl. 568 In which, by the process of garnishment, the rival claimant is brought into the suit.

garnishry (ˈgɑːnɪʃrɪ). *nonce-wd.* [f. GARNISH *sb.* + -RY.] Garnishment, adornment.

1835 BROWNING *Paracelsus* III. 62 Herdsmen..whose eyes..Saw in the stars mere garnishry of heaven. **1868** —— *Ring & Bk.* IV. 545 A meal all meat..no garnishry.

† **garnison**, *sb. Obs.* Forms: 4–6 **garnison, -yson,** 5 (? **gernyson**), **garnisoun, -esoin.** [a. OF. *garnison* (ONF. *warnison*: see WARNISON) defence, provision, garrison (= Pr. *g(u)arniso*, It. *guarnizione, guarnigione*, Sp. *guarnicion*), f. *garnir* to fit out, GARNISH.]

The word became obsolete in the 16th c., its place being taken by the synonymous GARRISON.

1. Defence: means of defence.

c **1386** CHAUCER *Melib.* ¶371 The gretteste and strongeste garnyson that a riche man may haue, as wel to kepen his persone as hise goodes, is that he be biloued amonges hys subgetz and with hise neighebores. *c* **1400** *Rom. Rose* 4204 Thus Ielousye hath enviroun Set aboute his garnisoun With walles rounde, and diche depe. **1483** CAXTON *Gold. Leg.* 276/1 Saynt Augustyn..fyghtyng in deffence of trouthe of feythe and of garnyson of the chirche, surmounted alle the other doctours of the chirche. **1489** —— *Faytes of A.* III. x. 187 A lorde sente a man of armes for the garnyson of som fortresse of his owne.

2. Stores of victual for an army, a besieged place, etc.

1481 CAXTON *Godfrey* cxviii. 177 The poure Cristen men that had not in theyr howses garnyson sufficiant for longe tyme they made them to voyde the toun. **1489** —— *Faytes of A.* I. xii. 31 Deffensable necessaryes and al maner of garnyson. ? *a* **1500** *Barbour's Bruce* XVII. 294 (ed. Hart 1616) With gret garnisoun [*Edin. MS.* warnysone, *Camb. MS.* varnysing] of vittale.

3. A body of men stationed in a fortress or other place for purposes of defence.

c **1386** CHAUCER *Melib.* ¶61 We conseille Þat in thyn hous thou sette sufficeant garnison so that they may as wel thy body as thyn hous defende. **1489** CAXTON *Faytes of A.* II. iii. 95 Hys garnysons shulde yssue out of the castelles and townes. **1528** ROY *Rede me* (Arb.) 49 Have they of angels eny garnyson Ye god knoweth many a legion Att all tymes theym to socoure. **1549** *Compl. Scot.* Ep. Ded. 5 He pat ane garnison of tua thousand men vitht in the toune of sanct quintyne. **1609** BIBLE (Douay) *1 Kings* xiv. 12 And the men of the garnison spake to Jonathas and to his esquier.

b. ? A stronghold or fortress occupied by armed forces. (Somewhat doubtful.)

c **1430** LYDG. *Hors, Shepe, & G.* 123 in *Pol. Rel. & L. Poems* 19 With-owtyn werr..wee may nat saue and kepe our Right, Oure garnesoins [*v.r.* garisouns] ne oure castellis olde. *c* **1500** *Melusine* xxi. 128 Telle vs what nombre of men may yssue out of all your garnysons the Fortresses alwayes kept. ? **1520** BARCLAY *Salust's Jugurth* xxxv. 46 On the other syde thinhabitauntes of the towne and garnyson resysted manly.

c. *in garnison* = in garrison (see GARRISON *sb.* 5).

1583 T. STOCKER *Civ. Warres Lowe C.* II. 30 a, Seuen of the Wallon Ensignes, of the nine, whiche laie in Garnison at Mastright.

† **garnison**, *v. Obs. rare.* In 7 **garnizon.** [f. prec. sb.] *trans.* To garrison (a place).

1583 T. STOCKER *Civ. Warres Lowe C.* I. 39 (margin), Count Mansfelde garnysoneth Antwerp. **1656** HARRINGTON *Oceana* (1658) 84 A Common-wealth Established in her rise upon Fifty such Towers, and so Garnizoned as are the Tribes of Oceana, containing one hundred thousand Elders upon the Annuall List, and yet but an out-guard.

garnissh(e, obs. form of GARNISH *v.*

garniter, var. GARNETER. *Obs.*

garniture (ˈgɑːnɪtjʊə(r)). [a. F. *garniture* (f. *garnir* vb.), which occurs in most of the senses of the Eng. word.]

1. a. Furniture, outfit, appurtenances.

1532 HERVET *Xenophon's Househ.* (1768) 38 Pannes, caudrons, and other garnitures of the kitchen. **1580** HOLLYBAND *Treas. Fr. Tong* s.v., *La garniture d'vn lict, d'vne espée, ou quelque chose*, the garniture or furniture of a bed, sword, or any other thing. **1854** MRS. OLIPHANT *Magd. Hepburn* III. 295 The table sparkles with silver cups and antique wealth of garniture. **1878** SCHILLER *Technol. Dict.* s.v., Garniture of a boiler, all apparatuses which serve for the safety of a boiler, all steam-pipes, stoking-tools, etc.).

b. Trappings, harness (of horses, etc.). ? *Obs.*

1670 G. H. *Hist. Cardinals* I. III. 77 The garniture of the Mules are but ordinary. **1821** SCOTT *Kenilw.* xxiv, A palfrey, with a side-saddle and all other garniture for a woman's mounting.

c. ***garniture de cheminée*** (see quot. 1960).

1900 F. LITCHFIELD *Pott. & Porc.* iv. 39 The famous Sèvres *garnitures de cheminées.* **1960** R. G. HAGGAR *Conc. Encycl. Cont. Pott. & Porc.* 203/2 *Garniture de cheminée,* a set of five vases, three baluster-shaped with covers, and two beakers with trumpet-shaped apertures called 'flutes', decorated *en suite.*

2. Ornament, trimming, etc., added to dress.

1667 DRYDEN *Maiden Queen* v. i. A man of garniture and feather is above the dispensation of the sword. **1684** J. LACY *Sir H. Buffoon* II. ii, My French garniture, a pox on 'em, is not yet arrived from Paris. **1706** PHILLIPS (ed. Kersey), *Garniture,* the trimming of a Suit with Ribbons, precious Stones, &c. as *a Garniture of Diamonds.* **1710** STEELE *Tatler* No. 116 ¶7 Stomachers, Caps, Facings of my Wastcoat-Sleeves, and other Garnitures suitable to my Age and Quality. **1753** HANWAY *Trav.* (1762) I. VII. xcv. 437 A garniture of saphirs, as buttons, sword, star, watch, snuff-box, &c. **1840** DICKENS *Old C. Shop* xxviii, A military surtout..which had once been frogged and braided all over, but was now sadly shorn of its garniture. **1897** *Globe* 18 Feb. 6/3 At the wrists the sleeves..are finished with a two-inch garniture of violets.

3. a. Ornament, embellishment generally.

1685 CROWNE *Sir C. Nice* III, I bestow some garniture on plays, as a song or a prologue. **1713** DERHAM *Phys. Theol.* IV. xii. 214 The suitableness of Animals Clothing; and Garniture and Beauty thereof. *a* **1716** SOUTH *Serm.* III. 131 Where real Kindnesses are done, the circumstantial Garnitures of Love (as I may so call them) may be dispensed with. **1762** FOOTE *Lyar* I. Wks. 1799 I. 283 A man is naturally permitted more ornament and garniture to his conversation than they will allow in this latitude. **1821** LAMB *Elia* Ser. I. *Mackery End,* She happily missed all that train of female garniture which passeth by the name of accomplishments. **1878** MORLEY *Carlyle* in *Crit. Misc.* 178 No verbal garniture of a transcendental kind.

b. Applied to natural objects (as trees, etc.) as ornaments of the landscape.

1684 T. BURNET *Th. Earth* II. 80 This destroying of the outward garniture of the earth is but the first onset. **1768** BEATTIE *Minstr.* I. ix, The pomp of groves, and garniture of fields. **1809** W. IRVING *Knickerb.* (1861) 56 To their right lay the sedgy point of Blackwell's Island, drest in the fresh garniture of living green. **1863** MRS. C. CLARKE *Shaks. Char.* ii. 60 The pomp and garniture of God's creation—the green fields and the forest glades.

4. Apparel, costume, dress.

1827 POLLOK *Course T.* VII, Gloomy garniture of purchased woe. **1853** KANE *Grinnell Exp.* xl. (1856) 365, I have never before alluded to the garniture of my outer man.

5. Trimming or dressing of a dish. Also *fig.*

1725 BRADLEY *Fam. Dict.* s.v. *Sturgeon,* It may be..set out with a Marinade, or other Garniture. **1761** WESLEY *Wks.* (1872) XIII. 393 This means nothing; it is mere garniture of the dish. **1862** GOULBURN *Pers. Relig.* i. (1873) 5 If he has skilfully dressed a rather spare dish of knowledge with the garniture of amusement. **1888** FRITH *Autobiog.* III. 134 A huge boar's head, with the usual garniture, was placed upon the table.

garnop, var. GARDNAP. *Obs.*

garnsdorfite (ˈgɑːnzdɔːfaɪt). *Min.* [f. *Garnsdorf* in Saxony, where it is found; named by Brooke and Miller in 1852.] A synonym of PISSOPHANITE.

1852 BROOKE & MILLER *Phillips' Min.* 544 Garnsdorfite.. is found in soft drops. **1861** BRISTOW *Gloss. Min.* 149 *Garnsdorffite,* a name for pissophane.

Garnsey (*violet*), var. GUERNSEY.

†**garnwin.** *Obs. rare.* [OE. *ʒearn-winde,* f. *ʒearn* YARN + *winde* = OHG. *winta* (G. *winde*) winding-wheel, f. *windan* to WIND; cf. Du. *garenwinder,* G. *garnwinde* (LG. *garwinne*), Icel. *garnvinda.* The ME. form has the northern (Scandinavian) GARN for *yarn.*] = next.

c **725** *Corpus Gloss.* 1735, *Reponile,* ʒearnuuinde. *a* **1000** *Gloss.* in Wr.-Wülcker 213/11 *Conductum,* ʒearnwinde. **14**.. *Metr. Voc.* Ibid. 628/1 Garne wyne, *Iurgillum.* ?**14**.. *Nominale MS.* (Halliw.) A par garnwyn, *girgillum.*

garnwindle, yarnwindle. *Obs.* exc. *dial.* Forms: 5 **garnwyndil, garwyndyl(le, (-elle), -wyngyll,** 6 **garnwindell,** 7, 9 **garnwindles (-winnles).** Also 5 **ȝarn-, yer-.** [f. GARN, YARN + *-windel* formed as instrumental noun to OE. *windan* to WIND; cf. OE. *windel* basket, G. *windel* swaddling-band, Sw. *vindel* whirl, spiral, ON. *vindill* wisp, *vindla* to wind. So Ger. *garnwindel* (15th c.) beside *-winde.*] A rotatory appliance, on which a skein of yarn is placed in order to be more easily wound into a ball.

c **1440** *Promp. Parv.* 188/1 Garwyndylle (*S.* garwyndyl, or ȝarnwyndyl, *P.* garwyngyll), *girgillus.* **1483** *Cath. Angl.* 150/2 A Garwyndelle (*A.* A Garne qweylle or A Ȝarnwyndylle), *deuolutorium, gergillus.* **1674–91** RAY *Collect. Words, Gloss. Northan.* 141 *Garn-Windles,* harpedone, Rhombus. **1878** *Cumbld. Gloss., Garn winnels,* a wooden cross from which yarn is wound off.

2. *Comb.,* as ***garnwindle blades, -stocks.***

14.. *Nom.* in Wr.-Wülcker 695/35 *Hoc iurgillum* [printed *nirgilium*], a par garnwyndil-blades. **1576** *Richmond. Wills* (Surtees) 260 A spinning whele..ij garnwindell stocks.

Garo (ˈgɑːrəʊ). Also **Garrow.** A member of one of a group of Mongoloid tribes of the Garo Hills, Assam; also, their language. Also *attrib.*

1872 E. T. DALTON *Descr. Ethnol. Bengal* 88 The Garo apology for a robe does not reach half down the thigh. **1880** *Encycl. Brit.* XII. 777/2 The following are the twenty principal dialects of the Tibeto-Burman group:—(1) Cáchári or Bodo, (2) Garo, [etc.]. **1883** *Ibid.* XV. 295/1 Of the aboriginal tribes [of Maimansinh] the most numerous are the Hajongs (24,936) and Gáros (10,997). **1898** C. M. YONGE *J. Keble's Parishes* v. 54 Among the Garrows, a people of Hindustan, the youngest *daughter* inherits the property. **1912** A. GORDON *Life A. H. Charteris* 339 The plains at the foot of the mountains—called the Dooars—are peopled by Mechis, Rajbunsis, and Garos. **1959** *Chambers's Encycl.* VII. 482 The Assam-Burmese group is represented in eastern India, chiefly in Assam. There is very great linguistic diversity in this area. Some of the more important languages are..Gārō, [etc.].

‖**garookuh, garrooka.** (See quots.)

1855 OGILVIE Suppl., *Garookuh,* a vessel met with in the Persian Gulf..In length it varies from 50 to 100 feet, and is remarkable for the keel being only one-third the length of the boat. **1867** SMYTH *Sailor's Word-bk., Garrooka,* a fishing-craft of the Gulf of Persia. Also in mod. Dicts.

garope, garoup(h)a, varr. GROUPER.

garotte: see GARROTTE.

†**garous,** *a. Obs. rare*⁻¹. [f. L. *gar-um* GARUM + -OUS.] Of or resembling GARUM.

1646 SIR T. BROWNE *Pseud. Ep.* III. iv. 114 A different and offensive odour, proceeding partly from it's food, that being especially fish, whereof this humor may be a garous excretion or a raucide [*sic*] and olidous separation.

garous(s)e, obs. form of CAROUSE.

gar-pike (ˈgɑːˌpaɪk). [formed after GARFISH: see PIKE.] = GARFISH.

1776 PENNANT *Zool.* III. 283 Garpike..this fish, which is found in many places, is known by the name of the Sea-Needle. **1849** *Zoologist* VII. 2395 The gar-pike of the western rivers. **1866** OWEN *Anat. Vertebrates* I. iv. 275 The Tench, the Garpike, and the common Eel. **1883** *Harper's Mag.* Mar. 515/2 The gar-pike of Western lakes.

attrib. **1872** C. KING *Mountain. Sierra Nev.* ix. 185 Savage fishes, of the garpike type.

†**garquince.** *Obs.*

a **1483** *Liber Niger* in *Househ. Ord.* (1790) 81 He resceyvyth..all manner of spyces to make confections, garquinces, plaates, sedes, and all other spycery nedefull.

garr, obs. form of GAR *sb.* and *v.*

garran: see GARRON.

garrapata, var. CARRAPATO.

garrat, obs. form of GARRET.

garrawse, obs. form of CAROUSE.

1617 F. MORYSON *Itin.* III. 152 Gentlemen garrawse onely in Wine.

†**garray.** *Sc.* and *north. Obs.* Also 7 **garry.** [? f. OF. *guerrei-er* to make war, to harry: see WARRAY *v.*] **a.** ? Armed force. **b.** Commotion, disturbance, noise, row.

c **1450** HENRYSON *Parl. Beistis* 270 As thay wer carpand in this cais with knakis, And all the court in garry, and in gam. *c* **1460** *Towneley Myst.* viii. 377 Full soyn he will shape vs to sheynd, And after vs send his garray. *Ibid.* xiii. 564 He made all the garray. *a* **1500** *Peebles to Play* ii. in *Wks. Jas. I* (1786) 100 For reiling thair micht na man rest, For garray and for glew. **1606** *N. Riding Rec.* (1884) I. 50 For making on two severall Saboath daies in June last drinkinges and garries, whereby above the number of cᵗʰ persons were assembled together with pipes and drummes and dancing all the time of Divine Service. **1725** in *Old Leeds* (1868) 70 Therefore none were to attend 'any such garrays or merry nights'.

†**garre,** *sb. Obs.* [Cf. GARGET, GARGIL.]

1678 PHILLIPS, *Garre,* a kind of disease incident to Hogs.

†**garre,** *v. Obs.* [Echoic, but suggested by L. *garrire*; ME. had also *ȝarren, ȝeorren,* OE. *ʒeorran,* of imitative origin (see YAR(R *v.*); cf. MDu., MLG., MHG. *garren* of similar meaning.] *intr.* To growl, snarl; to chatter, chide; to chirp, twitter. Hence ˈ**garring** *vbl. sb.* and *ppl. a.*

1382 WYCLIF *3 John* 10, I shal moneste his werkes, whiche he doith, garringe, or chidinge [L. *garriens*] in to us. **1387** TREVISA *Higden* (Rolls) II. 159 And som vseþ straunge wlafferynge, chiterynge, harrynge, and garrynge [L. *garritus*] grisbayting. *c* **1400** *Apol. Loll.* 95 Augurreris we calle þoo þat tentun to be garring & fliyng of briddus. **1587** M. GROVE *Pelops & Hipp.* (1878) 106 The foole..May sing and garre as doth the birde against a shower of raine.

garre, obs. form of GAR.

garret (ˈgærɪt), *sb.*¹ Forms: 4 **garite, -yte,** 5 **-ytte,** 5–6 **garett(e,** (5 **garet, gerret),** 6 **garrette, gar(r)it,** 6–8 **garrat,** 6– **garret.** [a. OF. *garite, guerite,* watch-tower (mod.F. *guérite* watch-tower, sentry-box, refuge) = Sp. *garita* (? from Fr.), Pg. *guarita*; of Teut. origin, connected with OF. *guarir, warir,* to preserve, guard, cure (mod.F. *guérir* to cure), ad. Teut. **warjan* to defend, protect; the precise formation of the sb. has not been satisfactorily explained.]

†**1.** A turret projecting from the top of a tower or from the parapet of a fortification; a watch-tower. *Obs.*

13.. *Sir Beues* (A.) 1658 He be-held forþer a lite To a chaunber vnder a garite. **1340** HAMPOLE *Pr. Consc.* 9101 þe garettes oboven þe yhates bryght Of þe ceté of heven, I lyken þus ryght, Tylle þe garettes of a cetè of gold. ? *a* **1400** *Morte Arth.* 562 There salle appone Godarde a garette be rerede. *a* **1450** *Knt. de la Tour* (1868) 88 She putte her in a garet to see the Kinge Josue passe. **1598** BARRET *Theor. Warres* IV. iv. 112 Garrits and watch houses, where the..Sentinels are to be placed.

2. A room on the uppermost floor of a house; an apartment formed either partially or wholly within the roof, an attic. ***from cellar to garret, from garret to kitchen,*** etc.: over the whole house.

1483 CAXTON *Cato* H v b, What shold auaylle..a garette ful of whete or a celer ful of wyn. **1577** B. GOOGE *Heresbach's Husb.* I. (1586) 43 In countreys that are very wette and watrishe, it is better to make them [corn lofts] in Garrettes as hie as may be. **1625** BACON *Apophth.* xvii. Wks. 1859 VII. 180 My Lord St. Alban said that wise Nature did never put her precious jewels into a garret four stories high: and therefore that exceeding tall men had ever very empty heads. **1645** MILTON *Colast.* Wks. (1851) 368 This is not for an unbutton'd fellow to discuss in the Garret, at his tressle. **1703** MOXON *Mech. Exerc.* 262 Two Stories high, besides Cellars and Garrats. **1712** ARBUTHNOT *John Bull* IV. viii, John Bull..ran upstairs and downstairs, from the kitchen to the garrets, and from the garrets to the kitchen. **1714** LADY M. W. MONTAGU *Let. to W. Montagu* 24 Sept., If it were possible to restore liberty to your country..by reducing yourself to a garret, I should be pleased to share so glorious a poverty with you. **1781** GIBBON *Decl. & F.* III. 219 The ..lodging-house, where the poet Codrus, and his wife, were permitted to hire a wretched garret immediately under the tiles. **1828** CARLYLE *Misc.* (1857) I. 231 The news of his arrival circulated from the cellar to the garret. **1849** MRS. CARLYLE *Lett.* II. 80, I was through all our house yesterday, from garret to kitchen. **1874** L. STEPHEN *Hours in Library* (1892) II. i. 11 His [Johnson's] happiest effort is a dissertation upon the advantage of living in garrets.

fig. **1812** H. & J. SMITH *Horace in Lond.* 132 We'll talk of our gambols..Till Phœbus looks out of his garret.

3. *slang.* **a.** The head; esp. in phrases ***to be wrong in one's garret, to have one's garret unfurnished,*** etc. **b.** (See quot. 1812.)

1796 *Grose's Dict. Vulg. Tongue, Garret,* or *Upper Story,* the head. His garret, or upper story, is empty, or unfurnished; i.e. he has no brains, he is a fool. **1812** J. H. VAUX *Flash Dict., Garret,* the fob-pocket. **1840** BARHAM *Ingol. Leg., Bagman's Dog,* What's called the claret Flew over the garret. **1869** *Lonsdale Gloss.* s.v., *To be wrang in yan's Garrets,* to be wanting in intellect, or suffering from temporary delirium.

4. *attrib.* and *Comb.,* as ***garret-poverty, -room, -stairs, -story, -window; garret-high*** adj.; ***garret-wise*** adv.; **garret-lock** (see quot.); **garret-master,** a cabinet-maker, lock-smith, etc. who works on his own account, selling his manufacture to the dealers direct (cf. CHAMBER-MASTER).

1684 DRYDEN *Prol. to Disappointment* 46 He hires some lonely room, love's fruits to gather, And *garret-high rebels against his father. **1848–52** *Dict. Archit.,* **Garret-lock,* the term applied to locks of the most inferior description, because they are made by men of small means who live and work in garrets. **1861** MAYHEW *Lond. Labour* II. 376/2 In the shoe trade..they are called 'chamber-masters', in 'the cabinet-trade' they are termed '*garret-masters'. *Ibid.* III. 223/2 The garret-masters are a class of small 'trade-working masters', supplying both capital and labour. **1894** *Westm. Gaz.* 6 June 2/3 Complaints made by the local Locksmith's Trades Union, as to the sub-letting of Navy contracts to garret-masters not under factory inspection. **17**.. *Addit. to Pope* (1776) I. 117 Again my *garret poverty is shown By the mean cov'ring of this Portland stone. **1671** J. DAVIES *Sibylls* I. viii. 23 There may be some brain which hath *garret-room to receive it. **1838** DICKENS *O. Twist* xxiv, It was a bare garret-room. **1859** W. COLLINS *Q. of Hearts* (1875) 69 My aunt came hastily up the *garret-stairs. **1806** FORSYTH *Beauties Scotl.* IV. 1 Most of them have now what the country-people call a loft; *i.e.* a *garret-story. **1611** COTGR., *Lucarne,* a *garret window, or window in the roofe of a house, etc. **1886** WILLIS & CLARK *Cambridge* II. 531 The rooms on the second floor are still arranged *garret-wise.

†**garret,** *sb.*²

1626 BACON *Sylva* §352 The Experiment of Wood that Shineth in the Darke..The Colour of the Shining Part, by Day-light, is in some Peeces White, in some Peeces inclining to Red; Which in the Countrey they call the White and Red Garret.

garret (ˈgærɪt), *v. Build.* [Of uncertain origin; cf. GALLET *v.*] *trans.* To insert small pieces of stone in the joints of (coarse masonry). Hence ˈ**garreting** *vbl. sb.* (see quots. 1845 and 1893).

1845 PARKER *Gloss. Archit.* (ed. 4), *Garretting,* small splinters of stone, inserted in the joints of course masonry; they are stuck in after the work is built. Flint walls are very frequently garretted. **1846** *Ecclesiologist* VI. 45 The old way of 'garreting' flint-work, that is, of inserting small flint-shivers in the mortar of the joints. **1893** *Surrey Gloss., Garreting,* a species of pointing of stonework with small chips of stone in the joints.

garreted (ˈgærɪtɪd), *ppl. a.* Also 6 **garyted,** 7–8 **garretted.** [f. GARRET *sb.*¹ + -ED².]

1. Provided with 'garrets' (see GARRET *sb.* 1).

1531 *Surv. Tower Lond.* in Bayley *Hist. Tower* I. (1821) App. p. ix, The whiche forsaide wall p'te of it to be ventyde, garyted, coped, lowped, and also crestyde. **1602** CAREW *Cornwall* 121 a, An uneasie landing place for boats..fenced with a garretted wall. *c* **1630** RISDON *Surv. Devon* §192 (1810) 202 A castle they have, garreted with turrets at every corner. **1675** OGILBY *Brit.* 55 East and West Looe..towards the Sea are fenc'd with a Garreted Wall. **1797** MATON *West. Count. Eng.* I. 262 A circular garretted wall, inclosing some traces of buildings.

2. Lodged in a garret. *rare*⁻¹.

1837 WORDSW. *Sonn. 'They who have seen the noble Roman's scorn'*, Laying down his head, When the blank day is over, garreted, In his ancestral palace.

garreteer (ˌgærɪˈtɪə(r)). Also (7 ? **garretteir**, ? **garitier**), 8–9 **garretteer**. [f. GARRET *sb.*[1] + -EER[1].] One who lives in a garret; *esp.* an impecunious author or literary hack.

[1650, 1653: Examples of these dates are prob. misprints; see GAZETTEER 1.] **1720** BENTLEY *Let.* 31 Dec. Wks. 1836–8 III. 538 Let other scribblers and garreteers take some caution from his example. **1739** P. WHITEHEAD *Manners* 15 Down, down, ye hungry Garretteers, descend. **1824** *Blackw. Mag.* XV. 325 If they be not garretteers, living out of the world, and never seeing a newspaper. **1887** MISS BETHAM-EDWARDS *Next of Kin* II. xviii. 248 The editorial 'I am very sorry'—how many garreteers has it driven to suicide?

attrib. **1815** W. H. IRELAND *Scribbleomania* 149 Sir Southey, now chang'd from his garretteer state, To write silly odes, and palaver the great.

garrhial, var. GAVIAL.

garri (ˈgærɪ). *W. Afr.* Also **gari**, **garry**. = CASSAVA 2.

1926 P. A. TALBOT *Peoples S. Nigeria* III. xxxvii. 908 Cassava grated up into 'Garri', or beaten into 'fufu', is becoming more and more general. **1946** FORDE & SCOTT *Native Economies of Nigeria* ii. 106 The high incidence of pellagra in association with a gari (cassava flour) diet was due not only to the lack of the anti-pellagric vitamin factor.. but to a lack of organic sulphur. **1962** *New Scientist* 27 Sept. 660 Gari, a meal made by fermenting cassava root. **1964** J. P. CLARK *Three Plays* 115 His.. sentence to a six-months' diet On beans and garri. **1968** *Guardian* 4 July 1/1 His official supply of nine bags of garry (an inert vegetable staple), two fish, and two cups of salt.

garrigue: see GARIGUE.

†**garrise**, *v. Obs. rare*⁻¹. [? back-formation from GARRISON.] *trans.* To station as a garrison. (Cf. GARRISON *v.* 3.)

1633 T. STAFFORD *Pac. Hib.* III. ii. 287 Your Lordship is to assemble your forces together.. and because they lye dispersed, for the more expeditions sake, to take them in your way Westward, as they are garrised.

garrison (ˈgærɪsən), *sb.* Forms: 3, 5–8 **garison**, 3, 6 **garyson(e**, 4 **garis(so)un**, **gareisoun**, **geryzoun**, 4–5 **garysoun**, 4–7 **garisoun(e**, (5 **garson(e**, 6–7 *Sc.* **garesone**, **-oun**, 7 **guarison**), 5–6 **garryson**, (6 **garrisoun**), 6– **garrison**. [a. OF. *garison*, *gareison*, *guerison* (ONF. *warison* WARISON), defence, safety, provision, store, f. *garir*, *guerir*, to defend, preserve, furnish, ad. OHG. *warjan* to defend (= OE. *wẹrian* WEAR *v.*[2]).

Senses 1 and 2 agree with the uses of the French word. The further development is app. due to confusion with F. *garnison* GARNISON, which had the same meanings of 'defence' and 'supplies', as well as that of 'garrison'. There is not sufficient evidence to show that the last was ever a common sense of F. *garison*: Godefroy gives only one quotation for it. It seems probable that the specially English sense of 'fortress', 'stronghold' (see 3), led to the identification of the two words and to the final adoption of 'garrison' in place of 'garnison'.]

†**1.** Store, treasure; donation, gift. *Obs.*

1297 R. GLOUC. (Rolls) 8461 þe king of Camele made pays & an amirail al so & ȝeue hom gret garison hom non harm to do. **13..** *Gaw. & Gr. Knt.* 1837 He nay þat he nolde neghe in no wyse Nauþer golde ne garysoun. *a* **1400–50** *Alexander* 1074 Geuys him garsons of gold & of gud stanes. *c* **1450** *St. Cuthbert* (Surtees) 6835 Of þir kyngs and þair garysouns, What þai gaf, landes and touns.

†**2.** Defence, protection; deliverance, safety; means of defence. *Obs.*

c **1320** *Cast. Love* 870 God.. nom flesch and blood of hire, to bringe His folk out of prisoun: þat was vre garysoun. *c* **1400** *Rom. Rose* 3248, I can nat seen how thow mayst go Other weyes to garisoun. **1549** COVERDALE, etc. *Erasm. Par. Cor.* 5 It is no weake and feble thing, but a thing of Gods owne doyng, muche more mightie and effectuall, than is any mans power and garrisons. **1561** T. NORTON *Calvin's Inst.* I. 46 He hath an innumerable gard to whome he hath geuen in charge to trauaile for our safetie, and that so long as we be compassed with a garrison and support of them.. we be without al reach of hurt.

3. †**a.** A fortress or stronghold (*obs.*). **b.** (from sense 4) A place in which troops are quartered for defensive or other military purposes; a garrison-town.

c **1430** LYDG. *Hors, Shepe, & G.* (Roxb.) 21 With oute werre.. We may not saue ne kepe our right Our garisouns [*v.r.* garnesoins] ner castellis olde. *c* **1440** *Promp. Parv.* 188/1 Garsone, stronge place (*H.* garysone, or garzone, strong holde), *municipium*. *c* **1450** *Golagros & Gaw.* 1144 Quhen that Gawyne.. Wes cummyn to the castel.. Gromys of that garisoune maid gamyn. **1483** *Cath. Angl.* 150/1 A Garison, *municipium*. **1494** FABYAN *Chron.* an. 1454 (1533) 200 a/2, Lord Talbot.. in defendynge of the kynge's Garysons, was beset with Frensh men at a place named Castyllyon. **1568** GRAFTON *Chron.* II. 280 The toune of New Castell upon Tyne, and in all other garrisons on the marches of Scotlande. **1654** EVELYN *Mem.* (1857) I. 314 Went by Newark-on-Trent, a brave town and garrison. **1743** CAPT. WOODROOFE in Hanway *Trav.* (1762) I. II. xx. 88 With directions to look for a proper place to build a garrison. **1759** ROBERTSON *Hist. Scot.* (1817) I. ii. 372 He.. with his own soldiers invested Werk Castle, a garrison of the English. **1799** *Med. Jrnl.* I. 462, I would propose that a ship of the line.. be employed as a lazaretto.. and stationed.. opposite the garrison.

4. †**a.** A body or troop of persons (*obs.*). **b.** A body of soldiers stationed in a fortress or other place for purposes of defence, etc.

In sense b the word has taken the place of the older GARNISON.

a. **1500–20** DUNBAR *Poems* xxxv. 35 Jonet the weido on ane bussome rydand Off wichiss with ane winder [*v.r.* wondrous] garesoun. **1526** *Pilgr. Perf.* (W. de W. 1531) 253 b, After this sentence all the garyson of the knyghtes and turmentours gathered aboute hym. *a* **1533** LD. BERNERS *Gold. Bk. M. Aurel.* (1536) D iiij, If I leade garrysons of menne of armes. **1535** STEWART *Cron. Scot.* III. 150 The nobillis all in ane greit garesone, For the most part passit out of the toun.

b. **1542** UDALL *Erasm. Apoph.* 161 b, When certain persones moued hym and would haue had hym to kepe the cites with garysons.. he saied [etc.]. **1587** HOLINSHED *Scot. Chron.* 237/1 He made the castle stronger, in which he placed a valiant garrison. **1639** DK. HAMILTON in *H. Papers* (Camden) 72 If att the same tyme the garisounes att Beruick and Carlyll mad inroods into the Countrie. **1725** DE FOE *Voy. round World* (1840) 280 Strong forts erected.. and strong garrisons maintained in them. **1801** WELLINGTON in Gurw. *Desp.* (1837) I. 347 The garrison could not remain in that fort opposed to the fire of a man of war. **1844** H. H. WILSON *Brit. India* II. 221 He.. gave orders that the forts demanded should be opened to British garrisons. **1874** GREEN *Short Hist.* i. §2. 15 The bulk of the garrison.. lay cantoned along the Roman wall.

fig. **1548** LD. SOMERSET *Epist. Scots* C j, Hauyng the sea for wall, the mutuall loue for garrison, and God for defence. **1598** DRAYTON *Heroic, Ep., Black Prince to C'tess Salisbury* 126 Thy virtuous thoughts.. Like carefull skouts, passe vp and down thy breast.. Whilst al the blessed garison do sleepe. **1644** MILTON *Divorce* (ed. 2) To Parl. Eng., To inslave the dignity of man, to put a garrison upon his neck of empty and overdignifi'd precepts. **1754** COWPER *Ep. to R. Lloyd* 18 A fierce banditti.. That.. daily threaten to drive thence My little garrison of sense.

†**c.** *place, town of garrison*: a garrison-town.

1591 SHAKS. *1 Hen. VI*, v. iv. 168 Onely reseru'd, you claime no interest In any of our Townes of Garrison. **1592** NASHE *P. Penilesse* Wks. (Grosart) II. 79 If he haue beene ouer, and visited a towne of Garrison. *a* **1613** OVERBURY *A Wife* (1638) 208 He learnt his trade in a Towne of Garison neere famish't. **1649** J. TAYLOR (Water P.) *Wandering to see the West* C iv, For at all places of Garison, there is very strict examinations of persons.

5. Phrases. *in garrison* [F. *en garnison*]: doing duty as a garrison or as one of a garrison. (*to go* or *be sent*) *into garrison*: to do garrison duty. *to keep garrison*: to maintain a force of armed men in a fortified place; to be 'in garrison'.

c **1489** CAXTON *Blanchardyn* lii. 200 Whan the souldyours, that Subyon had lefte there is garryson, herde [etc.]. **1548** HALL *Chron., Hen. IV*, 30 All the soldiers whiche the duke of Orleance had left there in garrison to defend the bridge. *c* **1550** *Deb. betw. Somer & Wynt.* 39 in Hazl. *E.P.P.* III. 35 They haue no wyll to labour, in felde nor in garysone. **1596** SPENSER *State Irel.* Wks. (Globe) 652/1 The Earl of Tyrone is nowe accoumpted the strongest; upon him would I lay 8000 men in garrison. **1607** DEKKER *Northw. Hoe* v. Wks. 1873 III. 69 My husband is in garrison i' the Low-Countries. **1707** *Lond. Gaz.* No. 4317/2 Part of their Troops.. are to remain in Garison there; the rest are to go into Garison at Mantua. **1719** DE FOE *Crusoe* II. xv, His soldiers keep garrison. **1730** A. GORDON *Maffei's Amphith.* 176 The Circus.. in which a certain Count kept garrison for his own Security. **1769** ROBERTSON *Chas. V*, VI. vi. 90 Those in garrison at Goletta threatened to give up that important fortress. **1802** C. JAMES *Milit. Dict.* s.v., The elite or flower of the Janissaries of Constantinople is frequently sent into garrison on the frontiers of Turkey.

6. *attrib.* and *Comb.*, as ***garrison-artillery***, ***-battalion***, ***-duty***, ***-guard***, ***-gun***, †***-man***, ***-preaching***, ***-soldier***; **garrison cap** *U.S.*, a peakless cap worn esp. as part of a military uniform; **garrison-carriage** (see quot.); **garrison-hack** *slang*, a woman who flirts indiscriminately with the officers of a garrison (Farmer); **garrison-hold**, possession or occupation by means of a garrison; **garrison state** (see quot. 1954); **garrison-town**, a fortified town in which a garrison is stationed; †so ***garrison-house***.

1872–6 VOYLE & STEVENSON *Milit. Dict.* (ed. 3), **Garrison Artillery*. **1809** *Char.* in *Ann. Reg.* 737/2 [He] was promoted to the rank of Major in the sixth *Garrison-Battalion then in Ireland. **1947** S. BELLOW *Victim* i. 6 A Negro janitor in a *garrison cap was washing the stairs. **1971** *U.S. Army Reg.* 670–5 (*Uniform & Insignia, Male Personnel*) Jan. 14 (*caption*) Distinctive unit insignia worn on garrison cap. **1872–6** VOYLE & STEVENSON *Milit. Dict.* (ed. 3) s.v. *Carriages*, **Garrison Carriages*, carriages constructed for such guns and howitzers as are not intended for transport, and which are generally placed on the ramparts of a fortress [etc.]. **1813** SOUTHEY *Nelson* i. 37 The few who were able to perform *garrison duty. **1800** *Asiat. Ann. Reg., Misc. Tracts* 206/2 No person under the dignity of a chief Rajah has.. the honour of being saluted by the *garrison guard. **1876** JAS. GRANT *One of the 600* i. 8 The *garrison hacks, or *passé belles*, whose names and flirtations are standing jokes. **1890** *Athenæum* 8 Feb. 176/1 The heroine is a 'garrison-hack'. **1888** W. CORY *Lett. & Jrnls.* (1897) 529 We are in danger if we relax our *garrison-hold of the adjacent island. **1677** W. HUBBARD *Narrative* II. 80 Yet were they able to surprize but one *garrison house. **1586** *Leycester Corr.* (Camden) 60 The poor *garrison-men.. suffer.. the greatest miserie. **1855** MOTLEY *Dutch Rep.* (1861) I. 226 Without undervaluing the influence.. of the *garrison preaching of the German military chaplains in the Netherlands. **1617** MORYSON *Itin.* I. 11 The Duke was at great charge in keeping *Garison Souldiers at Dresden. **1665** MANLEY *Grotius' Low C. Warres* 443 The rest of the Fortifications upon that Coast, the Garrison Souldiers that were therein, when they fled, did overthrow and destroy. **1937** H. D. LASSWELL in *China Q.* II. 643 In the *garrison state the specialist on violence is at the helm, and organized economic and social life is systematically subordinated to the fighting forces. **1941** —— in *Amer. Jrnl. Sociology* XLVI. 455 We are moving toward a world of 'garrison states'—a world in which the specialists in violence are the most powerful group in society. **1954** WEBSTER Add., *Garrison state*, a state dominated by military rather than by civilian personnel and policies, esp. one whose military preparations threaten to convert it into a totalitarian state. **1959** *Listener* 26 Mar. 553/2 Cultural activities, on the one hand, tend to become a commercial part of an overdeveloped capitalist economy or, on the other, an official part of the Science Machine of the Garrison State. **1648** *Art. Peace* ix. in *Milton's Wks.* (1847) 251/1 The disposal of the forts, castles, *garrison-towns. *a* **1656** BP. HALL *Rem. Wks.* (1660) 35 The Nights in those Guarison Towns.. brought me.. weakness. **1796** MORSE *Amer. Geog.* II. 346 A strong garrison town.

garrison (ˈgærɪsən), *v.* [f. prec. sb.]

1. *trans.* To furnish with a garrison, to place troops in (a fortress, town, etc.) for defensive purposes.

1569 STOCKER tr. *Diod. Sic.* III. v, After he had garrisonned Sycione. **1665** MANLEY *Grotius' Low C. Warres* 634 They Garrison'd Viseo. **1786** W. THOMSON *Watson's Philip III* (1839) 261 Garrisoning and fortifying such of the towns he had taken, as were most important for their situation and strength. **1840** THIRLWALL *Greece* VII. 315 He.. fortified the citadel and garrisoned the port. **1895** *Scot. Antiq.* X. 77 In the 'Forty-five, Burleigh Castle .. was garrisoned for King George.

fig. *a* **1856** H. MILLER *Paper on Cur. Suite Fossils* (1874) 348 Is bone a thing rather strongly garrisoned by vitality, than itself vital? **1876** GEO. ELIOT *Dan. Der.* VII. liv, His soul was garrisoned against presentiments and fears.

†**b.** 'To secure by fortresses' (J.); to protect with a garrison. *Obs.*

1693 G. STEPNEY in *Dryden's Juvenal* Sat. viii. (1697) 194 Those Forces join Which Garrison the Conquests near the Rhine. **1797** BURKE *Regic. Peace* iii. Wks. VIII. 372 We have been.. fortifying and garrisoning ourselves at home.

†**c.** *intr.* To establish a garrison or military post. *Obs. rare*⁻¹.

1726 CAVALLIER *Mem.* III. 163 He garrison'd in several Places, that he might be the more ready to disturb and deprive us of all Means of getting Provisions.

2. Of troops: To occupy as a garrison.

1645 LD. DIGBY in *Ludlow's Mem.* (1669) III. 381 Let them.. enquire before they put in, lest by any accident the Enemy should have Garisoned those Places before we come thither. **1673** RAY *Journ. Low C.* 23 No great Town, but well fortified and entrencht, garrison'd by three Companies of Foot. **1838** THIRLWALL *Greece* IV. 363 The other towns, which were garrisoned by the Greek mercenaries, refused to receive him. **1855** MACAULAY *Hist. Eng.* IV. xvii. 99 The fort was stormed. The soldiers who had garrisoned it fled in confusion to the city.

transf. and *fig.* **1646** J. HALL *Poems, The Call* 6 I'le keep off harms, If thou'l be pleas'd to garrison mine arms. **1647** COWLEY *Mistr.* lxvii, Since thou took'st it [my Heart] by Assault from Me, 'Tis Garison'd so strong with Thoughts of Thee. *a* **1711** KEN *Psyche* Poet. Wks. 1721 IV. 201 O Make my Heart thy Care.. No Rebels then will garrison my Breast. **1832** G. DOWNES *Lett. Cont. Countries* I. 439 The convent, although spacious, is garrisoned by only seven monks.

3. To put 'in garrison' or on garrison-duty; to station as a garrison. Also *fig.*

1596 SPENSER *State Irel.* Wks. (Globe) 651/2, I would wish the chief power of the armye to be garrisoned in one countrey that is strongest. **1614** RALEIGH *Hist. World* II. vii. §4. 347 Hippos or Hippion, a Citie so called of a Colonie of Horsemen, there garrisond by Herod. **1671** MILTON *Samson* 1497 Garrisoned round about him like a camp Of faithful souldiery. **1891** *Daily News* 30 Dec. 6/3 He was garrisoned .. in the highest of the French forts on the Savoy Alps.

Hence **ˈgarrisoned** (*town*), furnished with or defended by a garrison; also = *garrison* (*town*); **ˈgarrisoning** *vbl. sb.* and *ppl. a.* Also **ˈgarrisoner**, a garrison-soldier.

1658 W. BURTON *Itin. Anton.* 121 Much less let him marvel to find Baths in garrisoned Towns. **1681** NEVILE *Plato Rediv.* 241 The Second great Prerogative the King enjoys, is the sole Disposal and Ordering of the Militia.. Garrisoning and Fortifying places [etc.]. **1693** W. FREKE *Art of War* xiv. 278 Military Discipline is as necessary for Your Garrisoners in their Sallies, as Your Field Soldiers in their March. **1797** BURKE *Regic. Peace* iii. Wks. VIII. 374 A garrisoned sea-town. **1879** BARING-GOULD *Germany* I. 393 The garrisoning army.. consisted of 10,107 officers, 353,102 men. **1884** *Manch. Exam.* 27 Sept. 5/3 A specially recruited Indian army.. for the garrisoning of Egypt. **1894** *Athenæum* 29 Dec. 886/1 The Chouans attacked Teilleul, a garrisoned town.

†**garriˈsonian**, *sb.*[1] *Obs. nonce-wd.* [f. GARRISON + -(I)AN.] One who lives in a fort or garrison-town.

1773 MRS. GRANT *Lett. fr. Mount.* (1809) I. xxii. 172 All the spirit that diverted you in my description of our garrisonians, is evaporated. **1786** *Ibid.* (1809) II. xxiii. 118.

Garrisonian (gærɪˈsəʊnɪən), *a.* and *sb.*[2] [f. the proper name *Garrison* + -(I)AN.] **A.** *adj.* Pertaining to W. L. Garrison, a leader in the American anti-slavery agitation. **B.** *sb.* A follower or supporter of Garrison; an abolitionist.

1863 W. PHILLIPS *Speeches* vi. 111 Garrisonian antislavery movement. **1890** C. MARTYN *W. Phillips* 160 The Church.. had accused the Garrisonians of infidelity. **1892** *Nation* (N.Y.) 30 June 490/2 The Garrisonian abolitionists.

So **ˈGarrisonism**, the anti-slavery principles of Garrison; abolitionism.

1848 LOWELL *Lett.* (1894) I. 125 Theodore Parker's letter ..is full of Garrisonism from one end to the other. **1878** *N. Amer. Rev.* CXXVII. 98 The wires of Calhounism and Garrisonism were joined and the war began.

† **'garrisonize,** *v. Obs. rare*$^{-1}$. [f. GARRISON *sb.* + -IZE.] *trans.* To furnish with a garrison.

1657 EARL MONMOUTH tr. *Paruta's Pol. Discourses* 176 Not being able to garrisonise or furnish so many Fortresses with things necessary.

† **'garrisonment.** *Obs. rare*$^{-1}$. ? = GARRISON *sb.*[4].

1593 NASHE *Christ's T.* (1613) 44 Set some garisonment before the gate of thy Tabernacle, to oppugne the dispossessors of thy Tabernacle.

garrit, obs. form of GARRET.

† **garritour.** *Obs. Sc.* Also 6 garaitour, garitour. [f. OF. *garite* GARRET + *-our* -OR.] One who occupies a 'garret' or watch-tower; a watchman on a tower or wall.

1501 DOUGLAS *Pal. Hon.* III. lv, Than on the wall ane garitour I considder, Proclamand loud that did thair hartis swidder. **1560** ROLLAND *Crt. Venus* II. 857 On the walheid was gretest Garaitour Dame Chaistitie, in armis most actiue. **1580** *Inv. R. Wardr.* (1815) 301 And in the nedder hous thairof [the quhite toure] ane stand bed for the garritoure.

‖ **garrocha** (ga'rrotʃa). [Sp.] (See quots.)

1846 R. FORD *Gatherings from Spain* xxii. 301 The bull.. well remembers this *garrocha*, or goad, by which herdsmen enforce discipline. **1882** H. DE WINDT *On Equator* ix. 136 Each [picador] was armed with a *garrocha*, or spear, the blade of which..is only about an inch long, as the picadores are not allowed to kill the bull, but merely to irritate and goad him. **1910** *Encycl. Brit.* IV. 790 As the bull attacks the horse, the *picador*, who is armed with a short-pointed, stout pike (*garrocha*), thrusts this into the bull's back with all his force. **1957** R. CAMPBELL *Portugal* 110 The mounted *campinos* and grazers are skilled in the use of the *garrocha* or cattle-spear. **1967** MCCORMICK & MASCAREÑAS *Compl. Aficionado* vii. 215 Mounted men pursue the calves in order to upset them with the blunt pole, or garrocha, which they carry.

garron[1], **garran** ('gærən). Forms: 6–9 garran, (6 garrant, 6–7 garon, 7 guarrent, garroon(e, 7, 9 garrone, 7–8 gerran, 8–9 girran), 6– garron. [a. Gael. *gearran*, Irish *gearrán*.] A small and inferior kind of horse bred and used chiefly in Ireland and Scotland.

1540 *St. Papers Hen. VIII*, III. 169 That the saide Ferganamym shall pay yerely to our Soverayne Lorde the Kyng for every horse, mare, garrant, kowe, oxe, and bull.. 4*d* Irishe. **1586** J. HOOKER *Chron. Irel.* in *Holinshed* II. 156/2 His cariage horsses (which they terme garons) waxed faint. **1601** HOLLAND *Pliny* I. 466 Horses, Mules, and such laboring garrons. **1633** STAFFORD *Pac. Hib.* (1821) ii. 39 Three thousand Mares and Gerrans. **1672** PETTY *Pol. Anat.* (1691) 41 The Footmanship..is..almost quite lost.. everyman now keeping a small Garran to ride on. **1735–6** CARTE *Ormonde* I. 405 Men..whose horses were most of them no better than garrons. **1792** A. YOUNG *Trav. France* 209, I thought..that the Irish garrans had no rivals on the globe. **1846** MCCULLOCH *Acc. Brit. Empire* (1854) I. 299 Neither carts nor any other sort of carriage could be used, the whole inter-course of the country being carried on by means of Highland ponies or garrons. **1891** R. KIPLING *Light that failed* ii, The seediest, weediest Egyptian garron offered for sale in Cairo or Alexandria.

attrib. **1681** DINELEY *Jrnl. Tour Irel.* in *Trans. Kilkenny Archæol. Soc.* Ser. II. I. 175 The guarrent horses many going without shoos. **1792** A. YOUNG *Trav. France* 85 That province [Bretagne] is infested in every stable with a pack of garran poney stallions, sufficient to perpetuate the miserable breed that is every where seen. **1865** CARLYLE *Fredk. Gt.* XIII. xiii. V. 127 Thick-soled peasants..mount your garron plough-horses.

Hence **'garronly** *a.*, resembling the garron (breed).

1737 BRACKEN *Farriery Impr.* (1757) II. 58 Our ugly, crooked, garronly Breed.

garron[2] ('gærən). Also 6 *Sc.* garrown, garrone, garoun, 7 *Sc.* garroun. [? a. ONF. *garron = OF. *jarron* branch of a tree.]

† **1.** *Sc.* ? A beam of wood. *Obs.*

1543 *Aberdeen Reg.* V. 18 (Jam.) Greit treis, rwif sparris, garrownis. **1554–5** in *Burgh Recs. Edinb.* (1871) II. 307 Item, for uther thre garronis coft fra Robert Gray to be hand spaikkis vj*s*. **1612** *Bk. Customs* in *Halyburton's Ledger* (1867) 308 Garrones, single the hundreth xii. *li.*, dowble the hundreth xxiiii *li.* **1615** in Pitcairn *Crim. Trails* III. 276 Dang at his hall dur with ane garroun.

2. (More fully *garron-nail.*) A kind of large nail.

1552–3 in *Burgh Recs. Edinb.* (1871) II. 276 Item vij^{xx} garrone nalis thairto ix*s*. **1833** LOUDON *Encycl. Cottage Archit.* §1072 The rafters to be..chacked and spiked together with double garron nails.

garrooka: see GAROOKUH.

† **garrot**[1]. *Obs. rare*$^{-1}$. [a. F. *garrot* 'the Wythers of a horse, &c.; also, a wring, or pinch in the Wythers' (Cotgr.).] A disease of horses.

1600 SURFLET *Country Farme* I. xxviii. 193 For the garrot: plucke away the flesh that is dead with a sharpe instrument.

garrot[2] ('gærət). Also garrott. [a. F. *garrot* (1757 in Hatz.-Darm.).] A sea-duck of the genus *Clangula*; esp. the Golden-eye (*C. glaucion*). ***Harlequin garrot***: see HARLEQUIN 6.

1829 GRIFFITH *Cuvier's Anim. Kingd.* VIII. 609 We may, moreover, separate [from the Lobate Duck, Shaw] the Garrots, *Clangula*, Leach, whose bill is shorter and narrower in front. **1844** *Zoologist* II. 314 Golden eye, 'Garrot', *Clangula chrysophthalmos*.

garrot[3] ('gærət). [a. F. *garrot*: see next.]

1. *Antiq.* A lever used for winding a cross-bow. Only in mod. writers, with erroneous explanation.

1824 MEYRICK *Antient Armour* III. Gloss., *Garrotus*, the *garrot* or quarrel for the cross-bow. It was also used to imply a lever.

2. *Surg.* (See quot.)

1845 S. PALMER *Pentaglot Dict.*, *Garrot*, in Surgery, a small cylinder of wood, employed to tighten the circular band, by which the artery of a limb is compressed, in order to suspend the circulation of the blood in hæmorrhage from accident, amputation, or aneurism. (In mod. Dicts.)

garrotte, garote (gə'rɒt), *sb.* Also garrote, garrot. [a. Sp. *garrote* (the form now prevailing being through Fr. vb. *garrotter*: see GARROTTE *v.*) = *garrot* (from 13th c.) stick, *spec.* packing-stick, etc.; of obscure origin: cf. GARRON[2].]

† **1.** 'A cudgell to winde a cord as carriers do to packe their wantels with' (Minsheu). *Obs. rare.*

1629 J. M[ABBE] tr. *Fonseca's Dev. Contempl.* 236 Thou hast..rich furniture for thy horses, siluer Garrotes or Wrests to packe vp and fasten thy Sumpter vpon thy strong backed Mules. [**1826** *Blackw. Mag.* XX. 82 There is another kind of torture, employed by the Spanish Inquisition.. When the patient is placed in this apparatus, his arms, thighs, and ankles are made fast to the sides by means of small cords, which being tightened by means of *garrots*, or rackpins (called by some the *Spanish windlass*), in the same manner precisely as carriers tighten the ropes that fasten down the loads on their carts, cut into the very bone.]

2. The Spanish method of capital punishment by strangulation; the apparatus for inflicting this.

The cord was originally twisted by means of a *garrote* or packing-stick (see sense 1).

1622 MABBE tr. *Aleman's Guzman d' Alf.* I. 266 Throwing a cord about his necke, making vse of one of the corners of the Chayre, he gaue him the Garrote, wherewith he was strangled to death. **1832** SOUTHEY *Penins. War* III. 54 The man was hanged and quartered, the woman strangled by the *garrote.* **1837** MAJOR RICHARDSON *Brit. Legion* viii. (ed. 2) 210, I have no hesitation in pronouncing death by the garrot, at once the most manly, and the least offensive to the eye. **1878** *N. Amer. Rev.* CXXVI. 89 He next went to Cuba..was wounded and captured, but escaped the *garrote* to follow Walker to Nicaragua.

3. Highway-robbery performed by throttling the victim. ***to tip the garrotte***: (*slang*) to use this method of robbery.

1852 *Ann. Reg.* 78 The crime of robbery by means of suffocation, and known as 'garotte', from the Spanish mode of execution, has become exceedingly common. **1856** *Punch* XXXI. 194 The old 'Stand and deliver!' 's all rot; Three to one; hit behind; with a wipe round the jowl, boys, That's the ticket—and *Vive la Garotte*!..Let them cly-fake, we'll tip the *Garotte.*

4. *attrib.*, as ***garrotte-man, -robbery.***

1862 MAYHEW & BINNY *Crim. Pris. Lond.* 5 If India has its Thugs, London has its garotte men.

garrotte, garotte (gə'rɒt), *v.* Also 9 gar(r)ote. [ad. Sp. *garrotear*, f. *garrote*: see prec. The prevailing form is due to the equivalent F. *garrotter.*]

1. *trans.* To execute by means of the garrotte.

1851 *Gentl. Mag.* Oct. 418 Lopez..was publicly garroted at Havannah on the 1st of September. **1894** *Westm. Gaz.* 21 Nov. 4/3 The rule now is to garrotte culprits within the walls of the prison.

2. To throttle (a person) in order to rob him.

1858 [see GARROTTING *vbl. sb.*]. **1869** J. GREENWOOD *Sev. Curses Lond.* 201 A ruffian, committed for trial for garotting and nearly murdering a gentleman. **1890** *Spectator* 30 Aug., Young ruffians of the class who garotte their schoolfellows to rob them. **1896** *Boston* (Mass.) *Herald* 16 Feb. 11/8 A man was garrotted last night at Bayard Street, New York.

b. *transf.* and *fig.* To strangle.

1878 R. JEFFERIES *Gamekeeper at home* viii. 184 This happens when the loop..has slipped and seized the creature just at the gills. It then garottes the fish. **1893** K. GRAHAME *Pagan Papers* 38 Commercialism, whose name is Jerry, and who studs the hills with stucco, and garrotes the streams with the girder.

Hence **ga'rrotted** *ppl. a.*

1860 TYLOR *Anahuac* ix. 247 Garotted malefactors sitting bolt upright in the high wooden chairs they had just been executed in.

garrotter, garotter (gə'rɒtə(r)). [f. GARROTTE *v.* + -ER[1].] One who garrottes.

1859 SALA *Tw. round Clock* (1861) 290 Burkins, the garotter, who is now in hold in Pentonville for his sins. **1879** FARRAR *St. Paul* I. 496 We..cannot read without a shudder even of the flogging of some brutal garotter. **1885** *Law Times* 14 Mar. 348/1 Lord Bramwell..sentenced many a garrotter to the cat.

garrotting, garotting (gə'rɒtɪŋ), *vbl. sb.* [f. as prec. + -ING[1].]

1. Execution by means of the Spanish garrotte.

1890 *Pall Mall G.* 9 Aug. 6/1 In the way of executions, nothing so bad has been seen in Europe for a long time as the garotting of Higinia Balaguer, a Spanish murderess, at Madrid.

attrib. **1890** SAINTSBURY in *New Rev.* Feb. 136 You go to the gallows, the block, the garrotting chair.

2. The practice of throttling a person for the purpose of robbing him.

1858 R. S. SURTEES *Ask Mamma* xvi. 54 She pursued the even tenour of her way apparently indifferent to everything —even to a garotting. **1870** MISS BRIDGMAN *Ro. Lynne* II. vi. 134 The heaviest weapon of defence, bought in the days of garotting.

† **garrub.** *Obs. rare*$^{-1}$.

1696 J. F. *Merchant's Ware-ho.* 35 There is Silk Romals, there is Romals Garrub and Cotton Romals..The Garrub is the most deceitful of any, for they for the generallity wear like Dirt.

garrulance ('gærələns). *rare*$^{-1}$. [badly f. GARRUL-OUS + -ANCE.] = GARRULITY.

1890 MRS. HUNGERFORD *Born Coquette* I. vi. 48 With all the garrulance of youth.

† **garrulate,** *v. Obs. rare*$^{-1}$. [f. ppl. stem of late L. *garrulāre*, f. *garrul-us*: see GARRULOUS.] *trans.* To say or speak with garrulity.

1656 J. BOURNE *Def. Script.* 41 Whatsoever these Quakers garrulate to the contrary.

† **garruling,** *vbl. sb. Obs. rare*$^{-1}$. [ad. late L. *garrulāre*: see prec.] The action of chattering or talking volubly. In quot., of a bird.

1549 *Compl. Scot.* vi. 39 The garruling of the stirlene gart the sparrou cheip.

garrulity (gə'ru:lɪtɪ). [a. F. *garrulité*, ad. L. *garrulitātem*, f. *garrul-us*: see GARRULOUS.] The quality of being garrulous, loquaciousness.

1581 W. FULKE in *Confer.* III. (1584) O ij b, Such as are like to proceede from a Fryer, full of impudencie and garrulite. **1603** HOLLAND *Plutarch's Mor.* 28 Thou thy selfe ..with thy vaine babling and garrulitie troublest our eares. **1671** MILTON *Samson* 491 Let me here..expiate, if possible, my crime, Shameful garrulity. **1751** JOHNSON *Rambler* No. 141 ¶1 The prudence of a slave, or the garrulity of a woman, have hindered or promoted the most important schemes. **1788** H. WALPOLE *Remin.* i. 6, I am sensible of the garrulity of old age. **1834** PRINGLE *Afr. Sk.* vii. 247 All alive with the amusing garrulity of monkeys and paroquets. **1859** TENNYSON *Guinevere* 309 The novice crying..Shame on her own garrulity garrulously. **1869** PHILLIPS *Vesuv.* ii. 25 Nor is this reticence balanced by the garrulity of any other writer.

† **garru'lose,** *a. Obs.*$^{-0}$ = next.

1727 BAILEY vol. II, *Garrulose*, full of Talk, always prating.

garrulous ('gærələs), *a.* [f. L. *garrulus* talkative (f. *garrīre* to chatter, prattle) + -OUS.]

1. Given to much talking; fond of indulging in talk or chatter; loquacious, talkative.

c **1611** CHAPMAN *Iliad* III. Comm. 48 Where they were graue and wise Counsellors, to make them garrulous, as Grasshoppers are stridulous; that application holdeth not in these old men, though some old men are so. **1730–46** THOMSON *Autumn* 1231 Age..garrulous, recounts The feats of youth. **1788** H. WALPOLE *Remin.* vii. 46 Such anecdotes ..have not yet emerged into publicity from the *porte-feuilles* of such garrulous *Brantômes* as myself. **1820** W. IRVING *Sketch Bk.* II. 176 The house is shown by a garrulous old lady in a frosty red face. **1876** BLACK *Madcap V.* xviii. 162 The garrulous ancient was for once holding his tongue.

b. *transf.* Of birds and inanimate things: Chattering or babbling. [So L. *garrulus.*]

1854 TENNYSON *To F. D. Maurice* v, You'll..only hear the magpie gossip Garrulous under a roof of pine. **1854** PATMORE *Angel in Ho.* I. II. x. (1879) 239 Birds grew garrulous in the grove. **1877** L. MORRIS *Epic Hades* II. 177 The stream stayed Its garrulous tongue.

2. Of speech or talk: Characterized by garrulity; full of long rambling statements, wordy.

1838–9 HALLAM *Hist. Lit.* IV. i. IV. §16. 9 In a desultory and almost garrulous strain, Bentley pours forth an immense store of novel learning. **1847** DISRAELI *Tancred* II. ii. Colonel Brace was indulging in his garrulous comments. **1867** FREEMAN *Norm. Conq.* (1876) I. iv. 149 A..very discursive and garrulous history of the time. **1873** BLACK *Pr. Thule* (1874) 6 The tall and grave-faced keeper might have kept up his garrulous talk for hours.

Hence **'garrulously** *adv.*, **'garrulousness.**

1727 BAILEY vol. II, *Garrulousness*, Talkativeness, Pratingness. **1856** MISS MULOCK *J. Halifax* xvi, How I blessed Mrs. Jessop's innocent garrulousness. **1859** TENNYSON *Guinevere* 228 To whom the little novice garrulously, 'Yea, but I know' [etc.]. **1884** *Pall Mall G.* 12 Jan. 5/1 Garrulousness chastened into terseness.

garrupa, var. GROUPER.

Garry ('gærɪ). The name of Nicholas *Garry* (1781–1856), an officer of the Hudson's Bay Company, used attrib. to designate a species of oak, *Quercus garryana*, native to south-western British Columbia and the Pacific coast to the south.

1908 G. B. SUDWORTH *Forest Trees Pacific Slope* 283 Next to valley oak, Garry oak, known most commonly as 'white oak', is the largest oak in the Pacific coast region. **1926** *Daily Colonist* (Victoria, B.C.) 25 July 17/1 The Garry oaks rivetted his attention as the most beautiful trees he had ever seen. **1952** D. F. PUTNAM *Canad. Regions* xxi. 465/1 Around Victoria..such trees as madrona and Garry oak indicate a similarity to some Mediterranean environments.

garry, var. GARRAY. *Obs.*

garrya (ˈgærɪə). *Bot.* [mod.L. (D. Douglas 1834, in *Bot. Reg.* XX. 1686), f. the name of Nicholas *Garry* (see prec.).] An evergreen shrub of the genus so called, esp. *Garrya elliptica*, which is native to California and Oregon, and cultivated for the ornamental catkins it bears during the winter.

1834 *Bot. Reg.* XX. 1686 Garrya elliptica. Elliptic-leaved Garrya. **1854** *Explor. Route to Pacific* (*U.S. War Dept.*) *Botany* IV. 136 Colonel Frémont found on the Upper Sacramento, 'above the Great Cañon', in 1846, a Garrya nearly allied to this species. **1893** A. D. WEBSTER *Hardy Ornamental Flowering Trees & Shrubs* 50 There are male and female plants of the Garrya, and..the former is the more ornamental. **1937** C. H. MIDDLETON *Winter-flowering Plants* 61 Young Garryas do not transplant readily. **1963** *Oxf. Bk. Garden Flowers* p. viii, Garrya does best if grown on a wall or sunny bank.

Garryowen (ˌgærɪˈəʊən). *Rugby Football.* Also **garryowen.** [f. the name of an Irish Rugby club in Limerick.] = UP AND UNDER.

1965 *Times* 12 Apr. 4/6 Instead of the garryowen and swift follow up they preferred the diagonal kick. **1974** *Sunday Tel.* 9 June 35/1 He achieved a rather better contact than he did with his earlier Garryowen. **1978** *Times* 31 Oct. 8/1 All Munster rugby men are praying..that he will be on target.. as a hoister of garryowens, under which his forwards will advance like the hounds of hell. **1985** *Guardian* 4 Mar. 23/4 MacNeill pumped up Garryowens whenever he had the chance.

†**garse**, *sb. Obs.* Forms: 3 **garce**, 4 **gerse**, 5 **gaarce**, 6 **garsshe**, 3, 5–8 **garse**. See also GASH. [a. OF. **garse*, noun of action f. *garser* (see GARSE *v.*); cf. med.L. *garsa*, *gersa* incision, scarification.] A cut, incision, gash.

a **1225** *Ancr. R.* 258 þeo ilke reouðfulle garcen [*T.* garses] of þe luðere skurgen. *c* **1380** *Sir Ferumb.* 3693 þe dent of þat sper..Of ys skyn a litel hit nam. Richard gan grope to þat gerse. *c* **1440** *Promp. Parv.* 186/1 Gaarce, *scarificacio, sesura, inscisio, scissura.* **1530** PALSGR. 224/1 Garsshe in wode or in a knyfe, *hoche.* **1611** COTGR., *Chiqueture*, a cutting; a gash, cut, garse. [**1783** *Ainsworth's Lat. Dict.* (Morell) 11, *Incisura*, a cut, gash, or garse.]

†**garse**, *v. Med. Obs.* [a. OF. *garser*, *jarser* to scarify; in mod.F. *gercer* (dial. *jarcer*) to chap, open in cracks, in which sense Palsgr. has *garscher*. OF. *garser* glosses *caraxāre* (= *char-*), L. form of Gr. χαράσσειν to cut, incise: its identification with this word involves phonological difficulties, but is more plausible than the view of Diez that it represents a pop. L. type **carptiāre*, f. *carpĕre* to pull, pluck. The development of Eng. *garsh*, *gash* from *garse* is obscure; Palsgrave's French form is perhaps not to be relied on.] *trans.* To scarify, to make a series of cuts or incisions in. Also *absol.*

1398 TREVISA *Barth. De P.R.* VII. iii. (1495) 224 It is good to garse the legges byneth that the humours..may be drawe from the heed downwarde to the nether partyes. *c* **1400** *Lanfranc's Cirurg.* 18 A surgian vndoiþ þat þat is hool, whanne he letiþ blood, eiþer garsiþ, eiþer brenneþ. **1541** R. COPLAND *Guydon's Quest. Chirurg.* Qj b, Gyue it small fyllyps with your nayle and garse it a newe that it may blede well.

garse (measure for rice): see GARCE.

Garshuni (gɑːˈʃuːnɪ). Also **Carshuni**, **Karshuni.** [ad. Arab. *karšūnī.*] Arabic written in Syriac characters.

1856 T. H. HORNE *Introd. Holy Script.* (ed. 10) IV. 261 The propaganda at Rome issued an edition in 1703 in Syriac and Carshuni (i.e. Arabic in Syriac letters) for the use of the Maronites. **1902** *Daily Chron.* 13 Feb. 5/1 His accomplishments in this direction included the Karshuni alphabet, in which very few Orientalist professors are skilled. **1910** *Cath. Encycl.* IX. 685 The Maronite is a Syrian Rite, Syriac being the liturgical language, though the Gospel is read in Arabic for the benefit of the people. Many of the priests, who are not sufficiently learned to perform the Liturgy in Syriac, use Arabic instead, but Arabic written in Syriac characters (*Karshuni*). **1912** F. J. BLISS *Relig. Mod. Syria & Palestine* iii. 124 The books containing these are written or printed in Syriac character, this combination of Arabic words and Syrian form being known as Karshûni. **1922** J. HASTINGS *Encycl. Relig.* XII. 168/1 In Syria proper ..many of the prayers are said in an Arabic translation, so as to be intelligible to the people; they are then written in Syriac characters, and this combination of Syriac and Arabic is called Carshuni (Syr. *garshūnī*). **1948** D. DIRINGER *Alphabet* II. iv. 269 There are rare instances of Arabic being written in non-Arabic scripts, for instance, in *garshuni*, or *karshuni*, which is the Syriac script adapted to Arabic. **1957** P. K. HITTI *Lebanon in History* xxxi. 457 Introduced probably by some Maronite student of Rome, this establishment put out in 1610 the Arabic Psalms in Syriac characters (Garshūni).

ˈ**garsil.** *north. dial.* Forms: 4–5 **garsell(e**, 5 **gars(s)yl**, **gressell**, 7 **garzill**, 8–9 **garsil.** [For earlier **garthsel*, **gerthsel* = Da. *gjærdsel*, Sw. *gärdsel* fencing, fencing-stuff, brushwood, f. ON. *gerða* (Da. *gjærde*, Sw. *gärda*) to fence (f. *garð-r* fence: see GARTH) + -SEL as in HIRSEL, YEMSEL.] Brushwood used for fencing, or (mod.) for burning.

[**1396** *Mem. Ripon* (Surtees) III. 125 Et in garsell emp. pro clausura Ricardi quondam Roberti de Hundgate, 8*d.* **1453** *Ibid.* 160 De 11*d.* sol. pro j plaustrat. de gressell cum cariagio, empto pro orto ibidem. Et de 2*d.* sol. pro faccione j cepis ibidem.] **1483** *Cath. Angl.* 151/1 Garselle. [Not glossed.] **1674–91** RAY *N.C. Words* (E.D.S.), *Garzill*, hedging-wood. **1788** W. MARSHALL *Yorksh.* Gloss. (E.D.S.), *Garsil*, hedging-thorns, or other brushwood used in making dead hedges. **1876** *Whitby Gloss.*, *Garsil.*

†ˈ**garsing**, *vbl. sb. Obs.* [f. GARSE *v.* + -ING[1].] The action of the verb GARSE.

c **1440** *Promp. Parv.* 186/2 Garcynge, *scarificacio, inscisio.* *a* **1450** *MS. Bodl.* 423 lf. 208 a, By medicyn outher by bledynge Bledyng I say either by veyne or by garsyng. **1502** ARNOLDE *Chron.* (1811) 172 In that tyme [Winter] men shulde lete them bloode in ther bodys by garsinge. **1541** R. COPLAND *Guydon's Quest, Chirurg.* N iij a, Some [ventoses] be with garsynge and other without scaryfycacyon.

garsome, var. GERSUM. *Obs.*

garson(e, obs. form of GARRISON.

garson, -soon, -soun: see GARCION.

garss, -ie, obs. Sc. forms of GRASS, -Y.

garsshe, var. GARSE *sb. Obs.*

ˈ**garston**, ˈ**gerston.** *Obs.* exc. *dial.* and *Hist.* [OE. *gærstún*, f. *gærs* GRASS + *tún* enclosure: see TOWN.] A grassy enclosure; a paddock or field.

a **1000** *Laws of Ina* c. 42 (Schmid) Gif ceorlas gærs-tun hæbben ȝemænne. *a* **1377** in *Hist. MSS. Comm.* I. (1876) 560 [A..deed of Edward 3rd..grants to Ralph..a piece of ground..lying between the 'garston'..and the lane]. **1856** AKERMAN in *Archæol.* (1857) XXXVII. 140 The site, formerly a small paddock or garstun, called from a former owner of the land, Purbrick's Close. **1885** *Q. Rev.* Apr. 324 Yards (gerstuns or garstons) for rearing stock..were enclosed.

garsum(me, var. GERSUM. *Obs.*

gart(e, pa. t. of GAR *v.*

gartain, -an(e, -en, Sc. forms of GARTER.

garte, obs. form of GARTH[2].

garter (ˈgɑːtə(r)), *sb.* Forms: 5 **gartare, -ere, gardere, gart(o)ur**, 6 *Sc.* **gartan(e, -tain**, 6–9 *Sc.* **garten**, 4– **garter.** [a. OF. *gartier*, *jartier*, *jarretier* (also *jartiere*, F. *jarretière*, whence Sp. *jarretera*, It. *giarrettiera*), f. OF. *garet*, *jaret* (F. *jarret*) the bend of the knee (in men), the lower part of the leg (in animals) = Sp. *jarrete*, It. *garretto.* A form *jarre*, *garra*, in Fr. dialects answers to Sp. and Pg. *garra*, and may be of Celtic origin = Breton *gar*, Welsh *gâr* the ham or leg-bone; if so the words must have spread from OFr. to the other Romanic tongues. The substitution of *n* for *r* in the Scottish forms is not accounted for.]

1. a. A band worn round the leg, either above or below the knee, to keep the stocking from falling down.

1382 WYCLIF *Gen.* xiv. 23 Fro a threed of the weeft vnto a garter [**1388** layner] of a hoos. *c* **1440** *Promp. Parv.* 188/1 Gartere or gardere, *subligar.* **1539** in Pitcairn *Criminal Trials* (1833) I. *297 Beltes and gartanis of taffiteis. **1547** BOORDE *Brev. Health* 51 With ii garters I do bynde the wrestes of the armes. *c* **1630** RISDON *Surv. Devon* §63 (1810) 62 Lancelot..was found hanged in his bed-chamber, by his garter, to the bedstead. **1711** ADDISON *Spect.* No. 16 ¶ 1 A Pair of silver Garters buckled below the Knee. **1786** BURNS *Halloween* 24 The lads sae trig, wi' wooer-babs, Weel knotted on their garten. **1826** SCOTT *Woodst.* iii, Lasses leaping till you might see where the scarlet garter fastened the light-blue hose. **1865** MRS. CARLYLE *Lett.* III. 288, I have knitted myself a pair of garters.

†**b.** A similar band, worn as a belt or sash. *Obs.*

1598 SYLVESTER *Du Bartas* II. ii. IV. *Columnes* 271 From her right shoulder, sloaping over-thwart her, A watchet Scarf, or broad imbrodered Garter.

c. *Naut. slang.* Fetters, irons.

1769 FALCONER *Dict. Marine* (1780), *Iron Garters*, a cant word for bilboes, or fetters. **1867** in SMYTH *Sailor's Word-bk.*

2. a. *the Garter*, the badge of the highest order of English knighthood. Hence, membership of this order; the order itself.

The institution of the order is commonly (on the authority of Froissart) attributed to Edward III about the year 1344. By the time of Selden (1614) it was traditionally asserted that the garter was that of the Countess of Salisbury, which fell off while she danced with the King, who picked it up and tied it on his own leg, saying to those present *Honi soit qui mal y pense.* The Garter as the badge of the Order is a ribbon of dark-blue velvet, edged and buckled with gold, and bearing the above words embroidered in gold, and is worn below the left knee; garters also form part of the ornament of the collar worn by the Knights.

c **1350** *Wynnere & Wastoure* 63 And iche a gartare of golde gerede full riche Then were th[e]re wordes in þe webbe.. paynted of plunket..'hethyng haue the hathell þat any harme thynkes'. [**1388** in *Higden* (Rolls) IX. 155 A cause qil fuist chevalier del gartour.] **14..** HOCCLEVE *Min. Poems* (1892) 41 To yow, lordes of the garter 'flour Of Chiualrie' as men yow clepe and calle. *a* **1500** *Flower & Leaf* lxxv, Eek there be Knightes olde of the garter, That in hir tyme did right worthily. **1548** HALL *Chron., Hen. VI*, 108 b, Sir Jhon Fastolffe, the same yere for his valiauntnes elected into the ordre of the Garter. **1596** DALRYMPLE tr. *Leslie's Hist. Scot.* IX. 230 The king of Jngland with his Gartan..maid him illustre. *a* **1685** DRYDEN *Albion & Albanius* III. Wks. 1883 VII. 283 Record the Garter's glory; A badge for heroes, and for kings to bear. **1712–14** POPE *Rape Lock* I. 85 Peers, and dukes, and all their sweeping train, And garters, stars, and coronets appear. **1821** BYRON *Juan* IV. cix, Blue as the garters which serenely lie Round the Patrician left-legs. **1855** THACKERAY *Newcomes* I. 296 You might as well ask the prime minister for the next vacant garter.

b. *pl.* Knights of the Order of the Holy Ghost (in France), wearing a blue ribbon or garter (*cordon bleu*).

1670 COTTON *Espernon* III. ix. 468 The Dukes, and Peers of France, the Officers of the Crown, the blue Garters, and whoever of the highest quality of the Kingdom.

3. *Her.* **a.** (See quot. 1882, and cf. GARTIER.)

In some Dicts. the garter is explained as half of the bendlet.

1658 PHILLIPS, *Garter*..also half a bend in Blazon. **1882** CUSSANS *Her.* iv. (ed. 3) 57 The diminutives of the Bend are the Bendlet or Garter, which is half the width of the Bend.

b. A strap or ribbon buckled in a circle, with the free end hanging down.

1882 CUSSANS *Her.* xviii. (ed. 3) 244 Another badge is sometimes worn. This is a George within an inscribed Garter.

4. a. *transf.* A band which surrounds anything as a garter does the leg, or which resembles a garter in shape.

1556 in W. H. TURNER *Select. Rec. Oxford* 258 Item, for a garter for the sydes [of cucking stool]..iijd.

†**b.** *Printing.* (See quot.) *Obs.*

1683 MOXON *Mech. Exerc.* II. 65 The Garter (but more properly the Coller)..is the round Hoop incompassing the flat Grove or Neck in the Shank of the Spindle.

c. *techn.* A semicircular plate, fitting into a groove in the screw of a bench-vice, in order that the vice may open when unscrewed.

1874 in KNIGHT *Dict. Mech.* 943/1.

5. a. The belt or band used in the game of 'prick the garter' (see 7); the game itself.

1827 HONE *Every-day Bk.* II. 112 The profits gained by.. wheel of fortune, the garter, &c. **1833** MOIR *Mansie Wauch* xix. (1849) 140 Swindling folks at fairs by the game of the garter.

b. The tapes held up for a circus-performer to leap over.

1854 DICKENS *Hard T.* vi. 37 Jupe has missed his tip very often lately..Offered at the garters four times last night, and never done 'em once.

6. As abbreviation for: **a.** *Garter King of Arms* (see KING); **b.** *garter-snake* (see 8).

a. ? **1504** in *Trevelyan Papers* (Camden Soc.) III. 7 The armys off Carminow, Garter seth..came of the iij brotherys. When ye ware made knytt ther wher but iiij cottes off recorde yn Garterys booke. **1558** in Leland *Collect.* (1774) V. 321 [Interment of Q. Mary] Then the Executors. Then Garter. Then the chief Morner. **1614** SELDEN *Titles Hon.* 364 The Kings of England are Soueraigns of the Order, and Henrie V ordaind the King of Heralds, Garter, for it. **1724** *Lond. Gaz.* No. 6284/2 Garter carrying on a Crimson Velvet Cushion the Garter (the Ensign of the Order) and a Gold George in a Blue Ribbon. **1796** PEGGE *Anonym.* (1809) 366 The late excellent Garter, John Anstis, Esq. **1882** CUSSANS *Her.* xviii. (ed. 3) 245 In 1881, Garter, and the other officials, invested the King of Spain, in Madrid, in due and ancient form.

b. 1880 *New Virginians* I. 132 This rockery..will be a regular snake nursery! The garter and the copperhead will think you put it up on purpose for them.

7. Phrases. ***to cast one's garter***: (*Sc.*) to secure a husband; ***in the catching up of a garter***: in a moment; ***to fly the garter***: see FLY *v.*[1] 4 b; ***to have one's guts for garters***: see GUT *sb.* 1 b; ***pricking in the garter*** (also ***prick-the-garter***): a swindling game (see FAST-AND-LOOSE); see also PRICK *v.* 29.

1697 VANBRUGH *Relapse* IV. i, I'll do your honour's business in the catching up of a garter. **1815** *Sporting Mag.* XLV. 234 He had better lose his money in a more fashionable way than by pricking in the garter. **1826** R. T. in Hone *Everyday Bk.* II. 1309 Here is pricking in the garter. **1869** C. GIBBON *R. Gray* xi, 'Ye micht hae cast your gartens a hantle waur, guidwife.'

8. *Comb.*: **garter belt**, a suspender-belt; **garter-blue**, the colour (originally pale, now dark blue) of the ribbon worn by Knights of the Garter; **garter-fish**, the scabbard-fish (*Lepidopus caudatus*); **garter-knee**, the left knee, on which the Garter is worn; **garter-plate**, a plate of gilt copper, upon which the arms of a knight of the garter are engraved, and which is fixed in the stall of the knight in St. George's Chapel, Windsor (Elvin 1889); **garter-ring** (see quot.); **garter-robes**, the dress proper to Knights of the Garter; **garter-snake**, (*a*) *U.S.*, the name of various grass- or ribbon-snakes of the genus *Eutænia*; (*b*) *S. Afr.* the name of various banded snakes, as *Elaps lacteus*; **garter-stitch**, the simplest stitch in knitting, orig. used in making garters; also called *plain knitting*; **garter-vein** (see quot.); **garter-webbing**, 'a narrow elastic webbing enclosed in a covering of silk-ribbon, used for garters' (*Stand. Dict.*).

1959 W. BROWN *Cry Kill* viii. 76 Naked except for her dark nylon stockings and a *garter belt. **1963** *Time* 4 Jan. 40/3 No girdle or garter belt was needed [for leotards]. **1971** 'D. SHANNON' *Whim to Kill* ii. 30 Her white nylon panties and garter-belt had been ripped off. **1789** *Ann. Reg.* 252 The gown was white tiffany, with a *garter blue body. **1888** *Bookseller* 5 Sept. 915 The books were superbly bound in 'garter blue' crushed levant. **1774** GOLDSM. *Nat. Hist.* (1776) VI. 313 The *Lipidopus* [*sic*] or the *Garter-fish. The body sword-like; the head lengthened out. **1848** THACKERAY

Van. Fair xxxvii, A short man was his Lordship.. always caressing his *garter-knee. **1709** HEARNE *Collect.* 17 Nov. (O.H.S.) II. 310 In former times there were several Gold Rings made for the Use of Knights of the Garter, which they receiv'd at their first Installment... They had often the same motto with the Garter, and were therefore called *Garter-Rings, being cast into the Figure of Garters. **1716** *Lond. Gaz.* No. 5430/4 A Garter-Ring, with the Motto *Honi soit qui mal y pense.* **1702** *Eng. Post* 23 Mar., The late Duke of Gloucester in his *garter robes. **1775** A. BURNABY *Trav.* 10 Reptiles and insects are almost innumerable: some of them are indeed harmless and beautiful; such as the black-snake, the bead-snake, the *garter-snake, the fire-fly. **1789** W. PATERSON *Narr. Journeys Country of Hottentots* 163 The Kouse Band, or Garter Snake, is another of the poisonous reptiles of that country. **1885** C. F. HOLDER *Marvel Anim. Life* 131 One of the commonest of the non-poisonous snakes is the striped, or common garter snake. **1910** *East London Dispatch* 10 June 6/2 The *Garter Snakes* and the Vipers are the only snakes of South Africa which permit themselves generally to be closely approached without evincing much concern. **1931** R. L. DITMARS *Snakes of World* xiii. 165 Garter snakes or Coral snakes. **1947** J. STEVENSON-HAMILTON *Wild Life S. Afr.* xxxvi. 328 The various species of garter snakes (*Elaphechis* and *Homorelaps*) likewise are akin to the true cobra. **1909** *Daily Chron.* 8 Dec. 9/4 Sixty stitches are loosely cast on, and sixty rows of *garter-stitch knitted. **1970** M. HAMILTON-HUNT *Knitting Dict.* 8 Garter stitch is used for this corner. **1656** BLOUNT *Glossogr.* s.v. *Vein*, **Garter or gartering vein* is a fourth branch of the thigh vein, from which it descends.. unto the bought of the ham, where it gets this name.

garter ('gɑːtə(r)), *v.* Also 5 garteryn, 6 *Sc.* gartain. [f. prec.]

1. *trans.* To tie with a garter. Also with *on, up.*

c **1440** *Promp. Parv.* 188/1 Garteryn, *subligo.* **1509** HAWES *Past. Pleas.* xxx x, Her fete proper, she gartered well her hose. **1591** SHAKS. *Two Gent.* II. i. 83 Hee beeing in loue, could not see to garter his hose. **1601** —— *All's Well* II. iii. 265 Why dooest thou garter vp thy armes a this fashion? Dost make hose of thy sleeues? **1617** F. MORYSON *Itin.* II. 46 His leggs somewhat little, which hee gartered ever above the knee. **1673** WYCHERLEY *Gentl. Dancing-Mast.* IV. i, I have taken occasion to garter my stockings before him, as if unawares of him. **1717** ST. ANDRÉ in *Phil. Trans.* XXX. 580 Like as a Silk-Stocking, which when 'tis not gartered, falls upon the Foot. **1807** PIKE *Sources Mississ.* III. App. (1810) 36 A kind of leather boot of wrapper, bound round the leg .. and gartered on.

absol. **1791** LACKINGTON *Memoirs* (1792) 454 They.. put on their shoes and stockings, and garter up very deliberately. **1887** FRITH *Autobiog.* I. 241 Rob Roy.. was supposed to be able to garter below the knee without stooping.

†**b.** *Surg.* To bandage tightly. *Obs.*

1577 B. GOOGE *Heresbach's Husb.* III. (1586) 123 b, His medicine was this: Garter each leg immediately one handful above the knee with a liste, good and hard. **1607** MARKHAM *Caval.* IV. 8 Take soft linnen ragges, and therewithall to garter vppe the Foales hinder legs, three fingars aboue the cambrell. **1684** tr. *Bonet's Merc. Compit.* xvi. 565 They garter up the Skin about the twelfth vertebra of the Back.

c. *transf.* To fetter (cf. the sb. 1 c).

1604 DEKKER *Honest Wh.* Wks. 1873 II. 66, I charge you keepe the peace, or have your legs gartered with yrons.

2. *Her.* To surround with a garter (cf. the sb. 3 b).

1864 BOUTELL *Her. Hist. & Pop.* xiii. (ed. 3) 107 One is charged with Camoys only.. and is gartered.

gartered ('gɑːtəd), *ppl. a.* [f. prec. + -ED[1].]

1. Tied with a garter.

1745 *White Cockade* in *Jacobite Songs* (1871) 60 O leeze me on the philabeg, The hairy hough, and gartened leg.

2. Wearing the Garter, as a knight of that Order.

1718 POPE in *Lady M. W. Montagu's Lett.* (1887) I. 317 In this hall, in former days, have dined gartered knights and courtly dames. **1823** BYRON *Juan* XIII. lxviii, Steel barons, molten the next generation To silken rows of gay and garter'd earls. **1838** MACAULAY *Ess., Temple* (1887) 484 When he [Swift] stood in the Court of Requests, with a circle of gartered peers round him.

3. *Her.* Surrounded by a garter (cf. the sb. 3 b).

1823 RUTTER *Fonthill* 34 Seventy-two gartered shields contribute to give richness. **1864** BOUTELL *Her. Hist. & Pop.* xxiii. 394 Several slabs.. show traces of having once been enriched with gartered shields.

gartering ('gɑːtərɪŋ), *vbl. sb.* Also 6 gartoning. [f. as prec. + -ING[1].]

1. The action of the verb GARTER.

a **1529** SKELTON *P. Sparowe* 1176 Wherto shuld I disclose The garterynge of her hose. *a* **1634** RANDOLPH *Muses' Looking-Gl.* IV. i, Hogs go to bed in rest, and are not troubled .. With gartering, girdling, trussing, buttoning. **1702** FARQUHAR *Twin-Rivals* I. i, There is such a plague every morning, with buckling shoes, gartering, combing and powdering!

2. The material of which garters are made; in *pl.* = garters.

1571 *Wills & Inv. N.C.* (Surtees 1835) 362, vj pece of gartoning crewle iij^s—iij double peces of saye gartoning iij^s iv^d. **1577** *Richmond Wills* (Surtees) 269, viij yeards of gartering x . **1604** ROWLANDS *Looke to it* 17 You that weare Scarfs and Gart'rings for your hose. **1612** WOODALL *Surg. Mate* Wks. (1653) 19 A band made of worsted gartering is the best. **1709** F. HAUKSBEE *Phys.-Mech. Exp.* ii. (1719) 30 The Woollen.. was the coarsest sort of that which is commonly used for Gartering.

3. *Comb.*, as †**gartering-place**, the part of the leg where the garter is tied; **gartering-vein** = *garter vein* (see GARTER 8).

1583 STUBBES *Anat. Abus* I. (1877) 56 The Venetian-hosen, they reach beneath the knee to the gartering place to the Leg. **1627** *Vox Piscis* 7 Letters.. found in the gartering place of the Childes legge. **1658** A. FOX *Wurtz' Surg.* II. xxviii. 185, I took out the bone from the gartering place to the Ankle.

garth[1] (gɑːθ). Also 5 gerth, 5–6 garthe, 9 *dial.* gaath, gaith. [a. ON. *garð-r* (Da. *gaard*, Sw. *gård*) yard, courtyard, fence = OE. *ʒeard* YARD. The word is still current in the eastern and northern dialects of English, but is obsolete in Scottish.]

1. a. A small piece of enclosed ground, usually beside a house or other building, used as a yard, garden, or paddock; freq. with defining word, as ***apple-, barn-, church-, cloister-, field-, fold-, garden-, hall-, hemp-, kirk-, minster-, stack-, willow-garth***, q.v. under their initial element.

a **1340** HAMPOLE *Psalter* xxxvi. 2 þe kale, þat he says not ere of garthis bot of gressis. *c* **1420** *Pallad. on Husb.* I. 777 Yet is the chalk or cley lond forto eschewe, And from the rede also thy garth remewe. *c* **1470** HENRY *Wallace* I. 257 Throw a dyrk garth [**1570** gait] scho gydyt him furth fast. **1535** STEWART *Cron. Scot.* II. 39 In symmer syne, quhen euerie schaw wes schene, And euerie garth with gerss wes growand grene. *c* **1560** A. SCOTT *Poems* (S.T.S.) vii. 25 Sen in ȝour garth þe lilly quhyte May nocht remane amang þe laif. **1625** LISLE *Du Bartas, Noe* Ded. 5 See lad, quoth he, the house and garth well drest To morrow morn. **1701–2** A. DE LA PRYME *Diary* (Surtees) 249, I got it [*Aparine Plinii*] plentifully in a garth of Richard Rogison's of Broughton in Lincolnshire, amongst the corn. **1799** A. YOUNG *Agric. Linc.* 412 A garden for potatoes, of a rood or half an acre, called a garth. **1848** *Jrnl. R. Agric. Soc.* IX. I. 126 The most independent mode is for the cottager to rent a small garth or close. **1887** *York Herald* 16 Apr. 6/5 The party of Greek gipsies.. encamped in a garth close to the Gaol.

fig. **1530** LYNDESAY *Test. Papyngo* 57 In all the garth of Eloquence, Is no thyng left bot barrane stok and stone.

b. In recent use short for: Cloister-garth.

1884 *19th Cent.* Jan. 104 The open space [of the quadrangle] not roofed in was called the garth. **1890** *Daily News* 30 June 7/6 The central grassplot of the cloisters—the garth—offers a far better and more sanitary burialplace.

2. A fence or hedge. *rare.* Also with defining word, as *thorn-garth.*

a **1340** HAMPOLE *Psalter* lxxxviii. 39 Thou distroyd all his thorne garthis [Vulg. *sepes*]. **1483** *Cath. Angl.* 42/2 To breke garthe, *desepire. Ibid.* 151/1 A garthe, *sepes.* **1894** J. C. ATKINSON *Memorials of Old Whitby* 43 A *garth* is a fence of any kind,—earth, stones, turves, posts and rails. **1908** W. G. COLLINGWOOD *Scand. Brit.* 193 He made his *bær*, a group of buildings, in the *tún*, or homefield, which he manured and mowed for hay, and surrounded with a garth.

3. = FISHGARTH.

1609 *Sc. Acts Jas. VI* (1814) IV. 432/1 All & haill þe salmond fischeing.. Comprehending þe garthis and pullis vnder-writtin. **1708** *Termes de la Ley* 366 *Garth* is.. a Dam or Wear in a River for the catching of Fish, vulgarly called a Fish-Garth. **1873** *Act 36 & 37 Vict.* c. 71 Sched. 3 License Duties.. For each.. hangbaulk, garth, goryd, box, crib, or cruive £12 0. 0.

4. *attrib.* and *Comb.*, as *garth-end, -yard*; also †**garth-cress**, garden-cress (cf. ME. *toun-cresse*); **garth-man**, (*a*) †one who owns or works a fish-garth; (*b*) (see quot. 1877); †**garth-spade**, a garden-spade; **garth-stead** (see quot. 1877).

? **14..** *MS. Linc. Med.* lf. 292 (Halliw.) Tak a peny-weghte of *garthe cresse sede, and gyff hym at ete. **1565–73** *Durham Depos.* (Surtees) 226 He threatyned hir.. to cast hir over the wall at hys *garth end. **1740** J. CLARKE *Educ. Youth* (ed. 3) 22 The.. Fellow.. directed a Gentleman.. to go by his Father's Garth-End. **1389** *Act 13 Rich. II*, c. 19 Qe null peschour ne *garthman.. ne mette.. en les ewes de Thamise .. ascuns rees appelez stalkers. **1584** in *Descr. Thames* (1758) 63 No Fishermen, Garthmen, Petermen, Draymen or Trinkermen, shall.. set up any Wears, Engines [etc.]. **1865** *Stamford Mercury* in *Standard* 16 Sept., A man.. for 20 years garthman at Mr. Mason's, of Rigsby. **1877** *N.W. Linc. Gloss.*, *Garthman*, the man who attends upon the stock in a fold-yard. **1573** *Richmond Wills* (Surtees) 242 A gavelocke, ij hacks, iij peatspades, ij flainge spades a *garthspade, vij^s. [**1515** *Comp. Gild St. Mary, Boston* 9 b, Tenentes vnias Garthstede nuper Hugonis Madershall.] **1877** *N.W. Linc. Gloss.*, **Garth-stead*, a homestead; a stack-yard; a yard in which cattle is folded. **1890** W. A. WALLACE *Only a Sister* 78, I just stopped under the big ash-tree at the end o' the *garth-yard.

Hence †**garth** *v.*, to enclose with a fence. *rare*$^{-1}$.

1483 *Cath. Angl.* 151/2 To Garthe, *sepire, &c.*; *vbi* to close.

garth[2] (gɑːθ). *north. dial.* Forms: 5 garte, 5–7 garthe, 7– garth. [Northern form of *gerth* (see under GIRTH), a. ON. *giǫrð* fem., girth or hoop.]

1. A saddle-girth.

c **1425** *Thomas of Erceld.* 57 Hir garthes of nobyll sylke þay were.. Hir steraps were of crystalle clere. *c* **1425** *Voc.* in Wr.-Wülcker 665/34 *Hec singula*, a garthe. **1483** *Cath. Angl.* 151/1 A Garte of a hors (*A.* Garthe for A hors); *singula, ventrale.* **1617** MARKHAM *Caval.* II. 32 This done, with the help of another groome that may deliuer the girthes, let the saddle be girded on; at the first so gently that he may no more but feele the garths. **1888** *Sheffield Gloss.*, *Garth*, the strap which goes under a horse's belly to fasten the saddle to him.

2. A wooden hoop (e.g. for a barrel).

[**1424** *Mem. Ripon* (Surtees) III. 152 Item Thomæ Colleper pro v garthys ligneis, 5*d.*] **1483** *Cath. Angl.* 151/2 A Garthe for wesselle, *cinctorium, circulus.* **1523** FITZHERB. *Husb.* §134 If there be asshes in it, to sell the smalle asshes to cowpers for garthes [*printed* garches]. **1609** C. BUTLER *Fem. Mon.* (1634) 40 Then, with a round Belt or Garth, gird the Hackle close to the Hive. **1615** MARKHAM *Eng. Housew.* 168 Besides the wearing and breaking of Garthes, and Plugs. **1688** R. HOLME *Armoury* III. 424/2 Distilling Bag.. Its wide at the top and open, being kept so by an hoop or garth sowed about it. **1847–78** HALLIWELL, *Garth*, a hoop or band. *North.* **1888** *Sheffield Gloss.*, *Garth*, the rim or hoop of a barrel.

3. Girth, or measurement round about.

1684 R. H. *School Recreat.* 133 The largest in the Garth is the strongest Cock. The Dimension of the Garth is thus known: Gripe the Cock about [etc.]. **1725** BRADLEY *Fam. Dict.* s.v. *Cock*, He should be.. long from the Head to the Rump, thick in the Garth. **1755** JOHNSON, *Garth*, the bulk of the body measured by the girdle.

4. *Comb.*, as †**garth-web**, woven material for making saddle-girths (see GIRTH-WEB).

1523 FITZHERB. *Husb.* §10 Take a brode thonge, of ledder, or of garthe-webbe of an elle longe. **1617** MARKHAM *Caval.* IV. 43 Then you shall take a peece of garthwebbe.

Hence †**garth** *v.*, to fit with hoops. *rare*$^{-1}$.

1483 *Cath. Angl.* 151/2 To Garthe wesselle, *circulare.*

garthen, obs. form of GARDEN.

†**garther.** *Obs. rare*$^{-1}$. [f. GARTH[1] + -ER[1].] ? = *garthman* (see GARTH[1] 4).

1679 *Manch. Crt. Leet Rec.* (1888) VI. 93 John Williamson Garther.

garthing(e, -ynere, obs. ff. GARDEN, -ER.

†**gartie.** *Irel. Obs.* 'A ransom for felony' (?).

1533 *St. Papers Hen. VIII*, II. 162 The immoderate takeng of coyne and lyverey, withought order, after mennes awne sensuall appetites, cuddees, gartie, takeng of caanes for felonies, murdours and all other offences.

†**gartier(e.** *Obs. Her.* [a. OF. *gartier* GARTER.] A bendlet (see quots; cf. GARTER *sb.* 3).

1572 BOSSEWELL *Armorie* 12 A 'Gartiere' conteyneth halfe the bende aforesayde, and mayе not bee charged but with floures of leaues. **1610** GUILLIM *Heraldry* II. v. (1660) 61 That which containeth half the bend is called a Gartier.

gartion, var. GARCION. *Obs.*

Gartner ('gɑːtnə(r)). Also (erron.) Gärtner, Gaertner. The name of Herman Treschow *Gartner* (1785–1827), Danish anatomist, used to designate certain anatomical structures distinguished or described by him; as ***Gartner's canal*** or ***duct***, a vestigial part of the Wolffian duct in some female mammals, running from the parovarium through the broad ligament to the vagina. Hence **Gart'nerian** *a.*; esp. ***Gartnerian cyst*** (see quot. 1900).

1874 DUNGLISON *Dict. Med. Sci.* 447/2 *Gärtner, Canals or Ducts of.* The excretory ducts of the Wolffian bodies disappear in the human female, but in some of the lower animals, as the pig, they persist, and receive this name. **1876** *Quain's Elem. Anat.* (ed. 8) II. 821 In the sow and several ruminants.. the subdivided upper tubular part or epoophoron has disappeared, and the main part (middle part of the Wolffian duct) remains in the duct of Gaertner, a strong, slightly undulated tube. **1900** DORLAND *Med. Dict.* 188/1 *Gartnerian cyst*, a cystic tumor developed from Gärtner's duct. **1901** C. H. ROBERTS *Outl. Gynæcol. Path.* ii. 36 The Gartnerian (parovarian) duct can be actually recognised in some animals (cows and pigs) and traced to the vagina giving rise to cysts in those animals. **1908** J. CAMPBELL *Obstetr. & Gynaecol.* 233 In removing Gärtnerian cysts, damage to the ureters must be guarded against. **1957** M. F. CAMPBELL *Princ. Urology* vi. 125 Persistence of Gartner's duct explains ectopic ureteral opening into the vagina, cervix, or uterus. **1968** PASSMORE & ROBSON *Compan. Med. Stud.* I. xxxvii. 58/2 The rest of the mesonephric duct degenerates, although part of it may persist in vestigial form as Gartner's duct.

Gärtner: see GAERTNER[1], GAERTNER[2].

gartoning, north. var. GARTERING.

gartour, gartur, obs. forms of GARTER.

‖**garua** (gə'ruːə). [Peruvian Sp.]

= CAMANCHACA.

1840 *Penny Cycl.* XVIII. 3/1 From June to November, the sky is covered with a kind of fog, which is called the *garua.* **1847** T. ROSS tr. *Von Tschudi's Trav. Peru* ix. 248 In the oases the garuas are much heavier than in the adjacent wastes. **1914** C. R. ENOCK *Ecuador* 195 The Peruvian coast .. receives.. a light mist-drizzle, known as *garua.* **1927** W. G. KENDREW *Clim. Cont.* (ed. 2) 313 At Lima.. heavy showers are rare, the usual rain being a fine drizzle or a wet mist called Garua.

garuda ('gærədə). Also Garuda, Garuṛa. [Skr. *garuḍá.*] **a.** In Indian mythology, the name of a fabulous bird, half-eagle, half-man, ridden by the god Vishnu. **b.** The eagle in the official seal of Indonesia.

1882 M. LOCKWOOD tr. *Lenormant's Beginnings Hist.* (1883) ii. 89 There is a singular analogy between these symbolic beings and the *Garuda*, or rather *Garudas*, of the Aryans of India, genii, half men and half eagles. **1924** E. BEST *Maori* II. xxi. 574 The myth and representations of Vishnu and the two *garuda* birds that represent the powers of Good and Evil. **1952** W. D. P. HILL *Holy Lake of Acts of Rāma* 510 Garuṛa.. has the head, wings, talons and beak of an eagle or vulture and the body and limbs of a man. **1964** *Telegraph* (Brisbane) 19 Nov. 8 (*heading*) Cage me a garuda! *Ibid.*, The mythical garuda bird, Indonesia's national emblem.

‖**garum** ('gɛərəm). Also 6–7 garume. [a. L. *garum*, a. Gr. γάρον, earlier γάρος.] A sauce prepared from fermented fish, much used by the ancient Romans; in 16th and 17th c.

recommended (after classical writers) as a medicine for horses. Now only *Hist.*

1587 MASCALL *Govt. Cattle* (1600) 123 With a pint and a halfe of Garum, which I take to bee saltfish water with a pounde of oile oliue mixed together, and put into his left nostrill. **1607** TOPSELL *Four-f. Beasts* (1658) 437 Cure it by laying two linnen clothes, or by a pinte of the best Garum, and a pound of Oyl infused into the left nostril of the Mule. **1766** SMOLLETT *Trav.* 168 The famous pickle of the antients, called garum, was made of the gills and blood of the tunny. **1867** *Archæol.* XLI. 293 ff., *Classic Cookery* [The ancient method of its preparation is minutely described].

‖**Garus.** ? *Obs. rare*⁻¹. [Fr.; f. *Garus*, the inventor, a Dutch physician of the 17th c.] A medicinal liqueur.

1836 T. HOOK *G. Gurney* (1850) I. v. 107 He..prescribed a glass of garus, at that time the popular liqueur.

garvance, obs. form of CALAVANCE.

garvie ('garvɪ). *Sc.* Also 7 **garvine,** 8 **garvock.** [Origin uncertain. The form *garvock* is app. = Gael. *garbhag*, but the latter may be from Sc. The earliest quots. give *garvie-fishes* (see 2).]

1. A sprat.

1742 *De Foe's Tour Gt. Brit.* IV. 9, Soles, Flukes, Garvie, Eels are also caught on the Scotish Coasts in great Plenty. **1793** *Statist. Acc. Scotl.* VIII. 597 They are often very successful in taking the smaller fish, such as herrings, garvies or sprats, sparlings or smelts. **1794** *Ibid.* IX. 609 The fish caught on this coast are herrings, and garvocks or sprats. **1885** BERTRAM *Harvest of Sea* 56 The pilchard..ought to be the *Sardinia* of commerce, but its place is usurped by the sprat, or garvie as we call it in Scotland.

2. *attrib.* and *Comb.*, as ***garvie-fish, -fishery, -fishing***; **garvie-herring** (Ogilvie) = sense 1.

1680 SIR G. MACKENZIE *Sci. Her.* 61 Three Fishes called Garvine-fishes. **1681** COLVIL *Whigs Supplic.* (1751) 16 When men eat roasted hens and veal, And those at Forth eat Garvie fishes. **1870** *Pall Mall G.* 19 Apr., The fishermen themselves had rather a prejudice against garvie fishing. **1881** in *Fife Jrnl.* 13 Jan. 5/5 During a good season it is estimated that the 'garvie fishery' of the Forth yields £10,000.

garwyndelle, -dyl(le, -gyll, var. GARNWINDLE.

†**gary,** *a. Obs. rare*⁻¹. Cf. the older GERY. [f. GARE *sb.*²] Vehement, furious.

1609 HOLLAND *Amm. Marcell.* XIV. vi. 16 In the same gary braid [L. *eodem impetu*] they tyed Domitian likewise with his head forward to a sled or ladder.

†**garyable,** *a. Obs. rare*⁻¹. [ad. OF. (*guerre*) *guerriable, guerroyable.*] In ***war garyable***, a state of war in which active hostilities are suspended.

1523 LD. BERNERS *Froiss.* I. cclxxix. 418 They counsayled the duke of Aniou..to send all his people into garysons, and to warr garyable; sayeng howe they had done sufficyently for that tyme.

garyophyll(is), var. GARIOFLE, *Obs.*

garyte, -ytte, obs. forms of GARRET.

garzill, var. GARSIL.

gas (gæs), *sb.*¹ Pl. **gases** ('gæsɪz). Forms: 7–8 **gass,** 8–9 **gaz,** 7– **gas.** [A word invented by the Dutch chemist, J. B. Van Helmont (1577–1644), but avowedly based upon the Gr. χάος ('halitum illum *Gas* vocavi, non longe a Chao veterum secretum.' *Ortus Medicinæ*, ed. 1652, p. 59 a); the Dutch pronunciation of *g* as a spirant accounts for its being employed to represent Gr. χ; perh. suggested by Paracelsus's use of *chaos* for the proper element of spirits such as gnomes: see GNOME².

Van Helmont's statement having been overlooked, it has been very commonly supposed that he modelled his word on Du. *geest* spirit, an idea found at least as early as 1775 (Priestley *On Air* Introd. 3). Van H. also invented the term BLAS, which has not survived, while *gas* has been adopted (usually in the same form) in most European languages; the spelling in F. and Pg. is *gaz*, which was also employed by English writers for a time.]

†**1.** An occult principle supposed by Van Helmont to be contained in all bodies, and regarded by him as an ultra-rarefied condition of water (see quot. 1662). *Obs.*

1658 R. FRANCK *North. Mem.* (1694) 202 Insomuch, that neither Gass nor Blass, nor any nauseating suffocating Fumes, nor hardly Death it self can snatch them from Scotland. **1662** J. CHANDLER *Van Helmont's Oriat.* 69 Because the water which is brought into a vapour by cold, is of another condition, than a vapour raised by heat: therefore ..for want of a name, I have called that vapour, Gas, being not far severed from the Chaos of the Auntients..Gas is a far more subtile or fine thing than a vapour, mist, or distilled Oylinesses, although as yet, it be many times thicker than Air. But Gas it self, materially taken, is water as yet masked with the Ferment of composed Bodies. **1692** tr. *Blancard's Phys. Dict.* (1693) 99/2 *Gas*, a term used by Helmont, and signifies a Spirit that will not coagulate, or the Spirit of Life, a Balsom preserving the Body from Corruption. **1743** *Lond. & Country Brew.* II. (ed. 2) 154 Your Water never is to boil; for Boiling irritates and evaporates the subtile, fine, penetrating Gas or Spirit.

2. Any aeriform or completely elastic fluid; matter in the condition of an aeriform fluid. Usually applied only to those elastic fluids which remain such at ordinary atmospheric temperatures; the gaseous forms of substances ordinarily found solid or liquid being by preference called *vapours.*

1779 INGENHOUSZ in *Phil. Trans.* LXIX. 376 Account of a new kind of inflammable Air or Gass, which can be made in a Moment without Apparatus, and is as fit for Explosion as other inflammable Gasses in use for that Purpose. **1790** KERR tr. *Lavoisier's Elem. Chem.* 50 Gas, therefore, in our nomenclature, becomes a generic term, expressing the fullest degree of saturation in any body with caloric; being in fact, a term expressive of a mode of existence. **1791** HAMILTON *Berthollet's Dyeing* I. 6 The refracting power of the different gases. **1798** T. HINDERWELL *Scarborough* II. i. 187 Carbonic Acid Gaz, or Fixt air. **1808** J. BARLOW *Columb.* IV. 456 O'er great, o'er small extends his physic laws, Empalms the empyrean or dissects a gaz. **1831** T. P. JONES *Convers. Chem.* xxiv. 252 In its affinities also it [Iodine] is strikingly similar, decomposing water and forming with its hydrogen a gaseous acid, called hydriodic acid gas. **1878** HUXLEY *Physiogr.* 84 The specific gravities of the three gases which composed the atmosphere. **1891** RAMSAY *Inorg. Chem.* 97 The density of a gas which exists as a liquid at ordinary atmospheric temperatures is termed a vapour-density; there is no real distinction between the words gas and vapour.

3. *spec.* **a.** Gas of a kind suitable to be burnt for illuminating or heating purposes; originally = COAL-GAS, but now including (*a*) various artificial mixtures consisting chiefly of carburetted hydrogen, and distinguished by defining words indicating the source from which they are obtained, as ***water-gas, oil-gas,*** etc.; and (*b*) *natural gas* (see NATURAL *a.* 6 b).

The first experiments in the use of coal-gas for illumination are said to have been made by Dr. Clayton, rector of Crofton about 1688; the practical introduction of gas-lighting was due to Murdoch 1792–1808.

1794 COLMAN *Br. Grins, Epil. Open. Drury Lane Th.* 32 Our decorations [are] gossamer and gas. **1808** MURDOCH in *Phil. Trans.* XCVIII. 124 The whole of the rooms of this cotton mill..and the adjacent house of Mr. Lee, are lighted with the gas from coal. **1823** BYRON *Juan* XI. xxii, Here the lamplighter's infusion Slowly distill'd into the glimmering glass (For in those days we had not got to gas). **1833** HT. MARTINEAU *Loom & Lugger* I. i. 10 He turned on the gas in his back room to an unusual brightness. **1878** HUXLEY *Physiogr.* 39 As invisible as the air we breathe or the gas we burn.

b. *Coal Mining.* Firedamp mixed with common air, the mixture involving a danger of explosion.

1853 URE *Dict. Arts* II. 223 Carburetted hydrogen gas, which produces these dreadful explosions, is not explosive until it is united with a certain proportion of ordinary air.. Some coal mines supply a much greater quantity of gas than others, and these are commonly called 'fiery mines'.

c. The hydrogen, helium, or coal-gas employed to fill a balloon or airship. Also *fig.*

1792 WOLCOTT (P. Pindar) *Ep. to Ld. Macartney*, Such Soldiers! such rare generals! no Poltroons Swell'd by the gas of Courage to Balloons. **1793** M. CUTLER in *Life Jrnls. & Corr.* (1888) II. 279 His gas is now pretty well expended, and he has descended into universal contempt. **1800** T. JEFFERSON *Writ.* (1859) IV. 314 Their gass is nearly run out. **1871** GLAISHER *Trav. Air* ii. 42 The inflation of the balloon was proceeded with, and after three hours about 60,000 feet of gas had passed in.

d. Nitrous oxide gas, used as an anæsthetic, esp. by dentists. (Called also *laughing gas.*)

1894 *Times* 22 Feb. 7/6 The deceased came to consult him with reference to having a tooth extracted with gas.

e. *Path.* Vapour generated in the stomach or intestines. (So F. *gaz.*)

1882 ALLCHIN in *Quain's Dict. Med.* 369/1 All ill-smelling gases and excreta may be, indeed, indicative of the progress of putrefaction lower down in the canal.

f. Any of various gases used in warfare to cause poisoning, asphyxiation, irritation, etc., to the enemy; freq. preceded by defining word, as ***asphyxiant, asphyxiating, lachrymatory, mustard, nerve, poison, tear gas.***

1900 F. W. HOLLS *Peace Conf. Hague 1899* vii. 337 Concerning the prohibition of the use of projectiles containing asphyxiating gas. **1915** D. O. BARNETT *Lett.* 28 Apr. 124 You may like to know we've got a way of competing with asphyxiating gas. **1915** *War Illustr.* 8 May 282/1 Germans held back by their own gas. **1921** [see ASPHYXIANT *a.* and *sb.*]. **1959** *Chambers's Encycl.* III. 334/1 Gas was first used on a large scale in the first world war.

4. A jet of gas, used to light a room, etc.; a gas-light; also, a jet or jets of gas used for heating or cooking. Chiefly *colloq.*

1851 MRS. GASKELL *Let. c* 28 Mar. (1966) 147 They acted in the outer lobby, under the gas. **1872** BLACK *Adv. Phaeton* v. 60 The gases were lit in the spacious coffee-room. **1896** E. TURNER *Little Larrikin* xiv. 160 Several contrivances she saw about. One over the gas, for instance—a piece of hoop-iron, bent hook-wise.

5. a. *slang.* [Cf. 3 c *fig.*] Empty or boastful talk; showy pretence, bombast; humbug, nonsense.

1847 PORTER *Quarter Race*, etc. 120 The boys said that was all gas to scare them off. **1856** EMERSON *Eng. Traits, Religion* Wks. (Bohn) II. 102 Lord Shaftesbury calls the poor thieves together, and reads sermons to them, and they call it 'gas'. **1889** *Globe* 31 Oct. 4/4 (Farmer) It went on to state that the petitioner's talk about a divorce was all gas, and made a further appointment.

b. Colloq. phr. ***all*** (or ***everything***) ***is gas and gaiters***, everything is very satisfactory; (***all***) ***gas and gaiters***, pompousness, verbosity.

1839 DICKENS *Nickleby* xlix. 489 She is come at last—at last—and all is gas and gaiters! **1923** A. C. BENSON *Trefoil* iii. 26 My father was profoundly irritated by him, and..said something..about 'gas and gaiters' which seemed to us a harsh description of so pretty a man. **1925** A. CHRISTIE *Secret of Chimneys* xiii. 124 I've only got to get hold of dear old Stylptitch's Reminiscences..and all will be gas and gaiters. **1932** G. B. SHAW *Adv. Black Girl* 67 Its [*sc.* the Bible's] one great love poem is the only one that can satisfy a man who is really in love. Shelley's Epipsychidion is, in comparison, literary gas and gaiters. **1961** WODEHOUSE *Ice in Bedroom* ii. 21 She cries 'Oh, Freddie darling!' and flings herself into his arms, and all is gas and gaiters again.

c. Fun; a joke. *Anglo-Irish slang.*

1914 JOYCE *Dubliners* 24 He told me he had brought it [*sc.* a catapult] to have some gas with the birds. Mahony used slang freely. **1962** E. O'BRIEN *Lonely Girl* ii. 20 'Let's do it for gas,' Baba said. **1965** M. KENYON *May you die in Ireland* xxiii. 197 Gas is Irish for joke—gag, fun, having a wonderful time.

d. (Esp. prec. by indef. article.) Something or someone that is very pleasing, exciting, impressive, admirable, etc. Also *attrib.* or quasi-*adj.* Cf. GASSER 2. *slang* (orig. *U.S.*).

1957 J. BALDWIN in *Partisan Rev.* III. 357 Brand-new pianos certainly were a gas. **1962** *Austral. Women's Wkly.* Suppl. 24 Oct. 3/2 *Gas*, anything which is very good. **1963** *Guardian* 5 July 11/3 You can listen to his old records now and they are still a gas. **1963** L. DEIGHTON *Horse under Water* xxxii. 124 'Yeah,' he said, 'got me an E-type Jag: Cambridge blue—wire wheels—it's a gas.' **1964** 'J. WELCOME' *Hard to Handle* vii. 79 I'm bound to say I thought it rather gas at the time. **1967** *Melody Maker* 27 May 10/6 Altogether an indefinite sound except for a gas build-up in the middle. **1971** *Frendz* 21 May 16/1 The Stones..were a screaming, speeding, sexy gas.

6. *attrib.* and *Comb.* General relations: **a.** simple attrib., as ***gas-bubble, -fire, -flame, -jet, -lamp***; (sense 3 f) ***gas alert, attack, bomb, -bombardment, war, warfare***; **b.** instrumental, as ***gas-lighting; gas-charged, -driven, -filled, -heated, -laden, -lighted, -lit*** adjs.; **c.** objective, as ***gas-lighting, -maker, -making, -tester, -testing; gas-delivering, -producing, -yielding*** adjs.; **d.** limitative, as ***gas-tight*** adj.

1918 E. S. FARROW *Dict. Mil. Terms* 256 When conditions of atmosphere and wind are favorable for a gas attack preparations are made to meet it. This is known as **gas alert.* **1916** *King's Royal Rifle Corps Chron. 1915* 20 The Germans opened a burning *gas attack upon the front of the trenches we had captured from them ten days before. **1971** *Daily Tel.* 13 Sept. 1/5 Hundreds of New York State police prepared last night for a gas attack on 1,000 rebellious prisoners holding 38 hostages at Attica prison. **1915** *Sphere* 1 May 107/2 The Germans throw their *gas bombs with a species of sling. **1920** G. K. ROSE *2/4th Oxf. & Bucks. Lt. Infty.* 203 Throughout the night of August 7/8..a heavy *gas-bombardment was kept up. **1823** J. BADCOCK *Dom. Amusem.* 76 The *gas-bubbles ascend. **1896** *Daily News* 1 May 2/1 It is feared..that none of the men will have survived their long imprisonment in the *gas-charged workings. **1839–47** TODD *Cycl. Anat.* III. 819/2 A bent *gas-delivering tube. **1899** *Westm. Gaz.* 23 June 8/3 *Gas-driven cars, similar to those running from Blackpool to Lytham. *a* **1918** W. OWEN *Poems* (1963) 95 Gas-driven busses. **1907** *Jrnl. Soc. Arts* LV. 596/2 *Gas-filled airships have lately been so improved. **1919** *Conquest* I. 25/3 A modern half-watt gas-filled lamp. **1932** *Discovery* Oct. 319/2 The..introduction of thermionic valves containing mercury, called 'gas-filled relays' and 'thyratrons'. **1971** F. RAPHAEL *Who were you with Last Night?* 113 She's slowly turning blue in a gas-filled room. **1860** PIESSE *Lab. Chem. Wonders* 57 In this *gas-fire diamonds may be burned. **1877** RUSKIN *Fors Clav.* VII. 257 A sentence which..ought to be blazoned, in letters of stinking gasfire, over the condemned cells of every felon's prison in Europe. **1910** *Encycl. Brit.* XIII. 160/1 Gas fires, as a substitute for the open coal fire, have many points in their favour. **1815** ACCUM *Treat. Gas-Light* (ed. 2) 150 The great power of a *gas-flame does not appear when we try small quantities of it. *a* **1877** KNIGHT *Dict. Mech.* I. 946/1 *Gas-heated furnace. **1963** *B.S.I. News* Apr. 31 (*heading*) Gas-heated catering equipment. **1839** URE *Dict. Arts* 1139 A tube placed immediately above a row of *gas-jets. **1884** MRS. H. WARD *Miss Bretherton* 62 Only a few gas-jets were left burning round a pillar. **1879** MISS GIBERNE *Sun, Moon & Stars* (1880) 293 Sun and stars are solid burning bodies, sending their light through burning *gas-laden atmospheres. **1815** ACCUM *Treat. Gas-Light* (ed. 2) 143 The light of the parish *gas-lamps, is [etc.]. **1823** BYRON *Juan* VII. xlvi, O'er whom Suwarrow shone like a gas lamp. **1849** CLOUGH *Dipsychus* IX. 84 As the light of day enters some.. city..shaming the gas-lamps. **1862** LLOYD *Tasmania* xix. 472 The opulent city of Melbourne..its plate-glassed and *gas-lighted shops. **1838** *Penny Cycl.* XI. 85/2 This was a hint which..might have brought *gas-lighting into operation a century earlier. **1839** URE *Dict. Arts* 545 By the year 1822, gas-lighting in London had become the business of many public companies. **1874** KNIGHT *Dict. Mech.* 951/2 Devices for gas-lighting are matches [etc.]. **1837** LOCKHART *Scott* xli, Passing from a *gas-lit hall into a room with wax candles. **1883** BLACK *Shandon Bells* xii, He walked away down through the gas-lit streets to Fulham. **1839** *Proc. Inst. Civ. Eng.* 69 This coke..was of extreme disuse to the *gas-makers. *Ibid.* 69 The process of *gas-making. **1895** *Westm. Gaz.* 31 Dec. 6/3 Lothian producers of Cannel *gas-producing coal. **1893** *Dublin Rev.* July 652 The need of an efficient *gas-tester. *Ibid.* 654 The flame is then ready for *gas-testing. **1831** BREWSTER *Nat. Magic* v. (1833) 109 A short tube *d e*, moveable up and down within it, so as to be *gas-tight. **1931** 'MILES' (*title*) The *gas war of 1940. **1916** W. OWEN *Let.* Aug. (1967) 402, I am now as well up in **Gas* Warfare as can be. **1888** *Pall Mall G.* 29 Oct. 9/1 To test the coal..with respect to its *gas-yielding properties.

7. Special comb.: **gas alarm,** an apparatus (*a*) to give warning of the presence of gas, (*b*) to give an alarm by means of a slight explosion of gas; (*c*) *U.S.* an alarm device operated by gas; (*d*) a warning of the presence of poisonous gas; **gas amplification,** a process in which, in a strong electric field, an ion produced in a gas by ionizing radiation gives rise to further ions; also, the factor by which the total ionization is increased by this process; **gas analysis**, the measurement or estimation of the quantity of different gases in a mixture; = GASOMETRY; so *gas analyser*; **gas-apparatus**, the apparatus used in the making of gas; **gas arc**, an electric arc in any of the rare gases under high pressure; also, a lamp using a gas arc; **gas-balloon** = BALLOON *sb.*[1] 6; **gas barrel** (see quot. 1904); **gas-bath**, (*a*) a bath heated by gas; (*b*) (see quot.); **gas-battery**, a voltaic battery which operates by the inter-action of gases; **gas-bellows** (see quot.); **gas-bill**, (*a*) a bill in Parliament granting powers to manufacture and supply gas for lighting purposes; (*b*) an account rendered for gas consumed; **gas-black**, a pigment obtained by the burning of gas; **gas-bleaching**, 'the operation of bleaching by means of sulphur dioxide' (*Cent. Dict.*); **gas-blower**, a stream of gas from a coal-seam; **gas-boiler** (see quot.); **gas-bottle**, (*a*) a retort; (*b*) a vessel (of iron) to hold compressed gas, usually for anæsthetic or other medical purposes; **gas-bracket** = BRACKET *sb.* 4; **gas-buoy**, a buoy having one or more chambers filled with gas to supply the lamp which it carries; **gas-burner** (see BURNER 4); **gas-cape**, a cape for protection against poison gas; **gas-carbon** (see quots); **gas-cell**, a cell containing gas in an airship; **gas centrifuge**, a centrifuge for partially separating a mixture of gases, esp. gases that are isotopes of a single element or compounds of them; hence **gas-centrifuging** *vbl. sb.*; **gas chamber**, (*a*) (see quot. 1885); (*b*) a chamber in which gas masks are tested or demonstrated; (*c*) esp., one of the chambers used by the Germans in the 1939–45 war for exterminating groups of human beings by gas-poisoning; any place of execution by gas-poisoning; **gas-chandelier** = GASELIER; **gas-check**, a device used in ordnance to prevent escape of gas at the breech; **gas chromatogram, chromatograph** (see CHROMATOGRAM, CHROMATOGRAPH); **gas chromatography**, chromatography analogous to liquid chromatography but using a carrier gas as the moving phase, which carries the gaseous or vaporized sample through a column containing the solid or liquid stationary phase so that the sample emerges separated into its constituents; hence **gas-chromatographic** *a.*, relating to or involving gas chromatography; **gas-coal**, bituminous coal used in making gas; **gas-cock**, a tap fitted to a gas-pipe; **gas-coke**, the residuum (chiefly carbon) of coal employed in gas-making; **gas-company**, a company formed to make gas and supply it to the public; **gas-condenser**, an apparatus for freeing coal-gas from its tar; **gas-cooker**, a cooker in which the heat is supplied by the burning of gas; a gas-stove; so *gas-cooking*; **gas-cooled** *a.*, of a nuclear reactor, having a gaseous coolant; **gas-cylinder**, a cylinder in which pressurized gas is stored; **gas-detector**, a device for detecting the presence of poisonous gas; **gas-discharge**, applied *attrib.* to a gas-filled lamp, tube, etc., designed so that electric discharges may be produced in it; **gas-douche** (see quot.); **gas-drain** (*Coal-mining*), a heading for carrying off fire-damp; **gas-dregs**, the refuse of gas-making; **gas dynamics**, the study of the dynamic properties of gases; **gas-engine**, an engine in which the motive power is obtained by the production or the rhythmical combustion and explosion of gas in a closed cylinder; **gas-engineer**, one engaged in the making of gas, or in regulating its supply (esp. in theatres); **gas-escape**, a leakage of gas; **gas-field**, 'a region from which natural gas is obtained' (*Cent. Dict.*); **gas-fired** *a.*, heated by the combustion of gas; **gas-firing**, (*a*) a mode of firing a furnace so that the gaseous products of combustion are utilized as fuel; (*b*) a gas-fired system of heating; **gas-fixture**, 'a bracket or gaselier for gas, including burner and stop-cock' (Ogilvie); **gas-float** (see quot.); **gas-focused** *a.*, applied to a cathode-ray tube that makes use of the ionization produced in residual gas to focus the beam of electrons; **gas-furnace**, (*a*) a furnace for manufacturing gas; (*b*) a furnace heated by gas; **gas gangrene**, a rapidly spreading form of gangrene marked by the evolution of gas and usually resulting from the infection of deep wounds by *Clostridium* species; **gas-gauge** (see quot.); **gas-generator**, an apparatus for the production of gas; **gas-globe**, a globe of glass or porcelain used to shade a gas-light; **gas-gong**, a gong to give warning of a gas attack; **gas-governor** (see quots.); **gas-gun**, (*a*) (see quot. 1884); (*b*) a gun using gas as a propellant or as fuel; **gas-harmonicon** (see quot.); **gas-heater**, any apparatus in which gas is employed for heating purposes; **gas helmet** = *gas mask*; **gas-holder**, a vessel for storing coal-gas, a gasometer; **gas-house** (orig. *U.S.*), a gas-works, or a building forming part of a gas-works; also *attrib.* (U.S.), designating a run-down area or its inhabitants (see also quot. 1926); **gas-indicator**, (*a*) a device for showing the pressure of gas; (*b*) (see quot.); **gas-jar** (see quot. 1842); **gas kinetics**, the study of the kinetic properties of gases; so **gas-kinetic** *a.*; **gas-lantern**, the glazed frame of a gas-lamp; also, see quot. 1884; **gas laws** *Physics*, a group of laws (as Boyle's law, Graham's law) that describe the physical properties of gases in general; **gas-lighter**, (*a*) a device for igniting gas; (*b*) a cigarette-lighter in which the fuel is a gas; **gas-lime**, lime which has been used to purify coal-gas (it is used as a dressing for land); **gas-liquid** *a.*, designating or pertaining to a chromatographic process in which the moving phase is gaseous and the stationary phase is liquid; **gas-liquor, -main** (see quots.); **gas-mantle** = MANTLE *sb.* 5 g; **gas mask**, a mask used as a protection against poisonous gas; hence *gas-masked* adj.; **gas-meter**, an apparatus which registers the amount of gas consumed; **gas-microscope**, one in which the object is illuminated by oxyhydrogen light; **gas-motor**, a gas-engine; **gas-office**, the office of a gas-company; **gas officer**, an army officer responsible for the precautionary measures taken against gas attacks; **gas oil** (see quot. 1949); **gas oven**; (*a*) an oven powered by gas; also, with reference to its use as a means of committing suicide; (*b*) = *gas chamber* (c); **gas-pendant**, a gas-pipe suspended from the ceiling and fitted with one or more burners; **gas-pipe**, (*a*) a pipe for conveying gas; (*b*) jocular term for a gun of inferior quality; (*c*) = *gas-drain*; **gas-pipe chair**, a cantilever chair with legs and arms resembling gas-pipes; **gas-plate**, a steel disk, in the Krupp gun, to receive the direct force of the powder-gases (*Cent. Dict.*); **gas pliers** (see quot. 1940); **gas poker**, a hollow poker perforated with holes through which gas can be made to flow, and which on being lit provides heat for kindling a fire; **gas-producer, -purifier, -range, -register, -regulator, -retort** (see quots.); **gas-ring**, (*a*) a gas-check consisting of a thin perforated plate of metal; (*b*) a hollow iron ring with perforations or jets, supplied with gas from a pipe, and forming a kind of lamp or stove for heating a vessel placed above it; **gas-sand**, sandstone yielding a natural gas; **gas-service** (see quot.); **gas shell** (see quot. 1918); **gas show** [SHOW *sb.*[1] 5 c], a detected escape of natural gas at the surface, taken as indicating that oil may be present underground; **gas-spectrum**, a spectrum formed from the rays of an incandescent gas; **gas-spurt**, little heaps or lumps occurring on the surface of some strata, thought to be due to the intermittent escape of gas from decomposing organic matter; **gas starter** (see quot. 1935); **gas-stocks**, the capital of gas-companies as a means of investment; **gas-stoker**, one employed in the heating of gas-retorts; **gas-stoking**, the heating of gas-retorts; **gas storage**, the preservation of fruit and vegetables in carbon dioxide or other gases; so *gas stored* adj.; **gas-stove**, a stove in which the heat is supplied by gas; **gas-tap**, a gas-cock; **gas-tar**, COAL-TAR produced in the manufacture of coal-gas; hence **gas-tar** *v. trans.*, to coat with gas-tar; **gas thermometer**, one in which a column of gas is used as the expanding medium; **gas thread**, a standard form of screw-thread of relatively fine pitch, used on metal tubes; **gas trap** = TRAP *sb.*[1] 8 a; **gas-tube, -tubing**, narrow piping (of metal or india-rubber) for the transmission of gas; **gas-turbine**, a turbine in which the motive power is derived from a flow of gas; also (now more commonly), an internal combustion engine in which air is compressed, heated by combustion with fuel, and the expansion of the resulting hot gases used to power a turbine; also *attrib.*; **gas-vacuole** [a. G. *gasvacuole* (H. Klebahn 1895, in *Flora* LXXX. 252)], a type of vacuole found in certain bacteria and blue-green algæ, containing gas; **gas van**, a mobile gas chamber (senses b and c above); **gas-washer**, an apparatus for removing the ammonia from gas; **gas-water**, water through which coal-gas has passed to be purified; **gas welding**, fusion welding in which the metal is heated by the combustion of a gas; hence *gas-welded* adj.; **gas-well**, a boring in the earth, tapping a supply of natural gas; **gas-work**, now **gas-works**, an establishment for the manufacture of coal-gas; **gas-worker**, one employed in making gas. Also GAS-BAG, GAS-FITTER, GAS-FITTING, GAS-LIGHT, GAS-MAN, GAS-PLANT.

1866 *Rep. Comm. Patents 1864* (U.S.) I. 364 The construction of a *gas alarm, for the protection of property. **1874** KNIGHT *Dict. Mech.* 945/1 Another gas-alarm.. consists of a galvanic battery with a bell. **1915** D. O. BARNETT *Lett.* 183 There was a false gas alarm last night. **1938** Gas-alarm [see *gas-detector* below]. **1933** A. F. COLLINS *Exper. Telev.* iv. 82 This great increase in sensitivity and current-carrying power is due to what is called *gas amplification. **1950** D. H. WILKINSON *Ionization Chambers* vi. 143 When fewer electrons are released in the initial ionization.. the 'signal' must obviously be increased, and gas amplification may be resorted to. **1956** *Nature* 25 Feb. 391/1 The latter process, particularly photo-electric effects and positive ion bombardment of the cathode, have set an upper limit.. to the gas-amplification which has been practicable in single-stage devices. *a* **1884** KNIGHT *Dict. Mech.* Suppl. 378/1 **Gas analyzer*, an instrument for determining the presence and quantity of the gases obtained by the destructive distillation of coal. **1956** *Nature* 25 Aug. 407/1 A gas analyser depending on the variation of the velocity of sound with the nature of the gas. **1859** *Proc. R. Soc.* IX. 218 In Bunsen's admirable method of *gas analysis, considerable time and trouble are expended in observing the exact temperature and pressure to which the gas is subjected at the time of measurement. **1887** W. DITTMAR *Quant. Chem. Analysis* 155 Gas Analysis, in the customary acceptance of the term, comprises only the *gas volumetric* methods for the analysis of gaseous bodies. **1933** H. A. DAYNES (*title*) Gas analysis by measurement of thermal conductivity. **1938** *Thorpe's Dict. Appl. Chem.* (ed. 4) II. 687/1 The sensitiveness of spectroscopy as a method of gas analysis varies greatly according to the gas under test. **1808** MURDOCH in *Phil. Trans.* XCVIII. 128 The cost of attendance upon candles would be as much, if not more, than upon the *gas apparatus. **1949** *Trans. Illum. Engin. Soc.* XIV. 19 The radiation from the *Gas Arc is characterised by an intense continuum extending from the ultra violet through the visible region into the infra red. **1951** W. R. STEVENS *Princ. Lighting* v. 117 Xenon may be used in either air-cooled or water-cooled lamps (for example, the 'gas arc'). **1960** H. COTTON *Princ. Illumination* xv. 390 The gas arc is the name given to the discharge at heavy current-density through one of the rare gases at high pressure. *Ibid.*, Under gas-arc conditions there is an intense continuum covering the whole visible range. **1881** W. D. HAY *300 Years Hence* ix. 187 Supporting his car with a proportionately large *gas-balloon. **1914** H. M. BUIST *Aircraft in German War* i. 19 An airship is any form of gas balloon fitted with motors, propellers and steering gear. **1904** GOODCHILD & TWENEY *Technol. & Sci. Dict.* 247/1 **Gas barrel*, the wrought iron tube used for conducting gas from the large mains.. into buildings, and up to the point from which it is distributed by 'compo' pipes. **1937** *Archit. Rev.* LXXXI. 12 The heating in the cloak-rooms is by means of heating coils extending underneath boot lockers (which are constructed of welded gas-barrel) and behind seats under clothes pegs. **1885** *Syd. Soc. Lex.*, **Gas-bath*, the exposure of the body to the influence of a gas. *Ibid.*, **Gas-battery*, a galvanic battery devised by Grove. **1874** KNIGHT *Dict. Mech.* 946/2 **Gas-bellows*, a kindling device consisting of a hollow poker attached by a flexible tube with the gas-pipe. **1882** 'MARK TWAIN' *Stolen White Elephant* 22 Three month's unpaid *gas-bills taken. **1892** *Pall Mall G.* 6 Dec. 6/2 The first gas bill was passed in 1809. **1969** *Listener* 9 Jan. 59/1 In these first weeks of the New Year the TV consumer is receiving his quota of new programmes, which arrive as inevitably as the quarterly gas bill. **1883** R. HALDANE *Workshop Receipts* Ser. II. 261/2 A quicker way is to give the wood a coat of size and lamp-black, and then use *gas-black in your polish-rubber. **1839** URE *Dict. Arts* 1272 As soon as any district has ceased to be dangerous by the exhaustion of the *gas-blowers. **1884** KNIGHT *Dict. Mech.* Suppl. 380/1 **Gas Boiler*, a form of steam-boiler in which coal gas is used as fuel. **1800** HENRY *Epit. Chem.* (1808) 92 Introduce them into a small *gas-bottle or retort. **1883** *Fisheries Exhib. Catal.* 45 Gas bottle.. in which gas may be generated.. sufficient to inflate a good size balloon. **1874** KNIGHT *Dict. Mech.* 946/2 **Gas-bracket*, a branch proceeding from the wall, and having on its end a burner or burners. **1897** *Scientific Amer.* 18 Dec. 389/1 Experimental acetylene *gas buoy for New York harbor. **1815** in *Phil. Mag.* (1816) XLVII. 50 The *gas-burner and air-pipe.. may be united with the lantern by the screw. **1856** EMERSON *Eng. Traits, Ability* Wks. (Bohn) II. 43 Gas-burners are cheaper than daylight in numberless floors in the cities. **1941** *Illustr. London News* CXCVIII. 487 (*caption*) The men are all wearing *gas-capes. **1948** A. BARON *From City from Plough* 165 They sat in their shallow pits at the roadsides, huddled in their waterproof gas-capes. **1876** *Encycl. Brit.* V. 399/1 Coal-gas Charcoal, or *Gas-Carbon, is a dense and pure variety of charcoal.. which is deposited in the inside of gas-retorts. **1928** C. F. S. GAMBLE *N. Sea Air Station* xix. 334 Above us the *gas-cells are hanging limply down. **1950** *Chem. Abstr.* XLIV. 6694 (*heading*) Convection processes in the *gas centrifuge. **1955** *Sci. Abstr.* A. LVIII. 391/1 The fractions of xenon drawn off at the two ends of the rotor of a gas centrifuge are enriched respectively in the heavy and light isotopes. **1967** *New Scientist* 6 Apr. 17/1 Capital investment in a gas centrifuge plant would probably be favourable with that of the gaseous diffusion plant. **1960** *Times* 19 Oct. 15/3 The production of enriched uranium by *gas-centrifuging. **1885** *Syd. Soc. Lex.*, **Gas-chamber*, an apparatus used in microscopy for.. studying the action of different gases on structures or organisms. **1938** *Times* 12

Jan. 11/6 The only way to convince is to multiply the 40 Home Office gas-vans and allow anybody to put on a mask and enter the gas chamber. **1945** *Daily Mirror* 27 Sept. 8 The Germans knew what to do with women with white hair, or too exhausted to work. For them was the gas-chamber. **1953** *Encounter* Nov. 26/1 In the gas chambers of Auschwitz, Belsen, and other extermination camps, around six million human beings were put to death during the closing phase of the Second World War. **1969** *Listener* 3 July 11/3, I wanted to find out..what would have happened if Huey Newton had been sent to the gas chamber. **1828** *Blackw. Mag.* XXIV 636 The Festal Hall is seen illuminated ..with its *gas-chandeliers. **1879** *Man. Artillery Exerc.* 14 The use of copper *gas checks..gives an increase in muzzle velocity. **1880** *Times* 27 Dec. 9/4 A copper gas check—which is used to prevent windage and give rotation to the projectile —is next attached to the shell. **1952** J. GRIFFITHS et al. in *Analyst* LXXVII. 897 Recent work on various *gas chromatographic techniques in the authors' laboratory is described. **1965** PHILLIPS & WILLIAMS *Inorg. Chem.* I. xi. 416 More recently, gas chromatographic methods have been employed in which the hydrides are transferred in streams of oxygen-free hydrogen or nitrogen. **1952** J. GRIFFITHS et al. in *Analyst* LXXVII. 897 (*title*) Adsorption and partition methods. *Gas chromatography. **1961** *Listener* 7 Dec. 977/1 What is now called 'gas chromatography' allows mixtures of vapours to be analysed with the same degree of subtlety that is possible when liquids are being analysed by 'paper chromatography'. **1967** *New Scientist* 25 May 463/1 Present gas chromatography units (in which the components of a mixture are separated by diffusing at different rates through a porous solid). **1879** *Encycl. Brit.* X. 88/2 The cannel coals ..are specially recognized as '*gas coal'. **1843** *Proc. Inst. Civ. Eng.* 188 Any leakage..from a *gas-cock being inadvertently left open. **1827** FARADAY *Chem. Manip.* iv. 99 If common *gas-coke be used in this furnace. **1817** 'CANDIDUS' *Observ. Gas-Lights* 48 If the *Gas Companies wish to extend the introduction of their lights. **1853** URE *Dict. Arts* I. 876 By the use of the meter, gas companies are enabled to reduce the price of gas. **1874** KNIGHT *Dict. Mech.* 947/2 **Gas-condenser*. **1884** *Gas cooker [see COOKER 1]. **1935** *Discovery* Dec. 361/1 The allied gas, butane, compressed similarly in cylinders, is now in frequent use for gas-cookers etc. **1886** *Chambers's Jrnl.* 5th Ser. III. 63/2 Six hundred pounds is saved yearly since the introduction of *gas-cooking. **1949** C. GOODMAN *Sci. & Engin. Nuclear Power* II. x. 141 It is obvious that split-flow would be advantageous for *gas-cooled reactors... It would not be advantageous for liquid-cooled reactors. **1955** *Sci. Amer.* Oct. 58 Gas cooled reactor being built by British at Calder Hall is described as 'the slow-speed reciprocating engine of the reactor world'. **1965** *Listener* 2 Sept. 342/3 This will use the now famous advanced gas-cooled atomic reactor which can produce electricity more cheaply than any other in the world. **1904** GOODCHILD & TWENEY *Technol. & Sci. Dict.* 247/1 **Gas cylinders*. Compressed gases are sent out in steel cylinders. **1923** KIPLING *Irish Guards in Great War* I. 120 Recessions which they had been cutting out in the trenches for the reception of gas-cylinders. **1886** *Cassell's Fam. Mag.* Feb. 189/1 (*heading*) A miner's *gas detector. **1895** *Daily News* 17 Aug. 5/3 If the electric light could be combined in a portable form with a gas-detector. **1938** *Times* 11 Feb. 11/4 The sentry sat watching his gas-detector, and when it changed colour he sounded the gas-alarm. **1934** WEBSTER, *Gas-discharge lamp. **1940** *Chambers's Techn. Dict.* 367/1 *Gas-discharge tube*. Generally, any tube in which an electric discharge takes place through a gas. Specially, a tube comprising a heated cathode, a grid, and an anode enclosed in an atmosphere of gas at low pressure, generally mercury vapour, argon, or neon. **1960** *Times* 11 Mar. 16/1 Considered as a light source, they [*sc.* glow-worms] are about three times as efficient as a gas-discharge lamp. **1969** *Times* 29 May 12/8 Based on an orange-red wavelength of light emitted by an isotope of the inert gas krypton, when stimulated in a standardized gas discharge tube, the system gives precision to about one part in 100 million. **1885** *Syd. Soc. Lex.*, **Gas-douche*, the directing of a stream of gas to a part of the body. **1883** GRESLEY *Gloss. Coal Mining*, *Gas-drain. **1831** T. L. PEACOCK *Crotchet Castle* (1887) 50 Mud, filth, *gas-dregs, lock-weirs, and the march of mind..have ruined the fishery. **1949** O. G. SUTTON *Science of Flight* 138 Flow problems in which density variations are produced or accompanied by large variations in velocity are said to belong to the science of **gas dynamics*. **1874** KNIGHT *Dict. Mech.* 947/2 The first *gas-engines were gunpowder engines. **1853** URE *Dict. Arts* I. 435 A good *gas engineer will control the entire produce of his manufactory. **1890** *Monthly Packet* Christmas 184 She certainly was not troubled with either *gas-escapes or School Boards. **1940** W. EMPSON *Gathering Storm* 46 He makes no leak we ought to mend Or gas-escape that should not blow. **1889** GROVES & THORP *Chem. Technol.* I. 546 The *gas-fired boiler showed an evaporation of from 8·6 to 9·2 lbs. of water per lb. of coal. **1967** *Times* 17 Jan. 10/6 Heating units for gas-fired ..central-heating systems. **1879** *Encycl. Brit.* IX. 844/2 A more general remedy has been found in what is known as *gas-firing. **1961** *Listener* 12 Oct. 583/1 Dwellers in urban districts may find gas-firing has much to commend it. **1897** *Daily News* 26 May 7/3 A *gas float is a species of beacon, shaped at the bottom like a ship, and carrying on a lofty pyramid the light, which is fed from a gas cylinder placed in the hull. **1934** *Discovery* Nov. 324/2 Two classes of the [vacuum] tubes are made, hard and soft or *gas-focused tubes. **1959** RIDER & USLAN *Encycl. Cathode-Ray Oscill.* (ed. 2) i. 11/1 One of the first (1922) cathode-ray tubes developed..was the Western Electric 224, a gas-focused type of tube. **1874** KNIGHT *Dict. Mech.* 955/1 Croll's *gas-furnace..has an upper series of 6 clay retorts. **1879** *Encycl. Brit.* IX. 844/2 Gas Furnaces. **1874** KNIGHT *Dict. Mech.* 950/1 **Gas-gage*, an instrument for ascertaining the pressure of gas. **1914** *Jrnl. R. Army Med. Corps* XXIII. 514 There are some ten different organisms that have been isolated from cases of *gas gangrene in man. **1918** *Nomencl. Dis.* (ed. 5) 238 Bacillus œdematis maligni... The cause of malignant œdema and some cases of gas gangrene. **1939** AUDEN & ISHERWOOD *Journey to War* 93 The sweet stench of gas-gangrene from a rotting leg. **1944** *Ann. Reg. 1943* 359 The routine use of the sulphonamides have made wound infections and gas gangrene relatively infrequent. **1865** *Proc. Amer. Phil. Soc.* X. 9 Dr. Scheirz's *gas-generator for puddling and heating furnaces. **1924** R. H. MOTTRAM *Spanish Farm* III. 230 The *gas-gong hanging from a nail. **1842** FRANCIS *Dict. Arts*, etc. **Gas Governor*, a kind of gas-meter..for equalizing the pressure of gas previous to its issuing from the gasometer. **1890** *Anthony's Photogr. Bull.* III. 355 The observatory was well fitted with gas governors. **1884** KNIGHT *Dict. Mech.* Suppl. 388 **Gas-gun* , a signaling device, consisting of the explosion of gases in a pipe. **1896** W. W. GREENER *Gun & its Development* (ed. 6) 756/1 Gas guns. **1955** L. WESLEY *Air-Guns & Air-Pistols* ii. 18 The Giffard gas-gun created much interest when it first appeared on the English market. **1962** *Daily Tel.* 15 Nov. 1/7 A liquid or powder had been sprayed over them from a 'gas gun'. **1875** *Encycl. Brit.* I. 115/1 **Gas harmonicon* consists of a small flame of hydrogen or of coal gas, burning at the lower part of the interior of a glass tube, and giving out a very distinct note. **1874** KNIGHT *Dict. Mech.* 950/2 The *gas-heater is sometimes made to assume the forms of grate-bars or logs of wood. **1915** *Punch* 15 Dec. 488/3 Will officers please state how many *Gas Helmets they possess? **1916** A. BENNETT *Jrnl.* 1 June (1932) II. 164 The 'gas officer' came down yesterday to inspect gas-helmet efficiency of troops. **1802** WARWICK in *Phil. Mag.* XIII. 256 Description of an improved *gas holder. **1839** URE *Dict. Arts* 552 The upper floating cylinder [of a gasometer] called the gas-holder. **1880** G. N. LAMPHERE *U.S. Govt.* 227/1 The buildings connected with the hospital..are..*a gas-house [etc.]. **1923** T. S. ELIOT *Waste Land* iii. 15 Fishing in the dull canal..round behind the gashouse. **1926** WOOD & GODDARD *Dict. Amer. Slang* 20 *Gas-house district*, district in city unsuitable for living; abode of gangsters. **1952** B. CERF *Good for Laugh* 163 On the mound pitching for the old St. Louis Cardinal gas-house gang. **1884** KNIGHT *Dict. Mech.* Suppl. 389/1 **Gas Indicator*, a device specially intended to indicate the presence of fire-damp in collieries. **1842** FRANCIS *Dict. Arts*, etc., **Gas Jars*, glass jars for the holding of the gases during the progress of experiments. *c* **1865** J. WYLDE in *Circ. Sc.* I. 304/1 The gas jars are made of various sizes. **1929** J. A. RATCLIFFE *Physical Princ. Wireless* ii. 21 In a metal we suppose that there exist free electrons, which move about hither and thither in random directions with '*gas-kinetic' velocities. **1937** *Discovery* Dec. 394/2 The main topics include..gas kinetics, magnetic and electric moments. **1858** SIMMONDS *Dict. Trade*, **Gas-lantern maker*. **1884** KNIGHT *Dict. Mech.* Suppl. 389/1 *Gas Lantern*, the Parisian 'phare' burner. **1899** J. WALKER *Introd. Physical Chem.* iv. 29 These simple *gas laws..apply in strictness only to ideal or 'perfect' gases. **1966** BARNARD & MANSELL *Fund. Physical Chem.* iii. 108 These Gas Laws are really generalizations about the behaviour of gases to which most conform only approximately. **1971** J. HOWLETT in B. de Ferranti *Living with Computer* ii. 12 The gas laws tell how the volume of a gas varies with pressure and temperature. **1856** *Rep. Comm. Patents 1855* (U.S.) I. 514 Improved *Gas-Lighter. **1874** KNIGHT *Dict. Mech.* 790/1 It..is used as a gas-lighter, by developing a spark over the burner. **1962** R. JEFFRIES *Exhibit No. 13* ii. 15 He flicked open a gas lighter. **1966** J. B. PRIESTLEY *Salt is Leaving* iii. 45 He..lit his pipe again, using what seemed to be an outsize gas lighter. **1853** URE *Dict. Arts* I. 435 Foul *gas-lime or refuse, is somewhat more complex. **1882** *Garden* 1 Apr. 219/1 Any strong smelling preparation spread over the ground will be found very useful, such as gas-lime. **1951** *Biochem. Jrnl.* XLVIII. p. vii/1 A *gas-liquid partition chromatogram of similar efficiency to a liquid-liquid partition chromatogram should lead to a better separation of the two compounds. **1952** *Ibid.* L. 679/2 The theory of gas-liquid chromatography differs from that of liquid-liquid chromatography..only by virtue of the fact that the mobile phase is compressible and thus produces a gradient of gas velocity down the column. **1963** *Times* 22 May (Margarine Suppl.) p. vi/3 The analysis of these fatty acids has been revolutionized by the development of gas-liquid chromatography. **1842** FRANCIS *Dict. Arts*, etc., **Gas Liquor*. **1885** *Syd. Soc. Lex.*, *Gas-liquor*, the ammoniacal liquid contained in the condensing apparatus of gas-works. **1819** ACCUM *Descr. Manuf. Coal Gas* 243 All *gas mains laid in public streets should be placed [etc.]. **1842** FRANCIS *Dict. Arts*, etc., *Gas main*, the principal pipes which conduct the gas from the gas works to the places where it is to be consumed. **1900** *Jrnl. Soc. Arts* XLVIII. 460/2 The Incandescent *Gas Mantle and its Use. **1909** H. G. WELLS *Tono-Bungay* III. i. 282 The cerium and thorium alone were worth the money he extracted for the gas-mantles then in vogue. **1915** *War Illustr.* 4 Sept. 69 French soldiers wearing anti-poison *gas masks and respirators. **1917** *Ibid.* 17 Feb. 15/3 An Austro-Hungarian infantryman with gas-mask. **1971** *Daily Tel.* 13 Sept. 1/5 Following an appeal to the rioters to free their captives, guards in watchtowers began putting on gas masks. **1940** *War Illustr.* 5 Jan. 560 The *gas-masked gun crew are ready for all eventualities. **1815** *Specif. Clegg's Patent* No. 3968 Another part of my invention is a gauge or rotative *gas-meter. **1865** J. A. SYMONDS *Let.* 5 Oct. (1967) I. 575 On reading our gas meter I found that a huge quantity must have been wasted. **1867** THOMSON & TAIT *Nat. Phil.* I. I. §414 The train of wheel-work in a gas-meter counts the number of revolutions of the main shaft. **1906** M. H. BAILLIE-SCOTT *Houses & Gardens* xl. 116 Rows of little houses..each with its gas-meter under the stairs. **1837** DICKENS *Pickwick* xxxiv, 'A pair of patent double million magnifyin' *gas microscopes of hextra power.' **1871** tr. *Schellen's Spectr. Anal.* vi. 20 The oxyhydrogen light and the magnesium light are employed..in the gas microscope. **1882** MAIER tr. *Hospitalier's Electricity* iv. 264 **Gas motors*.. have rendered electric lighting economical. **1825** *Edin. Jrnl. Sci.* July 88 The boy was then sent to the *gas-office to give information there of the smell. **1882** 'MARK TWAIN' *Stolen White Elephant* 22 Gas office broken open here during night. **1916** *Gas officer [see *gas helmet*]. **1916** W. OWEN *Let.* *c* 23 July (1967) 401, I *may*, thus, become Gas Officer. **1901** *Jrnl. Soc. Chem. Ind.* Dec. 1257/1 Crude oil is now used instead of *gas oil in the making of gas. **1949** *Thorpe's Dict. Appl. Chem.* (ed. 4) IX. 390/2 Gas oil is the term broadly applied to petroleum distillates which distill between kerosene and lubricating oils... The term gas oil has been broadly applied to these distillates because of their use in carburetting water gas to raise its heating and illuminating value. However, they are widely used as domestic fuel oils and are in demand as cracking-plant charging oils. **1960** *Which?* Jan. 5/1 Larger burners, especially those for central heating boilers, use 'gas oil', sometimes marketed under proprietary names such as 'Domestic Fuel Oil'. **1884** KNIGHT *Dict. Mech.* Suppl. 390/1 **Gas oven*, one heated by gas jets. **1922** JOYCE *Ulysses* 482 Many..women also commit suicide by..asphyxiating themselves by placing their heads in gas ovens. **1939** G. GREENE *Confid. Agent* I. ii. 77 You've got to choose some line of action and live by it. Otherwise nothing matters at all. You probably end with a gas oven. **1945** 'G. ORWELL' *England your England* (1953) 54 Was it true about the German gas ovens in Poland? **1968** J. R. ACKERLEY *My Father & Myself* xv. 163 It was the kind of shock that people must receive when some old friend..goes home and puts his head in the gasoven. **1896** CORFIELD *Dis. & Defect. Sanit.* 30 Basement rooms with gas-brackets or *gas-pendants in them. **1815** ACCUM *Treat. Gas-Light* (ed. 2) 155 The *gas-pipe communicating with the burner. **1839** URE *Dict. Arts* 1271 He could confine..all the vitiated current to a mere gas-pipe or drift. **1883** *Daily Tel.* 9 July 5/7 The old Snider —the despair-breeding gaspipe of our Volunteers. **1897** MARY KINGSLEY *W. Africa* 238 These guns are not the 'gas-pipes' I have seen up north. **1937** 'G. ORWELL' *Road to Wigan Pier* xii. 223 No one.. who has not looked at a gaspipe chair and reflected that the machine is the enemy of life. *a* **1942** L. G. BLOCHMAN *See you at Morgue* (1946) iii. 30 One of the chrome-plated gaspipe chairs..in Pen's living-room. **1894** *Gas pliers [see *monkey-wrench* s.v. MONKEY *sb.* 18a]. **1940** *Chambers's Techn. Dict.* 367/2 *Gas pliers*, stout pliers with narrow jaws, the gripping faces of which are concave and serrated, to provide a secure grip on pipes, nipples, etc. **1940** H. BRIGHOUSE in *Best One-Act Plays 1940* 49 It's a *gas-poker... You light it and put it under the coals. **1962** *Which?* Feb. 60/1 The fire lighters using gas were of two kinds: the *gas poker*, which is put into the fuel, and the *underbar fire lighters*, which are used under the grate. **1881** RAYMOND *Mining Gloss.*, **Gas-producer*, a furnace in which combustible gas is produced, to be used as fuel in another furnace. **1842** FRANCIS *Dict. Arts*, etc., **Gas purifier*, a vessel into which the coal gas enters from the retorts..intended to deprive the impure gas of its sulphuretted hydrogen. **1884** KNIGHT *Dict. Mech.* Suppl. 391 **Gas-range*, a form of cooking-stove heated by gas-jets. **1842** FRANCIS *Dict. Arts*, etc., **Gas Register* is a simple instrument for indicating and registering the impurities of coal gas. **1874** KNIGHT *Dict. Mech.* 954/1 *Gas-register*, an instrument by which the pressure of gas is indicated and recorded. **1840** *Proc. Inst. Civ. Eng.* 61 A new *Gas Regulator..to regulate the supply of gas to burners. **1839** *Ibid.* 69 The incrustation on the interior of a *gas retort. **1842** FRANCIS *Dict. Arts*, etc., *Gas Retort*, a vessel used for holding the coal or other material of which gas of any kind is to be made. **1880** *Daily Tel.* 23 Dec., A *gas ring at the joint has been found..to prevent the escape of the powder gases on discharge [of the gun]. **1901** *Westm. Gaz.* 18 Dec. 1/3 You stirred them for five minutes on the gas-ring. **1954** T. S. ELIOT *Confid. Clerk* I. 20 Cooking a sausage on a gas ring. **18..** *Amer. Jrnl. Sc.* Ser. III. XXVI. 309 (Cent.) The Sheffield *gas-sand, the lowest in Warren Co., is of Chemung age. **1882** OGILVIE, **Gas service*, gas-fittings or fixtures. **1915** D. O. BARNETT *Lett.* 204 Coming through a district where they'd been using *gas-shells. **1918** E. S. FARROW *Dict. Mil. Terms* 257 *Gas shells*, ordinary shells from which the greater part of explosive has been taken and replaced by a poisonous liquid, which, when the shell bursts, turns into a poisonous vapor or gas. **1940** *Chambers's Techn. Dict.* 367/2 *Gas show. **1964** *Times Rev. Industry* Apr. 82/1 Shell once had a concession in the [Nile] delta and obtained some 'gas shows'. **1871** tr. *Schellen's Spectr. Anal.* xxiii. 76 A spectrum of bright lines, or a *gas-spectrum. **1879** *Encycl. Brit.* X. 294/1 *Gas-spurts. **1932** *Jrnl. R. Aeronaut. Soc.* XXXVI. 853 The R.A.E. Mark I. *gas starter was still doing very good service, particularly in civil aviation. **1935** C. G. BURGE *Compl. Bk. Aviation* 585/2 *Gas starter*, a device whereby an engine is rotated for starting, by supplying gaseous combustible mixture under pressure to the cylinders during the power stroke. **1895** *Daily News* 19 July 9/1 Several *gas stocks have improved. **1889** *Ibid.* 5 Dec. 6/2 Threatened strike of *gas stokers. **1889** *Times* (weekly ed.) 13 Dec. 3/2 To supply 1,000 soldiers to be taught *gas-stoking. **1935** *Economist* 19 Nov. 949/1 Remarkable progress has been made in the '*gas' storage of home-grown orchard fruit—i.e. storage in an atmosphere whose carbon dioxide content has been appreciably increased. **1935** *Ibid.* 25 May 1230/1 English *gas-stored Bramleys and imported boxes of apples have sold well. **1852** *Proc. Inst. Civ. Eng.* 477 A small portable asbestos *gas-stove for heating apartments. **1853** F. NIGHTINGALE *Let.* Dec. in C. Woodham-Smith *F. Nightingale* (1950) vi. 122 The whole flue of a new gas stove came down the second time of using it. **1861** MRS. BEETON *Bk. Househ. Managem.* 266 (*caption*) Gas-stove. **1919** V. WOOLF *Night & Day* x. 128 They sat..talking together over the gas-stove in Ralph's bedroom. **1967** K. GILES *Death & Mr Prettyman* viii. 157 Persuade Mrs Jewel to leave some stewy soup on the gas stove. **1897** *Westm. Gaz.* 18 Feb. 10/1 Mr. Green met his death through the *gas-tap being too loose. **1842** JOHNSON *Farmer's Encycl.* s.v. *Gas-Works*, *Gas Tar. This substance being..employed very commonly as a paint, has not been used as a manure to any extent. **1848** HARDY in *Proc. Berw. Nat. Club* II. No. 6. 321 Gas-tar is preferable as it leaves a strong..odour. **1880** SIR W. THOMSON in *Encycl. Brit.* XI. 574/1 We have accordingly designed a constant-pressure *gas thermometer. **1888** *Lockwood's Dict. Mech. Engin.* 158 **Gas thread*, a screw thread of fine pitch employed for wrought iron and brass tubes. **1902** Gas thread [see THREAD *sb.* 5]. **1882** 'M. HARLAND' *Eve's Daughters* 81 Nature scorns the use of patent *gas-traps. **1815** ACCUM *Treat. Gas-Light* (ed. 2) 156 The *gas-tube enters through one of the claw-feet of the pedestal. **1880** C. R. MARKHAM *Peruv. Bark* 443 India-rubber is necessary, too..for hose, *gas-tubing, and innumerable domestic purposes. **1904** *Proc. Inst. Mech. Engin.* Oct. 1061 (*heading*) A scientific investigation into the possibilities of *gas-turbines. *Ibid.* 1125 He did not see any immediate future for a gas-turbine, except in possibly utilizing the exhaust gases from reciprocating engines. **1930** *Engineering* 10 Jan. 38/2 The early development of what may possibly be the next important form of heat engine, the gas turbine. **1935** *Jrnl. R. Aeronaut. Soc.* XXXIX. 53 This invention relates to an aeroplane propelled by a constant pressure gas turbine, the exhaust gases of which are exhausted towards the rear at so high a velocity that their recoiling effect sustains or wholly replaces the propeller. **1948** *Jane's Fighting Ships 1947–48* 5 The first time gas turbines have ever been employed for the purpose of marine propulsion. **1957** *Times* 21 Dec. 5/3 Travel in the B.O.A.C. Britannia is..luxurious, and the low level of noise and vibration, which is a feature of gas turbine engined aircraft, makes a long journey less tiring. **1902** *Encycl. Brit.* XXV. 265/1 A *gas-vacuole..may be made to vary its volume with varying pressure. **1968** *New Scientist* 21 Nov. 437/1 Most planktonic blue-green algae possess gas-vacuoles, and the buoyancy that they confer tends to lead to the accumulation of the algae at the surface of natural waters in dense growths. **1938** *Gas-van [see *gas chamber* above]. **1946** *Ann. Reg. 1945* 185 Mass-murder by shooting, the gas-van or the crematorium. **1874** KNIGHT *Dict. Mech.* 958 Mr. Croll, an English gas-engineer, is credited with the invention of the *gas-washer now in use. **1848** HARDY in *Proc. Berw. Nat. Club* II. No. 6. 338 Waterings..of weak *gas-water..would ..be useful applications. **1951** *Archit. Rev.* CX. 394/2 The ring main is of cast iron; risers and supply pipes are of copper, *gas-welded. *a* **1877** KNIGHT *Dict. Mech.* I. 958 **Gas welding-furnace*, a heating jet, or cluster of jets, to heat pieces of metal locally, in order to bring them to a welding temperature. **1927** *Jrnl. Iron & Steel Inst.* CXV. 911 Gas welding has many applications, particularly to chrome-molybdenum steel. **1847** in *Proc. Amer. Phil. Soc.* IV. 366 An account of the inflammable *Gas-wells on the banks of the Kanawha river. **1885** *Public Opinion* 9 Jan. 44/1 The latest revelation of our subterranean treasures [is] the natural gas wells. **1819** ACCUM *Descr. Manuf. Coal Gas* title-p., Plans of the most improved sorts of apparatus now employed at the *Gas Works in London. **1863** LYELL *Antiq. Man* 43 In one part of the modern delta..a large excavation has been made for gas-works. **1898** *Pall Mall Mag.* Jan. 120 The water..smelt like the lee-side of a gas works. **1889** *Daily News* 5 Dec. 5/2 We are probably on the eve of a strike of *gas-workers in South London.

gas (gæs), *sb.*[2] *colloq.* (orig. *U.S.*). Abbrev. of GASOLENE (= petrol); ***to step, tramp*** or ***tread on the gas, to give it*** (or ***her***) ***the gas***: to accelerate a motor vehicle by pressing down the accelerator pedal; also *fig.*, to put on speed; to hurry.

1905 R. BEACH *Pardners* (1912) v. 125, I turned the gas into the tug, blowin' for the Wells Street Bridge. **1911** *Daily Colonist* (Victoria, B.C.) 22 Apr. 8/6 (Advt.), Having installed a new portable gasoline wagon we can supply you with 'gas' in record time from our Central Garage. **1916** H. L. WILSON *Somewhere in Red Gap* vii. 289 Once she'd tramped on the gas of a ninety-horse-power racer and socked him against a stone wall. **1918** E. M. ROBERTS *Flying Fighter* xvi. 236 We were to land the machines [*sc.* aeroplanes] to be refilled with gas and oil. **1920** C. W. HOFFMAN in C. L. Gregory *Condensed Course Motion Pict. Photogr.* xxii. 322 Any suggestion to him that—'He get a move on', or 'Step on the gas'. **1924** W. M. RAINE *Troubled Waters* viii. 81 Next moment she was pushing home the brake and shutting off the gas. **1926** A. HUXLEY *Jesting Pilate* IV. 297 Jazz it up. Keep moving. Step on the gas. **1929** *Times* 6 Nov. 15/4 The time may come when, to speed up the cause, he may tread on the gas with the best of them. **1932** *Atlantic Monthly* Mar. 314/1 The old Ford rocked and rattled as I gave it the gas. **1942** L. RICH *We took to Woods* (1948) 66, I remember shoving for dear life while Ralph gave her the gas. **1955** L. P. HARTLEY *Perfect Woman* xxviii. 249 Something that can keep people going and make them feel their value, which..is what we want to feel—without stepping on the gas and running people down. **1963** H. GARNER in R. Weaver *Canad. Short Stories* (1968) 2nd Ser. 36 He claimed he didn't have enough gas in his car to drive him to the hospital. **1965** PRIESTLEY & WISDOM *Good Driving* iii. 27 More gas means more speed. Less gas means less speed.

b. *attrib.* and *Comb.*, as ***gas-pump, rationing, tank***; **gas boat**, a boat driven by a petrol-engine; **gas guzzler** *U.S. slang*, a motor vehicle (esp. a large car) that uses fuel extravagantly; also *transf.*, one who drives such a vehicle; so **gas-guzzling** *a.*, making inefficient use of fuel; **gas pedal**, an accelerator pedal; **gas station**, a filling-station.

1910 *Our Navy* (U.S.) III. XI. 21/1 The *gas boat bumps and mutters. **1959** *Native Voice* (Vancouver) Jan. 2/5 Chief Assu had four fine sons, each of whom he set up with a house and gas boat. **1973** *Washington Post* 29 Apr. L1/4 Most of the *gas-guzzlers have big engines of 400 cubic inches or better. **1977** *TV Guide* (U.S.) 17 Sept. 70/2 Who really was off the beam..he..or I, the gas-guzzler? **1985** *Washington Post* 6 Nov. F1/3 The big American family sedan may be a gas-guzzler. But it can also be an insurance bargain. **1968** *Time* 16 Aug. 62/3 What George Romney called the Big Three's '*gas-guzzling dinosaurs'. **1979** *Tucson Mag.* Apr. 17/3 Volgy asked the city to buy him a used bug instead of a gas-guzzling sedan. **1961** A. MILLER *Misfits* xi. 116 Guido turns sharply with them—the truck leaning dangerously—and works brake and *gas pedal simultaneously. **1925** F. SCOTT FITZGERALD *Great Gatsby* i. 21 Garages, where new red *gas-pumps sat out in pools of light. **1968** *Globe & Mail* (Toronto) 17 Feb. 47/5 (Advt.), B-A Gas pumps,..good highway, busy fishing. **1951** in M. McLuhan *Mech. Bride* 116/1 You willingly put up with *gas rationing. **1932** E. WILSON *Devil take Hindmost* viii. 65 The city..cannot afford to have the *gas stations go broke. **1957** J. KEROUAC *On Road* (1958) 149 Dean was wearing his gas-station coveralls. **1926** *Daily Colonist* (Victoria, B.C.) 7 July 5/3 An extra ninety-gallon *gas tank has been installed in the Yorktown, giving her a non-stop cruising radius of 800 miles.

gas (gæs), *v.*[1] Inflected **gassing, gassed.** [f. GAS *sb.*[1]]

1. *trans.* **a.** To supply with gas. **b.** To light up (theatre scenes) with gas. *colloq.*

1886 *Pall Mall G.* 9 Dec. 4 The District trains are now 'gassed' only once a day. **1888** *Scribner's Mag.* Oct. 452/1 To 'gas' this act is an exceedingly difficult problem, for..a great variety of light-effects are introduced.

c. To inflate with gas.

1922 *Encycl. Brit.* XXX. 48/2 Airship harbours have facilities for gassing airships with hydrogen. **1934** J. A. SINCLAIR *Airships* x. 204 The whole work of gassing the ship fell to the crew.

2. To pass (a thread or textile fabric) through a gas-flame, in order to remove superfluous fibres.

1859 SMILES *Self-Help* iv. (1860) 91 The process of gassing lace and the bleaching of starch. **1890** PROSSER in *Dict. Nat. Biog.* XXIV. 87/2 He [S. Hall] took out patents in 1817 and 1823 for 'gassing' lace and net.

3. To impregnate (slaked lime) with chlorine, in the manufacture of bleaching-powder.

1880 [see *gassed, gassing*, below].

4. ***to be gassed***: to be poisoned by a gas. Also, to be subjected to a gas attack.

1889 *L'pool Daily Post* 19 Mar. 523/7 'Gassed' was the term used in the india-rubber business, and it meant dazed. **1896** *Westm. Gaz.* 6 Feb. 5/2 A man..shouted..that he was 'gassed' (poisoned by the sulphuretted hydrogen gas). **1914** GLAISTER & LOGAN *Gas Poisoning in Mining* viii. 145 Recognising the characteristic action of carbon monoxide as causing powerlessness of the limbs long before, perhaps, total loss of consciousness supervenes, it can readily be understood that men are sometimes placed in most perilous positions by being gassed. **1915** *Times* 7 May 9/4 The men in hospital..who were 'gassed'..on Hill 60. **1915** D. O. BARNETT *Let.* 9 June 168 Young had to go off this morning to a village a few miles back to be gassed. He (and a lot of staff men) were put in a trench and given a dose, with respirators on of course. *Ibid.* 14 June 178 They say that round Wipers the German infantry is rotten..[and] won't advance if there is any fire to hold them up, that is, unless we're gassed out. **1919** G. K. ROSE *2/4th Oxf. & Bucks Lt. Infty.* 203 The Colonel,..Regimental Sergeant-Major and many signallers and runners, all found that they were gassed. **1922** *Daily Mail* 11 Nov. 7, 18 Girls 'Gassed'. A number of employees were overcome by fumes..through a stopper flying from a cylinder of ammonia gas. *Ibid.* 14 Nov. 7 Army Officer Gassed in his Bath... Accidental Death, the result of poisoning by a gas escape from a geyser. *Ibid.* 20 Nov. 7 Residents of Horley, Surrey, complain of being 'gassed' by the fumes released in the breaking up of mustard gas shells at a dump near Gatwick Racecourse, about a mile and a half away.

5. *slang.* (Cf. GAS *sb.*[1] 5.) **a.** *trans.* To deceive or impose upon by talking 'gas'. Only *U.S.*

1847 *Sk. Williams Coll.* 72 (Hall *College Wds.*) Found that Fairspeech only wanted to 'gas' me, which he did pretty effectually. **1888** *Scribner's Mag.* Aug. 219 But in all the rest, he's gassin' you.

b. *intr.* To indulge in 'gas' or empty talk; to vapour, to talk idly or boastfully. orig. *U.S.*

1852 F. A. BUCK *Let.* 1 Jan. (1930) 95, I have been..doing the agreeable to the customers at the Hermitage Hotel..and gassing with travellers generally. **1875** *Chamb. Jrnl.* 25 Sept. 610 To 'gas' is to talk only for the purpose of prolonging a debate. **1878** BESANT & RICE *By Celia's Arbour* xliv, The half dozen who went across to the States to gas about their victory. **1893** R. KIPLING *Many Invent.* 38 I'm 'fraid I've been gassing awf'ly, sir.

6. Of a storage battery or dry cell: to give off gas.

1902 E. J. WADE *Second. Batteries* 332 When once the surfaces of a pure lead anode in an electrolyte of dilute sulphuric acid are peroxidised and gassing. *Ibid.* 335 As a rule the positives commence to gas almost immediately the current passes. **1907** R. W. VICAREY *Storage Batteries* 7 The charge must be continued until every cell in the whole battery has become milky or 'gasses freely'. **1950** G. W. VINAL *Primary Batteries* iv. 123 That dry cells do gas is well established, but..as the public normally uses them such gassing is negligible and the gas is of no concern. **1964** G. SMITH *Storage Batteries* iii. 45 Most of the charge is now being used in dissociating the water of the sulphuric acid solution into hydrogen and oxygen, and the cell begins to gas freely.

7. *trans.* To impress or please enormously; to excite or thrill. Cf. GAS *sb.*[1] 5 d. *slang* (orig. *U.S.*).

1949 L. FEATHER *Inside Be-Bop* vi. 44 Woody, after a year's retirement, had decided to come back with a band that would 'gas' everyone. **1958** *Sunday Express* 19 Oct. 7/6 Duke Ellington said the visit 'gassed' him—a swing expression which means that he was thrilled. **1967** *Crescendo* Mar. 6/2 A..cadenza at the end of 'Watermelon man' which really gassed me.

Hence **gassed** *ppl. a.*, **'gassing** *vbl. sb.*

1872 *Lond. Figaro* 14 Dec. (Farmer), There is no good to be got out of gassing about rallying around standards, uniting as one man to resist, etc. **1880** LOMAS *Alkali Trade* 279 Through them [manholes] samples of the bleaching powder can be withdrawn, and cognisance taken of the progress of the 'gassing' operation. *Ibid.* 280 That no gas, or damp, gassed material shall effect a lodgement. **1886** *Pall Mall G.* 9 Dec., The 'gassing' of such a train would occupy ten minutes. **1893** *Westm. Gaz.* 13 Nov. 7/3 The gassing process in silk mills is..very injurious to health.

gas (gæs), *v.*[2] *colloq.* (orig. *U.S.*). [f. GAS *sb.*[2]]

1. *trans.* To supply (a motor car) with petrol. Freq. const. *up*.

1934 J. M. CAIN *Postman always rings Twice* i. 18, I went to gas up a car. **1959** 'J. R. MACDONALD' *Galton Case* (1960) x. 78 The attendant..was busy gassing a pickup truck. **1962** E. AMBLER *Light of Day* ii. 25 You'd gone to gas up the car.

2. *intr.* To fill *up* the petrol tank of a motor car.

1962 E. S. GARDNER *Case of Blonde Bonanza* (1967) xiv. 161 One of the city police picked up Dillard at a service station..where he was gassing up. **1967** W. MURRAY *Sweet Ride* x. 170 They'll know at the station, on account of they gas up there sometimes.

gasalier, var. GASELIER.

'gas-,bag.

1. a. A bag in which gas is kept for use.

1827 FARADAY *Chem. Manip.* xv. 353 Gas-bags are made of oiled silk. *c* **1865** J. WYLDE in *Circ. Sc.* I. 194/2 Gasometers or gas-bags. **1871** tr. *Schellen's Spectr. Anal.* 17 Gas-bag for oxygen or hydrogen.

b. A balloon or airship; a bag inflated with gas, forming part of an airship or balloon.

1852 *Illustr. London News* 18 Sept. 224/2 Above us reeled the monster gas-bag like a monster peg-top. **1877** *Design & Work* III. 602 Science! indeed, to talk of propelling a flaccid gas-bag! **1897** *Aeronaut. Jrnl.* Jan. 6/2 The machine flew against the wind. There was nothing of the balloon nature about it. There were no gas bags to uphold it. **1912** *Rev. Reviews* XLVI. 61 Inside the frames go the gas-bags, sixteen or so in number. **1932** *Ann. Reg. 1931* 32 The liability of the gas-bags to chafing was the only weak spot in the airship. **1963** A. SMITH *Throw out Two Hands* (1966) iv. 43 Somehow I was unprepared for looking into the gas-bag above us,..and for seeing nothing.

2. An inflated bag used to plug a gas-main during repairs or alterations.

1884 in KNIGHT *Dict. Mech.* Suppl.

3. A flat circular bag of gas-tight material serving to keep a stock of gas for a gas-engine.

4. An empty talker, a 'windbag'.

1889 *Referee* 6 Jan. 1/4 That great gas-bag of modern days, John L. Sullivan. **1894** *Ch. Times* 16 Mar. 302 One who will prove a better guide to national eminence than the gas-bags who trade upon their weakest characteristics.

Gascogne, Gascoi(g)ne, obs. ff. GASCON.

gascoign, obs. form of GASKIN.

Gascoignader, obs. form of GASCONADER.

†**Gascoigny.** *Obs. rare*[−1]. [cf. F. *Gascogne* Gascony.] App. used for: Gasconading spirit.

1754 G. WASHINGTON *Lett.* Writ. 1889 I. 84 The summons is so insolent, and savours so much of gascoigny.

Gascon ('gæskən), *sb.* Forms: α. 4 **Gascoun**, 6 **Gascone**, 7-8 **Gascoon**, 6, 8- **Gascon.** β. 5 **Gaskin**, 6 **Gaskyn, -quine**, 7 **Gascogne, -coine, -coyne**, 7-8 **Gascoigne**, 7, 9 **Gascoygne.** [a. F. *Gascon*; the β forms seem to be influenced by *Gascogne* Gascony, or derived from the attributive use of this; cf., however, the OF. adj. *Gascuinz* (:—pop. Lat. type *-ōnius*).

The name is identical with L. *Vasco, Vascones*, whence BASQUE.]

1. A native of Gascony, a former province in south-western France.

α. **1375** BARBOUR *Bruce* x. 325 Schir Peris Lumbard, a Gascoun. **1687** [see GASCONISM]. **1709** *Tatler* No. 126 ¶4 A young Coquet Widow in France having been followed by a Gascon of Quality who [etc.]. **1849** THACKERAY *Pendennis* I. xxvii. 262 He is a Gascon, and comes from the borders of Spain. **1959** *Chambers's Encycl.* VI. 176/2 The Gascons were virtually independent under their national dukes until 1032.

β. **1603** FLORIO *Montaigne* II. viii. (1632) 214, I have seen diverse so inured to that vice [stealing] that..they would.. steale such things, as they would restore again. I am a Gascoine, and there is no vice wherein I have less skill. **1608** in *Crt. & Times Jas. I* (1849) I. 78 There be 800 Gascoignes at Dieppe, attending passage for Holland.

2. One who resembles a Gascon in character; a braggart, boaster (the natives of Gascony being notorious as such).

a **1771** SMOLLETT *Song* in Anderson *Brit. Poets* (1795) X. 959/1 A peacock in pride, in grimace a baboon, In courage a hind, in conceit a Gascoon. **1814** SIR R. WILSON *Priv. Diary* II. 345 He was exceedingly interesting, very candid, and by no means a Gascon for himself or his brethren in arms. **1826** SCOTT *Diary* 29 Aug. in *Lockhart*, They [the Irish] are the Gascons of Britain. **1836** W. IRVING *Astoria* I. 66 The Canadians especially, who..have a considerable dash of the gascon, were buoyant and boastful, and great braggarts as to the future. **1867** J. W. HALES in Furniv. *Percy Folio MS.* I. 58 Here..the King of Cornwall plays the gascon, not the King of Little Britain.

3. *attrib.* or *adj.* Pertaining to Gascony. †Formerly the designation of a kind of wine.

α. ?*a* **1550** *Freiris of Berwik* 158 in *Dunbar's Poems* 290 Thay hald ane gallone full of Gascone wyne. **1581** *Acc.-Bk. W. Wray* in *Antiquary* XXXII. 117 One dosse' brode gascon lace, iijs. iiijd.; and ij dosse' narow gascon lace, vs. **1849** JAMES *Woodman* ii, She did not altogether dislike a moderate portion of Gascon wine.

β. **1488** *Acta Dom. Conc.* (1839) 97/2 A pip of Gaskin wyne, xxj lb. **1556** *Nottingham Rec.* IV. 113 For sellyng of Gaskyn wyne..aboue the Statute. **1638** BAKER tr. *Balzac's Lett.* (Vol. II) 82 Being a Gascogne Doctour. **1765** STERNE *Tr. Shandy* VII. xliii. (1802) 101 'Twas a Gascoigne roundelay. *Viva la Joia!*

4. *ellipt.* for †**a.** Gascon wine (*obs.*); **b.** Gascon dialect.

1630 J. TAYLOR (Water P.) *Wks.* III. 65 No Gascoygne, Orleance, or the Chrystall Sherrant, Nor Rhenish from the Rheine would be apparant. **1813** A. BRUCE *Life Alex. Morus* ii. 14 Because they do not speak Gascon in Touraine. **1860** *All Year Round* No. 68. 420 The Basque and Béarnais along the Western Pyrenees, the Gascon throughout the regions of the Landes [etc.].

gasconade (gæskə'neɪd), *sb.* Also 8 **gasconnade.** [a. F. *gasconnade*: see prec. and -ADE.]

Extravagant boasting; vain-glorious fiction.

1709 STEELE *Tatler* No. 115 ¶5 That Figure of Speech which is commonly distinguish'd by the Name of Gasconade. **1748** SMOLLETT *Rod. Rand.* xliv. (1804) 287 He recounted his victory with many exaggerations and gasconades. **1776** J. Q. ADAMS *Wks.* (1854) IX. 400 The reports of fifty-five thousand men coming against us, are chiefly ministerial gasconade. **1818** SYD. SMITH *Wks.* (1859) I. 244/2 In their criticisms upon American gasconade, they forget that vulgar people of all countries are full of gasconade. **1874** GREEN *Short Hist.* x. §1. 736 The occasional gasconade of the young soldier of thirty-three.

attrib. **1841** LEVER *C. O'Malley* li. 261 The gasconade tone of the Frenchman would peep through.

gasconade (gæskə'neɪd), *v.* [f. prec. Cf. F. *gasconner*.] *intr.* To indulge in gasconades; to boast extravagantly.

1727 BOYER *Dict. Angl.-Fr.*, To Gasconade, *faire des Gasconnades*. **1778** J. Q. ADAMS in *Fam. Lett.* (1876) 352 The English reproach the French with gasconade, but they never gasconaded as the English do now. **1813** SIR R. WILSON *Priv. Diary* II. 442, I should hope that he was gasconading a little when he spoke to the officers. **1853** C. L. BRACE *Home Life Germany* 139 Though under a severe temptation..I did not gasconade, and they all listened courteously.

Hence **gasco'nading** *vbl. sb.* (also *attrib.*) and *ppl. a.* Also **gasco'nader**, a braggart, boaster.

1745 *Gentl. Mag.* 609/1 Notwithstanding their gasconading in the Caledonian Mercury, &c. the number of the rebels does not exceed six thousand. **1753** *Old & New Interest* 63 But then these Gascoignaders..Your Lands and Lives wou'd have. **1753** in *Scots Mag.* Apr. 198/1 A monument..with a gasconading inscription. **1793** A. YOUNG *Examp. France* (ed. 3) 119 Their gasconading decree of war..is an effort of despair. **1824** MISS MITFORD *Village* Ser. I. (1863) 174 The B. people..must have been braggers born— a whole parish of gasconaders. **1856** OLMSTED *Slave States* 302 The gasconading mountebank who was elected governor. **1859** THACKERAY *Virgin.* II. 337 We are in the habit of laughing at our French neighbours for boasting, gasconading, and so forth.

gasco'nado. *Obs. rare*[−1]. [Pseudo-Sp.: see -ADO.] = GASCONADE *sb.*

1809 W. IRVING *Knickerb.* VI. ii. (1849) 320 All his auditors knew them to be incontinent lies and outrageous gasconadoes.

gasconism ('gæskənɪz(ə)m). [f. as prec. + -ISM. F. *gasconisme* means only 'a Gascon peculiarity of speech'.] A spirit of boastfulness or vaunting.

[**1687** MIEGE *Gt. Fr. Dict.*, *Gasconisme*..a Gasconism, or Gascoons Expression.] **1807** PIKE *Sources Mississ.* I. App. (1810) 2 As I conceive him much of a hypocrite, and possessing great gasconism, I am happy he was not chosen for my voyage. **1822** *Blackw. Mag.* XII. 444 The old *maestro* ..was not devoid of a mixture of gasconism.

Gascoon, obs. form of GASCON.

gascoyne, obs. form of GASKIN[1], GASCON.

‖**gascromh, gascrome.** Incorrect forms of CASCHROM.

1822 SCOTT *Pirate* xiv, Even the savage Highlandmen.. can make more work..with their gascromh, or whatever they call it. **1846** WORCESTER (citing *Gentl. Mag.*), *Gascrome*.

gase, north. var. *goes* (see GO); obs. f. GAZE *v.*

gaseity (gæ'siːɪtɪ). [f. GASE-OUS + -ITY (see quot. 1852). Cf. GAZITY.] Gaseous character; the state or condition of being a gas.

1852 ROGET *Thesaurus* Introd. 22 *note*, I..having framed from the adjectives *irrelative*..and *gaseous*, the abstract nouns *irrelation*..and *gaseity*. **1864** *Athenæum* No. 1929. 500/3 Characteristic of gaseity. **1870** PROCTOR *Other Worlds* xii. 281 Some of these objects give the bright line spectrum indicative of gaseity.

gaselier (gæsə'lɪə(r)). Also **gasalier**. [f. GAS *sb.*[1] after CHANDELIER. The older name was *gas-chandelier*; see GAS *sb.*[1] 7.] An ornamental frame to hold a number of gas-burners, usually hung from the ceiling of a room.

1849 *Times* 29 Aug. 5/5 Above the orchestra hangs a circular gaselier formed of several small circles of gas burners. **1880** OUIDA *Moths* II. 32 The gilded gaseliers were glowing with light.

gaseline, var. GASOLENE.

†**gasement.** *Obs.* [var. of CASEMENT, f. GAZE, by popular etymology.]

1628 WITHER *Brit. Rememb.* IV. 413 None to their closed wickets made repaire; Their empty gasements gaped wide for ayre.

‖**gaseosa** (gæsɪ'əʊsə). [Sp., = soda-water.] An effervescing drink. Also *attrib.*

1927 D. H. LAWRENCE *Mornings in Mexico* 70 He had had a bottle of *gazoosa* [*sic*], fizz, with us. **1932** E. HEMINGWAY *Death in Afternoon* iii. 35 The vendors of cold beer and gaseosas. **1939** G. GREENE *Lawless Roads* viii. 199 There were stacks of empty 'gaseosa' bottles.

gase'osity. *rare*[−1]. [f. *gaseose adj. (= GASEOUS: see -OSE) + -ITY.] = GASEITY.

1802–12 BENTHAM *Rationale Jud. Evid.* (1827) III. 320 Solidity, liquidity, and gaseosity. *Ibid.* 327 In their several states of solidity, liquidity, and gaseosity.

gaseous ('gæsɪəs, 'geɪsɪəs), *a.* Also 9 **gazeous.** [f. GAS *sb.*[1] + -EOUS; cf. GAZOUS and F. *gazeux*.]

1. a. Having the nature, or in the condition, of gas.

1799 *Med. Jrnl.* I. 171 When it is exhibited to the senses in a gaseous state, it is then termed oxygenous gas. **1804** C. B. BROWN tr. *Volney's View Soil U.S.* 237 The sudden appearance of fever..may be owing to the action of some gazeous principle on the fluid which pervades the nerves. *c* **1860** FARADAY *Forces Nat.* iii. 85 Bodies in what we call the vaporous, or the gaseous state, are always perfectly transparent. **1878** HUXLEY *Physiogr.* 190 Associated with the steam are various gaseous exhalations.

fig. **1834** LANDOR *Imag. Conv.* (1846) II. 238/2 A word of honour is but the gaseous and volatile part of honour, which would blow up a true Frenchman if he tried to retain it within him. **1879** GEO. ELIOT *Theo. Such* iv. 94 His gaseous, illimitably expansive conceit.

b. ***gaseous diffusion***, the diffusion of gas (see DIFFUSION 5), esp. through a porous wall or membrane as a means of partially separating the gases in a mixture. Also *attrib.*

1846 *Phil. Trans. R. Soc.* CXXXVI. 623 The full elucidation of the transpiration of mixed gases, must await ..the further extension of our knowledge of the laws of gaseous diffusion. **1922** *Jrnl. Amer. Chem. Soc.* XLIV. 41 A possible cause of loss of efficiency in gaseous diffusion is local convective action, due to unevenness in the texture of the membrane. **1958** W. K. MANSFIELD *Elem. Nucl. Physics* i. 11 Separation using this fact occurs in gaseous diffusion plants.

c. ***gaseous gangrene*** = *gas gangrene* (see GAS *sb.*[1] 7).

1889 *Pacific Med. Jrnl.* XXXII. 469 That septic disease now generally called malignant œdema..is also called.. fulgurating gaseous gangrene. **1965** *Dorland's Med. Dict.* (ed. 24) 316/2 *C*[*lostridium*] *novyi*, a species which is an important cause of gaseous gangrene, being reported in 32 to 48 per cent of cases.

2. Relating to gases.

1805 W. TAYLOR in *Ann. Rev.* III. 511 The father of the gazeous philosophy [Priestley].

gaser, obs. form of GAZER.

gaseyn. Also **gayseyn.** [cf. OF. *gaisse* marsh (dial. *gasse* pool of water), *gacel*, *gacelet*, *gaçuel* marsh.] Marshy ground.

c **1420** *Pallad. on Husb.* I. 36 The watir out of gaseyn [*Bodl. MS.* gayseyn; L. *lacuna*] or of myre Be not ybrought.

'gas-,fitter. A tradesman or workman engaged in fitting up buildings with the apparatus necessary for the use of gas.

1858 SIMMONDS *Dict. Trade*, *Gas-fitter*, a workman who lays on pipes and fits burners for gas. **1863** P. BARRY *Dockyard Econ.* 83 The bricklayer, the carpenter, the plumber, the gasfitter, &c. **1885** *Instr. Census Clerks* 53 Gas fitter.

'gas-,fitting.

1. a. Chiefly *pl.* The apparatus (pipes, brackets, etc.) required for the employment of gas in a building. **b.** The action or occupation of fixing gas-appliances in a building.

c **1865** LETHEBY in *Circ. Sc.* I. 132/1 No one is allowed to make use of his gas-fittings until the gas-fitter has tested their soundness. **1883** *Eng. Illustr. Mag.* Nov. 89/2 Gas-fittings go from Birmingham all over the Globe.

2. *attrib.*, as ***gas-fitting trade***.

1893 *Daily News* 6 Mar. 7/4 The gasfitting trade continues dull.

gash (gæʃ), *sb.*[1] Also 6 **gashe.** [Later form of GARSE *sb.* *Garse* and *gash* are given side by side in Levins (quot. 1570), and Palsgrave has the intermediate form *garsshe*. The change may have been helped by the analogy of *slash* and similar words.]

1. A cut, slash or wound, relatively long and deep, made in the flesh; a cleft in any object, such as would be made by a slashing cut.

1548 UDALL, etc. *Erasm. Par. Luke* xxiv. 39 Touche and handle ye my syde, it hath the gashe of the speare. **1555** W. WATREMAN *Fardle Facions* II. ix. 193 Firste, with his knife he maketh in it a gashe rounde aboute in a circle, vndre the eares. **1563** SACKVILLE *Induct. Mirr. Mag.*, lvii, There hunge his targe with gashes depe and wyde. **1570** LEVINS *Manip.* 33/14 A garse or gashe, *incisura*. **1575** J. STILL *Gamm. Gurton* I. ii. in Dodsley *O. Pl.* II. 9 By the masse, here is a gashe, a shamefull hole indeade And one stytch teare furder, a man may thruste in his heade. **1601** HOLLAND *Pliny* I. 545 The same excessiue humor is let out of Fig trees by meanes of certaine light slits or gashes made in the barke. **1667** MILTON *P.L.* VI. 331 From the gash A stream of Nectarous humor issuing flow'd Sanguin, such as Celestial Spirits may bleed. **1706–7** FARQUHAR *Beaux' Strat.* V. iv. Wks. (Rtldg.) 664/2 Let me see your arm..O me! an ugly Gash upon my Word. **1807** G. CHALMERS *Caledonia* I. III. vii. 397 He at length received a mortal gash. **1878** BROWNING *La Saisiaz* 7 Scarce enough to heal and coat with amber gum the sloe-tree's gash. **1886** M. F. SHELDON tr. *Flaubert's Salammbô* 8 Through his tattered tunic could be seen on his shoulders the weals of long gashes.

transf. and *fig.* **1641** MILTON *Ch. Govt.* I. vi, Instead of healing up the gashes of the Church..fall to gore one another with their sharpe spires. **1643** —— *Divorce* II. xvii, Who hath taught you to mangle thus, and make more gashes in the miseries of a blamelesse creature. **1894** FENN *In Alpine Valley* I. 29 This wretched deep gash in a hideous Swiss mountain.

b. The act of making such a cut.

1829 HOOD *Eugene Aram* xv, Two sudden blows with a ragged stick And one with a heavy stone, One hurried gash with a hasty knife, And then the deed was done. **1853** KANE *Grinnell Exped.* l. (1856) 483 With a knowing gash of his knife, he makes a hole in the under jaw of the seal.

2. *U.S. slang.* The mouth.

1852 MRS. STOWE *Uncle Tom's C.* xxxviii, Shut your old black gash, and get along in with you. **1878** —— *Poganuc P.* xiv. 122 Ef Zeph Higgins would jest shet up his gash in town-meetin', that air school-house could be moved fast enough.

3. *attrib.*, as *gash-lobed* adj.; also **gash-vein** *Australian Mining* (see quot. 1869).

1846 DANA *Zooph.* (1848) 122 The margin..of the base is ..entire, undulating, gash-lobed. **1869** R. B. SMYTH *Goldf. Victoria* 612 *Gash-vein*, a wedge or V shaped vein. **1872** RAYMOND *Statist. Mines & Mining* 269 The almost incredible number of small gash-veins in the slates and greenstone have probably furnished most of the gold.

gash (gæʃ), *sb.*[2] *Sc.* [Prob. a transf. sense of *gash* 'a projection of the under jaw' (Jam.), whence GASH-GABBIT; cf. GASH *v.*[2]] 'Prattle', 'pert language'. ***to set up one's gash***, 'to talk pertly, give an insolent reply' (Jam.).

1810 *Cock's Simple Strains* 135 (Jam.) Wad ye set up your gash, nae faut, Ye crustie foul-mou'd tyke. **1813** W. BEATTIE *Fruits Time Parings* (1871) 43 Wi this the wife sets up her gash.

gash (gæʃ), *sb.*[3] *slang.* Also **gashing, gashion.** [Origin unknown; cf. Eng. dial. *gaishen* a skeleton, a silly-looking person, an obstacle (see E.D.D.).] Something superfluous or extra; waste, rubbish, garbage. Also *attrib.* and *Comb.*

1925 FRASER & GIBBONS *Soldier & Sailor Words* 103 *Gashions*, extra of anything. **1943** BAKER *Dict. Austral. Slang* (ed. 3) 34 *Gash*, a second helping of food; any surplus or residue. **1945** 'TACKLINE' *Holiday Sailor* 62 Gash can mean so many things. It is rubbish, waste... It can be supernumerary—a gash-hand who hasn't any particular job to do. **1953** SCOTT & FISHER *Thousand Geese* v. 54 James planned to tidy up the camp—dig a gash-pit. **1960** *Times* 2 Apr. 8/7 A disgusted stoker is emptying a bottle of best Demerara down the gash-shute. **1965** P. WAYRE *Wind in Reeds* xiv. 194 She [*sc.* a bear] has an unerring nose for what in the Navy was called 'the gash bucket', and..invariably went straight to the sink and turned out the contents of the garbage pail underneath.

gash (gæʃ), *a.*[1] Since 16th c. only *Sc.* [? back-formation from GASHFUL *a.* or GASHLY *a.* (but recorded earlier than these).] Dismal in appearance.

1589 GREENE *Tullies Love* (1609) Fiij, His friends.. noting..his sodaine starts, his gash lookes and his abrupt answeres judged the extremitie of his sicknesse had [etc.]. **1590** *Cobler of Canterburie* 71 He looked wan and gash. *a* **1774** FERGUSON *Poems* (1785) 235 The day looks gash, toot off your horn, Nor care yae strae about the morn. **1824** SCOTT *Redgauntlet* Let. xi, His face looked as gash and ghastly as Satan's. **1861** RAMSAY *Remin.* Ser. II. 42 'What gars the laird of Garskadden luk sae gash?' 'Ou', says his neighbour..'Garskadden's been wi' his Maker these twa hours'. **1864** J. BROWN *John Leech*, etc. (1882) 1 The French nun..who was observed by her sisters to sit suddenly still and look very 'gash' (like the Laird of Garscadden).

gash (gæʃ), *a.*[2] *Sc.* [cf. GASH *sb.*[2] and *v.*[2]]

1. Talkative, loquacious.

1721 RAMSAY *Ode to the Ph——*. iv, It [claret] makes a man baith gash and bauld.

2. quasi-*adv.* Fluently, loquaciously.

1721 RAMSAY *Elegy P. Birnie* ii, To see his snowt, to hear him play And gab sae gash.

gash (gæʃ), *a.*[3] *Sc.* [Of obscure origin: perh. a corruption of *sagacious*, in Sc. pronunc. (sə'gɑʃəs).]

1. Sagacious, wise.

1706 in J. Watson *Collect. Poems* I. 69, I Wily, Witty was, and Gash, With my auld felni packy Pash. **1721** RAMSAY *Poems*, Gloss., *Gash*, solid, sagacious. **1786** BURNS *Twa Dogs* 29 He was a gash an' faithfu' tyke.

2. Having an air of wisdom, dignity, or self-importance.

1826 J. WILSON *Noct. Ambr.* Wks. 1855 I. 192 Hae I been sittin wi' specs all the afternoon? You have, James, and very gash you have looked. **1858** M. PORTEOUS *Souter Johnny* 11 He was a gash, wee fodgel body Stood on his shanks baith tight an' steady.

3. Well-dressed and dignified.

1785 BURNS *Holy Fair* 55 Here farmers gash, in ridin graith, Gaed hoddin by their cotters. *Ibid.* 208 In comes a gaucie, gash Guidwife. **1788** R. GALLOWAY *Poems* 111 And gash they thought such country-man.

4. In adverbial use: Trimly, neatly, so as to have a good appearance.

1806 A. DOUGLAS *Poems* 147 The saft o'en cakes, in mony stack, Are set in order rarely, Fu' gash this night.

gash (gæʃ), *a.*[4] *slang.* [Origin unknown; cf. GASH *sb.*[3]] Superfluous, extra, spare; free.

1945 [see GASH *sb.*[3]]. **1946** R. HARLING *Steep Atlantick Stream* vii. 190 You can grab an oilskin from the wardroom and there's a gash lifebelt there. **1967** G. HAMMOND *Mud in his Eye* vii. 82 I've always said the big one [*sc.* shed] was gash, and the harbour might as well have the rent. **1968** *Guardian* 15 June 8/2 Would he like to go to London, all expenses paid..? Of course he would; a good gash trip. **1971** M. RUSSELL *Deadline* ix. 103 Cop-shop's stuffed with gash CID apprentices.

gash (gæʃ), *v.*[1] Also 6 **gashe, gassh, gayshe.** [For earlier *garsh*, GARSE; cf. GASH *sb.*[1]]

1. *trans.* To cut, slash or wound (the body).

1570 LEVINS *Manip.* 35/8 To Gashe, *incidere*. **1633** HEYWOOD *Eng. Trav.* II. Wks. 1874 IV. 40 This murdered Ghost appeared His body gasht, and all ore-stucke with wounds. **1659** *Termes de la Ley* s.v. *Hambling*, The custome was..to cut or gash Dogs in the hammes. **1715–20** POPE *Iliad* IV. 617 Then sudden waved his flaming falchion round, And gash'd his belly with a ghastly wound. **1816** BYRON *Siege Cor.* xxxii, With barbarous blows they gash the dead. **1856** KANE *Arct. Expl.* I. xxiii. 296 After skinning the old one they gashed its body. **1878** BOSW. SMITH *Carthage* 30 His worshippers gashed and mutilated them-selves in their religious frenzy.

absol. *a* **1694** TILLOTSON *Serm.* Wks. 1728 I. ii. 34 Wit is a keen instrument, and every one can cut and gash with it; but to carve a beautiful image and to polish it requires great art and dexterity.

b. To cut or tear *asunder*. (*nonce-use.*)
1884 TENNYSON *Becket* I. i, O Herbert, here I gash myself asunder from the King, Tho' leaving each a wound.

2. To make a cut or deep slash in any material object. (Chiefly in pa. pple.)
1562 [see GASHING *vbl. sb.*]. **1577** tr. *Bullinger's Decades* (1592) 239 And to what ende doe wee iagge and gash the garmentes? **1847** DISRAELI *Tancred* v. ii, They filled the stomachs of the animals with lemons gashed with their daggers.
transf. **1872** C. KING *Mountain. Sierra Nev.* ix. 204 Afar to the west lay the rolling plateau gashed with cañons.

3. *intr.* To open in a gash. *rare*$^{-1}$.
c **1750** SHENSTONE *Eleg.* xxii. 67 To see my limbs the felon's gripe obey? To see them gash beneath the daring steel?

Hence **'gashing** *vbl. sb.* and *ppl. a.* Also **'gasher**, one who gashes or cuts. *rare*$^{-0}$.
1562 TURNER *Herbal* II. 84 There may be taken out of the stalke and roote both a iuice by gasshyng and an other by pressyng. **1598** FLORIO, *Incisore*,..a gasher, a lancer, a grauer or cutter. **1834** M. SCOTT *Cruise Midge* (1863) 109 The clear axe..fell twice in heavy gashing thumps. **1888** J. INGLIS *Tent Life in Tiger Land* x. 161 With swift cutting blows of the cruel, gashing tusks.

gash (gæʃ), *v.*[2] *Sc.* [Perh. f. *gash* projecting under-jaw; see GASH *sb.*[2] Cf. also GASH *a.*[2]] *intr.* To talk, converse, gossip.
a **1774** FERGUSSON *Poems* (1845) II. 104 The couthy cracks begin whan supper's owre, The cheering bicker gars them glibly gash. **1785** BURNS *Halloween* xi, She lea'es them gashin at their cracks, An' slips out by hersel.

Hence **'gashing** *ppl. a.*
1819 W. TENNANT *Papistry Storm'd* (1827) 12 Crail town was up wi' gashin' gabs; Wabsters, throu' zeal, forgat their wabs.

gashed (gæʃt), *ppl. a.* [f. GASH *v.*[1] + -ED.]
†**a.** Produced by gashing (*obs.*). **b.** Slashed or cut; having large rents or openings; *spec.* in *Bot.* (see quot. 1793); also ***gashed in.***
1578 LYTE *Dodoens* I. lxxiii. 109 The leaues be long, hearie, and grayish, snipt and cut rounde aboute, but nothing so much or so deepely gaysht, as the two others. **1605** SHAKS. *Macb.* II. iii. 119 His gash'd Stabs look'd like a Breach in Nature. **1641** MILTON *Animadv.* (1851) 194 Your dissever'd principles were but like the mangl'd pieces of a gash't Serpent. **1652** CULPEPPER *Eng. Physic.* 39 Those that follow are gashed in on both sides of the leaves. **1657** W. COLES *Adam in Eden* cvi. 149 With broad grayish tough leaves diversly folded, crumpled, and gashed in on the edges. **1793** MARTYN *Lang. Bot.*, *Gashed leaf* (*Folium incisum s. dissectum*), having the sections or divisions usually determinate in their number; or at least more so than in the Laciniate leaf. The Gashed differs from the Cleft leaf (*fissum*) in having the sections extending but little beyond the edge (though deeper than in the crenate leaf); whereas in the cleft leaf they reach almost to the middle. **1865** *Sat. Rev.* 21 Jan. 86/2 He would hang about butchers' stalls..waiting an opportunity to put his mouth to the gashed throats of animals. **1883** OUIDA *Wanda* I. 2 There were a few stunted willows near the house, and a few gashed pines.

'gashful, *a. Obs.* exc. *dial.* [? alteration of GHASTFUL, through association with GASH *sb.*[1]: cf. GASH *a.*[1] and GASHLY.] Ghastly.
1620 QUARLES *Feast Wormes* H ij, Prodigall up-banding of thine eyes, Whose gashfull balls doe seeme to pelt the skyes. **1621** —— *Argalus & P.* (1678) 4 His gashful countenance swarthy, long and thin. **1651** CULPEPPER *Astrol. Judgem. Dis.* (1658) 157 Signs of death by the eyes are..when they are very moveable, gashful, staring up and down or sunk deep in the head. **1654** GAYTON *Pleas. Notes* III. i. 69 Come death, and welcome: which spoke, comes in a gashfull, horrid, meagre, terrible, ugly shape. **1823** MOOR *Suffolk Wds.*, *Gashful*, ghastly—or as in Nares 'horrid, frightful'.

gash-gabbit, *a. Sc.* [f. *gash* (see GASH *sb.*[2]) + *gabbit* (f. GAB *sb.*[2]).] Having a projecting chin.
1721 RAMSAY *Poems* Gloss. s.v. *Gash*, One with a long out chin, we call gash-gabet, or gash beard. **1813** D. ANDERSON *Poems* 125 (Jam.), A' teethless and gash-gabbit The hags that night.

gashing, gashion: see GASH *sb.*[3]

'gashly, *a. Obs.* exc. *dial.* [? Altered form of GHASTLY: cf. GASHFUL.] Ghastly, horrid.
1633 P. FLETCHER *Purple Isl.* VII. xxxi, Next Pharmacus, of gashly wilde aspect; Whom hell with seeming fear, and fiends obey. **1650** FULLER *Pisgah* IV. vii. 131 Their warm and wanton embraces of living bodies, ill agreed with their offerings *Diis manibus*, to gashly Ghosts. **1675** OTWAY *Alcib.* 54 Now there grim death his gashly Revels keeps. **1765** STERNE *Tr. Shandy* VIII. xi, By all that is hirsute and gashly! I cry. **1880** MRS. PARR *Adam & Eve* xiii. (1881) 65 See 'em stare and then give a gashly look at mother.

b. in adverbial use.
1893 *Wiltsh. Gloss.*, s.v. *Ghastly*, 'Thick hedge wur gashly high, but it be ter'ble improved now.' **1897** C. LEE in *Leisure Ho.* Dec. 98/1 Her strange calm face, her gashly coloured tresses, her noiseless movements about the room.

Hence **'gashliness,** ghastliness, dismalness.
1848 DICKENS *Dombey* viii, The general dulness (gashliness was Mrs. Wickam's strong expression) of her present life.

'gashly, *adv. Sc.* [f. GASH *a.*[2] + -LY[2].] Fluently, loquaciously.
a **1774** FERGUSSON *A Drink Eclogue* Poems (1845) 50 And courtiers aft gaed greinin for my smack, To gar them bauldly glower and gashly crack.

gashy ('gæʃɪ), *a.* [f. GASH *sb.*[1] + -Y[1].] Of the nature of or resembling a gash; full of gashes.
1814 *Witness* II. iv, The dead man's ghost..with its clotted locks and gashy head. **1814** *Sorceress* II. ii, Raw and bloody like a gashy wound. *Mod.* (heard in Suffolk). 'I was careless with my sickle, and got a gashy place in my arm.'

gasifiable ('gæsɪˌfaɪəb(ə)l), *a.* [f. GASIFY *v.* + -ABLE.] That can be reduced to a gaseous state.
1880 *Nature* XXI. 8 But at present we know the molecular weights of gasifiable bodies only.

gasification (ˌgæsɪfɪ'keɪʃən). Also **gasefication, gassification.** [f. GAS *sb.*[1] + -(I)FICATION.] The process of converting into gas.
1812 R. SAUMAREZ *Princ. Physiol. Sc.* 188 The process of evaporation and of gassification. **1839** URE *Dict. Arts* 547 When the cooling agency of gasefication has become feeble. **1883** *Nature* XXVII. 292 The latent heat of gasification..of any body.
fig. **1824** J. MCCULLOCH *Scotl.* II. 190 Poetry has rarely been subjected to such chemistry as this without the gasification and loss of its essence.

gasifier ('gæsɪfaɪə(r)). [f. GASIFY *v.* + -ER[1].] Any apparatus for manufacturing gas (see also quot. 1959).
1883 J. W. INGHAM *Brit. Pat. 2339* p. 2 An apparatus which I designate a Gasifier consisting of retorts chambers or pipes maintained at an elevated temperature and containing what is known as Soda Lime. **1959** *Times Rev. Industry* Jan. 60/1 A gasifier consists..of a single cylinder containing a pair of opposed pistons which reciprocate freely without connecting rods or crankshaft. On the working stroke they compress air... The air compressed, together with the exhaust gases, provides a flow of medium temperature gas which is used to drive a gas turbine. **1961** *New Scientist* 22 June 728/3 Steam and oxygen at high pressure are introduced at the lower end of the gasifier.

gasiform ('gæsɪfɔːm), *a.* [f. GAS *sb.*[1] + -(I)FORM.] In a gaseous form or state.
1800 *Med. Jrnl.* IV. 556 Dr. Ackermann treats..of the different gasiform fluids contained in the intestines. *c* **1865** J. WYLDE in *Circ. Sc.* I. 6 The laws of air or gasiform bodies. **1869** E. A. PARKES *Pract. Hygiene* (ed. 3) 123 Ventilation is, in fact, the problem of the removal of the gasiform excreta of the lungs and skin.
fig. **1824** J. MCCULLOCH *Scotl.* II. 352 Druids thus become visionary and gasiform.

gasify ('gæsɪfaɪ), *v.* [f. GAS *sb.*[1] + -(I)FY.]
a. *trans.* To render gaseous; to produce gas from. **b.** *intr.* To become gaseous.
1828 WEBSTER, *Gasify*, to convert into gas or an aeriform fluid by combination with caloric. **1833** N. ARNOTT *Physics* (ed. 5) II. 13 An exceedingly subtile fluid or ether pervading the whole universe, and softening or melting or gasifying bodies. **1881** *Sci. Amer.* XLIV. 324 Liquid ammonia gasifies under considerable pressure at ordinary atmospheric temperatures.

gasiness, var. GASSINESS.

gasing(e, obs. form of GAZING.

gasket ('gæskɪt). Also 7 **casket(te, gassit,** 8 **gaskett.** [Of obscure origin; It. *gaschetta* has the same sense, but is believed to be from Eng.; F. *garcette* plait of rope, rope's end (for flogging) is in some Dicts. said to mean also 'gasket', but it has not been found earlier than the 19th c. With the early form *casket* cf. Sp. *cajeta.*]
1. A small rope or plaited cord, which secures a furled sail to the yard, being wrapped several times round both. Chiefly in *pl.*
1622 R. HAWKINS *Voy. S. Sea* (1847) 188 His sayles repayred and sufficiently prevented with martnets blayles and caskettes. **1626** CAPT. SMITH *Accid. Yng. Seamen* 15 There is also diuerse other small cordage, as head lines, the knaulings, gassits or furling lines. **1633** J. TAYLOR (Water P.) *Navy Landships* Wks. I. 81/1 Her Gaskets, Martlines, Cables. **1711** W. SUTHERLAND *Shipbuild. Assist.* 16 The Lines that are drawn cross the Yards are call'd Rope-bands; they make fast the Sail to the Yard, and Gaskets furl them. **1762** FALCONER *Shipwr.* II. 94 Along the sail the gaskets are convey'd. **1825** H. B. GASCOIGNE *Nav. Fame* 49 In haste the binding Gaskets they unfold But yet the canvass in their arms they hold. **1894** HALL CAINE *Manxman* III. x, Her rudder was unshipped, her sails were torn from their gaskets.
2. a. A strip of tow, plaited hemp, or other material, used for packing a piston or for caulking a joint.
1829 R. STUART *Anecd. Steam Eng.* I. 270 Screwing this plate down to the projecting rim, the packing (or gasket) between them was pressed outwards, so tightly as not to allow steam to pass. **1859** RANKINE *Steam Eng.* (1861) 129 Round the body of the piston is wrapped the packing, consisting either of loose hemp, or of a soft loosely spun hempen rope called gasket, soaked with grease.
b. A flat sheet or ring of some relatively soft material made to be placed between adjoining metal surfaces so as to seal the joint against the pressure of gas or liquid; *spec.* one inserted between the cylinder-head and the cylinder-block in an internal-combustion engine.
1903 R. J. MECREDY *Dict. Motoring* 123 *Gasket*, a packing washer of asbestos, rubber, or other material used to make liquid, steam, or air-tight joints. **1915** *Autocar Handbk.* (ed. 6) ii. 59 This head is held down by a number of bolts, and a copper and asbestos gasket is interposed, so that a gas and watertight joint is obtained. **1925** *Morris Owner's Man.* 34 The cylinder head lifted, showing the valves, ports, waterways and the gasket. **1946** KUNS & PLUMRIDGE *Automobile Engines* 46 The cylinder-head gasket, of course, is a specially prepared gasket in all cases, of copper, bronze, and asbestos. **1963** C. CAMPBELL *Sports Car Engine* xiii. 291 Solid copper gaskets should always be used on an engine used for racing. **1969** *Which?* Aug. 229/2 Replace rubber plugs and gaskets [in pressure cookers] if they show signs of age.
3. *attrib.*, as ***gasket-work.***
1831 JANE PORTER *Sir Seaward's Narr.* I. 124 A fathom of this gasket-work, being fastened end to end.
Hence **'gasket** *v. trans.*, to fasten up with gaskets.
1892 STEVENSON & L. OSBOURNE *Wrecker* xiii. 207 The sails were gasketed and covered..and the decks tidied down.

gaskin[1] ('gæskɪn). Forms: 6 **gaskyn, -kyng, -coine, -coigne, gayshekoon,** 6–7 **gascoyne,** 7 **gaskoine, gasskin, gasking,** 7–8 **-coin,** 8 **-coign,** 6–9 **gaskin.** [Of uncertain origin; perh. due to a false analysis of GALLIGASKIN, to which the 'gallant gaskins' of the first quot. comes close in point of sound. On the other hand, as Cotgrave explains F. *grègues* by 'wide slops, Gregs, Gallo-gascoines, Venetians; a great Gascon or Spanish hose', it seems possible that such hose were actually worn in Gascony; if so, this word may have been a special use of GASCON, and have existed earlier than *galligaskin*.]
†**1.** A kind of breech or hose. Chiefly *pl. Obs.*
1573 G. HARVEY *Letter-bk.* (Camden) 6 His oun gai gallant gaskins, his kut dublets, his staring hare. **1577** *Wills & Inv. N.C.* (Surtees 1835) 423, j pair of gayshekoones broken iij[s]. iv[d]. **1591** GARRARD *Art Warre* 18 A straite brabantie and gascoine is to be worne. **1600** DEKKER *Gentle Craft* Wks. 1873 I. 18 Goe thy wayes thought I, thou maist be much in my gaskins, but nought in my neather stockes. **1611** BEAUM. & FL. *Knt. Burn. Pestle* II. ii, The child's a father-lesse child, and say they should put him into a streight paire of Gaskins..he would neuer grow after it. **1755** JOHNSON, *Gaskins*, wide hose, wide breeches. An old ludicrous word.
†**b.** *attrib.*, as ***gaskin breeches, hose.*** *Obs.*
1591 PERCIVALL *Sp. Dict.*, *Çaraguelles*, gascoigne hose, *femoralia.* **1604** *Lismore Papers* Ser. II. (1887) I. 105 Sattine to make yor Dublett and gaskoine hose. **1623** MINSHEU *Sp. Dict.* s.v., Gascoigne breeches, or Venetian hosen ..*greguéscos.*
2. (See quot. 1726.)
1652 COTTERELL *Cassandra* III. (1676) 43 And thrust him back upon his gaskins. **1726** *Dict. Rust.* (ed. 3), *Gascoin*, the hinder Thigh of a Horse, which begins at the Stiffle, and reaches to the Ply or bending of the Ham. **1827** *Sporting Mag.* XX. 159 Good hind legs and well spread gaskins are very essential points in a coach horse.
transf. **1678** DRYDEN *Limberham* IV. i, One of my Daughters is big with Bastard, and she laid at her Gascoins most unmercifully! every stripe she had, I felt it.

gaskin[2] ('gæskɪn). *rare.* Also **gasking.** [Alteration of GASKET; the ending may represent -ING[1].] = GASKET (in both senses).
1831 TRELAWNEY *Adv. Younger Son* III. 170 Both of them lashed on the yard by the gaskins. **1860** *Ure's Dict. Arts* I. 328 R, cover for kier; the flanch on which this cover rests is grooved a little to admit of 'gasking' being inserted, so as to form a 'joint'. **1880** *G. Wightwick's Hints Yng. Archit.* (Weale) 221 Socketted pipes to be..jointed with clay, tarred gaskin or cement. **1883** STEVENSON *Treas. Isl.* III. xv, This extraordinary patchwork was all held together by..loops of tarry gaskin.

Gaskin, obs. form of GASCON.

gasless ('gæslɪs), *a.* [f. GAS *sb.*[1] + -LESS.] Destitute of gas; not lighted by gas.
1872 'MARK TWAIN' *Innoc. Abr.* xiii. 87 The gasless room. **1883** P. HOOD *Scot. Char.* ix. 162 The lass with the lantern, the constant attendant of every lady..who might happen in those gasless days to be out after nightfall. **1889** *Catholic News* 7 Sept. 4/4 Whisperings of gasless cities and revolution, still hover in the air.

'gas-light. Also **gaslight. a.** The light produced by the combustion of gas, usually coal-gas.
1808 MURDOCH in *Phil. Trans.* XCVIII. 126 The time during which the gas light is used, may..be stated at least at two hours per day. **1838** *Penny Cycl.* XI. 86/2 The great success which attended gas-light in London has extended itself throughout Great Britain. **1857** MRS. CARLYLE *Lett.* II. 334, I had not been able to read then, by the gas-light, which dazzles my eyes.
b. A jet of burning gas; chiefly *pl.*
1808 MURDOCH in *Phil. Trans.* XCVIII. 125 A..standard for determining the advantages to be expected from the use of the gas lights under favourable circumstances. **1815** ACCUM *Treat. Gas-Light* (ed. 2) 145 The Church of St. John the Evangelist..has been illuminated with gas-lights for upwards of two years. **1831** T. P. JONES *Convers. Chem.* xv. 160 Such is not the case with the gas lights. **1865** DICKENS *Mut. Fr.* III. i, Gaslights flared in the shops with a haggard and unblest air.
c. *attrib.*, as ***gas-light company, manufactory.*** **gaslight paper,** a photographic printing-paper sufficiently insensitive to be usable in weak artificial light, without the necessity for a dark-room.
1809 J. VAN VOORST (*title*) Address to the Proprietors of the intended Gas Light and Coke Company. **1826** SCOTT *Mal. Malagr.* ii. 63 It would be supposing the blessed sun himself jealous of a gas-light manufactory. **1906** R. C. BAYLEY *Compl. Photogr.* 243 Gaslight papers, as their name implies, are sufficiently insensitive to be worked in gaslight. **1963** JOHN & FIELD *Textbk. Photogr. Chem.* ii. 24 Contact

papers have long been known under the alternative name of 'gaslight' papers, since they can be handled cautiously in a weak domestic gas or electric light.

'gas-ˌman. Also **gasman.**

1. a. One who is engaged in manufacturing or supplying gas. **b.** A collector of sums due to a gas-company for gas supplied.

1821 [T. Hickman, the pugilist, who fought with Neat on 11 Dec. 1821, was called 'the Gas man' or 'the Gas-light man'. See P. Egan *Boxiana* (1828) New series I. 33, 42.] **1842** THACKERAY *Fitz-Boodle's Conf.* Pref., The first gas-man was ruined. **1889** *Spectator* 14 Dec. 829 The public are willing that the gasmen should suffer, if only they may keep cheap light. **1889** *Voice* (N.Y.) 14 Nov., He..bowed the astonished gas-man into the presence of the amazed family.

c. A workman who installs or repairs equipment for supplying household gas.

1873 A. T. RITCHIE *Let.* (1924) viii. 151 Two gas-men in one room, a carpenter in another. **1971** *Guardian* 21 June 9/5 The North Thames Gas Board..dump and collect meters in vans and other gasmen have to use bicycles.

2. a. One who attends to the gas-lights in a theatre.

1865 *Sat. Rev.* 21 Jan. 80/2 Probably the gasman of a London theatre is, as a rule, equally incautious. **1893** F. F. MOORE *Gray Eye or So* III. 197 The actors, the carpenters, the gasmen, the firemen.

†**b.** A man who lights gas-lamps in the street. *Obs.*

1849 THACKERAY *Pendennis* I. xxxix. 379 The gasman came and lighted the lamps before Sir Francis's door. **1854** M. CUMMINS *Lamplighter* 520 The gas-man came quickly up the street, lit, as by an electric torch, the bright burners. **1863** S. C. MASSETT *Drifting About* 50 The narrow and gloomy passage slightly illuminated by one or two jets of gas, which 'Tom the Gasman'..had a few moments before lighted.

3. *Coal-mining.* (*U.S.*) One who examines the workings for fire-damp.

1883 in GRESLEY *Gloss. Coal Mining.*

gasogene, var. GAZOGENE.

gasolene, gasoline ('gæsəliːn). Also **gasoleine, gazoline.** [f. GAS *sb.*[1] + -OL (as in BENZOL) + -ENE, -INE.] **a.** A volatile inflammable liquid, one of the first products in the distillation of crude petroleum, employed for purposes of heating and illumination. **b.** Now usu. = PETROL *sb.* 3 (chiefly *U.S.*).

1865 *Appleton's Ann. Cycl. 1864* 669/2 Many refiners [of petroleum] separate first of all the lightest naphtha..; to this the name of *gasolene* has been given. **1871** J. R. NICHOLS *Fireside Sc.* 50 Benzine, benzoline, gasoleine, kerosolene. **1883** *Century Mag.* July 338/1 No fewer than ten substances are obtained from petroleum by the refining process..2nd, gasolene, used in artificial gas machines. **1895** *New Rev.* Oct. 392 Of the petroleum vehicle..it may be said that it owes much of its extreme lightness to its modesty in the matter of fuel. A few pints of gasolene or rectified petroleum will suffice it for five or six hours. **1897** *Westm. Gaz.* 25 June 7/3 Her engines are 20-horse power, and are driven by gasoline. **1914** DUCHESS OF SUTHERLAND *Six Weeks at War* iii. 39 The Germans seemed to be doing the whole of this campaign on gasolene—that is to say, they use motor transport throughout. **1951** *Manch. Guardian Weekly* 15 Feb. 5 Gasolene, kerosene, and other petroleum products are smuggled out.

attrib. **1881** *Harper's Mag.* May 815/1 The street hawkers, with gasoline torches, are crying their wares. **1890** *Pall Mall G.* 30 June 6/3 Cooking breakfast over a gasoline stove. **1895** *New Rev.* Oct. 390 Thirteen [vehicles] were driven by petroleum (or gasolene) motors. **1895** *Daily News* 22 Nov. 2/2 Both [vehicles] used gasolene motors. **1896** *Cosmopolitan* XX. 420/2 The practicability of the gasolene road vehicle. **1908** *Westm. Gaz.* 4 Aug. 10/1 The winner became unconscious..through the gasolene fumes. **1926** *Daily Colonist* (Victoria, B.C.) 13 July 1/3 Albert..attended the gasoline station of Corfield Motors. **1959** K. DAVIS *Human Society* 627 A change from horse-powered to gasoline-powered vehicles.

gasometer (gæ'sɒmɪtə(r)). Also **gazometer.** [ad. F. *gazomètre*, f. *gaz* GAS *sb.*[1] + *mètre*, ad. Gr. *μέτρον* measure.]

1. *Chem.* (See quot. 1831.) In later use (on analogy of sense 2) a vessel for holding gas.

1790 KERR tr. *Lavoisier's Elem. Chem.* 308, I give the name of *gazometer* to an instrument which I invented..for the purpose of a kind of bellows, which might furnish an uniform and continued stream of oxygen gas in experiments of fusion. **1793** BEDDOES *Let. to Darwin* 41 A construction not very dissimilar to that employed in the gazometers of Mr. Lavoisier and Dr. Van Marum. **1831** T. P. JONES *Convers. Chem.* Gloss., *Gasometer*, an air holder, so constructed that the quantity of gas which it contains can be ascertained or measured. **1874** tr. *Lommel's Light* 6 Through the middle of this runs a..narrow tube, which..conducts oxygen from an adjoining gasometer.

2. A large tank or reservoir in which illuminating gas is stored, to be distributed thence by means of pipes.

1808 MURDOCH in *Phil. Trans.* XCVIII. 125 The gas..is conveyed by iron pipes into large reservoirs, or gazometers, where it is washed and purified. **1819** ACCUM *Descr. Manuf. Coal Gas* 164 The name of gas holder, or as it is improperly called, gasometer is given to the vessel employed for collecting the gas and storing it up for use. **1879** *Cassell's Techn. Educ.* II. 99/2 Lastly, the gasometer with its tank into which the gas is finally received in a purified state.

gasometry (gæ'sɒmɪtrɪ). Also 8 **gazometry.** [f. GAS *sb.*[1] + Gr. -*μετρία* measurement: see -METRY.] The science of measuring gases, or of estimating the quantity of different gases in a mixture.

1790 KERR tr. *Lavoisier's Elem. Chem.* 304 Of Gazometry, or the Measurement of the Weight and Volume of Aëriform Substances. **1869** *Eng. Mech.* 19 Nov. 234/1 To work out any problem..in quantitative gasometry.

So **gaso'metric** *a.*, relating to gasometry.

1866 BRANDE & COX *Dict. Sci.* etc. II. 15 *Gasometric Analysis*, Eudiometry, or the process of separating and estimating the individual constituents of a gaseous mixture.

gasoscope ('gæsəskəʊp). [f. GAS *sb.*[1] + Gr. -*σκόπος* observer: see -SCOPE.] (See quot.)

1858 SIMMONDS *Dict. Trade, Gasoscope*..an apparatus for indicating the presence of bicarburetted hydrogen gas in buildings, mines, &c.

gasp (gɑːsp, -æ-), *sb.* Also 6–7 **gaspe.** [f. GASP *v.*]

1. A convulsive catching of the breath from distress, exertion, or the lessening of vital action; also, as a result of surprise.

1586 WARNER *Alb. Eng.* IV. xxi[i]. (1589) 94 [He] shortly gaue a quiet gaspe or twaine. **1727–32** GAY *Fables* II. xvi. 53 Can those [hoards] prolong one gasp of breath, Or calm the troubled hour of death? **1810** SCOTT *Lady of L.* I. vii, While every gasp with sobs he drew, The labouring stag strained full in view. **1840** DICKENS *Old C. Shop* iv, The old lady gave a gasp. **1879** BROWNING *Ivan Ivanovitch* 67 Then followed gasps and sobs, and then the steady flow Of kindly tears.

b. esp. (*one's*) *last gasp*: the final attempt to draw breath before the departure of life. *at the last gasp*: at the point of death. Also *fig.*

1577 HANMER *Anc. Eccl. Hist.* 147 Retayning a valiant and inuincible minde vnto the last gaspe. **1602** MARSTON *Ant. & Mel.* I. Wks. 1856 I. 17 Tell her the spirit of Antonio Wisheth his last gaspe breath'd upon her breast. **1611** SHAKS. *Cymb.* I. v. 53 His Fortunes all lye speechlesse, and his name Is at last gaspe. **1655** SIR E. NICHOLAS in *N. Papers* (Camden) II. 338 At this instant he [Cromwell] is like one at yᵉ laste gaspe, full of convulsions, laying hould on what commes next him. **1736** BUTLER *Anal.* I. i. Wks. 1874 I. 29 In those diseases..[there may be] the highest mental enjoyments and sufferings, even to the last gasp. **1846** TRENCH *Mirac.* vi. (1862) 184 He left her at the last gasp; he knew not whether to regard her as alive or dead. **1851** HUSSEY *Papal Power* iii. 158 The authority of the Augusti breathed on that day its last gasp in Rome.

2. *transf.* in various occasional uses.

c **1611** CHAPMAN *Iliad* XXIII. 380 But straite, more cleare appear'd the streight, Antilochus foresaw, It was a gaspe the earth gaue, forc't, by humours, cold and raw. **1710** CONGREVE *On Mrs. A. Hunt, Singing* Wks. III. 875 Let..ev'ry ruder Gasp of Breath Be calm, as in the Arms of Death. **1795** AGNES MUSGRAVE *Cicely* I. 20 The wish to see our new sister occupied every thought, and engrossed every gasp of conversation 'till we reached Raby. **1853** KANE *Grinnell Exp.* xxxi. (1856) 268 Winds nearly at rest, with the exception of a little gasp from the westward.

gasp (gɑːsp, -æ-), *v.* Forms: 4 **gaysp**, 4–7 **gaspe**, 7– **gasp.** [a. ON. *geispa* to yawn (Sw. *gäspa*), by metathesis from **geip-sa*, cf. *geip* idle talk, *geipa* to talk idly. The weak grade of the root, found in Sw. dial. *gispa*, Da. *gispe*, appears also in Sw. *mungipa* corner of the mouth, OE. *ȝipung* open mouth, f. *ȝipian* to yawn (only in pr. pple *ȝypiȝend* 'hiulcus' = OLow Frankish *gipendi* 'patens'). The root **gap-* (see GAPE *v.*), whence Ger. dial. *gapsen* to gape for breath, belongs to a different vowel-series, but the sense of 'opening' is apparently common to both.]

1. *intr.* To catch the breath with open mouth, as from exhaustion (esp. in the death-struggle) or astonishment.

1390 GOWER *Conf.* II. 260 And thries on the water there She gaspeth with a drecchinge onde. ? *a* **1400** *Morte Arth.* 1462 Thare ware gomes thurghe-girde with grundyne wapynes, Grisely gayspande with grucchande lotes! **1583** STANYHURST *Æneis* II. (Arb.) 61 Whilst I beheld Priamus thus gasping. **1645–6** MILTON *Sonn.* xi, Those rugged names to our like mouthes grow sleek, That would have made Quintilian stare and gasp. **1794** MAD. D'ARBLAY *Lett.* Apr., I almost gasped with impatience and revived old feelings. **1813** SCOTT *Trierm.* II. xxv, Already gasping on the ground Lie twenty of the Table Round. **1848** RUSKIN *Mod. Paint.* II. III. II. iii. §2. 155 He has taken our breath away, and leaves us gasping.

fig. **1579** SPENSER *Sheph. Cal.* Nov. 126 The flouds do gaspe, for dryed is theyr sourse.

2. *to gasp for* (occas. *after*): to pant for (air); *fig.* to long for, to desire eagerly (cf. GAPE *v.*[4]).

c **1586** C'TESS PEMBROKE *Ps.* LXIII. i, O God..How gaspes my soule for thy refreshing taste! **1684** T. HOCKIN *Gods Decrees* 333 Future happiness..nature it self does incessantly gasp and breath after. **1697** DRYDEN *Virg. Georg.* IV. 375 The sick, for Air before the Portal gasp. **1711** ADDISON *Spect.* No. 198 ⁋5 Seeing how dearly they loved one another, and gasped after their Liberty. **1833** L. RITCHIE *Wand. by Loire* 9 The doors and windows, as we passed, were all open, gasping for air. **1844** MRS. BROWNING *Drama of Exile* Poems 1850 I. 59 And gasp for space amid the Infinite.

3. *trans.* and quasi-*trans.* To exhale (*occas.* also, to inhale) with convulsive breathings, esp. *to gasp one's last, to gasp* (*life*) *away*. Also *to gasp out*: to utter with gasps. †*to gasp up*: to give up (the ghost).

1534 SIR T. MORE *Cumfort agst. Tribulation* (1573) 42 And long was it not ere they gasped vp the goste. **1599** SHAKS. *Hen. V*, V. ii. 149, I cannot looke greenely, nor gaspe out my eloquence. **1653** BAXTER *Chr. Concord* 97 We have no other way to revive the hopes of the Churches, now they seem to be ready to gasp their last. **1697** DRYDEN *Æneid* IX. 558 He staggers round, his Eyeballs rowl in Death, And with short sobs he gasps away his Breath. **1791** COWPER *Iliad* IV. 621 He..lay gasping life away. **1849** MACAULAY *Hist. Eng.* I. iv. 501 The poor girl..gasped out, 'May God save him, if it be God's will!' **1856** KANE *Arct. Expl.* II. xi. 113, I soon found myself gasping the ammoniacal steam of some fourteen..fellow lodgers.

'gaspant, *a. nonce-wd.* A mock-heraldic term for 'gasping'.

1831 T. L. PEACOCK *Crotchet Castle* i. (1867) 12 Arms, three empty bladders, turgescent, to show how opinions are formed..three barbers' blocks, gaspant, to show how they are swallowed.

gasper ('gɑːspə(r), -æ-). [f. GASP *v.* + -ER[1].]

1. One who gasps (in various *nonce-uses*).

1868 DICKENS *Lett.* 3 Feb. (1882) III. 245 Charles Dickens..whose surprising performances..on..the American catarrh, have won for him the well-merited title of the Gad's Hill Gasper. **1877** BLACKIE *Wise Men* 16 He bade them fling The finny gaspers back into the brine Wholesale. **1884** *Contemp. Rev.* June 817 The agonies of feudalism had changed some of the trembling gaspers into greedy graspers.

2. A cigarette, esp. a cheap or inferior one. *slang.*

1914 *Isis* 14 Feb. 5/2 Not only does he prefer the Irish-grown 'gasper' to all others, but he provides them for his Saxon guest. **1916** *Punch* 11 Oct. 261 'D'yer fink Jellicoe gits 'is share?' 'Course not, stoopid. Admirals don't smoke gaspers!' **1921** S. P. B. MAIS *Why we should Read* 32 Why should one prefer a Corona cigar to a 'gasper'? **1965** *Listener* 21 Oct. 624/3 'Gasper' commercials are with us still at every peak viewing hour.

gaspereau ('gæspərəʊ, gæspə'rəʊ). *Canad.* Also **gaspereaux, gasperot.** [Canadian F. *gaspareau, gasparot.*] = ALE-WIFE[2].

1703 tr. *Lahontan's New Voy. N. Amer.* I. 243 Gasperots, a small Fish like a Herring. **1890** in WEBSTER. **1912** *Sea Fisheries E. Canada* (*Commission of Conservation*) 105 The gaspereaux..is mostly used as a bait fish. **1938** *Nature* 5 Mar. 421/1 The gaspereau (Pomolobus pseudoharengus) spawns in the spring.

gaspergou (gæspə'guː). *local U.S.* Also **gaspar-goo, gaspergoo.** [f. Louisiana Fr. *casseburgau*, f. *casser* to break + *burgau* a species of shellfish.] The freshwater drum-fish, *Aplodinotus grunniens.*

1809 F. CUMING in R. G. Thwaites *Early Western Trav.* (1904) IV. li. 330 A fine dish of gaspar-goo, the best fish I had yet tasted of the produce of the Mississippi. **1831** W. B. DEWEES *Lett. fr. Texas* (1852) xv. 137 Up the country our rivers abound with various kinds of fish, such as cat, buffalo, perch and gaspergoos. **1947** B. W. DALRYMPLE *Panfish* 344 For years they've been catching Sheepshead and Gaspergou.

gasping ('gɑːspɪŋ, -æ-), *vbl. sb.* [f. GASP *v.* + -ING[1].] The action of the verb GASP, in various senses.

c **1440** *Promp. Parv.* 188/1 Gaspynge, *idem quod* Gapynge. **1494** FABYAN *Chron.* VII. 355 Then was the felde coueryd with deed bodyes, and gaspynge and gronynge was herde on euery syde. **1513** DOUGLAS *Æneis* VI. viii. 36 Thair clamour was full scant, The soundis brak with gasping or a gant. **1561** T. NORTON *Calvin's Inst.* IV. xviii. (1634) 705 This also Christ signified by his last saying and uttered among his last gaspings. *a* **1652** J. SMITH *Sel. Disc.* iv. 109 Those breathings and gaspings after an eternal participation of him are but the energy of his own breath within us. **1742** RICHARDSON *Pamela* IV. 256 To attend the dear Baby him-self—to see his last Gaspings, poor little Lamb. **1812** CRABBE *Tales in Verse, Confidant* 210 Some youthful gaspings for forbidden fruit. **1843** CARLYLE *Past & P.* IV. iii. Inarticulate gaspings.

attrib. **1802** T. BEDDOES *Hygëia* viii. 123 Those gasping-fits, which come on with greater and greater violence.

gasping ('gɑːspɪŋ, -æ-), *ppl. a.* [f. GASP *v.* + -ING[2].] That gasps, in various senses of the vb.

1509 HAWES *Past. Pleas.* I. xiii, At the last with a gaspyng nette Slouth my head caught with his whole purpose. **1579** SPENSER *Sheph. Cal.* Apr. 6 Quenching the gasping furrowes thirst with rayne. **1603** DEKKER *Wonderfull Yeare* B iij, In such a panting time, and gasping yeare, Victuals are cheapest, only men are deare. **1681** BAXTER *Apol. Nonconf. Min.* 1 Before the expiring of my gasping hopes. **1738** WESLEY *Ps.* XIII. v, Save, or my gasping Spirit dies. **1835** BROWNING *Paracelsus* 126 This arch-knave..dogs me As a gaunt crow a gasping sheep.

Hence **'gaspingly** *adv.*, in a gasping manner.

1816 BYRON *Prisoner of Chillon* xi, My breath came gaspingly and thick. **1834** *Fraser's Mag.* X. 111 The gills..are dilated gaspingly. **1879** 'ANNIE THOMAS' *Lond. Season* II. 214 Bertram and Daisy..gaspingly force a passage through the crowd.

'gas-ˌplant.

1. A name given to the plant *Dictamnus Fraxinella.*

In recent U.S. Dicts.

['It is said that the atmosphere surrounding this plant is in hot dry weather inflammable' (Lindley, *School Bot.*, ed. 1845, p. 49).]

2. The apparatus employed in the manufacture and supply of illuminating gas.

1889 in *Cent. Dict.*

gas-proof ('gæspruːf), *a.* [f. GAS *sb.*[1] + PROOF *a.* 1 b.] Impervious to poisonous gas.

1909 *Westm. Gaz.* 17 Feb. 7/2 Experts in the use of gas-proof apparatus. **1939** W. H. DAVIES *Loneliest Mountain* 17 Is it the Baby, three weeks old, That wears a gas-proof mask?

Hence as *v. trans.*, to render gas-proof; so **gas-proofed** *ppl. a.*, **gas-proofing** *vbl. sb.*

1936 *Lancet* 19 Dec. 1466/2 The [first-aid] posts would be structurally protected as far as possible and should certainly be gas-proofed. **1938** *Times* 11 Jan. 13/6 Will the materials be ready for gas-proofing rooms? *Ibid.* 12 Jan. 12/1 Southampton has a model gas-proofed house on a new estate. *Ibid.* 10 Mar. 15/4 A sudden interest in the gas-proofing of rooms.

gaspy (ˈgɑːspɪ, -æ-), *a. rare.* [f. GASP *sb.* + -Y¹.] Having a tendency to gasp.

1879 G. MEREDITH *Egoist* I. xiv. 255 The august great robes back-flowing and foaming over the gaspy page-boys.

Hence ˈ**gaspiness** (in quot. *fig.*).

1892 *Spectator* 9 Jan. 48 Gaspiness is one of the worst flaws in most English Hymns.

Gasquine, gass, obs. forms of GASCON, GAS.

gassampine, var. GOSSAMPINE.

gassed (gæst), *ppl. a.* [f. GAS *v.* 4.] **1.** Affected by poisonous gas.

1915 *Morn. Post* 29 May 7/7 The death of the gassed victims around Ypres. **1918** E. M. ROBERTS *Flying Fighter* 28 Several thousands of other wounded and gassed men followed us.

2. Drunk; intoxicated. *slang.*

1925 FRASER & GIBBONS *Soldier & Sailor Words* 103 *Gassed*, drunk. **1956** WALLIS & BLAIR *Thunder Above* (1959) xiii. 136 He's getting gassed already. We'd better steer him out of here. **1960** *Daily Mail* 22 Aug. 4/6 When I'm with people I laugh so much..they figure I'm 'gassed'. But I'm not. I don't drink.

Gassendist (gæˈsɛndɪst). [f. *Gassendi* + -IST. Cf. F. *Gassendiste.*] A follower of Gassendi, a French metaphysician, born 1592.

1821 D. STEWART *Diss. Prog. Philos.* II. §1 Wks. 1854 I. 230 *note*, [The word Reflection] expresses the peculiar.. doctrine by which his [Locke's] system is distinguished from that of the Gassendists and Hobbists. *a* **1834** COLERIDGE *Notes Eng. Divines* (1853) I. 280 Taylor was a Gassendist.

gasser (ˈgæsə(r)). [f. GAS *v.*¹ (sense 2) + -ER¹.]

1. (See quot.)

1892 *Labour Commission* Gloss., *Gassers*, those who work at the gassing machines.

2. = GAS *sb.*¹ 5 d. *slang* (orig. *U.S.*).

1944 C. CALLOWAY *Hepsters Dict.* 7. **1945** L. SHELLY *Jive Talk Dict.* 11 *Gasser*, show-stopper. **1955** L. FEATHER *Encycl. Jazz* 11, I wrote a piece of music for this scene... It was a gasser; real great, I confess it. **1962** *Radio Times* 17 May 43/3 Should he [*sc.* a jazz musician] 'blow' with feeling, or great excitement..he is..considered by one and all to be a 'gasser'. **1970** *Sunday Truth* (Brisbane) 26 Apr. 14/2 (*heading*) Ron's Friday night show was a gasser.

Gasserian (gæˈsɪərɪən), *a.* [Named by Hirsch in 1765, after his teacher Johann Laurentius *Gasser*: see -IAN.] ***Gasserian ganglion***, the ganglion on the sensory trunk of the fifth cranial nerve. See also CASSERIAN *a.*

1831 R. KNOX *Cloquet's Anat.* 461 The superior maxillary nerve arises from the middle part of the Gasserian ganglion. **1881** MIVART *Cat* 272 The larger root swells out into what is called the Gasserian ganglion.

gassiness (ˈgæsɪnɪs). *rare.* [f. GASSY + -NESS.] **a.** The state of being pervaded by gas. **b.** The possession of gaseous qualities.

1883 MABEL COLLINS *H. Modjeska* iii. 46 The theatre. Its stuffiness, its gassiness, all the abominations common to such buildings. **1888** *Cornh. Mag.* Jan. 37 Gas of such an.. unimaginable gasiness [*sic*] that millions of cubic miles of it might easily be compressed into a..pill-box.

gassit, obs. form of GASKET.

gassy (ˈgæsɪ), *a.* [f. GAS *sb.*¹ + -Y¹.]

1. Abounding in gas; of the nature of gas.

1757 tr. *Henckel's Pyritol.* 160 The volatile spirit will.. smell extremely quick, pungent and gassy. **1842** *Blackw. Mag.* LI. 173 A clear, gassy, sea-coal fire, puffing and fizzing in smiling welcome. **1878** F. FERGUSON *Pop. Life Christ* xviii. 174 The gassy spring at Kissingen begins to bubble up at about the same time every day. **1891** G. MEREDITH *One of our Conq.* III. xiii. 290 The gassy passages of the back of the theatre.

2. *slang.* Characterized by 'gas' or empty talk; given to 'gassing'.

1863 B. TAYLOR *H. Thurston* I. 139 Woodbury..was amused at the remarks of the crowd: 'He?—oh, he's a gassy old fellow'. **1875** WHITNEY *Life Lang.* ii. 17 As when we call an empty and sophistical but ready talker 'gassy'. **1892** LD. ROSEBERY in *Daily News* 24 June 5/8 The last development of the Irish question was a gassy meeting in St. James's Hall the previous night.

gast (gæst), *sb. Sc.* [f. GAST *v.*¹] A fright.

[Cf. quot. 1420 under GAST *ppl. a.*] *a* **1684** R. LAW *Mem.* (1818) 220 The woman in a gast..comes and tells her lady who had stollen her things. **1873** W. ALEXANDER *Johnny Gibb* (ed. 3) 96 'Aw never got sic a gast's aw got the nicht.'

gast (gæst), *a. dial.* [app. cognate with GEASON; cf. MDu. *gâst, gêst* (Du. *geest*), barren soil, GEEST.] (See quots. *a* 1825 and 1895.)

1729 *Corton Parish* (Suffolk) *Terrier*, Every Gast Beast, i.e. for every Heifer or young Steer. **1760** *Ibid.*, Barren or gast cattle. *a* **1825** FORBY *Voc. E. Anglia*, *Gast* or *Ghast-Cow*, a cow which does not produce a calf in the season. **1895** *E. Anglian Gloss.*, *Gast*..Also applied to mares.

†**gast,** *v.*¹ *Obs.* Forms: 1 gǽstan, 4 gaast, 6 ghast, 4–7 gast(e. [OE. *gǽstan* (only once):—OTeut. type **gaistjan*, app. cogn. w. Goth. *usgaisjan* to terrify, *usgeisnan* to be terrified. See GHOST.]

trans. To frighten, alarm, scare, terrify.

(In quot. *c* 1000 the sense seems to be rather 'to torture' or 'to destroy'.)

c **1000** *Juliana* 17 in *Exeter Bk.*, Hi..gæston godes cempan gare and lige. **1362** LANGL. *P. Pl.* A. VII. 129 To..Gaste crowen from his corn. **1382** WYCLIF *2 Kings* xxii. 19 Thi herte is gaastyde. **1412–20** LYDG. *Chron. Troy* I. v, And gasten men with sodeyn erth quaue. **1422** tr. *Secreta Secret.*, *Priv. Priv.* (E.E.T.S.) 215 Thou shalte haue many rynnynge engyns to make horribill Sownes to gasten thyn enemys. **1530** PALSGR. 560/2, I gaste hym as sore as he was these twelve monethes. **1592** STOW *Ann.* an. 1586. 1228 These men..were..so ghasted with feare..that they looked rather like to ghostes than men. **1605** SHAKS. *Lear* II. i. 57 Or whether gasted by the noyse I made, Full sodainely he fled. **1616** J. LANE *Cont. Sqr.'s T.* ix. 413 *note*, So Pirrus lookes in Argos gastes his ffoes.

†**gast,** *v.*² *Obs.* [? ad. OF. *gaster, guaster, waster*: see WASTE *v.* (But cf. quot. *c.* 1000 in prec.)] *trans.* ? To ruin, spoil.

a **1310** in Wright *Lyric P.* xxxi. 90 Whet helpeth the, my suete lemmon, my lyf thus forte gaste?

†**gast,** *ppl. a.* [pa. pple. of GAST *v.*¹] Terrified, afraid. ***for gast***: for fear.

13.. *Gaw. & Gr. Knt.* 325, I know no gome þat is gast of þy grete wordes. *c* **1340** *Cursor M.* 5814 (Trin.) He was gast So ferde þat he to fle bigon. **1382** WYCLIF *Jer.* viii. 9 Confoundid ben the wise men, gast and caȝt thei ben. *c* **1420** *Chron. Vilod.* 777 He durst not meve hurrself for gast. *Ibid.* 1006 When þuse ladyes weron areson up to han ygon.. Towarde herre chambers for gast every chon. **1500–20** DUNBAR *Poems* lxxiv. 19 Me think my spireit rynnis away full gast. **1575** *Mirr. Mag.*, *Nennius* xxxii, Thou neuer wast in all thy life so gast, Nor durst againe be euer halfe so bold.

gast, obs. form of GHOST.

gastaldite (gæˈstældaɪt). *Min.* [Named by Strüver in 1875 after Prof. B. *Gastaldi*: see -ITE.] A variety of glaucophane.

1882 DANA *Min.* App. iii. 52 A mineral closely related to glaucophane is called gastaldite.

gasteli, obs. form of GHOSTLY.

†ˈ**gaster,** *v. Obs.* [app. a frequentative f. GAST *v.*¹ (? and *v.*²): see -ER⁵.

Sense 2 may be a distinct word, a. F. *gaster* (infinitive) to waste, spoil (mod.F. *gâter*).]

1. *trans.* To frighten, scare, terrify.

1593 G. GIFFARD *Dial. Witches* E ij b, If they run at him with a spit red hot, they gaster him so sore, that his dame shal go her self, if she will, he will come no more there. **1614** BEAUM. & FL. *Wit at Sev. Weapons* II. iii, Either the sight of the Lady has gaster'd him or else he's drunk. **1675** BROOKS *Gold. Key* Wks. 1867 V. 92 He begun to be gastred with wonderful astonishment. **1721–1800** BAILEY, *Gastred*, frightened, astonished. **1787** GROSE *Prov. Gloss.*, *Gaster*, to startle, scare, or affright suddenly.

2. To destroy.

1609 BP. W. BARLOW *Answ. Nameless Cath.* 191 His Breue euen then gastring his Maiesties title and debarring his right. *Ibid.* 264 The best works haue attending on them two wormes, which gaster and infect the goodnes of them.

Hence **gastered** *ppl. a.*, ˈ**gastering** *vbl. sb.*

1642 ROGERS *Naaman* 138 That she might at last be wholly quit of all such callings upon, and gasterings. **1644** QUARLES *Sheph. Orac.* v, Feare not, said he, I come not to affright Thy gastered soule with terrours of the night.

gasteral (ˈgæstərəl), *a. jocular.* Also **gastral**. [f. Gr. γαστ(ε)ρ-, γαστήρ stomach + -AL¹.] Of or pertaining to the stomach.

1828 *Harrovian* 15 To recreate the gastral powers with the odorous sacrifice offered up on P——'s polished round table. **1854** *Chamb. Jrnl.* I. 178 One..represented Silenus with most extravagant gasteral development.

gasteromycetous (ˌgæstərəʊmaɪˈsiːtəs), *a. Bot.* [f. mod.L. *gasteromycēt-es* (f. Gr. γαστερ(ο)-, γαστήρ stomach + μύκητες pl. of μύκης fungus) + -OUS.] Of, belonging to, or relating to the *Gasteromycetes*, one of the orders of Fungi.

1861 BENTLEY *Man. Bot.* 387 Gasteromycetous Fungi. **1889** BENNETT & MURRAY *Cryptog. Bot.* 319 Gasteromycetous Lichens.

gasteropod, gastropod (ˈgæstərəpɒd, ˈgæstrəpɒd), *sb.* and *a.* Also 9 -pode. [ad. mod.L. *gasteropoda, gastropoda* neut. pl.: see next.]

A. *sb.* An animal of the *Gasteropoda* class or group of molluscs.

1826 KIRBY & SP. *Entomol.* IV. xlv. 235 Several Gasteropods can neither hear nor see. **1841** DOUGLAS in *Proc. Berw. Nat. Club* I. No. 9. 244 The most beautiful naked gasteropode we have seen. **1851–6** WOODWARD *Mollusca* 97 The gasteropods, including land-snails, sea-snails, whelks, limpets, and the like, are the types of the mollusca.

transf. **1854** OWEN *Skel. & Teeth* in *Circ. Sc.*, *Organ. Nat.* I. 231 They [seals] may be called 'gastropods,' in respect of their..mode of progression.

B. *adj.* Gasteropodous.

1836–9 TODD *Cycl. Anat.* II. 386/1 The Gasteropod Mollusca. **1850** JOHNSTON *Conchol.* 118 The small Gasteropod order which Cuvier has called Heteropods, are [etc.].

‖**gasteropoda, gastropoda** (gæstəˈrɒpədə, gæˈstrɒpədə), *sb. pl. Zool.* [mod.L., f. Gr. γαστ(ε)ρ(ο)-, γαστήρ stomach, + ποδ-, πούς foot.]

A class or group of molluscs (including the snails, limpets, etc.), so called from the ventral position of the locomotive organ.

1828 J. STARK *Nat. Hist.* II. 59 M. Cuvier has given the name of *Gasteropoda* to all the animals of this class which have a foot or muscular disc proper for crawling. **1851–6** WOODWARD *Mollusca* ii. 7 In the gasteropoda, or snails, the under side of the body forms a single muscular foot. **1878** BELL *Gegenbaur's Comp. Anat.* 319 These relations are different in the Gastropoda.

Hence **gast(e)ˈropodan** *a.* and *sb.* = GASTEROPOD; **gasteˈropodic** *a.* = next.

1876 F. HARRISON *Choice Bks.* (1886) 123 Your argument ..done into gasteropodic prose, is simply that the human kind have utterly gone backward since the statue was carved.

gasteropodous (gæstəˈrɒpədəs), *a.* Also **gastropodous.** [f. GASTEROPOD-A + -OUS.]

Belonging to the *Gasteropoda*; pertaining to or characteristic of a gasteropod.

1822–34 *Good's Study Med.* (ed. 4) I. 10 In the snail and some other gasteropodous mollusca. **1858** GEIKIE *Hist. Boulder* vi. 108 Among the higher gastropodous molluscs. **1872** W. S. SYMONDS *Rec. Rocks* vi. 182 Fossils are numerous, the gasteropodous shells occurring frequently. *jocular.* **1864** *Reader* 18 June, The Gasteropodous order of rifleman, who..go perpetually on their stomachs.

gastful: see GHASTFUL.

‖**gasthaus** (ˈgasthaʊs). Also **Gasthaus.** [G., = GUEST HOUSE.] A small German inn or hotel.

1834 F. B. HEAD *Bubbles from Brunnens* 254 At one of these solemn villages the postilion stopped at a 'gast-haus' to bait his horses. **1841** *Fraser's Mag.* June 710/1 If he has dined at an inn or restaurant, gasthaus, posada, albergo, or what not, [he] invariably inserts into his log-book the bill of fare. **1874** R. H. BUSK *Tirol* 86 Its principal inn..claims to be not merely a *Gasthaus*, but a *Gasthof*. **1936** R. LEHMANN *Weather in Streets* II. 252 Stopping in the evening at a small gasthaus. **1969** *Daily Tel.* 13 June 16/7 Most Europeans.. have always drunk in places which offer fairly broadly-based catering services, like the café or *gasthaus*.

‖**gasthof** (ˈgasthoːf). Also **Gasthof.** [G., f. *gast* guest + *hof* hotel, large house.] A German hotel (usu. a larger establishment than a GASTHAUS).

1832 J. H. STOCQUELER *15 Months' Pilgr. Khuzistan* II. iv. 106 A spacious gasthof, or public house. **1865** 'OUIDA' *Strathmore* v, A Bohemian Gasthof is about the only place.. where you see the doctrine of equality in absolute..practice. **1874** [see prec.]. **1960** B. K. WILSON *Lovely Summer* ix. 107 Time to stop at a wayside *Gasthof* for delicious hot chocolate topped with cream. **1969** A. GLYN *Dragon Variation* viii. 228 The boy and the rest of the British team were in a gasthof near the university, students' rooms.

gastlet. *Obs. rare.* [a. F. *gastelet* 'a little cake; also the name of an excellent Cyder-apple' (Cotgr.), dim. of *gasteau* (now *gâteau*) cake.] A kind of apple.

1600 SURFLET *Country Farme* III. xlix. 528 Such [apples] are those that followe, the heroet..fairewife, gastlet.

gastly, obs. form of GHASTLY, GHOSTLY.

†ˈ**gastness.** *Obs.* [f. GAST *ppl. a.* + -NESS.] Terrified condition or appearance; terror, dread.

c **1374** CHAUCER *Boeth.* III. pr. v. 59 (Camb. MS.) A tyraunt..shewede by symylytude the dredes of Reaumes by gastnesse of a swerd þat heng ouer the heued of hys famyler. **1382** WYCLIF *Josh.* ii. 9 ȝoure gastnes is faln into vs. —— *1 Sam.* xxxi. 4 And his squier wolde not; forsothe he was agaist with to mych gaistnes. *a* **1420** HOCCLEVE *De Reg. Princ.* 20 And of the brotilnesse of hir nature My tremlyng hert so grete gastnesse hadde, That [etc.]. **1604** SHAKS. *Oth.* v. i. 106 Looke you pale, Mistris? Do you perceiue the gastnesse of her eye. **1721** BAILEY, *Gasteness*, terror, dread.

‖**gastræa** (gæˈstriːə). [mod.L., f. Gr. γαστ(ε)ρ-, γαστήρ belly.]

1. = GASTRULA.

1877 HUXLEY *Anat. Inv. Anim.* i. 50 In the Porifera the terminal aperture of the gastræa becomes the egestive opening of the adult animal.

2. A primitive sac-like animal, whose existence is assumed by Haeckel, consisting of two layers of cells, an ectoderm and an endoderm. ***gastræa theory***, the theory which supposes this to have been the ancestral form of the whole animal kingdom.

1879 tr. *Haeckel's Evol. Man* I. 9 A very ancient ancestral form is represented by the two-layered Gastræa. *Ibid.* 250 These are the principles of the unified or monophyletic genealogy of the animal kingdom, as they present themselves, provisionally, according to the Gastræa Theory. **1892** *Nation* (N.Y.) 21 Apr. 309/2 The author is thoroughly permeated by the gastraea myth.

gastræad (ˈgæstriːæd). [ad. mod.L. *gastræad-es*, pl. form of prec.] One of the *Gastræades*, a division of sponges whose development does not go beyond that of a gastrula.

In recent Dicts.

gastral, var. GASTERAL.

‖**gastralgia** (gæˈstrældʒɪə). *Path.* [mod.L., f. Gr. γαστ(ε)ρ-, γαστήρ stomach + ἄλγος pain.] Pain in the stomach, *esp.* neuralgia of the stomach.

1822–34 [see GASTRODYNIA]. **1836** J. GULLY *Magis. Formul.* 87, I have given it [prussic acid] with the best effects in gastralgia. **1867** O. W. HOLMES *Guard. Angel* xxv. (1891) 296 Some lozenges for gastralgia. **1884** *Sat. Rev.* 7 June 741/1 A..state of political babyhood and political gastralgia.

Hence **gaˈstralgic** *a.*, pertaining to, affected with, or liable to gastralgia; also *sb.*, one who is subject to gastralgia.

1892 *Harper's Mag.* Nov. 862/2 Portly and gastralgic papas. **1897** ALLBUTT *Syst. Med.* III. 476 Gastralgics are also liable to asthma. *Ibid.* 477 Pains of gastralgic character.

gastrectomy (gæˈstrɛktəmɪ). [f. Gr. γαστ(ε)ρ-, γαστήρ stomach + ἐκτομή (n. of action f. ἐκτέμνειν to cut out) + -Y^3.] 'The removal of a part of the stomach, as the pylorus, in cancer of the organ' (*Syd. Soc. Lex.* 1885).

1886 *Braithwaite's Med. Retrospect.* XCII. 40 Duodenostomy, gastrostomy for the passage of a tube, and complete gastrectomy, should all be replaced by gastro-enterostomy.

gastric (ˈgæstrɪk), *a.* [f. Gr. γαστ(ε)ρ-, γαστήρ stomach + -IC.] **a.** Of or pertaining to the stomach; situated in, performed by or in, the stomach; of the nature of a stomach. ***gastric fever***, a term somewhat loosely employed, but now usually signifying enteric or typhoid fever. ***gastric patient*** (rare): one suffering from gastric diseases.

1656 BLOUNT *Glossogr.* s.v. *Vein, Gastrick vein*, the belly veine; a branch of the Port veine, from which it descends to the hallow part and backside of the ventricle. **1727–51** CHAMBERS *Cycl.*, *Gastric*..in anatomy, is applied to divers veins on account of their proceeding from the stomach. **1796** DUNCAN *Ann. Med.* I. 68 The author saw evidently gastric patients sinking under a load of the Peruvian bark. **1802** *Med. Jrnl.* VIII. 436 Symptoms that widely differ from those which are to be observed in gastric fevers. **1822–34** *Good's Study Med.* (ed. 4) I. 633 [Mild remittent fever] is..called by Professor Frank..gastric fever. **1830** R. KNOX *Béclard's Anat.* 12 In other animals..the gastric cavity has prolongations which extend into the mass of the body. **1834** McMURTRIE *Cuvier's Anim. Kingd.* 458 The domicile of the larvæ is of three kinds..cutaneous, cervical, and gastric. **1842** E. WILSON *Anat. Vade M.* 302 The Gastric Artery ascends between the two layers of the lesser omentum to the cardiac orifice of the stomach. **1850** *Fraser's Mag.* XLII. 540 They..have left on record gastric achievements to be envied by aldermen of the most giant appetite. **1854** CARPENTER *Princ. Phys., Gen. & Compar.* iii. 163 The great purpose of the gastric digestion appears to be, to dissolve the albuminous and gelatinous constituents of the food. **1872** BAKER *Nile Tribut.* viii. 106 My wife was prostrated by a severe attack of gastric fever. **1876** tr. *Wagner's Gen. Pathol.* 13 Gastric catarrh. **1877** HUXLEY *Anat. Inv. Anim.* iii. 152 The oral aperture of an Actinozoon leads into a sac, which, without prejudice to the question of its exact function, may be termed 'gastric'.

b. ***gastric juice*** (formerly also ***gastric acid, liquor***): thin, clear, almost colourless fluid, of an acid nature, secreted by certain glands in the stomach, where it is the chief agent in the process of digestion.

1730–6 BAILEY (folio), *Gastrick juice.* **1753** CHAMBERS *Cycl. Supp.*, *Bulimy*..is a disorder of the stomach seated in the fibres thereof, or in the gastric liquor. **1794–6** E. DARWIN *Zoon.* (1801) I. 439 There is at the same time a deficiency of gastric acid. **1799** *Med. Jrnl.* II. 79 The gastric juice of these birds. **1821** BYRON *Juan* v. xxxii, Intellects, whose use Depends so much upon the gastric juice. **1845** G. E. DAY tr. *Simon's Anim. Chem.* I. 85 Acetic acid has been found..in the gastric juice. **1889** M. FOSTER *Text-bk. Phys.* II. (ed. 5) 365 The essential property of gastric juice is the power of dissolving proteid matters.

c. ***gastric mill***, a framework consisting of movable calcareous or chitinous plates in the stomach of certain crustacea.

1897 PARKER & HASWELL *Text-bk. Zool.* I. 547 A gastric mill is present in Malacostraca. **1927** HALDANE & HUXLEY *Anim. Biol.* i. 7 Gastric mill, with grinding teeth and straining apparatus. **1967** *Oceanogr. & Marine Biol.* xv. 377 The masticatory apparatus or gastric mill.

gastricism (ˈgæstrɪsɪz(ə)m). [f. prec. + -ISM.] **1.** 'Stomach diseases generally' (*Syd. Soc. Lex.*).

1796 DUNCAN *Ann. Med.* I. 67 But now nothing is seen or heard of the use of neutral salts or resolvents, with a view to gastricism, or to prepare for evacuants.

2. (See quot. 1842.)

1842 DUNGLISON *Dict. Med.*, *Gastricism*, a name, by which is designated the medical theory, that refers all, or almost all, diseases to an accumulation of saburræ in the digestive passages.

gaˈstricity. ? *Obs. rare.* [f. GASTRIC *a.* + -ITY. So F. *gastricité.*] A state of gastric disturbance.

1796 DUNCAN *Ann. Med.* I. 69 But sometimes the author saw with astonishment the bark overcome the gastricity. **1885** in *Syd. Soc. Lex.*

gastriloquist (gæˈstrɪləkwɪst). [formed after the analogy of *ventriloquist*, replacing *ventri-* by *gastri-*, a combining form of Gk. γαστ(ε)ρ-, γαστήρ.] = VENTRILOQUIST. So **gastriˈloquial** *a.*, **gaˈstriloquism, gaˈstriloquous** *a.*, **gaˈstriloquy.**

1731 BAILEY vol. II, *Gastriloquous*, speaking out of the belly. **1785** REID *Int. Powers* II. xxii. 298 The deception.. which is said to be produced by Gastriloquists. **1831** HOOPER *Med. Dict.*, *Gastroloquism*: see *Ventriloquism.* **1848** CRAIG, *Gastriloquy*, a manner of speaking that seems to proceed from the belly. **1864** A. McKAY *Hist. Kilmarnock* 259 The greatest success has attended his..gastriloquial displays.

†**gastrimargism**(e. *Obs.*$^{-1}$ [f. as next + -ISM.] = next.

1607 WALKINGTON *Opt. Glass* v. 37b, Be not addicted to this foule vice of Gastrimargisme and belly chear.

†**gastrimargy.** *Obs.* [ad. Gr. γαστριμαργία f. γαστρίμαργος gluttonous (f. γαστήρ belly + μάργος raging mad).] Gluttony; voraciousness.

c **1430** *Pilgr. Lyf Manhode* III. xl. (1869) 156 And what is, quod j, Castrimargye [*sic*; so spelt also in Fr. original]? It is, quod she, plounginge and drenchinge of morselles that men mown fynde in goode housholdes. *a* **1625** BOYS *Wks.* (1629) 769 These foure Angels are the spirit of Luxurie, the spirit of Pride, the spirit of Gastrimargie, the spirit of Auarice.

gastrin (ˈgæstrɪn). *Physiol.* [f. GASTRIC *a.* + -IN^1.] A hormone that stimulates gastric secretion.

1905 J. S. EDKINS in *Proc. R. Soc.* B. LXXVI. 376 The active principle, which may be called 'gastrin', is not destroyed by boiling. **1955** *Sci. News Let.* 7 May 293/1 Gastric juice production is also caused by a hormone called gastrin, formed in the lower third of the stomach, the antrum, when this part of the stomach comes in contact with food. **1968** *New Scientist* 25 July 199/2 The hormone gastrin ..is produced by the wall of the stomach itself.

‖**gastritis** (gæˈstraɪtɪs). *Med.* [mod.L., f. Gr. γαστ(ε)ρ-, γαστήρ stomach + -ITIS.] Inflammation of the coats of the stomach.

1806 *Med. Jrnl.* XV. 412 This might be in reality a case of gastritis. **1859** TODD *Cycl. Anat.* V. 414/2 Acute gastritis.

gastro- (ˈgæstrəʊ), *rarely* before a vowel **gastr-**, combining form of Gr. γαστ(ε)ρ-, γαστήρ, belly, stomach, in many mod. terms of *Anat.*, *Path.*, etc. **ˌgastro-caˈtarrhal** *a.*, connected with gastric catarrh; **ˈgastrocele** [Gr. κήλη tumour] (see quot.); **gastro-ˈcolic** *a.* [Gr. κόλον the colon], pertaining to the stomach and to the colon; **gastroˈdiaphane** [Gr. διαφανής translucent], an instrument for illuminating the inside of the stomach in order that its outline may be seen through the abdominal wall; so **gastrodiˈaphany**; **ˌgastro-duoˈdenal** *a.*, pertaining to the stomach and to the duodenum; **ˌgastro-duodeˈnitis**, inflammation of the stomach and duodenum; **ˌgastro-duodeˈnostomy**, the surgical creation of a passage between the stomach and the duodenum; **ˌgastro-enˈteric** *a.*, pertaining to the stomach and intestines; **ˌgastro-enteˈritis**, inflammation of the stomach and intestines; hence **ˌgastro-enteˈritic** *a.*; **ˌgastro-enteˈrology**, the branch of medicine dealing with the stomach and intestines and their pathology; hence **ˌgastro-enteroˈlogical** *a.*; **ˌgastro-enteˈrologist**; **ˌgastro-enteˈrostomy** [Gr. ἔντερο-ν intestine + στόμ-α mouth + -Y^3], 'the formation of a permanent mouth, or fistulous opening, connecting the duodenum and the stomach, when the pylorus is obstructed' (*Syd. Soc. Lex.* 1885); **ˌgastro-enteˈrotomy**, 'the opening of the intestine through the abdominal walls' (*Syd. Soc. Lex.* 1885); **ˌgastro-epiˈploic** *a.*, pertaining to the stomach and to the epiploon; **ˌgastro-gaˈstrostomy** (see quot. 1900); **ˌgastro-heˈpatic** *a.*, pertaining to the stomach and to the liver; **ˌgastro-hysteˈrotomy**, the Cæsarean operation: see CÆSAREAN *a.* 2; **ˌgastro-ileˈostomy**, the surgical creation of a passage between the stomach and the ileum; **ˈgastro-inˈtestinal** *a.* = *gastro-enteric* adj.; **ˌgastro-jeˈjunal** *a.*, pertaining to or involving both the stomach and the jejunum; **ˌgastro-jejuˈnostomy**, the surgical creation of a passage between the stomach and the jejunum; **gastro-œsoˈphageal** *a.*, pertaining to or involving both the stomach and the œsophagus; **ˈgastropexy** [see -PEXY], an operation for restoring a prolapsed stomach to its proper position by suturing it to the abdominal wall; **ˌgastro-ˈphrenic** *a.*, pertaining to the stomach and to the diaphragm; **gastropliˈcation** [L. *plicāre* to fold], an operation for reducing the capacity of the stomach by sewing together folds made in the stomach wall; **ˌgastro-pneuˈmonic** *a.*, pertaining to the stomach and to the lungs; **gastroˈptosis** [PTOSIS], a downward displacement of the stomach; **ˌgastro-ˈpulmonary** *a.*, **-pulˈmonic** *a.* = prec.; **ˌgastro-ˈsplenic** *a.*, pertaining to the stomach and to the spleen; **gastroˈstaxis** [Gr. στάξις a dripping], oozing of blood through the mucous membrane of the stomach; **ˌgastro-ˈvascular** *a.*, pertaining jointly to the abdominal cavity and to a vessel.

1833 W. STOKES in *Cycl. Pract. Med.* II. 337/1 One of the most frequent forms of disease in Dublin is that which may be termed the *gastro-catarrhal fever. **1807–26** S. COOPER *First Lines Surg.* (ed. 5) 450 When a hernia contains a part of the stomach..it is sometimes named..*gastrocele. **1846** BUCHANAN *Technol. Dict.*, **Gastrocolic*, an epithet for the great omentum, because it passes from the gaster or stomach to the arch of the colon. **1892** M. MANGES tr. *Ewald's Dis. Stomach* ii. 63 The use of the *gastrodiaphane has been suggested by Einhorn. This instrument consists of a small electric light, which is introduced into the stomach; the contours of this organ are outlined by the light shining through the gastric wall and the abdominal parietes. **1894** GOULD *Dict. Med.*, **Gastrodiaphany*, a method of exploration of the stomach by means of the gastrodiaphane. **1896** A. E. MAYLARD *Treat. Surg. Alim. Canal* 156 Gastrodiaphany..has received up to the present but a very limited trial. **1904** *Nature* 4 Aug. 316/2 This includes the ordinary clinical methods and the examination by the Röntgen rays and by so-called gastro-diaphany. **1854** MAYNE *Expos. Lex.*, *Gastro-Duodenalis*..*gastro-duodenal. **1882** *Quain's Elem. Anat.* (ed. 9) I. 436 The gastro-duodenal artery descends near the pylorus behind the first part of the duodenum. **1897** ALLBUTT *Syst. Med.* II. 367 The jaundice was due..to gastro-duodenal catarrh. **1822–34** *Good's Study Med.* (ed. 4) II. 175 *note*, *Gastro-duodenitis may exist without jaundice. **1890** BILLINGS *Med. Dict.*, *Gastroduodenostomy. **1903** *Lancet* 29 Aug. 591/2 We rapidly considered the relative advantage of pyloroplasty.. and gastro-duodenostomy. **1833** W. STOKES in *Cycl. Pract. Med.* II. 343/1 *Gastro-enteric inflammation. **1854** MAYNE *Expos. Lex.*, *Gastrentericus*..gastrenteric. *Ibid.*, *Gastrenteriticus*..*gastrenteritic. **1861** T. J. GRAHAM *Pract. Med.* 629 We hear of..mucous, gastro-enteritic [fevers]. **1822–9** *Good's Study Med.* (ed. 3) II. 517 *Gastro-enteritis ..exists without any painful point when [etc.]. **1927** F. F. IMIANITOFF tr. *Rachet's Pract. Gastroscopy* p. vi, *Gastro-enterological endoscopy. **1935** *Jrnl. Amer. Med. Assoc.* 2 Feb. 402/2 This dictum of the *gastro-enterologists. **1904** *Appleton's Med. Dict.*, **Gastroenterology*, the pathology, etc., of the stomach and intestines. **1908** *Practitioner* Feb. 283 The student of gastro-enterology. **1952** F. A. JONES *Mod. Trends Gastro-enterol.* p. xiii, In many countries, as in Great-Britain, gastro-enterology is not an established speciality..but remains within the sphere of general medicine and surgery. **1886** *Gastro-enterostomy [see GASTRECTOMY]. **1893** *Brit. Med. Jrnl.* 1 Apr. 50/2 After gastro-enterostomy the contents of the stomach often pass into the..pyloric limb of the attached loop of intestine. **1876** *Clin. Soc. Trans.* IX. 109 *Gastro-Enterotomy (artificial anus in the small intestine). **1656** BLOUNT *Glossogr.* s.v. *Vein*, **Gastrepiploick vein.* **1835–6** TODD *Cycl. Anat.* I. 194/2 It [the hepatic artery] gives two..branches called the pyloric and the right gastro-epiploic. **1900** DORLAND *Med. Dict.*, **Gastrogastrostomy*, the formation of an anastomosis between the pyloric and cardiac ends of the stomach, performed for hour-glass contraction of the stomach. **1902** *Encycl. Medica* XI. 454 *Gastro-anastomosis or Gastro-gastrostomy* (Wölfler)..consists in making a free communication between the two compartments of an hour-glass stomach. **1921** J. SHERREN *Lect. Surg. Stomach & Duodenum* iii. 35 If there is a double hour-glass stomach,.. double gastrojejunostomy should be performed if this operation is indicated. Plastic operations on the stomach, such as gastro-gastrostomy, should not be done. **1835–6** TODD *Cycl. Anat.* I. 502/2 A defined margin terminates the *gastro-hepatic omentum on the right side. **1854** MAYNE *Expos. Lex.*, *Gastro-hysterotomia*..*gastro-hysterotomy. **1896** A. E. MAYLARD *Treat. Surg. Alim. Canal* 249 When the junction is with the ileum, it is strictly a *gastro-ileostomy. **1957** H. A. DAVIS *Princ. Surg. Physiol.* xvii. 453 The unintentional performance of a gastro-ileostomy often results in the development of an ileal ulcer or an ileitis. **1831** J. DAVIES *Manual Mat. Med.* 213 A lively irritation of the *gastro-intestinal surface. **1869** E. A. PARKES *Pract. Hygiene* (ed. 3) 485 Anything which causes gastro-intestinal disorder. **1908** *Practitioner* Sept. 450 The original posterior *gastro-jejunal opening had closed. **1891** *Lancet* 2 May 988/2 The growth having much increased and the stomach being greatly dilated, *gastro-jejunostomy was performed. **1921** Gastrojejunostomy [see *gastro-gastrostomy* above]. **1889** *Cent. Dict.*, *Gastro-esophageal. **1962** *Lancet* 1 Dec. 1178/2 He has made a particular study of gastroœsophageal disorders in children. **1896** A. E. MAYLARD *Treat. Surg. Alim. Canal* 225 An operation termed *gastropexy has been performed by Duret for certain cases of displacement and dilatation. **1908** *Practitioner* Sept. 440 For ptosis and atony of the stomach, gastro-enterostomy is preferable to gastropexy or gastroplication alone. **1854** MAYNE *Expos. Lex.*, *Gastro-phrenicus*..*gastro-phrenic. **1882** *Quain's Elem. Anat.* (ed. 9) II. 727 A small duplicature to the left of the œsophagus, named the gastro-phrenic ligament. **1896** A. E. MAYLARD *Treat. Surg. Alim. Canal* 248 Brandt also records a successful case [*sc.* of gastrorrhaphy] under the title of *gastroplication. **1903** RIEGEL & STOCKTON *Dis. Stomach* I. 284 The operation of Bircher consists in reducing the capacity of the stomach by constructing folds in the stomach-wall and sewing these reduplications together (gastroplication). **1893** DUNGLISON *Dict. Med. Sci.* (ed. 21) **Gastroptosis*, falling or dragging down of the stomach. **1900** *Encycl. Medica* V. 207 In dilatation and gastroptosis the location of the pain approaches nearer to the umbilicus. **1909** OSLER & MCCRAE *Syst. Med.* V. 608 Gastroptosis, although one of the less frequently recognized of the visceral ptoses, is one of the most important as regards symptomatology. **1927** S. WYARD *Handbk. Dis. Stomach* vii. 170 Gastroptosis..occurs as an isolated phenomenon or in association with a downward displacement of certain of the other viscera as well, e.g. intestines, kidneys, etc. **1856** *Ibid.* (ed. 6) I. p. ccli, The mucous membranes..may be reduced to two great divisions, namely the *gastro-pulmonary and the genito-urinary. **1854** BUSHNAN in *Circ. Sc.*, *Org. Nat.* II. 54 The first..is termed the *gastro-pulmonic membrane. **1844** HOBLYN *Dict. Med.*, **Gastro-splenic omenta*..the laminæ of the peritoneum, which are comprised between the spleen and the stomach. **1906** W. H. WHITE in *Lancet* 3 Nov. 1190/1 Sir Cooper Perry kindly suggested to me that the disease might be called *gastrostaxis. **1929** HURST & STEWART *Gastric & Duodenal Ulcer* III. iii. 82 Many cases of so-called 'gastrostaxis', i.e. gastric hæmorrhage without easily recognizable lesion, are due to bleeding from innumerable microscopic lesions. **1960** JONES & GUMMER *Clinical Gastroenterol.* xiii. 395 Patients with small acute ulcers, diffuse erosive gastritis, and also gastrostaxis with diffuse mucosal bleeding. **1876** tr. *Beneden's Anim. Parasites* 47 The Cydippe densa..lodges in its *gastro-vascular apparatus larvæ of annelids.

ˌgastroˈcnemial, *a.* [f. as next + -AL¹.] = next.
1889 in *Century Dict.*

gastrocnemian (ˌgæstrəʊˈkniːmɪən), *a.* Also **-knemian.** [f. next + -AN.] Of or pertaining to the gastrocnemius muscle.
1854 in MAYNE *Expos. Lex.* **1872** BROWNING *Fifine* lx, And ..duly sympathize With gastro-knemian grace.

‖**gastrocnemius** (ˌgæstrəʊˈkniːmɪəs). Pl. **-cnemii** (ˈkniːmɪaɪ). [mod.L. *gastrocnēmius*, f. Gr. γαστροκνημία the calf of the leg, f. γαστ(ε)ρ-, γαστήρ belly + κνήμη leg.] The chief muscle of the calf of the leg, which gives it a protuberant or 'bellying' form.
1676 J. COOKE *Marrow Surg.* 430 (*folding leaf*) The two Gastrocnemii. **1831** R. KNOX *Cloquet's Anat.* 382 The Gastrocnemius..is composed of two fleshy masses, called the outer and inner heads, resembling each other in form. **1863** KINGSLEY *Water-Bab.* viii. (1878) 339 The dog tackled them so sharply about the gastrocnemius muscle. **1871** W. A. HAMMOND *Dis. Nerv. Syst.* 65 A ballet-dancer, whose gastrocnemii muscles were the apparent starting-points of the disease.

gastrodisc (ˈgæstrədɪsk). *Embryol.* [ad. mod.L. *gastrodiscus*: see GASTRO- and DISC.] The germinal area of a mammal.
1881 MIVART *Cat* 320 That part where the two membranes coexist is the germ area, or gastrodisc.

‖**gastrodynia** (ˌgæstrəʊˈdaɪnɪə). *Med.* [mod.L., f. Gr. γαστ(ε)ρ-, γαστήρ stomach + ὀδύνη pain.] Pain in the stomach; = GASTRALGIA.
1804 *Med. Jrnl.* XII. 289 The Case, which I..request you will insert in your next Number, I have called Gastrodynia. **1822–34** *Good's Study Med.* (ed. 4) I. 121 *note*, Gastrodynia and gastralgia are terms frequently used almost synonymously with cardialgia. **1879** KHORY *Princ. Med.* 17 Gastrodynia is common in dyspeptics.

gastroid (ˈgæstrɔɪd), *a.* [f. Gr. γαστ(ε)ρ-, γαστήρ + -OID.] Having a belly-like dilatation.
1854 in MAYNE *Expos. Lex.* **1886** THOMAS *Med. Dict.*, *Gastroid*, resembling the belly, or stomach:—applied to parts of animals and plants.

gastrolater (gæˈstrɒlətə(r)). [ad. F. *gastrolatre* (Cotgr.), f. Gr. γαστρ(ο)-, γαστήρ belly + -λατρος serving.] A belly-worshipper.
1694 MOTTEUX *Rabelais* IV. lviii. 227 Pantagruel observ'd two sorts of..Apparitors..The first were call'd Engastrimythes, the others, Gastrolaters. *Ibid.* lix. 230 These lozelly Gulligutted Gastrolaters.
Hence †**gaˈstrolatrous** *a.*, belly-worshipping.
1694 MOTTEUX *Rabelais* IV. lviii. 229 The Variety we perceiv'd in the Dresses of the Gastrolatrous Coquillons.

gastrolith (ˈgæstrəlɪθ). [f. GASTRO- + Gr. λίθ-ος stone.] A calculus or stony concretion in the stomach; *spec.* = CRAB'S-EYE I.
1854 MAYNE *Expos. Lex.*, *Gastrolithus*..a stone or calculus in the stomach: a gastrolith. **1880** HUXLEY *Crayfish* 29 There are..found at the sides of the stomach two lenticular calcareous masses, which are known as 'crabs-eyes' or gastroliths.

gastrology (gæˈstrɒlədʒɪ). [ad. Gr. γαστρολογία, the title of a poem quoted by Athenæus (also γαστρονομία), f. γαστρ(ο)-, γαστήρ stomach + λόγος discourse.] The science of catering for the stomach; hence, cookery, good eating. Similarly **gaˈstrologer**, one versed in gastrology. **gastroˈlogical** *a.*, of or pertaining to gastrology. **gaˈstrologist** = *gastrologer*.
1810 W. TAYLOR in *Monthly Mag.* XXX. 48 Under the denomination of gastrology, to compile learned quartos on the science of enhancing the physical and moral pleasures of the palate. **1820** *Sporting Mag.* VI. 261 The gourmet.. deserves the higher appellation of gastrologer. **1822** *Edin. Rev.* XXXVII. 59 The Gastrologists will..not lay these things to heart. **1827** STEUART *Planter's G.* (1828) p. viii, What the Doctor learnedly calls 'the Science of Gastrology'. **1851** *Fraser's Mag.* XLIV. 208 The mechanical, physiological, and gastrological intricacies and differences of fish, flesh, and fowl. **1853** *Ibid.* XLVII. 682 A famous gastrologer was wont to affirm that the whole of an Athenian supper put together was not to be compared to it.

‖**gastromalacia** (ˌgæstrəʊməˈleɪʃ(ɪ)ə). *Path.* [mod.L., f. GASTRO- + Gr. μαλακία softness, f. μαλακός soft.] Softening of the coats of the stomach.
1855 in OGILVIE, Suppl. **1866** A. FLINT *Princ. Med.* (1880) 459 Strict proof of the development of gastromalacia during life.

gastromancy (ˈgæstrəʊmænsɪ). *Obs.* exc. *Hist.* [f. Gr. γαστρ(ο)-, γαστήρ belly + μαντεία divination (Gr. had γαστρομαντεύεσθαι 'to divine by the belly').] Divination by the belly.
1. (See quots.)
1610 HEALEY *St. Aug. Citie of God* 294 Hydromancy.. done..in a glasse bottle full of water, wherein a Childe must looke (and this is called Gastromancy of the glasses belly). **1613** PURCHAS *Pilgrimage* (1614) 366 Gastromancie procured answere by pictures, or representations in glasse-vessels of water, after the due Rites.
2. (See quot. 1652.)
1652 GAULE *Magastrom.* xix. 165 Gastromancy, [divining] by the sound of, or signes upon the belly. *a* **1693** URQUHART *Rabelais* III. xxv, Gastromancy, which kind of ventral fatiloquency was for a long time together used in Ferrara. [*a* **1836** E. SMEDLEY *Occ. Sc.* in *Encycl. Metrop.* (1855) 323 Gastromancy or divination from the belly, is now generally explained by ventriloquism.]

†**gastromantic** (gæstrəʊˈmæntɪk), *a. Obs.* [f. as prec. + Gr. μαντικ-ός soothsaying.] Pertaining to or practising gastromancy.
1646 GAULE *Cases Consc.* 28 The Gastromanticke, the Ventriloquist, or if you will the Bottle-bellyed Witch.

gastronome (ˈgæstrənəʊm). [a. F. *gastronome*, back-formation from *gastronomie* GASTRONOMY.] One versed in gastronomy; a judge of good eating.
1823 SCOTT *Peveril* xxvii, A conversation on the mysteries of the table, which..a modern gastronome might have listened to with pleasure. **1837** W. IRVING *Capt. Bonneville* III. 15. **1859** G. MEREDITH *R. Feverel* xxxv, Tears and shrieks accompany the descent of the gastronome.

gastronomer (gæˈstrɒnəmə(r)). [f. GASTRONOMY, after the analogy of *astronomer*.] = prec.
1820 *Sporting Mag.* VI. 261 The gormand unites theory with practice, and may be denominated gastronomer. **1852** *Blackw. Mag.* LXXI. 747 A philosophical gastronomer of European reputation.

gastronomic (gæstrəʊˈnɒmɪk), *a.* [ad. F. *gastronomique*, f. *gastronomie* GASTRONOMY.] Of or pertaining to gastronomy.
1828 H. ANGELO *Remin.* 292 Her ladyship proposed tickets or lots, which were inscribed each with some article for the supper-table..Nothing could exceed the amusement which this lottery gastronomic produced. **1841** D'ISRAELI *Amen. Lit.* (1867) 582 Being initiated into the gastronomic mysteries of the kitchens of the ancients. **1858** HAWTHORNE *Fr. & It. Jrnls.* (1872) I. 24 It would require less time to cultivate our gastronomic taste than taste of any other kind.
So **gastroˈnomical** *a.*, **gastroˈnomically** *adv.*
1809 W. IRVING *Knickerb.* VII. iii. (1849) 395 The gastronomical merits of terrapins. **1842** W. S. SETON-KARR in *Haileybury Observer* V. 10 Duly qualified as a graduate of the gastronomical College. **1875** DASENT *Vikings* II. 81 Gastronomically viewed, the whole feast was.. unsatisfactory.

gastronomist (gæˈstrɒnəmɪst). [f. GASTRONOMY + -IST.] = GASTRONOMER.
1825 *Q. Rev.* XXXII. 436 We may teach Beauvilliers, and all such gastronomists, that they are but men. **1828** *Blackw. Mag.* XXIII. 593 A true gastronomist will..shun diversity of food. **1845** STOCQUELER *Handbk. Brit. India* (1854) 30 The European gastronomist in India is materially a debtor to the Portuguese.

gaˈstronomous, *a. rare*⁻¹. [f. GASTRONOME + -OUS.] Devoted to gastronomy.
1828 *Examiner* 708/2 Fervent and gastronomous—he was the very apostle of gluttony.

gastronomy (gæˈstrɒnəmɪ). [ad. F. *gastronomie* (first occurring as the title of a poem by Berchoux 1801), a. Gr. γαστρονομία (the title of a poem quoted by Athenæus), f. γαστρ(ο)-, γαστήρ stomach, on the analogy of ἀστρονομία astronomy.] The art and science of delicate eating.
1814 SIR R. WILSON *Priv. Diary* II. 345 The banquet was according to all the rules of perfect gastronomy. **1837** M. DONOVAN *Dom. Econ.* II. 379 The march of improvement will induce the professors of gastronomy to elevate their calling. **1845** FORD *Handbk. Spain* I. 25 This trait of Spanish gastronomy was not lost on the author of Gil Blas.

gaˈstropathy. *rare.* [f. Gr. γαστρ(ο)-, γαστήρ stomach + πάθος feeling, suffering.] (See quot.)
1854 MAYNE *Expos. Lex.*, *Gastropathia*, term for disease of the stomach: gastropathy.

gastrophilanthropist. *nonce-wd.* A benevolent purveyor for the appetites of others.
1814 *Sch. Gd. Living* 161 The honour of recording them among the gastrophilanthropists of the present day.

gastrophile (ˈgæstrəʊfɪl). *rare.* [f. Gr. γαστρ(ο)-, γαστήρ stomach + φίλ-ος friend.] One who loves his stomach, or good eating.
1820 *Sporting Mag.* VI. 261 The glutton practises without any regard to theory; and we call him gastrophile.
So **ˈgastrophilism** [-ISM], the disposition of a gastrophile; love of good eating; **ˈgastrophilist** [-IST] = GASTROPHILE; **ˈgastrophilite** *a.* [-ITE], fond of good eating.
1814 *Sch. Gd. Living* 84 Which the modern gastrophilist cannot fail to admire. *Ibid.* 115 Let no one say that the spirit of gastrophilism never found its way within the walls of the Vatican. **1835** *Tait's Mag.* II. 459 The name..bringing at once to my mind..the Scrap-Stall, and gastrophilite hackney-coachman. **1850** *Fraser's Mag.* XLII. 548 The sturdy gastrophilist would not be baulked of his meal.

gastropod, gastropodous: see GASTER-.

gastrorrhaphy (gæˈstrɒrəfɪ). Also **gastroraphy.** [ad. F. *gastroraphie* (Cotgr.), ad. Gr. γαστρορραφία, f. γαστρ(ο)-, γαστήρ belly + root of ῥάπτειν to sew.] Suture of wounds in the abdomen.
1739 SHARP *Treat. Surg.* iii. 9 The Gastroraphy..though the word in strictness of etymology, signifies no more than sewing up any Wound of the Belly, yet in common acceptation it implies that the Wound of the Belly is complicated with another of the Intestine. **1767** GOOCH *Treat. Wounds* I. 158 Gastroraphy, for large extensive wounds in the abdomen. **1885** *Syd. Soc. Lex.*, *Gastrorrhaphy*.

gastroscope (ˈgæstrəʊskəʊp). [f. GASTRO- + -SCOPE.] An instrument which makes possible a visual inspection of the interior of the stomach when passed into it via the mouth and œsophagus.
1888 *Lancet* 7 July 35/1 A special means of examination introduced by Mikulicz—viz., the direct inspection of the gastric mucous membrane by means of a specially constructed gastroscope, to be termed *gastroscopy*. **1956** J. J. SPIRA *Gastro-duodenal Ulcer* v. xxii. 323 The duodenal lesion is obviously out of the area which can be seen through the flexible gastroscope. **1965** S. WOLF *Stomach* x. 209 The gastric mucous membrane as seen through the gastroscope is red and thickened.
Hence as *v. trans.*, to examine (a patient) with a gastroscope.
1937 R. SCHINDLER *Gastroscopy* 5 Many patients were gastroscoped repeatedly. **1970** H. M. SPIRO *Clin. Gastroenterol.* xv. 255 Some physicians recommend that all patients with upper digestive symptoms..be gastroscoped.

gastroscopy (gæˈstrɒskəpɪ). [f. Gr. γαστρ(ο)-, γαστήρ belly + -σκοπία inspection: see -SCOPY.]
1. (See quot.)
1855 OGILVIE, Suppl., *Gastroscopy*, an examination of the abdomen, in order to detect disease.
2. The practice and techniques of using the gastroscope; an examination of the stomach by means of the gastroscope.
1888 [see prec.]. **1927** F. F. IMIANITOFF tr. *Rachet's Pract. Gastroscopy* p. v, We have had the opportunity of watching several gastroscopies. **1956** J. J. SPIRA *Gastro-duodenal Ulcer* v. xxii. 323 Gastroscopy is restricted by its limited field of vision but may be useful as contributory evidence of a gastric lesion. *Ibid.*, 3 deaths in an unknown number of gastroscopies. **1967** S. TAYLOR et al. *Short Textbk. Surg.* xx. 267 Gastroscopy may help decide if a gastric ulcer is simple or malignant.
Hence **gastroˈscopic** *a.*; **gastroˈscopically** *adv.*, by means of a gastroscope; **gaˈstroscopist,** one skilled in the use of the gastroscope.
1888 *Lancet* 7 July 35/2 One case of pyloric cancer (not examined gastroscopically). **1892** M. MANGES tr. *Ewald's Dis. Stomach* ii. 63 Gastroscopic examination. **1937** R. SCHINDLER *Gastroscopy* 1 In most of the fundamental matters the gastroscopists are in complete accord. **1956** J. J. SPIRA *Gastro-duodenal Ulcer* v. xxii. 323 Gastroscopic examination is particularly useful in diagnosing mucosal atrophy..and early tumours. **1958** H. OGILVIE in Blackburn & Lawrie *Textbk. Surg.* xx. 533 The opinions offered even by expert gastroscopists on the nature of the lesion are more often wrong than right.

gastrosoph (ˈgæstrəʊsɒf). [f. Gr. γαστρ(ο)-, γαστήρ stomach + σοφ-ός wise.] One who is skilled in matters of eating. Hence **gaˈstrosopher** = GASTROSOPH; **gaˈstrosophy,** the science of good eating.
1824 *Blackw. Mag.* XV. 642 Your cooks and waiters have never turned away from their works of gastrosophy, to think of the neighbouring millions. **1855** *Househ. Words* XII. 288 The English..do not stand first-rate as gastrosophs. **1894** *Westm. Gaz.* 16 Apr. 8/2 There are many gourmets, but the number of gastrosophers is exceedingly small.

gastrostomy (gæˈstrɒstəmɪ). *Surg.* [f. GASTRO- + Gr. στόμα mouth + -Y³.] The operation of opening the stomach for the introduction of food when the gullet is closed.
1854 in MAYNE *Expos. Lex.* **1878** T. BRYANT *Pract. Surg.* I. 617 The advantages offered by gastrostomy for stricture of the œsophagus.

gastrotomy (gæˈstrɒtəmɪ). *Surg.* [f. GASTRO- + Gr. -τομία cutting.] **a.** The operation of opening the abdomen by incision. **b.** The operation of opening the stomach through the abdominal walls.
1656 in BLOUNT *Glossogr.* **1721** in BAILEY. **1857** BULLOCK *Cazeaux' Midwif.* 261 Gastrotomy alone would be practicable when [etc.]. **1878** T. BRYANT *Pract. Surg.* I. 616 When the foreign body is large and clearly cannot be passed, the surgeon should open the stomach by gastrotomy.
Hence **gastroˈtomic** *a.*, pertaining to gastrotomy.
1854 in MAYNE *Expos. Lex.*; and in recent Dicts.

gastrozooid (gæstrəʊˈzəʊɔɪd). *Zool.* Also **gastero-.** [f. GASTRO- + ZOOID *sb.*] A nutritive zooid in colony-forming Hydrozoa and Thaliacea.
1879 H. N. MOSELEY in *Phil. Trans. R. Soc.* CLXIX. 429 In all Stylasteridæ two forms of zooids are present. One form has a mouth and gastric cavity, the other is devoid of these and has a purely tentacular function. For the former the term 'gastrozooid' is here adopted, and for the latter that of 'dactylozooid'. **1932** BORRADAILE & POTTS *Invertebrata* v. 147 The manubrium has come to lie outside the medusa bell as the gastrozooid. *Ibid.* xix. 608 These [buds] of the lateral row become gasterozooids which gather food for the community. **1961** *Encycl. Brit.* XII. 3/2 In certain colonies

[*sc.* of polyps and medusæ], such as those of *Millepora* and *Hydractinia*.., the hydranths are not all alike. Some of them (*gastrozooids*) possess mouths as well as tentacles. **1967** E. J. W. BARRINGTON *Invert. Struct. & Function* xxi. 449 The differentiation of the colonial polyps into gastrozooids, concerned with feeding, and gonozooids (blastozooids) concerned with reproduction.

‖**gastrula** (ˈgæstrələ). *Embryol.* [mod.L. dim., f. Gr. γαστρ-, γαστήρ stomach.] That form of the metazoic germ which consists of a cup with two layers of cells in the wall.

1877 HUXLEY *Anat. Inv. Anim.* iii. 115 A gastrula is formed by invagination of the morula, the ectoderm of which has the structure of the endoderm of the adult. **1886** H. SPENCER in *19th Cent.* May 764 The two-layered 'gastrula'—the simplest ancestral form of the Metazoa.

attrib. **1878** BELL *Gegenbauer's Comp. Anat.* 111 This condition is simplest in the Gastrula form. **1880** *Gentl. Mag.* CCXLVI. 43 The opening which formerly led into the gastrula-body. **1880** HUXLEY *Crayfish* iv. 211 This is the gastrula condition of the embryo. **1887** A. C. HADDON *Introd. Embryology* ii. 24 The normal method of gastrula-formation.

Hence ˈ**gastrular** *a.*, pertaining to a gastrula or to gastrulation.

In recent Dicts.

gastrulation (gæstruːˈleɪʃən). *Embryol.* [f. GASTRULA + -ATION.] The formation of a gastrula.

1879 tr. *Haeckel's Evol. Man* I. viii. 199 The formation of the Gastrula, or gastrulation. **1887** A. C. HADDON *Introd. Embryology* ii. (*heading*), Segmentation and gastrulation.

gastruran (gæˈstruːərən), *a.* and *sb.* [f. mod.L. *Gastrūra* neut. pl., Gr. γαστ(ε)ρ-, γαστήρ stomach + οὐρά tail + -AN.] **A.** *adj.* Of or pertaining to the *Gastrura* or stomatopodous crustaceans. **B.** *sb.* An animal of this class. Similarly **gaˈstrurous** *a.*

In recent Dicts.

gat[1] (gæt). Also **gate.** [app. a. ON. *gat* (Da., Sw. *gat*) opening, passage: see GATE *sb.*[1]] An opening between sandbanks; a channel, strait; in Kent, an opening, natural or artificial, in the cliffs, serving as a landing-place.

1723 J. LEWIS *Hist. Tenet* (1736) 6 Through these chalky cliffs the inhabitants whose Farms adjoin to them have cut several gates or ways into the sea.. But these gates or passages they have been forced to fill up in the time of War. *a* **1805** A. CARLYLE *Autobiog.* 163 The three ships which took through the gat or opening between sand-banks, were almost out of sight before we ventured to sail. *a* **1825** FORBY *Voc. E. Anglia, Gat*, an opening in the great sand-bank which lies at the back of the Yarmouth Roads. **1847** LD. G. BENTINCK in *Croker Papers* (1884) III. xxv. 143 Louis Philippe sent all his war steamers to tug the French ships through the gat of Gibraltar. **1885** L. JACKSON *Our Caughmawagas in Egypt* 17, I had to use the tow-line at one place where there was a 'gate' (or channel), as we say in Canada.

gat[2] (gæt). *slang* (orig. *U.S.*). Also **gatt.** [Short for GATLING.] A revolver or other gun.

1904 'No. 1500' *Life in Sing Sing* xiii. 248/2 Gatt, a revolver. **1920** [see *cap-pistol*]. **1928** E. WALLACE *Gunner* xviii. 146 Why was a pistol called a gat, he wondered. Probably it was an abbreviation of gatling, and was obviously an Americanism. **1931** WODEHOUSE *Big Money* xiii. 283 He produced the gat.. and poised it in an unsteady but resolute grasp. 'Hands up!' he said. **1966** *Punch* 1 June 792/3 The dive he took us to.. was as bad as anything Akim Tamaroff ever ran through with his gat blazing.

gat, obs. f. GATE, GOAT; pa. t. of GET *v.*

gatch (gætʃ). [ad. Pers. *gach.*] A type of plaster used by Persian craftsmen.

1886 *Century Mag.* XXXII. 718 By the aid of *gatch* or plaster of Paris, the artisan of Teherân often transforms these mud structures into dreams of loveliness. **1934** F. STARK *Valleys of Assassins* 109 A slender piece of column moulded in a pattern of overlaid leaves, and probably once intended to be covered with metal, for it was made of very fragile 'gatch'.

[**gatchers.** Error for *catchers*, the after-leavings of tin, originating in the glossary to Pryce's *Mineralogia Cornubiensis.* Also **gatches** (*English Dialect Dictionary*).

1778 PRYCE *Min. Cornub.* 229 All dressers save the hinder stuff from the frame end, as it washes off in a pit by the name of Catchers. Gloss., *Gatchers*, the after leavings of Tin. **1849–50** WEALE *Dict. Terms, Gatchers*, the after-leavings of tin. [Hence **1890** in *Century Dict.*] **1882** JAGO *Anc. Lang. & Dial. Cornwall* 320 *Gatchers*, the after-leavings of tin ore. *Pryce.*]

gate (geɪt), *sb.*[1] Forms: *α.* 1 **ȝeat, ȝet** (*Northumb.* **ȝæt, ȝeat(t),** 2–4 **ȝeat,** (3 **giate),** 2–6 **ȝet,** 3–5 **ȝat(t)e,** 3–5, 6–9 *dial.* **yat(t)e,** 4–6 **yhate, -et, ȝett,** 5–6 **yet(e,** 7–9 *dial.* **yeat(t,** 6– *Sc.* **yett.** *β.* (1 *pl.* **gatu),** 2–6 **gat,** (4 **gatte,** 5 **gaytt,** 6 **gaat),** 3– **gate.** [OE. *ȝeat* str. neut., corresponds formally to OFris. *gat, jet*, hole, opening, OS. *gat* eye of a needle (LG. and Du. *gat* gap, hole, breach), ON. *gat* (see GAT[1]):—OTeut. type *gato[m]. The word is wanting in Goth. and HG.

The ulterior etymology is obscure. Some scholars refer the word to the root of GET *v.*, supposing the etymological sense to be either 'receptable' (hence 'cavity', 'hole', 'opening') or 'means of reaching' (hence 'way of access'). It is however very uncertain whether it is allied either to GET or to GATE *sb.*[2]

The original OE. declension was *gæt, gætes, gæte* in the sing., and *gatu, -a, -um* in the plur., according to the phonetic law by which *a* became *æ* exc. when a back vowel followed in the next syllable. Subsequently the *g* (= ɣ) before *æ* became palatalized, and the influence of the palatal ȝ caused the change of *æ* into *ea*. Hence the stem assumed the two forms *ȝeat-* and *gat-*, which are respectively represented by the *α* and *β* types in the later language. In late OE. the functional distinction between the two types was already disappearing through the operation of analogy, so that we find such forms as *gates, gate* (sing.) and *ȝeatu, ȝeatum* (pl.); in Mercian the forms *geatu, -um* (with guttural) are earlier, being due not to analogy but to the phonetic laws of the dialect. In ME. the *α* forms are universal in northern and in north- and west-midland writers, and also prevailed in the s.w. (Robert of Gloucester, the *South-Eng. Legendary*, etc.); the MSS. of Chaucer have *gate* in some passages and *ȝate* in others. Since the 16th c. *gate* has been the sole form in literary English; dialectally the forms with *y* remain in northern and north-midland districts, so far as they have not been displaced by the influence of the literary language; occasionally they are found surviving elsewhere, as in N. Devon and at Banbury (Ellis *Phonol. Eng. Dialects*).]

1. An opening in a wall, made for the purpose of entrance and exit, and capable of being closed by a movable barrier, the existence of which is usually implied; said with reference to a city or other enclosure, or the enclosure-wall of a large building, formerly also to the bulding itself, where *door* or *doors* is now commonly employed.

α. **778** *Charter* in Birch *Cartul. Saxon.* I. 315 Et eodem septo to hadfeld ȝeate. et eodem septo to baggan ȝete. *c* **900** tr. *Bæda's Hist.* III. ix. [xi.] (1890) 184 Ond heo sona þæt ȝeat þæs mynstres ontynde. *c* **1000** *Ags. Gosp.* Matt. vii. 13 Gangað inn þurh þæt nearwe ȝeat. *c* **1175** *Lamb. Hom.* 141 He com among his disciples þer þe ȝeten were ilokene. *a* **1225** *Ancr. R.* 424 þe oðer beo euer inne, ne wiðute þe ȝeate ne go heo wiðute leaue. **13..** *Guy Warw.* (A.) 4296 þe lyoun goþ to play wiþouten þe ȝat In pais wiþouten vilanie. *c* **1450** *Merlin* 78 We driven the remenaunt in at the yates. **1552** LYNDESAY *Monarche* 5964, I stude, naikit att ȝour ȝett. **1592** in Picton *L'pool Munic. Rec.* (1883) I. 98 Kepinge the yate of the church yeord open. **1695** A. DE LA PRYME *Diary* (Surtees) 77 You may go through this yate, and along the field side. **1802** ANDERSON *Cumbld. Ball., Impatient Lassie* v, He steeks the faul yeat softly tui. **1826** J. WILSON *Noct. Ambr.* Wks. 1855 I. 142 Across and recross, backwards and forrits, out ae yett and in at anither. **1865** G. MACDONALD *A. Forbes* III. 14 He's oot at the back yett and awa'!

β. **971** *Blickl. Hom.* 241 Hi betyndon þære ceastre gatu. *a* **1175** *Cott. Hom.* 231 Gief he fend were me sceolden anon eter [= at the] gat ȝemete mid gode repples. *c* **1330** R. BRUNNE *Chron.* (1810) 183 With grete duble cheynes drauhen ouer þe gate. **1393** LANGL. *P. Pl.* C. XIII. 47 And whan the peuple was plener come the porter vnpynnede the gate. *c* **1440** *Promp. Parv.* 188/2 Gate, or ȝate (*P.* yate), *porta.* **1577** B. GOOGE *Heresbach's Husb.* I. (1586) 9 b, I made a square wall.. with a great gate, for the bringing in of my cariages. **1601** SHAKS. *Jul. C.* III. ii. 274 Brutus and Cassius Are rid like Madmen through the Gates of Rome. **1670** COTTON *Espernon* II. VI. 244 The Ladies Coach so stopt the Gate, that the Duke's could not possibly pass. **1722** DE FOE *Plague* (1884) 179 You see here is a Gate, and.. we make them pay Toll. **1756** NUGENT *Gr. Tour* IV. 75 The gate of S. Martin was erected after the designs of Peter Bullet in 1674. **1861** M. PATTISON *Ess.* (1889) I. 47 The gates were closed at nine o'clock, and on no pretext opened after that hour.

2. In Biblical phraseology, after Hebrew; *ellipt.* for ***gate(s of the city*** as a place of judicial assembly.

c **825** *Vesp. Psalter* lxviii. 13 [lxix. 12] Ða ðe setun in ȝete. *c* **1000** *Ags. Ps.* (Th.) cxxvi. 6 [cxxvii. 5] þonne he on gaton greteð his grame feondas. **1382** WYCLIF *Isa.* xxii. 7 Knyȝtes shul sette ther setes in the ȝate. **1535** COVERDALE *Ruth* IV. i, Boos wente vp to yᵉ gate, and sate him downe there. **1656** J. HARRINGTON *Oceana* (1700) 161 Her Husband is known (by his Robes) in the Gates, when he sits among the Senators of the Land. **1837** GEN. P. THOMPSON *Exerc.* (1842) IV. 225 O for one hour of old Oliver, to talk with the royal miscreant in the gate! **1860** PUSEY *Min. Proph.* 194 The gate is the well-known place of concourse where judgment was given. **1865** J. FERGUSSON *Hist. Archit.* I. 175 Nor can it be doubted that this [ruin at Persepolis] is one of those buildings so frequently mentioned in the Bible as a 'gate', not the door of a city or buildings, but a gate of justice.

3. Phrases. **a.** ***at the gate***: fig., close at hand.

1340 HAMPOLE *Pr. Consc.* 2000 For when þe dede es at þe yhate, þan es he warned over late.

b. ***the gate(s of heaven, hell, paradise***, where the word may originally have been apprehended in a material sense. Also ***the gate(s of death***, used to denote a near approach to death (cf. DEATH *sb.* 14).

c **1000** *Ags. Gosp.* Matt. xvi. 18 Ofer þisne stan ic timbriȝe mine cyricean and helle gatu [*c* **1160** *Hatton Gosp.* gate] ne maȝon ongen þa. *c* **1175** *Lamb. Hom.* 41 He him sceawede haȝe treon eisliche beorninde et-foren helle ȝete. *c* **1200** *Trin. Coll. Hom.* 105 þe giate of paradis is opened to-genes hem. *a* **1300** *Cursor M.* 3783 Open him thoght þe ȝate of heuen. **1340** HAMPOLE *Pr. Consc.* 2127 þou ert he þat fra þe yhates of dede liftes me. *c* **1400** *Apol. Loll.* 56 þe ȝats of helle schal not be miȝty aȝen þe. *c* **1400** MAUNDEV. (Roxb.) viii. 29 þai er þe entreez and þe ȝ ates of hell. *c* **1460** *Towneley Myst.* vi. 40 And now is here none othere gate, Bot godis howse and heuens yate. **1662** *Bk. Com. Prayer* Collect Easter Even, That through the grave, and gate of death, we may pass to our joyful resurrection. **1678** LADY CHAWORTH in *12th Rep. Hist. MSS. Comm.* App. v. 50 Lord Rochester hath bin att the gates of death. **1820** KEATS *Hyperion* III. 126 Most like the struggle at the gate of death. **1871** MORLEY *Voltaire* (1886) 4 To each alike of the countless orthodox sects his name is the symbol for the prevailing of the gates of hell.

†**c.** ***the gate*** (***of the great Turk***): the Turkish court or government; the Porte. *Obs.*

1585 T. WASHINGTON tr. *Nicholay's Voy.* III. cxxi. 97 b, Followe the court of the great Lord (which they call the gate). **1599** HAKLUYT *Voy.* II. I. 129 *note*, The gate of the great Turke, is as much to say, as Constantinople: the which they call in the Turkish language Stanboll.

4. *transf.* An entrance into a country through mountains; a mountain-pass. Also *pl.* Cf. Gr. πύλη, L. *porta.*

1601 HOLLAND *Pliny* I. 121 They tooke it that those gates of Caucasus whereof we spake before, were the Caspian gates. **1697** POTTER *Antiq. Greece* I. xvi. (1715) 89 A strait narrow passage, and, as it were, a Gate, or Inlet into the Country. **1860** PUSEY *Min. Proph.* 393 The Easterns, as well as the Greeks and Latins, used the word 'gate' or 'doors' of the mountain-passes, which gave an access to a land, but which might be held against an enemy. **1877** C. D. WARNER *Levant* xii. 175 We dashed down the gate of a magnificent cañon.

5. *fig.* **a.** A means of entrance or exit; said e.g. of the five senses. Phrase ***to open a gate for*** or ***to***: to provide facility or opportunity for. ***the ivory gate, the gate of horn***: in Greek legend, those through which false and true dreams respectively come forth. Cf. DOOR 3.

c **1175** *Lamb. Hom.* 127 Hwet beoð þas .vii. ȝeate? Ðet beoð ure eȝan and ure neose and ure muð and ure earan. *a* **1300** *Cursor M.* 10146 (Cott.) þat mari, þat was þe gat [*other texts* ȝate, yate] of vr merci. **1390** GOWER *Conf. A.* III. 29 And thus min eye is made the gate, Through which the deinties of my thought Of lust ben to min herte brought. *c* **1416** HOCCLEVE *Poems* (1892) 62 Benigne lige Lord! o hauene and yate Of our confort. *c* **1440** *Jacob's Well* (E.E.T.S.) 274 þise arn þe wyndowys of þe body, & þe gatys of þe soule. *c* **1491** *Chast. Goddes Chyld.* 7 The yate of grace is opened to al that aske thenne to entree. **1526** *Pilgr. Perf.* (W. de W. 1531) 76 The hearynge, the touchynge, the tastynge, & the smellynge, whiche with yᵉ syght, be as fyue gates, by the whiche the ennemy sendeth in.. [his] messages .. to the soule. **1548** HALL *Chron., Hen. VI*, 187 Although the gate of a conquest were opened, yet it was shut agayn. **1599** SHAKS. *Much Ado* IV. i. 106 For thee Ile locke vp all the gates of Loue. **1603** KNOLLES *Hist. Turks* (1621) 690 Auria had don nothing but wisely & politickly, in.. opening a gate for a long war. **1623** DRUMM. OF HAWTH. *Cypress Grove* Wks. (1711) 117 What sweet contentments doth the soul enjoy by the senses! They are the gates and windows of its knowledge. **1625** BACON *Ess., Superstit.* (Arb.) 347 The Fauoring too much of good Intentions, which openeth the gate to Conceits and Nouelties. **1738** GLOVER *Leonidas* I. 153 To guard the gates of Greece, which open stand. **1781** GIBBON *Decl. & F.* II. 9 The Bosphorus and the Hellespont may be considered as the two gates of Constantinople. **1831** MACAULAY *Ess., Hampden* (1880) 204 Then he [Laud] dreamed that he turned Papist; of all his dreams the only one, we suspect, which came through the gate of horn. **1866** B. TAYLOR *Poems, Wayside Dream* 74 The gates of Slumber fold. **1870** MORRIS *Earthly Par.* I. Apol., Let it suffice me that my murmuring rhyme Beats with light wing against the ivory gate.

b. ***to get the gate***, to be dismissed, rejected or jilted; so ***to give*** (someone) ***the gate.*** *slang* (orig. and chiefly *U.S.*).

1918 *Diary* 26 Mar. in *Wine, Women & War* (1926) 52 Col. Y—— slated to get the gate. **1918** H. C. WITWER *From Baseball to Boches* iv. 143 'I wanna speak to you in private, Jeanne,' I says to her. 'Give this hick the gate!' **1922** S. LEWIS *Babbitt* viii. 119 If any of us were to indulge in it here, he'd get the gate so fast it would make his head swim. **1930** WODEHOUSE *Very Good, Jeeves!* x. 263, I don't believe there's a female in the world who could see Uncle George fairly often in those waistcoats without feeling that it was due to her better self to give him the gate. **1951** *Sat. Even. Post* 8 Dec. 44/1 There's no reason why he should be fired .. or given the gate. **1971** E. FENWICK *Impeccable People* viii. 47 She billed you for an extra month because Monnie gave her the gate.

c. The mouth. *slang.*

1937 in PARTRIDGE *Dict. Slang* 318/1 **1955** P. WILDEBLOOD *Against Law* 98 Eats sweets... Unwraps them as slowly as he can, and then pops them into his gate, all gloating like. **1963** 'A. GARVE' *Sea Monks* iii. 85 Macey pointed the gun at him... 'You keep your gate shut, big boy.' **1966** B. NAUGHTON *Alfie* viii. 54 Shut your big ugly gate at once.

d. [See quot. 1937, but perh. a shortening of *alligator.*] A person, esp. a jazz-musician; = CAT *sb.*[1] 2 c; freq. used as a form of address. *U.S. slang.*

1937 L. ARMSTRONG *Swing that Music* vii. 77 When I was a kid.. they started calling me 'Gate-mouth'... I started calling the other boys 'Gate' too... Then I got used to saying it and when I got into Kid Ory's band when the boys were all swinging good and hot, I would sing out, 'Swing it, Gate'.. and now 'Gate' is a word swing players use when they call out to one another in their own language. **1939** *Collier's* 8 Apr. 33/3 You've handicapped your tunes with stuff no gate wants to play. **1952** B. ULANOV *Hist. Jazz in Amer.* (1958) 351 *Gate*, once (and occasionally used after the swing era) synonymous with jazz musician.

6. a. The barrier itself; a framework of wood or iron either consisting of bars, gratings, etc., or with a solid face, turning on pivots or hinges, or sliding in a groove, and used either in a pair or singly. For *five-, six-bar(red gate* see FIVE C. 1, SIX.

c **1000** ÆLFRIC *Judges* xvi. 3 Samson.. ȝenam þa burȝ-gatu and ȝ ebær on his hricȝe mid þam postum. *a* **1300** *Cursor M.* 7185 Sampson, þat was selcuth wight.. bar þe yates o þe tun, And laid þam on a hei dun. **1543** *Ludlow Churchw. Acc.* (Camden) 13, ij. hasp for the same yatt. *c* **1600** SHAKS. *Sonn.* lxv, Rocks impregnable are not so stout, Nor gates of steel so strong, but Time decays. **1735** SOMERVILLE *Chase* II. 164 They strain to lead the Field, top the barr'd Gate, O'er the deep Ditch exulting Bound. **1762** GOLDSM. *Cit. W.* xiii, We made up to an iron gate, through which my companion told me we were to pass. **1805** G. M'INDOE *Million of Potatoes* 151 The laird look'd ower the yett. **1820** SCOTT *Monast.*

(1830) II. xvi. 250 It would be an unco task to mend the yetts. **1848** DICKENS *Dombey* vii, An immense pair of gates, with an immense pair of lion-headed knockers on them.

b. A contrivance for stopping or regulating the passage of water. (Cf. *flood-*, *lock-*, *sluice-gate*.)

1496 *Naval Acc. Hen. VII* (1896) 153 The Costes and Expences of makyng the Gates of the Dokke aforsaid. **1719** DE FOE *Crusoe* II. xii, This canal.. passes.. hills by the help of sluices and gates. **1874** KNIGHT *Dict. Mech.*, *Gate*, the valve which admits the water to the bucket of the Water-wheel.

c. *spec.* A starting-gate.

1928 *Daily Mail* 25 July 14/1 Drift has hitherto been a disappointment. She is bad at the gate. **1963** *Sunday Mirror* (Sydney) 20 Jan. 43/1 Gili.. was actually the first to hit the ground when the gates opened.

d. *Cricket.* The space between the bat and the batsman's body; formerly also, the wicket.

1851 W. BOLLAND *Cricket Notes* v. 108 His 'Gates' fell as flat as my hand. *Ibid.* 109 Upon the earliest appearance of the game in Ireland, the people applied the word Gate instead of Wicket. **1958** *Times* 17 Dec. 3/1 He [*sc.* the batsman] is on his way back to the pavilion bowled through the 'gate'. **1966** E. R. DEXTER *Ted Dexter Declares* ii. 22 If you're out, bowled through the gate.

e. A numbered entrance to the apron of an airport.

1956 J. STROUD *Famous Airports of World* v. 70 Each building will have one or two of these 'fingers' [*sc.* finger-like walkways] and each of these will have eight or more gates leading to the aircraft. **1969** J. ELLIOT *Duel* I. iv. 79 We're called at gate two; we might as well go over. **1971** F. RAPHAEL *Who were you with last night?* 168 We were standing around like passengers who've had their flight called but haven't been told which gate number.

7. Payment at a toll-gate.

1812 COL. HAWKER *Diary* (1893) I. 46 Coal.. 5*s.* 6*d.* a cart-load, free of gates and everything.

8. *techn.* **a.** (*Locksmithing*) One of the apertures in the tumblers for the passage of the stub.

1874 in KNIGHT *Dict. Mech.* I. 958.

b. A frame in which a saw or set of saws is stretched to prevent buckling. *U.S.*

1815 D. DRAKE *Cincinnati* iii. 145 The engine drives four saws in separate *gates*. **1874** KNIGHT *Dict. Mech.*, *Sash-saw*, a mill-saw strained in a gate, or sash, as it is sometimes called, from the resemblance of its stiles and rails to the frame of a window-sash.

c. *Lace-manuf.* (See quot.)

1839 URE *Dict. Arts* etc. 733 The term gauge, in the lace manufacture, means the number of gates, slits, or interstices, in one inch of the bolt-bar or comb.

d. An arrangement of slots, usu. in the shape of the letter **H**, through which the lever of a gear-box is moved to engage different gears. Freq. *attrib.* and *Comb.*

1906 *Westm. Gaz.* 23 Jan. 4/2 The advantage of the gate change is.. its simplicity and certainty. **1906** *Daily Chron.* 14 Nov. 9/3 The 'gate' system of gear changing. **1908** *Westm. Gaz.* 28 May 4/2 The two motions that an ordinary gate-quadrant necessitates. *Ibid.* 14 Nov. 15/2 Four speeds operated through a gate. **1928** *Daily Express* 11 Oct. 1/2 The gear lever can be shifted through the gate at will according to the road and traffic. **1956** C. MONDAY *Centre Lathe Work* i. 29 A yoke holds *B* and *C* in contact, and is extended to form an operating handle which fits into a gate on the outside of the gearbox. **1957** S. MOSS *In Track of Speed* xi. 137, I fumbled the five speed gear box until I got used to it. The reason for this was that the gate change was back to front to what was usual. **1967** A. DIMENT *Dolly Dolly Spy* i. 8 Only put the throttles through the gate in a dire emergency.

e. The mechanism in a cinematographic camera or projector that holds each frame momentarily behind the lens.

1909 *Statutory Rules & Orders* 12 The film gate shall be of massive construction and provided with ample heat radiating surface. **1915** B. E. JONES *Cinematogr. Bk.* i. 6 The radio of speed at which the film passes the gate will be found to be 50 ft. in one minute. *Ibid.* iii. 14 The function of the gate is to keep the film flat and steady during exposure. **1951** G. H. SEWELL *Amateur Film-Making* (ed. 2) iii. 22 The camera is an instrument whose function is to hold a supply of film, feed this to a position behind the lens known as the 'gate' of the instrument, move it intermittently past this gate, [etc.].

f. *Electronics.* An electrical signal that is used to trigger or control the passage of other signals in a circuit; a gate pulse.

1946 *Jrnl. Appl. Physics* XVII. 954/1 The ideal system would be to have an infinitesimal gate come right at the maximum of the rectified pulse. **1947** H. B. ABAJIAN in J. S. Hall *Radar Aids to Navig.* III. vii. 205 The timing circuits of the system.. provide a rectangular pulse, called a 'gate', coincident in time with the desired signal to switch on a normally cutoff section of the receiver. **1959** RIDER & USLAN *Encycl. Cathode-Ray Oscill.* (ed. 2) vii. 50/2 The control of the negative gate is such that for recurrent sweeps it is periodically applied to the pentode, where it causes a longer period of tube nonconduction as compared to tube conduction.

g. *Electronics*. A circuit with one output and a number of inputs, the output signal of which is determined by the combination of signals applied to the inputs.

1946 *Electronics* May 144/3 It is with the gate circuit, or switching unit, that the present discussion deals... The gate shown was simply substituted for the existing gate of the chronograph. **1948** *Ibid.* Sept. 114/3 A gate is essentially a device having two inputs and one output... Logically the gate detects the AND concept. **1964** C. DENT *Quantity Surveying by Computer* iii. 23 Multiplication and division are carried out in a similar manner, circuits employing such devices as 'gates'.. and 'flip-flops', being used to control and hold the binary digits.

h. *Electronics.* The material in a unipolar transistor forming the electrodes to which the input signal is applied, corresponding to the grid of a thermionic valve.

1952 W. SHOCKLEY in *Proc. Inst. Radio Engineers* Nov. 1368/1 The principles of operation of the unipolar transistor are substantially different from those of the bipolar types. For this reason, it seems appropriate to consider choosing a new set of names for the three terminals... The choice selected is 'source'.., 'drain'.., and 'gate' for the control electrodes that modulate the channel. One reason for selecting 'gate'.. is that the subscript '*g*' is reminiscent of 'grid' and the analogy is close between the two. **1959** J. N. SHIVE *Semiconductor Devices* xiii. 237 The gates act like the control grid wires in that the voltage applied to the gates determines the width of the channel through which source-to-drain current may flow. **1970** D. F. SHAW *Introd. Electronics* (ed. 2) xii. 304 In normal operation the gate [of a field effect transistor] must always be reverse biassed with respect to source and drain.

9. *University slang. pl.* ? The hour fixed for return to college. ? *Obs.*

1856 'C. BEDE' *Tales Coll. Life* i. 19 That's the ticket! that will just land me in time for Gates.

10. a. The total number of persons entering by payment at the gates, to see an athletic contest, football match, etc.

1888 *Leeds Even. Express* 10 Jan., Large football 'gates' are not an unusual thing in Yorkshire. **1890** *Whitby Gaz.* 24 Jan. 3/1 At the Hull match played on Saturday the gate was not half so large. **1894** *Times* 15 Sept. 6/4 They.. can rely on gates of 10,000 or more at every important match they play.

b. The amount of money thus received; = *gate-money* (see 13).

1891 *Daily Tel.* 21 Mar. 3/2 The leading clubs are now.. dependent for revenue on the 'gates' at the matches. **1894** *Times* 23 Mar. 10/2 The Middlesex executive determined to give the Whit Monday 'gate' to the famous Notts wicket-keeper.

11. Short for *Billingsgate*, *Newgate*, etc.

1722 DE FOE *Col. Jack* (1840) 44 The collier-masters generally sell their coals at the gate [? Billingsgate] as they call it. **1851** MAYHEW *Lond. Labour* I. 255 Of very ready sale are 'fish got from the gate' (stolen from Billingsgate). **1877** *Five Yrs.' Penal Servit.* i. 5 The 'steel', a slang name of the large metropolitan prisons, as the 'gate' is for Newgate.

12. *attrib.* and *Comb.*, as ***gate-bolt***, ***-opener***, ***-toll***, ***-tower***, ***-wright***; †***gatewise*** adv.

1845 BROWNING *How they brought*, etc. i. 3 'Good speed!' cried the watch, as the *gate-bolts undrew. **1826** T. MOORE *Mem.* (1854) V. 94, I.. was *gate-opener to the party all the way. **1892** *Daily News* 6 Apr. 5/4 They are known as 'through' or '*gate' tolls. **1842** SIR A. DE VERE *Song of Faith* 191 And *gate-towers, mouldering where the stream moans by. **1886** WILLIS & CLARK *Cambridge* III. 285 Every.. gate-tower in Oxford follows Wykeham's in the absence of angle-turrets.. with the sole exception of Christ Church. **1611** SPEED *Hist. Gt. Brit.* VII. xii. 267 A third stone somewhat of lesse quantity laid *gate-wise ouerthwart on their toppes. **1816** T. PARKER *Ess. Turnpike Gate* 20 The *gate-wright having planed and prepared the scantlings.

13. Special comb., as **gate-alms**, alms given by monks at the gate of a monastery; **gate-bill** (at the Universities of Oxford and Cambridge), a record of the times at which a man returns to college (or lodgings) after hours; also, the weekly account of fines charged against a man for staying out late; **gate-boot** (see quot. 1877 and cf. BOOT *sb.* II. 5 b); **gate-chamber** (see quot.); **gate-cheek** = CHEEK *sb.* II. 9; **gate circuit** = GATE *sb.*[1] 8 g; **gate city** *U.S.*, a city placed at the entrance to a district; *spec.* (with capital initials) applied to Atlanta, Keokuk, Kansas City, etc.; **gate-fine**, at a university, a fine imposed for failing to be within the College gates by a certain hour; **gatefold**, 'a folded insert (as a map) in a book or other publication larger in some dimension than the page' (1961 Webster); also, a similar piece of folded paper or other material; **gate-head** = GATEWAY; **gate-hook** (see quot.); **gate-leg**, **-legged** *a.*, designating a table with a leg or legs set in a gate-like frame which may be swung back to allow the leaves to be shut down; **gate-lodge**, a lodge (LODGE *sb.* 3) at the gate of the grounds belonging to a mansion, etc.; **gate pulse** *Electronics*, a pulse that allows a gate circuit to pass a signal; = GATE *sb.*[1] 8 f; **gate receipts** = *gate-money*; **gate(s-man**, a gate-keeper, esp. at level crossings on railways; **gate-meeting**, a race or athletic meeting to which admission is given on payment at the gate; **gate-money**, (*a*) money paid at the gates for admission to an athletic meeting, etc.; also *transf.*; (*b*) money charged on a gate-bill; **gate-net**, a net hung loosely across a gateway, for the purpose of catching hares driven at night; also *attrib.*; so **gate-netting** *vbl. sb.* and *pr. pple.*; **gate-penny**, 'a tribute paid by the customary tenants for leave to pass through one or more of their lord's gates' (Cassell); †**gate-room**, a lodge at the gate of an estate; **gate-saw** (see quot.); †**gate-stang** (see quot.); **gate-stead**, a gate-way; **gate-table**, a gate-leg table; **gate-valve**, a valve in which a sliding part controls the extent of the aperture; **gate-vein**, the *Vena portæ* (*obs.* exc. *fig.*); **gate-wheel**, a wheel operating the gates protecting a level crossing; **gate-works**, fortifications at the gate of a town, etc.

1896 T. BLASHILL *Sutton-in-Holderness* 56 Considerable gifts that had been settled on the monastery for the *gate-alms. **1803** *Gradus ad Cantab.* (1824) 128 To avoid *gate-bills he will be out at night as late as he pleases.. climb over the College walls, and fee his Gyp well. **1853** 'C. Bede' *Verdant Green* xi, Our freshman became aware of the mysteries of a gate-bill. **1716** in *N.W. Linc. Gloss.* s.v., To have, perceive, and take.. sufficient houseboot, hedge-boot .. *Gateboot, and Stakeboot. **1877** *Ibid.*, *Gateboot*, the right of cutting wood for making gates. **1874** KNIGHT *Dict. Mech.* 959/1 **Gate-chamber* (*Hydraulic Engineering*), a recess in the side wall of a canal-lock, which receives the opened gate, so that it shall not project into the lock-chamber. **1513** DOUGLAS *Æneis* VII. xi. 52 Strang *ȝet-cheikis of weirfayr and battale Straik dovne. *a* **1670** SPALDING *Troub. Chas. I* (1829) 12 He lodges in Andrew Haddentoun's at the yett-cheek. **1945** *Electronics* Dec. 135/1 The timing circuit is controlled by the counter and its associated *gate circuit. **1859** *Ladies' Repository* XIX. 51/2 Keokuk, Iowa, is the '*Gate City'—a translation, I believe, of its Indian name. **1865** *Atlanta Daily Intelligencer* 1 Oct. 2/1 Atlanta, the 'Gate City' of the South. **1887** *Courier-Journal* (Louisville, Ky.) 8 May 9/16 He enters the new South through the gate city. Louisville is to the South what Chicago is to the Northwest. **1909** 'O. HENRY' *Roads of Destiny* 348 In the Gate City of the South the Confederate Veterans were reuniting. **1898** *Chambers's Dict.* 377/2 **Gate-fine*, the fine imposed for disobedience to such orders. **1963** *Nation* 4 May 18/1 They were even less real than the *gatefold girls in 'Playboy'. **1963** 'E. MCBAIN' *Ten Plus One* (1964) ii. 19 There were seventy dollars in cash in the wallet... Carella found the photographs in the gatefold. **1965** *Spectator* 5 Mar. 308/3 The Consumer Council's eight-page gatefold leaflet on 'How to say "No" to a doorstep salesman'. **1968** *Punch* 6 Mar. 325/2, I don't think we are in danger of seeing a Modigliani in the gatefold pin-up section of *Playboy*. **1718** BP. HUTCHINSON *Witchcraft* 147 The cart was set fast in a *Gate-head, though it did not touch the Posts. **1847–78** HALLIWELL, *Thimble*, the boll of a *gate-hook on which the gate turns. *Staff.* **1874** KNIGHT *Dict. Mech.* 959/1 *Gate-hook*, a gate-hook is that part of a gate-hinge which is driven into the post and sustains the leaf attached to the gate. **1905** A. HAYDEN *Chats Old Furnit.* 25 **Gate-leg table.* This term is self-explanatory. The legs of this class of table open like a gate. They belong to Jacobean days and are sometimes spoken of as Cromwellian tables. **1924** 'J. SUTHERLAND' *Circle of Stars* viii. 64 An oak gate-leg table holding books and flowers. **1962** *Williamsburg Reproductions Catal.* 6/2 Among the most admired furnishings in the Governor's Palace is the oval gate-leg table in the supper room. **1903** *Connoisseur* V. xix (Advt.), Oak *gate-legged table. **1919** W. DEEPING *Second Youth* iii. 28 A gate-legged table in the hall. **1971** D. FRANCIS *Bonecrack* i. 13 The furniture.. consisted of an uninspiring three piece suite.., a gate-legged table, a standard lamp. **1922** JOYCE *Ulysses* 697 A baronial hall with *gatelodge and carriage drive. **1938** L. MACNEICE *Earth Compels* 8 A Yorkshire terrier ran in and out by the gate-lodge. **1796** MRS. M. ROBINSON *Angelina* I. 32 'Here's health and prosperity to all', said the old *gate-man. **1870** *Daily News* 19 Dec., Notwithstanding the efforts of the gate-man, the fellow succeeded in getting his horse and cart upon the line. **1884** *Pall Mall G.* 27 Dec. 4/1 The gate-men.. do not open their gates until the train has completely stopped. **1881** *Daily News* 14 July 5/3 Few of these athletes care to compete at *gate-meetings. **1820** *Sporting Mag.* VI. 190 Some demur took place respecting the division of what is termed the *gate money. **1887** *Times* 20 Sept. 9 We do not know exactly what control those who pocket the gate-money have over the performers. **1889** G. B. SHAW *London Music 1888–89* (1937) 118 A host of strangers who never did and never will contribute a farthing to the gate money upon which music depends for her living. **1920** *Hibbert Jrnl.* July 715 Now that paintings may only be seen behind barriers by paying gate-money, there is 'no demand for that sort of thing'. **1961** E. WILLIAMS *George* xix. 302 After.. 9.20 nobody's allowed out, and if we are out already, on our battels—our bills—we're charged gate-money, so much every half-hour, mounting till 12.20. **1598** MANWOOD *Lawes Forest* xviii. §9 (1615) 135 Any Buckstall or Engin, Hayes, *Gatenets [*printed* Gatenents], Pursenets, Ferrets or Conie-dogges. **1892** *Athenæum* 4 June 723/2 He was.. engaged in night poaching for hares with lurchers and gate-nets. **1892** *Autobiog. Eng. Gamekeeper* (J. Wilkins) 239 They poked their gate net stick into the ditch, and I felt it scrape over my legs. *Ibid.* 222 A great dodge in poaching used to be *gate netting. A hare on the prowl, started off a field when feeding, generally makes for the gate-run—that is to say, leaves the field by means of the gate—and, for this reason, one of the oldest methods of poaching is gate snaring or netting. *Ibid.* 224 They do not stop to touch the gate netting. *Ibid.* 250 When we caught two men gate netting at Gravel-Pits field. **1693** *Phil. Trans.* XVII. 691 He ends this Treatise with an Enumeration of the Quit-rents formerly paid out of the Weald, as Gavel-swine, Scot-ale, Pannage, *Gate-penny. **1945** *Electronics* Dec. 136/2 Upon firing the first round, the final trigger circuit shifts its state of equilibrium, initiating a negative *gate pulse. **1948** WOODWARD & WILLIAMS in J. A. Pierce et al. *Loran* II. vii. 227 The gate-pulse mixer is a double-triode coincidence mixer. **1914** G. V. HOBART *Boobs* v. 80 He.. proceeded to cover the *gate receipts with eager mitts. **1959** *Daily Tel.* 27 June 1/7 He now expected the crowd to reach 35,000 and gate receipts £178,500. **1702** *Lond. Gaz.* No. 3825/4 Two Copy-hold Estates, with a good House, Garden, and.. *Gate-rooms. **1874** KNIGHT *Dict. Mech.* 959/2 **Gate-saw*, a mill-saw which is strained in a gate or sash to prevent buckling. **1879** *Lumberman's Gaz.* 15 Oct., This was an improvement over the gate saw, almost as great as was the gate. **1611** COTGR., *Bonde*, the *yate-stang, or beame thats pulled vp, when a mill is to be set agate. **1610** *N. Riding Rec.* (1884) I. 201 For not making a sufficient *Yate stead being a common way in a place called Hurwood Yate. **1891** ATKINSON *Moorland Par.* 65 *note*, A brig-stone is a kind of rough conduit for water across a gate-stead. **1904** *Daily Chron.* 4 Feb. 8/1 Choose a *gate table in preference to any other, since after meals are over it is but a small matter to fold this and place it at one side. **1906** *Mag. Fine Arts* Apr. 443 Spiral-legged

Gate-table. *a* **1884** KNIGHT *Dict. Mech.* Suppl. 394/2 Jenkin's *gate valve has a disk of compressible packing held to its seat by a wedge-shaped follower. **1958** *Engineering* 11 Apr. 469/1 Hydraulically-actuated wedge gate valves.. have successfully met the rigorous specification. **1615** CROOKE *Body of Man* 99 The vpper branches which wee call the roots of the *Gate-veine.. are disseminated through the hollow part of the Liuer. **1622** BACON *Hen. VII*, 161 Hee could not endure to haue Trade sicke, nor any obstruction to continue in the Gate-vaine which disperseth that bloud. **1840** BROWNING *Sordello* I. 264 He, Gate-vein of this heart's blood of Lombardy.. is thine. **1903** *Jrnl. Inst. Electr. Engin.* XXXII. 620 In all cases where the gates and signals are worked from one point the *gate-wheel is interlocked with the signal levers. **1808** SCOTT *Marm.* VI. xi, *Gate-works, and walls, were strongly mann'd.

gate (geɪt), *sb.*[2] Now only *Sc.* and *north. dial.* Forms: *α.* 3- **gate**, (3, 5 **gatt(e**, 4-5 **gat**). *β.* 5-7 **gaite, gayte**, 4, 8 *Sc.* **get(e**, 8 *Sc.* **gaet**, 9 *dial.* **geeat**. See also GAIT. [a. ON. *gata*, wk. fem. (Sw. *gata*, Da. *gade*) = OHG. *gaȥȥa* (MHG. *gaȥȥe*, mod.Ger. *gasse* lane, whence early mod.Du. *gasse*, now dial. *gas*), Goth. *gatwô*:—OTeut. **gatwôn-*.

As to the ulterior etymology nothing has been ascertained. Connexion with the root of GET *v.* has been supposed for this as for GATE *sb.*[1]; some have assumed a root **ghad* meaning 'to go', on the ground of the OIr. *dia n-gaidh* he went. The spelling *gait* (*gayte*) first appears in the 15th c., but was almost confined to Sc. and northern writers until the beginning of the 17th c. It remains in the only sense of the word which is current in literary English: see GAIT *sb.* (A supposed example of this spelling has been found in the Cotton MS. of the *Cursor M.*, line 15278; but this is prob. a mistake: see GATE *sb.*[3])]

I. A way.

1. A way, road, or path.

α. *c* **1200** ORMIN 12749 An off þa tweȝȝen þatt comenn till þe Laferrd Crist þær he bi gate ȝede. *a* **1300** *Cursor M.* 8960 þar þis tre lai in hir gatt. *c* **1380** *Sir Ferumb.* 1801 On þe gate we mette of þyne stronge þeues seuene. *c* **1450** *St. Cuthbert* (Surtees) 5820 þai lete þair oxen in þe gate A while standdand rest. **1533** BELLENDEN *Livy* V. (1822) 425 Thay maid ane mine undir the erde, to mak ane gate be quhilk thay micht cum to the castell of Veos. **1590** SPENSER *F.Q.* I. i. 13 Wisedome warnes, whilest foot is in the gate To stay the steppe.

β. *c* **1450** HENRYSON *Mor. Fab.* 71 Where hee in length lay streiked in the gait. **1535** STEWART *Cron. Scot.* (1858) I. 83 Quhat freik befoir thame in thair gait tha fand, Tha gart him lig rycht law vponn the land. **1573** *Satir. Poems Reform.* xlii. 982 A lytill Eist the bra, Quhair that our gaittis partit in twa.

b. *fig.*

13.. *E.E. Allit. P.* A. 395 Of alle my Ioy þe hyȝe gate Hit is in grounde of alle my blysse. **1583** *Leg. Bp. St. Androis* 755 in *Satir. Poems Reform.* xlv, For greid of geir, and warldly graith, On baith the gaitis he grundis his fayth.

c. (*to find, lose, ask*, etc. *one's*) way.

1390 GOWER *Conf.* II. 35 That he be right ware.. That he mistake not his gate. *c* **1440** *Bone Flor.* 149 Evyr Speryng ther gatys gane Unto the Cyte of Rome. *c* **1746** J. COLLIER (Tim Bobbin) *Lanc. Dialect* (1862) 23, I mawkint, on lost meh gete ogen snap.

2. Phrases. ***to come, gang, go, ride a, the, his, her***, etc. ***gate***: see GANG *v.* and GO *v.* ***to take*** (***the***) ***gate***: to take the road, go away; to follow a path or course. † ***to be in gate to***: to be on the way to, be bound for. † ***to give gate to***: to give a road *to*, make way *for*. † ***to go to the gate***: to get into the current (of destruction), go to wrack. † ***to grant the gate***: to give leave to go. † ***to hold the gate***: to hold on one's way, hence, to prosper. † ***to put by the gate, to put*** (***lay***, etc.) ***out of the gate***: to put out of the way. ***this*** (***that***) ***gate***: used adverbially = this (that) way, in this (that) direction. ***some, any gate***: somewhere, anywhere.

α. *a* **1300** *Cursor M.* 6262 In þe see his wand he smat, It claue, and gaue þan redi gat. *c* **1320** *Sir Tristr.* 2091 þe duerwe toke þe gate. **1375** BARBOUR *Bruce* VI. 577 Ilk man a syndri gat is gane. **1426** AUDELAY *Poems* 14 That hath goon gatis ungayne. *c* **1435** *Torr. Portugal* 680 Owt of the watyr he toke the gate. *c* **1440** *York Myst.* xxx. 230 Here, ye gomes, gose a rome, giffe vs gate, We muste steppe to yone sterne of a-state. *Ibid.* 446 He graunte hym his gates for to gone. *a* **1542** WYATT *Of Courtier's life* 39 [Cato] that with his death did scape out of the gate. **1548** KEY *Erasm. Par. Mark* vi. 6-9 Yf he dyd take vitayle and a good summe of money with him, beyng in gate to the sandes of Afrike, or to summe nacion where as there is no ientle entertaynement.. of strangers [orig. *ad Libycas harenas aut inhospitalem gentem profecturus*]. **1577-87** HARRISON *England* I. xii. in *Holinshed* 55 After this confluence, it [the Test] taketh the gate to Kimbebridge. **1579** SPENSER *Sheph. Cal.* Epil., Goe, little Calender! thou hast a free passeporte; Goe but a lowly gate amongst the meaner sorte. **1583** *Leg. Bp. St. Androis* 639 in *Satir. Poems Reform.* xlv, To Londoun Lowrie tuke the geat. **1596** DALRYMPLE tr. *Leslie's Hist. Scot.* III. 192 The tyran Romack was put by the gate. **1637** RUTHERFORD *Lett.* (1894) 260 It is only best that ye set yourself apart, as a thing laid up and out of the gate, for Christ alone. *a* **1670** SPALDING *Troub. Chas. I* (1792) I. 113 Ilk ane of the rest rode a sundry gate. *Ibid.* 233 Monro took gate to Strathbogie. **1671** M. BRUCE *Good News in Evil Times* (1708) 9 Ye will go to the Gate, few or none of you shall be left. **1709** —— *Soul-Confirm.* 22 (Jam.) Hold ay your shoes on your feet, and in God's name I promise you ye shall hade the gate, fail who will. **1786** BURNS *Brigs of Ayr* 122 Crashing ice, borne on the roaring speat, Sweeps dams, an' mills, an' brigs, a' to the gate. *a* **1810** TANNAHILL *Poems* (1846) 55, I truly hate the dirty gate That mony a body taks. **1872** C. GIBBON *For the King* i, Come this gate. **1889** BARRIE *Window in Thrums* xix. 183 A notion 'at I had put it some gait. **1893** STEVENSON *Catriona* 12 Ye're no likely to gang far this gate.

β. *c* **1450** *Golagros & Gaw.* 791 The king grantit the gait to schir Gawane, And prayt to the grete God to grant him his grace. *c* **1470** HENRY *Wallace* I. 250 Thai left him swa, and furth thar gait can gang. **1535** STEWART *Cron. Scot.* I. 574 He tuke the gait towart Candalia. **1560** ROLLAND *Crt. Venus* IV. 524 He is gane ane vther gait. **1637** B. JONSON *Sad Sheph.* II. i, False gelden, gang thy gait And do thy turns betimes. **1692** *Scot. Presbyt. Eloq.* (1738) 114 They went a Gait of their own. **1795** BURNS *O Lassie, art thou sleeping yet?* Gae back the gait ye cam again. **1855** MRS. GASKELL *North & S.* xxviii, To keep me from going what gait I choose. **1855** MOTLEY *Dutch Rep.* II. v. (1866) 218 The man.. described himself to Granvelle as one who went his own gait. **1875** W. MCILWRAITH *Guide Wigtownshire* 38 It is now time for us to 'tak' the gait' again.

3. Length of way, distance. Chiefly in advb. phrases. ***half-gate***: half-way. *Obs.* exc. *Sc.*

? *a* **1500** *Peebles to Play* in Chambers *Pop. Hum. Scot. Poems* (1862) 7 They had not gane half of the gait, When the maidens cam upon them. **1536** BELLENDEN *Cron. Scot.* (1821) I. xlvi, Schort gait fra thir Ilis is Iona. **1597** MONTGOMERIE *Cherrie & Slae* 339 With earnest eye quhil I espye The fruit betwixt me and the skye, Halfe gaite almaist to hevin. **1795** MACNEILL *Will & Jean* I. xxix, Hame's now scarce a mile o' gate.

4. A street. Frequent in street-names of northern and midland towns (e.g. York, Nottingham, Leicester); as Gallowgate, Kirkgate, Micklegate, etc.

α. *c* **1470** HENRY *Wallace* V. 764 A nothir sone apon the hed strak he, Quhill chaftis and cheyff [*v.r.* cheik] vpon the gate can fle. **1571** in Tytler *Hist. Scot.* (1864) III. 341 *note*, He came running down the gate. **1607-8** *N. Riding Rec.* (1884) I. 99 Will. Kidd of Kirby Moreside for keeping disorder in the towne-gate. **1811** WILLAN *W. Riding Gloss.*, *Gate*, a street or road. **1876** *Whitby Gloss.*, *Geeat*, a course, street or thoroughfare.

β. *c* **1470** HENRY *Wallace* vi. 176 The worthi Scottis the gait left at the last. **1508** DUNBAR *Flyting w. Kennedie* 225 Than rynis thow down the gait, with gild of boyis, And all the toun tykis hingand in thy heilis. **1570** *Durham Depos.* (Surtees) 197 The sande pytt in the towne gait at Langnewton. *c* **1590** BUREL *Pass. Pilgr.* in J. Watson *Collect. Poems* (1706) II. 5 All curious pastimes and consaits.. Wes to be seen on Edinburgh gaits. **1609** *N. Riding Rec.* (1884) I. 171 The highe wayes throughe the town gayt in Morton upon Swayle, being the Kinges heigh street. **1788** W. MARSHALL *Yorksh. Gloss.*, *Gait*, street; as west-gait, castle-gait, the town-gait, the gait-door.

5. *Mining.* (See quot. 1881.)

1747 HOOSON *Miner's Dict.* G iij b, The Distance between the Nogs is the width of the Gate within the Timber. **1829** GLOVER *Hist. Derby* I. 47 The miners have driven a gate across under the river. **1881** RAYMOND *Mining Gloss.*, *Gate* ..a road or way underground for air, water, or general passage.

II. Act of going.

†**6.** A going, journey, course. *lit.* and *fig.* *Obs.*

α. *a* **1300** *E.E. Psalter* i. 6 Gate of wicked for-worth sal ai. *a* **1340** HAMPOLE *Psalter* xvii. 40 þou made brade my gatis vndire me. **1377** LANGL. *P. Pl.* B. XVIII. 241 Peter the apostel parceyued his gate, And.. wel hym knewe. *c* **1450** *Bidding Prayer* in *Lay Folks Mass Bk.* 69 We sall pray also for all trewe pilgrams.. þat god of his gudenes graunt þame parte of our gode prayers & us of þare gode gates. *c* **1450** *Bk. Curtasye* 201 in *Babees Bk.* 305 To sayntis yf þou þy gate hase hyȝt, Thou schalle fulfylle hit with alle þy myȝt. *a* **1547** SURREY *Æneid* II. 268 But they [the serpents] with gate direct to Lacon ran. *c* **1565** LINDESAY (Pitscottie) *Chron. Scot.* (1728) 42 Coming forward with a great army for the king's support, his gate was overset by Alexander, earl of Crawford. **1579-80** NORTH *Plutarch* (1676) 78 So grant the gods.. my ship and me good gate. **1600** HOLLAND *Livy* XXI. xxxvi. (1609) 413 That snow, being once within the gate of so many people and beasts upon it [L. *tot hominum jumentorumque incessu*], fretted and thawed. **1612** W. PARKES *Curtaine-Dr.* (1876) 29 Euen like this Cedar in times gate ile bring, Both him and such to fatall ruining. **1633** EARL MANCH. *Al Mondo* (1636) 96 Death.. thou art.. swifter in thy gate than the Roe or Hinde.

†**b.** Of a bird, *esp.* a hawk: Flight. *Obs.*

1340 HAMPOLE *Pr. Consc.* 7076 Als foghel fleghand in þe ayre als wynd, Of whase gate men may na trace fynd. **1575** TURBERV. *Faulconrie* 150 Get your hawke to a good gate above the fowle. **1611** MARKHAM *Countr. Content.* I. v. (1668) 32 When she [a hawk] is at the height of her gate. **1612** DRAYTON *Poly-olb.* i. 25 My verse with wings of skill may flie a loftie gate. **1677** N. COX *Gentl. Recreat.* (ed. 2) 201 When a high-flying Hawk, being whistled to, gathers upwards to a great Gate, you must continue her therein.

†**c.** ***gate-down***: going down, setting (of the sun, etc.). ***at the gate-down***: ready to tumble down.

c **1440** *Promp. Parv.* 188/2 Gate downe, *descensus*. *Ibid.*, Gate downe, or downe gate of þe sunne, or any oþer planete, *occasus*. *c* **1475** *Crabhouse Reg.* (1889) 61 The dortoure was at so grete mischeef and at the gate-downe the Prioresse.. took it downe for drede of more harmys.

†**d.** *fig.* Proceeding. *Obs.*

1602 SHAKS. *Ham.* I. ii. 31 We haue heere writ To Norway, Vncle of young Fortinbras (Who Impotent and Bedrid, scarsely heares Of this his Nephewes purpose) to suppresse His further gate heerein.

7. Manner of going. *Obs.* exc. in specific applications, for which see GAIT *sb.*

a **1637** B. JONSON *Elegie on my Muse* Wks. (1692) 581 She had a Mind as calm, as she was fair; Not tost or troubled with light Lady-air; But, kept an even Gate. **1735** SOMERVILLE *Chase* II. 172 Huntsman! her Gait observe, if in wide Rings She wheel her mazy Way.

†**b.** *Hunting.* Length of stride (of a deer) as shown by his footmarks. *Obs.*

1677 N. COX *Gentl. Recreat.* (ed. 2) 17 When Huntsmen.. finde a Hart by the Slot, &c. and then minde his step to know whether he is great.. they then say, they know him by his Gate. **1706** in PHILLIPS (ed. Kersey).

8. A right to run or pasturage for a cow, horse, etc. **a.** on a common field, representing a share of the joint ownership in the field; **b.** on private ground (let for an annual rent). Also ***beast-, cattle-, cow-***, etc. ***gate***. Cf. GANG *sb.*[1] 4c. (In north. and north-midl. English dialects.)

α. **1606** *Nottingham Rec.* IV. 281 The East Steyner shall go to 10 men att 3 kyne gate a peice att xiiij. li. rent. **1613** *Hibbaldstow, Lincolnsh., Court Roll*, That none shal lett any gates in the Inges but to those that haue gates of ther awne. **1641** BEST *Farm. Bks.* (Surtees) 118 Aboute a weeke before St. Hellen day, wee beginne to inquire and listen after gates for our younge beasts. **1665** *MS. Grassmens Bk. St. Giles', Durham*, Resaved for 2 gates .00. 02. 08. **1769** *Atwick Inclos. Act 2* Certain cattle gates, or pasture for cattle there. **1804** *Hull Advertiser* 4 Feb. 2/3 Six gates or common rights on a common called Wilfholme.

β. **1586** *Wills & Inv. N.C.* (Surtees 1860) 207 To my sister Swinburne's children the grasse or gaite of one milke-cowe. **1846** *Award, Apportionm. Tithes, Carnforth, Lancs.* 31 Dec., Four Gaits and one Claw in Bolton Highfield. **1887** *York Herald* 16 Apr. 2/1 The Gaits to be paid for before the animals are taken away. **1890** *Westmld. Gaz.* 8 Nov. 4/2 To be let.. Twelve Sheep Gaits on Appletree Fell.

III. Way, manner, method.

9. Way, manner, or method of doing or behaving; a peculiar habit. † ***at no gate***: nowise. *Obs.*

α. *c* **1200** ORMIN 12320 Whatt gate he wann Eve & Adam þurrh þise þrinne wæpenn. *c* **1375** *Sc. Leg. Saints, Ninian* 825 þai var richt besy ay aboute To fynd sum get hyme to grewe. *c* **1400** *Destr. Troy* 2239 Let oure gate be so gouernet, þat no grem folow. *c* **1450** HENRYSON *Mor. Fab.* 25 Unto the Tod this gate the Wolfe can tell. **1513** BRADSHAW *St. Werburge* I. 2399 Thefte, murthur, robry, were founde at no gate. **1633** RUTHERFORD *Lett.* (1862) I. 105, I have gotten now.. the gate to open the slote [etc.]. **1671** M. BRUCE *Good News in Evil Times* (1708) 2 They that are Faithful to Him will not want a Word, one Gate or another. *Ibid.* 30, I love not to be called Singular, and make a World's-wonder of that gate. **1787** BURNS *Death Poor Mailie* 35 An' may they never learn the gaets Of ither vile, wanrestfu' pets! **1816** SCOTT *Antiq.* vi, Dinna speak that gate o' the gentlemen volunteers. **1832-53** A. RODGER in *Whistle-Binkie* (Scot. Songs) Ser. I. 25 That's never the gate wi' blythe Jamie M'Nab.

β. **1793** BURNS *Let. to G. Thomson* Wks. (Globe) 537 Ilka man wears his belt his ain gait. **1808** MISS HAMILTON *Cottagers Glenburnie* xiii. 259 Aye, says she, we have new gaits now. *a* **1810** TANNAHILL *Poems* (1846) 42, I smile at your low trifling gaits, And could heartily lend you my prayers. **1835** MARRYAT *Jac. Faithf.* xi, Tom, Tom, I'll cut you into pork pieces, if you go on that gait. **1862** J. R. WISE *New Forest* 282 When a person has done anything foolish he says, 'this is a gait I have got'. **1886** ELWORTHY *W. Somerset Word-bk.*, *Gait*, any peculiar habit, such as a nervous twitching of the face; any antic or grimace performed habitually.

b. In combination with certain adjs. and advs., often with advb. genitive ending *-s*, as *any gate(s*. Also *algate(s, another gate(s, howgate(s, manygate(s, nogate(s, nonegate, othergate(s, sogate, thusgate(s*, for which see those words.

10. *attrib.* and *Comb.*, *as* † **gate-door**, a street door; **gate-end** *Coal-mining* (see quot.); † **gate-going** *vbl. sb.*, wayfaring; † **gate-law, -leave**, right of way; toll or rent paid for this (cf. *way-leave*); **gate-lips** *Coal-mining* (see quot.); **gate-road** *Coal-mining* = GATEWAY[2]; † **gate-row**, a street; † **gates-man**, one employed in a coal-pit to make the passages; † **gate-trip** (see GAIT *sb.*[1] c).

c **1460** *Towneley Myst.* xiii. 328 Go spar The *gaytt doore. **1891** *Labour Commission* Gloss., **Gate-end*, in the case of long-wall workings the end (nearest to the face of the coal) of the branch roadway leading from the main road to the coal face where the miners work. *a* **1555** BRADFORD *Wks.* (Parker Soc.) II. 293 Then came up visions, miracles, dead spirits, walking, and talking how they might be released by this mass, by that pilgrimage *gate-going. **1641** BEST *Farm. Bks.* (Surtees) 18 Such as are forced to goe to other townes for want of water att hoame, pay oftentimes 2*d.* a score for *gatelawe. **1769** *Hutton Cranswick Enclos. Act* 9 Money.. paid.. as and for a toll or gate law. **1325** *Charter penes W. Greenwell* (1897), Le dit Johan et ses heires.. trouerunt *Gateleue et Rivage pour touz les carbouns. **1891** *Labour Commission* Gloss., **Gate-lips*, the roof of the *gate-end*, that is, the place where the roof ceases to have been made high enough for horses to work in or the entrance to the face, divided from the gate-end by the 'ripping'. **1860** *Ure's Dict. Arts* III. 955 A '*gate-road' or horse-way is next driven in the bottom of the coal. **1897** *Daily News* 23 Apr. 3/1 Lord Dudley reserved a right to drive gate-roads through the coal. **1598** R. BERNARD tr. *Terence, Andria* I. i, A certaine woman ..came.. to dwell here in our neighbourhood or *gaterow. *a* **1649** *Sc. Acts Chas. I* (1870) V. 419/2 *Gaitesmen, who workes þe wayes and passages in þe saidis hewghes ar als necessar to þe owneres.. as þe coall-hewers.

† **gate**, *sb.*[3] *Obs. rare.* Also 3 **gait**, 5 **gayte**. [app. a. OF. *gait, gaite*, n. of action f. *gaiter* to watch.]

? The action of watching or lying in wait; a watch; an ambush.

a **1300** *Cursor M.* 15278 þat i ha luued, he sal me trai, þe gait it es al graid. [The other texts have *gate* and *weye*, showing that the scribes interpreted the word as GATE *sb.*[2]; but the spelling *ai* for *a* seems unexampled at so early a date, and the sense of 'ambush' seems to be required.] *c* **1435** *Torr. Portugal* 1605 To the I have fulle good gate; For thou slow my brother Cate—That thou shalte by fulle dere. **1494** FABYAN *Chron.* VII. 649 Y[t] he shulde be ware & haue hym selfe in good gayte.

gate (geɪt), *sb.*[4] *Founding.* Also **gat, geat, get, git.** [Of somewhat obscure origin; the Du. synonym is *gietgat*, f. *gieten* (= OE. *ȝéotan*) to pour, cast

+ *gat* = GATE *sb.*[1] Cf. OE. *gyte* sb., pouring out.]

1. †**a.** (See quot. 1683.) *Obs.* **b.** The opening or channel through which the molten metal flows into a mould.

1677 MOXON *Mech. Exerc.* I. 53 A *Geat*, is the hole through which the Mettal runs into the Mold. **1683** *Ibid.* II. 378 *Geat*, is the little Spout or Gutter made in the Brim of Casting Ladles. **1790** IMISON *School Arts* II. 154 When the git is filled up with the fluid metal. **1839** URE *Dict. Arts* etc. 520 The hydrostatic pressure produced by a high gate or filling-in aperture, contributes much to secure the soundness and solidity of the casting. **1893** *Northumberld. Gloss.*, *Git*, in a mould, the narrow neck or channel through which the metal is poured. It is generally applied as the term for the superfluous piece of metal which is left in the neck of the mould after a casting is made.

2. The waste piece of metal cast in the gate.

1839 URE *Dict. Arts* etc. 522 This excess [of metal] forms the gates, false seams, &c. **1862** MAYHEW *Lond. Labour* IV. 377 When you have your coin cast, there is a 'gat', or piece of refuse metal, sticks to it. **1879** *Cassell's Techn. Educ.* IV. 262-3 When cooled sufficiently they are.. broken off from the 'gets' which are thin strips of metal filling the connecting gutters. *Ibid.* 413/2 The blank is.. cut a little larger than is necessary in order to leave room for a 'get' or solid piece at the end of the prongs [of a fork] which is retained.. for the purpose of maintaining the requisite rigidity to keep the article in shape.

3. *attrib.* and *Comb.*, as **gate-piece** = 2 above; **gate-shutter** (see quot.).

1839 URE *Dict. Arts* etc. 520 This gate piece being superfluous is knocked off almost immediately after, or even before the casting cools. **1875** KNIGHT *Dict. Mech.*, *Gate-shutter*, a spade or paddle which closes the channel against the molten metal when the mold or bed is full, and turns it in another direction to other molds or beds.

gate (geɪt), *v.*[1] [f. GATE *sb.*[1]] **1.** *trans.* At the Universities of Oxford and Cambridge: To confine (an undergraduate) to the precincts of the college, either entirely or after a certain hour.

1835 *Snobiad* 62 in Whibley *Cap & Gown* (1889) 144 Two Proctors kindly holding either arm, Staunch the dark blood, and gate him for the term. **1861** HUGHES *Tom Brown at Oxf.* xii, [He] gave him a book of Virgil to write out, and then gated him for a fortnight after hall. **1881** SAINTSBURY *Dryden* 6 He was discommonsed and gated for a fortnight for disobedience and contumacy.

2. *Electronics.* To subject to the action of a gate (see GATE *sb.*[1] 8 f, g). **a.** To select those parts of (a signal) that occur within given time intervals or have amplitudes within given limits. **b.** To switch by means of a gate circuit. Usu. as **'gated** *ppl. a.*, or as *vbl. sb.* and *ppl. a.* (see below).

1946 *Jrnl. Appl. Physics* XVII. 968/1 The gated background audio-noise voltage. **1946, 1947** [implied in GATING *vbl. sb.*] **1950** LAWSON & UHLENBECK *Threshold Signals* ix. 253 In the aural method of detection one usually gates or strobes the incoming signals. **1957** R. F. SHEA *Transistor Circuit Engin.* x. 317 A transistor switching circuit which may be used to gate an input signal from a common input terminal to one of two output terminals. **1959** J. N. SHIVE *Semiconductor Devices* xiv. 255 (*caption*) This gating circuit not only performs the gating function but amplifies the gated signal as well. **1968** P. A. P. MORAN *Introd. Probability Theory* i. 44 An electric source producing random impulses.. was gated (switched on and off) once every second.

Hence **'gating** *vbl. sb.* and *ppl. a.*

1861 HUGHES *Tom Brown at Oxf.* xii, He.. then dismissed punishment and gating from his mind. **1883** LD. R. GOWER *My Remin.* I. xii. 221 Our tutor threatened to report us to the Head. However, we eventually got off without even a gating. **1946** *Jrnl. Appl. Physics* XVII. 953/2 Gating under such circumstances would result in a distortion of the pulse by shearing it fore and aft. **1947** H. B. ABAJIAN in J. S. Hall *Radar Aids to Navig.* III. vii. 205 (*caption*) Block diagram of the gating system. **1959** [see sense 2 above.] **1966** *McGraw-Hill Encycl. Sci. & Technol.* XI. 207/1 The counting circuit can operate a gating circuit which passes the clock pulses directly to the cathode-ray tube.

†**gate**, *v.*[2] *Obs. rare*$^{-1}$. [f. GATE *sb.*[2]] *intr.* Of an animal: To walk.

1583 STANYHURST *Æneis* (Arb.) 23 Three stags sturdye wer vnder Neere the seacost gating.

†**gate**, *v.*[3] *Obs. rare*$^{-1}$. [? a. OF. *gaiter*: see GATE *sb.*[3]] *intr.* To watch.

c **1590** BUREL *Pass. Pilgr.* in J. Watson *Collect. Poems* (1706) II. 33 Bot as the foular casts his cair, His catch for to preuent, So thay wer trapit in the snair.. Still waiting and gating, Quhyll thay wer all oretane.

gate (geɪt), *v.*[4] *Founding.* [f. GATE *sb.*[4]] *trans.* To provide (a mould, etc.) with a gate or gates (see GATE *sb.*[4] 1 b). Also *intr.*

1901 *Shop & Foundry Practice* (*Colliery Engineer Co.*) IV. xl. 5 It is usually better to gate a mold for a heavy casting as near the bottom as possible. **1950** J. S. CAMPBELL *Casting & Forming Processes* ix. 77 For many metals such as aluminum and magnesium it is good practice to gate into the castings at several places as a help in avoiding hot spots and in filling the mold cavity.

Hence **'gated** *ppl. a.*[2], provided with a gate or gates; **'gating** *vbl. sb.*[2], the action of providing gates; the arrangement of gates, runners, etc., through which molten metal enters a mould.

1906 F. W. BARROWS *Pract. Pattern-Making* I. i. 16 The moulder.. suggested the gating of the patterns, having noticed the castings as he dumped the mould, with their runners tying them all together, making one pattern of the flask full. *Ibid.* IV. i. 228 The moulding-machine manufacturers advertise that you can use your present patterns, whether of wood or metal, single or gated, on 'our' machines. **1907** J. G. HORNER *Encycl. Pract. Engin.* V. 88/2 *Gating*, signifies the channels, and formation of the same by which liquid metal enters a mould after it leaves the pouring basin. **1931** *Foundry Trade Jrnl.* 28 May 369/2 This gating is not so simple as the top one, and it requires a heavier weight of sprues. **1948** *Metals Handbk.* (*Amer. Soc. Metals*) 6/2 *Gated pattern*, mold patterns designed to permit two or more castings, joined by connecting channels, to be made in one mold.

gate, obs. form of GOAT.

-gate, *suffix.* orig. and chiefly *U.S.* [Part of the name *Watergate*: see note s.v. WATERGATE[3].] A terminal element denoting an actual or alleged scandal (and usually an attempted cover-up), in some way comparable with the Watergate scandal of 1972. Appended to: **a.** The name of the place where such a scandal (allegedly) occurred, or that of a place in some way associated with the scandal, as ***Dallasgate***, ***Hollywoodgate***, ***Irangate***, ***Koreagate***, etc.

1973 *National Lampoon* Aug. 27/2 There have been persistent rumors in Russia of a vast scandal... Implicated in 'the Volgagate' are a group of liberal officials. **1975** *Mod. People* 1 Oct. 1 (*heading*) Shocking Dallasgate revealed. **1976** *Guardian Weekly* 5 Dec. 6/2 The continually expanding scandal over the Park regime's influence peddling on Capitol Hill has already been called a 'Koreagate'. **1978** *Newsweek* 23 Jan. 55/3 Rumors of a coverup spread, and journalists scurried to investigate what some were already calling Hollywoodgate. **1978** *Maclean's Mag.* 9 Oct. 66 (*caption*) Thorpe and Whitehall-gate: how the Establishment works. **1986** *Independent* 10 Dec. 12/3 It is all too easy for Mr Reagan.. to see 'Irangate' purely in domestic American terms.

b. The proper name, nickname, etc., of a person or organization implicated in the scandal, as ***Billygate***, ***Floodgate***, ***Totegate***, etc.

1975 *Wall St. Jrnl.* 24 Apr. 1/6 (*heading*) Motorgate: how a floating corpse led to a fraud inquiry and ousters by GM. **1977** *N.Y. Times Mag.* 16 Oct. 38/1 Lancegate is no Watergate... The Carter men had hardly a month to plan.. a downplaying of Bert Lance's problems. **1978** *Time* 6 Mar. 21/2 Many friends of Flood's will probably be touched by the investigation, which is already becoming known as 'Floodgate'. **1978** *Observer* 10 Dec. 5/1 The South African Government easily defeated.. an attempt.. to force its resignation over 'Muldergate'—the Information Department scandal. **1979** *Ibid.* 29 July 4/1 'Totegate'.. centres on the Tote's practice of collecting off-course bets and sending them for inclusion.. at the racecourse up to five minutes after the result of the race is known. **1980** *Newsweek* 18 Aug. 81/1 The unfolding tale of Billy Carter and his Libyan connection—an affair that many big-city dailies still call 'Billygate'. **1983** *Tuscaloosa* (Alabama) *News* 11 July 4/2 It seems to me absurd—on the basis of what we know now—to equate 'Cartergate' with 'Watergate'. **1986** *Marxism Today* Sept. 41/3 The current deterioration of the Ulster environment will continue unabated.. if future developments significantly touch the RUC ('Stalkergate') or the judiciary.

c. A common noun (or occas. another part of speech) that specifies the commodity, activity, etc., at the centre of the scandal.

1973 *Saturday Rev. World* (U.S.) 20 Nov. 45/1 Inevitably, the brouhaha of Bordeaux became known as Wine-gate. **1975** *Time* 18 Aug. 67/2 The suspects allegedly falsified records, fed incriminating evidence through a paper shredder and conducted a cover-up so pervasive that one investigator calls it 'Ice Cream Gate'. **1976** *Tuscaloosa* (Alabama) *News* 11 Apr. D14/7 Farmers in Zuiderveen's Missaukee County have distributed bumper stickers that say 'PBB: Cattlegate bigger than Watergate.' **1978** *Time* 2 Oct. 43/1 The affair that Britons were dubbing 'Oilgate' threatened to reach into the highest places. **1983** *Wall St. Jrnl.* 8 July 20/2 'Hearingsgate' is now before the House ethics committee. **1983** *Tuscaloosa* (Alabama) *News* 2 Aug. 4/5 In their zeal to pump 'Altergate' into a full-blown scandal.. Gregg and Hiler charged that.. alterations had been made in the transcripts of.. other hearings.

‖**gâteau** (gato, 'gætəʊ). Also **gateau**. [F. *gâteau* cake:—OF. *gastel*: see WASTEL.] A cake or pudding; now usu. a large rich cake often filled with cream, or cream and fruit, and highly decorated; also, meat or fish baked and served in the form of a cake (see also quot. 1861). ***veal gâteau***: minced veal made up like a pudding, and boiled in a shape or mould.

1845 E. ACTON *Mod. Cook* xviii. 473 (*heading*) A French Rice Pudding, or Gateau de Riz. *Ibid.* 474 It will.. turn out.. having the appearance of a cake... An admirable variety of this Gâteau is made with cocoa-nut flavoured milk. **1849** THACKERAY *Pendennis* I. xxiv. 232 A basket containing little gateaux of apricots. **1861** MRS. BEETON *Bk. Househ. Managem.* 45 *Gâteau*, a cake, correctly speaking; but used sometimes to denote a pudding and a kind of tart. *Ibid.* 680 French rice pudding, or gateau de riz. **1883** *Cassell's Fam. Mag.* Sept. 602/2 Any dish that has a baked cake for its foundation, if served in its original shape, may be called a gâteau. **1897** *Home Notes* 16 Oct. 28 Veal Gâteau. **1906** MRS. BEETON *Bk. Househ. Managem.* lxvii. 1754 Gateau of minced meat. **1932** *Edinburgh Bk. Plain Cookery Recipes* 51 Gâteau of Fish. **1955** M. HASTINGS *Cork & Serpent* v. 64 Bread and butter, tea-cakes, and gateaux. **1960** C. DALE *Spring of Love* i. 16 Having something else—some gateau, an ice-cream?

gate-crasher ('geɪt,kræʃə(r)). [f. GATE *sb.*[1] + CRASHER 2.] One who enters a sports ground or a private party, reception, entertainment, etc., without an invitation or ticket; also *transf.* and *fig.* Hence **'gate-crash** *v. intr.* and *trans.*, to enter (a party, etc.) as a gatecrasher; **'gate-crashing** *vbl. sb.* and *ppl. a.*

1927 *Daily News* 28 June 5/3 'One-eyed Connolly', the champion American 'gate crasher' (one who gains admittance to big sporting events without payment). *Ibid.*, The Committee of the White Rose Ball.. dealt severely with a few cases of 'gate crashing'. **1928** *Sunday Dispatch* 15 July 1 The doom of the society gate-crasher is irretrievably fixed. *Ibid.* 5 Aug. 3/2 He was arrested for 'gate-crashing' over the frontier from Canada to America without a passport. **1929** *Daily Mail* 18 July 7/4 (*headline*) Gate-crashing woman. *Ibid.*, Helly Cozzonis.. was the gate-crasher at the Mansion House reception. **1930** *Morn. Post* 19 Aug. 12/1 A 'Political Gatecrasher'. **1931** E. MANNIN *Ragged Banners* viii. 80 Geoffrey Hayes is giving a party to-night—shall we gate-crash? **1933** D. L. SAYERS *Murder must Advertise* xi. 192 I'm sick of Slinker's parties.. let's go and gate-crash something really virtuous. *Ibid.* 198 'I had the pleasure of entertaining your cousin there one night.' 'Did he gate-crash on you? That is exactly what he would do.' **1957** D. ROBINS *Noble One* vii. 73 'Afraid I'm a gate-crasher,' he said. 'Your father heard me knock and let me in.' **1963** *Times* 23 May 4/7 The British women can be said to have gate-crashed the semi-final round.

gated ('geɪtɪd), *ppl. a.*[1] [f. GATE *sb.*[1] + -ED[2].] **a.** Furnished with a gate or with gates. **b.** (see GATE *v.*[1] 2).

c **1630** RISDON *Surv. Devon* §191 (1810) 200 There you may behold a.. pond, strong walled and gated. **1876** BROWNING *Shop* 27 Some suburb palace, parked about And gated grandly. **1880** L. WALLACE *Ben-Hur* 201 Broken at intervals by gated sluiceways.

gated, *ppl. a.*[2]: see after GATE *v.*[4]

gatehouse ('geɪthaʊs). [f. GATE *sb.*[1] + HOUSE *sb.*] **1.** A house (for a servant or gatekeeper) at or over the entrance of a park or other enclosure; a lodge.

c **1380** WYCLIF *Wks.* (1880) 15 Grete cost of kechenes and ȝate housis. **1458** *Visit. St. Paul's Churches* (Camden) 99 Vnum gattehous, et vnum hoghous. *c* **1543** in *Turner's Dom. Archit.* III. 79 The great quadrangle with a gatehous. **1625** K. LONG tr. *Barclay's Argenis* III. xvii. 205 The Gate-house and Hall swarmed with troupes. **1762–71** WALPOLE *Vertue's Anecd. Paint.* (1786) V. 298 The gate-house or tower of Layer-Marney-hall. **1835** W. IRVING *Newstead Abbey* Crayon Misc. (1863) 320 An arched way led through the centre of the gate-house. **1876** *Whitby Gloss.*, *Yat-house*, a lodge on an archway through which you drive into a court-yard.

fig. **1599** NASHE *Lenten Stuffe* (1871) 27, I would be loth to build a labyrinth in the gatehouse of my book, for you to lose yourselves in.

2. The apartment over the gate of a city or palace, often strongly built, and hence used as a prison; *spec.* that over the gate of the palace of Westminster.

1587 FLEMING *Contn. Holinshed* III. 947/2 The kings maiestie.. at that time sat in his new gatehouse at his palace of Westminster, where he viewed all the whole companie. **1637** *Documents agst. Prynne* (Camden) 87 As Doctor Bastwicke came from the gatehouse towards the pallace the light common people strowed herbes and flowers before him. **1641** in Rushw. *Hist. Coll.* III. (1692) I. 275 One Newton a Popish Priest was committed to the Gate-House. **1647** CLARENDON *Hist. Reb.* VII. §139 [The king's] messenger.. was.. by the Houses committed to the Gate-house. **1895** *Murray's Handbk. Hertfordsh.* etc. 81 [St. Alban's], The Abbey Gate House, the only other relic left of the monastery, stands about 50 yards W. of the Cathedral.

'gate-keeper. [f. GATE *sb.*[1] + KEEPER *sb.*] **1.** One who has charge of a gate.

1572 HULOET, Gate keeper, or a porter. **1712** *Lond. Gaz.* No. 5028/1 That the Gate-keepers give constant Attendance at the Gates. **1845** DISRAELI *Sybil* (Rtldg.) 323 The gate-keeper ought not to have let them pass. **1896** *Law Times Rep.* LXXIII. 615/2 There is no general duty on railway companies to place gatekeepers at level crossings.

fig. **1872** YEATS *Growth Comm.* 59 The products of every clime were thus brought to Rome, 'the gatekeeper of the world'.

2. A species of butterfly.

1819 G. SAMOUELLE *Entomol. Compend.* 240 *Hipparchia Megæra* (gate-keeper). *a* **1887** JEFFERIES *Field & Hedgerow* (1889) 227 The Gatekeeper butterfly is common.

gateless ('geɪtlɪs), *a.*[1] [f. GATE *sb.*[1] + -LESS.] Without a gate, destitute of gates.

1608 MACHIN *Dumbe Knt.* v. i, Gold hath power To enter without force a gateless tower. **1817** *Blackw. Mag.* I. 71 The horses pasturing through the range of gateless fields. **1849** LYTTON *K. Arthur* VII. lxxxii, Justice sits listening in her gateless halls. **1859** W. COLLINS *Q. of Hearts* (1875) 19 The chaise.. passed through the gateless gap in our rough enclosure wall.

Hence **'gatelessly** *adv.*

1880 RUSKIN in *19th Cent.* June 942 The lane itself.. is a deep-rutted, heavy-hillocked cart-road, diverging gatelessly into various brickfields.

†**'gateless**, *a.*[2] *Obs.* In 2–3 **gatelæs**. [f. GATE *sb.*[2] + -LESS.] Pathless.

c **1200** ORMIN 9211 Whærse iss all.. sharrp, & ruhh, & gatelæs þurrh þorrness & þurrh breress.

†**'gatelings**, *adv. Sc. Obs.* In 8 **gatelins**. [f. GATE *sb.*[2] + -LINGS.] Directly. Cf. GATEWARD(S *adv.*

1768 ROSS *Helenore* II. 96 An' mair attour his mind this monie a day, Gatelins to Nory there my lassie lay.

'gate-post. [f. GATE *sb.*[1] + POST *sb.*] **a.** One of the posts belonging to a gate, either that upon which it hangs, or that against which it shuts.

1522 *MS. Acc. St. John's Hosp., Canterb.*, For settyng vp of a gatepost ij d. **1614** RALEIGH *Hist. World* II. x. §2. 380 The Mountaines within this Tribe are few, and that of Sampson the chiefest: vnto which he carried the Gate-post of Gaza. **1708** MOTTEUX *Rabelais* v. xxviii. (1737) 128 As grave as an old Gate-Post. **1789** *Trans. Soc. Arts* VII. 11 Gate-Posts of the Spanish Chestnut. **1816** J. SMITH *Panorama Sc. & Art* II. 598 Stone is the most suitable for gate-posts. **1848** C. A. JOHNS *Week at Lizard* 257 Gate-posts ..are..often made of timber recovered in this way.

b. Colloq. phr. ***between*** (or †***betwixt***) ***you*** (***and***) ***me and the gate-post***, in strict confidence. Cf. BED-POST, POST *sb.*[1] 1 c.

1871 E. EGGLESTON *Hoosier Schoolmaster* (1872) xiv. 82 A-twix you and me and the gate-post, don't you never believe nothing that Mirandy Means says. **1875** BROWNING *Inn Album* ii. 39 A secret's safe 'Twixt you, me and the gate-post! **1884** 'C. E. CRADDOCK' *Where Battle was Fought* 152 Between you and me and the gate-post, old Walter Percy is a fool about everything in this world except money. **1959** P. H. JOHNSON *Humbler creation* xxxix. 265 Strictly between you and me and the gate-post, Colonel, I don't care for them.

†**gate'shodel.** *Obs.* Also 4 **-sadlis,** 5 **-schadylle, -schedelle, -shodil.** [f. GATE *sb.*[2] + ME. *scheadel (cf. OHG. *sceitila* parting of the hair), f. *scheaden*, OE. *sceádan* to part.] Parting of the ways; a cross-way.

c **1375** *Sc. Leg. Saints, Nicolaus* 993 He abad hyme..At a get-sadlis. *c* **1440** *Promp. Parv.* 188/2 Gate schadylle (*K.H.* gate shodel, *P.* gate shodil), *compitum.* Gate schadyl, yn-to twey weyys, *bivium.* *c* **1475** *Pict. Voc.* in Wr.-Wülcker 798/21-3 *Hic bivius, Hic trivius, Hic quatrivius*, a gate-schedelle.

'gate-ward, *sb. arch.* [f. GATE *sb.*[1] + WARD, keeper.] A gate-keeper.

c **1000** *Ags. Gosp.* John x. 3 þæne se ȝeat-weard læt in. *c* **1205** LAY. 18998 þe ȝæteward hit cudde ouer al. *a* **1300** *K. Horn* 1067 He com to þe gateward þat him answerede hard. *c* **1300** *Harrow. Hell* 139 Wer ys nou this ȝateward? **1393** LANGL. *P. Pl.* C. XIV. 92 Ther god is gatwarde hym-self. **1805** SCOTT *Last Minstr.* IV. iv, 'And by my faith', the gate-ward said, 'I think 'twill prove a Warden-raid'. **1849** JAS. GRANT *Kirkaldy of G.* iv. 35 The retinue of armed servants ..created no surprise in the mind of the gate-ward.

†**gateward(s,** *adv. Obs.* [f. GATE *sb.*[2] + -WARD(S.] By the direct road, directly.

1630-56 GORDON *Hist. Earld. Sutherl.* xxiii. (1813) 380 He returned back the same day gettward to Strathnaver. **1768** ROSS *Helenore* I. 26 They left me there, sae I but ony mair, Getwards alane, unto the glens can fare.

'gateway[1]**.** [f. GATE *sb.*[1] + WAY.]

1. A passage that is or may be closed by a gate; an opening through a fence or wall. ? *Obs.*

1707 MORTIMER *Husb.* 233 Gate-ways between their enclosures are so miry..that they cannot..Cart between one Field and another.

2. A frame or arch in which a gate is hung; a structure built at or over a gate, for ornament or defence.

1762-71 H. WALPOLE *Vertue's Anecd. Paint.* (1786) V. 299 View of an ancient gateway, dedicated to Nicholas bishop of Exeter. **1832** W. IRVING *Alhambra* I. 91 Having the most marvellous stories to relate of every tower, and vault, and gateway of the fortress. **1861** M. PATTISON *Ess.* (1889) I. 45 A lofty massive front with three fortified and portcullised gateways.
attrib. **1850** TENNYSON *In Mem.* viii, A happy lover..Who 'lights and rings the gateway bell. **1853** W. JERDAN *Autobiog.* IV. 53 He latterly occupied apartments at the top of one of the gateway-towers. **1886** WILLIS & CLARK *Cambridge* III. 283 A large gateway-arch flanked by a postern-arch. *Ibid.* 284 The gateway-tower..was..employed for the first time in collegiate architecture..at New College, Oxford, and..at Winchester.

3. *transf.* and *fig.* **a.** A means of egress or ingress. **b.** = GATE *sb.*[1] 4.

1842 TENNYSON *Locksley Hall* 157 At the gateways of the day. **1857** G. WILSON (*title*) The five gateways of knowledge. **1877** M. M. GRANT *Sun-Maid* i, In summer wrapt in a sunshine radiant and glorious as the gateway of heaven. **1878** B. TAYLOR *Deukalion* II. ii. 58 Say to the East, her gateway of return stands open. **1884** *Harper's Mag.* May 878/2 Snoqualmie Pass..is the lowest gateway of the Cascade Range. **1896** *Montreal Gaz.* 3 Dec. 5/3 The Canadian Pacific Railway having routed all its Northwest business through the Port-Arthur gateway.

4. *local.* = *gate*, GAT[1].

1794 J. BOYS *Agric. Kent* 32 Sloping passages in the cliff, called gate-ways, for the carts to go down to the sea.

'gateway[2]**.** [f. GATE *sb.*[2] + WAY.] *Mining.* = GATE *sb.*[2] 6.

1786 HARTLAND in Nicholls *Forest Dean* (1858) 76 Oak timber is necessary..for making what the miners call the gateway, or gangway, from the body of coal to the pit. **1888** W. E. NICHOLSON *Gloss. Coal Trade Terms* (*Northumbld. Gloss.*), *Gateway*, a roadway; in a pit, a passage through the goaf..for the purpose of bringing out coals worked on the long wall system.

Gath: see TELL *v.* 3 b.

Gatha ('gɑːta). Also with lower-case initial. [Zend; = Skr. *gāthá* song, verse, stanza.] Any of a number of psalms or versified sermons that form part of the Avesta. Also *attrib.*, esp. with reference to their language. Hence **Gathic** ('gɑːtɪk) *a.* [cf. F. *gathique*], of or pertaining to the gathas or the language in which they are written; *sb.*, the language itself, being the more archaic form of the Avestic language. Also **Gathaic** (gɑː'teɪɪk) *a.*

1862 M. HAUG *Ess. Parsees* iii. 136 The first Gâtha contains verses, each of which contains 48 syllables. **1867** —— *Old Zand-Pahlavi Gloss.* p. xliii, The difference of the Gâtha dialect (*gâsânîk*) from the common Avesta language is shown in the pronouns of the first and second persons. **1891** K. E. KANGA *Pract Gram. Avesta Lang.* p. iv, The examples, both Avestaic and Gâthâic..are such as are actually met with in the sacred writings. **1902** L. H. MILLS (*title*) A dictionary of the Gâthic language of the Zend Avesta. **1910** E. C. SYKES *Persia* 21 The entire copies of the Avesta and Gathas are believed to have been destroyed when Alexander burnt one of the palaces of Persepolis. **1961** *Times* 13 Apr. 14/7 As soon as they see the moon they worship her by chanting a gatha (psalm) in her honour. **1968** *Language* XLIV. I. 2 It is only the Later Avestan form; Gathic instead has..the aorist imperative.

gathamercy, var. GOD-A-MERCY.

gather ('gæðə(r)), *sb.*[1] [f. GATHER *v.*]

1. a. The amount gathered, crop, harvest. **b.** Contraction, drawing together. *rare.* **c.** The action of 'gathering' a ball (see GATHER *v.* 4 d).

1555 W. WATREMAN *Fardle Facions* II. i. 114 He that is lorde and gouernour among them, when the whole gather (of Cinamome) is brought together, deuideth out vnto euery man his heape. **1893** *Strand Mag.* VI. 188/1 There was no sign of agitation save the pitiful gather in the brows. **1921** E. H. D. SEWELL *Rugby Football* iii. facing p. 64 (*caption*) A 'gather' at full-speed..of a well-heeled ball.

2. a. Pl. ***the gathers***, that part of a dress which is gathered or drawn in (cf. the vb. 11 b).

1663 BUTLER *Hud.* I. iii. 925 Give us laws for pantaloons, The length of breeches, and the gathers, Port-cannons, perriwigs, and feathers. **1704** CIBBER *Careless Husb.* v. vi, Take and lay this Silver Plain all along the Gathers. **1768** STERNE *Sent. Journ.* (1778) II. 98 (*Temptation*) A stitch or two had broke out in the gathers of my stock. **1862** MRS. H. WOOD *Mrs. Hallib.* II. xxv. 301, I have done all the stitching and nearly the plain part of the bodies; I shall soon be at the gathers. **1889** *Daily News* 6 Jan. 3/1 A coffee-coloured lace skirt mounted in gathers at the waist, and falling straight to the feet.

b. In *sing. rare*[−1].

1880 *Plain Hints* 19 The take up of each gather should be lightly and neatly done.

c. ***out of the gathers***: 'out of order, in distressed circumstances' (Halliwell 1847-78).

3. *techn.* **a.** 'The inclination forward of an axle journal, or spindle, usually one-tenth of its diameter' (Knight *Dict. Mech.* 1874).

b. *Glass-making.* A mass of molten glass on the end of a punty or blowing-iron.

1934 in WEBSTER. **1944** *Electronic Engin.* XVII. 101 A portion of hot glass, called a gather, is made to drop into a mould in which the loose pins have previously been assembled. **1967** C. GASKIN *Edge of Glass* viii. 187 They blew a gather of glass into a mould.

4. *Comb.*: **gather-dam**, a dam for collecting water.

1768 J. GRAY *Refl. Inland Navig.* in J. Phillips *Hist. Inland Navig.* (1795) 307 Every reader may recollect what great quantities he has seen collected in gather-dams, or mill-ponds, by banks above their surface; and..it is..easy to form a string or chain of gather-dams from sea to sea.

†**'gather,** *sb.*[2] *Obs.* Forms: 6 **gader, gad(d)re, gaither, geither,** 7 **geather,** 6-8 **gather.** [Prob. a spec. sense of prec.; cf. PLUCK.] The pluck (heart, liver and lights) of an animal, esp. of a sheep or calf. Also *pl.*

1530 PALSGR. 223/2 Gaddre, as a calfes gadre or a shepes, *froissure de ueav ov de motton.* **1598** DELONEY *Jacke Newb.* viii. 103 The sheepes heads and the gathers, which you give away at your gate, might serve them well enough. **1616** SURFL. & MARKH. *Country Farme* 41 You must apply vpon the head of the patient the lungs of a Sheepe newly killed, or the whole Gather. **1678** J. PHILLIPS *Tavernier's Trav.*, *Persia* III. xii. 129 These three old men take a Sheep or a Goat..cut the throat of it..boil it whole, all but the Gathers. **1783** AINSWORTH *Lat. Dict.* (Morell) I. s.v. *Calf*, A calf's pluck, or gather, *exta vitulina.*

gather ('gæðə(r)), *v.* Forms: 1-2 **gad(e)rian, gæd(e)rian,** (1 **gadorian,** *Northumb.* **geadriȝa**), 3 **gaddren, gæderen,** 3-5 **gadir, gider, geder(e(n,** 3-6 **gader(e(n,** 4 **gadrie, gethur,** 4-5 **gedur, -yr, gedder, -ar, gadre,** 6 **geddur, gether, geather, gadder,** 6- **gather.** [OE. *gad(e)rian* = OFris. *gad(e)ria, gaduria* (mod.Fris. *gearjen*), MDu., Du. *gaderen* (*garen*), MLG. *gadern*, MHG. (Mid.Ger.) *gatern*:—WGer. type **gadurôjan*. The OE. form *gæd(e)rian*, whence the ME. *geder(en*, etc., and the wide-spread mod. dialectal pronunciation ('gɛðə(r)), is prob. due to the influence of the related OE. (*tó*)*gædere* TOGETHER, where the vocalism normally represents a WGer. type **gadurî*. Cf. OE. *gæder-, gader-* (in *gæder-tang* continuous), *ȝeador* together; also Du. *gader-*, *te gader* together; the OTeut. root is **gad-* as in OE. *gæd* union, *ȝegada* companion, *gædeling* GADLING.

There is no trace in ME. or dialects of any palatalization of the initial consonant in this or any of the related words. Until the 16th c. the words were, with few exceptions, spelt with *d*; for the change to *th* see FATHER.]

I. *trans.*

†**1.** (Only in forms with prefixed *ȝe-*.) To join or unite; to put together, form by union. *Obs.* since early ME.

c **725** *Corpus Gloss.* 512 *Compactis*, ȝegædradon. *c* **825** *Vesp. Hymns* xiii, Ðæt..ðu..usic to gode ȝegadrades [L. *conjunxeris*] ðo[r]h flæsces gemænnisse. *c* **950** *Lindisf. Gosp.* Matt. xix. 6 þæt forðon god ȝegeadrade [L. *coniunxit*], monn ne to-slite. *a* **1000** *Soul & Body* 160 Forðan wyt bioð ȝegæderode æt godes dome. *c* **1175** *Lamb. Hom.* 147 An is ..þet faire icunde þet is igedered bi-twene saule and licame. *c* **1230** *Hali Meid.* 27 Muche confort haueð wif of hire were þat beoð wel igedered.

2. a. To bring (persons, or *occas.* animals) together; to cause to assemble in one place or company; to collect (an army, a flock, etc.). Also ***to gather together*** (or †***samen***). In early examples also with *ȝe-* prefix.

a **975** *O.E. Chron.* (Parker MS.) an. 973 þær wæs preosta heap..gleawra ȝegaderod. *a* **1000** *Andreas* 1556 (Gr.) þa þær an ongann..folc gadoriȝean. *a* **1000** *Soul & Body* 51 On þam miclan dæȝe. þonne monna cynn se ancenda ealle ȝegædrað [*Verc.* ȝesamnað]. *a* **1121** *O.E. Chron.* (Laud MS.) an. 1117 Normandiȝ wearð swiðe ȝedreht..þurh fyrde þe se cing Henri þær onȝean gaderode. *c* **1175** *Lamb. Hom.* 89 þa weren þer igedered wiðinne þere buruh of ierusalem trowfeste men. *c* **1200** ORMIN 16462 He wollde..gaddrenn himm an haliȝ follc Off alle kinne lede. *c* **1275** LAY. 1863 Vppen one doune..þat folk was igadered. *a* **1300** *Cursor M.* 5784 Ga, gedir samen þin eldir men Of all þi folk of israel. *c* **1386** CHAUCER *Prol.* 824 Up roos our host..And gadrede us togidre, alle in a flok. *c* **1440** *Generydes* 947 This fals Stiward he had gaderid people grete. *a* **1533** LD. BERNERS *Huon* xciv. 305 Than Huon cryed his crye to gader his men togyther. **1591** SHAKS. *1 Hen. VI*, III. ii. 102 Gather we our forces out of hand And set vpon our boasting enemie. **1638** F. JUNIUS *Paint. Ancients* 132 The Lacedæmonians together with their confederates having gathered an Armie of forty thousand men. **1711** BUDGELL *Spect.* No. 77 ¶6 Will was standing in the midst of several Auditors whom he had gathered round him. **1802** MAR. EDGEWORTH *Moral T.* (1816) I. xv. 119 He saw a crowd of people gathered before the..window. **1874** GREEN *Short Hist.* ii. §2. 65 He at once gathered his forces and marched upon Gloucester.

†**b.** *refl.* To come together in a body, to assemble. *Obs.*

921 *O.E. Chron.* (Parker MS.) an. 921 Æfter þam ..ȝegadorode micel folc hit on Eadweardes cynges anwalde. *c* **1205** LAY. 4032 Gumen heom igaderen. *c* **1340** *Cursor M.* 11081 (Trin.) To gider gidered þei hem alle. *c* **1400** *Destr. Troy* 9044 Then the Grekes by a-grement gedrit hom somyn. **1535** COVERDALE *Josh.* xviii. 1 And all the multitude of the children of Israel gathered them selues together vnto Silo. **1611** BIBLE *Job* xvi. 10 They haue gathered themselues together against mee.

c. In the Biblical phrase ***to be gathered to one's fathers, to one's people***: to be buried with one's ancestors; hence, to die.

Although ***to be gathered to one's fathers*** is the form of the expression that has become proverbial, it occurs only in one passage of the canonical books and twice in the Apocrypha.

1382 WYCLIF *Gen.* xxv. 8 [Abraham] was gaderyd [L. *congregatus est*] to his puple. —— *Judg.* ii. 10 And al that generacioun is gedrid to her fadris [**1535** COVERDALE, gathered; **1611**, *id.*]. **1611** BIBLE *1 Macc.* ii. 69 So he blessed them, and was gathered to his fathers [*otherwise in earlier versions*]. **1842** TENNYSON *St. Sim. Styl.* 194 When I am gather'd to the glorious Saints. **1889** FROUDE *Two Chiefs Dunboy* viii, No change was to be made till MacFinnan Dhu had been gathered to his fathers.

d. ? *U.S.* with *in*: To receive into a religious community.

1880 HOWELLS *Undisc. Country* viii. 114 They looked like stage players to me; before I was gathered in I used often to see such folks.

3. a. To bring (things) together; to collect from different quarters into one mass or place; to acquire by such means, to amass. Also ***to gather together***.

c **1000** *Ags. Ps.* (Th.) xxxviii. 8 [xxxix. 6] Hy gaderiað feoh, and nyton hwam hy hyt gadriað. *c* **1200** *Vices & Virtues* (1888) 47 Se ðe gadereð mihtes [L. *qui virtutes congregat*] wiðuten eadmodnesse. *c* **1200** ORMIN 1484 þu..gaddresst swa þe clene corn all fra þe chaff togeddre. *a* **1225** *Ancr. R.* 146 Hercneð nu..hu god þinc hit is uorte..gederen ine þeosternesse..soule uode. *a* **1300** *Cursor M.* 6502 (Gött.) þair golden tresur gadrid þai samen. **1398** TREVISA *Barth. De P.R.* XIX. cxvi. (1495) 920 Many dyuers thynges gadryd togyder ben one: as many stonys makyth one hepe. *c* **1450** tr. *De Imitatione* I. xxiii. 32 Whiles þou hast tyme, gadre riches immortale. *a* **1533** LD. BERNERS *Huon* lii. 176 Huon had ynough to do to gather togyther the clothes. **1611** BIBLE *Prov.* xxviii. 8 He that by vsurie and vniust gaine increaseth his substance, he shall gather it for him that wil pity the poore. **1697** DRYDEN *Virg. Past.* VI. 52 How Seas, and Earth, and Air, and active Flame..were blindly gather'd in this goodly Ball. **1774** GOLDSM. *Nat. Hist.* (1776) V. 233 The place being thus determined upon, they begin to gather the materials for their nest. **1779-81** JOHNSON *L.P.*, *Gay*, He died without a will, though he had gathered three thousand pounds. **1825** LYTTON *Falkland* 14 We gather the honey of worldly wisdom, not from flowers, but thorns.
refl. **1664** POWER *Exp. Philos.* 145 The water..gathering it self into round bubbles..would fall to the ground. **1871** FREEMAN *Norm. Conq.* (1876) IV. xix. 417 A small town had gathered itself outside the episcopal precinct.

†**b.** *absol.* To accumulate wealth. *Obs.*

a **1225** *Ancr. R.* 222 [He] bringeð hire on to gederen and ȝiuen alre erest þe pure. *a* **1300** *Cursor M.* 26824 Quat bot on aside gadir til, And on anoþer side to spill. **1377** LANGL. *P. Pl.* B. XII. 53 Riche renkes riȝt so gaderen and sparen, And tho men that thei moste haten mynistren it atte laste. *c* **1440** *Gesta Rom.* lxix. 311 (Harl. MS.) When þat þei se a man gadery or purchesse [*v.r.* gadre richesse] thenne þei sey, 'loo! he is a carle'.

c. To pick up (a living).

1461 *Paston Lett.* No. 427 II. 71, I have as moche as I may to gader myn ownne lyfflode, and truli, cosyn, I can not gader that well. **1858** FROUDE *Hist. Eng.* III. xiv. 256 Sturdy vagrants whose living had been gathered hitherto at the doors of the religious houses.

4. a. To collect (flowers, fruit) from the place of growth; to cull, pick, pluck.

a **1000** *Phoenix* 193 in *Exeter Bk.*, þonne feor and neah þa swetestan somnað and gædrað wyrta wynsume and wudubleda. *a* **1300** *Cursor M.* 12523 He sent him to þe yerd..for to gedir þam sum cale. *c* **1386** CHAUCER *Merch. T.* 987 Whil that she gadered floures in the mede. **1489** CAXTON *Faytes of A.* III. i. 168 Take and gadre of the tree that is in my gardyn somme fruytes of whiche thou shalt use. **1577** B. GOOGE *Heresbach's Husb.* III. (1586) 135 b, Gather all these Hearbes in Sommer, and keepe them, and make them in powder. **1611** SHAKS. *Cymb.* I. v. 1 Whiles yet the dewe's on ground, Gather those Flowers. **1661** BOYLE *Style of Script.* (1675) 209 He [David] gathered bayes both on Parnassus and in the field of honor. **1715** [see GATHERED *ppl. a.*]. **1717** BERKELEY *Tour in Italy* Wks. 1871 IV. 552 A physician gathering simples in a field. **1820** W. IRVING *Sketch Bk.* I. 52 I've been gathering some of the most delicious strawberries. **1887** BOWEN *Virg. Eclog.* II. 18 White hedge flowers we abandon, to gather the hyacinth dark.

b. To collect (grain, fruit, etc.) as harvest or annual produce; also *to gather in*.

c **950** *Lindisf. Gosp.* Matt. xiii. 30 In tid hripes ic willo cuoeða ðæm hrippe-monnum, geadriʒes *vel* somniʒes [L. *colligite*] ærist ða unwæstma *vel* wilde ata. *a* **1100** *Gerefa* in *Anglia* IX. 261 Fela tilða ham gæderian. *c* **1175** *Lamb. Hom.* 135 Alse me saweð sed on ane time, and gedereð þet frute on oðer time. *a* **1300** *Cursor M.* 4060 He-self was on þe feld biside To geder corn in herueistide. *c* **1400** MAUNDEV. (Roxb.) vii. 26 Men of þat cuntree, what tyme þat felde sall be tilled, getes þam Cristen men for to tille it and to geder it. **1535** COVERDALE *Isa.* lxii. 9 But they that haue gathered in the corne, shal eate it. **1585** T. WASHINGTON tr. *Nicholay's Voy.* II. vi. 36 b, Out of these..cuttes proceedeth the Masticke by droppes as it were Gum, which they gather in the moneth of September. **1697** DRYDEN *Virg. Georg.* IV. 200 To quit his Care, he gather'd first of all In Spring the Roses, Apples in the Fall. **1816** J. SMITH *Panorama Sc. & Art* II. 694 Gather the remaining fruits. **1870** YEATS *Nat. Hist. Comm.* 2 We do not merely gather in the indigenous materials of the country where we live, but [etc.].

c. To cull or pluck (a single flower or fruit).

1588 [see GATHERED I b]. **1667** MILTON *P.L.* IV. 271 That faire field Of Enna, where Proserpin gathering flowrs, Her self a fairer floure, by gloomie Dis Was gathered. **1681** DRYDEN *Span. Friar* V. i, Like a Rose just gather'd from the Stalk. **1799** MRS. J. WEST *Tale of Times* I. 62 The rose grows so close to the thorn, that you cannot gather it without encountering a painful sensation.

transf. **1844** BP. S. WILBERFORCE *Hist. Protest. Episc. Ch. Amer.* (1846) 5 But the native thus cruelly gathered was not the only specimen they gathered.

d. To pick up. (See also 16 a.) Esp. to pick up (*a*) a ball in fielding at cricket or in rugby football, or (*b*) a shot bird.

1715 [see GATHERED *ppl. a.*]. **1838** *Sheffield Independent* 29 Sept., Gathered the ball. **1846, 1851** [see GAUNTLET[1] I, 5]. **1891** *Hurlingham Club Rules* 14 All birds must be gathered by the dog or trapper, and no member shall have the right to gather his own bird. **1892** W. W. GREENER *Breech-Loader* 225 If a wounded bird struggles in front of you from a companion's gun, drop it if you can. Explain to the first shooter that you did so to save time in gathering it. **1898** *Daily News* 7 Feb. 8/6 [Rugby Football] Having to gather the ball off the floor, instead of receiving it high up and fairly straight. **1925** D. J. KNIGHT *More Compleat Cricketer* 12 The ball must be gathered in the palm of the hand. *Ibid.*, Gather it off the ground with a kind of sweeping movement.

†**5.** To collect or bring together (literary matter); to compile. *Obs.*

a **1000** *Ags. Astron.* in *Treat. Science* (1841) 1 Of ðære bec þe Beda..ʒesette and gaderode of maneʒra wisa lareowa bocum. **1450–1530** *Myrr. our Ladye* 29 Thou gadrest and made many bokes out of holy scripture. **1482** *Monk of Evesham* (Arb.) 38 Some thynges y wylle gedur to gedur of some certeyn persons what they sufryd afore ther dethe and after ther dethe. **1562** TURNER (*title*) A Book of the natures and properties..of the bathes in England..Germany and Italy..gathered by William Turner Doctor of Physik. **1571** HANMER *Chron. Irel.* (1633) 40 What Bale hath formerly written, I find he hath gathered out of Vincentius, Antoninus [and others]. **1677** MIEGE *Dict. Eng.-Fr.* s.v., He gathered his lights from the most impartial authority's.

6. Of material objects: To be the means of bringing together or accumulating; to receive addition of.

a **1225** *Ancr. R.* 138 Wiðuten salt, fleshs gedereð wurmes. **1398** TREVISA *Barth. De P.R.* XIII. xxiii. (1495) 455 The see gadryth aboue a fome of smytynge and betynge of wawes. **1579** GOSSON *Sch. Abuse* (Arb.) 52 Standing streames geather filth; flowing riuers are euer sweet. **1611** BIBLE *Joel* ii. 6 All faces shall gather blacknesse. **1670** SIR S. CROW in *12th Rep. Hist. MSS. Comm.* App. v. 15 The silke sleizie and not Naples, which will soone grow rough, gather dust and sullie. **1687** MIEGE *Gt. Fr. Dict.* II. s.v., To gather Rust (*or* to grow rusty) as Steel and Iron does. **1821** CLARE *Vill. Minstr.* I. 131 Which the early-rising lass Climbs with milk-pail gathering cream. **1850** TENNYSON *In Mem.* ci, That beech will gather brown. **1885** *Athenæum* 23 May 669/1 The thick-standing trees gather golden and ruddy tints.

Prov. **1573–80** TUSSER *Husb.* (1878) 24 The stone that is rouling can gather no mosse.

7. a. To collect (money or other contributions) from a number of people. Now *rare*. Also *absol.* to make or take up a collection (*obs.* exc. *dial.*).

1389 in *Eng. Gilds* (1870) 3 Which wardeins schul gadere þ[e] qwarterage of bretheren & sustren. *c* **1440** *Jacob's Well* (E.E.T.S.) 24 Þei may neyther gaderyn here tythes, ne kepyn hem, ne fecchyn hem. **1532** *Privy Purse Exp. Hen. VIII* (1827) 257 Item the same daye paied to a woman that gathered for a Churche vijs. vj*d.* **1568** GRAFTON *Chron.* II. 202 This yere sayth Fabian, the king gathered the sixt penny of all temporall mennes goodes..which was graunted unto him in the aforesayd Parliament. **1600** J. PORY tr. *Leo's Africa* II. 171 Being vassals unto the king of Fez..out of which they yeerely gather ten thousand duckats. **1668** PEPYS *Diary* (1877) V. 156 While the sexton was gathering to his box, to which I did give 5*s.* **1710** PRIDEAUX *Orig. Tithes* iv. 167 This Law..enabled the Clergy to gather and recover Tithes. **1896** *Hetton-le-hole Gloss.*, *Gather*, make a collection ('gathering') in money.

†**b.** in indirect passive. *Obs.*

c **1592** MARLOWE *Jew of Malta* II. ii, Hoping to see them.. gather'd for in our Synagogue. **1615** DR. KING *Serm.* 57 (T.) Few Sundays come over our head, but decayed householders or shipwrackt merchants are gathered for.

8. To collect or summon up (one's energies); to gain or recover (breath, etc.). Also ***to gather oneself* (*together*)**.

c **1400** *Destr. Troy* 9860 All the grekes with grem gedret þere herttes. **1470–85** MALORY *Arthur* XIV. vi, Thenne he dyd of his helme for to gadre wynde, for he was gretely enchafed with the serpente. **1530** PALSGR. 561/1, I gather my spyrites to me, as one dothe that hath maters layde to his charge. *Ibid.*, I gather myselfe togyther as a man doth whan he intendeth to shewe his strength. **1545** *Act 37 Hen. VIII*, c. 17 §2 The People gathereth Heart and Presumption to do Evil. **1590** SPENSER *F.Q.* I. vi. 19 The lucklesse lucky mayd ..long time with that salvage people stayd, To gather breath in many miseryes. **1719** DE FOE *Crusoe* I. vi, While I was thus gathering Strength. **1768** ROSS *Helenore* I. 8 He had fa'en aswoon..But howsomever in a little wee Himsel he gathers, and begins to see. **1850** HAWTHORNE *Scarlet L.* xvii, He had almost gone by, before Hester..could gather voice enough to attract his observation.

9. To collect or acquire by way of increase; to gain. † ***to gather ground***: to gain ground, make progress. ***to gather head***: to acquire strength; also, to swell as a festering sore. ***to gather way***: 'to begin to feel the impulse of the wind on the sails, so as to obey the helm' (Adm. Smyth).

1590 MARLOWE *Edw. II*, II. ii, Meantime, my lord of Pembroke and myself Will to Newcastle here, and gather head. **1597** SHAKS. *2 Hen. IV*, III. i. 76 The Time will come, that foule Sinne gathering head Shall breake into Corruption. **1643** BAKER *Chron.* II. 21 No snow-ball ever gathered greatnesse so fast by rolling, as his Forces increased by marching forward. **1664** POWER *Exp. Philos.* 178 Then to gather Vent (as they call it) they straiten the Vault, and wall part of it up; so that the Ayr..gathers in strength, and runs more swiftly. **1667** MILTON *P.L.* XII. 631 As Ev'ning Mist..o're the Marish glides, And gathers ground fast at the Labourer's heel. **1687** MIEGE *Gt. Fr. Dict.* II. s.v., To gather Flesh, *grossir.* **1691** DRYDEN *Eleonora* 4 Soft whispers first..rise..then the sound Soon gathers voice and spreads the news around. **1693** —— *Ovid's Met.* I. 730 He gathers ground upon her in the chase. **1697** —— *Virg. Georg.* III. 693 Till the Core be found, The secret Vice is fed, and gathers Ground. **1774** GOLDSM. *Nat. Hist.* (1776) I. 373 As the descending fluid gathers velocity in its precipitation. **1832** TENNYSON '*You ask me why*' 13 Where faction seldom gathers head. **1866** R. M. BALLANTYNE *Shifting Winds* xiv. (1881) 148 A light breeze was blowing, and the ship..soon gathered way, and left the boat behind.

10. To collect (knowledge) by observation and reasoning; to infer, deduce, conclude. (= L. *colligere*: cf. COLLECT *v.* 5.)

1535 JOYE *Apol. Tindale* (Arb.) 23 Men gatherd that I denied the general reserreccion. **1556** RECORDE *Cast. Knowledge* 70 For this muche I may gether by that I haue learned already, that [etc.]. **1576** FLEMING *Panopl. Epist.* 17 So farre as I gather by the substance of your letters. **1664** POWER *Exp. Philos.* 72 The Physiologist also may gather something from the former Observations, touching the nature of Colours. **1744** BERKELEY *Siris* §23 Pliny supposed amber to be a resin..which he gathered from its smell. **1816** T. JEFFERSON *Writ.* (1830) IV. 297, I gather from his other works that he adopts the principle of Hobbes. **1893** *Law Times* XCV. 303/1 She..usually, as I gather from the evidence, associated her daughter's name with her own in her investments.

11. a. To draw (a garment) into smaller compass; to contract (the brow) into wrinkles.

1617 MORYSON *Itin.* III. 169 They gather the Vaile with their hands to cover all their faces, but onely the eyes. **1711** POPE *Temp. Fame* 240 Gath'ring his flowing robe he seem'd to stand, In act to speak. **1790** BURNS *Tam O'Shanter* 11 Gathering her brows like gathering storm, Nursing her wrath to keep it warm. **1887** BOWEN *Virg. Æneid* IV. 140 Golden the clasp that gathers her shining robe to her side.

b. *spec.* To draw together or pucker (part of a dress) by means of a thread.

1576 GASCOIGNE *Steele Glas* (Arb.) 68 How ere their gownes, be gathered in the backe, With organe pipes. **1617** MORYSON *Itin.* III. 169 They weare great large puffed breeches, gathered close above the knees. **1625** PURCHAS *Pilgrims* II. 1421 The women in Camienitz goe with their Coates close bodied, and the neather bodies gathered like a Frocke. **1711** STEELE *Spect.* No. 109 ¶4 You see, Sir, my Great Great Great Grandmother has on the new-fashioned Petticoat, except that the Modern is gather'd at the Waste. **1848** C. BRONTË *J. Eyre* I. xiv. 275 A dress of rose-coloured satin..as full in the skirt as it could be gathered. **1875** *Plain Needlework* 20 It is wiser, if the space into which the gathers are set be more than three inches, to gather only half or quarter [etc.].

c. *Arch.* To contract, close in or make narrower (a drain, chimney, etc.); also ***to gather over***.

1703, 1823 [see GATHERING *vbl. sb.* 1 c]. **1837** *Penny Cycl.* XII. 327/1 The flue is gathered over, or contracted to this size.

d. *nonce-use.* (See quot.)

1557 N. T. (Genev.) *1 Cor.* vii. 18 Is any man called beyng circumcised? let him not gather his vncircumcision. [*Note*, Which is, when the Surgeon by art draweth out the skyne to couer the part.]

†**12.** To put (the feet) together, keep from straying. *Obs.*

1671 M. BRUCE *Good News in Evil Times* (1708) 26 If the Storms ye are meeting with make you not walk more evenly and gather your Feet, ye shall get a new Storm to scald you, until you..gather your Feet better.

13. *techn.* **a.** *Glass-making.* To collect (a quantity of melted glass) on the end of the blowing-tube.

1839 URE *Dict. Arts* 581 The requisite ball of plastic glass is gathered..on the end of an iron tube. **1886** *Proc. R. Soc.* XXXIX. 100 [Glass] maintained..at a temperature barely sufficient to admit of its being 'gathered'.

b. To collect and place in their proper order according to signatures (the printed sheets of a book). Also *absol.*

1683 MOXON *Mech. Exerc.* II. 348 Till he has Gathered the last Sheet on his Right Hand..Thus he Gathers on, till one of all the Heaps Comes off..Having thus Gathered one Book, he Knocks it up, that is, he [etc.].

14. = ***gather on*** (see 21).

1834 J. WILSON in *Blackw. Mag.* XXXVI. 2 Gathering the shore, lo, the Barge! *Ibid.* 7 We had not proceeded above a hundred yards, fast gathering the Shuffler, till we heard.. loud cries.

15. In various phrases with advs. † ***to gather off***: to take off (a gown). ***to gather out***: to select or pick out.

c **1460** J. RUSSELL *Bk. Nurture* 957 Than his gowne ye gadir of, or garment of his estate. **1611** BIBLE *Isa.* lxii. 10 Cast vp the high way, gather out the stones. **1875** MANNING *Mission H. Ghost* i. 10 The world will go on until the last of that number has been gathered out and made perfect for the kingdom of God.

16. gather up. a. To pick up (from the ground).

a **1300** *Cursor M.* 13241 (Gött.) Pouder or bone þat þai fand þare, þai gedrid vp, and wid þaim bare. *c* **1375** *Sc. Leg. Saints, Johannes* 156 Small stanis of þe sand he gadderit vpe into his hand. **1576** FLEMING *Panopl. Epist.* 48 That I might gather up the gleanings of my labours, and sende money to Rome. **1617** MORYSON *Itin.* II. 188 The wearied foote cast away their Armes, which those of the Country gathered up. **1784** COWPER *Task* III. 286 What pearl is it..That learning is too proud to gather up. **1840** DICKENS *Old C. Shop* xlvi, The school-master took the child..and bidding the old man gather up her little basket..bore her away.

fig. **1606** HOLLAND *Sueton.* 71 Howbeit, in the ende he lost not much: but after his great losses gathered uppe his crummes pretily well by little and little.

b. To draw together, bring into smaller compass; to draw up (the limbs or person): in immaterial sense, to sum up, summarize. In agriculture, to plough a ridge in such a way that the earth is turned over towards the highest part of it.

1553 EDEN *Treat. Newe Ind.* (Arb.) 39 Thei came into such a tempeste that they were enforsed to gather vppe theyr sayles. **1616** BROWNE *Brit. Past.* II. iii. 72 A greene silke frock..Which at her middle gath'red vp in pleats, A loue-knot Girdle willing bondage threats. **1617** MARKHAM *Caval.* II. 48 It correcteth, if when he will not gether vp his hinder partes, you giue him a good Iert or two. **1677** N. COX *Gentl. Recreat.* IV. (ed. 2) 68 Within two foot of the bottom of the Rod there is..a Winde to turn with a Barrel, to gather up the Line and loose it at pleasure. **1686** *Ibid.* v. (ed. 3) 57 You may there gallop him..to teach him to lay out his Body, and to gather up his Legs. **1756** A. DICKSON *Treat. Agric.* (ed. 2) 282 At the next plowing this may be reversed, the ridge in the middle of the field gathered up, and the plough go round and round the ridge till the whole field is plowed. **1781** COWPER *Convers.* 867 But now to gather up what seems dispersed..May prove..best for the public. **1832** LANDER *Adv. Niger* II. xi. 146 Their legs, which had before been stretched out carelessly and comfortably..were now gathered up under them. **1846** *Jrnl. R. Agric. Soc.* VII. I. 56 They have thus for centuries continued to gather up the land. They gather up twice and split once. **1846** TRENCH *Huls. Lect.* Ser. II. i. 144 Such appears to me the title which will best gather up and present at a single glance..the subject. **1891** E. PEACOCK *N. Brendon* II. 377 She gathered herself up in a manner seldom seen off the boards of a third-rate theatre.

c. To compose (the features) *into* an expression.

1712 ADDISON *Spect.* No. 269 ¶10 Gathering up his Countenance into a more than ordinary Seriousness, Tell me truly, says he. **1831** LAMB *Elia* Ser. II. *Ellistoniana*, Gathering up his features into one significant mass of wonder, pity [etc.].

d. To collect or summon up (one's thoughts, strength, etc.) for an effort. Also *refl.*

1617 MORYSON *Itin.* I. 41 Wee gathering up strength went on. **1623** BEAUM. & FL. *Maid in Mill* III. i, Will you gather up your wits A little and hear me? **1644** LAUD *Wks.* (1854) IV. 369, I confess I was a little troubled. But after I had gathered up myself and looked up to God, I went on to the business of the day. **1847** L. HUNT *Men, Women, & B.* I. iii. 40 It only made him gather up his determination. **1848** THACKERAY *Van. Fair* lviii, Mr. Sedley started up, shaking a great deal, and gathering up his thoughts. **1887** RUSKIN *Præterita* II. 269, I have never been able to..gather myself up against the national guilt of war, seeing that such men were made by the discipline of it.

†**e.** To chide, reprove (L. *corripere*). *Obs.*

1577 HARRISON *England* II. ii. (1877) I. 52 The ladie Wake ..hearing the king hir cousine to gather vp the bishop so roundlie..dooth presentlie picke a quarrell against him.

II. *intr.* (chiefly = refl. uses of I).

17. Of persons: To come together into one place or assembly; to congregate, assemble.

a **891** *O.E. Chron.* (Parker MS.) 879 þy ȝeare ȝegadrode on [? *read* an] hloþ wicenga. *a* **1079** *Ibid.* (MS. D.) an. 1052 þæt landfolc him on ȝean ȝegaderode. *a* **1300** *Cursor M.* 14619 þar bigan þai for to rute And for to gadir him a-bute. *c* **1440** *Generydes* 2917 Anon withall thei gaderid on the playn. **1526** *Pilgr. Perf.* (W. de W. 1531) 253 b, How..all the garyson of the knyghtes and turmentours gathered aboute hym. **1580** SIDNEY *Ps.* III. iv, I will not be afraid, Though legions round be laide Which all against me gather. **1611** BIBLE *1 Esdras* viii. 91 There gathered vnto him from Ierusalem, a very great multitude of men, and women, and children. **1713** ADDISON *Cato* IV. iv, See where the corps of thy dead son approaches! The citizens and senators, alarm'd, Have gather'd round it, and attend it weeping. **1855** MACAULAY *Hist. Eng.* xiii. III. 275 His old soldiers were known to be gathering round him. **1894** J. T. FOWLER *Adamnan* Introd. 73 Having given his blessing to the monks who had gathered together.

† **18. a.** ? To apply oneself *to* something. *Obs.*

13.. *E.E. Allit. P.* C. 105 þay..Gederen to þe gyde ropes, þe grete cloþ falles. **13..** *Gaw. & Gr. Knt.* 777 þenne gederez he to Gryngolet with þe gilt helez.

† **b.** Of a hawk: ? To 'gather itself' (cf. 8), address itself to flight. *Obs.*

1677 N. COX *Gentl. Recreat.* (ed. 2) 201 When a high-flying Hawk, being whistled to, gathers upwards to a great Gate, you must continue her therein.

19. a. Of things: To collect, to come together in a mass; to form or increase by the coming together of material.

1390 GOWER *Conf.* I. 308 Hate is a wrathe nought shewend, But of long time gaderend. **1615** CROOKE *Body of Man* 308 A Male gathereth sooner and is sooner articulated. **1676** DRYDEN *Epil. Etherege's Man of Mode* 19 His bulky folly gathers as it goes, And, rolling o'er you, like a snow-ball grows. **1722** SEWEL *Hist. Quakers* (1795) II. vii. 18 Though darkness gather together on a heap. **1749** JOHNSON *Van. Hum. Wishes* 28 The dangers gather, as the treasures rise. **1825** SCOTT *Talism.* xviii, It seemed as if a tear..were gathering in his..eye. **1827–35** WILLIS *Child Tired of Play*, Twilight gathers, and day is done. **1860** MRS. CARLYLE *Lett.* III. 71 One knows how a story gathers like a snowball.

b. To accumulate and come to a head, as purulent matter in the body. Hence, of a wound, a sore, a wounded finger, etc.: To develop a purulent swelling. Also *to gather to a head* (in quots. *fig.*).

c **1000** [see GATHERING *vbl. sb.* 3]. **1610** SHAKS. *Temp.* v. i. 1 Now do's my Proiect gather to a head. **1804** ABERNETHY *Surg. Obs.* 81 A redness took place superficially in the skin, which gathered and burst. **1855** [see HEAD *sb.* 31].

20. a. To contract, to grow narrower (also *to gather in*). **b.** To form folds or wrinkles. *rare.*

1577–87 HARRISON *England* I. ii. in *Holinshed* 3 Like unto a triangle..being broadest in the south part, and gathering narrower and narrower. **1631** GOUGE *God's Arrows* IV. xv. 395 The garret..was within the roofe: and so gathered in narrower than the roome below it. [Or does this belong to 11 c?] **1816** SHELLEY *Alastor* 534 For, as fast years flow away, The smooth brow gathers, and the hair grows thin.

21. *Naut.* To make way (towards an object). *to gather on*: to gain on or draw nearer to, in following. *to gather into the wind*: to sail nearer to the wind.

1577–87 HARRISON *England* I. x. in *Holinshed* 77 From hence we cast about [sailing] gathering still towards the Northest. *a* **1608** SIR F. VERE *Comm.* 29, I plied onely to windward..by that means gathering nearer to the fleet. **1627** CAPT. SMITH *Seaman's Gram.* ix. 40 The longer your boords are, the more you worke or gather into the wind. *Ibid.* xii. 57 If you gather on him..hee will trie you before the wind. **1794** *Rigging & Seamanship* II. 250* A ship is said to *gather* on another, as she comes nearer to her.

22. *Mech.* Of the teeth of a cog-wheel, *to gather in upon*: to fit into. Also refl. *to gather itself into.* ? *Obs.*

1677 MOXON *Mech. Exerc.* I. 45 That the Teeth of the Worm-wheel may gather themselves into the grooves of the Worm in the Worm-spindle..the Teeth must be filed very square and smooth..which much helps the Teeth to gather in upon the Teeth of the Nut.

gatherable (ˈgæðərəb(ə)l), *a.* [f. GATHER *v.* + -ABLE.] Capable of being gathered or inferred.

1548 GEST *Pr. Masse* in H. G. Dugdale *Life* (1840) App. i. 75 Here upon gatherable it is [that] oure alone massing is a wyckednes uncomparable. **1616** HIERON *Wks.* II. 39 Many deare children of God..haue beene and are in great want..as is gatherable out of the parable of Lazarus. **1674** BOYLE *Excell. Theol.* I. i. 60 You will the more easily think the foreknowledge of the Divine Dispensations gatherable from Scripture to be highly valuable. **1820** *Examiner* No. 617. 84/1 It is easily gatherable from the anecdotes reported of him. **1877** RUSKIN *Fors Clav.* VII. lxxxi. 251, I will make this message, so far as I have yet been able to deliver it, clearly gatherable.

† **gather-bag.** *Obs.* [f. GATHER *sb.*[1] + BAG *sb.*] (See quot. 1616.)

1575 TURBERV. *Venerie* 39 The gatherbagge or mugwet of a yong harte is very medicinable also agaynst the byting of Serpentes. **1616** BULLOKAR, *Gatherbag*, the bag or skinne, inclosing a young red Deere in the Hyndes belly. **1706** in PHILLIPS (ed. Kersey).

gathered (ˈgæðəd), *ppl. a.* [f. GATHER *v.* + -ED[1].]

1. Collected, brought together; culled, picked.

1388 WYCLIF *Isa.* lvii. 13 Whanne thou schalt crie thi gederid *tresours* delyuere thee. *c* **1586** C'TESS PEMBROKE *Ps.* LXVIII. vii, Captyves store thou hast led up with thee, Whose gathered spoiles to men thou wilt impart. **1616** SURFL. & MARKH. *Country Farme* 608 The gathered grapes must be left in the ground at the least for a day or two. **1693** DRYDEN *Ovid's Met.* I. 309 About his lips the gather'd foam he churns. **1715** LEONI *Palladio's Archit.* (1742) I. 4 All dug Stones are better..than gather'd ones. **1816** BYRON *Siege Cor.* xxxiii, The jackal's troop, in gather'd cry, Bay'd from afar complainingly. **1871** C. E. MUDIE *Stray Leaves* (1872) 12 How can I, Lord, withhold Life's brightest hour From Thee; or gathered gold.

b. Of a single flower: Culled, plucked.

1588 SHAKS. *Tit. A.* III. i. 113 Then fresh teares Stood on her cheekes, as doth the hony dew Vpon a gathred Lillie almost withered.

2. Contracted, drawn together (esp. of dress).

1601 R. JOHNSON *Kingd. & Commw.* (1603) 26 One thousand Irishmen, all naked save their mantels and their thicke gathered shirts. **1617** MORYSON *Itin.* III. 175 The men weare a long coate to the knee, and upon it a long gowne with gathered sleeves. **1823** SCOTT *Quentin D.* xii, Louis..sent, from under his gathered and gloomy eyebrows, a keen look on all around. **1882** CAULFEILD & SAWARD *Dict. Needlework* s.v. *Gathering*, The gathered portion of material. **1894** *Daily News* 16 June 6/3 A white cloth skirt is made with a gathered vest to match.

3. Affected with a 'gathering' or purulent sore.

1894 *Times* (weekly ed.) 26 Jan. 79/3 In his opinion the boy's debilitated condition through a gathered finger had contributed to his death.

gatherer (ˈgæðərə(r)). [f. GATHER *v.* + -ER[1].]

1. One who gathers or collects (in general senses). Also *gatherer up*.

a **1200** *Moral Ode* 265 in *O.E. Misc.* (1872) 67 þe þat were gaderares of þisse worldes ayhte. **1382** WYCLIF *Prov.* xxx. 1 The wrdis of the gederere [L. *congregantis*]. **1768–74** TUCKER *Lt. Nat.* (1852) I. 596 Lion-skinned Free-thinking..ten times slays the slain, and claims to be the sole gatherer up of thy [Liberty's] spoils. **1807** A. KNOX *Rem.* (1844) I. 95 Of these [the ignorant, etc.] sects and societies have been, as it appears, the appointed..gatherers. **1868** MORRIS *Earthly Par.* I. 320 A gatherer-up of gold.

b. *esp.* A collector of money, often with defining word as *rent-*, *tax-*, *toll-gatherer* (now commonly *-collector*).

c **1460** *Towneley Myst.* xxx. 284 Rasers of the fals tax, And gederars of greyn wax. **1521** FISHER *Wks.* (1876) 318 They that were the gaderers of this trybute came to saynt Peter. **1572** in W. H. Turner *Select. Rec. Oxford* 342 To appoynt two gatherers..for the same money.

† **c.** A money-taker at a theatre. *Obs.*

c **1600** in *Alleyn Papers* (1843) 32 One Jhon Russell, that by youre apoyntment was made a gatherer with vs, but my fellowes finding [him often] falce to vs, haue many times warnd him from taking the box.

† **d.** One who gathers wealth (opposed to 'spender' or 'waster'); a miser. *Obs.*

1500–20 DUNBAR *Poems* xxvi. 59 Hud-pykis, hurdaris and gadderaris, All with that warlo went. **1564–78** BULLEYN *Dial. agst. Pest.* (1883) 133 The foolishe Prodigall waster, whiche commonlie succedeth the gatherer. **1592** GREENE *Groat's W. Wit* (1874) 13 Ah, Lucanio, my onely comfort, because I hope thou wilt, as thy father, be a gatherer, let me blesse thee before I die.

2. One who gathers flowers, fruit, or other produce.

1382 WYCLIF *Obad.* i. 5 Ȝif gadreris of grapis hadden entriden to thee. *c* **1449** PECOCK *Repr.* I. vi. 29 The feld is the fundament of the flouris, and not the hondis of the gaderers. **1567** MAPLET *Gr. Forest* 37 Celedonie is an Herbe..whose flower..dyeth and stayneth the gatherers hande. **1607** TOPSELL *Four-f. Beasts* 3 In Caucasus there are trees of Pepper and Spices whereof Apes are the gatherers. **1725** BRADLEY *Fam. Dict.* s.v. *Mulberry*, The Gatherer must have his Hands clean.

3. A collector of literary material; a compiler.

1387 TREVISA *Higden* (Rolls) I. 13 [þey] cleped him a gaderere of old wrytynges [L. *compilator veterum*]. **1579** FULKE *Heskins' Parl.* 183 He hath not redd the place in Augustine him selfe, but taketh it out of some collectour or gatherer. **1624** WOTTON *Archit.* Pref., I am but a gatherer and disposer of other men's stuffe. **1853** TRENCH *Proverbs* 10 Many collections include whatever brief sayings their gatherers have anywhere met with.

4. *techn.* **a.** *Bookbinding.* An operative who collects the sheets of a book in their proper order. **b.** *Glass-making.* (See quots.)

a. 1683 MOXON *Mech. Exerc.* II. 348 The Gatherer takes it [a Sheet] off with his Right Hand. **1874** KNIGHT *Dict. Mech.* 959/2 A more convenient way is to arrange the signatures on a long straight table..so that the gatherers may follow each other.

b. 1839 URE *Dict. Arts* etc. 578 One, called a gatherer, dips the end of an iron tube..into the pot of melted metal. **1888** *Daily News* 14 Feb. 6/6 In the ordinary process of bottle-blowing the..'gatherer', as he is called, gathers a charge of the molten metal from the furnace on the end of a blow-pipe.

5. One of the front teeth of a horse.

1696 SIR W. HOPE tr. *Solleysel's Parf. Mareschal* I. v. 19 There groweth then in the place of these four Foal-teeth which fell, four others which are called Nippers or Gatherers. **1797** *Sporting Mag.* X. 295 *Gatherers*, the two fore teeth. **1847–78** HALLIWELL, *Gatherers*, a horse's teeth by which he draws his food into his mouth.

ˈgathering, *vbl. sb.* [f. as prec. + -ING[1].]

1. a. The action of the verb GATHER, in various transitive senses. Also with *in*, *out*, *up*.

c **1050** *Byrhtferth's Handboc* in *Anglia* VIII. 312 For þære ripunge oððe for þære gaderunge. **1398** TREVISA *Barth. De P.R.* XVII. lxxiii. (1495) 647 Bein that gadre hony visyte and haunte floures by cause of gadrynge of hony. **1488–9** *Act 4 Hen. VII*, c. 5 Abbottes..quyte and discharged of gadryng of dysmes. **1597** HOOKER *Eccl. Pol.* v. vii. §2 The gathering of principles out of..particular experiments. **1617** MORYSON *Itin.* III. 242 [He] was much delighted in the gathering of antiquities. **1691** SIR W. HOPE *Fencing Master* (1692) 99 Of raising or Gathering up of your Adversaries sword. **1705** STANHOPE *Paraph.* II. 359 By this..we become capable of diffusing the Riches of that Knowledge in a Moment, the gathering whereof may have cost us the pains and study of many Years. **1842** MANNING *Serm.* xix. (1848) I. 274 In these words He foretells the gathering out and knitting together of His mystical body, which is the Church. **1875** WHITNEY *Life Lang.* xv. 312 Nothing will make dispensable the wide gathering-in of evidence.

† **b.** The action or practice of collecting wealth; miserly acquisition of money. *Obs.*

a **1225** *Ancr. R.* 286 Aȝeines ȝiscunge. Ich wolde þet oðre schuneden, ase ȝe doð, gederunge. **1340** *Ayenb.* 192 Elmesse þet is y-do of þyefþe..oþer of oþre kueade gaderinge, hit ne likeþ noþing god. *c* **1400** *Rom. Rose* 5782 [Thre] gret mischeves hem assailith, And thus in gadring ay travaylith. **1550** CROWLEY *Last Trump.* 252 Though the Lord geue the plentye..Be thou neuer the more gredy, Nor set thy mynd on gatheringe.

c. The action of drawing in or contracting; also, the result of this (see GATHER *v.* 11 b, 11 c, 16 b); *spec.* in *Building* (see quot. 1851).

1580 LYLY *Euphues* To Ladies Engl. (Arb.) 222 If a Tailour make your gowne too little, you couer his fault with a broad stomacher..if too long, with a false gathering. **1611** in Heath *Grocers' Comp.* (1869) 92 That none should wear..any ruff exceeding 4 yards in length before the gathering or setting in thereof. **1703** T. N. *City & C. Purchaser* 107 An apt falling-back of the Back, and convenient gathering of the Wings, and Brest of the Chimney. **1765** A. DICKSON *Treat. Agric.* (ed. 2) 308 Gathering keeps the crown and furrows of the ridge in the same place in which they were before. **1807** SIR R. C. HOARE *Tour Irel.* 198 The weight of this new building, pressed upon the gathering of the arches. **1823** P. NICHOLSON *Pract. Build.* 585 Gathering of the wings, in a chimney. **1846** *Jrnl. R. Agric. Soc.* VII. I. 57, I would soon endeavour to make the present heading or gathering as good, by deep ploughing and the application of manure. *Ibid.*, On these high-back lands..the gathering up, or centre of each land..has become dead, inert clay. **1851** *Dict. Archit.* s.v., Where the fireplace in one story is directly over another, and the flues go up in the jambs, the brickwork which oversails and forms the soffite of the with of the flue is called the gathering. Hence the term is loosely applied instead of gathering of the wings or gathering wings, to that part of a chimney funnel which is built inclined over the fireplace, so as to contract the sides to a union with the throat of the flue. **1880** *Plain Hints* 18 The depth of the material under the band above the gathering.

d. *in* (or *a*) *gathering* = being gathered. Also with omission of the preposition.

c **1400** *Destr. Troy* 11735 While this gode was in gederyng the grettes among. **1625** USSHER *Answ. Jesuit* 194 Yet were there certain sticks then agathering. **1693** SIR T. P. BLOUNT *Nat. Hist.* 54 The Cloves are gathering from September unto the End of February.

2. The action of coming together, uniting or combining; the result of this; union, accumulation. (In early instances also with *ȝe-*.)

c **900** tr. *Bæda's Hist.* I. xvi. [xxvii.] (1890) 82 Forðon ȝedafenað, þætte seo ælice ȝegadrung lichoman seo for intingan tudres. *c* **1230** *Hali Meid.* 3 þi folc he clepeð dauid þe gederunge inwið þe of fleschliche þohtes. *Ibid.* 27 Of wif & weres gederinge weorldes wele awakeneð. **1382** WYCLIF *Gen.* i. 10 The gaderyngis of watris he clepide, sees. **1398** TREVISA *Barth. De P.R.* v. xviii. (1495) 123 In the chynne of a beest is the moust strength of hardnes of the boon and harde gaderynge of synewes. **1553** EDEN *Treat. Newe Ind.* (Arb.) Ep. Rdr. 9 Ye gathering of many mens wittes into one mans head. **1724** DE FOE *Mem. Cavalier* (1840) 43 The gathering of this storm, which..began to threaten all Germany..determined me. **1726** LEONI *Alberti's Archit.* I. 47/2 To prevent the gathering of Dirt and Seeds, which might make Weeds grow in the Wall. **1870** L'ESTRANGE *Miss Mitford* I. vi. 168 But all this was but the gathering of the wind before a storm.

3. *spec.* An accumulation of purulent matter in any part of the body; a suppurated swelling.

c **1000** *Sax. Leechd.* I. 300 Wið cyrnlu & wið ealle yfele ȝegaderunga, ȝenim [etc.]. **1667** *Decay Chr. Piety* v. 105 No less happy than..the ease of a broken Imposthume, after the painful gathering and filling of it. **1753** J. BARTLET *Gentleman's Farriery* xxxii. 263 If a gathering forms on the opposite side, open it in the same manner. **1763** MRS. HARRIS in *Priv. Lett. Ld. Malmesbury* I. 102 Some say Mr. Wilkes is very well, others say they apprehend a gathering in his side. **1862** MRS. H. WOOD *Mrs. Hallib.* I. i. 3 I've a gathering come on my thimble finger. **1893** *Northumbld. Gloss.* s.v. *Gether*, An abscess is called a *getherin*.

4. a. A bringing together or coming together of people; an assembly or meeting. (In early examples also with prefixed *ȝe-*, *i-*.) *spec.* An assembly organized annually in various parts of the Scottish Highlands for contests in athletics, dancing, piping, etc.; = GAME *sb.* 4 d.

c **1000** *Ags. Gosp.* John v. 13 Se hælynd soþlice beah fram þære ȝegaderunge. *c* **1100** *Ags. Voc.* in Wr.-Wülcker 326/7 *Aecclesia*, cyrce, oððe ȝeleafful gaderung. **1154** *O.E. Chron.* an. 1137 þa þe king Stephne to Engla lande com, þa macod he his gadering at Oxeneford. *c* **1175** *Lamb. Hom.* 89 þe apostles speken to þes folkes igederunge. *a* **1300** *Cursor M.* 10703 Bot þar was nan at þat gedring, þat cuthe giue consail o þat thing. **1375** BARBOUR *Bruce* VI. 389 He maid a gaddering preuely Of thame that war of his party. *c* **1400** *Destr. Troy* 2922 Women..shunt not for shame to shake ouer lande, To glogh vppon gomes at gedering of folke. **1568** GRAFTON *Chron.* II. 141 Dyvers conventicles and gatherynges were made of the Citizens and other, that robbed in the Citie and did much harme. **1611** BIBLE *Ecclus.* xxvi. 5 The gathering together of an vnruly multitude. **1828** *Edin. Evening Courant* 16 Aug., The Athole Gathering or Highland Meeting was held..on Wednesday the 6th instant. **1828–40** TYTLER *Hist. Scot.* (1864) I. 259 *note*, Winton is in an error in making this gathering of the states in 1285. **1850** QUEEN VICTORIA *Jrnl.* 12 Sept. (1868) 123 We..went..to the Gathering at the *Castle of Braemar*. **1860** TYNDALL *Glac.* I. xii. 86 It was not the goodness of the conversation..which gave the charm to our gatherings. **1874** GREEN *Short Hist.* iv. §4. 191 In their beginnings our boroughs seem to have been mainly gatherings of persons engaged in agricultural pursuits. **1947** DUKE OF HAMILTON in H. W. Meikle *Scotland* xxxi. 244 Of the greater 'gatherings' the northern meeting at Inverness, the Braemar

Gathering on Deeside, and the Oban Games are the outstanding examples. **1969** M. Pugh *Last Place Left* xvi. 113 Always wanted to see a Gathering through local eyes.

b. A signal (by beat of drum, sound of pipes, etc.) for assembling.

1653 Urquhart *Rabelais* I. xlix, Immediately after the soldiers had done with eating and drinking..a gathering should be beaten for bringing them altogether. **1810** Scott *Lady of L.* II. xvii, The clan's shrill Gathering they could hear. **1847** J. Wilson *Recr. Chr. North* (1857) I. 167 Some old soldier, probably, playing a gathering or a coronach.

5. That which is gathered or brought together: *esp.* (*a*) a collection in money (now *dial.*); †(*b*) a conclusion or inference; †(*c*) a compilation (of literary matter).

c **1380** *Sir Ferumb.* 3339 To gadrie þat gold þay dude hure miȝt..On þe gadryngge þat þay made; þan þay by-gunne to fiȝte. *c* **1425** *Found. St. Bartholomew's* (E.E.T.S.) 39 We shall bere thedir..[a] collecte or gaderyng maade amongse vs offerynge yt to that chirche yn mynde of oure delyueraunce. **1508** *Pilton Churchw. Acc.* (Som. Rec. Soc.) 54 Item receved of the parish gathering for the coueryng of the rode loȝffte viij^{s}. ij^{d}. **1526** *Pilgr. Perf.* (W. de W. 1531) 191 b, For this colleccyon or gatheryng of the artycles of fayth..is the instruccyon of the faythfull people. **1552** Latimer *Serm. Lord's Prayer* vi. Wks. II. 91 Which you may perceive partly by that I have said, and partly by gatherings and conjectures. **1577** B. Googe *Heresbach's Husb.* II. (1586) 97 For setting and planting of Cheryes, you may read a great sorte of rules in the gatheringes of Constantine. **1579** Fulke *Heskins' Parl.* 314 His gathering is altogether fond & ridiculous. **1611** Bible *2 Macc.* xii. 43 When he had made a gathering throughout the company, to the sum of two thousand drachmes of siluer. **1709** Steele *Tatler* No. 44 ¶4 The Company here..had made a Gathering to purchase the Moveables of the neighbouring Play-house. **1751** Paltock *Peter Wilkins* (1884) I. 124 Some few new sorts of berries and greens were the gathering of that day. **1879** *Athenæum* 5 Apr. 445 This gathering [an exhibition of pictures] is, as a whole, by no means equal to some of its predecessors. **1887** *S. Chesh. Gloss.*, *Getherin*, a collection. The word is becoming obsolete.

6. *Bookbinding*: **a.** The arrangement of the loose sheets of a book in proper order; **b.** A certain number of leaves placed one inside another, making up a group or quire.

1683 Moxon *Mech. Exerc.* II. 348 Gathering of Books is to take one Sheet off every Heap, beginning at the last Heap first. **1824** J. Johnson *Typogr.* II. xvi. 568 The collater cannot be too attentive in observing whether the gathering be true. **1844** Lingard *Anglo-Sax. Ch.* (1858) II. App. 331 The last folio in the seventh gathering. **1893** J. H. Bernard in *Trans. R. Irish Acad.* XXX. 308 The gatherings in the original binding do not seem to have been made up uniformly of the same number of leaves.

7. *Glass-making.* = gather *sb.*[1] 3 b.

1908 W. Rosenhain *Glass Manuf.* vi. 88 The introduction of the gathering into the molten glass is each time liable to produce air bells which would spoil the whole mass of glass. **1925** Hodkin & Cousen *Textbk. Glass Technol.* xxxi. 403 It is not necessary to blow down the pipe, when this method is used, before the gathering is brought from the furnace.

8. *attrib.* and *Comb.*, as ***gathering-place***, ***-season***, ***-time***; also **gathering-board** *Bookbinding* (see quot.); **gathering-coal**, a large piece of coal, laid on the fire to keep it burning during the night; **gathering-cry**, a summons to assemble for war; **gathering-ground**, region from which the feeding waters of a river or a reservoir are collected; **gathering-hoop** (see quot.); **gathering-iron** *Glass-blowing*, the iron tube used in 'gathering' (see gather *v.* 13 a); **gathering-pallet** (or **piece**) (see quots.); **gathering-peat** (see quots.); **gathering-rod** = *gathering-iron*; **gathering-sound**, a signal for assembling; **gathering-table** (see quot.); **gathering-thread**, the thread used in making gathers in a dress, etc.

1874 Knight *Dict. Mech.*, **Gathering-board*, a horseshoe-shaped table on which signatures are laid to be gathered or assembled to form a book. **1808** Bald *Coal Trade Scotl.* iv. 60 Another demand for large blocks of coals is, for the servants to make what is termed *gathering-coals in the kitchen. **1816** Scott *Antiq.* xxvi, The matron of the family, having laid the gathering-coal upon the fire..retired to rest the last of the family. **1893** *Northumbld. Gloss.*, *Getherin coal.* **1817** Campbell *Reullura* 86 And no *gathering-cry rose yet O'er the isles of Albyn's sea. **1851** M. A. Denham *Slogans N. Eng.* 11 The Slogan, or Gathering-cry of the clan Fenwick was never heard in vain. **1877** A. H. Green *Phys. Geol.* iii. §2. 106 The table-land on which snow accumulates is called the *gathering-ground. **1895** E. A. Parkes *Health* 19 Dublin is supplied with water from gathering-grounds and a large 'impounding reservoir'. **1874** Knight *Dict. Mech.*, **Gathering-hoop*, one used by coopers to draw in the ends of the staves so as to allow the hoop to be slipped thereon. **1883** H. J. Powell *Princ. Glass-making* iii. 12 A part of the bulb remote from the *gathering-iron. **1850** E. B. Denison *Clock & Watch Making* §90 At every stroke of the hammer, it [a pinion] takes up the teeth of the rack one after another, and it is therefore called the **gathering piece* or *pallet.* **1884** F. J. Britten *Watch & Clockm.*, *Gathering Pallet*, a revolving finger that in striking clocks and repeating watches moves the rack one tooth for each blow struck. **1825–80** Jamieson, **Gathering-peat*, a fiery peat which was sent round by the borderers, to alarm the country in time of danger. **1882** Ogilvie, *Gathering-peat*, a peat put into the kitchen-fire at night..to preserve the fire till the morning. **1820** W. Irving *Sketch-Bk.* (1859) 42 In England ..the metropolis is a mere *gathering-place, or general rendezvous of the polite classes. **1883** H. J. Powell *Princ. Glass-making* iii. 12 If the *gathering rod be hollow. **1657** S. Purchas *Pol. Flying-Ins.* 289 The provident prudent Bee, finding a likely decay of the *gathering season, and observing that the Drones are only spenders..doe at last violently expell them. **1810** Scott *Lady of L.* III. i, Clamorous war-pipes yelled the *gathering sound. **1841** Savage *Dict. Print.*, **Gathering table*, a table..on which the printed sheets are arranged in the order of their signatures, in order to their being gathered into books. **1882** Caulfield & Saward *Dict. Needlework* s.v. *Gathering*, Care should be taken to conceal the *gathering thread. **1532** Huloet, *Gatherynge tyme or season when rype fruite is gathered, *vindemia*.

'gathering, *ppl. a.* [f. gather *v.* + -ing[2].]

1. That gathers, brings together, or accumulates.

a **1225** *Ancr. R.* 128 þus beoð þe gederinde ancren of god iþe gospelle to uoxes iefned.

2. That gathers or comes together in a mass; that contracts or draws together.

1697 Dryden *Virg. Past.* IX. 88 Or if e'er Night the gath'ring Clouds we fear, A Song will help the beating Storm to bear. **1703** Rowe *Ulyss.* II. i. 821 Dost thou dread the gath'ring Storm That grumbles in the Air. **1851** [see gathering *vbl. sb.* 1 c]. **1863** Geo. Eliot *Romola* II. xxii, The soldiers found themselves escorted by a gathering troop of men and boys. **1872** W. Black *Adv. Phaeton* xxx, We drive on in the gathering twilight.

gating: see gate *v.*[1], gate *v.*[4]

Gatling ('gætlɪŋ). [The name of the inventor.] *attrib.* in *Gatling gun*, a form of machine gun, with a cluster of barrels into which the cartridges are automatically loaded at the breech, invented by Dr. R. J. Gatling, and first used in the American civil war (1861–65). Also *Gatling* simply.

1870 *Daily News* 8 Sept. 6 A hundred more Gatling guns have been ordered in America. *Ibid.* 22 Sept., Yesterday two Gatling mitrailleuses were tried at Shoeburyness. **1872–6** Voyle & Stevenson *Milit. Dict.* (ed. 3) 259/1 This led to the introduction of the Gatling gun into the British army. *Ibid.* 259/2 Few Gatlings up to this date have been manufactured for the service. **1886** *Echo* 25 Sept. 4/3 The firing was continued with big guns, gatlings and rifles.

'gator ('geɪtə(r)). Also **gater**, **gator**. Colloq. abbrev. of alligator[2]. orig. *U.S.*

1844 *Knickerbocker* XXIII. 407 The 'gator is n't what you may call a han'some critter. **1886** *Outing* (U.S.) Apr. 60/2 The natives often feed their dogs and hogs boiled 'gator meat. **1890** C. W. Butler in G. O. Shields *Big Game N. Amer.* 563 This is not based upon the dog's love of 'Gator-hunting, but upon the 'Gator's love of dog-hunting. **1933** *Bulletin* (Sydney) 20 Sept. 33/2 Halifax (where the local pubkeeper used to keep a couple of 'gators chained up in the back yard like dogs). **1948** G. B. Shaw *Buoyant Billions* IV. 52 You cannot charm the rattlers and gators as I can. **1967** C. O. Skinner *Madame Sarah* viii. 168 Mr. Bell..managed to get hold of a baby 'gator, which was dumped into one of the lakes.

G.A.T.T., GATT, Gatt (gæt). [f. the initials of *General Agreement on Tariffs and Trade.*] A convention or organization established in 1947 to agree common rules for tariffs and to reduce trade restrictions.

1948 *Hansard Commons* 29 Oct. 3 Multilateral tariff negotiations should be held..to afford an opportunity to certain additional countries to adhere to the G.A.T.T. **1955** *Ann. Reg. 1954* 148 G.A.T.T.'s objective was to raise the standard of living of all peoples by means of the freest possible exchange of goods. **1957** *Economist* 19 Oct. 198/1 They have got to convince the members..that the common market does not conflict with GATT. *Ibid.* 2 Nov. 420/1 The question whether the common market treaty was compatible with Gatt.

gatt, obs. form of goat.

gatt(e, obs. form of *got*, pa. t. of get.

gatten: see gaiter *sb.*[2]

'gatter. *slang.* Beer; liquor generally.

1818 Maginn *Vidocq Versified* iv. Misc. I. 353 'Lots of gatter' quo' she, 'are flowing'. **1841** *Punch* I. 243/2 Gatter is but 3d. a pot, and that's the price of a reasonable 'pike ticket. **1851** Mayhew *Lond. Labour* I. 218 They have a 'shant of gatter' (pot of beer) at the nearest 'boozing-ken' (alehouse).

gatter(idge, gatton: see gaiter *sb.*[2]

gattine (gæ'tiːn). Also **gattina.** [Fr.] A disease of the silkworm; = pébrine.

1825 F. Rozier in tr. *Dandolo's Art of Rearing Silkworms* xii. 281 M. Dandolo..makes some observations on two diseases..called in Lombardy *calcinaccio*..and *gattine. Ibid.* 283 The change of the nature of the silkworm, when subject to the *gattina*,..is a real animal disease. *Ibid.*, By gattina is generally understood a worm that cannot accomplish the prescribed functions of nature. **1884** *Encycl. Brit.* XVII. 613/2 Owing to the ravages of *gattine*, the silk industry has greatly declined since 1864. **1888** E. A. Butler *Silkworms* v. 72 The most terrible of the diseases of the silkworm is *pébrine*, or pepper disease, which was formerly called *gattine.* **1954** E. Attwood *Louis Pasteur* x. 56 The silkworms were dying of a strange disease: they were covered with tiny black or brown spots, and they grew stiff and made little movements with their feet like a cat trying to scratch. One of the names given to this disease was gattine, from a word meaning a small cat.

†**gat-toothed**, *a. Obs. rare.* [app. = gap-toothed, f. gat *sb.* opening, gap.] Having the teeth set wide apart.

This is said to be popularly regarded as a sign that the person will be lucky and travel much (Skeat), and was perhaps so intended by Chaucer.

c **1386** Chaucer *Prol.* 468 She koude muchel of wandrynge by the weye; Gat tothed was she, soothly for to seye. —— *Wife's Prol.* 603 Gat tothed was I, and that bicam me weel.

‖**gatto'rugine.** [mod.Lat. (Willughby *Hist. Pisc.* 1686) a. alleged It. (Venetian) *gattoruggine*, 'quasi cattus rubiginosus' (!).] A species of blenny. Hence **gatto'ruginous** *a.*, epithet of this species.

1769 Pennant *Zool.* III. 181 [Blenny], Gattorugine.. This curious kind was discovered to be a British fish by the Rev. Mr. Williams, who found it on the Anglesea coast. **1818** Montagu in *Mem. Wernerian Nat. Hist. Soc.* II. 444 The shape of the species is somewhat similar to that of the Gattorugine. **1836** Yarrell *Brit. Fishes* I. 226 The Gattoruginous Blenny.

†**'gature.** *Obs. rare*$^{-1}$. [irregularly f. *gate* gait *sb.* + -ure.] Gait, mien.

1538 Bale *Thre Lawes* A vij, I thought so by your stature, And by your auncyent gature, Ye were of soch a rature.

gatwarde, obs. form of gate-ward.

‖**gau** (gaʊ). [G.] A territorial and administrative division of ancient Germany, including several villages or communities; in the Middle Ages, a larger division, over which, under Frankish rule, was placed a graf.

The word is a frequent final element of place-names, as Breisgau, Oberammergau.

1845 B. Thorpe tr. *Lappenberg's Hist. Eng.* I. 88 In the time of Charlemagne, they [*sc.* the Saxons] were in possession of..the 'gaus', or districts, of the later Upper and Lower Saxony. **1874** Stubbs *Const. Hist.* §26 The four [*sc.* marks] were in A.D. 804 made into a Gau, in which the archbishop of Bremen had the royal rights of Heerbann and Blutbann. **1916** E. G. A. Holmes *Nemesis of Docility* i. 19 The counts..were supposed to..keep order in their own *gaus* or 'shires'. **1959** *Chambers's Encycl.* VI. 257 The people looked for protection to the local ruler rather than the reigning prince, to the count of the district (Gau) and to the tribal duke.

gaub[1] (gɔːb). *Naut.* Also **gab, gob.** Only *attrib.* in **gaub-line, -rope** (see quots.).

1841 R. H. Dana *Seaman's Man.* 107 *Gob-line* or *Gaub-line*, a rope leading from the martingale inboard. The same as back-rope. **1867** Smyth *Sailor's Word-bk.*, *Gaub-line.* **1882** Nares *Seamanship* (ed. 6) 196 A gab rope is often fitted to a jib. It is a short piece of rope spliced into a thimble, about half-way along the foot of the sail, and rove through a block on the bowsprit cap.

‖**gaub**[2] (gɔːb). *Indian.* [Hindustani *gāb.*]

1866 *Treas. Bot.*, *Gaub*, an Indian name for the astringent medicinal fruit of *Diospyros Embryopteris.* **1897** Willis *Flowering Pl. & Ferns* II. 135 *Diospyros Embryopteris*, Pers., is the gaub tree of India; its fruit contains a sticky pulp, used for caulking seams in boats.

gaubart, var. galbart *Obs.*, gaberdine.

gauche (‖goʃ, gəʊʃ). *a.* [F. *gauche* skew, left (hand), left-handed, awkward.]

1. Wanting in tact or in ease and grace of manner, awkward, clumsy.

1751 Chesterf. *Let.* 10 May, Mr. **** is *gauche*; it is to be hoped that will mend with keeping company. **1806–7** J. Beresford *Miseries Hum. Life* (1826) x. cxxii, On going early to bed..finding..a gauche Dawdle just beginning to introduce the warming pan between the sheets. **1860** *All Year Round* No. 42. 363 He never does anything ludicrous, or gauche, or intrusive, or fussy, or vulgar.

2. *Math.* Skew, not plane (see quot.).

1879 Thomson & Tait *Nat. Phil.* I. I. §7 If various points of the line do not lie in one plane, we have in one case..a curve of double curvature, in the other a gauche polygon.

Hence **'gauchely** *adv.*, **'gaucheness.**

1883 *My Trivial Life* II. viii. 164 Never was more astonished than by Lady Arabella's gaucheness. **1891** Broughton & Bisland *Widower indeed* iii. (1892) 37 He enters gauchely, for he is a cub. **1936** Auden *Look, Stranger!* 55 O can you see precisely in our gaucheness The neighbour's strongest wish, to serve and love? **1937** *Discovery* July 226/1 Sixty-one excellent plates atone for any 'gaucheness' of the style. **1967** M. Wilding in *Coast to Coast 1965–6* 253 She liked him for his gaucheness.

‖**gaucherie** (goʃri). [Fr., f. *gauche*: see gauche *a.*] Want of tact or grace of manner, awkwardness; an instance of this, a 'gauche' proceeding.

1798 Charlotte Smith *Young Philos.* III. 35 Medora, when divested of a little of that *gaucherie*, which diffidence gave. **1823** *Edin. Rev.* XXXIX. 237 The known *gaucherie* of our cabinet in all sorts of Continental interference. **1826** Disraeli *Viv. Grey* I. viii, An elegant lively lad, with just enough of dandyism to preserve him from committing *gaucheries.* **1853** Kingsley *Misc. Th. Shelley & Byron* I. 324 Every conceited word and look, every gaucherie and rudeness. **1856** Miss Yonge *Daisy Chain* I. xxv. (1879) 263 The young lady contrived to make her exit, with the same amount of gaucherie as had marked her entrance.

gaucho (ˈgaʊtʃəʊ, ˈgɔːtʃəʊ). Also incorrectly Guacho. [Sp.; prob. from some native S. American lang.] (See quot. 1871.)

1824 B. HALL *Jrnl. Chili & Peru* (1825) I. iv. 151 Two mounted horsemen, Guassos as they are called in Chili, or Guachos in Peru. **1838** HALIBURTON *Clockm.* Ser. II. xxii. (1848) 182 A party of them Guachos.. galloped up to him.. and made him prisoner. **1851** MAYNE REID *Scalp Hunt.* xxxiii, The savage coiled the lasso with the dexterity of a gaucho. **1860** GOSSE *Rom. Nat. Hist.* 201 The Guachos are able to entangle them [birds] with the bolas. **1871** TYLOR *Prim. Cult.* I. 41 The Gauchos of the South American Pampas, a mixed European and Indian race of equestrian herdsmen.

gaucie, gaucy: see GAWSY.

gaud, *sb.*[1] *Obs.* exc. *Hist.* In quots. **gaude**. See also GAUDY *sb.* [Of somewhat uncertain origin.

Du Cange cites an Anglo-Latin document of 1415 which has *gaudia* (pl. of *gaudium* joy) in this sense. It does not appear that *gaudia* was so used on the continent, and in this example it is prob. only a latinization of the Eng. word. At the same time, it seems likely that the L. *gaudia* is really the source, and that the 'gauds' were so called as serving to mark the fifteen mysteries (the first five of which are 'joyful mysteries') to be meditated upon in reciting the fifteen decades of aves. An AF. *gaudes* pl., app. in this sense, occurs in a document of 1381 (Nichols *Royal Wills* (1780) 100). Cf. also 17th c. F. *gaudees*, explained in Oudin's *Fr.-It. Dict.* as 'prayers without attention' (Godef.).]

One of the larger and more ornamental beads placed between the decades of 'aves' in a rosary. (Called in Fr. *signaux* or *seigneaux*.)

1390 GOWER *Conf.* III. 372 A paire of bedes blacke as sable.. Upon the gaudes all without Was write of gold *pur reposer*. **1531** in Weaver *Wells Wills* (1890) 134 A pere of beydes of jette with sylver gaudes. **1570** *Durham Depos.* (Surtees) 164 She saith that she occupied her gaudes as many thowsand dyd. **1874** *Archæol. Assoc. Jrnl.* Dec. 440 In all probability this large and once beautiful bead formed the Gaude or 'Pater noster' of a rosary of the sixteenth century.

gaud (gɔːd), *sb.*[2] Forms: 4–9 **gaude**, 4–7 **gawde**, 4–7, 9 **gawd**, 6– **gaud**. [perh. an AF. sb. f. *gaudir* to rejoice, make merry, to jest, scoff at, ad. L. *gaudēre* to rejoice.]

†**1.** A trick, prank; often, a device to deceive, a piece of trickery, a pretence; also a game, sport, or pastime. *Obs.*

13.. *Seuyn Sages* (W.) 3957 For thi gaudes [*printed* gandes] and thy gilry I gif this dome that thou sal dy. *c* **1386** CHAUCER *Pars. T.* ¶577 Þay maken folk to laughe.. as folk doon at the gawdes of An Ape. *a* **1400–50** *Alexander* 2732 Sire vanite & vayne-glori & vices of pride þa ere þe gaudis, as I gesse þat all gods hatis. *Ibid.* 2966 Sone þis gouernour of grece is of þis gaude ware. *c* **1400** *Destr. Troy* XXII. 9279 Þat he.. with no gawdes me begile. *c* **1425** WYNTOUN *Cron.* VIII. x. 173 Bot þis King Edward all wyth gawdys Knakkyd Robert þe Brws wyth frawdis. *c* **1440** *York Myst.* xi. 37 What gawdes haue they begonne? **1513** DOUGLAS *Æneis* X. ii. 27 Quhat God amovit him with sic a gawd In his dedis to oys sik slychtis and frawd. *c* **1560** A. SCOTT *Poems* xxxiv. 85 Quhen thay begyn sic gawdis To leif thay ar most laith. **1576** GASCOIGNE *Steele Glas* (Arb.) 59 These Enterluds, these newe Italian sportes And euery gawde, that glads the minde of man. **1603** HARSNET *Pop. Impost.* 32 There was never Christmas Game performed with moe apish indecent slovenly Gawdes then your Baptising and Super-baptising Ceremonies are. *a* **1639** W. WHATELEY *Prototypes* II. xxvi. (1640) 22 Staying too long at your gawdes, following them such a space of time together, or with such great violence, that you be even tired and spent by them. *a* **1796** PEGGE *Derbicisms* (E.D.S.) 26 *Gawd*; an ugly gawd, a habit or custom. [**1882** *Lanc. Gloss.* s.v., *Goad*, a custom, a way of doing a thing.]

†**b.** A jest, scoff; also, an object of mockery. *Obs.*

c **1440** *Promp. Parv.* 188/2 Gawde or iape, *nuga*. **1538** BALE *Thre Lawes* 122 Without vayne gaudes or fables. **1563–83** FOXE *A. & M.* (1583) 2102 The sayde John Apowell mocked hym.. with contrary gaudes and flouting wordes. **1650** TRAPP *Comm.* Gen. xxi. 9 [Ishmael mocked] at that mystical name Isaac, as a gaud, or laughing-stock.

†**c.** A festivity, rejoicing. *Obs.*

1571 CAMPION *Hist. Irel.* II. vi. (1633) 89 Therefore at the decease of the Lord Iustice.. Bonfires and gawdes were solemnized in all the Land.

2. *concr.* A plaything, toy. Also (now always), something gaudy; a showy ornament, a piece of finery; a gewgaw. Now *rhetorical*. [Perh. influenced by GAUD *sb.*[1].]

c **1430** LYDG. *Min. Poems* 92 Where he [Sardanapalus] with wymmen satte and made his gawdes. **1550** BALE *Apol.* 119 b, A wonton gyglot maye cal men to sorrowfull repentaunce, whils she is yet in her gawdes, and the maystre of the stewes maye persuade men to chastyte. **1587** HARMAR tr. *Beza's Serm.* 82 To disburden her [the Church] of those stincking and defiled gawdes, to restore her vnto her natiue beuty. [Cf. *ante*, Which disguised hir with prophane trimmings & tifflings vp of her.] **1591** H. SMITH *Trump. of Soul* A vij b, Why Solomon maketh us fooles and giueth us gaudes to play withall. **1650** JER. TAYLOR *Holy Living* ii. §4 (1727) 96 Or should study hard and labour to cozen a child of his gauds. **1666** DRYDEN *Ann. Mirab.* ccvi, Some bound for Guinny, golden sand to find, Bore all the gawds the simple Natives wear. **1768** BEATTIE *Minstr.* I. xvi, Dainties he heeded not, nor gaude, nor toy. **1823** PRAED *Troubadour* Poems 1865 I. 121 A dazzling gaud of twisted gold. **1842** F. TROLLOPE *Vis. to Italy* I. xxii. 363 The gaud that most delights the ladies.. is the old lace. **1883** *Sat. Rev.* LV. 497 Otherwise than as gauds for a procession they [umbrellas] are not held in any great estimation.

fig. **1656** BAXTER *Reformed Pastor* 23 All the Rhetorical jingling writers they could meet with, were prest to serve them for the adorning of their stile, (and gawds were oft their chiefest ornaments). *a* **1839** PRAED *Poems* (1864) I. 308 And blazon honour's hapless wreck With all the gauds of guilt. **1850** WHIPPLE *Ess. & Rev.* (ed. 3) I. 235 They spurned at the old tricks and gauds of diction.

3. *pl.* Showy ceremonies, 'pomps and vanities'; gaieties. Now *rhetorical*.

1650 W. BROUGH *Sacr. Princ.* (1659) 66 The gawds and glories of an earthly court. *c* **1800** K. WHITE *Poems* (1837) 36 How insignificant do all the joys, The gaudes, and honours of the world appear! **1853** MOTLEY *Corr.* (1889) I. v. 157, I had hoped that Mary would have mustered up energy to send you a description of these fine doings.. I am not good at these gauds. **1866** FELTON *Anc. & Mod.Gr.* I. xiii. 249 Its bishops and patriarchs surrounded themselves with the pomps and gauds of this world.

b. *sing.* Idle display; showy ceremony.

1800–24 CAMPBELL *Poems, Poland* 93 Public Murder!—that with pomp and gaud And royal scorn of Justice walks abroad. **1835** LYTTON *Rienzi* IV. i, The pomp, the gaud.. strongly contrasted the patriarchal simplicity which marked his justice court.

4. *Comb.*, as †**gaud-glorious** *a.* [cf. the phrase *to gawde and glory*, GAUD *v.*[2]], very showy.

1555 W. WATREMAN *Fardle Facions* II. viii. L ij a, In their Toumbes.. very plaine and nothyng costlie: But in trimming and arraieng of their bodies, to, to, gaude glorious.

†**gaud**, *v.*[1] *Obs.* [f. GAUD *sb.*[1] (? and *sb.*[2])]

1. *trans.* To furnish with 'gauds' (see GAUD *sb.*[1], GAUDY *sb.* 1).

c **1386** CHAUCER *Prol.* 159 A peire of bedes gauded al with grene. **1500** *Will of Strudy* (Somerset Ho.), A payre of Corall bedys of fifty gawded with bedis of syluer and gilt. **1527** *Inv. Goods T. Cromwell* (Pub. Rec. Off.), ij payer of corall beds gauded with xxxviij gaudyes of sylver and gylte. **1552** *Bury Wills* (Camden) 144 My beades gauded gold.

2. To ornament, adorn, make showy.

1554 *Bury Wills* (Camden) 146 My best cassocke gawded wt velvet. **1559** BECON *Displ. Pop. Mass* Wks. 1563 III. 36 b, Thys your fooles cote, gayly gawded, signifieth youre pleasaunte fynenesse and womanly nicenesse.

Hence **ˈgauded** *ppl. a.*

1607 SHAKS. *Cor.* II. i. 233 Their nicely gawded Cheekes.

†**gaud**, *v.*[2] [? ad. OF. *gaudir* to rejoice, jest; or perh. f. GAUD *sb.*[2]] *intr.* To make merry; to sport, jest; to scoff (*at*).

1532 MORE *Confut. Tindale* Wks. 366/2 And yf [the battle] walke on your syde then [you] gawde and glory. **1563** *Homilies* II. *Cert. Places H. Script.* I. (1859) 373 More reasonable it were for vain man to learn and reverence the form of God's words, than to gaud at them to his damnation. **1566** PAINTER *Pal. Pleas.* I. 60 In carping, gauding, and iesting at young gentlemen, and specially olde men. **1570** LEVINS *Manip.* 43/32 To Gaude, scoffe, *scommari, nugari*. **1579–80** NORTH *Plutarch* (1676) 435 He was sporting and gauding with his Familiars.

Hence **ˈgauding** *vbl. sb.*

a **1553** UDALL *Royster D.* III. iv. (Arb.) 49 What gaudyng and foolyng is this afore my doore?

gaud, Sc. form of GAD *sb.*[1]

‖**gaudeamus** (gɔːdiːˈeɪməs). [The first word of the mod.L. students' song: *Gaudeamus igitur, juvenes dum sumus*, 'Then let us be merry while we are young'. (Similarly used in Fr. of 15th c.)] A college-students' merry-making.

1823 SCOTT *Fam. Lett.* (1894) II. 178 Our Bannatyne Club goes on *à merveille*, only that at our *gaudeamus* this year we drank our wine *more majorum*, and our new judge Lord Eldin had a bad fall on the staircase. **1894** *College Echoes* (St. Andrews Univ.) VI. 71 On Saturday evening the first Gaudeamus of the session was held in the Cross Keys Hotel. **1895** *Athenæum* 12 Oct. 487/2 A song sung at a public Gaudeamus [at Maynooth] in 1829.

†**gaude-flore**. *Obs.* A hymn beginning '*Gaude flore virginali*'.

1500–20 DUNBAR *Poems* lxxii. 7 Syne to his mother I did inclyne, Hir halsing with ane gaude-flore.

gaudery (ˈgɔːdərɪ). Forms: 6–7 **gauderie**, 7 **gaudry**, 6–7 **gawdry**, 7–8 **-ery**, 7– **gaudery**. [f. GAUD *sb.*[2] + -ERY.]

†**1.** Trickery. *Obs.*

a **1529** SKELTON *Agst. Garnesche* iv. 39 Garnyshe, ye gate [= you got] of Gorge with gawdry Crimsin velvet for your bawdry.

2. Gaudy or showy decoration, ostentatious show; finery, fine clothes; also, a fine or gaudy thing, a piece of finery.

1597–8 BP. HALL *Sat.* III. i. 63 But thou canst maske in garish gauderie. **1653** MANTON *Exp. James* ii. 2–4 We do not prize a horse for the gaudry of his saddle and trappings. **1663** *Unfort. Usurper* I. i, Vice.. trickt up with its alluring gauderies. **1713** ? DARRELL *Gentlm. Instructed* (ed. 5) 427 Set off with all the glittering gawdery of Silk and Silver. **1812** W. TENNANT *Anster F.* III. vii, Streams the red gaudery of flags in air. **1837** CARLYLE *Fr. Rev.* I. v. v, Tapestries enough, and gauderies; but of serviceable fighting-gear small stock! **1893** *Eng. Illustr. Mag.* X. 241/2 Women shameless in their gaudery.

†**gaudez**. *Obs. pl.* [a. F. *gaudez* (obs.), f. L. *gaudē* 'rejoice'. Cf. GAUDE-FLORE.] Prayers beginning with '*Gaude*'.

1653 URQUHART *Rabelais* II. xi. 77 The foresaid good woman, saying her gaudez and audinos.

ˈgaudful, *a. rare*⁻⁰. [f. GAUD *sb.*[2]] Joyful.

1855 in H. CLARKE *Dict.*; and in later Dicts.

†**ˈgaudibund**, *a. Obs. rare*⁻⁰. [ad. L. *gaudibund-us*, f. *gaudēre* to rejoice.] (See quot.)

1727 BAILEY vol. II, *Gaudibund*, full of Joy, very joyful.

†**gauˈdiloquent**, *a. Obs. rare*⁻⁰. [f. L. *gaudi-um* joy + *-loqu-us* speaking + -ENT.] So †**gauˈdiloquous** *a.* + [-OUS].

1656–81 BLOUNT *Glossogr.*, *Gaudiloquent*, he that speaks with joy. **1727** BAILEY vol. II, *Gaudiloquous*, speaking gladsom Things.

gaudily (ˈgɔːdɪlɪ), *adv.* [f. GAUDY *a.* + -LY[2].] In a gaudy manner; showily.

1611 COTGR., *Gorgiasement*, gorgeously, gaudily, gayly, gallantly. **1763** CHURCHILL *Gotham* III. (1764) 17 Nor, in one hand, fit emblem of thy trade, A Rod; in t'other, gaudily array'd A Hornbook, gilt and letter'd. *a* **1859** MACAULAY *Hist. Eng.* xxv. (1861) V. 297 It was soon discovered that these gaudily dressed horsemen were proclaiming James the Third. **1883** GILMOUR *Mongols* xxvi. 310 Dressed.. gaudily in yellow, blue, red, white, or green.

gaudiness (ˈgɔːdɪnɪs). [f. GAUDY *a.* + -NESS.] The quality of being gaudy.

1601 CHESTER *Love's Mart., K. Arthur* lxi, The ayre that struggles for to kisse The gaudinesse of faire King Arthurs blisse. *a* **1639** W. WHATELEY *Prototypes* I. xix. (1640) 240 When you have set up your selves with a deale of gaudinesse, such lace, such ruffes so in the fashion. **1762–71** H. WALPOLE *Vertue's Anecd. Paint.* (1786) III. 170 The gawdiness of the Romish religion. **1833** I. TAYLOR *Fanat.* iii. 67 The gaudiness of false sentiment. **1869** SPURGEON *Treas. Dav.* Ps. v. 4 Men may.. forget the wickedness of the battle in the gaudiness of the triumph.

†**ˈgaudious**, *a. Obs.* [f. med.L. *gaudiōs-us*, f. L. *gaudium* joy + -OUS.] Festive, joyful.

1570 LEVINS *Manip.* 226/2 Gaudiouse, *solennis*. *a* **1746** LEWIS in Gutch *Coll. Cur.* II. 176 Of which Mysteries [of the Rosary] the five first are called Gaudious; the second five Dolorous; and the third five Glorious.

†**ˈgaudish**, *a. Obs.* [f. GAUD *sb.*[2] + -ISH.]

a. ? Trivial, idle, scoffing (cf. GAUD *sb.*[2] 1). **b.** Gaudy, showy (*rare*⁻⁰; implied in the derivatives).

1538 BALE *God's Promises* Prol. in Dodsley *O.P.* (1780) I. 8 Ye may loke to have no tryfeling sporte In fantasyes fayned, nor such lyke gaudysh gere. **1563–87** FOXE *A. & M.* (1596) 212/1 [He] was woont to make manie rimes and gaudish prose to delight the eares of the multitude.

Hence **ˈgaudishly** *adv.*, **ˈgaudishness**.

1583 GOLDING *Calvin on Deut.* cxxvi. 773 If they vse any gaudishnes and make themselues to bee as gasing stocks. **1677** *Compl. Servant Maid* 114 It is more commendable to go decent and clean, than gaudishly fine.

ˈgaudless, *a. rare*⁻⁰. [f. GAUD *sb.*[2] + -LESS.]

1848 CRAIG, *Gaudless*, destitute of ornament. Hence in later Dicts.

gaudroun, obs. form of CAULDRON *sb.*

gaudsman, *Sc.* var. GADMAN *Obs.*

gaudy (ˈgɔːdɪ), *sb.* Also (6 **gaid-**, **galdye**), 6–7 **gaudye**, 6–8 **gawdy**. [ad. L. *gaudium* joy. In some senses the word may represent L. *gaudē* 'rejoice thou', as used in hymns or liturgies; and there may also be mixture of OF. *gaudie* n. of action f. *gaudir* to rejoice, make merry.]

†**1.** = GAUD *sb.*[1] *Obs.*

1434 *E.E. Wills* (1882) 102 A payre bedes of blak gaudys of siluer & gilt. **1483** in Arnolde *Chron.* (1811) 116 Item a pair of coral beedis the gawdies gilt wrythen. **1500** in Hearne *Collect.* 19 June 1706 (O.H.S.) I. 263 My Blake beds of jett with gaidyes of Gold. **1542** *Inv. R. Wardrobe* (1815) 62 Item ane pair of beidis of raisit wark with galdeis of aget. **1560** *Richmond Wills* (Surtees) 147, vj parr of beaddes with zigs and siluer gawdies.

†**2.** A taper (see quot. 1852). *Obs.*

1531 in Blomefield *Norfolk* (1739) I. 182, I gif half an Acr of Lond.. to find yerely evermore, v. Gawdyes Brenning before our Lady, in the Chancel of St. John Baptist. **1852** ROCK *Ch. of Fathers* III. I. 277 The tapers themselves, from being meant to commemorate the Virgin's five joys, were called 'gawdyes' from the Latin word 'gaude' which begins the hymn in memory of these five joys.

†**3.** A bright-coloured ornament; a toy, bauble, gewgaw; = GAUD *sb.*[2] 2. *Obs.*

1555 EDEN *Decades* 209 They make also little brasselets whiche they mengle with gaudies of golde.

†**4.** Rejoicing, joy; a festival, merry-making.

1535 JOYE *Apol. Tindale* (Arb.) 18 Hauyng no respecte.. to the gaudye and reioyse of our aduersaries. *Ibid.* 43. **1540** PALSGRAVE *Acolastus* I. iv. G iij b, That we maye make our tryumphe .i. kepe our gaudyes, or let vs sette the cocke on the hope, and make good chere. **1647** TRAPP *Comm. Matt.* ix. 10 When a sinner repents there are gaudies in heaven.

5. A grand feast or entertainment; *esp.* an annual dinner in commemoration of some event in the history of a college.

1651 RANDOLPH, etc. *Hey for Honesty* v. 40, I know Some that have spent whole Hecatombs of Beef To give the gods their gawdies. **1686** WILDING in *Collect.* (O.H.S.) I. 264 Towards a Gaudy..00 01 00. **1710** HEARNE *Collect.* (O.H.S.) III. 100 No Gaudy before as Dr. Crosthwait reported. [**1726** AMHERST *Terræ Fil.* xlix. 264 Sir William Paddy, knt. gave, by will.. twenty shillings for a feast (call'd in the university a *gaudium*) upon the anniversary day of his death.. This was given anno 1634.] *a* **1763** SHENSTONE *Charms Preced.* 32 What moves that scientific body, But the first cutting at a gawdy? **1803** *Gradus ad Cantab.* (1824) 122 Cut lectures.. give Gaudies and Spreads. **1823** LOCKHART *Reg. Dalton* III. i. (1842) 183 Such a scene as.. a College Gaudy was like to be. **1878** BESANT & RICE *Celia's Arb.* xv, We went home to a sort of Great Grand Day dinner, a Gaudy, a City Feast. **1882** T. MOZLEY *Remin.* I. lx. 380 One of the Oriel gaudies or festive anniversaries. *c* **1893** J. A.

SYMONDS in *Biogr.* (1895) I. 224 My father had recently sat next him at a Magdalen Gaudy.

†**b.** *pl.* 'Commons' for gaudy-days. *Obs.*

1618 in M. Burrows *Worthies All Souls* ix. (1874) 154 Whereas our Gaudyes on All Soules Day to the Side Tables in the Hall were but five dishes to every Messe. **1620** *Ibid.* viii. 139 This I doe not..to prevent any dues either of plate or gawdies usually to be paid. **1706** PHILLIPS (ed. Kersey), *Gaudies*, double Commons, such as are allowed on gaudy Days.

†**c.** Dainties, luxurious viands. *Obs.*

1622 MABBE tr. *Aleman's Guzman d'Alf.* II. 275 If at any time we had pease porrige (which was very seldome, that we had such Gau-dies [*sic*]).

6. *Comb.*, as †**gaudy-shop**, a shop for finery.

1620 MIDDLETON *Chaste Maid* I. ii, Embroderings, spanglings, and I know not what, As if she lay with all the gaudy Shops In Gressams Bursse about her.

ˈgaudy, *a.*[1] *Obs.* exc. *arch.* Also 4–5 **gaude**, 5 **gawdy**, 6 **gawdie**. [app. f. OF. *gaude* weld + -Y[1]; the form *gaude* may be the OFr. word adopted and used *attrib.*] Only in *Comb.* **gaudy-green**, green dyed with weld, yellowish green.

In the first quot. *gaudi of grene* may be a mistake for *gaudi grene*, or the word may be a sb. evolved from the combination.

13.. *Gaw. & Gr. Knt.* 167 Enbrauded abof, wyth bryddes & flyȝes, With gay gaudi of grene, þe golde ay in myddes. *c* **1386** CHAUCER *Knt.'s T.* 1221 In gaude grene hire statue clothed was. *c* **1420** LYDG. *Assemb. Gods* 320 Hyr gowne was of gawdy grene chamelet. *c* **1440** *Anc. Cookery* in *Househ. Ord.* (1790) 452 Colour hit gaude grene. *c* **1440** *Promp. Parv.* 189/1 Gawdy grene, *subviridis.* **1579** SPENSER *Sheph. Cal.* May 4 How falls it then, we no merrier beene, Ylike as others, girt in gawdie greene. **1590** GREENE *Never too Late* (1600) P 3 b, It was a valley gawdy greene. **1902** W. DE LA MARE *Songs of Childhood* 29 There's a ring gaudy-green in the dell.

gaudy (ˈgɔːdɪ), *a.*[2] Forms: 6 **gaudie**, **-ye**, 7–8 **gawdy**, 7 **-ie**, 6– **gaudy**. [Of somewhat uncertain formation. Sense 1 looks like an attributive use of GAUDY *sb.* 4; cf. quot. 1540 there. In senses 2 and 3 the word may have been apprehended as if f. GAUD *sb.*[2] + -Y[1].]

†**1.** Of fare: Luxurious. *Obs.* [Cf. OF. *gaudechere*, ? ad. Eng. 'good cheer'.]

1540 PALSGR. *Acolastus* IV. ii. S iij b, I haue good cause to set the cocke on the hope, and make gaudye chere. *a* **1550** *Hye Way to Spittel Ho.* 244 in Hazlitt *E.P.P.* IV. 35 Where they make reuell and gaudy chere. **1601** HOLLAND *Pliny* II. 554 The greatest exceeding..and gaudiest fare at a feast, was serued vp in three platters.

†**2.** Full of trickery. *Obs.* [Cf. GAUD *sb.*[2] 1.]

a **1529** SKELTON *Agst. Garnesche* ii. 36 Gup, Garnysche, gaudy fole. *Ibid.* iii. 120 Gawdy, gresy, Garnesche.

3. a. Brilliantly fine or gay, highly ornate, showy. Now chiefly in disparaging sense: Excessively or glaringly showy, tastelessly gay or fine.

1583 STUBBES *Anat. Abus.* II. (1882) 37 To the ende they may seeme gaudie to the eie, they must be stitched finelie. **1602** SHAKS. *Ham.* I. iii. 71 Costly thy habit as thy purse can buy; But not exprest in fancie: rich, not gawdie. **1655** FULLER *Ch. Hist.* IV. ii. §2 Scriveners use with gaudy flourishes to deck and garnish the initial characters of Copies. **1663** COWLEY *Verses & Ess., Hymn to Light* v, The Gawdy Heav'nly Bow. **1665** BOYLE *Occas. Refl.* IV. iii. (1845) 191 They..almost worship a Man for wearing a Gaudy suit of Cloaths. **1709** STEELE *Tatler* No. 151 ¶1 Gawdy Ribands and glaring Colours being now out of Use. **1720** GAY *Wks.* (1745) II. 181 There from the gawdy train select a dame. **1722** SEWEL *Hist. Quakers* (1795) I. III. 184 He wrote..against pride, gaudy apparel [etc.]. **1838** DICKENS *Nich. Nick.* vi, An intricate winding of gaudy colours. **1876** MISS BRADDON *J. Haggard's Dau.* II. vii. 154 The gaudy daffodils were flaunting everywhere.

b. said of immaterial things; *esp.* of diction, etc.; hence of a speaker or writer.

1647 CLARENDON *Hist. Reb.* VII. §235 A gaudy Letter of kindness and value, was sent to Colonel Massy. *a* **1674** *Ibid.* XI. §143 Those gaudy promises which the Cardinal had made. **1655** BAXTER *Quaker Catech.* 9 A late notable gawdy Orator. *a* **1701** SEDLEY *Poems* Wks. 1722 I. 58 In gaudy Dreams your Love and Beauty shine. **1726** BUTLER *Serm. Rolls* vi. 113 The florid and gaudy Prospects..which we are too apt to indulge. **1830** MACKINTOSH *Eth. Philos.* Wks. 1846 I. 45 The natural proneness of metaphysical speculations to degenerate into gaudy dreams. **1836** EMERSON *Nature, Prospects* Wks. (Bohn) II. 172 When the fact is seen under the light of an idea, the gaudy fable fades and shrivels. **1853** ROBERTSON *Serm.* Ser. III. xx. 262 When this gaudy world has ceased to charm.

c. *slang.* In negative sentences: Very good.

1884 H. SMART *From Post to Finish* II. ix. 130. I don't think they are likely to give him a very 'gaudy chance'. **1894** ASTLEY *Fifty Years Life* II. 96 They [the horses] were not a gaudy lot, and only fetched £3500.

4. *Comb.*, chiefly parasynthetic, as ***gaudy coloured***, ***-feathered***, †***hearted***, ***-minded***, ***-speckled*** adjs.

a **1680** BUTLER *Rem.* (1759) I. 140 As Indians use With *gawdy colour'd Plumes Their homely nether Parts 't adorn. **1824** 'H. L. HOWARD' *Joseph & Brethren* II. 123 The gaudy-colour'd story of his mind. **1921** W. DE LA MARE *Crossings* 67 Muffled up in a gaudy-coloured shawl. *a* **1668** DAVENANT *To the Queen* Poems (1673) 246 Your voice, which can allure, and charme the best Most *gawdy-feather'd Chaunter of the East. **1599** MIDDLETON & ROWLEY *Old Law* II. i. (1656) D 2 b, A cunning griefe, That's only fac'd with sables for a shew, But *gawdy hearted. **1742** YOUNG *Nt. Th.* VI. 238 Were they as vain, as *gaudy-minded man, As flatulent with fumes of self-applause. *a* **1631** DONNE *Elegy* xxi. 47 Shall I a *gawdie-speckled serpent kisse?

ˈgaudy, *v.* Also 6 **galdie**. [f. GAUDY *sb.* and *a.*[2]]

†**1.** *trans.* To furnish (a rosary) with 'gaudies'.

1482 *Paston Lett.* No. 861 III. 287 My peir bedys of calcidenys gaudied with silver and gilt. **1513** *Test. Ebor.* (Surtees) V. 40 On pair of corrall beydes gawdied wt silver. **1542** *Inv. R. Wardrobe* (1815) 62 Item ane pair of beidis of jaspe galdeit with gold.

2. To deck out, make smart or gaudy. *rare.*

1805 SOUTHEY *Madoc in W.* VII, Not half so gaudied, for their May-day mirth, All wreathed and ribanded, our youths and maids, As these stern Aztecas in war attire!

ˈgaudy-day. Also 6 **gaude-day** (9 **gaudé-**). [f. GAUDY *sb.* + DAY.] A day of rejoicing, a festival or gala day; *esp.* the day on which a college 'gaudy' is held (see GAUDY *sb.* 5).

1567 DRANT *Horace's Ep.* To Rdr., Their loue dayes, their gaude dayes. **1585** COGAN *Haven Health* cciii. 172 The full dyet..may be such, as is vsed at Oxforde vppon gaudie daies. **1624** MIDDLETON *Game at Chess* III. i. 42 Your foode shall be Black-beries, and vpon gawdy dayes A Pickled Spider. **1656** BLOUNT *Glossogr.*, *Gawdy*, or *Granddays*, in the Inns of Court there are four of these in the yeer, that is, one in every Term. **1710** HEARNE *Collect.* (O.H.S.) III. 100 St Thomas a Gaudy-Day in Queen's College. **1769** *De Foe's Tour Gt. Brit.* (ed. 7) I. 372, 13 Companies of incorporated Trades, who, on public Occasions, and on Gaudy-days, walk in the Mayor's Train. **1795–6** BURKE *Regic. Peace* iv. Wks. IX. 51 On this their gaudy day the new Regicide Directory sent for their diplomatick rabble. **1814** *Hist. Univ. Oxford* II. 261 This dress is worn..at dinners on gawdy days. **1830** T. WILSON *Pitman's Pay* III. (1843) 52 A gaudy-day myeks a' hands merry. **1864** SIR F. PALGRAVE *Norm. & Eng.* III. 161 It was a gaudy day for the burly London Citizens. **1884** *Edin. Rev.* Apr. 418 The annual gaudy day was especially a festivity of the Arts Faculty.

So **gaudy-night.**

1606 SHAKS. *Ant. & Cl.* III. xiii. 183 Come, Let's haue one other gawdy night: Call to me All my sad Captaines, fill our Bowles once more: Let's mocke the midnight Bell. **1935** D. L. SAYERS (*title*) Gaudy night. **1963** LOCKHART & WOODHOUSE *Rhodes* xxiii. 404 It happened to be the College's annual Gaudy night.

gaudy-green: see GAUDY *a.*[1]

gauffer, gauffre: see GOFFER.

‖**gauffrage** (gofraʒ). *Printing.* [ad. F. *gaufrage* embossing, f. *gaufrer* (see GOFFER *v.*).] = *blind printing* (BLIND *a.* 16).

1904 [see *blind printing*]. **1927** H. HUBBARD *Colour Block Print Making* 172 The Japanese call this 'gauffrage', but it is known amongst western artists as 'blind printing'. **1960** H. HAYWARD *Antique Coll.* 127/2 *Gauffrage*, blind-printing, producing an embossed effect without colour, and used in Japan from the late 18th cent. as a technique in making prints.

gaufre, var. GOFER[1].

gauge, gage (geɪdʒ), *sb.* Forms: 5–7 **gawge**, (6 *Sc.* **gadge**), 8–9 **guage**, 5– **gage**, **gauge**. [a. ONF. *gauge* (Central OF. and mod.F. *jauge*), of unknown origin; wanting in the other Rom. langs.

The OFr. word is found, along with the related vb. *gauger*, in the 13th c.; the earliest sense appears to be 'action or result of measuring', the sense 'instrument of measurement' being prob. derivative; the sb. is perh. f. the vb. Possibly there may be ultimate connexion with *jale* bowl, *galon* GALLON (so Littré), or with *jalon* stake to measure from (so Scheler). Horning's conjecture that the word represents Teut. **galgon-* (see GALLOWS *sb.*) in its assumed primary sense of 'rod' is not very satisfactory from the Teut. point of view; derivation from L. **æquālificāre* or *quālificāre* (Diez) is impossible.

The spelling *gauge* prevails in this country, except in sense 5. The more normal *gage* has been adopted in recent American Dicts. The form *guage* is a mere blunder.]

I. 1. a. A fixed or standard measure or scale of measurement, the measure to which a thing must conform; esp. a measure of the capacity or contents of a barrel, etc., the diameter of a bullet or the thickness of sheet iron.

[**1357** *Act 30 Edw. III*, Stat. I. c. 5 Les tonelx de vin duissent contenir certein nombre des galons solonc launciene gauge.] *c* **1450** *Mann. & Househ. Exp.* (Roxb.) 438 Eampylle of meatynge [of ashelers] after the gawge of xij. meten, in lengthe xviij. yerdes. **1491** *Act 7 Hen. VII*, c. 7 §1 Malmeseys..shalbe of full gauge conteynyng vjxx and vj galons at the lest in mesure. **1580** HOLLYBAND *Treas. Fr. Tong*, Iauge, as *poison de iauge*, an hogshead of gage. **1595** in *Munim. Irvine* (1891) II. 34 The gadge of Hering, quhitefische and Salmond the Hogheid was reduceit. **1638** PENKETHMAN *Artach.* D, From which weight is derived or drawne the Assise and Gawge of all manner of wet and dry measures. **1677** MARVELL *Let. to Mayor of Hull* Wks. I. 315 The gager shall always leave with the Brewer a note of his gage. **1793** SMEATON *Edystone L.* §239 *note*, The jumpers were kept to the same gauge by means of two brass rings..when the jumpers by wearing became too little, they were..made to their full size, by the hammer, according to the gauge ring referred to. **1858** GREENER *Gunnery* 137 A bullet of 50-gauge exceeding in range one of 25-gauge. **1871** YEATS *Techn. Hist. Comm.* 347 From the smallest mouse-tail file..to the square file..there is a multifarious diversity in shape, size, and gauge of cutting. **1892** *Workshop Receipts* Ser. v. 287 It is an advantage, with all sheets thicker than 20 gauge, to galvanise after corrugation.

b. *transf.* and *fig.* Capacity, extent; dimensions, proportions. Chiefly in phrase ***to take the gauge of***.

1655 FULLER *Ch. Hist.* VI. ii. 291 He needed to be a good Mathematician in the gages of mens bellies..proportioning it to their severall ages, labour..appetites, &c. **1780** BURKE *Sp. Bristol* 25 He [Howard] has visited all Europe..to take the gage and dimensions of misery, depression, and contempt. **1835** LYTTON *Rienzi* I. iv, Rienzi sat at the feast ..taking gauge and measurement of the intellect, policy, temperament, of every guest. **1860** HOLLAND *Miss Gilbert* xviii. (1880) 219 The old man looked up and around, apparently taking the gauge of the structure. **1863** KINGLAKE *Crimea* (1876) I. xiv. 219 His intellect..was much above the low gauge which people used to assign to it. **1876** GEO. ELIOT *Dan. Der.* I. viii. 157 The broadening of gauge in crinolines seemed to demand an agitation.

c. *Physics.* [tr. G. *maßstab* (H. Weyl 1918, in *Sitzungsber. d. Preuss. Akad. d. Wissensch.* 30 May 475).] A concept introduced by Weyl as a measure of the vector field that in his cosmology related length and position, represented mathematically by a potential funcion; hence, any function introduced as an additional term into the equations of the potentials of a field such that the derived equations of observable physical quantities are unaltered by the introduction. Freq. ***attrib.***

1920 A. S. EDDINGTON *Space, Time & Gravit.* xi. 169 The only possible course is to lay down (1) a mesh-system filling all the space and time considered, (2) a definite unit of interval, or gauge, *at every point of space and time. Ibid.* 176 The radius of curvature of the world provides a natural and absolute gauge at every point; and it will presumably introduce the greatest possible symmetry into our laws if the observer chooses this, or some definite fraction of it, as his gauge. **1923** —— *Math. Theory of Relativity* vii. 202 Change of gauge is a generalisation of change of unit in physical equations, the unit being no longer a constant but an arbitrary function of position. **1940** W. PAULI in *Physical Rev.* 15 Oct. 718/1 By 'gauge-transformation of the first kind' we understand a transformation $U \rightarrow Ue^{i\alpha}$ $U^* \rightarrow U^*e^{-i\alpha}$ with an arbitrary space and time function α. By 'gauge-transformation of the second kind' we understand a transformation of the type $\phi_k \rightarrow \phi_k - i(\partial\alpha/\partial x_k)/\epsilon$ as for those of the electromagnetic potentials. **1959** J. AHARONI *Special Theory of Relativity* I. 29 We draw an arbitrary Cartesian system x, t and prescribe along the axes two gauges of geometrical length g_1 and g_2, one to represent a unit of distance, the other a unit of time. **1961** *Encycl. Dict. Physics* III. 409/2 The gauge is chosen for convenience in a particular problem to bring about symmetry (gauge invariance) or a convenient form of equations involving the potentials. **1965** R. ADLER et al. *Introd. Gen. Relativity* iv. 106 The four-vector function $\phi\mu$ has no *direct* physical meaning; only its four-dimensional curl has physical meaning. It is thus clear that we may make a so-called gauge transformation on ϕ_μ; that is, we can add an arbitrary four-dimensional divergence..to ϕ_μ without altering $F_{\mu\nu}$ and therefore without altering the physical situation. *Ibid.* xiii. 405 Quantities and relations that do not change under gauge transformation are called gauge invariants.

†**2.** A limit of distance or extent. Also *fig. Obs.*

1600 HOLLAND *Livy* III. lxvii. (1609) 134 Neither we have any gage or stay of rule and command, nor [etc.]. **1601** —— *Pliny* I. 98 How high it [Nilus] riseth, is known by markes and measures taken of certain pits. The ordinary height of it is sixteen cubits. Vnder that gage the waters ouerflow not at all. **1606** —— *Sueton.* 103 That Corinthian vessels grew to an exceeding high rate..he grievously complained, and gave his opinion, that there should be a gage set and a mediocritie kept in houshold furniture.

3. *spec.* The distance between the rails of a railway, tramway, etc.; more fully ***gauge of way***; also, the distance between the opposite wheels of a carriage. ***mixed gauge***: a broad and narrow gauge laid down together. See also BROAD GAUGE, NARROW GAUGE.

1841 BREES *Gloss. Civ. Engin.*, *Gauge of Way* (as applied to railways), the width in the clear between the top flanches or rounded rims of the rails. **1846** MCCULLOCH *Acc. Brit. Empire* (1854) II. 57 The distance between the opposite rails, or width of gauge, which, of course, determines the width of the carriage. **1860** O. W. HOLMES *Prof. Breakf.-t.* v. (Paterson) 107 The engine-driver of our broad-gauge mail train. **1862** SMILES *Engineers* III. 165 When forming the road, the proper gauge had also to be determined. What width was this to be? The gauge of the first tramroad laid down had virtually settled the point. The gauge of wheels of the common vehicles of the country..which were first used on the tramroads—was about 4 feet 8½ inches. And so the first tramroads were laid down of this gauge. **1876** F. S. WILLIAMS *Midl. Railw.* 555 Formerly there was the mixed gauge for both broad and narrow gauge trains; but the outer rail has been removed. **1883** *Harper's Mag.* Jan. 198/2 The track is of the usual gauge.

4. *techn.* **a.** The length of projection of a slate or tile beyond that which overlaps it. Now also called the ***margin***. **b.** (See quot. 1847.)

1703 T. N. *City & C. Purchaser* 274 At 6 Inches Gage, about 800..Tyles will cover a Sprare; at 7 Inch Gage, 690. **1842** BRANDE *Dict. Sci.* etc., *Gage*, or *Gauge*, the length of a slate or tile below the lap. **1847–78** HALLIWELL, *Gage*, a measure of slate, one yard square, about a ton in weight. **1851** LAXTON *Builder's Price Bk.* 38 Pantiling per square. Laid dry, to a 10-inch gauge.

5. *Naut.* (Usually spelt *gage*.) **a.** The position of one vessel with reference to another and the wind. In phrase ***to have*** or ***keep the weather gage of***: to be to windward of; also *fig.* to get the better of. Subsequently also in ***lee gage*** (see quots. 1644, 1794).

1591 RALEIGH *Last Fight Rev.* (Arb.) 26 The rest..entred as far as the place permitted and their own necessities, to keep the weather gage of the enemy. **1644** MANWAYRING *Sea-mans Dict.* s.v., When one ship is to-weather of another, she hath, as they terme it, the weather-gage, but they never use to say, the Lee-gage. **1692** *Capt. Smith's Seaman's*

Gram. I. xvi. 78, *Weather Gage*, is when one Ship has the Wind (or is to Weather) of another. **1790** BEATSON *Nav. & Mil. Mem.* II. 57 They tacked, when at about two leagues distance, in order to gain the weather gage. **1794** *Rigging & Seamanship* II. 253 *Lee-gage, a ship or fleet to leeward of another is said to have the lee-gage. **1795** NELSON in Nicolas *Disp.* (1845) II. 14 Taken aback with a fine breeze at N.W. which gave us the weather-gage, whilst the Enemy's Fleet kept the southerly gage. **1818** JAS. MILL *Brit. India* II. v. v. 523 After a variety of movements in which Suffrein still kept the weather gage, the two fleets came to action. **1835–40** *J. M. Wilson's Tales Bord.* (1859) XX. 270 He has got the weather gage of them, and for us to run down to them would be to run ourselves into the lion's mouth. **1867** SMYTH *Sailor's Word-bk.*, *Lee-guage.*

b. The depth to which a vessel sinks in the water with a full cargo.

1644 MANWAYRING *Sea-mans Dict.* s.v., So many foote as she drawes, is called the ships gage. **1800** [see *Gauge-mark* in 15]. **1867** in SMYTH *Sailor's Word-bk.*

6. *Plastering.* (See quots.)

1842 BRANDE *Dict. Sci.* etc., *Gage*, or *Gauge*,.. the greater or less quantity of plaster of Paris used with the common plaster to accelerate its setting. **1849** WEALE *Dict. Archit.*, *Gauge*, a mixture of fine stuff and plaster, or putty and plaster, or coarse stuff and plaster used in finishing the best ceilings and for mouldings and sometimes for setting walls.

II. An instrument for measuring or testing.

†**7. a.** A gauging-rod. **b.** (See quot. *c* 1780.) *Obs.*

a. 1530 PALSGR. 224/2 Gauge to measure wyne with, *gauge*. **1611** COTGR., *Iauge*, a Gage; the instrument wherewith caske is measured. **1706** PHILLIPS (ed. Kersey), *Gage*, a Rod to measure Casks with.

b. 1635 in Nicholls *Forest Dean* (1858) 276 Implem^nts^..1 tuiron plate, 1 plackett, 1 gadge. *c* **1780** WYRRALL *Ibid.* 279 *Gage*, two rods of iron jointed in the middle with a ring for the filler to drop the shortest end into the furnace at the top, to know when it is worked down low enough to be charged again.

8. A graduated instrument or vessel for gauging or measuring the force or quantity of a fluctuating object, as a rainfall, tide, stream, wind, etc. Also ***rain-***, ***wind-gauge***, etc.: see RAIN, etc.

1688 BURNET *Lett. Pres. State Italy* 145 There is a Gage, by which they Weigh the Water, and so they know how the Evaporation advances; it is of Silver, and is so made, that according to the weight of the Water, it sinks in to such a depth; & so by the degrees markt upon it, they know how heavy the Water is. **1763** W. LEWIS *Commerc. Philos. Techn.* 286 A smiths bellows raised a mercurial gage about an inch so that it would have raised a water-gage about fourteen inches. **1830** SIR J. ROSS *Narr. 2nd Voy.* xxxv. (1835) 490 Nor is it an easy matter to measure the depth to which a fall of snow is equivalent; such is.. the difficulty of securing any thing like an average within the compass of any gauge that has yet been devised. **1851–9** HERSCHEL in *Man. Sci. Enq.* 135 One inch in depth of rain in the gauge will be measured by 100 inches of the graduated vessel. **1871** TYNDALL *Fragm. Sc.* (1879) I. iv. 115 They were followed by about three inches (measured by the mercurial gauge) of air. **1880** HAUGHTON *Phys. Geog.* ii. 31 The sea-waves were recorded on the self-registering tide gauges.

fig. **1856** EMERSON *Eng. Traits, Lit.* Wks. (Bohn) II. 110 [Bacon].. basked in an element of contemplation out of all modern English atmospheric gauges.

9. A contrivance attached to a vessel, esp. a boiler, to show the height or condition of its contents; more fully ***gauge-cock***, ***-glass***. Of an air-pump: An instrument which points out the degree of exhaustion in the receiver; usually with word prefixed specifying the form of gauge, as ***barometer***, ***siphon gauge***: see those words.

1794 G. ADAMS *Nat. Exp. Philos.* I. xi. 47 A cyphon-gage which is occasionally substituted for the barometer-gage. **1824** R. STUART *Hist. Steam Engine* 204 This temperature.. was ascertained by the common means of a gauge placed on the boiler. **1825** J. NICHOLSON *Operat. Mechanic* 376 The pipe G is a sort of gauge, by means of which, after the pulp rises to a proper height in the vessel L, the remainder of the water is carried off into the cistern C. **1839** R. S. ROBINSON *Naut. Steam Eng.* 125 Each boiler having its feed pipe, gauges, and blow-off pipes as before. **1876** ROUTLEDGE *Discov.* 12 The gauge is screwed into some part of the boiler, where it can always be seen by the person in charge.

10. An instrument for ascertaining and verifying dimensions, esp. for testing and sorting into trade sizes tools, sheet iron, wire, etc.; an instrument by which tools, parts of machinery, etc., are regulated, in process of manufacture, to standard dimensions.

1677 MOXON *Mech. Exerc.* I. 32 This plate, must be a gage to file your Worm and Groove to equal breadth by. **1712** ARBUTHNOT *John Bull* III. i, Timothy.. proposed to his mistress, that she should entertain no servant that was above four feet seven inches high; and for that purpose he prepared a gauge, by which they were to be measured. **1750** BLANCKLEY *Nav. Expos.* s.v., Gages are used by the Smiths for gageing Bolts, so as to make them of a true and right size. **1812–16** J. SMITH *Panorama Sc. & Art* I. 29 It is much easier to file correctly with the assistance of a guage than a pair of callipers. **1832** G. R. PORTER *Porcelain & Gl.* 46 Certain pegs are fixed as a gauge without the circumference of the revolving board, but placed in such a manner, that whenever the plastic clay is brought to coincide at the requisite points with the gauge the thrower knows that the article has attained the proper dimensions. **1841** BREES *Gloss. Civ. Engin.* s.v., It is very necessary, in the practical working of railways, to keep standard iron gauges, from which all those employed on the line should be made. **1863** TYNDALL *Heat* iv. 86 A cold bar which fits between the two sides of a gauge will not fit when heated.

11. An adjustable tool used by carpenters and joiners for marking lines parallel to the edge of a board. ***mortice gauge***: one for marking parallel lines for mortice-cutting.

1678 MOXON *Mech. Exerc.* I. 90 Of the Gage.. Its Office is to Gage a Line parallel to any straight side. **1751** CHAMBERS *Cycl.*, *Gage*, in joinery.. is made of an oval piece of wood, fitted upon a square stick, to slide up and down stifly thereon [etc.]. **1842–59** GWILT *Archit.* (ed. 4) §2120 The gauge is an instrument used for drawing or making a line on a piece of stuff to a width parallel to the edge.

12. a. *Printing.* A strip of anything used for measuring and regulating the length of a page or the width of a margin. **b.** *Type-founding.* A piece of hard wood or metal, variously notched, used to adjust the dimensions, slopes, etc. of the various sorts of letters.

1683 MOXON *Mech. Exerc.* II. 85 The Face-Gage is a Square Notch cut with a File into the edge of a thin Plate of Steel. Iron, or Brass.. There be three of these Gages made, for the Letters to be cut on one Body. **1841** SAVAGE *Dict. Print.* s.v., A Gauge, to regulate the margin, is used both by compositors and pressmen.. The pressmen require a gauge ..in order to keep the head lines of the pages of each sheet precisely at the same distance from the edge of the paper. **1880** *Print. Trades Jrnl.* No. 30. 13 There is a guage both at back and side to ensure absolute uniformity in folding. **1891** JACOBI *Printing* v. 69 The length of a page having been determined, a gauge should be made to the size.

13. A contrivance to limit or regulate the penetration of a cutting tool.

(? Always used in comb. with the name of the tool with which it is used or of the process in which it is employed, as ***auger-gauge***, ***boring-gauge***, except where the name may be supplied from the context.)

14. *fig.* A means of estimating or determining, a test.

1691 LOCKE *Consid. Lower. Interest* Wks. 1714 II. 31 If Money were.. to be had from the Owner himself,.. it might then probably be had at the Market Rate, and that Rate of Interest would be a constant gauge of your Trade and Wealth. **1728** YOUNG *Love Fame* iii. Wks. (1757) 102 Another judges by a surer gage, An author's principles, or parentage. **1842** EMERSON *Lect., Transcendent.* Wks. (Bohn) II. 292 Besides farmers, sailors, and weavers, there must be a few persons of purer fire kept specially as gauges and meters. **1848** H. ROGERS *Ess.* I. vi. 289 A standard or gauge of the highest and sublimest pitch to which the unaided intellect of man can aspire. **1868** M. PATTISON *Academ. Org.* iv. 71 The impracticability of any equitable gauge of property, either by testimonial or by enquiry, has been felt. **1884** *Century Mag.* July 430 The gauge of a pensioner's disability is always his unfitness to do manual work.

III. 15. *attrib.* and *Comb.*, as (sense 5 b) ***gauge-mark***; (sense 1) ***gauge-ring***; **gauge-book**, ? a book on star-gauging; **gauge box, brick** (see quots.); **gauge-cock** (see quot. 1849); **gauge-concussion**, 'the lateral rocking of railway carriages against the rails' (Ogilvie); **gauge-door** (see quot.); **gauge-field** *Astr.*, a restricted area of the sky photographed for the purpose of gauging the number and density of the stars in that region; **gauge-frame** (*a*) the frame of a gauge-weir; (*b*) a frame used to gauge the loading of railway trucks, so as to limit it to the size capable of passing through tunnels, etc.; **gauge function** *Math.* (see quot. 1965); **gauge-glass**, a strong glass tube attached to a boiler to indicate the height or agitation of the water in it; **gauge-knife**, a knife with some contrivance for regulating the amount cut off; **gauge-ladder, -lamp** (see quots.); **gauge-lathe**, a lathe for turning work to pattern or size, the depth of cut being regulated by a gauge or stop; **gauge-paddle**, a paddle or shutter used in a gauge-weir; †**gauge penny**, a gauger's fee or perquisite; **gauge-pile, -pin** (see quots.); †**gauge pipe** (cf. *gauge-cock*); **gauge-plate** (see quot.); **gauge-point**, a point marked on a gauging rod, slide rule, etc., to indicate the diameter of a cylinder one inch high containing a unit of a given liquid measure; also, the length marked by this point; **gauge-rod, -saw, -stuff** (see quots.); **gauge-weir**, a weir fitted with movable paddles or shutters (as distinguished from a solid weir); **gauge-wheel** (see quot.); **gauge-work** = *gauged work* (see GAUGED *ppl. a.* 2).

1872 PROCTOR *Ess. Astron.* iii. 35 Here.. are a few of his [Sir John Herschel's] notes respecting the lesser Magellanic Cloud: they are taken from the *Guagebooks. **1874** KNIGHT *Dict. Mech.*, **Gage-box for Shingles*, a box of a certain size in which shingles are laid to form bunches of a certain number. **1880** JEFFERIES *Gt. Estate* viii. 152 She knew when the oven was hot enough by the *gauge-brick: this particular brick as the heat increased became spotted with white, and when it had turned quite white the oven was ready. **1824** R. STUART *Hist. Steam Engine* 88 A cock to supply air to the receiver.. is also employed as a *gauge-cock. **1838** R. STEPHENSON *Descr. Steam Engine* 17 Two gauge cocks.. are fixed in the side of the fire box. **1849** WEALE *Dict. Archit.*, *Gauge-cocks*, two or three small cocks fixed in front of the boiler of a steam engine, for the purpose of ascertaining the height of the water. **1883** GRESLEY *Gloss. Coal Mining*, **Gauge-door*, a wooden door fixed in a mine in an airway for regulating the supply of ventilation necessary for a certain district, or number of men, &c. **1891** *Smithsonian Inst. Rep.* 107 A photographic *gauge-field on a small scale. **1791** R. MYLNE *Rep. Thames & Isis* 55 If weirs were raised with *gauge-frames, the Water could be penned over all the shoals. **1937** J. VON NEUMANN *Coll. Wks.* (1962) IV. 208 A familiar symmetric *gauge function is

$$\phi_p(u_1, .. u_n = \left(\sum_{i=1}^{n} |u_i|^p\right)^{1/p}$$

for $1 \leqslant p < +\infty$. **1965** *Pacific Jrnl. Math.* XV. 242 A function ϕ on a complex vector space is called a gauge function if $\phi(u) > 0$ when $u \neq 0$, $\phi(au) = |a|\phi(u)$ for complex a, $\phi(u + v) \leqslant \phi(u) + \phi(v)$. **1849** WEALE *Dict. Archit.*, **Gauge-glass*, in locomotive engines, a strong glass tube, connected with the boiler by two cocks attached to the gauge-cock pedestal. **1888** *Daily News* 29 Dec. 6/3 A lady.. was busily engaged with a *gauge knife slicing up the puddings into ha'penny pen'orths. **1874** KNIGHT *Dict. Mech.*, **Gage-ladder*, a square timber frame for raising the ends of wheeling planks in excavating. A horsing-block. **1849** WEALE *Dict. Archit.*, **Gauge-lamp*, in locomotive engines, a small lamp placed beside the gauge-glass at night. **1800** *Hull Pilot. Act* 22 Two *guage marks to be made and fixed on the stem and stern. **1795** J. PHILLIPS *Hist. Ireland Navig.* Add. 66 Not to pass any lock unless the water flows over the waste wire or *gauge paddle. **1444** *Act 23 Hen. VI*, c. 15 Le Roi ad ordeigne.. que le denier que est appelle le *gauge peny ne soit paie a le Gaugeor ne a ascun autre en son noune, tanque il ou son deputee eit gauge lez vinez. **1874** KNIGHT *Dict. Mech.*, **Gage-pile* (Pile-driving), a preliminary pile to mark the desired course. **1891** JACOBI *Printing* 285 **Gauge pins*, small steel pins with teeth, for securing the lay on small platen machines. **1702** SAVERY *Miner's Friend* 25 The design of a Servant to do Mischief.. is easily discovered by those *Guage Pipes. **1888** *Lockwood's Dict. Mech. Engin.*, **Gauge-plate*, an adjustable plate fixed to shearing, cropping, and cutting-off machines, for insuring the uniform length of short pieces.. to be cut off. **1721** BAILEY, **Gauge Point* of Solid Measure, is the Diameter of a Circle whose Area is equal to the solid Content of the same Measure. **1807** HUTTON *Course Math.* II. 82 On it are marked WG at 17.15, and AG at 18.95, the wine and ale gage points. **1842** BRANDE *Dict. Sci.* etc., *Gauge-point*, is a term used in Gauging to denote the diameter of a cylinder whose altitude is one inch, and its content equal to that of a unit of a given measure. **1793** *Gauge ring [see sense 1 above]. **1888** *Lockwood's Dict. Mech. Engin.*, **Gauge-rod*, a rod of iron from ¼ in. to ½ in. in diameter, and used for measuring the internal diameters of portions of work in cases where great accuracy is essential. **1874** KNIGHT *Dict. Mech.*, **Gage-saw*, a saw having an adjustable frame or clamp, which determines the depth of kerf. **1823** P. NICHOLSON *Pract. Build.* 372 Mortar, called *gauge-stuff, consists of about three-fifths of fine-stuff and one of Plaster of Paris. **1847** A. SMEATON *Build. Man.* 120 Gauge Stuff is chiefly used for mouldings and cornices which are run or formed with a wooden mould. **1791** R. MYLNE *Rep. Thames & Isis* 53 The Weir near the Lock should be rebuilt with a *gauge Weir. **1874** KNIGHT *Dict. Mech.*, **Gage-wheel*, one attached to the forward end of a plow-beam, to gage the depth of furrow. **1906** *Daily Chron.* 23 Aug. 2/5 *Gage-work window headings. **1920** *Conquest* Apr. 269/2 These slips of steel.. are much used in gauge work for building up bars of any desired thickness.

gauge, gage (geɪdʒ), *v.*[1] [a. ONF. *gauger* (Central F. *jauger*), related to *gauge*: see prec.]

†**1.** *trans.* To measure or measure off (a length or quantity). *Obs. rare.*

c **1420** *Pallad. on Husb.* I. 208 Too feet deep is good for corn tilage, And doubil that for treen, in depnes gage. *Ibid.* XI. 79 Or euery tre a stryke of askes gage.

2. To ascertain by exact measurement the dimensions, proportions, or amount of; applied *spec.* to the measurement of objects of standard size (e.g. wire, bolts); also to the measurement of fluctuating quantities such as rainfall and intensity of wind. In non-technical use, the commonest application is to the measurement of the depth of a liquid content.

c **1440** *Promp. Parv.* 189/1 Gawgyn depnesse, *dimentior.* **1523** LD. BERNERS *Froiss.* I. cclxix. 399 He gauged ye depnesse of the dyche with a speare. *a* **1547** SURREY *Æneid* II. 52 Capys.. Will'd.. to.. bore and gage the hollow caues uncouth. **1579–80** NORTH *Plutarch* (1676) 331 And when they gaged the foord, they found it impossible to wade through. **1618** E. ELTON *Compl. Sanct. Sinner* (1622) 156 Continually sounding and gaging the depth of it. **1725** BRADLEY *Fam. Dict.*, *Water-gage*, an Instrument to Gage or Measure the Profundity or Quantity of any Water. **1750** [see GAUGE *sb.* 10]. **1781** COWPER *Charity* 139 Who drive a loathsome traffic, gauge and span, And buy the muscles and the bones of man. **1828** CARLYLE *Misc.* (1857) I. 196 We are yet to learn by what arts or instruments the mind could be so measured and gauged. **1833** J. HOLLAND *Manuf. Metal* III. 347 Wire is gauged, or the diameter of each sort ascertained.. by inserting it into a nick filed in the margin of a steel plate containing a gradation of these nicks. **1852** MISS FOX *Jrnls.* 23 Aug., In six weeks.. they mean to begin gauging the heavens. **1853** PHILLIPS *Rivers Yorks.* iii. 44, I have gauged.. the river which washes the walls of York, and obtained.. the quantity of water in cubic feet per day. **1875** PROCTOR in *Encycl. Brit.* II. 821/2 Gauging the sidereal system on this principle, Sir W. Herschel deduced the inference that it is shaped like a cloven flat disc.

†**b.** ***to gauge a ship*** (see quot.). *Obs.*

1644 MANWAYRING *Sea-mans Dict.* s.v., When we would know how much water a ship drawes when she is a-floate we stick a naile into a pike or pole, and so put it downe by the Rudder, till this naile catch hold under the Rudder, and this we call gageing a ship.

3. To ascertain the capacity or content of (a cask or similar vessel) by combined measurement and calculation (usually performed by the instrument called a *gauging-rod*).

[**1353** *Act 27 Edw. III*, Stat. I. c. 8 Que tous vins.. soient bient & loialment gaugez par le Gaugeour le Roi ou son depute.] **1483** *Act 1 Rich. III*, c. 13 All the Vessels of Wine ..shall.. be well and truly gauged by the King's Gauger. **1531–2** *Act 23 Hen. VIII*, c. 7 Euery gaugeour within this realme shall truely and effectually..gauge all the said.. barrels. **1591** *Child Marriages* (E.E.T.S.) 155 Whiche wines Ralphe Allen and Richard Broster, Sheriffes..haue seased vpon as forfeited, because they were sold without, and before they were gauged. **1644** MANWAYRING *Sea-mans Dict.* s.v., We are to Gage our Cask, that we may see how great it is, or how much is leaked out; which we doe by putting downe a stick at the Boong, and that, by the wetnesse, will shew how much liquour is in it. **1712** ARBUTHNOT *John Bull* III. vii, He would slip into the cellar, and gauge the casks. **1850** CARLYLE *Latter-d. Pamph.* iii. (1872) 101 To break his heart among poor mean mortals, gauging beer! **1855** MACAULAY *Hist. Eng.* xix. IV. 483 They would collect the customs, and gauge the beer barrels.

absol. **1770** GOLDSM. *Des. Vill.* 210 And even the story ran that he could gauge.

b. *humorously.*

1589 NASHE *Ded. to Greene's Menaphon* (Arb.) 15 It is for a Poet, to examine the pottle pottes, and gage the bottome of whole gallons. **1600** ROWLANDS *Lett. Humours Blood* vi. 76 Where boone companions gage the pots apace.

4. *fig.*; esp. to 'take the measure' of (a person, his character, etc.).

1583 GOLDING *Calvin on Deut.* clxxxiv. 1143 What are the Judgmentes of God? Euen a deepe gulfe vnpossible to be gaged. **1596** SHAKS. *Merch. V.* II. ii. 208, I barre to night, you shall not gage me By what we doe to night. **1612** T. TAYLOR *Comm. Titus* i. 2 By these notes gage thy heart. **1716** POPE *Ess. Homer's Battles in Iliad* II. 326 That artful Manner of taking Measure or (as one may say) Gaging his Heroes by each other. **1807** CRABBE *Par. Reg.* III. 480 He who, by contract, all your paupers took, And gauges stomachs with an anxious look. **1870** E. PEACOCK *Ralf Skirl.* II. 61 She, on the contrary, was never able to gauge him. **1880** KINGLAKE *Crimea* VI. xi. 414 Can they gauge or record the alleviation of misery effected by care. **1888** BRYCE *Amer. Commw.* III. lxxxvi. 145 How is he to gauge the voting strength its advocates can put forth?

5. To render conformable to a given standard of measurement or dimensions; also *to gauge up*. Hence *fig.* to set bounds to, to limit.

1600 HOLLAND *Livy* XXXIII. xxiii. (1609) 489, I will myselfe limit and gage [L. *semodum inpositurum*] those things, which fortune, occasion of the times, and necessitie have made excessive and beyond all measure powerfull. **1601** —— *Pliny* I. 129 The voiage thither from the foresaid country was gaged within a lesse time. **1651–3** J. BARKER *Art of Angling* 8 Gage your line, bait your hook. **1678** MOXON *Mech. Exerc.* I. 105 By these Screws, and the Rabbet and Groove, your work will be evenly gaged all the way..under the edge of the Iron Q. **1713** DERHAM *Phys. Theol.* VII. i. (1727) 335 The Vanes as nicely gaug'd on each Side as made; broad on one Side, and narrower on the other. **1788** *Trans. Soc. Arts* VI. 200 Two steel chaps to guage the Cutter. **1891** JACOBI *Printing* vi. 90 When formes are sent to press or machine great care should be exercised in straight-edging after gauging-up the margins.

b. *spec.* To cut or rub (bricks or stones) accurately to a uniform size.

1750 LANGLEY *Lond. Prices* 130 in *Dict. Archit.* (1848–52) s.v., The workman must gauge and rub down the red-stock bricks, so that every five courses of them shall come level with every four courses of place-bricks. **1842–59** GWILT *Archit.* (ed. 4) §1917 The stones are guaged and dressed by the hammer. **1879** *Cassell's Techn. Educ.* I. 225/2 In bricks, they must either be 'gauged', that is, rubbed or cut to the shape required, or the difference must be made up by mortar.

6. To mark off or set out (a measurement or measured distance).

1678 MOXON *Mech. Exerc.* I. 79 Gage another line opposite to the first gaged line. **1725** W. HALFPENNY *Sound Building* 33 The Arch HD is drawn by gauging from the Arch GC. **1873** J. RICHARDS *Wood-working Factories* 25 A strong line may be stretched about 5 feet from the floor..to gauge the plumb-lines from. **1879** *Cassell's Techn. Educ.* IV. 206/1 The length of the spokes is then guaged.

7. *Plastering.* To mix (plaster) in the right proportions for drying rapidly or otherwise.

1686 PLOT *Staffordsh.* 173 When they seel or parge with it [alabaster], they wet it by degrees, which they call gageing. **1823** P. NICHOLSON *Pract. Build.* 372 When great expedition is required, the plasterers gauge all their mortar with Plaster of Paris. **1897** *Laxton's Builders' Price Bk.* (ed. 18) 255 When used as concrete it [Portland cement] has been gauged as poor as 10–1—*i.e.* 1 part of cement to 10 of sand and shingle or ballast.

8. *Dressmaking.* To draw up in a series of parallel gatherings. (See GAUGING *vbl. sb.*)

1881 MISS BRADDON *Asph.* xix. 210 Dresses—gaged, and puffed and pleated. **1883** *Myra's Jrnl.* Aug., The sleeves.. consist of a lace puff, gauged into the shoulder. **1896** *Daily News* 17 Oct. 6/5 The underbodice is in drawn muslin, gauged at the neck in several rows.

†**gauge**, *v.*² *Obs. rare.*$^{-1}$ [? Cf. OF. *jaugier* to break in (a door).] *trans.* ? To burst through.

1583 T. STOCKER tr. *Civ. Wars Low C.* III. 126a, They feared that the fielde bankes and ditches were not as yet gawged and cut [orig. F. *ne furent encore percé*], by reason they saw not the water come downe. *Ibid.*, The messengers ..had seene with their owne eyes the gawging and cutting downe of the field bankes or ditches.

gaugeable (ˈgeɪdʒəb(ə)l), *a.* [f. GAUGE *v.*¹ + -ABLE.] That may be gauged; liable to be gauged for excise duty.

1768–74 TUCKER *Lt. Nat.* (1852) 648 Does our God, as was fabled of the heathen Jupiter, distribute His mercies out of a gaugeable tun? **1809** *Chron.* in *Ann. Reg.* 329/1 The right of gauging all gaugeable matters within the city. **1824** *Act 5 Geo. IV*, c. 74 §25 Vessels of wine, oil, honey, and other gaugeable liquors.

gauged, gaged (geɪdʒd), *ppl. a.* [f. GAUGE *v.*¹ + -ED¹.]

1. Marked or measured with a gauge.

1678 MOXON *Mech. Exerc.* I. 79 Work your stuff down to those two Gaged Lines.

2. *Bricklaying.* Of bricks: Cut or rubbed accurately to a uniform size. *gauged arch*, an arch composed of gauged bricks. *gauged work*, work in which gauged bricks are used.

1823 P. NICHOLSON *Pract. Build.* 345 The fine red cutting bricks are used for ruled and gauged work. **1836** *Penny Cycl.* V. 410/1 The bricks for rubbed or gauged arches are cut with radiating lines. **1842–59** GWILT *Archit.* (ed. 4) §1897 It was formerly..the practice to face the front walls of houses with guaged or rubbed bricks. **1848–52** *Dict. Archit.* s.v., Gauged and rubbed brickwork. **1851** LAXTON *Builder's Price Bk.* 37 Arches..Mouldings in gauged and cut malms, set in putty.

3. *Plastering.* Mixed in the proper proportions for quick drying. *gauged stuff* = gauge-stuff (see GAUGE *sb.* 15).

1848–52 *Dict. Archit.* s.v. *Gauged stuff*, Lath plastered, floated, and set with gauged putty appears in the price books between 1830 and 1840..Mortar mixed with roman cement to accelerate the drying of the brickwork is also called gauged mortar. **1897** *Laxton's Builders' Price Bk.* (ed. 18) 253 Coarse plaster [is used] principally for what is called 'gauged work'.

4. *Dressmaking.* (Cf. GAUGE *v.* 8.)

1896 *Daily News* 17 Oct. 6/5 The long sleeves are also in gauged muslin.

5. Of a weir: Fitted with movable paddles or shutters.

1791 *Rep. Navig. Thames & Isis* Estim. 3 At Shifford's Wear, a new Pound Lock, a new gauged Wear and Cut, raising Banks, &c. £1200.

gauger (ˈgeɪdʒə(r)). Forms: 6 gagier, gaugeo(u)r, 7 gawger, -eo(u)r, gaudger, gajor, 6–8 gager, 9 guager, 5– gauger. [a. AF. *gaugeour*, agent-n. f. *gauger* GAUGE *v.*¹]

1. One who gauges, in senses of the vb.; esp. in sense 3, an exciseman.

1483, 1531 [see GAUGE *v.*¹ 3]. **1542** RECORDE *Gr. Artes* (1575) 206 How they do differ daily from their iust measure, yᵉ Gagiers can tell you better than I. **1608** R. NORTON tr. *Stevin's Disme* B iij b, To Land-Meaters, Gaudgers, Stereometers in generall. **1668** *N. Riding Rec.* VI. 125 Gajor to His Majesty for the duty of Excise. **1702** *Lond. Gaz.* No. 3790/5 Every Bushel of Malt, so conveyed from the Sight and View of the Gaugers. **1789** BURNS *To Dr. Blacklock* iv, But what d'ye think, my trusty fier, I'm turned a gauger. **1818** SCOTT *Rob Roy* iv, It's e'en because your English gaugers and supervisors..have taen up the trade of thievery over the heads of the native professors. **1887** STEVENSON *Underwoods* I. ii, The gauger walked with willing foot And aye the gauger played the flute.

fig. **1856** R. A. VAUGHAN *Mystics* (1860) I. 181 Entertained my jovial gauger of monks' bellies with the best cheer I had. **1874** WHITTIER *Hum. Sacr.* v, Calm gauger of the swelling tide Of mortal agony and fear.

†**2.** One who sells liquor. *Obs. rare*$^{-1}$.

c **1610** in Gutch *Coll. Cur.* II. 14 That no Tipler or Gauger sell by other measure than by gallon, pottel [etc.].

3. A gauging instrument, a measure.

1580 BABINGTON *Exp. Lord's Prayer* (1596) 200 As with a gager he gageth them by those blessings. **1612** WOODALL *Surg. Mate* Wks. (1653) 314 This Instrument, the Trafine.. needeth no rule or gager. **1858** SIMMONDS *Dict. Trade*, *Gauger*..an instrument used by leather cutters.

Hence ˈ**gaugership**, the office of a gauger.

1881 *Nation* (N.Y.) XXXIII. 1 Because he does not satisfy them with collectorships, gaugerships, and consulates.

†ˈ**gaugery.** *Obs. rare*$^{-1}$. In 7 gaudgerie. [f. GAUGE *v.*¹ + -ERY. In AF. *gaugerie.*] The action or process of gauging.

1608 R. NORTON tr. *Stevin's Disme* D iv, Gaudgerie is Stereometrie..but..all Stereometrie is not Gaudgerie.

gauging, gaging (ˈgeɪdʒɪŋ), *vbl. sb.* [f. GAUGE *v.*¹ + -ING¹.]

1. The action of the vb. GAUGE in various senses; *esp.* the action or method of determining by actual measurement the capacity of a vessel or the amount contained in it.

c **1440** *Promp. Parv.* 189/1 Gawgynge of depenesse, *dimencionatus.* **1570** DEE *Math. Pref.* 16 Of Wine..or Ale vessels, &c., the Measuring, commonly..is called Gaging. **1661** MARVELL *Corr.* xxxiv. Wks. 1872–5 II. 60 Your Patent for the gaging of wines. **1665** *Phil. Trans.* I. 65 For the Figure of the Tool in that way is presently vitiated by the working of the Glass, and without much gaging will not do any thing considerable. **1743** *Lond. & Country Brew.* II. (ed. 2) 127 A moving Consideration to an Officer to take Care of oppressing the Subject with Over-charges in Gaging. **1867** *Jrnl. R. Agric. Soc.* Ser. II. III. II. 476 Numerous gaugings and samplings of the sewage..have been undertaken.

b. The gauged part (of a thing). *rare*$^{-1}$. (Cf. GAUGE *v.*¹ 5.)

1725 W. HALFPENNY *Sound Building* 56 The two Gaugings of the Bow A are let into two level Pieces on each side the Puppet-head.

2. *Coal-mining.* (See quot.)

1883 GRESLEY *Gloss. Coal Mining*, *Gaging*, a small embankment or heap of slack or rubbish, made at the entrance to a heading, &c., as a means of fencing it off.

3. *Needlework.* (See quot. 1882.)

1882 CAULFEILD & SAWARD *Dict. Needlework*, *Gauging* or *Gaging*, a term applied to a series of close parallel runnings, which are all drawn up so as to make the material between them set full by gatherings. **1893** GEORGIANA HILL *Hist. Eng. Dress* II. 248 Sleeves made with several small puffs and gaugings. **1896** *Daily News* 6 June 8/4 The blouse is pink silk muslin, with a few gaugings across the chest to keep the folds in order.

4. *attrib.* and *Comb.*: **gauging-line**, a graduated line for gauging casks, drawn on a gauging-rod or slide-rule; **gauging-rod**, an exciseman's instrument on the principle of the slide-rule for measuring the capacity or contents of a cask or other vessel; **gauging-rule, -ruler, -stick** = prec.

1656 H. PHILLIPS *Purch. Patt.* (1676) 171 How to make this *Gauging-line, and to set it upon a Gauging-Rod. **1570** J. DEE *Math. Pref.* A iij b, By due applying of..*Gaging rod (or such like instrument) to the Length, Plaine, or Solide measured, to be certified, either of the length, perimetry, or distance lineall. **1635** SIR C. CAVENDISH in Rigaud *Corr. Sci. Men* (1841) I. 22, I thank you..for the way of calculating the divisions of your guaging rod. **1809–12** MAR. EDGEWORTH *Absentee* ix, And the gauging-rod even! who fears it? **1807** HUTTON *Course Math.* II. 82 On it are marked..the wine and ale gage points, to make this instrument serve the purpose of a *gaging rule. **1656** H. PHILLIPS *Purch. Patt.* (1676) 162 These *Gauging Rulers are made by Mr. Hayes. **1789** *Gauging stick [see EXCISEMAN].

gauk, var. GAWK.

Gaul (gɔːl), *sb.* and *a.* [f. *Gaul* (the name of the country), a. F. *Gaule*, an adoption (phonologically obscure) of L. *Gallia*, f. *Gall-us* a Gaul.]

A. *sb.* **a.** An inhabitant of ancient Gaul; also, in a more restricted sense, an individual of the 'Gallic' people or race, as distinguished from other peoples inhabiting Gaul. **b.** Used *poet.* and *humorously* for: A Frenchman (cf. the similar use of *Gaul* for 'France', GALLIC for 'French').

[**1563** WINZET tr. *Vincentius* (title), Vincentius Lirinensis of the natioun of Gallis. **1625** BACON *Ess.*, *Greatness of Kingd.* (Arb.) 485 The Galls, Germans, etc.] **1630** J. TAYLOR (Water P.) *Wks.* III. 112 (124) Where many a Mounsieur of the gallant Gaules, Vnnat'rally was slaine in ciuill braules. **1668** WILKINS *Real Char.* 9 The Gauls were wont often to pass over into Britain, to be instructed by the Druids. **1698** DRYDEN *Ep. to Motteux* 40 Let thine own Gauls condemn thee, if they dare. **1705** ADDISON *Campaign* 54 Delightful stream [the Moselle], had Nature bid her fall In distant Climes, far from the perjur'd Gaul. **1856** EMERSON *Eng. Traits, Race* Wks. (Bohn) II. 27 They [the Normans] had lost their own language, and learned the barbarous Latin of the Gauls. **1886** M. F. SHELDON tr. *Flaubert's Salammbô* 4, Gauls, with their long hair coiled up on the top of their heads.

†**B.** *adj.* Of or pertaining to Gaul, Gallic. *Obs.*

1601 HOLLAND *Pliny* I. 87 Seas..betweene it [Sequana] and Pyrenæus, the Gaule Ocean. **1606** —— *Sueton.* 22 He left Commentaries also of his owne Acts, to wit, as touching the Gaule-warre, and the Ciuill warre with Pompeius.

gaul(e: see GALL.

gaulding: see GAULIN.

gauleiter (ˈgaʊlaɪtə(r)). Also with capital initial. [G., f. *gau* GAU + *leiter* leader.] A political official controlling a district under Nazi rule; also *transf.* and *fig.*, a local or petty tyrant.

1936 A. HUXLEY *Eyeless in Gaza* xxxi. 413 Tyranny under commissars, tyranny under *Gauleiters*—it doesn't seem to make much difference. **1943** *Penguin New Writing* XVI. 9 Mr. Scollop, with his draper's shop and his councillorship, is by way of being the gauleiter of this town. **1949** L. P. HARTLEY *Boat* 299 Two bullies, gauleiters almost, from whom everyone fled in terror. **1958** *Times Lit. Suppl.* 4 Apr. 186/4 The Nazi gauleiters in occupied countries. **1970** *New Statesman* 23 Oct. 526/1 His friend Karl Hanke, the Gauleiter of Lower Silesia, visited him in a state of shock after he had been to Auschwitz concentration camp.

Gaulic (ˈgɔːlɪk), *a.* Now *rare.* [f. GAUL *sb.* + -IC.] = GALLIC *a.*¹ a.

1610 HOLLAND *Camden's Brit.* I. 21 The Gaulike Luca or League, conteineth..just so many paces. *c* **1645** HOWELL *Lett.* (1650) I. 457 There be divers old Gaulick words yet remaining in the French, which are pure British. **1844** MISS COSTELLO *Béarn & Pyrenees* I. 99 Numerous treasures of Gaulic and Roman and Middle-age art. **1846** H. TORRENS *Mil. Lit. & Hist.* I. 166 The old Gaulic habit of using the heavy wains of the army as..a rallying point.

gaulin (ˈgɔːlɪn). *Jamaica.* Also 8 gaulding, 9 gawling. A kind of egret.

a **1705** RAY *Synops. Avium* (1713) 189 *Ardea alba major nostras.* The largest White Gaulding..*Ardea cœruleonigra.* The Black or Blew Gaulding. **1725** SLOANE *Jamaica* II. 314 The largest white Gaulding. *Ibid.* 315 The Black Gaulding, or blue Gaulding. **1750** G. HUGHES *Barbadoes* 70 The Dark-coloured Gaulding..The whole bird is of the Crane kind and generally found feeding upon worms about the edges of ponds. *Ibid.* The Grey Gaulding. This bird is seldom seen in this island. **1756** P. BROWNE *Jamaica* 478 The grey crested Gaulding. **1847** GOSSE *Birds Jamaica* 335, I have observed in June, the white forms of many Gaulins studding the verdant meadows. **1870** *Gd. Words* June 381 A slate-blue heron, or gawling, as they call him here, rose lazily off a dead bough.

Gaulish (ˈgɔːlɪʃ), *a.* (*sb.*) [f. GAUL *sb.* + -ISH.]

A. *adj.* Of or pertaining to the ancient Gauls. Also used (chiefly *poet.* or *humorous*) for: French.

1659 B. HARRIS *Parival's Iron Age* 1 That Gaulish Hercules [K. Henry IV of France]. **1755** JOHNSON, *Galliard* (*gaillard*, French; imagined to be derived from the Gaulish *ard*, genius, and *gay*). **1756–7** tr. *Keysler's Trav.* (1760) I. 448 Not only in the old Gaulish language, but also in the Netherlands. **1766** SMOLLETT *Trav.* 246 Carracalla was the name of a Gaulish vestment which this prince affected to wear. **1830** LYELL *Princ. Geol.* I. 19 It was a dogma of the Gaulish Druids that the universe was immortal. **1845** GRAVES *Rom. Law* in *Encycl. Metrop.* 755/1 The destruction of monuments consequent upon the Gaulish invasion.

B. *sb.* The language of the Gauls.

1668 WILKINS *Real Char.* I. i. §3. 4 The old Gaulish, or British, which is yet preserved in Wales. **1727–51** CHAMBERS *Cycl.* s.v. *Romans*, A mixture..of half Latin, half Gaulish or Celtic, constituted the Romans [language]. **1893** *Nation* (N.Y.) 12 Jan. 32/3 In Gaulish the word would not be 'Allobroga'.

Gaullism ('gəʊlɪz(ə)m). [ad. F. *Gaullisme*, f. the name of General Charles de *Gaulle* (1890–1970), French military and political leader: see -ISM.] The principles and policies associated with General de Gaulle; adherence to or support of these principles. Also *transf.* (Cf. next.)

1950 *Chambers's Encycl.* IV. 61/1 The dual threats of communism and Gaullism. **1951** *20th Cent.* Nov. 400 (*title*) Aspects of Gaullism. **1955** *Times* 25 June 7/5 It is regrettable to consider either the history of the Armistice of 1940 or that of Gaullism and 'Free France' only with humour. **1959** *New Statesman* 7 Feb. 174/1 'Gaullism'..is a growing factor in Italian politics. **1968** *Listener* 21 Mar. 377/1 He was terrified by the effect Gaullism was having, and might have, on his own countrymen.

Gaullist ('gəʊlɪst), *a.* and *sb.* Also **Gaulliste**. [ad. F. *Gaulliste*, f. as prec.: see -IST.] **A.** *adj.* Supporting or pertaining to the principles and policies of General de Gaulle (see prec.). **B.** *sb.* One who supports General de Gaulle and his principles. Also *transf.* Cf. DE GAULLIST *a.* and *sb.*

1941 H. NICOLSON *Diary* 20 Jan. (1967) II. 139 De Gaulle says that he had received a long letter of the most Gaulliste nature. **1947** KOESTLER in *Partisan Rev.* XIV. 344 In the name of what principle do you prefer the Communist jail to Gaullist restricted freedom? **1952** *Ann. Reg. 1951* 206 Proportional representation would increase Communist and Gaullist representation. *Ibid.* 209 Gaullists and Communists were opposed to it and Socialists hesitant. **1958** [see BAND-WAGONER]. **1960** *New Statesman* 2 Apr. 471/1 In French eyes, Khrushchev has allowed himself to appear first and foremost as a Gaullist of the left. **1971** *Guardian* 7 Sept. 2/5 The election of June 1968, when it was hard for any candidate running under Gaullist colours to miss.

Gauloise (golwaz, 'gəʊlwɑːz). Also **Gaulois**, and with lower-case initial. [A proprietary name, f. Fr. *gaulois, -oise* Gallic.] A cigarette of a popular French brand.

1920 *Trade Marks Jrnl.* 17 Mar. 528, 20 Cigarettes Gauloises. **1926–7** *Army & Navy Stores Catal.* 76/2 Imported French cigarettes. Gauloises. **1933** *Trade Marks Jrnl.* 23 Aug. 1033 *Gauloises*. Cigarettes. Service d'Exploitation Industrielle des Tabacs..Ministère des Finances, Palais du Louvre. **1933** 'G. ORWELL' *Down & Out* v. 35, I even squandered two francs fifty on a packet of Gaulois Bleu, in anticipation of my wages. **1958** R. GODDEN *Greengage Summer* iv. 49 It's a Gauloise, a French cigarette. **1959** *Listener* 20 Aug. 285/3 She smoked Gauloises, but she prefered black Russian cigarettes with gold tips. **1960** *20th Cent.* Sept. 259 He sat in his truck smoking gauloises.

gault (gɒlt, -ɔː-), *sb. Geol.* Also 6 **galte**, 8–9 **golt**, **galt**. [Of obscure origin: cf. OSw. *galt* neut. of *galder* adj., barren.]

1. (See quot. 1833.) Also *gault clay*.

1575 TURBERV. *Venerie* 186 In grounde that is harde to dygge as in galte clay and stonye grounde. **1698** FRYER *Acc. E. India & P.* 332 The Element..vegetates, and takes upon it the Nature of Minerals, Stones, Gaults, or Clay. **1766** *Phil. Trans.* LVI. 12 This stratum of gravel is..surrounded with a bed of very dark blue golt. **1807** VANCOUVER *Agric. Devon* (1813) 285 *note*, The bottom of this drain was formed of a retentive clay or gault. **1833** LYELL *Princ. Geology* III. Gloss. 69 *Gault*, a provincial name in the east of England for a series of beds of clay and marl, the geological position of which is between the upper and the lower greensand. **1846** J. BAXTER *Libr. Pract. Agric.* (ed. 4) I. 339 Chalk marl and galt are the strata which appear immediately under the lower chalk and occupy a valley at the foot of the chalk hills. **1876** PAGE *Adv. Textbk. Geol.* xviii. 337 The argillaceous strata.. known by the provincial term 'gault' or 'golt'.

2. *Comb.*: **gault-mill**.

1889 *Athenæum* No. 3244. 883/1 Urchins who, like horses in a gault-mill, trotted beneath the structure in a circle and pushed it round.

gault (gɒlt, -ɔː-), *v. dial.* [f. prec. sb.] **a.** *trans.* To cover (soil) with clay obtained from the subsoil. **b.** *intr.* To dig gault for embankments.

Hence **'gaulting** *vbl. sb.* Also **'gaulter**, a labourer who digs gault.

1851 H. STEPHENS *Bk. of Farm* §2124 (ed. 2) The process of gaulting or claying the soil. **1885** *Instr. to Census Clerks* 86 Clay Banksman, Clay Miner..Gaulter. **1893** BARING-GOULD *Cheap-Jack Z.* II. 39, Gangers, clayers, bankers, gaulters. *Ibid.* 48 How should I be paid for my gaulting? and without gaulting there can be no banking.

‖**Gaultheria** (gɒl'θɪərɪə, -ɔː-). [mod.L., f. name of M. *Gaultier*, a Canadian botanist.] A genus of evergreen aromatic plants (N.O. *Ericaceæ*). The plant *Gaultheria procumbens*, known in the U.S. as Wintergreen, yields a volatile oil, used in the pharmacopœia, called *gaultheria oil*.

1848 in CRAIG. **1859** *Fownes' Chem.* 527 Gaultheria oil is isomeric with anisic acid. **1876** GROSS *Dis. Bladder* 49 Emulsion, prepared with gum Arabic, loaf-sugar, and oil of gaultheria. **1880** C. R. MARKHAM *Peruv. Bark* 140 Above the tambo there was a small thicket of gaultherias.

gaulty ('gɒltɪ, -ɔː-), *a.* In quots. **galty**. [? f. GAULT + -Y[1]. Cf. GOUTY and GALLY.] (See quots.)

1790 SIR J. CULLUM *Hist. Hawsted & Hardwick* iii. in *Bibl. Topogr. Brit.* V. 171 *Sand-Galls*, spots of sand in a field where water oozes: and lands where such spots are frequent, are called *galty* lands. **1823** MOOR *Suffolk Words*, *Galty*, wet, boggy, clayey land. **1841** *Jrnl. R. Agric. Soc.* II. II. 263 If the shoulders of the drain give way in a gravelly or galty place, bushes or stubble are placed under the turf.

gaum (gɔːm), *v.*[1] *Obs.* exc. *dial.* Also 7 **goam**. *trans.* To handle, esp. in some improper fashion.

1656 R. FLETCHER *Martial* etc. 230 Each Lad took his Lass by the fist, And when he had squeez'd her, and gaum'd her untill The fat of her face ran down like a mill He [etc.]. **1674–91** RAY *N.C. Words*, *Goam*, to grasp, or clasp. *a* **1700** B. E. *Dict. Cant. Crew*, *Gaum*, see Paume [= to *palm* (a die, etc.)]. **1738** SWIFT *Pol. Convers.* ii. Wks. (ed. Faulkner, Dublin) VI. 331 Don't be mauming and gauming a Body so. [Differently in other edd.] Can't you keep your filthy Hands to your self? **1886** *Chester Gloss.*, *Gawm.*, to grasp in the hand. **1894** *S.E. Worcs. Gloss.*, *Gaum*, to handle articles in a manner calculated to damage or mar their appearance.

gaum (gɔːm), *v.*[2] [Cf. GOME *sb.* = COOM *sb.*[2] 4.] *trans.* To smear with a sticky substance; to daub (something sticky) on a surface.

a **1796** PEGGE *Derbicisms* II. (E.D.S.) 102 *Gawm'd*, smeared. **1824** LAMB *Lett.* (1888) II. 120 Hope it won't clog his wings (gaum, we used to say at school). **1872** 'MARK TWAIN' *Innoc. Abr.* xx. 146 Those low savages..mix the.. grease and ashes..with tar, and 'gaum' it thick all over their heads. **1883** *Athenæum* No. 2885. 192 The greater part of the interior was gaumed with shellac in solution.

gaum (gɔːm), *v.*[3] *dial. intr.* To stare vacantly.

1674–91 RAY *N.C. Words*, s.v. *Goam*, We pronounce it *gaum* or *gauve*, and speak it of persons that unhandsomely gaze or look about them. **1839** *Cumbld. & Westmld. Dial.* 72 A body knaas better haw tae carry thersel when they er amang gentlefowk: yan leaks nit quite sae gawmin. **1877** *Holderness Gloss.*, *Gawm*, to stare vacantly. **1887** *S. Chesh. Gloss.*, *Gawmin*, foolish, awkward, rash.

gaum, dial. form of GOME, notice.

gaumbisoun, var. GAMBESON.

gaumeril, var. GOMEREL.

gaumless, dial. var. GORMLESS *a.*

'gaum-like, *a. dial.* [f. as *gaumless* GORMLESS *a.* + -LIKE.] Having an intelligent look.

1863 MRS. GASKELL *Sylvia's L.* II. 21 She were a poor, friendless wench..but honest and gaum-like.

gaumy ('gɔːmɪ), *a. rare.* Also **gormy**. [Cf. GAUM *v.*[2]] Of the nature of a daub or smear; of painting: coarsely executed, dauby.

1881 *Leicestersh. Gloss.*, *Gaumy*, gummy; sticky. **1888** *Athenæum* 25 Feb. 250/3 It shows Wilkie designing with admirable vigour, but the execution is vicious and 'gaumy'. **1907** W. DE MORGAN *Alice-for-Short* xxxii. 331 'What's his work like though, reely?' 'Footy stuff. Gormy colour. No drawin'!' **1919** —— *Old Madhouse* 306, I wish she wouldn't trot out her gormy daubs and ask my honest opinion of them.

gaun, Sc. f. *going*, ppl. of *gae*: see GO *v.*

†**gaunce**, *v. Obs. rare*[−0]. [Cf. F. *jancer* of the same meaning (only in Palsgr.).] (See quot.)

1530 PALSGR. 561/2, I gawance [*sic*] a horse up and downe upon the stones and make hym gambalde and flynge, *Je pourbondis*. And you gaunce your horse up and downe thus [etc.].

gauncely(e, gaunch, var. GANSEL, GANCH.

gaundies, -ise, obs. ff. JAUNDICE.

gaundre, obs. form of GANDER.

gaunsell(e, var. GANSEL. *Obs.*

gaunt (gɔːnt, gɑːnt), *a.* Forms: 5 **gawnt(e**, 6 **ga(u)nte**, 6–7, 9– (*U.S. dial.*) **gant**, 6– **gaunt**. [Of unknown origin: Prof. Skeat compares Norw. *gand* thin pointed stick, tall thin man (Aasen), and Sw. dial. *gank* a lean and nearly starved horse (Rietz).

All other words in *-aunt* (exc. *flaunt*) are of Fr. origin. The prevailing early use might suggest that the word was a graphic adoption of *gant* = OF. *gent*, GENT, elegant.]

†**1.** In favourable or neutral sense: Slim, slender, not fat. *Obs.*

c **1440** *Promp. Parv.* 189/1 Gawnt or lene, *maciolentus* [sic]. Gawnte or swonge (*K.* or slendyr), *gracilis*. **1546** *St. Papers Hen. VIII*, XI. 230 The King..was nothing so lusty nor so gaunte, when I saw him last, as He is nowe..I wold not haue beleved He had byne in so good case as He is nowe, if I had not sene Him myself. **1549** LATIMER *5th Serm. bef. Edw. VI* (Arb.) 154 Sodaynelye, she was gaunte agayne [after childbirth]. **1577** B. GOOGE *Heresbach's Husb.* III. (1586) 154 b, The Dogge that is for the folde, must neither be so gaunt nor swift as the Grayhounde, nor so fatte nor heavy as the masty. **1601** HOLLAND *Pliny* II. 152 They who feed ouermuch, and desire to be gant and slender..ought to forbear drinking at meales. **1657** W. COLES *Adam in Eden* cl. 229 It [groundsell] is much used to be given to tame Rabbets when they are pot-bellyed..to make them gaunt and healthfull. **1684** R. H. *School Recreat.* 10 If you would chuse a swift, light Hound..he ought to have a slender Head.. broad Back, gaunt Belly, small Tail..and in fine, of a Greyhound-like make. **1690** *Lond. Gaz.* No. 2572/4 One light grey Mare, comes 7, about 15 hands, a gant Body. **1703** THORESBY *Let. to Ray* (E.D.S.), *Gant*, lusty, hearty and healthful. [Cf. quot. 1546 above.] **1736** PEGGE *Kenticisms* (E.D.S.), *Gant*, of a greyhound, or a racehorse, being thin in the flanks. [**1848** THACKERAY *Van. Fair* lvii, He was quite well (though as gaunt as a greyhound) before they reached the Cape.]

2. Abnormally lean, as from hunger; haggard-looking; tall, thin, and angular in appearance.

c **1440** [see 1]. **1581** MULCASTER *Positions* xxxiii. (1887) 119 If the colour begin to faint, or the bodie to be gaunt. **1593** SHAKS. *Rich. II*, II. i. 74 Oh how that name befits my composition: Old *Gaunt* indeed, and gaunt in being old. *Ibid.* 82 Gaunt am I for the graue, gaunt as a graue. **1639** G. DANIEL *Ecclus.* xiii. 59 For what Alliance, what relation Hath the gant Wolfe wth the Innocent Lamb? **1697** DRYDEN *Virg. Georg.* IV. 144 Gaunt are his Sides, and sullen is his Face. **1815** SCOTT *Guy M.* ii, His tall, gaunt, awkward bony figure, attired in a thread-bare suit of black. **1882** OUIDA *Maremma* I. 17 A tall gaunt woman with blue eyes and snow-white hair.

fig. **1809** HEBER *Palestine* 261 Wide-wasting plague, gaunt famine, mad despair.

b. Hungry, greedy, ravenous. *rare.*

1746 SMOLLETT *Reproof* 125 Gorg'd with our plunder, yet still gaunt for spoil, Rapacious Gideon fastens on our isle.

3. *transf.* Of inanimate things: Grim or desolate of aspect; †(of a sound), suggestive of desolation.

1814 *Prophetess* I. v, Like the gaunt echo of a hollow tomb. **1840** DICKENS *Old C. Shop* i, I had, ever before me, the gaunt suits of mail with their ghostly silent air—the faces all awry. **1871** BESANT & RICE *Ready Money Mortiboy* i, Mortiboy's parlour is a gaunt cold room. **1874** MAHAFFY *Soc. Life Greece* xi. 349 Human art has been thrust..even into hostility with our stern and gaunt devoutness. **1876** T. HARDY *Ethelberta* (1890) 93, I am at present..surrounded by gaunt realities. **1886** HALL CAINE *Son of Hagar* II. xiv, Paul walked among the naked trees of the gaunt wood at the foot of Coledale.

4. *Comb.*, as ***gaunt-bellied, -looking*** adjs.

1629 GAULE *Holy Madn.* 324 Is he not mostly..Gaunt belly'd. **1860** TYNDALL *Glac.* I. xi. 70 Mounds of ice..split into high towers and gaunt-looking pyramids.

Hence **'gaunted** *a.*, made lean or meagre; starved.

1583 STANYHURST *Æneis* II. (Arb.) 55 Lyke rauening woolfdams vpsoackt and gaunted in hunger. **1887** *Scribner's Mag.* Oct. 475/2 Looks right puny an' ga'nted. **1890** D. S. CAGE in Shields *Big Game N. Amer.* 476 A gorged Wolf is not fast..but when properly 'gaunted', few horses can catch a Gray Wolf. **1909** R. A. WASON *Happy Hawkins* 333 His face was pale..an' he was ganted down in weight a little.

gaunt: see GANT.

†**gaunter**. *Obs. rare*[−1]. [a. F. *gantier*, f. *gant* glove.] A glover or glove-maker.

1415 in *York Myst.* Introd. 20 Gaunters (*glossed by* Glovers).

gauntlet ('gɔːntlɪt, 'gɑːntlɪt), *sb.*[1] Forms: 5 **gantelet**, **gauntelote**, 5–6 **gauntelette**, 6 **ga(u)ntlett**, 7 **gantlet**, 5– **gauntlet**. [a. F. *gantelet*, dim. of *gant* (OF. also *guant, want*) glove = Sp. *guante*, Pg. *guante* (gauntlet), It. *guanto*, med.L. *gantus, wantus*. The word is app. of Teut. origin, though found only in Scand. as ON. *vǫtt-r* (:—OTeut. **wantu-z*), dim. *vett-lingr*, OSw. *vanter*, Sw. Da. *vante*. MDu. *want* is prob. from OF.

Noreen suggests that the root may be related to ON. *vinda*, OE. *windan* to wind, by an interchange of *t* and *d* (= orig. *d, dh*) dating from the Indo-Eur. period.]

1. A glove worn as part of mediæval armour, usually made of leather, covered with plates of steel.

c **1420** LYDG. *Assemb. Gods* 346 Mynerue..All in curas clad, Gauntlettes on hyr handys. **1484** CAXTON *Chivalry* 64 The knyght with his gauntelotes handleth more surely the spere or his swerd. **1568** GRAFTON *Chron.* II. 377 He..cast away his Gauntlets, and his sworde to make him the lighter. **1658** COKAINE *Trappolin* III. ii, These hands, that wont to wave a dreadful sword, Instead of iron gauntlets now must wear Perfum'd gloves! **1762** HOOLE *Tasso* XI. 295 Wing'd with speed, the vengeful arrow flew: Swift thro' his better hand it held its course, Nor could the steely gauntlet stop the force. **1828** SCOTT *F.M. Perth* vi, I am not the man..to disparage the glover's mystery..I am myself a maker of gauntlets. **1860** TYNDALL *Glac.* I. ii. 20 The glacier resembles a vast gauntlet, of which the gorge represents the wrist.

b. used for CESTUS[2].

c **1697** DRYDEN *Æneid* v. 88 The strong with Iron Gauntlets arm'd shall stand, Oppos'd in Combat on the yellow Sand. **1700** —— *Pal. & Arc.* III. 1001 Who naked wrestled best.. Or who with gauntlets gave or took the foil. **1886** LEWIS & SHORT *Lat. Dict.*, *Caestus*..a gauntlet, boxing glove for pugilists.

c. ***to cast (out), fling out*** or ***down, throw (down) the gauntlet*** (= F. *jeter le gant*): to give a challenge, from the mediæval custom of throwing down a glove or gauntlet in challenging an opponent: cf. GAGE *sb.*[1] 2. ***to pick up, to take up, to gather*** (rare) ***the gauntlet***: to accept a challenge (F. *relever le gant*); to undertake the defence of a person or opinion.

1548 HALL *Chron., Rich. III* (1809) 376 Makynge a proclamacion, that whosoeuer would saie that kynge Richard was not lawefully kynge, he woulde fighte with hym at the vtteraunce, and threwe downe his gauntlet. **1590** NASHE *Pasquil's Apol.* I. D iv b, I cast them my Gauntlet, take it vp who dares. **1632** HEYWOOD *1st Pt. Iron Age* II. Wks. 1874 III. 297 See'st thou not Æacides Dart emmulous lookes on Kingly Diomed, Least hee should stoope to take his Gantlet vp. **1641** HINDE *J. Bruen* lxi. 205 And casting out as it were, his gantlet of defiance..he challengeth them all. **1647** WARD *Simp. Cobler* 72 Yee that fling out the gantlet to him that calls you Coward. **1784** KIPPIS *Biog. Brit.* III. Corrig. & Add. s.v. *Bentley*, This [challenge] the Poet communicated to some of his military friends; two or three of whom..took up the gauntlet. **1806** SURR *Winter in Lond.* (ed. 3) II. 204 The duchess of Drinkwater appeared upon the field of fashion, and threw down the gauntlet of defiance to Belgrave. **1851** GALLENGA *Italy* 363 This was a declaration of war to Mazzini, and he was not slow in gathering the gauntlet thus wantonly thrown. **1867** TROLLOPE *Chron. Barset* II. lxvii. 249 [She] had thrown down her gauntlet to him, and he had not been slow in picking it up. **1875** STUBBS *Const. Hist.* III. xviii. 146 The commons at once took up the gauntlet.

2. In recent use: A stout glove, covering part of the arm as well as the hand, used in driving or riding, fencing, wicket-keeping, etc.

1858 SIMMONDS *Dict. Trade*, *Gauntlet*, a long glove, worn by ladies or soldiers. **1865** *Dublin Univ. Mag.* Feb. 140 Her fur-trimmed driving-jacket showed a piquant figure—her white gauntlets a shapely little hand. **1872-6** VOYLE & STEVENSON *Milit. Dict.* (ed. 3) 160/2 A leather gauntlet is now used, in place of gloves, by the household cavalry. **1891** W. G. GRACE in *Outdoor Games & Recreat.* 7 Brown..is going to keep wicket; his gauntlets, or wicket-keeping gloves, are in his hand.

b. The part of a glove intended to cover the wrist.

1882 CAULFEILD & SAWARD *Dict. Needlework* s.v. *Gloves*, Thick white 'wash leather' gloves, with gauntlets, are worn by the Life Guards.

c. *Surg.* 'A sort of bandage which envelops the hand and fingers like a gauntlet or glove' (Ogilvie).

†**3.** The plant *Campanula Trachelium.* [So F. *gantelet.*] *Obs. rare*$^{-1}$.

1578 LYTE *Dodoens* V. xxxv. 596 The Marians Violet and the Gauntelet..are also of the kindes of Rampions.

4. *Naut.* 'A rope round the ship to the lower yard-arms, for drying scrubbed hammocks' (Adm. Smyth). [Perh. a distinct word.]

5. *attrib.* and *Comb.*, as ***gauntlet-cuff***, ***-gatherer***, ***-glove***, ***grasp***; also †**gauntlet-work**, ? imbricated plates.

1664 POWER *Exp. Philos.* I. 9 A Louse appears the bignesse of a large Crecket, with three legs on either side, and two horns in the Snout, all transparent and of Gauntlet-work, having here and there hairs and bristles. **1815** SCOTT *Ld. of Isles* VI. xv, The axe-shaft, with its brazen clasp, Was shiver'd in the gauntlet grasp. **1846** BROWNING *Soul's Trag.* I. Poet. Wks. 1896 I. 466 No general gauntlet-gatherer for the weak against the strong. **1895** *Daily News* 5 Feb. 6/6 The coat is cut half length and has old silver buttons at the waist and on the gauntlet cuffs.

Hence '**gauntleted** *a.*, covered or armed with a gauntlet; of a glove: having a gauntlet (see 2 b above); '**gauntlet** *v. trans.*, to strike with a gauntlet (*nonce-use*).

1810 SCOTT *Lady of L.* V. xxv, Such blow no other hand could deal, Though gauntletted in glove of steel. **1842** W. IRVING in *Life & Lett.* (1866) III. 260 He rode along the heads of the columns, saluting them with his gauntleted hand. **1885** TENNYSON *Balin & Balan* in *Tiresias* etc. 120, I smote upon the naked skull A thrall of thine..my hand Was gauntleted, half slew him. *Ibid.* 130 The thrall His passion half had gauntleted to death. **1902** C. MAJOR *D. Vernon* 38 He was drawing on his gauntleted gloves. **1924** 'J. SUTHERLAND' *Circle of Stars* iv. 37 Her loose gauntleted gloves of wash-leather.

gauntlet ('gɔːntlɪt, 'gɑːntlɪt), *sb.*[2] Forms: 7-9 gantlet, 8 ga(u)ntlett, 7- gauntlet [corrupted f. GANTLOPE, by assimilation with GAUNTLET *sb.*[1]] = GANTLOPE.

1676 I. MATHER *K. Philip's War* (1862) 137 They stripped them naked, and caused them to run the Gauntlet. **1704** T. POCOCK in *Torrington Mem.* (Camden) 187 One of the boatswain's mates ran the gantlett for stealing a shirt. **1778** SHERIDAN *Camp* I. i, You should..be forced to run the gauntlet, from Cox heath to Warley Common. **1830** SCOTT *Demonol.* vii. 214 Six-and-thirty of those who were young were forced to run the gauntlet. **1897** F. N. MAUDE *Volunt. v. Compulsory Service* 33 Scharnhorst..procured the removal [in the Prussian army] of all dishonouring punishments, such as running the gauntlet.

b. *transf.* and *fig.*

1661 GLANVILL *Dogmatizing* Pref., To print, is to run the gantlet, and to expose ones self to the tongues strapado. **1709** POPE *Let. to Wycherley* 17 May, Hitherto your miscellanies have safely run the gantlet, through all the coffee-houses. **1768** MAD. D'ARBLAY *Early Diary* (1889) I. 16 O what a gauntlet for any woman of delicacy to run! **1839** LD. BROUGHAM *Statesm. Geo. III, Eldon* (ed. 2) 254 The case had run the gauntlet of the courts. **1851** HT. MARTINEAU *Hist. Peace* (1877) III. IV. ix. 44 The premier had to run the gauntlet between the lines of objectors. **1858** O. W. HOLMES *Aut. Breakf.-t.* (1883) 138 They have run the gantlet of the years. **1880** PARKMAN *France & Eng. in Amer.* 12 They descended the Mississippi, running the gantlet between hostile tribes.

gauntly ('gɔːntlɪ), *adv.* [f. GAUNT + -LY[2].] In a gaunt manner.

1755 in JOHNSON. **1864** BLACKMORE *Clara Vaughan* xv, I beheld a man about fifty years old, of moderate stature, gauntly bodied, and loosely built. **1884** *Harper's Mag.* Nov. 888/1 One of them walked gauntly down to the post-office in the corner of the variety store.

gauntness ('gɔːntnɪs). [f. GAUNT + -NESS.]

1. The condition of being gaunt.

1607 TOPSELL *Four-f. Beasts* (1658) 288 It is known by the leanness of the Horse, and gantness of his belly. **1619** MIDDLETON *Inner Temple Masque* A 3, I know him by his gauntnes, his thin chitterlings. **1829** LYTTON *Devereux* I. ii, The total absence of all superfluous flesh would have given the lean gauntness of his figure an appearance of almost spectral emaciation. **1884** ROE *Nat. Ser. Story* xii, He was growing thin even to gauntness.

2. *fig.* Grimness, repulsive character.

1874 MAHAFFY *Soc. Life Greece* viii. 252 Compare all this humane and kindly feeling with the gauntness and horror of our modern executions.

gauntree, gauntrie, -y: see GANTRY.

gaup, gaupus, varr. GAWP, GAWPUS.

gaur (gaʊə(r)). Also gour, gore. [a. Hindustani *gaur.*] A large species of ox, *Bos gaurus*, found wild in various parts of India.

1806 ELPHINSTONE in Colebrooke *Life* (1884) I. 156 There is an account of a similar kind called the Gore; one distinction between it and the buffalo is the length of the hoofs. **1827** D. JOHNSON *Ind. Field Sports* 49, I have met with an account of Gayals..which appear..to be animals of the same species as the Gour. **1860** GOSSE *Rom. Nat. Hist.* 119, I need only advert to other colossal quadrupeds..the camel, the gaur, the gayall. **1893** R. LYDEKKER *Horns & Hoofs* 15 The gaur (*Bos gaurus*) the misnamed bison of Indian sportsmen.

†**gaure**, *v. Obs.* Also gawre(n, gowren, gare. [Possibly a frequentative f. GAW *v.*]

1. *intr.* To stare, gape, gaze in wonder or astonishment.

c **1374** CHAUCER *Troylus* II. 1108 (1157) And seide hir, caste it now a-wey a-non, þat folk may sen, and gauren on vs tweye. **1430-40** LYDG. *Bochas* IX. iii. (1554) 199 a, For very shame I did mine eyen close For them y[t] gaured and cast on me their sight. *a* **1529** SKELTON *Magnif.* 2275, I was your mayster..And nowe on me ye gaure and sporne.

2. To shout or cry (cf. GAPE *v.* 1 c).

1530 PALSGR. 561/2, I gaure, I krye, *je hue.* Howe he gaureth after his hauke: *comment il hue apres son oyseau.*

Hence '**gauring** *ppl. a.*; also ***gauring-stock***, a gazing-stock.

1558 PHAER *Æneid* VI. R j b, With fifty garing heads [L. *quinquaginta atris hiatibus*] a monstrous dragon stands vpright. **1559** *Mirr. Mag., Dk. York* xxi, As a gawring Stocke he sent it [the duke's head] to the Queen. **1579** TWYNE *Phisicke agst. Fort.* II. lxxv. 252 b, Thou art a notable garyng stocke for al men.

gaure, gaurish, obs. ff. GIAOUR, GARISH.

†**gausapine.** *Obs.*$^{-0}$. [ad. L. *gausapina* garment made of *gausapē* frieze, a Gr. γαυσάπης.]

1623 COCKERAM II, A Frize-jerkin, *gausapine.*

Hence **gausapinal** *a.*, made of frieze. *nonce-wd.*

1652 URQUHART *Jewel* Wks. (1834) 279 Bringing their persons to stand before them on penitentiary pews, like so many varlets, in mendiciary and gausapinal garments.

gause, obs. form of GAUZE *sb.*

gausie, gausy: see GAWSY.

†**Gausk.** *Sc. Obs.*$^{-1}$. [Cf. the Fife and Perthshire place-name *Gask*, of unknown origin and meaning.] (See quot.; possibly a mistranslation.)

c **1375** *Sc. Leg. Saints, Juliana* 131 Nocht-þane, scho drev hym to þe tone, & in a depe gausk [L. *latrinam*] kist hym done, þat ves a ful foule pyt, rycht vgly & ful ves It.

gauss (gaʊs). *Physics.* Also **Gauss.** [f. the name of a German mathematician and natural philosopher, Karl Friedrich *Gauss* (1777-1855).] The electromagnetic unit of magnetic induction (flux density) in the C.G.S. system, defined as the induction that exerts a force of one dyne on each centimetre of a straight wire carrying one e.m.u. (10 amp.) of current, when the induction is perpendicular to the wire. (In the International System of Units the gauss is replaced by the tesla, or weber per square metre, equal to 10,000 gauss.)

The name has been suggested for various magnetic units. The original sense was the C.G.S. unit of magnetic field strength (later called an *oersted*), and, because in the C.G.S. system the electromagnetic units of field strength and of induction have the same dimensions and *in vacuo* are numerically the same, the word has freq. been used for both indiscriminately.

1882 *Nature* XXVI. 391 Two other units may have to be added, the one expressing that of magnetic field..Sir W. Thomson suggested the former..and pointed out that it would be proper to attach to it the name of Gauss..A Gauss will then be defined as the intensity of field produced by a Weber at the distance of one centimetre. **1891** L. CLARK *Dict. Metric & Other Useful Measures* 38 *Gauss*, a unit [*printed* unity] of intensity of magnetic field, proposed by Prof. S. P. Thompson. = 10^8 C.G.S. units. Other values have also been suggested. **1893** *Electrician* 29 Sept. 579/1 Some attempt was made to secure the adoption of the name of 'gauss' for the C.G.S. unit of magnetic field. **1895** *Rep. Brit. Assoc.* 196 The Committee [*sc.* the British Association Committee on Electrical Standards]..recommend for tentative adoption the following terminology... That the c.g.s. unit of magnetic potential or of magneto-motive force be called a *gauss*... Hence the number of gausses round any closed curve linked on an electric circuit is equal to 1·2566 the number of ampère-turns in this circuit. **1913** C. W. C. BARLOW *Electr. & Magn.* xii. 241 The Gauss is the unit of Magnetic Induction and also of Field, the Gilbert of M.M.F... These names are not in common use. **1930** *Nature* 16 Aug. 252/2 The committee on nomenclature [of the International Electrotechnical Commission]..adopted the following names for the magnetic C.G.S. units. The unit of magnetic flux was called the 'maxwell' and the unit of flux density the 'gauss'. **1947** *Science News* IV. 116 The gauss is the unit of the magnetic field. It exerts unit force (1 dyne) on a unit magnetic pole placed in it. **1955** *Sci. Amer.* May 56/3 The earth's field near the poles is ·7 gauss. **1962** A. R. W. HAYES *Revision Physics* v. 170 In free space an applied field *H* oersted produces a flux density *H* gauss; in a magnetic medium the flux density is modified to a value *B* gauss which is the sum of the original flux and that due to magnetization of the medium. **1965** A. H. MORRISH *Physical Princ. Magn.* i. 2 The cgs unit of magnetic field is the oersted, although the term gauss is still frequently used.

Gaussian ('gaʊsɪən), *a.* [f. the name of K. F. *Gauss* (see GAUSS) + -IAN.]

a. Discovered or formulated by Gauss.

1874 *Rep. Brit. Assoc. 1873* 75 Gaussian logarithms have for their object to facilitate the finding of the logarithms of the sum and difference of two numbers whose logarithms are known, the numbers being themselves unknown. **1881** *Proc. Lond. Math. Soc.* XII. 187 On the Gaussian Theory of Surfaces. By Prof. Cayley. **1897** A. G. WEBSTER *Theory Electr. & Magn.* II. ix. 367 We may, when dealing with electrical quantities, assume that the dimensions of the electrical inductivity are zero. This gives the electrostatic system of units. We may.., when dealing with magnetic quantities, assume that the dimensions of the magnetic inductivity are zero. This gives the magnetic system. Both these systems are due to Gauss, and when we use both systems for their respective kinds of quantities, we shall say that the quantities are measured in *Gaussian* units. **1957** B. & B. I. BLEANEY *Electr. & Magn.* xxiii. 646 In electromagnetic theory Maxwell's equations involve both electrical and magnetic units, and in the c.g.s. system they are generally written in mixed or Gaussian units.

b. *Statistics.* Designating a curve, frequency distribution, or statistical process, etc., that is described mathematically by a function of the form exp $(-x^2/2\sigma^2)/\sqrt{(2\pi\sigma^2)}$, where x is the variable.

1905 K. PEARSON in *Biometrika* IV. 173 Many of the other remedies which have been proposed to supplement what I venture to call the universally recognised inadequacy of the Gaussian law..cannot..effectively describe the chief deviations from the Gaussian distribution. *Ibid.* 189 In writing for Germans I naturally spoke of the Gaussian curve. **1920** *Biometrika* XIII. 10 To get the Gaussian or normal curve we must..replace differences by differentials and we have $(dy/dx)/y = -x/\sigma_0^2$. *Ibid.* 15 The so-called Gaussian or normal curve was first introduced into statistics as a *rough and ready* solution for the sum of a certain number of terms in a definite hypergeometrical series. **1968** P. A. P. MORAN *Introd. Probability Theory* ix. 424 The homogeneous additive process in which the distribution of $x(t_1) - x(t_2)$ is always a normal distribution is known by various names as the Gaussian, normal, Wiener, or Brownian process.

'**gauster,** '**goster.** *v. dial.* Also goyster, gowster. [dial. survival of ME. GALSTRE.] *intr.* To behave in a noisy, boisterous, or swaggering fashion; to brag or boast; in some localities, to laugh noisily.

1674-91 RAY *N.C. Words, Gauster.* —— *S. & E.C. Words, Goyster*, to be frolick and ramp, to laugh aloud. **1825** CROKER *Fairy Leg.* (new ed.) 113 Some people used to wink and look knowing when Felix was gostering. **1847-78** HALLIWELL, *Gauster*, to laugh loudly; to be noisy; to swagger. **1879** WAUGH *Chimney Corner* 89 He began o' gosterin' an' talkin' about th' horses—he'd ha' this done, an' he'd ha' that done, or else [etc.].

Hence '**gauster** *sb.*, the action of the vb.; '**gaustering** *vbl. sb.* and *ppl. a.*

1703 THORESBY *Let. to Ray* (E.D.S.), *Gauster*, a hearty, loud laughter. **1736** LEWIS *Hist. Isle Tenet* (ed. 2) 37 *Goyster*, to laugh aloud; 'a goystering Wench', a Boy-maid, or a Lad-lass. *c* **1746** J. COLLIER (Tim Bobbin) *Lanc. Dialect* Wks. (1862) 71, I can mex'n, keem on fettle Tits os weel os onny one on um aw, tho theaw mey think its gawstring. **1824** *Craven Gloss.*, *Gaustering*, imperious, boasting. **1806-29** T. MOORE *Ballads* (Galignani 1829) 353 Poh, Dermot go along with your goster.

gaut(e, obs. f. GHAUT; var. GALT; dial. var. GOTE.

gauva, gauvey, vars. GUAVA, GABY.

gauze (gɔːz), *sb.* Forms: 6 *Sc.* gais (? 7 *Sc.* gadza), 7-9 gawse, 8 gause, gawz, 7- gauze. [a. F. *gaze*, of uncertain origin, app. first recorded in the 16th c. Hence also Sp. *gasa*, Du. *gaas.*

In 1279 (*Concilium Budense* lxi, quoted by Du Cange) *gazzatum* is mentioned among the stuffs which monks are forbidden to wear. This is usually identified with F. *gaze*, and Du Cange conjectures that it may have been named from Gaza in Palestine, but there is no evidence for either supposition.]

1. a. A very thin, transparent fabric of silk, linen, or cotton.

1561 *Inv. R. Wardr.* (1815) 159 Mair, ane litle pece of gais of silvir and quhite silk. **1612** *Sc. Bk. Rates* in *Halyburton's Ledger* (1867) 308 Gadza of all sortis without gold or siluer the eln, xvis. Gadza stript, with gold and siluer. **1688** R. HOLME *Armoury* III. 349/1 Housewifes Cloth made of Hemp or Flax..Holland, Tiffany, Gawse. **1720** SWIFT *Song* Wks. 1755 IV. I. 29 Brocados and damasks, and tabbies, and gawses, Are by Robert Ballentine lately brought over, With forty things more. **1754** *Songs Costume* (Percy Soc.) 235 A Vandyke in frize your neck must surround. Turn your lawns into gauze, let your Brussels be blond. **1831** G. R. PORTER *Silk Manuf.* 286 The weight of silk contained in a

yard of gauze is very trifling. **1878** BROWNING *Poets Croisic* 99 Breast and back Of this vivacious beauty gleamed through gauze.
fig. **1860** EMERSON *Cond. Life, Fate* Wks. (Bohn) II. 325 All the toys that infatuate men.. are the selfsame thing, with a new gauze or two of illusion overlaid. **1881** JOWETT *Thucyd.* I. Introd. 17 The good cloth of Herodotus or Thucydides or Xenophon is patched with the transparent gauze of Diodorus and Plutarch.

b. A similar fabric made of fine wire; usually with defining word, as ***wire-gauze***.

1842 PARNELL *Chem. Anal.* (1845) 14 A wire gauze is fastened over the top. **1867** W. W. SMYTH *Coal & Coalmining* 197 A cap of perforated copper within the wire gauze. **1871** TYNDALL *Fragm. Sc.* (1879) I. v. 132 The tube contained a roll of platinum gauze.

2. *transf.* A thin transparent haze.

1842 TENNYSON *Vision Sin* ii, Purple gauzes, golden hazes.. Flung the torrent rainbow round. **1860** LD. LYTTON *Lucile* II. i. 18 Like one of those light vivid things That glide down the gauzes of summer. **1871** L. STEPHEN *Playgr. Eur.* xi. (1894) 272 To the east a blue gauze seemed to cover valley by valley. **1876** T. HARDY *Ethelberta* II. xlviii. 273 A blue gauze of smoke floated over the chimney.

3. *Comb.* **a.** simple attrib., as ***gauze blind, curtain, dress, handkerchief, merino, ribbon, silk, suit, veil, wing, wire-cloth***. **b.** objective, as ***gauze-dresser, -dyer, -manufacturer, -weaving***; ***gauze-like*** adj. **c.** Special comb.: **gauze-lamp**, a safety-lamp in which the flame is surrounded by wire-gauze; **gauze-loom** (see quot.); **gauze ring** = *crape ring* (CRAPE *sb.* 3 b); **gauze-tree** (*West Indian*), the lace-bark tree, *Lagetta lintearia*.

1838 DICKENS *Nich. Nick.* xvi, It was a shop-front, fitted up with a *gauze blind and an inner door. **1859** —— *T. Two Cities* II. ix, He let his thin *gauze curtains fall around him. **1863** MISS BRADDON *J. Marchmont* II. i. 2 How pretty and fairy-like she looked in her white *gauze dress. **1858** SIMMONDS *Dict. Trade*, **Gauze-dresser*, a stiffener of gauze. *Ibid.*, **Gauze-dyer*, one who colours gauze fabrics. **1762** STERNE *Tr. Shandy* V. i, Throwing a thin *gauze handkerchief over her head. **1780** MARY FRAMPTON *Jrnl.* (1885) 3 Gauze handkerchiefs trimmed with blonde were worn on the neck. **1877** *Daily News* 25 Oct. 3/7 He worked with a *gauze lamp, and on a lad coming down beside him with a naked lamp he left. **1798** CHARLOTTE SMITH *Young Philos.* IV. 181 She wrapt the silk and *gauze-like what d'ye call it, that the women folks wear, over her pretty face. **1897** MARY KINGSLEY *West Africa* 570 The white, gauze-like mist comes down from the upper mountain towards us. **1858** SIMMONDS *Dict. Trade*, **Gauze-loom*, a loom in which gauze is woven. *Ibid.*, **Gauze-manufacturer*, a weaver of gauze. **1871** NAPHEYS *Prev. & Cure Dis.* I. 124 *Gauze merino [cloth]. **1833** HT. MARTINEAU *Loom & Lugger* I. i. 5 Instead of flaunting in silks and *gauze ribbons. **1858** SIMMONDS *Dict. Trade*, *Gauze-ribbon*, a thin kind of ribbon worn by ladies, made of gauze. **1867** G. F. CHAMBERS *Descriptive Astron.* VII. viii. 709 As a rule the *gauze ring must not be expected to be seen with any aperture below 4 inches. **1964** D. H. MENZEL *Field Guide Stars* ix. 297 Toward the inner edge the grains again thin out, producing a partially transparent ring, the gauze, or crepe, ring. **1852** R. S. SURTEES *Sponge's Sp. Tour* (1893) 89 Glorious calves swelling within his *gauze-silk stockings. **1759** *Compl. Lett.-writer* (ed. 6) 230 A fine French *Gauze Suit. **1864** GRISEBACH *Flora W. Ind. Isl.* 784 List of Colonial names.. *Gawse tree: *Lagetta lintearia*. **1860** TYNDALL *Glac.* I. xii. 87 The current was sufficiently strong to blow away the corner of my *gauze veil. **1838** *Penny Cycl.* XI. 97/1 The essential character of *gauze-weaving is that between each cast of the shuttle a crossing of the warp threads shall ensue. **1802** PALEY *Nat. Theol.* xix. 354 We see a white, smooth, soft worm, turned into a black, hard, crustaceous beetle with *gauze wings. **1839** URE *Dict. Arts*, etc., **Gauze wire cloth*; is a textile fabric, either plain or tweelled, made of brass, iron, or copper wire, of very various degrees of fineness and openness of texture. Its chief uses are for sieves, and safety lamps.

Hence **gauze** *v. trans.*, to cover with a thin veil of mist; to cover with or as with gauze; to veil; also *intr.*, to become gauzy or misty.

1876 *Gd. Words* 687 Every lone house and tree distincter stood Than in the sunny glare that gauzed the noon. **1902** B. BAYNTON *Bush Studies* 45 The wide plain gauzed into a sea on which the hut floated lonely. **1938** E. BOWEN *Death of Heart* II. vii. 292 Thickets of hazel gauzed over the distances inside.

gauzily ('gɔːzɪlɪ), *adv.* [f. GAUZY *a.* + -LY².] In a light, delicate manner; so as to resemble gauze.

1903 *Daily Chron.* 16 May 3/6 The black chiffon.. very gauzily and daintily treated. **1934** I. W. HUTCHISON *North to Rime-Ringed Sun* vii. 64 In the placid gold water.. the clouds were gauzily mirrored. **1970** *Daily Tel.* 21 Sept. 10, I don't see myself.. drifting gauzily about like Botticelli's Primavera. I just want a dress.

gauziness ('gɔːzɪnɪs). [f. GAUZY + -NESS.] The quality of being gauzy; the appearance or effect of gauze as an article of dress. Also *fig.*

1827 *Examiner* 581/1 Less excusable faults are to be found in.. a little gauziness of epithet, and unnecessary lengthiness of description. **1873** *Daily News* 25 Aug., A lady.. with.. a general gauziness and lightness of costume.

gauzy ('gɔːzɪ), *a.* [f. GAUZE *sb.* + -Y¹.] Of the nature of, or resembling, gauze.

1796 CHARLOTTE SMITH *Marchmont* II. 245 A gauzy mist hovered over the unruffled sea. **1801** SOUTHEY *Thalaba* III. xxxiii, His out-spread sails of green; His gauzy underwings. **1850** KINGSLEY *Alt. Locke* xxxvi, One vast thistle-bed, the down of which flew in grey, gauzy clouds before a soft, fitful breeze. **1888** *Times* 2 Jan. 7/4 Here Romney has not shrunk from the problem how to paint thin gauzy stuff.
fig. **1774** *Westm. Mag.* II. 453, I have seen a powdered coxcomb of this gawzy make value himself upon his success of speech. **1815** SCOTT *Guy M.* xvii, Tales which you can only enjoy through the gauzy frippery of a French translation. **18..** FORSTER *Ess.* (L.), The whole essay, however, is of a flimsy, gauzy, texture.

gavage (gæ'vɑːʒ). [Fr.] A method of forcible feeding by the use of a force-pump and a tube passed into the stomach.

1889 *Buck's Handbk. Med. Sci.* VIII. 102/2 Dr. Turnier, of Paris, has advocated the method of gavage in infants prematurely born. **1905** OSLER *Princ. Med.* (ed. 6) 511 When there is persistent anorexia, gavage may be necessary. **1963** L. DURRELL in *Holiday* Jan. 70/1 In goose country, where the practice of force-feeding geese (*gavage*) is in operation, there are always a goodly number of casualties.

ga'vaul, *v. Sc.* Also **gava(w)ll.** *intr.* To revel, carouse. (? Only in *pr. pple.* and *vbl. sb.*)

1822 GALT *Provost* xxiii. 170 Bailie McLucre.. one night in going from a gavawlling with some of the neighbours, was overtaken by an apoplexy. **1823** —— *Entail* III. 282 Thir jocose gavaulings are worthy o' the occasion. **1887** SERVICE *Dr. Duguid* xii. 74 Dyvours.. gavalling at the laird's expense.

gavel ('gævəl), *sb.*¹ *Obs.* exc. *Hist.* Forms: 1 gæbul, geabul, gebil, gafol, gaful, gafel; *north.* gæfil, 3, 5 govel, 5 govyl(l, gowle, 2–4, 8–9 gavel. [OE. *gafol* (:—OTeut. **gabulo-*) is not found in the cognate tongues, but is a deriv. of the common Teut. root **geb-* (OE. ȝiefan GIVE). Latinized forms of the word, as *gablum, gabulum, gavelum, gaulum*, are frequent in mediæval documents in England and France, and an OF. *gaule* is recorded. From *gabulum* is derived med.L. *gabella*, F. *gabelle*, GABELLE.]

1. Payment to a superior; tribute. Only OE. and early ME.

*c***725** *Corpus Gloss.* 813 *Exactio*, geabules monung. *a***800** *Erfurt Gloss.* 394 *Exactio*, gebles monung. *c***893** K. ÆLFRED *Oros.* I. i. §17 Hyra ar is mæst on þæm gafole þe ða Finnas him ȝyldað. þæt gafol bið on deora fellum [etc.]. *c***950** *Lindisf. Gosp.* Matt. xvii. 25 Cyninges eorðo from ðæm onfoas gæfil [L. *tributum*] *vel* penning-slæht? *c***1205** LAY. 6105 þat heo to Brut-londe nolden maren senden gold ne garsume ne gauel of þon londe. *c***1250** *Gen. & Ex.* 844 He.. gouen him gouel of here lond.

b. Rent. *to set to gavel*: to let out for a certain payment. OE. and *Hist.*

*a***1121** *O.E. Chron.* an. 1100 Ealle [þa biscop rices] he oððe wið feo ȝesealde, oððe on his aȝenre hand heold and to gafle gesette. **1872** E. W. ROBERTSON *Hist. Ess.* II. 94 A rent, or gavel of a penny. **1874** STUBBS *Const. Hist.* I. vii. 193 He was easily tempted to become a socager, paying rent or gavel.

†**2.** Interest on money lent; usury. *Obs.*

*a***700** *Epinal Gloss.* 115 *Ære alieno*, gæbuli. *c***1000** *Ags. Gosp.* Matt. xxv. 27 Hyt ȝeberede þæt þu befæstest min feoh mynyterum & ic name þænne ic come þæt min ys mid þam gafole [L. *cum usura*]. *c***1200** *Vices & Virtues* (1888) 77 After ðe hali writes, ealch miede is iteld for gauele; and þe gaueleres ne cumen neure into heueriche. *a***1225** *Ancr. R.* 326 Vor sunne is þes deofles feih þet he giueð to gauel, & to okere of pine. **1340** *Ayenb.* 35 Hi wylleþ rekeny tuyes oþer þries þet yer uor to arise þet gauel.. and makeþ ofte of þe gauel principale dette. *c***1440** *Promp. Parv.* 206/2 Gowle or vsury, *usura fenus*. *c***1485** *Digby Myst.* (1882) v. 604 Of govele and symonye though he bere the name. **1496** *Dives & Paup.* (W. de W.) VII. iv. 279/2 It is called usura, gouel or usure in englysshe.

3. *attrib.* in a number of compounds, chiefly legal terms relating to payments or services exacted from tenants, as ***gavel-bread, -corn, -dung, -earth, -gild, -land, -man, -mark, -mead, -rip, -sester, -swine, -timber, -wood, -work***.

A few of these are found in OE.; others occurring in later documents were collected by Somner in his *Treatise of Gavelkind* 1660, whence some of them have passed into Blount, Phillips, and later Dicts.

?*a***1300** in Somner *Treat. Gavelkind* (1660) 25 In pane ad *Gavelbred. **1706** PHILLIPS (ed. Kersey), *Gavel-bred*, provision of Bread or Corn reserv'd as a Rent, to be paid in kind by the Tenant. *c***1300** in Somner *Treat. Gavelkind* (1660) 22 De consuetudine extrahendi fimum debita per Custumarios tenentes.. quod servitium vocatur *Gaveldung. *c***1000** *Rect. Sing. Pers.* c. 4 §2 (Schmid) His *gafol-yrþe iii. æceras eriȝe, and sawe of his aȝanum berne. *c***1300** in Somner *Treat. Gavelkind* (1660) 17 Arabit unam dimidiam acram ad semen frumenti, & seminabit, & herciabit.. et vocatur istud opus Gavelerth. **1706** PHILLIPS (ed. Kersey), *Gavelerth*, the Duty or Work of Ploughing so much Earth or Ground, done by the Tenant for his Lord. **1275** in Dugdale *Monast. Angl.* (1673) III. 155 Idem Radulphus tenet unam toftam.. et non dat *Gavelgeld. **15..** *Yorksh. Chantry Surv.* (Surtees) II. 509 To the Erle of Rutland for gavill gild ijd. **1670** BLOUNT *Law Dict.*, *Gafold-gyld*, the payment or rendring of Tribute or Custom. Also Usury. *a***1000** *Laws Ælfred & Guthr.* c. 2 (Schmid) Buton þam ceorle þe on *gafollande sit. *c***1300** in Somner *Treat. Gavelkind* (1660) 189 Tenentes de Gavellond de octodecim Jugis pro cariagio triginta et sex carectatas feni de prato de Redhamme. **1670** BLOUNT *Law Dict.*, *Gafol-land*, alias *Gaful-land* (*Terra censualis*), land liable to Tribute or Tax; rented Land, or Land letten for Rent. **1...** in Somner *Treat. Gavelkind* (1660) 33 Villani de Terring, qui vocantur *Gavelmanni. **1741** T. ROBINSON *Gavelkind* I. i. 3 The Tenant from whom these Services were due was called Gavelman. *c***1300** *Battle Abbey Custumals* (Camden) 6 Et debet claudere v virgatas haiæ quæ vocantur *gavelmerke. **900** in Thorpe *Charters* (1865) 145 Healfne æcer *gaoulmæde. **1283** in Somner *Treat. Gavelkind* (1660) 21 Consuetudo falcandi, quæ vocatur Gavelmed. **1706** PHILLIPS (ed. Kersey), *Gavel-med*, the Duty or Work of mowing grass, or cutting Meadow-Land, requir'd by the Lord from his Customary Tenant. **1...** in Somner *Treat. Gavelkind* (1660) 19 De consuetudine metendi xl. acras & dimid. de *Gavel-rip in autumno. **1706** PHILLIPS (ed. Kersey), *Gavel-rep*, the Duty of Reaping at the Command of the Lord of the Manour. **1...** in Somner *Treat. Gavelkind* (1660) 24 De *Gavelsester cujuslibet bracini braciati infra libertatem maneriorum, viz. unam lagenam & dimidium cerevisiae. **1706** PHILLIPS (ed. Kersey), *Gavel-sester*, a Measure of Rent-Ale, one of the Articles anciently charg'd on the Stewards and Bailiffs of Manours, belonging to the Church of Canterbury. **1693** *Phil. Trans.* XVII. 691 He ends this Treatise with an Enumeration of the Quit-rents formerly paid out of the Weald, as *Gavel-swine, Scot-ale, Pannage. **900** in Thorpe *Charters* (1865) 145, iiii foðera aclofenas *gauolwyda. **1...** in Somner *Treat. Gavelkind* (1660) 23 De xviijs. iijd. ob. de fine cariandi Gavelwood de consuetudine. *c***1300** *Ibid.* 24 Arabit unam acram.. & metet unam acram.. de *Gavelwerk.

gavel ('gævəl), *sb.*² *Obs.* exc. *dial.* [a. ONF. *gavel*, masc., *gavelle*, fem. (mod. dial. *gavel, gaviau*), F. *javelle*, fem. = Pg. *guavella*, Sp. *gavilla*, Pg. It. *gavela*, fem., med.L. *gavellus*, masc., *gavella*, fem.

The early OFr. sense both of the masc. and the fem. sb. is 'heap' generally; mod.Fr. has *javeau* mud, etc. left by an inundation. The etymology of Rom. *gavello, -a* is obscure.]

1. A quantity of corn cut and ready to be made into a sheaf.

*c***1440** *Promp. Parv.* 189/1 Gavel of corne, *merges*. **1555** W. WATREMAN *Fardle Facions* App. 325 He that reapeth his corne.. let him leaue some of the gauelles vngathered: that the niedie maie finde, etc. **1611** COTGR., *Javelle*, a gauell or sheafe of corne. *a***1825** FORBY *Voc. E. Anglia*, *Gavel, Gavin*, a sheaf of corn before it is tied up. **1851** THOREAU *Autumn* (1894) 61 He used the word *gavel* to describe a parcel of stalks cast on the ground to dry.

2. ***to lie on the gavel*** († ***on the gavel heap***): to lie unbound.

The meaning 'ground' given in Johnson and later Dicts. rests on a misunderstanding of quot. 1707.

*c***1611** CHAPMAN *Iliad* XXI. 328 As fields that haue bene long time cloide With catching wether; when their corne lies on the gauill heape; Are with a constant North wind dried. **1707** MORTIMER *Husb.* 97 Let it [Rye] lie upon the ground or gavel [*printed* gravel], as they call it, after it is cut 8 or 10 days. **1797** A. YOUNG *Agric. Suffolk* 74 It [coleseed] is reaped, and left on the gavel till fit to thresh. **1799** ASHBY in *Ann. Agric.* XXXII. 258 Wheat reaped and not bound lies on the gavel.

gavel ('gævəl), *sb.*³ *Pseudo-arch.* [f. the first element of GAVELKIND.] A partition of land among the whole tribe or sept at the death of the holder, with reference to Celtic practice.

1827 HALLAM *Const. Hist.* (1876) III. xviii. 345 A gavel or partition was made on the death of every member of a family for three generations, after which none could be enforced. **1886** *Fortn. Rev.* Aug. 199 In the case of the death of the chief.. or even of any one of the clansmen.. the lands of all the sept were thrown into gavel and redivided.

b. *Comb.*: **gavel-act** or **gavel-law**, a statute of Ireland (2 Anne) enforcing the principle of (English) gavelkind on Irish Catholics.

[**1795** BURKE *Tracts Popery Laws* Wks. 1842 II. 431 The first operation of those acts.. was.. to take away the right of primogeniture; and.. to substitute and establish a new species of statute gavelkind.] **1803** C. BUTLER *Let. to Rom. Cath. Gentlem.* 13 Your estates were subject to odious gavel laws. **1818** CRUISE *Digest* (ed. 2) II. 536 The gavel act; which enacted that the lands of persons of that persuasion [Catholics] should descend to all the males, according to the custom of gavelkind. **1882** LECKY *Eng. in 18th C.* IV. 476 A repeal of the Gavel act, which breaks up the landed property of Catholics by an equal distribution among the children.

gavel ('gævəl), *sb.*⁴ *U.S.* **a.** 'A mason's setting maul' (Knight *Dict. Mech.*). **b.** A president's mallet or hammer.

1860 WORCESTER cites SHEPARD. **1866** *Nation* (N.Y.) 23 Aug. 153/1 Mr. Doolittle gave two or three raps with his gavel. **1895** JEWITT & HOPE *Corporation Plate* II. 538 The Mayor's gavel or mallet is of ivory with fluted handle.

2. *attrib.*, as ***gavel-stand***.

1892 *Sp. at Chicago* in *Times* 22 June 5/3 Two needs.. indispensable to our success—namely, unity and harmony. Of the one this chair and gavel-stand are the representatives.

†'**gavel**, *v.*¹ *Obs. rare.* [f. GAVEL *sb.*¹] **a.** *trans.* To rent (land). **b.** *intr.* To lend money on interest. **c.** *passive.* (See quot. 1824.)

997 *Cod. Dipl.* (Kemble) III. 305 Ic ȝeann ðarto tweȝra hida ðe Eadric gafelað. **1382** WYCLIF *Deut.* xxviii. 44 He shal oker [*v.r.* gauyl] to thee, and thow shalt not oker to hym. **1824** MANDER *Derbysh. Miner's Gloss.* s.v. *Gavelor*, a duty must be first paid by every Miner before he can enter his pit or Mine, and then his men are said to be Gavelled; which is the Peak language for Freeing.

gavel ('gævəl), *v.*² *Obs.* exc. *dial.* [f. GAVEL *sb.*²: cf. F. *javeler*.] *trans.* (See quot. *a* 1825; the statement in quot. 1611 is perh. an error.)

*c***1440** *Promp. Parv.* 189/1 Gavelyn corne, or oþer lyke, *manipulo, mergito*. **1611** COTGR., *Iaveler*, to swathe, or gauel corn; to make it into sheaues, or gauells. **16..** *Song* in R. Bell *Collect.*, When it [the barley] is well sown See it is well mown Both raked and gavelled clean And a barn to lay it in. *a***1825** FORBY *Voc. E. Anglia*, *Gavel, Gavin*, to collect mown corn into heaps in order to its being loaded. **1856** J. GLYDE *Suffolk* 364 They are to be seen making hay, gavelling, dressing corn.

gavel ('gævəl), *v.*³ *Pseudo-arch.* [f. GAVEL *sb.*³ Cf. DISGAVEL.] *trans.* To divide or distribute (land), according to the practice of gavelkind.

1875 MAINE *Hist. Inst.* vii. 206 They 'gavelled' the lands of Papists and made them descendible to all the children alike. **1884** MISS HICKSON *Irel. 17th C.* I. Introd. 32 The

poor and ignorant Irish, long accustomed to gavel and rundale the land as their fathers had done.
fig. **1828** MOORE *Irish Melod.* Pref. 195 So artfully has the harmonist (if I may thus express it) gavelled the melody, distributing an equal portion of its sweetness to every part.

gavel ('gævəl), *v.*[4] orig. and chiefly *U.S.* [f. GAVEL *sb.*[4]] To hammer with, or as with, a gavel (GAVEL *sb.*[4] b).
1925 T. DREISER *Amer. Tragedy* (1926) II. II. xxv. 313 And at once Oberwaltzer gaveling for order and ordering the arrest of the offender. **1934** *Words* Nov. 5/2 *To gavel* and *to yes* are new, and..obviously American. **1959** *Time* 23 Feb. 20/1 'The faces will be different,' said Arkansas' John McClellan as he gaveled his Senate labor-racketeering committee into session. **1966** D. F. GALOUYE *Lost Perception* v. 53 Radcliff strode..onstage, the determined *thuds* of his heels gavelling order among the assembly.

gavel, var. CAVEL *sb.*[1] (sense 3).
1827 J. HODGSON *Northumbld.* II. I. 188 *note*, Each proprietor's portion [of the town-fields] being made up of numerous gavels, ridges, and buts scattered and intermixed in a very inconvenient way.

gavel, north. var. GABLE.

†**gavelage.** *Obs. rare.* Also 5 **gaffelage.** [f. GAVEL *sb.*[1] + -AGE: cf. OF. *gabellage, gablage*, med.L. *gablagium.*] Rent, or other periodical payment.
c **1450** *Surtees Misc.* (1888) 63 Every Burgesse sshall gyff to ye Lord one tyme in y^e ȝere, a farme for hys tenement, the qwyche is called the gaffelage. **1697** A. DE LA PRYME *Diary* (Surtees) 126 The cryer crys thus..Whay! whay! whay! Pay your gavelage, ha! Between this and Michaelmas day, Or you'll be fined, I say..This is the true origin of the proverb [Scarburg Warning] for this custome of gavelage is a certain tribute that every house pays to the [*a word illegible*] when he is pleased to call for it, and he gives not above one day warning, and may call for it when he pleases.

gaveler(e, obs. form of GAVELLER.

†**gavelet.** *Law. Obs.* [f. GAVEL *sb.*[1]
The second element is obscure: perh. the word arose from some phrase in which OE. *gafol* occurred with *lǣtan* to LET, neglect.]
A legal process against a tenant for non-payment of rent; chiefly relating to lands held in gavelkind (see quots.).
1... in Somner *Treat. Gavelkind* (1660) 31 Et postea per quandam consuetudinem, quæ vocatur Gavelate, usitatam in comitatu isto de terris & tenementis de Gavelkinde, pro redditibus & servitiis quæ a retro fuerint de eisdem per plures annos devenerunt eædem terrae in manus cujusdam Abbatis, &c. ?**1317** *Act* [? *10 Edw. II*] in *Stat. Realm* (1810) I. 222 (*Statutum de Gaveleto in London*) Tunc ipsi tenentes inplacitentur de Gaveleto. **1419** in *Liber Albus* (Rolls) III. 186 De Gavellet. Item, en brief de Gaivelett les tenauntz averount troys somons et troys essones. **1607** COWELL *Interpr.*, *Gavelet* is a speciall and auncient kinde of Cessauit vsed in Kent, where the custome of Gavill kind continueth: whereby the tenent shall forfeit his lands and tenements to the Lorde of whome he holdeth, if he withdraw from him his due rents and seruices. **1741** T. ROBINSON *Gavelkind* II. vi. 253 Framed the Statute of Gavelet for Rents arrear in London. *Ibid.* Custum. Kent 292 If his escheate be by Gavelate.

gavelkind ('gævəlkaɪnd). *Law.* Forms: 3 gavelikind, -kende, gaulikend, gavelkend, 4-5 gavelkynde, 6-7 gavellkind, gavelkinde, 6- gavelkind. [The 13th c. form *gavel(i)kende* (latinized *-kenda*) seems to point to an OE. **gafolȝecynd*, sb. neut. (the *e* for *y* being a mark of Kentish dialect), f. *gafol* GAVEL *sb.*[1] + *ȝecynd* nature, species, KIND.
When the meaning of the word came to be misunderstood (see 2), attempts were made to assign to it an etymology expressive of the custom of equal division of a deceased person's land among his male children; favourite explanations in the 16th c. were 'give al kinde' (Rastell 1557), and 'give all kyn' (Lambarde 1576); sometimes the word was written in pseudo-etymological fashion as *gavealkin, gaveall-kind*. The application of the Kentish term to the Welsh and Irish system of succession led to the notion that the word was of Celtic origin: a Welsh derivation from *gafael* to take, and *cenedl* race, family, was proposed in the 16-17th c.; an alleged Irish *gabháil-cine* (from *gabháil* to take, taking, and *cine* tribe, sept) appears with the rendering 'gavelkind' in O'Reilly's Irish Dictionary.]
1. The name of a land-tenure existing chiefly in Kent.
The name implies that it was originally a tenure by 'gavel', i.e. by the payment of rent or fixed services other than military; by this agrees with the indentification of it with SOCAGE (quot. 1253). After the Conquest, the Kentish form of socage was distinguished by certain customs elsewhere generally disused (cf. quot. 1702). Of these the most conspicuous was the custom by which a tenant's land at his death was divided equally among his sons; hence, even in early times, 'gavelkind' and 'partible land' are used as equivalent terms.
1205 *Rotuli Chartarum* 160/1 In gavelikind. **1241** in Somner *Treat. Gavelkind* (1660) 179 Burga dicit quod prædictum manerium est Gauelkinde et partibile, et prior dicit quod prædictum manerium non est Gaulikend, neque partibile. **1253** *Close Roll 37 Hen. III* in C. J. Elton *Tenures Kent* (1867) 49 Terræ quæ tenentur in socagio vel gavelikende. ?**1324** *Prerogativa Regis* in *Stat. Realm* (1810) I. 227 Et in Kancia in Gavelkynde..ibidem omnes hæredes masculi participant hæreditatem; similiter omnes femine; set femine non participant cum masculis. **1495** *Act 11 Hen. VII*, c. 49 The Lordshippes..[shall] in no wise be of the nature of Gavelkynde ne departed ne departable amonges heires males. **1599** NASHE *Lent. Stuffe* Wks. (Grosart) V. 221 When hee firmed and rubrickt the Kentishmens gauill kinde of the sonne to inherite at fifteene. **1702** E. CHAMBERLAYNE *St. Gt. Brit.* I. I. iii. (1707) 19 The privileges of gavel-kind belonging to this Country [Kent] are threefold: 1. The Heirs Male share all the Lands alike. 2. The Heir is at 15 at full Age to sell or alienate. 3. Tho' the Father were convicted of Treason..yet the Son enjoys his Inheritance. **1703** *Stat. Ireland* 2 Anne c. 6 §10 That all lands..whereof any papist now is or hereafter shall be seized in fee-simple or fee-tail shall be of the nature of gavelkind [i.e. shall descend to all his sons equally]. **1846** MCCULLOCH *Acc. Brit. Empire* (1854) I. 199 All lands in Kent, unless specially exempted by an act of the legislature, are held by the tenure of gavelkind; descending, in the event of the father dying intestate, not to the eldest son, but to all sons alike in equal portions; and, if there be no sons, then they divide equally among the daughters.
2. From the 16th c., often used to denote the custom of dividing a deceased man's property equally among his sons, whether as an incident of the Kentish tenure or otherwise.
1531 *Dial. on Laws Eng.* I. x. (1638) 21 There is a custome in Kent that is called Gavelkind, that all the brethren shall inherit together, as sisters at the Common Law. **1577** HARRISON *England* II. ix. (1877) I. 202 *Gauellkind*, which is all the male children equallie to inherit, and continued to this daie in Kent. **1754-61** HUME *Hist. Eng.* I. App. i. 104 In the Saxon times, land was divided equally among all the male children of the deceased, according to the custom of Gavelkind. **1874** GREEN *Short Hist.* v. §4. 240 The law of gavel-kind..divided the inheritance of the tenantry equally among their sons.
fig. **1627** DONNE *Serm.* clvii. VI. 268 For God shall impart to us all a mysterious Gavel-kind, a mysterious Equality of fulness of Glory to us all. *a* **1639** T. CAREW *Poems* Wks. (1824) 80 But if thou bind By citie custome, or by Gavell-kind, In equal shares thy love on all thy race. *a* **1661** FULLER *Worthies* I. (1662) 2 Every County hath a Child's portion, as if God in some sort observed Gavel-kind, in the distribution of his fauours. **1838-9** HALLAM *Hist. Lit.* III. III. v. §7. 230 Their parental love forbids all preference, and an impartial law of gavelkind shares their page among all the offspring of their brain. **1869** LOWELL *Cond. in Foreigners* Pr. Wks. 1890 III. 223 All that is worth having in them is the common property of the soul,—an estate in gavelkind for all the sons of Adam. **1894** *N. & Q.* 24 Feb. 146/2 It would be hard to find another family in whom a literary taste has descended in gavelkind to such a degree.
3. *transf.* **a.** A Welsh custom of dividing property, similar to the Kentish practice.
The *Statutum Walliæ*, 12 Edw. I. c. 13 recounts that the Welsh custom of inheritance differs from the English, 'eo quod hereditas partibilis est inter heredes masculos'; the statute sanctions this custom, but provides that bastard sons shall no longer be entitled to share with those born in wedlock.
1542-3 *Act 34 & 35 Hen. VIII*, c. 36 That all manoures, landes..and other hereditamentes..in any of the said Shyres of Wales..be..holden as English Tenure..and not to be partable among heyres males after the custome of Gavel-kinde as heretofore in divers parties of Wales hath been used. **1584** POWEL *Lloyd's Cambria* 21 The diuision of the fathers inheritance amongst all the Sonnes, commonlie called Gauel kinde. Gauel is a Brytishe tearme, signifieng a hold. **1612** DAVIES *Why Ireland*, etc. 130 King Henrie the eight..among other Welsh Customes, abolished that of Gauel-kinde: whereby the Heyres-Females were vtterlie excluded, and the Bastards did inherit, as well as the Legitimate, which is the very Irish Gauelkinde. **1638** SIR T. HERBERT *Trav.* 357 The Annalls of those times..tell us That so soone as Owen..was dead; the custome of Gavel-kind..became a Subject of implacable hate amongst his sonnes. **1863** *Cambrian Jrnl.* 155 His family may have fallen by the usual custom of gavel-kind from its former respectability.
b. ***Irish gavelkind***: a system of tribal succession, by which land, on the decease of its occupant, was thrown into the common stock, and the whole area redivided among the members of the sept.
1612 DAVIES *Why Ireland*, etc. 166 By the Irish Custome of Gauellkinde the inferiour Tennanties were partible amongst all the Males of the Sept, both Bastards and Legittimate. **1827** HALLAM *Const. Hist.* (1876) III. xviii. 344 They held their estates by a very different and an extraordinary tenure, that of Irish gavel-kind. **1868** ROGERS *Pol. Econ.* xiii. (1876) 176 Tanistry and Irish gavelkind, as the system of electing the worthiest to the headship of the clan and re-dividing the estate among all the males of the sept on certain occasions were called, were..formerly recognised by the English law. **1875** MAINE *Hist. Inst.* vii. 185 The peculiar Irish custom called Gavelkind.
4. *attrib.*
1570-6 LAMBARDE *Peramb. Kent* (1826) 491 In this Inquisition some lands are denoted to be of Gavelkinde nature, which neverthelesse doe yeelde none other but money alone. *a* **1617** HIERON *Wks.* II. 10 We shall find poperie..to admit..as it were a gauel-kind custome, and to allow sharers with God in the things wherein He will endure no partners. **1624** in Rushw. *Hist. Coll.* (1659) I. 150 An Act for altering of Gavel-kind-Lands. *a* **1626** BACON *Max. & Uses Com. Law* (1636) 40 The custome of Kent is, that Gavelkind land is not forfeitable nor escheatable for felony. **1701** C. WOLLEY *Jrnl. N. York* (1860) 57 Henry..who abolished and repealed the Gavelkind custom whereby the Lands of the Father were equally divided among all the Sons. **1766** BLACKSTONE *Comm.* II. vi. 85 The gavelkind tenures holden of the fee of Canterbury. **1817** W. SELWYN *Law Nisi Prius* (ed. 4) II. 717 Declaration was for a moiety of land of gavelkind tenure, in Kent.
Hence **gavelkinder**, one who holds lands in gavelkind. *rare*$^{-1}$.
1570-6 LAMBARDE *Peramb. Kent* (1826) 491 The very Customall of Gavelkinde it selfe useth never a woord of Socage tenure, but of Gavelkynders.

gaveller ('gævɪlə(r)). Forms: 3-4 **gaveler, gouler,** 4 **gavelere,** 5 **govelere, gowlare,** 8-9 **gaveller.** [f. GAVEL *sb.*[1] + -ER[1].]
†**1.** A usurer. *Obs.*
c **1200** *Vices & Virtues* (1888) 77 Fullȝewiss hie bieð idemd for gouleres, and al swulch lean hie sculen ðarof habben alse gaueleres, ðat is, helle pine. *c* **1275** *XI Pains Hell* 130 in *O.E. Misc.* 150 Such is heore pyne þer Vor heo weren gauelers her. *a* **1300** *E.E. Psalter* cviii. 11 [cix. 10] (Horstm.) Ransake mote gaueler [L. *fenerator*] his aghte. **1340** *Ayenb.* 35 Þise byeþ gaueleres kueade and uoule. *c* **1440** *Jacob's Well* (E.E.T.S.) 124 A gouelere doth aȝens þe old lawe. *c* **1440** *Promp. Parv.* 206 *Gowlare*, or vserere, *usurarius.*
2. *Mining.* In the Forest of Dean: An officer of the Crown who grants 'gales' to the miners.
c **1692** PARSONS in Nicholls *Forest Dean* (1858) 56 The head Gaviler of the Forest. **1702** *Lond. Gaz.* No. 3810/5 We Your Majesties Gaveller, and Miners of the Forest of *Deane* in the County of *Glocester.* **1824** MANDER *Derbysh. Miner's Gloss.*, *Gavelor* or *Gaverler* or *Gafler*..an officer among the Miners, in the Forest of Dean. **1884** *Law Times* 31 May 78/2 A freeminer made an application to the gaveller for a grant to him of one of the two gales, on the ground that M. had forfeited them..by non-working. **1885** *Pall Mall G.* 26 June 3/2 A 'gaveller' has been appealed to..He is an officer whose functions arise out of the Royal forest.
3. *Hist.* One who pays 'gavel' for land rented.
1862 E. W. ROBERTSON *Scotl.*, etc. II. 270 Except in the case of the Gavellers of East Kent, military tenure seems to have prevailed with hardly any exception. **1872** —— *Hist. Ess.* Introd. 54 He made them..Gavellers.

†'**gavelling,** *vbl. sb. Obs. rare.* [f. GAVEL *v.*[1] + -ING[1].] Usury.
c **1250** *Kent. Serm.* in *O.E. Misc.* 31 Si lepre betokned þo grete sennen þet biedh diadliche, ase so is lecherie, spusbreche, gauelinge. **1340** *Ayenb.* 34 Of þe rote of auarice guoþ out manye smale roten..þet byeþ wel greate dyadliche zennes..þe uerste is gauelinge.

gavelock ('gævələk). *Obs.* exc. *Hist.* and *dial.* Forms: 1 **gafeluc, gaveluc,** 2-4 **gaveloc,** 4-6 **gavelok (gaw-),** 5 **gavilok, gavylok,** 6 **gaiflok,** 6-7 **gavelocke,** 9 **gav'loc(k), gowelock,** *dial.* **geavelock (-lick),** 4, 7- **gavelock.** [OE. *gafeluc* str. masc. has the form of a regular dim. of *gafel*, *ȝeafel* fork (see GABLE *sb.*); the senses, however, are somewhat difficult to account for on this view of the etymology: evidence is lacking for the supposition that the word originally meant a *forked* or barbed arrow (cf. FORK *sb.* 9) and a *forked* crowbar.
Words of closely similar form and meaning are ON. *gaflak, gaflok* neut. javelin (perh. adopted from Eng.), Welsh *gaflach* (said to mean 'bearded arrow'), Irish *gabhla* lance, ONF. *gavelot* (12th c.), *gaverlot, gavrelot, garlot* (= Central F. *javelot*, It. *giavelotto*) javelin, whence MDu. *gavelot, gaverloot*, MHG. *gabilôt*; see also GAFF *sb.*[1] The relation between the words is uncertain. Thurneysen, followed by most recent etymologists, regards the Romanic word as of Celtic origin; the OE. word may possibly be adopted from the OF. (though recorded earlier) or from its source.]
1. A spear for throwing; a dart, javelin.
c **1000** ÆLFRIC *Gloss.* in Wr.-Wülcker 143/6 *Hastilia*, gafelucas. *c* **1050** in Napier *O.E. Glosses* I. 4238 *Catapultas*, gauelucas. **1183** *Jocelin de Brakelonda* (Camden) 35 Baculum meum excussi ad modum teli quod vocatur *gaveloc.* *a* **1259** MATTH. PARIS an. 1256 (Rolls) V. 550 Frisones igitur..ipsum Willelmum cum jaculis, quae vulgariter gavelocos appellant, quorum maxime noticiam habent et usum..hostiliter insequebantur. *a* **1300** *E.E. Psalter* liv. 22 [lv. 21] (Horstm.) Nesched als oyle his saghs bene, And þai ere gauelokes [L. *jacula*] þam bitwene. *c* **1330** R. BRUNNE *Chron.* (1810) 297 Þe Waleis partie had vmbilaid þe brigge. With gauelokes and dartes suilk ore was non sene. *c* **1400** *Sowdone Bab.* 1426 Thai hurte him foule and slough his hors With gauylokes and wyth dartis. *c* **1450** *Merlin* 300, I saugh hem launche at hym knyves and gavelokkes and dartes. *a* **1650** *Merlin* 2138 in Furniv. *Percy Folio* I. 489 [He] bare a gauelocke in his hand. **1817** J. F. PENNIE *Royal Minstr.* v. 390 Two hundred spearmen, bearing each His gav'loc crown'd with a stern warrior's head.
†**2.** An artificial spur for a fighting cock. *Obs.* (Cf. GABLOCK 1, GAFF 3 a, GAFFLE 3, GAFFLET.)
1698 FRYER *Acc. E. India & P.* 175 Cocks as big as Turkies: which they Arm with Razors tied flat under the Claws, and faulched Two Inches, instead of Gavelocks.
3. An iron crowbar or lever. (Cf. GABLOCK 2.)
1497 in *Ld. Treas. Acc. Scotl.* (1877) I. 349 Item, giffin for xiij stane of irne, to mak grath to Mons new cradill, and gavilokkis to ga with hir. **1558** *Lanc. Wills* III. 80, viij. mylne pycke ij axes one gavelocke of iron. *c* **1632** in Brand *Hist. Newcastle* (1789) I. 370 *note*, One iron gavelock, and one swea tree with two rolles for taking and laying down lairstones. **1681** H. MORE *Exp. Dan.* i. 6 Thou sawest moreover a Stone cut out without hands, no man with Axe or Gavelock dissevering it. **1804** R. ANDERSON *Cumberld. Ball., Jeff & Job* ii, Nin leyke thee cud fling the geavelick. **1839** URE *Dict. Arts* 758 The greater part of the matters contained in the [lead] furnace is drawn over on the work-stone, by means of a large rake called a gowelock. **1855** ROBINSON *Whitby Gloss.*, *Geavelock*, a large iron crowbar for raising stone. **1880** *Antiquary* Apr. 187 On trying the ground on the north side of the fence with a gavelock, they came on the cover of a cist.

†'**gavelot.** *Obs. rare.* [a. OF. *gavelot*, F. *javelot*: see prec.] A javelin or casting-spear.
14.. *Voc.* in Wr.-Wülcker 596/23 *Missile*, a shafte and a shetel and a gauelot. **1674** BLOUNT *Glossogr.* (ed. 4) [Wrongly explained as 'a warlike Engine to shoot stones or darts; a great sling'. So **1726** in KERSEY].

'**gaverick.** *local* (*Cornwall*). The Red Gurnard.
1846 COUCH in *Zoologist* IV. 1402. (In recent Dicts.)

gavial ('geɪvɪəl). *Zool.* Also in more correct forms, **gar(rh)ial, gharrial, ghur(r)ial, ghuryal.** [a. F. *gavial* (recorded 1789) corruptly ad. Hindustani *ghaṛiyāl*.] A saurian inhabiting the Ganges, distinguished by its elongated muzzle from the American alligator and the African crocodile.

1825 HAMILTON *Handbk., Gavial.* **1830** LYELL *Princ. Geol.* I. 243 The Gangetic crocodile, or Gavial (in correct orthography, Garial) is confined to the fresh water. **1835** BURNES *Trav. Bokhara* (ed. 2) I. 115 The large alligator is unknown here; but the long-nosed animal called 'ghuryal' abounds. **1850** H. MILLER *Footpr. Creat.* xv. (1874) 284 There are fierce contests in their native jungles, on the banks of the Ganges, between the gavial and the tiger. **1854** OWEN *Skel. & Teeth* in *Circ. Sc., Org. Nat.* I. 98/1 The Gangetic crocodile, called 'garrhial' by the Hindoos. **1864** —— *Lect. Power of God* 40 Gharrials are confined to India; alligators are limited to America. **1878** P. ROBINSON *In my Indian Garden* 83 The ghurial is of a finer breed. **1905** *Kynoch Jrnl.* July-Sept. 152 On the sandbars Ghurrials in thousands basked in the sun. **1923** *Chambers's Jrnl.* Dec. 811/1, I had constant opportunity of seeing and observing the habits of the gharial. **1930** *Times Educ. Suppl.* 29 Nov. p. iv/3 The Zoo has received five young Eastern gharials from Borneo.

Hence **'gavialid**, a crocodile belonging to the same family as the gavial.

1889 in *Century Dict.*

gavotte (gə'vɒt). Also 7-8 **gavote**, 8-9 **gavot(t.** [a. F. *gavotte* (in Cotgr. *gavote*), ad. mod.Pr. *gavoto*, dance of the Gavots, a name given in Provence to the natives of the Alps.] **a.** A kind of dance, resembling the minuet, but requiring a more lively movement. **b.** The music used to accompany this dance; a piece of music in common time, moderately quick, and consisting of two parts, each of which is repeated; frequently forming one of the movements of the Suite.

1696 tr. *Du Mont's Voy. Levant* 284 The Greek Dances are..a sort of Country Dance..and.. a kind of Gavote or Branle, in which the Men and Women are mingl'd. **1727** POPE, etc. *Martin. Scriblerus* xii. (1741) 46 With the several modifications of this tune-playing quality in playing of Preludes, Sarabands, Jigs, and Gavotts. **1776** SIR J. HAWKINS *Hist. Mus.* IV. III. i. 389 The Gavot..is hardly to be traced further backwards than..about the year 1670. **1876** OUIDA *Winter City* iii. 65, I am certain he went to sleep one night after a gavotte with Montespan, and has just awakened. **1879** *Grove's Dict. Music* I. 586/1 The gavotte should always begin on the third beat of the bar, each part finishing, therefore, with a half-bar.

attrib. **1774** BURNEY *Hist. Mus.* (1789) I. vi. 82 It must not be imagined that in our simple airs of the gavot and minuet kind we have no musical rhythm.

Hence **ga'votte** *v.*, to dance a gavotte. *rare*$^{-1}$.

1819 H. BUSK *Vestriad* III. 62 In rusty gown gavotting at a ball.

‖**gavroche** (gavrɔʃ). [Fr., f. the name of a gamin in Victor Hugo's *Les Misérables*.] A street urchin or gamin, esp. in Paris.

1876 *Times* 2 Nov. 4/4 A Norwegian *gavroche* is balancing himself by a miracle of adroitness on the dorsal extremities of the slender shafts. **1882** *Pall Mall Gaz.* 8 Dec. 4/1 'Mosieu'..is..pronounced as 'm'sieu' in 1882, or, if one wishes to talk as a real *gavroche*, 'm'seu'. **1921** *Blackw. Mag.* Feb. 251/1 Beneath the demure exterior the Parisian *gavroche* lurked. **1964** *Guardian* 16 June 9/2 Paris..adopted her as a gavroche of the theatrical boulevards.

gaw (gɔː), *sb.*[1] *Sc.* [Of uncertain origin: perh. identical with *gaw* Sc. form of GALL *sb.*[2]; but the sense is not easy to account for on this supposition.] (See quots. 1793 and 1812.) Also *attrib.* in **gaw-cut** (whence **-*cutting***), **-fur** (= *furrow*): see quots.

1793 SIR J. SINCLAIR *Stat. Acc. Scotl.* IX. 352 *note*, Gaw is that slit or opening made by a plough or spade in the side of a pond, loch, or stagnated water, by which it is drained off. **1805** R. SOMERVILLE *Agr. Surv. E. Loth.* 172 As soon as a field is sown and harrowed, the gaw-furs, as they are provincially called, are neatly and perfectly cleaned with the spade and shovel. **1812** J. WILSON *Agric. Renfrewsh.* 130 Open drains, called sloped gaws. **1844** H. STEPHENS *Bk. of Farm* I. §779 In every variety of soil ploughed..for winter, care should be taken to have plenty of channels or gaws or grips, as they are usually termed, so as the surface water may find them at every point by which to escape..The precaution of gaw-cutting should never be neglected. *Ibid.* §854 The gaw-cuts, small channels cut with the spade, are carefully made through every natural hollow of the ground. **1888** *Sheffield Gloss., Gaw cut.*

gaw (gɔː), *sb.*[2] *rare*$^{-1}$. ? Short for GEWGAW.

1822 T. MITCHELL *Aristoph., Wasps* II. ii, Like this, with his hair Curling tier above tier, With his gauds and his gaws Do despite to the laws.

†**gaw**, *v. Obs.* Forms: 3 **gawen, gowen,** 5 **gou,** 6 **gawe.** [cf. ON. *gá* to heed.] *intr.* To gape, stare; to look intently.

c **1200** ORMIN 12233 And doþ itt [*sc.* hoarded money] te nan oþerr god Butan þatt tatt tu gowesst þæronne þa þu gast tærto. *c* **1300** *Seyn Julian* 125 Ne make þou namo men gawen on me! *c* **1420** *Anturs of Arth.* x. (Irel. MS.) The bryddus in the boes, That of [*other texts* on] the gost gous [*Thornton MS.* gewes, *riming with* bewes, clewes; *Douce MS.* glowes] Thay scryken. **1566** DRANT *Horace's Sat.* I. i. Ajb, Who gapes, who gawes, who pores, who pries, who proggs his mate but he? **1808–25** JAMIESON s.v., *To gawe*, to go about staring in a stupid manner. *Teviotd.*

gaw, Sc. var. GALL *sb.*[1], *sb.*[2], *v.*[1]

gawbardyne, -berdyne, obs. ff. GABERDINE.

†'**gawberd.** *Obs.* Also **-bert, -barte.** [Of obscure origin; the first element is perh. = OE. *gealȝ-* gallows, as in GALLOW(S-BALK. The word seems to have been confused inextricably with COBBARD.] (See quot. 1847-78.)

1483 *Cath. Angl.* 151/2 A Gawbert, *ipepurgium.* **1520** *Lanc. Wills* II. 10 All my iron broches gawbarte. **1591** GARRARD *Art Warre* 14 Or that for rost meat he makes a spit, wodden Gawberds [etc.]. **1847–78** HALLIWELL, *Gauberts*, iron racks for chimneys.

gawblimey, -blimy, varr. GORBLIMEY.

gawcie, -cy, vars. GAWSY *a.*

Gawd (gɔːd). Also **gaw, gawd.** Vulgar or slang pronunciation of GOD *sb.* So **Gawd-forbid** = *God-forbid* (GOD *sb.* 8 d); **Gawd-help-us, Gawdelpus**, a helpless or exasperating person.

1877 G. MEREDITH *Let.* 24 Nov. (1970) I. 553 Your Black Christian..appears to have been blest by *Gawd* recently. **1892** I. ZANGWILL *Childr. Ghetto* I. x. 223 'Is your Daniel in?' 'Yes.' 'Tank Gawd! I mean, can I see him?' **1896** A. MORRISON *Child of Jago* xxviii. 272 Run, for Gawd's sake, or the woman'll croak! **1908** H. G. WELLS *War in Air* iv. 115 'Gaw!' said Bert. 'We're going up!' **1911** L. STONE *Jonah* I. ix. 104 Gawd, 'e's stiffened 'im! **1912** A. N. LYONS *Clara* xv. 162 Look at all the Gawdelpuses ya see on the trams—cow-spirited, cocoa-faced makeshifts. **1928** 'SAPPER' *Female of Species* v. 76 'A lounge lizard. A ball-room snake. What matter that his Black Bottom is the best in London.' 'My Gawd! sir,' gasped the other. 'His 'ow much?' **1931** WODEHOUSE *If I were You* ix. 98 He had always been an ugly sort of Gawd-help-us. **1936** J. CURTIS *Gilt Kid* vii. 73 Why don't you take off your gawd-forbid? We're passing the Cenotaph. **1937** PARTRIDGE *Dict. Slang* 319/1 *Gawd forbid*, a variant of *God forbid* [= kid]. **1955** M. ALLINGHAM *Beckoning Lady* xiv. 204 You take 'Er Ladyship and the Gawd-ferbid to the party. **1961** WODEHOUSE *Ice in Bedroom* iii. 25 A potbellied baggy-trousered Gawd-help-us. **1967** L. WHITE *Crimshaw Memo.* (1968) v. 93 Gawd knows I got enough problems.

gawd, gawd-: see GAUD, GAUD-.

gawelok, obs. form of GAVELOCK.

gawf (gɔːf), *sb. Sc.* Forms: 6 **gawf(e, gaufe,** 7 **gaff.** [Onomatopœic.] A loud noisy laugh; only in phrase ***to give a gawf.*** Also ***gawf (of) laughter.***

1500–20 DUNBAR *Poems* lxxv. 22 'Tehe', quod scho, and gaif ane gaufe [*v.r.* gawf]. *a* **1572** KNOX *Hist. Ref.* Wks. 1848 II. 67 Sche gaif ane gawfe of lauchter, and said, 'Now will I go'. *Ibid.* 404 Sche first smyleit, and efter gaif ane gawf lauchter. **1678** SINCLAIR *Satan's Invis. World* 88 The Devil gave a great gaff of laughter.

gawf (gɔːf), *v. Sc.* Also **gaff, gauf.** [Connected with prec.] *intr.* To laugh noisily.

1719 RAMSAY *Ep. to Hamilton* III. 77 Gaffin they wi' sides sae sair [etc.]. **1721** —— *Elegy on Patie Birnie* 2 The famous fidler of Kinghorn, Who gart the lieges gawff and girn ay.

gawge, gawg-: see GAUGE, GAUG-.

gawin, Sc. f. GAIN *sb.*[1] *Obs.*

†'**gawish**, *a. Obs.* [? GAW *v.* + -ISH. In all the examples, conceivably a misprint for *gawrish, garish*; but the occurrence of GAW *v.* in Drant confirms the reading in the first quot.] Staring, gaping; showy, gaudy.

1567 DRANT *Horace's Ep.* II. i. G vj, A gawishe sort gredie to gase Not gredie to be tawght. **1567** J. SANFORD tr. *Epictetus* 11 a, What is our life? a gawish game, a sweete delighting play. **1589** L. WRIGHT *Displ. Dutie* 41 Your attyre..not gawish, but godly: as beseemeth Christianitie. **1603** H. CROSSE *Vertues Commw.* (1878) 74 The minde is set vpon fashions, fangles, and gawish cloathes, now one, and then another. **1616** T. ADAMS *Diseases of Soul* xvii. 65 A gawish Traueller that came to Sparta, who standing in the presence of Lacon a long time vpon one leg, that he might be obserued & admired, cryed at the last, 'O Lacon, thou' [etc.].

gawk (gɔːk), *sb.* [perh. f. next; but see GAWK *v.*] An awkward person; a fool; a simpleton.

Johnson, followed by later lexicographers, confounds this with GOWK, cuckoo, simpleton.

1837 HT. MARTINEAU *Soc. Amer.* I. 299 They [his sons] proved 'such gawks' that they were unable to learn. **1850** MRS. CARLYLE *Lett.* (1883) II. 114 That barenecked hooing gawk Stewart. **1894** HALL CAINE *Manxman* 10 The girl was by common judgment and report a gawk.

gawk (gɔːk), *a.* Also **gauk.** [Of difficult etymology; app. a contraction of a disyllabic word which appears in many north-Eng. dialects as *gaulick-, galloc-, gaulish- (hand, handed)*: see Ray *N.C. Words* 1674–91 (E.D.S.), Thoresby *Let. to Ray* 1703 (E.D.S.), and the Whitby and Mid-Yorks. glossaries.

The natural assumption that the word represents an adoption of a prehistoric form of F. *gauche* has grave difficulties: it is not certain that the etymon of the Fr. word had an *l* at all (see Hatz.-Darm., where it is assumed that the word has lost a nasal); and even on the common view that *gauche* represents an OLow Frankish **walki*, it would be expected that an Eng. adoption old enough to retain the *l* would have *w* as the initial.]

Left. Also in *Comb.*, as *gawk-handed.*

1703 THORESBY *Let. to Ray* (E.D.S.) *Gawk hand, Gallock hand*, [the] left hand. **1855** ROBINSON *Whitby Gloss., Gauk-handed*, left-handed. **1876** *Mid-Yorksh. Gloss., Gawk-hand*, the left hand.

gawk (gɔːk), *v. colloq.*, orig. *U.S.* or *dial.* Also **gauk.** [perh. f. the sb.; possibly, on the other hand, an iterative f. GAW *v.* (with suffix as in *tal-k, wal-k, lur-k*), in which case it may be the source of the sb.] *intr.* To stare or gape stupidly.

1785 M. CUTLER in *Life, Jrnls. & Corr.* (1888) II. 227 We ..do little else than sit in the chimney-corner, repeating over the same dull stories, or gawking at one another with sorry grimace. **1862** MRS. STODDARD *Morgesons* xiii. (1889) 68 The whole table stared as we seated ourselves..'How they gawk at you', whispered Temperance. *a* **1866** KEBLE in Sir J. Coleridge *Mem. K.* (1869) 111 Making one ashamed of going gawking as one is wont to do about the world. **1869** *Lonsdale Gloss., Gauk*, to stare vacantly. **1883** *Harper's Mag.* Sept. 528/1 I'd like t' know what you'd say if I went down thar and gawked around like you do up yere. **1890** *Gloucestersh. Gloss., Gawk*, to loiter and gape about. **1905** *Westm. Gaz.* 30 Mar. 8/1 Many of the audience turned round to 'gawk'—as he phrased it—at a poor fainting girl. **1959** 'M. AINSWORTH' *Murder is Catching* vii. 82 Everyone will come and gawk. **1965** C. D. EBY *Siege of Alcázar* (1966) ii. 58 Gawking in wonder at the falling bombs.

Hence **'gawking** *ppl. a.*

1892 STEVENSON & L. OSBOURNE *Wrecker* (ed. 2) 237 Unmindful of the gawking creatures that struggled and died among their feet.

gawkily ('gɔːkɪlɪ), *adv.* [f. GAWKY *a.* + -LY[2].] In a gawky or ungainly manner; like a gawk.

1812 L. M. HAWKINS *C'tess & Gertrude* IV. 39 'I suppose you read a great deal then,' said Lady Elma gawkily. **1928** *Daily Express* 13 Feb. 3 He is tall and almost gawkily built. **1928** *Oxf. Poetry* 38 These boughs..stretch gawkily above the cross-roads. **1944** W. S. MAUGHAM *Razor's Edge* iv. 153 She held herself gawkily as though she didn't know how to cope with the length of her limbs.

gawkish ('gɔːkɪʃ), *a.* [f. GAWK *sb.* + -ISH.] Like a 'gawk', awkward, clownish.

1876 *White Cross & Dove of Pearls* xlviii. 312 Some of the young women in these parts were quaint, gawkish, and from very shyness, awkward.

gawky ('gɔːkɪ), *a.* and *sb.* [f. GAWK *sb.* (? or *v.*) + -Y[1].]

A. *adj.*

1. Of persons: Awkward and stupid; ungainly.

1759 J. TOWNLEY *High Life below Stairs* I. i, Under the Form of a gawky Country Boy I will be an Eye-witness of my Servants Behaviour. **1786** BURNS *Ep. to M'Adam* ii, Now deil-ma-care about their jaw, The senseless, gawky million. **1806–7** J. BERESFORD *Miseries Hum. Life* (1826) XI. Sigh 15 A stupid gawky boy of about 14. **1860** THACKERAY *Lovel* ii, I should like to know who that great tall gawky.. girl in the passage is. **1862** MISS BRADDON *Lady Audley* iii, Her cousin looked round in gawky embarrassment.

2. *transf.* of things.

1821 GALT *Ayrsh. Legatees* x. 288 As for the town of Brighton, it's what I would call a gawky piece of London. **1832** L. HUNT *Sir R. Esher* (1850) 133 Never heard I in my life such an infernal noise as our great gawky ship made. **1843** LD. SHAFTESB. in *Life* xi. (1887) 263 The little church ..choked with high gawky boxes that they call pews.

B. *sb.* An awkward, foolish person; a lout, a simpleton.

1724 RAMSAY *Tea-t. Misc.* (1733) II. 163 What signifies how pawky, Or gentle-born ye be,—bot youth In love your but a gawky. **1762** *Lond. Chron.* XI. 263/2 Some wear their hats..pointed into the air; those are the Gawkies. *a* **1764** LLOYD *Fam. Ep. to Friend* 55 The great gawky Admiration, Parent of stupid Imitation. **1777** SHERIDAN *Sch. Scand.* II. ii, She is..an awkward gawky. **1863** MRS. C. CLARKE *Shaks. Char.* ii. 58 Audrey is the most perfect specimen of a wondering she-gawky. **1876** GEO. ELIOT *Dan. Der.* VI. xlviii, Nothing makes a woman more of a gawky than..showing tempers in public.

Hence **'gawkihood**, the condition, state, or period of being a 'gawky'; **'gawkiness**, the quality of being gawky.

1872 F. W. ROBINSON *Bridge of Glass* II. II. xxii. 285 It was like the Fanny Redbridge whom he had teased and jested with in her girlhood and gawkyhood. **1873** MISS BROUGHTON *Nancy* III. ii. 32 The crude gawkiness of the raw girl he has drifted into marrying. **1889** BARRIE *Window in Thrums* xiv. 127 The minister's wife..smiling good-humouredly at country gawkiness.

†**gawl**, *v. Obs. rare*$^{-1}$. [? echoic; cf. GOWL.] *trans.* ? To bawl *out.*

1592 GREENE *Disput.* 25 He..could gawll out many quaint and ribadrous Iigges and songs.

gawl, obs. form of GALL *sb.* and *v.*

gawlin ('gɔːlɪn). *Sc.* ? *Obs.* [Of obscure origin; Jamieson suggests ON. *gagl* goose.] (See quot.)

1703 M. MARTIN *West. Isl.* 71 The Gawlin is a Fowl less than a Duck; it is reckon'd a true Prognosticator of fair weather, for when it sings, fair..weather always follows.

gawling, var. GAULIN.

gawm, gawm(b)less: see GAUM, -LESS.

gawn (gɔːn). *Obs.* exc. *dial.* Also 7 **gawne.** See also GOAN. [contraction for GALLON.]

1. A gallon.

1565 in T. Sharp *Diss. Cov. Myst.* (1825) 50 It' payd for iij gawnes of ale in the pagiand. **1609** C. BUTLER *Fem. Mon.* iii. (1623) E iv, The abating of one inch in each dimension, abateth a gawne in the content. **1691** Wood *Ath. Oxon.* II. 379 His fare was course, his drink of a penny a gawn or gallon. **1886** *Chesh. Gloss.*, *Gawn*, a gallon.

2. (See quots.)

1688 R. Holme *Armoury* III. 320/2 A Gawn.. is a Vessel made after the form of a Piggen, but it hath a long handle or neck thereby to reach to the bottom of deep Brewing Vessels to fetch out the Liquor. **1841** Hartshorne *Salop. Antiq.* Gloss., *Gawn*, a small bucket chiefly used in brewing. **1881** *Leicestersh. Gloss.*, *Gawn*, a milking lade; any vessel for lading out a liquid. **1890** *Sale-Catal. Suffield House near Derby*, Two milk gawns. **1894** *S.E. Worc. Gloss.*, *Gawn*, a tub holding about a gallon, and usually having an handle projecting upwards on one side.

gawncel(y, var. GANSEL. *Obs.*

gawne, var. GAIN *v.*[1] *Obs.*

†**gawne,** *v. Obs.*−1 App. a late spelling of *gone* GANE *v.*

1563 B. Googe *Eglogs*, etc. (Arb.) 84, I take not I as some do take, To gape and gawne for Honours hye.

gawney ('gɔːnɪ). *dial.* or *colloq.* See also GONEY. [? Connected with GANE (*gone, gawn*) *v.*] A simpleton.

1842 Akerman *Wiltsh. Gloss.*, *Gawney*, a simpleton. —— *Wiltsh. Tales* 83 Leave m' 'lone y' great gawney! **1880** Jefferies *Gr. Ferne F.* 257 A hand-barrow, then—you gawnies!

gawp (gɔːp), *v.* Also 8 *Sc.* gap, 8–9 gaup. [dial. survival of GALP *v.*] *intr.* To yawn or gape; to gaze in astonishment. *to gawp up*: to devour. Also = GAWK *v.* Hence **'gawping** *vbl. sb.* and *ppl. a.*

1682 N. O. *Boileau's Lutrin* IV. 39 Methought I sat enthroned in the Quire, Where crowds of Choristers my Grace admire; There blest the gawping throng. **1704** F. Fuller *Med. Gymn.* (1718) 6 This is *Sneezing*; to which frequently is join'd *Gauping* or *Retching*. **1728** Ramsay *Fables & T., Daft Bargain* 12 Syne till't he fell, and seem'd richt yap His mealtith quickly up to gawp. **1819** W. Tennant *Papistry Storm'd* (1827) 18 Syk is the nature o' that grot To echoe sae, e'en should there not Be gaupin body on the spot. **1855** Robinson *Whitby Gloss.*, *To Gaup* or *Gauve*, 'He gaup'd and gloor'd at all he saw', gaped with wonder at new sights. **1881** *Leicestersh. Gloss.*, *Gawp*, to open eyes and mouth in stupid wonder. **1942** D. Powell *Time to be Born* (1943) vii. 175 You sit there gawping at him like some little goon. **1952** J. Cannan *Body in Beck* vii. 134 I'm here to get on with the job, not to gawp at the clients. **1959** J. Burke *Echo of Barbara* v. 42 Flauntin' yourself before a lot of gawpin' idiots.

gawp (gɔːp), *sb. dial.* and *colloq.* Also **gaup.** [f. prec.] A fool or simpleton. (See also GAWPUS.)

1825–80 [see GAWPY]. **1926** L. Coutts *Lyrics* 41 I've affin seen conceit in men But ee're the warst! Ye gawp! **1937** L. A. G. Strong *Swift Shadow* 155 Standing by like gawps to see bloody murder done. **1960** R. Williams *Border Country* 95 Country's not going to be run by a lot of young gawps.

gawpus ('gɔːpəs). *dial.* Also **gaupus.** [? f. GAWP *v.*] A silly person, simpleton.

1826 J. Wilson *Noct. Ambr.* Wks. 1855 I. 110 O ye gawpus! Ye great gawpus! It's me, man—it's me! **1853** Mrs. Gaskell *Ruth* II. iii. 44 The great gaupus never seed that I were pipeclaying the same places twice over. **1880** Mrs. Parr *Adam & Eve* xxvi. 362 The gawpuses have sooked it all in, and I'll be bound, raced off so fast as wind and tide 'ud carry 'em.

So **'gawpy,** of the same meaning.

1825–80 Jamieson, *Gaup*, a stupid person, other forms are *Gaupus, Gaupie.* Banffsh. **1843** Carlyle in Froude *Life* 1834–1881 (1884) I. 306 Those open-mouthed wondering gawpies, who lodge you for the sake of looking at you.

gawre(n, var. GAURE.

gawse, var. GAUZE *sb.*

gawsy ('gɔːsɪ), *a. Sc.* and *north. dial.* Forms: 8 gawcie, 8–9 gaucie, -cy, 9 gausie, -sy, gawcy, -sey, -sie, 8– gawsy. [Of unknown origin.] Of persons: Well-dressed and jolly-looking. Of things: Large and handsome.

1720 Ramsay *Edinb.'s Salut. to Ld. Carnarvon* iii, But since I have been fortune's sport, I look nae hauf sae gawsy. *a* **1774** Fergusson *Poems* (1814) II. 44 Pacing wi' a gawsy air In gude Braid Claith. **1785** Burns *Holy Fair* xxiv, In comes a gaucie, gash Guidwife. **1786** —— *Twa Dogs* 35 His gawcie tail, wi' upward curl, Hung owre his hurdies wi' a swirl. *a* **1810** Tannahill *Poems, Rab Roryson's Bonnet* (1846) 116 A braw gawcier bonnet there never was seen. **1818** Scott *Hrt. Midl.* xvi, Gawsie and grand he lookit, like ony queen in the land. *Ibid.* xxviii, Whilk is a dribble in comparison of our gawsie Scots pint. **1830** Galt *Lawrie T.* I. ii. (1849) 4 A decent, gausy, conversible carlin. **1888** *Glasgow Even. Times* 9 Aug. 2/5 Not so long ago it was quite orthodox to have a big gaucie midden in front of or near the house doors in Glasgow. **1894** Crockett *Raiders* 393 He cam' steppin' sae gawsy across the dry stanes at Sandy's Ford.

gay (geɪ), *a.*, *adv.*, and *sb.* Forms: 4–6 **gai(e,** 4–7 **gaye,** (9 *Sc.* **gaie**), 4– **gay.** [a. F. *gai* (recorded from 12th c.) = Pr. *gai, guai* (? *jai*), OSp. *gayo*, Pg. *gaio*, It. *gajo.*

The ulterior etymology is disputed: the view of Diez, that the word is a. OHG. *gâhi* swift, headlong (mod.Ger. *jähe*), is now generally abandoned. An etymon more satisfactory both with regard to sense and phonology is OHG. *wâhi* pretty (MHG. *wæhe*, mod. dial. *wæh*); but some scholars doubt whether the Rom. forms can represent a Ger. word with medial *h.* The sense 'slack, not closely fitting', which exists in all the Rom. langs. (though not recorded very early in any of them) may possibly be of etymological significance.]

A. *adj.* **1. a.** Of persons, their attributes and actions: Full of or disposed to joy and mirth; manifesting or characterized by joyous mirth; light-hearted, exuberantly cheerful, sportive, merry.

a **1310** in Wright *Lyric P.* xvi. 52 Heo is.. Graciouse, stout, ant Gay, Gentil, jolyf so the jay. *c* **1386** Chaucer *Miller's T.* 153 This Absolon, that iolif was and gay, Gooth with a sencer on the haliday. *c* **1440** *York. Myst.* xxix. 291 Boy, be not agaste if we seme gaye. **1514** Barclay *Cyt. & Uplondyshm.* (Percy Soc.) p. lii, Making the tapster come gay and feate. **1706** Stanhope *Paraphr.* III. 367 That gay insulting Man was particularly careful to distinguish himself from his poor dejected Companion. **1784** Cowper *Task* I. 493 Whom call we gay? The lark is gay. **1795–1814** Wordsw. *Excurs.* III. 507 The choir Of gay companions. **1812** J. Wilson *Isle of Palms* I. 58 Smiles wander o'er thy placid face As if thy dreams were gay. **1843** Lytton *Last Bar.* I. i, Edward was the handsomest, the gayest, and the bravest prince in Christendom. **1849** Macaulay *Hist. Eng.* iv. I. 431 He made an effort to converse with them in his usual gay style. **1880** Ouida *Moths* II. 123, I knew he was gay and careless.

transf. **1730–46** Thomson *Autumn* 705 Quick As is the wit it gives, the gay champagne.

absol. **1712** Pope *Ep. to Miss Blount* 16 And the gay mourn'd, who never mourn'd before. **1789** W. Buchan *Dom. Med.* (1790) 89 That greatest of human blessings [sleep].. visits the happy, the cheerful, and the gay. **1821** Craig *Lect. Drawing* viii. 440 To the youthful and gay, I would recommend these studies most particularly.

b. Of a horse: Lively, prancing. [So in Fr.] *rare*−1.

1826 Disraeli *Viv. Grey* VI. ii, As spruce a cavalier as ever pricked gay steed on the pliant grass.

c. With implied sense of depreciation: Airy, off-hand.

1779–81 Johnson *L.P., Pope* Wks. IV. 21 Fenton.. made him a gay offer of five pounds. *Ibid.* 99 Gay indifference.

†**d.** In poetry: Applied to women, as a conventional epithet of praise. *Obs.* (Cf. FREE *a.* 3.)

c **1350** *Will. Palerne* 816 Whan þe gaye gerles. were into þe gardin come, Faire floures þei founde. of fele maner hewes. *c* **1386** Chaucer *Miller's T.* 583 Some gay gerl.. Hath broght yow thus vpon the viritoot. **1599** Shaks. *Pass. Pilgr.* 225 The learned man hath got the lady gay. *a* **1802** *Prince Robert* in Child *Ballads* IV. 284 Prince Robert has wedded a gay ladye, He has wedded her with a ring.

e. *the gay science*: a rendering of *gai saber*, the Provençal name for the art of poetry.

1813 W. Taylor in *Monthly Rev.* LXX. 455 So little of an heroic or tragic cast had their effusions, that they termed poetry the *gay* science. **1855** Milman *Lat. Chr.* IV. 313 Not forbidding himself those amorous indulgences which were the reward of chivalrous valour, and of the 'gay science'.

f. Forward, impertinent, too free in conduct, over-familiar; usu. in phr. *to get gay. U.S. slang.*

1896 W. C. Gore in *Inlander* Jan. 147 *Get gay*, to joke boisterously; to show off; to act 'smart'. **1899** Ade *Fables in Slang* 109 The Copper, perceiving that he had come very near getting Gay with our First Families, apologized for Cutting In. **1901** Merwin & Webster *Calumet 'K'* xii. 226 He got gay one day. I warned him once, and then I threw him off the distributing floor. **1911** J. F. Wilson *Land Claimers* vi. 80 And I wouldn't get gay round her. **1915** Wodehouse *Something Fresh* iv, The flush on the little man's face deepened. 'Are you trying to get gay with me?' he demanded dangerously.

g. Of a dog's tail: carried high or erect.

1927 W. H. Dowling in C. C. Sanderson *Pedigree Dogs* 334 *Tail.*—Should be carried proudly, curved or plumed in a tight curl over and close to the back (never gay as in a 'Peke'). **1952** C. L. B. Hubbard *Pembr. Corgi Handbk.* 111 *Gay tail*, one which from root to tip is carried over the horizontal.

2. a. Addicted to social pleasures and dissipations. Often *euphemistically*: Of loose or immoral life. Esp. in *gay dog*, a man given to revelling or self-indulgence; *gay Lothario*: see LOTHARIO.

1637 Shirley *Lady of Pleasure* v. K 1 b, *Lord.* You'le not be angry, Madam. *Cel.* Nor rude, though gay men have a priviledge. **1700** T. Brown tr. *Fresny's Amusem. Ser. & Com.* 130 Every Dunce of a Quack, is call'd a Physician.. Every Gay thing, a Chevalier. **1703** Rowe *Fair Penit.* v. i, Is this that Haughty, Gallant, Gay Lothario? **1754** *Adventurer* No. 124 ¶7 The old gentleman, whose character I cannot better express than in the fashionable phrase which has been contrived to palliate false principles and dissolute manners, had been a gay man, and was well acquainted with the town. **1791** Burke *Let. to Member Nat. Assembly* Wks. VI. 36 The brilliant part of men of wit and pleasure, or gay, young, military sparks. **1798** Ferriar *Illustr. Sterne* ii. 40 The dissolute conduct of the gay circles in France is not of modern date. **1847** H. Rogers *Ess.* I. v. 214 For some years he lived a cheerful, and even gay, though never a dissipated life, in Paris. **1849** Macaulay *Hist. Eng.* vi. II. 103 The place was merely a gay suburb of the capital. **1851** Mayhew *Lond. Labour* I. 382 The principal of the firm was what is termed 'gay'. He was particularly fond of attending public entertainments. He sported a little as well, and delighted in horse-racing. **1891** E. Peacock *N. Brendon* I. 302 This elder Narcissa had led a gay and wild life while beauty lasted. **1897** J. Hutchinson *Archives Surg.* VIII. 224 My patient was a married man, who admitted having been very gay in early life. **1900** G. Swift *Somerley* 54 Oh! that first kiss! how proud of it we are, what gay dogs we feel! **1910** S. Kaye-Smith *Spell Land* xix. 221 He felt rather a gay dog.

absol. **1849** Macaulay *Hist. Eng.* ii. I. 196 On the vices of the young and gay he looked with.. aversion.

b. Hence, in *slang* use, of a woman: Leading an immoral life, living by prostitution.

1825 C. M. Westmacott *Eng. Spy* II. 22 Two sisters—both gay. **1857** J. E. Ritchie *Night Side Lond.* 40 The gay women, as they are termed, are worse off than American slaves. **1868** *Sund. Times* 19 July 5/1 As soon as ever a woman has ostensibly lost her reputation, we, with a grim inappositeness, call her 'gay'. **1885** *Hull & Linc. Times* 26 Dec. 8/4 She was leading a gay life.

c. Of a person: homosexual. Of a place: frequented by homosexuals. *slang.*

1935 N. Ersine *Underworld & Prison Slang* 39 *Geycat*,.. a homosexual boy. **1951** E. Lambert *Sleeping-House Party* vii. 74 In a way it was an odd threesome. It occurred to me that Esther rather hung round our two gay boys. **1955** P. Wildeblood *Against Law* I. 23 Most of the officers at the station had been 'gay'.. an American euphemism for homosexual. *Ibid.* III. 105 The place [*sc.* a prison] is *packed* with gay people who are in for something else. **1960** [see BENT *ppl. a.* 5 c]. **1963** A. Heron *Towards Quaker View of Sex* iii. 24 These may form the 'queer' society; these will frequent 'gay' bars.

absol. **1966** A. Firth *Tall, Balding, Thirty-Five* xv. 194 Would he ever dare, even if he wanted to, join the shrill freemasonry of the London gay? **1968** *Globe & Mail Magazine* (Toronto) 13 Jan. 6/1 A coffee shop frequented by the gay.

3. Bright or lively-looking, esp. in colour; brilliant, showy.

13.. *K. Alis.* 3204 Gret pruyde and gay gere. **13..** *E.E. Allit. P.* A. 260 In þis gardyn gracios gaye. *c* **1386** Chaucer *Prol.* 111, Vpon his arm he baar a gay bracer. *c* **1420** *Sir Amadace* (Camden) lvi, He come in als gay gere, Ryȝte as he an angelle were. **1463** *Bury Wills* (Camden) 41 My best gay cuppe of erthe. **1508** Dunbar *Tua mariit Wemen* 365 He grathit me in a gay silk, et gudly arrayis. **1539** *Will of Aslyn* (Somerset Ho.), My gaye potte of glasse. **1573** G. Harvey *Letter-bk.* (Camden) 6 His oun gai gallant gaskins do and wil descri it sufficiently. **1638** F. Junius *Paint. Ancients* 285 Too much cheerefulnesse of gay and flourishing colours. **1650** Bulwer *Anthropomet.* 260 The Brama's, who delight in such Gay-babbles. **1717** Lady M. W. Montagu *Let. to P'cess of Wales* 1 Apr., The perpetual spring.. makes everything gay and flourishing. **1797** Mrs. Radcliffe *Italian* i, In every gay carriage that passed, he hoped to see the object of his constant thought. **1834** Lytton *Pompeii* I. ii, They were now in that quarter which was filled with the gayest shops. **1860** Piesse *Lab. Chem. Wonders* (1869) 131 The Collinsia verna, a gay, dark purple flower. **1870** E. Peacock *Ralf Skirl.* III. 233 Their costumes were gay with ribbons.

absol. **1842** Miall in *Nonconf.* II. 1 The civil magistrate, dressed in his gayest, approached the altar.

4. Finely or showily dressed. Now *rare.*

c **1381** Chaucer *Parl. Foules* 234 Wommen y-nowe, of whiche somme ther were Faire of hem-self, and somme of hem were gay. **1387** Trevisa *Higden* (Rolls) IV. 241 Cleopatra made here gay. *c* **1475** *Rauf Coilȝear* 484 He is the gayest in geir, that euer on ground glaid. **1509** Barclay *Shyp of Folys* (1570) 27 Women.. sell their soules and bodyes to go gay. **1604** Shaks. *Oth.* II. i. 151 She that.. Neuer lackt Gold, and yet went neuer gay. **1801** Strutt *Sports & Past.* I. i. 7 The king was desirous of knowing the name of this gay gentleman. **1812** J. Wilson *Isle of Palms* III. 600 Vaunt not, gay bird! thy gorgeous plume. **1859** Tennyson *Enid* 284 The armourer.. seeing one so gay in purple silks.

5. In immaterial sense: Brilliant, attractive, charming. †Formerly also of reasonings, etc.: Specious, plausible.

1529 More *Dyaloge* III. Wks. 243/2 Those reasons semed.. gay and glorious at the first sight. **1548** Hall *Chron., Hen. VI*, 113 Thei with money, and gay promises, first corrupted a Miller. **1562** Cooper *Answ. Apol. Priv. Masse* 57 b, You will seeme with your gay gloses to glorifie the bloud of Christe. **1634** Milton *Comus* 790 Enjoy your dear wit, and gay rhetoric. **1638** Chillingw. *Relig. Prot.* I. vi. §5. 327, I would fain know what gay probabilities you could devise to disswade him from this Resolution. **1709** Pope *Ess. Crit.* 392 Let not each gay turn thy rapture move. **1779–81** Johnson *L.P., Pope* Wks. IV. 17 All the gay varieties of diction were ready at his hand.

†**6. a.** Brilliantly good; excellent, fine. *Obs.*

c **1470** Henry *Wallace* IX. 54 A gud gay wynd out off the rycht art com. **1533** Bellenden *Livy* II. vii. (1822) 127 Becaus vertew wes honorit in this wise, it gaif occasioun to wemen to do gay vassalege. **1540** Hyrde tr. *Vives' Instr. Chr. Wom.* (1592) N v, But looke in the same booke, how goodly and gay is the prais of a good woman. **1550** Latimer *Last Serm. bef. Edw. VI* (1562) 125 The concord of brethren, & agreeing of brethren is a gay thing. **1563** T. Wilson *Logike* 15 b, People, which haue moche dispraised all temporall lawes.. thinkyng it mete that all common weales, should onely haue the Gospell, and none other lawe at all. This maie seme to some, a gaie saiyng where as in deede, it is bothe foolishe, and wicked. **1573** Tusser *Husb.* xxxv. (1878) 80 The labour is little, the profit is gay. **1577** Harrison *England* Ded. (1877) I. p. cix, And thus with hope of good although no gaie successe. **1593** *Tell-Troth's N.Y. Gift* 38 It is a gay thing to come to dignity.

†**b.** *ironically. Obs.*

1581 J. Bell *Haddon's Answ. Osor.* 11 b, O gay payre of Byshops, which are so intangled in two examples onely, that [etc.]. **1582** G. Martin *Discov. Corrupt. Script.* vii. 120 If these later Rabbines be the Hebreues that Beza meaneth, and which these gay English translatours follow.

†**c.** *to have a gay mind*: 'to have a good mind', to be very much inclined.

1557 Pole in Strype *Eccl. Mem.* III. App. lxviii. 238 Yf you.. had suche a gay mynde to restore the ruynes of the Chyrches.

7. Of quantity or amount. Pretty good, 'tolerable', 'middling'. *Sc.* and *north.* Also GEY.

1796 W. Marshall *Yorksh.* Gloss. (ed. 2), *Gay*, considerable, middling, ordinary. **1801** Seward *Lonsdale Dial.* 54 (E.D.S. No. 76) Thau knaes it'tle be a gay dele, when it's o put tagidder. **1869** in *Lonsdale Gloss.* **1882** in *Lanc. Gloss.*

8. *dial.* In good health; well, convalescent.

1855 Robinson *Whitby Gloss.* s.v., I am quite gay I thank you. **1876** in *Mid-Yorksh. Gloss.* **1877** *N.W. Linc. Gloss.*

s.v., I heard thoo was badly, but thoo looks gay. **1887** *Kent. Gloss.* s.v., I don't feel very gay this morning.

9. *Comb.*, chiefly parasynthetic, as ***gay-coloured***, ***-flowered***, ***-hearted***, ***-humoured***, ***-looking***, ***-seeming*** adjs.; **gay cat** *U.S. slang*, a young or inexperienced tramp; a hobo who accepts occasional work; (see also sense 2 c); **gay deceiver**, (*a*) a deceitful rake (RAKE *sb.*[5]); (*b*) *pl. slang* = FALSIES *sb. pl.*; **gay-feather** *U.S.*, the name of a plant (see quot.); **Gay Gordons**, (*a*) (see quot. 1925); (*b*) a Scottish dance popular in old-time and modern dancing; **Gay Liberation (Front)** orig. *U.S.*, (a movement for) the liberation of homosexuals from social stigma and discrimination; also with lower-case initials, and abbrev. as **Gay Lib** (see LIB).

1897 'J. FLYNT' in *Forum* Feb. 741 Nothing arouses his [*sc.* the hobo's] scorn more than the dilettante, or '*gay-cat', as he calls him. **1901** J. LONDON *Let.* 6 Dec. (1966) 126 Wyckoff is a gay cat. That was his rating when he wandered over the States. **1926** J. BLACK *You can't Win* vi. 74 He must have been an awful gay cat to get into the end of a carload of planed lumber. It's suicide. **1950** R. CHANDLER *Let.* 18 May (1966) 78 A gay-cat is a young punk who runs with an older tramp and there is always a connotation of homosexuality. Again, he could be a 'look-out' (outside man) or a 'finder' (finger or finger man), but that is a derived or occasional meaning and not exact. **1866** HOWELL *Venet. Life* xx. 342 Brilliant tapestries and other *gay-coloured cloths. **1803** G. COLMAN *Love laughs at Locksmiths* (1823) II. 25 Says he, 'I am a handsome man, but I'm a *gay deceiver.' **1809** MALKIN *Gil Bl.* VII. i. III. 10, I..posted myself on the high road, where the gay deceiver was sure to be intercepted. **1898** J. D. BRAYSHAW *Slum Silhouettes* 44 Ah! he's a gay decaver, is Billy, like all the min. Sure I wouldn't trust my ould gran'mother wid him. **1942** D. POWELL *Time to be Born* (1943) x. 232 Her pink sweater..clung properly to the seductive curves of her Gay Deceivers. **1962** *Guardian* 12 Mar. 4/7 False bosoms..were known as 'gay deceivers'. **1880** *Libr. Univ. Knowl.* (N.Y.) VI. 493 *Gay-feather, the common name for the *liatris scariosa* and *spicata*. **1856** *Farmer's Mag.* Jan. 2 The *gay-flowered Senecio of the Canaries, known in gardens under the name of *Cineraria*. **1886** MRS. BURNETT *Little Ld. Fauntleroy* vi. (1887) 114 Everything was bright and cheerful with gay-flowered chintz. **1925** FRASER & GIBBONS *Soldier & Sailor Words* 185 **Gay Gordons, The*, The Gordon Highlanders. In particular the 2nd Battalion, the 92nd Highlanders. **1947** J. R. GILLESPIE *Old Tyme Dancing* 32 (*heading*) The Gay Gordons. **1955** J. I. M. STEWART *Guardians* III. iv. 238 The music of the Samba and the Gay Gordons. **1966** *Crescendo* Dec. 27/1 A musical chore to be dealt with grudgingly like the Veleta or the Gay Gordons. **1853** WHITTIER *Panorama* (1856) 33 *Gay-hearted Health. **1947** W. DE LA MARE *Coll. Stories for Children* 44 Fairies, sly, small, gay-hearted. **1883** F. M. PEARD *Contrad.* x, It was a fresh, *gay-humoured day. **1970** *Los Angeles Free Press* 6 Feb. 17 (*heading*) *Gay Lib Front meets. *Ibid.* 20 Feb. 18/3 The Pope hopes that all Gay organizations—Old line, Gay lib, motorcycle, and social—will join in the demonstration. **1986** *Guardian Weekly* 26 Jan. 12/4 The bars—since gay lib, their fronts are of transparent glass—do not have invitingly dim-lit backrooms. **1969** *Village Voice* (N.Y.) 18 Sept. 2/1 (Advt.), The *Gay Liberation Front sends love to all gay men and women in the homosexual community. **1969** *Berkley Barb* (San Francisco) 10 Oct. 12/2 A magazine devoted to gay liberation is shortly to be published. **1985** *Listener* 7 Feb. 28/3 To depict life from the standpoint of a male prostitute ..is to make a statement, if not to thump the tub for gay liberation. **1897** *Daily News* 21 Apr. 3/3 A *gay looking gig now put out from Palermo. **1595** SPENSER *Hymn Heavenly Beauty* 299 This vile world and these *gay-seeming things.

B. *adv.*

†**1. a.** Brightly, showily = GAILY 1. **b.** In a gay mood, joyously = GAILY 2. *Obs.*

1415 HOCCLEVE *To Sir J. Oldcastle* 414 Ymages..causen men honure The seint after whom maad is that figure, And nat worsshippe it how gay it be wroght. **1500–20** DUNBAR *Poems* xliii. 28 Send in ȝour steid, ȝour ladeis grathit vp gay. **1577** B. GOOGE *Heresbach's Husb.* I. (1586) 7 Nor seelyng garnisht gaye with Imagrye, Nor ritche attyre we see. **1633** BP. HALL *Occas. Medit.* (1851) 112 Not acknowledging any friend, but..the nurse, that dresses us gay. **1744** SARAH FIELDING *David Simple* II. 161 He was dressed very gay. **1754** J. SHEBBEARE *Matrimony* (1766) II. 140 This paid her Debts, and put some considerable Sum of Money in her Pocket, with which she lived as gay as before.

2. Very. Also in weaker sense: Considerably, 'pretty'. Frequent in *dial.* ***a gay few*** = ***a good few***: see FEW 2 d. Often written GEY.

1686 G. STUART *Joco-ser. disc.* Ep. Ded., Your Enemies (of which..yo've had a gay convenient number). **1807** SIR J. CARR *Caled. Sketches* xii. 212 It is a gaie (very) bonnie place to be out of the world. **1816** SCOTT *Old Mort.* vii, I ken I'm gay thick in the head. **1884** *Gd. Words* 229 There was a gay few folks waiting to cross.

3. *Comb.* Chiefly with pres. and pa. pples., as ***gay-beseen*** (see BESEE II), ***-careering***, ***-chirping***, ***-motleyed***, ***-painted***, ***-shifting***, ***-smiling***, ***-spent***, ***-spotted***, ***-throned***.

1549 CHALONER *Erasm. on Folly* O ij b, What saie you to Courtiers? these minion *gaibeseen gentilmen. **1596** SPENSER *F.Q.* VI. v. 38 Deckt with greene boughes, and flowers gay beseene. **1824** T. FENBY *4 Temperam.* I. 45 Thy *gay-careering soul. **1844** LD. HOUGHTON *Palm Leaves* 132 The sparrow *Gay-chirping by the door. **1742** COLLINS *Ecl., Abra* 17 *Gay-motley'd pinks and sweet jonquils she chose. **1777** WARTON *Poems* 36 The butterfly, *gay-painted soon, Explores awhile the tepid noon. **1728–46** THOMSON *Spring* 190 The downward sun Looks out effulgent from amid the flush Of broken clouds *gay-shifting to his beam. **1747** LD. LYTTELTON *Monody* Wks. (1774) 630 Ye lawns *gay-smiling with eternal green, Oft have you my Lucy seen! **1726–46** THOMSON *Winter* 1037 Those busy bustling days, Those *gay-spent festive nights. **1728–46** —— *Spring* 550 Nor broad carnations; nor *gay-spotted pinks. **1777** WARTON *Poems* 76 But since, *gay-thron'd in fiery chariot sheen, Summer has smote each daisy-dappled dale.

C. *sb.* [the *adj.* used *absol.*]

†**1.** A gay lady. Also, rarely of a man, a 'gallant'. *Obs.*

13.. *Gaw. & Gr. Knt.* 970 Gawayn glyȝt on þat gay, þat graciously loked. *c* **1400** *Destr. Troy* 2679 Parys was purpost with pouer to wende Into Grese for a gay, all on grete wise. *c* **1420** *Anturs of Arth.* (Camden) xli, Then gloppunt that gaye, Hit was no ferly in faye. *c* **1475** [see GAINAND].

2. a. Anything that looks gay or showy; an ornament; *esp.* one that is used to amuse a child. Now *dial.*

1399 LANGL. *Rich. Redeles* II. 94 But how the gayes han y-gon, God wotte the sothe, Amonge myȝtfull men alle these many ȝeris. *c* **1500** *Maid Emlyn* 330 in Hazl. *E.P.P.* IV. 94 This mannes name was Harry, He coude full clene cary, He loued prety gayes. **1519** HORMAN *Vulg.* 147 This baby hath many gayes hangyng at his necke. **1601** DENT *Pathw. Heaven* (1603) 41 As if a theefe should be proud of his halter, a begger of his cloutes, a childe of his gay. **1655** tr. *De Parc's Francion* II. 36 He..took pleasure in such Gayes, on purpose to be the more noted by wearing Cloathes out of the Common Mode. **1880** *W. Cornw. Gloss.*, *Gays*, children's toys: often, broken earthenware.

†**b.** *fig.* A 'toy', childish amusement. *Obs.*

1582 BRETON *Flourish Fancy*, etc. (Grosart) 28/1 Though (perhaps) most commonly each youth Is giuen in deede, to follow euery gaye. **1591** SYLVESTER *Du Bartas* I. iii. 1040 O how I grieve, deer Earth, that (given to gays) Most of best Wits contemn thee now a-dayes. **1667** L. STUCLEY *Gospel-Glass* xxiii. (1670) 232 Forraigners breed their Children..to work those gaies with their hands. **1694** F. BRAGGE *Disc. Parables* III. 83 It highly concerns us..no longer childishly to doat upon empty gayes and trifles.

3. A picture in a book. Now *dial.* (chiefly used by children).

1646 JENKYN *Remora* 30 'Tis the gay in the lesson, that makes the childe delight to learn. *a* **1657** R. LOVEDAY *Lett.* (1663) 149 Finding him still eager to put a gay before his book, I design'd him this which is now a cutting. **1698** MILBOURNE *Notes Dryden's Virg.* 4 Who, in the inscription to his fine Gay in the Front of the Book, calls it very honestly Dryden's Virgil. **1839** C. CLARK *J. Noakes & M. Styles* 157 (E.D.S. No. 76) At a stall, soon Mary bote A hume-book full ov gays. **1884** BARING-GOULD *Mehalah* xxxii. 322 'The master of Rest Hall is turning over a new leaf to-day.' 'Maybe—but I doubt it will be a blank one..It won't be a gay for him.'

4. *slang* (orig. *U.S.*). A homosexual, esp. a male homosexual. Cf. A 2 c above.

1971 E. MCGIRR *No Better Fiend* 69 Until the law was changed..there was a ring of roses around the gays, everybody extorting anything they could get. **1972** *Pride of Lions* (Columbia Univ.) Apr. 7/3 What about a program acceptable to gays, students and workers? **1974** K. MILLETT *Flying* (1975) I. 15, I talked at DOB in August, candid, one gay to another. **1975** *Whig-Standard* (Kingston, Ontario) 13 Aug. 43/5 The female gays in Ottawa are split into four main groups. **1977** *Time* 25 Apr. 52/3 Florida's former Miss America, Anita Bryant, took time out from her campaign against gays to oppose the ERA. **1980** E. WHITE in Michaels & Ricks *State of Lang.* 236 Many gays either were in therapy or felt they should be. **1985** *Sunday Tel.* 30 June 18/7 What about gays, one asks, and will there be facilities for them to relate significantly to each other?

gay, *v.* [f. the adj.] **a.** *intr.* To be gay. **b.** *trans.* To make gay; to give a bright and pleasant look to; to embellish. Usu. with *up*. Hence **gayed** *ppl. a.*

1581 MULCASTER *Positions* xxxviii. 170 Their natural towardnesse..doth call vpon vs, to see them [girls] well brought vp..Are not we to be condemned of extreme vnnaturallnes, if we gay not that by discipline, which is giuen them by nature? **1641** HINDE *J. Bruen* iv. 15 They are well contented that their children prove no wiser than themselves..nor have any skill in any arts but of Gaming, and Gaying. **1671** EACHARD *Obs. Answ. Grounds Cont. Clergy* (1705) 35 Children must have..gay'd and easie digestible Words. **1960** *News Chron.* 2 May 6/6 The charming effect of houses gayed up with these flower-filled boxes. **1968** 'E. TREVOR' *Place for Wicked* iii. 39 She called in with a geranium in a pot for them because they'd never think about gaying the place up for themselves.

‖**gayal** ('geɪəl, ga'jal). Also 9 **gayall**, **guyal**, **g(h)yal**. [Hindi *gayāl*.] A semi-domesticated kind of ox common in Burmah, Assam, and Bengal; by some believed to be a variety of the GAUR; by others regarded as a distinct species (*Bibos frontalis*).

1790 *Asiatic Res.* II. 188 When a rich man has made a contract of marriage, he gives four or five head of *gayáls* (the cattle of the mountains) to the father and mother of the bride. **1808** *Ibid.* VIII. 512 'The *Gayál*', says Dr. Roxburgh, 'is nearly of the size and shape of the English bull'. **1860** GOSSE *Rom. Nat. Hist.* 119 The gaur, the gayall, and other great wild oxen of India.

gāyatrī ('gajatri). [Skr., f. *gā* to sing.] **a.** An ancient twenty-four-syllable metre. **b.** A hymn, etc., composed in this metre; *esp.* the verse of the Rig-veda repeated daily as a prayer by Brahmins.

1843 *Penny Cycl.* XXVI. 177/1 The principal metres used in the hymns of the Vedas are the Jagatî, Gâyatrî, and Trishtup. **1845** *Encycl. Metrop.* XVI. 351/1 His father.., guided by the priest,..pronounces three times the Gáyatrí; 'let us meditate on the adorable light of the Divine Ruler, may it guide our intellects!' **1865** MAX MÜLLER *Chips* (1867) I. 19 The famous hymn, the Gâyatrî, which now for more than three thousand years has been the daily prayer of every Brahman. **1886** *Encycl. Brit.* XXI. 275/2 The *gâyatrî*..and other chiefly octosyllabic metres. **1916** A. A. MACDONELL *Vedic Gram.* 446 Gāyatrī triplets. **1965** *Language* XLI. 11 *Yaja* occurs at the end of a gāyatrī.

gaybine ('geɪbaɪn). [f. GAY *a.* + BINE.] A name of several showy twining plants of the genera *Ipomœa* (*Cent. Dict.*) and *Pharbitis*.

1866 *Treas. Bot.* 523/1 Gaybine, *Pharbitis*.

gaydiang ('geɪdɪæŋ). An Annamese vessel, somewhat resembling a Chinese junk.

1855 OGILVIE, Suppl., *Gay-diang*, a vessel of Anam, generally with two, but in fine weather with three masts.. with lofty triangular sails.

gayety: see GAIETY.

gayge, obs. form of GAGE.

gayhole, -holer, obs. ff. JAIL, JAILER.

†**gay horse.** *Obs.*[−1] [f. ? GAY *a.* + HORSE.] A bugbear or hobgoblin, carried about at plays and public shows, with wide jaws and great teeth.

1483 *Cath. Angl.* 147/2 A Gay horse, *manducus*.

gayish ('geɪɪʃ). [f. GAY *a.* + -ISH.]

1. Somewhat gay.

1824 J. WILSON in *Blackw. Mag.* XVI. 600 There's a gayish song on the subject.

2. *dial.* Fairly good or large; 'tolerable.'

1855 ROBINSON *Whitby Gloss.* s.v., 'A gayish crop'..'A gayish sample'. **1876** *Whitby Gloss.* s.v., 'It's a gayish step te gan', or it's 'gayish and far'.

gayity, gayitry: see GAIETY, GAYTRY.

gayl(e, gayler, -or, obs. ff. JAIL, JAILER.

†**gaylede.** *Obs.*[−1]

c **1430** *Two Cookery-bks.* I. 22 *Gaylede.* Take Almaunde Mylke and Flowre of Rys, and do þer-to Sugre or Hony, and Powder Gyngere; þen take figys, an kerue hem a-to, or Roysonys y-hole, or harde Wastel y-dicyd and coloure it with Saunderys, and sette it and dresse hem yn.

Gay-'Lussac tower (geɪ'lysæk). [See next.] (See quot. 1888.)

1888 W. W. FISHER *Elem. Chem.* vii. 72 In order to catch any nitric oxide which would otherwise pass away [in the manufacture of sulphuric acid], and be lost in the air, a tower, called a Gay-lussac's tower..filled with coke is interposed, and the gases from the chambers are passed through it. **1894** *Daily News* 4 Sept. 2/6 The defendants were having repacked a gay lussac tower.

gaylussite ('geɪlysaɪt). *Min.* [f. the name of *Gay-Lussac*, a celebrated French physicist + -ITE. Named by Boussingault in 1826.] A double carbonate of calcium and sodium, found in white or yellowish crystals.

1826 *Brande's Jrnl.* XXI. 406 New Mineral—the Gay-Lussite. **1892** DANA *Min.* 301 Gay-Lussite.

gayly, gayn-: see GAILY, GAIN-.

gayness ('geɪnɪs). [f. GAY *a.* + -NESS.] The quality, condition or state of being gay.

†**1.** Delight, merriment, pleasure. *Obs.*

1377 LANGL. *P. Pl.* B. x. 81 But in gaynesse and in glotonye..for-glotten her goode hem-selue, And breken nouȝte to the beggar. **1435** MISYN *Fire of Love* II. x. 97 Oftyms also odyr noys happyns þat gaynes & swetnes of lufars sturbyls. ? **15..** in Pinkerton *Anc. Scot. Poems* (1786) 192 The gaynis of my yeiris gent, The flouris of my fresche youtheid, I wait nocht how away is went.

†**2.** Gay appearance, brightness of colour, dressiness, display, pomp. *Obs.*

c **1449** PECOCK *Repr.* II. xviii. 255 For to speke and write tho wordis in sum gaynes and bewte..thei vsiden certein colouris of rethorik. **1561** T. NORTON *Calvin's Inst.* IV. xix. (1634) 727 Clerkes did everywhere sheare their heads, least they should seem to covet the gainesse of haire. *a* **1594** AYLMER in Strype *Life* xiii. (1701) 274 Oh! ye English ladies, learn rather..to make your Queen rich for your Defence, than your Husbands poor for your garish Gayness. **1602** MARSTON *Antonio's Rev.* I. ii, A modest eye forceth affection, Whilest outward gainesse light lookes but entice. **1660** S. FORD *Loyal Subj. Exhult.* 21 Such pomp and glory as declared how glad his Subjects were in their hearts, by the gayness of their habits. **1676** HOBBES *Iliad* (1677) 77 In Hyla ..he dwelt..And known was by the gayness of his belt.

†**b.** A decoration, distinction. *Obs.*

1670 WALTON *Lives* IV. 338 The Orator..takes place next the Doctors, is at all their Assemblies and Meetings and sits above the Proctors, is Regent or Non-regent at his pleasure, and such like Gaynesses. **1674** N. FAIRFAX *Bulk & Selv.* To Rdr., Those borrowed words & gaynesses, that Englishmen have pickt and cull'd from other Tongues.

3. = GAIETY 1.

1896 *Advance* (Chicago) Oct. 438 'There's many a slip 'twixt cup and lip', she quoted with a gayness that belied her own words.

gayole, gayre, obs. forms of JAIL, GEAR.

Gay-Pay-Oo (geɪpeɪ'u:). Also **Gay-Pay-U.** Phonetic representation of G.P.U. as pronounced in Russian (see G III. f).

1927 *Observer* 11 Dec. 21/2 The Gay-Pay-OO, or Political Police. **1928** *Punch* 18 Jan. 57/2 The Gay-Pay-Oo, it seems, is the name of the reorganised Russian Cheka. **1934** G. B. SHAW *Pref.* 359 The Russians were forced to set up an Inquisition or Star Chamber, called at first the Cheka and now the Gay Pay Oo (Ogpu). **1936** D. POWELL *Turn, Magic Wheel* III. 225 He yanked words out of the corner of his mouth..as..cautiously as if Gay-Pay-U men were all about.

gaysh(e, gaysling, obs. ff. GASH, GOSLING.

gaysome ('geɪsəm), *a.* Now *rare.* [f. GAY *a.* + -SOME.] **a.** Full of gaiety; blithe, buoyant, cheerful. **b.** Inspiring with gaiety; cheery; pleasant.

a. 1610 *Mirr. Mag., Robt. Normandie* vii, And fier'd with heat of gaysome youth did venter, With warlike troopes the Norman coast to enter. *c* **1611** CHAPMAN *Iliad* XI. 194 His breast was heightned with the fire Of gaisome youth. **1839** MOIR *Poems, To Bust of my Son* v, A gaysome elf, whose heart had ne'er Been tamed by grief.

b. 1633 FORD *Broken Heart* II. i, 'Island!' prison; A prison is as gaysome: we'll no islands. **1831** *Lincoln Gaz.* 14 Oct. 3/1 Oh, ask me not to sing to-night, Nor bid me touch the gaysome lute. **1854** W. WHITE *To Switz. & back* ii. (1855) 16 Paris..its dingy quarters as well as its gaysome places.

gayson, obs. form of GEASON.

gaysp, var. GASP.

gayte, obs. form of GATE *sb.*[2], GOAT.

†**'gaytry, 'gayitry.** *Obs.* [? altered from GAIETY, after *poetry, coquetry*, etc.] = GAIETY.

1655 FULLER *Pisgah* IV. vi. 111 A Bride (though never so mean a person, or silly servant) is decked and dressed in all gayitry lent unto her by her neighbours. **1685** CROWNE *Sir C. Nice* II. 11 He's the General Guitarre o' the Town, inlay'd with every thing Women fancy; Gaytry, Gallantry, Delicacy, Nicety, Courtesy.

gaytt, obs. form of GATE *sb.*[1]

gazabo (gə'zeɪbəʊ). *slang* (orig. and chiefly *U.S.*). Also **gazebo.** [Perh. f. Sp. *gazapo* a sly fellow; cf. GAZEBO.] A fellow, 'guy'; often with a pejorative connotation.

1896 ADE *Artie* v. 44 Who does I meet comin' out o' the house but a cheap gazabo that was with her the first time I see her. **1910** W. M. RAINE *B. O'Connor* 39 A big gazabo in a red wig held up Frost, the engineer. **1934** B. PENTON *Landtakers* (1935) I. i. 14 Aw, leave the old gazebo. He's drunk. **1953** H. MILLER *Plexus* (1963) vii. 262 But there was one thing he seldom did, queer gazabo that he was—he seldom asked questions.

gazabo, var. GAZEBO.

gazafylace: see GAZOPHILACE.

gazania (gə'zeɪnɪə). *Bot.* [mod.L. *Gazania* (G. Gaertner *De Fructibus Plantarum* (1791) II. 451), f. the name of Theodorus *Gaza* (1398–1478), a Greek scholar.] A plant of the genus of South African herbs so named, belonging to the family Compositæ and having showy yellow or orange flowers.

1813 W. T. AITON *Hortus Kewensis* (ed. 2) V. 140 Great-flower'd Gazania. **1844** MRS. LOUDON *Ladies' Flower-Garden Ornam. Perennials* II. 29 The Peacock Gazania.. only expands its flowers in broad daylight. *Ibid.*, The Golden-Flowered Gazania.. is a very pretty little plant, with golden yellow flowers. **1921** G. JEKYLL *Colour Schemes* 63 A few belated Orange Lilies have their colour nearly repeated by the Gazanias next to the path. **1966** E. PALMER *Plains of Camdeboo* xvii. 280 There are Nemesias and Gazanias.

gaze (geɪz), *sb.* Also 6 **gase.** [f. GAZE *v.*]

†**1.** That which is gazed or stared at. *Obs.*

(In the first quot. *gase* may be another word or an unmeaning invention.)

[*a* **1529** SKELTON *Garl. Laurell* 1206 This fustian maistres and this giggish gase.] **1542** UDALL *Erasm. Apophth.* 25 But this wise manne thought better to shewe of hymself an example of paciente suffreaunce, then to shewe a gase or sight for folkes to laugh at, in..contendyng wᵗ his wife. **1546** LANGLEY *Pol. Verg. de Invent.* VI. viii. 125 Outwarde apparell of the body, which is rather a gloriouse gase then anye godlye edifiying. *c* **1600** SHAKS. *Sonn.* v, Those howers that with gentle worke did frame The louely gaze where euery eye doth dwell. **1671** MILTON *Samson* 34 Made of my enemies the scorn and gaze. **1739** MELMOTH *Fitzosb. Lett.* (1763) 382 Who are more the gaze and admiration of the people in general? **1797** MRS. A. M. BENNETT *Beggar Girl* (1813) I. 223 His father lolled in his coach, and was the gaze of the village of Penry.

2. The act of looking fixedly or intently; a steady or intent look.

1566 DRANT *Horace's Sat.* I. vii. 205 For weryed with my bookishe gaze, I noynte with supple oyle My loytrous limmes. *c* **1590** GREENE *Fr. Bacon* x. 126 Fancy that slippeth in with a gaze, goeth out with a winke. **1712** STEELE *Spect.* No. 406 ¶6 In vain, you envious Streams, so fast you flow, To hide her from a Lover's ardent Gaze. **1718** *Entertainer* No. xxii. 148 Beauty such as mov'd the whole City to Gaze and Admiration. **1794** COLERIDGE *Death Chatterton* 66 Thy sullen gaze she bade thee roll On scenes that well might melt thy soul. **1822** W. IRVING *Braceb. Hall* xxvii. 244 Every event is a matter of gaze and gossip. **1849** MACAULAY *Hist. Eng.* ii. I. 235 The corpse..was exhibited during several days to the gaze of great multitudes. **1879** FARRAR *St. Paul* (1883) 138 Who was this to whom His followers turned their last gaze?

fig. **1814** CARY *Dante, Parad.* v. 129 The sun..when his warm gaze Hath on the mantle of thick vapours prey'd. **1841** BROWNING *Pippa* 13 Oh, Day, if I squander a wavelet of thee ..The least of thy gazes or glances.

3. Phrases. †**a.** ***at first gaze***: at first sight. ***to give*** (a person) ***the gaze***: to be a spectator of, look on at. (***to have***) ***in gaze***: in prospect. ***to set oneself at gaze***: to expose oneself to view, display oneself.

1577 STANYHURST *Descr. Irel.* in Holinshed (1587) II. 36/2 You must not thinke..that you were sent gouernour into Ireland..to pen your selfe vp within a towne or citie to giue rebels the gaze, to [etc.]. —— *Chron. Irel.* ibid. 83/2 One of the earle his capteins presented him a band of Kerns..and withall demanded of the erle in what seruice he would haue them imploied: Marie (quoth he) let them stand by and giue vs the gaze. **1632** BROME *Court Beggar* II. Wks. 1873 I. 206 To set your selfe at gaze to draw them on. *a* **1657** R. LOVEDAY *Lett.* (1663) 235 Repugnant to any apprehension that at first gaze did not appear a visible aid to the cause.

b. ***at gaze***, †***at a*** or ***the gaze***; said of a deer (now chiefly *Her.*: see quot. 1828–40), also of persons: in the attitude of gazing, esp. in wonder, expectancy, bewilderment, etc. So in ***to stand at*** (†***a, the***) ***gaze***, †***to set at the gaze***, etc. †***to hold at gaze***: to hold fascinated. Also with other preps. as †***in a gaze, on, upon the gaze***; †***to put to the gaze***: to puzzle, nonplus. See also AGAZE.

c **1430** [see AGAZE]. **1579** LYLY *Euphues* (Arb.) 78, I haue read..that the whole heard of Deare stand at the gaze, if they smell a sweete apple. **1594** GREENE & LODGE *Looking Gl.* (1598) A 4 Whose eye holds wanton Venus at a gaze. **1603** KNOLLES *Hist. Turks* (1638) 309 A shepheard.. strucken with the majesty of the man, stood at gaze vpon him. **1622** BACON *Hen. VII*, 137 Especially as many as were English: who were at a gaze looking strange one upon another. **1646** SIR C. CAVENDISH *Let. to Pell* in R. Vaughan *Protect. Cromwell* (1838) II. 374 The business is too difficult for me to judge of, for it puts our learned men here to the gaze. *a* **1657** R. LOVEDAY *Lett.* (1663) 140, I had still a likelyhood in gaze. *a* **1700** DRYDEN *Ovid's Epist.* Pref., Pindar is generally known to be a dark Writer, to want Connexion..to soar out of Sight, and leave his Reader at a Gaze. **1704** SWIFT *Tale of a Tub* ix, This vapour..had so long set the nations at a gaze. *a* **1715** BURNET *Own Time* (1823) I. 128 And when the time of setting out the fleet came on, all were in a gaze whither it was to go. **1736** BOLINGBROKE *Patriot.* (1749) 22 All indifferent men stood as it were at a gaze. **1817** CHALMERS *Astron. Disc.* iv. (1830) 139 There is nothing that can so set his adoring myriads upon the gaze. **1828–40** BERRY *Encycl. Her.* I. s.v., The hart, stag, buck, or hind, when borne in coat-armour, looking affrontée or full-faced, is said to be at gaze..but all other beasts in this attitude are called guardant. **1859** J. WHITE *Hist. France* (1860) 20 On this occasion all Europe was on the gaze. **1864** BOUTELL *Her. Hist. & Pop.* xix. §5 (ed. 3) 310 Vert, three Harts at gaze or. **1874** FARRAR *Christ* II. lxi. 407 The great body of the people seem to have stood silently at gaze.

c. ***at gaze***: by sight (said of a hunting-dog).

1865 G. F. BERKELEY *Life & Recoll.* II. 236, I called on my deer dog 'Thor' to help me, for he could run a deer by nose as well as at gaze.

gaze (geɪz), *v.* Also 5 **gaase,** 5–6 **gase,** 6 **gayse, gayze.** [Of unknown origin; possibly f. the same root as GAW *v.*, with an *-s-* suffix. Rietz gives a Sw. dial. *gasa* to gape, stare.]

1. *intr.* †In early use: To look vacantly or curiously about; also, to stare, open one's eyes (with astonishment). In modern use: To look fixedly, intently, or deliberately at something. Now chiefly *literary.*

c **1386** CHAUCER *Clerk's T.* 1003 The peple gazed vp and doun, For they were glad..To han a newe lady. *c* **1430** *Stans Puer* 9 in *Babees Bk.* 27 Be symple in cheer; caste not þi looke aside, Gase [*v.r.* gaase] not about, turnynge þi siȝt oueral. *c* **1530** H. RHODES *Bk. Nurture* 175 *ibid.* 76 Gase thou not to and fro as one thats voyde of curtesye. **1535** COVERDALE *Ecclus.* ix. 7 Go not aboute gasinge in euery layne of the cite. **1667** PEPYS *Diary* (1879) IV. 199, I did make them all gaze to see themselves served so nobly. **1674** N. COX *Gentl. Recreat.* (1677) 50 That the Hare-finder should give the Hare three Sohoe's before he put her from her Lear, to make the Grey-hounds gaze and attend her rising. **1700** DRYDEN *Cymon & Iphig.* 171 With trembling heart Gazing he stood, nor would nor could depart. **1774** GOLDSM. *Nat. Hist.* (1776) III. 117 He stops, gazes round him, and seems to recover his natural tranquility. **1812** J. WILSON *Isle of Palms* II. 507 Long, long they gaze with meeting eyes. **1869** FREEMAN *Norm. Conq.* (1876) III. xi. 71 Men gazed and wondered in every land.

b. Const. *at, on, upon.* Also in *indirect passive.*

1553 EDEN *Treat. Newe Ind.* (Arb.) 39 And stode gasinge on him and feling his apparell. **1583** STANYHURST *Æneis* II. (Arb.) 67, I ran too Priamus razd court, at castel I gazed. **1631** GOUGE *God's Arrows* v. Ded. 406 You have brought me forth into the open field, and set me up to be gazed on, and baited at. **1674** N. COX *Gentl. Recreat.* (1677) 57 The Hart ..when he is..not afraid, he wonders at everything he seeth and taketh pleasure to gaze at them. **1758** JOHNSON *Idler* No. 7 ¶3 The natives..gaze upon a tumbler. **1820** W. IRVING *Sketch Bk.* I. 40, I have often noticed the mute rapture with which he would gaze upon her in company. **1866** G. MACDONALD *Ann. Q. Neigh.* i. (1867) 15 The boy gazing at the red and gold and green of the sunset sky. **1870** MORRIS *Earthly Par.* II. III. 387 So up the long street then, Gazing about, well gazed at, went the men.

c. quasi-*trans.* with adv. or phrase expressing result.

1713 C'TESS WINCHELSEA *Misc. Poems* 12 The amazed Emperor, When Cleopatra anchor'd in the Bay..Like his own Statue stood, and gaz'd the world away. **1735** SOMERVILLE *Chase* III. 497 An obsequious Crowd, As if by stern Medusa gaz'd to Stones. **1792** S. ROGERS *Pleas. Mem.* I. 218 So Scotia's Queen, as slowly dawned the day, Rose on her couch and gazed her soul away.

2. *trans.* To stare at, look fixedly at. *poet.*

c **1591** DANIEL *Sonn.* xxvi. in Arb. *Garner* I. 593 When, if she grieve to gaze her in her glass..Go you, my verse! go tell her what she was. **1593** DRAYTON *Idea* 593 So doth the Plow-man gaze the wand'ring Starre. **1667** MILTON *P.L.* VIII. 258 Strait toward Heav'n my wondring Eyes I turnd, And gaz'd a while the ample Skie. **1839** BAILEY *Festus* xxii. (1848) 281 As who dare gaze the sun.

gazebo (gə'ziːbəʊ). Also 9 **gazeboo, gazeebo(o, gazabo.** [Commonly explained as a humorous formation on GAZE *v.*, imitating Lat. futures like *videbo* 'I shall see' (cf. LAVABO); but the early quots. suggest that it may possibly be a corruption of some oriental word.]

1. A turret or lantern on the roof of a house, usually for the purpose of commanding an extensive prospect; also, a similar erection in a garden or pleasure ground; a belvedere or look-out.

1752 W. & J. HALFPENNY *New Designs* IV. 2 The Elevation of a Chinese Tower or Gazebo. **1790** W. WRIGHTE *Grotesque Archit.* 7 The whole is lighted from the gazebo on the top. **1828** *Q. Rev.* XXXVII. 316 Kent and his followers had temples, obelisks, and gazabos of every description in the park. **1858** W. WHITE *Month in Yorksh.* 288, I was first led to the gazebo on the roof that I might enjoy the prospect of the town and neighborhood.

2. A projecting window or balcony.

1843 MRS. ROMER *Rhone, Darro*, etc. II. 354 The houses [at Valetta, Malta] are invariably built of stone, and provided with large projecting balconies or gazeebos covered and glazed, which open and close at pleasure. *a* **1871** A. B. GRANVILLE *Autobiog.* I. 223 Dwelling-houses.. present lofty walls without windows towards the street except here and there a single latticed gazebo.

gazee (geɪ'ziː). *nonce-wd.* [f. GAZE *v.* + -EE.] One who is stared at.

1853 DE QUINCEY *Autobiog. Sk.* Wks. I. 155 Such a group would relieve both parties—gazer and gazee—from too distressing a consciousness of the little business on which they had met.

†**'gazeful,** *a. Obs.* [f. GAZE *sb.* + -FUL; a Spenserian word.] That gazes intently.

1595 SPENSER *Hymn Heavenly Beautie* 12 The ravisht harts of gazefull men might reare To admiration of that heavenly light. **1596** —— *F.Q.* IV. x. 28 Which when as I.. beheld with gazefull eye, I thought there was none other heaven then this.

'gaze-hound. Also 6–7 **gase-hound.** [f. GAZE *sb.* + HOUND *sb.*] A species of dog used in hunting, which follows its prey by sight and not by scent. Now chiefly *Hist.*

1570 J. CAIUS *De Canibus Brit.* 11 Similiter a verbo nostrati gase, (quod fixius rem aliquam contueri est) Gasehunde appellatur nostris, quem ante Agasæum nominari diximus. **1610** W. FOLKINGHAM *Art of Survey* 9, English Mastiffes, Gase Houndes (or Lurchers) and Tumblers are in request. **1714** TICKELL in *Steele's Poet. Misc.* 178 See'st thou the Gaze-hound! how with Glance severe From the close Herd he marks the destin'd Deer! **1808** SCOTT *Marm.* II. Introd. 41 And foresters in green-wood trim, Lead in the leash the gazehounds grim. **1869** BLACKMORE *Lorna D.* xxii, I entered the house with some wrath upon me at seeing the gazehounds in the yard.

gazel, var. GHAZAL.

'gazeless, *a. rare*⁻¹. [f. GAZE *sb.* + -LESS.] Sightless, unseeing.

a **1819** WOLCOT (P. Pindar) *Progr. Admiration* 118 Desire lies dead upon the gazeless eye.

gazelle (gə'zɛl). Also 6–7 ? **gugelle,** 8 **ghazel,** 9 **gazel** (*erron.* **gazhal**). [a. F. *gazelle* (OF. *gazel*, recorded in 14th c.) = Sp. *gacela, gacele, gacel*, Pg. *gazella*, It. *gazzella*, ad. Arab. *ghazāl*, which prob. passed first into Sp. and thence to the other Rom. tongues.]

A small delicately-formed antelope, of which the typical species (*Gazella Dorcas*) is a native of Northern Africa; other varieties are found in various parts of Africa and Asia. The gazelle is especially noted for the grace of its movements and the softness of its eyes.

[**1582** N. LICHEFIELD *Castanheda's Discov. E. Ind.* ii. 6 b, Also they doe eate of beastes, which they call *Gazelas*.] **1600** J. PORY tr. *Leo's Africa* I. 39 Heere also, besides goates, sheepe, deere, Gugelle, conies..and ostriches. **1669** *Phil. Trans.* IV. 995 The Gazelle, or wild African Shee-goat (the same with the Dorcas or Strepsiceros). **1745** tr. F. BERNIER in *Harl. Misc.* II. 184 Likewise leopards, or panthers tamed, which they use in the hunting of Gazelles. **1807–8** W. IRVING *Salmag.* (1824) 382 The turtle-dove, the timid fawn, the soft-eyed gazel..resorted to its vicinity. **1813** BYRON *Giaour* 474. **1822** GOOD *Study Med.* I. 277 They [Bezoars] are white, yellow, or brownish; that of the gazhal is greenish blue. **1851** LAYARD *Pop. Acc. Discov. Nineveh* xiii. 352 Plenty of..gazelles, wild boars, and lions for the chase.

b. *attrib.* as ***gazelle-antelope***; ***gazelle-eyed*** adj.

1774 GOLDSM. *Nat. Hist.* III. iii. 72 A gazelle-eyed beauty is considered as the highest compliment that a lover can pay. **1850** SWAINSON *Quadrup.* §265. 256 The gazelle antelopes may, then, be said to have their horns lyre-shaped.

Hence **ga'zelline** *a.*, 'akin to the gazelle' (Cassell).

'gazement. *rare.* [f. GAZE + -MENT.] Stare, look, observation.

1596 SPENSER *F.Q.* V. iii. 17 Then forth he brought his snowy Florimele..Covered from peoples gazement with a vele. **1829** *Blackw. Mag.* XXV. 81 There he look'd with ceaseless gazement on its walls.

gazer ('geɪzə(r)). Also 6 **gaser.** [f. GAZE *v.* + -ER[1].]

1. One who gazes or looks steadily, esp. from motives of curiosity.

1548 UDALL, etc. *Erasm. Par. Luke* xix. 4 He [Zacheus] stood a lofte in a tree to bee a gazer vpon one man and no mo. **1552** *Bk. Com. Prayer, Commun.* 1st Exhort., If ye stand by as gasers and lokers on them that do communicate. **1590** GREENE *Never too late* (1600) 2 Lockes where loue did sit and twine Nets to snare the gazers eyne. **1649** MILTON *Eikon.* Pref. Wks. (1851) 332 The conceited portraiture before his Book..sett there to catch fools and silly gazers. **1742** YOUNG *Nt. Th.* VIII. 493 Fain would he make the world his pedestal; Mankind the gazers. **1818** BYRON *Ch. Har.* IV. clii, How smiles The gazer's eye with philosophic mirth. **1849** MACAULAY *Hist. Eng.* v. I. 625 Tower Hill was covered.. with an innumerable multitude of gazers.

2. The name of a fish.

1861 J. COUCH *Brit. Fishes* I. 68 Broad headed Gazer. *Polyprosopus macer*, Nobis.

†**ga'zet(t.** *Obs.* [a. F. *gazette* (obs.), a. It. *gazzetta.*] A Venetian coin of small value.

The earliest quots. give its value as about three farthings, but Cotgr. says of the F. *gazette*, 'scarce worth our farthing', and quot. 1682 agrees with this. Probably its worth varied in different places, as it was coined at Venice for circulation in the Levant.

1605 B. JONSON *Volpone* II. ii. (1607) E 2, What monstrous, and most painefull circumstance Is here, to get some three, or foure Gazets! Some three-pence i'th whole, for that 'twill come too. **1632** BROME *Novella* III. Wks. 1873 I. 143 *Pedro.* Take from my hand a peece of foure Gazetts. *Paulo.* That's three-pence sterling; you are bounteous, Sir. **1682** WHELER *Journ. Greece* I. 43 The owners sell the rest for two Gazets the pound, which is not a half-peny English.

gazette (gə'zɛt), *sb.* Forms: 7 **gazetta, gasetta** (pl. **gazetti, gazettaes**), 7–8 **gazet(t,** (7 **gaziette**), 8 **gazzette,** 7– **gazette.** [a. F. *gazette*, ad. It. *gazzetta*, pl. *gazzette* (whence the earliest forms in English), app. so called from the coin of that name (see GAZET), which may have been the sum paid either for the paper itself or for the privilege of reading it; but a derivation from *gazzetta*, dim. of *gazza* magpie, is not impossible.

In late 17th and early 18th c., the word came to be accented on the first syllable, and it is so marked by Johnson. Cowper (*Table Talk* 37) again accents it in the original fashion.]

1. A news-sheet; a periodical publication giving an account of current events. (Now only *Hist.*)

The *gazzetta* was first published in Venice about the middle of the 16th c., and similar news-sheets appeared in France and England in the 17th. The untrustworthy nature of their reports is often alluded to by writers of that period; thus Florio explains *gazzette* as 'running reports, daily newes, idle intelligences, or flim flam tales that are daily written from Italie, namely from Rome and Venice'.

1605 B. JONSON *Volpone* v. iv. (1607) M 3, O, I shall bee the fable of all feasts; The freight of the *Gazetti.* **1611** R. RICHMOND *Panegyr. Verses*, in Coryat *Crudities* e 2 b, For sure that Iew from Venice came, we finde it so recorded, In late Gazettas. **1623** *Accident in Blacke Friers* 15 Witnesse heauen and earth, &..those rediculous Italian Gazetts, that come from Rome, Millane, and Antwerp. *a* **1639** DONNE *Lett.* (1651) 234 Perchance you look not so low as our ordinary Gazetta. **1642** HOWELL *For. Trav.* (Arb.) 27 The Gazets and Courants hee should do well to reade weekly. **1646–8** G. DANIEL *Poems* Wks. 1878 I. 211, I will not speake of Feats, High Stories, to out-rant our dull Gazetts. *a* **1668** DAVENANT *News fr. Plymouth* IV. Dram. Wks. 1873 IV. 171 All's true, I assure you. Can the gazets lie? Or the courants fail? **1682** DRYDEN *Medal*, Ep. Whigs A 4 b, I am afraid it is not read so much as the Piece deserves, because the Bookseller is every week crying help at the end of his Gazette, to get it off. **1762** GOLDSM. *Cit. W.* iv, This universal passion for politics is gratified by daily gazettes. **1812** BYRON *Waltz* vi, She came..and with her certain sets Of true despatches, and as true gazettes. **1855** MACAULAY *Hist. Eng.* xxi. (1869) IV. 108/2 During a considerable time the unofficial gazettes, though much more garrulous and amusing than the official gazette, were scarcely less courtly.

b. Of a person: A news-monger. (So F. *gazette.*)

1702 FARQUHAR *Twin Rivals* I. i. (1703) 2 For that reason I communicate: I know thou art a perfect Gazette, and will spread the News all over the Town.

2. *spec.* One of the three official journals entitled *The London Gazette*, *The Edinburgh Gazette*, and *The Dublin Gazette*, issued by authority twice a week, and containing lists of government appointments and promotions, names of bankrupts, and other public notices. Hence sometimes used *gen.* for the official journal of any government. *to be in the gazette*: to be published a bankrupt.

The first official journal published in England was *The Oxford Gazette*, the first number of which appeared in Nov. 1665, when the Court was at Oxford on account of the plague. Nos. 22 and 23 were printed in London, and with No. 24 the title was changed to *The London Gazette*. *The Edinburgh Gazette* was first issued in 1690, *The Dublin Gazette* in 1705.

1665 WOOD *Life* (O.H.S.) II. 49, Oct...In this month gazets were first published at Oxon. **1685** LUTTRELL *Brief Rel.* (1857) I. 324 There is a reward of 100*l.* published in the Gazet for any one that shal apprehend the said col. Danvers. **1700** T. BROWN tr. *Fresny's Amusem. Ser. & Com.* 114 And you hear no more of our Goldsmith, till you find him in a Gazette, torn to pieces by a Statute of Bankrupt. **1762** FOOTE *Lyar* I. Wks. 1799 I. 290 I'll undertake to do more business by the single aid of the London Gazette, than by all ..that the whole race of rhymers have ever produced. **1805** WELLINGTON in Gurw. *Desp.* (1837) III. 617, I do not augur any thing unfavourable to your promotion, because it is not confirmed by the last gazettes. **1817** BYRON *Beppo* xlix, Our trifling bankruptcies in the Gazette. **1831** T. L. PEACOCK *Crotchet Castle* Conclus. 299 The great firm of Catchflat and Company figured in the Gazette, and paid sixpence in the pound. **1855** WYNTER *Curios. Civiliz., Advts.* 15 The London Gazette..is the only paper still in existence that had its root in those days. **1859** SALA *Tw. round Clock* (1861) 48 He sometimes goes into the 'Gazette', paying but an infinitesimal dividend in the pound. **1897** *Daily News* 16 Oct. 3/1 Last night's 'Gazette' contains the formal order that the city of Canterbury shall..be the place where assizes are holden for the County of Kent.

b. A report in an official gazette.

1801 SYD. SMITH in Lady Holland *Life* (1855) I. 50 If we were to read the gazette of a naval victory from the pulpit, we should be dazzled with the eager eyes of our audience.

3. *Comb.*, as *gazette-writer*; † **gazette-marks,** ? the points of a description in a 'lost or stolen' advertisement, or in a 'hue and cry'.

a **1678** MARVELL *Poems, Tom May's Death* 267 Must therefore all the world be set on flame Because a Gazette-writer missed his aim? **1687** CONGREVE *Old Bach.* II. ii, This rascally gazetwriter never so much as once mentioned me. **1703** DE FOE *More Reform.* 670 All men would say the Picture was thy own, No Gazet Marks were half so quickly known. **1807** *Hist. Eur.* in *Ann. Reg.* 241/2 Another appointment made by the late administration was, that of gazette-writer created by patent for Scotland with a salary of £300 per annum.

gazette (gə'zɛt), *v.* [f. prec. sb.] *trans.* To publish in a gazette. Chiefly pass. *to be gazetted*: to be the subject of an announcement in the official gazette; to be named in the gazette as appointed *to* a command, etc.; also, in early use, to be mentioned or discussed in the newspapers.

to be gazetted out: said of an officer whose resignation is announced in the gazette.

1678 MARVELL *Growth Popery* Wks. 1875 IV. 406 The Parliament being grown to that height of contempt, as to be gazetted among runaway servants, lost dogs, strayed horses, and highway robbers. **1748** H. WALPOLE *Corr.* (1837) II. cxcvii. 250 Mr. Villiers, you know, has been much gazetted, and had his letters to the King of Prussia printed. **1813** COL. HAWKER *Diary* (1893) I. 69 Received official information that I was gazetted out. **1831** LYTTON *Godolphin* 13 And very shortly afterwards, Percy Godolphin was gazetted as a cornet in the —— Life Guards. **1852** THACKERAY *Esmond* II. ix, During this winter Mr. Esmond was gazetted to a lieutenantcy in Brigadier Webb's regiment of Fusileers. **1885** *Law Times* LXXIX. 173/2 K.'s retirement was gazetted on the evening of the 18th Dec. **1897** *Daily News* 4 Mar. 7/1 The fees charged are on a uniform scale, settled and gazetted by the Government Department of Labour.

Hence **ga'zetted** *ppl. a.*, **ga'zetting** *vbl. sb.*

1808 MOORE *Corrupt.* ii, That courtly ear, Which..hears no news but W——rd's gazetted lies. **1852** W. JERDAN *Autobiog.* II. 159 After the Gazetting, another advertisement was substituted. **1856** LD. HOUGHTON in *Life* (1891) II. xii. 13, I do not know why Labouchere delays the gazetting of your knighthood. **1891** *Daily News* 4 Nov. 5/5 By a Resolution published in the 'Calcutta Gazette'..The skin and skull of each tiger..'should be retained until the arrival of a gazetted officer of the Sunderbuns Forest Department'.

gazetteer (gæzə'tɪə(r)). Also 7 **gazettier, gazetiere.** [a. F. *gazettier* (now written *gazetier*) = It. *gazzettiere*: see GAZETTE *sb.* and -EER[1].]

1. One who writes in a gazette; a journalist, a retailer of news. (Now only *Hist.*)

1611 DONNE *Panegyr. Verses* in Coryat *Crudities* d 3 Mount now to Gallo-Belgicus; Appeare As deepe a Statesman as a Gazettier [**1650** *Poems* p. 262 Garreteir]. **1653** BP. WEBBE *Pract. Quietnesse* xxvi. 249 Such Makebates, idle Garitiers [? *read* Gazitiers], and tatling News-carriers, are very rife every where in the world. **1664** EVELYN *Let.* 31 Oct. in *Diary* (1879) III. 295 He [Sorbiere] styles himself Historiograph du Roy, the mighty meede of the co'monest Gazetiere, as that of Conseiller du Roy is of every trifling petifoger. **1671** MARVELL *Corr.* Wks. 1872–5 II. 393, I address myself, which is all I am good for, to be your gazettier. **1693** [see 3 *note*]. **1771** SMOLLETT *Humph. Cl.* II. 10 June, Let. i, The flimsy reveries of an ignorant gazetteer. **1817** J. W. CROKER in *Croker Papers* 26 Nov. (1884) Those who go out do not call upon me, so that I am but a bad gazetteer. **1858** CARLYLE *Fredk. Gt.* IX. vi. II. 460 Gazetteers, who would earn their wages..had to watch with all eagerness the movements of King August.

b. A journalist appointed and paid by Government.

1711 SWIFT *Let.* 8 Nov. Wks. 1762 XIV. 70, I have got poor Dr. King who was some time in Ireland, to be Gazetteer, which will be worth 250*l.* per annum to him. **1738** POPE *Epil. Sat.* I. 84 No Gazetteer more innocent than I. **1755** JOHNSON, *Gazetteer*, it was lately a term of the utmost infamy, being usually applied to wretches who were hired to vindicate the court. **1843** MACAULAY *Ess., Addison* (1887) 792 Steele had been appointed Gazetteer by Sunderland. **1884** W. J. COURTHOPE *Addison* v. 85 The office of Gazetteer became henceforth a regular ministerial appointment.

†**2.** A newspaper, gazette. *Obs.*

1730–46 THOMSON *Autumn* 558 Glasses and bottles, pipes and gazetteers. **1742** FIELDING *J. Andrews* II. xvii, 'Gazetteers', answered Adams; 'What is that?' 'It is a dirty newspaper', replied the host. **1769** BURKE *Pres. St. Nat.* Wks. II. 13 They have drawled through columns of Gazetteers and Advertisers for a century together.

3. A geographical index or dictionary.

A work of this kind, by L. Echard (ed. 2, 1693), bore the title 'The Gazetteer's: or, Newsman's Interpreter: Being A Geographical Index'. 'The Title', he says, 'was given me by a very eminent Person, whom I forbear to name' (Pref. p. 1). In Part II, published in 1704, the author refers to the book as 'the Gazetteer' simply (see quot.).

1704 L. ECHARD *Gazetteer's or Newsman's Interpr.* II. Pref., The kind Reception the Gazetteer has met with in the World..[has] induced us to go on with a second Part. **1751** (*title*) England's Gazetteer, and accurate Description of all the Towns, Cities, Villages, &c. **1806** *Gazetteer Scotl.* (ed. 2) Introd. 20 Scotland has five Universities..of which an account will be found in the Gazetteer. **1853** (*title*) Dictionary of Geography, forming a complete Gazetteer of the world. **1875** LOWELL *Among my Bks.* Ser. II. (1876) 137 The 'Polyolbion' is nothing less than a versified gazetteer of England and Wales.

Hence **gaze'tteer** *v. trans.*, to describe geographically in gazetteers; **gaze'tteerage,** the class of gazette-writers; **gaze'tteering** *vbl. sb.*, the making of gazetteers; **gaze'tteering** *ppl. a.*, that writes in gazettes; **gaze'tteerish** *a.*, resembling the style of a gazetteer; **gaze'tteership,** the position of official gazetteer.

1799 *Spirit Publ. Jrnls.* (1800) III. 152 You and your partner, and gazetteering brother chip, are all of the same block. **1860** A. L. WINDSOR *Ethica* v. 221 An unlucky paper in his 'Tatler' lost Steele his gazetteership. **1865** CARLYLE *Fredk. Gt.* XXI. vi. X. 105 [He] saw..the general Gazetteerage everywhere, seized of this affair, and thrown into paroxysms at the size and complexion of it. **1875** LOWELL *Among my Bks.* Ser. II. (1876) 137 Neither of them [Drayton and Daniel] could make poetry coalesce with gazetteering or chronicle-making. **1890** *Chambers' Encycl.* V. 120 Few countries, if any, are more thoroughly gazetteered than France. **1891** *Review of Rev.* Jan. 77/2 A brief paper on 'Armour for Warships', which is somewhat gazetteerish and historical.

†**ga'zettist.** *Obs. rare.* [f. GAZETTE *sb.* + -IST.] The writer of an official gazette.

1625 W. B. *True School War* 10 He..was inuested with the titles of the Intelligencer and Gazettist of Rome and Spaine. **1626** *Raleigh's Ghost* 22 Gondomar..Gazetist of State, one of the consumers of the King's purse.

gazing ('geɪzɪŋ), *vbl. sb.* [f. GAZE *v.* + -ING[1].]

1. The action of the verb GAZE.

c **1502** in Grose *Antiq. Rep.* (1808) II. *286 It is sen, great resorte often to be made for wonderyng and pleasure in their owne sights, and in wolgar speche callid gasyngs, of the rud and unlernyd persons. *a* **1533** LD. BERNERS *Gold. Bk. M. Aurel.* (1546) L j b, Fro tauerne to tauerne, from one gasing to another. **1552** LATIMER *Fruitf. Serm.* (1584) 273 Theyr teaching..begate a wondering and a gazing. Euery body maruelled at it & was desirous to talke of it. **1598** MANWOOD *Lawes Forest* xx. § 10 (1615) 177 The noyse of their running together, and the gasing of those Deere, that are scarred.. will disturbe the quiet of those wild beasts. **1626** BACON *Sylva* § 944 The Aspects that procure Loue, are not Gazings, but Sudden Glances, and Dartings of the Eye. **1741** RICHARDSON *Pamela* II. 92, I wanted to be out of their gazing. **1860** PUSEY *Min. Proph.* 240 Malicious gazing on human calamity..is the worst form of human hate.

fig. **1587** GOLDING *De Mornay* xxxiii. 532 The vanitie of these contemplations or rather gasings, is plainely bewraied by the effect thereof. **1659** C. NOBLE *Answ. Cert. Queries* 5 Such reproachfull things may amuse and stagger some weak judgements, and put them to gazings, and to doubtfull standings in their thoughts.

†**b.** Something to gaze at; a spectacle. *Obs.*

1548 HALL *Chron., Hen. VII* (1809) 471 For yᵉ which cause thei be more fierce, more bolde & hardy then the other Irish-men, and thei be very desyrous of newe things, & straunge sightes, and gasynges.

2. *attrib.*, as *gazing-point*, *-sight.* Also GAZING-STOCK.

1563 *Homilies* II. *Place & Time Prayer* II. (1859) 349 They see the church altogether scoured of such gay gazing sights, as their gross fantasy was greatly delighted with. **1856** R. A. VAUGHAN *Mystics* (1860) I. 45 The monks of Mount Athos, whose mysticism was also of this most degraded type, substituted, as a gazing-point, the navel for the nose.

gazing ('geɪzɪŋ), *ppl. a.* [f. as prec. + -ING[2].]

That gazes, in senses of the verb.

1553 LATIMER *Fruitf. Serm.* (1584) 293 b, Nowe hee had a daughter called Dina, which gasing damsell went abroad to see the countryes. **1633** P. FLETCHER *Purple Isl.* X. xxxvi, Her rubie lips lock up from gazing sight. **1683** TRYON *Way to Health* 486 Neither do we deck our selves with rich Ornaments to draw unto us every Gasing Eye. **1711** STEELE *Spect.* No. 167 ¶ 3 Gazing Crowds have found their Passions work'd up into Rage, or soothed into a Calm. **1840** HOOD *Up Rhine* 310 So we..at last marched into Nichol, through a gazing population.

fig. **1791** COWPER *Odyss.* XXII. 457 The gazing sun dries all their life away.

Hence **'gazingly** *adv.*

1563 GRINDAL *Let. to Abp. Parker* Wks. (Parker Soc.) 267 If the communion be ministered in Paul's, it will be done so tumultuously and gazingly..that the rest of the action will be disordered.

'gazing,stock. [f. GAZING *vbl. sb.* + STOCK.] An object of the people's gaze; a person on whom others gaze or stare.

1535 COVERDALE *Nahum* iii. 7, I wil cast dyrte vpon yᵉ, to make the be abhorred, and a gasynge stocke. **1566** UNDERDOWNE *Thes. & Ariadne*, A fayre woman is nothynge but a gasynge stocke of ydell folkes. **1650** tr. *Caussin's Ang. Peace* 75 They are made gazing-stocks to others, and are formidable to themselves. **1751** *Phil. Trans.* XLVII. 189 He was the gazing-stock and admiration of all people. **1840** LADY C. BURY *Hist. of Flirt* xx, I am free, and not a gazing-stock for the world to jeer at.

†**'gazity.** *Obs. rare*[−1]. [f. *gaz* GAS + -ITY: cf. GASEITY.] A gaseous state or condition.

1799 SIR H. DAVY *Ess. Heat, Light*, etc. Wks. 1839 II. 8 The peculiar modes of existence of bodies, solidity, fluidity, and gazity, depend (according to the calorists) on the quantity of the fluid of heat entering into their Composition.

gazob (gə'zɒb). *Austral. slang.* [Origin unknown; perh. f. GAZABO.] A fool; a blunderer.
1906 E. DYSON *Fact'ry 'Ands* xii. 162 But I thought barrer-pushin' was er game fer gazobs? **1916** C. J. DENNIS *Songs Sentimental Bloke* 42 Ar! but 'e makes me sick! A fair gazob! **1966** BAKER *Austral. Lang.* (ed. 2) vi. 135 Fools of one kind and another..*gazob, gimp, gup,* [etc.].

gazogene ('gæzədʒiːn). Also **gasogene**. [a. F. *gazogène*, f. *gaz* GAS + *-gène*: see -GEN.] A gas-producer. **a.** An apparatus for the production of aerated waters. **b.** An apparatus used in the process of *gas-firing* (GAS *sb.*[1] 7).
a. 1853 *Pract. Mech. Jrnl.* VI. 87 Gaillard and Dubois' 'Gazogene' or Aerated Water apparatus. **1886** *Pall Mall G.* 23 June 12/1 Bright milk cans standing in rows, with baskets full of new-laid eggs, and gazogenes.
b. 1879 *Encycl. Brit.* IX. 844/2 In this case [when 'gas-firing' is used], the fireplace proper is replaced by a *gas-producer* or *gazogene*.

†'**gazolite.** *Obs.*$^{-0}$ An aerolite. (In mod. Dicts.)

gazolyte ('gæzəlaɪt). [a. F. *gazolyte*, f. *gaz* GAS + Gr. λυτός soluble.] **a.** (See quot.) **b.** 'A body which is resolvable into a gas. Ampère's term for those elementary bodies which by combination form gases' (*Syd. Soc. Lex.* 1885).
1842 FRANCIS *Dict. Arts*, etc., *Gazolyta* or *Gazolytes*, a name given by Berzelius to such simple gases as are permanently elastic. These are oxygen, nitrogen, and hydrogen.

gazometer, obs. form of GASOMETER.

†**gazon.** *Obs.* [a. F. *gazon* grass; *pl.* pieces of turf; a. OHG. *waso* (MHG. *wase*, G. *wasen*) sod, turf, damp soil, or mass of earth.] A sod or piece of turf, used in fortification (see quots.).
1704 HARRIS *Lex. Techn.*, *Gazons*, in Fortification, are pieces of fresh Earth covered with Grass, cut in form of a Wedge, about a Foot long, and half a Foot thick, to line parapets, and the Traverses of Galleries. **1759** STERNE *Tr. Shandy* II. v. 70, 'I would make the walls and parapets with sods too'. 'The best engineers call them gazons, Trim', said my uncle Toby. **1768** in SIMES *Milit. Medley* Dict. **1802** in C. JAMES *Milit. Dict.*
b. *attrib.*, as ***gazon-theatre***.
1699 EVELYN *Acetaria* (1729) 119 Gazon-Theatres, Amphi-theatres, Artificial Echos.

gazoo, gazooka, varr. KAZOO.

gazook (gə'zuːk). *slang.* [Origin unknown, but cf. GAZABO and GAZOB.] A fool; a stupid or unpleasant person.
1928 M. H. WESEEN *Crowell's Dict. Eng. Gram.* 266 *Gazook*, slang name applied contemptuously to any person who is disliked. **1936** B. PENTON *Inheritors* I. ii. 15 Look at that poor gazook, Sambo. He'd call your old man God Almighty even if he starved him to death.

gazoomph, var. GAZUMP *v.*

ga'zoon. App. an adapted form of GAZON, with mistaken sense. (Hogg app. took the word to mean 'a compact body of men', or something similar.)
1813 HOGG *Queen's Wake* 263 A close gazoon the horsemen made, Douglas and Morison the head, And through the ranks impetuous bore.

†**gazophilace.** *Obs. rare.* [a. OF. *gazophilace*, ad. late L. *gazophylacium*.] = GAZOPHYLACIUM.
13.. *E.E. Allit. P.* B. 1283 þe golde of þe gazafylace.. Wyth alle þe vrnmentes of þat hous, he hamppred to-geder. [**1583** FULKE *Def.* xxi. 507 Yea, I woulde gladly know, why among so many Greekish and Latine-like terms, Gazophylacium is not a Gazophilace but a 'treasurie'.]

†**gazophile.** *Obs. rare*$^{-1}$. [a. OF. *gazophile*, corruptly ad. late L. *gazophylacium*: see next. The quot. is a close translation from Octovien de S. Gelais, *Ep. d'Ovide*, quoted by Godefroy, s.v.]
A treasury, storehouse (in *fig.* sense).
1549 *Compl. Scot.* To Rdr. 7, I began to reuolue the libraryе of my vndirstanding, ande i socht all the secreit corneris of my gazophile.

†**gazophy'lacium.** *Obs.* [a. late L. *gazophylacium*, ad. Gr. γαζοφυλάκιον, f. γάζα treasure + φυλάσσειν to guard, keep.] The box in which offerings to the Temple were received; a strong-box or treasure-chest.
1377 LANGL. *P. Pl.* B. XIII. 197 Haued nouȝt..the pore widwe [more] for a peire of mytes Than alle tho that offreden in-to gazafilacium. [**1398** TREVISA *Barth. De P.R.* XIX. cxxviii. (1495) 934 Gazofilacium is an hutche in the whyche is put what is offrid in the Temple.] **1563-87** FOXE *A. & M.* (1596) 259/1 What monie was raised to the popes gazophylacium, I leaue to the estimation of the reader. **1681** J. STEPHENS *Procurations* 105 There seemed to be a kind of pious contention in the people..who should be first to bring in their offerings to this sacred *Gazophylacium.* **1697** EVELYN *Numism.* viii. 266 Blood who made that bold attempt on the Royal Gazophylacium in the Tower.

†'**gazous**, *a. Obs. rare*$^{-1}$. [f. *gaz* GAS *sb.*[1] + -OUS.] Of the nature of gas, gaseous.
1794 SULLIVAN *View Nat.* I. 272 Many naturalists, as well as he, conceived this substance to be neither animal nor vegetable, but to be merely an aerial or gazous scum.

‖**gazpacho** (gaθ'patʃo, gasp-). Also **gaspacho**. [Sp.] A cold Spanish soup (see quot. 1845).
1845 R. FORD *Hand-bk. Trav. Spain* I. i. 69 *Gazpacho*.. is a cold vegetable soup, and is composed of onions, garlic, cucumbers, *pepinos*, pimientas, all chopped up very small and mixed with crumbs of bread, and then put into a bowl of oil, vinegar, and fresh water. **1903** CONRAD & HUEFFER *Romance* I. iv, He spent his days cooking extraordinary messes,..making substitutes for eternal gaspachos. **1963** R. CARRIER *Great Dishes of World* 56/2 *Gazpacho* is traditionally served accompanied by individual small bowls of raw vegetables and garlic *croûtons*. **1969** *New Yorker* 20 Sept. 164/2 Gazpacho..should rest and 'marry' for a time before being eaten.

gazump (gə'zʌmp), *v. slang.* Also **gasumph, gazoomph, gazumph, gezumph**. [Origin uncertain.] *trans.* To swindle; *spec.* to act improperly in the sale of houses, etc. (see quots. 1971). Also as *sb.*, a swindle. Hence **ga'zumper**, a swindler.
1928 *Daily Express* 19 Dec. 2/7 'Gazoomphing the sarker' is a method of parting a rich man from his money. An article is auctioned over and over again, and the money bid each time is added to it. *Ibid.*, I 'gazoomphed' a friend of mine with complete success last night. **1932** G. S. MONCRIEFF *Café Bar* xvii. 185 'Ere 'e is..parasitin' on people all day.. and then 'e objects to a little *gasumph*! *Ibid.* 187 That's all we are, gasumphers an' researchers of tripe. **1934** P. ALLINGHAM *Cheapjack* xv. 189 Grafters speak a language comprised of every possible type of slang... Quite a number of words are Yiddish. These include 'gezumph', which means to cheat or to overcharge. *Ibid.* xxiii. 301 The whole gezumphing world seemed to have gathered together. *Ibid.* 319 *Gezumpher*, a swindler. **1961** *Daily Mail* 25 Feb. 9/2 M.P.s had admitted that they had been 'gazoomphed' by fast-talking racketeers. **1969** Y. CARTER *Mr. Campion's Farthing* xiii. 121 I've never known an offer from you that wasn't a *gezumph*. **1971** *Guardian* 8 Nov. 13/2 'Gazumping'—a system of profiteering by double selling and pushing prices up—is creeping into the property market... The word is car trade slang for selling to one buyer and then, as values rise, to a second buyer. **1971** *Times* 6 Dec. 4/1 A Bill to be presented to the Commons next week..would outlaw the raising of the price of a house before contracts are exchanged. The practice is known as 'gazumping'.

gazy ('geɪzɪ), *a. rare.* [f. GAZE *sb.* + -Y[1].] **a.** Affording a wide prospect. **b.** Given to gazing.
1745 MRS. DELANY *Life & Corr.* (1861) II. 382 Has he.. laid himself down upon the gazy hill, to take breath a little? **1883** HOLME LEE *Loving & Serving* II. ix. 161 The most gazy and dreamy and restless of the people had learnt to keep their heads straight.

gazzette, obs. form of GAZETTE.

geach, *sb. slang.* ? *Obs.* A thief. So **geach** *v. trans.*, to steal.
1821 HAGGART *Life* 56 He was a tolerable geach. *Ibid.* 70 We saw a conish cove..with his back to the wall, beset by a great number of geachs. *Ibid.* 73, I bought two wedge table-feeders..which I knew had been geached from the house of Mrs. Campbell.

geadephagous (dʒiːə'dɛfəgəs), *a.* Also erron. **geo-**. [f. mod.L. *Geadephag-a* (f. Gr. γῆ earth + ADEPHAGA) + -OUS.] Of or pertaining to the *Geadephaga*, a tribe of terrestrial and predaceous beetles.
1884 *Athenæum* 22 Mar. 381/2 Mr. E. A. Fitch exhibited a large geodephagous larva.

geagged, obs. form of JAGGED.

geal ('dʒiːəl), *a. rare.* [badly f. Gr. γῆ earth + -AL[1].] Of or pertaining to the earth regarded as a planet. ***geal tides***: tides (on the moon) due to the earth's attraction.
1883 WINCHELL *World-Life* II. iii. §2 (1889) 384 The geal tide on the moon will be about eighty times higher than the lunar tide on the earth.

geal (dʒiːl), *v. Obs.* exc. *dial.* In 5 **gell(yn**. [a. F. *gele-r*:—L. *gelāre* to freeze. Cf. CONGEAL.] *trans.* and *intr.* To stiffen as with cold, to congeal.
The examples are often difficult to separate from those of *geal*, GELL *v.* (with 'hard' *g*), to tingle as with cold.
c **1440** *Promp. Parv.* 190/1 Gellyn, or congellyn (togedyr), *gelat, congelat.* **1608** TOURNEUR *Rev. Trag.* v. i, Wks. 1878 II. 133 We found the Duke my father gealde in bloud. **1633** H. A. *Partheneia Sacra* 190 It [the mother-pearl] forms litle graines or seeds within it, which cleaue to its sides, then grow hard, and geale, as it were. **1804** TARRAS *Poems* 19 Wer't no for houp..Our very hearts wou'd geal.
Hence '**gealing** *ppl. a.*
1604 T. WRIGHT *Passions* v. §4. 229 Gealing frostes cause springs and welles..in the depth of winter to smoke with heate.

geale, gealous, obs. ff. JAIL, JEALOUS.

gean (giːn). Now chiefly *Sc.* Forms: (6 **guyne**, 7 **guind**, 8 **guigne, guynne**), 8-9 **gean, geen**, (9 **guean**). [a. F. *guigne* (in the 14th c. spelt *guine*). Of unknown origin: Sp. has *guinda*, Pg. *ginja* of similar meaning.
Some have suggested that the word may be connected with OSl. *višnja*, Lith. *vysna*, Roumanian *vişină*, mod.Gr. *βίσινον*, and more remotely with OHG. *wîhsala* (mod.Ger. *weichsel*), It. *visciola*; but this is very doubtful.]
The wild cherry (*Prunus avium*), tree and fruit.
a **1533** LD. BERNERS *Gold. Bk. M. Aurel.* (1546) Ccij, Whan the guynes come, the season of cheryes is not come. **1653** URQUHART *Rabelais* II. xxxiv. 221 In the season of cherries and guinds. **1765** EARL HADDINGTON *Forest-trees* 17 The Black Cherry. This is called the Geen here. **1839** JARDINE *Brit. Birds* II. 78 They [missel-thrushes] are remarkably fond of ripe geans. **1882** *Garden* 28 Oct. 382/1 The Gean..grows in rocky, dry woods.
attrib. **1793** *Trans. Soc. Arts* (ed. 2) V. 16 Birch, Geen-tree, and Mountain Ash. **1854** H. MILLER *Sch. & Schm.* x. (1857) 201 To strip the guean-trees of their wild cherries.

†**geance.** *Obs. rare*$^{-1}$. ? An imagined rustic pronunciation of *chance*.
1633 B. JONSON *Tale Tub* II. iv, Vaith, would I had a few more geances on't!

geand, geant, obs. forms of GIANT.

†**Geane.** *Obs.* Also 5 **geene, gene**, 5-7 **Jeane**. See also JEAN, JANE[1]. The English form of the name of Genoa (F. *Gênes*, It. *Genova*); used *attrib.* in designations of commodities imported thence. ***treacle of Geane***: see TREACLE.
c **1466** SIR J. PASTON in *Paston Lett.* No. 563. II. 293, I sende yow—iij. tracle pottes of Geane as my potecarie sweryth on to me, and mooreovyr that they weer never ondoo syns they come from Geane. **1466** *Mann. & Househ. Exp.* (Roxb.) 369 My mastyr toke his man to kepe a potte of geene to put in grene gyngyr. **1494** *Will of Astry* (Somerset Ho.), 50 bales of Jeane wood. **1545** *Rates Custom ho.* b iij b, Geane paper the reame. **1582** N. LICHEFIELD tr. *Castanheda's Conq. E. Ind.* v. 14 b, Some of them doe carrie with them compasses of Geane. *a* **1618** *Rates Merchandize* L iij, Treacle of Ieane the pound viij.d.

geanticlinal (dʒiːæntɪ'klaɪnəl), *a.* and *sb. Geol.* [f. Gr. γῆ earth + ANTICLINAL.]
A. *adj.* Of the nature of a general upward flexure of the earth's crust.
1879 DANA *Man. Geol.* (ed. 3) 818 Many mountains owe half or more of their elevation above the sea level to geanticlinal movements.
B. *sb.* A general upward flexure of the earth's crust.
187. DANA *Man. Geol.* (ed. 2) 752 (Cent.) The part of the force not expended in producing them carried forward an upward bend, or geanticlinal, of the vast Rocky Mountain region as a whole. **1879** *Ibid.* (ed. 3) 818 Geanticlinals or upward flexures in the crust that become permanent elevations. **1882** A. H. GREEN *Phys. Geol.* xiii. (ed. 3) 631 The squeezing up of this mass of rock into a geanticlinal.

geanticline (dʒiː'æntɪklaɪn). *Geol.* [f. Gr. γῆ earth + ANTICLINAL *sb.*] = GEANTICLINAL *sb.*
1895 J. D. DANA *Man. Geol.* (ed. 4) 389 A mountain range includes all the mountain ridges made over the area and border of a single geanticline. **1925** J. JOLY *Surface-Hist. Earth* vii, The first Rocky Mountains geanticline came into existence in closing Carboniferous (early Pennsylvanian) time. **1957** G. E. HUTCHINSON *Treat. Limnol.* I. i. 14 Lake Poso..is probably a remnant of an old surface that escaped the general Pleistocene uplift which affected two geanticlines east and west of the lake.

gear (gɪə(r)), *sb.* Forms: 3 **gære**, 4-5 **ger**, 4 **guere**, 5-6 **gheer(e**, 4-5 **gare**, 5-6 **gayre, gaire, geyre**, 4-9 **ge(e)r(e, geir(e**, 5-6 **geyer**, 6-8 **geare**, 6- **gear**. [ME. *gere*, prob. ad. ON. *gervi, gørvi* = OE. ⁎*ȝieru* (*poet.* in pl. *ȝearwe*, with pre-Eng. change of declension), OS. *garewi, gerwi*, OHG. *garawî, gar(e)wî*:—OTeut. ⁎*garwîn-* wk. fem., f. ⁎*garwu-* ready, YARE, whence ⁎*garwjan* to make ready, ON. *gerva, gørva, gera, gøra* to make, GAR *v.*
It is prob. unnecessary to assume as the source an ON. ⁎*geri* with a dropping of the *v* (*w*) similar to that in *gera, gøra*, the common prose forms of the verb *gørva*; there was app. in ME. a disposition to reduce *rw* to *r* after a stressed palatal vowel.]
I. Equipment. Cf. FURNITURE 4.
1. a. *collect. sing.* (†rarely *pl.*) Apparel, attire, dress, vestments. Now common in colloq. use.
a **1310** in Wright *Lyric P.* x. 36 Heo glystnede ase gold when hit glemede, ues ner gome so gladly on gere. **13..** *E.E. Allit. P.* B 1811 þat we gon gay in oure gere. **1390** GOWER *Conf.* II. 227 Let clothen in the same gere. **1450-70** *Golagros & Gaw.* 158 Ane girdill ourgilt, and vthir light gere. **1465** J. PASTON in *Paston Lett.* No. 526 II. 233, I beseche yow that this ger be not forget, for I have not an hole hose for to doon. **1484** *Churchw. Acc. Croscombe* (Som. Rec. Soc.) 13 Item for wayschyng of the church gare vi[s]. iiij[d]. **1526** SKELTON *Magnyf.* 776, I can devyse my gere after the courtly maner. **1530** *Nottingham Rec.* III. 363 For makyng the dawnsars gayre. **1563-87** FOXE *A. & M.* (1684) II. 38/1 They did it to shew their new gay geere. **1727** VANBR. & CIB. *Prov. Husb.* I. Wks. (1730) 295 My Lady's geer alone were as much as filld four portmantel trunks. **1776** MRS. DELANY *Life & Corr.* Ser. II. (1862) II. 196, I have put on all my birthday geer. **1792** A. YOUNG *Trav. France* 61 Dressed in holiday geers. **1807** WORDSW. *White Doe* III. 34 Noisy swarms of peasants in their homely gear. **1857** HOLLAND *Bay Path* xxiv. 278 Mr. Pynchon himself, in his rusty travelling gear. **1879** 'E. GARRETT' *House by Wks.* II. 206 She packed her own marriage gear..with her own hand. **1963** *Sunday Express* 22 Dec. 14/2 A designer of singularly *avant garde* 'gear' (men's wear to the uninitiated). **1966** *Listener* 3 Mar. 327/2 There was no dressing up—in case, presumably, the customers fled at the sight of the queer gear.
†**b.** Appendages to a (clerical) vestment. *Obs.*

1552 *Invent. Ch. Goods* (Surtees 1897) 37 Albes and other geir belonging to the afforesaid vestmentes. *Ibid.* 55 One old vestment..and one..boithe without geire.

†**c.** *pl.* Habits, manners. *Obs. rare.*

The earliest recorded sense: placed here as being possibly a forced application of sense 1, suggested by the L. *habitus*.

c **1200** *Trin. Coll. Hom.* 35 þe deuel..teð forð geres hwile after fox, hwile after wulue, hwile after leun, hwile after oðre, and on ech of hise deden is iefned to þe deore wuas geres he forðteoð. *Ibid.* 165 Hie..teð forð geres after wilde deore, sume after beore, sume after wulue, sume after oðer deor. *Ibid.* 209.

2. Armour, arms, warlike accoutrements. Rarely *pl.* Also ***fighting-gear***. *Obs.* exc. *arch.*

c **1205** LAY. 13679 On ich wulle mid mine gære. *a* **1300** *Cursor M.* 7533 'Dos awai', he [David] said, 'þis gere, Certes can i nan armes bere'. **1375** BARBOUR *Bruce* XVIII. 165 Thai ..fand Gib Harper in his ger. And, for sa gude his armys wer, Thai [etc.]. *c* **1420** *Avow. Arth.* xxiv, Quen thou art armut in thi gere, Take thi schild and thi spere. **1483** CAXTON *Gold. Leg.* 88 a/2 They made theyr geer redy and departed. **1513** *Act 5 Hen. VIII*, c. 6 Any Armour or defenceable Geer of War. **1546** in Tytler *Hist. Scotl.* (1864) III. 374 After yame came the young laird..and viii men with hym all in geir. **1837** CARLYLE *Fr. Rev.* I. v. v, Of serviceable fighting-gear small stock. **1864** SKEAT *Uhland's Poems* 376 The host comes slowly onward, equipped with warlike gear.

3. a. Accoutrements of a riding horse, or his rider. (†Formerly also *pl.*) Now always explicitly ***riding-gear***.

a **1400–50** *Alexander* 790* (Dublin) Grathez on þis gay gere, & þen a gilt sadyll. *c* **1420** *Sir Amadace* (Camden) xxxii, Ylke mon his owne schall have, That he syttes apon, Sadyll, brydyll, and oder geyre. **1535** COVERDALE *Zech.* xiv. 20 At that tyme shal the ryding geer of yͤ horses be holy vnto the Lorde. **1690** DRYDEN *Don. Sebast.* I. i. Wks. 1883 VII. 342 *Ant.* Thou wilt not make a horse of me? *Must.* Be advised, friend, and buckle to thy gears [makes him go down on all-fours, bridles him—'To your paces villain, amble, trot and gallop']. **1840** DICKENS *Barn. Rudge* xlvii, Bridles, top-boots, spurs, and such gear, were strewn about. **1871** YEATS *Techn. Hist. Comm.* 46 The Egyptians were skilful manufacturers of riding gear.

b. Harness for draught animals. Before the 19th c. chiefly *pl.*

a **1300** *Cursor M.* 6221 Sex hundreth cartes wit al þair geres. **1424** *E.E. Wills* (1882) 56 My cartes and my plowes, and all my hors þat longen to hem, whith all her gere. **1523** FITZHERB. *Husb.* §5 He muste haue..his oxen or horses, and the geare that belongeth to them; that is to say, bowes, yokes [etc.]. **1525** *Will* in *Ely Episcop. Rec.* (1891) 220 Yͤ best donge carte, and fyve gayres of yͤ best; and my best ploughe and the geyers. **1601** HOLLAND *Pliny* I. 221 When they [horses] are set in their geirs to draw the chariots, how they ioy when they are encouraged. **1695** *Lond. Gaz.* No. 3115/4 A Sorrel Mare..the Hair rub'd off her sides with Geers. **1751** JOHNSON *Rambler* No. 138 ¶11 She rises before the sun to order the horses to their geers. **1799** G. WASHINGTON *Lett.* Writ. 1893 XIV. 220 Not suffering the Ploughs, Harrows..and the Gears belonging to them, to be unnecessarily exposed. **1821** CLARE *Vill. Minstr.* I. 74 Cracking whip and jingling gears Recall'd the toils of boyish years. **1846** J. BAXTER *Libr. Pract. Agric.* (ed. 4) II. 129 Their gear or harness, including the cost of keeping it in repair, amounts to 25*s.* yearly. **1869** *Lonsdale Gloss.*, *Gear*, harness, tackle of any kind, furniture; as plough-gear, cart-gear, etc. **1886** *Chesh. Gloss.* s.v., 'What's Tom doing this wet day?' 'Mester, he's cleaning th' gears.'

†**4.** *fig.* (Prob. chiefly referring to sense 3 b.) (***ready***) ***in one's gears***: in harness, ready for work = L. ***in procinctu***. ***to put in, get into one's gears***: to set or get to work. ***right in one's gear***: in one's right senses. ***warm in one's gear(s***: settled down to work. ***out of one's gears***: out of sorts. *Obs.*

c **1460** *Towneley Myst.* xxi. 181 He is inwardly flayde, not right in his gere. **1642** FULLER *Holy & Prof. St.* III. xiii. 184 They think themselves not warm in their geeres, till they are all on fire. **1642** ROGERS *Naaman* 128 Iehu..being warme in his geare. *a* **1659** CLEVELAND *Gen. Poems*, etc. (1677) 134 Let him put himself in his Geers. **1664** ETHEREDGE *Com. Rev.* IV. ii. 67 Is Grace ready in her gears. *a* **1677** BARROW *Pope's Suprem.* (1687) 49 The Apostles were..*in procinctu*, ready in their gears to move whither Divine suggestions did call them. **1682** DRYDEN *Medal* 60 The Frauds he learnt in his Fanatick Years Made him uneasie in his Lawful Gears. **1683** PENN *Descr. Pennsylv.* 8 Of this more hereafter, being yet Raw and New in our Geer. *a* **1700** B. E. *Dict. Cant. Crew* s.v., *Out of his Gears*, out of sorts. **1711** SWIFT *Wks.* (1824) II. 463 Nuttal was surprised when they gave him bits of paper instead of money, but I made Ben Tooke put him in his gears. **1712–13** —— *Jrnl. to Stella* 8 Jan., I am in my geers..and I treat folks sometimes. **1780** JOHNSON *Let. to Mrs. Thrale* 4 July, Keep my master tight in his geers.

II. Apparatus.

5. a. Apparatus generally; appliances, implements, tackle, tools. †Also *pl.* toys.

a **1300** *Cursor M.* 24485 (Gött.) Joseph and nichodeme.. Wid þaim broght þai gere enogh, vte of his fete þe nail droght. **13..** *E.E. Allit. P.* B. 1505 Nov is alle þis guere geten glotounes to serue. **1375** BARBOUR *Bruce* XVII. 702 Iohne crab, that had his geir all ȝar, In his fagattis has set the fyre. *c* **1386** CHAUCER *Prol.* 352 Wo was his Cook but if his sauce were Poynaunt and sharpe and redy al his geere. *a* **1400–50** *Alexander* 1773 For ai a child mot him chese . to childire geris. **1461** *Paston Lett.* No. 391 II. 13 It were tyme your gere necessarye on that by halfe were purveyd fore. **1823** SCOTT *Peveril* xxxvi, The warders must bring their own gear [fetters] with them. **1832** J. HODGSON in J. Raine *Mem.* (1858) II. 260 All the quarry gear was swept away by one of the great floods. **1850** SCORESBY *Cheever's Whaleman's Adv.* iv. (1859) 60 An ingenious Frenchman.. had bladders and other gear to float dead whales. **1851** GREENWELL *Coal-trade Terms Northumb. & Durh.* 28 *Gear*, work-tools, consisting of picks, drills, maul and wedge, shovel, cracket, &c. **1883** *Fisheries Exhib. Catal.* p. xxxiv, Such sportsman's gear as rods, lines, artificial flies, and baits. **1885** *Act 48 & 49 Vict.* c. 70 §7 Injury..done by one sea-fishing boat to another, or to the nets, lines, and gear thereof. **1885** SIR J. C. MATHEW in *Law Times Rep.* LII. 265/1 The vessel..was sold as she lay with her gear and tackle. **1885** *Athenæum* 16 May 637/3 Pretending to work, amidst building stones and masons' gear, on a Paris *quai*.

b. The organs of generation. Now only *slang*.

1675 HOBBES *Odyssey* (1677) 280 To the dogs to eat they threw his gear. **1704** SWIFT *Tale of Tub* xi. 202. **1893** in FARMER *Slang*.

Comb. **1611** COTGR., *Chaude-colle*, saltnesse, leacherousnesse, geereitch.

†**c.** *Weaving.* A leaf of heddles. *Obs.*

1500 *Nottingham Corp. Rec.* 1380, 43 iij. lynen geyrs et j. lathe. **1523** *Ibid.* 1395, 7 Pro quodam instrumento textorum vulgariter dicto a lynen gegre [? *read* geyre]. **1780** A. YOUNG *Tour Irel.* I. 324 It [flax] is ready to be delivered to the weaver, with the reed and geers adapted to manufacturing it. **1813** T. MARTIN *Circle Mech. Arts* 239 in Bischoff *Wool. Manuf.* (1862) II. 407 The loom consists merely of two bamboo rollers, one for the warp, and another for the web, and a pair of geer. **1822** R. G. WALLACE *15 Yrs. Ind.* 298 The loom consists of a reed and geers, with a small beam, upon which the warp is rolled. **1839** URE *Dict. Arts* 1285 The Hindu..inserts his great toes into two loops under the geer, to serve him for treddles.

d. *Mining. pair of gears* = gallows-timber.

1851 GREENWELL *Coal-trade Terms Northumb. & Durh.* 28, *Pair of Gears*, see *Gallows Timber*.

e. ***that's*** (or ***it's***) ***the gear***: an expression of approval. Hence as *adj.*, good, excellent, 'great'. Also as *int. slang.*

1925 FRASER & GIBBONS *Soldier & Sailor Words* 103 *Gear*, apparatus generally... Also used as a colloquial term for anything giving satisfaction—*e.g.*, 'That's it, that's the gear!' **1951** *Sunday Pictorial* 29 Oct., If a guy is 'gear', as they call a smart boy, he will dress in a single-breasted.. drape jacket. **1963** *Guardian* 8 Oct. 9/1 The Liverpool Sound..put expressions like 'it's the gear' into the mouths of debs... How long has it been since a native expression ousted a transatlantic jargon import like gear did to crazy and judy to chick? **1963** *Today* 30 Nov. 15 (*caption*) They're gear! The Beatles leave for London after their triumphant tour of Sweden. **1964** J. BURKE *Hard Day's Night* iii. 71 'Gear!' John jumped up from his seat. 'Come on, girls, let's have a bit of a dance.' *Ibid.* iv. 89 Once we even all sat down and wrote those letters saying how gear she was and all that rubbish. **1967** W. MURRAY *Sweet Ride* vi. 88 Choo Choo, you're boss! Fab! Gear! Bitchin'!

6. *Machinery.* **a.** A combination of wheels, levers, and other mechanical appliances for a given purpose; *esp.* the appliances or furnishings connected with the acting portions of any piece of mechanism. Often with some defining word prefixed, as ***expansion-***, ***hand-***, ***steering-***, ***valve-***, ***winding-gear***: for which see those words.

1523 FITZHERB. *Surv.* xx. (1539) 42 And the mylner shall make all the coste, both of the hous and the goinge geyre. **1786** T. JEFFERSON *Writ.* (1859) I. 550 The consumption [of coal] will be increased by the additional geer. **1825** J. NICHOLSON *Operat. Mechanic* 44 Chains have been beneficially introduced as substitutes for straps in driving heavy geer. **1851** *Illustr. Catal. Gt. Exhib.* 135 Model of a steam crane, with travelling gear. **1882** *Knowledge* No. 19. 397/2 Being caught by the steering gear or front wheel. **1888** F. HUME *Mad. Midas* I. iii, The towers contained the winding gear. **1892** *Law Times Rep.* LXVII. 251/1 A steamship of 1074 tons net, fitted with steam steering gear.

fig. **1861** *Lond. Rev.* 20 Apr. 434/1 There is considerable friction in our parliamentary gear. **1889** LOWELL *Latest Lit. Ess.* (1892) 149 None of these set our thinking gear in motion to..good purpose.

b. Wheels working one upon another, by means of teeth, or otherwise. ***a train of gears***: a set of such wheels. Often preceded by some defining word, as ***bevel-***, ***crown-***, ***spur-gear***. ***double gear*** (see quot. 1874).

1829 *Nat. Philos.*, *Mechanics* II. vii. §70. 30 (U.K.S.) Wheels are denominated *spur*, *crown*, or *bevel gear*, according to the position or direction of the teeth. **1874** KNIGHT *Dict. Mech.* 726/1 *Double-gear*, the nests of variable-speed gear-wheels in the head-stock of a lathe. **1881** *Metal World* No. 22. 340 The moving of the car sets in motion a train of gears, which in turn gives motion to the pencil mechanism, which traverses crosswise of the paper, while the paper itself traverses from the pencil lengthwise at a uniform speed.

c. (See quot.)

1874 KNIGHT *Dict. Mech.*, *Gear*..the running parts of a wheeled vehicle, as the fore-gears, hind-gears, referring to the fore-axle and its wheels, the hind-axle and its wheels.

d. *Aeronaut.* Short for *landing gear*. *U.S.*

1931 J. E. YOUNGER *Airplane Constr. & Repair* iii. 48 Such a device is called a retractable landing gear. The method is quite practicable provided the pilot does not forget to unfold the gear before landing. **1936** *Jrnl. R. Aeronaut. Soc.* XL. 275 Call for a maximum permissible time for raising or lowering the undercarriage, although I understand that the U.S. Dept. of Commerce require that a gear should be lowered in 60 seconds or less. **1963** *Amer. Speech* XXXVIII. 118 This is accomplished by adding power, raising the gear and flaps, and climbing back to a safe altitude.

7. a. *Machinery.* The mechanical arrangements connecting a motor with its work; = GEARING. Hence ***in, out of gear***: in, out of connexion with the motor. So ***to get*** (***put, set, throw***) ***in, into, out of gear***.

1814 R. BUCHANAN *Mill Work* (1823) 451 When any particular part of machinery is set agoing, it is said among workmen to be set on, or put in gear; when stopped, set off, or put out of gear. **1839** R. S. ROBINSON *Naut. Steam Eng.* 103 To see what is to be the position of the eccentric pulley, relative to the crank when in gear. *Ibid.* 132 To work three or four strokes by hand prior to throwing the eccentric rod in gear. **1851** *Illustr. Catal. Gt. Exhib.* 233 For the purpose of moving the handles in and out of gear. **1869** *Eng. Mech.* 19 Mar. 574/2 The..lever..is reversed, so as to throw the shafts..into gear by the action of the..clutch. **1879** *Cassell's Techn. Educ.* II. 13/2 When wheels are in gear there are three teeth of each engaged. *Ibid.* IV. 307/2 The parts which they should hold in position get out of gear. **1885** *Law Rep. 15 Q. Bench Div.* 358 A wheel-factory, including the machinery and gear, was mortgaged to the plaintiffs. *Ibid.*, The..driving-belts..could be removed at pleasure when the machinery was thrown out of gear.

fig. **1849** H. MAYO *Pop. Superstit.* (1851) 79 The attention ..is unlinked from the other faculties, and they are put out of gear. **1860** KINGSLEY *Misc.* II. 11 An industrial system so out of gear. **1861** THORNBURY *Turner* (1862) I. 21 In a week or two he began to get into gear and work better in his new harness. **1874** GREEN *Short Hist.* v. §4. 241 The whole organization of labour was thrown out of gear. **1880** MISS BRADDON *Just as I am* xviii, I have been out of gear for my ordinary pursuits of late. **1886** W. HOOPER *Sk. Acad. Life* 56 He is quite thrown out of gear by every little anomaly.

b. Any of the several sets of gear-wheels in a motor vehicle, bicycle, etc., which can be used to alter the relation between the speed of the engine or driving mechanism and the speed or torque of the driven wheels; also, the relation between the number of revolutions made by a motor vehicle or cycle-wheel and the number of revolutions made by the gear-wheels; ***high*** (or ***low***) ***gear***: a gear affording a high (or low) ratio between the speed of the driven wheels and the speed of the driving mechanism, and consequently a high (or low) speed to the vehicle itself; ***top gear***: see *s.v.* TOP *sb.*[1] 34.

1888 *Encycl. Brit.* XXIII. 560 Two-speed gears [for tricycles] are becoming general. **1896** F. T. BIDLAKE *Cycling* 66 High gear for downhill, low gear for up. **1897** *Encycl. Sport* I. 268/1 The higher the gear, the further the machine travels at each stroke of the pedals. **1902** H. STURMEY in A. C. Harmsworth et al. *Motors* x. 203 When putting a lower gear into operation, as is necessary when climbing a hill. *Ibid.* 204 If the calculated speed of the second gear is, say, eighteen miles per hour. **1907** 'I. HAY' *Pip* II. ix. 283 Sometimes slowing through a village or changing gear up a hill. **1909, 1910** [see *top-gear* (b) s.v. TOP *sb.*[1] 34]. **1923** W. E. DOMMETT *Motor Car Mech.* (ed. 2) 185 On the top gear with the dog clutches engaged the speeds are equal. **1930** *Strand Mag.* May 348/1 Trout retired, top gear, into the distance. **1958** *Times* 19 Aug. 11/6 The three-speed gearbox with a comparatively low second gear which encourages the driver to stay in top.

8. *Naut.* Rigging in general; 'the rigging of any particular spar or sail' (Adm. Smyth).

1669 STURMY *Mariner's Mag.* I. 17 See that your main Hall-yards be clear, and all the rest of your Geer clear and cast off. **1833** MARRYAT *P. Simple* (1863) 366, I seized another [axe], and disengaged the..small gear about the mast. **1860** *Merc. Marine Mag.* VII. 279 The topsails were reduced by the patent gear to nearly close reefs.

III. Stuff.

9. a. Goods, movable property, household necessaries and utensils.

a **1300** *Cursor M.* 4938 Sargantz send i son on hand þat in þair gare mi god þai fand. *Ibid.* 13797 Do þe to ga, wit all þi ger. *c* **1380** WYCLIF *Serm.* Sel. Wks. I. 200 Freris and preestis þat..maken riche chirches and housis wiþ oþer gere. **1413** *Pilgr. Sowle* (Caxton 1483) I. xv. 9, I hald it best to cast awey this gere and shape my selue pryuely to fle. **1466** *Mann. & Househ. Exp.* (Roxb.) 436 Item, owenge to the chaundelere..for wode, candelles and odre gere for howsold, iij.s. xj.d. **1634** MILTON *Comus* 166 Some harmelesse Villager, Whom Thrift keeps up about his Countrie Geare. **1785** C. KEITH *Har'st Rig* 47 For he did gar her sweetly pay For crackit gear. **1865** LIVINGSTONE *Zambesi* x. 216 Then follow wife and daughters with bulky loads of household gear on their heads.

†**b.** *Sc.* and *north. dial.* Possessions in general, wealth, money. ***goods and gear*** = wealth, property. †***free gear*** (see FREE 28 b). *Obs.*

1535 STEWART *Cron. Scot.* III. 230 Siluer or gold or ony other geir. **1547** in Tytler *Hist. Scot.* (1864) III. 380, I judge him [Argyle] greedy of gear, desirous of authority. *c* **1565** LINDESAY (Pitscottie) *Chron. Scot.* (1728) 14 Spend his goods and gear. **1570** BUCHANAN *Ane Admonit.* Wks. (1892) 23 ȝe wer neuir desyrous of blude geir nor honour. **1609** HUME *Admonition* in *Wodrow Soc. Misc.* 586 A borrowing.. of uther mennis geir. **1637** B. JONSON *Sad Sheph.* II. i, I am na fay..But a good man, that lives o' my awn geer. **1637** RUTHERFORD *Lett.* (1862) I. 300, I had not so much free gear when I came to Christ's camp as to buy a sword. **1706** in J. Watson *Collect. Poems* I. 30 Which made the Laird take up more Gear Than all the Lands or Rigs could bear. **1706** SEMPILL *Piper Kilbarchan* xiii, His pipes..after wan him gear enough. **1712** ARBUTHNOT *John Bull* III. iv, Spending the goods and gear that his forefathers wan with the sweat of their brows [The speaker is Scotch]. **1725** RAMSAY *Gentle Sheph.* I. ii, His honour maunna want—he poinds your geer. **1775** BURNS '*Tibbie, I hae seen the day*' vi, Your daddy's gear maks you sae nice. **1808** MAYNE *Siller Gun* II. xxvi, Dingwall..Whase modest merit Was sae repres'd for want o' gear, Care crush'd his spirit! **1855** ROBINSON *Whitby Gloss.* s.v., 'Ill gotten gear', property unjustly obtained. **1884** ANNIE S. SWAN *Dorothea Kirke* vi. 58 That foolish, misguided sister of yours has married an old man for his gear!

c. Things. †Also in *plural. rare.*

a **1400** *Sir Perc.* 214 He wolde schote with his spere Bestes and other gere. **1556** J. OLDE tr. *Gualter's Antichrist* 124 The God whom his fathers knew not shall he honour with gold, and silver, and precious stones, and other costly gaires. **1817** SOUTHEY *Ess.* (1832) II. 13 The appetite for slander must be sharp-set, when it can prey upon such small gear.

†**10. a.** A material substance or stuff; in depreciatory sense, rubbish. *Obs.*

1489 Caxton *Faytes of A.* II. xxxvii. 159 A drinke myxte with suche manere of gere that aftre they had taken hyt they were alle dronken. 1549 Latimer *6th Serm. bef. Edw. VI* (Arb.) 165 Of decimations of Anets seade, and Cummyn, and suche gere. 1562 Turner *Herbal* II. 50 b, The sour gear that is within [the shell of the Citron] is colde and dry. 1578 Lyte *Dodoens* IV. xvi. 470 You shal finde much of this geare amongst Rye. 1603 Sir C. Heydon *Jud. Astrol.* vii. 187 That out of wheat there should spring vp darnell, solders, and smuttie geare. 1613 Purchas *Pilgrimage* (1614) 475 The Bramans marke themselves in their fore-heads.. with a kind of yellow geare which they grinde. 1691 Ray *N.C. Words* Pref. 5 *Gear*.. is also used for trumpery, rubbish, so as stuffe is. 1800 Larwood *Norfolk Dial.* 44 (E.D.S. No. 76) The thacker wou'd ha gin har some doctor's geer in a beaker. 1805 H. MacNeill *Poet. Wks.* (1812) II. 76 A bottle primed ..Wi' somewhat mair than half a gallon O' precious gear.

†**b.** Corrupt and foul matter; pus. *Obs.*

1562 Turner *Herbal* II. 131 b, It [Germander] scoureth out also thicke and watery gear out of the brest. 1596 Spenser *F.Q.* VI. xii. 28 That spat out poyson and gore-bloudy gere. 1632 tr. *Bruel's Praxis Med.* 223 Cholericke, sowre and stinking geere is voyded. 1653 H. More *Antid. Ath.* III. viii. (1712) 113 The wound of his throat gaping, but no gear nor corruption in it.

c. *Mining.* (See quots.)

1747 Hooson *Miner's Dict.* G ij b, *Dead*, where there is no Ore.. Deads are the Gear, or Work got in such dead Places. *Ibid.* I iv b, *Gear*, a general Name for all Deads, when cut out of the Wholes. *Ibid.* Q iij, We rise with these Pair upwards, drawing up the Gear, and teeming it round about them.

11. *fig.* = MATTER, STUFF, in various uses.

a. Discourse, doctrine, talk; also in depreciatory sense, 'stuff', nonsense. ? *Obs.* exc. *arch.*

1415 Hoccleve *To Sir J. Oldcastle* 159 Our fadres medled no thyng of swich gere. *a* 1529 Skelton *Sp. Parrot* 387 For drede ye darre not medyll with such gere. 1570 B. Googe *Pop. Kingd.* I. 13 b, I am ashamed here To weare my pen.. about such foolish gere. 1606 Day *Ile of Guls* III. i. (1881) 70 Was not this stinging geere? 1607 Rowlands *Guy, Earl Warw.* 55 Why turn me back to conn my gear again. 1624 Bedell *Lett.* vi. 101 No maruell if this geare could not passe the Presse at Rome. *a* 1654 Selden *Table-T.* (Arb.) 20 Lord, what Gear do they make of it! 1700 Dryden *Wife of Bath's T.* 24 For priests with prayers and other godly gear, Have made the merry goblins disappear. 1722 N. Mist *Lett. fr. Mist's Jrnl.* Pref. 12, I had a great deal more of this learned Gear from my Friend. 1875 Tennyson *Q. Mary* III. i, Have you had enough Of all this gear? 1895 *E. Anglian Gloss.*, *Gere*, unintelligible stuff; or a confused heap.

b. Doings, 'goings on'. *arch.* or *dial.*

c 1460 *Towneley Myst.* xvi. 370 This is well wroght gere that euer may be. *c* 1475 *Partenay* 276 Non may on the trust, ne in thy fals gere. 1546 *St. Papers Hen. VIII*, XI. 140 The French practises now a dayes be but bare geare to other mens practises. 1616 R. C. *Times' Whistle* v. 1883 Brave boyes, this gear doth cotten well. 1652 C. B. Stapylton *Herodian* IV. 31 Wee shall smart for this unruly geere. *a* 1806 K. White *Childhood* I. 119 To view our gambols, and our boyish geer. 1831 Scott *Cast. Dang.* i, Then I hardly see how your ladyship can endure this gear much longer. 1876 *Whitby Gloss.* s.v., He has now taken up with that kind of gear. 1881 Mrs. Lynn Linton *My Love* I. 273 We shall have such fun!.. It will be good gear, I can tell you!

†**c.** A matter, affair, business. *Obs.*

1545 Ascham *Toxoph.* (Arb.) 57 You handle this gere in dede. 1579–80 North *Plutarch* (1676) 160 Whilest this gere was a brewing. 1594 Greene & Lodge *Looking Gl.* Wks. (Rtldg.) 126/1 Master Lawyer.. I pray you to this gear. *a* 1625 Fletcher & Shirley *Nt. Walker* v. i, You wo' not to this geer of marriage then? 1636 James *Iter Lanc.* (Chetham Soc.) 97 This worck, this gheere.. Was done by daughters of great Charlemaine. 1823 Scott *Quentin D.* xxxi, I understand this gear better than you do.

IV. *attrib.* and *Comb.*, as (sense 6 b) ***gear-cutter***, ***-cutting***; (sense 7) ***gear-oil***, ***-shaft***, ***-sleeve***, ***-work***; ***gear-driven*** adj.; (sense 8) ***gear-block***; (sense 9 b) ***gear-gatherer***, ***-grasping***; **gear-box**, **-case**, the case enclosing the gearing of a bicycle, motor vehicle, etc.; hence ***gear-box-less*** adj.; **gear-change**, (*a*) the action of changing gear; (*b*) = *gear-lever*; so ***gear-changing***; **gear-lever**, the lever by means of which one changes gear; **gear-pump**, a pump in which liquid is drawn in by one gear-wheel and expelled by another gear-wheel in mesh with the first; **gear ratio**, the ratio between the rates at which the last and the first wheels of a train of gears rotate; **gear-shift** (orig. *U.S.*) = *gear-lever*; **gear-wheel**, (*a*) a cog-wheel; (*b*) in a bicycle, etc., the cog-wheel by means of which the motion of the pedals is transmitted to the axle.

1851 *Illustr. Catal. Gt. Exhib.* 340 Lower yards filled with inventor's slings and portable *gear-blocks. 1887 Visct. Bury & Hillier *Cycling* xiii. 385 Otherwise the effect of the same amount of resistance on each wheel will become unequally operative in the *gear-box. 1902 W. W. Beaumont in A. C. Harmsworth et al. *Motors* x. 208 Many cars have.. a secondary frame to which the motor and gear-box, &c., are attached. 1909 *Chambers's Jrnl.* Jan. 62/2 There is a centrifugal governor mounted on or driven from one of the rotating shafts behind the gear-box, and its speed of rotation is always in fixed relation to that of the road-wheels. 1957 *Times* 2 July (Agric. Suppl.) p. viii/4 Other new features [of the Ferguson 35 tractor] include the six-speed gear-box. 1909 *Westm. Gaz.* 14 Sept. 4/3 A *gear-box-less 'Sheffield-Simplex' car. 1963 Bird & Hutton-Stott *Veteran Motor Car* 45, A 45 h.p. 'gearbox-less' car came on the market. 1896 G. B. Shaw *Let.* 6 Mar. (1965) 608 Their net price, new, with *gear case, saddle &c, complete is £25. 1897 *Daily News* 16 Sept. 3/4 There was a black gear-case instead of a transparent one. 1902 H. Sturmey in A. C. Harmsworth et al. *Motors* x. 206 The gear-case should be kept sufficiently full of lubricant to enable the lower edges of the gear wheels to be constantly passing through it. 1912 *Motor Man.* (ed. 14) v. 169 (*heading*) A method for obtaining a 'silent' *gear change. 1955 *Times* 5 July 5/7 The excellent gearchange.. is effected by a short central lever. 1967 *Autocar* 5 Oct. 73/3 With the gearchange switched from the left of the cockpit to the right. 1909 *Westm. Gaz.* 23 Feb. 4/1 The beginner.. can practise the art of *gear-changing on the hill. 1884 Knight *Dict. Mech.* Suppl., **Gear Cutter* [a machine for cutting the teeth on gear-wheels]. 1874 *Ibid.*, **Gear-cutting Machine*, one for making cog-wheels by cutting out the interdental material. 1906 *Westm. Gaz.* 26 Mar. 10/2 A *gear-driven car. 1906 *Daily Chron.* 14 Nov. 9/3 The water circulates by a gear-driven pump. 1825–80 Jamieson, **Gear-gatherer*, a money-making man. 1819 W. Tennant *Papistry Storm'd* (1827) 40 He smasht and smote thae men o' sin For their *gear-graspin' greed. 1904 *Motor Man.* (ed. 6) ix. 97 Put the *gear lever on to the next speed. *a* 1951 D. Stewart in *Austral. Short. Stories* (1951) 409 Placing his hand on her knee as, doubtless in error for the gear-lever, he so often does. 1910 *Blackw. Mag.* Nov. 606/1 A black and glutinous compound, which I afterwards learned to recognise as *gear-oil. 1922 *Automobile Engineer Ref. Bk.* 202/1 *Gear pump. 1933 Rutherford in *Proc. R. Soc.* A. CXLI. 261 The plug.. is cooled by a rapid stream of transformer oil supplied by a gear-pump through insulating tubes. 1909 *Gear ratio [see *top-drive* s.v. TOP *sb.*[1] 34]. 1915 Young & Aston *Complete Motorist* (ed. 8) iii. 81 An arrangement of toothed pinions, which allow two, three or four different gear ratios to be employed as the case may be. 1959 '*Motor*' *Man.* (ed. 36) iv. 74 The gear ratios usually quoted.. take also into account the reduction in the final drive. *Ibid.* 91 Reference was made to an overdrive unit... Its purpose is to provide an extra gear ratio, higher than direct drive, so that quiet and economical cruising is possible. 1904 A. B. F. Young *Complete Motorist* iii. 59 Different sets of gearing, by means of which the *gear shaft transmits its motion to the road wheels in different ratios. 1927 *Glasgow Herald* 30 Nov. 11 The new model.. will be of the standard selective gearshaft type. 1926 *Amer. Speech* I. 686/2 American: *gear shift... English: change speed lever. 1959 *Observer* 12 Apr. 3/3 The steering-column gear-shift.. is partly cable-operated. 1908 *Westm. Gaz.* 20 Nov. 4/2 It is arranged with divided *gear-sleeve to enable short shafts to be used. 1874 Knight *Dict. Mech.*, **Gear-wheel*, any cog-wheel, whether crown, spur, internal-cogged, bevel, or lantern, is a gear-wheel. 1891 *Daily News* 6 June 6/1 The engine is a two-cylinder horizontal one, and drives a gear-wheel. 1892 *Dublin Rev.* Apr. 437 The mirror is fixed to a gear-wheel driven off the spindle of a small alternating electric motor. 1851 *Illustr. Catal. Gt. Exhib.* 220 Occasioning the rapid destruction of the *gear-work through which the power is transmitted.

gear (gɪə(r)), *v.* Forms: 3–5 gere, 5 *Sc.* geir, 7–9 geer(e, (7 geare), 6– gear. [ME. *geren*, f. *gere* GEAR *sb.* (OE. had *ȝierwan*, pret. *ȝierede* to equip, clothe, f. OTeut. **garwu-* ready, YARE).]

†**1.** *trans.* To adorn; to array; to dress. *Obs.*

c 1250 *Gen. & Ex.* 2441 Osep dede hise lich faire geren, Wassen, and riche-like smeren, And spice-like swete smaken. 13.. *E.E. Allit. P.* B. 1568 He schal be gered ful gaye in gounes of porpre. *c* 1350 *Parlt. 3 Ages* 122 He was gerede all in grene. 1674–91 Ray *N.C. Words* 30 *To Geer* or *Gear*, to dress. *Snogly geered*, neatly dressed.

2. To equip. *arch.*

13.. *Gaw. & Gr. Knt.* 791 Garytez ful gaye gered bitwene, Wyth mony luflych loupe. 1456 *Sc. Acts Jas. II* (1814) II. 45/2 It is ordanyt þt all maner of man þt has landis or gudis be redy horsit and geryt. 1833 *Fraser's Mag.* VIII. 650 We accordingly geared ourself, and switch in hand.. sallied out.

fig. 1480 *Robt. Devyll* (Percy Soc.) 56 He dyde helpe hym for to gere and fortefye the crysten fayth.

3. To harness (a draught animal). Also with *up*, and *absol.*

1638 F. Junius *Paint. Ancients* 319 Paine of the painter.. for it is no small trouble, in my opinion, to geare foure horses together, and not so much as to confound any of their legges. 1640 G. Abbott *Job Paraph.* 248 Canst thou tether or geere him like a horse? 1649 Blithe *Eng. Improv. Impr.* (1653) 197 The plough-man must have a little regard to his Teem or Draught, and to the well geering or ordering them. 1807 Pike *Sources Misss.* (1810) 50 *note*, My sleds were such as are frequently seen about farmers' yards.. in which two men were geared abreast. 1856 C. W. Upham *J. C. Frémont* ii. 55 (Funk) We were ready to depart; the tents were struck, the mules geared up, and our horses saddled. 1877 *Holderness Gloss.* s.v., It's about time we was off ti gear. 1886 *Chesh. Gloss.*, *Gear* or *gear up*, to put harness on a horse.

4. a. To put (machinery) into gear (see GEAR *sb.* 7); to connect by gearing. Also *fig.*, to adjust, correct or co-ordinate; *spec.* to adjust or adapt (something) *to* a particular system, situation, etc.; to bring into dependence, conformity or harmony; freq. in *pass.* ***to gear up*** (see quot. 1882); so ***to gear down***, ***level***.

1851 *Illustr. Catal. Gt. Exhib.* 1184 Another feature in the machine is for gearing and pulling out of gear the cogs. 1868 *Pall Mall G.* 15 July 10 The spindle is geared to a system of toothed wheelwork. 1879 Thomson & Tait *Nat. Phil.* I. I. 479 The several shafts, with their axes all parallel, are geared together. 1882 *Knowledge* 10 Mar. 397/2 About two years since, most of the tricycles which were driven by means of a chain were geared up—that is, the driving wheels were made to go round faster than the pedals.. Now, most of the best riders agree that tricycles should be geared down. 1883 *Ibid.* 22 June 368/1 For average riders these [tricycles] might be geared level. 1895 *Daily News* 15 May 7/4 Parts necessarily exposed for the purposes of cleaning, lubricating, gearing, or altering the arrangements of a machine. 1900 J. London *Let.* 21 Jan. (1966) 85 The tongue is too often geared at too high a pitch to adequately carry on its labors. 1937 *Time* 22 Feb. 26 That part of *John Meade's Woman* which is geared to these phenomena is an effectively written, well-photographed slice of U.S. industrial history. 1945 *Reader's Digest* July 13/1 Every country's production had been geared to an intricate system of German demands and supplies. 1958 *Spectator* 22 Aug. 249/1 This might have been effective in an entire [ballet] production geared to the Bolshoi interpretation. 1962 *Sunday Times* (Colour Suppl.) 10 June 10 Authors', composers' and other royalties are often closely geared to recording rights. 1969 *Times* 31 Jan. 11/8 The rate of the addition reaction is somehow geared to the rate of growth of the cell as a whole.

b. *intr.* Of a toothed wheel, or its teeth: To fit exactly *into*; to be in gear, so as to work smoothly *with*.

1734 *Phil. Trans.* XXXVIII. No. 434 Engrav., The loose Wallowers, whose turn'd rounds geer truly with ye Coggs in ye great Wheel. 1848 *Tait's Mag.* XV. 844 Carrying an angle-wheel, into which two others gear. 1870 *Eng. Mech.* 18 Mar. 652/3 This bevel gears with a horizontal bevel underneath the base. 1881 Anderson in *Nature* No. 626. 619 Two circular frames.. with teeth cut in their edges, are mounted, so that the teeth gear into each other, and they can rotate freely, but in opposite directions.

gear, *a.* See GEAR *sb.* 5 e.

gear(e, var. GERE, *Obs.*, whim, fit of passion.

geard, obs. form of GUARD.

geared (gɪəd), *ppl. a.* [f. GEAR *sb.* and *v.* + -ED.]

†**1.** Equipped; armed. *Obs.*

c 1470 Henry *Wallace* v. 806 Twa hundreth haill off weill gerit Inglismen.

†**2.** Provided with gear; ? with handles or other appendages. *Obs.*

1588 *Wills & Inv. N.C.* (Surtees 1860) 329, vj geared yockes 4*s.*, iiij yockes, vngeared, 16*d.*, v geard forkes 20*d.*, ij forkes, ungeared, 6*d.*

3. a. *Machinery.* Connected with the motor by gearing.

1868 *Gainsborough News* 27 June (N.W. Linc. Gloss.), Six double-geared slide and break lathes. 1881 *Eng. Mech.* 27 May 1/2 Back Geared Lathe, 4¼ in. centres, bed 3 ft. 6 in. long; per set £2 5*s.* 1884 Knight *Dict. Mech.* Suppl., *Geared Brace*, a boring tool in which the drill or bit is rotated by hand crank and bevel gear. *Ibid.*, *Geared Locomotive*, a locomotive in which the motion of the engine is conveyed by gearing to the travelling wheels. 1895 Earl Albemarle & Hillier *Cycling* xii. 303 The Geared Ordinary. This, a relatively new type, has not secured that measure of success which its friends hoped for it.

b. *Finance.* Of a company or its capital (see GEARING *vbl. sb.* 3 b).

1930 *Economist* 25 Oct. 768/2 Ordinary stocks.. by reason of the 'high geared' capital structure of the companies.. must always bear the jolts and jars of trade fluctuations. 1940 *Ibid.* 6 July 14/1 The relatively high income thus secured was indispensable for paying generous debenture interest and preference dividends on a highly geared paid-up capital. 1965 [see GEARING *vbl. sb.* 3 b].

gearing (ˈgɪərɪŋ), *vbl. sb.* [GEAR *sb.* and *v.* + -ING[1].]

1. *dial.* Harness.

1863 Mrs. Toogood *Yorksh. Dial.*, Put the gearing on t' hoses and go away to plough. 1877 *Holderness Gloss.*, *Gearin*, harness.

2. Working implements, 'plant'.

1825 Ld. Cockburn *Mem.* i. 76 Our colliers and salters belonged.. to their respective works with which they were sold as part of the gearing.

3. a. The action of fitting a machine with gear; the manner in which a machine is geared; *concr.* apparatus for the transmission of motion or power, *e.g.* a train of toothed wheels = GEAR *sb.* 7. Often preceded by some qualifying word, as ***bevel-***, ***spur-***, etc. ***gearing***; also with advs., as in ***gearing-down***, ***-up***. ***out of gearing***: out of gear.

1833 J. Holland *Manuf. Metal* II. 350 These wires pass through the gearing, between the bars of a reed, as in linen-weaving. 1851 *Illustr. Catal. Gt. Exhib.* 210 The speed requisite for the propeller is obtained by means of accelerating gearing. 1860 Maury *Phys. Geog. Sea* xviii. §740 It is so stable and true in its work that nothing can throw it out of gearing. 1862 Smiles *Engineers* III. 49 By an entire rearrangement of the gearing of the machine, he shortly succeeded in greatly lessening the wear and tear of the ropes. 1869 R. B. Smyth *Gold F. Victoria* 612 Gearing —A series of wheels working into each other whereby motion is transmitted. 1882 *Knowledge* 10 Mar. 397/2 When the gearing down is carried to a great extent, the pedals make two revolutions for one revolution of the driving-wheels. A machine so geared can be ridden up a steep hill easier than a bicycle.

b. *Finance.* (See quots.) Also *attrib.*

1932 H. Parkinson *Sci. Investment* ix. 88 Among the stocks shown in the table, the high gearing of the railways is conspicuous. 1936 *Economist* 14 Mar. 594/1 The 'gearing ratio' is the proportion borne by the total net assets of the company to the net assets available for the common stock. 1959 *Jrnl. Inst. Bankers* Apr. 149 The simplest form of gearing is the issue of two classes of shares of which one class gives a preferential right to a fixed percentage dividend before the holders of the other class receive anything. 1965 Seldon & Pennance *Everyman's Dict. Econ.* 193 *Gearing*, the proportion of a company's annual income allocated to 'prior charges' (interest on debentures and preference dividends), the remainder going to the ordinary shareholders. Where it is high the company is said to be highly geared, and conversely.

4. *Comb.*, as ***gearing-beam***, ***-chain***, ***-wheel***.

1835 J. H. Ingraham *South-West* II. 288 Two *gearing beams are laid across, for supporting the machinery. 1874 Knight *Dict. Mech.*, **Gearing-chain*, an endless chain transmitting motion from one toothed wheel to another. 1835 Ure *Philos. Manuf.* 109 Two eighty-horse steam-engines.. are mounted with their great *geering-wheels on the ground floor. 1876 Preece & Sivewright *Telegraphy* 81 Made to revolve by means of the 'gearing' or driving wheels.

gearksutite (dʒiːˈɑːksuːtaɪt). *Min.* [f. Gr. γῆ earth (from its earthy appearance) + ARKSUTITE. Named by Dana in 1868.] Hydrous fluoride of calcium and sodium, of a clay-like appearance.
1868 DANA *Min.* (ed. 5) 130 Gearksutite. Earthy, kaolin-like in aspect.

gearless (ˈgɪəlɪs), *a.* [f. GEAR *sb.* + -LESS.] Of a motor: Having no gear for the transmission of motion; acting directly.
1892 *Pall Mall G.* 4 July 7/1 They are mounted on two bogies, each having 200 h.p. gearless motor attached to it. **1906** *Westm. Gaz.* 15 May 4/2 The long-promised six-cylinder 'gearless' Napier car. **1951** *Catal. Exhibits, S. Bank Exhib., Festival of Brit.* 183/1 Gearless passenger lift to carry 20 persons. **1966** *Listener* 6 Oct. 515/3 Dr Donald Firth with his gearless car and revolutionary machine tools deserves far more urgent attention.

†ˈ**geason**, *a.* and *sb.* *Obs.* Forms: 1 **gǽsne, géasne**, 3 **geasne**, 4 **gesen(e**, 5–6 **geso(u)n**, 6 **ges(s)en**, 6–7 **gayson, geazon, geasone**, (6 **gai-, geison**, 7 **gey-, gheason**), 5–7 **geason**. [OE. *gǽsne, gésne* barren. Cf. OHG. *keisinî* barrenness.]
A. *adj.*
1. Producing scantily; barren, unproductive; exhausted. Const. in OE. with *gen.* or *on*; later *of*. Also, clear *of*.
a **1000** *Christ* 849 in *Exeter Bk.*, þæt we gæstes wlite ær þam gryre-broȝan on þas gæsnan tid ȝeorne biþencen. *a* **1000** *Juliana* 381 *ibid.*, He siþþan sceal godra gum-cysta geasne hweorfan. *a* **1000** *Andreas* 1084 (Gr.) Ah þær heorodreoriȝe hyrdas laȝan, gæsne on greote, gaste berofene. *a* **1121** *O.E. Chron.* an. 1116 þisȝear wæs swa gæsne on mæstene. **14..** *MS. Cantab. Ff.* ii. 38 lf. 23 (Halliw.) In werke they weren never so nyce, Ne of moo good liveres geson. *c* **1420** *Pallad. on Husb.* VIII. 5 Now make the feeldis wilde of busshis geson. *c* **1430** *Hymns Virg.* 64 Drunkelew folk ben goostli blinde, For faute of witt her lyf is gesoun.
2. Scantily produced; rare, scarce, uncommon. In the 16th c. sometimes with passive infinitive, as ***geason to be found, to be seen***, etc.
1377 LANGL. *P. Pl.* B. XIII. 271 My wafres there were gesen. *c* **1460** J. RUSSELL *Bk. Nurture* 803 Custade Costable, when eggis & crayme be geson. **1494** FABYAN *Chron.* VII. 588 Grotes and peas were geson. **1514** BARCLAY *Cyt. & Uplondyshm.* (Percy Soc.) 35 A good man is geason, not easy to be founde. *c* **1530** H. RHODES *Bk. Nurture* 116 in *Babees Bk.* 85 They that will not knowe howe to amend, their wits be very geason. **1548** UDALL *Erasm. Par.* Pref. 19 Precious stones that are gayson to bee founde. **1567** TURBERV. *Epit. & Sonn.* (1837) 295 Rich be thy robes, and geason to be had. **1577** HARRISON *England* II. xii. (1877) I. 239 In the houses of Knights.. it is not geson to behold generallie their prouision of tapistrie. **1583** STUBBES *Anat. Abus.* II. (1882) 51 Rare birds vpon the earth, and as geason as blacke swans. **1601** F. GODWIN *Bps. of Eng.* 380 Good knowledge in the Greeke toong.. in those daies was geason. **1601** HOLLAND *Pliny* II. 98 Ixine is a rare herb and geason to be seen. **1610** —— *Camden's Brit.* (1637) 536 Marle in this place is very geason or skant. **1674** RAY *S. & E.C. Words* 67 Geazon, scarce, hard to come by. *Ess.*
3. 'Rare', extraordinary, amazing.
1572 N. ROSCARROCKE *Prelim. Verses Bossewell's Armorie*, The siege of Thebes, the fall of Troy, in beaten massie golde, dan Vulcan hath set out at large, full geazon to beholde. **1583** STANYHURST *Æneis* II. (Arb.) 47 With weather astonyed, with such storms geason agrysed. *Ibid.* IV. 104 The duke Æneas with sight so geason agasted.
B. *sb.* Rarity, scarcity. *rare.*
1509 BARCLAY *Shyp of Folys* (1570) 124 Of them is no plentie but great geason. **1557** *Tottel's Misc.* (Arb.) 250 Good should by geason, earne no place, Nor nomber make nought, that is good.

geast, obs. form of GEST, GUEST, JOIST.

geast, geaster, var. GIST, GISTER.

geaster (dʒiːˈæstə(r)). [mod.L., f. Gr. γῆ earth + ἀστήρ star.] An earth-star (see EARTH- II).
1887 W. PHILLIPS *Man. Brit. Discomycetes* 213 Splitting into several lobes, like a *Geaster*.

geat(e, obs. form of GATE, GET, JET.

geather, obs. form of GATHER.

geaum, geaunt, obs. forms of JAMB, GIANT.

gebang (dʒɪˈbæŋ). Also **gebanga**. [Mal. *gĕbang*.] In full ***gebang palm***. A Malaysian fan palm, *Corypha elata*, the leaves of which are used for basket-work and thatching, while the pith of the trunk yields a sago.
1817 T. S. RAFFLES *Hist. Java* I. i. 37 Another species of palm, the *gebáng*, also yields valuable ropes. **1846** LINDLEY *Veget. Kingd.* 138 Employed.. in weaving into baskets and bags the young leaves of the Gebang Palm. **1952** 'W. MARCH' *October Isl.* x. 125 Lontar, gebanga, rattan and nipa. **1966** E. J. H. CORNER *Nat. Hist. Palms* xii. 300 The most widespread gebang palm of Malaysia, *C. elata*, is distributed from Bengal.. to north Australia.

gebat, gebbet, obs. forms of GIBBET.

gebbie (ˈgɛbɪ, ˈgɪbɪ). *Sc.* Also 8 **gabbie**. [Origin obscure: the pronunciation is against a connexion with GAB. Cf. Gael. *giaban* gizzard.] The crop of a fowl; *transf.* the human stomach.
a **1774** FERGUSSON *Poems* (1814) II. 15 She round the ingle wi' her gimmers sits, Crammin their gabbies wi' her nicest bits. **1843** BETHUNE *Sc. Fireside Stor.* 76 When your heads are filled wi' the horrors, your gebbies wi' wind, and your pouches wi' naething.

gebbit, gebbrish, obs. ff. GIBBET, GIBBERISH.

gebel, var. JEBEL.

geber, var. GUEBRE.

geberish, gebet(te, obs. ff. GIBBERISH, GIBBET.

‖**Gebrauchsmusik** (gəˈbraʊxsˌmuːziːk). Also **gebrauchmusik**. [G., f. *gebrauch* use + *musik* music.] Music intended primarily for practical use and performance, esp. music suitable for amateur groups and domestic playing.
1930 *Mod. Music* Feb.–Mar. 17 Present day 'Gebrauchsmusik' seems to be principally music for the dance, the sound films, [etc.]. **1932** *Music & Lett.* XIII. 43 Hindemith.. is young and impetuous enough to have one or two bees in his musical bonnet. These are known variously as *Gebrauchsmusik, Gemeinschaftsmusik*,.. and so on. **1934** C. LAMBERT *Music Ho!* IV. 249 Hindemith's music has been somewhat unduly saddled with the description of Gebrauchsmusik—bread-and-butter music, workaday, or utility music are perhaps the best equivalents. **1947** A. EINSTEIN *Mus. Romantic Era* ii. 11 Until late in the 18th century there was scarcely any music conceivable that was not utilitarian, *Gebrauchsmusik*, or that would not have served an immediate purpose. **1952** P. HINDEMITH *Composer's World* p. viii, A quarter of a century ago, in a discussion with German choral conductors, I pointed out the danger of an esoteric isolationism in music by using the term *Gebrauchsmusik*.. that ugly term showed a power of penetration and a vigor that would be desirable for worthier formulations. **1962** *Times* 14 Dec. 15/2 The now unfashionable category of *Gebrauchsmusik*.

gebur (gɪˈbʊə(r)). *Hist.* [OE. *ȝebúr* = OS. *gibûr*, OHG. *gipûr, gipûro*: see NEIGHBOUR.] A tenant-farmer (in the early English community).
[*c* **1000** *Laws of Ine* c. 6 §3 (Schmid) Gif he.. on ȝebures [huse] ȝefeohte. **1706** PHILLIPS (ed. Kersey), *Geburus*, a Country-Neighbour.] **1861** PEARSON *Early & Mid. Ages Eng.* 261 The tenants, cotsetlas, geburs, and geneats, were the highest among the semi-servile. **1892** F. SEEBOHM in *Eng. Hist. Rev.* July 459 The gebur himself is not a full freeman because he has services to perform on the lord's demesne, and cannot leave the land if he chooses.

gebyllot, obs. form of GIBLET.

gecarcinian (dʒiːkɑːˈsɪnɪən). [f. mod.L. *Gĕcarcin-us* (Gr. γῆ earth + καρκίνος crab; introduced by Dr. Leach in 1815) + -IAN.] A land-crab.
1838 *Penny Cycl.* XI. 99/1 The Land-crabs, or Gecarcinians, inhabit the warm countries of the New and Old World, and Australasia. **1847–9** TODD *Cycl. Anat.* IV. 330/2 The land-crabs or Gecarcinians.. are enabled to live as terrestrial animals.

gecimine, obs. form of JASMINE.

geck (gɛk), *sb.*[1] *Obs.* exc. *dial.* Forms: 6 **geke**, 7 **gecke**, 6, 9 **geck (geek)**. [app. a. LG. *geck*, = MDu. *gec(k, ghec(k*, Du. *gek* adj. and sb.; related (either as source or derivative) to *gecken* GECK *v.* From LG. the word passed into the HG. dialects, MHG. *geck(e*, G. *geck*, and into Scand., Da. *gjæk*, Sw. *gäck*, Norw. *gjekk*, ? Icel. *gikkr*.] A fool, simpleton; one who is befooled or derided, a dupe.
1515 BARCLAY *Egloges* I. (1570) A iij b, He is a foole, a sotte, and a geke also Which choseth.. the worst [way] and most of ieoperdie. **1601** SHAKS. *Twel. N.* V. i. 351 Why haue you suffer'd me to be imprison'd.. And made the most notorious gecke and gull That ere inuention plaid on? **1611** —— *Cymb.* V. iv. 67 To become the geeke [*sic*] and scorne o' th' others vilany. **1859** GEO. ELIOT *A. Bede* 83 If she's tackled to a geck as everybody's laughing at. **1876** *Whitby Gloss.*, *Gawk*, *Geek*, *Gowk* or *Gowky*, a fool; a person uncultivated; a dupe.

geck (gɛk), *sb.*[2] Chiefly *Sc.* [= Du. and G. *geck* vbl. sb. corresponding to *gecken* (see GECK *v.*) as in G. *gecken machen* to play tricks; *in geck sagen*, Du. *in gheck segghen* (Kilian), to say in jest.] A gesture of derision; an expression of scorn or contempt.
1500–20 DUNBAR *Poems* xxvi. 28 Than all the feyndis lewche, and maid gekkis. **1576** *Tyde tarryeth no Man* in Collier *E.E. Pop. Lit.* (1863–4) 29 And though I haue attire both costly and gay, Yet unlesse it be new, I shall haue but a geck. **1597** MONTGOMERIE *Cherrie & Slae* 1085 'Gudeman, gramercy for ȝour geck' Quod Hope, and lawly louts.
b. ***to get a geck***: to be deceived or tricked. ***to give one the geck***: to mock, trick, deceive one.
1568 *Satir. Poems Reform.* xlvii. 84 Now better war lat bee Nor to begin to gett ȝour selffis ane geck. **1583** *Leg. Bp. St. Androis* 898 *ibid.* xlv, The first merchant he cleane forsuike, Gave him the geck, and lat him gea. **1603** *Philotus* lxxviii, The Carle that hecht sa weill to treit ȝow, I think sall get ane geck. ? **16..** *Fair Janet & Sweet Will.* xx. in Child *Ballads* III. lxiv. (1885) 105/2 This day she has gien me the gecks, Yet she must bear the scorn. **1808–25** JAMIESON, s.v., *To gie one the geck*, to give him the slip; generally including the idea of exposing him to derision.

geck (gɛk), *v.* *Sc.* and *north. dial.* [app. a. LG. *gecken* = MDu. *ghecken*, DU. *gekken*, G. *gecken*: see GECK *sb.*[1], and cf. the echoic Ger. *gecken* to croak, cackle. Also in Scand. as Da. *gjække*, Sw. *gäcka*.]
1. *trans.* To mock, deceive, cheat.
1583 *Leg. Bp. St. Androis* 867 in *Satir. Poems Reform.* xlv, Hame to the prowest it was directit; But ye sall heir whow he was geckit.
2. *intr.* ***to geck at***: to scoff at, to use mocking language or gestures towards.
1603 *Philotus* ciii, I trow that all the warld euin Sall at ȝour guckrie geck. **1725** RAMSAY *Gentle Sheph.* I. i, She Bauldy looes.. But gecks at me, and says I smell of tar. **1775** BURNS '*Tibbie I hae seen*' i, Ye geck at me because I'm poor. **1837** R. NICOLL *Poems* (1843) 102 He'll geck e'en at the Minister An' joke wi' laird an' lady. **1876** *Whitby Gloss.*, *Geck*, to sneer or deride.
3. To toss the head, as in scorn; to look proudly. Also *trans.* ***to geck up the head***. [Possibly a distinct word.]
1724 RAMSAY *Evergreen* (1761) II. 15 Scho gecks as gif I meind her Ill. **1728** —— *Fables, Caterpillar & Ant* 9 The saucy Ant.. gecking up her head, quoth she 'Poor animal! I pity thee'. **1786** BURNS *Dream* viii, Adieu, my liege! may freedom geck Beneath your high protection. **1811** WILLAN in *Archæol.* XVII. 147 *Geck*, to toss the head.

gecko (ˈgɛkəʊ). Forms: 8 **(chacco, jackoa)**, **gekko**, 9 **geco, gecko**; *pl.* **geckos, -oes**. [a. Mal. *gēkoq* (the *q* is faint) an imitation of the animal's cry.
The note uttered by this lizard is imitated in other Malay names, as *gaguh, gōke, tōke*, etc. and similar forms occur in the Indian languages, to which the earliest examples in English are due. The statement made in quot. 1792, that the name is current in Egypt, is due to the translator and is apparently a blunder.]
A house-lizard, found in the warmer regions of both hemispheres, remarkable for its peculiar cry, and for its power of climbing walls.
[**1711** C. LOCKYER *Acc. Trade Ind.* iv. 84 Chaccos, as Cuckoos receive their Names from the Noise they make.. they are much like Lizards but larger. **1727** A. HAMILTON *New Acc. E. Ind.* II. xliv. 131 They have one dangerous little Animal called a Jackoa, in shape almost like a Lizard.. he seldom fails of giving Notice where he is, by a loud noise called Jackoa.] **1774** GOLDSM. *Nat. Hist.* VII. 142 Of all animals the Gekko is the most notorious for its powers of mischief. **1792** HERON tr. *Niebuhr's Trav. Arab.* II. 332 We saw several sorts of lizards, of which the only dangerous one was that called by the Egyptians Gecko. **1852** TH. ROSS *Humboldt's Trav.* II. xix. 199 All the stones were covered with an innumerable quantity of iguanas and geckos with spreading and membranous fingers. **1860** *All Year Round* No. 37. 247 There are the friendly geckoes which, by help of padded toes, can run up walls like a fly, climb glass and cross the ceiling. **1883** *Harper's Mag.* Jan. 189/1 The gecko, a lizard found along the Nile, has been observed to emit a brilliant light.

geckoid (ˈgɛkɔɪd), *a.* [f. prec. + -OID.] Resembling a gecko.
1887 *Proc. Zool. Soc.* 15 Feb. 153 On a new Geckoid Lizard from British Guiana.

ged[1] (gɛd). *north.* and *Sc.* Forms: 4 **gedde**, 4, 6 **gedd**, 7 **gid**, 8 **gidd**, 7–9 **ged**. [a. ON. *gedda* (= OSw. *gedde, gedda*, Sw. *gädda*, Da. *gjedde*), app. f. ON. *gadd-r* spike, GAD. (With respect to the etymological signification of the name, cf. PIKE.)] The fish *Esox lucius*; the pike or luce.
1324–5 *Durham MS. Cell. Roll*, In j Gedde et lx Lamprouns. **1375** BARBOUR *Bruce* II. 576 And with his handys quhile he wrocht Gynnys, to tak geddis & salmonys. **1572** SEMPILL in *Satir. Poems Reform.* xxx. 90 Thay beand beistis that hes bene men befoir, Compairit with Geddis that dois thair fry deuoir. **1680** SIR G. MACKENZIE *Sci. Her.* 61 Ged of that ilk. Azur, 3. Geds or Pyks hauriant argent. **1775** L. SHAW *Hist. Moray* 78 It [the river Lossie] abounds with Pykes or Gidds. **1787** BURNS *Tam Samson* vi, Eels well kend for souple tail, And Geds for greed. **1840** W. HAY in *Mod. Scot. Poets* XV. 131 Bullsegs will wave their nigger pows and geds will bite again. **1857** KINGSLEY *Two Y. Ago* III. 16 He is now eating like any ged. **1893** *Northumbld. Gloss.*, *Ged*, the pike fish.

†**Ged**[2]. [Minced pronunc. of GOD in oaths; cf. GAD.]
1697 VANBRUGH *Relapse* III. ii, O Ged—the devil's in you. **1753** *Scots Mag.* Oct. 491/1, I now advanced to *By Jove, 'fore ged, Geds curse it*, and *Demme*.

gedackt, gedact (gəˈdakt). Also **gedeckt**. [G. *gedackt*, old pa. pple. of *decken* to cover.] An organ flue-stop having its pipes closed at the top. So ***gedackt-work*** [G. *gedacktwerk*], such stops collectively; ***lieblich gedackt*** (see quot. 1938).
1855 E. J. HOPKINS *Organ* xxxviii. 304 To a 'Gedact of 8-feet tone' he introduced a 'Rohrflöte of 4-feet tone'. *Ibid.* 364 Lieblich Gedact. **1880** GROVE *Dict. Mus.* II. 601/2 In Schulze's organ the Gedact (No. 4) was formed of stopped wood pipes that produced a fuller tone than the usual Stopped Diapason. **1904** GOODCHILD & TWENEY *Technol. & Sci. Dict.* 252/2 *Gedact work*, those organ stops belonging to the flue work, which consist of closed pipes. **1938** *Oxf. Compan. Mus.* 668/2 *Lieblich Gedact* (literally 'lovely and covered' or 'lovely and lidded'). A Gedact of 8- or 4-foot length and pitch.

gedanite (ˈdʒɛdənaɪt). *Min.* [f. *Gedan-um*, the med. Lat. name for Dantzig + -ITE: named by Helm in 1878.] A mineral resin resembling amber.
1887 in DANA *Min. & Petrogr.* (ed. 4) 349.

‖**Gedankenexperiment** (gəˈdaŋkən ɛkspɛrɪˌmɛnt). *Philos.* [G., f. *gedanke* thought + *experiment* experiment.] An experiment carried out only in imagination or thought; an appeal to imagined experience; a *thought-experiment*.

1958 N. R. Hanson *Patterns of Discovery* vi. 137 The first presentation involves a *gedankenexperiment*; it supposes a super-microscope more powerful than any electronic microscope. **1966** *Amer. Philos. Q.* III. 306/2 The child in his [*sc.* Ayer's] *Gedankenexperiment* is taught the use of psychological concepts by a recorded voice.

geddar, -ur, geder, obs. forms of GATHER.

gedeling, ged(e)lyng, var. GADLING².

Gedinnian (dʒɛɪˈdɪnɪən), *a. Geol.* Also †**Gedinnien.** [ad. F. *gedinnien* (A. H. Dumont 1848, in *Mém. de l'Acad. R. des Sciences de Belgique* XXII. 4), f. *Gedinne*, name of a village in Belgium: see -IAN.] Pertaining to or designating the lowest division of the Devonian system in Europe, or the epoch or age during which it was deposited. Also *absol.*

1853 *Q. Jrnl. Geol. Soc.* IX. 25 The 'Gedinnian system' must be entirely separated from the Rhenane series with which..it has no organic remains in common. **1882** A. Geikie *Text-bk. Geol.* vi. ii. iii. 702 Gedinnien, comprising an upper group of shales and sandstones and a lower group of fossiliferous shales, quartzo-phyllades, quartzites, and conglomerates. **1928** E. Neaverson *Stratigr. Palaeont.* xi. 255 The Gedinnian fauna of Belgium is not well known, since it is often represented only by fragments of ostracoderm fish. **1955** G. G. Woodford tr. *Gignoux's Stratigraphic Geol.* iv. 119 The Gedinnian and Coblenzian are completely missing and the Devonian begins with a basal conglomerate..directly overlain by sandstones.

gedred, gedring, obs. ff. GATHERED, -ING.

gedrite (ˈdʒɛdraɪt). *Min.* [a. F. *gédrite* f. *Gèdre* (see below): see -ITE. Named by Dufrénoy *Ann. des Mines* Ser. III. X. 582 (1836).] An aluminous variety of anthophyllite, discovered by D'Archiac near Gèdre in the French Pyrenees.

1844 in Dana *Min.* (ed. 2) 524.

gedur, -yr, obs. forms of GATHER.

gedy, gedynes, obs. ff. GIDDY, GIDDINESS.

gee (giː), *sb.*¹ *north.* and *Sc.* A fit of bad temper or sullenness; usually in phrase ***to take the gee***: to take offence, become sulky.

a **1605** Montgomerie *Sonn.* xxv. 9 ȝe knau ill guiding genders mony gees And specially in poets. ?**17..** *Song* in Herd *Collect. Scot. Songs* (1829) 5 Lang or e'er that I cam hame, My wife had ta'en the gee. **1714** '*What's the matter wi' the Whigs*' in *Jacob. Songs* (1887) 82 When he takes on his good dame's gees He canna rule himsel', sir. **1768** Ross *Helenore*, etc. 143 When I speak to them that's stately, I find them ay ta'en with the gee. **1844** Henderson in *Proc. Berw. Nat. Club* II. No. 12. 101 The bride 'took the gee'..and would not proceed a foot further. **1878** *Cumbld. Gloss.* s.v., 'He's teaun t' gee', he has taken offence. **1893** *Northumbld. Gloss.*, *Gee*, a sudden turn, a pique.

gee (dʒiː), *sb.*² *colloq.* [f. GEE *int.*¹] A horse (orig. a child's word; cf. GEE-GEE).

1887 *Punch* 22 Oct. 192/3 Pray tell me why that frisky gee, Called Pegasus, should harnessed be? **1890** *Licensed Vict. Gaz.* 8 Feb. (Farmer) The gees were all broken to the stable. **1894** Astley *50 Years Life* I. 59, I was to pay forty pounds in case either of the hired gees died.

gee (dʒiː), *sb.*³ *slang.* [Origin unknown; cf. next, and GEE *v.*² 1 c.] The accomplice of a cheapjack or showman. Also ***gee-man***.

1898 *Bulletin* (Sydney) 17 Dec. (Red page), A gee is their outside confederate, who 'gees up' the mugs for them. **1928** *Daily Express* 19 Dec. 2/7 'Ricks' or 'gees': people who mingle with the crowd to arouse their enthusiasm. **1941** K. Tennant *Battlers* xiii. 141 'I'm geeing for him, and I'll fix it.' The busker's spirits fell again. In the show world a 'gee-man' or 'micky finn' was socially on the level of a duck's feet. He is the man who goes out in the crowd and touts for custom. **1959** *News Chron.* 16 Nov. 5/3 Strategically placed in the crowd, the 'gee men' started the bidding going.

gee (dʒiː), *sb.*⁴ *U.S. slang.* [f. the pronunciation of the initial letter.] = GUY *sb.*² 3 d.

1921 P. & T. Casey *Gay-Cat* 302/2 Gee, guy, gun, mug, plug, stiff, etc.—a fellow. **1930** [see GO *v.* 58 d]. **1931** *Flynn's* 24 Oct. 656/2 They tell me you've got a mortgage on the dump... I could find a gee with free money to stake you. **1968** S. Challis *Death on Quiet Beach* xii. 177 'Just a minute, this ain't O'Brien.' 'No. This is some other gee.'

gee (dʒiː), *sb.*⁵ The name of the letter G; *spec.* in *U.S. slang*, a thousand dollars (cf. G III. f).

1926 *Evening Standard* 12 July 3/2 If one branch of English society drops its initial aitches, and another branch ignores its terminal gees. **1936** L. Duncan *Over Wall* i. 21 A thousand-dollar bill was a Gee. **1946** M. Taylor in 'D. Stanley' *Treas. Sports Humor* 149 There's a hundred gees at stake.

gee (giː, dʒiː), *sb.*⁶ *slang* (orig. *U.S.*). [Origin uncertain; perh. f. GHEE.] Opium or some similar drug. Also *attrib.* Hence **geed-up** *a.*, drugged.

1936 *Amer. Speech* XI. 121/1 *Gee-yen*, opium which precipitates in very small quantities in the stem of the pipe. **1938** *Ibid.* XIII. 184/2 *Gee*,..smoking opium, especially refined or reworked opium. *Ibid.* 185/1 Geed up. *Ibid.*, *Gee-stick*, an opium pipe. **1939** *Flynn's* 18 Mar. 56/2 She fell from the doorway, either not knowing there were two steps down into the bathroom or else forgetting it on account of being so geed up. **1953** Anslinger & Tompkins *Traffic in Narcotics* 308 *Gee*, drugs, especially opium.

gee (dʒiː), *sb.*⁷ *Aeronaut.* Also **G.** [f. initial letter of *grid*.] A navigational radar system developed in the war of 1939–45 to guide bombers to their targets. Also *attrib.*

1945 *Electronic Engin.* XVII. 685/1 Gee. The navigational system which enabled our bombers to know exactly where they were at any time *en route* to or from Germany. *Ibid.* 713 'G' or 'Gee' as it is more often spelt as an abbreviation for 'Grid', relating to the grid map references used by R.A.F. navigators. **1947** Crowther & Whiddington *Science at War* Pl. x. (*caption*), The two boxes shown here contain the essential Gee receiver used on aircraft. **1959** *Times Lit. Suppl.* 3 Apr. 194/4 It could give the bombers a set of lattice-lines from which the navigator might infallibly determine his position on the way to the target up to a distance of about 400 miles. This was Gee.

gee (dʒiː), *v.*¹ *slang.* Also **ge.** [Of doubtful etymology: possibly f. GEE *int.*¹] *intr.* To 'go'; to fit, suit, etc. (only in negative phrases).

a **1700** B. E. *Dict. Cant. Crew* s.v., *It won't Gee*, it won't hit, or go. **1785** Grose *Dict. Vulg. Tongue* s.v., It won't gee, it won't hit or do, it does not suit or fit. **1850** Seaworthy *Nag's Head* v. 35 'It don't seem to gee!' said Isaac, as he was trying to adjust the stove.

b. Of persons: To behave as is desired; to agree, get on well (*together*).

1719 D'Urfey *Pills* V. 83 If Miss prove peevish, and will not gee, Ne'er pine..at the wanton Pug. **1803** S. Pegge *Anecd. Eng. Lang.* 13 In Yorkshire, in Lancashire, and other Northern parts of the kingdom..where things do not suit or fit each other or where neighbours do not accord, the expression is 'They do not Ge well together'. *a* **1825** Forby *Voc. E. Anglia* s.v., This does not ge well with that. He and she will never ge together. **1825** Britton *Beaut. Wiltsh.* III. 374, *Gee* or *Jee*, to agree; to go on well together. **1889** *Century Mag.* Dec. 225/2 Me and the president didn't gee. He hadn't no fault to find with me; but I didn't like his ways, and I quit.

gee (dʒiː), *v.*² [f. GEE *int.*] **1.** *trans.* **a.** *Sc.* = JEE *v.* 2.

1813 G. MacIndoe *Wandering Muse* 114 For me, I never geed my noddle, Nor car'd I Snip, or Tib a boddle. **1931** H. S. Roberton *Curdies* xxvi. 106 The same men widna gee their ginger to put a bane-teeth comb through a wean's heid to stop it frae scartin'.

b. To direct (a horse, etc.) by the call of 'gee'. Also *absol.*

1845 E. J. Wakefield *Adv. N.Z.* II. 133 He *geed* the bullocks and ploughed on. **1867** 'T. Lackland' *Homespun* II. 194 The regiment is somehow got back, by hawing and geeing, into line. *Ibid.* III. 286 The man..is turning up the sod with the gleaming share..while he 'gees' and 'haws' the yoke of cattle.

c. To incite, encourage; *spec.* to entice or encourage (the public) to patronize side-shows, etc., at a fair (cf. GEE *sb.*³). Also, to make (a person or animal) move more quickly. Freq. const. *up*. Cf. GEE-UP *v. slang.*

1898 [see GEE *sb.*³]. **1932** 'Ex-Convict No. ——' *Dartmoor from Within* iv. 86 Yells of encouragement were shouted from the cell windows by men in my own hall—'geeing' him on. **1936** J. Curtis *Gilt Kid* xxiii. 231 He could flash a few oncers before her eyes if he wanted to gee her up. **1941** [see GEE *sb.*³]. **1956** R. Fuller *Image of Society* v. 141 The directors of the company must be gee'd up. **1958** F. Norman *Bang to Rights* 64 With us still shouting and geeing the twirls up. *Ibid.* 130 My life I'm not geeing you up. **1967** L. Deighton *Expensive Place* ix. 67, I tried to decide whether she was geeing me up.

2. *intr. dial.* (chiefly *Sc.*) = JEE *v.* 1.

1835 D. Webster *Original Sc. Rhymes* 116 Gloomy clouds may dim the air, But winna mak my fancy gee. **1891** R. P. Chope *Dial Hartland* 47 To *gee* or *gee round* is to turn towards the right.

gee (dʒiː), *int.*¹ A word of command to a horse, variously (in different localities) used to direct it to turn to the right, to go forward, or to move faster.

1628 Earle *Microcosm.*, *Country Fellow* (Arb.) 49 He expostulates with his Oxen very vnderstandingly, and speaks Gee and Ree better then English. **1655** Heywood & Rowley *Fort. by Land & Sea* II. H.'s Wks. 1874 VI. 384 Come Ile go teach ye..gee and whoe. **1733** Fielding *Don Quixote in Eng.* II. xii, Gee, gee, boys, hup! **1806** Bloomfield *Wild Fl.* Poems (1845) 189 Gee, Bayard! move your poor old bones. **1868** Atkinson *Cleveland Gloss.*, *Gee*, the word of command to horses in a team to turn to the right, or from the driver: substituted for the older word *Ree*. **1871** C. Gibbon *Lack of Gold* xii, A steady-going old brown mare, which moved to and fro with mechanical regularity in obedience to the 'gee' and 'wo' of its driver.

gee (dʒiː), *int.*² orig. *U.S.* [Prob. a shortening of *Jesus!* (or *Jerusalem!*); cf. GEEWHILLIKINS *int.*, GEE WHIZ(Z *int.*] An exclamation of surprise or enthusiasm; also used simply for emphasis. Cf. JEE *int.*, JEEZ(E *int.*

1895 S. Crane *Red Badge of Courage* ii. 28 Gee rod! how we will thump 'em! **1901** S. E. White *Westerners* ii. 11 'Gee Christmas!' ejaculated Billy, and laughed loudly. **1902** *Captain* VII. 40 Gee! I thought the hair would come out of my head. **1906** *Amer. Illustr. Mag.* Apr. 701 'I guess he's tall and thin and homely and dark, gee,' he yowled explosively. **1909** E. Underhill *Runaway Place* 134 'Gee, I believe you're right!' he exclaimed. **1927** H. A. Vachell *Dew of Sea* 269 But gee! if she is downing you, she offs it. **1953** 'N. Shute' *In Wet* 91 'Gee,' said Wing Commander Dewar, 'this thing'll drive me nuts.'

gee, var. GHEE; dial. var. GIVE.

geebung (ˈdʒiːbʌŋ). Also **gibong, jibbong.** [Native Australian.] The fruit of various species of *Persoonia*, an Australian tree. (N.O. *Proteaceæ*.)

1827 P. Cunningham *2 Yrs. N.S. Wales* I. xiii. 221 The jibbong is another tasteless fruit. **1847** L. Leichhardt *Overland Exped.* xiv. 478 We gathered and ate a great quantity of gibong (the ripe fruit of *Persoonia falcata*). **1852** Mundy *Antipodes* vii. (1855) 176 The geebung, a native plum very woolly and tasteless. **1889** Boldrewood *Robbery under Arms* (1890) 255 You won't turn a five-corner into a quince or a geebung into an orange.

Geechee (ˈgiːtʃiː). *U.S. dial.* [f. the name of the *Ogeechee* River, Georgia.] (See quot. 1934.) Also, a derogatory term for a Negro of the southern United States. Cf. GULLAH.

1926 *Nat. Geogr.* Sept. 278 Among the negroes living on the Ogeechee River a patois, developed in ante bellum days, has persisted... The origin of 'Geechee', as the patois is called, is explained by the fact that slaves employed on the old rice plantations were more or less isolated and rarely conversed with their white owners, with the result that their knowledge of English words was slight and the pronunciation of them was bizarre. The 'Geechee' negro speaks in a sort of staccato and always seems excited when talking. **1934** Webster, *Geechee.* A dialect, originally of Negro slaves on the Ogeechee river, Georgia, formed of English and native African words. 2. One who speaks Geechee. **1940** E. Caldwell *Trouble in July* xiii. 208 He sounds like one of those Geechee niggers... That breed'll do anything to keep them from working. **1945** *New Yorker* 8 Sept. 20/2 Creecy was a Geechee..blacker than the soot in the fireplace.

gee-gee (ˈdʒiːˌdʒiː). *colloq.* [Reduplication of GEE *int.*¹] A horse (orig. a child's word; cf. GEE *sb.*²).

1869 Blackmore *Lorna D.* lxx, The 'great Gee-Gee'—as all the small ones entitled me. **1886** G. R. Sims *Ring o' Bells*, etc. xi. 242 To carry two heavy boys..on his back, pretending that he was a gee-gee. **1895** *Cornh. Mag.* Jan. 56 'Tell the fellow to drive faster'... 'My dear Datchet, the man's already driving his geegee off its legs.'

geegot, obs. form of GIGOT.

gee-ho (ˈdʒiːˈhəʊ), *int.* Also **gee-o.** [f. GEE *int.*¹ + HO *int.*] = GEE *int.*¹

1668–71 Skinner *Etymol.*, Ho, Gee Ho. **1697** J. Serjeant *Solid Philos.* 378 The Horses not hearing any cry Gee, ho, to urge them forwards, took their Opportunity to rest themselves, and stood still. **1801** *Sporting Mag.* XVIII. 110 And now, behold he cry'd 'Gee-ho' And now he jerk'd the rein. **1819** [see GEE-UP].

b. *attrib.*, in ***gee-ho-coach***: also *absol.* (quasi-*sb.*).

a **1704** T. Brown *Wks.* (1720) II. 316 Never..but ply close at Inns upon the coming in of Waggons and Gey-ho-Coaches. **1769** *De Foe's Tour Gt. Brit.* (ed. 7) II. 314 They draw all their heavy Goods here [Bristol] on Sleds, or Sledges, which they call Gee-hoes, without Wheels.

Hence **gee-(h)o** *v.*, **gee-(h)oing** *vbl. sb.*

1659 D. Pell *Impr. Sea* 93 Carmen that never leave jerking and *Geoing* of their horses till they hale the hearts of them out. **1858** Carlyle *Fredk. Gt.* ix. i. II. 384 The gee-ho-ing of an expert wagoner, who has got a fiery young Arab thoroughly tied into his dastard sandcart and has to drive him by voice. **1881** Ld. W. P. Lennox *Plays, Players*, etc. I. 203 The country lad who..had 'gee-ho-ed' and 'gee-up-ed' him [my horse].

geek (giːk). [Var. GECK *sb.*¹] *U.S. slang.* (See quots. 1954 and 1961).

[**1876**: see GECK *sb.*¹]. **1916** *Wells Fargo Messenger* Oct. 29/2 A new Wells agent struck our town the other week, and say—you never saw a more enthusiastic geek! **1954** Webster Add., *Geek*, a carnival 'wild man' whose act usually includes biting the head off a live chicken or snake. **1961** *Times Lit. Suppl.* 27 Jan. 62/2 He picks up waitress, a simple girl, and enslaves a 'geek', a dumb sideshow stooge whose daily routine consists of being exhibited in a pit which he has to dig for himself.

geelbek (ˈgiːlbɛk, ‖ˈxɪəlbɛk). *S. Afr.* Also **geelbec, geelbeck.** [Afrikaans, f. *geel* yellow + *bek* mouth, beak.] **1.** A marine fish, *Atractoscion æquidens*, of the family Sciænidæ, which has bright yellow edges to jaws and gill-cover and is found off the southern coasts of Africa and also of Australia, where it is called teraglin.

1853 L. Pappe *Edible Fishes Cape of Good Hope* 16 *Otolithus Æquidens*..(*Geelbeck*)..Common along the whole coast. **1900** *Trans. S. Afr. Phil. Soc.* 216 The name Cape Salmon..is now appropriated almost exclusively by the Geelbek. **1931** *Times Lit. Suppl.* 16 Apr. 301/2 Like so many of the Cape fish,..the geelbek..gets his name from the original Dutch settlers. **1953** J. L. B. Smith *Sea Fishes S. Afr.* (rev. ed.) 227 Sometimes the tails of cured Kobs are trimmed by dishonest vendors so as to resemble those of the more costly Geelbek.

2. A yellow-billed wild duck, *Anas undulata*, found in Eastern and Southern Africa.

1867 E. L. Layard *Birds S. Afr.* 352 *A*[*nas*] *Xanthorhyncha*..*Geelbec* of Colonists and Sportsmen. **1901** W. T. Black *Fish River Bush* i. 21 An occasional shot may be got at a Geelbec duck (*Anas*) as it flies low along the bush lining the river banks. **1957** McLachlan & Liversidge *Roberts's Birds S. Afr.* 48 Yellowbill. Geelbek.

‖**geelhout** ('xɪəlhəʊt). *S. Afr.* Also formerly **geele-houtt.** [Afrikaans, f. *geel* yellow + *hout* wood.] = YELLOW-WOOD.

1790 E. HELME tr. *Le Vaillant's Trav. Afr.* II. xiv. 288, I also remarked the *Geele-Houtt*, (yellow-wood) so called from its colour: which.. is very serviceable for planks, beams, and rafters. **1801** J. BARROW *Trav. S. Afr.* I. iii. 133 The most common was the *geel hout* or yellow wood, (*taxus elongatus*) erroneously called by Thunberg the *ilex crocea*. **1834** [see YELLOW-WOOD]. **1953** *Cape Argus* 25 Feb. 9/4 Eighty trees, including jakkalsbessie, geelhout, wild fig, .. have been planted along Table Bay boulevard. **1961** PALMER & PITMAN *Trees S. Afr.* 122 The common yellowwood, Outeniqua yellowwood, .. geelhout.

geen, var. GEAN.

geer(e, obs. form of GEAR, GEIR, JEER, GYRE.

geerish, var. GERISH. *Obs.*, whimsical.

geese, pl. of GOOSE.

geest (giːst). *Geol.* [a. G. *geest* (orig. LG.) dry or sandy soil, opposed to marsh-land.] Old alluvial matter on the surface of land; coarse drift or gravel.

1847 in CRAIG; and in mod. Dicts.

geest, obs. form of GEST, GUEST, JOIST.

gee-string, var. G-STRING 2.

geet, var. GETE *v.*, to keep; obs. f. GET, JET.

geet, obs. pl. of GOAT.

geete, var. GITE, dress.

gee-up ('dʒiːˈʌp), *int.* Also **gee-, je-hup.** [f. GEE *int.*[1] † HUP *int.* (confused with UP *adv.*).] = GEE *int.*[1]

1733 [see GEE *int.*[1]]. **1769** *Trinculo's Trip* 29 Yates a Carter, without a je-hup. **1819** 'R. RABELAIS' *Abeillard & Heloisa* 34 Cross Hounslow Heath, jee up! jee o! **1825** *Sporting Mag.* XVI. 332 A second 'Gee up' issued from behind a hedge. **1862** THACKERAY *Wks.* (1872) X. 225 Gee-up, carter. **1888** J. PAYN *Myst. Mirbridge* I. iii, Gee up, 'oss.

Hence **gee-(h)up** *v.*, *intr.* and *trans.*, to say 'gee-up' (to), also (of a horse), to obey this call.

1752 FOOTE *Taste* II. Wks. 1799 I. 19 May I.. be tumbled from my phaeton the first time I jehup my sorrels. **1816** SCOTT *Antiq.* xvii, He was only apprized of the arrival of the Monkbarns division by the gee-hupping of the postilion. **1824** *Blackw. Mag.* Oct. 442 Mr. Bubb ge-hupp'd in vain, and strove to jirk the rein, Nobbs.. wouldn't mend his pace. **1881** [see GEE-HO *v.*]. **1888** *Punch* 21 Apr. 186/1 'Gee-up!' he cried. The horse gee-up'd, To gallant G——'s joy.

geewhillikins (dʒiːˈwɪlɪkɪnz), *int.* orig. *U.S.* Also **ge-, je-, -whil(l)iken(s), -whil(l)ikin(s), -whit(t)aker(s).** [Perh. a fanciful substitute for *Jerusalem!*, but cf. next.] = GEE *int.*[2]

1851 'A. MISSOURIAN' in T. A. Burke *Polly Peablossom's Wedding*, etc. 52 Jewhilliken, how he could whip er nigger! **1856** *Town Talk* (San Francisco) 20 July 1/1 Gee-whitaker! what a kurchy she made, and bowed so low that I nearly fell outer my dickey onto the floor. **1857** *Knickerbocker* Nov. 435 (Th.), And great Gewhilikins! wasn't the snow peppering down! **1865** R. H. NEWELL *Orpheus C. Kerr Papers* ii. 31 Geewhillikins! how the critter did squawk and squeal. **1872** SCHELE DE VERE *Americanisms* 611 *Jerusalem!*, a favorite New England exclamation... In the West it is, as usual, improved to suit the louder taste of the people, and becomes Jewhillikin. **1884** 'MARK TWAIN' *Huck. Finn* xxxviii. 386 'Geewhillikins,' I says, 'but what does the rest of it mean?' **1906** E. NESBIT *Railway Children* xii. 251 When I tried to get up again I couldn't stand, so I sat down. Gee whillikins! it does hurt, though. **1932** E. WEEKLEY *Words & Names* viii. 112 Of similar origin [*sc.* euphemistic substitution] are *gee-whittakers, gee-whiz*, [etc.]. **1941** C. S. FORESTER *Capt. from Connecticut* xx. 261 'Geewhillikins, sir,' said Hubbard; the dark mobile face lengthened in surprise.

gee whiz(z (dʒiːˈwhɪz), *int.* orig. *U.S.* Also **gee whitz, gee wiz,** and with hyphen. [Prob. a corruption of prec. or a euphemism for *Jesus!*: cf. GEE *int.*[2] and WHIZZ, WHIZ *int.*] = GEE *int.*[2]

1885 W. T. GRAY *Bad Boy at Home* 8 (*at back*) Gee wiz! but they do put on stile in New York. **1888** *Judge* (U.S.) 1 Sept. 334 Geewhitz! **1904** *N.Y. Times* 21 Apr. 9 He appeared in the saloon and shouted: 'Gee whiz! The gas pipes is all leakin'.' **1908** *Westm. Gaz.* 9 May 6/1 The 'Raid on Prosperity' is what he calls his statement for the defence, and, gee-whiz!.. he goes for the Raiders in a way that is positively refreshing. **1940** 'R. CROMPTON' *William & Evacuees* vi. 164 'Gee whiz!' breathed William in ecstasy. **1957** J. D. SALINGER *Franny & Zooey* (1962) 86 Well, gee whizz. I'm only trying to make polite bathroom talk.

Geez ('giːɛz, giːz). Also **Geëz, Gheez, Giez, Giz.** [Ethiopic.] The ancient language of Ethiopia, still used as a liturgical language; = ETHIOPIC *a.* 2. Also *attrib.*

1790 J. BRUCE *Trav.* I. 424 Speaking of the Ethiopic at present, I mean only the Geez language, the language of the Shepherds, and of the books. *Ibid.* 425 The Geez is exceedingly harsh and unharmonious. **1839** *Penny Cycl.* X. 52/2 The antient Ethiopian, or Geez. **1867** [see ETHIOPIC 2]. **1883** R. N. CUST *Sk. Mod. Lang. Afr.* I. 74 The Written Characters of the old Ethiopic, or Giz. **1908** *Daily Chron.* 6 Mar. 3/5 Their Bible, which is in Gheez,.. contains all the books of our own Old Testament, except the Book of Esther. **1920** *Blackw. Mag.* May 676/1 A book in the Geez language. **1957** *Listener* 14 Nov. 774/1 Their recital of Geez texts and the copying of old manuscripts on the lives of Ethiopian saints. *Ibid.*, The priests are satisfied if the ordinary man says his prayers in Geez which he does not understand.

geez, geeze, varr. JEEZ(E *int.*

geezer ('giːzə(r)). *slang.* Also **geeser, geyser.** [A dial. pronunciation of GUISER.] A term of derision applied esp. to men, usu. but not necessarily elderly; a chap, fellow.

1885 'CORIN' *Truth about Stage* 16 If we wake up the old geezers we shall get notice to quit without compensation.. The two geezers, as Sandy styled the landlord and his wife. **1893** *Northumbld. Gloss.*, *Geezer*, a mummer; and hence any grotesque or queer character. **1897** *Westm. Gaz.* 17 Aug. 2/3 So an obliging firm of Liverpool solicitors, like the nice old geeser in the song, have just assured him. **1904** 'No. 1500' *Life in Sing Sing* 248/2 *Geezer*, a fellow. **1910** *Punch* 5 Oct. 243 'Old yer blooming rah, an' give the old geyser [*sc.* a lady singer] a charnst, cawn't yer? **1914** *Dialect Notes* IV. 201 The old geezer wouldn't let us play ball in his pasture. **1938** G. GREENE *Brighton Rock* II. i. 74 You're a grand little geezer. *Ibid.* II. ii. 90 A geezer can't have an alibi for every minute of the day. *Ibid.* IV. ii. 267 I'll tell you a thing or two, you bloody little geezer. **1958** [see BARON 2 c]. **1958** J. SYMONS *Gigantic Shadow* vii. 37 There's a geezer I know named Twisty Dodds, kind of a small-time crook you might call him. **1960** [see BIRD *sb.* 1 d]. **1965** [see CHINA[1] 7].

gef, obs. form of *gave*, pa. t. of GIVE; obs. f. IF.

gefe, gef(f)in, obs. forms of GIVE, *given*.

geffel, var. GAFFLE. *Obs.*

1668 J. WHITE *Rich Cab.* (ed. 4) 119 Therefore it is good to have certain strong cross-bowes, to bend either with a rack, or a geffel [*printed* gessel].

gefte, gegelotte, obs. ff. GIFT, GIGLET.

gefuffle (gəˈfʌf(ə)l), Altered form, occasionally found, of CURFUFFLE, KERFUFFLE.

1943 B. J. HURREN *Eastern Med.* ii. 32 The gefuffle created in the search for this stick was unbelievable. **1959** J. VERNEY *Friday's Tunnel* xxvi. 234 He made such a gefuffle of safety precautions and locked doors I couldn't imagine what was up.

‖**gefüllte fish** (gəˈfɪltə fɪʃ). Also **gefil(l)te, gefuellte, gefulte, gefülte fish** or **fisch.** [Yiddish, a. G. *gefüllt* filled, stuffed, f. *füllen* FILL *v.*] A Jewish dish of stewed or baked stuffed fish or fish-cakes, boiled in a fish- or vegetable-broth.

1892 I. ZANGWILL *Childr. Ghetto* I. I. iv. 114 There is even *gefüllte Fisch*, which is stuffed fish without bones. **1916** J. LAIT *Beef, Iron, & Wine* (1917) 15 That crowd of tired *hoi-polloi* fighting for a spot to stand to get their corned beef and cabbage, or *gefuellte* fish. **1931** D. RUNYON *Guys & Dolls* (1932) iv. 71, I am sitting in Mindy's restaurant putting on the gefillte fish. **1941** L. G. BLOCHMAN *See You at Morgue* (1946) ix. 61 Don't your Old Lady make gefüllte fish any more for Shabbath dinner? **1959** H. PINTER *Birthday Party* II. 26 The nicest piece of gefilte fish you could wish to find on a plate. **1962** *Coast to Coast 1961–62* 113 It was Friday, so I ran into *gefüllte* fish.

Gegenschein, gegenschein ('geɪgənʃaɪn). *Astr.* [G., f. *gegen* opposite + *schein* shine, glow; first used technically by T. J. C. A. Brorsen 1854, in *Unterhaltungen im Gebiete der Astron.* 17 May 156, after an earlier use in the same connection by F. H. A. von Humboldt *c* 1803, published in his *Kosmos* (1845) I. 144.] A patch of very faint nebulous light occurring in the ecliptic opposite the sun.

1880 *Amer. Jrnl. Sci.* CXX. 442 The gegenschein is an extremely faint spot of light some 7° in diameter, lying in the zodiacal band. **1888** [see COUNTER-GLOW]. **1968** *Observer* 22 Dec. 3/1 The astronauts.. have a heavy programme of photography, including an attempt to photograph the 'Gegenschein', the image of the sun faintly reflected back from dust and tenuous gas in space. **1971** *Nature* 30 July 323/1 Observations of the gegenschein are made best away from the Milky Way in February, March and April.

gegg (gɛg), *sb. Sc.* [Cf. GAG *sb.*[2]] A trick, hoax, practical joke.

1855 J. STRANG *Glasgow* (1856) 401 The cabalistic term gegg signifies a practical joke.

Hence **gegg** *v.*, to hoax, play a trick on; also **ge'ggee, 'gegger, 'geggery.**

1826 J. WILSON *Noct. Ambr.* Wks. 1855 I. 111 Sae sune as I turn the tables on you, gegg you, as they say in Glasgow. *Ibid.* 235 The rums were looking up, the punch was pleasant, and the people given to geggery, every house hospitable. **1855** J. STRANG *Glasgow* (1856) 327 That class loved fun and frolic, jest and song, geggery and gossip. *Ibid.* 403 The party to be gegged would be present. *Ibid.* 404 The whole party including the geggee were in the highest spirits. *Ibid.* 405 The geggers slipped silently behind.

gegg, obs. form of GIG *sb.*

†**gegge.** *Obs.* Also **gigge.** [Of obscure origin: app. not identical with GIG.] A term, apparently contemptuous, applied both to man and woman.

a **1300** *Floris & Bl.* (Hausknecht) 853 Twei gegges þe cupe bere. **1387** TREVISA *Higden* (Rolls) I. 403 Thus arraied gooþ þe geggis [*v.r.* gigges, *Caxton* segges], And alle wiþ bare legges.

gegger ('gɛgə(r)). *Sc.* Also **gagger.** [Of unknown origin.] The under-lip; also *gegger-lip*.

1825–80 JAMIESON, *Gegger*, the under lip. *To hing the geggers*, to let the under-lip fall, to be chop-fallen. **1826** G. BEATTIE *John o' Arnha'* in *Life* (1863) 232 The gagger lip o' Card'nal Beaton.

geggie ('gɛgɪ). *Sc.* Also **gaggie.** [f. GAG *sb.*[1]] A travelling theatrical show, usu. held in a tent. Cf. GAFF *sb.*[4]

1898 D. WILLOX *Poems & Sk.* 16 Glasgow Fair was then held in all its glory.. and.. young Willox sometimes neglected his duties to witness the glories of the 'geggie'. **1922** *Glasgow Herald* 17 July, The 'geggie', which to the children of the present day is little more than a name, if it is even that. **1931** A. J. CRONIN *Hatter's Castle* I. i. 23 This is the first night of Levenford Fair. I saw the start o' the stinking geggies on my way home. **1952** T. JOHNSTON *Memories* i. 14 The gaggie shed or theatre was built of wooden partitions.

gegilot, geglotry, obs. ff. GIGLET, -LETRY.

‖**Geheimrat** (gəˈhaɪmraːt). Also **Geheimer Rat.** [G.] In Germany, a privy councillor (see also quot. 1911).

1837 H. C. ROBINSON *Diary* 27 July (1967) 180, I called on Geheimrat Schlosser and had an interesting chat with him. **1911** *Encycl. Brit.* XXII. 373/2 The title.. of *Geheimer Rat* simply is very generally, *e.g.* in Prussia, given to high officials, usually with the addition of the branch of the service to which they belong, *e.g. Geheimer Finanzrat.* **1936** A. HUXLEY *Eyeless in Gaza* liii. 601 The sofas where the Geheimrats slept off the effects of noonday eating. **1943** H. L. MENCKEN *Heathen Days* vii. 91 Thus a plain Mister became Doctor, a Doctor became Professor, and a Professor became *Geheimrat*. **1971** AUDEN *Academic Graffiti* 19 The *Geheimrat* in Goethe Made him all the curter With *Leute* who were leery Of his Colour Theory.

‖**gehenna** (gɪˈhɛnə). [a. Eccl. Lat. *gehenna*, a. Hellenistic Gr. *γέεννα*, rendered 'hell' in the Eng. N.T. (also *γέεννα τοῦ πυρός* 'gehenna of fire', rendered 'hell fire'). In med.L. the word was used transf. for judicial torture: cf. GEHENNE.

The Gr. *γέεννα* was ad. post-Biblical Heb. *gēhinnōm* hell, place of fiery torment for the dead (whence Arab. *jahannam*), a figurative use of the place-name which occurs also in the fuller form *gē ben Hinnōm*, 'the valley of the son of Hinnom', denoting a place near Jerusalem where, according to Jer. xix. 5, etc., children were burnt in sacrifice to Baal or Molech. Cf. TOPHET.]

1. The place of future torment; hell.

1623 COCKERAM, *Gehenna*, Hell. **1627** HAKEWILL *Apol.* IV. i. §5. 281 A valley shadowed with wood, called Gehinnon [*sic*] or Tophet, from whence is the word Gehenna vsed for hell. [**1667** MILTON *P.L.* I. 405 [Moloch] made his Grove The pleasant Vally of Hinnom, Tophet thence And black Gehenna call'd, the Type of Hell.] **1854** MOTLEY *Corr.* (1889) I. vi. 166 The groans which occasionally ascended seemed as from a Gehenna. **1882** FARRAR *Early Chr.* II. 63 Making their proselytes ten-times-worse children of Gehenna than themselves. **1883** *Punch* 8 Sept. 119/1 A Gehenna of flaring gas-flames and a howling warder stop the way again.

2. *transf.* A place of torture; a prison.

1594 NASHE *Unfort. Trav.* Wks. 1883–4 V. 131, I [a Spaniard] winning haue the crownes, he losing is carried to the galleys. This is our custome, which a hundred times and more hath paid mee custome of crownes, when the poore fellowes haue gone to *Gehenna*, [and] had course bread and whipping chere all their life after. **1641** MILTON *Animadv.* (1851) 195 They had neither bin hal'd into your Gehenna at Lambeth, nor strappedo'd with an Oath *Ex Officio* by your bow men of the Arches.

Hence † **ge'hennical** *a.*, belonging to gehenna.

1599 *Broughton's Lett.* v. 18 As by his genealogicall glosses he hath abused *βίβλον γενέσεως*, so by his gehennicall cursings he might set on fire *τροχὸν γενέσεως* [cf. *Jam.* iii. 6].

†**ge'henne.** *Obs. rare.* Also 5 **gehyne.** [a. F. *gehenne*, ad. eccl. L. *gehenna*: see prec. The word was early confused with *gehine* confession, examination of accused persons by torture (mod.F. *gêne* discomfort), whence the form in quot. 1481.] **a.** A hell, place of torment. **b.** Judicial torture.

1481 CAXTON *Myrr.* II. xviii. 107 Thise ben the terryble gehynes stynkynge And there is the fyre so ouer moche ardaunt. **1646** BUCK *Rich. III*, III. 93 The fame was the Question or Gehenne was given Him [Perkin].

gehlenite ('geɪlənaɪt). *Min.* [f. name of A. F. *Gehlen* (1775–1815) + -ITE; named by Fuchs in 1815.] A silicate of aluminium, calcium and iron, of a greyish colour, chiefly found in the Tyrol.

1817 *Thomson's Ann. Philos.* IX. 70 Gehlenite.. occurs usually crystallized in four-sided rectangular prisms. **1869** PHILLIPS *Vesuv.* x. 291 Gehlenite is mentioned among the products of Pollena, on the slopes of Somma.

geibat, obs. form of GIBBET.

geic ('dʒiːɪk), *a.* [f. Gr. *γῆ* earth + -IC.] In *geic acid* (F. *acide géique*), a product of the conversion of wood into vegetable mould. Also called *humic* or *ulmic acid*.

1844 in HOBLYN *Dict. Med.* **1864** in WATTS *Dict. Chem.*

geier: see GEIR.

geierite *Min.*: see GEYERITE.

geif, obs. form of GIF, GIVE.

geig (dʒiːg), *v. Sc.* and *north. dial.* Also 8 jeeg, jig, gig, gike, jike, jeyk. [From the sound.] *intr.* To creak, make a creaking noise.

1513 DOUGLAS *Æneis* VI. vi. 62 Vnder the paysand and the hevy charge Gan grane or geig [*v.r.* grank] ful fast the jonit barge. **1721** KELLY *Scot. Prov.* 239 Lick thy Loof and lay't to mine, dry Leather gigs [Ramsay 1737 has *jeegs*] ay. **1781** HUTTON *Tour to Caves* (E.D.S.), *Gike* or *Jike*, to creak as wheels or doors do. **1808–25** JAMIESON, *Geig*, to make a creaking noise, as a door when the hinges need to be greased. **1878** *Cumbld. Gloss., Jeyk*, to creak like machinery requiring oil.

Geiger (ˈgaɪgə(r)). Also with lower-case initial. [The name of Hans *Geiger* (1882–1945), German physicist.] **Geiger counter** [COUNTER *sb.*² 3 b], an instrument for detecting and counting ionizing radiation, used esp. for measuring radioactivity; it consists essentially of a wire anode surrounded by a cylindrical cathode in a chamber containing gas at low pressure. Also ***Geiger-Müller counter***.

1924 *Sci. Abstr.* A. XXVII. 295 (*title*) The Geiger counter as a sensitive detector of X-radiation. **1926** *Physical Rev.* XXVII. 111 A study of Geiger counting chambers has been made. **1930** *Ibid.* XXXV. 651 (*title*) Multiple coincidences of Geiger-Müller tube-counters. **1945** *Electronic Engin.* XVII. 612/2 An improved circuit..for reading the rate of pulses from a Geiger-Müller counter. **1951** *New Biol.* X. 34 A single particle or γ-ray passing through a Geiger-Muller counter triggers off an electrical discharge which can be amplified to work an electrical and mechanical relay counter. **1956** 'N. SHUTE' *Beyond Black Stump* 1 A number of substances that are trapped in the earth's centre will influence a Geiger counter sufficiently to set it clicking. **1957** M. LOWRY *Let.* 4 Apr. (1967) 406 When the last old sourdough has traded in his divining rod and gold sifting pan for a geiger counter.

b. *fig.*

1957 *London Mag.* June 65 We do not feel inclined to treat political beliefs as geiger counters by which we can measure the significance of events as they occur. **1959** *Times Lit. Suppl.* 24 Apr. 246/5 Dr. Simon runs his Geiger counter over the writings of Bernard Shaw to detect the educationist beneath the playwright and pamphleteer. **1961** *John o'London's* 12 Oct. 423/3 A sadistic gangster story..at times, unless my moral geiger counter deceived me, rather slanted, sympathy-wise, towards the gang.

geikielite (ˈgiːkɪlaɪt). *Min.* [f. the name of Sir Archibald *Geikie* (1835–1924), Scottish geologist + -LITE.] A titanate of magnesium, with some magnesium replaced by iron, known only as brownish or bluish black rolled pebbles from Ceylon.

1892 *Nature* 27 Oct. 620/2 The pebbles were handed over to Mr. Allan Dick for chemical investigation. Quantitative analysis proved the mineral to be essentially magnesium titanate... To this interesting new species Mr. Dick..gave the name Geikielite, in honour of Sir Archibald Geikie,..in whose laboratory the analysis had been made. **1906** *Jrnl. Chem. Soc.* XC. II. 459 The ferric oxide shown in these analyses is in some cases primary (isomorphously replacing the geikielite molecule). **1944** C. PALACHE et al. *Dana's Syst. Min.* (ed. 7) I. 536 Ilmenite is $FeTiO_3$ with as much as 54 atomic per cent of Mg..and grading into geikielite, $(Mg,Fe)TiO_3$.

geiler, obs. form of JAILER.

geilfine (ˈgeɪlfɪnɪ). *Irish Hist.* Also **geilfhine**. [Ir.] One of the four divisions of the *fine*, comprising the chief and his four nearest male relatives. Cf. FINE *sb.*², IARFINE, INDFINE.

1869 W. N. HANCOCK et al. tr. *Anc. Laws Irel.* II. 161 The 'Geilfine'-tribe relationship in the direct line, such as the father, and the son, and the grandson, and the great grandson, and the great great grandson to the fifth generation. **1875** H. S. MAINE *Lect. Early Hist. Instit.* 211 A Geilfine class may consist of a father and four sons who are not in the same degree. **1882** C. G. WALPOLE *Short Hist. Kingdom Irel.* i. 9 The father and the four sons formed a family group of five households, which went by the name of the *Geilfine*. **1903** P. W. JOYCE *Soc. Hist. Anc. Irel.* I. vii. 188 The *Gelfine* system, under which four groups of persons, all nearly related to each other, held four adjacent tracts of land as a sort of common property. **1967** F. J. BYRNE in Moody & Martin *Course Irish Hist.* iii. 49 The brehon lawyers drew up a very elaborate scheme of the different degrees of relationship. The *geilfhine*, sometimes called *deirbfhine* was the normal family group—basically the relationship between a man and his brothers; but it was extended over five generations to include his own children, his father's brothers, his grandfather's brothers, and even his great-grandfather and *his* brothers!

geill (dʒiːl). *Sc.* and *north.* Also 6 **gylle**. [a. OF. *gel, giel* (vbl. sb. from *geler* to congeal) = *gelée* JELLY.] Jelly.

c **1450** HENRYSON *Mor. Fab.* 12 And main-flour fine shee brought in stead of geill. **1550** LYNDESAY *Sqr. Meldrum* 887 Gude Aquavite, Wyne, and Aill, With nobill Confeittis, Bran and Geill. **1819** W. TENNANT *Papistry Storm'd* (1827) 99 Pies and tarts, Rang'd here and there in sindry parts, And sauces, soups, and geills, and creams.

b. *Comb.*, as **geill-pock**, a jelly-bag.

1570 *Wills & Inv. N.C.* (Surtees 1835) 327 Item I gyve to John Robison ij° gylle pokes. *a* **1586** MAITLAND in Pinkerton *Anc. Scot. Poems* (1786) 326 Of fyne silk thair furrit cloikis With hinge and sleivis lyk geill pokkis.

geilt, var. GELT *sb.*¹

geily, Sc. var. GAILY.

gein¹ (ˈdʒiːɪn). *Chem.* Also **geine**. [f. Gr. γῆ earth + -IN; in F. *géine* (Berzelius *a* 1848).] A brown precipitate obtained by boiling mould or decayed vegetable matter with alkalies.

1844 HOBLYN *Dict. Med., Geine.* **1864** WATTS *Dict. Chem.*

gein² (ˈdʒiːɪn). [f. *Ge-um* + -IN; named by Buchner.] 'A bitter substance extracted from the root of *Geum urbanum*' (*Syd. Soc. Lex.* 1885).

gein, obs. form of GAIN *sb.*¹, GAIN-.

gein, Sc. var. *given*: see GIVE.

geing, var. GING *Obs.*, company, crew.

geinȝie, var. GANYIE. *Obs.*

1596 DALRYMPLE tr. *Leslie's Hist. Scotl.* (1890) II. 66 With gun and geinȝie.

†**geir**. *Obs.* Forms: 6–7 geire, geyre, 7 gier, geer, 7–8 geir, 7, 9 geier. [a. Du. *gier* = G. *geier*, MHG. *gîr, gîre*, OHG. *gîr, kîr*, not found in the other Teut. languages.] A vulture.

1565 COOPER *Thesaurus, Vultur*, a rauenous birde called a voulter or geyre. **1586** J. HOOKER *Girald. Irel.* in *Holinshed* II. 43/1 Argent three griphs or geires gules crowned gold: this griph or geire is a kind of an eagle. **1601** HOLLAND *Pliny* I. 353 The Vultures or Geires which flie from sweet ointments, are desirous yet of other odors and perfumes. **1615** T. THOMAS *Lat. Dict., Vultur*, a ravenous birde called a vulter, a geyre or grappe. **1721–1800** BAILEY, *Geir*, a Vulture.

b. *Comb.* **geir-eagle** (= G. *geier-adler*), used in the Bible of 1611 to render Heb. *rāhām*, supposed to be the *Neophron percnopterus*, a species of vulture.

1611 BIBLE *Lev.* xi. 18 The Swanne, and the Pellicane, and the Gier-eagle. —— *Deut.* xiv. 17 The Geer-eagle. **1835** BROWNING *Paracelsus* I. 19 Ask the gier-eagle [ed. 1888 geier-eagle] why she stoops at once Into the vast and unexplored abyss!

geir(e, obs. form of GEAR *sb.*

‖**geis** (gɛʃ, geɪʃ, giːʃ). Also **gaysh, geas**. Pl. **geasa, geise**. [Ir.] In Irish folklore: a solemn injunction, prohibition, or taboo; a moral obligation.

1880 S. FERGUSON *Poems* 63 This journey at this season was ill-timed, As made in violation of the *gaysh*. **1899** D. HYDE *Lit. Hist. Irel.* 344 He thought he saw Gradh son of Lir upon the plain, and it was a *geis* (tabu) to him to see that. *Ibid.* 373 Every man who entered the Fenian ranks had four *geasa* (gassa, *i.e.*, tabus) laid upon him. **1928** *Observer* 22 Jan. 5/4 Apparently a man could be either:—(1) Born under a 'geis' prohibiting certain actions on his part, or (2) Laid under 'geis' either at birth or any time during his life, either by divine or human agency. **1965** *New Statesman* 23 July 129/2 In a sense which most Irish people will know, this put Fallon under a *geas*, a moral compulsion, to say his bit.

geis(e, obs. form of *geese*, pl. of GOOSE.

geise, var. GIZZEN.

‖**geisha** (ˈgeɪʃə). Pl. **geisha, -as**. [Japanese.] A Japanese girl whose profession is to entertain men by dancing and singing; loosely, a Japanese prostitute.

1891 SIR E. ARNOLD in *Contemp. Rev.* Dec. 777 All Kyôto's geishas will be there. **1892** *Critic* (U.S.) 5 Mar. 139/2 Most of the illustrations illustrate that one-half of Japan which foreigners, including authors, usually meet in the *gei-sha* or singing-and-dancing girl. **1896** HALL & GREENBANK (*title*), The Geisha, a story of a tea house. A Japanese Musical Play. *Ibid.* 129 Geisha are we, Bidden to be Present to-day at the ceremonee. **1910** *Encycl. Brit.* XI. 553/2 *Geisha*.., strictly the name of the professional dancing and singing girls of Japan. The word is, however, often loosely used for the girls and women inhabiting Shin Yoshiwara, the prostitutes' quarter of Tokyo. **1922** JOYCE *Ulysses* 95 And they call me the jewel of Asia, Of Asia, The geisha. **1939** B. H. CHAMBERLAIN *Things Japanese* (ed. 6) 460 Up-to-date garb and manners make the geisha appear prim and old-fashioned.

attrib. **1887** *Pall Mall G.* 17 Nov. 5/1 My companion and I..entered a theatre, where we were regaled with a terribly realistic tragedy and geisha dancing. **1887** [see KIMONO]. **1895** 'C. HOLLAND' *My Japanese Wife* i. 2 A real mousmé, not a *geisha* girl with a past, an ambiguous present, and a who-knows-what future. **1910** *Chambers's Jrnl.* Sept. 617/1, I have heard of the geisha girls of Japan. **1947** J. BERTRAM *Shadow of War* VII. iii. 221 Omori..had enjoyed a certain reputation as a home of rather superior geisha-houses. If not quite a red-light district.., it was down in the guide-books as a 'pleasure-quarter' of Tokyo.

geison, obs. form of GEASON.

Geissler (ˈgaɪslə(r)). The name of Heinrich *Geissler* (1814–79), German mechanic and glass-blower, used attrib. (†or in the possessive) to designate certain apparatus invented by him, as **Geissler tube**, a sealed glass tube containing gas at low pressure and a pair of electrodes so designed that a luminous discharge can be produced between them.

1863 E. ATKINSON tr. *Ganot's Physics* §740. 706 Plücker has found that the light in Geissler's tubes does not depend on the substance of the electrodes. **1870** *Chem. News* 28 Jan. 45/2 Experiments made with perfectly pure gases enclosed in so-called Geissler tubes. **1883** *Encycl. Brit.* XVI. 31/1 As it takes a height of about 30 inches of mercury to balance the pressure of the atmosphere, a Geisler pump necessarily is a somewhat long-legged and unwieldy instrument. *Ibid.*, Even a Geisler's stop-cock requires to be lubricated to be absolutely gas-tight. **1930** W. M. DEANS tr. *Pohl's Electr. & Magn.* 219 Geissler tubes are being used to an increasing degree in practice for lighting. **1966** *McGraw-Hill Encycl. Sci. & Technol.* XII. 589/1 Modified forms of Geissler tubes containing helium, neon, argon, or mercury have become familiar to everyone as luminous signs or fluorescent tube lamps.

geissospermine (gaɪsəʊˈspɜːmɪn). [f. mod. L. *Geissosperm-um* (f. Gr. γεῖσσον, γεῖσον eaves, cornice + σπέρμα seed) + -INE.] An alkaloid derived from the bark of *Geissospermum læve*, a Brazilian plant. Also called *geissine* (*Syd. Soc. Lex.* 1885).

‖**Geist, geist** (gaɪst). [G., = spirit: see GHOST *sb.*] Spirit; spirituality; intellectuality; intelligence.

1871 M. ARNOLD *Friendship's Garland* i. 8 In Berlin we oppose 'Geist'—*intelligence*, as you or the French might say —to 'Ungeist'. *Ibid.* 9 France has 'Geist' in her democracy, and Prussia in her education. **1883** *19th Cent.* Aug. 274 So that the heaven to which we must look forward will be a heaven of pure *Geist*. **1958** *Times Lit. Suppl.* 10 Jan. 19/1 Papers acquire a certain temperament with time. They have their own *Geist*, their own quirks of personality. **1964** *Economist* 12 Dec. 1256/1 The main *geist* which rules the Treasury is that of amenability.

geist, obs. form of GEST; var. GIST.

geister, obs. form of JESTER.

‖**Geisteswissenschaft** (ˈgaɪstəsˌvɪsənʃaft). Pl. **Geisteswissenschaften**. [G., f. *geist* spirit (see GHOST *sb.*) + *wissenschaft* learning (*wissen* to know).] Usu. in *pl.*, the arts of humanities, opp. 'the sciences'. So **ˈGeistesˌwissenschaftler**, one who studies the arts or humanities.

1909 W. M. URBAN *Valuation* i. 10 Psychology..is the fundamental *Geisteswissenschaft*. **1925** *Phil. Rev.* XXXIV. 334 Dilthey held that for the mental sciences, which he called, following Mill, the *Geisteswissenschaften*, the natural scientific method is insufficient. **1931** M. R. COHEN *Reason & Nature* 371 We shall here concern ourselves only with the values which are the study of the *Geisteswissenschaften*. **1934** M. BLACK tr. *Carnap's Unity of Sci.* 31 Science..includes, in addition to the 'natural' sciences, Psychology and the *Geisteswissenschaften* (social sciences) generally. **1938** *Mind* XLVII. 114 Artists and 'Geisteswissenschaftler'..wishing to have a concentrated glimpse of the whole breadth and wealth of human thought.

†**geit**, *sb. Sc. Obs.* Also 6 jeit, get. [a. F. *get, giet, jet* etc., border.] A border on a garment.

1542 *Inv. R. Wardrobe* (1815) 100 Item, ane kirtill of tweldore with ane small geit of cramasy velvott.

Hence †**geit** *v.*, to trim, border.

1542 *Ld. Treas. Acc. Scotl.* in Pitcairn *Crim. Trials* I. 322* To jeit the Cote with thre vanis aboute the Taill. **1542** *Inv. R. Wardrobe* (1815) 88 Item, twa dowblettis of cramasy sating cuttit out upon reid taffate, getit with the self..Item ane dowblet of gray sating geitit and buttonit with the self.

geit(e, geitt, obs. ff. JET (mineral).

geither, var. GATHER *sb.*² *Obs.*

‖ˈ**geitje**. *South African.* ? *Obs.* [Du. *geitje*, lit. 'little goat'; perh. an etymologizing perversion of a native name.] A venomous African lizard.

1786 tr. *Sparrman's Voy. Cape G. Hope* II. 334 It is a fortunate circumstance, that the geitje is slow in its motions, and not of a very irritable disposition. **1812–15** ANNE PLUMPTRE *Lichtenstein's Trav. S. Afr.* II. 167 Poisonous lizards abound in old walls and forsaken houses. They are known by the name of geitjes. **1834** PRINGLE *Afr. Sk.* viii. 287 One species of lizard called the geitje..is considered very venomous.

geitonogamy (gaɪtəˈnɒgəmɪ). [f. Gr. γειτονο-, γείτων neighbour + -γαμία marriage.] (See quot.)

1880 GRAY *Struct. Bot.* 216 *note, Geitonogamy*, fertilization by pollen of other flowers of the same plant.

geiue, obs. form of GIVE.

gekko, obs. form of GECKO.

gel (dʒɛl), *sb.* [Orig. a suffix f. the first syllable of *gelatin* (as in ALCOGEL, HYDROGEL) and later used as an independent word.] **1.** *Chem.* A semi-solid colloidal system consisting of a solid dispersed in a liquid. Also *attrib.*

The invention of this word and of *sol* is ascribed by later writers to Thomas Graham (died 1869).

1899 W. B. HARDY in *Jrnl. Physiol.* XXIV. 164 Graham's nomenclature is as follows: The fluid state, colloidal solution, is the 'sol', the solid state the 'gel'. The fluid constituent is indicated by a prefix. Thus an aqueous solution of gelatine is a 'hydrosol', and on setting it becomes a 'hydrogel'. **1904** W. C. D. WHETHAM *Recent Devel. Phys. Sci.* iv. 137 The mass will solidify under certain conditions to form a solid which may be called a gel. **1918** *Nature* 28 Mar. 66/1 A very minute amount of electrolyte added to a stable colloidal solution may bring about complete precipitation or flocculation of the sol, the sol separating out in a gelatinous form known as a gel. **1922** *Encycl. Brit.* XXX. 591/1 On digestion with water the cellular tissue is transformed into a series of hydrated gel-products. **1926** *Ibid.* Suppl. I. 785 The Brownian movement affords a criterion of whether protoplasm is in the condition of a sol or a gel. **1930** *Engineering* 31 Jan. 142/3 Cement could be regarded as what in colloid chemistry is known as a rigid gel, which changes its physical properties..according to the variations of its moisture content. **1930** *Nature* 15 Mar. 432 Structure in very permeable collodion gel films and its significance in filtration problems. **1931** *Oxf. Univ. Gaz.* 17 June 693/2 The equilibria between (*a*) silica gel and water vapour, (*b*) silica gel and alcohol vapour, (*c*) iron oxide gel and alcohol. **1951** Williams & Alberty in Taylor & Glasstone *Treat. Physical Chem.* (ed. 3) II. v. 675 There is at present almost universal acceptance of the view that gels possess a ramifying, more or less coherent, framework that retains the liquid component and confers elasticity and rigidity upon the system as a whole. **1966** *McGraw-Hill Encycl. Sci. & Technol.* VI. 93/1 Commonly, gels have a low solid content, for example, 2–5% for ferric oxide, and as little as 0·1% for coagulated blood.

2. *Hairdressing.* A jelly-like substance used for setting or styling the hair, sold as a jelly.

1958 *Amer. Hairdresser* July 26/1 (Advt.), Contains miracle deprovinyllol/DEP/styling gel. *Ibid.* 26/1 DEP.. Not a spray...not a liquid. DEP is a silky gel. **1968** *Trade Marks Jrnl.* 11 Sept. 1518/1 Trugel..Preparations for the hair, all in gel form. Nicholas Products Limited, 225 Bath Road, Slough, Buckinghamshire; Manufacturers and Merchants.—2nd March, 1967. **1975** *Chem. Week* 26 Mar. 37/1 Beauty salon hair dressers and cosmeticians expect women to go in for fancier coiffures..which..will increase sales of chemical specialty products, such as permanent waves, hair-setting lotions and gels. **1984** *Daily Mail* 20 Oct. 12/2 Hair is expensively highlighted—blown and brushed back and worked over with gels.

gel (dʒɛl), *v.* [f. the sb.] *intr.* To become a gel. *fig.* = jell *v.* (*fig.*). Hence **gelled** *ppl. a.*, **'gelling** *vbl. sb.*

1917 *Sci. Amer. Suppl.* 22 Sept. 191/2 Ligno-cellulose fibre..does not gel so readily by cold mechanical treatment as does cellulose. **1924** H. B. Weiser in R. H. Bogue *Theory & Applic. Colloidal Behavior* I. xv. 390 A sol containing 1 per cent of pure gelatin does not gel until around 10°. **1933** Fischer & Hooker *Lyophilic Colloids* I. ix. 159 These explanations..do nothing to make clear why the silicic acid so frequently gels before being precipitated, or the relationship of the gelling process to the precipitation. **1953** Kirk & Othmer *Encycl. Chem. Technol.* XI. 162 It causes the ink to body up and finally to gel completely. **1970** *Nature* 25 July 371/1 The mixture gelled at T_0 °C. After 5 h..the cell was warmed a few degrees to make the gelled oil transparent.

fig. **1958** *Observer* 30 Mar. 14/3 The combination of drawingroom and documentary failed to gel. **1966** *Listener* 14 Apr. 549/1, I recognize the moment As when an awareness gels.

gelable ('dʒɛləb(ə)l), *a.* *rare*⁻⁰. [f. L. type *gelābilis*, f. *gelāre* to freeze.] (See quot.)

1727 Bailey vol. II, *Gelable*, capable of being frozen or congealed. **1847** in Craig.

gelada ('dʒɛlədə). [Native name.] In full *gelada baboon*. An Ethiopian baboon, *Theropithecus gelada*, characterized by a heavy mane in the adult male, and by a tufted tail.

1843 J. E. Gray *List of Mammalia in Brit. Mus.* 9 The Gelada. **1878** *Proc. Zool. Soc.* 1 A Family of Gelada Baboons. **1893** R. Lydekker *Royal Nat. Hist.* I. I. iv. 125 The aspect of the gelada forcibly suggests a large black poodle dog, with an unusually abundant mane. **1906** *Westm. Gaz.* 27 Aug. 10/2 A fine specimen of the Dusky Gelada. **1967** *Listener* 6 Apr. 459/3 Other ground-dwelling monkeys such as the patas monkey, the gelada baboon and the hamadryas baboon. *Ibid.*, The gelada is especially interesting.

Gelalæan (dʒɛlə'liːən), *a.* Also **Gelalean**, **Jalalæan**, **Jel(l)alæan**. [f. Arab. *Jalāl ad-dīn*.] Of or pertaining to Gelal-ed-Din, 'Glory of the Faith', a title of Malek Shah, Sultan of Khorasan, and reformer of the Persian calendar in 1079.

1780 *Encycl. Brit.* VI. 4009 *Gelalean* or *Jellalæan* Kalendar, is a correction of the Persian kalendar, made by order of sultan Gelaleddan, in the 467th year of the Hegira; of Christ 1089. **1838** H. Nicolas *Chronol. Hist.* (ed. 2) 25 The Gelalæan era..March 14. A.D. 1079. **1866** Brande & Cox *Dict. Sci.* etc., *Gelalæan Era*, the era of Yezdegird. **1910** *Encycl. Brit.* VI. 317/1 Era of Yazdegerd, or Persian or Jelalaean Era.

†**gelan(d.** *Obs.* Some kind of spice.

1714 *Fr. Bk. of Rates* 384 List of Merchandizes coming from the Levant..Gelan. **1725** Bradley *Fam. Dict.* s.v. *Waters*, Musk, Nutmeg, Clove, Geland, Spikenard.

Gelasian (gɪ'leɪzɪən), *a.* [f. *Gelasius* (see below): see -ian.] Of or pertaining to Pope Gelasius I (492–6 A.D.); esp. applied to liturgical books or prayers attributed to him.

a **1773** A. Butler *Feasts Cath. Ch.* (1839) II. i. 59 In the Gelasian liturgy..only five Sundays occur in Advent. **1832** *Archaeologia* XXIV. 10 The whole ancient Roman liturgy is comprised in the three books called the Leonine, Gelasian, and Gregorian Sacramentaries. **1915** F. E. Brightman *Engl. Rite* p. x, [The Leonine Sacramentary] contains much official matter, some of which recurs in the later Gelasian and Gregorian books.

†**gelasin.** *Obs.* Also **gelazin**. [a. F. *gelasin* (Cotgr.), ad. Gr. γελασῖνος, f. γελᾶν to laugh.] A dimple in the cheek, produced by smiling.

1630 Lennard tr. *Charron's Wisd.* (1658) 19 The cheeks somewhat rising, and in the middle the pleasant gelasin. **1697** Evelyn *Numism.* ix. 298 The charming Gelazin and dimple of the Cheek and Chin.

gelastic (dʒɪ'læstɪk), *a.* *rare.* [ad. Gr. γελαστικός, f. γελᾶν to laugh.] Serving the function of laughter, risible. Also (humorous *nonce-use*) as *sb. pl.*, remedies operating by causing laughter.

a **1704** T. Brown *Wks.* (1720) II. 167 My friendly Pill.. causes all Complexions to laugh or smile..which it effects by dilating and expanding the gelastic Muscles, first of all discover'd by my self. **1716** M. Davies *Athen. Brit.* II. 410 A rising Clergyman publishing a Sermon against uninspir'd Prophecies..Apologetically..seem'd to excuse that venerable Cambrian Prelate's Prophetick Vein..not without a Gelastick deference to so great a name. **1838** Southey *Doctor* V. 147 Happy man would be his dole, who, when he had made up his mind..to a dreadful course of drastics, should find that gelastics had been substituted.

†**gela'taneous,** *a.* *Obs.* *rare.* [f. It. *gelata* jelly.] Of the nature of jelly.

1763 *Char.* in *Ann. Reg.* 28/2 The *nostoch*, a singular plant, which appears only after hard rains in the summer, under a gelataneous form, and soon after disappearing.

gelate (dʒɛ'leɪt), *v.* [Back-formation f. gelation².] *intr.* = gel *v.* So **ge'lated** *ppl. a.*

1915 [see gelation²]. **1948** *New Biol.* V. 33 A reversible liquefaction of any gelated regions of the protoplasm. **1951** *Ibid.* X. 17 When this plasmasol reaches the tip of the pseudopodium we can imagine it gelating to form new pseudopodial wall.

†**ge'latia.** *Obs.* Also 4 **gelacia**. [perh. an etymologizing perversion (after L. *gelāre* to freeze) of L. *chalazias*, f. Gr. χάλαζα hail.] (See quot.)

1398 Trevisa *Barth. De P.R.* xvi. l. (1495) 570 *Gelacia* is a whyte precyous stone shapen as an heyll stone: and it is so calde that it neuer hetith wyth fyre. **1567** Maplet *Gr. Forest* 9. **1601** Chester *Love's Mart.*, *Dial.* lxxxvi, The Topaze, Turches, and Gelatia.

gelatification (ˌdʒɛlətɪfɪ'keɪʃən). [f. gelati-n + -fication.] (See quot.)

1860 Fowler *Med. Voc.*, *Gelatification*, the production of, or conversion into, gelatin or jelly. **1885** in *Syd. Soc. Lex.*

gelatigenous (ˌdʒɛlə'tɪdʒɪnəs), *a.* [f. gelati-n + -gen + -ous.] Producing or developing gelatin. *gelatigenous tissues* (see quot. 1855).

1854 *Eng. Cycl.*, *Nat. Hist.* I. 949 Gelatigenous substance is so widely diffused over the body that [etc.]. **1855** Ogilvie Suppl., *Gelatigenous tissues*, animal tissues which yield to boiling water gelatine. **1885** in *Syd. Soc. Lex.*

gelatin, gelatine ('dʒɛlətɪn, -(')iːn). [a. F. *gélatine*, orig. 'an excellent white broth made of the fish Maigre' (Cotgr.), ad. It. *gelatina*, f. *gelata* jelly. In medical Latin *gelatina* was adopted as a term for 'any sort of clear gummy juice, as the Juice of Fruits, the Jelly of Quinces, etc.' (Phillips, ed. Kersey 1706); in the 18th c. the F. *gélatine* was occasionally used in medical books in this sense, and with the rise of scientific chemistry came to be restricted to its present use. On the analogy of this and some other words, the suffix *-ine* (see -ine, -in) was adopted by chemists for forming names of 'extractive principles'. In popular use the spelling is commonly *gelatine*, and the pronunc. is often (dʒɛlətiːn); in chemical use consistency demands the form *gelatin*.]

1. a. The substance which is the basis of the jellies into which certain animal tissues (skin, tendons, ligaments, the matrix of bones, etc.) are converted when treated with hot water for some time. It is amorphous, brittle, without taste or smell, transparent, and of a faint yellow tint; and is composed of carbon, hydrogen, nitrogen, oxygen, and sulphur.

It is used in the preparation of soups, jellies, etc., and latterly in many photographic processes; it is also pressed into thin sheets for making transparent cards.

1800 Hatchett in *Phil. Trans.* XC. 366 That animal jelly ..which is distinguished by the name of gelatin. **1819** J. G. Children *Chem. Anal.* 304 Gelatine is usually prepared from the skin of animals. Common glue is gelatine contaminated with impurities, to which it owes its colour. Isinglass is gelatine nearly in a state of purity. **1858** Carpenter *Veg. Phys.* §329 Animal tissues containing gelatin (the material commonly known as glue, which forms a large part of the skin of most animals). **1878** L. Wingfield *Lovely Wang* 192 Soup..thickened by gelatine.

b. *vegetable gelatin*: one of the constituents of gluten, identical with animal gelatin.

1852 Th. Ross *Humboldt's Trav.* I. xi. 373 This principle accompanies gelatin, even in the bark of beech, alder, and nut-trees. **1885** Goodale *Physiol. Bot.* 363 The albumin-like matters. Ritthausen classifies these substances into (1) Albumin of plants; (2) Casein of plants; (3) Gelatin of plants.

c. In trade use: Short for *gelatin card*.

1851 Mayhew *Lond. Labour* I. 266 The principal traffic has lately been in 'gelatines' (gelatine cards). Those in the greatest demand contain representations of the Crystal Palace, the outlines of the structure being given in gold delineation on the deep purple..of the..shining gelatine.

2. The name given to an explosive compound (see quot. 1895). More fully, *blasting* or *explosive gelatin*.

1878 *Ure's Dict. Arts* (ed. 7) IV. 1015 *Blasting Gelatine*, this name has been given by Mr. Nobel..to a new explosive compound. **1887** *Pall Mall G.* 23 May 10/2 A..blast of 100,000 tons of rock took place at Llanberis Quarry..on Saturday, two tons of gelatine, equal to nineteen tons of powder, being employed. **1895** *Bloxam's Chem.* (ed. 8) 626 Blasting Gelatine is made by dissolving collodion-cotton in about nine times its weight of nitroglycerine.

3. *attrib.* and *Comb.*, as (sense 1) *gelatin capsule*, *film*, *lozenge*, *-maker*, *pellicle*, *size*; *gelatin-coated* adj.; (sense 2) *gelatin-shell*. Also **gelatine dry plate**, **gelatine dynamite** (see quots.); **gelatine emulsion**, 'an emulsion of gelatine containing a sensitive silver compound' (Woodbury *Encycl. Photogr.* 1890); also *attrib.*; **gelatine paper** *Photogr.*, paper coated with sensitized gelatin; **gelatine picture**, a photograph produced by the action of light on bichromated gelatine; **gelatine process**, any photographic process in which gelatine is employed; **gelatine sugar** = glycocoll.

1858 Simmonds *Dict. Trade*, **Gelatine-capsule Maker*, a manufacturer of small hollow soluble capsules, enclosing a few drops of nauseous medicines. **1895** *Pop. Sci. Monthly* Sept. 716 The lines are ruled..on a *gelatin-coated plate. **1890** Woodbury *Encycl. Photogr.*, **Gelatine dry plates*, plates usually of glass coated with a film of gelatine, containing sensitive silver bromide. **1889** Cundill *Dict. Explosives* 52 **Gelatine dynamite*..occupies a place mid-way between blasting gelatine and dynamite. It consists of a thin blasting gelatine mixed with other substances. **1885** G. Marlow in *Brit. Jrnl. Photogr.* 18 Dec. 804/1 The present makes of *gelatine emulsions. **1891** *Anthony's Photogr. Bull.* IV. 133 Negative enlargements on gelatine-emulsion paper. **1878** *Design & Work* 26 Jan. 121/2 The *gelatin film is then moistened with cold water. **1889** *Judge* (U.S.) 22 June 180/2 The gelatine film..is one two-thousandths of an inch in thickness. **1895** *Daily News* 22 Nov. 5/4 A fashionable trimming for ladies' black capes is now a *gelatine lozenge. **1858** Simmonds *Dict. Trade*, **Gelatin-maker*, one who boils and prepares glue and gelatin from animal tissues. **1851** *Illustr. Catal. Gt. Exhib.* 1463 Transparent sheets of *gelatine paper. **1885** J. Barker in *Brit. Jrnl. Photogr.* 6 Mar. 150/2 The published formulæ for gelatine paper. **1889** *Anthony's Photogr. Bull.* II. 152 Bromine is set free and metallic silver is deposited in minute particles in the *gelatine pellicle. **1875** Knight *Dict. Mech.* 962/1 The *gelatine picture from which the metallic mold was struck. **1860** *Photogr. News* 13 Jan. 228 The capabilities of the *gelatine preservative process. **1875** Knight *Dict. Mech.*, **Gelatine-process*. **1890** *Pall Mall G.* 3 Feb. 5/1 The *gelatine shell need not hit to be an effectual destroyer. **1934** H. Hiler *Notes Technique Painting* iii. 179 To the second series, the albumins, belong..the *gelatine-size glues. **1843** Pereira *Food & Diet* 215 *Gelatine sugar or glycicoll.

Hence **'gelatined** *a.*, coated with gelatin.

1879 *Cassell's Techn. Educ.* III. 326 The gelatined side of the paper..having a dark colour. **1894** *Brit. Jrnl. Photogr.* XLI. 69 A sheet of gelatined paper.

gelatinase (dʒɛ'lætɪneɪz, -eɪs). *Biochem.* [f. gelatin + -ase.] An enzyme which liquefies gelatin, occurring among bacteria, yeasts, etc.

1911 *Jrnl. Chem. Soc.* C. II. 810 The pancreas gelatinase differs from gelatinase *B. prodigiosus*, by the action of which glycine is formed. **1912** *Ibid.* CII. II. 283 The Gelatinase of Bacillus prodigiosus... The most active gelatinase preparations are obtained from bouillon cultures of the organism. **1949** H. W. Florey et al. *Antibiotics* I. xi. 514 In addition to the antibiotic, gelatinase was secreted. Metabolism solutions containing gelatinase lysed suspensions of heat-killing gram negative bacteria.

gelatinate (dʒɪ'lætɪneɪt), *v.* [f. gelatin (? or mod.L. *gelātīnus*: see next) + -ate.]

1. *intr.* = gelatinize 1.

1796 Kirwan *Elem Min.* (ed. 2) I. 279 It [Zeolite] is partially and slowly soluble in the three mineral acids without effervescence, and, if they be not in too great quantity, it *gelatinates* most commonly. **1808** Henry *Epit. Chem.* (1808) 305 Nor does it [mucilage] gelatinate, when its heated solution cools. **1826** —— *Elem. Chem.* II. 573 Certain minerals that gelatinate. **1828** in Webster; and in mod. Dicts.

2. *trans.* = gelatinize 2.

1828 Webster, *Gelatinate*, to convert into gelatin or into a substance resembling jelly. Hence in mod. Dicts.

Hence **gelati'nation** = gelatinization.

1796 Kirwan *Elem. Min.* (ed. 2) I. 42 Their solubility therein [in acids]..with or without heat..gelatination, &c. **1885** Goodale *Physiol. Bot.* 34 The principal modifications of the cell-wall are the following:—(1) Partial or complete conversion into mucilage (Gelatination).

†**'gelatine,** *a.* and *sb.* *Obs.* [f. L. type **gelātīnus*, f. assumed L. *gelāta* (= It. *gelata* jelly).]

A. *adj.* Of the nature of jelly, gelatinous.

1713 Derham *Phys.-Theol.* viii. vi. (1727) 382 That spermatick, galatine Matter in which they [insects' eggs] are reposited. *Ibid.* 383 *note*, In this gelatine, transparent Spawn, the Eggs are neatly laid.

B. *sb.* *Zool.* (See quot. 1855.)

1835 Kirby *Hab. & Inst. Anim.* I. vi. 195 Lamarck has divided this class [the Radiaries] into two orders, the Gelatines and the Echinoderms. **1855** Ogilvie, Suppl., *Gelatines*, the name given by Kirby to the Acalephæ of Cuvier, from the gelatinous consistency of their bodies.

gelatine: see gelatin.

gelatiniferous (dʒɪˌlætɪ'nɪfərəs), *a.* [f. gelatin + -(i)ferous.] Yielding gelatin.

1878 Foster *Phys.* II. i. 189 The proteid and gelatiniferous envelopes of the fat cells are dissolved. *Ibid.* (1879) 236 The gelatiniferous elements of the tissues.

gelatiniform (dʒɛlə'tɪnɪfɔːm), *a.* [f. as prec. + -(I)FORM.] Having the form, consistence, or appearance of gelatin.

1830 R. KNOX *Béclard's Anat.* 121 Gelatiniform mucus. **1845** BUDD *Dis. Liver* 308 Cells of gelatiniform cancer . . may . . become adherent to any part of the serous membrane with which they are accidentally brought in contact. **1877** ROBERTS *Handbk. Med.* (ed. 3) I. 275 Gelatiniform cancer.

gelatinify (dʒɛlə'tɪnɪfaɪ), *v. rare.* [f. GELATIN + -(I)FY.] *trans.* To render gelatinous.

1839-47 TODD *Cycl. Anat.* III. 644/2 Dilute acetic acid . . gelatinifies the bodies.

gelatinity (dʒɛlə'tɪnɪtɪ). [f. as GELATINE *a.* + -ITY.] The gelatinous state.

1881 *Eng. Mechanic* No. 874. 366/1 The general elastic cohesive rigidity, or gelatinity of the water.

gelatinizable (dʒɪ'lætɪˌnaɪzəb(ə)l), *a.* [f. GELATINIZE + -ABLE.] Capable of being gelatinized.

1809 PEARSON in *Phil. Trans.* XCIX. 344 Gelatinizable, or . . mucous fluids.

gelatinization (dʒɪˌlætɪnaɪ'zeɪʃən). [f. next + -ATION.] Conversion into a gelatinous state.

1843 PEREIRA *Food & Diet* 143 It also promotes the gelatinization of pectic acid. **1853** C. MORFIT *Tanning*, etc. 20 This gelatinization of the tissue is all-essential. **1882** A. H. GREEN *Phys. Geol.* ii. (ed. 3) 92 Gelatinization sometimes takes place without evaporation. **1887** tr. *De Bary's Fungi* 69 The gelatinisation of the lateral walls of the spores.

gelatinize (dʒɪ'lætɪnaɪz), *v.* [f. GELATIN + -IZE.]

1. *intr.* To assume the character of a jelly; to become gelatinous.

1809 HOME in *Phil. Trans.* XCIX. 186 It could not be brought to gelatinize by the usual method of evaporation. **1819** J. G. CHILDREN *Chem. Anal.* 305 Silica gelatinizes when hydrochloric acid is added to a solution of silicated potassa. **1867** *Fownes' Chem.* 550 The strained solution gelatinizes on cooling. **1890** ABNEY *Treat. Photogr.* (ed. 6) 115 Washing the whole bulk of the emulsion after allowing it to gelatinise by evaporation of the solvents.

2. *trans.* To render gelatinous or jelly-like.

1843 PEREIRA *Food & Diet* (L.) They are easily gelatinized. **1853** C. MORFIT *Tanning*, etc. 20 The tissue is gelatinized. **1881** ATKINSON in *Nature* No. 622. 509 By exposing the softened rice-grains to the action of dry steam . . the starch is gelatinised.

3. To coat with gelatin.

1890 [see GELATINIZED *ppl. a.*].

Hence **ge'latinized** *ppl. a.*; **ge'latinizing** *vbl. sb.*, the action of the vb., also *attrib.*

1819 J. G. CHILDREN *Chem. Anal.* 286 The acid is drained off from the gelatinized juice [of fruit]. **1853** URE *Dict. Arts* I. 895 It possesses a gelatinizing force superior even to isinglass. **1883** *Knowledge* 24 Aug. 120/2 The gelatinising of starch. **1890** *Anthony's Photogr. Bull.* III. 228 Collodion films require greater body than gelatinized surfaces.

gelatino- ('dʒɛləˌtiːnəʊ), comb. form of GELATIN, in words denoting the association of gelatin with other chemical substances, as ***gelatino-albuminous***, ***-sulphurous*** adjs.; also in certain photographic terms, as ***gelatino-bromide***, ***-chloride***, ***-citro-chloride***, used *attrib.* (with *emulsion*, *paper*, *process*) to denote preparations or processes in which silver bromide or chloride is employed with gelatin as a vehicle; sometimes used *ellipt.* in the same sense.

1835-6 TODD *Cycl. Anat.* I. 61/1 The *gelatino-albuminous principles employed in the nutrition of the several tissues. **1881** *Times* 4 Jan. 3/5 The *gelatino-bromide process. **1885** W. B. WOOD in *Brit. Jrnl. Photogr.* 20 Feb. 118/2 Gelatino-bromide for amateurs. **1891** *Adeline's Art Dict.*, *Gelatino-bromide* (Phot.), a process by means of which sensitive glass plates may be prepared in advance and kept in the dark for an indefinite period, both before and after being exposed in the camera. **1885** J. BARKER in *Brit. Jrnl. Photogr.* 6 Mar. 150/2 How to make *gelatino-chloride paper for printing out. **1890** WOODBURY *Encycl. Photogr.*, *Gelatino-chloride emulsion*, an emulsion of gelatine containing silver chloride. **1890** *Anthony's Photogr. Bull.* III. 218 Obernetter's paper and the aristotype, it is believed, are simply *gelatino-citro-chloride. **1882** OGILVIE, **Gelatino-sulphurous*, consisting of gelatine and sulphur.

gelatinoid (dʒɪ'lætɪnɔɪd), *a.* and *sb.* [f. GELATIN + -OID.]

A. *adj.* Resembling gelatin, jelly-like, gelatinous.

1866 ODLING *Anim. Chem.* 117 The acid or alkali merely enables the protein or gelatinoid substance to react with water H_2O. **1883** *Knowledge* 20 July 41/1 A few [Radiolaria] . . form compound gelatinoid masses at the surface of the sea.

B. *sb.* A substance resembling gelatin.

1882 TWINING *Less. Food & Nutr.* 23 The gelatinoids. This group takes its name from the substance so well known . . under the name of Gelatin. **1888** *Century Mag.* May 135 Gelatinoids, fats, and other substances . . Three-fourths was fat and the rest gelatinoids and the like.

gelatinous (dʒɪ'lætɪnəs), *a.* [ad. F. *gélatineux*, f. *gélatine*: see GELATIN.]

1. Having the character or consistency of a jelly; jelly-like.

1724-1800 BAILEY, *Gelatinous*, [in Anatomy] any thing that approaches to the consistence of a Jelly. **1766** PENNANT *Zool.* (1776) II. 453 The gelatinous substance, known by the name of Star Shot, or Star Gelly. **1767** ELLIS in *Phil. Trans.* LVII. 429 Some are stiff and gelatinous, others fleshy and muscular. **1874** COOKE *Fungi* 2 The early condition of the plant is pulpy and gelatinous. **1879** RUTLEY *Study Rocks* iii. 18 Holes through which the gelatinous occupants can protrude their filamentous processes.

fig. **1880** E. WHITE *Cert. Relig.* 85 It is by the infiltration of this solid element that the floating gelatinous soul rises in the scale of being. **1887** *Spectator* 22 Oct. 1407 The gelatinous suggestions to which we are accustomed in Church affairs.

2. Of, pertaining to, or consisting of gelatin.

1798 W. BLAIR *Soldier's Friend* 64 Gelatinous broths answer the purpose both of food and medicine. **1804** ABERNETHY *Surg. Obs.* 20 The gelatinous part of the blood. **1843** PEREIRA *Food & Diet* 212 A gelatinous tissue (that is, a tissue which by boiling is resolved into gelatine). **1873** A. FLINT *Nerv. Syst.* i. 25 The true gelatinous nerve-fibres.

3. *Comb.*, as ***gelatinous-like***, ***-looking*** adjs.

1835-6 TODD *Cycl. Anat.* I. 786/1 A gelatinous-looking membrane. **1849** D. CAMPBELL *Inorg. Chem.* 96 The gelatinous-like solution . . is placed on a linen filter.

Hence **ge'latinously** *adv.*, **ge'latinousness** (in recent Dicts.).

1872 H. C. WOOD *Fresh Water Algæ* 175 The membrane of the parent-cell becoming gelatinously softened.

gelation[1] (dʒɪ'leɪʃən). [ad. L. *gelātiōn-em*, f. *gelāre* to freeze.] Solidification by cold, freezing.

1854 MAYNE *Expos. Lex.*, *Gelatio* . . gelation. **1871** tr. *Schellen's Spectr. Anal.* lxvi. 369 Complete gelation and torpidity. **1875** RUSKIN *Deucalion* (1879) I. 44, I do not doubt but that wonderful phenomena of congelation, regelation, degelation and gelation pure without preposition, take place whenever a schoolboy makes a snowball.

gelation[2] (dʒɛ'leɪʃən). [f. GEL *sb.* + -ATION.] The process of becoming a gel.

1915 W. W. TAYLOR *Chem. Colloids* 11 There seems no escape from the adoption of the following terms:—gel, to gelate, gelation, sol, to solate, solation. **1950** *Thorpe's Dict. Appl. Chem.* (ed. 4) X. 56/2 Gelation is not necessarily due to the formation of very large molecules. *Ibid.*, Gelation occurs only when there is the possibility of unlimited growth in three dimensions. **1954** *Electronic Engin.* XXVI. 141 If gelation takes place before maximum expansion has been reached, the product will be much denser than expected.

geld (gɛld), *sb. Hist.* Also incorrectly **gelt**, **gheld**. See also GILD *sb.*[2] [ad. med.L. *geldum* (in Domesday Book), ad. OE. *ȝield*, *ȝeld*, *ȝyld*, str. neut., payment, tribute, also GUILD; = OFris. *geld*, *jeld* money, OS. *geld* payment (MDu. *gelt*, Du. *geld* money), OHG. *gelt* (MHG. *gelt*, mod.Ger. *geld*), ON. *giald* payment, reward (Sw. *gäld*, Da. *gjæld*), Goth. *gild* tribute:—OTeut. **geldo*^{m}, f. root of **gelþan*: see YIELD *v.*

In the 17th c. confused with GELT *sb.*[2] (which is in fact identical in ultimate etymology); hence the spelling *gelt*.]

1. The tax paid to the crown by English landholders before the Conquest, and continued under the Norman kings.

1610 HOLLAND *Camden's Brit.* I. 294 When Gelt was giuen in the time of King Edward. *a* **1645** HABINGTON *Surv. Worcs.* in *Worcs. Hist. Soc. Proc.* II. 147 Tenne of thease hydes are free from Geld by testimony of the County. **1655** FULLER *Walth. Abb.* 7 Free from all gelts and payments. **1759** B. MARTIN *Nat. Hist. Eng.* II. Suffolk 40 The First called the Geldable, because it paid Geld, or Tribute. **1864** SIR F. PALGRAVE *Norm. & Eng.* III. 558 Geld after Geld had been exacted from the people.

b. A district paying 'geld'. *rare*$^{-1}$.

1809 BAWDWEN *Domesday Bk.* 2 Within the geld of the city there are fourscore and four carucates of land to be taxed.

2. *Comb.*, as ***geld inquest***, ***levy***, ***roll***; also **geld-acre**, **-hide** (Domesday *acra*, *hida ad geldum*), the quantity of land which was reckoned as an acre or a hide for the purposes of 'geld'.

1878 R. W. EYTON *Key to Domesday* 4 The hidation prescribed by the then most recent Gheld-Roll,—that of Easter 1084. *Ibid.* 14 In Dorset the Gheld-hide was subdivided into four virgates. **1880** —— *Domesday Stud.* I. Pref. 2-3 The nature of the Gheld-Inquest may be told in a very few words. After Christmas 1083, King William levied a tax of six shillings on every hide of land. This was the Gheld-Levy of which we are now speaking. *Ibid.* 6 For so great a number of Gheld-acres would be expressed in other terms.

geld (gɛld), *a. Obs.* exc. *dial.* See also YELD. [a. ON. *geld-r* = OSw. *gald-er* (mod.Sw. dial. *gall*, *gåll*, Da. *gold*), OHG. *galt* (mod.Ger. *gelt*, said of a cow):—OTeut. **galdu-* (which, like other adj. *-u-* stems, has passed into the *-o-* and *-jo-* declensions).]

1. Of women or female animals: Barren. Now *dial.* in restricted application (see quot. 1869).

c **1230** *Hali Meid.* 33 Giff ha ne mei nawt teamen, ha is iclepet gealde. *a* **1300** *Cursor M.* 2600 Nan barns ber, þou seis, mai i . . For i am geld þat es me wa. *c* **1460** *Towneley Myst.* x. 134 Elesabeth, thi Cosyn, that is cald geld. **1641** BEST *Farm. Bks.* (Surtees) 9 A good gimmer shearinge goinge geld. **1869** *Lonsdale Gloss.* s.v., 'A geld cow or ewe' = a cow or ewe not with young at the usual time.

absol. *a* **1300** *Cursor M.* 12257 (Gött.) þat þe geld þair fruiting find. *a* **1300** *E.E. Psalter* cxii[i]. 9 þat geld in houses makes wonand, Moder ofe sones to be faineand.

b. *dial.* (See quot.)

1878 *Cumbld. Gloss.*, *Geld grund*, a mining term signifying ground devoid of minerals.

†**2.** Sexually impotent. (In quot. 1440 perh. var. GELT *ppl. a.*) *Obs.*

c **1325** *Old Age I* in *E.E.P.* (1862) 148 Elde makiþ me geld an growen al grai. *c* **1440** *Promp. Parv.* 190/1 Geldynge, or gelde horse, *canterius*.

†**3.** Profitless, yielding no satisfaction. Also, destitute *of*. *Obs.*

a **1310** in Wright *Lyric P.* 24 Of gomenes he mai gon al gelde. *Ibid.* 48 Alle myn godes me at-goht, myn gomenes waxeth gelde.

geld (gɛld), *v.*[1] Also 4-5 **gild(e**, 6-7 **gueld(e**. Inflected **gelt** and **gelded**. [a. ON. *gelda* (= MSw. *gälda*, mod.Sw. *gälla*, Da. *gilde*), f. *geld-r* GELD *a.* Cf. Ger. dial. *gelten* (Grimm s.v. *gelzen*); the Ger. *gelzen*, Du. *gelten* (obs.) may be more remotely connected.]

1. *trans.* **a.** To deprive (a male) of generative power or virility, to castrate or emasculate.

Obsolescent in general literary use; current in technical language with reference to animals.

a **1300** *Cursor M.* 26033 Samson . . bath was geldid and mad blind. **1382** WYCLIF *Matt.* xix. 12 Geldyngis that han geldid hem self, for the kyngdam of heuenes. *c* **1400** *Lanfranc's Cirurg.* 275 He mai ete . . of beestis þat ben gildid. *c* **1420** *Pallad. on Husb.* I. 1164 Toolis forto gelde, and clippe and shere. *a* **1535** *How the Plowman lerned*, etc. 7 in Hazl. *E.P.P.* I. 210 He coude . . Thresshe, fane, and gelde a swyne. **1555** EDEN *Decades* 3 Such chyldren as they take, they geld to make them fat. **1602** MIDDLETON *Blurt* II. ii. C 3 b, She threatens to geld me vnlesse I bee lustie. **1674** tr. *Scheffer's Lapland* xxviii. 131 Those [rein-deer] that are designed for labour they commonly gueld. **1727** SWIFT, etc. *Mem. P.P.* Misc. II. 275, I was sought unto to geld the Lady Frances her Spaniel, which was wont to go astray. **1775** JOHNSON in Boswell 6 Apr., A Judge may be a farmer; but he is not to geld his own pigs.

transf. (jocularly). **1602** *2nd Pt. Return fr. Parnass.* II. iii. 657 Is there no body heere will take the paines to gelde his mouth?

b. To extirpate the ovaries of (a female), to spay.

1557 TUSSER *100 Points Husb.* liii, Geld marefoles. **1607** TOPSELL *Four-f. Beasts* (1658) 521 The female also is gelt or splayed. **1621** BURTON *Anat. Mel.* III. iii. IV. ii. (1651) 623 The Lydians used to geld women whom they suspected. **1862** J. WILSON *Farming* 36 It seems to have been the practice . . to 'geld fillies' as well as colts. **1869** in *Lonsdale Gloss.*

†**2.** *transf.* and *fig.* To deprive *of* some essential part; to cut down the resources of, to impair the strength or force of, to weaken, enfeeble. *Obs.*

1508 DUNBAR *Tua marriit Wemen* 392 Quhen I that grome geldit had of gudis, and of natur. **1565** COOPER *Thesaurus* s.v. *Circuncido*, *Stipendia circuncidere* . . to deminish or gelde mennes wages. **1591** SPENSER *M. Hubberd* 520 Scarse can a Bishoprick forpas them by, But that it must be gelt in priuitie. **1593** SHAKS. *Rich. II*, II. i. 237 Bereft and gelded of his patrimonie. **1594** NASHE *Unfort. Trav.* Wks. (Grosart) V. 55 So would he that first gelt religion or Church-liuings had . . neuer liued. **1607** DEKKER & WEBSTER *Northw. Hoe* IV. F 2, Shee gelded my purse of fifty pounds in ready money. **1622** H. SYDENHAM *Serm. Sol. Occ.* (1637) 123 Who dwelling too critically upon God's *omnia potest*, went about to geld his omnipotence. **1630** B. JONSON *New Inn* I. iii. (1631) B 4, Or geld a iewell Of an odde stone, or so. **1651** CHARLETON *Ephes. & Comm. Matrons* II. Pref., You gave me good Wine, and then gelt it with Water. **1658** OSBORN *Q. Eliz.* 77 To keep the Church humble and quiet whilest she gelt their Sees by exchanges, and other mortifications of their power and estates. **1705** HICKERINGILL *Priestcr.* IV. Wks. 1716 III. 211 I'll take . . the Sting from the Tails of the Wasps, I'll Gueld them from doing Mischief.

†**b.** To mutilate (a book, a quotation, etc.) by excising certain portions, esp. objectionable or obscene passages; to expurgate. Cf. CASTRATE 4.

1579 FULKE *Heskins' Parl.* 338 Which . . he hath mangled and gelded, least the true sense might be gathered out of it. **1583** —— *Defence* xiii. 358 Thus you vse to gelde the Doctors sayings, when you rehearse them. **1648** JOS. BEAUMONT *Psyche* IX. cxcvi, They, by his authentick Copie know Both how to geld and to adulterate it. **1693** SALMON *Bates' Disp.* (1713) A iij, So that I could by no Means . . have gelt the Text, or obliterated any Part thereof, without a manifest Wrong and Injury to the Author. **1729** *Reliq. Hearn.* (1857) II. 696 Several covers of books . . have been discovered . . but the valuable contents gelt.

†**c.** To cut *out* (portions of a book). *Obs.*

1555 W. WATREMAN *Fardle Facions* I. v. 69 Who so . . in lettres and writinges . . should guelde out any thyng.

†**d.** To garble, remove the best part from. *Obs.*

1637 T. MORTON *New Eng. Canaan* (1883) 269 Meane time the skinnes were by the Wessaguscus men gelded, and the better halfe by them juggled away before the owner came.

3. In Gardening, Bee-keeping, etc. [In all the uses, after L. *castrare*.] †**a.** To cut, to prune or remove superfluous shoots, etc., from (a plant or tree); (see also quot. 1523). *Obs.*

1523 FITZHERB. *Husb.* §29 Loke that your sherers . . geld not your beanes, that is to saye, to cutte the beanes so hye, that the nethermoste codde growe styll on the stalke. **1601** HOLLAND *Pliny* I. 536 By the third yeare it must be quite cut in two (where before it was but guelded to the pith). **1615** W. LAWSON *New Orch. & Gard.* vii. (1623) 16 The second yeere in the Spring, geld his top. **1616** SURFL. & MARKH. *Country Farme* 386 For which cause good farmers are carefull to geld and weed out some of the boughes of such a Tree. **1658** EVELYN *Fr. Gard.* (1675) 153 The vines and superfluous shoots must be guelded. **1664** —— *Kal. Hort.* (1729) 199 Geld and prune Strawberries.

†**b.** To cleanse or remove the husks from (wheat). *Obs.*

1601 HOLLAND *Pliny* I. 563 The very pure corn of Campain wheat, which they cal guelded, *i.* wel husked and clensed. **1611** [see GELDED 2].

†**c.** To cut out the old comb from (a bee-hive); to take out (the comb). *Obs.*

1574 HYLL *Ord. Bees* xxiii, So that when they [the hives] shall be next gelded, the old combes rather then the new be taken forth. **1616** SURFL. & MARKH. *Country Farme* I. lxviii. 328 It will be good..at such times as their Combes are to be gelded, to smoake them. **1657** S. PURCHAS *Pol. Flying-Ins.* 135 If any Hive bee taken, driven, or gelded.

d. *dial.* To cut off the top of (an ant-hill) and throw the inside over the land.

1831 LOUDON *Encycl. Agric.* (ed. 2) 902 What is called 'gelding' ant-hills. **1839** *Herefordsh. Gloss* s.v., 'To geld anty tumps', is to cut off the tops of ant-hills, and to throw the inside over the land. **1848** [see GELDING *vbl. sb.*].

geld (gɛld), *v.*[2] *Hist.* Also *erron.* gelt; and see GILD *v.*[2] [f. GELD *sb.*[1]; after med.L. *geldāre.*]

1. *trans.* To charge with 'geld'.

c **1630** RISDON *Surv. Devon* §67 (1810) 64 This place was never gelded. **1891** P. G. STONE *Archit. Antiq. Isle of Wight* 129 It was gelted for half a hide.

2. *intr.* To pay 'geld'.

c **1630** RISDON *Surv. Devon* §228 (1810) 244 West Putford ..gelded after thirty shillings. **1890** GROSS *Gild Merch.* I. 258 Exeter 'gelded' when London, York, and Winchester 'gelded'.

geldable ('gɛldəb(ə)l), *a.*[1] *Hist.* Also GILDABLE. [ad. med.L. (Domesday) *geldābilis*, f. *geldāre*: see GELD *v.*[2]] Liable to pay 'geld'.

1610 HOLLAND *Camden's Brit.* I. 605 Foure hundred thirty and one houses were thus Geldable. *c* **1630** RISDON *Surv. Devon* §315 (1810) 328 It..was geldable on all services, by land or sea. **1774** E. JACOB *Faversham* 28 All which lands and tenements are geldable by the Abbot. **1869** MOLYNEUX *Burton-on-Trent* 39 There were then in the village six hides geldable. **1888** J. C. ATKINSON in *Whitby Gaz.* 5 Oct. 3/7 The very large amount at which Whitby is returned as geldable in the Domesday record.

Hence **gelda'bility**.

1878 R. W. EYTON *Key to Domesday* 9 A geldability at only 2 hides was a benefaction to the extent of from 3000 to 4000 per cent. in favour of the Cornish Manor.

geldable ('gɛldəb(ə)l), *a.*[2] *rare.* [f. GELD *v.*[1] + -ABLE.] That may be gelded or castrated.

1611 COTGR., *Chastrable*, geldable. **1727** in BAILEY vol. II. **1846** in WORCESTER; and in mod. Dicts.

geldant ('gɛldənt), *a. Hist.* [ad. med.L. *geldantem*, pr. pple. of *geldāre* GELD *v.*[2]] Paying 'geld'.

1897 MAITLAND *Domesday Bk. & Beyond* 461 They shuffled off large numbers of their geldant hides.

gelded ('gɛldɪd), *ppl. a.* Also GELT. [f. GELD *v.*[1] + -ED[1].]

1. Of a person or animal: Castrated. †*gelded-man*, a eunuch.

1387 TREVISA *Higden* (Rolls) V. 173 Iulianus put out of his court eunochos, gilded men, barboures and cokes. *c* **1475** *Pict. Voc.* in Wr.-Wülcker 758/24 *Hec nefrenda*, a geldyd sow. **1526** TINDALE *Acts* viii. 34 The gelded man answered Philip. **1553** BECON *Reliques of Rome* (1563) 28 No gelded person..shuld be made a priest. **1618** BOLTON *Florus* IV. ii. 278 By the counsel of gelded men. **1652** C. B. STAPYLTON *Herodian* 17 Gelded priests. **1705** HICKERINGILL *Priest-cr.* II. ii. 24 All the Qualification that St. Philip required of the guelded Blackamore.

b. Of meat: Derived from castrated animals.

1621 BURTON *Anat. Mel.* I. ii. II. i. (1651) 66 All gelded meats in every species are held best.

2. in *transf.* and *fig.* uses of the vb.

1599 MARSTON *Sco. Villanie* II. v. 196 His halfe-dozen gelded vicaries. **1611** FLORIO, *Castrato*,..a kind of well-husked, cleansed or gelded wheat.

†**3. gelded satyrion**, a kind of *Orchis. Obs.*

1597 GERARDE *Herbal* I. civ. 173 Gelded Satyrion hath leaues with nerues and sinewes like to those of Daffodil.

geldene, obs. form of GILDEN.

gelder ('gɛldə(r)). [f. GELD *v.*[1] + -ER[1].]

1. One who gelds or castrates (animals, etc.). Also in *Comb.*, as *dog-, horse-, sow-gelder.*

c **1440** *Promp. Parv.* 190/1 Geldere of beestys, *castrator.* **1598** FLORIO, *Castracane*, a dog gelder. **1655** MOUFET & BENNET *Health's Improv.* (1746) 143 Even Nature hath deprived some things of that which Gelders cut away. **1699** DAMPIER *Voy.* II. I. 82 He agreed with an expert Gelder to castrate him. **1709** *Brit. Apollo* II. Supern. No. 4. 4/2 Escaping the Gelder when he was a Lamb. *a* **1722** LISLE *Husb.* (1752) 314, I sent for the gelder..to cut this bull.

†**2.** *fig.* (See GELD *v.*[1] 2, 2 b.) *Obs.*

1564 BECON *Wks.* Pref. A vj, These impostors rather then pastors, minishers more truly than Ministers, gelders rather then elders. **1579** FULKE *Heskins' Parl.* 184 Heskins, the impudent falsifier, truncator, gelder..and lewd interpreter of Augustine.

gelder(s rose, obs. form of GUELDER ROSE.

†'**geldhead.** *Obs.* In 3 geldehede. [f. GELD *a.* + -HEAD.] Barrenness.

a **1300** *E.E. Psalter* xxxiv. [xxxv.] 12 Þai yhelde to me for goednes ille, Geldehede swa mi saule vntille.

†'**geldherd.** *Obs. rare.* [f. GELD *a.* + HERD[2].] One who tended the 'geld' cattle.

1317 *Compotus Bolton* in Whitaker *Craven* (1805) 338 Pro Geldherds [*note*, elsewhere called the *Pastores sterilium animalium*].

gelding ('gɛldɪŋ), *sb.* [a. ON. *gelding-r*, f. *geld-r* GELD *a.*; cf. *gelda* GELD *v.*[1]]

†**1.** A gelded person, a eunuch. *Obs.*

1382 WYCLIF *Gen.* xxxvii. 36 Putiphar, the geldyng of Pharao. **1483** *Cath. Angl.* 152/2 A Geldynge..*eunuchus.* **1548** UDALL, etc. tr. *Erasm. Par. Matt.* xix. 12 The gospell also hath his Eunuches very blessed, whiche be not geldynges of nature, nor gelded of men. **1579–80** NORTH *Plutarch* (1676) 741 Lysimachus..thought great scorn that Demetrius should reckon him a gelding. **1693** DRYDEN *Juvenal* vi. (1697) 151 The Venerable Guelding..O'er-looks the Herd of his inferiour Fry. **1785** GROSE *Dict. Vulg. Tongue*, *Gelding*, an eunuch.

2. A gelded or castrated animal, esp. a horse.

1380 *Test. Karleolensia* (1893) 134 Et qe Lawrence eit sie demure en vie un hakney bay geldyng et xl. s. **1420** *E.E. Wills* (1882) 53 Þat Acris Mersk haue þe grey geldyng. **1520** *Test. Ebor.* (Surtees) V. 116 My blak, trotting gelding wᵗ a white fote. **1634** HEYWOOD & BROME *Lanc. Witches* II. Wks. 1874 IV. 191 Give me the Key oth' Stable. I will goe see my Gelding. **1643** in Clarendon *Hist. Reb.* VII. §347 Six hundred light Geldings for Recruits. **1711** BUDGELL *Spect.* No. 116 ⁋7 The jolly Knight, who rode upon a white Gelding. **1815** SCOTT *Guy M.* ii, He..took his grey gelding and joined Clavers at Killiecrankie. **1860** FROUDE *Hist. Eng.* VI. 236 A grey gelding was led up for Philip.

3. With a mixture of senses 1 and 2.

c **1386** CHAUCER *Prol.* 691, I trowe he were a geldyng or a mare. *a* **1621** BEAUM. & FL. *Thierry & Theod.* I. i. (1621) B 2 b, Or curse me heauen If all your guilded knaues..Be not made ambling Geldings. **1749** FIELDING *Tom Jones* VI. x, As for Jones, he swore, if he caught him at his house, he would qualify him to run for the gelding's plate.

†**4.** Applied to a tree (see quot.). *Obs.*

1562 TURNER *Herbal* II. 75 a, As long as the tre is very yong the fruite hath no stone within him and therefore suche are called geldynges.

5. Used appositively (quasi-*adj.*).

a **1658** CLEVELAND *Gen. Poems*, etc. (1677) 65 A Gelding Earl. **1691** *Lond. Gaz.* No. 2638/4 A black Gelding Colt. **1693** DRYDEN *Persius* v. (1697) 485 Guelding Priests.

Hence **geldin'geity**, *nonce-wd.* [after *corporeity*, etc.], the quality of being a gelding.

1768–74 TUCKER *Lt. Nat.* (1852) II. 190 Colteity, horseiety, and geldingeity, must always continue themselves, in whatever beast inexisting.

gelding ('gɛldɪŋ), *vbl. sb.* [f. GELD *v.*[1] + -ING[1].] The action of the vb. GELD in various senses.

1398 TREVISA *Barth. De P.R.* XII. xvii. (1495) 424 Cocke hyghte Gallus and hath that name of geldynge. *c* **1440** *Promp. Parv.* 190/1 Geldynge of beestys, or fowlys, *castracio.* **1523** FITZHERB. *Husb.* §67 Than shall ye se the oxe calfe, ferre greatter euery waye, than the bull..there is noo cause, but the geldynge. **1577** B. GOOGE *Heresbach's Husb.* (1586) 182 b, This kind of gelding of your hives. **1656** SANDERSON *Serm.* (1689) 31 In gelding of good Authors by expurgatory indexes. *c* **1720** W. GIBSON *Farrier's Guide* II. lviii. (1738) 217 The Gelding of a Foal is an easy operation. **1848** *Jrnl. R. Agric. Soc.* IX. i. 25 Ant-hills..the other plan is, to throw them, or what is provincially termed 'gelding'. **1884** PHIN *Dict. Apic.*, *Prune*, to cut out old combs so that new may be built. Called by the older writers gelding.

attrib. **1591** PERCIVALL *Sp. Dict.*, *Castradera*, the cutting, or gelding knife.

†**gele**, *sb. Obs. rare*[−1]. [a. ON. *gæla* blandishment.] Blandishment, enticing speech.

c **1200** *Trin. Coll. Hom.* 198 Man mid his gele egged us and fondeð and forð-teð to idele þonke.

†**gele**, *v. Obs. rare.* **a.** *trans.* To retard, delay (OE. only). **b.** *intr.* To tarry, linger.

a **900** CYNEWULF *Elene* 692 (Gr.) Scealcas ne gældon. **971** *Blickl. Hom.* 191 Ne gæle ȝe minne sið, nu mine fet gongað on heofenlicne weȝ. **13..** *E.E. Allit. P.* A. 930 By þyse bonkeȝ þer I con gele & I se no by-gyng nawhere aboute.

gele, obs. form of JELLY.

geleflower, gelefre, obs. ff. GILLYFLOWER.

‖**Gelehrte(r** (gə'leːrtər). Also gelehrte(r. Pl. -ehrten. [G., f. *gelehrt* learned, *lehren* to instruct.] A learned person; a scholar or savant.

1836 MILL *Let.* 9 Jan. in *Wks.* (1963) XII. 292 Heaven knows whether our stupid public will read or buy a book by a German *gelehrte* who is neither prince nor minister & whom they never heard of. **1854** GEO. ELIOT *Jrnl.* Aug.—Oct. (1884) I. vi. 271 Sauppe is also a *Gelehrter*, Director of the Gymnasium, and Editor of a series of Classics. **1875** *Nation* 9 Sept. 169/2 These *Gelehrten* are not true Baconians. **1939** WYNDHAM LEWIS *Let.* Jan. (1963) 261 The theoretic basis was never very clearly understood, it seems, even by the Gelehrter. **1961** L. NAMIER *Eng. in Age of Amer. Revol.* (ed. 2) 15 No German *Gelehrter* was ever made a baron or a count.

†'**gelicide.** *Obs.*[−0] [ad. L. *gelicidium* frost, f. *gelum* frost + *cid-*, *cad-ĕre* to fall.] (See quot.)

1656–81 BLOUNT *Glossogr.*, *Gelicide*, a frost.

gelid ('dʒɛlɪd), *a.* [ad. L. *gelid-us* icy cold, f. *gelum* (*gelus*, *gelu*) frost, intense cold; for the cognate Teutonic words see COLD *a.*]

1. Extremely cold, cold as ice, icy, frosty.

In the first quot., *gelled* may be a ppl. adj. from GEAL *v.*

1606 MARSTON *Sophonisba* IV. i. E iv, If she find some life Yet lurking close, she bites his gelled lips. *c* **1611** CHAPMAN *Iliad* xv. 162 Like a mighty snow Or gelide haile, that from the clouds, the Northerne spirit doth blow. **1695** LD. PRESTON *Boeth.* I. 7 The Brightness of the Gelid Moon. **1747** HERVEY *Medit.* (1748) II. 278 Even the blooming Cheeks contract a gelid Hue; and the Teeth hardly forbear chattering. **1764** GOLDSM. *Trav.* 121 While sea-born gales their gelid wings expand. **1820** SCORESBY *Acc. Arctic Reg.* I. 298 As the air passes over the gelid surface of the ice. **1830** W. PHILLIPS *Mt. Sinai* I. 205 In gelid Zembla's chill domain. **1863** TYNDALL *Heat* vi. §228 (1870) 179 Sometimes ..large and deep valleys receive the gelid masses thus sent down.

b. *fig.*

1630 B. JONSON *New Inn* v. i. (1631) G 2 b, The masse of blood Within me is a standing lake of fire, Curl'd with the cold wind of my gelid sighs, That..shoot a February through my veines. **1681** COLVIL *Whigs Supplic.* (1751) 121 A gelid fear his heart possessed. **1827** *Blackw. Mag.* XXI. 791 Our gelid reception was owing not to dislike. **1866** HOWELLS *Venet. Life* 36 She sniffed and offered a gelid prayer.

2. In a weaker sense: Cold, chill. Often of water, etc.: Refreshingly cold.

1659 T. PECKE *Parnassi Puerp.* 84 Autumn shakes off the Leaves, and brings Fruit too: I wish we could like gelid Autumn doe. **1676** BEAL in *Phil. Trans.* XI. 601 Some thought, they perceived the luminous parts less gelid than the dark parts. *a* **1678** MARVELL *Poems, Bill-borow Hill* lxvii, As I carless on the bed Of gelid strawberryes do tread. **1727–46** THOMSON *Summer* 208 By gelid founts and careless rills to muse. **1755** SMOLLETT *Quix.* (1803) IV. 257 Drinking liquid chrystal from the gelid springs. **1869** *Daily News* 18 Aug., The sun down, the air is cool and gelid.

Hence '**gelidly** *adv.*, '**gelidness**.

1727 BAILEY vol. II, *Gelidness*, Coldness, Frozenness. **1848** WEBSTER, *Gelidly*, coldly. **1873** HOWELLS *Chance Acquaint.* vii. 152 Gelidly self-satisfied.

gelidity (dʒɪ'lɪdɪtɪ). ? *Obs.* [as if ad. L. **geliditāt-em*, f. *gelidus*: see GELID and -ITY.] Extreme cold, frigidity.

1656–81 BLOUNT *Glossogr.*, *Gelidity*, coldness, frostiness. **1721–92** in BAILEY. **1818** *La Belle Assemblee* No. 109. 132/6 Straw bonnets, notwithstanding the gelidity of the atmosphere, are in high estimation.

gelignite ('dʒɛlɪgnaɪt). [? f. GEL(ATINE) + L. *ign-is* fire + -ITE.] A variety of gelatine dynamite.

1889 CUNDILL *Dict. Explosives* 52 One [variety of Gelatine Dynamite] contains about 80, the other 60 per cent. of explosive. The last named is known as gelignite. **1897** *Daily News* 2 Sept. 3/5 A frozen consignment of gelatine dynamite and gelignite.

†'**geline.** *Cookery. Obs.* In 5 gelyne. [a. OF. *geline.*] A hen.

c **1430** *Two Cookery-bks.* I. 13 Gelyne in dubbatte.—Take an Henne, and [etc.]. *c* **1450** *Ibid.* II. 80 Gelyne in brothe ⁋Take rawe hennes [etc.].

gelinotte ('dʒɛlɪnɒt). Also gelinote. [a. F. *gelinotte*, dim. of *geline* hen (see GELINE).] The hazel-grouse or hazel-hen.

1777 G. FORSTER *Voy. round World* I. 85 The knorhan, which is not a gelinote or grous..but the African bustard. **1785** *Gentl. Mag.* Oct. 761/1, I observed a singular invention for taking great quantities of gelinottes. **1893** NEWTON *Dict. Birds*, *Gelinotte*..often used in English for what is otherwise called the Hazel-hen or Hazel-Grouse.

gell (gɛl), *v. Sc.* and *north. dial.* Also 8–9 geal. [Of unknown origin: cf. '*Gale*, to ache, to tingle as when frost-bitten' (Willan, *West-Yorkshire Words*, 1811).] *intr.* 'To tingle, thrill with intense pain' (Jam.); also, to ache or tingle with cold.

? **16..** *Sir Egeir* (1711) 13 Your wounds they will both glow and gell. **1781** HUTTON *Tour to Caves* (E.D.S.), *Geal*, to be benumbed with cold. **1788** PICKEN *Poems* 49 The growlan fish-wives hoise their creels, Set a' their banes a gelling. **1878** *Cumbld. Gloss.*, *Geall*, to ache with cold.

gelle, gellie, obs. forms of JELLY.

gelly ('dʒɛlɪ), *a. Sc.* [Of unknown origin: connexion with JOLLY is hardly possible.] Worthy, pompous, well-conditioned.

c **1560** A. SCOTT *Poems* (S.T.S.) ii. 181 Than gelly Johine come in a jak To feild quhair he wes feidit. **1573** DAVIDSON *Schort Disc. Estaitis* 23 in *Satir. Poems Reform.* xli, He..was als meit for sic Office As outher gellie Jok or Johne. **1648** R. BAILLIE *Lett. & Jrnls.* (1841) III. 32 Your nephew, I hope, shall prove a gelly lad. **1788** PICKEN *Poems* 180 To the west, thy gelly mouth Stood wide to a'.

gelly, gellywat(te, obs. ff. JELLY *sb.*[1] and *v.*, GALLIVAT.

gelly, var. JELLY *sb.*[2]

gelof(f)er, gelofre, obs. ff. GILLYFLOWER.

†**gelongs.** *Obs. rare.* A kind of Indian silk.

1696 J. F. *Merchant's Ware-ho.* 33 There is a sort more of the same nature, both for bredth and length, it is called Gelongs, it hath a few flowers up and down in it.

gelore, Sc. var. GALORE.

†**ge'loscopy.** *Obs.* Better GELOTOSCOPY. [f. Gr. γέλω-ς, γελωτ- laughter + -σκοπία looking.] (See quot.)

1730–6 BAILEY (folio), *Geloscopy*, a sort of divination performed by means of laughter; or a divining any persons qualities or character, by observation of the manner of his laughing.

gelose (dʒiː'ləʊs). *Chem.* [f. GEL-ATIN + -OSE.] (See quots.)

1864 WATTS *Dict. Chem.* II. 829 Gelose. **1878** *Ure's Dict. Arts* (ed. 7) IV. 402 *Gelose*, a gelatinous matter obtained from an alga growing in Cochin China. **1883** *Cassell's Fam. Mag.* Sept. 636/2 Algin..differs from..gelose in not gelatinising when cooled. **1885** *Syd. Soc. Lex.*, *Gelose*, an amorphous gelatinous substance obtained by Payen from Japan moss, chiefly *Gelidium corneum*.

gelosie, obs. form of JEALOUSY.

gelo'tometer. *nonce-wd.* [f. Gr. γέλως, γέλωτ- laughter + μέτρον measure: see -METER.] A gauge for measuring laughter.

1828 LANDOR *Imag. Conv.* III. 304 We may expect the Society for the Suppression of Vice to offer a reward for a gelotometre.

†**gelotoscopy.** *Obs.* Better form of GELOSCOPY.

1697 EVELYN *Numism.* ix. 337 Made Divinations by Gelotoscopy.

gelousy, obs. form of JEALOUSY.

gelover, gelowe floure, obs. ff. GILLYFLOWER.

gelows, obs. form of JEALOUS.

‖**gelsemium** (dʒɛl'siːmɪəm). [Mod.Lat., f. It. *gelsomino* JASMINE: the name 'jasmine' being in the U.S. misapplied to plants of this genus.]

a. With capital initial. A genus of twining shrubs of the NO. *Loganiaceæ*. **b.** The roots of a plant of this genus (*G. sempervirens*), or a preparation of them, used as a medicine; also called **gelseminum**. Hence **'gelsemine** (also **gel'seminine**), **gel'semic (acid)**: (see quots.).

1875 H. C. WOOD *Therap.* (1879) 356 The influence of gelsemium upon man is very marked. **1883-4** *Med. Ann.* 29/1 Esculine..is not taken up by ether which is the case with gelseminum. **1885** *Syd. Soc. Lex.*, *Gelsemic acid*, a crystalline substance obtained from the root of *Gelsemium sempervirens*. *Ibid.*, *Gelsemin*, a colourless, or in commerce a yellowish brown, inodorous, bitter alkaloidal substance obtained by [etc.]. **1892** *Pall Mall G.* 21 Jan 2/2 For the fever [of influenza] aconite is our remedy, and for the persisting pains gelseminin or eupatorium.

gelsomine, obs. form of JASMINE.

gelster. *rare.* An osier (see YOLSTER).

1670 EVELYN *Sylva* (ed. 2) xx. 88 The most usual names by which Basket makers call them [*sc.* osiers] about London ..are, the hard Gelster, the Horse Gelster, Whyning, or shrivell'd Gelster, the Black Gelster.

gelt (gɛlt), *sb.*[1] *rare.* Also 9 geilt. [a. Irish *geilt* a mad or frenzied person.

In the *Chron. Scot.* p. 122 the Irish *gealta* (pl.) is explained by *volatiles*. According to the Old Norse work *Konungs Skuggsjá* (*Speculum Regale*) c. 11, a *gelt* was one who went mad with fear in battle, and thenceforth lived in the woods like a wild beast. In ON. the phrase *verða at gjalti* 'to become frantic', is in frequent use (in Cleasby-Vigfusson wrongly placed under *gǫltr* boar), and two instances of the madness itself are described in *Eyrbyggja Saga*, the persons being Celts.]

A lunatic.

1596 SPENSER *F.Q.* IV. vii. 21 Like a ghastly Gelt whose wits are reaved. **1894** *Q. Rev.* Oct. 331 The vision of the long-haired, long-robed Geilt.

gelt (gɛlt), *sb.*[2] Also 7 **ghelt, guelt.** [a. Ger., Du. *geld* money: see GELD *sb.*] Money; in early use often with reference to the pay of a (German) army; now only *slang*. † *bare gelt* (= Ger. *baares geld*, Du. *baar geld*) ready money. † *passage gelt*: tr. of Ger. *fahrgeld* passage money.

a **1529** SKELTON *E. Rumming* 610 That nothynge had There of theyr awne Neyther gelt nor pawne. **1591** WOTTON *Let.* in *Reliq. Wotton.* (1685) 616 It..amounts to not above 12000 Fr. Rhenish, yearly, in bare gelt. **1629** MAXWELL tr. *Herodian* (1635) 343 The Germans..being very greedy of Ghelt. **1648** *Let.* in *Cromwelliana* (1810) 48 Sufficient to make any soldiers in the world that fights only for gelt, to sheath, and be gone. **1658** USSHER *Annals* 299 His whole army cryed out for gelt, and he promised them pay. *a* **1700** B. E. *Dict. Cant. Crew*, *Gelt*, money. There is no Gelt to be got. *a* **1712** W. KING *Ulysses & Tiresias* 16 Lineage and virtue at this push, Without the gelt, 's not worth a rush. **1745** *Lond. Mag.* 402 Both Natives and Foreigners are forced to pay passage Gelt. **1815** SCOTT *Guy M.* xxxiii, All the gelt was gone. **1875** *Whitby Gloss.*, *Gelt*, profit. **1876** *Mid-Yorksh. Gloss.* s.v., I smiled a bird yesterday..and while I was doing it..over went my egg-basket; so there weren't much gelt out of that. **1892** I. ZANGWILL *Childr. Ghetto* II. I. xxii. 165 Fourteen *Shtibbur's* a lot of *Gelt*. **1960** *Observer* 24 Jan. 7/1 Had I ever heard the underworld saying: No grass ever grasses for gelt alone? **1968** C. DRUMMOND *Death & Leaping Ladies* iv. 80 'The gelt?' said Reed... 'Four thousand dollars,' said Miss Pocket.

¶ In the following examples, perh. a pseudo-archaism for *gold*.

1538 BALE *Thre Lawes* 1832 Myght I haue bene stopped for syluer or for gelte. **1579** SPENSER *Sheph. Cal.* Feb. 65, I wonne her with a gyrdle of gelt.

gelt (gɛlt), *ppl. a.* [pa. pple. of GELD *v.*] Gelded, castrated. *lit.* and *fig.*

c **1440** *Promp. Parv.* 190/1 Gelt, *castratus*. *Ibid.*, Gelt mann, *spado*. **1599** MARSTON *Sco. Villanie* I. iii. 185 By chance..Hath got the farme of some gelt Vicary. **1626** BACON *Sylva* §852 Eunuchs and Gelt Creatures of all kindes. **1639** T. DE GREY *Compl. Horsem.* 219 A horse or mare-filly that is cut, gelt, or spla. **1659** FULLER *App. Inj. Innoc.* (1840) 287, I remembered the man who moved in chancery for a gelt-order, which should beget no more. **1682** SHADWELL *Medal* 3 An old gelt Mastiff has more mirth than thou. **1789** G. WHITE *Selborne* lxxiv, Gelt stags and bucks. **1800** *Asiat. Ann. Reg.*, *Misc. Tr.* 145/2 Unless the favour of the deity..were conciliated by the sacrifice of a gelt goat and a cock. **1810** *Provinc. Voc. Devon* in *Monthly Mag.* XXIX. 466/2 *Gelt bull*, an ox, a bull-stag.

gelt, obs. form of GELD *sb.*, GUILT.

gelt, var. GILT, young sow.

geluce, gelus, gely(e, obs. ff. JEALOUS, JELLY.

gem (dʒɛm), *sb.* Forms: α. **ȝim(m, ȝym(m**, 3 **ȝimme, ȝumme (y), (gim)**, 4 **gymme, ȝymme.** β. 3-8 **gemm(e**, 4-8 **jem(me**, 4- **gem.** [OE. *ȝim* str. masc. (whence prob. ON. *gim* neut.) = OHG. *gimma* fem., a. L. *gemma* bud, hence jewel, f. root *gen-* to produce. In ME. the word was adopted afresh in (or refashioned after) the F. form *gemme*.]

1. A precious stone of any kind, *esp.* when cut and polished for ornament; a jewel.

α. *c* **825** *Vesp. Psalter* cxviii. 127 Forðon ic lufade bibodu ðin ofer gold and ȝim. **971** *Blickl. Hom.* 11 He sealde his þone readan ȝim, þæt wæs his þæt haliȝe blod. *c* **1000** ÆLFRIC *Hom.* I. 64 Hi wurdon ȝehwyrfede to deorwurðum ȝymmum. *c* **1205** LAY. 6081 Heo makeden ane tunne of golde and of ȝimme. *c* **1250** *Gen. & Ex.* 2700 He carf in two gummes [? = *ȝümmes*] of pris Two likenesses. **13..** *K. Alis.* 3152 This koroune he the sent, Of gold and gymmes.

β. *c* **1374** CHAUCER *Former Age* 30 And in the Ryverys fyrst gemmys sowhte. *c* **1400** *Destr. Troy* 10585 A toure, triedly wroght..With Jemmes, & iuwells, & other ioly stonys. **1485** *Ripon Ch. Acts* (Surtees) 366 Duo anuli aurei cum j pro gemys. **1500-20** DUNBAR *Poems* xlviii. 153 Cum blowme of joy with jemis to be cround. **1601** HOLLAND *Pliny* I. 41 See how many sorts of jemmes there be still. **1702** ADDISON *Dial. Medals* (1727) 94 Th' Imperial standard..That Gold embroiders and that Gemms adorn. **1750** GRAY *Elegy* xiv, Full many a gem of purest ray serene The dark unfathom'd caves of ocean bear. **1832** G. R. PORTER *Porcelain & Gl.* 273 He made artificial rubies..which he sold, in the manner of real gems, according to their weight. **1860** C. W. KING *Ant. Gems* (1866) 6 The Romans..divided gems into males and females, according to the depth or lightness of their colour. **1886** M. F. SHELDON tr. *Flaubert's Salammbô* 15 On her neck she wore a collection of luminous gems.

†**b.** *slang.* (See quots.) *Obs.*

c **1700** *Street Robberies Consider'd*, Jem, Ring. **1725** *New Cant. Dict.*, *Jem*, a Gold Ring; *Rum-Jem*, a Diamond one.

2. *transf.* and *fig.* **a.** Said of persons; esp. in phrases, † *gem of chastity, jollity, virtue*, etc. (*obs.*).

c **1275** *Luve Ron* 163 in *O.E. Misc.* 98 Þis ilke ston þat ich þe nemne Mayden-hod icleoped is. Hit is o derewurþe gemme. *c* **1386** CHAUCER *Prioress' T.* 157 This gemme of chastite, this Emeraude, And eek of martirdom the Ruby bright. *c* **1410** HOCCLEVE *Mother of God* 106 Marie and Ion hevenly gemmes tweyne. **1500-20** DUNBAR *Poems* lxxxvi. 3 O gemme joynit in joye angelicall, In quhom Jhesu rejosit wes to dwell. **1554** in Strype *Eccl. Mem.* III. App. xx. 57 It is a most unworthy thing, that that gem of vertues should enlighten foreign nations. **1575** GASCOIGNE *Pr. Pleas. Kenilw.*, Delitefull dames and gemmes of jolitie. **1613** SHAKS. *Hen. VIII*, II. iii. 78 Who knowes..But from this Lady, may proceed a Iemme, To lighten all this Ile. **1678** *Yng. Mans Comf.* 384 Spains rod, Romes ruin, Netherlands relief..Englands jem. **1814** SCOTT *Ld. of Isles* IV. xxx, O what a gem lies buried here.

b. of things.

1618 BOLTON *Florus* To Rdr., Certaine gemmes as it were, and jewels of wise sentences, inserted by him with good advisement. **1781** COWPER *Friendship* 7 Every polish'd gem we find, Illuminating heart or mind. **1799** J. SCOTT *Bahar-Danush* II. xiii. 89 Shedding the valuable jems of remonstrance on his lap. **1872** JENKINSON *Guide Eng. Lakes* (1879) 79 The..vale of Grasmere..is a little gem in the diadem of the Lake District. **1893** SIR R. BALL *Story of Sun* 359 The beautiful star Vega, the most brilliant gem of the northern hemisphere.

c. An object of rare beauty or priceless worth; the choicest part *of* (anything). Now colloquially often with somewhat playful tone: Something greatly prized, a 'jewel', 'treasure'.

c **1560** A. SCOTT *Poems* (S.T.S.) xxvii. 1 In June the jem Of joy and geme. *a* **1605** MONTGOMERIE *Sonn.* xlix, The Margarit does merit mekle mare, As jem of jeuels, paragone but peir. **1647** N. BACON *Disc. Govt. Eng.* I. ii. 3 As if..the Lord of all the earth had found out one place that should be to him as the gemme of this Terrestrial globe. **1818** W. IRVING in *Life & Lett.* (1864) I. xxv. 407 A little cabinet picture..which will be quite a gem. **1870** MAX MÜLLER *Sc. Relig.* (1873) 384 Among the Hottentots..we find the following gem of a fable. **1875** BUCKLAND *Log-bk.* 1 The gem of the collection..was a picture representing [etc.]. **1895** *Pall Mall Mag.* Nov. 328 The new man seemed to be a gem.

3. A precious or semi-precious stone, bearing an engraved design either in relief or intaglio.

[**1638** F. JUNIUS *Paint. Ancients* 95, I cannot but remember the royal fame of a gem that same Pyrrhus had.. an Agathe wherein [etc.]. **1658** SIR T. BROWNE *Hydriot.* ii. 18 Great number of Gemmes with heads of Gods and Goddesses.] **1791** RASPE (*title*), A descriptive Catalogue of a general Collection of ancient and modern engraved Gems, Cameos, as well as Intaglios..cast..by J. Tassie. **1849** MACAULAY *Hist. Eng.* iii. I. 338 The cabinets were filled with a fine collection of gems purchased by that Earl of Arundel whose marbles are now among the ornaments of Oxford. **1860** C. W. KING (*title*), Antique Gems, their Origin, Uses, and Value.

attrib. **1838** *Penny Cycl.* XII. 498/1 *Intaglio*..is a term of art applied to small works of the gem class.

†**4.** A bud, esp. a leaf-bud. *Obs.*

1382 WYCLIF *Num.* xvii. 8 Swellynge the gemmes, breken out flowres. *c* **1420** *Pallad. on Husb.* III. 405 A graffes shaft Of vyne or tre with gemmes oon or too. **1526** *Pilgr. Perf.* (W. de W. 1531) 202 Yᵉ rodde of Aaron..in one day..brought forth fayre floures, gemmes & almondes. **1651** JER. TAYLOR *Serm.* I. ii. 13 Like the gem of a vine, or the bud of a rose. *a* **1688** DENHAM *Of Old Age* 576 From the joints of thy prolific stem A swelling knot is raised, called a gem. **1732** *Hist. Litteraria* IV. 158 Insects which terebrate the Gems of some Branches, and therein deposit their eggs. **1791** E. DARWIN *Bot. Gard.* I. 197 If prouder branches with exuberance rude Point their green gems. **1813** MARSHALL *Gardening* ii. 22 Those flowers that dare to continue above ground all the year have yet their gems carefully locked up.

5. *Zool.* = GEMMA 3.

1832 LYELL *Princ. Geol.* II. 112 The most frequent mode of transportation..consists in the buoyancy of their eggs or certain small vesicles which are detached and are capable of becoming the foundation of a new colony. These *gems*, as they have been called, may be swept along by a wave that breaks upon a coral reef.

6. A collector's name for the small geometrid moth *Camptogramma fluviata*.

1869 in E. NEWMAN *Brit. Moths* 172.

7. *Printing.* (See quot.; the size is little used.)

1888 JACOBI *Printer's Vocab.*, *Gem*, a size of type one size larger than Brilliant and one size smaller than Diamond.

8. *attrib.* and *Comb.* **a.** simple attrib., as † ***gem-mint, -pit, -ring, -work.*** **b.** objective, as ***gem-artificer, -cutting, -engraver, -engraving, -fancier, -polisher, -sculpture***; ***gem-bearing, -yielding*** adjs. **c.** instrumental, as ***gem-bedewed, -bedizened, -bespangled, -bossed, -bright, -knosped, -spangled*** adjs.; also ***gem-like*** adj. or adv. **d.** Special comb., as **gem-bed** (see quot.); **gem-peg** (corruptly *gim-peg*) (see quot.); **gem-salt** (*rare*), rock-salt = SAL-GEM; **gem-stick**, a stick on the end of which a gem is cemented while being cut.

1870 RUSKIN *Lect. Art* v. 136 Drawings of the *gem-artificers. **1894** *Westm. Gaz.* 27 Dec. 6/1 The property comprised 4000 acres of '*gem-bearing' land. **1886** *Daily News* 28 Dec. 5/4 The '*gem-bed', as it is called, or strata in which the rubies are found, varies considerably at different points in its depth. **1820** LANDOR *Heroic Idylls*, *Myrtis* 2 Her white wrist above it, *gem-bedewed. **1832** J. P. KENNEDY *Swallow B.* IV. (1860) 47 She rests her chin upon her *gem-bedizened hand. *a* **1794** SIR W. JONES *Hymn to Surya* Wks. 1799 VI. 349 The churn'd Ocean's *gem-be-spangled shore. **1879** GEO. ELIOT *Coll. Breakf. P.* 17 In *gem-bossed pyx and broidered chasuble. **1587** T. HUGHES *Misfort. Arth.* 14 O Cassiopæa, *gem-bright signe, Most sacred sight and sweet cælestiall starre. **1838** ELIZA COOK *Poet's Wreath* iii, On his temples a gem-bright rim. **1839** URE *Dict. Arts* 738 The operation of *gem-cutting. **1860** C. W. KING *Ant. Gems* (1866) 169 The earliest *gem-engravers. *Ibid.* p. xli, Under Augustus *gem-engraving in all its branches reached its very highest point. **1877** W. JONES *Finger-ring* 17 Xerxes, King of Persia, was a great *gem-fancier. **1818** MILMAN *Samor* 225 To break the glassy glories of this world? The *gem-knosp'd diadem, the ivory ball. **1859** TENNYSON *Enid.* 1047 A meadow *gemlike chased In the brown wild. **1592** G. HARVEY *Pierce's Super.* 136 His *gemmemint is not always current. **1853** O. BYRNE *Artisan's Handbk.* 210 The support..placed a little to the right and in advance of the lap, is called a **gim-peg*, or *germ-peg*..The gim-peg serves as a support for the arm of the workman in grinding the edges of small stones, but its principal use is to serve as a guide for the vertical angle in cutting facets. **1882** *Encycl. Brit.* XIV. 299/2 A very important substitute for the gim-peg-socket.. is the dial. **1889** *Ceylon Observer* 11 May, The find of a valuable sapphire on Rangwelletenne estate by a coolie woman near the mouth of an old *gempit. **1886** *Daily News* 28 Dec. 5/4 The lapidaries, or *gem-polishers, are in the capital, and not at the mines. **1864** BOUTELL *Her. Hist. & Pop.* xix. §5 (ed. 3) 312 Holding between the finger and thumb a *gem ring. **1852** TH. ROSS *Humboldt's Trav.* III. xxxii. 361 It is enlarged by the spurs of the Rio Beni, rich in *gem-salt. **1882** OGILVIE, **Gem-sculpture*, the art of.. representing designs upon precious stones, either in raised work or by figures cut into or below the surface. *a* **1847** ELIZA COOK *There would I be* i, A *gem-spangled crown. **1856** KANE *Arct. Expl.* I. iii. 37 Making the ice around us one great resplendency of *gem-work. **1887** *Pall Mall G.* 28 Dec. 5/2 Like most *gem-yielding regions..it is less attractive than the yellow sands.

Hence **'gemless** *a.*, devoid of gems.

1818 *Blackw. Mag.* II. 533 A casket gemless!

gem (dʒɛm), *v.* Inflected **gemmed, gemming.** Forms: α. 2-3 **ȝimmen.** β. 7-9 **jem**, 5- **gem.** [f. prec. sb.]

†**1. a.** *intr.* To put forth buds; to bud. **b.** *trans.* To put forth (a blossom, a fruit). *Obs.*

c **1150** *Fragm. Ælfric's Gr.* (Phillipps) 2 [Wintreowe] ȝimmeþ forþ in þe akeres. **1667** MILTON *P.L.* VII. 325 The stately Trees..spred Thir branches..or gemm'd Thir Blossoms. **1746-7** HERVEY *Medit.* (1818) 150 The tender twigs have scarce gemmed their future blessings.

2. To adorn with gems.

1610 G. FLETCHER *Christ's Vict.* II. lvi. 42 Kings, whose temples wear impal'd In goulden diadems, set here, and thear, With diamonds, and gemmed euery whear. **1741** H. BROOKE *Constantia* Wks. 1789 I. 289 All gem'd in ornaments of curious mode. **1808** J. BARLOW *Columb.* I. 39 Cold-hearted Ferdinand his pillow prest, Nor dream'd'..Of him who gemm'd his crown. **1877** M. M. GRANT *Sun-Maid* viii, Gemmed with rubies.

b. *transf.* and *fig.* To adorn as with gems.

1747 COLLINS *Passions* 72 Her buskins gemm'd with morning dew. **1798** S. ROGERS *Ep. to Friend* 156 When Frost ..gems with icicles the sheltering eaves. **1798** CANNING & FRERE *New Morality* 118 in *Anti-Jacobin* xxxvi. (1852) 205 The teardrop gems her eye. **1813** BYRON *Giaour* xiv, A speck of white That gemm'd the tide. **1824** T. K. HERVEY *Gondola* v, He looks to the stars Which are gemming the blue. **1835**

W. IRVING *Tour Prairies* 329 The prairies were all gemmed with frost. **1849–53** ROCK *Ch. of Fathers* III. ix. 341 Gemming.. the Virgin's name with every brightest epithet. **1859** TENNYSON *Enid* 339 A coppice gemm'd with green and red. **1863** HAWTHORNE *Our Old Home* (1883) I. 283 A ring.. thickly gemmed around with faces.

†**3.** *intr.* To shine as a gem; in quot. *to gem it.*

1652 BENLOWES *Theoph.* For Author Cj, Who jemm'st it in Ierusalem Above, Where all is Grace and Glory, Light and Love.

4. *trans.* To extract gems from; to excavate for the purpose of obtaining gems.

1889 *Ceylon Observer* 7 June, Everton estate.. has been 'gemmed' for over thirty years. *Ibid.* 28 June, The Government could have no objections to grant the right to gem the whole river.

Hence **'gemming** *vbl. sb.* Also **'gemmer**, one who seeks or digs for gems.

1859 TENNENT *Ceylon* 35 The season selected by them for 'gemming' is between December and March, when the waters are low. **1887** *Chamb. Jrnl.* 12 Mar. 166 Gemming has been carried on in that part of Upper Burmah for centuries. **1889** *Ceylon Observer* 8 June, Pits dug by ancient and modern gemmers.

‖**Gemara** (gɪ'mɑːrə). [Aramaic *gᵉmārā* completion, f. *gᵉmar* to be complete.] The later of the two portions of the Talmud, consisting of a commentary on the older part (the Mishna).

1613 PURCHAS *Pilgrimage* (1614) 169 The Mischnaios, and Gemara made up the whole Talmud. **1659** BP. WALTON *Consid. Considered* 6 The Mishna and Gemara, which are the integral parts of both the Talmuds, one being as the Text, and the other as the Comment. **1877** C. GEIKIE *Christ* II. xxxvi. 64 The commentaries of the Rabbis, now embodied in the Mishna and Gemara. **1891** J. E. H. THOMSON *Bks. wh. infl. Our Lord* I. x. 179 The Gemara is a commentary on the Mishna.

Hence **Ge'maric** *a.*, of, pertaining to, or concerned with the Gemara.

1723 MATHER *Vind. Bible* 217 The Gemarick doctors give this reason for it. **1882–3** D. MOORE in Schaff *Encycl. Relig. Knowl.* III. 2293 Rabbi Abina, who died in 498.. is regarded as the last of the Gemaric doctors.

‖**gematria** (giː'meɪtrɪə). Also 7 **gematry.** [Rabbinical Heb. *gēmaṭriyā*, a. Gr. γεωμετρία GEOMETRY. (The suggestion that it represents Gr. γραμματεία is unfounded.)] A cabbalistic method of interpreting the Hebrew Scriptures by interchanging words whose letters have the same numerical value when added.

1686 GOAD *Celest. Bodies* II. i. 156, I am perswaded.. that there may be something in Cabala, Gematry, something in the mysterious Force of Numbers, in Critical Days, Climacteric Years, &c. **1730–6** BAILEY (folio), *Gematria*, the first kind of arithmetical cabala, in use among the cabalistical Jews. **1884** GOW *Gr. Mathem.* 44 The supposed antiquity of *gematria* depends solely on a conjectural and improbable comment on Zechariah xii. 10. There is in fact no clear instance of *gematria* before Philo or Christian writers strongly under Philonic influence (e.g. Rev. xiii. 18; Ep. Barn. c. 9). **1892** *Edin. Rev.* July 77 Belief in the gematria or mystic value of letters in the Scriptures.

gematry(e, obs. form of GEOMETRY.

‖**Gemeinschaft** (gə'maɪnʃaft). Also with lower-case initial. [G., f. *gemein* common, general + *-schaft* -SHIP.] A social relationship between individuals based on affection, kinship, or membership of a community, as within a family or group of friends; contrasted with GESELLSCHAFT. So ***Gemeinschaft-like*** adj. [G. *gemeinschaftlich*].

[**1887** F. TÖNNIES (*title*) Gemeinschaft und Gesellschaft.] **1937** T. PARSONS *Struct. Social Action* xvii. 687 Both *Gemeinschaft* and *Gesellschaft* are what are sometimes referred to as positive types of social relationship. *Ibid.* 688 *Gemeinschaft*.. is a broader relationship of solidarity over a rather undefined general area of life and interests. **1940** C. P. LOOMIS tr. *Tönnies's Concepts Sociol.* 18 The essence of both *Gemeinschaft* and *Gesellschaft* is found interwoven in all kinds of associations. **1961** L. MUMFORD *City in History* x. 310 Both primary and secondary groups, both *Gemeinschaft* and *Gesellschaft*, took on the same urban pattern. **1964** GOULD & KOLB *Dict. Social Sci.* 281/2 *Gemeinschaft* is an ideal-type concept, and as such is most correctly applied in describing or analyzing social systems in its adjectival form, *Gemeinschaft*-like. *Gemeinschaft*-like social systems are those in which *Wesenwille* (natural or essential will) has primacy.

gemel ('dʒɛməl). Forms: 5–7 **gemell**, 6 **gemmell**, **-ull**, **gemoll**, 6–7 **gemmal**, 6, 9 **gemmel**, 4– **gemel**. Also GEMEW, GIMBAL, GIMMAL, GIMMER. [a. OF. *gemel* (later *gemeau*, whence GEMEW; mod.F. *jumeau* twin):—L. *gemellus*, dim. of *geminus* twin.]

†**1.** *pl.* Twins; said also of things associated in pairs. *Obs.*

1382 WYCLIF *Gen.* xxxviii. 27 Gemels apereden in the wombe. **1430–40** LYDG. *Bochas* I. (1554) 31 b, Toward him a great pace gan she goe And her brother Caunus came also And of one wombe as gemelles twayne. **1603** DRAYTON *Bar. Wars* To Rdr., The often harmonie thereof soft'ned the verse more then the maiestie of the subject would permit, vnlesse they had all been Gemmels [*printed* Geminels] or couplets.

†**b.** *attrib.* or *adj.* Twin. *Obs.*

1497 in *Ld. Treas. Acc. Scotl.* (1887) I. 376 Giffin to Walter Ogiluy, in payment for the reparatioun of the tua gemmel touris of Inuernes. **1513** DOUGLAS *Æneis* X. vii. 71 And ȝe alsso, stowt gemel brether twa. **1652** URQUHART *Jewel* Wks. (1834) 243 Then from the snow-white galaxy betwixt those gemel-monts, whose milken paths [etc.]. **1657** TOMLINSON *Renou's Disp.* 344 Because its roots were frequently gemmell [*printed* geminell] resembling two Leggs.

2. *Her.* in *pl.* Bars, or rather barrulets, placed together as a couple. Also in AF. form ***bar(re)s gemelles***: see BAR *sb.*[1] 6.

1592 WYRLEY *Armorie* 136 Three gemels finely set in Azurd shield. **1603** DRAYTON *Bar. Wars* I. To Rdr., The quadrin doth neuer double; or, to vse a word of Heraldry, neuer bringeth foorth Gemells. **1688** R. HOLME *Armoury* I. iii. 35 A Gemell ever goeth by Paires, or Couples, and not to be Seperated. **1706** PHILLIPS (ed. Kersey), *Gemelles* [in Heraldry], the bearing of Bars by Pairs or Couples in a Coat of Arms. *a* **1737** STRYPE *Life Smith* i. *note* (1820) 2 Two gemells unde, silver, between two griffins passant. **1864** BOUTELL *Her. Hist. & Pop.* v. 22 When Barrulets are placed together in couples.. each couple is entitled a pair of Bars Gemelles.

†**3.** ? 'A two-part harmony' (Jam.). *Obs. rare*$^{-1}$. Cf. *gymel* (GIMMAL 5) and GEMILLING.

1501 DOUGLAS *Pal. Hon.* I. xlii, In modulatioun hard I play and sing.. Cant organe, figuratioun, and gemmell.

4. A kind of finger-ring (much worn in the 16th c.) so constructed as to admit of being divided horizontally into two rings. Now only *Hist.* Also ***gemel-ring***. Cf. GIMMAL.

1572 HULOET, Gemoll or a gemmow, *stalagnium*, it is suche as the Egiptians vse to hange at their eares. *Ibid.*, Gemoll, or a litle rynge to weare on the finger, *annellus*. **1601** HOLLAND *Pliny* XXXIII. i, The manner was in old time to weare rings but upon one finger onely, but now adayes.. every joint by themselves must have some lesser rings and gemmals to fit them. **1877** W. JONES *Finger-ring* 313 The old matrimonial Gemmel, or Gemmow, ring was a kind of double ring, curiously made.

5. A hinge. Now only *spec.* in Comb. ***gemel-hinge*** (see quot. 1874).

1536 *Inv.* in W. Dodsworth *Hist. Acc. Salisbury* (1814) 229 Three.. chests.. with gemmels of siluer and gilt. **1556** *Yatton Churchw. Acc.* (Som. Rec. Soc.) 168 For thei locke and the gemmulls.. xij^d. **1613–16** W. BROWNE *Brit. Past.* II. iii. 82 The gemels beaten so That little strength could thrust it [doore] to and fro. **1875** KNIGHT *Dict. Mech.*, *Gemel-hinge* (*Locksmithing*), a hinge consisting of an eye or loop and a hook.

Hence **'gemelled** *a.* [-ED[2]] (see quot.).

1883 MOLLETT *Dict. Art & Archæol.*, Gemelled, double; thus a gemelled bay is one divided into two parts; gemelled arches, those which are joined two and two.

gemellion (dʒɪ'mɛlɪən). Also **gemellione**. [ad. med.L. *gemellio*, f. L. *gemellus* a twin.] One of a pair of basins used for washing the hands before meals, the water being poured over the hands from one basin and caught by the other; hence, any decorative basin; *spec.* in liturgical use (see quot. 1960).

1889 in *Cent. Dict.* **1920** *Proc. Soc. Antiq.* 18 Mar. 131 The enamelled basins known as gemellions. **1960** H. HAYWARD *Antique Coll.* 127/2 *Gemellion*, this term describes one of a pair of basins used for the liturgical washing of the hands at the Mass.

†**geme'lliparous**, *a. Obs.*$^{-0}$ [f. L. *gemelli-*, *gemellus* twin (see GEMEL) + *par-ĕre* to bring forth + -OUS.] Producing twins.

1727 in BAILEY vol. II. Hence in mod. Dicts.

†**ge'mellous**, *a. Obs.*$^{-1}$ [f. L. *gemell-us* (see prec.) + -OUS.] = GEMINATE *a.*

1697 in *Phil. Trans.* XIX. 435 A Tree Apocynum from the Canaries.. whose gemellous Pods stand opposite.

gemensye, obs. form of GEOMANCY.

†**'gement**, *a. Obs.*$^{-0}$ [ad. L. *gement-em*, pres. pple. of *gemĕre* to groan.] Groaning, lamenting.

1656 in BLOUNT *Glossogr.*

gemeny, obs. form of GEMINI.

gemeotre, gemetry, obs. ff. GEOMETRY.

†**gemew, gemow.** *Obs.* Forms: 4–6 **jemew(e**, **gemow**, (5 **gewmew**, **gemoose** *pl.*), **gymmew**, 5–6 **gymew(e**, **gymow(e**, 6 **gimew**, **jemowe**, **gymmow**, **gimmon**, 6–7 **gemew(e**, **gemowe**, **gim(m)ew**, (**jewmew**, **jemmow**, 6–8 **gemmow**, 7 **gemmey**). [a. OF. *gemeaus*, pl. of *gemel* (see GEMEL) twin. The Eng. sing. is prob. developed from the plural, though in some uses it may have been taken from the later Fr. form *gemeau*, *jumeau* of the singular.]

1. *pl.* Twins: see GEMEL 1.

1382 WYCLIF *Song Sol.* vii. 3 Thi two tetus as two ȝunge capretis, iemews of the she capret.

b. *attrib.* or *adj.* Of a door: Double. Of lines: Parallel. Cf. GEMEL 1 b.

1523 in Kirkpatrick *Relig. Ord. Norwich* (1848) 170 Within the White Freris, in Norwich, at the Jemowe dore. **1551** RECORDE *Pathw. Knowl.* I. Defin., Paralleles, or Gemowe lynes be suche lines as be drawen foorth still in one distaunce, and are no nerer in one place than in an other. **1674** JEAKE *Arith.* (1696) 613 A pair of Parallels or Gemowe Lines.

2. *Her.* in *pl.* (rarely *sing.*) = GEMEL 2.

1486 *Bk. St. Albans, Her.* Bj b, Collaterall is calde in armys the sonnys of the bretheren of the right heyre beryng the cotarmuris of theyr faderis with a dyfferans Jemews. **1572** BOSSEWELL *Armorie* II. 33 b, The fourth beareth Argent, three Barres Gemewes, Sable. **1610** GUILLIM *Heraldry* VI. vii. (1611) 274 A crowne Topaze or griffon's head with wings displaied pearle, gorged with a gemew ruby.

3. A double ring; = GEMEL 4. Also ***gemowe-ring***.

1497 *Will of Butside* (Somerset Ho.), A Jemewe of golde. **1552** HULOET, Gymmow or ringe to hange at ones eare as the Egyptians haue, *staloginum, inauris*. **1562** *Lanc. Wills* I. 181 On gemewe of silver wyre. **1572** *Ibid.* II. 262 My beste Jemewe rynge of golde. **1589** GREENE *Menaphon* (Arb.) 58 Twas a good world.. when a ring of a rush would tie as much loue together as a gimmon of gold. **1602** R. T. 5 *Goldie Serm.*, Silver, golde, jemmowes or jewells. **1611** COTGR., *Annelet*, a gimmew, or little ring for the finger. **1721** BAILEY, *Gemmow-Ring*, a double Ring in Links.

4. Any joint or fastening consisting of two parts fitting into each other.

? *a* **1400** *Morte Arth.* 2894 Joynter and gemows he jogges in sondyre! **1463** *Bury Wills* (Camden) 16 A bagge of grene silk with jemewys of green. **1530** PALSGR. 225/1 Gymewe of a gyrdell, *crochet dune troussovere*. **1611** COTGR., *Membret d'esperon*, the gimmew or ioint of a Spurre.

5. *Pl.* = *gimmals*. (See GIMMAL 5.)

1657 W. MORRICE *Coena* Def. §10 Huge Weights hang upon Gemmeys.

6. A hinge. Cf. GEMEL 5.

1396 *Mem. Ripon* (Surtees) III. 123 Et in ij paribus de gemus [*sic*] cum clav. emp. de Johanne de Sutton pro magno hostio in magn. clocher 13*d*. *c* **1440** *Promp. Parv.* 194/2 Gymowe of a sperynge [*K.* gymmew, *S.H.* gymew], *vert(i)nella, gemella*. **1447–8** *Durham MS. Alm. Roll*, j pare de lez Gemoose. **1510** in Willis & Clark *Cambridge* (1886) II. 197 A lokke with Gemows for another presse. **1573–80** BARET *Alv.* G 217 Gimew or henge of a dore. **1657** HOWELL *Londinop.* 393 That the Stalls.. be flexible, and moveable, viz. to hang by Jewmews or Garnets, so that they may be taken up, and let down.

Hence †**gemew** *v.*, in pa. pple. ***i-jemewd***, jointed.

1408 tr. *Vegetius De Re Mil.* IV. xxiii. MS. Roy. 18 A. XII. fol. 110 a, An Iren made as it wer a peir tonges I Iemewd [MS. Douce 291 fol. 106 b, I gymewed] as tonges in the myddes.

†**gemilling.** *Sc. Obs. rare*$^{-1}$. *Music.* (Meaning uncertain: cf. GEMEL 3.)

c **1450** HENRYSON in *Bannatyne MS.* (Hunter. Club) 934 With baiss tonis in ipotdorica, With gemilling in yporlerica.

[**geminal.** Explained as: a pair. Error founded on *geminels*, misprint for *gemmels*: see GEMEL 1, quot. 1603.

1871 in LATHAM (quoting Drayton). Hence in some later Dicts.

Similarly taken as *adj.* = geminate.

1657 TOMLINSON *Renou's Disp.* 344 Because its roots were frequently geminell [*read* Gemmell] resembling two Leggs.]

geminate ('dʒɛmɪneɪt), *a.* and *sb.* [ad. L. *gemināt-us*, pa. pple. of *gemināre* to double, f. *geminus* twin.]

A. *adj.* Duplicated, combined in pairs, twin, binate. ***geminate leaves***, leaves springing in pairs from the same node, one leaf beside the other.

1598 HAKLUYT *Voy.* I. 340 We desire of your Maiestie to.. continue the geminate disposition of your beneuolences, both generally to all our subiects, and also priuately to this our beloued seruant. **1829** LOUDON *Encycl. Plants* 1099 *Geminate*, doubled. **1872** OLIVER *Elem. Bot.* II. 213 Observe the frequently geminate leaves and extra-axillary inflorescence of the Order. **1880** GRAY *Struct. Bot.* 413/1. **1964** R. H. ROBINS *Gen. Ling.* iii. 103 Consonants can be long, or geminate, when the closure or obstruction is held momentarily before release. **1967** V. NABOKOV *Speak, Memory* (ed. 2) vii. 141 Spacious windows alternated with narrower ones, single or geminate, and some of these were of frosted glass.

B. *sb.* A doubled consonant.

1885 COOK tr. *Sievers' O.E. Gram.* (1887) 99 B.. occurs.. in medial and final positions as a geminate. **1958** *Archivum Linguisticum* X. 61 The question of 'subsidiary' syllables, perceptibility as against sonority, whispered speech, dipthongs and geminates. **1965** *Language* XLI. 449 Intervocalic *p t k* indicate a so-called short geminate; *pp tt kk* stand for overlong geminates.

Hence **'geminately** *adv.*, in pairs, doubly.

In recent Dicts.

geminate ('dʒɛmɪneɪt), *v.* [f. L. *gemināt-*, ppl. stem of *gemināre* (see prec.).] *trans.* To double. Also *pass.* of two contiguous teeth: To be united.

a **1637** B. JONSON *Eng Gram.* iii. (1640) 40 *W*, Is but the *V*. geminated in the full sound. **1670** BROOKS *Wks.* (1867) VI. 326 *Macon*.. is a Hebrew participle that signifies firm, constant, and established; and he geminates it, 'my heart is firm, constant, and established'. **1721** in BAILEY. **1881** COLEMAN in *Trans. Odont. Soc.* XIII. 9 It appeared to consist of the two central incisors geminated. **1885** COOK tr. *Sievers' O.E. Gram.* (1887) 100 F.. is.. a surd spirant.. when geminated in the medial position.

Hence **'geminated** *ppl. a.*, doubled, occurring in pairs.

1802 in *Spirit Publ. Jrnls.* (1803) VI. 100 They would run hooting about, bawling and dancing with geminated clamours. **1819** G. SAMOUELLE *Entomol. Compend.* 122 *Atypus*.. Eyes on each side geminated. **1859** J. TOMES *Dental Surg.* 43 Mr. Brookhouse.. sent me two examples of geminated teeth. **1885** COOK tr. *Sievers' O.E. Gram.* (1887) 123 The geminated consonants were often written long after the second had ceased to be pronounced.

gemination (dʒɛmɪˈneɪʃən). [ad. L. *geminātiōn-em*, n. of action f. *gemināre* to double.]

1. A doubling, duplication, repetition.

1597 BACON *Coulers Good & Evill* viii. (Arb.) 149 If the euill bee in the sence and in the conscience both, there is a gemination of it. 1646 SIR T. BROWNE *Pseud. Ep.* III. xv. 140 Men..admit a gemination of principall parts, which is not naturally discovered in any animall. 1655 FULLER *Ch. Hist.* IX. §61 This was conceived..a necessary gemination of a duty in that seditious age. 1700 BP. PATRICK *Comm. Deut.* xxxii. 5 There being a gemination..of a syllable in the latter of these two words. 1895 *Century Mag.* July 457/1 The 'gemination' of the canals [on Mars] has been observed at Mount Hamilton.

b. Of teeth: (See quot. 1878).

1859 J. TOMES *Dental Surg.* 241 A union or gemination of contiguous teeth. 1878 T. BRYANT *Pract. Surg.* I. 562 Gemination, or the union of contiguous teeth, due to the fusion of their pulps.

†**2.** *Rhet.* The immediate repetition of a word or phrase, or the using of a pair of synonymous expressions, for the purpose of rhetorical effect. *Obs.*

1650 FULLER *Pisgah* III. xii. 345 First putting forth his hand, My God; yea both his hands, My God, my God, claiming by that gemination a double interest in Gods fatherly affection. 1661 BOYLE *Style of Script.* (1675) 90 In all languages there are some customary geminations and expressions, which..are..oftentimes emphatical. 1666 J. SMITH *Old Age* (1676) 14 Here are two expressions that intimate unto us the unavoidable approach of these decrepit yeares, i.e. *come* and *draw nigh*; of which gemination, signifying the same thing, I may well say [etc.].

3. *Gram.* **a.** The doubling of an originally single consonant sound. **b.** The doubling of a letter in the orthography of a word.

1875 RENOUF *Egypt. Gram.* 8 The gemination of the letters is not expressed in writing. 1877 MARCH *Comp. Gram. Anglo-Saxon* 16 *Gemination* is the doubling of a consonant..A real gemination can not occur at the beginning or at the end of a word..nor is it easy after a long vowel.

geminative (ˈdʒɛmɪnətɪv), *a.* and *sb.* [f. L. *geminat-* (see GEMINATE *v.*) + -IVE.] **A.** *adj.* Characterized by gemination. **B.** *sb.* A geminated or doubled letter.

In recent Dicts.

1885 in *Trans. Amer. Philol. Assoc.* XVI. 161 The geminatives and diphthongs *ai*, *ay*, *ea* [etc.].

Gemini (ˈdʒɛmɪnaɪ). Forms: 4 **gemyni**, 6–7 **geminy**, (5 **gemeny**, 6 **gemyne**, 7 **gemony**, and (with plural ending) **geminies**, 5– **gemini**. Also (sense 3 only) 7 **gemony**, 9 **gemminy**, **jeminy**, **jimminy**, **jiminy**. [a. L. *geminī* (pl. of *geminus*) twins; also the name of the constellation.]

1. *Astron.* A constellation, otherwise 'Castor and Pollux'; also the third sign of the zodiac, with which this constellation was anciently identical.

c1391 CHAUCER *Astrol.* I. §21 Gemyni. 1413 *Pilgr. Sowle* (Caxton 1483) v. x. 100 The signe of gemini that ben cleped twynnes or doubles. 1426 *Pol. Poems* (Rolls) II. 139 Furious Mars, the ferfulle red sterre..Was two pocys passed of gemeny. 1503 HAWES *Examp. Virt.* i. (Arb.) 7 And Dyane entred was one degre Into the sygne of Gemyne. 1633 P. FLETCHER *Purple Isl.* x. xxiv, Not those [twins] in heaven, the flowery geminies, Are half so bright. 1695 CONGREVE *Love for L.* II. iii, She..was born under Gemini. 1797 *Encycl. Brit.* II. 521/1 From the shifting of the equinoctial points..those stars which were in Aries are now got into Taurus; those of Taurus into Gemini. 1855 TENNYSON *Maud* III. vi. 1 When..the starry Gemini hang like glorious crowns Over Orion's grave.

b. *Astrol.* A person born under the sign of Gemini. Also *attrib.* or as *adj.*

1894 E. KIRK *Influence of Zodiac upon Human Life* xi. 78 Gemini women are especially fond of color, and of flowers. 1927 [see TAURUS 1 c]. 1940, 1969 [see SAGITTARIUS 3]. 1972 V. C. CLINTON-BADDELEY *To study Long Silence* I. vi. 33 Davie was Gemini. Solemnly he consulted his fate. 1984 *Observer* 11 Mar. 12/8 Geminis spend most of their working time in corridors or other people's offices.

†**2.** Used for: A couple, a pair; *esp.* in pl. form, a pair of eyes. *Obs.*

1598 SHAKS. *Merry W.* II. ii. 8 Else you had look'd through the grate, like a Geminy of Baboones. 1633 P. FLETCHER *Purple Isl.* I. xxxi, Or, shine upon me with her Geminies? 1635 QUARLES *Embl.* II. iv, He that daily spies Twin babies in his mistress' Geminis. 1638 FORD *Lady's Trial* I. ii. (1639) C 1 b, Heres now the Gemini of wit. 1700 CONGREVE *Way of World* IV. ix, A gemini of Asses split, would make just four of you.

†**3.** *to play the gemini*: ? alluding to the twin gods (Castor and Pollux) who could never be both in heaven or both in Hades at the same time.

1622 COCKS *Diary* (1883) II. 295 God grant Tozayemon Dono do not play the jemeny with us.

4. A mild form of oath or exclamation. *vulgar.*

[Perhaps a distinct word. Cf. Ger. *gemine, jemine*, which Hildebrand (in *Grimm's D. Wb.*) regards as a corruption of *Jesu domine*; also Du. *jemenie, jemie.*]

1664 SCUDAMORE *Homer a la Mode* 99 O Gemony! neighbour, what a blisse is This, that [etc.]. 1666–7 DENHAM *Direct. Paint.* I. xx, Henceforth, O Gemini! two Dukes Command. 1681 OTWAY *Soldier's Fort.* II. i, Gemini! what wou'd become of me? 1694 CROWNE *Married Beau* II. 3, Oh Gemini! what a rare Complement Has she bestowed upon that ugly Fellow. 1704 ROWE *Biter* III. i, Oh gemini! I wou'dn't marry such a strange sort of an Old Fellow for all the world. 1780 MRS. COWLEY *Belle's Strat.* IV. ii, Oh Gemini! beg the Petticoat's pardon. Just saw a corner of it. 1798 MORTON *Secr. Worth Knowing* I. i, Oh gemini gig! how my poor bones do ache! 1833 M. SCOTT *Tom Cringle* i, Gemini! what is that now? quoth Tip again. 1863 READE *Hard Cash* I. iv. 124 O, jiminy! This polite ejaculation was drawn out by the speaker's sudden recognition of Alfred.

Hence **'Geminids** *pl.* [see -ID], the meteoric bodies forming the 'star-shower' that has its radiant point in Gemini.

1876 G. F. CHAMBERS *Astron.* 799 The example has been followed in designating other meteor showers by the constellations in which their radiant-points are situated; so that we have..the Geminids of December 12.

Geminian (dʒɛmɪˈnaɪən). *Astrol.* [f. GEMINI + -AN.] One born under the sign of Gemini: see GEMINI 1 b.

1911 I. M. PAGAN *From Pioneer to Poet* iii. 42 Geminians are more or less children as regards their health all their days. 1970 R. GARRETT *Run Down* 14 Born Stepney, June 3rd, 1935, and a *Geminian* to his fingertips. 1978 *TV Times* 28 Jan. 68/3 A link with a Geminian could be bitter-sweet.

geminiflorous (ˌdʒɛmɪnɪˈflɔərəs), *a.* [f. L. *gemini-*, *geminus* twin + *flōr-*, *flōs* flower + -OUS.] Having flowers in pairs.

1866 in *Treas. Bot.*

geminous (ˈdʒɛmɪnəs). *rare.* [f. L. *gemin-us*.] Double; occurring in pairs.

1646 SIR T. BROWNE *Pseud. Ep.* III. xv. 141 Christians.. have baptized these geminous births, and double connascencies with severall names. 1704 HARRIS *Lex. Techn.*, *Geminous Arteries*; so some call the two small Arteries which descend to the Joint of the Knee, between the Processes of the Thigh-bones. 1860 FOWLER *Dict. Med.*, *Geminate, Geminous.* In Nat. Hist. Twin; in pairs.

gemm, obs. Sc. f. GAME.

gemm(e, obs. form of GEM *sb.*

‖**gemma** (ˈdʒɛmə). Pl. **gemmæ**. [L.: see GEM.]

†**1.** (See quot.) *Obs.*[-1]

1691 RAY *Creation* II. (1701) 305 The Gemma or cicatricula of the egg contained in the Female ovary.

2. *Bot.* **a.** A leaf-bud as distinguished from a flower-bud.

1770 C. MILNE *Bot. Dict.* s.v. *Gemma*, Mr. Ray was the first who gave the name of Gemma to the bud, which had formerly been denominated germen. 1826 KIRBY & SP. *Entomol.* (1828) III. xxix. 60 A state analogous to that of the larva in the insect begins in the plant when it..is evolved from the gemma. 1872 CARPENTER *Anim. Phys.* xv. 552 The bodies of the first class are known as leaf-buds or gemmæ in the Flowering Plants. 1880 GRAY *Struct. Bot.* 413/1.

b. In mosses, liverworts, etc.: A small cellular body which becomes detached from the mother-plant and originates a new one.

1830 LINDLEY *Nat. Syst. Bot.* 325 In Jungermannia there is a third kind of reproductive matter, consisting of heaped clusters of little amorphous bodies, growing from the surface of the leaves, and called gemmæ. 1857 HENFREY *Bot.* §324 The Hepaticae produce cellular bulbels or gemmae. 1867 J. HOGG *Microsc.* II. i. 308 These plants are produced by spores and minute cellular nodules called gemmae or buds.

3. *Zool.* A bud-like growth upon animals of low organization, which becomes detached and develops into a new individual.

1841–71 T. R. JONES *Anim. Kingd.* (ed. 4) 123 The Alcyons..are reproduced..by gemmæ, which are developed around the preexistent polyps. 1851 RICHARDSON *Geol.* viii. 213 Small gemmæ, covered with cilia, which are free organisms during the first period of their existence.

gemmaceous (dʒɛˈmeɪʃəs), *a.* [f. L. *gemma* bud + -ACEOUS.] Pertaining to, or of the nature of leaf-buds.

1854 in MAYNE *Expos. Lex.*

gemmal, var. GEMEL.

gemman (ˈdʒɛmən). (Also written **gem'man**.) Vulgar pronunc. of GENTLEMAN; cf. GENTMAN.

c1550 *Dr. Doubble Ale* 197 Did it become a cobblers boy To shew a gemman such a toy? 1762 *Gentl. Mag.* 86 You're welcome Gem'men, kindly welcome Ladies. 1770 COLMAN *Oxon. in Town* I. i, I hope you left all the gemmin well at Oxford? 1795 WOLCOT (P. Pindar) *Lousiad* IV. Wks. 1812 I. 286 Which is the better gemman, I or you? 1823 BYRON *Juan* XI. xix. *note*, If there be any gemman so ignorant as to require a traduction. 1833 MARRYAT *P. Simple* (1863) 3 Bill, you must take this here young gem'man..to this here direction. 1850 KINGSLEY *Alt. Locke* v, Now I'll just tell you how that'll work, gemmen.

†**'gemmary**, *a.* and *sb.* *Obs.* [ad. late L. *gemmāri-us* (see -ARY[1]), f. *gemma* GEM.] **A.** *adj.* Of or pertaining to gems; concerned with or skilled in gems. **B.** *sb.* An engraver of gems, a jeweller.

1382 WYCLIF *Exod.* xxxix. 29 Thei graueden in it [the plate] with gemmary werk. *Ibid.* xxviii. 11 In the grauyng of the gemmarye [L. *cælatura gemmarii*] thow shalt graue hem. 1646 SIR T. BROWNE *Pseud. Ep.* II. i. 55 The principle and most gemmary affection is its Traluceny. a1682 —— *Tracts* (1684) 4 Gemmarie Naturalists reade diligently the pretious Stones in the holy City of the Apocalypse.

gemmary: see GEMMERY.

gemmate (ˈdʒɛmeɪt), *a.* *Bot.* and *Zool.* [ad. L. *gemmāt-us*, pa. pple. of *gemmāre*: see next.] Furnished with buds; reproducing by buds.

1846 DANA *Zooph.* (1848) 352.

gemmate (ˈdʒɛmeɪt), *v.* [f. L. *gemmāt-*, ppl. stem of *gemmāre*, f. *gemma* GEM.] †**a.** *trans.* To deck or set with gems (*obs.*). **b.** *intr.* To put forth buds; to propagate itself by buds. Hence **ge'mmated** *ppl. a.*, **ge'mmating** *vbl. sb.* or *ppl. a.*

1623 COCKERAM, *Gemmated*, bedeckt with precious stones. 1697 EVELYN *Numism.* ii. 29 These Regal Heads.. are commonly dress'd with a Diadem..Others we find Gemmated and Studded. 1846 DANA *Zooph.* iv. (1848) 72 The gemmating powers of the apical polyp.

gemmation (dʒɛˈmeɪʃən). [a. F. *gemmation*, n. of action f. L. *gemmāre*: see prec.]

1. *Bot.* **a.** The action of budding. **b.** The manner in which the young leaf is enfolded in the bud. **c.** The time when leaf-buds are put forth. **d.** The arrangement of buds on the stalk.

1760 LEE *Introd. Bot.* III. xv. 200 Gemmation is the Construction of the gem or Bud. 1794 MARTYN *Rousseau's Bot.* xxxi. 485 The gemmation, or various construction of the buds. 1880 GRAY *Struct. Bot.* 413/1 *Gemmation*, budding-growth; or the disposition of buds.

2. *Zool.* The process of reproduction by gemmæ or buds; the formation of a new individual by the protrusion and complete or partial separation of a part of the parent; budding.

1836–9 TODD *Cycl. Anat.* II. 142/1 The male has the appearance of a branch..sent off by gemmation. 1868 E. P. WRIGHT *Ocean World* iv. 84 In the next group the gemmation takes a spiral bias, producing the nautilus shape. 1883 *Chamb. Jrnl.* 142 The natural process of reproduction in the sponge is effected by gemmation or budding off.

gemmative (ˈdʒɛmətɪv), *a.* [f. L. *gemmāt-* (see GEMMATE *v.*) + -IVE.] Concerned with the production of offspring by gemmation.

1877 HUXLEY *Anat. Inv. Anim.* iii. 151 The medusoids which result from the gemmative process closely resemble the stock from which they are produced.

gemmed (dʒɛmd), *ppl. a.* [f. GEM *sb.* and *v.* + -ED.]

†**1.** Covered with buds. *Obs.*[-1]

c1420 *Pallad. on Husb.* IV. 10 With graffes sadde ygemmed thicke and rounde. 1513 DOUGLAS *Æneis* XII. Prol. 101 The lowkyt buttonis on the gemmyt treis.

2. Adorned with or as with gems.

a1240 *Wohunge* in *Cott. Hom.* 273 þu..leddes ham wið þe self to þi ȝimmede bur. 1813 BYRON *Corsair* II. xii, And auburn waves of gemm'd and braided hair. 1820 SCOTT *Abbot* xiii, The gemmed ring and jewelled mitre had become secular spoils. 1849 CLOUGH *Dipsychus* II. v, O beautiful, o'ervaulted with gemmed blue, This spacious court. 1875 PROCTOR *Expanse Heav.* 124 A cloud of light around the gemmed feet of Andromeda in the northern skies.

gemmel(l, var. GEMEL.

gemmeous (ˈdʒɛmɪəs), *a.* Also 7 **gemmeus**. [f. L. *gemme-us* (f. *gemma* GEM) + -OUS.] Of or pertaining to, of the nature of, or resembling a gem. *gemmeous dragonet*: the fish *Callionymus Lyra.*

1605 TIMME *Quersit.* III. 160 There are..in mans bodie.. of saltes..vitriolated, alluminous, niterous, and gemmeus. 1695 WOODWARD *Nat. Hist. Earth* IV. (1723) 191 The gemmeous Matter it self. 1765 C. SMART *Phædrus* III. xvii. (Bohn) 508 And what a blaze of gemmeous dies Shines from the plumage of your tail. 1766 PENNANT *Zool.* (1776) III. 145 *heading*, Gemmeous Dragonet. 1778 *Nat. Hist.* in *Ann. Reg.* 103/2 The fistular bones..are lined within with a crust of gemmeous spar. 1882 J. HARDY in *Proc. Ber. Nat. Club* IX. No. 3. 493 A specimen of the Gemmeous Dragonet.

gemmery (ˈdʒɛmərɪ). Also **gemmary**. [f. GEM *sb.* + -ERY; in sense 1 perh. f. Lat. type **gemmārium*: see -ARY.]

†**1.** A jewel-house. *Obs.*

1656 BLOUNT *Glossogr.*, *Gemmery*, a Jewel house, or place to keep Gems in, a Cabinet. 1721 BAILEY, *Gemmary.*

2. Gems as an object of connoisseurship. *rare.*

1840 POE *Cask of Amontillado* Wks. 1864 I. 346 In painting and gemmary Fortunato, like his countrymen, was a quack.

gemmiferous (dʒɛˈmɪfərəs), *a.* [f. L. *gemmifer* (f. *gemma* GEM *sb.* + *-fer* bearing) + -OUS. Cf. F. *gemmifère.*]

1. Producing gems.

1656 in BLOUNT *Glossogr.* 1721 in BAILEY. 1854 MAYNE *Expos. Lex.*, *Gemmiferous, Min.*, bearing gems, applied to the gravel among which diamonds are found.

2. Producing a gemma or bud; producing offspring by gemmation.

1804 CARLISLE in *Phil. Trans.* XCV. 5 A regular confirmation of which would improve the knowledge of animal generation by shewing that it is gemmiferous. 1856–8 W. CLARK *Van der Hoeven's Zool.* I. 89 Adhering by filiform gemmiferous stolons of the base.

Hence †**ge'mmiferousness**.

1727 BAILEY vol. II, *Gemmiferousness*, the Quality of producing Gems or Jewels.

gemmiparous (dʒɛˈmɪpərəs), *a.* [f. mod.L. *gemmipar-us* (f. *gemmi-*, *gemma* bud + L. *parĕre* to bring forth) + -OUS.] **a.** Of organisms: Producing new individuals by gemmation. **b.** Of or pertaining to the process of gemmation.

1793 MARTYN *Lang. Bot.*, *Gemmiparus*, Gemmiparous. Producing gems or buds. **1830** R. KNOX *Béclard's Anat.* 16 There is also an internal gemmiparous or suboviparous generation. **1835** KIRBY *Hab. & Inst. Anim.* I. xi. 322 The species..which he calls *Planaria tentaculata*..is oviparous in the spring and gemmiparous in the autumn. **1863** BERKELEY *Brit. Mosses* iii. 10 The production of the plant from the threads is rather gemmiparous than embryonic. **1877** HUXLEY *Anat. Inv. Anim.* x. 612 The generative blastema..from which the generative organs of the gemmiparous zooid have been developed.

Hence **ge'mmiparously** *adv.* Also **gemmi'parity**, the attribute of being gemmiparous.

1859 TODD *Cycl. Anat.* V. 117/1 An instance of 'internal gemmiparity' rather than the production of true ova. **1867** H. SPENCER *Princ. Biol.* II. 93 The resulting segments are so many gemmiparously-produced individuals.

gemmipore ('dʒɛmɪpɔə(r)). [ad. mod.L. *gemmipora*, neut. pl., f. L. *gemmi-*, *gemma* GEM *sb.* + late L. *porus* = Gr. πόρος passage.] One of the *Gemmipora*, a genus of madreporian corals.

1846 DANA *Zooph.* iv. (1848) 47 The gemmipores resemble these in general form, and in their fringe of short tentacles, but the disk is not striated.

gemmoid ('dʒɛmɔɪd), *a. rare*$^{-0}$. [f. GEMMA + -OID.] Having the nature or form of a gemma.

In some recent Dicts.

gemmologist (dʒɛ'mɒlədʒɪst). [f. GEMMOLOGY + -IST.] One who is skilled in gemmology.

1931 *(title of periodical)* The Gemmologist. **1937** R. WEBSTER *(title)* The gemmologist's pocket compendium. **1959** *Listener* 23 Apr. 706/2 The diamond is known to the gemmologist as the hardest..of all minerals. **1960** *Guardian* 11 July 4/2 A gemmologist's two-year course..includes the study of crystallography.

gemmology (dʒɛ'mɒlədʒɪ). [f. L. *gemm-a* GEM *sb.* + -(O)LOGY.] The science of gems.

1811 PINKERTON *Petral.* I. 12 The detached crystals of siderite..are properly topics of gemmology, or lithology, and not of petralogy. **1970** *Daily Tel.* 21 Sept. 19 My son is interested in gemmology and would like to be a diamond cutter.

†**ge'mmosity.** *Obs.*$^{-0}$ [f. L. *gemmōs-us* full of gems (f. *gemma* GEM *sb.*) + -ITY.] (See quots.)

1656-81 BLOUNT *Glossogr.*, *Gemmosity (gemmositas)*, abundance of Precious stones. **1755** JOHNSON, *Gemmosity*, the quality of being a jewel. **1775** ASH, *Gemmosity*, the quality of abounding in jewels; an exuberance of buds.

gemmow, var. GEMEW.

gemmule ('dʒɛmjuːl). [a. F. *gemmule*, ad. L. *gemmula*, dim. of *gemma* a bud, GEM.]

1. *Bot.* **a.** = PLUMULE.

1844 HOBLYN *Dict. Med.*, *Gemmule*, a term used synonymously with *plumule*, the growing point of the embryo in plants. **1861** BENTLEY *Bot.* 344 Thus we distinguish three parts in the embryo, corresponding to the root, stem, and leaves of the perfect plant; namely, a *radicle*, *plumule* or *gemmule*, and one or more *cotyledons*.

b. One of the reproductive cells of cryptogams.

1874 COOKE *Fungi* 55 Short germinating utricles shoot forth, which soon form themselves into rows of gemmules.

2. *Zool.* A small gem (see GEM *sb.* 5) or gemma; *spec.* a ciliated embryo of one of the *Cœlenterata*; an encysted mass of sponge-particles, from which new ones are produced. In Darwin's theory of pangenesis, one of the hypothetical units conceived of as capable of reproducing the part from which it is thrown off.

1845 *Zoologist* III. 955 This cell, or germ, or gemmule, is the origin of all existing animals. **1858** T. R. JONES *Aquar. Nat.* 34 These yellow granules are the rudiments of the eggs, or gemmules of the sponge. **1871** DARWIN *Desc. Man* I. viii. 280 According to this hypothesis, every unit or cell of the body throws off gemmules or undeveloped atoms. **1872** CARPENTER *Anim. Phys.* xv. 562 In this state it becomes clothed with cilia and is termed a gemmule. **1875** [see PANGENETIC *a.*]. **1877** W. THOMSON *Voy. Challenger* I. iii. 176 Small examples of the sponge, some of them not much beyond the condition of gemmules. **1913** *Q. Rev.* Oct. 376 No one now accepts Darwin's theory of gemmules or pangenesis. **1952** C. P. BLACKER *Eugenics* ii. 45 According to this provisional hypothesis,..the cells of the body throw off minute particles called *gemmules* which circulate freely throughout the blood-stream and multiply there.

fig. **1869** F. GALTON *Hered. Genius* 365 Young artisans, and other floating gemmules of English population.

gemmuliferous (dʒɛmjuː'lɪfərəs), *a.* [f. L. *gemmula* GEMMULE + -(I)FEROUS.] Bearing gemmules.

1846 DANA *Zooph.* (1848) 691 Gemmuliferous branchlets much branched. **1847-9** TODD *Cycl. Anat.* IV. 49/1 The gemmuliferous urns are, however, deciduous.

gemmull, var. GEMEL.

gemmy ('dʒɛmɪ), *a.* [f. GEM *sb.* + -Y[1].]

1. Abounding in, covered with, or set with gems, or something resembling gems.

c **1420** *Pallad. on Husb.* I. 625 The cok confesseth emynet Cupide When he is gemmy tayl bygynnyth splay. *a* **1649** DRUMM. OF HAWTH. *Poems* Wks. (1711) 12 Night westward did her gemmy world decline, And hide her lights that greater lights might shine. *a* **1749** PHILIPS *Pastorals* vi. 123 (1790) 37 Hast thou seen their king in rich array, Fam'd Oberon, with damask'd robe so gay, And gemmy crown. **1759** GRAINGER *Tibullus' Elegies* II. ii. 16 Not venal, you request no Eastern Stores, Where ruddy Waters lave the gemmy shores. **1832** TENNYSON *Lady of Shalott* iii, The gemmy bridle glitter'd free.

2. Gem-like; brilliant; glittering.

1675 EVELYN *Terra* (1776) 14 Rough crystals of which some were very transparent and Gemmy. **1735** THOMSON *Liberty* IV. 353 The flitting cloud, against the summit dash'd, And, by the sun illumined, pouring bright A gemmy shower. **1882** GROSART *Spenser's Wks.* I. 126 She has hairs half-golden, half-silvern, half-gemmy on her..head. **1883** *Good Words* 113 Birds of matchless plumage—green, gold, orange, and blue-tipped wings shedding gemmy light.

Hence **'gemmily** *adv.*, so as to resemble gems; **'gemminess**, the quality or state of being gemmy.

1864 WEBSTER, *Gemminess.* **1893** SYMONDS *In the Key of Blue* 53 Blots of *acqua-marina*—gemmily imposed upon the thick impasto of the dominant ochres.

gemoll, obs. form of GEMEL.

†**'gemonies.** *Rom. Antiq. Obs.* Also 7 *sing.* **Gemony.** [ad. L. *(scālæ) Gemōniæ*; of uncertain origin, the assumed connexion with *gemĕre* to groan having little probability, in spite of the existence of the synonymous form *Gemitōriæ*.] Steps on the Aventine Hill leading to the Tiber, to which the bodies of executed criminals were dragged to be thrown into the river.

1598 GRENEWEY *Tacitus' Ann.* III. ii. 67 They had drawne Pisoes images to the Gemonies; and broken them in peeces, if [etc.]. **1603** B. JONSON *Sejanus* v. i. (1605) K 2, Some your seruants; who..Slip't downe the Gemonies, and brake their neckes. **1626** MASSINGER *Rom. Actor* I. i. (1629) B 2 b, Noe day passes In which some are not fastend to the hooke, Or throwne downe from the Gemonies. **1656-81** BLOUNT *Glossogr.*, *Gemony (gemoniæ scalæ)*, a place in Rome where condemned persons were cast down by a pair of stairs headlong into the River Tiber.

¶ Misapplied *fig.* in the sense of 'tortures'.

1656 R. FLETCHER *Martial's Epigr.* etc. 174 The world, fame, honour, wealth & pleasure then Are the fair wrack and Gemonies of men. *a* **1683** OLDHAM *To Mem. C. Morwent* xxxiii. in *Rem.* (1684) 84 Anguish through every Member flies And all those inward Gemonies Whereby frail Flesh in Torture dies.

gemot(e (gɪ'məʊt). *Eng. Hist.* [repr. OE. *ȝemót*, f. *ȝe-* together, 'com-' (see Y-) + *mót* MOOT.] A meeting; an assembly (in England before the Norman Conquest) for judicial or legislative purposes. See also WITENAGEMOT.

c **1000** *Laws of Æthelstan* c. 20 (Schmid) ȝif hwa ȝemot forsitte. **1641** BAKER *Chron.* 27/1 Their Gemote..was a little court held monthly in every hundred. **1860** HOOK *Lives Abps.* I. v. 252 When the synod was concluded..the convention formed itself into a gemot. **1871** FREEMAN *Norm. Conq.* (1876) IV. xviii. 130 It was probably in the same Gemót that William for the first time exercised the power of bestowing an English bishoprick on one of his own countrymen.

gemow(e: see GEMEW.

‖**gemsbok** ('gɛmzbɒk). Also 8-9 **gemsbock**, (8 **gemse-bok**), 9 **gemsbuck**, **-boc.** [Du. *gemsbok* (properly chamois, but in S. Africa misapplied as below), a. Ger. *gemsbock*, f. *gemse*, fem., chamois + *bock* buck.] The name given in S. Africa to a large antelope (*Oryx capensis*).

1777 G. FORSTER *Voy. round World* I. 84 The Egyptian antelope..is here [at the Cape] called gems-bock or chamois. **1822** BURCHELL *Trav.* II. 23 A herd of antelopes of the species known among the boors by the misapplied name of Gemsbok. **1865** TYLOR *Early Hist. Man.* viii. 221 A gemsbock's horn attached to a slender stick. **1883** J. MACKENZIE *Day-dawn in Dark places* 48 The kukama (gemsbuck or oryx) fleetest of the antelopes.

gemshorn ('gɛmzhɔːn). [a. Ger. *gemshorn*, lit. chamois horn (cf. prec.).] An organ stop with tapering metal pipes, yielding a tone resembling that of the viola da gamba.

1825 DANNELEY *Encycl. Mus.*, *Gemshorn*, an organ-stop, of the flute species. **1852** SEIDEL *Organ* 21 In 1515..an organ in St. Mary's, at Danzic..contained..hohl-flute, gems-horn, nasal. **1869** *Eng. Mech.* 17 Dec. 332/2 Would a harmonic flute, or gems-horn, not be an improvement? **1876** HILES *Catech. Organ* ix. (1878) 67 *Gemshorn*, Goat-horn; [an organ stop] of tin or metal, pointed at the top..The tone is soft, and resembling a *horn* in quality.

gemster, obs. Sc. f. GAMESTER.

gemstone ('dʒɛmstəʊn). [f. GEM *sb.* + STONE; in OE. *ȝimstán*.] †**a.** In OE. and ME. = GEM 1. Also *fig.* **b.** A stone capable of being worked up into a gem.

a. *c* **1000** ÆLFRIC *Hom.* I. 62 þas ȝymstanas synd tocwysede. *c* **1175** *Lamb. Hom.* 135 Ne sculen ȝe nawiht ȝimstones leggen swinen to mete. *a* **1240** *Ureisun* in *Cott. Hom.* 193 Mid brihte ȝimstones hore krune is al biset. *c* **1290** *S. Eng. Leg.* I. 370/109 And with riche ȝimstones al-so.

fig. *a* **1175** *Cott. Hom.* 217 Heo is hefone liht..and all hiscefte ȝimston. *c* **1200** *Vices & Virtues* 95 Ðat faire scrud of charite all besett mid ȝimstanes of gode werkes.

b. **1883** A. H. CHURCH *Precious Stones* ii. 9 With an instrument so constructed the pleiochroism of the vast majority of gem-stones may be determined at a glance.

‖**gemütlich** (gə'myːtlɪç), *a.* [G.] Pleasant, cheerful; cosy, snug, homely; genial, goodnatured.

1852 QUEEN VICTORIA *Jrnl.* 11 Oct. (1868) 141 The view was so beautiful over the dear hills; the day so fine; the whole so *gemüthlich.* **1858** —— *Let.* 7 Apr. in R. Fulford *Dearest Child* (1964) 86, I like him very much, he is pleasant, gemütlich, accomplished. **1867** W. JAMES *Let.* 24 July in R. B. Perry *Tht. & Char. W. J.* (1935) I. 239 Young Thies is a great wit, to judge by a saying of his the other night that 'the Americans were almost as *gemütlich* as the Germans, at a fire.' **1934** A. HUXLEY *Beyond Mexique Bay* 180 Germany is to be made as remote from Europe as New Guinea... The result promises to be extremely *gemütlich.* **1958** A. WILSON *Middle Age of Mrs. Eliot* III. 427 A very roly-poly, chuckling gemütlich middle-aged German. **1960** *Times* 11 June 11/6 Those yellow Biedermeier villas which give the town its gemütlich atmosphere. **1965** T. CAPOTE *In Cold Blood* iv. 206 Their five-room apartment, with its *gemütlich* mélange of plump hassocks and squashy chairs.

‖**Gemütlichkeit, gemütlichkeit** (gə'myːtlɪçkaɪt). [G., cf. prec.] The quality of being *gemütlich*; geniality; cosiness; cheerfulness.

1892 W. JAMES *Let.* 18 Dec. (1920) I. 332 When *Gemüthlichkeit* is banished from the world, it will still survive in this dear and shabby old country [*sc.* Italy]. **1912** W. E. HOCKING *Meaning of God.* xxviii. 406 We must have ..music with beer, Gemütlichkeit, and a fine outlook. **1929** A. HUXLEY *Holy Face* 2 The *gemüthlichkeit*, the prettiness, the cosy sublimities of the Lake District. **1959** *Oxf. Mag.* 11 June 464/1 The 'cosiness' and 'Gemütlichkeit' of the Bodleian. **1969** H. MACINNES *Salzburg Connection* i. 9 The other lake offered..folk music and dancing and general Gemütlichkeit. **1971** *Times* 6 Nov. 14/5 The double stress on God's 'terrible' demands on men and on his loving-kindness revealed in Christ gives German piety a quality which not even Catholic *Gemütlichkeit* quite overcomes.

gemytre, obs. form of GEOMETRY.

gen (dʒɛn). *slang* (orig. *Services*'). [Perh. abbrev. of *general* in the official phrase 'for the general information of all ranks', or possibly from part of the words *genuine* or *intelligence*.] Information; facts. Also *attrib.*

1940 MICHIE & GRAEBNER *Their Finest Hour* iv. 60 Operations room, where I got my 'Gen' (R.A.F. slang for information, or instructions). **1943** C. H. WARD-JACKSON *Piece of Cake* 31 *Gen book*, note-book kept for jotting down useful bits of information. *Ibid.*, *Genwallah*, orderly room sergeant, or anyone else well-couched in..King's Regulations and Air Council Instructions [etc.]. **1944** *Penguin New Writing* XXII. 41 My mate Tich..gives me the 'gen' of the last nine days. **1950** M. KENNEDY *Feast* 46 He pretends to have the gen on the visitors, but no visitor would know so much as that. **1958** G. MITCHELL *Spotted Hemlock* ix. 84 I'll get you a brochure... Last season's will give you all the gen you need. **1970** *Daily Tel.* 10 Dec. 8/6 A vast amount of 'gen' is included, and this will be invaluable for settling arguments.

Hence as *v. intr.* (see quot. 1943); also *trans.*, to inform (const. *up*); so **,genned-'up** *a.*, informed; well supplied with information or facts.

1943 C. H. WARD-JACKSON *Piece of Cake* 31 *Gen-up, to*, to learn quickly, to swot—prior to a trade test board or some equally binding ordeal. **1945** PARTRIDGE *Dict. R.A.F. Slang* 29 *Genned up*, well supplied with information. **1958** E. HYAMS *Taking it Easy* I. i. 5 He wanted information; I had it. I was in a position to, as we said then, gen him up. I genned him up.

-gen (-dʒɛn), *suffix*, forming *sbs.* in mod. scientific use; ad. F. *-gène*, ultimately repr. Gr. *-γενής* (f. *γεν-* root of *γί-γν-εσθαι* to be born, become, *γεν-νάειν* to beget, *γέν-ος* kind, etc.: see KIN) an adjective suffix which has two different uses: (1) giving the sense 'born in a certain place or condition', as in *οἰκογενής*, *ἐνδογενής* born in the house (respectively f. *οἶκος* house and *ἔνδον* within); (2) giving the sense 'of a (specified) kind', as in *ὁμογενής* of the same kind, homogeneous, *ἑτερογενής* of another kind, heterogeneous. The F. *-gène* in scientific terms has two distinct applications (of different origin) both of which have been adopted in Eng.

1. *Chem.* In 1777-9 Lavoisier (*Œuvres* II. 249) proposed for the recently discovered element (till then known as 'dephlogisticated air', etc.) the alternative names *principe acidifiant* and *principe oxygine*, which he states to be etymologically synonymous. In G. de Morveau *Nomencl. chimique* 1787 (prepared in collaboration with Lavoisier and other chemists) the sbs. *oxygène* and *hydrogène* occur, and are explained to mean 'engendrant l'acide' and 'engendrant l'eau'; and in Lavoisier's *Traité de Chimie* 1789 the etymon of the suffix is said to be 'Gr. *γείνομαι*, j'engendre'. This etymology accounts for Lavoisier's original form *oxygine*; the change of *-gine* into *-gène* must have been due to the observation that *-gine* did not occur in Gr. derivatives, while *-gène*, from the same root, already existed in *hétérogène*, *homogène* (ad. Gr. words in *-γενής*: see above); the fact that the suffix *-γενής* in Gr. words was not capable of meaning 'that which produces' was overlooked or disregarded. The names *oxygène*, *hydrogène* were soon adopted into Eng. with the ending *-gene*, afterwards altered to *-gen*. On the analogy of these words, a considerable number of new terms have been added to the common (French and Eng.) vocabulary of chemistry, in which the ending *-gène*, *-gen* expresses the sense 'that which produces'; they are usually names of chemical substances, as *nitrogen*, *amidogen*, *cyanogen*, etc.; rarely of classes of substances, as *halogen*, †*amphigen*.

2. *Bot.* The botanical use of *-gène* was introduced in 1813 by Decandolle (*Théorie de Botanique* 210) in the words *endogène*, *exogène*, adjs. designating two classes of plants which respectively produce their new tissue internally (Gr. ἔνδο-ν within) and externally (Gr. ἔξω outside). The formation of the words was suggested by the older terms *endorhize*, *exorhize*. Decandolle gives as the etymon of the suffix 'γεναω [*sic!*], j'engendre, je crois'; app. his *-gène* was not a new adoption from Gr. -γενής, but a different application of the *-gène* already used in chemical terms, which he vaguely remembered to be derived from a Gr. root meaning 'to produce, to grow'. The adjs. *endogène*, *exogène* first came into Eng. in the adapted forms *endogenous*, *exogenous*; Lindley *c* 1845 formed from these the sbs. *endogen*, *exogen*; and he and others added many analogous terms denoting classes of plants, the first element indicating the part at which the new growth takes place, or some characteristic of their mode of growth, as *acrogen*, *amphigen*, *dictyogen*, *thallogen*. The suffix is also occasionally used in terms denoting plant tissues that give rise to particular kinds of cells, as *calyptrogen*, *dermatogen*, *phellogen*.

3. *Geol.* In the form **-gene**, used in terms indicating the type, method, or place of formation, as *tectogene*.

gena ('dʒiːnə). *Anat.* Pl. **genæ**. [L., see GENAL *a.*, GENIAL *a.*[2]] The cheek or lateral part of the head, *esp.* of insects.

1826 KIRBY & SPENCE *Introd. Ent.* III. xxxiv. 488 The cheeks of insects (*Genæ*) usually surround the anterior part of the eyes, and lie between them and the mandibles or their representatives. **1887** MARSHALL & HURST *Pract. Zool.* ix. 153 The genæ, or 'cheeks', are a pair of vertical plates covering the sides of the head, behind and below the eyes. **1911** *Encycl. Brit.* XXVII. 283/1 A lateral unsegmented plate, the *gena*, which carries the eyes [in Trilobites]. **1957** RICHARDS & DAVIES *Imms's Gen. Textbk. Ent.* (ed. 9) I. 20 The *gena*..forms the whole of the lateral area below and posterior to the eyes on each side. *Ibid.* III. 587 The *genae* (parafacials or cheeks) comprise the region lying between the face and the anterior margin of the eye on either side. **1964** C. J. GOODNIGHT et al. *Gen. Zool.* x. 198/1 The dorsal region [of the head of the grasshopper] is known as the vertex; the lateral, the genae, or cheeks.

gena-, obs. form of GENEA-.

genal ('dʒiːnəl), *a. Zool.* [f. L. *gena* cheek + -AL[1].] Pertaining to the cheek or cheeks.

1877 *Encycl. Brit.* VI. 660/1 (*caption*) Another of the same stage, in which the genal or cheek spines are developed. **1885** in *Syd. Soc. Lex.*

genappe (dʒɪ'næp). [f. *Genappe* in Belgium, the original place of manufacture.] (See quot. 1858.) Also ***genappe yarn***.

1858 SIMMONDS *Dict. Trade*, *Genappe*, a worsted yarn or cord used in the manufacture of braids, fringes, &c.; its smoothness enabling it to be well combined with silk. **1888** *Daily News* 16 July 2/7 Small purchases are made in a great variety of yarns, including cords, genappes, fustians, &c. **1892** HOLDEN in *Pall Mall G.* 7 June 7/2, I introduced a new manufacture, namely, that of genappe yarns.

b. *Comb.*, as ***genappe-spinner***.

1897 *Daily News* 5 Nov. 11/3 The worsted genappe spinners are all very busy.

genarch ('dʒɛnɑːk). *rare.* Anglicized form of next.

1879 HEARN *Aryan Househo.* vi. 145 To this original chief or genarch, the nearest in blood was the natural successor.

†**ge'narcha.** *Obs. rare.* [Lat. form of Gr. γενάρχης, f. γένος race + -άρχης ruler, founder, root of ἄρχειν to rule, to begin; cf. PATRIARCH.] The founder of a family or race.

1649 *Bounds Publ. Obed.* (1650) 17 We all derive from him, as from a *Genarcha*. **1650** B. *Discolliminium* 31 It is enough to prove they were our Political Parents, which the whole series of our English Chronicles make good, from a *Genarcha*.

Hence **ge'narchaship**, headship of a family or people.

1650 *Reply to Dr. Sanderson* 3 First it provides not for Peoples obeying a Capitall family in Genarchaship.

genatour, var. GENETOR *Obs.*

gencian, -yan(e, obs. forms of GENTIAN.

†**gend** (gɛnd). *Sc. Obs.* App.: Foolish, simple.

?*a* **1500** *Peebles to Play* iii, Scho was so guckit and so gend, That day ane byt scho eit nocht. **1508** DUNBAR *Poems* v. 1 My Gudame wes a gay wife, bot scho wes rycht gend. **15..** *Priests Peblis* (1603) C ij, For he as fule began guckit and gend, And ay the wyser man neirar the end.

gend, alleged var. GENT.

1676–1732 COLES, *Gend*, Gent, Neat.

‖**gendarme** (ʒɑ̃darm, dʒɛn'dɑːm). Forms: 8 **gens d'arm**, 9 **gendarme**; *pl.* 6 **gentzdarmes**, (7 **gend'arme**), 9 **gend'armes**, 7–9 **gens d'arm(e)s**, **gensdarmes**, **gendarmes**. [F. *gendarme*, a sing. formed from the pl. *gens d'armes* men of arms; hence a fresh pl. *gendarmes*. Some confusion between these forms is evident in English writers; in mod.Fr. the spelling *gens d'armes* is restricted to the historic sense.]

†**1.** (Chiefly *pl.*) In the older French army, a horseman in full armour, having several others under his command; in later times, a mounted trooper, esp. of the royal companies. *Obs.* exc. *Hist.*

c **1550** *Disc. Common Weal Eng.* (1893) 7 Whether gentzdarmes were necessarye here as in Fraunce. **1584** HUDSON *Du Bartas' Judith* v. 538 We come not here, my Lord, said they, with armes, For to resist the chok of thy Gens d'armes. **1644** EVELYN *Diary* 12 Apr. (1879) I. 73, I took coach, to see a general muster of all the *gens d'armes* about yᵉ Citty [Paris]. **1670** COTTON *Espernon* II. VII. 340 The man of the house.. was one of the Gend'arme [*margin*, Or *Cuirassiers*] of the King's own Troop. **1688** *Lond. Gaz.* No. 2375/3 The Gendarmes and Light Horse that formed the Camp of Acheres, and were returning to their Quarters, are countermanded. **1755** *Mem. Capt. P. Drake* II. i. 4 This I would by no Means suffer, assuring him that I could bear Fire and Water at least as well as he, or I was not fit to be a Gens d'Arm. **1864** BURTON *Scot Abr.* I. i. 48 The Scots Guard consisted of one hundred gensdarmes and two hundred archers.

2. a. A soldier, either mounted or on foot (F. *gendarme à cheval*, —— *à pied*), who is employed in police duties, esp. in France.

1796 HEL. M. WILLIAMS *Lett. France* (ed. 2) I. vii. 88, I proceeded on my journey haunted by the images of gens d'armes. **1815** SCOTT *Paul's Lett.* (1839) 266 The patroles of the modern gens d'armes, or military police. **1833** MARRYAT *P. Simple* (1863) 148 At this delightful town, we had unlimited parole, not even a gendarme accompanying us. **1880** OUIDA *Moths* II. 220 A few gendarmes had been sent to protect the fair during the night.

b. *fig.* (See quots.)

1883 *Sat. Rev.* 17 Feb. 208/2 One of those projecting pieces of rock which are called gendarmes; apparently from their frequently stopping travellers. **1895** *Westm. Gaz.* 13 Sept. 3/2 The formidable-looking ridge, bristling with innumerable 'gendarmes' or rock-towers..was inspected.

c. A policeman. *slang.*

1906 H. GREEN *At Actors' Boarding House* 204 She'll be cabling the old guy to set the gendarmes on us as we leave the boat. **1931** H. CRANE *Let.* 30 Mar. 367, I am to sail to *Mexico* (damn the gendarmes!) next Saturday.

3. *attrib.* in ***gendarme blue***, a colour like that of a French gendarme's uniform; also *absol.*

1884 *Girl's Own Paper* Jan. 200/2 That shade of blue called 'Gendarme'. **1891** *Daily News* 23 Mar. 2/2 One of these [bodices], in gendarme blue, has a vest of cornflower blue. **1895** *Ibid.* 20 Mar. 7/1 A new shade, suggesting gendarme and cornflower, but not precisely either.

Hence **gen'darming** *vbl. sb.* (*nonce-wd.*), the discharge of police duties.

1890 *Sat. Rev.* 13 Sept. 314/1 The German gendarmes should do their gendarming with more gentleness.

gendarmery (dʒɛn'dɑːmərɪ), ‖**gendarmerie** (ʒɑ̃darməri). Also **gens darmery**, **gens d'armerie**. [a. F. *gendarmerie* (f. *gendarme* GENDARME), first recorded in the 16th cent. The forms with *gens* are not recognized in French dictionaries.]

1. *Hist.* A corps or squadron of cavalry, esp. in the old French army, or of certain forces raised in England in the reign of Edward VI.

1551 EDW. VI *Jrnl.* 5 May in *Lit. Rem.* (Roxb.) II. 317 The muster of the gendarmery apointed to be the first of June, if it were possible; if not, the 8. **1630** *R. Johnson's Kingd. & Commw.* 144 His Forces, as well horse as foot, of which this Country [France]..vaunteth..to be the best and greatest Gens d'armerie of any Realme. *a* **1656** USSHER *Ann.* (1658) 35 Abner, who was formerly the chief of Sauls gendarmery. **1702** *Lond. Gaz.* No. 3836/2 The Enemy had there all their Gendarmerie. **1756** HUME *Hist. Eng.* (1761) II. xxxvii. 311 Some troops of French and Scotch gensdarmery. **1823** LINGARD *Hist. Eng.* VI. 107 Their gendarmerie..was broken by a strong body of Spanish musqueteers. **1860** FROUDE *Hist. Eng.* V. 347 The economy which had been attempted in the household had been more than defeated by the cost of the gendarmerie, as the force was called.

fig. a **1670** HACKET *Abp. Williams* II. §99 (1693) 102 Had the Gensdarmery of our great Writers no other Enemy to fight with?

2. a. A body of soldiers, mounted or unmounted, employed as police, esp. in France.

1792–6 HEL. M. WILLIAMS *Lett. France* IV. iv. (Jod.) Among the troops of the Convention were several of the gendarmerie. **1825** SCOTT *Fam. Lett.* 25 Aug., A very strict police, which reminds me more of the Gens-d'armerie of France than any other institution. **1866** *Daily Tel.* 5 Feb. 5/3 That useful body, the gendarmery, could..be retained at the infantry barracks. **1894** D. C. MURRAY *Making of Novelist* 144 Waiting for the formation of the Turkish gendarmerie under Colonel Valentine Baker.

b. The head-quarters of the gendarmes; the police-station.

1945 G. MILLAR *Maquis* vi. 131 We left our bicycles in the cabbage patch behind the Gendarmerie. **1955** J. THOMAS *No Banners* ix. 78 Well, try the *Gendarmerie*. They've got cells there. *Ibid.* xx. 191 Patrice was a British officer who had the bad luck to land by parachute on the roof of a *gendarmerie*. **1967** G. M. WILSON *Cake for Caroline* v. 61 Ring the gendarmerie... Ask somebody to meet me up there.

3. *attrib.*, as ***gendarmery barracks***, ***battalion***, ***officer***, ***station***.

1881 *Daily News* 14 Nov. 4/6 Our Correspondent in Constantinople telegraphs that it appears to be decided to dispense with the service of the gendarmery officers. **1893** *Ibid.* 16 Nov. 4/5 A bomb was exploded..outside the gendarmery barracks. **1897** *Ibid.* 14 May 5/4 A gendarmery battalion is to be formed, partly from Macedonians, partly from Thessaly. **1897** *Ibid.* 2 Oct. 2/3 There is no military post proper at Haffir, but it is one of the gendarmerie stations.

gender ('dʒɛndə(r)), *sb.* Also 4 **gendre**. [a. OF. *gen(d)re* (F. *genre*) = Sp. and Pg. *genero*, It. *genere*, ad. L. *gener-* stem form of *genus* race, kind = Gr. γένος, Skr. *jánas*:—OAryan ***genes-**, f. root γεν- to produce; cf. KIN.]

†**1.** Kind, sort, class; also, genus as opposed to species. ***the general gender***: the common sort (of people). *Obs.*

13.. *E.E. Allit. P.* B. 434 Alle gendrez so ioyst wern ioyned wyth-inne. *c* **1384** CHAUCER *H. Fame* I. 18 To knowe of hir signifiaunce The gendres. **1398** TREVISA *Barth. De P.R.* VIII. xxix. (1495) 341 Byshynynge and lyghte ben dyuers as species and gendre, for euery shinyng is lyght, but not ayenwarde. **1602** SHAKS. *Ham.* IV. vii. 18 The great loue the generall gender beare him. **1604** —— *Oth.* I. iii. 326 Supplie it with one gender of Hearbes, or distract it with many. **1643** PRYNNE *Sov. Power Parl.* App. 153 The Governour..is a servant of the Ship..neither differs he from a mariner in gender, but in kind. **1662** R. MATHEW *Unl. Alch.* §22. 15 Diseases of this gender are for the most part incurable. **1727** *Philip Quarll* 218 To strike in him that Terror which the Gender of Death he had fix'd upon could not. **1784** R. BAGE *Barham Downs* I. 274, I..am a man of importance, a public man, Sir; of the patriotic gender.

†**b.** ***the nervous gender***: the nervous system [= F. *le genre nerveux*].

1698 *Phil. Trans.* XX. 432 In other sorts of Distempers where the nervous Gender is attack'd.

2. *Gram.* Each of the three (or in some languages two) grammatical 'kinds', corresponding more or less to distinctions of sex (and absence of sex) in the objects denoted, into which substantives are discriminated according to the nature of the modification they require in words syntactically associated with them; the property (in a sb.) of belonging to, or (in other parts of speech) of having the form appropriate to concord with, a specified one of these kinds. Also, the distinction of words into 'genders', as a principle of grammatical classification.

In the Indo-European langs. there were originally three genders, the masculine and feminine, to which respectively belonged the great majority of nouns denoting male and female persons or animals; and the neuter, including chiefly nouns denoting things without sex. But great numbers of words denoting inanimate objects were of the masculine or feminine gender, without even any figurative attribution of sex; and in some cases the names of objects possessing sex were of the neuter gender. In Semitic, and in the Romanic langs., there are only two genders, masculine and feminine. In many langs. the adjectives, and in some langs. the verbs, have inflexions depending on the gender of the sbs. to which they syntactically refer. Mod. English has 'natural' as opposed to 'grammatical' gender; i.e. nouns are masculine, feminine or neuter according as the objects they denote are male, female, or of neither sex; and the gender of a noun has no other syntactical effect than that of determining the pronoun that must be used in referring to it. For *common*, *epicene gender*, see those words.

[The Eng. use in this sense follows the Lat. use of *genus*, which in its turn is a rendering of the equivalent Gr. γένος. The formulation of the three grammatical genders (τὰ γένη τῶν ὀνομάτων, ἄρρενα καὶ θήλεα καὶ σκεύη) is ascribed by Aristotle *Rhet.* III. v. to Protagoras.]

a **1380** *St. Theodora* 109 in Horstm. *Alteng. Leg.* (1878) 36 Hire name, þat was femynyn Of gendre, heo turned in to masculyn. **1387–8** [see 3]. **1509** HAWES *Past. Pleas.* v. xi, The Latyn worde whyche that is referred Unto a thynge whych is subtancyall, For a nowne substantyve is wel averred, And wyth a gender is declynall. **1581** SIDNEY *Apol. Poetrie* (Arb.) 70 Those cumbersome differences of Cases, Genders, Moodes, and Tenses, which I thinke was a peece of the Tower of Babilon's curse. **1612** BRINSLEY *Pos. Parts* (1669) 7 What is gender? *A.* The difference of nouns according to Sex..The difference, whereby a word is noted to signifie the male, or female, or neither; that is, either *he* or *she*, or neither of them. **1751** HARRIS *Hermes* I. iv. (1786) 61 Gender..descends to every Individual, however diversified. **1783** BLAIR *Lect. Rhet.* I. viii. 144 Gender, being founded on the distinction of the two sexes..can only find place in the names of living creatures, which admit the distinction of male and female. **1824** L. MURRAY *Eng. Gram.* (ed. 5) I. 76 Gender is the distinction of nouns, with regard to sex. There are three genders, the masculine, the feminine, and the neuter. **1887** EARLE *Philol. Eng. Tongue* (ed. 4) §383 In the English language as now current, the traditional Gender of ancient Grammar is entirely extinct.

b. By some recent philologists applied, in extended sense, to the 'kinds' into which sbs. are discriminated by the syntactical laws of certain languages the grammar of which takes no account of sex.

Thus the North American Indian languages are said to have two 'genders', animate and inanimate. With still greater departure from the original sense, the name 'genders' has been applied to the many syntactically discriminated classes of sbs. in certain South African langs.

3. *transf.* Sex. Now only *jocular*.

1387-8 T. USK *Test. Love* II. iii. (Skeat) 13 No mo genders been there but masculine, and femynyne, all the remnaunte been no genders but of grace, in facultie of grammer. *c* **1460** *Towneley Myst.* xxx. 161 *Primus demon.* Has thou oght writen there of the femynyn gendere? **1632** MARMION *Holland's Leaguer* III. iv, Here's a woman! The soul of Hercules has got into her. She has a spirit, is more masculine Than the first gender. **1709** LADY M. W. MONTAGU *Let. to Mrs. Wortley* lxvi. 108 Of the fair sex.. my only consolation for being of that gender has been the assurance it gave me of never being married to any one among them. **1896** *Daily News* 17 July 6/4 As to one's success in the work one does, surely that is not a question of gender either.

b. In mod. (esp. feminist) use, a euphemism for the sex of a human being, often intended to emphasize the social and cultural, as opposed to the biological, distinctions between the sexes. Freq. *attrib.*

1963 A. COMFORT *Sex in Society* ii. 42 The gender role learned by the age of two years is for most individuals almost irreversible, even if it runs counter to the physical sex of the subject. **1969** *Erickson Educ. Found. Newslet.* Spring 1/1 The Erickson Educational Foundation has been called upon to function in gender identity areas needing service not otherwise supplied. **1972** A. OAKLEY *Sex, Gender & Society* viii. 189 Sex differences may be 'natural', but gender differences have their source in culture. **1981** *Heresies* XII. 67/3 Our ideology and practice of sex roles construct.. two mutually exclusive categories, that is, genders. **1985** *Times Lit. Suppl.* 5 Apr. 378/4 Without threatening gender models, she produced poetry good enough to praise. **1985** *Times* 2 Sept. 12/5 It is the tradition.. that Christ is present and acts through all the sacraments, and is present and active also in various other ministrations of the church... There is nothing gender-specific to those. **1986** *Financial Times* 15 Apr. 8/4 It was most important.. that schools could intervene in and modify the education of a child regardless of race, gender or class background.

†**4.** Product, offspring, generation. *Obs. rare.*

1637 BASTWICK *Litany* II. 9 Such a gender of filth that great frog left behind him. **1662** R. MATHEW *Unl. Alch.* §57. 66 This is to shew how they have been, and may be abused, in doing of which a most accursed gender of hell is born into the World.

5. Special Comb.: **gender-bender** *slang*, a person (esp. a pop singer or follower of a pop cult) who deliberately affects an androgynous appearance by wearing sexually ambiguous clothing, make-up, etc.; freq. *attrib.*; hence **gender-bending**; also ***gender-blender***, ***-blending***; **gender gap** chiefly *U.S.*, the difference in (esp. political) attitudes between men and women; cf. GAP *sb.*[1] 6 a.

1980 *Economist* 27 Dec. 48 The cult hallows ambiguous sexuality: Mr David Bowie, the rock star '*gender bender', is a key hero. **1984** *Sunday Mirror* 22 Jan. 10/3 Gender Bender boys are mad about make-up and adore dressing up ... Gender Benders are anything but gay. They make up and dress up out of a sense of fashion. **1986** *Observer* 13 July 25/3 Boy George became ubiquitous, first announcing himself as an outrageous dresser of ambiguous sexuality—Gender Bender in Fleet-speak. **1984** *Ibid.* 11 Mar. 47/1 This '*gender-bending', as it has been dubbed, is not news in the world of popular music. **1983** *Washington Post* 6 Mar. H6/3 Boy George, with his urban beachcomber look and *gender-blender confusions, manages to fit in and stand out. **1985** *TV Guide* (Canada) 28 Sept. 12/1 *Tootsie*.. is one gender-blender comedy with more going for it than the standard drag gags. **1984** *Washington Post* 11 Mar. G1 Not to mention all those other socio-pop labels—*gender-blending, drag, cross-dressing—that have sprung up in the wake of Michael Jackson, Boy George [etc.]. **1977** D. MORRIS *Manwatching* 230 They argue that the *gender gap belongs to man's ancient past and is no longer relevant in the modern world. **1982** *Newsweek* 4 Oct. 19/2 The White House is opening the loophole to help close the 'gender gap'—data that show women are disproportionately dubious about administration policies.

gender (ˈdʒɛndə(r)), *v.* Forms: 4-6 gendre, 5 gendyr, 6 gendur, *Sc.* gen(n)er, 4- **gender**. [a. OF. *gendrer*, *genrer*, ad. L. *generāre* to beget, f. *gener-*, *genus* race, breed: see GENDER *sb.*]

1. *trans.* Of parents (male or female, or both): To beget, engender, produce (offspring). *arch.*

13.. *E.E. Allit. P.* B. 300 He had þre þryuen sunez.. þe Iolef Iapheth watz gendered þe þryd. **1382** WYCLIF *Hos.* v. 7 In the Lord thei trespassiden, for thei gendriden [L. *genuerunt*] Alien sonys. *a* **1450** *Knt. de la Tour* (1868) 66 And the squier had not gendered on her no childe. *c* **1500** *Melusine* xxxvi. 246 He faught ayenst a knight, that was gendred with a spyryte in a medowe nygh by Lusynen. **1583** STANYHURST *Æneis* I. (Arb.) 26 Heere thre hundred wynters shal raigne Knight Hector his ofspring, By Mars fyrye fatherd twyns tyl the Queene Ilia gender. **1757** W. WILKIE *Epigon.* I. 20 Pards gender pards; from tigers tigers spring. **1850** BLACKIE *Æschylus* I. 24 Fair Morn be gendered from boon mother Night!

absol. *c* **1330** R. BRUNNE *Chron. Wace* (Rolls) 7333 So waxynge folk.. In no lond scholde men fynde, Ne selcouþloker so to gendre, Ne haue so manye childre tendre. **1387** TREVISA *Higden* (Rolls) I. 81 þese Pigmei geten children and gendreþ [L. *generant*] in þe fourþe ȝere. **1398** —— *Barth. De P.R.* XIII. xxvi. (1495) 459 Though fysshe gendre and is gendred, yet no manere kynde of fysshe haue gendrynge stones. **1513** DOUGLAS *Æneis* x. Prol. 38 Quhilk souerane substans.. Nowther generis, generat is, nor doith proceid. **1577-95** *Descr. Isles Scotl.* in Skene *Celtic Scotl.* (1880) III. App. 431 Mony fisches resortis and hantis thairto and generis within the same. **1658** tr. *Porta's Nat. Mag.* I. xii. 18 An Hare.. genders every month.

†**2.** *intr.* To copulate. *Obs.*

1486 *Bk. St. Albans* E iv b, Then shall the Roobucke gendre with the Roo. *c* **1510** *Gesta Rom.* Add. Stor. xxviii. 442 Yᵉ nyghtyngale vsed to sytte vpon a tree.. where as her make.. came and gendred with her. **1526** *Pilgr. Perf.* (W. de W. 1531) 202 b, Yᵉ bee, which neuer gendreth with ony make of his kynde. **1599** H. BUTTES *Dyets drie Dinner* I vij, In the beginning of winter, the wilde swine gender; and about the prime of the spring they pigge. **1634** T. JOHNSON *Parey's Chirurg.* II. (1678) 40 [Elephants] never gender but in private, out of sight.

3. *trans.* †**a.** To produce by natural processes, generate (heat, odours, etc.). *Obs.* **b.** To give rise to, bring about, produce, engender (a feeling, state, etc.) *arch.*

a. **1398** TREVISA *Barth. De P.R.* XIX. iii. (1495) 861 Hete gendryth clerenesse and bryghtnesse. **1432-50** tr. *Higden* (Rolls) I. 151 The principalle floode of Lydia is callede Pactolus gendrenge [L. *gignens*] gravel of golde. **1450-1530** *Myrr. our Ladye* 303 There are gendered tempastes of weder and hayle. **1477** NORTON *Ord. Alch.* v. in Ashm. (1652) 71 And when Evill substance shall putrifie, Horrible Odour is gendred thereby. **1548** GEST *Let. to Cecil* in H. G. Dugdale *Life* App. (1840) 147 Every thing is genered by yᵉ wordes of God yᵗ he ones spoke, encrease & fill yᵉ earth. **1653** H. MORE *Antid. agst. Atheism* (1662) II. ix. 68 For what life or phansie has the Earth, which, as they say, gendred at first all Animals, some still?

b. *c* **1450** *Cov. Myst.* (Shaks. Soc.) 61 Yf thou use oftyn tyme to swere, It may gendyr custom in the. **1508** DUNBAR *Tua mariit Wemen* 316 Neuer bot in a gentill hert is generit ony ruth. **1549** *Compl. Scot.* v. 34 Oure smal resistance generis grit hardynes in the aduerse party of oure saul. **1611** BIBLE *2 Tim.* ii. 23 Foolish and vnlearned questions auoid, knowing that they doe gender strifes. **1813** SCOTT *Rokeby* v. xxxi, With all the agony that e'er Was gendered 'twixt suspense and fear, She watched the line of windows tall. **1856** JOS. YOUNG *Demonology* III. vi. 254 They are calculated to gender mental disquietude or slavish fear.

†**4.** *intr.* To be produced, come into being. *Obs.*

1722 SEWEL *Hist. Quakers* (1795) II. VII. 18 Though darkness gather together on a heap and tempests gender.

Hence **ˈgendering** *ppl. a.* Also †**ˈgenderable** *a.* = GENERABLE; **ˈgenderer**.

c **1330** R. BRUNNE *Chron. Wace* (Rolls) 7329 So waxynge folk.. Ne so gendryng [*v.r.* genderand], ne so plentyue.. In no lond scholde men fynde. **1382** WYCLIF *Zech.* xiii. 3 His fadir and modir, gendrers of hym [L. *genitores ejus*]. **1398** TREVISA *Barth. De P.R.* x. i. (1495) 371 Thinges that ben corruptible and genderable. **1854** Gendering [see GESTATE *a.*].

†**ˈgendering**, *vbl. sb.* *Obs.* [f. prec. + -ING[1].] The action of the verb GENDER; begetting, breeding. ***gendering again***: regeneration.

1382 WYCLIF *Matt.* xix. 28 In regeneracioun, or gendrynge aȝein.. ȝe shulen sitt on twelue setis. **1393** LANGL. *P. Pl.* C. XIV. 144 Reson ich seih sothliche suwen alle bestes In etynge, in drynkyng in gendrynge of kynde. *c* **1449** PECOCK *Repr.* I. vii. 34 We schulden be continent and mesurable in deedis of gendring. **1483** *Cath. Angl.* 153/1 A Genderynge, *genitura* (A. *coitus*).

attrib. **1387** TREVISA *Higden* (Rolls) II. 189 Plinius.. seiþ þat som men beeþ i-gete and i-bore wiþ gendrynge stones cleuynge togidres as it were al oon. **1880** *N. & Q.* 6th Ser. I. 311/2 It [a frog supposed to be in a woman's stomach] al'us started croakin' every spring at generin' time.

genderless (ˈdʒɛndəlɛs), *a.* *Gram.* [f. GENDER *sb.* + -LESS.] Without distinction of gender.

1887 *Advance* (Chicago) 6 Jan. 7 Literarians are still in search of a genderless pronoun of the third person singular. **1893** SAYCE *Higher Critic.* (1894) 96 Purat was formed like Ashtoreth by the addition of the Semitic feminine suffix (*-t*) from the genderless Accado-Sumerian Pura.

gendral, obs. form of GENERAL.

†**ˈgendrure**. *Obs.* [a. OF. *gendreure*, *(en)gendrure*, med.L. *generātūra*.] Engendering, begetting.

c **1330** R. BRUNNE *Chron. Wace* (Rolls) 7347 Mo childre þer are of oure gendrure þan bestes are in oure pasture. **1388** WYCLIF *Job* xl. 12 He [behemoth] streyneth his tail as a cedre, the senewis of his stones of gendrure [L. *testiculorum*] ben folded together.

gene[1] (dʒiːn). *Biol.* [a. G. *gen* (W. Johannsen *Elem. d. exacten Erblichkeitslehre* (1909) 124), irreg. f. Gr. γεν- (see -GEN).] Each of the units of heredity which (except for polygenes) may be regarded as the controlling agents in the expression of single phenotypic characters and are usu. segments of a chromosome at fixed positions relative to each other; they were orig. defined as ultimate units of mutation and recombination, but are now best regarded as sequences of nucleotides within nucleic acid molecules each of which determines the primary structure of some protein or polypeptide molecule.

The term *gene* is used indiscriminately for both a genetic locus and an allele.

1911 W. JOHANNSEN in *Amer. Naturalist* XLV. 132, I have proposed the terms 'gene' and 'genotype'.. to be used in the science of genetics. The 'gene' is nothing but a very applicable little word, easily combined with others, and hence it may be useful as an expression for the 'unit-factors', 'elements' or 'allelomorphs' in the gametes, demonstrated by modern Mendelian researches. **1917** T. H. MORGAN in *Ibid.* LI. 520 The linkage relations of genes.. have a very important bearing on the problem of the localization of genes in the germ plasm. **1925** *Nation* 3 Oct. 19/1 If.. in a given kind of plant there is a single 'factor' for flower colour and the flowers are blue or yellow, the gamete will bear either the blue factor (gene) or the yellow one, not both. **1930** G. R. DE BEER *Embryol. & Evol.* iii. 21 By introducing into an egg containing a weak female-producing gene a sperm containing a strong male-producing gene (as may be done by crossing moths of different races), it is possible to convert would-be females into males more or less completely. **1946** *Nature* 6 July 30/2 The evidence indicates that resistance to blight is controlled by major genes, though minor genes determine the degree of susceptibility in susceptible varieties. **1955** *Sci. Amer.* July 74/2 Heredity is determined by the chromosomes, the threadlike bodies in the nucleus of the cell, and by their subunits the genes. **1964** G. H. HAGGIS et al. *Introd. Molecular Biol.* x. 260 The functional genes turn out to occupy a much greater chromosomal length than the genes defined by mutation or recombination. **1971** *Sci. Amer.* Aug. 52/1 When we speak of genes, we usually have in mind the hereditary material —the DNA—in the chromosomes of the cell nucleus. Yet genes are also found outside the nucleus in the cytoplasm, notably in association with chloroplasts and mitochondria.

2. *attrib.* and *Comb.*, as **gene bank**, a collection of different kinds of living cells, plants, or animals maintained as a repository of genetic material, esp. for developing new varieties or breeds or safeguarding the survival of existing ones; **gene frequency** (see quot. 1968); **gene mutation**, a mutation in which the change is confined to a single gene; **gene pool**, the stock of different genes in a breeding population.

1964 *Nature* 11 Apr. 132/2 The Zoological Society of London.. has set aside an area.. to establish small flocks and herds which are to be bred under expert guidance... Great efforts will be made to ensure the success of this scheme—the *Gene Bank. **1971** *New Scientist* 13 May 413/2 With animals, zoos may provide a last gene bank for species which cannot be protected in their natural habitats. **1980** *Daily Tel.* 16 Jan. 8/3 A unique gene bank to prevent vegetable seeds with valuable disease resistance being lost for ever, is to be established in a joint Government-Oxfam venture. **1930** R. A. FISHER *Genet. Theory Nat. Selection* i. 10 Even relatively intense selection will change the ratio *p:q* of the *gene frequencies relatively slowly. **1968** R. RIEGER *Gloss. Genetics & Cytogenetics* 170 *Gene frequency*, the proportion of one particular type of allele to the total of all alleles at this genetic locus in a breeding population. **1928** *Daily Tel.* 11 Sept. 8/2 Whether X-rays could produce '*gene mutations'. **1930** R. A. FISHER *Genet. Theory Nat. Selection* iii. 49 Gene-mutation.. consists in a change in a single hereditary particle, or gene, into a gene of a new type. **1950** T. DOBZHANSKY in *Amer. Naturalist* LXXXIV. 404 Every sexual species accordingly possesses a *gene pool, in which each gene may be represented by a certain number of alleles, and each chromosome by one or more structural variants. **1959** *New Biol.* XXVIII. 90 Sexual reproduction provides such a mechanism in allowing gene-recombination; but.. if unlimited in its scope it would inhibit diversification by randomizing the 'gene pool' in each generation. **1970** *Times* 29 Dec. 10/6 There is a necessity to conserve a wide range of different genes in the 'gene pool' from which new strains can be selected.

‖**gêne**[2] (ʒɛn). [Fr., f. OF. *gehine* torture (*gehir* to confess under torture): cf. OHG. *jehan* to speak, say.] Constraint, embarrassment, discomfort.

1817 H. C. CAMPBELL *Jrnl.* 17 Oct. in *Journey to Florence* (1951) 108, I dislike seeing such things in a crowd particularly in an English one. There is a certain *gêne* which they always occasion. **1853** LYTTON *My Novel* II. VII. xxi. 283 This will prevent a great deal of *gêne* and constraint. **1914** WODEHOUSE *Man Upstairs* 257 The advent of an unbidden guest rarely fails to produce a certain *gêne*. **1953** R. A. KNOX *Off Record* p. ix, He is condemned to listen to one side of a telephone conversation, with something of the *gêne* which that exercise entails.

‖**gêné** (ʒene), *a.* Also fem. **gênée**. [Fr., pa. pple. of *gêner* to embarrass; cf. prec.] Constrained, embarrassed, discomforted. Also as *v. trans.*, to make (someone) feel *gêné*; so **gêné(e)d** *ppl. a.*

1806 *Wynne Diaries* (1940) III. 301 Mrs. Bishop seemed gênée, we played at Loo, and were very merry all the Evening. **1817** H. C. CAMPBELL *Jrnl.* 4 Oct. in *Journey to Florence* (1951) 102 A few people came in the evening. I felt geneed not having been in company for some time. **1823** BYRON *Don Juan* XIII. ciii. 106 But none were 'gêné'. **1851** E. RUSKIN *Let.* 25 Nov. in M. Lutyens *Effie in Venice* (1965) 219 He is very good and well bred and.. they don't see how gened he is. **1929** E. BOWEN *Last Sept.* I. viii. 91 She looked gênée, dispirited.

geneagenesis (ˌdʒɛniːəˈdʒɛnɪsɪs). [f. Gr. γενεά race, stock + γένεσις generation.] Alternation of generation (see ALTERNATE 2 b).

So **ˌgeneageˈnetic** [cf. GENETIC] *a.*, pertaining to geneagenesis.

1864 H. LAWSON tr. *De Quatrefages' Metamorph.* Transl. Pref. 8 In the following pages the author has.. reduced all the varieties of generation to one common law, which he has termed Genea-genesis. The expression itself, simply meaning the development of generations, does not involve a theory, although it is associated with one. *Ibid.* xvi. 166, I have been endeavouring to show how the knowledge of geneagenetic phenomena was gradually arrived at.

†**geneˈaloger**. *Obs. rare.* [f. Gr. γενεᾱλόγος (L. *geneālog-us*: see GENEALOGY) + -ER[1].] A genealogist.

1630-1 FULLER *Comm. on Ruth* i. 1. (1654) 2 One of the Ends is, to shew the Pedigree of our Saviour, otherwise Genealogers had been at a loss, for four or five Descents in the deducing thereof. *a* **1727** NEWTON *Chronol. Amended* Introd. (1728) 2 One of the best Genealogers.

† **genea·logial**, *a. Obs. rare*⁻¹. [f. GENEALOGY + -AL¹.] = GENEALOGICAL.

1447 BOKENHAM *Seyntys* (Roxb.) 45 For more cler undurstondynge Of this genealogyal descencyoun.

genealogic (ˌdʒɛniːəˈlɒdʒɪk, dʒiː-), *a.* [ad. F. *généalogique*, ad. med.L. *geneālogic-us*, a. Gr. γενεαλογικός, f. γενεαλόγ-ος: see GENEALOGY.] = GENEALOGICAL.

1765 H. WALPOLE *Vertue's Anecd. Paint.* III. i. 15 He [Hondius] also engraved a genealogic chart of the Houses of York and Lancaster. **1788** —— *Remin.* ii. 19 Genealogic purity of blood is the predominant folly of Germany. **1797** W. TAYLOR in *Monthly Rev.* XXIV. 189 The genealogic, and perhaps the medallic, parts of the history display accuracy. **1820** BYRON *Mar. Fal.* III. ii. 493 'Tis mine to.. strike the blow, Which shall..hew the highest genealogic trees Down to the earth. **1833** CARLYLE *Cagliostro* in *Misc. Ess.* (1888) V. 118 To get at those genealogic documents, he has been obliged to invent some story. **1879** HEARN *Aryan Househo.* v. 139 The pure genealogic clan which *bonâ fide* springs, or believes that it springs, from some common ancestor.

genealogical (ˌdʒɛniːəˈlɒdʒɪkəl, dʒiː-), *a.* [f. as prec. + -AL¹.] That belongs to genealogy, or that traces family descent. ***genealogical tree***: a table exhibiting the relation of ancestors to descendants under the form of a tree with spreading branches; also, a table showing the descent of animal species from a supposed common origin.

1577–87 HOLINSHED *Chron.* VI. x. I. 141 Which genealogicall recapitulation in their nationall families and tribes, other people also haue observed. **1610** HEALEY *St. Aug. Citie of God* 585 Hee begat the sonne who is enranked in this genealogicall rolle. **1685** BAXTER *Paraphr. N.T., Luke* iii. 23–38 The Genealogical Controversies I pass by. **1815** SCOTT *Guy M.* ii, His genealogical tree..bore heathen fruit of yet darker ages. **1818** COBBETT *Pol. Reg.* XXXIII. 70, I shall begin to trace backward the branches of my own genealogical tree. **1846** GROTE *Greece* I. xviii. II. 9 It bears every mark of being the primitive view originally presented by the genealogical poets. **1870** LOWELL *Among my Bks.* Ser. I. (1873) 212 There is a kind of genealogical necessity in the character..Hamlet seems the natural result of the mixture of father and mother in his temperament.

Hence ˌ**genea·logically** *adv.*

1656 J. HARRINGTON *Oceana* (1658) 146 Solon having found the Athenians neither Locally nor Genealogically, but by their different wayes of life divided into four Tribes ..instituted a new distribution of them. **1858** CARLYLE *Fredk. Gt.* x. iii. II. 615 After whom a second Brother, father of the now Serene Strelitzes;—who also is genealogically notable. **1865** MAX MÜLLER *Chips* (1880) I. i. 21 Languages are now classified genealogically, i.e. according to their real relationship.

genealogist (dʒɛniːˈælədʒɪst, dʒiː-). [f. as prec. + -IST.] One who traces the descent of persons, or who is interested in the study of genealogies.

1605 CAMDEN *Rem.* 125 Likewise Ralph Gernon marrying the daughter of Cavendish..left that name to his issue, as Th. Talbot, a learned Genealogist hath prooved. **1631** WEEVER *Anc. Fun. Mon.* 543 A great Genealogist. **1698** VANBRUGH *Æsop* III. xv, Sir, I'm a genealogist. **1725** *Lond. Gaz.* No. 6382/3 The Genealogist of the Order [of the Bath]. **1804** W. TENNANT *Ind. Recreat.* (ed. 2) I. 120 A person versant in their family genealogy, is employed by the parents on both sides..the rank and merits of each family, are fully discussed by these genealogists. **1845** DARWIN *Voy. Nat.* xviii. (1879) 430 One old man, who appeared a perfect genealogist, illustrated the successive possessors by bits of stick driven into the ground. **1873** BURTON *Hist. Scot.* VI. xlv. 34 The most expert genealogist could not have made a family-tree out of such materials.

genealogize (dʒɛniːˈælədʒaɪz, dʒiː-), *v.* [f. as prec. + -IZE.] **a.** *trans.* To draw up a genealogy of. **b.** *intr.* To trace the descent of persons or families; to make out genealogies.

1602 WARNER *Alb. Eng.* XIII. lxxvii. (1612) 318 How many pennes genealogize their Godheads from their bearthes? **1621** AINSWORTH *Annot. Pentat., Num.* i. 18 They declared their Genealogie, of what Tribe and family every man came: or, they were Genealogized, that is, were numbered. **1669** GALE *Crt. Gentiles* I. III. vi. 68 Deucalion and Pyrrha; of whom men are wont to Mythologise and Genealogise. **1794** T. TAYLOR *Pausanias* I. 341, I have perused..all that Cinæthon and Asius have genealogized in verse. **1837** SOUTHEY *Doctor* IV. 44 Leaving, however, Sir William Gell to genealogize, if he pleases, as elaborately as he has topographized [etc.]. **1861** F. HALL in *Jrnl. Asiat. Soc. Bengal* 147 If Professor Lassen had read, in Hiouen-Thsang, less than two pages after that in which Buddhagupta is genealogized, he would have seen reason [etc.].

Hence **gene·alogizing** *vbl. sb.*; **gene·alogizer**.

1774 WARTON *Hist. Eng. Poetry* (1778) II. 178 *note*, In the same rage of genealogising, Alban..framed the Descent of Jesus Christ from Adam. **1775** W. BUCHANAN *Inq. Anc. Scot. Surnames* (1820) 28 The more modern method of genealogising. **1846** GROTE *Greece* I. xi. I. 279 Two names.. appear to be mere duplication..placed there by genealogisers for the purpose of filling up what seemed to them a chronological chasm.

† **genealogue.** *Obs. rare*⁻¹. = GENEALOGY I.

1586 WARNER *Alb. Eng.* IV. xxii. (1589) 99 Of whose Coniunction in the Crowne, the Genealogue is thus.

genealogy (dʒɛniːˈælədʒɪ, dʒiː-). Forms: 3 genialogi, geneologi, -elogi, 4 -ologi, (5 genealogye, 6 -loge, -logy, *Sc.* genol(l)igie), 4–6 genelogie, (5 -gy), 6 genalogey, 4–7 genealogie, (5–6 -gye), 4– genealogy. [a. OF. *gene(a)logie* (F. *généalogie*), ad. late L. *geneālogia*, a. Gr. γενεαλογία tracing of descent, f. γενεαλόγος (whence L. *geneālogus*) genealogist, f. γενεά race, generation + -λόγος that treats of: see -LOGY.]

1. An account of one's descent from an ancestor or ancestors, by enumeration of the intermediate persons; a pedigree.

a **1300** *Cursor M.* 7846 Tuix abraham and king daui, Yee herken nov þe geneologi. **1382** WYCLIF *1 Tim.* i. 4 Nethir ȝyue tent to fablis and genologies withouten endes. *c* **1440** *York Myst.* xxv. 242 Of Juda come owre kyng so gent..þe Genolagye beres witnesse on. **1494** FABYAN *Chron.* VI. clxxiv. 170 And for the genelogy of Charlys the Conquerour ..maye the clerelyer appere..I shal [etc.]. **1589** PUTTENHAM *Eng. Poesie* I. xii. (Arb.) 43 The Poets first commended them [the gods] by their genealogies or pedegrees. **1683** *Brit. Spec.* Pref. 6 King James..whose genealogy from Cadwalladar I have here set down. *a* **1750** MIDDLETON *Reflections* Wks. 1752 II. 24 The two different genealogies of our Saviour's family. **1867** PEARSON *Hist. Eng.* I. 12 The early mention of genealogies in the Welsh laws is proof of the importance attached to noble birth. **1882** CUSSANS *Her.* xxi. (ed. 3) 281 A copious record..is commonly called a Genealogy; but when the names only are inserted..it is usually styled a Pedigree. Both words, however, are frequently used in the same signification.

fig. **1577** tr. *Bullinger's Decades* (1592) 486 Hee doth.. shew vs the genealogie, that is, the beginning and proceeding of sinne. **1793** BEDDOES *Math. Evid.* 170 They have reversed the progress of language, both in the formation of words and the genealogy of significations.

b. *Biol.* The line of development of an animal or plant from older forms.

1880 HAUGHTON *Phys. Geog.* vi. 284 The true Horse appears in the Upper Pliocene, and completes the genealogy of the horse.

† **2.** Lineage, pedigree, family stock. *Obs.*

a **1300** *Cursor M.* 5602 A man was of his genelogi Fro him bot to þe toþer kne. *c* **1440** *York Myst.* xxx. 29 Was nevir juge in þis Jurie of so jocounde generacion Nor of so joifull genolgie to gentrys enjoyned. **1447** BOKENHAM *Seyntys* (Roxb.) 29 Me thynkyth it best for me Ageyn to returne in to Italye..For ther is the issu of my genealogy. *a* **1533** LD. BERNERS *Huon* xiv. 38 With Amaury was is next frendes, all issuyd of yᵉ genalogey of Gannelon. **1549** *Compl. Scot.* Ep. 2 Illustir princes, engendrit of magnanime genoligie, & discendit of Royal progenituris.

† **3.** Progeny, offspring. *Obs.*

1513 DOUGLAS *Æneis* V. xii. 131 Thair sall thow lern all thi genealogy, And what cetie is to the destany. **1768** STERNE *Sent. Journ.* (1778) II. 187 *(Supper)*, Five or six sons and sons-in-law and their several wives, and a joyous genealogy out of them.

4. The investigation of family pedigrees, viewed as a department of study or knowledge.

1768–74 TUCKER *Lt. Nat.* (1852) II. 466 Genealogy and chronology can scarcely be called sciences.

Hence † **gene·alogied** *pa. pple.*, traced back in line of descent. *rare*⁻¹.

1611 BROUGHTON *Require of Agreem.* Ep. Ded. 9 Iesus, Mary, Ely are Luc. 3. genealogied, not Ioseph.

genearch (ˈdʒɛnɪɑːk). [a. Gr. γενεάρχης founder of a family, f. γενεά race + -άρχης: cf. GENARCHA.] The chief or head of a family or tribe.

1727 in BAILEY vol. II. **1860** in WORCESTER; and in mod. Dicts.

geneat (gɪˈniːt, jɛˈneːat). *Hist.* [repr. OE. *ȝenéat* = OS. *genôt* (Du. *genoot*), OHG. *ginôz* (MHG. *genôz*), also *ginôzo* (MHG. *genôze*, mod.Ger. *genosse*), ON. *nautr*:—OTeut. **ga-nauto-z*, f. **neut-* (OE. *néotan* to enjoy, use). The original sense is companion, follower, esp. in war; in OE. the word was also in use as a legal term = vassal, tenant.] A retainer, vassal; one who holds lands of a superior either by service or payment of rent.

[*a* **900** *O.E. Chron.* (Parker MS.) an. 897 Æðelferð cynges ȝeneat. *c* **1050** *Gloss.* in Wr.-Wülcker 422/20 *Inquilinis* [sic] ȝeneat. *Ibid.* 466/11 *Parasitis*, ȝeneatum, ȝesoþum (? *read* ȝesiþum).] **1861** PEARSON *Early & Mid. Ages Eng.* I. 201 The tenants, cotsetlas, geburs, and geneats, were the highest among the semiservile. **1872** E. W. ROBERTSON *Hist. Ess.* 101 The right of the husbandman was a share right, his name was Geneat or sharer in the vill.

b. *attrib.*, as ***geneat-land***.

[*c* **1000** *Laws of Eadgar* II. c. i. (Schmid), Æȝðer ȝe of þeȝenes in-lande ȝe of ȝeneat-lande.] **1892** F. SEEBOHM in *Hist. Rev.* July 458 In each manor there is the same division into land in demesne and land in villainage, the inland and the geneat land.

genecology (dʒɛn-, dʒiːniːˈkɒlədʒɪ). *Biol.* [f. Gr. γέν-ος race + ECOLOGY.] The study of genetic differences between related species, and populations of a species, in relation to the environment. Hence **geneco·logic**, **geneco·logical** *adjs.*

1923 G. TURESSON in *Hereditas* IV. 172 It seems appropriate for several reasons to denote this study of species-ecology by the term *genecology*..as distinct from the ecology of the individual organism, for which the old term autecology seems to be the adequate expression. **1928** B. D. JACKSON *Gloss. Bot. Terms* (ed. 4) 439/2 Genecological. **1947** R. F. DAUBENMIRE *Plants & Environment* x. 366 *(heading)* The genecologic classification. **1963** DAVIS & HEYWOOD *Princ. Angiosperm Taxon.* xii. 398 Genecological differentiation has been found to be especially common in trees. *Ibid.* 401 The basis of genecology..is the observation that this intra-specific variability can be demonstrated to be of genetic origin and is not randomly dispersed throughout the species range, but is distributed in such a way that neighbouring plants tend to resemble one another.

genelogi(e, geneologi, obs. ff. GENEALOGY.

† **geneoglosse**: see GENIO-.

geneper, genepre, obs. forms of JUNIPER.

gener, obs. Sc. form of GENDER *v.*

genera, pl. of GENUS.

generable (ˈdʒɛnərəb(ə)l), *a.* See also GENDERABLE. [ad. L. *generābilis* that may produce or be produced, f. *generāre*: see GENERATE *v.* and -ABLE.]

1. That may be generated or produced (chiefly in phrase ***generable and corruptible***).

[**1398**: see GENDERABLE.] *c* **1450** HENRYSON *Test. Cres.* 170 Juppiter..God of the starnis in the firmament And nureis to all thingis generabill. **1589** PUTTENHAM *Eng. Poesie* I. iv. (Arb.) 25 They [poets] were the first obseruers of all naturall causes and effects in the things generable and corruptible. **1628** JACKSON *Creed* VI. I. i. §1 If every particular man or body generable haue precedent causes of their beings, their whole generations must of necessity have some cause. **1692** BENTLEY *Boyle Lect.* vi. 196 The forms of particular worlds are generable and corruptible. **1822** T. TAYLOR *Apuleius* 262 For the generable and corruptible portion of the world is comprehended indeed by the lunar sphere. **1962** S. R. LEVIN *Ling. Struct. Poetry* ii. 11 Many poetic sequences are generable by the kind of grammar constructed for ordinary language, but some are not.

† **2.** That may generate or produce. *Obs. rare.*

1633 JASP. FISHER *Fuimus Troes* II. vi. D iij, Thou Queene of Heauen..the source of generable moysture.

Hence **genera·bility**, ·**generableness**. *rare.*

1708 H. DODWELL *Nat. Mortality Humane Souls* 7 The World, from the Generability and Corruptibility of which he proves the Mortality of Humane Souls. **1727** BAILEY vol. II, *Generableness*, capableness of being generated. **1800** J. JOHNSTONE *On Madness* Pref. 7 The genealogy of the passions, the origin of ideas, and the generability of mind.

generacio(u)n, -yon: obs. ff. GENERATION.

general (ˈdʒɛnərəl), *a.* and *sb.* Forms: 3–6 generale, 4–8 generall(e, (5 gendral), 3– general. [a. OF. *general* (mod.F. *général*), ad. L. *generāl-is*, f. *gener-* GENUS, class, kind, race. The word has been adopted in most of the European langs.: Pr., Sp. *géneral*, Pg. *general*, *geral*, It. *generale*, Ger. *general*, as sb. and in composition (with adj. sense), also *generell*, as adj., Du. *generaal*.

The primary sense of the Latin adj. is thus 'pertaining to the (whole) kind or class'. The word is somewhat rare in classical Latin; in the later lang., when *genus* and *species* (after the Aristotelian γένος and εἶδος) had become familiar as the technical terms for classes respectively of greater and less extension, *generalis* came to be often used in contrast to *specialis*; the antithetic use of the two words remains in all the European langs.]

A. *adj.*

1. a. Including, participated in by, involving, or affecting, all, or nearly all, the parts of a specified whole, or the persons or things to which there is an implied reference; completely or approximately universal within implied limits; opposed to ***partial*** or ***particular***. ***general average***: see AVERAGE *sb.*² 4. ***general health***, the state of health of the body as a whole, or of a community. ***general paralysis***: see PARALYSIS.

1340 *Ayenb.* 14 þe tuelfte article is to leue þe general arizinge of bodye. **1389** *Eng. Gilds* 52 Also ordeynd it was, be on assente of þe fraternite, þᵗ þe general day schulde ben helde [vppon] þe feste of reliques. **1398** TREVISA *Barth. De P.R.* XVIII. lxxxviii. (1495) 837 Wherto grete multytude is of lyce in a body it is ofte take of generall corrupcion. *c* **1400** *Sowdone Bab.* 295 Thai made assaite [*sic*] then generalle. **1583** STUBBES *Anat. Abus.* II. (1882) 86 The generall resurrection at the last day. **1659** B. HARRIS *Parival's Iron Age* 125 He wanted but the getting of one General Battel. **1665** MANLEY *Grotius' Low-C. Warres* 387 The Cities of the Netherlands, made it their general Request..that [etc.]. **1707** in Picton *L'pool Munic. Rec.* (1886) II. 9 The Earl of Derby being elected Mayor, the Aldʳmen and Councell signify'd the same to his Lordᵖᵖ by a general letter. **1712** ADDISON *Spect.* No. 523 ¶7 The time of a general peace is, in all appearance, drawing near. **1732** BERKELEY *Alciphr.* I. §15 Is not the general Good of Mankind to be regarded as [etc.]? **1738** SWIFT *Polite Conv.* i. 31 All the World knows, that Mr. Spruce is a general Lover. **1738** *Lucca's Mem.* 95 Those vast Lands or Hills of Gravel, were undoubtedly left by the general Deluge. **1771** MRS. GRIFFITH tr. *Viaud's Shipwreck* 47, I returned..and was received with a general shout of joy. **1786** BURKE *W. Hastings* Wks. 1842 II. 192 A general rebellion and revolt for the utter extirpation of the English nation. **1818** JAS. MILL *Brit. India* III. vi. i. 8 The remaining chiefs..immediately broke into general discord. **1819** in A. Clarke *Ess. Dis. Skin* (1821) v. 97 It does not seem to hurt my general health; my appetite is good. **1820** SCORESBY *Acc. Arctic Reg.* II. 359 A large whale, harpooned from a boat belonging to the same ship, became the subject of a general share. **1833** ALISON *Hist. Europe* i. §64 (1849–50) I. 108 Fruitless struggles of partial freedom with general servitude. **1847** GROTE *Greece* II. xlii. (1862) III. 504 He determined on a general battle forthwith. **1849** MACAULAY *Hist. Eng.* ii. I. 202 The English government, lately an object of general contempt. **1870** *Food Jrnl.* 1 Mar. 67 So numerous are the forms which charitable relief assumes, that it would be next to impossible to analyse their separate influence on the general health. **1874** GREEN *Short Hist.* v. §1. 212 The tendency to a general use of the national tongue told powerfully on literature. **1879** *Man. Artill. Exerc.* III. 69 Attentions to the comforts of the men will..add to their general health. **1899** *Daily News* 11 May 4/1 Although my general health, to use a well-known phrase, is wonderfully good, I seem indeed..to fear being kept here too long. **1903** *Westm. Gaz.* 26 Mar. 9/2 His leg wound did not heal well, and this, with his poor general health, greatly depressed him. **1951** E. M. GRAVELIUS *Brit. Red Cross Nursing Man.* (ed. 9) xx. 240 The general health plays an important part in the recovery from skin complaints.

†**b.** Pertaining in common to various persons or things. Const. *to*. *Obs.*

c **1380** WYCLIF *Wks.* (1880) 43 A general mynystre and seruaunt of al þe breþerhed. **1559** W. CUNNINGHAM *Cosmogr. Glasse* 47 Th' Earth is round, causing vs & them not to haue one generall Horizent. **1631** WIDDOWES *Nat. Philos.* (ed. 2) 2 Accidents are..generall to all things, as motion, time, and place, for these belong to all. **1667** MILTON *P.L.* IV. 144 Our general Sire. *Ibid.* 492 So spake our general Mother.

c. With collect. or pl. sb.: All, all collectively, whole. *Obs.* exc. in ***general body***.

1591 SHAKS. *1 Hen. VI*, IV. iv. 3 All our generall force, Might with a sally of the very Towne Be buckled with. **1605** —— *Lear* I. iv. 65 A great abatement of kindnesse appeares as well in the generall dependants, as in the Duke himselfe. **1606** —— *Tr. & Cr.* v. ii. 132 Criticks, apt without a theame For deprauation, to square the generall sex By Cressids rule. **1725** POPE *Odyss.* XXIV. 230 The gen'ral sex shall suffer in her shame. **1874** GREEN *Short Hist.* iv. §2. 171 A fixed sum ..apportioned by their own magistrates among the general body of the burghers.

2. a. Concerned with, or established for, the whole of a certain territory or organization; opposed to *local*, *sectional*, etc. In early use chiefly of deliberative bodies, as in ***general chapter***, ***council*** (see COUNCIL 2). ***general American***, a form of U.S. speech without marked dialectal or regional characteristics; ***General Certificate of Education***, an examination set by each of a group of examining boards for pupils in secondary school in England and Wales; also, the certificate awarded to those who pass this examination; cf. *G.C.E.* (s.v. G III); ***general circulation***, (*a*) (see quot. 1928); (*b*) 'circulation, as of a newspaper, among readers not confined to a narrow class in business or interests' (Webster 1909); ***general election***: one in which representatives are elected by every constituency; opposed to ***by-election***; ***general headquarters***, the headquarters of the commander-in-chief; ***general meeting***, a meeting which all members of a society or other organization may attend; ***general quarters***, in the navy, the stationing of all hands, and the making of preparations, as if for an encounter with the enemy; also *attrib.* (as ***general-quarter***); ***general reserve*** (see quot.); ***general semantics***, 'a doctrine and educational discipline due to Alfred Korzybski (1879–1950) intended to improve the habits of response of human beings to their environment and one another esp. by training in the better and more critical uses of words and other symbols' (Webster 1961); ***general strike***, (*a*) a strike of all the workers of one industry; (*b*) a concerted strike by workmen of all or most of the important trades and occupations of a country with a view to securing some common object by the stoppage of business; ***spec.*** that in Britain in 1926; ***general ticket*** (U.S.): the system by which the whole list of candidates for the representation, e.g. of a state or city, is voted upon by the undivided body of electors (= F. *scrutin de liste*).

1934 WEBSTER, Introd. p. xxvi/1 In America three main types of cultivated speech are distinguishable:..(3) the variously named Western, Midwestern, or General American. *Ibid.*, The fact that more speakers in the English-speaking world habitually use the General American than any other single type cannot vitiate the standing of the Southern British..for the educated Englishman. **1947** C. K. THOMAS *Introd. Phonetics Amer. Eng.* xxii. 171 Eastern New England, the New York City area, the South, and the General American area clearly speak according to..different standards. *Ibid.* 172 The New York City area..has a population verging on ten million; General American,..a population of over eighty million. **1964** *Listener* 16 Apr. 634/3 What is called general American —a more-or-less middle-western accent. **1947** *Examinations Secondary Schools* (Rep. Second. School Exam. Council) 6 It is because the 'Ordinary' and 'Advanced' papers have fundamentally the same qualifying purpose..and because we wish them to be available to candidates who are not 'at school' that we have proposed the single certificate and offered the title 'General Certificate of Education'. *Ibid.* 8 A 'General Certificate of Education' should be awarded showing the subjects (and the level—'Ordinary' or 'Advanced'—in each subject) in which the candidate has satisfied the examiners. **1955** *Times* 28 June 5/3 It is hoped to establish courses leading to the General Certificate of Education, for pupils who need the G.C.E. to qualify for professional training. *c* **1290** *Beket* 1498 in *S. Eng. Leg.* I. 149 Greye Monekes of Cistevs fram ȝere to ȝere A Chapitre makeden generale of Abbodes þat þere were; For euerech Abbod of greie Monekes to þulke chapitle cam. **1899** *Q. Jrnl. R. Meteorol. Soc.* XXV. 166 Schemes and discussions concerning the general circulation of the atmosphere. **1926** N. SHAW *Man. Meteorol.* I. 291 Dove rendered a signal service to the observational representation of the general circulation by producing monthly maps of isotherms of the globe. **1928** D. BRUNT *Meteorol.* iv. 26 When we draw charts on which are represented, at a large number of stations, the most frequently occurring wind directions.., we find the movement of the winds of the globe form a system which is much simpler in appearance than might have been expected by one accustomed only to the variability of weather in the British Isles. This system is called the 'general circulation' of the atmosphere. **1297** R. GLOUC. (Rolls) 10172 þis bissopes..conceil made general. **1538** STARKEY *England* I. iv. 124 Els we schold haue veray oft general counsellys. **1778** A. HAMILTON *Wks.* (1886) VII. 539 Arguments to you, Sir, need not be multiplied to enforce the necessity of having a good general council. **1813** WELLINGTON *Let. to Brisbane* 18 Aug. in Gurw. *Desp.* (1838) XI. 10, I have to inform the General court martial that [etc.]. **1872** CLODE *Milit. & Mart. Law* ii. 33 'For the better administration of Justice', the Code [of 1666] established.. a 'General Court-martial' for offences punishable with life or limb. *c* **1375** *Sc. Leg. Saints, Barnabas* 15 He callit paule ..& mad hyme doctor generale, to preche in þis varld hale. **1800** J. JAY *Corr. & Pub. Papers* (1893) IV. 266 The approaching general election in this State will be unusually animated. **1849** MACAULAY *Hist. Eng.* ii. I. 174 Early in 1661 took place a general election. **1791** G. WASHINGTON *Lett. Writ.* 1892 XII. 33 The States individually are omitting no occasion to intermeddle in matters, which belong to the general government. **1837** HT. MARTINEAU *Soc. Amer.* II. 66 The expenses of the general government are so small that [etc.]. **1859** *War in Italy* 54 The infantry of the guard followed general head-quarters to Castenedolo. *Ibid.*, General head-quarters..moved to Montechiaro. **1914** *Times* 3 Oct. 8/2 The Press Bureau..issued the following descriptive account, which has been communicated by an eye-witness present with General Headquarters. **1894** G. FINDLAY *Eng. Railway* 13 The executive management of the line is carried on by a General Manager, etc. **1782** R. GOADBY *Life B.M. Carew* 11 Their general meetings at stated times, which they are all obliged to be present at. **1812** *Dramatic Censor for 1811* 419 The Committee, therefore, might be left..to call a General Meeting when they might deem such a proceeding necessary. **1900** *Westm. Gaz.* 5 Mar. 9/2 On every 'general-quarter' day, in my last ship. **1919** W. LANG *Sea Lawyer's Log* vi. 61 When the bugle sounds 'General Quarters', the prelude to action. **1918** E. S. FARROW *Dict. Mil. Terms* 259 *General reserve*, a reserve retained in the hands of the general officer commanding of the whole force until required. **1933** A. KORZYBSKI (*title*) Science and sanity. An introduction to non-Aristotelian systems and general semantics. **1951** *Essays & Studies* IV. 119 The term 'General Semantics' was used by the late Alfred Korzybski for a kind of linguistic therapy quite unrelated to technical linguistics. **1670** *Act 22 Chas. II*, c. 14 Preamb., A Generall Sessions of Sewers holden at Spalding. **1810**, **1830** General strike [see STRIKE *sb.* 9]. **1902** *Encycl. Brit.* XXXIII. 26/1 In 1891 a general strike took place in the German printing trade. **1924** J. F. BRYANT *Gandhi & Indianisation* 72 His methods were tinged with the ideas of Passive Resistance and the General Strike. **1926** *Hansard, Commons* 3 May 71, I do not think all the leaders when they assented to ordering a general strike fully realised that they were threatening the basis of ordered government. **1952** *Chambers's Encycl. World Survey* 215 A general strike of textile workers took place in Bombay and towards the end of the period notice of a general strike on the Indian railways was given. **1954** B. & R. NORTH tr. *Duverger's Pol. Parties* I. i. 15 General Strikes of 1891 and 1893 in Belgium; of 1902 and 1908 in Sweden. **1971** A. BULLOCK *20th Cent.* iii. 72/1 The failure of the General Strike in 1926 marked the defeat of the militants in the British Labour movement. **1800** T. JEFFERSON *Writ.* (Ford) VII. 401 On the subject of an election by a general ticket, or by districts, most persons.. seem to have made up their minds. **1888** BRYCE *Amer. Commw.* I. I. xxv. 385 *note*, The presidential electors being now chosen, in each State, by 'general ticket', not in districts.

b. (*a*) ***General Post Office***, † ***General Letter Office***: the office established in London in 1660 for the collection and dispatch of letters to all parts of the three kingdoms.

[**1591**: cf. *Postes Generall* under 10.] **1660** *Act 12 Chas. II*, c. 35 §1 Whereas for the..prevention of many Inconveniences happening by private Posts severall publique Post Offices have beene heretofore erected..To the end thereof that the same may be managed soe that speedy and safe dispatches may be had, which is most likely to be effected by erecting one Generall Post Office..Be it therefore enacted..that there be from henceforth one Generall Letter Office erected and established in some convenient place within the City of London from whence all Letters..may be with speede..sent unto any part of the Kingdomes of England, Scotland and Ireland [etc.]. **1675** *Lond. Gaz.* No. 1006/4 A Post will go every night..from the General Post-Office in London to Windsor. **1676** *Ibid.* No. 1081/4 During His Majesties stay at Newmarket, a Post will go thither every Night about 10 a Clock from the General Letter Office in London. **1708** *Ibid.* No. 4451/3 The Post will go to and from the General Post-Office in London and Tunbridge every Day in the Week.

(*b*) ***General Post***: formerly, the post or mail that was sent from the General Post Office in London, originally on certain days, latterly once a day, to all the post offices in the kingdom (opposed to the local 'penny' or 'two-penny' post); hence the first delivery in the morning is still officially designated ***the G.P.*** or ***General Post delivery***. †Also *attrib.*, as ***general-post-day***, ***general postman*** (opposed to 'penny' or 'twopenny' postman), ***general post-office*** (an office which receives letters for the 'general post'). '***General Post***' is also the name of a game, in which each player is called by the name of a place to which letters are supposed to be sent; also *fig.*, a general and rapid exchange or interchange of positions, etc.

1707 [see POST *sb.*[2] 5 a]. **1755** *Man* No. 13. 5 That I may not interfere with the penny-post, the general-post, or the news-men, I propose to receive no parcel that does not outweigh a pound. **1767** BURKE *Corr.* (1844) I. 130 Have the goodness to write me a line on general-post days, how you all go on. **1806** R. CUMBERLAND *Mem.* (1807) II. 179 Between the arrival of the general post and its departure there is an interval of twelve hours. **1837** DICKENS *Pickw.* ii, Like a general postman's coat. *Ibid.* xxxiii, Sam not forgetting to drop his letter into a general post-office as they walked along. **1838** DICKENS *Nickleby* i. 2 There came one morning, by the general post, a black-bordered letter. **1839** THACKERAY *Fatal Boots* xi, I..became a general postman! **1889** K. GREENAWAY *Bk. Games* 63 General Post. One person is selected as 'postman' and blindfolded, the others all take the names of different places, except one, who is chosen the leader, and has a written list of the places chosen by the players. **1898** A. B. GOMME *Games for Parlour & Playgr.* 51 An occasional call of 'General Post' by the leader, when all players must change their seats, gives a good chance to the blind man. **1941** A. L. ROWSE *Tudor Cornwall* xii. 307 They were..instituted to other livings; in effect, it meant a sort of general post of the affected clergy. **1954** M. BERESFORD *Lost Villages* vi. 213 In this general post the land-use of much of the Midlands, the grassy shires, could be considered afresh. **1969** I. & P. OPIE *Children's Games* vi. 209 The party game known variously as 'General Post', 'Move All' [etc.].

c. *Mil.* ***general orders*** (see quot. 1867).

1867 SMYTH *Sailor's Word-bk.*, *General orders*, the orders issued by the commander-in-chief of the forces. **1879** TOURGEE *Fool's Err.* iv. 18 He has been..gazetted for gallant conduct, and general orders and reports have contained his name.

3. †= CATHOLIC 5 (*obs.*). Also, in the modern translations of the N.T., used for CATHOLIC 4, interpreted as meaning 'addressed to all'.

1380 *Lay Folks Catech.* (Lamb. MS.) 306 We schul trow þat þer ys general chirche. *c* **1394** *P. Pl. Crede* 816 In þe heiȝe holly gost holly y beleue, and generall holy chirche. **1611** BIBLE, The Generall Epistle of Iames.

4. a. Pertaining to, shared by, or current among the majority or a considerable part of the community; prevalent, widespread, usual.

1390 GOWER *Conf.* I. 364 Which sinne [homicide] is nowe so generall. *c* **1400** MAUNDEV. (Roxb.) Pref. 2 It es lang tyme passed sen þare was any general passage ouer þe see in to þe haly land. **1535** COVERDALE *Eccl.* vi. 1 There is yet a plage vnder yᵉ Sonne, and it is a general thinge amonge men. **1613** PURCHAS *Pilgrimage* (1614) 907 These dances are generall thorow America. **1623** in *Crt. & Times Jas. I* (1849) II. 369 It [the report] came to town on Tuesday night, and was general all Wednesday. **1750** JOHNSON *Rambler* No. 71 ¶9 This general forgetfulness of the fragility of life. **1752** MASON *Elfrida* Introd. Lett. ii. p. v, A Writer of Tragedy must certainly adapt himself more to the general taste. **1794** PALEY *Evid.* (1825) II. 377 It was a general but erroneous opinion of those times. **1822** R. G. WALLACE *15 Yrs. Ind.* Advt. 5 Arrowsmith's new map is now in such general circulation that [etc.]. **1856** FROUDE *Hist. Eng.* (1858) I. i. 65 A proof..of Henry's confidence in the general attachment of his subjects. **1875** FORTNUM *Majolica* iii. 34 The use of the white stanniferous enamel did not become general in Italy until [etc.]. **1885** *Manch. Exam.* 15 May 5/3 Lord R. Churchill's latest escapade..is the theme of general remark.

b. ***in a general way***: ordinarily, usually.

1745 P. THOMAS *Voy. S. Seas* 144 Nor does this Distemper, in a general Way, incline People to Indolence, till [etc.].

5. a. Not specifically limited or determined in application; relating or applicable to a whole class of objects, cases, or occasions.

In *general confession*, *general pardon* (see the sbs.) the adj. varies between this sense and sense 1.

c **1380** WYCLIF *Sel. Wks.* III. 441 þai say furst, þat speciale prayere aplied by hor prelatis is better þen generale. *c* **1391** CHAUCER *Astrol.* II. §2 This chapitre is so general euer in on, þat ther nedith no more declaracion. **1405** *Rolls Parlt.* III. 605/1 Henry Boynton [etc.] our generalls and specialls Attornes and Deputes. *c* **1449** PECOCK *Repr.* IV. ix. 471 In a larger and generaler fourme. **1581** SIDNEY *Apol. Poetrie* (Arb.) 33 The Historian..is..tyed..to the particular truth of things, and not to the general reason of things. **1628** WITHER *Brit. Rememb.* II. 839 From acts particular None should conclusions generall inferre. **1687** DRYDEN *Hind & P.* Pref. §1 No general characters of parties..can be so fully and exactly drawn, as to comprehend all the several members of'em. **1697** DAMPIER *Voy.* I. 27 After we had answered these general questions, they began to be more particular. **1727** DE FOE *Prot. Monast.* 6 He gave me a general Invitation to come one Day or other and take a Dinner with him. **1751** JORTIN *Serm.* (1771) VII. ii. 29 These are some of the general directions which reason suggests with respect to God and man. **1801** G. ROSE *Diaries* (1860) I. 293 The conversation was quite general. **1818** CRUISE *Digest* (ed. 2) II. 464 The first words being general, the putting afterwards of a particular case will make no difference. **1833** I. TAYLOR *Fanat.* v. 124 What is special we can see; what is general escapes our notice. **1841** MYERS *Cath. Th.* III. §3. 8 Divine communications of a form the most general and of a character the most direct. **1890** BOWEN in *Law Times Rep.* LXIII. 690/1 It seems to me that the judge really intended to give the plaintiff the general costs of the action.

b. Of a rule, law, principle, formula, description: Applicable to a variety of cases; true or purporting to be true for all or most of the cases which come under its terms. In late use often with implied opposition to *universal* (with which in the older examples it is nearly synonymous): True in most instances, but not without exceptions.

c **1391** CHAUCER *Astrol.* Contents ¶5 The general rewles of theorik in Astrologie. **1486** *Bk. St. Albans* B j a, Bot that other Rewle is gendral [*ed.* **1496** generall]. **1563** FULKE *Meteors* (1640) 2 b, It is a generall rule, that that which is once a thing, cannot by changing become nothing. **1638** F.

JUNIUS *Paint. of Ancients* 224 There is another generall rule for our Invention propounded by Tullie. **1657** R. LIGON *Barbadoes* (1673) 53 Yet no rule so general but hath his acception [*i.e.* exception]. **1732** POPE *Ess. Man* I. 142 The first Almighty Cause Acts not by partial, but by gen'rall Laws. **1853** LYTTON *My Novel* x. xx, I guess you are right there, as a general rule. **1891** *Law Times* XCI. 405/2 They ..should have general principles to guide them.

c. Of a word, name, etc.: Applicable to each of the individuals or species forming a class or genus; in *Logic* = COMMON 17 a. Of a concept, notion: Including only those features that are common to the individuals of a class, to the neglect of the points in which they differ.

1551 T. WILSON *Logike* C iij b, The Predicamentes, called in Englishe Generall wordes. **1581** E. CAMPION in *Confer.* III. (1584) Y, It must not be..taken for a speciall substance, but *genericè*, for a generall being. **1690** LOCKE *Hum. Und.* III. iii. (1695) 227 How came we by general Terms, or where find we those general Natures they are supposed to stand for? **1732** BERKELEY *Alciphr.* VII. §7 Words become general by representing an indefinite number of particular ideas. **1785** REID *Int. Powers* 432 Every substantive that has a plural number is a general word. **1803** *Naval Chron.* X. 111 In..India we feed our horses with a species of vetch..; Europeans call it by the general name of gram. **1822** I. TAYLOR *Elem. Th.* 31 An indistinct remembrance formed by several similar objects is called a general notion. **1843** MILL *Logic* I. ii. §3 A general name is one which can be predicated of each individual of a multitude. **1870** JEVONS *Elem. Logic* iii. 18 General terms..are applicable in the same sense equally to any one of an indefinite number of objects which resemble each other in certain qualities. **1875** FORTNUM *Majolica* ii. 20 The general term..Majolica, has long been and is still erroneously applied to all varieties of glazed earthenware of Italian origin.

d. *Law.* ***general issue, general tail*** (†***tail general***) (see quots.).

1574 tr. *Littleton's Tenures* 4 b, Tenant in taile general is, where landes or tenements been geeven to a man and to hys heires of his body begotten. **1628** COKE *On Litt.* 26 a, If tenements be giuen..to the heires of the body of the man; In this case the husband hath an estate in generall taile. **1768** BLACKSTONE *Comm.* III. 305 These pleas are called the general issue, because, by importing an absolute and general denial of what is alleged in the declaration, they amount at once to an issue.

e. *Math.*, *Cryst.*, etc. (See quots.)

1823 H. J. BROOKE *Introd. Crystallogr.* 258 General symbol $\mathrm{p}^{\mathrm{P}}_{\mathrm{A}}\mathrm{p}$, represents the classes *e*, *f*, & *g*. If $p > 1$, the symbol represents *class f*. [etc.]. **1858** TODHUNTER *Algebra* xxxvi. 291 This expression is called the general term, because by putting 1, 2, 3..successively for r, it gives us in succession the 2nd, 3rd, 4th..terms.

6. a. Prefixed to personal designations of function or employment: Not restricted to one department; concerned with, or skilled in, all the branches of one's business or pursuit: said, e.g. of a scholar, an artist. †Also, in 16–17th c., without any title of function: Widely accomplished (*obs.*). ***general dealer***: a merchant or shopkeeper who deals in many kinds of goods; similarly ***general merchant, agent***, etc. ***general practitioner*** (see quot. 1885); see also PRACTITIONER 1 b. ***general servant***: a maid-of-all-work.

1552 ASCHAM *Let.* 12 July in *Lett. Lit. Men* (Camden 1843) 12 Taking away such a general and onely man as Mr. Cheeke is. **1590** GREENE *Mourn. Garm.* 5 Thus wit augmented by experience, shall make me a generall man fitte any way to profite my common-wealth. **1601** HOLLAND *Pliny* II. 547 A general man he was like himselfe still, that is to say, his craftsmaster in all, and as good in one thing as another. **1655** STANLEY *Hist. Philos.* I. (1701) 51/1 Be general. **1658** W. SANDERSON *Graphice* 67 Hans Holbin who in all..Painting either in Oyle, Distemper, or Limning, was so generall an Artist, as never to follow any man, nor any one able to imitate him. **1697** DRYDEN *Virg.* Life (1721) I. 72 He became the most general Scholar that Rome ever bred. **1711** STEELE *Spect.* No. 2 ⁋3 A general Trader of good Sense, is pleasanter Company than a general Scholar. **1830** J. F. COOPER *Water Witch* II. i, A man whose misdeeds in commerce are as universally noted as the stoppage of a general dealer. **1844** G. RAYMOND *Mem. R. W. Elliston* I. xiv. 348 The general practitioner had an exceedingly pretty wife. **1859** DICKENS in *All Year Round* 13 Dec. 3/1 The general-dealer opposite..is opening his shop. **1879** *St. George's Hosp. Rep.* IX. 21 Nine females..were admitted for anæmia. Six were housemaids or general servants. **1885** *Syd. Soc. Lex.*, *General practitioner*, a medical practitioner who does not restrict himself to one branch of the profession. **1890** GROSS *Gild Merch.* I. 129 The company of merchants included both general dealers and such as traded in only one kind of wares. **1891** General dealer [see DEALER 3].

†**b.** Affable to all. (Associated with *free*; perh. a colloq. phrase.) *Obs.*

1596 *Edw. III*, II. i. 16 Bid her be free and general as the sun. **1611** B. JONSON *Catiline* I. i. C 4 a, Are you coying it, When I command you to be free, and generall To all? **1630** J. TAYLOR (Water P.) *Wks.* II. 107/1 She's generall, she's free, she's liberall Of hand and purse, she's open vnto all.

7. a. Not belonging to, or confined to, some limited or special class; miscellaneous. ***general knowledge***, knowledge of miscellaneous facts, information, etc. (cf. quot. 1860 under sense 8 a); ***general public***, the ordinary people; = PUBLIC *sb.* 1 b; ***general*** (***theory of***) ***relativity***: see RELATIVITY.

1639 tr. *Du Bosq's Compl. Woman* 23 To make good choice of those they meane to converse with more familiarly, and not to have a generall acquaintance with persons of al sorts. **1650** W. ROWE *Let. to Cromwell* 28 Dec. in Nickolls *St. Papers addr. Cromw.* (1743) 43, I have had some converse with him in general Society. **1808** J. WEBSTER *Nat. Phil.* 6 The general class of society has become more interested in its pursuit. **1820** HAZLITT in *London Mag.* II. 250/2 Books of liberal taste and general knowledge. **1822–34** *Good's Study Med.* (ed. 4) III. 297 Neither musk nor opium..has been found successful in general practice. **1824** SCOTT *St. Ronan's* vii, In general society, they are like commercial people in presence of their customers. **1834** G. CRABBE JR. in *Poetical Wks. G. Crabbe* I. iv. 97 The fund of general knowledge which my father gradually showed..much surprised his patron. **1851** *Illustr. Catal. Gt. Exhib.* 254 Platform weighing machine..Railways, and for general weighing in warehouses. **1854** J. E. MILLAIS *Let.* 10 May in M. Lutyens *Millais & Ruskins* (1967) 210 This is what a number of comfortable, portly, philosophers will say merely in direct opposition of the general public. **1862** H. SPENCER *First Princ.* I. iv. §24 Not very intelligible to the general reader. **1863** KINGSLEY *Water-Bab.* 316 Tom told him that he knew no general information. **1877** TYNDALL in *Daily News* 2 Oct. 2/4 Never..has this longing been more liberally responded to, both among men of science and the general public. **1895** *Law Times Rep.* LXXIII. 156/2 The Kirkmichael left Liverpool with a general cargo on board. **1906** *Daily Chron.* 25 Jan. 4/7 A Scriptural general knowlege paper. **1934** *Discovery* Nov. 317/2 When the general public finds that the railways are providing local services much faster and no dearer than motor bus companies,..it will begin to return..to the railway. **1938** F. B. YOUNG *Dr. Bradley Remembers* (1940) iii. 124 That same Act of Parliament..had decreed that a medical student, before registration, must first pass an examination in General Knowledge. **1952** G. RAVERAT *Period Piece* iv. 65 When I went away to school, [I] was asked in a General Knowledge Paper, which were my three favourite composers.

b. ***general shop, store*** (cf. *general dealer* in 6): one in which miscellaneous goods are sold. ***general ship*** (see quot. 1867).

1835 J. MARTIN *Descr. Virginia* 134 A neat village.. containing 16 dwelling houses, 3 general stores, 2 groceries. **1836** General shop [see STORE *sb.* 12 a]. **1851** *Lyttelton Times* (N.Z.) 17 May 7/3 He has opened a General Store. **1861** DICKENS *Gt. Expect.* I. vii. 92 Mr. Wopsle's great-aunt.. kept—in the same room—a little general shop. **1865** —— *Mut. Fr.* IV. vi. 206 At the general shop, at the butcher's and at the public house. **1867** SMYTH *Sailor's Word-bk.*, *General ship*, where persons unconnected with each other load goods on board, in contradistinction to a chartered ship. **1883** SIR W. B. BRETT in *Law Times Rep.* (1884) XLIX. 768/2 This.. is a ship taken up by the charterer for the purpose of carrying two or three different sorts of cargo, but it is not a general ship. **1948** *Bangor* (Maine) *Daily News* 28 July 1 Shopping at the general store here to replenish his food supply.

c. Freq. in phrases used *attrib.*, as ***general-fish, -produce, -purpose, -purposes, -utility.***

1860 *Leisure Hour* 10 May 294 These are the 'general utility' men, as they are sometimes facetiously called by those whose genius is not quite so versatile. **1888** J. C. HARRIS *Free Joe*, etc. 127 One of the many 'general-utility' men that improved methods enable the high schools and colleges to turn out. **1894** *Country Gentlemen's Catal.* 230/2 Patent general purpose drill. **1909** *Westm. Gaz.* 11 Feb. 3/3 The largest fruit and general produce merchants in New York. *Ibid.* 3 Apr. 16/4 As the president of this excellent club, he spoke of the good trout and general-fish waters it leased on the Surrey Wey. *Ibid.* 28 Aug. 16/4 The Thames is in good condition, and general-fish anglers are promised a continuance of sport. **1911** F. O. BOWER *Plant-Life* 58 It served as a general-purposes shoot. **1923** KIPLING *Land & Sea T.* 143 A general-utility shed. **1933** *Meccano Mag.* Mar. 193/1 It [*sc.* the 'Tiger' engine] has been designed for use in general purpose and torpedo-carrying aircraft. **1937** B. H. L. HART *Europe in Arms* x. 131 The plans of the General Staff were dominated by the idea of contributing a general-purpose force of three army corps to join the French field armies. **1966** *Listener* 3 Nov. 668/1 German's generation was content with one general-purposes 'olde' manner. **1968** FOX & MAYERS *Computing Methods* i. 7 The Runge-Kutta method..is a useful general-purpose routine for non-linear first-order equations.

8. a. Comprising, dealing with, or directed to the main elements, features, purposes, etc., with neglect of unimportant details or exceptions.

1563 FULKE *Meteors* (1640) 1 b, But first wee must be occupied a little in the generall description of the same, that afterward shall be particularly intreated of. **1580** SIDNEY *Arcadia* I. (1629) 21 Palladius hauing gotten his general knowledge of the party against whom, as he had already of the party for whom he was to fight, he [etc.]. **1590** SPENSER *F.Q.* Pref., The generall end therefore of all the booke is to fashion a gentleman or noble person in vertuous and gentle discipline. **1596** SHAKS. *1 Hen. IV*, II. iii. 23 My Lord of Yorke commends the plot, and the generall course of the action. **1651** HOBBES *Leviath.* II. xxvii. 160 The Law regardeth not the particular, but the general inclination of mankind. **1719** J. RICHARDSON *Art Criticism* 145 As in all the Stages of our Lives there is a General Resemblance. **1798** FERRIAR *Illustr. Sterne* iv. 119, I shall try to give the reader a general idea. **1820** SCORESBY *Acc. Arctic Reg.* I. 539 In its general form, it [the squalus borealis] very much resembles the dog-fish. **1851** *Illustr. Catal. Gt. Exhib.* 860 We should first obtain a general idea of the number and position of the several mountain ranges of India. **1860** TYNDALL *Glac.* I. xi. 74 A general knowledge was all that could be expected. **1865** MILL in *Morn. Star* 6 July, What I will do now is to give you an idea of the general tendency of my political opinions. **1880** GEIKIE *Phys. Geog.* v. 349 Climate..must follow the same general distribution over the earth's surface.

b. Not entering into details; indefinite, vague. Opposed to *precise*.

1601 J. MANNINGHAM *Diary* (Camden) 18 Counterfayting a letter as from his lady, in generall termes. **1729** BUTLER *Serm.* Wks. 1874 II. 135 Every man hath a general desire of his own happiness. **1824** SCOTT *St. Ronan's* v, Some general remarks on fishing and field-sports. **1884** *Manch. Exam.* 10 May 5/6 The dispute..was alluded to only in the most general and distant terms.

9. a. *Mil.* Prefixed to the designation of an officer to indicate superior rank and extended command. ***general officer***, one above the rank of colonel.

1576 J. SANFORD *Gard. Pleas.* 164 When Paulus Aemilius was generall Capytayne in Greece for the Romans. **1601** HOLLAND *Pliny* II. 483 Fabricius..forbad expressly, that any warriours and Generall captains should haue in plate more than one drinking boll or goblet, and a saltsellar. **1626** in Rushw. *Hist. Coll.* (1659) I. 303 General-Governor of the Seas and Ships of the said Kingdom. **1681** NEVILE *Plato Rediv.* 259 Chancellor, Judges, General Officers of an Army, and the like. **1710** *Lond. Gaz.* No. 4650/1 Then marched the Majors, Lieutenant-Colonels, Colonels, and General-Adjutants. **1781** in Simes *Mil. Guide* (ed. 3) 4 The inactivity of the greatest part of our General Officers, during a peace. **1844** *Regul. & Ord. Army* 53 The General Officers intrusted with the Command of Districts are responsible..for [etc.]. **1882** *Macm. Mag.* XLVI. 473 When the General Field-Marshal..was but a captain in the general staff.

b. Prefixed to the designation of a civil or legal functionary. *rare.*

1613 PURCHAS *Pilgrimage* (1614) 525 They have another generall Officer or chiefe Justice. **1714** *Fr. Bk. of Rates* 124 The 16th Article of the Lease of the General-Farmer as aforesaid.

10. Standing as the second member in many designations of military officers, as *adjutant-*, †*captain-*, *lieutenant-*, etc. *general*; of civil and legal officers, as *attorney-*, *controller-*, *governor-*, *master-*, *postmaster-*, *receiver-*, *solicitor-*, etc. *general*; also in *heir-general*, *States-General*, for all of which see the respective words; hence sometimes attached playfully to ordinary substantives.

1591 *Proclam.* in *App. Rep. Secret Committee P.O.* (1844) 36 Our Master of the Postes, or the Masters of the Postes Generall of those countreys. **1824** LADY GRANVILLE *Lett.* (1894) I. 285 The men are deplorable, which accounts for Mr. Chad being lover general at the Hague. **1878** MOULTON tr. *Winer's N.T. Gram.* III. liii. 543 The assumption that καί in the N.T., as ו in Hebrew, was the conjunction-general.

11. *absol.* in various adverbial phrases.

†**a. as to the general.** Generally. *Obs.*

1654 tr. *Scudery's Curia Pol.* 157 Although the Sea do give leave that some few Fountains do break up, and so water some places of the earth, yet she is unthankful as to the general, and leaveth many vast parts, for want of moisture, to be altogether steril and barren. **1744** ELIZA HEYWOOD *Female Spect.* (1748) I. 115 The maxim questionless is just as to the general, but [etc.]. **1745** *Ibid.* (1748) IV. 110 Now these reflections, however just as to the general, are certainly the contrary as to particulars.

†**b. for the general** (cf. Sp. *por lo general*). For the most part. *Obs.*

1615 SANDYS *Trav.* 77 The other halfe Iewes and Christians, and those for the generall Grecians. **1645** FULLER *Good Th. in Bad T.* (1841) 28 A loyal subject for the general, though he was no favourite in these particulars. **1751** WARBURTON *Lett.* (1809) 85 Booksellers..know mankind, for the general, better than authors. **1766** F. BLACKBURNE *Confessional* 31 The Doctors..for the general, have been so tame in the controversy, that [etc.].

c. in general. †(*a*) In a body, collectively; universally, without exception. *Obs.*

c **1374** CHAUCER *Troylus* I. 163 And to the temple, in al hir beste wyse, In general, ther wente many a wight. **1390** GOWER *Conf.* III. 1 The grete sinne originall, Which every man in general Upon his birth hath envenimed. *c* **1440** *Generydes* 1691 They dede his pleasure to obeye, Theder they came ichon in generall. *c* **1515** *Cocke Lorell's B.* (Percy Soc.) 7, I wyll reherse here in generall The indulgences that ye haue shall. **1576** FLEMING *Panopl. Epist.* 366 Let not the confidence of your friendes in general, be deceived. **1583** STUBBES *Anat. Abus.* II. (1882) 27 Commons..or free places of feeding for the poore and others, euen all in generall. **1606** SHAKS. *Tr. & Cr.* IV. v. 21 'Twere better she were kist in generall.

†(*b*) In all respects. *Obs.*

c **1374** CHAUCER *Troylus* v. 822 She..was..goodly of hir speche in general. **1608** SHAKS. *Per.* v. i. 185 Thou art a grave and noble counsellor, Most wise in general.

(*c*) Generally; with reference to the whole class of persons or things spoken of; with respect to a subject as a whole; opposed to *in particular*, *in special*.

1390 GOWER *Conf.* III. 170 As for to speke in generall. *c* **1491** *Chast. Goddes Chyld.* 2 As ferforth as I dare or know of temptacyons I will shewe you in specyall and in general. **1529** MORE *Dyaloge* I. Wks. 112/1 Somwhat wold I speke of Luther, & his secte ingenerall. **1570** BUCHANAN *Ane Admonit.* Wks. (1892) 22 Bayth to 3or l. [your lordships] in speciall and in generall to ye haill communitie. **1662** STILLINGFL. *Orig. Sacr.* II. vii. §1 Whether a Divine Law in generall, or the Law of Moses in particular may be abrogated. **1711** ADDISON *Spect.* No. 62 ⁋7 Which..is not so properly a Definition of Wit, as of good writing in general. **1712** W. ROGERS *Voy.* 318 The Air in general is mild, temperate and healthful. **1774** GOLDSM. *Nat. Hist.* (1776) VI. 317 Of Spinous Fishes in General. **1812** SIR H. DAVY *Chem. Philos.* 71 The expansive power of liquids in general is greater than that of solids. **1893** *Bookman* June 78/1 The appointment..gave great dissatisfaction to the English world of letters in general and to Cary in particular.

†(*d*) Without specific reference. *Obs.*

1621 BURTON *Anat. Mel.* I. iii. I. ii. (1651) 185 If two talk together..or tell a tale in generall, he thinks presently they mean him.

(*e*) For the most part; as a general rule; commonly, usually.

1726 G. SHELVOCKE *Voy.* (1757) 404 Our new visitors, who behaved themselves in general, very quietly. **1765** BLACKSTONE *Comm.* I. 191 It is in general hereditary, or descendible to the next heir, on the death or demise of the last proprietor. **1851** *Illustr. Catal. Gt. Exhib.* 963 The curled maple..is met with where the common or sugar maple grows, but in general more on rocky ground. **1863** H.

Cox *Instit.* III. viii. 703 Not [required] to serve abroad, nor in general to go out of their own counties.

d. in the general. Generally; in general terms; on a general view; in the main, without considering details or occasional exceptions; without specific reference or application. Somewhat *arch.*

1620 E. BLOUNT *Horæ Subsec.* 286 This course, in the generall, is to be esteemed..a prouident one. **1621** S. WARD *Happiness Pract.* (1627) 43 You haue said much in the generall of Doing: what say you in particular to this Nation? **1671** M. BRUCE *Good News in Evil Times* (1708) 4 As long as thou thinks [*sic*] it spoken in the General, or to another Person, thou can get no good of it. **1677** HALE *Prim. Orig. Man.* 289 This Opinion is in the general true. **1748** RICHARDSON *Clarissa* (1811) VII. 337 Your observation, in the general, is, undoubtedly, just. **1806** R. CUMBERLAND *Mem.* (1807) II. 203 It is only true in some partiuclar instances, not in the general. **1834** J. H. NEWMAN *Par. Serm.* (1837) I. xiii. 200 It is easy to speak of human nature as corrupt in the general. **1860** —— *Lett.* (1891) II. 105 What occurred in the event I recollect well enough in the general.

B. *sb.*

I. With reference to things, collective unities, etc.

†**1. a.** The adj. used *absol.* (see also A. 11): The total, the whole, or in weaker sense, the most part, the majority. *Obs.*

1606 SHAKS. *Tr. & Cr.* I. iii. 342 For the successe (Although particular) shall giue a scantling Of good or bad, vnto the Generall. **1608** TOPSELL *Serpents* (1658) 795 This must be understood of the general. **1670** G. H. *Hist. Cardinals* Pref. A iij, Nor is it to be expected the general will submit to a particular. **1771** MAD. D'ARBLAY *Early Diary* (1889) I. 131 The general of people at his time of life are confined by infirmities.

b. The people in general; the public; the multitude. *arch.*

1601 SHAKS. *Jul. C.* II. i. 12, I know no personall cause, to spurne at him, But for the generall. **1602** —— *Ham.* II. ii. 457 The Play I remember pleased not the Million, 'twas Cauiarie to the Generall. **1679** DRYDEN *Troilus* Ep. Ded., That which has been done already..must be digested into Rules and Method, before it can be profitable to the General. **1832** AUSTIN *Jurispr.* (1879) I. iv. 161 The.. individual persons who constitute that public or general to which my attention is directed. **1880** DISRAELI *Endym.* lxxviii, He..understood all about rolling stock and permanent ways, and sleepers and branch lines, which were then cabalistic terms to the general. **1897** *Sat. Rev.* 5 June 623/1 It has lessened the respect with which the House of Commons has hitherto been regarded by the general.

2. a. Something that is general; chiefly *pl.* general facts, notions, or principles; general propositions or statements, generalities; general points or heads; items of general news. Now *rare* (chiefly in express antithesis to *particulars*, etc.).

1566 T. STAPLETON *Ret. Untr. Jewel* III. 78 The deceitefull and wrangler walketh in generalles. **1581** CAMPION in *Confer.* II. (1584) H b, You must not bring a particular to ouerthrowe a generall. *a* **1598** ROLLOCK *Wks.* (Wodrow Soc.) II. ix. 107 No man will lay down fairer generals out of the Word of God. **1627** in *Crt. & Times Chas. I* (1848) I. 207 He desired to know his charge and accusers, but obtained no more at that time than this general, that [etc.]. *a* **1635** SIBBES in Spurgeon *Treas. Dav.* Ps. lxxxvii. 3 It is enough to give you the generals of the delights and excellencies of God's house. **1642** BRIDGE *Wound. Consc. Cured* i. 13 Then hee proceeds to propound three Generalls. **1646** A. HENDERSON in *Chas. I's Wks.* (1662) 173 Concerning the application of the Generalls of an Oath to the particular case now in hand. **1647** CLARENDON *Hist. Reb.* I. §11 Those Accusations..are commonly stuffed with many odious Generals, that the Proofs seldom make good. **1671** M. BRUCE *Good News in Evil Times* (1708) 57 Now there is only one General I shall here mark for a Preface, and it is this. That [etc.]. **1672** WILKINS *Nat. Relig.* 4 Reason..descendeth from generalles to specialles, and from them to particulars. **1703** PENN in *Pa. Hist. Soc. Mem.* IX. 270 To whom I refer thee as to generals and common news. **1754** RICHARDSON *Grandison* (1781) VI. xxii. 120 My memory serves but for a few generals; and those I will not trouble you with. **1773** MONBODDO *Language* (1774) I. I. i. 5 What therefore constitutes the essential part of language.. is the expression of generals, or ideas. **1793** BEDDOES *Math. Evid.* 43 That perversion of the human understanding, which the study of generals occasioned. **1794** J. HUTTON *Philos. Light*, etc. 142 The moment that an animal perceives in natural events a general, that moment natural philosophy is in his mind begun. **1804** W. TENNANT *Ind. Recreat.* (ed. 2) II. 183, I am abundantly sensible..of keeping too much to generals in my description of the Hindoo farming. **1838–9** HALLAM *Hist. Lit.* III. iii. III. §104. 90 It is by means of our knowledge of particulars that we ascend to generals. **1864** BOWEN *Logic* viii. 233 Individual truths are proved by deduction from these generals.

†**b.** A general view or description. *Obs.*

1611 SPEED *Th. Gt. Brit.* Index, Scotlands kingdome in one Generall.

†**c.** That which is common to all. *Obs.*

1606 SHAKS. *Tr. & Cr.* I. iii. 180 All our abilities, gifts, natures, shapes, Seuerals and generals of grace exact.

†**d.** *pl. Oxford University.* **to answer, do generals**: to take part in the disputations which corresponded to the examination now called Responsions. *Obs.*

1650 WOOD *Life* 5 Apr. (O.H.S.) I. 163 He answered Generals in the public schools, and James Bricknell opposed him. **1684** WILDING in *Collect.* (O.H.S.) I. 260 For doing Generalls..00 03 00. **1841** G. PEACOCK *Stat. Cambr.* 74 In the university of Oxford, before..1800..the *disputationes in Parviso* were called *doing generals.*

e. *U.S.* **great, small generals**: The general charges furnished respectively (*a*) by the owner of a fishing vessel, *e.g.* wood, water, knives, lights, salt, bait, etc.; (*b*) by the crew, *e.g.* provisions, lines, hooks, etc.

1889 in *Century Dict.*

†**3.** *Logic*, etc. = GENUS. *Obs.*

1551 T. WILSON *Logike* B v b, The chief general is so, that where as it is in the head of al & aboue al it can neuer become inferiour to be of any kinde or sort in thinges..The middle general, is the same that beyng comprehended betwixt the chief general and the lowest kinde or sort in thynges, maye be also some kynde or fourme it self. **1628** T. SPENCER *Logick* 131 The generall is either supreame, or inferior. The speciall is either middlemost, or lowest. **1705** C. PURSHALL *Mech. Macrocosm* 82 From the various Combinations..of these Particles..Result the Three Great Generals, viz. Animals, Vegitables, and Minerals.

†**4.** *Painting.* ? A ground colour. *Obs.*

1466 *Mann. & Househ. Exp.* (Roxb.) 212 My mastyr paid to the clerke of Herewyche for ij. li. generall to paynt wyth pavyses, iij. s. **1487–8** in Willis & Clark *Cambridge* (1886) I. 412, ij li de colore fuluo anglice generall. **1510** *Ibid.* II. 199 Certen coloures as in whiteled redled generall. **1545** *Rates Custom-ho.* B iij b, Generall the C pounde xs. *a* **1618** *Rates Merchandizes* D ij, Druggs vocat... Generall the pound vjd. **1662** *Stat. Ireland* (1765) II. 400 General the pound 1s.

5. *Mil.* Also in French form **générale, generale.** 'Formerly a beat of the drum for the assembly of all the troops preparatory to a march, battle, or action' (Voyle).

1706 PHILLIPS (ed. Kersey), A *General*..a Beat of Drum so call'd [etc.]. **1708** *Lond. Gaz.* No 4452/3 The French.. did not beat their General 'till three a Clock in the Afternoon. **1749** FIELDING *Tom Jones* VII. xv, But hark, the general beats. **1794** COLERIDGE *Robespierre* III, The dreadful generale Thunders through Paris. **1803** WELLINGTON *Let. to Marq. Wellesley* in Gurw. *Desp.* (1837) II. 394 *note*, The generale was beat at half-past four, the assembly at half-past five, and we marched immediately after. **1843** *Whistle Binkie* (Scot. Songs) (1890) II. 86 The drum has beat the General. *a* **1845** T. O. DAVIS *Battle-Eve of Brigade* 16 The *generale's* beating on many a drum.

II. As the designation of a person.

6. *Eccl.* The chief of a religious order.

More fully *superior-general* (q.v.); in early med.Lat. use we find *abbas generalis, magister generalis*, but the elliptical use of the adj. had already in the 12th c. given rise to *generalis* as a sb.

1561 DAUS tr. *Bullinger on Apoc.* (1573) 116 b, The master of the whole order [of Fryers minors], whom they call generall hath beene heard many tymes, to offer the Pope.. thirtie thousand fightyng men. **1579** FULKE *Heskins' Parl.* 382 He is an English man, generall or prouinciall of Friers preachers. **1601** *Imp. Consid. Sec. Priests* (1675) 70 It would seem a very strange matter to the Provincial or General of that Society. **1687** *Lond. Gaz.* No. 2263/1 The 6th Instant the Jesuits chose for the General of their Order, Father Thyrso Gonzales a Spaniard. *a* **1843** SOUTHEY *Comm.-pl. Bk.* Ser. II. (1849) 43 The blessed Jordan..who was the second general of the Dominicans [etc.]. **1869–70** H. VAUGHAN *Year Prepar. Vatican Council* iii. 17 After the Bishops came the mitred Abbots..with the Generals of the Religious Orders.

7. a. *Mil.* A general officer (see A 9); originally, the commander of the whole army, subsequently applied also to commanders of divisions. In mod. use, designating an officer as holding definite military rank, in which application it is also used as a title prefixed to the name (often written **Gen.**).

In the British army the word officially denotes an officer holding the rank next below that of field-marshal. In popular and untechnical use, it is extended to those of the two next lower grades LIEUTENANT-GENERAL and MAJOR-GENERAL; in these titles, and perh. in BRIGADIER-*general*, the second element of the compound is historically not the *sb.* but the *adj.*

1576 GASCOIGNE *Steele Gl.* (Arb.) 64 Pericles was..victor ..in nine great foughten fields, Wherof he was the general in charge. **1591** SHAKS. *1 Hen. VI*, v. ii. 7 Successe vnto our valiant Generall. **1601** —— *All's Well* III. iii. 1 The General of our horse thou art. **1646** BUCK *Rich. III*, II. 60 To..give the Earle, being Generall of his Forces, the Signall of a Combate. **1705** ADDISON *Campaign* 296 The War's old Art each private Soldier knows, And with a Gen'rals Love of Conquest glows. **1781** in Simes *Mil. Guide* (ed. 3) 5 Many of our Generals..are either dead, too old, or too infirm, to undergo the fatigues of war. **1824** W. IRVING *T. Traveller* I. 206, I was like a general looking down upon a place he expects to conquer. **1825** J. NEAL *Bro. Jonathan* III. 128 They spurred along..and led off their general in chief by main force from the field. **1886** SEELEY *Napoleon I*, vi. 228 It [Waterloo] was perhaps on both sides rather a soldiers' than a general's battle.

appositive. **1735** THOMSON *Liberty* IV. 699 Prevail'd the General-King, and Chieftain-Thanes.

transf. and *fig.* **1592** SHAKS. *Rom. & Jul.* v. iii. 219 Then will I be general of your woes, And lead you even to death. *c* **1600** —— *Sonn.* cliv, So the Generall of hot desire, Was sleeping by a Virgin hand disarm'd. **1613** PURCHAS *Pilgrimage* I. VII. iii. 560 The worthiest Generall..against Errour that ever we have had. **1893** FORBES-MITCHELL *Remin. Gt. Mutiny* 223 The provost-marshal's cat is the only general to restore order in times like those. **1897** *Pall Mall G.* 19 May 2/1 The fighting men in genuine strenuous party warfare are somebodies, and their generals understand and never fail to remember it.

b. With reference to the degree of skill in the command of an army; a tactician, strategist.

c **1615** FLETCHER *Mad Lover* I. i, A man indeed: a Generall Generall, A soule conceived a soldier. **1707** ADDISON *Pres. St. War* 23 The Generals on the Enemy's side..in the Eyes of their own Nation..are inferior to several that have formerly commanded the French armies. **1724** DE FOE *Mem. Cavalier* (1840) 271 He was a complete general. **1781** in Simes *Mil. Guide* (ed. 3) 5 It is experience that makes the General. **1843** PRESCOTT *Mexico* VII. v. (1864) 456 Cortez was certainly a great general. **1865** KINGSLEY *Herew.* xviii, He began praising his skill as a general.

c. General February, Fevrier, January, Janvier or **Winter**: personifications of wintry months, alluding to their effect upon military campaigns, etc.

1855 *Punch* 10 Mar. 95 Russia has two generals in whom she can confide—Generals Janvier and Fevrier. **1908** KIPLING *Lett. to Family* (1920) 159 Here, General January will stiffen him up. **1919** *Mr. Punch's Hist. Great War* 20 'General Janvier' is doing his worst, but our men are sticking it out though slush and slime. **1926** B. PARES *Hist. Russia* xviii. 339 Nicholas had placed his hopes in 'General January' and 'General February', that is to say in the severity of a Russian winter. **1966** A. FIRTH *Tall, Balding, Thirty-Five* v. 63 When the crunch came in 1941 he [*sc.* Stalin] owed a good deal to General Winter. **1967** D. G. CHANDLER *Campaigns Napoleon* XIV. lxxi. 815 Time was playing into the hands of the Russians by bringing 'General Winter' even closer.

d. The head of the Salvation Army; *spec.* General William Booth, its founder.

1883 *All about Salv. Army* 26 If the General were to be removed by death to-morrow, his successor, without a minute's delay, would step into his position. **1884** W. BOOTH *General's Lett.* (1890) 18 Go to the crowd of sinners, or spot them individually..because out of them you may make Lieutenants, and Captains, and Majors, and Generals. **1886** —— *Orders & Regul. Salv. Army* 165 The General must and will appoint his own successor—each successive General doing the same. **1959** *Chambers's Encycl.* XII. 177/1 The general..no longer has the right of nominating his successor.

†**8.** *Naut.* = ADMIRAL. Also **general of the sea, at (the) sea.** *Obs.*

1589 *Drake's W. Ind. Voy.* 5 The Generall commaunded all the Pinnaces with the ship boates to be manned. **1598** tr. *Linschoten* in Arb. *Garner* III. 15 A great navy of ships was prepared in Lisbon, whose General was the Marquis of Santa Cruz. **1600** E. BLOUNT tr. *Conestaggio* 25 Diego de Sosa was made generall at the sea. **1653** H. COGAN tr. *Pinto's Trav.* ii. 3 A Fleet of five Ships, whereof there was no General. **1660** CHAS. II in Clarendon *Hist. Reb.* XVI. §201 To Our Trusty and Well-beloved General Monk, and General Mountague, Generals at Sea, to be communicated to the Fleet. **1702** *Lond. Gaz.* No. 3829/2 The Count de Tholouse, Great Admiral of France, is made General of all the Naval Forces of Spain. **1717** tr. *Frezier's Voy. S. Sea* 198 The General of the Sea, or Admiral.

9. *colloq.* A general servant, a maid-of-all-work.

1884 *Pall Mall G.* 10 May 6/1 Poor little generals, fighting the daily fight against dirt and dust. **1889** *Athenæum* 2 Nov. 593/2 Liza is a true London 'general', not a Cornish lass, as her disloyalty to her young mistress shows.

general ('dʒɛnərəl), *v. rare.* (Cf. *out-general.*) [f. the sb.] *trans.* To act as a general to.

1849 C. BRONTE *Shirley* iii, Crime and the lost archangel generalled the ranks of Pharaoh. **1889** *Pall Mall G.* 1 Mar. 6/2 Mrs. Bancroft has not only arranged nearly every group, but she has literally generalled the whole into completeness.

generalate ('dʒɛnərəleɪt). Also 7 **general(l)at.** [f. GENERAL *sb.* + -ATE. Cf. F. *généralat.*]

1. The office of a general (ecclesiastical or military); the period during which a man holds this office.

1644 R. BAILLIE *Lett. & Jrnls.* (1841) II. 260 The House of Lords have passed the ordinance for Sir Thomas Fairfax's generallat. **1659** B. HARRIS *Parival's Iron Age* 124 Tilly takes the Generalate, against his will. **1858** FABER *Xavier* 410 With the intention..of resigning the generalate into his hands.

2. A district under the control or supervision of a general. Cf. GENERALSHIP 4.

1883 *Encycl. Brit.* XVI. 295/1 By the close of the 17th century there were three frontier 'generalates'—Carlstadt, Warasdin, and Petrinia.

generalcy ('dʒɛnərəlsɪ). [f. as prec. + -CY.]

a. Generals collectively. **b.** = GENERALATE 1.

1864 CARLYLE *Fredk. Gt.* IV. 7 A patent of Generalcy. **1865** *Ibid.* XVIII. vii. (1873) VII. 207 The high Generalcy.. mount in the highest haste. **1868** *Morn. Star* 10 Mar., The rebuff Mr. Johnson received from General George H. Thomas when he offered him a brevet-generalcy.

generale: see GENERAL B. 5 *sb.*

'**generaless.** *rare.* [f. GENERAL *sb.* + -ESS.]

1. A female general.

1837 CARLYLE *Fr. Rev.* I. VII. v, He hastily nominates or sanctions generalesses. **1883** *Harper's Mag* June 140/1 She forgot the..Amazons, and generalesses.

2. The wife of a general. *rare* (chiefly *jocular*).

1646 CROMWELL *Let.* 25 Oct., in *Carlyle* (1857) I. 212 My service and dear affections to the General and Generaless. **1888** *Univ. Rev.* Oct. 220 The Generaless had not long been dead when Bazaine..married a great Mexican heiress.

general hospital. [app. after F. *hôpital général*, the name of the hospital founded at Bicêtre, France, in 1656.] **a.** A hospital which does not confine itself to patients suffering from one particular class of disease or to those of a particular sex or age-group.

1737 (*title*) The plan and elevation of a new general hospital intended to be erected at Bath for the reception of 150 poor strangers. **1757** A. R. *Curiosities of Paris* iv. 62 General Hospital, is a small Distance from the City... They receive all Kinds of Patients upon Application, such as Women with Child, Foundlings, Orphans, and Lunatics.

1794 *Medical Extracts* II. 62 The air in the lowest ward in the General Hospital. **1803** *Guide Watering & Sea-Bathing Places* 44 The General Hospital..is open to the sick poor of the United Kingdom,..the inhabitants of Bath alone excepted. **1869** E. A. PARKES *Pract. Hygiene* (ed. 3) 333 In general hospitals a sanitary officer is to be appointed. **1880** *Encycl. Brit.* XII. 302/1 Hospitals are usually divided into General and Special. In General Hospitals cases of all kinds are admitted in some, whilst in others certain classes are excluded. **1966** R. P. SLOAN *Today's Hospital* i. 7 The trend is away from the 'special disease' hospital and toward the 'general' hospital assuming responsibility directly or indirectly for all physical or mental disabilities.

b. A military hospital receiving the sick and wounded from field hospitals.

1854 F. NIGHTINGALE *Let.* 15 Dec. in C. Woodham-Smith *F. Nightingale* (1950) ix. 183 The proportion of Roman Catholics..is already making an outcry... Dr. Menzies has declared that he will have two only in the General Hospital. **1863** *Good Words* Nov. 817/1 The army hospitals near Washington are of course full, and a general hospital has been lately established at Gettysburg. **1899** *Daily News* 27 Nov. 5/3 Large hospitals..known as 'general hospitals' (or 'base hospitals'), each accommodating 500 men and 20 officers... A large staff is necessary for the working of each 'general hospital'. **1914** *Times* 30 Oct. 10/1, 3rd Southern General Hospital, Oxford. **1964** W. R. M. DREW in F. N. L. Poynter *Evol. Hospitals in Brit.* 165 Altogether, there were nineteen bearer companies, twenty-eight field hospitals..and twenty-two general hospitals.

generali, obs. form of GENERALLY.

‖**generalia** (dʒɛnəˈreɪlɪə), *sb. pl.* [L., neut. pl. of *generālis* GENERAL *a.*] General principles.

1832 AUSTIN *Jurispr.* (1879) II. xliv. 784 Many or most of the generalia which are contained in the Law of Things are just as applicable to the status of governors as to any of those of the governed. **1843** MILL *Logic* II. VI. xi. §5. 620 A set of intermediate scientific truths..destined to serve as the generalia or first principles of the various arts.

ˌgeneraˈlific, *a. nonce-wd.* [f. GENERAL *a.* + -(I)FIC.] Making or producing what is general.

1825 COLERIDGE *Aids Refl.* (1848) I. 178 In strict and severe propriety of language I should have said *generalific* or *generific* rather than general.

generalism (ˈdʒɛnərəlɪz(ə)m). [f. GENERAL *sb.* + -ISM.] **a.** A general conclusion, generalization. **b.** A general statement, a platitude.

1809 D. P. WATTS in Southey *Life of A. Bell* (1844) II. 595, I offer my humble tribute of praise to your individual energy..and real patriotism; but 'one swallow makes no summer'. I refer to generalisms. **1861** R. F. BURTON *City of Saints* v. 319 He began with generalisms about humility, faithfulness [etc.]. **1862** THORNBURY *Turner* II. 348, I have also gathered together into one chapter as many as possible of his more valuable generalisms.

c. The fact or quality of generalizing; the actions, principles or qualities of a generalist (opp. SPECIALISM 1).

1908 *Times Lit. Suppl.* 13 Aug. 260/3 The essays..were, in their day, too good specimens of the best generalism to be of permanent value. **1963** *Times* 1 May 10/3 The Common Market was encouraging a European particularism..at just the time in history when speedy communications..required a free world generalism. **1968** *New Scientist* 3 Oct. 31/2 There is a need for a new brand of 'science-based generalism'.

‖**ˌgeneraˈlissima.** [*quasi*-It. fem. of next.] A female commander-in-chief.

1643 *Char. Oxf. Incend.* in *Harl. Misc.* (1745) V. 472/2 What, Henrietta Maria!.. The Irish Rebels call her their Generalissima. **1643** in *King's Cabinet Opened* (1645) 33 Harry Jermyn commands the forces which goe with mee.. Syr Alexander Lesley the foote under him..and her shee Majestie Generalissima. **1827** SOUTHEY *Penins. War* II. 682 The Valencians imputed their deliverance on this occasion to their Patroness and Generalissima, the Virgin. **1859** *Sat. Rev.* VIII. 71/1 The Virgin Mary..was appointed Generalissima.

‖**generalissimo** (dʒɛneraˈlissimo, ˌdʒɛnərəˈlɪsɪməʊ). [a. It. *generalissimo*, superl. of *generale* GENERAL.] The supreme commander of a combined force as well naval as military, or of several armies in the field.

1621 ROE *Let.* 7/17 Dec. in *Cabala* (1654) I. 158 They.. are returned to the Port, where Don Philibert of Savoy Generalissimo is present. **1647** E. BRABAZON *Let. to J. Moore* in *10th Rep. Hist. MSS. Comm.* App. IV. 83 Sr. Tho. Fairfax is lately voted Generalissimo of all the forces of England and Ireland. **1647** CLARENDON *Hist. Reb.* VIII. §258 That Commission of Generalissimo was likewise given to the Prince. **1756** NUGENT *Gr. Tour* III. 85 They chuse one of the nobility for generalissimo at sea. **1800** WEEMS *Washington* i. (1877) 6 His fame as Generalissimo of the armies and first President of the councils of his nation. **1878** SIMPSON *Sch. Shaks.* I. 90 Philip was then deeply engaged in the league against the Turk, of which his brother Don John of Austria was generalissimo.

transf. and *fig.* **1642** FULLER *Holy & Prof. St.* IV. xvii. 326 He acknowledgeth God the Generalissimo of all armies. **1645** PAGITT *Heresiogr.* (1647) 114 Mistris Hutchinson, the Generalissimo, the high Priestesse of the new religion. **1697** J. WOODWARD *Relig. Soc.* i. (1701) 11 The King..will enter the lists against profaneness and immorality, as the Generalissimo of those who join in this honourable work.

‖**generaˈlissimus.** *Obs.*$^{-1}$ [L., superl. of *generālis* GENERAL.] = prec.

1683 *Lond. Gaz.* No. 1803/2 It is said, That the Duke of Lorrain will command the Emperor's Forces this next Campaign, as Generalissimus. **1706** in PHILLIPS (ed. Kersey).

generalist (ˈdʒɛnərəlɪst). [f. GENERAL *a.* + -IST.] One who generalizes. †**a.** (See quot. 1611.) **b.** One who devotes himself to general studies (opposed to SPECIALIST).

1611 COTGR., s.v. *Poil, Fait au poil, & à la plume*, a Generalist; one thats fit for, or can make one in, any imployment, or sport. **1894** G. ALLEN in *Westm. Gaz.* 27 Feb. 2/1 The man, as a man, is wider, greater, happier, freer, in proportion as he is a generalist rather than a specialist. **1961** *Economist* 2 Dec. 938/1 The complacent belief that a well trained 'generalist' could turn his hand to anything. **1961** L. MUMFORD *City in Hist.* v. 123 Gifted generalists like Aristotle. **1964** R. WILKINSON *Gentlemanly Power* vi. 71 The backbencher was a generalist also; Parliament has made less use of specialized committees than have either the French or American legislature. **1968** *Listener* 26 Sept. 395/2 I've been asking some large questions—when you are a generalist you learn to look towards big patterns.

attrib. **1858** RUSKIN *Arrows of Chace* (1880) I. 112 The modern pictures of the generalist school..have nothing else but faults. [Cf. GENERALIZE 5.] **1964** R. WILKINSON *Gentlemanly Power* vi. 72 In British bureaucracy, the generalist backgrounds of the top men have shown an interesting relation to professional procedure. **1971** *Physics Bull.* Apr. 231/2 Scheme for an initial two year generalist course for the majority of students backed up by specialist courses for the further studies of the few.

generality (ˌdʒɛnəˈrælɪtɪ). Forms: 5 **generalyte**, 6 **generalite, -ytie**, 6–7 **general(l)itie**, 7 **genrality, generallity**, 6– **generality**. [ad. F. *généralité* (substituted for the older *generauté* GENERALTY), a. L. *generālitās*, f. *generālis* GENERAL.]

I. Senses related to those of GENERAL *a.*

1. The quality or fact of being general, in various senses of the adj.; now chiefly (of principles, propositions, etc.), applicability to a whole class of instances; (of statements) vagueness, indeterminateness. †Formerly also, prevalence, commonness; wide range (of studies), etc.

1587 FLEMING *Contn. Holinshed* III. 1027/1 So also was it generallie doone throughout all England, in which generalitie this citie was of a particularitie. **1597** HOOKER *Eccl. Pol.* v. i. §3 The generalitie of which perswasion argueth, that God hath imprinted it by nature. **1605** TIMME *Quersit.* Pref. 7 A generalitie in humane learning beseemeth a Diuine. **1615** MARKHAM *Eng. Housew.* (1660) 175 Oates.. are of all manner of graine the cheapest because of their generality. **1628** T. SPENCER *Logick* 256 As we found in a simple axiome, so shall we finde in a simple Syllogisme.. generalitie, and specialitie. **1659** PEARSON *Creed* To Rdr., To settle the words of each Article according to their antiquity and generality of reception in the Creed. **1692** RAY *Dissol. World* ii. (1732) 118 Save only the Generality of it [the Deluge]. **1775** BURKE *Corr.* (1844) II. 84 When an epitaph is very short, it is in danger of getting into a cold generality. **1784** WARING in *Phil. Trans.* LXXIV. 408 A resolution of algebraical equations, not inferior, on account of its generality and facility, to any yet published. **1796** BURKE *Regic. Peace* i. Wks. VIII. 142 We must not always judge of the generality of the opinion by the noise of the acclamation. **1802** LD. ELDON in *Vesey's Rep.* VII. 69 According to that case the generality of the gift made the effectuating it impracticable. **1830** HERSCHEL *Stud. Nat. Phil.* 102 We arrive at axioms of the highest degree of generality of which science is capable. **1831** BREWSTER *Newton* (1855) II. xiv. 23 He announced to his friends that he possessed a method of great generality and power. **1865** GROTE *Plato* I. i. 86 Handled in a spirit of empty generality, without facts or particulars. **1871** TYNDALL *Fragm. Sci.* (1879) I. iii. 87 Let us test the generality of this conclusion. **1883** SIR E. E. KAY in *Law Rep.* 23 Ch. Div. 718 The subsequent words..did not restrain the generality of the former words.

†**b.** *in* or *under* (*a, a certain, the*) *generality*: in general terms, in a general way, in outline; generally, in general. (The earliest recorded use.)

1482 *Monk of Evesham* (Arb.) 76 As y haue schortely aboue seyde vnder a certen generalyte. **1530** PALSGR. 149 This for an introduction & in a generalytie to shewe howe many partes of speche there be. **1570–6** LAMBARDE *Peramb. Kent* (1826) 1 Having thus before hand exhibited in generalitie, the names, scituation, and compasse of the realme [etc.]. **1589** PUTTENHAM *Eng. Poesie* I. xiv. (Arb.) 48 The new Comedy came in place, more ciuill and pleasant a great deale and not touching any man by name, but in a certaine generalitie glancing at euery abuse. **1655** DIGGES *Compl. Ambass.* 371, I can as yet deliver your Lordship no more, but this in generality. **1726** AYLIFFE *Parergon* 159 And these Certificates do only in the generality mention the Parties Contumacies and Disobedience.

2. quasi-*concr.* Something that is general; †a general class (*obs.*); a general point, principle, or law; a general proposition or statement; chiefly in *pl.*

1551 BP. GARDINER *Presence in Sacram.* 37b, It hath no apparaunce of lernyng in scriptures, to conclude vnder one consideration a specialtie, & a generalitie. **1561** T. NORTON *Calvin's Inst.* II. iv. (1634) 139 Under the example of one speciall sort he comprehendeth the whole generalitie. **1563–87** FOXE *A. & M.* (1684) III. 490 You do agree in generalities, but when it shall come to the particularities, you will far disagree. **1597** HOOKER *Eccl. Pol.* v. ix. §2 With ..popular capacities nothing doth more preuaile then vnlimited generalities. **1640** BP. HALL *Episc.* II. §11. 147 Lest any man should construe these words onely of a generality of reverent respects. **1791** BURKE *App. Whigs* Wks. VI. 102 It was always in his power to bring the questions from generalities to facts. **1822** HAZLITT *Table-t.* Ser. II. v. (1869) 120 Keep to your sounding generalities, your tinkling phrases and all will be well. *a* **1850** CALHOUN *Wks.* (1874) II. 469 Those opposed to us have dealt in such vague generalities. **1860** MOTLEY *Netherl.* (1868) I. ii. 63 He was very cautious to confine himself to generalities. **1868** ROGERS *Pol. Econ.* viii. (1876) 73 The illustration was, that food increases in an arithmetical, population in a geometrical ratio. This generality has been adversely commented on, and with justice. **1875** STUBBS *Const. Hist.* III. xviii. 120 Gloucester..as usual dealt in generalities.

†**b.** *pl.* The general course. *Obs.*$^{-1}$

a **1628** F. GREVILLE *Sidney* (1652) 221 Ever guiding the generalities of the Voyage.

3. The main body, the bulk, the greater part *of*. (Now only with *sb. pl.* or *collect.*) †Also, the general body; people in general; the majority.

1622 R. HAWKINS *Voy. S. Sea* (1847) 164 Whatsoever belongeth to her of tackling, sayles, or ordinance, is to bee preserved for the generalitie: saving a peece of artillery for the captaine. **1624** CAPT. SMITH *Virginia* IV. 119 Many will make hay whilst the sunne doth shine, how euer it shall faire with the generality. **1641** WILKINS *Math. Magick* I. xi. (1648) 70 The generality of men, especially the wisest sort amongst them. **1660** STANLEY *Hist. Philos.* IX. (1701) 351/1 His Country summoned him to some publick employment, that he might benefit the generality. **1660** WOOD *Life* (O.H.S.) I. 310 Some..were good scholars, but the generality dunces. *a* **1700** HOPKINS *Serm.* vii. (1708) 140 These Things the generality of Mankind..firmly believe. **1703** tr. *Casa's Galateo* 44 With such idle insignificant Stuff; for such the generality of Dreams are. **1722** DE FOE *Plague* (1754) 22 The Generality stay'd, and seem'd to abide the worst. **1734** T. SMITH *Jrnl.* 4 Apr. (1849) 266 As hot a day as the generality of summer. **1759** ROBERTSON *Hist. Scot.* (1817) II. III. 75 An hundred merks Scottish was the allowance which their liberality afforded to the generality of ministers. **1790** BEATTIE *Let.* in Sir W. Forbes *Life* ccxiii. (1824) 380 It is plain that the generality are actuated by a levelling principle of the worst kind. **1808** J. WEBSTER *Nat. Phil.* 156 The generality of clouds are suspended at about the height of a mile. **1876** MOZLEY *Univ. Serm.* iv. 84 The generality are sent into the world for their own moral benefit. **1897** F. HALL in *Nation* (N.Y.) LXIV. 396/2 The phrases here collected will reveal, to the generality who read this letter, that [etc.].

†**b.** *for, in* (*a, the*) *generality*: for the most part, mostly, in general. *Obs.*

1563 *Homilies* II. *Rogat. Week* III. (1859) 491 The world in generality is forgetful of God. **1588** in *Harl. Misc.* (Malh.) II. 77 The people of his country, in a generality, did amongst themselves determine, that [etc.]. **1647** MAY *Hist. Parl.* I. ii. 19 On which side the common people in the generality..stood. **1654** H. L'ESTRANGE *Chas. I* (1655) 19 The Country Captains of the Train-bands were (for the generality) very unskilfull. **1684** R. H. *School Recreat.* 10 If you would chuse a swift, light Hound, the York-shire one in the generality will please you. **1709** F. HAUKSBEE *Phys. Mech. Exp.* v. (1719) 203 Small Loadstones, for the generality, have a stronger attractive Power (in proportion to their bulk) than the large ones have. **1799** G. SMITH *Laboratory* II. 13 For the generality, they [the medals] are made of pure gold or silver.

II. In special senses of F. *généralité*.

†**4.** The dignity or office of general. *Obs.*

1686 F. SPENCE tr. *Varilla's Ho. Medicis* 99 They changed his generality and quality of Count into that of Duke.

†**5.** The general staff of an army. *Obs.*

1578 T. N. tr. *Conq. W. India* 99 The other Letter was firmed by the Generalitie and Chiefest of the armie. **1676** *Lond. Gaz.* No. 1094/1 The Imperial Generality is now broke up from Eslingen, and the whole Army marches towards the Rhine.

6. *Fr. Hist.* A fiscal and administrative division of the kingdom of France, under the control of an officer called *général des finances* or *intendant*.

1630 *R. Johnson's Kingd. & Commw.* 167 Of these Generalities are twenty and one in all France. **1714** *Fr. Bk. of Rates* 156 Forbidding also the Intendants and Governours of Provinces or Generalities..to deliver any.. Permits, for bringing any such Goods into France. **1792** A. YOUNG *Trav. France* 577 The kingdom was parcelled into generalities, with an intendant at the head of each. **1877** MORLEY *Crit. Misc.* Ser. II. 194 There were three different divisions of France in the 18th Century..third, the Generality, or a district defined for fiscal and administrative purposes.

generalizability (ˌdʒɛnərəˌlaɪzəˈbɪlɪtɪ). [f. GENERALIZABLE *a.* + -ILITY.] The fact or quality of being generalizable.

1951 T. PARSONS et al. in Parsons & Shils *Toward Gen. Theory Action* II. iv. 202 The very fact that they [*sc.* rewards] become the objects of competing claims..is in part evidence of their generalizability to cover the claims of different individuals. **1967** *Language* XLIII. 749 He has provided us with no criteria for determining generalizability from sets of pattern correlations of the type he considers.

generalizable (ˈdʒɛnərəˌlaɪzəb(ə)l), *a.* [GENERALIZE *v.* + -ABLE.] Capable of being generalized.

a **1834** COLERIDGE *Lit. Rem.* (1839) IV. 129 Extreme cases are *ipso nomine* not generalizable. **1886** MOMERIE *Personality* Introd. 10 The facts..are practically interpretable by the method..of physics; or, as I should rather say, *generalisable*, for physics does not profess to *interpret* anything.

generalization (ˌdʒɛnərəlaɪˈzeɪʃən). [f. GENERALIZE *v.* + -ATION. Cf. F. *généralisation*.]

1. The action or process of generalizing, i.e. of forming, and expressing in words, general notions or propositions obtained from the observation and comparison of individual facts or appearances; also, an instance of this.

1761 ADAM SMITH *Form Lang.* Ess. (1869) 310 The original invention of such words would require a yet greater effort of abstraction, and generalization, than that of nouns adjective. **1794** J. HUTTON *Philos. Light*, etc. 234 Here then is a generalisation of many facts respecting light and heat.

1825 MACAULAY *Ess., Milton* (1887) 3 Generalization is necessary to the advancement of knowledge. **1836–7** SIR W. HAMILTON *Metaph.* xxxv. (1870) II. 294 Generalisation is the process through which we obtain what are called general or universal notions. **1860** TYNDALL *Glac.* II. vii. 257 With that wonderful power of generalization which belonged to him [Newton]. **1874** SAYCE *Compar. Philol.* i. 4 Ready conclusions and rapid generalisations are wanted. **1876** TAIT *Rec. Adv. Phys. Sci.* iii. (ed. 2) 60 Hasty generalization is the bane of all science.

2. quasi-*concr.* A result of this process; a general inference.

1794 G. ADAMS *Nat. & Exp. Philos.* IV. li. 409 All physical laws, not excepting even those of gravity, are only generalisations. **1804** W. TAYLOR in *Ann. Rev.* II. 254 His generalizations, or theoretical inferences, are numerous and very ingenious. **1830** LYELL *Princ. Geol.* (1875) II. III. xxxv. 275 He availed himself of the generalizations of paleontologists. **1840** MILL *Diss. & Disc.* (1875) I. 404 All knowledge consists of generalizations. **1876** MOZLEY *Univ. Serm.* v. 108 The impalpable generalisation of the nation.. disperses itself in the air, and defies our grasp. **1885** F. TEMPLE *Relat. Relig. & Sci.* i. 9 The doctrine..had been a fair generalization and expression of the facts.

3. The process of becoming general, or spreading over every part.

1897 ALLBUTT *Syst. Med.* III. 71 The generalisation of an infective disease which in most instances remains localised may be due..to the dissemination of the specific organism.

generalize ('dʒɛnərəlaɪz), *v.* (Not in Johnson.) [f. GENERAL *a.* + -IZE. Cf. F. *généraliser.*] To make general.

1. *trans.* To reduce to general laws; also, to form into a general concept; to throw into a general form; to give a general character to.

a **1751** BOLINGBROKE *Ess. Hum. Knowl.* v. Wks. 1754 III. 432 The mind..makes it's utmost efforts to generalize it's ideas. **1776** G. CAMPBELL *Philos. Rhet.* (1801) I. I. v. 112 An original incapacity of classing and (if I may use the expression) generalising their perceptions. **1785** REID *Int. Powers* v. iii. 450 Sometimes the name of an individual is given to a general conception, and thereby the individual in a manner generalised. **1798** EDGEWORTH *Pract. Educ.* (1811) I. 373 By degrees we may teach children to generalize their ideas, and to perceive that they like people for being either useful or agreeable. **1812** SHELLEY *Proposals* Pr. Wks. 1888 I. 265 None are more interesting than those..that generalize and expand private into public feelings. **1820** SCORESBY *Acc. Arctic Reg.* 354 This fact is of much importance in generalizing our knowledge of the temperature of the globe. **1829** JAS. MILL *Hum. Mind* I. ix. 215 Generalizing those names, so as to make them represent a class. **1849** LEWIS *Infl. Author. Matt. Opin.* ix. §1. 286 Causes which do not admit of being generalized. **1864** BOWEN *Logic* viii. 245 Whilst the form of reasoning itself, to which it properly applies, has never been generalized. **1875** JOWETT *Plato* (ed. 2) V. 69 He [Plato] generalizes temperance, as in the Republic he generalizes justice.

b. To designate by a general name.

1842 *Tait's Mag.* IX. 210 It is not often marriages take place in a family where the daughters are only generalized as 'the So-and-So's'. **1855** H. REED *Lect. Eng. Lit.* xi. (1878) 541 The processes, which we generalize under the names of wit and humour.

2. *trans.* To infer (a conclusion, law, etc.) inductively from particulars.

1795 W. SEWARD *Anecd.* II. 342 Sir Joshua Reynolds (who with great propriety and acuteness called in the aid of metaphysics to generalize the principles of art). *a* **1834** COLERIDGE (Webst.), A mere conclusion generalized from a great multitude of facts. *a* **1862** BUCKLE *Civiliz.* (1873) III. v. 306 The object of the geometrician is to generalize the laws of space. **1885** HOWELLS *Silas Lapham* (1891) I. 10 It was from Lapham's answers that he generalised the history of his childhood.

3. To draw general inferences from; to base a general law or statement upon.

a **1828** NICHOLSON (Webster) Copernicus generalized the celestial motions..Newton generalized them still more. **1832** DE LA BECHE *Geol. Man* (ed. 2) 193 The presence of fossils in particular strata was instantly generalized; and it became a well received theory..that every formation.. contained the same organic remains, not to be discovered in those above or beneath. **1840** MILL *Diss. & Disc.* (1875) I. 406 Knowledge is experience generalized. **1855** *Cornwall* 105 Generalizing the various facts connected with the directions of the common faults. **1868** DICKENS *Lett.* (1880) II. 401 A remarkable power of generalising evidence and balancing facts.

b. *Math.* and *Philos.* To throw (a proposition, etc.) into a general form, of which the original becomes a particular case.

1812–16 PLAYFAIR *Nat. Phil.* (1819) I. 20 It is on this proposition, generalized..that the going of a clock or watch is taken for a measure of time. **1834** MCMURTRIE *Cuvier's Anim. Kingd.* 2 Generalising and connecting the laws of these properties. **1883** A. BARRATT *Phys. Metempiric* 216 This when generalised comes to be the question of the evolution of self-consciousness.

4. *intr.* To form general notions by abstraction from particular instances; to arrive at or express general inferences.

1785 [see GENERALIZING *vbl. sb.*]. **1792** D. STEWART *Hum. Mind* I. iv. §1. 158 This has led some philosophers to suppose..that we might have been so formed, as to be able to abstract, without being capable of generalising. **1837** WHEWELL *Hist. Induct. Sc.* (1857) I. 203 The particulars from which we are to generalize. **1871** TYLOR *Prim. Cult.* I. 10 We can drop individual differences out of sight, and thus can generalize on the arts and opinions of whole nations. **1874** SAYCE *Compar. Philol.* vii. 259 Some tribes..are unable to generalise as far as four. **1884** CHURCH *Bacon* iii. 59 He liked to observe, to generalise in shrewd and sometimes cynical epigrams.

5. *Painting.* To render the typical or general characteristics of (objects) rather than the individual peculiarities. Also *absol.*

c **1817** FUSELI in *Lect. Paint.* ix. (1848) 519 Titian..strove to generalise, to elevate or invigorate, the tones of nature. **1858** RUSKIN *Arrows of Chace* (1880) I. 111 There never was anybody who generalized, since paint was first ground, except Opie, and Benjamin West, and Fuseli, and one or two other such modern stars.

6. To render indefinite; to efface or soften down the special features of.

1809 HAN. MORE *Cœlebs* I. vii. 80 They were contented to generalize the doctrines of scripture. **1835** *Fraser's Mag.* XII. 279 Travelling tends to generalise and rub off local habits, prejudices, and peculiarity of ideas. **1838** GLADSTONE *State in Rel. Ch.* viii. §4 (1841) II. 267 We should first be called..to generalise and relax our obligation. **1889** LOWELL *Lett.* (1894) II. 381 The haze which softens and civilizes, perhaps I should say, artistically generalizes, all it touches.

7. *trans.* To bring into general use; to make common or familiar; to make generally known; to popularize. Also, to spread over the whole extent or surface in question.

1818 W. TAYLOR in *Monthly Mag.* XLVI. 403 A style of superstition which Rome..had deposited in the monastic libraries of Europe, was now generalized among the laity of the north by the efficacious industry of the press. **1824** *Blackw. Mag.* XV. 15 The last forty or fifty years..claim also the credit..of extending and generalizing the use of the potatoe. **1887** *Sat. Rev.* 3 Dec. 767 There has arisen a copious and very special literature..which has done much to generalize and enhance the public interest in the art and its professors. **1897** [see GENERALIZED *ppl. a.*].

8. *intr.* To attend to general considerations. (Opposed to *specialize.*) *rare.*

1833 MARRYAT *P. Simple* (1863) 108 You see, Mr. Simple, it's the duty of an officer to generalise, and be attentive to parts only in consideration of the safety of the whole.

generalized ('dʒɛnərəlaɪzd), *ppl. a.* [f. GENERALIZE *v.* + -ED[1].] In senses of the verb. Of a disease: That has extended itself to the system in general (so F. *généralisé*). ***generalized co-ordinates***: in *Theoretical Dynamics*, a set of variables by the values of which the position of a system at any time may be defined.

1842–3 GROVE *Corr. Phys. Forces* 45 A generalized relation will ultimately be established between heat, chemical affinity, and physical attraction. **1852** H. ROGERS *Ecl. Faith* (1853) 75 This is a proper translation, in a generalised form, of the phrase 'a book-revelation'. **1862** *Lond. Rev.* 16 Aug. 144 Nor are these mere abstract assertions; a little further on we have the actual instances, of which they are the generalized description. **1867** J. ALDEN *Intell. Philos.* xxi. 208 The axioms [of geometry] are generalized statements of self-evident truths. **1885** WATSON & BURBURY *Math. Th. Electr. & Magn.* I. 170 If *q* be any generalised coordinate defining the position of the system. **1885** *Athenæum* 14 Mar. 352/1 The generalized and inaccurate sketches he [Munkacsy] made for spectacular pictures. **1897** ALLBUTT *Syst. Med.* II. 32 In rabbits on the other hand, the kidneys are frequently affected in generalised tuberculosis. *Ibid.* 636 The injection of the lymph was followed by a generalized eruption.

generalizer ('dʒɛnərəlaɪzə(r)). [f. GENERALIZE *v.* + ER[1].] One who generalizes.

c **1792** BURKE in Leslie & Taylor *Sir J. Reynolds* II. x. 638 *note*, He was a great generaliser, and was fond of reducing everything to one system. **1827** LYTTON *Pelham* xv, Your countrymen are great generalisers in philosophy. **1864** DE MORGAN in *N. & Q.* V. 455 A very moderate power of dramatic narrative..will set four-fifths of the abstracters and generalizers reading a second-rate novel. **1882** *Sat. Rev.* 28 Jan. 99 Mr. Gladstone is nothing if not a generalizer.

generalizing ('dʒɛnərəlaɪzɪŋ), *vbl. sb.* [-ING[1].] The action of the vb. GENERALIZE.

1785 REID *Int. Powers* v. iii. 445 The first is by Philosophers called abstraction, the second may be called generalising; but both are commonly included under the name of abstraction. **1827** SCOTT *Jrnl.* 24 July, [He] has a turn for generalising, which renders him rather dull. **1869** J. D. BALDWIN in *Preh. Nations* ii. (1877) 54 Let it not be inspired entirely by the generalizings of physical speculation.

attrib. **1861** *Q. Rev.* Oct. CX. 393 Trace that belief..to a separate principle in the human mind; call it the generalizing principle or the inductive principle. **1885** *Athenæum* 3 Jan. 22/3 The generalizing habit of Sir Joshua's mind..deprived him at the same time of not a little insight and penetration.

generalizing ('dʒɛnərəlaɪzɪŋ), *ppl. a.* [-ING[2].] That generalizes; tending or given to generalize.

1793 BEDDOES *Math. Evid.* 153 A man need not possess a very observant eye, nor a very generalizing mind, to notice a few out of a multitude of facts..and to suspect some connection between them. **1820** SCORESBY *Acc. Arctic Reg.* I. 347 By continuing to register their observations..they will confer an important obligation on the generalizing meteorologist. **1822** T. MOORE *Mem.* (1853) III. 346 Nothing, certainly, profound or generalizing, or grand or electric. **1849** GROTE *Greece* II. lxviii. (1862) VI. 102 The conversation of Sokrates was often..of a more negative, analytical, and generalising tendency. **1882** VERN. LEE in *Contemp. Rev.* XLII. 847 To these purely personal explanations have gradually been added others more suited to the generalizing temper of our days.

generally ('dʒɛnərəlɪ), *adv.* [f. GENERAL *a.* + -LY[2].]

†**1.** So as to include every particular, or every individual; in a body, as a whole, collectively. *Obs.*

a **1300** *Cursor M.* 29118 Generali nu haf i tald þe pointes þat ar for to hald. **1340** *Ayenb.* 263 Ich y-leue ine þe holy gost, holy cherche generalliche, Mennesse of halȝen. **1375** BARBOUR *Bruce* XI. 208 In hy gert he Hys men be summond generaly. *c* **1530** LD. BERNERS *Arth. Lyt. Bryt.* (1814) 91 Than generallye all the ladyes and damoyselles came to themwarde. **1596** SHAKS. *Tam. Shr.* I. ii. 274 You must as we do, gratifie this Gentleman, To whom we all rest generally beholding. **1613** PURCHAS *Pilgrimage* (1614) 425 They embraced not the faith of Mahomet generally, but as everie man liked.

b. With respect to a country, etc.: In its whole extent.

1851 *Illustr. Catal. Gt. Exhib.* 164 The metalliferous mineral wealth of Great Britain generally.

†**2.** Universally; with few or no exceptions; with respect to every (or almost every) individual or case concerned. With a negative = *at all. Obs.*

c **1394** *P. Pl. Crede* 575 And also þis myster men ben maysters icalled, þat þe gentill Iesus generallyche blamed. **1398** TREVISA *Barth. De P.R.* XVI. xciv. (1495) 586 Salte hath generally vertue to vndo clense and waast rotyd humours. **1526** *Pilgr. Perf.* (W. de W. 1531) 227 Generally offryng for theyr satisfaccyon that was commaunded in the lawe. **1568** TILNEY *Disc. Mariage* C vj b, Neyther speake I this nowe generally against all women..I do but touch some shrewde wyfes. **1583** T. STOCKER tr. *Civ. Wars Low C.* II. 16 b, Wee agree..not one forraine Souldier to remaine there generally. **1613** SHAKS. *Hen. VIII*, II. i. 47 This is noted (And generally) who euer the King fauours, The Cardnall instantly will finde imployment. **1636** *Bk. Com. Prayer, Catechism* Two [sacraments] onely, as generally necessarie to salvation. *a* **1641** BP. R. MOUNTAGU *Acts & Mon.* (1642) 388 In no Author generally, sacred or profane. **1653** BAXTER *Chr. Concord* 112 He is a rare man that is generally excellent.

b. In weaker sense: With respect to the majority or larger part; for the most part, extensively.

c **1374** CHAUCER *Troylus* I. 86 It..generally was spoken, That Calkas traytor fals fled was, and allyed With hem of Grece. *c* **1400** MAUNDEV. (Roxb.) xxxii. 144 Generally all þe men of þat ile..er trewer and riȝtwiser þan er in oþer cuntreez. **1658** OSBORN *Q. Eliz.* 77 The Doctrine professed most generally in England bore in forraigne nations the name of Parliament-Faith. **1662** STILLINGFL. *Orig. Sacr.* III. iv. §10 This is now the substance of the generally received account. **1790** HAN. MORE *Relig. Fash. World* (1791) 39 Its weight is determined by some generally-allowed standard. **1808** SYD. SMITH *Wks.* (1859) I. 115/2 The troops are generally disaffected. **1820** SCORESBY *Acc. Arctic Reg.* I. 349 This is a fact now generally received. **1856** FROUDE *Hist. Eng.* (1858) I. i. 37 The people, not universally, but generally, were animated by a true spirit of sacrifice. **1871** MORLEY *Voltaire* (1886) 5 The plain men of the earth.. would generally approve the saying of Dr. Johnson. **1893** *Leeds Mercury* 17 May 5/3 The opinion of the meeting was generally favourable to the amendment.

3. In a general sense or way; without reference to individuals or particulars; opposed to *specially.*

1340 *Ayenb.* 16 Huer-of he be-gyleþ..generalliche ech manere of uolk, ac specialliche þe greate lhordes. **1481** CAXTON *Reynard* Epil. (Arb.) 119 Ther is no good man blamed herein, hit is spoken generally. **1526** *Pilgr. Perf.* (W. de W. 1531) 1 The fyrst boke sheweth generally, how the lyfe of euery chrystian is as a pilgrymage. **1574** tr. *Littleton's Tenures* 103 b, If hee will pleade the release generally. **1626** BACON *Sylva* §525 Generally, wee would not haue those, that read this our Worke of Sylua Syluarum, account it strange..that wee haue set downe Particulars vntried. **1818** CRUISE *Digest* (ed. 2) VI. 277 He gave all his lands to Richard, generally. **1867** FREEMAN *Norm. Conq.* (1876) I. App. 787 The crime is attributed to the Danes generally. **1875** JOWETT *Plato* (ed. 2) I. 16 In leaping and running, and bodily exercises generally. **1884** *Law Times* 29 Nov. 79/2 Three [cheques]..were crossed generally 'and Co.', and three were uncrossed.

b. in phrase ***generally speaking*** = 'in general'.

[*c* **1386** CHAUCER *Manciple's T.* 224 For a litel speche auysely Is no man shent, to speke generally.] **1687** DRYDEN *Hind & P.* To Rdr., Those who are driven into the fold are, generally speaking, rather made hypocrites than converts. **1722** DE FOE *Plague* (1754) 9 Men on Horseback, some alone, others with Servants, and generally speaking, all loaded with Baggage. **1845** W. H. IRELAND *Scribbleomania* 223 Generally speaking..if a grand idea happens to strike any living architect, it is not the effect of study.

4. As a general rule; in most instances, usually, commonly.

1654 R. WHITLOCK *Zootomia* 361 Preaching too generally being but the Art of flattery. **1717** tr. *Frezier's Voy. S. Sea* 21 Brandy, a Liquor they are very fond of, tho' they generally drink nothing but Water. **1718** ATTERBURY *Serm.* (1734) I. 18 And yet it so happens that Popish Miracles are generally done at Home, before Believers. **1766** GOLDSM. *Vic. W.* i, The temper of a woman is generally formed from the turn of her features. **1820** SCORESBY *Acc. Arctic Reg.* II. 398 Built generally of wood, but sometimes of brick. **1850** MCCOSH *Div. Govt.* III. iii. (1874) 425 Where there is hope, there will generally be some life. **1880** GEIKIE *Phys. Geog.* v. 352 Winds from the sea are usually moist, those from the land are generally dry.

†**5.** With *in*, forming a compound adv. (Cf. *in especially.*) *Obs.*

1557 NORTH tr. *Gueuara's Diall Pr.* 43 a/2 To all ingenerallye [*sic*, and elsewhere in this book] he gaue place, to reste them selues in.

generalness ('dʒɛnərəlnɪs). [f. GENERAL *a.* + -NESS.] The state, quality, or fact of being general, in various senses. Now *rare.*

1561 T. NORTON *Calvin's Inst.* III. xxiv. (1634) 471, I confuted their errour, which thinke that the generallnesse of the promises extendeth equally to all mankinde. **1580** SIDNEY *Arcadia* (1622) 21 They had with a generall consent (rather springing by the generalnesse of the cause..) set themselves in armes. **1639** LAUD *Wks.* (1849) II. 239 It is not necessary to the lawfulness and generalness of a council that all the bishops of the world should be actually present. **1683** W. CLAGETT *Answ. Dissent. Object. Bk. Com. Prayer* (1688) 4 They who Object the Generalness of our Confessions against us. **1894** *Temple Bar Mag.* CI. 13 Here is a generality in no degree inferior in generalness to his.

generalship (ˈdʒɛnərəlʃɪp). [f. GENERAL *sb.* + -SHIP.]

1. †**a.** The functions of a general (*obs.*). **b.** The discharge of those functions; conduct in command.

1591 GARRARD *Art Warre* 225 May be able worthily to performe his Lieutenant and Generalship. **1730** BOLINGBROKE *Lett. on Hist.* ii. (1752) I. 24 Cicero..laughs, indeed in one of his letters to Atticus, at his generalship. **1840** THIRLWALL *Greece* VII. 167 Leosthenes was provoked to ask, what benefit Athens had reaped from Phocion's generalship. **1884** H. SPENCER *Man v. State* 109 The civil head, ceasing to be the military head, does his generalship by deputy.

2. The office or dignity of general.

1623 BINGHAM *Xenophon* 105 These thoughts lifted him [Xenophon] vp to desire the Generall-ship. **1690** *Lond. Gaz.* No. 2540/1 *Don Marco Ottoboni* is gone to *Civita Vecchia*, to take possession of the Generalship of the Gallies. **1707** LUTTRELL *Brief Rel.* (1857) VI. 206 The prince of Nassau Frizeland has been advanced to the generalship of the Dutch infantry. **1855** MILMAN *Lat. Chr.* IX. vii. (1864) V. 370 A new power..had wrested the generalship and the direction of a Crusade from the hands of the most mighty prelate. **1870** *Pall Mall G.* 18 Aug. 4 He joined Garibaldi.. and was promoted to a generalship.

†**b.** The tenure of the office of general. *Obs.*

1610 HEALEY *St. Aug. Citie of God* 37 Regulus..in his generalship returned with divers noble victories unto the Romanes. *a* **1674** CLARENDON *Hist. Reb.* IX. §126 Those fifteen hundred horse which march'd northward...within very few days were brought to nothing; and the generalship of the Lord Digby to an end. **1677** CARY *Chronol.* II. I. I. xi. 123 Unto which 207 there being added 21 for the time of Cyrus his Generalship.

3. The distinctive qualities of a general; skill in the command and management of an army; strategy.

1770 LANGHORNE *Plutarch* (1879) I. 209/1 Hannibal gave great proofs of generalship. **1800** WEEMS *Washington* vi. (1877) 39 This was a bold stroke of generalship. **1839** JAMES *Louis XIV*, II. 412 Turenne was too well aware of the generalship of Condé to attempt to attack him in his retreat. **1867** FREEMAN *Norm. Conq.* (1876) I. v. 324 The plan which he formed seems to vouch for his generalship. **1871** *Daily News* 25 Sept., Of all our weak points, generalship is the weakest.

b. *transf.* Skilful management.

a **1768** STERNE *Pol. Romance* Wks. 1779 VI. 213 An artful stroke of generalship in Trim to raise a dust. **1812** *Examiner* 5 Oct. 637/1 He thanked them for this mode of undermining him, for it only shewed their own want of generalship. **1849** THACKERAY *Pendennis* lvii, The..actress..but for the Major's generalship, might now have been your daughter-in-law, ma'am. **1887** *Times* (weekly ed.) 18 Nov. 9/2, I have infinite confidence in your generalship.

4. = GENERALATE 2.

1762 tr. *Busching's Syst. Geogr.* V. 180 The abbey of Denkendorf, which gives its name to the generalship [orig. *das Generalat*].

†**ˈgeneralty.** *Obs.* Forms: 4-5 generalte, 5-6 generaltee, -tie, -tye, 6- generalty. [a. OF. *generalté (generauté), f. *general* GENERAL.]

1. The quality or fact of being general; = GENERALITY 1. ***of, in a generalty***: in general.

c **1380** WYCLIF *Serm.* Sel. Wks. I. 316 þis Cesare was moost in generalte and larges, and pees of his lordship. *c* **1449** PECOCK *Repr.* 130 Forwhi this firste parti of this present book and *The iust apprising of Holi Scripture* as in generalte schewen vndoutabli..that [etc.]. **1494** FABYAN *Chron.* VII. 666 One other cause was, whiche ensuythe of a generaltie, that for the more partie one mayer wyll nat fynesshe that thynge whiche that other begynneth. **1549** COVERDALE, etc. *Erasm. Par 1 Tim.* 6 In a generaltye it is not expedient that the state of the commune wealth shoulde be dysturbed by meanes of vs. **1570-6** LAMBARDE *Peramb. Kent* (1826) 159 The name of this place [Hyde], importing..by the generaltie thereof, some note of woorthinesse. **1642** W. BIRD *Mag. Honor* 52 In this our Common-wealth of England, me thinks that a Baron may be described in a generalty, answerable to every kind thereof in this manner. *a* **1676** HALE *Hist. Com. Law* ii. (1713) 24 The Municipal Laws..include in their Generalty all those several Laws which are allowed, as the Rule and Direction of..Judicial Proceedings.

2. A general statement, notion, term, etc.; = GENERALITY 2.

1533 MORE *Apol.* xlv. Wks. 916/1 This pacifyer will fall fro the bablyng of a generaltie..and come to the naming of any one persone special. **1567** MAPLET *Gr. Forest* 8 b, I must needes..speake of the Gem: for that we haue beene occasioned, and shall be hereafter to vse it as the generaltie or notion of the name. **1601** B. JONSON *Poetaster* v. i. (1602) K 2 b, Nor any long, or far-fetcht Circumstance Wrappt in the curious General'ties of Artes. **1609** DOULAND *Ornith. Microl.* 29 To proceed from generaltie to specialty is more naturall to vs.

3. The main body, greater part; = GENERALITY 3.

c **1380** WYCLIF *Wks.* (1880) 43 ȝif it seme ony tyme to þe generalte of mynystris prouyncial & custodis þat þer forseide mynyster is not sufficient to þe seruyce [etc.]. **1525** LD. BERNERS *Froiss.* II. ccxxviii. [ccxxiv.] 716 Ye ought rather to entertayne the generaltie of your realme than the ydell wordes of two knyghtes.

4. a. The dignity or office of general; = GENERALITY 4. **b.** The general staff of an army; = GENERALITY 5. **c.** (See quot. 1611) = GENERALITY 6.

1611 COTGR., *Generalité*..a generaltie; a place of generall receit of the finances. **1643** PRYNNE *Sov. Power Parl.* App. 178 The Earle of Egmont..by the advice of the Councell of Estate, and of the Generalty, had..been..sent into Spain. **1647** W. BROWNE tr. *Gomberville's Polexander* III. v. 147 The Emperour..put a terrible Army into the Field, divided the Generalty between Achomat and Haly Basha, and gave the command of the Janizaries to Solyman.

generant (ˈdʒɛnərənt), *sb.* and *a.* [a. L. *generant-em*, pr. pple. of *generāre* to GENERATE; cf. OF. *generant*.]

A. *sb.* That which generates or produces; a begetter, parent. †Also, a second cause (*obs.*).

1665 GLANVILL *Scepsis Sci.* iv. 14 Some believe It [the Soul] came from the Moon..some that 'tis made by God, some by Angels, and some by the Generant. **1686** GOAD *Celest. Bodies* I. i. 1 The Divine Word..produceth by a Second inferior Cause, or Generant. **1691** RAY *Creation* (1701) 321 The Sun..is supposed to be the equivocal Generant or Efficient by these Philosophers. **1885** F. GALTON in *Science* 25 Sept. VI. 272/2 By a regression of the values of the mid-parentages the true generants are derived.

b. *Math.* A point, line, or surface conceived as producing by its motion a line, a superficial or a solid figure respectively; = GENERATRIX.

1842 FRANCIS *Dict. Arts*, etc., s.v., A circle which revolves rapidly on any diameter generates a sphere; a line moved steadily along forms a surface. The circle and line are therefore generants.

B. *adj.* Generating, productive. *rare.*

1875 G. MACDONALD *Malcolm* III. x. 147 In her genial bosom the exhausted gathers life, the effete becomes generant.

generate (ˈdʒɛnərət), *ppl. a.* [ad. L. *generāt-us*, pa. pple. of *generāre*: see next.] = GENERATED.

1509 HAWES *Past. Pleas.* XLIV. xiv, These two the worlde dampned in certaynete..And all other than frome them generate. **1555** EDEN *Decades* 266 It noryssheth the fecunditie of thynges generate. **1615** CHAPMAN *Odyss.* XI. 842, I was generate By Ioue himselfe. **1616** R. C. *Times' Whistle*, etc. (1871) 113 There is a soule, not generate, but infusde. **1830** W. PHILLIPS *Mt. Sinai* I. 280 Nor such shadows they As those of waters generate, or of air. **1895** *Q. Rev.* Oct. 396 There is only one physician, of flesh and of spirit, generate and ingenerate, God in man.

generate (ˈdʒɛnəreɪt), *v.* [f. L. *generāt-*, ppl. stem of *generāre* to beget, etc., f. *gener-*, *genus* stock, race: cf. GENDER *sb.*, GENUS.]

First in pa. pple. *generate*.

†**1. a.** *trans.* To beget, procreate, engender (offspring). *Obs.*

1509 [see GENERATE *ppl. a.*]. **1526** *Pilgr. Perf.* (W. de W. 1531) 170 b, He that by naturall propagacyon hath generate or begoten vs. **1618** CHAPMAN *Hesiod's Bk. of Days* 75 The nineteenth day..Auspicious both to plant, and generate Both sons and daughters. **1660** R. COKE *Power & Subj.* 76 The person of the Son being only generated, the Fathers power can extend no further. **1697** tr. *Burgersdicius' Logic* I. xxxii. 126 Every mortal is generated, and therefore that which is not generated is not mortal.

b. *absol.* or *intr.* To produce offspring. (Now *rare.*) †Also, to copulate (*obs.*).

1626 BACON *Sylva* §758 Some Liuing Creatures generate but at certaine Seasons of the Yeare. **1656** RIDGLEY *Prac. Physick* 160 Living Creatures which are said to generate, not when they generate their young, but their Seed. **1660** R. COKE *Power & Subj.* 30 The parents must be supposed to generate, before they can have a power or right of command. **1774** GOLDSM. *Nat. Hist.* (1776) VI. 252 These fish generate in March and April. **1847** EMERSON *Poems, Threnody* Wks. (Bohn) I. 492 Blood is blood which circulates, Life is life which generates.

fig. **1670** CLARENDON *Contempl. Ps.* Tracts (1727) 673 The good man..leaves an ample progeny of just and charitable actions which generate when he is dead.

2. a. Of natural or material agencies or conditions: To bring into existence, to produce (substances, animals, plants, etc.). Chiefly in *passive*.

1563 FULKE *Meteors* (1640) 65 All agree, that all metalles are generated of Sulphur. **1641** WILKINS *Math. Magick* (1648) II. xii. 253 This cannot be said to foment or preserve the same fire, but onely to generate new. **1665** HOOKE *Microgr.* 127 As mushrooms may be generated without seed, so does it not appear that they have any such thing as seed. **1691-1701** NORRIS *Ideal World* I. vii. 413 When a thing is created or generated, 'tis not this essence of it that is either created or generated, because it was before. **1734** tr. *Rollin's Anc. Hist.* (1827) I. Pref. 11 Monsters generated from the agitation of the sea. **1834** T. MEDWIN *Angler in Wales* I. 238 A six-pound trout is a mere minnow to what the Rhone generates. **1862** TYNDALL *Mountaineering in 1861*, 36 Beyond the boundaries of his knowledge lay a region where rain was generated he knew not how. **1878** SIR G. SCOTT *Lect. Archit.* I. iii. 126 On the other hand, we were far less liberal in the use of sculpture, and we generated a purely moulded capital, which the French can scarcely be said to possess.

b. *esp.* To produce, evolve (steam, gas, etc.); also heat, force, friction, light, velocity, etc.).

1791 HAMILTON tr. *Berthollet's Dyeing* I. iii. 59 They [vegetable substances] undergo the effects of a slight combustion, which may generate an acid. **1794** J. HUTTON *Philos. Light*, etc. 159 If a single coal..cannot generate heat upon the whole..How is the union of those bodies to increase their heat? **1812-16** PLAYFAIR *Nat. Phil.* (1819) I. 269 The elastic fluid generated by the gunpowder. **1825** J. NICHOLSON *Operat. Mech.* 202 The steam generated is carried to the place intended by means of pipes. **1838** GREENER *Gunnery* 378 Generating 300 per cent. less friction than in the Whitworth rifle. **1869** PHILLIPS *Vesuv.* ix. 261 Heat in some way generates the force of the earth-wave. **1872** YEATS *Techn. Hist. Comm.* 325 The gases generated were employed as fuel for heating steel furnaces. **1878** HUXLEY *Physiogr.* 40 Steam is generated from the water in the boiler by the aid of artificial heat. **1881** BESANT & RICE *Chapl. of Fleet* 235 The walls were streaming with the heat generated by the presence of so many men and so much drink. **1884** tr. *Lotze's Logic* 339 We can sometimes observe how they balance each other, sometimes what velocities they generate.

c. *Math.* To produce or evolve (a line or figure); said chiefly of a point, line, or surface conceived as doing this by its motion.

1698 KEILL *Exam. Th. Earth* (1734) 275 If both the Ellipse and Circle were turned round the Axis AB there would also be a Spheroid and a Sphere generated. **1709** BERKELEY *Th. Vision* §154 The properties of lines generated by the section of a solid. **1831** BREWSTER *Optics* vi. 57 When these properties of the ellipse and hyperbola, and of the solids generated by their revolution, were first discovered. **1864** BOWEN *Logic* viii. 233 We know how a circle is generated. **1866** PROCTOR *Handbk. Stars* 12 If the figure were to revolve about SP it would generate a sphere. **1885** LEUDESDORF *Cremona's Proj. Geom.* 83 The pencils generated by *m and m'* are projective.

d. *Math.* and *Linguistics.* To produce (a set or sequence of items) by certain specified operations or by the repeated application of rules to some basic items.

1896 *Bull. Amer. Math. Soc.* III. 115 If *G* is generated by substitutions of order p^a it is self-conjugate. **1903** B. RUSSELL *Princ. Math.* xxiv. 200 The simplest method of generating a series is as follows. **1947** BIRKHOFF & MACLANE *Surv. Mod. Algebra* vi. 138 The group G is cyclic if it contains some one element x whose powers exhaust G; this element is said to generate the group. *Ibid.* xiv. 373, $x^2 + 4x + 2 = O$ has a root $-2 + \sqrt{2}$ which generates the same field $R(\sqrt{2})$, for any number in the field can be expressed in terms of this new generator. **1956** N. CHOMSKY in *IRE Trans. Information Theory* IT—2 Sept. 113/1 We investigate several conceptions of linguistic structure to determine whether or not they can provide simple and 'revealing' grammars that generate all of the sentences of English and only these. **1957** —— *Syntactic Structures* ii. 13 The grammar of L will thus be a device that generates all of the grammatical sequences of L and none of the ungrammatical ones. **1958** J. T. CULBERTSON *Math. & Logic Digital Devices* iv. 45 This rule for generating the integers applies to all systems regardless of radix. **1959** *Word* XV. 237 Even in this grammar, however, it would probably be foolish to generate such small and unproductive sets as the Turkish personal pronouns. **1965** PATTERSON & RUTHERFORD *Elem. Abstract Algebra* ii. 44 Every element *x* of a finite group *G* generates a cyclic subgroup whose order is a factor of the order of *G*. **1968** *Language* XLIV. 57 If the optional Noun deletion rule does not apply, *ma maison* is generated instead of *la mienne*. **1968** J. LYONS *Introd. Theoret. Ling.* iv. 156 When we say that a grammar generates the sentences of a language we imply that it constitutes a system of rules..which..yield.. a decision-procedure for any combination.

3. To bring about, give rise to, produce (a result, a state of things; in later use also, a state of mind, feeling, etc.).

1626 BACON *Sylva* §260 Both of them [visibles and audibles] seeme not to Generate or produce any other Effect in Nature [etc.]. **1665** HOOKE *Microgr.* Table 255 Earthquakes seem to be generated much the same way [by eruptions of vapours]. **1796** BP. WATSON *Apol. Bible* 279 The belief of that miracle did not generate conviction that Jesus was the Christ. **1800** COLQUHOUN *Comm. Thames* viii. 256 Offences were generated in consequence of the imperfections of the Law. **1821** J. Q. ADAMS in C. Davies *Metr. Syst.* III. (1871) 124 The same inconsistency of the statutes..generated a lawsuit between commerce and revenue. **1829** I. TAYLOR *Enthus.* i. (1867) 14 There are among us enthusiastic principles and practices..generated in a period of greater excitement than our own. **1841** W. SPALDING *Italy & It. Isl.* III. 288 This unhealthy atmosphere, and the diseases which it generates, prevail over the whole of the great Maremma. **1863** KINGLAKE *Crimea* (1877) I. iv. 70 The love of killing game generates a sincere wish to preserve it.

generated (ˈdʒɛnəreɪtɪd), *ppl. a.* [f. prec. + -ED[1].] That is produced or originated.

1552 HULOET, Generated, *generatus, genitus.* **1638** F. JUNIUS *Paint. Ancients* 19 He that maketh any thing after the example of things generated, shall never..attaine to what is perfectly beautifull. **1743** EMERSON *Fluxions* p. v, Any generated, flowing Quantity. **1828** J. M. SPEARMAN *Brit. Gunner* (ed. 2) 239 When a body falls by the force of gravity, the spaces descended are proportional to the squares of the generated velocities.

generating (ˈdʒɛnəreɪtɪŋ), *vbl. sb.* [f. as prec. + -ING[1].] The action of the verb GENERATE.

1605 BACON *Adv. Learning* II. Ded. §9. 3 As those which are ordained for generating and propagating of sciences. **1660** R. COKE *Power & Subj.* 263 Every Creature of it selfe [would be] in a like power of Generating, one as much as another. **1846** GREENER *Sc. Gunnery* 249 All these occurrences are perfectly dependant on a knowledge of the generating of the explosive force.

generating (ˈdʒɛnəreɪtɪŋ), *ppl. a.* [f. as prec. + -ING[2].] That generates, in senses of verb; esp. of geometrical magnitudes (***generating line, circle***, etc.) and (in modern use) of electric apparatus. ***generating function*** (see quot. 1838); ***generating station***, a power station for the generation of electricity; ***generating surface***, the heating surface of a boiler (Knight).

1706 W. JONES *Syn. Palmar. Matheseos* 260 The Cycloidal Space..between the Curve and the Circle is..= Generating Circle. **1807** HUTTON *Course Math.* II. 276 Hitherto the generating line, or plane, has been considered as of a constant and invariable magnitude. **1838** *Penny Cycl.*

XI. 113/1 The term *generating function* is a name given by Laplace to any function of *x*, considered with reference to the coefficients of its expansion in powers of *x*. **1849** D. CAMPBELL *Inorg. Chem.* 18 The small tube of the generating apparatus being bent straight passes down into the wash solution. **1854** CT. E. DE WARREN tr. *De Saulcy's Dead Sea* II. 127 The generating arch is not then quite half a circumference. **1875** BENNETT & DYER *Sach's Bot.* 156 The generating member, since it continues to grow during the branching, may form numerous lateral members. **1894** *Daily News* 6 Apr. 6/1 The supply being from storage batteries, it..is not affected by temporary stoppage of the generating plant. **1898** *Ibid.* 13 June 7/3 The Company are practically reconstructing their electrical generating station. **1959** *Chambers's Encycl.* V. 93/1 The capacities of some of the largest generating stations.

generation (dʒenəˈreɪʃən). Also 3–6 **-acion**, (6 **-yon**), 4–5 **-acioun**. [a. L. *generātiōn-em*, n. of action f. *generāre* to GENERATE. Cf. F. *génération*.]

I. The action of generating.

1. a. The act or process of generating or begetting physically; procreation; propagation of species. For *equivocal*, *spontaneous generation*, see the adjs.

c **1374** CHAUCER *Boeth.* III. pr. xi. 78 (Camb. MS.) þat þat nature desireth and requereth alwey, that is to sein the werk of generacion. *c* **1400** MAUNDEV. (1839) xix. 206 Thei han Membres of Generacioun of Man and Womman. *c* **1485** *Digby Myst., Mor. Wisd.* 460 Of lust and lykyng comyth generacion. **1535** *Act 27 Hen. VIII*, c. 6 §1 The generacion & breding of good and swyfte and strong horses. **1626** BACON *Sylva* §608 Generation by Copulation (certainly) extendeth not to Plants. **1660** R. COKE *Power & Subj.* 265 Nor are all Creatures at all times alike disposed to Generation, but apted and disposed thereunto from some exterior cause. **1752** HUME *Pol. Disc.* x. 159 There is in all men, both male and female, a desire and power of generation more active than is ever universally exerted. **1834** MCMURTRIE *Cuvier's Anim. Kingd.* 474 A little thread that appears to be an organ of generation. **1861** HULME tr. *Moquin-Tandon* II. I. 46 In the higher animals, the act of reproduction is accomplished by means of special organs: this is Generative Reproduction, or Generation.

b. In passive sense: The fact or manner of being begotten.

1390 GOWER *Conf.* II. 76 Of generacion..There may no gentilesse be. *c* **1440** *Gesta Rom.* xii. 41 (Harl. MS.) By the fadir, that is cause of oure generacion, is vndirstonde mekenesse or humilite. **1532** MORE *Confut. Tindale* Wks. 547/1 His generacion (that is to wyt his being borne of God by the seed of god..) doth preserue and kepe hym. **1576** FLEMING *Panopl. Epist.* 364 The condition of men, even from their generation, is, in their owne sweate to earne their owne meate.

c. Manner of descent: genealogy, pedigree. *rare.*

1382 WYCLIF *Matt.* i. 1 The boke of the generacioun of Jhesu Crist. **1611** BIBLE *ibid.* **1613** PURCHAS *Pilgrimage* (1614) 233 They derive their generation from the Cretan Jupiter. **1834** COLERIDGE *Table-t.* (1836) 308 The generation of the modern worldly Dissenter was thus: Presbyterian, Arian, Socinian, and last, Unitarian.

d. *Theol.* The origin of the Son from the Father. Cf. BEGET *v.*

1659 PEARSON *Creed* (1839) 200 The generation of Christ admits no regeneration, he becoming at once thereby God and Son and heir of all. *a* **1711** KEN *Hymnotheo* Poet. Wks. 1721 III. 355 Strange Generation this? Father and Son Co-eval, two distinct, and yet but one! **1720** WATERLAND *Eight Serm.* 107 The Arians..had some plausible things to urge, particularly in respect of the Generation of the Son. **1848** R. I. WILBERFORCE *Incarnation* v. (1852) 122 Origen introduced the phrase of the Son's 'eternal generation'.

2. a. Production by natural or artificial processes (as of plants, animals, substances, etc.). †Also, mode of formation, nature of origin (*obs.*).

In mediæval philosophy, following Aristotle, *generation* (γένεσις) and *corruption* (φθορά) are often mentioned as contrary processes, together comprehending all the changes which take place in the universe. Hence the frequent allusive use of the words, e.g. in quot. 1611.

c **1400** *Lanfranc's Cirurg.* 49 Wiþ þis poudre þe generacioun of þese poris may be mendid. **1519** *Interl. 4 Elem.* (Percy Soc.) 2 Of the generacyon and cause of stone and metall, and of plantis and herbys. **1563** FULKE *Meteors* (1640) 63 b, Sand..is of the same generation, consisting of many small bodies, which are congealed into stones. **1600** J. PORY tr. *Leo's Africa* II. 361 There cannot be a countrie more apt then this, for the generation and increase of all plants and creatures. **1611** MIDDLETON & DEKKER *Roaring Girl* III. E 4 Would you know a catchpoole rightly deriu'd, the corruption of a Cittizen is the generation of a serieant. **1663** POWER *Exp. Philos.* III. ii. 155 Those insensible Corpuscules which daily produce such Considerable effects in the generation and corruption of Bodies about us. **1673** RAY *Journ. Low C.* Rome 383 The Monks shew'd us..2 marble pillars..Their generation at first was of a mass or heap of small flints and pebbles united into one body by a cement. **1710** J. CLARKE *Rohault's Nat. Phil.* (1729) I 17 The Production of Something which before was not, we call Generation; thus we say Fire is generated, when we see Fire where the Wood was before. **1748** HARTLEY *Observ. Man* I. i. 50 Ideas, their Generations, Associations, and Dependencies on bodily States. **1797** GODWIN *Enquirer* I. i. 1 The true object of education..is the generation of happiness. **1832** LYELL *Princ. Geol.* II. 210 The generation of peat, when not completely under water, is confined to moist situations. **1847** CRAIG, s.v., In Geometry, generation or genesis is the formation or production of a geometrical figure or quantity. **1863** TYNDALL *Heat* ii. §22 (1870) 26 Liquefaction in this case will conclusively demonstrate a generation of heat.

b. *spec.* The production of electricity. Also *attrib.*

1886 W. WORMELL tr. *Urbanitzky's Electr. in Service of Man* 95 The generation of electricity is to be explained by the mere contact of bodies with each other. **1900** *Westm. Gaz.* 7 Mar. 9/1 The generation and distribution expenses for the year. **1901** *Ibid.* 14 Nov. 8/3 The generation plant for the first section of the new electric tramways. **1943** J. S. HUXLEY *TVA* i. 9 Flood-control could be readily tied up..with the profitable generation of electric power.

c. *Linguistics.* The process of deriving the grammatical sequences of a language from a basis that constitutes the grammar.

1959 *Word* XV. 234 Following through with a very condensed generation sequence (in which most irrelevant rules and choices are omitted), we might have something like this. *Ibid.* 237 A short sample idiom-generation might look like this. **1963** J. LYONS *Structural Semantics* ii. 31 In the learning and use of language there are two complementary factors to be reckoned with. These I shall call generation and recall... By 'generation' [I mean] the construction of a form by the individual speaker from elements which are themselves taken from 'storage'. **1965** N. CHOMSKY *Aspects of Theory of Syntax* i. 60 Both weak and strong generation are determined by the procedure.

II. That which is generated.

The use of the word in senses 3–6 is largely due to the frequent occurrence of *generatio* in the Vulgate. Translators were probably uncertain as to the exact meaning of it in certain passages, as *Isa.* liii. 8, to which the following seems to be the earliest reference in English.

13.. *E.E. Allit. P.* A. 827 Hys generacyoun quo recen con, þat dyȝed for vus in Iherusalem?

†3. a. Offspring, progeny. In early instances chiefly *to give* (*have*) *generation*. *Obs.*

1382 WYCLIF *Isa.* lxvi. 9 If I, that generacion to othere men ȝyue, bareyn shal be? seith the Lord thi God. **1422** tr. *Secreta Secret, Priv. Priv.* (E.E.T.S.) 197 This same ysaac had a wyfe barayne ycallid Rebecta, he Prayed god that he wolde yeue hym generacion. *c* **1477** CAXTON *Jason* 4 He had in mariage a right fayr lady but they were long to geder with oute hauyng generacion. **1526** TINDALE *Acts* xvii. 28 For we are also his generacion. **1540–1** ELYOT *Image Gov.* (1549) 93 His mother Mammea exhorted hym to take to his wyfe some mayden of a noble and auncient house, to the entent that he mought haue generacion. **1553** BECON *Reliques of Rome* (1563) 240 Al those y^t wearry or slea their generations, or their children destroye with drinkes. **1605** SHAKS. *Lear* I. i. 119 The barbarous Scythian Or he that makes his generation messes To gorge his appetite. **1674** tr. *Martiniere's Voy. N. Countries* 84 If he were discovered..he and his generation [should be] sent Slaves into Siberia.

†b. Descendants, posterity. *Obs.*

c **1400** MAUNDEV. (1839) xii. 140 This Machomete..was of the Generacioun of Ysmael, that was Abrahames Sone. **1535** COVERDALE *Job* xxi. 8 Their childers children lyue in their sight, and their generacion [**1611** offspring] before their eyes. **1623** LISLE *Ælfric on O. & N. Test.* Exod., Foure hundred yeeres after Jacob came thither with the generation of the Hebrewes. **1704** HEARNE *Duct. Hist.* (1714) I. 185 Which Land the Lord gave to Abraham and his Generation, and promised that in his Family all the Nations of the Earth should be Blessed.

†c. Fruit, produce (of the vine). *Obs. rare.*

A rendering of *genimen* (*vitis*) (Matt. xxvi. 29) = Gr. γέννημα (τοῦ ἀμπέλου). Wyclif and later translators use 'fruit'.

1483 CAXTON *Gold. Leg.* 244 b/2, I shalle not drynke of thys generacion of the vyne tofore I shalle drynke it newe wyth you [etc.]. **1565** JEWEL *Repl. Harding* (1611) 334, I will drinke no more of this Generation of the Vine.

4. a. The offspring of the same parent or parents, regarded as a single degree or step in the descent of a person or family from an ancestor; also, in wider sense, = DEGREE 3.

In reckoning genealogies, each generation is naturally restricted to one individual in the direct line, without regard to collateral descendants.

a **1300** *Cursor M.* 9262 Qua-so will se fra adam þe ald Hu mani knes to crist es tald, He sal find, wit-vten mistruns, Sexti hale generacions. **1387** TREVISA *Higden* (Rolls) II. 231 Caym his synne was i-punsched seuenfold, þat is in þe seuenþe generacioun; for Lamech was þe seuenþe from Adam in þat lyne. *c* **1460** FORTESCUE *Abs. & Lim. Mon.* ix. (1885) 129 Charles, discended off Carolus Magnus..by ix. or by x. generacions, was put ffrom the Kyngdome of Fraunce. **1595** SHAKS. *John* II. i. 181 The Canon of the Law is laide on him, Being but the second generation Remoued from thy sinne-conceiuing wombe. **1638** F. JUNIUS *Paint. Ancients* 95 When many generations issuing forth out of one man, who had a certaine marke, do constantly retaine the same marke in some part of their bodies. **1816** J. WILSON *City of Plague* II. v, I have known the family Three generations, and I loved them all. **1834** T. MEDWIN *Angler in Wales* I. 77 A family party, consisting of three generations; the last a numerous one. **1835** THIRLWALL *Greece* I. vii. 258 Ætolus, his ancestor in the tenth generation, had quitted Elis.

b. first- (or **second-**, etc.) **generation** *a.*, designating a member of the first (or second, etc.) generation of a family, *spec.* of descendants of immigrant parents, esp. in the United States; also, designating a naturalized immigrant (or a child, etc., of a naturalized immigrant). Also *transf.* and *fig.*

1896 S. A. BARNETT *Let.* Sept. in H. Barnett *Canon Barnett* (1918) II. 119 There are the usual Americans. One 'first-generation man', as he calls himself..has made a great fortune. **1946** J. O'HARA in *55 Short Stories from New Yorker* (1952) 199 Francis had his place at the bar, at the far corner, and it was his so long as he was present. First-generation Jimmy and second-generation Jimmy had seen to that. **1951** M. MCLUHAN *Mech. Bride* 67/1 First-generation immigrants who quickly made good. *Ibid.* 67/2 The father is just such a second-generation type. **1953** E. COXHEAD *Midlanders* vi. 153 Herself a second-generation college girl, she now under-valued the freedoms the pioneers had won. **1956** *Nature* 10 Mar. 489/2 Second-generation inbreds... Fourth-generation inbreds... F_1 hybrids between third-generation inbreds. **1960** *Guardian* 29 July 4/4 Deriabin, born in 1921, was a second generation Communist. **1960** *Ibid.* 5 Nov. 3/6 A second-generation Kenyan whose father was one of the pioneer settlers in the White Highlands. **1962** *Chem. Engin. Progress* Oct. 44 (*caption*) First generation (left) and improved (right) void-free laminates of phenolic resin and graphite fabric. **1968** L. BLACK *Outbreak* ix. 86 The number of notifications [of smallpox] will rise sharply, as second and third generation cases emerge from the incubation period.

c. Any of the recognized stages in the development of computers; freq. *attrib.*, designating or pertaining to the type of computer belonging to this stage. Usu. in ***first*(-), *second*(-)**, etc., ***generation***.

The consistently defined generations are the first (employing valves), the second (employing transistors), and the fifth (not yet realized, but planned to include the capacity for artificial intelligence).

1952 *Rev. Electronic Digital Computers* (Amer. Inst. Electr. Engineers) 109/3 In building the first generation of electronic digital computers, we have learned the magnitude of the engineering involved. **1958** *Computer Jrnl.* I. 105/2 Much depends on the intrinsic reliability achieved by the next generation of very fast digital computers. **1963** *Ibid.* VI. 144/1 It has recently become conventional to distinguish between 'first-generation computers' and 'second-generation computers'. The term *second-generation computer* has come to mean transistorized core-store computers, mostly with some sort of time-sharing routine. .. The third-generation computers..will be transistorized with magnetic-film stores or superconducting stores. *Ibid.* 153/2 The new fourth-generation computers will be limited mainly by the uncertainty principle associated with any form of wave motion. **1969** P. B. JORDAIN *Condensed Computer Encycl.* 529 Fourth-generation computers will employ very large capacity data storage files. **1971** E. F. SCHOETERS in B. de Ferranti *Living with Computer* viii. 71 Programmers ran into severe difficulties with second-generation equipment on comparatively simple routines. Users are naturally applying a 'softly-softly' approach, even with third-generation computers, which are so much more flexible and powerful. **1978** *Pract. Computing* July–Aug. 12/1 The result was that the first Apple..was quickly converted into a market research exercise for a properly-funded second generation machine. **1982** F. J. GALLAND *Dict. Computing* 112/2 Some writers have used the term 'fourth generation' with respect to computers with virtual storage and/or dispersed intelligence. **1982** LONGLEY & SHAIN *Dict. Information Technol.* 125/2 *Fifth generation computer*, the proposed series of computers, to be produced in the early 1990's, which will have radically new architectures to exploit the potential of AI developments. **1983** *Dict. Computing* 150/2 *Fourth generation* of computers, a designation covering machines that were designed after 1970 (approximately) and are characterized by use of integrated circuit technology and very large (more than one megabyte) main memory. In addition to these characteristics, fourth generation systems nearly all have extensive support for networking. *Ibid.* 360/1 Third generation of computers... Discrete transistors were used through most of this generation. *Ibid.* 360/2 The third generation saw the introduction of comprehensive operating systems that included support for multiprogramming, multiprocessing, and multiprocessors. **1984** *Listener* 1 Nov. 38/4 The fifth-generation computer will carry out 'parallel processing', imitating the human brain by trying many paths of reasoning at the same instant, and quickly finding the 'right' answer. **1984** *QL User* Dec. 18 A fifth-generation computer is an artificial intelligence machine, a super-expert system.

5. The whole body of individuals born about the same period; also, the time covered by the lives of these.

In reckoning historically by 'generations', the word is taken to mean the interval of time between the birth of the parents and that of their children, usually computed at thirty years, or three generations to a century.

a **1340** HAMPOLE *Psalter* xi. 8 þou lord sall ȝeme vs & kepe vs fra þis generacioun. **1535** COVERDALE *Mark* viii. 12 Why doth this generacion seke a token? Verely I saye vnto you: There shal no token be geuen vnto this generacion. **1577** B. GOOGE *Heresbach's Husb.* I. (1586) 28 Barley, accounted in the olde generations among the woorthyest sort of grayne, and not of small estimation at this day. **1611** BIBLE *Judg.* ii. 10 And also all that generation were gathered vnto their fathers: and there arose another generation after them. **1694** *Acc. Sev. Late Voy.* Introd. (1711) 24 Heaps of Rocks, broken Stones, and Ice heap'd up from many Generations. **1750** JOHNSON *Rambler* No. 77 ¶ 14 The hopes of the rising generation. **1781** GIBBON *Decl. & F.* II. xxvi. 48 The rising generation was not disposed to accept his advice. **1831** BREWSTER *Newton* (1855) II. xxiii. 306 His second objection to the new system relates to the length of generations, which he says is made only eighteen or twenty years. **1837** HT. MARTINEAU *Soc. Amer.* II. 151 The negroes of the next generation are not to be doomed to slavery for fear of somewhat more being inflicted on their parents. **1874** GREEN *Short Hist.* ix. §1. 591 It is in this group of scientific observers that we catch the secret of the coming generation.

†6. Family, breed, race; class, kind, or 'set' of persons. *Obs.*

c **1477** CAXTON *Jason* 4 Thenne his wyf conceyued of his seed and multeplied the generacion humayn of a right fayr sone. *c* **1511** *1st Eng. Bk. Amer.* (Arb.) Introd. 36/2 Sende to vs ayen a good knyght of ye generacyon of fraunce. **1556** *Aurelio & Isab.* (1608) F vij, Butte corsede be the generation, that dressethe all his thoughtes againste hus unto the worste parte. **1576** J. SANFORD *Gard. Pleas.* 48 Banished out of Rome, advocates, proctours, notaries, and that lyke generation. **1607** SHAKS. *Timon* I. i. 204, *Pain.* Y'are a Dogge. *Ape.* Thy Mothers of my generation: what's she, if I be a Dogge? **1638** SIR T. HERBERT *Trav.* 233 However as they are, they [their Physitians] passe for a generation usefull and requisite. **1641** TRAPP *Theol. Theol.* 140 There have beene a generation..that have attempted to take armes against Heaven. **1712** ARBUTHNOT *John Bull* II. iii, Then the whole generation of him are so in love with bagpipes and puppet-shews! **1724** DE FOE *Mem. Cavalier* (1840) 216 They could not brook the fighting in conjunction with this wicked generation [the Irish]. **1727** BOYER *Dict.*

Angl.-Fr., *Generation* (*or* a great many),.. there is a whole generation of them.

7. *attrib.* and *Comb.*, as ***generation-conscious*** adj.; **generation gap** (cf. GAP *sb.*[1] 6 a).

1930 R. MACAULAY *Staying with Relations* iv. 57 'I remember an air raid,' said Julian. 'They woke me up and carried me down to the basement. I am the air raid generation.' 'They're terribly generation-conscious,' Adrian explained. **1934** R. CAMPBELL *Broken Record* 50 Quarrelling with my father made me generation-conscious. **1967** *Boston Globe* 18 May 10/1 He acknowledged that the 'generation gap' is difficult both for the younger and the older generations. **1968** *Guardian* 25 Oct. 14/6 There is a generation gap in attitude but not in the way this family treat each other. **1969** W. GARNER *Us or Them War* xxi. 167 He said, 'Patti, whatever becomes of the generation gap?' She said, 'I jumped across...' **1971** K. DICK *Ivy & Stevie* 54 Generally, poets in her [*sc.* Stevie Smith's] age group.. do not escape criticism from what is journalistically termed 'generation-gap' censure.

Hence **geneˈrational** *a.*, pertaining to generations.

1894 *Atlantic Monthly* Jan. 116 At this stage in the development of the generational system, the parent gives but the beginnings of life. **1947** WELLEK & WARREN *Theory Lit.* xviii. 259 The largest reputations survive generational tastes: Chaucer, Spenser, Shakespeare.. and Tennyson have a permanent.. position. **1956** WYNDHAM LEWIS *Red Priest* xxvi. 217 You are younger than I am, and probably are in a different generational stream. **1964** *Punch* 9 Sept. 382/2 The generational gap is even more extended at student level. **1971** *Guardian* 9 Feb. 8/7 The generational outbursts against humanity.

generationism (dʒɛnəˈreɪʃənɪz(ə)m). [f. GENERATION + -ISM.] (See quot. 1876.)

1864 *Home & For. Rev.* Apr. 676 He [Frohschammer] published a work on the origin of the soul.. defending the theory of Generationism. **1876** W. ALEXANDER *Bampton Lect.* (1877) 213 One school held that not only the body but the soul came from the parents; and this doctrine was termed traducianism or generationism. **1893** *Tablet* 18 Feb. 257 It is not allowable to any loyal Catholic to hold spiritual traducianism or generationism.

generative (ˈdʒɛnərətɪv), *a.* [f. GENERATE *v.* + -IVE. Cf. F. *génératif.*]

1. Pertaining to generation or procreation; having the power or function of producing offspring.

1413 *Pilgr. Sowle* (Caxton 1483) IV. xxvii. 72 The sowle hath power vegetatif and generatif for to conseruen his kynde and multyplyen. **1594** PLAT *Jewell-ho.* I. 6 Neither is there any place.. where that generatiue vertue doth more abound.. then in the wide Ocean. **1628** GAULE *Pract. Theories* (1629) 76 Spirits are not vsually generatiue, nor are Virgines pregnant. **1660** PEPYS *Diary* 14 Dec., We.. had very good discourse concerning insects and their having a generative faculty as well as other Creatures. **1809** *Med. Jrnl.* XXI. 519 Complaints of the generative organs. **1871-2** H. MACMILLAN *True Vine* iv. 167 By preventing plants from reproducing, leaves and wood are produced instead of generative products. **1880** GÜNTHER *Fishes* 158 In the Cyclostomes the generative organ is single.

fig. *c* **1400** *Apol. Loll.* 55 Wen þei of þer office are gederers of euerlastyng lif, how euen þey are þus misusing þis generatif strengþe. **1597** HOOKER *Eccl. Pol.* V. l. §1 Not onely the Word, but the Sacraments, both hauing generatiue force and vertue. **1816** COLERIDGE *Statesm. Man.* (Bohn) 353 This state of mind.. is a mere balance or compromise of the two powers, not that living and generative interpenetration of both which would give being to essential religion. **1883** *Congregationalist* Mar. 190 That word is creative, generative, begets a new life which supplants and expels the old.

2. a. Having the power or function of generating (in senses 2 and 3 of the vb.); productive.

1611 SPEED *Hist. Gt. Brit.* IX. xx. §36 These causes, (being in their proper nature most generatiue of sedition, and of all sorts of ciuill furies). **1640** BP. REYNOLDS *Passions* xxviii. 294 Feare is a Multiplying and Generative Passion, ever producing motions of its owne Nature. **1686** GOAD *Celest. Bodies* I. ii. 6 What Meats are generative of Wind? **1750** tr. *Leonardus' Mirr. Stones* 21 We will affirm then that the effective or generative cause of stones, is a certain mineral virtue. **1799** *Med. Jrnl.* I. 495 This agent is known to be the generative cause of several diseases of the bones. **1876** BANCROFT *Hist. U.S.* VI. Index 533 The people.. yearn for fuller knowledge of the rules of right, as the generative principles of social peace.

b. *Linguistics.* Able to generate (in sense 2 d of the vb.); concerned with generation (2 c); ***generative grammar***: see quots. 1964 and 1965.

1959 *Word* XV. 233 A generative grammar, as Chomsky has shown, may be conveniently arranged in the form of a series of equation-like rules. **1960** *Language* XXXVI. 360 (*title*) The place of intonation in a generative grammar of English. **1964** E. BACH *Introd. Transformational Gram.* ii. 13 A (*generative*) grammar of a language is a theory or set of statements which tells us in a formal and explicit way which strings of the basic elements of the language are permitted. **1964** E. A. NIDA *Toward Sci. Transl.* iv. 60 A generative grammar is based upon certain fundamental kernel sentences, out of which the language builds up its elaborate structure by various techniques of permutation, replacement, addition and deletion. **1965** N. CHOMSKY *Aspects of Theory of Syntax* i. 8 By a generative grammar I mean simply a system of rules that in some explicit and well-defined way assigns structural descriptions to sentences. **1968** J. LYONS *Introd. Theoret. Ling.* iv. 139 Any linguistic description which has this capacity of describing actual utterances as members of a larger class of potential utterances, is said to be generative.

Hence **ˈgeneratively** *adv.*, by way of generation; **ˈgenerativeness**.

1643 R. O. *Man's Mort.* vi. 41 That which is immortall cannot generatively proceed from that which is mortall. **1727** BAILEY vol. II, *Generativeness*, generative or begetting Quality or Faculty.

ˈgenerativist. [f. GENERATIV(E *a.* + -IST.] One who employs the methods of generative grammar.

1965 *Amer. Speech* XL. 289 This seems to allow generativists a token amount of equal time, but it is clear that they are 'the other party'. **1967** *Word* XXIII. 47 Since generativists began to turn to the concept of deep grammar as input to the transformational rules that produce 'surface' sentences.

generator (ˈdʒɛnəreɪtə(r)). [a. L. *generātor*, masc. agent-n. f. *generāre*: see GENERATE *v.*]

1. One who generates or begets.

1646 SIR T. BROWNE *Pseud. Ep.* VI. x. 327 Imagination.. sometimes assimilates the Idea of the generator into a realty in the thing ingendred. **1814** CARY *Dante, Par.* VIII. 141 Nature, in generation, must the path Traced by the generator still pursue. **1841-4** EMERSON *Ess.* Ser. I. x. (1876) 252 Whilst the eternal generation of circles proceeds, the eternal generator abides.

2. Something which generates or produces; *esp.* an apparatus for the production of gases, steam, or electricity.

1794 G. ADAMS *Nat. & Exp. Philos.* I. xii. 493 The French writers term it hydrogene, that is, generator of water. **1825** HAMILTON *Handbk.*, *Generator* in Pneumatics, the high pressure boiler of Mr. Perkins's steam engine is thus named. **1854** RONALDS & RICHARDSON *Chem. Technol.* (ed. 2) I. 160 Generators are constructed either to work with or without a blast of air. **1879** TYNDALL *Fragm. Sc.* (ed. 6) II. xvi. 435 By it, in short, the electric generator is so far simplified, and reduced in cost, as to [etc.]. **1884** *Health Exhib. Catal.* 109/1 Hot Wind Generator, for ventilating houses and hospitals, and heating same. **1895** *Educ. Rev.* (U.S. Nov. 352 Dynamo, absolutely meaningless as at present found, is popularly used in place of generator.

3. a. *Chem.* 'A term used to denote the elements or compounds from which a more complex substance is obtained' (Cassell).

b. *Mus.* The 'fundamental tone' of a series of harmonics or of a chord.

1825 DANNELEY *Encycl. Mus.* s.v. *Sound*, The diatonic scale is therefore formed by the products of a sonorous body, generator or generating string. **1847** CRAIG, *Generator*, in Music, the principal sound or sounds by which others are produced. **1889** E. PROUT *Harmony* ii. §33 The division of any string into halves, quarters, eighths, or sixteenths, gives the various upper octaves of the 'generator', or 'fundamental tone', that is the note produced by the vibration of the whole length of the string.

4. a. *Geom.* = GENERANT A. b.

1863 *Phil. Trans. R. Soc.* CLIII. 455 The nodal generating lines or Nodal Generator. **1893** N. F. DUPUIS *Elem. Synthetic Solid Geom.* i. 7 The variable line N is called the generator, and the fixed guiding lines are directors. **1959** *Chambers's Encycl.* III. 837/1 Analytically, it is convenient to regard the generators of a cone (i.e. the lines joining the vertex to points on the base circle) as extending to infinity in both directions.

b. *Algebra.* Any of a subset of the elements of a set in terms of which all the other elements of the set can be represented, using specified operations.

1894 *Bull. Amer. Math. Soc.* I. 63 A substitution σ of Γ' is determined by the elements a', b', c' which it makes correspond to the generators a, b, c. **1940** C. C. MACDUFFEE *Introd. Abstract Algebra* ii. 53 A cyclic group has as its elements the powers of a single generator. **1947** BIRKHOFF & MACLANE *Surv. Mod. Algebra* xiv. 373 Any number in the field can be expressed in terms of this new generator.

c. *Computers.* A routine that enables a computer to construct from a set of parameters other routines or sub-routines with specific applications. Also *attrib.*

1953 *Computers & Automation* May 4 Editing is but one phase of the commercial and logistic problems which lend themselves to generator techniques. **1956** BERKELEY & WAINWRIGHT *Computers* viii. 344/2 *Generator*, a computer program which generates coding. **1958** GOTLIEB & HUME *High-Speed Data Processing* xiv. 293 Generators have also been written for editing, re-run procedures, tape checking, and moving records. **1962** HUSKEY & KORN *Computer Handbk.* xvii. 19 If memory space is not a problem the input information can be reduced to reasonable size by devising a generator code which is usually cyclic in character and can produce the linear code.

generatrix (dʒɛnəˈreɪtrɪks). [a. L. *generātrix*, fem. agent-n. f. *generāre*: see GENERATE *v.*]

†**1.** She that generates or produces; a female parent. (Only *fig.*) *Obs.*

1657 PINNELL tr. *Paracelsus' Philos.* II. 32 The element of fire is the generatrix of the Stars, Planets, and the whole Firmament. **1794** SULLIVAN *View Nat.* II. 278 Night was called the mother, the generatrix of all things. **1813** T. BUSBY *Lucretius Comm.* I. iii, This divine generatrix of every being and every blessing.

2. *Math.* = GENERANT A. b.

1840 LARDNER *Geom.* 176 A straight edge representing the directrix may be moved over a figure representing the generatrix [etc.]. **1871** TYNDALL *Fragm. Sc.* (1879) I. iv. 108 Blended to a screw surface with an inclined generatrix.

3. 'A dynamo-electric machine employed to generate an electric current' (*Cent. Dict.*). = GENERATOR 2.

generic (dʒɪˈnɛrɪk), *a.* and *sb.* [f. L. *gener-*, stem of *genus* kind + -IC: cf. F. *générique*, used by Descartes.] **A.** *adj.* **a.** Belonging to a genus or class; applied to a large group or class of objects; general (opposed to SPECIFIC or SPECIAL); esp. in ***generic character, name, term. generic image***, a mental image representing a class or genus of objects, whether formed (as is usually supposed) by blending images of several particular members of that class or by preventing an image from becoming fully determinate.

1676 GREW *Anat. Leaves* I. vi. §5 This Saline Principle.. is.. a Generik Name, under which divers Species are comprehended. **1678** GALE *Crt. Gentiles* III. 97 He makes it be only a remote concurse to the act considered in genere, in its generic nature, not to the individual particular act. **1724** WATTS *Logic* I. vi. §4 Though wine differs from other liquids in that it is the juice of a certain fruit, yet this is but a general or generic difference, for it does not distinguish wine from cyder or perry. **1789** BENTHAM *Princ. Legisl.* xviii. §35 The circumstance of fraudulency then may serve to characterize a particular species, comprisable under each of those generic heads. **1805-17** R. JAMESON *Char. Min.* (ed. 3) 2 The generic characters are certain properties of minerals used as characters, without any reference to their differences, as colour, lustre, weight. **1817** COLERIDGE *Biog. Lit.* v. 98 Des Cartes.. showed, in what sense not only general terms, but generic images (under the name of abstract ideas) actually existed. **1821** J. Q. ADAMS in C. Davies *Metr. Syst.* III. (1871) 208 The terms 'weight' and 'balance' were thus generic terms, without specific meaning. **1851** RICHARDSON *Geol.* viii. 208 The preservation of the generic and specific characters of fossil remains varies in different strata. **1878** W. JAMES *Noteb.* in R. B. Perry *Tht. & Char. of W. J.* (1935) II. 80 Generic images.. will be remembered as further instances of facts persistently denied by empiricists. **1882** F. GALTON in *Proc. R. Inst.* IX. 166 The generic images that arise before the mind's eye.. are analogues of these composite pictures. **1918** J. WARD *Psychol. Princ.* xii. 299 The generic image (*Gemeinbild* of German psychologists) constitutes the connecting link between ideation and conception. **1953** H. H. PRICE *Thinking & Exper.* ix. 292 Both Locke and Kant were talking about generic images, though they did not know it.

b. Of a name or designation (as for some type of product): that is used generally for the article, etc., that it describes, and is therefore not admissible as a trade mark; not protected by legislation, non-proprietary. *Law* (chiefly *U.S.*).

1849 WOODBURY & MINOT *Rep. Cases Circuit Court U.S.: First Circuit* II. 10 It was merely decided, that the Court would not enjoin one tradesman from using the same mark with another, a generic one, 'the Great Mogul'. **1884** *Rep. Cases Ohio Supreme Court* 2nd Ser. XLI. 135 It is further insisted, that there is no mechanical device [etc.].. to which the name could refer, and thus become, as it were, generic in its character.] **1901** *Supreme Court Reporter* (U.S.) XXI. 13/2 He should not have waited until the name 'Hunyadi' had become generic in this country, and indicative of this whole class of medicinal waters. **1937** *Federal Reporter* (2nd Ser.) LXXXV. 81/2 From the evidence it appeared that 'Eureka' to the dealers in shirts had become generic in referring to the style, but to the ultimate purchasers the word had reference to the plaintiff's own make. **1938** *Supreme Court* (U.S.) (1939) LXXXIII. 73/1 The original maker of an article acquires no exclusive right to the use as a tradename of the term by which it has become known, where the term is generic. **1967** *Times Rev. Industry* Mar. 40/1 A number of articles, particularly consumer goods, have acquired the mixed blessing of becoming not only household words but being spoken of as 'generic' names. **1984** *Executive Newslet.* (U.S. Trademarks Assoc.) No. 42. 3/2 Escalator, yo-yo, cellophane and aspirin were once attractive trademarks. They have all been found by courts to be generic and have been stripped of their trademark status.

c. *spec.* designating a drug name specially given in order that it may be freely used without legal restriction (esp. pharmacopœias), in contrast to the brand names of particular suppliers; also applied to a product sold under such a name.

1953 *Chem. & Engin. News* 7 Dec. 5117/1 The problem of applying to chemicals short names of a type called variously 'generic', 'nonproprietary', and 'coined common' is becoming increasingly important. **1973** *Sci. Amer.* Sept. 161/2 The general public is aware of and concerned about such issues as.. the debate over brand-name v. generic-name prescription writing. *Ibid.* 161/3 Ethical pharmaceuticals are.. subdivided into brand-name and generic products. **1975** *Chem. Week* 26 Mar. 17/3 Maintaining bioequivalency among various brands of a particular generic drug should not prove a problem. **1984** *Gainesville Sun* 28 Mar. 8A/4 (Advt.), Compare & save on your next prescription both ways: brand names & generic drugs.

d. Of groceries, etc.: not marked with the producer's brand-name, esp. when the product is one of a range of goods offered at lower prices because of plain, cheap packaging. orig. *U.S.* Cf. NO-NAME *a.* 1.

1977 *Time* 21 Nov. 80/3 Unlike the major brands, which usually demand top-grade foodstuffs, the generic products are the cheaper, 'standard' quality goods. **1979** *Globe & Mail* (Toronto) 25 June 14/1 Loblaw's has just introduced them as part of its no-name line of generic foods. **1980** *Australian* 23 June 4/6 Australia's biggest wholesaling group, Davids Holdings Ltd, has moved into the boom area of generic grocery retailing. **1985** *Times* 4 July 25/7 Another six months or a year could.. put Liggett out for good, leaving B & W in a strong position in the US generic cigarette market. **1986** *Business Rev. Weekly* 22 Aug. 81/2 When generic products started to take hold, many consumers began demanding better-quality branded products.

B. *sb.* **a.** *absol.*; also (*nonce-use*) as *sb. pl.* = 'generic questions.'

1807 T. SIKES in Southey *Life of A. Bell* (1844) II. 567, I requested you to give me the solution of two generics, which

..would suggest to me what *sort* of matter I should want for your satisfaction. **1817** COLERIDGE *Biog. Lit.* II. xxiii. 263 The ideal consists in the happy balance of the generic with the individual.

b. A generic word; *spec.* (see quot. 1961).

1961 WEBSTER, *Generic*, an element of a compound proper name that is general and often lowercased (as *river* in 'Mississippi River' and *store* in 'XYZ Store'). **1962** BURRILL & BONSACK in Householder & Saporta *Probl. in Lexicogr.* 184 The words *hope* and *folly*, encountered in some names, have a topographic meaning and are used as generics in England. **1964** *Language* XL. 49 Generics may be considered the name given to a particular interpretation of the definite article.

c. A generic drug or product. Cf. NO-NAME *sb.* 1.

1967 *Sci. News Let.* 4 Mar. 207 (*heading*) Senate backing of low cost generics could cut retail prices and open new competition between drugs. **1967** *Business Periodical Index 1966-7* 867/1 (*title*) Drug potency survey by FDA discloses trade-name products are nosed out by the generics. **1970** *Sat. Rev.* (U.S.) 30 May 25 A pharmacist speaks candidly. ..I am a firm believer in using brand name products or quality generics from reliable manufacturers. **1979** *Glaxo Group News* Apr. 1/4 Selling branded generics is the toughest job in the pharmaceutical industry. **1979** *Fortune* 26 Mar. 70/3 Generics originated in France in 1976 with the giant Carrefour supermarket chain. Carrefour called them *produits libres*..which it explained were as good as the branded products it sold but free from costly promotion and fancy packaging. **1979, 1982** [see NO-NAME *a.* 1].**1985** [see NO-NAME *sb.* 1].

generical (dʒɪˈnɛrɪkəl), *a.* [f. as prec. + -AL[1].] Belonging to, or having the character of, a genus; generic, general.

1432-50 tr. *Higden* (Rolls) I. 27 Mappa mundi is describede in the firste boke of this werke, in the maner of a diuision genericalle in to a diuision specificalle [L. *more divisi generis in species*]. **1650** FULLER *Pisgah* I. vii. 17 We must conceive such of them as are omitted to be implyed under the genericall name of Canaanites. **1680** BAXTER *Answ. Stillingfl.* xxiii. 35 The Generical Notion sure is not enough for the definition of each species. **1764** REID *Inquiry* iii. Wks. I. 116/1 A question, how all smells come to be considered as one genus, and all tastes as another? What is the generical distinction. **1843** MRS. CARLYLE *Lett.* I. 270 Holding some rank in the world, besides the generical rank of fool. **1865** LECKY *Ration.* (1878) II. 334 There was such an amazing, I might almost say generical, difference between those who were Christians and those who were not.

Hence **geˈnericalness.** *rare*[−1].

1708 A. COLLINS *Answ. Clarke's 3rd Def.* 43 The Question ..has no relation to the genericalness of the Objects on which we think, but to the genericalness of Thinking itself.

generically (dʒɪˈnɛrɪkəlɪ), *adv.* [f. as prec. + -LY[2].] **a.** With reference to genus.

1651 BAXTER *Inf. Bapt.* 76 If it determine not the kinde of good formally, nor virtually, nor contain it generically [etc.]. **1695** WOODWARD *Nat. Hist. Earth* (1723) 27 Genericaly allied. **1748** HARTLEY *Observ. Man* II. i. 30 We suppose other Beings generically the same, and yet numerically different. **1783** BLAIR *Rhet.* (1812) I. vii. 144 These two kinds of writing are generically and essentially distinct. **1868** PEARD *Water-Farm.* xv. 155 The tench..belongs to the carp family, and is separated from it generically on account of the size of the scales with which the body is covered [etc.]. **1894** H. DRUMMOND *Ascent Man* 140 Among the most ancient Carboniferous plants..are found certain forms generically identical with those now living.

b. In a generic or non-proprietary manner; without the protection of a patent or of trade-mark legislation. Chiefly *U.S.*

1967 *Times Rev. Industry* Mar. 41/1 Although Dictaphone was the first company to sell dictating machines, it no longer holds the pride of place in the market and the use of its name 'generically' in speech is now largely historical. **1973** *Sci. Amer.* Sept. 162/2 The pharmacist..is in a position to select the brand when the prescription is written generically. **1977** *Chicago Tribune* 2 Oct. I. 4/3 The law will have a bigger impact on costs in a few years when many more drugs lose their patent protection and can be made generically.

geˈnericism. *rare*[−1]. [f. GENERIC + -ISM.] Explained by the writer to mean: 'The systematic official adoption of generic as contradistinguished from specific phraseology'.

1840 G. S. FABER *Regen.* 342 The principle of Genericism pervades all the Offices of the Church of England.

genericness (dʒɪˈnɛrɪknɪs). [f. GENERIC *a.* + -NESS.] Generic quality or characteristics.

1939 P. CHRISTOPHERSEN *Articles* 33 *The* represents an aggregating genericness,..*a* is a singularizing form. **1939** *Mind* XLVIII. 150 Scales of kinds or sorts, which scales exhibit differences in degree of generic-ness or specific-ness.

generific (dʒɛnəˈrɪfɪk), *a. nonce-wd.* [f. L. *gener-* (see GENERIC) + -(I)FIC.]

1825 [see GENERALIFIC].

generification (dʒɛˌnɛrɪfɪˈkeɪʃən). *Logic.* [f. as prec. + -ATION.] (See quots. 1837, 1864.)

1837-8 SIR W. HAMILTON *Logic* xi. (1866) I. 191 The abstraction which carries up species into genera, is called, in that respect, Generification, or, more loosely, Generalisation. **1864** BOWEN *Logic* iv. 74 Generification is the process of rising, through the successive abstraction of Marks, from lower to higher Concepts. **1874** McCOSH *Scot. Philos.* li. (1875) 382 Mr. Grote and Mr. John Stuart Mill have tried to improve Mill's doctrine of generification.

generosity (dʒɛnəˈrɒsɪtɪ). [ad. L. *generōsitāt-em*, f. *generōs-us* GENEROUS.]

1. Excellence, goodness of race; nobility of birth or lineage. Now only *arch.*

1432-50 tr. *Higden* (Rolls) I. 49 Hit is to be holden that Asia is moste in quantite, Europa lesse in quantite, but egalle in the nummere generosite [L. *generositate*] of peple. **1572** BOSSEWELL *Armorie* 13 b, Sentences concerning generositie, collected out of sundrye Auctors, and firste certayne verses, made by G. Chaucer, teaching what is gentlenesse, or who is worthy to bee called gentle. **1579** LYLY *Euphues* (Arb.) 190 Nobilitie began in thy auncestors, and endeth in thee, and the Generositie that they gayned by vertue thou hast blotted with vice. **1650** BULWER *Anthropomet.* iii. (1653) 83 The ingenious Women are marked with certaine notes in the Forehead, which is accounted a kind of generosity. **1864** LOWELL *Biglow P.* Poet. Wks. (1879) 275 The Virginians especially lay claim to this generosity of lineage.

†**b.** Of animals: Excellence of breed; the spirit arising from this. *Obs.*

1575 LANEHAM *Lett.* (1871) 15 The foot men lookt well too the hors, and hee of Generositée soon callmd of him self. **1607** TOPSELL *Four-f. Beasts* (1658) 110 It weakeneth their bodies, and dulleth in them all generosity.

2. †High spirit, courage, nobility of conduct (*obs.*). Now only in the more restricted sense: Willingness to lay aside resentment or forgive injuries; magnanimity.

1623 COCKERAM, *Generosity*, noblenesse of minde, courage. **1659** B. HARRIS *Parival's Iron Age* 53 Their generosity is remarkable, in regard they grudge not to give praise to the vertue even of their enemies, when they deserve it. **1699** BENTLEY *Phal.* 236 His Judgment, like other mens Valour, has commonly the generosity to favour the weaker side. **1718** LADY M. W. MONTAGU *Let. to C'tess Bristol* (1887) I. 240 'Tis a degree of generosity to tell the truth. **1786** W. THOMSON *Watson's Philip III* (1839) 239 The part which sound policy required him to act, was consonant to the natural generosity of his temper. This magnanimous prince [etc.]. **1838** LYTTON *Alice* 41 Let me throw myself on your generosity. **1883** SIR T. MARTIN *Ld. Lyndhurst* v. 142 Generosity is never a characteristic of political party warfare.

3. Readiness or liberality in giving; munificence.

1677 WYCHERLEY *Plain Dealer* IV. i, They are of that vain number, who had rather shew their false generosity, in giving away profusely to worthless Flatterers, than in paying just Debts. **1712** HEARNE *Collect.* (O.H.S.) III. 337 My excellent Friend, to whose Generosity I owe my Education. **1750** JOHNSON *Rambler* No. 81 ¶9 The giver & receiver differ in their opinions of generosity. **1833** ALISON *Europe* (1849-50) I. iii. §93. 356 Generosity is nearly allied to extravagance.

4. *pl.* Instances of generosity (senses 2 and 3). *rare.*

1647 W. BROWNE tr. *Gomberville's Polexander* II. iv. ¶¶¶¶5 You love him even after he..without regarding so many generosities which should perswade him, hath done what in him lay to deprive you of your life. *a* **1715** BURNET *Own Time* (1766) I. 106 One that carried the generosities of friendship very far. **1833** LAMB *Elia II*, *Produc. Mod. Art*, The relish with which *his* Reading Public had received the fooleries of the man, more to their palates than the generosities of the master [Don Quixote].

†**5.** *the Order of Generosity*: a Prussian order of distinction, instituted in 1665, and superseded in 1740 by the Order for Merit. *Obs.*

1707 *Lond. Gaz.* No. 4359/1 His Majesty hath been pleas'd to give him the Cross of the Order of Generosity.

generous (ˈdʒɛnərəs), *a.* [ad. F. *généreux*, ad. L. *generōs-us*, f. *gener-*, *genus* stock, race; cf. Sp., It. *generoso*. The senses appear already developed in Fr. and for the most part in Latin.]

1. a. Of noble lineage; high-born. Also *absol.* = nobles (quot. 1610). Now only *arch.*

1588 SHAKS. *L.L.L.* v. i. 96 Most generous sir. **1603** KNOLLES *Hist. Turks* (1621) 1300 Many knights..of generous extraction. **1610** GUILLIM *Heraldry* III. vii. 116 The Ancient Generous made choice rather of such Herbes as grew in the Fields. *a* **1683** SIDNEY *Disc. Govt.* III. xxvii. (1704) 345 This has in several ages cost the Nation a vast proportion of generous blood. **1850** NEALE *Med. Hymns* 178 In a generous womb once dwelling. **1875** KINGSLEY *Lect. deliv. in Amer.* i. 3 That genial reverence for antiquity which I hold to be the sign of a truly generous—that is in the right sense of the grand old word—a truly high-bred nature.

†**b.** Of animals: Of good breed or stock. *Obs.*

1607 TOPSELL *Four-f. Beasts* (1658) 109 The generous Bitches have 12. [speans], other but 10. **1641** HINDE *J. Bruen* vii. 26, I have seene a Gentleman..very carefull to have his horse of a generous race. *a* **1680** BUTLER *Rem.* (1759) I. 71 Eagles try their Young against his Rays, To prove, if they're of generous Breed, or base. **1697** DRYDEN *Virg. Georg.* III. 119 The Colt that for a Stallion is design'd, By sure Presages shows his generous Kind. **1781** GIBBON *Decl. & F.* II. 57 The plains..bred a generous race of horses, renowned above all others in the antient world, for their majestic shape, and incomparable swiftness.

c. *transf.*

1749 *Power Pros. Numbers* 11 Of those which I call the generous or the noble Feet, some are more excellent than others.

2. a. Of actions, character, etc.: Appropriate or natural to one of noble birth or spirit; hence, †gallant, courageous (*obs.*); magnanimous, free from meanness or prejudice.

1588 SHAKS. *L.L.L.* v. ii. 632 This is not generous, not gentle, not humble. **1656** B. HARRIS *Parival's Iron Age* I. iii. 37 [He] made a generous resistance, and won a glorious victory. **1697** POTTER *Antiq. Greece* III. i. (1715) 1 The rapine of these [Flocks and Herds] was look'd on as a generous and heroical exploit. **1725** DE FOE *Voy. round World* (1840) 121 The gratitude they expressed..was a token of generous principles. **1823** SCOTT *Peveril* xii, This generous disposition to defy control. **1845** M. PATTISON *Ess.* (1889) I. 19 The spirit of timid reserve still kept the bishops silent, and this generous appeal met no response. **1880** McCARTHY *Own Times* IV. lxii. 398 It was an error indeed, but it was at least a generous error.

b. Of persons: †High-spirited, gallant, courageous (*obs.*); magnanimous, noble-minded.

1623 COCKERAM, *Generous*, valiant, noble. **1640** tr. *Verdere's Rom. Rom.* III. 8 This generous Warrior, that was not capable of fear in the greatest..dangers. **1656** B. HARRIS *Parival's Iron Age* 130 This generous Prince, being brought up in arms. *a* **1704** T. BROWN *Dk. Ormond's Recov.* Wks. 1730 I. 50 Neglected horses range along the plain, Their chariots broke, and generous riders slain! **1781** GIBBON *Decl. & F.* III. 261 The usurper..was tempted to place some confidence in so generous a conqueror. **1794** GODWIN *Cal. Williams* 9 The most generous Italian conceives that there are certain persons whom it would be contamination for him to call into the open field. **1876** MOZLEY *Univ. Serm.* ix. (1877) 195 He who is generous to an equal is generous at the risk of his own loss or fall by comparison.

†**c.** Of animals: Spirited. *Obs. rare.*

a **1661** FULLER *Worthies* (1890) III. 394 A generous creature a horse is, sensible in some sort of honour, made most handsome by pride. **1661** LOVELL *Hist. Anim. & Min.* Introd., Amongst the aforesaid living creatures, some are Solar, *sc.* those that are generous and lively, as the bull, goat, horse, lion.

3. a. Free in giving, liberal, munificent.

1696 tr. *Du Mont's Voy. Levant* 35 Since the Ladies here are no less Generous than Charming..there are many Intrigues form'd. **1704** ROWE *Ulyss.* Ded., The Restoring and Preserving any Part of Learning is so Generous an Action in it self, that it naturally falls into your Lordship's Province. **1768** STERNE *Sent. Journ.* (1778) II. 51 (Versailles) The king, he said, was the most generous of princes, but his generosity could neither relieve or reward every one. **1878** R. W. DALE *Lect. Preach.* viii. 248 A man may be generous with his money and ungenerous in his spirit. **1882** *Sat. Rev.* No. 1383. 533 He was himself generous as a giver, parting, indeed, with that which did not altogether belong to himself. **1896** *Scott. Notes & Queries* X. 22 These generous donations were afterwards supplemented.

b. *transf.* Of land: Rich, fertile. (Cf. F. *sol généreux.*)

1853 MERIVALE *Rom. Rep.* (1867) 3 Miles and miles of generous soil were abandoned to the boar and the buffalo. **1860** MOTLEY *Netherl.* (1868) I. i. 7 A generous southern territory, flowing with wine and oil.

4. a. Furnished liberally or without stint; hence, abundant, ample, copious.

1615 J. STEPHENS *Satyr. Ess.* 11 Clearkes and other knaves (Who with their generous ruffs the Court out-braves) Will take a pention, or a quarter-fee To make their friend from information free. **1790** J. B. MORETON *Mann. W. Ind.* 15 Yet they are fond to see strong liquors given in generous portions to the sailors. **1855** THACKERAY *Newcomes* I. 348 How great and liberal the houses are with generous casements and courts. **1886** O. W. HOLMES *Morb. Antip.* Introd. 21 His ample coat..with its broad flaps and many buttons and generous cuffs.

b. Of diet (with mixture of sense 5): Ample in quantity and rich in quality, strengthening. Also, with somewhat similar notion, of colour: Rich, full.

1833 PARIS in *Cycl. Pract. Med.* I. 568/2 Young children and growing youths generally thrive upon a generous diet of animal food. **1844** KINGLAKE *Eöthen* iii. (1878) 42 The glow of generous colour.

5. Of liquor, esp. wine: Rich and full of strength; invigorating; †also *absol.* as *sb.*

This use is originally due to L. *vinum generosum* (Horace) wine of a good class or stock. In Eng. (as in Fr.) it has associations derived from senses 2 and 3.

1630 *R. Johnson's Kingd. & Commw.* 285 The Neccar, whose bankes are inriched with the most generous Wines. *a* **1661** FULLER *Worthies* (1840) III. 486 It [Metheglin] is a most generous liquor. **1697** DRYDEN *Virg. Past.* v. 109 Two goblets will I crown with sparkling Wine, The gen'rous Vintage of the Chian Vine. **1740** E. BAYNARD *Health* (ed. 6) 11 Not that in general I condemn A Glass of Gen'rous now and then; When you are faint, your Spirits low. **1755** AMORY *Mem.* (1769) II. 98 He..perhaps had a bottle of generous in his stomach. **1768** BOSWELL *Corsica* iii. (ed. 2) 187 The juice of the Corsican grapes is so generous, that..it will always please by its natural flavour. **1826** DISRAELI *Viv. Grey* II. xvi, Drawing out, by the assistance of generous wine, their most kindly sentiment, and most engaging feelings. **1859** JEPHSON *Brittany* xiii. 223 Whose earliest nutriment was the generous wine of Béarn.

†**6.** Of remedies: Vigorous, strong, powerful. (Cf. HEROIC 4.) Also of a disease. *Obs.*

1665 BOYLE *Occas. Refl.* II. iv. (1845) 109 The Doctor thought himself this Day oblig'd to a quite contrary, and yet a more generous Remedy; and order'd, that, instead of giving me Drink, they should take away Blood. **1674** R. GODFREY *Inj. & Ab. Physic* 134 A..Doctor..being asked.. why he would not give such a Patient more generous remedies, seeing he grew so much worse under the use of common languid ones [etc.]. **1677** LADY CHAWORTH in *12th Rep. Hist. MSS. Comm.* App. v. 37 My Lord is still ill of the gout and the Duke of Buckingham hath had a generous fitt of itt.

7. *Comb.*, as ***generous-hearted***, ***-lipped***, ***-natured***, ***-souled*** adjs.

1813 JANE AUSTEN *Pride & Prej.* III. i. 10 He was always the sweetest-tempered, most *generous-hearted, boy in the world. **1856** WHITTIER *Panorama* 6 Wise-thoughted age, and generous-hearted youth. **1924** M. A. LOWNDES *Terriford Myst.* iii. 35 Her *generous-lipped mouth was too large for beauty. *Ibid.* vi. 68 She was the most devoted and *generous-natured of wives to me. **1907** *Daily Chron.* 9 Nov. 8/5 Like all *generous-souled men, her grandfather ran to extremes.

generously (ˈdʒɛnərəslɪ), *adv.* [f. prec. + -LY[2].]

†**1.** Highly in respect of birth. *Obs.*

1608 HEYWOOD *Lucrece* B, Tis pittie one so generously deriu'd Should be depriu'd: his best induements thus.

2. Nobly; †gallantly, bravely (*obs.*); unselfishly, magnanimously.

1591 PERCIVALL *Sp. Dict.*, *Generosamente*, generously, gentleman-like, *generosè*. **1640** tr. *Verdere's Rom. Rom.* II. 121 Rozalmond had generously slain two Giants. **1665** BOYLE *Occas. Refl.* (1845) 60 A Good Man, generously contending with ill Fortune. **1692** E. WALKER *Epictetus' Mor.* xxvii, Generously brave, Thou all their little Malice may'st defy. **1754** RICHARDSON *Grandison* III. xiv. 101 My dear Emily sat generously uneasy, I saw, for the trouble she had been the cause of giving. **1774** PENNANT *Tour Scotl. in* 1772, 249 A companion of the Saint generously offered himself. **1855** PRESCOTT *Philip II*, I. III. iv. 357 Granville now generously interceded in behalf of his ancient foe.

b. Of a horse: Bravely, gallantly.

1888 *Times* 26 June 11/6 The jockey Warne, who rode Success at Derby..stated that he made a good start.. Success ran, he said, generously.

3. Liberally; in an open-handed fashion.

1634-5 BRERETON *Trav.* (Chetham Soc.) 82 Here we rested the Lord's-day, and were very generously and nobly entertained. **1725** DE FOE *Eng. Tradesman* (1732) I. vii. 77 If his creditors will do anything generously for him, to enable him to go on again, well and good. **1766** GOLDSM. *Vic. W.* x, My wife always generously let them have a guinea each, to keep in their pockets. **1882** SIR R. TEMPLE *Men & Ev. my Time India* iii. 44 Though simple in his tastes and habits, he was generously hospitable.

4. With reference to diet (see GENEROUS 4 b).

1833 F. TWEEDIE in *Cycl. Pract. Med.* II. 210/1 If he [the patient] have been accustomed to live generously..the allowance of wine must be greater.

generousness (ˈdʒɛnərəsnɪs). Now *rare*. [f. as prec. + -NESS.]

1. Nobility of character, high spirit, magnanimity.

1611 HEYWOOD *Gold. Age* IV. H 4 a, Much haue I heard of his renowne in armes, His generousnesse, his vertues. **1695** *Whether Parl. be dissolved by Death P'Cess Orange* 58 What will Posterity say of us, if..we have not the Fortitude and Generousness, through the refusing to pay Taxes, to force the Case of this Parliaments being dissolved. **1871** SMILES *Charac.* iv. (1876) 164 The width, and depth, and generousness of their nature.

†**2.** Fertility, richness (of soil). *Obs.*

1695 MOTTEUX *St. Olon's Morocco* 38 The generousness of its Soil, that yields its Fruits almost without help.

genesial (dʒɪˈniːsɪəl), *a.* [f. GENESI-S + -AL[1].] Pertaining to generation. ***genesial cycle***: 'a period of ovarian, of uterine, and of mammary activity, into a series of which the reproductive life of the human female is divided' (*Syd. Soc. Lex.* 1885).

1882 in OGILVIE; and in later Dicts.

genesiology (dʒɪˈniːsɪɒlədʒɪ). [f. as prec. + -(O)LOGY.] The science of generation.

1882 in OGILVIE; and in later Dicts.

genesis (ˈdʒɛnɪsɪs). [a. L. *genesis*, a. Gr. γένεσις origin, creation, generation, f. *γεν- root of γίγνεσθαι to come into being, be born. Usu. with lower-case initial in mod. use (exc. sense 1).]

1. (With initial capital.) The first in order of the books of the Old Testament, containing the account of the creation of the world.

The name was given by the Gr. translators, and retained in the Vulgate; in quot. 1225 *Genesi* is the Latin ablative.

c **1000** ÆLFRIC *On O. & N. Test.* (Gr.) 3/18 Fif bec he awrat mid wundorlicum dihte. seo forme ys Genesis. *a* **1225** *Ancr. R.* 54 A meiden also het was, Jacobes douhter, hit telleð ine Genesi, eode vt uor to biholden uncuðe wummen. *c* **1250** *Gen. & Ex.* 2522 Ðe boc ðe is hoten genesis. **1362** LANGL. *P. Pl.* A. VII. 219 Go to Genesis the Ieaunt, engendrure of vs alle. **1533** GAU *Richt Vay* 33 It is writine in the first chaiptur of Genesis [etc.]. **1649** ROBERTS *Clavis Bibl.* 6 Genesis, i.e. Generation, so called by the Greek; partly because it sets forth the Generations of the heavens and of the earth, in their first creation; partly because it describes the Genealogie of the Patriarchs. **1682** DRYDEN *Medal, Epist. to Whigs*, He has damned me in your cause from Genesis to the Revelations. **1885** HUXLEY *Coll. Ess.* (1893) IV. 157 Those modern representatives of Sisyphus, the reconcilers of Genesis with science.

allusively (see 4). **1614** T. ADAMS *Wks.* (1861) I. 227 Every man that hath his Genesis must have his Exodus, and they that are born must die.

†**2.** *Astrol.* Nativity, horoscope. *Obs.*

c **1375** *Sc. Leg. Saints, Clement* 434 Inpossible thing is, þat ocht be done but genesis [L. *extra genesin*]. **1624** B. JONSON *Fortunate Isles* A 4 a, Hauing obseru'd your Genesis, He would not liue. **1652** GAULE *Magastrom.* 347 Vespasian being admonished, by the mathematicians, to take heed of Metius Pomposianus, because he had an imperiall genesis [etc.] [L. *genesim imperatoriam* Suet. *Vesp.* 14].

†**3.** = SYNTHESIS (orig. with reference to geometry, opposed to *analysis*; see Aristotle *Eth. Nic.* III. iii). Cf. quot. 1654 s.v. GENETICAL. *Obs.*

1612 BRINSLEY *Lud. Lit.* 108 Hereby schollars may haue daily much sure practice both of Analysis and Genesis; that is, resoluing and making Latine: which as was noted, all the learned doe acknowledge to bee almost all in all, in getting all learning. **1674** JEAKE *Arith.* (1696) 358 Thus much may suffice for the Genesis. Now for the Analysis.

4. Origin, mode of formation or production (very freq. in mod. usage, esp. with reference to the origin of the universe and its parts, or of natural and mental phenomena).

1604 R. CAWDREY *Table Alph.* (1613), *Genesis*, beginning. **1675** R. BURTHOGGE *Causa Dei* 380 A Custom bottomed upon the Great Originist, and that account he gives us of the Genesis and Rise of things. **1678** CUDWORTH *Intell. Syst.* I. iv. § 14. 238 All which genesis or generation of gods is really nothing but a poetical description of the cosmogonia. *a* **1734** NORTH *Exam.* I. ii. § 11 (1740) 36 It seems the Author himself was in the Dark as to the Genesis of this Speech. **1817** COLERIDGE *Biog. Lit.* 138, I shall now proceed to the nature and genesis of the imagination. **1831** CARLYLE *Sart. Res.* (1858) 49 To the Genesis of our Clothes-Philosopher, then, be this First Chapter consecrated. **1838-9** HALLAM *Hist. Lit.* III. viii. III. § 17. 404 Harriott arrived at a complete theory of the genesis of equations. **1864** BOWEN *Logic* v. 119 It explains only the genesis, not the nature, of the Categories. **1885** CLODD *Myths & Dr.* I. i. 5 The theory of evolution must embrace the genesis and development of mind.

†**b.** *Math.* = GENERATION. *Obs.*

1706 W. JONES *Syn. Palmar. Matheseos* 224 The Genesis of Solids may be exhibited in various ways. **1721** BAILEY, *Genesis* [in Geometry] is the Forming of any Figure, plain, or solid. **1726** tr. *Gregory's Astron.* I. 205 An Account of the Genesis, Nature and Uses of the Celestial Equinoctial.

Hence **geˈnesic** *a.*, pertaining to genesis or origin (cf. F. *génésique*); **Geˈnesiac, Geneˈsiacal, Geneˈsitic** *adjs.*, belonging to the Book of Genesis (cf. F. *génésiaque*).

1849-52 TODD *Cycl. Anat.* IV. 1236/1 Of the progress of the genesic phenomena, there is as yet but little clearly known. **1856** R. F. BURTON *El-Medinah* III. 335 The Genesitic account of the Great Patriarch has suggested to learned men the idea of two Abrahams. **1877** DAWSON *Orig. World* ii. 56 Before the 'waters' (and here is the peculiar error of the genesiacal bard) some of the ancients claimed the pre-existence of light [etc.]. **1892** E. C. STEDMAN in *Century Mag.* XLIV. 669 We then comprehend the full purport of the Genesitic record—'ye shall be as gods'. **1895** *Month* Nov. 372 She [the Church] has so far acquiesced in the larger interpretations of Genesiacal cosmogony that now the six-day theory would be very unsafe. **1896** *Tablet* 27 June 1014 The Genesiac days of creation.

-ˈgenesis, repr. Gr. γένεσις (see GENESIS) in various quasi-Gr. compounds used in modern science, denoting modes of generation, as *abiogenesis*, *biogenesis*, *parthenogenesis*, etc.

genet[1] (ˈdʒɛnɪt). Forms: 5 jonet, genete, 6 jennet, jenette, 7 ginnet, jenit, 6, 9 genette, 7- gennet, 8- genet. [a. OF. *gen(n)ete*, *-ette*, *jen(n)ette* (F. *genette*) = Sp. and Pg. *gineta*, med.L. *geneta* (mod.L. *genetta*), a. Arab. *jarnait*.]

1. A kind of civet-cat, a native of southern Europe, western Asia, and Africa. The common species (*Genetta vulgaris* or *Viverra Genetta*) is found in the south of France.

1481 CAXTON *Reynard* (Arb.) 79 Tho cam forth many a beest anon, as the squyrel, the musehout, the fychews..the genete. **1572** in Whitaker *Hist. Craven* (1812) 325 A black velvet gown..furred with squyrels, and faced with jenet's furr. **1619** MIDDLETON *Love & Antiq.* Wks. (Bullen) VII. 331 Those beasts bearing fur..The ounce, rowsgray, ginnet, etc. **1653** A. ROSS *Πανσέβεια* (1658) 345 Gennets, which are beasts like Spanish Cats in bigness, with long and slender snowts, their furres..do smell like those of Civit Cats. **1774** GOLDSM. *Nat. Hist.* (1862) I. xiv. 234 The Dog Kind..the Dog, the Wolf..the Genet. **1859** TENNENT *Ceylon* II. IX. vi. 523 The palmyra becomes the resort of the palm-cat and the glossy and graceful genet.

†**2.** *pl.* The skins of the animal employed as fur for garments. *Obs.*

1418 *E.E. Wills* (1882) 36 Also a gowne of gray russet furred wit Ionetis and wylde Catis. **1538** FITZHERB. *Just. Peas* 121 b, The lorde Chaunceller..may weare..any maner furres, except blacke genettes. **1551** EDW. VI in Strype *Eccl. Mem.* (1721) II. II. ix. 319 No man..under an earl, not to wear sables, or black jennets, or cloth of silver. **1688** R. HOLME *Armoury* III. 260/2 Sables, Jenits, Minks, and Filches [*sic*] are reckoned by the Timber, which is 4 Skins. **1694** E. CHAMBERLAYNE *St. Gt. Brit.* III. ii. 385 Of Furrs, Filches [*sic*], Grayes, Jennets, [etc.] 40 Skins is a Timber.

b. The fur obtained from the genet; also an imitation of this, usually made from cat's fur.

1882 in OGILVIE. **1890** *Daily News* 27 Dec. 2/2 The cheapest fur for lining coats is gennet, black in colour and low in price. **1891** *Ibid.* 24 Oct. 6/1 Lined with a less expensive fur, such as genet, musquash or squirrel.

3. *attrib.*, as ***genet-cat***, ***-skin***.

1607 TOPSELL *Four-f. Beasts* (1658) 179 Of the Gennet-cat, called Genetha. **1677** CHARLETON *Exercit. de Diff. Anim.* (ed. 2) 20 *Genetta*..the Genet, *aut* Genet-Cat. **1812-15** ANNE PLUMTRE tr. *Lichtenstein's S. Afr.* II. 15 The hyenas..eat up the carrion and diminish very much the thieving, mischievous apes, and the crafty genet-cats. **1890** *Daily News* 25 Jan. 7/2, 244 sable skins, nine genet skins, and a skunk skin.

genet[2] (ˈdʒɛnɪt). Also 8 gennit. [Perh. an abbreviation of JENNETING; cf. GENET-MOIL.] A kind of apple.

1706 PHILLIPS (ed. Kersey), *Gennit*, or *Genniting*, a kind of Apple which is ripe before any others. **1895** *Funk's Stand. Dict.*, *Jenneting*..2. [U.S.] A winter apple, Rawle's Genet.

genet, obs. form of JENNET.

†**geˈnethliac**, *a.* and *sb. Obs.* Also 6 genethliak, 7 -aque, -ake, 7-8 ack. [Ultimately ad. Gr. γενεθλιακός belonging to one's birth or birthday (= γενέθλιος, f. γενέθλη birth, breed, race, f. *γεν- to bear, bring forth), whence late L. *genethliacus*, F. *généthliaque*: from these the English forms are more immediately derived.]

A. *adj.* Relating to the casting of nativities. Also, relating to a birthday.

1614 SELDEN *Titles Hon.* 67 Euery King hath a singular starre for the Ruler of his Royall life, common persons hauing only the mixtures of seuerall influences, according to their Genethliaque figures. **1649** G. DANIEL *Trinarch.*, *Hen. V*, xviii, When these Genethliake Rages are made out The Sober Obiects of a well-taught Mind. **1686** GOAD *Celest. Bodies* I. xv. 98 Will not this let in all the Vanities of the Genethliaque pretension? *a* **1693** URQUHART *Rabelais* III. xxxviii. 320 Genethliack and Horoscopal fool. **1727-51** CHAMBERS *Cycl.*, *Genethliacum*, Genethliac poem, is a composition in verse, on the birth of some prince or other illustrious person..There are also genethliac speeches or orations; made to celebrate a person's birth-day.

B. *sb.*

1. One who calculates nativities (so L. *genethliacus*, Gr. γενεθλιακός).

1584 R. SCOT *Discov. Witchcr.* XI. xxiii. 214 *margin*, The follie of our genethliaks, or nativiti-casters. **1625** HART *Anat. Ur.* II. ix. 117, I adhere to none of your iuggling Genethliacks. **1664** BUTLER *Hud.* II. iii. 689 Strange turns in the World's affairs, Foreseen b' Astrologers, Southsayers, Chaldeans, Learn'd Genethliacks. **1840-4** W. H. MILL *Obs. Gospel* iii. § 1 (1861) 307 The subject-matter alike of the true science of astronomers and the false lore of genethliacs.

2. *pl.* = GENETHLIALOGY (so L. *genethliacē* = Gr. *γενεθλιακή); also, horoscopes, nativities.

a **1619** FOTHERBY *Atheom.* II. vii. § 3 (1622) 263 A kind of Destinie bestowed vpon those Cities, in their genethliacks, and natiuities, by the aspects and positure of the Stars. **1706** PHILLIPS (ed. Kersey), *Genethliacks*, treatises about Fortune-telling, or casting nativities. **1755** JOHNSON, *Genethliacks*, the science of calculating nativities, or predicting the future events of life from the stars predominant at the birth. Hence in later Dicts.

3. A birthday ode. (= GENETHLIACON.)

1687 WINSTANLEY *Lives Eng. Poets* 60 He [Leland] wrote, among many other volumes, several books of epigrams, his Cignea Cantio, a Genethliac of Prince Edward.

Hence †**genethliacism**, the casting of nativities.

1652 GAULE *Magastrom.* 60 Nothing is left of its own, or peculiar to it self [astrologie], but a bare goeticall genethliacism..or casting of Nativities.

genethliacal (dʒɛnɪθˈlaɪəkəl), *a.* [f. as prec. + -AL[1].] = GENETHLIAC *a.*

1613 PURCHAS *Pilgrimage* I. xii. 54 This..Judicial, Conjectural, Genethliacal Astrology..God and man have condemned. **1640** HOWELL *Dodona's Grove* 191 Slighting the art of those foolish Astrologers, and Genethliacall Ephemerists, that use to pry into the horoscope of Nativities. **1764** *Char.* in *Ann. Reg.* 30/2 He set himself about erecting the following genethliacal type in order to a presage of Thomas's future fortune. **1835** SOUTHEY *Doctor* III. xcv. 208 An astral alphabet for genethliacal purposes was published near the close of the fifteenth century, at Cracow. **1838** J. P. KENNEDY *Rob of Bowl* xvi. (1860) 187 This wonderful medicament is a great remedy..for all diseases, whether proceeding from terrestrial or genethliacal influences.

Hence **genethˈliacally** *adv.*

1652 GAULE *Magastrom.* 49 How shall it, then, be believed that a mans religion or religious qualities may be genethliacally prognosticated from the starres and their influentiall constellations? **1816** G. S. FABER *Orig. Pagan Idol.* II. 285 The whole human race may be resolved genethliacally into the triad. **1821** SCOTT *Kenilw.* xi, He was ..an adept, who read the stars, and expounded the fortunes of mankind, genethliacally, as he called it, or otherwise.

‖**genethliacon** (dʒɛnɪθˈlaɪəkɒn). [L. *genethliacon* = Gr. γενεθλιακόν.] A birthday ode.

1589 PUTTENHAM *Eng. Poesie* I. xxiii. (Arb.) 61 Others for magnificence at the natiuities of Princes children, or by custome vsed yearely vpon the same dayes, are called songs natall or *Genethliaca*. **1675** J. SMITH *Chr. Relig. App.* I. ii. § I. 5 That [Quire] which before his birth sang his Genethliacon. **1796** BURKE *Regic. Peace* iv. Wks. IX. 74 This year's Constitution, which was formed and its genethliacon sung by the noble Author, while it was yet in embryo. **1888** *Edin. Rev.* CLXVII. 478 The eclogue..is a genethliacon, or birthday ode.

genethlialogy (dʒɪnɛθlɪˈælədʒɪ). Also **genethliology**. [ad. Gr. γενεθλιᾱλογία (L. *genethliologia*), abstract sb. related to γενεθλιᾱλογεῖν to cast nativities; see GENETHLIAC and -LOGY.] The science of casting nativities.

1656 BLOUNT *Glossogr.*, *Genethlialogy*, telling or casting of Nativities. **1662** STILLINGFL. *Orig. Sacr.* I. iii. § 2 The Chaldeans did so hold to Astronomy still, that they wholly rejected Genethlialogy. **1850** LEITCH tr. *C. O. Müller's Anc. Art* § 186 (ed. 2) 168 The Chaldæan Genethliology. **1862** LEWIS *Astron. Anc.* v. 13 Herodotus makes no allusion to any connexion with the stars in the Egyptian genethlialogy of his time.

Hence **genethliaˈlogic, genethliaˈlogical** *adjs.*, pertaining to genethlialogy.

1860 *Sat. Rev.* X. 363/2 The third is a comparatively modern genethlialogic work. **1865** RAWLINSON *Anc. Mon.* III. v. 425 The Chaldee astrology was primarily and mainly, genethlialogical.

genethliaque, var. GENETHLIAC *sb.* and *a.*

†**genethliatic.** *Obs. rare*[−1]. [f. Gr. γενέθλια neut. pl. of γενέθλιος: see GENETHLIAC and -ATIC.] One who casts nativities (= GENETHLIAC *sb.* 1).

1649 DRUMM. OF HAWTH. *Fam. Ep.* Wks. (1711) 147 The genethliaticks have other observations than the stars; they conjecture by the disposition, temper..of the person [etc.].

genethlic (dʒɪˈnɛθlɪk), *a.* *rare*⁻¹. [f. Gr. γενέθλη birth + -IC; cf. Gr. γενέθλιοι θεοί.] (See quot.)

1846 ELLIS *Elgin Marb.* I. 244 The genethlic divinities, or those which preside over birth.

genethliology, var. GENETHLIALOGY.

genetic (dʒɪˈnɛtɪk), *a.* and *sb. pl.* [f. GENESIS, on the analogy of pairs of words like *antithesis, antithetic*.]

A. *adj.* **1. a.** Pertaining to, or having reference to, origin.

1831 CARLYLE *Early Germ. Lit.* in *Misc. Ess.* (1888) III 168 Our theories and genetic Histories of Poetry should henceforth cease. **1860** MARSH *Eng. Lang.* 281 In a historical sketch of the genetic development of the parts of speech, we should naturally begin with the Interjection. **1870** MAX MÜLLER *Sci. Relig.* (1873) 143 The only scientific and truly genetic classification of religions. **1878** FOSTER *Phys.* III. v. §3. 481 Regarded in a genetic aspect, the spinal cord is a series of cemented segments.

b. *Biol.* ***genetic affinity, connexion, relation(ship)***: one that is the result of a common origin.

1859 DARWIN *Orig. Spec.* iv. (1873) 101 If this had occurred, we should meet with the same form, independently of genetic connection, recurring in widely separated geological formations. **1880** GÜNTHER *Fishes* 373 There is no direct genetic relation between those fishes.

c. *Logic.* ***genetic definition***: one which defines a thing by describing the manner of its formation.

1837–8 SIR W. HAMILTON *Logic* xxiv. (1866) II. 13 In Genetic Definitions the defined subject is considered as in the progress to be, as becoming; the notion, therefore, has to be made, and is the result of the definition, which is consequently synthetic. **1884** tr. *Lotze's Logic* 167 'Let a straight line revolve in one plane about one of its extremities, and combine the successive positions of the other extremity':—that is a genetic definition of a circle.

d. *Bot.* ***genetic spiral*** (see quot.).

1875 BENNETT & DYER *Sachs' Bot.* 169 A line is imagined proceeding..in such a direction that, traversing the axis..it includes the points of insertion of all the successive lateral members according to their age; the horizontal projection of this line is called the Genetic Spiral; in reality it is a helix running round the stem more or less regularly.

e. ***genetic psychology*** (see quot. 1909[1]).

1909 *Cent. Dict.* Suppl. (s.v. *psychology*), *Genetic psychology*, that division of psychology which deals with the development of mind in the individual and with its evolution in the race. **1909** W. M. URBAN *Valuation* iii. 72 How such presuppositions arise is..a problem of genetic psychology. **1947** O. BARFIELD in *Essays presented to C. Williams* 106 What I am talking about is not poetic diction, but etymology or philosophy or even genetic psychology.

f. ***genetic fallacy***: the fallacy of judging the value of something, or the truth of a belief, by its origin.

1934 COHEN & NAGEL *Introd. Logic* xix. 388 (*heading*) The genetic fallacy. **1941** *Mind* L. 386 The 'scientific method of interpreting Spinoza's philosophy' must avoid both the 'normative fallacy' and the 'genetic fallacy'. **1959** I. G. MACCAFFREY *Paradise Lost as 'Myth'* 210 Milton never committed the genetic fallacy which claims that good and evil are rendered indistinguishable when they are seen to have a common source. **1965** *Philos.* XL. 351 To commit a Genetic Fallacy, the fallacy of supposing that an opinion is discredited when its causal origins are revealed.

g. Of or pertaining to genetics or genes; ***genetic code***: the system by which nucleic acid molecules store genetic information, now known to operate by means of triplets of nucleotides read in sequence.

1908 W. BATESON *Methods & Scope Genetics* 11 The conception..of the individual as composed of what we call presences and absences of all the possible ingredients..is the basis of all progress in genetic analysis. *Ibid.* 46 At last by genetic methods we are beginning to obtain such facts. **1936** *Discovery* May 161/1 Recently attention has been paid to..the interaction of genes with, what may be termed, the genetic environment. **1939** C. D. DARLINGTON (*title*) Evolution of genetic systems. **1941** J. S. HUXLEY *Uniqueness of Man* ii. 42 One and the same genetic outfit will give different effects in different environments. *Ibid.* 43 Our ignorance of the precise genetic constitution of human populations. **1947** H. J. MULLER in *Proc. R. Soc.* B. CXXXIV. 30 Practically every mutation, even a 'small' and non-lethal one, with the rarest of exceptions, requires finally a genetic death, that is, a failure to live or to breed, somewhere along the line of its descent, if the population would remain genetically at par. For each mutation, then, a genetic death. **1959** *New Biol.* XXVIII. 23 Diverse non-adaptive evolutionary changes as may be brought about in small isolated populations by the phenomenon of 'genetic drift'. **1961** S. A. SAND in *Amer. Naturalist* XCV. 242 Our concept of a genetic system storing information should not be restricted to the denotation of 'gene' or to limited aspects of DNA structure... We would then recognize more than one type of genetic code and several classes of genetic change. **1962** *Nature* 31 Mar. 1268/1 The correspondence between groups of nucleotides and amino-acids has come to be known as the 'genetic code'. **1963** *Times* 12 Jan. 8/1 New experiments have suggested that viruses may, in effect, be genes or 'genetic messengers', the report says. **1969** *Times* 6 Jan. 10/7 If man is indeed carrying a large number of such inactive or 'nonsense' genes, the implication is that he is using only a small fraction of the genetic information that his D.N.A. is capable of storing. **1969** *New Scientist* 28 Aug. 415/2 The day may be approaching when genetic engineering may make it possible to make a plant to order. **1970** *Guardian* 8 May 3/7 Most couples who seek genetic counselling come after they have had one or more defective children. **1971** *Ibid.* 8 Oct. 13/1 Human genetic engineering aimed at the elimination of genetic diseases.

¶**2.** Sometimes misused for: Generative, productive (= Gr. γεννητικός).

1838 *Blackw. Mag.* XLIV. 242 It points to a genetic or creative power. **1865** LOWELL *Thoreau* Pr. Wks. 1890 I. 366 Above all, there is the standard of genetic power, the test of the masculine as distinguished from the receptive minds. **1884** *Expositor* Dec. 464 This view of faith..assigns to it a genetic energy adequate to the production of the rich and manifold results of the Christian life.

B. *sb. pl.* **a.** The principles or laws of origination.

1872 F. HALL *Recent Exempl. False Philol.* 101 Nor are his notions of verbal genetics at all less superficial than his acquaintance with practical precedents.

b. That branch of biology which is concerned with the study of natural development when not complicated by human interference.

1897 L. F. WARD *Outl. Sociol.* 180 But there is a shorter adjective form *telic*, which is preferable to teleological and possesses the advantage of being converted into the name of a science, *telics*, as proposed by Dr. Small. These two words may be conveniently set over against *genetic* and *genetics*.

c. The scientific study of heredity and variation.

1905 W. BATESON *Let.* 18 Apr. in B. Bateson *W. Bateson* (1928) 93 The best title would, I think, be 'The Quick Professorship of the study of Heredity'. No single word in common use quite gives this meaning.., and if it were desirable to coin one, 'Genetics' might do. **1906** —— in *Nature* 14 June 146/1 May it be suggested that the branch of science should now receive a distinctive name? The physiology of heredity and variation is a definite branch of science... To avoid further periphrasis, then, let us say genetics. **1907** *Daily Chron.* 23 Feb. 9/3 The..International Conference on Genetics. **1908** W. BATESON *Methods & Scope Genetics* Pref., The physiology of Heredity and Variation, a study now spoken of as Genetics. **1930** R. A. FISHER *Genet. Theory Nat. Selection* p. viii, That an independent study of natural selection is now possible is principally due to the great advance which our generation has seen in the science of genetics. **1949** DARLINGTON & MATHER *Elem. Genetics* 15 These inborn causes..have to be defined as materials or processes whose behaviour and effects we can predict and control. This is the aim and scope of genetics. **1965** PEACOCKE & DRYSDALE *Molec. Basis of Heredity* i. 3 The development of modern genetics dates only from the rediscovery of Mendel's paper in 1900.

-ge'netic (see prec.), *suffix* forming adjectives, which correspond to sbs. in *-genesis* and *-geny*, as *biogenetic*, *cosmogenetic*, *phylogenetic*, *physiogenetic*. All of these are of recent formation, and only in use as scientific terms. See -GENY.

genetical (dʒɪˈnɛtɪkəl), *a.* [f. GENETIC + -AL[1].] = GENETIC *a.* †Also, in early use = SYNTHETIC (cf. GENESIS 3).

1654 WHITLOCK *Zootomia* Pref. A viij b, I love books that make use of Sciences, not compile them into their Geneticall, or Analyticall Parcels. **1831** CARLYLE *Sart. Res.* I. xi. (1858) 45 A complete picture and Genetical History of the Man and his spiritual Endeavour lies before you. **1841** EMERSON *Misc. Papers, Landor* Wks. (Bohn) III. 311 These are not plants and animals, but the genetical atoms of which both are composed. **1875** WHITNEY *Life Lang.* xiii. 277 That classification aimed at being a strictly genetical one. **1910** *Amer. Naturalist* XLIV. 108 (*title*) Genetical studies on Œnothera. Notes on the behavior of certain hybrids of Œnothera in the first generation. **1922** *Ibid.* LVI. 59 Genetical and cytological proof was obtained that these intersexes in *Drosophila* possess two X-chromosomes and three sets of autosomes. **1925** *Jrnl. Bot.* LXIII. 360 A greater knowledge of modern genetical work would save taxonomists from falling into some common errors. **1930** R. A. FISHER (*title*) The genetical theory of natural selection. **1959** *Listener* 26 Nov. 920/2 Nucleic acids are the substances that embody genetical information. **1971** *Nature* 30 Apr. 552/3 The pathogen is now open to much more detailed genetical and physiological examination.

genetically (dʒɪˈnɛtɪkəlɪ), *adv.* [f. prec. + -LY[2].]

a. With respect to genesis or origin.

1837–8 SIR W. HAMILTON *Logic* xxiv. (1866) II. 13 Only those notions can be genetically defined, which relate to quantities represented in time and space. **1856** EMERSON *Eng. Traits, Race* Wks. (Bohn) II. 23 Certain tribes..coming from one place, and genetically identical. **1869** J. D. BALDWIN *Preh. Nations* iii. (1877) 91 Genetically related dialects and forms of speech constitute one family group. **1883** A. ROBERTS *O.T. Revision* xii. 269 Our Authorised Version is genetically connected with all the previous English versions.

b. By the agency of genes; according to genetics.

1902 BATESON & SAUNDERS *Rep. Evol. Comm. R. Soc.* I. 134 An organism can be strictly defined as genetically sure if all its gametes when united with similar gametes reproduce the parent identically. **1932** S. ZUCKERMAN *Soc. Life Monkeys* ii. 27 If an impulse to live a herd life is a genetically determined response. **1968** *Times* 17 Oct. 18/5 An attempt to determine whether the capacity of the rats to convert a high proportion of cyclamate into chemicals is inherited genetically.

geneticist (dʒɪˈnɛtɪsɪst). [f. GENETIC *sb.* c + -IST.] An expert in, or student of, genetics.

1913 in DORLAND *Med. Dict.* (ed. 7). **1924** E. W. MACBRIDE *Study Hered.* vii. 186 This theory..uncritically accepted by many 'geneticists'. **1930** G. R. DE BEER *Embryol. & Evol.* 20 The geneticist who studies this distribution in hereditary transmission is really following the genes through two cell-generations only. **1932** *Discovery* Mar. 73/2 Plant geneticists learnt how to build up a plant almost to a specification. **1950** A. HUXLEY *Themes & Variations* i. 74 The issue between Soviet geneticists and the geneticists of the West is similar in essence to that which divided the Pelagians from the Augustinians. **1971** A. E. H. EMERY *Elem. Med. Genetics* (ed. 2) ix. 162 We will..limit our discussion to those problems which face the medical geneticist.

genetics: see GENETIC *a.* (and *sb.*) B.

genetive, obs. form of GENITIVE.

†**genet-moil.** *Obs.* Also 7 gen(n)et-moyle, ginet-moil. [f. GENET[2]; the second element may be *moyle* MULE, suggested by the coincidence in sound with JENNET.] A variety of apple.

1657 AUSTEN *Fruit Trees* I. 77 Gennet-moyle is accompted better then either for Cider. *a* **1680** BUTLER *Rem.* (1759) I. 8 Another of as great Renown, And solid Iudgment in the Moon; That understood her various Soils, And which produc'd best Genet-moyles. **1727** BRADLEY *Fam. Dict.* s.v. *Dwarf-trees*, Such Trees as are apt to put forth Roots..the Kentish Codling, Genet-moil [etc.].

†**'genetor, gennitair.** *Obs.* Forms: 4 genatour, 6 geneto(u)r, -ture, gennitair, gennetter. [OF. *geneteur* and *genetaire*, f. *genet* JENNET.] A soldier who rides a jennet.

?*a* **1400** *Morte Arth.* 2897 Than the genatours of Genne enjoynes att ones. **1523** LD. BERNERS *Froiss.* I. cccxxxvi. 336, I haue thre thousande barded horses..and I haue also seuen M. genetours. **1525** *Ibid.* II. li. 179 When Syr John Ferrant saw the geneture, he sayd to a squyer of his, galop forth thy genet, and assaye to speke with yonder geneture. **1579** FENTON *Guicciard.* (1618) 257 And Ferdinand with three hundred Lances, two thousand Gennitairs, and sixe thousand footmen. **1592** WYRLEY *Armorie* 77 Seuen thousand I haue armed head and feet Of genetors full twentie thousand more. **1600** E. BLOUNT tr. *Conestaggio* 213 In the first ranke whereof marched their Harquebusiers on horsebacke, in the second their gennetters, in the thirde their light horsemen.

genetrix, genitrix (ˈdʒɛnɪtrɪks). Now *rare.* Also 6 *Sc.* genetrice, 7 genitresse. [a. L. *genetrix, genitrix* female parent (cf. GENITOR), f. *gen-*stem of *gignĕre* to beget, give birth. The form *genitrice* is adopted from OF., while *genitresse* is a new formation from GENITOR.] A female parent, a mother. Also *fig.* applied to one's native country.

1500–20 DUNBAR *Poems* lxxxv. 63 Victryce of wyce, hie genetrice Of Jhesu, lord soverayne. **1562** A. SCOTT *Poems* (S.T.S.) i. 5 Welcum, oure jem and joyfull genetryce! **1610** HOLLAND *Camden's Brit.* II. 46 But praises all of this my genitresse That shee deserv's, no wit nor art is able to expresse. **1678** CUDWORTH *Intell. Syst.* I. iv. §19. 366 Omnipotent Jupiter..the progenitor and genitrix, the both father and mother, of those gods. **1878** B. TAYLOR *Deukalion* I. v. 44 Who else than she the genetrix of light, The mother of the morning? **1892** SIR F. COOK in *Mod. Rev.* I. 140 The typical mother can neither be a slave nor a genetrix of slaves.

genetta, genett(e, obs. forms of JENNET.

geneva[1] (dʒɪˈniːvə). Also 8 geneve, -er. [ad. Du. *genever, jenever* (the ending being assimilated to that of GENEVA[2]), ad. OF. *genevre* (F. *genièvre*):—L. *jūniperus* juniper.] A spirit distilled from grain, and flavoured with the juice of juniper berries; it is made in Holland, and is hence also called *Hollands*, formerly ***Hollands Geneva***. (Often written with capital G by confusion with GENEVA[2].)

In the shortened form GIN, the name chiefly denotes a spirit of British manufacture, originally an imitation of the Dutch spirit, and usually flavoured not with juniper but with some substitute; but the words are sometimes used indiscriminately. In many works of reference in the 18th c. and even later, *geneva* is explained as the name of a spirit distilled, or obtained by fermentation, from juniper berries; but it does not appear that this was ever correct.

1706 PHILLIPS (ed. Kersey), *Geneva*, a kind of strong Water so called. **1709** *Brit. Apollo* II. No. 22. 3/1 The Gypsie With Flip and Geneve got most Damnably Typsie. **1727** ARBUTHNOT *John Bull* Postscr. ch. xiv, He found the combatants drinking Genever in a Brandy-Shop. **1732** FIELDING *Mock Doctor* ix, Take one of these boluses..washing it down with six spoon-fuls of the best Holland's Geneva. **1751** SIR J. HILL *Mat. Med.* II. v. xxi. 487 We used to keep a distill'd spirituous Water of Juniper in the Shops, but..the making of it became the Business..of the Distiller, who sold it under the Name of Geneva; but at present only a better Kind [of] that is made with the Juniper Berry, what they commonly sell is made with no better an Ingredient than Oil of Turpentine..and with the coarsest Spirit they have. **1796** *Campaigns* 1793–4 I. I. Introd. 5 Geneva..was in great quantities served out to the French armies, whenever an engagement was expected. **1816** KIRBY & SP. *Entomol.* (1843) II. 187 Immediately I seized my prey, and not knowing how to destroy it, I immersed it in Geneva. **1831** *Lincoln Herald* 16 Dec. 3/4 If a poor boatman is found in possession of..a gallon of contraband geneva, he is fined. **1889** *Pall Mall G.* 13 Nov. 2/2 Of rum, alcohol, and Geneva 652,000 cwt. were exported in 1888.

attrib. **1718** [*Read's*] *Weekly Jrnl.* 4 Jan., Last Thursday morning a Woman..coming out of a Jenava Shop, in Red Cross Street, fell down.

Hence †**ge'nevaed** *ppl. a.*, drunk with geneva.

1755 YOUNG *Centaur* vi. Wks. 1757 IV. 251 These..gorgons, furies, harpies..on fire or quenched; genevaed or citroned..in tavern, bagnio, brothel.

Geneva[2] (dʒɪˈniːvə). The name of a town in Switzerland, used *attrib.* or quasi-*adj.* with the sense 'belonging to, made or originated at Geneva'; often with reference to matters of

Calvinistic doctrine or discipline, or of puritanical practice.

Geneva bands, clerical bands (see BAND *sb.*[2] 4b) resembling those worn by the Swiss Calvinist clergy. **Geneva bible**, the English translation of the Bible first printed at Geneva in 1560; so ***Geneva testament***. **Geneva convention** (see quot. 1910[2] and cf. CONVENTION 8a). **Geneva cross**, a red Greek cross on a white ground, used in war time as a badge to distinguish ambulances, hospitals, and the persons serving them. **Geneva gown**, a black gown such as was worn by the Calvinist clergy when preaching. †**Geneva hat**, a hat of the style regarded as distinctive of the Puritan clergy. †**Geneva print**, (*a*) the kind of type used in the Geneva bibles (in quot. *allusively*); (*b*) applied jocularly to the style of pleated linen worn by Puritan women. **Geneva Protocol** (see quot. 1970). †**Geneva set**, ? a small plain ruff worn by the Calvinist clergy (cf. quot. 1633). Geneva watch, a Swiss-made watch; also *ellipt.*

c **1570** in *Strype's Parker* App. 139 This Error is also in the Geneva Bible. **1623** MASSINGER *Dk. Milan* I. i. Bj b, If you meet An officer preaching of sobriety, Vnlesse he read it in *Geneua* print, Lay him by the heeles. **1628** EARLE *Microcosm., Shee precise Hypocr.* (Arb.) 63 Shee is a Nonconformist in a close Stomacher and Ruffle of Geneua Print. **1633** T. ADAMS *Exp. 2 Peter* ii. 5 You shall..find her [i.e. pride] as soon in a little Geneva-set, as in a great Spanish ruff. **1635** DAVENANT *News fr. Plymouth* IV. (1673) 23/1 And get more Charities by it From your little ruff'd Geneva-Man, or Flemming. **1637** LAUD *Let.* 28 Aug. in *Strafford Lett.* (1739) II. 100 They do not only sing the Psalms after the Geneva Tune but expound the text too in the Geneva sense. **1639** MAYNE *City Match* v. i, Who does he look like in that dresse? *New.* Hum? why Like a *Geneva Weaver*, in black. **1639** DRUMM. OF HAWTH. *Consid. to Parl.* Wks. (1711) 186 Church-men..shall have liberty to wear the old fashion of Geneva hats and apparel. **1640** GLAPTHORNE *Wit in Const.* I. Wks. 1874 I. 172 He has already spoyld His eyes with prying on Geneva prints. **1678** DRYDEN *Limberham* IV. i, Get thee hence, thou old Geneva testament: thou art a part of the ceremonial law, and hast been abolished these twenty years. **1820** SCOTT *Abbot* vi, It is like that..the mass and the cross will come up, and then down go pulpits, Geneva-gowns, and black silk skull-caps. **1844** C. M. YONGE *Abbeychurch* ii. 23 Above it hung a small Geneva watch. **1854** THACKERAY *Newcomes* II. xxvii. 250 Let us hope divine truths may be shining..which Geneva glasses cannot yet perceive, and are beyond the focus of Roman telescopes. **1860** EMERSON *Cond. Life, Behav.* Wks. (Bohn) II. 383 Men are like Geneva watches with crystal faces which expose the whole movement. [**1865** *Parl. Papers* LVII. 473 (*title*) Accession of the British Government to the Convention signed at Geneva, August 22, 1864, for the Amelioration of the Condition of the Wounded in Armies in the Field.] **1880** L. HERTSLET *Treaties & Conventions Gt. Brit. & Foreign Powers* XIV. 1164 The following is a list of the Parties who signed, or have acceded to, the Geneva Convention up to this date. **1882** EDNA LYALL *Donovan* xv, No clergyman in surplice and stole, or gown and Geneva bands, had ever preached to him. **1900** *Daily News* 21 Mar. 5/6 'Explosive bullets'..were..expressly condemned by the Geneva Convention. **1910** A. BENNETT *Clayhanger* III. xiv. 422 Edwin..drew out the silver Geneva. **1910** *Encycl. Brit.* XI. 592/1 *Geneva Convention*, an international agreement for the purpose of improving the condition of wounded soldiers of armies in the field, originally adopted at an international conference held at Geneva, Switzerland, in 1864, and afterwards replaced by the convention of July 6, 1906, also adopted at Geneva. This later agreement is the one now known as the Geneva Convention. **1933** [see BACTERIOLOGICAL *a.* b]. **1959** *Listener* 26 Feb. 392/1 The tradition of the Geneva convention. **1970** *Sat. Rev.* 6 June 28/3 The Geneva Protocol of 1925..banned the use in war of all 'asphyxiating, poisonous, or other gases' and of 'bacteriological methods of warfare'.

b. *Mech.* **Geneva drive, mechanism**, etc., a mechanism for converting a continuous rotatory motion into an intermittent rotatory motion, consisting of a driving wheel to which is attached a pin that engages with one of several radial slots in the driven wheel for part of each revolution; also *ellipt.*; **Geneva stop**, a stop (STOP *sb.*[2] 9d) consisting of a pair of gears in which the driven wheel lacks cogs or slots on part of its circumference.

1869 W. J. M. RANKINE *Man. Machinery & Millwork* 286 (heading) Intermittent gearing-counter-wheels-Geneva stop. **1873** Geneva stop [see STOP *sb.*[2] 9d]. **1913** F. A. TALBOT *Pract. Cinematogr.* iii. 26 The early types of camera were fitted with what is known as the Geneva stop movement. **1918** F. D. JONES *Mechanisms* vi. 154 The general type of intermittent gearing..is commonly known as the 'Geneva wheel', because of the similarity to the well-known Geneva stop used to prevent the over-winding of springs. **1949** *Tool Engineers Handbk.* (Amer. Soc. Tool Engineers) lxxviii. 1143 A special geneva drive is utilized to impart intermittent motion to the circular electrodes. **1953** L. J. WHEELER *Princ. Cinematogr.* vi. 179 The Geneva Movement, or Maltese Cross,..is now used almost exclusively throughout the industry. **1967** S. B. TUTTLE *Mechanisms for Engin. Design* iii. 35 The Geneva mechanism. *Ibid.* 37 The internal Geneva produces intermittent circular motion in which the dwell period is less than 40% of the elapsed time. **1970** R. M. PHELAN *Fund. Mech. Design* (ed. 3) xii. 286 The Geneva wheel..is satisfactory for relatively high-speed operation. *Ibid.* 287 The Geneva stop is a useful variation of the Geneva wheel in which one of the slots in the driven member is left closed, thus permitting only a certain number of revolutions.. before the pin hits the closed slot and stops the motion.

Genevan (dʒɪ'niːvən), †**Ge'nevian**, *a.* and *sb.* [f. GENEV-A[2] + -AN, -IAN.]

A. *adj.* Of or pertaining to Geneva, esp. to its ecclesiastical organization; Calvinistic.

1573 *New Custome* in *Dodsley's Coll.* (1825) I. 291 For since these Genevian doctours came so fast into this lande, Since that time it was never merie with Englande. **1637** HEYLIN *Answ. Burton* iv. 64 If by your Divines you meane the Genevian Doctors, Calvin and Beza. **1665** WALTON *Life Hooker* in *H.'s Wks.* (1888) I. 78 The..parson of Borne was sequestred..& a Genevian minister put into his good living. **1709** *True Answ. Sacheverell's Serm.* 8 The Genevian Discipline. **1804** *Ode to Rainbow* in *Miniature* No. 8 [She] quaffs Genevian streams. [A burlesque allusion to GENEVA[1].] **1853** MARSDEN *Early Purit.* 232 In 1577 Sandys Archbishop of York cited him upon several charges, the chief of which was his Genevan ordination. **1883** *Congregationalist* Nov. 900 His tall form graced with a rich Genevan gown.

B. *sb.* A native of Geneva; also, one who adheres to the doctrines of Geneva.

1564 ABP. PARKER *Let. Sir W. Cecil* in *Corr.* (1853) 215 Charging the Genevians and the Scottish of going too far in extremities. **1639** W. SCLATER *Worthy Communicant Rewarded* 5 *Whoso*, or, as the Genevians [i.e. translators of the Geneva Bible] render it, *Whosoever*. *c* **1719** *Lett. fr. Mist's Jrnl.* (1722) i. 160 By the Help of their Palatines and Genevians. **1843** LOWELL *Let.* 19 Sept. (1894) I. 80 The clergyman nowadays, to many a disciple of the cropt Genevan, stands instead of the images and pictures of old Rome. **1875** KNIGHT *Dict. Mech.* 2732 The drilling of jewels for the pivots was first done by Nicolas Facio, a Genevan, in 1700. **1878** *N. Amer. Rev.* CXXVII. 337 He throws little light on the Genevan's marvelous style.

Hence †**Ge'nevanism**, Calvinism.

1625 BP. MOUNTAGU *App. Cæsar.* 72 A..Schisme on foot to bring in Genevanisme into Church and State.

†**'Genevate**, *v. Obs.* [f. GENEV-A[2] + -ATE[3].] *trans.* To fashion after the Geneva model. Implied in **'Genevated** *ppl. a.*, **'Genevating** *vbl. sb.*

1593 ABP. BANCROFT *Daung. Posit.* I. 10 *heading*, Scottish Geneuating for Reformation. **1609** in *Crt. & Times Jas. I* (1849) I. 99 He terms deposing princes, [etc.,] to be either Jesuited or Genevated divinity.

Geneve, obs. form of GENEVA[1].

Genevese (dʒenɪ'viːz), *a.* and *sb.* [f. GENEV-A[2] + -ESE.] **A.** *adj.* Pertaining to Geneva; *spec.* designating a type of sauce for fish.

1826 E. CRAVEN *Mem. Margravine of Anspach* II. ii. 44 His house was built by a Genevese architect named Billion. **1845** E. ACTON *Mod. Cookery* Index, p. xv/1 Genevese Sauce, or *Sauce Genevoise*. **1857** C. BRONTË *Professor* xix. 67, I have one object before me now—to get that Genevese girl for my wife. **1871** BLACKIE *Four Phases* i. 79 The stern Genevese disciplinarian. **1875** LOWELL *Wordsworth* Prose Wks. 1890 IV. 409 The Genevese humorist, Toepffer.

B. *sb.* A native of Geneva. (Not now inflected in pl.)

1650 STAPYLTON tr. *Strada* II. VI. 26 In their passage over the Mountaines; on the one side by the French, on the other by the Geneveses and Swisse, they might easily be distressed and cut off. **1794** G. WASHINGTON *Lett.* Writ. 1891 XII. 489 The picture drawn in them, of the Genevese, is really interesting and affecting. **1818** MRS. SHELLEY *Frankenst.* i. (1865) 31 I am by birth a Genevese. **1832** G. DOWNES *Lett. Cont. Countries* I. 260 A neat Protestant church, erected by..the Genevese. **1876** BANCROFT *Hist. U.S.* IV. xxxv. 99 They sent to him Dunant, a Genevese, as a British emissary. **1881** A. GRAY *Lett.* (1893) 719 All these Genevese speak English well, except Madame De Candolle.

Genevian, obs. form of GENEVAN.

'Genevize, *v.* [f. GENEV-A[2] + -IZE.] *intr.* To imitate or introduce the doctrines or practice of the Genevan church. Implied in **'Genevizing** *vbl. sb.* Also †**'Genevizer**, one who 'Genevizes'.

1682 G. VERNON *Life of Heylin* Pref. A5b, The Genevizers, who affirm, that we had too little of the People, and too much of the Prince therein. **1692** SOUTH *Serm.* (1717) V. 253 It were easy to bring up the rear with our English Genevizers. **1843** *Ecclesiologist* II. 16 The Genevizing spirit introduced in the time of Elizabeth.

Genevois. Also 6 **Genevoyes.** Pl. **Genevois.** [a. F. *genevois.*] = GENEVESE *sb.* Also as *adj.* = GENEVESE *a.*

1558–68 WARDE tr. *Alexis' Secr.* 62a, To make Conserve or Confiture of Quinces..whiche also the Genevoyes doe use. **1705** ADDISON *Italy* 503 The Genevois have been very much refin'd, or, as others will have it, corrupted by the Conversation of the French Protestants. **1765** J. CONYERS *Let.* in E. Hamilton *Mordaunts* (1965) viii. 181 The Genevois being lovers of order and decency. **1845** [see GENEVESE A.]. **1959** *Times* 17 Nov. 16/5 The year in which the earlier Genevois, Jean Etienne Liotard, so detested by Reynolds, died. **1968** D. TORR *Treason Line* 100 The knot of early comers, all of them prominent Genevois bores.

†**geng**, *v. Obs.* [OE. **gengan*, wk. vb. (only in pa. t. *gengde* = Goth. *gaggida*):—OTeut. **gangjan* f. root of GANG *v.*[1]]

1. *intr.* To go, pass, move.

Beowulf (Z.) 1412 He feara sum beforan gengde wisra monna wong sceawian. *c* **1000** *Ags. Ps.* (Th.) cxiii[i]. 5 þu, Iordanen, forhwi gengdest on bæcling? *c* **1205** LAY. 12865 Hu forð gengden [*c* **1275** forþ geinde] þa quenen 3 eond wudes & 3end feldes. *a* **1250** *Owl & Night.* 376 3if hundes urneþ to him ward He [the hare] gengþ wel swiþe a wey ward.

2. With *dat.* of personal obj.: To assist.

c **1200** ORMIN 4160 Swa þatt itt muȝhe gengenn uss To berrȝhenn ure sawle.

geng(e, var. GING *Obs.*, company, crew.

†**genge**, *a. Obs.* [OE. *genge* (= OHG. *gengi*, MLG. *genge*, MDu. *ghenge*, ON. *gengr*), WGer. **gangjo-*, f. root of GANG *v.*[1]] Current, prevalent, valid.

c **900** tr. *Bæda's Hist.* III. x[ii]. (1890) 188 Ne wæs þæt þonne to wundrienne, þeah þe þæs cyninges bene..mid him swiðade & genge wæren. *a* **1000** *Guthlac* 765 in *Exeter Bk.*, þæt his soð fore us on his ȝiefena ȝyld genge weorðe. *a* **1250** *Owl & Night.* 802 Wat tharf he recche of a mo swenge, Wone the on him is swo genge. *Ibid.* 1063 Thi song mai bo so longe genge, That thu shalt wippen on a sprenge.

genȝeild, -ȝell, var. ff. GAINYIELD.

genȝie, var. GANYIE *Sc.*, *Obs.*, missile.

gengzeng, obs. form of GINSENG.

genial ('dʒiːnɪəl), *a.*[1] Also 6–7 **geniall**. [ad. L. *geniāl-is*, f. *genius*: see GENIUS. Cf. OF. *genial*; the mod.F. *génial*, pertaining to or characterized by genius, is a new formation after Ger. *genial*, *genialisch*.]

1. Of or pertaining to marriage, nuptial; also, pertaining to generation, generative. Of an angel or deity: Presiding over marriage or generation. ***genial bed*** = L. *lectus genialis*. Now *rare*.

1566 NUCE tr. *Seneca's Octavia* I. iii. B2b Neroes dreaded visage..Doth fear me that I dare not weepe..Ne suffers me this geniall face To dash with teares. **1595** SPENSER *Epithal.* 399 And thou, glad Genius! in whose gentle hand The bridale bowre and geniall bed remaine. **1652** GAULE *Magastrom.* xviii. 149 So many Geniall or Genitall Gods and Goddesses. **1667** MILTON *P.L.* IV. 712 What day the genial Angel to our Sire Brought her in naked beauty. **1703** MAUNDRELL *Journ. Jerus.* (1721) 61 The virtue of them was to help Conception, being laid under the Genial Bed. **1774** GOLDSM. *Nat. Hist.* (1776) IV. 323 The male and female [bear]..seldom are seen together but upon the accesses of genial desire. **1793** COWPER *Tale* iv, The spring drew near, each felt a breast With genial instinct filled. **1822–34** *Good's Study Med.* (ed. 4) IV. 12 The electric impulse given in the genial act to every portion of the solids and fluids of the body. **1864** TENNYSON *Lucretius* 97 The all-generating powers and genial heat Of Nature.

†**2.** Of or pertaining to a feast; festive. *Obs.*

1620 VENNER *Via Recta* viii. 183 If it be a geniall meale, or much larger then ordinarie, another draught of Wine is.. allowable. **1644** MILTON *Areop.* (Arb.) 49 Buried..in the genial cups of an Academick night-sitting. **1697** DRYDEN *Virg. Past.* v. 111 In Winter shall the Genial Feast be made Before the Fire; by Summer in the Shade. **1715** POPE *Iliad* I. 772 Thus the blest gods the genial day prolong In feasts ambrosial. **1762** C. JOHNSTON *Reverie* (1763) I. 151 No resolution is proof against the pleasures of a genial hour.

3. Conducive to growth. Const. *to.* Now chiefly of air, climate, sunshine, passing into the sense: Pleasantly warm, mild.

1647 COWLEY *Mistr., Written in Juice of Lemon* vi, But when a Genial heat warms thee within. **1705** MAIDWELL *Necess. Educ.* 31 The Soil was not Genial to the Seed. **1766** [ANSTEY] *Bath Guide* i. 2 Ye genial Springs! Pierian Waters, hail! **1794** MRS. RADCLIFFE *Myst. Udolpho* vii, And gives its incense to the genial air. **1809** *Med. Jrnl.* XXI. 426 A recovery which..may be attributed to the regular and genial warmth of the wards. **1814** SCOTT *Ld. of Isles* III. xiv, The wildest glen, but this, can show Some touch of Nature's genial glow. **1820** W. IRVING *Sketch Bk.* I. 169 In the genial month of May. **1834** L. RITCHIE *Wand. by Seine* 119 The northern hordes..would naturally seek a more genial climate. **1858** HAWTHORNE *Fr. & It. Jrnls.* (1872) I. 19 The soil is not genial to them. **1893** SIR R. BALL *Story of Sun* 319 Ice Ages and Genial Ages must have alternated in each hemisphere.

fig. **1856** EMERSON *Eng. Traits, Relig.* Wks. (Bohn) II. 98 Heats and genial periods arrive in history. *a* **1872** MAURICE *Friendship Bks.* ix. (1874) 255 Those years at Horton are undoubtedly the poet's most genial time, the one in which he produced with the greatest freedom and joy.

4. Cheering, enlivening, inspiriting.

1746 COLLINS *Odes, Evening* v, I hail Thy genial lov'd return. **1856** R. A. VAUGHAN *Mystics* (1860) I. 8 This is the genial hour. **18..** W. W. STORY *Giannoni* 53 When the great logs blazed with a genial roar.

5. Sympathetically cheerful, jovial, kindly.

1746 SMOLLETT *Reproof* 173 Let ev'ry polish'd dame, and genial lord Employ the social chair and venal board. **1774** WARTON *Hist. Eng. Poetry* (1840) I. Dissert. ii. p. cxxvi, The celebrated drinking ode of this genial archdeacon [Walter Map] has the regular returns of the monkish rhyme. **1840** CARLYLE *Heroes* (1858) 258 Napoleon in Saint-Helena is charmed with the genial veracity of old Homer. **1847** DICKENS *Lett.* I. 173 The most genial letter that ever was written. **1847** TENNYSON *Princess* Concl. vi, A great broad-shoulder'd genial Englishman. **1859** KINGSLEY *Misc.* (1860) I. 17 There is a great laugh in Raleigh's heart, a genial contempt of asses. **1882** J. H. BLUNT *Ref. Ch. Eng.* II. 291 A pious and genial pastor.

†**6.** Pertaining to 'genius' or natural disposition; natural. *Obs.* (In the later echoes of Milton's phrase *genial spirits*, the adj. is prob. taken in sense 4 or 5.)

1646 SIR T. BROWNE *Pseud. Ep.* I. v. 19 Naturall incapacity, and geniall indisposition. **1671** MILTON *Samson* 594 So much I feel my genial spirits droop. **1687** DRYDEN *Hind & P.* III. 1147 A theologue more by need than genial bent. **1802** COLERIDGE *Sibyl. Leaves* Wks. 1877 II. 217 My genial spirits fail. **1850** TENNYSON *In Mem.* Concl. xx, Let all my genial spirits advance.

7. Of or pertaining to genius (see GENIUS 5); characterized by genius. (Chiefly after Ger. *genial*, *genialisch*.)

[**1825** CARLYLE *Schiller* II. (1845) 116 (Translating Goethe.) Heinse's 'Ardinghello' and Schiller's 'Robbers'.. those performances of genial worth and wild form.] **1827–48** HARE *Guesses* Ser. II. (1848) 35 But a genial age, like a genial individual, is unconscious of its own excellence. **1847**

EMERSON *Repr. Men, Shaks.* Wks. (Bohn) I. 353 Great genial power, one would almost say, consists in not being original at all: in being altogether receptive. **1855** LEWES *Goethe* I. IV. iii. 344 *note,* It is difficult to find an English word to express the German *genial*, which means pertaining to genius. The genial period was the period when every extravagance was excused on the plea of genius.

8. *Comb.*, as ***genial-looking*** adj.

1871 MISS BRADDON *Fenton's Quest* I. i. 4 She was not alone; a portly genial-looking old man stood by her side.

genial (dʒɪˈnaɪəl), *a.*[2] *Anat.* [f. Gr. γένει-ον chin (f. γένυς jaw = L. *gena*) + -AL[1].] Of or pertaining to the chin, situated on or arising from the chin; = MENTAL *a.*[2] ***genial process, tubercle***: one of two pairs of small bony prominences behind the symphysis of the lower jaw, which give attachment to two pairs of muscles.

1831 R. KNOX *Cloquet's Anat.* 283 Genio-hyoideus. This muscle..arises from a small tendon inserted into the lower genial process. **1844** HOBLYN *Dict. Med.*, *Genio-*, *Genial processes*, the name of four eminences of the inferior maxillary bone, beneath the symphysis of the chin. **1885** *Syd. Soc. Lex.*, *Genial tubercles*, the Mental spines. **1890** HUXLEY in *19th Cent.* July 775 *note,* The importance attached by some to the presence or absence of the so-called 'genial elevations'.

geniality (dʒiːnɪˈælɪtɪ). [f. GENIAL *a.*[1] + -ITY, after L. *geniālitās*.] The quality of being genial.

†**1.** Festivity, joviality. *Obs.*$^{-1}$

1609 HOLLAND *Amm. Marcell.* xxx. i. 380 Such a reverent regard in that time of auncient justice carried the Genialitie [L. *genialitas*], even of an enemies table.

2. Agreeable warmth; mildness.

1870 PROCTOR *Other Worlds* vii. 170 The imagined geniality of his [Uranus's] summer weather.

3. Sympathetic cheerfulness, good-nature, kindliness. (The sense in quot. 1652 is obscure: possibly = 'temper, disposition'.)

1652 H. L'ESTRANGE *Americans no Jewes* Ep. to Rdr., If I have any waies erred in judgment..I refer my self to the Readers *ferula*, and offer, and pray to be pruned of riot and rankness, to an innocent, candid, geniality, and meaning. **1831** CARLYLE *Sart. Res.* (1858) 182 Thou..with thy vivacities and genialities..makest such strange work. **1837** TALFOURD *Mem. Lamb* (L.), He had a natural geniality of disposition that endeared him to his friends. **1850** KINGSLEY *Alt. Locke* ii, There was a geniality in the tone to which I was unaccustomed.

genialize (ˈdʒiːnɪəlaɪz), *v.* [f. GENIAL *a.*[1] + -IZE.] *trans.* To impart geniality to; to render pleasant or agreeable.

a **1864** HAWTHORNE *Grimshawe* xix. (1891) 247 Some Burgundy, of which it was the quality to warm the blood and genialize existence for three days after it was drunk. **1888** *Blackw. Mag.* Aug. 313 He had the well-known Wellington physiognomy, only greatly softened and genialised. **1891** G. MEREDITH *One of our Conq.* II. v. 107 It would have genialized him.

Hence ˈ**genializing** *ppl. a.*

1849 D. THOMAS *Crisis of Being* iii. (1850) 50 Personal religion is the chief good of man..How it..brings all its germinant powers under the genializing influence of truth!

genially (ˈdʒiːnɪəlɪ), *adv.* [f. GENIAL *a.*[1] + -LY[2].]

†**1.** By genius or nature; naturally. *Obs.*

1661 GLANVILL *Vanity Dogm.* xii. 111 Some constitutions are genially disposited to this mentall seriousness.

2. In a genial manner; pleasantly; agreeably; cheerfully, kindlily.

1751 HARRIS *Hermes* II. iii. (1765) 266 The splendid Sun ..genially warmeth..the fertile Earth. **1782** COWPER *Progr. Err.* 412 Clearer skies and softer air..Freshening his lazy spirits as he ran, Unfolded genially and spread the man. **1847** C. BRONTE *J. Eyre* II. vii. 192 To taste but of the crumbs he scattered to stray and stranger birds like me was to feast genially. **1870** LOWELL *Study Wind.* (1871) 1 This genially garrulous Fellow of Oriel. **1874** GREEN *Short Hist.* v. §1. 213 No poetry was ever more human than Chaucer's, none ever came more frankly and genially home to its readers.

genialness (ˈdʒiːnɪəlnɪs). [f. GENIAL *a.*[1] + -NESS.] = GENIALITY.

1727 BAILEY vol. II, *Genialness*, Festivalness, Merriness at Meat. **1888** BURGON *Lives 12 Gd. Men* I. I. 109 Humour he had, and a certain genialness of nature.

genian (dʒɪˈnaɪən), *a. Anat.* [f. as GENI-AL *a.*[2] + -AN.] = GENIAL *a.*[2]

1885 *Syd. Soc. Lex.*, *Genian apophysis*, the Mental spines.

genic (ˈdʒiːnɪk, ˈdʒɛnɪk), *a.* [f. GENE[1] + -IC.] Of or pertaining to genes.

1922 C. B. BRIDGES in *Amer. Naturalist* LVI. 57 Comparison..between the effects of haploidy for an autosome and the effects normally present in diœcious sex shows that they have similar genic bases—namely, each is due to differences in the ratio between two aggregates of genes. **1925** *Ibid.* LIX. 129 Each character of an individual is the index of the point of balance in effectiveness of a large but unknown number of genes... This conception of 'genic balance' was applied to the sex characters of the intersexes. **1937** *Nature* 11 Sept. 450/2 Differences in chromosome constitution..may..mean a difference in genic balance. **1956** *New Biol.* XX. 32 All developmental processes..are to some extent under genic control.

-genic (-ˈdʒɛnɪk), *suffix* [f. -GEN + -IC], forming adjectives with the meaning: 'of, pertaining to, or relating to generation or production'; *spec.* (*a*) generating, producing, as CARCINOGENIC, EPEIROGENIC, PATHOGENIC, PYROGENIC; (*b*) generated, produced, originating in, as BLASTOGENIC, CRYPTOGENIC.

b. After PHOTOGENIC *a.* used to form adjectives with the meaning 'well suited for reproduction or dissemination in a particular medium', as in RADIOGENIC, TELEGENIC.

†**genice.** *Obs. rare*$^{-1}$. In 5 **genyce.** [a. OF. *genice* (F. *génisse*) heifer.] A heifer.

1480 CAXTON *Ovid's Met.* XII. xi, Achylles hade made sacrefyce of a genyce unto Pallas for the vyctorye.

†ˈ**genicle.** *Obs. rare*$^{-1}$. [ad. L. *geniculum*, dim. of *genu* knee.] A joint in the stalk of a plant.

1657 TOMLINSON *Renou's Disp.* 246 A stalk..intercepted with some genicles.

geniculant (dʒɛˈnɪkjʊlənt), *a.* [irreg. f. L. *genicul-um* (see prec.) + -ANT.] = GENICULATING.

1852 DANA *Crust.* II. 1131 The right male antenna, though geniculant, is but little different from the others in.. number of joints.

geˈnicular, *a.* [f. L. *genicul-um* (see prec.) + -AR.] = next. Also, of or pertaining to the knee or a genu.

1802 *Spirit Publ. Jrnls.* (1803) VI. 347 Buboes, imposthumations, genicular nodes, and the like. **1902** H. MORRIS *Human Anat.* (ed. 3) v. 756 These fibres..at the genu constitute the genicular bundle. **1913** *Gray's Anat.* (ed. 18) 853 The point where it [*sc.* the facial nerve] changes its direction is named the geniculum; it presents a reddish gangliform swelling, the genicular ganglion, or nucleus of the sensory root of the nerve. **1951** P. THOREK *Anat. in Surgery* xlv. 837 The middle genicular arteries enter the knee joint through the posterior ligament. **1967** G. M. WYBURN et al. *Conc. Anat.* vi. 161/1 The descending genicular artery arises distally and descends to the knee joint.

geniculate (dʒɪˈnɪkjʊlət), *a. Nat. Hist.* [ad. L. *geniculātus*, f. *geniculum*: see GENICLE.] Having knots or joints like a knee; bent like a knee; knee-jointed; knotty. ***geniculate body*** (= L. *corpus geniculatum*): each of two knee-shaped structures near the optic thalami at the base of the brain. ***geniculate ganglion***: 'a small, reddish, triangular ganglion, at the genu of the optic nerve' (*Syd. Soc. Lex.* 1885).

1668 WILKINS *Real Char.* II. iv. §3. 75 A scarlet flower.. with a geniculate stalk. **1805** J. GALPINE *Brit. Bot.* (1806) 26 Cal. lanceolate; cor. awned at the base: awn geniculate. **1828** STARK *Elem. Nat. Hist.* II. 297 Antennæ..geniculate, and inserted on the proboscis. **1856** TODD & BOWMAN *Phys. Anat.* II. 38 The optic tracts are connected with the optic thalami chiefly through the geniculate bodies. **1857** BERKELEY *Cryptog. Bot.* §124. 153 The threads become geniculate, and unite at the two bends. **1875** BLAKE *Zool.* 308 The posterior [antennæ] are geniculate and pediform.

Hence **geˈniculately** *adv.*, in a geniculate manner.

1657 TOMLINSON *Renou's Disp.* 314 Geniculately circumvesting the internodia of the cauls.

geniculate (dʒɪˈnɪkjʊleɪt), *v.* [f. L. *geniculāt-*, ppl. stem of *geniculāre* to bend the knee, f. *geniculum*: see GENICLE.] *trans.* and *intr.* To bend like a knee; to form or be formed into joints.

1623 COCKERAM, *Geniculate*, to ioynt. In mod. Dicts.

Hence **geˈniculating** *ppl. a.*

1852 DANA *Crust.* II. 1040 The right male antenna alone of the first pair with a geniculating joint.

geniculated (dʒɪˈnɪkjʊleɪtɪd), *ppl. a.* [f. GENICULATE *a.* + -ED[1].] = GENICULATE *a.* Of a twin crystal (see quot. 1805–17).

1657 *Physical Dict.*, *Geniculated*, kneed, or knobbed, or full of joynts. **1664** POWER *Exp. Philos.* I. 31 The Water-Spider. She hath two hairy geniculated horns, knotted or joynted at several divisions like Knot-grass. **1728** WOODWARD *Fossils* II. 1 A Piece of some geniculated Plant seeming to be part of a Sugar-Cane. **1805–17** R. JAMESON *Char. Min.* (ed. 3) 226 Geniculated..when it is composed of two prisms, which are united at one end, and form a kind of knee. **1836–9** TODD *Cycl. Anat.* II. 862/1 The antennæ..are usually geniculated. **1882** SLADEN in *Jrnl. Linn. Soc.* XVI. No. 91. 238 The other [spine] rather longer but much less robust..and rather geniculated sideways.

geniculation (dʒɪˌnɪkjʊˈleɪʃən). [ad. late L. *geniculātiōn-em*, n. of action f. *geniculāre* to bend the knee.]

†**1.** The act of kneeling, genuflexion. *Obs.*

1611 CORYAT *Crudities* 2, I saw their Masse, but not with that superstitious geniculation and elevation of hands..that the rest used. **1652** SPARKE *Prim. Devot.* (1663) 81 Her knees were grown brawny, like the knees of Camels, with her pious geniculation. **1662** GUNNING *Lent Fast* 103 To prepare themselves by frequent prayers, fastings, geniculations and watchings.

2. The state of being geniculated.

1879 RUTLEY *Study Rocks* x. 149 Twinning is common, sometimes giving rise to geniculation.

b. *concr.* A geniculate formation; a kneed part or process.

(In recent Dicts.)

geniculum (dʒɪˈnɪkjʊləm). *Anat.* [L., dim. of *genū* GENU.] A small genu; an angular knee-like or knot-like structure.

1889 *Buck's Handbk. Med. Sci.* VIII. 131/1 The thalami and geniculums project caudad beyond the intersegmental line. **1913** [see prec.]. **1967** ANSON & DONALDSON *Surg. Anat. Temporal Bone & Ear* II. 115 The fascial canal.. passes horizontally lateralward, then bends at a right angle, forming the geniculum.

genie (ˈdʒiːnɪ). Also 8 **geny, (genii),** 9 **geni.** [a. F. *génie*, ad. L. *genius*.]

1. †**a.** A tutelary spirit. (= GENIUS 1.) *Obs.*

1655 tr. *De Parc's Francion* II. 53 My Conductor.. informed me, that they were the Genyes of mankind. **1702** ADDISON *Dial. Medals* (1727) 15 To these you may add the Genies of nations, provinces, cities, etc.

b. A JINNEE; one of the sprites or goblins of Arabian demonology.

[The word *génie* was adopted by the Fr. translators of the Arabian Nights as the rendering of the Arab. word which it resembled in sound and in sense. In Eng. *genie* has been commonly used in the sing. and *genii* (see GENIUS 2) in the plural.]

1748 SMOLLETT *Rod. Rand.* lii, If the plot..had been whispered by a genie, communicated by a dream, or revealed by an angel from on high. **1787** *Minor* 60 It is out of my power to assert whether it is a man or a beast, a genii, or a woman. **1825** SCOTT *Talism.* xx, His single lock of hair streamed upwards from his bald and shaven head, as if some genie upheld him by it. **1877** MORLEY *Crit. Misc.* Ser. II. 119 The horrible genie of civil murder. **1896** *Westm. Gaz.* 28 Dec. 3/1 The engagement of Cinquevalli, cleverest of jugglers, to act as geni of the lamp.

2. a. Natural bent or disposition. (= GENIUS 3 a.) (Common in A. Wood.)

1662 BP. GAUDEN *Let.* in Chr. Wordsworth *Doc. Suppl.* (1825) 35 Thereby drawing me, much against my genie, from a very happy privacy. **1691** WOOD *Ath. Oxon.* I. 177 He was very apt to learn, having a natural genie to good letters. **1692** *Ibid.* II. 292 But his genie..lead him in the pleasant paths of Poetry.

†**b.** A person of genius. (= GENIUS 6 a, 6 b.) *Obs.*

1676 ETHEREDGE *Man of Mode* IV. ii, He serv'd some time under Merille, the greatest Genie in the world for a Valet d'Chambré. **1685** *Gracian's Courtiers Orac.* 35 These Paramount Genies are Kings by merit. **1687** A. LOVELL tr. *Bergerac's Com. Hist.* I. 189 That way of dying is common to great Genies, and it is called, To crack with Wit.

genii, pl. of GENIUS.

genin (ˈdʒɛnɪn). *Chem.* [The ending of SAPOGENIN, SALIGENIN, used as a generic word.]

a. Any of various steroids that occur as aglycones in certain glycosides present in some plants and toad venoms. **b.** Occas. used as the name of specific compounds.

[**1874** O. SCHMIEDEBERG in *Arch. f. exper. Path. u. Pharm.* III. 24 So bildet sich ein schön krystallisirender Körper, den man in Analogie mit dem Sapogenin Digitogenin nennen kann.] **1915** *Chem. Abstr.* IX. 1336 Genin, $C_{21}H_{30}O_5$, wartlets from 15 parts of b.96% alc. **1925** *Jrnl. Chem. Soc.* CXXVIII. I. 1295 The genin is converted by cold, concentrated hydrochloric acid into 'dianhydrogitoxigenin', identical with digitaligenin from 'Digitalinum verum'. **1927** *Jrnl. Biol. Chem.* LXXIV. 789 The toxicities of the unhydrogenated 'genins' were of themselves not of the highest order. **1938** *Thorpe's Dict. Appl. Chem.* (ed. 4) II. 381/1 All these drugs are non-nitrogenous glycosides of plant origin yielding on hydrolysis various sugars and a number of structurally similar aglycones or 'genins'. **1959** L. F. & M. FIESER *Steroids* i. 4 The glycoside of which digitogenin is the aglycone, or genin, is a saponin. **1964** C. W. SHOPPEE *Chem. Steroids* (ed. 2) v. 367 Four aglycones: genin B, $C_{21}H_{30}O_4$, genin D, $C_{21}H_{30}O_5$, genin E, $C_{21}H_{30-32}O_5$ and genin F, $C_{21}H_{34}O_5$, isolated from *D. grandiflora*.., are probably digitenols.

†**genio.** *Obs.* [a. It. *genio*, ad. L. *genius*.]

1. = GENIUS 2.

1609 BIBLE (Douay) *Gen.* vi. Comm., Those whom Moyses here called Angels, the Philosophers called Genios ..which are living creatures with ayrie bodies. **1684** tr. *Tavernier's Trav.* II. 106 Numens, Genio's, Demons, Spirits.

2. = GENIUS 3, 4.

1612 *Benvenuto's Passenger* (N.) As humours and genioes so affections and judgement..doth vary and alter. **1710** STEELE *Tatler* No. 182 ¶6, I shall endeavour to make the Parts fit the Genio's of the several Actors.

3. = GENIUS 6 a, 6 b.

1709 STEELE *Tatler* No. 5 ¶10 It is not only to the general Bent of a Nation that great Revolutions are owing, but to the extraordinary Genio's that lead 'em. **1709** *Ibid.* No. 53 ¶1 There are some Genio's which are not capable of pure Affection.

genio- (dʒɪˈnaɪəʊ), combining form of Gr. γένειον (see GENIAL *a.*[2]), occurring in several anatomical combinations in the sense of pertaining to the chin or lower jaw and some other member. †**genioglosse** (in 7 **geneo-**), a muscle of the tongue, connected with the chin and hyoid bone [mod.L. *genioglossus*, F. *genioglosse*]; so **geˈnioglossal** *a.* [see GLOSSAL] = next. **geˌnioˈhyoglossal** *a.* [see HYOGLOSSAL], pertaining to the chin, the hyoid bone, and the tongue. **geˌnio-ˈhyoid** *a.* [see HYOID], pertaining to the chin and to the hyoid bone; also *absol.* quasi-*sb.* = *genio-hyoid muscle.* **geˌnio-ˈmental**

a. [see MENTAL²], pertaining to the lower jaw and the chin.

1669 HOLDER *Elem. Speech* 49 The Tongue being held in that posture, onely by the force of the Geneoglosse, or Myleoglosse Muscles. **1848** *Quain's Elem. Anat.* (ed. 5) I. 273 The genio-hyoid muscle. **1873** MIVART *Elem. Anat.* 287 The genio-hyoid is narrow, and goes from the hyoid to the mandible inside the symphysis. **1885** *Syd. Soc. Lex.*, *Geniohyoid nerve*, a branch given off by the hypoglossal nerve as it lies beneath the mylohyoid muscle. **1890** H. ELLIS *Criminal* iii. 72 The relative frequency is especially marked in zygomatic and genio-mental wrinkles.

genioplasty (dʒɪˈnaɪəʊplæstɪ). [f. Gr. γένειο-ν chin + πλαστ-ός moulded + -Y³.] 'A plastic operation for restoring the chin' (*Syd. Soc. Lex.* 1885).

genip (ˈdʒɛnɪp). *West Indian.* [? short f. next.] *attrib.* in **genip-tree**, a name applied to *Genipa americana*, a small tree of the N.O. *Rubiaceæ*; also to certain similar trees of the N.O. *Sapindaceæ*, esp. *Melicocca bijuga* and *paniculata*.

1756 P. BROWNE *Jamaica* 210 The Genip-Tree.. This tree was brought to Jamaica from Surinam. **1885** LADY BRASSEY *The Trades* 239 Shrubs or rather trees, with large glossy leaves and a single white flower, which I think must have been genip trees.

genipap (ˈdʒɛnɪpæp). Also 7 **genipapi**. [app. a native name.] The fruit of *Genipa americana*.

1613 PURCHAS *Pilgrimage* (1614) 835 The men and women ..make themselves blacke with the fruit Genipapi. **1885** LADY BRASSEY *The Trades* 239 These trees produce the delicious fruit called genipap, which resembles an orange.

genisarie, obs. form of JANIZARY.

Genist (ˈdʒiːnɪst). [ad. late L. *Genistæ* sb. pl., f. L. *gen-* to be born.] One of a sect of ancient Jews who took no foreign wives during the Babylonian captivity, and who therefore claim to be pure-blooded descendants of Abraham. So **ˈGenite**.

1613 PURCHAS *Pilgrimage* II. viii. 128 He there nameth.. diuers other sects if they may beare that name: as the Genites or Genists, which stood vpon their stocke and kindred. **1882** F. W. FARRAR *Early Chr.* II. 342 Even down to the fifth century there continued to be..'Genists', or Jews by race.

‖**genista** (dʒɪˈnɪstə). *Bot.* [L. *genista* broom.] A plant of the genus (N.O. *Leguminosæ*) represented by Dyer's Broom or Greenweed (*G. tinctoria*); the Common Broom (*Cytisus scoparia*) is by some referred to this genus, and is prob. the plant chiefly referred to in the early examples.

1625 PURCHAS *Pilgrims* II. VIII. 1379 A peculiar kind of Genista, and many other vnknowne plants. **1669** EVELYN *Kal. Hort.* (ed. 3) 19 Jasmines, Honey-suckles, Genista Hisp., Carnations [etc.]. **1774** GOLDSM. *Nat. Hist.* (1862) I. xii. 61 A rush, resembling the genista, but much more soft and flexible. **1825** SCOTT *Talism.* xi, The genista, or broom plant, was an emblem of humility. **1886** MRS. CADDY *Footsteps Jeanne D'Arc* xi. 220 The brisk air of the common-land odorous with thyme and the genista.

genistein (dʒɪˈnɪsteɪɪn, -stiːn). *Chem.* [f. GENIST(A + -EIN.] An isoflavone derivative, $C_{15}H_{10}O_5$, that is present in dyer's broom, *Genista tinctoria*, and some other plants and is a weak yellow colouring matter. Also called *prunetol*.

1900 PERKIN & NEWBURY in *Jrnl. Chem. Soc.* LXXV. 833 This new colouring matter, for which the name *genistein* is proposed, crystallises in long, glistening, colourless needles. **1943** A. H. COOK tr. *Mayer's Chem. Natural Coloring Matters* iv. 195 Genistein..is contained in dyer's broom (*Genista tinctoria*), together with luteolin, and in soybeans (*Soja hispida*) as the 7-glucoside. **1953** *Jrnl. Chem. Soc.* 871 Genistein (5:7:4′-trihydroxy*iso*flavone) is a pro-œstrogen, responsible for most of the œstrogenic activity of subterranean clover.

†**ˈgenitable**, *a.* *Obs. rare*⁻¹. [a. F. *genitable* (obs.), ad. L. *genitābil-em* capable of generating, f. *genit-* (see next).] = GENITAL *a.*

1634 T. JOHNSON *Parey's Chirurg.* XXIV. xxxix. 933 Although the seed be genitable. [Mistranslated from L. *His etsi semen genitale sit.*]

genital (ˈdʒɛnɪtəl), *a.* and *sb.* [ad. L. *genitāl-em*, f. *genit-*, ppl. stem of *gignĕre* to beget + *-ālem*: see -AL¹. Cf. F. *génital*, Sp. *genital*, It. *genitale*.]

A. *adj.* Pertaining to animal generation.

1382 WYCLIF *Num.* xxv. 8 [Phynees] stikide thurȝ both togidre..in the genytale places [*L. locis genitalibus*]. **1398** TREVISA *Barth. De P.R.* v. xlviii. (1495) 165 In the membre genycal [*read* genytal] god hath sette suche an appetyte insuperable that [etc.]. **1585** J. B. tr. *Viret's Sch. Beastes* D vj b, Some [fishes] which follow the females, and sprinkle the egges, with the genitall seed. **1599** H. BUTTES *Dyets drie Dinner* M iij b, The Wine wherein a Mullet is stifled drunke, depriveth men of all genitall vertue. **1607** TOPSELL *Four-f. Beasts* (1658) 18 The seed genital of an Asse is more frigid then an Horses. **1660** SHARROCK *Vegetables* 46 Into so many offsets shall the genitall vertue dispose itself. **1774** GOLDSM. *Nat. Hist.* (1776) IV. 310 The genital part of the male [camel] resembles that of the bull. **1845** BUDD *Dis. Liver* 390 A small depression, in which are the two genital pores. **1878** BELL *Gegenbaur's Comp. Anat.* 122 In all forms the lower wall of the canal forms the genital region.

†**b.** Presiding over generation or birth (L. *dii genitales*). *Obs. rare*⁻¹.

1652 GAULE *Magastrom.* xviii. 149 So many Geniall or Genitall Gods and Goddesses.

B. *sb.* The external organ or organs of generation.

†**a.** *sing.* (= L. *genitāle.*) *Obs. rare.*

c **1450** BURGH *Contn. Lydg. Secrees* 1764 With white wyn drynk it in the morwenyng, ffrom seknesse in genital kepith soget and kyng. **1607** TOPSELL *Four-f. Beasts* (1658) 154 The female [elephant] hath her genital betwixt her thighes. **1727** BRADLEY *Fam. Dict.* I. L vj b/1 The..Male's Genital.

b. *pl.* (= L. *genitālia*; OF. *genitailles.*)

1390 GOWER *Conf.* II. 156 Jupiter..his father bonde.. And kut of with his owne honde His genitals. ? *a* **1400** *Morte Arth.* 1123 Ewyne into inmette the gyaunt he hyttez, Just to þe genitales [*MS.* genitates], and jaggede þame in sondre! **1599** A. M. tr. *Gabelhouer's Bk. Physicke* 175/1 Applye it verye warme to your genitalles. **1610** HEALEY *St. Aug. Citie of God* 520 Some philosophers called Gymnosophists.. cover their genitals, whereas all the rest of their bodies are bare. **1682** T. GIBSON *Anat.* 23 The parts ministring to Procreation, are the Genitals both in Men and Women. **1789** W. BUCHAN *Dom. Med.* (1790) 333 If the genitals be immersed for some time in cold water, it will generally stop a bleeding at the nose. **1808** *Med. Jrnl.* XIX. 180 Case of Malconformation in the Genitals.

‖**genitalia** (dʒɛnɪˈteɪlɪə), *sb. pl.* [a. L. *genitalia*] = GENITALS (see prec. B. b).

1876 DUHRING *Dis. Skin* 121 Their common seat is upon the face, neck, breast and genitalia. **1877** HUXLEY *Anat. Inv. Anim.* iv. 196 As in most Trematoda, the genitalia form a large part of the viscera.

†**ˈgenited**, *ppl. a. Math. Obs.* [f. L. *genit-us*, pa. pple. of *gignĕre* to beget.] = GENERATED.

1704 J. HARRIS *Lex. Techn.*, *Generated* or *Genited Quantity*, in a very large sense, for whatever is produced either in Arithmetick, by the Multiplication, Division, or Extraction of Roots; or in Geometry, by the Invention of the Contents, Areas and Sides, or of extream and mean Proportionals, without Addition and Subtraction. **1751** in CHAMBERS *Cycl.*

geniting, obs. form of JENNETING.

genitival (dʒɛnɪˈtaɪvəl), *a.* [f. GENITIVE + -AL¹.] Belonging to the genitive case.

1818 *Monthly Mag.* XLVI. 322 Instead of the genitival and datival terminations, *of* and *to*, were prefixed to the nominative. **1872** LOWELL *Milton* Prose Wks. 1890 IV. 102 He occupies some ten pages..with a history of the genitival form *its*. **1884** *Sat. Rev.* 7 June 760/1 The genitival *an* so frequent in Anglo-Saxon place-names.

genitivally (dʒɛnɪˈtaɪvəlɪ), *adv.* [f. GENITIVAL *a.* + -LY².] In the genitive case; as a genitive.

1893 in *Funk's Stand. Dict.* **1966** G. N. LEECH *Eng. in Advertising* xiv. 133 In 'Kellogg's Rice Krispies great new card series', a whole product name 'Kellogg's Rice Krispies' is used genitivally, itself containing a further genitive ('Kellogg's').

genitive (ˈdʒɛnɪtɪv), *a.* and *sb.* Also 4 **genitif**, 5 **genetife**, 7 **genetive**. [ad. L. *genetīv-um*, *genitīv-um* belonging to birth or generation (f. **gen-* root of *gignĕre* to beget); *genetīvus* (*casus*) was used by Lat. grammarians to render Gr. γενική (πτῶσις), which however properly means 'generic case'. Varro's *patricus casus* is a similar mistranslation. The earliest Eng. forms may be a. OF. *genetif* (F. *génitif*, It. and Sp. *genitivo*).] **A.** *adj.*

1. ***genitive case***: a grammatical form of substantives and other declinable parts of speech, chiefly used to denote that the person or thing signified by the word is related to another as source, possessor, or the like, but in different languages also employed in a variety of idiomatic usages.

1398 TREVISA *Barth. De P.R.* XVII. xcvi. (1495) 663 Lens, that is a nytte, and is wryte wyth D. in the genitif case. *c* **1440** *Gesta Rom.* xci. 416 (Add. MS.) The seconde case is genetife case. **1520** WHITINTON *Vulg.* (1527) 11 b, The hauer or yᵉ owner gouerneth somtyme a genytyue case of the thynge that is had. **1562** TURNER *Herbal* II. 23 a, The poticaries.. call it [Iris] Irios in the genitiue case. **1645** DIGBY *Mans Soul* ii. 367 The Hebrewes do expresse this vnion..of two different apprehensions..by putting in the genitiue case, the word which expresseth one of them. **1711** J. GREENWOOD *Eng. Gram.* 51 Of the English Genitive Case, with a Note concerning Gender. **1771** SIR W. JONES *Gram. Pers. Lang.* Wks. 1799 II. 147 There is no genitive case in Persian. **1898** EARLE *Simple Gram. Eng.* 15 To express the Genitive Case of these plurals no further sound is added.

†**2.** Pertaining to generation (so OF. *genetif*, *parties genitives*). *Obs.*

1536 BELLENDEN *Cron. Scot.* (1541) Proheme Cosmogr. xv, As ane beist, so is ane man consaue Of seid infuse in membris genitiue. **1560** ROLLAND *Crt. Venus* IV. 44 He ordanit sum be of kind genitiue, And fill the warld efter thair qualitie. **1612** *Benvenuto's Passenger* I. 103 Sparage.. prouokes vrine, increaseth genetiue seed, cleanseth the reynes from sand [etc.]. **1656** BLOUNT *Glossogr.*, *Genitive*, natural, engendring, of an ingendring faculty, that hath power to ingender.

B. *sb.* = *genitive case*; also, a part of speech in the genitive case. **genitive absolute**, a construction in Greek similar to the Latin ablative absolute.

c **1620** A. HUME *Brit. Tongue* (1865) 29 Our genitive is alwayes joyned with an other noun, and is noated with of, or s. **1749** *Power Pros. Numbers* 71 The Concurrence of many Genitives with their Sign of prefixed, should be avoided as an inelegance. **1824** L. MURRAY *Eng. Gram.* (ed. 5) I. 266 When this plurality is neither intimated, nor necessarily supposed, the double genitive..should not be used. **1860** W. W. GOODWIN *Syntax Greek Verb* vi. 297 We sometimes find the Participle in the Genitive Absolute with ὡς. **1866** MASSON tr. *Winer's Gram. N.T. Dict.* 209 Even in Greek prose the Genitive is usually employed to denote separation or removal. **1892** EARLE *Philol. Eng. Tongue* (ed. 5) 547 The Cumulative or Double Genitive, a peculiarly English combination, where both the *of* and the *s* are retained, as 'that boy of Norcott's'. **1897** A. N. JANNARIS *Hist. Greek Gram.* III. 499 The Greek genitive absolute substantially corresponds to the Latin ablative absolute.

attrib. **1872** MORRIS *Eng. Accid.* 101 It is probable that the genitive ending was nothing more than an adjective termination.

ˈgenitively, *adv. rare.* [f. GENITIVE *a.* + -LY².] As a genitive.

1846 MONIER WILLIAMS *Sanscr. Gram.* ix. 161 Dependent Compounds, or Compounds Dependent in Case.. Genitively Dependent. Or those in which the relation of the first word to the last is equivalent to that of a genitive.

genito- (ˈdʒɛnɪtəʊ), modern combining form of L. *genitālis* genital, used in various physiological terms which refer to the genital organs in conjunction with other parts of the body, as ***genito-anal***, ***-crural*** (in ***genitocrural nerve*** = F. *nerf génito-crural*), ***-spinal***, ***-urinary*** (F. *génito-urinaire*).

1835-6 TODD *Cycl. Anat.* I. 384/2 This tunic is but a portion of the genito-urinary mucous membrane. **1844** HOBLYN *Dict. Med.*, *Genito-crural*, the name of a nerve proceeding from the first lumbar, and dividing into an *internal branch*, which accompanies the spermatic cord; and an *external*, which is distributed into filaments at the crural arch. **1876** GROSS *Dis. Bladder* 158 The blood may be derived from any portion of the genito-urinary mucous tract. **1878** T. BRYANT *Pract. Surg.* I. 486 The genito-crural nerve, which lies upon the vessel, should not be included in the ligature.

genitoir, var. GENITOR¹.

†**genitor¹**, **genitory**. *Obs.* Chiefly *pl.* Forms: *α.* 4 **geny-**, **gene-**, **genitras**, **-traces**, 4, 7 **gene-**, (5 **genytours**), 7 **genitoir(e)s**, 5 **geny-**, 6 **genitores**, 6–7 **geniturs**; *β.* 5 **genetoryes**, 6 **gene-**, **geny-**, 6–8 **genitories**. [a. OF. *genitoir* (usu. pl. *genitoirs*, *génitoires*), app. f. L. type **genitōrium*.] A testicle; *pl.* the testicles, but in later use = *genitals*. (Cf. GENITURE.)

13.. *Minor poems of Vernon MS.* xxxvii. 276 Men miȝte, ȝif his brech weore to-tore, seon his genitras [*rime* has]. **1387** TREVISA *Higden* (Rolls) VII. 315 Who þat took a womman by strengþ schulde lese his genitras [*v.r.* genitraces]. **1398** —— *Barth. De P.R.* VII. lv. (1495) 269 Yf it happe that thys Hernia is broke a grete deele of the bowels falle downe in to the codde of the genetours. **1481** CAXTON *Myrr.* II. vi. 73 Castours..whan they ben honted..byte wyth their teeth their owne genytoirs or ballocks and lete them falle. **1483** —— *G. de la Tour* E v, And they kyt awey the Genytoryes of the sayde monk. **1533** ELYOT *Cast. Helthe* (1541) 7 a, Of the genytories or stones of generation. **1574** HYLL *Conject. Weather* iv, If his right genitour be trussed up..then doth he beget a Ewe lambe. **1579** LANGHAM *Gard. Health* (1633) 309 The same..healeth all paine and swellings of the genitors or stones. **1603** KNOLLES *Hist. Turks* (1621) 276 His sonnes deprived of their sight, and spoiled of their genitoires. **1657** W. COLES *Adam in Eden* xcix. 137 The Ashes..are used..to cleanse and heal old ulcers and sores, as well in the Genitories as other parts of the body. **1708** MOTTEUX *Rabelais* IV. xlviii. (1737) 194 He has Genitories.

b. In adjectival use: ***members genitors***.

1483 CAXTON *Gold. Leg.* 223 b/2 Thys synne may in no wyse be forgyuen But yf he cutte of his membris genytores.

genitor² (ˈdʒɛnɪtər). Also 5 **genytur**, 6 **genitour**. [a. L. *genitor* begetter, parent, f. **gen-*, root of *gignĕre* to beget, bear. The earliest forms are a. F. *geniteur*, ad. L. *genitōr-em*.] **a.** A male parent, father; in *pl.* = parents. Now *rare*.

1447 BOKENHAM *Seyntys* (Roxb.) 156 These thre.. dyvydyd the possessyoun Of her genyturs. **1537** LATIMER *2nd Serm. bef. Convoc.* D ij, They..that were the wise fathers and genitours of this purgatorie, were, in my mynde, the wysest of all their generation. **1659** PEARSON *Creed* (1839) 57 Whosoever is generated is from him which is the genitor. **1665** HOOKE *Microgr.* 192 In those places are found all the convenient causes of their production, namely, genitors, or Parents [etc.]. **1818** KEATS *Endym.* I. 300 High genitors, unconscious did they cull Time's sweet first-fruits. **1846** LANDOR *Imag. Conv.* Wks. I. 90 A son, worthy of his august genitor, in happy hour is born to your Majesty.

b. *spec.* in *Anthropol.* (See quots.)

1949 E. E. EVANS-PRITCHARD in M. Fortes *Social Structure* 86 When, as often happens among the Nuer, the physiological father, the *genitor*, is a different man from the sociological father, the *pater*, his sons will not marry into his minimal lineage. **1963** *Brit. Jrnl. Sociol.* XIV. 24 We use the words *genitor* and *pater* to distinguish between the begetter of a child and its legal father.

Hence **geniˈtorial** *a.*, parental. *rare*⁻¹.

1847 MEDWIN *Shelley* I. 158 Sir Timothy was a man entertaining high notions of genitorial rights.

genitory: see GENITOR¹.

genitrise, var. GENTRICE.

genitrix: see GENETRIX.

geniture. [ad. L. *genitūr-am* begetting, etc., f. *gignĕre* to beget. Cf. OF. *geniture.*]

1. Begetting, generation; birth.

1641 M. Frank *Serm.* (1672) 228 Parents here under the notion of γονεῖς seems very strange, Joseph having no part in His geniture. **1650** Fuller *Pisgah* iv. ii. 27 God.. foretelleth that Moab should be made drunk, (haply alluding to his geniture, seeing he was begotten in a fit of drunkenness). **1759** Sterne *Tr. Shandy* I. 7 On the 25th of the same month in which I date my geniture. **1916** A. Quiller-Couch *Art of Writing* viii. 145 A man's lineage and geniture being reckoned, as a rule, among the things he cannot reasonably be asked to amend. **1931** A. J. Cronin *Hatter's Castle* 439 She had failed him in everything.., in the very geniture of her children.

†**2.** *Astrol.* Nativity, horoscope. (Cf. genesis 2.) *Obs.*

1621 Burton *Anat. Mel.* i. i. i. ii, He had the significators in his geniture fortunate, and free from the hostile aspects of Saturne and Mars. **1647** Lilly *Chr. Astrol.* civ. 528 In diurnall genitures.. you must ever regard the degree of the Ecliptick. **1721** Earl Nottingham *Answ. Whiston* 47 The Second (Origin) signifies his Geniture or Nativity. **1819** J. Wilson *Dict. Astrol., Geniture*, the Birth, the radical figure, the plan of a nativity.

†**3.** That which is generated; offspring, product. *Obs.*

1579 Fulke *Confut. Sanders* 620 He may deny a man to be a creature because he is a geniture, that is a thing begotten. **1603** Holland *Plutarch's Mor.* 1345 Saying, that he [the Sunne] is the issue and geniture proceeding from Apollo who is eternall, and who continually bringeth him foorth. **1678** R. Barclay *Apol. Quakers* xi. x. 368 The little Seed of Righteousness.. receives a place to arise, and becometh a holy Birth, and Geniture in Man. **1698** Fryer *Acc. E. India & P.* 320 The Pearl is supposed to be the Geniture of a Shell-fish called Margaritifer.

†**4. a.** The generative seed of animals. *Obs.*

1615 Crooke *Body of Man* 259 The Seed is called.. in Latine *semen, Genitura*.. And so we wil call it Seed and Geniture. **1620** Venner *Via Recta* ii. 29 The vse of them.. is.. an enemy to procreation, because they dry up the geniture. **1683** A. Snape *Anat. Horse* App. §1 (1686) 6 As to the efficient Cause of Generation, that is the geniture of the Male.

b. The prolific germ in vegetable seed. *Obs. rare*$^{-1}$.

1674 *Phil. Trans.* IX. 63 That part of a Seed, in which properly the prolifique vertue lodgeth, and which is strictly called the geniture.

†**5.** *pl.* = Genitals (OF. *genitures*). (Cf. genitor[1].) *Obs.*

1548 Hall *Chron.* (1809) 744 Every strete laye full of the privie members and genitures of the Cardinalles and holy prelates.

†**6.** *Math.* = factor *sb.* 6. *Obs. rare*$^{-1}$.

1718 J. Chamberlayne *Relig. Philos.* I. xvi. §19 That all the Co-efficients or Genitures of the Terms taken together .. yield the Quantity.

genius (ˈdʒiːnɪəs). Pl. genii (ˈdʒiːnɪaɪ), geniuses, (†genius's). [a. L. *genius*, f. **gen-* root of *gi-gnĕre* to beget, Gr. γίγνεσθαι to be born, come into being.

In Lat. the word has mainly the sense 1 below (the extended sense 2 occurs post-classically), and a fig. sense approaching 3. As a word of learned origin it is found in the Rom. langs.: F. *génie* (whence Ger. *genie*), It., Sp., Pg. *genio*, which have approximately the same senses as in Eng. To some extent the sense-development in Rom. has been affected by confusion with *ingenium* (see engine): cf. for example F. *génie civil* 'civil engineering'.]

1. With reference to classical pagan belief: The tutelary god or attendant spirit allotted to every person at his birth, to govern his fortunes and determine his character, and finally to conduct him out of the world; also, the tutelary and controlling spirit similarly connected with a place, an institution, etc. (Now only in *sing.*)

In the first two quots. *Genius* is the proper name of an allegorical person who in the *Rom. de la Rose* represents the native moral instincts of mankind as setting bounds to the range of sexual passion.

[**1390** Gower *Conf.* I. 48 O Genius min owne clerke Come forth and here this mannes shrifte. *c* **1400** *Rom. Rose* 4768 They.. Whom genius cursith, man and wyf, That wrongly werke ageyn nature.] **1513** Douglas *Æneis* ix. iv. 49 Gif that euery mannis schrewit desyre Be as his God and Genyus in that place. **1536** Bellenden *Cron. Scot.* (1541) Proheme Cosmogr. xii, Thair is na thing may be so odius To man, as leif in miserie and wo Defraudand god of nature genius. [Cf. Ter. *Phorm.* i. i. 10 and Hor. *Ep.* ii. ii. 188.] **1596** Drayton *Leg.* iv. 51 The pale Genius of that aged floud. **1605** Shaks. *Macb.* iii. i. 56 Vnder him My Genius is rebuk'd, as it is said Mark Anthonies was by Cæsar. **1612** Drayton *Poly-olb.* i. 10 Thou Genius of the place.. Which liued'st long before the All-earth-drowning Flood. *c* **1630** Risdon *Surv. Devon* §225 (1810) 237 Genii of the spring. **1647** R. Stapylton *Juvenal* 63 Any thing wherein the spirit or soule delighted, was called sacred or peculiar to the genius, especially feasting and marriage. **1663** Dryden *To Author* 55 in Charleton *Stone-heng*, Watch'd by the Genius of this Royal place. **1701** Rowe *Amb. Step-Moth.* i. i. 51 Let their Guardian Genii still be watchful. **1745** Collins *Ode Col. Ross* i, Britannia's Genius bends to earth. *c* **1800** K. White *Childhood* ii. 260 Kind genii of my native fields benign. **1831** Carlyle *Sart. Res.* (1858) 87 It was his guiding Genius (*Dämon*) that inspired him; he must go forth and meet his Destiny. **1843** Dickens *Christm. Carol* i, It seemed as if the Genius of the Weather sat in mournful meditation on the threshold. **1863** *Scotsman* 12 Aug., We are now able.. to thank our stars that the genius of red tape was so strong even in France. **1871** Farrar *Witn. Hist.* iii. 99 Christians.. who would die rather than fling into the altar-flame a pinch of incense to the Genius of the Emperors. **1887** Bowen *Virg. Æneid* v. 95 His sire's familiar, or genius haunting the shore.

†**b.** After Lat. use: This spirit viewed as propitiated by festivities; hence, one's appetite. *Obs.*

1605 B. Jonson *Volpone* i. i. B 2 a, What should I do, But cocker vp my Genius, and liue free To all delights, my fortune calls me to? **1693** Dryden *Juvenal* iv. 105 To your glad Genius sacrifice this Day; Let common Meats respectfully give way.

c. (*a person's*) *good, evil genius*: the two mutually opposed spirits (in Christian language *angels*) by whom every person was supposed to be attended throughout his life. Hence applied *transf.* to a person who powerfully influences for good or evil the character, conduct, or fortunes of another.

1610 Shaks. *Temp.* iv. i. 27 The strongest suggestion, Our worser Genius can. **1613** Purchas *Pilgrimage* (1614) 365 A tradition of two Genii, which attend every man, one good, the other evill. **1653** H. More *Antid. Ath.* iii. xiv. (1712) 130 The Pythagoreans were of opinion that every man has two Genii, a good one, and a bad one. **1660** J. S. *Andromana* iii. v. in Hazl. *Dodsley* XIV. 244 My better genius, thou art welcome as A draught of water to a thirsty man. **1702** Rowe *Tamerl.* iv. i. 1689 Thou.. art an evil Genius to thyself. **1770** Langhorne *Plutarch* (1879) II. 1006/2 Men had their evil genii, who disturbed them with fears, and distressed their virtue. **1868** Freeman *Norm. Conq.* (1876) II. vii. 24 It needed the intervention of his better genius in the form of Godwine.

†**d.** In astrological use the word survived, with some notion of its original sense, passing into a symbolical expression for the combination of sidereal influences represented in a person's horoscope. *Obs.*

1643 Milton *Divorce* i. x, But what might be the cause, whether each one's allotted Genius or proper star, or [etc.]. **1657** H. Pinnell *Philos. Ref.* 67 The other part therefore of Man, or this sydereall body is called the Genius of man, because it proceedeth from the Firmament; it is called *Penates*, because it is in our power and born with us, the shadow of the visible body, *Lar domesticus*, the good or bad houshold or private Angell.

e. The quasi-mythologic personification of something immaterial (e.g. of a virtue, a custom, an institution), esp. as portrayed in painting or sculpture. Hence *transf.* a person or thing fit to be taken as an embodied type of (some abstract idea).

1597 Shaks. *2 Hen. IV*, iii. ii. 337 Hee was the very Genius of Famine. **1875** B. Harte *Tales Argonauts, Baby Sylvester*, A golden lizard, the very genius of desolate stillness, had stopped breathless upon the threshold of one cabin.

2. A demon or spiritual being in general. Now chiefly in pl. *genii* (the *sing.* being usually replaced by genie), as a rendering of Arab. *jinn*, the collective name of a class of spirits (some good, some evil) supposed to interfere powerfully in human affairs.

c **1590** Greene *Fr. Bacon* ix. 71 Whereas the pyromantic genii Are mighty, swift, and of far-reaching power. **1646** Buck *Rich. III* Ded., To the common-rout, they.. are another kind of Genius, or *ignis fatuus*. **1653** Ld. Vaux *Godeau's St. Paul* 321 The worship of Angels or Geniuses [*printed* Genieuses]. **1655** Stanley *Hist. Philos.* ii. (1701) 83/1 They mock even the Genius of Socrates as a feigned thing. **1681** H. More *Exp. Dan.* ii. 25 The activity therefore of the Aerial Genii or Angels may be understood by these Winds. **1688** Mrs. Behn tr. *Van Dale's Hist. Orac.* (1718) 150 Evil Genii, and Spirits condemn'd to eternal punishment. **1756–82** J. Warton *Ess. Pope* (1782) II. x. 178 It seemed one of those edifices in Fairy Tales, that are raised by Genii in a nights time. **1779** Franklin *Wks.* (1889) VI. 261 Albumazar.. was visited nightly by genii and spirits of the first rank. **1832** W. Irving *Alhambra* I. 251 The genii, who watch over the place, were obedient to my magic power. **1879** Gladstone *Glean.* I. i. 32 The whole narrative really recalls the most graceful fictions of wise genii and gentle fairies.

3. †**a.** Of persons: Characteristic disposition; inclination; bent, turn or temper of mind. *Obs.*

1581 Sidney *Apol. Poetrie* (Arb.) 62 A Poet, no industrie can make, if his owne Genius bee not carried vnto it. **1599** B. Jonson *Ev. Man out of Hum.* ii. i. (1600) D 4 a, I cannot frame me to your harsh vulgar phrase, tis agaynst my Genius. **1663** Gerbier *Counsel* 36 Those things whereunto their Genius doth tend. **1686** *Observ. Chinese Char.* in *Misc. Cur.* (1708) III. 215 There have been various ways thought of for Expressing Significancy, according to the several Genii of the Persons that were the Inventors. **1690** Evelyn *Mem.* (1857) III. 318 Its being suitable to my rural genius, born as I was at Wotton, among the woods. **1697** tr. *C'tess D'Aunoy's Trav.* (1706) 83 He immediately discovered the Queens Genius, and easily made himself her Confident. **1713** Derham *Phys. Theol.* v. i. 312 There is the same Reason for the variety of Genii, or Inclinations of Men also. **1761** Hume *Hist. Eng.* III. lxi. 319 Men of such daring geniuses were not contented with the ancient and legal forms of civil government. **1780** Johnson *Let. to Mrs. Thrale* 10 July, Every man has his genius.. my genius is always in extremes. **1781** J. Moore *View Soc. It.* (1790) I. xvi. 188 The intriguing genius of Pope Julius. **1804** W. Tennant *Ind. Recreat.* (ed. 2) II. 162 Operations requiring no effort.. and on that account peculiarly suited to the genius of the indolent Bengalese.

b. With reference to a nation, age, etc.: Prevalent feeling, opinion, sentiment, or taste; distinctive character, or spirit.

1639 Fuller *Holy War* v. xix. (1640) 260 The warre-genius of the world is altered now-a-dayes, and supplieth number with policie. *c* **1645** Howell *Lett.* (1650) II. 74 Before I wean my self from Italy, a word or two touching the genius of the nation. **1665** Boyle *Occas. Refl.* 189 My Acquaintedness with the Genius of the Age had sadly taught me that I was to alter my Method. **1701** Swift *Contests Nobles & Comm.* Wks. 1755 II. i. 44 The people of England are of a genius and temper never to admit slavery among them. **1711** Addison *Spect.* No. 29 ¶9 A Composer should fit his Musick to the Genius of the People. **1754** Hume *Hist. Eng.* (1761) I. ix. 196 The barbarous and violent genius of the age. **1791** Burke *App. Whigs* Wks. 1842 I. 531 The genius of this faction is easily discerned. **1845** Stephen *Comm. Laws Eng.* (1874) I. 81 Owing perhaps to some peculiar averseness in the early genius of the country from change in its legal institutions. **1855** Prescott *Philip II*, I. i. i. 2 This flexibility was foreign to the genius of the Spaniard.

personified. **1871** Morley *Voltaire* (1886) 4 The rays from Voltaire's burning and far-shining spirit.. struck upon the genius of the time, seated dark and dead like the black stone of Memnon's statue.

c. Of a language, law, or institution: Prevailing character or spirit, general drift, characteristic method or procedure.

1647 N. Bacon *Disc. Govt. Eng.* i. xlix. (1739) 85 The right genius of this Law will also more evidently appear by the practice of those times. **1699** Bentley *Phal.* 244 The Genius and Constitution of Tragedy. **1705** Addison *Italy* 183 They are chiefly to be ascrib'd to the very Genius of the Roman Catholick Religion. **1755** Johnson *Dict.* Pref., Such [words] as are readily adopted by the genius of our tongue. **1765** Harris *Three Treat.* Advt., Those Treatises, being written in Dialogue, from their Nature and Genius admit not of Interruption. **1776** Adam Smith *W.N.* i. viii. (1869) I. 77 The genius of the British Constitution. **1791** Burke *Th. Fr. Affairs* Wks. VII. 15 They will examine into the true character and genius of some late events. **1814** T. Bell *View Coven. Wks.* 270 The Decalogue changed as it were its genius. *a* **1850** Calhoun *Wks.* (1874) III. 219 The genius of our constitution is opposed to the assumption of power. **1875** Jowett *Plato* (ed. 2) II. 17 He expresses the very genius of the old comedy. **1875** Stewart & Tait *Unseen Univ.* i. §36 (1878) 54 The whole genius of Christianity would appear to point towards a total submission.

d. With reference to a place: The body of associations connected with, or inspirations that may be derived from it. (Cf. 1 and 7.)

[**1681** Dryden *Prol. Univ. Oxf.* 25 By the sacred genius of this place.] **1823** Lamb *Elia* Ser. ii. *Tombs in Abbey*, Is the being shown over a place the same as silently for ourselves detecting the genius of it? **1844** Disraeli *Coningsby* iv. xv, In Palestine, I met a German student who was accumulating materials for the History of Christianity, and studying the genius of the place. **1844** Stanley *Arnold* I. iii. 101 Whatever peculiarity of character was impressed on the scholars whom it sent forth, was derived not from the genius of the place, but from the genius of the man.

†**e.** Of material things, diseases, etc.: The natural character, inherent constitution or tendency.

1675 Grew *Anat. Trunks* ii. vi. §6 Convolvula's do not wind by any peculiar Nature or Genius. **1697** Dryden *Virg. Georg.* i. 80 The Culture suiting to the sev'ral Kinds Of Seeds and Plants; and what will thrive and rise, And what the Genius of the Soil denies. **1725** Pope *Odyss.* ix. 152 Here all products and all plants abound, Sprung from the fruitful genius of the ground. **1728–30** —— in Spence *Anecd.* (1858) 9 In laying out a garden, the first thing to be considered is the genius of the place: thus at Riskins.. Lord Bathurst should have raised two or three mounts; because his situation is all a plain. **1747** Berkeley *Tar-water in Plague* Wks. III. 483 Fevers.. change their genius in different seasons.

4. Natural ability or capacity; quality of mind; the special endowments which fit a man for his peculiar work. (Now only with mixture of sense 5.)

1649 Milton *Eikon.* 241 To unsettle the conscience of any knowing Christian is a thing above the genius of his Cleric elocution. **1662** Evelyn *Chalcogr.* 74 Hugens.. so worthily celebrated for his.. universal Mathematical Genius. **1725** T. Hearne *Pref. to R. Brunne's Chron.* I. 27 For no Study can be more pleasant to Persons of a genius than that of our National History and Antiquities. **1729** Franklin *Ess.* Wks. 1840 II. 263 Different men have geniuses adapted to a variety of different arts and manufactures. **1759** Robertson *Hist. Scot.* I. i. 68 His genius was of that kind which ripens slowly. **1768** W. Gilpin *Prints* 125 Dorigny seems to have exhausted his genius upon it. **1831** Brewster *Newton* (1855) I. xii. 322 The peculiar genius of Newton has been displayed in his investigation of the law of universal gravitation. **1840** Thirlwall *Greece* VII. 71 A design certainly suited to Alexander's genius. **1853** Lytton *My Novel* ii. x, The Squire, whose active genius was always at some repair or improvement.

b. Natural aptitude, coupled with more or less of inclination †*to, for* (something). (Now only with mixture of sense 5.)

1643 Sir T. Browne *Relig. Med.* i. §6, I have no Genius to disputes in Religion. **1707** J. Archdale *Descr. Carolina* 11, I advise, That such Missionaries be well skill'd in Chymistry, and some natural Genius to seek the Virtues in Herbs, Metts and Minerals. **1727** De Foe *Syst. Magic* i. i. (1840) 7 One having a genius to this, another to that kind of knowledge. **1788** Priestley *Lect. Hist.* v. l. 381 A genius for science by no means depends upon climate. **1798** Ferriar *Illustr. Sterne* ii. 38 He had no great genius for poetry. **1818** Jas. Mill *Brit. India* II. v. viii. 684 He had no genius, any more than Clive, for schemes of policy including large views of the past. **1844** Mrs. Browning *Crowned & Buried* xxvii, He had The genius to be loved. **1871** Smiles *Charac.* vi. (1876) 183 Their genius for borrowing, in the long run, usually proves their ruin. **1878** R. W. Dale *Lect. Preach.* ii. 38 Mr. Gladstone has an extraordinary genius for finance. **1889** Lowell *Latest Lit. Ess., Walton* (1891) 80 Walton had a genius for friendships.

5. (Only in *sing.*) Native intellectual power of an exalted type, such as is attributed to those who are esteemed greatest in any department of art, speculation, or practice; instinctive and extraordinary capacity for imaginative creation, original thought, invention, or discovery. Often contrasted with *talent*.

This sense, which belongs also to F. *génie*, Ger. *genie*, appears to have been developed in the 18th c. (It is not recognized in Johnson's Dictionary.) In sense 4 the word had come to be applied with especial frequency to the kind of intellectual power manifested by poets and artists; and when in this application 'genius', as native endowment, came to be contrasted with the aptitudes that can be acquired by study, the approach to the modern sense was often very close. The further development of meaning was prob. influenced by association with senses 1 and 2, which suggested that the word had an especial fitness to denote that particular kind of intellectual power which has the appearance of proceeding from a supernatural inspiration or possession, and which seems to arrive at its results in an inexplicable and miraculous manner. This use, which app. originated in England, came into great prominence in Germany, and gave the designation of *Genieperiode* to the epoch in German literature otherwise known as the 'Sturm und Drang' period. Owing to the influence of Ger. literature in the present century, this is now the most familiar sense of the Eng. word, and usually colours the other senses. It was by the Ger. writers of the 18th c. that the distinction between 'genius' and 'talent', which had some foundation in Fr. usage, was sharpened into the strong antithesis which is now universally current, so that the one term is hardly ever defined without reference to the other. The difference between *genius* and *talent* has been formulated very variously by different writers, but there is general agreement in regarding the former as the higher of the two, as 'creative' and 'original', and as achieving its results by instinctive perception and spontaneous activity, rather than by processes which admit of being distinctly analyzed.

1749 FIELDING *Tom Jones* xiv. i, By the wonderful force of genius only, without the least assistance of learning. **1755** W. SHARPE (*title*), Dissertation on Genius. **1756–82** J. WARTON *Ess. Pope* (1782) II. viii. 21 It were to be wished that no youth of genius were suffered to look into Statius. **1783** BLAIR *Rhet.* iii. I. 41 Genius always imports something inventive or creative. **1801** FUSELI in *Lect. Paint.* i. (1848) 348 By Genius I mean that power which enlarges the circle of human knowledge; which discovers new materials of Nature, or combines the known with novelty. **1849** MACAULAY *Hist. Eng.* ii. I. 259 The genius of Halifax bore down all opposition. **1853** DE QUINCEY *Autobiog. Sk.* Wks. I. 198 *note*, Talent and genius..are not merely different, they are in polar opposition to each other. Talent is intellectual power of every kind, which acts and manifests itself..through the will and the active forces. Genius..is that much rarer species of intellectual power which is derived from the genial nature—from the spirit of suffering and enjoying—from the spirit of pleasure and pain..It is a function of the passive nature. **1858** CARLYLE *Fredk. Gt.* iv. iii. I. 407 Genius..means transcendent capacity of taking trouble, first of all. **1866** R. W. DALE *Disc. Spec. Occ.* vii. 241 The world hardly knew what music was, till the genius of Handel did homage to the Messiah. **1883** FROUDE *Short Stud.* IV. ii. iii. 195 A man of genius..is a spring in which there is always more behind than flows from it.

6. Applied to a person. **†a.** With qualifying adj.: One who has *great*, *little*, etc. 'genius' (sense 4) or natural ability. Also, one who has a 'genius' (sense 3) or disposition of a specified kind. *Obs.*

[**1647–1697**: see 6 b.] **1731** A. HILL *Adv. Poets* 18 Vulgar Genii, sowr'd by sharp Disdain. **1768** W. GILPIN *Prints* 237 With a little genius nothing sways like a great name. *Ibid.* 240 A trifling genius may be found, who will give ten guineas for Hollar's shells.

b. A person endowed with 'genius' (in sense 5). (Now only *geniuses* in pl.)

The earlier examples, in which the word is accompanied by a laudatory adj., probably belong strictly to 6 a.

1647 W. BROWNE tr. *Gomberville's Polexander* iv. iv. 294 Those great Genius's, on whom most Kings disburthen themselves of the government of their Estates. **1697** DRYDEN *Virg., Past.* Pref. (1721) I. 91 Extraordinary Genius's have a sort of Prerogative, which may dispense them from Laws. **1711** ADDISON *Spect.* No. 160 ¶1 There is no Character more frequently given to a Writer, than that of being a Genius. I have heard many a little Sonneteer called a *fine Genius*. **1755** AMORY *Mem.* (1769) I. 91 Such admirable genii as Burnet and Butler. **1762–71** H. WALPOLE *Vertue's Anecd. Paint.* (1786) II. 90 Under the direction of that genius [Inigo Jones] the King erected the house at Greenwich. **1793** BEDDOES *Math. Evid.* 61 Why are not geniuses for arts or sciences born among savages? **1800** LAMB *Lett.* (1888) I. 141 All poems are good poems to George; all men are fine geniuses. **1806** H. SIDDONS *Maid, Wife, & Widow* I. 173 Isaac was a good-dispositioned, industrious boy, but no genius. **1873** H. ROGERS *Orig. Bible* ix. (1875) 382 Certain transcendent geniuses—the Bacons, the Newtons, the Shakespeares, the Miltons.

7. *phr.* ‖**genius loci** [L. = 'genius of the place'], the presiding deity or spirit (see sense 1); but often used in the sense of 3 d.

1771 SMOLLETT *Humph. Cl., To Dr. Lewis* 8 Aug., The pleasure-grounds are, in my opinion, not so well laid out according to the *genius loci*. **1835** W. IRVING *Crayon Misc., Newstead Abbey* (1863) 286 A white marble bust of the *genius loci*, the noble poet, shone conspicuously from its pedestal. **1878** L. W. M. LOCKHART *Mine is Thine* xix. II. 50 The *genius loci* may be solemn and pensive, but we laugh at him.

8. *attrib.* and *Comb.*, as ***genius school***; ***genius-gifted***, ***genii-haunted*** adjs.; **genius-born** *a.*, born of genius; **†genius-chamber**, **bridal chamber** (see GENIAL *a.*[1]).

1894 MILN *Strolling Players in East* xxi. 194, I represented..the sweet meek maiden who was the *genius-born daughter of Shakespeare's pen. **1513** DOUGLAS *Æneis* iv. i. 36 War nocht also to me is displesant *Genyus chalmer or matrimone to hant. *a* **1851** MRS. SHERWOOD *Life* i. (1854) 17 My *genius-gifted and benevolent father. **1817** MRS. HEMANS *Mod. Greece* Poems (1875) 29 Or Tigris rolls his *genii-haunted wave. **1882** SEELEY *Nat. Relig.* (1883) 166 The point of close resemblance between the *genius school in art, and the anti-legal school in morals.

Hence (*nonce-wds.*) **'geniused** *a.* [-ED[2]], endowed with genius; **'geniusess** [-ESS], a female genius; **'geniuskin** [-KIN], a little genius.

1772 NUGENT tr. *Hist. Friar Gerund* I. 145 She was not a common woman, but a geniusess and an elegant writrix. **1880** S. LANIER *Poems* (1884) 108 Led by the soaring-genius'd Sylvester. **1882** H. C. MERIVALE *Faucit of B.* II. I. xvii. 21 He failed..to catch a single idea out of those words with which my geniuskin of song had inspired me.

genizah (gɛ'ni:zə). Also **geniza**. Pl. **genizoth**. [Heb., lit., a hiding, hiding-place, f. *gānaz* to set aside, hide.] A store-room or repository for damaged, discarded, or heretical books and papers and sacred relics, attached to many synagogues; also, the contents of a genizah.

1897 *Times* 7 Aug. 11/5 The honour of discovering the Genizah belongs to the 'nameless' dealers in antiquities of Cairo. **1903** *Jew. Encycl.* V. 612/1 The term 'genizah' is now applied almost exclusively to the hoard at the old synagogue of Fostat near Cairo. **1926** *Glasgow Herald* 24 Feb. 8 All the old prayer books or torn Bibles are reverently carried to the synagogues, where they are placed in what is called a Genizah... In these ancient Genizahs have been found some priceless old MSS. **1968** *Economist* 10 Aug. 36/1 Devout Jews in the Middle Ages believed that pieces of paper which bore the name of God should not be burned but be put aside in a special room or *geniza*.

gennel, ginnel ('dʒɛnəl, 'dʒɪnəl; elsewhere 'gɪnəl). *dial.* Also 7 **genn-, ginn-, gynnell**, 9 **jennel**. [Of obscure origin: sense 1 suggests that it may be a corruption of *chenelle* CHANNEL.]

†1. = CHANNEL 3 a. *Obs.*

1613 *Manch. Ct. Leet Rec.* (1885) II. 287 Roberte Charnocke..hath newlie erected a privie, the ffilthe whereof ffalleth into a certen Gynnell or gutt[r]. **1647** *Ibid.* (1887) IV. 11 M[r] John Marler shall cause the said Ginnell soe to bee clensed as it may not bee for the future preiudiciall to others.

2. *dial.* A long narrow passage between houses, either roofed or unroofed.

1669 *Manch. Ct. Leet Rec.* (1887) V. 98 W[m] Jackson hath made a Doore into A Ginnell belongeinge to Edm[o] Heywood. *a* **1804** J. MATHER *Songs* (1862) 33 in *Sheffield Gloss.* s.v., When Sancho was a raw-boned whelp And lived in yonder jennel. **1855** WAUGH *Lanc. Life* (1857) 111 Through th' ginnel, an' up th' steps.

gennemic (dʒɪ'nɛmɪk), *a.* [f. Gr. γέννημα product + -IC.] In phonetics, of or pertaining to speech sounds after they have been uttered. So **ge'nnemically** *adv.*

[**1921** G. PANCONCELLI-CALZIA *Experimentelle Phonetik* 7 Die experimentelle Phonetik behandelt ihren Stoff zuerst in bezug auf die erzeugende Tätigkeit, d.h. genetisch (ἡ γένεσις), und dann in bezug auf das durch diese Tätigkeit entstandene Erzeugnis, d.h. gennemisch (τὸ γέννημα).] **1949** R-M. S. HEFFNER *Gen. Phonetics* i. 3 The phonetician, in his effort to delimit and to describe the several distinct constituent speech sounds, can examine the movements of the speech organs which produce the sounds (genetic investigation), or he may examine the sounds as acoustic phenomena after they have been produced (gennemic investigation). **1953** L. F. BROSNAHAN *Some O.E. Sound Changes* 22 A vowel sound, considered gennemically, consists of a series of 'distinctive frequency regions'. **1967** *Word* XXIII. 254 These terms have been divided into three groups..(*a*) the first column refers to genetic ('articulatory'), (*b*) the second to gennemic (acoustic) and (*c*) the third to energemic (auditory) phonetics.

genner, Sc. and dial. form of GENDER *v.*

gennet, obs. form of JENNET; var. GENET[1].

gennete (gɛ'ni:t). *Gr. Antiq.* [ad. Gr. γεννῆται *pl.*, f. γέννα family.] (See quots.)

1838 THIRLWALL *Greece* II. 12 The *genos*, or house, was again made up of thirty *gennetes*, or heads of families. **1847** GROTE *Greece* II. x. III. 85 The gennetes or members of the same gens lived in the same canton.

genny (pepper): see GUINEA-.

Genoa ('dʒɛnəʊə). See GEANE. The name of a city of Italy. Used *attrib.* in names of articles connected with Genoa, as ***Genoa lettuce***, ***-velvet***. **Genoa cake**, a rich currant cake with almonds on the top; **Genoa jib**, a large jib used on racing yachts; **Genoa treacle** (see TREACLE); **†paste of Genoa**, a baked sweetmeat made of quinces, spices, and sugar. Also *absol.* = *Genoa jib*, *-velvet*.

1615 MARKHAM *Eng. Housew.* II. ii. (1668) 101 To make paste of Genoa. **1669** EVELYN *Kal. Hort.* (ed. 3) 103 You may yet sow Genoa Lettuce, which will last all the Winter. **1766** W. GORDON *Gen. Counting-ho.* 427, 2 pieces of black Genoa. **1839** URE *Dict. Arts* 1234 The figure represents a piece of velvet..of that kind which, being woven upon a tweeled ground, is known by the name of Genoa velvet. **1932** *Yachting* Aug. 66/2 Genoa jibs, as cut at present, are a doubtful blessing in ocean racing. *Ibid.* 74/2 Genoas and jib topsails were of very little use... One boat, *Vamare*, split her Genoa at the start. **1933** *Rudder* Apr. 51/1 You will find your Snipe class boat greatly improved in both speed and stability if you equip her with the new Genoa jib. **1961** P. MOYES *Sunken Sailor* iv. 50, I want a proper complement of sails. Storm jib, beating jib, a Genoa for reaching and a spinnaker.

†'Genoan, *a.* and *sb.* [see -AN.] = GENOESE.

1608 DAY *Law Trickes* v. (1881) 80 Hee's a Genoan marchant that with much suite ransom'd mee from the Turke. **1670** R. COKE *Disc. Trade* 62 The Genoans are forced to turn Usurers, upon what they had got before.

genoblast ('dʒɛnəʊblɑ:st, -æ-). [f. Gr. γένο-ς offspring + -BLAST.] The bisexual nucleus of the impregnated ovum. Hence **geno'blastic** *a.*, of or pertaining to a genoblast.

1877 H. D. MINOT in *Proc. Bost. Soc. Nat. Hist.* XIX. 170 The sexual generation may be called *genoblasts*. **1880** *Nature* XXI. 458 The history of the genoblasts and the theory of sex. **1886** A. HYATT in *Amer. Jrnl. Sci.* Ser. III. XXXI. 336 This statement includes all the basal facts of the genoblastic theory.

genocidal (dʒɛnə'saɪdəl, 'dʒɛn-), *a.* [f. next + -AL[1].] Of, pertaining to, or involving genocide.

1948 *Sat. Rev. Lit.* 3 Jan. 8 Belligerents would probably be producing atomic bombs—unless they found other genocidal weapons. **1951** *Scottish Jrnl. Theol.* IV. 419 A fundamentally dishonest casuistry to justify genocidal warfare. **1958** *Observer* 20 July 21/3 Scientists far more deeply involved in these genocidal problems. **1968** *Sunday Tel.* 20 Oct. 8/4 In Zanzibar this has involved a total and genocidal revolution.

genocide ('dʒɛnəsaɪd). [f. Gr. γένο-ς (see GENUS) + -CIDE 2.] The deliberate and systematic extermination of an ethnic or national group.

1944 R. LEMKIN *Axis Rule in Occupied Europe* ix. 79 By 'genocide' we mean the destruction of a nation or of an ethnic group. **1945** *Sunday Times* 21 Oct. 7 The United Nations' indictment of the 24 Nazi leaders has brought a new word into the language—genocide. It occurs in Count 3, where it is stated that all the defendants 'conducted deliberate and systematic genocide—namely, the extermination of racial and national groups...' **1951** *Amer. Jrnl. Psychiatry* Feb. 595/1 Genocide as defined by the United Nations is the direct physical destruction of another racial or national group. **1962** *Listener* 20 Sept. 452/2 One of the things the seventeenth century never achieved was genocide. **1969** *Peace News* 13 June 4/1 The government are ..conducting cultural genocide by destroying this Scottish (Gaidhlig) community.

Genoese (dʒɛnəʊ'i:z), *a.* and *sb.* Also 6 **genuese**. (See GENOVESE, GENOWAY.) [f. GENO-A + -ESE.]

A. *adj.* Of or pertaining to Genoa.

1741 M. W. MONTAGU *Let.* 15 Feb. (1966) II. 226 A Genoese Abbé, who..is resolved never to return to Genoa. **1756** BURKE *Vind. Nat. Soc.* Wks. I. 43 A Genoese, or a Venetian republick, is a concealed despotism. **1849** *Art Jrnl.* XI. 45/2 One of those light-sailing Genoese boats. **1967** *Times* 22 Mar. 13/7 The last remaining vines of the Coronata valley which used to provide the exact white wine to accompany Genoese fish.

B. *sb.* ***the Genoese*** (pl.): the Genoese people. (†Formerly also pl. *Genoeses.*) *sing.*, a native or inhabitant of Genoa; also, the Genoese dialect.

1553 N. WOTTON *Let.* 27 Oct. in Tytler *Eng. under Edw. VI* (1839) II. 252 It shall be time for the Genoeses to bestir themselves. **1594** BLUNDEVIL *Exerc.* v. v. (ed. 7) 541 This Ile is governed by the Genueses. **1677** *Govt. Venice* 290 No Age but will mention me, I having defeated the Genoeses, reduced Clodia, (or Chiozza) and delivered my Countrey from very great Dangers. **1818** W. MARSDEN tr. *Trav. of Marco Polo* II. lxxvii. 560 There is a diversity of dialect, similar to what is found between the Genoese, the Milanese, the Florentine, and the dialects of other Italian states. **1845** S. AUSTIN *Ranke's Hist. Ref.* II. 321 The Genoese feel that they cannot withstand the imperial crown. **1878** [see EMILIAN *a.* and *sb.*]. **1905** [see TUSCANIZE *v.*]. **1950** E. WHELPTON *By Italian Shores* i. 20 Columbus, a Genoese of Jewish origin, discovered America, though he went there on behalf of the king of Spain.

†Genoesian, *a.* and *sb.* *Obs.* [see -IAN.] = GENOESE.

1624 CAPT. SMITH *Virginia* I. 1 Christopher Cullumbus, a Genoesian. **1670–98** LASSELS *Voy. Italy* I. 64 You see..the armour of the Genoesian Amazons who went to the war in the Holy Land.

genologe, -logy, etc., obs. ff. GENEALOGY.

genome ('dʒi:nəʊm). *Biol.* Formerly also **genom** (-nəm). [a. G. *genom* (H. Winkler *Verbreitung u. Ursache d. Parthenogenesis* (1920) iv. 165), irreg. f. *gen* GENE[1] + *chromosom* CHROMOSOME.] A haploid set of chromosomes; the sum-total of the genes in such a set.

1930 *Cytologia* I. 14 Chromosomes from different sets (or genoms) of *Triticum vulgare* show affinity toward each other. **1930** [see ALLOPOLYPLOIDY]. **1932** *Proc. 6th Int. Congr. Genetics* I. 275 The inviability of deficient genomes in the haploid generation serves to some extent as an alternative distinction between mutation and deficiency. *Ibid.* II. 5 There are two species having genoms resembling *C. neglecta*. **1952** C. P. BLACKER *Eugenics* x. 243 The appearance of such terms as gene-complex and genome (denoting a set of chromosomes as a working unity) testify to the movement towards holism in genetics. **1965** A. M. SRB et al. *Gen. Genetics* (ed. 2) vii. 190 Among organisms with chromosomes, each species has a characteristic set of genes, or genome. In diploids a genome is found in each normal gamete. It consists of a full set of the different kinds of chromosomes. **1970** *Sci. Amer.* Oct. 19/1 The human genome..consists of perhaps as many as 10 million genes.

genomere ('dʒɛnəʊmɪə(r)). *Biol. Obs.* exc. *Hist.* [f. GEN(E[1] + -O + -MERE.] A hypothetical component of a gene.

1928 W. H. EYSTER in *Zeitschr. f. indukt. Abstamm. u. Vererb.* (Suppl.) I. 666 The gene is an organization of more elementary genetic units, the genomeres... The term genomere was suggested by Dr. P. W. Whiting. **1939** C. H. WADDINGTON *Introd. Mod. Genetics* xvi. 373 Eyster suggested that this might be due to the sorting out of sub-units (genomeres) of which the gene was supposed to consist. **1966** E. A. CARLSON *Gene* xxvi. 247 Demerec's enthusiasm for the study of the gene was not discouraged to the point of withdrawal when he was unable to find support for his genomere hypothesis in *Delphinium*.

genonema, genoneme (dʒɛnəˈniːmə, ˈdʒɛnəniːm). *Biol.* [f. GENE[1] + -O + Gr. νῆμα thread.] = CHROMONEMA.

1934 N. KOLTZOFF in *Science* LXXX. 313/1 The size of the chromosomes in the salivary glands is determined through the multiplication of *genonemes*. By this term I designate the axial thread of the chromosome, in which the geneticists locate the linear combination of genes; the cytologists call it generally the 'axoneme' or 'chromonema'. **1937** *Ann. Reg. 1936* 53 Chromosome study of plants tended to confirm the spiral chromonemata theory but giant salivary chromosomes seem to contain ring-shaped chromomeres connected by oblique genonemes. **1965** L. C. DUNN *Short Hist. Genetics* xiii. 137 The logical next step, asking what kind of molecule composed the gene string ('genonema', a new term for chromosome).

genosophis *pl.*: see GYMNOSOPHIST.

a **1400–50** *Alexander* 4022 þe gentill genosophis.

genotype (ˈdʒɛnətaɪp), *sb.*[1] *Biol.* [f. Gr. γένος GENUS + -TYPE.] The type-species of a genus.

1897 C. SCHUCHERT in *Science* 23 Apr. 639/2 Genotype applies to any typical material of the type species of a genus. **1923** *Times Lit. Suppl.* 15 Mar. 171/2 It is..necessary to fix on a single species as the standard of each genus, new or old; it is called the genotype. **1926** F. A. BATHER in S. S. Buckman *Type Ammonites* VI. 6 In establishing a new genus an author should fix on one species as the genotype (or genoholotype). **1953** E. MAYR et al. *Methods Syst. Zool.* xiv. 265 The International Commission (Paris, 1948) recommends that the term *genotype* not be used because of possible confusion with the same word as used in genetics.

genotype (ˈdʒɛnətaɪp), *sb.*[2] *Biol.* [ad. G. *genotypus* (W. Johannsen *Elem. d. exakten Erblichkeitslehre* (1909) ix. 130), f. GENE[1] + -O + -TYPE.] The genetic constitution of an individual, esp. as distinguished from its phenotype; the sum-total of the genes in an individual or group. Hence **genoˈtypic, -ˈtypical** *adjs.*; **genoˈtypically** *adv.*

1910 *Science* XXXII. 588/2 The general program will consist of a symposium on the subject of 'Genotypes or pure lines of Johannsen'. **1911** [see GENE[1]]. **1911** *Amer. Naturalist* XLV. 133 We are able to demonstrate 'genotypical' differences. *Ibid.* 140 'Genotypically' determined abnormalities. **1922** *Hereditas* III. 211 The genotypical response of the plant species to the habitat. **1925** D. F. JONES *Genetics Plant & Anim. Improvement* xv. 503 No one can injure a breed more than by permitting genotypically inferior animals to enter. **1930** R. A. FISHER *Genet. Theory Nat. Selection* 9 The genotypes are probably unequally fitted, at least to a slight extent, to their task of survival and reproduction. *Ibid.* 81 A change in the genotypic constitution of the species. **1964** G. H. HAGGIS et al. *Introd. Molecular Biol.* x. 245 It is necessary to distinguish between the assemblage of outwardly recognizable traits by which an individual is defined, known as its phenotype, and the assemblage of inherited factors which determine these traits, known as its genotype. **1971** *Nature* 2 Apr. 279/2 Skin grafts exchanged between genotypically identical siblings survive significantly longer than grafts made between non-identical siblings.

genotype (ˈdʒɛnətaɪp), *v.* [f. prec. sb.] *trans.* To investigate the genotype of.

1961 *Lancet* 9 Sept. 602/1 When the mother has rhesus antibodies..the husband should be genotyped. **1971** *Nature* 2 Apr. 279/2 Some monkey families could be genotyped and the antigens were found to segregate in a pattern consistent with a single complex system.

genouillere (ʒənujɛr). Also 4 **genyllere**, 9 **genouilliere**. [a. F. *genouillère*, f. OF. *genouil* (F. *genou*) knee:—pop. L. **genuclum*, f. *genu* knee.]

1. A flexible piece of armour for covering the knees, with joints like those of a lobster.

c **1380** *Sir Ferumb.* 5631 þe strok ys ferþer wente..And ful opon ys genyllere. **1850** BOUTELL in *Gentl. Mag.* CXX. II. 44 The knees are guarded by genouillières of peculiar form.

2. *Fortification.* (See quots.)

1802 in C. JAMES *Milit. Dict.* **1851** J. S. MACAULAY *Field Fortif.* 78 That part of the interior slope of the parapet immediately beneath the embrasures is called the genouillère. **1867** SMYTH *Sailor's Word-bk.*, *Genouillere*, that part of a battery which remains above the platform, and under the gun after the opening of the embrasure. Of course a knee-step.

-genous (-dʒɪnəs), *suffix*, [f. -GEN + -OUS] = -GENIC, as (*a*) ALKALIGENOUS, CALCIGENOUS, KALIGENOUS, PATHOGENOUS, PYROGENOUS 2; (*b*) PYROGENOUS 1.

Genovese (ˈdʒɛnəviːz), *a.* and *sb.* Now *rare*. Also 7 **Genoevais**, *pl.* **Genoveses**. [a. It. *Genovese*, f. *Genova* Genoa.] = GENOESE *a.* and *sb.*

1603 NORTH *Plutarch's Lives* (1612) 1176 The Pannonians, the Genoveses, and those of Piemont rebelling. **1638** DAVENANT *Fair Favourite* III. (1673) 97/1 Madam, I beg your goodness would procure The Genouesse may be dismiss'd without A Tax upon his Goods. *c* **1645** HOWELL *Lett.* (1650) II. 89 You have the Romane [dialect]..the Calabresse, the Genoevais, the Piemontez. **1684** *Lond. Gaz.* No. 1993/3 Several Galliots are fitting out..against the Genoueses. **1855** TENNYSON *Daisy* 40 The grave, severe Genovese of old.

†**ˈGenoway**, *sb.* and *a.* *Obs.* Forms: α. 6–7 **genowaie, -way(e**, (6 **genoae**, 7 **genowae, -wey, -wyaie**, 6 **geneway**). β. 5 **jan(e-, jenewey**, 5–6 **januay, -ey**. [Originally sb. pl. *Janeweys*, a. OF. *Genoueis*, ad. It. *Genovese*: see prec. Afterwards the sing. form was produced by omission of the *s*, and the word used *attrib.* as *adj.*]

A. *sb.* A native of Genoa.

c **1400** MAUNDEV. (1839) iv. 23 The Ile of Crete, that the Emperour ȝaf somtyme to Janeweys. **1480** CAXTON *Chron. Eng.* ccxlix. (1482) 319 A grete batail on the see bitwene the Jeneweys and the kyng of Aragon. **1529** RASTELL *Pastyme, Hist. Brit.* (1811) 219 A Januay that had the kepynge of y[e] Castell of Caleys. **1593** MUNDAY *Def. Contraries* 37, I shall see no more the prating Florentine..the vsuring Geneway. **1596** *Edward III*, III. iv. 3 The garrison of Genoaes, my Lorde, That cam from Paris. **1600** SURFLET *Countrie Farme* III. xxvii. 483 The Genowaes doe plant branches [of the fig tree] all the moneth of August. **1642** HOWELL *For. Trav.* (Arb.) 41 When a Jew..meeteth with a Genoway..he puts his fingers in his eyes fearing to be overreached by him.

B. *adj.* Of or pertaining to Genoa.

1603 KNOLLES *Hist. Turks* (1638) 296 Vsing..the Genoway marchants ships. *Ibid.* 344 Three tall Genoway ships..came with a faire winde for Constantinople.

‖**genre** (ʒɑ̃r). [F. *genre* kind: see GENDER.]

1. a. Kind; sort; style.

1816 LADY MORGAN *Flor. Macarthy* (1818) IV. iii. 144 But what is the *genre* of character..which, if in true keeping to life and manners, should not be found to resemble any body? **1840** T. MOORE *Mem.* (1856) VII. 273 Two very remarkable men..but of entirely different genres.

b. *spec.* A particular style or category of works of art; esp. a type of literary work characterized by a particular form, style, or purpose.

1770 C. JENNER *Let.* 5 May in *Private Corr. D. Garrick* (1831) I. 384 With regard to the *genre*, I am of opinion that an English audience will not relish it so well as a more characteristic kind of comedy. **1790** A. YOUNG *Jrnl.* 15 Jan. in *Travels* (1892) I. 301 It is a *genre* little interesting when the works of the great Italian artists are at hand. **1843** THACKERAY *Misc. Ess.* (1885) 23 If..some of our newspapers are..inclined to treat for a story in this *genre*. **1880** S. LANIER *Sci. Eng. Verse* viii. 245 The prodigious wealth of our language in beautiful works of this genre. **1856** GEO. ELIOT *Ess.* (1884) 84 In every *genre* of writing it [*sc.* wit] preserves a man from sinking into the *genre ennuyeux*. **1882** G. SAINTSBURY *Short Hist. Fr. Lit.* 50 A better notion of the *genre* may perhaps be obtained from a short view of the subjects of some of the principal of those Fabliaux whose subjects are capable of description. **1967** *Radio Times* 13 Apr. 10/5 *Laike Moussike*, the new genre which in the last eight years has given a new impetus..to Greek popular music.

2. a. A style of painting in which scenes and subjects of ordinary life are depicted.

1861 C. M. YONGE *Young Step-Mother* xvii. 232 'I used to be very fond of drawing.' '*Genre* is my style.' **1873** OUIDA *Pascarel* I. 66 It [a picture] was a pretty little bit of *genre*. **1885** *Athenæum* 12 Sept. 341/3 It [a picture] is a piece of genre, a capital study of colour. **1897** *Mag. Art* Sept. 246 The realism which induced Quintijn Massijs to paint genre was the development of the spirit of the age.

b. *attrib.*, as ***genre-painting***, etc. Also *transf.*, of music and literature.

1849 WILLMOTT *Jrnl. Summer in Country* 7 June 86 His apartments are crowded with rubbish, but he hangs some little genre piece in the corner. **1849** *Art Jrnl.* XI. 59/3 This picture is certainly one of the masterpieces of the English school of *genre* painting. *Ibid.* 108/1 Dietz, a genre-painter of merit. **1861** *Times* 16 Oct., Those vulgarisms of blue, red, and yellow which many of our own genre painters suppose to be telling colour. **1879** FOTHERGILL *Probation* I. xix. 193 A discriminating taste in the matter of genre paintings. **1885** E. C. STEDMAN *Poets Amer.* iv. 98 Just as we call those genre canvases, whereon are painted idyls of the fireside, the roadside, and the farm, pictures of 'real life.' **1920** G. B. SHAW *How to become Mus. Critic* (1960) 310 It would be so much easier if Cockaigne were *genre* music, with the Westminster chimes, snatches of Yip-i-addy, and a march of the costermongers to Covent Garden. **1931** *Times Lit. Suppl.* 21 May 406/3 The story settles down for a time into the methods of a *genre* novel of Shropshire life. **1934** C. LAMBERT *Music Ho!* iii. 200 They are..satirical genre pieces—over in a flash, but unerringly pinning down some particular aspect of popular music, whether foxtrot, tango or tarantella. **1937** *Burlington Mag.* Sept. 139/1 Frans Hals's genre-pictures. **1959** *Times* 13 Jan. 3/3 All three are genre-portrait groups.

Genro (ˈgɛnrəʊ). *Obs.* exc. *Hist.* [Jap., = principal elders, f. *gen* root + *ro* old.] The 'elder statesmen' of Japan, a former body of retired statesmen who were at times informally consulted by the emperor. Also, a member of this body.

1876 E. M. SATOW tr. *Shôzan Yashi's Kinsé Shiriaku* i. 10 He was generally nick-named 'the swaggering Chief Minister' (Bakko Genrô). **1880** E. J. REED *Japan* I. 364 The second of the governing bodies of the state is the Genro-In (house of seniors), or senate. **1921**, etc. [see *elder statesman* (ELDER *a.* 1 c)].

gens (dʒɛnz). Pl. **gentes** (ˈdʒɛntiːz). [a. L. *gens* (stem *genti-*), f. root **gen-* of *gi-gn-ĕre* to beget, Gr. γίγνεσθαι be born.] **a.** *Roman Antiq.* A clan or sept; a number of families united by the ties of a supposed common origin, a common name, and common religious rites. **b.** Hence employed to translate Gr. γένος of similar meaning, and to designate any similar aggregation of families.

1847 GROTE *Greece* II. x. III. 74 The Phratries and Gentes themselves were real ancient and durable associations among the Athenian people. **1855** LIDDELL *Hist. Rome* I. II. ix. 121 The whole Fabian Gens determined to leave Rome altogether. **1872** BAGEHOT *Physics & Pol.* (1876) 184 The aggregation of families into clans or gentes. **1883** *Sat. Rev.* 10 Mar. 313/1 We hazard a guess that the full name indicative of the *gens* may have been Kishori Chand. **1889** *Nature* 5 Dec. 100 The general history of the various gentes and sub-gentes.

gens d'armerie, gens d'armes, var. ff. GENDARMERY, GENDARMES.

‖**gens de (la) robe** (ʒɑ̃ də la rɔb), *sb. pl.* [Fr., lit. 'men of the (long) robe'.] Lawyers.

1679 H. SAVILE *Let.* 5 June in *Savile Correspondence* (Camden Soc., 1858) 93 All Protestants are turn'd out of all places except just the *gens de robe*. **1850** C. M. YONGE *Kenneth* xxii. 272 His own future..arrayed itself..in sombre colours, as regarding English lawyers, with all a young French soldier's contempt for the *gens de la robe*. **1886** *Athenæum* 10 July 47/2 Henri de Mesmes..was one of not a few *gens de robe* of whom L'Hôpital is the best known. **1967** L. NORTON tr. *Mem. St. Simon* ix. 130 The *gens de la robe* (men of the long robe) were despised because they sold their services to the state for money.

genseg, obs. form of GINSENG.

gent (dʒɛnt), *sb.* [Short for GENTLEMAN.]

a. = GENTLEMAN; now only *vulgar*, exc. as applied derisively to men of the vulgar and pretentious class who are supposed to use the word, and as used in tradesmen's notices.

Early prose examples are doubtful, as they may represent only the graphic abbreviation which was formerly common; 'Gents' may be an editorial misreading for 'Gent.' = *gentlemen*. Early in the nineteenth century the word was colloquial and slightly jocular; about 1840 its use came to be regarded as a mark of low breeding.

1564 in Heath *Grocers' Comp.* (1869) 12 To make a supper to divers gentlemen of Gray's Inne, for the great amitie betweene them and the Middle Temple gents. **1605** Z. JONES tr. *Loyer's Specters 32 margin*, Another Gent of the quality lived of late in Deven..who could not endure the playing on a Bagpipe. **1635** [GLAPTHORNE] *Lady Mother* I. ii. in Bullen *O. Pl.* II. 114 Hees not a gent that cannot parlee. I must invent some new and polite phrases. **1649** EVELYN *Mem.* (1857) III. 56 Noise and tumult occasioned by three or four wild gents in drink. **1783** *Gentl. Mag.* LIII. II. 577 The modern gent. is formed under the sage direction of a French dancer, or a Swiss renegado. **1785** BURNS *Ep. to J. Lapraik* 21 Apr. xi, Do ye envy the city Gent, Behind a kist to lie an' sklent. **1799** MRS. H. WASHINGTON *Let.* in *Athenæum* (1892) 17 Dec. 857/1 His lordship has invited sixteen gents here today. **1810** BENTHAM *Packing* (1821) 207 If the practice of the Courts..be to such a degree a secret to Great Law Officers, can it be wondered that they should be equally so to lay-gents, such as Sheriffs and Members of Parliament? **1815** C. LUCAS in *Monthly Mag.* XXXIX. 296 How little support Mr. Kemble received from these gents, in his right pronunciation of the word aches, must be in the recollection of most of your readers. **1817** BYRON *Ep. fr. Murray to Polidori* 59 My humble tenement admits All persons in the dress of gent., From Mr. Hammond to Dog Dent. **1827** *Sporting Mag.* XX. 51 The poor ladies on Farnham Common had little to thank the gents of the hunt for their gallantry. **1831** BEDDOES *Let.* Jan. in *Poems* p. xciv, The reading populace ought to be much obliged to me for my forbearance; 'tis a pity that other young rhyming gents are not equally economical of their tediousness. **1838** COL. HAWKER *Diary* (1893) II. 141 The gents watched him till I came. **1842** THACKERAY *FitzBoodle's Prof.* i, Gents..[an] affectionate diminutive..at present much in use among commercial persons. **1847** *Illustr. Lond. News* 16 Oct. 250/1 His whole bearing was rather that of the 'gent' than gentleman. **1878** BESANT & RICE *Celia's Arb.* xxxix. (1887) 284 London audiences of shop-boys and flashy gents. **1885** F. ANSTEY *Tinted Venus* 100 I'm not responsible, indeed, gents. **1901** *Daily Chron.* 10 Sept. 9/1 Hair Dresser.—First-class gent's junior wanted. **1921** *Dict. Occup. Terms* (1927) §920 Hairdresser's assistant; gents' or ladies' hand.

b. *pl.* = GENTLEMAN 4 e. *colloq.*

[**1933** R. STRACHEY *Many Happy Returns* I. 41 He let me build the Palace Pier too, and the gents' place on the front.] **1938** G. GREENE *Brighton Rock* I. ii. 28 He's just gone into the gents to have a wash. **1958** B. HAMILTON *Too Much of Water* viii. 75 The Gents on the lower deck..consisted of three water-closets, a urinal, a..shower, and two small rooms containing large baths. **1965** *Crescendo* Oct. 7/1 It was confirmed by conversation overheard in the interval along the aisles or in the Gents. **1968** *Listener* 1 Aug. 141/1 The only place you could talk to Harrer was in the gents, and even there not for long.

†**gent** (dʒɛnt), *a.* *Obs.* Also 4–5 **gente**, 4–5 **jent(e**. [a. OF. *gent*:—popular L. **gentum* for class. Lat. *genitum*, pa. pple. of *gignĕre* to beget.

From meaning simply 'born', as in class. Lat., the word came to mean 'well-born', 'noble', and by a further development, 'noble in conduct', 'graceful in manners or appearance', 'courteous', 'beautiful'. Cf. GENTLE.]

1. Noble, high-born; having the qualities attaching to high birth. Of men, esp. a knight or warrior: Valiant and courteous. (Cf. GENTLE.) In later use: Graceful in manners, well-bred, polite, gentle.

13.. *E.E. Allit. P.* A. 265 Bot Iueler gente if þou schal lose þy Ioy for a gemme þat þe watz lef. *c* **1386** CHAUCER *Sir Thopas* 4, I wol telle verrayment..Al of a knyght was fair and gent. *c* **1410** *Sir Cleges* 247 Sir Cleges, and his son gent, The right waye to Cardiffe went. *c* **1440** *York Myst.* xl. 19 Jesu so gente. *c* **1460** *Towneley Myst.* xxix. 396 *Maria.* peter, andrew, Iohn, and Iamys the gent..And all my brethere dere. **1570** LEVINS *Manip.* 66/14 Gent, gentle, *mitis*. **1585** JAS. I *Ess. Poesie* (Arb.) 31 For as into the wax the seals imprent Is lyke a seale, right so the Poët gent [Du Bartas: *le poëte sçauant*], Doeth graue so viue in vs his passions strange. **1590** SPENSER *F.Q.* II. xi. 17 The prowest and most gent, That ever brandished bright steele on hye! 1600 *Eng. Helicon* (Grosart) 217, I met a Woodman queint and gent. *a* 1643 W. CARTWRIGHT *Ordinary* III. i. (1651) 36 *Pot.* Who is't that cals? *Mo.* A Knight most Gent. 1672 VILLIERS (DK. BUCKHM.) *Rehearsal* IV. i. (Arb.) 103 Is not that now like a well-bred person, I gad? So modest, so gent.

absol. or quasi-*sb.* 13.. *K. Alis.* 3960 In bothe halve, mony gent, Wenten hom to heore tent.

2. Of women and children: Graceful, elegant, pretty. Before Spenser chiefly in poetical phrases, ***gent and small, fair and gent***, etc.

a 1225 *St. Marher.* 131 So gent þu were & hende. *a* 1250 *Owl & Night.* 204 Niȝtingale And oþer wiȝte, gente and smale. 1297 R. GLOUC. (Rolls) 562 þo vond he þere damaiseles gent and vair inoȝ. *a* 1300 *Cursor M.* 13138 His broþer doghter, gent and smal Com þaim be for al for to bale. *c* 1400 *Sowdone Bab.* 1628 Tho spake Roulande..To Floripe, that was bothe gente and fre. *c* 1460 *Emare* 191 Messengeres forth he sent Aftyr the mayde fayre and gent. 1513 DOUGLAS *Æneis* V. x. *heading*, How that Ascanius and zoung childir gent, Assailzeit wthir, in manir of turnament. 1572 *Lament. Lady Scotl.* in *Scot. Poems 16th C.* II. 250 Ane lawyers wyfe, baith trym and gent. 1590 SPENSER *F.Q.* I. ix. 27 He lov'd, as was his lot, a Lady gent. 1600 FAIRFAX *Tasso* II. xvii. 23 She that was noble wise, as faire and gent. 1736 W. THOMPSON *Nativity* x. 7 A joyous fellowship was seen Of ladies gent. 1824 BYRON *Juan* XVI. lxvi, Not nigh the gay saloon of ladies gent.

absol. *c* 1440 *Bone Flor.* 2135 They..thankyd them for that gente. 1737 OZELL *Rabelais* I. liv, The Gent, the Brisk, the Fair.

quasi-*adv.* 1513 DOUGLAS *Æneis* V. x. 22 The childer, arrayit fair and gent, Enterit in the camp all sammyn, schyning brycht.

3. Of the body or limbs: Elegant, shapely, slender. Of things: Tasteful in design, elegant, neat.

c 1300 *Beket* 1193 His lymes also he bihuld: hou gent hi were and freo. 13.. *E.E. Allit. P.* B. 1495 His iueles so gent wyth iaueles wer fouled. *c* 1381 CHAUCER *Parl. Foules* 558 The goos, with hir facounde gent..Shal telle our tale. *c* 1386 — *Miller's T.* 48 As eny wesil hir body gent and smal. *c* 1450 HENRYSON *Mor. Fab.* 17, I beheld your Fethers faire and gent. 1483 CAXTON *G. de la Tour* C iij b, I was woned to haue a faire bodye and gente. 1500–20 DUNBAR *Poems* xlviii. 44 Scho, this quene..enterit in a lusty gairding gent. *a* 1550 in *Dunbar's Poems* (1893) 305 That bird..That wes so fair, with fedderis gent. 1590 GREENE *Mourning garment* (1616) 12 Her middle was both small and gent. *a* 1605 MONTGOMERIE *Misc. P.* xxxv. 62 Hir middel gent and small. 1677 SIR T. HERBERT *Trav.* 65 Such a Monument, The Sun through all the world sees none more gent. 1688 R. HOLME *Armoury* III. 350/1 An High Heel shooe Pinked..is a Shooe of the Gentest fashion.

gental(l, obs. form of GENITAL *sb.*

† **gentee**, *a. Obs.* Also 7 jentee; and see JAUNTY. [ad. F. *gentil* (pronounced ʒɑ̃ti).] **a.** = GENTEEL *a.* 4. **b.** = GENTEEL *a.* 3.

1664 BUTLER *Hud.* II. i. 747 They are..So gentee, Alamode, and handsome. *a* 1680 — *Rem.* (1759) I. 148 Taught the wild Arabs on the Road To act in a more gentee Mode.

genteel (dʒɛn'tiːl), *a.* and *sb.* Forms: 6–8 **gentile**, 8 **gentil**, 7– **genteel**. [A re-adoption, at the end of the 16th c., of F. *gentil*, which had been previously adopted in the 13th c., and had assumed the form GENTLE.

The re-adoption first appears in the form *gentile*, distinguished from GENTILE (= non-Jewish) by retaining the Fr. pronunciation of the *i* and the stress on the last syllable. It is probable that it was originally fashionable to retain the Fr. nasal sound in the first syll.; hence the vulgar pronunciation represented by the spelling 'jonteel', which occurs in comic literature of the early 19th c. The fully anglicized spelling *genteel* came in at the end of the 17th c.; see also GENTEE, which corresponds more nearly to the pronunciation of the Fr. word, in which the *l* is silent. Another attempt to render the Fr. sound is JAUNTY.

A few years before the middle of the 19th c. the word was much ridiculed as being characteristic of those who are possessed with a dread of being taken for 'common people', or who attach exaggerated importance to supposed marks of social superiority. In seriously laudatory use it may now be said to be a vulgarism; in educated language it has always a sarcastic or at least playful colouring.]

A. *adj.*

1. Belonging to or included among the gentry; of a rank above the commonalty. (Cf. GENTLE A. 1.) *Obs.* or *arch.*

1628 PRYNNE *Love-lockes* 1 Vngodly Fashions..Transforme our Light and Giddie Females of the Superior and Gentile ranke. 1642 FULLER *Holy & Prof. St.* II. xviii. 116 Nor is a capacity to be gentile denyed to one Yeoman. 1673 RAY *Journ. Low C., Malta* 308 All the Knights are of noble or gentile extraction. 1691 WOOD *Ath. Oxon.* I. 49 Thomas Wyatt..was born of an ancient and gentile Family. 1862 MERIVALE *Rom. Emp.* (1865) VIII. lxiv. 80 A genteel mob assembled on the day of each promised performance. 1885 J. GILLOW *Bibliogr. Dict. Eng. Cath.* II. 226 *Faunt, Laurence Arthur*..of an ancient and genteel family.

2. Appropriate to persons of quality. Now chiefly with sarcastic implication.

a. Of dress, dwellings, etc.; formerly also of food, meals, hospitality, etc.: Stylish, fashionably elegant or sumptuous.

1599 B. JONSON *Cynthia's Rev.* I. (1601) C iij a, *Amor.* Your Rose too do's most grace-fully in troath. *Asot.* Tis the most gentile and receiu'd Weare now Sir. 1655 FULLER *Ch. Hist.* VI. iv. 326 To accoutre their eldest Sonnes in a gentile military equipage when Knighted by the King. 1659 *Gentl. Calling* (1696) 80 Nature affords not meat delicate enough for their palats; it must be adulterated with the costly mixtures of Art, before it can become Gentile nourishment. 1665 PEPYS *Diary* (1879) III. 135 We had here the genteelest dinner..I have seen many a day. 1678 WOOD *Life* (O.H.S.) II. 425 *note*, A tall man..gentile clothes, and rings and pendants in his eares. 1683 TRYON *Way to Health* 64 And then what Curiosity in Sawces? What fantastick Humors for Dressing? The more extravagant and unnatural, the more genteel..forsooth! 1753 *World* No. 4. 20 Knocking at the door of a genteel house over-against her. 1787 'G. GAMBADO' *Acad. Horsemen* (1809) 31 And observe; a single flapped saddle is the genteelest. 1788 V. KNOX *Winter Even.* III. VIII. xi. 171 The entertainment was sumptuous and genteel. 1790 BEWICK *Quadrup.* (1807) 339 It [the Dalmatian Dog]..is frequently kept in genteel houses, as an elegant attendant on a carriage. 1797 *Monthly Mag.* III. 204 Near the bath are two or three genteel inns. 1814 D. H. O'BRIEN *Captiv. & Escape* 167 He..conducted us to a genteel house, close to a glass manufactory. 1859 GEO. ELIOT *A. Bede* 60 Some coast-town that was once a watering-place, and is now a port, where the genteel streets are silent and grass-grown. 1865 TROLLOPE *Belton Est.* xiv, He was possessed of a genteel villa and ornamental garden.

b. Of employments, education, income: Suited to the station of a gentleman or gentlewoman. Of manners, habits of life, etc.: Characteristic of persons of quality; resembling what prevails in upper-class society.

1602 MARSTON *Antonio's Rev.* IV. i. G 1 b, A spitting Critick, whose mouth Voids nothing but gentile and vnuulgar Rheume of censure. 1635 QUARLES *Embl.* II. ii. (1718) 70 We made art servile, and the trade gentile [*rimes with* guile]. 1673 STILLINGFL. *Serm.* ii. 32 Till..the greatest slavery to sin be accounted but..a gentile compliance with the fashions of the world. 1674 S. VINCENT *Yng. Gallant's Acad.* 87 [The Gallant's] pleasures consist in fine Cloaths, gentile Oaths, as he calls them. 1688 S. PENTON *Guardian's Instr.* 36 Civil Law, was then proposed as a genteel sort of study. 1697 POTTER *Antiq. Greece* I. xxvi. (1715) 151 They, who can afford a gentile Education. 1727 *Philip Quarll* (1816) 34 She intended to have kept him, till he was by years and learning qualified for some genteel trade. 1766 [ANSTEY] *Bath Guide* xiii. 106, I the Muffins preferr'd To all the genteel Conversation I heard. 1788 V. KNOX *Winter Even.* II. VI. xi. 284 You went..to provide a genteel maintenance for our four little ones. 1801 MAR. EDGEWORTH *Gd. French Governess* (1832) 176 She considered her mother as an inferior personage, destitute of genteel accomplishments. 1804 W. TENNANT *Ind. Recreat.* (ed. 2) I. 318 A genteel business, such as jewellery, mercery, or perfumery. 1832 HT. MARTINEAU *Life in Wilds* iv. 46 He led a pretty genteel life as a shopkeeper. 1840 DICKENS *Old C. Shop* xxxi, The pupils cared little for a companion who had..nothing genteel to talk about.

3. Having the habits characteristic of superior station; that ranks or claims to rank above the commonalty on the ground of manners or style of living. †In early use: Polished, well bred (*obs.*). (Now chiefly with sarcastic implication.)

a 1648 LD. HERBERT *Hen. VIII* (1683) 552 Lenox was young, handsome, and gentile. 1657 COKAINE *Obstin. Lady* I. i. Poems, etc. (1658) 302 Houswifery is the superficies of a genteel female, and the Parenthesis of a Lady, which may well be left out. 1681 WOOD *Life* 2 Mar. (O.H.S.) II. 519 A gentile man but a presbyterian. 1710 M. HENRY *Exp. Numb.* xxv. (1725) III. 371/2 Zimri and Cosbi, Sinners of the first Rank, genteel Sinners. 1712 BUDGELL *Spect.* No. 404 ¶3 Valerio had an universal Character, was genteel, had Learning. 1751 CHESTERF. *Lett.* 13 June (1774) II. 168 And though you should be told that you are genteel still aim at being genteeler. 1752 LADY M. W. MONTAGU *Let. to C'tess Bute* 16 Feb., He appeared to me gentile, well bred, well shaped, and sensible. 1776 MRS. HARRIS in *Priv. Lett. Ld. Malmesbury* (1870) I. 342 The Duchess of Manchester says he [Tessier] is not a person fit to be admitted into genteel society. 1815 JANE AUSTEN *Emma* II. vii. 175 They were of low origin, in trade, and only moderately genteel. 1833 L. RITCHIE *Wand. by Loire* 63 A man..might be rich without being genteel, and poor without being vulgar. 1837 J. D. LANG *New S. Wales* II. 217 Despicable avarice..and the practice of downright injustice are by no means..banished even yet from the genteelest circles in New South Wales. 1841 THACKERAY *Sk., Lady in Opera-Box*, I was not genteel enough for her circle. 1842 MISS COSTELLO *Pilgr. Auvergne* I. 295 The actual existence is evident of a genteel middle class. 1885 MISS BRADDON *Wyllard's Weird* I. iii. 101 Very narrow are the straits of genteel poverty.

ellipt. 1864 J. H. FRISWELL *Gentle Life* 6 The genteel know only the genteel. 1867 DICKENS *Lett.* (1880) II. 270 A very small opinion of what the great genteel have done for us.

abst. (quasi-*sb.*) 1726 SHELVOCKE *Voy. round World* 392 His behaviour had something of the genteel in it. 1888 STEVENSON *Some Gentlem. in Fict.* in *Scribner's Mag.* III. 766 Mr. Adams, delightful as he is, has no pretension to 'the genteel'.

†b. Of behaviour: Courteous, polite, obliging.

1659 B. HARRIS *Parival's Iron Age* 53 French..They are of so gentile an humour, that they make themselves admired by strangers. 1688 CROWNE *Darius* Prol., Nay, do not damn him much, if he writes ill; For then he writes like you—that is Gentile. 1702 W. J. *Bruyn's Voy. Levant* vi. 18 The Merchant gave him as genteel a Denial as he could. 1711 STEELE *Spect.* No. 75 ¶4 The more Virtuous the Man is, the nearer he will naturally be to the Character of Genteel and Agreeable. 1773 JOHNSON in *Boswell* (1831) III. 105 The hospitable and genteel manner in which you were pleased to treat me. 1814 SCOTT *Let. to J. B. S. Morritt* 7 Jan. in *Lockhart*, The magistrates..have done the genteel thing (as Winifred Jenkins says)..and presented me with the freedom of the city.

†c. Liberal in money matters. Of a gift, etc.: Handsome. *Obs.*

1628 DIGBY *Voy. Medit.* 34 The captaine and marchant..sent me a gentile present. 1742 RICHARDSON *Pamela* III. 270 Proposes that Mr. Williams's present Living be supply'd by a Curate; to whom no doubt Mr. Williams will be very genteel. 1774 GOLDSM. *Grecian Hist.* II. 130 Philip..settled a very genteel stipend upon him [Aristotle]. 1790 BEATSON *Nav. & Mil. Mem.* I. 152 Giving..a genteel reward to the sailors for their bravery.

4. Of persons: Gentlemanly or ladylike in appearance; well-dressed. (Now *vulgar*, exc. in depreciatory sense: cf. *shabby-genteel*.)

1629 *Leather* 13 Some Citizens (out of a scorne not to be Gentile) goe euerie day Booted. 1696 LUTTRELL *Brief Rel.* (1857) IV. 125 A genteel person was seized at the exchequer picking a man's pocket. 1703 *Lond. Gaz.* No. 3917/4 John Hunt, smooth Fac'd, a genteel Man, aged about 25. *a* 1732 GAY *Rehearsal at Gotham* I. Wks. (1772) 343 The Girl is very Genteel tonight. 1773 GOLDSM. *Stoops to Conq.* II. Wks. (Globe) 657/2 Did not I work that waistcoat, to make you genteel?

quasi-*adv.* 1771 T. HULL *Sir W. Harrington* (1797) III. 202 David, being dressed tolerably genteel, ventured into the coffee-room.

5. Elegant or graceful in shape or appearance. (Now only with playful or sarcastic mixture of sense 2.)

1688 R. HOLME *Armoury* III. 349/2 In this square is the Figure of the genteel Punch. 1710 *Lond. Gaz.* No. 4635/4 A genteel round-barrel'd Gelding. 1719 LONDON & WISE *Compl. Gard.* 187 A very pretty good Expedient, but never looks Gentile nor Handsom. 1730 A. GORDON *Maffei's Amphith.* 283 The genteel manner by which the Steps were disposed. 1753 HOGARTH *Anal. Beauty* xi. 139 The longest of these [lines] is not quite sufficiently so, in proportion to the other, for a genteel man. 1754 HUME *Hist. Eng.* (1761) I. xix. 458 His countenance beautiful; his limbs genteel and slender. 1789 W. BUCHAN *Dom. Med.* (1790) 91 How a small foot came to be reckoned genteel, I will not pretend to say. 1794 MARTYN *Rousseau's Bot.* xxi. 303 The third is a taller, genteeler, later-flowering plant. 1818 M. G. LEWIS *Jrnl. W. Ind.* (1834) 157 A young girl, who exactly answered George Colman's description of Yarico, 'quite brown, but extremely genteel, like a Wedgewood teapot'. 1852 MRS. STOWE *Uncle Tom's C.* xi, A little walnut-bark has made my yellow skin a genteel brown.

†b. Of immaterial things: Graceful, refined, delicate. *Obs.*

1678 CUDWORTH *Intell. Syst.* I. iii. §30 That other Corporeal Theism seems to be of the two rather more generous and gentile, which supposes the whole world to be one Animal, and God to be a certain..etherial but intellectual Matter. 1679 SHADWELL *True Widow* II. Wks. 1720 III. 144 They like my songs too; they say they're so easie, so gentile, and well bred. 1692 DRYDEN *St. Evremont's Ess.* 193 Happy then is that Fancy, Noble and Genteel, which makes it self accepted by our greatest Enemies. 1711 SHAFTESB. *Charac.* Misc. III. i. (1737) III. 142 The natural and simple manner which conceals and covers Art, is the most truly artful, and of the genteelest, truest and best-study'd Taste. 1715 J. RICHARDSON *Theory Paint.* 196 Annibale Carracci was rather Great, than Gentile; tho' he was That too; and Guido's Character is Grace. 1728 T. SHERIDAN tr. *Persius' Sat.* v. (1739) 67 You are well skilled in shaming People out of their Vices, by your genteel Manner of Raillery. 1742 GRAY *Let. to West* 8 May, Wks. 1816 II. 136, I rejoice to see you putting up your prayers to the May: She cannot choose but come at such a call. It [West's *Ode to May*] is as light and genteel as herself.

6. *Comb.*, as ***genteel-like***, †***-looked***, ***-looking***, ***-shaped*** adjs.

1708 *Lond. Gaz.* No. 4327/16 Deserted..William Wakling, a very genteel look'd Man. 1741 RICHARDSON *Pamela* (1824) I. 219 Miss Goodwin..is..the genteelest-shaped child. 1749 FIELDING *Tom Jones* XII. xiv, A genteel-looking man, but upon a very shabby horse, rode up to Jones. 1765 FOOTE *Commissary* II. Wks. 1799 II. 24, I accost him, in a courteous, genteel-like manner.

B. *sb.* A genteel person; a gentleman. *Obs.* exc. in occasional use. (Cf. GENTLE B.)

In ed. 1692 of B. Jonson's *Ev. Man out of Hum.* Prol., and in ed. 1711 of Cowley's *Love's Riddle* v, *Genteels* (vocatively) is substituted for the original reading *Gentles*.

1675 COTTON *Burlesque upon Burlesque* Prol. 1 Gentiles, Behold a Rural Muse..Presents you old, but new translated News. 1719 D'URFEY *Pills* (1872) V. 349 Ye lofties, Genteels, who above us all sit. 1829 *Mechanics' Mag.* XII. 68 A party..denominated 'The Genteels' by the working classes because of their dislike to the term mechanic. 1892 *Athenæum* 21 May 660/3 He [Manning] was known for some years as the 'Apostle of the Genteels', so little had he then developed his all-absorbing interest in the masses.

Hence **gen'teelify** *v. nonce-wd., intr.*, to become genteel.

1834 *Tait's Mag.* I. 609 Mrs. Mark Luke had genteelified and absolutely refined more in one season, than in some half-a-dozen former years of stinted appliances.

genteelish (dʒɛn'tiːlɪʃ), *a.* [f. GENTEEL *a.* + -ISH.] Somewhat genteel.

1750 J. TUCKER *Ess. Trade* (ed. 2) 130 If a young Woman has a genteelish Education, and a small Fortune, she stands upon the Brink of Destruction. 1814 *Sporting Mag.* XLIV. 48 In person genteelish—behaviour quite easy. 1825 LOCKHART in Scott *Fam. Lett.* (1894) II. 341 A large assemblage of vulgar women and men,—little Quillinan, 'the heavy dragoon', the only genteelish figure.

genteelism (dʒɛn'tiːlɪz(ə)m). [f. GENTEEL *a.* + -ISM.] Genteel behaviour, attitudes or characteristics; *spec.* (see quot. 1926); also, a genteel word or expression; a genteel euphemism.

1908 *Westm. Gaz.* 24 Jan. 3/1 They are the marks of 'genteelism', as distinguished from gentility. 1926 FOWLER *Mod. Eng. Usage* 212/2 By *genteelism* is here to be understood the substituting, for the ordinary natural word that first suggests itself to the mind, of a synonym that is thought to be less soiled by the lips of the common herd, less familiar, less plebeian, less vulgar, less improper. *Ibid.*, The small selection of genteelisms offered below. 1934 *S.P.E. Tract* XLIII. 156 A collection of chocolates and sweets to which even the worst enemy of genteelisms could scarcely deny the epithet *recherchée*. 1949 *Archit. Rev.* CV. 248 To dismiss entirely the whole field of publicity when landscaping new towns would seem to be an act of genteelism reminiscent of the days when the designer ignored everything that didn't fall into line with his own private taste. **1957** E. GOWERS *H.W. Fowler* 9 When King Richard..asks for a mirror and Bolingbroke tells someone to go and fetch a looking-glass, the usurper was inflicting..the final humiliation of being corrected for using a genteelism. **1960** *Spectator* 19 Aug. 275 There is no end to the flood of genteelism that is eroding the language.

gen'teelize, *v. rare.* See also GENTILIZE. [f. GENTEEL *a.* + -IZE.] *trans.* To render genteel.

1767 STERNE *Tr. Shandy* IX. xiii, A man cannot dress, but his ideas get cloth'd at the same time: and if he dresses like a gentleman, every one of them stands presented to his imagination, genteelized along with him. **1865** *Athenæum* No. 1950. 351/2 It is proposed to 'genteelize'—as a friend calls it—one of the largest open spaces.

genteelly (dʒɛn'tiːllɪ), *adv.* [f. GENTEEL *a.* + -LY[2].] In a genteel manner. (Cf. senses of the adj.)

1637 HEYWOOD *Royal King* III. E iij b, Such onely gentile are that can maintaine gentily. **1665** GLANVILL *Scepsis Sci.* Addr. 14 Those that would be gentilely learned..need not purchase it, at the dear rate of being Atheists. **1668** PEPYS *Diary* (1877) V. 149 After dinner, my Lord Brereton very gentilely went to the organ. **1708** PRIOR *Turtle & Sparrow* 218 Well born she was, genteelly bred. *c*1710 CELIA FIENNES *Diary* (1888) 76 He has a very good house and genteely fitted good Hall and parlour. **1732** LAW *Serious C.* ix. (ed. 2) 121 A saint genteely dress'd is as great nonsense as an Apostle in an embroider'd suit. **1739** LADY M. W. MONTAGU *Let. to Wortley Montagu* 14 Oct., I can live here very genteelly on my allowance. **1753** HOGARTH *Anal. Beauty* x. 105 The whole horn acquires a beauty by its being thus genteelly bent two different ways. **1779** FORREST *Voy. N. Guinea* 217 The Rajah..entertained us very genteelly at supper. **1810** *Sporting Mag.* XXXVI. 195 The day was genteelly closed by a bull-baiting. **1817** BYRON *Beppo* xxiii, Time..treated her genteelly. **1841** THACKERAY *2nd Funeral Napoleon* iii, Bred up genteelly at Eton. **1876** MISS BRADDON *J. Haggard's Dau.* II. 8 If Cynthia had been less handy, things could not have gone off so genteelly.

genteelness (dʒɛn'tiːlnɪs). [f. GENTEEL *a.* + -NESS.] The state, quality, or fact of being genteel; an instance of the same.

1652 SIR A. COCKAINE tr. *Calprenède's Cassandra* 104 He ..gave many eminent testimonies of his gentilenesse and bravery. **1670** G. H. *Hist. Cardinals* I. III. 82 From their Civility and Gentileness they express to Strangers, they draw no small profit in Almes. **1718** *Freethinker* No. 24 ¶6 Let us be cautious how we innovate too much in Genteelnesses. **1752** MRS. DELANY *Let. to Mrs. Dewes* in *Life & Corr.* 92, I should rather see a little awkward bashfulness, than a daring and forward genteelness. **1752** HUME *Ess. & Treat.* (1777) II. 329 He must be unhappy, indeed..who has never perceived the charms of a..decent genteelness of address and manner. **1757** H. WALPOLE *Lett. H. Mann* cccvii. (1834) III. 223 Not but Twickenham has a romantic genteelness that would figure in a more luxurious climate.

concr. **1855** MOTLEY *Dutch Rep.* v. iv. 739 A..banquet of confectionary..and all kinds of genteelnesses in sugar.

genteleri, var. GENTLERY. *Obs.*

genthite ('gɛnθaɪt). *Min.* [f. *Genth*, the name of an American geologist + -ITE. Named by Dana in 1867.] A hydrous silicate of nickel and magnesium, found in applegreen incrustations and amorphous masses.

1867 *Amer. Jrnl. Sci.* Ser. II. XLIV. 256 Genthite. **1868** DANA *Min.* (ed. 5) 471 Genthite, Nickel-Gymnite.

gentian ('dʒɛnʃən). Forms: 4 jencian, 5 gencyan(e, 5–6 gencian, 6 gentiane, 6– gentian. [ad. L. *gentiāna*, so called (according to Pliny) after Gentius, king of Illyria.]

1. a. Any plant belonging to the genus *Gentiana* (cf. FELWORT); esp. *G. lutea*, the officinal gentian which yields the gentian-root of the pharmacopœia. ***fringed gentian*** = *G. crinita*.

*c*1000 [see FELWORT]. **1382** [see *gentian-tree* in 2]. *c*1400 *Lanfranc's Cirurg.* 61 Take þe pouder of crabbis brent vj parties, gencian iij parties..make poudre. **1516** *Life St. Bridget* in *Myrr. our Ladye* p. lii, Gencian whiche is a moch bytter erbe she helde contynually in hir mouth. **1597** GERARDE *Herbal* II. cv. (1633) 432 There be divers sorts of Gentians or Felwoorts. **1671** SALMON *Syn. Med.* III. xxii. 402 *Gentian*, the root resists poyson and Plague. **1794** MARTYN *Rousseau's Bot.* xvii. 225 The principal of the genus is the Great Yellow Gentian, which has a single stalk, three feet high. **1801** SOUTHEY *Thalaba* IV. xxiv, The herbs so fair to eye Were Senna, and the Gentian's blossom blue. **1830** LINDLEY *Nat. Syst. Bot.* 216 The intense bitterness of the Gentian is a characteristic of the whole order. **1844** LOWELL *Leg. Brittany* I. xvi, More sad than cheery, making in good sooth, Like the fringed gentian, a late autumn spring. **1882** *Garden* 3 June 385/3 The early flowering Gentians..have done badly as regards bloom.

b. Applied to plants of other orders and genera.

1879 BRITTEN & HOLLAND *Plant-n.*, *Gentian*..2. *Erythræa Centaurium*, L.—Suss.; Scotl., on the shores of the Moray Firth, where an infusion is drunk as a tonic. **1889** *Century Dict.* s.v., False gentian, *Pleurogyne Carinthiaca*, a gentian-aceous plant of Europe, northern Asia, and western North America. Horse-gentian, *Triosteum perfoliatum*, a capri-foliaceous plant of North America. Spurred gentian, *Halenia deflexa*, a gentianaceous plant of North America.

c. A bitter liquor made from the root of gentian. Also ***gentiane, gentian brandy, gentian spirit.***

1857 L. PAPPE *Floræ Capensis* p. vi, Different kinds of Sebæa..could..serve as a good substitute for Gentian. **1892** *Cornhill Mag.* XVIII. 615 The gentian spirit may be said to be the very elixir of life to the mountain folk. *Ibid.* 616 The smell of gentian brandy is not pleasant, especially if new, but with age the spirit greatly improves, mellows, and loses its disagreeable aroma. **1902** J. T. LAW *Grocer's Man.* 408/2 *Gentian Spirit*, a bitter liquor made from gentian root. **1966** P. V. PRICE *France* 65 A pre-prandial digestive of a herby type, such as gentian or *anisette*. **1967** I. MARDER *Paris Bit* ix. 151 'I haven't been able to think of a blue drink. Can you?' 'How about *gentiane?*'

2. a. *attrib.*, as in ***gentian-blue, -flower, -root, -tree, -violet, -water, -wine***; **gentian-bitter**, the tonic principle extracted from gentian root; **gentian-worts**, Lindley's name for the N.O. *Gentianaceæ*.

1882 OGILVIE, *Gentian-bitter. **1865** BARING-GOULD *Werewolves* vii. 85 Sand-hills..patched with *gentian-blue. **1856** BRYANT *Poems, November* 7 The blue *gentian flower, that, in the breeze, Nods lonely. **1873** OUIDA *Pascarel* I. 81 Their hands were full of blue gentian flowers. **1530** PALSGR. 224/2 *Gencyan rote, *gentian*. **1811** A. T. THOMSON *Lond. Disp.* (1818) 598 Take of gentian root, bruised, two drachms. **1382** WYCLIF *Jer.* xvii. 6 It shal ben as *iencian trees [L. *myricæ*] in desert. **1897** ALLBUTT *Syst. Med.* II. 3 It takes up the stain..of *gentian violet. **1727–51** CHAMBERS *Cycl.* s.v. *Water*, *Gentian-water. Take four pounds of gentian roots..mince them [etc.]. *a*1700 B. E. *Dict. Cant. Crew*, *Gentian-wine, Drank for a Whet before Dinner. **1845** LINDLEY *Sch. Bot.* 91 Gentianaceæ—*Gentianworts.

b. quasi-*adj.* Having the blue colour of the gentian; gentian-blue.

1908 *Westm. Gaz.* 7 Dec. 2/3 A gentian sky untinged By any haze its noontide blue outstretches. **1967** S. PAKENHAM *Sixty Miles from England* xv. 204 Lady Blanche, in her white mantilla and pussy-cat bow of gentian silk.

Hence **gentia'naceous** *a.* [-ACEOUS], of or belonging to the N.O. *Gentianaceæ*; **gentia'nesque** *a.* [-ESQUE], of or pertaining to the gentians or *Gentianaceæ*; **gen'tianic** *a. Chem.*, in ***gentianic acid*** (see quot.); **'gentianin** (formerly also *-ine*) = *gentianic acid*.

1854 MAYNE *Expos. Lex.*, *Gentianaceus*, gentianaceous. (And in recent Dicts.) *Ibid.*, *Gentianin*. **1864** WATTS *Dict. Chem.*, *Gentianic Acid, Gentianin*, an organic acid existing in the root of gentian..extracted by treating the powdered root with water [etc.]. **1896** *Daily News* 23 July 8/6 Its flower still betrays undoubted marks of its gentianesque descent.

gentianal ('dʒɛnʃənəl), *a.* (*sb.*) [f. GENTIAN + -AL[1].] Of or pertaining to the gentians. ***gentianal alliance***: Lindley's name for a group of plants including the *Gentianaceæ* and other Orders. Also *sb.*, a member of this alliance.

1846 LINDLEY *Veg. Kingd.* 594 *Gentianales*—The Gentianal Alliance..With Cortusals Gentianals come in contact through Ebenads. *Ibid.* 595 Gentianal Exogens.

gentianella (ˌdʒɛnʃə'nɛlə). [mod.L., dim. of L. *gentiāna*.] A name for several species of gentian, esp. *Gentiana acaulis*, bearing flowers of an intense blue colour.

In botanical Latin used by some authorities as the name of one of the two sub-genera into which they divide the genus *Gentiana* (the other sub-genus being *Eugentiana*).

1658 SIR T. BROWNE *Gard. Cyrus* iii. 52 Flowers of one leaf have often five divisions answered by a like number of calicular leaves; as *Gentianella* [etc.]. **1794** MARTYN *Rousseau's Bot.* xvii. 226 Gentianella..is singular for having its fine bell shaped azure flowers larger than the whole plant besides. **1803** *J. Abercrombie's Ev. Man his Own Gard.* 233 Thrift, London pride, gentianella, with most other sorts of the fibrous-rooted plants, may be..removed. **1848** C. A. JOHNS *Week at Lizard* 311 *Exacum filiforme*, Least Gentianella, is a minute plant. *a*1861 MRS. BROWNING *Hector in Gard.* ix, Eyes of gentianella's azure.

attrib. **1646** SIR T. BROWNE *Pseud. Ep.* VI. xii. 338 A deep and Gentianella blew.

gentianose ('dʒɛnʃ(ɪ)ənəʊs, -əʊz). *Chem.* [a. G. *gentianose* (A. Meyer 1882, in *Zeitschr. f. physiol. Chem.* VI. 135), f. GENTIAN + -OSE[2].] A trisaccharide found in the roots of various species of gentian.

1883 *Jrnl. Chem. Soc.* XLIV. 811 The other properties of gentianose would appear to place it near cane-sugar. **1948** KIRK & OTHMER *Encycl. Chem. Technol.* II. 879 Gentianose may be hydrolyzed by invertase or by dilute acids to D-fructose and gentiobiose.

gentil, obs. form of GENTEEL, GENTLE.

gentile ('dʒɛntaɪl, -tɪl), *a.* and *sb.* Forms: 4–7 gentil(l, 5–6 gentyle, (6 gentle), 5– gentile. Also 4 jentile. [a. or ad. F. *gentil*, ad. L. *gentīlis*, f. *gent-*, *gens* nation, GENS.]

A. *adj.* **I.** In applications derived from the Vulgate ('dʒɛntaɪl). Now usually written with capital initial.

1. Of or pertaining to any or all of the nations other than the Jewish. †Also *absol.* used as a collective sb. = the Gentiles.

*c*1400 *Apol. Loll.* 6 Constreyning þe gentil to be com Jewes in obseruaunce. **1686** J. SCOTT *Chr. Life* (1747) III. 51 A current Doctrine among the ancient Writers, both Gentile and Jewish. **1774** J. BRYANT *Mythol.* II. 118 There had been a true notion of the Deity transmitted by Zoroaster ..when the rest of the gentile world was in darkness. **1782** PRIESTLEY *Corrupt. Chr.* I. I. 6 The richer and more learned gentile christians. **1888** AMY LEVY *Reuben Sachs* xi. 156 A goodly contingent of Gentile dancing men..and a smaller band of Gentile ladies.

b. Similarly, as used by the Mormons: Of or pertaining to any outside the Mormon community.

1861 R. F. BURTON *City Saints* iv. 271 The Endowment House..and all appertaining to it is carefully concealed from Gentile eyes and ears. *Ibid.* 276 It rests on the best and fairest Gentile evidence.

†2. Heathen, pagan. *Obs.*

1494 FABYAN *Chron.* v. lxxxii. 60 Thyse straungers..were of yᵉ Gentyle or Pagan lawe. **1535** STEWART *Cron. Scot.* II. 137 Thai war withoutin men also, Of gentill faith, and also Cristis fo. **1542** UDALL in *Lett. Lit. Men* (Camden) 5 Scipio Africanus the elder (to whom the gentile histories dooe attribute this honourable testimonie). **1613** PURCHAS *Pilgrimage* (1614) 477 Twentie Gentile Kings are numbred in his Court. **1647** A. ROSS *Mystag. Poet.* xv. (1675) 377, I wonder not why the Gentile gods were so cruel and savage. **1695** WOODWARD *Nat. Hist. Earth* III. i. (1723) 132 The ancient Gentil Writers. **1789** BRAND *Hist. Newcastle* II. 51 *note*, The basilicæ of gentile Rome..were converted into churches on their conversion to Christianity.

II. Senses derived from cl. L. (Usually 'dʒɛntɪl.)

3. Pertaining to a nation or tribe. Now *rare*.

1513 DOUGLAS *Æneis* VII. iv. 56 That was the sett eik by thair gentill law Deput for hallowit feyst and mangeory. **1645** PAGITT *Heresiogr.* (1661) 196 Such a one as the Iewes call a National or Gentile Saint. **1677** W. HARRIS tr. *Lemery's Course Chym.* (1686) Ep. Ded., Who have spent so many years..in France and who is..a Great master of that Gentile Language. **1858** GLADSTONE *Homer* I. 419 Twice in the Catalogue Homer has occasion to use the Achæan name locally, and in its original or, so to speak, gentile sense.

b. *Gram.* Of a word: Indicating the country, locality, or nation to which anything belongs.

1818 TODD, *Gentile*, belonging to a nation; as British, Irish, German, &c., are gentile adjectives. **1854** R. G. LATHAM *Native Races Russian Emp.* 223 *Lainen* is the regular Finlandish termination for gentile nouns.

4. Of or pertaining to a gens or to gentes.

1846 GROTE *Greece* (1854) I. 465 There were in every gens or family special gentile deities. **1865** MERIVALE *Rom. Emp.* VIII. lxvii. 260 He combined in his own person the gentile names of several ancestors. **1876** FREEMAN *Norm. Conq.* V. xxiv. 462 In England where the gentile system died out so much sooner. **1881** MISS BUCKLAND in *Knowledge* No. 8. 158 These four women councillors select a chief of the gens from their brothers and sons, and this chief is the head of the gentile council.

B. *sb.* **I.** From A. I. ('dʒɛntaɪl). (Usually with capital G.)

1. One of any nation other than the Jewish.

*c*1380 WYCLIF *Sel. Wks.* III. 345 He [Petre] wolde not dele wiþ Gentiles for tendirnnesse of þe Jewis. **1490** CAXTON *How to Die* 4 Paynyms & gentylis as were Jobe, Raab, Ruth, Achior & other semblable. **1526** TINDALE *Matt.* x. 5 Goo nott into the wayes thatt leade to the gentyls. **1671** MILTON *P.R.* I. 456 No more shalt thou by oracling abuse The Gentiles. **1753** WARBURTON *Serm.* I. v. 145 The representation of Jesus's being made unto us Wisdom and Righteousness is particularly addressed to the Gentiles. **1878** J. P. HOPPS *Jesus* iii. 15 He would go and tell them that not only Jews but Gentiles were His children. **1892** WESTCOTT *Gospel of Life* 182 Zarathustra is not wholly unworthy to be placed as a Gentile by the side of Abraham.

b. Similarly, as used by Mormons: One outside the Mormon community; opposed to 'Saint'.

1847 PARKMAN *Oregon Tr.* (1872) 305 The Mormons.. began earnestly to..complain of the ill-usage they had received from the 'Gentiles'. **1861** *Times* 21 Aug., The 'Gentiles', as the people are termed who are without the pale of the Mormon community. **1861** R. F. BURTON *City Saints* viii. 417 Mr. Kennedy, an Irish Gentile.

2. A heathen, a pagan. Now *rare*.

1390 GOWER *Conf.* II. 170 The cronique..Saith that the gentils most of alle Worshippen her. *a*1533 LD. BERNERS *Gold. Bk. M. Aurel.* (1546) B iij, Neither all doctours among christen men, nor all the philosophers amonge the gentiles. **1600** J. PORY tr. *Leo's Africa* I. 33 They are Gentiles in religion. **1624** I. BARGRAVE *Serm. agst. Self Policy* 32 Ecebolius with false Julian..turned Gentill. **1673** TEMPLE *Observ. Unit. Prov.* Wks. 1731 I. 9 The Goths were Gentiles when they first broke into the Roman Empire. **1732** BERKELEY *Alciphr.* I. §6 One is a Christian, another a Jew, a third a Mahometan, a fourth an idolatrous Gentile. **1844** LINGARD *Anglo-Sax. Ch.* (1858) II. xii. 201 The church of St. Cuthbert..is given in prey to the gentiles.

†b. *spec.* Of a Hindoo, as distinguished from a Mahometan. (Cf. GENTOO.) *Obs.*

1555 EDEN *Decades* 233 *heading*, The prices of precious stones..as they are soulde bothe of the Moores and the gentyles. **1613** PURCHAS *Pilgrimage* (1614) 477 This King.. more trusteth and employeth the Gentiles in his affaires then the Moores. **1653** H. COGAN tr. *Pinto's Trav.* vi. 15 The Tyrant had..propounded unto this King of Batas, who was a Gentile, the imbracing of Mahomet's Law. **1727** A. HAMILTON *New Acc. E. Ind.* I. xiii. 148 The Customs in the Kings Books, are but 2 per Cent. for Mahometans, and 5 per Cent. for Gentiles.

II. From A. II. ('dʒɛntɪl).

3. *Gram.* A part of speech indicating the locality or nation to which anything belongs. (Cf. A. 3 b.)

1612 BRINSLEY *Pos. Parts* (1669) 25 *Q.* Why are they [*nostras* and *vestras*] called Gentiles? *A.* Because they properly betoken pertaining to some Countrey or Nation: to some Sect or Faction. **1889** *Century Dict.* s.v., The words, Italian, American, Athenian, are gentiles.

4. *Roman Law.* A member of the same gens.

1875 POSTE *Gaius* III. Comm. (ed. 2) 316 The patrician Claudii were the gentiles of the patron. **1880** MUIRHEAD *Gaius* III. §17 On failure of agnates, the gentiles..are called to the inheritance.

gentile, obs. form of GENTEEL, GENTLE.

gentiledom (ˈdʒɛntaɪldəm). [f. GENTILE *sb.* + -DOM.] **a.** The gentile world; the area over which gentile beliefs and practices prevailed. **b.** The state of being gentile in belief and practice.

a **1638** MEDE *Disc. Gen.* x. 5 Wks. (1672) I. 272 Isles of the Gentiles..that is, Gentildome full of Islands. **1869** J. KER *Serm.* (1874) 163 This prerogative Gentiledom possesses over Judaism. **1878** F. FERGUSON *Life of Christ* II. xv. 305 Unvisited tracts of Gentiledom.

gentilesse (ˌdʒɛntɪˈlɛs). *Obs.* exc. *arch.* [ad. F. *gentillesse*, f. *gentil*: see GENTEEL, GENTLE.]

1. The quality of being gentle; courtesy, politeness, good breeding; an instance of courtesy. Frequent in Chaucer, esp. in phrases ***of, for, through (one's) gentilesse.***

1340 *Ayenb.* 89 Þet is þe gratteste noblesse and þe heȝeste gentilesse þet me may to hopye: and clive. *c* **1386** CHAUCER *Clerk's T.* 537 This child to fostre in alle gentillesse. **1390** GOWER *Conf.* III. 299 And of his grete gentilesse His doughter..He bad to go on his message. ?*c* **1460** *Stans Puer* 65 in *Babees Bk.* 30 Whereso euer that thow dyne or soupe, Of gentilesse take salt withe thy knyf. *c* **1500** *Lancelot* 1847 Many o cetee..offerith them with-outen strok of spere.. But only for his gentilles that thei Have hard. **1647** CLARENDON *Hist. Reb.* I. §151 Who out of their gentilesses had submitted the difficulties and mysteries of the law to be measured by the standard of general reason. **1655** tr. *De Parc's Francion* I. 19 This pretty Confidence, and the Gentilesses she entertained me with..took me exceedingly. **1670** *Moral State Eng.* 145 This new Flame..spurred on the Youth to little Gallantries, and Gentilesses. [**1801** WORDSW. *Cuckoo & Night.* xxxi, All gentiless and honour thence come forth.] **1881** E. ARNOLD *Ind. Poetry* 119 'God shield you!' said the knight and dame. And Saladin, with phrase of gentilesse Returned.

b. *transf.* Of a graft: The fact of coming from a good stock.

c **1450** *Pallad. on Husb.* XI. 28 (Colchester MS.) This is a preef of graffes gentillesse.

2. Slenderness; elegance.

c **1386** CHAUCER *Sqr.'s T.* 418 A ffaucon..of fairnesse, As wel of plumage as of gentillesse Of shape.

gentilic (dʒɛnˈtɪlɪk), *a.* Also 7 **gentilique.** [f. L. *gentīl-is* GENTILE *a.* + -IC.] †**a.** Heathen, pagan (*obs.*). **b.** Tribal, national.

1604 J. GORDOUN *Serm.* 26 The Gentilique religion of the Druides. *Ibid.* 44 His Temple..was full of Gentilique Idolatrie. **1871** tr. *Lange's Comm., Jer.* xxxv. 306 The house of the Rechabites must be taken in a gentilic sense. **1879** FARRAR *St. Paul* II. xlvii. 435 *note*, If Lydia be merely a Gentilic name. **1893** SAYCE *Higher Criticism* (1894) 189 The gentilic Sheshai may perhaps represent the Shasu or Bedawin of Southern Canaan.

†**genˈtilical**, *a.* *Obs.* [f. as prec. + -AL¹.] Peculiar to the Gentiles; heathen.

1573 *Epit. Barnes' Wks.* 370 Who soeuer from hereticall malice, or gentilical superstitition..shal bee clensed by the grace of Christ. **1600** F. WALKER *Sp. Mandeville* 102 a, It is a wicked and Gentilical kind of speech.

gentilie, obs. form of GENTLY.

†ˈ**gentilish**, *a.* *Obs.* [f. GENTILE + -ISH.] Of Gentile nature, origin, or character; heathenish.

1550 HOOPER *Serm. Jonas* i. B ij, Thys Cytye of Niniue was Idololatrycall and Gentelyshe. **1577–87** HOLINSHED *Chron., Eng.* V. xxv. 108/2 There was in him..a settled perswasion in gentilish error. *a* **1598** ROLLOCK *Serm.* Wks. (Wodrow Soc.) I. 489 This Gentilish woman. **1641** MILTON *Ch. Govt.* I. ii, He leaves it..to be polluted with idolatrous and Gentilish rites and ceremonies. **1651** BIGGS *New Disp.* ¶¶ 50 The rubbish of gentilish and anarchicall principles.

gentilism (ˈdʒɛntɪlɪz(ə)m). [f. GENTILE *sb.* + -ISM.]

1. Heathenism, paganism; a heathen belief or practice. *Obs.* exc. as used *occas.* in opposition to *Judaism.*

1577 HANMER *Anc. Eccl. Hist.* (1619) 214 Licinnius, famous..for his fond opinions in gentilisme, hated yᵉ Christians. *a* **1592** H. SMITH *Arrow agst. Atheists* (1593) I 1 b, Mahomets Religion is a patched religion, mixt partly with Judaism, partly with Gentilism. *a* **1602** W. PERKINS *Cases Consc.* (1619) 214 The Masse..hath more affinitie with grosse Gentilisme, then with the Institution of our Sauiour Christ. **1645** WITHER *Vox Pacif.* 172 Remember to bewaile your Gentilismes. **1662** STILLINGFL. *Orig. Sacr.* II. x. (1702) 238 It appears in the whole history of Gentilism. **1776** R. CHANDLER *Trav. Greece* (1825) II. 57 The extirpation of gentilism at Athens seems to have been accomplished by Alaric and his Goths. *a* **1817** T. DWIGHT *Trav. New Eng.* etc. (1821) I. 127 The Spaniards in their furious zeal against Gentilism..destroyed a great multitude of these pictures. **1844** S. R. MAITLAND *Dark Ages* 149 The insinuation, modification, or extirpation of gentilisms in the Christian church. **1885** J. MARTINEAU *Types Eth. Th.* I. I. iii. 239 The inward loss of Judaism was an inward attraction towards Gentilism.

†**b.** *concr.* The gentile or heathen world; heathendom. *Obs.*

a **1638** MEDE *Apost. Lat. Times* x. Wks. (1672) III. 648 The outmost Court of the Temple of God should not only be prophaned, but troden down by Gentilism. **1654** WHITLOCK *Zootomia* 469 It is wel known, in Gentilisme their Divines were Poets.

2. The bond uniting together the members of the same gens. *rare.*

1847 GROTE *Greece* II x. III. 79 Gentilism is a tie by itself, distinct from the family ties. **1881** L. H. MORGAN *Houses & Ho.-Life N. Amer. Aborig.* 38 Gentilism arrested usurpation.

†**Gentilist.** *Obs.* [f. the name *Gentilis* + -IST.] A follower of John Valentine Gentilis (an Italian Socinian, executed at Berne in 1566).

1726 C. MATHER *Ratio Discipl.* 5, I cannot learn, That among all the Pastors of Two Hundred Churches, there is one Arminian: much less an Arian, or a Gentilist.

†**gentilitat(e**, *ppl. a.* *Obs. rare*⁻¹. [ad. L. type **gentīlitāt-us*, f. *gentīlis* (see GENTLE).] Having gentle or refined manners.

1632 LITHGOW *Trav.* v. 185 Sicily being the most ciuill Ile, and nobly gentilitat [**1640** *ed. has* Gentilitate].

gentilitial (dʒɛntɪˈlɪʃəl), *a.* Also 7 **gentilitiall**, (-icial). [f. L. *gentīliti-us*, incorrectly *gentīlīcius* (f. *gentīlis* GENTILE) + -AL¹.]

1. Of, pertaining to, or peculiar to, a nation; national.

1650 BULWER *Anthropomet.* 84 This figure of the Nose is now become gentilitial and native to the Persians. **1741** WARBURTON *Div. Legat.* (1845) II. 433 The first [relation of God to the Hebrew nation] was that of a tutelary Deity, gentilitial and local. **1877** RAWLINSON *Orig. Nat.* II. v. 218 Pathros, the local name, from which the gentilitial noun 'Pathrusim' is formed.

2. Of or pertaining to a gens or family; family. (Cf. FAMILY 9 c.)

1611 CORYAT *Crudities* 493 The Casimires, for that is the gentilitiall name of the Count Palatines family. **1660** WATERHOUSE *Arms & Arm.* 49 Though I say there be no distinct proof for Ensigns personal and gentilicial among them. **1828** J. HUNTER *Hist. S. Yorksh.* I. 32 Writers upon gentilitial insignia. **1838** *Blackw. Mag.* XLIV. 403 Their Gentilitial names, such as the Gens Horatia, Julia [etc.].

3. Of or pertaining to gentle birth; belonging to the gentry. [Perh. strictly another word, f. med.L. *gentilitia* = GENTILESSE.]

1816 SIR E. BRYDGES *Life J. Hall* in *Hall's Poems*, John Hall was born of gentilitial parents in Durham. **1837** SIR F. PALGRAVE *Merch. & Friar* iv. (1844) 153 The inherent, indelible dignity of a gentilitial aristocracy. **1866** E. PEACOCK *Eng. Ch. Furniture* App. xi. 240 He was sprung from an old gentilitial stock. *a* **1875** R. DAVIES *Walks through York* (1880) 133 One of the most antient and distinguished of our Yorkshire gentilitial families.

gentilitian (dʒɛntɪˈlɪʃən). [f. as prec. + -AN.] = GENTILITIAL 1.

1650 BULWER *Anthropomet.* 9 Their [Muscovite infants'] faces are explained or flatted by Art, and so directed to grow into this gentilitian forme. **1897** C. RAMPINI *Hist. Moray & Nairn* i. 8 In the Celtic family is to be found the germ of all his [the Caledonian Pict's] gentilitian and national peculiarities.

gentilitious (dʒɛntɪˈlɪʃəs), *a.* [f. as prec. + -OUS.]

†**1.** Characteristic of a 'gentile'; pagan. *Obs.*⁻¹

1613 SHERLEY *Trav. Persia* 30 Without any gentilitious adoration, but with those respects which are fit for the maiesty of a Prince.

2. Of, pertaining to, or characteristic of, a nation; national. (= GENTILITIAL 1.)

1646 SIR T. BROWNE *Pseud. Ep.* IV. x. 201 That an unsavoury odour is gentilitious or nationall unto the Jews.. we cannot well concede. **1831** *Blackw. Mag.* XXIX. 519 It is not the generic likeness of a breed—the gentilitious contour of a nation. **1845** FORD *Handbk. Spain* II. 295 An unsavoury odour seems gentilitious in the Hebrew, but not more so than in the orthodox Spanish Monk.

3. Of or pertaining to a gens or family. (= GENTILITIAL 2.)

1646 SIR T. BROWNE *Pseud. Ep.* VII. xvi. 373 Nor is it proved, or probable, that Sergius changed the name of Bocca di Porco, for this was his sirname or gentilitious appellation. **1834** *W. Ind. Sketch Bk.* II. 48 Many of them had no other than a gentilitious cognomination. **1839** T. STAPLETON *Pref. to Plumpton Corr.* (Camden) 2 A family whose members in former days were distinguished by their labours for the preservation of our gentilitious antiquities.

b. Of diseases, etc.: Hereditary. ? *Obs.*

1731 ARBUTHNOT *Aliments* vi. (1735) 195 The common Causes of this Distemper are a particular and perhaps a gentilitious Disposition of Body. **1885** in *Syd. Soc. Lex.*

gentility (dʒɛnˈtɪlɪtɪ). Forms: 4 **gentylete**, 6 **gentilite(e**, **gentil(l)ity(e**, (**gentyllitie**), 6–7 **gentil(l)itie**, 6– **gentility**. [ad. OF. and F. *gentilité* (now only in sense 1), ad. L. *gentīlitās*, f. *gentīlis*: see GENTILE, GENTLE, GENTEEL.

The word serves as noun of quality both to *Gentile* and *genteel*, and also to *gentle* in those senses which correspond to obsolete senses of *genteel*.]

I. In senses related to GENTLE, GENTEEL.

1. Gentle birth; honourable extraction; the fact of belonging to a family of gentle blood. Also, the personality of one who is well-born.

1340 *Ayenb.* 89 Hy ham yelpeþ of hare gentylete uor þet hy weneþ by of gentile woze. **1583** STANYHURST *Æneis* I. (Arb.) 22 What syrs? your boldnesse dooth your gentilitie warrant? *a* **1677** BARROW *Serm.* Wks. 1686 III. 244 Without which [Courage and Courtesie] gentility in a conspicuous degree is no more than a vain shew. **1697** COLLIER *Ess. Mor. Subj.* I. (1709) 61 An ancient Gentility does not necessarily convey to us any Advantage either of Body or Mind. **1791** BOSWELL *Johnson* xix. (1831) I. 507 A new system of gentility might be established. **1820** SCOTT *Abbot* v, We must have a screened seat for you in the chapel, that your gentility may be free from the eyes of common folks! **1877** MRS. OLIPHANT *Makers Flor.* iv. 105 He had no claim to gentility and was only..an Italian clown.

quasi-*personified.* **1641** *Lond. Love* 1 Gentility without wealth staggers like a sicke man. **1659** *Gentl. Calling* (1696) 1 Gentility has long since confuted Job's Aphorism, Man is born to labour. **1873** BROWNING *Red Cott. Nt.-cap* 945 In just the place..Where aboriginal gentility Will scout the upstart. **1874** MISS MULOCK *Thy Mother & I* (Tauchn.) 89 Well-to-do commonalty loves to patronise poor gentility.

†**b.** *concr.* People of gentle birth; gentlefolks. Also, ***the gentility***: the gentry. *Obs.*

a **1577** SIR T. SMITH *Commw. Eng.* (1609) 36 The Nobility, the rest of the gentilitie, & the yeomanrie. **1587** HARRISON *England* II. vi. (1877) I. 147 As..in the gentilitie, so in the wealthie commonaltie the like desire of glasse is not neglected. **1589** COGAN *Haven Health* iv. (1636) 27 Bread.. made in forme of Manchet, as is used of the Gentility. **1594** CAREW *Huarte's Exam. Wits* xiii. (1596) 209 A..law that all those of their order shall be issued from gentilitie, both on the fathers side and the mothers. **1622** T. SCOTT *Belg. Pismire* 27 Their breede is from the lazie scumme of counterfeit Gentilitie.

c. The rank or heraldic status of a gentleman.

1642 W. BIRD *Mag. Honor* 150 If one be a Gentleman by Office, and looseth his office, then he doth also lose his Gentility. **1827** HALLAM *Const. Hist.* (1876) I. vi. 361 Floyd was adjudged to be degraded from his gentility.

2. The quality of being gentle (in manners, etc.) or genteel.

†**a.** The manners, bearing, habits of life, etc., characteristic of a gentleman or gentlewoman; polish of manners, politeness. *Obs.*

1588 SHAKS. *L.L.L.* I. i. 129 A dangerous law against gentilitie. **1590** SPENSER *F.Q.* III. vi. 1 Such wilde woodes should far expell All civile usage and gentility.

b. Social superiority, rank above the commonalty, as evidenced by, or asserted on the ground of, manners or habits of life. Now chiefly in depreciative use. Occas. in pl. ***the gentilities.***

1650 BULWER *Anthropomet.* Pref., Their long Nails define Idle Gentilitie's assured Signe. **1800** MRS. HERVEY *Mourtray Fam.* I. 3 Barely adequate to keep up the appearance of gentility. **1822** HAZLITT *Table-t.* I. xvi. 376 Gentility is only a more select and artificial kind of vulgarity. **1832** HT. MARTINEAU *Life in Wilds* iii. 35, I see no gentility in such airs. **1850** L. HUNT *Autobiog.* I. iv. 158 My aunt.. was a mighty cultivator of the gentilities, inward as well as outward. **1857** RUSKIN *Pol. Econ. Art* 141 Once get the wealthy classes to imagine that the possession of pictures by a given artist adds to their 'gentility'. **1861** GEO. ELIOT *Silas M.* 64 Let him forsake a decent craft that he may pursue the gentilities of a profession. **1872** *Punch* 18 May 202/2 There is nothing so vulgar as gentility.

c. quasi-*personified.* Also *concr.* in *pl.* Genteel people; also, marks of gentility.

1840 DICKENS *Old. C. Shop* xv, Poor streets where faded gentility essayed..to make its last feeble stand. **1856** MISS MULOCK *J. Halifax* xvii. 175 She..left the already vanquished gentilities of Norton Bury to amuse themselves. **1856** LEVER *Martins of Cro' M.* 571 The..smartened-up gentilities which once were the glories of Bond-street. **1858** O. W. HOLMES *Aut. Breakf.-t.* viii. 70 Shabby gentility has nothing so characteristic as its hat. **1874** SPURGEON *Treas. Dav.* Ps. lxxxi. 1 The gentility which lisps the tune in wellbred whispers.

†**d.** Elegance, grace, refinement. *Obs.*

1753 HOGARTH *Anal. Beauty* xi. 138 The whole gentility of a figure..depends upon the first proportioning these lines ....properly to one another. **1782** V. KNOX *Ess.* xxviii. I. 137 There is a certain gaiety and gentility diffused over it [the World], which gives it a peculiar grace.

†**e.** *concr.* in *pl.* 'Nice' or agreeable things. *ironically.*

1796 BURNEY *Metastasio* III. 197 The last winter assailed me with rheumatism, tension of nerves, implacable hypochondria, and other gentilities.

II. In senses related to those of GENTILE.

†**3.** Gentile or heathen belief, doctrine, or practice; the state of being a gentile or heathen; heathenism, paganism. *Obs.*

1526 *Pilgr. Perf.* (W. de W. 1531) 38 b, She had left her gentilite, & leaned holle to the secte of þe sayd iewes. **1565** JEWEL *Repl. Harding* (1611) 302 The Heathens in their rude Gentilitie thought that Bacchus and Ceres had first found out..the vse of Bread and Wine. **1594** PARSONS *Confer. Success.* I. ix. 213 Two gentiles marryed together in ther gentility. **1650** BULWER *Anthropomet.* 153 Can either Gentility or Christianity be forgiven such an error?

†**b.** *concr.* The gentile, or heathen world; heathendom, heathen people. *Obs.*

1546 LANGLEY *Pol. Verg. de Invent.* I. iii. 6 b, Thus muche is of the Vaine Opinions of the Gentilitee. **1563** MAN *Musculus' Commonpl.* 150 b, It was showen many waies, which was the Churche of God, and which was Gentilitie. **1582** N. T. (Rhem.) Matt. ii. 11 *note*, These treasures are as it were the first fruits of those riches and giftes, which.. Gentility should offer to Christ.

4. Relationship between 'gentiles' or members of the same gens (cf. GENTILE B. 4); † the gens itself.

a **1577** SIR T. SMITH *Commw. Eng.* III. viii. (1589) 131 The surname is the name of the gentilitie and stocke which the sonne doth take of the father alwaies, as the old Romans did. **1883** MAINE *Early Law & Cust.* 283 The Romans, therefore, regarded 'gentility' as a kinship among men not essentially different from 'agnation'.

gentilize (ˈdʒɛntɪlaɪz), *v.*[1] *arch.* Also 6 **gentellise**, 7 **gentlelize, gentillize**, 9 **gentilise**. [f. *gentil* GENTLE + -IZE.]

1. *trans.* To make gentle; to raise to the position, or invest with the character, of a gentleman.

1581 PETTIE *Guazzo's Civ. Conv.* II. (1586) 86 b, [It] is most true, that gentry is the daughter of knowledge: and that knowledge doeth gentellise him that possesseth it. **1607** NORDEN *Surv. Dial.* 80 Some..of small rent, bring up their children too nicely, and must needs, forsooth, Gentlelize them. **1631** BRATHWAIT *Eng. Gentlew.* (1641) 360 Where is that in us that may truly gentilize us. *a* **1650** MAY *Satir. Puppy* (1657) 100 Those that are rich strive to Gentilize their Female Of-spring.

absol. **1830** COLERIDGE *Table-t.* 30 May, Religion is, in its essence, the most gentlemanly thing in the world. It will alone gentilise.

†**b.** *intr. to gentilize it*: to act the gentleman.

1607 NORDEN *Surv. Dial.* 231 But where the master standeth upon tearmes of his qualitie..and will refuse to put ..his eye towards the plow, he may..gentlelize it awhile. **1613** WITHER *Abuses Stript* (1615) 147 Our Yeomen too, that neuer Armes haue borne To Gentillize it make themselues a scorne.

†**c.** *trans.* To refine; civilize. *Obs.*

1635 A. STAFFORD *Fem. Glory* (1860) 44 It would have gentiliz'd Barbarisme it selfe.

†**2.** *trans.* To make mild, to lenify. *Obs. rare.*

1679 NEWBURGH in Evelyn *Pomona* 393 Two or three Eggs whole put into an Hogshead of Cider that is become sharp..sometimes rarely lenifies and gentilizes it.

Hence †ˈ**gentilizing** *vbl. sb.* Also **gentiliˈzation**.

1630 BRATHWAIT *Eng. Gentlem.* Ep. Ded., A gentleman, who professeth the true and new art of gentilizing. **1825** *New Monthly Mag.* XVI. 277 The gentilization of so homely and culinary a name as Bacon.

gentilize (ˈdʒɛntɪlaɪz, ˈdʒɛntaɪlaɪz), *v.*[2] [f. GENTILE + -IZE.]

1. *intr.* To live like a Gentile or heathen; to conform to Gentile customs or practices.

1593 BELL *Motives conc. Rom. Faith* Ded. (1605) 1 If Tertullian..erred montanizing..if S. Paul gentilizing [etc.]. **1596** —— *Surv. Popery* Postscr., To gentilize is nothing els but to play the part of a gentile. **1680** T. LAWSON *Mite into Treas.* 50 They began to Jewdaize, yea, and to Gentilize. **1814, 1819** [see GENTILIZING below].

2. *trans.* To give a gentile character to, make gentile; to paganize.

1827 [see GENTILIZED below]. **1883** A. SAPHIR in *Bible Soc. Rec.* Mar., [Scripture] must not be Paganised or Gentilised, or stripped of its Jewish character.

Hence ˈ**gentilized, gentiˈlizing** *ppl. adjs.*

a **1638** MEDE *Rem. Apoc.* iv. Wks. (1672) III. 588 How long the Church..was to be prophaned..by Gentilizing Idolatry? **1660** MILTON *Free Commw.* Wks. (1847) 449/1 This is not my conjecture, but drawn from God's known denouncement against the gentilizing Israelites. **1814** W. TAYLOR in *Monthly Rev.* LXXIII. 285 They were both gentilizing Jews and great travellers. **1819** G. S. FABER *Dispensations* (1823) II. 395 Many of the oriental gentilizing converts. **1827** —— *Sacred Cal. Prophecy* (1844) II. 231 The completely gentilised members of the Visible Church. **1873** G. RAWLINSON in *Speaker's Comm. Bible* III. 471/1 He is not a Gentilised Jew. **1893** J. MARTINEAU in *19th Cent.* June 924 In the midst of a Christianity preponderantly gentilised.

gentill-; see GENTEEL, GENTIL-, GENTLE, etc.

gentill(e, obs. form of GENTILE, GENTLE.

gentilliche, gentilly(e, obs. forms of GENTLY.

gentilrie, var. GENTLERY, *Obs.*

gentin(g, var. GHENTING, *Obs.*

gentiopicrin (dʒɛntɪəʊˈpɪkrɪn). [f. *gentio-* combining form of GENTIAN + Gr. πικρ-ός bitter + -IN.] 'The bitter principle of gentian, a colourless crystalline glycoside' (*Syd. Soc. Lex.* 1885).

1875 H. C. WOOD *Therap.* (1879) 55 The active principle is probably the gentiopikrin of Kromayer, a neutral, crystalline substance, of an intensely bitter taste.

gentiresse, obs. form of GENTRICE.

gentish (ˈdʒɛntɪʃ), *a.* [f. GENT *sb.* + -ISH.] Resembling, or characteristic of, a 'gent'.

1847 ALB. SMITH *Chr. Tadpole* xxix. (1879) 262 His clothes, although cut in a slangy gentish fashion, were of good materials and work. **1857** *Chamb. Jrnl.* VII. 369 However gentish and impudent its followers may previously have been. **1862** *Temple Bar Mag.* IV. 289 To disport himself in his gentish garments on..a river-steamer.

Hence ˈ**gentishness**.

1885 *Mag. of Art* Apr. 247 Women of excellence and originality, who had the courage to reprove the gentishness and snobbery by which they were surrounded.

gentisic (dʒɛnˈtɪsɪk), *a.* *Chem.* [arbitrarily f. GENTIAN: see -IC.] In *gentisic acid* = gentianic acid. So ˈ**gentisate** [-ATE], a salt of this acid. ˈ**gentisin** [-IN], a synonym of gentisic or gentianic acid.

1838 THOMSON *Org. Bodies* 166 Gentisin. Gentisate of soda. **1879** E. M. HOLMES in *Encycl. Brit.* X. 160/1 Gentianic acid..is also called gentianin, gentisin, and gentisic acid.

gentism (ˈdʒɛntɪz(ə)m). [f. GENT *sb.* + -ISM.] The habits, ideas, and practices of a 'gent'.

1862 *Temple Bar Mag.* IV. 288 This was the age of gentism, of 'fast' literature, and of coarse and vulgar amusements.

gentle (ˈdʒɛnt(ə)l), *a.* and *sb.* Forms: 3–6 **gentil(l, -yl**, 3, 6–7 **gentile**, 4 **jentel**, 4–5 **gentille, -yle**, 4–6 **gentel(l, jentil(l, jentylle**, 4–7 **gentyll**, 5 **gentylle, gyntyl**, 6 **jentle**, 5– **gentle**. [a. OF. *gentil*, *jentil*, etc. high-born, noble (mod.F. *gentil* elegant, GENTEEL) = Pr. Sp. *gentil*, It. *gentile*:—L. *gentilis* belonging to the same *gens* or race, f. *genti-*, *gens* race, family. The sense 'belonging to a good family' common to the Rom. tongues is not found in Latin. See also GENTILE.]

A. *adj.*

1. a. Of persons: Well-born, belonging to a family of position; originally used synonymously with *noble*, but afterwards distinguished from it, either as a wider term, or as designating a lower degree of rank. Also, in heraldic use: Having the rank or status of 'gentleman', the distinguishing mark of which is the right to bear arms. *Obs.* exc. in the archaic phrase ***gentle and simple***, and in Comb. GENTLEMAN, GENTLEFOLKS, etc.

a **1225** *Ancr. R.* 166 Noble men and gentile ne bereð nout packes. *a* **1240** *Wohunge* in *Cott. Hom.* 273 Ah noble men and gentile and of heh burðe ofte winnen luue lihtliche cheape. **13..** *E.E. Allit. P.* B. 1180 Þe gentylest of Iudee in Ierusalem biseged. *c* **1400** MAUNDEV. (1839) v. 39 The fairest and the nobleste of Birthe and the gentylleste Damyseles of his Contree. *c* **1440** *Promp. Parv.* 190/2 Gentyl, of awncetrye, *ingenuus*. **1483** CAXTON *Gold. Leg.* 148 a/2 Hyt apperteyneth not that one so gentyl a man as I am be seruant to hym. **1500–20** DUNBAR *Poems* xxii. 32 Quhen seruit is all vdir man, Gentill and semple of euery clan. **1581** PETTIE *Guazzo's Civ. Conv.* II. (1586) 90 b, Gentle of base are those who, extracted from low parentage, raise themselves to Gentrie by their vertue. *a* **1625** FLETCHER *Love's Pilg.* II. i, I am as gentle as your self, as free born. **1683** EVELYN *Mem.* (1857) II. 182, I dined at Mr. Houblon's, a rich and gentle French merchant. **1786** BURNS *Highland Lassie* i, Nae gentle dames, tho' e'er sae fair, Shall ever be my muse's care: Their titles a' are empty show.

absol. with plural sense.

13.. *E.E. Allit. P.* B. 1216 Þer watȝ Þe kyng kaȝt..& alle hise gentyle for-iusted on ierico playnes. *c* **1420** *Anturs of Arth.* xxxix, So jolyly thes gentille justede one were! Schaftis thay shindr [*v.r.* scheuer], in sheldes so schene. **1837** HOWITT *Rur. Life* I. i. (1862) 10 Making acquaintance with the dwellings, habits, and feelings of both gentle and simple. **1840** BARHAM *Ingol. Leg.*, *Hand of Glory* 64 Gentle and Simple, Squire and Groom, Each one had sought his separate room.

†**b.** An epithet applied to persons of distinction. *Obs.* (Mainly in alliteration.)

1362 LANGL. *P. Pl.* A. I. 159 James Þe gentel bond hit [*B.* jugged, *C.* juggeth] in his Book. *a* **1400–50** *Alexander* 705 Loo! ȝonder Þe gentill Iubiter, how lolyle he schynes. *Ibid.* 4022 And ȝit Þe gentill genosophis, Þam in Þe gest callis. *c* **1440** *York Myst.* xxx. 58 As ye are gentill juger and justice of Jewes. *c* **1450** *St. Cuthbert* (Surtees) 1108 Of gentil Juda machabe. **1567** *Satir. Poems Reform.* iii. 27 In deidis he soulde haue bene lyke Deiphoebus..or gentill Julius.

c. Of an animal: Of excellent breed or spirit; now only in ***gentle*** (also ***gentil***) ***falcon*** (cf. FALCON-GENTLE).

1340 *Ayenb.* 75 Hy uoryeteÞ alle oÞre guodes, ase deÞ Þe gentyl hond; huanne ha zyÞ his praye touore his eȝen. *c* **1386** CHAUCER *Nun's Pr. T.* 45 This gentil Cok hadde in his gouernaunce Seuene hennes. **1398** TREVISA *Barth. De P.R.* XII. i (Tollem. MS.) Þe gentel ffawcon and oÞer suche fowles. *Ibid.* XVIII. xxxix. (1495) 800 In gentyll horse noble men takyth hede of foure thynges, of shape and of fayrnesse, of wylfulnesse, and of colour. *c* **1420** *Pallad. on Husb.* IV. 799 Fed stalons faat goth now to gentyl maris. *c* **1435** *Torr. Portugal* 2033 [2133] The kyng of Nazareth huntid there Among the hertes, that gentill were. *c* **1470** *Abraham & Isaac* 368 in L. T. Smith *Bk. of Brome* (1886) 65, I haue browt here full smerte, Thys jentyll scheppe [the ram]. **1500–20** DUNBAR *Poems* lxi. 13 With gentill horss quhen I wald knyp, Thane is thair laid on me ane quhip. **1523** SKELTON *Garl. Laurel* 1436 A ientyll hownde shulde neuer play the kur. *a* **1547** SURREY in *Tottel's Misc.* (Arb.) 218 A Lion saw I late..Vpon the gentle beast to gaze it pleased me. **1612** SELDEN *Notes to Drayton's Poly-olb.* v. 82 The Falcon stout Which we the Gentill call. **1678** RAY *Willughby's Ornith.* 79 The frequent agitation of the Wings in flying shews the Hawk to be a Gentile Falcon. **1802** BINGLEY *Anim. Biog.* (1813) II. 55 The Gentil Falcon measures about two feet in length. **1833** R. MUDIE *Brit. Birds* (1841) I. 86 The female is the gentil or gentil falcon.

†**d.** Of things: Noble, excellent. *Obs. rare.*

13.. *E.E. Allit P.* A. 1015 Þe twelfÞe Þe gentyleste in vch a plyt, Þe amatyst purpre. **13..** *Gaw. & Gr. Knt.* 1022 Þe ioye of sayn[t] Ionez day watz gentyle to here. *c* **1386** CHAUCER *Wife's Prol.* 29 God bad vs for to wexe and multiplye; That gentil text kan I [wel] vnderstonde. *c* **1400** MAUNDEV. (1839) xix. 209 There growethe fulle gode Wyn, that men clepen Bigon, that is fulle myghty and gentylle in drynkynge. **1556** *Aurelio & Isab.* O ij, For the whiche [women] all gentill inventions and all goodes comes in to the worlde.

e. Enchanted or haunted by fairies. Also ***gentle people***, the fairies. (Cf. GENTRY 3 b.) *dial.*

1823 S. MCSKIMIN *Carrickfergus* (ed. 2) IV. 258 The large hawthorns growing singly..are deemed sacred to fairies, and are hence called *gentle thorns*. **1877** *Cornhill Mag.* Feb. 174 Woe betide the foolhardy person who ventures to raise an axe against one of these 'gentle bushes', as they are called. *Ibid.* 178 All the land was of excellent quality except half an acre of rocky ground, which was 'allowed' to be a very 'gentle place'. **1893** W. B. YEATS *Celtic Twilight* 94 In some more than commonly 'gentle' place. **1907** J. MASEFIELD *Tarpaulin Muster* xiii. 136 There's many places here is gentle. **1913** E. M. WRIGHT *Rustic Speech* xii. 207 Collective names [for Fairies] are: the Fair Folk..the Gentle People, or Gentry (Irel.).

2. a. Of birth, blood, family, etc.: Honourable, distinguished by descent or position, belonging to the class of 'gentlemen'. (Cf. 1.)

a **1300** *Cursor M.* 4250 Sir putifar wel vndirstod Þat ioseph was o gentil blod. **1340** *Ayenb.* 89 Hy ne lokeÞ naȝt huer-of ham comÞ Þe zoÞe noblesse, and Þe gentil kenrede. *c* **1440** *York Myst.* xli. 435 For he is come of gentyll kynde. *a* **1661** FULLER *Worthies* (1840) III. 217 Who no doubt was ..of gentle extraction, because her parents bestowed on her so liberal and costly education. **1808** SCOTT *Autobiog.* in *Lockhart* i, His birth being admitted as gentle, gave him access to the best society in the county. **1861** TULLOCH *Eng. Purit.* I. i. 57 On his father's side Cromwell was of a gentle and old family. **1870** E. PEACOCK *Ralf Skirl.* I. 6 The husband was known to be sprung of gentle blood.

b. Of occupations or pursuits: Suitable for one of gentle birth. ***the gentle craft*** (humorously): †(*a*) the trade of shoemaking (*obs.*); (*b*) with allusion to sense 8, the sport of angling; similarly ***the gentle art***, now often humorously used in transferred applications.

a **1592** GREENE *George-a-Greene* (1599) F 4 b, You shall be no more called Shoomakers. But you and yours to the worlds ende, Shall be called the trade of the gentle craft. **1592** NASHE *P. Penilesse* (ed. 2) 21 b, [If certain people walked instead of riding] the price of veluet and cloath would fall..and the gentle craft (alias the red herrings kinsmen) get more and drink lesse. **1600** DEKKER *Gent. Craft* i. (1610) B 3, As I am a true shoomaker, and a gentleman of the Gentle Craft. **1658** W. SANDERSON *Graphice* 28 If it be the generall Rule..that Children be taught some gentle Manu-facture [etc.]. **1688** R. HOLME *Armoury* III. 99/1 A Man on a Seat [a Shooe-maker].. exercising of the Gentle Craft. **1799** A. MATHER in *Life J. Bunting* (1859) I. vii. 102 A profession [the medical] that will be gentle bread at some not very distant period. **1834** T. MEDWIN *Angler in Wales* I. 6 It would have made unquiet the ghost of old Isaac Walton to hear Julian's disparagement of 'the gentle art'. **1844** J. T. HEWLETT *Parsons & W.* i, One of the gentle craft—so called, I presume, from their using gentles in their art. **1850** WHITTIER *Songs of Labor, Shoemakers* i, Ho! workers of the old time styled The Gentle Craft of Leather. **1890** J. MCN. WHISTLER (*title*) The Gentle Art of making Enemies. **1894** CROCKETT *Raiders* 54 All the seven big sons..were said to be deeper in the Gentle Traffic [smuggling], as it was called, than any others in the locality.

3. a. Of persons: Having the character appropriate to one of good birth; noble, generous, courteous. Freq. in the phrase ***a gentle knight***. Now only *arch.*

1297 R. GLOUC. (Rolls) 8689 Of vairost fourme & best maneres, & mest gentil and fre. *Ibid.* 11719 Sir henri is sone Þat so gentil kniȝt was. *c* **1330** R. BRUNNE *Chron.* (1810) 188 Gentille of norture, & noble of lynage. *c* **1386** CHAUCER *Prol.* 72. *c* **1440** *Generydes* 3 Ther was a kyng, Ientill, curteys, full trew in worde. **1463** *Bury Wills* (Camden) 18 They [tenants] haue be to me ryght gentil and good at alle tymes. **1529** MORE *Dyaloge* I. Wks. 170/2 Sithe I am so gentle to graunt you so many things, I trust ye wyl grant me this one. **1563** *Mirr. Mag.*, *Blacksmith* xv, His wanton wyl and lust that brydel can In dede is gentil both to God and man. **1590** SPENSER *F.Q.* I. i. 1 A gentle knight was pricking on the plaine. *a* **1661** FULLER *Worthies* (1840) II. 575 [Robin Hood] The gentlest thief that ever was. **1814** SOUTHEY *Roderick* III, With such short interchange of benison As each to other gentle travellers give. **1871** BROWNING *Balaust.* 2377 The son of Zeus, He was the gentle guest to entertain!

b. Used in polite or ingratiating address, or as a complimentary epithet. *Obs.* exc. as a playful archaism in 'Gentle Reader'.

1500–20 DUNBAR *Poems* xiii. 78 Keip this all secreit, gentill brother. **1542–5** BRINKLOW *Lament.* (1874) 84 Iudge thow gentle reader. **1591** SHAKS. *Two Gent.* I. ii. 14 What think'st thou of the gentle Protheus. **1601** —— *Jul. C.* III. ii. 77 You gentle Romans. **1615** CROOKE *Body of Man* 428 That would be irkesome to vs both Gentle Reader. **1687** MIEGE *Gt. Fr. Dict.* II, Gentle Reader, *Ami-Lecteur*. **1844** HALIBURTON *Attaché* Ser. II. II. 285 Gentle reader, having taken my leave of Mr. Slick, it is now fit I should take my leave of you.

†**c.** Of language, actions, character, etc.: Courteous, polite. (Often closely approaching sense 8.)

c **1385** CHAUCER *L.G.W.* 1090 *Dido*, And manye a gentil word sche spake hym to. *c* **1440** AGNES PASTON in *P. Lett.* No. 25 I. 39 She made hym gentil cher in gyntyl wise. **1526** *Pilgr. Perf.* (W. de W. 1531) 142 Than yf we be touched with a sharpe worde, we shal yelde a benigne & gentyll answere. **1561** T. NORTON *Calvin's Inst.* I. 37 They which geue gentill and open eares to the word of God. **1598** YONG *Diana* 122 She gaue him infinite thankes..for the gentle entertainment she had in his Castle. **1646** F. HAWKINS *Youth's Behav.* (1663) 13 And be thou assured that gentle affability towards thy inferiours, will fix to thy name the Epithite of courteous. **1653** H. COGAN tr. *Pinto's Trav.* iv. 9 This man with very gentle words gave an end to the sedition..which shews of what power courtesie is.

4. a. Of fruit, a tree, etc.: Cultivated, domesticated (opposed to *wild*). Now *rare.* (? *arch.*)

c **1420** *Pallad. on Husb.* III. 711 A gentil tre, Not wilde at all, withoute asperite. *c* **1430** LYDG. *Min. Poems, Chorle & Bird* (Percy Soc.) 192 The vintere tretethe of his holsom wynes, Of gentille frute bostethe the gardener. **1601** HOLLAND *Pliny* II. 429 The berries..much like..to the grains or fruit of the gentle garden Corneil tree. **1611** SHAKS. *Wint. T.* IV. iv. 93 We marry A gentler sien to the wildest stock. **1871** JOWETT *Plato* II. 431 Tending the gentle shoots, and preventing the wild ones from growing.

b. Of an animal: Tame, quiet, easily managed. **1532** HERVET *Xenophon's Househ.* (1768) 60 We call al these beastis gentyll, the whiche be goodly, great, and profitable, and be not fierse, but tame among men. **1562** LEIGH *Armorie* 178 A Barnacle..This is yᵉ Chiefest Instrument yᵗ the Smyth hath, to make the vntamed Horse gentile. **1613** SHAKS. *Hen. VIII*, v. iii. 22 Those that tame wild Horses Pace 'em not in their hands to make 'em gentle. **1687** MIEGE *Gt. Fr. Dict.* II, A gentle Horse (a Horse that gives exact Obedience to the Rider), *un Cheval loyal.* **1774** GOLDSM. *Nat. Hist.* (1776) II. 330 They are gentle and harmless enough while young; but as they grow up, they acquire their natural ferocity.

†**5.** Not harsh or irritating to the touch; soft, tender; yielding to pressure, pliant, supple. *Obs.* **1555** W. WATREMAN *Fardle Facions* II. ii. 120 Their garmentes..are verye softe and gentle clothe. **1578** LYTE *Dodoens* III. xciii. 448 These small pottes [of henbane] do growe and are inclosed in a rounde skinne, but the same is gentle and pricketh not. **1597** A. M. tr. *Guillemeau's Fr. Chirurg.* 14b/1 Nether must shee [needle] be of to hard a steele, but of gentle steele, because they might rather bende then break. **1607** TOPSELL *Four-f. Beasts* (1658) 239 Another charge of a Horse-keeper is to keep his Horses lips soft, tender, and gentle, so as he may more sensibly feel his bit. **1657** W. COLES *Adam in Eden* cxli. 212 (Camomile) White flowers with yellow thrums in the middle, very like unto Feather-few, but more soft and gentle in handling. **1697** W. DERHAM in *Phil. Trans.* XX. Enclose the Mercury with gentle Leather tied very fast round the Tube. **1756** *Phil. Trans.* XLIX. 847 The English soft or gentle Thistle. **1769** SIR J. HILL *Herb. Brit.* I. 80 Gentle thistle.

6. a. Of the weather, wind, etc.: Not stormy, violent, or severe. ***gentle gale*** (see quot. 1867). **1563** FULKE *Meteors* (1640) 18b, Kinde of winde, which is but a soft gentle and coole moving of the ayre, and commeth from no certaine place. **1585** J. B. tr. *Viret's Sch. Beastes* Dvjb, And the great rivers..give a sweete and gentle temperatenes and most pleasaunt to the fishes. **1592** SHAKS. *Ven. & Ad.* 189 Ile sigh celestiall breath, whose gentle winde Shall coole the heate of this descending sun. **1600** J. PORY tr. *Leo's Africa* I. 35 Those seas are..most pleasant.. to saile upon, with faire and gentle weather. **1634** SIR. T. HERBERT *Trav.* 2 We had verie raging Seas and tempests, but at night a gentle calme ensued. **1697** DRYDEN *Virg. Georg.* IV. 380 Soft Whispers then..are heard, As when the Woods by gentle Winds are stirr'd. **1781** COWPER *Truth* 419 Complacency has breathed a gentle gale O'er all his thoughts, and swelled his easy sail. **1850** TENNYSON *In Mem.* ix, Sleep, gentle heavens, before the prow; Sleep, gentle winds, as he sleeps now. **1867** SMYTH *Sailor's Word-bk.*, *Gentle gale*, in which a ship carries royals and flying-kites; force 4.

b. Of a river: Flowing smoothly; not rough or rapid. **1593** SHAKS. *Lucr.* 1118 Deepe woes roll forward like a gentle flood. **1638** SIR T. HERBERT *Trav.* (ed. 2) 219 It is watered by Tigris..somewhat broader than the Thames, but not so navigable nor gentle. **1739** LABELYE *Short Acc. Piers Westm. Bridge* 63 The Stream..would be gentler.. than the Stream of the River Seine. **1791** W. JESSOP *Rep. Riv. Witham* 5 Being penned up by Locks, its velocity would be greatly decreased, and it would almost become a gentle River. **1891** E. PEACOCK *N. Brendon* I. 273 The Skern was changed from a gentle stream to a raging torrent.

c. Of sound: Soft, low; not loud or harsh. **1605** SHAKS. *Lear* v. iii. 273 Her voice was euer soft, Gentle and low, an excellent thing in woman. **1709** STEELE *Tatler* No. 80 ¶5, I heard a very gentle Knock at my Door. **1742** COLLINS *Ecl.*, *Hassan* 42 The gentle voice of Peace. **1781** COWPER *Conversat.* 905 In gentle sounds it seems as it complained Of the rude injuries it late sustained. **1812** J. WILSON *Isle of Palms* II. 407 And gives to the storm as gentle notes As e'er through sunshine stole.

d. Of a medicine: Acting without violence; mild. **1576** FLEMING *Panopl. Epist.* 289, I would therfore, that a stronger remedie be prepared: for this emplaster is too gentle. **1790** J. B. MORETON *Mann. W. Ind.* 25 If you find yourself costive, take a gentle purge. **1835** *Cycl. Pract. Med.* IV. 587/2 By mild and frequently repeated doses of gentle aperients.

e. Of rule, punishment, etc.: Free from violence or severity; mild. **1647** CLARENDON *Hist. Reb.* II. §98 The Papists..being upon the matter absolved from the severest parts of the law and dispensed with for the gentlest. **1696** TATE & BRADY *Ps.* lxxii. 4 Shall rule with gentle Sway. **1751** JORTIN *Serm.* (1771) IV. i. 4 Especially where the legal punishment was gentle. **1752** HUME *Ess. & Treat.* (1777) I. 21 In every respect, a gentle government is preferable. **1828** SCOTT *F.M. Perth* xiii, If gentler methods will succeed better with these Earish knaves, do not blame Douglas for speaking his mind. **1879** O. W. HOLMES *Motley* xxi. 158 This gentle form of violence is well understood in diplomatic service.

7. a. Moderate in operation, intensity, rate, or the like; esp. ***a gentle heat.*** **1626** BACON *Sylva* §399 The Sunne, which is a Gentler Heat [*sc.* than Fire]. **1632** LITHGOW *Trav.* I. 14, I found abundance of all things..at so easie and gentle a rate, that [etc.]. **1687** MIEGE *Gt. Fr. Dict.* II, A gentle Fit of an Ague, *acces de Fiévre moderé.* **1699** EVELYN *Kal. Hort.* (ed. 9) 138 Closing the Double-shuts, (or Chasses rather) continue a gentle Heat. **1758** REID tr. *Macquer's Chym.* I. 138 Liquors ..evaporated by a gentle heat..are called Extracts. **1816** ACCUM *Chem. Tests* (1818) 70 The paper regains its original colour..by exposure to a gentle heat. **1840** DICKENS *Barn. Rudge* ii, Ride forward at a gentler pace, and good night.

b. Of a slope: Very gradual; not steep. **1697** DAMPIER *Voy.* I. 187 On the North side it declines with a gentle descent to the Sea. **1777** WATSON *Philip II* (1839) 467 He pitched his camp in a spacious plain, which is terminated by two hills of a gentle ascent. **1851** DIXON *W. Penn* xxxii. (1872) 302 The house itself stood on a gentle eminence. **1860** TYNDALL *Glac.* I. xviii. 124 A gentle snow-slope brought us to the base of a precipice.

8. Of persons: Mild in disposition or behaviour; kind, tender. Also of language, actions, etc. Freq. in phr. ***a gentle hint. the gentle(r) sex*** : the female sex. **1552** HULOET, s.v., To waxe Gentle, *exeuio, mansuesco.* **1583** STUBBS *Anat. Abuses* Evijb, Yet (such is yᵉ magnificency & liberalitie of that gentle sex) that I trust I shall not be vnrewarded at their hands. **1725** POPE *Odyss.* XX. 388 A long cessation of discourse ensued, By gentler Agelaus thus renewed. **1812** J. WILSON *Isle of Palms* II. 307 But to yon gentle Maiden turn, Who never for herself doth mourn. **1839–40** W. IRVING *Wolfert's R.* (1855) 83 It is somewhat remarkable that..the gentler sex should have been most frequently the subjects of these rude trials. **1870** ROGERS *Hist. Gleanings* Ser. II. 42 Princes are seldom gentle when crossed. **1875** JOWETT *Plato* (ed. 2) III. 226 You have grown gentle towards me and have left off scolding. **1896** J. C. HARRIS *Sister Jane* 32 Taking this as a gentle hint, I went out. **1922** JOYCE *Ulysses* 354 She just gave a gentle hint about its being late.

9. Used advb. = GENTLY (esp. in *comparative*). **1601** SHAKS. *Jul. C.* I. ii. 231 Hee put it by thrice, euerie time gentler then other. *a* **1611** BEAUM. & FL. *Philaster* IV. iv, Lay me gentle on his neck. **1671** MILTON *Samson* 788 Men may censure thine The gentler, if severely thou exact not More strength from me, than in thyself was found. **1844** MRS. BROWNING *Drama of Exile* Poems 1850 I. 19 He [God] Did roll His thunder gentler at the close.

10. *Comb.* (chiefly parasynthetic and adverbial), as ***gentle-born, -breathing, -eyed, -gliding, -handed, -hearted, -licking, -looking, -mannered, -minded, -natured, -sleeping, -voiced*** ppl. adjs. *c* **1385** CHAUCER *L.G.W.* 2090 *Ariadne*, Syn that ye ben as *gentil born as I. **1725** RAMSAY *Gentle Sheph.* v. ii, It's no my fau't that I'm nae gentler born. **1859** TENNYSON *Elaine* 762 The gentler-born the maiden, the more bound..to be sweet and serviceable. **1600** FAIRFAX *Tasso* XV. ix. 6 A *gentle breathing aire made eu'n and plaine The azure face of heau'ns smooth looking glass. **1830** SCOTT *Auchindrane* I. ii, A young man, gentle-voiced and *gentle-eyed. **1612** DRAYTON *Poly-olb.* To Rdr., Delicate embrodered Meadowes often veined with *gentle gliding Brooks. **1863** I. WILLIAMS *Baptistery* II. xxxii. (1874) 189 With *gentle-handed charities. **1593** SHAKS. *3 Hen. VI*, I. iv. 176 And heere's to right our *gentle-hearted King. **1869** TROLLOPE *He Knew*, etc. xiii. (1878) 71 She was very gentle-hearted in regard to the fishes. **1648** HERRICK *Hesper.*, *To Musique to becalme his Fever*, Thou sweetly canst convert the same From a consuming fire, Into a *gentle-licking flame. **1612** DRAYTON *Poly-olb.* v. 294 The swelling surge, that with his fomie head, The *gentler looking Land with furie menaced. **1876** G. ELIOT in *Life* (1885) III. 276 A gentle-looking, clear-eyed, neatly made man. **1824** MISS MITFORD *Village* Ser. I. (1863) 187 But he managed every body, as your *gentle-mannered person is apt to do. **1795** W. SEWARD *Anecd.* II. 227 This beautiful and *gentle-minded woman. **1579–80** NORTH *Plutarch* (1676) 45 He was a *gentle-natured man, and one that loved quietness and peace. **1594** SHAKS. *Rich. III*, I. iii. 288, I will not thinke but they ascend the sky, And there awake Gods *gentle sleeping peace. **1830** *Gentle-voiced [see *gentle-eyed* above].

B. *sb.*

1. One who is of gentle birth or rank.

a. *rare* in *sing.* *c* **1400** *Destr. Troy* 128 Eson..Hade a son..And Iason þat gentill aioynet was to name. *Ibid.* 437 This gentill [Medea] by Iason ioinet was to sit. **1576** GASCOIGNE *Steele Gl.* (Arb.) 67 Art thou a Gentle? liue with gentle friendes. *a* **1603** BRETON in Farr *S.P. Eliz.* (1845) I. 178 Constancie, A worthie budde..Which every gentle certeinlie Delightes to chuse of. **1604** ROWLANDS *Looke to it* 16 You that are sonne to him that held the Plow, Transform'd by Gold, into a Gentle now. **1826** DISRAELI *Viv. Grey* v. iii, There is a gentle's voice under a dark cloak. *a* **1845** HOOD *Bianca's Dr.* iii, Ladies seldom vex An amorous gentle with a needless frown.

b. in *pl. Obs.* exc. *arch.*, or as a comic vulgarism for GENTLEFOLKS. *c* **1386** CHAUCER *Pard. Prol.* 37 And right anon the gentils gonne to crye, Nay, lat hym telle vs of no ribaudye. *c* **1400** MAUNDEV. (Roxb.) xxvi. 123 þe gentils hase schorte swerdez scharpe on þe ta syde. **1494** FABYAN *Chron.* VII. ccxxx. 261 But the gentyllys and commonnis, herynge of this mooste shamefull murder, assembled them togyder. **1557** TUSSER 100 *Points Husb.* xvii, When gentiles vse walking, with hawkes on their handes, Good husbandes, with grasing doe purchase their landes. **1598** BARRET *Theor. Warres* v. ii. 141 Men of qualitie & Gentles of good birth. **1641** BROME *Joviall Crew* v. (1652) N4b, To Knight, to Squire, and to the Gentiles here, We wish our Play may with content appear. **1788** MAD. D'ARBLAY *Diary* 16 Aug., All Cheltenham was drawn out into the High-street, the gentles on one side and the commons on the other. **1816** SCOTT *Old Mort.* xxxv, What made them send for a puir body like me, sae mony braw lords and gentles? **1868** GEO. ELIOT *Sp. Gipsy* I. 41 'Tis very hard When gentles sing for nought to all the town. **1882** *Mrs. Raven's Tempt.* III. 8 The simples are not bound to pick up what the gentles throw away.

†**c.** Used in polite address. *Obs.* *c* **1590** GREENE *Fr. Bacon* x. 16 Now, courteous Gentles, if the Keepers girle Hath pleas'd the liking fancy of you both [etc.]. **1591** *Troub. Raigne K. John*, To Gentlem. Rdrs. (1611) 70 Gentles, we left King John repleate with blisse. **1599** B. JONSON *Ev. Man out of Hum.* (1600) Prol., Gentles, all I can say for him is, you are welcome. **1638** COWLEY *Love's Riddle* v, It's no matter for that; farewell gentles. **1641** MARMION *Antiq.* III. F4a, Gentles I would entreat you a courtesie.

d. *Comb.* *c* **1550** *Robin Consc.* 101 in Hazl. *E.P.P.* III. 233 Bvt this shalbe only my preparation, To liue and goe gentle-like, gallant and gay.

2. = FALCON-GENTLE. **1776** PENNANT *Zool.* I. 152 The gentil and the goshawk are found in Scotland. **1833** [see GENTLE *a.* 1c].

3. A maggot, the larva of the flesh-fly or blue-bottle, employed as bait by anglers. (Cf. A. 5.) **1578** LYTE *Dodoens* VI. lxviii. 746 A white worme lyke a gentill. **1594** PLAT *Jewell-ho.* III. 12 White and glib worms, which the Anglers call Gentils. **1688** R. HOLME *Armoury* II. 193/1 The Cloudy, or Blackish Fly..proceed from Maggots, or Gentills, that breed of Putrified Flesh. **1741** *Compl. Fam.-Piece* II. ii. 336 Gentles are a very good Bait. **1851** D. JERROLD *St. Giles* xxiv. 251 As alive and wriggling as an angler's box of gentles. **1894** *Blackw. Mag.* Sept. 426/2 A gentle is placed on the hook.

gentle ('dʒɛnt(ə)l), *v.* [f. prec.]

†**1.** *trans.* To ennoble, dignify. *Obs. rare.* **1387–8** T. USK *Test. Love* II. viii. (Skeat) I. 100 Better is it thy kinne to been by the genteled, then thou to gloryfye of thy kinnes gentillesse, and hast no desert therof thy selfe. **1599** SHAKS. *Hen. V*, IV. iii. 63 Be he ne're so vile, This day shall gentle his Condition. **1630** J. TAYLOR (Water P.) *Wks.* III. 12/1 And all this raking toyle..Is for his clownish.. heyre, Who must be gentled by his ill got pelfe.

2. a. To render gentle, mild, or pleasant. **1651** *Raleigh's Ghost* 307 The consideration of the reward ..doth so temper and gentle the bitterness thereof, as that it maketh it to seem sweet and to be desired. **1883** MISS BROUGHTON *Belinda* II. III. i. 174 A smile..sweetening and gentling the now habitual sullenness of her face. **1908** *Daily Chron.* 3 Feb. 3/3 Tragic circumstances that are put with all the vigour of a strong hand, yet gentled by a beautiful thread of love. **1936** 'R. HYDE' *Passport to Hell* 23 Horse-dung trodden into the mire and yet gentled with the smell of warm straw. **1958** *Engineering* 28 Feb. 258/1 Whether a few rounds in the ring did in fact gentle his condition I was never able to discover.

b. To tame, break in, render tractable. **1735** R. LEE in *Virginia Hist. Mag.* III. 356 Y'r colts have not been gentled any, so that Charles can't lead them up. **1862** A. K. H. BOYD *Recreat. Country Parson* 72 A long course of kindness has gentled you [a horse] as well as Mr. Rarey could have done. **1887** MRS. C. READE *Maid o' the Mill* II. xxxix. 311 He has had much to do, a colt to gentle, and some ewes to doctor. **1894** *Harper's Mag.* Feb. 354, I strolled out to the corrals to see the bulls 'gentled'. *fig.* **1888** R. KIPLING *Plain Tales fr. the Hills* (1891) 289 A Viceroy who knew how to 'gentle' a fractious big man.

c. To soften, mollify (a person). *rare.* **1795** tr. *Moritz' Trav. Eng.* (Nat. Libr.) 142, I endeavoured to gentle him a little by asking for a mug of ale and once or twice drinking to him. **1847** BUSHNELL *Chr. Nurt.* vii. (1861) 173 They will all be gentled together by the tender brotherhood of the little ones.

3. *intr.* To become gentle. *rare.* **1912** J. MASEFIELD in *Eng. Rev.* Oct. 388 When the light gentles and the wind is soft. **1953** V. BUCHANAN-GOULD *Vast Heritage* i. 2 For a short time..the African world gentled to soft femineity.

Hence **'gentling** *vbl. sb.* and *ppl. a.* **1883** MISS BRADDON *Gold. Calf* xix. 211 She was wild and wilful, and wanted more gentling before she was brought to the lure. **1906** *Westm. Gaz.* 10 Sept. 2/3 Above the vale, with its gentling tale Of a life that is lived for right. **1952** E. HYAMS *Soil & Civilization* 167 The gentling influence of the Atlantic allows deciduous trees to grow farther north. **1966** *New Statesman* 4 Feb. 172/2 Within his gentling limits, Mr Sucksdorff seems authentic.

†**'gentleboy.** *Obs. rare*$^{-1}$. A young gentleman. **1685** CROWNE *Sir C. Nice* v, But I wou'd not dress like a Gentleboy, lag at my years among those Children, to play with their Toys.

†**gentledame.** *Obs. rare*$^{-1}$. A gentlewoman. **1647** WARD *Simp. Cobler* 24 When I heare a nugiperous Gentledame inquire what dresse the Queen is in this week.

gentlefolk, -folks ('dʒɛnt(ə)lfəʊk, -fəʊks). [f. as GENTLE *a.* + FOLK. The sing. first appears in this cent.; earlier writers use the pl. *folks.*] Persons of good position and family. **1594** SHAKS. *Rich. III*, I. i. 95 The Queene's Kindred are made gentle Folkes. *a* **1732** GAY *Wks.* (1745) I. 236 When gentle-folks their sweethearts leave behind They can write letters. **1787** M. CUTLER in *Life, Jrnls. & Corr.* (1888) I. 288 Freeman and his wife seem to be what we call in our country [New England] very great Gentlefolks. **1848** THACKERAY *Lett.* 1 Aug., Many hundreds of gentle-folks of all nations were congregated in the public walk. **1867** TROLLOPE *Chron. Barset* I. ix. 78 The neglected children, who are learning not to be the children of gentlefolk. **1897** *Atlantic Mag.* LXXIX. 136 Her people are eighteenth century gentle-folk. *Proverb.* **1897** *Pall Mall Mag.* Aug. 523 So it was a case of 'Compliments fly when gentlefolk meet'.

'gentle-,heart. Name of some plant. **1648** HERRICK *Hesper.*, *Nuptiall Song Sir C. Crew*, Prick-Madam, and..Gentle-heart, And soft Maidens-blush.

gentlehood ('dʒɛnt(ə)lhʊd). [See -HOOD.] Position or character attaching to gentle birth. **1860** TROLLOPE *Framley P.* III. xiii. 250 He..knew well what changes gentlehood would have demanded from him. **1881** MRS. LYNN LINTON *My Love* III. 224 That was her sole answer to his assertion of gentlehood and honour. **1883** —— *Girl of Period* I. 289 Time was when cruelty and falsehood were essentially sins which vitiated all claims to gentlehood. **1888** BESANT *Inner House* x. 142 When we allowed gentlehood to be destroyed, gentle manners, honour, dignity, and such old virtues went too.

gentlely(e, obs. form of GENTLY.

gentleman ('dʒɛnt(ə)lmən). Forms: see GENTLE and MAN; also GENTMAN, GEMMAN. [f. GENTLE + MAN, on the model of OF. *gentilz hom* (F.

gentilhomme) = It. *gentiluomo*, Sp. *gentilhombre*.]

1. a. A man of gentle birth, or having the same heraldic status as those of gentle birth; properly, one who is entitled to bear arms, though not ranking among the nobility (see quot. 1882), but also applied to a person of distinction without precise definition of rank. Now chiefly *Hist.*

a **1275** *Prov. Ælfred* 706 in *O.E. Misc.* 138 Hic ne sige nout bi þan, þat moni ne ben gentile man. **1297** R. Glouc. (Rolls) 6618 Gentil men þat he vond in prison ek ydo..he boȝte hom out also. **1340** *Ayenb.* 190 A riche ientilman wes y-robbed of þieues. *c* **1440** *York Myst.* xxx. 169 Ther schall a gentilman, Jesu, vn-justely be juged. *c* **1477** Caxton *Jason* 6 These two worthy Gentilmenn Hercules and Jason ouerthrew their felaws and gate the felde. **1493** *Festivall* (W. de W. 1515) 109 b, And Poule for he was a gentylman borne for the more worshyppe they smote of his heed. *a* **1529** Skelton *Poems agst. Garnesche* iv. 69 Thow thou be a jantyll man borne, Yet jentylnes in the ys thred bare worne. **1596** Spenser *State Irel.* Wks. (Globe) 672/1 Yf he can derive himselfe from the head of a septe..then he holdeth himselfe a gentellman. **1614** Selden *Titles Hon.* Pref. B iv, Hee that is so both *Εὐγενής* and *Γενναῖος* i. both discended from truly Noble Parentage, and withal following their steps, or adding to their Name, is the Gentleman that may lawfully glorie in his Title. **1671** Lady M. Bertie in *12th Rep. Hist. MSS. Comm.* App. v. 22 There are no men of quality but the Duke of Monmouth, all the rest are gentlemen. **1791** Mrs. Radcliffe *Rom. Forest* i, Pierre de la Motte was a gentleman descended from an ancient house of France. **1882** Cussans *Her.* xvi. (ed. 3) 215 Gentlemen are all those who, lawfully entitled to Armorial distinction, are not included in any of the before-mentioned degrees [of nobility]. **1884** Freeman in *Encycl. Brit.* XVII. 540/1 Early in the 11th century the order of 'gentlemen' as a separate class seems to be forming as something new.

†**b.** Appended to the name of a man, as an indication of his rank; often abbreviated as *Gent. Obs.*; but see sense 4 c.

1425 *Newminster Cartul.* (Surtees) 190 Joh. de Mitforde —gentilman. **1481** in *Surtees Misc.* (1888) 39 John Stathom jentilman, William Belasys jentilman..beris witness. **1591** (*title*) The Geomancie of Maister Christopher Cattan, Gentleman. **1706** (*title*) The New World of Words.. Compiled by Edward Phillips, Gent. **1791** Boswell *Johnson* (1831) I. 1 His father is there styled Gentleman, [but]..the appellation of Gentleman..was commonly taken by those who could not boast of gentility.

c. Used (with more or less of its literal meaning) as a complimentary designation of a member of certain societies or professions. Chiefly *pl. Obs.* in ordinary use.

1537 Wriothesley *Chron.* (1875) I. 61 One being a gentellman of the Inner Temple in London. **1581** W. Blandy *Cast. Policy* 18 b, Captayne, Lieutenent, Auncient, Serieant of a Company, gentleman in a company or of the Rounde, Lance passado. These are speciall; the other that remaine, priuate or common Souldiars. *c* **1661** in *12th Rep. Hist. MSS. Comm.* App. v. 6 Gervise Lucas served George Earle of Rutland as gentleman of his horse some yeares. **1670–1** Sir J. Turner *Pallas Armata* (1683) 218 A Gentleman of the company is he who is something more than an ordinary Souldier, hath a little more pay, and doth not stand Centinel. **1677** Yarranton *Eng. Improv.* 34 Three worthy Gentlemen of the Long Robe. **1681** Luttrell *Brief Rel.* I. 101 The addresse of some gentlemen of the Middle Temple was presented on Sunday last. **1713** in *Lond. Gaz.* No. 5086/2 The Gentlemen of the Horse and Grenadier Guards..who are..on the Out-Pension. **1768** J. Byron *Narr. Wager* (1778) 138, I leave it to the decision of the gentlemen of the faculty. **1867** Smyth *Sailor's Word-bk.*, *Gentlemen*, the messmates of the gunroom or cockpit—as mates, midshipmen, clerks, and cadets.

2. *spec.* **a.** A man of gentle birth attached to the household of the sovereign or other person of high rank; frequently with defining term added, as ***gentleman in waiting***, ***of the*** (***King's***) ***Chamber***, ***of the Chapel Royal***, etc.

1463 *Bury Wills* (Camden) 16 Item to eu'y gentylman of my lord abbotte wiche be comyng and goyng as officeres and menyal men longyng to the houshold of my felashippe. **1503** *Privy Purse Exp. Eliz. York* (1830) 96 To Richard Brampton gentilman of the pantry with the Quene. **1520** *Caxton's Chron. Eng.* III. 26 b/1 The gentylmen of the kynges housholde and the gentylmen of the Erles housholde of London after meet wente togyder for to play. **1561** *Cheque Bk. Chapel Royal* (Camden) 1 The Subdeanes and Gentlemen succeedinge since the third yeare of the raigne of Queen Elizabeth. **1630** *R. Johnson's Kingd. & Commw.* 142 Those which were then called Chamberlaines, are now Gentlemen of the Chamber. **1791–1823** in D'Israeli *Cur. Lit.* (1866) 559/2 *note*, He then called for his gentleman (a kind of humble friend whom noblemen used to retain under that name in those days). **1849** Macaulay *Hist. Eng.* iii. I. 315 In the reign of Henry the Seventh, fresh meat was never eaten even by the gentlemen attendant on a great earl. **1884** F. M. Crawford *Rom. Singer* I. 24 Now and then one of the young gentlemen-in-waiting from the Vatican strolls in and says his prayers.

b. †***gentleman-pensioner***, now ***gentleman-at-arms***: one of forty gentlemen who act as guards or attendants to the sovereign on state occasions.

1630 *R. Johnson's Kingd. & Commw.* 398 Guards of the Prince: which though they be souldiers in time of warre, yet are they but like our Gentlemen pensioners..in time of peace. **1702** *Lond. Gaz.* No. 3822/4 His Grace the Duke of St. Albans Captain of the Band of Gentlemen-Pensioners. **1706** Phillips (ed. Kersey) s.v. *Pensioner*, *The Queen's Pensioners*, or *Gentlemen-Pensioners*, a Band of Gentlemen so call'd, who are arm'd with Partisans, and attend as a Guard upon the Queen's Person in her Palace: They were first appointed A.D. 1539 and their Salary is 80 Pounds Sterling per Annum. **1859** A. de Fonblanque *How we are governed* 101 *note*, The corps of 'Gentlemen-at-arms' consists of a captain..and forty gentlemen. **1889** *John Bull* 2 Mar. 149/2 Her Majesty's Body Guard of the Hon. Corps of Gentlemen-at-Arms was on duty in the State saloons.

c. ***gentleman-at-large***, †a gentleman attached to the court but having no special duties assigned to him (*obs.*); hence jocularly in mod. use (after sense 4 c), one who is out of work.

1692 *Lond. Gaz.* No. 2809/3 The Gentlemen at large. **1862** Mrs. H. Wood *Mrs. Hallib.* II. iv. 168 You'd rather be a gentleman at large.

3. a. A man in whom gentle birth is accompanied by appropriate qualities and behaviour; hence, in general, a man of chivalrous instincts and fine feelings.

In this sense the term is frequently defined by reference to the later derived senses of 'gentle'.

c **1386** Chaucer *Melib.* ¶675 And certes he sholde nat be called a gentil man, that..ne dooth his diligence and bisynesse, to kepen his good name. *c* **1400** *Rom. Rose* 2197 Who so is vertuous, And in his post nought outrageous..he is gentil bycause he doth As longeth to a gentilman. **14..** *Qual. Gentlem.* in *Rel. Ant.* I. 252 Trauthe, pettee, fredome, and hardynesse..Off thisse virtues iiij. who lakkyth iij., He aught never gentylmane called to be. **1548** Hall *Chron.*, *Hen. VI*, 183 b, In this acte the lord Clyfford was accompted a tyraunt, and no gentelman. **1553** *Primer*, *Sundry godly prayers* P iv b, That as they be called gentle menne in name, so they maye shewe them selues in al theyr doinges gentle, curteous, louyng..vnto theyr inferiours. **1604** Dekker *1st Pt. Honest Wh.* (1635) K iv b, A soft, meeke, patient, humble, tranquill spirit; The first true Gentleman that ever breath'd. **1653** Walton *Angler* i. 13, I would rather prove my self to be a Gentleman, by being learned and humble, valiant and inoffensive, vertuous, and communicable, then by a fond ostentation of riches. **1710** Steele *Tatler* No. 207 ¶4 The Appellation of Gentleman is never to be affixed to a Man's Circumstances, but to his Behaviour in them. **1743** Appleton *Serm.* 153 The Gentle-Man will treat every Man with due Respect, and will be friendly, yielding, condescending, obliging, and ready to do a Kindness. **1821** Byron *Juan* III. xli, With such true breeding of a gentleman, You never could divine his real thought. **1834** T. Medwin *Angler in Wales* II. 287 Judges of the Exchequer were designated thus: one as a gentleman and a lawyer; another as a lawyer but no gentleman. **1894** Blackmore *Perlycross* 320 Because he is a gentleman..which a nobleman sometimes is not.

b. *transf.* In racing phrases, ***quite a gentleman***, etc., as a laudatory description of a horse.

1889 *Daily News* 27 Dec. 2/4 A trained and massive bay carthorse..who in pacing, prancing and stepping to music proved himself every inch a gentleman. **1891** *Field* 7 Mar. 334/1 Quite a gentleman, too, is the Compton Stud Company's Marioni..there is so much quality about him. **1894** *Daily News* 7 June 7/2 He [Ladas] is a gentleman all over.

4. a. A man of superior position in society, or having the habits of life indicative of this; often, one whose means enable him to live in easy circumstances without engaging in trade, a man of money and leisure. In recent use often employed (*esp.* in 'this gentleman') as a more courteous synonym for 'man', without regard to the social rank of the person referred to. *spec.* in *Cricket*: a non-professional player (opp. PLAYER[1] 2 c). Also *transf.* (See also FINE GENTLEMAN.)

1583 Hollyband *Campo di Fior* 233 He hath set his minde to keepe horses in stable, and to follow hunting: Thinking that he can not be a gentelman by other wayes. **1599** B. Jonson *Ev. Man out of Hum.* I. (1600) C 1 a, I haue lande and money, my friendes left mee well, and I will be a gentleman whatsoeuer it cost me. **1636** E. Dacres tr. *Machiavel's Disc. Livy* I. 219 Those are call'd gentlemen, that live in idlenesse yet deliciously of the profits of their estates, without having any care to cultivate their lands. **1700** S. L. tr. *Fryke's Voy. E. Ind.* 15 This old Gentleman was the first I saw buried after the Sea-fashion. **1727** De Foe *Eng. Tradesman* (1732) II. vi. 168 The rich Tradesman.. laid the Tradesman down and commenc'd Gentleman. **1762** Goldsm. *Nash* 209 The great error lies in imagining every fellow with a laced coat to be a gentleman. **1791** Hampson *Mem. J. Wesley* III. 114 Though gentlemen are often above being religious themselves, they seem generally to have agreed, that it is very proper for the vulgar. **1806** in F. Lillywhite *Cricket Scores & Biographies 1746–1826* (1862) I. 328 This being the first match between the Gentlemen and the Players. **1879** M. J. Guest *Lect. Hist. Eng.* lvi. 571 Gentlemen and tradesmen came forward to act as special constables. **1884** *Lillywhite's Cricket Ann.* 29 The two matches between the Gentlemen and Players. **1891** [see PLAYER[1] 2 c]. **1897** *Daily News* 30 Mar. 6/2 All shopkeepers are now 'young gentlemen' and 'young ladies'. **1966** *Listener* 25 Aug. 265/2 The social split..which I have described as the amateur and gentleman *versus* the professional and player. **1971** A. Price *Alamut Ambush* xii. 140 That calculated..amateurishness of his—the flouting of the rules to prove that he was a gentleman rather than a player.

b. In *pl.* used as a polite term of address to a company of men of whatever rank (corresponding to 'Sir' in sing.). †Also in *sing.* to one man.

1579 Lyly *Euphues* (Arb.) 49 Gentleman and friend, the tryall I haue had of thy manners [etc.]. *Ibid.* 205 *To the Gentlemen Readers.* I was driuen into a quandarie, Gentlemen, whether [etc.]. **1590** Shaks. *Mids. N.* III. i. 187 Your name, honest Gentleman? **1669** Dryden *Tyrannic Love* Epil. 3, I come, kind gentlemen, strange news to tell ye. *Ibid.* 25 But farewell, gentlemen. **1743** Bulkeley & Cummins *Voy. S. Seas* 93 The Captain said, Very well, Gentlemen, you have caught me Napping; I do not see any of you in Liquor. **1808** Grose *Antiq. Rep.* II. 405 All public addresses to a mixed assembly of both sexes, till sixty years ago, commenced Gentlemen and Ladies: at present it is Ladies and Gentlemen. **1851** *Househ. Words* No. 45. 436 'Aha!' exclaimed the director, '..This way, gentlemen!' **1872** Ruskin *Eagle's N.* §170 Gentlemen,—the word by which I at this moment address you [etc.]. **1897** *Westm. Gaz.* 15 July 7/1 Lady Henry Somerset..made a speech ..'Gentlemen and ladies,'—[etc.].

c. In legal documents used as the designation of a socially respectable person who has no specific occupation or profession. Cf. 1 b.

1862 *Daily Tel.* May, In the bill of sale..dated the 29th January, 1861, it was stated to be given by 'J. D... gentleman', Mr. Serjeant Petersdorff..called witnesses to show that Mr. D. was not 'a gentleman' at the time..and.. contended..that the misdescription vitiated the deed. Mr. Justice Willes: A gentleman is described in law as a person who has no occupation.

d. jocularly. ***to be a gentleman***: to have no work to do.

1859 Darwin *Let.* 23 Oct. in *Life & Lett.* (1887) II. 175 Now I am so completely a gentleman, that I have sometimes a little difficulty to pass the day.

e. *pl.* Designation of a public convenience for male persons. Freq. ***gentlemen's***, and with capital initial. Cf. GENT *sb.* b.

1929 'H. Green' *Living* xviii. 213 'You go and leave them in the Gentlemen.' 'Leave 'em in the lavatory?' **1933** S. Frazer *Acorned Hog* 78 Over on that platform's the general waiting-room,..and over there's the Gentlemen's, and, any'ow, everythink's written up. **1934** E. Waugh *Handful of Dust* iii. 117 'I tell you what I must do, is to telephone. Where is it?' ' D'you mean really the telephone or the gentlemen's?' **1941** J. Cary *Herself Surprised* xliv. 108 There are quays there and lamps and some squares of grass; a ladies and gentlemen, and a cinema.

5. a. In contemptuous or humorous uses; esp. ***old gentleman*** = old fellow, spec. the devil. ***my gentleman*** = 'the fellow'. Also a euphemism for a smuggler.

1622 Mabbe tr. *Aleman's Guzman d' Alf.* I. 55 But afterwards perceiuing, that..this piece of hangings came to be seene..the copy of my Gentlemans countenance was quickly altered, and began suddenly to looke blanke. **1698** Fryer *Acc. E. Ind. & P.* 311 That destructive custom of drinking Ice with their Liquors; which the Old Gentleman [Hippocrates] takes notice of to be of no good consequence. **1708** Yalden *Bickerstaff detected* in *Swift's Wks.* (1755) II. I. 163, I..was surprized to find my gentleman mounted on a table with a two-foot rule..measuring my walls. **1726** Shelvocke *Voy. round World* (1757) 402 Our ship was in an instant full of these swarthy gentlemen quite naked. **1727** De Foe *Hist. Appar.* (1729) 364 The Devil is not so black as he is painted, but that you may form such images of the old gentleman [etc.]. **1728** Vanbr. & Cib. *Prov. Husb.* IV. i. 88 *C. Bas.* Well, the Devil fetch me [etc.]. *Myr.* And may the Black Gentleman tuck me under his Arm at the same time. **1810** Anne Plumptre *Resid. France* I. xvii. 210 There is a certain old gentleman, whose name, we say in England, must not be pronounced in the hearing of polite ears. **1887** G. R. Sims *Mary Jane's Mem.* 57 How the old gentleman am I to earn my living? **1893** Earl Dunmore *Pamirs* II. 69 Nine rams..one of which had a very fine pair of horns, so I turned my particular attention to this old gentleman. **1906** Kipling *Puck of Pook's Hill* 251 Watch the wall, my darling, while the Gentlemen go by! **1929** G. Greene *Man Within* I. iv. 92 'You know who I am?'..'One of the Gentlemen.' **1966** E. & M. A. Radford *Death of 'Gentleman'* xxii. 188 A smuggler ..engaged in the Gentlemen's trade.

Phrase. **1785** Grose *Dict. Vulg. Tongue* s.v. *Churl*, To put a churl upon a gentleman; to drink malt liquor immediately after having drank wine.

b. ***gentleman's gentleman***: a valet.

1725 De Foe *Everybody's Bus.* (1841) 20 The complaints against the maids are as well masculine as feminine, and very applicable to our gentlemen's gentlemen. **1771** Smollett *Humph. Cl.* (1857) 35, I took down the name from his gentleman, Mr. O'Frizzle. [Said by a maid servant.] **1775** Sheridan *Rivals* II. ii, You gentlemen's gentlemen are so hasty. **1820** Lady Granville *Lett.* (1894) I. 186 The gentlemen's gentlemen and two impudent Englishmen had been examined. **1848** Thackeray *Van. Fair* xliv, The footman told the circumstance as a good joke to Lord Steyne's coachman; that officer imparted it to Lord Steyne's gentleman, and to the servants' hall in general. **1886** Mallock *Old Order Changes* I. 193 'Here's grandeur!' said Mrs. Harley. 'Maids, cockades, footmen and gentlemen's gentlemen!'

c. In humorous or slang phrases. †***gentleman of the first head***, ***of the first house***: used as terms of contempt. ***the*** (***old***) ***gentleman in black***: the Devil. ***the gentleman in black velvet***: a mole (a Jacobite phrase, referring to the belief that the death of William III was caused by his horse's stumbling over a mole-hill). ***gentleman in brown***: a bed-bug. ***gentleman in red***: a soldier. ***gentleman of fortune***: a pirate. ***gentleman of the road***: (*a*) a highwayman; also *ellipt.* as *gentleman*; (*b*) a commercial traveller; (*c*) a gypsy. ***gentleman of the short staff***: a constable. ***gentleman of the three outs*** (see quots. 1785, 1830). †***the gentleman that*** (or ***who***) ***pays the rent*** (Obs.): a pig.

1611 Cotgr., *Gentilhomme de ville*, a Gentleman of the first head, an vpstart Gentleman. *a* **1625** Fletcher *Wom. Prize* IV. i, But to be made..a Gentleman o' the first house For all my kindness to her. **1663** Dryden *Wild Gallant* III. i, I have not yet spoke with the gentleman in the black pantaloons; you know he seldom walks abroad by day-light. **1681** —— *Sp. Friar* v. ii, *Ped.* Gomez, give way to the old gentleman in black [the friar]. *Gom.* No! the t'other old gentleman in black shall take me if I do; I will speak first! **1718** *Entertainer* 294 The Gentlemen of the Pad, and those that Rob on the Road, shall die at the Tree for Actions trifling..with respect to these. **1728** Gay *Begg. Op.* III. xvi. 57 The fine Gentlemen imitate the Gentlemen of the Road. **1774** Lee in *Burke's Corr.* (1844) I. 513 We gentlemen in red never chose to remember that..the provincials never led the flight. **1778** J. Wedgwood *Let.* 19 Mar. (1965) 218, I got some knowledge of the gentlemen..and sent some of my people in pursuit of them who soon brought me in two of the robbers. **1785** Grose *Dict. Vulg. Tongue, Gentlemen of three outs*, i.e. without money, without wit, and without manners. **1805** Mrs. Burke *Secr. Cavern* II. 29 Lady Letitia..had been bred in the stable with her brother's grooms, and carried the manners..the attitudes and looks of those gentlemen of the whip into all the circles where her rank gained her admittance. **1809** [see road *sb.* 5 b]. **1814** Scott *Wav.* xi, The little gentleman in black velvet who did such service in 1702. **1830** Lytton *P. Clifford* iv, A gentleman of three outs—'out of pocket, out of elbows, and out of credit'. **1839** H. Ainsworth *J. Sheppard* I. ii, In the language of the gentleman of the short staff. **1855** Mrs. Gaskell *Squire's Story* in *Novels & Tales* (1873) IV. 228 Kate Hearn's husband collected his rents on the highway, like many another 'gentleman' of the day. **1869** Trollope *Vicar of Bullhampton* v. xxix. 184 They had no coffee room at the Bull, and strangers who came that way were of necessity shown into that in which the gentlemen of the road were wont to relax themselves. **1883** Stevenson *Treas. Isl.* II. xi, By a 'gentleman of fortune' they plainly meant neither more nor less than a common pirate. **1885** Sala in *Daily Tel.* 14 Aug. 5/3 Bed bugs..are the disagreeable insects known in modern polite English as 'Norfolk Howards', or 'gentlemen in brown'. **1907** G. B. Shaw *J. Bull's Other Island* IV. 80 The gintleman that pays the rint... They call a pig that in England. **1969** K. Giles *Death cracks Bottle* viii. 96 'A survival of the gentlemen of the road—all little cads.. today.'..'I should say..that Mr Rumly is the best in the business of selling wines.' **1969** *Radio Times* 3 Apr. 9/1 Gentlemen of the Road—a study of the Gypsy way of life.

6. *transf.* **a.** An apparatus used in soldering circular pewter ware (see quot.).

1875 Knight *Dict. Mech.* 2241 The work is supported on a revolving pedestal *b*, termed the *gentleman*, which may be adjusted by a side-screw to any desired hight.

b. The gannet or solan goose (*Sula bassana*).

1884–5 *Riverside Nat. Hist.* (1888) IV. 188 Other names bestowed upon these birds [gannets] are 'gentleman' or 'Jan van Gent'.

7. *attrib.* and *Comb.*: **a.** used *appositively* in various designations referring to pursuits, professions, etc. to denote that the person so styled is of superior rank to those who ordinarily follow the same occupation; also as attribute (often contemptuous or sarcastic) to any personal designation; as ***gentleman-adventurer***, ***-agent***, ***-atheist***, ***-beggar***, ***-cadet***, ***-covenanter***, ***-dependant***, ***-harbinger***, ***-jailer***, ***-jockey***, ***-lacquey***, ***-lodger***, ***-murderer***, ***-porter***, ***-priest***, ***-ranker***, ***recusant***, ***-rider***, ***-scholar***, ***-sewer***, ***tradesman***, ***-volunteer***, ***-waiter***; ***gentleman-cricketer***, ***-player***; see also GENTLEMAN-COMMONER, -FARMER, -USHER; **b.** humorously for 'male', as in ***gentleman-hound***, ***-turkey***; **gentleman friend**, a beau; a boy-friend.

1726 Shelvocke *Voy. round World* Pref. 25 [Capt. Clipperton] often express'd himself with the greatest contempt of the *Gentlemen-Adventurers, who had entrusted him with so large a share in the conduct of so promising an Expedition. **1896** R. Kipling *Seven Seas, Last Chantey*, Then said the souls of the gentlemen-adventurers ..'Ho, we revel in our chains O'er the sorrow that was Spain's.' **1711** Shaftesb. *Charac.* (1737) III. 337 'Tis not immediately from God Himself, but thro' the magistrate.. that these *gentlemen-agents are appointed..and set over us. **1664** H. More *Myst. Iniq.* 508, I averre no more to the *Gentleman Atheist..touching the resurrection than [etc.]. **1843** H. Gavin *Feigned Dis. Soldiers* 11 This class comprehends the professed mendicant, whether vagrant or stationary, whether gipsy or *gentleman-beggar. **1775** *Gentleman cadet [see cadet 3]. **1840** in A. Ponsonby *H. Ponsonby* (1942) 19 Every one of the Masters speaks of Gentleman Cadet Ponsonby in very favourable terms. **1953** E. Smith *Guide Eng. Traditions* 7 Up to 1939 those who gained high enough positions in the annual entrance examinations received (at their own expense) special military training as Gentleman Cadets at Sandhurst and Woolwich. **1639** Drumm. of Hawth. *Consid. to Parlt.* Wks. (1711) 187 That it shall be lawful for all *gentlemen-covenanters to kiss all gentle-women at all assemblies. **1885** F. Gale *Life R. Grimston* vi. 64 The M.C.C. was a small club..containing only from three to four hundred members, who were..all good *gentlemen cricketers. **1886** W. J. Tucker *E. Europe* 174 When persons they consider their equals are beneath their roof, they have a strange way, peculiarly their own, of snubbing the *gentleman-dependent. **1829** M. B. Smith *Let.* 27 Nov. in *Forty Yrs. Washington Soc.* (1906) 307 We have at least 6 or 7 young *gentlemen friends, who are frequently with us. **1894** Somerville & 'Ross' *Real Charlotte* III. xxxvi. 50 She respected him, an emotion not hitherto awakened by a varied experience of 'gentlemen friends'. **1935** Marsh & Jellett *Nursing-Home Murder* xii. 187, I hope you were not very shocked at what my gentleman-friend said..? **1970** R. Rendell *Guilty Thing Surprised* v. 58 My gentleman friend come in about seven. **1548** W. Patten *Exped. Scotl.* H viij a, *Gentleman harbynger of ye armie. **1843** Lytton *Last Bar.* I. viii, The patient Mongrel carries off the bone from the *gentlemen-hounds. **1864** A. McKay *Hist. Kilmarnock* 75 They were led to the bar accompanied by the *gentleman-jailer. **1829** *Sporting Mag.* XXIII. 265 That *gentleman-jockey..Lord George Germaine. **1726** Amherst *Terræ Fil.* I. 2 We do not find upon record one instance of any *gentleman-lacquey, who was turn'd out of doors upon this account. **1678** Dryden *Limberham* III. i, There might be some *gentleman-lodger in the house. **1897** *Daily News* 2 Dec. 8/1 Young Nicholson's dinner at Cabul with a company of *gentleman-murderers. **1823** M. R. Mitford in *Lady's Mag.* July 386/1 A set match at Lord's ground for money..between a certain number of *gentlemen players, as they are called—people who make a trade of that noble sport. **1832** P. Egan *Bk. Sports* 346/1 Who can beat twenty-two, with some wickets to spare, Of the gentlemen-players. **1906** A. E. Knight *Compl. Cricketer* ix. 299 The real gentleman player has no love for these miserable..labels and distinctions. **1642** in Rushw. *Hist. Coll.* III. (1692) I. 783 Drake and his Party went up to the *Gentleman-Porter, and demanded the Keys of the Gates. **1602** T. Fitzherbert *Apol.* 5 a, Two rare *gentlemen Priests and religious learned fathers Southwel and Walpoole. **1890** R. Kipling *City Dreadf. Nt.* 30 He who knows their composition [Calcutta European Police] knows some startling stories of *gentlemen-rankers. **1627** in *Crt. & Times Chas. I* (1848) I. 285 We hear that the *gentlemen recusants of the loan shall shortly be set at liberty. **1843** Lever *J. Hinton* ix. (1878) 56 That singular anomaly in our social condition, a *gentleman rider, ready upon any occasion to get into the saddle for any one that engaged his services. **1586** W. Webbe *Eng. Poetrie* (Arb.) 34 The learned company of *Gentlemen Schollers, and students of the Vniuersities, and Innes of Courte. **1748** Chesterf. *Lett.* (1792) II. clxiv. 93 Those who have read the most Latin, write the worst; and this distinguishes the Latin of a gentleman scholar from that of a pedant. *a* **1618** Raleigh *Rem.* (1644) 134 Demophon, which was *Gentleman-Sewer to Alexander. **1727** De Foe *Eng. Tradesman* (1732) I. xii. 146 It is the ordinary excuse of the *gentlemen tradesmen of our times, that they have good servants. **1855** S. A. Hammett *Adv. Capt. Priest* xvi. 111 A pugnacious *gentleman turkey. **1800** *Asiat. Ann. Reg., Char.* 35/2 He.. received the allowance of a *gentleman volunteer, a character at this time common in Portugueze India. **1630** *R. Johnson's Kingd. & Commw.* 142 They which were wont to be called Pantlers, Tasters and Carvers, are now called *Gentlemen Wayters of the Court.

c. gentlemen's (or **-man's**) **agreement** orig. *U.S.*, an agreement which is not enforceable at law, and which is only binding as a matter of honour; **Gentleman's Relish**, the proprietary name of a savoury paste (paste *sb.* 1 d).

1929 Wodehouse *Mr. Mulliner Speaking* vi. 201 What we had better do is to have a gentleman's agreement. **1930** *Times Lit. Suppl.* 27 Feb. 153/3 By a gentleman's agreement —if one may use such a term when speaking of ruffians who now have not even courage to commend them—rival gangs enjoyed the monopoly of trade in different districts. **1931** J. K. Winkler *Morgan the Magnificent* vii. 107 In 1886..was the first of a series of memorable dinner-table conferences. At them were formulated so-called 'gentlemen's agreements'. **1971** Lord Avon in *Listener* 7 Oct. 472/1 I'd made an agreement with Mussolini which he'd dubbed 'the Gentlemen's Agreement', by which we were both going to observe certain conditions about Spain. **1907** *Trade Marks Jrnl.* 17 Apr. 676 *Patum Peperium The Gentleman's Relish*... For Toast, Biscuits, &c. London. Potted Meat. Charles Augustus Osborn..Manufacturer. **1918** H. G. Wells *Joan & Peter* ix. 291 Perhaps a sandwich, Gentleman's Relish or shrimp paste. **1950** *Trade Marks Jrnl.* 6 Dec. 1033/1 *The Gentleman's Relish.* Food pastes consisting principally of anchovy extracts. C. Osborn & Company Limited.. Manufacturers. **1966** 'K. Nicholson' *Hook, Line & Sinker* v. 61 There was woodcock pâté, Gentleman's Relish, home-made black cherry jam.

Hence '**gentlemaning** *vbl. sb.*, the action of playing the gentleman; '**gentlemanism**, 'the state of being a gentleman, the affectation of gentlemanliness' (Ogilvie 1882); '**gentlema,nize** *v.*, to make into a gentleman. *nonce-wds.*

1833 *Fraser's Mag.* VIII. 709 Our nobility must have their menials all gentlemanised. **1885** Howells *S. Lapham* ii, Yes; gentlemaning as a profession has got to play out in a generation or two. **1898** G. B. Shaw in *Sat. Rev.* 29 Jan. 139/1 The dream-fed gentlemanism of the age which Shakespear inaugurated in English literature.

'gentleman-'commoner. [commoner 6.]

1. One of a privileged class of undergraduates formerly recognized in the Universities of Oxford and Cambridge.

Gentlemen commoners were distinguished from ordinary commoners by special academic dress, by dining at a separate table, by various immunities with respect to lectures, etc., and by the payment of higher fees. The term is now practically obsolete, but certain graduates of Christ Church, and three members of St. Mary Hall, are entered in the *Oxford University Calendar* (1898) under this title.

1687 Wood *Life* 7 Feb. (O.H.S.) II. 210 Mr. Edw. Hales, a gent. commoner, spake at a desk an eloquent English speech. **1709** Steele & Swift *Tatler* No. 71 ¶8, I believe a Gentleman-Commoner would as soon have the heels of his Shoes red as his Stockings. **1733** Humphreys *Life Prior* in *P.'s Poems* III. 3 To accomplish such a generous Intention this Noble Lord sent him, as a Gentleman-Commoner to St. John's College in Cambridge. **1791** Boswell *Johnson* 31 Oct. an. 1728, They were both entered, Corbett as a gentleman commoner and Johnson as a commoner. **1846** McCulloch *Acc. Brit. Empire* (1854) II. 347 This college [Brasenose] usually holds in residence a small number of gentlemen commoners, and about 100 commoners. **1884** M. Pattison *Mem.* (1885) 68 A goodly array of silk gowns— gentlemen-commoners, as they are invidiously called.

2. *slang.* An empty bottle.

1785 in Grose *Dict. Vulg. Tongue.*

'gentleman-'farmer. A country gentleman engaged in farming, usually on his own estate; a farmer who holds a better social position than the generality of his class.

1749 Fielding *Tom Jones* VIII. xi, My father was one of those whom they call gentlemen-farmers. He had a little estate of about 300*l.* a year. **1802** *Edin. Rev.* I. 111 The scarcity was produced by the higher order of farmers, whom he calls Gentlemen-farmers. **1864** Knight *Passages Work. Life* I. i. 19 The 'yeoman' of those days..would now be recognised as 'gentleman-farmer'.

gentlemanhood ('dʒɛnt(ə)lmənhʊd). [-hood.] The position or character of a gentleman.

1767 Cowper *Let.* 3 Apr., Wks. 1835 I. 193 When he hears me called 'That fellow Cowper'..he may be able..to assert my gentlemanhood. **1827** Lamb *Lett.* (1888) II. 187 What do I miss in him, then, of the essentials of gentlemanhood? **1889** Hamerton *French & Eng.* 250 Why not leave gentlemanhood and ladyhood to rich people, and why not be content with simple manhood and womanhood?

gentlemanlike ('dʒɛnt(ə)lmənlaɪk), *a.* and *adv.* [f. gentleman + like.] **A.** *adj.*

1. Of character, actions, pursuits, etc.: Appropriate or natural to a gentleman.

1557 North tr. *Gueuara's Diall Pr.* (1619) 626/2 Wearing that that is comely and Gentlemanlike. **1650** Bulwer *Anthropomet.* 22 Hard-head and Block-head..would be taken for terms of honour and Gentleman-like qualifications. **1709** Steele *Tatler* No. 37 ¶2 The most accomplish'd Man in this Kingdom for all Gentleman-like Activities and Accomplishments. **1792** *Munchausen's Trav.* iii. 9, I was..at liberty to sport away my time and money in the most gentlemanlike manner. **1838–9** Hallam *Hist. Lit.* III. vii. III. §30. 370 We have nowhere in our early writers ..an absence of quaintness, pedantry, and vulgarity, so truly gentlemanlike. **1882** Miss Braddon *Mt. Royal* II. ix. 170 It would have been more gentlemanlike to hold my tongue.

absol. **1864** Lowell *Fireside Trav.* 71 The gentleman-like pervaded even his prayers.

2. Of persons: Resembling a gentleman in appearance or conduct.

1581 Pettie *Guazzo's Civ. Conv.* II. (1586) 87 For the more good parts be in a man, the more Gentlemanlike he is saide to bee. **1669** Pepys *Diary* 14 May, It was a mockery by one Cornet Bolton, a very gentleman-like man. **1759** *Compl. Lett.-writer* (ed. 6) 226 He was elegantly dresst and Gentleman-like. **1808** Scott *Fam. Lett.* 4 Mar. (1894) I. 99 He is a well-educated and gentleman-like man. **1879** Froude *Cæsar* xxviii. 483 He [Cæsar] was quiet and gentlemanlike, with the natural courtesy of high breeding.

3. *Comb.*, as ***gentlemanlike-looking*** adj.

1823 T. Moore *Mem.* (1853) IV. 103 Knocklofty, a very gentlemanlike-looking place.

†**B.** *adv.* After the fashion of a gentleman.

1542 Udall *Erasm. Apoph.* 44 a, When certain persones did by ye waye of reproche cast in his teeth that he liued gentlemanlike and passyng deintyly. **1602** Rowlands *Greenes Ghost* 13 How manie haue we about London, y^t to the disgrace of Gentlemen liue gentlemanlike of themselues hauing neither mony nor land. **1606** Day *Ile of Guls* Prol., You should not deale gentleman-like with us els.

Hence '**gentlemanlikeness** (*nonce-wd.*).

1849 Thackeray in *Scribner's Mag.* I. 674/2 Go I must, to be killed by his melancholy gentlemanlikeness.

gentlemanliness ('dʒɛnt(ə)lmənlɪnɪs). [f. next + -ness.] The attribute of being gentlemanly.

1580 Hollyband *Treas. Fr. Tong, Generosité*, gentlemanlinesse, courage. **1611** Cotgr., *Noblesse*, nobilitie, gentrie, generousnesse, gentlemanlinesse. **1831** Arnold *Let.* in Stanley *Life & Corr.* (1844) II. App. C. 389 A spirit of unaffected kindness..which the spirit of gentlemanliness has doubtless greatly dulled in the Church of England. **1866** Geo. Eliot *F. Holt* xxxvi, To behave to Esther with a frank gentlemanliness.

gentlemanly ('dʒɛnt(ə)lmənlɪ), *a.* and *adv.* [f. gentleman + -ly.] **A.** *adj.*

1. Of persons: Having the character, behaviour, or appearance of a gentleman.

1433 Lydg. *S. Edmund* II. 128 This said Lothbrok was.. riht gentilmanly in al his demenyng. **1454** W. Paston in *P. Lett.* No. 216 I. 303 He is countyd a jantyllmanly man and a wurshepfull. **1548** Udall, etc. *Erasm. Par. Luke* xv. 127 b, He must be a ientilmanly disciple of the ryght makyng orels none at all. **1615** J. Stephens *Satyr. Ess.* 215 But fooles of his owne fashion praise him, for a..gentlemanly Fellow. **1720** Swift *Fates Clergymen* Wks. 1755 II. II. 25 The better scholar, and more gentlemanly person of the two. **1882** Ballantine *Recoll. Barrister* I. 78 He [Sir F. Roe] was a tall, handsome, gentlemanly man.

†**b.** Of race or family: Having the position of gentlefolks. *Obs. rare.*

1587 Fleming *Contn. Holinshed* III. 282/1 Simon Sudburie..descended of a gentlemanlie race. *Ibid.* 378/2 The gentlemanlie familie of the Theobalds.

2. Natural or appropriate to a gentleman.

1581 Pettie *Guazzo's Civ. Conv.* II. (1586) 90 Those who not onelie want the gentlemanlie instinct, but besides liue dissolutely. **1581** Studley tr. *Seneca's Hippol.* 55 The gentlemanly pastime of hunting. **1615** W. Lawson *Orch. & Gard.* (1626) 17 In so good, Gentlemanly, Scholerlike, and profitable a Faculty. **1712** Steele *Spect.* No. 490 ¶8 The Word *Consort*..would..give a more Gentlemanly Turn to the Epigram. **1818** *Gentl. Mag.* LXXXVIII. II. 247 These lectures are highly beneficial, both in diffusing among the votaries of the severer studies a gentlemanly portion of general information [etc.]. **1826** Croker in *C. Papers* (1884) I. xi. 352 The Duke often expressed a high opinion of what we call the gentlemanly spirit. **1861** Hughes *Tom Brown* i, We keep very gentlemanly hours.

3. *Comb.*, an ***gentlemanly-looking*** adj.

1861 Neale *Notes Dalmatia*, etc. 97 A portly, gentlemanly-looking Canon. **1897** Mary Kingsley *W. Africa* 232 One of them is a gentlemanly-looking man, who wears a gray shirt.

B. *adv.* As befits a gentleman. Now *rare.*

1412–20 Lydg. *Chron. Troy* I. v. So gentylmanly they demeaned were. **1440** in *Lett. Illustr. Wars in France* (Rolls) II. 307 Also Y pray ȝoue that ȝe wylle sende me worde.. what yt costyth; for trwly Y wulle chentylmanly aquyte ȝoure labour. **1534** More *Let. to Marg. Roper* Wks. 1429/1 Maister doctour Wilson..was..gentilmanly sent streight vnto the towre. **1586** *Cyv. & Vncyv. Life* To Gentlem. Rdrs., Euery Gentleman wil gentlemanly iudge of all things. **1834** T. Medwin *Angler in Wales* II. 284 Like Horace's Satires, where the *ridiculum* and *acre* are so gentlemanly combined.

†**'gentlemanry.** *Obs. rare*⁻¹. [-RY.] = GENTLEMANHOOD, GENTLEMANSHIP.

1550 BECON *Fortr. Faithful* Wks. 1560 II. 129 They thynke all nobilitie to consist in the abundaunce of worldlye goodes..And to set fourth this their gentlemanry they polle they pyl, they wake, they rake [etc.].

gentlemanship ('dʒɛnt(ə)lmənʃɪp). [-SHIP.]

1. Gentlemanhood; the position, character, or conduct of a gentleman.

1541 PAYNEL *Catiline* xix. 34b, Sometyme his newe gentilmanshyp was objected agaynste hym. **1613** R. CAWDREY *Table Alph.* (ed. 3), *Gentilitie*, gentry, nobilitie, gentlemanship. **1790** COWPER *Let. to Lady Hesketh* 7 July, Wks. 1836 IV. 198 Princes and peers reduced to plain gentlemanship. **1870** *Athenæum* 22 Oct. 523 He had, by right of Irish gentlemanship, been living at free quarters wherever he could thrust himself. **1881** BLACKIE *Lay Serm.* vi. 216 The normal type of manhood, gentlemanship [etc.].

2. The office of a gentleman (-in-waiting, etc.).

a **1613** OVERBURY *A Wife*, etc. (1638) 120 The last yeare of his gentlemanship. **1864** CARLYLE *Fredk. Gt.* IV. 252 Gentlemanship of the Chamber.

'gentleman-'usher. A gentleman acting as usher to a person of superior rank. ***Gentleman-usher of the Black Rod*** (see BLACK ROD).

1485 *Rot. Parl. 1 Hen. VII*, VI. 372/2 Oon of oure Gentilmen Hushers. **1503** *Privy Purse Exp. Eliz. York* (1830) 91 Item to John Whiting gentilman huissher of the chambre with the Kinges grace, xls. **1549** COVERDALE, etc. *Erasm. Par. 1 John* 47 What appeare they to be elles than Antichristes gentilmen husshers. **1609** DEKKER *Guls Hornbk.* v. 22 Walk vp and downe by the rest as scornfully and as carelesly as a Gentleman Vsher. **1621** BURTON *Anat. Mel.* III. i. II. iii. (1651) 422 Our old Poets..made Mercury the Gentleman-usher to the Graces. **1701** *Lond. Gaz.* No. 3714/1 The Commons were sent up for by Mr. Aston, Deputy Gentleman-Usher of the Black Rod. **1714** SWIFT *Pres. St. Aff.* Wks. 1755 II. I. 209 Many of them required no more abilities than would serve to qualify a gentleman-usher at court. **1840** DICKENS *Barn. Rudge* xxvii, He announced him in the voice of a gentleman-usher.

†**'gentlemany,** *a. Obs.* = GENTLEMANLY.

The first quot. perh. may not be an example of this word.

1489 *Paston Lett.* No. 908 III. 352 It were best for yow to purvey yow of some gentyl meny thynges ageyns the Kyngs comyng. **1694** SIR W. HOPE *Swordman's Vade-Mecum* [several times]. **1714** —— *New Method Fencing* 47 Those I formerly published upon this Gentlemany Subject. *Ibid.* 6. **1719** *Sc. Presbyt. Eloquence* (ed. 3) 135 One Mr. Thomas Ramsay..said in a Sermon..there is a Gentlemanny Preaching, and a Common-manny preaching.

gentleness ('dʒɛnt(ə)lnɪs). [f. GENTLE + -NESS.]

†**1.** One's inherited nature. *Obs.*⁻¹

a **1300** *Cursor M.* 28562 Þi smale sinnes..comand of vr gentilnes.

†**2.** The state or condition of being gentle in respect of birth or social position. *Obs.*

c **1450** *Merlin* 99 Gentilnesse ne richesse shall haue no power a-gein the wille of Ihesu criste. **1572** [see GENEROSITY 1]. **1671** F. PHILLIPS *Reg. Necess.* 208 A ready way to honour and gentleness, or the bearing of armes.

†**b.** In animals: Excellence of breed. *Obs.*

1398 TREVISA *Barth. De P.R.* XVIII. c. (1495) 846 The gentylnesse of the bulle is knowe..by sterne face and full eeres: and in hornes and in face dysposyd to fyghtyng.

3. The state or condition of being gentle in temper and conduct; †good breeding, courtesy, affability (*obs.*); kindliness, mildness.

c **1374** CHAUCER *Compl. Mars* 175 My lady is the verrey sours and welle Of beaute, luste, fredam, and gentilnesse. *c* **1400** *Rom. Rose* 3746 Graunte hym a kis, of gentilnysse! *a* **1450** *Le Morte Arth.* 1083 His gentilnesse was alle a-way, Alle churlysshe maners he had in wone. **1509** FISHER *Funeral Serm. C'tess Richmond* Wks. (1876) 296 For the straungers..what labour she of her veray gentylenes wolde take with them to bere them maner and company. **1548** HALL *Chron., Hen. V*, 34b, The kyng..required the prelates that if he were a straied shepe, rather by gentlenes then by rigoure to reduce hym to his olde flocke. **1581** PETTIE *Guazzo's Civ. Conv.* III. (1586) 171 Nothing maketh the servant more insolent and glorious, then ye over great gentlenesse of the maister. **1670–1** MARVELL *Corr.* Wks. 1872–5 II. 364 And had not the gentlenesse of the House prevailed, one or two of their own members were in great danger. **1743** APPLETON *Serm.* 152 By Gentleness we may understand..a sweet, soft, pleasant, obliging Temper. **1855** MACAULAY *Hist. Eng.* xvii. IV. 36 His eloquence, his probity, and the singular gentleness of his temper and manners, had made him the favourite of the Londoners. **1875** JOWETT *Plato* (ed. 2) IV. 287 He is full of gentleness, and flows on silently like a river of oil.

4. The state of being gentle (in other senses of the adj.); freedom from harshness or violence, etc.

1614 MARKHAM *Cheap Husb.* I. v. (1668) 40 Having scop't him a little, walk him with all gentleness home. **1626** BACON *Sylva* §610 And that (no doubt) is caused, by the Supplenesse and Gentlenesse of the Iuyce of that Plant. **1661** J. CHILDREY *Brit. Bacon.* 5 Its Maritime scituation is the cause of the gentleness of the Winter. **1693** SALMON *Bates' Disp.* (1715) 460/1 It operates with a world of gentleness, and therefore may be given to the most delicate ..Constitution. **1765** A. DICKSON *Treat. Agric.* (ed. 2) 214 The gentleness of its [a plough's] sloping towards the head.

†**b.** *pl.* Elegancies. *Obs.*⁻¹

1609 B. JONSON *Sil. Wom.* IV. i, I loue measure i' the feet, and number i' the voice: they are gentlenesses, that oft-times draw no lesse then the face.

'gentle-,people. = GENTLEFOLK.

1862 MRS. H. WOOD *Mrs. Hallib.* I. xxiv. 128 The trials..of the poor..are as nothing compared with the bitter lot of reduced gentlepeople. **1863** KINGSLEY *Water Bab.* vii. (1878) 288 So that gentlepeople's hunting is all spoilt.

†**'gentlery.** *Obs. rare.* Also 3 genteleri, 5 gentlore, 7 gentilrie. [f. GENTLE *a.* + -RY.] **a.** = GENTLEHOOD, GENTLESHIP. **b.** = GENTRY.

a **1275** *Prov. Ælfred* 708 in *O.E. Misc.* 138 Þuru þis lore and genteleri, he amendit huge companie. *c* **1420** *Liber Cocorum* (1862) 35 Heroun rostyd..Þat a knyȝt is called for gentlore. **1609** HOLLAND *Amm. Marcell.* XIV. vi. 13 The Nobilitie and Gentilrie.

attrib. *c* **1460** *Towneley Myst.* xiii. 18 We ar so hamyd.. We ar mayde hand tamyd, with thyse gentlery men.

gentleship ('dʒɛnt(ə)lʃɪp). *rare.* [-SHIP.] The condition or quality of being a gentleman.

a **1568** ASCHAM *Scholem.* I. (Arb.) 60 Som, in France, which will nedes be Ientlemen..and haue more ientleshipe in their hat, than in their hed. **1821** *New Monthly Mag.* II. 303 That part of the present generation which is growing up in real gentleship around me.

gentlewoman ('dʒɛnt(ə)lwʊmən). [f. GENTLE *a.* + WOMAN, after OF. *gentilfemme, gentifemme.*]

1. A woman of good birth or breeding.

c **1230** *Hali Meid.* 9 Biset uuele as gentille wimmen mest alle nu oworlde. **13..** *Coer de L.* 1574 As I am gentylwoman, Kyng Rychard wol do yow but good. **1377** LANGL. *P. Pl.* B. XI. 240 Ihesus Crist on a Iewes doghter lighte Gentil womman though she were Was a pure pore mayde. *a* **1450** *Knt. de la Tour* (1868) 20 For a gentille woman shuld haue no wrathe in hem, for thei aught to haue gentille herte, and faire and softe in ansuere. **1544** PHAER *Pestilence* (1553) Nj b, [A] goodly pomaunder for gentlewemen and ladies. **1580** LYLY *Euphues* (Arb.) 352 Here Gentlewomen you may see, how iustly men seeke to entrap you. *Ibid.* 370 Ladyes and Gentlewomen. **1625** HART *Anat. Ur.* I. i. 8 As for you, Ladyes and Gentlewomen..let me intreate you, not to be too officiously busie. *a* **1748** WATTS *Improv. Mind* (1801) 325 The good old gentlewoman trained them up precisely in the forms in which she herself was educated. **1801** VINCE *Elem. Astron.* xxi. (ed. 2) 191 Some Gentlewomen in the country saw more than 16 stars. **1890** BESANT *Demoniac* iv. 45 You are not fit to associate with gentlemen or to marry a gentlewoman!

fig. **1649** DAVENANT *Love & Hon.* v. 34/1 What thinke you of the stars now Caladine? Doe these small twinkling Gentlewomen Looke to their business well?

b. *old gentlewoman*: in humorous or derisive sense; cf. *old lady*.

1699 BENTLEY *Phal.* 517 There is not one Word in all the Epistles relating to the Old Gentlewoman. *a* **1715** in Amherst *Terræ Fil.* xv. (1726) 73 'Our holy mother [the church] was not permitted to take counsel for herself'. Poor old gentlewoman! What a sad thing that was!

2. A female attendant (orig. a gentlewoman by birth) upon a lady of rank. Now only *Hist.*

1432–50 tr. *Higden* (Rolls) V. 373 Rosamunda entrede in to a bedde of a gentilwoman [L. *domicilla*] longynge to her. **1535** COVERDALE *Nahum* ii. 7 The quene hir self shal be led awaye captyue, and her gentilwomen shall mourne. *c* **1661** in *12th Rep. Hist. MSS. Comm.* App. v. 6 In this attendance he and Lady Rutland's waiting gentlewoman married. **1673** *Rules Civility* (ed. 2) 31 In visiting a Lady..it is not enough to salute her, but her Gentlewoman also, if she be then present. **1770** FOOTE *Lame Lover* II. Wks. 1782 III. 49 For tho' I am..but a commoner, no gentlewoman's gentlewoman, has a prettier set of acquaintance. **1854** MRS. OLIPHANT *Magd. Hepburn* II. 9 Himself and Mistress Isobel, her gentlewoman, were to accompany the lady.

†**3.** *Comb.*: appositive., as ***gentlewoman-boy***, ***-heir***, ***-widow***.

1340 *Ayenb.* 190 A gentil wymman wodewe zente to þe uore yzede Ion uif hondred pond of gold. **1608** ARMIN *Nest Ninn.* (1842) 36 The gentlewoman-boy tooke him by the heeles, and pulled him out. **1641** BROME *Joviall Crew* IV. ii. Wks. 1873 III. 431 We must finde a young Gentlewoman-Heire among you.

Hence **'gentlewomanhood**, the character or disposition natural to a gentlewoman.

1848 THACKERAY *Van. Fair* xlviii, What a high and noble appreciation of Gentlewomanhood. **1887** MRS. C. READE *Maid o' the Mill* II. xxxiii. 185 Her chastity, her Christian gentlewomanhood.

gentlewomanlike ('dʒɛnt(ə)lwʊmən,laɪk), *a.* [f. prec. + LIKE.] **a.** Of persons: Having the manners, appearance, or air of a gentlewoman. **b.** Of conduct, etc.: Appropriate to a gentlewoman.

1591 HORSEY *Trav.* (Hakluyt Soc.) 213 A gentilweomanlike maiden..delivered me a curious white wraught hand-kercher. **1632** BROME *North. Lasse* I. iv. Wks. 1873 III. 9 And what a Minister she hath procur'd! A Devil in a most Gentlewoman-like apparition. **1748** RICHARDSON *Clarissa* (1768) VI. i. 4, I will provide for Dorcas Martindale in a gentlewoman like manner. **1832** GREVILLE *Mem. Geo. IV* (1874) II. 335 He afterwards married the daughter of an innkeeper, who proved as gentlewomanlike as the other had been the reverse. **1862** MISS YONGE *C'tess Kate* x. (1880) 117 You will write a proper and gentlewomanlike note.

gentlewomanly ('dʒɛnt(ə)lwʊmənlɪ), *a.* [f. as prec. + -LY¹.] = GENTLEWOMANLIKE.

1824 MISS MITFORD *Village* Ser. I. (1863) 217, I imbibed ..a love of strong green tea, for which gentlewomanly excitation Mossy had a remarkable predilection. **1831** JANE PORTER *Sir E. Seaward's Narr.* I. 289, I saw her restored to her former gentlewomanly condition. **1891** B. HARTE in *Black & White* 9 May 454/1 Low-voiced, gentlewomanly, with the pallor of ill-health.

Hence **'gentlewomanliness**.

1808 M. WILMOT *Jrnl.* 16 Aug. (1934) III. 368 He had felt ..the Gentlewomanliness of her manners. **1867** *Pall Mall G.* 21 Feb. 3 The education of the shop tends to superinduce the exterior signs of gentlewomanliness and gentlewomanliness. **1873** B. HARTE *Episode of Fiddletown* Wks. 1880 III. 59 She had..a certain languid grace which passed easily for gentlewomanliness.

gently ('dʒɛntlɪ), *adv.* Forms: 4 gentil(l)ich(e, gentel(l)iche, 4–6 gentilly(e, (5 jentilly), 5–6 gentylly, gentel(l)y, 6 gentlelye, gentlie, -lye, 6– gently. [f. GENTLE *a.* + -LY².]

1. †**a.** As befits one of gentle birth; generously, nobly, courteously; elegantly (*obs.*). **b.** In the condition of gentle birth (only in ***gently born***: see 4).

13.. *Guy Warw.* (A.) 4545 Wele he was y-armed gentilliche. *c* **1330** R. BRUNNE *Chron.* (1810) 134 Þe sonne cam also suiþe, & cried his fader mercy, Þe kyng Þerof was bliþe, forgaf him gentilly. **1362** LANGL. *P. Pl.* A. III. 13 Gentiliche with Ioye the Iustise soone Busked him into the bour. *c* **1440** *Sir Gowther* 41 Knyghtes and squyres..On steedes hem gentely to play. **1509** HAWES *Conv. Swearers* 22 And yf ye dyde ye wolde full gentylly Obeye my byddynge. **1572** BOSSEWELL *Armorie* II. 85 Couetous persons or niggardes, such as would not gently, or liberally departe from any of their goodes or substance. **1635** R. N. *Camden's Hist. Eliz.* I. an. 9. 67 Oxford and Cambridge, which gently envyed one another. **1864** TENNYSON *Sea Dreams* 1 A city clerk, but gently born and bred.

2. In a quiet, moderate, or subdued fashion; slowly, softly.

1559 MORWYNG *Evonym.* 201 Bake the bread therof gentlelye in an oven. **1578** LYTE *Dodoens* I. xix. 29 The whole herbe is not of so strong a sauour, but smelleth more gentilly, and pleasantly. **1600** E. BLOUNT tr. *Conestaggio* 288 They sailed gently towards the Iland. **1657** R. LIGON *Barbadoes* (1673) 3 The general Landscape of the Hills seemed to us very beautiful, gently rising and falling, without Rocks or high precipices. **1665** HOOKE *Microgr.* 78 Thus have I by gently mixing Vermilion and Bise dry, produc'd a very fine Purple. *a* **1683** SIR T. RAYMOND *Rep.* (1696) 212 Manning..was burned in the hand; and the Court directed the Executioner to burn him gently. **1709** ADDISON *Tatler* No. 116 ¶5 They gently touched upon the Weight and Unweildiness of the Garment. **1776** *Trial of Nundocomar* 76/2 His writer went close to him, and read it gently to him: I was at a distance, and did not hear it. **1823** F. CLISSOLD *Ascent Mt. Blanc* 22 A soft breath of wind spread its folds, and floated it gently in the air. **1833** *Cycl. Pract. Med.* I. 369/1 Tamarind-pulp, although an agreeable laxative, yet operates too gently..when given alone. **1855** MACAULAY *Hist. Eng.* xiii. III. 353 A highway..ascends gently from the low country to the summit of the defile. **1870** E. PEACOCK *Ralf Skirl.* II. 161 He pushed it gently open.

b. Used as an expression of remonstrance.

1806–7 J. BERESFORD *Miseries Hum. Life* VI. (1826) 116 Gently, Mr. Testy.

3. Mildly, tenderly, kindly.

1548 UDALL, etc., tr. *Erasm. Par. John* iv. 17 Here Jesus.. gentelly reprouyng the womans lyfe, saith vnto her. **1681** DRYDEN *Absol. & Achit.* To Rdr., That I can write severely with more ease than I can gently. **1711** LADY M. W. MONTAGU *Let. to Wortley Montagu* 9 Apr., I can bear being told that I am in the wrong, but tell it me gently. **1766** GOLDSM. *Vic. W.* xxvi, I gently rebuked their sorrow. **1836** J. H. NEWMAN *Par. Serm.* (1837) III. viii. 122 Feeling gently, even when we have reason to act severely. **1866** G. MACDONALD *Ann. Q. Neighb.* ii. (1878) 22 The little fellow looked at me..and then put his arms gently round my neck.

4. *Comb.*, as ***gently-aperient***, ***-born***, ***-breathing***, ***-falling***, ***-moulded***, ***-rising***, ***-soothing***, ***-swelling***, ***-wafted***, ***-waving***, ***-whistling*** adjs.

1835 *Cycl. Pract. Med.* IV. 586/1 *Gently aperient medicines. **1859** TENNYSON *Enid* 1040 They themselves [horses] like creatures *gently born But into bad hands fall'n. **1887** *Spectator* 2 July 901/2 Refinement and truth, which are still the distinguishing marks of the gently-born Briton. **1839** LONGF. *Terrest. Paradise* 7 A *gently-breathing air that no mutation Had in itself. **1776** MICKLE tr. *Camoens' Lusiad* 300 While to the lute the *gently-falling oar Now breaks the surges of the briny tide. **1839** TALFOURD *Fate of Macdonalds* III. ii, Through cluster'd piles Of *gently-moulded columns. **1718** ROWE tr. *Lucan* v. 1016 Speedy the Latian Chiefs unfurl their Sails, And catch the *gently-rising Northern Gales. **1768–74** TUCKER *Lt. Nat.* (1852) II. 360 It is like the tide flowing in waves upon a gently rising shore. *Ibid.* 139 Whatever goes beyond that *gently soothing content..is needless. **1885** *Truth* 28 May 850/2 Violent curves where there should be only *gently swelling lines. **1876** GEO. ELIOT *Dan. Der.* IV. liv. 111 This floating, *gently-wafted existence. **1748** THOMSON *Cast. Indol.* I. xl, The *gently waving wind. **1703** ROWE *Ulyss.* II. i, While Neptune smooths his Waters for their Passage, And *gently whistling Winds invite their Sails.

Hence **'gentlying** *vbl. sb.* (see 2b above).

1852 R. S. SURTEES *Sponge's Sp. Tour* (1893) 349 There were such climbings on, and clutchings..and gentlyings, and who-hoo-ings, and questionings if 'such a horse was quiet?'

†**'gentman.** *Obs.* Also **jentman.** Shortened form of GENTLEMAN: cf. GEMMAN. Hence **gentmanly** = GENTLEMANLY (in quot. *adv.*).

a **1553** UDALL *Royster D.* III. ii. (Arb.) 41 It is gentmanly spoken..But what gentman is it, I pray you tell me plaine, That woweth so finely? *Ibid.* III. iii. 44 Bawawe what ye say (ko I) of such a ientman.

Gentoo (dʒɛn'tuː), *sb.*¹ and *a. Obs.* exc. *Hist.* Forms: 7 Gentou, -tu(e, Jentew, 8 Gentow, Jentoo, 7– Gentoo. [Anglo-Indian ad. Pg. *gentio* GENTILE.] **A.** *sb.*

1. A pagan inhabitant of Hindostan, opposed to Mohammedan; a Hindoo; in South India, one speaking Telugu.

1638 SIR T. HERBERT *Trav.* (ed. 2) 110 Three hundred slaves whom the Persians bought in India; Parsees, Jentews ..and others. **1697** DAMPIER *Voy.* I. 507 Moors..calling the Idolaters, Gentous. **1727** A. HAMILTON *New Acc. E. Ind.* I. xx. 239 The Inhabitants of the Island..were all Gentows, or Gentiles. **1776** *Trial of Nundocomar* 47/1 Are not the customs of burying Mussulmen and Gentoos very different? **1834** LAMB *Lett.* (1888) II. 300 What a supreme felicity to the author..to meet a smutty Gentoo ready to burst with laughing at the tale of Bo-Bo!

2. The language of the Gentoos.

1698 FRYER *Acc. E. Ind. & P.* 33 Their Language they call generally Gentu. **1767** J. RENNELL *MS. Let.* (Y.), The original Language of this Countrey..is the Bengala or Gentoo.

B. *attrib.*, passing into *adj.* Of or pertaining to the Gentoos.

1686 *Lond. Gaz.* No. 2142/1 From thence we set forward with this numerous Company of People through the Gentue Town. **1763** SCRAFTON *Indostan* (1770) 11 In justice to the Gentoo religion and customs, I must say [etc.]. **1779** FORREST *Voy. N. Guinea* 282 The women tie their hair behind, and plait it like the Jentoo dancing girls at Madrass. **1807** J. HALL *Trav. Scotl.* II. 591 The Gentoo physicians give a patient an emetic. **1841** EMERSON *Ess.* Ser. I. iv. 163 The poor mind does not seem to itself to be any thing, unless it have an outside badge,—some Gentoo diet, or Quaker coat ..to testify that it is somewhat.

gentoo (dʒɛnˈtuː), *sb.*[2] [perh. a use of prec.] A kind of penguin (*Pygoscelis papua* or *tæniata*) frequenting the Falkland Islands. Also *gentoo penguin*.

1860 ABBOT in *Ibis* Oct. 337 This bird [*Eudyptes papua*] is called in the Falklands the Gentoo Penguin: whence the name I leave others to conjecture... They [Rock-hoppers] are also, like the Gentoos, continually going to and returning from the salt water.

gentre, gentre(i)s, obs. ff. GENTRY, GENTRICE.

gentrice, *sb.* and *a. Obs.* exc. *arch.* (*Sc.*) Forms: 3–6 gent(e)ris(e, 4–6 gentryce, -s(e, (4 gentiresse, 5 gentriose, gentrys(s, 6 gentre(i)s, gentriss, 7 gentryes), 4– gentrice. [ad. OF. *genterise*, var. of *gentelise*, f. *gentil* GENTLE.]

A. *sb.*

1. Gentle birth, noble descent or rank.

1297 R. GLOUC. (Rolls) 1313 He adde reuþe of him & uor is gentrise Hadde is pes wiþ þemperour. *c* **1300** *Seyn Julian* 52 And þench on hire heie kunne; and hire owe gentrise. *c* **1450** *St. Cuthbert* (Surtees) 4806 He spared na man of gentryse. **1893** STEVENSON *Catriona* 154 He supposed I would set up to be gentry..'My gentrice has nothing to do with where I lie', said I.

b. *concr.* Nobility, nobles; also, splendid attire.

13.. *E.E. Allit. P.* B. 1159 Þe gentryse of Iuise & Iherusalem þe ryche Watz disstryed with distres. *c* **1650** *Sir Lambewell* 461 in Furniv. *Percy Folio* I. 159 Every man had greet desire ffor to behold their gentryes.

2. Gentle or honourable feeling; kindness, generosity, clemency, courtesy.

a **1225** *Ancr. R.* 168 We wulleð folewen þe iðe muchele genterise of þine largesse. *c* **1300** *Cursor M.* 28940 (Cott. Galba) Þis 'gentrise' will vs lede Till doghty at do oure almus dede. *c* **1375** BARBOUR *Troy-bk.* I. 319 The noble kinge, þat neuir-mare For3 het walde hys Inborne gentryce. *c* **1475** *Rauf Coilȝear* 370 It is not my counsall..To do ȝow in his gentrise. **1500–20** DUNBAR *Poems* xxi. 26 All gentrice and nobilitie Ar passit out of he degre. *c* **1565** LINDESAY (Pitscottie) *Chron. Scot.* (1728) 44 Humbly..to render himself—in his [the king's] hands, will and gentrice. **1596** DALRYMPLE tr. *Leslie's Hist. Scotl.* x. 327 Steirit vp thair hartes meikle to that gentrise.

3. Gentility, good breeding.

1824 SCOTT *Redgauntlet* Let. xi, That may come of idleness as weel as gentrice.

B. *adj.* **a.** Of gentle birth. **b.** Genteel, elegant.

1508 DUNBAR *Tua Mariit Wemen* 69 My self suld be full semlie with silkis arrayit; Gymp, jolie, and gent, richt joyous, and gentryce. *c* **1560** A. SCOTT *Poems* (S.T.S.) iv. 81 Moir gentrice is to jott Vndir ane silkin goun Nor ane quhyt pittecott And reddyar ay boun. **1894** CROCKETT *Raiders* 165 'We're honest, honest—and gentrice to the back o' that'.

gentrifiˈcation. [f. next: see -IFICATION.] The process by which an (urban) area is rendered middle-class. Also *transf.*

1973 *Times* 26 Sept. 19/3 The switch to owner-occupation has shifted overcrowding to the north of the borough which already suffered acutely before the 'gentrification' process began. **1977** *Time Out* 7 Jan. 49/5 Some time ago the Chalcot Cafe became the Chalcot Bistro—keeping up with the gentrification of the neighbourhood. **1982** BARR & YORK *Official Sloane Ranger Handbk.* 8/1 Sloane gentrification isn't the same as trendy intelligentsia gentrification... You don't really *understand* The North (the *established* arty intelligentsia areas—Islington, Highgate and Hampstead). **1985** *Listener* 11 Apr. 7/1 An awful lot of gentrification is taking place in the Borough of Hackney.

gentrify (ˈdʒɛntrɪfaɪ), *v.* [f. GENTRY + -IFY.] *trans.* To renovate or convert (housing, esp. in an inner-city area) so that it conforms to middle-class taste; to render (an area) middle-class.

1972 J. I. M. STEWART *Palace of Art* i. 11 The humbler dwellings..were well-groomed rather than neat, and their little gardens had been gentrified as effectively as had their low parlours. **1975** *Observer* 7 Dec. 13/4 Sound housing..of the type which today would be rehabilitated (or gentrified by the owner-occupying middle classes). **1977** *N.Y. Times* 22 Sept. A2/3 Newcomers are 'gentrifying' working-class Islington and should be resisted, not welcomed. **1984** *Listener* 19 Apr. 8/2 In those days, this part of North London had not yet been gentrified. **1985** *Observer* 29 Dec. 20/8 Accountants and graphic designers busily gentrifying the shell-shocked terraces are just as hungry for pleasure.

Hence **ˈgentrified, ˈgentrifying** *ppl. adjs.*

1976 *Times* 17 Dec. 30/3 Labour's class of '71 was..a gentrified council, dominated by professional people from Putney rather than people from the working-class areas. **1977** *Economist* 20 Aug. 21/2 He then..attacks his gentry for underusing their newly gentrified houses. **1977** *Evening Standard* 29 Apr. 8/4 The 'spoilers' in the urban mosaic of Islington are the borough's growing population of 'intellectuals' and 'trendies' who are now spreading their 'gentrifying' tentacles through even the borough's most decrepit areas. **1984** *Listener* 15 Mar. 34/1 Gather together a group of latter-day Bright Young Things just down from Oxford, congregate them in a communally shared, lavishly gentrified house in SW2. **1986** *Sunday Times* 9 Feb. 24/2 But then the middle classes spread, like gentrifying locusts. Before long it was 'fashionable Fulham' in all the property adverts.

gentry (ˈdʒɛntrɪ). Forms: 4–5 gent(e)ry(e, 4–6 gentre, 4–7 gent(e)rie, (5 gentri), 4– gentry. [app. an altered form of GENTRICE, the final sound of which may have been taken as a plural ending. But cf. GENTLERY.]

1. Rank by birth (usually, high birth; *rarely* in neutral sense). *Obs.* exc. *arch.*

c **1386** CHAUCER *Wife's T.* 296 He wole han pris of his gentrye ffor he was born of a gentil house. *c* **1440** *Promp. Parv.* 190/2 Gentry, of awncetrye..*ingenuitas*. **1603** B. JONSON *Sejanus* v. x. (1605) M 1 b, We haue raised Seianus from obscure, and almost vnknowne Gentry. **1647** A. ROSS *Mystag. Poet.* xiv. (1675) 362 'Tis madness to presume too much upon our birth and Gentry. **1815** SCOTT *Guy M.* xxxviii, MacCasquil..feeling the propriety of asserting his superior gentry in the presence of Mr. Pleydell and Colonel Mannering.

b. The quality or rank of gentleman. *arch.*

1447 BOKENHAM *Seyntys* (Roxb.) 243 Crystys servage ys grettest genterye. **1570–6** LAMBARDE *Peramb. Kent* (1826) 8 Yeomen..that will not..change their condition, nor desire to be apparailed with the titles of gentrie. **1592** GREENE *Groat's W. Wit* (1617) 3 What is Gentry if wealth bee wanting, but base servile beggery. *a* **1613** OVERBURY *A Wife*, etc. (1638) 179 His gentry sits as ill upon him, as if he had bought it with his penny. **1651** HOBBES *Leviath.* (1839) 81 This kind of honour, commonly called gentry, hath been derived from the ancient Germans. **1828** SCOTT *F.M. Perth* xvi, The Provost told me..that our acquaintance, the Devil's Dick, was to wave his gentry.

†**c.** What is characteristic of a gentleman; polish of manners, good breeding; also courtesy, generosity; an instance of good-breeding, a gentlemanlike action. *Obs.*

c **1380** WYCLIF *Wks.* (1880) 205 Sumtyme curtesie & genterie was vertuouse lif & honest..but now it is turned in-to vanyte & nysete. *c* **1385** CHAUCER *L.G.W.* Prol. 380 Of his [the lion's] genterye, Him deyneth nat to wreke him on a flye. *c* **1386** —— *Pars. T.* ⁋ 527 Hem þat..holden it a gentrie or manly dede. **14..** *Sir Beues* (MS. M.) 211 For thy genterye, Thus cowardly let me nat dye. *c* **1435** *Torr. Portugal* 283 Wolddes thow for thy gentrie, Do the lyonnys downe lye. **1513** DOUGLAS *Æneis* XI. iii. 7 That he wald..thame restor agane, of hys gentre. **1595** GOSSON *Quips Upst. Gentlew.* 240 in Hazl. *E.P.P.* IV. 260 They are but puppets richly dight: True gentrie they have put to flight.

†**d.** A practice, style of dress, etc., characteristic of gentle-folks; 'the fashion'. *Obs.*

c **1325** *Poem temp. Edw. II* (Percy) liii, That is now the gentry In chawmbre & eke in halle. *c* **1400** MAUNDEV. (Roxb.) xxxiv. 154 Þat think þaim es a grete noblay and a grete gentry. And þe gentry of wymmen þare es to hafe smale fete.

2. People of gentle birth and breeding; the class to which they belong; in modern English use *spec.* the class immediately below the nobility.

c **1585** *Faire Em* I. 100 Our foes, That seek to root all Britain's Gentry [up]. **1611** SHAKS. *Cymb.* v. i. 18, I am brought hither Among th' Italian Gentry. *a* **1635** NAUNTON *Fragm. Reg.* (Arb.) 44 He..despised his Jury— tho' of the Order of Knighthood, and of the speciall Gentry—claiming the privilege of trial by the peers and baronage of the realm. **1661** LOVELL *Hist. Anim. & Min.* 10 The fore-feet [of the Bear]..are a dish for the Gentry. **1673** *Lady's Call.* I. v. §30 This seems to be the persuasion of many of our female gentry. **1709** STEELE *Tatler* No. 18 ⁋2 The common People are loud for Want of Bread, the Gentry have lost all Spirit and Zeal for their Country. **1796** MORSE *Amer. Geog.* II. 119 Montague-house, in Bloomsbury, with a number of others of the nobility and gentry. **1807** WORDSW. *White Doe* III. 36 Grave Gentry of estate and name. **1833** HT. MARTINEAU *Loom & Lugger* I. v. 90 Perceiving how the gentry of England are apparelled in smuggled goods. **1856** EMERSON *Eng. Traits, Relig.* Wks. (Bohn) II. 98 It is the church of the gentry; but it is not the church of the poor.

b. quasi-*adj.* (Cf. GENTRICE B.)

1893 STEVENSON *Catriona* 154 Saying he supposed I would set up to be gentry.

†**c.** Gentlemen. *Obs.*

1645 EVELYN *Mem.* (1857) I. 191 Pleasant walks..where the gentry and ladies used to take the air.

3. In playful or contemptuous use: People, folks.

1717 PRIOR *Lucius* Epil. 22 The many-colour'd gentry there above, By turns are rul'd by tumult, and by love. **1759** DILWORTH *Pope* 21 Not so eager and greedy as most of the Parnassian gentry. **1794** NELSON 9 July in Nicolas *Disp.* (1845) I. 431 My Agamemnon's Carpenter at Bastia made us much better platforms than these gentry. **1807–8** W. IRVING *Salmag.* (1824) 35 We have determined to let these crusty gentry know what kind of satisfaction they are to expect from us. **1810** *Sporting Mag.* XXXVI. 145 A tolerable muster of amateurs and boxing gentry. **1864** BURTON *Scot Abr.* I. v. 261 For these gentry [the students] imbibed a great amount both of restlessness and capriciousness.

trans. **1876** GEO. ELIOT *Dan. Der.* IV. xxix, The broken discourse of poultry and other lazy gentry in the afternoon sunshine.

b. ? *Anglo-Irish.* The fairies. Also *attrib.*

1880 *Antrim & Down Gloss.*, *Gentry*, the fairies. *Gentry bushes*, 'fairy thorns', etc. They are sacred to the 'good people', and are therefore let alone. **1894** W. B. YEATS *Celtic Twilight* 94 The night-capped heads of faery-doctors may be thrust from their doors to see what mischief the 'gentry' are doing.

4. *attrib.* and *Comb.*, as ***gentry-man*** (dial.), ***-state***; ***gentry-fashioned*** adj.; **gentry cove, mort** *thieves' slang* (see quot. 1567).

1563 *Mirr. for Mag.*, *Buckingham* lxxv. 3 To gentrye state auauncing him from nought. **1567** HARMAN *Caveat* (1869) 84 *A gentry cofe*, a noble or gentleman, *a gentry morte*, a noble or gentle woman. **1610** ROWLANDS *Martin Mark-all* E ij b, Gentry mort, a Gentlewoman. **1641** BROME *Joviall Crew* II. Wks. 1873 III. 388 And Scraps of the Dainties of Gentry Cofe's Feast. **1785** GROSE *Dict. Vulg. Tongue*, *Gentry mort.* **1837** DISRAELI *Venetia* I. xiv, The gentry cove will be romboyled by his dam. **1873** BROWNING *Red Cott. Nt.-cap* 132 The..gentry-fashioned, old-style haunts of sleep. **1881** BLACKMORE *Christowell* ii, Why, Parson Tom Short was the only gentry-man.

gentu(e, obs. form of GENTOO *sb.*[1] and *a.*

genty (ˈdʒɛntɪ), *a. Obs.* exc. *Sc.* [var. of GENTEE.] Neat; pretty; graceful; genteel.

1721 RAMSAY *Genty Tibby* 2 Her genty Shape our Fancy warms. **1724** —— *Tea-t. Misc.* (1733) I. 57 White is her neck, saft is her hand, Her waste and feet's fu genty. **1794** BURNS *My Lady's Gown* iv, Sae sweetly move her genty limbs, Like music notes o' lover's hymns. **1819** *Blackw. Mag.* V. 735 His waistcoat, coat and breeches, were all cut off the same web, of a beautiful snuff-colour, or a modest genty drab. **1863** J. L. W. *By-gone Days* 175, I wonder where she got sic genty ways as she had.

Hence †**ˈgentiness**, *Obs.*

1673 *Rules Civility* (ed. 2) 2 The Gentiness and plausibility, of which you desire information, is..but the modesty and decorum to be observed by every one.

gentyl(e, obs. form of GENTILE.

gentyl(l(e, obs. form of GENTLE.

‖**genu** (ˈdʒiːnjuː). *Anat.* [L. *genū* knee.]

a. The name given to a knee-like bend or curved part in various organs of the body.

1854 MAYNE *Expos. Lex.*, *Genu*, *Anat.*, the knee. **1882** *Syd. Soc. Lex.*, *Corpus geniculatum externum*, a mass of grey matter..lying on the outer side of the genu of the tractus opticus. **1885** *Ibid.* s.v., *Geniculate ganglion*, a small, reddish, triangular ganglion at the genu of the facial nerve.

b. In certain mod.L. terms, with the sense 'knee', as **genu recurvatum**, 'a backward curvation of the knee-joint' (Dorland 1900); **genu valgum**, knock-knee; **genu varum**, bow-legs.

In classical Latin *valgus*, *vārus* meant respectively 'bow-legged', 'knock-kneed'.

1887 *Encycl. Brit.* XXII. 691/2 During the last few years ..other deformities, such as knock-knee or *genu valgum* and bow-leg or *genu varum*, have been remedied by operation. **1910** *Practitioner* Mar. 348 Genu-valgum (with genu-recurvatum). **1936** BAILEY & LOVE *Short Pract. Surg.* (ed. 3) xli. 920 Genu Varum is less common than knock-knee, and is usually due to rickets. **1954** J. CYRIAX *Textbk. Orthopaedic Med.* (ed. 2) I. xxi. 559 Nowadays genu valgum due to vitamin-D deficiency is almost as rare as venal rickets. **1968** S. TAYLOR et al. *Short Textbk. Surg.* (ed. 2) xlii. 563 Patients are rarely disabled by genu recurvatum, and operative treatment is therefore seldom needed.

genual (ˈdʒɛnjuːəl), *a.* [f. L. *genū* knee + -AL[1].] Of or pertaining to the 'genu' or knee.

1861 J. BLACKWALL *Spiders* I. Introd. 3 The first part of the shank, or the genual joint, is usually short. **1874** MOGGRIDGE *Suppl. Ants & Spiders* 256 The genual joints of the third pair have some strongish spines on the outer side.

genuant (ˈdʒɛnjuːənt), *a. Her.* [f. L. *genū* knee + -ANT.] Kneeling, in a kneeling posture.

1688 R. HOLME *Armoury* II. 11/1 In some Coats you shall find Arch-Angels and Angels genuant or Kneeling. **1828–40** BERRY *Encycl. Her.* I, *Genuant*, in a kneeling posture, as an angel genuant, or kneeling.

genuclast (ˈdʒɛnjuːklæst). *Surg.* [f. L. *genū* knee + Gr. -κλαστής breaker.] (See quot.)

1885 *Syd. Soc. Lex.*, *Genuclast*, an instrument for breaking down adhesions, whether osseous or fibrous, in the knee-joint. **1890** in GOULD *New Med. Dict.*

Genuese, obs. form of GENOESE.

genuflect (ˈdʒɛnjuːflɛkt), *v.* [f. med.L. *genūflect-ĕre*, f. L. *genū* knee + *flectĕre* to bend.] *intr.* To bend the knee, esp. in worship. †Also *trans.*

1630 J. TAYLOR (Water P.) *Laugh & be fat* Wks. II. 80/1 With hands erected, with knees genuflected. **1850** J. H. NEWMAN *Diffic. Anglic.* 235 A feeble old woman, who.. genuflects before the Blessed Sacrament. **1884** *Catholic Dict.* s.v. *Genuflexion*, The priest repeatedly genuflects at Mass in adoration of the Eucharist, also at the mention of the Incarnation in the Creed, &c.

fig. **1881** A. AUSTIN in *Macm. Mag.* XLIII. 406 The poet before whom Mr. Swinburne..bows and bobs and genuflects an almost countless number of times in the course of the paper on which I am commenting—to wit, M. Victor Hugo.

Hence ˈ**genuflecting** *ppl. a.*

1872 O. W. HOLMES *Poems*, *Organ-blower* 14 His large obeisance puts to shame The proudest genuflecting dame.

genuflector (dʒɛnjuːˈflɛktə(r)). [f. GENUFLECT + -OR.] One who 'genuflects'.

1869 *Daily News* 22 Nov., The 'bowing to the altar' is not yet satisfactory at this church.. At present it looks as though the genuflectors were ashamed of themselves.

genuflectory (dʒɛnjuːˈflɛktərɪ), *a.* [f. as prec. + -ORY.] Pertaining to genuflexion or kneeling.

1861 THACKERAY *Four Georges* iii. (1862) 168 Misfortunes would occur in these interesting genuflectory ceremonies of royal worship. **1872** J. C. JEAFFRESON *Wom. in Spite of Herself* I 1. xi. 179 A course of genuflectory practice.

genuflex (dʒɛnjuːˈflɛks), *v. rare.* = GENUFLECT.

1879 *Daily News* 22 Mar. 5/7 The donna seconda, a strapping young woman, who genuflexed, slowly rotated, and waved her arms about.. as she sang.

Hence **genuˈflexed** *ppl. a.*

1885 *Syd. Soc. Lex.*, *Genuflexed*, bent at the knee, bent like a knee, bent at a joint.

genuflexion, genuflection (dʒɛnjuːˈflɛkʃən). [ad. med.L. *genūflexiōn-em*, n. of action f. *genūflectĕre*: see GENUFLECT. Cf. F. *genuflexion* (Cotgr.).] The action of kneeling or bending the knee, esp. in worship.

1526 *Pilgr. Perf.* (W. de W. 1531) 237b, With genufleccyons or knelynges.. to aske the mercy of god. **1611** J. DAVIS *Panegyr. Verses* in *Coryat's Crudities*, With cap in hand and lowly 'genuflexion'. **1660** BURNEY *Κέρδ. δῶρον* (1661) 51 He does not controvert the Genuflexion at the Supper of the Lord. **1741** WARBURTON *Div. Legat.* II. 188 The very way the learned Author so much insists upon, namely genuflexion. **1820** SCOTT *Ivanhoe* v, After many genuflections and muttered prayers. **1861** MUSGRAVE *By-Roads* 75 Our fast mare.. nearly pitched me on to the splashboard.. by a genuflection, which broke both her knees. **1884** *Catholic Dict.* s.v., A double genuflexion—i.e. one on both knees—is made on entering or leaving a church, where the Blessed Sacrament is exposed.

b. *Surg.* A forcible bending of the knee as a curative measure in popliteal aneurysm.

1870 HOLMES *Syst. Surg.* (ed. 2) III. 602 Before other severer measures are tried, genuflexion ought undoubtedly to be attempted. **1885** *Syd. Soc. Lex.* s.v., *Forcible Genuflexion*, the forcible bending of the knee-joint.

genuflexuous (ˌdʒɛnjuːˈflɛksjuːəs), *a.* [f. L. *genū* knee + FLEXUOUS.] (See quots.)

1889 *Century Dict.*, *Genuflexuous*, in *bot.*, geniculately bent; zigzag. **1894** GOULD *Dict. Med.*, *Genuflexuous*, in biology, zig-zag, with knee-like bendings.

genuform (ˈdʒɛnjuːfɔːm), *a.* [f. L. *genū* knee + -FORM.] Having the form of a knee, knee-shaped.

1847–9 TODD *Cycl. Anat.* IV. 555/2 The.. ganglionic nature of the genuform intumescence.

†**genuinal**, *a. Obs. rare*[−1]. [f. L. *genuīnus* GENUINE + -AL[1].] = GENUINE.

1599 THYNNE *Animadv.* (1875) 61 The genuynall sence hereof is, 'When' [etc.].

genuine (ˈdʒɛnjuːɪn), *a.*[1] [ad. L. *genuīn-us*, f. pre-L. **genwo-* (cf. *ingenuus* native, free-born, etc.: see INGENUOUS), f. Aryan root **gen-* to beget, produce, be born: see KIN.]

†**1. a.** Natural, not foreign or acquired, proper or peculiar to a person or thing, native. *Obs.*

1596 DRAYTON *Leg.* iv. 212 Strongly attracted by a Genuine light. **1612** —— *Poly-olb.* IX. 14 A constant Mayden still she onely did remaine, The last her genuine lawes which stoutly did retaine. **1630** PRYNNE *Anti-Armin.* 138 The self-same things in the same degrees admit no inequality in their genuine and natiue operations. **1644** BULWER *Chiron.* 118 This genuine blemish and epidemicall disease. **1664** H. MORE *Myst. Iniq.* 87 This wicked Antichristianism, whose Image we are now setting out in its genuine colours. **1703** tr. *Casa's Galateo* 98 Since it is necessary to use Genuine and proper Words in Discourse. **1712** W. ROGERS *Voy.* 1, I rather chuse to keep to the Language of the Sea, which is more genuine, and natural for a mariner.

†**b.** *genuine to*: germane to, closely connected with, arising out of. *Obs.*

1658–9 *Burton's Diary* (1828) III. 344 Let us debate this. It comes orderly before you; is genuine to your question.

2. Pertaining to the original stock, pure-bred.

1728 NEWTON *Chronol. Amended* ii. 203 Egypt at this time was therefore under the Government of the genuine Egyptians. **1774** J. BRYANT *Mythol.* II. 60, I am.. sprung from the genuine and respectable race of Sons. **1834** T. MEDWIN *Angler in Wales* I. 21 The race of our bull-dogs is getting fast extinct, and it is rare to see one now of a pure and genuine breed. **1842** PRICHARD *Nat. Hist. Man* 171 The towns and their vicinity are occupied by the genuine Persian race. **1871** FREEMAN *Norm. Conq.* (1876) IV. xviii. 295 Another grantee was William of Percy, the founder of a great name, whose genuine bearers soon passed away.

3. Really proceeding from its reputed source or author; not spurious; = AUTHENTIC 6.

The distinction which the 18th c. apologists attempted to establish between *genuine* and *authentic* (see quot. 1796) does not agree well with the etymology of the latter word, and is not now recognised.

1661 BRAMHALL *Just Vind.* v. 90 If any of those Canons which bear their names be genuine. **1719** J. RICHARDSON *Art Criticism* 145 When we have fix'd a few of the Works of the Masters as Genuine. **1756–7** tr. *Keysler's Trav.* (1760) III. 365 The impossibility that all the three *præputia* should be genuine reliques. **1779–81** JOHNSON *L.P.*, *Butler* Wks. II. 183 Two volumes more.. indubitably genuine. **1796** BP. WATSON *Apol. Bible* ii. 33 A genuine book, is that which was written by the person whose name it bears, as the author of it. An authentic book, is that which relates matters of fact, as they really happened. **1833** CRUSE *Eusebius* III. iii. 83 As to the writings of Peter, one of his epistles called the first is acknowledged as genuine. **1847** EMERSON *Repr. Men, Plato* Wks. (Bohn) I. 289 This range of Plato instructs us what to think of the vexed question concerning his reputed works—what are genuine, what spurious. **1882** FARRAR *Early Chr.* II. 530 *note*, The fragment.. is of very doubtful genuineness, and even if genuine proves nothing.

4. a. Having the character or origin represented; real, true, not counterfeit, unfeigned, †unadulterated. *(the) genuine article*: see ARTICLE *sb.* 14 d.

a **1639** CAREW *To my Friend G.N.* 18 We use No.. compounds that are Adulterate, but, at Natures cheap expence, With farre more genuine sweets refresh the sense. **1660** R. COKE *Justice Vind.* Ep. Ded. 1 The true and genuine causes. **1664** H. MORE *Myst. Iniq.* 214 What the genuine sense is I shall take notice in its proper place. **1712** PARNELL *Spect.* No. 501 ⁋6 The whole Vault had a genuine Dismalness in it. **1736** BUTLER *Anal.* II. i. Wks. 1874 I. 154 Christianity.. teaches natural Religion in its genuine simplicity. **1781** GIBBON *Decl. & F.* III. 37 Maximus now displayed his genuine character. **1845** M. PATTISON *Ess.* (1889) I. 25 Such a genuine expression of paternal regard. **1876** MOZLEY *Univ. Serm.* iv. 95 They had no genuine belief in any world which was different from theirs.

absol. **1639** tr. *Du Bosq's Compl. Woman* 34 The modesty of the simple and genuine is wholy in the hart.

b. Properly so called; that is such in the proper sense.

a **1682** SIR T. BROWNE *Tracts* 36 The true and genuine Sycamore.. which is a stranger in our parts. **1692** BENTLEY *Boyle Lect.* i. 3 This latter part to a genuine Atheist is meer Jargon. **1751** HARRIS *Hermes* (1841) 138 The genuine pronoun always stands by itself. **1758** JOHNSON *Idler* No. 9 ⁋7 There is no mark more certain of a genuine idler than uneasiness without molestation. **1850** SCORESBY *Cheever's Whalem. Adv.* vi. 76 None but a genuine son of the sea.. could make these characteristic rhymes. **1852** H. ROGERS *Ecl. Faith* (1853) 316 A genuine sceptic, as I am. **1879** *St. George's Hosp. Rep.* IX. 63 A piece of genuine false-membrane was coughed out.

5. Of persons: Free from affectation or hypocrisy.

[**1840, 1853**: Implied in GENUINENESS 3.] **1890** *Spectator* 28 June, He is a very great and genuine personage in many ways, but he has his peculiarities like other men.

†ˈ**genuine**, *a.*[2] *Obs.*[−0] [ad. L. *genuīn-us*, f. **genu-s* = *gena* cheek.] ***genuine teeth***: the back teeth.

1706 PHILLIPS (ed. Kersey), *Genuine Teeth*, the same as *Dentes Sapientiæ*.

genuinely (ˈdʒɛnjuːɪnlɪ), *adv.*[1] [f. GENUINE *a.*[1] + -LY[2].] In a genuine manner.

1640 BP. REYNOLDS *Passions* xv. 144 The goodnesse of the Law that doth kindly and genuinely restraine the violence.. of our defiled nature. *a* **1763** BYROM *Rem. Pamphl.* 49 This coxcombically mingling Of Rhimes.. For Numbers genuinely British, Is quite too finical, and skittish. **1820** BYRON *Blues* II. 159 For 'tis then that our feelings most genuinely—feel. **1875** JOWETT *Plato* (ed. 2) V. 36 They are genuinely and naturally good. **1890** BOLDREWOOD *Col. Reformer* (1891) 363 He.. enjoyed his.. whist or billiards, as genuinely as if he had not a debt in the world.

genuineness (ˈdʒɛnjuːɪnnɪs). Also 8 genuiness. [f. GENUINE *a.*[1] + -NESS.]

1. The quality or fact of being genuine or what it is represented to be, reality, trueness.

1647 H. MORE *Song of Soul* Notes 414 The fitnesse and genuinenesse of the Hypothesis it self. **1664** BOYLE *Exp. Colours* III. xxxvi. 282 It not being Essential to the Genuineness of a Colour to be Durable. **1715** tr. *Pancirollus' Rerum Mem.* I. I. xii. 31 The greatest Indication of the Genuiness of it [Juice], is the curdling of it. **1729** BUTLER *Serm.* Wks. 1874 II. 128 Truth, and.. integrity, carry along with them a peculiar consciousness of their own genuineness. **1817** BENTHAM *Parl. Ref. Catech.* (1818) 25 To secure genuineness, to prevent spuriousness. **1881** W. G. PALGRAVE in *Macm. Mag.* XLV. 22 A whole company of learned monks.. thoroughly qualified to pronounce authoritatively on the genuineness of the prodigy.

2. *esp.* The quality of being what it professes to be in origin or authorship; = AUTHENTICITY 3.

See GENUINE *a.* 3, and the note there.

1699 BURNET 39 *Art.* vi. (1700) 82 The full Testimony that they [the Books of the New Testament] give to the Books of the Old Testament, does sufficiently prove their [sc. the latter's] Authority and Genuineness. **1706** HEARNE *Collect.* 12 Jan. (O.H.S.) I. 161 Yᵉ Genuiness of yᵉ Fragment. **1738** WARBURTON *Div. Leg.* I. 111 The Genuineness of these Remains. **1752** MISS TALBOT *Let.* 17 Dec. (1808) 317 Madame de Maintenon's letters.. have all marks of genuineness, but no vouchers. **1796** BP. WATSON *Apol. Bible* ix. 334 The genuineness of Paul's Epistles proves their authenticity. **1864** BOWEN *Logic* xiii. 426 The age and genuineness of the document must first be proved. **1867** FREEMAN *Norm. Conq.* (1876) I. App. 786 Two charters of very doubtful genuineness.

3. Of persons, character, sentiments, etc.: Honesty, freedom from affectation or hypocrisy.

1840 CARLYLE *Heroes* (1858) 234 One would say the primary character of the Koran is this of its *genuineness*, of its being a *bona fide* book. **1853** DICKENS *Lett.* (1880) I. 314, I was greatly pleased with his genuineness altogether.

genuinity (dʒɛnjuːˈɪnɪtɪ). *rare.* [f. GENUINE *a.*[1] + -ITY.] Genuineness.

1894 *Thinker* VI. 450 The genuinity, integrity, and credibility of the sacred books.

†**geˈnuity.** *Obs.*[−1] [a. F. *génuité*, acc. to Littré a false form for *génuinité*.] Simplicity.

1603 FLORIO *Montaigne* I. xxx. 102 They could not imagine a genuitie so pure and simple, as we see it by experience; nor ever beleeve our societie might be maintained with so little arte and humane combination.

genupectoral (dʒɛnjʊˈpɛktərəl), *a.* [f. L. *genū* knee + *pector-*, *pectus* breast + -AL[1].] Of posture: Resting on the knees and breast.

1889 J. M. DUNCAN *Dis. Women* (ed. 4) Index 532 Genupectoral position.

‖**genus** (ˈdʒiːnəs). Pl. ‖**genera** (ˈdʒɛnərə). Also 7–8 genuses, 7 genus's. [L. *genus*, *-eris*, birth, race, stock, kind, genus = Gr. *γένος*, *-εος* (same meanings), Skr. *jánas*, f. Aryan root **gen-* to beget, produce, be born: see KIN.]

1. *Logic.* A class or kind of things which includes a number of subordinate kinds (called SPECIES) as sharing in certain common attributes; a general concept. (One of the five PREDICABLES, q.v.)

Each species is distinguished from all the others in the genus by the possession of some peculiar attribute or group of attributes, called its 'specific difference' or DIFFERENTIA. ***highest genus*** (L. *summum genus*), one which does not become subordinated as species to a higher genus; ***subaltern genus***, one which is also a species of some higher genus.

1551 T. WILSON *Logike* B v a, Genus is a general word, the which is spoken of many that differ in their kind.. Or els thus, Genus is a general worde, vnder the whiche diuers kindes or sortes of things are comprehended. **1581** SIDNEY *Apol. Poetrie* (Arb.) 34 Tell mee if you haue not a more familiar insight into anger, then finding in the Schoolemen his Genus and difference. **1586** SIR E. HOBY *Pol. Disc. Truth* Ep. ⁋iij b, In the first, all vertues handled, the trueth, as it were genus vnto them.. in the other, is intreated of all kinde of vices, and lying accounted as genus thereunto. **1616** *Rich Cabinet* 135 Souldier is a name of that honour, that it is the genus of vallure and valiant men. **1644** DIGBY *Nat. Bodies* xiv. 118 Rarity and Density.. can not change the common nature of Quantity, that is, their Genus, which by being so to them, must be vniuocally in them both. **1651** HOBBES *Govt. & Soc.* vii. §1. 109 We have already spoken of a City by institution in its Genus; we will now say some-what of its species. **1654** JER. TAYLOR *Real Pres.* 222 Substance is the highest Genus in that Category. **1668** WILKINS *Real Char.* 22, I shall first lay down a Scheme or Analysis of all the Genus's or more common heads of things belonging to this design; and then shew how each of these may be subdivided by its peculiar Differences. **1690** LOCKE *Hum. Und.* III. iii. (1695) 228 This may shew us the reason, why, in the defining of Words.. we make use of the Genus, or next general Word that comprehends it. **1725** WATTS *Logic* III. iii. §3 So substance is the remote genus of bird or beast; because it agrees not only to all kinds of animals, but also to things inanimate.. But animal is the proximate or nearest genus of bird, because it agrees to fewest other things. **1827** WHATELY *Logic* (1850) Index, *Genus*, a Predicable which is considered as the material part of the Species of which it is affirmed. **1851** MANSEL *Prol. Log.* 183 The Highest Genus in any special science is the general class, comprehending all the objects whose properties that science investigates.. In Geometry, for example, under the *summum genus* of magnitudes in space, we find [etc.]. **1862** BURTON *Bk. Hunter* (1863) 38 You individualise your object by showing in what it differs from the others of the genus.

2. a. *Zool.* and *Bot.* A classificatory group comprehending a number of species (sometimes a single species) possessing certain common structural characteristics distinct from those of any other group.

The determination of genera, and of what characteristics are to be considered generic, is more or less arbitrary and empirical, and admits of continual alteration according to current knowledge of facts and ideas of classification in the respective sciences. The genus ranks next under the family or sub-family, and above the species; it is sometimes divided into sub-genera. The generic and specific names (always in Latin or considered as Latin) together form the scientific proper name of an animal or plant, the generic name standing first and being written with an initial capital. (The zoological term ***the genus Homo*** is popularly current as a somewhat flippant or jocular synonym for 'mankind' or 'the human race'.)

1608 TOPSELL *Serpents* (1658) 682 Because there be many kinds of Crocodiles, it is no marvel although some have taken the word 'Crocodilus' for the genus; and the several species they distinguish into the Crocodile of the Earth, and the Water. **1683** RAY *Corr.* (1848) 134 The description.. is scarce sufficient to determine to what genus it belongs, much less whether it be a nondescript species. **1691** —— *Creation* I. (1692) 203 The greatest and most luxuriant Species in most Genera of Plants are Native of the Mountains. **1755** *Gentl. Mag.* XXV. 33 When the shells are distributed according to their proper classes and tribes, nothing remains but to remark their less essential differences, by which they are subdivided into genuses and species. **1807** J. E. SMITH *Phys. Bot.* 404 *Lychnis dioica* has the Stamens on one plant, the Pistils on another, though the rest of the genus has them united in the same flower. **1834** T. MEDWIN *Angler in Wales* I. 97, I was speaking of adders some time back: do you consider them of one genus? **1859** DARWIN *Orig. Spec.* ii. (1873) 47 The larger genera.. tend to break up into smaller genera. **1860** *Once a Week* 22 Sept. 353/2 Peter.. may turn out a magnificent specimen of the *genus homo*.

Comb. **1851–6** WOODWARD *Mollusca* Pref. 2 The blundering and bad spelling of English and French genus-makers.

†**b.** Similarly used in classifications of other sciences (see quots.). *Obs.*

[**1599** THYNNE *Animadv.* (1875) 41 'Porpherye' yᵒᵘ expounde 'marble', whiche marble ys genus, but purpherye is species.] **1666** G. HARVEY *Morb. Angl.* v. (1672) 13 If minerals are not convertible into another Species, though of the same Genus, much less can they be surmised reducible into a Species of another Genus. **1807** T. THOMSON *Chem.* (ed. 3) II. 630 The genus sulphates contains several salts of considerable importance. **1811** PINKERTON *Petral.* I. p. i, Hence in mineralogy some eminent writers entirely reject Genera; while others, with Daubenton, say that there are no Species. **1816** ACCUM *Chem. Tests* (1818) 207 This fluid precipitates many of the genera of metals. **1830** R. KNOX *Béclard's Anat.* 53 M. Chaussier has arranged the organs under twelve genera, the twelfth comprehending the viscera or compound organs.

3. *Mus.* Each of the three scales in ancient Greek music.

1763 J. BROWN *Poetry & Mus.* v. 62 The three Genera or Kinds of the Greek Melody. **1842** BRANDE *Dict. Sci.*, etc., *Genus* in Music, the general name for any scale of music. If a scale proceed by tones, it is called the *diatonic* genus; if between the tones semitones are introduced, it is called the *chromatic* genus. When the subdivisions are smaller, as quarter tones, it is called the *enharmonic* genus. **1867** MACFARREN *Harmony* i. 5 The true genera of the Greek system.

4. *gen.* A kind, class, order, tribe, etc. (Often with reference, more or less explicit, to sense 2.)

1649 J. COOKE *K. Charles' Case* 9 It seems to me, that the Lord renounces the very Genus of such Kings as are there mentioned. **1691** RAY *Creation* I. (1692) 6 Animate Bodies are divided into four great Genera or Orders, Beasts, Birds, Fishes and Insects. **1768–74** TUCKER *Lt. Nat.* (1852) II. 356 We cannot think it for the good of the human species, or the animal genus. **1789** BENTHAM *Princ. Legisl.* xviii. §13 Let us ..branch out the several divisions of that class as above exhibited into their respective genera. **1816** T. L. PEACOCK *Headlong Hall* i, Other varieties of the same genera, namely, men of taste and philosophers. **1818** MOORE *Fudge Fam. Paris* i. 5 'A Dandy' describes what I mean, And Bob's far the best of the genus I've seen. **1820** *Edin. Rev.* XXXIV. 136 The following short passage contains a picture of one, we trust, of the lost genera of the native Irish. **1844** DISRAELI *Coningsby* IV. v, The days of the genus Jawster Sharp were over in this borough. **1880** *Manch. Guard.* 25 Oct., The proprietors 'rarely or never resident in Ireland' are only one species of the genus absentee.

5. ***genus irritabile* (*vatum*)** [after Horace, *Ep.* II. ii. 102], the irritable or over-sensitive race or class (of poets).

1721 SWIFT *Let. to Young Poet* 23 These of your Profession have been call'd *Genus irritabile vatum.* **1818** KEATS *Let.* (1958) I. 386 That matter.. which is accounted so acceptable in the 'genus irritabile'.. **1838** DICKENS *Let.* (1965) I. 398 Your great patience is so exemplary and peculiar that I fear you will never make an author, as you can never be one of the *genus irritabile.* **1940** 'N. BLAKE' *Malice in Wonderland* vii. 86 The Mad Hatter realized he was of the *genus irritabile* of singers, so he doped the piano for him, knowing it would make him fly off the handle.

-geny, *suffix* = mod.F. *-génie*, in mod. scientific language appended to Gr. stems to form sbs. with the general sense 'mode of production (of something specified)', as in *anthropogeny, biogeny, cosmogeny, geogeny, ontogeny, phylogeny, physiogeny*, etc. Most of these sbs. have either corresponding sbs. in -GENESIS, or adjs. -GENETIC (in many instances both of these).

[The suffix may be regarded as representing Gr. *-γένεια*, the ending of abstract sbs. f. adjs. in *-γενής* (as in *ὁμογένεια*, f. *ὁμογενής*): see -GEN. But in all probability it was actually f. the root *gen-* in *genesis*, etc. (vaguely apprehended as meaning 'to produce') + -Y[3], F. *-ie*.]

Genymade, obs. form of GANYMEDE.

genyplasty (ˈdʒɛnɪplæstɪ). *Med.* [f. Gr. *γένυ-ς* jaw, cheek + *πλαστ-ός* moulded + -Y[3].] An operation for restoring the cheek when it has been destroyed or is congenitally imperfect.

1857 in DUNGLISON *Med. Lex.* **1885** in *Syd. Soc. Lex.*

genysaryes, obs. form of JANIZARIES.

geo, gio (gjoː). *dial.* Also goe. [a. ON. *gjá*.] In Orkney and Shetland: A gully, a creek. Also, in wider use: a long, narrow, steep-sided cleft or inlet formed by erosion in coastal cliffs, and typically represented by the geos of Orkney.

1793 *Statist. Acc. Scotl.* VIII. 159 A deep hollow, called, in the dialect of the parish, the Wolf's geo. **1822** SCOTT *Pirate* xix, By air and by wick, and by helyer and gio. **1856** EDMONSTON *Sk. & Tales Shetland Isles* iii. 30 Many a wild geo and shattered crevice. **1882** GEIKIE *Geol. Sk.* 41 Gios, or narrow steep-walled gullies, or inlets, by which the sea-cliffs are indented. **1883** *Standard* 21 Mar. 3/7 They came ashore ..in a small goe on the west side of Ronsay. **1934** E. LINKLATER *Magnus Merriman* xxxiv. 346 The waves.. drove another [*sc.* trawler]..hard ashore in a Westray geo. **1960** WILLIAMSON & BOYD *St. Kilda Summer* x. 102 The route rises to the right following a series of ledges into the geo. **1961** L. D. STAMP *Gloss. Geogr. Terms* 208/1 *Geo*.. has been adopted by geomorphologists to describe coastal clefts, often marking joints, faults or dikes from which material has been removed by wave action. **1970** R. J. SMALL *Study of Landforms* xii. 449 In plan the cliffs are usually complex and regular, with inlets and geos developed along joints and faults.

geo- (ˈdʒiːəʊ-, dʒiːˈɒ-), repr. Gr. *γεω-*, comb. form of *γῆ* earth; in compounds formed in Greek itself, as *geography γεωγραφία*, and in many of mod. formation; as **'geoblast** [-BLAST] (see quot.); **geobo'tanic** *a.*, geobotanical; **ˌgeobo'tanical** *a.*, of or pertaining to geographical botany; **geo'botany** = PHYTOGEOGRAPHY; so **geo'botanist**; **ˌgeo'chronic** *a.*, of or pertaining to geological time (Funk); **ˌgeochro'nometry**, (*a*) an extension of geometry conceived as taking time into account as the fourth dimension; the 'geometry' of space-time; (*b*) absolute geochronology, in which events are assigned (approximate) dates in relation to the present instead of to other events; **ˌgeo'clinal** *a. nonce-wd.* [Gr. *κλίν-ειν* to lean + -AL[1]], (see quot.); **geoco'rona**, an envelope of gas surrounding the earth, resembling the sun's corona and consisting chiefly of ionized hydrogen; **geo'cratic** *a.* [Gr. *-κρατία* rule + -IC], (*a*) applied to earth-movements which reduce the area of the earth's surface covered by water: opp. HYDROCRATIC *a.*; (*b*) of or pertaining to the predominant influence of the natural environment on man; **ˌgeo'cyclic** *a.*, of or pertaining to the revolutions of the earth; also (see quot.) ***geocyclic machine*** (see quot.); **ˌgeody'namic** *a.*, of or pertaining to the (latent) forces of the earth; so **ˌgeody'namical** *a.*; **ˌgeody'namics**, the study of geodynamic forces; **ge'ogenous** *a.* [Gr. *-γεν-ής* born, produced + -OUS], (said of certain fungi) growing or springing directly from the ground; **ˌgeo'isotherm**, an underground isotherm (Funk); **ˌgeomor'phogeny**, the science dealing with the genesis of the physical features of the earth's surface; so **ˌgeomorpho'genic** *a.*, **ˌgeomor'phogenist**; **ˌgeonavi'gation**, 'a term proposed for that branch of the science of navigation in which the place of a ship at sea is determined by referring it to some other spot on the surface of the earth—in opposition to *Cœlo-navigation*' (Ogilvie 1882); **ge'onomy** [Gr. *-νομία* arrangement], 'the science of the physical laws relating to the earth, including geology and physical geography' (Ogilvie 1882); hence **ˌgeo'nomic** *a.*; **ˌgeophysi'ognomy** (see quot.); **ˌgeopla'narian** [L. *plānus* flat + -ARIAN], one who believes the earth to be flat, a 'flat-earther'; **geopo'tential**, the work that must be done against gravity to raise unit mass to a given point from sea level; **ˌgeose'lenic** *a.* [SELENIC], relating to the earth and the moon; **'geosphere**, any of the more or less spherical concentric regions that together constitute the earth and its atmosphere; **ˌgeo'static** *a.* [Gr. *στατικ-ός* causing to stand], only in ***geostatic arch***, an arch of a construction suited to bear the pressure of earth (Ogilvie 1882); **geostatics** *pl.*, 'the statics of rigid bodies' (*Cent. Dict.*); **geo'stationary** *a.*, of, pertaining to, or designating an artificial satellite that revolves round the earth in one day and hence remains above a fixed point on the earth's surface; **geo'strategy**, strategy as applied to the problems of geo-politics, 'global strategy'; hence **ˌgeostra'tegic(al)** *adjs.*; **geo'taxis** *Biol.*, a taxis (see TAXIS 6) in which the external stimulus is the force of gravity; so **geo'tactic** *a.*; **geo'technic** *a.*, of or pertaining to geotechnics; **geo'technics**, the art of modifying and adapting the physical nature of the earth to the needs of man; **geotech'nology**, 'the application of scientific methods and engineering techniques to the exploitation and utilization of natural resources (as mineral resources)' (Webster 1961); **ˌgeotec'tonic** *a.* [Gr. *τεκτονικ-ός* skilled in building, f. *τέκτων* a craftsman], of or pertaining to the structure of the earth; structural; **ˌgeotec'tonical** *a.* [f. prec. + -AL[1]] = prec.; **ˌgeo'thermal** *a.*, of or pertaining to the internal heat of the earth; **ˌgeo'thermic** *a.* = prec.; **ˌgeother'mometer** (see quot.).

1880 GRAY *Struct. Bot.* 413/1 *Geoblast, a plumule which in germination rises from underground, such as that of the Pea. **1904** *Pop. Sci. Monthly* May 71 The immense region.. on *geo-botanic maps..has not the uniformity which one would be inclined to attribute to it. **1888** *Nature* 12 Apr. 570 M. Kuznetsoff will continue his *geo-botanical work on the northern slope of Caucasus. **1901** *U.S. Dept. Agric. Bur. Plant Industry Bull.* III. 18 The most thorough investigations have been given to the Chernozem soils by Russian *geo-botanists. **1960** *Times* 24 Sept. 19/2 A geobotanist has been included..on all major geological expeditions. **1904** *Pop. Sci. Monthly* May 68 (*title*) The geology and *geo-botany of Asia. **1956** *Nature* 17 Mar. 520/2 Geobotany, geochemistry and geophysics of all the central and eastern African lakes. **1923** C. D. BROAD *Sci. Thought* xii. 457 A sense-history and the physical world are both four-dimensional spatio-temporal wholes, and we must therefore talk of their *geo-chronometry rather than their geometry. **1949** *Mind* LVIII. 219 The alternative 'geochronometries' developed in mathematical physics convey little or no information about the ultimate nature of time. **1960** *Bull. Geol. Soc. Amer.* LXXI. 223/1 Despite the major advances in the technique of geochronometry the establishment of the absolute age of the geological, i.e. paleontological, time scale has proceeded very slowly. **1970** *Nature* 2 May 473/1 In practice..potassium-argon geochronometry does not always reveal the initial age of crystallization. **1863** DANA *Man. Geol.* 722 These great valleys or depressions..may be called **geoclinal*, the inclination on which they depend being in the mass of the crust, and not in its strata. **1960** *Aeroplane* 8 July 53/1 Analysis of data obtained from the Soviet space-probe, Lunik II,..has shown that the Earth is enveloped in a '*geo-corona' of ionized gas. **1962** *New Scientist* 12 July 94/3 This region composed essentially of protons..is called variously the exosphere, hydrogen geocorona or..the magnetosphere. **1969** *Nature* 20 Dec. 1187/1 The solar Lyman-α radiation.. is scattered by the geocorona into the dark hemisphere of the Earth. **1898** *Geogr. Jrnl.* Feb. 133 Hydrocratic and *geocratic movements alternated during Jurassic times. **1951** G. TAYLOR *Geogr. 20th Cent.* i. 5 Humboldt..thus developed what I have been accustomed to call a '*Geocratic*' type of geography, which suggests that the earth (i.e. Nature) itself plays a great part in determining the type of life which develops in a particular area. **1847** CRAIG, **Geocyclic*, circling the earth periodically. **1884** *Cassell's Encycl. Dict.*, *Geocyclic machine*, a machine for exhibiting the simple processes by which day and night and the seasons are produced. **1885** *Harper's Mag.* Feb. 494/1 The Central *Geodynamic Observatory at Rome. **1887** G. H. DARWIN in *Fortn. Rev.* Feb. 271 A '*Geodynamical Observatory'. **1885** *Nature* 22 Oct. 609/2 Full scope was given to seismology, vulcanology, and *geodynamics. **1958** A. E. SCHEIDEGGER (*title*) Principles of geodynamics. **1896** *Nature* 18 June 147/1 After the *geomorphogenic introduction, two lessons are given to geological principles. **1904** *Amer. Geologist* Mar. 159 Very few of the *geomorphogenists have carried their new science forward into a geographical relation. **1894** A. C. LAWSON in *Univ. Calif. Bull. Dept. Geol.* I. VIII. 241 (*title*) The *geomorphogeny of the coast of Northern California. **1909** W. B. SCOTT *Introd. Geol.* (ed. 2) 435 It would be an advantage in clearness and precision of nomenclature, if Geomorphogeny could be substituted [for Physiography or Physiographical Geography]. **1854** MAYNE *Expos. Lex.*, *Geonomia*, *geonomy. **1896** *Pop. Sci. Monthly* Apr. 819 The significance of landscape contours or *geophysiognomy. **1930** *Proc. Arist. Soc.* XXX. 114, I am thinking, say, of the earth as flat, as when I want to refute a geoplanarian. **1914** V. BJERKNES in *Q. Jrnl. Meteorol. Soc.* XL. 161 It should be borne in mind that in dynamical meteorology gravity-potential (or **geopotential* as it is now proposed to call it) has to be used as a *co-ordinate.* **1939** *Meteorol. Gloss.* (*Met. Office*) (ed. 3) 97 The zero of potential is taken as at sea level. .. Points with the same geopotential may be said to be at the same level. By using geopotential rather than height for specifying the position of parts of the atmosphere, the consideration of the air movements is simplified. **1970** *Nature* 9 May 494/2 The theory of the determination of the geopotential from satellite tracking data is not fully understood. **1860** WORCESTER, **Geoselenic.* **1898** W. J. MCGEE in *Nat. Geogr. Mag.* IX. 436 The atmosphere..is one of the *geospheres, the outermost of the four. *Ibid.* 437 The earth has an interior portion much denser than the known exterior; and this..may conveniently be called a centrosphere—the innermost of the four geospheres. **1913** J. MURRAY *Ocean* x. 227 Our earth..is composed of concentric spheres or shells of matter in the gaseous, liquid, and solid or 'trans-solid' states. These have been called Geospheres, viz., the atmosphere, the hydrosphere, the lithosphere, the biosphere, the tektosphere, and the great centrosphere. **1961** *Aeroplane* CI. 16/2 Raising a communication satellite from a low-circular orbit into a *geostationary orbit at 22,300 miles. **1967** *New Scientist* 25 May 456/3 How difficult, if not impossible, it is to ensure that a so-called geostationary satellite is truly stationary. **1968** *New Statesman* 13 Dec. 828/1 The existence of geo-stationary satellites and the enormous investment in world-wide communications will increase the flow of information and disseminate it on a scale that almost defies the imagination. **1944** G. B. CRESSEY *Asia's Lands & Peoples* ii. 32 The function of *geostrategy is to understand a nation's problems and potential and to suggest a program of internal development and international cooperation that will be of mutual value. **1957** *Encycl. Brit.* X. 182H/1 In theory a branch of geopolitics,..geo-strategy treated warfare as total, embracing the entire populations and resources of the contesting states... It helped to make Germany the first country to realize that airpower could take a position alongside seapower and landpower. **1958** *New Statesman* 26 Apr. 517/1 Pearl Harbour, indeed, provides the point of departure for American geostrategy. **1899** *Natural Sci.* Apr. 329 The negatively *geotactic organism should become positively geotactic in solutions of greater specific gravity than its own. *Ibid.*, The tendency that some Infusorians have to collect near the surface of the water in which they live has been regarded as a reaction to the force of gravity, —a negative *geotaxis. **1908** C. DAVENPORT *Exper. Morphol.* v. 117 On warm days the typical geotactic phenomena are often absent. **1962** *New Scientist* 6 Dec. 545/2 Common observation indicates that moths fly towards a light ('positive phototaxis') and flies climb up a window pane ('negative geotaxis')... The response of the fruitfly *Drosophila melanogaster* to gravity ('geotaxis') was tested in an ingenious vertical maze. **1964** *Oceanogr. & Marine Biol.* II. 476 The marked geotactic orientation of lamellibranch molluscs is well known. *Ibid.*, The animals orient with a positive geotaxis in the sand or mud. **1914** GEDDES & THOMSON *Sex* x. 241 Our aims are not only synthetic, as men-philosophers say, but applied—that is *geotechnic, as with practical women, who, as the anthropologists confess, had the first word in cultivation. **1924** *Glasgow Herald* 15 Nov. 4/2 Man..indulges in big geotechnic operations such as cutting a Panama Canal. **1927** A. DEFRIES *Interpreter* ix. 217 Neotechnics has its physical science, *geotechnics its vital sciences, its synthetic aims. **1968** *New Scientist* 19 Sept. 607/1 The geotechnics division of the station is well-known for its studies of civil engineering enterprises. **1942** *Sci. News Let.* 12 Dec. 370 A new word, '**geotechnology*', has been coined to include all the mineral arts and sciences from metallurgy to ceramics. **1961** *Times* 7 Mar. 2/5 Engineering Pedologist/Geologist.. with.. post-graduate research experience in pedology, sedimentary geology or geotechnology. **1882** GEIKIE *Text-bk. Geol.* IV. 474 *Geotectonic (Structural) Geology, or the architecture of the earth's crust. *Ibid.* IV. vii. 537 The characters by which an eruptive (igneous) rock may be distinguished are partly lithological and partly geotectonic. **1881** *Nature* XXIV. 363 The study of the *geotectonical conditions of the localities where they [earthquakes] occur. **1875** J. H. BENNET *Winter Medit.* I. i. 13 The peculiar mildness of the winter may also be partly accounted for on *geothermal..grounds. **1940** *Chambers's Techn. Dict.*, 374/1 *Geothermal gradient* (Mining), the rate at which the temperature of the earth's crust increases with depth. **1955** *Times* 5 July p. ii/3 An interesting possibility is the exploitation of geothermal steam—steam generated naturally below the surface of the earth. *Ibid.* 14 July 14/6 The large heavy water plant which will form part of the scheme for using the steam from the geothermal springs in New Zealand. **1971** *Nature* 29 Jan. 300 An unsuccessful attempt to develop geothermal power in a known geothermal area. **1882** OGILVIE, **Geothermic*. **1855** *Ibid.* Suppl., **Geothermometer*, an instrument for measuring the degree of terrestrial heat at different places, especially in mines and artesian wells.

geocentric (dʒiːəʊˈsɛntrɪk), *a.* (*sb.*) [f. GEO-: see CENTRIC. Cf. F. *géocentrique*. Opposed in both senses to HELIOCENTRIC.]

1. Referred to the earth as centre; considered as viewed from the centre of the earth: as the ***geocentric latitude, longitude, place***, etc. of a planet, i.e. that in which it would appear to an observer placed at the centre of the earth.

1686 *Phil. Trans.* XVI. 196 One of his [♃'s] Geocentrick places. **1726** tr. *Gregory's Astron.* I. 15 Its Geocentric Latitude will be measured by the Angle ♂ *T E*. **1784** HERSCHEL in *Phil. Trans.* LXXIV. 256 Our next business will be to reduce these two geocentric observations to a heliocentric measure. **1816** PLAYFAIR *Nat. Phil.* II. 161 If the planet's elongation from the Sun, and its geocentric latitude be observed, the inclination of the orbit may be found. **1868** LOCKYER *Elem. Astron.* 167 This latitude and longitude may be either heliocentric or geocentric, that is reckoned from the centre either of the Sun or Earth respectively. **1880** *Nature* XXI. 315 The apparent retardation of the eclipses as affected by the geocentric position of Jupiter.

2. Having, or representing, the earth as centre.

1696 PHILLIPS (ed. 5), *Geocentrick*, any Orb or Planet that has the Earth for its Center, or the same Center with the Earth. **1834** [see HELIOCENTRIC 2]. **1859** MILL *Liberty* 66 Some geocentric theory instead of heliocentric. **1865** GROTE *Plato* I. i. 14 *note*, The original system proposed by Protagoras was a geocentric system. **1880** M. PATTISON *Milton* xiii. 180 In the universe of being the difference between a heliocentric and a geocentric theory is of..small moment.

fig. **1854** DE QUINCEY *Autobiog. Sk.* Wks. II. 54 Wheel into a new centre your moral system; geocentric has that system been up to this hour—that is, having earth and the earthly for its starting-point. **1871** H. MACMILLAN *True Vine* i. 36 Regarded from this heliocentric position, difficulties and mysteries, insoluble from the geocentric position, are cleared away.

3. *sb.* An adherent of the geocentric theory.

1667 A. NOWEL in Josselyn *Voy. New Eng.* (1674) 48 This assertion is not expugned by Geocentricks who produce sense and Antiquity to support their suppositions.

Hence **geoˈcentrical** *a.* [+ -AL[1]] = prec.; ˌ**geoˈcentrically** *adv.*, as viewed from the centre of the earth; **geoˈcentricism**, the geocentric theory.

1727 BAILEY vol. II, *Geocentrically*. **1775** ASH, *Geocentrical*. **1882** F. HALL in *Nation* (N.Y.) XXXV. 340/3 And did not he [Bacon] cling to geocentricism, which was still prevailingly current in his day? **1885** W. W. ROBERTS *Pontif. Decrees* Introd. 53 In 1742..Geocentricism as a scientific theory was dead.

geochemistry (dʒiːəʊˈkɛmɪstrɪ). [f. GEO- + CHEMISTRY; cf. G. *geochemie* (C. F. Schönbein 1838, in *Ann. d. Physik. u. Chem.* XLV. 281).] The chemistry of the earth; the study of the chemical composition of the earth.

1903 *Carnegie Inst. Yearbk.* 1902 27 The problems of geophysics and geochemistry involve the applications of pure physics and pure chemistry from the minutest parts of the earth to the mass of the earth as a whole. **1952** *New Biol.* XIII. 122 The science of geochemistry, with its emphasis on the dynamic exchange of molecules and ions between lithosphere, hydrosphere, biosphere, and atmosphere.

So **geoˈchemical** *a.*, of or pertaining to geochemistry; **geoˈchemically** *adv.*; **geoˈchemist**, an expert in, or student of, geochemistry.

1888 *Jrnl. Soc. Chem. Industry* VII. 338 (*title*) Geochemical studies. **1918** WEBSTER Add., Geochemist. **1946** *Nature* 6 July 31/1 Some conclusions which may be of interest to oil- and water-geologists, geophysicists and geochemists. **1957** *Times* 20 Dec. 13/1 Developments in geochemical prospecting—the use of chemical analyses of soil to detect underlying deposits of minerals. **1957** G. E. HUTCHINSON *Treat. Limnol.* I. viii. 559 This Rb:K ratio is by no means geochemically impossible. **1965** G. J. WILLIAMS *Econ. Geol. N.Z.* x. 156/2 Miss X. F. Williams has reported copper and nickel geochemically in this region. **1970** *Nature* 17 Oct. 273/2 Geochemical studies indicate that the weathering of 100 tons of average continental surface rock supplies about 0·9 ton of sodium to the hydrological cycle.

geochronic: see GEO-.

geochronology (ˌdʒiːəʊkrəˈnɒlədʒɪ). [f. GEO- + CHRONOLOGY.] The chronology of the earth; the measurement of geological time and the ordering of past geological events. (The term *geochrone* introduced by Prof. H. S. Williams to designate a unit of geological time does not seem to have been widely adopted.)

1893 H. S. WILLIAMS in *Jrnl. Geol.* I. 294 In all these studies in which the geological time-scale is applied to the evolution of the earth.., the time concerned is not human chronology but is what may be called geochronology. For this purpose we need a standard time-unit or geochrone. **1934** *Discovery* Mar. 66/2 The high upper limits are supported by the geochronology of the Swedish geologist, de Geer. **1957** G. CLARK *Archæol. & Society* (ed. 3) v. 133 Geochronology, the chronology based on the natural changes recorded in the geological sequence, depends on many branches of natural science. **1965** F. J. MONKHOUSE *Dict. Geogr.* 1/2 *Absolute age*, in geochronology, the dating of rocks in actual terms of years.

Hence ˌ**geochronoˈlogical** *a.*, of or pertaining to geochronology; ˌ**geochronoˈlogically** *adv.*; ˌ**geochroˈnologist**, an expert in, or student of, geochronology.

1934 *Antiquity* VIII. 245 A geochronological investigation of the ice-lake sediments. **1936** *Proc. Prehist. Soc.* II. 169 The absolute geochronological scale which has been established by Scandinavian workers. **1958** F. E. ZEUNER *Dating Past* (ed. 4) 4 There are several geochronological methods, each capable of covering not more than a limited range of time. *Ibid.* iv. 109 Fromm's (1938) geochronologically dated pollen-diagrams from Angermanland provide the remainder of dates in the Scandinavian sequence, and Welten's work in Switzerland may become important as a second pollen-time-scale. **1960** *New Scientist* 14 July 137/3 The latest method in the repertoire of the geochronologist is the rubidium-strontium method. **1970** *Nature* 24 Oct. 320/1 The matching of discrete geochronological zones across the boundaries of continents thought to be adjacent before the onset of continental drift. *Ibid.* 320/2 Other pre-drift configurations have not been so well documented geochronologically.

geocian, -cie, mistakes for GOETIAN, GOETY.

geoclinal: see GEO-.

geocronite (dʒiːˈɒkrənaɪt). *Min.* [f. GEO- + Gr. Κρόν-ος the god identified with Saturn (in alchemy associated with lead) + -ITE. Named by Svanberg in 1839.] A sulphide of lead and antimony.

1844 DANA *Min.* (ed. 2) 493 Geocronite comes from the silver mines of Sala..Sweden. **1883** *Encycl. Brit.* XVI. 395/2.

geocyclic: see GEO-.

geodæsia: see GEODESY.

geode (ˈdʒiːəʊd). Also 8–9 **geod**. [a. F. *géode*, ad. L. *geōdes* = Gr. γεώδης earthy, f. γῆ earth.] A concretionary or nodular stone, containing a cavity usually lined with crystals or other mineral matter.

[**1619** R. C. *Table Alph.*, *Stones*, *Geodes*, a stone being hollow, having earth within the hollownesse thereof, and being put to a mans eare, it maketh a kinde of sound.] **1676–1732** COLES, *Geode*, the Earth-stone. **1774** STRANGE in *Phil. Trans.* LXV. 41 A hard ferruginous substance, of a dark-brown colour, much resembling some common ferruginous geodes I have seen. **1811** PINKERTON *Petral.* I. 436 Infiltrated geods of quartz and calcareous spar. **1839** MURCHISON *Silur. Syst.* I. vii. 107 Each geode being enveloped in red shale. **1860** O. W. HOLMES *Prof. Breakf.-t.* 71 An aphorism..has been forming itself in one of the blank interior spaces of my intelligence, like a crystal in the cavity of a geode. **1883** L. OLIPHANT *Haifa* (1887) 37 A plateau..abundantly strewn with geodes.

b. The cavity itself, together with the crystal or mineral formation therein contained. Also any similar formation.

1849 DANA *Geol.* iv. (1850) 298 Small geodes of stilbite and analcime were found in pebbles. **1831** RAYMOND *Mining Gloss.*, *Geode*, a cavity, studded around with crystals or mineral matter.

Hence **geoˈdiferous** *a.* [-(I)FEROUS], producing or abounding in geodes; ˈ**geodize** *v.* [-IZE], *trans.*, to convert into a geode; ˈ**geodized** *ppl. a.*

1847 CRAIG, *Geodiferous*. **1885** *Amer. Jrnl. Sci.* Ser. III. XXX. 376 The geodized fossils of the Keokuk limestone.

geodephagous, erroneous for GEAD-.

geodesia; see GEODESY.

†**geodesian.** *Obs.* Also 7 **geodecian, geodetian.** [f. mod.L. *geōdæsi-a* (see GEODESY) + -AN.] One who measures land; a land-surveyor.

1656 BLOUNT *Glossogr.*, *Geodesian*, a measurer of Land. **1669** STURMY *Mariner's Mag.* A4 The Geodecian, in this Book, may have Rules to Survey his Land. **1690** LEYBOURN *Curs. Math.* 205 For by the Rules hereof the Geodetian may measure..your Lands.

geodesic (dʒiːəʊˈdɛsɪk), *a.* [f. GEODES-Y + -IC. Cf. F. *géodésique*.] Of or pertaining to geodesy. ***geodesic curve***, a geodesic line on a curved surface; ***geodesic dome***, a dome built according to the principles of geodetic construction (see quot. 1959) enunciated by the American designer and architect, R. Buckminster Fuller (b. 1895); ***geodesic line*** (see quot. 1886). Also *sb.*, a geodesic line or curve.

1821 J. ROBSON (*title*), Treatise on Geodesic Operations, or County Surveying, Land Surveying and Levelling. **1853** TH. ROSS *Humboldt's Trav.* III. xxxii. 298 The combined means of barometric and geodesic measurements. **1881** CAYLEY in *Proc. Lond. Math. Soc.* XII. 187 The torsion of the same geodesic curve. **1883** BALL in *Encycl. Brit.* XV. 659/1 These lines being what we would call geodesics. **1886** W. S. ALDIS *Solid Geom.* xiii. (ed. 4) 219 A geodesic line on a surface is such that every small element *PQ* is the shortest line that can be drawn on the surface between *P* and *Q*. **1950** [see next]. **1959** *Times* 20 Mar. 3/5 The geodesic dome combines the structural advantages of the sphere (which encloses the most space within the least surface, and is strongest against internal pressure) with those of the tetrahedron (which encloses least space with most surface and has the greatest stiffness against external pressure). **1960** R. W. MARKS *Dymaxion World of B. Fuller* 58/1 In modern geometry, as we have seen, any arc of a great circle is called a 'geodesic'. **1968** *Listener* 26 Sept. 394/1 The key invention that emerged from these speculations was the geodesic dome..made up of a triangulated web of short struts. He developed the geodesic principle with countless experimental structures.

geodesical (dʒiːəʊˈdɛsɪkəl), *a.* Also 9 *erron.* **geodesiacal.** [f. prec. + -AL[1].] = prec.

1818 *Blackw. Mag.* III. 466 The war..has given to geodesiacal operations..the extreme perfection which they have acquired. **1853** DE QUINCEY *Autobiog. Sk.* Wks. I. 335 In geodesical operations, one part is referred to heaven, and one to earth. **1866** *Athenæum* 23 July 835/1, I desired to make some geodesical observations.

geodesist (dʒiːˈɒdɪsɪst). [f. GEODES-Y + -IST.] One versed in geodesy; a geodetic surveyor.

1840 HERSCHEL *Ess.* (1857) 525 In conjunction with M. Carlini, he [M. Plana] also carried on that extensive and important triangulation of the Savoy Alps, which have made his name celebrated as a geodesist. **1877** *Encycl. Brit.* VII. 597 The next geodesist, Willebrord Snell, took an immense step in the right direction. **1883** *Athenæum* 14 July 52/3 The principal triangulation of India..has occupied the geodesists continuously since the beginning of the century.

geodesy (dʒiːˈɒdɪsɪ). Also 6–9 **geodesie**, 7 **geodæsie**; and 8–9 in mod.L. form **geodæsia**, **-esia**. [ad. F. *géodésie*, ad. mod.L. *geōdæsia*, Gr. γεωδαισία, f. γεω-, γῆ earth + δαίειν to divide.]

†**a.** Land surveying; the measuring of land (*obs.*). **b.** In mod. use: That branch of applied mathematics which determines the figures and areas of large portions of the earth's surface, and the figure of the earth as a whole.

1570 DEE *Math. Pref.* 16 Of these Feates..is Sprong the Feate of Geodesie, or Land Measuring. **1664** V. WING *Art Surv.* 111 Geodæsie or Land-measure. **1755** JOHNSON, *Geodæsia* [citing HARRIS]. **1766** B. MARTIN *Surv. by Goniom.* 6 With regard to Geodesia or Land Surveying, and all kinds of Longimetry, the natural eyesight ought to be assisted. **1853** HERSCHEL *Pop. Lect. Sc.* v. §13. (1873) 189 'Geodesy' as distinct from mere mensuration and surveying. **1855** J. B. WILLIAMS (*title*), Practical Geodesy, comprising chain surveying and the use of surveying instruments. **1881** M. MERRIMAN (*title*), Figure of the Earth: an Introduction to Geodesy.

geodete (ˈdʒiːəʊdiːt). [back-formation from next, after words like ATHLETE.] = GEODESIST.

1887 *Pop. Sci. Monthly* XXX. 244 (Cent.) Dangerous ascents and solitary life on the top of high mountains..are common occurrences for the geodete.

geodetic (dʒiːəʊˈdɛtɪk), *a.* and *sb.* Also 7 **geodaetick.** [as if ad. L. **geōdætic-us*, a. Gr. *γεωδαιτικός, f. γῆ earth + δαίειν to divide.]

A. *adj.* **a.** Of or pertaining to geodesy. ***geodetic line*** (see quot. 1879).

1834 *Nat. Philos., Astron.* xiii. 253/1 (U.K.S.) Those great geodetic operations which have been undertaken to determine the figure of the earth. **1879** THOMSON & TAIT *Nat. Phil.* I. i. §132 If the shortest possible line be drawn from one point of a surface to another, its plane of curvature is everywhere perpendicular to the surface. Such a curve is called a Geodetic line. **1880** *Nature* XXI. 197 Geographical and topographical work such as had been carried on by the Coast and Geodetic Surveys and the Land Office.

b. ***geodetic construction*** (see quot. 1950); ***geodetic dome*** = *geodesic dome*.

1936 *Jrnl. Aeronaut. Sci.* Dec. 78/1 The multitudinous fittings employed in the geodetic construction..add much to the weight and cost of the structure. **1950** *Gloss. Aeronaut. Terms* (*B.S.I.*) 3105 *Geodetic construction*, a method of making curved space frames in which the particular structural members follow geodesics in the surface, the curves being designed in such a manner that the forces set up in the members are either tension or compression. **1958** *New Scientist* 15 May 27/2 The airship embodied Wallis's first essay in geodetic construction, and it was a complete success. **1959** *Times Lit. Suppl.* 6 Nov. p. xxx/5 With his geodetic domes and his synergetic geometry ..he [*sc.* Buckminster Fuller] is designing..methods of enclosing space that others may one day make into an architecture. **1970** K. PLATT *Pushbutton Butterfly* (1971) viii. 84 The house..was a series of geodetic domes clustered igloo-like beneath the main house.

B. *sb.* (the adj. used absolutely).

†**1.** *pl.* 'Geodetical' numbers: see GEODETICAL 2.

1674 JEAKE *Arith.* (1696) 62 The smaller Geodaeticks arise from such of the greater as admit of subdivisions.

2. A geodetic line (see quot. 1879 in A).

1879 THOMSON & TAIT *Nat. Phil.* I. i. §137 There must.. be tortuosity in every geodetic of the closed polygon.

3. in pl. form **geodetics** = GEODESY.

In mod. Dicts.

geodetical (dʒiːəʊˈdɛtɪkəl), *a.* Also 7 **geodeticall**, 7–8 **geodaetical.** [f. as GEODETIC + -AL[1].]

1. †**a.** Of or pertaining to land-measuring or surveying (*obs.*). **b.** Of or pertaining to geodesy.

1610 W. FOLKINGHAM *Art of Survey* II. iv. 53 The second is retriued with Plaine-Table, Theodelite, Sector, Circumferentor, Geodeticall-Staffe, etc. **1755** JOHNSON, *Geodætical*, relating to the art of measuring surfaces; comprehending or showing the art of measuring land. **1790** ROY in *Phil. Trans.* LXXX. 216 This new spheroid, founded immediately on the recent geodetical measurements and observations of the pole-star. **1800** *Ibid.* XC. 636 The longitudes and latitudes of places on its surface might be accurately computed, provided their geodetical situations were correctly ascertained. **1863** *Edin. Rev.* Oct. 380 Astronomical and geodetical science. **1887** J. BALL *Nat. in S. Amer.* 377 The true amount of atmospheric refraction found by day in geodetical observations.

†**2.** ***geodetical number***: used by Jeake app. in the sense of 'concrete number'. Also as sb. pl. *geodeticals*. *Obs.*

Jeake explains that the term, which he admits is not accurately expressive, is used in its etymological sense, all 'denominations' admitting of being regarded as 'measures.. according to the standard of earthly dimensions'.

1674 JEAKE *Arith.* (1696) 61 Numbers generally Contract are Geodaetical or Figural. Geodaeticals include all numbers contracted by Vulgar Names or Denominations according to the common and usual distinctions, divisions, dimensions or legal institutions customs or usages of Nature or Nations, as Men, Women, Horses, Sheep, Weights, Measures, etc. **1721** BAILEY, *Geodætical Numbers.*

Hence † **geo'detically** *adv.*

1674 JEAKE *Arith.* (1696) 232 To turn Common Signs into Physical, half them, or reduce Geodaetically by 30, the Signs into Degrees.

geodic (dʒiː'ɒdɪk), *a.* [f. GEODE *sb.* + -IC.] Of or pertaining to a geode; resembling a geode.

1851 S. JUDD *Margaret* II. iii. 221 Man, like this stone, is geodic. **1878** LAWRENCE tr. *Cotta's Rocks Class.* 9 Adularia is 'frequently found in the geodic cavities of granitic rocks'. **1889** HOUSTON in *Jrnl. Franklin Inst.* Nov. 361 They resembled the projecting crystals that form so common a lining in geodic masses.

geodite ('dʒiːəʊdaɪt). [f. GEODE + -ITE.] = GEODE.

1802-3 tr. *Pallas's Trav.* (1812) I. 182 Were partly hollow, and contained sand not unlike regular geodites.

geodize *v.*: see s.v. GEODE.

geoduck ('dʒiːəʊdʌk). [? American Indian.] A large edible clam (*Glycineris generosa*) from the Pacific coast of the U.S.

1883 *Echo* 2 May 1/6 The bivalve in question is found principally at Olympia, Washington Territory, and is locally known to the boys of the district as the 'geoduck'.

geodynamic, -al: see GEO-.

Geoffroy (ʒɔfrwa). [tr. *Felis geoffroyi* (D'Orbigny & Gervais 1844, in *Extr. Proc.-Verb. Soc. Philomathique Paris* 40), f. the name of Étienne *Geoffroy* Saint-Hilaire (1772–1844) or his son Isidore (1805–1861), both French zoologists.] ***Geoffroy's cat***: a South American species of cat, *Felis geoffroyi*.

1870 *Proc. Zool. Soc.* LIII. 796 A fine specimen of Geoffroy's Cat (*Felis geoffroii*),..obtained from Paraguay. **1906** *Westm. Gaz.* 30 Apr. 4/3 A nice example of Geoffroy's Cat may now be seen in the Small Mammals' House at the Zoo. **1961** G. DURRELL *Whispering Land* (1965) v. 124 It was a baby Geoffroy's cat, a small species of wild cat which is getting increasingly rare in South America. Its basic colouring was a pale fawny yellow, and it was dappled all over with neat, dark brown spots.

geogenic (dʒiːəʊ'dʒɛnɪk), *a.* [f. GEOGEN-Y + -IC.] Pertaining to geogeny; earth-forming or producing.

1854 MAYNE *Expos. Lex.*, *Geogenicus*, geogenic. **1882** T. S. HUNT in *Pop. Sci. Monthly* XXII. 170 They are the geogenic agencies which have molded the mineral mass of the earth.

geogenous: see GEO-.

geogeny (dʒiː'ɒdʒɪnɪ). Also 9 geogenie. [f. Gr. γεω- GEO- + -GENY.] That branch of geology which treats of the formation of the earth's crust.

1855 H. SPENCER *Princ. Psychol.* (1870) I. 138 Geology (or rather Geogeny let us call it, that we may include all those mineralogical and meteorological changes which the word Geology, as now used, recognizes but tacitly). **1876** A. H. GREEN *Phys. Geol.* ii. 11 Historical Geology or Geogenie.

geognosis (dʒiːəg'nəʊsɪs). [Incorrectly for GEOGNOSY, after Gr. γνῶσις.] = GEOGNOSY.

1872 GEO. ELIOT *Middlem.* (1878) I. I. 120 He has no bent towards exploration, or the enlargement of our geognosis.

geognosist (dʒiː'ɒgnəsɪst). [f. GEOGNOS-Y + -IST.] = next.

1851 MAYNE REID *Scalp Hunt.* xli, The eye of the geognosist could not be mistaken in the character of its atmosphere.

geognost ('dʒiːəgnɒst). [ad. F. *géognoste* (Werner 1802), f. Gr. γεω- GEO- + γνώστ-ης one who knows.] One versed in geognosy; one who has a knowledge of the structure of the earth.

1804 *Edin. Rev.* V. 67 The next generation may perhaps overwhelm.. Geognosts with the same contempt of which professors of alchemy have been the victims. **1854** *Fraser's Mag.* XLIX. 141 The microscopist and the geognost are daily revealing wonders. **1897** GEIKIE *Anc. Volcanoes Gt. Brit.* I. p. ix, Werner's disciples loved to call themselves by their teacher's term 'geognosts'.

geognostic (dʒiːəg'nɒstɪk), *a.* [f. prec. + -IC.] Of or pertaining to geognosy.

1796 KIRWAN *Elem. Min.* (ed. 2) I. Pref. 13 The third part is called geognostic or geological. **1814** T. THOMSON in *Ann. Phil.* IV. 410 Geognostic Map of the Counties of Northumberland, Durham and part of Cumberland. **1849** E. C. OTTÉ tr. *Humboldt's Cosmos* II. 543 Geognostic conjectures regarding the connection of mountain chains. **1880** A. R. WALLACE *Isl. Life* ix. 181 The knowledge of a mountain's geognostic character.

geognostical (dʒiːəg'nɒstɪkəl), *a.* [f. prec. + -AL[1].] = prec.

1791 J. HAILSTONE *Plan Lect. Min.* Pref., [The author apologises for the defects in] the Geognostical part [of the Syllabus]. **1814** J. THOMSON in *Ann. Phil.* IV. 410 A Geognostical Sketch of the Counties of Northumberland, Durham and parts of Cumberland. **1853** KANE *Grinnell Exp.* vii. (1856) 47 Its general geognostical structure is determined by a great green-stone dike.

Hence **geo'gnostically** *adv.*, with reference to geognosy.

1853 TH. ROSS tr. *Humboldt's Trav.* III. xxxii. 364 Geognostically speaking, these two regions of east and west form only one basin.

geognosy (dʒiː'ɒgnəsɪ). [ad. F. *géognosie*, f. Gr. γεω- GEO- + γνῶσις knowledge.]

1. A knowledge of the structure of the earth, its strata, their relative position and the probable condition of the interior. Often used as nearly equivalent to GEOLOGY.

1791 J. HAILSTONE *Plan Lect. Min.* Pref., Geognosy, or the knowledge of the Earth's internal structure. **1804** *Edin. Rev.* V. 66 We shall venture..to inform them, that.. Geognosie is synonymous with geology. **1831** CARLYLE *Sart. Res.* (1858) 1 Of Geology and Geognosy we know enough. **1870** LOWELL *Study Wind.* 123 Voltaire, Diderot, Mirabeau and others, who had hitherto been measured by the usual British standard of their respect for the geognosy of Moses. **1882** GEIKIE *Text-Bk. Geol.* 4 Geognosy.

2. In a more restricted sense: **a.** (See quot. 1830). **b.** Local geology; the geology of a certain district.

1811 *Edin. Rev.* XVIII. 93 The Geognosy of this celebrated mineralogist [Werner]. **1822** *Proc. Werner. Soc.* IV. 91 Geognosy of Germany. **1830** LYELL *Princ. Geol.* I. 55 Werner..directed his attention..to what he termed 'geognosy', or the natural position of minerals in particular rocks, together with the grouping of those rocks, their geographical distribution, and various relations. **1839** R. J. H. CUNNINGHAM (*title*), On the Geognosy of the Isle of Eigg.

geogony (dʒiː'ɒgənɪ). [f. Gr. γεω- GEO- + -γονία production.] The theory of the formation of the earth. Cf. GEOGENY. Also quasi-*concr.* an account of the origin of the earth.

1828 in WEBSTER. **1847** in CRAIG. **1870** *Eng. Mech.* 28 Jan. 480/3 The laws of Cosmogony, Astrogony, and Geogony, should be given. **1882-3** SCHAFF *Encycl. Relig. Knowl.* III. 2552/1 It is, indeed, a geogony, and not a cosmogony, which is given in the first chapter of Genesis.

Hence **geo'gonic, geo'gonical** *adjs.*, of or pertaining to geogony.

In mod. Dicts.

†**'geograph.** *Obs.* Also 6 in Latin form **geographus.** [ad. med.L. *geōgraphus*, a. Gr. γεωγράφος, f. γεω- GEO- + -γραφος, f. γράφ-ειν to write. Cf. F. *géographe*.] A geographer.

[**1547** HOOPER *Declar. Christ* viii. Ij, The Geographus conceiueth and comprehendithe all the worold in his hed.] **1639** HORN & ROBOTHAM *Gate Lang. Unl.* lxxix. §783 A Geograph in a map deciphereth..the situation..of countries.

geographer (dʒiː'ɒgrəfə(r)). Also 6 -ier. [f. med.L. *geōgraph-us* (see prec.): see -ER *suffix*[1] 4.] One who is versed in, or writes upon, geography. ***geographer-general*** (cf. GENERAL *a.* 10).

1542 UDALL *Erasm. Apoph.* 203 There wer also other tounes mo then one or twain of the same name elswhere, as testifien the Geographiers. **1559** W. CUNNINGHAM *Cosmogr. Glasse* 21 The Geographers name them Antipodes. **1576** FLEMING *Panopl. Epist.* 190 *note*, Dionysius..a geographer of Corynthus. **1632** LITHGOW *Trav.* III. 106, I come forth.. to have a single bout with the ignorant malice of an imperious and abortive Geographer. **1668** DRYDEN *Even. Love* III. i, I am not so ill a geographer. **1733** SWIFT *Poetry* 179 Geographers, in Afric maps, With savage pictures fill their gaps. **1790** A. HAMILTON *Wks.* (1886) VII. 51 The surveyor-general shall also have in charge all the duties committed to the geographer-general by the resolutions and ordinances of Congress. **1827** MAGINN *Red-nosed Lieut.* in *Forget-me-not* 107 Soldiers are no great geographers. **1845** FORD *Handbk. Spain* I. 1 The general comprehensive term 'Spain', which is convenient for geographers and politicians, is calculated to mislead the traveller. **1872** PROCTOR *Ess. Astron.* xxiii. 296 The construction of these figures..would form an instructive employment for the young geographer.

geographic (dʒiːəʊ'græfɪk), *a.* and *sb.* [ad. Gr. γεωγραφικ-ός, f. γεωγράφος GEOGRAPH. Cf. F. *géographique*.] **A.** *adj.* = GEOGRAPHICAL. Now somewhat *rare*, exc. in ***geographic latitude***: the angle made with the plane of the equator by a perpendicular to the surface of the earth at any point. (In quot. 1630 = versed in geography.)

1630 DAVENANT *Just Ital.* I. C 1 b, The Geographicke Captaine shall no more Studie the Town Mappe. **1655** STANLEY *Hist. Philos.* I. I. (1701) 60/1 He first set forth a Geographick Table. **1669** GALE *Crt. Gentiles* I. III. ii. 31 The Geographic descriptions, which the ancient Pagan Historians give of the dispersion of Noah's Posteritie. **1719** HALLEY in *Phil. Trans.* XXX. 985 So that in a round Number we may conclude it to have been just 60 Geographic or 69 Statute Miles above the Earth's Surface. *a* **1797** H. WALPOLE *Mem. Geo. II* (1847) III. ii. 35 When the affairs of this little spot, which we call Britain, shall appear of no more importance than our island itself in a geographic picture. **1853** TH. ROSS *Humboldt's Trav.* III. xxxii. 381 *note*, The 'geographic stones' (piedras mapajas) of the Orinoco..contain streaks of dark green mica irregularly disposed. **1879** NEWCOMB & HOLDEN *Astron.* 203 It will be observed that it is the geocentric and not the geographic latitude which gives the true position of the observer relative to the earth's centre.

B. *sb.* pl. **geo'graphics** *rare* (Gr. τὰ γεωγραφικά), geographical science; †a treatise on this.

1610 HOLLAND *Camden's Brit.* II. *Irel.* 65 You may see if you list to compare his Geographicks with his booke of Great Construction. **1831** CARLYLE *Sart. Res.* (1858) 108 Statistics, Geographics, Topographics came, through the Eye, almost of their own accord.

geographical (dʒiːəʊ'græfɪkəl), *a.* [f. as prec. + -AL[1].] Of or pertaining to geography; of the nature of geography. ***geographical mile***: a measure of length = 1′ of longitude on the equator.

1559 W. CUNNINGHAM *Cosmogr. Glasse* 138 A greate Circle, and devide it into 360 partes, as your Geographicall plaine Sphere is. **1600** J. PORY tr. *Leo's Africa* Ded., Vouchsafe therefore..to accept of this Geographicall Historie. **1674** tr. *Martiniere's Voy. N. Countries* 151 There having fallen into my hands several Geografical Charts. **1768** BOSWELL *Corsica* Introd. (ed. 2) 9 A Geographical and Physical description of the island. **1823** SCORESBY *Whale Fishery* 107 Its distance, by calculation..being 140 geographical, or 160 English miles. **1852** MRS. STOWE *Uncle Tom's C.* vii, Andy looked up innocently at Sam, surprised at hearing this new geographical fact. **1862** HUXLEY *Lect. Wrkg. Men* 21 Geographical Distribution of Animals.. Geographical Distribution of Plants.

b. Fancifully used for: Resembling a map. (Cf. quot. 1853 s.v. GEOGRAPHIC.)

1885 LADY BRASSEY *The Trades* 145 One variety..is called the 'geographical tree', or sometimes the 'picture-tree', because it is said to be always possible to be able to trace in imagination a map or a picture upon the surface of each leaf. **1897** ALLBUTT *Syst. Med.* III. 350 Wandering rash (Geographical tongue; Ringworm of the tongue; Lichenoid..).

geo'graphically, *adv.* [f. prec. + -LY[2].] In a geographical manner or sense; with respect to geography or geographical position.

1617 F. MORYSON *Itin.* I. 270 Wherein these Kingdomes are Geographically described out of Camden. **1646** SIR T. BROWNE *Pseud. Ep.* VI. x. 326 Geographically the clime is not intemperate. **1725** BROOME in *Pope's Odyss.* XIII. 299 *note*, Here he introduces Minerva to let Ulysses into the knowledge of his country. How does she do this? She geographically describes it to him. **1796** MORSE *Amer. Geog.* I. 39 There are, geographically speaking, two horizons, the sensible and the rational. **1837** *Fraser's Mag.* XV. 635 Baden is only geographically German. **1862** ANSTED *Channel Isl.* I. (ed. 2) 4 Geographically, no doubt, the Channel Islands belong to the continent and to France. **1884** SIR W. B. BRETT in *Law Times' Rep.* LI. 739/2 England is divided geographically into counties.

geographize (dʒiː'ɒgrəfaɪz), *v.* *rare.* [f. GEOGRAPH-Y + -IZE.] **a.** *intr.* To study geography; to make geographical researches. **b.** *trans.* To determine the geography of; to describe geographically; to reduce to geographical order. Hence **ge'ographizing** *ppl. a.*

1818 SOUTHEY in *Life* (1850) IV. 306 The amateur geographising 'gentlemen of England who sit at home at ease'. **1870** *Athenæum* 8 Oct. 470/3 By which time [1881] the Registrar-General will have completed two more decades of mortuary records..and these, with the one..which Mr. Haviland had geographized, will form a foundation for all future inquiry. **1886** BUNBURY in *Encycl. Brit.* XX. 96/1 Strabo was fully alive to the importance of the great rivers and mountain chains which (to use his own expressive phrase) 'geographize' a country.

geography (dʒiː'ɒgrəfɪ). Also 6-7 geographie. [a. F. *géographie*, ad. L. *geographia*, a. Gr. γεωγραφία, f. γεω- GEO- + -γραφία writing.]

1. a. The science which has for its object the description of the earth's surface, treating of its form and physical features, its natural and political divisions, the climate, productions, population, etc., of the various countries. It is frequently divided into ***mathematical, physical,*** and ***political geography.*** † ***subterranean geography*** = GEOLOGY.

1542 UDALL *Erasm. Apoph.* 285 b, Strabo in his werke of geographie, that is to saie, of the descripcion of the yearth, writeth, that [etc.]. **1599** HAKLUYT *Voy.* Pref. *4 Hauing.. by the helpe of Geographie, and Chronologie.. referred ech particular relation to the due time and place. **1646** SIR T. BROWNE *Pseud. Ep.* VI. viii. 315 The City of Rome is magnified by the Latins to be the greatest of the earth; but time and Geography enforme us, that Cairo is bigger then ever it was. **1727** ARBUTHNOT *Coins* 255 According to antient Fables the Argonauts..sail'd up the Danube, and from thence passed into the Adriatick, carrying their Ship Argo upon their Shoulders: a Mark of great Ignorance in Geography among the Writers of that time. **1786** WHITEHURST *Theory Earth* Pref. 2 A competent knowledge of subterranean geography. **1834** *Nat. Philos., Math. Geog.* i. 1/2 (U.K.S.) Mathematical Geography is that branch of the general science which is derived from the application of mathematical truths to the figure of the earth. **1858** *Sat. Rev.* 14 Aug. 158/2 The new term—Physical Geography of the Sea—devised to include all that relates to the physical condition of the watery surface of the globe [etc.]. *a* **1862** BUCKLE *Misc. Wks.* (1872) I. 304 The first Greek prose is on geography. **1880** GEIKIE *(title)* Physical Geography.

attrib. **1782** T. VAUGHAN *Fashionable Follies* I. 84 His figure [was]..just such a one as it may be supposed heaven would bestow on a geography master. **1857** RUSKIN *Arrows of Chace* (1880) I. 42 Precision of touch should be cultivated by map-drawing in his geography class.

b. The study of a subject in its geographical aspects. ***linguistic geography*** (see LINGUISTIC *a.*); ***dialect geography*** (see DIALECT 2 b).

1643 SIR T. BROWNE *Relig. Med.* I. §2 There being a Geography of Religions as well as Lands.

c. The subject-matter of geography; the geographical features of a place or region; the range or extent of what is known geographically.

1737 *Pope's Lett.* Contents, Letter lxxxv. Of the Map of the Geography of Homer, done by the Author. **1784** COOK *3rd Voy.* III. xii. II. 221 The islands in the Pacific Ocean, which our late voyages have added to the geography of the globe, have been generally found lying in groups and clusters. **1854** EMERSON *Lett. & Soc. Aims, Resources* Wks. (Bohn) III. 198 We have seen the railroad and telegraph subdue our enormous geography. **1859** LEVER *Davenport Dunn* i. 2 Science has been popularized, remote geographies made familiar, complex machinery explained.

d. ***the geography (of the house)***, the arrangement and position of the rooms, staircases, and other internal features of a house; hence as a jocular euphemism for lavatory, water-closet. *colloq.*

1864 C. M. YONGE *Trial* II. xiii. 239 The little gentleman showed himself minutely acquainted with the whole geography of the house, knew all the rooms and pictures. **1920** 'SAPPER' *Bull-Dog Drummond* ii. 65 He wanted to get the geography of the house firmly imprinted on his mind. **1927** R. GRAVES *Lars Porsena* (ed. 2) 68 For a man to show a woman the way to the lavatory..an evasive phrase had to be used:..'Have you been shown the geography of the house?' **1930** A. LYALL *It isn't Done* 59 It is all very baffling for the uninitiated foreigner..who when his host offers to 'show him the geography of the house' finds that his tour begins and ends with the smallest..room. **1958** 'A. BRIDGE' *Portuguese Escape* ix. 154 Will you excuse me if *I* show you the geography?.. There—that's the gentlemen's bathroom. **1963** L. MEYNELL *Virgin Luck* v. 117 'That's the bathroom,' she said, explaining the upstairs geography of the place, 'with the loo just beyond it.' **1967** *Listener* 21 Dec. 802/2 The Business Man Jocular: 'I say, where's the geography, old son?'

2. A treatise on this science.

1559 W. CUNNINGHAM *Cosmogr. Glasse* 5 Ptolomæus in his geographie defineth it in this sorte. **1646** SIR T. BROWNE *Pseud. Ep.* IV. xi. 206 Strabo..hath largely condemned it as a fabulous story in the first of his Geographie. **1658** W. BURTON *Comm. Antonius' Itin.* 162 The elder [Marcianus].. wrote a Geography, called also Περίπλους, in Iambic Greek verse. *a* **1854** E. FORBES *Lit. Papers* viii. (1855) 218 Districts, the accounts of which in our geographies are lamentably inaccurate and imperfect. **1882** W. H. BISHOP in *Harper's Mag.* Dec. 61/2 A high flat-topped peak..of the type of those we used to see in our geographies, rises out of it.

3. *transf.* The similar descriptive science relating to any other body resembling the earth.

a **1898** *Mod.* The geography of Mars.

geoid ('dʒiːɔɪd). [ad. Gr. γεοειδής, adj., earthlike, f. γεο-, γῆ earth + εἶδος form: see -OID.

First used in German (*geoide*) by Listing, *Ueber unsere jetzige Kenntniss der Gestalt u. Grösze der Erde* (1872).]

A geometrical solid, nearly identical with the terrestrial spheroid, but having the surface at every point perpendicular to the direction of gravity.

1881 M. MERRIMAN *Fig. Earth* 79 The word *Geoid* is used to designate the actual figure of the surface of the waters of the earth.. The geoid, then, is an irregular figure peculiar to our planet. **1883** *Nature* 15 Mar. 471 The geoid (or the true figure of the earth's surface, as determined by the directions of the pendulum) nearly corresponds with the spheroid on the shores of the Black Sea.

¶ Misused for GEODE.

1839 BAILEY *Festus* xx. (1848) 261 And even when their looks are earthy, still If opened, like geoids, they may be found Full of all sparkling sparry loveliness.

Hence **ge'oidal** *a.*, of or pertaining to a geoid.

1881 M. MERRIMAN *Fig. Earth* 79 The second definition determines that our geoidal surface to be investigated is that coinciding with the surface of the great oceans.

geoisotherm: see GEO-.

geol, obs. form of JOWL.

geolatry (dʒiː'ɒlətrɪ). *rare.* [f. GEO- + -LATRY.] Earth-worship.

1860 *Lit. Churchman* VI. 3/1 We cannot but express our gratitude for such a protest, in such a place..against the 'geo-latry' of a small party. [The word here means 'the idolizing of geology'.] **1870** G. W. COX *Mythol. Aryan Nat.* I. 95 To this succeeded astrolatry in the East, and geolatry in the West.

geologer (dʒiː'ɒlədʒə(r)). Now *rare.* [f. GEOLOG-Y + -ER[1].] = GEOLOGIST.

1822 *Blackw. Mag.* XII. 637 Geologers all, great, middling, and small. **1837–9** HALLAM *Hist. Lit.* I. iii. I. §113. 222 The very theories of recent geologers are anticipated by Da Vinci. **1893** LELAND *Mem.* II. 78 'Got any [oil-]land over?'..'Yes, first-rate; geologer's certificate; can you put it on the market?'

geologian (dʒiːəʊ'ləʊdʒɪən). Now *rare.* [f. GEOLOG-Y + -IAN.] = GEOLOGIST.

1837 SIR F. PALGRAVE *Merch. & Friar* (1844) 204, I never found a geologian who did not shirk the questions upon the answers to which all his theories depend. **1864** PUSEY *Lect. Daniel* Pref. 3 The unbelieving school of Geologians had done their worst. **1872** M. COLLINS *Pr. Clarice* II. ix. 109 It is a sleepy village..with many curious relics both for antiquary and geologian. **1884** *Punch* 8 Mar. 118/1 A.. writer, equally trustworthy as theologian and geologian.

geologic (dʒiːəʊ'lɒdʒɪk), *a.* [f. GEOLOG-Y + -IC.]

1. a. Of, pertaining to, or derived from geology; such as is described, investigated, or ascertained by geology. ***geologic time*** = *geological time* (see next); chiefly *U.S.*

There is now a slight distinction in usage between *geologic* and *geological*: the former tends to be used only as an epithet of things forming part of the subject-matter of the science: we may say *a geologic epoch*, but hardly *a geologic student*, *a geologic theory*.

1799 KIRWAN *Geol. Observ.* 56 The most unequivocal geologic proofs of a general deluge. **1830** *Blackw. Mag.* XXVIII. 248 Descriptive sketches of our planet..with reference to its geologic structure. **1856** EMERSON *Eng. Traits, Land* Wks. (Bohn) II. 18 It is written only in the geologic strata. **1861** GOLDW. SMITH *Lect. Mod. Hist.* 19 The vast length of geologic..time. **1863** J. G. MURPHY *Comm. Gen.* i. *ad fin.*, The last of those geologic changes which our globe has undergone. **1872** W. S. SYMONDS *Rec. Rocks* iv. 104 In far later geologic epochs, new volcanic vents poured forth their lavas. **1886** MALLOCK *Old Order Changes* II. 193 Found in some curious geologic formation. **1955** *Sci. Amer.* Mar. 82/1 Throughout geologic time, as far back as we can read the rocks, the continents have repeatedly been invaded by the oceans. **1968** DAYHOFF & ECK *Atlas Protein Sequence & Structure 1967–68* 74/1 *Geologic time*, a time scale related to, and comparable with, the age of the earth. It is sometimes used vaguely to refer to times of many millions of years, sometimes specifically referring to the dated occurrences of various geologic events or eras.

b. Of persons: Fond of geology.

1854 H. MILLER *Sch. & Schm.* (1858) 526 It was often explored by geologic tourists.

2. *transf.* with reference to bodies analogous to the earth.

1868 LOCKYER *Guillemin's Heavens* 153 These singular markings date from the last period of geologic change on the lunar surface.

geological (dʒiːəʊ'lɒdʒɪkəl), *a.* [f. prec. + -AL[1].] = GEOLOGIC (but see the note under GEOLOGIC 1). ***geological time***: time as measured in terms of geology; also, the time which has elapsed since the formation of the earth, or the stretch of time between the formation of the earth and the beginning of the historical period.

1795 J. HUTTON *Theory Earth* I. 203 Our author begins by examining a geological operation. **1808** in *Cobbett's Pol. Reg.* XIII. 1014/2 One of the most able engineers, who was also possessed of a vast geological knowledge. **1816** KEATINGE *Trav.* (1817) I. 31 Those extensive speculations, to which geological studies..lead. **1837** WHEWELL *Hist. Induct. Sc.* (1857) II. 389 The various facts..belong in general to geological science. **1851** *Illustr. Catal. Gt. Exhib.* 123 Geological map of England, showing the extent and position of the Bristol basin. **1863** LYELL *(title)* The Geological Evidences of the Antiquity of Man. **1875** J. CROLL *Climate & Time* xix. 326 It is..impossible to form an adequate conception of the length of geological time. **1876** PAGE *Adv. Text-bk. Geol.* ii. 31 Hypotheses..which are sometimes advanced to account for geological phenomena. **1881** RAYMOND *Mining Gloss., Geological formations*, groups of rocks of similar character and age are called formations. **1904** GOODCHILD & TWENEY *Technol. & Sci. Dict.* 253/2 *Geological time*, a chronological measure (of a somewhat indefinite character) which bears the same kind of relation to the measures of time used in history that the distances of the stellar bodies do to the ordinary standard of terrestrial measurement. **1911** *Jrnl. Chem. Soc.* C. II. 570 The Measurement of Geological Time. **1923** L. D. STAMP *Introd. Stratigr.* i. 5 Geological time is divided into five great Eras, and into a number of Periods. **1971** S. SMITH in K. Dick *Ivy & Stevie* 50 It is heaven to think of geological time.

Hence **geo'logically** *adv.*, in a geological manner or respect; with reference to geology.

1802 PLAYFAIR *Illustr. Hutton. Th.* 151 He therefore endeavours to ascertain the distinguishing characters of each, considered geologically. **1816** KEATINGE *Trav.* (1817) I. 66 Rocks of this conformation..are not picturesque; but geologically their outlines claim an interest. **1859** DARWIN *Orig. Spec.* x. (1873) 270 Only a small portion of the surface of the earth has been geologically explored. **1876** PAGE *Adv. Text-bk. Geol.* xxiii. 482 The best map of the district he can procure, and if coloured geologically so much the better.

geolo'gician. *rare.* [f. GEOLOGY, after LOGICIAN.] = GEOLOGIST.

1817 SOUTHEY *Lett.* (1856) III. 76 *note*, Hans Roth..Is an excellent guide; A geologician, A metaphysician, To search out how causes proceed. **1836** *Blackw. Mag.* XL. 701 'Munch', quoth the grave geologician, 'munch'.

geologist (dʒiː'ɒlədʒɪst). [f. GEOLOG-Y + -IST.] One versed in geology; one who pursues geological investigations.

1795 J. HUTTON *Theory Earth* I. 269 The opinions of other geologists should be clearly stated. **1813** J. TOWNSHEND *Char. Moses* I. 420 The skilful geologist will detect the origin of these springs. **1830** LYELL *Princ. Geol.* I. 3 The geologist and those who study natural history or physics stand in equal need of mutual assistance. **1855** SINGLETON *Virgil* I. 400 Their very existence would have remained unknown, except for the geologist and the fossil.

Hence **geolo'gistical** *a.*, *nonce-wd.*, jocularly used for GEOLOGICAL.

1831 *Fraser's Mag.* III. 334 Superabundant proofs of his having made a careful, moral, political, geologistical, and gravely quizzical survey of that wonderful region.

geologize (dʒiː'ɒlədʒaɪz), *v.* [f. GEOLOG-Y + -IZE.]

1. *intr.* To make geological researches.

1831 DARWIN in *Life & Lett.* (1887) I. 185 During Midsummer geologized a little in Shropshire. **1861** WILSON & GEIKIE *Mem. E. Forbes* v. 156 Out of doors his happiest days were spent in botanizing, geologizing, dredging, or sketching. **1887** in *Darwin's Life & Lett.* I. 365 *note*, While geologizing in a railway cutting..he [Strickland] was run over by a train.

2. *trans.* To examine geologically; to study as a geologist does.

1834 DARWIN *Jrnl.* 14 Aug. (1845), I set out..for the purpose of geologising the basal parts of the Andes. **1872** W. S. SYMONDS *Rec. Rocks* viii. 272 A gentleman who geologised the Ilfracombe district obtained many specimens. **1883** R. BROWN in *Fortn. Rev.* 1 Sept. 393 The world is so rapidly getting geologized and botanized.

Hence **ge'ologizing** *vbl. sb.* and *ppl. a.*

1880 BP. GOODWIN in *Macm. Mag.* No. 246. 478 Geologising and hunting were put on the same footing as regards risk to horseflesh. *Ibid.*, The present writer never joined the geologising party.

†**'geologue.** *Obs.* [a. F. *géologue*, f. Gr. γεω- GEO- + -λόγος one who discourses.] A geologist.

1800 PICTET in *Phil. Mag.* VIII. 53 The geologue, the mineralogist and the mere amateur repair thither [to Switzerland] with avidity. **1809** G. LANDT *Feroe Isl.* (1810) 130 The truth..I shall leave to the determination of geologues and astronomers. **1847** WHEWELL in Todhunter *Acc. W.'s Wks.* (1876) II. 342, I am still discontented with the want of justice towards you which our geologues have shewn.

geology (dʒiː'ɒlədʒɪ). [ad. med.L. *geōlogia*, f. Gr. γεω- GEO- + -λογία discourse: see -LOGY.

The med.L. word was used, perhaps for the first time, by Richard de Bury (14th c.) in the peculiar sense 'science of earthly things', applied to the study of law as distinguished from the arts and sciences which are concerned with the works of God. In 1687 *geologia* appears as the title of a work in Italian by F. Sessa, intended to prove that the 'influence' ascribed by astrologers to the stars, really proceeded from the earth itself. A work entitled *Geologia Norwegica*, containing a description of Hecla, is referred to in 1686 by Plot *Staffordshire* iii. 145; but, so far as is at present known, the use of the word as a name for a distinct branch of physical science occurs first in English.]

†**1.** The science which treats of the earth in general (see quots.). *Obs.*

[**1690** E. WARREN *(title)* Geologia: or, A Discourse concerning the Earth before the Deluge.] **1735** B. MARTIN *Philos. Gram.* 11 Geology, which treats of the Nature, Make, Parts and Productions of the Globe of Earth on which we live. *Ibid.* 12 Geology is..divided into the following subordinate Branches, viz.:—(i) Geography, which treats of the Earth or Land; (ii) Hydrography, which treats of Water; (iii) Phytography..(iv) Zoography. **1736** BAILEY (folio) Pref., *Geology*, a Treatise or Description of the Earth. **1755** JOHNSON, *Geology*, the doctrine of the earth; the knowledge of the state and nature of the earth.

2. The science which has for its object the investigation of the earth's crust, of the strata which enter into its composition, with their mutual relations, and of the successive changes to which their present condition and positions are due.

1795 J. HUTTON *Theory Earth* I. 216 A person, who has formed his notions of geology from the vague opinion of others. **1813** BAKEWELL *Introd. Geol.* Pref. (1815) 4 In the order of succession, mineralogy and geology are the last of the natural sciences. **1842** H. MILLER *O.R. Sandst.* ii. (ed. 2) 58 Geology, of all the sciences, addresses itself most powerfully to the imagination. **1874** LYELL *Elem. Geol.* v. 47 It..appeared clear as the science of 'Geology' advanced that [etc.]. **1880** GEIKIE *Phys. Geog.* iv. 189 To describe these [rocks] and trace their origin and history forms the subject of the science of Geology.

b. The geological features of a district.

1816 KEATINGE *Trav.* (1817) I. 38 The geology as well as the botany of the Pyrenees ought to repay all the patience.. of the enthusiasts in those sciences.

geomagnetism (dʒiːəʊ'mægnɪtɪz(ə)m). [f. GEO- + MAGNETISM.] The study of the magnetic properties of the earth and related phenomena; terrestrial magnetism.

1938 S. CHAPMAN in *Terrestr. Magn.* XLIII. 321 Workers on the science of the Earth's magnetism..should regularly adopt the title *geomagnetism*, and the corresponding adjective *geomagnetic*, in place of the more usual *terrestrial magnetism* and *terrestrial magnetic*. **1940** CHAPMAN & BARTELS *(title)* Geomagnetism. **1956** *Encycl. Brit. Ann.* 354/2 Geomagnetism has broad and basic implications in the study of the ionosphere, radio-wave propagation, [etc.]. **1968** W. M. KAULA *Introd. Planetary Physics* iii. 137 The fields..are..represented as vector spherical harmonics, with spheroidal (in geomagnetism called 'poloidal') and toroidal parts.

So **geomag'netic** *a.*, of or pertaining to geomagnetism; **geomag'netically** *adv.*; **geomagne'tician**, **geo'magnetist**, an expert in, or student of, geomagnetism.

1903 *Sci. Amer. Suppl.* 19 Sept. 23177/1 The geomagnetist Paulins..essayed to supply the..organs of the plants with this life and vigor-giving excitement. **1904** *Nature* 21 Apr. 581/1 Everyone who has ever been engaged in geomagnetic investigations. **1938** *Geogr. Jrnl.* XCII. 386 The position of the Earth's magnetic axis when the distorting effects caused by local conditions of the Earth's crust are eliminated..is known as the Geomagnetic Pole. **1955** *Sci. Amer.* Sept. 152/1 As a famous geomagnetician of the early 19th century, Christopher Hansteen, truly said: 'The earth speaks of its internal movements through the silent voice of the magnetic needle.' **1956** *Nature* 7 Jan. 29 (*heading*) Observations of whistling atmospherics at geomagnetically conjugate points. **1970** *Ibid.* 23 May 740/1 The contribution of ionospheric currents should predominate at both stations on days which are not geomagnetically disturbed.

geomalic (dʒiːəʊ'mælɪk), *a.* [f. Gr. γεω-, γῆ earth + ὁμαλός level, even + -IC.] Pertaining to geomalism.

1880 HYATT in *Proc. Amer. Assoc. Adv. Sci.* 541, I shall call this tendency to equalize the form in the direction of a horizontal plane, *geomalic*. *Ibid.* 542 The geomalic growth of the ventral side.

geomalism (dʒiː'ɒməlɪz(ə)m). *Biol.* [f. as prec. + -ISM.] The tendency of an organism to grow symmetrically in a horizontal plane. So also **ge'omaly**.

1884-5 *Riverside Nat. Hist.* (1888) I. 50 Geomalism appears in its primitive aspect among the sponges since they are comparatively soft and supported by a pliable and primitively fragmentary internal skeleton. **1889** *Century Dict.*, *Geomaly*.

†**'geomance**, *sb. Obs. rare*⁻¹. In 4 **geomaunce**. [a. f. *géomance.*] = GEOMANCY.

1390 GOWER *Conf.* III. 45 The craft, which that Saturnus fonde, To make prickes in the sonde, That geomaunce cleped is.

'geomance, *v. nonce-wd.* [Back-formation from GEOMANCY.] *intr.* To practise geomancy.

1889 *Sat. Rev.* 16 Feb. 175/1 No one can geomance successfully who has not plenty of faith and geomantical aptitude.

geomancer ('dʒiːəʊ,mænsə(r)). [f. GEOMANC-Y + -ER¹.] One who practises geomancy.

c **1400** *Apol. Loll.* 95 And þus are callid geomanceris, þat werkun bi þe ȝerþ. **1603** SIR C. HEYDON *Jud. Astrol.* viii. 199 Making them to hitte the truth by chance..and so the Astrologer no better then the Chiromancer, or Geomancer. **1646** SIR. T. BROWNE *Pseud. Ep.* I. iii. 12 Fortune tellers, Juglers, Geomancers, and the like incantatory impostors.. doe daily and professedly delude them. **1814** CARY *Dante, Purg.* XIX. 4 The geomancer sees His Greater Fortune up the east ascend. **1878** J. H. GRAY *China* I. xii. 297 The selection of a site for a tomb is entrusted to a geomancer.

†**geomancien**. *Obs. rare*⁻¹. [a. F. *géomancien.*] = GEOMANCER.

1591 SPARRY tr. *Cattan's Geomancie* 20 Although that it be not requisite that the Geomancien vnderstand..the Astrologe.

geomancy ('dʒiːəʊ,mænsɪ). Also 4 **gemensye, geomesye**, 4-6 **geomancie**, 5 **geomantie**, 7 **-manty**. [a. F. *géomancie*, ad. L. *geōmantīa*, a. late Gr. *γεωμαντεία, f. γεω-, comb. form of γῆ earth + μαντεία divination.] The art of divination by means of signs derived from the earth, as by the figure assumed by a handful of earth thrown down upon some surface (see also quot. 1569). Hence, usually, divination by means of lines or figures formed by jotting down on paper a number of dots at random.

1362 LANGL. *P. Pl.* A. XI. 153 Astronomye is hard thing.. Gemetrie and gemensye [B. geomesye] is gynful of speche. *c* **1386** CHAUCER *Pars. T.* ⁋531 What seye we of hem that bileeuen in diuynailes as..by Geomancie [etc.]. *c* **1400** MAUNDEV. (Roxb.) xxv. 115 Sum of geomancy, sum of pyromancy, sum of ydromancy. **1477** NORTON *Ord. Alch.* vi. in Ashm. (1652) 100 Trust not in Geomantie that superstitious Arte. **1569** J. SANFORD tr. *Agrippa's Van. Artes* 51 b, There is also an other kind of Geomancie..the which doth diuine by certaine coniectures taken of similitudes of the crakinge of the Earthe [etc.]. **1591** SPARRY tr. *Cattan's Geomancie* 1 Geomancie is a Science and Art which consisteth of points, prickes, and lines, made in steade of the foure Elements. **1622** J. TAYLOR (Water P.) *Water Cormor.* Wks. (1630) III. 12/2 By Water he knowes much in Hidromanty And by the Earth hee's skilled in Geomanty. **1774** WARTON *Hist. Eng. Poetry* (1775) II. 22 All the renowned authors..in alchemy, astrology, magic, palmistry, geomancy, and other branches of the occult philosophy. **1820** W. IRVING *Sketch Bk.* (1859) 177 Certain colleges in old times, where judicial astrology, geomancy, necromancy, and other forbidden and magical sciences were taught. **1878** J. H. GRAY *China* I. i. 10 The houses are built according to the principles of geomancy.

geomant ('dʒiːəʊ,mænt). *rare*. Also **geomaunt**. [App. a. It. *geomante.*] = GEOMANCER.

1870 ROSSETTI *Poems* 262 A foul beast unknown, Hell-birth of geomaunt and teraphim. **1880** A. J. BUTLER *Dante, Purg.* XIX. 4 In the hour..when the geomants see their Greater Fortune in the east before the dawn.

geomantic (dʒiːəʊ'mæntɪk), *a.* and *sb.* Also 7 **geomantique, -mantick**. [ad. med.L. *geōmanticus*, f. *geōmantīa* GEOMANCY. Cf. F. *géomantique.*]

A. *adj.* Belonging to geomancy.

c **1590** GREENE *Fr. Bacon* ix. 50 Those geomantic spirits, That Hermes calleth *terræ filii*. **1608** DAY *Law Trickes* IV. ii. (1881) 64 The pretious soule Of Geomantique spells and Characters. **1700** DRYDEN *Palamon & A.* 1224 Two geomantick figures were display'd Above his head, a warriour and a maid. **1816** SCOTT *Antiq.* xxiii, You have used neither..magic mirror, nor geomantic figure. **1855** SMEDLEY *Occult Sciences* 314 The geomantic figures obtained by inspecting the chance lines or dots. **1892** *Times* (weekly ed.) 7 Oct. 6/4 The Chinese..think..that the geomantic influences are affected injuriously to them.

†B. *sb.* A geomancer. *Obs.*

1642 ROGERS *Naaman* 591 To them that whisper out of the earth (Geomantics). **1652** GAULE *Magastrom.* xxvi, The pointing Geomantick will cast unhappy figures, and project for me a prison and sorrow.

geomantical (dʒiːəʊ'mæntɪkəl), *a.* Also 6-7 **-all**. [f. as prec. + -AL¹.] = GEOMANTIC *a.*

1569 J. SANFORD tr. *Agrippa's Van. Artes* 25 b, The Geomantical Diuination. **1593** R. HARVEY *Philad.* 21 Bladud found the hote Bathes in this Iland by his Geomanticall and Hydromanticall skill and subtiltie. **1647** LILLY *Catast. Mundi* (1683) 4 A third sort is a geomantical or terrestrial divination in which from certain voluntary pricks or points made by the hand at adventure certain figures are raised. **1889** [see GEOMANCE *v.*].

Hence **geo'mantically** *adv.*

1775 ASH, *Geomantically*, according to the geomantic art.

geometer (dʒiː'ɒmɪtə(r)). [ad. L. *geōmetra*, *-metrēs*, a. Gr. γεωμέτρης land-measurer, geometrician, f. γεω- GEO- + -μέτρης measurer. Cf. F. *géomètre.*]

1. One who studies, or is skilled in, geometry.

1483 *Cath. Angl.* 153/2 A Geometer (*Add. MS.* Gemitrician), *geometer*. **1553** GRIMALDE *Cicero's Offices* III. (1558) 126 The Geometers ar wont not to proue all but to require yt certein things be graunted. **1597-8** BP. HALL *Sat.* V. ii, Like to the plane of many-sided Squares, That wont be drawn out by geometers. **1610** GUILLIM *Heraldry* II. vii. (1611) 70, I know the learned geometer will find many more lines heere then I doe mention. **1709** BERKELEY *Th. Vision* §155 The manner wherein geometers describe a right line or circle. **1812** SIR. H. DAVY *Chem. Philos.* 37 Cavendish.. reasoned with the caution of a geometer upon the results of his experiments. **1837** WHEWELL *Hist. Induct. Sci.* (1857) I. 150 The idea of parallax..was indeed too obvious to be overlooked by geometers at any time. **1893** SIR. R. BALL *Story of Sun* 4 As a geometer would express it, an ellipse of high eccentricity.

b. ***subterraneous geometer*** (nonce-use) = DIALLER I.

1777 *Phil. Trans.* LXVII. 423 A twisted brass wire..two puncheons, a semi-circle, and a compass, are all the instruments made use of by the subterraneous Geometer.

†**2.** ? A gauger, inspector of measures. *Obs.*

1635 M. PARKER *Robin Consc.* B j, In stead of the quart pot of Pewter I fill small Jugs, and need no Tutor: I Quarteridge giue to the Geometer most duely.

†**3.** *U.S.* ? A government surveyor. *Obs.*

1802 in A. Ellicott *Jrnl.* (1803) 51 The geometer, and other officers that are to be employed, are already on their way from New Orleans.

4. The name of a class of caterpillars (see quots.).

1816 KIRBY & SP. *Entomol.* (1817) II. 292 Their name of geometer was given them..because they seem to measure the surface they pass over, as they walk, with a chain. **1869** E. NEWMAN *Brit. Moths* 49 The Second Great Division or Tribe of Moths are called Geometers (in science Geometræ), from the peculiar attitude which the caterpillars assume in walking.

attrib. **1897** *Daily News* 13 Sept. 6/2 The larvæ of the geometer moths..are widely known as 'stick caterpillars'.

†**geometral**, *a. Obs. rare.* [a. F. *géométral*, f. L. *geōmetra*: see -AL¹.] Geometrically drawn; showing the plan or section of a building.

1687 MIEGE *Gt. Fr. Dict.* I. s.v., *Un Plan Geometral*, a Geometral Draught. **1755** in JOHNSON ('pertaining to geometry'); and so in later Dicts.

†**geometrer**. *Obs. rare*⁻¹. Also **gemetrer**. [f. L. *geōmetr-a* + -ER¹.] = GEOMETER I.

1382 WYCLIF *Ep. St. Jerome* 66, I holde my pees of.. retorikis, filo[so]feris, geometrers [**1388** gemetreres].

†**geometrial**, *a. Obs. rare.* [f. GEOMETRY + -AL¹.] = GEOMETRICAL.

1549 *Compl. Scot.* vi. 66 None of them kepit moir geomatrial mesure nor thir scheiphyrdis did in ther dansing. **1563-87** FOXE *A. & M.* (1596) 1367/1 Upon his head he had a Geometriall, that is, a foure squared cap, albeit that his heade was rounde.

†**geometrian**. *Obs. rare.* Also 4-5 **geometrien**, 5 **gemetrien**. [ad. OF. *geometrien.*] = GEOMETRICIAN.

c **1374** CHAUCER *Boeth.* III. pr. x. 71 (Camb. MS.) Thyse geometryens..ben wont to bryngen in thynges þat they clepyn porysmes. **1430-40** LYDG. *Bochas* I. ii. 200 Making his masons for to compasse and casten their deuises, Gemetriens in theyr diuisions. **1590** RECORDE, etc. *Gr. Artes* 34 What causeth Geometrians so highly to be enhaunced? **1635** PERSON *Varieties* I. 44 If once a Geometrian give up the infallible number of the Miles which the Earth will reach to in compasse.

geometric (dʒiːəʊ'mɛtrɪk), *a.* [ad. L. *geōmetricus*, a. Gr. γεωμετρικός, f. γεωμέτρ-ης GEOMETER. Cf. F. *géométrique.*] **a.** = GEOMETRICAL.

1630 DEKKER *2nd Pt. Honest Wh.* C 1 a, Of Geometricke figures the most rare, And perfect'st are the Circle and the square. **1669** GALE *Crt. Gentiles* I. I. ii. 16 The overflowing of Nilus..required a Geometric Art for the Division of their lands, when the floud was over. **1706** W. JONES *Syn. Palmar. Matheseos* 57 In any Geometric Proportion, when the Antecedent is less than the Consequent, the Terms may be express'd by *a* and *ar*. **1814** CARY *Dante, Par.* XXXIII. 123 As one, Who versed in geometric lore, would fain Measure the circle. **1837** WHEWELL *Hist. Induct. Sci.* (1857) II. 422 The elasticity proceeds in a geometric series. **1864** BOWEN *Logic* x. 339 Thus, the numberless properties of every geometric figure are reduced.

b. †***geometric jasper***: ? some mineral with geometrical markings (*obs.*). ***geometric caterpillar*** = GEOMETER 4. ***geometric spider***, a spider which constructs a web of a geometrical form.

1681 GREW *Musæum* III. 291 A Geometrick jasper. **1815** KIRBY & SP. *Entomol.* I. 414 The nets of the geometric spiders are in favourable weather renewed either wholly, or at least their concentric circles, every twenty-four hours. **1851-6** WOODWARD *Mollusca* 138 They walk by contracting the space between their lips and foot, like the geometric caterpillars (Gray). **1878** *Daily News* 24 Oct. 6/4 The common garden or geometric spider is now to be seen abundantly.

c. Designating or pertaining to a style of English architecture preceding or corresponding to the decorated style (see DECORATED *ppl. a.* b).

1889 *Cent. Dict.* s.v. *decorated*, The Decorated style has been divided into two periods: namely, the Early or Geometric Decorated period, in which the ornament consists especially of simple curves and lines and combinations of them; and the Decorated style proper. **1899** R. GLAZIER *Man. Hist. Ornament* 39 Decorated or geometric period. *Ibid.*, The aisle windows with mullions and bold geometric tracery. **1957** *Times Lit. Suppl.* 25 Oct. 636/3 So far as architecture is concerned the book covers three periods, Early English, Geometric, and Early Decorated.

d. Designating a period, the 'Geometric Age', of ancient Greek culture lasting from *c* 900 to *c* 700 B.C., or objects belonging to that period, esp. the pottery, characterized by the use of geometrical forms in decoration.

1902 *Encycl. Brit.* XXV. 572/1 In the remains of the Geometric Age we may trace the influence of the Dorians. *Ibid.* 572/2 (*caption*) Geometric vase from Rhodes. **1939** J. D. S. PENDLEBURY *Archaeol. Crete* vi. 319 The Geometric pottery of Crete never attained the high standard of the Attic school. *Ibid.* 323 The most probable dating for the end of the true Geometric Period is about 700 in the East, and about 750 in Crete. **1950** H. L. LORIMER *Homer & Monuments* p. viii, The salient features of the Late Geometric age with which the Early Iron Age terminates had become known..through the exploration of the Dipylon cemetery. *Ibid.* ii. 70 Vases in the shape of a pomegranate are fairly frequent in Greek Geometric art.

geometrical (dʒiːəʊ'mɛtrɪkəl), *a.* [f. as prec. + -AL¹.]

1. a. Belonging to geometry; determined or constructed according to the methods of geometry; *spec.* = GEOMETRIC *a.* c. ***geometrical staircase*** (see quot. 1842-59). ***geometrical tracery***, tracery in which the openings are of geometrical form (circles, trefoils, etc.).

The name of ***geometrical figures*** was formerly restricted to those whose construction involved only the straight line and circle, all other curves being called *mechanical*.

1552 HULOET, Geometricall description, *ichnographia*. **1562** COOPER *Answ. Def. Truth* 52 b, To apointe a geometricall measure of place..that may serue for all churches..is far aboue our reache. **1576** FLEMING *Panopl. Epist.* 225 He shall learne to be skilfull in the art Geometrical. **1638** F. JUNIUS *Paint. Ancients* 282 Geometricall lines; which are nothing else but a length without breadth. **1695** ALINGHAM *Geom. Epit.* 114 Upon a given right line as *a d*, to make a Geometrical square. **1772** NUGENT tr. *Grosley's Lond.* II. 43 This hospital [Greenwich] has a great staircase of that sort which the English call Geometrical. **1817** T. RICKMAN *Architecture* 74 The figures ..are all worked with the same moulding, and do not always regularly join each other, but touch only at points. This may be called geometrical tracery. **1838** THIRLWALL *Greece* III. xviii. 59 A new town was built, with geometrical regularity. **1842-59** GWILT *Archit.* §2184 A Geometrical Staircase is one whose opening is down its centre..in which each step is supported by one end being fixed in the wall or partition. **1848** RICKMAN *Archit.* p. xxxvi, The heads of two windows ..affording very good examples of geometrical tracery. **1848** [see DECORATED *ppl. a.* b]. **1849** E. SHARPE *Treat. Decorated Window Tracery in Eng.* I. ii. 8, I propose..to name these three styles of Window tracery, Geometrical, Curvilinear, and Rectilinear. *Ibid.* II. i. 89 Towards the close of the Geometrical Period there occurred some singular attempts at originality in the designs of Window Tracery. **1850** PARKER *Gloss. Archit.* I. 230 *Geometrical tracery*: this epithet was applied by Rickman to distinguish the early forms of tracery, in which the figures, such as circles, trefoils, &c., do not always regularly join each other, but touch only at points. **1875** *Encycl. Brit.* II. 425/2 Edward I, 1272 to 1307. Transition from Early Pointed to Complete, or Geometrical Pointed. **1879** LUBBOCK *Sci. Lect.* v. 160 The ornamentation..consists of geometrical patterns—straight lines, circles, triangles, etc. **1942** N. PEVSNER *Outl. Europ. Archit.* iii. 51 The kind of tracery which is called flowing as against the geometrical tracery of 1230 to about 1275.

? quasi-*adv.* **1593** *Rites & Mon. Ch. Durh.* (Surtees) 2 A goodly faire round window..havinge in it twenty-four lights verye artificially made, as it is called geometricall.

fig. **1790** BURKE *Fr. Rev.* 80 Is every land-mark of the country to be done away in favour of a geometrical and arithmetical constitution?

b. *geometrical ratio* (now usually *ratio* simply, as the expression *arithmetical r.* is obsolete): that kind of relation between two quantities which is expressed by dividing the first by the second; the quotient expressing this. (The term survives chiefly in the phrase ***at a geometrical ratio***, loosely used for *in geometrical progression*.) ***geometrical proportion***: a proportion which involves an equality of geometrical ratio in its two parts, as 1:3::4:12. ***geometrical progression***: a series in which the ratio between the successive quantities is constant, as 1:3:9:27:81, etc.

arithmetical progression, †*proportion*, †*ratio*, etc. (see ARITHMETICAL *a.*) relate to differences instead of quotients. The term *geometrical* points to the fact that problems involving multiplication were originally dealt with by geometry and not by arithmetic.

1557 RECORDE *Whetst.* G ij, You can haue no progression Geometricalle, but it must be made either of square nombers, or els of like flattes. *Ibid.* Kkij, I knowe the propertie of those nombers in proportion Geometricall to bee soche, that the multiplication of bothe the extremes is equalle to the square of the middell terme. **1594** BLUNDEVIL *Exerc.* I. xiii. (ed. 7) 39 What is Progression Geometricall? It is that wherein every number exceedeth his fellow by like Proportion, for as six contayneth three twice, so doth twelve contayne six twice, &c. **1690** LEYBOURN *Curs. Math.* 144 Thus in .. the following Table, the Numbers in Geometrical Proportion are 1, 2, 4, 8, 16, &c. **1806** HUTTON *Course Math.* I. 110 Of these two numbers 6 and 3, the difference, or arithmetical ratio, is 6 − 3 or 3, but the geometrical ratio is $\frac{6}{3}$ or 2. **1859** DARWIN *Orig. Spec.* iii. (1873) 52 All plants and animals are tending to increase at a geometrical ratio. **1885** WATSON & BURBURY *Math. Th. Electr. & Magn.* I. 121 The distances of the images from the common centre are in geometrical progression.

†**c.** ***geometrical cubit, foot, mile, pace***: measures of length, some of which are app. fixed by geographical computation (1 degree = 60 miles, 1 mile = 1000 paces, 1 pace = 5 feet). *Obs.*

Originally perh. with reference to the literal sense of *geometry* = 'land-measuring'.

1559 W. CUNNINGHAM *Cosmogr. Glasse* 56 Table .. A Geometricall Pase conteyninge in it 5 Five foote. **1620–55** I. JONES *Stone-Heng* (1725) 23 In height one hundred twenty one Geometrical Feet (which of our Measure makes one hundred thirty six Feet). **1668** WILKINS *Real Char.* 163 The Ægyptian Geometrical cubit, each of which (say they) did contein six of the vulgar cubits, namely, nine foot. **1677** PLOT *Oxfordsh.* 10, 456 Geometrical paces, or 2280 feet. **1697** DAMPIER *Voy.* (1729) I. 287 Italian or Geometrical miles (at the rate of 60 to a degree). **1727** POPE, etc. *Art of Sinking* 122 A stage as large as the athenian, which was near ninety thousand geometrical paces square. **1843** *Penny Cycl.* XXVII. 198 In the second work, he [Fernel] says that five of his own paces, or those of ordinary men, make six geometrical paces.

d. *ellipt.* as *sb. pl.* Numbers or magnitudes which stand to each other in geometrical proportion. *rare.*

1807 HUTTON *Course Math.* II. 114 The reciprocals of geometricals are also geometricals, and in the same ratio.

e. ***geometrical optics***: the branch of optics which deals with the geometrical analysis of the paths of light in refraction and reflection.

1838 W. N. GRIFFIN *Treat. Optics* i. 1 In Geometrical Optics the circumstances of the transmission and modification of light are computed on certain laws established by experiment; in Physical Optics these laws are accounted for on hypotheses of the structure of bodies. **1936** *Discovery* Nov. 364/1 The Physical Society's report on the teaching of Geometrical Optics.

2. That works by the methods of geometry. *rare.* ***geometrical spider*** (cf. GEOMETRIC b).

a **1682** SIR T. BROWNE *Tracts* 6 Geometrical and Architectonical Artists look narrowly upon the description of the Ark. **1815** KIRBY & SP. *Entomol.* I. 413 The geometrical spiders. **1853** KANE *Grinnell Exp.* xl. (1856) 366 You remember the geometrical artist of Laputa. **1879** JEFFERIES *Wild Life in S. Co.* 317 Towards the latter part of September the geometrical spiders become conspicuous, spinning their webs on every bush.

geometrically (dʒiːəʊˈmɛtrɪkəlɪ), *adv.* [f. prec. + -LY².] In geometrical manner; according to geometry. ***geometrically proportional*** (also †***proportioned***): standing in geometrical proportion.

1555 EDEN *Decades* 360 The same is more easely and redely found geometrically by the globes. **1564–78** BULLEYN *Dial. agst. Pest.* (1888) 14 The fine knottes are doen in good arte, Geometrically figured. **1583** BABINGTON *Commandm.* viii. (1637) 74 What spoile so ever is got .. ought .. to be disposed to every man Geometrically, that is, according to every mans service and worthinesse; not Arithmetically, that is, to every man alike. **1643** HERLE *Answ. Ferne* 36 Nor matters it whether this coordination .. be arithmetically or geometrically proportioned. **1654** WHITLOCK *Zootomia* 458 Praise .. becometh their Due on whom it is bestowed (if not Geometrically squared to their Desert). **1717** tr. *Frezier's Voy.* 129 The Plan of the Bay of Coquimbo, on the Coast of Chili .. taken Geometrically. **1819** G. SAMOUELLE *Entomol. Compend.* 105 The animals composing this genus inhabit the sea .. moving geometrically like the larvæ of the *Phalænadæ*. **1885** WATSON & BURBURY *Math. Th. Electr. & Magn.* I. 125 We have thus constructed a new electrical system, in which every conductor *S* of the original system is represented geometrically by a surface *S′*.

geometrician (dʒiːˌɒmɪˈtrɪʃən). Also 5 gemitrician, 6 gemetricion. [f. L. *geōmetric-us* + -IAN.]

1. One who studies geometry. Now *rare.*

1483 [see GEOMETER 1]. **1547** BOORDE *Introd. Knowl.* i. (1870) 121 Certayne great stones .. lyeng and hangyng, that no Gemetricion can set them as they do hange. **1594** BLUNDEVIL *Exerc.* II. (ed. 7) 102 Our modern Geometricians have of late invented two other right lines belonging to a Circle, called lines Tangent, and lines Secant. **1691** NORRIS *Pract. Disc.* 228 Says Plato, God acts the part of Geometrician, does all things exactly and regularly. **1796** MORSE *Amer. Geog.* II. 158 While Maclaurin pursued this new career, a geometrician no less famous distinguished himself in the sure .. track of antiquity. *a* **1862** BUCKLE *Civiliz.* (1869) III. v. 306 The object of the geometrician is to generalize the laws of space.

†**2.** One who measures the earth or land; a land-surveyor. *Obs.*

1583 GOLDING *Calvin on Deut.* clxxxi. 1124 As if he [God] had beene some Geometrician, that should haue butteled and bounded the whole world. **1616** SURFL. & MARKH. *Country Farme* 517 The Art of measuring Grounds doth more properly belong vnto the Geometrician. **1676** W. HUBBARD *Happiness of People* 37 The Sovereign power is not tyed to the judgement of Physitians in the case of a wound, nor of a Geometrician in the measuring of Land.

geometrid (dʒiːˈɒmɪtrɪd), *a.* and *sb. Ent.* [f. L. *Geōmetra* mod. name for a genus of moths + -ID.]

A. *adj.* Belonging to the family of moths of which *Geometra* is the typical genus: see GEOMETER 4. **B.** *sb.* A moth of this family.

1876 A. S. PACKARD (*title*) A monograph of the Geometrid moths or Phalænidæ of the United States. *Ibid.* 37 The times of appearance of our geometrids. **1963** V. NABOKOV *Gift* i. 30 The four lovely gauze wings of the softest Geometrid moth in the world. *Ibid.* ii. 109 A tropical geometrid coloured in perfect imitation of a species of butterfly infinitely removed from it in nature's system.

So **geome'trideous** *a.*

1865 *Trans. Entomol. Soc.* 3rd Ser. II. i. 89 The imago of a species of an undetermined Geometrideous genus.

geometriform (dʒiːəʊˈmɛtrɪfɔːm), *a.* [f. *Geōmetra* (see prec.) + -FORM.] 'Resembling in form a moth of the family *Geometridæ*' (*Cent. Dict.*).

geometrine (dʒiːˈɒmɛtrɪn), *a.* [f. as prec. + -INE.] Pertaining to the *Geometridæ* (*Cent. Dict.*).

geometrist (dʒiːˈɒmɪtrɪst). *rare*⁻¹. [f. GEOMETRY + -IST.] A geometrician.

1864 BURTON *Scot Abr.* I. iv. 166 *note*, Every observing onlooker, seeing the compasses in the hand, pronounces it to be the portrait of an architect or a geometrist.

geometrize (dʒiːˈɒmɪtraɪz), *v.* [f. GEOMETR-Y + -IZE.] **a.** *intr.* To work by geometrical methods. **b.** *trans.* To form geometrically.

The word is almost exclusively employed with direct or indirect reference to Plato's phrase ἀεὶ γεωμετρεῖν τὸν θεόν. F. *géométriser* (rare) has the same origin.

1603 HOLLAND *Plutarch's Mor.* 768 The said matter .. refusing to be thus geometrized, that is to say, reduced to some finit and determinate limits. **1658** SIR T. BROWNE *Gard. Cyrus* iii. 54 Some resemblance there is of this order in the Egges of some Butterflies .. which .. doth neatly declare how nature Geometrizeth. **1661** BLOUNT *Glossogr.* (ed. 2) sig. S6ᵛ/2 To *geometrize*, to play the Geometrician, to hold a due proportion, to observe order. **1680** BOYLE *Produc. Chem. Princ.* I. 49 Chrystalls .. as if nature had at once affected variety in their figuration and yet confin'd herself to Geometrize. **1823** DE QUINCEY *Lett. Educ.* i. (1860) 15 Knowing that God geometrizes eternally. **1888** G. MACDONALD *Elect Lady* xi. 102 Do I meet God in my geometry? When I so much enjoy my Euclid, is it always God geometrizing to me? **1931** E. H. W. MEYERSTEIN *Let.* 28 Oct. (1959) 137 Even to try to geometrize *faith* was the inspiration of a Prophet.

Hence **ˌgeometriˈzation**; **ˈgeometrized**, **ˌgeomeˈtrizing** *ppl. adjs.*

1672 BOYLE *Ess. Gems* 71 As to the exquisite uniformity of Shape, which is so admir'd in Gems, and is thought to demonstrate their being form'd by a .. Geometrizing Principle. **1832** S. TURNER in *Fraser's Mag.* VI. 332 Our earth, and its finely gravitating and geometrised system. **1927** *Observer* 13 Nov. 15/5 Geometrisation is carried much further by Mr. Claude Flight in his Futurist essay entitled 'Holland' .. a jumble of curves, straight lines, and acute or obtuse angles. **1931** *Jrnl. Philos.* XXVIII. 19 The real basis of Meyersonian causalism is in geometrization... He seems satisfied .. if he can show relativity to be a 'reduction' of physics to geometry. **1933** *Antiquity* VII. 365 The progressive geometrization to which their ceramic decoration is subject.

geometry (dʒiːˈɒmɪtrɪ). Forms: 4–6 **gemetry**, (4 **-ttry**, **-trie**, 5 **-trye**, **gemytre**, **gem-**, **ghem-**, **jematry**, **-trye**, **gemeotre**), 4–7 **geometrie**, (5 **-trye**, **gewmatry**, 6 **geomatry**, 7 **gymitrie**), 5– **geometry**, (8 *vulgar* **jommetry**). [a. F. *géométrie*, a. L. *geōmetria*, a. Gr. γεωμετρία, f. γεω-, comb. form of γῆ earth + -μετρία measuring.]

1. a. The science which investigates the properties and relations of magnitudes in space, as lines, surfaces, and solids.

In early quots. geometry is chiefly regarded as a practical art of measuring and planning, and is mainly associated with architecture.

13.. *Seuyn Sag.* (W.) 185 Musike, and astronomie, Geometrie, and arsmetrike. **1390** GOWER *Conf.* III. 90 Geometrie, Through which a man hath the sleight Of length, of brede, of depth, of height. *c* **1400** *Destr. Troy* 8394 Foure ymages full fresshe, all of fyn gold .. With gematry Iustly aioynet to gedur. *c* **1450** *Cov. Myst.* (Shaks. Soc.) 189 Also of augrim & of asmatryk Of lynyacion that longeth to jematrye. **1513** BRADSHAW *St. Werburge* II. 605 They sende for masons vpon euery syde, Counnynge in geometrie. **1547** BOORDE *Brev. Health* Pref. 2 b, Every phisicion ought .. to have Geomatry to ponder and way the dregges or porcions the whiche ought to be ministred. **1570** DEE *Math. Pref.* 16 Geometrie .. is the Arte of Measuring sensible magnitudes, their iust quantities and contentes. **1631** R. BYFIELD *Doctr. Sabb.* 10 This is a plaine *non-sequitur*, and can not hold together by all the Geometry in the World. **1726** tr. *Gregory's Astron.* I. II. 289 'Tis certain from Geometry, that thirteen Spheres can touch and surround one in the middle equal to them. **1825** J. NICHOLSON *Operat. Mechanic* 673 Geometry is that branch of mathematics which treats of the description and properties of magnitudes in general. **1876** TAIT *Rec. Adv. Phys. Sci.* i. (ed. 2) 4 Geometry, which may be designated the science of pure space.

transf. **1674** S. VINCENT *Yng. Gallant's Acad.* 98 A man he is well poized in all humours, in whom nature shewed most Geometry. **1874** *Edin. Rev.* No. 285. 174 The geometry of the human form, as conceived by Phidias.

b. Applied to the relative arrangement of objects or constituent parts, as specified by geometrical quantities.

1933 H. B. HOWARD *Stresses in Aeroplane Structures* viii. 175 The loads in such frames do not depend on the elastic properties of the members, provided only that the extensions of those members do not materially alter the geometry of the frame. **1934** *Physical Rev.* XLV. 598/1 Earlier results .. showed the same trend .., but with a slightly lower value of collision area, as would be expected from the geometry. **1955** *Rev. Sci. Instr.* XXVI. 126/1 This was a 'good geometry' experiment, so that an aperture of, say, 90 percent of the total opening gave a photo-cell reading of 80 percent. **1962** *Jrnl. Geophys. Res.* LXVII. 5077/2 Next, we consider the geometry of the experiment... The spin axis of the spacecraft .. was at an angle of approximately 52·50° to the *z* axis... At the same time, the angle between .. the projection of the spin vector in the *xy* plane and the positive *x* direction was 43°. **1970** *Sci. Jrnl.* Apr. 56 (*caption*) Leyland 2S/350R powerplant is here illustrated in the form of exterior and cutaway views, slightly simplified but having the correct geometry. **1971** *E. Afr. Standard* (Nairobi) 10 Apr. 8/6 Suspension is fully independent all round, incorporating automatic ride-height control and anti-lift geometry.

†**2.** In etymological sense: The art of measuring ground. *Obs.*

1588 FRAUNCE *Lawiers Log.* I. i. 4 Geometrie (teacheth) to measure ground, not to purchase grounde. **1614** RALEIGH *Hist. World* II. (1634) 272 For Geometry, which is by interpretation measuring of grounds, was usefull unto them. **1621** G. SANDYS *Ovid's Met.* I. (1626) 4 The Ground, as common earst as Light, or Aire, By limit-giuing Geometrie they share.

†**3.** ***to hang by geometry***: app., to hang in a stiff, angular fashion (said of clothes). *Obs.*

1622 FLETCHER *Span. Curate* III. ii, And the old Cutworke Cope, that hangs by Gymitrie. **1633** ROWLEY *Match at Midnt.* III. i, Looke yee, here's Iarvis hangs by Geometry, and here's the Gentleman. **1661** DAVENPORT *City Nt.-Cap* IV. 37, I am a Pander, a Rogue, that hangs together, like a beggers rags, by geometry. **1738** SWIFT *Pol. Conv.* i. 85 *Miss.* Lord! my Petticoat! how it hangs by Jommetry. *Neverout.* Perhaps the Fault may be in your Shape.

ˌgeoˈmorphic, *a.* [f. Gr. γεω- GEO- + μορφή form + -IC.] **1.** Resembling the earth in form or fashion. *nonce-wd.*

1894 L. A. TOLLEMACHE in *Jrnl. Educ.* 1 Jan. 61/2 Our posthumous selves are likely to be less anthropomorphic, and heaven .. less geomorphic, than .. we are apt to expect.

2. Of or pertaining to the natural features of the earth's surface; geomorphological.

1893 [see next]. **1894** *Bull. Dept. Geol. Univ. Calif.* I. 242 The present geomorphy is the result of .. the advance in the new geomorphic cycle to a stage of late adolescence or early maturity. **1934** *Jrnl. R. Anthropol. Inst.* LXIV. 344 Geomorphic studies in Uganda reveal an arid climate in late Pliocene times. **1954** W. D. THORNBURY *Princ. Geomorphol.* i. 11 His [*sc.* W. M. Davis's] concept of the geomorphic cycle .. is the idea that in the evolution of landscapes there is a systematic sequence of land forms. **1969** *Nature* 15 Mar. 1005/2 These [projects] include .. the preparation of geomorphic, geological and vegetation maps.

Hence **geoˈmorphically** *adv.*

1969 *Nature* 15 Mar. 1005/1 Geomorphically, Aldabra consists of a peripheral narrow ridge 8 m above sea level, with a lower terrace cut into its seaward face.

geomorphology (ˌdʒiːəʊmɔːˈfɒlədʒɪ). [f. GEO- + Gr. μορφή form + -λογία: see MORPHOLOGY.] The branch of geology dealing with the origin, evolution, and configuration of the natural features of the earth's surface or a particular region of it.

1893 W. J. MCGEE in *Congrès Géol. Internat. 1891* 199 The systematic examination of land forms and their interpretation as records of geologic history introduces a new branch of geologic science, called 'physical geography' or 'physiography' by different writers, which has been designated 'geomorphic geology' by Powell and the 'new geology' or 'geomorphology' by the writer; but the term 'geomorphy', first employed in a somewhat different connection by Sir William Dawson, though never extensively used with this meaning, is preferable. **1896** *Pop. Sci. Monthly* XLVIII. Apr. 815 The new phase of geography, which is sometimes known as physiography, and later, as geomorphology. **1898** J. GEIKIE *Earth Sculpture* p. viii, Prof. A. De Lapparent's *Leçons de Géographie Physique* —a most instructive and comprehensive outline of geomorphology. **1931** L. D. STAMP in W. Rose *Outl. Mod.*

Knowl. 818 The underlying structure, in so far as it determines the character of the land surface, is obviously important, and at the present day forms a subject of its own known as geomorphology. **1932** J. A. STEERS (*title*) The unstable earth. Some recent views in geomorphology. **1946** *Nature* 31 Aug. 300/1 He has made considerable contributions to the geomorphology of Wales. **1946** F. E. ZEUNER *Dating Past* IV. xi. 339 The reaching by an area of the senile stage of geomorphology requires many millions of years. **1969** *Nature* 15 Mar. 1005/1 The results of the first eight months of the expedition..chiefly concerned..the distribution of terrestrial groups, with basic studies of geomorphology, climate and vegetation.

Hence **ˌgeomorphoˈlogical** *a.*, of or pertaining to geomorphology; **ˌgeomorphoˈlogically** *adv.*,; **geomorˈphologist**, an expert in, or student of, geomorphology.

1896 *Nature* 26 Nov. 76 (*title*) Geomorphological speculation. **1928** *Funk's Stand. Dict.*, Geomorphologist. **1935** *Geogr. Jrnl.* LXXXVI. 98 The group of glaciers which are geomorphologically characterized by extending in a continuous sheet in which the ice moves outwards in all directions. **1936** *Ibid.* LXXXVIII. 301 Geographers, geologists and geomorphologists..want accurate maps. **1946** F. E. ZEUNER *Dating Past* III. v. 113 Ridges of pressure-moraines are formed which sometimes are most prominent geomorphological features. **1960** B. W. SPARKS *Geomorphol.* i. 1 The geomorphologist does not study all aspects of the evolution of landforms. *Ibid.* 3 Geomorphological laboratories help greatly in understanding some processes. **1970** *Nature* 4 July 97/1 French geomorphologists are very interested in the effect of climate on landforms.

geomorphy (ˈdʒiːəʊmɔːfi). *rare.* = prec. So **geoˈmorphist**, a geomorphologist.

1889 in *Century Dict.* **1893** [see GEOMORPHOLOGY]. **1894** [see GEOMORPHIC *a.* 2]. **1904** *Amer. Geologist* Mar. 175 The geomorphist who is satisfied with the study of land forms as a finality.

geonavigation, geonomic, -nomy: see GEO-.

geonoma (dʒiːˈɒnəmə). *Bot.* [mod.L. (C. L. Willdenow 1804, in *Mémoires de l'Académie Royale des Sciences de Berlin* 37), f. Gr. γεωνόμος a colonist, in allusion to its rapid propagation.] A tree of the genus of small palms so named, natives of South and Central America.

1849 R. SPRUCE *Notes of Botanist on Amazon & Andes* (1908) I. i. 11 The roofs were..made by tying several of the broad flat fronds of a small palm called Ubim (Geonoma) on to a stick so as to closely overlap each other. **1871** *Jrnl. Linn. Soc. Bot.* XI. 104 The fine Geonomas discovered by Wendland in Central America are not always represented in the Kew Herbarium by specimens perfect enough to enable one to classify them with certainty. **1910** *Daily Chron.* 12 Mar. 8/4 Other graceful plants for our rooms are the Latania, the Grevillea, the Kentia, the Geonoma, the Rhapis, and the Dracæna. **1966** E. J. H. CORNER *Nat. Hist. Palms* xii. 307 If one wanted to study thoroughly the minutiae of palm-evolution..*Geonoma* should be the choice.

geophagy (dʒiːˈɒfədʒɪ). [ad. Gr. *γεωφαγία the eating of earth (γεωτραγία is found in this sense), f. γεω- comb. form of γῆ earth + φαγεῖν to eat.] The practice of eating earth; also **ˈgeophagism**. So **ˈgeophagist**, one that eats earth.

1850 LYELL *2nd Visit U.S.* II. 7 A diseased appetite.. prevails in several parts of Alabama, where they eat clay. I heard various speculations on the origin of this singular propensity, called 'geophagy' in some medical books. **1880** *Libr. Univ. Knowl.* (N.Y.) VI. 593 (*title*) Geophagism, the custom of dirt-eating, indulged in by the lowest order of savages, most particularly in Terra del Fuego. **1885** *Syd. Soc. Lex.*, *Geophagist.* **1897** ALLBUTT *Syst. Med.* II. 1040 Earth deliberately eaten by the geophagist. *Ibid.* 1043 Perverted appetite—pica or geophagy, as it is sometimes called—is a common occurrence in..intestinal helminthiasis.

geophilous (dʒiːˈɒfɪləs), *a.* *Zool.* and *Bot.* [f. mod.L. *Geōphilus* (a. Gr. *γεώφιλος earth-loving) + -OUS.] Belonging to one of the genera named *Geophilus* or *Geophila*.

1854 in MAYNE *Expos. Lex.* s.v. *Geophilus.* **1885** in *Syd. Soc. Lex.*

geophone (ˈdʒiːəʊfəʊn). [f. GEO- + -PHONE.] A device or instrument used to detect vibrations such as sound-waves or shock-waves in the ground.

1919 *Engin. & Min. Jrnl.* 17 May 872/1 The geophone, a 'listening' instrument invented by the French to detect enemy sapping and underground mining operations..is now being used by the Bureau of Mines..in establishing the location of miners who have been entombed after a disaster. **1922** *Encycl. Brit.* XXXII. 526/2 The *geophone* is an instrument for direction-finding of sounds proceeding through the earth, and its particular use during the war was for localizing the sound of picks, etc. used in tunnelling and land mining. **1933** *Discovery* Dec. 375/2 The geophones.. such as were used by the sappers in the war to localize enemy saps. **1953** *Sci. News* XXIX. 15 Ashore, use is made of moving coil instruments, called geophones, which respond to the velocity with which the ground surface moves after an explosion. **1965** *New Scientist* 4 Feb. 271/1 The largest seismic array in the world..will contain 525 geophones (a kind of seismometer).

geophyllous (dʒiːəʊˈfɪləs), *a.* [mod. formation f. Gr. γεω-, γῆ earth + φύλλ-ον leaf + -OUS.] 'Having leaves, or leaflets of an earthy colour'.

1854 in MAYNE *Expos. Lex.* s.v. *Geophyllus.* **1885** in *Syd. Soc. Lex.*

geophysical (dʒiːəʊˈfɪzɪkəl), *a.* [See GEO- and cf. GEOPHYSICS.] Of or pertaining to geophysics.

1888 *Science* XI. 181/2 The geophysical problems which geological history has to treat. **1894** *Pop. Sci. Monthly* Sept. 720/1 A company..proposes to devote twenty thousand dollars to the erection of a geophysical observatory. **1946** *Nature* 28 Dec. 931/2 (*title*) Geophysical prospecting and English oilfields. **1955** *Sci. Amer.* Sept. 49/1 During the Geophysical Year scientists of many disciplines will observe all the large-scale aspects of the earth: its interior, the oceans and glaciers, the lower and upper atmosphere, gravity and magnetism, and the extraterrestrial forces which profoundly influence these interacting features. **1970** *Earth-Sci. Rev.* VI. 275 Geophysical zones (e.g., electric-log zone, velocity zone, radioactivity zone).

geophysicist (dʒiːəʊˈfɪzɪsɪst). [f. next + -IST.] An expert in, or student of, geophysics.

1903 *Amer. Jrnl. Sci.* Dec. 402, I shall, leaving the consideration of the pre-fossil period to the geo-physicist, mention but briefly several associated theories of an astronomical or physical nature. **1934** *Times* 18 Sept. 9/1 The Swedish geophysicist who introduced one method of locating metals by electrical means. **1957** *Technology* Dec. 359/3 Work carried out by..a geophysicist..made use of an optical technique for measuring the temperature in..the upper atmosphere. **1970** *Sci. Jrnl.* May 32/3 The geochemical theories..do not seem to meet the geophysicist's requirement that extra mass must find its way into the basins to give a gravity excess.

geophysics (dʒiːəʊˈfɪzɪks). [f. GEO- + PHYSICS.] The science or study of the physics of the earth, esp. of its crust; the application of the principles, methods, and techniques of physics to the study of the earth.

1889 in *Cent. Dict.* **1906** *Nature* 12 July 258/1 The problems of geo-physics..are..intimately connected with each other. **1929** EVE & KEYS (*title*) Applied geo-physics in the search for minerals. **1964** *Oceanogr. & Marine Biol.* II. 37 This is usually the case for other types of density current in geophysics.

geophyte (ˈdʒiːəʊfaɪt). *Bot.* [ad. G. *geophyt* (F. W. C. Areschoug 1896, in *Acta Univ. Lundensis* XXXI. 1), f. GEO- + -PHYTE.] A plant that produces its perennating buds below the surface of the ground. Hence **geoˈphytic** *a.*

1900 B. D. JACKSON *Gloss. Bot. Terms* 110/2 *Geophytes*, applied by Areschoug to those plants which produce underground buds, without partial development there. **1913** *Jrnl. Ecol.* I. 17 Cryptophytes include plants with their dormant parts subterranean in the case of geophytes with bulbs, rhizomes, tubers on stem and root, and root-buds. **1952** P. W. RICHARDS *Tropical Rain Forest* i. 10 While in temperate forests the herbaceous ground flora includes a large proportion of..geophytes, in the rain forest.. geophytes are only rarely present. **1956** *Nature* 4 Feb. 214/2 The Pteridophyta..include only such plants as show a geophytic habit or are aquatic annuals.

geo-politics, geopolitics (dʒiːəʊˈpɒlɪtɪks). [ad. Sw. *geopolitisk* geopolitical (R. Kjellén 1900, in *Ymer 1899* XIX. 283), f. GEO(GRAPHY + POLITICS.] **a.** The influence of geography on the political character of states, their history, institutions, and esp. relations with other states; also, the study of this influence. **b.** A pseudo-science developed in National-Socialist Germany, which regarded the state as an organism with 'powers of action independent of and superior to the human groups or individuals who constitute it' (*Encycl. Brit.*, 1957).

1904 E. REICH *Found. Mod. Europe* i. 8 History, in Europe, and still more outside Europe, is written largely, if not wholly in characters of that geography, or, as we prefer to call it, geo-politics, that has..determined the trend and tenor of decisive events. **1931** *Geogr. Jrnl.* LXXVIII. 186 The rôle he assigns to 'geopolitics' is..the estimation of the strength and direction of geographical, economic, and political influences in the past, and their probable development in the future. **1942** H. BEUKEMA in A. Dorpalen *World of Gen. Haushofer* p. xii, Geopolitics is the science of the earth relationships of political processes. It is based on the broad foundations of geography, especially on political geography... Geopolitics sets out to furnish the tools for political action and the directives for political life as a whole. Thus, geopolitics becomes an art, namely, the art of guiding practical politics. **1961** *Listener* 16 Mar. 475/2 In terms of geo-politics, China and the United States are less compatible powers than the Soviet Union and the United States.

So **geo-poˈlitical** *a.*, of or pertaining to geo-politics; **geo-poˈlitically** *adv.*; **geo-poliˈtician**, a supporter or exponent of geo-politics.

1902 E. REICH in *Monthly Rev.* Nov. 124 Geographical, or rather geo-political, influences of an abiding character. *Ibid.* 131 History is made by minorities of men, if by majorities of geo-political factors. **1938** *German Life & Lett.* II. 261 Geo-politically the South Tyrol under Austrian rule, represented an enormous fortified bastion. **1942** A. DORPALEN *World of Gen. Haushofer* i. 16 Germany had to be schooled geopolitically. *Ibid.* ii. 75 Geopolitical action is to rely on a careful, detailed analysis of any given political situation. This implies a minute study of geographic, social, economic, and many other factors. **1942** D. WHITTLESEY *German Strategy of World Conquest* 96 This attribute the geopoliticians claim for Nazi Germany with eager pride. **1945** *Times* 21 Aug. 3/2 He emphasized Norway's geopolitical significance in the Scandinavian sphere. *Ibid.* 15 Dec. 4/7 The Nuremberg Tribunal to-day entered upon the maze of geo-political theories by which the Nazi State.. attempted to change the face of the conquered territories of Europe. **1946** 'G. ORWELL' *James Burnham* 15 If totalitarianism triumphs and the dreams of the geo-politicians come true, Britain will disappear as a world power. **1957** J. MASTERS *Far, Far the Mountain Peak* 227 That mission was being studied in secret on a geopolitical level.

geoponic (dʒiːəʊˈpɒnɪk), *a.* and *sb.* Also 7 -ique, 7–8 -ick. [ad. Gr. γεωπονικός, f. γεωπόνος husbandman, f. γεω-, γῆ earth + πον-, ablaut var. of πεν-, root of πένεσθαι to labour. Cf. F. *géoponique*.]

A. *adj.* Relating to the cultivation of the ground; agricultural. Also *humorously* rustic, countrified.

1663 in BULLOKAR. **1675** EVELYN *Terra* (1776) 2 But for a description of the rest..I shall refer the critical Reader to the old Geoponic authors. **1792** A. YOUNG *Trav. France* 283 In respect to the geoponic division of the soils of the kingdom, the rich calcareous plain of the north-eastern quarter first calls for our attention. **1827** STEUART *Planter's G.* (1828) 21 The Remains of the Greek Geoponic writers. **1848** LOWELL *Biglow P.* Poems 1890 II. 7 [Burlesquing Carlyle] A brown, parchment-hided old man of the geoponic or bucolic species. **1860** O. W. HOLMES *Elsie V.* xii. (1891) 166 Two or three notabilities of Rockland, with geoponic eyes.

B. *sb.*

†**1.** A writer on agriculture. *Obs. rare.*

1612 SELDEN *Notes to Drayton's Poly-olb.* VI. 99 Naturalists, Historians and Geoponiques, as Varro, Columel, Pliny, Trogus and Solinus. *Ibid.* x. 165.

2. *pl.* The science of agriculture or husbandry; a treatise on this subject (= Gr. τὰ γεωπονικά).

1608 TOPSELL *Serpents* 111 Which kind of fishing fraude, if you would better be instructed in, I must referre you to Tarentinus in his Geoponicks. **1699** EVELYN *Acetaria* (1729) 115 Of Herbs and wholesome Sallets, and other plain and useful parts of Geoponicks. **1705** HEARNE *Collect.* 16 Nov. (O.H.S.) I. 78 A Book..of the Geoponicks. **1893** *Contemp. Rev.* Jan. 3 Erroneous theories of the 'science of geoponics'.

Hence **geoˈponical** *a.*, **geoponiˈcality** *nonce-wd.* So also †**geˈoponist**, a student of geoponics; **geˈopony**, agriculture (Gr. γεωπονία; F. *géoponie*).

1646 SIR T. BROWNE *Pseud. Ep.* VI. iii. 286 Authors Geoponicall, or which have treated *de re Rustica*, as Constantine, Marcus Cato, Columella, Palladius and Varro. **1716** M. DAVIES *Athen. Brit.* III. *Diss. Physick* 12 Such were call'd at first variously *pro re natâ*, as Magists..Nurserists, Geoponists, Hygeists. **1753** *Gentl. Mag.* June 267 A good geoponical reason may certainly be assign'd for it. **1814** *Last Act* I. i, Posterity will call it the Twistonian system of geoponicality. **1882** *St. James's Gaz.* 11 Mar. 6 They may even have the effrontery to be acquainted with georgics or geopony, commonly called agriculture.

georama (dʒiːəʊˈrɑːmə). ? *Obs.* [a. F. *géorama*, f. Gr. γῆ earth + ὅραμα view.] (See quot. 1847.)

1847 CRAIG, *Georama*, an ingenious invention, of French origin, for exhibiting a very complete view of the different seas, lakes, rivers, and mountains on the earth's surface. It is formed in the shape of a hollow sphere. **1851** *Illustr. Catal. Gt. Exhib.* 1188 Georamas and uranoramas, used as lamp-shades. **1897** *Athenæum* 9 Jan. 52/3 The..first works ..of L. V. de St.-Martin..were an elementary atlas and a georama (1826), the first globe of the kind seen in Paris.

Geordie (ˈdʒɔːdɪ). *Sc.* and *north. dial.* Also **Geordy, Jordie.** [dim. of GEORGE.]

†**1.** (*yellow*) *Geordie*: a guinea. (Cf. GEORGE 4 b.)

1786 BURNS *Twa Dogs* 58 He draws a bonie, silken purse ..whare thro' the steeks, The yellow letter'd Geordie keeks. **1790** SHIRREFS *Poems* Gloss., *Geordie*, a guinea. **1893** JAS. SKINNER *Autobiog. Metaphys.* xxxvi. 193 A man..who has only to put his hand in his pocket, and out come the yellow Geordies.

2. a. A coal-pitman. **b.** A collier-boat. **c.** (See quot. 1881.)

1876 C. M. DAVIES *Unorth. Lond.* 353 A 'Geordie', or pitman. **1881** RAYMOND *Mining Gloss.*, *Geordie*, the miners' term for [George] Stephenson's safety-lamp. **1884** W. C. RUSSELL *Jack's Courtship* xliv, You thought..of the Channel aswarm with just such vessels as she—Geordies deep with coal. **1889** R. KIPLING *In Black & White* 53 Oh for a decent, rational Geordie! **1897** in *Daily Mail* 13 Oct. 7 A North-country 'Geordie' that was coolly snugging-down and outweathering the fierce squall.

3. a. A native or inhabitant of Tyneside. Also in slightly *transf.* senses. Also *attrib.* or as *adj.* *colloq.* **b.** A Scotsman. *Austral.* and *N.Z. colloq.*

1866 C. NORDHOFF *Young Man-of-War's Man* iv. 69 The sailors belonging to the ports on the north-eastern coast of England are called Jordies. **1872** T. & G. ALLAN *Tyneside Songs* (1891) 416 Where's a' his funny sayin's, that set a' the Geordies in a roar? **1890** 'R. BOLDREWOOD' *Miner's Right* I. ix. 227 Whose yer friend; a Geordie, most like? **1892** R. O. HESLOP *Northumberland Words* I. 196 The men who went from the lower Tyneside to work at the pits in South Tynedale were always called 'Geordies' by the people there. **1943** *Amer. Speech* XVIII. 89 [In New Zealand] a Scotsman is a *Geordie*, and an Irishman, as in vulgar American, a *Mick*. These synonyms are also current in Australia. **1955** 'C. H. ROLPH' *Women of Streets* iv. 56 A large rough Geordie woman in her mid-thirties. **1959** 'M. AINSWORTH' *Murder is Catching* 11 He had a faint Geordie twang. *Ibid.* 12 'Have a heart,' said the Geordie. **1971** *Listener* 12 Aug. 201/2 There's a people's culture in Geordieland—it was the last place in England to have its own circuit of music halls.

George (dʒɔːdʒ). [ad. L. *Geōrgius*, a. Gr. Γεώργιος name of a saint said to have been a prince of Cappadocia, and to have suffered martyrdom in the reign of Diocletian.

St. George, who at an English synod of 1222 was placed only among saints of the second rank (*Conc. Oxon.* viii. in

Conc. Collect. Paris 1644 XXVIII), has been recognized as the patron saint of England from the time of Edward III, perh. because of his being adopted as patron of the Order of the Garter, and his encounter with the dragon is frequently represented on coins, medals, etc. Hence are derived various secondary uses of the name, with or without the prefixed *Saint.*]

I. Saint George.

1. a. A cry formerly used by English soldiery.

1594 SHAKS. *Rich. III*, v. iii. 270 God, and Saint George, Richmond, and Victory. **1627** CAPT. SMITH *Seaman's Gram.* xiii. 62 So sound Drums and Trumpets, and Saint George for England. **1704** PRIOR *Let. To Boileau Despreaux* 164 Anne and St. George! the charging hero cries.

b. A form of lance-exercise.

1833 *Regul. Instr. Cavalry* I. 166 [The exercise is described at length].

2. *St. George's day*: the festival day in honour of St. George, April 23. ***St. George's cross***: an upright and a horizontal bar of red, crossing each other in the centre. ***St. George's colours***: colours bearing a St. George's cross (so also ***St. George's ensign, flag, jack***). ***St. George's guard*** (see quot. 1802).

1611 BARRY *Ram Alley* IV. i, By Dis I will be Knight, Weare a blew coate on great Saint Georges day. *a* **1642** SIR W. MONSON *Naval Tracts* III. (1704) 365/2 All Admirals.. were wont to carry anciently the St. George's Flag in the Head of the Top-Mast. **1773** *Naval Chron.* XXII. 186 Lord Edgcumbe.. hoisted the St. George's flag at the fore-top. **1802** *Ibid.* VII. 449 The men of war shifted the blue ensigns to St. George's colours. **1802** C. JAMES *Milit. Dict., St. George's Guard*, a guard of the broadsword or sabre, used in warding off blows directed against the head. **1806** A. DUNCAN *Nelson* 72 The squadron wore the white, or St. George's ensign. —— *Nelson's Funeral* 17 The St. George's jack.. was lowered half-mast high. **1867** SMYTH *Sailor's Word-bk.* s.v. *Flag*, The white field, with the red St. George's cross.. is now alone used in the British navy.

II. George.

3. The jewel which forms part of the insignia of the Order of the Garter (see quot. 1672). ***greater, lesser George*** (cf. quots. 1672, 1724).

1506 *Paston Lett.* No. 953 III. 404 A cheyn with a joerge of dyamondes. **1593** SHAKS. *2 Hen. VI*, IV. i. 29 Looke on my George, I am a Gentleman. **1672** ASHMOLE *Order Garter* 221 At the middle of the Collar before, is to be fastned the Image of St. George armed, sitting on Horseback, who having thrown the Dragon upon his back, encounters him with a tilting Spear. This Jewel is not surrounded with a Garter, or row of Diamonds, as is the lesser George, but made according to the representation in the Plate above, and called the Great George. **1675** *Lond. Gaz.* No. 1026/4 Lost or stolen.. an order of the Garter, or George, being a Cerdonix Stone.. with a George engraven on the one side of the Onix, and a George enameled on the other side. **1724** *Ibid.* No. 6284/2 Garter on his knee presented to the Sovereign the Blue Ribbon with the Gold or Little George, which His Majesty.. put over the Left Shoulder of his Lordship.. athwart under his Right Arm. **1788** *New Lond. Mag.* IV. 167 A convict under sentence of transportation.. for stealing a George set with diamonds. **1849** MACAULAY *Hist. Eng.* v. I. 615 At Chedzoy he stopped a moment to mount a fresh horse and to hide his blue riband and his George.

†**4.** *slang.* A coin bearing the image of St. George: **a.** A half-crown; **b.** (*yellow*) *George*, a guinea.

a. 1659 *Pol. Ballads* (1860) I. 138 When the Georges are flown, Then the Cause goes down. **1688** SHADWELL *Sqr. Alsatia* II. Wks. 1720 IV. 48, I make bold to equip you with some Meggs, Smelts, Decus's and Georges. *a* **1700** B. E. *Dict. Cant. Crew* s.v., He tipt me Forty Georges for my Earnest, he paid me Five Pounds for my Share or Snack. **1719** D'URFEY *Pills* I. 313 Let's give 'em a George. **1785** GROSE *Dict. Vulg. Tongue, George*, a half-crown piece.

b. 1784 BURNS *Ep. Rankine* xii, An' baith a yellow George to claim, An' thole their blethers! **1785** GROSE *Dict. Vulg. Tongue* s.v., Yellow George, a guinea. **1812** *Sporting Mag.* XXXIX. 139 A smart and scientific boxing match took place ..for a George betwixt a gallant knight of the thimble ..[and] Power the celebrated Pugilist.

5. (See quot.) ? *Obs.*; but cf. BROWN GEORGE I.

1755 JOHNSON, *George*, a brown loaf. Of this sense I know not the original. **1791** LD. JEFFREY in Cockburn *Life* (1852) II. 3 (*Let. from Queen's College, Oxford*) Most of us choose to walk till nine o'clock, at which hour a George (that is to say a round penny roll) is served up, with a bit of butter.. into each of our chambers.

6. a. *by George* (earlier †*before, for, fore George*): used as a mild oath, or as a mere exclamation. Also simply *George!*

1598 B. JONSON *Ev. Man in Hum.* II. i, Well! he knows what to trust to, for George [cf. III. i, By St. George]. **1678** DRYDEN *Limberham*, v. i, Before George 'tis so. **1700** T. BROWN tr. *Fresny's Amusem. Ser. & Com.* 135 Before George I think our Family's made of Iron. **1731** FIELDING *Grub St. Opera* III. vii, By George, I will make an Example of him. **1837** CAPT. BOLDERO *Sp. Ho. Com.* 19 Apr., By George I would, if I had the opportunity, serve him the same! **1885** F. ANSTEY *Tinted Venus* 49, I mean what I say, by George I do! **1888** A. C. GUNTER *Mr. Potter* i, George! isn't it horribly lonely?

b. Colloq. phr. ***let George do it***: let someone else do the work or take the responsibility. orig. *U.S.*

1910 *Bookman* May 293/2 What's going to happen when Lovey asks papa to hold Snookums and that hitherto devoted parent replies, 'Let George do it.' **1942** WODEHOUSE *Money in Bank* (1946) xvi. 140 He was not familiar with the fine old slogan, Let George Do It. **1948** *Chicago Tribune* (Grafic Mag.) 10 Oct. 8/1 Producers have a way of saying 'Let George do it' whenever a particularly difficult villain role turns up. **1971** P. G. WODEHOUSE in *N.Y. Times Encycl. Almanac 1971* 448 It is the old, old story. Overconfidence. We tell ourselves, 'Oh, I can't be bothered getting a divorce. They'll be plenty without me. Let George do it.'

c. Used as a familiar form of address to a stranger; *spec.* in Services' slang: (*a*) an airman; (*b*) an automatic pilot in an aircraft.

1925 FRASER & GIBBONS *Soldier & Sailor Words* 104 *George*, a colloquial term for an airman, corresponding to 'Jack' for bluejacket, and 'Tommy' for a soldier. Also used sometimes in the Air Force in addressing any stranger. **1931** *Flight* 30 Oct. 1082 'George' is the automatic pilot about which there has been so much talk lately. **1943** C. H. WARD-JACKSON *Piece of Cake* 31 In the early days of the Great War soldiers and sailors came to refer to any airman as 'George'. .. Airmen thus came to address any strange fellow by the same name. **1961** *Shell Aviation News* No. 282, 5/2 Even if powered controls do all the physical work, if 'George' does all the 'steering',.. the test pilot is the man who bears the responsibility, and is still irreplaceable.

7. *Comb.*, as **George Cross, George Medal**, decorations for gallantry in civilian life instituted by King George VI; **George guinea** = sense 4 b; †**George-noble**, a gold coin worth 6*s.* 8*d.*; †**George-ring** (see quot. 1709); also **Georgemas** = St. George's Day.

1597-8 BP. HALL *Sat.* IV. vi. 31 Whiles his George-Nobles rusten in his chest. **1695** W. LOWNDES *Amendm. Silv. Coin* 21 Masters and Workers, Covenanted to make Two sorts of Gold Coins to wit.. Rialls, Angels, George-Nobles. **1709** HEARNE *Collect.* (O.H.S.) II. 310 Having on them the Image of St. George they were call'd George Rings. **1805** *Edin. Rev.* VII. 270 Henry VIII.. coined george-nobles of 6*s.* 8*d.* **1830** JAMES *Darnley* xxxv, He was to take the lady, the chaplain, and the waiting-maid, to Boulogne, for ten George nobles. **1868** *Jrnl. R. Agric. Soc.* IV. II. 349 Buying.. wether hoggs at the Georgemas tryst. **1905** *Westm. Gaz.* 25 May 7/3 The finding of George guineas. **1940** *N. & Q.* 5 Oct. 235/1 In the broadcast.. which he delivered on Sept. 23, His Majesty the King.. announced that.. he has decided to create at once a new mark of honour for men and women in all walks of civilian life. 'I propose,' he said, 'to give my name to this new distinction, which will consist of the George Cross, which will rank next to the Victoria Cross, and the George Medal for wider distribution.' **1941** H. BRIGHOUSE in J. W. Marriott *Best One-Act Plays of 1940* 293 *Philip.* You can take it as official that you'll be recommended for the George Cross. *Alfred.* Crimes! That's the civilian V.C. **1959** *Daily Tel.* 24 Apr. 13/4 (*heading*) George Medal man gaoled. **1966** *Whitaker's Almanack* 772/1 Malta was.. besieged in the last war and again withstood the attacks... In recognition of the part played by the Maltese people, King George VI awarded the George Cross to the island.

georgette (dʒɔːˈdʒɛt, ʒɔːˈʒɛt). [Fr., f. the name of Mme *Georgette* de la Plante, French modiste.] A thin, semi-transparent, plain-woven crêpe made from fine, hard-twisted silk or other yarns. Also *georgette crêpe.*

1915 *Sphere* 22 May p. vi/1 A deep yoke and front composed of plain forget-me-not blue *chic* Georgette. **1920** *Glasgow Herald* 29 Nov. 15 Silk georgette. **1922** *Daily Mail* 10 Nov. 8 The bride's gown of gold embroidered georgette. **1927** A. MILLER *Colfax Bk.-Plate* xiii. 161 My negligée.. was made of georgette and satin. **1960** *Which?* Feb. 42/1 *Georgette*, fine, light, open, plain woven fabric with a crêpe yarn. Often silk, but other fibres as well.

Georgian (ˈdʒɔːdʒɪən), *a.*[1] and *sb.*[1] [f. *George* + -IAN.]

A. *adj.* **1. a.** Belonging to the time of the Georges, as Kings of Britain. *spec.* Of or resembling the style of architecture, esp. domestic architecture, characteristic of the reigns of the first four Georges (1714–1830). ***Georgian group***, the name of a society formed to advocate the preservation of examples of this style.

1855 in OGILVIE, Suppl. **1861** BERESF. HOPE *Eng. Cathedr. 19th C.* 119 We do not require.. evidence to prove the low morals of a large mass of the clergy in the Georgian or first præ-Georgian days. **1875** GEO. ELIOT *Let.* 14 Aug. (1955) VI. 165 Our house here is rather a fine old red brick Georgian place. **1879** JAS. GRANT in *Cassell's Techn. Educ.* IV. 291/1 Discoveries which distinguished him as one of the greatest astronomers of the Georgian era. **1883** *Harper's Mag.* July 166/2 There is a good old Georgian church at Hornsey. **1896** B. & B. F. FLETCHER *Hist. Archit.* 280 At this time, there grew up a vernacular style, most of the less important houses being erected in the useful and modest Queen Anne and Georgian type of square house. **1940** N. MITFORD *Pigeon Pie* vi. 99 They were going to pull it down and build a block of flats. (The Georgian Group, wrapped in dreams of Federal Union, stirred in its sleep on hearing this.) **1945** J. SUMMERSON *Georgian London* v. 53 With the general adoption of parapet-roofs and sash-windows with recessed frames, the characteristic Georgian town house had arrived. **1961** W. GÉRIN *B. Brontë* xvi. 236 A double-fronted Georgian house in the centre of the village. **1967** *Observer* 9 July 32/3 She wants to buy a house in Regent's Park, St. John's Wood or Chelsea—modern, but in Georgian style.

b. Belonging to or characteristic of the reign of George V (1910–36) or VI (1936–52). In literary criticism applied *spec.* to writers or writing of the first years of George V's reign, and esp. to contributors to five anthologies of 'Georgian Poetry' published between 1912 and 1922.

1910 P. GIBBS in *Lady's Realm* July 272 Under the new regime of Georgian England. **1912** E. H. MARSH (*title*) Georgian Poetry 1911–1912. **1921** R. LYND in *Anthol. Mod. Verse* Introd. p. xxx, The Georgian poets, like the Lake poets, are re-establishing the claim of familiar experiences to poetical treatment in familiar language. **1924** V. WOOLF *Mr. Bennett & Mrs. Brown* 19 The Georgian writer had to begin by throwing away the method that was in use at the moment. **1927** [see EDWARDIAN *a.* 3]. **1963** J. I. M. STEWART *Eight Mod. Writers* i. 14 The Georgian poets.. included a writer of unique vision in Walter de la Mare, a genius in D. H. Lawrence, and a dark horse in Robert Graves.

†**2.** ***Georgian planet*** = GEORGIUM SIDUS. *Obs.*

1787 *Phil. Trans.* LXXVII. 125 An Account of the Discovery of Two Satellites revolving round the Georgian Planet. By William Herschel, LL.D., F.R.S. **1812** WOODHOUSE *Astron.* xii. 101 The same method therefore will not apply to bodies more distant from us than the sun; neither to Jupiter, nor Saturn, nor the Georgian Planet.

3. ***Georgian green*** (see quot. 1949).

1934 *Historical Colours* (Thos. Parsons & Sons) 39 It is likely that William and Mary as well as Georgian greens were derived.. from the vert pomme or apple green of our French neighbours.. as intercourse in those times (*circa* 1757) was greater than generally credited. **1942** J. CARY *To be a Pilgrim* lxxvi. 171 She showed me the paint. 'Is this the colour, uncle. Georgian green they called it.' **1949** *British Colour Council Dict. Colours Int. Decoration* III. 12 *Georgian green*, one of the most typical of the slightly yellowish greens found in wall decoration, hangings and woven upholstery fabrics of many kinds during the period covered by the first four Georges, Kings of England, 1714–1830.

B. *sb.* One belonging to the time of the Georges, kings of England; *spec.* a writer of the early part of the reign of George V (see A. 1 b above).

1901 *Sketch* 28 Aug. 249/2 The arid stucco of the unimaginative Georgians and Early Victorians. **1913** R. BROOKE *Let.* 24 July (1968) 493 Send photographs of a Georgian or two.. to Canadian & American papers, when the book [sc. *Georgian Poetry*] goes for review. **1916** *Q. Rev.* Oct. 386 From such a catastrophe, the humour, commonsense, and the artistic judgment of the best of the new 'Georgians' will assuredly save their generation. **1924** V. WOOLF *Mr. Bennett & Mrs. Brown* 4 Mr. Forster, Mr. Lawrence, Mr. Strachey, Mr. Joyce, and Mr. Eliot I will call the Georgians. **1943** *English Studies* XXV. 1 After the War the Georgians still commanded a large public.

Georgian (ˈdʒɔːdʒɪən), *a.*[2] and *sb.*[2] [f. *Georgi-a* + -AN.] **A.** *adj.*

1. Belonging to Georgia, a district in the Caucasus, its inhabitants, or their language.

1607 TOPSELL *Four-f. Beasts* (1658) 79 These beasts are plentiful in Ethiopia, India, and the Georgian region, which was once called Media. *a* **1791** WESLEY *Serm.* Wks. 1811 IX. 234 Bodies of Georgian, Circassian, Mengrelian Christians. **1842** PRICHARD *Nat. Hist. Man* 172 The personal beauty for which the modern Persians are noted is inherited from Circassian and Georgian concubines. **1844** H. H. WILSON *Brit. India* III. 220 Some desultory incursions.. on the Georgian frontier.. had terminated in the discomfiture of the Persians.

2. Belonging to the State of Georgia, one of the United States of America.

1762 WESLEY *Jrnl.* 27 May (1827) III. 91 We had another Georgian day. **1775** ROMANS *Hist. Florida* 174 Cattle can hardly yield profit where the Carolinian or Georgian method of killing at two, three, and four years old obtains. **1835** URE *Philos. Manuf.* 113 The second experiment was made on a Georgian cotton, which sticks strongly to the seeds.

B. *sb.*

1. a. A native of Georgia in Asia. **b.** The language of that country.

c **1400** MAUNDEV. (1839) x. 121 There ben othere, that men clepen Georgyenes, that seynt George converted. **1625-6** PURCHAS *Pilgrims* II. 1269 There is also a warlike people dreadfull to the Saracens, called Georgians, of Saint George.. whom they worship. **1635** PAGITT *Christianogr.* I. ii. (1636) 54 The Georgians inhabite the Countrie that was antiently named Iberia. **1796** MORSE *Amer. Geog.* II. 471 The Georgians in general are by some travellers said to be the handsomest people in the world. **1838** *Penny Cycl.* XI. 173/1 The Georgian is full of Greek, Latin, Persian, Arabic, Turkish, and other foreign words.

2. An inhabitant of Georgia in America.

1741 P. TAILFER, etc. *Narr. Georgia* 72 In and about the Town of Charles-Town alone, this Autumn, above Fifty Georgians died in Misery and Want. **1850** LYELL *2nd Visit U.S.* II. 13 These Georgians seemed.. to be as insensible to the frost as some Englishmen the first winter after their return from India. **1868** *Spectator* 14 Jan. 37 It afforded strong support to those Georgians and Alabamians who were meditating on the means of rejoining the Union.

Georgianism (ˈdʒɔːdʒɪənɪz(ə)m). [f. GEORGIAN *a.*[1] + -ISM.] The qualities or characteristics of Georgian architecture, poetry, etc.

1914 R. BROOKE *Let.* 6 July (1968) 597 Marsh has got Georgianism on the brain, & will shortly issue a series of Georgian poker-work. **1929** *Daily Tel.* 15 Jan. 9/2 (*caption*) The best traditions of Georgianism inspire this most modern of.. dining-rooms. **1933** *Scrutiny* Dec. 300 It isn't the wordy debility of Georgianism that needs reacting against to-day. **1954** *Essays & Studies* VII. 83 'Georgianism' has for some time now been a term of implicit rebuke. **1970** *English Studies* LI. 271 That most fitting showpiece of Central Georgianism, his 'Weekend' sequence.

georgic (ˈdʒɔːdʒɪk), *a.* and *sb.* [ad. L. *geōrgic-us*, a. Gr. γεωργικός, f. γεωργός husbandman, f. γεω-(γῆ) earth + root ἐργ- of ἔργον work, ἔρξω used as fut. of ἔρδειν to work. Cf. F. *géorgique.*]

A. *adj.* Relating to agriculture. *Obs.* exc. in semi-humorous use = agricultural, rustic.

1711-20 GAY *Rural Sports* 67 Here I peruse the Mantuan's Georgic strains, And learn the labours of Italian swains. **1774** T. WEST *Antiq. Furness* Ded., These environs find the good effect of your taste and judgment in the useful parts of Georgic studies. **1875** G. MACDONALD *Sir Gibbie* xviii. 100 The idea was abroad in the mind bucolic and georgic.

B. *sb.*

†**1.** A husbandman, tiller of the soil. *Obs. rare*⁻¹.

1703 T. N. *City & C. Purchaser* Pref. 2 Adam in the Garden of Eden.. was.. to perform the Office of a Georgic (or Husband-man).

2. *pl.* **a.** The science of land-culture (= Gr. τὰ γεωργικά).

1802 ACERBI *Trav.* I. 144 The elements of botany, horticulture and other branches of georgics.

b. The title of Virgil's poetical treatise on husbandry, in four books; hence sometimes in *sing.* a poem dealing with rustic occupations.

1513 DOUGLAS *Æneis* VI. Prol. 101 Octavian, in his Georgikis, ȝe may se, He [Virgil] consalis nevir lordschip in hell desyre. **1586** W. WEBBE *Eng. Poetrie* (Arb.) 28 He [Virgil] immitateth Homer in that worke, so dooth he likewyse followe.. Hesiodus in his Georgicks or bookes of Husbandry. **1665** BOYLE *Occas. Refl.* Pref. (1845) 21 Such passages do.. make the style of his Georgicks, as well Noble.. as that of his Æneids. *a* **1719** ADDISON *On Virgil's Georgics* Wks. 1721 I. 250 A Georgic therefore is some part of the science of husbandry.. set off with all the Beauties and Embellishments of Poetry. **1753** GRAY *Lett.* Wks. 1884 II. 249 Today it is in the North, clear sunshine, but cold and a little wintry: and so ends my Georgick in prose. **1877** MORLEY *Crit. Misc.* Ser. II. 110 His Supreme Being—a mere didactic phrase, the deity of a poet's georgic.

georgical ('dʒɔːdʒɪkəl), *a.* Now *rare.* [f. as prec. + -AL¹.] Agricultural.

1660 BURNEY Κέρδ. δῶρον (1661) 42 Men wil sweat upon certain ground in georgical affairs, and venture themselves upon uncertain ground in warlike exploits. **1686** PLOT *Staffordsh.* 255 A Question scarce started before.. amongst the Philosophers, or Georgical writers. **1777** A. HUNTER (*title*) Georgical Essays. **1792** A. YOUNG *Trav. France* 304 My library abounds more with French georgical authors.. than any other I have had the opportunity to examine. **1824** G. CHALMERS *Caledonia* III. v. §7. 475 Such was the georgical state of Ayrshire. **1832** *Blackw. Mag.* XXXII. 174 Next follows the Georgical part of the Works.

georgina (dʒɔː'dʒiːnə). *rare.* [mod.L.; cf. Ger. *Georgine.*] = DAHLIA. Also in *Comb.*, as **georgina paper**, a kind of test-paper formerly used (see quot. 1863); it was of a violet colour, turning red with acids and green with alkalies.

1830 B'NESS BUNSEN in Hare *Life* I. ix. 351 At the Palace of Portici, I was delighted with a whole grove of Georginas. **1837** *Penny Cycl.* VIII. 285 Some attempts have been made of late years to substitute the name of Georgina for that of Dahlia. **18..** B. SILLIMAN Jr. in Dana *Geol.* v. (1850) 324 *note*, Alone in a test tube it gives off water copiously which is neutral to georgina paper. **1863** NOAD *Chem. Anal.* I. 42 Georgina paper.. is prepared by dipping paper into the coloured infusion of the petals of the *Georgina purpurea.*

†**'Georgite.** *Obs. rare*⁻¹. [f. *George* + -ITE.] A supporter of the Georges, or the Hanoverian dynasty, opposed to JACOBITE.

1726 AMHERST *Terræ Fil.* vii. 34 Oxford is just the same in its antient and in its present state; whigs and tories, Georgites and Jacobites, orthodox and unorthodox are not the only distinctions.

‖**Georgium sidus** ('dʒɔːdʒɪəm 'saɪdəs). [mod.L. *Geōrgium*, neut. f. L. *Geōrgius* George + L. *sīdus* star.] One of the greater planets (now called Uranus), so named by its discoverer, Sir William Herschel, in honour of George III (see quot. 1783).

1783 HERSCHEL in *Phil. Trans.* LXXIII. 2, I cannot but wish to take this opportunity of expressing my sense of gratitude, by giving the name Georgium Sidus.. to a star, which (with respect to us) first began to shine under His auspicious reign. **1788** —— *Ibid.* LXXVIII. 369 The Georgium Sidus, therefore, in bulk, is 80,49256 times as large as the earth.

†**ge'oscopy.** *Obs.*⁻⁰ [ad. Gr. *γεωσκοπία, f. γεω- earth + -σκοπία observation. Cf. F. *géoscopie* geomancy.] (See quot.) Hence **geo'scopic** *a.*, 'pertaining to geoscopy' (*Cent. Dict.*).

1727–51 CHAMBERS *Cycl.*, *Geoscopy*, a kind of knowlege of the nature and qualities of the ground, or soil; gained by viewing and considering it... *Geoscopy* is only conjectural; but its conjectures are very well grounded. **1847** in CRAIG; and in later Dicts.

geoselenic, -static, etc.: see GEO-.

geostrophic (dʒiːəʊ'strɒfɪk), *a.* [f. GEO- + Gr. στροφή a turning, f. στρέφειν to turn + -IC.] Of, pertaining to, or caused by the Coriolis force (see CORIOLIS); usu. applied to a wind (or a current of water) in which there is a balance between the Coriolis force and the horizontal pressure gradient (cf. *gradient wind* s.v. GRADIENT *a.* and *sb.* B. 6).

1916 N. SHAW in *Nature* 4 May 210/1 The motion of air.. is persistent because the pressure-gradient is balanced by the centrifugal action of the earth's rotation, which we may call the geostrophic component, and of the curvature of the path over the earth's surface, which we call the cyclostrophic component. *Ibid.* 211/2 We call the wind computed according to the first term the geostrophic wind, and regard it as generally representing the actual wind of temperate and polar regions. **1928** D. BRUNT *Meteorol.* vii. 66 The value of the gradient wind which is derived when the curvature of the path is neglected is called the *geostrophic wind.* **1933** *Jrnl. R. Aeronaut. Soc.* XXXVII. 314 The ground wind is rarely the same in direction as the geostrophic wind which blows at 1,500 feet above the surface, and in which the airman is more likely to be flying. **1957** *Times Survey Brit. Aviation* Sept. 7/3 Up to about 20,000 ft. the classical 'geostrophic balance' between the pressure and motion fields holds fairly well. **1966** [see *gradient wind* s.v. GRADIENT *a.* and *sb.* B. 6]. **1970** *Sci. Jrnl.* Mar. 56/1 In most ocean currents the horizontal pressure gradient is found to be in balance with coriolis force. Such currents are called geostrophic or 'Earth-balanced' currents.

geosynclinal (dʒiːəʊsɪŋ'klaɪnəl), *a.* and *sb. Geol.* [f. GEO- + SYNCLINAL.]

A. *adj.* Forming a large depression in the surface of the earth, from the lowest point of which there is a gradual rise to either side, even although the continuity of this is broken by smaller depressions. The opposite of *geanticlinal.*

1879 DANA *Man. Geol.* (ed. 3) 817 Flexure implies both upward and downward bendings, geanticlinal and geosynclinal, the one a complement to the other. **1882** A. H. GREEN *Phys. Geol.* xiii. (ed. 3) 630 After the geosynclinal mass had accumulated the state of things stood thus.

B. *sb.* A geosynclinal dip or depression in the earth's surface.

1873 DANA in *Amer. Jrnl. Sci.* Ser. III. V. 430 The making of the Alleghany range was carried forward at first through a long-continued subsidence—a geosynclinal (not a true synclinal). **1882** A. H. GREEN *Phys. Geol.* xiii. (ed. 3) 629 To the great trough-shaped mass of rock which was thus accumulated Dana has given the name of a Geosynclinal. *Ibid.* The geosynclinal of a mountain-chain.

geosyncline (dʒiːəʊ'sɪŋklaɪn). *Geol.* [Back-formation from GEOSYNCLINAL *sb.*] = GEOSYNCLINAL *sb.*

1895 J. D. DANA *Man. Geol.* (ed. 4) 389 A mountain system includes all ranges in a region made in different, more or less independent, geosynclines at the same epoch. **1925** J. JOLY *Surface-Hist. Earth* v. 85 The geosyncline wherein the Cordilleras of N. America were cradled extended from the Gulf of Mexico to the Arctic Ocean. **1954** M. P. BILLINGS *Struct. Geol.* (ed. 2) iii. 55 A geosyncline is a large basin in which many thousands of feet of sediments accumulate. **1965** A. HOLMES *Princ. Physical Geol.* (ed. 2) xxx. 1122 The modified form *geosyncline* came into general use.

geotectonic, -thermal, etc.: see GEO-.

[**geotic,** *a.* Error for GOETIC: see note s.v. GOETY.

1755 JOHNSON, *Geotic*, belonging to the earth; terrestrial. *Dict.* [But **1727** BAILEY vol. II. (followed by **1730–6** folio) has '*Geotick*, a sort of Magick, performed by the assistance of a Dæmon, the same as Geomancy '.] Hence in **1864** WEBSTER, and some later Dicts.]

geotropic (dʒiːəʊ'trɒpɪk), *a. Bot.* [f. Gr. γεω- GEO- + τροπικ-ός, f. τροπή turning.] Pertaining to, characterized by, or of the nature of, geotropism.

1875 BENNETT & DYER *Sachs' Bot.* 756 Internodes with an upward geotropic curvature. **1880** C. & F. DARWIN *Movem. Pl.* 81 As soon as the confluent petioles protrude from the seed they bend down, as they are strongly geotropic, and penetrate the ground. **1881** McNAB *Bot.* vi. §266. 147 The main root with the concave side of the bent portion downwards is positively geotropic, the stem with the concave side upwards is negatively geotropic. **1891** F. DARWIN in *Nature* 27 Aug. 409 Roots and other positively geotropic organs bend owing to plasticity. **1897** WILLIS *Flower. Pl.* I. 21 We express this property of the root [to assume its original downward progress in growing when forcibly deflected from its course, e.g. by a stone] by saying that it is positively geotropic.

Hence **geo'tropically** *adv.*

1882 F. DARWIN in *Nature* 27 Apr. 616 The central portion of the root.. is capable of bending geotropically downwards. **1882** VINES *Sachs' Bot.* 873 Geotropically curved stems and nodes of Grasses. **1891** *Athenæum* 27 June 832/3 The protoplasm of heliotropically and geotropically curving cells and hyphæ.

geotropism (dʒiː'ɒtrəpɪz(ə)m). *Bot.* [f. as prec. + -ISM. First used in Ger. form *geotropismus* by A. B. Frank *Beitr. z. Pflanzenphysiol.* (1868).] A collective term for the phenomena of irritability presented by various parts of plants in relation to the action of gravity. ***positive geotropism***: the tendency (of roots, etc.) to grow towards the centre of the earth. ***negative g.***: the tendency (of stems, etc.) to grow away from the centre of the earth.

By C. and F. Darwin (1880) the word was used in a narrower sense, as synonymous with the 'positive geotropism' of other writers, the term APOGEOTROPISM being substituted for 'negative geotropism'. DIAGEOTROPISM, the tendency (of leaves) to grow at right angles to the vertical, is a third variety of 'geotropism' in the original (and still prevalent) wider sense of the word.

1875 BENNETT & DYER *Sachs' Bot.* 758 The positive or negative character of geotropism depends as little as that of heliotropism on the morphological nature of the organ. **1880** F. DARWIN in *Nature* XXXIII. 179 The phenomena might result from the ordinary forms of heliotropism and geotropism acting in concert.

So also **ge'otropy.**

1889 in *Century Dict.*

geoul, obs. form of JOWL.

gep, var. GIP *int.*, *Obs.*

gephyrean (dʒɛfɪ'riːən), *a.* and *sb.* [f. mod.L. *Gephyrea*, sb. pl. (f. Gr. γέφῡρα bridge) + -AN.]

A. *adj.* Of or pertaining to the *Gephyrea*, a class or group of the *Vermes* or worms. **B.** *sb.* A worm of this class.

1881 CARPENTER *Microsc.* §596. 701 This was discovered by Krohn in 1858 to be a Gephyrean Worm. **1887** *Athenæum* 7 May 611/3 A report on the gephyreans of the Mergui Archipelago, by Prof. E. Selenka, of Erlangen, was read. **1893** *Ibid.* 29 Apr. 541/2 A communication was read from Mr. A. E. Shipley, on the anatomy and histology of two gephyrean worms of the genus Sipunculus.

gephyrocercal (ˌdʒɛfɪrəʊ'sɜːkəl), *a. Ichthyol.* [f. Gr. γέφυρα bridge + κέρκος tail + -AL.] Having the caudal fin formed by the meeting of the dorsal and anal fins. So **gephyrocercy** (ˌdʒɛfɪrəʊ'sɜːsɪ), gephyrocercal condition.

1886 J. A. RYDER in *U.S. Comm. Fish Rep. 1884* 983 *Gephyrocercy* and *gephyrocercal* are terms which will apply to the type of caudal structure appearing normally in only a few forms, such as *Mola* and *Fierasfer*. *Ibid.* 991 Gephyrocercy.—This type of tail appears to be normally met with in only two forms, of Teleosts, namely, *Mola* and *Fierasfer*. *Ibid.*, The interval so bridged by a secondary process of development leads to the formation of what we may call a gephyrocercal tail. **1939** *Nature* 18 Mar. 455/2 The gephyrocercal tail with protruding axial supplement, the normal first dorsal,.. and the form of the dermal armour of the head, are all typically cœlacanthid. **1955** E. H. COLBERT *Evol. Vertebrates* v. 68 Both these modern genera [of lungfishes] are characterized by gephyrocercal tails.

gepoun, var. GIPON, *Obs.*

ger, obs. form of GAR *v.*, GEAR, YEAR¹.

geraflour, obs. Sc. form of GILLYFLOWER.

gerah ('gɪərə). *Heb. Antiq.* Forms: 6 ge(e)ra, 7– gerah. [a. Heb. *gērāh*. Rendered in Vulgate *Exod.* xxx. 13 by *obolus.*] A Hebrew coin and weight, the twentieth part of a shekel.

1534 TINDALE *Wks.* (1573) 11/1 Geeras, in weight as it were an English halfepeny, or somewhat more. **1611** BIBLE *Exod.* xxx. 13 A shekel is twenty gerahs.

Geraldton wax ('dʒɛrəldtən wæks). *Austral.* [f. *Geraldton*, a town in W. Australia + WAX *sb.*¹] An evergreen shrub of Western Australia, *Chamælaucium uncinatum*, of the family Myrtaceæ. Also *attrib.*

1920 *Jrnl. & Proc. R. Soc. W. Austral.* VI. 42 Geraldton Wax-plant, Ornamental shrub. **1921** E. H. PELLOE *Wildflowers W. Austral.* iv. 42 From Geraldton.. southward almost to Fremantle blooms.. the well-known 'Geraldton Wax-flower'. **1934** *Bulletin* (Sydney) 14 Nov. 26/3 The Geraldton wax especially can be trimmed to any shape to get a better effect, since the blooms are carried along the stems. **1955** A. ROSS *Australia 55* 44 The foggy mauve of Geraldton wax.

geranial (dʒə'reɪnɪəl). *Chem.* [a. G. *geranial* (F. W. Semmler 1891, in *Ber. d. Deut. Chem. Ges.* XXIV. 201), f. *geraniumaldehyde.*] A fragrant colourless oil present in many essential oils (as lemon-grass oil) and used extensively in perfumery as citral, of which it is the *trans* form; it is the aldehyde, $C_{10}H_{16}O$, corresponding to geraniol.

1899 *Jrnl. Chem. Soc.* LXXVI. I. 67 Crystals are obtained which yield geranial.. when they are freed from oil. **1953** E. H. RODD *Chem. Carbon Compounds* IIB. xii. 498 The aldehyde citral.. occurs in two geometrical forms, citral-a (geranial) and citral-b (neral).

geranin (dʒə'reɪnɪn). Also **geraniin.** [f. GERANIUM + -IN.] An astringent principle obtained from *Geranium maculatum.*

1864 *New Syd. Soc. Year-bk. for 1863*, 440 Geranin. **1890** BILLINGS *Nat. Med. Dict.*, *Geraniin.*

geraniol (dʒə'reɪnɪɒl). *Chem.* [a. G. *geraniol* (O. Jacobsen 1871, in *Ann. d. Chem. und Pharm.* CLVII. 234), f. GERANI(UM + -OL.] A colourless oil with a fragrance of roses that is present in many essential oils (as geranium oil and rose oil) and is used extensively in perfumery; it is an open-chain primary alcohol of the terpene series, $C_{10}H_{18}O$.

1871 *Jrnl. Chem. Soc.* XXIV. 261 By repeated fractional distillation.. a liquid was obtained.. called by the author geraniol. **1906**, etc. [see *citronellal, -ol* s.v. CITRONELLA]. **1923** *Nature* 29 Dec. 952/1 Of active principles, australol, geraniol, citral, and piperitol gave coefficients of 22·5, 21, 19·5, and 13 respectively. **1949** E. GUENTHER *Essential Oils* II. 173 Geraniol serves extensively in the perfume, cosmetic, soap, and flavor industries. **1971** *Sci. Amer.* May 6/2 Chemical stereoisomers, whose molecules are mirror-images of one another, often taste and smell different from one another. For example, geraniol smells like roses while its stereoisomer smells like fresh oil.

geranium (dʒə'reɪnɪəm). Also 6–7 -ion. [a. L. *geranium*, *-ion*, a. Gr. γεράνιον, f. γέρανος crane.]

1. A genus of herbaceous plants or undershrubs (N.O. *Geraniaceæ*, of which it is the type), growing wild in temperate regions, and bearing a fruit similar in shape to the bill of a crane; a plant of this genus or its flower.

1548 TURNER *Names of Herbes* D iij, Geranium is of two kyndes. The one kynde is called Pinke nedle or Cranes byl. **1578** LYTE *Dodoens* I. xxxii. 45 The first kinde of Geranion or Storckes bill, his leaues are cut and iagged in many peeces. **1601** HOLLAND *Pliny* II. 259 The herb Geranion, which some call Myrrhis, others Merthrys, is like vnto Hemlocke. **1664** EVELYN *Kal. Hort.* 67 May..Flowers in Prime, or yet lasting..Gladiolus, Geranium [etc.]. **1725** BYROM *Lit. Rem.* (1854) I. I. 163 Mr. —— produced the plants from Chelsea Garden, all geraniums, neatly pasted on sheets of white paper. **1794** MARTYN *Rousseau's Bot.* xxiii. 332 A fruit composed of five grains and beaked; whence its names of Geranium and Crane's bill. **1863** KINGSLEY *Water-Bab.* 15 Among blue geranium and golden globe-flower.

2. A plant of the genus Pelargonium (N.O. *Geraniaceæ*), natives of S. Africa, of which many varieties are cultivated in Great Britain, esp. the Scarlet Geranium and the so-called Fancy Geranium or Pelargonium.

1760 SHENSTONE *Wks. & Lett.* III. 315 An antique vase is introduced with a flower and two or three leaves of the scarlet Geranium. **1796** C. MARSHALL *Garden.* (1813) 386 Shifting geraniums should generally take place once a year from smaller pots into..bigger. **1809** HAN. MORE *Cœlebs* I. xii. 160 Snatching up a wreath of various coloured geraniums. **1873** MRS. H. KING *Disciples, Ugo Bassi* (1877) 65 The red geraniums blazed in banks breast-high. **1890** 'LYTH' *Golden South* 155 Geraniums are grown as hedges.

3. *Med.* (*U.S. Pharm.*) The rhizome of *G. maculatum* used as an astringent (Mayne *Expos. Lex.* 1854).

4. The colour of the scarlet geranium.

1842 MISS COSTELLO *Pilgr. Auvergne* II. 158 Rich coloured aprons and handkerchiefs, scarlet and geranium prevailing amongst them. **1895** *Westm. Gaz.* 22 Apr. 1/2 Colour seemed chiefly to run on that blending of purple and geranium which was even a little overdone last year.

5. With defining word, applied to plants of other genera (see quots.).

1866 *Treas. Bot.* 528/2 *Indian Geranium*, a term used by perfumers for *Andropogon Nardus*. *Nettle Geranium*, a popular name for *Coleus fruticosus*.

6. *attrib.* and *Comb.*, as ***geranium-coloured***, ***-red***.

1836–9 DICKENS *Sk. Boz* (1850) 184/2 Mrs. Bloss..was dressed in a geranium-coloured muslin gown. **1894** *Daily News* 29 Sept. 6/5 The whole of this overlapping front is in black fretwork over geranium red.

Hence **ge'raniumed** *ppl. a.* [+ -ED[2]], having the colour of a scarlet geranium.

1819 'R. RABELAIS' *Abeillard & H.* 76 Pouting and geranium'd lips.

†**gerarchie.** *Her. Obs.* [? a use of *gerarchie* HIERARCHY, in allusion to the *nine* orders of the three hierarchies of angels.] (See quot.; substituted by Ferne for GERERI.)

1586 FERNE *Blaz. Gentrie* 206 The Armes called Quadrates, were nine in number..The first of the Quadrates finall, was called Gerearrie, or rather gerarchie: and that was when the feeld was deuided, into nine diuers quarters, or partes, meeting in the Fesse point of the Shielde.

gerarchie, -y(e, obs. forms of HIERARCHY.

†**gerard.** *Obs.* Also 4 gerarde, gerrard. [Of obscure origin; app. pronounced with (g) and with stress on the first syllable.] A villain.

a **1300** *Cursor M.* 7487, I sal vnder-tak þe fight, Agains yon gerard [Goliath] þat es sa grim. *Ibid.* 11811 Þat gredi gerard [Herod] als a gripe his vn-rightes biginnes to ripe! *Ibid.* 22308 Þai sal wene crist at vnderfang, And sal receiue þe gerard [Antichrist] strang. *c* **1350** *Leg. Rood* (1871) 64 Þe gerrard [the Devil] þus gan hir bigile, And me also, allas þat while!

‖**Gerardia** (dʒə'rɑːdɪə). [mod.L., named after John Gerarde the herbalist (1545–1612).] A genus of plants (N.O. *Scrophulariaceæ*) consisting of American herbs or undershrubs, with yellow or rosy-purple flowers.

1851 THOREAU *Autumn* (1894) 70 Still, purplish asters, late golden-rods..purple gerardia, etc.

†**gerate**, *v. Her. Obs.* Also 5–6 ger(r)at(t. [Of unknown origin.] *trans.* To powder or strew (a coat) with minor charges. Hence **gerat(t)ed**, †**i-geratt** *ppl. adjs.*; **gerat(t)ing** *vbl. sb.*

1486 *Bk. St. Albans, Her.* B iij b, His cootarmure ynyat or ellis I geratt with preciouse stonys. *Ibid.* B iij b, Gerattyng haue .ix. bagges of cootarmuris. **1562** LEIGH *Armorie* (1597) 37 When they may bee numbred, then it is called of old Herehaughtes geratting. *Ibid.* 37 b, You shall see at this daie fields of cote Armour gerated with diuers other thinges. **1586** FERNE *Blaz. Gentrie* 207 Coates Geratted of crosses might be geratted but of these foure seuerall sorts of crosses. **1864** BOUTELL *Her. Hist. & Pop.* xv. §14 (ed. 3) 200 The charges in geratted shields are poudrées or semées—poured over their fields. **1869** W. S. ELLIS *Antiq. Her.* x. 224 The composite coats of Conyers and Romara are an early testimony to the practice of gerating.

†**gerately**, *adv. Her. Obs.* [f. *gerate*, pa. pple. of prec. + -LY[2].] (See quots.)

1486 *Bk. St. Albans, Her.* B iij, Geratly is calde in armys whan the cootarmure is powderd. **1562** LEIGH *Armorie* (1597) 133 b, A chemise blanke, powdred and spotted with mullets Sable, which of the old Herehaughts is termed Gerately.

geratology (dʒɛrə'tɒlədʒɪ). [f. Gr. γηρατ-, γῆρας old age + -λογία discoursing: see -LOGY.] The science of the phenomena of decadence, esp. those characteristic of a species or other group of animals approaching extinction.

1884 A. HYATT in *Science* III. 147/2 We may trace the death of an entire order, and show that it takes place in accordance with the laws of geratology.

Hence **gerato'logic** [-IC], **gera'tologous** [-OUS] *adjs.*, of or pertaining to geratology. **gera'tologist** [-IST], one who studies geratology.

1884 A. HYATT in *Science* III. 124/1 These shells appear ..among the geratologous and pathological types.

†**geraty**, *a. Obs.* Also 6 gerattie. [f. *gerate*, pa. pple. of GERATE *v.* + -Y[1].] = GERATED.

1586 FERNE *Blaz. Gentrie* 207 The third quadrat, of the finals, was called gerattie when the coat armour was charged or powdered..with anye small deade thinge. **1869** W. S. ELLIS *Antiq. Her.* x. 238 Some of our earliest arms are *geraty* with cross crosslets..we don't find any coats geraty of crescents or escallops.

gerbe (dʒɜːb). Also 9 gerb, jerb. [a. F. *gerbe* (in the same senses): see GARBE *sb.*[1]]

†**1.** A wheat-sheaf. (Cf. GARB *sb.*[1] I.) *Obs.*[−1]

1808 J. BARLOW *Columb.* VII. 749 As when the toiling swains Heap their whole harvest on the stubbly plains, Gerb after gerb the bearded shock expands.

2. Something resembling a sheaf of wheat.

†**a.** A combination of jets in an ornamental fountain (*obs.*). **b.** A kind of firework (see quots.).

1698 M. LISTER *Journ. Paris* (1699) 208 Here are some Gerbes of a singular fashion, with a Circle of a great number of large Pipes. **1765** R. JONES *Fireworks* iii. 101 The cases for gerbes are made very strong, on account of the strength of the composition. **1801** STRUTT *Sports & Past.* IV. iii. 332 Exhibitions..consisting chiefly in fire-trees, jerbs, and rockets. **1833** *Philos. in Sport* xix. 401 Gerbes, a species of firework, which throws up a luminous and sparkling jet of fire. **1886** O. MASSON in *Encycl. Brit.* XX. 136/1 Gerbes are choked cases, not unlike Roman candles, but often of much larger size. Their fire spreads like a sheaf of wheat.

transf. **1802** T. BEDDOES *Hygeia* vi. 53 When once kindled, it [the fire of malignant fever] may justly be regarded as rising in a gerbe. **1862** G. P. SCROPE *Volcanos* 33 By a sudden vehement boiling up, it [the lava] almost reaches the upper rim, and then discharges a gerb of red-hot stones. **1869** tr. *Renan's Apostles* iv. 82 The atmosphere is furrowed as it were..with gerbes of flame.

gerbera ('dʒɜːbərə, 'gɜːbərə). *Bot.* [mod.L. (J. F. Gronovius 1737, in Linnæus *Corollarium Generum Plantarum* 16), f. the name of T. *Gerber* (died 1743), German naturalist.] A plant of the genus so named, of the family Compositæ; *spec.* the Transvaal daisy. Also ***gerbera daisy***.

1889 *Garden* 12 Oct. 341/1 The Gerbera may be planted outside for the summer. As a pot plant it is perfectly charming. **1949** H. E. BATES *Jacaranda Tree* i. 6 Fringes of heliotrope and gerbera daisy, mauve and pink and orange. **1956** J. HEARNE *Stranger at Gate* xv. 119 He got up and shifted the hose..to a bed of gerberas. **1960** [see BARBERTON].

gerbille ('dʒɜːbɪl). Also gerbil. [a. F. *gerbille*, ad. mod.L. *gerbillus*, dim. of *gerbo* JERBOA.] Any animal belonging to the genus *Gerbillus*.

1849 *Sk. Nat. Hist., Mammalia* IV. 47 The Indian gerbille is common in Hindustan, and seems to be gregarious. **1873** TRISTRAM *Moab* viii. 145 A pair of a beautifully marked Gerbille, with a fine squirrel-like tail.

gerbo, gerckem, obs. ff. JERBOA, GHERKIN.

gerd, gerd-, gerdel(l, -dle: see GIRD, GIRD-, GIRDLE, GRID-, GRIDDLE.

gerdon(e, gerdoun, obs. forms of GUERDON.

†**gere.** *Obs.* Forms: 4–6 geer(e, gere, 6 gier, 6–7 gear(e. See also GARE *sb.*[2] [Of obscure origin: the sense has some affinity to that of MDu. *gere, gaer, gare*, desire, zeal, passion, but the adoption of such a word from Du. is unlikely. At the beginning of 17th c. superseded by GARE *sb.*[2]]

A sudden fit of passion, feeling, transient fancy, or the like; a wild or changeful mood in which a loose is given to the feelings of the moment.

c **1369** CHAUCER *Dethe Blaunche* 1257 For-why I loved hir in no gere. *c* **1386** —— *Knt.'s T.* 673 Into a studie he fil sodenly, As doon thise louers in hir queynte geres. **1414** BRAMPTON *Penit. Ps.* lxi. (Percy Soc.) 23 Wysse me fro my wylde gerys. **1548** PATTEN *Exped. Scotl.* B viij a, Men may some time do y[t] hastely in a gere, whereof after they mai soon repent them. **1563** MAN *Musculus' Commonpl.* 284 b, The Anabaptistes also of our dayes, upon a mad gier, doe rebaptize them, which haue been allready baptised. **1579–80** NORTH *Plutarch* (1676) 140 This was not for a little while, nor in a geer of favour, that should continue for a time. **1609** HOLLAND *Amm. Marcell.* XXXI. xii. 421 The Emperour in a certain geare [*v.r.* gare] and violent heat..made hast to encounter them.

gere, obs. form of GAR *v.*, GEAR.

gereed, obs. form of JEREED.

gerefa (gɪ'riːfə, jɛ'reɪvə). *O.E. Antiq.* [a. OE. *ȝeréfa, ȝerǽfa*: see REEVE.] An administrative officer under the Old English kings.

1833 SOUTHEY *Lives Admirals* I. 66 Ethelwurd and Leofwin..were two of the king's high gerefas. **1863** H. COX *Instit.* II. iii. 384 *note*, In each township among the Saxons, there was a Gerefa, Tun-Gerefa, or Reeve. **1872** E. W. ROBERTSON *Hist. Ess.* 117 The King's Graphio or Gerefa.. exercised the royal prerogatives within..his shire.

†**geremumble**, *v. Obs. rare*[−1]. [Prob. onomatopœic; the initial sound seems to be (dʒ): cf. Sc. *jurmummle* 'to crush, disfigure; to bamboozle', given by Jam. with quots. from Hogg.] *trans.* ? To garbage (fish).

1599 NASHE *Lenten Stuffe* 55 With that speech hee.. deliuered him the king of fishes teaching hym how to geremumble it, sawce it, and dresse it.

gerent ('dʒɪərənt), *sb.* and *a. rare.* [ad. L. *gerent-em*, pres. pple. of *gerĕre* to manage.]

A. *sb.* One who holds an office; a manager, ruler. Also *attrib.*

1576 FLEMING *Panopl. Epist.* 80 *note*, He meaneth the Augurship wherein they were both Gerents at one Time. **1833** MRS. BROWNING *Prometh. Bound* Poems 1850 I. 182 Such a marriage-rite..Shall thrust him headlong from his gerent seat.

fig. **1882** STEVENSON *Fam. Stud.* 111 And so sympathy pairs with self-assertion, the two gerents of human life on earth.

B. *adj.* (See quot.)

1656 BLOUNT *Glossogr.*, *Gerent*, bearing or carrying. **1721** in BAILEY.

gerenuk ('gɛrɛnuːk). Also geranook, gerenook. [Somali name.] A long-necked gazelle-like antelope of East Africa, *Litocranius walleri*.

1895 H. G. C. SWAYNE *17 Trips through Somaliland* 312 The Gerenuk is the commonest and most widely distributed of the Somali Antelopes. **1895** [see DIK-DIK]. **1915** ROOSEVELT & HELLER *Life-hist. Afr. Game Animals* II. xviii. 610 The gerenuk was first described by Sir Victor Brooke [in 1878]. **1965** *New Scientist* 26 Aug. 505/1 Arid-country species like gerenuks never need to drink water. **1970** *Ibid.* 24 Sept. 639/2 A famous zoo breeding group of gerenuk or giraffe-necked antelope are now failing to be as productive.

†**gereri**, *a. Her. Obs.* Also 6 gerearrie. (See quots.; the two explanations in 1486 do not agree.)

1486 *Bk. St. Albans, Her.* B iij a, Gereri is called in armys whan cootarmuris ar ix quarteris dyuerse colowris. *Ibid.* B v b, Gereri is whan iij cheffrounce be to gedur or moo. **1586** [see GERARCHIE].

gerfalcon, var. of GYRFALCON.

†**gerfaunt.** *Obs.*[−1] [app. alteration of Arab. *zarāfah* GIRAFFE, assimilated to *elefaunt*.] A giraffe.

c **1400** MAUNDEV. (1839) xxviii. 289 In Arabye thei [orafles] ben clept Gerfauntz [*Roxb.* gyrfauntz]..he hath the necke a 20 Cubytes long.

†**'gerful**, *a. Obs.* [f. GERE + -FUL.] = GERISH.

c **1374** CHAUCER *Troylus* IV. 258 (286) (Harl. MS.) But euere more lo þis is thy manere To reue a wyght þat moost is to hym dere To preue in þat thi gerful [*Campsall MS.* greful, *MS. Gg.* 4. 27, gery] violence. *c* **1386** —— *Knt.'s T.* 680 (Ellesm. MS.) Right as hir day Is gereful [*Corpus MS.* geerful; *other MSS.* gerful] right so chaungeth she array.

gergeis, var. GREGEIS *Obs.*

gergon, obs. form of JARGON.

gerhardtite ('gɛəhɑːtaɪt). *Min.* [Named in 1885 by Wells and Penfield after Prof. C. F. *Gerhardt* of Strasburg: see -ITE.] Basic nitrate of copper occurring in small dark green crystals.

1885 *Amer. Jrnl. Sci.* Ser. III. XXX. 50 Gerhardtite and Artificial Basic Cupric Nitrates.

geriatric (dʒɛrɪ'ætrɪk), *a.* and *sb.* [f. as next.]

A. *adj.* **a.** Of or pertaining to geriatrics; designed for use by old people.

1926 *Med. Rec. of Revs.* XXXII. 193/1 We will publish a special geriatric number which will cover the field of diseases of old age. **1947** *Times* 20 June 5/4 Small, long-stay annexes, under the direct control of the 'geriatric' departments, for patients in need of constant nursing care. **1956** W. HOBSON *Mod. Trends in Geriatrics* xiv. 345 The organization of a geriatric unit requires..a flexible attitude of mind towards the rearrangement of the hospital. **1963** *Times* 16 Feb. 5/6 A new and deceptive form of restraint which has appeared in certain mental hospitals to fill the vacuum left by the strait-jacket—the geriatric chair.

b. In weakened use, esp. contemptuously: old or senile. *colloq.*

1968 *Time* 26 Jan. 78/2 This character was a geriatric loser with a Yiddish accent who invented the wheel but made it square. **1972** *Times* 24 Oct. 18/4 Invention only too easily becomes bizarre. Yet without vigorous encouragement the whole thing becomes..'geriatric'. **1977** *Western Mail* (Cardiff) 5 Mar. 8/4 The Welsh pack was led by the superb Bunner Travers, getting his ninth cap after an interval of 10 years! In one sense, the geriatric brigade was out again. **1978** *Insight* Nov. 8/1 For President Chiang Ching-kuo and his mainly geriatric advisers in the all-powerful Kuomintang 30 years of exile is but a temporary phase. **1981** *Times* 10 Feb. 9/3 Geriatric judges with 19th century social and political prejudices only bring the rule of law into disrepute. **1982** *Financial Times* 15 Feb. 6/8 What the work force consider a 'geriatric' 98 series engine. **1984** *Observer* 4 March 7/7 I hear and read such phrases as 'geriatric old twit': an expression which would hardly have sprung to the lips of the pious Aeneas.

B. *sb.* **a.** An old person receiving geriatric care; a patient in a geriatric ward or institution.

1974 *New Statesman* 25 Jan. 105/2 Ban all hospital treatment for miners, and send geriatrics and mental defectives back to their pit villages. **1980** *Guardian* 1 Oct. 2/5 Nurses and..patients..barricaded themselves inside a ward..in protest at the proposed mixing of geriatrics with surgical patients.

b. In weakened use: an old or senile person. Also *transf.*, anything old or outdated. *colloq.*

1977 P. Johnson *Enemies of Society* viii. 105 Old people are senior citizens, or, worse, geriatrics. **1978** *Economist* 4 Mar. 7/2 The greater pain has suddenly become the tendency for statesmen to flee from the old sensible ideas..to older, more foolish ones like..pre-Keynesianism or infant industry protection for dying geriatrics like British Shipbuilders. **1982** *Spectator* 18 Sept. 3/3 Hua Kuo-feng was replaced by Teng Hsiao-ping but a number of geriatrics remained. **1983** *Observer* 5 June 3/4 A sparse audience of geriatrics listened in polite mystification to Mr Powell's anti-nuclear thoughts. **1985** *Financial Times* 23 Nov. I. 8/8 The US stock market rally is already a geriatric at 39 months old.

geriatrics (dʒɛrɪˈætrɪks). [f. Gr. γῆρας old age + ἰατρικός (see iatric *a.*), after pædiatrics.] The branch of medicine, or of social science, dealing with the health of old people.

1909 I. L. Nascher in *N.Y. Med. Jrnl.* 21 Aug. 358/2 Geriatrics, from geras, old age, and iatrikos, relating to the physician, is a term I would suggest as an addition to our vocabulary, to cover the same field in old age that is covered by the term paediatrics in childhood. **1919** M. W. Thewlis (*title*) Geriatrics. A treatise on senile conditions, diseases of advanced life, and care of the aged. **1939** *Nature* 25 Nov. 902/2 Courses in geriatrics should be established in the medical schools to give future physicians a better understanding of the effects of mental attitudes on the bodily ailments of the aged. **1967** *New Scientist* 19 Jan. 160/2 There is in Britain only one university chair in geriatrics, and none in gerontology.

Hence **geria'trician**, an expert in geriatrics.

1934 in Webster. **1968** *Guardian* 9 May 7/2 Most progressive geriatricians now want to keep old people out of hospital beds at all costs.

†**gering.** *Obs.* [Cf. gerard.] ? A villain.

c **1290** *S. Eng. Leg.* I. 257/44 'ȝe,' þouȝte he, 'þis is mi wijf, and sum gering is i-comen hire to.

†**'gerish,** *a.* [f. gere + -ish.] Changeful, fitful; wild, wayward.

c **1430** Lydg. *Min. Poems* (Percy Soc.) 243 In gerysshe Marche toward the ariete. *Ibid.* 245 Now gerysshe glad, and anoon aftir wrothe. *Ibid.* 254 The sesoun of my yeerys greene..The gerisshe sesoun, straunge of condiciouns, Dispoosyd to many unbridlyd passiouns. **1430-40** —— *Bochas* vi. i. 53 And as a swalowe gerissh of hir flight Twene sloughth & swyft nowe croked nowe vpright. **1530** Palsgr. 312/2 Gerysshe wylde or lyght heeded, *farouche*. **1547** Boorde *Brev. Health* xliii. 13 b, *The Extravagante*, Madnesse that doth infest a man ones in a mone the whiche doth cause one to be geryshe, and waverynge witted, not constant, but fantasticall.

Hence †**'gerishness,** wildness, waywardness.

1494 Fabyan *Chron.* 4 Of Walys Gerysshnesse and of theyr lyght dotage. **1583** Golding *Calvin on Deut.* xiii. 75 As for this diuelish geerishnesse which the wicked haue to ouerthrowe Gods Children withall.

gerkin, gerland, obs. ff. gherkin, garland.

†**gerlaundesche.** *Obs. rare*[−1]. [a. OF. *garlande(s)che* garland.] A garland.

c **1230** *Hali Meid.* 23 A gerlaundesche schinende schenre þen þe sunne.

gerle, gerlond, obs. ff. girl, garland.

germ (dʒɜːm), *sb.* Also 7-9 **germe.** [a. F. *germe*:—L. *germen* sprout, of doubtful etymology; referred by some to the root **gen-* of *gignĕre* to beget, by others to the root *ges-* of *gerĕre* to bear.]

1. That portion of an organic being which is capable of development into the likeness of that from which it sprang; a rudiment of a new organism.

germ- is often used *attrib.* by mod. biologists for the female reproductive element, in opposition to *sperm-*; see 5 and 6.

a. in vegetables.

1644 Digby *Nat. Bodies* xxiv. 217 Can these germes choose but pierce the earth in small stringes, as they are able to make their way? **1777** Priestley *Matt. & Spir.* (1782) I. xvii. 201 Mr. Bonnet supposes..that all the germs of future plants..were really contained in the first germ. **1784** Cowper *Task* III. 521 Then rise the tender germes, upstarting quick And spreading wide their spongy lobes. **1802** Paley *Nat. Theol.* xx. 396 The germ grows up in the spring, upon a fruit stalk, accompanied with leaves. **1843** Lowell *Prometh.* 124 Good, once put in action or in thought, Like a strong oak, doth from its boughs shed down The ripe germs of a forest. **1873** Symonds *Grk. Poets* i. 1 What made the Jew a Jew, the Greek a Greek, is as unexplained as what daily causes the germs of an oak and of an ash to produce different trees.

b. in animals.

1650 [see gallature]. **1793** Holcroft *Lavater's Physiog.* xxiv. 120 We can easily conceive that defective juices may produce defective germs. **1816** Kirby & Sp. *Entomol.* (1828) I. 345 The germe of a future assassin of the larva that is to spring from that deposited by its side. **1841-71** T. R. Jones *Anim. Kingd.* (ed. 4) 72 Upon the outer aspect of the newly-formed germ a little spherical body may be detected. **1878** Huxley *Physiogr.* xv. 257 Coral-polypes..can also multiply by means of germs, which are thrown off from the parent as free-swimming bodies.

c. *gen.*

1798 Malthus *Popul.* i. i. (1806) I. 3 The germes of existence contained in the earth. **1836** Macgillivray tr. *Humboldt's Trav.* xvii. 222 The idea of those great inundations which for some time extinguished the germs of organic life upon the globe. **1858** Carpenter *Veg. Phys.* §6 Every organised structure..had its origin in another, which produced a germ capable of living and growing. **1862** Goulburn *Pers. Relig.* i. (1873) 10 Who could have believed that the germs of all the fair objects which we behold in nature were in that void and formless earth?

2. †**a.** In the Linnæan nomenclature: The ovary (*obs.*). **b.** The seed. *lit.* and *fig.*

a. 1759 B. Stillingfl. *Wks.* (1762) Introd. 30 An oblong thickish substance with six furrows along its sides. This contains the seed, and is called the germen or germ. **1794** Martyn *Rousseau's Bot.* i. 23 The swollen base, with three blunted angles, called the germ or ovary. **1829** Togno & Durand *Materia Medica* 93 Germ [of Crane's Bill Geranium] Egg-shaped.

b. 1823 Scott *Peveril* xx, The germs of her wilful and capricious passions might have been sown during her wandering and adventurous childhood. **1848** Lytton *Harold* x. iii, Does the new ground reject the germs of the sower?

3. In early use, vaguely, the 'seed' of a disease. In mod. use, a micro-organism or microbe; often, one of the microbes which are believed to cause disease.

1803 *Med. Jrnl.* IX. 484 The vaccine virus must act in one or other of these two ways: either it must destroy the germe of the small-pox..or it must neutralize this germe. [A passage translated from Fr.] **1871** Tyndall *Fragm. Sc.* (1879) II. xiii. 210 No germ from the kitchen air had ascended the narrow necks. **1897** Muir & Ritchie *Bacteriology* i. 2 Other general words, such as germ, microbe, micro-organism, are often used as synonymous with bacterium, though, strictly, they include the smallest organisms of the animal kingdom.

4. *fig.* That from which anything springs or may spring; an elementary principle; a rudiment. ***in germ***: in a rudimentary form.

1777 W. Dalrymple *Trav. Sp. & Port.* lxxi, Thereby to eradicate every germe of liberty. **1786** T. Jefferson *Writ.* (1859) I. 605 The only germ of dissension, which shows itself at present, is in the quarter of Turkey. **1810** Wellington in Gurw. *Desp.* (1838) V. 537 We ought to..encourage to remain here all the gentlemen of the country, as a germ of insurrection. **1816** Keatinge *Trav.* (1817) I. 222 An apathy..nips all efforts at action in their germ. **1846** Wright *Ess. Mid. Ages* II. xi. 38 Every country has possessed, in its own primeval literature, the first germ of romance. **1868** M. Pattison *Academ. Org.* v. 227 The idea exists in germ in the University itself. **1879** Farrar *St. Paul* (1883) 543 His keen eye marked the germs of coming danger.

5. *attrib.* and *Comb.*, as (sense 1 a) ***germ-case, -filament, -form, -forming, -life, -particle***; (sense 3) ***germ-breeder, -cloud, -nursery, -sac, -stage***; also ***germ-caused, -free, -like, -proof*** adjs.

1895 *Westm. Gaz.* 7 Aug. 2/1 There is no *germ-breeder like an outcast. **1859** Todd *Cycl. Anat.* V. 31/2 The more general appellations of *germ-cases or germ-sacs may be more appropriate. **1931** J. S. Huxley *What dare I Think?* i. 10 The numerous brood of *germ-caused diseases. **1884** *19th Cent.* Feb. 331 The disease-germs..rising in *germ-clouds and wafted by air-currents. **1889** Bennett & Murray *Cryptog. Bot.* 20 An inner endospore..which bursts through the exospore on germination, producing the *germ-filament. **1879** tr. *Haeckel's Evol. Man* I. 192 This highly important and interesting *germ-form is called the germ-cup, or the intestinal larva (Gastrula, Fig. 22). **1859** Todd *Cycl. Anat.* V. [124]/1 The separation of the *germ-forming and yolk-forming portions from each other. **1933** D. L. Sayers *Murder must Advertise* iv. 69 We spend our whole time asking intimate questions of perfect strangers...'Are you *Sure* that your Toilet-Paper is *Germ-free?' **1951** M. McLuhan *Mech. Bride* 61/1 When scrubbed, deloused, germ-free,..then she is lovely to love. **1969** *Times* 28 Jan. 6/7 The apparatus for the germ-free birth..is designed to make possible a cure for a deficiency disease of the body's immune defence system. **1875** E. White *Life in Christ* iii. xx. (1878) 288 Here we are thrown back upon some considerations on the phenomena of *germ-life in general. **1793** Holcroft *Lavater's Physiog.* xxiv. 122 To me it appears that something *germ-like..must previously exist in the mother. **1894** C. S. Ashley in *Pop. Sci. Monthly* XLIV. 458 Industrial society, like all other organisms, begins with a simple germ-like state. **1897** *Daily News* 1 June 3/2 The lack of any sort of attempt at efficient sanitation, must, I think, have made of the place a *germ nursery [etc.]. **1889** H. Campbell *Causation of Disease* 135 The slightest dislocation of the ultimate *germ and sperm-particles will modify the entire future development of the embryo. **1902** *Daily Chron.* 12 July 5/2 A *germ-proof house is the latest addition to the hygienic terrors of life. **1940** *Illustr. London News* 23 Mar. 376/1 (*caption*) Nurses in germproof clothing sealing the bottles. **1859** *Germ-sac [see *germ-case*]. **1885** *Syd. Soc. Lex.*, *Germ-sac*, the vesicular blastoderm of mammals. **1882** Bastian in *Quain's Med. Dict.* 533/1 The different kinds of contagia..may in essence be..cast-off micro-organisms of a low type, either in their 'finished' condition or in a *germ-stage.

6. Special comb.: **germ-area** (see quot.); **germ bomb**, a bomb containing germs, used in germ warfare; **germ-cell** (see quot.); also ***germ-cellule***; **germ-centre** [tr. G. *keimcentrum* (W. Flemming 1884, in *Arch. f. mikrosk. Anat.* Sept. 55)], a group of pale-staining cells forming the central area of a lymphatic nodule; **germ-cone**, a rudimentary volcanic cone; **germ-cup**, a gastrula; **germ-disk** = *germ-area*; **germ-force** (see quot.); **germ-gland**, one that produces germs; **germ-layer** = *germinal layer*; **germ-line** = *germ-track*; **germ-mass** (see quot.); **germ-membrane** = blastoderm; **germ-plasm**, the protoplasm peculiar to a germ or ovum (see quots.); *spec.* [tr. G. *keimplasma* (A. Weismann *Über die Vererbung* (1883) 15)] that part of the germ-cell which, according to Weismann's theory of heredity, bears the factors determining the transmission of characters from parent to offspring and is itself transmitted unchanged from generation to generation; = id[1], idioplasm; also ***germ-plasma***; **germ-polyp**, a polyp produced by gemmation; **germ-pore, -shield** (see quots.); **germ-spot** = *germinal spot*; **germ-stock** (see quot.); **germ-theory**, 'the theory of the origin of many diseases in the morbific influence of certain fungi, which are introduced into the organism by means of their germs or spores' (*Syd. Soc. Lex.* 1885); **germ-track** (see quot. 1949); **germ-tube**, the tube-like growth emitted from a spore in germination; **germ-vesicle** = *germinal vesicle*; **germ warfare**, the deliberate dissemination of disease-germs among an enemy as a weapon of war; = *bacteriological warfare*; **germ-yolk** (see quot.).

1879 tr. *Haeckel's Evol. Man* I. 292 The small, circular, dull whitish spot which lies at a particular point on the outer surface of the..'intestinal germ-vesicle'..is the 'intestinal germ-disc'..Sometimes..it was called the 'germ-disc'..more usually the *germ-area. **1934** *Archit. Rev.* LXXV. 98/2 But I visualize poison, explosive, incendiary and *germ bombs in an air-fleet attack. **1954** *Ann. Reg. 1953* 133 American airmen who, as prisoners, had confessed to using 'germ bombs' had retracted their confessions. **1855** Owen *Comp. Anat. Invertebr.* (ed. 2) 673 **Germ-cell*, the first nucleated cell that appears in the impregnated ovum, after the reception of the spermatozoon and the disappearance of the germinal vesicle. **1868** Carpenter *Microsc.* §251. 335 The Sexual distinction of the Generative cells into 'Sperm-cells' and 'Germ-cells'. **1846** Dana *Zooph.* v. §89 (1848) 92 This new *germ-cellule enlarges. **1898** E. A. Schäfer *Essentials Histology* (ed. 5) xxv. 152 Active multiplication of the lymph-cells by karyokinesis is..the cause of the formation of nodules in the tissue... On this account the nodules are sometimes termed **germ-centres*. **1906** *Practitioner* Nov. 708 The tonsils are composed of lymphoid tissue, which, besides being diffused throughout the whole organ, is collectd at various intervals into small nodules, in which the lymphocytes are closely packed... These nodules are sometimes spoken of as *germ-centres*. **1956** Yoffey & Courtice *Lymphatics, Lymph & Lymphoid Tissue* (ed. 2) v. 269 There is increased activity of the lymphoid tissues in response to bacterial injections, and..the main site of the reaction is the germ centre. **1849** Dana *Geol.* vii. (1850) 362 They illustrate the *germ-cone, proceeding from eruptions by overflowings, and through fissures. **1879** tr. *Haeckel's Evol. Man* I. 192 *Germ-cup [see *germ-form* in 5]. **1857** Dunglison *Med. Lex.*, **Germ-force*, plastic force. **1878** Bell *Gegenbaur's Comp. Anat.* 185 The excretory ducts of the paired *germ-glands are, in both sexes, united with the hind-gut. **1879** tr. *Haeckel's Evol. Man* I. 13 For example, the sexual organs of the human embryo..appear to originate from the middle *germ-layer. **1925** E. B. Wilson *Cell* (ed. 3) iv. 312 In some animals the germ-cells are set aside from the somatic cells at a very early stage in the ontogeny, so that we can actually trace their line of ontogenic descent or **germ-line* backwards to early stages of development. **1968** R. Rieger *Gloss. Genetics & Cytogenetics* 204 *Germ line*, a lineage of 'generative' cells..ancestral to the gametes..which, during the development of an organism (particularly in animals), are set aside as potential gamete-forming tissues. **1855** Owen *Comp. Anat. Invertebr.* (ed. 2) 673 **Germ-mass*, the material prepared for the formation of the embryo, consisting of the derivative germ-cells and the yolk which they have assimilated. **1879** tr. *Haeckel's Evol. Man* I. 197 The *germ-membrane, or blastoderm. **1889** Mivart in *Dublin Rev.* Oct. 282 It is only the *germ-plasm which has the power of reproducing an organism. **1889** S. Schönland tr. *Weismann's Continuity of Germ-Plasm* in *Ess. upon Heredity* 168, I propose to call it the theory of 'The Continuity of the Germ-plasm', for it is founded upon the idea that heredity is brought about by the transference from one generation to another, of a substance with a definite chemical, and above all, molecular constitution. I have called this substance 'germ-plasm'. **1890** G. Allen in *Academy* 1 Feb. 84/1 The germ-plasm is the essential part of the germ-cell, and determines the nature of the individual that arises from it. **1890** Billings *Med. Dict.* I. 577/2 *Germ plasma*, the substance from which the sexual products are developed. According to the theory of Weismann, a portion of the ovum is preserved, unaltered in constitution, to give rise to the sexual bodies, while the rest of the ovum is altered to produce the tissues of the body. **1893** Germ-plasm [see 1 d]. **1905** *Westm. Gaz.* 30 Mar. 2/1 The germ-plasm is the hereditary substance of the germ-cell, or the primary constituent substance of the whole organism. **1957** *Encycl. Brit.* XIII. 608/1 The continuity of the germ-plasm..suffices to account for the inheritance of the great majority of characters common to all individuals of a species without the need of postulating contributions from the body-cells. **1846** Dana *Zooph.* iv. §61 (1848) 63 *Germ-polyps differ essentially in their mode of increase. **1887** tr. *De Bary's Fungi* iii. 100 Many of these pores serve as places of exit for the tubular outgrowths from the spore at the time of germination, and may therefore be termed *germ-pores. **1879** tr. *Haeckel's Evol. Man* I. 297 The dull-coloured shield-shaped spot itself is the first rudiment of the dorsal portion of the embryo. We will call it briefly the '*germ-shield' (*notaspis*). **1861** J. R. Greene *Man. Anim. Kingd.*, *Cœlent.* 60 Some furnished with germ-vesicle and *germ-spot, others in a more advanced stage of development. **1885** *Syd. Soc. Lex.*, **Germ stock*, the term applied to the part of the body from which budding takes place in those animals in which a distinct special area is set apart for the purpose of generation by gemmation. **1871** Tyndall *Fragm. Sci.* (1879) I. v. 138 The *germ-theory of epidemic disease. **1893** Parker & Rönnfeldt tr. *Weismann's Germ-Plasm* vi. 184

The transmission of the germ-plasm from the ovum to the place of origin of the reproductive cells.. takes place in a regular manner, through perfectly definite series of cells which I call *germ-tracks. **1906** *Rep. Brit. Assoc. 1905* 434 In *Ascaris*.. there are two chromosomes in the fertilised egg, and in all the nuclei in the 'germ-track'. **1949** DARLINGTON & MATHER *Elem. Genetics* 394 *Germ track*, the lineage of cells in the development of an organism, particularly in animals, which are potential ancestors of germ cells, as opposed to somatic cells. **1890** BILLINGS *Nat. Med. Dict.*, **Germ-transmission*, inheritance from the Mother as opposed to Sperm-transmission. **1887** tr. *De Bary's Fungi* iii. 109 In nutrient solutions it [the spore] usually puts out *germ-tubes. *Ibid.* 110 This the first product of germination is accordingly known as the germ-tube. **1855** OWEN *Comp. Anat. Invertebr.* (ed. 2) 673 **Germ-vesicle* or Germinal vesicle. **1861** HULME tr. *Moquin-Tandon* II. I. 48 The Egg is essentially composed of the germ-vesicle or cicatricula, and of a protecting envelope. **1938** *Harper's Monthly* Mar. 367 Lurid descriptions of death rays, rocket planes, *germ warfare. **1940** BLUNDEN *Poems 1930–1940* 228 Revival of germ warfare. **1953** *Encounter* Oct. 15/2 The stories of germ warfare in Korea. **1963** *Ann. Reg. 1962* 395 Porton, a British Government Research establishment set up 20 years before to study germ warfare. **1855** OWEN *Comp. Anat. Invertebr.* (ed. 2) 673 **Germ-yolk*, that portion of the primary yolk of the egg which is assimilated by the germ-cells in the formation of the germ-mass. In some animals the whole yolk is so assimilated, in others (sepia *e.g.*) only a small portion, the remainder being the 'food-yolk', and absorbed by the future embryo or young animal.

germ (dʒɜːm), *v.* [in early use, ad. F. *germe-r*, f. *germe* GERM; the current word is f. GERM *sb.*]

1. *intr.* To put forth germs or buds; to bud, sprout. Now only *fig.*

1483 CAXTON *Gold. Leg.* 391 b/2 Whan the brannches been cutte of the knotte that remayneth.. It germeth and bryngeth forth newe buddes in al the places of the cuttyng. **1500–20** DUNBAR *Poems* lxxxvii. 3 Fresche flour of ȝouthe, new germyng to burgeoun. **1797** W. TAYLOR in *Monthly Rev.* XXIII. 572 Liberty may germ there, prolong its roots, and come to timber. **1863** MRS. C. CLARKE *Shaks. Char.* xiv. 346 He almost constantly allows a dormant passion to germ and sprout forth, and effloresce by slow degrees. **1885** *Longm. Mag.* VI. 539 Dreaming of some new project germing in his ever fertile brain.

2. *trans.* To cause to germinate. *rare*⁻¹.

1841 CATLIN *N. Amer. Ind.* (1844) I. iii. 18 The mud and soil in which they [trees] were germed and reared has been washed out from underneath them.

Hence **'germing** *vbl. sb.* (in quot. *attrib.*); **'germing** *ppl. a., fig.* that is 'in the bud', rudimentary, undeveloped.

1872 BLACKIE *Lays Highl.* 19 And the present fades from vision On the germing future bent. **1880** KINGLAKE *Crimea* VI. vi. 165 As yet unrelieved by any germing sense of security. **1883** *Contemp. Rev.* June 827 The aboriginal savage, with whose germing æsthetics we started these remarks. **1894** *Liberal* 1 Dec. 69/2 With no soft places in his soul for better and holier influence to find a germing ground.

germain(e, obs. form of GERMAN *a.*

german ('dʒɜːmən), **germane** (dʒə'meɪn, 'dʒɜːmeɪn), *a.*[1] and *sb.*[1] Forms: 4-5 **germeyn(e**, 4-6 **germayn(e**, 4-7 **germain(e**, (6 **jarman**, 7 **jermaine**), 4- **german**, 5- **germane**. [a. OF. *germain* (= senses 1-2 below), ad. L. *germān-us* (sense 1, also 'genuine, real'), whence Pr. *german*, *girman*, and the sbs. Sp. *hermano*, Pg. *irmão*, Catal. *germá*, brother.] **A.** *adj.*

I. Closely akin.

1. Having the same parents; 'own' (brother or sister). *Obs.* exc. in BROTHER-GERMAN (q.v. for some variations of sense), SISTER-GERMAN.

1340 [see BROTHER-GERMAN]. **1382** WYCLIF *1 Kings* xi. 19 He ȝaf to hym a wijf, the sister germayn of his wiif Taphnes, the queen. *c* **1460** *Towneley Myst.* v. 29 Iacob, that is thyne awne germane brother. **1530** [see BROTHER-GERMAN]. **1626** SANDYS *Ovid's Met.* VI. 117 For him the Nymphs, and german Satyres [L. *Satyri fratres*] weepe. **1663** BLAIR *Autobiog.* ii. (1848) 21 A Christian friend, was my german brother.. finding me in this case. **1751, 1882** [see BROTHER-GERMAN].

2. That is the child of a 'german' brother or sister of either of (one's) parents; = 'first' or 'own' (cousin). *Obs.* exc. in COUSIN-GERMAN.

13.. *Guy Warw.* (A.) 912 He is mi germain cosyn. *c* **1380**, *c* **1450** [see COUSIN-GERMAN]. **1502** *Ord. Crysten Men* (W. de W. 1506) IV. xiii. 204 Of the whiche degrees, the broder and syster make the fyrst, the chyldren the whiche ben germayne make the seconde. **1555**, etc. [see COUSIN-GERMAN].

fig. *a* **1555** RIDLEY *Treat, agst. Transubst.* (1556) 51 This kind of oblation standeth vppon transubstantyacion his germayne coosyn. **1615** CROOKE *Body of Man* 158 Hippocrates sayth that milke is German Cousen to the menstruous blood.

†**3.** Closely related; akin. *Obs.*

1470–85 MALORY *Arthur* II. xi, Basdemegus was his cosyn and germayn vnto kynge Uryence. **1607** SHAKS. *Timon* IV. iii. 344 Wert thou a Leopard, thou wert Germane to the Lion. **1611** —— *Wint. T.* IV. iv. 802 Those that are Iermaine to him.. shall all come vnder the Hang-man.

fig. **1657** W. MORICE *Cœna quasi Κοινή* Def. §23. 232 For their dear brethren, and such as are germane to them in principles, are most engaged in that guilt [etc.].

4. Closely connected; appropriate; relevant; pertinent. Const. *to*.

This sense arises from allusion to the Shaks. passage (quot. 1602), which is merely a fig. example of sense 3. The mod. form varies between *'german, ger'mane*, and *'germane*; the spelling *germain* has been used by some writers.

1602 SHAKS. *Ham.* v. ii. 165 The phrase would bee more Germaine [*so* **1623** (Fo. 1); **1603** (Qº1) *has* more cosin german; **1604** (Qº2) more Ierman; *mod. edd.* more german] to the matter: If we could carry Cannon by our sides. **1816** SCOTT *Antiq.* xxviii, Edie.. did not venture to repeat a query which was so little germain to the matter. **1840** MRS. TROLLOPE *Widow Married* xxxiv, A piece of intelligence more well-timed, or more completely germane to the subject of her thoughts. **1863** J. G. HOLLAND *Lett. to Joneses* vii. 102 Men who have.. resisted all evidences germane to the subject. **1865–6** H. PHILLIPS *Amer. Paper Curr.* II. 96 The document.. is not sufficiently germane to be reproduced in this place. **1870** HUXLEY *Lay Serm.* iv. (1874) 57 Those studies which are immediately germain to physic. **1877** SPARROW *Serm.* xxi. 274 An argument.. not pertinent or germain to the subject. **1886** *Illustr. Lond. News* Summer No. 24/3 The illustration was hardly germane to the case.

II. 5. Genuine; true; thorough. *Obs.* or *arch.*

1382 WYCLIF *Phil.* iv. 3, I preie thee, german felowe, helpe thou the ilke wymmen that traueliden with me in the gospel. **1542** BECON *Potat. for Lent* Pref., Sincere, germane and true learning. **1642** NETHERSOLE *Consid. upon Affairs* 3 The miserable Distractions of this divided Kingdom, threatning a Germane desolation thereof. **1678** CUDWORTH *Intell. Syst.* I. iv. §36. 575 Arius was a German or Genuine Disciple of Plato's. **1864** J. H. NEWMAN *Apol.* 7 That to be a pure, german, genuine Catholic, a man must be either knave or fool.

†**B.** *sb.* One sprung from the same stock; a brother, a near relative. *Obs.*

1491 CAXTON *Vitas Patr.* (W. de W. 1495) I. xxiii. 23 b/2 The whyche were not oonly bredren carnalle, but also in lyf, in religyon & in vertues they were germayns. **1590** SPENSER *F.Q.* I. v. 13 Goe now, proud Miscreant, Thyselfe thy message do to german deare. **1604** SHAKS. *Oth.* I. i. 114 You'le haue Coursers for Cozens: and Gennets for Germaines. **1721** BAILEY, *Germain*, a Brother or Sister by the same Father and Mother.

Hence **ger'manely** *adv.*, in a germane manner; pertinently.

1844 *Blackw. Mag.* LVI. 84 An embassy from the willow-wearers all—or to speak more germanely to the matter, of the Basket-bearers.

German ('dʒɜːmən), *a.*[2] and *sb.*[2] Also 6 **germayne**, 6-7 **germaine**, **germane**. [ad. L. *Germān-us*, used, as adj. and sb., as the designation of persons belonging to a group of related peoples inhabiting central and northern Europe, and speaking the dialects from which the 'Germanic' or 'Teutonic' languages have been developed.

The name does not appear to have been applied to these peoples by themselves, or to be explicable from Teut. sources. A view widely held is that it was the name given by the Gauls to their neighbours; the Celtic derivations suggested are from OIr. *gair* neighbour (Zeuss) and from Irish *gairm* battle-cry (Wachter, Grimm). According to Müllenhoff, *Germani* was originally the name of a group of Celtic peoples in north-eastern Gaul, was transferred from these to their Teutonic conquerors, and afterwards extended to all the Teutonic peoples.]

The pronunciation ('dʒɑːmən), for which cf. *clerk*, *sergeant*, *Hertford*, was formerly fashionable, but now survives only as *dial.* or *vulgar*.

In English use the word does not occur until the 16th c., the sb. appearing in our quots. earlier than the adj. The older designations were ALMAIN and DUTCH (DUTCHMAN); the latter, however, was wider in meaning.

A. *adj.*

1. Of or pertaining to Germany or its inhabitants.

The precise signification depends on the varying extension given to the name *Germany*.

German Ocean: transl. of Ptolemy's Γερμανικὸς Ὠκεανός, the sea to the east of Great Britain, the North Sea; also *German Sea*.

1552 HULOET, German or of germanye, *Germanus.* **1581** MULCASTER *Positions* xxxviii. (1887) 168 The Germaine or French gentlewymen. **1598** SHAKS. *Merry W.* IV. v. 70 They ..set spurres, and away; like three Germane-diuels, three Doctor Faustasses. **1618** *Owle's Alman.* 7 The German Fencer cudgell'd most of our English Fencers now about a moneth past. **1635** J. VAN LANGEREN *Direction for Eng. Traveller*, 'Northfolke' Germain-sea-N[orth]. *a* **1661** FULLER *Worthies* (1662) I. 317 Essex hath.. the German Ocean on the East. *Ibid.* II. 307 This had.. the German-Sea at the same distance. **1658** SIR T. BROWNE *Hydriot.* ii. 26 That burning the dead was.. the old Germane practise is also asserted by Tacitus. **1685** COOKE *Marrow Chirurgery* (ed. 4) I. §1. i. 2 [Some instruments are] of Horn, as Cups used at German Baths. **1705** BOSMAN *Guinea* 190 They are as Impertinent and Noisie as the.. German Jews at their Synagogue at Amsterdam. **1786** BURNS *Twa Dogs* 165 Then bouses drumly German water, To mak himsel look fair and fatter. **1814** [see OCEAN *sb.* 2]. **1816** KEATINGE *Trav.* (1817) II. 143 Fitted up with German stoves, the only powers of heat sufficient for.. this climate. **1845** S. AUSTIN *Ranke's Hist. Ref.* I. 11 It would be impossible to speak of a German nation, in the proper sense of the word, during the preceding ages. **1879** ESCOTT *England* I. 53 We at last reach the point where it discharges itself into the German Ocean. **1882** FREEMAN in *Longm. Mag.* I. 94 'German', which people used to sound 'Jarman'—as in the memorable story of the Oxford University preacher who wished the 'Jarman theology' at the bottom of the 'Jarman Ocean'.

b. with limiting word as in B. 1 b; the combination indicating the dialect or language spoken by the persons in question.

1726 AMHERST *Terræ Fil.* viii. 39 His fingers.. will not suffer him to keep any money between them, as he once told an High-German artist. **1887** SKEAT *Princ. Eng. Etym.* Ser. I. ii. §9 Taking English to represent the native speech of the Low-German conquerors of England.

2. *transf.* **a.** Marked by the characteristics of a German; German-like. **b.** Friendly to the Germans, biased in favour of German interests.

1861 M. PATTISON *Ess.* (1889) I. 47 Peace and order were maintained by police regulations of German minuteness and strictness. **1864** LD. MALMESBURY *Mem.* II. 318 As Lord Bath was there and is very German, of course Lord Derby did not feel himself on safe ground.

3. As the designation of a language (see B. 2). Hence of words, etc.: Belonging to the German language. Of literary compositions, etc.: Written or spoken in the German language.

Partly an attrib. use of the sb.: as in *German grammar*, *German master* (= one who teaches the language), etc.

1748 CHESTERF. *Let.* 1 July (1892) I. 124, I desire that you will not fail to write a German letter, in the German character, once every fortnight, to Mr. Grevenkop. —— *Let.* 5 Sept. I. 139 You will also desire your German master to teach you [etc.]. **1755** JOHNSON *Dict.* Pref., Of words undoubtedly Teutonick the original is not always to be found in any ancient language, and I have therefore inserted Dutch or German substitutes. **1817** COLERIDGE *Biogr. Lit.*, *Satyrane's Lett.* (Bohn) 266, I inquired.. concerning the history of German poetry and the older German poets. **1817** SIR J. SINCLAIR *Corr.* (1831) II. 324, I received several communications from him, chiefly written in the German language. **1888** H. A. STRONG tr. *Paul's Princ. Hist. Lang.* iv. 85 The correspondence of the function fixes the name in the German word *feder* for 'steel pen'. *Ibid.* xii. 260 This is the origin of the German possessive pronoun *ihr*.

b. with limiting words as in B. 2 b.

1872 MORRIS *Hist. Outl. Eng. Accid.* i. 5 The Low German dialects of the Continent are yielding to its [High German] influence. **1891** TRECHMANN *Hist. Gram. Germ. Lang.* I. v. 34 A person who understands *Hochdeutsch* is.. less able to understand the Low German than the Middle and South German dialects.

4. In names of things of actual or attributed German origin (sometimes written with a hyphen), as **German band**, an instrumental band of street musicians, properly of German extraction; **German bezoar** (see BEZOAR 2); **German bit, chest** (see quots.); **German Catholic**: see CATHOLIC *sb.* 3 b; **German clock**, in 16–17th c. chiefly one of elaborate construction, often containing automatic figures of persons or animals; **German collie** (see quot. 1933); **German congreve**, a kind of lucifer match; †**German devil** [cf. quot. 1598 in 1], ? a sort of screw-jack or similar contrivance; **German duck** (see quot.); **German flute** (see FLUTE *sb.*[1] 1); **German gamba, gold, hone** (see quots.); †**German Lombard**, a kind of paper; **German mile**, a distance of between 4 and 5 English miles; **German paste, process, sarsaparilla** (see quots.); **German sausage**, a large sort of sausage, the stuffing of which is meat spiced and partly cooked; usually sold in portions by weight; **German sheep-dog, shepherd (dog)**, a strong breed of dog, originally from northern Europe, frequently used as a guard-dog and for police work; = ALSATIAN *a.* and *sb.* B. 2; **German sheet**, a kind of sheet-glass; **German sixth** *Mus.*, a chord consisting of a note with its major third, fifth, and augmented sixth; **German steel, stitch** (see quots.); **German text**, a black letter resembling old English or modern German; also *attrib.*; **German tinder** = AMADOU; **German watch** (cf. *G. clock*); **German wool** = *Berlin wool* (see BERLIN 4). Also GERMAN SILVER.

[**1830** LADY WILLIAMS WYNN *Let.* 27 July (1920) 377 The *German Band is all disbanded.. & throughout His Household he has dismissed every Foreigner.] **1851** J. D. LEWIS *Across Atlantic* 100 Immediately after dinner, an excellent German band, of a dozen performers, plays for a couple of hours. **1898** H. G. HUTCHINSON *Golfing Pilgr.* 25 The German bands of our Margates and our Ramsgates. **1906** B. KENNEDY *Wander Pict.* 190 At first I thought it was a Salvation Army band, but it turned out to be an awful German band that was making the town hideous. **1875** KNIGHT *Dict. Mech.*, **German-bit*, a wood-boring tool adapted to be used in a brace. *Ibid.*, **German-chest* (*Metallurgy*), a long box into which the slimes are carried gradually by a stream of water. The heavier portions settle near the head of the box, and the lighter towards the lower end. **1588** SHAKS. *L.L.L.* III. i. 192 A woman that is like a *Germane Cloake [*i.e.* clock], Still a repairing; euer out of frame. **1609** B. JONSON *Sil. Wom.* IV. ii, Shee takes her selfe asunder still when shee goes to bed.. and about next day noone is put together againe, like a great Germane Clocke. *a* **1643** W. CARTWRIGHT *Ordinary* I. v. (1651) B iij, Let us try To win that old Eremit thing, that, like An Image in a German clock, doth move, Not walke. **1933** L. G. D. ACLAND in *Press* (Christchurch, N.Z.) 21 Oct. 15/7 **German collie*, a variety of sheepdog which is blue (black and white spots). He usually has one or both wall eyes. **1934** J. LILICO *Sheep Dog Mem.* 3 She was what is known in New Zealand as a German collie but on the Borders they were called 'Bilton Blues'. **1851** MAYHEW *Lond. Labour* I. 432 The *German congreves' were soon after introduced. **1670** EVELYN *Sylva* (1679) 23 That small Engine, which by some is call'd the *German-devil, reform'd, after this manner, and duely applied, might be very expedient for this purpose [the extirpation of Roots]. **1796** *Grose's Dict. Vulg. Tongue* (ed. 3), **German Duck*, half a sheep's head boiled with onions. **1754** CHESTERF. in *World* No. 101 (end), Upon the same shelf with their *German flute, their powder-mask and their four-horse-whip. **1880** C. A. EDWARDS *Organs* (1881) 157 *Viol-di-Gamba.* This stop is not to be confounded with the German Gamba... The *German Gamba, or Gamba proper, is a stop of louder intonation and somewhat larger scale. **1889** *Century Dict.*, **German gold*, an inferior gold powder prepared from gold leaf. **1893** *Funk's Stand. Dict.* s.v. *Hone*, **German hone*, a soft, smooth, yellow slate especially adapted for razor-setting. **1712** *Act 10 Anne* in

Lond. Gaz. No. 5018/3 For all Paper called..*German Lombard 1s. per Ream. **1559** W. Cunningham *Cosmogr. Glasse* 56 A comon *Germaine mile Conteyninge in it 32 Furlonges. **1594** Blundevil *Exerc.* ii. (ed. 7) 110 Foure Italian miles do make but one Germane mile. **1838** *Murray's Hand-bk. N. Germ.* 465/1, 3½ German miles = 17 English miles. **1858** Simmonds *Dict. Trade*, *German-paste, a food sold for..cage birds..made of pea-meal, hemp-seed, maw-seed, lard, and honey or treacle. **1881** Raymond *Mining Gloss.*, *German process, in copper smelting, the process of reduction in a shaft-furnace, after roasting, if necessary. **1882** Ogilvie, *German-sarsaparilla, a name given to the roots or rhizomes of *Carex arenaria, C. disticha*, and *C. hirta*, from their being occasionally used in Germany as a substitute for sarsaparilla. [**1837** Dickens *Pickw.* xxxi. 334 The ham (which was also from the *German sausage-shop round the corner).] **1839** C. Sinclair *Holiday House* xv. 334 Perigord pies, German sausages, cold fowls, pastry, and fruit. **1850** German sausage [see sausage 1]. **1858** Simmonds *Dict. Trade, German-sausage*, a polony, a bladder or cleaned gut stuffed with meat partly cooked. **1823** P. Nicholson *Pract. Build.* 421 *German Sheet is another species of glass much esteemed. **1922, 1926** *German sheepdog, Shepherd Dog [see Alsatian *a.* and *sb.* B. 2]. **1959** H. Neilsen *Fifth Caller* i. 17 A man..decided to take his German shepherd for a walk. **1825** Danneley *Encycl. Mus.*, *German sixth. **1875** Ouseley *Harmony* xi. 127 We produce a discord, which has been called..the 'German sixth'. **1799** *Nicholson's Jrnl. Nat. Philos.* II. 65 The steel obtained immediately from the ore by simple fusion, is called natural steel. It is likewise distinguished by the name of *German steel, because it comes principally from Germany. **1875** Knight *Dict. Mech., German-steel*, a metal made of charcoal-iron obtained from bog-iron or the sparry carbonate. **1882** Caulfeild & Saward *Dict. Needlework* 30/1 *German stitch, this is a stitch formed from a tapestry and a tent stitch being worked alternately in a diagonal line across the canvas. **1861** M. Pattison *Ess.* (1889) I. 45 Over each [gateway] was an inscription in the *German text. **1763** W. Massey *Origin Letters* ii. 28 A neat and correct alphabet of the german text capitals. **1851** Mayhew *Lond. Labour* I. 433 At one time, indeed, they were announced as '*German tinder'. **1866** *Treas. Bot., German tinder*, the Soft Amadou, *Polyporus fomentarius*. **1611** Middleton & Dekker *Roaring Girl* H j b, Here take my Germane watch, hang't vp in sight, That I may see her hang in English for't. **1847** A. Brontë *Agnes Grey* vii. 103 The elder girl..was trifling over a piece of canvas and a basket of *German wools. **1858** Geo. Eliot *Scenes Clerical Life* II. 88 Beaded urn-rugs and chair-covers in German wool.

b. In the names of various plants, as **German camomile, German iris, German ivy** (see ivy *sb.* 2), **German knotgrass, German larch, German lilac, German madwort, German millet, German rice, German tamarisk** (see quots.); **German wallflower** (see wallflower).

1884 *Cassell's Encycl. Dict.*, *German camomile, the flower-heads of *Matricaria chamomilla*. **1882** *Garden* 6 May 317/2 The earliest purple *German Iris. **1879** Britten & Holland *Plant-n.*, *German Knotgrass, *Scleranthus annuus*. **1838** H. Colman *1st Rep. Agric. Mass.* 116 The Larch referred to in the text and there called the German Larch, is the common or White Larch. **1877** *N.W. Linc. Gloss.*, *German Lilac, valerian. **1818** Withering *Brit. Plants* II. 316 *Asperugo procumbens*..Trailing Catchweed, *German Madwort. **1861** Miss Pratt *Flower. Pl.* IV. 59 (*German Madwort*)..This little prostrate annual plant..is found more or less all over Europe. **1832** *Veg. Subst. Food* 115 *German Millet, *Sitaria germanica*..This variety was ..imported from India, and acclimatized in Germany. **1839** *Penny Cycl.* III. 463/2 *Hordeum Zeocriton*; also called *German rice, or rice barley. **1882** *Garden* 22 July 73/3 The *German Tamarisk..a slender upright-growing shrub.

c. ***German measles***: A contagious disease, resembling measles in a mild form.

1875 tr. *Ziemssen's Cycl. Med.* II. 129. **1890** *Syd. Soc. Lex.*, s.v. *Roseola, epidemic*, German measles, *Rubella*... Symptoms, mild headache and chills, muscular pains; there may be some coryza. The rash appears usually on the first day on the face, chest, and afterwards over the body. **1894** *Lancet* 3 Nov. 1046 The council of the Medical Officers of Schools' Association have issued a circular to the members of the association, asking for their opinions upon the characteristics of measles and German measles.

Hence **'Germanly** *adv.*, in a German manner.

1799 Southey in C.C. Southey *Life* II. 19 As fine a Germanly compounded word as you may expect to see. **1854** G. Eliot in *Life* (1885) I. 350 He is a man of real culture, kindliness, and polish (Germanly speaking).

B. *sb.*

1. A native of Germany.

1530 Tindale *Practyse of Prelates* F vj a, When the empyre was translated vnto the Germaynes..there was moch stryfe. **1545** Brinklow *Compl.* 37 O noble Germanys, God hath made yow a lyght vnto all rulers in the world. **1691** Hartcliffe *Virtues* 121 Neither among the old Germans did any one bear Arms until he was honored with a Spear and Target in their State-Assemblys. **1781** Gibbon *Decl. & F.* III. 245 The Germans were less corrupt than the Italians. **1855** Motley *Dutch Rep.* Introd. ii. (1866) 5 The truculent German..considered carnage the only useful occupation.

b. With limiting word. ***High German***: one who speaks the High German language.

1611 Middleton & Dekker *Roaring Girl* E iv b, A name which Ide teare out From the hye Germaines throat.

c. One who is versed in the German language; a German scholar.

1809 Southey *Lett.* (1856) II. 183, I, who am no German, have heard enough read, and seen enough translated by his [Klopstock's] admirers, to be convinced that he is full of buckram and bombast.

2. The German language.

When used without defining word or contextual indication, the word is understood to denote High German (until the 18th c. called High Dutch).

1748 Chesterf. *Let.* 13 Feb. (1892) I. 84, I am very willing that you should take a Saxon servant, who speaks nothing but German; which will be a sure way of keeping up your German, after you leave Germany. **1798** Coleridge *Satyrane's Lett.* ii. in *Biog. Lit.* (1882) 249 See how natural the German comes from me, though I have not yet been six weeks in the country! **1841** Elphinstone *Hist. Ind.* I. 325 The two idioms are more nearly allied than English and German. **1886** Ruskin *Præterita* I. 314 At that time it was thought very fine and poetical to study German.

b. With limiting words. ***High German***: the variety of Teutonic speech, originally confined to 'High' or southern Germany, but now accepted as the literary language throughout the whole of Germany; its chief characteristic is that certain consonants have been altered by what is called the 'second sound-shifting' from their original Teut. sounds, which the other dialects in the main preserve. ***Low German***: properly = 'Plattdeutsch', the general name for the dialects of Germany which are not High German; but also applied by philologists to all the West Germanic dialects except High German (including, e.g. English, Dutch, Frisian); and formerly in a still wider sense including also Gothic and Scandinavian.

1838 *Penny Cycl.* XI. 192 The German or Teutonic language may be divided into two great branches..the High German, or the language of Southern Germany; and the Low German, or Saxon. **1872** Morris *Hist. Outl. Eng. Accid.* i. 5 Luther..made the High German the literary language of all German-speaking people. **1887** Skeat *Princ. Eng. Etym.* Ser. i. vi. §55 The West Teutonic branch includes..Saxon or Low German. **1897** *Nation* (N.Y.) 9 Dec., Of versions earlier than Chaucer's two into High German and French are of the greatest linguistic importance.

3. In various senses resulting from elliptical uses of the adj.

a. Short for *German cotillon* (see cotillion *sb.* 1); also, a dancing party where this is the chief dance.

[**1860** Motley *Netherl.* (1868) I. ii. 36 If I am ever caught dancing the German cotillon.] **1863** A. D. Whitney *Faith Gartney* x, Who danced with who at the ' German' last night. *Ibid.* xiii, It was very agreeable..to dance the German with the nicest partner in the Monday class. **1879** *Scribner's Mag.* XIX. 683/1 It is a dance they call the German. **1881** Howells *Fearful Respons.* (1882) 153 In the German..there was a figure fantastically called the symphony. **1886** *Ogontz Mosaic* Jan. 7/1 Tuesday evening a German was given in the amusement room by Prof. Asher's dancing class.

b. *pl.* Articles (defined by context) imported from Germany.

1891 *Daily News* 20 Oct. 2/7 Eggs..There has been a rise of 6d. on second Italians..and 1s. on Germans.

c. = *German sausage*.

1865 Dickens *Mut. Fr.* I. ii. viii. 240 Circumstances.. interpose obstacles between yourself and small germans. **1883** Greenwood *Odd People* 220 The sausage-eater may.. continue to munch his 'german' with a relish.

d. *Coal-mining*. (See quot.)

1883 Gresley *Gloss. Coal Mining, German*, a straw filled with gunpowder to act as a fuze in blasting operations.

C. *Comb.* as ***German-built, -made, -occupied, -owned, -speaking*** adjs.; also **German-Italian** *a.*, **German-Jewish** *a.*, **German-Swiss** *a.* and *sb.*; **German-American**, an American of German ancestry; also *attrib.* or as *adj.*

1824 I. Candler *Summary View Amer.* 333 Natives of Germany all told the *German Americans of their bad language. **1880** *Harper's Mag.* Sept. 567 A German-American School..is kept over a disreputable little grog-shop. **1919** *Mr. Punch's Hist. Great War* 134 Perhaps he over-estimated the strength of the German-American and Pacifist elements. **1941** Wyndham Lewis *Let.* Jan. (1963) 284 You, as a German-American, can feel little sympathy for poor old England. **1897** *Daily News* 7 Dec. 5/3 This *German-built, German-owned steamer has easily eclipsed all previous performances. **1936** H. Nicolson *Diary* 4 July (1966) 268 The French foresee and dread a *German-Italian alliance. **1876** G. Eliot in *Life* (1885) III. 290 Part of the scene at the club is translated into Hebrew in a *German-Jewish newspaper. **1851** Mayhew *Lond. Labour* I. 361 The tools..are sometimes displayed on a small barrow, sometimes on a stall, and are mostly *German-made. **1896** *Westm. Gaz.* 25 Sept. 3/1 German manufacturers, who ..'improve the occasion to offer other German-made wares'. **1940** W. S. Churchill *Into Battle* (1941) 169 In German-occupied Poland the most hideous form of terrorism prevails. **1964** M. Gowing *Britain & Atomic Energy* vi. 180 Outside German-occupied Europe, the main source of supply open to Germany was Portugal. **1872** *German-speaking [see B. 2 b]. **1919** C. Mackenzie *Sylvia & Michael* i. 31 She asked if the other two women spoke English, and Miss Savage told her that one was a *German-Swiss. **1934** E. Waugh *Ninety-two Days* v. 119 The monk was a German-Swiss. **1955** J. Thomas *No Banners* xx. 190 Two elderly German-Swiss gentlemen.

germander (dʒə'mændə(r)). Forms: (5 **germawnder**, 5, 7 **germandir**, 6 **germandre**, **germaunder**, **jarmander**, 7 **jermander**), 6– **germander**. [ad. med.L. *germandra, -drea* (F. *germandrée*), altered form of *gamandrea, -ia* (whence Ger., Du. *gamander*), corruptly ad. late Gr. χαμανδρυά, which is itself a corruption of Gr. χαμαίδρυς, lit. 'ground oak', f. χαμαί on the ground + δρῦς oak.

Another corrupt form based on the late Gr. word is It. *calamandrea*. The correct Gr. form was adopted in med.L. as *chamædrys*, whence It. *camedrio*, Sp. *camedréo*.]

The name of the plants of the genus *Teucrium*, esp. *T. Chamædrys*, the Common or Wall Germander. **garlic** or **water germander** = *T. Scordium*. **wood germander** = *T. Scorodonia*. In the U.S. applied to *T. Canadense* (Cent. Dict.). Also applied to certain species of *Veronica*, now chiefly in the compound names **germander chickweed** (*Veronica agrestis*); **germander speedwell** or **wild germander** (*Veronica Chamædrys*).

In early quots. it is often uncertain what plant is meant. The attrib. use in Tennyson refers to the beautiful blue colour of the flowers of *Veronica Chamædrys*.

c **1440** *Promp. Parv.* 190/2 Germawnder, herbe, *germandra*. **1548** Turner *Names of Herbes* (1881) 26 Chamedrys called..in englishe Germander or englishe Triacle. **1578** Lyte *Dodoens* i. lxxv. 111 Of Scordium or water Germander. *Ibid.* i. lxxvi. 112 Of Teucrion or wilde Germander. **1587** Harrison *England* ii. xx. (1877) i. 326 Our common germander or thistle benet is..of..great power in medicine. **1597** Gerarde *Herbal* ii. cciii. 534 Tree Germander is called in..Latine Teucrium: in English great Germander, vpright Germander, and Tree Germander. **1607** Topsell *Four-f. Beasts* (1658) 269 Take of Jermander four ounces, of Gumdragant, and of dryed Roses. **1688** R. Holme *Armoury* ii. 109/1 Tree Germander hath the Flowers..white, in a round pointed husk. **1741** *Compl. Fam.-Piece* ii. iii. 380 There are several other Trees and Shrubs which are now in Flower, as..Tree Germander, Lupine. **1789** Pilkington *Derbysh.* (1803) I. 325 *Veronica chamædris*, Wild germander. **1811** A. T. Thomson *Lond. Disp.* (1818) 398 Wall germander has been accounted tonic, stomachic [etc.]. **1860** Gosse *Rom. Nat. Hist.* 6 The germander speedwell, with its laughing blue eyes, spangling every hedge-bank. **1865** —— *Land & Sea* (1874) 15 The wood germander, or bitter sage, whose wrinkled leaves were used during the scarcity of the last war as a substitute for tea.

attrib. **1712** tr. *Pomet's Hist. Drugs* I. 82 Divided into five Leaves, as the Germander Flower. **1864** Tennyson *Sea Dreams* 4 They, thinking that her clear germander eye Droopt in the giant-factoried city-gloom, Came, with a month's leave given them, to the sea.

germane: see german *a.*[1]

germanesque (ˌdʒɜːmə'nɛsk), *a.* [f. German + -esque.] Marked by German characteristics.

1825 *New Monthly Mag.* XV. 28 The fair writer..has even rendered her tragedy more Germanesque than that wild and singular production.

Germanhood ('dʒɜːmənhʊd). [f. German + -hood.] The quality of being German.

1827 Carlyle *German Romance* Pref., They are German Novelists, not English ones; and their Germanhood I have all along regarded as a quality, not as a fault.

Germanic (dʒə'mænɪk), *a.*[1] and *sb.* [ad. L. *Germānic-us*, f. *Germānus* German *a.*[2] Cf. F. *germanique*.] **A.** *adj.*

1. a. Of or pertaining to Germany or to the Germans, German. Now chiefly *Hist.* in ***Germanic Confederation, Germanic Empire***.

1633 in *Crt. & Times Chas. I* (1848) II. 214 Setting up the Germanic liberty, and levelling of the House of Austria. **1652** Benlowes *Theoph.* v. xlix, Fifty milions of Germanick leagues. **1756–7** tr. *Keysler's Trav.* (1760) IV. 217 The association of the Germanic states would not be a sufficient security to the empire against a foreign enemy. **1777** Watson *Philip II* (1839) 13 He laboured..to establish concord among the several princes of the Germanic body. **1845** S. Austin *Ranke's Hist. Ref.* III. 251 Least of all could the German nation boast that the Germanic empire had recovered its ancient character and powers.

b. Marked by German characteristics. ***Germanic region*** (see quot.).

1851–6 Woodward *Mollusca* 383 Germanic Region. The whole of Northern Europe and Asia, bounded by the Pyrenees, Alps, Carpathians, Caucasus, and Altai.

2. Of or pertaining to the Teutonic race, or any of the Teutonic peoples. With reference to language, often used by philologists as = 'Primitive Germanic'. Also with limiting word, in the designations of the subordinate groups into which the Germanic family of langs. is divided: the ***East Germanic***, including Gothic (and some langs. of which only traces remain, as Burgundian, Vandal), the ***North Germanic*** = 'Scandinavian' (by some treated as a subdivision of East Germanic), and the ***West Germanic***, including High and Low German, English, Frisian, Dutch, etc.

Now tending to supersede *Teutonic* in scholarly work.

a **1773** A. Butler *Moveable Feasts Cath. Ch.* (1839) iii. 80 Roman conquerors often took names..from countries which they had subdued,..as the African,..the Germanic, ..&c. **1774** R. Henry *Hist. Gt. Brit.* ii. iii. 215 But though these Germanic nations differed very much from one another..yet they appear to have sprung from the same origin. **1841** W. Spalding *Italy & It. Isl.* II. 26 The Roman empire during the Germanic invasions. **1842** B. Thorpe *Codex Exoniensis* 513 To suppose it a translation from another Germanic dialect, would be giving..credit for a kind of knowledge hardly..in existence among our simple fore-fathers. **1879** Sir G. Scott *Lect. Archit.* I. 6 [Gothic] is the architecture of the Germanic nations. **1888** J. Wright *Old High-Ger. Primer* §70 The Germanic combination *kw* was represented in Franconian by *qu*, and in Upper German by *chu*. **1894** *Trans. Philol. Soc. 1891–4* 383 Germanic verse occasionally allows the freedom that syllables which in the spoken language are short, are, for the purposes of versification, treated as long. **1909** F. B. Gummere *Oldest Eng. Epic* p. viii, These two poems [sc. *Deor* and *Widsith*]..

contain many references to persons and stories of Germanic heroic legends. **1928** W. W. LAWRENCE *Beowulf & Epic Trad.* 4 Anglo-Saxon verse..was..rooted in the traditions of professional singers, the main features of whose craft were shared by the poets of the other peoples of Germanic stock. **1948** *Mod. Philol.* XLVI. 73, I shall not try to relate this meter to that of other Anglo-Saxon poetry or of the poetry in the other early Germanic dialects. **1963** R. W. V. ELLIOTT in S. B. Greenfield *Stud. in Honor of A. G. Brodeur* 64 Originality of invention was not the Germanic scop's aim.

B. *sb.* The language of the Germanic people; Teutonic: see A. 2.

1892 J. WRIGHT *Primer Gothic Lang.* §108 From an Indo-Germanic point of view the series I–V belong to one and the same series which underwent in Germanic various modifications upon clearly defined lines.

germanic (dʒəˈmænɪk), *a.*[2] *Chem.* [f. GERMAN(IUM + -IC.] Of, pertaining to, or containing germanium in the quadrivalent state. So **germanous** (-ˈmeɪnəs) *a.*, of, pertaining to, or containing germanium in the bivalent state; †also **gerˈmanious** (*obs.*).

1888 BLOXAM *Chem.* (ed. 6) 306 Germanium..forms two series of compounds, the germanious and germanic. **1895** *Ibid.* (ed. 8) 418 White germanic sulphide, GeS_2... Germanous oxide, GeO. **1962** P. J. & B. DURRANT *Introd. Adv. Inorg. Chem.* xviii. 621 Germanous sulphide, GeS, is made by the reduction of germanic sulphide, GeS_2, with germanium. **1966** *Kirk-Othmer Encycl. Chem. Technol.* (ed. 2) X. 522 Ionic germanic salts of the common inorganic oxy-acids..are not known.

Germanical (dʒəˈmænɪkəl), *a. rare.* [f. GERMANIC *a.*[1] + -AL[1].] = GERMANIC *a.*[1]

1560 BP. SANDYS *Let.* 24 Oct. in *Abp. Parker's Corr.* 125 Ye will not utterly condemn all Germanical natures. **1833** *Fraser's Mag.* VII. 602 Whose Germanical jabber Master Ben..put into English.

Hence **Gerˈmanically** *adv.*, in a Germanical manner.

1833 *Fraser's Mag.* VII. 706 The round-about, hubble-bubble, rumfustianish..roly-poly growlery of style, so Germanically set forth. **1854** DE QUINCEY in H. A. Page *Life* (1877) II. xviii. 87 That is, speaking Germanically, and therefore pedantically.

Germanicism (dʒəˈmænɪsɪz(ə)m). [f. GERMANIC *a.*[1] + -ISM.] A Germanic characteristic, idiom, etc.; Germanic quality.

1905 *Daily Chron.* 14 Sept. 3/2 Mr. Zilliacus's translator, who gives us..sch's for j's, w's for v's, and other Germanicisms. **1947** PARTRIDGE *Usage & Abusage* 94/2 Attempting to rejuvenate it [*sc.* the literary language] with Gallicisms, Germanicisms, Grecisms and Latinisms. **1964** *Listener* 2 Apr. 559/2 The style in which he painted and the school to which he so loosely belonged were tainted with the labels of vulgarity and Germanicism—the two qualities the English can least abide.

Germanify (ˈdʒɜːmənɪfaɪ), *v.* [f. GERMAN *a.*[2] + -(I)FY.] *trans.* To make German in form or character, imbue with German qualities, render German-like. Hence **Gerˈmanified** *ppl. a.*

1871 *Mad. Simple's Invest.* v. in *Old & New* in *Casq. Lit.* I. 312/1 That sounds Germanified. **1888** *Atlantic Monthly* Feb. 281 The Germanified ghost of the dead language is raised in the baccalaureate oration of my second son.

Germanish (ˈdʒɜːmənɪʃ), *a.* [See -ISH.] Having German characteristics, savouring of Germanism.

1796 R. BAGE *Hermsprong* viii, It sounds monstrous Germanish. **1819** SOUTHEY *Lett.* (1856) III. 124 The letter is Germanish enough, in all conscience. **1829** *Westm. Rev.* X. 197 Kellerman's name sounds Germanish.

Germanism (ˈdʒɜːmənɪz(ə)m). [f. GERMAN *a.*[2] + -ISM. Cf. F. *Germanisme.*]

1. An idiom or mode of expression peculiar to the German language; esp. one used by a speaker or writer in some other language.

1611 CORYAT *Crudities* 39 After I had duly considered this prety Germanisme. *a* **1773** CHESTERF. (T.), It is full of Latinisms, Gallicisms, Germanisms, and all isms but Anglicisms. **1832** GEN. P. THOMPSON *Exerc.* (1842) II. 2 Besides, it [the 'Tour of a German Prince'] lacks Germanity; the Germanisms in the whole are not greater than might be collected in a three years' residence. **1853** MISS SHEPPARD *Ch. Auchester* I. 324 The mere Germanisms of the novel rests and signs appalled me. **1892** *Nation* (N.Y.) 26 May 401/1 Many-jointed Germanisms stretch their unwieldy length and sprawl over every page.

2. a. German ideas; German modes of thought or action. **b.** Attachment to German ideas or institutions.

1841 *Blackw. Mag.* L. 154 Thou art alone practical, and despisest idealism, and mysticism, and Germanism. **1864** *Daily Tel.* 11 May, The advance of Germanism, as it was styled, was retarded, if not checked. **1884** *Jrnl. Educ.* XIX. 24 What our country needs of Germanism in education is the profound, accurate, broad, and genial habits.

3. Affectation of what is German; a disposition to adopt German modes of thought or expression.

1807 W. TAYLOR in *Ann. Rev.* V. 507 A something of Germanism clings about the style of these two first cantos. **1845** J. H. NEWMAN *Developm. Chr. Doctr.* 71 The same philosophical elements, received into a certain sensibility or insensibility to sin, and its consequences, leads [*sic*] one mind to the Church of Rome; another to what, for want of a better word, may be called Germanism. **1857** CHURCH *Let.* 26 Jan. in *Life* (1894) 149 How very much without real knowledge has been a great deal of the broad abuse of Germanism that goes on.

Germanist (ˈdʒɜːmənɪst). [f. GERMAN *a.*[2] + -IST.] **a.** One who has a knowledge of Germany and of the German language. **b.** One versed in Germanic or Teutonic philology. **c.** One influenced by German thought.

1831 CARLYLE *Let.* 29 Aug. in Froude *Life* (1882) II. 188 We are all to meet, along with a certain Mrs. Austin, a young Germanist..and breakfast some day in the Templar's lodgings. **1851** RUSKIN *Let. to Stillman* in *Pall Mall G.* (1887) 23 Dec. 11/2 Above all avoid German books—and all Germanists except Carlyle. **1880** A. H. HUTH *Buckle* II. 241, I..hope to take back the boys good Germanists. **1885** G. H. SCHODDE in *Homil. Rev.* May 395 The greatest of Germanists, Jacob Grimm..says that..Luther's language must be regarded as the foundation of modern German.

Germanistic (ˌdʒɜːməˈnɪstɪk), *a.* [f. prec. + -IC.] Pertaining to the study of Germanic philology and antiquities.

1881 *Athenæum* 30 July 143/2 The second volume of the admirable *Jahresbericht* on Germanistic philology..has reached us. **1883** *American* VI. 313 Cheap Germanistic texts.

†**germanity**[1]. *Obs.* [ad. L. *germānitātem*, f. *germānus* GERMAN[1].] The quality of being 'german' or closely related; near kinship.

1594 BP. J. KING *Jonas* (1618) 70 Thus was germanity and brotherhood broken betwixt the Thebans. **1637** R. HUMPHREY tr. *St. Ambrose* I. 81 The germanity and neerest blood of brotherhood. **1647** TRAPP *Comm. 2 Cor.* viii. 8 The germanity, the naturalnesse, legitimatenesse opposed to bastardlinesse. **1663** F. HAWKINS *Youth's Behav.* 105 Germanity, brotherhood. **1721** in BAILEY.

Germanity[2] (dʒəˈmænɪtɪ). [f. GERMAN *a.*[2] + -(I)TY.]

1. The characteristic qualities of Germany or the Germans.

1832 [see GERMANISM 1]. **1855** *Fraser's Mag.* LI. 700 The inhabitants [of Weimar] seemed to us to have more than the usual heaviness of Germanity. **1857** DE QUINCEY *Goethe* Wks. 1862 XII. 216 One other part of this lady's conduct merits notice for its exquisite Germanity.

2. Devotion to German interests.

1870 *Pall Mall G.* 25 Nov. 10 That they are slightly demoralized by success no one not directly inspired with 'Germanity' can doubt.

germanium (dʒəˈmeɪnɪəm). *Chem.* [mod.L., f. *Germānus* GERMAN *a.*[2]] A hard, brittle, semi-metallic element, greyish-white in colour, which has chemical properties intermediate between those of silicon and tin and is used esp. as a semiconductor in transistors and other solid-state devices. Atomic number 32; symbol Ge.

1886 *Athenæum* 13 Mar. 364/2 Prof. Clemens Winkler, in the *Berichte* of the Berlin Chemical Society, describes a new element—to which he has given the name of 'Germanium'—in a mineral named Argyrodite..Germanium appears to take a place between antimony and bismuth. **1948** *Bell Lab. Record* XXVI. 323/1 In semi-conductors, such as silicon and germanium,..there may be as few as one current-carrying electron for every million atoms. **1954** H. R. HARNER in C. A. Hampel *Rare Metals Handbk.* ix. 163 Commercial recovery of germanium has..been chiefly from zinc ores, germanite, and flue dust (from coals). *Ibid.*, Production of germanium in England was started in 1950. **1955** *Sci. News Let.* 19 Feb. 119/3 The germanium transistor, versatile little crystal substitute for the radio tube. **1959** [see ARGYRODITE]. **1970** D. F. SHAW *Introd. Electronics* (ed. 2) xi. 236 To manufacture a *P-N* junction diode using germanium, the crystal is grown from *N*-type germanium (i.e. germanium with arsenic or antimony as impurity).

Germanize (ˈdʒɜːmənaɪz), *v.* [f. GERMAN *a.*[2] + -IZE.]

1. *trans.* To translate into the German language.

1598 SYLVESTER *Du Bartas* II. ii. II. *Babylon* 624 The Dutch, hath him who Germaniz'd the story Of Sleidan. **1793** BÖTTIGER *Let.* in *Mem. Dalzel* (1862) 107, I have got a vast liking to Germanise them myself. **1814** W. TAYLOR in *Monthly Rev.* LXXIII. 354 Several of whose odes have been as happily Germanized by Ramler as his epistles have been by Wieland.

2. To make German in character, appearance, etc.

1609 HEYWOOD *Lucrece* III. iv. Wks. 1874 V. 205 The first health shall be impos'd on you Valerius, and if ever you have beene Germaniz'd, let it be after the Dutch fashion. **1751** FRANKLIN *Ess.* Wks. 1890 II. 320 Aliens, who will shortly be so numerous as to Germanize us instead of our Anglifying them. **1790** *By-stander* 350 [Thus did Handel] Germanize us out of the little taste which, previous to his misty appearance, had begun to glimmer on us. **1812** VISCT. FOLKESTONE *Sp. Ho. Com.* 10 Dec., He had seen our..officers adopting German dresses, and Germanizing themselves as much as possible. **1862** LATHAM *Channel Isl.* III. xiv. (ed. 2) 329 The process by which Normandy was Germanized. **1891** *Athenæum* 22 Aug. 250/2 She [Japan] has endeavoured in turn to anglicize, americanize, gallicize, and germanize herself.

3. *intr.* To adopt German manners and customs; to become German (in style, tastes, habits, sympathies, etc.).

1665 LOCKE *Let.* in Fox Bourne *Life* (1876) I. iii. 112 Our landlord, who is wont sometimes to germanize. **1801** *True Briton* in *Spirit Publ. Jrnls.* (1802) V. 123 For, though our troops might fraternize, They'd poltrons be to Germanize. **1821** SHELLEY *Let. to C. Clairmont* in Dowden *Life* II. 391 You are indeed Germanizing very fast.

Hence **ˈGermanized** *ppl. a.*, **ˈGermanizing** *vbl. sb.* Also **ˌGermaniˈzation**, the action or process of Germanizing; **ˈGermanizer**, one who Germanizes.

1743 *Lond. Mag.* 89 He might..have described himself as a Germanized Englishman. **1760** FOOTE *Minor* I. Wks. 1799 I. 240 Who knows whether this Germaniz'd genius has parts to comprehend..thy merit. **1817** COLERIDGE *Biog. Lit.* 100 A Latin word with a Germanized ending. **1825** SYD. SMITH *Speeches* Wks. 1859 II. 209/2 We should..have been..about as free as Denmark, Sweden, or the Germanised States of Italy. **1850** H. ROGERS *Ess.* II. iv. 213 The Germanised style..consists..in an absurd imitation of German idiom and construction. **1850** *Fraser's Mag.* XLII. 689 Should the Governments of Prussia and Austria persist in their present system of Germanization. **1860** *Lit. Churchman* VI. 3/1 The maudlin and unavowed scepticism of one or other of these classes of Germanizers. **1879** FROUDE *Caesar* xvi. 261 The Germanising of Gaul would lead..to fresh invasions of Italy. **1881** *Scribner's Mag.* XXII. 97/1 The vague..notion that his [Carlyle's] style consists in a mere Germanising of English may be dismissed at once. **1889** *Times* 14 Jan. 5/6 The Bill would tend to the Germanization of Hungary. **1895** *Pop. Sci. Monthly* Sept. 720 Incidents..illustrative of the people's concealing French hearts under their Germanized exteriors.

ˈGermano-, used as the combining form of 'German' in various formations, as **ˈGermano-Coleˈridgian** *a.*, used by Mill as an epithet designating opinions derived from German writers through Coleridge, or from the Germans and Coleridge jointly; **ˌGermano-ˈmania**, a mania for things German; **Gerˈmanophil(e)** *a.* and *sb.* (see -PHIL, -PHILE); so **Germaˈnophily**; **Germaˈnophilist**, one who is friendly to, or excessively fond of, the Germans; **Gerˈmanophobe** *a.* and *sb.* (see -PHOBE); **ˌGermanoˈphobia**, a morbid dread of Germany and of everything German.

1840 MILL *Diss. & Disc.* (1875) I. 403 The *Germano-Coleridgian doctrine is..the result of..a reaction. *Ibid.* 425 The Germano-Coleridgian school..saw beyond the immediate controversy. **1893** *Nation* (N.Y.) 11 May 350/3 One is almost tempted to wish that Dr. Minot had..intrusted the preparation of an American translation to some one not yet incurably affected by *Germano-mania. **1898** *Daily News* 14 Dec. 5/7 M. Barthélémy-St.-Hilaire, 'the only *Germanophile Frenchman then living'. **1906** *Outlook* 15 Sept. 338/2 Those whom the *Deutsche Revue* describes as 'very Germanophil Ministers'. **1911** *Q. Rev.* July 254 The editor of one of the greatest Russian newspapers, who is at one time a strong Germanophil, and at another an equally strong Germanophobe. **1946** R. CAPELL *Simiomata* III. 204 The second prime minister of the occupation..was..a convinced Greek Germanophil. **1961** *Guardian* 29 Sept. 6/4 The irrationalism and anti-rationalism of the Germanophiles. **1864** FURNIVALL in *Reader* 11 June 744 Whether you believe in Diez as an oracle as some *Germanophilists do, or doubt him as some English sceptics have done. **1910** *Westm. Gaz.* 16 Feb. 8/2 That champion of *germanophily. **1903** *N. Y. Tribune* 15 Apr. 8/3 The extreme *Germanophobes of England. **1904** *Daily Chron.* 22 Oct. 3/2 In this story he is neither Francophil nor Germanophobe. **1905** *Ibid.* 10 Jan. 5/5 The Germanophobe attitude of the English Press. **1964** *Economist* 12 Dec. 1225/2 A noisy handful of Germanophobes. **1887** *Germanophobia [see -PHOBIA]. **1894** *Forum* (U.S.) Dec. 398 There is no Germanophobia to be detected in his attitude.

ˈGerman ˈsilver. A white alloy consisting of nickel, zinc, and copper, originally obtained from an ore found at Hildburghausen.

1830 *Mech. Mag.* XIII. 96 The German silver..is now coming into vogue. **1851** *Illustr. Catal. Gr. Exhib.* 1052 A gun..in a case of rosewood, mounted in German silver. **1873** F. JENKIN *Electr. & Magn.* (1883) 200 The coils (of the differential galvanometer) are sometimes made of German silver instead of copper.

attrib. **1870** LOWELL *Study Wind.* 58 The beggars were a kind of German-silver aristocracy.

ˈGermantown. *U.S.* [The name of a suburb of Philadelphia.] A one-horse covered vehicle used in country districts: more fully ***Germantown wagon.***

1885 H. C. MCCOOK *Tenants Old Farm* 322 Farmers came in their buggies, germantowns and farm-waggons.

germarium (dʒəˈmɛərɪəm). *Zool.* Pl. **-aria.** [mod.L., f. L. *germen* germ.] In certain invertebrates, the ovary proper, as distinguished from the vitellarium; also, the corresponding part of a testis.

1877 T. H. HUXLEY *Man. Anat. Invert.* 178 A single or double *germarium*, having nearly the same structure as the ovary of *Macrostomum*. **1888** ROLLESTON & JACKSON *Forms Anim. Life* 646 The germarium is always single, usually globular or elongate, and even folded on itself. **1925** A. D. IMMS *Gen. Textbk. Ent.* 145 The germarium is the region containing the primordial germ cells or spermatogonia which undergo multiplication. **1970** D. GILMOUR et al. in *Insects Austral.* (C.S.I.R.O.) ii. 69 The germarium is situated at the apex of each ovariole.

gerˈmatic, *a. Biol. rare.* [Badly f. GERM *sb.*, on the analogy of *spermatic.*] Pertaining to a germ.

1889 H. CAMPBELL *Causation of Disease* 135 We have seen that the spermatic and germatic E[nvironment] cannot possibly be the same for any two germs or sperms.

germe, var. JERM, Turkish vessel.

germen ('dʒɜːmɛn). Also 7 **germaine**, 7–9 **germin**. [a. L. *germen* (pl. *germina*): see GERM *sb.*]

1. The rudiment of an organism, a germ. Now only *fig.* (Cf. GERM *sb.*)

1605 SHAKS. *Lear* III. ii. 8 And thou all-shaking Thunder, Strike flat the thicke Rotundity o' th' world, Cracke Natures moulds, all germaines spill at once That makes ingratefull Man. —— *Macb.* IV. i. 59. *a* **1691** BOYLE *Chr. Virtuoso* II. Wks. 1772 VI. 794 The cicatricula of an egg, or the germen in the seed of a plant, being, in reality, a model of the animal, or plant, to be produced from it. **1807** VANCOUVER *Agric. Devon* (1813) 123 Although that may cleanse the body of the grain, it will not carry off the down from its end, and which is reasonably supposed to contain the germin of smut. **1814** CARY *Dante, Purg.* xvii. 100 Love is germin [orig. *sementa*] of each virtue in ye. **1824** GALT *Rothelan* II. v. vi. 294 Many thought and feared some new evil was confusing the germins of nature.

†**2.** A shoot or sprout, a young branch or sucker.

1628 COKE *On Litt.* 53 a, If tenant cut down timber trees ..or suffer the young germins to be destroyed. **1669** WORLIDGE *Syst. Agric.* (1681) 326 *Germins*, young shoots of Trees. **1671** GREW *Anat. Plants* I. iv. §1 The Parts of the Germen and Branch, are the same with those of the Trunk. **1714** SCROGGS *Courts-leet* (ed. 3) 208 If..he destroys the young Germins, or stub up the same by the Roots. **1725** BRADLEY *Fam. Dict.* s.v. *Palm*, The Palm-Tree has a tender Germen, from whence other small Shoots proceed by Intervals. **1786** W. GILPIN *Mount. & Lakes* I. 227 Fruitful nature, making..unremitting efforts to vegetate, could not here produce a single germin.

3. *Bot.* The rudiment of a seed-vessel, an ovary.

1759 B. STILLINGFL. *Wks.* (1762) Introd. 30 Upon opening the flower leaves there will appear in the very center, at the bottom an oblong thickish substance..This contains the seed, and is called the germen or germ. **1776–96** WITHERING *Brit. Plants* (ed. 3) I. 3 The Seed-vessel. In the newly-opened flower, this part was called the Germen; but when it enlarges, and approaches to maturity, it is called the Seed-vessel. **1807** J. E. SMITH *Phys. Bot.* 274 The Germen appears under a variety of shapes and sizes. It is of great moment..to observe whether it be superior, that is, above the bases of the calyx and corolla..or inferior, below them. **1854** S. THOMSON *Wild Fl.* III. (ed. 4) 179 The bodies..are considered abortive germens, or seed-vessels. **1877** DARWIN *Forms of Fl.* iii. 83 The germens of these 12 flowers all swelled, and ultimately six fine capsules and two poor capsules were produced.

germicidal ('dʒɜːmɪˌsaɪdəl), *a.* [f. as next + -AL[1].] Destructive to germs, germ-killing.

1888 *Times* 24 Dec. 3/5 By first drawing the tobacco smoke through water, it was found to have lost its germicidal properties. **1891** *Review of Rev.* 14 Mar. 278/1 The great germicidal antidote of the future.

germicide ('dʒɜːmɪsaɪd), *sb.* (*a.*) [f. GERM *sb.* + -CIDE I.]

1. That which kills germs; *spec.* an agent used to destroy disease-germs.

1881 *Times* 17 Jan. 5 Neither oil nor glycerine is a germicide or a disinfectant. **1881** G. M. STERNBERG tr. *Magnin's Bacteria* (1883) 209 By germicides we mean agents which have the power to destroy the vitality of the various species of bacteria known to us.

2. quasi-*adj.* Destructive to germs, germicidal.

1880 MAC CORMAC *Antisept. Surg.* 106 Certain germicide agents absolutely arrest their power of reproduction. **1885** *Syd. Soc. Lex.*, *Germicide*, having power to kill germs.

germiculture ('dʒɜːmɪkʌltjʊə(r)). [f. GERM *sb.* + CULTURE; after *horticulture*, etc.] 'The artificial cultivation of the microscopical organisms (bacteria) connected with certain diseases' (*Cent. Dict.*). Hence **germi'culturist**, one who practises germiculture; a bacteriologist.

18.. *Med. News* LII. 640 (Cent.) The third point—the antiseptic value of these bodies—still remains for the germiculturist to determine.

germiduct ('dʒɜːmɪdʌkt). [f. GERM *sb.* = L. *duct-us*; after *aqueduct.*] 'The efferent canal of the germigene' (*Syd. Soc. Lex.* 1885).

germigene ('dʒɜːmɪdʒiːn). *Biol.* [f. GERM *sb.* + *-gene*, -GEN.] 'The gland of the female generative apparatus of cestoid and Trematode worms in which the germinal vesicles are formed' (*Syd. Soc. Lex.* 1885).

So **ger'migenous** *a.*, that produces germs.

1859 TODD *Cycl. Anat.* V. [136] In..Cestoid Entozoa there are distinct germigenous..organs. **1870** ROLLESTON *Anim. Life* Introd. 125 Besides other accessory organs, vitelligenous exist independently of germigenous glands. **1885** *Syd. Soc. Lex.* s.v. *Gland, Germigenous gland*, the germ-producing structure or ovary of cestoid worms; the structure which produces the germinative vesicles.

germin ('dʒɜːmɪn), *v. arch.* Also 5 **germyne**. [ad. L. *germin-āre*: see GERMINATE *v.*] *intr.* To put forth shoots, to bud. Of the earth: To begin to produce vegetation. Also *trans.* To bud or shoot forth into.

c **1420** *Pallad. on Husb.* XII. 48 For Columelle affermyth in that ioynt To germyne, and in veer therout to stare Mater thy vyne al newly to repare. **1483** CAXTON *G. de la Tour* A iv b, The swete dewe of Maye..pleseth moche unto the erthe and attempreth it swetely in making to germyne and fructyfye. —— *Gold. Leg.* 231 b/1 Thre thynges ben founden in seed germynyng. **1484** —— *Ryall Bk.* M iv, A dewe whyche maketh hym to germyne a swete rote and ryȝt wel atempred, that is good love. **1814** CARY *Dante, Par.* xxxiii. 10 The love Reveal'd, whose genial influence makes now This flower to germin in eternal peace.

germin, var. GERMEN.

germinable ('dʒɜːmɪnəb(ə)l), *a.* *rare*$^{-1}$. [as if ad. L. **germinābilis*, f. *germināre*: see GERMINATE *v.* and -ABLE.] Capable of germination.

1878 OGLE tr. *Kerner's Flowers* iv. 79 Visits.. indispensable for the production of germinable seeds.

‖**Germinal** (ʒɛrminal, 'dʒɜːmɪnəl), *sb.* [Fr., f. L. *germin-*, *germen*: see GERM *sb.*] The seventh month of the French revolutionary calendar.

1802 C. WILMOT *Diary* 25 Apr. (1920) 60 Three days in this month of Germinal, it is the custom for all the world to drive four miles out of Town in State, and return back again. **1833** NICOLAS *Chronol. Hist.* (1838) 171 French Revol. Calend., Germinal (Budding Month) Mar. 21–Apr. 19.

germinal ('dʒɜːmɪnəl), *a.* [ad. mod.L. *germinālis*, f. L. *germin-*, *germen*: see GERM *sb.*] Of or belonging to a germ or to germs; of the nature of a germ.

germinal cell, disc = *germ cell, disc* (see GERM *sb.* 6). ***germinal layer***, each of the three layers of cells into which the blastoderm divides. ***germinal matter***, a term applied by Beale to vitally active matter (see quot. 1870). ***germinal membrane*** = BLASTODERM. ***germinal pole***, 'the part or pole of the egg where lies the germinal spot' (*Syd. Soc. Lex.* 1885). ***germinal spot***, the nucleolus of the permanent ovum, situated in the germinal vesicle. ***germinal vesicle***, the nucleus of the permanent ovum of animals.

1825 COLERIDGE *Aids Refl.* 172 Relatively taken..the germinal power of every seed might be generalized under the relation of Identity. **1836, 1859** Germinal membrane [see BLASTODERM]. **1845** G. E. DAY tr. *Simon's Anim. Chem.* I. 118 Capillary vessels are developed by the stellated union of a certain set of blastodermic or germinal cells. **1851–6** WOODWARD *Mollusca* iv. 51 On one side of the yolk is a pellucid spot, termed the germinal vesicle, having a spot or nucleus on its surface. **1861** BEALE *Protoplasm* I. iii. (1874) 93 In all living beings the matter upon which existence depends is the germinal matter (Bioplasm). **1863** HUXLEY *Man's Place Nat.* II. 61 A mass of viscid nutritive matter, the 'yelk', within which is enclosed..the 'germinal vesicle'. In this, lastly, lies a more solid rounded body, termed the 'germinal spot'. **1870** BEALE *Protoplasm* (ed. 2) 36 It [living matter] alone possesses the power of growth and of producing matter like itself out of materials differing from it materially in composition, properties, and powers. I therefore called it *germinal* or *living matter*, to distinguish it from the *formed material*, which is in all cases destitute of these properties. **1870** ROLLESTON *Anim. Life* Introd. 36 The three layers into which the germinal membrane divides itself in the embryo. **1871** TYNDALL *Fragm. Sci.* xi. 306 The plague-corpuscles..might also be germinal in the worm, and still baffle the microscope. **1878** BELL *Gegenbaur's Comp. Anat.* 35 The so-called germinal layers, which make up the embryonic body. **1880** HUXLEY *Crayfish* iv. 206 The protoplasmic substance of the yelk..constituting a germinal layer. *Ibid.* 209 A whitish patch..termed the germinal disk. **1888** J. T. GULICK in *Linn. Soc. Jrnl.* XX. 237 Germinal Segregation is caused by the propagation of the species by means of seeds or germs any one of which, when developed, forms a community.

b. *transf.* Of non-material things: That is in the germ or in the earliest stage of development.

1808 W. TAYLOR in *Ann. Rev.* VI. 360 In our second volume..was noticed the germinal pamphlet, of which this quarto volume may be considered as the matured expansion. **1855** H. SPENCER *Princ. Psychol.* (1872) II. VI. xvi. 220 In what order do these germinal ideas arise? **1867** LEWES *Hist. Philos.* II. 367 It is needless..to point out the defects of this system. All we have to note here is its logical development of Condillac's germinal error. **1873** SYMONDS *Grk. Poets* i. 10 The artistic sentiment, indeed, exists in Homer..but it is germinal, not organized and expanded as it will be. **1874** SIDGWICK *Meth. Ethics* iii. 427 The germinal form of morality. *a* **1878** LEWES *Study Psychol.* (1879) 40 A forecasting tendency, germinal in animals and savages, conspicuous in the civilized man. **1885** CLODD *Myths & Dr.* II. i. 147 Indications of germinal ideas about an after-life are present in the contents of tumuli.

c. *humorously.* Rudimentary, undeveloped.

1866 GEO. ELIOT *F. Holt* xxii, Job was a small fellow, about five, with a germinal nose.

d. *fig.* Capable of development; productive of new ideas, influences, etc.; = SEMINAL *a.* 4 a.

1934 H. G. WELLS *Exper. Autobiogr.* I. iii. 136 The European country houses and chateaux that were so alive and germinal, mentally, in the seventeenth and eighteenth centuries, stand now mere empty shells. **1935** J. R. MOORE *Defoe & Mod. Econ. Theory* ii. 5 He was one of the rare germinal minds in literature. **1936** C. S. LEWIS *Allegory of Love* IV. i. 157 The *Romance of the Rose* is one of the most 'successful' books, in the vulgar sense, that have ever been written... As a germinal book during these centuries [*sc.* the later Middle Ages] it ranks second to none except the Bible and the *Consolation of Philosophy*.

Hence **'germinally** *adv.*

1869 MISS HARWOOD tr. *de Pressensé's Early Years Chr.* II. iii. 203 The old economy germinally contains the new.

germinance ('dʒɜːmɪnəns). *rare.* [f. L. *germināre*: see GERMINATE *v.* and -ANCE.] The act of germinating or putting forth shoots.

1841 MYERS *Cath. Th.* IV. xxviii. 312 When the fulness of time was come for the germinance and growth of..the plant.

germinant ('dʒɜːmɪnənt), *a.* [ad. L. *germinant-em*, pr. pple. of *germināre*: see GERMINATE *v.*] That develops like a germ; germinating, sprouting; also, having the potentiality of life or development. *rare* in literal sense.

1605 BACON *Adv. Learn.* II. iii. §2 Prophecies..are not fulfilled punctually at once, but haue springing and germinant accomplishment throughout many ages. **1727** BAILEY vol. II, *Germinant*, sprouting, budding, blossoming, &c. **1833** *Fraser's Mag.* Nov. 574/2 They are sowing the spiritual seed of immortal emulation..Such seed is germinant with quenchless vitality. **1841** MYERS *Cath. Th.* III. xxvii. 102 He destroyed subordinate errours by simply proclaiming germinant truths. **1846** DANA *Zooph.* v. §88 (1848) 91 Thus we trace out the beginning of the germinant process. **1870** BALDW. BROWN *Eccl. Truth* 266 The ideas were germinant and fruitful. **1878** *N. Amer. Rev.* CXXVI. 354 A seedcorn that has under genial influences been warmed into the first movings of germinant life. **1881** W. R. NICOLL *Incarnate Saviour* viii. 148 The teaching of Christ was not exhaustive but germinant.

b. *fig.* of the ground.

1848 R. I. WILBERFORCE *Doctr. Incarnat.* ii. (1852) 23 The dry ground of man's nature is spoken of as germinant with the plant of our salvation. **1856** P. FAIRBAIRN *Prophecy* ii. 32 The germinant soil out of which predictions were ever springing forth.

germinate ('dʒɜːmɪneɪt), *v.* [f. ppl. stem of L. *germināre*, f. *germin-*, *germen*: see GERM *sb.*]

1. *intr.* To sprout, put forth shoots, begin to vegetate. Said properly of a seed or of a spore; hence, also, of a plant: To bud and develop shoots and branches.

1663 BULLOKAR, *Germinate*, to bud out. **1667** *Phil. Trans.* II. 424 Whether seeds..will germinate and thrive in the exhausted Receiver. **1671** GREW *Anat. Plants* I. i. §39 'Tis now time for the Plume to rouze out of its Cloysters, and germinate too. *a* **1687** H. MORE *Def. Philos. Cabbala* App. xi. (1713) 196 God caused the Trees to germinate out of the Earth. **1707** *Curios. in Husb. & Gard.* 157 There is in one single Grain of Corn, that has throughly germinated, wherewith to feed the five Thousand Men. **1846** J. BAXTER *Libr. Pract. Agric.* (ed. 4) I. 107 When the agriculturist wishes his seeds to germinate, he should not bury them very deep. **1866** ROGERS *Agric. & Prices* I. xxii. 572 A kind of cloth woven of hair was used for drying the malt after it had been made to germinate. **1874** COOKE *Fungi* 27 The spores which produce spermatia are not at all apt to germinate. **1875** BENNETT & DYER *Sachs' Bot.* 138 The persistent buds of many trees (Aesculus), bulbs (Tulip), and corms (Crocus, &c.), formed in the summer and germinating in the spring after long rest in winter.

b. *fig.*

1647 H. MORE *Poems* 267 Lust and Vengeance..from one seed do germinate. **1660** JER. TAYLOR *Duct. Dubit.* I. iv. rule x. §2 (1676) 124 The Church was then a garden of the fairest flowers, it did daily germinate with blessings from Heaven, and Saints sprung up. **1758–65** GOLDSM. *Ess.*, *Cultiv. Taste* Wks. (Globe) 319/1 The preceptor will sow the seeds of that taste which will soon germinate, rise, blossom, and produce perfect fruit. **1849** ROBERTSON *Serm.* Ser. I. iii. (1866) 56 The soul requires room to germinate. **1849** H. COLERIDGE in *Encycl. Metrop.* 3 From the first, or initiative Idea, as from a seed, successive Ideas germinate. **1862** H. SPENCER *First Princ.* I. i. §5 (1875) 18 The sciences..severally germinate out of the experiences of daily life. **1889** JESSOPP *Coming of Friars* vi. 282 A wise man acts upon a hint, and it germinates.

2. *trans.* To cause to shoot or sprout.

1610 D. PRICE *Creat. Prince* E ij, In this Paradise is..the tree of goodnesse which is..watered by grace, germinated by godlines, will waxe greene by hope [etc.]. **1803** *Edwin* III. 264 The gentle influence of Spring began to spread the verdant carpet of Nature, and germinate the bursting buds. **1870** DISRAELI *Lothair* xii, The impassioned eloquence of that lady germinated the seed which the Cardinal had seemed so carelessly to scatter.

b. *fig.* To cause to issue or develop, to produce.

1796 BURNEY *Metastasio* II. 245 Some new composition flatters my vanity in fulfilling my predictions, and germinating fresh hopes of your future poetical fame. **1837** CARLYLE *Fr. Rev.* III. IV. i, Several French departments germinate a set of rebellious paper-leaves, named Proclamations. **1849** COBDEN *Speeches* 32 Those boundary questions which, we were assured, were to germinate a war for a quarter of a century. **1892** HALL CAINE in *Times* 19 Sept. 4/1 A crowd of people gathered in the Street and germinated alarming rumours.

3. *intr.* Of a salt, etc.: To effloresce. ? *Obs.*

1626 BACON *Sylva* §696 The Chalcites, which hath a Spirit that will put forth and germinate, as we see in Chymicall Trialls. **1774** BROWNRIGG in *Phil. Trans.* LXIV. 482 Which salt also germinates in great abundance in the same colliery. *Ibid.* 490 The stone on which the native alum ..germinates is black and shining. **1796** KIRWAN *Elem. Min.* (ed. 2) II. 9 It [Glauber's Salt] also, not unfrequently, germinates from, and adheres to, the walls of recent buildings.

Hence **'germinating** *vbl. sb.* (*attrib.*) and *ppl. a.*

1751 N. COTTON *Vis.* viii. 40 Infant roses, ere they blow, In germinating clusters grow. **1845** DARWIN *Voy. Nat.* xx. (1873) 454 The seeds retain their germinating power. **1854** GILFILLAN *Life Blair* in *B.'s Wks.* 128 Books..full of suggestive and germinating thought. **1863** FR. A. KEMBLE *Resid. in Georgia* 87 A young shoot is produced at the germinating season. **1884** BOWER & SCOTT *De Bary's Phaner.* 198 The root of the germinating seed.

germination (dʒɜːmɪ'neɪʃən). [ad. L. *germinātiōn-em*, n. of action f. *germināre*: see GERMINATE *v.* Cf. F. *germination.*]

1. The action or process of germinating, sprouting, or putting forth shoots; also, an instance of this. Used properly of a seed; hence of a plant, and also of the similar development of the spore in cryptogams.

1594 PLAT *Jewell-ho.* I. 23 It helpeth toward the generation and germination of all seeds. **1627-77** FELTHAM *Resolves, Lett.* v. 67 Can the Sun shine, and the dew fall, and not the Earth return her Germinations? **1646** SIR T. BROWNE *Pseud. Ep.* III. xxv. 178 Herein we finde no security to prevent its germination, as having made tryall in graines whose ends cut off have notwithstanding suddenly sprouted. **1692** BENTLEY *Boyle Lect.* 251 The whole globe would be one frigid zone..there would be no life, no germination. **1707** *Curios. Husb. & Gard.* 135 Salts are not absolutely necessary to the Germination of Plants. **1776** BP. WATSON *Apol. Chr.* i. 22 Any one phænomenon in nature, from the rotation of the great orbs of the universe to the germination of a blade of grass. **1830** M. DONOVAN *Dom. Econ.* I. 81 Germination would then proceed with dangerous rapidity in that part [of a heap of grain]..while in other parts the vegetation would not have commenced. **1846** J. BAXTER *Libr. Pract. Agric.* (ed. 4) II. 170 The germination which converts the acorn into an oak. **1872** OLIVER *Elem. Bot.* I. iv. 44 The essentials to germination are found by experience to be a certain amount of moisture, warmth, and air. **1875** BENNETT & DYER *Sachs' Bot.* 362 The spore.. increases in size as soon as germination commences..and divides into two cells.

fig. **1653** H. MORE *Conject. Cabbal.* 65 The sundry Germinations and Springings up of the works of Righteousness in him are a delectable Paradise to him. **1818** HALLAM *Mid. Ages* (1872) II. 268 We see the germination of that usurpation. **1875** STUBBS *Const. Hist.* II. xvii. 623 A time of germination in religious history.

2. *transf.* Used for: Efflorescence, ebullition.

1665 HOOKE *Microgr.* 128 Excrescencies or Ebullitions in the snuff of a Candle, partly from..a kind of Germination or Ebullition of some actuated unctuous parts which creep along. *Ibid.* 130 Why may not the Phænomena of Ebullition or Germination be in part..from the levity of an impregnated liquor. **1774** BROWNRIGG in *Phil. Trans.* LXIV. 483 Various other kinds of salts formed by germination, assume this fibrous texture.

germinative ('dʒɜːmɪneɪtɪv), *a.* [f. L. *germināre*: see GERMINATE *v.* and -ATIVE. Cf. F. *germinatif, -ive.*] **a.** Of or belonging to germination. **b.** 'Having power to bud or sprout, or to develop' (Mayne *Expos. Lex.* 1854).

1707 *Curios. in Husb. & Gard.* 155 Any Agent, indu'd with a germinative Power. *Ibid.* 230 Among the common Water there is another which I call germinative, for Plants. **1841-71** T. R. JONES *Anim. Kingd.* (ed. 4) 865 The blastoderm or germinative membrane. **1862** F. HALL *Hindu Philos. Syst.* 67 *note*, The germinative power of a seed..is destroyed by fire. **1883** *American* VII. 89 The germinative portion of the egg.

fig. **1821** *Blackw. Mag.* X. 334 [It] could not fail to weaken the germinative principles of popular disaffection. **1857** I. TAYLOR *World of Mind* 379 The 'Social Institution' by which such usages are sanctioned is itself a crime, and it will be germinative of crimes. **1865** *Reader* 18 Mar. 309/1 Any vital or germinative truth.

germinator ('dʒɜːmɪneɪtə(r)). [f. GERMINATE *v.* + -OR.] That which causes or promotes the growth (of a seed or plant). Also *spec.*, an appliance for testing the germinating power of seed.

1890 *Daily News* 26 June 6/1 Messrs. Sutton..have a most ingenious germinator on view, a device by which the buyer of seed may..test the germinating power of what he buys. **1895** *Voice* (N.Y.) 16 May 62 This infernal bottle..is a veritable germinator of misery and sin.

germi'niparous, *a.* *rare*$^{-1}$. [f. L. type **germinipar-us* (f. GERMEN + *parĕre* to bring forth, after *ōviparus, vīviparus*) + -OUS.] Bringing forth seeds; producing offspring through seeds.

1827 H. T. COLEBROOKE in *Trans. R. Asiat. Soc.* (1830) II. 36 The threefold division..is, 1st. viviparous..2d. oviparous..3d. germiniparous.

germless ('dʒɜːmlɪs), *a.* [f. GERM *sb.* + -LESS.] Containing no germs (see GERM *sb.* 3).

1883 H. DRUMMOND *Nat. Law in Spir. W.* (1884) 62 If the air were absolutely germless and pure, would the..life appear? **1887** C. DENISON in *Trans. 9th Internat. Med. Congress Washington* 8 Sept., He will never forget the noiselessness of that insectless and germless locality.

germon ('dʒɜːmən). [a. F. *germon* (see Littré *Suppl.*).] A fish of the genus *Orcynus*, esp. *Orcynus alalonga* the Long-finned tunny.

1860 YARRELL *Brit. Fishes* 2nd Supp. 15. **1861** COUCH *Brit. Fishes* II. 100 Germon. Long-finned Tunny. The name of Germon has been applied to more than one species, but we confine it to that to which in our opinion it more properly belongs.

germo(u)nt, obs. Sc. form of GARMENT.

germy ('dʒɜːmɪ), *a.* [f. GERM *sb.* + -Y^1.] Full of germs; unclean, polluted.

1912 P. A. AMOS *Processes Flour Manuf.* xxi. 202 Flaking ..is especially noticeable upon soft, damp, or germy stock. **1933** DYLAN THOMAS *Let.* (1966) 70 Remember this: each rose is wormy. And every lovely woman's germy. **1935** M. DE LA ROCHE *Young Renny* xiv. 123 Mary has washed this child's offering. It will put these new germy ideas in his head. **1970** *Guardian* 6 Apr. 9/2 A natural slut can languish unwashed, hairy, germy and odorous.

†**gernative**, *a.* *Obs.*$^{-1}$ [? f. *gern* GIRN *v.* + -ATIVE.] ? Addicted to 'girning' or grumbling.

1608 MIDDLETON *Trick to Catch Old One* IV. v, Out, you gernatiue queane.

gernet(t, obs. form of GARNET^1 and ^{2}.

gern(i)er(e, obs. form of GARNER.

†**'gernut**. *Obs.* [? mistake for *yir(d)nut, ernut*, EARTH-NUT; but cf. F. *gernotte* or *jarnote* (Littré s.v. *Terre-noix*), which recalls the Sw. *jordnöt.*] (See quot.)

1693 ROBINSON in *Phil. Trans.* XVII. 826 The Roots of our *Bulbocastanum*..commonly call'd Pig-nuts and Gernuts in the North, lie very deep, and fatten Hogs.

†**gero'comical**, *a.* *Obs.*$^{-1}$ [f. Gr. γηροκομικ-ός, f. γηροκομία (see next) + -AL^1.] Pertaining to the treatment of the aged.

1666 J. SMITH *Old Age* (ed. 2) 257 It is my earnest desire that Physicians would study the Gerocomical part of Physick more than they do.

gerocomy (dʒɪə'rɒkəmɪ). *rare.* [ad. Gr. γηροκομία, f. γηρο-, γῆρας old age + -κομία tending.] The science of the treatment of the aged.

1818 in TODD. **1885** FOTHERGILL *Dis. Sedent. Life* xxxii.

gerofleis, obs. form of GILLYFLOWER.

Geronomite (dʒə'rɒnəmaɪt). Also **Geronymite**. [a. Sp. or It. *geronomita*, repr. med.L. *Hierōnymīta.*] = HIERONYMITE.

1754 FIELDING *Voy. Lisbon* Wks. 1882 VII. 118 Close by ..is a large convent of Geronymites. **1782** R. CUMBERLAND *Anecd. Em. Painters* (1787) I. 70 A monk..of the order of Geronimytes [*sic*]. **1868** LD. HOUGHTON *Select. fr. Wks.* 228 A grey Geronomite This answer to his ecstacy returned.

gerontarchical (ˌdʒɛrən'tɑːkɪkəl), *a.* *rare.* [f. Gr. γεροντ-, γέρων old man + -αρχ-ος ruling + -IC + -AL^1. (In this and the three following words, many scholars would pronounce the initial letter as (g), not as (dʒ).)] Pertaining to, of the nature of, government by old men.

1884 *Med. Times* May 669/2 It [the Apothecaries' Company] preferred to retain its gerontarchical constitution.

gerontic (dʒə'rɒntɪk), *a.* [f. as prec. + -IC. Also in erroneous form *geronic*, from the Gr. nom. case.] Of or pertaining to old age, senile.

1885 FOTHERGILL *Dis. Sedent. Life* xxxii. 279 There are a large series of geronic troubles from which old ladies are free. **1885** *Syd. Soc. Lex.*, *Gerontic.*

gerontocracy (ˌdʒɛrən'tɒkrəsɪ). [f. Gr. γεροντ-, γέρων old man + -κρατία government. Cf. F. *gerontocratie.*] The system of government by old men. Also, a governing body consisting of old men.

1830 *Examiner* 643/1 The adjustment of the qualification of candidates involves the entire question between the gerontocracy and the young men. **1877** R. LOWE in *Fortn. Rev.* 1 Oct. 445 By making a Parliament already too old older, and already too rich richer—a plutocracy, and a gerontocracy.

gerontocratic (dʒɛˌrɒntəʊ'krætɪk), *a.* [f. GERONTOCRACY: see -CRAT and -IC.] Of, pertaining to, or characteristic of a gerontocracy.

1950 *African Studies* Dec. 159 Some anthropologists are of the opinion that gerontocratic age-groups are an invention of the Negro. **1957** P. WORSLEY *Trumpet shall Sound* ii. 40 Many youths looked forward to migrant labour as an exciting liberation from parental and gerontocratic control. **1957** V. W. TURNER *Schism & Continuity in Afr. Soc.* iii. 81 Grandparents..belong to the generation which exerts gerontocratic political and jural authority in the matrilineal village.

gerontogeous (dʒərɒntəʊ'dʒiːəs), *a.* Also **-gæous**. [f. Gr. γεροντ-, γέρων old man + γαῖα, γῆ earth + -OUS.] Of plants, etc.: Belonging to the Old World (i.e. the eastern hemisphere).

1880 GRAY *Struct. Bot.* 413/1 *Gerontogœous* [sic], belonging to the Old World. **1884** in *Cassell's Encycl. Dict.*, *Gerontogeous.* **1885** in *Syd. Soc. Lex.*, *Gerontogæous.*

gerontology (ˌdʒɛrən'tɒlədʒɪ). [f. Gr. γεροντ-, γέρων old man + -O + -LOGY.] The scientific study of old age and of the process of ageing.

1903 [see THANATOLOGY]. **1954** *Medical Press* 25 Aug. 180/1 The science of gerontology..includes the medical and biologic, the psychologic and sociologic, the economic and philosophic aspects of ageing. **1967** [see GERIATRICS].

Hence **geˌronto'logical** *a.*, of or pertaining to gerontology; **ˌgeron'tologist**, an expert in, or student of, gerontology.

1941 *Time* 22 Sept. 48 First problem facing the gerontologists is to get funds for research. **1944** *Science* 8 Dec. 508 Thus McCay, referring to gerontological work, expressed the need [etc.]. **1954** *Medical Press* 25 Aug. 180/1 No such science as a 'science of ageing' has actually been constituted—even, apparently, where most attention has been given to gerontological studies. **1955** *New Biol.* XVIII. 29 The gerontologist, with the prolongation of human life in mind, is interested in something..which is in no sense comparable with the evolution of sight. **1966** *Listener* 21 Apr. 573/1 Muscle aging is of particular interest, however, for gerontologists—people, that is, who are working on the nature and control of age changes. **1967** *New Scientist* 19 Jan. 160/1 The relatively small numbers engaged in gerontological research in Britain.

gerontomorphic (dʒəˌrɒntəʊ'mɔːfɪk), *a.* [f. Gr. γεροντ-, γέρων old man + -O + μορφή form + -IC.] Of, pertaining to, or designating anatomical specialization most fully represented in the mature male of a species.

1939 C. S. COON *Races of Europe* iv. 85 It represents a gerontomorphic or sexually differentiated Mediterranean or Galley Hill form. **1959** J. D. CLARK *Prehist. S. Afr.* iv. 86 These two fossils..are, however, not the only remains of this gerontomorphic, proto-Australoid type from Africa, for fragments of three fossil crania were found in 1935. *Ibid.* 88 'Proto-Australoid' type with fully adult anatomical features (gerontomorphic).

gerontophil (dʒə'rɒntəʊfɪl), *a.* [f. Gr. γεροντ-, γέρων old man + -O + -PHIL.] Loving or favouring old people, esp. old men; desiring sexual relations with old people. So as *sb.* So **geronto'philia; geronto'philic** *a.*; **geron'tophilism; geron'tophily**.

1918 E. JONES *Papers on Psycho-Analysis* (ed. 2) xxxviii. 655 Some of the resultants of the 'grand-father-complex' may now be mentioned. The most striking is the tendency to gerontophilia—i.e., a special fondness for old people. **1937** M. HIRSCHFELD *Sex Anomalies* II. v. 90 The third category of psycho-sexual infantilism, in which the individual seeks the object of his desire..among older people (gerontophilia). **1939** JOYCE *Finnegans Wake* 115 Speaking anent Tiberias and other incestuish salacities among gerontophils. **1945** E. WAUGH *Brideshead Revisited* I. vii. 162 Among Julia's friends there was a kind of gerontophilic snobbery; young men were held to be gauche and pimply. **1959** *Listener* 23 July 146/3 She seems to share the gerontophilism which Mlle Sagan has made so popular. **1963** *Times Lit. Suppl.* 18 Jan. 35/1 The English..are notoriously gerontophil, and the surest road to success for a writer or a painter..is to survive to a venerable age. **1964** *Listener* 15 Oct. 603/1 Sado-masochism, gerontophily, a whiff of incest. **1965** *Ibid.* 25 Nov. 869/1 Robin, one of those gerontophil types described by Proust as being so fortunately provided by Nature for the exclusive gratification of old men. **1965** F. SARGESON *Memoirs of Peon* v. 113 It's not that I suspect you of gerontophilia.

geroom. ? *Obs.* *West Indian.* Some kind of fish.

1713 RAY *Syn. Pisc.* 159 [Fishes of Jamaica] *Harengus major*..a Geroom. **1725** SLOANE *Jamaica* II. 282 A Geroom. This was twelve Inches long and two broad..The Snout is longer and sharper than that of a Herring, and the Fins and Tail are larger.

‖**geropiga** (dʒɛrəʊ'piːgə). Also **jerupiga** and (in Dicts.) **gero-, jerupigia**. [a. Pg. *geropiga* = HIERAPICRA.] A mixture of grape-juice, brandy, sugar, and red colouring-matter, manufactured in Portugal, and used in the adulteration of port-wine.

1858 HOMANS *Cycl. Comm.* 814/2 Geropiga or Jerupiga. **1864** *Daily Tel.* 14 Sept., It gets..copper in its pickles, and geropiga in its port wine. **1877** BLACKMORE *Cripps* (1887) 58 The common-room cellars which cannot have too much geropiga.

-gerous, in actual use always **-igerous** (-'ɪdʒərəs), an adjectival suffix f. L. *-ger* bearing (f. root of *gerĕre* to bear) + -OUS. It occurs in a few words representing actual Latin formations, as *cornigerous, florigerous*, and in mod. scientific language is added freely to Latin stems, as in *frondigerous*.

gerraflour, obs. form of GILLYFLOWER.

gerran, gerrard, vars. GARRON^1, GERARD.

gerre, gerret, obs. ff. GAR *v.*, JAR, GARRET.

gerrymander (gɛrɪ'mændə(r), 'dʒɛrɪ-), *sb.* *U.S.* [f. the surname *Gerry*: see quot. 1881.] (See quot. 1868.) Also, one elected by gerrymandering. Also *attrib.*

1812 *Columbian Centinel* 23 May 2/3 The sensibility of the good people of Massachusetts is..awakened to this 'Gerrymander'. **1812** *Massachusetts Spy* 4 Nov. (Th.), Gerrymander Senate. **1813** *Ibid.* 12 May (Th.), An official statement of the returns of voters for senators give[s] twenty nine friends of peace, and eleven gerrymanders. **1868** *Nat. Encycl.* I. 619 *Gerrymander*, a method of arranging election districts so that the political party making the arrangement will be enabled to elect a greater number of representatives than they could on a fair system, and more than they should have in proportion to their numerical strength. **1881** *Mem. Hist. Boston* III. 212 In 1812, while Elbridge Gerry was Governor of Massachusetts, the Democratic Legislature, in order to secure an increased representation of their party in the State Senate, districted the State in such a way that the shapes of the towns forming such a district in Essex county brought out a territory of regular outline. This was indicated on a map which Russell the editor of the 'Continent' hung in his office. Stuart the painter observing it added a head, wings, and claws, and exclaimed 'That will do for a salamander!' 'Gerrymander!' said Russell, and the word became a proverb. **1884** *Times* (weekly ed.) 17 Oct. 17/2 The Ohio Democrats had made a partisan gerrymander of certain districts in order to retain power. **1891** G. W. CURTIS in *Harper's Weekly* 28 Mar. (Funk), Mr. McKinley ..was defeated only by a gerrymander.

gerrymander (gɛrɪ'mændə(r), 'dʒɛrɪ-), *v.* Also *erron.* (in England) **jerrymander**. [f. the sb.] *trans.* To subject (a state, a constituency) to a gerrymander. Also *transf.*, esp. in sense: To manipulate in order to gain an unfair advantage.

1812 *Salem Gaz.* 22 Dec. 2/4 So much..for *War* and *Gerrymandering*. **1812** *N.Y. Post* 28 Dec. 3/1 They attempted also to *Gerrymander* the State for the choice of Representatives to Congress. **1859** BARTLETT *Dict. Amer.*

(ed. 2) Introd. 24. **1862** T. WINTHROP *E. Brothertoft* II. ii. (1876) 111 A great scope of fertile plain, gerrymandered into farms. **1884** *Times* (weekly ed.) 17 Oct. 4/1 A question how the constituencies can be gerrymandered. **1887** SMYTH in *Trans. Amer. Philol. Assoc.* XVIII. 123 Gerrymandering dialect phenomena cannot but hurt a domain of philology that is sadly in lack of material with which to operate. **1890** *Spectator* 20 Sept. 367/2 They either had been 'gerrymandered' or thought they had been 'gerrymandered' out of their fair share of representative power. **1893** *Times* 26 Apr. 9/3 Mr. C—— described Mr. B—— as a political puritan who had grossly gerrymandered the Lancashire bench [of magistrates].

Hence **gerry'mandered** *ppl. a.*; **gerry'-mandering** *vbl. sb.*; also *attrib.* Also **gerry'-manderer**, one who gerrymanders (a constituency, etc.).

1848 BARTLETT *Dict. Amer.*, *Gerrymandering.* **1872** *N.Y. Sunday Merc.* 31 Mar. (Farmer), The Legislature of Ohio intends to prove itself a veritable master in the Gerrymandering business. **1883** *Q. Rev.* Jan. 271 In 1832.. some very remarkable feats of 'jerrymandering' were performed by the Whig Party. **1884** *Ibid.* Oct. 577 It would enable ministers to appeal to a gerrymandered constituency. **1884** *Pall Mall G.* 18 July, We do not think the astutest gerrymanderer could turn the scale. **1893** *Times* 27 Apr. 8/1 He [Mr. Trevelyan] was admirably equipped for passing a gerrymandering Bill of this sort.

gers(s, gers-: see GRASS, GRASS-.

gersdorffite ('gɜːzdɔːfaɪt). *Min.* [Named by Löwe in 1842 after Von Gersdorf, the proprietor of the mine where it was first found.] A sulpharsenide of nickel.

1849 J. NICOL. *Min.* 459 Gersdorffite is used as an ore of nickel. **1892** *Dana's Min.* 90 With normal gersdorffite are classed a number of minerals.

gerse, obs. form of GARSE *sb.*

gerston: see GARSTON.

'gersum, *sb. Obs.* exc. *Hist.* Forms: 1 gær-, gersum(a, 2–6, 9 *Hist.* gersum, 3 garsum, gersom, 5 grassum, 5–6 gersome, girsum(me, gressome, 6 gersumme, -sowme, gyrsome, -soome, -soume, grassumme, gressam, -um, grissume, -ome, 6–7 garsome, 3, 7 gersume, (8 garsom). [OE. *gærsum*, *gersum*, str. masc. and neut. *gærsuma*, *gersuma*, wk. masc. = ON. *gørsimi*, wk. fem., MSw. *görsam.*]

1. A treasure, precious possession; a costly gift.

c **1045** *O.E. Chron.* (MS. C) an. 1035 Harold.. let niman of hyre ealle þa bestan gærsuma. *a* **1100** *Ibid.* (Laud MS.) an. 1047 For neah man sceolde to brecan his stef, ȝif he [Vlf] ne sealde þe mare gersuman. *c* **1175** *Lamb. Hom.* 91 Þa com þe mon mid his gersume to þan apostolum. *a* **1225** *Ancr. R.* 350 Þe gode pilegrim.. ne bereð no garsum. *a* **1300** *Floriz & Bl.* 419 Þureȝ.. þis gersume Ihc am nu þi man bicume. *a* **1300** *Cursor M.* 6753 If theif na gersum has ne gifte. *c* **1420** *Anturs of Arth.* 697 (Thornton) He weddid his wyfe.. Withe gyftes and gersoms [*Douce MS.* garsons: *see* GARRISON]. *c* **1475** *Rauf Coilȝear* 936, I rek nocht of thy riches.. Thy God [? *read* gude] nor thy Grassum set I bot licht.

2. Chiefly *Sc.* A premium or fine paid to a feudal superior on entering upon a holding.

1389 in C. Welch *Tower Bridge* (1894) 79 [An example of a] gersum [for a shop on the bridge occurs in the accounts of 1389]. *c* **1450** HENRYSON in *Bannatyne MS.* (Hunter. Club) 977 Syne vexis him, or half the terme be gane, With pykit querrellis, for to make him fane To flitt, or pay the girsum new agane. **1500–20** DUNBAR *Poems* xvii. 13 Mailis and gersomes rasit ouir hie. **1530** *Test. Ebor.* (Surtees) V. 288 In recompense of fynes and garsomes that I toke of his tenementes. **1560** ROLLAND *Seven Sages* (ed. Laing) 221 His maillis, gersowmes, and daylie rent. **1610** HOLLAND *Camden* 474 It paieth.. an hundred shillings for a Gersume to the Queene. **1682** HICKERINGILL *Wks.* (1716) II. 5 Except the Place might cost somewhat at the entrance and admittance for a Garsome or Fine. **1703** THORESBY *Let. to Ray* (E.D.S.), *Garsom*, 'a garsom', a foregift at entring a farm, a Gods-penny. **1708** *Termes de la Ley*, *Gersuma* is an obsolete Word, for a Fine or Sum of Money. **1851** SIR F. PALGRAVE *Norm. & Eng.* I. 592 According to the feudal system a gersum was rendered to the Seigneur upon the vassal's death.

attrib. **1567** in *Maitland's Hist. Edinb.* (1753) 211 The Interess and Gersome Silver yat sal happin to be obteinit yairfore.

† **'gersum**, *v. Obs.* [f. the sb.] *trans.* To subject to a fine, impose a fine upon. *to gersume in*: to admit to possession of in consideration of a fine or rent.

1483 *Cath. Angl.* 151/1 To Garsumme (*A.* Gersome), *gressummare.* **1502** *Will of T. Martyn* (Somerset Ho.), To my son.. as many acres of land as he is garsumed in of myn own lande.

gert, dial. form of GREAT.

gertcha ('gɜːtʃə), *int.* Also gercha, gertcher. Vulgar corruption of *get away* (or *along*) *with you*, etc., used esp. as a derisive expression of disbelief.

1937 PARTRIDGE *Dict. Slang* 323/1 Gertcher, get out of it, you! **1937** C. DAY LEWIS *Starting Point* 204 Gurtcher! If Voycey was to let 'imself go, Sid'd wake up in 'ospital. **1939** 'J. BELL' *Death at Half-Term* vii. 132 'Go down to the Old Vic sometime and see the real thing for yourself.' 'Gercha!' said Inspector Mitchell. **1949** J. B. PRIESTLEY *Delight* xxxii. 89 'One of the most energetic and prolific of our authors...' Gertcha! **1963** 'G. CARR' *Lewker in Norway* ii. 30 'Gertcha!' The orator.. elbowed him away.

gerth(e, gertt(e, obs. ff. GIRTH, GREAT.

gerund ('dʒɛrʌnd, -ənd). [ad. L. *gerund-ium*, app. f. *gerundum* = *gerendum*, gerund of *gerĕre* to carry on.] A form of the Lat. vb. capable of being construed as a sb., but retaining the regimen of the vb. Hence applied to forms functionally equivalent in other langs., e.g. to the Eng. verbal noun in *-ing* when used rather as a part of the vb. than as a sb.

1513 LILLY *Introd. Gram.* (1549) Bijb, There be moreouer belongyng to the infinitiue mode of verbes certayn voyces called gerundes.. whiche haue bothe the actyue and passiue significacion. **1591** PERCIVALL *Sp. Dict.* Cjb, There is only one Gerund ending in *do.* **1668** WILKINS *Real Char.* 446 Gerunds and Supines are unnecessary inflexions of Verbs, the notion of them being expressible by the Infinitive Mode, whose Cases they are. **1762** LOWTH *Eng. Gram.* 111 The Participle with a Preposition before it, and still retaining its Government, answers to what is called in Latin the Gerund. **1826** SYD. SMITH *Wks.* (1859) II. 100/1 He is driven to absolute despair by gerunds. **1872** MORRIS *Hist. Outl. Eng. Accid.* xiii. 179 We usually abridge sentences containing the verbal substantive, so that it looks like a gerund.

b. *Comb.* (used derisively), as **gerund-grinder**, one who instructs in Latin grammar; a pedantic teacher; **gerund-grinding**, instruction in Latin grammar; pedantic instruction generally; **gerund-grindery**, a classical school; **gerund-stone**, the imaginary grindstone of a 'gerund-grinder'.

1710 *Fanatick Feast* 6 The next was Cl——s, the walking Gerund-grinder, a noisie wrangling Sophist. **1762** STERNE *Tr. Shandy* V. xxxii, Here is the glass for pedagogues.. gerund-grinders, and bear-leaders, to view themselves in. **1827** HONE *Every-day Bk.* II. 33 Gerund-grinding and parsing are usually prepared for at the last moment. **1831** CARLYLE *Sart. Res.* (1858) 64 An inanimate, mechanical Gerund-grinder. **1864** *Reader* 1 Oct. 410/3 With less enthusiasm and tenderness, the author would probably have consented to wield his tawse and turn the 'gerundstone' in time-honoured style. **1882** *Macm. Mag.* XLV. 232 The man of theory will always continue to think and speak of the professed pedagogue as a 'gerund-grinder'. **1887** *Ch. Times* 20 May, How can it be right for clergymen to earn hundreds or even thousands a year, say, by gerund-grinding or by managing a great gerund-grindry?

gerundial (dʒɪ'rʌndɪəl), *a.* [f. L. *gerundi-um* (see GERUND) + -AL¹.] Pertaining to or of the nature of a gerund. Also quasi-*sb.*, *ellipt.* for *gerundial infinitive.*

1846 WORCESTER cites LATHAM. **1862** MARSH *Eng. Lang.* 47 The English.. dropped the characteristic ending of the gerundial, thus reducing it to the infinitive form. **1872** MORRIS *Hist. Outl. Eng. Accid.* xiii. 177 The infinitive had a dative form expressed by the suffix *e*, and governed by the preposition *to.* This is sometimes called the gerundial infinitive.

Hence **ge'rundially** *adv.*

1860 MARSH *Lect. Eng. Lang.* xxix. 655 The Icelandic active participle is used gerundially as a passive.

gerundie, obs. var. GYRONNY. *Her.*

gerundival (dʒɛrən'daɪvəl), *a.* [f. L. *gerundīvus* (see next) + -AL¹.] Of or pertaining to a gerundive; of the nature of a gerundive.

1884 WHITNEY in *Trans. Amer. Philol. Assoc.* XV. 119 The line between the gerundival and the more ordinary adjective use is in other cases not always easy to draw... Never having any other than a gerundival meaning.

gerundive (dʒɪ'rʌndɪv), *a.* and *sb.* [ad. late L. *gerundīvus (modus)*, f. *gerundium* GERUND. Cf. F. *gérondif.*]

A. *adj.*

1. Pertaining to, akin to, or of the nature of, a gerund. (Cf. B. 2.)

1612 BRINSLEY *Pos. Parts* (1615) 23 Is it then properly a Participle of the future in *dus*, when it signifieth Actiuely? *A.* No. It is rather an Adjectiue Gerundiue. **1868** MAX MÜLLER *Stratif. Lang.* 30 In Sanskrit.. the so-called gerundive participle.. signifies that a thing is necessary or proper to be done. **1885** SIR P. PERRING *Hard Knots* 307 This use of the Gerundive participle will hardly be disputed. **1894** W. M. LINDSAY *Lat. Lang.* 543 The origin of the Gerundive suffix still remains doubtful.

2. *humorous nonce-use.* Having to do with gerunds; crammed with gerunds.

a **1616** BEAUM. & FL. *Wit at Sev. Weap.* I. ii, That Gerundive [printed *Gerundine*] maw of yours, that without *Do* will end in *Di* and *Dum* instantly.

B. *sb.*

1. = GERUND. (So F. *gérondif.*)

1483 *Cath. Angl.* 154/2 A Gerundyfe, *gerundium.* **1520** WHITINTON *Vulg.* (1527) 3 Somtyme quis qui is gouerned.. of yᵉ gerundyue. **1851** G. BROWN *Gram. of Eng. Gram.* (1873) 466 *Gerundives* are participles governed by prepositions; but, there being little or no occasion to distinguish these from other participles, we seldom use this name. **1896** TOYNBEE *Brachet's Hist. Gram. Fr. Lang.* §553.

2. In Latin grammar, a verbal adjective, of the nature of a passive participle, expressing the idea of necessity or fitness: its suffix is the same as that of the gerund. Hence applied to forms of like meaning in other languages.

1706 in PHILLIPS (ed. Kersey), *Gerundive* (in Grammar) an Adjective made of a Gerund. **1721–1792** in BAILEY. **1847** KENNEDY *Elem. Lat. Gram.* 174 For signifying Necessity Passively, the Gerundive is used Impersonally in the Neuter Gender. **1881** BRADLEY *Arnold's Lat. Prose* §391 The use of the gerundive is confined to transitive verbs, including deponents.

3. *Comb.*, as ***gerundive-making*** adj.

1892 WHITNEY *Max Müller* 71 The gerundive-making suffixes *tavya* and *anīya.*

Hence **ge'rundively** *adv.*, in the manner of a gerund; as, or in place of, a gerund.

1849 J. W. GIBBS *Philol. Studies* (1857) 92 The participle used gerundively does not differ, in external form, from the ordinary participle.

gerusia (gɛ'ruːzɪə). [a. L. *gerūsia*, Gr. γερουσία, f. γέρων old man.] An assembly of elders, *spec.* the senate in Sparta and other Dorian cities.

1838 THIRLWALL *Greece* II. xi. 41 The old Athenian council came nearer in numbers to the Spartan *gerusia.* **1852** GROTE *Greece* II. lxxxi. (1856) X. 549 Aristotle assimilates.. the Gerusia of Carthage.. to that of Sparta. **1835** tr. *Wellhausen's Proleg. Hist. Israel* 514 At the side of the high priest stood the gerusia of the town of Jerusalem.

Gervais (ʒɛrve). [f. the name of Charles *Gervais*, French cheese-maker (1830–92).] In full ***Gervais cheese.*** The proprietary name of a soft, creamy cheese.

1896 LONG & BENSON *Cheese* v. 60 The Gervais cheese is a delicate little luxury produced.. by M. Gervais and M. Pommel... Gervais is a mixture of cream and milk. **1902** [see BONDON]. **1950** J. G. DAVIS *Dict. Dairying* 120 *Gervais cheese.* This is a popular French soft cheese and is usually made from two parts of whole milk and one of thin cream. **1951** E. DAVID *French Country Cooking* 197 Pound 6 ozs. of *Petit Suisse* (Pommel) or *Demi-Sel* (Gervais) cheeses with ½ teacup of cream or milk.

† **'gery**, *a. Obs.* [f. GERE + -Y¹.] Changeable, fitful, capricious.

c **1386** CHAUCER *Knt.'s T.* 678 Right as the friday, soothly for to telle, Now it shyneth, now it reyneth faste, Right so can geery Venus ouer caste The heirtes of hir folk. **1399** LANGL. *Rich. Redeles* III. 130 Gyuleris, Ioyfful, ffor here gery Iaces. **1412–20** LYDG. *Chron. Troy* I. iv, This gery fortune, this lady recheles. *c* **1430** —— *Min. Poems* (Percy Soc.) 24 A gery march his stondis doth disclose. **1430–40** —— *Bochas* III. vii. (1554) 80 The gery Romains, stormie and vnstable. *a* **1529** SKELTON *Ware The Hawke* 66 His seconde hawke waxid gery, And was with flying wery.

Hence † **'geriful** *a. Obs.*⁻⁰ (see quot.; perh. mistake for GERFUL); also † **'geriness**, changeableness.

1412–20 LYDG. *Chron. Troy* I. v, By gerinesse of this her reuolution. *a* **1420** HOCCLEVE *De Reg. Princ.* 69, I was adredde so of hir gerynesse. **1616** BULLOKAR, *Gerifull*, changeable: sometime cruell.

Gerzean (gə'ziːən), *a. Archæol.* [f. El *Gerzeh*, name of a district in Egypt + -AN.] Of, pertaining to, or designating the middle period of the ancient pre-Dynastic culture in Egypt.

1925 *Catal. Antiquities at Badari* (*Brit. Sch. Archæol. in Egypt*) 3 Approximate Dates. 13,000 B.C... Badarian Age, 10,000 B.C... Amratian Age, 9,000 B.C... Gerzean Age. **1928** BRUNTON & CATON-THOMPSON *Badarian Civilisation* I. i. 1 By 'Predynastic' is meant the age.. which has been subdivided into the three divisions of Early (or Amratian), Middle (or Gerzean), and Late (or Semainian). **1949** W. F. ALBRIGHT *Archæol. of Palestine* iv. 70 There was a large village and cemetery of Middle Gerzean date, roughly from about the third quarter of the fourth millennium.

ges, gesant(e, obs. forms of GUESS, JESSANT.

‖ **Gesamtkunstwerk** (gə'zamtkʊnstvɜːk). [G., f. *gesamt* total + *kunstwerk* work of art.] In the æsthetic theory of Richard Wagner (1813–83), an ideal work of art in which drama, music, and other performing arts are integrated and each is subservient to the whole.

1939 B. FLES tr. *Křenek's Music Here & Now* 223 Wagner went so far as to lower his orchestra into a cavity below the audience's line of vision to emphasize the illusionary character of his *Gesamtkunstwerk*, or 'symbiosis of the arts'. **1947** A. EINSTEIN *Mus. Romantic Era* xix. 356 In his *Gesamtkunstwerk* all the individual arts were supposed to give up something of their own nature in order to create a higher unity. **1948** L. SPITZER *Linguistics & Lit. Hist.* iv. 160 The nephew.. lends his voice to imitating an orchestra.. and impersonating a Wagnerian-like *Gesamtkunstwerk.* **1966** *Listener* 6 Oct. 517/3 Whether Gascoyne saw his poem in the light of a *Gesamtkunstwerk* I'm not qualified to say.

gesarne, geserne: see GISERNE.

‖ **Gesellschaft** (gə'zɛlʃɑːft, -æ-). Also with lower-case initial. [G., f. *gesell(e)* companion + *-schaft* -SHIP.] A social relationship between individuals based on duty to society or to an organization; contrasted with GEMEINSCHAFT. So ***Gesellschaft-like*** adj. [G. *gesellschaftlich*].

1887, etc. [see GEMEINSCHAFT]. **1964** GOULD & KOLB *Dict. Soc. Sci.* 286/1 *Gesellschaft*-like social systems are those in which rational will (*Kürwille*) has primacy.

gesem, -en, gesian, vars. GESINE, *Obs.*

gesier, obs. var. GIZZARD.

† **gesine**. *Obs.* Forms: 3–4 gesen, -in, geysene, gisin, 4–5 gesine, gesyn(e, 5 gysyn(e, gesem, jasane, jesaine, jesyne, gesian, 6 *Sc.* gissane,

jesing, 8 *Sc.* gizzen, jizzen. [a. OF. *gesine*, f. *gesir* to lie:—L. *jacēre*.] Childbed.

a 1300 *Cursor M.* 8594 On a night bath lighter war þai, At ans bath in gesen lai. *c* 1425 WYNTOUN *Cron.* v. i. 19 The modyr held bed in gysyne. *a* 1450 *Knt. de la Tour* (1868) 109 Moder vnto the said Joseph, of whom she deyed in gesyne. *c* 1450 *Cov. Myst.* (Shaks. Soc.) 150 The for to comforte in gesyne this day, Tweyn gode mydwyvis I have brought here. 1480 CAXTON *Chron. Eng.* cxxxiii. 112 William swore by God that whan he were aryse of his gysyn he wold lyght a thousand candels to the kyng of fraunce. ? *a* 1500 *Chester Pl.* (E.E.T.S.) ix. 246 (Harl. MS.) He that made vs meete on playne and offer to Mary in her Iesaine [*Addit. MS.* jasane]. 1576 *Pitcairn's Crim. Trials* I. 51 And sche new rissine out of gissane. 1596 DALRYMPLE tr. *Leslie's Hist. Scot.* IX. 151 The Quene in Jesing sair seik. 1785 FORBES *Dominie Depos'd* 30 (with *Poems in Buchan Dial.*) She made poor Maggy lie in gizzen.

attrib. 1768 Ross *Helenore* (1789) 13 The jizzen-bed wi' rantry leaves was sain'd.

ge'sith. *O.E. Antiq.* [OE. *ȝesīþ* companion = OS. *gisīð*, OHG. *gi-sind* (Ger. *gesind*).] An attendant or companion of a king; hence, like med.L. *comes* COUNT, used as a designation of rank.

1861 PEARSON *Early & Mid. Ages Eng.* 72 Dependent on the king, and on the nobles, were the gesith or thanes. 1881 *Athenæum* 17 Sept. 360/2 The personal followers, the gesiths or thegns, on the one hand, and on the other the independent nobility and the national militia.

b. *attrib.*, as **gesith-socn**, an alleged Old English division of the county.

(But the word is spurious: see Stubbs *Sel. Charters* Glossary s.v. *Sithessocna*, and Bosw.-Toller s.v. *Scip-fylleð*.) 1872 E. W. ROBERTSON *Hist. Ess.* 118 Every county was at this time divided into Hundreds and Gesith-socns.

gesling, -lyng, obs. forms of GOSLING.

‖**Gesnera** (ˈdʒɛsnərə). *Bot.* Also **gesneria** (the spelling preferred by Linnæus and now the accepted form). [mod.L., named after *Conrad von Gesner*, a naturalist and scholar of Zürich, of the 16th c.] A genus of tropical plants (N.O. *Gesneraceæ*); also a plant of this genus.

[1737 LINNÆUS *Genera Plantarum* 179 *Gesneria*. Gesnera *Plum*.] 1845 *Bot. Mag.* LXXI. Tab. 4152 *Schiede's Gesneria* .. is another lovely addition to the many beautiful *Gesnerias* now cultivated in our stoves. 1858 GLENNY *Gard. Every-day Bk.* 186/1 Some of the taller Gesneras may require a slight support. 1882 *Garden* 11 Nov. 420/2 There are not many stove plants more valuable than Gesneras. 1901 G. NICHOLSON *Dict. Gard.* Suppl. II. 389/1 *Gesnera*. According to the 'Index Kewensis' the correct spelling is that of Linnæus—*Gesneria*. 1956 *Dict. Gardening* (R. Hort. Soc.) (ed. 2) II. 886/1 The Gesnerias being tropical, need stove conditions. 1961 *Amat. Gardening* 14 Oct. Suppl. 23/3 The gesneras are related to the gloxinias and require very much the same conditions.

gesneraceous (ˌdʒɛsnəˈreɪʃəs), *a. Bot.* [f. prec. + -ACEOUS.] Of or pertaining to the order *Gesneraceæ* (of which GESNERA is the type).

1882 *Gard. Chron.* XVII. 43 Lysionotus serrata, an Indian Gesneraceous plant, is a pretty addition to stove plants.

gesnerad (ˈdʒɛsnəræd). [f. as prec. + -AD: see -AD 1 d.] A plant of the genus GESNERA.

1882 *Garden* 4 Feb. 74/1 It is well known that most of the Gesnerads are easily increased by means of leaf cuttings.

gesning, var. GESTENING.

gespen, var. GISPIN, *Obs.*

gess(e, obs. f. GUESS, and of *guests* pl. of GUEST.

gess, gessant, obs. forms of JESS, JESSANT.

gessemine, -my, obs. ff. JASMINE, JESSAMY.

gessera(i)n, -a(u)nte, -en, -on, vars. JAZERANT.

gessling, -lyng, obs. forms of GOSLING.

‖**gesso** (ˈdʒɛsəʊ). Also 8–9 **gess(e**. [a. It. *gesso*:—L. *gypsum*: see GYPSUM.]

1. Plaster of Paris; gypsum. †**a.** in the native state (*obs.*). **b.** as prepared for use in painting and sculpture.

1596 W. P. *Bk. Secr.* D iij a, Fill the vessell halfe full and stop it well with Gesso. *Ibid.* E j b, Gesso when it is first put into the wine maketh it bitter. 1698 in *Phil. Trans.* XX. 306 There are found with it Red-bole .. and Plaister Gypsum or Gesso. 1851 RUSKIN *Stones Ven.* (1874) I. App. 370 No colour is so noble as the colour of a good painting on canvas or gesso. 1859 GULLICK & TIMBS *Paint.* 7 The Venetians .. took the precaution of spreading the composition of size and gesso as thinly as possible. 1874 J. FERGUSSON in *Contemp. Rev.* Oct. 756 A coating of gesso—*vulgo* plaster—was to be applied. 1886 *Athenæum* 6 Feb. 207/2 These decorations have been modelled or 'raised' in gesso.

c. A prepared surface of plaster as a ground for painting.

1860 J. HEWITT *Anc. Arm.* III. 497 This [shield] .. is formed of wood .. faced with canvas, on which is laid a gesso to receive the painting and gilding.

†**2.** A work of art executed in plaster. *Obs.*

1758 *Chron.* in *Ann. Reg.* 84/2 Any painter, sculptor .. or other artist to whom the study of these gesses may be of use, will have liberty to draw or model at any time.

3. *attrib.*, as ***gesso figure, ornament, work.***

1745 H. WALPOLE *Let. to Mann* 4 Jan. (1857) I. 336, I must tell you that I have at last received the cases; three with gesse figures, and one with [etc.]. 1881 *Athenæum* 7 May 626/3 The design of the gesso ornaments [of the Painted Chamber], with their colours, gilding, and decoration, could still be made out. 1890 *Archæol.* LII. 693 In the centre a gold ring of gesso work with slightly raised bosses.

gest (dʒɛst), *sb.*[1] Forms: 3–5, 8–9 **geste**, (4–6 **jeste**), 4–5 **geest**, (4 **jeest**), 6 *Sc.* **geist**, 4– **gest**, (4–7 **jest**). See also JEST. [a. OF. *geste*, *jeste* (fem.), action, exploit (chiefly *pl.*), romance; ad. L. *gesta* actions, exploits, neut. pl. of *gestus*, pa. pple. of *gerĕre* to carry on (war, etc.), perform.]

1. *pl.* Notable deeds or actions, exploits (later also *sing.*, a deed, exploit); esp. the deeds *of* a person or people as narrated or recorded, history. *Obs.* exc. *arch.*

There seems to be no certain example in ME. of the sing. *gest* = an action. In the passages quoted by Mätzner from the *Destruction of Troy* (620, 3286) the alliteration proves that the *g* is hard, and the words are really *gift* (*gyfte* misread as *gyste*) and *guest*.

a 1300 *Cursor M.* 123, I sal .. tell sum gestes principale; For all may na man haue in talle. *a* 1340 HAMPOLE *Psalter* xlvii. 12 That ȝe tell .. til all þat will here þe gestis of halymen. *c* 1350 *Will. Palerne* 2780 þe hert .. fayn was a-way to fle for fere of mo gestes. *a* 1450 *Knt. de la Tour* (1868) 40 Hit is conteyned in the gestis of Athenes that there was an holy hermite. 1494 FABYAN *Chron.* v. lxxvi. 55 Turpinus that wrote the Gestes of the great Charles, saythe [etc.]. 1534 WHITINTON *Tullyes Offices* I. (1540) 35 The noble iestes at home by policy be not inferyor to the valyaunt actes in warre. 1558 PHAER *Æneid* I. B iij, He seeth among them all the iestes of Troy, and stories all And wars. 1591 SPENSER *M. Hubberd* 978 Fond Ape .. into whose brest Never crept thought of honor, nor brave gest. *a* 1656 USSHER *Ann.* VI. (1658) 121 [Diodorus] hudling together the gests of 2 years into one [etc.]. 1762–71 H. WALPOLE *Vertue's Anecd. Paint.* (1786) I. 35 He had .. rather employ master William and Edward of Westminster to paint the gestes of the kings of Antioch. 1816 *Monthly Mag.* XLII. 326 He also wrote *De Re Navali*, and a poem on his father's gests. 1834 SIR H. TAYLOR *2nd Pt. Artevelde* v. iii, I .. put to sea, Errant for geste and enterprise of wit. 1844 MRS. BROWNING *L.E.L.'s Last Quest.* iv, When knightly gestes and courtly pageantries Were broken in her visionary eyes. 1876 BESANT & RICE *Gold. Butterfly* xxxvii, Her bosom heaved when she heard of heroic gest.

b. In general sense: Action, performance. *rare.*

c 1460 J. RUSSELL *Bk. Nurture* 857 Now have y shewyd yow, my son, somewhat of dyuerse Iestis þat ar remembred in lordes courte þere as all rialte restis.

2. A story or romance in verse: also simply (in later use), a story, tale. ***in gest*** = in verse, in the manner of a metrical romance. ***the English gest, the French gest***: metrical chronicles of England, of France. *Obs.* exc. *Hist.*

a 1300 *K. Horn* 522 Murie was þe feste Al of faire gestes. *a* 1300 *Havelok* 2328 þer mouthe men se .. Romanz reding on þe bok; þer mouthe men here þe gestes singe. 13.. *K. Alis.* 30 Now pais holdith .. And ye schole here a noble jeste, Of Alisaundre, theo riche kyng. *c* 1330 R. BRUNNE *Chron. Wace* (Rolls) 38 After þe Bretons þe Inglis camen, þe lordschip of þis land þai namen .. þat calle men now þe Inglis gest. *c* 1386 CHAUCER *Melib.* Prol. 15 Lat se wher thou kanst tellen aught in geeste Or telle in prose somwhat at the leeste. *c* 1400 MAUNDEV. (1839) xx. 220 Mynstrelles, that syngen Songes and tellen Gestes. 14.. *Sir Beues* (MS. N) 4313 + 245 Men tellith bothe in gest & ryme, Thei were leide in maner of shryne. *c* 1440 *Partonope* 405 Thus tellyth now the french geest. 1494 FABYAN *Chron.* VII. ccxxxviii. 278 The bonys of King Arture, and his wyfe Gueynour .. were founden by a synger of gestys. 1500–20 DUNBAR *Poems* lviii. 4 Ay is the ouir-word of the geist, Giff thame the pelffe to pairt amang thame. 1565 GOLDING *Ovid's Met.* VII. (1593) 180 Duke Cephal weeping told this tale to Phocus and the rest, Whose eies were also moist with teares to heare the piteous jest. 1577–87 HOLINSHED *Chron.* I. 69 2 The tales of Robin Hood, or the gests written by Ariost the Italian in his booke intituled *Orlando furioso*. 1828–40 TYTLER *Hist. Scot.* (1864) I. 298 We know .. that there were gests and historic ballads written upon the story of Wallace. 1858 DORAN *Crt. Fools* 89 The harper probably only accompanied the reciter of the Gest.

†**3. a.** A satirical utterance, lampoon. **b.** An idle tale. *Obs.* with this spelling: for examples of the later use (16–19th c.) see JEST *sb.*

1387 TREVISA *Higden* (Rolls) I. 315 þere [in Sicily] was commedya, song of gestes, firste i-founde. *Ibid.* IV. 229 Cithero made gestes in blame of Salustius [L. *invectiones*]. *c* 1470 HENRY *Wallace* VI. 93 Fy on fortoun, fy on thi frewall quehyll: .. His plesance her till him was bot a gest.

†**gest,** *sb.*[2] *Obs. rare.* [a. OF. *geste*.] Race, kind, family; company.

13.. *K. Alis.* 6413 Ther byside, on the north-est, Buth men off selcouthe gest. *c* 1330 R. BRUNNE *Chron. Wace* (Rolls) 8917 þen dide þe kyng make somons Of bischopes, erles, & barons, & oþer lordes of þe nobleste [*v.r.* folk of noble geste]. —— *Chron.* (1810) 315 þei & all þer geste þat dome salle doute & rew.

gest (dʒɛst), *sb.*[3] *Obs.* exc. *arch.* Also 6, 9 **geste**, 6 **jest**. [ad. F. *geste*, ad. L. *gestus*, masc. (*u*-stem) gesture, bearing, f. *gerĕre* to bear, deport (oneself).]

1. Bearing, carriage, mien.

1509 BARCLAY *Shyp of Folys* (1570) 19 Ye fooles .. Of euill behauiour, gest and countenaunce. 1568 *Knt. of Courtesy* 394 He went .. With wofull mone and sory jest. 1590 SPENSER *F.Q.* III. viii. 8 Him needed not instruct .. how to speake, ne how to use his gest. 1844 MRS. BROWNING *Vis. Poets* xcv, Look and geste Of buried saint, in risen rest. 1890 *Cornh. Mag.* June 638 You eat and drink with mincing geste.

2. A movement of a limb; an action, gesture.

a 1521 *Helyas* in Thoms *Prose Rom.* (1858) III. 65 Well manered in all his gestes. 1534 WHITINTON *Tullyes Offices* I. (1540) 85 Some iests [L. *gestus*] of players be not without follyes. 1683 D. A. *Art Converse* 6 That outward and proud Behaviour either in Gests or Speech. 1717 GARTH tr. *Ovid's Met.* XIV. Appulus, The bold Buffoon .. Their Motion mimicks, but with Gests obscene. 1781 JUSTAMOND *Priv. Life Lewis XV*, IV. 181 Count Lally, whom the Chancellor pointed out by a gest [orig. *d'un geste*] to the King. 1844 MRS. BROWNING *Rom. Page* xxxv, Had the knight looked back to the page's geste, I ween he had turned anon.

†**gest,** *sb.*[4] *Obs.* Also 6 **jest(e,** *pl.* **jesses,** 7 **geast, jeyst, ghest,** *pl.* **gesses.** [Later form of GIST[1].] *pl.* The various stages of a journey, esp. of a royal progress; the route followed or planned.

1550 EDW. VI *Jrnl.* in *Lit. Rem.* (Roxb.) 275 The gestis of my progres wer set fourth, wich were thes; from Grenwich to Westmuster [etc.]. 1597 H. MAYNARD in Ellis *Orig. Lett.* Ser. I. II. 274 By that time the Queen meaneth to be with you, if the iestes hold, wch after manie alteracions is so sett downe .. to be with you on Wednesdaie night. 1601 HOLLAND *Pliny* I. 125 Diogneus and Beton .. set down all the geasts and iournies of that prince. 1611 SPEED *Hist. Gt. Brit.* VII. xlii. (1632) 405 The like custome vsed hee in the winter season in his ieysts, and circuits throughout his Country. 1650 FULLER *Pisgah* v. iii. 147 Though in Iacobs Gests, Succoth succeeds the next place to Peniel, yet it follows not, that Iacob with his train went so far in one day. 1654 H. L'ESTRANGE *Chas. I* (1655) 126 His [the king's] gests and motions were much fore-slowed by his making so many halts. 1755 JOHNSON (citing Hanmer) *Gest*, the roll or journal of the several days and stages prefixed, in the progress of our kings.

transf. and *fig.* 1596 J. NORDEN (*title*), A Progresse of Pietie, whose Jesses lead into the Harborough of heavenly Hearts-ease. 1645 QUARLES *Sol. Recant.* VII. 52 Let .. salvage brutes trade there, and lay their Gests Of progresse. 1646 SIR T. BROWNE *Pseud. Ep.* II. ii. 58 It takes not away this vertue of the earth, but more distinctly sets downe the gests and progresse thereof. 1649 H. HAMMOND *Chr. Oblig.* iii. 66 When God hath designed the crosse, the constant post and stage in our gesses to Heaven.

b. *sing.* The time allotted for a halt or stay.

1611 SHAKS. *Wint. T.* I. ii. 41 Ile giue him my Commission To let him there a Moneth behind the Gest Prefix'd for's parting.

†**gest,** *v.*[1] *Obs.* Also 4 **geest**, 4, 6 *Sc.* **geste**. See also JEST *v.* [f. GEST *sb.*[1]] *intr.* To tell a tale, to recite a romance.

c 1340 *Cursor M.* 7256 (Trin.) Whenne þei were gladdest at þe feest Sampson coude wel geest. *c* 1386 CHAUCER *Pars. T.* Prol. 43, I kan nat geeste, Rum, Ram, Ruf by lettre. *c* 1425 *Leg. Rood* (1871) App. 211, I haue ioye forto gest Of þe lambe of love with-oute oþe. 14.. *Sir Beues* (MS. N) 2244 Als feire a man as thei myȝt gest. *c* 1440 *Promp. Parv.* 191/1 Gestyn' yn romawnce, *gestio*.

b. To play or sing as a professional 'gester'.

1508 KENNEDIE *Flyting w. Dunbar* 507 Tak the a fidill, or a floyt and geste.

Hence †**ˈgesting** *vbl. sb.*

c 1440 *Promp. Parv.* 191/2 Gestynge, or romawncynge, *gesticulatus, rythmicatus*.

†**gest,** *v.*[2] *Obs. rare.* [f. L. *gest-*, ppl. stem of *gerĕre* to carry on.] *trans.* To perform; only in phrase ***gested and done.***

1523 LD. BERNERS *Froiss.* Author's Pref. 1 With what labours, daungers, and peryls they [auncyent actes] were gested and done. 1541 PAYNEL *Catiline* xxxii. 50 b, Supplications ware alwey decreed for a thinge prosperously gested and done against an ennemie.

gest, obs. f. JESS; obs. pa. t. of GUESS.

gest(e, obs. form of GUEST, JEST, JOIST.

gestagen (ˈdʒɛstədʒən). Also **gestogen.** [f. GESTA(TION + -GEN.] Any substance, such as the sex hormone progesterone, having progestational effects. Hence **gestaˈgenic** *a.*

1948 K. MIESCHER in *Rec. Progr. Hormone Res.* III. 47 The class of sexogens comprises the estrogens, the androgens, and the gestagens, as we propose to call the compounds with progestational action. 1949 L. F. & M. FIESER *Nat. Prod. related to Phenanthrene* (ed. 3) iv. 300 There are two types of female sex hormones, exemplified by the estrogens: estradiol, estrone, and estriol; and by progesterone, the sole natural progestational hormone or gestogen. 1958 *Jrnl. Clin. Endocrinol. & Metabolism* XVIII. 338 It has been generally supposed that progesterone is the only naturally occurring substance with a primarily gestagenic effect. 1962 *Lancet* 2 June 1176/1 The addition of œstrogens to the commercial preparations of orally active gestagens has enhanced their efficacy in contraception.

Gestalt, gestalt (gəʃˈtalt). [G., = form, shape.] A 'shape', 'configuration', or 'structure' which as an object of perception forms a specific whole or unity incapable of expression simply in terms of its parts (*e.g.* a melody in distinction from the notes that make it up); cf. CONFIGURATION 6. Freq. *attrib.*, as **Gestalt psychology**, a school of psychology which holds that perceptions, reactions, etc., are Gestalts; also *ellipt.*

[1890 C. VON EHRENFELS in *Vierteljahrsschrift für wissenschaftliche Philosophie* XIV. 249 (*title*) Ueber 'Gestaltqualitäten'.] 1922 K. KOFFKA in *Psychol. Bull.* XIX. 531 The *Gestalt*-psychologists proper. *Ibid.* 574 The *Gestalt* theory is fundamentally incompatible with the associationist's principles. 1924 tr. K. Koffka in *Psyche* V. 80 Gestalt-Psychology has so far got a number of important answers to its questions. *Ibid.* 81 Gestalt-Theory. *Ibid.* 84 Prof. Wertheimer, in his lectures, has treated personality as a Gestalt. 1926 *Encycl. Brit.* Suppl. I. 45/1 The work of the

Gestalt school with its stress upon the unity of psychic processes. *Note*, The Gestalt theorists. **1930** W. Köhler (*title*) Gestalt psychology. **1931** M. Belgion *Human Parrot* i. 15 The Behaviourists and the apostles of *Gestalt*. **1936** A. J. Ayer *Lang., Truth & Logic* ii. 57 The Gestalt psychologists who of all men talk most constantly about genuine wholes. **1941** Auden *New Year Let.* i. 19 A true gestalt where indiscrete Perceptions and extensions meet. **1959** *Times* 13 Feb. 13/5 Webern..eliminates not only rhythm but the *Gestalt* of a melodic line and all traces of coherence by tonality. **1962** [see after-image].

Hence **Ge'staltism**, Gestalt psychology; = configurationism; **Ge'staltist**, one who accepts or practises the principles of Gestalt psychology; a Gestalt psychologist; also as *adj.* Also in loan-words from German: **Gestalt-psychologie**, Gestalt psychology; **Gestalt-qualität**, the quality of a Gestalt; **Gestalt-theorie**, Gestaltism.

1909 E. B. Titchener *Lect. Exper. Psychol. of Thought-Processes* i. i. 32 We may speak of general attributes of sensation, as Ebbinghaus does: or we may speak of *Gestaltqualität*, form of combination, funded character. **1925** I. A. Richards *Princ. Lit. Crit.* iv. 25 There are very many problems of psychology, from those with which some of the exponents of *Gestalt theorie* are grappling to those by which psycho-analysts are bewildered. *Ibid.* xxii. 183 The exponents of *Gestalt-psychologie*. **1931** *Psyche* July 6 The rise of Gestaltists, hormic psychologists and many other varieties. **1933** *Times Lit. Suppl.* 16 Nov. 786/2 His own fivefold scheme of opposed viewpoints (Structure and Function, Association and *Gestaltqualitat*, Introspection and Behaviourism, Mechanism and Teleology, Conscious and Unconscious). **1938** *Mind* XLVII. 377 If Associationism may be regarded as Psychological Enemy No. 1, cannot Gestaltism put in a claim to be at any rate No. 2? **1938** *Amer. Speech* XIII. 295 Mr. Firth's gestaltist chapter on meaning ('Context of Situation') makes excellent sense. **1938** *Brit. Jrnl. Psychol.* July 77 Prof. Spearman's general theory of visual perception must of necessity lead him into conflict with the protagonists of the *Gestalttheorie*. **1951** H. McCloy *Alias Basil Willing* vii. 65 The Gestaltists believed in studying a complete picture of every psychiatric situation.

gestant ('dʒɛstənt), *a.* $rare^{-1}$. [ad. L. *gestant-em*, pres. pple. of *gestāre* to go with young.] Pregnant; in quot. *fig.*

1851 Mrs. Browning *Casa Guidi Wind.* 104 Cannons rolling on, Like blind, slow storm-clouds gestant with the heat Of undeveloped lightnings.

Gestapo (gə'stɑːpəʊ, gɛ-). [G., acronym f. the initial letters of *Ge*heime *Sta*ats-*Po*lizei, Secret State-Police, set up by Hermann Göring in Prussia, 1933, and extended to the whole of Germany in January 1934.] The secret police of the Nazi regime in Germany. Also *transf.*

1934 *New Republic* 18 July 249/2 The names and significance of the..semi-military organizations in Germany..are:..The *Geheime Staats Polizei*, usually called the *Gestapo*, the secret state police of Prussia. **1937** *N.Y. Times Mag.* 21 Nov. 1/3 The spokesmen of the regime,..are taking every opportunity..to ridicule the idea that every German servant girl abroad is a disguised Gestapo agent or a spy. **1940** *Mind* XLIX. 222 Morality..becoming nothing more than subservience to the decrees of a dictator with his Ogpu or Gestapo at his back. **1944** G. B. Shaw *Everybody's Political What's What?* xxiv. 224 The municipal statesman sends his sanitary Gestapo into an unhealthy private house and prosecutes the tenant. **1966** L. P. Davies *Psychogeist* xii. 109 My private Gestapo has already brought the news.

gestar, var. gester, *Obs.*

gestate ('dʒɛsteɪt), *a.* [ad. L. *gestāt-us*, pa. pple. of *gestāre*: see next.] In course of gestation.

1854 Syd. Dobell *Balder* xxiv. 169 The gendering caves and secrets where thy spring Is gestate, and the summer yet to be Seethes dark.

gestate ('dʒɛsteɪt, -'steɪt), *v.* [f. L. *gestāt-*, ppl. stem of *gestāre* to carry, to go with young.] *trans.* To carry in the womb during the period between conception and birth. Also *fig.*

1866 *Pall Mall G.* 31 May 1 There are mammals..whose progeny leave the womb half gestated. **1886** T. Frost *Remin. Country Journalist* x. (1888) 116 [His] mind was then gestating a work of the most original character.

gestation (dʒɛ'steɪʃən). Also 6 -acion. [ad. L. *gestātiōn-em* (n. of action f. *gestāre* to carry) found esp. in sense 1. Cf. F. *gestation* (Cotgr.).] The action of bearing or carrying.

1. A carrying or being carried, e.g., on horseback or in a carriage, regarded as a kind of exercise. Now *rare*.

1533 Elyot *Cast. Helthe* (1541) 49b, There is also another kynde of exercise, whiche is called Gestation..as.. sytting in a chaire, whiche is caried on mens shulders with staves..or syttynge in a boate or barge, whiche is rowed, rydyng on a horse [etc.]. **1562** Bulleyn *Def. agst. Sickness, Vse of Sicke Men* 67b, *Gestacion*, that is to be caried of an other thyng, without any trauaill of the bodie it self. **1606** Holland *Sueton.* 214 He never went forth any iourney (were it but for exercise by way of Gestation), but [etc.]. **1661** Lovell *Hist. Anim. & Min.* Introd., Gestation, increaseth heat..and causeth sleep. **1806** R. Cumberland *Mem.* (1807) II. 238 He..took his morning's circuit on horse-back at a foot's-pace; for his infirmity would not admit of any strong gestation. **1808** *Med. Jrnl.* XIX. 429 Moderate gestation, and a temperate course of diet, will be found to answer the purpose of promoting convalescence. **1822–34** *Good's Study Med.* (ed. 4) III. 251 Gestation, pure air, sea-bathing and every other kind of tonic..are also of the utmost importance. **1871** Sir T. Watson *Lect. Princ. Med.* (ed. 5) II. li. 245 Gestation in a carriage or in a boat, has the same good effects [as equitation] but in a less degree. **1885** in *Syd. Soc. Lex.*

†**2.** The practice of wearing (a ring). *Obs.* $rare^{-1}$.

1646 Sir T. Browne *Pseud. Ep.* iv. iv. 185 Affirming that the gestation of rings upon this hand and finger, might rather be used for their conveniency and preservation, then any cordiall relation.

3. The action or process of carrying young; the condition of being carried in the womb during the period between conception and birth.

Applied by extension to processes somewhat similar, e.g. *dorsal, oral, mammary* or *pouch gestation*.

1615 Crooke *Body of Man* 336 You shall reconcile Hippocrates to himselfe, if you say, that the end of the tenth moneth is the absolute and longest limit of gestation. **1661** Lovell *Hist. Anim. & Min.* Introd., The gestation is various also, the woolf goeth a month or forty daies, the bitch nine weeks. **1751** Smollett *Per. Pic.* (1779) I. i. 38 The comfort of her sister-in-law, during her gestation. **1786** Gilpin in *Mrs. Delany's Life & Corr.* Ser. ii. III. 340 Naturalists tell us, that the noblest animals are the longest in gestation. **1818** Cruise *Digest* (ed. 2) VI. 573 The words 'born in due time afterwards.' Such words, in the case of a man's own children, mean the time of gestation. **1821** *Sporting Mag.* IX. 4 The gestation and foaling, upon which so much has been already written. **1826** Kirby & Sp. *Entomol.* IV. xlii. 162 As to the period of gestation, most insects begin to lay their eggs soon after fecundation has taken place. **1868** Darwin *Anim. & Pl.* I. i. 29 It has been objected that our domestic dogs cannot be descended from wolves or jackals, because their periods of gestation are different.

fig. **1691–1701** Norris *Ideal World* i. Pref. 1 Measuring the perfection of the birth by the presumed time of the gestation [of a literary work]. **1837** Carlyle *Fr. Rev.* III. ii. v, How this Question of the Trial grew laboriously, through the weeks of gestation,..were superfluous to trace here. **1851** R. R. Madden *Shrines Old & New World* II. 606 The work was conceived in prison, and the whole process of gestation was accomplished there. **1879** Geo. Eliot *Theo. Such* xiii. 229 He has a trying gestation of every speech.

gestative ('dʒɛstətɪv), *a.* [ad. L. type **gestātīv-us*, f. *gestā-re* to carry.] Of or pertaining to gestation.

1828 Sir D. Le Marchant *Rep. Claims Barony Gardner* 90 To interfere with and to protract the gestative process.

gestatorial (ˌdʒɛstə'tɔərɪəl), *a.* [f. as next + -al[1].] *gestatorial chair*: a chair in which the Pope is carried on certain occasions. (So F. *chaise gestatoire*; in late L. *sella gestātōria* was used for 'sedan-chair'.)

1864 *Times* 6 Apr. 10/1 Pius IX once more was borne through the nave [of St. Peter's] in his 'gestatorial' chair. **1889** *Catholic Household* 2 Nov. 5/3 His Holiness, carried in the gestatorial chair, entered the hall.

gestatory ('dʒɛstətərɪ), *a. rare.* [ad. L. *gestātōri-us*, f. *gestātōr-em*, *gestātor*, one who carries, f. *gestā re* to carry.] †**a.** Adapted for carrying or wearing (*obs.*). **b.** Of or pertaining to carrying as a form of exercise.

a **1682** Sir T. Browne *Tracts* (1684) 90 The Crowns and Garlands of the Ancients were either Gestatory, such as they wore about their Heads and Necks [etc.]. **1804** *Edin. Rev.* IV. 190 We shall now take leave of Dr. Jackson and his gestatory plan of cure. **1882** *Antiq.* May 187 Gestatory garlands worn round the neck.

†'**gested**, *ppl. a. Obs.* [f. gest $sb.^3$ + -ed[2].] Accompanied with gestures.

1587 Fleming *Contn. Holinshed* III. 1323/1 This answer so smoothlie deliuered, and with such coie lookes and protestation of action gested, that [etc.]. **1731** Fielding *Grub St. Op.* ii. viii, From lips and eyes with gested grace In vain she keeps out charming him.

†**gestelin**. *Obs.*

1591 *Treasurie of Hidden Secrets* ix. A viij, And when it is cold, lay a larde of Quinces in your glasse (called a gestelin glasse) or an earthen pot well glased.

†'**gesten**, *v. Obs.* Forms: 3–4 gestin(e, gistne(n, gestne(n, 4–5 gestyn(ne, 3–5 gesten(e, (9 *dial.* guesten, guessen). [f. *gest* guest + -en[5], but perh. a back-formation from gestening.]

1. *intr.* To receive hospitality; to be entertained as a guest, to lodge.

a **1225** *Ancr. R.* 402 Elie..gistnede mid hire þet he iuond þe two treon gederinde i Sarepte. *a* **1300** *Cursor M.* 14082 He gestind wit þir sisters tua. *a* **1440** *Sir Degrev.* 935 How thei gestened that nyȝt Carp wyll we mare. *c* **1450** *St. Cuthbert* (Surtees) 1259 He gestynd at a huswyf house. *a* **1800** *Fray of Suport* ii. in Scott *Minstrelsy Scott. Bord.* (1802) I. 187 But Tobbet Hob o' the Mains had guesten'd in my house by chance.

2. *trans.* To receive as a guest, lodge, entertain.

a **1300** *Cursor M.* 2712 He..gestend þam wit him þat night. *c* **1315** Shoreham 13 Wanne hi beth deede, In hevene hi beth i-gistned. *c* **1440** *Gesta Rom.* lxi. 257 (Harl. MS.) A semly yonge knyȝte, that was gestenid with me in myn house al this nyȝt. *c* **1450** *St. Cuthbert* (Surtees) 1404 To gestyn commers fra ferr and nere. **1807** Stagg *Poems* 16 The blythe pair..War guessend up i' the loft Reeght snug that neeght.

Hence †'**gestener**, a guest.

c **1375** *Sc. Leg. Saints, Machor* 1186 Lowe we all god, my breþir dere, þat has ws send a gud gestenere.

†'**gestening**, '**gestning**. *Obs.* Also 3–5 gesning, -yng, 4 gistning, gistenynge, gistynnyng. [Of Scandinavian origin: cf. OSw. *gästning*, *gis(t)-*, *ges(t)-*, etc., f. *gästa* v. to lodge as a guest, f. *gäst-er* = ON. *gest-r* guest; in ON. only *gisting* (f. *gista* vb.) is found.] Entertainment as a guest, lodging, hospitality. Also, a banquet, feast.

c **1200** *Trin. Coll. Hom.* 93 þis dai haueð ure drihten ..ȝiarked þat holie gestninge þe he offe specð þus queðinde, *Ecce prandium meum paratum*. *a* **1300** *Floriz & Bl.* 82 Floriz ..hopede come to þat gesninge. *a* **1300** *Vox & Wolf* 256 To colde gistninge he was i-bede. *c* **1340** *Cursor M.* 11750 (Fairf.) þer þai fande na knawinge of quam þai muȝt aske gesteninge. *a* **1400** in *Pol. Rel. & L. Poems* 241 Matheu hat mad a grete gestenyng te Ihesu at home in his whonyyng. *c* **1425** Wyntoun *Cron.* vi. xv. 1638 The Kyng tuk wyth the mylnare hys gesnyng. *c* **1475** *Rauf Coilȝear* 975 That all that wantis harbery Suld haue gestning. **1513** Douglas *Æneis* x. viii. 56, I the beseyk, thou mychty Hercules, Be my faderis gestnyng. **1535** Stewart *Cron. Scot.* (1858) I. 250 King Caratac that gestnyng bocht rycht deir. **1584** Hudson *Du Bartas' Judith* vi. 108 Go fear not again: Wilt thou the sacred gestning then prophane?

†'**gester**. *Obs.* Forms: 4–5 gestour(e, (gestiour, jestour, 5 gestowre), 5 gester. See also jester. [f. gest $v.^1$ + -er[1].] A professional reciter or singer of romances.

c **1380** *Antecrist* in Todd *3 Treat. Wyclif* 128 þei sitten in castels & townes wiþ mynstralcie & lauȝ tur, wiþ tregetours & tomblers, wiþ gestours & japeres. *c* **1384** Chaucer *H. Fame* iii. 108 All manner of minstrales, And jestours, that tellen tales. **1387** Trevisa *Higden* (Rolls) IV. 101 Poetes and gestoures [L. *carminatores*] uppon a pulpet rehersede poysees, gestes and songes. *c* **1440** *Promp. Parv.* 191/2 Gestowre, *gesticulator*. *c* **1460** *Launfal* 430 Launfal..Fyfty fedde povere gestes..Fyfty clodede gestours. **1496** *Dives & Paup.* (W. de W.) i. iv. 36/1 His dedes ben tolde of heraudes and gestours.

gester, obs. form of gesture, *v.*

†**gester(o)n**. *Obs.* Also 5 gestron(e. [Corrupt form of jesserant.] A coat of mail.

1469 *Mann. & Househ. Exp.* (Roxb.) 538 My master paid ..fore werkemaneshipe of a gestrone of maylle, xs. **1509** *Will of Shoo* (Somerset Ho.), My litell gestern. **1522** *Test. Ebor.* (Surtees) V. 148 Coottes of plate, gestrons [etc.]. **1524** *Ibid.* 176 A gesteron covered with buke-skyns.

Comb. **1517** *Nottingham Rec.* III. 140 Roberto Stabuls, gestronmaker.

†'**gestible**, *a. Obs.*$^{-0}$ That may be borne.

1623 Cockeram ii, To be Borne, *Gestible*.

gestic ('dʒɛstɪk), *a.* [f. gest $sb.^3$ + -ic.] Of or pertaining to bodily movement, esp. dancing.

Todd (1818) explains *gestic* in quot. 1764 as 'legendary, historical' (from gest $sb.^1$), and this sense of the word is given in most mod. Dicts. even when the quot. is placed under the proper sense.

1764 Goldsm. *Trav.* 253 And the gay grandsire, skill'd in gestic lore, Has frisk'd beneath the burden of threescore. **1807–8** W. Irving *Salmag.* (1824) 119, Matrons..unskilled in 'gestic lore'. **1823** Scott *Peveril* xxx, He bore time to her motions with the movement of his foot..and seemed.. carried away by the enthusiasm of the gestic art.

†'**gestical**, *a. Obs.* [f. as prec. + -al[1].] = prec.

1607 Topsell *Four-f. Beasts* (1658) 83 She beggeth, playeth, leapeth—sometimes creeping, sometimes lying on the back..with divers such gestical actions.

gesticulacious ('dʒɛstɪkjʊˌleɪʃəs), *a.* $rare^{-1}$. [f. gesticul-ate *v.* + -acious.] Given to gesticulation. (Cf. gesticularious and quot. there.)

1834 *W. Ind. Sketch Bk.* II. 373 The French people, always so amusing, so gesticulacious and frisky.

gesticulant (dʒɛ'stɪkjʊlənt), *a. rare.* [ad. L. *gesticulant-em*, pres. pple. of *gesticulāri* to gesticulate.] Exhibiting gestures; gesticulating.

1877 Ruskin *Fors Clav.* VII. lxxv. 89 The poor gesticulant orator. **1887** Blackmore *Springhaven* (ed. 4) I. xvi. 157 The figure of the ungainly foe..huge against the waves like Cyclops, and like him gesticulant.

gesticular (dʒɛ'stɪkjʊlə(r)), *a.* [f. late L. *gesticul-us* a gesture + -ar.]

1. Of or pertaining to gesticulation.

1850 Leitch tr. *C. O. Müller's Anc. Art* §335 (ed. 2) 397 The comparison of the gesticular language of the modern Neapolitans..is interesting. **1861** *Temple Bar* I. 186 The deficiency of true genius and genuine gesticular humour in the mimics of our stage.

2. *nonce-use.* Full of quick and lively motion.

1856 Emerson *Eng. Traits* xiii. 231 Electricity cannot be made fast;..it is passing, glancing, gesticular.

gesticularious (dʒɛstɪkjʊ'lɛərɪəs), *a.* [f. late L. *gesticulāri-us* a pantomime, f. *gesticul-us* (see next) + -ous.] Given to gesticulation.

1830 *Fraser's Mag.* I. 291 It is that [snuff] which makes him [the Frenchman] so lively, so gesticularious, so frisky.

gesticulate (dʒɛ'stɪkjʊleɪt), *v.* [f. L. *gesticulāt-*, ppl. stem of *gesticulāri*, f. *gesticulus*, dim. of *gestus* action, gesture (see gest $sb.^3$).]

1. *intr.* To make lively or energetic motions with the limbs or body; esp. as an accompaniment or in lieu of speech.

1613 R. Cawdrey *Table Alph.* (ed. 3), *Gesticulate*, vse much or foolish gesture. **1638** Sir T. Herbert *Trav.* 235 Their hands, eyes..gesticulating severally, and swimming round, and conforming themselves to a Dorique stilnesse. **1783** Blair *Lect. Rhet.* vi. I. 111 A Frenchman both varies his accents, and gesticulates while he speaks, much more than an Englishman. **1815** SCOTT *Guy M.* iv, The gipsy remained on the shore, reciting or singing, and gesticulating with great vehemence. **1863** GEO. ELIOT *Romola* I. xvi, Men ..were standing in close couples gesticulating eagerly.

2. *trans.* To indicate or express by gestures or gesticulations.

1601 B. JONSON *Poetaster* Apol. Dial., To act the crimes, these Whippers reprehend, Or what their servile apes gesticulate. **18..** BAKER *Heart of Africa* 227 (Cent.) The whole day passed in shouting and gesticulating our peaceful intentions to the crowd assembled on the height on the opposite side of the river. **1871** MORLEY *Voltaire* (1886) 9 Muffled phantoms of debate are made to gesticulate inexpressible things in portentously significant silence.

Hence **ge'sticulated** *ppl. a.*, accompanied or varied by gesticulation; **ge'sticulating** *ppl. a.*, that gesticulates.

1623 COCKERAM II. A4b, Done with Actiuity or Wantonly. *Gesticulated.* **1791–1823** D'ISRAELI *Cur. Lit.* (1859) II. 117 Italy, both ancient and modern, exhibits a gesticulating people of comedians. **1816** KEATINGE *Trav.* (1817) I. 225 The group began a wild, and to our ideas extravagantly gesticulated dance. **1853** KANE *Grinnell Exp.* xiii. (1856) 97 Rounded hill slope and gesticulating tree. **1858** DE QUINCEY *Fr. & Eng. Mann.* Wks. IX. 105 A gesticulating nation cannot be a dignified nation.

gesticulatingly (dʒɛ'stɪkjʊˌleɪtɪŋlɪ), *adv.* [f. GESTICULATING *ppl. a.* + -LY².] With gesticulations. Also **ge'sticuˌlatively** *adv.*

1893 F. ADAMS *New Egypt* 22 Strolling about, noisily and gesticulatingly. **1898** E. P. EVANS *Evol. Ethics* vii. 223 He can..express the number of objects lying before him gesticulatively with his fingers.

gesticulation (ˌdʒɛstɪkjʊ'leɪʃən). Also 7 jesticulation. [ad. L. *gesticulātiōn-em*, n. of action f. *gesticulārī* to GESTICULATE.] The action or process of gesticulating. Also, an instance of this (chiefly in *pl.*).

1603 HOLLAND *Plutarch's Mor.* 1195 He liked well enough to see the daunces and gesticulations of yong boies. **1616** BULLOKAR, *Gesticulation*, a moouing of the fingers, hands, or other parts, eyther in idle wantonnesse, or to expresse some matter by signes, in dauncing, singing, or other such like exercise. **1657** R. LIGON *Barbadoes* (1673) 16 Their wanton smiles, and jesticulations. **1713** STEELE *Guardian* No. 42 ¶3 Story-telling..is not perfect without proper Gesticulations of the Body. **1764** REID *Inquiry* i. §6. 103 One may see a puppet make variety of motions and gesticulations. *a* **1784** JOHNSON in *Boswell* lxx. (1848) 662/2 He has no grimace, no gesticulation, no bursts of admiration on trivial occasions. **1824** W. IRVING *T. Trav.* I. 104 Their conversation was.. carried on with Italian vivacity and gesticulation. **1846** GROTE *Greece* I. xvi. (1862) II. 402 Dancing or rhythmical gesticulation. **1865** LIVINGSTONE *Zambesi* xxi. 436 Making various savage gesticulations. **1876** W. MATHEWS *Words* i. 25 Persons skilled in gesticulation can communicate by it a long series of facts and even complicated trains of thought.

gesticulative (dʒɛ'stɪkjʊlətɪv), *a.* [ad. L. type **gesticulātīvus*, f. *gesticulārī.*] Given to, or characterized by, gesticulation.

1795 W. TAYLOR in *Monthly Rev.* XVIII. 540 The people of that island are lively and gesticulative. **1865** CARLYLE *Fredk. Gt.* XIII. vii. V. 83 One hears..nasal eloquence from antique gesticulative mustachio-figures, witty and indignant. **1879** FARRAR *St. Paul* I. 474 *note*, He testifies to their disorderly and gesticulative fits of rage.

gesticulator (dʒɛ'stɪkjʊleɪtə(r)). [a. L. *gesticulātor*, f. *gesticulārī* to GESTICULATE.] One who gesticulates; one who uses gestures or gesticulations; an actor.

a **1693** URQUHART *Rabelais* III. xix. 157 He is such a fine Gesticulator. *a* **1800** PEGGE (T.), King Alfred..took upon him the character of a mimick, a dancer, a gesticulator, a jack-pudding. **1852** J. H. NEWMAN *Callista* (1890) 230 Mummers, bacchanals, satyrs and gesticulators.

gesticulatory (dʒɛ'stɪkjʊlətərɪ), *a.* [as if ad. L. **gesticulātōri-us*, f. *gesticulārī*: see GESTICULATE and -ORY.] Full of, consisting in, or of the nature of, gesticulation.

1774 WARTON *Hist. Eng. Poetry* vi. (1775) I. 249 Farcical and gesticulatory representations. **1830** PUSEY *Hist. Enquiry* II. 203 *A.* Or the action? *B.* About that I am indifferent, if it be only quiet and not gesticulatory. **1834** MRS. STOWE *Let.* in *Life* iii. (1889) 74 He sprung up all lively and oratorical and gesticulatory.

†**ge'sticulose**, *a. Obs.*⁻⁰ [f. L. *gesticul-us* gesture + -OSE.] 'Full of Gesture or Motions of the Body' (Bailey vol. II. 1727).

†'**gestient**, *a. Obs.* [ad. L. *gestient-em*, pres. pple. of *gestīre* to be excited (*lit.* use passionate gestures), f. *gestus* GEST *sb.*³] Restlessly excited.

1644 BULWER *Chiron.* 145 All juvenile gestient pompe and ostentation laid aside. **1649** —— *Pathomyot.* II. ii. 125 After that manner as men are shooke together, are gestient, tremble, or cannot abide in a place.

gestin(e, var. GESTEN, *Obs.*

gestion ('dʒɛstɪən, 'dʒɛstʃən). [ad. L. *gestiōn-em*, n. of action f. *gerĕre* to carry on. Cf. F. *gestion.*]

1. A carrying on or out; conduct, management. †Also, working order.

1599 CHAPMAN *Hum. Dayes Mirth* Plays 1873 I. 78 Is she a woman that objects this sight, able to worke the chaos of the world into gestion? **1656** BLOUNT *Glossogr.*, *Gestion*, a doing of a thing. **1801** T. JEFFERSON *Writ.* (1830) III. 486 That participation in the gestion of affairs which his office made incumbent on him. **1818** H. T. COLEBROOKE *Obligations & Contracts* I. 131 Of this [quasi-contract] there are five chief sorts. 1st. Gestion of another's affairs without a commission. **1851** H. D. WOLFF *Pict. Span. Life* 57 Myrmidons of evil, stand ready to furnish more instruments for the gestion of this torment. **1876** BROWNING *Pacchiarotto* x, Like landlord in house he had sublet Resuming of guardianship gestion.

2. *Sc. Law.* The conduct of one who acts as an heir: = L. *gestio pro hærede.*

1674 FOUNTAINHALL in M. P. Brown *Suppl. Dict. Decis. Crt. Session* (1826) III. 39 That disponing or selling of lands is a *gestio pro hærede*..but it is doubted by some, if the renouncing a reversion, legal or conventional, for a sum of money, be a gestion or not.

gestiour, var. GESTER, *Obs.*

gestnen, gestning, vars. GESTEN, -ING, *Obs.*

gestogen, var. GESTAGEN.

†**gestonye.** *Obs. rare.* [var. GESTENING, of obscure formation.] Feast; entertainment.

c **1435** *Torr. Portugal* 2374 They held a gestonye, With alle maner of mynstralsye. *Ibid.* 2627 The Emperoure of Rome, To that gestonye he come.

gestor, -our(e, var. GESTER, *Obs.*

gestron(e, var. GESTER(O)N, *Obs.*

†'**gestuose**, *a. Obs.*⁻⁰. [ad. L. *gestuōs-us*, f. *gestu-s* gesture.] 'Full of gesture' (Bailey vol. II. 1727). Hence **gestu'osity**, 'Apishness in Gestures' (ibid.).

gestural ('dʒɛstjʊrəl), *a.* [f. next + -AL¹.] Of or pertaining to gesture; consisting of gestures. *spec.* Designating or pertaining to the theory that human speech originated in oral imitation of bodily gestures. Hence '**gesturally** *adv.*

1613 F. ROBARTS *Revenue Gosp.* 23 The verball or gesturall honour which many men..performe to Ministers, is the very same which the Iewes or Iudas did to Christ. **1837** *Penny Cycl.* VIII. 329/1 Thus it is with the naturally deaf, the radical idea is all that their gestural language is capable of expressing. **1895** J. D. WRIGHT in *Proc. 14th Convent. Amer. Instruct. Deaf* 233 In the cases [deaf and blind] in the New York Institution, gestural signs were used to some extent combined with the manual alphabet. **1930** R. PAGET *Babel* iii. 84 The American twang..is mainly due to a tightening of the pharynx, and has nothing to commend it on gestural or phonetic grounds. *Ibid.*, Each word should, so far as possible, be gesturally appropriate to its meaning. **1941** D. EFRON *Gesture & Environment* II. iii. 95 This gestural vocabulary comprehends no less than 125 manual 'words', implying definite meaningful associations. **1949** *Trans. Philol. Soc. 1948* 49 The Gestural Theory is largely linked with the name of Sir Richard Paget. **1957** D. L. BOLINGER in *Publ. Amer. Dial. Soc.* XXVIII. 11 *Wonder* is a borderline case when it precedes. Gesturally it is often treated as a Q[uestion], but intonationally it usually is not. **1966** *Listener* 2 June 814/3 The *Sette peccati*..represents each of the seven deadly sins gesturally on the stage.

gesture ('dʒɛstjʊə(r)), *sb.* Also 6–7 jesture. [ad. med.L. *gestūra*, n. of action f. *gerĕre* to carry.]

†**1. a.** Manner of carrying the body; bearing, carriage, deportment (more fully, ***gesture of the body***); *rarely* in *pl. Obs.* (merged in 3).

c **1410** *Sir Cleges* 483 He was a knyght of yours full trewe, And comly of gesture. **1509** FISHER *Funeral Serm. C'tess. Richmond* Wks. (1876) 292 In wordes, in gesture, in euery demeanour of herself, so grete noblenes dyde appere, that [etc.]. **1532** BECON *Pomander Prayer* Wks. 1560 II. 211 b, That I may reuerence and honoure my father and mother, not onely with outwarde gestures of my body, but also with the vnfayned affeccyon of the hart. **1548–9** *Bk. Com. Prayer, Baptism*, By his outwarde gesture and dede he declared his good wyll towarde them. **1577** tr. *Bullinger's Decades* (1592) 160 To behaue himselfe decently in his going, and gesture of his bodie. **1587** TURBERVILE *Trag. Tales* (1837) 127 Hee usde his gestures so unto this gallant dame..that she at length his friend in love became. **1600** SHAKS. *A.Y.L.* v. ii. 69 If you do loue Rosalinde so neere the hart, as your gesture cries it out. **1651** HOBBES *Leviath.* II. xxix. 168 In gesture and habit of a mad-man. **1756** BURKE *Subl. & B.* I. iii, The fashion of the countenance and the gesture of the body on such occasions is so correspondent to this state of mind. **1770** *Junius Lett.* xxxviii. 188 [He] had a voice to persuade, an eye to penetrate, a gesture to command. **1786** W. THOMSON *Watson's Philip III* (1793) II. v. 119 The voice, the looks, and gestures of the young king made an impression. **1810** SCOTT *Lady of L.* I. xxi, Yet seemed that tone, and gesture bland, Less used to sue than to command.

†**b.** Grace of manner. Also *pl. Obs.*

1579 LYLY *Euphues* (Arb.) 51 Lest he should seeme to want gestures, or to be dashed out of conceipt with her coy countenance. **1704** STEELE *Lying Lover* III. (1747) 46, I haue a Kindness for her, but she has no Gesture in the least.

†**2. a.** Manner of placing the body; position, posture, attitude, *esp.* in acts of prayer or worship. Also, a specified posture. *Obs.*

1533 COVERDALE *Treat. Lord's Supp.* (1540) c vij b, The olde congregacion..dide in theyr gesture & ricte figurate a certayne ymage of a sacrifice. **1560** BECON *Catech.* Wks. 1564 I. 480 As concerning syttyng at the Lordes table..I could alowe that gesture best. **1581** MARBECK *Bk. of Notes* 852 Some foolishly imagine that praier is made either better or worse, by the jesture of our bodyes. **1613** PURCHAS *Pilgrimage* (1614) 154 What position of body hee was in the Sabbath morning, in the same hee ought to continue all that day, without change of gesture or place. **1646** SIR T. BROWNE *Pseud. Ep.* v. vi. 241 As for their gesture or position, the men lay downe leaning on their left elbow. **1676** ALLEN *Address Nonconf.* 178 Gesture in Prayer, such as is kneeling, lifting up hands and eyes, and the like. **1729** BURKITT *On N.T.* Mark iv. 2 Observe our Saviour's gestures in preaching: *he sat*, it being the custom of the Jewish Church to do so.

†**b.** (See quot.) *Obs.*

1612 BRINSLEY *Pos. Parts* (1669) 72 What call you verbs of gesture? *A.* Verbs of bodily moving, going, resting, or doing. *Ibid.* 72 *note*, They are called verbs of Gesture, because they signifie some special gesture of the body.

3. †**a.** In early use: The employment of bodily movements, attitudes, expression of countenance, etc., as a means of giving effect to oratory (*obs.*). **b.** Now in narrower sense, as a generalized use of 4: Movement of the body or limbs as an expression of feeling.

1545 ASCHAM *Toxoph.* I. (Arb.) 56 No man can wryte a thing so earnestlye, as whan it is spoken wyth iesture. **1553** T. WILSON *Rhet.* 118 Gesture is a certaine comely moderacion of the countenaunce and al other partes of mans body, aptely agreeyng to those thynges whiche are spoken. **1597** HOOKER *Eccl. Pol.* v. xxii. §12 To put life into words by countenance, voice, and gesture. **1607–12** BACON *Ess.*, *Seeming Wise* (Arb.) 216/1 Some helpe themselves with countenance, and gesture, and are wise by signes. **1697** EVELYN *Numism.* ix. 303 The Tongue spake to Men's Ears, but it was the Gesture which spake to their eyes. **1712** ADDISON *Spect.* No. 407 ¶1 Our Orators are observed to make use of less Gesture or Action than those of other Countries. **1791** BOSWELL *Johnson* 15 Apr. an. 1758 His unqualified ridicule of rhetorical gesture, or action. **1804** *Med. Jrnl.* XII. 510 She seized the ice, and rubbed her face, neck, and arms with it, signifying by gesture the ease it afforded. **1875** JOWETT *Plato* (ed. 2) V. 106 Gesture is the imitation of words.

4. a. A movement of the body or any part of it. Now only in restricted sense: A movement expressive of thought or feeling.

1551–6 R. ROBINSON tr. *More's Utop.* (Arb.) 141 Theire armoure or harneys..is..handsome for all mouinges and gestures of the bodye. **1555** EDEN *Decades* I. VI. (Arb.) 89 They signified also by certeyne scorneful gestures that they nothyng esteemed perles. **1583** HOLLYBAND *Campo di Fior* 115, I shall name these letters. Looke well what gesture I make with my mouth. **1607** TOPSELL *Four-f. Beasts* 325 That at certain signes and tokens, he [a Horse] be taught of his owne accord to performe diuers and sundry jestures. **1626** BACON *Sylva* §717 The Shaking of the Head..is a Gesture of slight refusal. **1662** J. DAVIES tr. *Olearius' Voy. Ambass.* 220 An Oration, intermixt with more Faces and Gestures than any Player can shew on the stage. **1717** LADY M. W. MONTAGU *Let. to Abbé Conti* 17 May, Two buffoons ..diverted the mob with their antic gestures. **1814** SCOTT *Ld. of Isles* III. xxxi, His speechless gesture thanks hath paid. **1843** PRESCOTT *Mexico* II. v. (1864) 98 The natives supplied the deficiency..by their uncommon vivacity and significance of their gestures,—the hieroglyphics of speech. **1878** M. A. BROWN *Nadeschda* 62 She took a seat, And with a gesture, motioned her son to his.

b. *transf.* and *fig.*; *spec.* [after F. *geste*; cf. BEAU GESTE] a move or course of action undertaken as an expresssion of feeling or as a formality; esp. a demonstration of friendly feeling, usu. with the purpose of eliciting a favourable response from another.

1916 *Daily News* 2 Feb. 4/4 The cost of museums and galleries ought to be considered as part of the cost of the war. .. To shut them is a mean and shabby gesture before the whole world. **1921** *Times* 18 Oct. 10/4 The gift of your Medal of Honour to a British comrade in arms, whose tomb in Westminster Abbey stands for all our best endeavour and hardest sacrifice in the war, is a gesture of friendly sympathy and good will which we will not forget. **1921** *Daily News* 9 Nov., The hope that Sir James Craig might make a generous gesture. *Ibid.* 24 Nov., You cannot quite get that gesture from Mr. Balfour. **1922** *Daily News* 9 Nov. 9 So far as the movement against Prohibition is concerned, the victory of Mr. Edwards, Governor of New Jersey, is only a gesture. As Governor he promised to make the State as wet as the Atlantic. *Ibid.* 16 Dec. 9 The United States Cabinet to-day sat..to consider a world gesture which is intended..to assist Europe and to allay discontent at home. **1922** *Westm. Gaz.* 20 Dec., The semi-official gestures of Greece towards a reconciliation with this country. **1933** BLOOMFIELD *Lang.* ix. 147 Vocal gestures, serving an inferior type of communication, occur not only outside of speech, as in an inarticulate outcry, but also in combination with speech-forms. **1959** *Listner* 8 Oct. 563/2, I do not advocate, instead, an imitation of the gestures of the new 'Holy Trinity' of European music: Stockhausen, Boulez, and Nono. **1963** *Ibid.* 7 Mar. 418/2 The Lijnbaan..would be a very long, completely straight two-storey street for pedestrians were it not for a single formal gesture which acts like a magic wand, providing canopies across the Lijnbaan as well as along it. **1964** *Ann. Reg. 1963* 253 France did not sign the test ban treaty, described..as 'a purely platonic gesture'.

5. *attrib.*, as ***gesture language, -sign, -speech, -syntax***; **gesture theory**, a theory of the origin of language (see GESTURAL *a.*); hence ***gesture-theorist.***

1865 TYLOR *Early Hist. Man.* ii. 15 The Gesture Language, or Language of Signs. *Ibid.* 19 The educated deaf mutes can tell us from their own experience how gesture-signs originate. *Ibid.* iv. 64 The leading principle of the gesture-syntax. **1885** CLODD *Myths & Dr.* II. ix. 199 A girl who was a deaf-mute as well as blind..telling a dream in gesture language. **1889** MIVART *Orig. Hum. Reas.* 139 The gesture-speech of mankind. **1930** R. PAGET *Babel* ii. 54 The gesture theory of human speech is not new. *Ibid.* 62 To the gesture-theorist it is a natural consequence of the fact that every tongue- and lip-gesture can be construed in a variety of ways.

Hence '**gestureless** *a.*, without gesture.

1847 in CRAIG. Hence in mod. Dicts.

gesture ('dʒɛstjʊə(r)), *v.* Also 6 **jester, jesture,** 6–8 **gester.** [f. the sb.]

1. *intr.* To make or use gestures, to gesticulate.

1542 UDALL tr. *Erasm. Apoph.* 253 b, Augustus settyng twoo iesters together forto plaie their merie partes in gesturyng the one after the other by course. **1565** CALFHILL *Answ. Treat. Cross* 93 b, Whosoeuer hath ye vse of eyes or his right wits, wil see & consider, that there is meant, no priest gesturing, but holy ghost working. **1609** R. BARNERD *Faithf. Sheph.* 85 Some in meditating doe vse to speake and gesture. **1837** CARLYLE *Fr. Rev.* III. I. vi, The Mayor speaking and gesturing his persuasivest. **1890** *Harper's Mag.* Feb. 417/1 They peered for white faces at windows..gesturing with knives as if opening fish.

b. *Sc.* To walk proudly, to swagger.

a **1783** J. SCOTT *Poems* 339 (Jam.) The like o' me they'll har'ly own, But geck their head, and gester on.

2. *trans.* †**a.** To order the attitudes or movements of (the body, oneself). *Obs.*

1542 [see *vbl. sb.*]. *a* **1639** WOTTON *Dk. Buckhm., Reliq. W.* (1651) 110 His young Nephew, Lord Viscount Fielding.. undertaking so to gesture and muffle up himself in his hood, as the Duke's manner was to ride in cold weather, that none should discern him, from him.

b. To express by gestures; †to accompany with or emphasize by gestures.

1589 NASHE *Anat. Absurd.* E ij b, They have leisure to gesture the mislike of his rudenes. **1597** HOOKER *Eccl. Pol.* v. xxvii. §1 It is not orderly read nor gestured as beseemeth. **1607** *Schol. Disc. agst. Antichr.* II. x. 141 The player hath no purpose to commit the acte of adulterie: his sinne is in that he gestureth and expresseth the dalliances of it. **1890** *Pall Mall G.* 12 Apr. 7/2 He..gestured his intention of throwing the baby to the ground if anybody attempted to approach him.

c. in *nonce-uses.*

1879 G. MEREDITH *Egoist* III. x. 221 He swept his arm to Vernon, and gestured a conducting hand to Clara. **1885** HOWELLS *S. Lapham* (1891) I. 248 His father made an offer to rise. 'Don't go', said Lapham, gesturing him down again.

Hence **'gestured** *ppl. a.*, expressed by gestures; **'gesturing** *vbl. sb.* and *ppl. a.* Also **'gesturer**, one who gestures.

1542 UDALL tr. *Erasm. Apoph.* 344 a, Ye accion or pronunciacion comprehendeth..the gesturyng or conueighaunce of all the whole bodye. **1553** T. WILSON *Rhet.* 3 We must..folowe the moste wise and learned menne, and seke to fashion..their speache and gesturyng. **1561** T. NORTON *Calvin's Inst.* IV. xviii. (1634) 713 There is eachwhere too much of pompes, ceremonies and gesturings. **1576** NEWTON *Lemnie's Complex.* II. ii. 101 Counterfaiters, Skoffers, Tumblers, and Gesturers. **1609** HOLLAND *Amm. Marcell.* XIV. vi, 13 No meane furniture for gesturing actors and stage players. **1644** BULWER *Chiron.* 114 This doth usually appeare in many in the gesturing and skipping motions of joy. **1651** J. F[REAKE] *Agrippa's Occ. Philos.* 226 By whose gesturings the Magicians did silently signifie words unknown by sound. **1879** W. L. LINDSAY *Mind in Lower Anim.* I. 355 Not only does it [the dog] understand man's gestured threat, but [etc.]. **1889** *Amer. Ann. Deaf* July 202 When the educated gesturer is compared with the deaf-mute as he was before the invention of the gesture language.

†**'gesturement.** *Obs.*$^{-1}$ [f. GESTURE *sb.* + -MENT.] = GESTURE *sb.* 3 b.

1597–8 BP. HALL *Sat.* I. iii. 46 Meanwhile our poets in high parliament Sit watching euerie word, and gesturement.

†**'gesturous,** *a.* [f. GESTURE *sb.* + -OUS.] Addicted to gestures.

1576 NEWTON *Lemnie's Complex.* II. ii. 97 Some be as toyinge, gesturous, and counterfeicting of any thing by ymitacion as Apes.

†**'gestyll,** *v. Obs. rare.* [? var. of JOSTLE, JUSTLE.] **a.** *trans.* (Meaning obscure; cf. GAUNCE *v.*). **b.** *intr.* = JOSTLE.

1530 PALSGR. 562/1, I gestyll a horse to and fro in the stabyll, *je jance*.. I gestyll agaynste a thynge, I touche it with movynge, *je heurte.*

gestyn(ne, var. GESTEN, *Obs.*

‖**gesundheit** (gə'zʊnthaɪt), *int.* [G., lit. 'health'.] An exclamation used to wish good health to a person, esp. to someone who sneezes.

1914 *Everybody's* Feb. 484 'Saved your life,' he murmured mechanically, as one suffixes 'Gesundheit' to a sneeze. **1942** O. NASH *Good Intentions* 124 Mr. Weaver said 'A cashew', and the man said '*Gesundheit*'. **1959** H. PINTER *Birthday Party* II. 37 *Goldberg* (lifting his glass). Gezunteheit [1960 ed.: Gesundheit]. **1961** L. PAYNE *Nose on my Face* xvi. 252 Saunders sneezed suddenly. '*Gesundheit*,' said Jim.

ges-warp, var. GUESS-WARP.

gesyne, var. GESINE, *Obs.*

get (gɛt), *sb.*[1] Forms: 4–5 **gete,** 4–5 (6–9 *Sc.* and *north.*) **gett,** 4– **get.** Also *Sc.* (sense 2 b) 8 **geet,** 9 **gait(t.** [f. GET *v.*]

1. a. What is got; gain, booty, earnings. *Obs.* exc. *dial.*

13.. *Gaw. & Gr. Knt.* 1638 Alle my get I schal yow gif agayn, bi my trawþe. **1606** HOLLAND *Sueton.* 142 The gets ..and takings of common strumpets. **1647** TRAPP *Mellif. Theol.* in *Comm. Ep.* 625 The day-labourer must give somewhat out of his gets, the servant out of his wages. **1893** *Northumbld. Gloss.*, *Gets*, the nett payment received by a blacksmith under the Crowley system of working.

b. *Coal Mining.* (See quot. 1883.) ***good gets***: ? seams that are easily worked.

1829 GLOVER *Hist. Derby* I. 60 Grey stone with many coal stripes, good gets. **1883** GRESLEY *Gloss. Coal Mining*, *Get*.. The produce or output, in tons, of a colliery or mine during a certain period.

c. The action of returning the ball, esp. a difficult shot, in lawn tennis. *colloq.*

1927 *Daily Tel.* 22 Mar. 15/6 One does not remember seeing Hake play better, and some of his gets were most spectacular. **1969** *Sunday Times* 6 July 20/1 He was broken only once, in the third game as a result of an amazing 'get' by the champion.

2. a. What is begotten; an offspring, child. Also *collect.* progeny. Now only of animals.

c **1320** R. BRUNNE *Medit.* 817 Myn owne gete [*v.r.* gete sone] ys fro me take. *a* **1400–50** *Alexander* 391 Þus begylid he this gude wyfe & makis hire to wene It ware na gett of na gome bot of god ane. *c* **1460** *Towneley Myst.* vi. 124, I pray the, lord, as thou me het, thou saue me and my gete. **1513** DOUGLAS *Æneis* x. i. 67, I, thy blude, thi get, and douchter schene. **1783** BURNS *Mailie's Elegy* 31 She was nae get o' moorland tips. **1786** —— *Dream* 57 Will's a true guid fallow's get. **1795** J. HALDANE in J. Robertson *Agric. Perth* App. (1799) 534 Some of his [a ram's] gets were of the best country kind. **1815** *Sporting Mag.* XLVI. 118 The Stradling or Lister Turk..proved his high blood, by the racers, his immediate get. **1889** *Even. Post* 9 Feb., The winnings of his get in 1888 were $120,000.

b. orig. *Sc.* and *north.* In contemptuous use = brat. Also *spec.* a bastard; hence as a general term of abuse: a fool, idiot. (Cf. GIT.) Now *dial.* and *slang.*

1508 DUNBAR *Flyting w. Kennedie* 244 Fals tratour, feyndis gett. **1567** SEMPILL in *Satir. Poems Reform.* viii. 11 Blasphemus baird and beggeris get! *a* **1572** KNOX *Hist. Ref.* Wks. 1846 I. 236 [John] Leslye, preastis gett, Abbot of Londorse and Bischope of Ross. **1706** in W. Cramond *Court Bks. Regality of Grant* (1897) 20 Gregor Burgess protested against the said Allane that called him a witch gyt or bratt. **1725** RAMSAY *Gentle Sheph.* I. ii. Song 5, Whingeing getts about your ingle side. **1768** ROSS *Helenore* I. 248 They've gotten a geet that stills na night nor day. **1818** SCOTT *Hrt. Midl.* xxxi, A' the gaitts o' boys and lasses wad be crying at Madge Wildfire's tail. **1822** J. GALT *Provost* ix. 65 A donsie mother that could gie no name to her gets. **1880** W. H. PATTERSON *Gloss. Antrim & Down* 43 *Get*, an opprobrious term used in scolding matches. **1887** J. SERVICE *Life Dr. Duguid* vi. 42 Gibby a ne'er-do-weel hellicate thing that was the get o' a son who was deid. **1893** *Northumbld. Gloss.*, *Getts*, young children. **1908** J. MASEFIELD *Capt. Margaret* xi. 325 He's a mother's joy, the Portuguese drummer's get. **1922** JOYCE *Ulysses* 319 The bloody thicklugged sons of whores' gets! **1934** 'L. G. GIBBON' *Grey Granite* 126 The woman said of all the whoreson's gets she'd ever met he was the worst. **1940** *Daily Mail* 7 Sept. 3/8 Here are some current military phrases interpreted:..*get*, chump, fool. **1965** *Listener* 24 June 949/1, I would..define him as a daft old get. **1967** 'H. CALVIN' *Nice Friendly Town* viii. 101 Put something on him, the stupid get!

3. Begetting, procreation. *Obs.* exc. in sporting use. Also †birth, hereditary right.

c **1375** *Sc. Leg. Saints, Baptista* 186 Iohne is..borne of woman thru get kindly, bot criste of maydine is þe birth. *Ibid.* 915 ȝet ware herodis ma þan he, þat be get cane til hym succede. *c* **1460** *Towneley Myst.* x. 115, I cam neuer by man's syde, Bot has avowed my madynhede, ffrom fleshly gett. **1807** *Sporting Mag.* XXIX. 149 The foals of Ruzio's get, only one year old, are near fourteen hands high. **1892** *Field* 18 June 904/3 The dog fox..will cater for all the cubs of his own get.

4. A getaway; a hasty retreat; esp. in phr. ***to do*** (or ***make***) ***a get.*** Cf. GET *v.* 31 d. *Austral.* and *N.Z. slang.*

1898 *Bulletin* (Sydney) 28 May 31/2 Their inquisitiveness ..compelled Jim to kill his stud-sluts and growing stock, and do a timely 'get'. **1906** E. DYSON *Fact'ry 'Ands* ix. 117 They thort his jills had done er get. **1909** T. H. THOMPSON *Ballads about Business* 92, I..prepared to do a get. **1914** A. A. GRACE *Tale of Timber Town* v. 32, I must make a git. So-long.

get, *sb.*[2] [App. a readoption of F. (*get*) *jet*, JESS.] The jess of a hawk.

1607 HEYWOOD *Wom. Kilde w. Kindn.* B ij, Now she hath seis'd the Foule, and gins to plume her: Rebecke her not, rather stand still and checke her: So: seise her Gets, her Iesses and her Bels. **1957** T. HUGHES *Hawk in Rain* 33 Grubbing his get among your lilies.

get (gɛt), *sb.*[3] Also **gett.** [Aramaic.] Among the Jews, a written 'bill of divorcement' prepared according to a prescribed form; also, the divorce itself.

1892 ZANGWILL *Childr. Ghetto* I. I. iv. 122 'He must give her *Gett*!' 'Of course!..I divorce her at once!' **1960** L. P. GARTNER *Jewish Immigrant in England* vi. 168 Social pressure and legal adjustments in the *ketubah* (marriage document) could force the most recalcitrant of husbands to grant his estranged wife a *get* (divorce). **1963** *Listener* 17 Jan. 123/1 The husband delivered a Jewish letter of divorce, called a *gett*, to his wife.

get (gɛt), *v.* Pa. t. **got** (*arch.* **gat**). Pa. pple. **got** (**gotten**). Pres. pple. **getting.** Forms: *Infin.* 3–4 **geten,** (5 **getyn**), 3–6 **gete,** (4 **geit, geyt, gite,** *Sc.* **gat(e,** 4–5 **gyte,** 6 *Sc.* **gait**), 3–7 **gett,** (4–6 **gette,** 4 **gitte,** 5 **gytt,** 9 *dial.* **git**), 3– **get.** *Pa. t.* 3–7 **gate,** (3 **gait,** 4 **get,** *pl.* **gaten, geton, -yn, geetun, getton,** 5 **geten**), 3–6 **gatt,** (4–6 **gatte**), 3– **gat,** 6– **got,** (6 **got(t)e**). *Pa. pple.* **a.** 3–5 **geten,** (3 **ȝeten, getun,** 4 **getin, geteyn, giten, -in, gyten, -in,** 4–6 **getyn,** 5 **geton**), 3–5 **getten,** (4–5 **gettyn,** 5 **getton,** 6 **gitten**), 4–6 **gete,** (4 **i-gete,** 5 **y-gete, gyte**), 4–6 **gette,** (5 **y-gette**), 5–6 **gett,** (5 **get**). β. 3–4 **gotin,** 3– 6 **goten,** (4 **gotyn, gote,** 5 **y-goten, goton, gothen**), 4–6 *Sc.* **gottin, -yn,** 5–7 **gotton,** 6– **gotten, got,** (6 **y-got**).

[a. ON. *geta* (*gat, gátum, getenn*) to get, obtain, to beget, also, to guess (Sw. *gitta*, Da. *gide* to be able or willing, MSw. *gäta*, Da. *gjette* to guess) = OE. *-ʒietan* (only in the compounds *a-, be-, for-, ofer-, on-, under-ʒietan*: see BEGET, FORGET), OFris. (*ur-, for-*)*jeta*, OS. (*bi-, far-*)*getan* (MDu. *ver-gheten*, Du. *ver-geten*), OHG. *geʒʒan*, *keʒʒan* (once in pple. *keʒʒendi*, 'adeptus', otherwise only in *bi-, int-, ir-, fer-geʒʒan*; MHG. *er-, ver-geʒʒen*, mod.G. *ver-gessen*), Goth. (*bi-*)*gitan*:—OTeut. **getan, gat-, gêtum, getono-*. The OAr. root **ghed*, **ghod* 'to seize', 'take hold of', is found also in L. *præda* (:—**præ-hĕda*) booty, *prædium* an estate, perh. also in *hedera* ivy (literally the 'clinger'); and with inserted nasal in L. *prehendere* to catch, lay hold of, Gr. χανδάνειν (aor. ἔχαδον) to hold, contain, to be able.

Of the compounds of *-ʒietan* which existed in OE. (see above), only *beʒietan* and *forʒietan* survive in the modern language, and the normal equivalents *beyet* and *foryet* were displaced in later ME. in favour of BEGET and FORGET. Gower is app. the last author who employs *beȝet*; *forȝet* disappears in the 15th c. except in Sc., where it is not yet extinct. This change was prob. due to the influence of the simple verb. Conversely, the solitary example in ME. of *ȝeten* without prefix (sense 26) may be referred to the influence of *biȝeten*.

The forms of the pa. pple. retaining the original vowel (ON. *getenn*) are found in literature down to the 16th c., and in the north midlands and Yorkshire *getten* is still the dialectal form. From the beginning of the English history of the vb., however, it has, like most verbs with ME. open *e* in the present stem, tended to assume the conjugation of vbs. of the *e, a, o* series (originally confined to roots ending in a liquid); thus in the 13th c. we find *geten, gat, goten* parallel with *stelen, stal, stolen*. In the 16th c. the pa. t. was often *got*, by assimilation to the pa. pple.; in the 17th c. this became the usual form, though *gat* is used in the Bible of 1611 and still occurs in archaistic poetry. In England the form *gotten* of the pa. pple. is almost obsolete (exc. *dial.*) being superseded by *got*; in U.S. literature *gotten* is still very common, although Webster 1864 gave it as 'obsolescent'.]

I. *trans.* To obtain, procure.

1. a. To obtain possession of (property, etc.) as the result of effort or contrivance.

c **1200** ORMIN 10219 Forr whase itt iss þatt grediȝ iss To winnenn erþlic ahhte, Aȝȝ alls he mare & mare gett Aȝȝ lisste himm affterr mare. *c* **1330** R. BRUNNE *Chron.* (1810) 276 Þider ȝe alle salle ride, a faire prey salle ȝe gete. *c* **1400** MAUNDEV. (Roxb.) xxxiii. 150 On þis wyse þai get grete plentee of þis gold. **1489** CAXTON *Faytes of A.* III. xxi. 218 Noo good euyl goten can not be longe..kept of hym that geteth hit. **1508** FISHER *7 Penit. Ps.* li. Wks. (1876) 133 He caused the ryghtwyse man Naboth to be slayne and by gyle gate his vyneyarde. **1639** T. BRUGIS tr. *Camus' Mor. Relat.* 252 After so many difficulties of getting, what he so greatly desired, hee enjoyed it..surpassing expression. **1678** WANLEY *Wond. Lit. World* v. ii. §61. 471/2 Andronicus Comnenus by ambitious practices and pretence of reformation, got the Empire. **1737** POPE *Hor. Epist.* I. i. 79 Get Money, Money still! And then let Virtue follow if she will. **1858** G. MACDONALD *Phantastes* i. (1878) 5 Perhaps I was to find only the records of lands and moneys, how gotten and how secured. **1870** EMERSON *Soc. & Solit., Dom. Life* Wks. (Bohn) III. 47 Men are not born rich; and in getting wealth the man is generally sacrificed.

Proverb. **1523** LD. BERNERS *Froiss.* I. ccccxiii. 722 Sir..he that nothyng aduentureth nothynge getteth.

b. With advs.: To acquire or obtain in a certain way, esp. in ppl. combinations, ***well-, ill-gotten.***

c **1440** *Jacob's Well* (E.E.T.S.) 209 A ryche man wyth fals gotyn good seyde to a preest þat he wolde ȝyue all þat he had falsely gett to pore folk. *a* **1533** LD. BERNERS *Huon* lxviii. 235 Al that rychys was not wel goten. **1622** R. HAWKINS *Voy. S. Sea* (1847) 163 If one happen upon a bag of gold, silver, pearle, or precious stones, it is held well gotten, provided it be cleanly stolne. **1871** FREEMAN *Norm. Conq.* (1876) IV. xvii. 79 We are assured that it was all honourably gotten and was designed to be honourably spent.

Proverb. **1546** J. HEYWOOD *Prov.* (1867) 62 Soone gotten, soone spent, yll gotten yll spent. **1548** in Strype *Eccl. Mem.* (1721) II. App. Q. 51 Evil gotten, worse spent. **1591** HORSEY *Trav.* (Hakl. Soc.) 206 Eyll gotton soen lost.

c. *absol.* To acquire wealth or property.

1573 J. SANFORD *Hours Recreat.* (1576) 129 They are suspected to tende rather to get than to give. **1635** QUARLES *Embl.* IV. Epig. xii. 231 Wisdome not onely gets, but got, retaines. **1677** EVELYN *Diary* 10 Sept., Whilst he was Secretary of State..he had gotten vastly, but spent it as hastily. **1864** BURTON *Scot Abr.* I. iv. 213 The Church.. ever getting and never giving up, was eating away the territorial wealth of the temporal barons.

d. with epexegetic phrase, ***to get into one's hand, to get into one's possession.***

1548 HALL *Chron., Hen. VI*, 161 He..determined to get into his possession, the duchie of Acquitayne. **1571** *Satir. Poems Reform.* xxvii. 60 The Newhawin thay gatt into þair hand.

e. ***I wish you may get it, don't you wish you may get it?***: ironical colloq. expressions implying the speaker's doubt of, or lack of desire for, another's success.

1836 DICKENS *Sk. Boz* I. 42 An 'I wish you may get it' sort of expression in his eye. **1837** —— *Pickw.* xxvi. 274 'But the plaintiff must get it,' resumed Mrs. Cluppins... 'Vell,' said Sam... 'All I can say is, that I wish you *may* get it.' **1842** BARHAM *Ingol. Leg.* 2nd Ser. 245 Ah, ha! my good friend! —don't you wish you may get it? **1848** THACKERAY *Van. Fair* xiii, 'There's one of the greatest men in the kingdom wants some.' 'Does he?' growled the senior. 'Wish he may get it.' **1851** MAYHEW *Lond. Labour* I. I. 56 I've heard people say when I've cried 'all a-growing' on a fine-ish day, 'Aye, now summer's a-coming.' I wish you may get it, says I to myself; for I've studied the seasons. **1857** Hughes *Tom Brown* I. ix, Don't you wish you may get it?

2. a. To obtain as the proceeds of one's business or employment; to earn.

c **1300** *Havelok* 792 Ich am wel waxen, and wel may eten More than euere Grim may geten. **1362** Langl. *P. Pl.* A. vii. 238 He that get his fode her with trauaylinge in treuthe, God ȝiueth him his blessyng that his lyflode so swynketh. *a* **1533** Ld. Berners *Huon* liii. 177 Thy myster hath nothynge but that he geteth with his vyal. **1600** Shaks. *A.Y.L.* iii. ii. 78, I earne that I eate: get that I weare. **1701** De Foe *True-born Eng.* 27 And what they get by Day, they spend by Night. **1779–81** Johnson *L.P., Pope* Wks. IV. 46 If the money with which he retired was all gotten by himself.

absol. **1540** Hyrde tr. *Vives' Instr. Chr. Wom.* (1592) T viij, They compell their husbandes unto shamefull crafts to get by. **1806** Wordsw. *Sonn., 'The world is too much'*, Late and soon Getting and spending, we lay waste our powers.

b. in phr. ***to get a living*** or ***livelihood***.

c **1420** *Chron. Vilod.* 4377 [He]..leuede..In gode prosperite & in gode hele & wt his trauell his lyf-lode kat. **1530** *Act 22 Hen. VIII*, c. 12 If any man..be vagrant, and can gyue no rekenynge howe he doth lefullye get his lyuynge. **1634** Peacham *Gentl. Exerc.* 3 The Emperour Constantine got his living a long time by painting. **1711** Addison *Spect.* No. 94 ¶8 He set himself to think on proper Methods for getting a Livelihood in this strange Country. **1893** *Law Times* XCV. 4/2 There was no allegation against the mother's conduct or her means of getting a livelihood.

3. a. To obtain (much, little, nothing, etc.) by way of profit; to be benefited or advantaged to the extent of; to gain.

1490 Caxton *Eneydos* liii. 148 We that dyde fyghte ayenst the Troyens..Gatte nor wanne therby nothynge. **1568** Grafton *Chron.* II. 356 When he had made the best agreement with them that he could, he gate but little by them. **1599** Shaks. *Much Ado* i. i. 65 They never meet, but there's a skirmish of wit between them. *Beat.* Alas, he gets nothing by that. **1677** Miege *Dict. Eng.-Fr.*, I got nothing by it, *je n'y ai rien gagné*. **1841** Gen. P. Thompson *Exerc.* (1842) VI. 244 Is it that I have ever gotten anything by taking the manufacturers' side?

†**b.** *absol.* To derive profit; to gain, be a gainer, esp. *by* a thing. *Obs.*

1591 Shaks. *1 Hen. VI*, iv. iii. 32 We mourne, France smiles; We loose, they dayly get. **1679** Penn *Addr. Prot.* ii. 156 Doing as ill Gamesters are wont to do, get by using false Dice. *a* **1687** Waller *Poem, Night-piece* 22 Like jewels to advantage set, Her beauty by the shade does get. **1727** A. Hamilton *New Acc. E. Ind.* I. xxv. 315 Whether our East-india Company got or lost by that War, I know not. **1748** Richardson *Clarissa* (1768) V. 164 People who keep lodgings at public places expect to get by every one who comes into their purlieus. **1762** Goldsm. *Cit. W.* xiii, The guardians of the temple, as they got by the self delusion, were ready to believe him too.

†**c.** Of a clock: To gain in time. *Obs.*

1761 Maskelyne in *Phil. Trans.* LII. 440 The clock got 4m 1s, upon mean time, in two days.

†**4.** To capture, gain possession of (a fortress, etc.). *Obs.*

a **1400–50** *Alexander* 1453 Þen..Gais him furth to Gasa ..& sesis it be-lyue; And quen þis Gasa was geten he [etc.]. **1477** Sir J. Paston in *P. Lett.* No. 798 III. 192 The Frenshe Kynge hathe gothen many off the towns off the Duk of Burgoyne. **1548** Hall *Chron., Hen. VI*, 161 b, Without spedy aide..the whole countrey were like to be gotten from his possession. **1598** Grenewey *Tacitus' Ann.* xiv. viii. 208 Neuerthelesse the Kings fortresse..was not gotten but by fight. **1676** Hobbes *Iliad* i. 159 And when the city Troy we shall have got.

5. a. To gain, win (a victory). Now *rare*. Also †***to get a battle, the day, the field, the gree***.

c **1300** *Cursor M.* (Cott. Galba) 25367 He þat victori may gete Sall be corond [with] wirschippes grete. **1377** Langl. *P. Pl.* B. xviii. 98 The gree ȝit hath he geten for al his grete wounde. **1520** *Caxton's Chron. Eng.* i. 7/1 Ye chyldren of Israel gate ye victory agaynst Jabyn. **1579** Gosson *Sch. Abuse* (Arb.) 47 Tydinges was broughte him that his Souldiers gotte the day. **1659** B. Harris *Parival's Iron Age* 266 Had Charles gotten the Battel, it is very probable, that England had been the price of the victory. **1705** Bosman *Guinea* 40 Their small Force behaved themselves so well, that they had certainly got the Day if [etc.]. **1737** L. Clarke *Hist. Bible* (1740) I. ix. 580 For Lathyrus having gotten the Victory, pursued it to the utmost.

b. To obtain (a position of superiority or advantage over another person); in phrases ***to get the upper*** (†***over***, †***better***) ***hand*** (***of***); ***to get the start, the advantage***, etc. (***of***); ***to get the sun, the wind, of***; ***to get the better of*** (formerly also simply †***to get the better***); †***to get a good hand against***. ***to get anything*** (or ***something***) ***on*** (a person), to gain or possess incriminating information about (someone); to have an advantage over; cf. on *prep.* 21 b, d.; (*colloq.*, orig. *U.S.*).

a **1300** *Cursor M.* 2508 Þai lete þairs was þe land Fra þai had geten þe ouer-hand. **1530** Palsgr. 563/2, I get the upper hande of one, I overcome hym, *je vaincs*. **1548** Hall *Chron., Edw. IV*, 218 Thei had fought from mornyng almoste to noone, without any part gettyng avauntage of other. **1563** *Homilies* ii. *Resurrection* (1859) 434 He [Christ] hath..overcome the devil, death, and hell, and hath victoriously gotten the better hand of them all. **1568** Tilney *Disc. Mariage* D v b, By conquest getting ye upper hande. **1588** Shaks. *L.L.L.* iv. iii. 369 Be first aduis'd In conflict that you get the sunne of them. **1600** Holland *Livy* vii. vii. 253 The other armie..got a good hand against their enemies. **1601** Shaks. *Jul. C.* i. ii. 130 It doth amaze me A man of such a feeble temper should So get the start of the Maiesticke world. *Ibid.* ii. i. 326, I will strive with things impossible, Yea get the better of them. **1613** Purchas *Pilgrimage* (1614) 400 These reeds would fight together, and the victorie should remaine with him whose reede got the better. **1653** H. Cogan tr. *Pinto's Trav.* xix. 68 Like an old Soldier as he was, and verst in the trade of Pyrat, he got the wind of us. **1748** *Anson's Voy.* ii. viii. 221 They at last got so far the better of their aversion, as to be persuaded to taste it. **1872** Freeman *Gen. Sketch* xxi. §19 (1874) 230 Casimir the Fourth finally got the better of the Teutonic Knights. **1885** F. Anstey *Tinted Venus* 157 Supposing the police don't nip in and get the start of her. **1919** *Detective Story Mag.* 25 Nov. 129 He gave me the slip... Maybe it's just as well since I haven't got anything on him yet. **1923** L. J. Vance *Baroque* vii. 42 You haven't got any thing on me. **1946** T. Jones *Skinny Angel* 85 Those fellows are trying to get something on someone. **1960** 'W. Haggard' *Closed Circuit* iii. 31 Get something on the men who counted. Then you could do almost as you pleased. It was astonishing how most of the men who counted had something to hide.

†**c.** (Cf. gain *v.* 8.) ***to get ground***: to make progress, advance. So also ***to get head*** (cf. head *sb.* 52). ***to get ground of***: to encroach upon, obtain the mastery of; to draw away from (pursuers).

1529 S. Fish *Supplic. Beggers* (E.E.T.S.) 4 The Turke.. shulde neuer be abill to get so moche grounde of cristendome. **1597** Shaks. *2 Hen. IV*, ii. iii. 53 If they get ground, and vantage of the King, Then ioyne you with them. *c* **1611** Chapman *Iliad* xxiii. 399 This, the horse fear'd, and more powre Put to their knees, straite getting ground. **1640** tr. *Verdere's Rom. Rom.* i. 127 Being better mounted then they, he quickly got a great deal of ground of them. **1662** R. Mathew *Unl. Alch.* §31. 26 If one Fever have got head before this Pill be taken. **1680** H. More *Apocal. Apoc.* 209 The ancient zeal..will be much relaxated, and wickedness will get head again. **1700** T. Brown tr. *Fresny's Amusem. Ser. & Com.* 92 A Feaver..that press'd hard upon a Sick Man, and every Minute got Ground of him. **1737** Whiston *Josephus, Antiq.* Dissert. iii. v, The rest of their institutions..got ground by their pravity.

†**d.** *absol.* ***to get of***: to gain advantage over; also, to outstrip in speed; to gain upon in pursuing.

1525 Ld. Berners *Froiss.* II. xxi. 43 Euery day they ymagined by what subteltie they coulde gette one of another by dedes of armes. **1548** Hall *Chron., Edw. IV*, 209 The kynges shyp was good with sayle, and so much gat of the Easterlinges, that she came on the coast of Holland. **1599** Hakluyt *Voy.* II. i. 246 Notwithstanding, they get of the Persians, and make castles and holds in their countrey. **1628** Digby *Voy. Medit.* (1868) 37 It was her boate which I tooke vp, that they had cutt of because my sattia got so mainely of her.

e. *Racing.* To hold out for, to stay (a specified distance).

1898 A. E. T. Watson *Turf* vii. 148 There are not a few horses that cannot fairly 'get' even five furlongs. **1898** *Daily News* 17 Oct. 3/3 He will..be opposed by plenty of candidates who can get the Cambridgeshire course. **1907** *Daily Chron.* 14 Nov. 3/3 Only a wonder of a horse can 'get' those four miles and a half of ditches and fences.

6. a. To earn, win, acquire (fame, credit, glory, renown, love, favour, etc.).

a **1300** *Cursor M.* 2546 Mikel it was þat luffeword þan þat abram gat o mani man. **1362** Langl. *P. Pl.* A. x. 206 Fyndlynges and lyȝers, Vn-gracios to gete loue or eni good elles. *c* **1375** *Sc. Leg. Saints, Mathou* 415 He fawndyt myn wil for to gate. **1485** Caxton *Paris & V.* (1868) 3 Bothe..wente euer to-gyder there as they knewe ony Ioustyng..for to gete honour. **1500–20** Dunbar *Poems* lxxxii. 70 That ȝe may gett ane bettir name. **1568** Grafton *Chron.* II. 40 He gat himselfe thereby small or little favour. **1596** Shaks. *Tam. Shr.* ii. i. 120 If I get your daughter's loue, What dowrie shall I haue. **1639** T. Brugis tr. *Camus' Mor. Relat.* 188 No more approach her..much lesse get the good will of her friends. **1680** Otway *Orphan* i. i. 71 To send them forth where Glory's to be gotten. **1693** *Humours of Town* 36 By large Quotations..borrowed from *Burton's Melancholy*.. get the Reputation of profound Scholars.

b. In various games: to make (a certain score); to score (so many points, runs, goals, etc.); in *Cards*, to take (so many tricks). Also, in *Cricket*, to take (a wicket), to take the wicket of.

1548, **1553** [see goal *sb.* 3 a]. **1710** [see odd *a.* 1]. **1731** in H. T. Waghorn *Cricket Scores* (1899) 4 The Duke's hands came in first, and got 79 before they were out. **1778** *Miss Wicket & Miss Trigger (caption of print)*, Miss Trigger you see is an excellent Shot, And forty five Notches Miss Wicket's just got. **1857** Hughes *Tom Brown* ii. viii. 387 We haven't got the best wicket yet. *Ibid.* 397 Only seventeen runs to get with four wickets—the game is all but ours! **1901** *Encycl. Sport* I. 231/2 Many a bad ball gets a wicket. **1912** A. A. Lilley *Twenty-four Years Cricket* (1914) x. 164 The substantial support Trumper received..left us 194 to get to win. **1930** C. V. Grimmett *(title)* Getting wickets. **1971** *Sunday Express* 31 Oct. 31/3 He could not get the goal he sought so eagerly.

7. a. To acquire (knowledge, etc.) by study or experience.

1388 Wyclif *Prov.* iv. 7 In al thi possessioun gete thou [1382 purchace] prudence. *c* **1400** *Cato's Mor.* 209 in *Cursor M.* App. 1672 Þe man þat is harde witte gode clergis mai gitte, wiþ-in lite ȝeres. **1535** Fisher *Wks.* (1876) 388 Much comfortable knowledge and sweetnesse this Prophette gate by this booke. **1577** Harrison *England* Pref. (1877) i. p. cx, I gat some knowledge of things by letters and pamphlets. **1651** Hobbes *Leviath.* i. v. 21 Reason is not..gotten by Experience onely. **1732** Berkeley *Alciphr.* vii. § 11 Some old ideas may be lost, and some new ones got. **1864** Swinburne *Atalanta* 297 In such wise I gat knowledge of the Gods. **1868** C. Clarke *Relig. & Duty* 255 That knowledge which is gotten at school.

b. ***to get knowledge*** (***intelligence***, †***wit***, etc.) ***of***: to learn of, receive information of. For ***to get wind of***, see 15 b.

a **1557** *Diurn. Occurr.* (Bannatyne Club) 45 The governour gettand witt therof, past with his cumpany and saigit the samyn. **1639** S. Du Verger tr. *Camus' Admir. Events* 128 His wife had already gotten some small knowledge of this matter. **1761** Hume *Hist. Eng.* II. xlii. 461 The duke of Parma, who had gotten intelligence of their approach. **1762** Kames *Elem. Crit.* xix. (1833) 349 King Richard having got intelligence [etc.].

c. To learn, ascertain. *rare.*

1638 F. Junius *Paint. Ancients* 122 He findeth that the unlearned and carelesse multitude hath got his name. **1737** L. Clarke *Hist. Bible* (1740) I. i. 51 Abraham having got the price, never offers to beat it down.

d. To understand (a person or statement). Also *absol. colloq.* (orig. *U.S.*).

[**1892** 'Mark Twain' *Amer. Claimant* xiii. 101, I don't know that I quite get the bearings of your position.] **1907** M. C. Harris *Tents of Wickedness* i. iii. 33 'I don't get her,' she murmured, as if Leonora was a telephone number. **1913** J. London *Valley of Moon* i. vii, When I go after anything I get it, an' if anything gets in between it gets hurt. D'ye get that? **1918** Wodehouse *Piccadilly Jim* xi. 114, I get you not, friend. Supply a few footnotes. **1937** 'J. Bell' *Murder in Hospital* vii. 136 'I'd go about it rather quietly if I were you. ..' 'I get you,' said Thornton. **1948** —— *Wonderful Mrs. Marriott* xxi. 273 Oh, I get. The Condover Court lady. **1956** I. Bromige *Enchanted Garden* ii. ii. 93 Fiona broke into peals of laughter and became quite helpless for a few moments. 'Don't get it,' said Julian. **1966** 'M. Innes' *Change of Heir* ii. 14 Okay, okay. I get. Norval. My name is Norval.

e. To notice, look at (a person, esp. one who is conceited or laughable); usu. as *imp.* with a pronoun as object. *colloq.*

1958 *News Chron.* 22 May 4/4 If he is conceited the girls mutter get *yew!* **1967** H. Dalmas *Fowler Formula* (1968) i. 16 It was almost like hearing himself say, 'Get me! I had a special invitation to the Universal party this afternoon.'

8. To learn (a lesson, †a language, etc.), commit to memory; esp. ***to get by heart*** (see heart *sb.* 32); ***to get by rote*** (see rote *sb.*); †***to get without book***.

1582 N. Lichefield tr. *Castanheda's Conq. E. Ind.* xxxi. 77 One of those..after that hee had gotten the Arabian language, went by lande. **1597** Morley *Introd. Mus.* 3 You must get it perfectly without booke, to saie it forwards and backwards. **1612** Brinsley *Pos. Parts* (1669) 38 Which do you account the speediest way of all to get and keep these verbs. **1666** J. Davies *Hist. Caribby Isl.* 185 And he had such an excellent memory, that he had got their Language in perfection. **1692** Burnet *Past. Care* ix. 115 A whole Discourse is got by heart. **1749** Chesterf. *Lett.* (1792) II. 251 Those principles, which you then got, like your grammar rules, only by rote. **1761** Churchill *Rosciad* 248 Without the least finesse of art He gets applause!—I wish he'd get his part. **1834** T. Medwin *Angler in Wales* I. 123, I had got almost all Watts' hymns by heart. **1891** *Longm. Mag.* Oct. 647 What she said was never very profound, unless she had got it by heart.

9. To find out, ascertain by calculation or experiment; to obtain as a result of arithmetical or other processes.

1559 W. Cunningham *Cosmogr. Glasse* 97 It is not so easie ..to trie th' eleuation of the Pole: but it is as harde, and laborus, to get the Longitude. **1887** 'L. Carroll' *Game of Logic* i. §2. 28 By taking *x* as subject, we get 'all *x* are *y*'. **1888** *Times* 2 Oct. 3/2 A trial sand-loaded projectile was first fired in order to get the range. **1891** *Chamb. Jrnl.* 20 June 400/1 Dividing this by three hundred and sixty we get 364,609·13 feet as the length of a mean degree.

10. a. Without reference to agency on the part of the subject: To become possessed of; to receive, e.g. as one's share in a division, as a gift, wages, or as a payment of any kind.

c **1250** *Gen. & Ex.* 1497 'Broðer,' quad he, 'sel me ðo wunes, ðe queðen ben ðe firme sunes, ðat ic ðin firme birðehe gete. *c* **1300** *Havelok* 908 Wel is set þe mete þu etes And þe hire þat þu getes. *c* **1320** *Sir Tristr.* 545 Wheþer hem leuer ware Win or ale to gete. *c* **1330** R. Brunne *Chron.* (1810) 159 Loke ȝe be me nehi, fulle gode giftes gete [so *MS.*; *printed* ȝete] ȝe. **1500–20** Dunbar *Poems* lxi. 46 Quhen uther horss had bran to byt I gat bot griss. **1567** *Satir. Poems Reform.* vii. 192 Donald the fyft, he gat the same reuaird. **1593** Shaks. *2 Hen. VI*, iv. x. 29 Thou wilt betray me, and get a 1000 Crownes of the King. **1636** Finch *Law* ii. xvii. 177 If.. within the yeare it [a stray] strayeth againe, and another Lord getteth it, the first Lord cannot take it againe. *a* **1639** W. Whateley *Prototypes* i. xix. (1640) 189 Julius, by being courteous to Paul..gave his life and the life of his soldiers for a reward. **1834** H. Miller *Scenes & Leg.* xv. (1857) 230 Pictures of little boys and girls, which, in every case, the little boys and girls got to themselves. **1844** Lady G. Fullerton *Ellen Middleton* (1854) II. x. 26 She told me she had got a note from Henry. **1890** *Blackw. Mag.* CXLVIII. 717/2 They get from 10*s.* to 12*s.* a-week for their eggs alone. **1892** *Chamb. Jrnl.* 1 Oct. 625/2 As to salaries, an officer.. usually gets sixty pounds.

b. To obtain (a name). Also ***to get the name of***: to have the reputation of (being so-and-so).

1662 J. Davies *Mandelslo's Trav.* 89 Cuncam, for so it is more commonly called, though from its Metropolis it somtimes gets the name of Visiapour. **1741** Monro *Anat. Bones* (ed. 3) 17 The first [Vertebra], from its Use of supporting the globular Head, has got the Name of *Atlas*. **1832** Austin *Jurispr.* (1879) II. xxxii. 592 Laws which have gotten the specious name of natural.

11. a. To obtain by way of concession or favour, or by means of pressure, insistence, or entreaty; e.g. ***to get mercy, forgiveness, grace, leave, permission***; ***to get an answer, information***, etc. Const. *from*, *of*, *out of*.

a **1300** *Cursor M.* 460 (Cott.) O me seruis sal he non gette. *a* **1300** *Ibid.* 484 (Gött.) Merci getis he neuer mare. *a* **1300** *Ibid.* 19605 (Cott.) O prince o preistes, gatt he leue. *c* **1350** *Will. Palerne* 1592 Þe gracious graunt þei gaten of here herande. **1362** Langl. *P. Pl.* A. vi. 126 Thou maiȝt gete grace ther, so that thou go bi-tyme. *c* **1375** *Sc. Leg. Saints, Bertholomeus* 24 Of þare god gat þai nan answere. *c* **1386** Chaucer *Manciple's Prol.* 102 Of that mateere ye gete namoore of me. *c* **1450** *St. Cuthbert* (Surtees) 5042 He gettes here forgifnes. *c* **1470** Henry *Wallace* i. 116 He gat ymage

[= homage] of Scotland swne. **1480** CAXTON *Descr. Brit.* 31 And prayde to haue a place to duelle inne and myght none gete. **1535** J. AP RICE in *Four C. Eng. Lett.* 33 As touching the convent, we coulde geate litle or no reportes. **1568** GRAFTON *Chron.* II. 209 Who with muche adoe gate leave to depart from his brother the Erle. **1602** SHAKS. *Ham.* IV. iii. 13 Where the dead body is bestow'd.. We cannot get from him. **1612** T. TAYLOR *Comm. Titus* iii. 2 Is there no iustice to be gotten at the Magistrats hand? **1651** in *Fuller's Abel Rediv., Pareus* 578 At last through Gods mercy, by importunity he gat his fathers consent. **1709** STEELE *Tatler* No. 194 ¶3, I knocked and called, but could get no Answer. **1738** *Lucca's Mem.* 17 Examining the Woman first, to get what we could from her. **1804** W. TENNANT *Ind. Recreat.* (ed. 2) I. 280 To.. get permission to enter into [his] service. **1814** D. H. O'BRIEN *Captiv. & Escape* 119 Asked if I could have a bed? I could get no answer. **1839** *36 Yrs. Seafaring Life* 263 A Frenchman never gets a word of French from me .. till I see it serves my purpose.

†**b.** with clause as object. *Obs. rare.*

1483 CAXTON *Gold. Leg.* 223b/1 Seynt James.. gate that he shold be restored to his lyf. **1556** *Aurelio & Isab.* (1608) M iv, At that tyme was it easey inoughe to gette that the deathe was not geven unto Isabell.

12. a. To obtain, come to have, attain (some immaterial thing desired or aimed at); e.g. ***to get rest, sleep, comfort; to get one's sight, health, liberty***, etc.; also ***to get one's end, one's will, one's own way***, etc.

a **1300** *Cursor M.* 12259 (Cott.) A commament nu mak i here.. þat þe poueral get sum bote. *a* **1300** *Ibid.* 13553 (Gött.) He went and weisse his eien þare, And gat [*Cott.* tok] his sight. *c* **1375** *Sc. Leg. Saints, Bertholomeus* 108 Parfyte hele þe madyne gate. *Ibid., Mathou* 412 [He] cessis nocht to threte ws al bot gyf his wil he gate. *c* **1470** HENRY *Wallace* IV. 47 Thow gettis no mendis. **1530** PALSGR. 563/1, I trust in God I shall get my desyre of hym. *a* **1547** LATIMER in Strype *Eccl. Mem.* (1733) I. II. 262 What rest hath he gotten, that is removed from the Stocks in Newgate to the Rack in the Tower? ? *a* **1550** *Freiris Berwik* 589 in *Dunbar's Poems* (1893) 304 Alesone on na wayiss gat hir will. **1581** SIDNEY *Astr. & Stella* xlv, Pitie.. gate in her breast such place, That [etc.]. **1618** RALEIGH in *Four C. Eng. Lett.* 38 When I had gotten my libertye. **1671** LADY MARY BERTIE in *12th Rep. Hist. MSS. Comm.* App. v. 22 It was so hard to get room that wee were forced to goe by four a clocke. **1674** S. VINCENT *Yng. Gallant's Acad.* Ep. Ded. A ij b, The other laughs at us when he hath got his ends. **1693** *Humours of Town* 2, I could scarce get one sound nap. **1734** tr. *Rollin's Anc. Hist.* (1827) I. 113 In what manner this passion.. got such a footing upon our stage. **1792** *Gentl. Mag.* Jan. 12/1, I got a very comfortable nap between London and St. Albans. **1860** TRENCH *Synon. N.T.* Ser. I. (ed. 5) 75 Any benefit which he could have gotten from his books. **1885** *Manch. Exam.* 8 June 4/7 If they do not get their own way they will resign.

b. Frequently with noun of action as obj.: To succeed in doing, obtain opportunity to do, what the sb. implies. Also in phrases ***to get (a) sight (a glance, glimpse, peep***, etc.) ***of, to get (a) hold of*** (†***on***, †***upon***), ***to get possession of***, etc.

a **1300** *Cursor M.* 22570 Vp to þe lift rise sal þe see, þar wit strenght to get entre. **1375** BARBOUR *Bruce* xix. 785 The discurrouris.. Of athir host has gottin sicht. **1535** COVERDALE *Ps.* cxiv. [cxvi.] 3 The paynes of hell gat holde vpon me. **1568** TILNEY *Disc. Mariage* C iv b, See I pray you .. how soone this Ladie, hath gotten holde of that sentence. **1613** PURCHAS *Pilgrimage* (1614) 32 Like men drowning, that get hold on euery twig. **1615** J. STEPHENS *Satyr. Ess.* 240 You get acquaintance with him by a bare salutation. **1699** DAMPIER *Voy.* II. II. 34 And though we followed the Blood a good way, yet did not come up with him.. to get a second shot. **1700** T. BROWN tr. *Fresny's Amusem. Ser. & Com.* 55 We made hard shift to get now and then a Glance at some of them. *a* **1703** BURKITT *On N.T.* Luke iv. 37 Where Satan has once gotten a hold.. how unwilling he is to be cast out of possession. **1748** *Anson's Voy.* II. viii. 222 We were.. in hopes of getting sight of the Gloucester. **1761–2** HUME *Hist. Eng.* (1806) V. lxvii. 64 Their enemies they thought.. had gotten possession of their sovereign's confidence. **1834** T. MEDWIN *Angler in Wales* I. 202 To the west we got a peep.. of Swansea Bay. *c* **1860** H. STUART *Seaman's Catech.* 47 As soon as the buntlines are bent get a pull of them. **1889** *Times* (weekly ed.) 13 Dec. 14/1 Every effort was made.. to get speech of the Emperor.

†**c.** ***to get a stomach***: to procure an appetite. (Also said of the means employed.)

[**1682**: see 18b. **1684** tr. *Bonet's Merc. Compit.* I. 16 Peaches eaten before Meals get a stomach, if it be lost through a hot cause.] **1688** C. HOOLE *School-Colloq.* 29 So also we shall get a stomach to our meat. **1725** WATTS *Logic* I. iv. §6 When we say.. to get a stomach, and to get a cold, etc.

d. ***to get religion*** (orig. U.S.): to be converted.

1772 in *D.A.* **1802** *Methodist New Connexion Mag.* Nov. 432 A number, too, are wrought upon in the usual way, and hopefully get religion without any of these extraordinary appearances. **1857** C. W. ELLIOTT *New Engl. Hist.* I. 460 Capt. Underhill killed his neighbor's wife, and 'got his religion on a pipe of tobacco'. *a* **1882** J. P. QUINCY *Figures of Past* (1883) 6 We had come to Andover to get religion. **1952** *Manch. Guardian Weekly* 9 Oct. 7 It is sad news for his publishers that he has got religion.

13. a. To acquire, to come to have (a quality, power, custom, etc.).

c **1600** SHAKS. *Sonn.* lxxviii, Euery Alien pen hath got my vse. **1611** —— *Cymb.* IV. ii. 236 Let vs.. though now our voyces Haue got the mannish crack, sing [etc.]. **1626** BACON *Sylva* §352 After two Nights.. it [a root] got a Shining. **1629** R. HILL *Pathw. Piety* (1849) I. 182 They have gotten a custom of sinning. **1640** FULLER *Joseph's Coat* Comm. I Cor. xi. 25 (1867) 62 Wine was then subject to spilling; it hath not since gotten a more liquid or diffusive quality. **1676** SHADWELL *Libertine* II, It's nothing but a way of speaking, which young amorous fellows have gotten. **1736** BUTLER *Anal.* I. v. Wks. 1874 I. 91 By accustoming ourselves to any course of action, we get an aptness to go on.

b. To come to have (a notion, impression, etc.). Also ***to get into one's head***; often ***to get (it) into one's head that***, etc.

1677 WYCHERLEY *Plain Dealer* IV. ii, *Jer.* How? what quirk has she got in her head now? **1762** GOLDSM. *Cit. World* lxxviii. ¶2 The people, it seems, have got into their heads that they have more wit than others. **1876** GEO. ELIOT *Dan. Deronda* I. vii, Anna had got it into her head that you would want to ride after the hounds this morning. *a* **1898** *Mod. colloq.*, Don't let him get the idea that you care nothing about it. If he gets it into his head that he is a genius, he will be intolerable.

14. a. To catch, contract (an illness).

1610 SHAKS. *Temp.* II. ii. 68 This is some Monster.. who hath got (as I take it) an Ague. **1710** STEELE *Tatler* No. 234 ¶15 To you I apply my self for Redress, having gotten.. a Cold on Sunday was Sevennight. **1765** STERNE *Tr. Shandy* VIII. vi, Art thou not tormented with the vile asthma that thou gattest in skating against the wind in Flanders? **1805** *Med. Jrnl.* XIV. 363 When a person.. gets a catarrh [etc.]. **1892** *Black & White* 13 Aug. 182/1 Horses get glanders and men get cholera.

b. *colloq.* ***to get*** (a person or thing) ***on the brain, on one's nerves***: to be crazy about, or morbidly affected by the thought of.

c. ***to have got 'em (bad)***: to have the D.T.'s, to have 'the horrors'; also in milder sense, to have a fit of nerves. *slang.*

1893 FARMER & HENLEY *Slang* III. 188/1 A very sick person, especially a patient in the horrors, is said to have *got 'em bad*. **1936** P. M. CLARK *Autobiogr. Old Drifter* xiii. 184 Another fellow who 'got 'em' was 'Taffy'. He got 'em so badly one night that he ran from the Old Drift, clad only in his nightshirt.

d. ***to have got it bad(ly)***: to have fallen love; to be infatuated. *slang.*

1911 G. B. SHAW *Getting Married* in *Doctor's Dilemma*, etc. 263 You seem to have got it pretty bad. **1921** W. J. LOCKE *Mountebank* xiii. 163 'She's got it rather badly,' Charles murmured to me. **1941** WEBSTER & ELLINGTON (*song-title*) I got it bad and that ain't good. **1969** D. CLARK *Nobody's Perfect* v. 148 Take it from me he's got it badly. He couldn't even hear me mention your name without wanting to talk about you.

15. a. ***to get wind***, † ***air*** (cf. AIR *sb.* 11), ***vent***: to get abroad, to become known to others.

1722 DE FOE *Plague* (1884) 10 It had gotten vent. **1726** *Adv. Capt. R. Boyle* 166 But my Story getting Air, I was made the Scoff of every Body. **1776** *Trial of Nundocomar* 90/2 It got wind, and a great many people asked me: I told them. **1828** *Life Planter Jamaica* 340 That it may get vent is not improbable, for these black fellows are as inquisitive [etc.]. **1884** MRS. PIRKIS *Judith Wynne* III. xi. 126 It's getting wind in the neighbourhood that the child is lost.

b. Hence (after 7b), ***to get wind of***: to hear of, become acquainted with.

1840 THACKERAY *Paris Sk.-bk.* (1867) 32 If my old aunt gets wind of it, she'll cut me off with a shilling. **1885** *Century Mag.* XXX. 380/2 If that sweet little Rose were to get wind of it, I believe she'd faint.

16. a. To receive, meet with, suffer (a fall, blow, defeat, etc.); †also (with omission of object) to be struck on a specified part of the body (constr. *on, over*, etc.). Phr. ***to get the worst of it*** (cf. 5b).

c **1375** *Sc. Leg. Saints, Peter* 585 Sike ane fall þane he gat. *c* **1475** *Rauf Coilȝear* 698 As he gat ben throw He gat mony greit schow [shove]. **1508** *Dunbar's Flyting* 48* Iuge.. quha gat the war. *a* **1550** *Christis Kirke Gr.* xx, Thay gat upon the gammis. **1597** MONTGOMERIE *Cherrie & Slae* 214, I gat sik chek Quhilk I micht nocht remuif nor nek. **1601** SHAKS. *All's Well* IV. i. 41, I must giue my selfe some hurts, and say I got them in exploit. **1632** J. HAYWARD tr. *Biondi's Eromena* 91 Who.. had (without this succour) for all his valour gotten the worst of the day. **1697** COLLIER *Ess. Mor. Subj.* I. (1703) 80 Many persons.. in the crowd and tumult of the action, get nothing but blows for their pains. *a* **1732** T. BOSTON *Crook in Lot* (1805) 163 Several of the saints have gotten on the finger ends by this means. **1738** SWIFT *Pol. Conversat.* 6, I hope you are up for all Day?—Yes, if I don't get a Fall before Night. **1809** WINDHAM *Let.* 16 Sept. in *Parl. Speeches* (1812) I. 113 A slight hurt which I got here in riding. **1888** RIDER HAGGARD *Col. Quaritch* III. i. 1 Cossey had only got the outside portion of the charge of No. 7.

b. To receive, suffer, by way of punishment.

In Sc. the obj. is often a pl. sb. with poss. pron., as ***to get one's rages***, to get a scolding (cf. quots. 1508, 1567, 1785).

1508 DUNBAR *Flyting w. Kennedie* 70 Throw all Bretane it salbe blawin owt, How that thow.. gat thy paikis. **1567** *Satir. Poems Reform.* v. 38 It war weill wairit he gat his quhippis. **1654** WHITLOCK *Zootomia* 144 And thus they get Credit among some, for which at Schoole they should have got a whipping. **1785** BURNS *Ep. to W. Simson* Postscr. 39 Monie a fallow gat his licks. **1790** —— *Tam o' Shanter* 201 Ah, Tam! ah, Tam! thou'll get thy fairin! **1889** J. K. JEROME *3 Men in Boat* 238 We did not want to overdo the thing and get six months.

c. ***to get it*** (colloq. or slang): to receive a punishment, scolding, or the like; to 'catch it'. Also ***to get it hot; to get it in the neck***: see NECK *sb.*[1] 1 e.

1872 *Figaro* 22 June 389/1 The German Emperor, Bismarck, and Earl Granville also 'got' it, but not quite so hotly. **1898** *Westm. Gaz.* 14 Jan. 4/3 You will get it hot before you are done.

d. In various *slang* phrases: ***to get the sack (bag, boot, bounce***, etc.): to be dismissed from a situation. ***to get the mitten***: to be rejected as a suitor. ***to get the lead***: to be shot. (For quots. see the sbs.)

e. ***to get his*** (or ***theirs***): to be killed. *slang.*

a **1910** 'O. HENRY' *Rolling Stones* (1913) iii. 65 Clifford Wainwright being shot by a squad of soldiers... Oh, yes, it was rum that did it. He backslided and got his. **1913** KIPLING *Diversity of Creatures* (1917) 288 He'd got *his*. I knew it by the way the head rolled in my hands. **1928** E. WALLACE *Flying Squad* xiii. 110 He'll get his one of these days. **1938** F. D. SHARPE *Sharpe of Flying Squad* viii. 107 The other women leave her alone because they know that if they don't—they'll get theirs from Johnny. **1959** N. MAILER *Advts. for Myself* (1961) 66 He was going to get his, come two three four hours. That was all right, of course, you didn't live forever.

17. a. To procure or obtain (a required thing or person); to seek out and take, to cause to come or be supplied.

a **1300** *Cursor M.* 26129 If he in suilk a nede be tan, þat he ne get man bot curst an [etc.]. **13..** *Gaw. & Gr. Knt.* 1625 þe goude ladyez were geten, & gedered þe meyny. *c* **1385** CHAUCER *L.G.W.* 1123 *Dido*, Ther nas coursere.. That in the lond of Libie may be gete. *c* **1400** *Destr. Troy* 13477 Two spies full spedely he sped hym to gete. **1465** MARG. PASTON in *P. Lett.* No. 500 II. 179, I have gyte a replevyn. **1523** FITZHERB. *Husb.* §124 Gette thy quycke-settes in the woode-countreye. ? *a* **1550** *Freiris Berwik* 247 in *Dunbar's Poems* (1893) 293 Scho stertis vp and gettis licht in hy. **1559–60** *Act 2 Eliz.* in Bolton *Stat. Irel.* (1621) 271 The bookes concerning the said services.. shall be attained and gotten before the said feast of St. John. **1585** T. WASHINGTON tr. *Nicholay's Voy.* I. xxii. 29 Moreover, we got a pilote being of the yle of Chio, in place of him that was dead. **1590** SHAKS. *Com. Err.* II. ii. 37 And you vse these blows long, I must get a sconce for my head. **1647–8** COTTERELL *Davila's Hist. Fr.* (1678) 23 Few people were to be gotten there abouts. **1700** S. L. tr. *Fryke's Voy. E. Ind.* 197 So I went up to the Village, and got a Praw, which I sent to bring him over to me. **1748** *Anson's Voy.* II. xiv. 288 We could not have failed of getting whatever numbers [of sailors] we pleased. **1818** J. W. CROKER in *C. Papers* (1884) I. iv. 113 At last I have gotten the warrant for searching for the old regalia of the Scottish Crown. **1849** MACAULAY *Hist. Eng.* iii. I. 380 The coach sometimes reached the inn so late that it was impossible to get supper.

b. with immaterial object.

1814 D. H. O'BRIEN *Captiv. & Escape* 179 Dr. B. got a lift in a waggon for three or four miles. **1879** *Lond. Soc.* Christm. No. 61/1, I went into a little shop to get a shave. **1892** H. R. MILL *Realm Nat.* xi. 61 To get Greenwich time in remote places is more difficult.

c. To obtain in marriage. *Obs.* exc. as a contextual use of 17.

1390 GOWER *Conf.* II. 242 She muste than algate faile To geten him, whan he were dede. **1611** SHAKS. *Cymb.* II. iii. 9 If I could get this foolish Imogen, I should haue Gold enough. **1738** SWIFT *Pol. Conversat.* 82, I wonder why such a handsome.. young Gentleman as you do not get some rich Widow.

†**d.** To gain, bring over to one's side; to win (a woman). *Obs.*

c **1385** CHAUCER *L.G.W.* 1753 *Lucretia*, For wel, thoghte he, she sholde nat be geten. *c* **1470** HENRY *Wallace* III. 31 It war the best for King Eduuardis awaill, Mycht he him get to be his steidfast man For gold or land.. Me think before he may nocht gottyn be. **1653** HOLCROFT *Procopius, Vandal Wars* II. xiii. 46 Maximinus.. had gotten many of those mutiners with a design to usurp.

18. With dat. of the person for whom the specified object is obtained or procured.

a. With dat. of refl. pronoun (†occas. with *to* or *unto*): To obtain, procure for oneself.

a **1300** *Cursor M.* 4607 (Cott.) Do gett þe a god purueur þat in þis nede þe mai socur. *c* **1340** *Ibid.* 21094 (Fairf.) Thomas.. preiched.. for to gite him heiuen to mede. *c* **1375** *Sc. Leg. Saints, Cristofore* 517 Gais & gettis ȝou lechis fele, ȝoure brokine godis fore to hele. *c* **1385** CHAUCER *L.G.W.* 2160 *Ariadne*, [He] gat him ther a newe barge anoon. *a* **1400–50** *Alexander* 794 Kest hym on þis yong knyght to gett hym a name. **1548** HALL *Chron., Edw. IV*, 237b, You .. by your.. noble feates have gotten to you, in maner an immortall fame. **1597** GERARDE *Herbal* I. iv. §2 (1633) 6 This water grasse doth get vnto it selfe some new rootes. **1628** HOBBES *Thucyd.* (1629) 70 A man of Argilus.. got him a Seale like to the Seale of Pausanias. **1690** EVELYN *Mem.* (1857) III. 315, I have now gotten me a pair of new horses. **1797** HAN. MORE in Lady Chatterton *Mem. Ld. Gambier* (1861) I. 320 This young lady has got her a husband. **1842** TENNYSON *Locksley Hall* 18 In the spring the wanton lapwing gets himself another crest.

b. To obtain or procure for others. Chiefly with simple dat. of personal pronoun, but also (in later writers) with *to* and *for*.

a **1300** *Cursor M.* 3502 (Gött.) Ay was he bone, To gete [*Cott.* fete] his fadir venisun. *a* **1300** *Ibid.* 7293 (Cott.) Gett vs a king. *c* **1350** *Will. Palerne* 644 Melior.. preide hire prineli.. to gete hire þat gode gras as sone as sche miȝt. *c* **1385** CHAUCER *L.G.W.* 1649 *Hypsip. & Medea*, [She] gat him greet name as a conquerour. *c* **1430** *Syr Tryam.* 454 A norse they gatt hyt [a child] untylle. *a* **1550** *Freiris Berwik* 255 in *Dunbar's Poems* (1893) 294 Ga, gait me cheiss and breid. **1559** W. CUNNINGHAM *Cosmogr. Glasse* 1 This was it which gat him so many victories. **1596** SHAKS. *Tam. Shr.* I. i. 123 *Gre.* What's that, I pray. *Hor.* Marrie sir to get a husband for her Sister. **1600** in *Shaks. C. Praise* 36 Promysyng to gete them xls. more then their ordynary to play yt. **1682** SHADWELL *Lanc. Witches* 11, Coursing had gotten me a woundy stomach, and I eat like a Swine. **1690** LOCKE *Hum. Und.* I. ii. §15 They are lodg'd in the Memory, and Names got to them. **1890** SIR A. KEKEWICH in *Law Times Rep.* LXIII. 683/2 The landowner requires a carriage for his own use, and he asks the estate agent to get it for him.

19. a. To procure by hunting or fishing; to catch. Now somewhat *rare*.

a **1300** *Cursor M.* 3522 Bath on fer and ner he soght, Bot þat dai wayth þan gatt he noght. *c* **1300** *Havelok* 1393 He wore yare, Grimes sones, for to fare In-to þe se, fishes to gete. **13..** *Gaw. & Gr. Knt.* 1171 þe gre-hounde ȝ so grete, þat geten hem [the deer] bylyue. *c* **1450** *St. Cuthbert* (Surtees) 4345 Elfride men fared fysshe to gete. **1694** *Acc. Sev. Late Voy.* II. (1711) 12 On the 9th we got another male whale, being the eighth. **18..** KINGSLEY *Poems, Sands of Dee* 17 Was never salmon got [*v.r.* yet] that shone so fair.

b. To bring in, gather, secure (a crop).
1523 FITZHERB. *Husb.* §25 Shorte hey, and leye hey is good for shepe, and all maner of catell if it be well got. **1657** AUSTEN *Fruit Trees* I. 5 From the time that fruits come to be worth getting, till they be ripe. **1773** *Phil. Trans.* LXIII. 222 The crop of wheat where it was well gotten was tolerable good. **1858** *Jrnl. R. Agric. Soc.* XIX. I. 230 Hay secured before the 27th of June was got without a drop of rain. **1891** *Blackw. Mag.* CXLIX. 817/1, I remember well the fustiness of that haystack (it must have been 'got' after oceans of rain).

c. To obtain (coal, ore, etc.) by mining.
1664 POWER *Exp. Philos.* 172 The Roof and Seat is the Top and Bottom of the Works, wherein they get Coles. **1671** J. WEBSTER *Metallogr.* i. 18 The Pits or Shafts where Ores are usually gotten. **1841** *Collieries & Coal Trade* (ed. 2) 244 In proceeding to get the coal, the collier, whenever he can do so, works upon the face of the bed. **1885** *Law Times* LXXIX. 119/2 The 'butties'..paid him his wages out of the 2*s.* 3*d.* per ton which they received for getting the coal.

†**20.** To take hold of (something) in one's hands.
c **1375** *Sc. Leg. Saints, Baptist* 1100 þis tyrand..in hand a knyfe can gete. *c* **1400** *Melayne* 104 His swerd in his hand he gat. **1592** R. D. *Hypnerotomachia* 88 Getting him by the winges, she was about to plucke of his fethers.

21. a. To get hold of, capture (a person); also (in recent colloquial use, esp. in perf. and pa. t.), to have an advantage over (another), to 'corner'. Also, to puzzle, perplex, nonplus. So ***to get*** (someone) ***where one wants him*** (or ***her***): to have at one's mercy; to render subservient, dependent, etc.
1596 SPENSER *State Irel.* Wks. (Globe) 624/1 Many of them be such losells and scatterlings, as that they cannot easely by any sheriff..be gotten. **1607** SHAKS. *Cor.* V. iv. 39 The Plebeians haue got your Fellow Tribune, And hale him vp and downe. **1868** *Harper's Mag.* Mar. 538/2 Scratching his head a minute, Benjamin F. replied: 'Well, I confess your Honor's got me there!' **1879** 'CAVENDISH' *Card Ess.* 198 Second hand put on knave, saying, 'Now I've got you!' **1887** F. FRANCIS Jr. *Saddle & Mocassin* xiii. 236 Who was Navajo? Ah, that's where you've got me, young man. Heaven knows. **1888** H. F. LESTER *Hartas Maturin* III. vi. 157 Yes..I did. I don't deny it. You've got me there. **1906** W. CHURCHILL *Coniston* I. xiv. 171 'What's the name of your gal?' 'Well,' said Mr. Hopkins, 'I guess you've got me. We did christen her Lily, but she didn't turn out exactly Lily... I guess her name's Cassandra.' **1936** W. DE LA MARE *Wind blows Over* 32 'That's Mistaken Point,' he said. 'Why was it mistaken?' He shook his head... 'That's got me, miss,' he replied. **1939** A. THIRKELL *Before Lunch* iii. 76 You only want to get her where you want her. Most people are like that. **1968** A. CLARKE *Darkened Room* iii. 41 Silly young fool, I thought angrily; he's got you where he wants you.

b. colloq. ***what has got*** (——)?: what has befallen or happened to, what has become of (——)?
1823 SCORESBY *Whale Fishery* 124 They all at once, on looking round..enquired what had got Carr.

c. To succeed in taking or catching (a person or animal); *spec.* (orig. *U.S.*) to succeed in killing or injuring; to shoot or kill.
1853 'P. PAXTON' *Yankee in Texas* 118 [A Texan] does not kill his game, he *saves* or *gets it*, or *makes it come*. **1887** F. FRANCIS *Saddle & Mocassin* vii. 138 They'll get you one of these days, Colonel, when you are driving around in your wagon. **1899** B. TARKINGTON *Gentlemen fr. Indiana* ix. 160 Wiley,..you don't think they've got him? **1900** E. GLYN *Visits Eliz.* 50 She did not hit any rabbits, but she got a gardener in the leg. **1908** *Daily Chron.* 16 Sept. 7/5 This climate is sure to get a white man sooner or later. **1917** 'S. ROHMER' *Hand of FuManchu* (1920) viii. 65, I turned, dizzily, to see Fletcher sinking to his knees, one hand clutching his breast. 'She got me...with the knife,' he whispered. **1932** [see AGENT *sb.* 4b]. **1951** R. CAMPBELL *Light on Dark Horse* xxiii. 334 He never told me whether he was implicated in the attempt to 'get' Guillermo, or not.

d. To exercise, worry, annoy. *colloq.* (orig. *U.S.*).
1867 B. HARTE *Condensed Novels* 280 To have let bigger things go by, and to be taken in by this cheap trick..is what gets me. **1904** W. H. SMITH *Promoters* xii. 190, I wish to the Lord he hadn't been so quick about it. That's what gets me. **1926** W. DEEPING *Sorrell & Son* xxix, 'Do you think he minds?' 'I know he doesn't. But it gets me.' **1960** B. COBB *Don't lie to Police* ix. 149 It got me—her talking that way.

e. To enthral, attract, appeal to; to touch emotionally, to obsess. *colloq.*
1913 R. BROOKE *Let.* 20 Nov. (1968) 532 It's the *Rhythm* that gets you. **1916** *To-Day* 11 Nov. 50/3 The 'curtain' on that dog walking across the stage and sticking his cold nose into the hand of his lonely master always used to get me. **1928** F. N. HART *Bellamy Trial* i. 6 'It [*sc.* murder]'s always interested me more than anything else.'..'Well, don't let it get you. I'd just keep it as a hobby.' **1938** G. GREENE *Brighton Rock* II. i. 68 'It gets you,' the Boy said, 'it gets you,' surrendering himself to the huge brazen suggestion. **1958** B. HAMILTON *Too Much of Water* xi. 243 'How was it that the '*Dichterliebe*' made you cry?' 'I can't answer that. Somehow it got me.'

22. a. To succeed in finding (what is required).
1615 J. STEPHENS *Satyr. Ess.* 297 Like a Trumpeter in the fields, that shifts places to get an eccho. **1670** NARBOROUGH *Jrnl.* in *Acc. Sev. Late Voy.* (1711) 114, I caused the Lead to be cast forth, but could not get ground at eighty Fathom. **1748** *Anson's Voy.* II. x. 242 To stand no farther to the northward than is..necessary for the getting a westerly wind. **1865** KINGSLEY *Herew.* xxx, Driving them mad and desperate just that you may get a handle against them. **1873** BLACK *Pr. Thule* xxvi, Her father..wondered what he could get to scold her about.

b. To obtain an audible signal from (a radio or television transmitter or station); to 'pick up'.
1899 *Windsor Mag.* X. 145/2 Another station can always get us in a few minutes. **1921** *Wireless World* XI. 571/1 To ensure that the signals be picked up if it is at all possible to get them. *Ibid.* 586/2 If it be possible to get the Dutch concerts..with this three-valve set. **1924** *Wireless Ann.* 25 Hello, did you get me? 8 XY standing by. **1947** M. LOWRY *Under Volcano* vi. 162 Hugh..turned the radio dial back and forth, trying to get San Antonio. **1965** H. C. WOODRUFF *Short Wave Listener's Guide* (chapter for U.K. readers), Although one may expect to be able to get the majority of the stations in this list, the frequencies..may well be different from those quoted..for American reception.

c. To get in touch by telephone with (a person or place).
1907 [see sense 7d, above]. **1908** G. B. SHAW *Let.* 1 July (1956) 126, I have just telephoned Stella... I tried to get Mrs. Pat herself... I also tried to get Forbes..but he was out. **1958** WODEHOUSE *Cocktail Time* xxi. 174 He took up the receiver... 'I hear you've been trying to get me. What's your trouble?'

d. To answer (a telephone, door-bell, etc.); usu. ***to get it.***
1941 THURBER & NUGENT *Male Animal* I. 29 (Doorbell rings.).. *Tommy* (going to door). I'll get it.

23. *colloq.* To take, 'have', eat (one's dinner, etc.).
1888 *Sheffield Gloss.* s.v., Come and get your tea with us. **1892** 'J. S. WINTER' *Mere Luck* i, Here, get your dinner, my lad.

24. The perfect tense is used in familiar language in senses equivalent to those of the present tense of *have* or *possess*. (Cf. Gr. κεκτῆσθαι to possess, lit. to have acquired.) So (*colloq.* or *vulgar*) in recent use ***to have got to*** = 'to have to', to be obliged to (see HAVE 7); also (orig. *U.S.*) in the sense of 'must', 'to be certainly'.
[**1596** SHAKS. *Merch. V.* II. ii. 99 What a beard hast thou got; thou hast got more haire on thy chin, then Dobbin my philhorse has on his taile.] **1607** —— *Timon* I. ii. 26 Fie, th' art a churle, ye haue got a humour there Does not become a man. **1699** T. C[OCKMAN] *Tully's Offices* (1706) 234 But I, who han't got such a strength of Genius. **1712** J. JAMES tr. *Le Blond's Gardening* 144 They have got a Custom of heading it from Time to Time. **1738** SWIFT *Pol. Conversat.* 68 Miss, you have got my Handkerchief; pray, let me have it. **1775** JOHNSON *Let. to Boswell* 23 Dec., I have just now got a cough; but it has never yet hindered me from sleeping. **1839–40** THACKERAY *Catherine* v, He has..got C. R. in blue upon his right arm. **1865** 'L. CARROLL' *Alice in Wonderland* iv. 54 The first thing I've got to do is to grow to my right size again. *Ibid.* 57 I'd nearly forgotten that I've got to grow up again. **1875–7** RUSKIN *Morn. Florence* (1882) 129 Quite 'from the heart'—such hearts as the people have got. **1875** 'MARK TWAIN' in *Atlantic Monthly* Mar. 283/2 This has got to be learned. **1876** RUSKIN *Fors Clav.* VI. lxx. 315, I am very doubtful..whether you have wit enough to understand a word more of what I have got to say this month. **1878** JEVONS *Primer Pol. Econ.* 12 As a general rule the banker has not got in his possession the money which he owes to his customers. **1887** A. BIRRELL *Obiter Dicta* Ser. II. 125 What ..has the general public got to do with literature? **1889** MRS. C. CARR *Marg. Maliphant* II. xvii. 42 The thing has got to be fought out. **1919** E. JORDAN *Girl in Mirror* (1925) iv. 79 You'll have to see me every day. I've got to look after you. **1968** *Amer. N. & Q.* Mar. 104/1 If there's cockfighting today it's got to be in the bluegrass around Lexington, Kentucky. **1968** L. O'DONNELL *Face of Crime* (1969) ix. 125 Now I was really appalled. 'You've got to be kidding.' **1969** R. AIRTH *Snatch!* vi. 61 He said to Morland, 'This guy has got to be a comedian.'

¶The pa. pple. is also used *colloq.* with omission of (*I*) *have*. Cf. GOTCHA, GOTCHER, GOTTA.
1849 *Knickerbocker* XXXIV. 12 They got no principles. They got no platform to stand onto. **1857** *Quinland* I. 1 Got an hour to spare—thought I'd just run in and see what you were all about. **1884** [see GET-OUT 1]. **1887** M. E. WILKINS *Humble Romance* 370 What you got there, grandma? **1911** R. D. SAUNDERS *Col. Todhunter* i. 11 Oh, of course, you got to laugh at me. **1911** J. F. WILSON *Land Claimers* ix. 118 But I got several plans, and I need ye. **1941** [see sense 14d]. **1967** [see GAWD.].

†**II. 25.** To gain, reach, arrive at (a place).
a **1300** *Cursor M.* 12382 Forþ in þes he bad þam ga.. Til þai had geten þair herd a-gain. *a* **1375** *Joseph Arim.* 523 Hedde þei geten þat holt..þei mihten haue do muche harm. *a* **1547** SURREY *Æneid* II. 264 With sound of broken waves they gate the strand. **1578** T. N. tr. *Conq. W. India* 31 The fleete sayled to get the coast of Yucatan. **1613** PURCHAS *Pilgrimage* (1614) 504 The men saved themselves, and.. built a Carvall, wherein to get the Continent. **1712** W. ROGERS *Voy.* App. 2 If the Wind blows strong out, and you cannot get the Harbour, you must anchor.

III. 26. To beget, procreate (said of the male parent); now *rare* exc. of animals, esp. horses. Const. *on*, *upon*. †In early use *occas.* of both parents.
[Quot. 1300 is the only instance in our material in which the word begins with ȝ instead of *g*; as the sense is here identical with that of *biȝeten*, BEGET *v.*, the word seems to be either a shortening of the native compound vb. or an assimilation of the adopted Scandinavian simple vb. to the form of the compound.]
c **1300** *Leg. Gregory* 132 He miȝt se þe sinnes sore, Hou he was ȝeten and of wham. *c* **1300** *Havelok* 495 Sweren y wole, þat bircabein Neuere yete me ne gat. *c* **1330** R. BRUNNE *Chron.* (1810) 27 Fourtene childre he gate opon tuo wifes. **1382** WYCLIF *Ecclus.* iii. 8 He shal serue to them that geeten hym. *c* **1400** *Destr. Troy* 290 Ercules was getton of a god on a gret lady. *c* **1450** *Merlin* 213 On hir he gat a doughter the same nyght that he had geten Gonnore on his wife. **1523** FITZHERB. *Husb.* §68 It is a horse foole, bycause a horse gate it. **1594** *2nd Pt. Contention* (1843) 143 Whosoeuer got thee, there thy mother stands. **1676** HOBBES *Iliad* I. 265 Though you be strong and on a Goddess got. *c* **1704** PRIOR *Henry & Emma* 136 What groom shall get, and 'squire maintain the child. **1727** ARBUTHNOT *John Bull* II. iv, Hocus loved her best, believing her to be his own, got upon the body of Mrs. Bull. **1760** R. HEBER *Horse Matches* ix. 144 Bay Horse..sure in getting stock. **1845** FORD *Handbk. Spain* I. 53 It means strictly speaking the foal of an ass got by a horse. **1859** *Jrnl. R. Agric. Soc.* XX. II. 350 Thoroughbred Stallions for getting hunters. **1923** R. GRAVES *Feather Bed* 23 We are his sons Got on she-furies of our Northern gales.
fig. **1691** T. H[ALE] *Acc. New Invent.* 19 If they were under any disbelief themselves, or aimed at the getting any in others, touching the Truth of Fact now discoursed upon [etc.]. **1733** *Islington* Pref., This Pamphlet..'Twas got, conceived and born in six Hours' space.

IV. With compl. indicating some change effected in the position or state of the object.

27. Followed by a prep. or adv. of place: **a.** To succeed in bringing, conveying, putting, causing to come or go (*to*, *from*, *into*, *out of* a place, *through*, *over*, etc. a space).
As *get* may be apprehended as the equivalent of *come to have*, a static prep. is sometimes used, e.g. 'If I can get the key *in* the hole.'
[*c* **1350** *Will. Palerne* 2895 þe grettest of þe grim bestes he gat to prison sone.] *c* **1450** *St. Cuthbert* (Surtees) 6024 þare was a monke of durham To helpe to kary þis bell hame.. he did his bisynes ilk a dele to durham it to gett. **1568** E. TILNEY *Disc. Marriage* E iv b, If you perceive him in such case..speake hym faire..till you get him to bed. **1627** CAPT. SMITH *Seaman's Gram.* ix. 38 He commands them to get the sailes to the yards. **1669** STURMY *Mariner's Mag.* 17 Go hawl down the Yeard, and get the Sail into the Ship. **1712** W. ROGERS *Voy.* 25 We were forc'd to get a Rope from the Ship to the watering-place. **1748** *Anson's Voy.* II. ii. 133 We bent the cable to the spare anchor, and got it over the ship's side. **1793** SMEATON *Edystone L.* §318 The wind..blowed too fresh for her to be gotten into the Gut. **1859** JEPHSON *Brittany* ii. 11 The next point was to get my little knapsack through the custom-house. **1888** A. DE G. STEVENS *Miss Hildreth* II. iv. 74 The same powerful influence that got her out of Russia..has now sent her back.

b. *refl.* To betake oneself to or convey oneself away from a place; to make one's way, to go; esp. in imperative phrases, as ***get thee*** (***you***) ***away***, ***hence***, ***in***, ***out***, etc. (Cf. 28c.) Now only *arch.*
1513 MORE in Grafton *Chron.* (1568) II. 765 [She] got her selfe in all the hast possible..out of the palace of Westminster. **1530** PALSGR. 562/1 Get the hence. *Ibid.* 562/2, I get me hence..I get me out of the waye..I get me a syde. **1579** GOSSON *Sch. Abuse* (Arb.) 54 Shut vp the Schoole, and get you home. **1591** SHAKS. *Two Gent.* IV. iv. 64 Goe, get thee hence, and finde my dog againe. **1603** KNOLLES *Hist. Turks* (1621) 53 [He] got him up into the highest tower of the pallace. **1700** S. L. tr. *Fryke's Voy. E. Ind.* 17 Early the next morning I got me above Deck. **1733** FIELDING *Intrig. Chambermaid* I. iii, Hist! hist! get you both about your business. **1828** HAWTHORNE *Fanshawe* iv. (1883) 115 The elderly men..gat themselves silently to their steeds, and hied homeward. **1886** G. T. STOKES *Celtic Ch.* (1888) 128 He got himself back to his beloved Iona.

c. To bring, succeed in bringing (oneself, another person, a thing) into or out of a certain position or state. ***to get with child***: to make pregnant. ***to get*** (a person) ***upon***: to bring (him) to talk about (a subject).
As in a, the preposition may be of static import.
1530 PALSGR. 562/2, I get a wenche with chylde, *je engrosse*. **1592** SHAKS. *Rom. & Jul.* V. i. 84 Buy food, and get thy selfe in flesh. **1601** —— *Jul. C.* I. i. 34 To weare out their shooes, to get myselfe into more worke. **1607** —— *Timon* III. i. 30 Honesty is his [fault]. I ha told him on't, but I could nere get him from't. **1608** —— *Per.* I. i. 168 If I can get him within my Pistols length, Ile make him sure enough. **1659** B. HARRIS *Parival's Iron Age* 94 Having gotten on foot, a fresh Army of sixteen thousand men. **1712** W. ROGERS *Voy.* 32 A wild Ass, which after a long Chase they got within shot and wounded. **1715** LEONI *Palladio's Archit.* (1742) II. 59 Sylvia being soon after got with child. **1748** *Anson's Voy.* II. iv. 161 We exerted ourselves in getting our ships in readiness for the sea. **1802** MAR. EDGEWORTH *Moral T.* (1806) I. xv. 121 He was sorry to find that Forester had gotten himself into such a scrape. **1822** G. W. MANBY *Voy. Greenland* (1823) 19 He ..got the ship under close-reefed topsails. **1823** SCORESBY *Whale Fishery* 289 Having..got our prizes in tow, we stretched about a league to the east-ward. **1875** JOWETT *Plato* (ed. 2) I. 26 A difficulty into which I have got myself. **1891** MISS DOWIE *Girl in Karp.* ix. 111 We fell a-talking about one thing and another. Very soon I got him upon legends and tales of the district. **1896** *Law Times* C. 508/1 Mr. Justice Grantham succeeded in getting the animal under control.

d. ***to get*** (someone) ***at it***: to have (a person) 'on', to make fun of. *slang.*
1958 F. NORMAN *Bang to Rights* III. 136 You see I did this on perpose just to get her at it. *Ibid.* 151 He had half sused that the boggie was getting him at it.

28. With pa. pple. as complement: **a.** To cause, or succeed in causing, the specified action to be performed upon (a person or thing). Also *refl.*, and (rarely, with intentional quaintness) in *passive*.
1500–20 DUNBAR *Poems* xliii. 43 Thay get indoist Alhaill thair evidens. **1548** *Invent. Ch. Goods* (Surtees) 119, I can get no such some [= sum] confessed. **1560** WHITEHORNE tr. *Machiavelli's Arte of Warre* (1573) 73 b, The first thing that he ought to doo is to get described and paincted oute all the countrie. **1628** HOBBES *Thucyd.* (1822) 127 Without gifts there was nothing to be gotten done amongst them. **1689** *Tryal Bps.* 134 These Declarations which they were commanded to take care of getting read. **1768** STERNE *Sent. Journ.* (1778) II. 120 (*Le Dimanche*), La Fleur..had got himself so gallantly array'd, I scarce knew him. **1779** R. GRAVES *Columella* I. 184 Poor Barty..had applied, and got himself appointed a writer to the..East India Company. **1843** CARLYLE *Past & Pr.* IV. i, The Bravest men..had here ..been got selected. **1870** —— *Corr. w. Emerson* (1883) II. 331, I am by no means certain..that the whole of this amendatory programme will get itself performed to equal satisfaction. **1876** RUSKIN *Fors Clav.* VI. lxvii. 234, I have

more to say when my lecture on Jewels can be got published. **1877** MISS YONGE *Cameos* Ser. III. I. 3 The difficulty was, not in making laws, but in getting them obeyed. **1877** MRS. OLIPHANT *Makers Flor.* Introd. 12 One of the most costly, splendid, and elaborate structures in the world..got itself built.

b. To incur or suffer some specified injury to (something belonging to one, a part of the body).

1787 T. JEFFERSON *Writ.* (1859) II. 249, I got my right wrist dislocated. **1790** J. B. MORETON *Mann. W. Ind.* 23 To avoid heats and colds..as well as getting your feet wet. **1889** DOYLE *Micah Clarke* vi. 47 You might chance to get your own skin beaten.

c. *to get oneself gone*: to take oneself away, go, be off; esp. *get thee (you) gone.* (Cf. 27 b.) Now only *arch.*

1590 SHAKS. *Com. Err.* III. i. 84 Go, get thee gon, fetch me an iron Crow. **1632** J. HAYWARD tr. *Biondi's Eromena* 85 Repose your selfe on your pillow, or I will get me gone. **1678** OTWAY *Friendship in F.* 26 *Sir Nob.* Well, get thee gone for an Arch-wagg. **1712** ARBUTHNOT *John Bull* I. xii, Get you gone into the country, to look after your mother's poultry. **1891** *Illustr. Lond. News* 21 Mar. 382/2 He was recommended to get him gone.

29. With adjective: To bring into the specified state; esp. in *to get ready*.

1590 SPENSER *F.Q.* I. i. 19 He..knitting all his force, got one hand free. **1605** SHAKS. *Lear* I. iv. 8 Let me not stay a iot for dinner, go get it ready. **1639** T. BRUGIS tr. *Camus' Mor. Relat.* 247 The maid runnes against the chamber door, gets it open [etc.]. **1674** tr. *Martiniere's Voy. N. Countries* 22, I caused the Horses and break-fast to be got ready. **1712** W. ROGERS *Voy.* 133 This morning we..got every thing ready to depart. **1818** M. G. LEWIS *Jrnl. W. Ind.* (1834) 129, I visited the hospital while breakfast was getting ready. **1847** MARRYAT *Childr. N. Forest* xi, Let us first get him all right again. **1889** J. MASTERMAN *Scotts of Bestminster* II. viii. 27 The boats were got ready and the passengers collected.

30. a. With an infinitive (now always preceded by *to*): To induce, prevail upon (a person), succeed in causing (a thing), *to* do something; in weaker sense, to cause or set (a person) *to* do something for one.

c **1460** *Towneley Myst.* xxi. 218 And so myght we gett hym som word for to say. **1596** SHAKS. *Tam. Shr.* I. ii. 38, I bad the rascall knocke vpon your gate, And could not get him for my heart to do it. **1598** —— *Merry W.* II. ii. 76 They could neuer get her so much as sippe on a cup with the prowdest of them all. **1612** DRAYTON *Poly-olb.* i. 443 Their King Groffarius [they] get to raise his powerfull force. **1647** W. BROWNE tr. *Gomberville's Polexander* III. v. 134 Get him be propitious to thee. *Ibid.* IV. v. 339 By the helpe of a great tumult which he heard in the lower towne, hee got slide some troopes into the enemies intrenchments. **1662** J. DAVIES *Olearius' Voy. Ambass.* 83 The women..got their husbands to sit down again. **1701** W. WOTTON *Hist. Rome, Marcus* i. 9 His Mother had much ado to get him but to cover the Bed..with Skins. **1771** MRS. GRIFFITH tr. *Viaud's Shipwreck* 51 It would be impossible to get them to listen to reason. **1791** 'G. GAMBADO' *Ann. Horsem.* x. (1809) 108 The horse..went oddly; and I got the hostler..to get up instead of me. **1807–8** W. IRVING *Salmag.* xvii. (1860) 389 At such times there was no getting Will to join in our walks. **1887** A. BIRRELL *Obiter Dicta* Ser. II. 75 He promptly got a bookseller to pirate Curll's edition.

†**b.** With passive infinitive: To cause to undergo the specified action. *Obs. rare.* (Cf. 28 a.)

c **1592** MARLOWE *Jew of Malta* III. iii, *Abig.* I am bold to sollicite thee. *Fry.* Wherein? *Abig.* To get me be admitted for a Nun. **1681** H. MORE *Exp. Dan.* 166 Laodice..got him to be poisoned. **1736** LEDIARD *Life Marlborough* I. 20 His Father got him to be made Page of Honour.

V. *intr.*

31. a. To succeed in coming or going, to bring oneself *to, from, into, out of*, etc. (a place or position), *through, over*, etc. (a space, an intervening object); also, in weaker sense, to come in the course or at the end of a journey *to*. †Of land: to stretch, extend (*obs.*). Used with any of the preps. which usually follow vbs. of motion, also with advs. of motion to or from a place, as *hither* (*here*), *thither* (*there*), *hence, thence*, and adverbial and prepositional phrases, as *to get as far as, to get the length of*. Formerly conjugated with *be*.

For *fig.* phrases, as *to get to the bottom of, root of, windward of*, see the sbs.

a **1300** [see *get away* (61), *get out* (72)]. *a* **1375** *Joseph Arim.* 497 Þei han geten on hem þe lengþe of a gleyue. **1375** BARBOUR *Bruce* XVIII. 454 Thai bar thaim swa That thai ar gottyn aboun the bra. *a* **1400** *Sir Perc.* 2225 Be that so nere getis he, That scho myghte nangatis fle. *a* **1533** LD. BERNERS *Huon* lxi. 212 Yf they perceyue vs, we shal neuer get hense. **1548** HALL *Chron., Hen. V*, 74 Many..[were] apprehended before they could get to the castel. **1585** T. WASHINGTON tr. *Nicholay's Voy.* I. xx. 25 b, He found meanes to recover a barke, intoo the which he and his men got. **1593** SHAKS. *Lucr.* 549 From earths dark womb some gentle gust doth get. **1598** B. JONSON *Ev. Man in Hum.* II. ii. (1601) D 4 a, S'lid I am afeard they will know me, would I could get by them. **1639** T. BRUGIS tr. *Camus' Mor. Relat.* 192 Basse or Low-Brittaine, is a corner of the earth which gets farre into the Ocean. **1647** W. BROWNE tr. *Gomberville's Polexander* IV. v. 326 Assoone as she was gotten into a grove of Orange-trees..she call'd for Palantus. **1667** MILTON *P.L.* IX. 594 Amid the Tree now got..to pluck and eat my fill I spar'd not. **1693** *Humours of Town* 18 Let us get into the most airy Room of the House. **1701** W. WOTTON *Hist. Rome, Alexander* iii. 510 Maximus was got as far as Ravenna. **1728** NEWTON *Chronol. Amended* i. 181 Hercules that year got into Italy. **1793** SMEATON *Edystone L.* §262 The buss..had got a considerable distance from the buoy;..we had really got out of the accustomed place. **1820** SOUTHEY *Life Wesley* II. 452 No less than ninety persons set out in pursuit of him; but he was got beyond their reach. **1847** MARRYAT *Childr. N. Forest* v, We never can get across this patch of clear grass without being seen. **1849** MACAULAY *Hist. Eng.* v. I. 609 The drums of Dumbarton's regiment beat to arms; and the men got fast into their ranks. **1867** HOWELLS *Ital. Journ.* 71 We were got no further than Porto Longone.

b. To reach, attain, come *to* an end aimed at, or a condition towards which progress has been made. *to get to blows*: to come to blows, to begin to fight.

1626 BACON *Sylva* §744 Those that are very Cold, and especially in their Feet, cannot get to Sleepe. **1701** SWIFT *Contests Nobles & Com.* Wks. 1755 II. I. 30 The Carthaginians were declining, because the balance was got too much on the side of the people. **1751** PALTOCK *Peter Wilkins* I. xxvi. 257 He..got to champing the Blade. **1798** T. JEFFERSON *Writ.* (1859) IV. 205 The scene has not yet got to its height. **1888** MCCARTHY & MRS. PRAED *Ladies' Gallery* III. xv. 298 He..succeeded in getting to speech of a police officer. **1891** *Leeds Mercury* 27 Apr. 4/4 The hostile parties got to blows and stone-throwing. **1895** *19th Cent.* Aug. 322, I don't think that I get quite as far as having views of my own.

c. *colloq.* or *slang. where has it got to*: what has become of it. *to get there*: (*U.S.*) to attain one's object, be successful in an undertaking. *to get nowhere, not to get anywhere*: not to reach any goal or object; to make no progress; to achieve nothing. *to get somewhere*: to be successful; to make some progress.

1887 F. FRANCIS Jr. *Saddle & Mocassin* viii. 144 He said as he'd been gambling, and was two hundred dollars ahead of the town. He 'got there with both feet' at starting. **1888** *N.Y. Herald* 29 July (Farmer), Although not a delegate he got there all the same. **1889** J. K. JEROME *3 Men in Boat* 242 Muttering something about its being extraordinary where his umbrella could have got to. **1891** *Daily News* 18 Nov. 5/1 As the humorous American phrase goes, 'he gets there all the same'. **1923** H. C. WITWER *Fighting Blood* i. 18 I'm going to *get* somewhere! Right now I ain't got no more idea than a baby of what I'm going to be. **1925** *New Yorker* 14 Nov. 13/3 If he was sharper, this Sandburg, he'd get nowhere. **1932** W. CATHER *Obscure Destinies* i. 84 Mrs. Rosen felt that she was not getting anywhere. **1940** E. H. W. MEYERSTEIN *Let.* 4 June (1959) 242 Even when Jews 'get somewhere'—if they marry Englishwomen they are condemned by their wives. **1960** C. DAY LEWIS *Buried Day* viii. 174 Unless you get inside their ring you will get nowhere. **1961** *Guardian* 4 Nov. 7/6 Talking alone will get nowhere.

d. *colloq.* (orig. *U.S.*) (often in form *git*): To be off, 'clear out'. Also = sense 80 g.

1864 *Harper's Mag.* Oct. 565/2 Belaboring the mules till he was tired, and telling them to 'git' till he was hoarse. **1874** 'MARK TWAIN' *Sk.* 12/1 Then he says, 'one-two-three-*git!*' **1884** *Graceville* (Minn.) *Transcript* 25 Aug., He presented a cocked revolver and told them to get, and they got. **1887** F. FRANCIS Jr. *Saddle & Mocassin* iv. 83 A captain and a full company appeared, but this brave man 'made them get'. **1888** 'R. BOLDREWOOD' *Robbery under Arms* II. xi. 190 'I reckon you're bound to git.' 'Yes, Bill, sharp's the word.' **1889** H. O'REILLY *50 Yrs. on Trial* 170, I therefore thought discretion the better part of valour, and the sooner I 'got' the better. **1892** H. NISBET *Bushranger's Sweetheart* xxiii. 176 None of your damned impertinence. Get. **1893** MCCARTHY *Red Diamonds* I. 66 He got up and gitted before we struck ile. **1895** *Blackw. Mag.* Aug. 282 Our team proceeded with many a 'git' and whip crack from their dusky Jehu. **1907** *Daily Chron.* 21 Nov. 5/1 In other words, as the Americans said, 'That fleet can get.' **1938** G. GREENE *Brighton Rock* II. i. 81 Turn out the light and get. **1959** 'D. BUCKINGHAM' *Wind Tunnel* viii. 72, I want you out of the way—so git. And what's more—git quickly. **1967** K. GILES *Death & Mr. Prettyman* ii. 62 Anybody in a room either gets or pays for another twenty-four hours.

†**e.** quasi-*trans. to get one's way(s*: to go away, take oneself off. *Obs.*

1375 BARBOUR *Bruce* XIX. 683 The fox scathless gat his way. **1606** BIRNIE *Kirk-Buriall* (1833) 18 Either God must get his way, or be content to dwell in a dedicate Innes to Idoles. **1815** *Woman's Will* III. ii, Well, get thy ways for an incorrigible coxcomb.

f. *to get by oneself*: to escape from company.

1863 MRS. C. CLARKE *Shaks. Char.* iii. 65 Inexpressibly affecting is that eagerness he betrays to get by himself.

g. To reach the point or stage where; freq. in *U.S.* const. *so. colloq.*

1906 E. DYSON *Fact'ry 'Ands* viii. 98, I got I could pick 'em out in me sleep. **1944** E. S. GARDNER *Case of Crooked Candle* (1947) xviii. 193 You get so you know your way around. **1967** *Boston Sunday Globe* 23 Apr. B. 41/5 It's getting so now that real estate news is getting 'daily space'.. to match the Vietnam war stories.

32. a. Followed by infinitive (with *to*): To attain, reach, secure an opportunity of (being or doing something), to come (to be or do); to acquire a habit of (doing).

1583 STUBBES *Anat. Abus.* II. (1882) 79 Then get they to be chaplines to honorable and noble personages. **1591** SHAKS. *1 Hen. VI*, I. iv. 25 By what meanes got's[t] thou to be releas'd. **1649** J. ECLISTON tr. *Behmen's Ep.* xxxii. (1886) 15 All those that shall get to read them. **1664** POWER *Exp. Philos.* 21 We..could never get to see it quick in the Microscope. **1701** W. WOTTON *Hist. Rome* 272 By the Interest of Laetus..he got to be sent into Illyricum, to command the Legions there. **1833** *New Monthly Mag.* XXXVII. 22 They get to look upon every law as a mere conventional enactment. **1856** RUSKIN *Mod. Paint.* IV. v. xix. §32 The evil that God sends to warn us gets to be forgotten, and the evil that He sends to be mended by us gets left unmended. **1891** *Blackw. Mag.* CXLIX. 103/1 It is not quite two years since we got to be friends.

b. Followed by pr. pple. (or, formerly, by a gerund governed by *on*, which is now omitted, so that the two constructions are no longer distinguishable): To come to be (doing something). Also *Sc.*, to find opportunity for (doing something).

1727 *Wodrow Corr.* (1843) III. 298 Probably I'll scarce get writing, the Assembly will sit so late. **1759** WARBURTON *Lett.* (1809) 288 And now I am got on transcribing, I will send you a passage or two from some late letters. *a* **1810** TANNAHILL *Barrochan Jean* Poems (1846) 117 Naething got growing for Barrochan Jean. **1872** RUSKIN *Fors Clav.* xix. 10 Instead of looking at the sun, I got thinking about the dry bed of the stream, just beneath. **1889** MRS. H. MARTIN *Common Clay* III. ix. 144 When they got talking together it was Greek to me.

c. *to get going*: to begin; to start talking, acting, etc., vigorously; to get into full swing; to 'get a move on'. Also *trans.*, to start; to render (someone) excited, talkative, etc. See also *to get cracking* s.v. CRACK *v.* 22 b.

1897 O. W. HOLMES *Pollock-Holmes Lett.* (1942) I. 77 He is really fine when he gets going on the Church of England. **1898** E. N. WESTCOTT *David Harum* 391 David is not only living, but appears almost no older than when we first knew him, and still just as likely to 'git goin'' on occasion. **1920** S. LEWIS *Main St.* xxviii. 326 She kidded him along, and got him going. **1932** 'A. BRIDGE' *Peking Picnic* iv. 38 She's rather a character, you know, when you get her going. **1956** A. H. COMPTON *Atomic Quest* i. 8 If this task is as important as you men say..we must get going. *Ibid.* iii. 189 To get the Hanford plant going.

33. a. With adjective (or equivalent phrase, or, occasionally, a descriptive sb.) as complement: To make oneself; to become, or succeed in becoming; to grow (with comparatives). *to get better, get well*: to recover from an illness. *to get drunk*: to become intoxicated. *to get clear of, quit of, rid of, shut of*: see CLEAR, etc. *to get left*: see LEAVE *v.*[1] 7 d; *to get lost* (*slang*, orig. *U.S.*), to go away; to take oneself off (freq. *imp.*); *to get next to*: see NEXT *a.* 13 c.

1596 SHAKS. *Merch. V.* I. i. 134 How to get cleere of all the debts I owe. **1659** B. HARRIS *Parival's Iron Age* 169 Having, with very much adoe, gotten loose from their Enemies [etc.]. **1662** J. DAVIES *Olearius' Voy. Ambass.* 220 They were both gotten sufficiently Drunk. **1700** S. L. tr. *Fryke's Voy. E. Ind.* 179 He..got past me before I could get aware of him. **1768** STERNE *Sent. Journ.* (1778) II. 158 (*Paris*), I had got master of my secret just in time. **1776** *Trial of Nundocomar* 23/1 He was at first very ill, then got better; he is now worse. **1810** *Sporting Mag.* XXXVI. 60 After which he [a horse] got lame. **1821** KEATS *Isabella* xxiv, [He] went in haste, to get in readiness, With belt, and spur, and bracing huntsman's dress. **1834** T. MEDWIN *Angler in Wales* I. 227 He will smoke himself into a mummy, for he gets thinner day by day. **1857** RUSKIN *Pol. Econ. Art* 20 They get all wrong in their experiments. **1862** *Temple Bar* V. 254, I am getting an old man, and I'm ailing. **1874** DASENT *Half a Life* III. 88 You must not suppose we got very great friends with Honora Tailby all at once. **1878** HUXLEY *Physiogr.* 55 Almost everything gets smaller as it is cooled. **1885** *Bookseller* July 650/1 Retail bookselling seems to be getting a less remunerative business every day. **1890** TOUT *Hist. Eng. fr. 1689*, 24 France..got ready to resist invasion. **1891** *Illustr. Sporting & Dram. News* 10 Jan. 581/3 He worked hard, and soon got chums with the swells. **1947** F. WAKEMAN *Hucksters* v. 66 If Kimberly were to walk in tomorrow..I'd tell him to get lost. **1959** *Times* 25 Sept. 9/2 Tell him to get lost. **1961** 'B. WELLS' *Day Earth caught Fire* ix. 145 'Cut that out, man,' the beatnik said... 'Get lost, man,' replied Pete. **1962** 'H. CALVIN' *System* xiii. 179 The last time Carabine came in I told him to get lost. **1967** WODEHOUSE *Company for Henry* v. 80 Can I have a word with you?.. In private. Get lost, young Jane.

b. *how —— can you get?*: a colloq. phr. implying that the person referred to has an extreme amount or an excess of the quality described by the adjective.

1951 H. WOUK *Caine Mutiny* VII. 488 How unconscious can you get? Don't you know to-day's Navy Day? **1966** 'A. GARVE' *Murderer's Fen* II. iii. 84 Damn it, the writer himself admits he isn't sure.—How vague can you get? **1967** J. FLEMING *No Bones about It* 80 Ben! How old-fashioned can you get? **1968** 'P. HOBSON' *Titty's Dead* xii. 125 There's been an affair... And I never twigged it. How dim can you get?

34. With pa. pple.

a. With intransitive pa. pple.: To accomplish or complete an action. Now only *colloq.* (*rare*).

1716 *Wodrow Corr.* (1843) II. 117 If we could get fled I would remove all my family from this. **1768** STERNE *Sent. Journ.* (1778) I. 2 By three I had got sat down to my dinner.

b. With passive pple.: To cause or procure oneself to be treated in a certain way or to undergo a certain action; also, in weaker sense, to come to be the object of a certain action. Often taking the place of *be* as a passive-forming auxiliary where a continuous state is not intended to be expressed.

1652 GAULE *Magastrom.* 361 A certain Spanish pretending Alchymist..got acquainted with foure rich Spanish merchants. **1793** SMEATON *Edystone L.* §266 We had got (as we thought) compleatly moored upon the 13th of May. **1814** D. H. O'BRIEN *Captiv. & Escape* 113, I got supplied with bread, cheese and a pint of wine. **1823** SCORESBY *Whale Fishery* 183 We got entangled among a quantity of heavy drift-ice. **1826** DISRAELI *Viv. Grey* II. i, His Lordship was voted a bore, and got shelved. **1848** J. H. NEWMAN *Loss & Gain* 264 'The taste, I suppose, is peculiar'..'Just at first', answered Campbell; 'but one soon gets used to it'. **1867** FREEMAN *Norm. Conq.* (1876) I. iii. 128 The different tenures got confounded. **1881** *Dr. Gheist* 190 You will be astonished to hear that I am going to get married. **1887** RIDER HAGGARD *Jess* vi, I..got caught in the storm.

1891 *Nation* (N.Y.) 19 Nov. 389/3 It may leave on your readers an impression unfair to Prof. Royce if nothing more gets said.

c. Similarly ***to get done with*** = to have done with. (Cf. *to be done*, DO *v.* B. 8 b.)

1827 CARLYLE *German Rom.* III. 156 To get the sooner done with it, he had used to begin his devotion..before leaving that place where [etc.].

VI. *intr.* With preps., in specialized senses.

(For unspecialized uses see sense 31 and the preps.)

†**35. get above** ——. To rise superior to, surmount, overcome; to recover from (an illness, etc.). *Obs.* Cf. *get over*, 46.

1705 STANHOPE *Paraphr.* II. 315 Contempt of the World, Heavenly Mindedness, Subduing our Appetites and Passions, suppose us present with the Creatures and the Passions we get above. **1754** RICHARDSON *Grandison* V. xxviii. 175 Religion..required, as she thought, that she should get above all regards for me.

36. get across ——. See ACROSS B. 1 c and 2 b.

37. get around ——. = *get round* —— (47 a, b). *U.S.*

1849 G. A. F. RUXTON *Life in Far West* 89 One from the Land of Cakes..sought to 'get around' (in trade) a right 'smart' Yankee, but couldn't 'shine'. **1875** MRS. STOWE *We & Neighbors* iii. 38 Eva is my girl; I sha'n't let anyone get around her. **1875** 'MARK TWAIN' in *Atlantic Monthly* Mar. 283/2 This has got to be learned; there isn't any getting around it. **1894** —— *Those Twins* iv. 362 There is no getting around proof like that.

38. get at ——. Also in *indirect passive*.

a. To get hold of, come at, reach, arrive at.

1771 MRS. GRIFFITH tr. *Viaud's Shipwreck* 33 We gave him all our handkerchiefs, and what line we could get at. **1833** HT. MARTINEAU *Brooke Farm* x. 117 A ledge of rock which cannot be got at but by his companions letting him down by a rope. **1840–1** DE QUINCEY *Style* Wks. XI. 175 Augustus was much of a blockhead; a truth which we utter boldly, now that none of his thirty legions can get at us. **1893** *Law Times Rep.* LXVIII. 302/1 The pipe could not be seen or got at without removing a portion of the cargo.

b. To attain to knowledge of, to find out, ascertain, learn.

1793 J. B. BURGES in *14th Rep. Hist. MSS. Comm.* App. v. 488 Baron Jacobi called; his sole intention appeared to be to get at the nature and extent of Lord Malmesbury's instructions. **1847–9** HELPS *Friends in C.* Ser. I. (1851) I. 10 To get at the truth of any history is good. **1873** SYMONDS *Grk. Poets* iii. 89 There are no means of getting at the thoughts of men. **1883** *Law Times* 20 Oct. 412/1, I cannot see..the process by which the court will get at the facts on which its judgment is to hinge.

c. *colloq.* or *slang.* To tamper with; to influence by underhand means, to corrupt, bribe; to practise dishonest tricks on (a horse, etc.) in order to prevent (it) from winning. Also, to solicit or pester; to try to influence.

1865 J. S. MILL in *Morn. Star* 6 July, That part of the electors whose minds are to be got at by money—who are to be reached by trickery. **1870** *Spectator* 23 Apr. 514/2 That, of course, makes it profitable..for scoundrels to 'get at' horses. **1871** *Sat. Rev.* 9 Sept. 329/2 It is quite clear that some of them [imported artisans] have been 'got at', and it is easy to conceive the terrorism, which [etc.]. **1880** *Daily News* 18 Dec., A bulldog can be 'got at' in this way. **1888** BRYCE *Amer. Commw.* II. II. xxxix. 78 The legislator can be 'got at', the people cannot. **1952** W. SPROTT *Social Psychol.* (1964) vii. 123 We are all 'propaganda conscious' in the sense that we put up a resistance if we feel we are being 'got at'. **1958** *Times Lit. Suppl.* 31 Jan. 57/1 We resent, as the Victorians did not, being 'got at' by the social or religious moralist.

d. *slang.* (*a*) To attack, assail. (*b*) To banter, make game of. (Farmer *Slang* 1893).

1823 J. CONSTABLE *Let.* 2 Aug. (1964) II. 283, I fear my great coat is got at by moths, as I find my father's is that I am come down here with. **1891** *Ally Sloper's Half Holiday* 3 Jan. 7/1 'Your family don't seem to get on, missie?'.. '*On!* Who're ye gettin' at?' **1893** *Nat. Observer* 1 July 176/2 The author's burning anxiety to 'get at' capital, his profligate disregard of national prosperity. **1895** *Punch* 14 Dec. 227/1 Smart women..delight In 'getting at' you in a shameful way. **1957** J. OSBORNE *Entertainer* iii. 30 Don't look hurt. I'm not getting at you. I love you very much.

e. To begin; to start work on; to turn one's attention to. *U.S. colloq.*

1884 'MARK TWAIN' *Lett. to Publishers* 14 Apr. (1967) 173 Get at your canvassing early, and drive it with all your might. **1923** H. CRANE *Let.* 6 Feb. (1965) 118, I have been so rushed around..that I have not yet got at the review for your study.

f. To mean or intend; to hint, imply; usu. in phr. ***what are you getting at?*** *colloq.*

1899 D. BELASCO *Naughty Anthony* II, in *Heart of Maryland* (1941) 294 What are you getting at? What do you refer to when you call me the husband? **1921** *Collier's* 26 Mar. 22/1 'Say, what are you gettin' at?' says the kid, interested at last. **1931** N. COWARD *Post Mortem* vi. 75, I wish I knew what you were getting at.

39. get by ——. To succeed in getting past (someone); to evade. *colloq.*

1904 S. E. WHITE *Blazed Trail Stories* II. v. 199 How he had gotten by the office boy Brown could not conceive. **1919** H. CRANE *Let.* 13 Dec. (1965) 27, I am thoroughly confident about the thing itself since it has got by the particular, hierarchic Josephson.

†**40. get from** ——. To escape from. *Obs.*

1639 DU VERGER tr. *Camus' Admir. Events* 130 He leapes upon his Mule, and spurring him hard to get from the bawling woman [etc.]. **1699** HACKE *Collect. Voy.* II One of the three [Indians]..got from our men, and run to the Town. **1771** T. HULL *Sir W. Harrington* (1797) III. 201, I hope she got from him innocent. *Ibid.* IV. 27, I did get from him, however, and ran to the door.

41. get inside ——. To penetrate; to investigate closely; to achieve a deep or intimate understanding of.

1875 *Athenæum* 14 Aug. 222/2 More important..is the power of getting inside a character and revealing it to the public. **1959** *Listener* 16 July 112/3 No need to stress the good qualities of William Parsons as a vocalist or his ability to get inside a song and really interpret it. *Ibid.* 23 July 146/1 No one, not even Thurber, ever got inside Harold Ross. *Ibid.* 150/1 Mr. Denis Constanduros's *As Far as the Flagstaff*..got inside the doldrum life of a retired engineer.

42. get into ——.

a. To come to be, result in being, in (a certain state or condition).

For special phrases as *to get into full swing*, *deep* (*hot*) *water*, see the sbs.

1662 J. DAVIES *Olearius' Voy. Ambass.* 81 When they are once got into Wine they mind nothing else. *Ibid.* 284 The King who was got into a pleasant Humour, only Laugh'd at it. **1692** LOCKE *Educ.* §131 Wks. 1714 III. 60 Lying is..so much in fashion among all sorts of People, that a Child..can scarce be kept, without great Care, from getting into it. **1709** STEELE *Tatler* No. 82 ¶1 When one is got into such a Way of Thinking. **1771** MRS. GRIFFITH tr. *Viaud's Shipwreck* 151 They were got into full cry before we heard them. **1787** 'G. GAMBADO' *Acad. Horsemen* 40 Before ever your horse gets into motion, clap both your spurs into him pretty sharp. **1801** tr. *Damberger's Trav. Africa* 57, I had got into a sort of scrape. **1833** *Act 3 & 4 Will. IV*, c. 46 §104 Where any..spouts, shores, or pipes, drains or common sewers..shall get into disrepair. **1862** *Temple Bar* VI. 401 He used to get into a frightful passion. **1887** RIDER HAGGARD *Jess* iv, He very soon got more or less into the swing of the thing.

b. To make one's way *into* (business, favour, office, etc.); to succeed in obtaining.

1598 tr. *Linschoten's Voy.* 3, I..vsed all meanes I could to get into his seruice. **1693** *Humours of Town* 88 Your Physicians Discourse is..as if they..are pretending mighty Practice to get into Practice. **1704** J. PITTS *Acc. Mahometans* 47 Slaves in such places do always strive to get into the Childrens Affections. **1790** J. B. MORETON *Mann. W. Ind.* 93 When a young man gets into a good employ. **1890** T. F. TOUT *Hist. Eng. fr. 1689*, 182 Trade grew much more active after he got into office.

c. *colloq.* To put on (clothes, etc.).

1690 W. WALKER *Idiomat. Anglo-Lat.* 151 He is gotten into a new dress. **1813** LADY BURGHERSH *Lett.* (1893) 38 By that time I shall 'get into my shoes' here.

d. To become occupied with, to 'land in'. Also, to become interested, involved, or absorbed in; to specialize in (sometimes with mixture of sense 42 e).

1712 STEELE *Spect.* No. 479 ¶6 Instead of..Displaying Conjugal Love in its natural Beauties.. I am got into Tales to the Disadvantage of that State of Life. **1938** E. HEMINGWAY *Fifth Column* (1939) 220 'What are you reading?' '*Richard Feveral.*' 'I couldn't get into it.' **1966** 'C. KEITH' *Elusive Epicure* (1968) v. 69 He did advise me one time to get into Early American antique furniture. **1969** *It* 11–24 Apr. 11/2 What sort of things are you getting into musically now?

e. To penetrate by inquiry, to get knowledge of.

1788 T. JEFFERSON *Writ.* (1859) II. 376, I endeavored to get, as well as I could, into the state of national credit there.

f. Of liquor: To take effect upon; render confused or unsteady.

1834 T. MEDWIN *Angler in Wales* I. 145 This ale gets into my noddle. **1894** *Pall Mall Mag.* Dec. 576 Ever since I've been holding off from the whisky the least drop gets into my walk.

g. To take possession of; to 'come over'.

1876 'MARK TWAIN' *Tom Sawyer* iii. 37 All through supper his spirits were so high that his aunt wondered 'what had got into the child'. **1937** I. BAIRD *John* xiv. 163 You, too? Why, what's got into you tonight? **1946** D. STIVENS in *Austral. Short Stories* (1951) 386, I dunno what's got into you to-night.

h. To have sexual intercourse with (a woman).

c **1888–94** *My Secret Life* in S. Marcus *The Other Victorians* (1966) iv. 166, I felt as if I was wicked in getting into her, almost as if I was going to poke my mother. **1922** F. HARRIS *My Life & Loves* I. iii. 61 Again I dreamed of Lucille and again I was trying, trying in vain to get into her when again the spasm of pleasure overtook me. **1957** J. KEROUAC *On Road* (1958) 44 I've just got to get into her sister Mary tonight.

43. get off ——. (Cf. 70.)

a. To dismount from (a horse). Also (*U.S.*) to alight from (a train).

1890 *Century Mag.* July 349/1 When I got off the train, I found myself on a moss-grown platform.

b. To be disinclined for, to give up. **c.** To obtain release from.

a **1806** K. WHITE *Lett.* (1837) 329, I never get quite off study. **1835** J. CONSTABLE *Let.* 12 Sept. (1967) V. 27, I wish I could get off going there to lecture. **1893** SIR R. ROMER in *Law Times Rep.* LXVIII. 443/1 It appears to me impossible to say that the defendants can get off the contract.

44. get on ——. (Cf. *get upon*, 51; also 71.)

a. To mount (a horse, etc.). ***to get on one's high horse***: see HORSE.

1613 PURCHAS *Pilgrimage* (1614) 502 When the keeper employeth him [the elephant] in any burthen, hee getteth first on his necke. **1662** J. DAVIES *Olearius' Voy. Ambass.* 220 He got on Horse-back and departed. **1856** WHYTE MELVILLE *Kate Cov.* v, Aunt..really is very formidable when she gets on her high horse.

†**b.** To produce an effect on. *Obs.*

1647 W. BROWNE tr. *Gomberville's Polexander* II. IV. 270 This discourse got somewhat on the slave, but not enough to bring him wholly to himself.

c. *Sport.* To come upon, meet with (a fox, etc.).

1694 *Acc. Sev. Late Voy.* II. (1711) 94, I got on him [a Bird] the 11th of July.

d. To enter upon (a subject), esp. by chance.

1705 BOSMAN *Guinea* 158 Since we are got on this Subject, I must not forget to inform you that [etc.].

e. ***to get on one's feet*** or ***legs***: to assume a standing position, *esp.* for the purpose of speaking in public.

1727 BOYER *Dict. Angl.-Fr.* s.v., To get on one's feet, *se lever.* **1857** HUGHES *Tom Brown* I. vi, The pounding and cheering..becoming deafening when old Brooke gets on his legs. **1887** LOWELL *Democr.* 30 Before the authorized and responsible debaters get on their legs.

f. *Racing.* To stake money upon (a horse).

1884 *Punch* 18 Oct. 181/1 There is all the difference between getting on an ordinary hack and 'getting on' the favourite for the Derby.

g. To affect in such a way as to harass or obsess; to become a source of worry to; esp. in phr. ***to get on one's nerves*** (see NERVE *sb.* 8 e).

1920 R. MACAULAY *Potterism* III. ii. 127 'Never mind Arthur,' she said. 'I wouldn't let him get on my mind if I were you, mother.'

45. get outside ——. To eat (occas., to drink). Also, ***to get outside of***. *slang.*

1886 GREEN & HALL *Jack in Box* 15 Here, get outside some grub. **1886** P. G. EBBUTT *Emigr. Life Kansas* 182 Directly he got outside of a few glasses of whisky, his manner was very different. **1909** S. WATSON *Wops the Waif* xi. 26 So git outside your scran as quick as yer knows how. **1927** WODEHOUSE *Meet Mr. Mulliner* viii. 256 He lay there in a sort of delirium, picturing himself getting outside a medium-cooked steak smothered in onions. **1967** D. CAMPBELL in *Coast to Coast 1965–6* 21 It takes me half an hour to get outside the mixed grill and the ice-cream and coffee.

46. get over ——. (Cf. 74.)

a. To overcome, surmount (a difficulty); to evade the force of (evidence); to cease to be troubled or surprised by.

1687 MIEGE *Gt. Fr. Dict.* II. s.v., They cannot get over the Prejudice of Education. **1701** W. WOTTON *Hist. Rome, Alexander* ii. 469 [This] was Alexander's great difficulty, which for many years he happily got over. **1764** GIBBON *Misc. Wks.* (1814) IV. 376 Yet the name of slave was not to be got over. **1783** *Ainsworth's Lat. Dict.* (Morell) IV. s.v. *Bellerophontes*, He conquered them, and got safe over several other dangers. **1848** J. H. NEWMAN *Loss & Gain* 264 All such substances, milk, butter, cheese, oil, have a particular taste at first, which use alone gets over. **1850** *Tait's Mag.* XVII. 597/1 We have happily got over the prejudice of last century. **1889** DOYLE *M. Clarke* x. 80 No explanation or excuse could get over the fact that the man was dead. *a* **1898** *Mod. colloq.* I can't get over his being a married man.

b. To recover from (a shock, injury, illness, etc.).

1712 C. MORDAUNT *Let.* in E. Hamilton *Mordaunts* (1965) iv. 83, I hope she may be in no great danger but got over the Measles as easily as I did. **1769** GOLDSM. *Roman Hist.* (1786) II. 357 These excesses..brought on a violent fever, which his constitution was sufficiently strong to get over. **1791** DE FOE *Crusoe* I. xvi, He was..gotten over his fright. **1839** *Thirty-six Yrs. Seafaring Life* 219 Such was his state, that no one supposed he ever could get over it [an amputation]. **1877** MISS YONGE *Cameos* Ser. III. xxx. 306, I shall get over this hurt. **1892** *Gd. Words* May 341/2 A shock that he never got over. **1966** *Listener* 13 Jan. 77/1 'I shall never get over her death..,' he said, over eighty years later.

c. To cover (a distance).

1857 HUGHES *Tom Brown* I. i, You can get over a couple of thousand miles of ground for three pound ten. **1883** FENN *Middy & Ensign* xxxii. 193 Ten miles were got over that evening.

d. To finish, accomplish (an action); to get through with, have done with.

1872 BLACK *Adv. Phaeton* xxvii, The inn..had clearly got over its day's labour. **1889** MRS. C. CARR *Marg. Maliphant* II. xxiv. 191, I had got over my visit quite safely.

e. To while away, succeed in passing (time). (Cf. 48 c.)

1890 *Temple Bar* XC. 147 He never is quite clear afterwards how he gets over the hours that intervene.

f. *slang.* To take advantage of, circumvent.

1840 H. COCKTON *Life Valentine Vox* viii. 49 And as the old boy's not always exactly wide awake, he's to be got over just in the same way. **1862** *Temple Bar* VI. 418 If any possible swindle had been intended, they had not got over me. **1891** F. W. ROBINSON *Her Love & His Life* II. IV. ix. 210 You'll have to get up early to get over me.

g. ***to get over the footlights*** = to get across (see ACROSS B. 2 b). *U.S.*

1915 *Munsey's Mag.* Aug. 515/1 Shaw was generally considered altogether too wild to stand a chance of getting over the footlights.

47. get round ——. (Cf. 75.)

a. To circumvent, get the better of, cajole.

1849 RUXTON *Life in Far West* 106 One from the Land of Cakes..sought to 'get round' (in trade) a right 'smart' Yankee, but couldn't 'shine'. **1885** F. ANSTEY *Tinted Venus* 40, I must..ask her for the ring, very polite and civil, and try if I can't get round her that way. **1890** *Harper's Mag.* Nov. 963/2 She probably managed to get round him in various ways.

b. To evade.

1896 *Westm. Gaz.* 24 July 1/2 With every change in the rules comes a fresh ingenuity in getting round them.

48. get through ——. (Cf. 76.)

a. To reach the end of, bring to a conclusion, accomplish (a task, etc.).

1661 MARVELL *Corr.* Wks. 1872–5 II. 76 We are not yet got through the Bill of Corporations to have it ingrosd. **1850** *Tait's Mag.* XVII. 463/2 He managed to get through four good meals. **1860** GEO. ELIOT *Mill on Fl.* II. i, He got through his supines without mistake. **1889** J. MASTERMAN *Scotts of Bestminster* I. vi. 194 He therefore got through his business as quickly as he could.

b. Of legislative measures: to be passed by (Parliament, the Commons or Lords). Also, ***to get through the court***: to receive one's 'discharge' as a bankrupt.

1855 COSTELLO *Stor. Screen* 82 As to the Court, if you did get through it..you'd be worse off when you came out than when you went in. **1890** T. F. TOUT *Hist. Eng. fr. 1689*, 168 A new Reform Bill had got through the Commons by more than a hundred majority.

c. To succeed in passing (time); *esp.* to find occupation for (a period of time), so as to escape ennui. (Cf. 46 e.)

1768 STERNE *Sent. Journ.* I. 17 (*The Monk*), Those who.. have no other plan in life, but to get through it in sloth and ignorance. **1847–9** HELPS *Friends in C.* (1851) II. 7 How do you get through the day? **1890** *Temple Bar* Oct. 145 He gets through the morning tolerably well with letter-writing.

49. a. get to ——. (Cf. 77.) To begin, settle down to.

1861 HUGHES *Tom Brown at Oxf.* Introd., Tom was.. beginning to feel that it was high time for him to be getting to regular work again. **1889** F. C. PHILIPS *Yng. Ainslie's Courtship* II. v. 52 You and I will get to business with due solemnity.

b. To bribe. *U.S. slang.*

1927 *Dialect Notes* V. 447 *Get to one*, to bribe. **1930** E. D. SULLIVAN *Chicago Surrenders* i. 10 Gangsters can't operate on a satisfactory scale anywhere until they have 'got to someone'.

c. To worry, depress, or obsess; = sense 44 g above. *U.S. slang.*

1961 in WEBSTER. **1968** *New Yorker* 28 Dec. 42/2 It depresses me, but I don't let it get to me. *Ibid.*, You can't excuse yourself that way, any more than you can let drunks and such get to you.

d. To get across to (an audience, etc.) (see ACROSS B. 2 b). *U.S. colloq.*

1968 *Globe & Mail* (Toronto) 13 Jan. 28/6 They didn't even realize that they were hearing a great man in Teagarden ..even though we always got to them by the end of the evening.

50. get under ——. *Naut.* ***to get under sail***: to set sail. ***to get under way***: to begin to move.

1748 *Anson's Voy.* II. vii. 207 We got under sail from the road of Paita..about midnight. **1772–84** COOK *Voy.* (1790) V. 186 In the mean time the ships were got under way. **1823** SCORESBY *Whale Fishery* 42 The sails were instantly set, and the ship got under-way.

51. get upon ——. (Cf. *get on*, 44.)

a. To assume a position upon; to rise to (one's feet); to mount (a horse, etc.).

1581 PETTIE *Guazzo's Civ. Conv.* I. (1586) 12 All beastes so soone as they are delivered from their dam get upon their feete, and are able to stand a high alone. **1720** MRS. MANLEY *Power of Love* I. 123 With much Difficulty he got upon his Knees. **1826** in Cobbett *Rur. Rides* (1885) II. 270 Getting upon a good strong horse, and riding about the country, has no merit in it.

b. To begin or proceed to talk of.

1852 H. ROGERS *Ecl. Faith* (1853) 38 If you find us getting upon these topics, join us.

†52. get within ——. *Obs.*

a. To succeed in coming within the defences of (an adversary).

1580 SIDNEY *Arcadia* II. (1590) 211 b, I had in a short space gotten within him, and (giuing him a sound blowe) sent him to feede fishes. **1590** SHAKS. *Com. Err.* v. i. 34 Some get within him, take his sword away. **1659** B. HARRIS *Parival's Iron Age* 279 Got within shot of the enemy, who fearing that by degrees the English Fleet would get within them; set up their sailes [etc.].

b. To succeed in deceiving, or in winning confidence with (a person).

1640 SANDERSON *Serm.* I. 303 By this very means he got within our grandmother Eve. **1660** *Trial Regic.* 154, I should so much sympathize with him, to get within him to know his intentions.

VII. With adverbs.

53. get aboard. (See ABOARD.)

a. *trans.* (sense 27).

1590 SHAKS. *Com. Err.* IV. iv. 162 Therefore away, to get our stuffe aboord. **1712** W. ROGERS *Voy.* 40 We had got a great deal of Water and Wood aboard.

b. *intr.* (sense 31).

1611 SHAKS. *Wint. T.* III. iii. 7 Go get a-boord, Looke to thy barke. **1697** DAMPIER *Voy.* I. 116 They knew not how to get aboard. **1780** COXE *Russ. Disc.* 58 They had no sooner got aboard than a violent gale of wind..broke the cable. **1849** [see ABOARD A. 1 b].

54. get about.

a. *intr.* To make one's way about, go from place to place: also, to begin to walk (after an accident, illness, etc.).

1857 HUGHES *Tom Brown* II. vi, You're getting well..But you'll get about now directly, won't you? **1889** F. C. PHILIPS *Yng. Ainslie's Courtship* I. xiii. 171 Not even a cab can get about in December for the snow. **1890** *Sat. Rev.* 1 Nov. 510/1 Mr. Hare might offer more help as to the means of getting about.

b. Of rumours, reports, etc.: To be circulated, become generally known, to obtain currency.

1816 JANE AUSTEN *Emma* III. xii. 219 Mr. Weston..did not conceive..that it would be of any consequence; for 'such things..always got about'. **1848** J. H. NEWMAN *Loss & Gain* 244 When the report got about, Sheffield said that he was not surprised at it. **1889** F. C. PHILIPS *Yng. Ainslie's Courtship* II. i. 8 Paine's 'Age of Reason', for instance, gets about. **1890** F. BARRETT *Betw. Life & Death* III. l. 298 The rumour..had got about that the timber was not his.

55. get abroad.

†a. *refl.* (See sense 27 b, and ABROAD 3.) *Obs.*

1568 GRAFTON *Chron.* II. 107 He gate him abroade and prated thereof at large.

†b. *trans.* (See quot.) *Obs.*

1687 MIEGE *Gt. Fr. Dict.* II. s.v., To get a Thing abroad, to publish it.

c. *intr.* Of rumours, etc.: To become current.

1687 MIEGE *Gt. Fr. Dict.* II. s.v., When such Things get abroad. **1825** T. JEFFERSON *Autobiog.* Wks. 1859 I. 32 Should the idea get abroad..it will damp the minds of the people. **1849** MACAULAY *Hist. Eng.* viii. II. 327 As soon as the questions got abroad, a form of answer..was circulated all over the kingdom. **1885** *Manch. Exam.* 6 Nov. 5/2 A suspicion has got abroad that they are meditating a reimposition of the tax on corn.

56. get across. See ACROSS A. 4 and B. 2 b.

1913, etc. [see ACROSS B. 2 b]. **1923** U. L. SILBERRAD *Lett. J. Armiter* vi. 148 Sorry—my fault—one fails to get across. **1928** *Observer* 1 Apr. 6 His verse..in spite of all the efforts of his friends and admirers..has not really 'got across' eleven years after his death. *Ibid.* 17 June 8 Something, somehow, fails to get across. For it cannot be denied that the actual story..is a little slow. **1930** *Times* 24 Mar. 15/5 He can 'get his words across' as Gilbert intended.

57. get again. *trans.* To recover, obtain a second time.

a **1300** *Cursor M.* 8677 Bot moght i neuer gete hider-til, Mi child a-gain. **1362** LANGL. *P. Pl.* A. VI. 106 Thus maihtou leosen his loue..Bote gete hit aȝeyn bi grace. *c* **1400** *Destr. Troy* 5899 Then the grekes agayne getou þere hertes, And myche comford kaght of his come þen. *c* **1430** *Pilgr. Lyf Manhode* IV. lxiii. (1869) 206 þe flesh shal first be roten, and newe geten ayen at þe general assemblee. **1548** HALL *Chron., Edw. IV*, 218 b, It was to her declared, how that kyng Edward had gotten again the garland. **1678** BUNYAN *Pilgr.* I. 47 When he had gotten his Roll again.

58. get ahead. *intr.* To make progress, meet with success. ***to get ahead of***: to clear oneself from (a debt).

1807 SOUTHEY in Robberds *Mem. W. Taylor* II. 190, I have better hopes than I ever yet had of getting ahead. **1851** MAYHEW *Lond. Lab.* I. 380 There are many who have incurred a tally debt, and have never been able to 'get a-head of it', but have been kept poor by it all their lives.

59. get along.

a. *intr.* (See sense 31 and ALONG.)

1768 STERNE *Sent. Journ.* I. 19 (*The Monk*), I have only just set out upon my travels; and shall learn better manners as I get along. **1889** MRS. C. L. PIRKIS *At Moment Vict.* III. x. 158 She gets along faster in the wind than Havelock.

b. To succeed, find no insurmountable difficulties; to get on, fare (well, ill); to manage, esp. *without* something. (Cf. *get on*, 71 g, h.)

1830 [see ALONG *adv.* 2 a]. **1837** HT. MARTINEAU *Soc. Amer.* II. 204 But there is no bringing glass over a corduroy ..road; and those who have no other highways must 'get along' with such windows as it may please the weather..to leave them. **1850** [see ALONG *adv.* 2]. **1868** DICKENS *Lett.* (1880) II. 365 Some of these halls turn out to be smaller than represented, but I have no doubt, to use an American expression, that we shall 'get along'. **1868** G. DUFF *Pol. Surv.* 145 You are wanted there, and we can get along without you! **1890** *Cornh. Mag.* Oct. 376 If one's soul passes out of one's reach, one has to get along without it.

c. To agree, act, or live harmoniously *together*; also, ***to get along well with*** (cf. 71 i).

1875 B. L. FARJEON *Love's Vict.* xi, You and Mr. Barton do not seem to get along well together. **1885** *Harper's Mag.* Mar. 501/2 If they wished to get along well with him they must let him have his own way.

d. *imp.* ***get along with you*** = go away; also *fig.* let be, have done, be quiet. *colloq.*

1837 DICKENS *Pickw.* xiv. **1840** —— *Barn. Rudge* xxii, Leave me. Get along with you.

60. get around.

a. ***to get around to*** = to get round to (sense 75 c).

1887 M. E. WILKINS *Humble Romance* 35 There has been a good many things I haven't got around to. **1936**, **1952** [see AROUND *adv.* 4].

b. To go round; to circulate; *spec.* to go out a great deal; to visit many places. Chiefly *U.S.*

1928 *Amer. Speech* III. 219 *Get around*, to..have many desirable dates. 'Mary Jane sure did get around last semester.' **1951** M. MCLUHAN *Mech. Bride* 60/2 The news got around fast. **1959** *Times Lit. Suppl.* 20 Mar. 159/3 Still, Mr. Donnelly has got around... He makes his way to places like Tashkent, Samarkand and Alma Ata.

61. get away.

a. *intr.* To escape, succeed in departing. Also (usu. with a negative), to disregard or escape *from* (a fact, implication, etc.). Also, in *Hunting* and *Racing*: to start.

a **1300** *Cursor M.* 7902 In batail sua he suld be sette, þat he awai suld neuer gette. **1375** BARBOUR *Bruce* XIV. 223 The lordis war gottin all avay. **1535** COVERDALE *Job* i. 17 The Caldees..haue..slayne the seruauntes with the swearde: and I only am gotten awaye, to tell the. **1638** F. JUNIUS *Paint. of Ancients* 131 David..had leisure enough to get away whilest the Kings messengers were so deceived. **1707** *Curios. in Husb. & Gard.* 15 They escap'd from the City, as from a Prison, and got away into the Country. **1818** COBBETT *Pol. Reg.* XXXIII. 13 He came out of the Tower, or, rather, got away out of it somehow or other. **1875** WHYTE MELVILLE *Riding Recoll.* ii, Exhaust, therefore, all your knowledge of woodcraft to get away on good terms with the hounds. **1885** F. ANSTEY *Tinted Venus* 56 All our party was glad to get away. **1912** T. DREISER *Financier* lvii. 601 A jail is a jail; and there is no getting away from that. **1930** A. CHRISTIE *Murder at Vicarage* xi. 84 It's his pistol—you can't get away from that.

b. *imp.* = go away, be off. Also as a colloq. expression of astonishment or incredulity = 'go on', you don't say (so). Also ***get away with you*** = 59 d.

1796 JANE AUSTEN *Pride & Prej.* xlix, Take whatever you like, and get away. **1848** THACKERAY *Van. Fair* xxii. 190 'Don't trifle with her affections, you Don Juan!' 'Get away,' said Jos Sedley, quite pleased. **1960** H. PINTER *Dumb Waiter* 124 *Ben.* The lorry started and ran over him. *Gus.* Go on! *Ben.* That's what it says here. *Gus.* Get away. **1969** 'D. CORY' *Night Hawk* 16 'Do you speak Spanish?' 'Of course I do. I *am* Spanish.' 'Get away.' 'I am. I can prove it.'

c. ***to get away with***: (*U.S. slang*) to get the better of, to beat in a contest. Also (*colloq.*, orig. *U.S.*), to carry off successfully; to succeed in winning or stealing; to do (something) with impunity; freq. in phr. ***to get away with it***: to succeed in what one tries; to act without being detected or punished; so ***to get away with murder***: to get away with anything; to do whatever one wishes.

1878 J. H. BEADLE *Western Wilds* ii. 41 More'n once the robbers would tackle some gritty man that was handy with his 'barkers', an' he'd get away with two or three of 'em. **1886** *Boston Jrnl.* 18 Dec. 2/4 They got away with the pennant three successive seasons. **1887** A. A. HAYES *Jesuit's Ring* 227 The boys got away with the..road agents. **1892** *Congress. Rec.* 13 Dec. 122/2 [These gentlemen] will have to be content with the pitiful $240,000 that they have already 'got away with'. **1908** *Dialect Notes* III. 314 You can't get away with me. **1912** *Maclean's Mag.* Oct. 56/2 In the Elizabethan days you could assault the watch..and have a jolly set-to with the blades in any convenient angle of a wall and 'get away with it'. **1921** *Collier's* 26 Mar. 25/1 The Kid loved her enough for her to get away with murder—which he undoubtedly did. **1923** A. HUXLEY *Antic Hay* x. 145 He had no sense of time or of order. But he got away with it, as he liked to say. **1926** *Amer. Speech* I. 292/2 This stable has been getting away with murder. **1939** *Chatelaine* Sept. 19/2 Usually she's young enough and amusing enough to 'get away with murder'. **1945** E. WAUGH *Brideshead Revisited* 12 He would sometimes say of the ways of the Army in pay and supply and the use of 'man-hours': 'They couldn't get away with that in business.' **1958** *Times* Oct. 3/3 A film set in Ireland and relying upon whimsical comedy can get away, if not with murder, at least with weaknesses. **1967** J. CAIRD *Murder Scholastic* viii. 98 George gets away with murder... I mean, he does things in his own way. **1968** *Listener* 8 Aug. 164/3 Nobody can quite believe that Mr Dubcek is being allowed to get away with it.

d. *trans.* and *refl.* (See sense 27 and AWAY.) *spec.* in *Cricket.* To hit (the ball) past the fieldsman, so as to make a run or runs; also with the bowler as object.

c **1375** *Sc. Leg. Saints, George* 883 Men..gat away prywely of his relykis a party. *c* **1400** *Destr. Troy* 11765 The kyng..hade hit goten, Paladian the pure god, pertly away. *c* **1430** *Syr Tryam.* 479 Ther myght no man gete hym [greyhound] away. **1585** T. WASHINGTON tr. *Nicholay's Voy.* I. xx. 25 b, There was no remedy to get them [prisoners] away, but by great presents. **1640** tr. *Verdere's Rom. Rom.* III. 27 Taking a little courage to her, she got her speedily away. **1687** MIEGE *Gt. Fr. Dict.* II. s.v., He has got away my Customers..She got away the best Things in the House, *elle a soustrait* [etc.]. **1868** *Bailey's Mag.* July 128 The two first-named..exhibited splendid defence; but they could not get the ball away. **1903** C. F. WOOD in H. G. Hutchinson *Cricket* xii. 379 Scoring is out of the question. You may stop the ball as long as your patience lasts, but you can't get it away. **1955** *Times* 12 May 4/4 Phillips was one of five freshmen to bowl. He is tall and an awkward man to get away by reason of his length.

†e. *trans.* To shake off, get rid of (a cold).

1676 LADY CHAWORTH in *12th Rep. Hist. MSS. Comm.* App. v. 34 The season continues so seveere I cannot get away my ill cold nor goe out of the house.

f. *intr.* To begin; to start quickly; esp. of a plant, to start growing vigorously or well.

1930 *Forestry* IV. 113 If the oak got away quickly it would soon be out of reach of the weeds. **1933** *Jrnl. R. Hort. Soc.* LVIII. 99 You wish to ensure the roots getting away quickly into the new soil. **1950** *N.Z. Jrnl. Agric.* Oct. 295/1 There would be danger of fires getting away on sunny faces when the vegetation was very dry. **1957** *Jrnl. R. Hort. Soc.* LXXXII. 370 If the ground is broken into rubble the roots can get away and the plant will flourish. **1960** F. C. STERN *Chalk Garden* xv. 163 It is advisable to put them in as small plants as they get away much quicker than large plants. **1967** R. MACKAY *House & Day* 86 'The trees are quite big.' ..'Yes. They've got away well now.'

62. get back.

a. *intr.* To effect a return. Also *refl.*

1605 SHAKS. *Ant. & Cl.* III. xiii. 139 Get thee backe to Cæsar. **1664** PEPYS *Diary* 22 Nov., They have no victuals to keep them out, and it is likely they will be frozen before they can get back. **1707** *Curios. in Husb. & Gard.* 22 If any Disgrace..drive any one away, he is never at rest till he get back again. *a* **1847** MRS. SHERWOOD *Lady of Manor* I. iv. 99 Perhaps you hoped I was got back to England. **1862** *Temple Bar* V. 315 Get you back to your inn, good youth. **1889** *Univ. Rev.* Nov. 360 It was an attempt on the artist's part to get back to nature.

b. *trans.* To recover. (Cf. *get again*, 57.) ***to get one's own back***: to revenge oneself; to get even with someone.

1808 'CERVANTES HOGG' *Miss-led General* 161 Another considerable estate..was rattled away in one night; but the good old lord contrived to get it back. **1872** FREEMAN *Gen. Sketch* xiii. §7 (1874) 245 Venice got back nearly all that she had lost. **1890** T. F. TOUT *Hist. Eng. fr. 1689*, 189 Austria got back its hold on Italy. **1910** J. DRISCOLL *Ringcraft* 17 He wanted to get his own back, and..he fancied he saw his chance. **1914** G. B. SHAW *Pygmalion* iv, *Higgins*... You have wounded me to the heart. *Liza*... I'm glad. I've got a little of my own back. **1920** 'IXION' *Motor Cycle Remin.* 124

Whenever he met me I was able to get my own back. **1922** *Westm. Gaz.* 28 Nov., Busby said that he did it to 'get his own back'.

c. *to get back at* (or *on*): to retort or retaliate upon. *colloq.* (orig. *U.S.*).

1888 *Chicago Inter-Ocean* (Farmer), The open letter writers are getting back at Sam for his fondness for tobacco. **1907** *Daily Chron.* 17 Oct. 3/3 You cannot afford to be rude to a journalist. Some day he will get back on you. **1923** WODEHOUSE *Inimitable Jeeves* ix. 90 A lesser man might easily have snatched at the chance of getting back at me a bit by loosing Cyril into by bedchamber. **1972** *Guardian* 11 Feb. 1/6 For most of question time.. Mr Thorpe tried to get back at the.. Prime Minister.

63. get before. *intr.* (See 31 and BEFORE.)

1662 J. DAVIES *Olearius' Voy. Ambass.* 7 The Boat-men.. forbearing ever and anon to row, purposely to let the Amabssadors get before.

64. get by. *intr.* To be successful in escaping or evading something; to succeed, get along, 'manage'; to pass muster, be acceptable; to get away *with*. *colloq.* (orig. *U.S.*)

1908 J. M. SULLIVAN *Crim. Slang* 12 *Getting by*, living without doing any hard work. **1918** in *Wine, Women & War* (1926) 24 Absorbing what's useful in foreign methods.. just getting by, myself... Too damned technical. **1922** H. CRANE *Let.* 2 Apr. (1965) 83 It has enough in it to 'get by' on the first reading with a rather pleasing effect. **1926** *S.P.E. Tract* XXIV. 122 That chap could get by with murder. **1939** WODEHOUSE *Uncle Fred in Springtime* i. 12 Polly thinks I can get by all right. **1952** A. WILSON *Hemlock & After* I. i. 20 *Our* old bus will get by with a new engine. **1968** *Listener* 14 Nov. 663/3 The pseudo-metaphysical jargon that gets by as art criticism today.

65. get down.

a. *intr.* (See sense 31 and DOWN.) Also *refl.*

1581 PETTIE *Guazzo's Civ. Conv.* I. (1586) 28 b, Then they tell the wall, and the waie, whereby her lover got downe. **1700** S. L. tr. *Fryke's Voy. E. Ind.* 43 The day being come ..he gets down.. leaving his dead Companion upon the Tree. **1757** FOOTE *Author* Prol., Sirrah! get down, and let your father ride. **1857** HUGHES *Tom Brown* I. iv, Then one of the biggest [boys] gets down [from the coach] and begs his pardon. **1865** DICKENS *Mut. Fr.* I. vi, Bob, get ye down to your supper. **1887** *Westm. Rev.* June 361 We have now got down to the fifteenth century.

b. *trans.* (See sense 27 and DOWN.)

15.. *Mylner of Abyngton* 382 in Hazl. *E.E.P.* III. 114 Stout strokes was them betweene; The milner was the more keene, And gat the clarke downe. **1662** J. DAVIES *Olearius' Voy. Ambass.* 142 If, through weaknesse.. he be not able to get down the bread. **1669** STURMY *Mariner's Mag.* I. 17 Shall we get down our Topmasts? **1712** ARBUTHNOT *John Bull* III. ii, Even when Master had got her down, she would scratch and bite like a tiger. **1793** SMEATON *Edystone L.* §266 We returned to the buss about noon to get down our moorings. **1843** MACAULAY *Lays Anc. Rome, Virginia* 271 Small chance was his to rise again, if once they got him down.

c. *to get down on* (someone): to develop a dislike for or grudge against; to be hostile or oppressive to. *U.S. colloq.*

1875 'M. QUAD' *Quad's Odds* 381 The adult male population of the village got down on John Anderson Tompkins. **1898** E. N. WESTCOTT *David Harum* 105 Dave got down on him fer some little thing or other.

d. *intr.* To settle down *to* (something); to turn one's attention *to*; freq. in phr. *to get down to it*: to get started; to begin work seriously or energetically. See also *to get down to brass tacks* (BRASS *sb.* 5 b), *to get down to cases* (CASE *sb.*[2] 1 d).

1892 'MARK TWAIN' *Amer. Claimant* xiv. 108 You've got to get right down to it and amuse your mind. **1924** *Sunday Times* 30 Mar. 6/2 The Bishop of Beauvais, the Earl of Warwick, and Chaplain de Stogumber assemble round a table and 'get down to it'. **1930** J. B. PRIESTLEY *Angel Pavement* viii. 413 Then come back here, bring your notebook, and we'll get down to it. **1957** K. M. KENYON *Digging up Jericho* 39 The first stages of a dig.. start long before one actually gets down to excavating.

e. *trans.* To depress or weary (someone). Cf. DOWN *adv.* 18.

1930 C. V. GRIMMETT *Getting Wickets* v. 115 There is quite enough to worry about on the field without allowing the troubles of the game to 'get you down' when you leave it. **1932** N. COWARD *Cavalcade* III. ii. 137 Blues, Twentieth Century Blues, are getting me down. **1953** 'N. SHUTE' *In Wet* v. 171 It's just being cooped up in the office gets you down a bit.

66. get forth. *intr.* (See sense 31 and FORTH.)

c **1475** *Rauf Coilȝear* 603 He saw the King was engreuit, and gat furth glaid. **1639** tr. *Du Bosq's Compl. Woman* 30 This Musing is a Maze, where one easily looseth himselfe, and whence without great difficulty he gets not forth. **1796** MACNEILL *Will & Jean* v. viii, Will got forth; On a cart, or in a waggon, Hirplin aye towards the north.

67. get forward. (See senses 27 and 31, and FORWARD.)

a. *intr.*

1583 HOLLYBAND *Campo di Fior* 281 Get forward, for I will come after you a foote. **1651** *Life Father Sarpi* (1676) 10 He was already gotten so forward in all the Sciences, that [etc.]. **1796** COLERIDGE *Watchman* No. 2 ¶5 They who act up to my precepts, will.. be precluded from all the customary means of getting forward in the world. **1815** CHALMER in *Life* (1851) II. 8, I.. got forward in the coach with Mr. Paul. **1857** *Jrnl. R. Agric. Soc.* XVIII. I. 19 The mares are indulged a little as they get forward with foal.

b. *trans.*

1712 W. ROGERS *Voy.* 5 We lengthen'd our Mizen-Mast ..got our Fore-Mast forward.

68. get in.

a. *intr.* (See sense 31 and IN.)

a **1533** LD. BERNERS *Huon* lix. 206 He.. went toward the posterne the whiche, with muche payne, they gatte in there at. ? *a* **1550** *Freiris Berwik* 94 in *Dunbar's Poems* (1893) 288 Our ȝettis ar closit that we may nocht in gett. **1613** SHAKS. *Hen. VIII*, v. iv. 18 *Port.* How got they in? *Man.* Alas I know not, how gets the Tide in. *a* **1691** BOYLE *Hist. Air* (1692) 84 Although the bar of Porta Nova proved more.. dangerous than we were informed; yet our ship got safe in thither. **1782** COWPER *Gilpin* 38 Three doors off the chaise was stayed, Where they did all get in. **1803** JANE PORTER *Thaddeus* xiv. (1831) 129 He was in hopes to have gotten in as he had stolen out. **1850** *Tait's Mag.* XVII. 722/2 The chaise having arrived.. Trotter got in.

b. To be elected or chosen to represent a constituency in parliament, etc.

1700 J. VERNEY *Let.* 10 Nov. in M. M. Verney *Verney Lett.* (1930) I. x. 159 The Coll. may carry it for the County, & Sir T. Lee get in at Aylesbury. **1861** *Temple Bar* II. 395 [He] is trying to get in for Wylminstre at the next election.

c. In *Falconry*. (See quots.)

1879 *Encycl. Brit.* IX. 7 To go up to a hawk when she has killed her quarry is to 'get in'. **1891** HARTING *Bibl. Accipitr.* 223 *Get in*, to reach the hawk as soon as she has killed.

d. *trans.* (See sense 27 and IN.). *spec.* To bring in or buy; to get a stock of.

1593 SHAKS. *3 Hen. VI*, IV. vii. 25 When the Fox hath once got in his Nose, Hee'le soone finde meanes to make the Body follow. **1793** SMEATON *Edystone L.* §158 In getting in the bridle cable by means of its buoys. **1869** MRS. H. WOOD *Roland Yorke* II. xx. 125 She [*sc.* the landlady] gets things in for us, and wants to be paid for them. **1893** *Chambers's Jrnl.* 1 July 414/2, I fetched water, got in sticks, cleaned boots. **1907** R. BROOKE *Let.* July (1968) 92 The Mrs Chaffey, the lady who will land us, wanted to know what food to get in. **1932** A. J. WORRALL *Eng. Idioms* ix. 72 Most shopkeepers are getting in their Christmas goods. **1962** *Oxford Mail* 22 June 4/7 So long as I can earn enough to pay the rent and get in the odd bottle, I'm happy.

e. To gather in, secure (harvest produce).

1628 EARLE *Microcosm., Country Fellow* (Arb.) 50 For Death hee is neuer troubled.. if hee get in but his Harueſt before. **1699** *Poor Man's Plea* 7 In all these Three Counties the Crop was good, and the Corn well got in. **1762** FOOTE *Orators* I. Wks. 1799 I. 195 It would be difficult.. to get in even our harvests, without the aid of hands.. from Ireland. **1855** COSTELLO *Stor. Screen* 61 A summons to assist in getting in the vintage.. wholly prevented him. **1889** MRS. C. CARR *Marg. Maliphant* II. xxi. 107 We had to get the hay in.

f. To collect, gather (contributions of money, esp. sums due).

1687 MIEGE *Gt. Fr. Dict.* II, To get in his Debts, *se faire payer.* **1754** J. HILL (*title*) The Young Secretary's Guide.. with a true method every honest dealer should take to get in what is owing to him. **1884** 'C. POWER' [Grant Allen] *Philistia* I. viii. 217 The poor landlords can't get in their rents. **1886** *Law Times* LXXX. 132/1 Some of the assets had been got in by the receiver, and had never come to her hands at all.

g. *Printing.* To set close (see quot.).

1676 MOXON *Print Lett.* 10 If.. you are pinched for room, you may leave no Space between Letter and Letter; and then one or two Spaces between a Word will serve. This by Printers is called Getting in, or Setting close.

h. To sow, plant (seed).

1843 *Jrnl. R. Agric. Soc.* IV. II. 566, I find it [a roller].. useful in getting-in my spring corn, when the ground is dry and rough. **1853** *Ibid.* XIV. I. 192 April is the usual time for getting in the seed.

i. To yoke, harness (horses, etc.); to bring or drive (cattle) into the stock-yard.

1887 RIDER HAGGARD *Jess* xxii, I will tell the boy to get your horses in. **1890** BOLDREWOOD *Col. Reformer* (1891) 217 A portion of the herd he thought he could get in.

j. To succeed in doing certain work (esp. within a specified time).

1838 MRS. GASKELL *Lett.* 17 July (1966) 19, I had engaged a girl.. to help in all the extra work, & meant to get all sorts of things in. **1890** *Jrnl. Educ.* 1 Sept. 479/1 We are not bound to get in a certain period [of history] by a certain date.

k. To succeed in delivering (a blow).

1891 *Chamb. Jrnl.* 21 Nov. 750/1 The youngster got in a nasty blow, drawing streams of blood from his opponent's face.

l. *to get one's hand in*: to become skilful by practice (see HAND 53). *to get in a word* (*edgeways*): to succeed in saying something in a pause of another's talk (see also EDGEWAYS).

1832 HT. MARTINEAU *Life in Wilds* vi. 78 It was some time before she got her hand in, as we say. **1835** H. C. ROBINSON *Diary* 12 Nov. (1967) 143 Rogers.. said in his sneering way: 'Can Mrs. Masquerier get in a word?' **1863** KINGSLEY *Water Bab.* vii, She was running on, while Tom tried to get in a word edgeways. **1888** LADY D. HARDY *Dang. Exper.* II. xi. 222 You have given me no time to get in a word. **1891** T. HARDY *Tess* II. xv, 'I'll begin milking now, to get my hand in', said Tess.

m. *to get in bad* (or *wrong*): to incur dislike; to get into trouble; also *trans.*, to bring (someone) into disfavour; to get (someone) into trouble; cf. BAD B. 1 c; so *to get in good.* Freq. const. *with.* *colloq.* (orig. *U.S.*).

1910 O. JOHNSON *Varmint* xi. 152 Dink, you're getting in wrong again. **1913** *Dialect Notes* IV. I. 26 *Get in bad*, to make a mistake or a false move. **1920** F. SCOTT FITZGERALD *This Side of Paradise* (1921) I. iv. 139 People are beginning to think he's odd... He certainly is getting in wrong. **1921** S. FORD *Inez & Trilby May* iii. 56 So much prattle about a rich uncle who couldn't be produced was bound to get us in wrong sooner or later. **1928** *Observer* 19 Feb. 16/2 Young Woodley.. prefers poetry to cricket. That, of course, 'gets him in bad' with his house-master. **1928** *Sunday Dispatch* 22 July 22/3 It will be he who will get in bad with the fans. **1931** *Kansas City Star* 7 Nov., The husband, jumping at a chance to 'get in good' came home from work the next day with a bundle of books. **1966** *Listener* 27 Oct. 622/2 The speech he made in Chicago which got him in bad with the organizers of Negro protest marches.

69. get in with.

†**a.** *trans.* To bring (a person) into favour with.

1628 EARLE *Microcosm., Yng. Rawe Preacher* (Arb.) 23 His fashion and demure Habit gets him in with some Town-precision, and maks him a Guest on Fryday nights.

b. *intr.* To become familiar with, attain to intimacy or favour with.

1687 MIEGE *Gt. Fr. Dict.* II. s.v., To get in with one, to scrue himself into his Friendship. **1700** S. L. tr. *Fryke's Voy. E. Ind.* 215 He so contrived his Business as to get in with our Men. **1705** HEARNE *Collect.* 24 Aug. (O.H.S.) I. 34 He is got in with the Whigs. **1744** SARAH FIELDING *David Simple* II. 284, I got in with a Set of Sharpers, and.. was admitted to share some Part of the Booty. **1887** *Old Man's Favour* II. III. iii. 186, I couldn't get in with him at all;.. he's tremendously reserved.

c. *Naut.* To come close up to.

1671 NARBOROUGH *Jrnl.* in *Acc. Sev. Late Voy.* (1711) 177 At 6 at night we got in with the Land. **1748** *Anson's Voy.* III. i. 302 We were extremely impatient to get in with the nearest Island. **1797** SIR J. JERVIS 15 Feb. in Nicolas *Disp. Nelson* (1845) II. 333, I was fortunate in getting in with the Enemy's Fleet before it had time to connect. **1823** SCORESBY *Whale Fishery* 67 The wind falling, and veering to the westward, we tacked, to get in with the ice.

70. get off.

a. *intr.* (See sense 31 and OFF.) To escape, get away; to start on a journey, or in a race. Also, to succeed in falling asleep; to fall asleep. Cf. sense 70 m. *to get off to sleep*: to succeed in falling asleep. *to get off from*, † *of* = 'to get off' (43 a, c).

1607 SHAKS. *Cor.* II. i. 141 They fought together, but Auffidius got off. **1687** MIEGE *Gt. Fr. Dict.* II, To get off from his Horse, *descendre de Cheval.* **1693** *Mem. Cnt. Teckely* IV. 61 The Right Wing of the Christian Army, having.. abandoned its attack.. gave opportunity to the Janizaries.. to get off on this side. **1748** *Anson's Voy.* II. iii. 146 The crazy condition of the ship.. prevented her from getting off to sea. **1749** DODWELL *Free Answer* 109, I was wondering.. how he would get off of this difficulty. **1891** *Cassell's Fam. Mag.* Mar. 212/1, I find I can get off to sleep by trying to count up to 100. **1897** A. MORRISON *Dorrington Deed-box* i, We.. got off comfortably by the ten o'clock train from Euston. **1922** V. WOOLF *Jacob's Room* i. 17, I thought he'd never get off—such a hurricane. **1934** L. A. G. STRONG *Corporal Tune* III. iv. 267 If you find you can't get off tonight .. don't lie awake. Ring your bell, and ask sister to give you my ' A' drink. **1969** A. LASKI *Dominant Fifth* v. 182 The doctor gave me some very good sleeping-pills and said I must take one every evening, and so I did, though not until I'm sure Tess has got off.

b. To escape from punishment, defeat, etc., either entirely or *with* or *for* a specified loss or penalty; to be acquitted in a criminal trial.

1640 tr. *Verdere's Rom. Rom.* I. 81 The Christians got off with the losse of two thousand men. *Ibid.* I. 146 The Christians having got off for seventy two thousand horse, and two and twenty thousand of their infantry. **1690** BURY in W. Nicholls *Answ. Naked Gospel* (1691) B 4 b, But perhaps the Trinitarians will not so easily get off here. **1724** DE FOE *Mem. Cavalier* (1840) 271 He got off for 4000*l.* **1759** DILWORTH *Pope* 98 By this artful compliment Mr. Pope got off. **1840** DICKENS *Barn. Rudge* II. xv, He had got off very well with a reprimand. **1881** MRS. LYNN LINTON *My Love* III. iv. 79 The Pennefathers got off with fewer rebukes than usual. **1889** DOYLE *M. Clarke* xxxvi. 408 The leaders of the insurrection got off much more lightly than their followers.

†**c.** *to get off with.* To get rid of, have done with *Obs.*

1719 DE FOE *Crusoe* II. vi, I thought to have gotten off with my young priest by telling him [etc.].

d. *trans.* (See sense 27 and OFF.)

1662 J. DAVIES *Olearius' Voy. Ambass.* 35 To get off our Ship from among those Rocks. **1712** W. ROGERS *Voy.* 42 Two men waiting.. by the Shore, for a Portuguese Canoe to get 'em off. **1731** *Gentl. Mag.* I. 32/2 The Samuel.. ran ashore.. but 'twas thought might be got off.

e. To remove, take off.

1662 J. DAVIES *Olearius' Voy. Ambass.* 314 This colour will not be got off in fifteen dayes, though they wash their hands several times a day. **1687** MIEGE *Gt. Fr. Dict.* II. s.v., To get his Coat off, *tirer son Justaucorps.* **1702** *Act 1 Anne* Stat. II. c. 19. [22.] §2 If any Person or Persons.. shall.. fraudulently cut, tear, or get off any Mark or Stamp from any Piece of Vellum [etc.].

f. To deliver (a person) from punishment, or procure a modified penalty for.

1725 DE FOE *Voy. round World* (1840) 43, I will see and get you off if I can. **1862** *Temple Bar* V. 452 He promised to get my master off on payment of a fine. **1885** *Times* 18 May 5 Riel's friends were powerful enough to get him off with five years' banishment.

g. To learn, commit to memory. Also *to get off by heart* (cf. sense 8).

1709 HEARNE *Collect.* (O.H.S.) II. 308 He would always make them set about his own [Grammar], and spend time in getting it off intirely. **1861** *Temple Bar* III. 141 Read the *Times*.. and get off by heart that portion.. devoted to the news of the money-market. **1883** GILMOUR *Mongols* xvii. 201 Our religious system has no set form of liturgy to be got off by heart and repeated.

h. To 'get off one's hands'; to find sale for (goods); *colloq.* to get (one's daughters) married. Also *intr.*, to get married or engaged to be married.

1710 [see OFF *adv.* 3 b]. **1724** SWIFT *Drapier's Lett.* i. (1730) 13 Wood.. to get them [his Half-Pence] off, offered an Hundred Pounds in his Coin for Seventy or Eighty in Silver. **1801** M. EDGEWORTH *Belinda* I. ii. 41 There's no less than six of her nieces, whom she has *got off* within these four winters—Not one of 'em now, that has not made a catch-match. **1868** F. C. BURNAND *Hit & 'Miss'* i. 14 You should have got her off as she's a daughter—Why, noblemen in numbers must have sought her. **1915** B. RUCK *Courtship of Rosamond Fayre* iii, 'Miss Urquhart's got off herself.' 'She has and she hasn't. Her chap's always away.' **1923** E. Bowen *Encounters* 116 It had been difficult to get poor Cicely off.

i. To succeed in uttering (*esp.* a joke).

1849 *Yale Lit. Mag.* XIV. 187 There is the writing of one who tried to 'get off', as the boys say, something comic on every occasion. **1858** J. G. Holland *Titcomb's Lett. to Yng. Men* vii. (1873) 58 Have you a good set of teeth, which you are willing to show whenever the wit of the company gets off a good thing? **1886** Mrs. Macquoid *Sir J. Appleby* II. vi. 83 If [he] had to speak at any public occasion, he could never get a sentence off without hesitation. **1891** *Chamb. Jrnl.* 618/1 They would..get off their jokes on him and insult him.

j. ***where one gets off***: the point beyond which one is not competent, entitled, or required to go; esp. in phr. ***to tell*** (someone) ***where he gets*** (or ***to get***) ***off***: to rebuke for presumption or interference; to 'tell off'. *colloq.* (orig. *U.S.*).

1900 Ade *More Fables* 163 He said he was a Gentleman, and that no Cheap Skate in a Plug Hat could tell him where to Get Off. **1922** S. Lewis *Babbitt* vii. 93 Once in a while I got to assert my authority, and... I told him just exactly where he got off. **1932** A. J. Worrall *Eng. Idioms* 73, I told him where he got off. **1953** J. Trench *Docken Dead* vi. 90 I'm sure you knew how to deal with the police. Told them where they got off, I expect. **1963** D. Lessing *Man & Two Women* 128 If just for once she told us where to get off.

k. *intr.* To become acquainted or friendly *with* (one of the opposite sex), esp. with amorous intentions. *colloq.*

1915 [see click *v.*¹ 1 d]. **1925** Fraser & Gibbons *Soldier & Sailor Words* 104 *Get off with, to*, to make the acquaintance of or 'pick up' with anyone, usually some girl, without the formality of an introduction. **1925** F. Lonsdale *Spring Cleaning* I. 13 What fun it would be if one of us could get off with him. **1936** Auden *Look, Stranger!* 35 The lady who admires us, you Have thought you're getting off with too.

l. Of a jazz musician: to improvise skilfully. *U.S. slang.*

1933 *Fortune* Aug. 47/1 Returning to Trombonist Brown, he can *get off*, *swing it*, *sock it*, *smear it*, or *go to town* (all of which mean syncopate to beat the band). **1955** R. Blesh *Shining Trumpets* (ed. 3) xii. 289 The present-day solo is esteemed modern and full of ideas in direct proportion to the more unrecognizable it makes the melody. Such 'getting off' conceals lack of true invention.

m. *trans.* To succeed in getting (a child) to go to sleep. *colloq.* Cf. sense 70 a.

1951 N. Mitford *Blessing* I. iii. 25 Well, I only hope he won't overexcite the poor little fellow. You know what it's like getting him off, evenings. **1968** A. Laski *Keeper* ii. 23 Gavin's been playing up; teeth; I think she may have just about got him off.

n. Used as an exclamation expressing impatience or incredulity; = sense 61 b. *colloq.*

1958 J. Wain *Contenders* 29 'Get off,' I said. I should explain that 'Get off' is an expression much used in North Staffordshire as an ironic rejoinder to obvious remarks.

o. *slang.*: (*a*) orig. *U.S.*, to become intoxicated with drugs; to get 'high'; (*b*) to achieve sexual satisfaction; to experience an orgasm; cf. *to get one's rocks off* s.v. rock *sb.*¹ 2 i; (*c*) orig. *N. Amer.*, to experience an emotional 'high'; to enjoy or be 'turned on' by something. Also const. *on*. Cf. sense 70 l.

(*a*) **1969** R. D. Lingeman *Drugs from A to Z* 82 *Get off*, to inject heroin. **1980** A. Kukla in Michaels & Ricks *State of Lang.* 521 Did you get off on that acid you took last night? (*b*) **1973** D. Lang *Freaks* 30 Another time..Annie got off on her own fingers while describing exactly what it felt like to her ex-husband on the telephone. **1976** N. Thornburg *Cutter & Bone* ii. 55 And the shrink getting off on it all, sitting there with one hand stuck in his fly. (*c*) **1973** *Globe & Mail* (Toronto) 11 May 43/3 Yeah, there are hockey chicks, girls who get off on jocks. **1973** *Rolling Stone* 8 Nov. 20/3, I remember buying their album and getting off. **1977** C. McFadden *Serial* (1978) ii. 10/2 She really got off on weddings. **1977** *Time* 23 May 51/3, I really get off on dancing. It's a high. **1984** N Mailer *Tough Guys don't Dance* ii. 29, I could get off on my plans for the day if only the dream that I was in Prison would not persist.

71. get on.

a. *trans.* To put on, don (an article of dress); to place (a kettle, etc.) on the fire.

1597 Shaks. *2 Hen. IV*, v. iii. 137 Get on thy Boots, wee'l ride all night. **1605** —— *Macb.* II. ii. 70. **1650** Trapp *Comm. Gen.* xli. 14 And should not we get on our best [raiment], when we are to come before God? **1839** *Thirty-six Yrs. Seafaring Life* 332 We soon lit a good fire not far from the tent, got the kettle on, had supper. **1891** L. Malet *Wages of Sin* III. VI. i. 63 As the vulgar little boys say, Carr has 'got 'em all on' to-night, hasn't he?

b. To put on, succeed in acquiring (speed). Often *to get a move on*: see move *sb.* 6.

1891 *Field* 21 Nov. 770/1 Their forwards often got on a good deal of pace, but were never really dangerous.

c. *refl.* To advance one's own interests.

1890 T. F. Tout *Hist. Eng. fr. 1689*, 18 Using men as his tools to get himself on.

d. *slang.* To lay (a bet) on (a horse). Also *intr.*

1836 *Spirit of Times* (N.Y.) 5 Mar. 20/1 Other parties were anxious to 'get on' at this price, but could not succeed. **1869** E. Farmer *Scrap Bk.* (ed. 6) 53 When a 'sov' or 'fiver' can be got on, We're game to risk it.

e. *intr.* To advance, move forward; to make haste (in movement).

1768 Sterne *Sent. Journ.* (1778) I. 131 (*Postilion*) Then, prithee, get on—get on, my good lad, said I. **1777** Sir M. Hunter *Jrnls.* (1894) 25 The guns got on so slowly that we did not arrive at Brunswick before ten the next morning. **1891** *Leisure Hour* Jan. 151/2 Let us get on and lose no time.

f. To advance, make progress (*with* a work or business). Said also of the work itself. Freq. in phr. *to get on with it*: to continue with one's affairs; to pursue one's course.

1798 Southey in *Life* (1849) I. 347 The more the work gets on, the better does it please me. **1805** —— *Lett.* (1856) I. 328 Don Manuel cannot get on for want of such knowledge and of a book of the roads. **1822** *Ibid.* III. 353, I am getting on with the 'Book of the Church'. **1813** T. Moore in *Mem.* (1853) I. 350, I am more anxious than I can tell you to get on with it [my poem]. **1823** Scoresby *Whale Fishery* 446 We began to flench; but..we only got slowly on. **1932** R. Fraser *Marriage in Heaven* II. vi. 161 I've always just let people get on with it, especially men, if they didn't like what I said or did. **1955** J. Bingham *Paton Street Case* v. 91, I started out with some idea of serving the community and bunk like that, and now the community can get on with it as far as I'm concerned. **1962** *Listener* 8 Feb. 242/1 The only thing for France was to get out and leave Guinea to get on with it on its own.

g. To prosper, succeed; esp. ***to get on in the world***: to acquire wealth and position. Also, to fare (in some specified way, or with suggestion of some success or progress).

1785 J. Trusler *Mod. Times* I. 115 So it is in society, we labour to get on and become conspicuous. **1809** [see on *adv.* 9 a]. **1813** T. Moore in *Mem.* (1853) I. 342 She had to come down and see how her crocuses and primroses before the window were getting on. **1833** Ht. Martineau *Brooke Farm* i. 5 The grocer has got on in the world considerably. **1852** Dickens *Bleak Ho.* II. xii, Not the way to get on in life, you'll tell me? **1861** Hughes *Tom Brown at Oxf.* i, According to promise, I write to tell you how I get on up here. **1883** [see world *sb.* 17 b]. **1885** *Manch. Exam.* 13 Apr. 5/2 Mr. Courtney seemed to get on swimmingly till he got to Bodmin. **1911** G. B. Shaw *Getting Married* Pref., in *Doctor's Dilemma*, etc. 124 It used to be said that members of large families get on in the world.

h. To manage *without* (something viewed as helpful), *with* (something deemed inadequate).

1857 Hughes *Tom Brown* II. vii, Be a good fellow, and let's try if we can't get on without the crib. **1875** Jowett *Plato* (ed. 2) III. 47 A State may get on without cobblers. **1889** F. C. Philips *Yng. Ainslie's Courtship* I. xiii. 173 The universe could get on very well without them.

i. To attain intimacy or maintain friendly relations *with* (a person); to agree, harmonize, fraternize (*together*).

1816 Lady Granville *Lett.* (1894) I. 101 His manner is brusque and short, and I got on but little with him. **1844** Lady G. Fullerton *Ellen Middleton* (1854) I. 177 We entered into conversation, and *got on* (as the phrase is) very well. **1852** Dickens *Bleak Ho.* II. vii, They get on together delightfully. **1885** F. Anstey *Tinted Venus* 36 You can see for yourself that we shouldn't be likely to get on together. **1888** J. Payn *Myst. Mirbridge* (Tauchn.) II. xxviii, 283 [She] had none of the usual misgivings about getting on with her mother-in-law. **1889** F. C. Philips *Yng. Ainslie's Courtship* II. xv. 163, I am an easy sort of fellow to get on with.

j. ***to be getting on for*** (***to, towards***): to be advancing towards, coming close to (a certain age, time, number, etc.).

1861 Mayhew *Lond. Labour* III. 183, I was about getting on for twelve when father first bought me a concertina. **1861** *Temple Bar* III. 145 It's getting on for eleven. **1874** Dasent *Tales fr. Fjeld* 64 When it was getting on towards gray dawn in the morning, down fell snow. **1892** *St. Nicholas Mag.* XIV. 502/2 Lott was taller than ever. 'He's getting on for six feet', said Tom. **1892** *Review Rev.* 15 Mar. 301/1 We have an overcrowded population getting on to 40,000,000.

k. To advance, move onwards (of time). ***to get on in years*** or ***life***: (of persons) to become aged.

1882 Besant *Revolt of Man* ii. (1883) 52 He took out his watch and remarked that the time was getting on. **1885** L. Malet *Col. Enderby's Wife* (ed. 3) I. II. i. 102 As one gets on in years. **1891** *Temple Bar* Oct. 149 He was getting on in life, whereas his fiancée was not yet twenty.

l. With *to*: to grasp the meaning, truth or significance of; to understand; to detect or find. *colloq.* (orig. *U.S.*).

1880 *Chicago Inter-Ocean* 2 June 6/3 The visitors taking kindly to Ward's curves, Dunlap and McCormick especially getting on to him in fine style. **1889** J. W. Riley *Pipes o' Pan* 28 Get onto that position for a poet! **1893** 'Johnston Smith' *Maggie* xv. 130 Do yehs want people ter get onto me? **1923** Wodehouse *Inimitable Jeeves* ix. 97, I knew there wasn't a chance of my being able to work this stage wheeze in London without somebody getting on to it and tipping off the guv'nor. **1930** J. B. Priestley *Angel Pavement* vi. 277 That was a bit of smart thinking on your part... There aren't many men about here who could have got on to it like that. **1940** E. Percy in *Best One-Act Plays 1940* 70 It's very fortunate I got on to it in time. I'm sure I've saved Ann a great deal of unhappiness.

m. With *to*: to get into touch or communication with (someone).

1895 W. B. Yeats *Let.* 3 Mar. (1954) II. 252, I am beginning to think of getting on at Roscommon to Douglas Hyde. I shall go from that to Dublin. **1955** *Times* 30 June 9/5 Then later I read the body was to be exhumed. This thing got on my nerves, so I got on to the police.

72. get out.

a. *intr.* (See sense 31 and out.) ***to get out from under***: see under *adv.* 4 b.

a **1300** *Cursor M.* 17350 Þai..did to sper þe dors fast..Þat he suld noþer-quar get vte. **1665** Hooke *Microgr.* 121, I found them [vegetable growths] just gotten out, with very little or no stalk. **1700** S. L. tr. *Fryke's Voy. E. Ind.* 19 Seven more got out after me, and 35 before, so that 43 of us only escaped.

b. *imp.* = 'Go away', 'be off' (expressing disbelief, dissent, or a desire to hear no more). *colloq.*

1711 Ld. Molesworth tr. *Hotman's Franco-Gallia* (1721) 136 You have nothing to do here (said she): get out! **1840** Dickens *Old C. Shop* x, Kit only replied by bashfully bidding his mother 'get out'. **1851** Seaworthy *Bertie* vii. 78 Thrue as the tin commandhers! Git aout! **1887** *Blackw. Mag.* Dec. 763/2, 'I shan't, then', said the boy sulkily..'He belongs to my father—you get out'.

c. Of the weather: To turn out, become (fine, etc.).

1852 *Jrnl. R. Agric. Soc.* XIII. II. 336 The afternoon got out very fine.

d. To leak out, become known.

1891 *Boston* (Mass.) *Jrnl.* 28 Nov. 2/3 The fact that this step was to be taken did not get out till the charges were safe in the hands of the Governor.

e. *slang. Racing.* (See quot. 1884.) *Stock Exchange.* To get rid of one's shares in any venture.

1884 H. Smart *Fr. Post to Finish* xlii, Johnson..had taken more than one opportunity of what is termed 'getting out', that is, backing the horse against which he had previously laid. **1887** *Daily News* 21 July 6/1 Until they shall have retailed their wares, and, to use the expressive slang of the Stock Exchange, 'got out'.

f. *trans.* (See sense 27 and out.)

a **1400** *Sir Perc.* 2064 Then Percevelle the gode Hys swerde owt he get. **1442** *Cursor M.* 9652 (Bedford) A! þat wrech Frende withoute, þat non frende gete may hym oute. **1662** J. Davies *Olearius' Voy. Ambass.* 123 Much after the manner that Fell-mongers beat their Furs, to get out the Worms. **1691** T. H[ale] *Acc. New Invent.* 46 Some of them were gotten out by the Caulkers with their Spike-Irons. **1712** W. Rogers *Voy.* 105 It falling calm, we both got out our Oars. **1762** Foote *Lyar* I. Wks. 1799 I. 283 My dear Miss Godfrey, what trouble I have had to get you out! **1801** R. Cecil *Wks.* (1811) I. 138 He was led to invent an instrument for transferring the form of the model to the marble (technically called getting out the points). **1849** Thackeray *Pendennis* xliii, That rascal Blackland got the bones out, and we played hazard on the dining-table. **1857** Hughes *Tom Brown* II. iii, You've been making all these foolish marks on yourself, which you can never get out. **1884** *Milit. Engin.* I. II. 67 The excavation in which the shaft is placed is got out.

g. To draw out (information), elicit, find out by inquiry.

1530 Palsgr. 563/1, I get out the truthe of a mater that is in doute, *je saiche* and *je espluche*. **1611** Bible *Ecclus.* xiii. 11 Smiling vpon thee [he] will get out thy secrets. **1662** J. Davies *Mandelslo's Trav.* 230 They endeavour to get out the truth by fair means. **1861** *Temple Bar* II. 139 In cross-examination I had 'got out' some facts.

h. To publish (a book). Also *intr.*

1786 T. Jefferson *Writ.* (1859) II. 6 A bad French translation which is getting out here. **1846** Geo. Eliot *Let.* Mar. in J. W. Cross *Life* (1885) I. ii. 141, I wish we could get the book out in May. **1870** D. G. Rossetti *Let.* 3 Feb. (1965) II. 787, I suppose I cannot get out till April.

i. To succeed in bringing out (a sound).

1834 T. Medwin *Angler in Wales* I. 269, I could not find it in my heart to get out a negative. **1842** Tennyson *Gard. Dau.* 89 The lark could scarce get out his notes for joy.

j. *Cricket.* To put out, dismiss (a batsman or side). Also *intr.*, to be put out. So ***to get oneself out***: to be dismissed, to be got out, freq. with the implication that one is oneself largely to blame.

1833 J. Nyren *Young Cricketer's Tutor* 89 They were devilish troublesome customers to get out. **1836** [see out *adv.* 4 c.]. **1897** K. S. Ranjitsinhji *Jubilee Bk. Cricket* iv. 178 People get themselves out off slow bowling more often than the bowler gets them out. **1908** E. P. Oppenheim *Missioner* I. vi. 62 Stephen is in now... If he gets out, the match is over. **1912** A. A. Lilley *24 Yrs. Cricket* x. 137 He [*sc.* Victor Trumper]..never gave one the remotest suggestion that he would ever get out. **1926** J. B. Hobbs *My Cricket Mem.* xvi. 214 We did well to get them out for this total.

k. To succeed in solving or finishing (a puzzle, game, etc.). *colloq.*

1924 B. Dalton *Games of Patience* 34 Lady Betty.. The game..is not easy to get out. **1928** R. Knox *Footsteps at Lock* xvi. 158 He had 'got it out'. 'The cipher?' 'No, the patience.' **1931** N. Coward *Post Mortem* II. 16 Lady Cavan is seated at a bridge table playing Canfield Patience... *Lady C.* I got it out yesterday. **1951** C. P. Snow *Masters* III. xli. 328 I've got it out!.. I've got the answer to the slow neutron business.

73. get out of.

a. *intr.* To issue or emerge from, to succeed in doing so; to escape from; to leave, quit. ***to get out of bed***: to rise. ***to have got out of bed on the wrong side***: a jocular explanation of bad temper.

a **1533** Ld. Berners *Huon* xxi. 64 Or he can gete out of the wood he wyll cause reyne and wynde. **1585** T. Washington tr. *Nicholay's Voy.* I. xx. 25 b, Some of them before they coulde gette out of the barke were stripped intoo their shyrtes. **1639** Du Verger tr. *Camus' Admir. Events* 89 The Marquesse to get out of the confusion, and to avoyd the tumult..retired to his Castle. **1662** J. Davies *Olearius' Voy. Ambass.* 92 The Bride..gets out of bed, gets on a morning Gown [etc.]. **1726** *Adv. Capt. R. Boyle* 64, I told him they might do as they thought fit, but I would get out of the Way. **1748** *Anson's Voy.* II. v. 187 He was..all in rags, being but just got out of Paita goal. **1849** Macaulay *Hist. Eng.* v. I. 600 Before they got out of the lane more than a hundred of them had been killed or wounded. **1887** G. R. Sims *Mary Jane's Mem.* 203, I never lived in a family that so often got out of bed on the wrong side, to use a homely expression.

b. To get beyond, esp. ***to get out of sight, reach***; ***to get out of one's depth*** (see depth); ***to get out of hand***: †to advance beyond the necessity for instruction or guidance (*obs.*); (of horses) to break away from control.

1632 J. Hayward tr. *Biondi's Eromena* 73 The Galley.. got quit out of their sight. **1748** *Anson's Voy.* II. v. 171 They flattered themselves they were got out of his reach. **1765** FOOTE *Commissary* II. Wks. 1799 II. 22 We have at our school two..that were full half a year before they could get out of hand. **1892** *Pall Mall G.* 19 Jan. 4/3 He remained three hours in the water, afraid to move, lest he should get out of his depth. *Mod.* The horses got completely out of hand and dashed down the hill.

c. To give up, leave off (a fashion, etc.). Of things: To begin to go out of (fashion).

1711 ADDISON *Spect.* No. 119 ¶7 The Rural Beaus are not yet got out of the Fashion that took place at the time of the Revolution. **1742** RICHARDSON *Pamela* III. 193 And between the one Character, which she wants to get into, and the other she dares not get out of, she trips up and down mincingly. **1834** T. MEDWIN *Angler in Wales* I. 214 Those classical wigs..that I am sorry to see getting out of fashion, yclept bobs.

d. To evade, escape from, avoid.

1885 SIR N. LINDLEY in *Law Times Rep.* LIII. 479/1, I do not see how to get out of the language of the Act. **1888** J. PAYN *Myst. Mirbridge* (Tauchn.) I. xxiii. 282 He is like a schoolboy in getting out of things that are disagreeable to him. **1893** EARL DUNMORE *Pamirs* I. 228 He tried to evade the question and..he attempted to get out of giving a direct reply.

e. *trans.* To draw out, elicit (information) from (a person); also, to succeed in obtaining (money, work, etc.) from one.

1632 J. HAYWARD tr. *Biondi's Eromena* 189 The Queene, perceiving well what he meant..yet resolved to get it plainly out of him. **1676** WYCHERLEY *Pl. Dealer* v. ii, I told you 'twas in vain to think of getting money out of her. **1720** DE FOE *Capt. Singleton* xi. (1840) 202 This was the account we got out of them. **1737** [S. BERINGTON] *G. di Lucca's Mem.* 17 We resolv'd to try what we could get out of him by his own Confession. **1857** HUGHES *Tom Brown* II. ii, You won't get anything out of him worth having.

f. To extract (juice, etc.) from (any substance).

1662 J. DAVIES *Mandelslo's Trav.* 84 Opium..is nothing but the juice which is got out of poppy, by an incision made therein.

g. *to get out of hand*: to finish (a piece of work).

1793 SMEATON *Edystone L.* §284, I found..six pieces..unset, but which were scarcely got out of hand, when the swell came on so violent.

74. get over.

a. *intr.* (See sense 31 and OVER.)

1597 SHAKS. *2 Hen. IV*, I. i. 171 You knew he walk'd o're perils, on an edge More likely to fall in, then to get o're. **1677** W. HUBBARD *Narrative* I. (1865) 89 Capt. Henchman..as soon as he could get over with six Files of Men..followed after the Enemy. **1705** BOSMAN *Guinea* 259 They [Camelions] have also several times been sent to Europe, and got over alive. **1881** HENTY *Cornet of Horse* xiii. (1888) 134 Fascines had to be laid down, and the rivulets filled up, before guns could get over.

b. *trans.* (See sense 27 and OVER.)

1700 S. L. tr. *Fryke's Voy. E. Ind.* 197 So I told him, I would get him over, and bid him stay there.

c. To finish with, have done with (esp. something troublesome or disagreeable). Also, ***to get it over with.***

1813 JANE AUSTEN *Let.* 15 Sept. (1952) 323 At nine we are to set off for Grafton House, and get that over before breakfast. **1861** J. RUFFINI *Dr. Antonio* xi, Yes, let us get it over at once. **1889** J. MASTERMAN *Scotts of Bestminster* III. xx. 248 The sooner you get the interview over the better. **1890** I. D. HARDY *New Othello* II. ix. 207 He had made these three engagements for the one day so as to get them all over together. **1935** *Punch* 4 Sept. 262/2 Already from Australia I hear of 'meet up', 'rest up', and 'get it over with'. **1947** R. ALLEN *Home Made Banners* iii. 18 Figure I might as well sign up tomorrow and get it over with.

†**d.** To win over, gain to one's side. *Obs.*

1799 *Spirit Publ. Jrnls.* (1800) III. 395 John has got over most of her servants..and he has made large promises to others.

e. *trans.* and *intr.* = *get across* (see ACROSS B. 2b).

1916 *Picture-Play* III. 122 If he works from characters and uses..bits of effective business to 'get his plays over', he [*sc.* the scenario writer] should keep such material in handy files. **1920** WODEHOUSE *Jill the Reckless* xviii. 261 Dramatic critics..were telling each other that 'The Rose of America' was just another of those things but it had apparently got over. **1921** H. A. VACHELL *Blinkers* viii. §3 Mrs. Merrytree, delighted to perceive that she had, in stage parlance, 'got over', held the situation firmly. **1928** *Sunday Express* 29 Apr. 5/6 Her friendliness 'gets over'.

75. get round.

a. *intr.* (See sense 31 and ROUND.)

1748 *Anson's Voy.* II. iv. 160 Pizarro's squadron..had got round into these seas. **1812–16** J. SMITH *Panorama Sci. & Art* I. 528 When the planet has got round to B, its projectile force is as much diminished..as it was augmented.

b. To recover from illness, get well.

1857 HUGHES *Tom Brown* II. vi, Thompson died last week? The other three boys are getting quite round, like you. **1885** MRS. C. L. PIRKIS *Lady Lovelace* III. xli. 64 She would get round fifty times as quickly in the lighter, brighter room.

c. With *to*: to succeed in finding the time, energy, or inclination for (doing something); to come to the point of dealing with.

[**1902** W. D. HOWELLS *Lit. & Life* 155 The high banks of the seasonable Christmas-week snow, which the street-cleaners had heaped up there till they could get round to it with their carts.] **1946** K. TENNANT *Lost Haven* (1947) xiv. 221 Everything in Lost Haven was put off until someone should have enough time to 'get round to it'. **1961** J. SEYMOUR *Fat of Land* viii. 106 Our neighbour Richard cans hares, but we never got round to that. **1967** K. GILES *Death in Diamonds* viii. 145 He must take Elizabeth there for a weekend, he resolved, with a slight undertone of sadness at the thought he would probably never get round to it.

76. get through.

a. *intr.* (See sense 31 and THROUGH.) **b.** To reach a destination. **c.** Of a bill: To pass in parliament. **d.** To succeed in an examination.

1694 *Acc. Sev. Late Voy.* II. (1711) 13 The Ice was already-fixed to the Land, so that we could but just get through. **1854** 'C. BEDE' *Verdant Green* II. xi. 100 So you see, Gig lamps, I'm safe to get through!—it's impossible for them to plough me, with all these contrivances. **1885** U. S. GRANT *Pers. Mem.* I. 411 Troops after a forced march of twenty miles are not in a good condition for fighting the moment they get through. **1890** T. F. TOUT *Hist. Eng. fr. 1689*, 175 The Irish Tithe Bill..got through at last, though much cut about by the Opposition. **1895** A. F. WARR in *Law Times* XCIX. 547/1 An articled clerk of average sharpness may rely upon getting through with three month's coaching.

e. *to get through with*: to succeed in accomplishing, enduring, or the like.

1839 A. CONSTABLE *Let.* 4 Feb. in *J. Constable's Corr.* (1962) 306 Your Uncle Golding's affairs I have not got through with yet. **1870** BRET HARTE *Luck of Roaring Camp*, Bets were freely offered and taken..that 'Sal would get through with it'. **1878** *Scribner's Mag.* XV. 866/1 You would be surprised to know the number of books young girls manage to get through with. **1888** MCCARTHY & MRS. PRAED *Ladies' Gallery* II. xii. 234, I must have had pretty well all the heart-throbs a sinful man could get through with. **1893** *Punch* 29 Apr. 199 Don't know how I should get through with my work, if I were tied down to eight hours a day.

f. *trans.* To secure the implementation of (a bill or other political measure).

1873 'MARK TWAIN' & WARNER *Gilded Age* xx. 190 The Senator..favored the appropriation and he gave the Colonel..to understand that he would endeavor to get it through.

g. *intr.* To establish communication by radio or telephone. Also *trans.*, to send or receive (a message) by radio or telephone.

1895 A. R. BENNETT *Teleph. Syst. Europe* 11 The delay and uncertainty in getting through would probably deter him from using the telephone at all. **1902** BEERBOHM in *Sat. Rev.* 27 Dec. 805/1 We feel..that he has rung up a messenger-boy after failing to 'get through' on the telephone. **1916** 'BOYD CABLE' *Action Front* 188 The signallers leaped to their instruments, buzzed off the call, and getting through, rattled their messages off. *Ibid.* 189 They haven't had time since they got my message through. **1954** G. DURRELL *3 Singles to Adv.* ix. 85, I tried to contact McTurk to let him know that we were coming, but I could not get through.

h. With *to*: to reach the attention or understanding of (someone); to communicate with. *colloq.*

1961 in WEBSTER. **1962** J. BRAINE *Life at Top* iii. 54 He had defeated me; I couldn't think up any way to get through to him. **1969** A. HUNTER *Gently Coloured* ii. 14 You don't have to answer them, but you can do. Am I getting through to you, Osgood?

77. get to. *intr.* To begin eating. (Cf. 49.)

1827 CARLYLE *Germ. Rom.* I. 57 The traveller's appetite was gone. The host endeavoured to encourage him. 'Why do you not get to? Come, take somewhat for the raw foggy morning.'

78. get together.

a. *trans.* To collect, gather together (persons and things).

c **1400** *Destr. Troy* 11782 The golde was all gotyn, & the grete sommes Of qwhete, & of qwhite syluer, qwemly togedur. **1548** HALL *Chron., Edw. IV*, 222 He gat together a great navy of shippes. **1600** SHAKS. *A.Y.L.* I. iii. 136 Let's away And get our Iewels and our wealth together. **1639** DU VERGER tr. *Camus' Admir. Events* 50 Betooke himselfe to spend foolishly, what he had so unjustly gotten together. **1662** J. DAVIES *Mandelslo's Trav.* 184 They get together fourscore of the handsomest young Women. **1771** MRS. GRIFFITH tr. *Viaud's Shipwreck* 52 There never was so small a number of persons got together oppressed with so many misfortunes. **1848** MRS. JAMESON *Sacr. & Leg. Art* (1850) 278 Seven of the wisest masters that could be gotten together. **1890** T. F. TOUT *Hist. Eng. fr. 1689*, 42 Argyll had got together a fair-sized army.

b. *intr.* To meet, assemble. Also, to confer; to meet in friendly conference; to agree.

1694 *Acc. Sev. Late Voy.* II. (1711) 118 They got together in great numbers..so that we were forced to flee. **1700** S. L. tr. *Fryke's Voy. E. Ind.* 25 They use commonly to get together near to the Sea-shore in the morning. **1816** JANE AUSTEN *Emma* II. iii. 47 It is such a happiness when good people get together. **1889** *Judge* (U.S.) 10 Aug. 282/1 Five Men..are to be hanged on the same day. In other words, they will follow Mr. Dana's advice and get together. **1889** *Puck* (U.S.) 14 Aug. 418/2 'I saw you conferring with Congressman Shouter this morning.'..'Why, yes; he said that we ought to get together.' **1904** *N.Y. Times* 23 Dec. 1 The jury was unable to get together, and the Presiding Justice had ordered them locked up for the night. **1923** *Illustr. London News* 1 Sept. 418/3 So widely divergent are the standpoints that I wonder the police authorities do not get together..and formulate a standard practice.

c. *trans.* In *Rowing*, to cause (a crew) to work together. Also *intr.*

1876 E. D. BRICKWOOD *Boat Racing* I. viii. 97 If the progress made by the crew is satisfactory, and they have got well together, a regular racing outrigger may be substituted for the tub. **1888** W. B. WOODGATE *Boating* xii. 170 The other days are long-course days of long grinds, to get men together, and to reduce weight. **1898** *Encycl. Sport* II. 280/2 As the day of the race..draws near, the attention of the coach must be given entirely towards getting the crew absolutely together.

d. To organize, harmonize, put in order. *slang* (orig. *U.S.*).

1962 *Down Beat* 12 Apr. 22, I guess I was on my way in '57, when I started to get myself together musically. **1969** *It* 4–17 July 10/3 The promoters just hadn't got things together at all and would have made an immense loss.

79. get under. *trans.* To subdue, overcome (esp. a fire).

1752 *Convent-Garden Jrnl.* 23 June 3/2 Yesterday Morning..a Fire happened at the Swan Alehouse..but three Engines coming immediately, it was soon got under. **1791** *Chron.* in *Ann. Reg.* 4* The fire was got under. **1799** in *Spirit Publ. Jrnls.* (1800) III. 387 Advices from Lime-house mention that a violent quarrel broke out between Mr. and Mrs. Tarpaulin, which was not got under when the post came away. **1806–7** J. BERESFORD *Miseries Hum. Life* (1826) II. xviii, The assault is continued..till every meadow is completely got under. **1884** *Manch. Exam.* 8 Apr. 4/7 The fires fortunately were got under before much damage had been done.

80. get up.

a. *intr.* To rise, raise oneself to a sitting or (more commonly) a standing posture; esp. to rise from bed or rise to one's feet. Colloq. phrases: ***to get up and get*** (U.S.), ***to get up and go***: to start moving quickly or acting energetically; to make haste; ***to get up early (in the morning)***: to be alert, wide awake, or quick.

c **1340** *Cursor M.* 3721 (Fairf.) 'Fader', he saide, 'gete vp in bedde; wiþ þis mete þou sal be fedde'. ? *a* **1550** *Freiris Berwik* 561 in *Dunbar's Poems* (1893) 303 In ane myr he fell ..ȝeit gat he vp. **1583** HOLLYBAND *Campo di Fior* 5 Get up, get up, out of the idle fethers. **1632** J. HAYWARD tr. *Biondi's Eromena* 22 He could not possibly cause him [a horse] to get up on his feet. **1662** J. DAVIES *Olearius' Voy. Ambass.* 290 The king was so incens'd..that as soon as he got up the next morning [etc.]. **1738** SWIFT *Pol. Conversat.* 98 If you fall by the Way, don't stay to get up again. **1806–7** J. BERESFORD *Miseries Hum. Life* (1826) VI. xxii, Getting up for a journey with a racking headache. **1841** LANE *Arab. Nts.* I. 107, I got up immediately, and followed her until she had quitted the palace. **1864** B. COTTON *Songster* 10 Monsieur will be invited to just 'get up and get'. **1870** 'MARK TWAIN' *Lett. to Publishers* (1967) 39 Have written first four chapters of the book, and I tell you the 'Innocents Abroad' will have to get up early to beat it. **1884** [see EARLY *adv.* 1 a]. **1885** *Manch. Weekly Times* 6 June 5/5 As soon as a long-winded orator gets up the members wisely retire. **1903** J. FOX *Little Shepherd* xxii, A voice bellowed from the rear..'Git up and git, boys!' That was the order for the charge. **1940** F. L. ALLEN *Since Yesterday* iv. 79 They were exhibiting the same emotional willingness to get up and go, they knew not where, that was being exhibited in Germany by multitudes of men and women. **1960** J. MORTIMER *Lunch Hour* 150 Well, you didn't pin it on Sammy Noles. Oh, no. Sammy gets up too early in the morning for that little carry on.

b. To ascend, mount, climb up: esp. to mount on horseback; also in *fig.* phrases, to ascend, rise in dignity; to rise *to* a certain level.

1530 PALSGR. 563/2, I get up upon a ladder or any hyghe thyng, *je monte.* **1548** HALL *Chron., Hen. VI*, 149 b, This Marques thus gotten vp, into fortunes trone..was shortely erected to the estate and degree of a Duke. **1553** EDEN *Treat. Newe Ind.* (Arb.) 16 When you attempt to geat vp to ryde on them. **1629** EARLE *Microcosm., Emptie Wit* (Arb.) 81 A verse or some such worke he may sometimes get vp to, but seldome aboue the stature of an Epigram. **1658** *Trad. Mem. K. Jas.* G ij, By what steps the Puritans got up, and the old Clergy degenerated. **1700** S. L. tr. *Fryke's Voy. E. Ind.* 189 After this they took a Ladder..one of the other four got up to the top of it. **1791** [see 30 above]. **1844** DICKENS *Mart. Chuz.* viii, The coach stopped and went on..Passengers got up and passengers got down. **1847** MARRYAT *Childr. N. Forest* v, He used to get up into the trees.

c. To come up, come close *to*.

1659 B. HARRIS *Parival's Iron Age* 279 The wind coming at North and by West, they could not get up to them. *Ibid.* 280 The rest were not able to get up being to the lee-ward. **1700** S. L. tr. *Fryke's Voy. E. Ind.* 179 This made us the more Earnest to get up to 'em. **1796** NELSON 25 Apr. in Nicolas *Disp.* (1845) II. 162 The batteries..opened on our approach and the fire was returned as our Ships got up.

d. Of fire, wind, the sea: To begin to show action or movement; to increase in force or violence.

1556 in W.H. Turner *Select. Rec. Oxford* (1880) 246 The fire got up. **1834** T. MEDWIN *Angler in Wales* II. 136 The wind got up with the sun. **1890** S. LANE-POOLE *Barbary Corsairs* I. xi. 121 The wind was getting up, the sea rising.

†**e.** Of health: ***to get up again***: to reach its former (good) condition. *Obs.*

1788 NELSON 6 May in Nicolas *Disp.* (1845) I. 273 My health is got up again, after the Doctors telling me they could do nothing for me.

f. Of game: To rise from cover.

1834 T. MEDWIN *Angler in Wales* I. 43 Traversing one of our untrodden wildernesses, with..hogs..quail and partridges, getting up on all sides. **1850** *Tait's Mag.* XVII. 614/1 He never missed anything that got up within range.

g. *colloq.* As a command to a horse = Go! go ahead!

1887 F. FRANCIS Jr. *Saddle & Mocassin* vii. 123 Get up! —get up..he says..and once more the horses resume their gait.

h. *Cricket.* Of the ball: To rise off the pitch higher than usual.

1828 *Sporting Mag.* Feb. 244/2 Straight-armed bowlers are invariably slow bowlers. Their balls, indeed, get up fast, but they never come fast to the long stop. **1881** *Sportsman's Year-bk.* 139 A ball got up and smashed his hand. **1888** A. G. STEEL in *Cricket* (Badm.) 163 Should the ball 'shoot' or 'get up'.

†**i.** *refl.* To rise up (preparatory to action).

1535 COVERDALE *2 Chron.* xiii. 6 But Ieroboam..gat him vp [**1611** is risen vp] & fell awaye from his lorde. **1737** WHISTON *Josephus, Antiq.* I. vii. §2 But after a long time he got him up and removed from that country.

j. *trans.* (See sense 27 and UP.)

1662 J. DAVIES *Olearius' Voy. Ambass.* 157 We at last made a shift to get up the great [anchor]. **1697** DAMPIER *Voy.* (1729) I. 416 Having fine handsom weather we got up our yards again. *a* **1732** T. BOSTON *Crook in Lot* (1805) 107 The man naturally bends his force to get off the weight, that he may get up his head. **1735** J. PRICE *Stone-Br. Thames* 6 The rest of the Piers..are all got up to the Stones abovementioned. **1822** G. W. MANBY *Voy. Greenland* (1823) 12 All the crew were called to get up the whale-boats. **1876** WHYTE MELVILLE *Katerfelto* v. 60 Show me where the deer is harboured. The Lord have mercy on him, for I will not, when once I get him up to bay.

k. To prepare, make ready, organize, set on foot, bring into existence.

1593 ABP. BANCROFT *Daung. Posit.* IV. i. 136 The Puritanes in Scotland haue got-vp their discipline. **1728** NEWTON *Chronol. Amended* i. 179 Minos..got up a potent fleet. **1771** SMOLLETT *Humph. Cl.* 8 Nov., We have got up several farces. **1806-7** J. BERESFORD *Miseries Hum. Life* (1826) VI. xxix, A mob of red-hot cooks and scullions.. getting up two or three large dinners. **1831** *Hist.* in *Ann. Reg.* (1832) 153/1 Petitions to the magistrates in his favour were gotten up by his friends. **1840** E. E. NAPIER *Excurs. S. Africa* II. 291 It was deemed more than probable that he would 'get up a fight'. **1850** *Jrnl. R. Agric. Soc.* XI. ii. 681 It is..more easy to get up a good breed than to keep it up. **1868** FREEMAN *Norman Conq.* II. x. 499 It was affirmed that the revolt had been..got up by the secret practices of Harold.

l. To dress (linen), make ready for wearing.

1750 JOHNSON *Rambler* No. 12 ¶3 There would be nothing to do but to clean my mistress's room, get up her linen [etc.]. **1834** T. MEDWIN *Angler in Wales* I. 77 Hard at work..at what is called getting up frills. **1884** G. GISSING *Unclassed* II. III. iv. 86, I was in the laundry nearly six months, and became quite clever in getting up linen.

m. To dress (the person, hair, etc.) in a certain way; to produce or 'turn out' in a (specified) style as regards externals; said with reference to the mounting of a play, the binding, print, and paper of a book, etc. Chiefly in pa. pple. *got up.* Also *intr.* for *refl.*

1782 MRS. THRALE *Let. to Johnson* 16 Feb., I am told the new plays this year *are got up* (as the phrase is) very penuriously. **1800** in *Spirit Publ. Jrnls.* (1801) IV. 388 The principal novelty is a piece called the Confederacy..which is getting up in great style. **1823** J. BADCOCK *Dom. Amusem.* 51 Instead of two reflectors, this instrument may be got up with three or more such planes. **1828** L. HUNT *Ess.* (Camelot) 13 The pocket-books that now contain any literature are 'got up', as the phrase is, in the most unambitious style. **1858** R. S. SURTEES *Ask Mamma* iii. 7 Miss Willing was extremely well got up. **1863** [HEMYNG] *Eton Sch. Days* xviii. (1864) 207 He felt confident in his power of 'getting up' so that no one would recognise him. **1879** F. POLLOK *Sport Brit. Burmah* I. 8 The hair is taken great care of and tastefully got up à la Chinois. **1890** *Sat. Rev.* 22 Nov. 603/2 The book is prettily got up.

n. To make good, recover (an expense, a deficiency, loss, arrears).

1607 MIDDLETON *5 Gallants* I. i, Tis got vp at your house in an after-noone ifaith, the hire of the whole month. **1622** WESTON in Bradford *Plymouth Plant.* (1856) 115 Mr. Beachamp and myselfe bought this little ship..partly to gett up what we are formerly out. **1687** MIEGE *Gt. Fr. Dict.* II. s.v., I am so much a Loser, I must get it up another Way. **1872** BLACK *Adv. Phaeton* xv, The afternoon was spent in getting up arrears of correspondence.

†**o.** To collect, raise (money). *Obs.*

1639 T. BRUGIS tr. *Camus' Mor. Relat.* 314 Having gotten up a good summe of money, hee stole away. **1697** DAMPIER *Voy.* I. Introd. 3, I was willing to get up some money before my return, having laid out what I had at Jamaica.

p. To cause to rise; to lift up, raise from a stooping position; also, to improve (one's health). *to get one's* or *another person's back up*: to become or make angry (cf. BACK *sb.* 24 f.).

1674 tr. *Martiniere's Voy. N. Countries* 106, I awaked at the noise the Master made to get up his Family. *a* **1708** BEVERIDGE *Thes. Theol.* (1711) III. 410 It is a good while, before we can get up our hearts from earth to heaven. *a* **1732** T. BOSTON *Crook in Lot* (1805) 152 God will..remove the weight so long hung at them..and let them get up their back long bowed. **1815** M. J. CLAIRMONT in Dowden *Shelley* (1887) I. 521 Don't you think Papa and Mamma will go down to the seaside, to get up their health a little? **1887** RIDER HAGGARD *Jess* ii, 'I'm your brother.' 'Are you?' I said, beginning to get my back up.

q. *to get up steam*: to produce sufficient steam to work the engine; often *fig.*

1832 MARRYAT *N. Forster* xl, I have..a way of going ahead, by getting up the steam..—and the fuel is brandy. **1844** DARWIN in *Life & Lett.* (1887) I. 301 Get up your steam, if this weather lasts, and have a ramble in Wales. **1883** FENN *Middy & Ensign* xxxix. 237 Every effort being made by the firemen to get up steam.

r. To work up, create in one's self (an emotion or feeling).

1837 J. HALLEY in Arnot *Life* (1842) 81 Let him beware of getting up (ὡς εἰπεῖν) certain emotions as due to his views.. of the sacred office. **1860** *Temple Bar* I. 68 She got up a spurious affection for the creature. **1885** MRS. PRAED *Affin.* I. ii. 42 These are the only subjects about which she ever gets up any excitement.

s. To acquire a knowledge of (a subject) for a special purpose or by a special effort.

1828 ALFORD in *Life* (1873) 32 Getting up the Georgics, reading trigonometry. **1866** CARLYLE *Inaug. Addr.* 172 There is a process called cramming..that is, getting-up such points of things as the Examiner is likely to put questions about. **1887** A. BIRRELL *Obiter Dicta* Ser. II. 157 He would..devote studious hours to getting up the subjects to be dicussed.

t. To harvest (a crop); also, to stack (corn).

1844 *Jrnl. R. Agric. Soc.* V. I. 68 The crops having been got up, the land is..sown with wheat. **1876** *Encycl. Brit.* IV. 266 If 'got up' damp, it [barley] is liable to generate excessive heat.

VIII. *Comb.* **81.** *Comb.* (forming substantive and adjective phrases). **a.** The *trans.* verb with an object, as †**get-nothing**, one who earns nothing, an idler; †**get-penny**, something which brings in money (cf. CATCHPENNY). **b.** The *intr.* verb with an adv., as GET-AWAY; **get-off**, (*a*) an evasion, subterfuge; (*b*) = TAKE-OFF *sb.* 3 b; (*c*) the action of 'getting off' in jazz (see 70 l); an improvisation or 'break'; also *attrib.*; **get-on**, one who 'gets on'; a successful person; also *attrib.*; **get-there** (orig. *U.S.*), energy, ambition; also *attrib.* **c.** **get-overable** *a.* (*nonce-wd.*), that may be won over or got round.

1607 MIDDLETON *5 Gallants* I. i, That face will get money ifaith; twill bee a get peny I warrant you. **1614** B. JONSON *Barth. Fair* v. i, The Gunpowder-plot, there was a get-penny! I haue presented that to an eighteene or twenty pence audience, nine times in an afternoone. *a* **1625** BOYS *Wks.* (1629) 55 As a spend-all so a get-nothing is a theefe to his estate. **1655** R. YOUNGE *Agst. Drunkards* 4 Drunkards are not onely lazie get nothings but they are also riotous spend alls. **1684** S. G. *Angl. Spec.* 481 'London Lick-penny' ..there is no less Truth in this 'London Get-penny'. **1832** *Chambers's Jrnl.* I. 121/2 As a get-off, she commences a eulogy on her butter. **1848** J. H. NEWMAN *Loss & Gain* 80 'But it is an illegal declaration or vow', said Willis, 'and so not binding'. 'Where did you find that get-off?' said Charles; 'the priest put that into your head.' **1853** G. JOHNSTON *Nat. Hist. E. Bord.* I. 256 Pooh! that explanation won't do. A mere get-off! **1886** J. K. JEROME *Idle Thoughts* 26 A belted earl may be..get-overable by flattery; just as every other human being is. **1898** E. N. WESTCOTT *David Harum* xix. 169 He hain't got much 'git there' in his make-up. **1901** *Daily Chron.* 22 June 10/5 Their style of rowing.. is certainly the 'get there' style. **1908** *Westm. Gaz.* 10 Mar. 14/2 A little weary of this 'get on' gospel being continually dinned in their ears. **1908** *Daily Chron.* 13 Mar. 4/6 Prophetically numbered by Landor among the 'ons' who are get-ons. **1916** H. BARBER *Aeroplane Speaks* 50 The Pilot turns the Aeroplane in order to face the wind and thus secure a quick 'get-off'. **1932** *Melody Maker* July 593 There is an abundance of trumpet-playing of the first order from the local 'get-off' man. **1935** *Vanity Fair* Nov. 71 Breaks are sometimes known as *get-offs* or *take-offs*. **1956** M. STEARNS *Story of Jazz* (1957) xvi. 180 The formula consisted of importing one or two 'hot' soloists, or 'get-off' men, letting them take a chorus once in a while.

d. The *intr.* verb with an adj., forming compound adjectives, as **get-tough**; **get-well**, esp. designating cards or other forms of message sent to a sick person to express good wishes for his recovery.

1959 *Daily Mail* 1 Apr. 7/2 The United States wants to force its 'get tough' line on the other Western Powers. **1960** *News Chron.* 14 Oct. 1/5 The Government's get-tough policy follows a growing demand..to 'teach the natives a lesson'. **1971** *Guardian* 19 Nov. 14/3 Criminal Justice Bills tend to be miscellaneous collections of proposals... The current one..is a sweet-and-sour concoction, with several 'get tough' provisions. **1956** B. CLEARY *Fifteen* (1962) x. 145 She looked over the get-well cards in Woodment's stationery store. **1966** *Guardian* 29 Dec. 7/4 Mrs. Kennedy ..sent him a 'get-well' telegram.

geta ('geɪtə), *sb. pl.* [Jap., f. *ge* lower, under + *ta* footwear.] Wooden shoes worn by the Japanese, with thongs between the big toe and the small toes.

1884 tr. *Rein's Japan* 416 He leaves his geta or zôri at the door, so as not to soil the beautiful mats. **1897** *Outing* (U.S.) XXX. 214/2 Their wooden geta clattering and slapping their soles as they go. **1904** *Daily Chron.* 13 June 8/5 Some of the 'geta' worn by little girls are painted in many colours. **1905** *Westm. Gaz.* 16 Mar. 2/1 The Yorozu are artistic to the stilts of their wooden geta. **1947** J. BERTRAM *Shadow of War* 334 If the youngest tot stumbled in his *geta* he was bullied unmercifully.

get-at-able (get'ætəb(ə)l), *a.* Also **getatable**. [f. the phrase *get at* (see GET *v.* 38) + -ABLE; cf. COME-AT-ABLE.] That may be got at, reached, or obtained; accessible, attainable.

1799 SOUTHEY in Robberds *Mem. W. Taylor* I. 275 The book is not get-at-able. **1896** *Rep. B. & F. Bib. Soc.* 244 The people are more get-at-able than in China.

Hence **get-at-a'bility**, **get-'at-ableness**, the state or quality of being get-at-able.

1863 SMILES *Industr. Biog.* 292 The pyramidal form of this engine, its great simplicity and get-at-ability of parts.. have rendered it a universal favourite. **1890** *Pall Mall G.* 2 July 4/2 Most of the dancing men preferred the get-at-ableness of Grosvenor-place.

get-away, getaway ('getəweɪ). [GET *v.* 81.] The action of getting away; *spec.* (*a*) the breaking cover of a fox; (*b*) an escape; a method or chance of escape; esp. of thieves with their booty (often *to make one's get-away*); (*c*) the start of a race. Also *attrib.*, esp. designating a vehicle in which thieves make their get-away.

1852 R. S. SURTEES *Sponge's Sp. Tour* (1893) 131 The quick find, the quick get away. **1890** BOLDREWOOD *Col. Reformer* (1891) 173 There is some get away, if anything broke, short of your neck. **1893** L. W. MOORE *His Own Story* xlviii. 622 Only three [prisoners] had made their escape. Mrs. Keene had prevented a clean 'get-away' for many more. **1907** C. E. MULFORD *Bar-20* xv. 166 We'll have to make our get-away plumb sudden or we'll never go. **1922** *Punch* 1 Nov. 423/1 Quickly removing the ball from my toe I crawled under the net and made a get-away in the referee's car. **1923** *Motor Cycling* 26 Sept. 657/2 No one failed to start, although in general the getaways were not so fast or neat as in the case of the trade riders. **1924** [see BEAN *v.*]. **1930** E. H. LAVINE *Third Degree* (1931) iv. 38 He will make his getaway before the fun starts. *Ibid.* xi. 129 The stolen get-away Cadillac car. **1966** M. R. D. FOOT *SOE in France* x. 325 Robert Benoist, arrested in the street three days after his brother, made the first sensational get-away of a splendid run of escapes. **1968** 'L. MARSHALL' *Blood on Blotter* xxvi. 174 You provided the job, you cased it, took care of the law, provided the get-away car.

†**gete**, *sb. Obs.* [cogn. w. next; cf. ON. *gætr* (pl.) heed, *gætiliga* heedfully.] Heed, attention.

a **1200** *Fragm. Ælfric's Gram.* (1838) 6 Nulleþ heo nimen gete.

Hence †**'geteless** *a.*, careless, heedless.

c **1200** ORMIN 6190 Forr ȝiff þatt ȝho iss gætelæs & eȝȝelæs & wilde ȝho gilleþþ sket.

†**gete**, *v. Obs.* Forms: 3 **gætenn, geaten, geite,** 3-4 **get(t,** 4 **geet,** 3-5 **gete.** *Pa. t.* 3-4 **geit, gett(e.** *Pa. pple.* 3-4 **get, gett(e,** 4 **gate.** [a. ON. *gæta* (pa. t. *gætte*, pa. pple. *gǽtt-r*) to watch, tend:—orig. **gátjan*, f. *gát, gǿt* fem., heed, attention, believed by some scholars to represent an OTeut. type **ga-ahtâ*, f. **ga-* (OE. *ȝe-*, Y-) + **ahtâ* (OHG. *ahta*, Ger. *acht*) attention.

The word is chiefly northern, being especially frequent in the *Cursor Mundi*, in the later texts of which *keep* is sometimes substituted.]

1. *trans.* To watch, guard, take charge of (a person or place); to tend (cattle or sheep).

c **1200** ORMIN 3765 Forr þatt teȝȝ sholldenn hirdess ben To ȝemenn hemm & gætenn. *a* **1225** *Ancr. R.* 50 Witeð þer our eien [*T.* wel itachet, & geateð wel þer owre ehne]. *a* **1300** *Cursor M.* 28279 Quare I was scheperd..To reckelesly i geit my schepe. *c* **1300** *Havelok* 2960 [He] bad Ubbe..þat he sholde on ilke wise Denemark yeme and gete so, þat no pleynte come him to. *c* **1330** R. BRUNNE *Chron. Wace* (Rolls) 648 Loke wel þat þy schip be get; Lat non come vnder þy telde [etc.]. **1375** BARBOUR *Bruce* xv. 264 The castell tuk he in his hand..and has set A gud wardane it for to get. *c* **1400** *Destr. Troy* 2113 Our goddes with grace get vs þerfro! *c* **1420** *Avow. Arth.* lix, He gafe me a castelle to gete With alle the lordschippus grete.

2. To keep, observe (a holy-day).

a **1300** *Cursor M.* 28261 Þe festes þat in kyrk ar sette Ic haue þam soth ful iuel gette.

Hence †**'geter**, keeper, guardian. [= ON. *gætir*.]

c **1400** *Destr. Troy* 972 Ʒet merueld hym more how Mars was distroyed, Geter of his good and a god holdyn. *Ibid.* 11739 Thoantes..he heght þat was geeter of the god.

gete, obs. f. GET, JET; obs. pl. of GOAT.

getee, obs. form of JETTY.

geten, var. GETON, *Obs.*, banner.

†**getenly**, *adv. Obs. rare*$^{-1}$. In 2 **getenluker** (*comparative*). [App. f. **geten* careful (a. ON. *gætenn*, f. *gæta* GETE *v.*) + -LY[2]; cf. ON. *gætiliga* carefully.] Carefully, diligently.

c **1200** *Trin. Coll. Hom.* 121 Men bien swo wiðerfulle. þat swo he getenluker clepeð hem to him, swo hie wiðere turneð froward him.

geterne, obs. form of GITTERN.

†**gethe**. *Obs. rare.* Also 6 *Sc.* **gayth.** [? repr. OE. **géhð(u* = OHG. *gâhida*:—OTeut. type **gaŋhiþâ*, f. **gaŋhjo-* (OHG. *gâhi* mod.G. *jähe*) hasty, precipitate.] Haste, hurry.

c **1440** *Bone Flor.* 1607 Before hur bedd lay a stone, The lady toke hyt up anon, And toke hyt yn a gethe. **1572** *Satir. Poems Reform.* xxxi. 13 To send this Sedull in a gayth That nane of ȝow kep ony skayth For laik of Premonitioun.

†**'gether**, *adv. Obs.* Short for TOGETHER.

1589 R. ROBINSON *Gold. Mirr.* (Chetham Soc.) 18 He layes not gether poor men's grounds He is no country stroyer.

†**gethicall.** 'Vile, wicked' (Cockeram 1623).

Gethsemane (geθ'seməni:). [ad. L. (Vulgate) *Gethsemani*, Gr. Γεθσημανῆ, ad. Aramaic *gath shemānī(m)* oil-press.] The name of a 'garden' or enclosure on the Mount of Olives, scene of the agony of Christ (*Matt.* xxvi. 36-46). Hence **a.** A representation in painting or sculpture of Christ's agony in the garden. **b.** A scene of spiritual or mental anguish; an instance of such anguish.

1901 *Westm. Gaz.* 26 July 2/1 A great, sad, German-looking Gethsemane, its big white figures shining mysteriously behind a grating. **1913** D. H. LAWRENCE *Love Poems* 16 And I at the foot of her cross did suffer My own gethsemane. **1923** —— *Birds, Beasts & Flowers* 53 See it [*sc.* an almond-tree] come forth in blossom..Sweating his drops of blood through the long-nighted Gethsemane Into blossom.

geting, obs. form of GETTING.

†**'getless**, *a. Obs. rare*$^{-1}$. [f. GET *sb.*[1] + -LESS.] Having got nothing, empty-handed.

? *a* **1400** *Morte Arth.* 2728 Ʒif we gettlesse goo home, the kyng wille be grevede.

getling ('getlɪŋ). *Sc.* Also 8-9 **gytlin(g.** [f. GET *sb.*[1] 2 + -LING.] A child, brat. Also *attrib.*

1718 RAMSAY *Christ's Kirk Gr.* III. xix, The wives and gytlings a' spawn'd out O'er middens, and o'er dykes. **1736** —— *Epist. to J. Wardlaw* 19 That the getlings prove na fools

They maun be hawden att the schools. **1804** TARRAS *Poems* 119 Daft gytlin thing! what gypitness is this?

†**geton.** *Obs.* Forms: 4-5 geten, 5 geto(u)n, gettorne, guytorne, gyton(e, gytton, gyttorne, 5-6 gitton, 6 getton, getorn. [Of obscure origin: the sense would suggest identity with F. *guidon* (see GUIDON), which is recorded only from the 16th c.; but the form is difficult to explain.] A small flag: see quot. *c* 1500.

1392 *Earl Derby's Exp.* (Camden) 152 De ij getens de armis Sancti Georgii. **1420** *Siege Rouen* 1214 in *Archæol.* XXII. 380 There was many a getoun gay, With mychille & grete aray. *c* **1420** LYDG. *Assemb. Gods* 970 Penowns & guytornes many a score. **1437** in Dugdale *Antiq. Warwicksh.* (1656) 327 Item, a Gyton for the Shippe of viij yerdis longe. *c* **1440** *Promp. Parv.* 197/1 Gytone, *conscisorium.* ? *c* **1500** *MS. Harl.* 838 in *Archæol.* XXII. (1829) 396 Euery baronet ..shal haue hys baner displeyd in ye field yf he be chyef capteyn, euery knyght his penoun, euery squier or gentleman hys getoun or standard.. A stremer shal be slyt & so shal a standard as well as a getoun; a getoun shall berr ye lenght of ij yardes, a standard of iii or 4 yardes, & a stremer of xii. xx. xl. or lx yardes long. **1525** LD. BERNERS *Froiss.* II. clxix. [clxv.] 478 Great pleasure it was..to se their standardes, getorns, and penons, wauynge in the wynde. **1548** HALL *Chron., Hen. VIII*, 17 The Baners, Penons, Standerdes, and Gittons.

get-out. *colloq.* [f. GET *v.* 72 and 73.]

1. Phr. *as* or *like* (*all*) *get-out*, used to indicate a high degree of something.

1838 J. C. NEAL *Charcoal Sks.* 12 We look as elegant and as beautiful as get out. **1869** W. C. HAZLITT *Eng. Proverbs* 60 As common as get out. *Cornw.* **1881** J. SARGISSON *Joe Scoap's Jurneh* 119 He glooart at meh as impident as *git oot.* **1884** 'MARK TWAIN' *Huck. Finn* xxxviii, We got to dig in like all git-out. **1916** H. L. WILSON *Somewhere in Red Gap* v. 197 When I got into the parlour she had them on, pleased as all get-out. **1959** M. STEEN *Tower* I. ii. 35 By then I was as drunk as all-get-out. **1967** V. CANNING *Python Project* vii. 146 They looked as comfortable as all get-out.

2. An escape from a difficult position; an evasion, withdrawal.

1899 E. W. HORNUNG *Amateur Cracksman* 115, I ask you, was there ever a better get-out? **1909** *Westm. Gaz.* 4 June 7/3 I'm entirely in your hands. I have got no get-out. **1932** *Economist* 30 Jan. 221/2 An orderly 'get-out' from their German commitments. **1968** *Listener* 4 Jan. 27/2 The lads didn't know what they wanted to say and fell on the magic and mystery idea as an unanswerable get-out.

3. *Theatr.* The total weekly cost of a theatrical production; orig., the ability of a touring company to leave a town after paying all expenses; the amount of box-office takings required to assure this. Also *attrib.*

1952 GRANVILLE *Dict. Theatr. Terms* 88 *Get out*, the ability to leave a town with all expenses paid... *Get-out figure*, the weekly running cost of a touring show. **1959** P. BULL *I know Face* iii. 54 In actual fact we should have been sitting pretty, as the get-out was only £663 a week. *Ibid.* 55, I was able to get the 'get-out' figure down to £500 a week. **1961** *Times* 3 Jan. 3/7 The 'get-out' for Brecht's *Galileo* (cast of 40) was £1,920 a week, for eight performances a week.

get-rich-quick, *a.* orig. *U.S.* [GET *v.* 33 and QUICK *adv.*] Characterized by attempts at, or hopes of, acquiring wealth rapidly. Hence **get-rich-quicker**, a person who desires to make quick profits.

[**1902** O. WISTER *Virginian* xxxi, He's disturbed over getting rich quick and being a big man in the Territory.] **1904** 'O. HENRY' in *McClure's Mag.* Aug. 360/1 A get-rich-quick—excuse me—gang giving back the boodle! Oh, no. **1910** *Daily Chron.* 22 Apr. 1/6 Tales of the get-rich-quick order are quite common. **1914** *Chambers's Jrnl.* Feb. 144/1 California passed from the 'get rich quickers' into the hands of scientific exploiters. **1940** J. BUCHAN *Memory Hold-the-Door* v. 114 The get-rich-quick offscourings of European capitals. **1957** *Sat. Rev.* 8 June 25 As a businessman, yes; as a private enterpriser, a get-rich-quicker, of course. **1960** *Times* 5 Dec. 4/2 The Government..had made things far too easy for the get-rich-quick boys. **1971** D. POTTER *Brit. Eliz. Stamps.* i. 15 Stamps were solemnly discussed in the financial columns,..and get-rich-quick operators joined in the *mêlée.*

getron, obs. form of GITTERN.

gett, var. GET *sb.*[3]

gettable ('gɛtəb(ə)l), *a.* Also 6 gettabill, -ible, 8-9 getable. [f. GET *v.* + -ABLE.] That can be got.

1555 *Extracts Aberd. Reg.* (1844) I. 289 Gyf the same be ..nocht gettabill in the sam forme as it ves. *a* **1605** MONTGOMERIE *Sonn.* xlix, Wald God if it wer gettible for geir! **1611** COTGR., *Gaignable*, gettable..to be got. **1769** H. WALPOLE *Corr.* (1837) II. 432, I..shall employ a little collector to get me all [prints] that are getable. **1796** COLERIDGE *Lett.* (1895) 184, I wish that little cottage by the road-side were gettable. **1867** FURNIVALL *Babees Bk.* Introd. 74 Getting all that was gettable out of them. **1871** *Echo* 21 June, Sufficient economically gettable coal exists in Great Britain and Ireland to last from 800 to 1,000 years. **1882** OGILVIE, *Gettable, Getable.* **1884** CASSELL, *Getable, Gettable.*

gette, obs. form of GET *v.*, GHAUT, JETTY.

getter ('gɛtə(r)), *sb.* Also 4 gettare, 5 getare. [f. GET *v.* + -ER[1].] One who gets.

1. a. One who gets or obtains; *esp.* one who acquires wealth.

c **1440** *Promp. Parv.* 192/1 Getare of goodys, *adquisitor.* *c* **1510** BARCLAY *Mirr. Gd. Manners* (1570) G iv, Vile lucre.. causeth the getter oft time his purpose ban. **1548** HALL *Chron., Hen. V*, 81 Experience teacheth that there is no lesse praise to be geuen to the keper then to the getter. **1596** BELL *Surv. Popery* I. II. iv. 84 After great getters come great spenders. **1667** J. CORBET *Disc. Relig. Eng.* 25 They are not the Great Wasters, but mostly in the number of Getters. **1707** ROWE *Pythagoras' Gold. Vers.* 44 Revolve the Getter's Joy and Loser's Pain, And think if it be worth thy while to gain. **1853** TRENCH *Proverbs* 141 Unrighteous gains are sure to disappoint the getter. **1880** L. WALLACE *Ben-Hur* 238 He will have need of getters and keepers.

b. One of a class of coal-miners. (Cf. also *coal-getter, stone-getter.*)

1839 URE *Dict. Arts* 979 (*Pitcoal*) The set who succeed the holers are called getters. **1871** *Trans. Amer. Inst. Mining Eng.* I. 305 Beginning at the far end of his work the getter knocks out or loosens the spragς that had protected the holers, retreating as he operates. **1883** *Manch. Exam.* 27 Nov. 5/5 The drawers at the Whinney Hill Pit..struck work for an advance of wages, and, as the getters can do nothing without the drawers, the mine is stopped.

c. A substance used to remove residual gas from an evacuated enclosure by chemical or other action. Also *attrib.* and *Comb.*

1922 *Proc. Inst. Radio Engin.* X. 469 By 'getter' we mean the substances such as phosphorus, arsenic, sulphur and so on. These substances, when applied to metals and volatilized by heating them, trap the gases. **1943** J. YARWOOD *High Vacuum Technique* iv. 38 These 'getters' during volatilization combine with the residual gases in the vessel and they are fixed as chemical compounds deposited on the walls of the tube. **1944** *Light Metals* Jan. 34/1 Getters are used in all radio valves..and in cathode-ray-oscillograph bulbs. **1959** *New Scientist* 26 Mar. 708/3 In other types of getter-ion pumps, the getter film is produced by sputtering—that is, by knocking atoms out of the bulk getter metal by bombarding it with the ions of the residual gas.

2. One who begets; a procreator, begetter (*obs.* exc. of horses); in 14th c. Sc., a parent.

c **1375** *Sc. Leg. Saints, Machor* 116 It is mast sorow of ane barne to be fra þe gettare sa tane. *Ibid., Baptista* 643 & þe lofinge of his getteris Ine to fyfe thinge wele aperis. **1607** SHAKS. *Cor.* IV. v. 240 Peace is..a getter of more bastard Children, then warres a destroyer of men. **1632** SHERWOOD, A getter or begetter, *engendreur.* **1798** in *Spirit Publ. Jrnls.* (1799) II. 298 It is well known the getter of him [a charger] was engaged in almost every review during the last war.

3. In comb. with advs., as *getter-on, getter-up*; also *getter to bed*; **getter-in** (*Agric.*), ? a machine for reaping and binding.

1820 W. IRVING *Sketch Bk.* (1859) 54, I recognized in him a diligent getter-up of miscellaneous works. **1834** *New Monthly Mag.* XLII. 330 A getter-up of fights, a second of the fighters. **1837** *Ibid.* LI. 186 Sunshine for me..and gas-shine for late getters to bed. **1849** MARRYAT *Valerie* viii, Your aunt..has resided there..as a clear-starcher and getter-up of lace. **1866** *Athenæum* No. 2025. 208/1 A getter-on, born in the Glasgow gutter. **1873** H. SPENCER *Stud. Sociol.* xv. (1877) 363 Getters-up of bubble-companies. **1884** *W. Sussex Gaz.* 25 Sept., An American getter in.

getter ('gɛtə(r)), *v.* [f. GETTER *sb.*] *trans.* **a.** To remove (gas) by means of a getter. **b.** To evacuate (an enclosure) by means of a getter. So **'gettered** *ppl. a.*; **'gettering** *vbl. sb.*, freq. *attrib.*

1922 *Brit. Pat.* 187,055 3/1 The present invention.. depends upon the process of 'gettering'. **1925** F. H. NEWMAN *Prod. & Measurem. Low Pressures* vii. 133 In the 'gettered' lamp a solution of red phosphorus in alcohol was painted on the leads below the filament. **1933** *Phil. Mag.* XVI. 673 Gettered hydrogen may be re-evolved from magnesium owing to a 'vapour pressure' exerted by the cleaned-up gas. *Ibid.* 674 Hydrogen may be gettered by and reliberated from magnesium. **1943** J. YARWOOD *High Vacuum Technique* v. 51 Gettering is carried out at the lowest possible pressure, and the magnesium or barium pellet reduces the pressure in the valve to less than 10^{-5} mm. Hg. **1967** WARD & BUNN *Introd. High Vacuum Technol.* iii. 65 The gettering process..can obviously be used to remove gas from a system and hence produce a pumping action.

getter, var. JETTER, braggart.

gettible, gettie, obs. ff. GETTABLE, JETTY.

getting ('gɛtɪŋ), *vbl. sb.* [f. GET *v.* + -ING[1].]

1. The action of the verb GET in various senses.

1398 TREVISA *Barth. De. P.R.* XVIII. i. (1495) 737 Beestes haue redynesse of wytte in sekynge and getynge of meete and of nourysshynge. *c* **1430** *Pilgr. Lyf Manhode* I. cxlv. (1869) 74 For litel is woorth thing ygoten, if after þe getinge it ne be kept. **1548** HALL *Chron., Hen. V*, 74 After the gettyng of the toune, the castle..denied to rendre, and so it was strongly besieged. *a* **1639** W. WHATELEY *Prototypes* II. xxvi. (1640) 36 Yea but I am sure that his getting hinders my gains. **1726** LEONI *Alberti's Archit.* I. 69/1 The Cornishes ..by their projection hinder the getting into the Town from scaling Ladders. **1772** MACKENZIE *Man World* I. iv. (1773) I. 46 With Annesly, the getting of a lesson, or performing of an exercise, was a privilege. **1839-40** THACKERAY *Catherine* viii, He had not the genius for getting. **1882** OUIDA *Maremma* I. 63 Wood was to be had for the getting.

b. In comb. with advs., esp. *getting-in, -out, -up*; **getting-on races** (Cambridge University), races in which the winning boat obtains the right to row in the Lent races.

c **1380** WYCLIF *Wks.* (1880) 369 þis lawe of getynge in of þes temporaltes. **1596** SHAKS. *Merch. V.* III. v. 41, I shall answere that better to the Commonwealth, than you can the getting vp of the Negroes bellie. **1626** BACON *Sylva* §328 The Getting forth, or spreading of the Spirits. **1649** BP. GUTHRIE *Mem.* (1702) 60 This Emergent made those at home more eager for getting up of an Army. **1663** COWLEY *Ess., Dang. Procrast.* (1669) 141 Begin; the Getting out of doors is the greatest part of the Journey. **1748** *Anson's Voy.* III. i. 299 The only step to be taken was, the..getting out of her [the ship] as much as was possible before she was destroyed. **1791** NEWTE *Tour Eng. & Scot.* 122 The whole country being turned into pasture land..has prevented the wood from getting up. **1825** HONE *Every-day Bk.* I. 435 Expenses attending the 'getting-up' of the representations. **1856** RUSKIN *Mod. Paint.* IV. v. ii. §15 That extraordinary road, and its goings on, and gettings about. **1873** H. SPENCER *Stud. Sociol.* v. 82 Like the getting-up of companies, the getting-up of agitations..is..a means of advancement. **1892** *Pall Mall G.* 23 Feb. 2/3 The getting-on races took place last week.

2. *concr.* (usually in *pl.*). That which is got or acquired; gains, earnings. Now only *arch.*

c **1425** *Eng. Conq. Irel.* 26 The englysh hoste, wyth grett gettynges & with rych yiftes, turned ayeyne yn-to leynestre. **1473** WARKW. *Chron.* (Camden) 4 By whiche he hade grete getynge. **1577-87** HOLINSHED *Chron.* I. 187/2 Certeine Danish rovers..spoile the coast..make sale of their gettings, and returne to their countrie. **1614** RALEIGH *Hist. World* III. (1634) 103 He..was desirous to be soone at home, that he might freely enjoy his gettings. **1726** SWIFT *Gulliver* I. vi, A small monthly share of their gettings, to be a portion for the child. **1760** FOOTE *Minor* II. Wks. 1799 I. 253 Your gettings should be added to his estate. **1891** G. MEREDITH *One of our Conq.* I. i. 16 They dispossess him of his greedy gettings.

3. Begetting, procreation, generation. *arch.*

a **1300** *Cursor M.* 22035 In his geting þe feind of hell sal crepe in his moder to duell. **1387** TREVISA *Higden* (Rolls) V. 279 Of Merlyn his fantastik getynge [L. *genitura*]. *c* **1440** *Jacob's Well* (E.E.T.S.) 140 þe chylderyn of mannys gettyng vnder þi weengys..in hope schul be gyed. **1494** FABYAN *Chron.* VI. cxli. 129 The sayd Sergius was accusyd or defamyd of ye gettyng of a chylde. **1601** SHAKS. *All's Well* III. ii. 44 That's the losse of men, though it be the getting of children. *c* **1825** BEDDOES *Poems, 2nd Brother* II. ii, Better thou wert the brother of his foe Than what thou art, a man of the same getting.

†**4. a.** Used to render L. *generatio* = generation; produce. *Obs.*

a **1300** *E.E. Psalter* xiii. 6 [xiv. 5] (Horstm.) For lauerd night and dai In rightwise getinge es he ai. *a* **1340** HAMPOLE *Psalter* ix. 28, I sall noght be stired fra getynge in getynge wiþout ill. **1382** WYCLIF *Ecclus.* vi. 20 In the werk forsothe of it a litil thou shal trauailen, and soone thou shalt ete of the getingus of it [**1388** the generaciouns therof].

†**b.** = Genesis, nativity. *Obs.*

c **1375** *Sc. Leg. Saints, Clement* 385 Fore of my-self & [of] my wyf..þe gettyne [L. *genesin*] kene I wondir wele.

5. *Comb.*: **getting-rock** (see quot.).

1883 GRESLEY *Gloss. Coal Mining, Getting-rock*, clay ironstone in the roof of a coal-seam, which is worked in conjunction with the coal.

getting ('gɛtɪŋ), *ppl. a.* [f. GET *v.* + -ING[2].]

1. That gets or acquires.

1634 RAINBOW *Labour* (1635) 29 A Science, if not more thriving, yet more getting than any of the Liberall ones. **1703** COLLIER *Ess. Mor. Subj.* II. 138 As for the getting part, a covetous man never troubles himself with the niceties of morality. **1744** BERKELEY *Siris* §331 The most knowing as well as the most getting part of mankind.

2. That begets, or favours begetting.

1632 RANDOLPH *Jealous Lovers* v. ii, You were born Under a getting constellation—A fructifying star.

'get-to,gether. *colloq.* (orig. *U.S.*). [GET *v.* 78 b.] A meeting, gathering; an informal conference; *esp.*, an informal social gathering. Also *attrib.* Hence **,get-to'getherness.**

1911 *Springfield Weekly Republican* 9 Feb. 12 It was the biggest get-together the organization has ever held. **1932** *News Chron.* 23 Sept. 5/2 All passengers greatly enjoyed the Get Together Dance last night. **1935** WODEHOUSE *Luck of Bodkins* xv. 173 Brother Bodkin said as much last time we were having one of our get-togethers. **1936** 'J. TEY' *Shilling for Candles* xv. 169 The article..finished with a real Hopkins touch of get-togetherness. **1958** *Punch* 1 Jan. 60/3 Accepting one of his hostess's 'specials' at one of her now-famous 'get-together' parties. **1959** J. ARDEN *Party* I. i, in J. C. Trewin *Plays of Year* XVIII. 238 You know Richard, how he really loves a get-together. A party, eh, on Wednesday? **1962** *Times Lit. Suppl.* 30 Nov. 938/3 An era of political and ecclesiastical get-togetherness. **1966** J. CAIRD *Perturbing Spirit* xv. 161 She normally dislikes crowds and jollity and get-togetherness.

getton, gettorne, vars. GETON, *Obs.*, banner.

gettour, var. JETTER, braggart.

Getulian (gɪ'tju:lɪən), *a.* and *sb.* Also Gætulian, Getulan. [f. L. *Gætūli, Gētūli*, ad. Gr. Γαιτοῦλοι, perh. from Berber root.] **A.** *adj.* Of or pertaining to the ancient nomadic Berber people inhabiting the desert region to the south and east of Numidia or to the region under their control.

1607 TOPSELL *Four-f. Beasts* 659 This Getulian or Barbarian Squirrell, is of mixt colour, as it were betwixt black and red. **1697** DRYDEN *Virgil's Æneis* IV. 56 Getulian Cities here are spread around. **1850** W. SMITH *Dict. Gr. & Roman Biogr.* II. 636/1 Some of the Gaetulian tribes were at the same time subjected to his sway. **1935** A. TOYNBEE *Study Hist.* I. 241 An infiltration of 'Getulan' Nomadic hunters from North-West Africa. **1950** *Chambers's Encycl.* X. 126/1 A new kingdom of Mauritania now limited Numidia in the west, as did a confederacy of free Gaetulian tribes in the south.

b. *Archæol.* (See quots.)

1927 PEAKE & FLEURE *Hunters & Artists* iv. 40 It [the Capsian industry]..seems to occur in two cultural regions, an eastern or *Getulian*, and a western or *Ibero-Maurusian*, each of which displays characteristic differences. **1932** *Antiquity* June 193 In North Africa the Upper Palaeolithic industries are known as *Capsian* (Early and Late, or *Getulian*).

B. *sb.* One of the Getulian people.

1607 TOPSELL *Four-f. Beasts* 201 The *Getulians* fought with them with Speares and Dartes. **1854** W. SMITH *Dict. Gr. & Roman Biogr.* I. 925/2 The ancients clearly recognised the distinction between the Gaetulians and the Negro peoples who dwelt S. of them. **1910** *Encycl. Brit.* I. 360/1 The Berber tribes..bore in ancient times the generic names of Numidians, Gaetulians and Moors or Maurusiani. **1928** V. G. CHILDE *Most Anc. East* iii. 48 And others [*sc.* migrants], conveniently termed Getulans, remained in North Africa.

get-up. [See GET *v.*]

1. Style of equipment or costume.

1847 LD. CANNING in Ld. Malmesbury *Mem.* (1884) I. 200 He is just like Lord Combermere in face, figure, and get-up, but a little bigger. **1852** SMEDLEY *L. Arundel* ii. 26 Studying with the air of a connoisseur the 'get-up' of a spanking team of greys. **1856** LEVER *Martins of Cro' M.* 315 There was an ostentatious pretension in the 'get-up' of this gentle-man. **1889** MRS. PRAED *Rom. of Stat.* 88 Dressed in a well-made tweed suit, that contrasted with the careless get-up of the bushmen round.

2. Style of production or finish, esp. of a book.

1865 *Sat. Rev.* 28 Dec. 795 Very superior both in get-up and illustration to any of our S.P.C.K. books. **1867** *Art Jrnl.* XXIX. 123/2 The general 'get up' of the picture is pleasing. **1884** *Bookseller* 6 Nov. 1180/2 The get-up of the book is in every respect satisfactory and displays great taste of design and finish.

3. A meeting 'got up' or arranged. *nonce-use.*

1833 *Fraser's Mag.* VIII. 30 We attended this hole and corner get up, and can therefore give a correct report of its proceedings.

4. Inclination to get up and be active; energy, enterprise, determination. Also ***get-up-and-get, get-up-and-go***, etc. (cf. GET *v.* 80 a). *colloq.* (orig. *U.S.*).

1841 'Dow, JR.' *Short Patent Sermons* 86 It flats right down, and stays there, like a junk of dough—no get up to it. **1863** *Ladies' Repository* Aug. 477/1 In vain I tried to convince him that there was some 'get-up' in the animal. **1884** G. W. PECK *Peck's Boss Book* 183 The adjutant..felt that his position demanded a horse that had some git-up-and-git. **1889** *Kansas Times & Star* 2 Dec., It's not wealth, nor birth, nor state, But get-up-and-get, that makes cities great. **1907** N. MUNRO *Daft Days* xvi. 142, I wish to goodness folk here had a little git-up-and-go to them! **1910** W. M. RAINE *B. O'Connor* 223 When it comes to the get-up-and-hustle, she's there. **1915** WODEHOUSE *Something Fresh* x, He'll make a name for himself one of these days. He's got get-up in him. **1947** J. STEINBECK *Wayward Bus* 123 It's a pleasure to talk with a man with some get-up and go. **1962** *Punch* 11 Apr. 573/2 Tortoises are not easy to race because they are devoid of get-up-and-go. **1964** MRS. L. B. JOHNSON *White House Diary* 12 Jan. (1970) 42 Lyndon went to church... I am sorry I did not have the get-up-and-get to go with him.

getyrne, obs. form of GITTERN.

Geu, geugaw, obs. forms of JEW, GEWGAW.

geules, obs. form of GULES.

‖**geum** (dʒiːəm). [mod.L. use of L. *gēum*, ? Herb Bennet.] A genus of rosaceous plants, the best-known species of which are *G. urbanum* Avens or Herb Bennet, and *G. rivale* Water Avens.

1548 TURNER *Names of Herbes*, *Geum* is called in englishe Auennes. **1562** —— *Herbal* II. 9 b, Geum..this rote..put..in to wyne..maketh it pleasant both in smellinge & taste. **1849** C. STURT *Exp. Centr. Austr.* I. 353 Geum and many other minor plants. **1882** *Garden* 10 June 404/3 A big mass of the scarlet Geum. **1892** *Pall Mall G.* 10 Feb. 3/1 Geums, forget-me-nots, and primulas.

geve, var. GIF, GIVE.

gew, obs. form of JAW.

gewe, obs. form of GIF, GIVE.

gewegawe, obs. form of GEWGAW.

geweling, gewel(l, obs. ff. JAVELIN, JEWEL.

gewgaw, gew-gaw (ˈgjuːgɔː). Forms: 3 giuegoue, 5–8 gugaw, (5 gwgawe, 7 gugawe, guga), 6–8 guegaw, 6 gue gaw, guy-gaw, 7 guegaye, gugau, guigaw; 6–7 gew(e)gawe, 7 gewgai(e, gew-gaude, 8 geugaw, 9 *dial.* gewgow, geegaw, 6– gewgaw, gew-gaw. [Etymology and primary sense uncertain; a reduplicated formation such as is commonly found in words of contemptuous signification. If the original application be to a musical instrument, the word may have been invented as an imitation of the sound; cf. Du. *giegagen* to 'hee-haw', bray. On the other hand, if the primary notion was that of 'a gaudy object', the suggestion may have come from the vb. GAW, with its variants or synonyms *gow, gew.* It is not impossible that the word as applied to a musical instrument may be an independent formation. The mod.Du. *giegauw*, recorded once in the sense 'flourish, scalloped border', and now preserved only in a phrase of obscure origin belonging to the game of merels, is supposed by the Du. lexicographers to be an adoption of the Eng. word.

The commonly accepted view has been that the earliest form, which is written *giuegoue* (Ancren Riwle) should be read as *givegove*, and that the word is a reduplicated formation from the root of GIVE *v.* On this supposition it would be identical with GIFF-GAFF and the MDu. *ghiveghave*, of which a single example is known. But if this were the etymology, the initial would have been ȝ, not *g*, in the southern texts of the *Ancren Riwle* (unless indeed these texts have been transcribed from an original in northern dialect). Further, the proposed explanation does not account plausibly for the recorded senses, and it is doubtful whether the assumed development of *givegove* into *gugaw* (15th c.), *guygaw* (16th c.), *gewgaw*, is phonetically possible. The probability is that the *u* in *giuegoue* is a vowel.]

1. A gaudy trifle, plaything, or ornament, a pretty thing of little value, a toy or bauble.

a **1529** SKELTON *Sp. Parrot* 474 So myche tournyng on the cooke stole for every guy-gaw. **1630** *R. Johnson's Kingd. & Commw.* 60 With gewgaies of copper and latton about their armes and necks. **1631** R. H. *Arraignm. Whole Creature* iv. 24 Which feed the Soule as much as Guegayes, or painted Plumes..can feed the bodies of beasts, or birds. **1693** DRYDEN *Juvenal* x. (1697) 248 A heavy Gugaw, (call'd a Crown,) that spred About his Temples. **1720** WELTON *Suffer. Son of God* I. xi. 289 Every childish Gugaw,..takes Possession of me. **1807–8** W. IRVING *Salmag.* (1824) 280 He who has most ribands and gew-gaws on his coat. **1845** R. W. HAMILTON *Pop. Educ.* x. (ed. 2) 318 The toy and the gewgaw no more can divert. **1861** DICKENS *Gt. Expect.* lvi, The sheriffs with their..civic gewgaws and monsters.

b. *fig.* A paltry thing of no account, a trifle. In *pl.* also, 'vanities'.

a **1225** *Ancr. R.* 196 Worldes weole, & wunne, & wurschipe, & oðer swuche giuegouen [*v.rr.* giuegaue(n, gyuelgowue]. *a* **1529** SKELTON *Ware the Hauke* 157 Of the spiritual law They made but a gewgaw. **1574** tr. *Marlorat's Apocalips* 11 Free will, purgatorie, and such other gew-gawes wherby the bloud of gods sonne is troden vnder foote. **1639** MASSINGER *Unnat. Combat* I. B 3, This is indeed great businesse—mine a gugawe. **1702** *Eng. Theophrast.* 289 Philemon wants none of those curious gewgaws which make all the accomplishments of our modern beaux. *a* **1754** FIELDING *Remedy Afflict.* Wks. 1775 IX. 260 All the trash and trifles, the bubbles, bawbles, and gewgaws of this life. **1832** J. W. CROKER in *C. Papers* 15 Aug. (1884) If, in the storm-portending times in which we live, the gewgaws of art or literature are worth a thought. **1879** 'E. GARRETT' *House by Wks.* II. 168 Her accomplishments had not been the mere gewgaws which accomplishments so frequently are.

c. Used depreciatingly of a person.

1634 FORD *P. Warbeck* I. i, Ireland The common stage of Noveltie, presented This *gewgaw* to oppose vs. **1638** —— *Fancies* I. ii, Th'art..a citterne headed gew, gaw. **1735** POPE *Donne's Sat.* IV. 209 Such painted puppets! such a varnish'd race Of hollow gew-gaws, only dress and face! **1790** J. B. MORETON *Mann. W. Ind.* 105 Creoles..when deprived of the advantage of an European education, are..awkward, ignorant guegaws. **1876** *Mid-Yorksh. Gloss.*, *Gewgow*..also used figuratively, of a simpleton.

2. †**a.** A disparaging term for a flute or pipe.

c **1440** *Promp. Parv.* 168/1 Flowte, pype..*Pastor sub caula bene cantat cum calamaula* The scheperd vndyr þe folde syngythe the well wythe his gwgawe þe pype.

b. *Sc.* and *north. dial.* A Jews'-harp.

1788 W. MARSHALL *Yorksh.* II. Gloss. (E.D.S.) *Gewgaw*, a Jew's harp. **1855** ROBINSON *Whitby Gloss.*, *Gewgow*, a Jew's harp; any nick-nack or trifle.

3. *attrib.* passing into *adj.*: Of the nature of a gewgaw, resembling gewgaws; hence *fig.* 'splendidly trifling, showy without value' (J.).

1631 BRATHWAIT *Eng. Gentlew.* 20 What a shop of guga nifles hang vpon one backe! **1678** DRYDEN *All for Love* II. i, Give to your Boy, your Cæsar, This Rattle of a Globe to play withal, This Gu-gau World. *a* **1680** EARL ROCHESTER *Poems* (1705) 15 But if you are fond of Baubles, be, and starve, your guegaw Reputation still preserve. **1714** ROWE *J. Shore* III. i, The Dainty gew-gaw Forms dissolve at once, And shiver at the Shock. **1732** LAW *Serious C.* xii. (ed. 2) 196 The gugaw-happiness of Feliciana. *Ibid.* xix. 350 If many women are vain, light, gugaw creatures, they have this to excuse themselves. **1754** RICHARDSON *Grandison* (ed. 7) II. 174 His quality! Gewgaw. What is a Scottish peerage? **1762** CHURCHILL *Ghost* IV. 992 The gew-gaw robes of Pomp and Pride. **1812** H. & J. SMITH *Rej. Addr.* v. Introd., The gewgaw fetters of rhyme. **1855** TENNYSON *Maud* I. x. 18 Seeing his gewgaw castle shine New as his title, built last year. **1888** RIDER HAGGARD *Col. Quaritch* xvi, Looking..at the gee-gaw ornaments.

b. *Comb.*, as ***gewgaw-girl.***

1631 BRATHWAIT *Whimzies* II. *Pedler* 19 Here the Guga-girles gingle it with his neat nifles.

gewgawed (ˈgjuːgɔːd), *ppl. a.* [f. GEWGAW + -ED[2].] Dressed out or adorned with gewgaws.

1871 ROSSETTI *Last Confess.* 387 Before some new Madonna gaily decked, Tinselled and gewgawed. **1879** W. JONES *N. Test. Illustr.* 705 We shall leave our gewgawed devotees to reconcile humiliation in worship with vanity in dress.

gewgawish (ˈgjuːgɔːɪʃ), *a. nonce-wd.* [f. GEW-GAW + -ISH.] Gaudy, showy.

1857 HAWTHORNE *Eng. Note-Bks.* (1870) II. 414 It [the Guildhall] looked rather gewgawish..being hung with flags of all nations, and adorned with military trophies.

So **gewgawry** [see -RY], vain show; **gewgawy** *a.* [see -Y[1]], gewgaw-like, gaudy.

1858 HAWTHORNE *Fr. & It. Jrnls.* (1883) 35 The interior loftiness of Notre Dame..gives it a sublimity which would swallow up anything that might look gewgawy in its ornamentation. **1882** *Pall Mall G.* 1 July 2/2 Fond of fine uniforms and gewgawry.

gewles, obs. form of GULES.

gewmew, var. GEMEW, *Obs.*

gey (geɪ), *a.* and *adv. Sc.* [A variant of GAY.]

A. *adj.* Considerable, 'tolerable', 'middling': *esp.* of quantity or amount. Cf. GAY *a.* 7.

1815 SCOTT *Guy M.* i, Kippletringan was distant at first 'a gey bit'; then the 'gey bit' was more accurately described, as 'aiblins three mile'.

b. quasi-*adverbially* in *gey and* followed by an adj.: Considerably, 'pretty'.

1725 RAMSAY *Gentle Sheph.* I. i. Song i, Last Morning I was gey and early out. **1884** *Illustr. Lond. News* 24 May 510/3 You're gey and wet.

B. *adv.* Very; considerably, 'pretty'. Cf. GAY *adv.* 2.

1816 SCOTT *Old Mort.* vii, I ken I'm gey thick in the head. **1868** G. MACDONALD *R. Falconer* I. 65 He was a gey (*considerably*) auld man than. **1893** STEVENSON *Catriona* 22 I've seen him colloguing with some gey queer acquaintances. **1896** BARRIE *Sentim. Tommy* 34 A woman that was gey gruel to me.

geyan (ˈgeɪən), *adv. Sc.* [= *gey and*: see prec. A. b; but cf. GAIN *adv.*] Tolerably; considerably.

1826 J. WILSON *Noct. Ambr.* Wks. 1855 I. 68 Music's a subject I could get geyan tiresome upon. **1837** R. NICOLL *Poems* (1843) 299 We two are geyan young yet.

geyaunt, geylefat, obs. ff. GIANT, GYLE-VAT.

geyerite (ˈgaɪəraɪt). *Min.* [f. *Geyer* the place in Saxony where it was first found + -ITE. Named by Breithaupt in 1866.] = LOELLINGITE.

1868 DANA *Min.* (ed. 5) 78 The 4th [analysis] is between this species and mispickel, and has been called geyerite.

geyn, geyn-: see GAIN, GAIN-.

geyre, obs. form of GEAR.

geysan: see GIZZEN.

geysene, var. GESINE, *Obs.*

geyser (ˈgeɪsə(r), ˈgaɪsə(r), ˈgaɪzə(r), ˈgiːzə(r)). Also 9 geysir. [a. Icel. *Geysir*, proper name of a particular hot spring in Iceland; literally 'gusher'; related to *geysa*, ON. *gøysa* to gush.

By non-Icelanders the word has been used as an appellative to denote any of the springs of this kind in Iceland, and hence it has been extended to similar springs in other parts of the world.]

1. An intermittent hot spring, throwing up water, etc. in a fountain-like column.

[**1763** *Ann. Reg.* VI. (1768) *Characters* 95/1 Geyser, a wonderful spring in the valley of Haukadal, is but a few miles from Skaa[l]holt.] **1780** tr. *Von Troil's Iceland* (ed. 2) 256 Among the hot springs in Iceland, several of which bear the name of geyser, there are none that [etc.]. **1813** BAKEWELL *Introd. Geol.* (1815) 323 It can scarcely be doubted that the Geysers in Iceland..are occasioned by the subterranean fires which extend under that island. **1860** G. H. K. *Vac. Tour* 122 Mrs. Rory's hot room, that makes one steam like a Geyser. **1885** LADY BRASSEY *The Trades* 476 The Azores..abound in geysers.

fig. **1857** KINGSLEY *Two Y. Ago* I. 163 Ere the Geyser could explode, Tom had continued, in that dogged nasal Yankee twang which [etc.]. *c* **1883** FARRAR *Nation's Curse* 8 Any man who calls himself a Christian, would have been..afraid to swell those geysers of curse and ruin. **1884** A. SMITH *Pref. Burns' Wks.* (Globe) 14 But years after from a sudden geysir of impassioned song we learn that through all that time she had never been forgotten.

2. The name given to an apparatus for rapidly heating water attached to a bath. Also for the heating of water for use in wash-basins, sinks, etc. (See also GEEZER.)

1878 *Gas Engineer* Feb. 184 (Advt.), The instantaneous water heater; or Maughan's Patent Geyser..so constructed that any quantity of hot water can be drawn from it with the utmost facility. **1891** *Daily News* 9 Apr. 7/1 What the cost of reinstating a 'geyser' would be he could not tell. **1897** *Oxford Chron.* 30 Oct. 7/4 The geyser or gas apparatus for heating the bath was turned full on. **1920** L. C. HALE *American's London* viii. 109 The aristocratic landlady was telling me of the advantage of her own particular geezer... I moved closer to descry the lettering on the cylinder, and lo! it was a geyser. I suppose the word is universally mispronounced over here because they have not been brought up in a geyser country. **1929** *S.P.E. Tract* XXXII. 400 The mechanical device for heating bath-water made *geyser* a household word, and though the introducers gave it the vowel of *grey*, the pronunciation as in *key* gained ground. **1965** G. MCINNES *Road to Gundagai* v. 83 A crude precursor of the 'Ascot' gas heater—known to various Lady Helps as the geezer, the gayzer or the guyzer.

3. *attrib.*, as ***geyser-flood, -tube.***

1866 G. MACDONALD *Ann. Q. Neighb.* xxvi. (1878) 454 The boiling *geyser-floods of old affection rush from the hot deeps of the heart. **1863** TYNDALL *Heat* iv. §150 (1870) 128 Stopping our model *geyser-tube with corks.

ˈ**geyseric**, *a.* [f. GEYSER + -IC.] 'Pertaining to or of the nature of a geyser' (*Cent Dict.*).

geyserite (ˈgeɪsəraɪt). *Min.* [f. GEYSER + -ITE. Named by Delamétherie in 1812.] A variety of opal, of concretionary form, found deposited about the orifices of geysers.

1814 T. ALLAN *Min. Nomen.* 22 Geyserite [*printed* Geyerite.]. **1826** EMMONS *Min.* 220 Quartz..recent deposit from hot springs..Geyserite. **1879** RUTLEY *Stud. Rocks* xiv. 303 Geyserite is a snow-white silicious sinter..which occurs incrusting the pipes of geysers.

geyson, var. GEASON *a. Obs.*, scarce.

geyt, obs. form of GET, JET.

gezumph, var. GAZOOMPH *v.*

ghaffir ('gɑːfɪər). Also ghafir, etc. [ad. Arab. *ġafīr*.] A native Egyptian policeman; a guardian, watchman.

a **1817** J. L. Burckhardt *Notes on Bedouins* (1831) I. 366 The Arab guardian was called *ghafeyr*. **1856** R. F. Burton *Narr. Pilgr. El-Medinah* I. 231 Without guns or gunners, it [*sc.* the fort] is occupied by about a dozen Fellahs, who act as hereditary 'ghafirs', (guardians). **1883** D. M. Wallace *Egypt* 216 At the bottom of the communal organisation stand the Gaffirs or village watchmen. **1923** *Glasgow Herald* 19 Feb. 9 The whole distance was guarded.. by 'ghaffirs', or watchman. **1928** *Blackw. Mag.* Feb. 248/1 A canal watchman, known as a Ghaffir. **1938** w. B. Ziff *Rape of Palestine* 421 Even the Jewish *Ghaffirs* and supernumerary constables were usually armed with truncheons only. **1971** G. Household *Doom's Caravan* iv. 169 The naval stores were.. guarded by Arab ghaffirs.

ghaist, Sc. form of ghost.

Ghanaian (gɑːˈneɪən), *sb.* and *a.* Also (as short-lived variants) **Ghanan, Ghananian, Ghanian.** [f. *Ghana* + -ian.] **A.** *sb.* A native or inhabitant of Ghana, a West African state formerly known as the Gold Coast. **B.** *adj.* Of, pertaining to, or characteristic of Ghana or its people.

1949 *Accra Even. News* in B. Timothy *K. Nkrumah* (1955) vii. 81 Kwame Nkrumah.. Born a true Ghanaian for Ghana. **1957** *Evening Standard* 9 Apr. 4/6 After dinner the Ghanians, wearing national costume, will give a dancing display. **1957** *Economist* 31 Aug. 671/1 The two Muslims were Ghanaians. **1957** *Times* 17 Dec. 9/6 The C.P.P.'s greatest handicap has been failure to capture the sympathy of the Ghanaian middle classes. **1964** P. Strevens *Papers in Lang.* (1965) vi. 81 There are well-known accents of English.. as a second language (such as Ghanaian's English accent or Urdu-speaker's English accent). **1966** *Daily Tel.* 29 Dec. 9/1 A ship, ordered by the Nkrumah régime and apparently not wanted by the present Ghanaian Government. **1966** *Transition* (Uganda) XXVI. 17/2 But by the tragedy of his domestic excesses *after* independence, Nkrumah fell short of becoming a great Ghanaian.

ghanta ('gantə). Also **gunté.** [Hind. *ghaṇṭā*.] A bell or gong, used as an instrument in Indian music.

1865 *Proc. R. Irish Acad.* IX. i. 108 (*Gunté*).—Bell. As a musical instrument, the bell is used somewhat in the same manner as the cymbals. **1954** *Grove's Dict. Mus.* (ed. 5) IV. 459/2 The conch (*śaṅkha*), of few but mellow notes, is used in the temple, as also the bell (*ghaṇṭa*).

ghap (gɑːp). Also **ghaap, ghab, guaap, ngaap.** [Nama name.] A South African carrion flower belonging to the genus *Trichocaulon*, esp. *T. piliferum.*

1819 *Rees Cycl.* XXXIII. (s.v. *Stapelia pilifera*), The Hottentots are said to eat it, knowing it by the name of *Guaap.* **1857** L. Pappe *Floræ Capensis* (ed. 2) 29 *Stapelia pilifera*.. is eaten by the natives, who call it *Guaap*, for the purpose of quenching their thirst. **1878** *Trans. S. Afr. Philos. Soc.* I. 24 Here we find stunted Mesembryanthemums, numerous kinds of Euphorbias, the peculiar *Ghap* (Stapelia) in at least a half dozen varieties. **1913** Pettman *Africanderisms* 186 *Ghab*.. *Stapelia pilifera* (as well as others of these Carrion-flowers as they are called), is known by this name in the Karoo. [**1932** Watt & Breyer-Brandwijk *Medicinal & Poisonous Plants S. Afr.* 151 Natives formerly ate the stem of *Stapelia pilifera* L., Nama *guaap*, as a thirst quencher. The Namas still use it for this purpose.] **1962** *Ibid.* (ed. 2) 138 The Trichocaulons, known generically to the Hottentots as *ngaap* (the spiny-stemmed species) are mostly edible in the raw state.

gharana (gəˈrɑːnə). Also **gharwana.** [Hind. *gharānā*.] In Indian music, a school of players who practise a particular style of interpretation.

1957 O. Gosvami *Story Indian Mus.* xxiv. 260 These [groups] came to be known as *Gharwanas* or schools of interpretations [*sic*]. **1967** B. V. Keskar *Indian Mus.* i. 20 The tendency to run down the music of other *gharanas* increased. There was great rivalry between these various *gharanas.* **1968** *Indian Mus. Jrnl.* V. 33 Though based on the traditional Gwalior *Gharānā* he evolved his own individual style. **1969** *Cultural News fr. India* Nov. 30 The active society Raag Rang brought us Mushtaq Hussain Khan's son Ishtiaq and grandson Sharafat in a splendid programme of the Rampur gharana.

gharial, gharrial, varr. gavial.

‖**gharry** ('gærɪ, 'gʌrɪ). *Anglo-Indian.* Also gari, gharee, gharrie, g'horry. [Hindi *gāṛī* a cart or carriage.] (See quots.)

1810 Williamson *E. Ind. Vade M.* I. 329 The common g'horry.. is rarely, if ever, kept by any European; but may be seen plying for hire in various parts of Calcutta. **1849** Judson in *Wayland's Mem. J.* (1853) II. 267 She drives out every morning in a gharry. **1866** Trevelyan *Dawk Bungalow* in *Fraser's Mag.* LXXIII. 384 Where my husband was to have met us with the two-horse gharee. **1887** Fife-Cookson *Tiger Shooting* 5 The gharrie is a box-like vehicle with small wheels. It rather resembles a bathing-machine.

b. *Comb.*, as *gharry-driver.*

1883 Mrs. Bishop in *Leisure Hour* 204/1 My gharrie-driver took me to see a.. pepper-plantation.

ghasel, var. ghazal.

Ghassulian (gæˈsuːlɪən), *a. Archæol.* [ad. Fr. *Ghassoulien* (R. Neuville 1930, in *Jrnl. Palestine Oriental Soc.* X. 202), f. the site Teleilat el-*Ghassul* near Jericho in Jordan: see -ian.]

Of, pertaining to, or designating a chalcolithic culture of which remains have been found at Teleilat el-Ghassul. Also as *sb.*, an inhabitant of this area in the chalcolithic age.

1931 *Bull. Amer. Sch. Oriental Res.* Apr. 15 Then comes the characteristic Chalcolithic of Palestine, the Ghassulian. **1949** W. F. Albright *Archaeol. of Palestine* ii. 45 The new Ghassulian culture was at first dated much too low by the excavators. *Ibid.* iii. 64 The Ghassulian graves excavated by Stekelis were dug in the ground and lined with stones. **1952** V. G. Childe *New Light on Most Anc. East* (ed. 4) xi. 229 The Ghassulians in Transjordan were buried individually in stone cists, sometimes covered by round barrows supported by a circular kerb of boulders. **1966** R. de Vaux in *Cambr. Anc. Hist.* (ed. 3, 1970) I. ix(b). 523 The name 'Ghassulian' has sometimes been applied to everything which is regarded as 'Chalcolithic' in Palestine. This usage is inaccurate, but there are certain sites, especially in the southern half of the country, which were related to Ghassūl and were almost contemporary with it.

ghast (gɑːst, -æ-), *a. arch.* or *poet.* [A back-formation from ghastful or ghastly.] = ghastly *a.*

1622 Bp. Andrewes *Serm., Of Repent.* vi. (1631) 233 The looke of a wilde-beast.. grimme and ghast. **1807** Byron *Elegy Newstead Abb.* xxi, There many a pale and ruthless robber's corse, Noisome and ghast, defiles thy sacred sod. **1844** Mrs. Browning *Drama of Exile* Poems 1850 I. 37 How doth the wide and melancholy earth Gather her hills around us, grey and ghast. **1866** S. Bamford *Wild Rider* in Harland *Lanc. Lyrics* 15 Fearfully ghast was the light which it threw.

ghast, var. gast *v.*[1], *Obs.*, to frighten.

ghastful, gastful ('gɑːstfʊl, -æ-), *a. Obs.* or *arch.* Forms: α. 4-8 **gastful(l,** 5-6 **gasteful(l.** β. 6-7 **ghastfull,** 6-9 **ghastful.** [f. gast *v.*[1] + -ful.]

1. Full of fear, timid, scared.

1388 Wyclif *Deut.* xx. 8 Who is a ferdful man and of gastful herte? **1422** tr. *Secreta Secret., Priv. Priv.* (E.E.T.S.) 221 An hare and a sheppe bene ful gastefull. *a* **1586** Sidney *Arcadia* I. (1590) 51 b, Musidorus had gathered his spirites together and yet casting a gastfull countenaunce vpon him. **1603** Harsnet *Pop. Impost.* xxi. 137 The.. fond Gastful opinions of all the other Dottrels arise out of one of these two rootes. **1708** Ozell tr. *Boileau's Lutrin* v. 103 The Prelate saw their Fall with ghastful Eyes.

2. Dreadful, frightful, terrible.

α. **1398** Trevisa *Barth. De P.R.* xviii. lxxvi. (1495) 830 He makyth a ruthefull noyse and gastfull whan one profryth to fyghte wyth a nother. *c* **1449** Pecock *Repr.* ii. xiii. 224 Hou gastful is this place! **1519** Horman *Vulg.* 57 b, His loke is horryble and gastfull. **1566** Drant *Horace's Sat.* i. i. A v b, Those goodes That.. brings of feare suche gastfull fluddes. **1579** Spenser *Sheph. Cal.* Aug. 170 Here will I dwell apart In gastfull groue. **1616** J. Lane *Cont. Sqr.'s T.* ix. 365 This gastfull dreame.. soone awooke him. **1658** tr. *Bergerac's Satyr. Char.* xii. 43 After many gastfull contortions. **1714** Fortescue-Aland *Fortescue's Abs. & Lim. Mon.* 4 Gastful.. came to signify any thing that look'd frightful.

β. *a* **1586** Sidney *Arcadia* ii. (1590) 132 With a ghastful noise. **1606** J. Carpenter *Soloman's Solace* xxv. 101 They were.. subdued vnto ghastfull death. **1702** Dennis *Monument* xxix. 24 The joining Squadrons.. make one ghastful Charnel of the Field. **1891** H. C. Halliday *Someone must suffer* III. xi. 196 Goblin shapes.. grinning and gibbering in ghastful fashion.

3. = ghastly *a.* 3.

1720 Gay *Dione* ii. i, What pious care my ghastful lid shall close?

Hence **†ˈg(h)astfully** *adv.*, **†ˈgastfulness.**

1398 Trevisa *Barth de P.R.* vii. xliii. (1495) 256 The heere of the hede arysyth and stondeth vppe for some fere and gastfulnesse. *c* **1449** Pecock *Repr.* iv. i. 421 Scripture.. seith ful gastfulli thus. *a* **1586** Sidney *Arcadia* iv. (1629) 405 A solitarie darknesse.. naturally.. breeds a kind of irke-some gastfulnesse. **1664** Dryden *Rival Ladies* iv. iii, He looks so ghastfully, Would I were past him. **1713** Swift etc. *Frenzy J. Dennis* Wks. 1755 III. i. 138 He often stares ghastfully. **1726** De Foe *Hist. Devil* (1822) 246 A ghastfully frightful fellow.

'ghastily, *adv. rare.* [as if f. *ghasty adj. (f. gast *v.*[1] + -y[1]) + -ly[2].] = ghastlily or ghastly *adv.*

1829 T. Hook *Bank to Barnes* 124 When fifty skel'tons, all of a row, Right ghastily did grin. **1844** Mrs. Browning *Drama of Exile* Poems 1850 I. 85 The drear-white steed.. ghastily champeth the last moon.

ghastlily ('gɑːstlɪlɪ, -æ-), *adv.* [f. ghastly *a.* + -ly[2].] In a ghastly manner: **a.** Frightfully, horribly. **b.** With a deathlike appearance; drearily, dismally.

a. 1830 *Blackw. Mag.* XXVIII. 637 He.. stood fear-fully and ghastlily conspicuous. **1884** G. Allen *Str. Stor.* i. 15 She lay unconscious upon the bed, her eyes open, staring ghastlily.

b. 1829 J. Wilson in *Blackw. Mag.* XXV. 383 Each [cheek].. collapsed into a perpendicular hollow, shooting up ghastlily from chin to cheek-bone. **1882** E. O'Donovan *Merv Oasis* I. iv. 63 The walls and domes.. now stand ghastlily amid the waste.

ghastliness ('gɑːstlɪnɪs, -æ-). [f. ghastly *a.* + -ness.] The quality or condition of being ghastly.

1591 Spenser *Daphn.* xlvii, Let ghastlinesse And drery horror dim the chearfull light. **1628** Wither *Brit. Rememb.* iii. 700 Deaths fearfull gastlinesse. **1726** Swift *Gulliver* iii. x, They acquired an additional Ghastliness in proportion to their number of Years. **1842** J. Wilson *Chr. North* (1857) I. 243 A night of shipwreck did strew with ghastliness a lee seashore.

ghastly, † gastly ('gɑːstlɪ, -æ-), *a.* Forms: α. 4-5 **gast(e)lich(e, -lych,** 4-7 **gastlie,** 4-8 **gastly;** β. 6- **ghastly.** [f. gast *v.*[1] + *-lich*, -ly[1].]

1. a. †In early use: Causing terror, terrible (*obs.*). In mod. use (cf. 2): Suggestive of the kind of horror evoked by the sight of death or carnage; horrible, frightful, shocking.

α. *c* **1305** *St. Christopher* 147 in *E.E.P.* (1862) 63 He was so gastliche & so moche þat hi þerste vneþe him iseo. *c* **1330** *Arth. & Merl.* 1494 A gastlich best he was to mete. **1390** Gower *Conf.* III. 250 He [Phœbus].. With gastly vois, that all it herde, The Romains in this wise answerde. *c* **1430** *Pilgr. Lyf Manhode* ii. cxxiv. (1869) 124 Oothere tweyne.. as gastlich as she, or more. **1523** Skelton *Garl. Laurell* 1316 By Hecates bowre.. In Plutos gastlye towre. **1583** Stanyhurst *Æneis* iii. (Arb.) 78 On the typ of rockish turret stood gastlye Celæno Vnlucky prophetesse. **1681** Cotton *Wond. Peak* 31 Having with terror, here beheld.. The gastly aspect of this dang rous place.

β. **1590** Spenser *F.Q.* iii. ii. 29 As one with vew of ghastly feends affright. **1658** A. Fox *Wurtz' Surg.* i. iii. 8 Every stitch causeth [a scar].. which after healing sheweth ghastly. *a* **1677** Barrow *Serm.* Wks. 1716 I. 15 He standeth exposed to.. horrid and ghastly dangers. **1704** Swift *T. Tub* viii. (1709) 100 Certain ghastly notions which have served them pretty tolerably for a devil. **1812** J. Wilson *Isle of Palms* ii. 403 The ghastly dreams, That haunt the parting soul. **1855** Prescott *Philip II*, I. iii. v. 370 His bloody head was set up opposite to that of his fellow-sufferer. For three hours these ghastly trophies remained exposed. **1889** Jessopp *Coming of Friars* ii. 80 The ghastly frequency of the punishment by death tended to make people savage.

b. *colloq.* Said *hyperbolically* of persons or things objectionable on various grounds: Shocking, 'frightful'.

1861 Thackeray *Four Georges* ii. (1862) 88 There never was such a ghastly farce. **1865** Dickens *Mut. Fr.* ii. i, This pretence, much favoured by the lady-visitors, led to the ghastliest absurdities. **1890** Saintsbury in *New Rev.* Feb. 138 A most ghastly act of high treason is being committed. **1896** *Daily News* 21 July 3 To take measures to prevent the session being a ghastly failure. **1931** F. Grierson *Mystery in Red* iv. 70 Don't be a ghastly idiot. **1960** N. Mitford *Don't tell Alfred* vii. 76 Then he'd never have heard of this ghastly Yanky. *Ibid.* 81, I bought her [*sc.* a tortoise] from those ghastly children. **1969** C. Fremlin *Possession* i. 9, I know his mother, and she's *frightful*! She really is, Clare, I promise you: she's *ghastly*!

2. a. (Influenced by ghost: cf. quot. 1711.) Like a spectre, or a dead body; death-like, pale, wan. Of light: Lurid.

1581 A. G. *XII. Patr.* 14 b, Euen in sleepe some spice of imagined malice gnaweth hym.. makyng his body gastly, and his mynde afrighted with trouble. **1603** Knolles *Hist. Turks* (1621) 331 And striving with the pangs of death halfe a day, he then breathed out his gastly ghost. **1638** Baker tr. *Balzac's Lett.* II. 83 That his watchings and abstinence had dried up his blood and made him looke gastly. **1700** Dryden *Cock & Fox* 231 His Friend.. with a ghastly Look and doleful Cry Said help me Brother, or this Night I die. **1711** J. Greenwood *Eng. Gram.* 276 *Gastly*.. like a Ghost, or like a dead Corps; for a gastly Look is chiefly said of the Countenance of a dying Person. **1712** Addison *Spect.* No. 303 ¶ 15 That ghastly Light, by which the Fiends appear to one another in their Place of Torments. **1718** Prior *Power* 334 Ghastly with wounds, and lifeless on the bier. **1844** Mrs. Carlyle *Lett.* I. 280 Touched by compassion for my ghastly appearance. **1860** Tyndall *Glac.* i. iii. 30 A ghastly gleam rested upon the summit of the Ortler.

b. of a smile, a grin.

1576 Lambarde *Peramb. Kent* (1826) 325 She tolde him, that there was lately buried (neare to the place where she was honoured) a sinfull person, which so offended her eie with his ghastly grinning, that [etc.]. **1832** Lytton *Eugene Aram.* i. vi. 32 'What eavesdropping', said he, with a ghastly smile. **1837** —— *E. Maltravers* 31 With a ghastly grin.

c. said of immaterial things.

1821 Shelley *Prometh. Unb.* i. i. 244 Unlike the voice With which our pallid race hold ghastly talk. **1860** Hawthorne *Marb. Faun* (1879) I. xxv. 251 A ghastly emotion rose up out of the depths of the young count's heart. **1879** McCarthy *Own Times* II. xxv. 257 A ghastly semblance of faith in the possibility of a peaceful arrangement. **1884** *Punch* 18 Oct. 190/1 The grim refrain to their ghastly minstrelsy.

†3. Full of fear, inspired by fear. *Obs.*

1590 Spenser *F.Q.* iii. i. 62 The Dame, halfe dedd Through suddein feare and ghastly drerihedd. **1602** Marston *Ant. & Mel.* iii. Wks. 1856 I. 32 Gastly amazement, with upstarted haire, Shall hurry on before, and usher us. **1610** Shaks. *Temp.* ii. i. 309 Why are you drawn? Wherefore this ghastly looking? **1634** Sir T. Herbert *Trav.* 207 In great hast and feare with gastly amazed lookes.

ghastly, † gastly ('gɑːstlɪ, -æ-), *adv.* [f. the adj.]

1. Qualifying a vb.: **a.** Frightfully, horribly; with a deathlike look. **b.** In a frightened manner, timidly.

a. 1593 Shaks. *2 Hen. VI*, iii. ii. 170 His eye-balles.. Staring full gastly, like a strangled man. **1813** Shelley *Q. Mab* vii. 192 My murdered children's mute and eyeless sculls Glared ghastly upon me. **1837** Marryat *Dog-fiend* xxx, Vanslyperken grinned ghastly.

b. 1589 R. Robinson *Gold. Mirr.* (Chetham Soc.) 4 And at the gase I gastly quaking stood. **1599** *Warn. Faire Wom.* ii. 706 Why stop you on the sudden? why go you not? What makes you looke so gastly towards the house? *a* **1628** F. Greville *Sidney* (1652) 145 He saw a poor Souldier carryed along.. gastly casting up his eyes at the bottle. **1681** H. More *Expos. Dan.* 92 None understood what the matter was with me, that I lookt so sadly and ghastly on it.

2. Qualifying an adj. *ghastly pale*: deathly pale. *ghastly sick*: †sick unto death; also, frightfully sick.

1653 H. More *Antid. Ath.* iii. x. (1712) 118 His Nose was entire and full, not sharp, as in those that are gastly sick, or quite dead. **1824** W. IRVING *T. Trav.* I. 28 Her face was ghastly pale, and perhaps rendered more so by the bluish light of the fire. **1862** MRS. CARLYLE *Lett.* III. 127, I am less ghastly sick.

ghaur, var. GIAOUR.

‖**ghaut, ghat** (gɔːt). *Anglo-Indian.* Forms: 7 gaot, 7–8 gate (guate), 8–9 gaut, (8 gette), 9 ghât, 8– ghaut. [Hindi *ghāt.*

The senses are here placed in the order of their occurrence in English. The order of development, however, is as follows: 1. A path of descent to a river; hence a landing-stage, a quay, the place of a ferry. 2. A path down from a mountain; a mountain pass. 3. In *pl.*, the name erroneously given by Europeans to the mountain ranges parallel to the east and west coasts of India.]

1. *the Ghauts*: the name applied by Europeans to two chains of mountains along the eastern and western sides of southern Hindostan, known as the Eastern and Western Ghauts.

1603 R. JOHNSON *Kingd. & Commw.* 200 Narsinga..lieth Between the mountain Gate and the gulfe of Bengala. **1698** FRYER *Acc. E. India & P.* 49 All along here the Top of Gates is seen above the Clouds. **1762** J. RENNELL *MS. Let.* 21 Mar. (Y.), The Mountains of Gate (a string of Hills in ye country). **1844** H. H. WILSON *Brit. India* III. 342 Thickets which clothe the skirts of the eastern ghats where they approach the sea. **1879** R. H. ELLIOT *Writ. on Fore-heads* II. 5 The ravines..which run down into the forest at the foot of the ghauts.

2. a. A mountain pass or defile.

1698 FRYER *Acc. E. India & P.* 126, I sent to the Havaldar, to know when he would Pass us up the Gaot. **1800** *Asiat. Ann. Reg., Misc. Tr.* 261/1 At the different gauts or passes into the mountains, duties..are levied. **1803** WELLINGTON *Let. to Murray* 26 Apr. in Gurw. *Desp.* (1837) I. 520 The ghaut I am informed is exceedingly bad. **1834** MEDWIN *Angler in Wales* II. 36 This tigress had been the terror of the country, having long infested the Gaut. **1876** JAS. GRANT *Hist. India* I. lxi. 309/2 The army descended the Ghauts. *attrib.* **1876** *Ind. Forester* III. 465 The whole forest region below is now pierced by easy ghât roads..In the lower ghât forests we can offer *Castilloa elastica* a habitat quite as unhealthy as its own in America.

b. *transf.*

1807 J. HALL *Trav. Scot.* I. 198 Not a house or hut is to be seen in this gloomy gaut.

3. A passage or flight of steps leading to the river-side; hence, *gen.* a landing-place, the place of a ford or ferry.

1783 RENNELL *Mem. Map Hindostan* Introd. (1788) 128 Gaut or Ghaut signifies..a landing-place on the bank of a river. **1793** W. HODGES *Trav. India* 60 Several Hindoo temples greatly embellish the banks of the river, and are all ascended to by Gauts, or flights of steps. **1834** CAUNTER *Orient. Ann.* xi. 142 He descended the Gaut, and entered the water with his long hair trailing upon the steps behind him. **1842** BP. D. WILSON in *Life* (1860) II. 195 Lord Auckland ..walked..to the ghât at the river side. **1862** *Rep. Direct. E. Ind. Railw. Comp.* 25 The following materials have been delivered at the Ghauts on the Ganges, in the neighbourhood of the line. **1888** INGLIS *Tent Life Tigerland* 25 In the afternoon we stopped near Pokureea *Ghat* (ferry) to have some *tiffin*. *Ibid.* 136 'Look out, boys! there's a ghat on ahead'; and..we descried one of those cart-tracks worn down the face of the bank, and leading to a ford.

4. In full *burning-ghat.* A level spot at the top of a river ghat on which Hindus burn their dead; a funeral pyre.

1877 *Encycl. Brit.* VI. 567/1 To erect cinerators on the burning ghat or ground. **1885** KIPLING *Life's Handicap* (1891) 328 A woman's corpse going down to the burning-ghat. **1908** *Daily Chron.* 14 Nov. 5/4 At the ghat, or funeral pyre, a mixture of milk and cocoanut water..was poured into the mouth of the corpse. **1937** L. BROMFIELD *Rains Came* I. i. 12 He came frequently along these paths to the ghats after nightfall. There was a kind of macabre beauty about the place, and in the spectacle of the cremation itself there was a kind of faith and certainty. **1964** A. SWINSON *Six Minutes to Sunset* ii. 33 The corpses were taken to the burning *ghats* outside the city.

ghawazee (gəˈwɑːziː), *sb. pl.* Also **ghawâzi, ghowazee.** [ad. Arab. *ğawāzī*, pl. of GHAZEEYEH.] Egyptian dancing-girls.

1799 W. G. BROWNE *Trav. Afr.* vi. 86 The last are the female dancers or *ghawasié*. **1836** E. W. LANE *Mod. Egypt* I. 240 The *Ghawa'zee* (or public dancing-girls). *Ibid.* II. 95 The Ghawa'zee perform, unveiled, in the public streets, even to amuse the rabble. **1845** R. FORD *Hand-bk. Trav. Spain* I. 188 The *ghowazee* of the Egyptians. **1924** 'S. ROHMER' *Grey Face* iv, Her hair, which was dressed in the fashion of the dancing girls who pose for ever upon the Egyptian monuments, and which is preserved in life to this day by the ghawâzi of Keneh. **1964** W. G. RAFFE *Dict. of Dance* 198/1 *Ghawazee* or *Ghazeeyeh* (Egypt, Modern Arabian), the professional public dancing girls.

‖**ghazal** (ˈgæzæl). Also **gazel, ghazel, ghasel, ghazul.** [Pers., Arab. *ghazal.*]

1. A species of Oriental lyric poetry, generally of an erotic nature, distinguished from other forms of Eastern verse by having a limited number of stanzas and by the recurrence of the same rhyme.

1800 *Asiat. Ann. Reg., Acc. Bks.* 17/1 The Arabs, Persians, and Turks, celebrate in their gazels the praises of love and wine. **1813** MOORE *Post-bag* vi. 69 The tender Gazel I enclose Is for my love, my Syrian Rose. **1835** *Athenæum* 14 Nov., Ghazi Gherai clothed in Ghazels his official complaint to the Sultan's preceptor. **1884** J. PAYNE *1001 Nts.* IX. 333 The great city on the Tigris is the theme of many an admiring ode or laudatory ghazel. **1888** *Edin. Rev.* July 134 Another Persian metre much used by him was the ghazal. **1892** *Q. Rev.* Jan. 48 The whole range of these singing and dancing ghasels is nothing if not ironical.

2. *Mus.* (See quot.)

1876 STAINER & BARRETT *Dict. Mus. Terms, Ghazel* (Arab.) a term used by Dr. Hiller to describe a piece in which a simple theme is constantly recurring.

ghazeeyeh (gəˈziːjeɪ). Also **ghazie.** [ad. Arab. *ğāziya.*] An Egyptian dancing-girl.

1819 T. HOPE *Anastasius* I. xv. 325 A knot of ghazie distorted their limbs into as uncouth postures as if they had been frogs themselves. **1877** *Encycl. Brit.* VII. 727/1 The Ghawázee (sing. Gházeeyeh) form a separate class. **1964** [see prec.].

‖**Ghazi** (ˈgɑːziː). Also 8 **gazi,** 9 **ghazee.** [Arab. *ghāzi*, pr. pple. of *ghazā* to fight.] A champion, esp. against infidels; also used as a title of honour. In modern use, chiefly applied to Mohammedan fanatics who have devoted themselves to the destruction of infidels. Hence **ˈGhazism**, the practice of the Ghazis.

1753 HANWAY *Trav.* (1762) II. VI. i. 144 The most potent Sultan Achmed, Khan Gazi. **1835** BURNES *Trav. Bokhara* (ed. 2) I. 123 [They] entertain such hatred for the infidel Seiks, that they often declare themselves 'ghazee', and devote their lives to their extinction. **1884** *Men of the Time* (ed. 11), Osman Pasha (Ghazi)..In October [1877] he received from the Sultan the title of 'Ghazi', or 'Victorious'. **1885** T. P. HUGHES *Dict. Islam* 139 In the Turkish Empire the title of Ghazi implies something similar to our 'Field Marshal'. **1897** *Daily News* 2 Sept. 5/3 The outrage is regarded as an act of pure 'Ghazism', as the victims were Hindus. **1898** *Blackw. Mag.* Feb. 211/2 The houses..were attacked by a mob of Ghazis.

ghea, gheber, -bre, vars. GHEE, GUEBRE.

gheason, var. GEASON, *Obs.*

gheblee, var. GIBLI.

‖**ghee** (giː). Also 7 **gee,** 7–9 **ghi.** [Hindi *ghī*, Skr. *ghrta*, f. *ghr* to sprinkle.] **a.** Butter made from buffalo's or cow's milk, clarified by boiling, so as to resemble oil in consistency.

1665 SIR T. HERBERT *Trav.* (1677) 100 Butter, Gee, or Moccon. **1698** FRYER *Acc. E. India & P.* 33 But they will drink Milk and boil'd Butter, which they call Ghe. **1732** PIKE in *Phil. Trans.* XXXVII. 233 Take the White of five or six Eggs, and four Ounces of Ghee. **1816** 'QUIZ' *Grand Master* II. 51 [He] begs 'from master a rupee, To go to the bazar for ghee'. **1830** MACAULAY *Ess., Montgomery* (1854) 122 He asked pardon of him who carried the dog, and bought it for a measure of rice and a pot of ghee. **1873** H. BLOCHMANN tr. *Abul Fazl 'Allami's Ain i Akbari* I. 130 Most of them get..4*s.* of g'hí, and half a *man* of rice. **1879** E. ARNOLD *Lt. Asia* v. 130 Bright tongues of flame Hissing and curling as they licked the gifts Of ghee and spices. **1939** M. PALLIS *Peaks & Lamas* ii. 21 In most districts the village shop can be relied on for flour, rice, lentils, *ghi* (clarified butter), sugar, onions and pepper. **1957** *Encycl. Brit.* X. 323/2 *Ghee*... The best is prepared from butter of the milk of cows, the less esteemed from that of buffaloes. **1959** *Times* 31 Dec. 10/6 A ramshackle bus which smelt of packed humanity, spiced with garlic, *ghi*, [etc.]. **1967** SINGHA & MASSEY *Indian Dances* iv. 59 A small diva (oil-lamp) which burnt ghee (clarified butter) was placed on a salver. **1971** *Illustr. Weekly India* 4 Apr. 31/3, I tried to retaliate by objecting to his eating spiced food cooked in ghee.

b. *attrib.* and *Comb.*, as *ghee-bowl, -pot*; *ghee-fed* adj.

1835–6 TODD *Cycl. Anat.* I. 545/2 Its ventricose body firmly imbedded in a ghee-bowl. **1845** STOCQUELER *Handbk. Brit. India* (1854) 180 The slim, wasted form of a New-market jockey elbowing a fat ghee-fed Baboo. **1889** *Voice* (N.Y.) 7 Mar., We would let go the drop of ghee rather than upset the gheepot.

†**gheereaguar.** *Obs. rare.*

1658 W. SANDERSON *Graphice* 68 Having therefore laid the ground of silver burnisht, the bignesse of the Rubie, take gheereaguar of the best and purest wagron mixt. *Ibid.* 69 For Saphire, and all kind of blew stones the same Gheereaguar tempered with ultra-marine is excellent.

gheet, obs. form of JET.

Gheez, var. GEEZ.

Gheg (gɛg). Also **Geg, Gegde, Gheghe, Ghegide, Ngeghe.** A people of Northern Albania; a member of this people; also, the language spoken by this people. Also *attrib.* and as *adj.*

1812 BYRON *Ch. Har.* 129 Though they have some cavalry amongst the Gegdes, I never saw a good Arnaout horseman. **1835** W. M. LEAKE *Trav. N. Greece* I. ii. 61 The only important divisions of the Albanians are four: the Ngégh̨e, Tóshkę, Liápę and Tjamę. **1851** E. LEAR *Jrnls. Landscape Painter in Albania* 110 These Gheghes are all armed. *Ibid.* 125 The Gheghe Albanians..are still allowed the privilege of carrying arms. **1891** *Trans. Philol. Soc. 1888–90* 355 the Gheg or Central Albanian of Albania. **1954** PEI & GAYNOR *Dict. Linguistics* 83 *Gheg*, one of the two predominant dialects of Albanian, spoken in northern Albania and parts of Dalmatia. **1958** P. KEMP *No Colours or Crest* v. 77 The rivalry of Gheg and Tosk and the age-long hatred of both for their Slav and Greek neighbours. *Ibid.* 78 A stocky, granite-faced, illiterate Gheg from Krujë in the Mati country. *Ibid.*, Gheg tribesmen from Kossovo and his own territory of Mati. **1971** P. DRISCOLL *White Lie Assignment* ix. 73 My method has kept me safe for twenty years against stupid Ghegs like him.

†**ghells.** *Obs.* 'The game of trip.'

1790 in GROSE *Prov. Gloss.* (ed. 2). **1847** in HALLIWELL.

ghematry, obs. form of GEOMETRY.

Ghent (gɛnt). *Hort.* The name of a city in Belgium (Flemish *Gent*, French *Gand*), used *attrib.* to designate any of a number of hybrid azaleas first developed by P. Mortier of Ghent between 1804 and 1834.

1841 J. LOUDON *Ladies' Companion* 23/1 The kinds called the Ghent Azaleas, are hybrids and varieties raised in Belgium. **1882** LINDLEY & PAXTON *Paxton's Flower Garden* I. 65 Blooming somewhat later than the Ghent varieties. **1889** W. ROBINSON *Eng. Flower Garden* (ed. 2) 769/2 The hardy Azaleas, called Ghent azaleas, have sprung chiefly from the wild azaleas that grow in North America. **1963** *Oxf. Bk. Garden Flowers* 56 *Azalea pontica*..is one of the species used in developing the first 'Ghent' azaleas.

†**ˈGhenting.** *Obs.* Also **gentin(g.** [f. *Ghent* (see prec.) a city in Belgium (Flanders) + -ING. Cf. CAMBRIC.] A kind of linen, originally made at Ghent. Also *attrib.*

a **1700** B. E. *Dict. Cant. Crew* s.v. *Wiper*, He Pickt-pockets of a broad, or narrow, Ghenting, Cambrick, or Colour'd Handkerchief. **1712** E. COOKE *Voy. S. Sea* 363, 2 Bales of Ghenting. **1721** C. KING *Brit. Merch.* I. 284 Gentins 2021 Pieces. **1750** *Lond. Mag.* 341 To encourage the consumption of ghentings, cambricks, &c.

†**ˈGhentish,** *a.* and *sb.* [f. as prec. + -ISH.] **A.** *adj.* Applied to certain textile fabrics originally made at Ghent. **B.** *sb.* Used as a name for these.

1545 *Rates Custom-ho.* A vij, Carpettes called gentisshe the pece. **1583** *Ibid.* C ij b, Gentish cloth the peece. **1758** FRANKLIN *Let.* Wks. (1887) III. 7 Also..forty-three ells of Ghentish sheeting Holland.

gherao (gɛˈraʊ). [f. Hind. *gherna* to surround, besiege.] A form of harassment in labour disputes in India and Pakistan, whereby workers detain their employers or managers on the premises, refusing to let them depart until their claims are granted. Hence as *v. trans.*, to detain (a person) in this manner.

1967 *Statesman* (Calcutta) 7 Apr. 1 (*heading*) Gheraos must be declared illegal, say employers. *Ibid.*, There had been 'gheraos' on minor issues like the quality and quantity of food to be supplied by a canteen. **1967** *Economist* 9 Dec. 1049/2 Hospitals were gheraoed; so were the Calcutta city government and the West Bengal assembly. **1968** *Ann. Reg. 1967* II. iv. 79 Industrial labour diminished production by frequent organization of *gheraos* or forceful confinement of the managers. **1969** *Times* 22 Mar. 1/5 Pakistan workers.. have 'gheraoed' (put pressure upon) two Scottish executives. **1969** *National Herald* (New Delhi) 29 July 3/2 They threatened Academic Council members with gherao. **1969** *Amrita Bazar Patrika* 5 Aug. 5/5 More than 50 students of Bengal Veterinary College gheraoed the Director of Veterinary Services..and other officers of the department in the New Secretariat building for three hours on Monday.

gherkin (ˈgɜːkɪn). Also 7–8 **ger-, girkin,** (7 **gerckem, gurchen**), 9 **gurken.** [a. early mod.Du. ***gurkkijn**, ***agurkkijn** (now *gurkje, augurkje*), dim. of *agurk, augurk* (also shortened *gurk*), cucumber; the proximate source is uncertain (cf. Ger. *gurke*, earlier also *gurchen*, Sw. *gurka*, Da. *agurk*), but the word must have been indirectly adopted from some Slav. lang.: cf. Slovenish *ugorek, angurka*, Polish *ogurek, ogorek*, Czech *okurka*, Serbian *ugorka* (the Hungarian *ugorka*, Lith. *agurkas*, Lettish *gurkjis*, are adopted from Slav.); these words have a diminutive suffix, which is replaced by another suffix of like function in the Russian *ogurets*, Church Slav. *ogouritsĭ*. The primary form is not recorded in Slav., but appears in late Gr. ἀγγούριον, ἀγκούριον (mod.Gr. ἀγγοῦρι), whence It. *anguria* a kind of cucumber, F. *angourie, angurie* (Cotgr.), Sp. *angúrria* (obs.) water-melon: see ANGURIA.

The ultimate origin is unknown. Arabic has *ḳajūr* cucumber, but Lane regards this as adopted from Gr. The Persian *angūr* is sometimes given as the etymon, but it means 'a grape'.]

A young green cucumber, or a cucumber of a small kind, used for pickling.

1661 PEPYS *Diary* 1 Dec., We..opened the glass of girkins ..which are rare things. **1693** *Phil. Trans.* XVII. 684 The Fruit is..eaten with Rice and other Meats, as we do Gurchens and Olives. **1712** tr. *Pomet's Hist. Drugs* I. 7 There is another kind of Fennel..which we make Vinegar off to sell in Winter with girkins. **1834** LANDOR *Exam. Shaks.* Wks. 1846 II. 290 One of these Greeks methinks thrown into the pickle-pot, would be a treasure to the house-wife's young gherkins. **1837** *Penny Cycl.* VIII. 211/2 The best sorts of cucumbers are, for gurkens, the *Russian* [etc.]. **1860** DELAMER *Kitch. Gard.* 126 Gherkins, or young cucumbers for pickling, are mostly, in England, half-grown, late-produced fruit.

attrib. **1882** *Garden* 1 Apr. 222/1 Gherkin Cucumber beds.

ghess(e, ghest, obs. forms of GUESS, GHOST.

‖**ghetto** (ˈgɛtəʊ), *sb.* Also 7 **gheto.** [Of uncertain etym., perh. f. It. *getto* foundry, as the first ghetto founded in Venice in 1516 was on the site of a foundry.]

1. The quarter in a city, chiefly in Italy, to which the Jews were restricted.

1611 CORYAT *Crudities* 230 The place where the whole fraternity of the Iews dwelleth together, which is called the Ghetto. *Ibid.* 234 Walking in the Court of the Ghetto, I casually met with a Iewish Rabbin that spake good Latin. **1756–7** tr. *Keysler's Trav.* (1760) II. 76 A particular part of the city, noted for houses of ill-fame, was assigned by Cosmo I. to the Jews, for their particular quarter, or ghetto. **1879** FARRAR *St. Paul* I. 5 The crowded ghetto of a Pagan capital. **1887** DOWDEN *Shelley* II. vii. 277 An obscure quarter of Rome, hard by the gate of the Ghetto.

2. *transf.* and *fig.* A quarter in a city, esp. a thickly populated slum area, inhabited by a minority group or groups, usu. as a result of economic or social pressures; an area, etc., occupied by an isolated group; an isolated or segregated group, community, or area.

1892 I. ZANGWILL *Children of Ghetto* I. I. 2 The particular Ghetto that is the dark background upon which our pictures will be cast is of voluntary formation. **1897** *Literature* 27 Nov. 180/1 The Farringdon-road collection of barrows has become the veriest Ghetto of bookland. **1908** J. LONDON *Martin Eden* (1910) xxxvi. 310 They dismounted and plunged off to the right into the heart of the working-class ghetto. **1909** *Westm. Gaz.* 20 Aug. 8/3 The people..have grown superior to the banal excitement and cheap attractions of the densely crowded areas. The day on which the tramways went over Westminster Bridge recorded the unlocking of the London ghettos. **1937** *Times* 6 Oct. 13/7 Part of the benches [in the Warsaw Polytechnic] have been marked for students belonging to a union almost exclusively controlled by 'Aryans', and others for the Jewish students' union, while a few seats for non-union students are left unmarked... The establishment of the 'bench ghetto' is an important precedent, unknown even in Germany. **1957** *Times Lit. Suppl.* 29 Nov. 713/3 On records the Coloured jazz musicians still played largely for their race; in life they played for the immigrants into the Negro city ghettoes. **1961** L. MUMFORD *City in History* xvi. 493 The suburb..was a segregated community..a sort of green ghetto dedicated to the elite. **1961** *Listener* 7 Dec. 1000/3 [The television programme] 'Bookstand', (November 30), capriciously shifted to the Tuesday ghetto, had one memorable item. **1966** *Ibid.* 29 Sept. 454/1 The ghetto is one of two in which most of Chicago's Negroes, who make up a quarter of the city's population, are forced to live. **1968** *N.Y. Rev. Books* 11 July 34/1 The 'breakdown of the Catholic ghetto' is a good thing, but the breakdown of intellectual ghettos at M.I.T. and Harvard might be, educationally, an even better thing.

3. *attrib.* and *Comb.*

1892 I. ZANGWILL *Childr. Ghetto* (1893) 2 The Ghetto.. becomes only a swarming-place for the poor and the ignorant... Such people are their own Ghetto gates. **1903** *Daily Chron.* 5 Aug. 5//2 What he calls the Ghetto face and the Ghetto eye, observable enough in immigrants, cannot be detected after a generation or two on American soil. **1908** J. LONDON *Martin Eden* (1910) xxxviii. 328 Tell them why you don't want Socialism. Tell them what you think about them and their ghetto ethics. **1941** KOESTLER *Scum of Earth* 48 The country which was the first to introduce yellow ghetto benches in its schools. **1949** —— *Promise & Fulfilment* II. iv. 251 The victory of the new type of Israelis grown on Palestine soil over the obstinate fanaticism of ghetto-bred politicians. *Ibid.* III. I. 294 The same ghetto-heritage of suspicion. **1968** *Guardian* 24 Oct. 10/2 Those ancestors of today's ghetto-dwellers came to areas where, unlike the South, there was no discrimination. **1969** *Ibid.* 17 Sept. 10/2 Catholics are not going to abandon the ghetto mentality which the events of the past month have created unless Stormont shows some belated signs of having the stomach for dealing with Protestant extremists. **1971** *Radio Times* 16 Sept. 37/5 Social workers are becoming increasingly worried by the 'ghetto mentality' in the deprived areas of our cities.

b. Special Comb. **ghetto blaster** *slang* (orig. *U.S.*), a large portable stereo radio (and cassette player), esp. one on which (Black) popular music is played loudly.

[**1982** *N.Y. Times* 30 May 46/3 He and his sextet, the Ghetto Blasters, brought their mixture of harmonized Southern rock and rhythm-and-blues to the Bottom Line.] **1983** *Times* 27 May 10/3 The growing high-street popularity of Sony Walkmans and portable stereo cassette players ('*ghetto blasters'). **1983** *Daily Mirror* 4 June 13/1 A beat throbbing from a ghetto-blaster—a giant, portable stereo system. **1983** *Christian Science Monitor* 27 Sept. 21 Six feet tall, 16 years old, and carrying a 'ghetto blaster'.

ghetto ('gɛtəʊ), *v.* [f. the sb.] *trans.* To put or keep (people) in a ghetto. So **'ghettoed** *ppl. a.*; **'ghettoize** *v. trans.*; also **ghettoi'zation**.

1936 *Times* 15 Feb. 11/3 Jews, who are ghettoed under the racial legislation. **1939** *Jewish Standard* (Toronto) Apr. 13 An element of ghettoization, self demoralization. **1939** *Canadian Jewish Chron.* 4 Aug. 3 Arcand's attempt..to ghettoize a minority. **1964** M. A. GALAMISON in J. H. Clarke *Harlem* 225 It is a land of ghettoized human beings: men denied creative work. **1965** *Listener* 15 Apr. 543/1 We don't ghetto them or keep them out of work. *Ibid.* 545/2 The immigrant can be ghettoed psychologically. **1970** *Guardian* 27 Oct. 11/8 Skilled white workers are moving South from the ghettoed and polluted cities of the North.

ghi, var. GHEE.

ghiaour, ghibber, vars. GIAOUR, GIBBER.

Ghibelline ('gɪbəlɪn, -aɪn), *sb.* and *a.* Also 6 Gibiline, 7–8 Gibel(l)ine, 7 Ghibelin, 9 Ghi-, Guibeline. [ad. It. *Ghibellino*, commonly stated to be a corruption of Ger. *Waiblingen*, the name of an estate belonging to the Hohenstaufen family; the Ger. name is said to have been used as a war-cry by the partisans of the Hohenstaufen emperor Conrad III at the battle of Weinsberg 1140.]

A. *sb.* One of the emperor's faction in the Italian states, as opposed to the Pope's faction: see GUELPH.

1573 G. HARVEY *Letter-bk.* (Camden) 112 Nether hard-hearted Gibiline nor desperate Guelphe Made ever profession of so wicked pelfe. **1602** *Metam. Tabacco* (Collier) 49 The inhumane designes of furious Guelphes and warlike Gibellines. **1639** DRUMM OF HAWTH. *Prophecy* Wks. (1711) 181 Thence arose the Guelfs and Gibellines, imperialists against papists. **1663** DRYDEN *Wild Gallant* I. i, Thy doublet and breeches are Guelphs and Ghibelins to one another. **1705** ADDISON *Italy* (1766) 88 Their republic was torn into the divisions of Guelphs and Gibelines. **1837** *Penny Cycl.* VIII. 302/2 The Bianchi in their reverses joined the Guibelines. **1872** LOWELL *Dante* Pr. Wks. 1890 IV. 129 The nobles..were commonly Ghibellines, or Imperialists.

B. *adj.* Of or adhering to the Ghibellines.

1826 K. DIGBY *Broadst. Hon.* (1829) I. 1. 270 The Ghibelline party aimed at nothing but the establishment of merely worldly dominion. **1861** M. PATTISON *Ess.* (1889) I. 34 The weakness of Henry III would not suffer him to commit himself heartily to a Ghibelline policy.

Ghibellinism ('gɪbəlɪnɪz(ə)m). [f. GHIBELLINE + -ISM.] The policy and principles of the Ghibellines; adherence to the Ghibelline party.

1826 K. DIGBY *Broadst. Hon.* (1829) I. I. 270 Frederick Schlegel justly objects to Dante's perpetual Ghibellinism. **1855** MILMAN *Lat. Chr.* XI. v. (1864) VI. 453 Nicolas..died accused by the Guelfs of unpapal Ghibellinism. **1865** *Cornh. Mag.* Aug. 249 Ghibellinism did not exclude a republican form of government.

ghilgai, var. GILGAI.

ghillie, var. GILLIE[1].

Ghilzai ('gɪlzaɪ). Also **Ghilji**. The name of one of the most famous of the tribes of Afghanistan. Also *attrib.*

1826 LEYDEN & ERSKINE tr. *Mem. Zehir-Ed-Din* 220 Plundering and beating up the quarters of the Ghiljis. **1842** C. MASSON *Narr. var. Journeys* II. 207 The Ghiljis, although considered, and calling themselves, Afghâns..are undoubtedly a mixed race. **1875** *Encycl. Brit.* I. 235/1 On the British invasion the Ghilzais showed a rooted hostility to the foreigner. **1920** *Blackw. Mag.* Aug. 172/2 Information at hand pointed to the Ghilzais from Afghanistan. **1971** *Whitaker's Almanack* 815/2 The most numerous race [of Afghanistan] is the Pathan.., the main divisions being the Durranis, from whom the Royal family springs, and the Ghilzais.

ghimner, obs. form of CHIMER[1], a loose robe.

1614 CAMDEN *Rem.* 231 The ghimners, Rochets, Miters of Bishops, with the Archbishop's Palle.

ghing, var. GING, *Obs.*

ghinschenn, obs. form of GINSENG.

Ghiordes (giː'ɔːdəz). The name of a town (Gördes) in western Turkey, used *attrib.* or as *adj.* to designate a fine type of Turkish rug, or a kind of knot used in weaving some oriental carpets (see quots.).

1900 J. K. MUMFORD *Oriental Rugs* x. 147 In some Ghiordes rugs the main border is made up of a pattern which..suggests a comb. *Ibid.* 159 The Ghiordes knot is used [in new Meles rugs]; the warp is of two- or three-strand wool. **1957** *Encycl. Brit.* IV. 918/1 There are two different kinds of knot employed, the Ghiordes or Turkish, and the Senne or Persian; the tufts of yarn in the former coming in pairs between the two warp threads. **1967** R. JEFFRIES *Deadly Marriage* ii. 28 Cabbot.., correctly identified it as a Ghiordes prayer mat.

ghirland, -lond, obs. forms of GARLAND.

ghittar, ghittern: see GUITAR, GITTERN.

ghoast, obs. form of GHOST.

gholam (gəʊ'lɑːm). Also **gholaum, ghulam, goulam.** [Arab.] A courier, messenger.

1820 M. TANCOIGNE *Narr. Journey Persia* 251 The military household of the king of Persia..is composed of a certain number of cavalry, who are called goulams, or slaves. *Ibid.* 252 The goulams always escort the king when he appears in public, or when he leaves the city to hunt. **1840** J. B. FRASER *Trav. Koordistan* I. i. 21 'What am *I* to do then, your Excellency?' roared out some Gholaum or Beg. **1882** E. O'DONOVAN *Merv Oasis* I. 319 We had with us a *gholam*, or courier, belonging to the British Legation at Teheran.

ghole, var. GHOUL.

ghoont (guːnt). Also **ghounte, goont, gunt.** [Hind.] A Himalayan pony.

1625 PURCHAS *Pilgrims* I. IV. iv. 438 Heere is the great breed of a small kind of Horse, called *Gunts*, a true trauelling scalecliffe beast. **1834** tr. *Jacquemont's Journ. India* II. 12 In Cashmere, I shall buy, without regard to price, the best *ghounte* in Tibet. **1858** SIMMONDS *Dict. Trade, Ghoont*, a small surefooted Indian pony, used in the mountain ranges as a pack or saddle-horse. **1871** E. BALFOUR *Cycl. India* (ed. 2) II. 312/2 During winter the ghoont live on the roots of the stunted bushes, and are very expert at scraping the snow from off them with their fore feet.

Ghoork(h)a, varr. GURKHA.

ghoos, ghoost, obs. ff. GOOSE, GHOST.

ghospel(l, ghossip, etc.: see GOSPEL, GOSSIP.

ghost (gəʊst), *sb.* Forms: 1 gást, gǽst, 2–5 gast(e, 3–6 gost(e, 4–6 goost(e, 6 *Sc.* goast, goist, 5–6 ghoste, ghoost, (6 ghoast, 8 ghest), 5– ghost, 6– *Sc.* g(h)aist. [Common WGer.: OE. *gást* (also *gǽst*) str. masc. = OFris. *gâst*, OS. *gêst* (Du. *geest*), OHG. (MHG., mod.Ger.) *geist*:—OTeut. type **gaisto-z*.

Although the word is known only in the WGer. langs. (in all of which it is found with substantially identical meaning), it appears to be of pre-Teut. formation. The sense of the pre-Teut. **ghoizdo-z*, if the ordinary view of its etymological relations be correct, should be 'fury, anger'; cf. Skr. *hēḍas* neut. anger, Zend *zōižda-* ugly; the root **gheis-*, **ghois-* appears with cognate sense in ON. *geisa* to rage, Goth. *usgaisjan* to terrify (see GAST *v.*); outside Teut. the derivatives seem to point to a primary sense 'to wound, tear, pull to pieces'.

The OE. form *gǽst* is constant in the Exeter Book, and occurs 49 times in the Hatton MS. and 3 times in the Bodl. MS. of Alfred's transl. of Gregory's *Pastoral Care*; it is app. not known elsewhere. The occurrence of *gǽst*:—**gaisti-* beside *gást*:—**gaisto-* is explained by Sievers (*Ags. Gram.* ed. 3) as indicating that the word, though recorded only as masc., was orig. a neut. *-os*, *-es* stem: it would thus correspond formally to the Skr. word quoted above.

The spelling with *gh-*, so far as our material shows, appears first in Caxton, who was probably influenced by the Flemish *gheest*. It remained rare until the middle of the 16th c., and was not completely established before about 1590.]

1. The soul or spirit, as the principle of life; also *ghost of life*. *Obs.* exc. in phrase ***to give up*** (†earlier ***to give, give away, yield up***) ***the*** (†***one's***) ***ghost***: to breathe one's last, expire, die.

a **900** in *O.E. Texts* 178 Se casere hio heht ȝemartyria(n), & God wuldriende heo aȝeaf hire gast. *a* **1000** *Cædmon's Gen.* 1281 (Gr.) He wolde..forleosan lica ȝehwilc, þara þe lifes gast fæðmum þeahte. *c* **1205** LAY. 23986 þa feol Frolle folde to grunde..his gost he bi-læfde. *a* **1225** *Juliana* 59 As ha ȝeide to godd & walde aȝeouen hire gast in to his honden. *a* **1300** *Cursor M.* 5188 His gast bigan to quiken egain. *c* **1305** *St. Lucy* 171 in *E.E.P.* (1862) 106 Wiþ þe laste word heo ȝaf þe gost. **13..** *E.E. Allit. P.* B. 325 Alle þat glydez & gotz, & gost of lyf habbez. **1377** LANGL. *P. Pl.* B. xv. 141 By lered, by lewed þat loth is to spende þ us gone her godes be þe goste faren. **1388** WYCLIF *Matt.* xxvii. 50 Jhesus eftsoone criede with a greet voyce and ȝaf vp the goost. *c* **1400** *Destr. Troy* 8216 He gird to the ground & the gost past. *c* **1450** *Mirour Saluacioun* 4833 Thow herde hym his goost commende til his fadere on the crosse. *c* **1460** *Towneley Myst.* xvi. 155, I wote I yelde my gast, so sore my hart it grefys. *c* **1510** MORE *Picus* Wks. 8/2 He might ere he gaue vp yͤ goste, receiue his full draught of loue and compassion. **1574** *Mirr. Mag., Albanact.* lxviii, He gasped thryse, and gaue away the ghost. *a* **1586** SIDNEY *Arcadia* (1622) 275 But when indeede shee found his ghost was gone, then Sorrow lost the witte of utterance. **1598** GRENEWEY *Tacitus' Ann.* VI. x. 136 Being fallen downe and yeelding vp his ghost. **1746–7** HERVEY *Medit.* (1818) 13 It was his last wish..He breathed it out, and gave up the ghost. **1816** J. WILSON *City of Plague* II. iii. 143, I have seen for two months past some score i' the day Give up the ghost. **1879** F. POLLOK *Sport Brit. Burmah* I. 127 A tiger..shot through the heart..is still capable of killing half-a-dozen men before giving up the ghost.

fig. **1892** *Idler* Sept. 220 The old mill..has tumbled down and given up the ghost.

†**2.** Used as the conventional equivalent for L. *spiritus*, in contexts where the sense is *breath* or *a blast*. *Obs.*

c **825** *Vesp. Psalter* x[i]. 7 Gast ysta [Vulg. *spiritus procellarum*]. *c* **1000** *Ags. Ps.* (Spelm.) cxxxiv. 17 Ne ne..is gast on muðe heora. *a* **1340** HAMPOLE *Psalter* x. 7 Gast of stormes. **1340** —— *Pr. Consc.* 4610 þe boke says, alswa, þat he, Thurgh þe gast of Goddes mouthe slayn sal be. ? *a* **1500** *Chester Pl.* (E.E.T.S.) ii. 95 Fowles in the ayer flying and all that ghoste hath. **1625** GILL *Sacr. Philos.* VIII. 113 The word Ghost in English..is as much as *athem*, or breath; in our new Latine language, a Spirit.

3. a. The spirit, or immaterial part of man, as distinct from the body or material part; the seat of feeling, thought, and moral action. Also, in New Testament language, the SPIRIT or higher moral nature of man; opposed to *flesh*. *Obs.* exc. in *nonce-uses*.

a **1000** *Cædmon's Exod.* 447 (Gr.) Folc wæs afæred; flodeȝsa becwom gastas ȝeomre. *c* **1000** *Ags. Gosp.* Matt. xxvi. 41 Witudlice se gast is hræd & þæt flæsc ys untrum. *c* **1200** *Trin. Coll. Hom.* 189 Ðe lichame winneð toȝenes þe gost. *c* **1220** *Bestiary* 550, I mene ðe stedefast in riȝte leue mid fles and gast. *a* **1250** *Owl & Night.* 1396 Sum a-rist of the flesches luste, An sum of the gostes custe. *a* **1300** *Cursor M.* 18602 Quils his licam lai vnder stan In gast es he til hell gan. *a* **1325** *Prose Psalter* I. 18 [li. 17] Trubled gost is sacrifice to God. *c* **1460** *Towneley Myst.* xi. 50 My gost gladys with luf, In god that is my hele. *c* **1500** *Lancelot* 1031 Deuoydit was his spritis and his gost. **1596** SPENSER *Hymn Beautie* 24 Whose faire immortall beame Hath darted fyre into my feeble ghost. **1674** N. FAIRFAX *Bulk & Selv.* 12 It will be a good step towards the knowledg of what the world ought to be to us, who are body and ghost together. **1850** TENNYSON *In Mem.* xciii, Descend, and touch..That in this blindness of the frame, My Ghost may feel that thine is near. **1855** LONGF. *Hiaw.* xvii. 164 The ghost, the Jeebi in him, Thought and felt as Pau-Puk-Keewis.

b. Philos. ***the ghost in the machine***: Gilbert Ryle's name for the mind viewed as separate from the body (see quots.).

1949 G. RYLE *Concept of Mind* i. 15 Such in outline is the official theory. I shall often speak of it, with deliberate abusiveness, as 'the dogma of the Ghost in the machine'. *Ibid.* 22 The dogma of the Ghost in the machine..maintains that there exist both bodies and minds; that there are mechanical causes of corporeal movements and mental causes of corporeal movements. **1960** J. O. Urmson *Conc. Encycl. Western Philos.* 350/1 We are inclined to construe the concept of mind as of an extra object situated in the body and controlling it by a set of unwitnessable activities; this is what he [*sc.* Ryle] calls the dogma of the ghost (the mind) in the machine (the body). Ryle regards this picture as totally misleading. **1961** *Mind* LXX. 103 Certainly he [*sc.* Teilhard de Chardin] imports a ghost, the entelechy or *élan vital* of an earlier terminology, into the Mendelian machine. **1967** Koestler (*title*) The ghost in the machine.

†**4.** A person. Cf. the similar use of soul, spirit.

a **1000** *Guthlac* 690 in *Exeter Bk.*, þæt se leofesta gæst ȝeȝearwad in godes wære on ȝefean ferde. *c* **1305** *Pol. Songs* (Camden) 70 The Kyng..Brohte from Alemayne mony sori gost to store Wyndesore. **1387** Trevisa *Higden* (Rolls) VI. 253 Aigolandus was a lewed goost and lewed-liche i-meved as þe devel hym tauȝte. **1399** Langl. *Rich. Redeles* I. 25 Graceles gostis gylours of hem-self..sawe no manere siȝth saff solas and ese. **1590** Spenser *F.Q.* II. viii. 26 No knight so rude, I weene, As to doen outrage to a sleeping ghost.

†**5. a.** An incorporeal being; a spirit. ***local ghost*** = L. *genius loci. Obs.*

1297 R. Glouc. (Rolls) 2750 þe clerkes sede..þat þer beþ in þe eyr an hey, ver fram þe grounde, As a maner gostes ..þat men clupeþ eluene. *c* **1600** Shaks. *Sonn.* lxxxvi, That affable familiar ghost Which nightly gulls him with intelligence. **1618** Bolton *Florus* I. xiii. (1636) 39 When they beheld the purple-cloathed Senatours sitting in their chayres of state, they worship them at first as gods or locall ghosts.

†**b.** A good spirit, an angel. *Obs.*

c **900** tr. *Bæda's Hist.* III. xiv. [xix.] (1890) 214 Heo..eft mid þæm engelicum gastum to heofonum hwurfen. *a* **1000** *Cædmon's Gen.* 2430 (Gr.) Aras þa metodes þeow gastum toȝeanes. *a* **1240** *Sawles Warde* in *Cott. Hom.* 261 Ich biseh to þe engles..iblescede gastes þe beoð a biuore godd. *c* **1485** *Digby Myst.* III. 601, I am þe gost of goodnesse þat so wold ȝe gydde.

†**c.** An evil spirit. ***the loath, foul, wicked ghost***: the Devil. *Obs.*

a **1000** *Christ & Satan* (Gr.-Wülk.) 126 Se wereȝa gast. *c* **1000** *Ags. Gosp.* Matt. xii. 43 Se unclæna gast utfærþ fram menn. *c* **1200** Ormin 8064 Herode king maȝȝ swiþe wel þe laþe gast bitacnenn. *c* **1200** *Trin. Coll. Hom.* 87 Swiche hertes fondeð þe fule gost deies and nihtes. *a* **1300** *Cursor M.* 170 How iesus quen he long had fast Was fondid wit þe wik gast. *a* **1350** *Life Jesu* (Horstm.) 232 þou luþere gost and doumb..def and vn milde, Ich hote þe þat þov wende hasteliche fram þe childe. **1377** Langl. *P. Pl.* B. XVIII. 431 May no grysly gost glyde þere it shadweth. *c* **1420** *Anturs of Arth.* (Thornton) 163 Nowe I am a grisely gaste, and grymly graue With Lucefere. **1529** More *Comf. agst. Trib.* II. Wks. 1178/1 Oure wrestlynge is..against the spiritual wicked gostes of the ayre.

6. Formerly used in the sense of spirit (of God). Now only in Holy Ghost, the usual designation of the Third Person of the Trinity in liturgical and dogmatic language.

'Thy Ghost' for 'Thy Holy Ghost' in quot. 1871 is merely a nonce-use.

c **825** *Vesp. Psalter* cxxxviii[i]. 7 Hwider gongu ic from gaste ðinum. *c* **1000** *Ags. Gosp.* John xiv. 26 Se haliȝa frofre gast. *c* **1050** *Byrhtferth's Handboc* in *Anglia* VIII. 310 On þam dæȝe godes gast com to mancynne. *a* **1300** *Cursor M.* 26041 He has couerd þe seuen Giftes o þe gast of heuen, þe quilk he had al forwit tint. **13..** *E.E. Allit. P.* B. 1598 A haþel..þat hatz þe gostes of god þat gyes alle soþes. **1340** *Ayenb.* 53 þe zixte [libbeþ] be þe goste and be þe loue of god. *c* **1386** Chaucer *Prioress' T.* 18 O mooder mayde!..That rauysedest doun fro the deitee, Thurgh thyn humblesse, the goost þat in thalighte. *c* **1400** Maundev. (Roxb.) xv. 68 Ihesu Criste was þe worde and þe gaste of Godd. *c* **1440** *York Myst.* xxi. 14 He schall giffe baptyme more entire in fire and gaste. *c* **1550** Cheke *Mark* i. 10 He saw yͤ heavens departed, and yͤ ghoost to come down lijk a doov on him. **1552** Latimer *Fruitf. Serm.* (1584) 330 The onely remedy, is to call vpon God to endue thee with the Holy Ghost..Call I say vppon almighty God for this Ghost [**1607** *ed.* helpe]. **1647** H. More *Song of Soul* I. II. xci, God's Spirit is no private empty shade But that great Ghost that fills both earth and sky. **1871** G. Macdonald *Sonn. conc. Jesus* iv, 'Tis man himself, the temple of thy Ghost.

†**7.** The soul of a deceased person, spoken of as inhabiting the unseen world. In later use only = manes; sometimes *pl. Obs.*

a **800** in *O.E. Texts* 149 To ymbhycggannae..huaet his gastae..aefter deothdaege doemid uueorth[a]e. *c* **835** *Charter* ibid. 448 þonne foe se hlaford to & ða hiȝan æt kristes cirican, & hit minum gaste nytt ȝedoen. *c* **1200** *Trin. Coll. Hom.* 169 Witeð ȝie awariede gostes in to eche fur. *c* **1290** *St. Brandan* 525 in *S. Eng. Leg.* I. 234 Heo i-seiȝe onouewarde..A wrechche gost, naked and bar. *a* **1300** *Cursor M.* 18603 His bodi here, his gast was þar, His goddhede wanted noþer-quar. **1606** G. W[oodcocke] tr. *Justin's Hist.* 126 He did sacrifice to his Wiues Ghost. **1654** R. Codrington tr. *Justin's Hist.* 470 He took Gryphina, the wife of Gryphus, prisoner, who killed her sister, and by her death did parentate to the Ghosts of his wife. *a* **1674** Clarendon *Hist. Reb.* XI. §124 To take full vengeance for the loss of Rainsborough, to whose Ghost he design'd an ample sacrifice.

8. a. The soul of a deceased person, spoken of as appearing in a visible form, or otherwise manifesting its presence, to the living. (Now the prevailing sense.)

c **1385** Chaucer *L.G.W.* 1295 *Dido*, This night my fadres gost Hath in my sleep so sore me tormented. **1430–40** Lydg. *Bochas* VI. xi. (1554) 157 a, Crye of goostes in cauernes and kaues. **1513** Douglas *Æneis* VI. xi. 35 Fadir, thi drery gost Sa oft apperand, maid me seik this cost. *a* **1550** *Christis Kirke Gr.* xviii, He grainit lyk ony gaist. **1599** Massinger, etc. *Old Law* IV. i. (1656) H 1 b, I'le bury some money before I die, that my ghost May hant thee after-ward. **1602** Shaks. *Ham.* I. v. 126 There needs no Ghost my Lord, come from the Graue, to tell vs this. **1691** Norris *Pract. Disc.* 180 We should be no more concerned with the things of this World, than a Ghost is, that only comes to do a Message of Providence. **1742** Collins *Odes, Fear* 60 Ghosts, as cottage-maids believe, Their pebbled beds permitted leave. **1794** Mrs. Radcliffe *Myst. Udolpho* xxii, Now you would persuade me you have seen a ghost. **1838–9** Hallam *Hist. Lit.* IV. iv. IV. §21. 162 The canonists and casuists have vanished like ghosts at the first daylight. **1897** Mary Kingsley *W. Africa* 488 Between five and six weeks..the widow remains in the hut, armed with a good stout stick, as a precaution against the ghost of her husband.

transf. and *fig.* **1764** Foote *Patron* III. Wks. 1799 I. 358 If I go to the bar, the ghost of this curs'd comedy will follow, and haunt me in Westminster-hall. **1819** G. Peacock *Flux. & Diff. Calc.* 20 To represent a fluxion as the limit of the increment..is to reduce it..in the language of Berkly, to the ghost of a departed entity. **1849** Thackeray *Pendennis* xli, The ghost of the dead feeling came back as he mused. **1897** Mary Kingsley *W. Africa* 522 In front of us a spear's ghost used to fly across the path about that time in the afternoon.

b. Phrases. ***to lay a ghost***: to cause it to cease appearing. ***to raise a ghost***: to cause it to appear. Both also *fig.* ***the ghost walks*** (Theat. slang): there is money in the treasury, the salaries are forthcoming.

1716, etc. [see lay *v.*[1] 3 b]. **1826** [see raise *v.*[1] 21 a]. **1833** R. Dyer 9 *Yrs. of Actor's Life* 53 If I played with applause, it was a matter of indifference whether 'the ghost' walked on Saturday or not. **1853** *Househ. Words* 24 Sep. 77/1 When no salaries are forthcoming on Saturday the 'ghost doesn't walk'. **1857** Hughes *Tom Brown* I. i, Where the last ghost was laid by the parson. **1883** *Referee* 24 June 3/2 An Actor's Benevolent Fund box placed on the treasurer's desk every day when the ghost walks would get many an odd shilling or six-pence put into it. **1884** tr. *Lotze's Metaph.* iii. 63 We are fighting here against ghosts raised by ourselves. **1889** J. C. Coleman in Barrere & Leland *Slang* 405 Instead of enquiring whether the treasury is open, they generally say —'Has the ghost walked?'

c. An apparition; a spectre.

1592 Shaks. *Ven. & Ad.* 933 'Hateful divorce of love'—thus chides she Death—'Grim-grinning ghost, earth's worm.' **1651** Hobbes *Leviath.* III. xxxiv. 208 A Ghost, or other Idol or Phantasme of the Imagination. **1658** Manton *Exp. Jude* 16 We are not to..fight with ghosts and antiquated errors, but to oppose with all earnestness the growing evils of the world. **1727** De Foe *Hist. Appar.* v. (1840) 50 An apparition is vulgarly called by us a ghost. **1852** Mrs. Stowe *Uncle Tom's C.* xxxix. 344 They won't come there to inquire after us. If they do, I'll play ghost for them.

†**9.** A corpse. *Obs.* (Cf. L. *mānes*.)

1567 Fenton *Trag. Disc.* B b j, Kissyng every parte of his senceles ghoste. **1593** Shaks. *2 Hen. VI*, III. ii. 161 Oft haue I seene a timely-parted Ghost, Of ashy semblance, meager, pale, and bloodlesse.

10. In allusion to the pale, shadowy and unsubstantial appearance attributed to ghosts.

a. Applied to a person in a state of extreme emaciation; 'a shadow of his former self'.

1590 Sir J. Smyth *Disc. Weapons* I. *** iv, Great numbers of miserable and pitiful ghosts, or rather shadowes of men. **1698** Fryer *Acc. E. India & P.* 218 By their unmerciful bleeding him; insomuch that he seemed to have little more left than would suffice to make him a walking Ghost.

b. A shadowy outline or semblance, an unsubstantial image (of something); hence, a slight trace or vestige, esp. in phrase (***not***) ***the ghost of a chance***. Cf. shadow.

1613 Purchas *Pilgrimage* (1614) 40 That Berosus which we now have, is not so much as the ghost, or carkasse..of that famous Chaldean Author. **1731** A. Hill *Adv. Poets* Ep. 13 Things, without Wit, or Meaning, and which are not so much, as the Ghosts of good Poetry. **1818** Moore *Fudge Fam. Paris* iii. 43 There, Dick, what a breakfast!—oh, not like your ghost Of a breakfast in England. *a* **1845** Hood *Workhouse Clock* iii, The Sempstress, lean, and weary, and wan, With only the ghosts of garments on. **1851** Ruskin *Stones Ven.* (1874) I. x. 121 The arch line is the ghost or skeleton of the arch. **1857** Hughes *Tom Brown* II. v, Williams hadn't the ghost of a chance with Tom at wrestling. **1869** *Mayne Reid's Mag.* June 509 But to secure him, this whale did not give us the ghost of a chance. **1887** Rider Haggard *Jess.* viii, Her breath rested for a second on his cheek like the ghost of a kiss.

c. An impression of a signature made by folding the paper over while the ink is still wet.

1929 *Sotheby's Catal.* 4–7 Nov. 82 On the back of one 'ghost' there is a note in the Author's hand.

11. *Optics*, etc.

†**a.** A name for Ramsden's eye-piece for the microscope, which is so constructed that the image formed by the objective lies below instead of above the field-glass. *Obs.*

1793 Wollaston in *Phil. Trans.* LXXXIII. 139, I approve much of Mr. Ramsden's ghost, as it is called, where it can be used with safety.

b. A bright spot or secondary image appearing in the field of a telescope, produced by some defect, temporary or permanent, in one of the lenses of the eye-piece.

1867 Smyth *Sailor's Word-bk.*, *Ghost*, a false image in the lens of an instrument. **1870** *Eng. Mech.* 7 Jan. 397/3 What opticians call 'a ghost', or internal reflection from the lenses of the eye-piece.

c. *Photogr.* = flare, *sb.*[1] 3.

1864 J. Towler *Silver Sunbeam* xlviii. (1870) 451 You will perceive one, two, three, etc., illuminated circles move across the field of vision over the picture—these are ghosts. **1868** [see flare *sb.*[1] 3].

d. *Spectroscopy.* A spurious spectral line produced by periodic errors in a diffraction grating.

1879 C. S. Peirce in *Amer. Jrnl. Math.* II. 330 (*heading*) On the ghosts in Rutherford's diffraction-grating. *Ibid.* 338 The positions of some of these 'ghosts', or repetitions of the principal spectrum, have been carefully measured. **1882** *Nature* XXVII. 95 Professor Rowland's plates..were free from 'ghosts' caused by periodicity in the ruling. **1963** R. W. Ditchburn *Light* (ed. 2) vi. 188 Every fifth line [of a diffraction grating] slightly displaced has the effect of superposing a 'grating' of spacing five times the true spacing and gives a 'ghost' whose apparent wavelength is $\lambda/5$.

e. *Biol.* A cell wall or cell membrane, esp. of a red blood corpuscle, that has lost its protoplasmic contents; also, in extended use, a bacteriophage with an empty 'head'.

1890 *Jrnl. Chem. Soc.* LVII. 499 The parenchymatous tissue of the endosperm portions..is completely disintegrated, the cell-walls either entirely disappearing or remaining in a much swollen and altered form as mere 'ghosts'. **1902** *Jrnl. Exper. Med.* VI. 267 Whether this increase of permeability persists when the corpuscles have been reduced to ghosts by the escape of hæmoglobin I am unable to say. **1951** *Jrnl. Bacteriol.* LXI. 753 The ghosts have a host range specificity similar to that of the virus from which they were derived. [*Note*] The word 'ghost' has been used because of its obvious relationship to the red cell ghost produced in a somewhat similar manner. It consists of the deflated head and the tail. **1959** Garen & Kozloff in Burnet & Stanley *Viruses* II. 207 Ghosts of a T1..and a staphylococcal phage have been seen in electron micrographs. **1970** *Nature* 31 Oct. 415/1 At least 50 per cent of the protein in red cell ghosts is present in this form.

f. *Metallurgy.* A faint band on the surface of steel due to the segregation of certain of its constituents.

1905 *Trans. Inst. Naval Archit.* XLVII. II. 369 All [these micrographs], however, showed lines which are technically known as 'ghosts', namely lines of metal high in sulphur and phosphorus. *Ibid.* 380 The well-marked 'ghosts' in the micro-structure. **1945** Greaves & Wrighton *Pract. Microsc. Metallogr.* x. 173 A ghost is due to local segregation of impurities during the solidification of the ingot.

g. *Television.* A displaced repeated image on a television screen caused by a duplicate signal travelling by a longer path.

1927 *Bell Syst. Techn. Jrnl.* VI. 646 When marked fading occurred, the normally clear [television] reproduction was accompanied by 'ghosts' or additional images which faded in and out. **1929** Sheldon & Grisewood *Television* xiii. 143 The 'ghosts' represented energy which had traveled from the transmitter upward to the Heaviside..whence it was reflected to the receiver. **1967** *Guardian* 24 June 1/3 After a rain storm of static and a flutter of television 'ghosts' we were able to recognise LBJ.

h. *Cinemat.* (See quots.)

1940 *Chambers's Techn. Dict.* 375/2 *Ghost*, vertical streaks on high-lights in a projected picture, arising from incorrect phasing of the rotary shutter with respect to the moving film. **1959** W. S. Sharps *Dict. Cinematogr.* 100/1 In film projection, a ghost is an extension above or below the main images on the screen and is caused by faulty synchronization between the shutter and intermittent mechanisms of the projector.

i. A spurious signal on a radar screen that does not correspond to a target at the indicated location.

1945 *Amer. Speech* XX. 309/2 *Ghost*, echoes which do not follow normal characteristics and for which definite targets cannot be found. **1961** D. J. Povejsil et al. *Airborne Radar* vi. 331 In a two-PRF system, two targets would yield four possible range values: two correct ranges and two 'ghosts'. **1969** Barton & Ward *Handbk. Radar Measurement* i. 12 Common examples are ambiguities in range and Doppler measurements..and the ghosts produced by scanning with two fan beams which are oriented at right angles to each other.

12. *Sc.* 'A piece of dead coal, that instead of burning appears in the fire as a white lump' (Jam.).

1824 Miss Ferrier *Inher.* xvii, Mr. R. sat by the side of the expiring fire, seemingly contemplating the gaists and cinders which lay scattered over the hearth.

13. One who secretly does artistic or literary work for another person, the latter taking the credit.

1884 *Pall Mall G.* 23 June 8/2 Plaintiff said he had heard of the expression 'A sculptor's ghost'..a few months ago, and understood it to mean that a person who was supposed to do a work did not do it. **1889** *Ibid.* 12 Jan. 6/1 The only persons who make no secrecy about their ghosts are American millionaires, one of whom in..advertising once for a private secretary stated that the chief duties of the post would be to issue all his invitations and to write all his speeches. **1896** *Daily News* 17 Feb. 6/3 Van Dyck was probably one of his master's 'ghosts'.

14. *attrib.* and *Comb.* (Sense 8 only.) **a.** simple attrib., as ***ghost-apparition***, ***-appurtenance***, ***-ballad***, ***-haunt***, ***-hero***, ***-hour***, ***-house***, ***-land*** (also *attrib.*), ***-lore***, ***-story*** (also *attrib.*), ***-world***. **b.** objective, as ***ghost-fear***, ***-hunter***, ***-lover***, ***-monger***, ***-seer***, ***-service***, ***-worship***; ***ghost-seeing*** vbl. sb. and ppl. adj.; ***ghost-compelling***, ***-fearing*** ppl. adjs. **c.** instrumental, as ***ghost-filled***, ***-haunted***, ***-poisoned***, ***-ridden***, ***-trod*** ppl. adjs. **d.** similative, as ***ghost-dim***, ***-white*** adjs.; ***ghost-wise*** adv.

1829 Carlyle *Misc.* (1857) I. 276 Murders, duels, *ghost-apparitions. *Ibid.* 274 Other *ghost-appurtenances. **1830** Scott *Demonol.* x. 360 Mat Lewis published it with a *ghost ballad which he adjusted on the same theme. **1742** Francis *Horace's Odes* I. xxiv. 27 The *Ghost-compelling God..will not..unbar the Gates of Death. **1850** Mrs. Browning *Poems* II. 298 What angel, but would seem To sensual eyes, *Ghost-dim? **1892** *Proc. Amer. Miss. Assoc.* 62 Superstition ..in the form of *ghost-fears..pervades every community of..the Afro-Americans in the South. **1840** Gen. P. Thompson *Exerc.* (1842) V. 130 Your modern Indian..is no *ghost-fearing wretch. **1627** MAY tr. *Lucan* IX. 42 From thence they saile away To *ghost-fill'd Tænarus. **1845** G. MURRAY *Islaford* 179 The *ghost-haunt of guilt. **1884** *Littell's Living Age* CLXI. 91 He might easily imagine it to be one of those weird, grey, *ghost-haunted castles. **1838** CARLYLE *Misc.* (1857) IV. 142 An impersonal *ghost-hero. *a* **1847** ELIZA COOK *Old Man's Marvel* v, The orb that maketh the *ghost-hour fair. **1844** LADY G. FULLERTON *Ellen Middleton* (1884) 56 The ruins of the old hall, which my maid used to call the '*ghost-house'. **1894** LANG *Cock Lane*, etc. 234 Wodrow, a great *ghost-hunter. **1853** HAWTHORNE *Eng. Note-bks.* (1883) I. 468 *Ghostland lies beyond the jurisdiction of veracity. **1897** MARY KINGSLEY *W. Africa* 555 The rain is too thick for one to see two yards in any direction, and we seem to be in a ghost-land forest. **1893** H. R. HAWEIS in *Fortn. Rev.* Jan. 120 Literature is deeply dyed with *ghost-lore. **1827** HARE *Guesses* Ser. I. (1873) 184 This should be borne in mind by political and philosophical *ghostseers, *ghostlovers, and *ghostmongers. **1880** G. MEREDITH *Trag. Com.* (1881) 67 Hamlet was poisoned—*ghost-poisoned. **1897** *Edin. Rev.* Apr. 451 The one was *ghost-ridden, the other fancy free. **1886** M. GRAY *Silence Dean Maitland* I. x. 272 Dr. Everard, what prescriptions have you for young ladies who take to *ghost-seeing? **1894** *Westm. Gaz.* 5 Sept. 2/1 The great *ghost-seeing age is between twenty and twenty-nine. **1817** SCOTT *Harold* IV. vii, With a *ghost-seer's look when the ghost disappears. **1862** JAS. GRANT *Capt. of Guard* x, Lord abbot, talk to this old ghostseer, and assure him that there can be no such thing in nature as the spectre of a living man. **1819** BYRON *Juan* I. cxxxv. (*MS. reading*), Supper, punch, *ghost-stories, and such chat. **1897** *Westm. Gaz.* 6 July 2/3 The visitor awoke with the true ghost story 'feeling of chilliness' and an impression that there was 'something' in the room. **1870** MORRIS *Earthly Par.* III. IV. 225 Over the empty *ghost-trod way. **1893** KIPLING *Seven Seas* (1896) 61 A sloop-of-war, *ghost-white and very near. **1954** L. MACNEICE *Autumn Sequel* III. 27 Two great swans, ghost-white. **1905** *Daily Chron.* 16 May 4/5 He weeps, *ghost-wise, at the auctioneer's bills in his bedroom. **1924** *Public Opinion* 11 July 48/3 Your nearness gathers ghostwise down the room. *a* **1849** J. C. MANGAN *Poems* (1859) 121 Mine inner sense upwakes to see The *ghost world's clear and wondrous deep. **1891** *Month* LXXIII. 77 The attention that has been given of late years to Animism, or *ghost-worship.

e. Special comb., as **ghost-bird** (*U.S. local*), 'the American yellow-breasted chat (*Icteria virens*)' (Funk); **ghost-candle**, one of a number of candles kept burning round a corpse to scare away ghosts; **ghost-coal** *Sc.* = sense 12; **ghost-dance**, a fanatical observance among the North-American Indians; hence ***ghost-dancer***; **ghost-demon**, a human spirit that has become a demon (see DEMON[1] 1), and is worshipped as such; **ghost-family**, the family of a ghost-marriage; **ghost-form** = *ghost-word*; **ghost-god** = *ghost-demon*; **ghost-gum** *Austral.*, a species of *Eucalyptus* (cf. WHITE-GUM[2]); **ghost image**, applied to various kinds of spurious or false images (see quots. and sense 11); **ghost-light**, ? = CORPSE-CANDLE 2; **ghost line** = sense 11 f; **ghost-marriage** (see quots.); **ghost-moth**, a nocturnal moth (*Hepialus humuli*); **ghost-name** (see *ghost-word*); **ghost-plant**, the tumble-weed (*Amarantus albus*); **ghost-raiser**, one who 'raises a ghost' (see 8 b); **ghost-soul**, in folk-lore, a double or apparition of a person; **ghost-swift** = *ghost-moth*; **ghost town** orig. *U.S.*, a town partially or completely devoid of its inhabitants; **ghost train**, (*a*) (see quot. 1884); (*b*) a train of cars at a fun fair that travels through dark tunnels in which there are ghost-like effects; (*c*) a train run during the night to keep the track clear in periods of heavy snowfall or severe frost; **ghost-word** (see quot. 1886); **ghost writer** orig. *U.S.*, a hack writer who does work for which another person takes the credit (cf. sense 13); hence **ghost-write** *v. trans.* and *intr.* = GHOST *v.* 4; ***ghost-writing*** vbl. sb.; ***ghost-written*** ppl. adj.

1885 E. PEACOCK in *Academy* 26 Sept. 204/2 So we lighted the *ghost-candles round her bed. **1824** MACTAGGART *Gallovid. Dict.*, *Gaistcoal, a coal that when it is burned becomes white. **1890** *Daily News* 25 Nov. 6/3 All the western tribes..are dancing the *Ghost Dance, and looking forward to the coming of the Great Leader. **1890** *Boston* (Mass.) *Jrnl.* 29 Nov. 2/3 The sudden metamorphosis of a great number of the *ghost dancers..into cattle-stealers. **1677** GALE *Crt. Gentiles* III. 105 It was their custome to build Shrines or Temples at such places where the bodies or ashes of their *Ghost-Demons lay entombed. **1871** TYLOR *Prim. Cult.* II. 103 Ancient and modern European tales of baleful ghost-demons. **1951** E. E. EVANS-PRITCHARD *Kinship & Marriage among Nuer* iii. 110 The family that develops out of a ghost-marriage may be called a *ghost-family in acknowledgement of the ghostly status of the pater of the children. It consists of a ghost, his wife, his children born in the union of marriage, and the kinsman who begat these children and acts as father to them. **1933** BLOOMFIELD *Lang.* xxvii. 487 Chaucer's phrase *in derring do that longeth to a knight* 'in daring to do what is proper for a knight', was misunderstood by Spenser, who took *derring-do* to be a compound meaning 'brave actions' and succeeded in introducing this *ghost-form into our elevated language. *a* **1638** MEDE *Wks.* I. xliii. (1672) 242 In Religious graves and sepulchres..they hoped to find their *Ghost-gods. **1954** Y. HILLMAN in *Coast to Coast* 45 It was a good pelt and as white as a *ghost gum. **1954** G. DUTTON *Ibid.* 152 The chalky ghost-gums. **1959** *Listener* 7 May 785/1 On the slopes, and in the valleys too, grow ghost-gums—a species of eucalyptus with drooping, dark-green leaves and smooth sculpted trunks of an exquisite pallor. **1902** *Daily Chron.* 19 June 4/4 'The "Grubs" Collimating Telescope Gun Sight', an optical contrivance arranged so that a vertical or *ghost image is made to appear as if projected upon the object aimed at. **1904** J. MCINTOSH *Photogr. Ref. Bk.* (ed. 2) ii. 43 The ghost image is a reflection of the bright object in front of the camera reflected from the back lens upon the front lens, and finally transmitted to the plate. **1940** *Chambers's Techn. Dict.* 375/2 *Ghost image*, the image arising from a mirror when the rays have experienced reflection within the glass between the surface and the silvering. **1953** L. J. WHEELER *Princ. Cinematography* vi. 185 If the shutter is out of phase with the pull-down a 'ghost image' will be seen on the screen. **1897** *Folk-Lore* Sept. 215 A. F. says that he himself saw what they call a *ghost-light. **1926** *Jrnl. Iron & Steel Inst.* CXIII. 109 When the ascending segregates are impeded by the growing crystals, they tend to elongate and form typical stringlike formations of segregate known as '*ghost lines'. **1951** E. E. EVANS-PRITCHARD *Kinship & Marriage among Nuer* iii. 109 A very common feature of Nuer social life is a union I have called *ghost-marriage. If a man dies without legal male heirs, a kinsman of his..ought to take a wife to his name. **1964** GOULD & KOLB *Dict. Soc. Sci.* 388/1 *Ghost Marriage*, the custom of marrying a girl to the name of a dead brother or other relative. **1831** LOUDON *Encycl. Agric.* (ed. 2) 1116 The *ghost moth (*Hepialus humuli*, F.) deposits its eggs near the roots of the hop plant, upon which the larva or caterpillar feeds, some-times doing them considerable injury. **1896** *Daily News* 3 Jan. 5/2 Grampians is a *ghost-name, derived from a mis-reading of Tacitus's Mons Graupius. **1887** *Science* IX. 32/2 Dr. Newberry has told us that it [*Amarantus albus*] is also known as the '*ghost-plant', in allusion to the same habit, bunches flitting along by night producing a peculiarly weird appearance. **1886** J. K. JEROME *Idle Thoughts* 166 Memory is a rare *ghost raiser. **1908** *Daily Chron.* 30 June 3/1 An efficient new ghost-raiser presents himself. **1871** E. B. TYLOR *Prim. Cult.* I. 451 The notion of a *ghost-soul animating man while in the body. **1924** W. B. SELBIE *Psychol. Relig.* 29 As formulated by Professor Tylor this theory of a quasi-material ghost-soul is to be regarded as the typical and almost universal source of religious ideas and practices. **1869** E. NEWMAN *Brit. Moths* 20 The *Ghost Swift (Male) (*Hepialus humuli*)..So called from the white colour of the male. [**1875** *Cincinnati Enquirer* 2 July 5/1 The deserted mining towns, like the ghosts of their departed prosperity.] **1931** G. F. WILLISON *Here they dug Gold* 71 Today all lie *ghost towns smelling of the long slow processes of ruin and decay. **1944** F. CLUNE *Red Heart* 6 Then Broken Hill will be a Ghost Town..like White Cliffs which once boomed on opals. **1952** H. INNES *Campbell's Kingdom* I. iii. 51 Come Lucky was a rotten clutter of empty shacks. It was my first sight of a ghost town. **1967** *Times* 18 July 1/3 Qantara, after the Middle East war, has been turned into a ghost town, as not more than 1,000 of its 8,000 people remain. **1884** *Q. Rev.* July 94 On some lines, freight trains are frequently run of which no account is given, the profits going to the officials and the *employés*. They are technically known as '*ghost trains'. [**1925** A. RIDLEY (*title of play*) The Ghost Train.] **1936** AUDEN & ISHERWOOD *Ascent of F6* II. iii. 100 The *Ghost Train and the switchback did not always disappoint. **1958** A. SILLITOE *Sat. Night* xi. 157 Winnie clamoured for the Ghost Train. **1968** *Daily Express* 10 Jan. 1 (*headline*) Ghost trains fight big freeze. **1886** SKEAT in *Trans. Philol. Soc.* (1885–7) II. 350–1 Report upon '*Ghost-words', or Words which have no real Existence..We should jealously guard against all chances of giving any undeserved record of words which had never any real existence, being mere coinages due to the blunders of printers or scribes, or to the perfervid imaginations of ignorant or blundering editors. **1888** —— in *N. & Q.* 7th Ser. V. 504/1 The word meant is *estures*, bad spelling of *estres*; and *eftures* is a ghost-word. **1927** *Editor & Publisher* 18 June 9/1 When he isn't *ghost-writing [he] is a member of the European staff of the New York Times. **1932** *New Republic* 10 Feb. 347 The autobiographical boloney ghost-written by Samuel Crowther for Ford. **1938** J. HILTON *To you, Mr. Chips* i. 37 The kind..whose autobiography, written or ghost-written, exudes the main idea that 'school made him what he was'. **1951** WODEHOUSE *Old Reliable* iii. 40 I'm ghostwriting the story of her life. **1956** AUDEN *Making, Knowing & Judging* 9 And end up by ghost-writing poems for him which he was too busy to start or finish. **1927** *Lit. Digest* 30 July 27 A *ghost-writer may do all the work. **1928** J. P. MCEVOY *Show Girl* 77, I told you I was one of them there ghost writers doing my bit for belle lettres. **1964** G. A. WILLIAMSON *World of Josephus* xvii. 261 Ghost writers are always with us. **1927** *Editor & Publisher* 18 June 9/1 *Ghost-writing originated very naturally in the field of sports. **1964** M. MCLUHAN *Understanding Media* II. xxi. 212 Modern ghost-writing, teletype, and wire services create an insubstantial world of 'pseudo-events'.

Hence **'ghostdom**, the region or domain of ghosts; **'ghostified** *ppl. a.* [see -FY], having the aspect of being haunted by ghosts; **'ghostite** [-ITE], one who believes in ghosts; **'ghostlet** [-LET], a little ghost.

1855 SMEDLEY *H. Coverdale* v. 29 A dark archway..which ..looked jolly queer and ghostified. **1882** *Pall Mall G.* 24 Oct. 2 Here, sir, is an offer for the ghostites. **1890** *Nature* 20 Feb. 376 Their tiny fleets of medusa-buds, watery ghost-lets, flitting away. **1892** *Pall Mall G.* 23 July 3/1 More Glimpses of Ghostdom. **1893** J. SKINNER *Autobiog. Metaphysician* xxix. 144 His belief in and familiarity with supernatural appearances, particularly imps and ghostlets.

ghost (gəʊst), *v.* [f. prec. sb.]

†**1.** *intr.* **a.** To give up the ghost, expire.

a **1586** SIDNEY (J.), Euryalus taking leave of Lucretia, precipitated her into such a love-fit, that within a few hours she ghosted. **1689** G. HARVEY *Curing Dis. by Expect.* vii. 51 A day or two after..the Lad having been miserably tortured, Ghosted.

2. a. *trans.* To haunt as an apparition.

1606 SHAKS. *Ant. & Cl.* II. vi. 13 Iulius Cæsar Who at Philippi the good Brutus ghosted. **1621** BURTON *Anat. Mel.* Democr. to Rdr. 19 Aske not with him in the Poet..what madnesse ghostes this old man, but what madnesse ghostes vs all? **1879** H. N. HUDSON *Hamlet* 10 The being thus ghosted was held to be no such trifling matter as we are apt to consider it.

b. To scare with pretended apparitions.

1813 E. S. BARRETT *Heroine* (1815) III. 196 'Can he be ghosting her all this time?' said Betterton. [Cf. quot. under GHOSTING *vbl. sb.*]

3. a. *intr.* To flit about, prowl as a ghost. Also ***to ghost it***. ***to ghost away***: to steal away like a ghost.

1833 *Fraser's Mag.* VIII. 577 Doomed to wither..and, after ghosting it about for an hour..be buried. **1880** *Antrim & Down Gloss.*, *Ghost*, to haunt a person or place for the purpose of importuning for money or anything else.

b. Of a sailing vessel: to make relatively good progress when there is very little wind.

1891 *Field* 26 Dec. 967/2 On the second day..the Dragon again ghosted away from the trio. **1921** *Glasgow Herald* 6 July 8 The Lady Anne's remarkable facility for what is known as ghosting was undoubtedly the means of falsifying all forecasts of the issues. **1926** D. BYRNE *Brother Saul* xvii. 450 Every inch of sail was set as they ghosted along. **1954** W. G. ARNOTT *Orwell Estuary* i. 1 We ghosted into the harbour in the gloom of an autumn evening. **1962** A. G. COURSE *Dict. Naut. Terms* 87 The British clippers, such as the *Cutty Sark*, were the best ever at ghosting. **1971** E. FENWICK *Impeccable People* iv. 24 They took an evening sail down the coast..and came ghosting back near shore in the quiet dark.

4. *trans.* and *intr.* To write (something) as a ghost-writer; to act as a 'ghost' (see GHOST *sb.* 13).

1922 *Glasgow Herald* 11 Oct. 3 'A certain general' for whom he did some 'ghosting'. **1925** T. E. LAWRENCE *Let.* 21 Apr. (1938) 474 A very distinguished person's wife once asked me if I would care to edit or 'ghost', her husband's diary. **1932** *Times Lit. Suppl.* 1 Sept. 609/1 The articles which he 'ghosted' for Jerry Turnbull, a millionaire with literary ambitions. **1954** KOESTLER *Invis. Writing* 338, I enjoyed fussing over her, ghosting her dispatches. **1959** M. CUMBERLAND *Murmurs in Rue Morgue* viii. 57 A man of talent who has failed—to the point where he is ready to ghost for a man like Galotin.

Hence **'ghosted** *ppl. a.*, that has become a ghost, deceased, departed; **'ghosting**, *vbl. sb.*

1813 E. S. BARRETT *Heroine* (1815) III. 183 The Baron Hildebrand..had adopted the ghosting system (so common in romances) to frighten me into his schemes. **1834** AIRD *Churchyard Eclogue* 149 Rise, my ghosted love, and testify Against the harsh decree that such must die.

ghoster ('gəʊstə(r)). *Naut.* [f. GHOST *v.* 3 b + -ER[1].] (See quots.)

1956 E. C. HISCOCK *Around World in Wanderer III* ii. 20 Such is the property of really light large sails, the ghoster gave us steerage way. *Ibid.* 267 *Ghoster*, a sail similar to a genoa but made of very light material for use in light airs. **1962** *Guardian* 28 June 5, I had my 'ghoster' (large Genoa rig) set this afternoon.

ghostess ('gəʊstɪs). *nonce-wd.* [f GHOST *sb.* + -ESS.] A female ghost.

1842 BARHAM *Ingol. Leg.*, *Old Wom. in Grey*, That she, The said Ghostess, or Ghost, as the matter may be, From 'impediment', 'hindrance', and 'let' shall be free, To sleep in her grave.' **1896** *Westm. Gaz.* 29 Feb. 8/1 Ever the fair child-hostess Heaved a sepulchral sigh—Sighed like a care-worn ghostess!

ghosthood ('gəʊsthʊd). [f. GHOST *sb.* + -HOOD.] The state of being a ghost. Also *attrib.*

1889 *Daily News* 12 Dec. 5/3 It is difficult for a ghost to become a man, because it has fallen to ghosthood, and because it has lost manhood. **1890** B. L. GILDERSLEEVE *Ess. & Stud.* 416 From my childhood up, as in ghosthood now, I've felt an invincible horror of spiders.

attrib. **1884** *Sat. Rev.* 22 Nov. 651/1 How long are we to wait for Ghosthood Suffrage and Haunted Electoral Districts?

ghostiness ('gəʊstɪnɪs). [f. GHOSTY *a.* + -NESS.] The quality or state of being ghosty.

1895 G. MACDONALD *Lilith* xi. 69 What a night I found it! How shall I make my reader share with me its wild ghostiness? **1904** *Westm. Gaz.* 1 Jan. 2/2 The ghostiness of these faded, frail old men gliding and whispering about in the old house.

ghostish, *a.* [f. GHOST *sb.* + -ISH.] Somewhat like a ghost. Hence †**'ghostishly** *adv.*, in a ghostish manner.

c **1580** J. JEFFERE *Bugbears* IV. ii. in *Archiv Stud. Neu Spr.* (1897) XCVIII, Did you marke, Amedeus, how gostishly the[i] dyd dawnse. **1911** D. H. LAWRENCE *White Peacock* II. iii. 245 It's rather ghostish to have the road suddenly smudged out. *Ibid.* vi. 306 You do see yourself a bit ghostish.

'ghostism. *rare.* [f. GHOST *sb.* + -ISM.] Ghostly characteristics.

1782 MRS. E. BLOWER *G. Bateman* II. 55 Something so contrary to all their ideas of ghostism. **1798** ANNA SEWARD *Lett.* (1811) V. 176 The bell tolling over the heath, is still a fine, though somewhat hacknied, accompaniment to ghostism.

ghostless ('gəʊstlɪs), *a.* [f. GHOST *sb.* + -LESS.] †**a.** Devoid of spirit or life; without strength or virtue (*obs.*). **b.** ? Void of belief in ghosts (*rare*).

a **1000** *Elene* 874 (Gr.) Meniʒo cwom folc unlytel and ʒefærenne man brohton on bære..ʒingne, gastleasne. *a* **1603** T. CARTWRIGHT *Confut. Rhem. N.T.* (1618) 219 A Ghostly Father is hard to finde amongst you, where Priests can for the most part do nothing but giue the visited a little ghostlesse oyle. *a* **1634** R. CLERKE *Serm.* (1637) 473 Workes are the breath of Faith..they are the pulse of Faith..If you feele them not, the Faith is ghostlesse. **1651** N. BACON *Disc. Govt. Eng.* II. xxxiii. (1739) 151 But let the Laws be never so severe, if they have not free liberty to walk at large, they are soon ghostless. *a* **1849** J. C. MANGAN *Poems* (1859) 287 To warn and wake a ghostless, godless age.

ghostlike ('gəʊstlaɪk), *a.* and *adv.* [f. GHOST *sb.* + -LIKE.]

A. *adj.* Resembling a ghost or its qualities; like a place haunted by ghosts.

1611 COTGR., *Havé*, . . also, dreadfull, wild-looking, ghastlie, ghost-like. **1637** NABBES *Hannibal & Scipio*, Their Ghost to Auth. A 3 Thy thinne cheeke, hollow eye, And ghostlike colour. **1639** FULLER *Holy War* II. ix. (1647) 56 The ghost-like ghastliness of their famished faces. **1835** WILLIS *Melanie* 291 Her majestic trees stand ghostlike in the Cæsars' home. **1877** A. B. EDWARDS *Up Nile* xiii. 382 The four colossi came out, ghostlike, vague, and shadowy, in the enchanted moonlight. **1884** Q. VICTORIA *More Leaves* 80 It looks very ghostlike, and reminds me a little of Holyrood Chapel.

B. *adv.* In the manner of a ghost.

1859 TENNYSON *Guinevere* 600 Himself became as mist Before her, moving ghostlike to his doom. **1873** MISS BRADDON *L. Davoren* Prol. ii, The brief days flit by ghostlike.

ghostliness ('gəʊstlɪnɪs). [f. GHOSTLY *a.* + -NESS.] The quality or state of being ghostly.

1. †**a.** Spirituality, spiritual-mindedness; in early use quasi-*concr.* Spiritual matters (*obs.*). **b.** *nonce-use.* The condition or quality of being a 'ghostly' or ecclesiastical person. *arch.*

a **1300** *Cursor M.* 6449 To þaa [*sc.* wranges] þat gret birþin bar, Namli þat fel to gastli-nes, Suld vissed be thoru moyses. *c* **1440** HYLTON *Scala Perf.* (W. de W. 1494) II. iv, Other chaungyng felyst þou none fro flesshlynes into ghostlines. **1526** *Pilgr. Perf.* (W. de W. 1531) 1 b, Shall be ryght delectable & pleasaunt, specially to all them that loueth goostlynes. **1799–1805** WORDSW. *Prelude* VI. 428 That frame of social being, which so long Had bodied forth the ghostliness of things In silence visible and perpetual calm. **1893** J. BALDW. BROWN *Stoics & Saints* v. 122 This intrusion of a ghostly man of an inferior order of ghostliness, would cause some soreness in the monastery.

2. The quality or condition of being a ghost, of resembling a ghost or its qualities, also, of being filled with ghosts.

1853 KANE *Grinnell Exp.* xxxi. (1856) 266 One of them . . told me, with an utter unconsciousness of his own ghostliness, that I was the palest of the party. **1871** TYLOR *Prim. Cult.* II. 72 There are conceptions of an abode of the dead characterised not so much by dreaminess as by ghostliness. **1883** *Harper's Mag.* June 131/1 Here among these hills with all their ghostliness she would haunt me. **1896** JESSOPP *Frivola* x. 164 Think of the accumulation of facilities for ghostliness here.

ghostly ('gəʊstlɪ), *a.* Forms: see GHOST and -LY^1. [OE. *gástlic*, f. *gást* GHOST + *-lic*, -LY^1.]

1. Pertaining to the spirit or soul; spiritual. Opposed to *bodily* or *fleshly*; occas. to *natural*. Now purely *literary* and *arch.*

c **1000** ÆLFRIC *Hom.* II. 588 He [Crist] is se grundweall þære gastlican cyrcan. *c* **1050** *Byrhtferth's Handboc* in *Anglia* VIII. 303 Heræfter we moton us ȝeȝearwian mid gastlicum wæpnum. *c* **1175** *Lamb. Hom.* 105 Ure wununge is on heuene, þider we sculen hihȝen of þissere erfeðnesse mid gastlichere blisse. *a* **1225** *Ancr. R.* Pref. 23 Fleschliche fondunges. And gastliche baðe. **1303** R. BRUNNE *Handl. Synne* 1534 Also ys slagheter gostly To vse to speke vyleyny. *c* **1380** WYCLIF *Wks.* (1880) 49 Gostely matrimonye bitwixi Crist and Cristen mennus soulis. *c* **1430** LYDG. *Min. Poems* (Percy Soc.) 7 Thes thre ladyes . . Three gostly giftes . . Unto the kyng . . did present. **1549** LATIMER *Ploughers* (Arb.) 25 So doeth the souls pyne a way for default of gostly meate. **1649** JER. TAYLOR *Gt. Exemp.* II. Ep. Ded., I shall beg of God that your honour may receive . . Ghostly Strength in the reading this booke. **1820** SCOTT *Ivanhoe* xxv, Qualified to administer both worldly and ghostly comfort. **1844** LINGARD *Anglo-Sax. Ch.* (1858) II. xiii. 286 It may have a literal, but it has also a 'ghostly', a spiritual signification. **1865** MOZLEY *Mirac.* iii. 60 A miracle . . has a ghostly force and import which nature has not. **1877** TYNDALL *Fragm. Sci.* (1879) II. xiv. 362 How many disorders, ghostly and bodily, are transmitted to us by inheritance?

b. (With mixture of sense 4.) (*Our*, etc.) ***ghostly enemy***, †***foe***: the Devil.

1447, 1526 [see ENEMY *sb.* 1 b]. **1526** SKELTON *Magnyf.* 2357 Remedy principall Agaynst all sautes of your goostly foo. **1603** *Catechism* in *Prayer-bk.* N 7 That hee will keepe vs . . from our ghostly enemy.

c. (With mixture of sense 3.) ***ghostly father***: a father confessor. So ***ghostly adviser***, ***director***, etc.; also ***ghostly comfort***, ***counsel***, etc., used *esp.* with reference to what is rendered by a priest to a penitent or one near death.

a **1225** *Ancr. R.* 178 Gostlich cumfort. *c* **1290** *Becket* 1015 in *S. Eng. Leg.* I. 135 'Sire', he seide, 'ore gostliche fader þov were here-bi-fore'. **1387** TREVISA *Higden* (Rolls) VI. 457 His goostly fader Donstan. **1536** R. BEERLEY in *Four C. Eng. Lett.* 34 Wych no man may know but my gostly fader. **1552** *Prayer Bk.*, *Communion* (Whytchurche) N iij b, That he may receiue such gostly counsail, aduise and comfort, as hys conscience maye be releued. **1592** SHAKS. *Rom. & Jul.* III. iii. 49 A Ghostly Confessor. **1651** C. CARTWRIGHT *Cert. Relig.* I. 63 We ought to confesse our sinnes unto our Ghostly Father. **1712** ARBUTHNOT *John Bull* Pref., When thou gavest ghostly Counsel to dying Felons. **1748** RICHARDSON *Clarissa* (1811) VIII. lxxix. 380 He had refused ghostly attendance. **1798** FERRIAR *Illustr. Sterne* v. 155 Her ghostly directors thought it very edifying to punish her contumacy, by refusing her the Sacrament. **1839–40** W. IRVING *Wolfert's R.* (1855) 129 A ghostly instructor was soon found, ready to accomplish his conversion in the shortest possible time. **1871** G. MEREDITH *H. Richmond* xxiv. (1889) 215 We shall not be the worse for a ghostly adviser at hand.

†**2.** Of persons and their actions: Spiritual, devout, religious. *Obs.*

a **1340** HAMPOLE *Psalter* cxxxvi. 9 All fleschly men are enemys til gostly. *c* **1450** *St. Cuthbert* (Surtees) 999 For to lyue slike gastely lyfe. **1481** CAXTON *Reynard* (Arb.) 48 Ye be of good condicions, and goostly of your lyuyng. **1483** —— *Gold. Leg.* 60 a/2 Therfore we ought . . to cesse of the werkes of synne & tendende to doo ghoostly werkes.

3. Concerned with sacred things, or with the church; belonging to an ecclesiastical order or to a member of such an order; *spiritual* as opposed to *lay*, *secular*, or *temporal*. *arch.* Also †***ghostly day***: a day set apart for worship.

c **900** tr. *Bæda's Hist.* I. xvi. [xxvii.] (1890) 84 þæt hwæðre on oðre wisan þæt gastlice folc is onȝeotonde under þam ilcan ondȝete, þe we forespreceende wæron. *c* **1175** *Lamb. Hom.* 11 þet we maȝen on þisse gastliche daȝen ibeten ure sunne. *a* **1300** *Cursor M.* 27837 O couaitise . . cums . . symoni, als gastli thing to selle or byi. **1390** GOWER *Conf.* I. 17 Their gostly staf is then awey, Wherof they shulde her flock defende. **1530** *Proper Dyaloge* (Arb.) 141 Refusynge any labour to do Because they are people gostely. **1597** HOOKER *Eccl. Pol.* v. lxii. § 13 To settle our hearts in the loue of our ghostly Superiors. **1632** LITHGOW *Trav.* x. 429 A ghostly Wife [a Bishop's wife], shall be still Madam Lady with me. **1651** HOBBES *Leviath.* II. xxix. 171 And set up . . a Ghostly Authority against the Civill. **1835** I. TAYLOR *Spir. Despot.* iii. 93 [The Hebrew religion] afforded fewer means of sustaining ghostly power than perhaps any other system ancient or modern. **1858** HAWTHORNE *Fr. & It. Jrnls.* (1872) I. 14 Snatching with ghostly hands at sceptres. **1859** TENNYSON *Elaine* 1094 Father . . bid call the ghostly man Hither, and let me shrive me clean, and die. **1868** FREEMAN *Norm. Conq.* (1876) II. ix. 405 He laid aside his chrism and his rood, his ghostly weapons.

†**4.** Of the nature of a spirit, incorporeal. *Obs.*

c **1440** *Boctus* (Laud MS. 559) lf. 8 O god of gostely substaunce is. **1674** N. FAIRFAX *Bulk & Selv.* 28 That ghostly being which enlivens the body of man.

5. Of or pertaining to, or issuing from, a ghost, disembodied spirit, or spectre; resembling a ghost, spectral, shadowy; occas., haunted by ghosts.

c **1000** *Gosp. Nicodemus* xxvii, Gastlic hream. *a* **1300** *Cursor M.* 18076 A gastli uoice criand ful fast. ? *a* **1600** *Dunbar's Flyting w. Kennedie* 175 (MS. Reidpeth) Thy ghaistly luke fleys folkis that pas the by. **1730–46** THOMSON *Autumn* 494 The retreating horn Calls them to ghostly halls. **1829** POLLOK *Course T.* VII, Thy ghostly shape, O Death, Stood in his avenues of fairest hope. **1839** DE QUINCEY *Recoll. Lakes* Wks. 1862 II. 28 Duties so suddenly revealed amidst terrors ghostly as well as earthly. **1844** LD. BROUGHHAM *Brit. Const.* xv. (1862) 237 This ghostly body (commonly called Barebones' Parliament). **1850** LYNCH *Theo. Trin.* xi. 212 His visage and form were ghostly. **1864** SKEAT *Uhland's Poems* 179 The ghostly voices in silence died. **1865** KINGSLEY *Herew.* xix, Martin chuckled a ghostly laugh as he [etc.]. **1871** B. TAYLOR *Faust* (1875) II. II. iii. 104 Ghostly 'tis in vale and hollow, Spectral all that we discover. **1873** LONGF. *Wayside Inn* III. Interl. i, Forbear to-night your ghostly legends. **1884** TENNYSON *Becket* III. ii, How ghostly sounds that horn in the black wood! **1887** RUSKIN *Præterita* II. 156 Ghostly ranges of incredible mountains.

Hence **'ghostlify** *v.* [-FY], to render ghostly; †**ghostlihead** [-HEAD], spirituality; in quot. quasi-*concr.*, spiritual things; **'ghostlily** *adv.* [-LY^2], in a ghostly manner.

c **1440** *Jacob's Well* (E.E.T.S.) 282 He louyth no gostly-hede, he desyreth no swetnesse of heuenly thynges. **1841** *Tait's Mag.* VIII. 7 Think of finding yourselves ghostlified in surplices. **1857** NEALE *Theod. Phranza* (1879) 58 The wind sang more mournfully; the oaks whispered more ghostlily.

ghostly ('gəʊstlɪ), *adv.* Now *rare.* [OE. *gástlíce*, f. *gást* GHOST *sb.* + *-líce*, -LY^2.] † In a ghostly or spiritual manner or sense; opp. to *bodily* or *carnally*; in spirit, as a spirit. *Obs.* In mod. use *rarely*: As a ghost.

c **1000** ÆLFRIC *Hom.* I. 34 þæt haliȝe husel is gastlice Cristes lichama. *c* **1175** *Lamb. Hom.* 7 þa wise witega þe beoð nu ouer þe halie chirche and libbed gastliche heore lif. *c* **1200** ORMIN 985 Hu Cristess þeoww birrþ lakenn Crist Gastlike i gode þæwess. *a* **1300** *Cursor M.* 25054 þat we gastli wit him ded suld be. **1357** *Lay Folks Catech.* 455 Dedli synnes . . gastely sla ilk mannes saule. *c* **1400** MAUNDEV. (1839) xii. 136 The Jewes . . undirstonde not the Lettre gostly, but bodyly. *c* **1449** PECOCK *Repr.* v. xv. 561 Ech man schal fare weel goostli oonli bi hise owne gode deedis. **1508** FISHER 7 *Penit. Ps.* Prol., The gloryous Trynyte . . preserue ghostly and bodyly my foresayd lady. **1548** UDALL, etc. *Erasm. Par. Mark* vi. 43 We maye lyue ghostlie in heauen. **1548** LATIMER *Ploughers* (Arb.) 25 So muste we haue also the other for the satisfaction of the soule, or elles we canne not lyue longe gostly. **1619** DONNE *Serm.* xiv. 139 The Sword of the Lord . . cuts bodily and it cuts ghostly. **1642** ROGERS *Naaman* 438 Of Naaman both bodily and ghostly. **1827** POLLOK *Course T.* III, Meagre all, and ghostly thin.

ghostology (gəʊ'stɒlədʒɪ). [badly f. GHOST *sb.* + -(O)LOGY.] Ghost-lore.

1824 J. MCCULLOCH *Scotland* II. 222 The mere ghostology being of a neutral character might escape all dangerous criticism. **1853** *Tait's Mag.* XX. 417 Clairvoyants, rappists, connoisseurs in ghostology, and such-like mystery-mongers. **1864** HAWTHORNE *S. Felton* (1883) 294 More unaccountable than if it had been a thing of ghostology and witchcraft. **1869** *Contemp. Rev.* X. 295 There are Mormonisms and spirit-rappings and ghostologies without end.

ghostship ('gəʊstʃɪp). [f. GHOST *sb.* + -SHIP.] The condition or quality of being a ghost. Also *humorously*, the personality of a ghost.

1826 J. WILSON in *Blackw. Mag.* XX. 107, I became somewhat too much hand-in-glove with his ghostship. **1830** MISS MITFORD *Village* Ser. IV. (1863) 297 Neither Kate nor her father or mother had ever seen the spectre, although such near neighbours to his ghostship. **1855** MISS YONGE *Lances of Lynwood* viii. (1864) 117 You believed in our ghostship as fully as any of them. **1891** *Daily News* 10 Aug. 4/7 First the worship of the ancestral ghost, simply as a ghost; next the development of his ghostship into godship.

ghosty ('gəʊstɪ), *a. jocular.* [f. GHOST *sb.* + -Y^1.] Concerned with ghosts; resembling a ghost.

1866 *Examiner* 8 Dec. 774 Mr. Dickens tells a good ghosty story of the Signal Man. **1880** MISS BROUGHTON *Sec. Th.* II. III. viii. 244 Lucent pebbles underfoot, a ghosty moon overhead.

Hence **'ghostily** *adv.*, in a ghost-like manner.

a **1849** BEDDOES *Song on Water* i, Night's dumbness breaks, rolling Ghostily. **1871** G. MACDONALD *Wks. Fancy & Imag.* III. 43 The thin-voiced firs are calling Ghostily.

ghoul (gu:l). Also 8–9 goul(e, 9 gho(o)l, gho(u)le, g(h)owl. [a. Arab. *ghūl*, from a verbal root meaning 'to seize'.] An evil spirit supposed (in Mohammedan countries) to rob graves and prey on human corpses.

1786 tr. *Beckford's Vathek* (1868) 71 All the stories of malignant Dives and dismal Goules thronged into her memory. **1817** MOORE *Lalla R.*, *Veiled Proph.* 114 No church-yard Ghole, caught lingering in the light Of the bless'd sun. **1870** LOWELL *Among my Bks.* Ser. I. (1873) 84 It sucks with the vampire, gorges with the ghoule.

transf. and *fig.* **1812** SOUTHEY in *Q. Rev.* VII. 53 These human ghowls were not content . . to let their friends die a natural death before they ate them. **1824** W. IRVING *T. Trav.* I. 73 He was, in a manner, a literary goul, feeding in the charnel-house of decayed literature. **1831** CARLYLE *Sart. Res.* (1858) 180 Two immeasurable Phantoms, Hypocrisy and Atheism, with the Gowl, Sensuality, stalk abroad over the Earth. **1841** LANE *Arab. Nts.* I. 36 The term 'Ghool' is applied to any cannibal. **1855** THACKERAY *Newcomes* I. 312 Ghouls feasting on the fresh corpse of a reputation. **1885** MISS BRADDON *Wyllard's Weird* I. iii. 95 What ghouls people must be to gloat over such a subject.

b. *attrib.* and *Comb.*, as ***ghoul-eye***, ***-head***; ***ghoul-haunted***, ***-like*** adjs.

1844 DISRAELI *Coningsby* VIII. vi, Her natural pallor aggravated into a ghoul-like tint. *a* **1849** POE *Poems*, *Ulalume*, In the ghoul-haunted woodland of Weir. **1858** G. MACDONALD *Phantastes* vi. (1878) 104 His ghoul-eyes and his ghastly face fascinated me. **1884** J. PAYNE *Tales fr. Arabic* II. 280 She . . told him . . that which had betided her with the Ghoul-head, whenas it appeared to her in the garden. **1896** *Westm. Gaz.* 26 May 8/1 The typhoid statistics of the Brisbane Hospital show a remarkable triumph of pioneering work in what the *Sydney Herald* calls the 'ghoul-haunted swamps of medical conservatism'.

ghoulish ('gu:lɪʃ), *a.* [f. GHOUL *sb.* + -ISH.] Of the nature of, resembling, or characteristic of ghouls.

a **1845** HOOD *Open Quest.* vi, The spirit of the place . . Turns fell hyæna of the ghoulish race? **1875** MISS BRADDON *Str. World* I. ix. 150 They had done nothing but talk about the murder all the morning with a ghoulish gusto.

Comb. **1881** BLACK *Sunrise* III. vii. 99 These dusky shadows lent something ghoulish-looking to his head, and face, and sparkling black eyes.

Hence **'ghoulishly** *adv.*, in a ghoulish manner.

1844 *Blackw. Mag.* LV. 550 The difference is nearly as great as between Lady Amine eating rice with a bodkin, and the same fair one battening ghoulishly upon the cold meat in the cemetery. **1890** *Voice* (N.Y.) 20 Feb., It ghoulishly dug up some of George's [Washington's] personal weaknesses.

'ghoulishness. [-NESS.] Ghoulish nature or quality.

1910 H. WALKER *Lit. Victorian Era* II. vii. 505 Her poetry altogether escapes the taint of ghoulishness. **1928** *Weekly Dispatch* 24 June 12/4 What is there in poor human nature . . that creates this ghoulishness? **1954** *New Yorker* 15 May 92 One of the best-known facts about him . . has gained currency simply by virtue of its ghoulishness.

'ghoulism. [-ISM.] Ghoulish characteristics or quality.

1959 I. & P. OPIE *Lore & Lang. Schoolch.* ii. 32 *Ghoulism.* When children are about ten years old they enter a period in which the outward material facts about death seem extraordinarily funny. **1959** *20th Cent.* Dec. 426 In ghoulism the necrophiliac traffic is one way, as it were.

ghuest, obs. form of GUEST.

ghur(r)ial, ghuryal, varr. GAVIAL.

ghurry ('gɜ:rɪ). *Anglo-Indian.* Also 7 gree, 8 gurry, -ie, 9 garri, ghur(r)ie, -ee. [a. Hindi *gharī* a water-clock consisting of a perforated floating cup which fills and sinks in a fixed time, usually 24 minutes.]

1. A space of time: **a.** In old Hindoo custom, 24 minutes, the 60th part of a day of 24 hours; **b.** In Anglo-Indian usage, an hour.

1638 W. BRUTON *Newes fr. E. Ind.* 12 This stroak or parcell of time they call a Goome, the small pot being full they call a Gree, 8 Grees maketh a Par, which Par is three houres by our accompt. **1776** *Trial J. Fowke* I. 3/2 About two gurries afterwards, the said Gentleman, the Maha Rajah, &c. came out and got into their palanquins. **1803** in Gurw. *Wellington's Desp.* (1844) I. 585 If you are resolved on having an audience, come tomorrow, when only two ghurees of the day shall remain. **1832** G. A. HERKLOTS tr. *Cust. Moosulmans India* 37 *note*, When two ghurrees of the night are still wanting.

2. A metal plate on which the hours are struck.

1816 'QUIZ' *Grand Master* VII. 194 The bramin, when the ghurry's sound Told one, was with the idol found. **1879**

Low *Afghan War* ii. 177 Not a sound was heard in camp, save the ghurries striking the hours.

b. 'A clock or other time-piece' (*Cent. Dict.*).

ghyll: see GILL *sb.*²

G.I. ('dʒi:aɪ). (Stress variable.) **1.** Abbrev. of *galvanized iron*, used chiefly in ***G.I. can***: (*a*) *slang*, a German artillery shell; (*b*) a galvanized-iron can; a rubbish-bin.

1928 *Papers Mich. Acad. Sci. & Arts* X. 294 *G.I. cans*, German heavy shells, so called because of their similarity to the galvanized cans found around hospitals. **1929** F. A. Pottle *Stretchers* (1930) 38 An army 'G.I. can' is identical with a civilian ash can. **1930** *Amer. Speech* V. 381 *G.I. can*, a German shell. *Ibid.* 384 *G.I. can or boiler*, galvanized iron utensil made for army cooking. **1951** *Word Study* May 8/1 Navy men of World War II will recall that on every ship and station big garbage cans were invariably referred to as G.I. cans.

2. Abbrev. of *government* (or *general*) *issue*.

a. Used *attrib.* of equipment designed or provided for members of the armed forces of the U.S. and hence applied to things belonging to or associated with American servicemen; ***G.I. bride***, a foreign woman married by an American serviceman while he is on duty abroad; ***G.I. Joe***, an American soldier.

1936 *Amer. Speech* XI. 51 *G.I.* soap is government issue soap. **1940** *Ibid.* XV. 211/1 The boys are equipped with *Government Issue* materials—abbreviated to *G.I.* These include *G.I. shoes* and *clothes*, *G.I. trucks* and, if necessary, *G.I. pills*. *Ibid.*, An official camp dance is a *G.I. stomp*. **1942** E. Colby *Army Talk* 92 The girls whom kindly chaperones bring to an army dance..they call..'G.I. girls', and the dance a 'G.I. Hop'. The soldier calls peace-time maneuvers as 'G.I. War' and a close military haircut a 'G.I. haircut'. **1842** D. Breger in *Yank* 17 June 24 (*strip-cartoon title*) G.I. Joe. **1945** *News Chron.* 17 May 2 Four G.I. Joes calmly playing dice. **1945** *Evening Standard* 20 Dec. 3/2 (*headline*) Ships soon to take G.I. brides. **1947** Auden *Age of Anxiety* (1948) i. 26 Bringing to all John Doakes and G.I. Joes tidings of great joy. **1956** A. H. Compton *Atomic Quest* v. 337 The eagerness with which young men who had served in World War II accepted the educational opportunities offered by the GI Bill of Rights was not surprising. **1961** *Guardian* 18 May 8/3 A group of GI brides was asking Tracy for his autograph.

b. As *sb.* An enlisted member of a U.S. armed force.

1943 *Time* 15 Nov. 11, I am surprised that you ask for 'a name for soldiers who also serve—behind the front'... That term, of course, is 'G.I.' **1944** *Spectator* 5 May 400/2 Relations between British other ranks and their equivalents, the American G.I., notoriously vary. **1945** *Manch. Guardian* 8 Aug. 3 The appearance of American soldiers in uniform, 'G.I.'s' or officers, as 'guest' book-sellers in British bookshops. **1957** J. Braine *Room at Top* vi. 55 The G.I. who drove the jeep he crashed into.

‖**giallo antico** ('dʒallo an'tiko). Also 8-9 in semi-anglicized form **giall(o antique**. [It., lit. 'ancient yellow'.] A rich yellow marble found among ruins in Italy, and employed as a decoration; identified by some with the *marmor Numidicum* of the ancients. Also *attrib.* or *adj.*

1741 Lady Pomfret *Lett.* (1805) II. 310 Pillars and pilasters of giallo antique. **1771** H. Walpole *Lett.* (1857) V. 290 He..inhabits that most sumptuous of all palaces at Rome with door-cases *giallo antico*. **1773** Brydone *Sicily* xxxvii. (1809) 354 Marbles..little inferior to the giall and verd antique. **1789** Mrs. Piozzi *Journ. France* II. 130 The granites, in giall antique, have an undescribable effect. **1850** Mrs. Jameson *Leg. Monast. Ord.* (1863) 445 He lies on a couch of *giallo-antico*. **1859** J. C. Hobhouse *Italy* II. 108 One of the giallo-antico columns.

‖**giallolino** (dʒallo'lino). ? *Obs.* Also 8 **gialolina**. [It. *giallolino* (Florio), now by dissimilation *giallorino*, dim. of *giallo* yellow.] A fine yellow pigment (see quots.).

1728 Woodward *Meth. Foss.* 4 *Gialolina*..Earth of a bright Gold Colour, found in the Kingdom of Naples, very fine, and much valued by painters. **1847** Craig, *Giallolino*, A fine yellow pigment, much used under the name of Naples yellow. In mod. Dicts.

giambeux, Spenser's artificial sp. of JAMBEAUX.

†**gianet(t)on**. *Obs. rare.* [a. It. *giannettone*, augmentative of *giannetta* a kind of lance.] A kind of lance.

1562 J. Shute *Two Comm.* II. 42b, When anye beaste came forthe of the woodes to the playne, the kinge vsed to apointe some noble man to sley it with his sharpe Gianetton. *Ibid.*, Withoute..taking anye Gianeton with him.

giant ('dʒaɪənt), *sb.* and *a.* Forms: 3-6 **geant**, 4-5 **ge-, jea(u)nd(e, -a(u)nt(e**, 4-6 **ge-, gi-, gyaunt(e**, (5 **ge-, gi-, gyaw(u)nt, gyand, geant**, 6 **geyaunt, gyane**), 5-8 **gyant(e**, 6- **giant**. See also GIGANT. [ME. *geant* (afterwards with the first syll. influenced by the Lat. form), ad. OF. *géant*, *jéant*, *gaiant* (mod.F. *géant*):—popular Lat. **gagantem*, corrupted form of classical Lat. *gigantem* (nom. *gigās*), a. Gr. γίγαντ-, γίγᾱς.

The Gr. word and its Lat. transliteration appear in classical use (chiefly in *pl.*) as the name of a mythical race of beings of enormous stature and strength, represented as the sons of Gæa (Earth) and of Uranus (Heaven) or Tartarus (Hell), and as having warred with the Gods, by whom they were in the end destroyed. The LXX, and (hence) the Vulgate, used the word in passages of the Bible which refer to men of extraordinary stature and strength, and it thus obtained the wider sense in which it is current in the Rom. langs. and in Eng. The etymology of Gr. γίγας, like that of many other mythological names, is obscure; the hypothesis of connexion with the root *γα-, γεν- to be born, to beget, is hardly tenable.]

A. *sb.*

1. a. One of the supposed beings in human form but of superhuman stature, who occur frequently in mythic or pseudo-historical traditions and in romantic fiction. In Greek mythology, used *spec.* (chiefly in plural, with initial capital) as the rendering of Gr. γίγας (see above in the etymology).

1297 R. Glouc. (1724) 15 So strong..of honde, þat hym ne myȝte no mon ne geant at stonde. *c* **1325** *Chron. Eng.* 54 in Ritson *Met. Rom.* II. 272 To wrastle wyth that foule thing, That was the geaundene kyng. *c* **1330** R. Brunne *Chron. Wace* (Rolls) 1754 In þat tyme wer here non hauntes Of no men bot of geauntes. (Geaunt ys more þan man.. Lyke men þey ar in flesche & bon..Of membres haue þey liknes þe lymes alle þat in man ys.) *c* **1450** Henryson *Bludy Serk* 44 The king gart seik baith fer and neir..Off ony knycht gife he micht heir, Wald fecht with that Gyand. **1500-20** Dunbar *Poems* xxxviii. 20 He..as gyane raxit him on hicht. **1553** Eden *Treat. Newe Ind.* (Arb.) 11 The Gyaunte Atlas beareth the worlde on hys shoulders. **1649** Jer. Taylor *Gt. Exemp.* III. xiv, A hundred weight to a gyant is a light burden. **1706-7** Farquhar *Beaux Strat.* v. iii, I'm none of your Romantick Fools, that fight Gyants and Monsters for nothing. **1726** Leoni *Alberti's Archit.* I. 7/2 Typho the Gyant being buried in the Island of Prochyta. **1810** Scott *Lady of L.* I. iv, The Cavern, where, 'tis told, A giant made his den of old. **1838** *Penny Cycl.* XI. 209 The fabulous stories of the giants and pygmies of antiquity, the former of whom are said to have made war against Jupiter.

b. *fig.* Applied to some influence or agency of enormous power. Sometimes prefixed as a title to names of personified qualities, in imitation of Bunyan's allegorical 'Giant Despair'.

a **1631** Donne *Poems* (1650) 54 If you dare be brave.. First kill th' enormous Gyant, your Disdaine. *a* **1658** Lovelace *Poems* (1864) 175 Is there such a trifle as honour, the fools gyant. **1880** G. Meredith *Trag. Com.* (1881) 175 Giant Vanity urged Giant Energy to make use of Giant Duplicity. **1893** *Daily News* 3 Mar. 5/4 Americans are now styling electricity 'our docile giant'.

c. *Econ.* A large or powerful industrial company; a business that dominates its market. Freq. with indication of product, branch of industry, etc., prefixed.

1958 *Spectator* 4 July 15/3 One of the soap giants, Unilever, is a British firm. **1969** *Times* 6 Mar. 23/3 The bitter exchanges between the two French glass giants. **1975** J. de Bres tr. *Mandel's Late Capitalism* x. 338 The World Bank and other international organizations have promoted common projects linking many of the most important industrial giants of the world. **1979** J. Harvey *Plate Shop* xxiii. 111 He would become..Managing Director of a giant. **1986** *Economist* 14 June 18/2 The government was worried about the bid..for Allied-Lyons, a British food-and-drinks giant.

2. a. A human being of monstrously or abnormally high stature; often used *hyperbolically*.

1559 W. Cunningham *Cosmogr. Glasse* 202 Here Magelanus founde a Giaunt x. fote in length. **1571** Campion *Hist. Irel.* vii. (1633) 22 Nemrod, worthily tearmed a gyant, as one that in bodily shape exceeded proportion. **1653** H. Cogan tr. *Pinto's Trav.* xl. 160 They were followed by twelve huge tall men, that seemed to be Giants, clothed with Tygers skins as wild men are used to be painted of them. **1840** Dickens *Old C. Shop* iii, His head and face were large enough for the body of a giant. **1884** J. Hall *A Chr. Home* 176 As there are dwarfs, giants, and albinos, so there are exceptional natures.

b. *transf.*

1834 T. Medwin *Angler in Wales* I. 289 The salmon, which was a giant of the species, did not..find more than depth for his huge body to swim in. **1891** H. Herman *His Angel* x. 202 Five or six mighty elms clustered at the side of the house, hoary giants.

c. *Astr.* One of the class of larger diffuse stars, as distinguished from the dwarfs (see DWARF *sb.* 2b).

1912 *Proc. Amer. Philos. Soc.* LI. 573 The naked-eye stars of this class are all 'giants'. **1925** F. J. M. Stratton *Astronomical Physics* ix. 126 For a given spectral type, the giants are redder or have lower effective temperatures than the dwarfs. **1956** H. S. Jones in A. Pryce-Jones *New Outl. Mod. Knowl.* 114 Some stars are so large that their diameters are several hundreds of times greater than the Sun's... Such stars are called giants.

3. One distinguished by the possession of intellect, strength, valour, etc. in extraordinary amount or degree.

1535 Coverdale *Ps.* cxxvi[i]. 4 Like as the arowes in the honde of the giaunt, euen so are the yonge children. **1680-90** Temple *Ess., Learn.* Wks. 1731 I. 159 There may be Gyants in Wit and Knowledge, of so over-grown a Size, as not to be equalled again in many Successions of Ages. **1851** Robertson *Serm.* Ser. II. x. (1864) 135 Many a spiritual giant is buried under mountains of gold. **1868** J. H. Blunt *Ref. Ch. Eng.* I. 426 The schoolmen were mental giants. **1871** E. F. Burr *Ad Fidem* xiv. 278 Giants of faith.

4. *U.S. Mining.* A discharge-pipe through which great volumes of water are sent for the washing of ore.

1877 Raymond *Mines* 62, 97. **1882** *Rep. Proc. Met. U.S.*, From the distributor the streams are piped on to the 'monitors', or 'giants'.

5. *attrib.* and *Comb.* **a.** simple attrib., as ***giant-brood, -land, -race, -world***; **b.** objective, as ***giant-crusher, -killer, -queller, -slayer***; ***giant-killing*** adj.; **c.** instrumental, as ***giant-hurled*** adj.; **d.** similative, as ***giant-great, -huge, -vast*** adjs.; **e.** appositive, as ***giant-hunter*** (passing into adj.: see B).

1612 Drayton *Poly-olb.* xiv. 84 Since Gomer's *Giant-brood inhabited this Ile. **1671** Milton *Samson* 1247, I dread him not, nor all his giant brood. **1842** Sir A. de Vere *Song of Faith* 91 Communities are as the Giant-brood Fabled by poets old. **1891** Atkinson *Last of Giant-Killers* 79 The Dalesfolks seldom called him anything but the Wolf-queller or the *Giant-crusher. **1871** B. Taylor *Faust* (1875) II. III. 171 Stalking marvellous figures *Giant-great. **1866** Howells *Venet. Life* viii. 126 The gondoliers' spectral shadows *giant-huge. **1725** Pope *Odyss.* xi. 704 There huge Orion of portentous size, Swift thro' the gloom a *Giant-hunter flies. **1871** H. King tr. *Ovid's Met.* xi. 707 If ..the mass Of Pindus or of Ossa, *giant-hurled, Fell sheer in middle-sea. **1726** Amherst *Terræ Fil.* x. 46 History professors, who never read any thing..but Tom Thumb, Jack the *giant killer [etc.]. **1873** Symonds *Grk. Poets* x. 330 Heracles, a Jack the Giant-Killer in his cradle. **1781** Cowper *Conversat.* 244 Guy, Earl of Warwick..Or *giant-killing Jack would please me more. **1766** H. Walpole *Acc. Giants* Wks. 1798 II. 102, I hope..that nobody will beg a million of acres of *giant-land. **1884** S. E. Dawson *Handbk. Dom. Canada* 322 It is a veritable giant-land. **1751** (*title*) Last Speech of John Good, vulgarly called Jack the *Giant Queller. **1813** Scott *Rokeby* iv. i. *note*, Thor was the Hercules of the Scandinavian mythology, a dreadful giant-queller. **1820** Keats *Hyperion* ii. 200 Then their first-born, and we the *giant-race Found ourselves ruling new and beauteous realms. **1879** Sir G. Scott *Lect. Archit.* I. 38 The *giant-slayers of old romance. *a* **1849** J. C. Mangan *Poems* (1859) 48 *Giant-vast [flames]. **1595** Shaks. *John* v. ii. 57 Commend these waters to those baby-eyes, That neuer saw the *giant-world enrag'd. **1889** R. B. Anderson tr. *Rydberg's Teut. Mythol.* 132 The giant-world's wintry agents.

6. Special comb., as **Giant's causeway** (see CAUSEWAY 1); **giant-cell** (see quot. 1881); hence **giant-celled** *a.*, consisting of giant cells; **giant cement**, an extremely tenacious cement; **giant-disc** *v. trans.* (N.Z.), to cultivate by means of a machine with very large disc-cutters; †**giant-dwarf**, a dwarf with the power of a giant; **giant fibre** *Zool.*, an enlarged and modified nerve-fibre esp. in certain invertebrates; **giant's grave** (see quot.); **giant's kettle**, one of the numerous very large pot-holes (moulins) on the coast of Norway; **giant-powder**, also simply ***giant*** (see quot. 1875); **giant racer**, a large switchback at a fun fair; also *fig.*; †**giant rude** *a.*, rude as a giant; **giant('s) stride**, a gymnastic apparatus, consisting of an upright pole with a revolving head, to which ropes are attached, by holding which, one is able to take gigantic strides round the pole; (cf. quot. 1862 for B. 1 a); **giant-swing** (see quot.).

1779 Sir W. Hamilton in *Phil. Trans.* LXX. 48 Lava's regularly crystallized, and forming what are vulgarly called *Giants Causeways. **1876** *Ziemssen's Cycl. Med.* V. 644 A *giant-cell. **1881** *Syd. Soc. Lex.*, *Cells, giant*, large protoplasmic masses..without cell wall, and containing many roundish nuclei.. They are found in tubercle. Also,.. certain large ganglionic cells found in the frontal and the ascending parietal convolutions of the brain. **1886** T. Holmes *Syst. Surg.* (ed. 3) I. 279 Myeloid or *giant-celled sarcoma. **1884** R. Jefferies in *Longm. Mag.* IV. 258 All Brighton chimneys are put on with *giant cement. **1951** *Landfall* V. 175 Billy's going to cut out that manuka so I can *giant-disc it and put in a crop of turnips. **1963** *Weekly News* (Auckland) 3 July 37/2 We climbed a hill giant-disced to grey dust with chopped vegetation showing through. **1588** Shaks. *L.L.L.* iii. i. 182 This wimpled, whyning, purblinde waiward Boy, This signior Iunios *gyant dwarfe don Cupid. **1888** *Giant-fibre [see *neurochord* s.v. NEURO-]. **1897** Parker & Haswell *Text-bk. Zool.* I. x. 438 Running longitudinally through the ventral cord in many forms are certain *giant fibres* of very large size. **1963** R. P. Dales *Annelids* vi. 111 Giant fibres have been known for some time, but their nervous nature was not at first appreciated. *Ibid.* 116 The giant-fibre system has been evolved for the rapid conduction of impulses. **1880** *Antrim & Down Gloss.*, **Giant's Graves*, cromlechs and kistvaens. **1882** Geikie *Text-bk. Geol.* iii. ii. ii. §5. 415 On the ice-worn surface of Norway singular cavities of this kind, known as '*giants' kettles', exist in great numbers. **1872** Raymond *Statist. Mines & Mining* 34 The company consume about 25 pounds of *giant powder weekly for blasting purposes. **1875** Knight *Dict. Mech.*, *Giant-powder*, a form of dynamite, consisting of infusorial earth saturated with nitro-glycerine. **1882** *Century Mag.* XXV. 221/2 'They sets a kag o' that Giant on..it, and it goes off on 'em and tears everything to pieces.' **1934** G. Greene *It's Battlefield* iv. 203 Marriage was the switchback, the *giant racer,..the guarantee that one would never be alone. **1949** 'J. Tey' *Brat Farrar* ix. 79 Lost in contemplation of the Giant Racer. **1600** Shaks. *A.Y.L.* iv. iii. 34 Womens gentle braine Could not drop forth such *giant rude inuention. **1863** Crown Princess of Prussia *Let.* 11 May in R. Fulford *Dearest Mama* (1968) 210 Having a swing, a see-saw and a *giant stride put up for little and big children. **1883** *Pall Mall G.* 14 Nov. 1/2 Give them a giant's stride, give them a climbing or leaping pole, and see what a change you will bring into their life. **1906** M. H. Baillie-Scott *Houses & Gardens* 121 The woodwork of the swing and giant's stride is painted in gay colours. **1963** C. Mackenzie *My Life & Times* II. 29 A giant-stride is a column of wood from a revolving horizontal wheel at the top of which depend about a dozen ropes with small wooden bars at the end of them. **1889** *Century Dict.*, **Giant-swing*, in gymnastics, a revolution at arm's length around a horizontal bar.

B. *adj.* [developed from the attrib. and appositive use of the sb.]

1. a. Of extraordinary size, extent, or force; gigantic, huge, monstrous.

1480 CAXTON *Descr. Brit.* 17 Grete palayses, gyantes toures, noble bathes. **1602** MARSTON *Antonio's Rev.* II. iii, Pigmie cares Can shelter under patience shield; but gyant griefes Will burst all covert. **1613** SHAKS. *Hen. VIII*, I. ii. 199 A gyant Traytor [l. 216 hee's Traytor to th' height]. **1649** DRUMM. OF HAWTH. *Poems* Wks. (1711) 45 Such gyant moods our parity forth brings, We all will nothing be, or all be kings. **1699** BENTLEY *Phal.* xi. 225 He was a Gyant Tragedian, rather than a Fairy one. **1725** POPE *Odyss.* IX. 274 His giant voice the echoing region fills. **1747** COLLINS *Odes, Liberty* 19 With heaviest Sound a Giant-statue fell. **1777** WARTON *Poems* 43 More horrible and huge her giant-shape she rear'd. **1812** BYRON *Ch. Har.* II. xxii, Mauritania's giant-shadows frown. **1851** HELPS *Comp. Solit.* ix. (1874) 155 Near the land some giant reeds rose up from the water. **1852** ROBERTSON *Serm.* Ser. III. xvii. 220 Passion in its giant might. **1861** GEN. P. THOMPSON *Audi Alt.* III. clxvii. 189 Adam Smith, a giant authority. **1862** MRS. H. WOOD *Mrs. Hallib.* III. xviii. (1888) 409 When old age approaches then time moves with giant strides. **1888** F. HUME *Mad. Midas* I. Prol., Above which could be seen giant mountains with snow-covered ranges.

b. In the names of plants and animals.

[**1578–1848**: see FENNEL-GIANT.] **1845** *Florist's Jrnl.* 29 The sort of asparagus at present most generally grown is known under the name of the Giant. **1861** MISS PRATT *Flower. Pl.* III. 339 *Campanulaceæ*..(Giant Bell-flower). **1864–5** WOOD *Homes without H.* i. 42 The Giant Armadillo (*Priodonta gigas*) is so determined a burrower that [etc.]. *Ibid.* v. 109 The Giant Teredo (*Teredo gigantea*)..produces a shell more than five feet in length. **1882** *Garden* 4 Feb. 75/3 The Giant Orache (*Atriplex hortensis*) attains a height of 6 ft. or upwards. *Ibid.* 20 May 353/2 For planting by the side of water..there are few..equal to the Giant Fennels. **1897** *Daily News* 9 Sept. 8/7 Giant seed rye is scarce and firm. **1911** C. E. W. BEAN *'Dreadnought' of Darling* xiii. 130 The giant emu, giant kangaroo, alligator, tortoise, and giant wombat. **1937** *Discovery* Jan. 27/1 The first Giant Panda to be captured alive was taken by Mrs Ruth Harkness, on a recent expedition into the frontier country between South-Western China and Tibet. *Ibid.* Oct. 308/2 The giant squid is certainly the largest invertebrate animal. **1947** I. L. IDRIESS *Isles of Despair* xxxv. 234 We must show you the giant clam. **1947** J. STEVENSON-HAMILTON *Wild Life S. Afr.* xxxiv. 300 The giant kingfisher (*Megaceryle masima*), attains a total length of close on eighteen inches. **1969** *Nature* 21 June 1126/1 In the wild, giant pandas are usually alone; except for mothers with cubs they have rarely been seen in company.

c. Applied to a star (see the sb., sense 2 c).

1912 *Proc. Amer. Philos. Soc.* LI. 571 The existence of these two series was first pointed out by Hertzsprung, who has called them by the very convenient names of 'giant' and 'dwarf' stars—the former being of course the brighter. **1913** *Observatory* Aug. 328 Giant stars must either have low density or great surface-brightness, and the reverse is true of the dwarf stars. **1959** *Listener* 3 Dec. 971/1 We have red giant stars which are accompanied by bluish-green companions.

2. *Comb.*, as ***giant-bodied, -factoried, -treed*** adjs.

1624 R. DAVENPORT *City Nt. Cap* III. (1661) E 1, Her little pedling sins..will shew in my book as foils to her *giant-bodied vertues. **1864** TENNYSON *Sea Dreams* 5 The *giant-factoried city gloom. *c***1865** O. W. HOLMES *Hunt after 'Captain'* in *Pages Old Vol. Life* (1891) 76 Springfield, the wide-meadowed..*giant-treed town.

b. Special collocation. **giant order** *Archit.*, an order whose columns extend through more than one storey; also called *colossal order*.

1945 J. SUMMERSON *Georgian London* vi. 72 Gibbs adopted the reverse policy of starting with a *giant order. **1961** N. PEVSNER *Northamptonshire* 269 The giant order of pilasters, a motif derived from Delorme's St Maur of 1541–4 and illustrated in his *Architecture* in 1567. **1979** E. H. GOMBRICH *Sense of Order* vii. 178 'The giant orders' which Michelangelo introduced in his design of the Capitol.. presented such a bold departure because normally each storey of a building was assigned its own order.

giantesque (dʒaɪən'tɛsk), *a.* [f. GIANT *sb.* + -ESQUE, after F. *gigantesque.*] Having characteristics of a giant, gigantic.

1909 in WEBSTER. **1929** *Sunday Express* 20 Jan. 9 You gloat over their giantesque sins and sorrows.

giantess ('dʒaɪəntɪs). Forms: see GIANT. Also 5 geaunesse. [f. GIANT *sb.* + -ESS.] A she-giant; a woman of abnormal bulk and height.

*c***1380** *Sir Ferumb.* 4663 Amyote hure damme, a geauntesse. *c***1400** *Sowdone Bab.* 2943 This Barrok was a geaunesse. **1590** SPENSER *F.Q.* III. vii. 37 He spide far off a mighty Giauntesse. **1627** HAKEWILL *Apol.* III. v. §4. 202 The woman Gyantesse before mentioned ws so strong, that shee would lift vp in either hand a barrell full of Hamborough beere. **1663** COWLEY *Ess., Greatness* (1669) 121 He kept a Concubine that was a very Gyantess. **1825** J. NEAL *Br. Jonathan* III. 447 'Who are you?' cried Savage; throwing himself at her, as if she were a giantess.

transf. and *fig.* **1640** HOWELL *Dodona's Gr.* 71 Which were shee entirely subject to the Cedar, would..bee able of her selfe to make head against that huge Giantess Alcarona. **1841** W. SPALDING *Italy & It. Isl.* I. 249 The giantess [Rome] had grown old and weak; but the life-blood still circled through her veins. **1865** *Sat. Rev.* 25 Mar. 337 Intellectual giantesses are still rarer than intellectual giants. **1896** *Westm. Gaz.* 3 Nov. 6/3 A magnificent giantess [a chrysanthemum] of pure white.

gianthood ('dʒaɪənthʊd). [f. GIANT *sb.* + -HOOD.] **a.** The nature or characteristics of a giant; hugeness. **b.** *concr.* The race of giants.

1840 CARLYLE *Heroes* (1858) 199 A kind of vacant hugeness, large awkward gianthood, characterises that Norse System. **1859** GEN. P. THOMPSON *Audi Alt.* II. lxxxii. 45 The strong-limbed gianthood of the olden time.

giantish ('dʒaɪəntɪʃ), *a.* [f. GIANT *sb.* + -ISH.] Resembling a giant or his qualities.

*a***1634** RANDOLPH *Muses' Looking Gl.* v. i, Their stature neither Dwarfe nor Gyantish. **1755** SMOLLETT *Quix.* (1803) II. 27 The boon she asks..is a mere trifle; no more than slaying a giantish sort of fellow.

giantism ('dʒaɪəntɪz(ə)m). [f. GIANT *sb.* + -ISM.] **a.** The quality or state of a giant; the practices of a giant or of the Giants.

1639 CHAPMAN & SHIRLEY *Chabot* III. ii, The improvement of his estate in so few years, from a private gentleman's fortune to a great duke's revenues, might save our sovereign therein an orator to enforce and prove faulty, even to giantism, against heaven. **1665** J. WEBB *Stone-Heng* 31 It appears most apt to sustain any the heaviest Weight; and therefore hath much of Giantism in it. **1730** FIELDING *Tom Thumb* I. iii, Oh! happy state of giantism. **1855** P. LANDRETH *De Quincey* in *Stud. Mod. Lit.* (1861) 275 Goliath is associated with giantism.

b. *Phys.* and *Biol.* Abnormal development in size. Also *spec.* (see quot. 1885).

1885 *Syd. Soc. Lex.*, *Giantism*, a condition of excess of developement in which a young living thing precociously attains the size and appearance of adult life, but does not go on to surpass the average. **1895** J. HUTCHINSON *Archives Surg.* VI. 74 Inherited tendency to Giantism. Mr. E——, of D——, aged 29, who stood six feet seven inches, told me that his paternal grandfather had attained the same height.

c. *transf.* and *fig.*

1936 M. ALLIS *Eng. Prelude* xxiv. 176 London remains the great metropolis, but those of the Midlands give an impression of giantism London lacks. **1952** *Archit. Rev.* CXI. 127/3 Giantism in classical architecture is a well-known phenomenon. **1961** L. MUMFORD *City in History* xv. 456 The more units in a given area, the more efficient was the source of power: hence the tendency towards giantism. **1967** *Economist* 7 Jan. 4 Before succumbing to a philosophy of industrial giantism you must answer this question.

giantize ('dʒaɪəntaɪz), *v. rare.* [f. GIANT *sb.* + -IZE.] †**a.** *intr.* To play the giant. *Obs.*$^{-0}$ **b.** *trans.* To give the appearance of a giant to.

1611 COTGR., *Geantiser*, to Giantize; to make as big as a Giant; also, to play the Giant. **1864** *Daily Tel.* 28 Dec. 5/2 Their anxious parents ply them with gin until they stop at a size which enables them to giantise every competitor.

giantlike ('dʒaɪəntlaɪk), *a.* [f. GIANT *sb.* + LIKE.] Resembling a giant or what pertains to a giant; gigantic.

1571 GOLDING *Calvin on Ps.* lvi, Heathnish persons are puffed up with Giant-lyke presumptuousnes. **1590** SHAKS. *Mids. N.* III. i. 197 Good master Mustard seede..that same cowardly gyant-like Oxe beefe hath deuoured many a gentleman of your house. **1618** BOLTON *Florus* (1636) 201 Those Gyantlike bodies..were..the fairer mark for a sword, or dart to hit. *a***1680** CHARNOCK *Attrib. God* (1834) II. 625 Winds have..a giant-like force. *a***1716** SOUTH *Serm.* (1737) I. vi. 231 All their giant-like objections against Christian religion shall presently vanish and quit the field. **1847** LD. LINDSAY *Chr. Art* I. 28 The duomo..with its giant-like procession of columns, is singularly beautiful. **1878** L. P. MEREDITH *Teeth* 188 A person almost giantlike in strength and stature may faint at the thoughts of the operation.

'giantling. [f. GIANT *sb.* + -LING.] A young giant.

1871 H. F. SHEPPARD in *Sacristy* I. 340 Gayant was a married giant, with a wife and three giantlings.

giantly ('dʒaɪəntlɪ), *a.* and *adv.* [f. GIANT *sb.* + -LY.]

A. *adj.* = GIANTLIKE. Now *rare.*

1561 DAUS tr. *Bullinger on Apoc.* (1573) 77 Idle men.. peruerte and wrest Gods word after their wonted giantly boldenes. **1607** WALKINGTON *Opt. Glass* 11 The massier and more gyantly body must be maintained with large..diet. **1613** PURCHAS *Pilgrimage* (1614) 862 The lower Mountaines ..although they bee for their height wonderfull, yet..they have more Giantly-overlookers. **1636** DAVENANT *Witts* v. iii, Our hopes grow strong and giantly. **1659** *Gentl. Calling* viii. (1679) 131 Great Mens vices are of a yet more giantly frame, they proclaim solemn War with Heaven. **1809** W. IRVING *Knickerb.* VI. ii. (1849) 315 Governor Risingh, notwithstanding his giantly condition, was, as I have hinted, a man of craft.

†**B.** *adv.* In a giantlike manner. *Obs.*

1625 T. JACKSON *Orig. Vnbeliefe* vii. 61 His picture as Euripides hath taken it, is more Gyantly vast. **1719** D'URFEY *Pills* III. 44 Bacchus giantly bestrid A Strong Beer Barrel.

†**'giantness.** *Obs.*$^{-0}$

1611 FLORIO, *Gigantaggine*, giantness, or greatnesse or quality of a Giant.

giantry ('dʒaɪəntrɪ). *rare.* [f. GIANT *sb.* + -RY.] **a.** The race of giants; giants collectively. **b.** Tales about giants; giant-mythology.

1611 COTGR., *Geanterie*, giantrie; the generation, race, kind, or brood, of Giants. **1784** H. WALPOLE *Lett.* (1820) IV. 380 The flimsy giantry of Ossian has introduced mountainous horrors. **1816** SOUTHEY *Poet's Pilgr.* IV. 21 The Giantry of old their God defied.

'giantship. [f. GIANT *sb.* + -SHIP.] **a.** The state of being a giant. **b.** The personality of a giant.

1671 MILTON *Samson* 1244 His giantship is gone somewhat crest-fallen. **1761** *Brit. Mag.* II. 603 Even their giantships Gog and Magog seemed to be almost animated. **1819** MOTHERWELL *Harp Renfrewshire* Pref. 52 In this his Giantship is miserably deceived. **1847** *Blackw. Mag.* LXI. 590 He stands, a modern Gulliver, pre-eminent in moral giantship amidst surrounding pigmies.

‖**giaour** (dʒaʊ(r)). Forms: 6–8 gower, 7 gaur(e, gawar, (ghaur), gour(e, 7–8 giaur, jaour, (7 dgiahour, 9 ghiaour, jour, yaoor), 7– giaour. [Pers. *gaur, gōr*, pronounced by the Turks (gyaur), var. *gebr*: see GUEBRE.] A term of reproach applied by the Turks to non-Mussulmans, esp. Christians.

1564 JENKINSON in Hakluyt *Voy.* (1599) I. 349 He [the Sophy of Persia] reasoned with mee much of Religion, demaunding whether I were a Gower, that is to say, an vnbeleeuer, or a Muselman, that is of Mahomets lawe. **1609** W. BIDDULPH in T. Lavender *Trav.* 85 In words they [Turkes] reuile them as the Egyptians did the Israelites, and call them Gours, that is, Infidels. **1654** tr. *Scudery's Curia Politiæ* 28 Have you never heard them call the Christians, *Jaours*, that is, Doggs? **1676** tr. *Guillatiere's Voy. Athens* 329 The Eunuch..set him..to threaten the Christian [Corsaire], incouraging him as soon as they came within distance to call them *Giaours*. **1682** WHELER *Journ. Greece* II. 199 He..was reproachfully sent away with the Name of Goure, or Infidel. **1786** tr. *Beckford's Vathek* (1868) 14 Accursed Giaour! what comest thou hither to do? **1813** BYRON *Giaour* 745 Who falls in battle 'gainst a Giaour Is worthiest an immortal bower. **1881** *Harper's Mag.* LXIII. 248 An unadulterated Arab place of entertainment, seldom profaned by the presence of giaours.

giaunt(e, giaw(u)nt, obs. forms of GIANT.

gib (gɪb), *sb.*[1] *Obs.* exc. in *Comb.* Forms: 4–7 gibb(e, 6–7 gyb, 5– gib. [A familiar abbreviation of *Gilbert.*]

1. A familiar name given to a cat. ***to play fy gib*** (? to say 'fie' to the cat), to utter threats, to look threateningly.

*c***1400** *Inscr.* in *Proc. Soc. Antiq.* (1886) 11 Mar., Gret: wel: gibbe: oure: cat. *c***1400** *Rom. Rose* 6204 For right no mo than Gibbe [Fr. *Tibers*] our cat. *c***1450** HENRYSON *Mor. Fab.* (1832) 13 Scantly had they drunken once or twise, When in came Gib-Hunter our joly Cat. *a***1529** [see CAT 1 b]. **1575** *Gamm. Gurton* I. v, Gyb our cats two eyes..Gyb shut her two eyes. *Ibid.* III. iii, Mary fy on thee, thou old gyb, with al my very hart. **1640** BASTWICK *Lord Bps.* viii. I j, He playes fy gib with his thunderbolt of Excommunication.

2. A cat, *esp.* a male cat (cf. *Gib* a male ferret in *Chester Gloss.*); in later dialectal use, one that has been castrated. ***to play the gib***: (of a woman) to act the cat (see CAT AND DOG).

1561 *Schole-ho. Wom.* 508 in Hazl. *E.P.P.* IV. 124 Nature she foloweth, and playeth the gib, And at her husband dooth barke and ba[w]ll, As dooth the Cur. **1600** *Dr. Dodypoll* III. ii. in Bullen *O. Pl.* III. 129 This is Melpomene, that Scottish witch, Whom I will scratche like to some villanous gibb. **1602** SHAKS. *Ham.* III. iv. 190 Who..Would..from a Bat, a Gibbe, Such deere concernings hide? *a***1616** BEAUM. & FL. *Knt. of Malta* v. ii, Wee'l call him Cacodemon, with his block gib there. **1668** WILKINS *Real Char.* II. viii. §1. 199 Male..Dog, Gib, Cock, [etc.]. **1804** J. DUNCUMB *Herefordsh.* I. 213 *Gib*, a male cat, castrated.

3. A term of reproach, esp. for an old woman.

*a***1529** SKELTON *E. Rummyng* 99 She is a tonnish gyb. **1598** DRAYTON *Heroic. Ep.* xiii. 104 Call me, Beldam, Gib, Witch, Night-mare, Trot. **1611** MIDDLETON & DEKKER *Roaring Girl* IV. ii, 'Faith gib, are you spitting? I'le cut your tayle pus-cat for this. *a***1687** COTTON *Poet. Wks.* (1765) 122 And humbly the old Gib beseeches To shew her utmost Skill and Cunning.

4. *gib-cat* = sense 2. Now only *arch.* and *dial.*

1596, 1667, 1785 [see CAT 1 b]. **1820** LAMB *Elia* Ser. I. *S. Sea Ho.*, Melancholy as a gib-cat over his counter all the forenoon. **1895** CROCKETT *Men of Mosshags* 103, I declare I purred like our gib cat.

Hence †**'gibship** *jocular*, the personality of a cat. (In quot. applied to a woman.)

1616 BEAUM. & FL. *Scornf. Lady* v. i, Bring out the Cat hounds, Ile make you take a tree whore, then with my tyller Bring downe your Gibship.

†**gib**, *sb.*[2] *Obs.* Also 5 gybbe. [a. OF. *gibbe, gibe*, ad. L. *gibba.*]

1. A hump.

*c***1440** *Promp. Parv.* 280/1 Knobbe yn a beestys backe or breste, þat ys clepyd a gybbe. **1638** SIR T. HERBERT *Trav.* 192 Camells..varie according to the Countrie they breed in: in..Persia they have but one gib or bunch, the Arabian is doubled.

2. A bale (of cloth, etc.).

1526 in Dillon *Calais & Pale* (1893) 81 Item, of a gybbe of Wollen clothe outwardes ij^{d}.

gib (gɪb), *sb.*[3] Also 6 gibbe, 9 gibb. [Of obscure origin; cf. KIP, KEBBIE.]

†**1.** An iron hook. *Obs.*$^{-1}$

1567 *Wills & Inv. N.C.* (Surtees 1835) 278 A rosting Iron, a pair of gibbes, iij pair of pott clipps.

2. (See quots.)

1788 W. MARSHALL *Yorksh.* II. Gloss. (E.D.S.) *Gib* (the g hard, as in gild), a hook; a gibby stick, a hooked stick. **1855** ROBINSON *Whitby Gloss.*, *Gib*, a wooden hook... *A nutting gib*, a nutting hook.

3. The hooked gristle which grows at the end of the lower jaw of a male salmon after spawning; = KIP. Also *Comb.*, as **gib-fish**, a salmon with a 'gib'. (Otherwise explained in quot. 1867.)

1818 *Sporting Mag.* I. 290 At the end of his lower chop, there grows a hard boney gib, from which they are then called the gib-fish. **1867** SMYTH *Sailor's Word-bk.*, *Gibb*, the beak, or hooked upper lip of a male salmon. *Ibid.*, *Gib-fish*, a northern name for the male of a salmon.

4. *Comb.*, as †**gib-crook** = sense 1; **gib-staff** (see quots.); **gib-stick** = sense 2.

1564 *Wills & Inv. N.C.* (Surtees 1835) 223 One payre of toynges, *gibcrokes, rakincroke, and racks xx^d. **1674–91** RAY *N.C. Words* (E.D.S.), **Gibstaff*, a quarter-staff. **1721** in BAILEY. **1847** CRAIG, *Gibstaff*, a staff to gauge water or to push a boat; formerly, the name of a weapon used in fighting beasts on the stage. **1876** *Whitby Gloss.* s.v., *A *gib stick*, a stick that is bent-headed.

gib (dʒɪb), *sb.*[4] *slang.* [Said to be short form of GIBRALTAR.] A prison.

1877 5 *Yrs.' Penal Servit.* iii. 221, I did a lagging of seven, and was at the Gib. three out of it.

gib (dʒɪb, gɪb), *sb.*[5] [Of obscure origin; cf. JIB *sb.*[2], GIBBET *sb.*[1]] **1.** A piece of wood or metal employed to keep something else, *e.g.* some part of a machine, in place. **a.** A bolt, pin, or wedge for insertion in a hole, to fasten the adjoining parts more tightly together.

gib and cotter, *gib and key*: a two-part contrivance, consisting of a fixed and a movable wedge, used to tighten the strap at the end of a connecting rod.

1795 W. FELTON *Treat. Carriages* II. 221 *Gib*, a small half round wedge, which keeps the pole from rising. **1838** *Civil Engin. & Arch. Jrnl.* I. 150/1 The corners were secured by a strong iron strap with a gib and key. **1839** R. S. ROBINSON *Naut. Steam Eng.* 78 The rectangular hole for the gib and cutter. *a* **1865** SMYTH *Sailor's Word-bk.* (1867) 339 *Gib*, a forelock. **1880** *Encycl. Brit.* XIII. 732/1 The pin is sometimes rectangular in section, and tapered or parallel lengthwise. 'Gibs' and 'cottars' are examples of the latter. **1887** D. A. LOW *Introd. Machine Draw.* 49 The gib is provided with horns at its ends to keep it in its place. **1888** *Lockwood's Dict. Mech. Engin.* 91 The gib and cottar arrangement is that in which the cottar is formed in two parts, whose outer faces are parallel with each other, the requisite taper being given to their inner or sliding faces.

b. A bearing surface to reduce friction, or a wedge to take up wear at a sliding contact.

1873 J. RICHARDS *Treat. Wood-working Machines* 13 Gibs of lignum vitæ will be found to wear well. *a* **1877** KNIGHT *Dict. Mech.* 650/1 The box has two taper-cheeks *a a* and two taper-gibs *b b* adjustable by screws, so as to set up the boxing to the wrist and the cheeks to the guides in the cross-head.

c. (See quot.)

1902 *Encycl. Brit.* XXX. 402/2 The extractor [in a Maxim gun] is recessed to take a movable plate termed a 'gib', behind which is a spring.

2. *Mining.* A piece of wood used to support the roof of a coalmine.

1847 in HALLIWELL. **1879** G. F. JACKSON *Shropsh. Word-bk.* 172 *Gib*, a wooden prop used to support the coal when being 'holed'. **1883** GRESLEY *Gloss. Coal-m.*, *Gib*, a short prop of timber by which the coal is supported whilst being holed or undermined.

3. *attrib.* and *Comb.*: **gib-head**, a head (of a rod, pin, etc.) with projecting shoulder(s); **gib-headed key** (see quot.).

1854 RONALDS & RICHARDSON *Chem. Technol.* (ed. 2) I. 152 The opposite ends of the connecting-rods are provided ..with gib-heads. **1887** D. A. LOW *Introd. Machine Draw.* 23 When the point of a key is inaccessible the other end is provided with gib-head. **1888** *Lockwood's Dict. Mech. Engin.*, *Gib-headed key*, a key having a set-off standing at right angles with the thicker end, for convenience of drawing it back in situations where the use of a drift is not practicable.

†**gib**, *v.*[1] *Obs.*$^{-0}$ [f. GIB *sb.*[1]] *intr.* To behave like a gib or cat. Hence †'**gibbing** *vbl. sb.*

1621 BEAUM. & FL. *Wild-Goose Chase* IV. iii. (1652) 44 Out Kitlings What Catterwalling's here? what gibbing?

gib (gɪb), *v.*[2] [var. GIP.] *trans.* To disembowel (fish); = GIP. Also *Comb.*, as **gib-tub** (see quot.). Hence '**gibber**, one who disembowels fish.

1883 *Chamb. Jrnl.* 271 In the centre another man gibbing or eviscerating the fish. **1893** *Funk's Stand. Dict.*, *Gib-tub*, a tray in which fish are laid to be gibbed or disemboweled.

gib (dʒɪb, gɪb), *v.*[3] [f. GIB *sb.*[5]] *trans.* To provide or secure with a gib or gibs. Hence **gibbed** *ppl. a.*

a **1884** KNIGHT *Dict. Mech.* Suppl. 398/1 *Gibbed lathe*, a lathe, the carriage of which has a bar which grips beneath the overhang of the bed, beneath which it is secured by a wedge known as a *gib*, to prevent the riding up of the carriage. **1893** *Funk's Stand. Dict.*, *Gibbed way*, a guiding surface provided with gibs for adjustment.

gib, var. JIB *sb.* and *v.*

gibaltar: see GIBRALTAR 2.

gibb(e, obs. form of GIB, JIB.

gibbed cat. [orig. var. *gib-cat* (GIB *sb.*[1] 4); but *gibbed* was afterwards taken as pa. pple. of an assumed vb. **gib* to geld.] = *gib-cat*, GIB *sb.*[1] 2.

1633 W. ROWLEY *Match Midn.* II. i, *Iohn.* Looke Mistresse, how they stare one at another? *Iar.* Yes, and swell like a couple of gib'd Cats. **1651** RANDOLPH, etc. *Hey for Honesty* II. iii, Some gib'd Cat that died issuelesse has adopted thee for her Heire. **1670** RAY *Prov.* 206 As melancholy as a gibd cat. **1687** SEDLEY *Bellamira* V. i, I had as live drink with a gib'd cat. **1824** W. IRVING *T. Trav.* I. 293 The melancholy of a gibed cat.

gibber ('dʒɪbə(r), 'gɪbə(r)), *sb.*[1] [f. GIBBER *v.*[1]] Rapid and inarticulate utterance.

1832 J. P. KENNEDY *Swallow B.* iii. (1860) 38 The gibber of ducks and chickens and turkeys. **1835** BROWNING *Paracelsus* II. 43 The blank space 'twixt an idiot's gibber And a mad lover's ditty. **1859** KINGSLEY *Misc., Plays & Purit.* II. 131 He has none of the obscene gibber of the ape.

‖**gibber** ('gɪbə(r)), *sb.*[2] [L. *gibber.*] (See quots.)

1857 *Dunglison's Med. Lex.*, *Gibber*, hump. **1866** *Treas. Bot.*, *Gibber*, a pouch-like enlargement of the base of a calyx, corolla, etc. **1880** [see s.v. GIBBEROSE]. **1885** *Syd. Soc. Lex.*, *Gibber*, a hump, a hunch.

gibber ('gɪbə(r)), *sb.*[3] *Australian.* Also 9 **gibba, ghibber.** [aboriginal Australian.] **a.** A large stone; a boulder.

1834 L. E. THRELKELD *Austral. Gram.* p. xi, Barbarisms ..*Gibber*, a stone. **1847** [A. HARRIS] *Settlers & Convicts* ix. 159 He did not object to stow himself by the fire-side of any house he might be near, or under the 'gibbers' (overhanging rocks) of the river. **1889** BOLDREWOOD *Robbery under Arms* (1890) 39 There was a kind of gully that came in, something like the one we came in by, but rougher, and full of gibbers. **1896** B. SPENCER in *Rep. Horn Exped.* I. 11 Our course lay across..upland plains covered with 'gibbers'.

b. *attrib.* and *Comb.*, as **gibber country**, **-*field***, **-*plain***; **gibber-gunyah**, an aboriginal cave-dwelling.

1894 B. SPENCER in *Argus* 1 Sept. 4/2 (Morris) Our track led across what is called the *gibber country. **1896** —— in *Rep. Horn Exped.* I. 27 Even the Stony *gibber-field becomes green with herbage. **1847** [A. HARRIS] *Settlers & Convicts* xi. 211, I coincided in his opinion that it would be best for us to camp for the night in one of the *ghibber-gunyahs. These are the hollows under overhanging rocks. **1863** R. W. VANDERKISTE *Lost, but not for Ever* (ed. 2) 210 Our home is the gibber-gunyah. **1891** R. ETHERIDGE *Rec. Austral. Museum* I. VIII. 171 Notes on 'Rock Shelters' or 'Gibba-gunyahs' at Deewhy Lagoon. **1933** *Bulletin* (Sydney) 27 Sept. 20/4 A well-found homestead..set in a howling wilderness of bare *gibber plain. **1953** *Sci. News* XXVII. 9 In cases where the initial rock surface is harder.. stone-desert surfaces are commonly formed. These are known as hamada in Africa, gobi in Mongolia, and gibber-plains in Australia.

gibber ('dʒɪbə(r), 'gɪbə(r)), *v.*[1] Also *rarely* **jibber.** [Onomatopœic; cf. GABBER, JABBER.

Probably ('dʒɪbə(r)) and ('gɪbə(r)) are originally independent words of parallel formation, not merely divergent interpretations of the written form.]

intr. To speak rapidly and inarticulately; to chatter, talk nonsense. Said also of an ape.

1604 SHAKS. *Ham.* I. i. 116 (Qo. 2) The graues stood tenantlesse and the sheeted dead Did squeake and gibber in the Roman streets. **1791** COWPER *Odyss.* XXIV. 11 The ghosts Troop it downward, gibbering all the dreary way. **1833** HT. MARTINEAU *Cinnamon & Pearls* iii. 56 Monkeys..hung by one arm from the boughs overhead, gibbering and chattering. *a* **1845** HOOD *Forge* II. xix, Meanwhile the demons, filthy and foul, Are not contented to jibber and howl. **1857–8** SEARS *Athan.* 23 Not a spectre can rise and gibber. **1871** RUSKIN *Fors Clav.* x. (1896) I. 196 Those who work and do not gibber. **1877** V. L. CAMERON *Across Africa* xv. (1885) 209 They chattered and gibbered at the strange sight of a boat.

†**gibber**, *v.*[2] *Obs.*$^{-1}$

1602 *Life Cromwell* E b, I faith ile gibber a ioynte, but ile tell him his owne.

gibberellic (dʒɪbə'rɛlɪk), *a.* [f. next + -IC.] *gibberellic acid*: one of the gibberellins, a tetracyclic lactonic acid ($C_{18}H_{21}O_4COOH$) produced by the fungus *Gibberella fujikuroi.*

1954 CURTIS & CROSS in *Chem. & Ind.* 28 Aug. 1066/1 In attempting to isolate gibberellin A from culture filtrates of this fungus we have instead isolated another compound with similar biological properties. We propose to call this compound gibberellic acid. **1956** *Wall St. Jrnl.* 13 Dec. 1/1 In tests, gibberellic acid made such plants as sunflowers, roses, petunias and asters grow up to three times the height of untreated plants in three to four weeks. **1962** C. A. WEST in Florkin & Stotz *Comprehensive Biochem.* XI. ix. 152 An exchange of samples and a comparison of properties soon showed the identity of gibberellic acid, gibberellin A_3 and gibberellin X. **1968** *New Scientist* 21 Mar. 651/1 Gibberellic acid, the principal gibberellin, is known to be responsible for inducing the synthesis of the enzyme..in barley seed..that breaks down the starch food reserve within the seed during germination.

gibberellin (dʒɪbə'rɛlɪn). [f. mod.L. *Gibberell-a* (generic name of the fungus *G. fujikuroi*, from cultures of which gibberellin was first isolated), dim. of the generic name *Gibbera*, f. L. *gibber* hump: see -IN[1].] Any of numerous compounds which are chemically related to gibberellic acid and which are present in many higher plants as growth regulators; their characteristic effects include elongation of the stem and other parts of the plant and the promotion of germination and flowering.

1939 YABUTA & HAYASHI in *Jrnl. Agric. Chem. Soc. Japan* (*Eng. Abstr.*) Mar. 41 (*heading*) Isolation of 'gibberellin', the active principle which makes the rice seedlings grow slenderly. **1958** *Science News* XLVII. 9 Plants treated with a few micrograms of gibberellin became much longer. **1961** *Q. Rev.* XV. 59 The gibberellins are used to stimulate swelling of fruits, e.g., grapes and tomato. **1965** BELL & COOMBE tr. *Strasburger's Textbk. Bot.* (new ed.) III. 498 *Gibberella fujikuroi*, which causes a disease of rice in Japan, yields the growth substance gibberellin, now much used in plant physiological researches. **1968** *New Scientist* 21 Mar. 651/1 Some 23 gibberellins, each with a slightly different physiological action and chemical structure, have so far been recognized.

gibberi(d)ge, obs. form of GIBBERISH.

gibbering ('dʒɪb-, 'gɪbərɪŋ), *vbl. sb.* [f. GIBBER *v.*[1] + -ING[1].] The action of the vb. GIBBER[1].

1786 tr. *Beckford's Vathek* (1868) 32 Stunned by their gibbering. **1857** BIRCH *Anc. Pottery* (1858) II. 35 Like the twittering and gibbering of the 'Birds' of Aristophanes. **1872** MINTO *Eng. Prose Lit.* I. iii. 161 Full of screechings and gibberings.

gibbering ('dʒɪb-, gɪbərɪŋ), *ppl. a.* [f. as prec. + -ING[2].] That gibbers or takes the form of gibbering; unmeaning; unintelligible.

1711 *Lond. Gaz.* No. 4850/4 Pretending to be a Fortune Teller, talking after a gibbering manner. **1820** W. IRVING *Sketch Bk.* (1859) 127 We almost fancy we hear the gibbering yell of triumph bursting from the distended jaws of the spectre. **1859** SALA *Tw. round Clock* (1861) 377 Gibbering forms of men and women in filthy rags. **1881** P. BROOKS *Candle of Lord* 265 They saw Him face the gibbering maniac among the tombs.

gibberish ('dʒɪbərɪʃ, 'gɪbərɪʃ), *sb.* and *a.* Forms: 6–8 **geb(b)-, gib(b)-, g(h)yb(b)rish, gib(b)r-, gib(b)eridge, -ige,** (7 **geberish, guibbridge,** 8 **gibbirish),** 6– **gibberish.** [? f. GIBBER *v.*[1] (though that word appears later in our quots.), after names of langs. in -ISH.]

A. *sb.* Unintelligible speech belonging to no known language, and supposed to be of arbitrary invention; inarticulate chatter, jargon. Often applied contemptuously to blundering or ungrammatical language, to obscure and pretentious verbiage, etc.

c **1554** *Interl. Youth* A ij b, What me thynke ye be clerkyshe For ye speake good gibbryshe. **1579** E. K. *Ded. to Spenser's Shep. Cal.*, Other some..if they happen to here an olde word..crye out streightway, that we speak no English, but gibbrish. **1603** HARSNET *Pop. Impost.* 46 They are agreed of certaine uncouth non-significant terms which goe current among themselves as the Gipsies are of Gibridge, which none but themselves can spell without a paire of Spectacles. **1612** DRAYTON *Polyolb.* xii. 200 His little infant neere in childish gibbridge showes What addeth to his griefe. *a* **1656** USSHER *Ann.* VI. (1658) 523 They all the while crying quarter in their barbarous gibbridge. **1673** DRYDEN *Marr. à la Mode* II. i, It may keep the field against a whole army of lawyers, and that in their own language, French gibberish. **1700** *Paper to W. Penn* Pref. A ij, The Books of the Quakers..were generally set at nought as Gibberish. **1748** SMOLLETT *Rod. Rand.* xxx, He repeated some gibberish, which by the sound seemed to be Irish. **1790** BURKE *Fr. Rev.* Wks. V. 197 Their language is in the patois of fraud; in the cant and gibberish of hypocrisy. **1803** *Edin. Rev.* II. 377 The admixture of the gibberish used by the negroes. **1835** MACAULAY *Ess.*, *Mackintosh* (1887) 350 A state trial was a murder preceded by the uttering of certain gibberish and the performance of certain mummeries. **1884** STEPNIAK in *Contemp. Rev.* Mar. 333 The aborigines speak an unintelligible gibberish.

Comb. **1653** URQUHART *Rabelais* II. xi. The babling tattle, and fond fibs, seditiously raised between the gibblegablers, and Accursian gibberish-mongers.

†**B.** *adj.* Of or pertaining to gibberish, expressed in gibberish; unintelligible, unmeaning. *Obs.*

1598 FLORIO, *Balchi*, a..roguish, gibbrish word, vsed for money. **1612** tr. *Benvenuto's Passenger* I iii 3 b, The frauds, deceits, lyes, gibbrish language of roagues. **1648** MILTON *Tenure Kings* (1650) 3 That old entanglement of iniquity, their gibrish Lawes. *a* **1691** BAXTER in Sir J. Stephen *Eccl. Biog.* (1850) II. 47 By his gibberish derision, persuading men that we deserve no other answer than such scorn and nonsense as beseemeth fools. **1704** *Proclam.* 24 Feb., in *Lond. Gaz.* No. 3996/1 The Key or Cypher, whereby Four Letters written in Gibbirish Language..may be.. explained. **1764** *Mem. G. Psalmanazar* 173 A kind of gibberish prose and verse. **1821** CLARE *Vill. Minstr.* I. 122 How oft I've bent me o'er her fire and smoke, To hear her [the gipsy's] gibberish tale so quaintly spoke.

Hence †'**gibberish** *v. intr.*, to talk gibberish; also *trans.*, to speak the 'gibberish' of.

1577–86 STANYHURST *Descr. Irel.* i. in Holinshed *Chron.*, One demanded merilie whie Oneile..would not frame himselfe to speake English? What (quoth the other) in a rage, thinkest thou that it standeth with Oneile his honor to writh his mouth in clattering English? and yet forsooth we must gag our iawes in gibbrishing Irish? **1625** BP. R. MOUNTAGU *App. Cæsar.* xviii. 248 You understand not the state of *Limbus Patrum*, nor the depth of the Question, but scumme upon the surface, and gibberish you cannot tell for what.

gibberose (,gɪbə'rəʊs), *a.* *rare*$^{-0}$. [ad. L. *gibberōs-us*, f. *gibber* a hump.] 'More convex or tumid in one place than another' (*Treas. Bot.* 1866). Hence **gibbe'rosity.**

1727 BAILEY vol. II, *Gibberosity.* **1880** GRAY *Struct. Bot.* 413/1 Gibbous..swelling out on one side into a gibber or gibberosity.

†'**gibbert.** *Obs.* Also 7 **gibbartas, gibbarta,** 7–9 **gibbar**; and see JUBARTES. [ad. F. *gibbar* in the same sense.] A kind of whale, a FINNER.

1602 R. DOLMAN tr. *Primaudaye's Fr. Acad.* (1618) III. lxiii. 782 And in this number is the whale, of which the ancients write, and whome some moderns call Gibbar (because that the common whale, which some take for the Musculus of Aristotle, doth not answere to the description of this), which is of incredible hugenes. **1620** J. MASON *New-found-land* (Bannatyne Club 1867) B, What should I speake of a kinde of Whales called Gibberts? **1658** SIR T. BROWNE *Pseud. Ep.* III. xxvi. (ed. 3) 214 Mariners..called it a Jubartas, or rather Gibbartas. The name Gibbarta we find also given unto one kind of Greenland Whales. **1843**

Zoologist I. 34 It..is well known among fishermen and mariners generally by the names of finner..and gibbar.

gibbet (ˈdʒɪbɪt), *sb.*[1] Forms: 3-8 gibet(t, 3-5 gebet(t, 4-6 gyb(b)ate, -et(te, jebat, (4 gebat, 6 *Sc.* geibat, geobet, gibbot), 5-6 jub(b)et(t, 5-7 jeb(b)et(t, 6 gyb(b)yt(te, gebbit, jebytt, 6-7 jeb(b)it, jibbet(t, jeobet(te, -it, 7-8 gibbit, 6- gibbet. [a. OF. *gibet* gallows, gibbet, in early use, staff or cudgel, dim. of *gibe* staff, club: see JIB. The It. *giubbetto* of the same meaning is believed to be from Fr., influenced in form by *giubbetto*, *-etta*, dim. of *giubba* cloak.]

1. Originally synonymous with GALLOWS *sb.*, but in later use signifying an upright post with projecting arm from which the bodies of criminals were hung in chains or irons after execution.

a **1225** *Ancr. R.* 116 Me were muchele dole leouere þet ich iseie ou alle þreo..hongen on a gibet uorte wiðbuwen sunne. **13..** *K. Alis.* 4722 Heore feet men kneotte theo hors to. To the gybet al quyk men tare, Hygh they weore an-honged thare. **1382** WYCLIF *Deut.* xxi. 22 Whanne a man..were hongid in the gebet, the careyn of hym shal not abide in the tree. *a* **1450** *Knt. de la Tour* (1868) 64 She was atyred with highe longe pynnes lyke a iebet, and so she was scorned of alle the company, and saide she bare a galous on her hede. **1509** BARCLAY *Shyp of Folys* (1570) 8 Their bodyes to the ieobet solempnly ascende Wauing with the wether while their necke will holde. *a* **1529** SKELTON *Sp. Parrot* 75 The iebet of Baldock was made for Jack Leg. **1572** *Nottingham Rec.* IV. 141 Payd to Bate for takyng of Cranwell downe of the jebytt xij d. **1625** *Gonsalvio's Sp. Inquis.* 48 The lines that tye both his hands and thumbes to a certaine Pullie which hangeth on the Ieobit. **1642** FULLER *Holy & Prof. St.* IV. ii. 248 Haman inherits the gibbet of Mordecai. **1705** HICKERINGILL *Priest-cr.* I. (1721) 37, I never saw any spiritual Highway-Man..according to their Merits, hang'd upon Gibbets. **1727-41** CHAMBERS *Cycl.*, *Gibet*, a machine in manner of a gallows, whereon notorious criminals after execution, are hung in irons, or chains, as spectacles, in terrorem. **1770** GOLDSM. *Des. Vill.* 318 There, the black gibbet glooms beside the way. **1818** SCOTT *Hrt. Midl.* ii, Several groups..gazed on the scaffold and gibbet. **1865** KINGSLEY *Herew.* xxi, You shall see a row of gibbets from here to Deeping.

fig. c **1440** *Gesta Rom.* I. i. 5 (Harl. MS.) Now þan most a prelate honge the wif—what bymenyth that? Farsoth þat ..þe flesh be hongyd on þe iebet of penaunce. **1600** HEYWOOD *1st Pt. Edw. IV*, Wks. 1874 I. 34 Hast thou ensnar'd our heedlesse feet with death, And brought vs to the Iibbet of defame? **1650** TRAPP *Comm. Gen.* vi. 17 God hath hang'd up the old world in gibbets, as it were, for our admonition. **1742** YOUNG *Nt. Th.* VI. 264 Heart-merit wanting, mount we ne'er so high, Our height is but the gibbet of our name. **1806** FESSENDEN *Democr.* I. 15 Expos'd on satire's gibbet high, To frighten others of the fry.

†**b.** Applied to the Cross. *Obs.*

c **1450** *Mirour Saluacioun* 4666 On the Gibet of the crosse deignyng for me to dye. **1535** FISHER *Wks.* (1876) 416 On the gebbit of the Crosse.

c. ***Halifax Gibbet***: an instrument for beheading criminals, similar to the Scotch maiden or French guillotine, formerly in use at Halifax in Yorkshire.

1650 in J. Watson *Halifax* (1775) 219 To suffer death, by having their heads severed, and cut off from their bodies, at Halifax Gibbet. **1775** J. WATSON *Ibid.*, The said Abraham Wilkinson and Anthony Mitchell were..conducted to the said gibbet, and there executed in the usual form.

†**d.** ***to ride the gibbet***: to be carried on a pole round the town. Cf. *to ride the stang*. *Obs.*$^{-1}$

1519 *Surtees Misc.* (1888) 34 She shalnot chyde ne flyte wᵗ eny neghtburez..oppen ridyng of the jebit, or thew, aboute the towne.

2. The punishment of death by hanging.

1751 JORTIN *Serm.* (1771) VII. xi. 218 The..wickedness of many is such, that nothing but..jails and gibbets can keep civil society in..order. **1814** SCOTT *Ld. of Isles* II. v, Some poor criminal..from the gibbet..Respited for a day. **1872** C. GIBBON *For the King* xiii, The gibbet and the musket are the only lawgivers of the hour.

fig. **1502** *Ord. Crysten Men* (W. de W. 1506) II. iv. 91 And to be condempned unto the gybet of hell.

3. †**a.** A short beam projecting from a wall, having a pulley fixed at the end (*obs.*). **b.** The projecting arm of a crane; also called JIB. **c.** *Sc.* A chimney crane for hanging a pot over the fire.

a. 1502 ARNOLDE *Chron.* (1811) 127 The said wardens.. haue made in the stede of yᵉ said crane a gibet hanging on a wall not able to take any thingis out of the watir of Thamyse. **1545** *Act 37 Hen. VIII*, c. 12 §9 Houses, with Key or Wharf, having any Crane or Gibet belonging to the same. **1570** DEE *Math. Pref.* 35 All Cranes, Gybbettes, and Ingines to lift vp.

b. 1729 DESAGULIERS in *Phil. Trans.* XXXVI. 194 The Crane must be a fix'd one, and only the Gibbet moveable, from which the Weight hangs. **1806** O. GREGORY *Mech.* (1807) II. 197 Gibbet or jib of a crane, the projecting beam upon the extremity of which is fixed a pulley. **1875** in KNIGHT *Dict. Mech.*

c. 1477 *Extracts Aberd. Reg.* (1844) I. 408 A brewyne fat, a hemmyr stand, a bukket, and a gybbate that it hang by. **1887** [see *gibbet-pan* in 5 below].

†**4.** A cudgel. *Obs.*

c **1600** DAY *Begg. Bednall Gr.* v. (1881) 108 Give me but an ashen Gibbet in my hand, an I do not dry bang them both, I'll be bound to eat hay with a horse, so will I. **1674-91** RAY *S. & E.C. Words* 100 A *Gibbet*; a great Cudgel, such as they throw up Trees to beat down the Fruit.

5. *attrib.* and *Comb.*, as ***gibbet-chain***, ***-foot***, ***-irons***, ***-law***, ***-tree***; ***gibbet-carrier***, ***-maker***; ***gibbet-wise*** adv.; also **gibbet-gab**, **-pan**, *Sc.* (see quots.); **gibbet-thief**, a thief who is hanged on a gibbet.

1731 ARBUTHNOT *Treat. Scolding* 20 You did not love Cruelty, you Kennel-raker, you *Gibbet-carrier. *a* **1847** ELIZA COOK *Song of Wind* vi, I had swung the *gibbet-chains against the bleaching bones. **1826** SCOTT *Woodst.* xxx, Keep your scurrile jests for the *gibbet-foot. **1887** JAMIESON, Suppl. s.v. *Gibbet*, The largest pots were hung on the swee itself, or were attached to it by a strong double hook called the *gibbet-gab. **1898** *Daily News* 13 Sept. 5/1 A complete set of *gibbet irons. **1708** S. MIDGLEY (*title*) Hallifax, and its *Gibbet-Law placed in a true Light. **1838** *Penny Cycl.* XII. 13/2 The 'Halifax Gibbet Law' was not alone exercised for the protection of clothiers, but it was also used for the punishment of other felonies. **1588** SHAKS. *Tit. A.* IV. iii. 80 What sayes Iupiter? *Clowne.* Ho the *Iibbetmaker, he sayes that he hath taken them downe againe, for the man must not be hang'd till the next weeke. **1887** JAMIESON, Suppl., **Gibbet-pan*, a name given to the largest pot or pan used in cooking: so called because it generally hung on the gibbet or swee. **1700** CONGREVE *Way of World* III. v, I hope to see him hung with Tatters, like a long Lane Pent-house, or a *Gibbet-thief. **13..** *St. Cristofer* 668 in Horstm. *Altengl. Leg.* (1881) 462 Myne eldirs.. sloughe hym on a *gebete-tree. **1808** SCOTT *Marm.* I. xii, We saw..on the gibbet-tree, reversed, His foeman's scutcheon tied. **1622** MABBE tr. *Aleman's Guzman d'Alf.* I. 266 Putting a piece of Timber *Gibbet-wise into that hole in the Wall.

†ˈ**gibbet**, *sb.*[2] *Obs.* [Perh. a. OF. *juppet* (occurring in the sense 'distance to which one can shout'), f. *jupper*, *juper* to whoop, cry out.]

A note on the horn, a call or whistle as a signal to a dog or hawk. Hence †ˈ**gibbeting** *vbl. sb.*, the utterance of such a signal.

1590 SIR T. COCKAINE *Hunting* C iv b, Being sure it is his owne Deere, he may giue one gibbet at euery imprime, and no more. **1615** MARKHAM *Country Contentm.* I. viii. 93 If your Hawke..rake and gase after euery checke, neither respecting whooping nor gibbeting, in this case you must [etc.]. **1616** SURFLET & MARKHAM *Country Farme* 668 The cries of the hounds, the winding of hornes, or the gibbetting of the huntsmen. **1621** MARKHAM *Hunger's Prevent.* (1655) 49 Your Water-dogge..vpon the least gybbet or call to come running vnto you. **1730** SIR W. YONGE *Norfolk Garland*, Tolle Aux! then Callet cry'd And gave a gibbet shrill.

gibbet (ˈdʒɪbɪt), *v.* [f. GIBBET *sb.*[1]]

†**1.** *intr.* To hang as on a gibbet. *Obs.*

1597 SHAKS. *2 Hen. IV*, III. ii. 282 Hee that gibbets on the Brewers Bucket.

2. *trans.* To put to death by hanging.

1726 AMHERST *Terræ Fil.* viii. 37 Starving, burning, and gibetting, one year, all persons holding such opinions. **1851** DIXON *W. Penn* xxvii. (1872) 246 He was..found guilty, and gibbeted in front of his own house in Cheapside. **1881** BLACKIE *Lay Serm.* viii. 239 The Stuarts gibbeted the Covenanters because they denied the rights of a civil sovereign to frame liturgies [etc.].

b. To hang (a carcase) on a gibbet by way of infamous exposure. Also with *up*.

1752 [see 3]. **1761** *Brit. Mag.* II. 669 This murderer.. under-standing that he was to be gibbeted..was greatly enraged. **1790** BURKE *Fr. Rev.* 209 Wickedness..walks abroad; it continues its ravages; whilst you are gibbeting the carcass, or demolishing the tomb. *c* **1820** S. ROGERS *Italy, Adventure* II. xiv. (1828) 87 Soon should I..limb by limb, be mangled on a wheel, Then gibbeted to blacken for the vultures. **1828** SCOTT *F.M. Perth* xxiii, Away with that convict to the gallows, and gibbet him alive an you will. **1866** ROGERS *Agric. & Prices* I. iv. 88 All the culprits were hanged; according to Walsingham, were gibbetted in chains.

c. *transf.* To hang up (a bird, a thing) on or as on a gibbet.

1749 FIELDING *Tom Jones* I. i, The same animal..may perhaps be degraded in another part, and some of his limbs gibbetted, as it were, in the vilest stall in town. **1777** BRAND *Pop. Antiq.* 389 Some Inns still gibbet their Signs across a Town. **1822** W. IRVING *Braceb. Hall* xxv. 212 They [the crows] are gibbetted in every corn-field. **1866** HOWELLS *Venet. Life* vii. 111 A long crane with villainous pots gibbeted upon it.

3. *fig.* To hold up to infamy or public contempt. Also with *up*. ***to gibbet into***: to bring into (an ignominious position) as by hanging on a gibbet.

1646 J. WHITAKER *Uzziah* 5 God doth..gibbet his open adversaries. *a* **1683** OLDHAM *On Printer* 44, I mean to hang and Gibbet up thy Name. **1752** WARBURTON *Let. to Balguy* in Hurd *Life* (1794) 65, I had gibbeted up Julian, and he comes by night to cut him down. **1762** GOLDSM. *Cit. W.* xii, Thus [he] unknowingly gibbeted himself into infamy, when he might have otherwise quietly retired into oblivion. **1836** SOUTHEY in *Cowper's Wks.* II. 26 This reviewal of Cowper's first volume is one of those defunct criticisms which deserve to be disinterred and gibbeted for the sake of example. **1848** ASHLEY in Hodder *Ld. Shaftesbury* II. xvii. 274 Poor Melbourne died yesterday, and to-day he is, of course, gibbeted in the Times. This is 'one of the new terrors of death'. **1886** T. FROST *Remin. Country Journalist* v. (1888) 59 Everybody..[was] apprehensive of being morally gibbeted in its pages.

Hence ˈ**gibbeted** *ppl. a.*, ˈ**gibbeting** *vbl. sb.* (in quot. *attrib.*).

1756 L. C. in *Old Maid* (1764) No. 34 ¶4 Thus I hung suspended in the air..a terrible gibbeted example of curiosity. **1825** SCOTT *Talism.* xiv, I shall be a gibbeted and dishonoured corse. **1858** CARLYLE *Fredk. Gt.* VII. v. II. 291 Your road horribly decked with gibbeted thieves hanging aloft. **1875** W. HOUGHTON *Sk. Brit. Ins.* 105 Stomachs of the gibbeted moles. **1891** *Pall Mall G.* 7 Sept. 7/2 It seems to be by the merest accident that any gibbeting irons have been preserved for our gratification, since they were left to perish with the bodies they contained.

†**gibbeˈtation.** *Obs.*$^{-1}$ In 7 gibitation. [f. GIBBET *v.*[1] + -ATION.] The action of gibbeting.

1689 in Ld. Campbell *Chancellors* (1857) IV. cii. 412, I, George Jeffreys, being in sound and perfect memory, of high commissions..gibitations, barbarity, butchery, etc., do make my last will.

gibbey, gibbi, gibbier, vars. GIBBY, GIBIER.

gibbirish, gibbit, obs. ff. GIBBERISH, GIBBET.

gibble-gabble (ˈgɪb(ə)lˈgæb(ə)l). Also 7 gible-gable. [Reduplication of GABBLE *sb.* Cf. FIDDLE-FADDLE.] Senseless chatter.

1600 DEKKER *Gent. Craft* (1610) C 3 Hee's some vplandish workman, hire him good maister, that I may learne some gibble, gabble, twill make vs worke the faster. **1615** J. TAYLOR (Water P.) *Siege Jerus.* Wks. (1630) 10/2 Such Gibrish Gibble Gabble all did iangle. **1769** *Trinculo's Trip* 41 Soon was heard a gibble-gabble, Neither harmony or sense. **1889** *N.W. Linc. Gloss.* (ed. 2), *Gibble-gabble*, silly chatter.

attrib. a **1693** URQUHART *Rabelais* III. xxii. 178 The Gibble gabble Gibbrish of this odious Error and Heresie. **1745-6** MRS. DELANY in *Life & Corr.* (1861) II. 424 A strange gibble-gabble woman has plagued me all the morning.

Hence †ˈ**gibble-ˈgabble** *v.* Also †ˈ**gibble-ˈgabbler.**

1653 Gibblegablers [see GIBBERISH *sb. Comb.*]. **1775** SHIRREFS *Poems* (1790) 211 They said the grace as fast as able, Syn a' yok'd to to gibble-gabble, And mak a din. *c* **1785** *J. Thompson's Man* 11 She will gibble-gabble like a Goose.

gibbon[1] (ˈgɪbən). *Zool.* [a. F. *gibbon* (Buffon), alleged to be an Indian word, but it has not been found in any Indian language.] A name common to the long-armed apes of the genus *Hylobates*, but applied esp. to the species *Hylobates lar* which inhabits the islands of the Indian Archipelago.

[**1770** *Gentl. Mag.* XL. 402 This Monkey, the Editor thinks is the same that M. Buffon has described under the name of Gibbon.] **1774** GOLDSM. *Nat. Hist.* IV. 206 Of this kind also is the Gibbon..or the Long Armed Ape. **1834** MᶜMURTRIE *Cuvier's Anim. Kingd.* 45 The Gibbons have the long arms of the true Ourangs, and the low forehead of the Chimpansé. **1867** WOOD *Pop. Nat. Hist.* 12 The Agile Gibbon is not a very good walker on its hinder feet. **1882** *Contemp. Rev.* Mar. 422 A gibbon will hang for hours suspended from a branch.

gibbon[2] (ˈgɪbən). *dial.* [a. Manx. *gibbin* (Kelly) = Irish *goibin* (O'Reilly).] A sand eel.

1868 *Nat. Encycl.* I. 627 In the Isle of Man the two species are distinguished from each other as the Gray Gibbon and Red Gibbon. **1883** *Fisheries Exhib. Catal.* (ed. 4) 131 One Sand Eel or Gibbon Grip. One Pair of 'Corran Gibbon' or Sand Eel Sickles.

Gibbonian (gɪˈbəʊnɪən), *a.* [f. the name *Gibbon* (see def.) + -IAN.] Relating to or resembling the style or opinions of the historian Edward Gibbon (1737-94).

1794 *Crit. Rev.* XI. 60 That sneering infidelity, which after times, perhaps, will distinguish by the epithet of Gibbonian. **1892** A. BIRRELL *Res Judicatae* 46 Is it not sometimes a relief to exchange the quips and cranks of some of our modern writers..for the stately roll of the Gibbonian sentence? **1939** A. TOYNBEE *Study Hist.* IV. 149 Great Britain..could congratulate herself, in Gibbonian language, upon having survived..a fluctuation in the Balance of Power. **1970** *Daily Tel.* 6 Aug. 6/2 [J. G.] Frazer's Gibbonian style [in *The Golden Bough*]..does not make for exactly easy reading.

gibbose (gɪˈbəʊs), *a.* [ad. L. *gibbōs-us*, f. *gibbus* hump.]

1. = GIBBOUS *a.* 1, 1 b, and 1 c.

1674 GREW *Anat. Plants, Lect. Mixture* iii. §8 (1682) 226 When two Atomes meet, which are globular or other-wise gibbose. **1695** WOODWARD *Nat. Hist. Earth* VI. (1723) 280 Reducing those [shells] that are concave and gibbose to a flat. **1714** DERHAM *Astro-Theol.* v. i. (1726) 113 Even Mars, too, in its Quadratures, becomes Gibbose. **1851-6** WOODWARD *Mollusca* II. 228 Atrypa reticularis..Shell impunctate..dorsal valve gibbose. **1866** *Treas. Bot.* 530/2.

2. = GIBBOUS *a.* 2.

1721 in BAILEY.

gibbosity (gɪˈbɒsɪtɪ). [ad. F. *gibbosité*, f. L. *gibbōsus*: see prec.]

1. The state, quality, or condition of being gibbose or gibbous.

1547 BOORDE *Brev. Health* cviii. 41 A backe the which may have many infirmities, as debylytie, and wekenes, curvytie, and gybbositie. *a* **1646** J. GREGORY *Maps & Charts* in *Posthuma* (1650) 305 This way of Description rendreth the face of the Earth upon a Plain in its own proper Figure Spherically, as upon the Globe it self, the gibbositie onely allowed for. **1691** RAY *Creation* II. (1701) 194 What should take away the sight of these ships from each other, but the gibbosity of the interjacent water? **1794-6** E. DARWIN *Zoon.* (1801) I. 159 It is by suggestion, that the gibbosity of the tree and the moss, that fringes its trunk, appear before us. **1853** ERICHSEN *Surg.* 624 When they have fallen together and very considerable gibbosity has resulted, anchylosis more readily takes place. **1872** PROCTOR *Ess. Astron.* iv. 63 When Mars is in quadrature his gibbosity is not very remarkable.

2. A swelling; a protuberance.

c **1400** *Lanfranc's Cirurg.* 224 Apostym wiþoutforþ aboute þe spaudis and þe gibbositees. **1545** RAYNOLD *Byrth Mankynde* I. (1634) 72 The gybosite or swelling seate of the liuer. **1638** WILKINS *New World* viii. (1707) 60 The brighter parts [of the Moon] are full of rugged Gibbosities and Mountains. *a* **1794** SIR W. JONES *Select Ind. Plants* Wks. 1799 II. 105 Some with an acute point, dark green above, paler beneath with a gibbosity at the insertion of the petiols. *a* **1813** WILSON *Amer. Ornith.* (1814) VIII. 77 The edges of the upper and lower gibbosities have each twenty-three indentations, or strong teeth, on each side. **1826** KIRBY & SP. *Entomol.* III. 145 In some..this anal horn is replaced by a gibbosity. **1870** HOOKER *Stud. Flora* 138 Acute or acuminate, the gibbosity close to the stem. **1875** LYELL *Princ. Geol.* I. II. xxv. 641 Such gibbosities are caused by the abrupt termination of viscous streams.

gibboso- (gɪˈbəʊsəʊ), modern combining form of L. *gibbōsus* GIBBOUS, in terms denoting combination of the gibbous form with some other: see quots.

1846 DANA *Zooph.* (1848) 268 Incrusting and prominently gibbous or gibboso-lobate. *Ibid.* 342 Coarse gibboso-glomerate and angular. *Ibid.* 495 Subcespitose..gibboso-subramose. *Ibid.* 563 Gibboso-subglobose. Corallum having the cells shallow.

gibbot, obs. form of GIBBET *sb.*[1]

gibbous (ˈgɪbəs), *a.* Also 7 gibbouse. [f. L. *gibbus* hump + -OUS.

The guttural (g) in this and the related words is contrary to the ordinary rule for the pronunciation of Latin derivatives, but there is no evidence that (dʒ) was ever used.]

1. Convex, rounded, protuberant.

c **1400** *Lanfranc's Cirurg.* 167 In oon side he is gibbous, & in þe toþer side he is more playn. **1548–77** VICARY *Anat.* viii. (1888) 69 The forme of the lyuer is gibbous or bunchy on the back side. **1615** CROOKE *Body of Man* 636 The exterior superficies of this gristle is conuex or gibbous. *a* **1646** J. GREGORY *Maps & Charts* in *Posthuma* (1650) 307 The Globe of the Moon..is as solid and gibbous as that of this Earth and Water. **1677** PLOT *Oxfordsh.* 117 In Cowley-common we meet only with the gibbous, and not the flat shell of the petrified Oyster. **1737** *Gaudentio di Lucca* 101 All the new Philosophers allow the Earth to be Spheroidal and Gibbous towards the Equator. **1766** PENNANT *Zool.* (1768) I. 213 The gibbous substance on their head. **1849** MURCHISON *Siluria* ix. 195 That section..which has both valves gibbous. **1881** G. BUSK in *Jrnl. Microsc. Sc.* Jan. 8 The outer border..sharp and nearly straight, and the inner as it were gibbous.

b. *Bot.* ‘Very convex or tumid..this term should be restricted to solid convexities’ (Lindley).

1757 *Phil. Trans.* L. 66 The calyx is a gibbous permanent periantheum. **1805** J. GALPINE *Brit. Bot.* (1806) 274 Calyx gibbous. **1845** LINDLEY *Sch. Bot.* vi. (1858) 103 Corolla without a spur, gibbous at the base. **1861** MISS PRATT *Flower. Pl.* V. 327 Order Pistiaceæ..(Gibbous Duck-weed). Fronds inversely egg-shaped, hemispherical beneath. **1872** OLIVER *Elem. Bot.* II. 136 Observe [in Common Fumitory] the irregular corolla, one of the petals being gibbous at the base.

c. *Astr.* Said of the moon or a planet when the illuminated portion exceeds a semicircle, but is less than a circle.

1690 LEYBOURN *Curs. Math.* 449 She is liable to the same variety of changes as the Moon, sometimes almost Full, at other times Gibbous. **1755** B. MARTIN *Mag. Arts & Sci.* 122 She is then said to be gibbous; and this Phase or Aspect increases till she comes to the Situation E, where she is in Opposition to the Sun. **1834** SIR H. TAYLOR *2nd Pt. Artevelde* v. iii, The gibbous moon was in a wan decline. **1879** *Cassell's Techn. Educ.* IV. 3/1 Mars likewise appears gibbous when near the quadratures of the sun.

Comb. **1839** BAILEY *Festus* xix. (1848) 198 Many moons and planets full, crescent, or gibbous-faced.

2. Of persons and animals: Hunch-backed; having a hump. Of a part of the body: Hump-shaped. ***gibbous wrasse***, a fish (see quot. 1769).

1646 SIR T. BROWNE *Pseud. Ep.* VI. x. 329 How Oxen in some Countries began and continue gibbous or bunch back'd? *a* **1661** FULLER *Worthies, Cambridgesh.* I. (1662) 150 A Camel passeth in the Latine proverb, either for gibbous and distorted, or for one that undertaketh a thing awkely or ungeenly. **1769** PENNANT *Zool.* (1776) III. 219 *Gibbous Wrasse*..of a very deep and elevated form, the back being vastly arched, and very sharp or ridged. **1791** COWPER *Iliad* II. 266 His gibbous shoulders o'er his breast Contracted. **1810** CRABBE *Borough* v. 54 Is there of all your kindred some who lack Vision direct, or have a gibbous back? **1822–34** *Good's Study Med.* (ed. 4) I. 482 Lommius asserts after Hippocrates, that if a person become gibbous before puberty in consequence of asthma, he dies. **1879** DIXON *Windsor* I. iv. 38 Shrivelled in his loins, he [William de Longchamp] had a gibbous chest [etc.].

Hence ˈ**gibbously** *adv.*, in a gibbous manner; ˈ**gibbousness**, the state of being gibbous.

1692 BENTLEY *Boyle Lect.* viii. (1693) 37 Because of the distance, the convexity and gibbousness would vanish away; he would only see below him a great circular Flat, as level to his thinking as the face of the Moon. **1846** DANA *Zooph.* (1848) 497 Bearing above a few very stout erect stems, gibbously divided and tuberose, never angular. **1880** WATSON in *Jrnl. Linn. Soc.* XV. No. 82. 108 Spire sharply but slightly convexly and a very little gibbously conical.

gibbridge, gibbrish, obs. ff. GIBBERISH.

gibbsite (ˈgɪbzaɪt). *Min.* [named after George *Gibbs*, an American mineralogist: see -ITE.] Aluminium hydrate found in stalactitic forms, often as an incrustation.

1822 CLEAVELAND *Min.* 783 Dr. Torrey..has proposed for this mineral the name of Gibbsite, in honor of Col. George Gibbs. **1873** *Proc. Amer. Phil. Soc.* XIII. 373 A pseudomorph of gibbsite after corundum.

gibby (ˈgɪbɪ). Also 9 gibbey. [dim. of GIB *sb.*[3]]

a. Short for *gibby-stick*.

1852 R. S. SURTEES *Sponge's Sp. Tour* l. 286 Fine, straight hollies, fit either for gibbeys or whip-sticks.

b. *Comb.*, as **gibby-stick**, (*a*) a stick with a bent or hooked handle; (*b*) a kind of sweetmeat made in the form of a gibby-stick.

1788 W. MARSHALL *Yorksh.* Gloss. (E.D.S.) s.v. *Gib*, A *gibby stick*, a hooked stick. **1832** W. STEPHENSON *Gateshead Local Poems* 103 Here's barley sugar sweet, Gibby sticks and kisses. **1852** R. S. SURTEES *Sponge's Sp. Tour* xlix. 275 All the gibbey sticks were bundled out. **1893** *Northumbld. Gloss.*, *Gibby-stick*, a stick with the end bent for a handle.

gibbyhorse: see JIBBYHORSE.

gibe, jibe (dʒaɪb), *sb.*[1] Also 6–9 **gybe**, 6 **jybe**, 6– **gibe**. [f. the vb.] A scoffing or sneering speech; a taunt, flout, or jeer.

1573 G. HARVEY *Letter-bk.* (Camden) 8 Besides sum other trim iests and iybes of his. **1602** SHAKS. *Ham.* v. i. 209 Alas poore Yorick..Where be your Jibes now? **1642** MILTON *Apol. Smect.* Wks. (1847) 76/2 To be girded with frumps and curtall gibes. **1712** STEELE *Spect.* No. 300 ¶1 Their aversion would be too strong for little Gibes every moment. **1757** DYER *Fleece* (1807) 65 They..cast about their gibes. **1812** BYRON *Ch. Har.* I. lxix, Provoking envious gibe from each pedestrian churl. **1835** MARRYAT *Jac. Faithf.* iv, Many were the bitter gibes and inuendoes which I was obliged to hear. **1874** DISRAELI *Sp.* 5 Aug. in *Hansard's Debates* CCXXI. 1358 He is a great master of gibes, and flouts, and jeers. **1885** BLACK *White Heather* i, The jibes that seemed to form their farewells for the night.

† **gibe**, *sb.*[2] *Obs.*[−1] [shortened form of GIBBET.] A gibbet.

1590 FENNE *Frutes, Hecuba's Mishaps* D d b, They his body ript, And naked on a gibe they hang for Troyans there to see.

gibe, jibe (dʒaɪb), *v.* Also 6 **jybe**, 6–9 **gybe**, (7 **ghybe**). [Of obscure origin: perh. ad. OF. *giber*, explained by Godef. (who refers to mod. dial. *giber* to kick) as meaning to shake, *trans.* and *intr.* (‘secouer, s'agiter’), but in the examples app. meaning ‘to handle roughly in sport’, ‘to use horseplay’. Cf. JIB *v.*]

1. *intr.* To speak sneeringly; to utter taunts; to jeer, flout, scoff. Const. *at*, †*with*. Also *dial.* to scold.

1567 TURBERVILE *Epit.*, etc. 68 Speake fayre, and make the weather cleere To him that gybes with thee. *a* **1592** GREENE *Alphonsus* III. Wks. 1831 II. 33 You shall perceive Medea did not gibe. *a* **1639** W. WHATELEY *Prototypes* I. vi. (1640) 72 Wicked wittes will never cease gybing at those good things that crosse their sense and reason. **1674–91** RAY *N.C. Words* (E.D.S.), *Gibe, Ghybe*, to scold. **1722** DE FOE *Moll Flanders* (1840) 5 Well, madam, forsooth, says she, gibing at me; you would be a gentle-woman. **1821** GALT *Ann. Parish* xxxv. (1895) 133 The rising generation were taught to jibe at its [the Christian religion's] holiest ordinances [etc.]. **1851** THACKERAY *Eng. Hum.* vi. (1876) 347 The old fiddler gibed at him for his ugliness. **1874** L. STEPHEN *Hours in Library* (1892) I. ii. 58 Richardson..is always gibing at Fielding.

2. *trans.* To address with scoffs and sneers; to flout, taunt.

1582 T. WATSON *Centurie of Loue* lxvii. in *Poems* (Arb.) 103 When other whiles he passeth Lemnos Ile, Vnhappy boy he gybes the Clubfoote Smith. **1606** SHAKS. *Ant. & Cl.* II. ii. 74 You..with taunts Did gibe my Misiue out of audience. **1666** WOOD *Life* (O.H.S.) II. 90 The deane..would be alwaie gibing him at meales. **1733** SWIFT *Legion Club* Wks. 1755 IV. I. 208 Draw the beasts as I describe them From their features, while I gibe them. **1825** C. M. WESTMACOTT *Eng. Spy* I. 273 Gibe him for a dolt. **1852** HAWTHORNE *Blithedale Rom.* viii. (1883) 394 Zenobia soon saw the truth, and gibed me about it, one day. **1893** JESSOPP *Stud. by Recluse* i. 33 Evil demons might chatter and gibe and twit him at his prayers.

gibe, var. JIBE *U.S.*, to chime in (*with*).

gibel (ˈgɪbəl). [a. G. *gibel, giebel*.] The Prussian or Crucian Carp, *Carassius* (formerly *Cyprinus*) *gibelio* (see CARP *sb.*[1] 2). Also *gibel carp*.

1841 YARRELL *Brit. Fishes* (ed. 2) I. 358.

gibelet(te, Gibel(l)ine, obs. ff. GIBLET, GHIBELLINE.

†**giben.** *Obs. Hebrides.* [? a use of Gael. *giaban* gizzard.] (See quots.)

1697 MARTIN in *Phil. Trans.* XIX. 729 This Giben is the Fat of Sea Fowls preserved in the Stomach. **1700** [see BROCHAN]. **1746** *Brit. Mag.* 134 Gibben is the Fat in the Stomach of a Sea-Fowl, and it is a sovereign Remedy for Coughs and green Wounds.

Gibeonite (ˈgɪbɪənaɪt). [f. *Gibeon* + -ITE.] One of the inhabitants of Gibeon who were condemned by Joshua to be ‘hewers of wood and drawers of water’ for the Israelites (*Josh.* ix. 27). Hence, a menial, a drudge.

1798 BLOOMFIELD *Farmer's Boy, Spring* 223 A Gibeonite, that serves them all by turns.

giber, jiber (ˈdʒaɪbə(r)). [f. GIBE *v.* + -ER[1].] One who gibes; one who utters gibes and taunts.

1563 *Homilies* II. *Inform. Cert. Places Script.* II. (1859) 379 Provoke him not to pour out his wrath now upon you, as he did then upon those gibers and mockers. **1607** SHAKS. *Cor.* II. i. 91 You are..vnderstood to be a perfecter gyber for the Table, then a necessary Bencher in the Capitoll. **1612** SHELTON *Quix.* I. iii. 16 The Oast, who, as we noted before, was a great giber. *a* **1745** SWIFT *Char. Sir R. Walpole* in *Lett. C'tess Suffolk* (1824) II. 32 Of virtue and worth by profession a giber; Of juries and senates the bully and briber. **1881** *Daily News* 8 Aug. 5/1 The most relentless jiber at the amusements of Congresses will hardly refuse to admit that [etc.].

gibett, obs. form of GIBBET.

‖**gibier** (ʒibje). Now *rare*. Also 8 **gibbier**. [Fr.] Game; wild-fowl.

1514 in *Rutland Papers* (Camden) 27 Item, iiij pieces of gibier or wildfowle, that is to say, ij perdryches and ij.. woodcocks, and at some tyme other gybier. **1704** ADDISON *Italy* (1733) 126 The Fowl and Gibbier are tax free. **1827** LYTTON *Pelham* xix, An excellent restaurateur's..where one gets irreproachable *gibier*, and meets no English. **1872** [EARL PEMBROKE & G. H. KINGSLEY] *S. Sea Bubbles* v. 129 A small whistling parrot, with a purple back and white throat, which I am told is the king's favourite gibier.

gibing, jibing (ˈdʒaɪbɪŋ), *vbl. sb.* [f. GIBE *v.* + -ING[1].] The action of the verb GIBE.

1579 G. HARVEY *Letter-bk.* (Camden) 61 What but.. notorious or auricular iybinge on every hande? **1672** MARVELL *Reh. Transp.* I. 196 Mr. Bayes..might..have spared his jibing at that day. **1864** CARLYLE *Fredk. Gt.* XI. iii. IV. 54 There was no end to his jibings and bitter pleasantries.

gibing, jibing (ˈdʒaɪbɪŋ), *ppl. a.* [f. GIBE *v.* + -ING[2].] That gibes; mocking, taunting, sarcastic.

1574 WHITGIFT *Def. Answ.* II. 96 Yet is it also your pleasure to spende your gibing and iesting eloquence vpon me. **1579** LYLY *Euphues* (Arb.) 92 Euphues..answering his taunts in these gibing termes. *a* **1680** ROCHESTER *Sat. agst. Man.* 49 This gibing, gingling Knack, call'd Wit. *a* **1687** COTTON *Poet. Wks.* (1765) 12 With a gibing kind of Nay-word. **1704** SWIFT *T. Tub* xi. (1709) 128 He would tell the gibing prentices. **1792** R. CUMBERLAND *Calvary* (1803) II. 7 Never yet Lur'd I the popular ear with gibing tales. **1887** *Spectator* 3 Sept. 1175 The gibing tone of the German Press.

Hence ˈ**gibingly** *adv.*, in a gibing manner.

1602 FULBECKE *Pandectes* 66 Whose childish humour Iuuenall gibingly toucheth. **1787** *Minor* 229 The curate grin'd, and gibingly asked whether [etc.]. **1855** *Chamb. Jrnl.* III. 96 He once gibingly asked what was the difference.

gibitation, var. GIBBETATION. *Obs.*

giblet (ˈdʒɪblɪt). Forms: 4–5 **gibelet(te**, (4 **gyblot**, 5 **gebyllott**, **giblott**, 5–6 **jeblet**, 7 **giblit**, **gublett**, 9 **jiblet**), 5–7 **gyb(e)let(t**, 6– **giblet**. [a. OF. *gibelet*, app. a stew or ragout of game; cf. Walloon *giblè d'awe* goose-giblets (Littré), mod.F. *gibelotte* rabbit-stew.

The order of senses below is that of their appearance in Eng., and may possibly coincide with the order of development; the culinary sense is, however, the only one recorded in Fr., and Hatz-Darm. regard the word as cognate with *gibier* game.]

†**1.** An unessential appendage. *Obs.*

1303 R. BRUNNE *Handl. Synne* 4273 A messe ys ynoghe for þe þe touþer gyblot [F. *tut l'autre gybelot*], late hyt be. **1387** TREVISA *Higden* (Rolls) VII. 403 þey putteþ non giblettes [L. *appendicia*] to þe houres of Goddes service.

2. †**a.** *sing.* Garbage, entrails. *Obs.*

14.. *Metr. Voc.* in Wr.-Wülcker 627/21 *Exta*, a gibelet. *c* **1440** *Promp. Parv.* 193/1 Gybelet, *idem quod* Garbage.

b. *pl.* rarely *sing.* The portions of a goose that are taken out or cut off before cooking, the liver, gizzard, etc., with the pinions and feet.

1539 [see HARE *sb.* 2]. **1591** PERCIVALL *Sp. Dict.*, *Pepitoria*, the giblets of a goose, or anie bird. **1623–4** MIDDLETON & ROWLEY *Sp. Gipsy* II. ii. (1653) D 3 a, It was mine own Goose, and I laid the Jiblets upon an other Coxcombs trencher. **1731** FIELDING *Grub St. Op.* III. iii, Take particular care of the giblets, they bear a very good price in the market. **1812** SCOTT *Let. to Morritt* 29 Nov. in *Lockhart*, How shall I send you the entire goose which will be too heavy to travel the same way with the giblets? *a* **1845** HOOD *Irish Schoolmaster* viii, Eyes of gizzard hue, That inward giblet of a fowl.

c. *transf.* with reference to a human being. †*to levy one's giblets*: ? to summon up one's courage. †*to join giblets*: to marry.

1651 CLEVELAND *Poems* 28 Pym and the Members must their giblets levy T'incounter Madam Smec. **1672** MARVELL *Reh. Trans.* I. 130 The Entremesses shall be of a Fanaticks Giblets. **1681** HICKERINGILL *Wks.* (1716) I. 399 Oh! there's no Ho when Power makes Court'sey to Revenge, and joyns Giblets together. *a* **1693** URQUHART *Rabelais* III. ix, Yet in that case should it go worse with me, if I did not..bethwack her Giblets [*printed* Gillets: orig. *la petite oye*], to wit, her Arms, Legs, Head, Lights, Liver and Milt, with her other Intrails. **1769** *Stratford Jubilee* II. i. 29 If your ladyship's not engaged, what's the reason but we may join giblets without any pribble-prabble? **1845** BROWNING *Flight Duchess* xvii. 20 My heart's blood..Is pumped up brisk now, through the main ventricle, And genially floats me about the giblets.

d. *fig.* (*pl.*) Things of little value, odds and ends. Now chiefly *dial.* †Also as a term of contempt applied to a person. (Cf. sense 1.)

1638 FORD *Fancies* III. ii, Oh fie upon 'em giblets! **1647** WARD *Simp. Cobler* 26 Which are the very pettitoes of infirmity, the gyblets of perquisquilian toyes. *a* **1659** CLEVELAND *Wks.* (1687) 53 They fear the Giblets of his Train, they fear, Even his Dog, that four-leg'd Cavalier. **1839** COL. HAWKER *Diary* (1893) II. 161 The great ladies with their grace, lace, and giblets. **1887** *Kent. Gloss.*, *Giblets*, rags, tatters.

3. *attrib.*, as *giblet-pie*, *-porridge*, *-soup*.

1693 DRYDEN *Persius* vi. (1697) 498 Shall I my Houshold-Gods and Genius cheat, That he..When I am laid, may feed on *Giblet-Pie? *a* **1845** HOOD *Drowning Ducks* xiii, A duckling turned to giblet pie! **1674** DRYDEN in Johnson *L.P.* (1868) 136 It is a kind of *giblet porridge, made of the giblets of a couple of young geese. **1806** *Culina* 262 A *Giblet Soup.

1817 Col. Hawker *Diary* (1893) I. 150 In order to make me a substitute for giblet soup.

'giblet-'check. *Sc.* Also giblet-, jiblet-cheque, -cheek. [Etymology and correct form uncertain.] (See quot. 1842.) Hence **giblet-checked** *ppl. a.*

1842 Gwilt *Archit.* Gloss., *Giblea* [sic] *Cheque*, a term used by Scotch masons to denote the cutting away of the right angle formed by the front and returns of the aperture of a stone door-case, in the form of a rebate or reveal, so as to make the outer side of the door or closure flush with the face of the wall. **1849** H. Stephens *Bk. of Farm* (ed. 2) I. 306/1 It..should have a giblet-checked outer door to open outwards. **1882** Ogilvie, *Giblet-check, Giblet-cheek.*

gibli ('gɪblɪ). Also gheblee, gibleh, qibli, etc. [ad. Arab. *kiblī* south wind.] A local name in Libya for the sirocco.

1821 G. F. Lyon *Narr. Trav. N. Afr.* 94 Nothing can be more overpowering than the south wind, El Gibli. **1848** J. Richardson *Travels* I. 17 A *ghiblee* day. The wind from The Desert is coming with a vengeance. **1853** —— *Narr. Mission Cent. Afr.* 61 Under the enervating influence of the gheblee, or hot wind. **1857** H. Barth *Trav. N. & Cent. Afr.* 652 A heavy gibleh. **1902** *Encycl. Brit.* XXXIII. 481/2 It is very wind-swept and parched in summer by the terrible south wind (*qibli* or 'sirocco'). **1927** W. Kendrew *Clim. Cont.* (ed. 2) xxxi. 240 The Sirocco..has naturally received local names, in south-east Spain levèche, in Algeria sirocco, in Tunis chili, in Tripoli gibli, [etc.]. **1966** *Punch* 29 June 965/3 Her steadfastly sunny outlook even in the middle of a *ghibli* (khamsin or sirocco, by any other name as blinding and painful). **1968** *Encycl. Brit.* VII. 792/1 The khamsin of Egypt (or gibleh of Libya).

†**giblin.** *Obs.* [? Cf. G. *giebel.*] ? A gable.

1613–39 I. Jones in Leoni *Palladio's Archit.* (1742) I. 72 The Giblins are to be at the narrow Ends of the Building.

gibong, var. geebung.

Gibraltar (dʒɪ'brɒltə(r), -ɔː-). Forms (see 2 below).

1. The name of a fortified town on the south coast of Spain, since 1704 a British possession. Used *fig.* for: An impregnable stronghold.

1856 Emerson *Eng. Traits, Manners* Wks. (Bohn) II. 50 In this Gibraltar of propriety, mediocrity gets intrenched, and consolidated.

†**2.** (In corrupted forms *gibaltar, giberaltar*). ? A Gibraltar-monkey. *Obs.*

1592 G. Harvey *Pierce's Super.* 158 Asse, and worse then a Cumane Asse, and foole, and dolt, and idiot..and dodipoul, and Gibaltar. **1608** *Merry Devil Edmonton* (1617) B 2 b, Let me cling to your flanks, my nimble Giberalters.

3. A kind of sweetmeat; a piece of this. More fully *Gibraltar rock.*

1831 Hawthorne in *Hawthorne & Wife* (1885) I. 126, I send Susannah's Gibraltars. There were fourteen of them originally. **1851** Mayhew *Lond. Labour* I. 203 Gibraltar rock and Wellington pillars used to be flavoured with ginger, but these 'sweeties' are exploded. **1883** *Harper's Mag.* Aug. 460/1 The gibraltars and the silver pieces that Mr. Morley ..bestowed upon him. **1886** Mrs. Bates (Eleanor Putnam) *Old Salem, Two Salem Inst.* 64 The Gibraltar..is a white and delicate candy, flavored with lemon or peppermint.

4. *attrib.* and *Comb.* In names of things belonging to Gibraltar, as **Gibraltar ape**, the Barbary ape, *Macaca sylvana*, esp. a member of the colony of these animals living on the rock of Gibraltar; **Gibraltar-monkey, -stone, -swift** (see quots.).

1770 G. White *Selborne* xxxiii. 88 Scopoli seems to me to have found the *hirundo melba*, the great Gibraltar swift, in Tyrol, without knowing it. **1884** *Cassell's Encycl. Dict.*, Gibraltar-monkey, *Inuus ecaudatus*, an originally African monkey, a colony of which is wild on the rocks of Gibraltar. *Ibid.*, *Gibraltar stone*, stalagmite from a cavern in the rock of Gibraltar. **1932** S. Zuckerman *Soc. Life Monkeys* iii. 49 The young of the Gibraltar ape, *Macaca sylvana*, are born in spring and early summer. **1968** *Sunday Tel.* 20 Oct. 3/5 He has had to be content with Gibraltar apes.

Hence **Gibral'tarian, Gi'braltarine,** an inhabitant or native of Gibraltar.

1883 *Athenæum* 7 Apr. 438/3 Tangier..has long been one of the holiday haunts of the Gibraltarines. **1896** J. Thomson *Afr. Explorer* ix. 209 Fortunately he fell in with a Gibraltarian.

Gibson[1] ('gɪbsən). The name of C. Dana *Gibson* (1867–1944), American artist and illustrator, used *attrib.* to designate a type of girl fashionable in the late 1890s and early 1900s, or dress, etc., characteristic of this type of girl.

1901 *Cosmopolitan* June 120/1 It is a saying among artists that nine out of ten models who come..seeking employment say they are the original 'Gibson girl' or the 'Diana of the Garden'. **1902** *Encycl. Brit.* XXVI. 590/1 American men.. impart as much importance and humour to his [*sc.* Gibson's] pages as his 'Gibson girls' give realistic. **1904** *Daily Chron.* 11 Apr. 8/4 The lean-limbed, lantern-jawed American.. accompanied by a Gibson girl, who calls him 'poppa'. **1905** *Ibid.* 1 Mar. 6/6 A Gibson girl..is a lady with a perfect figure and a perfectly-fitting dress... Miss Hardren, a handsome brunette in black, with a black picture hat, criticised the Gibson dress unsparingly. *Ibid.* 13 Mar. 8/1 Gibson pleats starting from the shoulder line and brought in symmetrical lines to the waist. **1942** D. Powell *Time to be Born* (1943) x. 221 Miss Finkelstein..had swept her sleek black locks into a Gibson girl pompadour.

Gibson[2] ('gɪbsən). In full *Gibson cocktail.* A cocktail consisting of gin and vermouth garnished with pearl onions.

1930 H. Craddock *Savoy Cocktail Bk.* I. 75 *Gibson cocktail.* ½ French Vermouth. ½ Gin. **1951** H. McCloy *Alias Basil Willing* x. 121 Two double Gibsons, very dry..icy, oyster-white liquid that was almost pure gin with only a dash of vermouth. **1968** 'J. Welcome' *Hell is where you find It* iv. 51 He busied himself with a martini jug. I supposed that he was making a Gibson.

gibus ('dʒaɪbəs). [f. *Gibus* the name of the first maker.] An opera or crush hat. Also *gibus-hat.*

1848 Thackeray *Bk. Snobs* xviii, With his gibus-hat and his little glazed pumps. *a* **1854** E. Forbes *Lit. Papers* viii. (1855) 214 No man in a gibus ever commanded public awe or private respect. **1888** *Daily Tel.* 28 Apr. 5/2 The collapsible crush hat or Gibus.

gicks, var. kex.

gid[1] (gɪd). [short form of giddy *sb.*] Giddiness; *spec.* a brain-disease of sheep, caused by the hydatid *Cœnurus cerebralis.* Also giddy.

1601 Holland *Pliny* II. 218 This healeth the gid or woodeuill in sheep. *Ibid.* 230 The party who hath the cutting of them, had need first to annoint his head all ouer and his nosthrils with oile..for feare of the gid. **1750** W. Ellis *Mod. Husbandm.* IV. 107 The other Day you lost a Sheep by the Gid, or Giddiness. **1780** A. Young *Tour Irel.* II. 224 Rot.. with the gid, (a sudden giddiness)..are the chief distempers. **1869** E. A. Parkes *Pract. Hygiene* (ed. 3) 187 The so-called 'gid', 'sturdy', or 'turnsick', is caused by the development of the Cœnurus cerebralis.

†**b.** ? *transf.* ? A whim, 'maggot'.

1556 J. Heywood *Sp. & Flie* lxxvii. 5 As gidds cum and go, so flies cum and are gone.

gid[2]. ? *Obs.* A provincial name for the Jack Snipe (*Limnocryptes gallinula*).

1674 Ray *Words, Water Fowl* 89 The Gid or Jack-snipe, *Gallinago minima.* **1678** —— *Willughby's Ornith.* 291 The Gid or Jack-Snipe or Judcock.

gid, obs. form of guide.

gid(d, obs. form of ged[1].

giddap ('gɪdæp, gɪ'dæp), *v.* (Chiefly in *imp.*) *colloq.* (orig. *U.S.*). Also **giddy-ap, -up.** [Colloq. pronunc. of *get up.*] **A.** *int.* = get *v.* 80 g. **B.** *v. intr.* To move quickly; also *trans.*, to urge (a horse) forward.

1925 T. Dreiser *Amer. Trag.* (1926) I. I. xviii. 133 'Giddap, horsey,' she played. 'Giddap.' **1938** D. Runyon *Furthermore* xiv. 293 Princess O'Hara..tells Gallant Godfrey to giddap, and Gallant Godfrey is giddapping very nicely. **1938** O. Nash *I'm Stranger here Myself* 136 Then giddy-ap, Napoleon! Giddy-ap, Gideon! **1948** D. W. Ballantyne *Cunninghams* (1963) I. xviii. 82 Another joker giddaped a horse. **1954** *Manch. Guardian Weekly* 24 June 7 He harnessed the brawling Pennsylvanians and with a twinkling 'giddy up' drove them into the Eisenhower camp.

giddea, gidya ('gɪdiːə). Also gidgee, -jee, gydya. [Native Australian; 'the original meaning is probably *small*' (Morris).] **1.** A species of Acacia (*A. homalophylla*). Chiefly *attrib.*

1885 Mrs. C. Praed *Austr. Life* 51 Gidya shrubs. **1890** Boldrewood *Col. Reformer* II. xvii. 88, I sat..watching the shadows of the gydya trees lengthen. **1896** B. Spencer in *Rep. Horn Exped.* I. 23 The Stinking Acacia or Giddea.

2. A long spear made from this wood, used by Australian Aborigines.

1878 *Catal. Objects Ethno-typical Art in Nat. Gallery, Melbourne* 46 *Gid-jee*, hardwood spear, with fragments of quartz set in gum on two sides and grass-tree stem. Total length, 7 feet 8 inches. **1966** W. S. Ramson *Austral. Eng.* vi. 117 *Gidgee* (also *gidya* or *giddea*)..is used..of a long spear made from the wood of this tree.

†**'gidded,** *a. Obs. rare.* [? f. **gid* vb. (back-formation from giddy *v.*) + -ed[1].] ? Seized with giddiness.

1563 *Mirr. Mag., Ld. Hastings* xxxv, In hast they runne, and mids theyr race they staye, As gydded roe.

giddeliche, obs. form of giddily.

giddify ('gɪdɪfaɪ), *v.* [f. giddy *a.* + -fy.] *trans.* To render giddy, to daze. Hence **'giddifying** *ppl. a.*

1628 Wither *Brit. Rememb.* 146 And otherwhile so strangely giddifies The Reason..That..we doe not know What in our selves to like, or disallow. **1645** —— *Vox Pacif.* 181 That Clergie-bane Which hath your Clergie, lately, giddifi'd. **1818** T. Moore *Mem.* (1856) VIII. 246 In such a giddyfying labyrinth of bustle, acclamation, hurrahs, &c. **1888** *Roots: a Plea for Tolerance* 86 My young friend was a very giddifying person to talk to.

†**'giddihead.** *Obs.* [f. giddy *a.* + -head.] Giddiness, folly.

c **1275** *Duty Christ.* 60 in *O.E. Misc.* 143 Vre gydihede. *c* **1305** *St. Katherine* 13 in *E.E.P.* (1862) 90 Here gydihede Heo seȝ honoure þe maumetz.

giddily ('gɪdɪlɪ), *adv.* [f. giddy *a.* + -ly[2].] In a giddy manner (see the senses of the adj.); †insanely, madly, foolishly; †carelessly. Now chiefly, Dizzily, with vertigo; so as to cause dizziness; also, thoughtlessly.

a **1250** *Owl & Night* 1280 Nu thu miȝt wite readliche, That eavere thu spekest gideliche. **1599** Shaks. *Much Ado* III. iii. 140 Seest thou not..what a deformed thiefe this fashion is, how giddily a turnes about all the Hotblouds. *a* **1631** Donne *Poems, To R. Woodward* 29 To roame Giddelie and be euery where but at home, Such freedom doth a banishment become. *a* **1729** Congreve *Judgm. Paris* 67 Lost in Amaze, I giddily gaze. **1801** Southey *Thalaba* IX. vii, Giddily, giddily, still she whirls. **1864** *Realm* 25 May 1 When Home Secretaries' private secretaries become giddily excited. **1873** Ouida *Pascarel* I. 151 It all swam giddily before my sight.

giddiness ('gɪdɪnɪs). [f. giddy *a.* + -ness.]

1. The condition of being giddy or dizzy, vertigo or swimming in the head, dizziness.

1398 Trevisa *Barth. De P.R.* VII. viii. (1495) 228 Gedynes is false dome..for by that dome it semeth that al thyng gooth abowte. **1562** Turner *Baths*, Names Siknesses A iij a, The dusenes or gydenes in the heade. **1592** tr. *Junius on Rev.* xvii. 4 Bringing upon them a deadly giddiness. **1655** Culpepper, etc. *Riverius* I. Pref., Giddiness, or swimming of the Head, called Vertigo. **1718** Lady M. W. Montagu *Let. to C'tess Bristol* 10 Mar., They..turn round with an amazing swiftness..without..shewing the least appearance of giddiness. **1804** Abernethy *Surg. Obs.* 176 The sudden motion of his head in any direction occasioned no giddiness. **1870** Dickens *E. Drood* ii, A dimness and giddiness crept over him. **1871** L. Stephen *Playgr. Europe* xiii. (1894) 331 Upon this ridge..one can hardly stand without giddiness.

b. Bewildering rapidity of flight.

1657 R. Ligon *Barbadoes* (1673) 5 The pleasure she gives the eye, is by the giddiness of her flying.

2. Thoughtless folly, flightiness; fickleness, instability.

a **1290** *Signs of Doomsday* 112 in *Cod. Digby* 86 (Stengel) We hit [i.e. heaven] forloren þoru sottes dede, þoru gidinesse and þoru misdede. **1561** T. Norton *Calvin's Inst.* I. 20 Although they be vexed with extreme madnesse, yet I think they are not caried with such giddinesse. **1625** Bacon *Ess., Truth* (Arb.) 499 Certainly there be, that delight in Giddinesse; And count it a Bondage, to fix a Beleefe. **1756** Burke *Vind. Nat. Soc.* 57 Their Giddiness might make the People condemn where they meant to acquit. **1801** Southey *Thalaba* IX. xvi, The Tyrant..Seeks in the giddiness of boisterous sport Short respite from the avenging power within. **1863** W. Phillips *Speeches* ii. 32 A few mere giddiness hurries to ruin.

b. A foolish or flighty action, etc.

1593 Donne *Sat.* I. 51 Thou..doest repent Theese vanityes and giddinesses. **1859** Dickens *T. Two Cities* II. xii, The mincing vanities and giddinesses of empty-headed girls.

†**'giddish,** *a. Obs. rare.* [f. gidd-y *a.* + -ish.] Giddy, fickle, foolish.

1566 Drant *Horace's Sat.* II. iii. F vij, The people cawle thee giddishe mad, why, all the worlde is so.

giddy ('gɪdɪ), *sb.* [f. the adj.] = gid[1].

1603 Harsnet *Pop. Impost.* xxi. 136 If any of you haue a sheepe sicke of the giddies, or an hogge of the mumps, or [etc.]. **1805** R. W. Dickson *Pract. Agric.* (1807) II. 705 The Turn or Giddy is a disorder with which these animals [sheep] are often seized. **1888** *Berksh. Gloss.*, *Giddy*, a disease of the brain in sheep.

giddy ('gɪdɪ), *a.* Forms: 1 gidiȝ, 3 gidi(e, gidy, gydi(e, (guydi), 4–5 gedy, 6–7 giddie, gyddy, 6– giddy. [OE. *gidiȝ* insane, is shown by its guttural initial to be a graphic variant of **gydiȝ*:—prehistoric **gudīgo-*, app. f. OTeut. **gudo*[m] god. The primary sense thus appears to be 'possessed by a god, ἔνθεος'; cf. OE. *ylfiȝ* insane, lit. 'elf-possessed', similarly f. *ælf* elf.]

†**1. a.** Mad, insane, foolish, stupid. *Obs.*

c **1000** *O.E. Gloss.* (Napier) I. 5009 *Limphaticum*, þæne gidiȝan. *c* **1200** *Winteney Rule St. Benet* vii. (1888) 41 Se gidie [L. *stultus*] on his hleæhtre his stefene onhefð. *a* **1250** *Owl & Night.* 290 Hi hit seggeþ wel ilome þat me ne chide wiþ þe gidie. **1297** R. Glouc. (Rolls) 1542 He [Nero] bicom sone þer after pur gidy & wod. *a* **1300** *Leg. Rood* (1871) 58 þou gidi [*v.r.* wode] hound quaþ Seint quiriac.

b. *dial.* Mad with anger, furious.

1674 Ray *N.C. Words* 21 *Giddy*, mad with anger. *a* **1787** Pegge *Derbicisms* (E.D.S.), *Giddy*, mad; as a giddy horse, one that is wild or untam'd. **1828** *Craven Gloss.*, *Giddy*, furious, heated with anger. **1847–78** in Halliwell.

2. a. Having a confused sensation of swimming or whirling in the head, with proneness to fall; affected with vertigo, dizzy.

[This sense appears to be first exemplified in the compound turngiddy.]

1570 Levins *Manip.* 97/23 Gyddie, *vertiginosus.* *c* **1586** C'tess Pembroke *Ps.* LX. ii, Dull horror was our drink, We drinking giddy grew. *a* **1649** Drumm. of Hawth. *Jas. V*, Wks. (1711) 110 His brains having been a little giddy (like one looking from a great height) by his advancement to honours and place in court. **1665** Boyle *Occas. Refl.* IV. xviii. (1845) 277 My Head began to grow giddy. **1732** Berkeley *Alciphr.* II. §26 They seem to me drunk and giddy with a false notion of liberty. **1821** Praed *Poems* (1864) I. 51 The Monk is as straight as a poplar tree, Gog is as giddy as Gog may be! **1860** Tyndall *Glac.* I. xi. 78 For the first time during the journey he grew giddy. **1875** Jowett *Plato* (ed. 2) I. 154, I felt at first giddy and faint, as if I had received a blow from the expert hand of a boxer.

†**b.** *transf.* Of a ship: Staggering as if dizzy.

1700 Dryden *Ceyx & Alcyone* 198 The giddy ship ran round. **1725** Pope *Odyss.* IX. 79 Now here, now there, the giddy ships are born.

c. Causing or apt to produce dizziness or swimming in the head, rendering dizzy.

1585 Abp. Sandys *Serm.* iii. 49 If thou sowe the giddie darnell of humane traditions, looke for like fruites. **1594** Shaks. *Rich. III*, I. iv. 17 As we pac'd along Vpon the giddy footing of the Hatches. **1597** —— *2 Hen. IV*, III. i. 18 Vpon the high and giddie Mast. **1676** Dryden *Aurengz.* IV. i, Time these giddy Vapours will remove. **1718** Prior *Power*

124 The giddy precipice, and the dangerous flood. **1781** COWPER *Hope* 187 From infancy through childhood's giddy maze. **1847** EMERSON *Poems, Woodnotes* I. 92 Whose giddy top the morning loved to gild. **1871** L. STEPHEN *Playgr. Europe* iii. (1894) 81 The giddy cliffs which surround them.

d. Whirling or circling round with bewildering rapidity.

1593 SHAKS. *Lucr.* 952 To..turne the giddy round of Fortunes wheele. *a* **1652** J. SMITH *Sel. Disc.* ix. 454 With swift and giddy motions. **1715–20** POPE *Iliad* XVIII. 695 So whirls a wheel, in giddy circle toss'd. **1764** GOLDSM. *Trav.* 417 While above the giddy tempest flies. *a* **1793** G. WHITE in *Selborne* (1854) 8 The happy schoolboy brings transported forth His long-forgotten scourge and giddy gig. **1810** SCOTT *Lady of L.* II. xxxi, Amid his senses' giddy wheel. **1842** TENNYSON *Sin* 29 The strong tempestuous treble..Ran into its giddiest whirl of sound. **1890** R. BRIDGES *Shorter Poems* IV. 13, I lean across the paddock pale And gaze upon the giddy mill.

e. *dial.* Of a sheep: Affected with the 'gid'. ***giddy mutton*** (see quot. 1881).

1847–78 HALLIWELL, *Giddy*,..a term applied to sheep that have hydatides on the brain. **1881** *Leicestersh. Gloss.* s.v., Lambs and sheep are said to be *giddy* when they take to turning round in an aimless sort of way..When the animal is killed as it generally is on manifesting this gyratory tendency, the meat is known as 'giddy lamb', or 'giddy mutton'.

3. a. Of persons, their attributes and actions: Mentally intoxicated, 'elated to thoughtlessness' (J.); incapable of or indisposed to serious thought or steady attention; easily carried away by excitement; 'light-headed, frivolous, flighty, inconstant. ***to play the giddy goat***: see GOAT 3 b; ***to play the giddy ox***: to behave foolishly or frivolously; to play the fool.

Chiefly *transf.* from sense 2; but some of the uses may descend directly from sense 1.

a **1547** SURREY *Æneid* II. 33 So diuerse ranne the giddy peoples minde. **1561** T. NORTON *Calvin's Inst.* II. 81 Such as do alway sauor of a certaine giddy imagination. **1591** SHAKS. *1 Hen. VI*, III. i. 83 [They] Doe pelt so fast at one anothers Pate, That many haue their giddy braynes knockt out. **1626** BACON *Sylva* §698 It may be Gnats and Flies haue their Imagination more mutable and giddy. *a* **1631** DONNE *Poems* (1650) 118 Giddie fantastique Poets. **1643** MILTON *Divorce* Wks. (1847) 158/2 Many they shall reclaim from obscure and giddy sects. **1681** DRYDEN *Abs. & Achit.* I. 216 Govern'd by the Moon, the giddy Jews Tread the same Track when she the Prime renews: And once in twenty Years..By natural Instinct they change their Lord. **1713** STEELE *Guardian* No. 5 ¶6 The giddy part of her sex will have it she is in love. **1766** GOLDSM. *Vic. W.* xix, She said twenty giddy things that looked like joy. **1779** MAD. D'ARBLAY *Diary* Oct., A mere playful, giddy, romping child. **1822** HAZLITT *Table-t.* Ser. II. xv. (1869) 301 Art.. still allures our giddy admiration. *a* **1839** PRAED *Poems* (1864) II. 26 And giddy girls of gay fifteen Mimic his manner and his mien. **1845** DISRAELI *Sybil* (1863) 257 She ..thinks she is gay when she is only giddy. **1892** *Ally Sloper's Half-Holiday* 19 Mar. 91/2 Fanny Robinson was flighty; she played the giddy ox—I mean, heifer. **1915** W. S. MAUGHAM *Of Human Bondage* xiii. 47 Don't play the giddy ox. **1922** JOYCE *Ulysses* 9, I don't want to be debagged! Don't you play the giddy ox with me!

absol. **1807** CRABBE *Par. Reg.* I. 282 'Twould warn the giddy and awake the gay. **1838** LYTTON *Alice* 55 She seemed born, not only to captivate the giddy, but to turn the heads of the sage.

b. Used (often ironically) as an intensive; also used in the expression of surprise ***my giddy aunt*** (cf. AUNT 5).

1896 KIPLING *Seven Seas* 171 'E's a kind of a giddy harumfrodite—soldier an' sailor too! **1899** —— *Stalky & Co.* 28 King'll have to prove his charges up to the giddy hilt. *Ibid.* 112, I spoke the giddy truth... I said I didn't know. *Ibid.* 142 Hullo. What's the giddy jest? **1915** J. BUCHAN *39 Steps* iv. 97 A giddy lot Scudder's friends cared for peace and reform. **1919** 'W. N. P. BARBELLION' *Jrnl. Disappointed Man* 268 Oh my giddy aunt! **1924** A. J. SMALL *Frozen Gold* iii. 92 The giddy part of it is that our strike isn't up north at all.

4. *Comb.*, as ***giddy-brain, -head*** (said of a person); ***giddy-brained, -drunk, -headed, -paced, -pated, -witted*** adjs.; **giddy-gander** *dial.* = GANDERGOOSE; **giddy-go-round**, something that revolves with giddy rapidity, *esp.* a 'merry-go-round' or 'roundabout'; **giddy-goating** *vbl. sb.*, acting the 'giddy goat', fooling about; †**giddy-lumpishness**, heaviness and dizziness (of the head).

a **1652** BROME *Covent Gard.* I. Wks. 1873 II. 17 This kicksy wincy *Giddibrain will spoil all. **1796** *Plain Sense* I. 199 Lady Almeria was a little giddy-brain. **1561** T. NORTON *Calvin's Inst.* I. 19 Certain *giddy brained men. **1682** OTWAY *Venice Preserved* III. i, Useless, giddy-brain'd Ass! **1784** *Denouement* 108 A foolish penchant for a little giddy brained girl. **1827** COLERIDGE *Let.* in *Mem. H. F. Cary* (1847) II. 176 Even as a man *giddy-drunk throws his arms about, and clasps hold of a barber's block for support. **1847–78** HALLIWELL, *Giddygander, the orchis. *Dorset.* **1863** BARNES *Dorset Gloss.*, *Giddygander*, the early purple orchis (*orchis mascula*)..and other common species of orchis. **1883** MRS. EWING *Jackanapes* iii. 20 His friend could not..ride in the *giddy-go-round. **1893** R. KIPLING *Many Invent.*, *My Lord the Elephant* 65 He put his arm round av' me an' I came into the sun, the hills an' the rocks skippin' big giddy-go-rounds. **1891** SARAH J. DUNCAN *Amer. Girl Lond.* 79 A little *giddy-goating does nobody any harm. **1641** 'SMECTYMNUUS' *Vind. Answ.* ii. 29 Before he.. condemne those for *giddyheads that will not take his word for proofs. **1698** FRYER *Acc. E. India & P.* 106 The Heir of Bantam is..of little Credit, being a Giddy-head. **1575** TURBERVILE *Faulconrie* 148 So much the greater ought your bells to be by how much more you see your hawke *gyddy headed. **1639** G. DANIEL *Vervic.* 395 Oh the sickly tast Of giddie-headed Popularitie. **1748** SMOLLETT *Rod. Rand.* xlvi, Dangling after a parcel of giddy-headed girls. **1678** *Yng. Man's Call.* 389 He [prince Henry] grew more pale than formerly..yet he did not much complain, but only of *giddy-lumpishness in his forehead. **1601** SHAKS. *Twel. N.* II. iv. 6 These most briske and *giddy-paced times. **1604** R. ARMIN *Ded.* in *G. Dugdale's Disc. Pract. Eliz. Caldwell* A ij, We haue many *giddie pated Poets, that coulde haue published this Report with more eloquence. **1830** SCOTT *Demonol.* viii. 240 These enthusiastic and giddy-pated girls. *c* **1830** R. SULLIVAN in *Casquet Lit.* V. 173/1 Betty was a reckless, *giddy-witted baggage.

giddy ('gɪdɪ), *v.* Also 7 **gyddy.** [f. the adj.]

1. *trans.* To make or render giddy.

1602 WARNER *Alb. Eng.* IX. li. (1612) 232 Your Darnell giddieth so. **1617** COLLINS *Def. Bp. Ely* II. viii. 317 So are you gyddied and hurled vp and downe, with euery blast of vaine doctrine. **1638** SIR T. HERBERT *Trav.* 28 Betele.. giddies the braine. **1710** *Acc. Last Distemp. T. Whigg* II. 44 After he had giddy'd his Guests by a Chase of various Meanders and winding ways. **1799** COLERIDGE *Lett.* (1895) 284 Oh this strange..scene-shifter, Death!—that giddies one with insecurity. **1889** C. EDWARDES *Sardinia* 163 That he may not be giddied by his perpetual rotations.

2. *intr.* To become giddy.

1845 S. JUDD *Margaret* vi. (1871) 28 My head swims, my brain giddies.

†**3.** ? To turn *round* with giddy movement.

1615 CHAPMAN *Odyss.* IX. 135 Had not..a sodaine North-wind fetcht, With an extreame sea, quite about againe, Our whole endeuours; and our course constraine To giddie round; and with our bowd sailes greete Dreadfull Maleia.

Hence **'giddying** *ppl. a.*, that makes giddy.

1820 MRS. STARKE *Direct. Trav. on Cont.* ii. (1823) 34 The Chapeau, a giddying eminence opposite to Montanvert. **1844** LD. HOUGHTON *Mem. Many Scenes, Illum. St. Peter's* ii. 135 At last that giddying sight took form. *a* **1882** LONGF. *Mich. Angelo* I. iv, You think..my head Swims with the giddying whirl of life about me. **1886** T. HARDY *Mayor Casterbr.* xxvii, One that creeps into the maiden heart like the giddying worm into the sheep's brain.

giddy-ap, -up: see GIDDAP *v.*

†**giddy gaddy.** *Obs.* Some old game.

1609 *Manch. Court Leet Rec.* (1886) II. 248 A game, or games vsed in the towne of Manchestr called giddye gaddye.

giddyish ('gɪdɪɪʃ), *a.* [f. GIDDY *a.* + -ISH.] Somewhat giddy, dizzy.

1711 SWIFT *Jrnl. to Stella* 26 Jan., My head..is not absolutely ill, but giddyish. *Ibid.* 21 Apr., To be giddyish three or four days together mortified me.

gide, obs. f. GUIDE; var. GITE, *Obs.*, gown.

Gideon ('gɪdɪən). *U.S.* [f. the name of an Israelite leader (see Judges vi. 11 ff.).]

A member of a Christian organization of American commercial travellers, founded in 1899. ***Gideon Bible***, a Bible purchased by this organization and placed in a hotel room, Pullman car, etc.

1906 *Springfield Weekly Republican* 13 Sept. 11 The religiously-minded commercial travelers, known as Gideons, have four prosperous camps in cities of New York state. **1920** *Atlantic Monthly* July 88 He replied in words that may still be read, thanks to the Gideons, in any hotel room. **1922** *Bookman* Feb. 552/2 He has stolen, to date, fifty-eight Gideon Bibles, twenty-seven from the Hotel Astor alone, and presented them to friends. **1956** 'N. SHUTE' *Beyond Black Stump* 17 He had nothing to read till he discovered the Gideon Bible in the drawer of the bedside table. **1961** K. VONNEGUT *Sirens of Titan* (1967) iii. 53 He took the Gideon Bible that was in his room, and he started with the first sentence in Genesis.

gidgee, var. GIDDEA, GIDYA.

gidya: see GIDDEA.

gief, gieft, obs. forms of GIVE, GIFT.

giela(i)nger, var. GILENYER, *Obs.*

gier-eagle: see GEIER-.

gierfalcon, gierle, obs. ff. GYRFALCON, GIRL.

gieroglife, -gliphick, obs. ff. HIEROGLYPH, -IC.

gieseckite ('giːsəkaɪt). *Min.* [Named by Stromeyer in 1819 after Sir Chas. *Giesecke*, who brought it from Greenland: see -ITE.] A variety of pinite, believed to be a pseudomorph after nephelite.

1821 R. JAMESON *Man. Min.* 323 Gieseckite, *Stromeyer, Sowerby.* **1868** DANA *Min.* (ed. 5) 479 *Gieseckite*..In 6-sided prisms.

†**'giesetrye.** *Obs.*⁻¹ [ad. OF. *gieziterie*, f. med.L. *giezita* (St. Bernard) (see GYESITE), f. *Giezi*, L. (Vulgate) equivalent of Heb. *Gehazi*.] The crime of selling some sacred thing; a correlative of SIMONY.

c **1430** *Pilgr. Lyf Manhode* III. xxv. (1869) 149 Who so wole propirliche speke, whan it selleth, Giezitrye, and whan it biggeth, Symonye it is seyd.

giest(e, obs. form of JOIST.

gieve, var. GIVE, GYVE.

gif (gɪf), *conj.* *Sc.* and *north. dial.* Forms: 5–6 **giff(e, gyf(fe**, (5 **gyve**, 6 **geif, geve, gewe, giwe**), 6 **giue**, 5– **gif.** [An alteration of ME. *ȝif*, IF.

It has not been certainly traced beyond the 15th c. (the MSS. of Barbour having been written in 1487–9). Probably it was due to the influence of GIVE, in which a form with a guttural similarly took the place of an earlier form with a palatal. Cf. GIN *conj.*]

1. Introducing a condition: = IF. Also *gif that.* Now *rare.*

1375 BARBOUR *Bruce* I. 12, I wald fayne set my will, Giff my wyt mycht suffice thartill. *c* **1425** WYNTOUN *Cron.* VIII. v. 107 Gyve þai couth, þai suld declere Of þat gret dystans þe matere. *c* **1470** HENRY *Wallace* I. 391 Gentill men gif ȝe be, Leiff ws sum part, we pray for cheryte. **1556** LAUDER *Tractate* 89 Geue that thare ony places be More creuell than vthers in degre [etc.]. **1563–83** FOXE *A. & M.* 4/2 And giue he were so holy, yet [etc.]. **1588** A. KING tr. *Canisius' Catech.* 15 b, Giue nothinge be iugit mair sueit and plaisant thane þis lyfe..how mekil [etc.]. *c* **1620** A. HUME *Brit. Tongue* (1865) 21 Gif they speak not soe, I wald understand quhy they wryte not as they speak. **1786** C. KEITH *Har'st Rig* 47 Gif like your tongue were your twa hands, Nae help you'd need. **1826** J. WILSON *Noct. Ambr.* Wks. 1855 I. 354 Gif it was the last word I was ever to speak in this world, it was God's truth. **1858** M. PORTEOUS *Souter Johnny* 29 Gif bless'd wi' freedom, ye can flee Wi' angel haste Through heaven's starr'd empire ye will be A prying ghaist. **1876** *Mid Yorksh. Gloss.*, *Gif*, if. A casual form, mostly heard in Nidderdale.

†**2.** Introducing an object clause: = WHETHER. Also *gif that.* *Obs.*

1535 STEWART *Cron. Scot.* II. 206, I can nocht tell gif that he wes his bruther. **1567** in Tytler *Hist. Scotl.* (1864) III. 247 [Bothwell] is minded to..bring her [the queen] to Dunbar. Judge you gif it be with her will or no?

gif(e, giff, obs. forms of GIF, GIVE.

giff (gɪf). *Sc.* [Formed by analysis of GIFF-GAFF.] In phrase ***the giffs and the gaffs***: the givings and the takings, the gains and the losses. Cf. GIFF-GAFF.

1821 GALT *Ann. Parish* xliii. 161, I think that the giffs and the gaffs nearly balance one another.

giff-gaff ('gɪf-gæf). *Sc.* and *north. dial.* Also 6 **giffe-gafe, gyffe-gaffe**, 8 **giff-goff**, 9 **gif-gaf(f.** [reduplication of GIVE *v.* Cf. MDu. *ghivegave.*]

1. Mutual giving, mutual help; give and take.

1549 LATIMER *3rd Serm. bef. Edw. VI* (Arb.) 89 Some what was geuen to them before, and they muste nedes geue somewhat againe, for giffe gafe was a good felow, this gyffe gaffe led them clene from iustice. **1624** BP. R. MOUNTAGU *New Gagg* 92 Giff-gaff is a good fellow. **1787** GROSE *Prov. Gloss.* s.v., Giff-goff makes good fellowship. **1790** SHIRREFS *Poems* Gloss., *Giff-gaff*, open-heartedness, familiarity, frankness, or mutual condescension. **1815** SCOTT *Guy M.* xl, I played at giff gaff with the officers. **1818** —— *Hrt. Midl.* xvi, Gif-gaf makes gude friends, ye ken. **1824** —— *Redgauntlet* xii, You must give me your [word] to be private in the matter—giff-gaff, you know. **1895** *Dundee Advertiser* in *Daily News* 22 Mar. 7/2 The 'giff-gaff' principle of making friends.

2. Interchange of remarks; promiscuous talk. (Cf. GAFF *sb.*²)

1787 GROSE *Prov. Gloss.*, *Giff-gaff*, unpremeditated discourse. **1855** ROBINSON *Whitby Gloss.*, *Giff-gaff*, the random conversation which strangers fall into when they meet in going the same road. **1894** CROCKETT *Lilac Sunbonnet* 45 The shrill 'giff-gaff' of their colloquy.

Hence †**giff-gaffing** *vbl. sb.* = sense 1.

1606 BIRNIE *Kirk-Buriall* (1833) 35 The which gif-gaffing with God is the verie simoniacal sin of Anani and Saphira.

gift (gɪft), *sb.* Forms: α. 1 **ȝift, ȝyft**, 2–5 **ȝift(e**, (4 **ȝiefte**), 3–5 **ȝeft**, 4 **ȝyft(e**, 4–6 **yeft(e**, (5 **ȝefft, yeffe, yifte, yyft, yft**, 6 **yeffte**). β. 4 **yefþe, -the**, 5 **ȝyfth.** γ. 3–6 **gifte, gyft(e**, 6 **gyfft**, (3 **giuete**, 4 **gifit, giftt**, 6 **gefte, gieft**), 3, 6, 7 **guift(e**, 3– **gift.** [Com. Teut.: OE. *ȝift* str. fem. (recorded only in the sense 'payment for a wife', and in the plural with the sense 'wedding') corresponds to OFris. *jeft* fem., gift, MDu. *gift(e* (Du. *gift* fem., gift, *gift* neut., now more commonly *gif*, poison), OHG. *gift* fem., gift, poison (MHG., mod.G. *gift* fem., gift, neut., poison), ON. *gift*, usually written *gipt* gift (Sw., Da. *-gift* in compounds), pl. *giptar* a wedding, Goth. *-gifts* in compounds:—OTeut. **gifti-z* fem., f. root **geb-* GIVE *v.*

The OE. sense does not appear to have survived into ME.; the α. and β. forms are perh. new formations from the vb., while the γ. type, to which the mod. Eng. form belongs, is prob. (as the guttural seems to show) adopted from ON.]

I. Giving.

1. a. The action of giving, an instance of the same; a giving, bestowal. †*of gift*: as a gift, gratuitously, for nothing; also *of free gift.* (***I would not have it) at a gift*** (colloq.): at the price of nothing; even as a gift. †***of a person's gift***: of his giving, as his gift. Also, the power or right of giving, in phr. ***in*** (†***of***) ***a person's gift.***

α. *c* **1300** *K. Alis.* 4682 [Laud MS.] What wiþ ȝifte what wiþ queyntise Alle he wan hem to his seruyse. *c* **1340** *Cursor M.* 5090 (Trin.) ȝoure sackes shal I fille of ȝift [*Cott.* o gift]. *c* **1400** *Rom. Rose* 3663, I wolde gladly..Have a cos therof freely Of your yeft. **1475** *Bk. Noblesse* (1860) 22 William..

was righte duke of Normandie by yeft of Charlys the symple, king of Fraunce. **1503** *Churchw. Acc. Croscombe* (Som. Rec. Soc.) 28 Of the yefte of Alsun Abbot a payr of beds of jett.

γ. *a* **1300** *Cursor M.* 28760 Þe thrid almus es gift of hand, or elles in word or werk helpand. **1357** *Lay Folks Catech.* 25 Thai had it of goddes giftt at thaire begynnyng. **1523** FITZHERB. *Surv.* 29 It is to be enquered of all ye churches that belong to the lordes gyft how many there be & where they be & what they be worthe. **1583** HOLLYBAND *Campo di Fior* 109 But canst thou not haue of gifte the filth which is painted on thy handes and necke? **1589** C. OCKLAND in *Lett. Lit. Men* (Camden) 71 For thei be of my Lorde of Warwikes gyfte. **1596** SPENSER *F.Q.* v. x. 14 Therefore these two, her eldest sonnes, she sent To seeke for succour of this Ladies gieft. **1650** FULLER *Pisgah* III. i. 359 This floor David bought of Araunah the Jebusite, from whom he would not take it of gift. **1651** HOBBES *Leviath.* II. xxi. 108 When we say a Guift is Free, there is not meant any Liberty of the Guift, but of the Giver. **1675** SOUTH *Serm.* (1737) I. xi. 406 No man has any antecedent right or claim to that which comes to him by free-gift. **1679–88** *Secr. Serv. Money Chas. & Jas.* (Camden) 27 To $Lieu^t$ Anthony Heyford, as of free guift 30*li.* 0*s.* 0*d.* **1785** COWPER *Lett.* Wks. (1876) 220 A gift of bedding to the poor of Olney. **1837** DISRAELI *Venetia* I. iv, The rich living was in the gift of the Herberts. *a* **1854** H. REED *Lect. Eng. Lit.* iv. (1878) 126 Language always makes gift of its best wealth to a great poet. **1857** HUGHES *Tom Brown* I. ix, Wouldn't have them at a gift. **1888** BRYCE *Amer. Commw.* II. lxv. 486 The minor appointive offices which lie in his own gift.

Prov. **1583** FULKE *Defence* xv. 403 The prouerb is, what is so free as gift?

†**b.** *to give a gift* (= earlier *to give a give*): to give assurance *that*. *Obs.* (See GIVE *v.*)

2. *Law.* **a.** The transference of property in a thing by one person to another, voluntarily and without any valuable consideration.

α. **1480** *Waterf. Arch.* in *10th Rep. Hist. MSS. Comm.* App. v. 314 The saide feftments, yefts, graunts, and lesses. **1483** *Act 1 Rich. III*, c. 1. §1 Every astate feoffement yeft relesse graunte lesis and confirmacion of landys.

γ. *c* **1471** in *Paston Lett.* No. 679 III. 21 A box with the dede of gyfft off J.P. **1558** *Extracts Aberd. Reg.* (1844) I. 314 Be this our letter of gyft and donatioune. **1590** SWINBURNE *Testaments* 16 Of gifts in case of death there be three sortes. *c* **1590**, **1613** Deed of gift [see DEED *sb.* 4]. **1767** BLACKSTONE *Comm.* II. 440 Gifts are always gratuitous, grants are upon some consideration or equivalent. **1838** *Penny Cycl.* XI. 217/2 To complete a gift of goods and chattels delivery is absolutely necessary.

fig. **1729** E. ERSKINE in Agnew *Theol. Consolat.* (1881) 109 There is a deed of gift or grant made by the Father to all the hearers of the Gospel.

b. (See quots. 1818, 1876.)

1818 CRUISE *Digest* (ed. 2) IV. 63 A gift, *donatio*, is properly applied to the creation of an estate tail; as a feoffment is to that of an estate in fee simple. **1827** JARMAN *Powell's Devises* II. 295 The word 'against' was construed *without*, to make it alternative to the other gift. **1876** DIGBY *Real Prop.* x. §1. 378 A feoffment was technically confined to an estate in fee simple, the conveyance of an estate tail by the same process was technically called a gift.

II. The thing given.

3. a. Something, the possession of which is transferred to another without the expectation or receipt of an equivalent; a donation, present. Also preceded by qualifying words, as ***Christmas-***, ***Easter-***, ***New Year's***, etc. ***gift***.

Grecian gift (see Virg. *Æn.* II. 49): some seeming favour or concession on the part of an enemy, suspected to be offered with sinister motive.

α. *c* **1250** *Gen. & Ex.* 1416 Ðe broðer and de moder oc Riche ȝiftes eliezer ðe toc. *c* **1275** LAY. 1790 Þo hafde Brutus þe ȝeft: þat Dyanne him bi-hehte. *c* **1350** *Will. Palerne* 5357 Sterne stedes & strong, & oþer stoute ȝiftes. **1401** *Pol. Poems* (Rolls) II. 27 Why make ye not your feasts to poore men, and yeveth him yefts, as yee done to the rich. **1483** CAXTON *G. de la Tour* C ij, I pray yow alle that it plese yow to graunte me a bone and a yefte.

β. **1447** BOKENHAM *Seyntys* (Roxb.) 46 Be nathan david sone also ȝyfth or thynge ȝoven is signyfyed.

γ. *a* **1300** *Cursor M.* 3319 He hir gaue a gift onan, A gold ring. *Ibid.* 3339 Ilkan gaue he giftes sere. *c* **1460** *Launfal* 67 The quene yaf gyftes for the nones..Her curtasye to kythe. **1539** TAVERNER *Erasm. Prov.* (1552) 26 The mynde of giftes is best. **1548** HALL *Chron., Hen. VIII*, 67 Also that you..shall confesse that you receive the citie as a gift, and not rendred as a right to the kyng your Master. **1585** T. WASHINGTON tr. *Nicholay's Voy.* III. xxii. 112 [They] went through the city demanding their new yeres gifts of al those they met. **1632** SANDERSON *Serm.* 491 The one eye vpon the guift and the other vpon the Giver. **1667** MILTON *P.L*, IV. 735 Both when we wake, And when we seek, as now, thy gift of sleep. **1781** COWPER *Hope* 115 Life is His gift, from whom whate'er life needs, And every good and perfect gift, proceeds. **1832** S. R. MAITLAND *Albig. & Waldenses* iii. 66 The candour of Gibbon is..so remarkable that I wonder Milner did not reject the Grecian gift. **1884** BROWNING *Ferishtah* (1885) 38 Giving is giving, gift claims gift's return.

Proverbs. *c* **1460** *How Gd. Wif taught hir Dau.* 70 in Hazl. *E.P.P.* I. 185 Bounden he is that ȝifte takithe, my dere childe. **1546** J. HEYWOOD *Prov.* (1867) 30 Throw no gyft agayne at the geuers head.

b. Something of value proceeding from a specified source, quasi-personified as a giver.

1796 H. HUNTER tr. *St.-Pierre's Stud. Nat.* (1799) I. 252 These precious gifts of the Waters [fisheries] are presented to all Nations. **1871** MORLEY *Voltaire* (1886) 4 The ever-living gifts of Grecian art and architecture and letters.

†**c.** A fee for services rendered. $Obs.^{-1}$

1477 *Paston Lett.* No. 808 III. 214 Hery Cook wold goo with your swanes, for hys yefte chuld be vj*s.* viij*d.* and there fore he wold yeffe you his labore, be so ye payd for his costes.

†**d.** *pl.* Applied to almshouses founded by a specified person. *Obs.*

1651 T. BARKER *Art of Angling* Epist., I live in Henry the 7th's Gifts.

e. In kindergartens, one of a series of educative toys designed to develop the child's powers of observation, etc.

1855 E. VON WICKERODE tr. *von Marenholtz's Woman's Educ. Mission* 19 The little gymnastic games for the hands and fingers connected with the 'First Gift', answer the triple end of amusing, occupying, and educating the infant. **1892** C. M. YONGE *That Stick* II. xxxix. 195 The elder children ..were busied..in building up coloured cubes, 'gifts' in Kindergarten parlance. **1892** —— *Old Woman's Outlook* 80 Children are supposed to learn multiplication rationally by proof on the abacus frame, or by the 'gifts' of the Kindergarten. **1905** J. H. BOARDMAN *Educ. Ideas of Froebel & Pestalozzi* iv. 48 According to the general definition of the term, there are altogether twenty Gifts, although most Kindergartners now limit the name to the first six or seven.

4. An offering to God or to a heathen deity.

α. **1382** WYCLIF *Matt.* v. 24 Leeue there thi ȝift before the auter. *c* **1489** CAXTON *Sonnes of Aymon* xvii. 390 He..offred a riche yefte vpon the awter.

γ. *a* **1300** *Cursor M.* 10218 Ilkan þan to þe temple broght Sirekin gift after þai moght. **1597** HOOKER *Eccl. Pol.* v. xxxiv. §3. 70 Gifts are offered vnto God not as supplies of his want. **1611** BIBLE *Matt.* v. 23, 24. **1895** *Daily News* 30 Oct. 4/7 The Deodand, or gift to God.

5. Something given with a corrupting intention; a bribe. *Obs.* as a specific sense.

The existence of this sense seems to be implied *a* **1300** in *Cursor M.* 17464 (Gött.) Þai war for gifte [*read* forgifte, *bribed*] þe soth to hele.

α. **1362** LANGL. *P. Pl.* A. III. 90 Fuir schal falle and brenne atte laste þe houses and þe homes of hem þat desyreþ For to haue ȝiftes. **1382** WYCLIF *Deut.* xvi. 19 Thou shalt not accept persone, ne ȝiftis, for ȝiftis blynden eyen of wise men.

γ. **1549** LATIMER *3rd Serm. bef. Edw. VI* (Arb.) 89 Wo worth these giftes, they subuert iustyce euerye where. **1594** WILLOBIE in *Shaks. C. Praise* 10 For giftes the wysest will deceave. **1611** BIBLE *2 Chron.* xix. 7 There is no iniquitie with the Lord our God..nor taking of gifts.

6. a. A faculty, power, or quality miraculously bestowed, e.g. upon the apostles and other early Christians; a Christian virtue looked upon as an emanation from the Holy Ghost; extended further to endowments bestowed by heathen deities or some supernatural agent; occas. in sense of inspiration. ***the gift of tongues***: see TONGUE.

α. *c* **1175** *Lamb. Hom.* 69 We ne maȝen þe fond from us driue, ne mid sworde ne mid kniue, bute hit beo þurh godes ȝifte. *a* **1225** *Ancr. R.* 28 Uor ðe seoue ȝiftes of ðe Holi Goste, ðet ich mote habben ham. **1382** WYCLIF *Acts* viii. 20 Thou gessidist the ȝifte of God for to be had..by money. *c* **1449** PECOCK *Repr.* 181 The ȝiftis of gracis, the glories of heuen bihiȝt ben to alle Cristene passyng greete benefetis.

β. **1340** *Ayenb.* 200 Nou we willeþ zigge uerst of þe yefþe of onderstondinge be þan þet þe holy gost wile ous teche.

γ. *a* **1300** *Cursor M.* 19007 Of haligast þe giftes sere, Gin us he has als yee se here. *a* **1533** LD. BERNERS *Huon* lxxxiv. 265 Amonge other [ladyes of ye fayrye] there was one that gaue me ye gyft to be suche one as ye se that I am. **1605** CAMDEN *Rem.* (1637) 6 That admirable gift hereditary to the anointed Princes of this Realme, in curing the Kings Evill. **1667** MILTON *P.L.* IV. 715 Pandora, whom the Gods Endowd with all thir gifts. **1704** NELSON *Fest. & Fasts* xxi. (1739) 258 Having a Power to impart the same Gift to others. **1709** STRYPE *Ann. Ref.* (1824) I. xxv. 254 He did begin to write, but he could bring nothing to pass: his gift was not come to him. **1732** BERKELEY *Serm. S.P.G.* Wks. 1871 III. 241 We have not the gift of miracles. **1834** J. H. NEWMAN *Par. Serm.* I. i. 13 To obtain the gift of holiness is the work of a life. **1875** MANNING *Mission H. Ghost* xiii. 359 Now the gift of intellect or understanding is precisely that gift of the Holy Spirit which enables us to understand the meaning of what we believe. **1876** MOZLEY *Univ. Serm.* xi. (1877) 216 Faith is not only an excellent gift, a sublime gift, but it is a gift full of present happiness.

b. A natural endowment, faculty, ability, or talent. Also ***natural gift***, ***gift of God*** or ***nature***. ***gift of the gab***: (*colloq.*) see GAB 1 b.

a **1300** *Cursor M.* 23892 Sum for mar and sum for less, Efter þat vr giftes ess. **1504** ATKYNSON tr. *De Imitatione* III. lx. 252 Gyftes of nature be gyuen Indyfferentlye to good folke and euyll. **1573** J. SANDFORD *Hours Recr.* (1576) Ep. Ded. A 5 Hir vertues and giftes of minde. **1588** J. UDALL *Demonstr. Discip.* xi. (Arb.) 49 For some hath an excellent gift in doctrine, and not in application. **1597** MORLEY *Introd. Mus.* 115 Imagining that all the guiftes of God should die in themselues, if they should bee taken out of the worlde. **1647** N. BACON *Disc. Govt. Eng.* I. v. (1739) 12 Austin had also a gift or trick of working miracles. **1693** S. HARVEY in *Dryden's Juvenal* ix. (1697) 231 The Gifts of Nature, what will they avail? **1710** S. SEWALL *Diary* 2 Dec. (1879) II. 294, I have heard he had a good Gift in Prayer. **1711** ADDISON *Spect.* No. 128 ¶1 As Vivacity is the Gift of Women, Gravity is that of Men. **1769** *Junius Lett.* i. 8 Nature has been sparing of her gifts to the noble lord. **1814** WORDSW. *Excurs.* I. 78 Endowed with highest gifts, The vision and the faculty divine. **1849** MACAULAY *Hist. Eng.* vii. II. 229 He was in the habit of exercising his spiritual gifts at their meetings. **1856** SIR B. BRODIE *Psychol. Inq.* I. i. 29 The faculty of reasoning correctly..is for the most part a natural gift. **1871** FREEMAN *Norm. Conq.* (1876) IV. xvii. 99 He was displaying in Normandy the gifts of the wise lawgiver and firm administrator. **1882** PEBODY *Eng. Journalism* xix. 144 The precise gifts that are needed in a special correspondent. **1888** BRYCE *Amer. Commw.* II. liii. 328 [Hamilton's] countrymen seem to have never..duly recognized his splendid gifts.

7. *slang.* (See quots.)

1832 *Examiner* 187/2 [They] asked him if he would join them in a good thing, which was to carry away a landlord's till of money, and that it would be a 'gift' (an easy task). **1859** *Slang Dict.*, *Gift*, any article which has been stolen and afterwards sold at a low price.

8. A white speck on the finger-nails, supposed to portend a gift.

1708 *Brit. Apollo* No. 17. 2/1 *Q.* What is the Cause of little white Spots, which sometimes grow under the Nails of the Fingers? And what is the reason they say they are Gifts? *A.* The reason of their being call'd Gifts is as Wise an one as that of Letters, Winding Sheets, &c. in a Candle. **1796** in *Grose's Dict. Vulg. Tongue* (ed. 3). **1854** KNIGHT *Once upon a Time* II. 269 We showed each other the gifts on our nails. **1886** in *Chesh. Gloss.*

9. *attrib.* and *Comb.* **a.** simple attrib., as ***gift-copy***, ***-money***, ***-package***, ***-picture***. **b.** objective, as ***gift-bearer***, ***-giving***, ***-taker***; †***gift-greedy*** adj. **c.** instrumental, as ***gift-laden*** adj. Also **gift-book**, a book given as a present; a book published in an attractive form, such as is suitable for a present, a school prize, etc.; **gift coupon**, a coupon issued with certain commodities, a specified number of which entitles the holder to a free gift; **gift-enterprise** *U.S.* (see quot.); **gift-exchange** (see quot. 1963); **gift-food**, food given in charity; **gift-horse**, a horse given as a present: see also HORSE *sb.* 21; **gift-house** (see quot.); †**gift-sermon**, a sermon that is paid for by an endowment; **gift shop** orig. *U.S.*, a shop dealing in articles suitable for gifts; also with pseudo-archaic spelling, ***gifte-shoppe***; **gift-token** or **voucher**, a voucher (intended to serve as a gift) for a sum of money to pay for the purchase of an article; **gift-wrap** *v. trans.* (orig. *U.S.*), to wrap (an article intended as a gift) attractively; also *absol.* and *fig.*; hence ***gift-wrapped*** ppl. adj.; ***gift-wrapping*** vbl. sb. (also *attrib.*).

1483 *Cath. Angl.* 155/2 A *Gift berer, *doniferus*, *munifer*. **1834** *Knickerbocker* III. 113 It is, I believe, your standing *gift-book. **1842** (*title*) The royal gift book for the young. **1848** D. VEDDER (*title*) The pictorial giftbook of lays and lithography. **1868** *Publisher's Pref. to Watts' Improv. Mind*, As a gift-book to advanced scholars it is most appropriate. **1886** T. FROST *Remin. Country Journalist* viii. (1888) 94 They..wished to use them [engravings] in the production of a gift-book. **1832** MRS. TROLLOPE in L'Estrange *Friendsh. Miss Mitford* (1882) I. 238 Mr. Howe told him that all the *gift copies were already sent. **1931** *Morning Post* 18 Feb. 6/5 The '*Gift' Coupon system. **1933** D. L. SAYERS *Murder must Advertise* iv. 54 It only needed the alteration of a sentence and the introduction of a panel about gift-coupons. **1893** *Funk's Stand. Dict.*, **Gift-enterprise*, a business that offers gifts to secure patrons or purchasers. **1936** R. LINTON *Study of Man* 144 All trade was phrased in terms of *gift exchange. **1951** R. FIRTH *Elem. Social Organiz.* i. 21 Such diverse social relations as buying and selling, gift-exchange, [etc.]. **1963** *Brit. Jrnl. Sociol.* XIV. 26 *Gift exchange*.. describes a type of transaction which formally consists in the making of a gift and its repayment by another. **1865** *Daily Tel.* 6 Dec. 4/5 The danger was..that the dangerous habit of living upon *gift-food would demoralise the recipients. **1937** M. MEAD *Cooperation & Competition among Primitive Peoples* i. 22 All this importation is phrased as *gift giving between devoted friends. **1949** —— *Male & Female* 408 The fish were then exchanged in a gift-giving context. **1959** I. & P. OPIE *Lore & Lang Schoolch.* xii. 236 Sometimes..the older children take advantage of the gift-giving and play tricks. *c* **1611** CHAPMAN *Iliad* IV. 118 With this, the mad-*gift-greedie man, Minerua did perswade. **1663** BUTLER *Hud.* I. i. 490 He ne'er consider'd it, as loth To look a *Gift-Horse in the mouth. **1837** W. IRVING *Capt. Bonneville* II. 249 The Captain..put spurs to his very fine gift-horse. **1893** FARMER *Slang*, **Gift-house* (or *Gift*), (printers'), a club; a house of call; specifically for the purpose of finding employment, or providing allowances for members. **1895** *Daily News* 27 Dec. 2/5 A giant Christmas tree, constituted of some hundreds of the *gift-laden firs of the nursery. **1548** UDALL, etc. *Erasm. Par. Mark* i. 12–15 Thou haste receyued the holy ghoste as it were *gifte money, a bond, and an earnest penye of thy salarye. **1897** BAILEY *Fruit-growing* 416 In all the finest fruits the grower should use nothing but a *gift-package, that is, one which is given away with the fruit when it is sold. **1862** THORNBURY *Turner* II. 128 Men never valued *gift pictures so much as those in which they had invested money. **1766** ENTICK *London* IV. 64 Here is a *gift-sermon every Tuesday..well endowed by lady Cambden. **1918** C. WELLS *Vicky Van* i. 10 Little faddly prize bags of *gift-shop novelties are her stakes. **1929** Gift shop [see ART $v.^2$ 5]. **1932** E. BOWEN *To North* xxi. 229 There are too many shops... Especially gift shops. **1948** J. CANNAN *Little I Understood* xi. 136 Expensive and financially unstable gifte shoppes. **1549** LATIMER *3rd Serm. bef. Edw. VI* (Arb.) 94 He was no *gyfte taker, he was no wynker, he was no bywalker. **1963** *She* Dec. 51 Best leg forward in 1964 with a *gift token for nylon stockings. *Ibid.*, Make life easier for a hard-working house-wife whose feet are killing her with a Scholl *Gift Voucher entitling her to one or a set of foot massaging sessions. **1969** *Times* 17 Dec. 18/5 (Advt.), Who's lucky? Everybody who gets a gift voucher for two tickets. **1936** *Amer. Speech* XI. 101/1 During the holiday season many department stores advertised, 'We *Gift-Wrap Here.' **1948** in *Amer. Speech* (1956) XXXI. 210 Ready to gift-wrap your package. **1958** *Economist* 20 Dec. 1083/2 Whatever he buys will be professionally gift-wrapped for him. **1969** *New Yorker* 11 Oct. 146/3 (Advt.), We gift wrap and ship everywhere. **1964** *Punch* 16 Dec. 936/3 People..pile them [*sc.* cars] up with *gift-wrapped presents. **1949** *Word Study* May 8/1 (*caption to cartoon*) *Gift Wrapping. **1963** M. MCCARTHY *Group* xi. 240 They also sold..Valentines and gift-wrapping paper.

gift (gɪft), *v.* [f. GIFT *sb.*]

1. *trans.* To endow or furnish with gifts (see chiefly GIFT *sb.* 6); to endow, invest, or present *with* as a gift.

15.. *Wife in Morel's Skin* C j b, The friendes that were together met He [*printed* Be] gyfted them richely with right good speede. **1608** W. SCLATER *Malachy* (1650) 197 See how the Lord gifted him above his brethren. **1621** SANDERSON *12 Serm.* (1637) 396 If God have not gifted us for it, he hath not called us to it. **1677** W. HUBBARD *Narrative* (1865) I. 61 He was better gifted than any other of the Indian Nation. **1749** FIELDING *Tom Jones* I. v, Nothing but the inspiration with which we writers are gifted can possibly enable anyone to make the discovery. **1826** E. IRVING *Babylon* II. VIII. 282 When they were gifted with the self same Spirit with which Moses had been gifted. **1834** T. MEDWIN *Angler in Wales* I. 290 How admirably Nature had provided.. by gifting it [the salmon] with a form of all others the best adapted for [etc.]. **1844** MRS. BROWNING *Swan's Nest*, The world must love and fear him Whom I gift with heart and hand. **1884** ROGERS *6 Cent. Work & Wages* I. 126 Many settlements, which afterwards grew into towns, were gifted subsequently with parliamentary representation.

b. To invest with a charm; to impart a fascination to. *rare*$^{-1}$.

1853 G. JOHNSTON *Nat. Hist. E. Bord.* I. 141, I may not dwell on scenes and events which the pen of Scott has gifted.

2. To bestow as a gift; to make a present of. Const. with *to* or dative. Also with *away*. Chiefly *Sc.*

1619 SIR J. SEMPILL *Sacrilege* 31 If they object, that tithes, being gifted to Levi, in official inheritance, can stand no longer than Levi [etc.]. *a* **1639** SPOTTISWOOD *Hist. Ch. Scot.* v. (1677) 278 The recovery of a parcel of ground which the Queen had gifted to Mary Levinston. **1711** in A. McKay *Hist. Kilmarnock* (1880) 98 This bell was gifted by the Earl of Kilmarnock to the town of Kilmarnock for their Council-house. **1754** ERSKINE *Princ. Sc. Law* I. (1809) 51 Where a fund is gifted for the establishment of a second minister, in a parish where the cure is thought too heavy for one [etc.]. **1801** RANKEN *Hist. France* I. 301 Parents were prohibited from selling, gifting, or pledging their children. **1829** J. BROWN *New Deeside Guide* (1876) 19 College of Blairs.. having been gifted to the Church of Rome by its proprietor. **1839** ALISON *Europe* xlii. §71 (1849–50) VII. 155 Thus did Napoleon and d'Oubril gift away Sicily. **1878** J. C. LEES *Abbey of Paisley* xix. 201 The Regent Murray gifted all the Church Property to Lord Sempill.

Hence **'gifting** *vbl. sb.* and *ppl. a.*

1619 SIR J. SEMPILL *Sacrilege* App. 4 Was Abraham so idle in gifting? Jacob so superstitious in vowing? **1671** *True Nonconf.* 163 Our Lords most gracious gifting. **1796** T. TOWNSHEND *Poems* 32 Where once thy gifting hand did weave Garlands of glory for the poet's head. **1875** WHITNEY *Life Lang.* xiv. 302 A gifting of man, at his birth, not with capacities alone.

gifted ('gɪftɪd), *ppl. a.* [f. GIFT *v.* + -ED^{2}.]

1. Endowed with gifts (see GIFT *sb.* 6); talented.

1644 *Minutes Westm. Assembly* (1874) 38 It is one thing to say a gifted man may preach, but another thing to say a ruling elder.. by virtue of his office may do it. **1677** W. HUBBARD *Narrative* (1865) II. 201 Such of the Women as were gifted at knitting and sewing [etc.]. **1711** G. CARY *Phys. Phylactick* 241 This is a Text that the Gifted Brethren have often urged. **1794** MATHIAS *Purs. Lit.* (1798) 212 No patriot weeps, when gifted villains die. **1839** A. GRAY *Lett.* (1893) 100 The famous Christopher North.. a gifted genius. **1875** JOWETT *Plato* (ed. 2) III. 376 The most gifted minds, when they are ill-educated, become the worst. **1892** ZANGWILL *Bow Myst.* 92 It's a grand thing to be gifted, Tom.

absol. **1828** CARLYLE *Misc.* (1857) I. 231 Men felt and knew that here also was one of the Gifted! **1850** ROBERTSON *Serm.* Ser. III. ix. 114 The gifted of their species.

b. said of an utterance and of a frame of mind.

1678 BUTLER *Hud.* III. ii. 635 Where had they all their Gifted Phrases, But from our Calamies and Cases? **1850** ROBERTSON *Serm.* Ser. III. ii. 26 Genius in its most gifted hour.

†**2.** Given, bestowed. *Obs.*$^{-1}$

1671 MILTON *Samson* 36 Why was my breeding ordered and prescribed.. To grind in brazen fetters under task With this heaven-gifted strength?

Hence **'giftedness**, the condition, quality, or state of being gifted. Also quasi-*concr.*, a gift.

1660 tr. *Paracelsus' Archidoxis* II. 149 The things of nature are not so alike graduated as Diseases are, as in relation to the Dose or Guiftedness. **1671** EACHARD *Observ. Answ. Grounds Cont. Clergy* 116 Not endued with the sublimest giftednesses of our Separatists. *a* **1734** NORTH *Lives* (1826) III. 312 He was very illiterate, but thought to supply that defect by extraordinary giftedness. **1875** H. JAMES *R. Hudson* ii. 64 Rowland.. felt more and more the fascination of what he would have called his giftedness.

gifter, var. GIFTURE, *Obs.*

giftie ('gɪftɪ). *Sc.* [dim. f. GIFT *sb.*: see -Y^{4}.] Playfully used for GIFT *sb.* 6 b.

1787 BURNS *To a Louse* viii, O wad some Pow'r the giftie gie us To see oursels as others see us! **1791** A. WILSON *Laurel Disputed* Wks. (1876) II. 22 [He] shows at twenty-twa as great a giftie For painting just, as Allan did at fifty.

†**'giftishness.** *Obs. rare.* [f. **giftish* (f. GIFT *sb.* + -ISH) + -NESS.] Giftedness, talent.

1654 WHITLOCK *Zootomia* 78 An old Trot (that boasteth of her Giftishnesse in Waterology). *Ibid.* 158 Such whose Giftishnesse in Exhortation amounteth to a perswasive power.

giftless ('gɪftlɪs), *a.* [f. GIFT *sb.* + -LESS.]

1. That has no gift to offer. *giftless gifts* = gifts that are no gifts (after Gr. ἄδωρα δῶρα).

1390 GOWER *Conf.* I. 193 This messanger was yefteles. **1614** D. DYKE *Myst. Selfe-Deceiving* 15 As in the proverbe, there are giftlesse gifts. **1650** TRAPP *Comm.* Gen. xv. 6 *Abraham gave gifts.* So doth God to reprobates; but they are giftless gifts: better be without them. **1870** MORRIS *Earthly Par.* I. I. 245 Fair lords, be still awhile, And say no ill about this giftless guest.

2. That receives or has received no gift.

c **1435** *Torr. Portugal* 415 Yftles schall they not be, That dare I sothely sey. **1751** CAMBRIDGE *Scribleriad* IV. 161 But not unhonour'd shall he halt away, Or giftless mourn this unauspicious day. **1870** MORRIS *Earthly Par.* I. I. 297 O righteous man, we leave this land, Nor leave thee giftless for the welcoming Thou gav'st us erst.

3. Devoid of mental endowments; without talent.

1894 *Daily News* 13 July 6/4 An industrious, and by no means giftless, Welsh scholar.

giftling ('gɪftlɪŋ). *nonce-wd.* [f. GIFT *sb.* + -LING.] A small gift.

1860 THACKERAY *Round. Papers* x. (1863) 151 The kindly Christmas tree.. may you have plucked pretty giftlings from it.

gift-over ('gɪftəʊvə(r)). [f. GIFT *sb.* + OVER *adv.*] The act of making over as a gift.

1927 *Daily Mail* 8 July 7/1 That the gift-over, by which the property might pass away from the children on account of the son's marriage, was void. **1929** *Glasgow Herald* 8 July 8 The gift-over whereby the estate would go elsewhere than to the children.

†**'gift-rope.** *Naut. Obs.* [The first element is prob. corrupt; perh. the word may be spurious, evolved by a misprint or misreading from *gest-rope*.] = GUEST-ROPE, GUESS-WARP.

1704 HARRIS *Lex. Techn.*, *Gift-rope* is the Boat-Rope, which is fastened to the Boat when she is swifted, in order to her being towed at the Stern of a Ship. **1753** CHAMBERS *Cycl. Supp.*, *Chest-rope*, in a ship, is the same with the guest or gift-rope. **1867** SMYTH *Sailor's Word-bk.*, *Gift-rope* (synonymous with *guest-rope*), a rope for boats at the guest-warp boom. [Not known to two nautical experts consulted.]

†**'gifture.** *Obs.* Also 6 yefture, 6–7 gifter. [f. GIFT *v.* + -URE.]

1. The action of giving; also the right of giving. Cf. GIFT *sb.* I. *upon gifture*: gratuitously.

1503 *Will of Lady Hastings* in *Test. Vetusta* II. 452 A faire prymmar, which I had by the yefture of Queen Elizabeth. **1583** STUBBES *Anat. Abus.* II. (1882) 79 In whome doth the patronage, right, and gifture of these ecclesiastical promotions and benefices consist? **1634** W. WOOD *New Eng. Prosp.* II. (1865) 5 The English will not be so liberall as to furnish them upon gifture.

2. A gift; a prize.

1592 WYRLEY *Armorie, Ld. Chandos* 63 Willing the gifter to some other wight. **1615** R. CLEAVER *Prov.* 48 The wealth of the godly is the peculiar gifture of wisedome.

3. *attrib.*, as *gifture-banquet*; **gifture-ore**, a quantity of ore given as a customary due.

1609 HOLLAND *Amm. Marcell.* XIX. vi. 12 Solemn doles, or gifture banquets. **1631** *Star Chamb. Cases* (Camden) 90 The Deputy Barre Masters.. would not measure their oare unlesse they would pay them their gifter oare. **1632** *Ibid.* 98 There was some given to the Deputy Barre Masters for their paines, and it is called therefore gifter oare.

gig (gɪg), *sb.*^{1} Forms: 3–8 gigg(e, 4–5 gygge, (6 ghyg), 6– gig. [Perh. onomatopœic; the identity of the word in all senses is very doubtful.]

I. Something that whirls.

†**1.** A whipping-top. *Obs.*

c **1440** [see WHIRLIGIG]. **1570** BILLINGSLEY *Euclid* XI. def. xvi. 317 This solide [Cone] of many is called Turbo, which to our purpose may be Englished a Top or Ghyg. **1588** SHAKS. *L.L.L.* v. i. 70 Thou disputes like an Infant: goe whip thy Gigge. **1644** in *N. & Q.* Ser. I. IX. 422/1 For four giggs and scourge sticks *is.* *a* **1657** LOVELACE *Poems* (1864) 159 H' has left his apish jigs, And whipping hearts like gigs. **1692** LOCKE *Educ.* §130 Play-things which are above their Skill to make, as Tops, Gigs, Battledors, and the like. **1719** D'URFEY *Pills* V. 109, I told her I'd give her a Whip for her Gig. *a* **1793** [see GIDDY *a.* 2 d].

fig. **1630** J. TAYLOR (Water P.) *Wks.* II. 79/2 For hee's the gigge of time, Whom sharpest wits haue whipt with sportful rime. *Ibid.* 144/1 Thou Tauerne, Alehouse, Whorehouse, Gig of time, That for a groat wilt amongst Tinkers rime.

†**2.** A set of feathers arranged so as to revolve rapidly in the wind, for the purpose of attracting birds to a net. *Obs.*

1621 MARKHAM *Prev. Hunger* (1655) 115. *a* **1698** BLUNDELL *Cavalier's Note-bk.* (1880) 272 A great help.. for bringing in of larks about your net, is a gigg of feathers.. which twirleth swiftly round on the least breath of wind. **1727** BRADLEY *Fam. Dict.* s.v. *Day-net.*

3. = GIG-MILL.

1842 BRANDE *Dict. Sci.*, *Gigs*, or *gig machines*, are rotatory cylinders covered with wire-teeth, for teazling woollen cloth. **1886** ELWORTHY *W. Somerset Word-bk.* s.v., *Gig, Gig-mill*, the machine by which the shag or nap is raised upon blankets and other cloth; also applied to the building in which the machine is worked.. 'Where's your Tom now? Au! he do worky down to factory—he 've a-worked to the gig's two year'.

II. Applied to persons.

†**4.** A flighty, giddy girl. *Obs.*

a **1225** *Ancr. R.* 204 Hunten þer efter.. mid gigge leihtre, mid hor eien, mid eni lihte lates. *c* **1395** *Plowman's T.* (Skeat) 759 Some spend hir good upon [hir] gigges, And finden hem of greet aray. *c* **1430** *How Gd. Wyf tauȝte hir Dau.* 55 in *Babees Bk.* 38 Fare not as a gigge, for nouȝt þat may bitide, Lauȝe þou not to loude, ne ȝane þou not to wide. **1594** WILLOBIE *Avisa* (1880) 41 Thou selfewill gig that doth detest My faithfull loue, looke to thy fame. *a* **1700** B. E. *Dict. Cant. Crew*, s.v., A young Gig, a wanton Lass. **1780** MAD. D'ARBLAY *Diary* June, Charlotte L—— called, and the little gig told all the quarrels.. she led in her family.

5. A queer-looking figure, an oddity; *dial.* a fool. Chiefly *Eton slang.* Cf. GECK *sb.*^{1}, GEGGE.

1777 in *Life Hugh Eliot* iv. (1868) 124 Upon my word, Hugh, you are the greatest gig in the world. **1797** G. COLMAN *Heir at Law* IV. ii, What a damn'd gig you look like. *a* **1825** FORBY *Voc. E. Anglia*, *Gig*, a trifling, silly, flighty fellow. **1825** *Blackw. Mag.* XVII. 416 O, France is the region of caricature, And a regular Frenchman's a gig to be sure With his apple-green breeches [etc.]. **1832** MACAULAY in *Life & Lett.* (1880) I. 265 Be you Tories, be you Whigs, You must write to sad young gigs. **1836** T. HOOK *G. Gurney* I. 193 They were what Mr. Daly.. called uncommon gigs. **1856** WHYTE MELVILLE *Kate Cov.* xiv, Such a set of 'gigs', my dear, I never saw in my life.. not a good-looking man amongst them.

III. **6.** †**a.** A fancy, joke, whim. *Obs.*

1590 NASHE *Pasquil's Apol.* I. C ij b, A right cutte of the worde, without gigges or fancies of hæreticall and newe opinions. **1600** J. LANE *Tom Tel-troth* 118 New gigges for a countrie clowne. **1607** *Schol. Disc. agst. Antichr.* I. i. 16 It is a common gigge to shift of all things brought against this filthee Idoll. *a* **1625** FLETCHER *Hum. Lieuten.* IV. iv, I must go see him presently, For this is such a gig. **1642** ROGERS *Naaman* 204 Any idle tale, or gigge of a geering, gibing wit. **1724** RAMSAY *Tea-t. Misc.* (1733) III. 321 They put a gigg in the gravest scull And send their wits to gather wool. **1821** *Joseph the Book-Man* 111 One talk'd of life's most funny rigs, And much enlarg'd on pleasing gigs.

b. Fun, merriment, glee. *in high gig, on the (high) gig*: in a state of boisterous hilarity; also *dial.* eager, impatient. Now *dial.*

1777 MAD. D'ARBLAY *Early Diary* (1889) II. 201 The girls, Betsy and Beckey, were upon the *high gig* all the time, for they enjoyed seeing me thus whisked about. **1807** *Oracle* in *Spirit Publ. Jrnls.* (1809) XII. 45, I tells you Common Garden's the gig, the go, and the finish. **1813** MOORE *Post Bag* iii. 21 We were all in high gig—Roman Punch and Tokay Travelled round, till our heads travelled just the same way. **1819** 'R. RABELAIS' *Abeillard & H.* 36 Being so full of gig and glee Begins her speech with He! He! He! *c* **1830** in Besant *50 Yrs. Ago* 134 A laughter-loving lass of eighteen who dearly loved a bit of gig. **1876** *Mid-Yorksh. Gloss.*, *Gig*, a state of flurry; 'He's on the gig to be off.'

c. *Comb.* **gig-fair** *local* (see quot.) ? *Obs.*

1829 GLOVER *Hist. Derby* I. 271 Fairs for shows, ribands, toys, &c. commonly called holiday or gig fairs.

gig (gɪg), *sb.*^{2} [Transferred sense of GIG *sb.*^{1} I.]

1. A light two-wheeled one-horse carriage.

1791 'G. GAMBADO' *Ann. Horsem.* v. (1809) 89 Airing *en famille*, in a gig, accompanied with a husband and three children. **1796** in *Grose's Dict. Vulg. Tongue* (ed. 3). **1809** WINDHAM *Sp. Parl.* 26 May 24 Let the former riders in gigs and whiskeys and one-horsed carriages continue to ride in them. **1838** HAWTHORNE *Jrnl. Solit. Man* in *Tales & Sk.* (1879) 84 Spruce gigs rattling past. **1855** THACKERAY *Newcomes* I. 51 In the carriage, mind you, not in the gig driven by the groom. **1889** G. N. HOOPER in *Driving* (Badm.) 379 Gigs are considered equally suitable for London and country use.

2. *Naut.* A light, narrow, clinker-built ship's boat, adapted either for rowing or sailing. Also ***cutter-, whale-gig.***

(Not in Falconer *Dict. Marine* 1780.)

1790 WOLCOT (P. Pindar) *Adv. Fut. Laureat* Wks. 1812 II. 338 That by its painter drags the Gig or Yawl. **1801** in Nicolas *Disp. Nelson* (1845) IV. 325 Lord Nelson repaired in his gig (his usual conveyance) on board of our Ship. **1816** 'QUIZ' *Grand Master* I. 24 Tis number sixty-five—a wig—O d——n the number! man the gig. **1860** L. OLIPHANT *Earl Elgin's Mission to China* I. 71 Customhouse guards.. have a proper respect for a British man-of-war's gig. **1875** BEDFORD *Sailor's Pocket Bk.* vi. (ed. 2) 213 Cutter Gig, Whale Gig, Whale Gig-Life[boat].

b. A modified form of the ship's gig, used, esp. on the Thames, as a rowing boat, chiefly for racing purposes.

1865 [see *gig eight* sense 4]. **1881** *Sportsman's Year Bk.* 100 A heavy pair-oared gig. **1882** *Times* (weekly ed.) 16 June 2/1 The steam-launches and gigs of the Thames police may with noiseless vigilance patrol the waters. **1888** W. B. WOODGATE *Boating* xi. (Badm.) 143 Many regattas offered prizes for pair oars with coxwains in outrigged gigs.

c. Short for *gigsman* (see 4).

1833 M. SCOTT *Tom Cringle* xv, One of the Captain's gigs, the handsome black already introduced on the scene.

3. A wooden box or chamber, with two compartments, one above the other, used by miners in ascending and descending a pit-shaft. Also = KIBBLE.

1881 RAYMOND *Mining Gloss.*, *Gig.* See *Kibble*.. *Kibbal* or *Kibble* (*Corn. & Wales*), an iron bucket for raising ore. **1883** *B'ham Weekly Post* 18 Aug. 4/3 Thirteen men placed themselves in the gig to be drawn to the surface from a depth of about 1,300 feet.

4. *attrib.* and *Comb.* **a.** simple attributive, as (sense 1) ***gig-apron, -cushion, harness, -horse, -house, -umbrella, -whip***; ***gig-ways*** adv.; (sense 2 b) ***gig-eight, -race, -sculling.*** **b.** similative, as (sense 2 b) ***gig-built*** adj. Also **gig-bishop**, a bishop who rides in a gig instead of a carriage; **gig-box**, a box in the seat of a gig; **gigsman**, one of the crew of a ship's gig; **gig-pair**, a gig fitted for two rowers; **gig-road, -saddle, -tree** (see quots.); **gig-work**, practice in rowing in a gig.

1869 *Daily News* 10 Dec., Stetham and Co. have gutta percha in the shape of *gig-aprons and dumb jockeys. **1852** S. G. OSBORNE in *Times* 3 Nov., Divide the dioceses into manageable districts, and have what I will call '*gig bishops'. **1897** *Tablet* 4 Sept. 384 The Suffragans, or 'gig-bishops', as the late Mr. Rogers used to call them. **1833** M. SCOTT *Tom Cringle* vii. (1859) 143 Fyall ordered Jupiter to bring a case from his *gig box containing some capital brandy. **1896** *Daily News* 5 Aug. 3/3 Mr. J. E. M... happened to be with some friends in a large *gig-built boat close by. **1843** HALIBURTON *Attaché* I. xi. 195 The lawyer took a stretch for it on the bench, with his *gig cushions for a pillar. **1865** *Pall Mall G.* 23 May 110 We may imagine.. the raws and blisters that he endured, ere he was qualified to progress from the coaching tub to a seat in the *gig eight. **1886** ELWORTHY *W. Somerset Word-bk.*, *Gig-saddle*, the saddle belonging to a set of single-horse carriage or *gig-harness. **1835** BOOTH *Analyt. Dict.* 304 Coach-horse,

Carriage-horse, *Gig-horse, &c. **1882** OGILVIE, *Gig-horse*, a horse that draws a gig. **1829** D. CONWAY *Norway* 151 There was also attached..a coach or *gig-house and a garden. **1869** *Echo* 9 Feb., He daily has one or two out in the *gig-pairs. **1888** W. B. WOODGATE *Boating* xi. (Badm.) 144 This system ..caused *gig races to be fruitful sources of squabbles. **1824** *Times* 7 Jan. 3/5 That is the *gig-road toward's Batler's-green. **1883** *Standard* 9 Nov. 2/2 The road is not a working road, but what they call a gig road. **1875** KNIGHT *Dict. Mech.*, **Gig-saddle*, a small saddle used with carriage-harness, and carrying the terrets for the driving-reins and the check-hook for the bearing-rein. **1887** *Sporting Life* 30 June 4/6 No sculling boats had been engaged for the scratch *gig sculling race. **1875** KNIGHT *Dict. Mech.*, **Gig-tree*, the frame of a gig or harness saddle. **1883** READE *Tit for Tat* in *Harper's Mag.* Jan. 252/2 The lady..came out to her, and a servant and a *gig umbrella. **1832** J. HODGSON in J. Raine *Mem.* (1858) II. 258 If you come *gig-ways pray bring with you *Raine's Testamenta.* **1830** *Chron.* 24 Aug. in *Ann. Reg.* (1831) 137/2 Captain Smith, having jumped out of it, with the *gig-whip in his hand. **1843** M. J. HIGGINS *Ess.* (1875) 39 Albert..takes up a gig-whip, but does not use it. **1898** *Daily News* 20 Jan. 3/4 All the candidates indulged in long bouts of *gig work.

Hence **gig-ful**, as many as a gig will hold.

1848 J. MACKINTOSH *Diary* in Macleod *Mem.* vi. (1854) 154 Two gigfuls of fishers passed me.

†**gig**, *sb.*[3] *Obs. rare*[−1]. In 4 **gyge**. [Of obscure origin; perh. echoic; cf. Sc. *gig*, GEIG *v.*, to squeak.] ? A squeaking noise.

c **1384** CHAUCER *H. Fame* III. 852 (Fairfax MS.) And euer mo so swyft as thought This queynt hous about went..And al thys hous..was made of twigges..That for the swough and for the twynges [*read* twyges] This house was also [= as] ful of gyges And also ful eke of chirkynges As [etc.].

gig (gɪg), *sb.*[4] [Shortened from FISHGIG or FIZGIG.] A kind of fish-spear; = FISHGIG, FIZGIG 4. Also *U.S.*, 'An arrangement of four barbless hooks, fastened back to back, and attached to a hand-line, used for catching fish by dragging it through a school' (*Funk's Stand. Dict.*).

1722 R. B. *Hist. Virginia* 131 At each End of the Canoe stands an Indian, with a Gig, or pointed Spear, setting the Canoe forward with the Butt-end of the Spear, as gently as he can, by that Means, stealing upon the Fish, without any Noise. **1774** COOK *Voy.* (1777) II. III. vii. 91, I did not see that they had any other weapon but darts and gigs, intended only for striking of fish. **1807** P. GASS *Jrnl.* 228 Two men are trying to take some of the fish with a gig. **1877** G. GIBBS *Tribes Washington* 195 The spring salmon are taken..in the small streams either with the scoop-net or with a gig.

†**gig**, *sb.*[5] *Obs.* Also 7 **gigg(e**. (See quots.)

1688 R. HOLME *Armoury* III. 106/1 A Gigge is a hole in the Ground where Fire is made to dry the Flax. **1706** PHILLIPS (ed. Kersey) *Gigge.*

gig (gɪg), *sb.*[6] *colloq.* [Origin unknown.] An engagement for a musician or musicians playing jazz, dance-music, etc.; *spec.* a 'one-night stand'; also, the place of such a performance. Also *transf.* and *attrib.* Hence **ˈgigster**, one who does 'gigs'.

1926 *Melody Maker* Sept. 7 One popular 'gig' band makes use of a nicely printed booklet. **1927** *Ibid.* May 457/3 This seven-piece combination does many 'gigs' in S.E. London, but is hoping to secure a resident engagement at Leamington in the near future. **1934** S. R. NELSON *All about Jazz* vi. 113 Jack runs numerous bands which play 'gig' work—i.e. private engagements or public work. In his office, he has a file in which some hundreds of 'gig' musicians are listed. **1939** *Melody Maker* 9 Sept., When King George died there was terrible confusion, especially among gigsters, as to whether they should fulfil their gigs or not. **1964** L. HAIRSTON in J. H. Clarke *Harlem* 287 Pa—knockin' hisself out on a mail-handler gig at the Post Office where the pay is so lousy he's gotta work a part-time gig. **1965** G. MELLY *Owning-Up* vii. 80 Another Proustian gig was the Civic Hall, Nantwich. We played there fairly regularly right through the 'fifties. **1969** *Observer* 12 Jan. 31/5 Leading groups will be given two hours in which to play what they want, without the limitations imposed by commercial gigs.

†**gig** (gɪg), *v.*[1] [f. GIG *sb.*[1] (sense 1).] **a.** *intr.*; **b.** *trans.* (sense obscure: see below).

The verb seems literally to denote the action of some kind of 'gig' or whipping-top of peculiar construction, having inside it a smaller 'gig' of the same shape, which was thrown out by the effect of rapid rotation. Hence *to gig* (*out*) appears to be used *fig.* with the sense 'to throw out or give rise to (a smaller repetition of itself)'. The Dicts., on the ground of the Dryden quot., have plausibly, but erroneously, explained the transitive vb. as meaning 'to engender,' assigning to it a derivation from L. *gignĕre*.

1651 CLEVELAND *Poems* 44 No wonder they'l confesse no losse of men; For Rupert knocks 'em, till they gig agen. **1658–9** in *Burton's Diary* (1828) IV. 185 One question gigs out another. We shall never end. **1677** I. L. *Ded. to Cleveland's Poems* A iv, How many of their slight productions may be gigged out of one of his pregnant Words? **1690** DRYDEN *Amphitryon* Prol. 21 Yet in lampoons you libel one another. The first produces still a second jig; You whip them out, like school-boys, till they gig; And with the same success..For every one still dwindles to a less. *Ibid.* III. i, *Sosia.* You, my Lord Amphitryon, may have brought forth another You my Lord Amphitryon..and our Diamonds may have procreated these Diamonds.. *Phædra.* If this be true, I hope my Goblet has gigg'd another Golden Goblet.

gig (gɪg), *v.*[2] [perh. onomatopœic; there may be connexion with prec.]

†**1.** *intr.* ? To move to and fro. *Obs. rare.*

1693 DRYDEN *Juvenal* vi. (1697) 138 The rank Matrons, dancing to the Pipe, Gig with their Bums.

2. *trans.* To move backwards and forwards. Chiefly *U.S.*; also *techn.* in *to gig back* (the carriage of a sawmill after the cut is made). Cf. JIG *v.*

1815 *Niles' Weekly Reg.* 16 Sept. 36/1 The carriages run upon cast racks, are propelled by the improved short hand and gigged backwards by bevel wheels, in the manner of the best mills. **1874** W. M. BAINES *Narr. E. Crewe* viii. 180 This carriage [to the frame-saw] could be 'gigged' backwards or forwards or fed forwards. **1875** KNIGHT *Dict. Mech.* s.v. *Gig-saw*, The motion is imparted by the crank and pitman, and the spring above gigs back the saw, keeping it strained on its upward stroke. **1877** *Lumberman's Gaz.* 8 Dec. 362 These gangs [i.e. of saws]..convert whole logs into lumber as they pass through—thus obviating the necessity of 'gigging back'. **1886** HOTCHKISS in *Encycl. Brit.* XXI. 345/1 A rope..passing over pulleys in the floor to a drum beneath, so arranged as to be under the control of the sawyer in its feeding movement or in reversal to 'gig' the carriage back to its first position. **1887** *Microscope* VII. 333 Gently gig the glass back and forth.

3. *Comb.*, as **gig-back, gig-saw** (see quots.).

1875 KNIGHT *Dict. Mech.*, *Gig-saw*, a thin saw to which a rapid vertical reciprocation is imparted. **1893** *Funk's Stand. Dict.*, *Gig-back*, a device by which a sawmill carriage is run back after the cut has been made, usually much more rapidly than during the forward motion.

Hence **ˈgigging** *vbl. sb.*; in quot. *attrib.*

1887 *Microscope* VII. 335 The..diatoms are again transferred to the crystal gigging glass.

gig (gɪg), *v.*[3] [? Back-formation from GIG-MILL.] *trans.* To raise the nap of (cloth) with a gig. Also in *Comb.*, as *gig-drum, -machine, -wheel.* Hence **ˈgigging** *vbl. sb.*; also *attrib.*, as *gigging-machine, -mill.* Also **ˈgigger**, one who works a gigging-machine.

1789 *Trans. Soc. Arts* VII. 195 Mills, called here Gigging-Mills..worked by men turning them backward and forward, till the wool is sufficiently opened for use. **1839** URE *Dict. Arts* 1320 Several French schemes have been mounted for making the gig-drum act upon the two sides of the cloth. **1842** FRANCIS *Dict. Arts*, *Gig Wheel*, a mill in which the nap of woollen cloth is raised by the application of teasles. **1842** [see GIG *sb.*[1] 3]. **1875** KNIGHT *Dict. Mech.*, *Gigging-machine*, a machine for dressing woolen cloth by subjecting it to the action of teasels, whose fine hooks draw the loose fibres to the surface. **18..** *Fibre & Fabric* V. 20 (Cent.) A man who can take charge of dyeing, scouring, fulling and gigging in a small country mill.

†**gig**, *v.*[4] *Obs.*[−1] *trans.* ? To befool, hoax.

1795 *Poetry* in *Ann. Reg.* 153 *Gigg'd by their neighbours, gull'd of all their cash.

gig (gɪg), *v.*[5] [f. GIG *sb.*[4]] **a.** *trans.* To spear (fish) with a gig. **b.** *intr.* 'To fish with a gig or fishgig' (Webster 1828–32).

1816 *Chron.* in *Ann. Reg.* 569 The Indians sometimes gig them [porpoises].

gig (gɪg), *v.*[6] [f. GIG *sb.*[2]] *intr.* To ride or travel in a gig. Also *to gig it.*

1807 T. MOORE *Mem.* (1856) VIII. 65 To-day I gig it to Ashby. **1823** LADY GRANVILLE *Lett.* 17 Oct. (1894) I. 229, I am enchanted, I have gigged round the new road. **1829** COL. HAWKER *Diary* (1893) II. 3 Lost the coach, and had to gig it home. **1860** *All Year Round* No. 38. 280 A young doctor gigging it at an express-train velocity. **1836** SOUTHEY *Lett.* (1856) IV. 479 We had first two miles' walk, then two miles' gigging.

gig (gɪg), *v.*[7] *colloq.* [f. GIG *sb.*[6]] *intr.* To do a 'gig' or 'gigs' (see GIG *sb.*[6]); freq. to ***gig around*** (see quot. 1939). Hence **ˈgigging** *vbl. sb.*

1939 C. E. SMITH in Ramsey & Smith *Jazzmen* (1940) xiii. 267 To gig around meant to play for small parties, week-end engagements, and the like. **1949** L. FEATHER *Inside Be-Bop* III. 77 [He] gigs around New York with Chubby Jackson, Lennie Tristano, Benny Goodman. *Ibid.* 92 Settling in California, [he] gigged with Boyd Raeburn, [etc.]. **1952** B. ULANOV *Hist. Jazz in Amer.* (1958) xviii. 227 He had the usual Gotham gigging beginning. **1959** 'F. NEWTON' *Jazz Scene* xii. 222 He had to earn his living as a blueprint inspector, occasionally gigging in his spare time. **1967** *Crescendo* Feb. 12/2 Buy Professor Jacko's 'Gig-Book For All Occasions'. Gives melody line, chords and starting note for complete evening's gigging.

gig: see JIG.

gig(g by geoul: see CHEEK *sb.* 5.

‖**giga** (ˈdʒiga). *Mus.* [It. = F. *gigue.*] = GIGUE.

1730–6 in BAILEY (folio). **1879** [see GIGUE].

giga- (dʒ-, ˈgaɪgə; dʒ-, ˈgɪgə), *pref.* An arbitrary derivative of Gr. γίγας giant, prefixed to the names of units in the metric system to form the names of units 1000 million (10^9) times greater. Abbrev. G.

1947 *Compt. Rend. de la 14me Conf.* (Internat. Union of Chem.) 115 The following prefixes to abbreviations for the names of units should be used..G giga- 10^9×. **1951** *Symbols, Signs, & Abbrev.* (R. Soc.) 15/1 Prefixes to abbreviations for the names of units indicating multiples.. giga (× 10^9). **1960** *Gloss. Terms Telecomm.* (*B.S.I.*) 179 Frequencies of 1,000 Mc/s and above are sometimes expressed in gigacycles per second (Gc/s). 1 Gc/s = 1000 Mc/s. **1964** *New Scientist* 30 Jan. 286/1 An extraordinarily high output (from megawatts to gigawatts). **1966** *Electronics* 3 Oct. 171 It will relay aircraft transmissions..over existing 4-gigahertz and 6-Ghz satellite frequencies. **1966** AUDEN *About House* 17 Translated in a nano-second To a c.c. of poisonous nothing In a giga-death. **1968** *Nature* 19 Oct. 311/2 CIPM at its meeting in 1958 recommended the prefix giga (pron. jĭga; symbol G) for the multiple 10^9.

‖**gigalira** (dʒigaˈlira). [It.; f. *giga* fiddle + *lira* lyre.] A kind of wood harmonicon.

1889 *Century Dict.*, *Gigelira.* **1892** *Daily News* 22 Jan. 6/2 Performances on the gigilira [*sic*], dulcimer, and piano.

†**gigant**, *sb.* and *a.* *Obs.* Also 5 **gigante**, 6 **gygant**. [ad. L. *gigant-em*, *gigās*: see GIANT. The Lat. word had been adopted in OE. as *ȝigant.*] = GIANT *sb.* and *a.*, in various senses.

[**971** *Blickl. Hom.* 31 Þa nam he [Dauid] fif stanas on his herdebeliȝ &..mid anum he þone ȝigant ofwearp.] **1432–50** tr. *Higden* (Rolls) I. 95 That cite callede Babylon whom Nemproth the gigante made. **1538** LELAND *Itin.* I. 61 Waddes Grave, whom the People there say to have beene a Gigant and owner of Mougreve. **1565** COOPER *Thesaurus*, *Anguipes*, a gygant that had crooked feete like a serpent. **1610** HOLLAND *Camden's Brit.*, II. *Irel.* 154 A day was appointed betweene these Gigants or Champions, namely betweene John Curcy and the other. **1658** ROWLAND *Moufet's Theat. Ins.* 1007 The stalk of Fennel gigant would scarse contain this when he is grown great.

†**gigantal**, *a.* *Obs.* [a. OF. *gigantal*, f. L. *gigant-*, *gigās*: see GIANT.] = GIGANTIC *a.*

1616 DRUMM. OF HAWTH. *Urania* I Gigantal frames, held wonders rarely strange, Like spiders' webs, are made the sport of days. **1653** URQUHART *Rabelais* II. xxx. 193 This Gigantal victory being ended, Pantagruel withdrew himself to the place of the flaggons.

gigantean (dʒaɪgænˈtiːən), *a.* [f. L. *gigantē-us* (ad. Gr. γιγάντειος, recorded only in late Gr., f. γίγαντ-: see GIANT) + -AN.] = GIGANTIC *a.*

1611 CORYAT *Crudities* 420 An exceeding huge Gigantean Switzer. **1647** H. MORE *Poems* 318 When the strong Fates with Gigantean force Bear thee in iron arms. **1670–98** LASSELS *Voy. Italy* 121 Near the gates..stand two statues of more than Gygantean bulk. **1715** M. DAVIES *Athen. Brit.* I. 255 They can't reach up to that wicked Pitch of Jesuitical Gigantean Heights therein. **1818** J. H. FRERE *Whistlecr. Nat. Poem* III. xlix, Had he so done, the gigantean corps Had sack'd the convent on that very day. **1865** *Athenæum* No. 1955. 524/2 The desire for gigantean buildings.

gigantesque (dʒaɪgænˈtɛsk), *a.* [a. F. *gigantesque*, ad. It. *gigantesco*, f. *gigante*, ad. L. *gigant-em* GIANT.] Having the characteristics of a giant; befitting a giant.

1834 *New Monthly Mag.* XLI. 468 Everything..was gigantesque and awful. **1858** HAWTHORNE *Fr. & It. Jrnls.* I. 302 How gigantesque the campanile is in its mass and height. **1875** *Contemp. Rev.* XXVII. 66 All gigantesque, eccentric, distorted, extravagant art is barbarous. **1888** W. H. PAYNE tr. *Compayré's Hist. Pedagogy* 95 Rabelais wrote for giants, and it is natural that he should demand gigantesque efforts of them.

absol. **1821** *New Monthly Mag.* II. 123 This play abounds with two vices..ringing changes upon words, and a disposition to the unnatural and gigantesque. **1871** L. STEPHEN *Playgr. Europe* ii. (1894) 59 The expressions savour rather strongly of the gigantesque.

gigantic (dʒaɪˈgæntɪk), *a.* [f. L. *gigant-*, *gigās* (see GIANT) + -IC. (Gr. had γιγαντικός of equivalent formation.)]

†**1.** Of, pertaining to, or characteristic of, a giant or giants. *Obs.*

1612 DRAYTON *Poly-olb.* i. 10 Thou Genius of the place.. Which liued'st long before the All-earth-drowning Flood, Whilst yet the world did swarme with her Gigantick brood. **1667** MILTON *P.L.* XI. 659 On each hand slaughter and gigantic deeds. *a* **1677** BARROW *Serm.* (1686) III. 472 There are some persons of that wicked and Gigantick disposition.. that..would be ready to say with Polyphemus in Homer [etc.]. **1774** J. BRYANT *Mythol.* II. 178 He was the son of Uricus, and of the gigantic race.

2. Of persons or their stature: Having the proportions of a giant; resembling a giant in size, etc.

1651 HOBBES *Leviath.* IV. xlvii. 386 The Fairies..have their enchanted Castles, and..Gigantique Ghosts. **1762** H. WALPOLE *Vertue's Anecd. Paint.* (1765) II. i. 10 Jeffery.. had many squabbles with the King's gigantic porter. **1796** MORSE *Amer. Geog.* II. 172 The gigantic bones found in many burial places here, give room to believe, that the former inhabitants were of larger size than the present. **1828** SCOTT *F.M. Perth* xi, One who had never seen the Black Douglas, must have known him by his swart complexion, his gigantic frame [etc.].

3. Hence of things material or immaterial, actions, etc.: Greatly exceeding ordinary dimensions; huge, enormous.

1797 MRS. RADCLIFFE *Italian* xiii, Vivaldi pointed out to Ellena the gigantic Velino in the north. **1801** STRUTT *Sports & Past.* Introd. 45 The evils complained of by these writers ..have in the present day attained to a gigantic stature. **1802** BINGLEY *Anim. Biog.* (1813) II. 293 The Gigantic Crane is an inhabitant of Bengal and Calcutta. **1812–16** J. SMITH *Panorama Sci. & Art* I. 494 Facing this gigantic telescope. **1849** MACAULAY *Hist. Eng.* iii. I. 315 The ancestors of the gigantic quadrupeds, which all foreigners now class among the chief wonders of London, were brought from the marshes of Walcheren. **1861** M. PATTISON *Ess.* (1889) I. 42 The gigantic spirit of enterprise which was kindled in England and Spain. **1878** E. WHITE *Life in Christ* V. xxviii. (ed. 3) 468 The hell believed in is thought too dreadful for all except gigantic offenders.

Hence **giˈganticness.**

1727 in BAILEY vol. II; and in mod. Dicts.

†**giˈgantical**, *a.* *Obs.* [f. GIGANTIC *a.* + -AL[1].] = GIGANTIC *a.*, in various senses.

1604 MIDDLETON *Black Bk.* C j b, A pair of Corpulent Gigantical Andirons. **1614** RALEIGH *Hist. World* I. v. §8. 81 Goropius Becanus, an Antuerpian (who thought his owne wit more Giganticall then the bodies of Nimrod and

Hercules) hath written a large discourse. **1621** BURTON *Anat. Mel.* II. ii. III. (1651) 242, I would see.. whether there be.. gigantical Patagones in Chica. **1678** CUDWORTH *Intell. Syst.* I. ii. §3. 62 A gigantical and Titanical Attempt to dethrone the Deity.

gigantically (dʒaɪˈgæntɪkəlɪ), *adv.* [f. GIGANTICAL *a.* + -LY².] In a gigantic manner or degree; after the manner or proportions of a giant; enormously.

1678 CUDWORTH *Intell. Syst.* I. ii. §3. 62 Though this monster.. strut and stalk so gigantically. **1797** *Monthly Mag.* III. 509 The fountains of barbarous and gigantically daring impiety. **1845** [MISS J. ROBINSON] *Whitehall* xxxviii. 260 A gigantically tall porter. **1852** J. WILSON in *Blackw. Mag.* LXXII. 375 You do not habitually think thus gigantically of angels. **1864** LOWELL *Fireside Trav.* 271 [He] felt so gigantically good-natured that he could not keep his face sober. **1870** *Daily News* 13 Dec., Prince Edward—our Guardsman—loomed almost gigantically through the fog on the morning of Inkermann.

giganticide¹ (dʒaɪˈgæntɪsaɪd). [f. L. *gigant(i)-*, *gigās* GIANT + -CIDE I.] A giant-killer.

1806 SOUTHEY *Let.* 17 June in *Life & Corr.* III. xii. 43 Jack the Giganticide's leathern bag. **1883** *Times* 20 Dec. 9 The young preferred to live in Fairyland, among fairy godmothers, giganticides, genii good or bad.

giganticide² (dʒaɪˈgæntɪsaɪd). [f. as prec. + -CIDE 2.] The killing of giants.

1860 in WORCESTER (citing HALLAM). *a* **1876** G. DAWSON *Serm. Disp. Points* (1878) 184 The wonderful hero who ascended into an invisible land and took to giganticide.

Hence **gigantiˈcidal** *a.*

1891 S. MOSTYN *Curatica* 55, I had become familiar in childhood with the giganticidal precocity of beanstalks.

gigantify (dʒaɪˈgæntɪfaɪ), *v.* [f. as prec. + -FY.] *trans.* To cause to develop gigantically. Hence **giˈgantifying** *vbl. sb.*, in quot. *attrib.*

1841 *Tait's Mag.* VIII. 332 The gigantifying art, to coin a word, is more beneficially applied to fir-trees.

†**gigantine**, *a. Obs.* [a. F. *gigantin* (Cotgr.), f. L. *gigant-*, *gigās* GIANT.] = GIGANTIC, in various senses.

1605 BACON *Adv. Learn.* II. xxi. §1. 74 That Gygantine state of mind which possesseth the trowblers of the world.. who.. would giue fourm to the world according to their owne humors (which is the trewe theomachie), pretendeth [etc.]. **1664** EVELYN tr. *Freart's Archit.* ii. 10 The heroick and gigantine manner of this Order. **1696** tr. *Du Mont's Voy. Levant* 3 A Man of such Gigantine Stature.

Hence †**gigantinism**, gigantic development.

1606 BIRNIE *Kirk-Buriall* Ded., Such vigorous talnes in statur and strength.. that.. by a grace-full Gygantinisme, the commonly doughty are become your dwarfes.

gigantism (ˈdʒaɪgæntɪz(ə)m). *Biol.* [f. L. *gigant-*, *gigās* + -ISM.] Abnormal or monstrous size. *spec.* **a.** In man, excessive size due to an increase in the supply of growth hormone caused by overactivity of the anterior lobe of the pituitary gland. **b.** In plants, excessive size due to polyploidy. Also *fig.* Cf. GIANTISM.

1885 in *Syd. Soc. Lex.* **1899** *Q. Rev.* CXC. 279 Disease may.. lead to.. acromegaly, or gigantism. **1927** *Bot. Gaz.* LXXXIV. III. 314 An aberrant form of *Potentilla anserina* was characterized by gigantism, sterile pollen, and lack of fruit formation. **1932** C. D. DARLINGTON *Chromosomes & Plant-Breeding* xi. 57 Gigantism is a normal and perhaps universal property of those tetraploids which can be compared directly with the diploids from which they have arisen. **1932** J. S. HUXLEY *Prob. Rel. Growth* v. iv. 130 Some cases of dwarfing gigantism. *Ibid.* 131 Simple pituitary gigantism is associated with relatively long limbs. **1944** *Science* 16 June 481/1 In the case of *Gigantopithecus* the gigantism reaches a new climax. **1953** *Encounter* Nov. 9/1 The prosperous gigantism of the Japanese papers is based.. on the high.. literacy rate of the population. **1965** C. D. DARLINGTON *Cytology* I. vi. 222 Simple doubling [of chromosomes].. is usually accompanied by more or less gigantism. **1970** R. GORER *Devel. Garden Flowers* ii. 42 Gigantism is one of the commonest phenomena in cultivated plants.

†**gigantive**, *a. Obs.* [Badly f. L. *gigant-* GIANT + -IVE.] Mistake for, or synonym of, GIGANTINE.

1638 SIR T. HERBERT *Trav.* 146 The walls are cut into Gygantive Images. *Ibid.* 159 His gigantive shape [**1677** *reads* gigantick; *elsewhere* (p. 149) *Herbert has* gigantine]. **1656** HEYLIN *Journeys* vii. 91 What minded King Lewis to make his father of so gigantive a stature, I cannot tell.

gigantize (ˈdʒaɪgæntaɪz), *v.* [f. GIGANT-IC + -IZE.] *trans.* To cause to appear gigantic.

1630 RANDOLPH *Paneg. Verses Shirley's Gratef. Serv.* A iij, I cannot.. straine Garagantuan lines to Gigantize thy veine. **1848** *Blackw. Mag.* LXIV. 152 The former humanising the divine, the latter, if not deifying, gigantising humanity. **1865** *Spectator* 30 Sept. 1084 The comparison with dwarfs never makes average men seem unnaturally tall, never gigantizes them, though giants dwarf them.

gigantoblast (dʒaɪˈgæntəʊblɑːst, -æ-). *Med.* [f. Gr. γιγαντο-, γίγας giant + βλαστός embryo, germ.] A particularly large erythroblast.

1898 A. C. COLES *Blood* 176 Large nucleated erythrocytes—megaloblasts or gigantoblasts.. are occasionally seen. **1935** WHITBY & BRITTON *Disorders of Blood* ix. 180 Gigantoblasts, or very large cells of megaloblastic type, may be met with.

gigantolite (dʒaɪˈgæntəlaɪt). *Min.* [f. Gr. γιγαντ(ο)-, γίγᾱς GIANT + -LITE. Named by Bonsdorff 1832.] A pseudomorph after iolite occurring in large six or twelve sided crystals, a variety of pinite.

1835 SHEPARD *Min.* II. II. 325 Gigantolite, a mineral composed of alumina, lime, and iron.

gigantology (dʒaɪgænˈtɒlədʒɪ). [a. F. *gigantologie*, f. Gr. γιγαντ(ο)-, γίγᾱς GIANT + -λογία: see -LOGY.] Discussions or treatises about giants.

1773 PATERSON *Bibl. West.* p. vi, Astrology, Geomancy, Sorcery, Gigantology and other Marvellous History. **1811** DIBDIN *Bibliomania* (ed. 2) 503 *note*, The word 'Gigantology' first introduced by Mr. Paterson.. was used by the French more than two centuries ago. **1865** *Reader* 14 Oct. 419/2 There is but little material to fill up the history of gigantology between the men of renown and the giants of romance.

gigantomachy (dʒaɪgænˈtɒməkɪ). Also ‖**gigantoˈmachia**. [a. and ad. Gr. γιγαντομαχία, f. γιγαντ(ο)-, γίγᾱς GIANT + μάχη battle.]

1. a. The war of the giants against the gods. **b.** A contest resembling this.

1606 BIRNIE *Kirk-Buriall* (1833) 31 In a Gigantomachy they prease to commix the heauen with the hell. **1678** CUDWORTH *Intell. Syst.* I. i. §19. 18 There had been always .. a kind of gigantomachy betwixt these two parties or sects of men. **1681** COLVIL *Whigs Supplic.* (1751) 148 This with our church monomachie Ends with a gigantomachie. **1710** HUME *Sacr. Success.* (1716) 308 Its former gigantomachy drove our Church into the wilderness. **1855** SMEDLEY *Occult Sc.* 127 The Tartarus, which he prepares for the defeated Titans, after the Gigantomachia. **1885** *Illustr. Lond. News* 11 Nov. 492 So 'tall' were the scores.. that it was a veritable 'gigantomachia', or 'battle of the Anakim'.

2. A representation of the same.

1820 T. S. HUGHES *Trav. Sicily* I. i. 19 In the pediment, however, of the eastern portico was sculptured in high relief the Gigantomachia, or Assault of Heaven by the Titans. **1852** *Meanderings of Mem.* I. 128 One is the sculptor, of the statue nice, Or Gigantomachies of rock and ice.

Hence †**giganˈtomachize** *v. Obs.*⁻¹ *intr.* To rise in rebellion like the giants against heaven.

1599 B. JONSON *Ev. Man out of Hum.* v. iv, The.. Goggle-ey'd Grumbledories would ha' Gigantomachiz'd.

gigantopithecus (dʒaɪˌgæntəʊˈpɪθɪkəs, -ˈθiːkəs). [mod.L. (G. H. R. von Koenigswald 1935, in *Proc. Sect. Sci. K. Nederl. Akad. Wetensch.* XXXVIII. 874), f. Gr. γιγαντο-, γίγας giant + πίθηκος ape.] A large fossil primate, sometimes considered hominid, belonging to the genus so called, which is known from bones found in China.

1943 *Palaeont. Sinica* (Ser. D) x. 271 *Gigantopithecus* is to be considered not only as true anthropoid but as a type very close to the hominids. **1944** *Science* 16 June 481/2 We seemingly do not know more of the provenance of the *Gigantopithecus* teeth than the fact that they were gathered from drawers of a chemist's shop. **1950** D. P. QUIRING *Funct. Anat. Vertebr.* xiii. 509 The third lower molars of Gigantopithecus have a mass about six times larger than those of modern man. **1965** M. H. DAY *Guide to Fossil Man* III. 263 The fossil bones discovered with the new mandibles confirm that *Gigantopithecus* formed a part of this fauna. *Ibid.* 262 (*heading*) The 'Gigantopithecus' Teeth.

†ˈ**gigar**. *Obs.*⁻¹ [a. med. or mod.L. *gigart-um*, ad. Gr. γίγαρτ-ον.] A grape-stone.

1657 TOMLINSON *Renou's Disp.* 257 With small, brown, compressed seeds, like Gygars [L. *gygartis similibus*].

gigas (ˈdʒaɪgəs), *a. Bot.* [a. Gr. γίγας: see GIANT.] Of or designating a polyploid form of a plant which is larger and more vigorous than the normal form.

1915 *Amer. Naturalist* XLIX. 703 Both *gigas* forms are more persistently biennial in habit than their parents. **1939** SINNOTT & DUNN *Princ. Genetics* (ed. 3) xiv. 321 A case in mosses (*Bryum*) where an autotetraploid (2*n* gametophyte, 4*n* sporophyte) showed gigas characters. **1946** *Nature* 22 June 843/2 Isolations were made from these large-spored colonies and 'gigas' lines established. **1967** BRIGGS & KNOWLES *Introd. Plant Breeding* xxi. 268 Plant organs may show some increase in size, termed *gigas* characteristics. **1970** R. GORER *Devel. Garden Flowers* i. 39 The leaf, or any other part of a gigas plant, contains not only larger cells than the wild type, but also more of them.

gigelot(te, obs. form of GIGLET.

‖**gigerium** (dʒɪˈdʒɪərɪəm). [sing. of L. *gigeria* cooked entrails of poultry.] = GIZZARD I a.

1875 *Encycl. Brit.* III. 726/1 A proventriculus, connected by a narrow neck with the gizzard (*gigerium*). **1884** E. COUES *N. Amer. Birds.* (ed. 2) II. 213 The gizzard, *gigerium*, or muscular division of the stomach. **1956** A. N. WORDEN *Funct. Anat. Birds* vi. 31 The gizzard (known also as the *gigerium* or *ventriculus bulbosus*) or second part of the stomach, usually follows immediately after the proventriculus.

gigg(e, obs. form of GIG, JIG.

giggambob(b, var. JIGGAMBOB.

†**gigge**, *v. Obs.*⁻¹ [f. *gigge*, GUIGE.] *trans.* To fit the guige or arm-strap to (a shield).

c **1386** CHAUCER *Knt.'s T.* 1646 Squieres.. Giggynge of sheeldes, with layneres lacynge.

giggelot, obs. form of GIGLET.

gigger¹ (ˈgɪgə(r)). [f. GIG *v.*³ + -ER¹.] One who works a gigging-machine.

1889 in *Century Dict.*

gigger² (ˈgɪgə(r)). *U.S.* [f. GIG *v.*⁵ + -ER¹.] 'A fisherman who uses the gig as a means of capturing fish; a gigman' (*Cent. Dict.*).

gigger, var. JIGGER *sb.* and *v.*

giggering. *Book-binding.* See JIGGER *v.*⁵

gigget(t, obs. form of GIGOT.

giggish (ˈgɪgɪʃ), *a.*¹ Also 6 giggisse. [f. GIG *sb.*¹ (sense 6) + -ISH.] Lively, flighty, wanton.

1523 SKELTON *Garl. Laurel* 1206 This fustiane maistres and this giggisse gase. **1596** COLSE *Penelope* (1880) 167 Thy giggish tricke, thy queanish trade, A thousand Bridewel birds hath made. **1642** ROGERS *Naaman* xxii. 844 Our giggish heads have not the gift to observe a Promise. **1795** WOLCOT (P. Pindar) *Tales of Hoy* Wks. 1812 IV. 398 Come, come, something giggish, something merry. **1882** BERESF. HOPE *Brandreths* I. xvi. 254 A giggish widow.

Hence ˈ**giggishness**.

1781 BENTHAM *Wks.* (1843) X. 100 There is a sort of giggishness about him, too.

giggish (ˈgɪgɪʃ), *a.*² [f. GIG *sb.*² + -ISH.]

a. Resembling a gig. **b.** Directed towards driving a gig.

1837 *New Monthly Mag.* L. 532 They would not accuse it [his one-horse chaise] of ever having been too giggish even for a doctor of divinity. **1846** MRS. GORE *Eng. Char.* (1852) 121 It was now his ambition to drive a pair. He had outlived his giggish propensities.

giggit (ˈgɪgɪt), *v. U.S. colloq.* [Cf. GIG *v.*²]

a. *trans.* To convey rapidly. **b.** *intr.* To move rapidly.

1862 MRS. STOWE in *N.Y. Independent* 27 Feb. (Cent.), He nearly like to have got her eat up by the sharks, by giggiting her off in the boat out to sea, when she warn't more 'n three years old. **1869** —— *Oldtown Folks* 56 While the wagon and Uncle 'Liakim were heard giggiting away.

giggle (ˈgɪg(ə)l), *sb.* Also 7 gigle. [f. the vb.]

†**1.** = GIGLET 1 b. *Obs.*

1611 COTGR., *Gadrouillette*, a minx, gigle, flirt.

2. a. A giggling laugh.

a **1677** BARROW *Serm.* xiv. Wks. 1687 I. 202 A small transient pleasure a tickling the ears, wagging the lungs, forming the face into a smile, a giggle, or a humme, are not to be purchased with a grievous distaste and smart. **1771** SMOLLETT *Humph. Cl.* 12 June, 'My family is much obliged to your ladyship', cried Tabby, with a kind of hysterical giggle. **1815** JANE AUSTEN *Emma* I. viii, You have cured her of her schoolgirl's giggle. **1843** JOHNSTON in *Proc. Berw. Nat. Club* II. No. 11. 48 The solitude is disturbed by the giggle of pic-nic parties. **1881** *Academy* 15 Oct. 289 There is much humour—here and there, however, tending to degenerate into 'a fit of the giggles'—in Miss Tytler's representation of [etc.].

b. An amusing person or thing; a joke; fun; ***no giggle***: no joke (see JOKE *sb.* 3). *colloq.*

1936 J. CURTIS *Gilt Kid* x. 108 It's no giggle being in the nick. **1958** F. NORMAN *Bang to Rights* 117 There was one geezer who was a right giggle. **1959** C. MACINNES *Absolute Beginners* 152 Wiz told the tale as I've just done, for giggles, but even he didn't seem to think it all that laughable, I could see. **1963** 'A. GARVE' *Sea Monks* vi. 169 Prob'ly have the Home Secretary on the line next... What a giggle, eh? **1963** *Sunday Express* 29 Sept. 17/1 As the gang burst in.. one warned: 'This is no giggle, I will shoot you.' **1966** D. FRANCIS *Flying Finish* ii. 21 It's all very well you taking on Peter's job for a bit of a giggle but you surely can't mean to go on with it permanently? **1968** J. RATHBONE *Hand Out* iv. 24 He enjoyed the course, which was mostly rather a giggle.

3. [Cf. GAGGLE *sb.* 1.] A group of girls or young children. *colloq.*

1940 B. RUCK *Pennies from Heaven* xxix. 236 He had picked her out of the whole giggle of Society débutantes. **1957** J. BRAINE *Room at Top* iii. 28 A giggle of schoolgirls round a pile of brightly-coloured rayon underwear. **1967** *Evening News* 12 Sept. 8/3 At Mitcham.. a blue M.G.B... impressed a giggle of schoolgirls.

4. *attrib.* and *Comb.*, as **giggle-house** *Austral.* and *N.Z. slang*, a mental hospital; **giggle-pants, -suit** *Austral. Services' slang*, working trousers, clothes; overalls; **giggle-water** *slang*, intoxicating liquor.

1919 W. H. DOWNING *Digger Dial.* 26 *Giggle-house*, lunatic asylum. **1943** N. MARSH *Colour Scheme* iv. 72 When I've taken over this joint the resemblance to a giggle-house will fade out. **1944** K. LEVIS in *Meanjin Papers* III. 1. 32 The Lieutenant.. was a young fellow with deep blue eyes, and fresh-creased giggle pants. **1942** A. G. MITCHELL in *Southerly* Apr., *Gigglesuit*, a fatigue dress. **1945** J. B. BLAIR in *Coast to Coast* 133 Always smart and spruce in his Field Service uniform, Wang never looked his best in giggle-suits. **1929** *Amer. Speech* IV. 386 Some of the common names for whiskey.. *giggle water, nose paint,* [etc.]. **1946** G. HACKFORTH-JONES *Sixteen Bells* I. i. 32 Drop o' gin'll go down nicely on top of that giggle-water [*sc.* champagne cocktails]. **1962** *John o' London's* 14 June 571/1 Giggle-water is any unseemanlike drink.

giggle (ˈgɪg(ə)l), *v.*¹ Also 6 gygyll, 6–7 gigle. [Echoic; cf. the synonymous Du. *giggelen*, *giegelen*, *gi(e)chelen*, MHG. *gickeln*, mod.Ger. *gichelen*, *gickeln*, *gichern*, *kichern*; also various other imitative words in Eng. with the frequentative suffix -LE, as *gaggle*, *cackle*.

(Johnson 1755 remarks 'It is retained in Scotland'; but there is no scarcity of examples in English writers of the 18th c.)] *intr.* To laugh continuously in a manner not uproarious, but suggestive either of foolish levity or uncontrollable amusement. Cf. *snigger*, *titter*. Also with *on*, *out*.

1509 BARCLAY *Shyp of Folys* (1874) I. 63 Some gygyll and lawgh without grauyte. **1566** DRANT *Wayl. Hieremie* i. Kib, Her enmies..Dyd scorne her sacred sabboth day, And gyggle out theyr fyll. **1580** LYLY *Euphues* (Arb.) 473 If when thou laughest she [thy wife] weepe, when thou mournest she gigle. **1635** QUARLES *Embl.* I. viii. (1718) 34 Fool, giggle on, and waste thy wanton breath. **1706** *Reflex. upon Ridicule* 128 We see them..in the Park walking, giggling with their sparks. **1770** GRAY *Lett.* Wks. 1884 III. 374 Lady Maria did not beat me, but giggled a little. **1777–1836** J. MAYNE *Siller Gun* II. 125 Wee things giggling in the arms O' their fond mithers. **1827** SCOTT *Jrnl.* 5 Oct., A quiet day..giggling and making giggle among the kind and frank-hearted young people. **1851** D. JERROLD *St. Giles* xv. 154 All men in the court laughed, and the pretty ladies giggled. **1874** L. STEPHEN *Hours in Library* (1892) I. x. 365 The striking scene ..when the House of Commons was giggling over some delicious story of bribery and corruption.

b. quasi-*trans.* To utter with a giggle. Also *to giggle out* (*time*): to waste in giggling. *to giggle away*: to do away with by giggling.

1649 G. DANIEL *Trinarch.* To Rdr. 10 These pass the glass about; the Conclave set, Giggle applause. *a* **1704** *Compl. Servant-Maid* (ed. 7) 56 Be modest in your deportment or behaviour..not giggling or idling out your time. **1837** SYD. SMITH *Let. to Archd. Singleton* Wks. 1859 II. 278/1 He was always on the heel of pastime..he would giggle away the Great Charter.

†**'giggle**, *v.*[2] *Obs.* In 6 gigle. [f. GIG *sb.*[1] + -LE.] *trans.* ? To turn rapidly; make giddy. Hence **'giggled** *ppl. a.*

1577 HANMER *Anc. Eccl. Hist.* (1585) 348 They auouch that tidings (being coyned in the closet of their gigled braine).

gigglement ('gɪg(ə)lmənt). [f. GIGGLE *v.*[1] + -MENT.] The action of giggling.

1820 *Blackw. Mag.* VIII. 198 Gaping gigglement surrounds the fire. **1847** L. HUNT *Men, Women, & B.* I. ii. 22 He..is first made aware of the delicacy of his position by the gigglement of the two young ladies.

giggler ('gɪglə(r)). Also 7–8 gigler. [f. GIGGLE *v.*[1] + -ER[1].] One who giggles.

1633 G. HERBERT *Temple, Church-Porch* xlii, The gigler is a milk-maid, whom infection, Or a fir'd beacon frighteth from his ditties. **1716** STEELE *Town-Talk* No. 9, I have known a very giggler express an air of satisfaction when he has been speaking plain sense. **1835** SOUTHEY in *Cowper's Wks.* (1835) I. 41 His fellow idler and giggler in former days. **1881** MRS. LYNN LINTON *My Love* I. 224 Flying over the country with a parcel of giddy gigglers.

gigglesome ('gɪg(ə)lsəm), *a.* [f. GIGGLE *v.*[1] + -SOME.] Prone to giggling.

1893 MARY HULLAH *Aunt Constantia Jane* ii. 66 When you are once gigglesome the least thing sets you off again.

gigglet, obs. form of GIGLET.

giggling ('gɪglɪŋ), *vbl. sb.* [f. GIGGLE *v.*[1] + -ING[1].] The action of the vb. GIGGLE.

c **1510** BARCLAY *Mirr. Gd. Manners* (1570) Eiv, Loude gigling and laughing is but a foolishe signe And euident token of maners feminine. **1786** COWPER *Lett.* 17 Apr., Wks. (1876) 231 There was I, and the future Lord Chancellor, constantly employed from morning to night in giggling and making giggle. **1824** W. IRVING *T. Trav.* II. 19 Such giggling and bantering about the church-door. **1872** EARL PEMBROKE & G. H. KINGSLEY *S. Sea Bubbles* iii. 72 After infinite wrigglings, gigglings, and whisperings.

giggling ('gɪglɪŋ), *ppl. a.* [f. GIGGLE *v.*[1] + -ING[2].] That giggles.

1611 COTGR., *Ricaneux*, tighying, giggling, euer sporting, dallying, or playing the wanton. *a* **1625** FLETCHER *Nice Valour* v. i, A gigling waiting wench for me, That shewes her teeth how white they be. **1709** STEELE *Tatler* No. 49 ¶4 If therefore the giggling Leucippe could but see her Train of Fops assembled. **1775** MAD. D'ARBLAY *Let. to Crisp* 8 May in *Early Diary*, A parcel of young giggling girls laugh'd her out of it. **1820** W. IRVING *Sketch Bk.* II. 47 You have glances on every side of fresh country faces and blooming giggling girls. **1887** JESSOPP *Arcady* vii. 210 The giggling fool, who is the butt of the harvest field.

†**b.** *transf.* of a brook. *Obs.*

1640 J. GOWER *Ovid's Fest.* III. 54 A giggling brook doth on much gravel fall.

c. said of laughter, tone of the voice, etc.

1576 NEWTON *Lemnie's Complex.* I. vi. 36 To gygling laughter geeuen was Democritus alway. **1658** GURNALL *Chr. in Arm.* verse 15. ix. §2 (1669) 143/2 The Saints joy and peace, is not such a light gigling joy as the Worlds. **1733** P. DRAKE *Grotto* 11 And looks diviner graces tell, Which dont with giggling muscles dwell. **1824** MISS FERRIER *Inher.* xlvi, A weak giggling laugh. **1848** THACKERAY *Van. Fair* xlvi, She ..in a faint genteel giggling tone, cackled to her sister about her fine acquaintance.

'gigglish, *a.* [f. GIGGLE *v.* + -ISH.] Disposed to giggle.

1671 MRS. BEHN *Amor. Prince* IV. iv, For all the maids I meet with are so giglish And scornful. **1900** E. GLYN *Visits Eliz.* 22 [She] got rather gigglish.

giggly ('gɪglɪ), *a.* [f. GIGGLE *sb.* + -Y[1].] Addicted to giggling.

1866 CARLYLE *Edw. Irving* 175 Miss Augusta, tall, shapely, airy, giggly, but a consummate fool. **1881** COLVIN *Landor* vi. 118 His young women..are..apt..to comport themselves in a manner giggly, missish, and disconcerting.

giggombob, var. JIGGAMBOB.

giggot, obs. form of GIGOT.

†**giggs, gigs**, *sb. pl. Obs.* Also 6 gigges, 7 jigs. [Of obscure origin; cf. the various words spelt JIG.] A mouth-disease in horses (see quots.).

1580 BLUNDEVIL *Curing Horses Dis.* xl. 18b, Of the bladders in a horses mouth, which our old Ferrers were woont to call the Gigges. The Italians call them Froncelle. **1607** TOPSELL *Four-f. Beasts* 362 The Gigs..be litle soft swellings or rather pustuls with blacke heads, growing in the inside of his lips, next vnto the great iaw-teeth. **1623** MARKHAM *Cheap Husbandry* (ed. 3) 75 The Iigs. **1639** T. DE GREY *Compl. Horsem.* 211 Having the lampes, barbs, giggs, blisters, bloudy rifts. **1727** BRADLEY *Fam. Dict.* s.v., These Giggs proceed from foul Feeding, either of Grass or Provender. **1753** J. BARTLET *Gentleman's Farriery* xliv. 320 There are frequently observed on the inside the lips and palate, little swellings or bladders, called Giggs.

'gig-lamp. [f. GIG *sb.*[2] + LAMP.]

1. One of the lamps at either side of a gig.

transf. **1888** FROUDE *Eng. W. Ind.* xv. 248 Fireflies..with two long antennæ, at the point of each of which hangs out a blazing lanthorn. The unimaginative colonists call them gig-lamps.

2. *pl.* Spectacles. *slang.*

1853 'C. BEDE' *Verdant Green* iii, 'Looks ferociously mild in his gig-lamps!' remarked a third, alluding to Mr. Verdant Green's spectacles. **1887** *Punch* 30 July 45/1 Jack's a straw-thatched young joker in gig-lamps.

gigle, gigler, obs. forms of GIGGLE, -ER.

giglet, giglot ('gɪglɪt, -ət). Forms: 4 gigelot(te, (4 gegelotte, gegilot, 5 giggelot), 5–6 gyg(e)lot, 6 giglott(e, 6–7 gigget, -lot, 6– giglot, giglet. [Of obscure origin; the 14th c. form *gigelot(te* seems to point to a Fr. (or AFr.) etymon, but nothing satisfactory has been found. Cf. GIG *sb.*[1] (sense 4), which is prob. in some way connected. The less unfavourable sense (1 b) which the word assumed in later use seems due to association with GIGGLE *v.*[1]]

1. †**a.** Originally, a lewd, wanton woman (*obs.*). **b.** A giddy, laughing, romping girl.

a **1340** HAMPOLE *Psalter* xliv. 7 Here he praysis him of his wife þat is na gigelot. *c* **1380** WYCLIF *Serm.* Sel. Wks. II. 233 Poul moveþ not here to joie, as joien unstable men in gegilotis. *c* **1430** *How Gd. Wyf tauȝte hir Dau.* 82 in *Babees Bk.* 40 Go not to þe wrastelinge..As it were a strumpet or a giggelot. **1590** GREENE *Never too late* (1600) K 3 a, Marry gep Giglet, thy loue sits on thy tongs end. **1603** SHAKS. *Meas. for M.* v. i. 352 Away with those Giglets too, and with the other confederate companion. **1603** B. JONSON *Sejanus* v. iv, And I be brought, to doe A peeuish Giglot rites? **1632** MASSINGER & FIELD *Fatal Dowry* III. G 2 a, If this be The recompence of striuing to preserue A wanton gigglet honest. **1725** RAMSAY *Gentle Sheph.* I. ii. Song v, Some young giglet on the green, Wi' dimpled cheeks and twa bewitching een. **1820** *Lond. Mag.* June 631/1 Hump-backed giglots, scrimply arrayed in two guineas' worth of trumpery British muslin. **1865** W. WHITE *E. Eng.* I. 97 A party of showy giglots, who have come from Norwich, to take part in the fortunes of the day. **1885** *Chamb. Jrnl.* 758 Why should female clerks in the postal service consist of pert giglets hardly out of their teens?

†**c.** Applied to a man: One excessively given to merriment. *Obs. rare.*

1529 MORE *Comf. agst. Trib.* II. Wks. 1171/1 Of trouth.. my selfe am of nature euen halfe a gigglot.

2. *attrib.* and *Comb.* Chiefly appositive and quasi-*adj.*, as in *giglet-flirt*, *-fortune*, *giglot-wench*; *giglot-like*, *-wise* advs. Also **giglet-fair**, a statute fair for hiring servant-girls (but cf. *gig-fair*).

1890 BARING-GOULD *Old Country Life* 296 The farm-servants..were hired at certain fairs..; in the West of England these are called *giglet fairs. **1562** PHAER *Æneid* IX. Eeiv, Your stody chief is daunse in pampring feasts w[t] *giglet flirts. **1611** SHAKS. *Cymb.* III. i. 31 The fam'd Cassibulan, who was once at point, (Oh *giglet Fortune) to master Cesars Sword. *c* **1450** HENRYSON *Test. Cres.* 83 And go amang the Greikis air and lait Sa *giglot-lyk. *a* **1577** GASCOIGNE *Flowers, Herbs*, etc. Wks. (1587) 70 Ask him what made her leave her woful aged sire And steale to Athens gyglot like. **1550** BALE *Eng. Votaries* II. Gij, A sort of wanton *gyglot wenches. **1591** SHAKS. *1 Hen. VI*, IV. vii. 41 Yong Talbot was not borne To be the pillage of a Giglot Wench. **1577** tr. *Bullinger's Decades* 224 The wife that gadds not *gigglot wise, with euerie flirting gill. **1600** FAIRFAX *Tasso* VI. lxxii, That thou wilt gad by night in giglet wise.

Hence †**'gigletry**, lasciviousness.

1387 TREVISA *Higden* (Rolls) III. 161 Oþer men wifes were a slepe and som aboute gigelotrie [L. *circa lascivias occupatis*]. **1487** *How Gd. Wife taught her Dau.* 159 in *Barbour's Bruce* 530 Nocht leif to vantoune giglotrise.

†**'gigly**, *a. Obs.*[−1] [f. GIG *sb.*[1] + -LY[1].] Lascivious.

1482 CAXTON *Higden* III. xx, Thou hast right wantoon gygly eyen [Higd. *oculos corruptoris*; Trev. *an horlyng his eiȝen*; MS. Harl. *unchaste eien*].

gigman[1] ('gɪgmən). [f. GIG *sb.*[2] + MAN.] One who keeps or uses a gig; whimsically used by Carlyle for one whose respectability is measured by his keeping a gig; a narrow-minded person belonging to the middle class, who views 'respectability' as the chief concern of life, a 'Philistine'.

Invented by Carlyle, who gives (*Miscell.* (1857) III. 56) the following quotation in explanation of its origin. '*Q.* What do you mean by "respectable"? *A.* He always kept a gig. (Thurtell's trial).' This is taken from *Q. Rev.* XXXVII. (1828) 15, where the writer says 'We quote from memory'. In the *Times* report of the trial (3 Nov. 1823) the passage reads: 'He always maintained an appearance of respectability, and kept his horse and gig.'

1830 CARLYLE *Misc.* (1857) II. 144 This was not a nobleman, or gentleman, or gigman, but simply a man! **1840** HOOD *Up the Rhine* 5 The doctor, be it said, is a respectable gigman, who also likes a fast horse. **1884** R. BUCHANAN in *Harper's Mag.* Sept. 603/2 The gigman..spells God with a little 'g'.

Hence many nonce-wds. of obvious meaning used by Carlyle or his imitators: **'gigmaness, 'gigmanhood, gig'mania** [with play on MANIA], **gig'manic** *a.*, **gig'manically** *adv.*, **'gigmanism, gig'manity.**

1830 CARLYLE in Froude *Life* (1882) II. 122 The gig and gigmania must rot. **1831** *Ibid.* 185 As Gigmaness you could not have lived. *Ibid.* 199 Frivolous gigmanity. **1832** *Ibid.* 233 A..person of considerable faculty, which, however, had shaped itself gigmanically only. —— *Ess.* iv. (1872) 150 Consider what this Gigmanhood issues in. **1835** MRS. CARLYLE *Lett.* I. 42 Educated in the school of country gigmanism. **1931** *Times Lit. Suppl.* 12 Feb. 112/3 The sculptor's abandonment of exotic delights and infidelity to return to swaggering Sicilian gigmanity. **1966** *New Statesman* 16 Dec. 908/3 The style..was suitable for the full-souled, for the gigmanity and for those in office.

'gigman[2]. *U.S.* [f. GIG *sb.*[4]] One who fishes with a gig; = GIGGER[2].

1889 in *Century Dict.*

gig-mill. [f. GIG *sb.*[1] + MILL.] **a.** A machine for raising a nap on cloth by the use of teazles or wire-cards. **b.** A building in which such machines are used.

1551–2 *Act 5 & 6 Edw. VI*, c. 22 Milles called Gigge Milles, for the perchinge and burlinge of Clothe. **1556** *Lease* in Jeanes *Catal. Berkeley Chart.* (1892) 215 His two mylles under one roffe that is to say a corne myll and a giggmyll. **1670–81** BLOUNT *Glossogr.*, *Gig-mills*, were Mills used in the Fulling of cloth, which with Iron cards are prohibited by the Statutes of 3 Ed. 6 2, 5 Ed. 6 22. **1780** A. YOUNG *Tour Irel.* II. 34 A gigg mill for glossing, smoothing, and laying the grain. **1816** *Chron.* in *Ann. Reg.* 6/1 He [a cloth-dresser] having been employed in Ireland on a species of machinery called gig mills. **1849** C. BRONTË *Shirley* ii, A gig-mill was burnt to the ground. **1879** *Cassell's Techn. Educ.* IV. 342/2 The teazles are arrayed in frames..The whole machine is called a gig-mill.

gignate ('dʒɪgneɪt), *v. jocular.* [badly f. L. *gignĕre* to beget + -ATE[3].] *trans.* To produce, be the author of.

1819 *Blackw. Mag.* VI. 239 Whatever be the name of the supposed father—Tims or Tomkins—Johnny Keates [*sic*] gignated these sonnets. **1827** *Ibid.* XXII. 546 Why then may not men who are not blockheads..go on for a long time gignating productions, that [etc.].

gignitive ('dʒɪgnɪtɪv), *a. rare*[−1]. [f. L. *gignĕre* to produce; cf. OF. *gignitif.*] Productive of something else.

1837 SOUTHEY *Doctor* Interch. xiv. IV. 57 The first [Interchapter] gignitive but not generated; the second and third both generated and gignitive, the fourth generated but not gignitive.

gigolo ('ʒɪgələʊ, 'dʒɪ-). [Fr., formed as masc. correlative of *gigole* tall thin woman, woman of the streets or public dance-halls.] A professional male dancing-partner or escort; a 'kept' man (see KEPT *ppl. a.* 1 a), esp. a young man supported financially by an older woman in return for his attentions.

1922 *Woman's Home Companion* Nov. 7/1 A gigolo, generally speaking, is a man who lives off women's money. In the mad year 1922..a gigolo, definitely speaking, designated one of those incredible and pathetic male creatures,..who, for ten francs..would dance with any woman wishing to dance..in the cafés, hotels, and restaurants of France. **1927** *Daily News* 21 May 5/4 The audience was delighted with the grannies' dance with gigolos—as lounge lizards are called. **1927** *Daily Express* 24 Oct. 10/4 The Riviera wakes up... Well-known mannequins, dance partners, gigolos, and barmen..have once more returned to their place in the sun. **1928** *Daily Tel.* 27 Mar. 6 Similar indulgence, perhaps, would not be extended to her adoption of a 'gigolo'. **1933** N. COWARD *Design for Living* I. 21 I'd forgotten about your French accent and the the way you move your hands, and the way you dance. A sleek little gigolo! **1961** P. USTINOV *Loser* x. 226 The role of Captain Val di Sarat..has been consigned to a superannuated gigolo.

gigot[1] ('dʒɪgət). Forms: 6–7 gigget(t, -ot, (6 gygget, gygot, jigotte), 7–9 jigget, (7 geegot, jegotte, 9 jigot), 7– gigot. [a. F. *gigot*, of unknown origin.]

1. A leg or haunch of mutton, veal, etc. prepared for table. ? *Obs.*

1526 in *Househ. Ord.* (1790) 174 Giggots of Mutton or Venison, stopped with Cloves. **1615** MARKHAM *Eng. Housw.* 57 To roast a Gigget of Mutton which is the legge splatted and halfe part of the loine together; you shall [etc.].

1657 R. LIGON *Barbadoes* (1673) 11 Turkies and Hens we had roasted; a gigget of young goat. **1725** BRADLEY *Fam. Dict.* s.v. *Veal*, A Gigot of Veal may be..eaten with Sauce made of Vinegar, Pepper, &c. **1766** ST. JOHN in J. H. Jesse *G. Selwyn* (1882) II. 102, I hope to be in town on New Year's day in order to have your company over a *gigot*, and a bottle of claret. **1834** M. SCOTT *Cruise Midge* (1863) 194 A good practical sermon should be like a jigot o'..mutton, short in the shank and pithy and nutritious. **1860** J. C. JEAFFRESON *Bk. ab. Doct.* viii. (1862) 96 On the table the only viands were barons of beef, jiggets of mutton [etc.].

b. *humorously*. The knee. Cf. MARROW-BONE.

1687 A. LOVELL *Bergerac's Com. Hist.* 117 So that he falls upon his Geegots.

†**2.** A slice, a small piece. *Obs.*

c **1611** CHAPMAN *Iliad* I. 452 They eat the inwards; then in giggots cut the other fit for meat. *c* **1618** FLETCHER *Double Marr.* III. ii, Cut the slaves to giggets.

transf. *a* **1626** MIDDLETON *Mayor Queenb.* II. iii. (1661) C 4 b, Your Roman Gallants, that cannot wear Good Suits but they must have them cut and slasht in giggets.

†**b.** A minced meat, a sausage. *Obs.*

1553 EDEN *Treat. Newe Ind.* (Arb.) 29 Keping it in a certayne pickle as we do iegottes or sausages. **1656** W. D. tr. *Comenius' Gate Lat. Unl.* §365 Of flesh shred small he maketh a gallimafery, pies, giggots.

3. *Comb.*, as **gigot-sleeve** = 'leg of mutton sleeve'. Also simply *gigot*.

1824 LADY GRANVILLE *Lett.* (1894) I. 310 The sleeve will not disgrace it. Gigot at the top, *un seul pli*, and then innumerable little furrows. **1837** GEN. P. THOMPSON *Exerc.* (1842) IV. 347, I cannot say positively whether he ever touched her face..he certainly touched the *gigot* sleeves. **1848** THACKERAY *Van. Fair* li, Ladies wore gigots, and large combs..in their hair. **1853** MRS. GASKELL *Cranford* (1886) 2 The last gigot, the last tight and scanty petticoat in wear in England, was seen in Cranford and seen without a smile. **1859** TENNENT *Ceylon* II. VII. v. 207 A..dress of stiffened white muslin with gigot sleeves.

†**'gigot**[2]. *Obs.* [a. F. *gigot.*] A small piece of money; the later French liard.

1530 PALSGR. 851 Not a gygot, *pas vng nycquet*.

†**gigour.** $Obs.^{-1}$ [ad. OF. *gigueour*, f. *gigue* fiddle: see JIG.] A fiddler.

a **1300** *K. Horn* 1472 Hi sede hi weren harpurs, And sume were gigours.

gigs: see GIGGS.

gigster ('gɪgstə(r)). [f. GIG *sb.*[2] + -STER.] A horse suitable for drawing a gig.

a **1812** MALONE *MS. Note* in Bodl. copy of *Beattie's Scoticisms* (1787) 13 Roadster, Gigster, vulgar English. **1861** WALSH & LUPTON *Horse* vii. 112 Our gigsters and phaeton-horses are of all kinds. **1863** *Riding & Driving* 78 Gigsters of all kinds are the refuse of the hunting-stock or of the racing-stud.

‖**gigue** (ʒig). *Mus.* See also JIG. [F. *gigue* = It. *giga*, orig. a fiddle or lute (whence Ger. *geige* fiddle).] A piece of music, of a lively character, in two strains or sections, each of which is repeated; usually employed as the last movement of the Suite.

1685 *Lond. Gaz.* No. 2081/4 Airs for the Violin: To wit, Preludes, Fuges, Allmands, Sarabands, Courants, Gigues. **1823** ROSCOE tr. *Sismondi's Lit. Eur.* I. v. 170 To adapt a gigue so as to enliven the psaltry. **1879** GROVE *Dict. Mus.* I. 595/2 *Gigue* or *Giga*.

gil, obs. form of GILL *sb.*, GUILE.

Gila, gila ('hiːlə). [The name of a river in New Mexico and Arizona.] In full ***Gila* (or *gila*) *monster***. A large venomous lizard, *Heloderma suspectum*, found in the southwestern United States.

1877 H. C. HODGE *Arizona* 226 There is one variety [of saurian lizard], however, peculiar to Arizona..and locally known as the Gila monster. **1890** *Chamber's Jrnl.* 8 Mar. 158/2 The Gila Monster..which lives in the valleys and sandy plains of Arizona and Sonora, is called by the native Mexicans *Escupion*, which means 'Spitter'. **1902** C. E. MULFORD *Bar-20* v. 60, I only had th' main show—Gilas, rattlers an' toads. **1930** *Times Educ. Suppl.* 9 Aug. p. iv/2 The Zoo has bought six examples of the Arizona poisonous lizard known as the Gila monster. **1969** A. BELLAIRS *Life of Reptiles* I. vi. 228 Others such as the Gila monster and many geckos and snakes are principally nocturnal.

†**'Gilbert**[1]. *Obs.* $rare^{-1}$. A proper name, used as the appellation of a male cat (cf. *Tom*). Usually shortened to GIB.

c **1450** HENRYSON *Mor. Fab.* 338 in *Anglia* IX. 352 Scho [the mouse] clam sa hie, that Gilbert mycht not get hir.

gilbert[2] ('gɪlbət). *Physics.* [The name of William *Gilbert* (1544–1603), English physician and natural philosopher.] The electromagnetic unit of magnetomotive force in the C.G.S. system of units, equal to $10/4\pi$ ampere-turns.

1893 *Trans. Amer. Inst. Electr. Engin.* X. 364 The four units—gilbert, weber, oersted and gauss—have been suggested by the Committee of the Institute. **1930** *Nature* 16 Aug. 252/2 The committee on nomenclature [of the International Electrotechnical Commission]..adopted the following names for the magnetic C.G.S. units... Magnetomotive force... The 'gilbert'. **1967** *Hanbk. Chem. & Physics* (ed. 48) F-79 Magnetizing force is measured by the space rate of variation of magnetic potential and as such its unit may be the gilbert per centimeter.

Gilbertese (gɪlbə'tiːz), *a.* and *sb.* [f. *Gilbert* (see below) + -ESE.] **A.** *adj.* Of or pertaining to the Gilbert Islands in the mid-Pacific. **B.** *sb.* **a.** Collectively, the people of the Gilbert Islands; also, one of these people. **b.** The language of the Gilbert Islands.

1908 H. BINGHAM (*title*) A Gilbertese-English dictionary. *Ibid.* Pref., Such Gilbertese as desire to acquire a knowledge of English. *Ibid.*, The spiritual and social uplift of the Gilbertese people. **1945** H. LUKE *From South Seas Diary* ix. 101 A South Gilbertese, neither young nor beautiful, but none the less plagued by a jealous husband. *Ibid.* 112 Mrs Maude is doing valuable work in developing Gilbertese arts and crafts. **1964** M. DICKSON *World Elsewhere* v. 195 I've been staying among the Gilbertese who've been settled here.

Gilbertian (gɪl'bɜːtɪən, gɪl'bɜːʃən), *a.* [f. the name of W. S. *Gilbert* (1836–1911), librettist of the Gilbert and Sullivan operas + -IAN.]

Of, pertaining to, or characteristic of W. S. Gilbert or his work; *spec.* resembling or reminiscent of the ludicrous or paradoxical situations characteristic of the Gilbert and Sullivan operas. Hence **Gil'bertianism**.

1879 *Scribner's Monthly* Oct. 909/1 'Thespis' ran one hundred nights. Of course the plot unfolds a Gilbertian conceit. **1887** *Graphic* 29 Jan. 107 All do their duty, and, to borrow a Gilbertian phrase, 'do it very well'. **1891** *Strand Mag.* Oct. 331/2 There is a perfect home farm on the Gilbertian land. **1894** P. FITZGERALD *Savoy Opera* 13 The 'Gilbertian' topic of the English traveller 'turning up his nose' at everything he sees abroad. *Ibid.* 14 A sort of 'Gilbertian humour'. **1906** *Daily Chron.* 16 Nov. 6/7 The Gilbertian question whether a Lord Chancellor could bring himself to justice for contempt of his own court..is equalled in the quality of Gilbertianism by the puzzle of Baton Rouge, Indiana. **1918** T. H. WARD *Eng. Poets* V. 540 His peculiar quality of topsy-turvydom, which has perhaps added the word 'Gilbertian' to the language. **1929** *Times* 18 July 15/2 A Gilbertian situation arose in which a Government pledged to attack and an Opposition pledged to defend private enterprise simply exchanged roles. **1961** *Sunday Times* 30 Apr. 12/6 Might one deduce a coming Gilbertian revival? There seems no reason why that difficult Gilbertian morality should not appeal to the connoisseur like contemporary wax-fruit and beadwork.

Gilbertine ('gɪlbətɪn, -aɪn), *a.* and *sb.* *Obs.* exc. *Hist.* Also 6–7 **Gilbertin.** [ad. med.L. *Gilbertīnus*, f. *Gilbert-us* Gilbert: see -INE.]

A. *adj.* Of or belonging to Gilbert of Sempringham in Lincolnshire, or to the religious order founded by him (*c* 1140), which included both men and women. **B.** *sb.* A canon or nun of the Gilbertine order.

c **1540** *Pilgr. T.* 156 in *Thynne's Animadv.* (1875) App. i. 81 There be other that be anthonyn, but he whom I salute was gylbertin. **1631** WEEVER *Anc. Funeral Mon.* 148 Thirteene religious houses of the same Order.. had in them seuen hundred Gilbertin Brethren, and eleuen hundred Sisters. **1693** tr. *Emilianne's Hist. Monast. Ord.* xiv. 133 His Followers, who, for his Name, were called Gilbertines. **1725** HEARNE *R. Brunne's Chron.* Pref. (1810) 32 He [Robert Manning] lived for some time in the House of Sixhill..a Gilbertine Priory in Lincolnshire. **1885** *Catholic Dict.* (ed. 3) 907/2 The habit of a Gilbertine canon was a black cassock with a white cloak over it, and a hood lined with lambskin.

gilbertite ('gɪlbətaɪt). *Min.* [named by Thomson in 1835 after Davies *Gilbert* (1767–1839): see -ITE.] A silky micaceous mineral closely allied to kaolinite.

1835 SHEPARD *Min.* II. II. 228 Gilbertite..occurs at St. Austle in Cornwall. **1868** DANA *Min.* (ed. 5) Suppl. 798 *Gilbertite*,..Perhaps an impure kaolinite.

gil-clear: see GYLE.

gil-cup, dial. var. *gilt-cup*: see GILT *ppl. a.* 3.

†**gild,** *sb.*[1] *Sc. Obs.* [perh. connected with ON. *gialla* to YELL.] Noise, clamour.

1508 DUNBAR *Flyting w. Dunbar* 225 Than rynis thow doun the gait, with gild of boyis, And all the toun tykis hingand in thy heilis. **1533** BELLENDEN *Livy* (1822) 274 Appius, herand the huge noyis and gilde rissin haistelie amang the pepill..rais fra his sait. **1599** A. HUME *Day Estivall* 225 Throw all the land great is the gild Of rustik folks that crie.

gild (gɪld), *sb.*[2] *Hist.* Also **guild.** [ad. med.L. *gildum*, ad. OE. *ȝield*; cf. GELD *sb.*[1]] A payment or tax.

1656 BLOUNT *Glossogr.*, *Gild* alias *Geld*, signifies a Tribute, or sometime an amercement. **1658** PHILLIPS, *Geld*, money or tribute, it is also called Gild, or Guild. **1839** KEIGHTLEY *Hist. Eng.* I. 123 They laid guilds (taxes) evermore on the towns. **1890** GROSS *Gild Merch.* II. 314 Johanna Hughettes was allowed to give her gild to her husband.

†**gild,** *a.* *Sc. Obs. rare.* [a. ON. *gild-r* of full value or growth (OSw. *gilder*, mod.Sw. *gill*).]

1. Of an ox: Full-grown, of full value. (Orkney: so Sw. *en gill oxe.*)

1597 SKENE *De Verb. Sign.* s.v. *Serplaith*, Ane gild Oxe is apprised [in Orkney] to 15 meales, & ane Wedder is four meales.

2. *transf.* (See quot.)

1710 RUDDIMAN *Gloss. to Douglas' Æneis*, Thus Scot. we say a *gild laughter* i.e. loud, a *gild rogue*; i.e. a great wag or rogue.

gild (gɪld), *v.*[1] Inflected gilt and gilded. Forms: *Infin.* 4 gilden, 5 gyldyn, gilde, 6 gyld, 6–8 guild, 6– gild. *Pa. t.* 7 guilt, 7– gilt, 9 gilded. *Pa. pple.* 4 gilde, y-guld, gildid, gilt(e, gylt, y-gelt, 6–8 guilded, 8 gild, guild, 6– gilded, gilt. [Represents OE. *gyldan* (found in pa. pple. *ȝegyld* (see GILDED *ppl. a.*), otherwise only in the combinations *begyldan*, *ofergyldan*) = ON. *gylla*:—OTeut. **gulþjan*, f. **gulþom* GOLD.

In the earliest examples only the pa. pple. is found.]

1. *trans.* To cover entirely or partially with a thin layer of gold, either laid on in the form of gold-leaf or applied by other processes.

13.. *E.E. Allit. P.* B. 1344 þay [goddes] ar gilde al with golde & gered wyth syluer. *c* **1380** *Sir Ferumb.* 1330 þe celynge with-inne was siluer plat & with red gold ful wel yguld. **1382** WYCLIF *Exod.* xxvi. 29 And thilke tablis thou shalt gilden [**1388** ouergilde]. **1535** STEWART *Cron. Scot.* II. 367 The image als quhilk wes of Sanct Androw, Wes gilt with gold for to compleit his vow. **1580** FRAMPTON *Dial. Yron & Steele* 148 They gyld them [iron and steel], they silver them, & there is given to them other coulors. **1601** HOLLAND *Pliny* II. 477, I see that now adaies siluer only.. is guilded by the means of this artificiall Quicksiluer. **1684** *Contempl. State Man* II. v. (1699) 168 He spent many days in finding out..how much Gold would serve to guild a Crown of Silver. *a* **1711** KEN *Sion* Poet. Wks. 1721 IV. 316 A Pile magnificent..Which by devout Imperial Helen build, Was richly by her Son adorn'd and gild. **1775** JOHNSON *Diary* 11 Oct. in *Boswell*, One of the rooms was gilt to a degree that I never saw before. **1806** R. CUMBERLAND *Mem.* (1807) I. 184 Its magnificent owner..had gilt and furnished the apartments with a profusion of luxury. **1816** J. SMITH *Panorama Sc. & Art* II. 800 Articles of iron or steel may..be instantly gilt by dipping them into this auriferous ether. **1875** KNIGHT *Dict. Mech.* 967/1 Porcelain or glass is gilded by a magma of gold [etc.].

fig. **1340** *Ayenb.* 233 þanne byeþ þe þri cornes of þe lilye wel y-gelt mid þe golde of charite. *c* **1340** *Cursor M.* 27603 (Fairf.) I-nogh mai we finde of þa [men] þat wiþ-in is rotin as molde & wiþ-oute gilt as golde [*Cott. MS.* ouergilt with gold]. **1705** HICKERINGILL *Priest-cr.* I. (1721) 64 The first Cause..was open'd by the Plaintiff's Council, who..laid on Tongue enough to gild a rotten Sign-Post.

b. *fig.* ***to gild the pill***: to soften or tone down something unpleasant (from the practice of gilding a bitter pill so that it may be more easily swallowed).

1674 BOYLE *Excell. Theol.* I. iii. 88 The inward gratulations of conscience for having done our duties is able to gild the bitterest pills. **1685** *Gracian's Courtier's Orac.* 189 Princes are not cured by bitter Medicines. It requires art to guild their Pill. **1857** TROLLOPE *Barchester T.* xxvi, It gilded the pill which Mr. Slope had to administer.

†**c.** To cover with (a specified) metal (see quot.). *Obs.*

1623 COCKERAM II, To Gild with golde, *inaurate*: to Gild with siluer, *inargentate*.

d. Used *transf.* for To smear (with blood). Common in 16–17th c.

1595 SHAKS. *John* II. i. 316 Their Armours that march'd hence so siluer bright Hither returne all gilt with Frenchmens blood. **1605** —— *Macb.* II. ii. 56 If he doe bleed, Ile guild the Faces of the Groomes withall, For it must seeme their Guilt. **1615** MARKHAM *Pleas. Princes* (1635) 42 That Cocke..every time he..draweth blood of his adversary, guilding (as they terme it) his spurres in blood. **1632** HEYWOOD *2nd Pt. Iron Age* III. E 4 b, We haue guilt our Greekish armes With blood of their owne nation. **1816** BYRON *Siege Cor.* xxv, Swords with blood were gilt.

†**2.** *Alch.* To impregnate (a liquid) with gold. Also *intr.* for *refl.* *Obs.*

1460–70 *Bk. Quintessence* 7 The science how ȝe schule gilde..by brennynge watir or wiyn..wherby þe water or þe wiyn schal take to it myȝtily þe influence & þe vertues of fyne gold. **1666** BOYLE *Orig. Formes & Qual.* 373, I dropp'd into the Yellow Liquor afforded me by the Elevated Gold, a convenient quantity of clean running Mercury, which was immediately colour'd with a Golden colour'd Filme, and shaking it to and fro, till the Menstruum would guild no more, when [etc.]. **1684–5** —— *Min. Waters* Contents, A Mineral Water..considered as being gilt in its Channel or Receptacles.

3. *fig.* To supply with gold or money; *esp.* (with mixture of sense 5) to make reputable or attractive by supplying with money.

1584 R. SCOT *Discov. Witchcr.* II. x. 35 There is no waie to escape the inquisitors hands..but to gild their hands with monie. **1596** SHAKS. *Merch. V.* II. vi. 49, I will make fast the doores and guild my selfe With some more ducats. **1603** DEKKER *Grissil* (Shaks. Soc.) 14 I'll gild that poverty, and make it shine With beams of dignitie. **1875** MERIVALE *Gen. Hist. Rome* xxvi. (1877) 185 The missions of proconsuls and propraetors..were gilded, not indeed, with fixed salaries, but by gifts from states and potentates. **1890** BESANT *Demoniac* iii. 29 The Thanets are new people, as everybody knows. Yet not so very new; and their novelty is gilded.

b. said of the money itself.

c **1613** ROWLANDS *Paire Spy-Knaves* 1 Their gold and siluer gildeth them so well, They are the best in Parish where they dwell. **1842** TENNYSON *Locksley Hall* 62 Cursed be the gold that gilds the straitened forehead of the fool.

4. To cover or tinge with a golden colour or light (said esp. of the sun).

1588 SHAKS. *Tit. A.* II. i. 6 The golden Sunne..hauing gilt the Ocean with his beames Gallops the Zodiacke. **1616** CHAPMAN *Musæus* 391 No torches gilt the honor'd nuptial bed. **1697** DRYDEN *Virg. Georg.* I. 503 Stars..shooting through the darkness, guild the Night With sweeping Glories, and long trails of Light. **1792** S. ROGERS *Pleas. Mem.* II. 25 Memory..Like yon fair orb, she gilds the brow of night With the mild magic of reflected light. **1821** BYRON *Juan* III. *Isles of Greece* i, Eternal summer gilds them yet, But all, except their sun, is set. **1856** KANE *Arct. Expl.* II. iii. 47 The crests of the northeast headland were gilded by true sunshine.

b. To adorn with a golden colour or appearance.

1703 MAUNDRELL *Journ. Jerus.* (1721) 40 The walks are shaded with Orange Trees..They were..guilded with Fruit. 1821 CLARE *Vill. Minstr.* I. 140 Cowslips are gilding the plain.

5. *fig.* To adorn with a fair appearance or show of beauty: esp. to give a specious brilliance or lustre to (actions or things) by the use of fair words.

1596 SHAKS. *1 Hen. IV*, v. iv. 162 If a lye may do thee grace Ile gild it with the happiest tearmes I haue. 1635 QUARLES *Embl.* I. iv. (1718) 18 Proclaiming bad for good, and gilding death with pleasure. 1660 HICKERINGILL *Jamaica viewed* (1661) 77 All plausible Pretexts that witty usurpation doth use to colour and gild blacker Designes. 1713 *Lond. Gaz.* No. 5127/5 Poisonous Prefaces (..gilded with the specious Pretence of Zeal). 1775 SHERIDAN *Rivals* Epil., Love gilds the scene. 1822 SHELLEY *Hellas* 454 A rebel's crime gilt with a rebel's tongue! 1862 MERIVALE *Rom. Emp.* (1865) V. xlii. 147 Such a death at least doubly gilds his virtues. 1879 FROUDE *Cæsar* xii. 148 Cicero had prepared a speech in which he had gilded his own performances with all his eloquence.

†**6.** To impart a brilliant colour or flush to (the face; cf. quots. 1618, 1683 in sense 7). *Obs.*

1610 SHAKS. *Temp.* v. i. 280 Trinculo is reeling ripe: where should they Finde this grand Liquor that hath gilded 'em.

7. *to gild over*: to cover with gilding, so as to conceal defects; chiefly *fig.* (= sense 5). †Also, to make somewhat drunk (cf. sense 6).

1597 SHAKS. *2 Hen. IV*, I. ii. 169 Your daies seruice at Shrewsbury hath a little gilded ouer your Nights exploit on Gads-hill. 1618 FLETCHER *Chances* IV. iii, *Duke.* Is she not drunk too? *Con.* A little gilded o'er. 1648 *Hunting of Fox* 45 Counterfeit coyn, sleightly gilded over. 1677 GILPIN *Demonol.* (1867) 161 Satan's second care for the advancement of error..is to gild it over with specious pretences. 1683 KENNETT tr. *Erasm. on Folly* 1 All their countenances were guilded o're with a liuely, sparkling pleasantness. 1815 *Hortensia* I. iii, Beauty gilds Her vices o'er, which more securely harm.

†**gild**, *v.*² *Hist. rare.* Also guild. [var. GELD *v.*²: see GILD *sb.*²] *intr.* To pay taxes.

a 1645 HABINGTON *Surv. Worc.* in *Worc. Hist. Soc. Proc.* II. 254 William de Bellicampo in Eastwood..Gildeth..Of the demeanes syx Acres which gyld not. 1746 S. SIMPSON *Compl. Eng. Traveller* I. 300 This Town [Ilfracombe], in the Confessor's Days, guilded after one Hide, and one Farthing of Land.

gild(e, var. GUILD; obs. f. GELD *v.*¹, GILDED *ppl. a.*

gildable ('gɪldəb(ə)l), *a.* and *sb. Hist.* Also guildable. [f. GILD *v.*² + -ABLE; cf. GELDABLE.]

A. *adj.* Subject to taxation.

1495 *Act 11 Hen. VII*, c. 9 §1 The seid lordshippe..[shall be] from hensforth gildable and parte of the Shire of Northumbreland aforeseid. 1556 in W. H. Turner *Select. Rec. Oxford* (1880) 254 The seid strete is..wᵗ in the liberties ..and..gildable. 1681 BURNET *Hist. Ref.* II. 125 Commissions were next given to examine the state of the chantries and guildable lands. 1766 ENTICK *London* I. 275 Southwark is guildable.

B. *sb.* An area subject to taxation.

1602 FULBECKE *2nd Pt. Parall.* 40 That which was within the bayliwicke of the Shirife namelie in guildable, himselfe caused to be extended by parcels. 1639 *Nuisance to Priv. Houses* 31 The Statute doth not distinguish betweene the ancient Demesne and the Guildable in these cases. 1766 ENTICK *London* IV. 384 It contains three liberties or manors, viz. the great liberty, the guildable, and the king's manor. 1837 SIR F. PALGRAVE *Merch. & Friar* (1844) 69 Not being shire-land or guildable.

gilded ('gɪldɪd), *ppl. a.* Also 1 ʒegyld, 4 gyld, 4–5 gild. [f. GILD *v.* + -ED¹; the early forms show the syncopation usual in the pa. pples. of verbs of this type. See also GILT *ppl. a.*]

1. Overlaid wholly or in parts with a thin coating of gold. *Gilded Chamber*: the House of Lords. *gilded spurs*: one of the emblems of knighthood.

In mod. use *gilded* has more dignified associations than *gilt*, and hence is the form employed in fig. and poet. uses.

α. *a* 1000 *Ags. Ps.* (Spelm.) xliv. 11 [xlv. 9] On ʒyrlan ʒegyldum [Vulg. *in vestitu deaurato*]. *c* 1000 ÆLFRIC *Gloss.* in Wr.-Wülcker 154/22 *Crisendeta* gyldena *uel* ʒegylde fatu. 13.. *Gaw. & Gr. Knt.* 569 Miche watz þe gyld gere þat glent þer alofte. *c* 1369 CHAUCER *Dethe Blaunche* 338 (Fairf. MS.) Throgh the glas the sonne shon..With many glade gilde stremys. *c* 1400 *Destr. Troy* 3989 Gilde hores hade þat gay, godely to se. *c* 1460 J. RUSSELL *Bk. Nurture* 231 þan emperialle [apparel] þy Cuppeborde with Siluer & gild fulle gay.

β. *c* 1566 J. ALDAY tr. *Boaystuaw's Theat. World* sig. I 5 Their goodly gilded cups and goblets. *a* 1586 SIDNEY *Arcadia* v. (1598) 462 When the marchant hath set out his guilded baggage. 1621 BURTON *Anat. Mel.* II. ii. IV. (1651) 271 Two or three hundred guilded Gallies on the water. 1668 DAVENANT *Man's the Master* v. i, Having first swallowed the gilded pill of love, it prepares the stomach for any thing. 1717 LADY M. W. MONTAGU *Let. to Abbé Conti* 17 May, In one corner is a little Gallery, inclosed with gilded lattices. 1799 G. SMITH *Laboratory* I. 98 To give gilded work a fine colour. 1808 SCOTT *Marm.* I. vii, Behind him rode two gallant squires..They burned the gilded spurs to claim. 1855 MACAULAY *Hist. Eng.* xix. IV. 317 The display of jewels, plumes, and lace, led horses and gilded coaches, which daily surrounded him. 1894 J. BURNS in *Daily News* 12 Feb. 6/3 The House of Lords had ceased to be the stronghold of a high type of statesmanship..The 'Gilded Chamber' was a misnomer.

2. Tinged with a golden colour.

1588 SHAKS. *Ant. & Cl.* I. iv. 62 Thou did'st drinke The stale of Horses, and the gilded Puddle Which Beasts would cough at. 1698 J. FRYER *E. Ind. & Persia* 49 Fishes..some gilded like Gold. 1736 BAILEY *Househ. Dict.* 35 Apples are wholesome and laxative..and the more they are gilded, the more wholesomer they are. 1784 COWPER *Task* VI. 922 Like summer birds Pursuing gilded flies. 1860 TYNDALL *Glac.* I. v. 39 It remained the only gilded summit in view.

3. *fig.* in various uses: see GILD *v.*¹ 3, 5.

1601 CORNWALLYES *Disc. Seneca* (1631) Nn, Setting vp.. wealth against honesty, guilded honour aboue reall. 1626 C. POTTER tr. *Sarpi's Hist. Quarrels Paul V* 404 In those things which he desired, men vsed guilded or disguised words. 1649 JER. TAYLOR *Gt. Exemp.* II. Ad §12. 91 Poverty of Spirit; that is..a divorce of our affections from those guilded vanities [etc.]. 1784 COWPER *Task* VI. 39 Allur'd By every gilded folly. 1827 SOUTHEY *Penins. War* II. 574 Gilded disasters were called splendid victories. 1831 SCOTT *Ct. Robt.* iv, His respect..would prove more truly flattering, than the gilded assent of the whole court. 1868 FARRAR *Silence & V.* iii. (1875) 63 When the old iron discipline had yielded to an effeminate luxury and a gilded pollution.

4. *gilded youth*: fashionable young men belonging to wealthy families: a rendering of F. *jeunesse dorée.* (See GILT.)

1882 FARRAR *Early Chr.* I. 9 The old warlike spirit of the Romans was dead among the gilded youth of families in which [etc.]. 1885 MABEL COLLINS *Prettiest Woman* ix, He was invited to dine with some of the gilded youth of the city at a certain club that same evening.

†'**gilden**, *sb. Obs.* [a. OF. *geldon.*] A pikeman.

c 1440 *Partonope* 1236 An hundred thousand withouten arblasters Withoute gyldenes and archers.

†'**gilden**, *a. Obs.* Forms: 1 gylden, 3–4 gulden(e, g(u)ylden, 4–5 gyldyn, 5 gildin, geldene, 6 guilden, -in, 3–7 gilden. [OE. *gylden* = OFris. *gulden*, *gelden*, OS. *guldîn* (MDu. *guldin*, *gulden*, Du. *gulden* arch.), OHG. *guldîn* (MHG. *guldîn*, *gülden*, mod.G. *gülden* arch.), ON. *gullenn* (Sw. *gyllen*, Da. *gylden*), Goth. *gulþein-s*:—OTeut. **gulþino-*, f. **gulþom* GOLD. See -EN *suffix*⁴, and cf. GOLDEN.]

1. Made of gold, golden.

Beowulf 2809 [He] dyde him of healse hring gyldenne. *a* 1000 *Cædmon's Dan.* 204 (Gr.) þæt hie þider hweorfan wolden..to þam gyldnan ʒylde. *c* 1200 ORMIN 8179 Onn hiss hæfedd wærenn twa Gildene cruness sette. *c* 1205 LAY. 14298 Heo bar an hir honde ane guldene [*c* 1275 goldene] bolle. *c* 1290 *S. Eng. Leg.* I. 417/505 For-to ȝyue þis pouere Man bote ane guyldene ring. *a* 1300 *Cursor M.* 6632 (Gött.) þai þat war in godes half..honurd noght þat gilden calf. 1340–70 *Alex. & Dind.* 522 þe guldene ger þat þi gomus vsen Wiþ þe blasinge ble blenden þe sonne. *a* 1440 *Sir Degrev.* 279 Gleves gleteryng glente Opone geldene scheldus. *c* 1450 *Cov. Myst.* viii. (Shaks. Soc.) 76 Whan thou come to Iherusalem, to the gyldyn gate.

fig. a 1225 *Ancr. R.* 336 þe middel weie of mesure is euer guldene. *a* 1240 *Sawles Warde* in *Cott. Hom.* 225 Bituhhe muchel ant lutel is in euch worldlich þing þe middel wei ȝuldene [*read* guldene].

b. In renderings of χρυσόστομος ('Chrysostom') 'golden-mouthed', the posthumous cognomen of the great preacher John archbishop of (Constantinople *died* 407).

a 1300 *Cursor M.* 11380 Iohn gilden-moth sais wit þis dome þat [etc.]. 1340 HAMPOLE *Pr. Consc.* 5360 For Johan, wyth þe gilden mouth, þos says [etc.]. *c* 1430 *Pilgr. Lyf Manhode* IV. xxix. (1869) 192 þe which, as Gildene mouth seith, mown lede þe ship to hauene.

2. Of the colour of gold; golden.

1580 SIDNEY *Arcadia* II. (1622) 123 The next morning began a little to make a gilden shew of a good meaning. 1591 SYLVESTER *Du Bartas* I. iii. 611 Never mine eyes in pleasant Springs behold The Azure Flax, the gilden Marigold.

¶**3.** From the 16th c. occasionally misapprehended as a strong pa. pple. of GILD *v.*¹, and used instead of GILDED.

1530 TINDALE *Answ. More* Wks. (1573) 251 When he layth Timothe vnto my charge..then he weneth that he hath wonne his gilden spurres. 1573 TWYNE *Æneid* XI. Hhjb, Their helmets fayer into the fier, and guilden swordes they threw. 1596 SPENSER *F.Q.* VII. vii. 33 His hornes were gilden all with golden studs. 1601 HOLLAND *Pliny* I. 59 The gilden piller Milliarium, erected at the head or top of the Rom. Forum. 1640 [see GILTED quot. 1563]. 1880 STODDARD *Castle in Air* ii. 40 My barges ride With gilden pennons blown from side to side.

gilder ('gɪldə(r)), *sb.*¹ *Obs.* exc. *north.* Also 4 gildir(e, gilder, 5 gildre, 8 giller, 7–8 gildard, 9 gildert. [a. ON. *gildra* fem., *gildre* neut., of a snare, trap (OSw. *gildra* fem., *gildre gilder* neut., mod.Sw. *giller* neut.).]

1. A snare, esp. for catching birds (see quot. 1855).

a 1300 *E.E. Psalter* ix. 31 In his gilder [*Surtees* gildert] night and dai Meke him-seluen sal he ai. *a* 1340 HAMPOLE *Psalter* xxxvi. 33 Godis luf and godis word..sall kepe him fra þe gildire of þe deuele. *c* 1450 *Mirour Saluacioun* 256 Gods modire is oure protectrice Ageyns goddes ire the fendes gildres and fraude of this worlds uice. 1535 COVERDALE *Job* xviii. 9 His fote shalbe holden in the gilder and the thurstie shal catch him. 1674–91 RAY *N.C. Words* (E.D.S.), *Gilders*, snares. *c* 1746 J. COLLIER (Tim Bobbin) *View Lanc. Dial.* Wks. (1862) 44, I know him weel enough ..for honging o Hare e some hure [hair] Gillers. 1788 W. MARSHALL *Yorksh.* II. Gloss. (E.D.S.), *Gilders*, hair nooses for catching small birds. 1807 J. STAGG *Poems* 62 T'wards heame they kevvel'd yen and a' Nor ventur'd yen an a—ewards luik, For fear he'd in the gilders fa'. 1855 ROBINSON *Whitby Gloss.*, *Gilderts*, slip loops or nooses of horse-hair stretched upon lines for catching birds on the snow. The bread bait is attempted through the loops, which entangle the birds' legs when they rise to fly off. [In *Lanc.*, *Cumbld.* & *Northumbld. Gloss.* s.v. *Gildert.*]

2. *Angling.* (See quots.)

1681 CHETHAM *Angler's Vade-m.* ii. §6 (1689) 10 When you makes lines, especially 4 or 5 of the lowermost links, Gildards or toughts. 1787 BEST *Angling* (ed. 2) 168 *Gildard*, the link of a line. 1818 WILBRAHAM *Gloss. Chesh.* 17 *Giller*, or, rather, *Guiller*, several horse hairs twisted together to compose a fishing line.

gilder ('gɪldə(r)), *sb.*² [f. GILD *v.*¹ + -ER¹.] One who gilds, *esp.* one who practises gilding as an art or trade.

1550 BALE *Image Both Ch.* III. Bbviij, No conninge artificer, caruer, painter, nor gylder [etc.]. 1609 B. JONSON *Sil. Wom.* I, You see guilders will not worke, but inclos'd. They must not discouer, how little serues, with the helpe of art, to adorne a great deale. 1675 HOBBES *Odyss.* (1677) 33 Another bid the gilder hither come, To gild the sacred heifers horns with speed. 1753 *Scots Mag.* May 220/2 The gilders have coated a piece of metal. 1806 SURR *Winter in Lond.* III. 144 My brother is a carver and gilder. 1873 HAMERTON *Intell. Life* IX. ii. (1875) 305 A certain quantity of gold is necessary for the work of the gilder.

†**gilder**, *v. Obs. rare.* [a. ON. *gildra* to snare, f. *gildra* GILDER *sb.*¹] *trans.* To catch in a snare.

a 1300 *Cursor M.* 9479 Now es man gildred in iuels all, His aun sin has mad him thrall. *a* 1340 HAMPOLE *Psalter* xxx. 10 þe deuel þat gildirs men wiþ couaitis of life. 1483 *Cath. Angl.* 155/2 To Gilder, *laqueare, illaqueare, irretire.*

gilder, obs. f. GUILDER, GUELDER(-ROSE).

Gilderoy ('gɪldərɔɪ). Chiefly *U.S.* The name of a Scottish robber, used in the colloq. phr. *higher than Gilderoy's kite*: extremely high; out of sight.

1869 'MARK TWAIN' *Innoc. Abr.* (1870) xxv. 192 The first time she took her new toy into action she got it knocked higher than Gilderoy's kite—to use the language of the Pilgrims. 1888 E. C. BREWER in *N. & Q.* 7th Ser. V. 357/1 To be 'hung higher than Gilderoy's kite' means to be punished more severely than the very worst of criminals... The ballad says: Of Gilderoy sae fraid they ware They bound him mickle strong, Tull Edenburrow they led him thair, And on a gallows hong; They hong him high abone the rest, He was so trim a boy. They 'hong him high abone the rest', because his crimes were deemed to be more heinous. So high he hung, he looked like 'a kite in the air'. 1903 G. BROWN *How to beat Game* 53 This theory, however, like many others, is often knocked higher than Gilderoy's kite when put to the test of practice. 1934 H. COREY *Crime at Cobb's House* iii. 35 The colt threw him higher'n Gilderoy's kite.

gilderoy, obs. form of GILLAROO.

gilding ('gɪldɪŋ), *vbl. sb.* [f. GILD *v.*¹ + -ING¹.]

1. The action of the verb GILD.

c 1440 *Promp. Parv.* 193/2 Gyldynge wythe golde, *deauracio.* 1480 *Wardr. Acc. Edw. IV* (1830) 125 For bynding gilding and dressing of a booke called Titus Livius. 1537 *Bury Wills* (Camden) 128, I geve to the gyldyng of the ij angells on the candelbeme xxvj s. viij d. 1613 *Organ Specif. Worc. Cath.*, The guilding and painting 77ˡ 8ˢ. 1776 ADAM SMITH *W.N.* I. v. (1869) I. 47 The continual waste of them [gold & silver] in gilding and plating. 1866 ROGERS *Agric. & Prices* I. xxi. 533 The art of gilding was familiarly known to our forefathers.

2. The golden surface which is produced by the process of gilding.

1634–5 BRERETON *Trav.* (Chetham Soc.) 32 In the second story the beauty of the rooms is the gilding on the roof, which seems to be very rich. 1676 DRYDEN *Aurengz.* IV. i, The Metal's base, the Guilding worn away. 1776 ADAM SMITH *W.N.* I. xi. II. (1869) I. 183 No paint or dye can give so splendid a colour as gilding. 1819 BYRON *Juan* II. cxxvii, It was a spacious building Full of barbaric carving, painting, gilding. *a* 1859 MACAULAY *Hist. Eng.* xxiii. V. 112 The streets were crowded with gazers who admired the painting and gilding of his Excellency's carriages.

b. *transf.* and *fig.*

1663 COWLEY *Ess., Dang. Procrast.* (1684) 142, I well content the Avarice of my sight, With the fair gildings of reflected Light. 1672 WILKINS *Nat. Relig.* I. vi. (1675) 80 There are such inimitable gildings and embroideries in the smallest seeds of Plants. 1728 YOUNG *Love Fame* I. (1757) 87, I envy none the gilding of their woe. 1792 A. YOUNG *Trav. France* 257 These laughable adventures, with the gilding of a bright sun, made the day pass pleasantly.

c. 'A rich golden colour imparted to herrings by the use of hard wood only in smoking them' (*Cent. Dict.*).

3. *Comb.*, in various technical terms, as *gilding-cage*, *-cap*, *-metal*, *-press*, *-size*, *-tool*, *-wax* (see quots.).

1838 *Penny Cycl.* XI. 219/2 The '*gilding-cage' is made in a cylindrical form..It is formed of coarse iron-wire gauze [etc.]. *Ibid.* 220/1 The '*gilding-cap', which is a white felt hat of a peculiar sort and shape. 1842 FRANCIS *Dict. Arts*, **Gilding Metal*, an alloy composed of 4 parts of copper, 1 part of Bristol old brass, and 14 ounces of tin, to every pound of copper. 1884 KNIGHT *Dict. Mech.*, Suppl., **Gilding-press*, a book-binder's press for gilding covers and edges of books. 1830 *Edin. Encycl.* X. 279/1 The *gilding size which is to cement the gold leaf, is now applied hot. 1875 KNIGHT *Dict. Mech.* 967/1 Fig. 2216, Bookbinders' *Gilding Tools. 1838 *Edin. Encycl.* X. 278/1 *Gilding wax is compounded of bees wax and red chalk in equal quantities, with French verdigris and alum or green vitriol..The use of the wax seems to be only to flow, and carry the other ingredients to every part of the surface, and to determine the proper degree of heat to be applied.

gildren, obs. form of GUILDER.

gild-taile, obs. var. GILT-TAIL.

gile, obs. form of GILL *sb.*¹

gile, obs. f. GUILE *sb.* and *v.*, GYLE.

gileflower, obs. form of GILLYFLOWER.

†**gilenyer.** *Sc. Obs.* Forms: 8 gileynour, giela(i)nger, 9 golinger. [f. next + -ER¹.] A cheat, a swindler.

1721 KELLY *Scot. Prov.* 307 The greedy Man and the Gileynour are soon agreed. **1728** RAMSAY *On seeing Archers divert themselves* 79 Gielaingers, and each greedy wight, You place them in their proper light. **1737** —— *Scot. Prov.* (1750) 93 The greedy man and the gielainger are well met. **1808–80** JAMIESON, *Golinger*, a contemptuous term, the meaning of which is uncertain.

†**gilenyie.** *Sc. Obs.* Forms: 6 *pl.* galenȝeis, gillenȝies, golinȝies. [Cf. OF. *Gilain*, *Ghillain*, a quasi-proper name designating a swindler, with allusion to *guiler* to deceive: see GUILE.] A device, trick, dodge.

1533 BELLENDEN *Livy* III. (1822) 235 Than the consullis sett thame be galenȝeis [L. *cavillari*] to exoner and discharge the pepill of the aith be thame maid. **1560** ROLLAND *Seven Sages* (Bannatyne Club) 123 Ane kingdome thow wald quell, thow grounder of gillenȝies. **1595** DUNCAN *App. Etymol.* (E.D.S.), *Meander, fluvius Phrygiae*, bout-goings, guillenȝies: *ambages, amfractus*. **1681** COLVIL *Whigs Supplic.* (1751) 138 They bring but bout-gates, and golinȝies, Like Dempster disputing with Menzies.

‖**gilet** (ʒile). [F. *gilet* waistcoat.] In dressmaking: A bodice shaped like, or in imitation of, a man's waistcoat.

1883 *Cassell's Fam. Mag.* Sept. 619/1 A most favourite style of bodice is the gilet, which is either a positive waistcoat or merely a plastron.

gilgai (ˈgɪlgaɪ). *Austral.* Also **ghilgai, gilgie, gilguy.** [Native name.] A saucer-like depression forming a natural reservoir for rainwater. Also *attrib.*

1898 MRS. K. L. PARKER *More Austral. Legendary Tales* 7 A..shower fell,..filling the gilguy holes on the plain. **1898** MORRIS *Austral Eng.* 160/1 Ghilgais vary from 20 to 100 yards in diameter, and are from five to ten feet deep. **1930** V. PALMER *Men are Human* v. 41 They watched the gilgais turn to mud on the blacksoil plains. **1933** *Bulletin* (Sydney) 28 June 20/3 They found the old girl bogged to the belly in a gilgai. **1959** A. UPFIELD *Bony & Black Virgin* xv. 135 Bony was led to a gilgie hole amid the scrub trees.

gilguy (ˈgɪlgaɪ). *Naut.* **1.** (See quot.)

1867 SMYTH *Sailor's Word-bk.*, *Gilguy*, a guy for tracing up, or bearing a boom or derrick. Often applied to inefficient guys.

2. A 'thingummy', a 'what-d'ye-call-it'. *Naval slang.*

1886 [see GADGET]. **1918** *Chambers's Jrnl.* May 291/2 The placing on board of the various engines, machines, and fittings,—boilers, turbines,..and a hundred and one other gilguys. **1926** [see GIMMICK].

giliflour, -flower, obs. ff. GILLYFLOWER.

giling, obs. form of GUILING.

†**gilk.** *slang. Obs. rare*⁻¹. (See quot. and cf. GILT *sb.*³ 2.)

1610 ROWLANDS *Martin Mark-all* E 2 b, Gilkes for the gigger, false keyes for the doore or picklockes.

gill (gɪl), *sb.*¹ Chiefly *pl.* Forms: 4 gile, 5 gyle, 5–6 gylle, 5–7 gille, 7 gil, guil(l, (gild), 6– gill. [Of obscure origin; Sw. *gäl* (MSw. *gel* masc.), Da. *gjælle*, which agree in meaning, do not account for the form of the English word.

An ON. *gjǫlnar*, explained as 'gills' in Cleasby-Vigfusson, is of uncertain meaning; the word occurs only as a poetic name for the whiskers of the Fenris-wolf.]

1. a. The organ of respiration in fishes and other water-breathing animals, which is so arranged that the venous blood is exposed to the aerating influence of water. In fishes, the gills are situated on each side of the neck: in other aquatic animals their position and structure is very varied.

In scientific use the term *gills* is applied only to the branchial lamellæ attached to the gill-arches: in popular language the word denotes the whole breathing apparatus, including the gill-covers.

13.. *E.E. Allit. P.* C. 269 He [Jonah] glydez in by þe giles [of the whale], þurȝ glaymande glette. **1388** WYCLIF *Tobit* vi. 4 Take thou his gile *ether iowe* [Vulg. *branchiam*; **1382** fin] and drawe hym to thee. *c* **1440** *Promp. Parv.* 194/1 Gylle of a fysche, *branchia, senecia*. **1483** in *Cath. Angl.* 156/1. **1519** HORMAN *Vulg.* 277 b, Fysshes breth at theyr gyllys. **1601** HOLLAND *Pliny* I. 237 They..suppose..that no fishes hauing guils, do draw in and deliuer their wind again to and fro. **1660** BOYLE *New Exp. Phys. Mech.* Digress. 370 Their Gills seem somewhat Analogous (as to their use) to Lungs. **1667** MILTON *P.L.* VII. 415. ?**1705** W. KING *Fisherman* 22 Till they, of farther Passage quite bereft, Were in the Mash with Gills entangl'd left. **1774** GOLDSM. *Nat. Hist.* (1776) II. 299 The amphibia are furnished with lungs; the fishes, with gills. **1813** SIR H. DAVY *Agric. Chem.* (1814) 212 Atmospheric air taken into the lungs of animals, or passed in solution in water through the gills of fishes, loses oxygene. **1872** MIVART *Elem. Anat.* xii. (1873) 461 The gills or *branchiæ*. These are delicate processes of skin richly supplied with blood, and capable of absorbing oxygen.

b. The branchiæ or respiratory organs of certain worms and arachnids.

1878 BELL tr. *Gegenbaur's Comp. Anat.* §190. 247 The wings [of insects] must be regarded as homologous with the lamellar tracheal gills. **1884** *Syd. Soc. Lex.* s.v., In Vermes many of the Chætopoda have external tufted gills attached to the dorsal parapoda.

2. Applied to various organs, etc. resembling the gills of a fish. **a.** The wattles or dewlap of a fowl.

1626 BACON *Sylva* §852 The Turky-Cocke hath great and Swelling Gills, the Hen hath lesse. **1681** R. KNOX *Hist. Ceylon* 27 It is black with yellow gills about the bigness of a Black-Bird. **1726** SHELVOCKE *Voy. round World* 184 Here are also plenty of Guanoes and Carrion-crows, which, with their red gills..bear the exact resemblance of a Turkey. **1785** TRUSLER *Mod. Times* III. 18 Her face was as red as the gills of a turkey cock.

†**b.** In quadrupeds: (see quot.). *Obs.*

1787 BEST *Angling* (ed. 2) 88 Furs, off the squirrel, especially his tail..a martern particularly from off the gills, or spots under the jaws.

c. The radiating plates arranged vertically in the under side of the cap or pileus of fungi.

1715 *Phil. Trans.* XXIX. 350 He could never find them to produce any Seed either in their Gills or other Parts. **1743** PICKERING *Ibid.* XLII. 595 The Gills, as they are called, are no other than Capsulæ, or Pods for the Seed. **1835** KIRBY *Hab. & Inst. Anim.* I. v. 179 Channels, separated from each other by elevated processes resembling the gills of a mushroom. **1868** HERSCHEL in *People's Mag.* Jan. 62 Mushrooms and 'toadstools', furnished at their under side with gills, or radiating plates or laminæ, set edgewise.

d. *Aeronaut.* (See quot. 1949.)

1949 *Gloss. Aeronaut. Terms (B.S.I.)* II. 13 *Gills*, a set of movable flaps at the rear of a cowling to control the flow of air. **1971** D. N. JAMES *Gloster Aircraft* 229 The engine was an 840 hp Bristol Mercury IX..with a leading-edge exhaust collector ring and controllable cooling gills.

3. Attributed to persons: †**a.** with jocular allusion to the capture or holding of a fish by the gills.

1589 *Pappe w. Hatchet* 3 Martin beware your gilles, for Ile make you daunce at the poles end. **1599** MINSHEU *Span. Dial.* (1623) 67/2 He throwes againe the dice, and he drew vp all, and so he left me hanging on the gill [*marg.* as a fish], without a farthing. *a* **1616** BEAUM. & FL. *Wit at Sev. Weap.* II. ii, And when thou hast him by the amorous gills, Think on my vengeance.

b. with allusion to sense 2 a: The flesh under the jaws and ears; esp. in phrases ***to be rosy about the gills***, to look in good health; ***to be white, blue, yellow about the gills***, to look dejected or in ill health; ***to turn red in the gills***, to show signs of anger or indignation.

1626 BACON *Sylva* §872 Anger..maketh both the Cheekes and the Gills Red. **1632** B. JONSON *Magn. Lady* I. i, He..draws all the parish wills, designs the legacies, and strokes the gills Of the chief mourners. **1681** DRYDEN *Span. Friar* II. ii, He says he's but a friar, but he's big enough to be a pope; his gills are as rosy as a turkey-cock. **1798** CHARLOTTE SMITH *Young Philos.* III. 274 'My dear Sir!' replied Sir Appulby, in visible confusion, his fat gills quivering, and his swollen eye-lids twinkling [etc.]. **1812** *Sporting Mag.* XXXIX. 102 [He] grew white about the gills. **1816** WOLCOT (P. Pindar) *Wks.* I. 8 Whether you look all rosy round the gills, Or hatchet-fac'd like starving cats so lean. **1842** C. WHITEHEAD *R. Savage* (1845) II. viii. 277 You won't run away with her, I hope, and leave my old gills to be cuffed, will you? **1855** THACKERAY *Newcomes* II. 58 He looks a little yellow about the gills. **1893** 'Q.' [Couch] *Delect. Duchy* 168 He..looked very yellow in the gills, though clearly convalescent. **1894** DU MAURIER *Trilby* (1895) 236 How red and coarse their ears and gills and cheeks grew, as they fed!

4. *slang.* Only in *pl.* The corners of a stand-up shirt-collar.

1826 H. N. COLERIDGE *West Ind.* 253 Your shirt collars should be loose round the neck, and the gills low. **1852** R. S. SURTEES *Sponge's Sp. Tour* xxxvi. 196 He wore no gills. **1859** SALA *Tw. round Clock* 223 With a red face..with gills white and tremendous, with a noble white waist-coat. **1884** *Daily Tel.* 8 July 5/4 Lord Macaulay wore, to the close of his life, 'stick-ups', or gills.

5. *attrib.* and *Comb.* **a.** General combinations (attrib. and objective), as ***gill-bearer, -branch, -filament, -fin, -intestine, -muscle, -tuft; gill-like*** adj.; ***gill-bearing, -covering*** ppl. adjs. **b.** Special combinations: **gill-arch, -bar**, one of the cartilaginous arches to which the gills of fishes are attached; **gill-artery** (see quot.); **gill-basket**, the cartilaginous framework protecting the gills in the lamprey and allied species; **gill-book**, the lamellate respiratory organs of the king crabs which form the order Xiphosura; **gill-breather** (see quot.); **gill-cavity, -chamber**, the cavity or compartment in which the gill is contained; **gill-cleft** = *gill-opening*; **gill-comb** = CTENIDIUM; **gill-cover**, the bony case covering and protecting the gills of fish; **gill-fishing**, fishing with a gill-net (*Cent. Dict.*); **gill-fissure** = *gill-opening*; **gill-flap** (see quot.); **gill-footed** *a.* = BRANCHIOPODOUS; **gill-lamella, -leaf, -leaflet** = *gill-plate*; **gill-lid** (see quot.); **gill-membrane** (see quot.); **gill-net**, a fishing-net so constructed that the fish are caught by the gills; **gill-netter**, 'one who owns or uses gill-nets' (*Cent. Dict.*); **gill-netting**, the material of which gill-nets are made; **gill-opening** (see quot.); **gill-plate**, one of the vascular lamellæ forming part of the gills of fishes, molluscs, etc.; **gill-plume** = *gill-comb*; **gill-pore**, a small pore between the gill-pouch and the exterior in acorn worms of the class Enteropneusta; **gill-pouch**, (*a*) a pouch into which the gills of acorn worms open; (*b*) a pouch enclosing the gills in fishes of the subclass Cyclostomata; (*c*) *Embryol.*, a pouch present during part of the development of all vertebrate embryos; **gill-raker**, one of a line of cartilaginous or bony projections on the inner side of a gill-arch; **gill-slit** = *gill-opening*; †**gill-stone**, a kind of fossil; **gill-vein** (see quot.).

1879 tr. *Haeckel's Evol. Man* I. ix. 266 These vascular *gill-arches pass along the gill-openings, and directly accomplish respiration. **1885** *Syd. Soc. Lex.*, *Gill-artery*, the artery which..travels along the base of each gill in fishes and breaks up into capillaries, by means of which the blood is exposed to the water and undergoes oxidation. *Ibid.* s.v. *Gill*, In Cyclostomi the gills are a series of six or seven pouches..with an outer cartilaginous frame-work or *gill-basket. **1883** *Gd. Words* Sept. 589/1 These *gill-bearers are, however, but one order in this extensive division of plants. **1851** OGILVIE, *Gill-bearing*, producing gills. **1885** *Syd. Soc. Lex.* s.v., In Teleostei the gills..are covered by a gill-bearing operculum. **1881** *Q. Jrnl. Microsc. Sci.* XXI. 541 The lamellæ of the *gill-books of Limulus are..delicate flattened bags with a setose free border. **1902** *Encycl. Brit.* XXV. 521/2 The leaves (some 150 in number) of the gill-book..correspond to the tooth-like processes of the pectens of Scorpio. *Ibid.*, The gill-books of Limulus. **1932** BORRADAILE & POTTS *Invertebrata* xv. 445 The gill books are stated to be the most primitive respiratory organs. **1881** *Nature* XXV. 136 The theory which considers the limbs and their girdles to be transformed and translocated *gill-branch elements. **1889** *Century Dict.*, *Gill-breather*, that which breathes by means of gills; spec. one of the *Caridea* or *Crustacea* as distinguished from any tracheate arthropod or tube-breather. **1846** OWEN *Comp. Anat.* I. 259 In a common *gill-cavity which has a single outlet. **1851–6** WOODWARD *Mollusca* 65 The hectocotyle of tremoctopus was discovered by Dr. Kölliker at Messina, in 1842, adhering to the interior of the *gill-chamber and funnel of the poulpe. **1872** MIVART *Elem. Anat.* 478 The gill-chamber is further protected by a membranous fold which lies within the opercular flap. **1890** *Dublin Rev.* Oct. 448 Certain *gill-clefts in the embryos of higher animals. **1883** *Gill-comb [see CTENIDIUM]. **1776** PENNANT *Zool.* III. 223 The edges of the *gill-covers serrated. **1872** NICHOLSON *Palæont.* 310 The only portions of the skull which require special mention are the bones which form the gill-cover or operculum. **1769** PENNANT *Zool.* III. 30 Which bones are called the Radii Branchiostegi, or the *Gill-covering Rays. **1847** CARPENTER *Anim. Phys.* 249 The *gill-filaments themselves are so arranged that they do not clog together. **1676** COTTON *Complete Angler* II. xii, A Bullhead, with his *gill-fins cut off. **1681** CHETHAM *Angler's Vade-m.* iv. §22 (1689) 54 His guill-fins being cut off. **1879** tr. *Haeckel's Evol. Man* I. i. 18 Nearly the whole of the front half of the body consists of a shapeless head without a face, on the sides of which are seen *gill-fissures and gill-arches as in Fishes. **1828–32** WEBSTER, *Gill-flap*, a membrane attached to the posterior edge of the gill-lid, immediately closing the gill-opening. **1854** BADHAM *Halieut.* 241 A palm-tree, which it climbed by hooking its spinous gill-flaps into the inequalities of the bark. **1846** PATTERSON *Zool.* 76 In one division [of the crustacea] termed '*gill-footed', the surface of the legs is extended. **1879** tr. *Haeckel's Evol. Man* I. x. 280 At a very early period the intestinal tube is divided into a *gill-intestine and a stomach-intestine. **1878** BELL tr. *Gegenbaur's Comp. Anat.* 336 Each *gill-lamella is developed from a row of processes which bud out close to one another. **1865** GOSSE *Land & Sea* (1874) 208 The entire *gill-leaf [of a Mussel] is formed out of a single thread. **1885** *Syd. Soc. Lex.*, *Gill-leaflets*, the delicate layer of connective tissue..on which the gill-arteries ramify. **1828–32** WEBSTER, *Gill-lid*, the covering of the gills. **1852** DANA *Crust.* I. 5 Certain *gill-like organs. **1889** *Century Dict.*, *Gill-membrane*, the membranous covering of the foremost branchiostegal arch of the branchial skeleton of ordinary fishes. **1839–47** TODD *Cycl. Anat.* III. 507/2 In some fishes..the *gill-muscles are red. **1796** MORSE *Amer. Geog.* I. 369 The fishermen turn the course of the river..or compress it into a narrow channel, where they fix their *gill nets. **1883** G. B. GOODE *Fish. Indust. U.S.* 12 The introduction of the Norwegian gill-net into the winter cod fisheries. **1894** *Times* 17 Aug. 9/2 Flax *gill netting, nets, webs, and seines. **1828–32** WEBSTER, *Gill-opening*, the aperture of a fish or other animal by which water is admitted to the gills. **1880** GÜNTHER *Fishes* 35 The boundary between the first and second being generally indicated by the gill-opening. **1878** BELL tr. *Gegenbaur's Comp. Anat.* 336 Owing to this union of the flattened filaments or lamellæ, which have their surfaces directed towards one another, a *gill-plate is formed. **1894** *Wrkg. Men's Coll. Jrnl.* Dec. 139 The larvæ..bear at the extremity of the abdomen three delicate leaf-like gill-plates. **1902** *Encycl. Brit.* XXVI. 85/1 Each gill-slit may be said to open into its own..gill-pouch; this in its turn opens to the exterior by a minute *gill-pore. **1967** P. A. MEGLITSCH *Invert. Zool.* xii. 427/1 The gill pores are usually guarded by sphincter muscles. **1888** *Gill-pouch [see POUCH *sb.* 3 a]. **1888** ROLLESTON & JACKSON *Forms Anim. Life* 590 New gill-pouches appear to be constantly added throughout life. **1895** B. DEAN *Fishes Living & Fossil* ii. 18 There has been a general tendency to press closely together the gill pouches. **1914** W. E. KELLICOTT *Outl. Chordate Devel.* iv. 269 There is a pair of lateral extensions of the foregut [of the chick]..marking the positions of the future first gill pouches. **1931** J. R. NORMAN *Hist. Fishes* iii. 37 The gill-pouches are large in the lamprey. **1932** BORRADAILE & POTTS *Invertebrata* xix. 663 A pair of collar pores open backward from the collar cavities into the first gill pouch. **1959** L. H. HYMAN *Invertebrates* V. xvii. 111 In *Stereobalanus canadensis*..all the gill pouches on each side are fused. **1960** B. I. BALINSKY *Introd. Embryol.* i. 10 The formation of gill pouches in the ontogenetic development of all vertebrates. **1962** K. F. LAGLER et al. *Ichthyology* iii. 82 Some hag-fishes have numerous gill pouches on a side. **1880** GÜNTHER *Fishes* 59 On the inner side they support horny processes called the *gill-rakers. **1846** OWEN *Comp. Anat.* I. 258 Each *gill-sac receives..its proper artery. **1885** *Syd. Soc. Lex.*, *Gill-sac*, the flattened cavities, each having a separate internal and external orifice, containing the gill, in the Myxine. **1854** OWEN *Skel. & Teeth* in *Circ. Sci.*, *Organ. Nat.* I. 173 The two vertical fissures behind are called '*gill-slits', or branchial or opercular apertures. **1880** E. R. LANKESTER *Degener.* 44 Secondly, the throat perforated by gill-slits. **1708** in *Phil. Trans.* XXVI. 78 *Branchiale*, The *Gill-stone. **1848** CARPENTER *Anim. Phys.* 250 A similar action goes on, still more energetically, on the *gill-tufts of the Annelida. **1885** *Syd. Soc. Lex.*, **Gill-vein*, the vessel situated at the base of each gill which returns the blood after it has been aerated to the dorsal aorta in fishes.

gill (gɪl), *sb.*^{2} Forms: 5 gille, 5-6 gyll(e, 6 gil, 8-9 ghyll, 5- gill. [a. ON. *gil* a deep glen (cogn. w. *geil* of the same meaning); further relations are uncertain.]

The spelling *ghyll*, often used in guide-books to the Lake district, seems to have been introduced by Wordsworth.

1. A deep rocky cleft or ravine, usually wooded and forming the course of a stream.

In dialect use in the northern counties, also in Kent and Surrey.

1400 *Destr. Troy* 13529 As he glode thurgh the gille by a gate syde, There met he tho men. *c* **1440** *Bone Flor.* 1419 They came downe in a depe gylle. **1535** STEWART *Cron. Scot.* III. 98 Onto the number of ten thousand men, Dalie he led ouir mony gill and glen. **1667** *Relation of Teneriffe* in Sprat *Hist. R. Soc.* 208 The Canary-birds..breed in the Barancos or Gills, which the Water hath fretted away in the Mountains. **1787-9** WORDSW. *Even. Walk* 54, I wandered where the huddling rill Brightens with water-breaks the hollow ghyll. **1820** SCOTT *Monast.* xiii, I have..led the chase when the Laird of Cessford and his gay riders were all thrown out by the mosses and gills. **1886** JEFFERIES *Field & Hedgerow* (1889) 157 In the dells, the 'gills', as these wooded depths are called. **1887** *Kent Gloss.*, *Gill*, a little, narrow, wooded valley with a stream of water running through it; a rivulet; a beck.

2. A narrow stream, a brook or rivulet.

1625 GILL *Sacr. Philos.* VI. 84 The great rivers are nothing else but the gathering together of waters from many smaller fountains and gilz. **1703** T. N. *City & C. Purchaser* 55 Any Brook, Gill, or small River. **1752** in *Philos. Mag.* Jan. (1866) XXXI. 80 We ran to look at the Gill; and we directed our sights (by the noise that it made) the right way. **1778** *Eng. Gaz.* (ed. 2) s.v. *Gillisland*, 'Tis a tract much embarrassed with brooks, here called Gilles. **1853** PHILLIPS *Rivers Yorksh.* iii. 51 The rivulets (called gills) which run in these branches have very elevated summits. **1866** SEDGWICK in *Philos. Mag.* XXXI. 79 Hence the *becks*, or mountain-streams, are often greatly swollen, and the *gills*, or lateral branches, frequently descend in brawling torrents from the mountain-side into the lower valley through deep ravines and lateral valleys.

3. *attrib.*, as ***gill-brack*** (see BRACK *sb.*^{1} 8), ***-edge***, ***-runnel***, ***-stream***.

a **1400-50** *Alexander* 3231 Girdid out as gutars . in grete gill-stremes. **1855** ROBINSON *Whitby Gloss.* s.v., *A gill runnel*, a rivulet or thread of water coursing along a deep dell. **1863** BARING-GOULD *Iceland* 121 He was raised on a litter, and carried to a gill edge. **1890** CLARK & HUGHES *Life A. Sedgwick* I. i. 7 It was in this hamlet [Kirthwaite] that a destructive avalanche—or, as they would have said in Dent, a 'gill-brack'—took place in January, 1752.

gill (dʒɪl), *sb.*^{3} Forms: 4 gille, jille, 4-5 gylle, 6 gyll, 7- gill, (9 jill). [a. OF. *gille*, *gelle* in med.L. *gillo*, *gellus*, the name of a vessel or measure used for wine. The relation between these forms and those cited under GALLON is obscure.]

1. A measure for liquids, containing one fourth of a standard pint.

In many districts the gill is equivalent to a half-pint, the quarter-pint being called a *jack*.

1275 in *Mun. Gildhallæ* (Rolls) III. 432 Mensuræ quæ vocantur schopinas et gilles. **1362** LANGL. *P. Pl.* A. v. 191 Til Gloten hed i-gloupet a galoun and a gille. **1590** *Wills & Inv. N.C.* II. (Surtees 1860) 199 For j gyll of veolarium 5^{s}. 4^{d}. *a* **1719** ADDISON *Playhouse* 75 Till, freed at length, he.. to some peaceful brandy-shop retires; Where in full gills his anxious thoughts he drowns. **1773** JOHNSON in Boswell *Tour Hebrides* 20 Sept., Each man called for his own half-pint of wine, or gill, if he pleased. **1824** CARLYLE in Froude *Life* (1882) I. 263 His [Irving's] philosophy with me is like a gill of ditch-water thrown into the crater of Mount Ætna. **1862** ANSTED *Channel Isl.* IV. App. A. (ed. 2) 566 The smaller divisions are into pots (half-gallon), quarts, pints, gills (quarter of a pint), and noggins (an eighth of a pint).

b. A measure used for tin (see quot.).

1602 CAREW *Cornwall* 13 b, They measure their black Tynne, by the Gill, the Toplippe, the Dish and the Foote, which containeth a pint, a pottell, a gallon, and towards two gallons.

2. A vessel holding a gill.

c **1440** *Promp. Parv.* 194/1 Gylle, lytylle pot, *gilla, vel gillus*. *c* **1800** W. B. RHODES *Bomb. Fur.* iv. (1830) 25 O was I a quart, pint or gill To be scrubb'd by her delicate hands. **1864** *Lond. Gaz.* No. 1989/4 Several Silver Spoons mark'd T.J.M., a Silver Gill with the same Letters.

3. *attrib.*, as ***gill-glass***, ***-house***, ***-stoup***.

1673 DRYDEN *Marr. à la Mode* III. i, Who..opens her dear bottle of *mirabilis* beside, for a gill-glass of it at parting. **1728** POPE *Dunc.* III. 139 Thee shall each Ale-house, thee each Gill-house mourn. **1799** *Spirit Publ. Jrnls.* (1800) III. 349 With a bottle of gin in her right hand, and a gill glass in her left. **1820** *Blackw. Mag.* VI. 569 Having paid our respects to the gill-stoup at Lamington.

gill, jill (dʒɪl), *sb.*^{4} Also 5-6 gille, 6 gyll, 6-7 gil. [Abbreviation of GILLIAN.]

1. a. A familiar or contemptuous term applied to a woman; a lass, wench.

c **1460** *Towneley Myst.* iii. 219 *Noah* [to his wife]. Haue at the, gill. **1465** J. PASTON in *P. Lett.* No. 528 II. 238 My Lord Persy and all this house..wysshe ye had be here stille For the sey ye are a good gille. **1577** tr. *Bullinger's Dec.* 224 The wife that gadds not gigglot wise with euerie flirting gill. **1577-87** HOLINSHED *Chron.* III. 1159/2 She is a princesse, and the daughter of a noble king, and it euill becommeth thee to call her a gill. **1665** J. WILSON *Project.* I. Dram. Wks. (1874) 228 *Mrs. Got.* Sirrah..look out and mind your business..*Got.* Good faith, I do. *Mrs. Got.* Yes, among your gills too much! What was that you said to our maid t' other night? **1938** *Times Lit. Suppl.* 8 Oct. 638/4 She was a rolling-stone and an ignorant Jill-of-all-trades. **1942** BERREY & VAN DEN BARK *Amer. Thes. Slang* §382/2 A female, esp. a girl or young woman,..*gill*,..*Jill*.

attrib. **1635** QUARLES *Embl.* I. x, Close by the jack, behold, jill Fortune stands To wave the game.

b. A female ferret, polecat, or weasel. *colloq.* or *dial.*

1851 *N. & Q.* III. 461/2 The name by which the male ferret is known in the midland counties is the *hob*: the female is called the *jill*. **1875** G. C. DAVIES *Rambles School Field-Club* xxviii. 210 A..'hob', or male ferret, and..a 'jill', or female. **1902** W. E. DE WINTON in C. J. Cornish *Naturalist on Thames* 72 The female, or 'Jill', changes her entire coat directly she has young.

2. a. ***Jack and Gill*** = lad and lass; also in proverb ***Every Jack must*** (or ***will***) ***have his Gill***. See also JACK *sb.*^{1} 1 b.

c **1460** *Towneley Myst.* iii. 336 For Iak nor for gill. *a* **1529** SKELTON *Magnyf.* 290 What auayleth lordshyp, yourselfe for to kylle With care and with thought howe Iacke shalle haue Gyl. **1566** DRANT *Horace's Sat.* I. i. A vj a, Thy cheefe acquaintaunce all, Thy iacke, thy gille, thy kith, thy kinne doth prosecute thy fall. **1588** SHAKS. *L.L.L.* v. ii. 885 Our woing doth not end like an old Play: Iacke hath not Gill. **1621** B. JONSON *Gipsies Metam.* (1640) 93, I can..Give you all your fill, Each Iack with his Gill. *a* **1700** B. E. *Dict. Cant. Crew*, *Gill*,..a homely Woman. Every Jack must have his Gill. [*Nursery Rime*, Jack and Gill went up the hill, To fetch a pail of water.]

†**b.** With punning allusion to GILL *sb.*^{3} *Obs.*

1619 H. HUTTON *Follies Anat.* Epigr. xlvi, Fill me a quart (quoth he) I'me called Will. The prouerbe is, Each Iack will haue his Gill.

†**3.** A name for a mare. Cf. GILLOT 2. *Obs.*

1650 B. *Discolliminium* 16 If my Mare hath the Scratches on her hinder Heeles, I must not cut off her four legs..if I doe, I shall wrong my poor Gyll.

4. a. *dial.* Short for *gill-go-by-ground* (see 5). ?*Obs.*

1727 [see 5 b]. **1742** SHENSTONE *Schoolmistr.* xi, The lowly gill, that never dares to climb. **1760** LEE *Bot.* App. 303 Gill, *Glechoma* [in the Linnaean system]. **1846** BUCHANAN *Techn. Dict.*, *Gill*, the plant ground-ivy.

b. Short for *gill-ale* or *gill-beer*.

1755 JOHNSON, *Gill*, a malt liquor medicated with ground-ivy. **1828-64** in WEBSTER; and in recent Dicts.

5. *attrib.* and *Comb.* **a.** In phraseological *Comb.*, as †***gill-burnt-tail***, †***gill-o'-th'-wisp***, will-o'-the-wisp (see GILLIAN); ***gill-creep-*** (or ***go-***) ***by-ground***, ***gill-go-over-the-ground***, ***-run by-the-ground***, dialect names for Ground Ivy (*Nepeta Glechoma*); †***gill-run-by-the-street***, Common Soap-wort (*Saponaria officinalis*). †**b.** *attrib.* (sense 4), as ***gill-ale***, ***-beer***, ***-tea***. Also GILL-FLIRT.

a. **1597** GERARDE *Herbal* II. ccc. 705 It is commonly called ..ground Iuie, Alehoof, Gill creepe by ground [(1633) 856 Gill go by ground]. **1640** PARKINSON *Theat. Bot.* v. lxxix. 642 The countrey people in Kent and Sussex call it [Sopewort] Gill run by the street. **1654** GAYTON *Pleas. Notes* III. v. 97 Will with the Wispe, or Gyl burnt tayle. **1749-50** LADY BRADSHAIGH *Let.* 21 Feb. in Richardson *Corr.* (1804) IV. 367 Looking, as I knew, for a certain gill-o'-th'-wisp, who, I have a notion, escaped being known by you. RICHARDSON *Ibid.* 372. **1864** THOREAU *Cape Cod* v. (1894) 118 There were yellow-dock, lemon balm, hyssop, Gill-go-over-the-ground, and other plants. **1877** *N.W. Linc. Gloss.*, *Gill run by th' grund*, ground ivy. **1883** *Hampsh. Gloss.*, *Gill-go-by-ground*.

b. *a* **1700** B. E. *Dict. Cant. Crew*, *Gill-ale*, Physic-ale. **1710** SWIFT *Lett.* (1767) 19, I was forced to..dine for tenpence upon gill-ale, bad broth, and three chops of mutton. **1727** BRADLEY *Fam. Dict.*, *Gill-Ale*, Ale, &c. where Ground-ivy or Gill is infused. **1737** G. JONES *Lett. to Miss Bevan* 527 Am now to confine my self to Gill Tea and few other simple things. **1807** MARTYN *Miller's Gard. Dict.* s.v. *Glechoma*, The leaves [of Ground Ivy] were formerly thrown into the vat with ale to clarify it, and to give it a flavour. This was called Gill-ale. **1889** *Century Dict.*, *Gill-beer*, malt liquor medicated with the leaves of the gill or ground ivy.

†**gill**, *sb.*^{5} *Obs. rare*$^{-1}$. In 5 gylle. [? A use of GILL *sb.*^{4} (or of the proper name *Gill*); cf. *mawkin*.] ? An apron.

c **1440** *Promp. Parv.* 194/1 Gylle, fowle clothe (*H.*, *P.* fulclothe), *melota*, *vel melotes*.

gill (dʒɪl), *sb.*^{6} *dial.* Also 9 jill. [Of uncertain origin; cf. GILL *sb.*^{4} 3.] (See quot. 1895.)

1787 W. MARSHALL *Norfolk* (1795) II. 380 *Gill*, a pair of timber-wheels. **1843** MARRYAT *M. Violet* xliv, A couple of powerful oxen yoked to a gill, employed to drag out the stumps of old trees. **1894** *E. Daily Press* 11 June 5/2 Forty or fifty timbers were drawn up the hill one at a time on a single jill by a traction engine. **1895** *E. Angl. Gloss.*, *Gill*, a vehicle for conveying timber, consisting of two wheels, a strong axle-tree supporting a very stout bar, on which the timber is slung, and shafts.

gill (gɪl), *sb.*^{7} *slang.* A fellow, 'chap', 'cove'.

1812 J. H. VAUX *Flash Dict.*, *Gill*, a word used by way of variation, similar to *cove*, *gloak* or *gory*; but generally coupled to some other descriptive term as a *flash-gill*, a *toby-gill*. **1812** *Sporting Mag.* XXXIX. 142 Come list ye all, ye fighting Gills And Coves of boxing note, sirs. **1834** H. AINSWORTH *Rookwood* III. v, High Pads and Low Pads, Rum Gills and Queer Gills.

gill (gɪl), *sb.*^{8} *techn.* [Conceivably a transferred use of GILL *sb.*^{1}] A flax-comb (see quots.).

1839 URE *Dict. Arts* 499 The machine commonly called the gill, employed for preparing, drawing, and roving flax and hemp, and for combing and spinning long wool. **1853** *Ibid.* I. 763 The use of 'gills' became general about thirty years since. **1875** KNIGHT *Dict. Mech.*, *Gill*, a hackle. A series of points which divide the ribbons of flax fibre into finer parallel filaments ready for drawing and spinning.

b. *attrib.* and *Comb.*

1839 URE *Dict. Arts* 501 Fig. 454 is a horizontal representation of a gill machine. **1851** *Illustr. Lond. News* (1854) 5 Aug. 118 Gill-maker and presser. **1853** URE *Dict. Arts* I. 758 This part of the machine..is generally termed the 'gill-frame' or 'gill-head'. *Ibid.*, gill-spreader. *Ibid.* 759 The screws or worm shaft for carrying the gill-bar. *Ibid.* 764 Gill-sheet. Gill-teeth. **1879** *Cassell's Techn. Educ.* IV. 378/2 These gill-combs are heated by travelling over jets of gas. **1882** *Worc. Exhib. Catal.* III. 31 Wool goes to Gill Box..to be gilled. **1885** *Census Instr.* 43 Gill Maker, Gill Bars Maker, Gill Stock Maker. *Ibid.* 65 Gill-setter.

gill (gɪl), *v.*^{1} Also 5 gylle, gyllyn, 6 gyll. [f. GILL *sb.*^{1}]

1. *trans.* To gut or clean (fish). †Formerly also, to eviscerate (beasts) (cf. GILLER, quot. 14..).

14.. *Voc.* in Wr.-Wülcker 581/13 *Euiro* [read *eviscero*], to gylle. *c* **1440** *Promp. Parv.* 194/1 Gyllyn, or gylle fysche, *exentero*. **1530** PALSGR. 566/1, I gyll fysshe, *je oste la branche*. **1881** DU CHAILLU *Land Midnt. Sun* II. 149 Here the fish are gilled, which is done by making a cut with a sharp knife over the throat of the herring, whereupon the windpipe and entrails are drawn out.

†**2.** To handle the gills of, take hold of by the gills. *Obs.*$^{-1}$

1613 PURCHAS *Pilgrimage* (1614) 335 The fishes in the Lake of Venus..presented themselves, enduring to be scratched, gilled, and mens hands to be put in their mouthes.

3. To cut away the gills of a mushroom.

1728 E. SMITH *Compl. Housew.* (ed. 2) 75 Take the large Mushrooms..cut off the Stalks, but do not peel or gill them.

4. To catch or entangle (fish) by the gills in a gill-net. Said also of the net.

1884 ROE *Nat. Ser. Story* v, A bass of nine pounds weight can be..'gilled' in the ordinary manner. **1892** *Graphic* 13 Aug. 194/1 Another system of pilchard-fishing..is carried on much further from shore, by means of drift or driving nets, in the meshes of which the fish become entangled or gilled..The shore-seines do not gill the fish, having much smaller mesh.

Hence **gilled** *ppl. a.*; **'gilling** *vbl. sb.*; also *Comb.*, as ***gilling-knife***, ***-thread***.

c **1440** *Promp. Parv.* 194/1 Gyllynge of fysche, *exenteracio*. **1615** E. S. *Brit. Buss* in Arb. *Garner* III. 631 Tools and Implements used in drying and packing of Herring[s]. Gipping or Gilling knives. **1883** *Fisheries Exhib. Catal.* 36 Netting Threads..Gilling Threads..Flax Threads.

gill (dʒɪl), *v.*^{2} *local.* [f. GILL *sb.*^{3}] Hence **'gilling** *vbl. sb.* (See quots.)

1795 AIKIN *Manchester* 183 The bad custom of gilling, or drinking white wine as a whet before dinner. **1855** ROBINSON *Whitby Gloss.* s.v. *Jilling*, 'He goes jilling about', drinking his half-pints at different places, as the toper. **1855** STRANG *Glasgow* (1856) 123 Forenoon gilling prevailed through the whole range of the different craftsmen.

gill (gɪl), *v.*^{3} *techn.* [f. GILL *sb.*^{8}] *trans.* To dress (flax or wool) by means of a gill. Hence **gilled** *ppl. a.*; **'gilling** *vbl. sb.* (in quot. *attrib.*).

1882 *Worc. Exhib. Catal.* III. 31 [Exhibit No.] 18. Wool goes to Gill Box..to be gilled. 19. Machine for Gilling the tops. 21. Winds the gilled balls. **1875** KNIGHT *Dict. Mech.*, *Gilling-machine*, a gill-frame.

gillaroo (gɪlə'ruː). Also 8 gilderoy, 9 gilleroo. [a. Irish *giolla ruadh* (*giolla* lad, fellow + *ruadh* red).] A species of trout found in certain Irish rivers and lakes (see quot. 1833).

1773 BARRINGTON in *Phil. Trans.* LXIV. 118 The poke of the Gillaroo seems to perform the office of a gizzard. **1776** R. TWISS *Tour Irel.* 111 A species of trout, called gilderoy, are caught here [in the Shannon and lakes near]. **1833** J. RENNIE *Alph. Angling* 39 Trouts, which are called gillaroo, are found in Loch Melvin, near Ballyshannon, and Loch Con, near Ballina..and differ little from the common trout, except in being of a bright golden yellow on the belly and fins, with more red spots on the sides, and somewhat broader and thicker in form. **1867** F. FRANCIS *Angling* vii. (1880) 257, I was having great sport with the gillaroos. **1880** *Antrim & Down Gloss.*, *Gillaroo trout*, a large lake trout, commonly said to have a gizzard like that of a fowl.

gilled (gɪld) *ppl. a.* [GILL *sb.*^{1}] Having gills.

[**1823** *Spirit Publ. Jrnls.* (1824) 76 Remember the deeds of Sir Billy the Fat, That rosy-gill'd Alderman bold.] **1895** ST. G. MIVART in *Harper's Mag.* Mar. 634/2 The experiment of removing such young gilled tadpoles of the land salamander from the body of the mother in order to see whether they would then breathe in water. **1895** *Daily News* 4 Nov. 3/3 Specimens of gilled fungi.

gillenȝie: see GILENYIE *Sc. Obs.*

gillenia (dʒɪ'liːnɪə, gɪ'liːnɪə). *Bot.* [mod.L. (C. Moench *Methodas Plantas Suppl.* (1802) 286), f. the name of Dr. Arnold *Gille*, or *Gillenius*, a seventeenth-century German botanist.] A member of a small genus of herbaceous plants belonging to the family Rosaceæ; also the root of these plants, used as an emetic.

1820 J. BIGELOW *Amer. Med. Bot.* III. 17 Some authors have attributed a tonic power to the Gillenia, when administered in small doses. **1848** Dunglison *Med. Lex.* (ed. 7) 390/2 The root of this shrub,—*Gillenia*,.. is a safe and efficacious emetic. **1901** W. Robinson *Eng. Flower Garden* (ed. 8) 575 The Gillenias have a distinct and delicate beauty all their own. **1951** *Dict. Gardening* (R. Hort. Soc.) II. 891/1 Gillenias are hardy, easily grown plants.

giller ('gɪlə(r)). [f. GILL *v.*[1] + -ER[1].] One who guts or cleans fish. †Formerly also, one who eviscerates beasts.

14.. *Voc.* in Wr.-Wülcker 560/4 *Abestis* [sic: ? read *ab extis*] *intestina hostiarum aspiciens*, a gyller of bestys. **1881** Du Chaillu *Land Midnt. Sun* II. 149 Two skilled gillers can clean and fill thirty barrels a day.

giller, obs. form of GILDER *sb.*[1]

gillery, gillet, vars. GUILERY, GILLOT.

gill-flirt ('dʒɪlflɜːt). Also 7-8 Jil(l)-flirt. [f. GILL *sb.*[4] + FLIRT *sb.* 5; cf. FLIRT-GILL.] A young woman or girl of a wanton or giddy character. Now only *arch.*

1632 Sherwood, A Gill, or gill-flirt [Cotgr. 1611 has 'gill, flirt', s.v. *Gaultiere*]. **1673** Wycherley *Gentl. Dancing-Mast.* III, 'Tis your dainty Minx, that Jillflirt your Daughter here. **1754** Foote *Knights* II. Wks. 1799 I. 84 How! gill-flirt! —none of your fleers! I am glad here's a husband coming that will take you down. **1822** Scott *Nigel* v, She is a dutiful girl to her godfather, though I sometimes call her a jill-flirt. **1865** Carlyle *Fredk. Gt.* V. 609 A beautiful gillflirt of the court (*minaudière*).

attrib. **1824** Miss Mitford *Village* Ser. I. (1863) 203 No brazen-faced gipsy, like Sally Wheeler..or the jill-flirt Phœbe. **1870** Lowell *Study Wind.* 91 How much has she not owed of late to the tittle-tattle of her gillflirt sister Thalia? **1881** Duffield *Don Quix.* II. 405 Thy skull is.. empty; mine is more pregnant than ever was the gill-flirt drab which bore thee.

So †**gill-flirting** *ppl. a.*

1696 Southerne *Oroonoko* IV. i, The young jil-flirting girls, forsooth, believe no Body must have a husband but themselves.

gill-hooter ('dʒɪl,huːtə(r)). *dial.* Also 7 gill-houter, 8-9 gilli(e)-, gilly-hooter, -howter, 9 jill-, jilly-hooter. [f. the female name *Gill* (see GILL *sb.*[4]) + HOOTER[1].] An owl; esp. the barn-owl (*Strix flammea*).

1674 Ray *N.C. Words* 26 *A Gill-houter*, Chesh., an Owl. *c* **1746** J. Collier (Tim Bobbin) *Lanc. Dialect* Wks. (1862) 34 Thoose ot connaw tell a Bitter-bump fro a Gillhooter. **1828** H. Angelo *Remin.* I. 492 If the lout who was pointed out to me just now, be he, I never beheld..such a scare-crow, such a long-legged gilly-hooter. **1856** F. E. Paget *Owlet Owlst.* 8 Not a leaf of ivy to shelter a gilliehowter. **1895** *E. Angl. Gloss.*, *Jill-hooter, jilly-hooter*.

†**gillian.** *Obs.* [a. F. *Juliane*, a. L. *Jūliāna*, f. *Jūlius*, a Roman gentile name.] A girl, wench. (= GILL *sb.*[4])

1618 [see FLIRT-GILL]. **1625** Fletcher & Shirley *Nt. Walker* II. iii, De'e bring your Gillians hither? nay, she's punish'd, you[r] conceal'd love's cas'd up? *c* **1685** *Bagford Ball.* (1878) App., Seeing this Al-a-mode wear of the Town, by Gillians is practis'd so common, It is high time that it now was laid down by every Honest Woman.

b. *gillian-flirt* = GILL-FLIRT. (Cf. *flirt-gillian*.)

1592 G. Harvey *Pierce's Super.* 146 Yet was she not such a roinish rannell, or such a dissolute gillian-flurtes as this wainscot-faced Tomboy.

c. *gillian-a-burnt-tail* (see quot. and cf. *gill-burnt-tail*, GILL *sb.*[4] 5). *gillian-spend-all*: an unthrifty woman.

1573 Tusser *Husb.* xxiii. (1878) 64 Some Gillian spendal so often doth go For hogs meat and hens meat [etc.]. **1654** Gayton *Pleas. Notes* IV. xx. 268 An *Ignis Fatuus*, an exhalation, and Gillion a burnt taile, or Will with the wispe.

gillian-bower, var. JULIAN-BOWER.

gillie ('gɪlɪ), *sb.*[1] Also 6 cuille, geilȝie, 8 gaelly, 8-9 gilly, 9 ghillie. [a. Gael. *gille* a lad, servant = Irish *gille, giolla*.]

1. *Hist.* **a.** An attendant on a Highland chief.

[**1596** Spenser *State Irel.* Wks. (Globe) 641/2 Next after the Irish Kearne, me seemes the Irish Horse-boyes or Cuilles (as they call them) would come well in order. *a* **1605** Montgomerie *Misc. Poems* liv. 2 Fyndlay McConnoquhy.. Cativilie geilȝie with ye poik-braik.] *c* **1730** Burt *Lett. N. Scotl.* (1754) II. 158 It is very disagreeable to an Englishman over a Bottle, with the Highlanders, to see every one of them have his Gilly; that is, his Servant standing behind him all the while, let what will be the Subject of Conversation. **1771** Smollett *Humph. Cl.* 3 Sept., We were attended by a.. number of *Gaellys*, or ragged Highlanders. **1814** Scott *Wav.* xix, From the jargon, therefore, of the Highland gillies, I pass to the character of their Chief.

†**b.** *gillie-wetfoot*, a rendering of Gael. *gillecasfliuch* (f. *cas* foot + *fliuch* wet); a contemptuous name among Lowlanders for the follower of a Highland chief; *spec.*, the servant who carried the chief across a stream (see quot. *c* 1730). Also in adapted form *gillie-casflue*.

1681 Colvil *Whigs Supplic.* (1751) 84 Like gilliwetfoots purging states By papers thrown in pocks or hats [**1751** *Note*, Gilliwetfoots, the attendants on highland chieftans]. [*c* **1730** Burt *Lett. N. Scotl.* (1754) II. 158 *Gillie-casflue* carries him [the Chief] when on Foot over the Fords.] **1755** Johnson s.v. *Sorehon*, Whenever a chieftan had a mind to revel, he came down among the tenants with his followers, by way of contempt called in the lowlands giliwitfitts, and lived on free quarters. **1814** Scott *Wav.* xiii. *note*, A bare-footed Highland lad is called a gillie-wet-foot. [**1815** Mrs. Johnstone *Clan Albin* v, Roban's father had been Gillie-casflue to the old Laird.]

transf. **1808-80** Jamieson, *Gilliewetfoot*,..a worthless fellow, a swindler, one who gets into debt and runs off. Loth[ian], almost obsolete.

2. One who attends a sportsman in hunting or fishing in the Scottish Highlands.

1848 Clough *Bothie* III. 130 They had run, and beaten the gillies of Rannoch. **1873** Black *Pr. Thule* (1874) 5 The tall gillie patiently waited until his master had exhausted his passion. **1884** Marq. Lorne in *Pall Mall G.* 10 May 2/1 The moral life of a ghillie in a deer forest is a most virtuous one.

3. A type of shoe (see quots.).

1934 Webster, *Gillies*, low-cut sport shoes or ties with laces wound about the ankles. **1939** A. Keith *Land below Wind* xiii. 220 We had tried lace boots, gillies, short riding boots. **1950** H. McCloy *Through Glass Darkly* (1951) vi. 57 And brown shoes. The sort with no tongues and criss-cross laces that they call 'gillies'.

gillie ('dʒɪlɪ), *sb.*[2] *Sc.* [dim. of GILL *sb.*[3]] A gill of liquor.

1786 Burns *On a Scotch Bard* 59 I'll toast ye in my hind-most gillie Tho' owre the sea. **1790** A. Wilson *Ep. W. Mitchell* xi, Owre a pint or gillie.

gillie ('dʒɪlɪ), *sb.*[3] *rare.* [dim. of GILL *sb.*[4]; cf. GILLOT, JILLET.] **a.** A giddy young woman; = GILL *sb.*[4] 1, GILLOT 1. **b.** A mare; = GILL *sb.*[4] 3, GILLOT 2.

a **1529** Skelton *Elynour Rummyng* 390 Of folys fylly That had a fole wyth wylly, With Iast you, and gup, gylly. **1603** *Philotus* xcvii, Sho is a gillie, Scho is a Colt-foill, not a fillie. **1822** Hogg *Perils of Man* I. iv. 54 'I wad ride fifty miles to see ony ane of the bonny dames'..'Twa wanton glaikit gillies, I'll uphaud', said Pate.

gillie ('gɪlɪ), *v.* [f. GILLIE *sb.*[1]] *intr.* To act as gillie. Hence **'gillying** *vbl. sb.*

1905 *Daily Chron.* 2 Mar. 3/2 Contriving during the long vacation of six months to make enough money—by teaching, gillying or field-labour—to keep himself at the University for another year. **1926** *Chambers's Jrnl.* Mar. 153/1 Archie usually gillied for me. **1927** *Scots Observer* 9 Apr. 10/1 Nor is it intended to have classes in gamekeeping and ghillie-ing.

gilli(e)howter, var. GILL-HOOTER.

gilliefloure, -flower, obs. ff. GILLYFLOWER.

gilling ('gɪlɪŋ). *dial.* [Of obscure origin; perh. a var. of GIRLING.] (See quot.)

c **1640** J. Smyth *Hundred of Berkeley* (1885) III. 319 The salmon growes by theis degrees and ages: vz. 1 a pinke; 2 a botcher; 3 a salmon trout; 4 a gillinge; 5 a salmon. **1880** Buckland *19th Rept. Salmon Fish.* 58 *Gilling*, a salmon on his second return from the sea is sometimes called a gilling in the Severn District.

gillingite ('gɪlɪŋaɪt). *Min.* [f. *Gillinge* in Södermanland, Sweden, where it is found; named by Hisinger in 1826: see -ITE.] Hydrous silicate of iron, found in amorphous black masses.

1850 Dana *Min.* (ed. 3) 441 Hermann names the Gillinge ..mineral Gillingite. **1885** Erni *Min. Simplif.* 274 Gillingite..and Xylotile..are fusible with difficulty.

gillion ('gɪlɪən, 'dʒɪlɪən). [Blend of GIGA- and MILLION.] A name sometimes used for 1000 million by writers wishing to avoid the ambiguity of 'billion'.

1961 N. W. Pirie in *New Scientist* 11 May 331/3 A name is needed for 10^9... Because G is the symbol, gillion would be the logical word. **1966** V. A. Firsoff *Facing Universe* III. ii. 95 The number of galaxies within the observable universe ..is estimated at about 3 gillion (3×10^9). **1971** *Nature* 12 Mar. 133/2 The difficulty with N. W. Pirie's proposal of 'gillion' and 'tillion'..is—where do we go after 'giant' and 'monster'.

gilliver: see GILLYFLOWER.

gill-less ('gɪllɪs), *a.* [f. GILL *sb.*[1] + -LESS.] Unprovided with gills.

1846 Owen *Comp. Anat.* I. 267 Such arches are, therefore, gill-less.

†**gill-master.** *Obs. rare.* [? a. Du. *gildemeester* guild-master, i.e. head of one of the 'guilds' or companies of bowmen, gunners, etc. See *Wb. der Nederl. Taal*, s.v. *Gilde*.] The title of a military officer (see quot. 1598).

1598 Barret *Theor. Warres* v. iv. 136 A Gill Maister, or Lieutenant to the Mayorall, ouer euery 200 horses or beasts. **1622** F. Markham *Bk. War* v. vii. 188 Under the command of the master of the Ordnance is the Cariage master..the Steward, a Gilmaster, a Provost.

gillofer, -flower, -fre, obs. ff. GILLYFLOWER.

gillore, obs. form of GALORE.

†**'gillot.** *Obs.* Also 4-6 gillet, 6 gillat, gylat. [prob. a dim. of the female name *Gill* (cf. GILL *sb.*[4]); '*Gillet*, a woman's name' (Phillips 1658, who connects it with *Giles*).]

1. A loose or wanton woman (cf. JILLET).

1557 *Tottel's Misc.* (Arb.) 211 What though a gyllot sent that note, By cocke and pye I meant it not. **1561** *Schole-ho. Wom.* 559 in Hazl. *E.P.P.* IV. 126 The fairer woman the more gillot. **1579-80** North *Plutarch* (1676) 757 In honest mens houses..he would haue..these tumbling gillots lodged.

2. *Sc.* A mare.

c **1375** *Sc. Leg. Saints, Justina* 112 þarfor be his nygramancy He wald wirk mony ferly, As to gere a womane apere As scho ane wgly gillet were [L. *matronas in jumenta convertere videbatur*]. *c* **1450** Henryson *Mor. Fab.* 898 in *Anglia* IX. 369 The jolie gillet and the gentill steid, The asse, the mule, the hors of euerie kynd. **1494** *Acta Dom. Conc.* (1839) 321 Gillot wt sadill and Ryding gere price v crovnis. **1508** Dunbar *Tua mariit wemen* 114 He feppillis like a farcy aver, that flyrit on a gillot [*Maitland MS.* gylat].

gill-o'-th'-wisp: see GILL *sb.*[4] 5.

gillover, gillowflower, obs. ff. GILLYFLOWER.

gillry, obs. form of GUILERY.

gilly ('dʒɪlɪ). *dial.* [Short form of GILLYFLOWER.] A wallflower.

1892 *B'ham Weekly Post* 24 Dec. 5/6 Some nice little bunches of wall-flowers, or gillies as we call them here.

gilly: var. GILLIE *sb.*[1]

gillyflower ('dʒɪlɪ,flaʊə(r)). Forms: α. 4 geloffer, 4-5 gil-, gylofre, 5 gyllofyr, (-fre), gelefre, ielopher, 5-6 gelofer, (-fre), 6 gillo(w)fer, gill-, gelouer, (gelopere), 6-7 gilofer, 7 gillofre, (-over), gillyvor, 9 gilliver, (jilliver, gilver). β. *Sc.* 5 gerafloure, 6 ger(r)aflour; *pl.* 5 iorofflis, 6 gerofleis. γ. 6 gely-, iele-, gil(l)ifloure; 6 gilo-, 7 gillyflowre; 6 gile-, gili-, jilli-, 6-7 gillo(w)-, 6- gilli-, gillyflower. δ. 6- July-flower. [a. OF. *girofle, gilofre* clove; for the history of the forms see CLOVE-GILLYFLOWER.]

†**1.** A clove (cf. CLOVE-GILLYFLOWER 1); also *attrib.* in ***sauce gilofre***, clove sauce. *Obs.*

13.. *K. Alis.* 6796 Theo gilofre, quybibe, and mace. **13..** *E.E. Allit. P.* A. 43 Gilofre, gyngure & gromylyoun. *c* **1430** *Two Cookery-bks.* I. 15 Maces, Gelofres an Galyngale. *c* **1485** *Digby Myst.* (1882) III. 1363 þe Ientyll Ielopher a-ȝens þe cardyakylles wrech. **1513** *Bk. Keruynge* in *Babees Bk.* 279 Befe with sauce gelopere [*sic*].

2. Applied to native plants having flowers scented like a clove, esp. to the clove-scented pink (*Dianthus Caryophyllus*) = CLOVE-GILLYFLOWER 2, and hence to other plants more or less resembling this.

In those dialects in which the word is still current, it is commonly applied either to the wallflower (*Cheiranthus Cheiri*; see *wall-gillyflower*) or to the white stock (*Matthiola incana*; see *stock-gillyflower*).

α. **14..** *Voc.* in Wr.-Wülcker 586/2 *Gariofilata*, auens *vel* gilofre. **1509** Hawes *Past. Pleas.* xxvi. iii, The gentyl gelofer his odoure renued. **1688** R. Holme *Armoury* II. 64/1 The Julyflower as they are most properly called (though vulgurly Gilliflower and Gilofer). **1876** *Mid. Yorksh. Gloss.*, *Jilliver*, wallflower. **1883** *Almondbury Gloss.*, *Gilliver*, a kind of pink clove or carnation. **1894** Hall Caine *Manxman* v. xxi. 347 In one hand she carried a huge bunch of sweet-smelling gilvers.

fig. **1597** A. M. tr. *Guillemeau's Fr. Chirurg.* 6 b, They may gather..fragrant gillowfers of Chyrurgicall operations.

β. **1423** Jas. I *Kingis Q.* clxxviii, Of red Iorofflis..A fair[e] branche. *Ibid.* cxc, Gerafloure. **1500-20** Dunbar *Poems* lxxxviii. 20 London..Of royall cities rose and geraflour. **1570** *Satir. Poems Reform.* xv. 14 ȝe Baselik and Ionet flouris, ȝe Gerofleis so sweit.

γ. **1551** Turner *Herbal* I. H ij a, The herbe that wee call in Englyshe Gelouer or a Gelyfloure. **1589** Greene *Menaphon* (Arb.) 38 He that grafteth Iillyflowers vpon the Nettle, marreth the smell. **1621** Quarles *Div. Poems, Esther* (1638) 117 As when a Lady (walking Flora's Bowre) Picks here a Pink and there a Gilly Flowre. **1629** Parkinson *Parad.* (1656) 306, I account those that are called Carnations to be the greatest, both for leaf and flower, and Gilloflowers for the most part to be lesser in both. **1664** Evelyn *Kal. Hort.* (1679) 21 Gilly-flowers and Carnations. **1779** Sheridan *Critic* II. ii, The striped carnation, and the guarded rose, The vulgar wallflower, and smart gilly flower. *a* **1851** Moir *Poems, May-day* vi, The gillyflower raises its stem on high, And peeps on heaven with its pinky eye. **1877** *N.W. Linc. Gloss.*, *Gilly-flowers*, wall-flowers. Stocks are called *Stock-gilliflowers*.

δ. **1584** G. Peele *Arraignm. Paris* I. iii. A iij b, Julie flowers. **1605** Sylvester *Du Bartas* II. iii. I. *Vocation* 18 Som July-flowr or som sweet Sops-in-wine. **1612** Drayton *Poly-olb.* xv. 241 The braue Carnation then, with sweet and soueraigne power So of his colour call'd, although a Iuly-flower. **1649** Lovelace *Poems* (1864) 62 The July-flow'r that hereto thriv'd..straight sheds her leaves. **1721** Bailey, *Gilliflower* (q.d. *July-flower*, because it Flourishes in that Month), a Flower of a grateful Scent. **1855** [see b.].

b. *dial.* Applied to a woman (see quots.).

a **1797** Pegge *Derbicisms* (E.D.S.), *Gilliver*, a light-heel'd dame. **1855** Robinson *Whitby Gloss.*, *A Jilliver*, a wanton woman in the last stage of her good looks. A 'July flower', or 'the last rose in summer'. **1882** *Lancash. Gloss.*, *Jilliver*, a termagant. **1883** *Almondbury Gloss.*, *Gilliver*, sometimes used as Jezebel, a term of reproach to a woman.

3. With various distinguishing attributes, used (mainly in early botanical works) to denote varieties of the pink, the wallflower, and other plants related to or resembling these, as **African gillyflower**, the African marigold (*Tagetes erecta*); **dame's gilliflower** (see DAME'S-VIOLET); **English gillyflower**, the carnation; **feathered gillyflower**, *Dianthus plumarius*; **mock-gillyflower**, soap-wort (*Saponaria officinalis*); **single gillyflower**, *Dianthus plumarius*; **striped gillyflower**, a variety of *Dianthus Caryophyllus*; **yellow gillyflower**, wallflower. See also *castle-, cuckoo-, garden-, lea-, marsh-, queen's-, rogue's-,* sea-, stock-, *Turkey-*, *wall-*, *water-*, *Whitsun-*, *winter-gillyflower*; CLOVE-GILLYFLOWER.

1578 LYTE *Dodoens* II. iii. 151 The yellow Gillofer or Wall floure groweth vpon olde walles & stonehilled houses. *Ibid.* vii. 155 The Pynkes, and small feathered Gillofers, are like to the double or cloaue Gillofers in leaues, stalkes, and floures, sauing they be single and a great deale smaller. *Ibid.* 156 The second sorte..may well be called..in English single Gillofers, whereof be diuers sortes..& are called in Englishe by diuers names, as Pynkes, Soppes in Wine, feathered Gillofers. *Ibid.* xxv. 176 We do call this floure Turkie Gillofers, and French Marygoldes..or Aphrican Gillofers. *Ibid.* III. xiii. 335 Some do also take it [Sopewort Gentian] for *Struthion*, but it is nothing lyke: we may call it in English Soopewort: some call it Mocke Gillofer. **1693** EVELYN *De la Quint. Compl. Gard.* II. 155 We sow the Seed of Pannacht or striped Gilliflowers upon Hot Beds..to replant them in May. **1727** BRADLEY *Fam. Dict.*, *Carnation*, otherwise called English Gilly-Flower.

4. A variety of apple; also ***gillyflower-apple***.

1657 AUSTEN *Fruit Trees* I. 54 The Queen Apple is a great bearing fruit and good. So the Gillofloure. **1664** EVELYN *Kal. Hort.* (1729) 203 Apples..Russetting, Gilly-flower-Apples. **1741** *Compl. Fam. Piece* II. iii. 410 Apples [Dec.] Wheeler's Russet..Hautbonne, Winter Gilliflower. **1884** in HOGG *Fruit Manual* 85.

5. *attrib.*, as †*gillyflower-grass*.

1640 PARKINSON *Theat. Bot.* XIII. xiii. 1161 *Gramen Carophylleum Rabinum* the principall Gilloflower grasse. **1685** AUBREY *Nat. Hist. Wilts* (1847) 49 A blew grasse they call July-flower grasse, which cutts the sheepes mouthes.

gilly-gaupus (ˌgɪlɪˈgɔːpəs). *Sc.* Also **gilly-gap(o)us, -gacus, -gawpy.** [cf. GAUPUS; the first part of the compound is obscure.] A foolish or awkward person. Also *attrib.*

1719 RAMSAY *Answ. Hamilton* III. 44 Sweet Flaccus, Wha nane e'er thought a gilly-gacus. **1728** —— *Fables & T.*, *Monk & Miller's Wife* 136 Think ye this Youth's a Gilly-gawpy. **1755** R. FORBES *Jrnl. fr. Lond.* 29 Our great gillegapous follow o' a coach-man. **1785** GROSE *Dict. Vulg. Tongue*, *Gilly gaupus*, a Scotch term for a tall awkward fellow. *a***1791** —— *Olio* (1796) 112 You careless gilly gaupus, you break more lime ware than your head's worth. **1823** W. TENNANT *Cdl. Beaton* 26 The Cardinal's ain lang gilly-gapus dochter, Tibbie Beaton.

gilmin, obs. form of GUILLEMIN.

gilofer, obs. form of GILLYFLOWER.

gilore, obs. form of GALORE.

gilour(e, -ous, var. GUILER, -OUS.

gilpy (ˈgɪlpɪ), *sb.* and *a. Sc.* Also **gilpey, -ie.**

A. *sb.* †**a.** A frolicsome young fellow (*obs.*). **b.** A lively young girl.

a. 1718 RAMSAY *Christ's Kirk Gr.* III. xviii, A gilpy that had seen the faught I wat he was nae lang [etc.].

b. 1785 BURNS *Halloween* 129, I was a gilpey then, I'm sure I was na past fyfteen. **1816** SCOTT *Old Mort.* v, I mind, when I was a gilpy of a lassock, seeing the Duke. **1854** MRS. OLIPHANT *Magd. Hepburn* II. 7, I hear the lady has just as good a chance of a man as ony gilpie gaun.

B. *adj.* Sportive.

1863 JANET HAMILTON *Poems & Ess.* 297 Lassocks gilpie.

gilravage (gɪlˈrævɪdʒ), *sb. Sc.* Forms: 8 **gulravage**, 9 **gilravage, -ravatch, -raivitch, galravage, (goravich, girrebbage).** [? f. the vb.] Riotous or uproarious conduct; noisy romping.

1785 BURNS *Ep. to M'Math* 3 While at the stook the shearers cow'r..Or in gulravage rinnin scowr To pass the time [etc.]. **1818** *Edin. Mag.* Sept. 155 Muckle din an' loud gilraivitch was amang them, gaffawan an' lauchan. **1863** R. PAUL *Let.* in *Mem.* xviii. (1872) 269 An after-dinner galravage with the children.

gilˈravage, *v. north.* and *Sc.* Also **gill-, gal-, guleravage, gilraivitch, galravitch, (-atch, -erge), -revitch.** [Of unknown origin; ? connected with RAVAGE.]

1. *intr.* To feast or make merry in an excessive degree or in a riotous fashion.

1822 GALT *Provost* xliii. 316 At all former..banquets, it had been the custom..to galravitch both at hack and manger, in a very expensive manner to the funds of the town. **1887** J. SERVICE *Life Dr. Duguid* iii. 16 Galrevitchin' at my grandfather's honey-kaimbs, I had gotten the colic.

2. To gad about.

1863 MRS. GASKELL *Sylvia's L.* (ed. 2) I. 108 This lass o' mine..thinks as because she's gone galraverging, I maun ha' missed her.

Hence **gilˈravaging** *vbl. sb.* Also **gilˈravager.**

1818 SCOTT *Rob Roy* xxiii, Ye had better stick to your auld trade o' theft-boot, black-mail, spreaghs, and gillravaging. *Ibid.*, And wha's this?..Some gillravager that ye hae listed, I daur say. **1822** —— *Nigel* xxx, Our gracious master is auld, and was nae great gillravager amang the queens even in his youth. **1848** J. RAMSAY *Poems, Eglinton Park Meeting*, Great Was the galravagin and fun. **1893** *Northumbld. Gloss.*, *Gilravishin*, a tumult, a row.

gilry, gils(e, var. GUILERY, GRILSE.

Gilsonite (ˈgɪlsənaɪt). Also **gilsonite.** [f. the name of S. H. *Gilson* (see quot. 1888): see -ITE[1].] The proprietary name of an exceptionally pure variety of asphalt, found in Utah and Colorado as a brittle, brilliant black solid with a high softening temperature; it resembles glance pitch and grahamite.

1888 J. M. LOCKE in *Trans. Amer. Inst. Mining Eng.* XVI. 162 Gilsonite or Uintahite, a new variety of Asphaltum from the Uintah mountains, Utah. The discovery of this asphaltum was made by S. H. Gilson, of Salt Lake, and since then the material has borne the local name of Gilsonite. **1921** *Brit. Mus. Return* 160 Basalt coated with asphalt, and gilsonite, from Vera Cruz, Mexico. **1929** H. ABRAHAM *Asphalts* (ed. 3) x. 166 Gilsonite is one of the most valuable asphalts for manufacturing paints and varnishes. **1938** J. S. MILLER in A. E. Dunstan et al. *Sci. Petroleum* IV. 2724/1 Because of its brown undertone, Gilsonite is used widely in printing-inks. **1960** K. STERN in *Industr. Min. & Rocks* (ed. 3) xxxiii. 635/1 Gilsonite's high dielectric strength, heat-resisting qualities and its resistance to acids and alkalies makes it of great value as a waterproofing and weather-resisting agent.

gilt (gɪlt), *sb.*[1] Also 5 **gylte**, 6-7 **guilt.** [from GILT *ppl. a.* in the phrases *silver and gilt*, etc.]

†**1.** Gilt plate. *Obs. rare*$^{-1}$.

1492 *Bury Wills* (Camden) 74 My best standyng pece of gylte, and my best doseyn syluer sponys.

2. Gilding; the thin layer of gold with which anything is gilt. Also *fig.* in phr. ***to take the gilt off the gingerbread*** (see GINGERBREAD 2).

1593 SHAKS. *Rich. II*, II. i. 294 Wipe off the dust that hides our Scepter's gilt. **1610** G. FLETCHER *Christ's Vict.* II. xliii, For her tresses Marigolds wear spilt: Them broadly shee displaid, like flaming guilt. **1642** in Willis & Clark *Cambridge* (1886) II. 51 For guilt for y[e] Diall o. 4. 6. *c***1880** 'SALADIN' *Woman* I. xvii. 141 The gilt of the big Bible gleams on the window-sill. **1893** E. F. BENSON *Dodo* (1894) 372 It was to be bound in white vellum, with their arms in gilt upon the outside.

Comb. **1858** SIMMONDS *Dict. Trade*, *Gilt-jeweller*, a manufacturer of gilded ornaments to represent gold.

3. a. Gold; money. Now only *slang*.

Perhaps due to a confusion with GELD, GELT *sbs.*

1598 MARSTON *Sco. Villanie* I. iii. 156 D i a, Now nothing, any thing, euen what you list, So that some guilt may grease his greedy fist. **1608** MIDDLETON *Mad World* II. ii. C i b, Tho guilt condemnes, tis gilt must makes vs glad. **1637** R. MONRO *Exp. Scots Regim.* I. 7, I have seene other Nations call for Guilt being going before their enemie to fight, a thing very disallowable in either Officer or Souldier, to preferre a little money to a world of credit. **1708** *Mem. J. Hall* 18 And from thence conducted (provided he has Gilt) over the Way to Hell. **1885** *Daily News* 25 May 3/1 Disputatious little mobs grouped together to discuss whether Charrington or Crowder had the most 'gilt'.

b. A gilt-edged security.

1936 W. B. M. FERGUSON *Somewhere off Borneo* vi. 37 If he could get free board and travel.., it would mean just so much more towards another 'gilt' for his private collection. **1953** *Economist* 14 Nov. 508/1 (*heading*) Spotlight on gilts. **1967** *Times Rev. Industry* June 93/1 They went into equities largely because the scope for gilts had been mostly exhausted by three cuts in Bank rate.

gilt (gɪlt), *sb.*[2] Forms: 5 **gilte, gylte**, 6-7 **gylt**, 7-8 **guilt, guelt**, 8 **gelt**, 7- **gilt.** [a. ON. *gylt-r* (OSw. and mod.Icel. *gylta*) young sow:—OTeut. type **gultjâ*, related by ablaut to ON. *gǫlt-r* (:—OTeut. type **galtu-z*) boar, GALT.

Of the same origin, but of different formation, are OHG. *galza*, MHG. *galz(e* (also mod.G. dial.):—OTeut. **galtôn-*; also, OE. *ȝilte*, OHG. *gelza* (MHG. and mod.G. *gelze*), MDu. *gelte* (Du. *gelt(e)*:—OTeut. **galtjôn-*. The OE. form is found only in Ælfric's Gloss., but must have remained current in southern dialects; it appears as *yelte*, *jelte*, in 15th c. vocabularies (*Wr.-Wülcker* 614/30, 624/32), and as *ilt* about 1746 (*Exmoor Scolding*). *Gilt* on the other hand belongs to the eastern and northern dialects. Connexion with GELD *v.* has been suggested, but the meaning of 'spayed pig' seems to be accidental, though it is the common sense in Ger. and Du. The late spellings *gelt*, *guelt* are prob. due to a popular etymology of this kind.]

A young sow or female pig.

The precise application of the term varies in different districts; see quots. 1788-1886.

*c***1440** *MS. Linc. Med.* f. 312 (Halliw.) Tak unto the mane the galle of the galte, and to the womane the galle of the gilt. *c***1440** *Promp. Parv.* 194/2 Gylte, swyne, *idem quod* Galte. **1483** *Cath. Angl.* 156/1 A Gilte, *suella*. **1570** *Wills & Inv. N.C.* (Surtees 1835) 354 A sowe and a gylt vj[s]. **1601** HOLLAND *Pliny* II. 319 The grease of a young guelt which neuer had pigs. **1616** SURFL. & MARKH. *Country Farme* I. xxiv. 106 Let not youre Gylt goe to Bore, till she be past a yeare old. **1707** MORTIMER *Husb.* 185 The spaid Guilts, as they call them, they steem the more profitable. **1788** W. MARSHALL *Yorksh.* II. Gloss. (E.D.S.) *Gilts*, young female pigs, whether open or spayed. **1877** *N.W. Linc. Gloss.*, *Gilt*, a female pig before she has had a litter. **1886** *S.W. Linc. Gloss.*, *Gilt*, a female pig, called by this name till it has had a second litter, when it is called a sow. **1959** *Chambers's Encycl.* X. 724/2 Well-grown gilts can be put to the boar at eight months. **1967** *Oxf. Times* 27 Oct. 11/6 A Large White pig from Burford Grammar School's farm was very highly commended in the carcase class (gilts).

gilt, *sb.*[3] *slang.* ? *Obs.*

1. A thief or burglar. (Cf. GILTER[2].)

1620 MELTON *Astrolog.* 10 Leauing not a Pick-pockets, Gilts, Lifts, Decoyes, or Dyvers Hose unsurueyed. **1673** *Char. Quack Astrol.* B 3, He maintains..a correspondence with Gilts and Lifters. **1785** in GROSE *Dict. Vulg. Tongue.*

2. A pick-lock, skeleton key. (Cf. GILK.)

1673 R. HEAD *Canting Acad.* 94 The *Gilt*..with his Gilts (from whence he takes his name)..will readily find out one that shall fit any Lock. **1839** H. AINSWORTH *J. Sheppard* II. xviii, We shall have the whole village upon us while you're striking the jigger. Use the gilt, man!

gilt (gɪlt), *ppl. a.* Also 4 **gult**, *Kentish* **y-gelt**, 4-5 **gylt(e**, 4-6 **gilte**, 6 **guylt**, 6-7 **guilt(e.** [f. GILD *v.*[1], as *built* from BUILD.]

1. a. = GILDED *ppl. a.* (in literal sense).

13.. *K. Alis.* 927 Mony a riche gult scheld That day schon apon the feld. *a***1340** HAMPOLE *Psalter* xliv. 11 Þe quene vpstode at þi rightside in gilt clathynge. *a***1400-50** *Alexander* 1873 Þou..sittis..To-gedire with þi grete gods and on a gilt trone. **1480** CAXTON *Chron. Eng.* cclv. (1482) 331 He toke his brigantyns smyten ful of gylt naylen and also his gylt spores. **1597** *1st Pt. Return fr. Parnass.* v. i. 1480 Farewell, base carle clothed in a sattin sute, Farewell, guilte ass, farewell, base broker's poste! **1647** N. BACON *Disc. Govt. Eng.* I. xii. [xvi.] 56 A Helmet, a Coat of Mail, and a guilt sword. **1759** SYMMER in *Phil. Trans.* LI. 376 The gilt paper happened to lie with its gilded side upper-most. **1847** TENNYSON *Princess* Prol. 169 As a parrot turns Up thro' gilt wires a crafty loving eye. **1879** G. W. KITCHIN in *Encycl. Brit.* IX. 544 Four thousand gilt spurs were hung as trophies in Courtrai cathedral.

b. placed after the substantive.

1340 *Ayenb.* 26 Zuiche clepeþ oure lhord: berieles ypeynt and y-gelt. *c***1380** *Sir Ferumb.* 5493 Þe kyng ful ded of ys sadel y-gylt. **1434** *E. E. Wills* (1872) 102 A peyre of bedes of siluer with a crucifix of siluer and y-gilt. **1480** *Wardr. Acc. Edw. IV* (1830) 119, lxx bolyons of coper and gilt. **1533** *Act 24 Hen. VIII*, c. 13 And that no man shall weare..any maner aglettes, buttons, broches of golde or silver gilte. **1568** GRAFTON *Chron.* II. 383 Two Basons of Syluer and gylt. **1660** *Act 12 Chas. II*, c. 4 *Sched.* s.v. *Boxes*, Touch-boxes of iron or other mettal, guilt, the dozen. **1717** LADY M. W. MONTAGU *Let. to Abbé Conti* 17 May, Under the large lamp is a great pulpit of Carved wood, gilt. **1796** MORSE *Amer. Geog.* II. 91 Nine towers, covered with copper double gilt. **1833** J. HOLLAND *Manuf. Metals* II. 80 The guard..is..most commonly of brass, gilt. **1858** HAWTHORNE *Fr. & It. Jrnls.* (1872) I. 28 A gold or silver gilt ..image.

2. *fig.* ***gilt*** (now ***gilded***) ***youth***: a rendering of F. *jeunesse dorée*, app. first applied to the young men of wealthy families who assisted in the downfall of Robespierre in 1794.

1837 CARLYLE *Fr. Rev.* III. VII. ii, Young men of what they call the *Muscadin* or Dandy species! Fréron, in his fondness, names them *Jeunesse Dorée*, Golden or Gilt Youth. *Ibid.*, Let any one..think what an element, in sacred right of insurrection, this Gilt Youth was!

3. *Comb.* **a.** with sbs., as ***gilt-head*** (attrib.), ***-latten***; **gilt-bronze** (see quot. 1889); also *fig.*; cf. ORMOLU; **gilt-char** (see quot.); **gilt-cup** (also *dial.* gil-cup), the buttercup; **gilt-edge** *a.* = *gilt-edged*; also *absol.*, a gilt-edged security; †**gilt-leaf**, gold-leaf; **gilt-metal worker** (see quot.); †**gilt-paper**, writing paper with gilt-edges; **gilt-poll** = GILT-HEAD; **gilt tooling** (see TOOLING *vbl. sb.* 2 b); **gilt toy** (see quot. 1862); **giltwood** *a.*, made of wood and decorated with gilding.

1889 *Cent. Dict.*, **Gilt-bronze*, a gilded metal much used for decorative objects, either real bronze, or often brass, latten, or some similar yellow metal. **1906** F. TREVES *Highways & Byw. Dorset* iv. 43 A track made of gilt-bronze moss. **1936** *Burlington Mag.* Nov. p. xix/2 Various candelabra in gilt-bronze. **1787** BEST *Angling* (ed. 2) 4 The English fishes that we have in our ponds, rivers, &c. are as follow: Carpio Lacus Benaci, the Guilt or *gilt Charr. **1610** R. VAUGHAN *Herefordsh. Waterworks* Q 2, Medowground.. that takes more pride in the company of the Cowslipp, then the *gilt-cupp which carrieth the garland from the rest. **1864** W. BARNES in *Macm. Mag.* Oct. 476 Where the barn-vloor wer a-sheenen do vall The cwold zummer dew; an' gilcups be bright. **1818** KEATS *Let.* 21 Sept. (1931) I. 236 A dissertation on letter writing... *Gilt edge [paper] Dandies in general, male female and literary. **1895** *Brewer's Dict. Phr. & Fable* 519/2 *Gilt-edge investments*, a phrase introduced in the last quarter of the 19th century..for investments in which no risks are incurred. **1901** *Westm. Gaz.* 28 Aug. 7/1 The Demand for Gilt-Edges. **1905** G. WILSON *Ann. Glover Incorp.* 24 What is termed a gilt-edge security. **1847** TENNYSON *Princess* I. 19 Our great court-Galen poised his *gilt-head cane. **1900** S. R. GARDINER *Student's Hist. Eng.* 314 *Gilt-latten effigies of Richard Beauchamp. **1759** SYMMER in *Phil. Trans.* LI. 378 Any thin metallic substance, such as *gilt-leaf, or tin-foil. **1858** SIMMONDS *Dict. Trade*, **Gilt-metal worker*, one who over-lays metals with gold; an electro-plater. **1660** M. R. *Acc. Receipts Comm. Safety* 4 Ten *gilt Paper-books..for his Lady to write in at Church. **1772** *Gentl. Mag.* XLII. 192 He's the gilt paper which apart you store And lock from vulgar hands in the scrutore. **1713** RAY *Syn. Pisc.* 131 *Aurata*..The Gilt-head or *Gilt-poll. **1740** R. BROOKES *Art of Angling* II. lxxiii. 193 The Gilt-Head or Gilt Poll..is broad and flat, being in some respects like a Bream. **1907** *Yesterday's Shopping* (1969) 442/1 Russia leather, with *gilt tooling. **1930** G. H. BUSHNELL *University Librarianship* viii. 50 Marking books permanently by gilt tooling. **1839** URE *Dict. Arts* 571 Supposing the articles desired to be gilded be brass or copper buttons, or small articles for *gilt toys, or ornaments of dress. **1851** *Illustr. Catal. Gt. Exhib.* III. III. 629/1 Much of the Birmingham jewellery and gilt toys are produced by means of dies or steel blocks, with impressions of articles to be sunk therein. **1862** *Chambers's Encycl.* IV. 754/2 *Gilt toys*, this term is known in trade as a designation for small articles which are gilded, but is chiefly applied to the cheap jewellery which is almost exclusively manufactured at Birmingham. **1939** *Burlington Mag.* LXXV. 32/1 A set of *giltwood chairs by Thomas Chippendale. **1958** *Times* 2 Dec. 20/7 A pair of Italian giltwood side tables with rustic tree supports, 18th century. **1970** *Daily Tel.* 18 Apr. 10/5 A suite of 14 pieces of George I giltwood furniture was bought..for £19,000.

b. parasynthetic, as ***gilt-framed***, ***-handled***, ***-headed***, ***-knobbed***, ***-robed***, ***tooled***; also **gilt-edged**, *lit.* of writing-paper or books: applied *fig.* to 'paper' (i.e. bills) or securities of exceptionally high value, and occasionally to specially expensive qualities of any commodity; also used to denote something of very high quality, richness, elegance, etc.; *absol.*, gilt-edged securities.

1818 MOORE *Fudge Fam. Paris* xii. 61 There his Julie he wrote,—Upon paper *gilt-edged, without blot or erasure. **1851** *Ord. & Regul. R. Engineers* ix. 48 No Gilt-edged Paper is allowed. **1892** *Spectator* 17 Sept. 374/1 Colonial and Indian Securities, and other gilt-edged Stocks. **1894** *Daily News* 20 Sept. 3/1 'Gilt-edged' butter in New York realises 4s. a pound. **1867** *Galaxy* July 278 He decidedly should not honor any more drafts unless secured by previous deposits of specie, gilt-edged paper endorsed with two good names, or U.S. or solvent State stocks. **1872** *Vermont Board Agric. Rep.* I. 163 The high prices reported to be paid in the Boston market for what is called 'gilt-edged butter'. **1897** KIPLING *Capt. Cour.* x. 230 Pastors of great, gilt-edged congregations, at the seaside for a rest. **1913** E. WHARTON *Custom of Country* ix. 113, I don't want to break into your gilt-edged crowd. **1930** *Economist* 10 May 1038/2 Gilt-edged were fairly steady after a shaky start, but little business was done. **1952** KOESTLER *Arrow in Blue* ii. 16 Dr. Bedoe's eyes flashed and he broke into his gilt-edged smile. **1958** *Times* 11 Jan. 12/1 While gilt-edged took the news of the new £500m. Exchequer stock issue in their stride, the equity markets turned dull on the Stock Exchange yesterday. **1965** *New Statesman* 9 Apr. 588/2 There is to be no [tax] exemption..for gilt-edged. **1854** THOREAU *Walden* 48 A..*gilt-framed looking-glass. **1936** *Discovery* Dec. 386/2 The Coffee House, where once the little gilt-framed poster had found so fit a home. **1686** *Lond. Gaz.* No. 2100/4 Little *Gilt-handled Swords. **1858** *Skyring's Builder's Prices* (ed. 48) 7 *Gilt-headed screws double..the above prices. **1859** SALA *Gas-light & D.* xxvi. 301 The silken calves and *gilt-knobbed sticks of the splendid footmen. **1825** D. L. RICHARDSON *Sonn.* 135 A *gilt-robed villain came, With heartless guile her hopes betrayed And triumphed o'er her shame. **1926-7** *Army & Navy Stores Catal.* 431/2 Leather photograph frames... Crushed calf, *gilt tooled. **1936** *Burlington Mag.* Apr. 198/2 Small gilt-tooled ornament.

† **gilt**, *v. Obs.* Also 6 **gylte**, 6–7 **guilt**. [f. GILT *ppl. a.* by extension of the participial form to other parts of the verb.] = GILD *v.*[1] in various senses.
c **1375** *Sc. Leg. Saints, Seven Sleepers* 478 Sume men sais, þe emperoure gert gilt þair bare. **1382** WYCLIF *Exod.* xxxvi. 34 And thilk tablid thingis he giltide. **1483** *Cath. Angl.* 156/1 To Gilte, *aurare*. **1503** HAWES *Examp. Virtue* vi. (Arb.) 21 Her towre was gylted full of sonne bemys. *a* **1533** LD. BERNERS *Gold. Bk. M. Aurel.* (1546) B iij b, This aunciente worlde..was not golde by the sages that dyd gylte it. **1590** L. LLOYD *Diall Daies* 92 The sonne of this Scythian dead man causeth his father's head..to be guilted over. **1623** COCKERAM, *Inargentate*, to gilt or couer with siluer. **1641** MILTON *Prel. Episc.* 11 We doe injuriously..with these [rags] deformedly to guilt, and interlace the..robe of Truth.

gilt(e, obs. form of GUILT, JILT.

'**gilted**, *ppl. a. Obs.* exc. *dial.* Also 6–7 **guilted**. [f. GILT *v.*] = GILDED, GILT *ppl. adjs.* (in early examples placed after the sb.).
1460-70 *Bk. Quintessence* 7 þerfore vse wiyn or brennynge watir giltid, so þat 3e may be hool. *c* **1475** *Reg. Gild Corp. Xti. York.* (1872) 295 Harnest thorowoute with sternes gylted. *c* **1507** in *Etoniana* (1865) 214 Coats of blacke clothe duble garded with gilted leather. **1509** HAWES *Past. Pleas.* VII. iii, O sterre of famous eloquence, O gylted goddesse of hyghe renowne. **1563** *Homilies* II. *Idolatry* III. Yy iii b, To spreade vs abroade these goodlye caruen and gylted [**1574** gylten, **1582** gilten, **1640** gilden] bookes. **1570** *Wills & Inv. N.C.* (Surtees 1835) 328 It'm I gyue & bequithe vnto my cosinge John Haveloke my gylted dagger. **1634** *Malory's Arthur* VII. xv, Their..gilted [**1485** gylt] spurs upon their heels. *a* **1649** DRUMM. OF HAWTH. *Poems* Wks. (1711) 27 Why, worldlings, do ye..lean to guilted glories which decay? **1877** *N.W. Linc. Gloss.*, *Gilted*, gilded. 'His shop's gotten gret gilted letters ower th' door.'

gilteles, obs. form of GUILTLESS.

† '**gilten**, *a. north.* and *Sc. Obs.* Also 6 **gilting**. [Prob. due to a confusion between GILT and GILDEN.] Gilt, gilded; golden.
c **1400** *Melayne* 1098 Many lay stekede vndir stedis In gilten gere. *a* **1400-50** *Alexander* 3456 þai gone agraythen vp þaire gods on gilten segis. **1501** DOUGLAS *Pal. Hon.* I. x, A diademe maist plesandlie polite, Set on the tressis of her giltin hair. **1513** —— *Æneis* VII. iii. 82 With fyry sparkis, lyke to goldin bemys Or twynkland sprayngis with thair giltin glemys. **1539** *Inv. R. Wardr.* (1815) 53 Twa harnessingis of grene reid and quhite velvett with gilting bukkillis. **1574-82** [see GILTED, quot. 1563].

† '**gilter**[1]. *Obs.* [f. GILT *v.* + -ER[1].] A gilder.
1565 COOPER *Thesaurus, Bractearius*,..a gilter. **1620** THOMAS *Lat. Dict.*, *Aurarius*,..a gilter, or worker in gilt.

† '**gilter**[2]. *slang. Obs. rare*$^{-1}$. [f. GILT *sb.*[3] + -ER[1].] (See quot.)
1676 *Warn. Housekprs.* 3 The first sort [of Thief] is called a Gilter. This Gilter is one that hath all sorts of Picklocks and false Keys.

gilter, var. GUILTER, *Obs.*

'**gilt-head.** ? *Obs.* [f. GILT *ppl. a.* + HEAD.] A name given to various fishes which have the head marked with golden spots or lines: The striped tunny or bonito; the dorado or dolphin (*Coryphæna hippuris*); the cunner or golden wrasse (*Crenilabrus melops* or *tinca*).
1555 EDEN *Decades* 203 These flyinge fyshes and the fyshes named gylte heades. **1565** COOPER *Thesaurus, Aurata* ..A fish, thought of some to be called a giltheade. **1591** R. TURNBULL *St. James* 102 They are not vnlike the fish Scarus, which some take to be the Gilthead or Goldenie. **1600** HAKLUYT *Voy.* III. 520 Of these [flying fish] wee sawe ..a hundred in a company.. chased by the gilt-heads, otherwise called the bonitoes. **1601** HOLLAND *Pliny* I. 337 All fishes be toothed like saws, saue only the guilt-head Scarus. **1620** VENNER *Via Recta* iv. 76 The Guilt-head or Goldine is whiter, and not..of so hard a substance as the Allowes. **1623** WEBSTER *Devil's Law Case* I. i, It may be, whiles he hopes to catch a gilt-head, He may draw up a gudgeon. **1674** RAY *Collect.*, *Sea Fishes* 105 Gilt-Heads, *Aurata*, Chrysophrys. **1705** BOSMAN *Guinea* 278 Here are.. Giltheads and other large Fish. **1725** BAILEY *Erasm. Colloq.* 579 Don't think that any Lucullus sups more pleasantly upon his..Gilt-heads, Sturgeons or Lampreys. **1769** PENNANT *Zool.* III. 197 The Gilt-head..takes its name from its predominant colour; that of the forehead and sides being as if gilt. *Ibid.* 198 No praise, no price a Gilt-head e'er will take, Unfed with oysters of the Lucrine lake. **1774** GOLDSM. *Nat. Hist.* VI. 305 The Ophidium, or Gilthead..is by sailors called the dolphin, and gives chace to the flying-fish. **1836** YARRELL *Brit. Fishes* I. 97 *Chrysophrys aurata*. The Gilt-head. *Ibid.* 293 The Gilt-head, Connor, Golden Maid. *Crenilabrus tinca*.
b. *toothed gilthead* = *Sparus dentatus*.
1832 JOHNSTON in *Proc. Berw. Nat. Club* I. No. 1. 7 The most remarkable..were..the toothed gilt-head, the sea perch.

† '**gilting**, *vbl. sb. Obs.* [f. GILT *v.* + -ING[1].] = GILDING *vbl. sb.*
1460-70 *Bk. Quintessence* 2 þer be manye werkis in þe whiche gold and siluir be meyngid, as in giltynge of vessel & Iewellis. **1483** *Cath. Angl.* 156 A Giltynge, *apocrisis, deauracio*. **1529** MORE *Dyaloge* viii. a/2 Yᵉ gold yᵗ is quyte cast away about yᵉ gilting of kniuis, swordis, sporys, arrace, & paynted clothes. **1611** CORYAT *Crudities* 145 Sixe very precious sockets made indeede but of timber worke, but flowrished over with a triple gilting. **1682** A. BEHN *City Heiress* 33 Gilting and Hypocrisie cheat the world best.

giltless(e, obs. form of GUILTLESS.

'**gilt-tail.** Also 7 **gild-tail**. [f. GILT *ppl. a.* + TAIL *sb.*]
1651-7 T. BARKER *Art of Angling* (1659) 42 A little short worme..called a Gild-taile. **1653** WALTON *Angler* iv. 95 The marsh-worm, the tag-tail..the gilt-tail. **1787** BEST *Angling* iii. 13 Brandlings, Gilt-tails, and Red worms. Found in old dunghills [etc.].

gilty(f, gilver, obs. ff. GUILTY, GILLYFLOWER.

Gilyak ('gɪljæk). A people of the northern part of Sakhalin Island or the adjacent part of Siberia; a member of this people; the language of this people. Also *attrib.* or as *adj.*
1858 *Jrnl. R. Geogr. Soc.* XXVIII. 389 One hundred and seventy miles below Pul, one finds the dwelling places of the Gilyaks. *Ibid.*, The Gilyak villages passed were Mangal, Dengdala,..and Tyr. **1861** E. G. RAVENSTEIN *Russians on Amur* xx. 391 A Gilyak would not..permit any fire to be taken from his hut. **1890** J. G. FRAZER *Golden Bough* II. iii. 105 The Gilyaks, a Tunguzian people of Eastern Siberia, hold a bear festival. *Ibid.* 107 The Gilyak custom of leading him from house of house. **1933** BLOOMFIELD *Lang.* iv. 70 *Gilyak* is spoken in the northern part of Sakhalin Island and round the mouth of the Amur River. **1956** J. WHATMOUGH *Language* 32 Grouped together with Kamchadal and Gilyak, as 'Hyperborean'. **1958** E. A. ARMSTRONG *Folklore of Birds* i. 6 The Ainu and the Gilyak treat the bears they slay with great reverence. **1968** CHOMSKY & HALLE *Sound Pattern Eng.* 305 In Ubykh, as in many other languages, such as Gilyak..the difference between velar and uvular points of articulation is paralleled by the difference between nonstrident and strident.

gim (dʒɪm), *a. Obs.* exc. *dial.* Also 6 **gym**, 8 **jim**. [perh. a var. of JIMP *a.*] Smart, spruce.
1513 DOUGLAS *Æneis* XII. Prol. 161 The payntit povne, pasand with plomys gym, Kest vp his taill. *c* **1560** A. SCOTT *Poems* (S.T.S.) v. 14 In May gois gentill wemen gymmer, In gardynis grene thair grumis to glaid. **1705** VANBRUGH *Confed.* I. iii, He's as fine as a prince, and as gim as the best of them. **1755** in H. Walpole *Let.* 17 July, Corr. 1820 I. 422 Though Surry boasts its Oatlands, And Claremont kept so jim. **1812** W. TENNANT *Anster F.* II. xxi, Lasses..Gay as May-morning, tidy, gim, and clean. *a* **1825** FORBY *Voc. E. Anglia*, *Gim, Gimmy*, spruce, neat, smart.

gimal, obs. form of GIMMAL.

gimbal ('dʒɪmbəl, 'gɪmbəl). Forms: 6–7 **gimbol(e**, (8 **jimbol**), 7, 9 **gimball**, 8 **gimbel**, 9 **gimble**, (**jimble**), **gimbald**, **gymbal**, 8– **gimbal**. [altered form of GIMMAL.]
† **1.** = GIMMAL 1. *Obs.*
1605 J. DOVE *Confut. Atheism* 37 Three gimballes compacted together are one ring, and yet three as they be disioyned. **1711** J. GREENWOOD *Eng. Gram.* 190 *Gimbal*, i.e. a doubled or twisted Ring.
† **2.** *pl.* Joints, connecting links (in machinery); = GIMMAL 2. Chiefly *fig. Obs.*
1577 STANYHURST *Descr. Irel.* in Holinshed *Chron.* (1807-8) VI. 15 Truly this argument hangeth together by verie strange gimbols. **1599** HAKLUYT *Voy.* II. II. 195 The ship..they found fraighted with all sorts of small yron-worke, as horse-shoes..boults, locks, gimbols, & such like. *a* **1652** BROME *Damoiselle* III. ii, I can yet bowe my Haunches ..My Gimboles don't complain for want of Oyle yet.
† **3.** (See quot. 1736.) *Obs.*
1727 BRADLEY *Fam. Dict.* s.v., To prepare Gimbels, take a Quartern of Flower [etc.]. **1736** BAILEY *Househ. Dict.*, *Gimbel*, a kind of pastry work that is hard, about the thickness of one's little finger, form'd round, and made in the shape of a ring.
4. *pl.* A contrivance by means of which articles for use at sea (esp. the compass and the chronometer) are suspended so as to keep a horizontal position. It usually consists of a pair of rings moving on pivots in such a way as to have a free motion in two directions at right angles, so as to counteract the motion of the vessel.
1780 in *Falconer's Dict. Marine*. **1787** CAVALLO *Magnetism* 60 Notwithstanding the contrivance of the jimbols. **1794** G. ADAMS *Nat. & Exp. Philos.* IV. lii. App. 490 The frame of the instrument is suspended on gimbals near to the centre of gravity. **1816** J. SMITH *Panorama Sc. & Art* II. 184 The ring of the gimbals rests with its pivots on a semicircle, the foot of which turns in a socket. **1858** T. R. JONES *Aquar. Nat.* 372 That the body may be poised, and capable of moving freely in all directions, as though suspended on gimbals. **1870** KENNAN *Tent-life Siberia* ii. (1871) 13 The cabin lamp swung uneasily in its well-oiled gimbals. **1884** F. J. BRITTEN *Watch & Clockm.* 115 The object of the gymbals is to keep the chronometer level.
5. *attrib.* and *Comb.*, as *gimbal-joint*; also, in sense of supported or suspended on gimbals, as *gimbal-compass*, *-lamp*, *-table*. Also **gimbal-jawed** *a.* (see quot.); **gimbal-ring** (see quot.).
1859 BARTLETT *Dict. Amer.*, **Gimbal-jawed* or *Jimber-jawed*, one whose lower jaw is loose and projecting. **1875** KNIGHT *Dict. Mech.*, **Gimbal-joint*, a two part joint having articulations on axes at right angles to each other. **1883** *Fisheries Exhib. Catal.* 31 Collection of *Jimble and Cabin Lamps. **1875** KNIGHT *Dict. Mech.*, **Gimbal-ring*, a single gimbal by which the cock-eye of the upper mill-stone is supported on the spindle to permit vibration. A rynd. **1851-9** *Man. Sci. Enq.* 91 The apparatus when used at sea is placed in a *gimball table by which the motion of the vessel is greatly counteracted.
Hence '**gimballed** *ppl. a.*, fitted with or supplied with a gimbal.
1875 R. H. R. *Rambles Istria* 47 *note*, She has a powerful electric light..gimballed, so as to allow it to be thrown in any direction. **1876** *S. Kens. Mus. Catal.* No. 1148 (ed. 3) 289 This instrument is..placed on a properly constructed gimballed table.

gimbri ('gɪmbrɪ). Also **gunibri**, **gunibry**. [ad. Arab. *gunbrī*.] A small Moorish guitar played by plucking the strings with a piece of dry palmetto leaf; also, a player of this instrument.
1876 STAINER & BARRETT *Dict. Mus. Terms* 214/1 The resonance-body of the Gunibry is made of a bottle-pumpkin cut longwise, and covered with sheep skin. **1894** G. MONTBARD *Among Moors* 7 He sings in a sad broken voice, ..accompanying the song on a sort of square guitar, a *gimbry*. **1903** *Westm. Gaz.* 18 Feb. 2/3 The slender fanatical singer, Whose fingers were skilled on the gimbri. **1907** F. CAMPBELL *Shepherd of Stars* xv. 177 The Gimbri wagged his [head] from side to side. **1954** *Grove's Dict. Mus.* (ed. 5) V. 506/2 Those [instruments] of popular acceptance are the pandore (*gunibri*), [etc.].

gimcrack ('dʒɪmkræk), *sb.* and *a.* Forms: α. 4 **gybe-**, **gibecrake**, 7 **jibcrack**. β. 7 **gimcracke**, **gincracke**, 8 **jem-**, **jimcrack**, 9 *dial.* **gimcrank**, 7– **gimcrack**. [The 14th c. form *gibecrake* is perh. connected with OF. *giber* to shake (see JIB *v.*); the primary sense may have been 'a slight or flimsy ornament'. (For the change to the nasalized forms, cf. mod.F. *regimber* = OF. *regibber* to kick.) The second element may be connected in some way with CRACK *sb.* or *v.* Sense 3 is perh. in part due to association of the word with GIM *a.* and CRACK *sb.* 11 and 14.]
A. *sb.*
† **1.** App. applied to some kind of inlaid work in wood. *Obs.*
1360 *Acc. William de Rothewelle* in *Pipe Roll* No. 204 m. 42 d, Et Eustachio de Glastonia..in precio j tabule cum j piler et Gibecrake bordura cum minutis peciis diversi coloris..j ta ula de quercu j piler et Gybecrake de Buxo, xvjs. viijd.
2. † **a.** A fanciful notion; also, a 'dodge', underhand design (*obs.*). **b.** A mechanical contrivance; also *pl.* scientific apparatus. **c.** Now usually applied to a showy, unsubstantial thing; esp. to a useless ornament, a trumpery article, a knick-knack.
1635 SHIRLEY *Coronat.* II. (1640) D ij, Such spectacles Are rare ith' Court, and they were to skirmish naked Before her, then there might be some excuse, There is some gimcrackes in 't, the Queen is wise Above her yeares. **1639** CHAPMAN & SHIRLEY *Ball* IV. H iij, *Luc.* There remaines to take away one scruple. *Co.* Another gimcracke. *Luc.* I have none, tis your doubt sir. **1676** WALTON *Angler* I. xxi. (ed. 5) 263 Ribbins, and Looking-glasses, and Nut-crackers, and Fiddles, and Hobbyhorses, and many other gim-cracks..and all the other finnimbruns that make a compleat Country Fair. **1709** STEELE *Tatler* No. 34 ¶5 My Eye was diverted by Ten Thousand Gimcracks round the Room. **1712** ARBUTHNOT *John Bull* III. vi, What a Devil! is the meaning of all these trangrams and gimcracks [surveying instruments] gentlemen? **1772** MUDGE *Let.* 2 June in *Descr. Time-keeper* (1799) 23, I am prosecuting my gimcrack with all the vigour I am able, and hope I shall have an opportunity of shewing it to you going (but I fear without the balance spring). **1778** MISS BURNEY *Evelina* xxiii. (1784) 191 Lord Orville.. changed the subject to Cox's Museum, and asked what he thought of it? 'Think!' said he, 'why I think as how it i'n't worth thinking about. I like no such jemcracks.' **1820** EARL DUDLEY *Lett.* 3 Apr. (1840) 243 This gimcrack [the Brighton Pavilion] is the only monument of the greatest sovereign in Europe. **1849** THACKERAY *Pendennis* II. iii, She praised the lovely breloques or gimcracks which the young gentleman wore at his watch-chain. **1871** BESANT & RICE *Ready Money Mort.* xix, Get me good things: no gim-cracks. **1887** A. GRAY *Lett.* (1893) 796 Weisner's physiological laboratory I had an hour or two in, and saw all his gimcracks.
attrib. **1855** THACKERAY *Newcomes* ix, No shops so beautiful to look at as the Brighton gimcrack shops.

†**3.** An affected showy person, a fop; in later use applied to women. (A term of contempt.) *Obs.*

1618 FLETCHER *Loyal Subj.* IV. ii, Enter second Servant .. *Theod.* These are fine gim-cracks. Hey! here comes another; A flagon full of wine in's hand, I take it. **1623** MASSINGER *Dk. Milan* IV. iii, He's come. What gimcrack have we next? *a* **1625** FLETCHER *Wom. Prize* IV. i, But to be made a whim-wham, A Jib-crack, and a Gentleman o' th' first house For all my kindness to her. —— *Elder Bro.* III. iii, Lady, I pitie you .. this [fellow] is a Gincracke, That can get nothing but new fashions on you. **1706** MRS. CENTLIVRE *Basset-Table* II, I don't think any woman I haue seen since I came ashore worth fighting for. The philosophical gimcrack I don't value of a cockle-shell. **1785** GROSE *Dict. Vulg. Tongue, Gimcrack* or *jimcrack*, a spruce wench.

4. (See quots. 1785 and 1854.) Now only *dial.*

1766 FRANKLIN *Let.* Wks. 1887 III. 458 There is also a gimcrack corkscrew, which you must get some brother gim-crack to show you the use of. **1785** GROSE *Dict. Vulg. Tongue* s.v., A gimcrack also means a person who has a turn for mechanical contrivances. **1854** MISS BAKER *Northampt. Gloss., Gimcrack*, or *Gimcrank*, an universal mechanic, a Jack of all trades. 'He's quite a gimcrank, he can turn his hand to anything.'

B. *adj.* Trivial, worthless; showy but unsubstantial; trumpery.

1750 CHESTERF. *Lett.* (1792) III. ccxxviii. 91 Your reading should be chiefly hstorical; I do not mean of remote, dark, and fabulous history; still less of jimcrack natural history of fossils, plants [etc.]. **1812** H. & J. SMITH *Rej. Addr., Hampsh. Farmer's Addr.*, You are now (thanks to Mr. Whitbread) got into a large, comfortable house. Not into a gim-crack palace .. but into a plain, honest, homely, industrious, wholesome, brown, brick playhouse. **1837** HOWITT *Rur. Life* II. v. (1862) 140 This gimcrack tenement would be crushed in before the brawny hand of a thief. **1844** ALB. SMITH *Adv. Mr. Ledbury* xxxiii. (1886) 99 Some new gimcrack invention, that was to give ten times the light of ordinary oil. **1874** MICKLETHWAITE *Mod. Par. Churches* 340 The cheap church is generally a gimcrack affair. **1883** *Pall Mall G.* 6 Sept., A veritable battle of Armageddon seems to be impending in Zululand, and the gimcrack arrangement set up .. seems already to have collapsed utterly. **1890** W. C. RUSSELL *Ocean Trag.* I. iv. 70 Soberly clothed, with nothing more jimcrack in the way of finery upon him than a row of brass waistcoat-buttons.

gimcrackery ('dʒɪmkrækərɪ). [f. GIMCRACK *sb.* + -ERY.] Gimcracks collectively.

1779 FRANKLIN *Let.* Wks. 1889 VI. 422, I am glad the enemy have left something of my gimcrackery that is capable of affording you pleasure. You are therefore very welcome to the use of my electrical and pneumatic machines as long as you think proper. **1812** MOORE *Horace, Odes* I. xxxviii, I hate all nick-nackeries, Fricassees, vol-au-vents, puffs and gim-crackeries. **1846** D. JERROLD *Chron. Clovernook* Wks. 1864 IV. 397 The gimcrackery of woe that libels death. **1884** *Times* 14 June 7 Insist on having plain but handsome buildings without the Gimcrackery of modern architecture.

¶ With punning alteration of form (after *crockery*).

1862 THACKERAY *Round. Papers, Notch on Axe* I, In that little back parlour .. there is .. Worcester, Amstel, Nankin and other jimcrockery.

†'**gimcracking,** *vbl. sb. Obs.* [f. GIMCRACK *sb.* + -ING[1].] Dealing in gimcracks. Also *attrib.*

1709 *Brit. Apollo* II. No. 22. 3/1, I .. find now in spight of all Gimcracking Labors, Vert'oso's are Cuckolds as well as their Neighbors. *Ibid.* No. 56. 3/1 For tho' Gimcracking's my chief Labor, I'd fain be thought as wise as Neighbour.

gimcracky ('dʒɪmkrækɪ), *a.* [f. GIMCRACK *sb.* + -Y[1].] Of the nature of a gimcrack.

1820 C. EDWARDS in *Blackw. Mag.* (1824) XVI. 661/1 How the gardens of the Thuilleries were commended to me! —with their .. parterres .. gaudy white statues, and water in basins thirty feet superficial—All so fine prepense, and formal, and well swept and cleaned, and gimcracky. **1860** *All Year Round* No. 74. 571 This cheap looking-glass, a foolish gimcracky sort of article. **1892** MARIANNE NORTH *Recoll. Happy Life* I. 312 A little house full of curiosities, quite under the shade of the Temple Garden, and close to its pretty lake with its gimcracky balustrade.

gime (gaɪm). *dial.* Also gyme. [cf. ON. *gíma* 'a vast opening' (Vigf.); f. Teut. root *gī-: see GANE *v.*] (See quot. 1877.)

1697 A. DE LA PRYME *Diary* (Surtees) 167 It being impossible that such vast waters should be contained in such short and small bounds, it burst a huge gime close by Gore Steel, near Thorn, where there had been a vast gime formerly, and so drounded all the whole Levels. **1877** *N.W. Linc. Gloss., Gyme*, a hole washed out of the ground by the rushing water, when an embankment gives way.

gimew, var. GEMEW, *Obs.*

gimlet ('gɪmlɪt), *sb.*[1] Forms: 5 gym(e)lot, 5–6 gymlet, (6 gymlocke), 7–9 gimblet, 7– gimlet. [a. OF. *guinbelet, guimbelet* (later *guibelet*, mod.F. *gibelet*), a dim. of the word (unrecorded in the Rom. langs.) which appears in Eng. as WIMBLE.]

1. a. A kind of boring-tool (see quot. 1859).

c **1420** LYDG. *Assemb. Gods* 357 Then came the good Bachus .. On hys hede he had a thredebare kendall hood; A gymlot and a fauset thereopon stood. *c* **1440** *Promp. Parv.* 194/2 Gymelot, *penetral.* *c* **1460** J. RUSSELL *Bk. Nurture* 67 A gymlet sharpe to broche & perce sone to turne & twyne. **1530** PALSGR. 188 *Foret*, a gymlet. **1577** HARRISON *England* I. viii. 19/1 in *Holinshed*, The salte rilles .. doe so seperate the one of them from the other, that they resemble the slope course of the cutting part of a skrew or gimlet, in very perfite maner. **1616** B. JONSON *Devil an Ass* I. i, From thence shoot the Bridge, childe, to the Cranes i' the Vintry, And see, there the gimblets, how they make their entry! **1720** DUDLEY in *Phil. Trans.* XXXI. 27 You must also Tap the Tree with a small Gimblet .. so as to draw the Liquor off. **1774** GOLDSM. *Nat. Hist.* (1776) V. 252 Some have affirmed that the animal [the woodpecker] uses its tongue, as a gimblet, to bore with. **1833** MARRYAT *P. Simple* (1863) 158 Six large pieces of iron, about eighteen inches long, with a gimlet at one end of each, and a square at the other, which fitted to a handle. **1859** GWILT *Archit.* (ed. 4) Gloss., *Gimlet*, or perhaps more properly *Gimblet*, a piece of steel of a semi-cylindrical form, hollow on one side, having a cross handle at one end and a worm or screw at the other. **1881** YOUNG *Every Man his own Mechanic* §263. 98 Gimlets are of two kinds, plain and twisted. **1881** H. JAMES *Portr. Lady* liv, She paused, with a gaze like a gimlet.

b. *fig.*

1925 HARDY *Human Shows* 34 In the waves they bore their gimlets of light. **1946** *John Bull* 18 May 14/4 Crowthers was .. a little gimlet of a man with glasses.

c. A cocktail, usu. consisting of gin and lime-juice.

1928 D. B. WESSON *I'll never be Cured* III. 73 The 'Gimlet' we were introduced to .. at the Golf Club: and it proved to be the well and flavorably known ricky, but described as 'gin, a spot of lime, and soda'. **1937** N. COWARD *Present Indicative* IX. 378 Standing about in the ward-room accepting with gracious melancholy 'gimlet' after 'gimlet'. **1953** R. CHANDLER *Long Good-Bye* (1959) iii. 18 A real gimlet is half gin and half Rose's Lime Juice and nothing else.

2. (See quot.)

1769 ELLIS in *Phil. Trans.* LIX. 150 Fig. 5. is the *volvox terebrella*, or the gimblet. This animal .. moves along swiftly, turning itself round as it swims, just as if boring its way.

3. *attrib.* and *Comb.*, as ***gimlet-borer, -maker***; **gimlet-eye,** (*a*) a squint-eye, (*b*) a sharp or piercing eye; hence **gimlet-eyed** *a.*, having a gimlet-eye; **gimlet-hole,** a hole made by a gimlet.

1872–6 VOYLE & STEVENSON *Milit. Dict.* (ed. 3) s.v. *Borer*, A new pattern hand *gimlet borer has been introduced into the service .. to be used instead of the hook borer. **1825** BROCKETT *N.C. Words*, *Gimlick-eye, a squint, vulgo, cock-eye. **1861** HUGHES *Tom Brown at Oxf.* iii, [A] head .. from which one lively little gimlet eye went glancing about. **1894** CROCKETT *Raiders* 238 'What said ye yer name was?' said the old dame again, looking at me with her gimlet eyes. **1752** FOOTE *Taste* I. (1781) 10 She has a Sister at Hampton-Court .. she had but one Eye, indeed, but that was a Piercer .. we were called the *gimlet-ey'd Family. **1785** GROSE *Dict. Vulg. Tongue, Gimblet eyed*, squinting. **1876** *Whitby Gloss., Gimlet-eyed*, squint-eyed or 'swivel-eyed'. **1948** WYNDHAM LEWIS *Let.* 30 Jan. (1963) 429 A gimlet eyed rat steeped in classical learning. **1956** *Observer* 18 Mar. 15/2 'All for Love, or the World Ill Lost' is the message that issues from Shakespeare's gimlet-eyed indictment of Helen and Cressida. **1727** SWIFT *Gulliver* II. ii, A few *gimlet-holes to let in air. **1830** M. DONOVAN *Dom. Econ.* I. 315 The cider .. is to be drawn off the lees by boring a gimlet-hole at the bottom of the cask. **1858** SIMMONDS *Dict. Trade*, **Gimlet-maker, Gimblet-maker.*

Hence '**gimletize** *v. trans.*, to pierce with a gimlet (*nonce-wd.*).

1861 DUTTON COOK *P. Foster's D.* ii, A private detective, ready to peer into anybody's cupboards and gimletise anybody's doors, upon the slightest provocation.

†'**gimlet,** *sb.*[2] *Obs.* Forms: 4 gymlotte, 6 gymley, gymlett, 7 gymblett. [app. an altered form (with substitution of -*lotte*, -LET, for the equivalent -LING) of *gimlin(ge*, KIMLIN.] A large shallow tub, used for salting bacon and for other purposes.

c **1391** *Earl Derby's Exp.* (Camden) 86, j scope et ij gym-lottes, xiijs. j ferdkyn (pr. iiijd.) pro nauibus. *c* **1562** *Richmond. Wills* (Surtees) 163 One showill and one gymley, xijd. **1574** *Ibid.* 251 Two gymletts for salting of fleshe in the larderhouse. **1610** *Althorp MS.* in Simpkinson *Washingtons* App. 7 Itm formes ij, Itm tunnell dishes iij, Itm gymbletts j.

gimlet ('gɪmlɪt), *v.* [f. GIMLET *sb.*[1]]

1. *trans.* To pierce with or as with a gimlet.

1840 DICKENS *Barn. Rudge* xiii, The purple-faced vintner .. stood transfixed, or morally gimleted as it were, to his own wall. **1841** MARRYAT *Poacher* xxxvii, We should rather say .. gimleting, as it were, a hole in your side. **1896** JULOC *Boarding Ho. Remin.* 137 He had dark, piercing black eyes that simply gimleted you.

2. *refl.* To thrust oneself or bore one's way like a gimlet. *nonce-use.*

1842 DE QUINCEY *Pagan Oracles* Wks. 1862 VII. 206 The artist had but to excavate a peck or two of earth with his trowel; a rabbit's burrow was large enough; this he soon improved and widened, using his own body as a gimlet; and very soon he had gimleted himself down amongst the family rats.

3. *Naut.* (See quot.)

1828 WEBSTER, *Gimblet* .. to turn round an anchor by the stock; a motion resembling that of the turning of a gimblet. **1846** in WORCESTER; and in later Dicts.

Hence '**gimleting** *vbl. sb.* and *ppl. a.*

1769 FALCONER *Dict. Marine, Gimbleting*, a term particularly applied to the anchor, to denote the action of turning it round by the stock, so that the motion of the stock appears similar to that of the handle of a gimblet. **1867** in SMYTH *Sailor's Word-bk., Gimbleting.* **1875** MISS BIRD *Sandwich Isl.* (1880) 104 The most persistent, unwinking, gimleting stare I ever saw.

gimlety ('gɪmlɪtɪ), *a.* Also **gimletty.** [f. GIMLET *sb.*[1] + -Y[1].] Of eyes: piercing like a gimlet.

1899 *Daily News* 3 Jan. 5/6 Small, gimlety eyes. **1900** *Ibid.* 3 May 7/2, I can see the black, beady, gimletty, oblique eyes of his opponent glitter. **1919** J. BUCHAN *39 Steps* 13 Small gimlety blue eyes. **1955** *English Digest* June 44/2 Corporal of Horse Pomfret .. subjected us to a dispassionate scrutiny. His gimlety eye fell on me.

gimmal ('dʒɪməl). Forms: 6 **gymell, gemoll,** 6–7 **gimal, gimmall, gim(m)ol,** 7 **gimmoule, jim(m)al,** 7–9 **gymmal(l, gimmal,** (9 **gimmel**). See also GIMBAL. [an altered form of GEMEL.]

1. *Antiq.* A finger-ring (*rarely* an ear-ring) so constructed as to admit of being divided into two (sometimes into three) rings. Also ***gimmal-ring***, † ***ring of gimmals.*** Cf. GEMEL 3.

a **1607** BREWER *Lingua* II. iv, Anamnestes his Page, in a graue Sattin sute Purple .. a Garland of Bayes and Rosemary, a gimmall ring with one linke hanging. **1622** FLETCHER *Beggar's Bush* IV. ii, *Huh.* Sure I should know that Gymmal. *Jac.* 'Tis certain he; I had forgot my ring too. **1641** J. JACKSON *True Evang. T.* III. 199 We must be as a thred, or gimmal ring about their finger to put them in mind of their sin. **1648** HERRICK *Hesper., Jimmall Ring*, Thou sent'st to me a true-love-knot; but I Return'd a ring of jimmals. **1711** J. GREENWOOD *Eng. Gram.* 190 Gimmal .. a doubled or twist'd Ring. **1820** SCOTT *Ivanhoe* xxxiii, The treasure he hath already robbed me of—gold chains and gymmal rings to an unknown value. **1863** SALA *Capt. Dangerous* I. i. 6 Diamond gimmels on skeleton hands.

†**2.** *pl.* Joints, links, connecting parts (in machinery) esp. for transmitting motion (as in clockwork). (Rare in *sing.*) *Obs.*

1598 GOSSON *Trump. War* F 5, Man is compared in the ps[alms] to a watch, he hath a great many gimols appertaining to him to mooue him. **1599** SANDYS *Europæ Spec.* (1632) 168 Their fashion is when their gimmalls are all in tune for a Miracle, to enjoyne [etc.]. **1636** W. SAMSON *Vowbreaker* B, My acts are like the motional gymmalls Fixt in a watch. **1644** DIGBY *Mans Soul* viii. 413 His answeres do not proceed vpon sett gimals or stringes, whereof one being struck, it moueth the rest in a sett order. **1867** SMYTH *Sailor's Word-bk., Gimmel*, any disposition of rings, as links, device of machinery.

†**3.** ? A hinge; = GIMMER 2. *Obs.*

1605 T. HUTTON *Reasons for Refusal* 76 A point that hangs strangely, as it were by gimmols.

†**4.** *pl.* The voussoirs of an arch. *Obs. rare.*

1613–39 I. JONES in Leoni *Palladio's Archit.* (1742) II. 46 The Gimals and Key-stone, is less than the Rustic of the Asler, so as drawing the Asler first all of a height, and then divide the Gimals and key-stone of the Arch drawn to the Center.

†**5.** = GIMBAL 4. *Obs.*

1623 J. TAYLOR (Water P.) *Very Merry Wherry Voy.* Wks. (1630) II. 8/1 An Hostesse with a Tongue As nimble as it had on Gimmols hung. **1793** WOLLASTON in *Phil. Trans.* LXXXIII. 137 The construction of these Ys is peculiar: they hang, as it were, in gimmals.

†**6.** A duet. *Obs. rare.*

1530 PALSGR. 225/1 Gymell song, *jumeau.*

Hence †'**gimmaled,** *ppl. a.* (in 6–7 gymould, jymold), made with gimmals or joints; consisting of two similar parts hinged together.

1596 *Edw. III*, I. ii, Neuer shall .. rust in canker, haue the time to .. lay a side their Iacks of Gymould mayle. **1599** SHAKS. *Hen. V*, IV. ii. 49 And in their pale dull mouthes the Iymold Bitt [*mod. edd.* gimmal bit] Lyes foule with chaw'd-grasse, still and motionlesse.

gimme ('gɪmɪ). Also gi'me. Colloq. contraction of *give me* (occas. of *give it to me*).

1883 [see IDIOTICON]. **1884** 'MARK TWAIN' *Huck. Finn.* v. 44 Don't gimme no sass. **1888** 'R. BOLDREWOOD' *Robbery under Arms* xi. 131 Now gimme some grub, for I've had nothing since sunrise. **1892** KIPLING *Many Invent.* (1893) 163 Gimme a light—gimme a light! **1918** H. G. WELLS *Joan & Peter* viii. 230 'Gimme my cane, someone,' said Mr. Mainwearing. **1923** WODEHOUSE *Adv. Sally* xv. 185 'Will you have a whisky and soda, Uncle Donald?' .. 'Yes,' said his relative... 'Gimme.' **1958** E. NEL *Mr. Churchill's Secretary* ii. 30 If the Prime Minister said 'Gimme Pug' I must fetch General Ismay. *Ibid.*, If he merely stretched out his hand and said 'Gimme' I must place in his hand whatever he needed.

Hence as *sb.*, acquisitiveness; greed; a desire for gifts; freq. *pl.*, in ***to have*** or ***get the gimmes.*** Also *attrib. slang.*

1927 WODEHOUSE *Meet Mr. Mulliner* v. 166 Boy, I use bank-notes for summer underclothing, and I don't care how bad you've got the gimme's if only you'll sign on the dotted line. **1928** *Sunday Dispatch* 2 Sept. 7/3 The vamp .. is what the Americans call a 'Gimme Girl'. **1963** C. MORRIS *I bought Newspaper* ii. 19 One could only write him off as a victim of our acquisitive, thrusting, philosophy of get and 'gimme'.

gimme, obs. form of or mistake for next.

gimmer[1] ('dʒɪmə(r)). *Obs.* exc. *dial.* Forms: 6–9 **jimmer,** (6 ? **gimme,** ? **gymme, jemer, gimer, gimmor, gymmer,** 7 **jemmar**), 6, 9 **gemmer,** (6 **gemmerce** *pl.*), 6– **gimmer.** [Corrupt form of GIMMAL, GEMEW.]

†**1.** = GIMMAL 1. *Obs. rare.*

1570 *Durham Depos.* (Surtees) 234 The said Elizabeth did onc writhe a gimer of[f] this defendants fynger, and put yt upon hir owne.

2. A hinge. *Obs.* exc. *dial.*

c **1520** *Mem. Ripon* (Surtees) III. 206 Item for j par of gemmers to the sayd dorith, 16*d.* **1593** NASHE *Christ's T.* 27 b, The East-gate .. (the dry rusty creeking of whose hookes and gymmes as it was in the opening, might be heard a myle of). **1593** *Rites & Mon. Ch. Durh.* (Surtees) 26 A merveylous lyvelye and bewtifull Immage of the picture of our Ladie .. which picture was maide to open with gymmers [*v.r.* two leaves] from her breaste downd-ward. *Ibid.* 28 Also the fore parte of the said porch .. ther was a dore with two brode leves to open from syde to syde .. which dore did hing all in gymmers, and clasps in the insyde to claspe them.

a **1603** T. CARTWRIGHT *Confut. Rhem. N.T.* (1618) 191 You haue need of some Vulcan to make the gimmers that should hold these together. **1629** GAULE *Holy Madn.* 91 His Cloake displayd (as a Flagge) vpon his arme, his Doublet hanging by Gimmers vpon his shoulders. **1637** GILLESPIE *Eng. Pop. Cerem.* IV. vi. 25 Vulcans owne gimmers could not make his answer and the Bishops to sticke togither. **1674-91** RAY *N.C. Words* 39 *Jimmers*; Jointed Hinges: in other parts called Wing-hinges. **1869** *Lonsdale Gloss.*, *Gemmer, Gimmer*, a small hinge for a closet or desk door.

†**3.** = GIMMAL 2. (Rare in *sing.*) *Obs.*

1591 SHAKS. *1 Hen. VI*, I. ii. 41, I thinke by some odde Gimmors or Deuice Their Armes are set, like Clocks, still to strike on. *a* **1656** BP. HALL *Sel. Thoughts* Wks. 1808 VI. 249 When I saw my precious watch.. taken asunder.. so as here lay a wheel, there the balance; here one gimmer, there another. **1658** GURNALL *Chr. in Arm.* II. xiv. II. xvii. 183 Drest up like a Puppet, in the outward shape of a man, that moves by the jimmers which the workman fastens to it.

transf. and *fig.* *a* **1603** T. CARTWRIGHT *Confut. Rhem. N.T.* (1618) 37 Diuorced.. both from the body and marrow bones of the Popish Masse, as also from the jimmers and trinkets thereof. **1664** POWER *Exp. Philos.* I. 2 His [the Flea's] head, body, and limbs also, be all of blackish armourwork.. with jemmar's, most excellently contrived for the nimble motion of all the parts. **1668** H. MORE *Div. Dial.* I. viii. (1713) 17, I have been prone to conclude with myself that the Gimmers of the World hold together not so much by Geometry as some natural Magick.

Hence †'**gimmer** *v. Obs. rare*$^{-1}$, to furnish with 'gimmers' or joints.

1658 BROMHALL *Treat. Specters* IV. 256 The.. fragments of that brazen Ship being diligently sought up, and gimmer'd and set in their proper places.

gimmer[2] ('gɪmə(r)). *Sc.* and *north. dial.* Forms: 5 **gymbyre, -bure, gymmer,** 6 **gymmar, gylmyr, gimer,** 6- **gimmer.** [a. ON. *gymbr* a ewe lamb one year old (mod.Icel. *gimbur*, Da. *gimmer-lam*); cf. *gymbell* he-lamb.

Ulterior connexions unknown; the vowel of the ON. word seems to forbid the supposition of some etymologists, that it contains some form of the Indogermanic word **gheim-* (*ghjem-, ghim-* etc.) winter, and is thus cognate with Gr. χίμαρος masc., χίμαιρα fem., goat one year old.]

1. A ewe between the first and second shearing. ***gelt gimmer***, a barren ewe.

1424-1549, etc. [see DINMONT]. *c* **1425** *Voc.* in Wr.-Wülcker 638/36 *Hic gargia*, gymbure. *Ibid.* 698/23 *Hec bidua*, gymbyre. **1584** *Vestry Bks.* (Surtees) 18 Item at Shearborne a dinmont, a gimer, & thre lams. **1691** RAY *N.C. Words* 31 A *Gelt-gimmer*, a barren Ew. **1804** SCOTT *Let. to Ellis* 19 May in Lockhart, Long sheep and short sheep and tups and gimmers and hogs and dinmonts had made a perfect sheep fold of my understanding. **1849** H. STEPHENS *Bk. of Farm* (ed. 2) I. 594/2 A young ewe or gimmer is apt to be shy to her first lamb. **1883** *Trans. Highland Soc. Agric.* XV. App. B. 73 Ewes and Gimmers.. in pens of three.

2. 'A contemptuous term for a woman' (Jam.). Also *rarely* for a mare.

[Perh. a different word, formed by association of GAMMER and KIMMER. Cf. '*Gimmer*, a mistress. "My Gimmer always wore those blue and white checked aprons"' (*Kent. Gloss.* 1887).]

a **1774** FERGUSSON *Poems* (1814) II. 15 She round the ingle wi' her gimmers sits, Crammin' their gabbies wi' her nicest bits. **1788** R. GALLOWAY *Poems* 90 The mim-mou'd gimmers them misca'd. **1807** J. STAGG *Poems* 136 See Sawney.. Gallin the gimmer wi' a gad, Tho' leyke a porpoise peighan; He warrant's her soun' win' a' lim', As onny o' the hill. **1893** *Northumbld. Gloss.*, *Gimmer*, a low woman.

3. *attrib.* and *Comb.*, as ***gimmer mutton, -pet***; **gimmer-hog**, a ewe of not more than one year old; **gimmer-lamb**, a female lamb that has not been shorn.

1546 *Wills & Inv. N.C.* (Surtees 1835) 124 It'm I gyff to Yssabyll my dowghter.. v youes or els v *gymmars hoggs. **1870** *Daily News* 6 Dec., Sheep stocks in East Yorkshire.. consist chiefly of breeding ewes and wether and gimmer hogs. **1641** BEST *Farm. Bks.* (Surtees) 2 From lambinge time ..till clippinge time.. they [ewes] are called *gimmer lambes. **1886** *S.W. Linc. Gloss.* s.v., So in Contracts—so many stone of Wether or *Gimmer mutton. **1785** BURNS *Death & Dr. Hornbk.* xxvii, Twa guid *gimmer-pets.

gimmew, gimmon, vars. GEMEW, *Obs.*

gimmick ('gɪmɪk). orig. *U.S. slang.* [Origin unknown, but see quot. 1936.] A gadget; *spec.* a contrivance for dishonestly regulating a gambling game, or an article used in a conjuring trick; now usu. a tricky or ingenious device, gadget, idea, etc., esp. one adopted for the purpose of attracting attention or publicity.

1926 MAINES & GRANT *Wise-Crack Dict.* 8/2 *Gimmick*, device used for making a fair game crooked. **1926** *Amer. Speech* II. 62/1 Every snipe endeavors to impress the poor swabbos with his talk of gillguys, gadgetts, and gimmicks. [**1936** *Words* Nov. 12/2 The word *gimac* means 'a gadget'. It is an anagram of the word *magic*, and is used by magicians the same way as others use the word 'thing-a-ma-bob'.] **1948** J. THURBER *Beast in Me* (1949) 77 The wisecrack and the gag, the leg pull and the hotfoot, the gimmick and the switcheroo. **1951** *Manch. Guardian Weekly* 5 July 3/1 Washington has suspected that a political 'gimmick' might be wrapped up in the Malik offer. **1952** M. MCCARTHY *Groves of Academe* (1953) iv. 70 The perfect college they hinted at might exist on paper but it would never attract students, for it would have no selling-point, no gimmick, as they said in advertising. **1954** *Economist* 21 Aug. 602/1 Completely new 'gimmicks', such as the aerosol can, which is packed under pressure and blows its contents out as required, have opened up new fields for the tin-plate container. **1957** *Observer* 8 Sept. 9/5 Diamond.. is unalarmed by Tory *élan.* His publicity gimmick, a small red diamond, is to be seen all over the city, sometimes stuck up in very curious places. **1958** I. BROWN *Words in our Time* 58 Many comedians have their gimmicks, either as catch-phrase, theme-song, or bit of 'business', which they exploit in most of their appearances. **1959** 'P. QUENTIN' *Shadow of Guilt* xvii. 163 This was his new gimmick, his new device for making himself seem absolutely harmless. **1960** V. NABOKOV *Invitation to Beheading* xii. 122 There are.. all sorts of marvellous gimmicks. I remember, for instance when I was a child, there were objects called '*nonnons*' that were popular. **1969** *Daily Tel.* 1 Mar. 16/3 There is a growing tendency to use sport as a publicity gimmick for business. **1970** *New Society* 5 Mar. 385/2 It's a market that ..boomed briefly in the mid-sixties with gimmicks like paper dresses.

b. *attrib.* and *Comb.*

1953 *Economist* 30 May 595/2 Some of Professor Triffin's colleagues at the conference were innately suspicious of what they called 'gimmick solutions' of this kind. **1958** *Spectator* 14 Feb. 197/1 A weekly devoted to one blind purpose—the promotion of a single, gimmick-geared pattern of love and marriage. **1961** *New Left Rev.* Jan.-Feb. 34/2 The speculators and gimmick-mongers. **1967** *Punch* 29 Mar. 441/2, I am inviting fellow revolutionaries to *refuse* to buy all goods with attached gimmick offers.

Hence '**gimmick** *v. trans.*, to provide with a gimmick; to alter or tamper with; hence ***gimmicked*** ppl. adj.; '**gimmickless** *a.*, devoid of or free from a gimmick or gimmicks; '**gimmick(e)ry**, the use of gimmicks; gimmicks collectively; an abundance of gimmicks; '**gimmicky** *a.*, employing or characterized by gimmicks; designed to attract attention or publicity.

1952 *Astounding Sci. Fiction* Feb. 55, I could gimmick your machine. **1952** *N.Y. Times* 9 Sept. 2/2 Senator Johnson's subcommittee also had attacked what it called excessive 'gimmickery and gadgetry' on today's war-planes. *Ibid.* 26 Oct. VI. 49/1 The Kennedy tea parties are a unique addition to the campaign gimmickry of one of the most spirited and critical Senatorial contests of the year. **1957** *Times* 2 Dec. 7 (Advt.), What I thought I'd do was write a gimmicky ad with a screwy drawing, and people would be bound to read it. **1958** *Observer* 28 Apr. 15/1 A Shakespeare play can be ripped apart by the twin steel claws of naturalism and gimmickry. **1959** *News Chron.* 18 Nov. 6/7 Eisenhower's own favourite speech writer, the master ghost of those gimmicked years. **1959** C. MACINNES *Absolute Beginners* 55 I'm not sure I care for that gimmicky girl. **1962** *Times* 9 Mar. 13/4 To declare oneself gimmickless is in these times to assert straightforward procedure. **1963** *Punch* 16 Oct. 576/2 A good, straight, gimmickless lecture on painting. **1964** *New Statesman* 6 Mar. 354/3 US policy in Vietnam has been a compote of gimmickry, half-truth and self-deception. **1966** I. ASIMOV *Fantastic Voyage* xiii. 151 He knows the ship. He designed it. He can best gimmick its controls. **1970** D. BAGLEY *Running Blind* ix. 202, I wasn't stupid enough to search Slade's luggage... He would have gimmicked it so that he could tell at a glance whether a suitcase had been opened. **1970** *Amat. Photographer* 11 Mar. 27/2, I don't therefore go along with those who condemn elaboration in cameras and projectors as futile gimmickry.

†**gimnasse.** *Obs. rare*$^{-1}$. [anglicized form of GYMNASIUM. Cf. F. *gymnase.*] A gymnasium.

1652 STAPYLTON *Herodian* IV. xxxiii, A Gimnasse [*marg.* An Activity Court] also and a stately Bath He did erect.

gimp, gymp (gɪmp), *sb.*[1] Also 7-9 **guimp.** [Of obscure origin; Du. *gimp* in the same sense appears already in Jacob Cats (died 1660), and so is earlier than our first example of the Eng. word; some mod.Ger. Dicts. have *gimpe, gimpf*; recent Fr. has *guimpe* in this sense. The Eng. word corresponds in meaning nearly to F. *guipure*, f. *guiper* to 'whip' or wrap (a cord, etc.) with thread or silk.]

1. Silk, worsted, or cotton twist with a cord or wire running through it. Now chiefly applied to a kind of trimming made of this (see quot. 1882); sometimes covered with beads or spangles.

1664 J. WILSON *Cheats* II. iv, I have three or four as rich Suits, for Flanders Lace, Gimp, and Embroidery, as any in the Town. *a* **1704** *Compl. Servant-Maid* (ed. 7) 63 Open it betwixt the gimp or over-cast, likewise into every Ilit-hole. *a* **1717** PARNELL *Elegy to an old Beauty* 62 Unmov'd by Tongues, and Sights he walk'd the place, Thro' Tape, Toys, Tinsel, Gimp, Perfume, and Lace. *c* **1800** MISS KNIGHT *Autobiog.* I. 121 To another lady I was in the habit of writing in the millinery style giving descriptions of gimps and ribands. **1874** T. HARDY *Far fr. Madding Crowd* I. xxiv. 271 The military man's spur had become entangled in the gimp which decorated the skirt of her dress. **1881** YOUNG *Ev. Man his own Mechanic* §798 The kneeling stool may be finished with fringe or gimp round the edge. **1882** CAULFEILD & SAWARD *Dict. Needlework*, *Gimp* or *Gymp*, an openwork trimming, used on both dress and furniture, and in coach lace making. It is made of silk, worsted, or cotton twist, having a cord or a wire running through it. The strands are plaited or twisted, so as to form a pattern.

2. A fishing-line composed of silk, etc., bound with wire to strengthen it.

1827 *Blackw. Mag.* XXI. 819 Pass your gymp in at the fish's mouth. **1867** F. FRANCIS *Angling* xiv. (1880) 508 Bright brass gimp is very easily seen by the fish. **1873** G. C. DAVIES *Mount. & Mere* xxiii. 199 The brass wire of the ordinary gorge hook is cut away, and the gimp fastened to the thickest part or shoulder of the lead.

3. In *Lace-making*: The coarser thread which forms the outline of the design (see quot. 1882).

1839 *Penny Cycl.* XIII. 264 [The pattern of lace depends] partly upon the introduction of a thicker thread, called gymp, which is used for the formation of figures, flowers, and other ornaments. **1882** CAULFEILD & SAWARD *Dict. Needlework*, *Gimp*.. is the shiny, or coarse glazed thread used in Honiton and other Pillow Laces, to mark out and slightly raise certain edges of the design, as a substitute for Raised Work.

4. *attrib.*, as ***gimp cord, lace, -machine, -maker, manufacturer, nail, pin, -work***; †also quasi-adj. = 'trimmed with gimp', as ***gimp petticoat.***

1874 T. HARDY *Far fr. Madding Crowd* I. xxiv. 271 The rowel of the spur had.. wound itself among the *gimp cords [of a lady's dress]. **1661** PEPYS *Diary* 9 June, My wife put on her black silk gowne, which is now laced all over with black *gimp lace, as the fashion is. **1875** KNIGHT *Dict. Mech.*, **Gimp-machine*, a narrow-ware loom having devices at the edge of the warp to catch the woof and form loops or patterns, the gimp cords of various sizes being carried by independent shuttles or needles. **1892** *Daily News* 16 Apr. 6/3 The daughter of a *gimp-maker. **1851** in *Illustr. Lond. News* (1854) 5 Aug. 118 *Gimp manufacturer. **1875** KNIGHT *Dict. Mech.*, **Gimp nail*, a small forged nail with a rounded head, used by upholsterers. **1673** DRYDEN *Marr. à la Mode* III. i, Take my *Guimp Petticoat for that truth. **1882** *Worc. Exhib. Catal.* III. 51 *Gimp pins. **1755** *Gimp-work [see GIMP *v.*[2]].

gimp (gɪmp), *sb.*[2] [a. F. *guimpe*, repr. OF. *guimple*, WIMPLE.] A neckerchief or stomacher (worn by a nun).

1747 *Gentl. Mag.* 571/1 Sisters in grey.. with swarms of idle drabs and wenches in gimps, [*Guimps*, a nun's neck-kerchief] dispersed all over the kingdom. **1847** FABER *Life St. Rose of Lima* 152 To prevent them from cutting her habit, her veil, and her gimp.

gimp (gɪmp), *sb.*[3] *slang.* [Origin uncertain.] Courage, 'guts'; 'stuffing' (STUFFING *vbl. sb.* 2 d).

1901 *Munsey's Mag.* XXIV. 567/2 Sort of took the gimp out of you, didn't it? **1906** E. DYSON *Fact'ry 'Ands* xiii. 164 Ther wearer wouldn't have sufficient gimp t' get up off er tack. **1962** J. POTTS *Evil Wish* xii. 159 She didn't even have the gimp to make the break herself.

gimp (gɪmp), *sb.*[4] *slang* (orig. *U.S.*). [Origin uncertain; perh. a corruption of GAMMY *a.* 3.] A cripple; a lame person or leg; a limp. Also as *vb.*, to limp, hobble (1961 in Webster). So '**gimpy** *sb.*, a cripple; *adj.*, lame, crippled.

1925 *Flynn's* 31 Jan. 306/2 *Gimp*, a lame leg. **1925** G. H. MULLIN *Adv. Scholar Tramp* xiii. 194 On the Road a lame man is a gimpy. **1929** *New Yorker* 9 Feb. 38/1 Eat-'em-up Jack McManus would never hit a cripple. He'd just kick a gimp in the good leg and leave him lay. **1931** G. IRWIN *Amer. Tramp & Underworld Slang* 85 *Gimpy*, lame; crippled. **1931** D. RUNYON *Guys & Dolls* (1932) viii. 160 She walks with a gimp in one leg, which is why she is called Madame la Gimp. **1965** J. PHILIPS *Twisted People* iv. 77 Now I know you've got a gimpy leg. **1969** P. CRAIG *Gate of Ivory* (1970) xii. 161, I gimped back on deck.

gimp (dʒɪmp), *v.*[1] *rare* in literary use; *colloq.* in north. and midl. districts. [Of obscure origin; the mod. Dicts. erroneously assign to it the pronunciation (gɪmp), and confuse it with next.] *trans.* To give a scalloped or indented outline to.

1697 A. DE LA PRYME *Diary* (Surtees) 152 [A] woman's bust with the aforesaid strang head-dress on onely a little more waved and gimp'd. **1756** COWPER in *Connoisseur* No. 134 ⁋7 A Trollope or Slammerkin, with treble ruffles to the cuffs, pinked and gymped. **1846** WORCESTER, *Gimp*, to jag; to indent; to denticulate. **1878** *Thompson's Gardener's Assistant* 705 Leaves narrow, beautifully gimped along the margins.

gimp (gɪmp), *v.*[2] [f. GIMP *sb.*[1]]

1. *trans.* To trim with gimp.

1755 SCOTT *Bailey's Dict.*, *Gimp*, to make gimp-work, or to work in gimp. **1881** MISS BRADDON *Asph.* II. 232 Every one of the dresses is.. festooned and fringed and gimped.

2. To 'whip' or twine (wire, or the like) *into* a plait or twist of some softer material.

1885 W. L. CARPENTER *Soap & Candles* 275 The candles were made self-snuffing, by means of plaiting the wick, and 'gimping' strings of wire, or other fibrous material, into the plaits, with the object of bending the wick outwards, so that the end of it should reach the oxidizing part of the flame, and thus be destroyed.

gimp: see JIMP *a.*

†**gimpanado.** *Obs. rare*$^{-1}$.

1593 NASHE *Strange News* To Gentlem. Rdrs., Wks. (Grosart) II. 185 A certayne Theologicall gimpanado, a demie diuine, no higher than a Tailors pressing iron.

gim-peg, var. *gem-peg* (GEM *sb.* 8 d).

†'**gimping.** *rare*$^{-1}$. = GIMP *sb.*[1] 1.

1755 in Fawkes *Odes Anacreon* (1760) 74 Ornament it well with gimping, Flownses, Furbelows, and crimping.

gin (dʒɪn), *sb.*[1] Forms: 3-7 **ginne, gynne,** 3-6 (also 9 in sense 8) **gyn,** 5 **gyne,** (4-5 **gen**), 7 **gynn,** 7-8 **ginn,** 3- **gin.** [Aphetic form of OF. *engin*, ENGINE (q.v.).]

†**1.** Skill, ingenuity. Also in a bad sense: Cunning, craft, artifice (cf. ENGINE 2). ***quaint of gin***: clever in contriving or planning; also of things, curiously contrived. *Obs.*

c **1200** ORMIN 7087 Upwitess swiþe wise, þatt.. unnderrstodenn maniȝwhatt þurrh snoterr gyn bi sterrness. *a* **1250** *Owl & Night.* 765 Mid lutle strengþe þurȝ ginne Castel and burȝ me mai iwinne. *a* **1300** *Fragm. Pop. Sci.* (Wright) 2 Oure Loverd, that al makede i-wis, queynte is of ginne. *a* **1300** *Vox & Wolf* 72 in Hazl. *E.P.P.* I. 60 To one putte wes water inne, That wes i-maked mid grete ginne.

1340-70 *Alisaunder* 1135 Therfore þe Kyng had cast too keepe þat steede, In þat caue craftely enclosed with gynne. c1410 *Chron. Eng.* 180 in Ritson *Metr. Rom.* (1802) II Feole thinges ther beth ynne Craftilich ymad with gynne. c1470 HARDYNG *Chron.* LXVII. viii, By subtelte and his sleyghty gyn.

†2. An instance or product of ingenuity; contrivance, scheme, device. Also a cunning stratagem, artifice, trick (cf. ENGINE 3). *Obs.*

c1205 LAY. 1336 Brutus iherde siggen..of þan ufele ginnen þe cuðen þa mereminnen. a1300 *Floriz & Bl.* 131 Hu he miȝte mid sume ginne His lemman blauncheflur awinne. 1340-70 *Alisaunder* 644 By ginnes of Gemetrie hee ioifully telles Bothe þe date & þe daie. c1380 *Sir Ferumb.* 4352 Wan we buþ wyþ such a gynne þe brigge-ȝates al wyþ-ynne, þan wol y blowe myn horn. c1450 *Cokwolds Daunce* 149 in Hazl. *E.P.P.* I. 44, I wyll asey with a gyne All the cokwolds that here is yn, To knaw them wyll I fond. 1535 STEWART *Cron. Scot.* II. 543 So be no way, be ony wyle or gyn, Withoutin leif mycht no man wyn thairin. 1590 SPENSER *F.Q.* III. vii. 7 The Hag she found, Busie (as seem'd) about some wicked gin. 1650 BULWER *Anthropomet.* Pref., Indeliable tincture; which rub'd in The Gallants doe account their bravest gin. 1723 *Trickology* 16 They have an incurable Itch to intermeddle with their secret and profound Gins.

†b. Loosely used for; Affair, thing.

c1320 *Sir Tristr.* 2867 Her hors apolk stap in þe water her wat ay whare; It was a ferly gin, So heye vnder hir gare It fleiȝe.

3. A mechanical contrivance or device; a machine. (Cf. ENGINE 4.) *Obs.* exc. *arch.*

13.. *E.E. Allit. P.* B. 491 þen watz þer ioy in þat gyn [the ark] & much comfort in þat cofer. c1386 CHAUCER *Sqr.'s T.* 314 Trille another pyn, For ther-in lith theffect of al the gyn. — *Can. Yeom. Prol. & T.* 612 This false gyn Was nat maad ther, but it was maad bifore. c1425 *Seven Sag.* (P.) 2035 To ordayn and dyvyse a gyne, Forto holde the piler upryght. 1610 HEALEY *St. Aug. Citie of God* (1620) 542 He meaneth of all the gins in instruments, it is too tedious to stand reckning them here. 1662 HOBBES *Consid.* (1680) 54 Not every one that brings from beyond Seas a new Gin, or other janty device is therefore a Philosopher. 1820 SHELLEY *Let. to Maria Gisborne* Poet. Wks. (1891) 369/1 To breathe a soul into the iron heart Of some machine portentous, or strange gin.

†b. An instrument, a tool. *Obs.*

13.. *K. Alis.* 607 Neptanabus byhalt his gynne And saide [etc.]. 1570 BILLINGSLEY *Euclid* VI. Introd. 153 Instruments of..drawing huge thinges incredible to the ignorant, and infinite other ginnes. a1616 BEAUM. & FL. *Custom Country* I. i, Yet if you play not faire play and above boord too, I have a foolish gin here [*Rtldg.* Laying his hand upon his sword], I say no more. c1618 FLETCHER *Q. Corinth* III. i, I should curse my fortune Even at the highest to be made the ginne To unscrew a mother's love unto her son. 1624 CAPT. SMITH *Virginia* I. 3 Their Boats are but one great tree..burnt in the forme of a trough with gins and fire.

†c. A spring or similar piece of mechanism.

1592 GREENE *Art Conny Catch.* II. 5 His stirhops are made with vices and gins, that one may put them in a paire of glooues. 1613 BP. ANDREWES 96 *Serm.* (1641) 462 There goeth search and enquiry to it; paines and diligence are requisite; we shall not come thither, with the turning of a ginne. 1616 *Ibid.* 694 Of our selves, to move: not wrought to it, by any gin, or vice, or skrew made by art. 1621 T. WILLIAMSON tr. *Goulart's Wise Vieillard* 49 Idolles, and Statues, which artificially are moued by vises & gynnes.

4. *spec.* A contrivance for catching game, etc.; a snare, net, trap, or the like. (Cf. ENGINE 5 c.)

c1220 *Bestiary* 645 [The hunter] him seluen sit olon, bihalt, Weðer his gin him out biwalt. 1375 BARBOUR *Bruce* II. 576 With his handys quhile he wrocht Gynnys, to tak geddis & salmonys. c1400 MAUNDEV. (Roxb.) xxiii. 105 He may wylde fewle slayne with hawkes and dere slaen with hundes or oþer gynnez. 1484 CAXTON *Fables of Æsop* I. xviii, I am take & bound with this gynne. 1530 PALSGR. 225/1 Gynne to take quayles with, *ronnelle*. 1603 DRAYTON *Heroic. Ep.* I. 120 The little Fishes..With fearefull nibbling flye th' inticing Gin. 1637 HEYWOOD *Dial.* II. Wks. 1874 VI. 115 They onely shall lost labor win, Who seeke to catch an old Fox in a gin. 1664 BUTLER *Hud.* II. iii. 277 He made a Planetary Gin Which Rats would run their own heads in. 1712 ARBUTHNOT *John Bull* III. App. iii, A noose that slipped as glib as a bird-catcher's gin. 1781 CRABBE *Library* Wks. 1834 II. 48 Her subtile gin, that not a fly escapes! 1815 *Sporting Mag.* XLVI. 4 He discovered the defendants setting gins or engines to catch hares. 1879 JEFFERIES *Wild Life in S. Co.* 250 These animals get caught, too, in the gins. *fig.* 1340 *Ayenb.* 28 Hyre guodes to loȝy þe enuious agrayþeþ alle his gynnes. ?a1366 CHAUCER *Rom. Rose* 1620 His gynnes hath he [Love] sett withoute, Ryght for to cacche in his panters These damoysels & bachelers. 1484 CAXTON *Curiall* 2 b, For to make the grete and myghty to falle and ouerthrowe she [Fortune] setteth gladly her gynnes. 1563 *Mirr. Mag., Blacksmith* ii. 7 Caught in gyn wherein is layd no bayt. 1639 FULLER *Holy War* v. x. (1640) 247 Satan, the master juggler, needeth no wires or ginnes to work with, being all ginnes himself. 1677 F. SANDFORD *Geneal. Hist.* 128 So strong was the conceit of a Prophecy of Merlin (that Ginn of Error) That Llewellin should one day possess the Diadem of Brute. 1721 R. KEITH tr. *T. à Kempis' Solil. Soul* x. 174 For many are the Gins for that Soul which loveth to gad abroad. 1763 *Brit. Mag.* IV. 548 Beware the Wheel of Fortune—'tis a gin, You'll lose a dozen times for once you win. 1873 E. J. BRENNAN *Witch of Nemi* 17 That ye may shun the gins that trap to hell.

†5. An engine of torture, the rack. (Cf. ENGINE 5 b.) *Obs.*

a1225 *Leg. Kath.* 1980 þis pinfule gin wes o swuch wise iginet þæt te twa turnden eiðer wiðward oðer. 1526 SKELTON *Magnyf.* 2283, I bequeth hym the gowte and the gyn. 1590 SPENSER *F.Q.* I. v. 35 Typhœus joynts were stretched on a gin. 1592 LODGE *Euphues Shadow* (1883) 14 Trying vanitie in the gin, attyring Vertue with the garland.

†b. A fetter. *Obs.*

1663 BUTLER *Hud.* I. ii. 968 To keep from flaying scourge thy skin, And ancle free from iron gin.

†6. A machine or instrument used in warfare for casting stones or other missiles. (Cf. ENGINE 5.)

1297 R. GLOUC. (Rolls) 11435 Hii þat wiþinne were þe castel wuste vaste Mid arblast and mid oþer ginnes, vaste aȝen hom caste. a1300 *Cursor M.* 9890 (Gött.) þis castel.. may neyhe na warld wiht, Ne na maner gin [*Cott. MS.* engine] of were May cast þar-till it for to dere. c1320 *Cast. Love* 680 He stont on heiȝ roche and sound..þat þer ne mai wone non vuel þing, Ne derue no gynnes castyng. 1387 TREVISA *Higden* (Rolls) IV. 429 Iosephus þrewe out brennynge oyle uppon alle her gynnes and smoot al her gynnes. c1400 *Rom. Rose* 4176 They dredde noon assaut Of gynne, gunne, nor skaffaut. 14.. *Pict. Voc.* in Wr.-Wülcker 784/13 *Hoc mangnalium*, a gyn. 1500-20 DUNBAR *Poems* xlii. 67 Than Bissines the grit gyn bend, Straik doun the top of the foir tour. a1650 *Merline* 1854 in Furniv. *Percy Folio* I. 480 When they to the castle came wylde fyer soone them nume & cast itt in with a gynne.

†7. A device for fastening or securing a door, window, etc.; a bolt, bar, or the like. *Obs.*

a1300 *Cursor M.* 1759 þe windou was wit suilk a gin Men moght it open þat loked wit-in. c1320 *Cast. Love* 803 þe ffoure smale toures abouten..Euerichon wiþ a ȝat wiþ ginne þat may non vuel come þer-inne. ?c1475 *Sqr. lowe Degre* 97 Every wyndowe..On eche syde had there a gynne, Sperde with many a dyvers pynne. 1581 J. BELL *Haddon's Answ. Osor.* 398 b, The barres and gynnes beyng forced backe. 1710 RUDDIMAN *Gloss. to Douglas' Æneis*, *Gyn*, the bolt or lock of a door.

†b. *to know the gin*: to know the way or trick of opening (a door, etc.). *Obs.*

1514 BARCLAY *Cyt. & Uplondyshm.* (Percy Soc.) p. lv, Of our poore houses men soone may knowe the gin So at our pleasure we may go out and in. 1535 STEWART *Cron. Scot.* II. 523 Donewald..knew weill the gyn of euerilk chalmer duir. 16.. *Rattling Roaring Willie* in *Berw. Nat. Club* (1886) 475 Sae weel as I ken the gate, And far better the gin. a1650 *Old Robin of Portingale* 88 in Furniv. *Percy Folio* I. 239 About the Middle time of the Night came 24 good knights in, Sir Gyles he was the formost man, soe well he knew that ginne.

8. a. A mechanical apparatus used for hoisting heavy weights, a crane; now usually a tripod in form, one leg being movable for variations in height, and the other two a certain distance apart, with a winch or drum between them round which the rope is wound.

1447-8 in Willis & Clark *Cambridge* (1886) I. 399 Ropes Barowes gynnes herdelles. 1497 *Naval Acc. Hen. VII* (1896) 91 Resing gynne of xiij peces with apparell. 1512 in Willis & Clark *Cambridge* I. 608 Gynnes, wheles, cables. 1706 PHILLIPS (ed. Kersey), *Gin*..an Engine for raising or lifting up of great Guns. 1769 FALCONER *Dict. Marine* (1789), *Cabre*, a sort of gin, or machine resembling the sheers of a ship. 1779 FORREST *Voy. N. Guinea* 9 She had for a mast an artillery triangle (gin or tripod) made of three stout bamboos. 1788 *Trans. Soc. Arts* VI. 208 The Gin will not hoist it on such soft ground. 1868 KINGLAKE *Crimea* (1877) IV. iii. 60 The cranes, the gins, the engines of all kinds. *fig.* 1651 N. BACON *Disc. Govt. Eng.* II. iii. (1739) 16 The Privy Council of Kings hath been an old Ginn of State, that at a sudden lift could do much to the furthering of the present estate of publick Affairs.

b. *Mining.* An apparatus for hoisting, pumping, etc., usually a drum or windlass worked by horse- or wind-power.

1686 PLOT *Staffordsh.* 148 They draw it [the water] up by Gin..the Gin is always work't by Horses. 1708 J. C. *Compl. Collier* (1845) 23 [The Blast] may tear up your Timber Work and shatter the Gins. 1794 *Nat. Hist.* in *Ann. Reg.* 328 With these ginns or vertical wheels both water and coals were drawn from the pits. 1804 W. TENNANT *Ind. Recreat.* (ed. 2) II. 168 The cattle are not driven in a gin as ours, but retire away from the well, and return to its mouth. 1841 HARTSHORNE *Salop. Antiq.* Gloss., *Gin*, a wooden perpendicular axle, which has arms projecting from its upper part, to which a horse is fastened. A common mode of drawing materials out of a coal-pit when a work is in its infancy. 1862 SMILES *Engineers* III. 9 The gin consists of a large drum placed horizontally round which ropes attached to buckets and corves are wound, which are thus drawn up or sent down the shafts. 1875 KNIGHT *Dict. Mech.*, *Gin*, 2. A pump operated by windmill.

9. A machine for driving piles. ? *Obs.* exc. *U.S.*

1682 [see *gin-boat* in 12 b]. 1828-32 in WEBSTER. 1889 in *Century Dict.*

10. A machine for separating cotton from its seeds. Also called a ***cotton-gin*** (see COTTON *sb.*[1] 10).

1796 [see COTTON *sb.*[1] 10]. 1807 PIKE *Sources Mississ.* (1810) III. App. 22 One of Nolan's men constructed the first cotton gin they ever had in the province. 1817 J. BRADBURY *Trav. Amer.* 271 There are public gins established in almost every part, to which a planter may take his cotton, and have it cleaned and packed. 1854 HOOKER *Himal. Jrnls.* II. xxvi. 237 The cotton is cleansed here, as elsewhere, by a simple gin. 1879 *Cassell's Techn. Educ.* I. 306 A mill, where by means of a peculiar apparatus called a gin, the cotton is separated from them.

11. *Naut.* (See quot. 1867.)

c1860 H. STUART *Seaman's Catech.* 38 Topsail sheets when made of chain are rove through gins instead of quarter blocks. 1867 SMYTH *Sailor's Word-bk.*, *Gin*, a small iron cruciform frame, having a swivel-hook, furnished with an iron sheave, to serve as a pulley for the use of chain in discharging cargo and other purposes. 1882 NARES *Seamanship* (ed. 6) 73 The chain is led through a gin.

12. *attrib.* and *Comb.*, as (senses 8 and 11) ***gin-block, -pulley, -rope, -sheers, -tackle***; (sense 4) ***gin-net, -trap***; (sense 10) ***gin-mill, -roller***.

1875 KNIGHT *Dict. Mech.*, *Gin-block, a tackle block with a hook to swing from the gib of a crane or from the sheer of a gin. 1891 STEVENSON & L. OSBOURNE *Wrecker* (1892) 3 The astute Scotch engineer of the *gin-mill. 1883 *Contemp. Rev.* Sept. 355 He may dexterously and quickly lay a *gin-net. 1888 *Lockwood's Dict. Mech. Engin.*, *Gin Pulley, the pulley of a gin block. 1875 KNIGHT *Dict. Mech.* 969/2 Another [gin] has a roller-knife acting in combination with a *gin-roller. 1497 *Naval Acc. Hen. VII* (1896) 91 *Gynne rope with an hoke of iren. 1547 *Privy Council Acts* (1890) II. 447 Gynne ropes, j coyle. 1879 *Man. Artillery Exerc.* 639 *Gyn sheers, with or without lengthened prypole. 1859 F. A. GRIFFITHS *Artil. Man.* (1862) 317 A *gyn tackle consists of one triple and one double block: the fall is fixed to the double. 1843 *Zoologist* I. 223 A *gin-trap was set.

b. Special comb.: **gin-beam** *Mining* (see quot.); †**gin-boat**, a boat carrying a pile-driver; †**gin-hole**, ? a hole in the ground where a gin (sense 8 or 9) has stood; **gin-horse**, a horse that works a gin (sense 8 b), a mill-horse; **gin-house**, a building where cotton is ginned; **gin-pit** (see quot.); **gin-pump** = GIN *sb.* 8 b; **gin-race, -ring**, the circle or track in which a gin-horse moves; **gin-saw** (see quot.); **gin-wheel**, (*a*) the wheel or drum of a gin used for hoisting, etc.; (*b*) a wheel in a cotton gin.

1883 GRESLEY *Gloss. Coal Mining*, *Gin-beam, a timber cross-bar carrying the pully-wheels over the top of a gin-pit. 1682 J. COLLINS *Salt & Fishery* 21 Of Banking in, and Recovering the Ground. This is to be performed by aid of *Ginn-Boats, to drive into the Mud rows of Trees, and Posts sharpened at the Lower end. 1632 J. TAYLOR (Water P.) *On Thame Isis* B iv, And Sunning locke the groundsill is too high, Besides two *Gin-holes that are very bad And Sunning bridge much need of mending had. 1789 *Trans. Soc. Arts* (ed. 2) II. 217 They are like a parcel of old *gin-horses, that cannot be drove out of their pace. 1794 BURNS *Wks.* II. 435 There is a species of the human genus that I call the gin-horse class..Round and round they go..without an idea or wish beyond their circle. 1828 CARLYLE *Misc.* (1857) I. 240 This orbit may be..the circle of a gin-horse. 1852 MRS. STOWE *Uncle Tom's C.* xxxiv, In an old forsaken room of the *gin-house. 1880 C. R. MARKHAM *Peruv. Bark* 474 The engine-house, gin-house, and ware-houses stand about a hundred yards from the river. 1883 GRESLEY *Gloss. Coal Mining*, *Gin-pit, a shallow mine or pit-shaft..worked by a gin. a1728 WOODWARD *Nat. Hist. Fossils* (1729) I. 165 The *Gin-pump of Mostyn Coal-pits. 1862 SMILES *Engineers* III. 9 Buckets and corves..which are thus drawn up or sent down the shafts by a horse travelling in a circular track or "*gin-race". 1841 HARTSHORNE *Salop. Antiq.* Gloss., *Gin-ring. 1875 KNIGHT *Dict. Mech.*, *Gin-saw, one used in a cotton-gin for drawing the fibers through the grid, leaving the seed in the hopper. 1839 URE *Dict. Arts* 185 This machine moulds 30,000 [bricks] in a day's work of 12 hours, with the help of one horse, yoked to a *gin wheel. 1862 SMILES *Engineers* I. 323 The old methods of the gin-wheel and tub, and the chain pump had been tried. 1875 KNIGHT *Dict. Mech.*, *Gin-wheel*, a wheel in a cotton-gin. It may mean a wheel with curved pointed teeth or claws, which act as the teeth of the usual saws in drawing the fiber through the grid; or the brush-wheel, which cleans the lint from the said wheel or saw.

gin (dʒɪn), *sb.*[2] Also 8 jin. [Abbreviation of GENEVA[1].]

1. a. An ardent spirit distilled from grain or malt; see GENEVA[1] and the note there.

1714 MANDEVILLE *Fab. Bees* (1723) I. 86 The infamous Liquor, the name of which deriv'd from Juniper-Berries in Dutch, is now, by frequent use..from a word of midling length shrunk into a Monosyllable, Intoxicating Gin. 1728 SWIFT *Jrnl. Mod. Lady* Wks. 1755 III. II. 194 Their chatt'ring makes a louder din Than fish-wives o'er a cup of jin. 1738 POPE *Epil. Sat.* I. 130 This..hurls the Thunder of the Laws on Gin [*Note.* A spirituous liquor, the exorbitant use of which had almost destroyed the lowest rank of the People till it was restrained by an act of Parliament in 1736]. 1839 CARLYLE *Chartism* iv. 132 Gin..liquid Madness sold at ten-pence the quartern. 1862 SIR B. BRODIE *Psychol. Inq.* II. iii. 95 It is under the influence of gin and brandy, much more than of beer or wine, that bodily diseases arise. 1875 BUCKLAND *Log-bk.* 85 She was full length, in water as clear as gin.

b. A drink or glass of gin.

1922 JOYCE *Ulysses* 236 A small gin, sir. 1938 C. MORGAN *Flashing Stream* I. i. 54 Time for a gin before they come. 1938 G. GREENE *Brighton Rock* I. i. 5 He only felt his loneliness after his third gin. *Ibid.* III. i. 98 I'll have a gin.

c. *ellipt.* Gin rummy. *colloq.*

1956 E. AMBLER *Night-Comers* viii. 175, I was able to persuade her to..begin another game of gin. 1959 M. DOLINSKY *There is no Silence* i. 5, I was trying to salvage an incredible gin hand.

2. a. *attrib.* and *Comb.*, as ***gin-bottle, -case, -drinker, -riot, -sutler***; ***gin-drinking*** vbl. sb. and ppl. a.; ***gin-smuggling*** vbl. sb.; ***gin-bright, -clear, -sodden, -ward*** adjs.; and in the names of drinks, as ***gin-and-bitters, gin-and-orange, gin-and-tansy, gin-and-tonic, gin-and-water*** (also *attrib.*), ***gin-and-wormwood, gin-cocktail, -fizz, -grog, -punch, -straight, -toddy, -twist***; also ***gin-and-French*** (see FRENCH B. 3).

a1833 J. T. SMITH *Bk. for Rainy Day* (1845) 168 She had taken her morning dose of *gin and bitters. 1835 DICKENS *Sk. Boz* (1836) 2nd Ser. 148 A couple of ladies.., having imbibed the contents of various 'three-outs' of gin and bitters. 1872 RUSKIN *Fors Clav.* xiv. 18 If they had been bad old women they would have wanted gin and bitters for breakfast. 1950 J. CANNAN *Murder Included* i. 5 He himself took a sip of *gin-and-orange. 1865 'ARTEMUS WARD' *Interview w. Pr. Napoleon*, Did he perfoom her bedroom at an onseasonable hour with *gin and tanzy? 1880 *Barman's Man.* 56 [Recipe for making] Gin and Tansy. 1935 S. Box in *Best One-Act Plays of 1935* 56 Waiter! That will be two whiskies, and a *gin and tonic. 1949 J. B. PRIESTLEY *Delight* 29 Just gin and tonic and some potato crisps. 1838 DICKENS *O. Twist* xxxvii, Mr. Bumble..drank his *gin-and-water in silence. 1874 JEFFERIES *Toilers of Field* (1892) 28 Some towns have only what is called a 'gin-and-water' market;

that is, the 'deal' is begun and concluded.. at a inn over a glass of spirits and water. **1894** J. DALE *Round the World* x. 169 He had a full-moon sort of face, with a gin-and-water nose and cod-fish eyes. **1880** *Barman's Man.* 53 [Recipe for] *Gin and Wormwood. **1824** MISS MITFORD *Village* Ser. I. (1863) 102 Our drover could never resist the seduction of the *gin-bottle. **1893** *Westm. Gaz.* 3 June 7/1 The Thames is '*gin-bright', and many of the fish are in a very sickly condition. **1897** MARY KINGSLEY *W. Africa* 474 An empty *gin-case. **1894** *Daily News* 15 Oct. 3/5 The Suffolk Stour is '*gin-clear', and fish are off the feed there. **1852** HAWTHORNE *Blithedale Rom.* xxi. (1883) 520 He..being famous for nothing but *gin-cocktails. **1755** *Man* No. 13 ¶8 She proving a vixen, a gilt, and a *gin-drinker. **1839** CARLYLE *Chartism* ii. 117 The labourer's..unrest, recklessness, *gin-drinking. **1859** LD. LYTTON *Wanderer* (ed. 2) 292 That *gin-drinking hag. **1891** *Month* LXXII. 17 You take your luncheon-snack.. or '*gin-fiz'. **1823** *Blackw. Mag.* XIV. 514 The fumes of last night's *gin-grog. **1857** HUGHES *Tom Brown* I. ix, Flashman had been regaling himself on *gin-punch. **1839** CARLYLE *Chartism* iv. 132 A murky-simmering Tophet, of copperas-fumes, cotton-fuz, *gin-riot, wrath and toil. **1897** MARY KINGSLEY *W. Africa* 278 The prevention of *gin smuggling. **1886** J. K. JEROME *Idle Thoughts* (1889) 83 That dull-eyed *gin-sodden lout. **1880** *Barman's Man.* 57 [Recipe for] *Gin Straight. **1809** W. IRVING *Knickerb.* (1861) 218 A brawny *gin-suttler. **1840** BARHAM *Ingol. Leg.* Ser. I. *Execution* 72 My Lord Tomnoddy is drinking *gin-toddy. **1826** J. WILSON in *Blackw. Mag.* XIX. 395/2 Truth should be like *gin-twist, half and half. **1849** THACKERAY *Pendennis* xxxix, The gin-twist and devilled turkey had no charms for him. **1829** *Edin. Rev.* XLIX. 381 With characteristic sagacity, the legislators, justices, and parsons of the land join together.. to augment the *ginward bias.

b. Special comb.: †**gin-act**, the act of 1736 which, by an increased duty, restrained the sale of gin (cf. 1, quot. 1738); **gin and fog** *colloq.*, a hoarse or broken-down voice; also *attrib.*; **gin and it** (or It), gin and Italian vermouth; **gin-and-Jag(uar)**, colloq. phr. used *attrib.* to denote upper-middle-class people or areas; **gin-berry**, a juniper-berry; **gin-crawl** (see CRAWL *sb.*[1] 1 b); **gin-door** (*nonce-wd.*), the entrance to a gin-palace; **gin-drinker's liver**, 'a term applied to atrophic cirrhosis of the liver, from its frequent cause' (*Syd. Soc. Lex.* 1885); **gin-house** = GIN-SHOP; **gin-liver** = *gin-drinker's liver*; **gin-mill** *U.S.*, a drinking saloon (hence *gin-miller*); **gin rummy** orig. *U.S.*, 'a form of rummy in which a player who has cards that count no more than ten may "knock" in an effort to win the number of points by which his opponent's unmatched cards exceed his own' (D.A.); **gin-soaked** *a.*, soaked in gin; given to drinking large quantities of gin; **gin-spinner**, (*a*) a distiller; (*b*) a dealer in spirituous liquors; **gin-trap** *slang*, the mouth. Also GIN-PALACE, GIN-SHOP, GIN-SLING.

1752 FIELDING *Covent-Garden Jrnl.* No. 49. 1 Of this it is easy to give many instances, particularly in the case of the *gin-act some years ago. **1777** in *Chesterfield's Misc. Wks.* I. 242 Lord Chesterfield's first speech on the Gin act, February 21, 1743. **1907** *Westm. Gaz.* 18 May 7/1, I am badly bored by the man who, having an inclination to murder somebody, walks up and down the stage dissecting his inclination in what is known, I believe, as a '*gin and fog' voice. **1947** C. WITTING *Let X be Murderer* xiii. 133 His voice was of the hoarse variety known as gin-and-fog. **1932** B. WORSLEY-GOUGH *Public Affaires* xiv. 257 As I was sipping my *gin-and-it before lunch. **1933** *Punch* 15 Mar. 289/1 Soothed by many a gin and It. **1960** K. AMIS *Take Girl like You* xix. 229 Her lighter and chocolates and gin-and-its with two cherries on sticks. **1969** *Sunday Tel.* 16 Mar. 3/3 (*headline*) The '*gin and Jag' rebels. *Ibid.*, The working-class boy is a dedicated and motivated student. It is students from the gin-and-Jaguar belt who often lack any sense of what a university is for. **1839** Z. LEONARD *Adv.* (1904) 170 On the South side, where grows a kind of Juniper or Gin shrub, bearing a berry tasting similar to gin. Here we passed the night without any thing to eat except these *gin berries. **1960** *Spectator* 18 Nov. 795/3 People.. will turn and rend you.. if you say you've put a couple of juniper berries in the sauce for the pork chops. Why can't we change juniper.. to gin-berry? **1850** MRS. BROWNING *Poems* II. 191 The *gin-door's oath, that hollowly chinks Guilt upon grief. **1845** BUDD *Dis. Liver* 116 These forms of disease are.. most frequent.. among the poorer classes, many of whom spend great part of their earnings in gin; and for this reason the granular and the hob-nail liver.. has been familiarly termed by English practitioners, the *gin-drinkers' liver. **1848** J. H. NEWMAN *Let.* (1962) XII. 301 The owner of the *Gin House has put off till Monday next to decide whether he will accept £90. **1822–34** *Good's Study Med.* (ed. 4) I. 357 *note*, In what is termed the *gin-liver white lines are seen traversing it. **1872** *Belgravia* Dec. 251 He.. then goes off to rejoin his comrades, to adjourn to the nearest '*gin-mill' where a drink can be had on the sly. **1888** *Voice* (N.Y.) 9 Aug., A social organization named after that *gin-miller and Republican 'boss'. **1941** W. S. MAUGHAM in *Writer's Notebook* (1949) 317 After a good dinner.. she suggests a game of *gin-rummy. **1942** O. NASH *Good Intentions* 49, I love you more than gin rummy is a bore. **1965** M. SPARK *Mandelbaum Gate* vii. 253 She found her playing gin rummy with Ruth Gardnor. **1785** GROSE *Dict. Vulg. Tongue*, **Gin spinner*, a distiller. **1813** *European Mag.* Jan. 69 The distillers, alias Gin Spinners, have.. advanced the price of gin. **1827** EGAN *Anecd. of Turf* 179 Just as she was about to toddle to the gin-spinner's for the ould folks, and lisp out for a quartern of max. **1862** SALA *Accepted Addr.* 186 A strong team of gin-spinners' horses.. led by distillers' draymen. **1899** *Daily News* 15 Apr. 2/1 Lurid accounts of *gin-soaked Africa. **1908** *Daily Chron.* 20 Aug. 4/4 The gin-soaked grandmother. **1827** EGAN *Anecd. of Turf* 67 Never again could.. he feel his ivories loose within his *gin-trap.

gin (dʒɪn), *sb.*[3] *Australian.* Also ginn, jin. [Native word.] A female Australian aboriginal; a native woman or wife.

[**1798** D. COLLINS *Acc. N.S. Wales* 612 *Din*, a woman.] **1827** P. CUNNINGHAM *N.S. Wales* II. 16 He once looked into one of their *gins'* (wives') bags, and found [etc.]. **1831** TYERMAN & BENNET *Voy. & Trav.* II. xxxvii. 166 They [New Holland aborigines] answered.. 'We are poor men; we have no jins'. **1863** BEVERIDGE *Gatherings* 65 The camp where lay last night the youthful Gin. **1885** MRS. C. PRAED *Head Station* 21 The gins, or elder women.. lay basking in the sun.

b. *transf.* A female kangaroo.

1833 BRETON *Excurs. N.S. Wales* 254 The flying gin (gin is the native word for woman or female) is a boomah, and will leave behind every description of dog.

†**gin**, *sb.*[4] *Obs.* Also ginn, jinn. [Appellative use of *Ginn*, a female name (Shaks. *Com. Err.* III. i. 31), prob. = *Jenn, Jenny*.]

1. A female ferret (cf. GILL).

1688 R. HOLME *Armoury* II. 136/1 A Ferret, the Hob the Male, Ginn, or Jinn, the female.

2. *a gin of all trades*, the female equivalent of *Jack of all trades*.

1705 VANBRUGH *Confed.* I. iii, *Dick.* Who is this good Woman? *Flip.* A Gin of all Trades; an old daggling Cheat.

†**gin** (gɪn), *v.*[1] *Obs.* exc. *arch.* Forms: 4, 6–7 **gin**, 4–6 **ginn(e, gynne, (4 gyn)**. *Pa. t. sing.* 3 **gann**, 3, 5 **gane**, 4–7 (9 *arch.*) **gan**, (4 **gen**), 5–6 **ganne**; *plur.* 2 **gunnen**, 3–6 **gan**, (4 **gane**), 3–4 **gonne**, 4 **gonnen**, 3–5 **gun**, 3–4 **gunne**, (5 **gun**), 4–5 **gon**. *Pa. pple.* 3 **gunnen**, 4 **gonnen**. [Aphetic form of BEGIN (in early instances perh. rather of ONGIN); in ME. chiefly used in the pa. t. *gan*, also in the form CAN *v.*[2] In modern archaistic use sometimes written *'gin*.]

1. *intr.* To begin, followed by inf. active, with or without *to*; rarely *for to*. In ME. poetry the pa.t. *gan* was commonly used in a weakened sense, as a mere auxiliary (= the modern *did*) serving to form a periphrastic preterite; the altered form CAN *v.*[2] became, however, more frequent in this use.

a **1200** *Moral Ode* 272 Þo þe.. gunnen here gultes beter and betere lif leden. *c* **1200** ORMIN 3274 He gann þennkenn off himm sellf. **1297** R. GLOUC. (Rolls) 7653 Þer hii gonne abide. *a* **1300** *Cursor M.* 12129 (Gött.) 'O ho!' alle þan gan þai cri. **13..** *K. Alis.* 2540 Feole ascapith and gen to fleon. *c* **1330** *Arth. & Merl.* 1329 That so loude and sore ginneth wepe. *c* **1330** *Amis & Amil.* 1161 To bed thai gun go. **1387** TREVISA *Higden* (Rolls) VI. 203 Þe belles of þe citee gonne to rynge by hem self. *c* **1430** *Hymns Virg.* 56 Seynt iohun þat.. for ihesus loue to deeþ gan goon. *c* **1460** *Play Sacram.* 502 In woodnesse I gynne to wake. *a* **1529** SKELTON *Ware Hauke* 119 This fauconer gan showte. **1575** CHURCHYARD *Chippes* (1817) 91 Like as the bore, his brissels ginnes to shake When hee is chafte. **1581** J. BELL *Haddon's Answ. Osor.* 271 b, This troublesome tempest, which ganne spread itselfe abroad in every coast. **1601** WEEVER *Mirr. Mart.* E vij b, Thus ill at worst doth alway gin to mend. **1611** SHAKS. *Cymb.* II. iii. 23 The Larke at Heauens gate sings And Phœbus gins arise. **1791** COWPER *Retired Cat* 92 He 'gan in haste the drawers explore. **1883** R. W. DIXON *Mano* I. xiv. 13 Forth from that evil house gin they proceed.

b. followed by inf. passive. *rare.*

1579 SPENSER *Sheph. Cal.* Mar. 10 The grasse nowe ginnes to be refresht.

2. *absol.* To begin, commence; to have or make a beginning. Also *to gin at*.

c **1330** R. BRUNNE *Chron.* (1810) 77 Þe flode bigan to gynne, & klosed it [the island] aboute. **1382** WYCLIF *Eccl.* Prol., Heere gynneth the prologe in the boc of Ecclesiastes. *Ibid.* i. *heading*, Heer gynneth the booc. **1430–40** LYDG. *Bochas* Prol. (1544) 20 He.. Ginneth at Adam and endeth at King Iohn. *c* **1590** GREENE *Fr. Bacon* ii. 159 You shall to Henley to cheer up your guests 'Fore supper gin. **1839** BAILEY *Festus* x. (1848) 105 Earth's tale is told in Heaven, Heaven's told in earth. Since either gan one only faith hath been, The faith in God of all.

b. To begin speaking, to speak. *rare*[−1].

13.. *K. Alis.* 3006 Tofore heom alle thus he gan.

3. *trans.* To begin (something).

a **1300** *Cursor M.* 7792 (Gött.) Dauid had gunen a batayl kene. *c* **1330** R. BRUNNE *Chron.* (1810) 167 Þe grete lordes Inglis, þat þe werre had gonnen. *c* **1350** *Will. Palerne* 1929 Now listenes, lef lordes þis lessoun þus i ginne. *c* **1400** *Cato's Mor.* 167 in *Cursor M.* App. iv. 1671 For wisest and mast of maine, ginin childis witte a-gaine, quen þai ar vn-welde. **1591** *Troub. Raigne K. John* (1611) 19, I am bold to make myselfe your Nephew.. And with this Prouerb gin the world anew, Help hands, I haue no lands, Honor is my desire. **1605** SHAKS. *Macb.* I. ii. 25 Whence the Sunne gins his reflection.

gin (dʒɪn), *v.*[2] [f. GIN *sb.*[1]; cf. ENGINE *v.*]

1. *trans.* To catch in a gin or trap, to ensnare.

a **1625** FLETCHER *Nice Valour* III. iii, So, so, the Wood-cock's gin'd; Keep this doore fast, brother. **1781** P. BECKFORD *Hunting* (1802) 340, I would not gin him though —too good a sportsman for that. **1833** CARLYLE *Cagliostro* in *Misc. Ess.* (1888) V. 123 Destiny has her nets round him.. too soon he will be ginned. **1868** G. DUFF *Pol. Surv.* 221 Men are stationed with lassos to gin you dexterously.

2. To remove the seeds of (cotton) with a gin.

1789 *Trans. Soc. Arts* I. 256 It is the easiest of all Cotton to gin. **1863** F. C. BROWN *Supply Cotton fr. India* 10 The latest home-improved gins for ginning cotton. **1879** SIR G. CAMPBELL *White & Black* 157 Northern dealers gin and buy their [negroes'] cotton.

b. *U.S. slang. to gin her up*: to work things up, to make things 'hum', to work hard.

1887 F. FRANCIS Jr. *Saddle & Mocassin* vii. 124 The Apaches were out to beat hell.. And they *were* ginning her up, and making things a bit lively, that's a fact!

Hence **ginned** *ppl. a.* (sense 2), **'ginning** *vbl. sb.* (sense 1). See also GINNING *vbl. sb.*[2]

1825 *Sporting Mag.* XVII. 28 The art of snaring and 'ginning' as it is called. **1883** *Daily News* 11 Oct. 2/7 'Good' machine ginned Broach is raised 1–1*6d.* per lb.

gin (dʒɪn), *v.*[3] *colloq.* [f. GIN *sb.*[2]] *intr.* To drink gin or other intoxicating liquor; to become drunk; usu. with *up*. Hence **'ginned (up)** *a.*, intoxicated.

1894 *Midwinter Appeal* (San Francisco) 17 Feb. 4/5 As for jags, he held that he can gin up when he likes. **1900** W. F. DRANNAN *31 Yrs. on Plains* 121 This man Shewman got pretty well ginned up. **1905** H. A. VACHELL *Hill* iii. 53 They're pretty well ginned-up, I can tell you. **1924** *T. P.'s & Cassell's Weekly* 6 Sept. 631/1 He danced with a good many girls who had whisky breaths. One girl clung to him.. and whispered, 'Hold me up, kid; I'm ginned.' **1964** P. M. HUBBARD *Picture of Millie* x. 103 He always drinks a good deal... I have seen him more or less ginned-up.

gin (gɪn), *prep. Sc.* [= GAIN *prep.* 3, with vowel-shortening due to want of stress.] Against or by (a certain time).

?**17..** *Sweet William* xi. in Motherwell *Minstrelsy* (1827) 309 And gin the morn gin twelve o'clock, Your love shall married be. *a* **1765** *Chield Morice* xxxiv. in Child *Ballads* IV. lxxxiii. (1886) 271/2 This lady she died gin ten o'clock, Lord Barnard died gin twall. **1768** ROSS *Helenore* (1789) 88 Gin night we came unto a gentle place. **1788** E. PICKEN *Poems* 176 The lines, that ye sent owre the lawn.. Gin gloamin hours reek't Eben's haun.

gin (gɪn), *conj. Sc.* and *dial.* [Of obscure origin; app. in some way related to GIF.

One supposition is that *gif* was apprehended as identical with the imperative of GIVE, and that *gin* = *given* was substituted for it. The pa. pple. *given*, used in the absolute construction, comes very close in sense to the hypothetical conj., so that this view is plausible, though lacking confirmation. Some think that the conj. originated from GIN *prep.*]

If; whether.

1674 RAY *N.C. Words* 21 *Gin, gif*: In the old Saxon is Gif, from whence the word If is made. **1724** RAMSAY *Tea-t. Misc.* (1733) I. 23 Fast to the door I rin To see gin ony young spark Will light and venture but in. **1794** BURNS *Collier Laddie* iii, Ye shall gang in gay attire.. Gin ye'll leave your Collier Laddie. **1816** SCOTT *Old Mort.* xliv, Follow me, gin ye please, sir, but tak tent to your feet. **1842** J. D. PHELPS *Collect. Gloucestr.* (Glouc. Gloss.), *Gin*, if. **1864** TENNYSON *North. Farmer* (O.S.) xvii, An' gin I mun doy I mun doy. **1865** G. MACDONALD *A. Forbes* 9 Gin the warst cam' to the warst. **1878** *Cumbld. Gloss.*, Gin ye'll gan I'll gan.

gin, var. GING, *Obs.*

gincracke, obs. form of GIMCRACK.

ginestra (dʒɪ'nɛstrə). [It., = broom.] = BROOM *sb.* 1.

1899 *Daily News* 25 Feb. 5/1 The glorious ginestra, or mountain broom. **1921** *Q. Rev.* Jan. 52 Thou, Fragrant Ginestra, joyful in the wild, Scatterest thy solitary tufts around.

ginet, obs. form of JENNET.

ginet-moil, var. GENET-MOIL, *Obs.*

gineve, obs. f. GNEEVE, an Irish land measure.

†**'ginful**, *a. Obs. rare*[−1]. [f. GIN *sb.*[1] + -FUL.] Guileful, treacherous, deceitful.

1362 LANGL. *P. Pl.* A. XI. 153 Gemetrie and gemensye is gynful of speche.

†**ging**, *sb. Obs.* Forms: 1 **genge**, 2–5 **geng(e**, (4 **geing**, 6 **gin**), 3–6 **gyng(e**, 4–7 **ginge**, 6–7 **ghing**, 3–7 **ging**. Also 1 **ȝegenge**, 2 **i-geng**. [OE. *genge*, ? str. neut., troop, company (also = GONG *sb.*[1]), *latrina*, in which sense it has a wk. gen.pl. *gengena*); corresponding formally to ON. *gengi* success, help, support, value, currency; f. root of GANG *v.* The word in the senses explained below is prob. to be regarded as an abbreviation of the fuller form *ȝegenge*, which etymologically expresses the notion of 'a going together'; cf. *ȝegenga* masc., companion; the ON. word has prob. in like manner lost the OTeut. suffix *ga-* = OE. *ȝe*, Y-.]

1. A company of armed men, a troop, army, host.

a **1100** *O.E. Chron.* an. 1070 Hereward & his genge. **1154** *Ibid.* an. 1138 [Hi] sloghen suithe micel of his genge. *c* **1175** *Lamb. Hom.* 87 God bisencte þa þe pharaon and al his genge. **13..** *K. Alis.* 922 Alisaunder, in the mornyng, Quyk hath armed al his gyng. *c* **1400** *Destr. Troy* 1225 He.. Gedrit all his gynge And his grounde held. *a* **1400–50** *Alexander* 3618 And he was graythid [with] a ging of grekis kniȝtis.

2. The retinue of a great personage; a family, household, train of servants. Also *pl.* One's followers or 'people'; people in general.

c **1205** LAY. 11159 Þa læuedi Ælene.. to Jerusalem wende mid richere genge. *a* **1300** *Cursor M.* 2378 Abram went and wit him loth, His geing, his catel, ilk crot. *c* **1300** *Havelok* 786 Him and his genge wel he fedde. *a* **1330** *Roland & V.* 49 He sende him grace him to slo, Þat had y-wrouȝt so michel wo, & slawe godes ginges. *c* **1400** *Destr. Troy* 2882 He offert onestly in honour of Venus, A gobet of gold, þat gyngys might se. *a* **1400–50** *Alexander* 1648 (Ashm.) Þan gas he furth with his gingis [*MS. Dubl.* gyng] to godis awen temple. **1508** DUNBAR *Test. of A. Kennedy* 98, I will nane haif bot our avne gyng. **1601** MUNDAY *Downf. Earl Huntington* III. i. in Hazl. *Dodsley* VIII. 145 For all your dagger, wert not for your ging, I would knock my whip-stock on your addle-head. *c* **1626** *Dick of Devon* I. ii. in Bullen *O. Pl.* II. 13 The mermaydes of those Seas..when they by Drake And his brave Ginges were ravishd.

3. *gen.* A company; a gang, pack, set, train.

c **1200** ORMIN 3918 Þatt teȝȝre [angels] genge shollde ben Wiþþ gode sawless ekedd. **13..** *E.E. Allit. P.* A. 455 Þat dysplesez none of oure gyng, For ho is quene of cortaysye. *c* **1350** *Will. Palerne* 1600 Þis gaye genge of grece to rome gunne ride. *a* **1400–50** *Alexander* 2435 For-þi bees glad now, all þe gingis ȝe sall na gref haue. **1598** B. JONSON *Ev. Man in Hum.* II. ii, Let mee not liue, an I could not find in my heart to swinge the whole ging of 'hem, one after another. **1627** DRAYTON *Agincourt*, etc. 147 Rollo..Who still led the Rusticke Ging. *a* **1652** BROME *Damoiselle* I. i. Wks. 1873 I. 383 Could I but dream..his youthfull Ghing Could stretch to get him out. *a* **1653** MIDDLETON & ROWLEY *Span. Gipsy* III. i. M.'s Wks. (1885) VI. 161 Welcome, poet, to our ging!

transf. **1642** MILTON *Apol. Smect.* (1851) 274 Proceeding furder I am met with a whole ging of words and phrases not mine.

b. *spec.* The crew of a ship or boat. Cf. GANG.

1594 CAREW *Tasso* (1881) 54 So hardy ging of Marriners forth blowne, In venture to deskry some straungy shore. **1633** T. JAMES *Voy.* 56 The Cock-swaine with his ging, were to goe in the Boate. **1670** COTTON *Espernon* II. VIII. 408 The Ghing of all the Gallies in the Harbour being drawn out every night to water this Cours.

attrib. **1635** J. HAYWARD tr. *Biondi's Banish'd Virg.* 173 Doing himselfe the office of Boatsonne, ghing-captaine.

c. In depreciatory sense: A crew, rabble; rout.

a **1175** *Cott. Hom.* 243 Se forme is se deofel and his igeng. *c* **1325** *Body & Soul* 92 in *Map's Poems* (Camden) 348 Fare awey the foule Swyke ant thi cursede genge. **1592** GREENE *Upst. Courtier* E 2, What a Ging was here gathered together, no doubt Hell is broke loose. **1625** GILL *Sacr. Philos.* II. 173 Ebion, Cerinthus, Photinus, and the rest of that ging. **1659** TORRIANO, *Ciurmatore*, one of the basest crue or ghing.

4. Used to translate L. *gentes*: Nations, heathen.

a **1300** *E.E. Psalter* ii. 8 (Horstm.) Aske ofe me, and .i. to þe sal Giue genge wele mare with-al. *a* **1340** HAMPOLE *Psalter* ii. 1 Whi gnaistid þe genge & þe folke thoght vnnayte thyngs.

† **ging**, *v.*[1] *Obs. rare*[−1]. [Echoic; cf. JINGLE.] *intr.* To jingle, tinkle.

1570 LEVINS *Manip.* 135/34 Ging, *tinnire.*

ging, *v.*[2] *Mining.* ? *Obs. trans.* (See quots.) Hence **'ginging** (*dial.* **gingonin**) *vbl. sb.*

1747 HOOSON *Miner's Dict.*, *Ging up a Shaft.* Where the Oages lye not far of from the Day; in old Shafts, the Miner, by ordinary Timber and Stoprice, or sometimes by Walls from the Top of the Oagues, makes a wary and frugal Shift to support it. **1802** MAWE *Min. Derbysh.* Gloss. (E.D.S.), *Gingonin*, sb., walling up a shaft, instead of timbering, to keep the loose earth from falling. **1824** MANDER *Derbysh. Miners' Gloss.*, *Ging up a Shaft*, that is climbing up a Shaft. [Prob. an erroneous guess.] *Ibid.*, *Ginging a Shaft* is also arching the mouth of an old useless Shaft, which is usually done with stone in order to prevent Cattle falling therein. **1847** in CRAIG. **1883** GRESLEY *Gloss. Coal Mining*, *Ginging*, the walling or lining of a pit-shaft.

gingall, jingall ('dʒɪŋgɔːl). Also gingal, -jal(l, jingal, -gol, -jal(l. [ad. Hind. *janjāl*.] A heavy musket fired from a rest; or a light gun mounted on a swivel, sometimes on a carriage. Used in China and India.

1818 ELPHINSTONE in Sir T. E. COLEBROOK *Life* (1884) II. 31 There is much and good sniping from matchlocks and gingals. **1829** SHIPP *Mem.* III. 40 They fired their long ginjalls, which kill a mile off. **1841** *Ann. Reg.* 253 Exposed to a heavy fire from the guns and gingals [of the Chinese]. **1864** *Daily Tel.* 15 Aug., Your Talookdar..lived in a mud fort, mounted with jingalls and wall-cannon. **1878** W. H. G. KINGSTON *Mate of 'Lily'* iii. 67 We had several on either side of us blazing away with their gingalls.

b. Short for *gingall-ball*.

1879 LOW *Afghan War* i. 100*, I picked up a five pound shot and a six ounce jinjall both of hammered iron.

c. *attrib.*, as *gingall-ball*, *-battery*, *-fire*.

1834 T. MEDWIN *Angler in Wales* II. 57 He fell dead by a 'gingall' ball. **1857** S. OSBORN *Quedah* xv. 201 The gingal battery fired away manfully. **1880** E. OPPERT *Forbid. L.* viii. 255 The barrels, about one foot and a half long, threw a good-sized gingall-ball. **1884** A. FORBES *Chinese Gordon* ii. 47 The gunners were covered from musket and gingall fire by large wooden mantlets.

gingam, obs. form of GINGHAM.

gingambob, obs. form of JIGGAMBOB.

gingbreade, obs. form of GINGERBREAD.

ginge, var. GING, *Obs.*

gingebrar, -bras, etc., obs. ff. GINGERBREAD.

gingebred, Sc. var. GINGERBREAD.

gingell, -el(l)i, -el(l)y, var. JINGLE, GINGILI.

gingel(l)ine, var. GINGERLINE, *Obs.*

ginger ('dʒɪndʒə(r)), *sb.* and *a.*[1] Forms: 1 ȝingiber, ȝingifer(e, 3 gingivere, (3 gingevir, 4 gyngure, gyngyvre), 4–6 gynger(e, 5 gingere, gyngour, gyngevere, (zenzyber, gingivre, -ver, gyngangre, -yre), 4– ginger. [The OE. *ȝingiber*, *ȝingifer(e* are directly a. late L. *gingiber* = the earlier *zingiber(i*, a. Gr. ζιγγίβερις, app. a. Prakrit *siṅgabēra*:—Skr. *çṛṅgavēra*, which has the appearance of a compound of *çṛṅga* horn and *vēra* body, but is supposed by Yule to be an etymologizing perversion (suggested by the antler-like form of the root) of a Dravidian name, a prehistoric form of the Malayalam synonym *inchi-ver* (f. *inchi* root). The ME. forms seem to be readoptions chiefly through OF. *gimgibre*, *gingimbre* (mod.F. *gingembre*) = Pr. *gingibre*, *gingebre*, Sp. *gengibre*, *agengibre*, Pg. *gengivre*, It. *zenzevero*, *zenzero*, *gengero*, *gengiovo*.

Other forms of this widely diffused word are Arab. *zanjabīl* (already in the Koran); MDu. *gengber* (from Sp. or Pg.) whence Du. *gember*; also (with loss of the initial consonant as in Ger. *enzian* from L. *gentiāna*) MHG. *ingewer* (Ger. *ingwer*), MLG. *engewer*, Da. *ingefær*, Sw. *ingefära*.]

A. *sb.*

1. The rhizome of the tropical plant *Zingiber officinale*, remarkable for its hot spicy taste; used when dried and ground in cookery and as a medicine; also preserved in syrup or candied as a sweetmeat. ***black ginger***: the unscraped root, from the E. Indies. ***white ginger***: the scraped root, from Jamaica, often artificially bleached. ***green ginger***: the undried root, usually in preserve.

ginger colombyne (quot. *c* 1460), ginger from Quilon (L. *Columbum*); ***g. valadyne*** and ***g. maydelyn***, mentioned in the same quot., have not been identified.

c **1000** *Sax. Leechd.* II. 56 Wiþ seaðan recels lytel swefl, sweȝles æppel weax ȝingifer. *c* **1205** LAY. 17745 Muchel canele & gingiuere & licoriz he hom lefliche ȝef. *c* **1305** *Land Cokaygne* 73 in *E.E.P.* (1862) 158 Þe rote is gingeuir and galingale. *c* **1366** *Durham MS. Cell. Roll*, In Ginger emp. in villa, xxd. **1398** TREVISA *Barth. De P.R.* XVII. cxcv. (1495) 731 Gynger hyghte Zinziber: and is the rote of an herbe. *c* **1430** *Two Cookery-bks.* I. 21 Þenne take whyte Gyngere, and Galyngale, & Canel fayre y-mynced. *c* **1460** J. RUSSELL *Bk. Nurture* 131 Good gynger colombyne is best to drynke and ete. Gynger valadyne & maydelyn ar not so holsom in mete. **1463** in *Bury Wills* (1850) 40 My silvir forke for grene gyngour. **1562** TURNER *Herbal* II. 90 Ginger is not the roote of pepper as som haue iudged. **1599** BUTTES *Dyets drie Din.* O ij b, Greene Ginger, condite with hony, warmes olde mens bellyes. **1601** SHAKS. *Twel. N.* II. iii. 126 Yes by S. Anne, and Ginger shall bee hotte y' th mouth too. **1611** —— *Wint. T.* IV. iii. 50, I must have..a Race or two of Ginger. **1676** GREW *Anat. Plants, Exper. Luctation* i. §11. 240 Ginger makes a small Bullition with Aqua fortis, only observable by a Glass. **1707** *Lond. Gaz.* No. 4319/3 With Annotto, lower'd to 8*d.* per lb. and Black Ginger to 15*s.* per C. **1769** MRS. RAFFALD *Eng. Housekpr.* (1778) 243 To candy Ginger. **1811** A. T. THOMSON *Lond. Disp.* (1818) 420 Dried ginger has a pungent aromatic odour, and a hot biting taste. **1870** YEATS *Nat. Hist. Comm.* 151 Jamaica ginger is considered to be the best.

2. a. The plant *Zingiber officinale*.

? *a* **1366** CHAUCER *Rom. Rose* 1369 Ther was eek wexing many a spyce..Gingere, and greyn de paradys. **1553** EDEN *Treat. Newe Ind.* (Arb.) 20 Ginger groweth in *Calicut*. **1599** HAKLUYT *Voy.* II. 265 The ginger groweth like vnto our garlike. **1794** MARTYN *Rousseau's Bot.* xi. 118 This order contains several interesting plants, such as ginger, etc. **1879** *Cassell's Techn. Educ.* I. 91 Ginger..is an elegant, reed-like tropical plant.

b. applied to plants of other species.

1838 T. THOMSON *Chem. Org. Bodies* 894 *Amomum granum paradisi.* The fruit of this species of ginger, known by the name of grains of paradise, is used in India. **1866** *Treas. Bot.* 531/2 Amada Ginger, *Curcuma Amada.* Egyptian Ginger, *Colocasia esculenta.* Indian Ginger, *Asarum canadense.* Mango Ginger, *Curcuma Amada.* Wild Ginger, *Asarum canadense.* Wood Ginger, an old name for *Anemone ranunculoides*.

3. *slang.* **a.** *fig.* Mettle, spirit.

1843 HALIBURTON *Attaché* I. xv. 261 Curb him [a horse], talk Yankee to him, and get his ginger up. **1889** A. C. GUNTER *That Frenchman!* xvi, Look at her eyes—see 'em flash now—there's ginger for you! **1890** —— *Miss Nobody of Nowhere* 124 If father objects send him to me, I'll take the ginger out of him in short order!

b. A showy, fast horse.

1825 WESTMACOTT *English Spy* I. 86 If you want to splash along in glory with a ginger. [Explained in a footnote.]

4. *dial.* and *slang.* **a.** A light sandy colour, resembling that of ginger.

1865 DICKENS *Mut. Fr.* I. ii, Mature young gentleman; with..too much ginger in his whiskers. **1889** *N.W. Linc. Gloss.* (ed. 2), *Ginger*, a light red or yellow colour, applied to the hair.

b. A cock with reddish plumage; also, a red-haired or sandy-haired person.

1785 GROSE *Dict. Vulg. Tongue* s.v. *Ginger-pated*, Red cocks are called gingers. **1797** *Sporting Mag.* IX. 338 In cocking, I suppose you will not find a better breed of gingers. **1857** H. AINSWORTH *Spendthrift* xvi. 109 Examining the cocks, and betting with each other..this backing a grey, that a ginger. **1885** in *Eng. Illustr. Mag.* June 605 There is..'Ginger', the red-haired, who [etc.].

5. (*by*) *ginger!*: a mild expletive. *U.S.*

1865 LOWELL *Lett.* (1894) I. 348 There, by ginger! I meant to give the merest hint of a sentiment, and I have gone splash into a moral.

6. *attrib.* and *Comb.* **a.** simple attributive, as ***ginger biscuit***, ***-colour***, ***-cookie***, ***-jar***, ***-root***, ***-sauce***, ***-tea***; **b.** objective, as ***ginger-drinking***, †***-grate***; **c.** parasynthetic and similative, as ***ginger-coloured***, ***-faced***, ***-hackled***, ***-haired***, ***-red*** adjs.

1845 E. ACTON *Mod. Cookery* (ed. 2) xxiii. 519 Cheap *ginger biscuits. **1969** D. GRAY *Murder on Honeymoon* xvi. 98 A plate piled with ginger biscuits. **1552** HULOET, *Gynger coloure, after a whyte russet, *melinus.* **1880** *Harper's Mag.* Mar. 576/1 Aunty'll give you *ginger-cookey this very minute! **1930** J. DOS PASSOS *42nd Parallel* 445 He started to think about the smell of gingercookies. **1894** *Daily News* 10 July 6/2 *Ginger-drinking is also a new form of alcoholomania. **1897** *Ibid.* 30 Sept. 6/3 Mr. Bigelow has nothing but contempt for the '*ginger-faced' Portuguese. **1530** PALSGR. 225/1 *Gynger grate, *ratisseur a gingembre.* **1839** H. AINSWORTH *J. Sheppard* II. xii, Somebody may be on the watch—perhaps that old *ginger-hackled Jew. **1895** *Daily News* 10 Dec. 5/1 She is usually what an old writer calls 'a *ginger-haired hussy'. **1895** *Times* 4 Feb. 4/6 A thousand pounds has been given for a *ginger jar. **1811** *Sporting Mag.* XXXVIII. 63 The cocks are in colour, all alike, what sportsmen call *ginger-red. **1831** J. DAVIES *Manual Mat. Med.* 153 Long pepper and *ginger root. *c* **1460** J. RUSSELL *Bk. Nurture* 537 *Gynger sawce to lambe, to kyd, pigge, or fawn in fere. **1822–34** *Good's Study Med.* (ed. 4) I. 491 The beverage [should] consist chiefly of coffee, *ginger tea and acidulated waters.

d. *attrib.* or as *adj.* Applied to a group, person, etc., which provides the 'ginger', spirit, or stimulus of a party or movement; esp. in ***ginger group***.

1923 G. D. H. COLE *Workshop Organiz.* 37 A 'ginger' organization within the Trade Union movement. **1927** *Punch* 9 Mar. 269/1 The 'ginger group' of Conservative social reformers. **1944** H. CROOME *You've gone Astray* ii. 18 This little ginger group campaigning for better houses. **1958** *Manch. Guardian* 1 Aug. 6/7 (*headline*) Ginger grouper. *Ibid.*, One of a small ginger group of Left-wing Catholics. **1965** *Economist* 29 May 1039/1 The Ministry of Public Building and Works was reorganised into a ginger-ministry designed to co-ordinate Britain's industrial building systems. **1970** *New Society* 5 Feb. 210/2 The appearance of ginger groups to fight specific proposals, is not necessarily a bad thing—particularly if the established bodies aren't prepared to fight.

7. Special comb., as **ginger-ale**, an effervescing beverage flavoured with ginger; **ginger-brandy**, a cordial prepared by steeping bruised ginger in brandy; **ginger-cake**, a cake flavoured with ginger; gingerbread in the form of a cake; †**ginger-comfit** [a. OF. *gingebre confit*], preserved ginger; **ginger-cordial** (see quot.); hence ***ginger-cordial*** vb.; **ginger-fern**, a kind of fern growing in Jamaica; **ginger-grass**, (*a*) *Andropogon Nardus*, an aromatic East Indian grass, yielding an essential oil with a strong smell of ginger; (*b*) *Panicum glutinosum*, a coarse grass of Jamaica; **ginger lily** = *garland-flower* (*b*); **ginger-mad** *a.* ? *nonce-wd.*, hotly excited; **ginger-nob** *slang*, a red-haired person; also, the head of such a person; **ginger-nut** = GINGERBREAD-NUT; **ginger-plant** = GINGER *sb.* 2; see also quot. 1880; **ginger-race**, a root of ginger; **ginger-snap**, (*a*) a thin brittle cake flavoured with ginger, (*b*) (*U.S.*) a hot-tempered person, esp. one with carroty hair; **ginger-spice** = GINGER *sb.* 1; **ginger-suck**, a kind of sweetmeat flavoured with ginger; **ginger-wine**, a popular British wine, made by the fermentation of sugar, water, and bruised ginger (Cassell); **ginger-work** = *gingerbread-work*; **ginger-wort**, the name given by Lindley to the order *Zingiberaceæ*. Also GINGER-BEER, GINGER-POP.

1886 *Advt.*, *Ginger ale. **1894** *Westm. Gaz.* 27 June 8/1 The only time he was ever the worse for liquor was when he indulged in three bottles of a temperance drink called ginger ale. **1864** TOVEY *Brit. & For. Spirits* 284 *Ginger Brandy is the best cordial stomachic that is made. **1771** R. DRUMMOND *Let.* 23 Feb. in *Corr. Garrick* (1831) I. 414, I have sent you the receipt for the *ginger-cakes. **1824** J. PICKERING *Jrnl.* 25 Dec. in *Emigration* (1830) ii. 11, I was presented..with ginger-cake, and a cake with raisins in it, which is their 'Christmas cake'. **1843** W. T. THOMPSON *Major Jones' Courtship* 43 I'm jest as good for old Miss Stallionses consent as a thrip is for a ginger cake. **1936** LUCAS & HUME *Au Petit Cordon Bleu* 172 Ginger cake (A 2-lb. cake). **1334–5** *Gingebr' confit [see COMFIT *sb.* 1]. **1365** *MS. Hostill. Roll, Durham*, Octo coffynz de Anys comfytt genger comfytt et geloffers, viij[s]. **1401–2** *Mem. Ripon* (Surtees) III. 208 In ij unc. gingergumfet et annes, 6*d.* **1882** OGILVIE, **Ginger-cordial*, a liqueur made from raisins, lemon-rind, ginger and water, occasionally strengthened with whisky or brandy. **1853** READE *Chr. Johnstone* xi. 141 Flucker ginger-cordialed him; his sister bewitched him. **1847** GOSSE *Birds Jamaica* 381 Large ponds, in which tall and thick bulrushes densely grow, or masses of the great *ginger-fern. **1864** GRISEBACH *Flora W. Ind.* 784 *Ginger-grass, *Panicum glutinosum.* **1866** *Treas. Bot.* 531/2 *Ginger-grass oil*, an essential oil obtained from *Andropogon Nardus.* **1900** L. H. BAILEY *Cycl. Amer. Hort.* II. 717/2 Hedychium. ..*Ginger Lily. **1926** M. LEINSTER *Dew on Leaf* 8 A sickly odour of ginger-lilies. **1969** 'J. MORRIS' *Fever Grass* xxi. 189 The thick clumps of ginger lilies. **1802** COLERIDGE *Lett.* (1895) 413 The whole kingdom is getting *ginger-mad. **1907** J. MASEFIELD *Tarpaulin Muster* iv. 68 It wouldn't give me no pleasure..to have that *ginger-nob in my chest. **1959** I. & P. OPIE *Lore & Lang. Schoolch.* ix. 170 Red heads attract a barrage of nicknames:..gingernob, [etc.]. **1856** KANE *Arct. Expl.* II. xxviii. 276 Which a good aunt of mine had filled with *ginger-nuts two years before. **1832** *Veg. Subst. Food* 357 The *ginger plant has been cultivated in this country as a stove exotic since..1600. **1880** BRITTEN & HOLLAND *Plant-n.* 206 Ginger-plant, *Tanacetum vulgare.*

1889 LUMHOLTZ *Cannibals* (1890) 297 If the leaves of the ginger-plant are used, they give the food a peculiar piquant flavour. *a* **1659** CLEVELAND *Agst. Ale* iii, That Lover was in pretty Case, That trimm'd thee with a *Ginger-race. **1868** MRS. PHELPS *Gates ajar* xii, P'r'aps I'll have some strawberries too, and some *ginger-snaps. **1530** PALSGR. 225/1 *Ginger spyce, *gingembre*. **1880** BESANT & RICE *Seamy Side* i. 7 'You can't have eaten all that!' 'Every penny, mother—parliament, toffee, and *ginger-suck.' **1857** HUGHES *Tom Brown* I. ii, A 'feast-cake' and a bottle of *ginger or raisin wine. **1614** B. JONSON *Bart. Fair* III. i, Hence with thy basket of Popery, thy nest of Images: and whole legend of *ginger-worke. **1846** LINDLEY *Veg. Kingd.* 166 Formerly the *Gingerworts and Marants were united in one tribe called Canneæ.

B. *adj. dial.* Of hair: Having the colour of ginger. Of a person: Sandy-haired. Of a cock: Having red plumage.

a **1825** FORBY *Voc. E. Anglia*, *Ginger*, of a pale red colour, particularly applied to hair. **1834** T. MEDWIN *Angler in Wales* I. 35, I perceive a fine red or ginger game-cock in the yard. **1886** *Chesh. Gloss.*, *Ginger*, sandy-haired. 'He's a bit ginger.' **1897** *Daily News* 10 Sept. 2/6 Complexion and hair brown, moustache ginger.

'ginger, *a.*[2] *Obs.* exc. *dial.* [Back-formation from GINGERLY.] = GINGERLY *a.* in various senses.

1600 *Hosp. Incur. Fooles* 8 This man is verie ginger, & dangerous of himselfe, vpon his traine of three or foure raggie heeld followers. [*Orig.* Chi và in brodetto e in geladina da se stesso per hauer la coda di quattro scalzi attorno.] **1675** COTTON *Burl. upon Burl., Venus and Cupid* 41 But yet was not the Squelch so ginger, But that I sprain'd my little Finger. **1882** *W. Worc. Gloss.*, *Ginger*, careful, tender, light of touch.

ginger ('dʒɪndʒə(r)), *v.* [f. the sb.]

1. *trans.* To put ginger into (a drink); to flavour with ginger.

1825 [see the *ppl. a.*].

2. To treat a horse with ginger; = FEAGUE *v.* 2 b.

1823 *Spirit Publ. Jrnls.* (1824) 246 A horse has sore legs, Goes on three or four legs, Whether he's ginger'd, Spavin'd, gall'd, or injur'd. **1877** *Daily News* 13 Dec. 2/5 Captain Scot .. did not instruct the defendant to ginger his horses.

b. *fig.* To put mettle or spirit into; to spirit *up*.

1849 DISRAELI 11 Mar. in *Corr. w. Sister* (1886) 221 Whether they were gingered up by the articles in the 'Times' or not I can't say. **1879** *Punch* 22 Mar. 123 It is quite wonderful how dead the House is! It wants something to 'ginger' it. **1897** *Daily News* 20 July 5/1 The Duke is not, to put it mildly, proud, and he cannot apparently be 'gingered' into the semblance of a manly attitude.

Hence **'gingered** *ppl. a.*, **'gingering** *vbl. sb.*

c **1825** *Houlston Tracts* II. No. 47. 8 Thanks to .. Mrs. Pritchard's gingered ale! **1897** *Daily News* 22 Mar. 3/3 The practice of gingering was very common and very cruel. **1897** *Westm. Gaz.* 6 Aug. 3/3 The suffering of the poor gingered screws who go blindfold to their fate.

gingerade (ˌdʒɪndʒə'reɪd). [f. GINGER after *lemonade*.] An aerated drink flavoured with ginger.

1882 in OGILVIE. **1887** *Illustr. Lond. News* 24 Dec. 732 Gingerade is really not the liquor with which roast beef and plum-pudding ought to be associated.

ˌginger-'beer. [f. GINGER + BEER.] **1. a.** An aerated drink made of cream of tartar, lemon juice, sugar, yeast, and water, and flavoured with ginger.

1809 A. SHERO (*title*) [Watt *Bibl. Brit.*] A Practical Treatise on Brewing..; with an Appendix, containing Directions for making Ginger Beer [etc.]. **1813** L. HUNT *Corr.* (1862) I. 87, I am at present trying a composition called ginger-beer, which has all the pleasantness and usefulness of soda-water, without striking cold upon one. **1826** LAMB *Lett.* (1888) II. 149 There's a capital farm-house two thirds of the way to the Lover's Seat, with incomparable plum cake, ginger-beer, etc. **1845** MRS. CARLYLE *Lett.* I. 319 Like a bottle of ginger-beer bursting the cork. **1875** A. R. HOPE *My School-boy Fr.* 136 We had a bottle of ginger-beer each.

attrib. **1838** DICKENS *O. Twist* viii, A candle, stuck in a ginger-beer bottle. **1840** THACKERAY *Gt. Hoggarty Diamond* x, In the beginning of 1824, the Jamaica Ginger Beer Company shut up shop. **1871** MRS. A. EDWARDS *Ought we to visit her?* III. viii. 131 Among the ginger-beer stalls and Aunt Sallies of the back regions.

b. *ginger-beer plant*, a mixture of a yeast (*Saccharomyces pyriformis*) and a bacterium (*Bacillus vermiformis*) used to ferment sugar solution to make ginger-beer.

1892 H. M. WARD (*title*) The ginger-beer plant and the organisms. **1953** J. RAMSBOTTOM *Mushrooms & Toadstools* xviii. 213 The old English Ginger-Beer plant is a globular gelatinous white mass usually about the size of a pea and is used for fermenting sugary fluids.

2. Rhyming slang for 'queer': a homosexual; also as *adj.* Also *ellipt.* as *ginger*.

1959 E. MANNIN *Blue-Eyed Boy* I. i. 14 There were blokes .. that were definitely ginger-beer—that never had a fancy for the opposite sex, but plenty for their own. **1964** C. ROUGVIE *Medal from Pamplona* vii. 91 'There are too many ginger beers in the place.' 'Well, if you don't like queers .. what are you doing here with that fellow?' **1968** A. WILLIAMS *Brotherhood* i. 38 'Unless you prefer ginger.' 'Ginger?' 'Beer, dear.' .. 'You ever meet an Aussie who was queer?'

Hence **ginger'beery** *a.*, resembling the effervescing or 'popping' of gingerbeer.

1852 DICKENS *Househ. Words* 31 July 454/1 A brisk, ginger-beery sort of speech. **1858** —— *Lett.* 23 Aug. (1880) II. 58 He went off in the absurdest little gingerbeery giggle. **1948** J. BETJEMAN *Coll. Poems* (1958) 151 And ginger-beery surf hissed 'Christabel!'

gingerbread ('dʒɪndʒəbrɛd). Forms: α. 3 gingebrar, 4 -bras. β. 4 gingebreed, gyngebrede, 5, 8–9 *Sc.* gingebred, 6 gingbreade, gynbred. γ. 5 gyngerbrede, 6– gingerbread. [ad. OF. *gingembras*, *gingimbrat* (whence MDu. *gingebraes*, *-baers*, late ON. *gingibráð*, in Dicts. erron. *-brauð*) preserved ginger, ad. med.L. **gingi(m)brāt-um*, neut. ppl. a. (perh. in pharmaceutical use for some medicinal preparation; Du Cange has the form *gingibretum*), f. med.Lat. *gingiber* GINGER. The 3rd syllable was early confounded with *bread*, and the insertion of an *r* in the 2nd syllable completed the semblance of a compound word.]

1. †**a.** In early examples app.: Preserved ginger. **b.** From the 15th c. onwards: A kind of plain cake, compounded with treacle, and highly flavoured with ginger. Formerly made into shapes of men, animals, letters of the alphabet, etc., which were often gilded.

1299 *Durham MS. Burs. Roll*, In ij Gurdis de Gingebrar, xxvjs. viijd. **1302–3** *Ibid.*, In vij pixidibus de Gingebras. **1352–3** *Ibid.*, Et in duabus copulis de Pynyonade et de Gyngebrede. *c* **1386** CHAUCER *Sir Thopas* 142 They sette hym Roial spicerye And Gyngebreed. *c* **1430** *Two Cookery-bks.* I. 35 Gyngerbrede. Take a quart of hony .. Safroun, pouder Pepir .. gratyd Brede [etc.; ginger is not mentioned]. **1555** MACHYN *Diary* 99 Dyssys of spyssys and frut, as marmelad, gynbred. **1573–80** BARET *Alv.* C. 10 A kinde of cake or paste made to comfort the stomacke: ginger bread, *mustaceum*. **1613** BEAUM. & FL. *Coxcomb* IV. vii, Fetch two or three grating loaves out of the kitching, to make gingerbread of. **1663** BUTLER *Hud.* I. ii. 546 Some cry'd the Covenant instead Of Pudding-pies and Ginger-bread. **1708** W. KING *Cookery* 346 The enticing gold of ginger-bread. **1771** SMOLLETT *Humph. Cl.* 3 June, She don't yet know her letters .. but I will bring her the A B C in gingerbread. **1782** COWPER *Table T.* 555 As if the poet, purposing to wed, Should carve himself a wife in ginger-bread. **1795** *Times* 27 Oct. 3/1 Several young Gentlemen of the Guards .. have sent for the Alphabet, in gingerbread. **1833** MARRYAT *P. Simple* ix, The white tents and booths, the sun shining so bright, and the shining gilt gingerbread. **1851** MAYHEW *Lond. Lab.* I. 200 The principal .. toy ginger-bread that is vended is the 'cock in breeches'; a formidable looking bird, with his nether garments of gold. **1886** J. K. JEROME *Idle Thoughts* 158 Our boyish days look very merry to us now, all nutting, hoop, and gingerbread.

2. *fig.*, esp. as the type of something showy and unsubstantial. †*knight, lord, man of gingerbread* (obs.): app. terms of burlesque or ironical laudation. *cake and gingerbread*: something easy and pleasant. *to take the gilt off the gingerbread*: to deprive something of its attractive qualities.

1605 *Tryall Chev.* IV. i. in Bullen *O. Pl.* III. 326 *Anticke*; thou lyest: and thou wert a knight of ginger-bread I am no Anticke. **1664** J. WILSON *Cheats* IV. v, If I marrie, I promise you it shall not be Tyro, 'Tis such a piece of Ginger-bread! **1690** CROWNE *Eng. Friar* II, Oh! lead me to her, Ile behave my self like any Ginger-bread. **1763** CHURCHILL *Ghost* IV. Poems I. 311 Who, quite a man of Gingerbread, Savour'd in talk, in dress and phyz, More of another world than this. **1789** WOLCOT (P. Pindar) *Ep. to falling Minist.* Wks. 1812 II. 125 Those Lords of Gingerbread, a gaudy crew. **1841** LEVER *C. O'Malley* vi. 32 The marshalling a room full of mandarins was 'cake and gingerbread' to ushering a Galway party in to dinner. **1884** *Pall Mall G.* 9 Sept. 3/2 By the time the Germans have undertaken one or two of those punitive police expeditions .. a good deal of gilt will be rubbed off the gingerbread with which they are at present so overjoyed.

3. a. A local name for a kind of ironstone (see quot. 1829). **b.** A local (Sc.) name for a kind of tansy.

1829 GLOVER *Hist. Derby* I. 61 Ironstone, in finger-shaped nodules, consisting of concentric laminæ (Gingerbread). **1882** *Proc. Berw. Nat. Club* IX. 461 The Rev. I. F. Bigge found .. a form of the common tansy with much subdivided foliage .. In Scotland it is called 'gingerbread'.

4. *slang.* Money.

a **1700** in B. E. *Dict. Cant. Crew.* **1785** in GROSE *Dict. Vulg. Tongue.* **1834** H. AINSWORTH *Rookwood* II. III. v. 362 Your old dad, Sir Piers .. had the gingerbread, that I know. **1864** *Standard* 13 Dec. 3/2 We do not find .. the word 'gingerbread' used for money, as we have heard it both before and within the last six months.

5. *attrib.* and *Comb.* **a.** simple attributive, as *gingerbread-cake*, *-dog*, *-horse*, *-letter*, *-nut*, *-stand*, †*-temse*. **b.** objective, as *gingerbread-baker*. **c.** similative, as *gingerbread-complexion*; *gingerbread-gilt* adj. Also **gingerbread-nut**, a small round button-like cake of gingerbread; †**gingerbread-office**, a privy; **gingerbread-palm**, **gingerbread-tree**, (*a*) = DOUM-PALM; (*b*) *Parinarium macrophyllum*, a West African fruit-tree with a farinaceous fruit; **gingerbread-plum**, the fruit of *Parinarium macrophyllum*; also the tree itself; **gingerbread-trap** (*slang*), the mouth.

1760 FOOTE *Minor* I. Wks. 1799 I. 236 A patriot *gingerbread-baker from the Borough. **1855** MOTLEY *Dutch Rep.* (1861) III. 290 A man .. eminent both as a gingerbread baker and a sword-player. **1737** WESLEY *Wks.* (1872) I. 68 Having had no food all day, except a *gingerbread cake. **1839–40** W. IRVING *Wolfert's R.* (1855) 26 He was of a large frame, a *ginger-bread complexion, strong features. **1841–4** EMERSON *Ess.*, *Nature* Wks. (Bohn) I. 23 The child .. abandoned to a .. lead dragoon, or a *gingerbread dog. **1855** *Cornwall* 63 Stiff Madonnas with *gingerbread-gilt aureoles. **1844** EMERSON *Misc. Papers*, *Tantalus* Wks. (Bohn) III. 319 A gilt *gingerbread horse. **1769** *Public Advertiser* 15 Sept. 3/4 Go to the Nursery, and there teach little Misses to read *Gingerbread Letters. **1775** J. JEKYLL *Corr.* (1894) 38 We .. beg the receipt of your *gingerbread nuts. **1859** JEPHSON *Brittany* xvi. 271 Country-people .. were playing at a sort of roulette for gingerbread-nuts and macaroons. *a* **1643** W. CARTWRIGHT *Lady-Errant* v. i, There's no great need of souldiers; their Camp's No larger than a *Ginger-bread-office. **1863** SPEKE *Discov. Nile* v. 101 The rich flat district of Mininga, where the *gingerbread-palm grows abundantly. **1824** J. SABINE *Edible Fruits of Sierra Leone* in *Trans. Hort. Soc.* V. 452 *Gingerbread Plum, *Parinarium macrophyllum*. **1780–1808** MAYNE *Siller Gun* II. xvii, Craems, *ginge-bread-stawns .. And raree-shows, Entic'd young sparks to entertain And treat their joes. *c* **1562** *Richmond Wills* (Surtees 1853) 163 One *gynger breade tempes, vjd. **1865** DICKENS *Mut. Fr.* I. v, To bait his *gingerbread-trap. **1829** LOUDON *Encycl. Plants* 298 *Parinarium macrophyllum*, *Gingerbread Tree. **1866** *Treas. Bot.* 531/2.

6. *attrib.* passing into *adj.*: Resembling the figures made of (gilt) gingerbread; hence, showy, tawdry. *gingerbread work*: orig. applied by sailors to the carved and gilded decorations of a ship; hence to architectural or other ornament of a gaudy and tasteless kind; cf. *ginger-work* (GINGER *sb.* 7).

1748 SMOLLETT *R. Random* III, Lookee .. if you come athwart me, 'ware your gingerbread-work; I'll be foul of your quarter, d——n me. **1766** —— *Trav.* Let. xxx. II. 104 Yet the rooms are too small, and too much decorated with carving and gilding, which is a kind of gingerbread work. **1804** *Naval Chron.* XI. 408 As the sailors term it, there is an abundance of gingerbread work. **1807** SIR R. WILSON *Jrnl.* 9 July in *Life* (1862) II. viii. 302 Marshals of France; but disguised by their gingerbread clothes. **1807–8** W. IRVING *Salmag.* ii. (1811) I. 38 Two of those strapping heroes of the theatre, who figure in the retinues of our ginger-bread kings and queens. *Ibid.* v. 87 The gingerbread finery of a sword-belt. **1813** HODGSON & LAIRD *Beaut. Eng. & Wales* XII. I. 89 Little remains of this ancient bulwark except a strong gate-way. the approach to which has been lately flanked with bastions, in the true gingerbread style. **1816** J. GILCHRIST *Philos. Etym.* 197 Such paste-board, gingerbread fortifications of the *Monkish Theory*. **1826** in Cobbett *Rur. Rides* (1885) II. 105 New gingerbread 'places of worship', as they are called. **1833** LAMB *Lett.* (1888) II. 286 What can make her so fond of a gingerbread watch? **1836** T. HOOK *G. Gurney* ii, Gingerbread pantomimes, culled from Mother Bunch. **1840** R. H. DANA *Bef. Mast* xxii. 66 There was no foolish gilding and gingerbread work to take the eye of landsmen and passengers. **1870** H. MEADE *N. Zealand* 289 A gingerbread stockade of posts and coral. **1873** MRS. WHITNEY *Other Girls* vi. (1876) 97 A little enticing gingerbread work about the eaves and porch. **1874** LISLE CARR *Jud. Gwynne* I. i. 38 Some people would have crammed it full of gingerbread upholstery, all gilt and gawdy.

Hence **'gingerbread** *v. trans.*, to provide gingerbread for; in quot. *fig.* **'gingerbready** *a.*, (*a*) of or pertaining to gingerbread; (*b*) gingerbread-like, in a trivial and showy style.

1844 TUPPER *Heart* xiii. 135 His distant relative's good feeling .. served indeed to gild the future, but did not avail to gingerbread the present. **1867** MOTLEY *Corr.* 19 Sept. (1889) II. 292 But it is altogether too smart, gilt gingerbready, for my taste. **1881** WHITEHEAD *Hops* 70 The peculiar sweet gingerbready smell. **1883** *World* 3 Oct. 14/1 A monument to the Duke, which is the most gingerbready and *rococo* thing in Europe.

ginge'rette. [f. GINGER *sb.* + -ETTE.] An effervescing beverage resembling gingerade.

1895 *Advance* (Chicago) 31 Oct. 632/1 The ladies fanned themselves and lemonade and gingerette were passed.

gingerish ('dʒɪndʒərɪʃ), *a.* [f. GINGER *a.*[1] + -ISH.] Somewhat ginger in colour.

1910 W. DE LA MARE *Three Mulla-Mulgars* 85 In this tree grows a small round, gingerish nut. **1959** *Listener* 23 July 129/1 A gingerish moustache.

†**'gingerline.** Also 7 gingel(l)ine, gingioline. [app. a perversion (after GINGER) of It. *giuggiolino* of similar meaning; a transferred use of *giuggiolino* GINGILI.] The name of a colour; ginger colour. Also *attrib.*

1611 FLORIO, *Zalolino*, a kind of colour, which some take to be the gingerline colour. **1626** MIDDLETON *Anything for Quiet Life* II. ii, Your Nutmeg hue, or Gingerline. **1657** R. LIGON *Barbadoes* (1673) 83 Sky colour, and Orange tawny, Gridaline, and Gingeline, white and Philyamort. **1666** DAVIES *Caribby Isl.* 255 Other colours, as Black, White, Chestnut, Gingioline, Blew.

'gingerliness. [f. GINGERLY *a.* + -NESS.] The quality of being gingerly.

Misprinted *gingerness* in the 1585 ed. of Stubbes, whence this erroneous form appears in Latham (who took it from Abp. Trench) and in later Dicts.

1583 STUBBES *Anat. Abus.* I. (1879) 78 Their minsednes in woords and speaches, their gingerlynes in trippinge on toes like yong goats [etc.]. **1884** A. FORBES in *Eng. Illustr. Mag.* Dec. 148 The day came it could go no further, and then it let itself down with all its wonted gingerliness.

gingerly ('dʒɪndʒəlɪ), *adv.* and *a.* [f. **ginger* (of obscure origin) + -LY[2]; the adj. appears a few years later than the adv., and may possibly be derived from it.

It seems conceivable that *ginger-* may represent an adoption of OF. *gensor* (*gentchur*, *gentior*, *genzor*, etc.), properly the comparative of *gent*, GENT *a.*, but used also as a positive, 'pretty, delicate'. The form presents no difficulty, as the word would naturally be assimilated to GINGER *sb.* The sense of the OF. word agrees closely with that of *gingerly* in the earliest examples both as adj. and as adv., though the Eng. word was almost entirely confined to one specific application (perh. as a techical term in dancing), which easily developed into a sense very remote from that of the suggested etymon.

It does not appear that any other plausible conjecture has yet been offered. The usual comparison of Sw. dial. *gingla*, *gängla*, to totter, is inadmissible, both on account of the sound (dʒ) instead of (g) in both syllables of the Eng. word, and for other reasons; and derivation from GINGER *sb.* would not account for the 16th c. sense.]

A. *adv.* †**a.** In early use: Elegantly, daintily. Chiefly with reference to walking or dancing: With small elegant steps. (Originally in favourable or neutral sense, but subsequently with reproachful implication: Mincingly, effeminately.)

1519 *Interlude Four Elem.* (Percy Soc.) 49 And I can daunce it gyngerly. **1523** SKELTON *Garl. Laurel* 1203 With, Gingirly, go gingerly! her tayle was made of hay; Go she neuer so gingirly, her honesty is gone away. **1530** PALSGR. 836/1 Gyngerly, *a pas menu*, as *allez a pas menu*, *ma fille.* **1577** HANMER *Eccl. Hist.* 90 It is seemly for a Prophete neatly to pyncke and gingerly to sett forthe himselfe? **1583** STUBBES *Anat. Abus.* II. (1882) 33 Their dansing minions, that minse it ful gingerlie..tripping like gotes, that an egge would not brek vnder their feet. **1607** J. WEBSTER *Westward Ho* II. ii, Oh! she lookes so sugredly, so simpringly, so gingerly, so amarously, so amiably..Shees..such an intycing shee-witch.

b. From the 17th c. recorded with application to bodily movements or manipulation in general: With extreme caution, so as to avoid making a noise, hurting oneself, or injuring something touched or trodden upon; also, with the appearance of reluctance or distaste (as in handling some disagreeable object).

1607 R. C. tr. *Estienne's World of Wond.* 350 He tooke off the taffata very gingerly wherein the coffer was wrapped. **1624** MASSINGER *Parl. Love* v. i. Wks. (1805) II. 307 Prithee, gentle officer, Handle me gingerly, or I fall to pieces. **1647** TRAPP *Comm. Eph.* iii. 15 And when we walk, to tread gingerly, step warily. **1667** PEPYS *Diary* 3 July, But Lord! How gingerly he answered it. **1762** STERNE *Tr. Shandy* V. v, My mother was going very gingerly in the dark along the passage as my uncle Toby pronounced the word wife. **1768-74** TUCKER *Lt. Nat.* (1852) II. 123 It must be handled gingerly at first, or we shall run a hazard of cutting ourselves. **1825** LAMB *Refl. in Pillory*, Ketch, my good fellow..adjust this new collar to my neck gingerly. I am not used to these wooden cravats. **1837** DISRAELI *Venetia* II. ii, She held a taper in her hand, and came tripping gingerly in. **1851** W. COLLINS *Rambles beyond Railw.* i. (1852) 3 Touch him gingerly, or he will fall to pieces. **1871** CARLYLE in *Mrs. Carlyle's Lett.* I. 14 About July I cautiously, gingerly, stept up to the affair again. **1885** STEVENSON *Dynamiter* 191 [He] gingerly transported the explosive to the far end of the apartment. **1891** BARING-GOULD *In Troubadour-Land* xvi. 230 The boats..are all flat-bottomed, and the men have to row gingerly, lest their oars strike the bottom.

B. *adj.* †**a.** Of persons and their movements: Dainty, delicate (*obs.*). **b.** Of manner of walking or handling: Extremely cautious or wary; showing fear of making a noise, hurting oneself, or injuring what is touched or trodden upon.

1533 UDALL *Flowers Lat. Speak.* 99 We staye and prolonge our goinge with a nyce or tendre and softe, delicate, or gingerly pace [L. *tenero ac molli passu*]. **1563** *Jack Jugler* (Roxb. 1820) 9 We vse to call her at home, dame Coye A pretie gingerlie pice, god saue her and saint Loye. **1573** G. HARVEY *Letter-bk.* (Camden) 115 All ye rest of my trimmest, tricksiest, gingerliest ioyes. **1611** COTGR. s.v. *Larron, Pas de larron*, a gingerlie tread. **1754** J. SHEBBEARE *Matrimony* (1766) II. 223 Like those Ladies who affect to shew all the World they are accustom'd to a Coach, by their gingerly Stepping. **1862** MRS. H. WOOD *Mrs. Hallib.* II. ix, Tim treading with gingerly feet past his own door. **1871** L. STEPHEN *Playgr. Europe* iv. (1894) 103 We crept along in as gingerly a fashion as might be. **1876** MISS BRADDON *J. Haggard's Dau.* I. 187 Taking up the soft flaxen tresses in a gingerly manner. **1887** *Chr. World* 24 Jan. 53/3 Told in the most mincing and gingerly fashion.

[**gingerness**: a spurious word; see GINGERLINESS.]

gingerous ('dʒɪndʒərəs), *a.* [f. GINGER + -OUS.] Of hair: Ginger-coloured, sandy.

1865 DICKENS *Mut. Fr.* I. x, Mr. Lammle takes his gingerous whiskers in his left hand, and..frowns furtively at his beloved, out of a thick gingerous bush.

ˌginger-ˈpop. [f. GINGER + POP *sb.*[1]]

1. A colloquial term for GINGER-BEER I.

1827 *Blackw. Mag.* XXI. 829 Sauterne, swizzle, imperial, ginger-pop, soda-water, or lemonade. **1852** R. S. SURTEES *Sponge's Sp. Tour* ix. (1893) 44 Champagne, which went 'pop, pop, popping—and bang, bang, banging', just as ginger-pop goes between the acts on a hot night at a theatre. **1882** *Society* 11 Nov. 22/2 Let..the toasts be drunk in filtered water, or, at most, 'ginger-pop'.

Comb. **1859** CORNWALLIS *New World* I. 5, Two ginger-pop looking fountains playing with a most sickly effort.

2. *slang.* A policeman.

1887 'DAGONET' in *Referee* 6 Nov. 7/3 Ere her bull-dog I could stop, She had called a 'ginger-pop'.

gingery ('dʒɪndʒərɪ), *a.* [f. GINGER + -Y[1].] **a.** Of the complexion or hair: Ginger-coloured, sandy. **b.** Spiced with ginger, hot-spiced; in quots. *fig.*

a. **1852** DICKENS *Bleak Ho.* xix, The very learned gentleman who has cooled the natural heat of his gingery complexion in pools and fountains of law. **1879** MISS BRADDON *Clov. Foot* iv. 41 The landlady was a lean-looking widow, with a false front of gingery curls.

b. **1894** *Columbus* (Ohio) *Disp.* 3 Oct., The reply filed this morning is gingery. **1896** *Daily News* 7 Jan. 4/7 The copy sent from the central office is said to be 'gingery' and 'snappy'.

gingham ('gɪŋəm). Also 7 **gingam**, 8 **ginghem**, **guingam**. [a. F. *guingan*, *guingamp* = Sp. *guinga*, *guingon*, Pg. *guingão*, It. *gingano*, *ghingano*, *guingano*, Du. *ging(g)ang*, Ger., Da., Sw. *gingang*, ultimately a. Malay *ginggang* gingham, originally an adj. meaning 'striped'. See C. P. G. Scott *Malayan Words in English*, 1897.]

1. A kind of cotton or linen cloth, woven of dyed yarn, often in stripes, checks, and other patterns. In *pl.* fabrics of this kind.

1615 COPPINDALL *Let.* in *Cocks' Diary* (Hakluyt Soc.) II. App. 272 Capt. Cock is of opinion that the ginghams, both white and browne..will prove a good commodity in the Kinge of Shashma his cuntry. **1687** *Lond. Gaz.* No. 2269/3 19176 pieces of divers sorts of Ginghams. **1727** W. MATHER *Yng. Man's Comp.* 411 Ginghams, Taffaties, Beads of all sorts, Buckshawes. **1763** *Brit. Mag.* IV. 406 Ladies of taste are prodigiously fond of the Ginghams manufactured there [Manchester]. **1834** HT. MARTINEAU *Farrers* iv. 73 The quality of wear of a piece of gingham or calico. **18..** THOMPSON in J. G. Wilkinson *Manners Anc. Egypt.* (1837) III. 123 Had this pattern..been repeated across its whole breadth, it would have formed a modern gingham. **1858** LYTTON *What will He do* I. vi, Only a little commonplace child in dingy gingham.

2. *colloq.* An umbrella (properly, one covered with gingham).

1861 MISS BRADDON *Trail Serpent* I. vii, Mr. Peters..took immediate possession, by planting his honest gingham in a corner of the room. **1889** *Sportsman* 2 Feb. (Farmer), It would really put a premium on the many little mistakes of ownership concerning ginghams at present so common.

fig. **1884** *Blackw. Mag.* Mar. 422/2 The umbrella cannot be got to go up at the right moment, which seems to be generally the case with the Government 'gingham'.

3. *attrib.*, as ***gingham-frock***, ***-manufacturer***, ***-mill***, ***-umbrella***, ***-waistcoat***.

1793 H. BOYD *Indian Observer* No. 14 ¶7 Even the ginghem waistcoats, which striped or plain have so long stood their ground, must I hear, ultimately give way to the stronger kerseymere. *a* **1845** BARHAM *Ingol. Leg.*, *Blasphemer's Warn.*, A good stout Taglioni and gingham umbrella. **1851** in *Illustr. Lond. News* (1854) 5 Aug. 118 Gingham manufacturer. **1853** MISS SHEPPARD *Ch. Auchester* xi. (1875) 45 She wore a pink gingham frock, ill made to a degree. **1860** EMERSON *Cond. Life, Power* Wks. (Bohn) II. 342 In the gingham-mill, a broken thread or a shred spoils the web through a piece of a hundred yards.

Hence (*nonce-wds.*) **ˈginghamed** *a.*, dressed in gingham; **ˈginghammy** *a.*, addicted to wearing gingham.

1831 JAS. WILSON *Let.* in *Mem.* (1859) IV. 136 All our other pets are well, both the feathered..and the ginghamed. **1856** *Tait's Mag.* XXIII. 215 Recommended to you by snubby seniors and ginghammy old maids.

gingiber, obs. form of GINGER.

gingili ('dʒɪndʒɪlɪ). Also 8 **gingerly**, 8-9 **gingel(l)i**, **gingel(l)y**, 9 **gengeley**, **gingilie**, **jinjili**. [a. Hindi and Mahratta *jinjalī*, according to Yule prob. of European introduction; ultimately repr. Arab. *juljulān*, in Spanish Arab. *jonjolin*, whence (with Arab. article) Sp. *aljonjolí*, It. *giuggiolino*, Pg. *girgelim*, F. *jugeoline* (with other forms in all the Rom. langs.] An East Indian plant (*Sesamum indicum* or *orientale*) the seeds of which yield a bland oil. Also the oil itself. Also *attrib.*

1704 *Collect. Voy.* (Churchill) III. 654/2 Nely, Rice, Gingely-seeds. **1727** A. HAMILTON *New Acc. E. Ind.* I. xi. 128 The men are bedawb'd all over with red Earth, or Vermilion, and are continually squirting gingerly Oyl at one another. **1807** T. BUCHANAN *Journ.* I. 8 The oil..of Sesamum, by the English called Gingeli, or sweet oil. *c* **1865** LETHEBY in *Circ. Sc.* I. 105/1 Sessamum or Gingilie oil is procured from the Sessamum orientale, of which there are several varieties cultivated in India for the oil which they yield. **1885** HUNTER *Imp. Gaz. Ind.* II. 63 Gingelli. **1897** WILLIS *Flower. Pl.* II. 351 Sesamum indicum L. is largely cultivated in India &c., for the oil expressed from its seeds (gingili, gingelly, sesame, etc.).

gingioline, var. GINGERLINE, *Obs.*

gingival (dʒɪnˈdʒaɪvəl), *a.* [ad. mod.L. *gingīvālis*, f. L. *gingīva* gum: see -AL[1]. Cf. F. *gingival.*]

1. Of or pertaining to the gums. ***gingival line***: 'the red line at the free edge of the gums seen in phthisical persons' (*Syd. Soc. Lex.* 1885).

1669 HOLDER *Elem. Speech* 71 P. and B. are Labial..T. and D. are Gingival. *Ibid.* 78 The Italians..make the Occluse Appulse, especially the Gingival, softer than we do. **1720** HALE in *Phil. Trans.* XXXI. 8 From the Buccal, Labial, and Gingival Glands, the Saliva flows from all parts of the Mouth without the Teeth. **1872** COHEN *Dis. Throat* 139 The tumor began at 14 years of age, following the spontaneous opening of a gingival abscess. **1875** HUXLEY in *Encycl. Brit.* I. 762/2 The gingival surfaces of the premaxillæ and of the dentary elements of the mandible.

2. quasi-*sb.* (See quot.)

1874 W. WRIGHT *Arabic Gram.* i. (1896) 4 The gingivals, in uttering which the tongue is pressed against the gums.

gingiver(e, obs. form of GINGER.

gingivitis (ˌdʒɪndʒɪˈvaɪtɪs). [f. L. *gingīva* + -ITIS.] Inflammation of the gums.

1874 JONES & SIEV. *Pathol. Anat.* 539 Ulcerative Stomatitis, or Gingivitis..is common, rarely fatal. **1892** *Pall Mall G.* 6 May 5/2 The *Lancet* thinks it was not a case of poisoning at all, but merely an attack of simple gingivitis.

gingivostomatitis (ˌdʒɪndʒɪvəʊstɒməˈtaɪtɪs). *Path.* [f. GINGIV(ITIS + -O + STOMATITIS.] Gingivitis combined with stomatitis.

1935 PRINZ & GREENBAUM *Dis. Mouth* vii. 102 The disturbances of the oral mucosa may be conveniently divided into gingivitis, stomatitis and gingivo-stomatitis. **1964** M. HYNES *Med. Bacteriol.* (ed. 8) xxv. 396 Primary infection with the herpes virus may be symptomless, but in childhood usually causes an acute gingivostomatitis.

gingivre, obs. form of GINGER.

gingko, var. GINKGO.

gingle, obs. form of JINGLE.

gingles, var. SHINGLES.

1655 FULLER *Ch. Hist.* IX. i. §60 It is observed of the Gingles, or St. Anthony his fire, that it is mortall if it come once to clip and encompasse the whole body.

ginglimoid, var. GINGLYMOID.

ginglyform ('gɪŋ-, 'dʒɪŋglɪfɔːm), *a.* *Anat.* [f. GINGLY-MUS + -FORM.] Hinge-shaped.

1847 in CRAIG. **1881** MIVART *Cat* 122 A more complex kind of articulation is called a Hinge or Ginglyform joint.

ginglymate ('gɪŋ-, 'dʒɪŋglɪmeɪt), *v.* *rare.* [f. GINGLYM-US + -ATE[3].] *intr.* To form a hinge.

1826 KIRBY & SP. *Entomol.* (1828) III. xxxiv. 403 Its articulation even where the joints ginglymate consists of pieces connected by the internal ligament.

ginglymoid ('gɪŋ-, 'dʒɪŋglɪmɔɪd), *a.* *Anat.* Also 9 **ginglimoid**, **ginglymoide**. [f. as prec. + -OID.] Resembling a hinge; hinge-like.

1669 HOLDER *Elem. Speech* 162 The Malleus lies along fixed to the Tympanum; and on the other end is joyned to the Incus by a double or Ginglymoid joynt. **1835-6** TODD *Cycl. Anat.* I. 251/1 In ginglymoid joints they [the ligaments] are always placed on the sides. **1861** HULME tr. *Moquin-Tandon* II. II. 57 Limbs perfect, with ginglymoid articulations.

So **ginglyˈmoidal** *a.* [+ -AL], ginglymoid.

1847 in CRAIG; and in mod. Dicts.

ginglymus ('gɪŋ-, 'dʒɪŋglɪməs). *Anat.* Also 7 **gynglimos**. [mod.L. *ginglymus*, a. Gr. γίγγλυμος hinge.] 'A diarthrodial joint having some likeness to a hinge, in that its motion is only in two directions, as the elbow-joint' (*Syd. Soc. Lex.* 1885). ***angular, lateral ginglymus*** (see quot. 1831).

1657 *Physical Dict.*, Gynglimos, is a joyning of a bone when the same bone receiveth another, and is received by another. **1721-1800** in BAILEY. **1784** ANDRÉ in *Phil. Trans.* LXXIV. 276 A complete joint is formed, of that kind called by anatomists *ginglymus*, that is, where the projecting parts of one bone are received by corresponding cavities in the other. **1802** PALEY *Nat. Theol.* viii. (ed. 2) 121 The ginglymus, or hinge-joint, does not..admit of a ligament of the same kind with that of the ball and socket joint. **1831** R. KNOX *Cloquet's Anat.* 169 Angular Ginglymus, or Hinge, of which the motions are commonly reduced to flexion and extension..Lateral Ginglymus, or Rotatory Diarthrosis, in which rotation is the only possible motion, and which is double, when a bone turns on another by two given points.

attrib. **1802** PALEY *Nat. Theol.* viii. (ed. 2) 122 Another no less important joint, and that also of the ginglymus sort, is the ankle. **1840** G. ELLIS *Anat.* 716 The knee, the largest and most complex ginglymus joint in the body.

gingo, var. GINKGO.

†**gingran.** *Obs.*[−1] [app. a. Welsh *gingroen* (by O. Pughe misrendered 'toad-flax, a kind of stinking mushroom').] ? A kind of toadstool.

1660 JER. TAYLOR *Duct. Dubit.* I. ii. rule iii. §32. 51 If you put in nothing but mushromes, or eggeshels, or the juice of coloquintida, or the filthy gingran, you must expect productions accordingly.

†**gingreate**, *v.* *Obs.*[−0] [? f. L. *gingrīre* to cackle like a goose + -ATE[3].] *intr.* 'To chirp as birds do' (Cockeram 1623).

gingumbob, obs. form of JIGGAMBOB.

ginimony. *Obs. rare*[−1].

1607 DEKKER & WEBSTER *Westward Ho* I. i. A 3 b, Heere is Ginimony likewise burnt, and puluerized, to be mingled with the iuyce of Lymmons, sublimate Mercury, and two spooneful of the flowers of Brimstone, a most excellent receite to cure the flushing in the face.

giniper, obs. form of JUNIPER.

gink (gɪŋk). *slang* (orig. *U.S.*). [Of obscure origin.] A fellow; a man. (Freq. pejorative.)

1910 *Sat. Even. Post* 22 Oct. 12/3, I don't believe that all these ginks have got coin enough to support one good game. **1919** WODEHOUSE *Damsel in Distress* ii, I'm certain this gink is giving her a raw deal. **1927** *Sunday Express* 6 Feb. 4 One of America's noblemen, a great pirate, a gink with nerve.

1930 G. MITCHELL *Myst. Butcher's Shop* xiv. 164 When I 'ears silly ginks in this 'ere bar talking about 'im doin' this 'ere murder, I says to 'em [etc.]. **1957** L. P. HARTLEY *Hireling* 134 Hughie was a heel or a gink or anything you liked to call him. **1961** *Times* 19 Dec. 7/7 There are ginks running these schools and interfering with small boys. **1970** A. DRAPER *Swansong for Rare Bird* viii. 71 George wasn't the most talkative gink alive.

ginkgo ('gɪŋkgəʊ, 'gɪŋkəʊ). Also **gingko, gingo, ginko.** [Jap., f. Chinese *yinhsing* silver apricot.] The maidenhair tree (*Ginkgo biloba*) native to China and Japan and cultivated elsewhere, with wedge-shaped leaves and yellow flowers, the only living species of the order Ginkgoales which flourished in the Mesozoic era. Also *attrib.*, as ***ginkgo-nut, -tree.***

[**1727** J. G. SCHEUCHZER tr. *Kæmpfer's Hist. Japan* ix. 116 Another sort of nuts, call'd Ginau.. grow very plentifully.. on a fine tall tree.] **1773** [see *maidenhair-tree* s.v. MAIDENHAIR 6]. **1808** *Pict. London* 349 Gingo trees, three fine cedars, a cork-tree, a black walnut. **1858** O. W. HOLMES *Aut. Breakf-t.* xii. (1891) 277 One of the long granite blocks used as seats was hard by,—the one you may still see close by the Gingko-tree. **1863** FORTUNE *Yedo & Peking* ix. 139 Dried fruits for sale were numerous.. such as oranges, pears, gingko nuts (*Salisburia adiantifolia*). **1883** *Harper's Mag.* Apr. 726/1 Towering up above its neighbors.. is a tall ginko. **1888** DAWSON *Geol. Hist. Plants* v. 180 Those elegant fan-shaped leaves characteristic of but one living species, the *Salisburia*, or gingko-tree of China. **1912** A. CONAN DOYLE *Lost World* x. 166 One huge gingko tree, topping all the others, shot its great limbs and maidenhair foliage over the fort which we had constructed. **1955** *Sci. News Let.* 26 Mar. 207/2 There are a lot of young ginkgos growing in Battery Park, New York. China is the native home of the ginkgo tree. **1957** R. CARRINGTON *Mermaids & Mastodons* xiii. 175 Ginkgos are exceptionally resistant to fire.

ginle, var. GINNLE.

ginn, ginnel, vars. JINN, GINNLE.

ginn(e, obs. form of GIN *sb.*[1] and *v.*[1]

ginnel, var. GENNEL.

† '**ginner**[1]. *Obs.* [f. GIN *v.*[1] + -ER[1].] A beginner.

c **1374** CHAUCER *Boeth.* v. pr. i. 150 þei ne vndirstoden ne moeueden it nauȝt by god prince and gynner [*Camb. MS.* bygynnere] of wirkyng. *c* **1385** —— *L.G.W.* 1231 *Dido*, This was the firste morwe Of hire gladnisse & gynnere of hire sorwe.

ginner[2] ('dʒɪnə(r)). [f. GIN *v.*[2] + -ER[1].] One who 'gins' cotton. Also ***cotton-ginner.***

1873 W. CORY *Lett. & Jrnls.* (1897) 304 A cotton ginner. **1879** SIR G. CAMPBELL *White & Black* 360 Merchants and ginners look a good deal after the quality of the seed.

So '**ginnery**, a place for 'ginning' cotton.

1896 *Living Topics Cycl.* (N.Y.) II., Crude oil mills.. refineries.. cotton ginneries.

'**ginners**, *pl.* (rarely *sing.*) *Obs.* exc. *dial.* Also local Sc. **ginnles.** [Of obscure origin; ? connected with ON. *gin-* wk. root of *gína* to yawn.] The gills of a fish.

1483 *Cath. Angl.* 156/2 A Ginner of yͤ fysche, *branchia.* **1781** HUTTON *Tour to Caves* 90 Ginners, the gills of a fish. **1824** MACTAGGART *Gallovid. Encycl.* s.v., He had swallowed the bait greedily, the huik was sticking in his 'ginners'. **1869** *Lonsdale Gloss., Ginners*, the gills of a fish.

ginnery ('dʒɪnərɪ). *nonce-wd.* [f. GIN *sb.*[2] + -ERY. Cf. GROGGERY.] A gin-palace.

1859 SALA *Gas-light & D.* vi. 71 Here.. is a Gin Palace —a 'ginnery' in full swing.

† **ginnet.** *Obs. rare*$^{-1}$. A carpenter's adze (see quot.).

1688 R. HOLME *Armoury* III. ix. 365/2 The Ginnet is used to cut and take off Irregularities in all sorts of work lying under hand or flat, which the Axe or Hatchet cannot be handled to touch: Some term it an Addice or Adz.

ginnet, obs. form of JENNET.

ginney, ginnie, obs. forms of GUINEA.

'**ginnified**, *ppl. a. nonce-wd.* [f. GIN *sb.*[2] + -(I)FY + -ED[1].] Showing traces of gin-drinking.

1852 R. S. SURTEES *Sponge's Sp. Tour* (1893) 78 His cadaverous ginnified face.

† '**ginning**, *vbl. sb.*[1] *Obs.* [f. GIN *v.*[1] + -ING[1].] = BEGINNING.

c **1330** R. BRUNNE *Chron.* (1810) 38 Als alle þis sorow & wo was in þe gynnyng, Died S. Dunstan. **1340** *Ayenb.* 234 Ase ine þe rounde figure, þe ende went ayen to his ginninge. **1429** *Pol. Poems* (Rolls) II. 143 The gynning of his roial noblesse. **1463** *Bury Wills* (Camden) 40 Annexid to the same rolle in the gynnyng.

So † '**ginningless** *a.*, having no beginning.

c **1420** *Pallad. on Husb.* IX. 212 On Endles Ende, o gynnyngles Gynnynge.

ginning ('dʒɪnɪŋ), *vbl. sb.*[2] [f. GIN *v.*[2] + -ING[1].] The action of GIN *v.*[2] (sense 2); the operation of separating the seeds of cotton from the fibre.

1789 *Trans. Soc. Arts* I. 255 Much of the moss also rubs off in ginning, and mixes with the cotton. **1839** URE *Dict. Arts, Ginning*, the operation by which the filaments of cotton are separated from the seeds. **1885** *Standard* 30 Jan. 5/3 The new fibre will require no ginning.

b. *Comb.* (in sense of 'used in' or 'for ginning cotton'), as ***ginning-cylinder, -house, -machine, -mill.***

1875 KNIGHT *Dict. Mech.* 969/1 The *ginning-cylinder. **1884** J. COLBORNE *Hicks Pasha* 15 M. Marquet, is erecting a *ginning-house for the preparation of cotton. **1888** *Pall Mall G.* 22 June 12/1 A *ginning machine which has been introduced into China from Japan. **1879** SIR G. CAMPBELL *White & Black* 150 Many hands.. find employment in the *ginning mills.

ginniting, obs. form of JENNETING.

ginnle (gɪn(ə)l), *v.* Also **ginle, ginnel.** [f. *ginnles* local Sc. var. GINNERS.] *trans.* To tickle (the gills of a fish); to tickle (trout), catch by tickling the gills, etc.

1819 RENNIE *St. Patrick* III. ii. 42 Ye.. took me aiblins for a black-fisher it was gaun to ginle the chouks o' ye. **1885** LD. BLACKBURN in *Law Rep.* 10 App. Cas. 388 The boy who was ginneling trout would observe.. that.. there was then no bridge, but a deep pool. **1887** J. SERVICE *Life Dr. Duguid* xiii. 88, I sighed.. for a lang simmer's day.. to ginnle trouts with John Paiks in the Roughburn.

ginnles, Sc. form of GINNERS.

† '**ginnous**, *a. Obs. rare*$^{-1}$. [f. GIN *sb.*[1] + -OUS. Cf. GINFUL.] Crafty, guileful.

c **1425** *Master of Game* MS. Bodl. 546 lf. 36 Hit is a wonder gynnous beest, and conynge and fals more þan any oþer beest.

Hence † '**ginnously** *adv.*

c **1425** *Master of Game* MS. Bodl. 546 lf. 35 b, 3if men se hem [were wolfes] þei wole come vp on hym gynnously þat wiþ greet payne þe man may ascape.

† '**ginny**, *sb. Thieves' slang. Obs.* Also 7 **jenny.** [f. *Ginny, Jenny*, female name. Cf. JEMMY.] A housebreaker's tool (see quots.).

1673 R. HEAD *Canting Acad.* 191 The ninth is a Ginny to lift up a Grate, If he sees but the Lurry, with his hooks he will bate. *a* **1700** B. E. *Dict. Cant. Crew, Ginny*, an Instrument to lift up a Grate, the better to steal what is in the Window. [Also s.v. *Jenny.*] **1725** in *New Cant. Dict.* **1785** in GROSE *Dict. Vulg. Tongue.*

† '**ginny**, *a.*[1] *Obs. rare.* [f. GIN *sb.*[1] + -Y[1].] Cunning, ensnaring, seductive.

1615 A. NIXON *Scourge Corrupt.* 17 These fellowes, with their ginny phreeses, and Italionate discourses, to set a fire the brauing thoughts of our yong gentlewomen.

'**ginny** *a.*[2] [f. GIN *sb.*[2] + -Y[1].] Affected by gin; resembling, addicted to, or characterized by gin.

1888 *Times* 19 Oct. 5/6 A 'ginny' kidney, that is to say one that belonged to a person who had drunk heavily. **1926** S. T. WARNER *Lolly Willowes* 39 A hot ginny churchyard smell. **1948** G. GREENE *Heart of Matter* III. iii. i. 294 His ginny breath. **1964** R. BRADDON *Year Angry Rabbit* vi. 58 Suddenly he felt very tired, and very reluctant to endure the ginny *bonhomie* of a wardroom.

ginny-carriage ('dʒɪnɪkærɪdʒ). *dial.* Also jenny-. (See quot. 1841.)

1824 MRS. CAMERON *Marten & 2 Scholars* ii. 12 On Sunday morning he looked so clean.. that nobody would have thought he had been driving a jenny-carriage all the week. **1841** HARTSHORNE *Salop. Antiq.* Gloss., *Ginny carriage*, a stout wooden or sometimes iron carriage, used for conveying materials along a rail road. **1875** KNIGHT *Dict. Mech., Ginny-carriage*, a railway car for conveying materials.

So **ginny-rails** (see quot.).

1841 HARTSHORNE *Salop. Antiq.* Gloss., *Ginny rails*, iron rails along which small wooden carriages (ginny carriages) are drawn, laden with coal, iron-stone [etc.].

ginormous (dʒaɪ'nɔːməs), *a. slang.* Also **gi-normous.** [f. GI(GANTIC *a.* + E)NORMOUS *a.*] Very large, simply enormous; excessive in size, amount, etc. (esp. in comparison with one's expectation).

1948 in PARTRIDGE *Dict. Forces' Slang.* **1962** W. GRANVILLE *Dict. Sailors' Slang* 53/2 *Ginormous*, acronymous adjective descriptive of something really impressive: a brush with the enemy; a raid upon the enemy's shipping or coastline, or merely a particularly 'heavy' party in the mess. **1970** A. REID *Confessions of Hitch-hiker* vi. 45 We went to a posh café... The prices were ginormous. **1976** *Scotsman* 20 Nov. 10/2 How about froggies filled with pot-pourri from small to gi-normous, as Just Us describe them. **1977** *Economist* 8 Oct. 98/3 The state company Egam, declared bust last spring,.. is going to cost considerably more than the £500 billion.. earmarked by the government last June, probably a ginormous £1,700 billion. **1986** *Sunday Express* (Colour Suppl.) 23 Mar. 70/3 Since Brands Hatch, doors have opened and it's possible to make gi-normous money.

† **ginour.** *Obs.* In 3 **ginnur,** 4 **gin-, gynour.** [f. GIN *sb.*[1] + *-our*, -OR.] An engineer, esp. one who manages war-engines (cf. ENGINEER 5 a).

a **1300** *Floriz & Bl.* 324 Wend tomoreȝe to þe Tur Also þu were a gud ginnur. **13..** *Coer de L.* 5221 The gynours mangeneles bente, And stones to the cyte they sente. **1375** BARBOUR *Bruce* XVII. 690 The gynour than gert bend in hy The gyne, and swappit out the stane.

'**gin-,palace.** [f. GIN *sb.*[2]] A gaudily decorated public house. (An opprobrious term.)

1834 *Oxf. Univ. Mag.* I. 327 The gin palaces, (as they have been not inaptly called). **1835** MARRYAT *Olla Podr.* xxi, Gin palaces, like hell, ever open. **1874** HELPS *Soc. Press.* iii. 56 It would probably counteract the attractions even of the gin-palace.

ginseng ('dʒɪnsɛŋ). Forms: (7 **genseg, ginsem**), 8–9 **ginsing, jin(g)sing,** (8 **gengzeng, ghinschenn**), 7– **ginseng.** [a. Chinese *jên shên*; the first word means 'man', the second is of obscure meaning; Giles suggests that the compound means 'image of man', and alludes to the forked shape of the root.]

1. A plant of either of two species of the genus *Aralia* or *Panax*, found in Northern China and Nepaul, also in Canada and the eastern United States.

1691 RAY *Creation* I. (1692) 195 The Cotton Trees.. the Nisi, or Genseg; the Numerose Balsam, and Gum-trees. **1713** *Phil. Trans.* XXVIII. 239 The Tartars often bring us the Leaves of Gin-seng instead of Tea. **1765** J. BROWN *Chr. Jrnl.* 155 In Tartary's barren soil, grow the medicinal jingseng and the vegetable lamb. **1812** J. SMYTH *Pract. of Customs* (1821) 94 *Ginseng*, the dried roots of this plant, as commonly imported, are about the thickness of the little finger. **1836** J. F. DAVIS *Chinese* I. iv. 131 The wild plant ginseng, long a monopoly of the Emperor in the Manchow country, has been imported in large quantities by the American ships to Canton. **1883** *Q. Rev.* Jan. 176 In the north the famous 'jinseng' (*Panax quinquefolium*) is found both wild and cultivated.

2. The root of the plant; a preparation of this used as a medicine.

1654 tr. *Martini's Conq. China* 9 The root cal'd Gimsem, so much esteemed amongst the Chineses. **1771** SMOLLETT *Humph. Cl.* 14 June, I took some of the tincture of ginseng. **1788** M. CUTLER in *Life*, etc. (1888) I. 402 Here we met a Packer with ten pack-horses, loaded principally with ginseng in barrels. **1819** JAS. WILSON *Dict. Astrol.* 268 Three or four cups of Ginseng taken every day, for a week, would soon remove most of her complaints. **1861** C. P. HODGSON *Resid. Japan* 32 Mushrooms, ginseng, gall-nuts and vermicelli are some of the articles which go to China. **1897** WILLIS *Flower. Pl.* II. 28 The root of the Aralia Ginseng.. is the source of the famous Chinese medicine Ginseng.

3. *attrib.* and *Comb.*, as ***ginseng-digger, -farm, -gatherer, -root, -tree.***

1758 *Michmakis & Maricheets* 77, I could never find any ginseng-root. **1791** D'ISRAELI *Cur. Lit.* (1834) I. 363 The ginseng tree is noticed for the same appearance. **1888** *Times* (weekly ed.) 6 Apr. 3/2 Ginseng gatherers who dwell.. in this.. land. **1891** *Pall Mall G.* 8 Sept. 3/3 A ginseng farm is a peculiar-looking affair. **1894** *Westm. Gaz.* 21 Nov. 2/1 Amélie Rives is introducing Virginian ginseng-diggers to politely-scandalised New York society.

'**gin-shop.** [f. GIN *sb.*[2]] A dram-shop retailing chiefly gin.

1714 MANDEVILLE *Fab. Bees* (1723) I. 340 [She] never did any thing to remedy her Wants in good earnest, but bewailing them at a Gin-shop. **1773** JOHNSON in *Boswell* 13 Apr., What is there in any of these shops, (if you except gin-shops) that can do any human being any harm? **1801** *Sporting Mag.* XVII. 20 The bar of a small gin-shop. **1854** MRS. GASKELL *North & S.* xvii, The more ill-looking of the men.. hung about on the steps of the beer-houses and gin-shops.

Hence **gin-shopper**, the keeper of a gin-shop.

1831 *Lincoln Her.* 1 July 4/5, I will drag them out one by one whether publican or sinner.. sugar-shopper, or gin-shopper.

ginsing, var. GINSENG.

gin-sling. [f. GIN *sb.*[2] + SLING *sb.*[2]] An American cold drink composed of gin, etc. flavoured and sweetened.

1790 J. BAXTER *Jrnl.* 19 Feb. in *Amer. Speech* (1965) XL. 199 Drank a gin sling with him at fat Simmon's. **1837, 1843** [see COCKTAIL 3 a]. **1839** MARRYAT *Diary Amer.* Ser. I. I. 105 Punch, gin slings, cocktails, mint julips. **1864** TOVEY *Brit. & For. Spirits* 105 The American summer drink, Gin Sling is prepared thus: Gin and water, sweetened with pounded white sugar, in which are stuck leaves of fresh gathered mint. **1938** G. GREENE *Brighton Rock* v. i. 192 They use their own eggs in the gin slings. **1943** N. COWARD *Middle East Diary* 15 Aug. (1944) 49 Sipping Gin-Slings and cocktails.

Hence **gin-slinger**, (*a*) a bar-tender, from his mixing the drinks; (*b*) a gin-drinker.

1887 *N.Y. Voice* Extra 1 Sept., Saloon-keepers and white-aproned gin-slingers stood in the doors of the saloons. **1889** FARMER *Americanisms, Gin slinger*, a tippler whose favorite beverage is gin.

ginzo ('gɪnzəʊ). *U.S. slang.* Also **guinzo.** [perh. ad. GUINEA 1 b.] In contemptuous use: a person of Italian extraction; also as *adj.*

1931 *Amer. Mercury* Dec. 413/1 He's a Roumanian or some kinda guinzo. **1964** W. MARKFIELD *To Early Grave* (1965) vii. 125, I have a boss, a ginzo—though he speaks a great Jewish. **1967** H. HARRISON *Technicolor Time Machine* (1968) v. 51 I'm *Americano*, but I got ginzo relatives all around the Bay of Naples.

gio, var. GEO, gully, creek.

giobertite (dʒəʊ'bɜːtaɪt). *Min.* [named by Beudant 1824 after G. A. *Gioberti*, an Italian chemist (1761–1834): see -ITE.] = MAGNESITE.

1835 C. U. SHEPARD *Min.* II. I. 228 *Giobertite* (see *Magnesite*). **1868** DANA *Min.* (ed. 5) 687 Beudant, in 1824, gave the name *giobertite* to the carbonate.

Gioconda (dʒ(ɪ)ə'kɒndə). [It., fem. of *giocondo* (see JOCUND *a.*).] The name of a painting (in full La Gioconda; also known as the *Mona Lisa*) by Leonardo da Vinci (1452–1519), used allusively attrib. to describe an enigmatic smile resembling that of the woman in this painting.

1921 A. HUXLEY in *Eng. Review* XXXIII. 89 Miss Spence was smiling too: her Gioconda smile, he had once called it. .. Miss Spence..always tried to live up to the Leonardo standard. **1964** T. HELMORE *Affair at Quala* iv. 113 She looked at me and gave me a Gioconda smile. **1967** L. PETERS *Riot '71* 110 Smith smiled again, putting a slightly mysterious, Gioconda quality into it this time.

gioconde, giornal, obs. ff. JOCUND, JOURNAL.

‖**giocoso** (dʒo'koso). *Mus.* [It. = merry.] A direction denoting that a composition is to be executed merrily. Also *transf.*

1828 T. BUSBY *Mus. Man.* 81 *Giocoso*, in a gay and joyous style. **1960** *Times* 25 July 3/1 It grew steadily more sinister, further from the *giocoso* drama of its title. **1962** *Times* 16 Feb. 15/5 The *giocoso* element [in *Don Giovanni*] was quite excessively overshadowed.

Giorgi ('dʒɔːdʒɪ). [The name of Giovanni *Giorgi* (1871–1950), Italian physicist, who first proposed the system in *Atti dell' Assoc. elettrotecn. ital.* (1901) V. 402–18.] ***Giorgi system***: a system of units based on the metre, the kilogramme, the second, and one other (electrical) unit; now *spec.* a system in which the electrical unit is the ampere.

1905 *Jrnl. Inst. Electr. Engin.* XXXIV. 179 The Giorgi system is a rational one (in the Heaviside sense). **1933** *Bull. Nat. Research Council* No. 93, 103 Like the Giorgi system, it could be adopted either unrationalized or rationalized. **1934** *Nature* 21 Apr. 597 (*heading*) The Giorgi (M.K.S.Ω) system of units. **1964** *Internat. System (SI) Units (B.S.I.)* 6 This system, called the MKSA or Giorgi System, was adopted by the International Electrotechnical Commission in 1950. **1969** *Nature* 8 Nov. 581/2 Physically all four of E, H, D and B act as 'force vectors'. Thus a dimensional difference between the members of each pair, as in the Giorgi systems, results in distortion.

Giorgionesque (dʒɔːdʒ(ɪ)ə'nɛsk), *a.* [f. *Giorgione* + -ESQUE.] Resembling the style of the Italian painter *Giorgione* Barbarelli (1478–1510).

1906 *Westm. Gaz.* 19 Dec. 10/3 Mr. Lane's beautiful Giorgionesque half-length portrait of a young man. **1929** *Daily Tel.* 8 Jan. 8/5 The rich, almost Giorgionesque modelling, of the Diana. **1956** K. CLARK *Nude* iv. 119 The most beautiful of Titian's Giorgionesque nudes is in the picture known as Sacred and Profane Love. *Ibid.* vii. 271 One of them..looks unbelievably Giorgionesque.

Giottesque (dʒɒ'tɛsk), *a.* and *sb.* [f. *Giotto* + -ESQUE.]

A. *adj.* Resembling the style of the Tuscan painter Giotto (13–14th c.). B. *sb.* The style founded by Giotto; also, an artist belonging to the school, or imitating the style, of Giotto.

1854 RUSKIN *Lect. Archit.* iii. 159 This whole range of landscape may be conveniently classed in three divisions, namely Giottesque, Leonardesque, and Titianesque; the Giottesque embracing nearly all the work of the 14th.. century. **1864** CROWE & CAVALCASELLE *Hist. Paint. Italy* I. 386 It would be difficult to say in what respect this poor Giottesque differs as to quality from the older art which was previously called Byzantine. *Ibid.* II. 1 (*heading of chapter*) Declining school of Giottesques. **1880** E. LEE-HAMILTON *God's Saints & Men* Pref. 6 A half effaced giottesque fresco. **1896** *Advance* (Chicago) 20 Aug. 253 Giotto..became the greatest artist of his time, and the founder of quite a new style of paintings called the Giottesque.

giour, var. GUYOUR, guide.

†**gip**, *sb.*[1] *Obs. rare*⁻¹. [? a. OF. *gip, gippe*; cf. GYPSE.] = GYPSUM.

1658 tr. *Porta's Nat. Magick* XIII. x. 312 Pliny saith, That Iron is preserved from rust, by Ceruss, Gip, and liquid Pitch.

gip (dʒɪp), *sb.*[2] Abbreviation of GIPSY.

a **1840** *Gipsey Davy* i. in Child *Ballads* VII. (1890) 72/1 There was a gip came o'er the land.

gip (gɪp), *v.* Also 7 **gipp(e**, 9 **gyp**; and see GIB *v.*[2] [Of unknown origin: the pronunc. (dʒɪp) given in most Dicts. is erroneous, at least so far as regards the Whitby dialect.] *trans.* To clean (fish) for curing (cf. quots. 1812–1876).

1603 HARSNET *Pop. Impost.* 55 He must gippe the Gudgin, and hit the Woodcocke on the bill, and the other scuruie crue of Exorcists must hold him the candell. **1641** S. SMITH *Herring Buss Trade* 8 Gip, salt and packe all the Herrings before they set on the Kettle. *a* **1700** in B. E. *Dict. Cant. Crew.* **1812** *Chron.* in *Ann. Reg.* 505/1 Immediately after the nets are hauled in..the crew begin to gyp the fish, that is, to cut out the gill, which is followed by the float or swim. **1867** SMYTH *Sailor's Word-bk.*, *Gip*, to take the entrails out of fishes. **1876** *Whitby Gloss.* s.v. *Gipping*, 'They're gipping herrings', i.e. they are taking out the gills, &c.; when preparing to cure them.

b. *Comb.*, as **gip-tub** = *gib-tub*.

1889 in *Century Dict.*

Hence **gipped** *ppl. a.*; '**gipping** *vbl. sb.*, in combination ***gipping-knife***, the knife used in gipping fish. Also '**gipper**.

1615 E. S. *Brit. Buss* in Arb. *Garner* III. 631 Gipping or Gilling Knives, 24, at fourpence. **1641** S. SMITH *Herring Buss Trade* 8, 2 dozen of gipping knives. *Ibid.* 9, 9 Gippers which cut their [the Herrings] throats, and takes out the Guts. **1883** *Fisheries Exhib. Catal.* 72 Samples of Gipped Herrings in barrel.

†**gip**, *int. Obs.* Also 6 **gyp(pe**, 6–7 **gep**. [The alliteration with *Gill, Gillian*, shows initial (dʒ); prob. formed as an involuntary exclamation; cf. GEE-(H)UP and GUP. The exclamation *Marry gip* (see MARRY *int.*) prob. originated from *By Mary Gipcy* = 'by St. Mary of Egypt'; but it became confused with this word.] a. An exclamation of anger or remonstrance addressed to a horse. b. An expression of surprise, derision, or contempt addressed to a person; = 'get out', 'go along with you'.

1530 PALSGR. 598 What gyppe gyll with a galde backe begynne you to kycke nowe: hey, de par le diable Gilotte [etc.]. **1592** GREENE *Upst. Courtier* B 4, Clothbreeches.. with a skorneful kind of smiling made this smooth replie: 'Mary gyp goodman vpstart, who made your father a gentleman?' —— *Disput. Connycatchers* Wks. (Grosart) X. 270, I would then say, gip fine soule, a yoong Saint will prooue an old diuel. **1600** HEYWOOD *1st Pt. Edw. IV*, IV. iv, Gep, Goodman Tanner, are ye so round? **1603** DEKKER *Batchelars Banq.* Wks. (Grosart) I. 196 Now gip with a murrin (quoth she) you are not troubled with them. *a* **1616** BEAUM. & FL. *Faithf. Fr.* III. ii, Money? Marry, gip! You might have stood there till moss had grown o' your heels. **1638** FORD *Fancies* III. iii. 41 Gip to your beauties, you would be faire forsooth. **1638** BROME *Antipodes* IV. ii. Wks. 1873 III. 298 Gip gaffer Shotten, fagh, Take that for your coy Counsell. *Kicks.* **1660** *Prince d'Amour* 71 Sweet Lady.. One friendly look impart, Gep Gillian, I will frounce you.

gip, var. GYP *sb.*[1,3] or *v.*

gipciere, var. GIPSER.

†**gipe**. *Obs. rare*⁻¹. In 4–5 **gype**. [a. OF. *gipe, gippe*, var. *jupe*, etc.: see JUPE, JUPON.] A tunic, smock-frock, cassock.

In the quot. the allusion is app. to the folds or gathers of the tunic.

c **1400** *Rom. Rose* 7262 High shoes knopped with dagges, That frouncen lyke a quaile pype, Or botes rivelyng as a gype.

gipe, var. GYPE *Sc.*

†**gipel**. *Obs. rare.* In 5 **gipell, gypell**. [a. OF. **gipel, jupel* (later *jupeau* GIPPO[1]), f. *gipe, jupe* GIPE.] A short tunic worn under the hauberk.

1460 *Lybeaus Disc.* (Kaluza) 248 þey caste on him of selk A gipell [*v.r.* gypell, gippon] whit as melk. *Ibid.* 1230 His fomen wer well boun To perce his aketoun, Gipell, maile and plate.

gipon. *Obs.* exc. *arch.* Forms: 4 **gypo(u)n, gepoun**, 4–5 **gipoun**, 5 **gippon**, 4, 9 **gipon**, (9 **gipion**). [a. OF. *gip(p)on, jup(p)on*, tunic, JUPON, f. *gipe, jupe* GIPE.] A tunic, frequently worn under the hauberk.

c **1386** CHAUCER *Prol.* 75 Of ffustian he wered a gypon [*v.r.* iopoun] Al bismotered with his habergeon. **1387** TREVISA *Higden* (Rolls) I. 403 Wiþ oute sorcot, gowne, coote, kirtelle; Wiþ gipoun [*v.r.* iopen], tabard, cloke, and belle [L. *sine supertunicis, collobiis et tunicis*]. *a* **1400** *Octouian* 1029 The hauberk was all reed of rust..Thaugh the gypon were full of dust Hyt was nat wykke. *c* **1420** LYDG. *Thebes* II. 499 And Tideus aboue his Habergeoun A gipoun hadde. **1616** BULLOKAR, *Gippon*, a doublet: a light coat. **1813** SCOTT *Trierm.* III. xviii, With nought to fence his dauntless breast But the close gipon's under-vest. **1843** JAMES *Forest D.* I. iii, Under his coat he had a gipon of sendull fit for a king.

gipp(e, obs. form of GIP *v.*

gipper, var. JIPPER.

†**gippo**[1]. *Obs.* Also 7 **gippoe, jippo**. [a. F. *jup(p)eau* (obs.), earlier *jupel* GIPEL.]

1. A short tunic, cassock, or jacket worn by men, later also by women.

1617 MORYSON *Itin.* III. IV. i. 170 He wore a loose gippoe of blacke veluet, sparingly adorned with gold lace. **1650** A. B. *Mutat. Polemo* 10 Horsemans Frock, or Serving-mans Livery..or a Pulpit-thumping Presbyters Jippo. **1654** WHITELOCKE *Jrnl. Swed. Emb.* (1772) II. 181 Her habit was blacke silke stuffe for her coates, and over them a blacke velvet jippo, such as men use to weare. **1679** *Marr. Charles II*, 6 Her Jippo was edged like her Gown.

2. *transf.* A scullion, varlet. Cf. GYP.

1651 RANDOLPH, etc. *Hey for Honesty* IV. i, The veriest Gippo in the house will not drink a degree under Muscadine. *Ibid.* v, For a rib of beef, Though it smelt of every Gippo's scabby fingers, May any Scullion be chief Cook of heaven.

gippo[2] ('dʒɪpəʊ). *slang* (chiefly *Services*'). Also **gippy, gyp(p)o, gypoo**. [Var. JIPPER, JIPPO.] (See quots.)

1914 *Times* 23 Dec. 3/2 You take your mess-tin, [and] empty out..the greasy 'gyppo' (that means stew). **1916** *Daily Mail* 1 Nov. 4/4 'Gipoo' (gravy or grease). **1925** FRASER & GIBBONS *Soldier & Sailor Words* 105 Gippo (also *gypo*), gravy. Bacon fat. Butter. Any greasy sauce.—*e.g.*, 'Is there any Gippo?'

gippy ('dʒɪpɪ). *slang.* Freq. with capital initial. Also **gippo, gypo, gyppie, gyppo, gyppy**. [f. GIP(SY *sb.* + -Y[6], infl. by EGYPTIAN *a.*] 1. An Egyptian, esp. a native Egyptian soldier. Also *attrib.* or as *adj.*

a **1889** *World* (Barrère & Leland), Colonel Kitchener will probably stick to his original intention of having only *gippies* (as they call the Egyptian soldiers here) at Suakim. **1915** V. HORSLEY in S. Paget *Sir V. Horsley* (1919) III. ii. 308 The Gippy himself has his points. **1916** *Anzac Bk.* 137 The erstwhile Land of Jacko did breed much 'flue' and 'pneu', and it did seem as though the plagues of the ancient Gyppos had descended upon them. *Ibid.* 138 And it came to pass that while they yet warmed their hands there was heard a mighty crash, and of the 'Gyppies' that remained were picked up seven stretchers full. **1919** *Athenæum* 8 Aug. 727/2 'Gypos' for Egyptians. **1925** FRASER & GIBBONS *Soldier & Sailor Words* 105 The 'Gyppie' Army was the common colloquial term for the native force organized by Sir Evelyn Wood and Lord Kitchener. *Ibid.*, *Gippy bint*, an Egyptian girl. **1928** *Papers Mich. Acad. Sci. & Arts* X. 297 *Gypos*, the Egyptian army; Egyptian laborers. **1929** C. MACKENZIE *Gallipoli Mem.* iii. 26 A captain of the Gyppy Army with a pleasant oblong face. **1942** C. BARRETT *On Wallaby* iv. 62 Marmalade was a luxury, which, on four-day old Gyppo bread, you spread as thinly as tinfoil. **1955** E. WAUGH *Officers & Gentlemen* 208 'What's to stop him coming round the other side?' asked Tommy. 'According to plan—the Gyppos,' said the Brigadier.

b. An Egyptian cigarette.

1920 *Punch* 7 Apr. 270 I'll smoke with pleasure if they're Gyppies. Can't *stand* gaspers. **1926** W. S. MAUGHAM *Constant Wife* (1927) II. 122 When you once get the taste for them, you prefer them to gippies.

c. ***gippy tummy***: diarrhœa suffered by visitors to hot countries.

1943 A. MOOREHEAD *Year of Battle* i. 22 Few set foot in Egypt without contracting 'Gyppy Tummy' which is a mild stomach disorder lasting usually a couple of days. It recurs at irregular intervals and it makes you feel terrible. **1948** PARTRIDGE *Dict. Forces' Slang* 89 *Gyppy tummy*, a sharp griping pain, accompanied by diarrhœa, very common in Egypt. **1960** C. MACKENZIE *Greece in my Life* xiii. 190 Both of them besides the usual gyppy tummy had had bad colds. **1961** G. EGMONT *Art of Egmontese* iv. 71 Always take.. whatever is your favourite antidote to gippy tummy when you go abroad. **1970** *New Scientist* 8 Jan. 47/1 The commonest ailment experienced by modern-day Marco Polos is an intestinal attack known as gyppy tummy..in the Middle East.

2. A gipsy. Also *attrib.* or as *adj.*

1902 E. G. HAYDEN *From Thatched Cott.* xi. 95 Dally-oh if Jim ha'n't..left the place fur tramps an' gippoes to walk in. **1912** *English Rev.* Oct. 476 He could get some one else, perhaps a half gypo, or a lad, to take my place. **1913** *Chums* 13 Dec. 253/2 'What's your name, sonny?'..'No idea,' answered the gipsy with a soft laugh. 'I'm generally called Gippy in England. I've got other names in France, and Spain, and Italy.' **1924** KIPLING *Debits & Credits* (1926) 126 There's no sayin' what Gippos know. *Ibid.* 127 What the Gippo girl 'ad told 'er. **1953** DYLAN THOMAS *Under Milk Wood* (1954) 21 Ducking under the gippo's clothespegs.

gips, var. GIPSIES *pl.*, intermitting springs.

gips(e, var. GYPSE, *Obs.*, gypsum.

gip'seian, *a. nonce-wd.* [f. *gipsey* GIPSY + -AN.] Belonging to gipsies. (Cf. EGYPTIAN A. 4.)

1749 FIELDING *Tom Jones* XII. xii, That profound respect which Jones paid to the King of the Gypsies..was sweeter to his Gypseian majesty [etc.].

gipsen, obs. form of GIPSY *sb.*

gipser ('dʒɪpsə(r)). *Obs.* exc. *arch.* Forms: 4 **gipciere**, 5 **gypcyere, (-cer, -sere), gipser**, 9 **gipsire, (gyp-)**. [ad. OF. *gibecier(e, gibessiere, gibacier, gibassier(e* purse, pouch (mod.F. *gibecière* game or provision bag), of uncertain origin.

The suggestion made by Diez that *gibecière* is connected with F. *gibier* game, the chase (cf. also OF. *gibecer* to go hunting) is accepted by Littré and Hatz.-Darm., but is not supported by the sense of the word in OF. For other conjectures see Körting.]

A purse, pouch, or wallet, suspended from a belt or girdle.

c **1386** CHAUCER *Prol.* 357 An Anlass and a gipser al of silk Heeng at his girdel. **1443** in Rymer *Foedera* XI. 76/2 A gipser of gold garnished with rubies and perle. **1463** *Bury Wills* (Camden) 37 My best gypcer, wᵗ iij bagges, the jewews and the rynges of sylvir. **1614** CAMDEN *Rem.* 234 They had also about this time a kinde of Gowne called a Git..a pouche called a Gipser. **1834** PLANCHÉ *Brit. Costume* 176 A gypsire of purple velvet garnished with gold. **1855** W. WHITE *To Switzerld. & back* xv. 187 Schoolboys, equipped with knapsacks and gipsires. **1881** E. ARNOLD *Indian Poetry* 114 All habited in garbs that merchants use, With trader's band and gipsire.

attrib. **1403** *Act 5 Hen. IV*, c. 13 §1 Pleuseurs des loialx artificers..font de jour en autre firmalx anelx bedes chandelers gipsserrynges [etc.].

gipsey, var. GIPSY.

gipsies, †**gips**, *sb. pl.* [Prob. only the proper name of the particular springs near Bridlington, now called the *Gipsy race*. (Perh. to be compared with OF. *eaux gypsées*, waters containing gypsum, petrifying springs.)] Intermitting springs.

c **1198** W. OF NEWBURGH *Hist. Angl.* (Rolls) I. 85 In provincia Deirorum, haud procul a loco nativitatis meæ, res mirabilis contigit..Est vicus aliquot a mari orientali milliariis distans, juxta quem famosæ illæ aquæ, quas vulgo Gipse vocant, numerosa scaturigine e terra prosiliunt, non quidem jugiter, sed annis interpositis [etc.]. **1644** DIGBY *Nat. Bodies* (1645) 189 Like those eruptions of water, which in the Northern parts of England they call Gypsies. **1674–91** RAY *N.C. Words* 33 *Gipsies*, springs that break forth sometimes on the Woulds in Yorkshire. They are look'd upon as a Prognostic of Famine or Scarcity. **1692** —— *Dissol. World* II. ii. (1732) 111 The spirting Gips or natural jets d'Eaus. **1727** DE FOE *Tour Gt. Brit.* III. I. 185 The Country People have a Notion that whenever those Gipsies or, as some call 'em, Vipseys, break out, there will certainly ensue either Famine or Plague. **1828** G. YOUNG *Geol. Surv. Yorks.* 25 This ebbing and flowing fountain might have some connection with the intermitting springs called Gipsies. **1856** H. C. HAMILTON *W. of Newburgh* I. 77 *note*,

The village of Wold Newton, near Hunmanby, in the East Riding of Yorkshire, is remarkable for the occurrence in wet seasons of a sudden eruption of cold, clear water, locally called the 'Gipsies,' or the 'Gipsey-race'.

† **gipsiety.** *nonce-wd.* The gipsy character.

1768–74 TUCKER *Lt. Nat.* (1852) II. 190 A mob of.. sturdy gypsies..may be pressed into a regiment: but gypsiety and regimentality can never be turned into one another.

gipsify, gipsire, var. GIPSYFY, GIPSER.

gipsisme, gipson, obs. ff. GIPSYISM, GIPSY.

gipsous, var. GYPSOUS.

gipsy, gypsy ('dʒɪpsɪ), *sb. Pl.* gipsies, gypsies. Forms: α. 6 gipcyan, gip-, gyptian, -sion, (jeptyon, -syon), gipson, -sen. β. 7 gypsey, -ee, 7–8 gypsie, 8–9 gipsey, 9- gypsy, 7- gipsy; *pl.* 7 gypsees, -ties, 9 gipseys, 7- gypsies, gipsies. [The early form *gipcyan* is aphetic for EGYPTIAN (B. 2); the change to *gipsy* may be due to influence of the suff. -Y³, or perh. of L. *Ægyptius*. Skelton (*a* 1529) has 'By Mary Gipcy', by St. Mary of Egypt.

From the quotations collected for the dictionary, the prevalent spelling of late years appears to have been *gipsy*. The plural *gypsies* is not uncommon, but the corresponding form in the sing. seems to have been generally avoided, prob. because of the awkward appearance of the repetition of *y*.]

1. a. A member of a wandering race (by themselves called *Romany*), of Hindu origin, which first appeared in England about the beginning of the 16th c. and was then believed to have come from Egypt.

They have a dark tawny skin and black hair. They make a living by basket-making, horse-dealing, fortune-telling, etc.; and have been usually objects of suspicion from their nomadic life and habits. Their language (called Romany) is a greatly corrupted dialect of Hindi, with large admixture of words from various European langs.

α. [**1514** see EGYPTIAN B. 2.] **1537** LD. CROMWELL in Ellis *Orig. Lett.* Ser. I. II. 101 The Kings Maiestie, about a twelfmoneth past, gave a pardonne to a company of lewde personnes within this realme calling themselves Gipcyans, for a most shamfull and detestable murder. **1589** NASHE *Martins Months Minde* 32 Hee wandring..in the manner of a Gipson..was taken, and trust vp for a roge. **1591** SPENSER *M. Hubberd* 86 Or like a gipsen, or a Iuggeler.

β. **1600** SHAKS. *A.Y.L.* v. iii. 16 Both in a tune like two gipsies on a horse. *a* **1641** BP. R. MOUNTAGU *Acts & Mon.* 232 Like our canting rogues or Gypties. *Ibid.* 519 Gypsies. **1642** MILTON *Apol. Smect.* (1851) 305, I perceave him to be more ignorant in his art of divining then any Gipsy. **1711** ADDISON *Spect.* No. 130 ¶1 We saw at a little Distance from us a Troop of Gipsies. **1722** SEWEL *Hist. Quakers* (1795) I. III. 170 She was put to lodge one night among a great company of gypsies. **1837** HOWITT *Rur. Life* III. i. (1862) 182 The true gipsies are readily distinguished by their..jet-black hair, black sparkling eyes, Indian complexions, and their genuine oriental language. **1875–7** RUSKIN *Morn. in Florence* (1883) 165 The gipsy who is mending the old schoolmistress's kettle on the grass.

¶ Allusively identified with *Egyptian*.

1607 SHAKS. *Ant. & Cl.* IV. xii. 28 Oh this false Soule of Egypt!.. Like a right Gypsie hath at fast and loose Beguil'd me. **1615** W. HULL *Mirr. Maiestie* 60 In this Gypsy [Pharaoh's daughter], the wife of Salomon.

b. Gipsy language, Romany.

1800 W. WHITER (*title*) Etymologicon Magnum..with illustrations drawn from various languages:..Sanscrit, Gipsey, Coptic, etc. **1841** BORROW *Zincali* I. ii. 53 We have found this beautiful metaphor both in Gypsy and Spanish. **1875** SMART & CROFTON *Dial. Eng. Gypsies* 276 Tell me, old fellow, what the sun is in Gypsy. *Ibid.*, I see you know plenty of Gypsy, and I dare say you know more words than any of us. **1930** J. SAMPSON *Wind on Heath* x. 277 (*heading*) One Use Of Gypsy.

2. *transf.* † **a.** A cunning rogue. *Obs.*

1627 E. F. *Hist. Edw. II* (1680) 88 This Overture being come to the Queens ear, and withal the knowledge how this Gipsie [Spenser] had marshall'd his cunning practice,..she seem'd wondrously well-pleas'd. *a* **1635** NAUNTON *Fragm. Reg.* (Arb.) 30 Beware of the Gipsie, meaning Leicester, for he will be too hard for you all.

b. A contemptuous term for a woman, as being cunning, deceitful, fickle, or the like; a 'baggage', 'hussy', etc. In more recent use merely playful, and applied esp. to a brunette.

1632 SHIRLEY *Love in a Maze* IV. 51 *Yon.* I heard You court another Mistris, that did answer it with entertainment. *Thor.* She was a very Gipsie. You were no sooner parted, but she us'd me Basely. **1673** KIRKMAN *Unlucky Cit.* 165 Cursing her [his Mother-in-law] for a dissembling hypocritical Gypsie. **1682** N. O. *Boileau's Lutrin* II. 14 Thus did the Gypsey flutter up and down Through City, Country, Village, and good Town. **1709** E. W. *Life Donna Rosina* 60 The cunning Gipsy, pretending she did not understand his meaning, returned him a civil Answer. *a* **1721** PRIOR *Dutch Proverb*, A slave I am to Clara's eyes: The gipsy knows her power, and flies. **1790** MORETON *W. Ind. Isl.* 127 Keep your employer's bosom-gipsy modestly at a distance [The reference is to a coloured mistress]. **1828** MONCRIEFF *Tom & Jerry* I. vi, Confound the little gipsey, she has fairly given us the slip, by Jupiter. [**1858** GEO. ELIOT *Janet's Repentance* vii, 'I've a capital idea, Gypsey!' (that was his name for his dark-eyed wife when he was in an extraordinarily good humour).]

c. *U.S. slang.* (See quots.)

1942 BERREY & VAN DEN BARK *Amer. Thes. Slang* §766/6 *Gypsy*, an out-of-town truck with no terminal in its destination city. **1954** *Ibid.* (ed. 2) §765/5 *Gipsy*, an independent truckman. *Ibid.* §766/6 *Gipsy*, an independently owned truck. **1967** *Boston Sunday Globe* 23 Apr. A. 36/1 The primary violators among truck drivers are the so-called 'gypsies' who operate independently.

3. Short for ***gipsy-bonnet, -hat, -moth, -winch*** (see 6).

1808–25 JAMIESON, *Gipsy*, a woman's cap, or mutch, plaited on the back of the head. **1819** G. SAMOUELLE *Entomol. Compend.* 431 *Liparis dispar.* The Gipsy. **1823** J. F. COOPER *Pioneers* xli, Concealing her raven hair under her gipsy. **1869** E. NEWMAN *Brit. Moths* 37 The caterpillar of the Gipsy has the ground-colour black. **1889** *Century Dict.*, *Gipsy* 4. *Naut.* a small winch or crab used on board ship; same as gipsy-winch.

4. *attrib.* and *Comb.* **a.** simple attrib., as ***gipsy-encampment, -fair, -prediction.*** **b.** appositive, as ***gipsy-boy, -brat, -devil, -Jewess, -lassie, -man, -mountebank, -musician, -wench.*** **c.** instrumental, as ***gipsy-ridden*** ppl. a. Also ***gipsy-like*** adj. and adv., ***gipsy-looking*** adj., ***gipsy-wise*** adv.

1807 CRABBE *Hall of Just.* I. 56 When first I loved—the *Gipsy-Boy. **1768–74** TUCKER *Lt. Nat.* (1852) II. 150 Two bundles of rags with a *gipsy brat in each of them. *a* **1661** HOLYDAY *Juvenal* 272 Conjecture did attribute it [the sound] to magick: and this *gypsie-devil continued this trick till the coming of our Saviour. **1830** CARLYLE in Froude *Life* (1882) II. 88 The 'Scottish History'..looks like that of a *gipsy encampment. **1881** FREEMAN *Sk. Venice* 57 The traveller who comes on the right day may come in for a *gipsy fair at Duino. **1693** DRYDEN *Juvenal Sat.* VI. (1697) 153 A *Gypsie Jewess whispers in your Ear, And begs an Alms. **1840** LONGF. *Sp. Stud.* III. v, God send the *Gypsy lassie here, And not the Gypsy man. **1651** RANDOLPH, etc. *Hey for Honesty* I. i, Troth, and he may tell you your fortune, *Gypsie-like, and all out of your pockets too. **1652** WHARTON *Ded. to Rothomanne's Chirom.*, The Rarity of the Subject, and the Gipsy-like Esteem it hath amongst the Vulgar [etc.]. **1855** MACAULAY *Hist. Eng.* xxi. IV. 610 The heath was fringed by a wild gipsy-like camp of vast extent. **1824** MISS MITFORD *Village* Ser. I. (1863) 20, I never saw any one who so much reminded me in person of..Meg Merrilies..as dark, as *gipsy-looking. **1840** *Gipsy man [see *Gipsy Lassie*]. **1677** R. CARY *Palæol. Chron.* II. I. xx. 145 Those..*Gipsie Mountebank Assertors of Tradition. **1886** W. J. TUCKER *E. Europe* 219 How is it that those ragged *gipsy musicians don't wash themselves? **1849** DE QUINCEY *Eng. Mailcoach* Wks. 1862 IV. 295 Some *gipsy prediction in his childhood. **1727** DE FOE *Syst. Magic* iii. (1840) 62 The whole world, or great part of it, has been *gipsey-ridden by them, even to this day. *a* **1627** MIDDLETON & ROWLEY *Sp. Gipsy* IV. i, Our *Gipsie Wenches are not common. **1895** *Daily News* 12 Dec. 6/2 Setting forth on his travels *gipsy-wise.

5. *attrib.* passing into *adj.* Resembling what is customary among or characteristic of gipsies; often applied to open-air meals or pic-nics, as ***gipsy breakfast, dinner, party,*** etc.

c **1630** DONNE *Serm.* lxxxv. (1649) II. 34 Never ask wrangling Controverters that make Gypsie-knots of Mariages;—ask thy Conscience and that will tell thee that thou wast maried till death should depart you. **1654** SIR E. NICHOLAS in *N. Papers* (Camden) II. 89, I had a gipsie visit of a mother and her children, bag and baggage. **1790** BURKE *Fr. Rev.* 22 The delusive, gypsey predictions of a 'right to choose our governors'. **1816** JANE AUSTEN *Emma* III. vi. 87 There is to be no form or parade—a sort of gipsy party. **1838** LYTTON *Alice* II. ii, Getting up an impromptu dance or a gipsy dinner. *a* **1839** PRAED *Poems* (1864) II. 46 With gipsy talent they foretell How Miss Duquesne will marry well. *a* **1845** HOOD *To St. Swithin* vi, Why spoil a Gipsy party at their tea, By throwing your cold water upon hot? **1849** E. E. NAPIER *Excurs. S. Africa* II. 294 This little gipsy tent, weighing about twenty pounds..is about three feet high. **1850** R. G. CUMMING *Hunter's Life S. Afr.* (ed. 2) I. 34 We set about preparing our gipsy breakfast.

6. Special combs.: **gipsy-bonnet**, a woman's hat or bonnet with large side-flaps; **gipsy-flower**, the wild scabious; **gipsy-gold** (see quot.); **gipsy-greyhound**, some species of greyhound; **gipsy-hat** = *gipsy-bonnet*; **gipsy-herb** = *gipsy-wort*; **gipsy-herring**, the pilchard; **gipsy-moth**, *Ocneria dispar*; **gipsy-onions** (see quot.); **gipsy-ring** (see quot.); **gipsy-rose**, the wild and garden scabious (*Scabiosa arvensis* and *atropurpurea*); **gipsy('s) pig**, the hedgehog; **gipsy('s) pork**, the flesh of the hedgehog; **gipsy-straw**, straw for making gipsy-bonnets; **gipsy's warning**, a cryptic or sinister warning; **gipsy table**, a light round table supported on three crossed sticks; **gipsy-winch** (see quot.); **gipsy-wort**, modern book-name for *Lycopus europæus* (and for the whole genus).

1855 TENNYSON *Maud* I. xx. 1 The frock and *gipsy bonnet. **1620** MARKHAM *Farew. Husb.* viii. 60 The weeds which are most incident thereunto, are..Thistles, Harebottles and *Gipsie flowers. **1883** JEFFERIES in *Longm. Mag.* June 189 Red sorrel spires..stand the boldest, and in their numbers threaten the buttercups. To these in the distance they give the *gipsy-gold tint—the reflection of fire on plates of the precious metal. **1695** *Lond. Gaz.* No. 3082/4 Lost or stolen..a small blue *Gipsy Grayhound, 16 Inches high. **1805** EMILY CLARK *Banks of Douro* III. 325 She..tied on a white chip *gipsy-hat. **1827** HONE *Every-day Bk.* II. 190 The woman [has] a gipsy-hat jerked up behind. **1727** THRELKELD *Synops. Stirp. Hib.* G 2 b, Some call this [Water-horehound] the *Gipsy-herb, because those stroling Cheats called Gipsies do dye themselves of a blackish Hue with the Juice of this Plant. **1803** WALKER in *Prize Ess. Highland Soc. Scotl.* II. 271 The pilchard..is known among our fishers by the name of the *gipsey herring. **1883** *Daily News* 7 Sept. 2/1 A stranger..might imagine that the great shoals of 'gipsy herrings' had already arrived. **1819** G. SAMOUELLE *Entomol. Compend.* 246 *Liparis dispar* (*gipsy moth). **1882** KIRBY *Europ. Butterflies & Moths* 110 *Ocneria Dispar* (Gipsy Moth). **1897** BAILEY *Princ. Fruit-growing* 24 The codlin-moth, Hessian-fly, gipsy-moth, and a score of other pests. **1847–78** HALLIWELL **Gipsy-onions*, wild garlic. **1928** *Sunday Disp.* 2 Sept. 3/3 'Gypsy Pork.' Hedgehogs are succulent this month. September is the month when the 'gypsies' pig' is plump and tender. **1880** BREWER *Reader's Handbk.* (1885) 385/1 **Gipsey Ring*, a flat gold ring, with stones let into it, at given distances. So called because the stones were originally Egyptian pebbles—that is, agate and jasper. **1892** BLACK *Three Feathers* 220 The purchasing of a gipsy-ring. **1824** MISS MITFORD *Village* Ser. I. (1863) 97 Wild scabious, or, as the country people call it, the *gipsy-rose! **1795** *Hull Advertiser* 29 Aug. 3/1 Fashions for August. Bonnet of cottage *gypsey straw. **1880** MISS BRADDON *Just as I am* vii, The middle-aged lady..with a lamp and a work-basket on the *gipsy table before her. **1918–19** *T. Eaton & Co. Catal.* 369/2 Vocal records... The *Gipsy's Warning (Tenor). **1923** W. J. LOCKE *Moordius & Co.* viii. 113 Bid him beware of Peter Moordius... The gipsy's second warning. **1928** D. L. SAYERS *Unpleasantness at Bellona Club* xi. 126 'What price the gipsy's warning now?' said Lord Peter. **1941** 'P. WENTWORTH' *Danger Point* (1942) xvi. 100, I expect Robson's got you taped... And that being so, suppose you listen to the gypsy's warning. **1967** A. CHRISTIE *Endless Night* xiii. 112 'You'll have to fend for yourself.' 'Cut out the gipsy's warning, Santonix,' I said. **1875** KNIGHT *Dict. Mech.*, **Gipsy-winch*, a small winch having a drum, ratchet, and pawl, and attachable to a post. **1786** WITHERING *Brit. Plants* (ed. 2) I. 19 *Lycopus*, *gypsie-wort. **1854** S. THOMSON *Wild Fl.* III. (ed. 4) 297 The lycopus, or gipsy-wort, is said to derive its English name from being employed by the wandering tribe to stain their skins of a dark colour.

Hence **gipsi'ologist, gipsy'ologist** (*rare*), one who makes a special study of gipsies (also *gipsologist*); **'gipsyhood**, gipsydom; **'gipsyish** *a.*, somewhat gipsy-like; **'gipsyless** *a.*, free from gipsies; **'gipsyness**, gipsy-like appearance or character; **'gipsyry**, a gipsy encampment.

1863 *Chambers's Encycl.* V. 172/1 The facile princeps of all *Gypsologists is Professor Pott of Halle. **1875** F. HALL in *Nation* (N.Y.) XX. 116/2 We are not certain that the observation of Gypsyologists has been sufficiently accurate to leave no room for doubt on this head. **1894** *Athenæum* 6 Oct. 454/2 'Scottish Gypsies under the Stewarts' should find many readers outside the small company of gipsiologists. **1885** *Ibid.* 18 July 78 So accomplished a gipsologist..must know that Meg Merrilies as a gipsy is entirely a fancy portrait. **18..** WHITTIER *Yankee Gypsies* Prose Wks. 1889 I. 342 It has been said..that their ancestors were indeed a veritable importation of English *gypsyhood. **1890** *Athenæum* 4 Oct. 441/2 Valentine is both handsome and piquant in her *gipsyish way. **1894** *Harper's Mag.* Jan. 277/1 Painters..are proverbially gypsyish in their habits. **1826** MISS MITFORD *Village* Ser. II. (1863) 436 We have stocks in the village, and a treadmill in the next town; and therefore we go *gipsyless. **1874** HELPS *Ivan De Biron* v. ii. 263 They had been pleased and amused at the *gypsyness, as they had called it, which had always been visible in Azra's costume. **1874** BORROW *Romano Lavo-Lil* 251 What may be called the grand Metropolitan *Gypsyry is on the Surrey side of the Thames. **1882** LELAND *Gypsies* 362 Near the city [Philadelphia] are three distinct gypsyries.

gipsy ('dʒɪpsɪ), *v.* [f. the sb.] *intr.* To live or act like gipsies, esp. to have meals in the open air, to picnic. Chiefly used in *gerund* and *pres. part.*

a **1627** MIDDLETON & ROWLEY *Sp. Gipsy* IV. i, For so well I love you That I in pitty of this Trade of Gipsying..offer you A state to settle you..so I may call you My Husband. **1834** *W. Ind. Sketch Bk.* II. 184 An occasional marooning, or gipsying party. *c* **1840** RANSFORD *Song*, In the days when we went gipsying, A long time ago. **1847** ALB. SMITH *Chr. Tadpole* xlix. (1879) 418 As cold weather came..he could no longer go on with his gipsying mode of life. **1856** KANE *Arct. Expl.* II. xxv. 249 The whole nation is gypsying with us upon the icy meadows. **1860** EMERSON *Cond. Life* ii. 61 Hunting lion..in South Africa; gipsying with Borrow in Spain and Algiers. **1887** F. FRANCIS Jr. *Saddle & Mocassin* i. 20 It is a delightful climate there in summer, and a glorious country for gipsying. **1890** *Sat. Rev.* 13 Sept. 327/1 Buy a dozen ash rods, a pine ridge-pole, and some red blankets, and set forth gipsying and to gipsy.

b. quasi-*trans.* *to gipsy away*: to filch, steal.

1886 SIR F. H. DOYLE *Remin.* 98 Besides gipsying away a good many lines, he quietly conveyed Macaulay's notes, *totidem verbis*, into his manuscript.

gipsydom ('dʒɪpsɪdəm). [f. GIPSY: see -DOM.] **a.** Life after the gipsy fashion. *rare.* **b.** The collective body of gipsies.

1860 GEO. ELIOT *Mill on Fl.* xi, Her misery had reached a point at which gypsydom was her only refuge. **1865** *Sat. Rev.* 30 Dec. 827 Gipsydom, in fact, is a vast secret society. **1873** LELAND *Eng. Gipsies* ix. 143 There is a strange goblinesque charm in Gipsydom. **1888** *Cornh. Mag.* Aug. 194 [They] adhere to the old traditions of gipsydom.

gipsyfy ('dʒɪpsɪfaɪ), *v.* Also **gipsify.** [f. GIPSY *sb.* + -FY.] *trans.* To make gipsy-like in appearance or character. Also (rarely) *intr.* To become a gipsy. Hence **'gipsyfied** *ppl. a*

1623 MIDDLETON *More Dissemb. Besides Wom.* IV. i, Which hoping you'll observe, to try thee With rusty Bacon thus I gipsifie thee. *a* **1627** MIDDLETON & ROWLEY *Sp. Gipsy* II. ii, *Soto.* Come then, wee'l be Gipsified. *San.* And tipsified too. **1873** LELAND *Eng. Gipsies* I. 4 He may be, of his kind, a quadroon or octoroon, or he may have 'gipsified' by marrying a Gipsy wife. **1882** T. MOZLEY *Remin.* II. lxxix. 68 [She was] very gipsyfied in her manner and style. **1884** TENNYSON *Becket* IV. ii, I will hide my face, Blacken and gipsyfy it; none shall know me.

gipsyism ('dʒɪpsɪɪz(ə)m). Also 7 gyp-, gipsisme. [f. GIPSY *sb.* + -ISM.] The life and pursuits of gipsies, or what resembles this.

a **1613** OVERBURY *A Wife* (1638) 128 Some foule sunne-burnt Queane, that since the terrible statute recanted

Gypsisme, and is turned Pedleresse. *a* **1634** RANDOLPH *Poems* (1640) 48 Live not the Magi that so oft reveal'd Natures intents? is Gipsisme quite repeal'd? Is Friar Bacon nothing but a name? **1826** MISS MITFORD *Village* Ser. II. (1863) 458 There are some hopes that in process of time her sin of gipsyism may be forgiven. **1841** BORROW *Zincali* (1843) I. 28 Gypsyism was denounced as felony by various royal statutes. **1874** BORROW *Romano Lavo-Lil* 266 Strange wild guests..who, without being Gypsies, have much of Gypsyism in their habits.

giptian, obs. form of GIPSY.

giraffe (dʒɪ'rɑːf, -æf). Forms: α. 6 **gyraffa**, 6–9 **giraffa**. β. 7 **giraf(f)le**, **gyraff**, **jarraff**, **ziraph**, 7–8 **giraff**, 6– **giraffe**. [Ultimately ad. Arab. *zarāfah*, whence also It. *giraffa*, Sp. and Pg. *girafa*, F. *girafe*; earlier adoptions of the word are found in OF. as *giras* (pl.), *orafle* and *giraffle*, in ME. as GERFAUNT, ORAFLE; also OSp. *azorafa*. The forms used by English writers have varied at different periods according to their immediate sources. The It. form *giraffa* was common in the 16–17th c., but some writers of 17th c. use *giraff*, app. following Gesner. The modern *giraffe* is from F., though the spelling in that language is now *girafe*. *Jarraff* and *ziraph* (17th c.) are independent adoptions from Arab. or some other oriental language.]

1. A ruminant quadruped found in Africa, remarkable for the length of its neck and legs, and for having its skin spotted like that of a panther; also called CAMELOPARD.

α. **1594** BLUNDEVIL *Exerc.* v. ix. (ed. 7) 551 This beast is called of the Arabians, Gyraffa. **1617** MORYSON *Itin.* I. III. v. 263 Another beast newly brought out of Affricke..is called..Giraffa by the Italians. **1688** R. HOLME *Armoury* II. 130/2 Beasts..Such as chew the Cud, and are not Horned, as Camelopard Giraffa. **1787** P. BECKFORD *Lett. Italy* (1805) I. 137 In the Piazza..was once seen a Giraffa alive, sent as a present to Lorenzo dei Medici..in 1487. **1822–33** tr. *Malte-Brun's Geog.* (1834) 539 (Stanf.) The Giraffa or the camelopard.

β. **1598** SYLVESTER *Du Bartas* I. vi. 104 Th' horned Hirable [**1605** *marg.* alias Giraffe, **1608** *marg.* Alias Gyraffa]. *c* **1600** SANDERSON in Purchas *Pilgrims* II. (1625) 1619 The admirablest and fairest beast that euer I saw, was a Iarraff. **1603** KNOLLES *Hist. Turks* (1621) 988 A live Giraffle (which is a beast like a Cammell and Panther). **1625** PURCHAS *Pilgrims* II. 1381 There wee saw a Ziraph speckled white and higher than any beast I had euer seene. **1665** SIR T. HERBERT *Trav.* (1677) 205 In Gesner's History of Quadrupeds the Gyraff is..mentioned. **1739** E. BROWN *Trav.* 289 There is likewise in this country the Giraff, an animal capable of striking with wonder the most incurious spectator. **1773** *Gentl. Mag.* XLIII. 17 Description of the Giraffe, or Camelopardus. **1857** LIVINGSTONE *Trav.* iii. 56 The presence..of the giraffe..is always a certain indication of water being within a distance of seven or eight miles.

appos. **1892** *Times* (weekly ed.) 25 Nov. 8/1 There my driver shot a fine giraffe-cow.

2. *Astr.* The constellation CAMELOPARD 2.

1836 [see CAMELOPARD 2]. **1868** LOCKYER *Guillemin's Heavens* (ed. 3) 320.

3. *Mining.* (See quots.)

1881 RAYMOND *Mining Gloss.*, *Giraffe*, a car of peculiar construction to run on an incline. **1884** KNIGHT *Dict. Mech.* Suppl., *Giraffe*, a form of cage or truck used on inclines in mines of the Pacific slope.

†**4.** A kind of upright spinet.

1876 in STAINER & BARRETT *Dict. Mus. Terms.*

5. Special Comb.: **giraffe acacia, tree** *S. Afr.*, names occas. used for the camel-thorn tree.

1896 H. A. BRYDEN *Tales of S. Afr.* 44 Groves of giraffe acacia (*kameel doorn*). **1815** A. PLUMPTRE tr. *Lichtenstein's Trav. S. Afr.* II. xlix. 288 A tall and wide spreading giraffe tree, the *acacia giraffæ* of Wildenow.

giraffid (dʒɪ'ræfɪd), *a.* and *sb.* [f. GIRAFFE + -ID³.] **A.** *adj.* Belonging to the family Giraffidæ; like or resembling a giraffe. **B.** *sb.* A member of the family Giraffidæ. So **gi'raffine, gi'raffoid** *a.* and *sb.*

1889 in *Cent. Dict.* **1891** FLOWER & LYDEKKER *Introd. Stud. Mammals* ix. 332 A gradual diminution..can be traced from the more Giraffoid to the more Bovoid forms. **1901** *Proc. Zool. Soc.* II. 280 [The skull] showed itself to be that of a Giraffine animal, and not that of a Bovine. **1902** *Rep. Brit. Assoc. Adv. Sci.* 623 The African Okapi..is a giraffine, horned in the male. **1945** G. G. SIMPSON *Princ. Class. Mammals* III. 266/2 The giraffid resemblance seems to be the result of..common ancestry. *Ibid.* 268/2 The giraffids..are a distinctive and fairly compact family unit. **1965** M. H. DAY *Guide to Fossil Man* III. 120 The fossil mammalian fauna..includes..several bovids and giraffids. **1968** C. A. SPINAGE *Bk. of Giraffe* i. 15 The earliest giraffid appeared in the Miocene. *Ibid.* ii. 28 It [*sc.* an animal in a rock painting] is walking with a giraffid gait.

‖**girandola** (dʒɪ'rændələ). Also 7 **gyrondola**, 8 **girondola**. [a. It. *girandola* GIRANDOLE, f. *girare* to turn in a circle, a. L. *gȳrare*, f. *gȳrus*, a. Gr. γῦρος circle.]

1. A kind of revolving firework; a discharge of rockets, etc. from a revolving wheel.

1670 LASSELS *Voy. Italy* II. 250 The *Girandola* and fire works upon S. Peter's Eve. **1684** EVELYN *Diary* 15 Nov., Being the Queene's birth-day, there were fire-works on the Thames before White-hall, with pageants of castles, forts, and other devices of gyrondolas, serpents..all represented in fire. **1845** FORD *Handbk. Spain* II. 670 Rockets were let off, starring again this Campus Stellæ with a St. Peter's *Girandola* on a small scale. **1887** DOWDEN *Shelley* II. vi. 259 They witnessed..the fireworks at the Castle of St. Angelo, which exhibited, in addition to the customary girandola, the Mausoleum of Hadrian in a fiery restoration.

2. A revolving jet of water, or a series of jets in an ornamental fountain.

1644 EVELYN *Diary* 1 Apr., A dolphin that casts a girandola of water neere 30 foote high. **1645** *Ibid.* 6 May, In the midst of these stands a Janus quadrifons, yᵗ cast forth 4 girandolas. **1673** RAY *Journ. Low C.* 366 The Girandola and other water works. **1756–7** tr. *Keysler's Trav.* (1760) II. 438 The *girondola*, or dragon fountain, throws up a vast column of water to the height of twenty *palmi*.

girandole ('dʒɪrəndəʊl). Also 7 **gironell**, **girondel**, 8 **girandel**. [a. F. *girandole*, a. It. *girandola*: see prec.]

1. A species of firework; = GIRANDOLA 1.

1634 J. BATE *Myst. Nat.* 77 How to make Gironells, or fire wheeles. **1749** *Phil. Trans.* XLVI. 132 The greatest height of any of those fired in the grand Girandole was about 615 yards. **1868** *Morning Star* 29 June, The whole wound up with a girandole of two thousand rockets.

transf. **1766** SIR W. HAMILTON in *Phil. Trans.* LVII. 195 The mouth of the volcano threw up every minute a girandole of red hot stones, to an immense height.

2. A revolving fountain-jet; = GIRANDOLA 2.

1813 J. FORSYTH *Rem. Antiq. Italy* 273 Rock-work and girandoles of water.

3. A branched support for candles or other lights, either in the form of a candlestick for placing on a table, etc., or more commonly as a bracket projecting from a wall.

1769 *Public Advertiser* 10 June 3/3 Sconce Glasses and Girandoles. **1804** *Sporting Mag.* XXIII. 281 A bill of sale of the sofas, pier glasses and girandoles. **1844** DISRAELI *Coningsby* I. iii, It led into a vestibule..hung with Venetian girandoles. **1880** MISS BRADDON *Just as I am* xi, The walls white and gold, with large oval mirrors at intervals, and old crystal girandoles.

4. An ear-ring or pendant, esp. one which has a large central stone surrounded by smaller ones.

1825 LADY GRANVILLE *Lett.* (1894) I. 347 She had my.. second-best earrings, the girandoles, and second-best necklace. **1852** MRS. SMYTHIES *Bride Elect* xiii, When the tiara was on her head, the girandoles in her ears [etc.].

5. *attrib.*, as **girandole-chest**, **-ornament**.

1799 G. SMITH *Laboratory* I. 17 The girandel chest is made of wood, of what size you think proper, according to the number of rockets you design to fire at once. **1828** *Ladies Pocket Mag.* I. 143 The neck-lace is formed of two rows of gold beads..with a girandole ornament of turquoise stones.

girant: see GYRANT.

gira pigra, obs. form of HIERA PICRA.

girar, obs. form of JEERER.

girasol(e ('dʒɪrəsɒl, -səʊl). Also 6 **girosol**, 8 **gyrasole**. [a. It. *girasole* (whence also F. *girasol*), f. *gira-re* to turn + *sole* the sun. Cf. HELIOTROPE.]

†**1.** A sunflower. *Obs. rare*⁻¹.

a **1586** SIDNEY *Arcadia* I. (1598) 91 With grazing lookes, short sighes, vnsetled feet He stood, but turn'd, as Girosol, to Sun.

2. A variety of opal which reflects a reddish glow in a bright light; called also *fire-opal*.

1588 PARKE tr. *Mendoza's Hist. China* 403 Diamonds, rubies, & other stones yᵗ are called *girasolis*. **1611** COTGR., *Girasole*, a Girasole; or precious stone, of the kind of Opalls, that yeelds an eye-like luster, which way soeuer you turne it, vnlesse it be towards the sunne; for then it casts forth beames like the sunne. **1662** MERRET tr. *Neri's Art of Glass* lxxiv, Some..were of a fair Opal colour, and some of the Girasole. **1796** KIRWAN *Elem. Min.* (ed. 2) I. 253 To this family (Oriental Sapphire) we may also annex the stone called Gyrasole. **1804** *Phil. Trans.* XCIV. 42 Girasol..I have long since adopted this word..to distinguish the substance to which Mr. Werner gives the general name of opal, and to which the Abbé Hauy gives the name of *quartz resinite*. **1853** KANE *Grinnell Exp.* xxxiv. (1856) 309 In the midst of which, like a huge girasole, flashes the round sun. **1868** DANA *Min.* (ed. 5) 198 Girasol. Bluish-white, translucent, with reddish reflections in a bright light.

girba ('gɜːbə). Also **gerba(h)**, **gurba**. [ad. Arab. *ḳirba* waterskin.] A water-vessel made of leather.

1790 J. BRUCE *Trav.* IV. VIII. iv. 334 A girba is an ox's skin squared, and the edges sewed together very artificially by a double seam. **1821** G. F. LYON *Narr. Trav. N. Afr.* 33 Our road was through very difficult passes in the mountains, where we found some rain water, with which we filled our gerbas, or water-skins, with a sufficient supply for three days. **1864** J. A. GRANT *Walk across Africa* 418 We had twenty Seedees, and each required to have two goatskins, or 'girba', to carry his drinking-water. **1866** S. W. BAKER *Albert Nyanza* I. iv. 150 This is the unexceptional rule in African travelling—'fill your girbas before starting'. **1925** W. J. H. KING *Myst. Libyan Desert* viii. 97 A *gurba*, raised slightly off the ground in this way, so that the air can circulate round it, keeps the water much cooler.

gircken, obs. form of JERKIN, falcon.

gird (gɜːd), *sb.*¹ *Obs.* exc. *north.* Also 9 *Northumb.* **gord**. [var. of GIRTH, perh. influenced by GIRD *v.*; but cf. *erd*, *yird* = EARTH.]

1. †**a.** A girdle (*obs.*). **b.** †A strap or band of any kind (*obs.*); a saddle-girth.

13.. *K. Alis.* 2272 Glitoun..smot Tauryn..On the helm with the sweord, That the dynt stod at the gird. **1566** in D. H. Fleming *Mary Q. of Sc.* (1897) 499 Tway skenyeis of girdis to bind up the bedde. *a* **1613** OVERBURY *A Wife* (1638) 167 He hath, as it were, put a gird about the whole world. **1653** URQUHART *Rabelais* I. v, What! Drink so shallow? It is enough to break both girds and pettrel. **1825–80** JAMIESON, *Gird, Girdan*, the girth of a saddle. *Perths.*

2. A hoop for a barrel, or one used as a child's plaything. (Cf. GIRR, GIRTH *sb.*¹ 2.)

1612 *Sc. Bk. Rates* in *Halyburton's Ledger* (1867) 308 Girds of Irone for punsheones or pypes the hundreth weght, viii *li.* **1622** *Vestry Bks.* (Surtees) 294 For fower gerdes for the runlets, 4*d.* **1791** NEWTE *Tour Eng. & Scot.* 413 This chain of rocks is called, by the country people, one of the Girds of the Earth. *a* **1800** *Fair Annie* xxvii. in Scott *Minstr. Scott. Bord.*, Has your wine barrels cast the girds, Or is your white bread gone? **1893** *Northumbld. Gloss.*, *Gord*, a hoop. 'The gords is all comin' off the rain-tubs.' 'The bairns hez all getten gords ti play wi'.'

3. *Comb.*, as †**girdsting**, a piece of wood for making hoops. (Cf. *girth-sting*, GIRTH *sb.*¹ 8.)

1534 *Aberd. Reg.* V. 19 (Jam.) Ane thousand half girdstingis and viᶜ haill gridstingis. **1612** *Sc. Bk. Rates* in *Halyburton's Ledger* (1867) 308 Girdstingis the hundreth, xxs.

gird (gɜːd), *sb.*² Also 4 **gyrd**. [f. GIRD *v.*²]

†**1.** A sharp stroke or blow. *Obs. rare.*

1375 BARBOUR *Bruce* v. 629 The brothir that the hand-ax bar..A gyrd rycht to the king can mak. **1570** *Satir. Poems Reform.* xxii. 60 With hir to sport and play, With fauldit neif, and tak hir mony gird. **1579** TOMSON *Calvin's Serm. Tim.* 79/1 When hee toucheth them to the quicke, when hee giueth them girdes with yᵉ spurre.

†**b.** *fig.* A stroke of policy. *Obs. rare*⁻¹.

1513 DOUGLAS *Æneis* VII. vii. 51 Was it nocht evin be sik a fenȝeit gyrd, Quhen Paris..Socht to the citie Laces in Sparta, And thar the douchtyr of Lydea stal awa.

2. A sudden movement or jerk, a spurt of action; chiefly in phrases ***at a gird, for a gird, by fits and girds*** (cf. FIT *sb.*² 4 c); also ***in a gird***: (dial.), in a trice. *Obs.* exc. *dial.*

1545 ASCHAM *Toxoph.* (Arb.) 149 Lowsynge muste be..so quycke and hard yat it be wyth oute all girdes. *c* **1570** *Marr. Wit & Sci.* I. A iv, Agayne, with labor by it selfe, great matters compaste bee, Euen at a gyrde in very lyttel time or none wee see. **1633** T. ADAMS *Exp. 2 Peter* ii. 18 The devotion of worldlings is all for a gird. **1672** MARVELL *Reh. Transp.* I. 56 All that he saith either by fits and girds of Calvin, or in his justest narratives. **1825–80** JAMIESON, *Gird*, a very short space of time, a moment. 'I'll be wi' you in a gird.' **1887** *S. Chesh. Gloss.*, *Gird*, only in the phrase 'by fits an' girds' = by fits and starts.

3. A spasm of pain, sudden pang. Now *dial.*

1614 T. ADAMS *Devil's Banq.* 213 What is..the torment of the reynes, to the stiches, girds, and gripes of an aking Conscience? **1667** SOUTH *Serm.* (1823) I. 371 Old age comes attended with many painful girds and achings. **1714** STEELE *Lover* No. 7 My Heart relented, and gave me several Girds and Twitches. **1876** *Mid-Yorksh. Gloss.* s.v., A poorly person will say, in humorous reference to his weak condition, 'I's middling at meal-times, but I've hardish girds between.'

4. A sharp or biting remark directed against a person; a gibe, 'dig', 'hit'. In common use *c* 1580–1700; now somewhat *arch.*

1566 DRANT *Horace's Sat.* a iv b, Those that wyll them [satires] write With taunting gyrds & glikes and gibes must vexe the lewde. **1676** MARVELL *Mr. Smirke* Wks. 1875 IV. 25 Many a dry bob, close gird, and privy nip has he given him. *a* **1734** NORTH *Lives* (1826) III. 390 For his girds were oblique, and touched to the quick, but not directly exceptionable. **1834** SIR H. TAYLOR *Artevelde* II. IV. iii. (1849) 218 Lois of Sanxere, I ask thee in this presence, Fling'st thou these girds at me? **1881** *Contemp. Rev.* Dec. 894, I mean no gird at this tendency.

b. with punning allusion to GIRD *sb.*¹

1593 NASHE 4 *Lett. Confut.* 72 Thou shalt be double girt with girds.

5. *dial.* An outburst (of laughter).

c **1746** J. COLLIER (Tim Bobbin) *View Lanc. Dial.* Wks. (1862) 42 Th' fly'ring Karron seet up o Gurd o Leawghing. **1790** MRS. WHEELER *Westmld. Dial* (1821) 103 She fetched up a girt gird a laffin, an sed [etc.].

gird (gɜːd), *v.*¹ Inflected girded and girt. Forms: 1 **gyrdan**, *Northumb.* **ȝi-gyrde**, 4–6 **gerd(e**, 4–7 **girde**, (5 **gyrdyn**, **gurde**, 6 **gyrde**), 6– **gird**. *Pa. t.* α. 1 **gyrde**, 3–4 **gurde**, (4 **gurd**, **gerd**), 4–5 **girde**, (5 *pl.* **gurdene**), 6 **gyrd(e**. β. 4 **girdede**, 5–6 **gyrded**, 6 **gerded**, 6– **girded**. γ. 4 **gyrt**, **gert**, **girt(e**, 5 **gyrte**, 7– **girt**. *Pa. pple.* α. 1 **gyrded**, 4 **gyrdid**, *Sc.* **girdit**, 6 **ger-**, **gyrded**, 6– **girded**. β. 3 **i-gurd**, 4 **gurde**, 4–6 **gird(e**, 5–6 **gyrd(e**. γ. 4 **gert**, 5 **girte**, 6 **gerte**, **gyrte** (**gyrthe**), 3– **girt**. [OE. *gyrdan* = OS. *gurdian* (Du. *gorden*), OHG. *gurten* (MHG. and mod.G. *gürten*), ON. *gyrða* (OSw. *giorþa*, Sw. *gjorda*, Da. *gjorde*) to gird:—OTeut. **gurdjan*. To other grades of the same root belong Goth. (*bi-*, *uf-*)*gairdan* to gird, *gairda* girdle; see GIRTH, GARTH²; some scholars connect also Goth. *gard-s* house, corresp. to GARTH¹, YARD.

Throughout its whole history the English word is chiefly employed in rhetorical language, in many instances with more or less direct allusion to biblical passages.]

1. *trans.* To surround, encircle (the waist, a person about the waist) with a belt or girdle, esp. for the purpose of confining the garments and allowing freer action to the body. Chiefly *refl.* or *pass.*; also, after Biblical phrase, ***to gird one's loins, reins***, etc. Also ***to gird up, about.***

c **950** *Lindisf. Gosp.* John xxi. 18 Mið-ðy [þu] uere ȝiungra ðu waldes ðec ȝigyrde..miððy uutudlice ðu bist ȝeuintrad..

oðer ðec gyrdeð. a 1225 *Ancr. R.* 418 ȝe schulen liggen in on heater, and i-gurd. c 1250 *Gen. & Ex.* 3149 Sod and girt, stondende, and staf on hond. c 1330 R. BRUNNE *Chron. Wace* (Rolls) 1804 Coryneus first vp he stirt, & wyþ a cloþ his body gyrt. 1382 WYCLIF *Exod.* xii. 11 ȝe schulen girde about ȝoure reynes. —— *Tobit* v. 5 Tobie..fond a ȝung man stondende, ful faire, gird [1535 COVERDALE gyrded vp], and as redi to gon. c 1430 *Syr Gener.* (Roxb.) 7054 The lauendres kirtel on she cast, She gird hir, and tukked hir fast. 1483 CAXTON *Gold. Leg.* 432 b/2 For gyrdle he gyrded hym on his bare flesshe wyth a corde. 1535 COVERDALE 2 *Kings* iv. 29 Girde vp thy loynes, and take my staffe in thy hande, and go thy waye. —— *Luke* xii. 35 Let youre loynes be gerded aboute. 1667 MILTON *P.L.* IX. 1113 Those Leaves They gathered..And..together sowd, To gird thir waste. 1782 COWPER *Truth* 82 In shirt of hair, and weeds of canvas dressed, Girt with a bell-rope that the Pope has blessed. 1810 SCOTT *Lady of L.* III. vii, He girt his loins and came. 1865 DICKENS *Mut. Fr.* III. iv, She girded herself with a white apron. 1872 [EARL PEMBROKE & G. H. KINGSLEY] *S. Sea Bubbles* vii. 176 They girded him with strange belts.

b. *fig.* To prepare (oneself) for action; to brace up (oneself) *for*, *to*, or *to do* something. Often with *up*.

c 1450 tr. *De Imitatione* I. xix. 22 Girde þe as a man ayenst þe fendes wickednes. 1592 tr. *Junius on Rev.* xiv. 1 As ready gird to doe his office in the midst of the Church. 1672 CAVE *Prim. Chr.* I. iii. (1673) 49 The mind is strengthened and girt close by indigence and frugality. 1781 COWPER *Conversat.* 702 [They] one in heart, in interest, and design Gird up each other to the race divine. 1822 HAZLITT *Table-t.* Ser. II. vi. (1869) 126 To gird themselves up to any enterprize of pith or moment. 1860 MOTLEY *Netherl.* (1868) I. i. 15 He was already girding himself for his life's work.

†**c.** To clothe *with* or *in* a garment confined by a girdle. *Obs. rare.*

1382 WYCLIF 2 *Sam.* vi. 14 Dauid is gird [Vulg. *accinctus*; 1388 clothed; 1611 girt] with a surplees. 1697 DRYDEN *Æneid* VII. 258 Girt in his Gabin Gown the Heroe sate.

†**d.** To bind (a horse) with a saddle-girth. (Cf. GIRTH *v.* 2.) *Obs.*

c 1330 *Arth. & Merl.* 3985 Adoun þai liȝt & her hors girten. c 1420 *Anturs of Arth.* xxxix. 495 Gawayne and Galerone gurdene [*v.r.* dyghtis] here stedes. 1509 BARCLAY *Shyp of Folys* (1570) 25 He is a foole..That to his saddle would leape on hye Before or he haue girt his horse. c 1566 *Merie Tales* in *Skelton's Wks.* (1843) I. p. lxv, Skelton commaunded the ostler to sadle his mare, & the hosteler did gyrde the mare hard. 1677 MIEGE *Dict. Eng.-Fr.*, To gird a Horse, *cengler un cheval.*

2. *fig.* To invest or endue *with* attributes, esp. (after biblical phrase) *with strength*, *power*, etc.

c 1000 *Ags. Ps.* (Th.) xvii. 31 [xviii. 32] Se god me ȝegyrde mid mæȝnum, and mid cræftum. a 1300 *E.E. Psalter* xvii. 33 [ibid.] (Horstm.) Lauerd þat girde me with might. 1388 WYCLIF *Ps.* xvii. 33 [ibid.] God that hath gird me with vertu. *Ibid.* lxiv. 7 [lxv. 6] Thou makest redi hillis in thi vertu, and art gird with power. a 1450–1530 *Myrr. our Ladye* 126 The vyrgyn mari in whome thou hast cladde the in fayrnesse and gyrthe the in strengthe. 1580 SIDNEY *Ps.* XVIII. ix, This God then girded me in his all-mighty pow'rs. 1667 MILTON *P.L.* VII. 194 The Son On his great Expedition now appeer'd, Girt with Omnipotence. 1812 S. ROGERS *Columbus* I. 49 Sent forth to save, and girt with God-like power. 1821 SHELLEY *Prometh. Unb.* I. 643 The sights with which thou torturest gird my soul With new endurance. 1874 BLACKIE *Self-Cult.* 14 Without carrying away any living pictures of significant story which might..gird them with endurance in a moment of difficulty.

3. To equip (oneself or another) *with* a sword suspended from a belt fastened round the body; sometimes with reference to investing a person with the sword of knighthood.

a 1000 *Cædmon's Gen.* 2865 (Gr.) Hine se halȝa wer gyrde græȝan sweorde. 1297 R. GLOUC. (Rolls.) 3615 Mid is suerd he was igurd, þat so strong was & kene. c 1350 *Will. Palerne* 3291 þe kniȝt..gerd him wiþ a god swerd. c 1450 *Merlin* 322 Gonnore hir-self girde hym with his swerde. 1568 R. GRAFTON *Chron.* II. 95 Upon Easter day..he was gyrde with the sworde of the Duke of Briteyn. 1641 BAKER *Chron.* (1660) 127 And because he had not yet received the Order of Knighthood, he was by Henry Earl of Lancaster girt solemnly with the sword. 1663 BUTLER *Hud.* I. ii. 742 Was I for this entitled Sir, And girt with trusty sword and spur. 1848 GALLENGA *Italy Past & Pr.* I. p. xxv, They gave her a standard; they girt her sons with the weapons of war.

4. a. To fasten (a sword or other weapon) to one's person by means of a belt. Const. *on*, *upon*, *to*. Also with *on* adv.

c 1000 *Ags. Ps.* (Th.) xliv. 4 [xlv. 3] Gyrd nu þin sweord ofer þin þeoh [L. *super femur tuum*] þu Mihtiȝa. a 1300 *E.E. Psalter* ibid. (Horstm.) Girde þi swerde of iren and stele Ouer þi thee. 1480 CAXTON *Chron. Eng.* cc. 181 Andrew of herkela..worthely arrayed and with a swerd gurt aboute hym. a 1533 LD. BERNERS *Huon* xliii. 146 He dyd on his helme and gyrte on his sword. 1555 EDEN *Decades* 270 Hauynge theyr quyuers of arrowes gerte to them. 1667 MILTON *P.L.* VI. 713 My Bow and Thunder, my Almighty Arms, Gird on, and Sword upon thy puissant Thigh. 1718 PRIOR *Knowledge* 247 The combatant too late the field declines, When now the sword is girded to his loins. 1781 GIBBON *Decl. & F.* II. xlv. 689 A trusty sword was constantly girt to their side. 1832 LYTTON *Eugene A.* I. iv, His pistols were still girded round him. 1840 DICKENS *Barn. Rudge* iii, Girt to his side was the steel hilt of an old sword without blade or scabbard. 1883 STEVENSON *Treas. Isl.* v. xxii, The doctor took up his hat and pistols, girt on a cutlass ..and..crossed the palisade.

b. To secure (clothing, armour, etc.) on the person by means of a girdle; also *to gird on*, *up*.

1297 R. GLOUC. (Rolls) 8962 þo caste þis gode mold hire mantel of anon & gurde aboute hire middel a uair linne ssete. c 1380 WYCLIF *Wks.* (1880) 316 ȝif þise cloþis ben gurde & more large in widnesse, þei beren on hem more synne. 1535 COVERDALE *John* xxi. 7 Simon Peter..gyrde his mantell aboute him & sprange in to ye see. 1583 STUBBES *Anat. Abus.* II. (1882) 109 An old gowne girded to him with a thong. 1611 BIBLE *1 Kings* xx. 32 So they girded sackcloth on their loynes. 1667 MILTON *P.L.* VI. 542 Let each His Adamantine coat gird well. 1791 COWPER *Iliad* XI. 17 Bade the Greeks Gird on their armour. 1814 SCOTT *Ld. of Isles* V. xxxiv, Warn Lanark's knights to gird their mail. 1835 W. IRVING *Tour Prairies* 45 He rode with his finely shaped head and breast naked, his blanket being girt round his waist. 1855 KINGSLEY *Heroes* II. (1868) 24 So Perseus arose, and girded on the sandals and the sword. 1877 J. NORTHCOTE *Catacombs* I. v. 71 With his tunic girt high about his loins.

c. To put (a cord, etc.) *round* something. *rare.*

1726 SWIFT *Gulliver* I. i, Very strong cords..which the workmen had girt round my neck, my hands, my body, and my legs.

5. *transf.* and *fig.* †**a.** To surround as with a belt; to tie firmly or confine. Also ***to gird up***, ***in***, ***about***, ***together***. *Obs.*

c 1600 SHAKS. *Sonn.* xii, Sommers greene all girded up in sheaues. 1602 MARSTON *Antonio's Rev.* II. v. Wks. 1856 I. 103 Then I Catch straight the cords end; and..offer a rude hand As readie to girde in thy pipe of breath. 1611 BIBLE *Ecclus.* xxii. 16 As timber girt and bound together in a building [etc.]. 1657 R. LIGON *Barbadoes* (1673) Index to Plate 84 Two stantions of timber which are girded together in several places, with wood or Iron. 1667 MILTON *P.L.* VIII. 82 How [they will] gird the Sphear With Centric and Eccentric scribl'd o're. 1674 N. FAIRFAX *Bulk & Selv.* 128 For I take the seed..to be a cluster of bubbles wryed up snug, or a bottome of hoops or springs closely girt or knit together.

b. To encircle (a town, etc.) with an armed force; to besiege, blockade.

1548 HALL *Chron. Hen. VI*, 153 b, He..determined to get the town of Vernoyle in perche, and gyrd it round about with a strong seage. 1590 GREENE *Orl. Fur.* (1599) C, But trust me, Princes, I haue girt his fort, And I will sacke it. a 1627 HAYWARD *Four Y. Eliz.* (Camden) 66 But the French was so streightly girt up within Lieth, that no supplies were brought unto them. 1814 CARY *Dante, Inf.* XIV. 64 This of the seven kings was one, Who girt the Theban walls with siege. 1867 DICKENS *Lett.* (1880) II. 284 The whole place is secretly girt in with a military force.

c. To fasten tightly, draw close (as a fetter or bond) upon a person. *rare.*

1732–8 NEAL *Hist. Purit.* IV. 139 His Highness girt the laws close upon the Papists.

6. Said of that which surrounds: To encircle, enclose, confine.

c 1290 *S. Eng. Leg.* I. 206 Some of þe naddrene biclupten heom so faste al a-boute þat heom þouȝte heo scholden to-berste so streite heo gurden heom with-oute. 1375 BARBOUR *Bruce* XVII. 616 Gret flaggatis tharof thai maid, Gyrdit with Irne-bandis braid. 1749 SMOLLETT *Regicide* V. ix, An iron crown intensely hot, shall gird Thy hoary Temples. 1781 COWPER *Retirement* 243 Girt with a chain he cannot wish to break His only bliss is sorrow for her sake. 1822–34 *Good's Study Med.* (ed. 4) IV. 444 A discoloration..which extended..over the loins and very nearly girded the body. 1843 CARLYLE *Past & Pr.* III. ii. (1858) 187 Girt with the iron ring of Fate. 1864 TENNYSON *En. Ard.* 157 Then first since Enoch's golden ring had girt Her finger [etc.]. 1868 FREEMAN *Norm. Conq.* (1876) II. viii. 197 A mighty mound girded by a fosse.

b. of natural surroundings or barriers, esp. of rivers.

1593 SHAKS. 3 *Hen. VI*, IV. viii. 20 Like to his Iland, girt in with the Ocean. 1601 R. JOHNSON *Kingd. & Commw.* (1603) 14 The navigable rivers, whereof some (as it were) gird in the whole realme. 1667 MILTON *P.L.* IV. 276 That Nyseian Ile Girt with the River Triton. 1809 PINKNEY *Trav. France* 27 This lawn..was girded entirely around by a circle of lofty trees. 1853 G. JOHNSTON *Nat. Hist. E. Bord.* I. 13 The range thus girds in and defines the plain. 1870–4 J. THOMSON *City Dreadf. Nt.* I. iv, A river girds the city west and south.

c. of a ring or crowd of people; chiefly *refl.* or *passive*.

1671 MILTON *Samson* 1415 Your company along I will not wish, lest it perhaps offend them To see me girt with friends. 1807 WORDSW. *White Doe* III. 133 On foot they girt their Father round. a 1839 PRAED *Poems* (1864) II. 37 Girt with a crowd of listening Graces, With expectation on their faces. 1864 TENNYSON *Boadicea* 5 Boadicea..Girt by half the tribes of Britain.

d. of immaterial surroundings (chiefly *passive*).

1629 MILTON *Nativity* 202 Ashtaroth..Now sits not girt with tapers' holy shine. 1671 —— *P.R.* I. 120 So to the coast of Jordan he directs His easy steps, girded with snaky wiles. 1833 TENNYSON *Pal. Art* 273 Shut up as in a crumbling tomb, girt round With blackness as a solid wall. 1836 H. HOLLAND *Med. Notes* (1839) 274 It is well worthy of note.. how long in fact it [life] may continue, thus narrowed and girt in on every side. 1847 L. HUNT *Jar Honey* ix. (1848) 120 Unheard was shepherd's song, And silence girt the woods.

e. To move round. *rare.*

1688 PRIOR *On Exod.* iii. 14, 51 Why does each consenting Sign With prudent Harmony combine..To gird the Globe, and regulate the Year? 1812 WOODHOUSE *Astron.* v. 20 They [Navigators] must therefore have surrounded, or girded the Earth.

†**7.** *intr.* Of a string: To have a grip *upon* what it encircles. *Obs.*

1680 MOXON *Mech. Exerc.* I. 187 The String..will touch and gird more upon the Groove of the Work, and consequently..will the better command the Work about.

gird (gɜːd), *v.*[2] Forms: 4 **girden, gerde, gorde,** 4–5 **gyrd, gurd(e,** 4–6 **girde,** 5–6 **gyrde,** (7 **guird-, guerd**), 4– **gird.** *Pa. t.* 3 **gurde,** 4 **gert(e,** 4–5 **girde, girt,** 4–6 **gird, gyrd;** 4 *pl.* **girdiden,** 5 *Sc.* **girdit,** 6– **girded,** (7 **guirded**). *Pa. pple.* 3 **gurd,** 4 **y-girt,** 4–5 **gird(e,** 5 **gurt,** (7 **gurde**), 6– **girded.** [Of obscure origin.

Derivation from OE. *ȝierd* rod, YARD, is impossible on account of the initial guttural, and indirect connexion with that word appears also inadmissible, as WGer. *ar-* from *az-* has no corresponding weak grade *ur-*.]

†**1.** *trans.* To strike, smite. Often with advb. compl. describing the effect of the stroke, as ***to gird down***, ***off***, ***out***, also ***to gird in two***, ***to death***, ***to ground***, etc. Also of pain: To touch sharply (*rare*).

c 1205 LAY. 1596 He gurde suard on þat hæfd þat he grund sohte. 13.. *K. Alis.* 2299 A-two peces he hadde him gurd, No hadde Glitoun y-come. c 1350 *Will. Palerne* 1240 Grimly wiþ gret cours eiȝþer gerdeþ oþer, & William wiþ god wille so wel þe duk hitt [etc.]. c 1400 *Destr. Troy* 177 Girde out the grete teth of the grym best. a 1400–50 *Alexander* 2474 Settis all þe gailis on gledis & girdis doun þe wallis. c 1450 HENRYSON *Mor. Fab.* 35 With that the Meir gird him vpon the gumes. c 1460 *Towneley Myst.* xiii. 622 If I trespas eft, gyrd of my hede. 1606 BP. HALL *Medit. & Vows* I. §92. 107 When therefore some sodain stitch girds me in the side. 1612 W. MARTYN *Youth's Instruct.* 91 The horseman..with a stiffe..cudgel so guirded and laced the backe..of his..master. 1618 LATHAM *2nd Bk. Falconry* (1633) 49 That will cause her [the hawk] to gird and master them, as it were, at the sowce.

b. *absol.* To deliver a blow. Also Sc. ***to let gird*** (cf. *to let drive*).

13.. *Gaw. & Gr. Knt.* 2062 [Gawayn] gordez to Gryngolet with his gilt helez. a 1400–50 *Alexander* 1219 Gers many grete syre grane & girdis þurȝe maillis. 1450–70 *Golagros & Gaw.* 105 The grume..leit gird to schir Kay, Fellit the freke with his fist flat in the flure. a 1550 *Christis Kirke Gr.* xv, Thay girnit and lait gird with grainis, Ilk gossip uder grievit.

†**2.** To impel or move hastily or rudely; to thrust *in*, cast *up*, drive *back*, pull *out*, throw *down*; to fire (a gun) *to* (= at). *Obs.*

13.. *Coer de L.* 1086 In at hys [the lion's] throte hys arme he gerte, Rent out the herte. 1377 LANGL. *P. Pl.* B. v. 379, I Glotoun girt it [food] vp, er I hadde gone a myle. c 1400 *Destr. Troy* 10370 But the grekes were so grym, þai gird hom abake. a 1400–50 *Alexander* 2227 Sum with gunnes of þe grekis girdis vp stanes. 1450–70 *Golagros & Gaw.* 848 Thai ..girdit out suerdis on the grund grene. a 1650 *Scot. Field* 93 in Furniv. *Percy Folio* I. 216 Many a gaping gunn was gurde to the walls, where there fell of the first shott manie a fell ffooder.

3. *intr.* To move suddenly or rapidly; to rush, start, spring. Also ***to gird forth***, ***forward***, ***out***, ***together***, ***up***. *Obs.* exc. *dial.*

13.. *E.E. Allit. P.* B. 911 þe grounde of gomorre [schal] gorde into helle. 1375 BARBOUR *Bruce* II. 417 With that come gyrdand, in A lyng, Crystall off Seytoun. a 1400–50 *Alexander* 1243 Ane Beritinus..Come girdand out of Gadirs, out of þe grete cite. 1513 DOUGLAS *Æneis* X. xiv. 161 Eneas gyrd abufe hym with a brayd. 1565 GOLDING *Ovid's Met.* II. (1593) 32 They girded forth, and cutting through the clouds..they overflue the easterne winde apace. 1579 GOSSON *Sch. Abuse* (Arb.) 58 The freest horse, at the whiske of a wand, girdes forwarde. 1601 HOLLAND *Pliny* II. 428 No sooner hangs he by the hooke, but he runneth and girdeth with it in his mouth too and fro. 1887 *S. Chesh. Gloss.*, *Gird*, to push, hurry about. The word is common in the phrase 'runnin' an' girdin'.'

4. *fig.* **a.** *absol.* To make 'hits' *at*, to jest or gibe *at* (rarely *against*, *upon*). Also in indirect passive. (The current sense.)

1546 BALE *Eng. Votaries* I. (1560) 52 Let the gogle eied Gardiner of winchester gyrde at it tyll his rybbes ake. 1608 MIDDLETON *Fam. Love* II. iii, I wonder why many men gird so at the law. a 1639 W. WHATELEY *Prototypes* I. xix. (1640) 173 You must labour to jest, scoff, and gird, or raile against such and such sinnes. 1679 J. GOODMAN *Penit. Pardoned* III. vi. (1713) 371 Why doth he not reprove debauchery..rather than..be always guerding at the sanctified party? 1823 LAMB *Let. to Southey* Corr. (1868) I. 212 You are always girding at what some pious..folk think to be so [religion]. 1862 SALA *Seven Sins* I. vi. 123 The clubmen talked club scandal and girded at the Committee. 1891 *Times* 11 July 11/2 Not only is each member of the Triple Alliance denounced and girded at in turn, but [etc.].

b. *trans.* To assail with jest or sarcasm; to sneer or scoff at. ? *Obs.*

1573 G. HARVEY *Letter-bk.* (Camden) 29 Sum..he hath spitefully girdid behind there backs. 1628 EARLE *Microcosm.*, *Discontented Man* (Arb.) 28 His life is a perpetuall Satyre, and hee is still girding the ages vanity. 1721 STRYPE *Eccl. Mem.* I. xxvi. 191 He girded him as he had done the Archbishop of York, telling him he looked for a new world. 1850 L. HUNT *Autobiog.* xi. 184 The Examiner had been long girding him on incompetency.

Hence †**gird-off** *ppl. a.*, struck off, severed.

1382 WYCLIF 2 *Kings* xx. 22 Thanne she wente into al the puple, and spak to hem wiseli, the which the gird of heed of Siba..casten forth to Joab.

gird-brew, var. GIRT-BREW.

girde, obs. form of Gird.

girded (ˈgɜːdɪd), *ppl. a.* [f. GIRD *v.*[1] + -ED[1].] In senses of the vb.

Beowulf (Z.) 2078 He fyrmest læȝ, gyrded cempa. 1599 SHAKS. *Hen. V*, III. Prol. 27 Behold the Ordenance on their Carriages, With fatall mouthes gaping on girded Harflew. 1627 MAY *Lucan* I. 649 But by the guirded Sacrificers strength..orecome..holds forth his conquer'd necke. 1877 BRYANT *Poems*, *Little People of Snow* 62 With trailing garments through the air they came, Or walked the ground with girded loins. 1882 J. ROBERTSON tr. *Müller's Heb. Synt.* §97 Six hundred girded men. 1889 *Sat. Rev.* 16 Mar. 319/2 The young lord with his *hakama* (silk trousers) and girded sword.

girdel, -er, obs. forms of GIRDLE, GIRDLER.

girder ('gɜːdə(r)), *sb.*[1] Also 7 gerder. [f. GIRD *v.*[1] (sense 5) + -ER[1].]

1. a. A main beam in a framed floor, supporting the system of joisting that carries the flooring.

Sometimes (erroneously) used instead of BREASTSUMMER.

1611 COTGR., *Solive*, the peece of timber called a Girder, or Joist (betweene two Summers). **1631** GOUGE *God's Arrows* iv. §15. 399 Two girders were by tenents and mortaises let into the midst of it [the maine Summier]. **1679** MOXON *Mech. Exerc.* I. 137 The Girders are also to be of the same Scantlins the Summer and Ground-Plates are of. **1770** THORPE in *Phil. Trans.* LXI. 157 When I repaired the old house at Nettlested,..in sawing off the end of the main girder, it was decayed at heart. **1820** T. TREDGOLD *Carpentry* (1853) 80 Framed floors differ from double floors only in having the binding joists framed into large pieces of timber, called girders. *Ibid.* 83 Framed floors consist of girders, binding joists, bridging joists, and ceiling joists.

b. An iron or steel longitudinal beam employed for a similar purpose; esp., a latticed, plate, or other compound structure used to form the span of a bridge.

The main transverse beams of a girder bridge, corresponding to the 'binding-joists' of a framed floor, are termed 'cross-girders'.

1853 SIR H. DOUGLAS *Milit. Bridges* (ed. 3) 344 IG and HK are vertical rods of wrought-iron which connect a great girder of the road-way with the tube AB. **1869** *Latest News* 5 Sept. 16 So fierce was the fire, that the glass in the roof melted; but the iron girders remained in their places. **1889** G. FINDLAY *Eng. Railway* 63 Forty-two girders, each thirty-two feet in length, were required, and the plates and angles for each girder were rolled in one length.

†**2.** In masonry (see quots.). *Obs.* **a.** A bondstone. **b.** A bonding-course.

a. 1726 LEONI *Alberti's Archit.* I. 47/2 Among the Girders we reckon those courses of large stones which tie the outward Shell to the inward.

b. 1726 LEONI *Alberti's Archit.* I. 48/1 But..there are other Girders besides..which run the whole length of the Wall to embrace the Corners. These other Girders..we call Cornices.

3. *attrib.*, as **girder-bridge**, a bridge whose superstructure consists of longitudinal girders carrying the platform or roadway; **girder-rail**, a form of tramway rail, introduced about 1860, and so called from the resemblance of its section to that of the ordinary iron girder used in construction.

1854 WEALE *Engineer's Pocket-bk.* 389 The excess of strength that should be given to Girder Bridges. **1856** H. HAUPT *Bridge Construct.* 265 The manner of constructing trussed girder bridges. **1861** *Times* 7 Oct, These persons were engaged..in the erection of a girder bridge across the River Ouse. **1894** *Daily News* 25 Oct. 6/3 Metal ways with girder rails and simple connections are the form most favoured.

Hence '**girderage**, girders collectively.

1880 *Standard* 5 Jan. 5 The whole top mass of girderage, without giving way in detail, may have been blown off the piers.

†'**girder**, *sb.*[2] *Obs. rare.* [f. GIRD *v.*[2] + -ER[1].] One who sneers or cavils.

1584 LYLY *Campaspe* III. ii, What is a quip? *Manes.* We great girders cal it a short saying of a sharp witte, with a bitter sense in a sweete word. **1609** DEKKER *Guls Horne-bk.* 138 By sitting on the stage, you..may lawfully presume to be a girder, and stand at the helm to steer the passage of scenes. **1611** COTGR., *Lardonneur*, a girder, flowter.

girder ('gɜːdə(r)), *v.* [f. GIRDER[1].] *trans.* To support or strengthen with or as with a girder; freq. *fig.* So '**girdered** *ppl. a.*

1934 DYLAN THOMAS *18 Poems* 32 Strong As motor muscle on the drill, driving Through vision and the girdered nerve. **1938** L. MACNEICE *Mod. Poetry* i. 18 There is a chance for poets..to girder it [sc. *élan vital*] with a structure supplied partly by reason. **1956** D. BARNHAM *One Man's Window* 19 The hangar is a vast girdered cavern. **1969** *Observer* 12 Jan. 27/1 A vision in which titanic masonry enveloped mankind like the girdered belly of a whale.

girding ('gɜːdɪŋ), *vbl. sb.*[1] [f. GIRD *v.*[1] + -ING[1].]

1. The action of the vb. GIRD[1], in various senses.

c **1400** MAUNDEV. (1839) x. 122 Othere there ben, that men clepen Cristene men of Gyrdynge: for thei ben alle gyrt aboven. *c* **1592** STOW *Eng. Chron.* an. 1340. 362 The king created him at Westminster by the girding of a sword. **1626** BACON *Sylva* §419 To make Roses, or other Flowers come late..The Seuenth [Meanes] is, the Girding of the Body of the Tree about with some Pack-threed. *a* **1716** SOUTH *Serm.* (1737) X. iv. 117 Patience is (as it were) the girding up of the soul, which like the girding up of the body gives it both strength and decency too.

2. That which girds; esp. †**a.** A girdle. (Also *girding-up*) (*obs.*). **b.** *dial.* A saddle-girth. †**c.** A girder (*obs.*).

1388 WYCLIF *Isa.* xi. 5 And riȝtfulnesse schal be the girdil of hise leendis, and feith schal be the girdyng of hise reynes. *c* **1430** *Syr Gener.* (Roxb.) 4224 Laces and stringes he kerue on twoo, and the girding of the shelde also. **1535** STEWART *Cron. Scot.* III. 402 Scho come sic speid, Than in the girding grittar ay scho growis. **1577** HARRISON *England* II. xii. (1877) I. 233 Groundsels..transoms, and such principals, with here and there a girding, wherevnto they fasten their splints or radels. **1689** tr. *Buchanan's De Jure Regni apud Scotos* 59 Are not Saddles, Girdings and Spurs made for Horses? **179.** BURNS *Weary fa' you, Duncan Gray*, The girdin brak, the beast cam doun.

3. *Comb.*, as **girding-beam** = GIRDER *sb.*[1] 1; **girding-place**, the part of the body round which the girdle or girth is fastened.

1751 CHAMBERS *Cycl.*, *Girding-beams. **1601** HOLLAND *Pliny* II. 274 It must (they say) be..kept fast bound neere vnto the middle or *girding place of the patient. **1682** *Lond. Gaz.* No. 1727/8 A large Chesnut Gelding..between 15 and 16 hands high..a white Rim under the Belly near the girding place.

'**girding**, *vbl. sb.*[2] [f. GIRD *v.*[2] + -ING[1].] The action of the verb GIRD[2]. †**a.** Discharging, firing (of cannon) (*obs.*). **b.** Jeering, gibing.

a. *a* **1650** *Scot. Field* 323 in Furniv. *Percy Folio* I. 228 There was gurding forth of gunns: with many great stones.

b. 1605 VERSTEGAN *Dec. Intell.* v. (1628) 130 He fell to taunting and girding at them. *a* **1663** SANDERSON *Serm.* II. 159 Bitter invectives, unmannerly jeers, petulant girding at those that are in authority. **1863** MRS. C. CLARKE *Shaks. Char.* ii. 37 Shakespeare..never misses an opportunity of girding at your pompous and affectedly pensive character.

'**girding** *vbl. sb.*[3] *dial.* [f. GIRD *sb.*[1] + -ING[1].] The action of fitting (barrels) with hoops.

1609 *Vestry Bks.* (Surtees) 289 For girding of barels, ijd. *c* **1817** HOGG *Tales & Sk.* IV. 17 John Jardine, the cooper, chanced to come to Knowe—back in the course of his girding and hooping peregrinations.

girding ('gɜːdɪŋ), *ppl. a.*[1] [f. GIRD *v.*[1] + -ING[2].] That girds, in senses of the vb.

1655 GURNALL *Chr. in Arm.* xiv. §1 (1669) 54/2 Walk (Christian) in the view of God's Omniscience, this is a girding consideration. **1708** OZELL tr. *Boileau's Lutrin* iv. 79 So, Abandon'd by its Girding Wood, Sinks an old Roof, which had for Ages stood. **1762–9** FALCONER *Shipwr.* II. 915 To cut the girding stay they run. **1822–34** *Good's Study Med.* (ed. 4) III. 246 The use of stiff and girding stays. **1853** KANE *Grinnell Exp.* (1856) 543 The Russo-Siberians gave us vaguely a girding-line of ice. **1869** BLACKMORE *Lorna D.* xxix, 'Tis the ripening of the oats! All the day they have been dancing..Waiting for the girding hook.

girding ('gɜːdɪŋ), *ppl. a.*[2] [f. GIRD *v.*[2] + -ING[2].] That girds, scoffs, or jeers.

a **1617** BAYNE *On Eph.* (1658) 168 Prophane, filthy, and girding jests. **1691** tr. *d'Emilianne's Observations* 126 The Receiver..told us, in a very girding manner, that [etc.]. **1882** *Spectator* 2 Dec. 1535 They..believe in girding speeches as foolish Communists believe in petroleum.

girdiron, obs. form of GRIDIRON.

girdle ('gɜːd(ə)l), *sb.*[1] Forms: 1 gyrdel, 2, 4, 6 gerdell(e, 3 girrdell, 3–4 gurdel, (5 -il), 4 girdel, -ul, 4–5 girdil, 5–6 gir-, gyrdel(l(e, -ill(e, -yl(l(e, 5–7 gyrdle, 6 girddel, girthell, guyrdell, 4– girdle. [OE. *gyrdel* (f. *gyrdan* to GIRD: see -LE) = MDu. *gurdel, gordel* (Du. *gordel*), OHG. *gurtil* masc., *gurtila* fem. (MHG. and mod.G. *gürtel*), ON. *gyrðill* (OSw. *giordel*, Sw. *gördel*); the OE. *gyrdels* (=OS. *gurdisl*), f. the same grade of the root with a different suffix (see -ELS), is found earlier than *gyrdel*, but did not survive into ME.]

1. a. A belt worn round the waist to secure or confine the garments; also employed as a means of carrying light articles, esp. a weapon or purse.

In the general sense now only literary (the colloquial word being BELT), but still commonly used for a cord or the like tied round the waist and having the ends hanging down.

c **1000** *Ags. Gosp.* Matt. iii. 4 Se iohannes witodlice hæfde reaf of olfende hærum & fellenne gyrdel [*c* **1160** *Hatton Gosp.* gerdel] embe hys lendenu. *c* **1200** ORMIN 3210 Hiss girrdell wass off shepess skinn Abutenn hise lendess. *c* **1290** *S. Eng. Leg.* I. 58/150 In stude of is gurdel al-so; with rope he him bond. **1340** *Ayenb.* 236 Þe gerdel aboue be-tocneþ chastete of bodie. *c* **1386** CHAUCER *Miller's T.* 64 By hire girdel heeng a purs of lether. **1463** *Bury Wills* (Camden) 16 My girdyl of ledir barryd with siluir with bokyll and pendaunth. **1525** LD. BERNERS *Froiss.* II. xlviii. 167 Gyrdelles of chaynes of golde and syluer. **1598** BARRET *Theor. Warres* v. ii. 143 A purse at his girdle, with bullets, and his other necessaries. **1619** BOYLE in *Lismore Papers* (1886) I. 216, I paid my cozen..for an embroydered girdle and Hangers. **1709** STEELE & ADDISON *Tatler* No. 147 ¶ 3 This Cestus was a fine Party-coloured Girdle. **1756** NUGENT *Gr. Tour* III. 83 The nobility..wear also a black girdle about four fingers broad, and garnished with plates and buckles of silver. **1819** SHELLEY *Cenci* v. iv. 160 Here, Mother, tie My girdle for me, and bind up this hair. **1863** GEO. ELIOT *Romola* I. xx, Her white silk garment was bound by a golden girdle. **1881** JOWETT *Thucyd.* I. 5 The combatants at boxing and wrestling matches wear girdles. **1890** *Draper's Circular*, Girdles are being used for all sorts and conditions of dresses for day wear.

b. *spec.* (*Eccl.*) (See quot. 1866.)

1519 *Churchw. Acc. St. Giles, Reading* 7 For frankensence ed iiij girdles iiij[d]. **1566** in Peacock *Eng. Ch. Furniture* (1866) 49, ij vestementes..a girdell a fruntall and 3 albes. **1866** *Direct. Angl.* (ed. 3) 354 *Girdle*, the cord that girds the alb, usually made of white cotton about three yards long.

c. in various phrases and proverbial sayings. ***girdle of chastity*** = ***chastity belt***; ***girdle of Venus***: See VENUS[1] 9.

Many of these refer to the practice of wearing keys hung at one's girdle. (***to have, hold***) ***under one's girdle***: in subjection, under one's control. †***ne'er an M by your girdle?*** = Haven't you the politeness to say 'Master'? †***to give up the girdle***: to confess oneself beaten. †***to turn one's girdle***: ? to find harmless outlet for one's anger (see Schmidt and the commentators).

a **1400–50** *Alexander* 181 Bot gefe þaim vp þe girdill vs gaynes noȝt ellis. *Ibid.* 758 And oþir recouyre me þi rewme or reche vp þe girdill. *c* **1530** R. HILLES *Common-Pl. Bk.* (1858) 140 All the keys hange not by one manys gyrdyll. **1541** BARNES *Wks.* (1573) 203/2 If hee bee in Rome, and hath all Princes neckes vnder hys gyrdell. *a* **1553** UDALL *Royster D.* III. iii. (Arb.) 48 Neare an M by your girdle? **1598** R. BERNARD tr. *Terence's Andria* I. i. (1607) 11 Iwis it is long hence I must liue after anothers pleasure, with my head vnder anothers girdle. **1599** PORTER *Angry Wom. Abingt.* (Percy Soc.) 104, I know you are as good a man..as was ere girt in a girdle. **1599** SHAKS. *Much Ado* v. i. 143 *Prince.* I thinke he be angrie indeede. *Claud.* If he be, he knowes how to turne his girdle. **1612** WOODALL *Surg. Mate* Wks. (1653) Pref. 12 In whose Opinion they onely have the Keyes of Art at their girdles. **1660** BURNEY *Κέρδ. Δῶ ρον* (1661) 80 He is curst in his Mothers Belly that would overtop such Princes, and bring their heads under his Girdle. **1667–8** PEPYS *Diary* 14 Feb., Thereby [by allowing £70,000 a year for 'intelligence'] Cromwell carried the secrets of all the princes of Europe at his girdle. **1706** FOWLER in Hearne *Collect.* 20 Jan. (O.H.S.) I. 166 He depended upon none, and..would not be under any one's Girdle. **1802** tr. *Pallas's Trav. S. Prov. Russ. Empire* I. 399 Their girls..are provided with laced stays, or a broad girdle made of untanned leather: this singular coat of mail is among the common people tightly sewed round the waist, but in the higher classes it is fastened with silver hooks, so that they are obliged to wear it till their wedding-night... Besides the girdle of chastity above mentioned there is another circumstance which contributes to preserve the elegant shape of the girls: they are sparingly nourished. **1858** GEN. P. THOMPSON *Audi Alt.* II. lxxvii. 31 A leader who carries half the Scottish Church under his girdle.

d. = CORSET 2; *spec.* a corset, usu. elasticated, that does not extend above the waist. orig. *U.S.*

1925 *Eaton's News Weekly* 24 Oct. 19 Brassiere of rayon jersey silk and girdle of mercerized cotton and silk brocade with panels of elastic. **1928** *Delineator* Mar. 109 (Advt.), Girdle. **1932** *Daily Mail* 3 Oct. 10/1 A two-way stretch elastic girdle. **1942** D. POWELL *Time to be Born* (1943) xi. 266 Go out and get yourself a girdle. **1957** H. ROOSENBURG *Walls came tumbling Down* 14 The girdle certainly didn't support her kidneys; it flapped..loosely around her. **1963** *Punch* 20 Mar. 426/3 His elevation from girdle ads to the glossies.

†**2. a.** The part of the body round which the girdle is fastened; only in phrases ***beneath, above, up to, the girdle***. *Obs.*

c **1205** LAY. 1325 Þe merminnen þæt beoð deor of muchele ginnen, wifmen hit þunchet fuliwis, bi-neoðe þon gurdle hit þuncheð fisc. **13..** *K. Alis.* 6449 Eren they haveth an ellen long, That byneothe theo gurdel hit hongith. **1526** *Pilgr. Perf.* (W. de W. 1531) 3 A persone syttyng in the trone of god whiche from ye gyrdell downwarde was all lyke fyre. **1624** LORD KEEPER WILLIAMS in *Fortesc. Papers* (Camden) 203 And allreadye up to the gyrdle in his grave. **1632** *Womens Rights* 315 It was greater shame to strike vnder the girdle than it is now. **1691** HARTCLIFFE *Virtues* 75 It was a favourable and merry Conceit of a Cardinal of Rome, that there was no Law beneath the Girdle. *a* **1734** NORTH *Lives* (1826) I. 124 This great man..married his own servant maid and then for excuse, said there was no wisdom below the girdle.

b. *transf.* and *fig.*

1607 *Puritan* III. i, Ere the day Be spent to th' Girdle, thou shalt be set free. **1860** TYNDALL *Glac.* II. xi. 291 The atmosphere cleared, and showed the mountains clothed to their girdles with snow.

3. *transf.* uses of 1. **a.** That which surrounds, as a girdle does the body; †a zone. †***the girdle of the world***; the ecliptic, the equator. Also of immaterial surroundings.

c **1000** *Sax. Leechd.* III. 260 We hataþ on leden quinque zonas, ðæt synd fif gyrdlas. **1559** W. CUNNINGHAM *Cosmogr. Glasse* 63 Five..zones..we may aptly call them equidistant places, or Girdles. **1599** SHAKS. *Hen. V*, Prol. 19 Suppose within the Girdle of these Walls Are now confined two mightie Monarchies. **1626** BACON *Sylva* §398 The Great Brizes, which the Motion of the Aire in great Circles, (such as are vnder the Girdle of the World) produceth. **1665** MANLEY *Grotius' Low C. Warres* 416 The Rhiphean Mountains encompass them..which..they call the Girdle of their Land. **1697** DRYDEN *Virg. Georg.* I. 322 Five Girdles bind the Skies, the torrid Zone Glows with the passing and repassing Sun. *c* **1700** J. LAWSON in *Harper's Mag.* (1883) Feb. 419/1 A delicious country..placed in that girdle of the world which affords wine, oil, fruit. **1781** COWPER *Expost.* 20 The billows roll, From the world's girdle to the frozen pole. —— *Charity* 86 Trade is the golden girdle of the globe. **1836** MACGILLIVRAY tr. *Humboldt's Trav.* xvii. 219 The horizon was bounded by a girdle of forests. **1847–8** H. MILLER *First Impr.* viii. (1857) 133 The quick, smart patter of hammers sounds incessantly, in one encircling girdle of din. **1875** MERIVALE *Gen. Hist. Rome* (1877) i. 5 The Palatine hill..the first nucleus of the Roman Empire, lay in the centre of a girdle of eminences. **1879** FARRAR *St. Paul* (1883) 321 Among good and holy men love would still be the girdle of perfectness.

†**b.** ***to put*** (***make, cast***) ***a girdle*** (***round***) ***about***: to go round, make the circuit of (the earth). *Obs.*

1590 SHAKS. *Mids. N.* II. i. 175 Ile put a girdle about the earth, in forty minutes. **1612** DEKKER *If it be not good* Wks. 1873 III. 277 About the world My trauailes make a girdle. **1621** MIDDLETON *Sun in Aries* Wks. (Bullen) VII. 342 Sir Francis Drake..did cast a girdle about the world. *c* **1626** *Dick of Devon* II. v. in Bullen *O. Pl.* II. 43 They would have thought Themselves as famous as their Country-man That putt a girdle round about the world.

c. That which confines or binds in; a restraint, limit.

a **1616** BEAUM. & FL. *Faithf. Friends* IV. iv, To all Thy thoughts, thy wishes, and thine actions, No power shall put a girdle. **1641** J. JACKSON *True Evang. T.* I. 38 The sixt Persecution..[was] limited..to a short time, (for it was precinct with a triennial girdle). **1645** MILTON *Tetrach.* (1851) 221 But suppose it any way possible to limit sinne, to put a girdle about that Chaos. **1833** I. TAYLOR *Fanat.* vi. 193 The iron girdle of a solemn and irrevocable oath.

4. *spec.* **a.** A kind of sea-weed, *Laminaria saccharina.*

1548 TURNER *Names Herbes* (E.D.S.) 27 Cingulum.. maye be named in englishe, fysshers gyrdle or sea gyrdel. **1551** —— *Herbal* I. K iv b, Ther is a certayne kynde of sewrake with a brode leafe, of a grene color, to the whyche sum geue the name of a leeke, other call this gyrdell.

b. *Anat.* Applied to various parts in the structure of animal bodies; in modern use chiefly of the bony supports for the upper and lower limbs, which in Vertebrata are respectively called the ***shoulder*** (or ***pectoral***) and ***pelvic*** (or ***hip***) ***girdle***.

1601 *Househ. Ord.* 296 The cheife clerke of the kitchen hath for his fee all the girdles of fresh sturgeon spent within the house. **1634** T. JOHNSON *Parey's Chirurg.* III. i. (1678) 56 Under the region of the navel, lies the girdle or upper part of the Kall. **1711** *Phil. Trans.* XXVII. 352 The last is very like our English Hedge Snail, but without Girdles, and has a small Navel. **1831** R. KNOX *Cloquet's Anat.* 109 As a powerful bony girdle, it [the pelvis] affords articulation to the abdominal extremities. **1861** HULME tr. *Moquin-Tandon* II. III. iv. 138 When a leech is impregnated, an enlargement takes place around the sexual apertures, which has received the name of the girdle or clitellum. **1883** MARTIN & MOALE *Vertebr. Dissect.* II. 119 The Shoulder Girdle is made up of a *coracoid, clavicle*, and *scapula* on each side. *Ibid.* 122 The Pelvic Girdle is composed of the ilium, ischium, and os pubis on each side. **1891** *Science* (N.Y.) 21 Aug. 107/2 The fins, girdles, gill arches, scales, and membrane bones are all imperfectly developed or wanting [in eels].

c. The line or rim dividing the two faces of a brilliant (see quots.).

1819 REES *Cycl., Girdle*, among Jewellers, the line which encompasses the stone parallel to the horizon; or which determines the greatest horizontal expansion of the stones. **1861** *Macm. Mag.* III. 184/2 The rim where the setting takes hold, or, as we have described it, the junction of the bases of the pyramids, is called the girdle. **1883** A. H. CHURCH *Precious Stones* iii. 21 The 'girdle' or edge bounding the widest part of the stone, divides the crown from the base, and is concealed in part.. by the mounting or setting.

d. *Arch.* (See quot. 1842.)

1727 BOYER *Dict. Angl.-Fr., Ceinture*, The Cincture, or Girdle of a Pillar. **1751** CHAMBERS *Cycl., Girdle*, in Architecture. See *Cincture*. **1842** FRANCIS *Dict. Arts, Girdle*, a small circular band around the shaft of a column.

e. *Mining.* A stratum or bed of stone or other substance occurring irregularly. (Cf. BAND *sb.*[2] 12.)

1819 REES *Cycl., Girdle*, in Mining, is the name used in Cumberland, and some other counties, to denote the uncertain strata, or chance beds, of stone or different substances that are met with in some districts. **1893** *Northumbld. Gloss., Girdles*, in mining, are beds from about three inches to two feet or more in thickness; but the term is usually applied to beds varying from three inches to nine or ten inches thick.

f. *Bot.*

1875 BENNETT & DYER *Sachs' Bot.* 368 When the growth is normal.. the three segments which form a cycle always become arranged into a disc transverse to the stem, their outer surfaces thus forming an annular zone or girdle. **1884** BOWER & SCOTT *De Bary's Phaner.* 381 The border of tracheides of each leaf is expanded into a low wing, which runs to meet that of the opposite leaf, and unites with it to form a transverse girdle.

g. A belt or ring made round the trunk of a tree by the removal of the bark (cf. GIRDLE *v.* 2).

1825 J. LORAIN *Pract. Husb.* 63 All of them eventually die, provided the girdle be carefully cut through the sap into the heart-wood of the tree. **1896** P. A. BRUCE *Econ. Hist. Virginia* I. 150 The method employed by the Indians for the removal of the forest.. consists in running a girdle around the trunks of the largest trees by cutting away the bark.. the object of this being to intercept the flow of the sap. **1897** BAILEY *Princ. Fruit-growing* 289, Fig. 45 shows a deposit of woody matter above a girdle caused by a label wire.

5. ***pin and girdle***: a swindling game, 'prick the garter' (see GARTER *sb.* 5, 7).

1710 PALMER *Proverbs* 209 'Tis astonishing that a young gentleman, bred five or six years in our own universities, shou'd.. be drawn in.. by those common known cheats of the pin and girdle.

6. *attrib.* and *Comb.*, as ***girdle-bell, -belt, -buckle, -compass, -maker; girdle-like, -shaped*** adjs.; also **girdle-bed, -bone** (see quots.); †**girdle-glass**, a mirror carried at the girdle; **girdle-hanger** (see HANGER[2] 4 b); **girdle-pains** = *girdle-sensation*; **girdle-sensation, -wheel** (see quots.).

1880 C. T. CLOUGH in *Geol. Mag.* 443 **Girdle Beds.*—Alternations of thin sandstones and sandy shales. **1810** SOUTHEY *Kehama* XIV. viii, The sweet music of their *girdle-bells. **1697** DRYDEN *Æneid* IX. 488 Nor did his [Euryalus] Eyes less longingly behold The *Girdle-Belt, with Nails of burnish'd Gold. **1871** HUXLEY *Anat. Vertebr. Anim.* 175 The Frog's skull is characterised by the development of a very singular cartilage bone, called by Cuvier the *os en ceinture* or *girdle-bone. **1790** *Chron.* in *Ann. Reg.* 207/1 A *girdle-buckle about the bigness of a crown-piece was also dug up. **1552** HULOET, *Girdle compasse, or in the compasse, or wyth the compasse of a gyrdle, *zotim* [? read *zonatim*]. *a* **1652** BROME *New Acad.* IV. ii. (1658) 85 How his [the man's] pocket-combe.. and her [the woman's] *Girdle-glasse, To order her black pashes, came together. **1921** *Brit. Mus. Return* 66 Anglo-Saxon iron *girdle-hanger from Cliffe, near Rochester. **1923** C. FOX *Archaeol. Cambr. Region* vi. 271 Girdle hangers. The simplest forms are a close copy in bronze of the housewife's keys of iron (a Roman type), the possession of which they doubtless symbolized. **1892** *Pall Mall G.* 23 June 1/3 It has a smart bodice, with.. a *girdle-like arrangement of cord in front. **14..** *Nom.* in Wr.-Wülcker 686/20 *Hic corrigiarius*, *gyrdil-maker. **1897** HUGHES *Mediterr. Fever* iii. 122 Mental irritability and sleeplessness are combined with.. *girdle-pains [etc.]. **1885** *Syd. Soc. Lex.*, **Girdle-sensation*, the feeling of having a string or a broad band tied round the body or one of the limbs. **1897** *Allbutt's Syst. Med.* II. 977 It was followed by atrophy of the muscles, impairment of vision.. girdle sensation [etc.]. *Ibid.* III. 521 The ulcer [of the stomach] is.. occasionally, if of very long-standing, *girdle-shaped. **1688** R. HOLME *Armoury* III. 287/1 *The Girdle Wheel is a [Spinning] Wheel so little that a Gentle-woman may hang it at her Girdle.. and Spin with it, though she be walking about.

girdle ('gɜːd(ə)l), *sb.*[2] *north.* and *Sc.* Forms: 6 girdil(e, -ill, (kyrdill), gyrdle, 6– girdle, (9 *dial.* gurdle). [var. GRIDDLE by metathesis of *r*.] A circular plate of iron which is suspended over the fire and upon which cakes are baked or toasted. (Cf. GRIDDLE *sb.*).

a **1400** *Burgh Laws* cxvi. (*Sc. Stat.* I), Alsua he sall hafe.. a brasyn pot a pan a rostyng yrne a girdill [etc.]. **1477** *Extracts Aberd. Reg.* (1844) I. 408 A gyrdil, a bakbrede, a brewyne fat. **1533** *Ibid.* 451 Ane kamery stok, ane girdill, ane baik bread. **1563** *Richmond. Wills* (Surtees 1853) 169 A gyrdle, a brandrett. **1596** DALRYMPLE tr. *Leslie's Hist. Scotl.* I. 95 Thay make breid after casting it vpon the girdle. **1681** COLVIL *Whigs Supplic.* (1751) 106 Oatmeal.. which girdles hot bakes And turns to bannocks, and to oat cakes. **1708** S. MOLYNEUX in *Phil. Trans.* XXVI. 39 A large Girdle about 20 Pounds Weight.. was found lying on the Floor. **1859** ATKINSON *Walks & Talks Schoolboys* (1892) 343 Bilberry jam, and flaky cakes hot from the girdle. **1886** STEVENSON *Kidnapped* xx. 196 We lay on the bare top of a rock, like scones upon a girdle.

b. Phrase. ***like a hen on a het*** (***hot***) ***girdle***: indicating a state of great uneasiness or discomfort.

1787 BURNS *Let. to W. Nicol* 1 June, It's true she's.. tipper-taipers when she taks the gate first, like.. a hen on a het girdle. **1814** SCOTT *Wav.* lxxi, The Bailie.. had all this while shifted from one foot to another with great impatience 'like a hen', as he afterwards said, 'upon a het girdle'. [**1849** C. BRONTË *Shirley* xxxi. 448 His gait.. emulated that of a hen treading a hot girdle.]

c. *Comb.*, as ***girdle-cake*** (cf. *griddle-cake*), ***-maker, -making, -smith.***

1802 R. ANDERSON *Cumberld. Ball.* 25 Aunt Ester spoil'd the *gurdle ceakes. **1852** MISS YONGE *Cameos* (1877) I. xlii. 361 Each man had.. a plate of metal on which he could bake his girdle-cakes. **1885** RUNCIMAN *Skippers & Sh.* 49 We had a girdle cake for tea. **1599** *Charter Jas. VI*, The *girdelmakers inhabitants within the bruch of Culross. **1833** CARLYLE *Cagliostro* II. *Misc.* (1840) IV. 376 She was the daughter of a Girdle-maker. **1885** D. BEVERIDGE *Culross & Tulliallan* II. xix. 93 The *girdlemaking monopoly. **1661** *Culross Town Rec.*, Patrick Sands *girdle-smythe.

Hence **'girdleful**, as much as a girdle can hold.

1895 J. WOOD in *Scot. Antiq.* X. 76 The goodwife was baking, and had a girdleful of bannocks on the fire.

girdle ('gɜːd(ə)l), *v.* [f. GIRDLE *sb.*[1]]

1. a. *trans.* To surround with a girdle. Also *to **girdle about, in, round.*** (Chiefly *transf.* and *fig.*)

1582 N. LICHEFIELD tr. *Castanheda's Conq. E. Ind.* xv. 39 Silke.. even such wherewith he was accustomed to girdle himselfe. **1591** SHAKS. *1 Hen. VI*, IV. iii. 20 Spurre to the rescue of the Noble Talbot, Who now is girdled with a waste of Iron, And hem'd about with grim destruction. **1598** BARRET *Theor. Warres* VI. i. 184 There is set down.. how many shot will girdle or impale the battell of pikes. **1607** SHAKS. *Timon* IV. i. 2 O thou Wall That girdles in those Wolues, diue in the earth, And fence not Athens. **1635** BARRIFFE *Mil. Discip.* xcv. (1643) 306 The Hollow Square, girdled with shot, is a figure to bee used in times of necessity. **1712** J. JAMES tr. *Le Blond's Gardening* 196 Wooden Pipes.. are ferriled and girdled with Iron. *a* **1782** COWPER *Heroism* 6 No thunders shook with deep intestine sound The blooming groves that girdled her around. **1808** SCOTT *Marm.* II. ix, The tide did now its floodmark gain, And girdled in the Saint's domain. **1848** C. BRONTË *J. Eyre* (1857) 106 The bright and velvet lawn closely girdling the grey base of the mansion. **1858** HAWTHORNE *Fr. & It. Jrnls* (1871) I. 252 That circumference of blue hills which stand afar off, girdling Rome about. **1871** FARRAR *Witn. Hist.* ii. 55 Let us mark how the hills that girdle them are scattered with the ruined engineery of assaults. **1888** ALICE MEYNELL in *Art Jrnl.* LI. 139/2 A tea-gown, waistless, and girdled low down.

b. To travel round. Cf. GIRDLE *sb.*[1] 3 b.

1901 F. H. BURNETT *Making of Marchioness* II. vi. 180 Agatha Norman, at present joyously girdling the globe with her bridegroom.

2. a. To cut through the bark of a tree in a circle extending round the trunk, or to remove a certain breadth of bark in a similar circle, either for the purpose of killing the tree or for that of rendering it more fruitful; sometimes in *passive* of injuries caused accidentally, e.g., by a tight wire or by the gnawing of rabbits. Also with *round.*

1662 WINTHROP in Birch *Hist. Roy. Soc.* (1756) I. 101 Several trials have been made.. by girdling the tree (as they call it) cutting off some of the bark round, and a little into the wood of the tree, about six feet from the ground. **1766** J. BARTRAM *Jrnl.* 11 Feb. in Stork *Acc. E. Florida* 65 There still remain.. great trees girdled round to kill them, which are now very sound, tho' above 60 years since they were cut. **1792** BELKNAP *Hist. New Hampsh.* III. 211 If the trees were girdled and left to die standing, the timber would be much superior to any which is cut whilst alive. *a* **1817** T. DWIGHT *Trav. New Eng.* etc. (1821) II. 459 They accordingly cut down some trees, and girdle others. **1871** H. MACMILLAN *True Vine* v. (1872) 212 The barren branch is girdled or ringed—that is, a narrow strip of its bark is removed all round the branch. **1897** BAILEY *Princ. Fruit-growing* 288 Trees which are girdled should have the injured parts pared down to live tissue.

b. *Surg.* (See quot.)

1883 WILDER & GAGE *Anat. Techn.* 197 (Cent.) When the skin, especially of a limb, is divided by an incision encircling the part, the latter is said to be girdled.

Hence **'girdled** *ppl. a.*

a **1817** T. DWIGHT *Trav. New Eng.* etc. (1821) II. 126 There is a sufficient number of girdled trees standing.. to give the new settlements a disagreeable appearance. **1883** E. P. ROE in *Harper's Mag.* Dec. 56/1 Girdled trees soon made it evident that rabbits were the depredators. **1888** [see GIRDLE *v.* 1]. **1940** E. S. GARDNER *Case of Silent Partner* xii. 196 Her tightly girdled, snappily dressed figure. **1961** A. SMITH *East Enders* vii. 119 Women with plucked eyebrows and men with girdled waists.

girdler ('gɜːdlə(r)). [f. GIRDLE *sb.*[1] + -ER[1].]

1. A maker of girdles.

c **1400** *Destr. Troy* 1584 Goldsmythes, Glouers, Girdillers noble. **1428** in *Surtees Misc.* (1888) 1 Ye crafte of Girdelers in ye cite of York. **1532–3** *Act 24 Hen. VIII*, c. 1 The wardens of the felowshippe of Saddellers, gyrdelers, coryers, or any other of the kynges subiectes. **1613** BEAUM. & FL. *Honest Man's Fort.* I. i, Do you heare? Talke with a Girdler, or a Milner. **1671** F. PHILLIPS *Reg. Necess.* 373 The Kings Grocer, Brewer.. Bookseller, Girdler, (a Trade now altogether disused). **1723** *Lond. Gaz.* No. 6189/4 John Sewell.. Sword-Cutler and Girdler. **1807** W. TAYLOR in *Ann. Rev.* V. 296 There are useless articles in this work, such as that of girdler, which is no longer a separate trade. **1872** *City Press* 20 Jan., The court of the Girdlers' Company dined at the hall.

2. One that surrounds or encompasses. ***girdler of the earth*** = Gr. γαιήοχος.

1879 BUTCHER & LANG *Odyss.* 33 Hear me, Poseidon, girdler of the earth.

girdlestead ('gɜːd(ə)lˌstɛd). *Obs.* exc. *arch.* [f. as prec. + STEAD *sb.*] That part of the body round which the girdle passes; the waist.

c **1330** *Arth. & Merl.* 5216 Þat at þe girdel stede it stode. ? **1366** CHAUCER *Rom. Rose* 826 Hise shuldris of a large brede, And smalish in the girdilstede. *c* **1420** LYDG. *Assemb. Gods* 340 Aboute hym, in hys gyrdyll stede, hyng fysshes many a score. **1583** STUBBES *Anat. Abus.* I. (1877) 60 Some [clokes] short, scarcely reaching to the gyrdle-stead, or wast. **1653** H. COGAN tr. *Pinto's Trav.* ix. 29 We walked a whole day along by the Isle of Sumatra, in the ouze up to the girdle-stead. **1696** AUBREY *Misc.* (1721) 94 An Antient Man.. having a long and broad white Beard, hanging down to his Girdle Steed. **1870** MORRIS *Earthly Par.* III. IV. 57 One gleaming lock of gold.. Fell far below her girdlestead.

b. Used for 'lap'.

1882 SWINBURNE *Tristr. of Lyonesse* vi. 51 There fell a flower into her girdlestead Which laughing she shook out.

girdling ('gɜːdlɪŋ), *vbl. sb.* [f. GIRDLE *v.* + -ING[1].]

1. The action of the verb GIRDLE in various senses. Also ***girdling in.***

1792 BELKNAP *Hist. New Hampsh.* III. 131 The method is that of girdling; which is done by making a circular incision through the bark, and leaving them to die standing. **1836** ARNOLD *Let.* in Stanley *Life & Corr.* (1844) II. viii. 48 The girdling in of the mountains round the valley of our home is.. an image.. of the encircling of the everlasting arms. **1897** BAILEY *Princ. Fruit-grow.* 291 Girdling or ringing to set trees into bearing is an old and well-known practice.

2. The material of which girdles are made.

1719 D'URFEY *Pills* VI. 248 Gartering, Girdling, Tape.

3. *attrib.*, as ***girdling-place.***

1658 BROMHALL *Treat. Specters* I. 118 He was become so weak and feeble below his girdling place or middle.

girdling ('gɜːdlɪŋ), *ppl. a.* [f. GIRDLE *v.* + -ING[2].] That girdles or surrounds.

1598 BARRET *Theor. Warres* III. ii. 71 The girdling shot to discharge at 20 pases off, and not farther. **1624** *Trag. Nero* III. iii. in Bullen *O. Pl.* I. 52 The girdling flame doth with unkind embraces Compasse the Citie. **1818** BYRON *Ch. Har.* IV. 174 Where yon bar Of girdling mountains intercepts the sight. **1821** JOANNA BAILLIE *Metr. Leg., Columbus* xxxvii, Mountains.. Whose frozen peaks.. Above the girdling clouds rear'd far in upper air. **1837** CARLYLE *Fr. Rev.* I. VI. iii, The Château Polignac still frowns aloft.. amid the blue girdling mountains of Auvergne. **1863** GEO. ELIOT *Romola* II. iv, Florence with its girdling stone towers.

gire, var. GYRE.

girefalcon, obs. form of GYRFALCON.

‖**girella**. *rare*[−1]. [It., dim. of *gira*, f. *girāre* to turn.] A vane or weather-cock.

1720 STRYPE *Stow's Surv. Lond.* I. 149/2 A lofty Tower with a Clock and Chimes: and at the top of it a Grashopper for the Vane, or Girella. **1790** BAILEY, *Girella*, a Vane, Weathercock. *Ital.*

girg, var. JARG *Sc.*, *v.* to creak (and *sb.*).

girk, obs. form of JERK *sb.* and *v.*

girkienet, var. JERKINET.

girkin, obs. form of GHERKIN.

girking, var. JERKIN, a kind of hawk.

girl (gɜːl), *sb.* Forms: 3 gurle, 4–6 gerl(e, 4–7 girle, gyrle, (6 guirle, gierle, gyrll, 7 garle), 9 *dial.* gal, gell, 7– girl. [Of obscure etymology.

A conjecture favoured by many scholars (Möller, Noreen, Luick) is that the word represents OE. **gyrela* masc., **gyrele* fem.:—OTeut. types **gurwilon-, -ōn-*, a dim. of **gurwjo-z, -jâ* (found in LG. *gœre*, boy, girl):—Aryan **ghʷrghʷ-*, presumed to be represented in Gr. παρθένος virgin. This involves some uncertain phonological assumptions, and the late appearance of the Teut. words gives additional ground for doubt, the ME. *gürle* being recorded only from the end of the 13th c., and the LG. *gœre* from the 17th c. It may be noted that *boy*, *lad*, *lass*, and the numerous synonyms in the mod. Scandinavian langs., are all of difficult etymology; probably most of them arose as jocular transferred uses of words that had originally a different meaning.]

†**1.** A child or young person of either sex, a youth or maiden. Chiefly in *pl.*: Children, young people. ***knave girl***: a boy. ***gay girl***: applied to a young woman. *Obs.*

c **1290** *S. Eng. Leg.* I. 108/76 And suyþe gret prece of gurles and Men: comen hire al-a-boute. **13..** *K. Alis.* 2802 Men myghte ther y-seo hondis wrynge.. Women scrike, girles gredyng. *c* **1350** *Will. Palerne* 816 And whan þe gaye gerles were in-to þe gardin come, Faire floures þei founde. **1362** LANGL. *P. Pl.* A. XI. 131 Gramer for gurles I gon furste to write, And beot hem with a baleys but ȝif thei wolde lernen. *c* **1386** CHAUCER *Prol.* 666 In daunger hadde he at his owne gyse The yonge girles of the diocyse, And knew hir counseil, and was al hir reed. *c* **1450** *Bk. Curtasye* 328 in *Babees Bk.* 308 Ne delf þou neuer nose thyrle With thombe ne fyngur, as ȝong gyrle. *c* **1450** *Cov. Myst.* (Shaks. Soc.) 181 Here knave gerlys I xal steke.

2. a. A female child; commonly applied to all young unmarried women.

1530 PALSGR. 922 A gyrle [F. *garce*] havyng laughyng eyes. *c* **1530** REDFORDE *Play Wit & Sc.* (Shaks. Soc.) 17 *Idelnes*. Thow [Recreacion] art occacion, lo! of more evyll Then I, poore gerle, nay, more then the dyvyll! **1546** HEYWOOD *Prov.* (1874) 50 The boy thy husband, and thou the girle, his wife. **1591** SHAKS. *Two Gentl.* v. iv. 134, I hold him but a foole that will endanger His Body, for a Girle that loues him not. *a* **1652** BROME *Queene's Exch.* I. ii. Wks. 1873 III. 467 What's that my Girle? **1679** *Hatton Corr.* (1878) 197 *note*, One of his sisters.. announces the birth of a very lusty garle. **1709** STEELE *Tatler* No. 75 ¶1 The Girl is a Girl of great Merit.. she converses with me.. like a Daughter. **1760** C. JOHNSTON *Chrysal* II. I. ii. 11, I will lay you, and you shall lose, my girl, if it was ten times as much. **1784** COWPER *Task* II. 227 As smooth And tender as a girl, all-essenced o'er With odours. **1855** BROWNING *Fra Lippo* 214 You should not take a fellow eight years old And make him swear to never kiss the girls. **1859** GEO. ELIOT *A. Bede* 62 To think of a gell o' your age wanting to go and sit with half-a-dozen men. **1863** LANDOR *Heroic Idylls, Theron & Zoe* 27 Girls often say More than they mean: men always do. **1894** H. GARDENER *Unoff. Patriot* 329 No girl is ever quite good enough to marry any mother's son.

Prov. **1683** TRYON *Way to Health* 628 The Proverb is certainly true.. He that Marries a Girl, marrs a Woman.

¶ ***old girl***: Applied *colloq.* to a woman at any time of life, either disrespectfully or (occas.) as an endearing term of address, *spec.* one's mother or wife; also, a former pupil of a girls' school or college; also *attrib.* Similarly, to a mare, etc.

1826 T. CREEVEY *Let.* 22 Aug. in J. Gore *Creevey* (1948) xvii. 266 The old girl has a jointure of £5,000 a year. **1837** DICKENS *Pickwick* xiv, 'Cheer up, old girl', said Tom, patting the bay mare on the neck.. 'Soho, old girl—gently—gently'. **1848** C. BRONTË *J. Eyre* ii. (1890) 19 He called his mother 'old girl', too. **1853** DICKENS *Bleak Ho.* xxvii. 272 You know me. It's my old girl that advises. *Ibid.* 273 'Old girl,' says Mr. Bagnet, 'give him my opinion.' **1875** C. M. YONGE *Let.* 6 Apr. in C. Coleridge *C. M. Yonge* (1903) 262 Fifty-four mothers had tea in the school... So many are my own old girls. **1898** J. D. BRAYSHAW *Slum Silhouettes* 220 He lets aht that Liz an' 'er ole gal was going ter the Crystal Palace. **1947** D. M. DAVIN *Gorse blooms Pale* 55 'Poor old girl,' he said as he leg-roped her [*sc.* a cow]. **1954** E. JENKINS *Tortoise & Hare* ix. 89 It was Old Girls' Week-end at her school. **1954** G. SMITH *Flaw in Crystal* x. 95 One hears these things on the old-girl network. **1967** E. LEMARCHAND *Death of Old Girl* ix. 109 She said she might still be held up at some Old Girls' supper.

b. A maid-servant. Also in ***girl-of-all-work***.

1668 PEPYS *Diary* 24 Aug., My wife is upon hanging the long chamber, where the girl lies, with the sad stuff that was in the best chamber. **1812** A. ADAMS in *J. Adams' Lett.* (1848) 409 Seven o'clock. Blockheads not out of bed. Girls in motion. Mean, when I hire another man-servant, that he shall come for one call. **1875** *Scribner's Monthly* X. 287 But all this time we had no girl, and.. at last I determined to go and get a girl myself. So one day at lunch-time I went to an intelligence office in the city. **1882** MRS. ALEXANDER *Freres* I. ii. 19, I [a landlady] must look to it myself, for I never yet see a gurl I could trust with a hegg. **1883** S. C. HALL *Retrospect* II. 139 A dirty, slipshod girl-of-all-work bawled at me from the area.

c. A sweetheart, lady-love. Also (*U.S. colloq.* or *slang*) ***best girl***. Similarly, one's wife.

1648 HERRICK *Hesper.* 24 Some ask'd how Pearls did grow, and where? Then spoke I to my Girle, To part her lips, and shew'd them there The Quarelets of Pearl. **1772** J. WEDGWOOD *Let.* 4 Oct. (1965) 137 Your good Lady is really recovering her health.., though more slowly than we could wish, which is exactly the case of my poor Girl. **1791** 'G. GAMBADO' *Ann. Horsem.* vii. (1809) 97, I may lose my dear girl for ever. **1887**, etc. [see BEST *a.* 2 c]. **1899** W. BESANT *Orange Girl* I. v. 59, I drew my girl closer and kissed her. **1912** T. DREISER *Financier* v. 54 Before leaving to call on his girl, Marjorie Stafford. **1917** *Punch* 15 Aug. 125/2 And when the War is over, some knight or belted earl, What's survived from killin' Germans, will take 'er for 'is girl. **1940** L. MACNEICE *Last Ditch* 23 Life in a day: he took his girl to the ballet. **1952** M. R. RINEHART *Pool* xxviii. 249 He even had a girl, although he said he wouldn't marry her until he was cleared of the murder charge.

d. († More fully, ***a girl about*** or ***of the town***, ***a girl of ease***): a prostitute. † ***a kind girl***: a mistress.

1711 STEELE *Spect.* No. 187 ¶2, I know not whether you have ever heard of the famous girl about Town called Kitty: This Creature.. was my Mistress. **1712** ADDISON *Ibid.* No. 486 ¶1, I am very particularly acquainted with one who is under entire Submission to a kind Girl, as he calls her.. No longer than Tuesday last he took me with him to visit his Mistress. **1756** *Demi-Rep* 6 The Men of pleasure, and the Girls of ease. **1815** W. H. IRELAND *Scribbleomania* 141 Lewis, of monkish renown, Who tickled the fancies of girls of the town. **1851** MAYHEW *Lond. Labour* I. 477 The 'gals' are sure to be beaten cruelly.. by their 'chaps'.

†**e.** A black woman. *U.S. colloq. Obs.*

1835 J. H. INGRAHAM *South-West* II. 242 They always address them [*sc.* the slaves] as 'boy' and 'girl', to all under forty years of age. **1879** A. W. TOURGÉE *Fool's Errand* x. 42 You must remember that all colored women are 'girls'.

f. Colloq. phr. (***all***) ***girls together***, on terms of close friendship with another girl or girls; also *attrib.* (hyphened).

1931 R. FERGUSON *Brontës went to Woolworth's* xii. 141 It would be terrible if she wanted to be all-girls-together with me about him. **1946** 'S. RUSSELL' *To Bed with Grand Music* viii. 101 She seemed more than willing to re-establish a girls-together relationship with Deborah. **1959** J. BRAINE *Vodi* xiv. 185 That would-be refined, all-girls-together voice. **1961** A. CHRISTIE *Pale Horse* xii. 128, I got her softened up... Girls-together stuff.

g. ***les girls***, girls collectively; *spec.* chorus girls.

1938 S. BECKETT *Murphy* ix. 193 The sceptic rut that places the objects of its curiosity on the level of Les Girls. **1955** E. WAUGH *Officers & Gentlemen* 178 He had come to the bar for stimulus, for a spot of pleasantry with 'les girls'. **1967** J. PORTER *Chinks in Curtain* ix. 89, I haven't seen hide or hair of him. He's probably still shacked up with les girls.

h. (***the***) ***girl next door***, the girl in a conventional romance; a trusting, sweet, and faithful but usu. unimaginative young woman.

1961 *Sunday Express* 28 May 18/5 June Thorburn.. has been trying.. to break away from her usual 'girl next door' film roles. **1962** C. N. PARKINSON *In-Laws & Outlaws* 37 It is the itch to marry the girl next door which is the mark of those predestined for merely average success. **1963** *Listener* 24 Jan. 165/1 She had all the physical equipment of the vamp, but the spirit of the girl next door. **1968** *Times Educ. Suppl.* 23 Feb. 602/2 Diana Quirk's Ophelia was very much the girl-next-door.

†**3.** A roebuck in its second year. *Obs.*

1486 *Bk. St. Albans* E iv b, The first yere he [the Roobucke] is a kyde.. The secunde yere he is a gerle.. The thirde yere an hemule. **1576** TURBERV. *Venerie* 236 A Rowe, the which is called the first yeare a Kidde, the second Gyrle, the third an Hemuse. **1660** HOWELL *Parley Beasts* 62 Those pretty Fawns, Prickets, Sorrells, Hemuses, and Girls.. which I [a Hinde] brought into the world. **1726** *Dict. Rust.* (ed. 3), *Girle* (among Hunters) a Roe-buck of 2 Years.

4. *attrib.* and *Comb.* **a.** appositive, indicating sex, as ***girl-child***, ***-clerk***, ***-friend***, ***-graduate***, ***-miser***, ***-sculler***, ***-soldier***, ***-sorter***, ***-warrior***, ***-worker***; or youthfulness, as ***girl-bride***, ***-mother***, ***-queen***, ***-widow***, ***-wife***, ***-woman***; **b.** simple attrib., as ***girl-life***, ***-nature***, ***-tragedy***; **c.** objective, as ***girl-confining*** adj.; ***girl-crazy***, ***-shy*** adjs. ***girl-like*** adj. and adv. Also **girl-boy**, ? a girlish boy; **girl friend**, **girl-friend**, a female friend; *spec.* a sweetheart; a man's favourite female companion; **girl guide**: see GUIDE *sb.* 2 d; **girl scout** *U.S.*, a girl guide.

1589 WARNER *Alb. Eng.* v. xxvi. (1597) 129 *Girle-boyes, fauouring Ganimede. **1598** DRAYTON *Heroic. Ep.* 18/2 And in my place vpon this regal throne, To set that girle-boy wanton Gaueston. **1884** BLACK *Jud. Shaks.* ix. in *Harper's Mag.* Mar. 542/2 My father used to call him the girl-boy. **1847** C. BRONTË *J. Eyre* II. ix. 220 Young Mrs. Rochester—Fairfax Rochester's *girl-bride. **1935** *Burlington Mag.* Mar. 143/2 Quite a young man by the side of his girl-bride. **1886** *Longm. Mag.* 646 A very great number of the *girl-children of the State have found happy homes in Canada. **1901** *Daily Chron.* 29 May 3/6 No redeeming feature of *girl-clerk labour. **1902** *Ibid.* 1 Sept. 3/6 The market is vastly overflooded with incapable girl-clerks, who can just manipulate a machine, at 10s. or 12s. a week. **1908** *Westm. Gaz.* 17 June 9/3 A girl-clerk does not expect to obtain an engagement without the necessary knowledge of shorthand and typing. **1798** SOTHEBY tr. *Wieland's Oberon* (1826) I. 55 The guardian of these *girl-confining walls. **1930** I. GERSHWIN (*title*) *Girl crazy. **1948** G. VIDAL *City & Pillar* (1949) x. 251 He was girl crazy, too, I guess. **1859** *Harper's Mag.* Aug. 337/1 A demure little widow, much more gay and girlish than any of her *girl-friends when she chose to forsake her rôle. **1892** F. J. FURNIVALL *Hoccleve's Minor Works* p. iv (*dedication*), To the memory of Teena Rochfort Smith my much-respected and deeply-regretted girl-friend. **1896** *Westm. Gaz.* 19 May 4/2 The 'Wedding March' was whistled by twelve girl-friends of the bride. **1907** A. WOOLLCOTT *Let.* 22 June (1946) 11 My best girl friend is the daughter of the big Grace Church in Utica. **1926** H. FIELDS (*title*) The girl friend. **1928** R. MACAULAY *Keeping up Appearances* xi. 118 Daphne seems quite to have become Raymond's girl friend again. **1962** 'C. E. MAINE' *Darkest of Nights* v. 67 Mom made up her mind to tolerate his girl friends years ago. **1847** TENNYSON *Princ.* Prol. 142 Sweet *girl-graduates in their golden hair. **1888** *Athenæum* 26 May 659/3 A well meaning.. story of *girl-life. **1852** ROCK *Ch. of Fathers* III. I. 269 The *girl-like maiden-mother bowed down before the crib. *a* **1861** T. WOOLNER *My Beautiful Lady* (1863) 124 Years before.. girllike she Adored a youth with sparkling genius graced. **1865** DICKENS *Mut. Fr.* I. vi, I saw you sitting there, like the ghost of a *girl-miser in the dead of the night. *a* **1861** T. WOOLNER *My beautiful Lady* (1863) 95 What art thou whispering lowly to thy babe, O wan *girl-mother? **1897** *Edin. Rev.* Oct. 393 The girl-mother of Amadis. **1876** BLACK *Madcap V.* xxvi. 242 Was it not true, he had to admit, that he knew nothing of *girl-nature? **1882** J. H. BLUNT *Ref. Ch. Eng.* II. 189 The *girl-'Queen'—she was only sixteen years of age. **1909** *Daily Chron.* 27 July 4/7 The *girl-scout has arrived... This writer saw six of them.. on Saturday—neat blue serge skirts, straw hats, haversacks, and poles. **1959** *Listener* 1 Oct. 542/3 A small contribution from Henry Miller and the Girl Scouts. **1925** T. DREISER *Amer. Trag.* (1926) I. xi. 71 He, at once girl-hungry and *girl-shy, held himself nervously aloof. **1895** 'MARK TWAIN' in *Harper's Mag.* July 232 To see and listen to the wonderful *girl-soldier [*sc.* Joan of Arc]. **1944** BLUNDEN *Shells by Stream* 34 Girl-soldiers hasten. **1894** *Daily News* 28 Mar. 3/1, 10,000 notices of withdrawal .. are handed to a roomful of '*girl sorters'. **1876** GEO. ELIOT *Dan. Der.* I. xvii. 342 His mind glanced over the *girl-tragedies that are going on in the world. **1894** *Dublin Rev.* Oct. 309 Leaders to whom the triumphs of the *girl-warrior were a reproach. **1837** HAWTHORNE *Twice-Told T.* (1851) I. xix. 285 Inflamed to madness by the coquetry of the *girl-widow. **1857** MRS. CARLYLE *Lett.* II. 321 The young *girl-wife who lives there is very lovely. **1876** MISS BRADDON *Dead Men's Shoes* I. i. 1 A *girl-woman alone on Battersea Bridge. **1895** *Tablet* 20 July 108 The *girl-workers taking their wages home.

girl, *v.*[1] [f. the sb.] **1.** *trans.* in *nonce-uses*. **a.** To furnish with girls. **b.** Jocularly substituted for 'to *man*', where the agent is a girl.

a **1635** CORBET *Poems* (1807) 126 Nor hast thou in his nuptiall armes enjoy'd Barren imbraces, but wert girl'd and boy'd. **1886** J. A. STERRY *Lazy Minstr.* (ed. 2) 53 She oft Quite longs.. to 'girl the boats'.

2. *intr.* To consort with women. Hence **'girling** *vbl. sb.*, usu. in phr. ***to go*** (***a-***)***girling***.

1787 *Sessions Papers* 10 Jan. 325/2 The maid said two men were missing, and the others said, G——d d——n them, they are gone a girling,.. but we will pay for them. **1922** JOYCE *Ulysses* 537 No girl would when I went girling. **1931** L. STEFFENS *Autobiogr.* I. I. i. 8 Cowboys.. used to come shouting on bucking bunches of bronchos into town to mix with the teamsters, miners, and steamboat men in the drinking, gambling, girling, fighting, of those days.

girl (gɜːl), *v.*[2] *Sc.* Also **girrel**. [onomatopœic.] *intr.* To thrill, whirl.

1820 HOGG *Wint. Even. T.* I. 336 Ye hae gart a' my flesh girrel, John. *Ibid.* II. 64 Its no deth it feirs me, but the efterkum garis my hert girle. **1894** IAN MACLAREN *Bonnie Brier Bush* VI. ii. 222 Juist like the threshing mill at Drumsheugh scraiking and girling till it's fairly aff.

girland, -ond, obs. forms of GARLAND.

girldom ('gɜːldəm). [See -DOM.] The domain or world of girls; girls collectively.

1864 D. W. THOMPSON *Day Dreams of Schoolmaster* x. 111 Frittering away the time and intellects of all subsequent generations of girldom. **1896** J. ASHBY-STERRY *Tale of Thames* ii. 20 Because.. you choose to quarrel with a girl.. there is no reason whatever that you should declare war against entire girldom. **1955** *Time* 29 Aug. 57 His house.. was ringed all day and half the night by gazing girldom. **1968** *Newsweek* 12 Aug. 80 While he is playing a specific Mr. Singer, she is playing all young girldom.

girleen ('gɜːliːn). *Anglo-Irish.* [f. GIRL *sb.* + *-een*, dim. suffix (= Irish *-ín* as in COLLEEN): cf. *squireen*, *buckeen*.] A young girl.

1836 H. F. CHORLEY *Mem. Mrs. Hemans* (1837) II. 213 The light-hearted gossoons and girleens of Dublin. **1882** MRS. ALEXANDER *Freres* I. ii. 22 You were just a slip of girleen then, and now you are an elegant young lady.

'girlery. [f. GIRL *sb.* + -ERY.] Girls collectively.

1805 LAMB *Let. to Wordsworth* Lett. 1888 I. 215 There were two young girls—the very head and sum of the girlery was two young girls. **1826** J. WILSON *Noct. Ambr.* Wks. 1855 I. 196 When one considers from what originals he painted his portraits of Edina's girlery.

girl Friday (,gɜːl 'fraɪdɪ). Also **Girl Friday**. [After the man *Friday* in Defoe's *Robinson Crusoe*: cf. MAN *sb.*[1] 10 a.] A resourceful young woman assistant (to a man).

1940 *Time* 10 June 66/3 Irna is assisted in her work by two secretaries and a pair of literary Girl Fridays. **1940** *Times* 29 July 6/7 (Advt.), Cary Grant, Rosalind Russell in His Girl Friday. **1951** C. W. MILLS *White Collar* p. x, There are a dozen kinds of social engineers and mechanical technicians, a multitude of girl Fridays. **1958** *Woman* 5 July 19/1 What's it like to be Girl Friday to a Very Important Person? **1967** *Times* 5 Apr. 25/6 (Advt.), Secretary/Girl Friday required for principal of professional firm in Mayfair. **1971** *Petticoat* 17 July 38/1 They could be earning several pounds more, as Girl Fridays, personal assistants or private secretaries to rising executives.

'girlfully, *adv. nonce-wd.* [f. GIRL *sb.* + -FUL + -LY[2].] With the energy characteristic of a girl.

1886 J. A. STERRY *Lazy Minstr.* (ed. 2) 156 But still the two maidens tramp girlfully on. **1895** CROCKETT *Sweeth. Trav.* 206 Defending herself girlfully with a branch of bramble. *Foot-note*, Why should not one say 'boyfully', 'girlfully', if one can say 'manfully'?

girlhood ('gɜːlhʊd). [f. GIRL *sb.* + -HOOD.] The state of being a girl; the time of life during which one is a girl; *concr.* girls collectively.

1785 ANNA SEWARD *Let. Boswell* 25 Mar. Lett. I. x. 38 My mother passed her days of girlhood with an uncle at Warwick. **1831** LYTTON *Godolph.* 1 Not a trace of the bloom or the softness of girlhood could be marked on her countenance. **1862** TROLLOPE *Small Ho. at Allington* in *Cornh. Mag.* VI. 568 The sportiveness and kitten-like gambols of girlhood. **1866** ANNIE THOMAS *Played Out* I. xv. 285 A group of girlhood. **1880** DIXON *Windsor* III. xiii. 118 The great queen, who had known him from her girlhood. **1883** L. OLIPHANT *Altiora Peto* I. 213 If the girlhood of the Pacific slope are half as innocent as they are insolent [etc.].

girlie ('gɜːlɪ), *sb.* [f. GIRL *sb.* + -IE, -Y[4]: cf. *birdie*.] A little girl. (A term of endearment.)

1860 *Artist & Craftsm.* 433 The little half-clad girlies ran off to hide themselves. **1877** P'CESS ALICE 28 July in *Mem.* (1884) 357 The two little girlies are so sweet. **1894** DOYLE *S. Holmes* 52 She is my own dear little girlie.

girlie ('gɜːlɪ), *a. colloq.* [f. GIRL *sb.* + -IE; cf. GIRLIE; GIRLY *a.*] Denoting a publication, entertainment, etc., featuring young women, esp. scantily clothed or in the nude.

1942 H. Felsen *He's in Submarines Now* 65 Being rather partial to girlie pictures. **1950** *N.Y. Times* 9 July II. 1/1 Mr. Todd..has produced a colossal spectacle and girlie show. **1952** B. Malamud *Natural* 104 It's a night club with a nice girlie show. **1953** *Books* Mar. 38/2 The only purpose of the 'girlie' magazine..was 'pictorial prostitution'. **1959** *Encounter* Jan. 94/1 The picture magazines known to the trade as 'girlie books'. **1969** V. Gielgud *Necessary End* v. 44 The barman, completely absorbed in the pages of a 'girlie' magazine. **1970** G. Greer *Female Eunuch* 35 Buttock fetishism is comparatively rare in our culture, although Kenneth Tynan did write a connoisseur article for a girlie mag..not so long ago. **1970** C. Whitman *Death out of Focus* vii. 92 All I printed for Forley were the usual girlie pictures.

girling (ˈgɜːlɪŋ). [Cf. GILLING.] A young salmon.

1861 *Act 24 & 25 Vict.* c. 109 §4 All migratory fish of the genus salmon, whether known by the names hereinafter mentioned, that is to say..kelt, laurel, girling, grilse..or by any other local name.

girlish (ˈgɜːlɪʃ), *a.* [f. GIRL *sb.* + -ISH[1].] Of or pertaining to a girl or to girlhood; characteristic of or like a girl.

1565 Cooper *Thesaurus*, *Puellaris*, propre to girles.. girlish. **1596** Drayton *Leg.* I. 937 She.. To other speech, and Girlish laughter fell. **1603** Holland *Plutarch's Mor.* 682 These chaplets of flowers be girlish gaudes. **1788** Burns *Let. to Mrs. Dunlop* 16 Aug., An old grand-uncle, with whom my mother lived a while in her girlish years. **1816** J. Scott *Vis. Paris* (ed. 5) 200 Girlish feeling prompts this anticipation of satisfaction. **1863** Geo. Eliot *Romola* II. xxvii, She had been very foolish and ignorant in her girlish time. **1875** W. S. Hayward *Love agst. World* 3 Walter was ..more girlish than either of the others.

Hence ˈ**girlishly** *adv.*, ˈ**girlishness**.

1623 Cockeram, *Puellaritie*, Girlishnesse. **1727** Bailey vol. II, *Girlishly*, like a Girl. **1824** Landor *Imag. Conv.* II. 279 Thou art still girlishly fond of those dried cherries! **1833** Browning *Pauline* 231 Autumn has come—like Spring returned to us, Won from her girlishness. **1875** A. R. Hope *My School-boy Fr.* 164 The elegance and girlishness for which we laughed at Philip. **1885** M. Pattison *Mem.* 123 Of all beyond I was girlishly ignorant.

girlism (ˈgɜːlɪz(ə)m). *nonce-wd.* [-ISM.] Girls, or their characteristics, collectively.

1788 Anna Seward *Lett.* (1811) II. 186 The prejudices of girlism. **1795** *Ibid.* IV. 70 With her sister, Miss Bowater, I passed some of the sprightly days of girlism.

girl-less (ˈgɜːllɪs), *a.* [GIRL *sb.* + -LESS.] Without or devoid of a girl or girls.

1903 *Daily Chron.* 15 Apr. 5/1 If 'Harper's Weekly' may be trusted, the girlless telephone will soon be as familiar as the horseless carriage or the boneless sardine. **1929** J. Masefield *Hawbucks* 147 It's a very girl-less neighbourhood.

girlls, obs. form of GRILSE.

girly (ˈgɜːlɪ), *a.* [f. GIRL *sb.* + -Y[1].] Characteristic of or befitting a girl; girlish.

1886 J. A. Sterry *Lazy Minstr.* (ed. 2) 127 Her laugh is light, Her figure slight and girly. **1891** G. Meredith *One of our Conq.* I. iii. 31 The silly girly sugary crudity has given way to womanly suavity.

Hence ˈ**girliness**, girlishness.

1886 J. A. Sterry *Lazy Minstr.* (ed. 2) 60 A white, white dress that artlessly reveals..The pouting beauty of her fair young form; In all its dainty, dimpled girliness.

girly-girly (ˈgɜːlɪˈgɜːlɪ), *a.* and *sb. colloq.* [f. GIRLY *a.*] **A.** *adj.* Girlish in an exaggerated or affected manner; effeminate.

Girly-girly was the name of a music-hall song *c* 1900.

1883 'Mark Twain' *Life on Mississippi* xlvi. 467 The very feature that keeps it [*sc.* Mardi Gras] alive in the South—girly-girly romance. **1891** *Outing* (U.S.) Dec. 246/1 They despised dancing as 'girly-girly' and silly. **1900** H. Lawson *On Track* 73 She'd..make a sweet little girly-girly dive for her chair. **1927** *Daily Express* 20 June 8 Typical girly-girly 'romp' stuff.

B. *sb.* A girl; a little girl.

1888 *Puck* 17 Oct. 123/2 The rusticator sighs, With a strange look in his eyes: 'Oh, where's my girly-girly of the Summer?' **1899** G. M. Cohan *Dear Little Girly, Girly*, Most ev'ry fellow tells about a little girly girly..with teeth so white and pearly.

girn (gɜːn), *sb.*[1] *Sc.* Also 4–6 gyrne, 6 girne. [var. of GRIN *sb.*[1]]

1. a. †A noose (*obs.*). **b.** A snare or trap for catching animals or birds, made of hair, wire, or the like, with a running noose.

c **1375** *Sc. Leg. Saints, Paulus* 1140 He a stalowart gyrne can ma To hang hym-self with be þe hals. **1535** Stewart *Cron. Scot.* (1858) I. 108 With falsheid he thame fed, As quha wald set ane girne befoir ane gled. **1536** Bellenden *Cron. Scot.* (1821) I. 186 He commandit, that na haris be slane..nor yet tane be nettis or girnis. **1721** *Court Bk. Barony of Urie* (1892) 119 Killed with guns..girns or other ingines. **1824–7** Moir *Mansie Wauch* (1833) xxiv. 186 The vagabond's girn was set.

2. *fig.* A snare, trap, wile.

c **1375** *Sc. Troy-bk.* II. 999 The quhilkes frome gyrnes of dede Ware eschapede. **1552** Abp. Hamilton *Catech.* 61 b, Thai that will be riche, fallis into temptatioun and in the gyrne of the deuil. **1596** Dalrymple tr. *Leslie's Hist. Scotl.* x. 462 Thame selfes skairse could defend from the girnes of this Edicte. **1721** Ramsay *Rise & Fall of Stocks* 35 Stock-jobbers, brokers..Wha set their gowden girns sae wylie, Tho ne'er sae cautious, they'd beguile ye.

girn (gɜːn), *sb.*[2] *Obs.* exc. *Sc.* [f. GIRN *v.*[1]]

1. The act of showing the teeth, a snarl.

1535 [see GAPE *sb.* 1]. **1602** Marston *Ant. & Mel.* III. ii, Euen so the Duke frownes for all this Cursond world: oh that gerne kils, it kils. *a* **1861** T. Woolner *My beautiful Lady* (1863) 107 A poring spectre shall be seen With livid stare and girn. **1870** in Ramsay *Remin.* (ed. 18) p. xxxiii, His girn's waur than his bite. **1883** Annie Swan *Aldersyde* iii. 51 A smile..afterwards described as resembling the 'girn o' a rat'.

b. *Sc.* A snarling tone.

1826 J. Wilson *Noct. Ambr.* Wks. 1855 I. 161 Lettin out the dry dusty moral apothegms wi' ae continued and monotonous girn.

†**2.** = GRIN *sb.*[2] *Obs. rare.*

1636 Davenant *Witts* IV. *ad fin.*, This is at least a girne of Fortune, if Not a faire smile. **1711** E. Ward *Quix.* I. 67 Scoff'd him, unseen, with Winks and Girns.

girn (gɜːn), *v.*[1] Forms: 4–6 gyrn(e, 5–6 girne, 6 gern(e, 6–7 gearne, 8 guern, 6– girn. [var. GRIN *v.* with metathesis of *r.*]

1. *intr.* To show the teeth in rage, pain, disappointment, etc.; to snarl as a dog; to complain persistently; to be fretful or peevish. Also *to girn at.* Now only *north.* and *Sc.*

1375 Barbour *Bruce* IV. 322 Than lukit he awfully thame to, And said, gyrnand, 'hangis & drawis!' *c* **1440** *York Myst.* xxxiii. 23 þat gome þat gyrnes or gales, I myself sall hym hurte full sore. **1513** Douglas *Æneis* IX. ii. 65 The wyld wolf ..Abowt the bowght, plet all of wandis tyght, Bayis and gyrnis. **1529** More *Comf. agst. Trib.* III. Wks. 1254/1 The bitch had founde the foote agayn: & on she came gerning. **1590** Spenser *F.Q.* I. iii. 15 His face was ugly and his countenance sterne..And gaped like a gulfe when he did gerne. *a* **1693** Urquhart *Rabelais* III. xvii, The old Trot for a while remained silent, pensive, and girning like a Dog. **1724** Ramsay *Tea-t. Misc.* (1733) I. 31 We hang our lugs and wi' a gloom, Girn'd at stockjobbing ane and a'. **1790** A. Wilson *1st Ep. to J. Dobie* Poet. Wks. (1846) 18 While chaunrin' critics girn and growl, And curse whate'er they light on. **1837** R. Nicoll *Poems* (1843) 133 She's girnin' at e'enin'—she's girnin' at morn—a' hours o' the day in my flesh she's a thorn. **1855** Browning *Old Pictures Florence* ix, The mastiff girns And the puppy pack of poodles yelp. **1863** Kingsley *Water-Bab.* v, How she [the otter] did grin and girn when she saw Tom. **1886** Stevenson *Kidnapped* vi. 50 He's a wicked auld man, and there's many would like to see him girning in a tow.

b. quasi-*trans.*

1894 Crockett *Raiders* (ed. 3) 120, I could only girn my teeth at him.

c. *trans.* To utter in a snarling tone.

1847 E. Brontë *Wuthering Heights* xvii. 148 'Isabella, let me in, or I'll make you repent!' he 'girned' as Joseph calls it.

†**2.** To show the teeth in laughing; to grin. *Obs.*

1552 Latimer *Serm. Lincolnsh.* v. 105 They goe with the corses girning and fleering, as though they went to a beare-bayting. **1593** *Pass. Morrice* (1876) 80 After that girne like a monkie that sees her dinner. **1602** Marston *Antonio's Rev.* I. iii. B ij, Laugh not..When thou dost girne, thy rusty face doth looke Like the head of a rosted rabbit. **1617** F. Moryson *Itin.* I. 247 The rascall multitude..ceased not to girn and laugh at our sighes and teares. *a* **1711** Ken *Edmund* Poet. Wks. 1721 II. 299 Curs'd Satan guerning stood, the while he spake.

girn (gɜːn), *v.*[2] *Sc.* Also 4 gyrne. [f. GIRN *sb.*[1]] *trans.* †**a.** *fig.* To ensnare (*obs.*). **b.** To catch in a girn or trap (cf. quot. 1825–80).

c **1375** *Sc. Troy-bk.* II. 366 But he, gyrnede syne atte last Inne ȝharnynge of the golde so rede. **1825–80** Jamieson, *Girn*, (1) to catch by means of a girn; (2) to catch trouts by means of a noose of hair. **1866** T. Bruce *Summer Queen* 320 I'll make sure To girn him like a hare. **1896** Crockett *Cleg Kelly* xiii. 96 As if he had been 'girning' sticklebacks and 'bairdies' in the shallow burns.

girnel (ˈgɜːnɛl), *sb. Sc.* Also 5 gyrnall, 6 girnall, 6–7 girnell, girnal. See also GARNEL. [variant of GARNEL.] A granary; also, a large chest for meal.

1452 *Sc. Acts Jas. II*, §4 (1814) II. 41/2 Item it is ordanyt þat na maner of wittail be haldin in gyrnall be ony persone forther þan is needfull. **1568** Lauder *Godlie Tractate* 490 ȝe cloise ȝour Girnallis frome the puris. *a* **1572** Knox *Hist. Ref.* Wks. (1846) I. 361 The Bischopis girnell was keapt the first nycht by the laubouris of Johne Knox. *a* **1670** Spalding *Troub. Chas. I* (1829) 114 They..brake up girnels, and baked good bannocks at the fire. **1791** Newte *Tour Eng. & Scotl.* 104 Another wooden house..of twenty feet square, which serves at present for a granary or girnal, as they pronounce it, for their oatmeal. **1834** H. Miller *Scenes & Leg.* xvii. (1857) 258 Each proprietor, too, had his storehouse or girnal—a tall, narrow building, the strong-box of the time. **1860** J. Grant *Mary of Lorraine* ii, Large oak chests, girnels, and almries, the receptacles of linen.

b. *Comb.*, as †*girnel river* (= breaker).

1508 Dunbar *Flyting w. Kennedie* 246 Muttoun dryver, girnall [*v.r.* garnale] ryver, ȝadswyvar, fowll fell the.

†**girnel** (ˈgɜːnɛl), *v. Sc. Obs. rare.* [f. prec. sb.] *trans.* To store up in a girnel or granary.

1609 Skene *Reg. Maj.* 153 Victuall suld not be girnelled, bot suld be brocht to the market. *a* **1670** Spalding *Troub. Chas. I* (1792) II. 167 There was victual girnelled in store to help to find the soldiers by way of plundering.

Hence ˈ**girnelled** *ppl. a.*, ˈ**girnelling** *vbl. sb.*

1481 in Maitland *Hist. Edin.* I. i. (1753) 9 For a Girnel of Corn, Two Bags..and the same from all girnelled goods. **1597** *Acts Parl. Scotl.* 34 b, Girnalling of victuallis is forbidden. **1637–50** Row *Hist. Kirk* (Wodrow Soc.) 173 Not thrashing victuall in due tyme, girnalling of it when it is threshen, and not bringing of it to the mercat.

girning (ˈgɜːnɪŋ), *vbl. sb.* [f. GIRN *v.*[1] + -ING[1].] The action of the verb GIRN[1].

1375 Barbour *Bruce* XIII. 157 Ther wes..Sic gyrnyng, granyng; and so gret A noyis, as thai can othir bet. **1580** North *Plutarch* (1676) 841 The Greyhound..at the first began to answer them with a soft girning; but when they came by the Tower where he lay, he barked out aloud. *a* **1693** Urquhart *Rabelais* III. xiii. 106 He..was.. environed about so with the barking of Curs..girning of Boars. **1792** A. Wilson *Watty & Mag* xxxviii, Owre the seas I march this morning, Listet, testet, sworn an a', Forc'd by your confounded girning. *a* **1810** Tannahill *Poet. Wks.* (1846) 105 Wi' girning her neb's like the gab o' the fleuk.

girning (ˈgɜːnɪŋ), *ppl. a. Sc.* and *dial.* Also 6 girnand, gerning. [f. GIRN *v.*[1] + -ING[2].]

1. *Sc.* That 'girns'; ill-humoured, snarling.

1447 Bokenham *Seyntys* (Roxb.) 86 Julyan..to hir seyd wyth chere gyrnyng Now [etc.]. *c* **1450** Henryson *Mor. Fab.* 85 With girnand teeth and awfull angrie luke. **1508** Dunbar *Tua mariit wemen* 290 Quhen that the chuf wald me chid, with girnand chaftis. **1785** Burns *To W. Simpson* xxviii, I've even seen them greetin Wi' girnin' spite. **1824** Scott *St. Ronan's* xxxi, The cappernoity, old girning ale-wife may wait long enough or I forward it.

†**2.** Grinning. *Obs. rare*[−1].

1599 Marston *Sco. Villanie* III. xi. 227 That iest-mounging youth Who nere did ope his Apish gerning mouth But to retaile and broke anothers wit.

‖**giro**[1] (ˈdʒiro). [It. *giro* a round, circuit:—L. *gyrus*, a. Gr. γῦρος circle: cf. GYRATE.] A tour, circuit; a 'turn'.

1670 Lassels *Voy. Italy* Pref. a vj, And no man understands Livy and Cæsar..like him who hath made exactly the *Grand Tour* of France and the *Giro* of Italy. **1823** Lady Morgan *Salvator Rosa* iii. (1824) I. 100 Nearly all his biographers have alluded to this early and singular *giro.* **1841** Motley *Corr.* (1889) I. iv. 93 From the library you reach the ante-chamber, thus completing the *giro* of one of the prettiest houses in St. Petersburg. **1880** Geo. Eliot *Let.* 9 June in *Life* (1884) III. 357 Afterwards we have a *giro* in our gondola.

giro[2] (ˈdʒaɪrəʊ). [G., a. It. *giro* circulation (of money).] **1.** A system whereby credits are transferred between banks, post offices, etc.; *spec.* a system operated by the British Post Office for the banking and transfer of money. Freq. *attrib.*

1896 P. des Essars in *Hist. Banking* III. ix. 384 Germany has a slight advantage arising from the fact that in that country cheques and transfers (giro accounts) are more in use than in France and Belgium. **1896** R. van der Borght *Ibid.* IV. III. i. 199 It will be perceived that the Amsterdam Bank was originally a bank of deposit and 'giro', in the primary sense of the word. **1907** *Westm. Gaz.* 17 Sept. 10/2 Invoices, note headings, &c., bearing in the the corner the words 'Reichsbank Giro-konto', indicate to all that accounts due to that firm may be paid to their credit by cash or transfer (i.e., Giro) at any branch of the Reichsbank. **1930** *Economist* 27 Sept. 562/1 Other suggestions are concerned with the increased use of cheques, post-office banking facilities, giro transfers, clearings, etc. **1959** *Rep. Comm. Working Monetary System* xi. 331 in *Parl. Papers 1958–9* (Cmnd. 827) XVII. 389 The method of operation of a 'giro' operated by the post office is very briefly as follows. **1961** *Daily Tel.* 10 May 15/8 To provide a simple method for transferring payments a 'Giro' system, similar to that used in some continental countries, may soon be introduced by the Post Office, Mr Bevins, Postmaster-General, said yesterday. **1963** *Economist* 29 June 1375/1 On the Continent nearly all letter heads and invoices carry a giro number. **1968** *Listener* 22 Aug. 255/1 The Post Office Giro..will probably open in the first week of October. Basically, the Giro banks money for you, which you can draw out for yourself, or which you can instruct the Giro to transfer to other people.

2. giro cheque, order: a cheque or money order issued through the giro system; in Great Britain, used for (and therefore esp. associated with) social security payments. Also *ellipt.*, as *giro.*

1972 *Banker* May 661 (*table*) Crossed giro cheques. **1975** *Economist* 9 Aug. (Brit. Banking Survey Suppl.) 42/1 If the retailer then uses giro cheques to pay his supplier he can become completely reliant on giro. **1976** *Southern Even. Echo* (Southampton) 11 Nov. 14/4 A 31-year-old woman told the Department of Health and Social Security she had not received her giro cheque. **1976** *Weekend Echo* (Liverpool) 4/5 Dec. 4/8 Police were informed when a 22-years-old man presented an altered giro order at a post office. **1981** *Sunday Times* 12 July 54 If it's a Wednesday I check straight away that I've got my Giro.—A. Benson, unemployed. **1982** *Times* 27 Jan. 2/3 Fraud involving girocheques sent through the Post Office for payment of social security benefits is 'extremely prevalent'. **1983** J. Kelman *Not, not while Giro* 200 All I'm fucking asking is regular giros and punctual counter clerks. **1985** *Telegraph & Argus* (Bradford) 25 May 6/4 Take £27 a fortnight out of a giro for £45 or £50 and you're not left with much.

giromancy, obs. form of GYROMANCY.

giron: see GYRON *Her.*

‖**Gironde** (ʒirɔ̃d, dʒɪˈrɒnd). [see GIRONDIST.] The Girondist party.

1795 H. M. Williams *Lett. Politics of France* I. v. 126 This calumny..formed the basis of the accusation which was framed against the Gironde. **1876** Gladstone in *Contemp. Rev.* June 11 They are apt to disappear..like Lafayette before the Gironde. **1943** J. B. Sirich *Revolutionary Committees* ii. 15 There were, however, still other enemies in Paris which the Gironde had to fear—the committees of surveillance.

girondel, obs. form of GIRANDOLE.

Girondin (dʒɪˈrɒndɪn), *sb.* (*a.*). [Fr. (see GIRONDIST).] = GIRONDIST *sb.* (*a.*).
1837 CARLYLE *Fr. Rev.* III. III. i. 160 As for the Girondin Formula, of a respectable Republic for the Middle Classes, all manner of Aristocracies being now sufficiently demolished, there seems little reason to expect that the business will stop there. *Ibid.* 166 The Girondins have left Memoirs, which are too often little other than long-drawn Interjections, of *Woe is me* and *Cursed be ye.* **1890** [see next]. **1965** M. J. SYDENHAM *Fr. Rev.* vii. 185 Thus the trial fulfilled its purpose, and the mythical 'Girondin party' was finally imposed on history. **1968** P. O'BRIAN tr. *Faÿ's Louis XVI* III. ix. 375 The Girondins, more eloquent and greedy than intelligent, wanted to compel the king to give them back their ministerial posts.

Girondism (dʒɪˈrɒndɪz(ə)m). [ad. F. *Girondisme*, f. *Gironde* (see GIRONDIST) + *-isme*, -ISM.] The doctrine or practice of the Girondists.
1837 CARLYLE *Fr. Rev.* III. III. ii. 173 Bourdeaux demands a reign of Law and Respectability, meaning Girondism, with emphasis. **1890** E. B. BAX *Story Fr. Rev.* xv. 66 All the leading Girondins, including the twelve forming the Commission, were placed under arrest... Thus perished Girondism.

Girondist (dʒɪˈrɒndɪst), *sb.* (*a.*) [ad. F. *Girondiste* (now *Girondin*), f. *Gironde* (see def.) + *-iste*, -IST.] A member of the moderate republican party (in the French assembly 1791–1793); its leaders were the deputies from the department of the Gironde (cf. quot. 1833). Also *attrib.* or *adj.*
1795 H. M. WILLIAMS *Lett. Politics of France* I. iv. 68 But we need not here recur to conspiracies either of Jacobins or Girondists to discern the motives of Dumourier's conduct. **1801** GIFFORD *Louis XVI*, 649 The Girondists, or moderate party, were reduced to a singular dilemma. **1827** SCOTT *Napoleon* Introd., Wks. 1870 IX. 113 The Girondist party. **1833** ALISON *Hist. Europe* (1847) II. 277 The Girondists, so called from the district near Bordeaux called the Gironde, from whence the most able of their party were elected. **1943** J. B. SIRICH *Revolutionary Committees* ii. 14 The minds of the Girondists were not far from the enemies of the interior, the demagogues, the anarchists.

gironell, obs. form of GIRANDOLE.

gironny: see GYRONNY *Her.*

‖**girouette** (ʒirwɛt). [F. *girouette*, obscurely connected with *gire-r*:—L. *gȳrāre* to revolve. It. has *giroetta* from Fr.] A weather-cock. Also *fig.*
1822 L. SIMOND *Switzerland* I. 323 You might as well pretend to stigmatize Talma or Mademoiselle Mars, with the name of *girouettes*, for not acting every night the same part, as our French politicians and philosophers, for changing sides and principles from day to day. **1831** JEKYLL *Corresp.* (1894) 2/4 He is no ordinary girouette. **1857** SIR F. PALGRAVE *Norm. & Eng.* II. 232 However nicely the weather-cock may be poised.. some breeze must breathe.. to make the girouette spin round.
Hence **girouettism**, constant changing of opinions or principles. [Cf. F. *girouetterie*.]
1825 *New Monthly Mag.* XIV. 109 Girouettism is the natural vice of revolutionary times and political consistency the rarest.. of virtues.

girr (gɪr). *Sc.* [var. GIRTH *sb.*[1]] A hoop for a barrel. Also, a child's hoop. Cf. GIRD *sb.*[1] 2, GIRTH *sb.*[1] 2.
1611 in *Glasgow Burgh Rec.* (1876) I. 322 Na firlot to be sealit bot sik as hes yron girris about the mowth. **1796** BURNS *Cooper o' Cuddie*, The cooper o' Cuddie cam here awa, And ca'd the girrs out owre us a'. **1821** *Blackw. Mag.* Aug. 35 Rowing girrs (rolling hoops) forms another healthy exercise to the boys of Edinburgh. **1887** J. SERVICE *Life Dr. Duguid* xxix. 185, I was a happy wee callan caing the girr on the street.
b. A hoop used to keep a pair of water-cans apart so that they may be more easily carried.
1832–53 A. A. RITCHIE *Whistle-Binkie* (Scot. Songs) Ser. III. 69 As our kimmer Nell, Wi' her stoups and her girr, was gaun down to the well [etc.].

girrebbage, var. GILRAVAGE *sb.*

girrock. ? *Obs.* (See quot.)
1674 RAY *Words, Sea Fishes* 103 *Girrock*, Acus major, called elsewhere Horn-Fish and Needle-Fish.

†**girse.** *Obs.* [var. GIRTH *sb.*[1], prob. from pl. *gir(th)s*.]
1. A saddle-girth; = GIRTH *sb.*[1] 1.
[**1417–18** *Abingdon Acc.* (Camden) 88 Et in frenis, capistris, singulis, gurs' emptis.. iiijs. viijd.] **1591** HARINGTON *Orl. Fur.* XXIII. lxvi, Orlando.. With all his strength bestrides the saddle fast, Yet did the Pagan heave him with such strength That all his gyrses broken were at length. **1613–18** DANIEL *Coll. Hist. Eng.* (1626) 46 All strooke his horse together with their Launces; as they brake pectorall, girses, and all. **1623** J. TAYLOR (Water-P.) *Praise Hempseed* Wks. III. 69/2 As Sadlers for their elks haire to stuffe their sadles And girses, and a thousand fidle fadles. **1655** E. TERRY *Voy. E. India* 151 His great Elephants.. carry, each of them, one iron gun, about five foot long, lying upon a strong frame of wood, made square, that is fitted to a thick broad Pannel fastned about him with very strong and broad Girses or Girts.
2. A band or hoop; = GIRTH *sb.*[1] 2.
1591 PERCIVALL *Sp. Dict.*, *Cincha*, a girse, the iron that bindeth a wheele, *Cingulum, orbita ferrea, canthus.*
3. *Comb.*, as *girse-web* = GIRTH-WEB.
1697 R. PEIRCE *Bath Mem.* I. ii. 29 Laying him upon a kind of a Cradle, bottom'd with Girse-web, letting it down, by degrees, into the Bath.

girse, dial. var. GRASS.

girsill, obs. form of GRILSE.

girsle, girstle, dial. var. GRISTLE.

girss, obs. Sc. f. GRASS.

girst, var. GRIST.

girt (gɜːt), *sb.* [var. GIRTH *sb.*[1], in use chiefly in the 17th and 18th c.]
1. A saddle-girth; = GIRTH *sb.*[1] 1. *Obs.* exc. *dial.*
1563 FULKE *Meteors* (1571) 30 b, Her horse laye dead with his bridle and girtes vntied. *a* **1616** BEAUM. & FL. *Wit without M.* II. v, Ile give um leave to cut my girts, and flay me. **1665** MILTON *University Carrier*, Here lies old Hobson; Death hath broke his girt And here, alas! hath laid him in the dirt. **1760–72** tr. *Juan & Ulloa's Voy.* (ed. 3) I. 432 It is with great difficulty they are first brought to suffer the girts to be put round their bodies. **1795** WOLCOT (P. Pindar) *Pindariana* Wks. 1812 IV. 240 Rapture's a Charger; often breaks his girt, Runs off and flings his Rider in the dirt. **1867** ROCK *Jim & Nell* 74 (E.D.S. No. 76) An' girts, a guide-strap, hayvor-seed.
†**b.** A surgical bandage. *Obs.*
1676 WISEMAN *Surg.* VII. v. 487 The most common way of Bandage is by that of the Girt, which Girt hath a Boulster in the middle, and the ends are tackt firmly together. **1743** tr. *Heister's Surg.* 169 There must also be fastened another Napkin, Sling, or Girt.
c. *Printing.* (See quot., and cf. GIRTH *sb.*[1] 1 d.)
1683 MOXON *Mech. Exerc.* II. 72 Girts are Thongs of Leather, cut out of the Back of an Horse-hide [etc.]. Two of them are used to carry the Carriage out and in.
2. A small girder. Now only *U.S.*
1579 in Willis & Clark *Cambridge* (1886) I. 311, ij girts xj foote longe, vj vnch thicke, ix vnch brod. **1665** *Ibid.* II. 531 For girt, sparrs, ioists.. and carriage of timbers for the Library roofe. **1796** MORSE *Amer. Geog.* I. 405 Each pier is composed of seven sticks of oak timber, united by a cap-piece, strong braces and girts. **1875** KNIGHT *Dict. Mech.*, *Girt*, a small girder, used in roofs or bridge-frames.
b. = FILLET *sb.* 11 b.
1823 in P. NICHOLSON *Pract. Build.* 585. **1842** in FRANCIS *Dict. Arts.*
3. = GIRTH *sb.* 3. Also, in technical use, measurement across or around a surface which is not flat (e.g. a moulded cornice) taking into account all elevations and depressions.
1664 in Willis & Clark *Cambridge* (1886) I. 156 The said Cornice.. to be measured by the girt. **1679** EVELYN *Sylva* xxii. 106 The Girt, or Circumference below is thirteen foot. **1703** MAUNDRELL *Journ. Jerus.* (1732) 142, I measur'd one of the largest, and found it twelve yards six inches in girt, and yet sound. **1716** ADDISON *Freeholder* No. 22 ¶2 He is a lusty, jolly fellow, that lives well, at least three yards in the girt. **1793** *Trans. Soc. Arts* (ed. 2) IV. 227 The girt of the old tree .. is five feet six inches. **1825** J. NICHOLSON *Operat. Mech.* 627 The number of square feet produced, by multiplying the girts of the roof by the length of the slates at the eaves. **1828** HUTTON *Course Math.* II. 87 In these articles, the content of a roof is found by multiplying the length of the ridge by the girt over from eaves to eaves. **1842–59** GWILT *Archit.* (ed. 4) §2372 Cornices are measured by obtaining their girt, and multiplying by their length for the quantity of moulded work in them. **1846** J. BAXTER *Libr. Pract. Agric.* (ed. 4) II. App. 446 If the girt be taken in inches, and the length in feet [etc.]. **1883** R. HALDANE *Workshop Receipts* Ser. II. 438/1 Surfaces under 6 in. in width or girt are called 6 in.
fig. **1647** N. BACON *Disc. Govt. Eng.* I. vii. (1739) 15 For long before Boniface his time Archbishops were swoln beyond the girt of the Canon.
b. (See quot.; loosely used for 'quarter-girt'.)
1842–59 GWILT *Archit.* (ed. 4) Gloss., *Girt*.. in timber measuring, according to some, is taken at one fourth of the circumference of the tree.
4. *attrib.* and *Comb.* **a.** simple attrib., as *girt-buckle, -line, -measure, -piece, -spot, -web, -wheel.* **b.** instrumental, as *girt-galled, -marked* adjs. Cf. *girth-buckle, -galled* (GIRTH *sb.*[1] 8), GIRTH-WEB.
1701 *Lond. Gaz.* No. 3746/4 Lost.. a brown Gelding above 14 hands,.. the Hair chafed off by the *Girt-buckle. *Ibid.* No. 3693/4 Lost.. a bay Gelding about 14 hands,.. and a little *Girt-galled. **1720** STRYPE *Stow's Surv. Lond.* (1755) II. 645/2 To give the Bounds or *Girt line of this Parish, I shall begin at Cecil-street. **1687** *Lond. Gaz.* No. 2282/8 A dark bay brown punch Nag.. with saddle marks, and *girt mark'd under the Belly. **1663** GERBIER *Counsel* 78 *Girt measure of Timber is the best for the buyer, because there is more in the circular measure then in the square. **1770–4** A. HUNTER *Georg. Ess.* (1804) II. 195 The *girt-pieces six inches by five. **1688** *Lond. Gaz.* No. 2314/4 No white, unless some Saddle or *Girt Spots. **1665** *Sir T. Roe's Voy. E. Indies* 384 Those Coaches will carry four persons.. but two may lie at ease.. upon quilts.. upheld by *girt-web, with which they are bottom'd. **1841** SAVAGE *Dict. Print.*, *Wheel.* Also called *girt wheel, and drum; a cylinder of elm wood, with two flat broad grooves turned in it on which the two girts wind and unwind alternately, as the carriage is run in and out.

girt (gɜːt), *v.* Now *rare.* [Two formations: (1) Altered from GIRD *v.*[1], perh. after the pa. pple. *girt.* (2) f. GIRT *sb.*
(The imperative *gyrt þe* occurs *Ags. Gosp., Luke* xvii. 8, but the form is prob. due to the nature of the initial consonant of the following word.)]
1. *trans.* = GIRD *v.*[1] in various senses.
c **1400** *Destr. Troy* 5118, I bid.. þat he.. pas fro this place o payn of his lyfe,.. And gyrt on no grete wordis to greue vs no more. **1579** GOSSON *Sch. Abuse* (Arb.) 49 If the enemy beseege vs.. preuent forrain aide, girt in the city [etc.]. **1602** MARSTON *Ant. & Mel.* I. Wks. 1856 I. 12 Weele girt them with an ample waste of love. **1631** GOUGE *God's Arrows* II. §22. 160 Girting and besieging their townes and cities, so as they can not go abroad. **1683** KENNET *Erasm. on Folly* (1709) 113 They will pick a quarrel.. for such poor provocation as the girting on a coat the wrong way. **1688** *Lond. Gaz.* No. 2311/1 The Inauguration Ceremony, which consisted only in Girting the Grand Signior with a Sword. **1726** LEONI *Alberti's Archit.* I. 44/1 The middle parts, which girt and surround the Wall. **1799** *Naval Chron.* II. 177 The whole was by them girted and surrounded. **1823** *Examiner* 106/2 [It] looks like a bright cincture girting the earth. **1895** *Daily News* 13 Feb. 6/6 The primeval forest which girts the mountain.
2. To secure with a girth (cf. GIRTH *v.* 3).
1663 GERBIER *Counsel* 8 Hasten with the Packet-Maile to the Post Office, be it never so ill girted, whereby it oft falls in the mid-way? **1841** CATLIN *N. Amer. Ind.* (1844) II. xli. 60 A buffalo skin girted on its back.
3. To surround with a cord or measuring-line in order to ascertain the girth; to take the girth of.
1663 GERBIER *Counsel* 81 Measured flat in square yeards, without girting the work with a line. **1727** BRADLEY *Fam. Dict.* s.v. *Felling*, By girting the middle of the tree with a line and taking a quarter part of the girt for the square. **1828** HUTTON *Course Math.* II. 86 For the Surrounding Architrave, girt it about the uppermost part for its length [etc.]. **1883** R. HALDANE *Workshop Receipts* Ser. II. 438/1 Surface painting is measured by the superficial yd., girting every part of the work covered.
b. *intr.* To take a measurement by drawing a string round the object to be measured. Said also of the string.
1825 J. NICHOLSON *Operat. Mechanic* 627 All mouldings in plaster work are measured.. by girting over the mouldings with a line. *Ibid.* 642 The dimensions must be taken with a line, that girts over the mouldings, breaks, etc.
4. Of trees, etc.: To measure (so much) in girth or girt (= GIRTH *v.* 5).
1750 G. HUGHES *Barbadoes* 175 This divides into five branches, each equal to a large tree, some of them girting round about eight feet. **1805** FORSYTH *Beauties Scotl.* (1806) IV. 262 There are larches.. which at five feet high girted, in 1792, full eight feet. **1828** HUTTON *Course Math.* II. 88 The cornice, which girts 8½ inches. **1858** O. W. HOLMES *Aut. Breakf.-t.* xii. (1891) 288 The tree 'girts' eighteen and a half feet, and spreads over a hundred.
5. *to girt against*: to press against (said of a ship's cable). [Cf. GIRT *ppl. a.* 2 and GIRD *v.*[1] 7.]
1794 *Rigging & Seamanship* II. 310 The ship, driving to leeward.. causes the cable to girt against the lee bow.
Hence **ˈgirting** *vbl. sb.* In quots. *attrib.*, as **girting-place**, (*a*) that part of a horse's body where the girth is worn; (*b*) that part of the trunk where a tree is girthed or measured; **girting-stead** = GIRDLESTEAD; **ˈgirting** *ppl. a.*
1607 TOPSELL *Four-f. Beasts* (1658) 113 They which are small in their girting stead about their loins, do much love hunting. **1676** *Lond. Gaz.* No. 1108/4 A large brown bay Mare.. with a hole on her ribs.. near the girting place. **1727** BRADLEY *Fam. Dict.* s.v. *Felling*, To know the Value of a Tree standing, you may girt it, allowing for the Bark, and so much as you think it will measure less in the girting Place than at the Butt [etc.]. **1867** D. G. MITCHELL *Rural Stud.* 190 But with us, who have no girting walls [etc.].

girt (gɜːt), *ppl. a.* Also 7 **gert.** [pa. pple. of GIRD *v.*[1]; see GIRDED *ppl. a.*]
1. In sense of the vb.
1791 COWPER *Lett.* 23 June, It is an old house with *girt* casement windows. **1870** MORRIS *Earthly Par.* I. I. 413 And how herself, with girt gown, carefully She went betwixt the heaps. *Ibid.* II. III. 173 Her panting breast and girt-up gown.
2. *Naut.* (See quots.)
1627 CAPT. SMITH *Seaman's Gram.* vii. 30 *Gert*, is when the Cable is so taught that vpon the turning of a tide, a Ship cannot goe ouer it. **1704** HARRIS *Lex. Tech.* s.v. *Girding-girt*, The Seamen say a Ship is Girt or hath a Girding-girt, when her Cable being so tite, or strained, that upon the turning of the Tide she cannot go over it with her Stern-post, but will lie a-cross the Tides. **1780** FALCONER *Dict. Marine*, *Girt*, the situation of a ship which is moored so strait by her cables, extending from the hawse to two distant anchors, as to be prevented from swinging or turning about. **1867** in SMYTH *Sailor's Word-bk.*

girt, dial. var. GREAT, GRIT.

†**ˈgirt-brew.** *Obs. rare.* Also gert-, gird-brew. [f. *girt* GRIT + BREW *sb.*[1]] (See quot. 1620.)
1620 MARKHAM *Farew. Husb.* (1625) 134 Gertbrew.. is somewhat more course, and less pleasant than washbrew, having both the branne and hulls in it, yet is accounted a food of very good strength. **1725** in BRADLEY *Fam. Dict.* s.v. *Oatmeal* (copying MARKHAM), *Gird-brew.*

girth (gɜːθ), *sb.*[1] Forms: 4–5 gerth(e, (5 gerreth), 5–6 gyrth, 6 gurth, 4– girth. See also GARTH[2], GIRD *sb.*[1], GIRR, GIRSE, GIRT *sb.* [a. ON. (**gerðu*) *gjǫrð* girdle, girth, hoop (Sw., Da. *gjord*) = Goth. *gairda* girdle:—OTeut. **gerdâ.* To different grades of the same root (**gerd-*, *gard-*, *gurd-*) belong GARTH[1], GIRD *v.*[1], GIRDLE *sb.*]
1. a. A belt or band of leather or cloth, placed round the body of a horse or other beast of burden and drawn tight, so as to secure a saddle, pack, etc. upon its back.

13.. *Coer de L.* 5733 Brydyl and peytrel al to-brast Hys gerth, and hys stiropes alsoo. **1377** LANGL. *P. Pl.* B. IV. 20 Sette my sadel vppon Suffre-til-I-se-my-tyme, And lete warrok it well with Witty-wordes gerthes. **1463** *Mann. & Househ. Exp.* 227 Item, payd there for gyrthys and a horskombe, and for mendyng of a tronke sadylle, viij.*d.* **1523** FITZHERB. *Husb.* §142 Thymble, nedle, threde, point, lest yᵗ thy gurth breke. **1580** SIDNEY *Arcadia* I. (1590) 75 b, The saddle with broken girthes was driuen from the horse. **1602** SEGAR *Hon. Mil. & Civ.* III. xiv. 130 He who falleth by the default of his horse, the breaking of Girthes, or any such like accident. **1716** SWIFT *Progr. Poetry* 29 The steed, oppress'd, would break his girth, To raise the lumber from the earth. **1787** 'G. GAMBADO' *Acad. Horsemen* (1809) 45 See that your girths are tight. **1841** ELPHINSTONE *Hist. Ind.* II. 425 Rája Rúp Sing..running up to Aurangzib's elephant, began to cut away the girths with his sword. **1867** LADY HERBERT *Cradle L.* viii. 206 One more vigorous kick, having cut the girths which held one of the saddles, the lady found herself suddenly under her steed.

b. ***to run (a horse) head and girth***: to keep pace with in racing.

1809 *Brit. Press* in *Spirit Publ. Jrnls.* (1810) XIII. 62 The mare ran him head and girth nearly the first half mile.

†**c.** (See quot.) *Obs.*

1706 PHILLIPS (ed. Kersey), *Girth*.. a saddle that is buckled and compleat for use.

d. *Printing.* (See quot. 1823.)

1823 CRABB *Technol. Dict.*, *Girth*, leather thongs belonging to the carriage of a printing press, by which it is let in and out. **1841** SAVAGE *Dict. Print.*, *Girths*.. They are sometimes made of Girthweb. **1851–82** in OGILVIE.

†**2.** A hoop of wood or iron, esp. for a barrel. *Obs.*

c **1356** *Durham MS. Burs. Roll*, Et in ccc girthes querculinis empt. pro cuvis et doleis in officio bracine, xvjs. *a* **1400–50** *Alexander* 5536 þan gert he gomes for to gang, and grayth him a tonn Of grene glitterand glas with gerrethis of iren. **1483** *Cath. Angl.* 157/1 A Gyrthe of a vesselle, *instata* (*A.*).

3. Measurement round the circumference of any object, of which the section is approximately circular, as the human body, the trunk of a tree, etc.

With quot. 1706 cf. GARTH[2] 3.

1644 EVELYN *Sylva* xxix. 92 Then cleanse the Boal of the Branches which were left, and saw it into lengths for the squaring, to which belongs the Measure and Girth (as our Workmen call it) which I refer to the Buyer. **1706** PHILLIPS (ed. Kersey), *Girth*,..a Term us'd by Cock-Masters, for the Compass of a Cock's Body. **1791** COWPER *Odyss.* XXIII. 223 Within the court a leafy olive grew Lofty, luxuriant, pillar-like in girth. *a* **1798** PENNANT *Zool.* (1812) III. 86 A fish.. its length was twenty-four feet; but the girth did not exceed twelve. **1827** STEUART *Planter's G.* (1828) 243 A strong but soft rope, of perhaps four inches in girth. **1869** E. A. PARKES *Pract. Hygiene* (ed. 3) 521 There must also be a special girth of the chest. **1887** RUSKIN *Præterita* II. 403 Walnuts, with trunks eight or ten feet in girth.

4. *Mining.* (See quot., and cf. GIRT *sb.* 2.)

1881 RAYMOND *Mining Gloss.*, *Girth*, in square-set timbering, a horizontal brace in the direction of the drift.

5. *transf.* That part of a horse's body where the girth is fastened.

1846 J. BAXTER *Libr. Pract. Agric.* (ed. 4) I. 413 The girth or brisket.

6. *fig.* Something that encircles.

1871 J. MILLER *Songs Italy* (1878) 36 The ripened fields drew round a golden girth. **1872** BLACKIE *Lays Highl.* 10 His soul this self-same moment From the girth of purging fire Leaps redeemed. **1876** SWINBURNE *Erechth.* 1442 That is girdled about with the round sea's girth As a town with its wall.

7. *U.S.* (See quots.)

1864 WEBSTER, *Girth*, a small horizontal beam [**1890** brace] or girder. **1889** *Century Dict.*, *Girth*, in *car-building*, a long horizontal bracing-timber on the inside of the frame of a box-car.

8. *attrib.* and *Comb.*, as ***girth-buckle, -groove, -strap***; also ***girth-deep, -high*** adj., ***girth-galled*** ppl. a. (hence ***girth-gall*** vb.); †**girth-sting**, †**-tree**, a piece of wood suitable for making into hoops; **girth-stretcher** (see quot.). Cf. *girt-buckle, -galled* (GIRT *sb.* 4); *gird-sting* (GIRD *sb.*[1] 3).

1385–6 *Durham MS. Sacr. Roll*, In tribus paribus de *Girthbokyls, vjd. **1851** MAYNE REID *Scalp Hunt.* iv, Back went the girth buckles with a 'sneck'. **1882** E. O'DONOVAN *Merv Oasis* I. 322 The horseman suddenly finds himself *girth-deep in a torrent. **1682** *Lond. Gaz.* No. 1720/8 The other a bright Bay, no white but a slip on the off-side as if he had been *Girth-gall'd. **1897** *Cavalry Tactics* ii. 11 Some horses are inclined to brush, others to girth gall. **1923** C. FOX *Archaeol. Cambr. Region* iii. 92 Cineraries of hard paste with burnished *girth-grooves. **1950** *Oxoniensia* XV. 48 A typical Oxford-style tripod-pitcher, with tubular spout and wavy applied vertical strips over rather irregular girth grooves. **1908** *Daily Chron.* 29 Aug. 7/2 They rode *girth-high through the grass. **1936** R. CAMPBELL *Mithraic Emblems* 166 Girth-high, the poppies and the daisies To brush the belly of my mule. **1496** in *Ld. Treas. Acc. Scotl.* (1877) 282 Item, to that samyn man, for xˣˣ and x *girthstingis viijs. ixd. **1534** *Aberd. Reg.* XVI. 523 (Jam.) The balyes chargyt Robert Stewart pay Archᵈ Stewart, &c. iiij lb. for I. M. gyrchtstingis. *Ibid.* 656 Three hundreyth gyrthstingis. **1897** *Westm. Gaz.* 8 Oct. 2/1 On the near [side] a latigo or *girth strap eight feet long is looped twice through the girth buckle. **1884** KNIGHT *Mech. Dict.* Suppl., **Girth-stretcher*, a frame in which saddle-girths are suspended and held taut 'to take the stretch out of them', as it is called. **1344–5** *Durham MS. Burs. Roll*, In *Girthetres emp. pro vas. Cellar. et Bracinæ, iiijs. vjd.

girth, *sb.*[2], sanctuary, protection: see GRITH.

girth (gɜːθ), *v.* [f. GIRTH *sb.*[1]]

1. *trans.* To gird, surround, encompass.

c **1450** *Merlin* 178 Ha now god yeve me grace to do so moche that he may me girthe with my swerde. **1513** DOUGLAS *Æneis* XII. xiii. 49, I suld, gyrthit [L. *cincta*] with flambis reid Stowtly haue standyn in ȝon batale steid. **1535** COVERDALE *Ezek.* xvi. 9, I gyrthed yᵉ aboute with white sylcke, I clothed the with kerchues. **1819** SCOTT *Ivanhoe* x, Within the four seas that girth Britain. **1848** LYTTON *K. Arthur* VII. lix, They whom the seas of fabled Sirens girth.

2. To fit or bind (a horse, etc.) with a girth.

1580 HOLLYBAND *Treas. Fr. Tong*, *Cengler vn cheval*, to girthe a horse. **1687** MIEGE *Gt. Fr. Dict.* II, To Girth a Horse..You girth him too hard. **1835** W. IRVING *Tour Prairies* xxii, 'For God's sake help me to girth this horse!' cried another. **1898** *Speaker* 1 Jan. 20/2 The horse is up and saddled: Girth the old horse tight.

3. To secure (a saddle, etc.) by means of a girth; also, ***to girth on, up***.

1819 KEATS *Otho* III. ii, O that..Thy girdle [were] some fine zealous-pained nerve To girth my saddle! **1851** MAYNE REID *Scalp Hunt.* xxvii, The animals are led in and watered; they are bridled; the robes are thrown over them and girthed. **1866** FROUDE *Hist. Eng.* IX. 43 Troopers were girthing up their saddles. **1875** W. S. HAYWARD *Love agst. World* 93 Her saddle seemed loosely girthed on.

absol. **1876** JAS. GRANT *One of the 600* li. 428 When we halted to girth up I threw myself on the rich grass.

†**4.** (See quot.)

1688 R. HOLME *Armoury* III. 97/1 Girth it [a Stool or Chair], is to bottom it with Girth Webb stret drawn and crossed.

5. To draw (a string) close round a surface which is being measured. Also *absol.*

1825 J. NICHOLSON *Operat. Mechanic* 544 Cornices are measured by girthing round the moulded parts. *Ibid.* 545 The measurer..girths round the string to the internal angle at the top of the string.

6. *intr.* To measure (so much) in girth.

1858 *Jrnl. R. Agric. Soc.* XIX. II. 575 Some of the carrots girthed nearly 20 inches. **1868** *Ibid.* Ser. II. IV. II. 288 He girthed 8 feet.

Hence **'girthed** *ppl. a.*, **'girthing** *vbl. sb.*

1805 SCOTT *Last Minstr.* III. vi, Down went the steed, the girthing broke. **1826** KIRBY & SP. *Entomol.* III. xxx. 207 Those which suspend themselves horizontally by means of a thread girthed round their middle. **1870** *Daily News* 31 Aug. 2 This [new pack saddle] together with a new mode of girthing, professes to prevent the rolling motion which generally galls the backs of animals.

'girth-,web. [f. GIRTH *sb.* + WEB *sb.*] Woven material of which girths are made; a strong broad tape used by upholsterers and others; a band made of this material.

1381–2 *Durham MS. Hostill. Roll*, In Girth Webbys Capistris flokkys [etc.]. **1410** *Nottingham Rec.* II. 84, j. gerthweb, *jd.* **1571** *Wills & Inv. N.C.* (Surtees 1835) 361 In Ye Great Shoppe ij groce of gyrthwebe and xv peces at vijˢ. ijᵈ. ye groce. **1634** SIR T. HERBERT *Trav.* 149 The better sort sleepe upon Cots, or Beds two foot high, matted or done with girth-web. **1763** WESLEY *Wks.* (1872) III. 149 He sent for some girth-web, with which he fastened her arms to her sides. **1798** EDGEWORTH *Pract. Educ.* (1822) II. 125 A piece of girth-web, which is used instead of a cord, because a cord would be unsteady.

b. *Comb.*, as ***girthweb-belt, -weaver***.

1762 *Gentl. Mag.* 204 The use of what the country people call a Girth-web-belt..would prevent it. **1885** *Census Instr.* 73 Girth Web Weaver.

So **'girth-,webbing**.

1794 W. FELTON *Carriages* (1801) I. 31 The roof-pieces.. are nailed to the Slats, by means of strong Manchester tape, called girth-webbing.

'girt-,line. *Naut.* (See quots.) Cf. GANTLINE.

1769 FALCONER *Dict. Marine* (1780), *Girt-line*, a rope passing through a single block, on the head of the lower masts, to hoist up the rigging thereof..The girt-line is therefore the first rope employed to rig a ship [etc.]. **1840** R. H. DANA *Bef. Mast* viii. 18 A long piece of rope..is taken up to the mast-head from which the stay leads, and rove through a block for a girt-line, or, as the sailors usually call it, a gant-line. *Ibid.* xviii. 50 Some got girt-lines up for riding down the stays and backstays. **1867** in SMYTH *Sailor's Word-bk.*

Girtonian (gə'təʊnɪən). [f. *Girton* + -IAN.] One who is, or has been, a student at Girton College, one of the two Cambridge colleges for women.

1887 *Athenæum* 25 June 833/2 The head mistress..was.. an early Girton student. She was immediately succeeded by ..another Girtonian. **1896** *Westm. Gaz.* 5 Dec. 2/1 On the Newnhamites and Girtonians.

So **'Girtonite**. Also **'Girtonish** *a.*, somewhat resembling the tone or style of Girton students.

1888 *Pall Mall G.* 3 Oct. 3/1 The first number of the new volume of *Atalanta* can certainly not be reproached with being 'too Girtonish'. **1894** SIR E. SULLIVAN *Woman* 58 Their reply would have been a little 'Girtonish', I fancy. **1894** *Athenæum* 24 Nov. 721/1 The plump and fair 'Girtonite'..provided herself with the 'Pensées' of Pascal.

†**gis, jis.** *Obs.* Forms: 6 **jys(se, jis, gisse, gys,** 6–7 **gis.** [Mincing pron. of *Jesus* or *Jesu*.] An oath or exclamation, *By Gis!*

1528 ROY & BARLOWE *Rede me* (Arb.) 56 They regarde it no more be gisse Then waggynge of his mules tayle. **1549** CHALONER tr. *Erasm. on Folly* Q ii b, Cherishyng them (by iysse) a little better than they are wont to dooe these frounyng philosophers. **1562** J. HEYWOOD *Prov. & Epigr.* (1867) 112 Ich can not one woord of it by Iis. Iack is nere his wit, by gis. **1602** SHAKS. *Ham.* IV. v. 58 By gis, and by S. Charity, Alacke, and fie for shame. **1655** tr. *De Parc's Francion* vii. 6 A hundred times and more, by Gis, I would have laid [etc.].

gisarme (gɪ'zɑːm). *Obs.* exc. *Hist.* Forms: α. 3–4 **gisharm(e,** 4–7 **gysarm(e,** 5 **gesarme, guysarme,** 9 **guisarme,** 3–5, 7, 9 **gisarme.** β. 4 **giserne,** 5 **gesarne, geserne, guysarne, gysyryne,** 5–6 **gys(s)erne,** 6 **gyssarn,** 7, 9 **gisarine,** (7 **gisaring**). Also 5 **gyser.** [a. OF. *g(u)isarme, gisarne*, etc. (also *jusarme*), = Pr. *gus-, jusarma*, It. *giusarma*, OSp. *bisarma*, of unknown origin. The Eng. pronunciation with (g) seems to be authenticated by the alliteration in ME. poetry.]

A kind of battle-ax, bill, or halberd, having a long blade in line with the shaft, sharpened on both sides and ending in a point.

c **1250** *Gen. & Ex.* 4084 Ðurȝ and ðurȝ boðen he stong wið hise gisarme sarp & long. **13..** *Gaw. & Gr. Knt.* 288, I schal gif hym of my gyft þys giserne ryche, þis ax, þat is heue innogh. **1460** *Lybeaus Disc.* 1094 Tho dyghte they hem all to armes, Wyth swerdes and wyth gysarmes. **1664** *Floddan F.* II. 11 Some did their grizly gisarings grind. **1843** LYTTON *Last Bar.* I. iii, Hob Yeoman turns gisarme and bill into plough shares. **1863** KINGSLEY *Water-Bab.* 198 A whole cutler's shop of lances, halberts, gisarines.

attrib. **1513** DOUGLAS *Æneis* VIII. xi. 45 In thair hand wyththaldand, euery knycht, Two javilling speris, or than gyssarn stavis.

So **gi'sarmier** [OF.], one armed with a gisarme.

1834 PLANCHÉ *Brit. Costume* 217 The general habits of the archers, bill-men, and guisarmiers.

gise (dʒaɪs), *v. dial.* Also 7 **juice.** [var. or back-formation from GIST *v.*] (See quots. 1695, 1869.)

1695 KENNETT *Par. Antiq.* Gloss. s.v. *Agistator*, To gise or juice ground is when the Lord or tenant feeds it not with his own stock, but takes in other cattle to agist or feed in it. **1706** in PHILLIPS (ed. Kersey). **1869** *Lonsdale Gloss.*, *Gise*, to put cattle out to grass at a sum agreed on per head. **1876** *Mid-Yorks. Gloss.* s.v. *Gise*, He's some oxen gising in Twenty-lands.

So **gise-taker** = *gist-taker*.

1848 WHARTON *Law Lex.*, *Gisetaker*, a person who takes cattle to graze.

gise, obs. f. GUISE; obs. pl. form of JOIST.

†**'gisel.** *Obs. rare*⁻¹. [a. ON. *gísl* (Sw. *gislan*, Da. *gidsel*) = OE. *ȝísel* YISEL.] A hostage.

a **1300** *Cursor M.* 5009 Coth iacob, 'how es þis, þat o mi childir an i misse?' 'Sir, he es in egypt'..'þar vs tok þe hei baili, To scap wit gisel war we fain'.

gisement[1] (dʒaɪzmənt). Also 7 **juicement.** [var. GISTMENT.] (See quot. 1848.)

1695 KENNETT *Par. Antiq.* Gloss. s.v. *Agistator*, Hence our Grasiers now call the foreign cattel, which they take in to keep by the week, Gisements or Juicements. **1829** [see *gisting* vbl. sb. *s.v.* GIST *v.*]. **1848** WHARTON *Law Lex.*, *Gisement*, cattle which are taken in to graze at a certain price; also the money received for grazing cattle.

‖**gisement**[2] (ʒizmɑ̃). [F. *gisement* position, f. *gis-, gésir* to lie.] The way in which something lies, position.

1864 *Reader* 9 Apr. 463/3 The main part of the evidence lies, of course, in the gisement of the vein. **1897** *Archæol. Jrnl.* Dec. 333 Rows of relics arranged in cases, without regard to their gisement, are of no use for educational purposes.

giser, obs. form of GIZZARD.

giserne, var. GISARME, GIZZERN.

gisily, gisin, var. GUISILY, GESINE, *Obs.*

gismo ('gɪzməʊ). *U.S. slang.* Also **gizmo.** [Origin unknown.] A gadget, gimmick, 'thingumajig' (see quots.).

1943 *Time* 19 July 69/1 Gizmo—a term of universal significance, capable of meaning 'gadget', 'stuff', 'thing', 'whozis' or almost anything else the speaker wants it to. **1949** R. A. HEINLEIN *Red Planet* iii. 26 Now what is this gismo? When you brought it aboard I thought it was a volley ball. **1954** C. WILLIAMS *Touch of Death* (1955) i. 7 She was working the strap of the halter gizmo up between her arm and her side. **1967** *Observer* 21 May 21/2 To help him 'shoot' [photographs], he used..a 'gismo'—a small cardboard tube which he presses against the camera lens. **1970** *New Yorker* 1 Aug. 26/3 Every gismo that made use of a clothes hanger will be demonstrated by its inventor.

gismondine, gismondite (gɪz'mɒndɪn, -aɪt). *Min.* [Named in 1817 by Leonard after Prof. Gismondi, who first described it: see -INE, -ITE.] A hydrous silicate of aluminium and calcium, found near Rome.

1823 W. PHILLIPS *Min.* (ed. 3) 211 Gismondine..is of a greyish-white color. **1837** DANA *Min.* 301 Gismondine.. occurs in white translucent crystals coating cavities of lava at Capo di Bove, near Rome; and in small purple colored crystals in the drusy cavities of ice spar and other volcanic minerals, at Vesuvius. **1869** PHILLIPS *Vesuv.* x. 295 Zeagonite, or gismondine, in ejected blocks and dykes of Somma. **1882** DANA *Man. Min. & Lith.* 296 *Gismondite*.. a hydrous lime-aluminum silicate, occurring in trimetric crystals resembling square octahedrons.

†**'gispin.** *Obs.* Forms: 6 **guispin, gyspen,** 7 **gespen, gespin, gispin.** [Of obscure origin: Godefr. quotes a 14th c. Fr. document which mentions 'quatre *guippons* d' yaue benoite', but

he interprets the word as = *goupillon*, asperser.] A leathern pot or cup.

1530 PALSGR. 225/1 Gyspen potte, *pot de cvir.* **1550** in Strype *Eccl. Mem.* (1721) II. II. xxxiii. 538 A pair of pinsons, a little pot, and a guispin. **1636** D. LLOYD *Leg. Capt. Jones* (1648) 2 Then up starts Jones, Calls for sixe Gispins, drinkes them off at once. **1641** S. SMITH *Herring Buss Trade* 23 Throwne into the barrels with panniers or gespen. *c* **1660–80** *Househ. Ord.* (1790) 374 A pott and a gespin .. for ale and wyne for the said watch.

gissane, Sc. var. GESINE, *Obs.*

† **'gissard.** *Obs. rare.* [? popular pronunc. of **geese-ward* or *-herd.*] (See quots.)

1584 R. SCOT *Disc. Witchcraft, Disc. diuels & spirits* xxiiij. 528 The Thebans had not a better shepherd than S. Wendeline, nor a better gissard to keepe their geese than Gallus. **1688** R. HOLME *Armoury* III. 193/1 St. Gallus the Patron of Gissards, or Keepers of Geese.

gisse, var. GIS, *Obs.*

† **gist**, *sb.*[1] *Obs.* Also 3–7 **giste**, 6 **geist**. [a. OF. *giste* (F. *gîte*) resting- or stopping-place, etc., vbl. sb. related to *gis-*, *gésir* to lie. In the 16th and 17th cents. the more usual form is GEST *sb.*[4]]

1. A stopping-place or lodging. Also *pl.* a list of stopping-places or stages in a monarch's progress.

a **1225** *Ancr. R.* 350 He ne etstont nout ase foles doð, auh .. hieð toward his giste. **13..** *Geburt Jesu* (Horstm.) 587 Oure ledi .. leide him on awisp of hei; þer was apore giste. *c* **1470** HARDING *Chron.* CCXL. Add. st. (Harl. MS.), I make you a kalende Of all the waie to Edenbourgh expres, And wher your giste ech nyght may well extend. **1528** GARDINER *Let. to Wolsey* (P.R.O.), I sende your Grace also the King's Gists. **1600** HOLLAND *Livy* XXXVIII. xli. 1009 From this giste they made but one daies journey to Apollonia. **1619** VISC'T DONCASTER in *Eng. & Germ.* (Camden) 144 According to the gistes I found there of King Ferdinand his coming on to the election [etc.]. **1706** PHILLIPS (ed. Kersey) s.v. *Giste*, Gists or Gests of the Queen's Progress, *i.e.* a Bill or Writing that contains the Names of the Towns or Houses where she intends to lie upon the Way.

b. said of birds and their halting-places.

1545 JOYE *Exp. Dan.* Ded. Aij, The same sea y[t] harbouretb these fowles thus sytting upon theyr egges wyl be so cawme and styll to her geistes for xiiii dayes, that men may suerly sayle withoute peryl upon her. **1601** HOLLAND *Pliny* x. xxiii, These Quailes have their set gists, to wit, ordinarie resting and baiting places.

2. ? Refreshment.

a **1290** *Kindh. Jesu* (Horstm.) 180 þo dronk Marie .. of þat welle .. And Josep maude al so gret feste, More him likede þat ilke giste þan ani flechs i oþur i rost.

† **gist**, *sb.*[2] *Obs.* Forms: 5 **geyst**, 6 **gyest**, 7 **geast**, **jeast**, **giste**, 8 **joist**. [f. GIST *v.*] A right of pasture or 'feed' for cattle by payment or otherwise, AGISTMENT. Also *cow-gist*.

1493 *Will R. Drury* in Cullum *Hawstead* (1784) 119 Also I will that William my sone have all suche shepe as I have at geyst at my dethe. **1558** *Scotter Manor Roll* (N.W. Linc. Gloss.), Richarde Hollande hathe taken of straungers vj beas gyest in y[e] Lordes commene. **1641** BEST *Farm. Bks.* (Surtees) 119 Such beasts as are thus taken into any pasture to bee kept are (hereaboutes) called geasters .. and theire gates soe many severall jeastes. *Ibid.* 120 Her nowtheards wage is 20 *s.* in money, the milke of a cowe, and a cowe-geast.

b. *Comb.*, as **gist-cattle**, **-horses**, animals agisted; **gist-money** (see quot.); **gist-taker** = AGISTOR.

1784 CULLUM *Hawsted* 119 *note* *Joist cattle .. the cattle of other people taken to pasture at so much a week or month. **1598** *Scotter Manor Roll* (N.W. Linc. Gloss.), De Thoma Easton quia cepit le *giste-horses in commune pastura iijs. iiijd. **1876** *Whitby Gloss.*, **Gist money*, the payment for pasturage of cattle that are agisted or fed at a stipulated price. **1626** SPELMAN *Gloss.* s.v. *Fenatio* [says that the Eng. versions of *Charta de Foresta* mistranslate *forestarii et viridarii* by] *Gyst-takers or walkers.

gist (dʒɪst), *sb.*[3] Also (sense 1 only) in 8–9 later F. form **gît**, corruptly **gite**, **gîte**, and JET *sb.*[4]. [a. OF. *gist* (F. *gît*), 3 sing. pres. ind. of *gésir* to lie, *gésir en* to consist in, depend on, used in the AF. law phrase (*cest*) *action gist*, '(this) action lies', which occurs 1502–3 in *Kelvey's Rep.* (1688) lf. 50a, and is common in law-books.]

1. *Law.* The real ground or point (of an action, indictment, etc.).

α. **1711** 5 *Modern Reports* (1794) 305 (*Gatehouse* v. *Row*) Because it is the very gist of the action. **1769** BLACKSTONE *Comm.* IV. 333 These charges .. are the points and very *gist* of the indictment. **1791** BURKE *App. Whigs* Wks. 1842 I. 501 This is the great gist of the charge against him. **1834** P. BINGHAM *New Cases* I. 72 The gist of the action being the assault and battery. **1875** POSTE *Gaius* IV. (ed. 2) 502 The gist (gîte) of the civil action of Condictio .. was the increase of the defendant's fortune or patrimony by the reduction of the plaintiff's patrimony without any consideration or equivalent gain to the plaintiff.

β. **1726** SIR J. STRANGE *Rep. Cases* I. 666 Where the special damage is the *git* of the action, this sort of evidence is allowed. **1795** CHRISTIAN in *Blackstone's Comm.* (1809) III. 140 The gît or foundation of the action is held to consist in the husband's loss of the comfort and society of his wife. **1823** DE QUINCEY *King of Hayti* Wks. 1862 XI. 41 The *gite* of the lawyer's reasoning.

2. The substance or pith of a matter, the essence or main part.

1823 in Cobbett *Rur. Rides* (1885) I. 339 This is the gist. Here lies the whole of it. **1861** T. A. TROLLOPE *La Beata* II. xii. 52 The gist of the fun is to demand the production of the green sprig .. at the most .. unexpected times. **1864** BOWEN *Logic* xi. 363 The gist of the reasoning does not depend upon any Maxim or First Principle.

gist (dʒaɪst), *v. Obs.* exc. *dial.* Also 5 **geyst**, 8 **joist**. [Aphetic form of AGIST; cf. also GISE *v.*]

1. *trans.* To take in or put out (cattle) to pasture at so much per head: = AGIST *v.* 1.

1483 *Cath. Angl.* 157/1 To Giste, *agistare.* **1492** *Plumpton Corr.* (Camden) 103 A neighbour of myne .. which geysted with two of your servants in Haywras x bests. **1695** KENNETT *Par. Antiq.* Gloss. s.v. *Agistator, Agister* .. to receive in cattel to be so pastur'd or gisted [etc.]. **1799** A. YOUNG *Agric. Linc.* 325 They are forced to .. joist their sheeders in the spring. **1869** *Lonsdale Gloss.*, *Gist*, to agist, to pasture out cattle on hire.

† **2.** *intr.* Of cattle: To remain and feed for a specified time: = AGIST *v.* 2. *Obs.*

1519 in *Surtees Misc.* (1888) 33 For takynge viij swyn to gist, xijd. **1601** FULBECKE *1st Pt. Parall.* 31 Whatsoeuer is gained by .. the harrowing of horses, or the letting to gist of kine.

Hence † **'gisted** *ppl. a.*; **'gisting** *vbl. sb.*

1794 PRINGLE *Agric. Surv. Westmld.* 21 Every occupier of land .. having it in his power to keep .. cattle through the months of summer, upon joisted fields .. at a cheap rate. **1829** BROCKETT *N.C. Words* (ed. 2), *Gisting*, the feeding of cattle, which in some places are called gisements. **1869** *Lonsdale Gloss.*, *Gisting*, the agistment of cattle.

gist(e, obs. form of GUEST, JOIST.

† **'gister.** *Obs. rare.* Also 7 **geaster**. [Aphetic form of AGISTOR: in sense 2 prob. f. GIST *v.* + -ER[1].]

1. = AGISTOR.

1483 *Cath. Angl.* 157/1 A Gister, *agistator.*

2. A cow, etc. feeding on hired pasture.

1641 [see GIST *sb.*[2]].

† **'gistment.** *Obs. rare.* Also 6 **joyssement**; and see GISEMENT. [Aphetic form of AGISTMENT.] = AGISTMENT 1.

1511 *MS. Acc. St. John's Hosp., Canterb.*, It. for þe gystment off ij drey Kyne. **1545** *Statem. Accts.* in *Paston MSS.* (B.M.) VIII, For the joyssement of ccxx shepe at Beckham .. at iijd. the shepe. lxvs. **1695** KENNETT *Par. Antiq.* Gloss. s.v. *Agistator*, Tenants within the forest, who had free gistment.

gistne(n, **gistning**, var. GESTEN, GESTENING.

git (gɪt). *slang.* [var. GET *sb.*[1]] In contemptuous use: a worthless person.

1946 *Penguin New Writing* XXVIII. 171 Chalky! You idle git! **1960** H. PINTER *Caretaker* I. 9 Who was this git to come up and give me orders? **1967** *Listener* 3 Aug. 136/3 That bald-headed, moon-faced, four-eyed git Garnett gristling on about Harold Wilson. **1967** *Observer* 24 Sept. 36/6 The girl scarcely turned her head: 'Shutup yerself yer senseless git!'

git, var. GATE *sb.*[4]; dial. f. GET *v.*; obs. f. GITH.

gît, git: see GIST *sb.*[3]

Gitane (ʒitan). [Fr. *gitane* gipsy woman.] A cigarette of a proprietary French brand. Also *attrib.*

1933 *Trade Marks Jrnl.* 6 Sept. 1095 *Gitanes.* Cigarettes. Service d'Exploitation Industrielle des Tabacs... Paris. **1937** *Tobacco World Ann.* 1 (Advt.), Cigarettes: Elegantes, Gauloises, Celtique, Gitanes. **1961** E. HYAMS tr. *Crespi's Cigarette* i. 8 A certain way of offering a packet of cigarettes to a departmental head—filter-tip Gitanes Bleues, or American cigarettes .. may enable a man to raise his prices by from twenty to a hundred per cent. **1967** V. CANNING *Python Project* viii. 157 Blowing a cloud of Gitane smoke, he went on, 'Your Prime Minister is not a wealthy man, is he?' **1968** N. FLEMING *Counter Paradise* iv. 58 'Here, have a Gitane,' he said, tossing the pack over to Jake. **1969** S. COULTER *Embassy* xxi. 237 A thick-set man smoking a yellow-paper Gitane cigarette.

‖ **gitano** (dʒɪ'tɑːnəʊ; in Sp. xi'tano). [Sp. repr. a popular Lat. type **Ægyptānus* Egyptian.] A male (Spanish) gipsy. So **gi'tana**, a female gipsy.

1834 W. H. AINSWORTH *Rookwood* III. i, Her father was a Spanish Gitano. **1845** FITZBALL *Maritana* II. ii. 22 Hear me swear, too fair Gitana, This fond heart beats but for thee. **1876** JAS. GRANT *One of the 600* I. iii. 42 Her thick wavy hair .. her ever-sparkling eyes, were black as those of a Spanish gitano [*sic*] or a Welsh gipsy.

gitarr(e, obs. form of GUITAR.

† **gite**[1], **gide**. *Obs.* Forms: α. 4–6 **gyte**, 5–7 **gite**, 7 **git**. β. 5 **gide**, **gyde**, (**guyde**). [app. a. OF. *guite*, some article of clothing (according to Godef., a hat).] A kind of dress or gown.

α. *c* **1386** CHAUCER *Reeve's T.* 34 She cam after in a gyte of reed. *c* **1450** HENRYSON *Test. Cres.* 260 (Thynne) Hir gyte was gray, and full of spottis blak. *a* **1529** SKELTON *El. Rummyng* 68 Whan she doth her aray And gyrdeth in her gytes: Stytched and pranked wyth pletes. **1567** TURBERV. *Epit. & Sonn.* (1837) 295 Thy brodred gyte makes thee a gallant gyrle. **1600** FAIRFAX *Tasso* XIII. liv. 245 Phœbus .. left his golden weed, And dond a gite in deepest purple dide. **1614** CAMDEN *Rem.* 234 They had also about this time a kinde of Gowne called a Git.

β. **13..** *Minor Poems of Vernon MS.* xxxvii. 281 þis wymmen þat muchel haunteþ pride .. Heore reuersede gydes on hem are streyt drawe. *c* **1420** *Anturs of Arth.* 366 Here gide was glorious and gay, of a gresse green. *c* **1470** HENRY *Wallace* I. 213 Likle he was, richt byge and weyle besyne, In till a gyde of gudly ganand greyne. ? *a* **1500** *Chester Pl.* (Shaks. Soc.) II. 187 Fie on pearles! fie on pride! Fye on gowne! fye on guyde.

¶ Used by Peele for: Splendour, magnificence.

1589 PEELE *Tale Troy* Wks. (Rtldg.) 558/1 Done is thy pride, dim is thy glorious gite, Slain is thy prince in this unhappy fight. *a* **1597** —— *David & Bethsabe* II. iii, So dim is David's glory and his gite.

‖ **gite**[2] (ʒiːt). Also **gîte**. [F. *gîte* (OF. *giste*: see GIST *sb.*[1]), vbl. sb. related to *gésir* to lie.]

1. a. A stopping-place, lodging.

1798 CHARLOTTE SMITH *Young Philos.* IV. 37 Would I had any pretensions to so happy a *gite!* **1809** SCOTT *Fam. Lett.* (1894) I. 140 This small farm .. will .. furnish a better *gîte* than any of the Inns on the road. **1841** JAMES *Brigand* xii, The village was too small to have a regular inn, or *gîte*.

b. In France (and French-speaking countries): a furnished or self-catering holiday home, usu. in a rural district.

1964 G. B. SCHALLER *Year of Gorilla* (1965) v. 97 At night we stayed at one of the many rest-houses, or *gîtes*, which lie scattered over the country [*sc.* the Congo.] The *gîtes* are simple houses, sparsely furnished with a bedstead, a table, and some chairs. **1971** *Daily Tel.* 20 Mar. 12 Almost nestling under the shadow of the Puy-de-Dome, our *gîte* had probably been an old farmhouse. Now it was converted into two flats. **1984** *Listener* 16 Aug. 15/2 Holidays are taken in the Dordogne, on remote Greek islands, in rural gites and in distant Kashmir. **1987** *Sun* 21 Feb. 19/1 The trend started when the French opened up their government-assisted self-catering gites to Britons.

2. The place where a fish lies. *rare.*

1854 BADHAM *Halieut.* 41 The gîtes of fish are very various, some lying on a bed of sand, some ambushed in mud [etc.].

† **gite**[3]. *Obs. rare*[−1]. [a. OF. *giet*, *jet*, etc.; cf. GET *sb.*[2] and JESS.] A strap (of a shield).

c **1440** *Partonope* 2241 He vndide the gyte of hys Sheelde And from hym cast hit into the feelde.

gite, gîte: see GIST *sb.*[3]

gitern(e, obs. form of GITTERN *sb.*

gith (gɪθ). Forms: α. 4, 6 **gitte**, 6–7 **git**. β. 7 **githen**, 4– **gith**. [a. L. *gith*, *git*, *gicti*, of unknown origin.] A name for plants of the genus *Nigella*, esp. *N. sativa*. **damask gith** = *N. damascena*.

α. *a* **1387** *Sinon. Barthol.* (Anecd. Oxon.) 16 *Ciminum Ethiopicum*, gitte. **1548** TURNER *Names of Herbes*, Git is named .. in englishe herbe Git or Nigella romana. **1608** TOPSELL *Serpents* (1658) 775 Take of the seeds of Git or Nigella ten drams.

β. **1382** WYCLIF *Isa.* xxviii. 27 Forsothe not in sawes shal he throsshe gith. **1398** TREVISA *Barth. De P.R.* XVII. lxxxii. (1495) 652 Gyth is a manere potage moche lyke to Comyn .. and growyth amonge corne wyth smalle sede .. and some meaneth that the herbe Gyth is Nigella. *c* **1420** *Pallad. on Husb.* x. 155 And gith is last eke in this mone ysowe. **1577** B. GOOGE *Heresbach's Husb.* (1586) 53 The onion and gith. **1611** COTGR., *Gith*, Hearbe githen, Nigella Romana. **1661** LOVELL *Hist. Anim. & Min.* 268 They may be driven away .. by the smoake of gith and hemlock. **1713** PETIVER in *Phil. Trans.* XXVIII. 207 Double flowered or Damask Gith. **1822** *Hortus Anglicus* II. 37 Small Fennel Flower, Herb Gith. **1869** BLACKMORE *Lorna D.* xxii, If thou would keep thy Son, See that bine and gith have none.

b. Applied to the Corn-cockle, *Lychnis Githago.*

1597 GERARDE *Herbal* II. ccccxxviii. 927 Cockle .. is called Gith .. yet not properly. **1866** *Treas. Bot.*, *Gith*, the Corn Cockle, *Agrostemma Githago.*

gitie, **gittar**, obs. ff. JETTY, GUITAR.

gitter ('gɪtə(r)). *Optics.* [Ger. = lattice, grating.] A diffraction grating.

1876 *Harper's Mag.* Jan. 210 The earliest gitters were prepared by Fraunhofer, and were ruled through leaf metal or thin coatings of grease on glass. **1881** C. S. PIERCE in *Nature* 21 July 262/2 It will be possible to deduce from the minimum deviation of this line produced by any given gitter, the mean width of that gitter.

gittern ('gɪtən), *sb. arch.* Forms: 4–5 **gitern(e**, 4–6 **gytern(e**, (5 **getarne**, **-erne**, **-yrne**, **gittyrn**), (6 **getron**, **githorn**, **guthorne**), 6–7 **gitterne**, (7 **gittron**, **gytterne**), 7, 9 **ghittern**, 8 **guiterne**, 6– **gittern**. [a. OF. *guiterne*, *guisterne*, etc. (obs. since 16–17th c.) of obscure formation. The form *guiterre* also occurs; usually believed to represent an altered form of Gr. κιθάρα CITHARA. Cf. GUITAR and CITHERN.] An old instrument of the guitar kind strung with wire, a cithern.

1377 LANGL. *P. Pl.* B. XIII. 233, I can noither tabre ne trompe .. ne synge with the gyterne. *c* **1410** *Sir Cleges* 101 Of harpis, luttis, and getarnys. **1571** *Satir. Poems Reform.* xxviii. 67 Quhair I begouth with guthorne for to dance. **1613** LEIGHTON *Teares or Lament.* 70 With Drumes & Fife & Shrillest shalmes, with Gittron and bandore. **1633** HEYWOOD *Eng. Trav.* II. Wks. 1874 IV. 29 A fourth, bestrides his Fellowes, thinking to scape, As did Arion, on the Dolphins backe, Still fumbling on a gitterne. **1693** SOUTHERNE *Maid's last Prayer* III. iii, Where's my Gittern? **1792** *Minstrel* (1793) II. 100 Elizabeth .. played incomparably on the guiterne. **1816** SCOTT *Old Mort.* xxiii, The same hand .. can touch a tinkling lute, or a gittern, to soothe the ears of the dancing daughters of perdition in their Vanity Fair. **1879** TENNYSON *Falcon*, You know that I can touch The ghittern to some purpose.

b. *attrib.*, as *gittern-head* (cf. *cittern-head* in CITHERN 2), *-wire*.

1599 MASSINGER, etc. *Old Law* IV. i. (1656) 47 The Heads of your Instruments differ, yours are Hogs-heads their Cittern and Gittern heads. **1662** *Irish Act 14 Chas. II*, c. 8 Bk. Rates, Wire called.. Virginal and Ghittern wire.

† '**gittern**, *v. Obs.* [f. prec. sb.] *intr.* To play on the gittern.

c **1380** [see the *vbl. sb.*]. *c* **1400** *Rom. Rose* 2322 To harpe and gitterne, daunce and play. *c* **1525** *Tale of Basyn* 82 in Hazl. *E.P.P.* III. 47 He harpys and gytryns and syngs well ther-too. *a* **1674** MILTON in Birch *Life* (1738) I. 44 Each evening every one with Mistress or Ganymed, gitterning along the Streets.

Hence † '**gitterning** *vbl. sb.*

c **1380** WYCLIF *Wks.* (1880) 9 Knackynge and harpynge, gyternynge & daunsynge & oþere veyn triflis. *c* **1386** CHAUCER *Miller's T.* 177 He syngeth in his voys gentil and smal.. Ful wel acordaunt to his gyternynge.

† '**gitterner.** *Obs.* A player on the gittern.

13.. *E.E. Allit. P.* A. 91 Bot sytole stryng & gyternere Her reken myrþe moȝt not retrete. **14..** *Nom.* in Wr.-Wülcker 693/44 *Hic gigator*, getyrnere.

gittie, giuegoue, obs. ff. JETTY, GEWGAW.

giulio, var. JULIO.

1909 *Westm. Gaz.* 17 Mar. 5/1 A.. purse containing twenty-five giulii.

giuncus, pl. **giunchi,** obs. form of JUNK.

‖ **giunta** ('dʒʊnta). *Hist.* See also JUNTA. [It. *giunta*, f. *giugnere* to JOIN.] In the Venetian republic, a number of patricians chosen to act as assessors to the Council of Ten in special emergencies; later, the name given to the 60 co-opted members of the council of *pregadi*, by which the affairs of the state were administered.

1673 RAY *Journ. Low C.* 167 In the number of the 60 *Pregadi* there can be but three of one and the same family, and if there be three in the *Pregadi* there can be but two in the *Giunta*. **1820** BYRON *Mar. Fal.* v. i, The Giunta Will hear you.

† **giunto,** quasi-It. spelling of JUNTO.

1641 *Jrnls. Ho. Commons* II. 118 A Giunto of the Privy Council for the Scotch affairs.

giuntur, obs. form of JOINTURE.

Giuoco Piano (dʒʊ'əʊkəʊ 'pjɑːnəʊ). *Chess.* [It., lit. 'plain game'.] (See quots.)

1813 J. H. SARRATT *Wks. Damiano, Ruy-Lopez & Salvio* 214 An opening, denominated by Salvio, and by all Italian Players, Giuoco Piano; that name being given to all openings in which *no Pawn is sacrificed* for the sake of an attacking position. **1860** 'OXFORD AMATEUR' *Hand-bk. Chess* viii. 32 If each player then brings his King's Bishop to QB 4th, we have the Giuoco Piano—a deservedly favourite opening with many players. **1965** I. A. HOROWITZ *Chess Openings* v. 25 Together with some related openings, the Giuoco Piano was extremely popular for many years; but the gradual change of insight.. tended more and more to a lasting initiative rather than a splurge of brief fireworks and has slowly replaced the Giuoco Piano and the King's Gambit with the Ruy Lopez and the Queen's Gambit.

† **giust.** Spenser's quasi-It. spelling of JOUST.

1579 SPENSER *Sheph. Cal.* Oct. 39 And sing of bloody Mars, of wars, of giusts. **1590** —— *F.Q.* I. i. 1 Knightly giusts and fierce encounters. **1808** SCOTT *Marm.* I. xiv, Seldom hath pass'd a week but giust Or feat of arms befel.

† **give,** *sb.*[1] *Obs.* Forms: α. 1 **ᵹi(e)fu, ᵹyfu, ᵹeofu,** 2 **ȝife, ȝieve,** 2–3 **ȝive, ȝe(o)ve, ȝefe,** 4 **yeve.** β. 3 **gife, give, gyve.** [Com. Teut.: OE. *ᵹiefu* str. fem. = OFris. *geve, jeve*, OS. *geba, giba* (MDu. *geve*), OHG. *geba, gepa, kepa* (MHG. *gebe*), ON. *gjǫf*, Goth. *giba*:—OTeut. **gebâ*, f. **geb-* to GIVE.

The β-forms, with initial *g* for ȝ, are northern and prob. due to the influence of the verb, q.v.]

1. Something given; = GIFT *sb.* 3.

The combination *ȝeres-ȝive*, New Year's gift (see YEAR[1]) occurs later, e.g. in 1377 text of *P. Plowman* B. x. 47. With the OE. *tó ᵹiefe*, as a gift, cf. Du. *te geef*, as a gift, gratis (now only in the sense 'dirt cheap').

α. *Beowulf* 1884 Þa wæs on gange ᵹifu Hroðgares oft ᵹe-æhted. *c* **888** K. ÆLFRED *Boeth.* xli. §2 Þam he ᵹeaf micle ᵹife freodomes. *c* **1000** *Ags. Gosp.* Matt. x. 8 Ge onfengun to ᵹyfe, syllað to ᵹyfe [L. *gratis*]. *a* **1200** *Moral Ode* 45 Þer ne þerf he habben kare of ȝefe ne of ȝelde. *c* **1205** LAY. 1790 Þa hefde Brutus þa ȝeue þat Diana hi bi-heihte. *Ibid.* 20494 Heo sculden habbeon ȝiuen gode. *c* **1300**, *c* **1330** [see GIVE *v.* B 8].

β. *c* **1300** *Havelok* 357 That he ne moucte no more liue, For gol ne siluer, ne for no gyue.

b. Something given by God; a divine gift, grace; = GIFT *sb.* 6.

α. **971** *Blickl. Hom.* 31 Ealra þara ᵹifa þe he middan-ᵹearde forᵹeaf þurh his tocyme, nis næniᵹ mare mæᵹen.. þonne [etc.]. *c* **1000** *Ags. Gosp.* Luke ii. 40 Þæt cild weox.. & godes ᵹyfu wæs on him. *c* **1200** *Vices & Virtues* 53 Full of godes ȝiues. *c* **1200** ORMIN 5482 Þe firrste ȝife iss witt & skill Inn heofennlike þingess. *c* **1200** *Trin. Coll. Hom.* 107 Swiche ȝiues [*MS.* giues] and none iuele sendeð lemene fader mankin. *c* **1230** *Hali Meid.* 11 Meidenhad is tat an ȝeoue iȝettet te of heouene.

β. *a* **1300** *Cursor M.* 23370 Þe sele þat sal leng in heuen, In bodi sal haf gifes seuen.

2. The action of giving; = GIFT *sb.* 1.

c **1205** LAY. 401 He heold þe stronge castles þurh staðele his fader ȝefe. **1340** *Ayenb.* 23 Lozengerie, simulacion, folliche yeue: uor þet me ssel him hyealde corteys and large.

3. *Comb.*, as **ȝeve-custi** [OE. *cystiᵹ* bountiful], bountiful in gifts.

c **1205** LAY. 4862 Nes he noht ȝælpinde ah he wes ȝeue- [*so MS.*; *printed* geue-] custi.

give (gɪv), *sb.*[2] [f. GIVE *v.*] The action, fact, or quality of 'giving' (cf. sense 40 of the vb.); a yielding, giving way.

1868 G. M. HOPKINS *Jrnl.* 15 Sept. (1959) 189 They look like the swaling or *give* of water in a river when you look across it. **1887** *Cassell's Fam. Mag.* Summer No. 62 The dead pull (so different to the spring and give of the rod). **1893** *Pall Mall G.* 4 Jan. 4/3 Notwithstanding the apparent 'give' in the weather yesterday, at no time.. did the thermometer rise above 31 degrees. **1921** *Daily Colonist* (Victoria, B.C.) 11 Mar. 2/3 One member in our business structure alone lacks 'give'—labor. If there is no 'give' something is going to smash. **1970** *Times* 13 Mar. 13/1 They began levelling the pitch at 8 a.m. this morning and if the weather stays fine we should have a fair surface with some give in it.

give (gɪv), *v.* Forms and Inflexions: see below. [A Common Teutonic str. vb.: OE. *ᵹiefan* (*ᵹeaf, ᵹéafon, ᵹiefen*) = OFris. *geva, jeva*, OS. *geban* (MDu. and Du. *geven*), OHG. *kepan, geban* (MHG. and G. *geben*), ON. *gefa* (Sw. *gifva*, Da. *give*), Goth. *giban*:—OTeut. **geban, gaf, gǣbum, gebono-*. By some the root is identified with that of Lith. *gabénti* to bring, OIrish *gabim* I take.

In OE. the strictly West Saxon forms of the infinitive and the pa. pple. show the influence of initial ᵹ in the substitution of *ie* (commonly *i, y*) for the original *e* of the root; thus *ᵹiefan, ᵹifan, ᵹyfan* for *ᵹefan*. In other dialects the *e* was normal, except where it passed into *eo* (northern *ea*) by *u-* or *o-* umlaut; but *i* occurs very frequently, perh. owing to the analogy of the 2nd and 3rd pers. sing. pres. ind.; on the other hand, the regular *i* of the last-mentioned forms is often replaced by the *e* of the infinitive. In midland and southern ME. there are three main forms: *ȝiven, ȝeven* and *ȝeoven*. The third of these is rare, and disappears *c* 1200. The relation of the other two forms is obscure, as both sometimes occur in the same text (e.g. in Layamon, where the earlier version favours *ȝeven*, the later *ȝiven*, but neither is consistent). In such cases the difference may be merely graphic, and due to an indeterminate vowel. Some texts, however, show an exclusive use of one or other of the forms; thus *ȝiven* is regular in the Ancren Riwle, while the Ayenbite has only *ȝeven*. The forms with initial guttural are first recorded in the Ormulum (? north-east midland, *c* 1200), though the forms with ȝ are much more frequent. (Apparent earlier instances with initial *g-* occur only in MSS. which confuse *g* and ȝ.) The *g* forms, however, certainly originated in the north (though the want of 12th c. northern texts renders direct proof impossible); and, as they do not admit of being (like the guttural *g* of *begin*) explained as the products of analogy, it seems most probable that they are due to Scandinavian influence. The regular form of the infinitive in early northern texts is *gif, give*, which rather corresponds to Sw. *gifva*, Da. *give*, than to ON. *gefa*. On the other hand, the pa. pple. is at an early date written with *e* as well as *i* (*gefin, gifin*, etc.; see the forms below), and *e* also appears in some contracted forms as *ges* (= gives). In the 15th and 16th c. the form *geve* (*geif*, etc.) is common both in English and Scottish writers; Levins (1570) places it along with *grieve, sleeve*, etc. In the 14–15th c. the northern forms extended themselves gradually to the midland dialects. Havelok (*c* 1300) has, like the Ormulum, both the ȝ and the *g* forms; R. Brunne's *Handlyng Synne* (1303) has only the former, but his Chronicle (*c* 1330), according to the two existing MSS., has always *g*. Langland has both types, well attested by the alliteration, but Chaucer seems to have always written *yeve, yaf*, and throughout the greater part of the 15th c. the palatal forms predominate in midland (including East Anglian) as well as in southern writers. The MSS. of Fortescue have *g*, which is common also in the London documents after 1430 (Morsbach, *Eng. Schriftsprache* 98). About 1500 the palatal forms disappear entirely from the literary language, and have left only very faint traces in the modern dialects.

In the 14th–15th c. the pa. pple. was sometimes conformed to the analogy of the *e, a, o* vbs. with *-l, -r* roots (cf. GET); this took place with both the midland and northern forms, but *ȝoven* is found more frequently than *goven*.]

A. Inflexional Forms.

1. *Infinitive.*

a. *Simple Infinitive* **give** (gɪv). Forms: α. 1 **ᵹeo-, ᵹiofan, ᵹiaban,** *Northumb.* **ᵹeafa,** 2 **ȝevan,** 3 **ȝeoven, ȝefve(n,** 3–4 **ȝeve(n,** 4 **ȝef,** 4–6 **yeve,** 5 **yeff(e, yew.** β. 1 **ᵹi(e)fan, ᵹyfan,** 2 **ȝyven, ȝiefe,** 2–4 **ȝyfen, ȝifen,** 3 **ȝifve(n,** *Orm.* **ȝifenn,** 3–4 **ȝi(e)ve(n, ȝyve,** 4 **ȝif, if,** 5 **ȝiffe, yiffe, yive.** γ. 3 *Orm.* **gifenn,** 4–5 **gyf(f(e, gif(f)e,** 4–7 **gif(f,** 4–6 **gyve, gyf(e(n,** 4–7 **geve,** (5 **gywe,** 6 **geive, ge',** *Sc.* **gewe,** 7 *Sc.* **giwe),** 8–9 *dial.* **gie, gi',** 4– **give.** (Also 6 **y-geve,** *Sc.* **gevin.**)

α. *Beowulf* (Z.) 2973 Ne meahte se snella sunu Wonredes ealdum ceorle hondslyht ᵹiofan. [*c* **831** *Charter* 39 in *O.E. Texts* 445 Hwet man.. aᵹiaban scel. *c* **950** *Lindisf. Gosp.* Matt. xxvii. 58 Pylatus.. ᵹeheht aᵹeafa lichoma.] *c* **1175** *Lamb. Hom.* 13 Ic eou wille ȝeuan wela. *c* **1205** LAY. 4779 He him wolde ȝeuen al þat gold. *c* **1230** *Hali Meid.* 19 Schulle.. ȝeouen ham stude & nome betere þen sunen & dohtren. *c* **1400** *Apol. Loll.* 7 He may ȝef non indulgence noiþer to man in purgatori, neiþer to hem þat are prescit. *c* **1440** *Gesta Rom.* xxxi. 113 (Harl. MS.) Eny man, that my fadir wolle ȝeve me to. **1477** *Paston Lett.* No. 808 III. 214 He wold yeffe you his labore, be so ye payd for his costes.

β. *a* **1000** *Cædmon's Gen.* 671 (Gr.) Hwa meahte me swelc ᵹewit ᵹifan. **1154** *O.E. Chron.* an. 1137 Þe uurecce men ne hadde nan more to ᵹyuen. *a* **1175** *Cott. Hom.* 231 Me hine sceolde.. ȝiefe him his formemete. *a* **1200** *Moral Ode* 64 in *Trin. Coll. Hom.*, Þar me sal.. ȝieuen us ure werkes lean after ure erninge. *c* **1200** ORMIN 10476 Forr þatt he wollde ȝifenn uss To brukenn eche blisse. *c* **1340** *Cursor M.* 23218 (Trin.) Peynted fire.. ȝyue liȝt neuer hit may. *c* **1350** *Will. Palerne* 2963 Þi douȝti sone schal þi dere douȝter ȝiuen Þe kinges sone of spayne. *c* **1400** *Apol. Loll.* 79 And if þe sentens to sle þe innocent. **14..** *MS. Fairfax* 16 (Halliw.) To.. yiffe hem audience. *c* **1430** *Pilgr. Lyf Manhode* II. cxliii. (1869) 132 With his yrened foot he shulde yiue me in þe visage. **1485–6** *Plumpton Corr.* (Camden) 49 All maner patayns, ȝeftys, offyȝs, that he dyd ȝiffe.

γ. *c* **1200** ORMIN Ded. 248 Þurrh þatt he shall o Domess daȝȝ Uss gifenn heffness blisse. *a* **1300** *Cursor M.* 145 (Cott.) How god bigan þe law hym gyfe. *c* **1330** R. BRUNNE *Chron. Wace* (Rolls) 2281 He þoughte his doughtres gyue hosebandes. *c* **1340** *Cursor M.* 13714 (Fairf.) Þou sal hir gif iuggement. *c* **1375** *Sc. Leg. Saints, Peter* 133, I sall gyf gud leif hym till. *c* **1400** *Destr. Troy* 11469 What godes þai wold gyffe to the gret harmes. *c* **1400** *Sowdone Bab.* 1760 Gode counsaile we shal you gyfen. **1483** *Cath. Angl.* 155/1 To Gife, *donare*. *Ibid.*, To Giffe to kepe, *commendare*. **1513** DOUGLAS *Æneis* v. vi. 39, I sall ȝow gevin ilk man.. twa schort speris. **1521** FISHER *Wks.* (1876) 313 Euery true christen man sholde gyf assured fayth. *a* **1533** LD. BERNERS *Huon* xliv. 147, I shall gyue the my syster in maryage. **1535** STEWART *Cron. Scot.* III. 56 Tua thousand merkis.. He had with him king Richart for to gewe. **1566** DRANT *Horace's Sat.* I. F, Some one or other wyll to thee thy fatall wounde ygeve. **1575** *Gamm. Gurton* III. iii. C iij b, Where is the strong stued hore, chil ge'ar a hores marke. **1609** BIBLE (Douay) *Zeph.* iii. 5 In the morning he wil geve his judgment into light. **1825** J. NEAL *Bro. Jonathan* I. 369 He was a-goin' to gi' me the lie. **1863** ROBSON *Bards of Tyne* 294 Aw'll gie them a' the sack.

b. *Dative Infinitive* (with *to*) **to give** (tʊ gɪv); in OE. **tó ᵹe(a)fanne, ᵹifenne, ᵹyfene,** ME. **to ȝifene, ȝivende, yevene.**

c **950** *Lindisf. Gosp.* Matt., Contents 16/15 To brenganne *uel* to ᵹeafanne. **1154** *O.E. Chron.* an. 1109 Ðær wurdon.. þa aðas ᵹesworene his dohter þam Casere to ᵹifene. *c* **1160** *Hatton Gosp.* Matt. xiv. 7 Ða be-het he mid aþe, hire to ȝyfene swa hwæt swa hyo hine bæde. *c* **1200** *Trin. Coll. Hom.* 119 Fir haueð on him þre mihtes, on to ȝiuende hete, oðer to ȝiuende liht [etc.]. **1340** *Ayenb.* 114 Oure guode fader þet is zuete and milde uor to yeuene.

2. *Indicative Present.*

a. *1st pers. sing.* **give.** Forms: α. 1 **-ᵹefo, -ᵹeofu,** 3 **ȝefve, ȝeove,** 3–5 **ȝeve.** β. 1 **ᵹife, ᵹiefe,** 2–3 **ȝife,** 3–5 **ȝive,** 4–5 **yive, ȝif.** γ. 3–6 **gif,** 6 **gyve, geve,** 4– **give.**

α. [*c* **825** *Vesp. Psalter* xxi. 26 Gehat min dryhtne ic aᵹeofu. *c* **950** *Lindisf. Gosp.* Matt. xviii. 21 Ic forᵹefo him wið sefo siða.] *a* **1225** *Juliana* 19 Nawiht ne ȝeoue ich for inc nowðer. *c* **1275** LAY. 9513 Mine dohter ich him ȝefue Genuis to sehte and to sibbe. **1393** LANGL. *P. Pl.* C. xv. 89 Ich ȝeue [B. XII. 146 ȝif] þe fyue shyllinges.

β. *a* **900** CYNEWULF *Christ* 478 in *Exeter Bk.*, Ic.. eow meaht ᵹiefe. *a* **1000** *Cædmon's Gen.* 679 (Gr.) Gife ic hit ðe ᵹeorne. *c* **1205** LAY. 29243 Ich ȝiue þe ane eorldom. **1297** R. GLOUC. (Rolls) 283 Þe þridde del mi kinedom ich ᵹiue þe to be mi fere. *c* **1385** CHAUCER *L.G.W.* Prol. 31 To hem yive I feyth.

γ. *a* **1300** *Cursor M.* 1930 (Gött.) Til ȝou.. Min brod benisun i giue [*Fairf.* geue]. *Ibid.* 15252 (Cott.) Þe gift þat I yow here gif nu. *c* **1375** *Sc. Leg. Saints, Peter* 16 To þe I gyff þe keys of hewyne. **1500–20** DUNBAR *Poems* xxxi. 134, I gif him to the Devill of hell. *a* **1533** LD. BERNERS *Gold. Bk. M. Aurel.* (1546) H v b, I gyue me to all men. **1535** COVERDALE *Gen.* xxiii. 11 As for the felde.. I geue [**1611** giue] it the.

b. *2nd pers. sing.* **givest** ('gɪvɪst). Forms: α. 1 *Northumb.* **-ᵹefes,** 3 **ȝevest,** 4 **yefst,** 4–5 **yevest, ȝees,** 5 **yeves.** β. 1 **ᵹifest, ᵹifst,** 2–3 **ȝifst,** 3 **ȝivest,** 4 **ȝyvest.** γ. 4 **gifes, gives, gyffis, gis,** 4–5 **ges,** 6 **gevest,** 7– **givest.**

α. [*c* **950** *Lindisf. Gosp.* Luke ii. 29 Nu forletes *uel* forᵹefes esne ðin.] *a* **1240** *Ureisun* in *Cott. Hom.* 185 Þu þet ȝeuest hire liht. **1340** *Ayenb.* 93 Þine zuetnesse þet þou.. yefst to þine uryendes. *c* **1420** *Anturs of Arth.* xiv, Those at thou ȝees [*Douce MS.* Of that þou yeues] at thi ȝate.

β. *c* **1000** *Ags. Ps.* lxxix. 5 Þu.. us drincan ᵹifest. *c* **1000** ÆLFRIC *Gen.* xv. 2 Hwæt ᵹifst þu me? *c* **1200** *Vices & Virtues* (1888) 77 Ȝif ðu ȝifst ðo manne ðe gaf [*sic*: ? *read* ȝaf] ðe. *c* **1340** *Cursor M.* 971 (Trin.) Lord he seide þou ȝyuest al. **1382** WYCLIF *Deut.* xv. 13 Whom with freedam thow ȝyuest.

γ. *a* **1300** *Cursor M.* 971 (Gött.) 'Lauerd', he said, 'þu gifes [*Fairf.* ges] all'. *Ibid.* 16106 (Cott.) Quin giues þou þaim answar? *c* **1375** *Sc. Leg. Saints, Magdalena* 315 Þu.. nocht gyffis þame of þi gud. *c* **1400** *Destr. Troy* 2089 Thow ges matir to men mony day after, fforto speke of þi spede. **1535** COVERDALE *Ps.* cxliv. [cxlv.] 15 Thou geuest [**1611** giuest] them their meate in due season.

c. *3rd pers. sing.* **gives** (gɪvz), *arch.* **giveth** (gɪvɪθ). Forms: α. 1 **-ᵹefes,** 2–3 **ȝeveð, ȝefeð,** 4–5 **ȝefþ(e, ȝev-, yeveth, -ys, -yth, -yþ.** β. 1 **ᵹiefeþ, ᵹifeþ, ᵹifþ,** 3 **ȝiefð,** *Orm.* **ȝifeþþ,** 3–4 **ȝif(þ, ȝiveþ,** 4 **ȝyveth.** γ. 3 *Orm.* **gifeþþ,** 4 **geves, gif(e)s, -ith, giffis, gis(e, givis, -ys, gyves,** 5 **gyfez,** 6 **geves, ghewys, gyvs,** 5–6 **gev-, gyveth, -yth,** 9 *Sc.* and *dial.* **gies,** 5– **giveth,** 4– **gives.**

α. [*c* **950** *Lindisf. Gosp.* Matt. vi. 15 Ne fader iuerre forᵹefes synna iuerre.] *c* **1175** *Lamb. Hom.* 19 Nimað ȝeme.. hwilche ȝife he us ȝefeð. *Ibid.* 137 Ure lauerd god almihten.. ȝeueð him his blescunge. *c* **1340** *Cursor M.* 9645 (Laud) To eche man she yevyþ wille Right to haue good and ille. *c* **1420** *Chron. Vilod.* st. 239 And ryȝt as þis lampe ȝefth gret lyȝt. *c* **1440** *Partonope* 3213 Precious stones she yeuys [*printed* yenys] me. *Ibid.* 8736 Leve to wende He yeuyth [*printed* yenyth] hem thurgh the Rewme of fraunce. *c* **1449** PECOCK *Repr.* 264 The seid preier of Iohun ȝeuith to me the seid xx[ti]. pound.

β. *a* **900** CYNEWULF *Christ* 604 in *Exeter Bk.*, He us æt ᵹiefeþ. *c* **1000** *Ags. Ps.* lxvii[i]. 12 God ᵹifeð gleaw word godspellendum. *c* **1175** *Lamb. Hom.* 97 He.. ȝifð heom forȝifnesse.. Summe Men he ȝif wisdom and speche. *a* **1200** *Moral Ode* 146 in *Trin. Coll. Hom.*, Al to diere he hit abuið þe ȝiefð þ ar-fore his swiere. *c* **1200** ORMIN 2795 Drihhtin ȝifeþþ haliȝ witt þa menn þatt wel himm follȝhenn. *c* **1230** *Hali Meid.* 7 Þis ure lauerd ȝiueð ham her as on erles of þe eche mede þat schal cume þrafter. **1377** LANGL. *P. Pl.* B. vii. 80 He that ȝiueth. **1393** —— *Ibid.* C. iv. 341 The ȝifte that god ȝyueth.

γ. c1200 Ormin 11314 Forr ȝure wuke gifeþþ ȝuw Aȝȝ sexe werrkedaȝȝess. a1300 *Cursor M.* 18650 (Cott.) He gifs his quelpe lijf to rise. *Ibid.* 29240 (Cott.) Pape allan, On man he gise [*Cotton Galba* gifes] til his pouste. *Ibid.* 24751 (Edin.) þat gifes me lust of hir to rede. 1375 Barbour *Bruce* i. 227 Fredome all solace to man giffis. a1400-50 *Alexander* 1662 He..Gyfez þaim garisons of gold & of god stanez. 1483 Caxton *G. de la Tour* D iib, He gyueth us it both by writynges and by lawe. 1485 —— *Paris & V.* 11 Myn hert giveth it me. 1500-20 Dunbar *Poems* xvi. 6 Sum gevis for pryd and glory vane. *Ibid.* 36 Sum givis to strangeris. 1503 *Kalender of Sheph., Pater Noster*, The qwych ghewys vs certaynte of the way of salwt. 1538 Starkey *England* i. ii. 45 Then vertue..gyuyth to man hye felycyte. 1602 Shaks. *Ham.* ii. ii. 73 Old Norwey..Giues him three thousand Crownes. 1780-1808 J. Mayne *Siller Gun* i, To show what diff'rence stands 'Tween him that gets and gies commands.

d. *plural* **give.** Forms: α. 1 -ȝeafað, -ȝefæs, 4 yeven, 5 ȝeveþ. β. 1 ȝifað, 3 *Orm.* ȝifenn, 4 ȝyve, ȝyveþ, -en, 5 yive. γ. 4 gif(s, gyven, 5 giffen, gife, gifves, gyffon, 5-6 gyve, -eth, 6 ge(e)ve, 6- give.

α. [c950 *Lindisf. Gosp.* Mark xiv. 12 Ðonne..eostro asægcas *uel* aȝeafað. *Ibid.* Luke xi. 4 Gif..we forȝefæs..scyldȝe us.] 1387-8 T. Usk *Test. Love* Prol. 18 Afterward the sight of the better colours yeven to hem more joye for the first leudnesse. 1460-70 *Bk. Quintessence* 17 Experience techiþ þat colerik men ȝeueþ to summe ymagynaciouns.

β. a1000 *Hymns* vii. 102 (Gr.) Swa we her [some] ȝifað earmon mannum. c1200 Ormin 15380 þæraffterr ȝifenn þeȝȝ þe follc ȝet werrse win to drinnkenn. c1340 [see γ]. c1380 Wyclif *Serm.* Sel. Wks. I. 67 þei ȝyve to symple men. c1394 *P. Pl. Crede* 114 And in pouertie praien for all oure parteners þat ȝyueþ vs any good. c1400 *Rom. Rose* 5788 With sorwe they bothe dye and live, That to richesse he hertis yive.

γ. a1300 *Cursor M.* 3114 To lare o godd gif [*Gött.* giue] þai na tent. *Ibid.* 5148 þai ar cled in riche pall And gifs [1340 *Fairf.* gyuen; *Trin.* ȝyuen] þair giftes ouerall. c1400 *Destr. Troy* 3668 To Agamynon þai giffen þe gouernaunce hole. *Ibid.* 12002 The grekys full glad gyffon to red. 1450-1530 *Myrr. our Ladye* 18 The prynces of the worlde gyueth worldly rewarde to her prayzers. ?1476 *Plumpton Corr.* (Camden) 35 The judges gifues [*printed* gifnes] her no favour, for they say [etc.]. a1533 Ld. Berners *Huon* lxviii. 235 It is a sayenge that they that gyue are euer welcome. 1548-9 (Mar.) *Bk. Com. Prayer, Communion*, Wee geue thankes to thee for thy greate glory. 1562 Phaer *Æneid* ix. A a ij b, The Troyans dastard harts..neither geeue them dare in open field, nor fierce outbreake In armes. 1589 Puttenham *Eng. Poesie* iii. xxiv. (Arb.) 292 With vs the wemen giue their mouth to be kissed.

3. *Indicative Past.*

a. *1st* and *3rd pers. sing.* **gave** (geɪv). Forms: α. 1 ȝæf, 2 iaf, 3-5 ȝaf(f(e, (4 ȝave, ȝof), 4-6 yaf(e, 4-5 yave, (5 yove). β. 1 ȝeaf, 2 ȝiaf, 2-4 ȝef, 4 yeaf. γ. 4 (9 *dial.*) gov, 4-5 gaf(e, gaaf(f, -ffe, gaffe, 5 geaf, 4, 6 *Sc.* gef, 4-6 geve, 6 gayf, *Sc.* gaif, 8 *Sc.* gae, 4- gave. Also *weak form* 7-8, 9 *dial.* gived, 8-9 *Sc.* gied.

α. [c950 *Lindisf. Gosp.* Luke ix. 42 [He] ȝehælde ðone cnæht & Aȝæf hine fæder his.] c1000 *Ags. Ps.* (Spelm.) lxvi. 5 Eorþan sealde [*v.r.* ȝæf] wæstm his. 1154 *O.E. Chron.* an. 1132 And te king iaf ð(et) abbotrice an prior of S' Neod. c1200 Ormin 15498 þe blinde ȝaff he wel to sen. c1300 *Beket* 296 As God ȝaf that cas. c1340 *Cursor M.* 3912 (Trin.) þe grace þat god him ȝof. 1413 *Pilgr. Sowle* (Caxton 1483) iv. xxv. 71 He yaue hym vnderstandyng. c1420 *Chron. Vilod.* 273 Of oþer wordelyche honour ȝaff he ryȝt nouȝt. c1440 *Partonope* 2740 He yafe golde, selver, and also coine. c1508 *Syr Lamwell* in *Laneham's Let.* (1871) Introd. 30 Sir landevale..yaf yeftes largely.

β. a1000 *Elene* 365 (Gr.) Eow dryhten ȝeaf dom unscyndne. a1175 *Cott. Hom.* 223 þat wif..ȝiaf hire were and he æt. a1240 *Ureisun* in *Cott. Hom.* 197 Ich..ȝef ðe al mi suluen. 1297 R. Glouc. (Rolls) 2600 The kyng ȝef is men grete ȝiftes. 1340 *Ayenb.* 81 Al þe uayrhede þet þet body heþ: þe zaule hit yeaf.

γ. a1300 *Cursor M.* 603 He gafe him..a luuesum land. *Ibid.* 4393 Sco gaue a cri þat all moght here. *Ibid.* 15228 Vp he lift his hali hand, and gaf [*Gött.* geue] þe benisun. 13.. *Gaw. & Gr. Knt.* 370 He..lyfte vp his honde, & gef hym goddez blessyng. c1375 *Sc. Leg. Saints* Prol. 112 God gaff þame sic mycht. c1380 Wyclif *Sel. Wks.* III. 458 Criste willefully gafe tribute to þo emperoure. a1400-50 *Alexander* 5157 Scho gaffe skirmand skrikis. c1489 Caxton *Sonnes of Aymon* xi. 282 Whan he had sayd this he..gaaffe hym the monkes hode vpon his hede. a1550 *Christis Kirke Gr.* xxiii, He..gaif them bayth their paikis. 1579 Fenton *Guicciard.* (1618) 21 The Pope..gaue shew that there could be laid no firme ground of their reconciliation. 1776 C. Keith *Farmer's Ha'* 35 The bridegroom gae me great commands To bring ye down. 1871 C. Gibbon *Lack of Gold* xxvi, He gied me a letter for Annie.

b. *2nd pers. sing.* **gavest.** Forms: α. 1 ȝéafe, ȝéfe, 2 ȝef, 4 ȝeve. β. 4 ȝaf, ȝave, yave, ȝavest. γ. 4 gaf(s, gave, 6- gavest.

α. c1000 *Ags. Ps.* (Th.) lxviii[i]. 27 Hi..ehtan ongunnon ðe þu him earfoðu ænig ȝeafe. a1240 *Wohunge* in *Cott. Hom.* 271 þu ȝef þe seluen for me to lese me fra pine. c1300 *Harrow. Hell* 92 The appel that thou ȝeve hym.

β. c1340 *Cursor M.* 10485 (Fairf.) þou..a worþy sonne hir yaue [*Trin.* ȝaue, *see also* γ]. 1382 Wyclif *Gen.* iii. 12 The woman whom thow ȝaue me felow, ȝaue to me of the tree. —— *Ezek.* xvi. 21 Thou..ȝauest hem.

γ. a1300 *Cursor M.* 971 'Lauerd!' he said, 'þou gafs [? gaf us] al'. *Ibid.* 14056 To mi fete þu gaf [c1340 *Fairf.* gaue, *Trin.* ȝaf] water nan. 1535 Coverdale *Gen.* iii. 13 The woman which thou gauest me. 1591 Shaks. *Two Gent.* i. i. 99 *Pro.* But do'st thou heare: gau'st thou my Letter to Iulia?

c. *plural* **gave.** Forms: α. 1 ȝéafon, ȝéfon, 3 *Orm.* ȝæfenn, 3-5 ȝe(e)ve(n, (3 ȝefven, ȝeove). β. 2 iafen, 3-5 ȝouen, yaf(f, 4-5 ȝaf, ȝave(n, (ȝofen), 5 ȝavun. γ. 3 *Orm.* gæfenn, 4-6 gaf(e, 5-6 gaff(e, 4-5 gef(e, geven, -yn, goven, 6 *Sc.* gaif, 4- gave. Also *wk. forms* 7-9 as in a γ.

α. a900 Cynewulf *Christ* 1354 in *Exeter Bk.*, þonne ȝe hyra hulpon and him hleoð ȝefon. c1200 Ormin 12732 And teȝȝ himm þa þuss ȝæfenn sware onnȝæness. c1205 Lay. 5469 ȝisles heo him ȝeoue sone. *Ibid.* 21247 Heo bittere swiþen ȝefuen mid axes & mid sweordes. c1305 *St. Christopher* 180 in *E.E.P.* (1862) 64 þis wimmen ȝeue him liȝt ansuere, as hi ne ȝeue of him noȝt.

β. 1154 *O.E. Chron.* an. 1137 And did ælle in prisun til hi iafen up here castles. c1250 *Gen. & Ex.* 844 He..ȝouen him gouel of here lond. c1340 *Cursor M.* 19582 (Trin.) Whenne seyntis ȝaf her malisoun þei ȝaf hit noon bi euel wille. c1375 *Ibid.* 17440 (Laud) A somme of pens gadird they And yaff to knyghtes. 1382 Wyclif *Matt.* xiii. 8 Other seedis felden in to good lond, and ȝauen fruyt. 1398 Trevisa *Barth. De P.R.* iii. iv. (1495) 51 In this matere olde Phylosophers yaaf dyuers and as it were contrary domes. a1400 *Prymer* (1891) 38 Thei ȝofen hym drinke galle. c1449 Pecock *Repr.* 459 The Apostlis ȝauun sum wey or ground wherbi [etc.].

γ. c1200 Ormin 8211 þeȝȝ gæfenn heore shorrte lif Forr eche lifess blisse. a1300 *Cursor M.* 13708 All þai gaf him list ilkan. *Ibid.* 19043 At þair gain come mete þai gaue [*Gött.* gaf; c1340 *Fairf.* yaff, *Trin.* ȝaue]. c1375 *Sc. Leg. Saints, Thomas* 659 þan al þe prestis gef a ȝell. c1400 Maundev. (Roxb.) ii. 5 þe spounge and þe rede of whilk þe Iewes gafe oure Lord to drynke. c1400 *Destr. Troy* 6436 Mony strokes, in þat stoure, þo stithe men hym gefe. a1400-50 *Alexander* 1070 Sagittarius forsoth men gafe it to name. *Ibid.* 2327 All europe to my empyre enterly þai geven. 1785 Burns *Address to the Deil* xvi, Ye..gied the infant warld a shog.

4. *Subjunctive Present* **give.** Forms: α. 1 ȝefe, ȝeofe, 2 ȝefe, 2-5 ȝeve, 3-4 ȝef, yeve. β. 1 ȝife, 3 *Orm.* ȝife, 3-4 ȝyve, 4 ȝif, yive. γ. 3 *Orm.* gife, 4 gif, *Sc.* giff, 5-6 geve, 4- give.

α. [c825 *Vesp. Psalter* lx[i]. 9 Ðaet ic aȝefe ȝehat min. 871-89 *Charter* 45 in *O.E. Texts* 452 þonne aȝeofen hio þa ilcan elmessan.] c950 *Lindisf. Gosp.* John xvi. 2 He uoenas [þæt] ȝeafa..he ȝefe *uel* ȝeselle gode. c1000 *Ags. Ps.* (Th.) lviii[i]. 1 Nymð þu me ræd ȝeofe. c1175 *Lamb. Hom.* 67 God us ȝefe mihte and deden. a1310 in Wright *Lyric P.* xix. 59 Iesu Crist, heovene kyng, ȝef us alle god endyng. c1375 *Cursor M.* 9763 (Laud) He hem yeve his beneson That gladly heryþ this sermon. c1380 Wyclif *Sel. Wks.* III. 328 ȝif God ȝeve him beyng and sustenaunce to his lif.

β. a1000 *Andreas* 388 (Gr.) Weoruda waldend..ðe wist ȝife heofonlicne hlaf. a1200 *Moral Ode* 395 Crist ȝyue us leden her swilc lif and habben her swilc ende. 13.. *Seuyn Sag.* (W.) 1450 Dame, God yive the howe!

γ. c1200 Ormin 9293 Gife he þatt an summ oþerr mann þatt iss wiþþutenn kirrtell. a1300 *Cursor M.* 1947 To doghty thues lok þou þe gif. *Ibid.* 4946 If yee giue [*Trin.* ȝyue] dome, þan sal þai hing. c1375 *Sc. Leg. Saints, Machor* 1358 Quhill god..þi full far crowne þe giff in hewine to þi werdoune. c1435 *Torr. Portugal* 2767 He geve us his blessing!

5. *Subjunctive Past* **gave.** Forms: 3 *Orm.* ȝæfe, 4 gof, gove.

c1200 Ormin 12015 Alls iff þe Laferrd ȝæfe þuss Anndswere onnȝæn þe deofell. c1350 *Will. Palerne* 1648 So god for his grace gove i hadde. *Ibid.* 2348 God for his grete grace gof i hadde now here horse and..harneys.

6. *Imperative* **give.**

a. *sing.* Forms: α. 1 ȝef, ȝief, 2 ȝief, 2-4 ȝef, 4-5 yef, 5 ȝe(e)ve, ȝe, yeve. β. 1-2 ȝif, 3 *Orm.* ȝiff, 3-5 ȝif, 4-5 ȝyve, 5 yf. γ. 4-5 gif(f(e, gyf(f, 6 geve, gyve, 8-9 *Sc.* and *dial.* gie, 4- give.

α. [c825 *Vesp. Psalter* xxvii. 4 Aȝef edlean heara him.] c950 *Lindisf. Gosp.* Matt. v. 39 Gif hua ðec slaes in suiðra ceica ðin, sel *uel* ȝef him & ðy oðera. c1000 *Hymns* v. 10 (Gr.) Ðu us freodom ȝief. c1205 Lay. 26075 Lauerd ȝef me grið. c1420 Lydg. *Assemb. Gods* 41 Yeue thy cruell iugement ageyn thys traytour. c1420 *Chron. Vilod.* 122 Syre Kyng..Some meyte ȝemme for charyte. c1420 *Pallad. on Husb.* i. 547 Yef hem comyn ynough, & baume her pennys. c1430 *How Wise Man tauȝt Son* 34 in *Babees Bk.* 49 ȝeeue þee not to ydilnesse. 1460-70 *Bk. Quintessence* 12 Sette it wiþinne a pott of watir, and ȝeue vndirneþe a fier til þe watir of blood be distillid.

β. c1050 *Byrhtferth's Handboc* in *Anglia* VIII. 303 Nim þa þreo þe þær synt to lafe, & ȝif maio. c1200 *Trin. Coll. Hom.* 27 ȝif [*MS.* gif] us to dai ure daihwamliche bred. c1200 Ormin 5224 ȝiff me nu þatt twifalde gast. c1340 *Cursor M.* 3293 (Trin.) Mayden, he seide, ȝyue me drynke. 1426 Audelay *Poems* 7 The hungre ȝif mete. c1450 *Guy Warw.* (C.) 2758 Yf me thy cowncell nowe.

γ. c1300 *Cursor M.* 968 (Cott.) O þi winning giue [*Gött.* gif; *Trin.* ȝyue] me þe tend. 1389 in *Eng. Gilds* (1870) 111 Yat gyff yam grace to ouer-come ere enmys. a1400-50 *Alexander* 4184 Giffe þam siluer. 1539 Tonstall *Serm. Palm Sund.* (1823) 97 Gyue you to prayer. 1548-9 (Mar.), *Bk. Com. Prayer*, Geue us this daye oure dayly bread. 1785 Burns *Death & Dr. Hornbook* xi, Come gie's your news.

b. *plural.* Forms: α. 1 -ȝeafas, 3-5 yeveth, ȝeveth, 5 yeve. β. 1 -ȝifað, 2 -ȝyfeð, 4-5 ȝyve(þ, ȝife(th. γ. 4 geves, gis, gives, 5 ges, 6- give.

α. [c950 *Lindisf. Gosp.* Mark xi. 25 Forletas *uel* forȝeafas ȝif huæt ȝie habbað wið huelc huone.] a1300 *Havelok* 911 But yeueþ me inow to ete. c1420 Lydg. *Assemb. Gods* 77 Consyder the cryme, and yeue your sentence.

β. [c1000 *Ags. Gosp.* Mark xi. 25 Forȝifaþ [*Hatton MS.* forȝyfeð] ȝif ȝe hwæt aȝen æniȝne habbað.] c1340 *Cursor M.* 6138 (Trin.) Gooþ & ȝyueþ [*Fairf.* geues] me ȝoure benesoun. 1382 Wyclif *Acts* viii. 19 ȝyue [*v.r.* ȝiue, ȝifeth] ȝe to me and this power.

γ. a1300 *Cursor M.* 5189 (Cott.) 'Gis [*Fairf.* giues] me mi clathes,' þan he said, 'And hastelik þa we be graid.' c1400 *Destr. Troy* 13553 Bes gracius, for goddes loue, ges me som part. 1599 Shaks. *Hen. V*, iii. iii. 3 This is the latest Parle we wil admit: Therefore to our best mercy giue your selues.

7. *Present Participle* **giving.** Forms: α. 1 ȝeafend, 5 ȝeving. β. 1 ȝifend, 4 ȝyvynge. γ. 4-6 gif-, gyfand(e, 6 geving, gewing, geavinge, gyvynge, 6- giving.

α. c950 *Lindisf. Gosp.* Matt. Prol. 16/3 ȝebreingendum *uel* ȝeafendum. c1400 *Apol. Loll.* 9 Dubli grauntid & dubli ȝeuing.

β. a1000 *Gloss.* in Wr.-Wülcker 244/7 *Frugalis largus*, ȝifend. 1382 Wyclif *Num.* xi. 25 Takynge of the spiryt that was in Moses, and ȝyvynge to the seuenty men.

γ. a1300 *Cursor M.* 18544 To þe wode gifand þair hele. c1340 Hampole *Prose Tr.* (1866) 1 *note*, þis name es swete, & Ioyful gyfand sothfast comforth vnto mans hert. 1533 Wriothesley *Chron.* (1875) I. 22 And the residue geavinge among the lordes and ladies. 1570 *Satir. Poems Reform.* xxiii. 21 Ay geuing the quhat thing that thow wald haif.

8. *Past Participle* **given** (gɪv(ə)n). Forms: α. 1 ȝeben, 3 yȝeve, 4 yef, ȝefun, 3-5 (i-)ȝeve(n, -in, -un, 4-5 (ȝe)ȝevyn, (y)-yove(n, -yn, ȝove(n, -un, yevyn(e, (5 ? ȝeifin, yewyn), 5-6 yeve(n). β. 1 ȝibaen, ȝifen, ȝyfen, 2 ȝyven, 3 *Orm.* ȝifenn, 3-5 iȝive(n, 4-5 ȝiv-, yive(n, yȝif. γ. 3 *Orm.* gifenn, 4 *Sc.* gefin, -yne, geffine, gevine, gewin(e, geyffine, gyfine, gyffine, -yne, 4-6 geve(n, gevyn(e, gifen, giffen, -yn, gifhen, give, -in, gyffen, gyven, -yn, (4 geen, gewyn, gin, 5 gefyn, geyn, 6 geaven, *Sc.* geif, gein, 7 *Sc.* gevin, giwin), 4-5 (y)gove(n, -yn, (6 gave, gwovyn), 8-9, *Sc.* gien, 9 *dial.* geen, gin, 4- given.

α. c725 *Corpus Gloss.* 1086 *Inpendebatur*, ȝeben wæs. [c825 *Vesp. Psalter* lxiv. 2 Ðe bið aȝefen ȝehat.] c1205 Lay. 26986 þer wes moni dunt iȝeuen. ?a1300 *Salomon & Sat.* 273 Betere is appel yȝeue þen y-ete, quoþ Hendyng. c1300 *Harrow. Hell* 179 Ich have ȝeve mi lyf For the. 13.. *Guy Warw.* (A.) 980 þe dome was ȝouen sikerliche. c1340 *Cursor M.* 16727 (Laud) The dome that is yovyn [*Cott.* giuen] to vs we haue yt with right. 1387 Trevisa *Higden* (Rolls) VIII. 73 þenke and have mynde what oure Lorde haþ y-ȝeve the. c1410 Love *Bonavent. Mirr.* iii. (Gibbs MS.), ȝyftes of grace that sche hadde herde ȝeuen to hyre þat neuere weren ȝouen to creature byfor. 1415 T. Walwayn in *E.E. Wills* (1882) 20 þat other half be ȝeifi [? *read* ȝeifin] to the maryage of yonge pore wommen. c1449 Pecock *Repr.* 74 What..power of heering hath God ȝoue to man. 1473 Warkw. *Chron.* 10 Kynge Edwarde hade..yevyne to hym the erledome. c1485 *Digby Myst.* (1882) v. 578 Kynde nobley of kynred me yovyn hase.

β. *Beowulf* (Z.) 1678 Ða wæs gylden hilt gamelum rince,..on hand ȝyfen. a700 *Epinal Gloss.* 525 *Inpendebatur*, ȝibæn uuæs. a900 Cynewulf *Christ* 877 in *Exeter Bk.* 56 Beorht and bliþe him weorþeð blæd ȝifen. c1200 Ormin 4018 Drihhtin haffde ȝifenn himm Swillc blettcinng. a1225 *Ancr. R.* 114 Hwar was euer iȝiuen to eni blodletunge so poure pitaunce? a1250 *Owl & Night.* 551 Ich the habbe i-ȝive ansvare. c1380 Wyclif *Sel. Wks.* III. 434 God forbede þat lordship ȝyven of þe emperor shulde chaunge or destrie þis lawe of Crist. c1385 Chaucer *L.G.W.* 1538 As wolde almighty god that I had yive [*v.r.* iyive] My blood and flesh. c1400 *Rom. Rose* 6686 A man..That al his good to pore hath yiven.

γ. c1200 Ormin 19827 Herodian..þatt fra Filippe ræfedd wass..& gifenn till Herode. a1300 *Cursor M.* 1502 Til caym was spused calmana, Als giuen [*Fairf.* gyuen] to seth was delbora. *Ibid.* 3938 Till he had gin him his blissing. *Ibid.* 16814 + 14 Pilat send & told þe Iews He hade geen his body. *Ibid.* 21923 Ful iuel-hail es gifen vs wiit. 13.. *E.E. Allit. P.* A. 1189, I..ȝerned no more þen watz me geuen [*rimes with* dryuen]. c1375 *Sc. Leg. Saints, Barnabas* 76 To preche goddis word as is gefyne vs. *Ibid., Lawrence* 633 Thre housis, þat gewine ware [etc.]. *Ibid., George* 106 His douchtir..to þe dragone suld be gyffine. 1375 Barbour *Bruce* i. 317 His landis halyly War gevyn to the Clyffurd. c1400 *Destr. Troy* 11978 Myche good hase þe gyffen of his gold red. *Ibid.* 12053 þe prise kyng Achilles, Was grauntid to be grauyn, & gyuyn to his toumbe. a1400-50 *Alexander* 1883 So þat if be gefyn me þe gre grete glory is my awne. c1420 *Anturs of Arth.* xxiii, Thou hase..Gifhen hom to Syr Gauan. c1460 *Towneley Myst.* ii. 446 That god of heuen my master has giffen; Browke it well. *Ibid.* xix. 270 Ful mekill grace is to the geyn. 1469 *Plumpton Corr.* (Camden) 22 The punishment will be grevieous to them, for it is gyffin by a statute. c1489 Caxton *Sonnes of Aymon* iii. 102 Whan Reynawde had gyven that stroke, he wente his waye. 1503 *Act 19 Hen. VII*, c. 14 §11 Lyvere to be giffyn by any serjauntes at the Lawe at ther makyng. 1513 Douglas *Æneis* ix. xii. 31 Geif into drowry. 1538 Wriothesley *Chron.* (1875) I. 75 That the said offring might be geaven incontynent to poore people. 1556 *Chron. Gr. Friars* (Camden) 30 A generall pardone was gevyne unto theme alle that came that tyme. 1567 *Satir. Poems Reform.* vii. 147 God has gein to thame baith strenth & mycht. a1568 Ascham *Scholem.* ii. (Arb.) 133 Liberallie geuen by others. 1592 Wyrley *Armorie* 129 Sense to daintie pleasure quite is giue. 1592 Shaks. *Ven. & Ad.* 571 O had she then gaue ouer Such nectar from his lips she had not suckt. 1595 in Picton *L'pool Munic. Rec.* (1883) I. 92 The pavements shalbe wth all conveniente expedicion geve in hand wth all. 1609 Skene *Reg. Maj.* 127 To reduce decretes wrangouslie gevin be all inferiour Commissars. 1786 Burns *On a Scotch Bard* 5 Our billie's gi'en us a' a jink. 1824 Scott *Redgauntlet* let. x, The gentleman may hae gien ye siller. 1855 Robinson *Whitby Gloss.* s.v. *Gin*, I think he has almost gin again about it.

B. Signification.

General sense: To make another the recipient of (something that is in the possession, or at the disposal, of the subject).

The verb seems, from the evidence of Goth., OHG., and OS., to have primarily denoted the placing of a material object in the hands of another person. This application (sense 6 below), however, does not occur in OE., and is not very frequent in ON.; the usual sense (which is found in all the Teut. langs.) is that of freely and gratuitously conferring on a person the ownership of a thing, as an act of bounty. When the notion of 'free gift' was not prominent, the word used was usually SELL (OE. *sellan*, ON. *selja*); it may be remarked that according to Prof. Cook's glossary to the Northumbrian gospels, the Lat. *dare* is never rendered by *ȝeafa* or its compounds, but always by (*á-*, *ȝe-*) *sella*. In early ME. the vb. *sell* became obsolete except in the limited sense = L. *vendere*, and its meanings passed over to *give*. While, however, *give* thus acquired a widened sense (for the process of development of which cf. F. *donner* to give:—L. *dōnāre* to present), it retained at the same time the specific meaning which it had in OE. In mod.Eng. both the wider and the narrower senses are still current, so that while *give* may be used as an antithesis of *sell*, *pay*, or *lend*, it may also be contextually equivalent to any of those vbs.

The construction, wherever nothing is said to the contrary, is with *to* (*unto*) or *dative*.

I. *trans.* To bestow gratuitously.

1. a. To hand over (a thing) as a present; to confer gratuitously the ownership of (some possession) on another person (with or without actual delivery of the object).

Beowulf (Z.) 1719 [He] nallas beaᵹas ᵹeaf Denum æfter dome. **c 1160** [see A 1 b]. **c 1205** LAY. 136 Muche lond he him ȝef. **a 1225** *Ancr. R.* 384 þauh ich ȝefde [? *read* ȝefe; L. *distribuero*] poure men al þet ich hefde. *Ibid.* 396 Þi luue, he seið, urre Louerd, oðer heo is forto ȝiuen allunge, oðer heo is forto sullen. **1297** [see A 3 a β]. **1389** in *Eng. Gilds* (1870) 16 Euery brother and sister shal yeuen ye pouer brother or syster a ferthyng in ye woke. **1480** *Waterf. Arch.* in *10th Rep. Hist. MSS. Comm.* App. v. 315 That no parson..yeve, sill, or lende..ony crosbow. **1538** [see A 8 γ]. **1596** SHAKS. *Merch. V.* IV. i. 443 Good sir, this ring was giuen me by my wife. **1711** STEELE *Spect.* No. 107 ¶3 A fine Woman, who distributed Rewards and punishments in giving becoming or unbecoming Dresses to her Maids. **1827** JARMAN *Powell's Devises* II. 21 The giving lands to a corporation for their own benefit barely as an aggregate body, is not a charitable use. *Mod.* I won't *give* you the book, but I will either lend it you, or sell it you, whichever you like.

absol. **c 1200** *Vices & Virtues* 11 Ac ðat we sculen bliðeliche ȝiuen and leanen. **a 1225** *Ancr. R.* 330 He is so unimete large þet him nis no þing leouere þen þet he muwe ivinden ancheisun uorto ȝiuene. **1388** WYCLIF *Prov.* xxi. 26 He that is a iust man schal ȝyue and shal not ceesse. **c 1430** *How Gd. Wijf* 20 in *Babees Bk.* 37 ȝeue of þin owne good, and be not to hard. **a 1500** *Syr Peny* 70 in Hazl. *E.P.P.* I. 164 Peny may both rede and gyffe. **1603** SHAKS. *Meas. for M.* I. iv. 81 When Maidens sue Men giue like gods. **1613** PURCHAS *Pilgrimage* (1614) 256 If you cannot give, be daily in prayers. **1664** H. MORE *Antid. agst. Idol.* To Rdr. §12 The Knight put his hand into his pocket, and gave them liberally. **1856** RUSKIN *Mod. Paint.* IV. v. vii. §4 The whole heart of Nature seems thirsting to give. **1877** MISS YONGE *Cameos* Ser. III. xxxii. 331 She gave largely to hospitals, and decorated churches.

b. To render (a benefit or service) without payment.

1719 DE FOE *Crusoe* II. xiii, We gave him his passage, that is to say, bore his charges. *Mod.* He has charged only for the material; he has given his labour.

2. a. To confer, grant or bestow (a favour, honour, office, privilege, etc.). Also in *indirect passive*.

1154 [see A 3 a α]. **1297** R. GLOUC. (Rolls) 8866 All þee bissopriches..he ȝef al clene þere, & alle þe abbeies þer to so that iȝiue me nuste So vale neuere at o tyme. **a 1300** *Cursor M.* 9373 Hu he gaf vs his pardun Scorteli i sall yow tell resun. **1388** WYCLIF *Prov.* xxvii. 24 But a coroun schal be ȝouun to thee in generacioun and in to generacioun. **1473** WARKW. *Chron.* (Camden) 2 He..confermyd alle the ffraunsches yeve to citeis and townes. **1548** HALL *Chron., Edw. IV*, 227 The rome of Gartier was never geven to no estraunger. **1584** POWEL *Lloyd's Cambria* 127 He gaue to the aforesaid Eneon the Lordship of Senghennyth. **1671** in *12th Rep. Hist. MSS. Comm.* App. v. 24, I have only to begg of your Lordship..to give me the liberty of waiting on you at my returne from Newmarket. **1766** ENTICK *London* IV. 189 Queen Elizabeth gave them another charter to take four human bodies, executed at Tyburn, to anatomize. **1858** W. PORTER *Knts. Malta* II. xix. 173 Any Maltese who desired to free himself from his allegiance to the Grand-master was given a patent. **1888** BRYCE *Amer. Commw.* II. II. lii. 306 Under such a charter the mayor is given power and opportunity to accomplish something.

b. To bestow on or accord to another (one's affection, confidence, etc.). ***to give one's heart*** (see HEART *sb.* 10).

1592 SHAKS. *Rom. & Jul.* IV. ii. 26, I..gaue him what becomed Loue I might. **1607** —— *Timon* I. ii. 10 You mistake my loue, I gaue it freely euer. **1859** TENNYSON *Elaine* (Song), Sweet is true love tho' given in vain, in vain. *Mod.* He does not readily give a stranger his confidence.

3. a. Of a higher power, esp. of the Deity: To bestow (a faculty, quality, a physical or mental endowment, a blessing or advantage). Also, to grant *to be* (so and so) or *to do* (something), or *that*, etc. Often in passive and quasi-impersonal.

a 1000 *Sal. & Sat.* 56 (Gr.) Him scippend gaf wuldorlicne wlite. **c 1175** *Lamb. Hom.* 19 Crist us ȝef moni freo ȝeue. *Ibid.* 49 He haueð ȝeuen us to beon mud freo. **c 1200** *Trin. Coll. Hom.* 35 Adam..forleas þe fiffeald mihten þe god him ȝef þo þe he him shop. **a 1225** *Ancr. R.* 234 'Louerd', cweð heo, 'ȝif me strencðe uorto wiðstonden'. **a 1300** *Cursor M.* 9275 Þe gast þat giues giftes sere. **1382** WYCLIF *John* vi. 66 [65] No man may come to me, no but it were ȝouun to him of my fadir. **1389** [see A 6 a γ]. **a 1400** *Prymer* (1891) 47 ȝif to thi seruawntes that pees: that the world may nouȝt ȝeue. **c 1430** LYDG. *Min. Poems* 47 Clerkys recorde, by gret auctoryte, Hornes wer yove to bestys for dyffence. **c 1460** *Towneley Myst.* xix. 270 Where so thou gone, fful mekill grace is to the geyn. **1483** *Vulgaria abs Terentio* 9 a, Itt is gouyn to hym that all that he dothe plesith. **a 1533** LD. BERNERS *Huon* lxxxiv. 265 She gaue me agayne that I sholde be the moost fayrest creature of the worlde. **1548** UDALL, etc. *Erasm. Par. John* 39 a, So hath he also geuen to his sonne to haue in himselfe the fountayne of all lyfe. **1553** T. WILSON *Rhet.* (1580) 166 Is not the tongue given for this ende, that one might knowe what an other meaneth? **1624** QUARLES *Div. Poems, Sion's Sonn.* iii. 1 Hee takes pleasure in those gifts, hee gave. **1645** FULLER *Good Th. in Bad T.* (1841) 8 If this day be obscure..give me to make it memorable in my soul. **1714** C. JOHNSON *Country Lasses* v, Gives us an antepast of joys above. **1742–3** *Observ. Methodists* 15 God gave me to wrestle with him for my Friends. **1794** V. KNOX *Antipolemus* Wks. 1824 V. 434 She [Nature] gave him [man] alone the power of laughing. **1803** *Pic Nic* No. 11 Give me to feel thy cheering ray. **1851** ROBERTSON *Serm.* Ser. III. xi. 135 It was given to the Apostle Paul to discern that this was the ground of unity.

b. Used in the expression of a wish, ***God, Christ give***, etc. †Also, when the wish is beyond granting = Would that...!

a 1000, **a 1200**, **13..** [see A 4 β]. **c 1300** *Beket* (Percy Soc.) 1723 God ȝeve hit were so. **a 1310** [see A 4 a]. **1458** in *Turner's Dom. Archit.* III. 44 Now God geve us grace to folowe treuthe even. **1484** CAXTON *Fables of Æsop* v. ix, Sayenge to hym in this manere Syre kynge god yeue good helthe. **1583** HOLLYBAND *Campo di Fior* 35 God geve thee all felicitie my sonne. **1601** SHAKS. *Twel. N.* I. v. 14 Well, God giue them wisdome that haue it.

c. ***give me***: used as an expression of strong preference or approbation; = 'what I would have is ——', 'I am for ——', 'commend me to ——', etc.

1596 SHAKS. *1 Hen. IV*, II. iv. 167 Giue me them that will face me. **1633** HERBERT *Temple, Church, Content* iv, Give me the pliant minde, whose gentle measure Complies and suits with all estates. **1700** T. BROWN tr. *Fresny's Amusem. Ser. & Com.* 43 Let what will happen on't, give me for my Money the Female Sollicitor. **1775** P. HENRY *Sp.* Mar. in Wirt *Life* (1818) 123, I know not what course others may take; but as for me, give me liberty, or give me death! **a 1873** LYTTON (Ogilvie), Give me the good old times! **1884** W. C. SMITH *Kildrostan* 89, I hate a boisterous life. Give me the calm of Tempe where no wind Blows on the vine-stocks roughly.

4. To assign the future ownership of (property) by testament; to bequeath or devise. (In legal documents conjoined with synonymous vbs.: ***to give and bequeath, to give and devise.***)

1420 in *E.E. Wills* (1882) 45, I ȝewe to Iohn Forster my godsonne a becure of seluer y-keueryd. **c 1430** *Syr Gener.* 7398 His yongest sonne, after his day He hath yoven him Tharse without nay. **1538** STARKEY *Will* in *Lett.* (1878) 8 *note*, I geve to..my lorde Montague, foure pounds. **1784** JOHNSON *Will* Codicil, To Bennet Langton, Esq., I give and bequeath my Polyglot Bible. **1818** CRUISE *Digest* (ed. 2) VI. 199 With respect to the words necessary to create a devise, the proper and technical words are, *give and devise*.

5. Of a parent or guardian: To sanction the marriage of (a daughter or female ward). Now only more explicitly ***to give in marriage***; formerly also †***to give in hand***. Cf. *give away*. [A prominent Com. Teut. sense: cf. OE. ᵹifta pl., marriage: see GIFT.]

a 855 *O.E. Chron.* an. 853 Ond þæs ofer Eastron ᵹeaf Æþelwulf cyning his dohtor Burᵹrede cyninge of Wesseaxum on Merce. **1154** [see A 1 b]. **a 1300** [see A 8 γ]. **a 1300** *Cursor M.* 12694 Was anna giuen to salomas. **c 1350** [see A 1 a β]. **c 1435** *Torr. Portugal* 933, I have a dowghttyr that ys me dere..I wille geve here in hande. **c 1440** [see A 1 a α]. **c 1548** HALL *Chron., Hen. VII*, 22 Because the lady was of that age, that she coulde neither be geven nor yet taken in mariage. **1592** DAVIES *Immort. Soul* VII. ix, Angels ..marry not, nor are in Marriage giv'n. **? c 1600** *Ballad, Merch. Daughter Bristow* II. in Arb. *Garner* VIII. 409 Her gentle Master she desired To be her Father, and at church to give her then. **1613** PURCHAS *Pilgrimage* (1614) 257 Take not a wife of another Law nor give your daughters to men of another Law. **1877** MISS YONGE *Cameos* Ser. III. xxvii. 270 He would not give his daughter in marriage to a stranger.

II. To deliver, hand over (without reference to change of ownership).

6. a. To deliver or hand (something) to a person, so that he takes it; to put (food or drink) before a person.

For figurative colloquial phrases, *to give the bag, the mitten, the sack*, etc., see the sbs.

a 1175 [see A 3 a β]. **1297** R. GLOUC. (Rolls) 4920 + 7Þe byssop yt nolde grante, ac outlych yt wyþ seyde To ȝyue hym þulke holy þyng [the sacrament]. **a 1300** [see A 6 b γ]. **1375** BARBOUR *Bruce* I. 565 The Endentur till him gaf he. **c 1400** *Destr. Troy* 804 And þan sho gafe hym a glasse with a good lycour. **1483** *Cath. Angl.* 155/1 To Gife a drynke, *potare*. **1564** HARDING *Answ. Jewel's Challenge* ii. 46 The custome was in some places to geue the Sacrament to infantes..by powring the bloude in to their mowthes. **1591** [see A 3 b γ]. **1597** SHAKS. *2 Hen. IV*, II. iv. 197 Giue me some Sack. **1617** MORYSON *Itin.* I. 37 The Letters you gave me to deliver at Breme. **1871** [see A 3 a γ].

b. With ellipsis of obj. before an *inf.*, ***to give to eat, drink***, †***suck***. Now only *literary*.

c 1000 [see A 2 b β]. **1340** HAMPOLE *Pr. Consc.* 6191 And yhe wald noght gyfe me at ete. **c 1375** *XI Pains Hell* 280 in *O.E. Misc.* 219 Of aysel and gal ȝe ȝeuen me drenkyn. **1382** WYCLIF *John* iv. 7 Jhesu seith to hir, ȝyue to me for to drynke. **c 1400** [see A 3 c γ]. **1483** CAXTON *G. de la Tour* C viij b, Loue and honoure thy husbond and lord as thou didest this brest that gaf the to sowke. **1862** *Temple Bar* IV. 313, I have given mine enemy to eat when he was a-hungered, and to drink when he was athirst. **1890** *Univ. Rev.* Dec. 503 Having no other way whereby they might give to eat to the children.

c. To administer, 'exhibit', as a medicine.

1577 B. GOOGE *Heresbach's Husb.* IV. (1586) 192 b, A sponefull of it given in Wine..wonderfully helpeth the hard labours of Women. **1636** DEKKER *Wonder. Kingd.* IV. Wks. 1873 IV. 269 Must I give you a Glister? **1811** A. T. THOMSON *Lond. Disp.* (1818) 414 The quantity..to be given, and the proper period of exhibiting it, require to be regulated with much judgment.

d. With immaterial object: To deliver (a message, etc.). So ***to give*** a person (some one's) ***compliments, love, kind regards***, etc.

1611 SHAKS. *Wint. T.* V. i. 140, I..from him Giue you all greetings, that a King (at friend) Can send his Brother. **1765** W. HUNTER in *Life W. Cullen* (1832) I. 554 Pray give my best respects to Mrs. Cullen. **1855** THACKERAY *Newcomes* I. vi. 61 Give my love to Clive.

e. ***give me*** ——: form of words used as a request by a telephone-user to be connected with a specified person, number, etc.

1887 J. M. W. YERRINGTON *H.K. Goodwin* 26 I heard him call, 'Give me police station.' **1908** *Sears, Roebuck Catal.* 199/1 Vocal Solos..Hello, Central: Give Me Heaven (sentimental). **1914** *Bell Telephone News* Mar. 19/1 Subscriber: 'Give me 1000.' Operator: 'What office, please?' **1928** HECHT & MACARTHUR *Front Page* II. 72 Endicott calling. Gimme a rewrite man.

7. To commit, consign, entrust. Often more fully in fig. phrase ***to give into the hands of***; also ***to give to keep, to give into the care*** or ***custody of***. ***to give in charge*** (see CHARGE *sb.* 13 b); ***to give into custody***, in recent use, to direct a policeman to take (a person) as a prisoner.

a 1000 *Cædmon's Dan.* 5 (Gr.) On Moyses hand wearð wiᵹ ᵹifen, wiᵹena mænieo. **c 1205** [see A 3 c β]. **c 1380** WYCLIF *Sel. Wks.* III. 511 Cristis reule ȝoven to apostlis. **c 1400** [see A 8 γ]. **c 1430** LYDG. *Chichev. & Byc.* in Dodsley *O. Pl.* XII. 334 We may wele syng and seyn, allas That we gaf hem the sovrante. **1483** [see A 1 b γ]. **1553** T. WILSON *Rhet.* (1580) 146 You have plaied the verie foole, to give the bestowing of so muche money to a straunger. **1617** MORYSON *Itin.* II. 63 Having already given the governement of Leax to Sir Richard Moryson. **1636** E. DACRES tr. *Machiavel's Disc. Livy* I. Contents, The power of stopping the publique actions of the city, should not be given in the hands of one Counsell, or one Magistracy. **1689** LOCKE *Governmt.* I. §94 If the Agreement and Consent of Men first gave a Scepter into any ones hands, or put a Crown on his Head, that also must direct its descent and conveyance. **1697** DRYDEN *Virg. Georg.* IV. 567 This Neptune gave him, when he gave to keep His scaly Flocks, that graze the wat'ry deep. **1869** HUGHES *Alfred Gt.* xii. 145 He gave it into the custody of his son-in-law. **1890** *Chamb. Jrnl.* 17 May 318/1 He was given into custody.

8. To hand over as a pledge. Also *fig.* (often with mixed notion of branch VI), to pledge (one's word, honour, etc.). † ***to give a give*** or ***gift*** (***that***): to give a pledge or assurance (that).

c 1300 *Havelok* 2880 For ich giue þe a giue, þat euere more hwil ich liue, For hire shal-tu be with me dere [etc.]. **c 1330** R. BRUNNE *Chron. Wace* (Rolls) 13481 Þorow þem ys Rome ..Halden hed of al þe werd, & so schal be, y gyue ȝow a gyue, Al so longe as y may lyue. **c 1350** *Will. Palerne* 536, I..leye my loue on þat lud lelly for euere. To god here i gif a gift, it gete schal neuer oþer. **a 1400** *Sir Perc.* 85 And therfore gyffes he a gyfte..That he scholde quyte hym that dynt. **a 1586** SIDNEY *Arcadia* II. (1633) 143, I giue you my word, he for me shall maintaine this quarrell against you. **1621** BP. MOUNTAGU *Diatribæ* 121 We must speake, unless we will give hands to be such as you blazon us for. **1724** RAMSAY *Tea-t. Misc.* (1733) I. 75 I'll..gi'e my thumb I'll ne'er beguile thee. **1742** H. WALPOLE *Corr.* (1837) I. xxxv. 143, I give you my honor I repeated it over and over to his mother. **1849** MACAULAY *Hist. Eng.* vii. II. 241 What guarantee could he give that he would adhere to his bargain? **1889** DOYLE *Micah Clarke* xxxiv. 378, I gave them the word of a sailor. **1893** *Law Times* XCV. 79/2 After the pledge which had been given by the Government, he thought [etc.].

III. To make over as a matter of exchange or debt.

9. a. To make over to another in exchange for something else, in discharge of a debt or obligation, or with the intention of obtaining some equivalent; to pay (a sum of money); to sell (a thing) for a price.

c 1200 [see A 3 c γ]. **c 1200** *Trin. Coll. Hom.* 213 Þe beggere ecneð his bode, and swereð þat he nele more ȝeuen. **a 1225** *Ancr. R.* 398 Nolde a mon, uor on of þeos, ȝiuen al þet he ouhte? **c 1250** *Gen. & Ex.* 1500 Quad esau, 'ful bliðelike', And ȝafe it him wel sikerlike. **c 1320** R. BRUNNE *Medit.* 331 Euyl for gode þey haue me ȝoue. **c 1340** *Cursor M.* 15409 (Fairf.) Quat wil ȝe me to mede giue? **1377** LANGL. *P. Pl.* B. VI. 201 And put hem to werke And ȝaf hem mete as he myȝte aforth and mesurable huyre. **1501** *Bury Wills* (Camden) 84, I will jt be gwovyn to a pryst to synge for me. **1577** B. GOOGE *Heresbach's Husb.* IV. (1586) 168 Yea at this day in our time, hath beene seene given for a paire of Pigions X. li. Flemish. **1611** BIBLE *Gen.* xxiii. 9 For as much money as it is worth he shall give it me. **1617** MORYSON *Itin.* I. 287 An Imperiall Dollar..at my being there [in Germany] was given for eighteene batzen. **1689** LOCKE *Governmt.* II. §46 He would give his Nuts for a piece of Metal. **1816** SCOTT *Antiq.* xxiv, The least ye can do is to gie him that o't that's left behind for his labour. **1861** M. PATTISON *Ess.* (1889) I. 46 A rare Livonian falcon for which the English noble was ready to give any price.

b. Phrases. ***to give*** (***one***) ***as good as he brings*** or ***one gets***, ***to give*** (***one***) ***his own*** or ***his due*** (see DUE *sb.* 2 b), ***to give a Roland for an Oliver***.

1691 DRYDEN *Pref. to Walsh's Dial. Conc. Women* A 4 To give Mankind their own, and to tell them plainly that [etc.]. **1703** CIBBER *She would & she would not* I, If I don't give you as good as you bring. **1713** STEELE *Guardian* No. 145 ¶3 Having dispatched this combatant, and given him as good as he brings, I proceed. **1738** SWIFT *Pol. Conv.* 45 She and I had some Words..; but I think I gave her her own. **1773** N. FROWDE *Life, Adv., Voy.* 132 We resolved to give him a Rowland for his Oliver, if he attacked us. **1884** *Graphic* 15 Nov. 519/3 To which he replied, as if to give me a Roland for an Oliver, that [etc.]. **1952** M. LASKI *Village* vii. 123 If there was only someone she could talk to who could give her as good as they got. **1956** A. L. ROWSE *Early Churchills* 408 She answered her grandmother back, gave as good as she got. **1967** A. CHRISTIE *Endless Night* xv. 131 We went on, hammer and tongs..and I pretty well gave her as good as I was getting. Told her she was a bossy, interfering female.

c. Often in hyperbolical statements: ***one would give the world***, etc. ***to give one's ears***: see EAR 1 c.

1749 FIELDING *Tom Jones* v. iv, Many's the Man would have given his Head to have had my Lady told. **1855** THACKERAY *Newcomes* xxxviii, Many a girl would give the world to have such a complexion. **1885** F. Anstey *Tinted Venus* 32 He would have given worlds for courage to show it the door. **1893** *Family Herald* 217/1 They'd give their heads at Scotland Yard for a chance of running you to earth.

†**d.** *to give* (*little, nought*, etc.) *of*: to value (at little, etc.), care (little, etc.) for. Also, *to give no force of, no charge of*. *Obs.*

The origin of these phrases is not clear. Cf. the synonymous Ger. (*nichts* etc. *um*, now usually *auf, etwas geben*) Du. (*niets, weinig* etc. *om iets geven*) ON. *gefa sèr* (*mikit, litit*) *um*, which, however, are not formally equivalent. Perh. *give* (in sense 9) was substituted in these phrases for other vbs. (as *tell, hold*), the original construction being retained.

c **1300** *Havelok* 468 Ther offe yaf he nouth a stra. **1303** [see force *sb.* 21]. *c* **1305** [see A 3 c α]. *c* **1300** R. Brunne *Chron.* (1810) 65 Of þe kirke gaf þei leste. *c* **1340** *Cursor M.* 1834 (Fairf.) In time þai soȝt him of na grace, and litel gaf of goddis manace. *c* **1400** Maundev. (1839) xxix. 292 Thei ȝive no charge of Aveer ne of Ricchesse. *c* **1420** *Chron. Vilod.* 864 Of his commandyng þey ȝeve ryȝt nouȝt. *c* **1430** [see force *sb.* 21]. **1530** Palsgr. 567/1, I gyve no force of a thing, I set no store by it, *je ne tiens compte*.

e. Used in negative contexts with various complements to indicate indifference or unconcern, as in *not to give a curse, damn*, etc.; = care *v.* 4 a(*a*). Cf. damn *sb.* 2.

1672 [see button *sb.* 1 b]. **1763** [see curse *sb.* 2 ¶]. **1895**, etc. [see damn *sb.* 2]. **1900** *Westm. Gaz.* 6 Nov. 1/3 Conductors who don't give a curse for the public. **1922**, **1960** [see bugger *sb.* 2 d]. **1969** *Advertiser* (Adelaide) 12 May 5/4, I don't give a bucket of dandruff for a bloke's lingo.

10. To hand over to a superior (what is due, or is demanded); to pay (taxes, tithes, etc.). *Obs.* exc. with reminiscence of the Biblical use.

1154 [see A 1 a β]. *a* **1300** *Cursor M.* 3104 To godd his tend þar gafe he lele. **1388–9** in *Wyclif's Sel. Wks.* III. 468 Hit ys not to gife dymes. **1526** Tindale *Matt.* xxii. 17 Is it lawfull to geve tribute vnto Cesar or not? [and so **1611**.]

IV. To sacrifice, devote, dedicate.

11. a. To sacrifice, offer up, submit to the loss of (one's life or possessions) for some object. Also *refl.*

a **1240** [see A 3 b β]. *c* **1275** in *O.E. Misc.* 186 To deþe he ȝef him for us alle. *a* **1300** *Christ on Cross* 22 in *E.E.P.* (1862) 21 Ic mi lif ȝef for þe and i-hang was on tre. *a* **1300** *Cursor M.* 13861 Til þai his suete bodi had schedd, And gin him self for vs in wedd. **1475** *Bk. Noblesse* 81 Youre saide citesins.. wille withe here bodies and goodes largelie depart to be yoven forto resist them. *a* **1586** Sidney *Arcadia* ii. (1633) 129 To reuenge those two seruants of theirs, of whose memorable faith, I told you.. in willingly giuing themselues to be drowned for their sakes. **1871** Freeman *Norm. Conq.* (1876) IV. xvii. 56 The Abbots of Peterborough and New Minster.. had given their lives in the cause of England.

b. *refl.* Of a woman: to devote (herself) completely *to* (a man); *spec.* to accept sexual intercourse.

1860 J. W. Palmer tr. *Michelet's Love* ii. ix. 130 She aspires only to give herself to you, to belong to you still more entirely. **1895** Hardy *Jude* (1896) i. ii. 10 Under the hedge which divided the field from a distant plantation girls had given themselves to lovers. **1926** R. Macaulay *Crewe Train* iii. i. 263 Barbara.. gives herself to a young fisherman in Cornwall. **1967** *Times* 6 Apr. 9/2 A youngish woman making a last bid for emotional adventure, gives herself to a lonely old man in an empty Jamaican hotel.

12. To dedicate, devote, give up, surrender. Also, to 'consign' (by way of imprecation) *to* (the devil, etc.), to commend *to* (God).

a **1300** *Cursor M.* 10661 To godd þan haue i giuen me. *a* **1400** *Octavian* (Percy Soc.) 400 To the worlde y wylle me never yeve. **1535** Coverdale *1 Sam.* i. 11, I wil geue him vnto the Lorde all his life longe. **1573** J. Sanford *Hours Recreat.* (1576) 163 He.. was mynded desperately to gyve himselfe to the Devill. **1598** Shaks. *Merry W.* v. v. 156 Do you thinke though wee would haue.. giuen our selues without scruple to hell, that [etc.]. **1606** —— *Ant. & Cl.* iii. ii. 64 Heere I haue you, thus I let you go, And giue you to the Gods. **1611** —— *Wint. T.* ii. iii. 8 Say that she were gone, Giuen to the fire. **1855** Dickens *Dorrit* ii. vii, On his imparting the news to Gowan, that Master gave Mr. Dorrit to the Devil with great liberality. **1879** M. J. Guest *Lect. Hist. Eng.* ix. 79 He made a resolution to give to God the half of his services.. the half of his time, and the half of his money.

13. a. To apply exclusively, devote *to* (an action, pursuit, etc.); to addict, devote (oneself) *to*. (Cf. given 2.)

a **1300** *Cursor M.* 3116 To foli giues him man to dai. *c* **1340** Hampole *Prose Tr.* 25 þei shuld oo tyme yevene hem to besynes and worldely thyngis att resonable nede. **1415** [see A 8 α]. *c* **1430** [see A 6 a α]. **1480** Caxton *Chron. Eng.* ccxxxviii. 263 Whan he was yeue to ony occupacion he left al other thyng for the mene tyme and tendid therto. **1579** Gosson *Sch. Abuse* (Arb.) 41, I gaue my self to that exercise. **1615** Chapman *Odyss.* xxii. 545 There were twelve that gave Themselves to impudence and light behave. **1688** Burnet *Lett. Italy* 22 Many nuns.. began.. to give themselves much to the practice of Mental Prayer. **1814** Cary *Dante, Par.* vi. 24 To my great task.. I gave me wholly. **1855** Browning *Fra Lippo* 102 Trash, such as these poor devils of Medici Have given their hearts to. **1879** M. J. Guest *Lect. Hist. Eng.* xi. 100 The priests were bidden to.. give all their time to their sacred work. **1889** M. Gray *Reproach Annesley* i. ii. iv. 205 It was important.. to give his mind entirely to political affairs.

†**b.** To apply or set oneself *to do* something.

a **1300** *Cursor M.* 10478 Sco gaf hir al to murn and care. **1509** Hawes *Past. Pleas.* xxvi. vi, Towarde the gate [he] gave hym selfe to hast. **1526** *Pilgr. Perf.* (W. de W. 1531) 2 b, Gaue them selfe to subdue the passyons of theyr bodyes. **1583** Hollyband *Campo di Fior* 233 He hath given him selfe to keepe horses. **1686** R. Parr *Life Abp. Ussher* 90 A certain English Mechanick.. gave himself to read what Books of Practical Divinity he could get.

V. To put forth from oneself.

14. a. With obj. a transitive act viewed as a thing 'given' by the agent, and 'received' by the person or thing affected by it: e.g. *to give a kiss, a blow, kick, look, push*, etc.: also with sbs. of gerundial formation, *to give a beating, a scolding*, etc.

c **1205** [see A 8 α]. **13..** *E.E. Allit. P.* A 174 Bot baysment gef myn hert a brunt. *c* **1400** [see A 3 c γ]. *a* **1550** [see A 3 a γ]. *c* **1566** J. Alday tr. *Boaystuau's Theat. World* O, Did give him so many strokes with yᵉ Hay forke, that [etc.]. **1593** Shaks. *2 Hen. VI*, iv. vii. 91 Giue him a box o' th' eare, and that wil make 'em red againe. **1661** Boyle *Style of Script.* (1675) 91 Though in all the.. stroaks the busie hammer gives the act be still the same yet [etc.]. **1687** A. Lovell tr. *Thevenot's Trav.* i. 262 Giving the Rasor a philip, [he] opens the Vein very neatly. **1701** Norris *Ideal World* i. iv. 191 This.. will give a rude shock to the prejudice of vulgar minds. **1847** Marryat *Childr. N. Forest* xx, Humphrey's only reply was giving a lash to Billy, which set him off at a gallop. **1891** *Pall Mall G.* 23 Nov. 6/1, I gave him one over the head with my umbrella.

b. *Sword exercise. to give the point*: to make a direct thrust. *to give 'third point'*: see point.

1833 *Regul. Instr. Cavalry* i. 125 Advance the body and give 'Third Point'. **1893** Forbes-Mitchell *Remin. Gt. Mutiny* 213 MacBean made a feint cut, but instead gave the point, and put his sword through the chest of his opponent.

c. *to give a broadside, a volley, a shot*: see the sbs. *to give fire*: see fire *sb.* 14. Also *to give a gun*: to order a gun to be fired; sometimes const. *dat.* (or †*to*), implying that it is done as an honour, as a help (occasionally as a hostile demonstration). Colloq. phr. *to give* (*her, it*, etc.) *the gun*: to cause (a vehicle) to accelerate; to open the throttle of (an engine). orig. *U.S.*

1605 *Journ. Earl. Nottingham* in *Harl. Misc.* (Malh.) II. 541 His Lordship gave many pieces of ordnance, which were again received and answered from the town and forts. **1626** Capt. J. Smith *Accid. Yng. Sea-men* 24 Wind vp the slaine.. giue three peeces for their funerals. **1634** Sir T. Herbert *Trav.* 21 We gave them a-sterne, two Gunnes as warning peeces of great danger, and tackt about. **1660** Pepys *Diary* 22 May (Chandos) 34 Nothing in the world but giving of guns almost all this day [in honour of the king's health]. **1694** Motteux *Rabelais* iv. lxvi. 266 The Gunners.. gave every one a Gun to the Island. **1836** Marryat *Three Cutters* iv, Give her a gun. **1917** B. K. Adams *Let.* 10 Oct. (1918) 35 He.. saw that he wasn't going to even reach the aerodrome, so he gave her the gun, but the engine wouldn't pick up. **1919** *Red Cross Mag.* Feb. 30/2 He 'gave her the gun'—speeded up the engine—but the altimeter told him instantly that he was falling fast. **1945** G. Casey in *Coast to Coast 1944* 6 He gave it the gun and went ahead. **1968** 'G. Bagby' *Corpse Candle* iv. 47 She slid behind the wheel, gave her hearse the gun, swung it around.

d. *absol.* (*ellipt.*) or *intr.* To deal a blow, make an attack or charge (*at, on, upon*). *Obs.* exc. in pugilistic language.

c **1430** [see A 1 a γ]. *c* **1489** Caxton *Sonnes of Aymon* ii. 64 He.. gaaff me wyth his fyst vpon my vysage. **1523** Ld. Berners *Froiss.* I. clxxxvii. 222 John Mayllart gaue him with an axe on yᵉ heed that he fyll downe to the yerthe. **1598** R. Bernard tr. *Terence, Phormio* Prol., Thus he gives at him. **1617** Moryson *Itin.* ii. 159 Being not fit to make good an entrenched campe, and much lesse fit to give upon a breach. **1640** tr. *Verdere's Rom. R.* II. 141 Merodiana's Knights.. gave so furiously on the enemy, that.. they layd above three hundred on the earth. **1653** Holcroft *Procopius, Goth. Wars* iii. 80 John furiously giving upon the Enemy with a great shout, one of his life guard was slain by a dart. **1814** *Sporting Mag.* XLIV. 71 His antagonist gave with his left.

e. To punish (a person) for (doing something), freq. with reference back to what the other person has just said. *slang.*

1906 E. Dyson *Fact'ry 'Ands* ii. 23 'I'll give yeh whisperin' an' tisperin',' cried Annie. *a* **1930** D. H. Lawrence *Phoenix II* (1968) 136 Hark at her clicking the flower-pots, shifting the plants. He'd give her shift the plants! He'd show her!

f. To play music, esp. jazz, excitingly or enthusiastically; also with *out*. *slang* (orig. *U.S.*).

1936 *Esquire* June 92 The singer with the outfit can do with his or her voice just what the soloist can do with his instrument, he can *give*. **1952** B. Ulanov *Hist. Jazz in Amer.* (1958) 351 *Give* or *give out*, swing parlance for 'let yourself go'. **1955** Shapiro & Hentoff *Hear me talkin' to Ya* x. 141 We would give out with such tunes as *Tiger Rag*. **1958** *Woman's Own* 19 Feb. 22/1 You feel that you're in a real jam session with everybody giving, the joint jumping.

15. (Without indirect object.) To make, esp. suddenly (some bodily movement or gesture); to put forth, emit (a cry, a sound, a sigh, etc.); †to make (an attempt). Also in ME. †*to give one's end*: to die.

c **1200** Ormin 3219 Till þatt he ȝaff hiss ende. *a* **1300** *Cursor M.* 14350 On lazaro he gaf a cri, þat all it herd þat stod him bi. *a* **1340** Hampole *Psalter* xvii. 15 þe heghest gaf his voice. *c* **1450** *Merlin* 229 He yaf a sore sigh. **1576** Fleming *Panopl. Epist.* 280 [They] clapped with their hands and gave a shout. **1583** T. Stocker tr. *Civ. Warres Lowe C.* i. 64 a, He greatly presumed that the banished Lords.. woulde giue an attempt to returne into their possessions. **1611** Speed *Theat. Gt. Brit.* i. (1614) 2/1 Julius Cæsar was the first Romane which ever gave an attempt to conquer it. **1663** H. Power *Exp. Philos.* 177 If a Pistol be shot off in a head remote from the eye of a pit, it will give but a little report. **1666** J. Davies *Caribby Isl.* 260 They are wont to give a little hem at the end of every three or four periods. **1822** G. W. Manby *Voy. Greenland* (1823) 16 They.. gave three cheers. **1825** *New Monthly Mag.* XVI. 132 His teeth gave a short chatter of ridicule. **1835** Alison *Europe* xiii. §115 (1849–50) III. 124 His foot struck against a body, which gave a groan. **1850** Tennyson *In Mem.* cxxv, Some bitter notes my harp would give. **1859** H. Kingsley *Geoff. Hamlyn* iv, Sometimes she gave a stitch or two; but then followed a long gaze out of the window. **1884** May Crommelin *Brown-Eyes* vii. 78 Her heart gave some beats so quick and loud under her brown bodice. **1889** M. Caird *Wing of Azrael* II. xx. 76 Geoffrey gave a rueful whistle.

16. a. To put forth in words; to address (words) *to*; to make (a reply, answer); to impose and make known, to issue (a command, law, order, direction, etc.); to pronounce (a blessing, curse).

c **1200** Ormin 10665 Ure Laferrd.. ȝaff himm anndswere & seȝȝde. **1250** [see blessing 2]. *a* **1300** *Cursor M.* 28359 þis sin es cald presumpcioun, þat crist gaf til his malisun. *a* **1300** [see A 8 γ]. **1340** *Ayenb.* 5 Almiȝti god yaf ten hestes ine þe laȝe of iewes. **1497** Bp. Alcock *Mons Perfect.* A ij, Gaaf his elect & belouid dyscyples his blessynge. **1548** Hall *Chron., Hen. VIII*, 19 A Spanyard gave evill language to the Englisheman. **1553** T. Wilson *Rhet.* (1580) 137 They.. make hym at his wittes ende, through the sodaine.. frumpe given. **1576** Fleming *Panopl. Epist.* 80, I being armed, gave language to mine adversarie, much misliked. *a* **1586** Sidney *Arcadia* ii. (1633) 149 Giuing order by a secret message. **1600** Holland *Livy* xxvi. xli. 616 He had given direction.. that the legions.. should there meete together. *a* **1626** Bacon *Max. & Uses Com. Law* vii. (1636) 31 If I give a man slanderous words, whereby I damnifie him in his name and credit [etc.]. **1687** Wood *Life* 5 Sept. (O.H.S.) III. 239 The base and scurrilous language given to Mr... Walker and.. Massy. **1720** De Foe *Capt. Singleton* xvi. (1840) 282 Give them good words. **1725** *Lond. Gaz.* No. 6390/1 A.. Mob.. gave them abusive Language. **1884** *Brit. Q. Rev.* Apr. 329 He gave the command 'right face about'. **1890** *Chamb. Jrnl.* 10 May 300/1 Suddenly the word of command is given.

†**b.** Of a law: To prescribe *that*. *Obs.*

c **1305** *Pilate* 197 in *E.E.P.* (1862) 116 And lawe ȝifþ þat alle suche me scholde bringe of dawe.

c. To tell (a person); to offer for acceptance; esp. to tell or offer (a person) something incredible or unacceptable. Also *absol.* as *imp.*, speak! tell me! *colloq.* (orig. *U.S.*).

1883 J. Hay *Bread-Winners* xviii. 275 'Why, what are you givin' me now?' 'I'm a-givin' you truth and friendship.' **1889** 'Mark Twain' *Yankee* 6 What are you giving me?.. Get along back to your circus, or I'll report you. **1956** E. Pound tr. *Sophocles's Women of Trachis* 48 Thazza good tough start. Give. **1960** N. Hilliard *Maori Girl* 123 He drew down the corners of his mouth. 'Don't give me that.' **1968** 'P. Hobson' *Titty's Dead* xvii. 165 'Come on. Give.' 'That ruddy policeman went digging things up and he found out I'd written my own testimonials.'

17. The elliptical use of the 3rd pers. subj. in complimentary wishes, as in *give you joy* for *God give you joy*, seems to have been interpreted as an ellipsis of the pronoun of the first person, so that *give* has the sense of 'to wish'. So in *to give* (*a person*) *good morning, good day, good evening, a merry Christmas*, etc. (now *obsolescent*). Hence (now chiefly *dial.*), *to give the* (*time of*) *day* (*to*): to salute with 'good morning', 'good evening', etc. (as the case may be). [Cf. F. *donner le bonjour*.]

c **1340** *Gaw. & Gr. Knt.* 668 Gawan.. gef hem alle goud day. **1593** Shaks. *2 Hen. VI*, iii. i. 14 In the Morne, When euery one will giue the time of day. **1613–16** W. Browne *Brit. Past.* i. ii, Sweetly she came and with a modest blush Gave him the day, and then accosted thus. **1640** Shirley *Constant Maid* v. iii, Is there any more Worke for the Priest? Then give you joy before hand, And let us celebrate the day together. **1642** —— *Sisters* v. ii. (1652) 57 Give you joy, Sir, my most illustrious Nephew. **1647** W. Browne tr. *Gomberville's Polex.* iv. ii. 195 Zabaim and the foure Princes thought they had time sufficient to give the Ladies the good night. **1666** Pepys *Diary* (1879) VI. 38 Both of whom I did give joy. **1674** tr. *Martiniere's Voy. N. Countries* 92 Discerning we were strangers, [he] saluted us in Dutch, gave us the time of the day. **1765** W. Hunter *Let.* in *Life W. Cullen* (1832) I. 553, I thank the young advocate, and give him joy and all good wishes. **1822** Scott *Nigel* xxxiv, Bravely done—nobly imparted! Give ye good-den. **1843** Dickens *Christm. Carol* ii, He heard them give each other Merry Christmas. **1855** Thackeray *Newcomes* I. ii. 15 The pokes in the waistcoat administered by the wags to Newcome, 'Newcome, give you joy, my boy'; 'Newcome, new partner in Hobson's' [etc.].

18. a. Of a judge, a tribunal: To deliver authoritatively (a decision, judgement, verdict, sentence, etc.); to award (costs, damages) *to, against*.

a **1300** *Cursor M.* 29512 Quen man wit iuel mode.. gis his sentence on ani man. ? **1429** in *Wetheral Reg.* (1897) 431 The Bishopp oppynly gaffe a decre and a sentence to all thame that [etc.]. *c* **1465** *Eng. Chron.* (Camden 1856) 60 The justice that yaf on him jugement livid not longe aftir. *a* **1533** Ld. Berners *Huon* lxxxi. 242 It is not possyble to gyue ony trewe Iugemente. **1553** T. Wilson *Rhet.* (1580) 106 The Judge is wholly bent to give sentence with hym. **1568** Grafton *Chron.* II. 59 The Archebishop.. by vertue of his Apostolike auctoritie gave censure upon these lawes.. of the king. **1603** Shaks. *Meas. for M.* ii. ii. 106 So you must be yᵉ first that giues this sentence, And hee, that suffers. **1676** Lady Chaworth in *12th Rep. Hist. MSS. Comm.* App. v. 28, I heard.. of Lord Shaftesberys having a 1000*l.* damages given against Lord Dighby for scandalum magnatum. **1700** Tyrrell *Hist. Eng.* II. 719 This Arrest or Sentence of the Peers of France was given against King John. **1818** Cruise *Digest* (ed. 2) VI. 483 Judgment was given in the courts of Exchequer.. for the plaintiff Fox. **1855** Macaulay *Hist. Eng.* xvii. IV. 39 Judgment had been given against him. **1888** *Spectator* 28 Apr. 561/1 A decision which must be given next week. **1890** Sir C. S. C. Bowen in *Law Times Rep.* LXIII. 690/1 It seems to me that the judge really intended to give the plaintiff the general costs of the action.

b. *to give the case* (idiomatically *to give it*): to decide *for* or *against* a litigant; †also absol. *to give with* or *against*. In Cricket, of the umpire: To declare (a batsman) *out, not out*, etc.

1573 G. HARVEY *Letter-bk.* (Camden) 2 Sir Lawhern pretendid that he would give with none unless al might go out, but indeed intendid to give against me. **1762** GOLDSM. *Cit. W.* xxxiii, The whole company..gave it unanimously against me. **1816** W. LAMBERT *Instr. & Rules Cricket* 23 Such Umpire..is authorized to *give him out*, for thus impeding the progress of the Ball towards the Wicket. **1890** *Field* 31 May 789/1 At 216 he was given out l b w. **1890** *Murray's Mag.* Dec. 828 He..has had the case given against him. **1891** GRACE *Cricket* 329 He had changed his mind and given me out. **1891** *Longm. Mag.* Oct. 661 The umpire gave it out. **1892** *Standard* 20 June 6/7 Smith was then given run out.

19. In imitation of Latin usage (see DATE *sb.*[2]) the pa. pple. is used in official documents for: Dated.

1443 in Willis & Clark *Cambridge* (1886) I. 386 Yoven the day and the yere abouesaid. **1485** in *Paston Lett.* No. 887 III. 325 Goven at Long Stratton the xx day of October. **1533** in Picton *L'pool Munic. Rec.* (1883) I. 25 Yeven at our said Paloys the xxviii[th] day of Iune. **1602** in Moryson *Itin.* II. (1617) 150 Given under our Signet..in the fortie three yeere of Our Raigne. **1726** SWIFT *Gulliver* I. iii, Given at our Palace at Belfaborac. **1885** *Times* (weekly ed.) 27 Feb. 6/4 Given under my hand at the War Office, Pall-mall, this 18th day of February, 1885. Hartington.

20. To provide as a host (an entertainment, a ball, dinner, etc.). Often with added notion of sense 1 or 2 (const. *to* or *dat.*), to do this in honour of, or for the gratification of, some person or persons. Also in *indirect passive*.

1523 LD. BERNERS *Froiss.* I. cccciii. 283 b, He gaue dyuers suppers and banketes to ladyes and damosels. **1562** in W. H. Turner *Select. Rec. Oxford* 299 A breckfast geven to Mr. Norres. **1712–14** POPE *Rape Lock* III. 12 In various talk th' instructive hours they past Who gave the ball, or paid the visit last. **1766** GOLDSM. *Vic. W.* viii, Intended that night giving the young ladies a ball. **1855** TENNYSON *Maud* I. xx. 2 Our ponderous squire will give A grand political dinner To half the squirelings near. *a* **1873** DEUTSCH *Rem.* (1874) 260 Frederick of Austria gave a tournament. **1885** *Truth* 2 July 2/1 Their Royal Highnesses also intend to give a dance as a wind-up to the season. **1892** *Cornh. Mag.* July 2 The school children were being given a treat.

VI. To present, expose, offer.

21. To present or expose to the action of a person or thing; to hold out (one's hand) to be taken. *to give a back*: see BACK *sb.*[1] 24 e.

c **950** [see A 6 a α]. **1382** WYCLIF *2 Kings* x. 15 He seith, ȝeue me thin honde. The whiche ȝaue to hym his hond; and he rerede hym to hym in to the chaar. —— *Isa.* l. 6 My bodi I ȝaf to the smyteres, and my chekes to the pulleris. **1589** [see A 2 d γ]. **1613** PURCHAS *Pilgrimage* (1614) 649 The mothers use to beare their children at their backs..they give them the brest over their shoulders. **1617** MORYSON *Itin.* II. 88 Because I had a white horse, I gave the Rebels a faire marke. **1697** DRYDEN *Æneid* VII. 553 All..Give to the wanton Winds their flowing Hair. **1711** *Fingall MSS.* in *10th Rep. Hist. MSS. Comm.* App. v. 133 The army was..to marche..by the river, giving their right flanck to the front of the enemy. *c* **1820** S. ROGERS *Italy, Brides Venice* 70 Their sails out-spread and given to the wind. **1837** HAWTHORNE *Twice-Told T.* (1851) I. ix. 160 He holds out his hand; she gives her own. **1855** DICKENS *Dorrit* I. xxxii, 'Give me a back, Mr. Rugg—a little higher, sir—that'll do!'

†**22. a.** Of (one's) 'heart', mind, conscience, etc.: To suggest (to one) *that*; in unfavourable sense, to misgive. Also, to prompt (one) *to* do something. Also, quasi-impersonal, *it gives me* = I have a foreboding. *Obs.*

1297 R. GLOUC. (Rolls) 9762 He bihuld & nuste þulke foure þere Is herte him ȝef anon wuderward hii wende. *c* **1375** BARBOUR *Bruce* XIX. 97 Myne hert giffis me no mor to be With ȝow duelland in this cuntre. *Ibid.* 107. *c* **1380** *Sir Ferumb.* 1450 Myn herte me ȝifþ þat ȝif he..takeþ þat iornee, þat þou ne seest hym no more. **1488** *Will of Sir E. Shaa* (Somerset Ho.), My conscience geueth me to make restitucion. **1523** LD. BERNERS *Froiss.* I. ccclvii. 577 My hert gyueth me that ye mater wyll nat reste longe in the case that it is nowe in. **1542** UDALL *Erasm. Apophth.* II. 200 a, Full well did it geue this prudent & wise prince in his mynde tofore, that [etc.]. **1551** ROBINSON tr. *More's Utop.* I. (Arb.) 67 To speke truelye as my mynde geueth me. **1600** HEYWOOD *2 Pt. Edw. IV*, I. iv, Somewhat, it giues me, you will bring from thence Worthy the noting. **1650** T. B. *Worcester's Apoph.* 91 The Marquess had a Daughter whose mind gave her to be a Nun. **1690** W. WALKER *Idiomat. Anglo-Lat.* 206 It gave me in my mind I should lose my labour in going. **1748** RICHARDSON *Clarissa* (1811) II. xiv. 95 My heart strongly gives me, that if once I am compelled to leave this house, I never shall see it more. **1820** SCOTT *Ivanhoe* xxviii, Therefore, do as thy mind giveth thee.

¶ **b.** In Malory the locutions ***my heart giveth*** (***me***) ***that*** sometimes have a further sense of inclining towards a person, expressed by a construction with *unto*. In some instances the obj. clause is dropped, so that the vb. assumes the intr. sense 'to incline, be kindly disposed'.

(Perh. quot. *c* 1330 may be an older example of this sense; on the other hand, it is possible that *Edward*, not *heart*, is the subject.)

[*c* **1330** R. BRUNNE *Chron.* (1810) 253 Sir Edward..His herte gaf tille dame Blanche, if her wille wer þerto.] **1470–85** MALORY *Arthur* VII. ii, My herte geueth me to the gretely that thou arte come of men of worshyp. *Ibid.* XVII. xiii, Moche my hert gyueth vnto yow. **1870** MORRIS *Earthly Par.* III. IV. 93 My heart giveth to thee.

23. a. To expose or offer to view or observation; to 'set' (an example); to show (a sign, token); to present or set forth (a statement, fact, proposal, reason, etc.) for acceptance or consideration; to mention, include in a list or enumeration. † *to give show*: to intimate.

c **1200** ORMIN 1239 Forr þe to ȝifenn bisne, þatt [etc.]. *a* **1225** *Ancr. R.* 68 þat oðer [ancheisun] is, uorte ȝiuen þe oðre uorbisne. *a* **1300** *Cursor M.* 12620 He gaf þaim rede all resun. *c* **1449** [see A 3 c β]. **1470–85** [see EXAMPLE *sb.* 6]. **1548** HALL *Chron., Edw. IV*, 235 b, A white Dove..came thether as a token, geven by God. **1559** W. CUNNINGHAM *Cosmogr. Glasse* 93, I..will shew you how to find the height of the Pole euery day, for whiche thinge I will geue you two sondrye wais. **1576** FLEMING *Panopl. Epist.* Epit. A, Give me the sundrie kindes of Epistles. **1579** [see A 3 a γ]. **1596** SHAKS. *Merch. V.* IV. i. 59 As there is no firm reason to be rendered..So can I giue no reason. **1613** PURCHAS *Pilgrimage* (1614) 20 Some giving one etymologie and derivation of the word, and some another. **1693** DRYDEN *Juvenal* Ded. (1697) 75 Thus have I given the History of Satire, and deriv'd it from Ennius to your Lordship. **1711** ADDISON *Spect.* No. 59 ⁋4 Among innumerable Instances that may be given of this Nature. **1736** LEDIARD *Life Marlborough* III. 376 The Queen gave some Signs of Life. **1769** GOLDSM. *Rom. Hist.* (1786) II. 382 As if he [Commodus] gave the example, very few of his successors escaped a violent death. **1796** H. HUNTER tr. *St.-Pierre's Stud. Nat.* (1799) III. 51 The account of it is given in the Mercury of France. **1821** KEATS *Isabella* iii, He knew whose gentle hand was at the latch, Before the door had given her to his eyes. **1889** M. GRAY *Reproach Annesley* I. I. i. 6 The far-off farms..gave no sign of life. **1892** R. C. LEHMANN *Billsbury Elect.* 196 A daily newspaper gave a head-lined account of the speech. *Mod.* Such words ought not to be given in a dictionary.

b. To indicate as existing; to state *at* a certain quantity). Of a measuring instrument: To show, indicate (a certain quantity).

1665 SIR T. HERBERT *Trav.* (1677) 15 Albeit Ptol. after him gives no further extendure of land south, than 12 deg. **1856** *Jrnl. R. Agric. Soc.* XVII. II. 445 He gives the average monthly amount..at 0·81 lbs. **1890** *Harper's Mag.* Nov. 815/1 The hydrometer [*sic*] gives a humidity as high as seventy-four. **1891** *Longm. Mag.* Oct. 600 The sounding-line..gave at last but six fathoms.

†**24.** To display as an armorial bearing; to bear (such or such a cognizance, etc.). *Obs.* Cf. *to give arms*, s.v. ARM *sb.*[2] 15.

1548 HALL *Chron., Hen. VII*, 59 The Emperour Maximilian..at that tyme gave an Egle in his armes. **1576** FLEMING *Panopl. Epist.* 388 *note*, He bare the name and gave the badge or cognisaunce of the same. **1591** SHAKS. *1 Hen. VI*, I. v. 29 Teare the Lyons out of Englands Coat;..giue Sheepe in Lyons stead. **1598** —— *Merry W.* I. i. 16 All his Ancestors (that come after him)..may giue the dozen white Luces in their Coate. *a* **1626** MIDDLETON *More Dissemblers* I. iii, I give the flaming heart, It is my crest. **1640** SHIRLEY *Doubtful Heir* I. (1652) 7 Her sweet Heart, that gives Cupid in his crest.

25. To represent, describe, portray, report. Now *rare*. †Also *refl.* with complement: To appear, present itself as. *Obs.*

1607 SHAKS. *Cor.* I. ix. 55 Too modest are you: More cruell to your good report, than gratefull To vs, that giue you truly. **1631** SHIRLEY *Traitor* III. iii. (1635) F 3 Your brother gave you more Desirous of the sport. **1634** SIR T. HERBERT *Trav.* 12 The Land at twenty leagues distance gave itselfe very high. **1638** *Ibid.* (ed. 2) 230 Many other things give themselves note-worthy. **1850** TENNYSON *In Mem.* lxxv, What practice howsoe'er expert..Hath power to give thee as thou wert?

26. To read, recite, sing, act (anything) in the presence of auditors or spectators; to perform, produce (a play, etc.); to deliver (a lecture, etc.). Cf. F. *donner*.

c **1460** *Towneley Myst.* xiii, 183, I wold, or we yode, oone gaf vs a song. *a* **1533** LD. BERNERS *Huon* lix. 207 Take thy vyall, and geue vs a songe. **1834** MEDWIN *Angler in Wales* I. 198 He promised to give us another chapter out of his book, on another occasion. **1855** THACKERAY *Newcomes* I. xiii. 134 Who will give us a song? **1879** TROLLOPE *Thackeray* i. 46 The piece was all given by memory. **1887** *Times* (weekly ed.) 24 June 14/4 The Russian Imperial hymn, given on the organ. **1889** *Cornh. Mag.* Dec. 625 Havard's play of 'Charles I' was being given at York. **1890** *Illustr. Lond. News* 26 Apr. 536/1 The opera was given again in 1864.

27. To offer, propose as a sentiment or toast.

1728 RAMSAY *On seeing Archers divert themselves* 96 Neist, sir, you name; I give you Basil's handsome dame. **1793** BURNS *On Rodney's Victory* 1 Instead of a Song, boys, I'll give you a toast. **1816** J. WILSON *City of Plague* I. iv, I rise to give, most noble President, The memory of a man well known to all. **1837** DICKENS *Pickw.* xxxvii, 'Gentlemen', said the man in blue..'I'll give you the ladies, come'. **1891** *Standard* 10 Nov. 3/3 The Lord Mayor next gave 'The Health of the Lord High Chancellor'.

VII. To make partaker of.

28. a. To communicate, impart to a person or thing (some quality, state, etc. belonging to the subject).

a **1470** TIPTOFT *Tulle on Friendsh.* (Caxton) iv, The gretest fruyte of naturel vertue..is thenne taken whan it is youen and departed to theym that be next in frendship & good wille. *c* **1566** J. ALDAY tr. *Boaystuau's Theat. World* F iij, For the father can give to the child but fraile and mortall fleshe. **1590** SIR J. SMYTH *Disc. Weapons* 18 The match also if it bee not..kept verie drie..it giveth no fire to the touchpowder. *Mod.* I hope I have not given you my sore throat.

b. Of a place, a thing: To supply, be the source or origin of (a name, title).

1639 T. BRUGIS tr. *Camus' Mor. Rel.* 144 This Castle giveth name unto a Family sufficiently knowne. *a* **1671** LD. FAIRFAX *Mem.* (1699) 84 The place was Marston fields, which afterwards gave the name to this battel. **1845** M. PATTISON *Ess.* (1889) I. 11 The Loire, its banks still clad with the broom which gives their title to the Plantagenets.

29. a. To impart (knowledge, information); to impart the knowledge of (a fact, a name, one's opinion or intention). † *to give part* [= Sp. *dar parte*, F. *faire part*]: to apprise a person *of*. *to give* (a person) ***a piece of one's mind***: (*colloq.*) usually, to give emphatic expression to one's disapprobation.

c **1449** PECOCK *Repr.* 68 Bi teching and informacioun of sum sad clerk ȝouun to thee. **1558** Q. ELIZ. in Strype *Ann. Ref.* (1709) I. App. i. 2 We do publish and give knowledge by this our proclamation to all maner peple. **1617** MORYSON *Itin.* I. 41 In giving my name, I wrote my selfe an Englishman. **1643** *Order Parlt.* in *Milton's Areop.* (Arb.) 26 By way of revenge for giveing information against them. **1652** NEEDHAM tr. *Selden's Mare Cl.* 481 This is the real and Roial design of this Fleet, whereof you may give part..to our good neighbors. **1661** BOYLE *Style of Script.* (1675) 36 Our great Antiquary..both in familiar discourse, and in his excellent tract on the Syrian Deities gave me first a hint. **1687** A. LOVELL tr. *Thevenot's Trav.* II. 59 Tales..which I shall give as cheap as I had them. **1785** [see A 6 a γ]. **1861** DICKENS *Gt. Expect.* v, Would you give me the Time? **1865** —— *Mut. Fr.* IV. xiii, The room in which she had given him that piece of her mind at parting. **1885** *Century Mag.* XXX. 79 I In a few words Captain Schley gave me an inkling of his plans. **1886** *Manch. Exam.* 23 Jan. 5/3 The policy given in outline in the Queen's Speech ensures the opposition of the Parnellites. **1887** HALL CAINE *Deemster* xxxiii. 216 The men gathered close about T... T. gave his plan. **1889** F. BARRETT *Under Strange Mask* II. xvi. 109, I gave him my name.

b. *to give to the world, to the public*: to publish (a literary work, a discovery, etc.).

1757 W. CULLEN in *Life* (1832) I. 531 When those parts that are finished shall be given to the public. **1825** *New Monthly Mag.* XV. 461 The results of these enquiries have been given to the world. **1892** *Temple Bar* Dec. 481 'Marmion' was given to the world in 1808.

c. *to give* (a person) *to believe, know, note, understand*, etc.: to impart to him information that will lead him to believe (etc.). Also in *indirect passive*.

c **1566** J. ALDAY tr. *Boaystuau's Theat. World* R b, The whiche giveth us to understande that man is the verie chiefe worke of God. **1586** Q. ELIZ. in *Corresp. Earl Leicester* (Camden Soc. 1844) 210 So we think mete the counsel of state be geven to understand. **1586** EARL LEICESTER *ibid.* 246 It is secretly and assuredly giuen me to vnderstand [etc.]. **1586** MARLOWE *1st Pt. Tamburl.* V. ii, I..Shall give the world to note..That virtue solely is the sum of glory. **1623** LISLE *Ælfric on O. & N. Test.* M iij a, He doth moreouer giue vs to vnderstand the number of the Sermons that he translated. **1661** R. L'ESTRANGE *State Divinity* 44, I am given to understand that [etc.]. **1778** J. LAURENS in Sparks *Corr. Amer. Rev.* (1853) II. 170 We have given them to understand that the frigate..is to push out of the Sound. **1786** T. JEFFERSON *Writ.* (1859) I. 539 Our report..they may be given to know, cannot be formed without decisive information. **1811** C'TESS BERKELEY *Addr. to Peers* 19, I met him when he gave me to believe that his intentions were honourable. **1849** MACAULAY *Hist. Eng.* vi. II. 82 Four of the Judges gave him to understand that they could not, on this occasion, serve his purpose. **1875** H. KINGSLEY *No. Seventeen* xxii. 167 'How did you lie?' 'Not at all in words, but I gave him to think that' [etc.]. **1889** M. CAIRD *Wing of Azrael* III. xxxvi. 129 Adrienne was given to understand that this..was entirely her doing.

VIII. To allot, apportion, assign.

30. a. To allot, apportion; to cause to have as one's share. † *to give to lot* (see LOT *sb.*). Also in *indirect passive.* †In *pa. pple.* with *adv.* = Dowered.

c **1050** [see A 6 a β]. *c* **1230** *Hali Meid.* 9 Hwen þus is of þe riche hwat wenes tu of the poure þat beoð wacliche iȝeouen. *a* **1300** *Cursor M.* 16767 + 118 Him was not geue so mikel plas, War-on he miȝt dee fayre. *Ibid.* 28724 O crist..We find he gaf na penance mare. **1382** [see A 3 b α]. *c* **1450** *St. Cuthbert* (Surtees) 7082 þe bischop penance þan him gaue. **1579** SPENSER *Sheph. Cal.* Apr. 114 Let that rowme to my Lady be yeuen. **1599** JAS. I *Βασιλ. Δωρον* (1603) 91 Æquitie in thinges arbitrall, giueth euery one that which is meetest for him. **1667** MILTON *P.L.* VIII. 339 Not onely these fair bounds, but all the Earth To thee and to thy Race I give. **1771** GOLDSM. *Hist. Eng.* II. 15 It was soon after united to the kingdom of England, made a principality, and given to the eldest son of the crown. **1885** J. MARTINEAU *Types Eth. Th.* II. I. i. §2. 156 The states in question being given to the respective subjects. **1890** *Lippincott's Mag.* Feb. 217, I was given a hut in Hope Town. **1891** *Murray's Mag.* Apr. 524 He was given the contract.

b. To assign or impose (a name); †to appoint, fix (a day, time).

c **1250** *Gen. & Ex.* 232 Adam abraid, and saȝ ðat wif, Name he ȝaf hire ðat is ful Rif. *c* **1320** *Cast. Love* 615 þeos beþ þe nomen..þat þe prophetes him ȝeeuen. *c* **1450** MYRC 138 Then may the fader wyþoute blame Crysten the chylde and ȝeue hyt name. **1461** *Paston Lett.* No. 394 II. 18 To gyve them that ar chosyn knyghtes of the shire, day after Michelmesse. *a* **1533** LD. BERNERS *Huon* xlix. 165 He..gaue them day to be with him within .xv. dayes. **1559** W. CUNNINGHAM *Cosmogr. Glasse* 3 For rewarde wherof vertu also gave you that name. **1570–6** LAMBARDE *Peramb. Kent* (1826) 259 A thing worthy..of reformation when God shal give time. **1613** PURCHAS *Pilgrimage* (1614) 622 The women wash the childe all over with water, and give the name. **1630** in Rushw. *Hist. Coll.* (1659) I. 45 The Court..gave day to joyn in Demurrer this Tearm. *a* **1715** BURNET *Own Time* II. 175 They were bound..to proceed according to the rules of parliament, which was to commit the person so impeached and then give a short day for his trial.

†**c.** To appoint to an office or function. *Obs.*

1535 COVERDALE *1 Chron.* vii. [vi.] 48 As for their brethren the Leuites, they were geuen to all the offices in the habitacion of the house of the Lorde. **1611** BIBLE *Eph.* iv. 11 He gaue some, Apostles; and some, Prophets.

d. To allow (a person) a specified period of time in which to do something; to predict a certain period remaining for (a person's life, a marriage, etc.). *colloq.*

1835 DICKENS *Let.* 30 Dec. (1965) I. 114, I give Cruickshank 'till Saturday:—I hope we shall have something to look at by that time. **1881** STEVENSON *Virg. Puerisque* 181 By all means begin your folio; even if the doctor does not give you a year.., make one brave push and see what can be accomplished in a week. **1913** F. L. BARCLAY *Broken Halo* xviii. 217 'How long do you give me, Sir James?' she asked, in a very quiet voice. **1962** WODEHOUSE *Service with Smile* vii. 107 'Well, all right,' said Lord Ickenham, rising. 'I can give her five minutes.' **1972** *Observer* 20 Feb. 8/5 The wiseacres..gave Charles Chaplin and Oona O'Neill's marriage six months. It's lasted decades.

31. a. To attribute in thought or speech; to ascribe, assign. †Formerly often, to ascribe (a literary work) to a person as author. *Obs.*

1559 W. CUNNINGHAM *Cosmogr. Glasse* 12 The Ægiptians ..gave to the seven Planetes .vij. heavens. **1603** FLORIO *Montaigne* II. iv. (1632) 200, I do..give pricke and praise [F. *je donne la palme*] unto Jaques Amiens. **1605** SHAKS. *Macb.* I. iii. 119 Those that gaue the Thane of Cawdor to me, Promis'd no lesse to them. **1613** —— *Hen. VIII*, III. ii. 262 From all That might haue mercie on the fault, thou gau'st him. **1624** BP. MOUNTAGU *Gagg* 42 He gave too much to traditions. **1756–82** J. WARTON *Ess. Pope* II. ix. 60 On its first publication, Pope did not own it, and it was given by the public to Lord Paget, Dr. Young, Dr. Desaguliers, and others. **1770** BURKE *Corr.* (1844) I. 243, I have lately read a good part..of a pamphlet on the late verdicts... They give it to Lord Camden. **1777** SHERIDAN *Sch. Scandal* I. i, I don't wonder at people giving him to me for a lover. **1797** *Morn. Chron.* 13 Nov., The translation of the *Diatribe* against England, which has been given to the pen of M. de Talyrand. **1812** *Brit. Bibliographer* II. 392 George Pettie. [*note*] Warton calls him William, but I have A. Wood's authority for giving him the name of George. **1879** M. J. GUEST *Lect. Hist. Eng.* xxxiv. 342 Henry..gave all the glory to God. **1885** *Manch. Exam.* 10 July 5/1 It is proper to give full weight to the exculpatory evidence adduced.

†**b.** *to give for*, also simply *to give* (chiefly with adjs. or pples. of condition): To account, consider, set down as. Cf. *to give over, up for*. *Obs.*

1606 SHAKS. *Ant. & Cl.* I. iv. 40 Mens reports Giue him [Pompey] much wrong'd. **1613** *Voy. Guiana* in *Harl. Misc.* (Malh.) III. 177 We descried her to leeward of us, contrary to our expectation, having given her for lost. **1622** BEAUM. & FL. *Span. Cur.* IV. iv, If, ere the sun be set, I see you not, give me dead. *a* **1625** FLETCHER *Hum. Lieutenant* II. ii, Nay, give 'em lost, I saw 'em off their horses. *c* **1645** HOWELL *Lett.* (1655) I. v. xxx. 226 Greek I perceiv'd it was not, nor Latin or English; So I gave it for meer gibbrish. **1646** FULLER *Wounded Consc.* (1841) 342 Pensive parents solicitous for the souls of their children have even given them for gone. **1671** MARVELL *Corr.* Wks. 1872–5 II. 392 The Dutchess of York is dead. All gave her for a Papist. **1711** ADDISON *Spect.* No. 130 ¶4 The Parents, after a long Search for him, gave him for drowned in one of the Canals. *a* **1715** BURNET *Own Time* II. 144 The party against the court gave all for lost. **1740** tr. *de Mouhy's Fort. Country-maid* (1741) I. 191, I gave myself for lost.

†**c.** *to give for granted*: to take for granted, consent to assume. *Obs.*

1637 HEYLIN *Antid. Linc.* II. vii. 81 Which given for granted we proceed, and will shew some reasons [etc.]. **1657** R. LIGON *Barbadoes* (1673) 25, I shall easily be led..to give for granted, that Carlisle Bay [etc.]. **1692** R. L'ESTRANGE *Josephus, Antiq.* III. v. (1733) 61 The Hebrews..fell into a Consternation giving it for granted that God in his wrath had taken away Moses.

32. The pa. pple. is used, esp. in an absolute clause, with the sense: Assigned or posited as a basis of calculation or reasoning. Cf. GIVEN *ppl. a.*

1667 PRIMATT *City & C. Build.* 159 How to draw a Perpendicular Line from any Point, to any Line given. **1828** J. H. MOORE *Pract. Navig.* (ed. 20) 109 The Difference of Latitude and Departure given, to find the Course, Distance, and Difference of Longitude. **1885** *Manch. Exam.* 5 May 5/1 Given a reasonable amount of variety and quality in the exhibits, an exhibition..is sure to attract large numbers.

IX. To yield as a product or result.

33. To yield, supply, furnish, as a product.

c **1200** [see A 1 b]. *a* **1225** [see A 8 β]. *a* **1300** *Cursor M.* 22326 Þe erth sal giue o frut plente. **1382** [see A 3 c a]. *c* **1420** [see A 2 c a]. **1548** HALL *Chron. Edw. IV*, 200 b, All the whole Province of Yorke, gave yerely to this Hospitall certain measures of corne. **1577** B. GOOGE *Heresbach's Husb.* III. (1586) 150 She requireth greater quantity of meate, whereby she may give the more milke. **1617** MORYSON *Itin.* I. 91 The same family hath given three Dukes..and three Patriarkes, and twelve Procurators of Saint Marke. **1628** DIGBY *Voy. Medit.* 41 Trees that giue aromatike gummes. **1641** J. JACKSON *True Evang. T.* II. 121 The Cow..which was so fruitfull at the Paile, that for the abundance of milk she did give, the owner might eate butter. **1756** C. LUCAS *Ess. Waters* I. 146 The washings..bubbled, subsided, and gave lime, like the rest. **1792** *Descr. Kentucky* 39 This establishment gives already 2,000 yards of sail-cloth a week. **1841** *Jrnl. R. Agric. Soc.* II. I. 121 The 241 lbs. of wheat should have given 189 lbs. of flour. **1852** *Ibid.* XIII. I. 26 The cow..gave in the evening 5 quarts of milk. *Ibid.* 38 Cream on milk, a little acescent, will 'give' the butter with less labour in churning than when the milk or cream is void of acidity. **1890** *Harper's Mag.* Oct. 770/1 This second brewing will give a darker liquid. **1891** *Strand Mag.* Jan. 96/1 The lamps gave an uncertain light.

†**34.** To fetch, be worth (a price). *Obs.*

a **1575** *Diurn. Occurr.* (Bannatyne Club) 306 The Meill gaif xij shillings the peck. **1634** SIR T. HERBERT *Trav.* 41 A Spanish shilling gives twenty five Pice, a Riall of eight gives five Mammoodees. **1681** W. ROBERTSON *Phraseol. Gen.* (1693) 663 Let him sell oyl, if it give anything. **1761** EARL HADDINGTON *Forest-trees* (1765) 8 In other countries it gives a great price. **1799** J. ROBERTSON *Agric. Perth* 258 The country would be so much overstocked with timber, that it would give no price.

35. To yield as the result of calculation or measurement.

1634 SIR T. HERBERT *Trav.* 91 The Garden..has six severall discents, each part giving eightie paces, and seventie broad. **1727** ARBUTHNOT *Table Anct. Coins*, etc. 240 The number of Men being divided by the number of Ships, gives four hundred and twenty-four Men a-piece. **1739** tr. *Algarotti on Newton's Theory* (1742) II. 149 Two multiplied by itself gives Four. **1858** *Jrnl. R. Agric. Soc.* XIX. I. 172 An analysis of the guano..gave the following results. **1890** *Longm. Mag.* July 282 [His] name in Hebrew characters gives us 666—the mystic number of the Antichrist.

†**36.** Of experience, reasoning, etc.: To yield the conclusion *that*. Also of a name: To import, signify. *Obs.*

c **1449** PECOCK *Repr.* III. v. 306 Experience hath ȝouun bifore these daies that grete lordis [etc.]. **1481** CAXTON *Myrr.* II. i. 64 Raison and nature gyue that alle the worlde be rounde. **1552** LATIMER *Serm. Lincolnsh.* ix. (1562) 144 b, The time giueth it that Christ shoulde come. **1567** MAPLET *Gr. Forest* 22 Taraxippus the stone, as the name giueth, doth signifie the Horse his trouble and disquietnesse. **1627–77** FELTHAM *Resolves* I. xxx. 52 The same reason gives it: for, *Optima corrupta pessima*. **1677** HALE *Prim. Orig. Man.* I. iii. 88 This Instance gives the impossibility of an eternal Existence in any thing essentially alterable or corruptible.

X. To cause to have.

37. a. With direct and indirect obj.: To cause to have (a possession); to cause to receive (anything material or immaterial, a benefit or injury); to produce in a person or thing (a state, condition, feeling); to invest or endow with (a quality, a right, a power); to restore (one's health, sight, etc.). Said both of persons and things. † *to give one the worse*: to worst, defeat.

a **1300** *Cursor M.* 539 Þe ouer fir gis man his sight. *c* **1340** [see A 7 γ]. *c* **1380** WYCLIF *Serm.* Sel. Wks. I. 333 To sich folk wolde Crist ȝeue blisse. **1387–8** [see A 2 d a]. *c* **1400** *Destr. Troy* 10404 He greuit þe greke, and geue hym þe worse. *c* **1420** *Chron. Vilod.* 710 þt suche a meracule for hurre hadde wrouȝt, And ȝeve, for hurre love, þt bysone mon his syȝt. **1513** MORE in Grafton *Chron.* (1568) II. 781 The ieoperdy so well passed, it gave him great pleasure to talke with him thereof. **1548** HALL *Chron., Hen. V*, 55 b, To geve men a courage for to go furth, money was fyrst gathered. **1590** SIR J. SMYTH *Disc. Weapons* 18 b, Whereby [a wad] the whole charge of powder being restrained may..give the more force to the bullets. **1610** BP. CARLETON *Iurisdiction* 163 When the pope was able to meet the Emperour in battell and give him the worse. **1617** MORYSON *Itin.* II. 75 Finding the Army a meere Chaos, he had given it forme. **1653** H. COGAN tr. *Pinto's Trav.* lxxix. 319 On the death which I hope to give to this Fish, my perfect content depends. **1674** tr. *Martiniere's Voy. N. Countries* 32 Which they distil.. putting in a certain grain which gives it the same strength and intoxication as ours. **1726** G. ROBERTS *4 Years Voy.* Ded. A iij b, A Person whose Profession and Opportunities have not given him those Advantages which others may boast. **1728** MORGAN *Algiers* II. iii. 247 It gives me the Vapours to find People miscalled. **1754** RICHARDSON *Grandison* II. xxiii. 168, I give you emotion, madam. Forgive me. I have performed my promise. **1773** MRS. GRANT *Lett. fr. Mount.* (1813) I. xiii. 108 Another far-seen object gives sad variety to the prospect. **1803** *Pic Nic* No. 4 (1806) I. 122 Her restless ambition continues to give alarm in every quarter. **1817** W. SELWYN *Law Nisi Prius* (ed. 4) II. 1183 This, in Lord Kenyon's opinion, gave the plaintiff a title to the whole. **1862** TYNDALL *Mountaineering* vi. 32 Its deep seclusion gives it a peculiar charm. **1874** GREEN *Short Hist.* iv. §3. 176 The King..wept bitterly at the news of his father's death, though it gave him a crown. **1883** *Manch. Exam.* 22 Nov. 5/4 Currency is given..to a rumour that the Parcel Post is being conducted at a loss of something like £10,000 a week. **1884** W. C. SMITH *Kildrostan* 88 Clumsy oars—faugh! they give blisters first And then a horny hand. **1890** T. F. TOUT *Hist. Eng. fr. 1689* 115 Burke gave the tone to the mass of English opinion.

b. with dat. of person and infinitive.

1768 *Woman of Honor* II. 187 Your knowing one gives you to know the whole mutton-headed species. **1803** MARY CHARLTON *Wife & Mistress* I. 52 Each despairing struggle only gave her to experience the full force of her bonds. **1841** J. H. NEWMAN in *Apologia* (1864) 273 The last miserable century..has given us to start from a much lower level.

c. With dative of refl. pronoun in various uses: To impose on oneself (trouble); to cause oneself to have (a possession, privilege, etc.); to assume, pretend to. † *to give oneself wonder*: to be astonished. *to give oneself airs*: to assume a bearing offensively or ludicrously indicative of belief in one's own superiority.

c **1500** *Melusine* xxx. 223, I gyue me grete wonder what folke they may be. **1676** tr. *Guillatiere's Voy. Athens* 5 Looking gravely, to give myself Authority [etc.]. **1704**, **1734** [see AIR *sb.* 15 b]. **1726** G. ROBERTS *4 Years Voy.* 22 Without giving myself any further Trouble. **1836** LANE *Mod. Egypt.* I. 146 She went to his shop, riding on an ass, to give herself consequence, and said [etc.]. **1843** BETHUNE *Sc. Fireside Stor.* 13 She gave herself no airs to procure it. **1875** JOWETT *Plato* (ed. 2) II. 409 We ought not to give ourselves airs. **1886** *Law Times* LXXXII. 77/2 A tribunal cannot give itself jurisdiction by erroneous findings of fact.

d. *to give of oneself*: to devote oneself unselfishly; to give one's time and energy to some specified thing.

1926 G. HUNTING *Vicarion* xiii. 222 She had come here to him that she might find a way to give of herself, her love, her loyalty, in the time of his need. **1961** R. & C. WINSTON tr. *Mann's Genesis of Novel* xi. 118, I gave too much of myself. **1964** *Bull. Amer. Library Assoc.* Jan. 49/2 I'm not sure I want to give of myself that way. *Ibid.* 52/2 People will still rise out of their fast-paced lives and give unstintingly of themselves when they are shown a worthy project.

¶**38.** *to give to reflect, think*: to furnish material for reflexion or thought. (A Gallicism.) Esp. in phr. *to give (one) furiously to think* [tr. F. *donner furieusement à penser*], to set (a person) thinking very hard or seriously; to give (one) much food for thought; to puzzle.

1890 *Globe* 7 Aug. 1/4 That pronouncement 'gives to reflect', as the French say. **1891** *Sat. Rev.* 24 Oct. 477/2 It is..likely to achieve a lasting popularity.. and to 'give to think'..to certain members of the House of Commons. **1910** W. J. LOCKE *Simon* i. 8 This gives one furiously to think. **1920** A. CHRISTIE *Mysterious Affair at Styles* xiii. 280 This attitude of his gave me furiously to think, and I was slowly forced to the conclusion that Alfred Inglethorp wanted to be arrested. **1926** H. W. FOWLER *Mod. Eng. Usage* 210/1 If writers knew..how furious is the thinking that 'give furiously to think' stirs in the average Englishman, they would leave such paltry borrowings alone for ever. **1936** 'J. TEY' *Shilling for Candles* iv. 32 That Jammy Hopkins should stay without moving for more than three consecutive minutes argued that he was being given furiously to think.

XI. 39. a. To allow a person or thing to have or take; not to withhold or withdraw; to concede, yield. *to give* (a person) *best*: to acknowledge oneself defeated by (*slang*).

1548 HALL *Chron., Hen. V*, 75 The kyng of Englande gevyng the upper hande to his father inlawe through the greate citee of Paris. *Ibid., Hen. VII*, 23 b, They never gave their enemies one daye to repose. **1583** HOLLYBAND *Campo di Fior* 377, I yealde unto thee..Without any more a doe, I give thee the victorie at this passe-time. *c* **1611** CHAPMAN *Iliad* I. 272 Atrides, give not stream to all thy power. **1687** A. LOVELL tr. *Thevenot's Trav.* III. 97 The common People give their Wives great Liberty. **1697** DRYDEN *Virg. Georg.* IV. 275 They give their Bodies due Repose at Night. **1711** W. KING tr. *Naude's Ref. Politics* iii. 121 To give a freer range to his passions. **1803** *Pic Nic* No. 3 (1806) I. 104 Give but time to this experiment, and it will work its end. **1821** SCOTT *Kenilw.* xxx, The gigantic warder..resigned his keys, and gave open way to the Goddess. **1836** E. HOWARD *R. Reefer* xxvi, If you'll give me five-and-twenty yards, I'll run you three hops and a step a hundred yards for another crown. **1848** THACKERAY *Van. Fair* ix, She said she would never give the *pas* to a tradesman's daughter. **1883** R. BUCHANAN *Love me for Ever* II. iii. 87 Give me a little time. *a* **1889** W. COLLINS *Blind Love* (1890) III. xlix. 82 Give yourself an hour to get from station to station. **1889** BOLDREWOOD *Robbery under Arms* vii, I could hardly stand for laughing, till the calf gave him best and walked. **1894** BARING-GOULD *Deserts S. France* I. 131 She is..given a long rest in the middle of the day.

†**b.** *absol. imper. give ye* = allow the remark, with your permission. *Obs.*

1662 J. CHANDLER *Van Helmont's Oriat.* To Rdr., Ye seek not the Poor, but (Give Ye) ye resemble Beggars.

†**c.** *give me myself*: let me go, leave me at liberty. *Obs.*

a **1616** BEAUM. & FL. *Valentinian* II. iii, Give me myself or, by the gods, my friend, You'll make me dangerous!

d. *to give and take*, (*a*) to exchange repartee, blows, etc.; (*b*) to make mutual allowances, concessions, or compromises. Cf. GIVE AND TAKE *sb.*

1519 W. HORMAN *Vulgaria* f. 63v A man muste somtyme gyve and somtyme take. **1594** SHAKES. *Rich. III* v. iii. 6 We must both giue and take my louing Lord. *a* **1661** FULLER *Worthies* (1662) III. 96 The King [*sc.* Henry VIII], who in this kind would give and not take, being no Good Fellow in tart Repartees, was..highly offended. **1853** T. C. HALIBURTON *Sam Slick's Wise Saws* II. xii. 300 Give and take, live and let live, that's the word. You can't do without me, for you hante got no pilot, and I can't do without you, for I want your cash. **1963** *Higher Educ.* xv. 225 in *Parl. Papers 1962–3* (Cmnd. 2154) XI. 639 The habit of informal conference and a disposition to give-and-take.

e. *give or take*: to subtract or add (a period of time, a quantity, a sum of money, etc.): an indication that the estimate is to be considered as approximate. *colloq.*

1958 'P. BRYANT' *Two Hours to Doom* 11 Estimate Lakenheath twelve thirty hours. Give or take a few minutes. **1960** 'R. SIMONS' *Frame for Murder* v. 59 The account ..[has] stayed more or less the same, give or take a few pounds. **1962** N. FREELING *Love in Amsterdam* i. 15 'What time would that have been..?' 'Don't know; about a quarter to ten maybe, give or take. Who's dead?' he joked. **1967** M. WADDELL *Otley Pursued* xii. 109 It was 6.42 by my Petticoat Lane watch, give or take ten minutes or so.

f. *I('ll) give you that*: I admit that; I concede the truth of what you say. *colloq.*

1917 [see *bone-head* s.v. BONE *sb.* 17]. **1966** *Daily Mail* 7 Nov. 4/5 He..savoured the flavour with great deliberation. 'Sort of salty mate, but tasty, I'll give you that.'

40. *intr.* To yield, give way.

a. To yield to pressure or strain.

1577 B. GOOGE *Heresbach's Husb.* II. (1586) 109 The Oliue ..will give and bende, and so will the Poplar, the Willow. **1687** A. LOVELL tr. *Thevenot's Trav.* I. 267 If that Cable had given as the other Two did, the Ship must unavoidably have been lost. **1715** LEONI *Palladio's Archit.* (1742) I. 9 If..the Walls should happen to sink, or give more on one side than the other [etc.]. **1827** *Chron.* in *Ann. Reg.* 193/1 When..the bricks were removed down nearly to the ends of the ties, these 'gave'. **1872** S. BUTLER *Erewhon* v. 32 My boots had begun to give, for I had been going on rough ground for more than three weeks. **1879** JEFFERIES *Wild Life in S. Co.* 72 The wood..'gives' a little and does not jar when struck. **1889** STEVENSON *Master of B.* ix. 240 The rail of the fence gave suddenly under his weight. **1890** *Univ. Rev.* Aug. 616 The harness of officialism..gave a little at the joints. **1890** *Tablet* 25 Oct. 650 When it begins to give and part it will be too late to cement the union. **1890** *Illustr. Lond. News* 1 Nov. 554/1 My head spun and throbbed, and my feet felt the world give under them. 1892 *Black & White* 2 Jan. 21/2 The great hayrick is giving. They're all out trying to prop it up. 1893 *Longman's Mag.* Apr. 551 The lock did not give.

b. Of a joint, the nerves: To lose tension, to become relaxed, to fail.

1892 *Field* 29 Oct. 656/2 Rendered worse than useless by his knee giving. 1897 *Pall Mall Mag.* Nov. 335 My nerves began to give.

c. (Of persons): To accommodate one's attitude *to*; (of a dress) to adjust itself *to* (the varying curves of the figure). Also, to allow free play, yield *to*. Also, to give ground, draw back.

1823 J. Badcock *Dom. Amusem.* 166 Persons..giving..to the motion of the vessel, like outside passengers by a stage-coach. 1850 Tennyson *In Mem.* liii, Dare we to this fancy give? 1866 A. Thomas *Played Out* II. ii. 40 Miss Lethbridge's habit..Fitting her splendidly, 'giving' to every curve and line of her supple figure. 1886 Rider Haggard *Solomon's Mines* xiv. 222 The Greys ceased to give.

d. To be affected by atmospheric influences; (*a*) of colours, to fade; (*b*) to deliquesce, effloresce, soften, or deteriorate, from the effect of damp; (*c*) to become damp, (appear to) exude moisture, as a stone floor after a thaw (see eve *v.*[2]); (*d*) of timber, to shrink from dryness.

(*a*) 1546 P'cess Eliz. in Ellis *Orig. Lett.* Ser. I. II. 147 From the grace of the pictur the coulers may fade by time, may giue by wether, may be spotted by chance.

(*b*) 1677 Grew *Colours Pl.* iii. §27 There are some Salts, which will not give in the least. 1707 Mortimer *Husb.* 26 Be sure before you carry your large Cocks [of hay] in, to open them once, and to spread them in the Sun, because 'tis apt to give in the Cock. 1745 Mrs. Delany *Let.* 3 Oct. in *Life & Corr.* (1861) II. 391 The damp weather made the cement give. 1890 *Standard* 9 Aug. 2/7 The wicket was in fine condition all day, and at present shows no signs of giving.

(*c*) 1590 Sir J. Smyth *Disc. Weapons* 21 Some moyst weather hath..caused the powder to give and danke. 1643 T. Goodwin *Trial Christian's Growth* 126 As we see against rainy weather, before the raine begins to fall, the stones will give, as we use to say, and grow danke. 1758 Reid tr. *Macquer's Chem.* I. 293 It will keep long without giving or calcining. 1894 'A. St. Aubyn' *Orchard Damerel* II. ix. 188 The old stones in the aisles were 'giving', as the sexton used to say in his homely way of describing mildew and damp. 1961 *Countryman* LVIII. iii. 468 'The walls are giving' does not mean that they are collapsing, but that they are moist. *fig.* 1607 Shaks. *Timon* iv. iii. 491 Flinty mankinde: whose eyes do neuer giue But thorow Lust and Laughter.

(*d*) 1627 tr. *Bacon's Life & Death* (1651) 8 Planchers of Houses, which at first lay close together but after they are dried, gave. 1633 G. Herbert *Temple, Vertue* iv, Onely a sweet and vertuous soul, Like season'd timber, never gives; But though the whole world turn to coal, Then chiefly lives.

e. Of frosty weather: To relax its severity, to become mild; to thaw.

1678 Wood *Life* 9 Dec. (O.H.S.) II. 426 Frosty, dry, and dusty..and then the weather gave, but no raine followed. 1709 Luttrell in *Collect.* (O.H.S.) II. 436 The weather began to give and the snow to melt. 1840 Spurdens *Suppl. to Forby, Give*, to thaw. 'It is beginning to give.' The frost is going. 1843 Lefevre *Life Trav. Phys.* II. ii. ix. 287 About Christmas the weather generally gives. 1895 *Times* 11 Feb. 6/3 The frost..did not 'give' at all in the last-named regions.

f. ***what gives?***: what is happening? (freq. as a question or merely as a form of greeting); so ***what gives with*** (someone or something)? = what is happening to?; what is (he, etc.) doing? (Cf. G. *was gibt's?*) *colloq.* (orig. *U.S.*).

1940 J. O'Hara *Pal Joey* 133 What gives, I asked her. 1952 S. Kauffmann *Philanderer* (1953) iv. 56 'What gives?' 'I don't know, he didn't tell me,' said Rose. 1953 F. Robb *Sea Hunters* vi. 80 George, whistle those lubbers again and ask them what gives. 1963 J. N. Harris *Weird World Wes Beattie* (1964) viii. 101 What gives with this cottage anyway? 1969 *Private Eye* 28 Mar. 14 What gives with this sheilah?

†XII. 41. In various obsolete uses, where *put* or *set* would now be used; e.g. ***to give (an) end, a period, a date, a stop to.*** Also ***to give in hand, to give fire to*** (see fire sb. 1 f).

1460–70 [see A 6 a a]. *c* 1489 Caxton *Sonnes of Aymon* xvii. 396 Reynawd..wyll not gyve noo yrens to your nevewe. *c* 1489 [see A 3 a γ]. *a* 1533 Ld. Berners *Gold. Bk. M. Aurel.* (1546) B, Tyme gyuethe ende to that suffrethe ende. 1595 [see A 8 γ]. 1617 Moryson *Itin.* iii. 253 His death gave an end to that warre in the yeere 1477. 1624 Heywood *Gunaik.* iii. 160 To give date unto that which hath..afflicted me. *a* 1641 Spelman *Sacrilege* (1698) 121 King Henry I..dying afterward without Issue Male, in the year 1135, gave a period to this Norman Family. *a* 1677 Barrow *Serm. Pleasantn. Relig.* Wks. 1687 I. 3 The imperceptible course of nature..may..give an end to our businesses and lives together. 1677 Hale *Prim. Orig. Man.* ii. i. 132 To give some stop to those Atheistical and Epicurean Opinions. 1712 J. James tr. *Le Blond's Gardening* 108 Placing..Barrels of Powder at the Foot of them, to which they give Fire, by Trains laid for that purpose.

XIII. *intr.* To have a (specified) direction.

†42. Of the sun: To direct its rays, shine. *Obs.*

1616 Surfl. & Markh. *Country Farme* 80 Her troughes may be in the ayre, and where the Sunne giueth.

43. To look, open, lead; afford a view or passage. Const. *into, off, on, on to, over, to, upon.* (A Gallicism: cf. F. *donner sur.*)

1840 T. Hook in *New Monthly Mag.* LX. 434 The back windows..to use a French phrase, give to the gardens. 1860 Dickens *Uncomm. Trav.* iii, The Refractories were picking oakum, in a small room giving on a yard. 1867 Miss Broughton *Cometh up as Flower* xxiii. (1878) 267 The verandah upon which the salon gives. 1872 Lever *Ld. Kilgobbin* xxviii. (1875) 165 Kate Kearney's room..'gave' by a window over the leads of a tower. 1872 Howells *Wedd. Journ.* 107 A narrow corridor gave into a wide festival space. 1885 *Times* (weekly ed.) 2 Oct. 17/4 No window giving on to the Street. 1889 Mrs. Lynn Linton *Thro' Long Night* I. i. vi. 83 Bed-room, dressing-room and boudoir, all gave off the first landing. *Ibid.* III. iii. xv. 268 It was the road which gave on to the highway.

XIV. In idiomatic phrases consisting of verb and object.

44. give birth to. a. To bear; bring forth. **b.** *fig.* To produce; result in.

1712 Addison *Spect.* No. 267 ¶6 Æneas's Settlement in Italy produced the Cæsars, and gave Birth to the Roman Empire. 1828 Scott *F.M. Perth* xxvi, His wife, then near the time of giving birth to an infant, fled into the forest. 1861 *Temple Bar* II. 327 His mother..dies in giving him birth. 1862 Stanley *Jew. Ch.* (1877) I. xii. 231 A fit receptacle of a nation which was to give birth to the Sacred Book of all lands.

45. give ground. a. To retire before a superior force; †*rarely* with indirect obj. **b.** *fig.* To yield; to relax effort. **†c.** To yield precedence (*obs.*).

a. 1593 Shaks. *3 Hen. VI*, i. iv. 15 And when the hardyest Warriors did retyre, Richard cry'de, Charge, and giue no foot of ground. 1640 tr. *Verdere's Rom. Rom.* i. 81 His arrivall stayed the fury of the Pagans in such sort, as they began to give him ground. *Ibid.* iii. 181 The Pagans [began] to give ground. 1709 Steele *Tatler* No. 6 ¶9 They are once again forced to give ground. 1855 Macaulay *Hist. Eng.* xxii. IV. 433 The enemy was beginning to give ground.

b. 1645 Pagitt *Heresiogr.* To Rdr., Hereupon is he persecuted, reviled, &c...he gave not ground for all this, but bore up manfully. 1705 Stanhope *Paraphr.* II. 258 Though the giving ground in such Cases be what we are apt rather to pity than to condemn. 1888 Mrs. H. Ward *R. Elsmere* xvi, As a man wavers in a wrestling match when his opponent unexpectedly gives ground.

c. 1652–62 Heylin *Cosmogr.* i. (1682) 130 Valleys of great fertility, not giving ground for fruitfulness to the best in Europe.

46. give it. a. With *dat.* or *to*: To make an attack either with blows or words. Also *colloq.*, ***to give it hot.*** **b.** *slang.* With *to*: To rob, defraud. **†c.** = *to give tongue* (see tongue) (*obs.*).

a. 1588 Shaks. *Tit. A.* iv. iii. 64 Now Maisters draw, Oh well said Lucian: Good Boy in Virgoes lap, giue it Pallas. 1612 Chapman *Widowes T.* i. C 2, Ile giue it him home. 1831 Macaulay *Lett.* 30 May, 'I am glad you put that in' [an apology for using the word *constituency*], said her ladyship [Lady Holland]. 'I was just going to give it you. It is an odious word.' 1872 *Punch* 27 Apr. 169/1 The Commander-in-Chief has given it to the offenders rather hot. 1878 *Scribner's Mag.* XVI. 191/1 Now he is giving it to him!

b. 1812 J. H. Vaux *Flash Dict., Give it to*, to rob or defraud any place or person, as, I gave it to him for his reader, I robb'd him of his pocket-book.

c. 1600 Cornwallyes *Ess.* xiv, How well Iumball gaue it in such a dry path, he hath a Nose cries one, like a Beagle, and yet a verie deepe mouth.

47. give place (const. *to*). **†a.** To give ground, yield to pressure or force (*obs.*). **b.** To quit one's place to make room (for another); to yield precedence; †*fig.* to be inferior, 'yield' to. **†c.** To yield or defer (to advice) (*obs.*). **d.** To be succeeded or superseded (by another person or thing).

[In the first two senses the phrase is a literal rendering of L. *dare locum*, Gr. τόπον διδόναι.]

a. 1382 Wyclif *Judg.* xx. 36 The which thing biholdynge the sones of Yrael ȝeuen to hem place to flee. 1413 *Pilgr. Sowle* (Caxton 1483) i. iii. 4 Right as the fletyng ayer yeuyth place to the flyght of byrdes..so was al this erthe passyble to spirites. 1559 *Mirr. Mag., Dk. Suffolk* xxii, Which must perforce geve place vnto the wave. 1582 N. Lichefield tr. *Castanheda's Conq. E. Ind.* lviii. 121 The enimies were driuen to giue place.

fig. 1382 Wyclif *Rom.* xii. 19 Gyue ȝe place to ire. 1603 Knolles *Hist. Turks* (1621) 605 Although he were glad to depart and give place to his evill fortune for a time [etc.]. 1638 J. Hayward tr. *Biondi's Erom.* 5, I am resolved to give fortune place.

b. 1382 Wyclif *Luke* xiv. 9 He comynge that clepide thee and him, seye to thee, Ȝyue place to this. *a* 1557 Ld. Vaux *Aged Lover* 24 in *Tottel's Misc.* (Arb.) 174 Limpyng age will hedge him now Where youth must geue him place. 1576 Fleming *Panopl. Epist.* 69 Giving place to none that is neere unto you for auncientnesse of acquaintaunce. 1634 Sir T. Herbert *Trav.* 91 A House and Garden of the Kings, giving place to few in Parthia. 1756–7 tr. *T. Keysler's Trav.* (1760) IV. 350 The body of Henry, which lay on the right hand, immediately moved to the left, and gave place to his imperial consort. 1871 R. Ellis tr. *Catullus* lxiv. 268 Thessaly's youth gave place to the Gods high-throned in heaven.

c. 1578 Timme *Caluine on Gen.* xv. 324 The wicked..do at no hand giue credite to his promises: but the godly..they giue place lest they stop the way to the word of God. 1633 Bp. Hall *Hard Texts, N.T.* 115 If ye had given place to that saving word of mine which hath beene delivered unto you.

d. 1555 J. Hooper in Coverdale *Lett. Mart.* (1564) 153 His enemies both of the body and soule..when death commeth they shal auoide and geue place to such ioyes as be prepared for vs in Christ. 1711 Steele *Spect.* No. 49 ¶3 These Gentlemen..give place to Men who have Business or good Sense in their Faces. 1849 Macaulay *Hist. Eng.* ii. I. 158 The liturgy gave place to the Presbyterian directory. *a* 1889 W. Collins *Blind Love* (1890) III. lx. 240 Autumn had given place to winter.

48. give rise to. To be the origin of; to produce; to result in.

1777 Sheridan *Sch. Scand.* i. i, Very trifling circumstances have often given rise to the most ingenious tales. 1798 Ferriar *Illustr. Sterne* ii. 25 The birth and education of Pantagruel evidently gave rise to those of Martinus Scriblerus. 1863 E. V. Neale *Anal. Th. & Nat.* 93 The answer to these questions gave rise to the systems of Heraclitus, Empedocles, and Anaxagoras. 1879 M. J. Guest *Lect. Hist. Eng.* xlviii. 480 His whole previous career had given rise to the gravest distrust.

49. give way.

a. Of fighting men: = *give ground.* To retreat before an advancing force; to break rank. Also *transf.* and *fig.* Const. *to.*

1413 *Pilgr. Sowle* (Caxton 1483) iv. xxx. 78 The chyuetayns haue at the moost nede of socour yeuen weye to their enemyes and made the peple proye to them. 1485 Caxton *Chas. Gt.* 193 They..made so grete bruyt that the moost hardyest of the paynyms gaf them waye. 1704–5 Atterbury *Serm.* (1726) I. 369 With how much greater Difficulty, every time that we give way, we recover our Ground. 1804 W. Tennant *Ind. Recreat.* (ed. 2) II. 383 Our troops..by some strange mismanagement gave way on the right. 1879 M. J. Guest *Lect. Hist. Eng.* lv. 567 The Guards, fighting gallantly, began to give way nevertheless.

†b. To make way; leave the way clear. In early use often ***to give the way.*** Const. *to. Obs.*

a 1533 Ld. Berners *Huon* xxxviii. 122 They gaue hym way, nor durst aproche nere hym. 1606 Holland *Suetonius* 102 He himselfe would arise up unto the said consuls and give them the way [L. *decedere via*]. 1617 Moryson *Itin.* iii. 55 The coaches comming downe from the upper parts, give the way to those that come up. 1687 Boyle *Martyrd. Theodora* vii. (1703) 90 Such sentiments..as made them with great respect give her way. 1697 Dryden *Æneid* i. 822 Scarce had he spoken, when the Cloud gave way, The Mists flew upward, and dissolv'd in day. 1828 Scott *F.M. Perth* ii, A common feeling of respect induced passengers to give way to the father and daughter.

c. To make room for; be superseded by. Const. *to.*

1713 Steele *Englishm.* No. 12 Sophistry must give way to Learning. 1852 H. Rogers *Ecl. Faith* (1853) 70 My early Christian faith has given way to doubt. 1885 M. Linskill *A Lost Son* 275 The surliness had given way to something deeper.

†d. To allow free scope, opportunity, or liberty of action *to*. Also in indirect passive, and ***to give way*** (***to*** a person) ***to do, that***, etc. *Obs.*; passing into f. and g.

a 1586 Sidney *Arcadia* i. (1633) 5 And knowing that the violence of sorrow is not at the first to be striven withall..they gave way unto it for that day and the next. 1597 Shaks. *2 Hen. IV*, v. ii. 82, I gaue bold way to my authority, And did commit you. 1605 Bacon *Adv. Learn.* i. vii. §7 Antoninus Pius..not only ceasing persecution, but giving way to the advancement of Christians. 1611 Bible *Transl. Pref.* 1 Certaine..could not be brought..to giue way to good Letters. 1631 *Star Chamb. Cases* (Camden) 15 This is not to be given way to. 1632 J. Hayward tr. *Biondi's Erom.* 133 Giving thereby rather way and encouragement to the Infante, to demand her. 1633 Hall *Hard T.* 610, I will give way to a shepheard not more foolish than wicked to arise in my Church. *a* 1657 Bradford *Plymouth Plantat.* (1856) 134 At length, after much debate of things, the Gov[r]..gave way that they should set corne every man for his owne perticuler. 1793 Burke *Corr.* (1844) IV. 143 They who, through weakness, gave way to the ill-designs of bad men [etc.]. [1818 Jas. Mill *Brit. India* v. v. II. 517 From that moment the General gave way to his spirit of dissatisfaction and complaint.]

e. Of things, material and immaterial: To yield, be dislodged, break down (under pressure or violence). †Const. *to* (*obs.*). Of the health, mental powers, etc.: To break down, fail.

1640 tr. *Verdere's Rom. Rom.* iii. 2 All the skill and courage the Marriners had were faine to give way to the violence of this tempest. 1665 Manley *Grotius' Low C. Warres* 683 Their Cannon being neither raised nor well planted, by their own weight and force were fixed, until at last the Sands giving way, they were removed. 1697 Dryden *Æneid* i. 170 The stoutest Vessel to the Storm gave way, and suck'd through loosen'd Planks the rushing Sea. 1726 G. Roberts *4 Years Voy.* 123 If any Thing gave Way, we could better mend it..by Day. 1820 W. Irving *Sketch Bk.* (1859) 163 The bashfulness of the guests soon gave way before good cheer and affability. 1849 *Tait's Mag.* XVI. 269/2 His health gave way to the attacks of disease. *Ibid.* 316/2 He rung the bell till the rope gave way. 1860 Tyndall *Glac.* i. xvi. 116 Once upon a steep hard slope Bennen's footing gave way. 1877 Miss Yonge *Cameos* Ser. iii. xxvii. 264 His strength gave way under repeated wounds. 1885 Sir J. Hannen in *Law Rep.* 10 Prob. Div. 90 Her health evidently gave way soon after her marriage. 1889 Mrs. Kennard *Landing a Prize* III. ii. 33 Neither knot nor gut gave way under the tremendous strain. 1889 M. Caird *Wing Azrael* ii. xvi. 19 Her voice shook and gave way at the last word.

f. Of persons: To yield under solicitation or insistence; to make concessions; to defer to the will of another. Const. *to.*

1758 Ld. Kames in *Life W. Cullen* (1832) I. 601 If you give way to every patient..you will never stir from Edinburgh. 1821 J. W. Croker in *Diary* 30 July (1884), When he gives way..he does it with so bad a grace [etc.]. 1874 Green *Short Hist.* iii. §2. 120 At the very moment of apparent triumph John suddenly gave way. 1875 Jowett *Plato* (ed. 2) III. 132 He gives way to a sentiment which in his own case he would control.

g. To abandon oneself *to* (anger, grief, etc.).

[1818: see 49 d.] 1822 Scott *Nigel* xxxvi, Here the dame was..inclined to give way to a passion of tears. 1880 McCarthy *Own Times* III. xxxii. 70 He never gave way either to anger or alarm. 1891 *Strand Mag.* May 552/2 Don't give way to despair so quickly.

h. To allow one's self-control or fortitude to be broken down.

1879 Miss Braddon *Vixen* III. 150 'The fact is, she *gives way* too much', exclaimed active little Mrs. Scobel, who had never *given way* in her life. 1879 Edna Lyall *Won by Waiting* xvii, Her old courage kept her from quite giving way.

i. Of stocks and shares: To fall in price.

1883 *Manch. Exam.* 30 Nov. 4/1 Mexican Ordinary at the morning was $1\frac{1}{4}$ up, but it afterwards gave way, the final price being $65\frac{1}{2}$ ex. div.

j. *Naut.* (See quot. 1867.)

1802 *Trans. Soc. Arts* XX. 327 The steersman should.. encourage the rowers to give way. 1840 R. H. DANA *Bef. Mast* xxv. 79 Give way boys! Give way! Lay out on your oars, and long stroke! 1867 SMYTH *Sailor's Word-bk.*, *Give way*, the order to a boat's crew to renew rowing, or to increase their exertions if they were already rowing. To hang on the oars. 1883 STEVENSON *Treas. Isl.* xvi. 134 The next moment..we had shoved off and given way.

XV. Used *intr.* with prepositions in specialized senses. (See also senses 14 d and 43.)

†**50. give against** ——. To impinge against; to attack, assault, run counter to. *Obs.*

1646 EARL MONM. tr. *Biondi's Civill Warres Eng.* II. vi.-ix. 152 They gave against the Standard, slew Sir William Brandon, the Standard-bearer. 1650 —— tr. *Senault's Man become Guilty* 20 Christian Religion may truly boast, that all her Maxims are Paradoxes, which agreeing with truth, give against humane reason. *Ibid.* 356 He gives against Gods Providence..who obeys those creatures which are inferiour to him. *Ibid.* 374 It was very just..that they which fill our Sailes should make our designes give against the rocks.

†**51. give into** ——. [After F. *donner dans*.] To enter into, give adhesion to, fall in with (an idea, project, etc.); to engage deeply in (a business); to fall into (an error, a snare). Now superseded by *give in to* (see 59 b). *Obs.*

1692 LOCKE *Toleration* III. ii. 69, I began presently to give into your method. 1702 ROWE *Tamerl.* Ded., At so Critical a Juncture as this is..your Lordship ought to give intirely into those Public Affairs which at this time seem to Demand you. 1705 ADDISON *Italy* 96 The Venetians, who are naturally Grave, love to give into the Follies and Entertainments of such Seasons. 1732 BERKELEY *Alciphr.* VI. §15 Some things are so manifestly absurd that no authority shall make me give into them. 1742 RICHARDSON *Pamela* III. 40 So that the poor Girl, divided between her Inclination for him, and her Duty to her designing Mother, gave into the Plot upon him. 1761 HUME *Hist. Eng.* II. xxv. 94 They gave into the snare prepared for them. *a* 1797 H. WALPOLE *Mem. Geo. II*, I. 57 Mr. Pitt gave strongly into a Parliamentary Inquiry. 1825 T. JEFFERSON *Autobiog.* Wks. 1859 I. 6 Marshall has given into this error. 1846 MCCULLOCH *Acc. Brit. Empire* (1854) II. 35 The country bankers gave into the infatuation.

XVI. Idiomatically combined with adverbs.

52. give about.

†**a.** *trans.* To encompass; surround. [translating L. *circumdare*.] *Obs.*

1382 WYCLIF *Ezek.* iv. 8 Loo! y ȝaue about [or cumpasside] thee with boondis. 1483 *Cath. Angl.* 155/1 To Giffe abowtte, *circumdare, circumstipare*.

b. To distribute, circulate (writings); to spread (a rumour).

a 1715 BURNET *Own Time* II. 348 He [Ferguson] gave about most of the pamphlets writ of that side: and with some he passed for the author of them. 1724 SWIFT *Drapier's Lett.* Wks. 1755 V. II. 74 It hath been given about for several days past, that somebody in England empowered a second somebody [etc.].

53. give again.

a. *trans.* To give back, restore; to give in return. Also † *to give againward*.

a 1300 *Cursor M.* 16476 Here i yeld yow yur mone, ges me a-gain mi war. *c* 1400 A. DAVY *Dreams* 19 No strook ne ȝaf he aȝeinward. 1483 *Cath. Angl.* 155/1 To Gife a-gayne, *redonare*. 1530 PALSGR. 566/2, I gyve agayne,..*je rens*.

b. *intr.* To soften; to yield. *lit.* and *fig.* Cf. 40 d, e. *Obs.* exc. *dial.*

1617 MORYSON *Itin.* III. 80 Minerall Salt..is..lesse subject to giving againe, then our boiled salt. 1623 MARKHAM *Country Contentm.* vii. 215 (Vnlesse the place where it is kept be like a Hot-house) it will so danke and give againe, that it will be little better then raw Malt. 1855 [see A 8 γ]. 1869 *Lonsdale Gloss.*, *Give again*, to thaw, to yield, of a frost; to relax through damp or fermentation. 1877 *Holderness Gloss.* s.v., Bread is said to give-ageean when it loses its pristine crispness, and becomes soft and moist.

54. give away.

a. *trans.* To alienate from oneself by gift; to dispose of as a present, as alms, or in any way gratuitously. Also (usu. in pa. pple.) ***given away with a pound of tea***: (of an article, usually something of little value) given, or as if given, free with a pound of tea; esp. in derisive use.

a 1400 *Sir Perc.* 1983 Thou hase giffene thi part of bothe away. *a* 1586 SIDNEY *Arcadia* II. (1633) 169 The more he gat, the more still he shewed that he (as it were) gave away to his new mistresse, when he betrayed his promises to the former. 1650 JER. TAYLOR *Holy Living* iv. §3 Charity 249 Love gives away all things that so he may advance the interest of the beloved person. [1709 ATTERBURY *Serm.* (1726) II. 227 Whatsoever we employ in Charitable Uses, during our Lives, is given away from ourselves; what we bequeath at our Death is given from others only.] 1831 BREWSTER *Newton* (1855) II. xxvii. 411 He used to remark that they who gave away nothing till they died, never gave at all. 1888 MRS. RIDDELL *Nun's Curse* II. iv. 89 He gave away most of his income. *a* 1899 *Mod.* The prices realised were wretchedly low; the goods were almost given away. 1890 *Punch* 28 June 306/2 But Shopman Salisbury, why should he stand And advertise goods of his master J. B. As 'Given away with a Pound of Tea'? 1937 D. L. SAYERS *Busman's Honeymoon* xix. 314 They would not have it if it were given away with a pound of tea. 1958 *Times* 4 Dec. 13/4 It used to fall to the lot of some hapless object to be 'given away with a pound of tea'. 1966 'L. LANE' *ABZ of Scouse* 40 *Given away wid a pound of tea*, said of something considered tawdry and worthless such as a very cheap engagement-ring.

b. To perform the ceremony of handing over (a bride) to the bridegroom at a marriage.

1719 DE FOE *Crusoe* II. vii, I..gave her away. 1826 LAMB *Elia* Ser. II. *Fallacies* xiii, The bride..presented to him as her father—the gentleman that was to give her away. 1879 MISS YONGE *Cameos* Ser. IV. xx. 215 Mary was given away ..by the Marquis of Winchester.

†**c.** To sacrifice (another's interests or rights).

1548 HALL *Chron., Hen. VI*, 155 b, Yea, said the capitain, so that you geve away no mannes right, but his, whose aucthoritie you have. 1604 SHAKS. *Oth.* III. iii. 28 Be merry Cassio, For thy Solicitor shall rather dye, Then giue thy cause away. 1711 C'TESS DORCHESTER in *15th Rep. Hist. MSS. Comm.* App. IV. 681 Represent to her Majesty that this would be giving away my Lord's rank, who is an older Lieutenant General than Lord Orkney.

d. orig. *U.S. slang.* To betray, expose (oneself, another person) to detection or ridicule; to let slip (a secret), esp. through carelessness or stupidity. See also SHOW *sb.*[1] 16.

1878 *Scribner's Mag.* XV. 812/1 Ye went back on her, and shook her, and played off on her, and gave her away—dead away! 1883 F. M. CRAWFORD *Dr. Claudius* ii, I thought he would give himself away. 1889 *Answers* 20 Apr. 326 My closely cropped hair, however, 'gave me away'. 1891 *Boston* (Mass.) *Jrnl.* 20 Feb. 4/1 General Sherman would not be told a secret. He said he would give it away to the first person he met. 1914 G. B. SHAW *Pygmalion* (1916) I. 114 They want to drop Kentish Town; but they give themselves away every time they open their mouths. 1922 D. H. LAWRENCE *England, my England* 132 He'd burn your letters for fear they'd give him away.

e. To distribute.

1889 PHILIPS & WILLS *Fatal Phryne* I. iii. 59 Then the old vicaire gave away the prizes. 1891 *Cornh. Mag.* Oct. 393 She gives away tracts, addresses meetings.

¶ **f.** *intr.* Misused for *give way* (? = *give a way*). Latterly *U.S.*

1611 SPEED *Hist. Gt. Brit.* IX. xii. §96. 579 The whole power of the French gaue away, and sought to saue it selfe by flight. 1747 SARAH FIELDING *David Simple* (1752) I. 37, I have continually languished for Impossibilities, and given away to Desires as madly as if [etc.]. 1816 U. BROWN *Jrnl.* in *Maryland Hist. Mag.* (1916) XI. 232, I was Just going to pay the Chain carriers & dismiss them, James gave away, Although full 6 feet high & well made. 1833 H. BARNARD *Ibid.* (1918) XIII. 305 He spoke about an hour and a half, and gave away on account of a sudden dizziness in his head and failure of voice. 1893 *Boston* (Mass.) *Weekly Transcript* 27 Jan. 4/2 His death is as though one of the sheet anchors of society had suddenly given away. 1903 R. T. ELY *Stud. Evol. Industr. Soc.* 42 The cattle-raising frontier has given away continually to higher stages.

g. *trans.* To give up, resign, surrender. *rare.*

1850 TENNYSON *In Mem.* iv. 1 To Sleep I give my powers away.

h. Esp. ***to give it away***. To abandon, give up, stop. *Austral. slang.*

1949 L. GLASSOP *Lucky Palmer* iii. 37 It's about time you mugs woke up to yourself. You're not in the race to get in without a ticket. Why don't you give the game away? 1950 'N. SHUTE' *Town like Alice* v. 148 'I've changed my mind,' he said. 'I'm going to give it away... I won't be writing any letter.' 1955 J. CLEARY *Justin Bayard* v. 72 When I spoke to you.., you didn't say you'd given the idea away. 1961 P. WHITE *Riders in Chariot* ix. 260 He was at that time driving a truck for a firewood contractor, though he was thinking of giving it away and starting a line in poultry manure. 1968 D. IRELAND *Chantic Bird* iii. 28, I only hit him a few times, then I gave it away for the night.

55. give back.

a. *trans.* (See simple senses and BACK.) To restore; to surrender again; to reciprocate; to reflect, to echo, etc.

a 1586 SIDNEY *Arcadia* II. (1633) 142 With that he gave her back the paper. 1601 SHAKS. *Twel. N.* IV. iii. 18 Take, and giue backe affayres. 1709 PRIOR *Despairing Sheph.*, He gave 'em back their friendly Tears, He sigh'd, but wou'd not speak. *a* 1732 ATTERBURY *Serm.* (J.), 'Till their vices perhaps give back all those advantages which their victories procured. 1823 *Douglas, or Field of Otterburn* I. xi 146 [He] defied my threats, and gave back my reproaches. 1831 FR. A. KEMBLE in *Rec. of Girlhood* (1878) II. ix. 249 It is the still, deep, placid element that gives back the images. 1889 J. MASTERMAN *Scotts of Bestminster* II. viii. 43 The sandy tracks gave back no rumble.

†**b.** *intr.* To retreat, fall back. *Obs.* or *arch.*

1548 HALL *Chron., Edw. IV*, 218 By reason of whiche succors, kyng Edwardes parte gaue a litle backe. 1597 DANIEL *Civ. Wars* III. lxxv, Now backe he giues, then rushes-on amaine. 1678 BUNYAN *Pilgr.* I. 108 So they [Fiends] gave back, and came no farther. 1814 *Theodora* IV. ii, Give back—make way—Room for the prisoner's witness. 1870 MORRIS *Earthly Par.* II. III. 484 Slowly then Did he give back face foremost from the men.

†**c.** Of a surface: To recede. *Obs.*

1723 tr. *Le Clerc's Archit.* I. 86 The Entablature is sometimes made to give back or retreat a little between the Columns.

†**d.** To yield to pressure. *Obs.*

1674 N. FAIRFAX *Bulk & Selv.* 71 As if he should thrust it against some hard body at rest, of too stout a withstanding to yield way or give back. 1678 BUNYAN *Pilgr.* I. 185 Christian..began to try at the Dungion door, whose bolt (as he turned the Key) gave back.

†**56. give by.** *intr.* To stand aside. *Obs.*

1633 MARMION *Fine Comp.* v. i, Give by Crochet, till I question them.

57. give down. *trans.* Of a cow; To let flow (milk). Also *absol.*

1699 DRYDEN *Ovid's Met.* xv. Fables (1700) 509 And daily to give down the Milk she bred, A Tribute for the Grass on which she fed. 1847 MARRYAT *Childr. N. Forest* vi, In the course of ten days she gave down her milk. 1878 *Scribner's Mag.* XV. 382 Give down! Give down—my crumpled brown!

58. give forth.

†**a.** *trans.* To offer; to hold out. *Obs.*

1584 R. SCOT *Discov. Witchcr.* III. i. 40 The diuell giueth foorth his hand.

b. To emit.

a 1586 SIDNEY *Arcadia* II. (1633) 122 All the sparkes of vertue..were so blown to giue forth their vttermost heat. 1859 GEO. ELIOT *A. Bede* 81 We do not hear that Memnon's statue gave forth its melody at all under the rushing of the mightiest wind. 1878 *Scribner's Mag.* XVI. 510/2 The fields ..give forth an odor of spring. 1886 ADEL. SERGEANT *No Saint* II. i. 15 An owl gave forth..a long, weird, melancholy note.

c. To spread abroad, publish; to report, rumour.

1611 BIBLE *Transl. Pref.* 1 He gaue foorth, that hee had not seene any profit to come by any Synode. *a* 1627 HAYWARD *Edw. VI* (1630) 84 Soone after it was giuen forth, and beleiued by many that the King was dead. 1629 BRENT *Counc. Trent* 774 By this he was forced to giue foorth his Oration, and sent a copie of it to Rome [etc.]. 1727 OLDMIXON *Clarendon* 272 It was given forth to be by Commission from the King, and there is great reason to suspect it. 1879 M. J. GUEST *Lect. Hist. Eng.* xlii. 430 The king gave forth a proclamation. 1880 FOWLER *Locke* iv. 59 Locke..then gave forth a series of works in rapid succession.

59. give in.

a. *intr.* To yield; to give up the contest; to acknowledge oneself beaten; *occas.* (*colloq.*) to admit under pressure of argument (*that*).

1616 S. WARD *Coale from the Altar* (1627) 16 They tire, giue in, and end in the flesh. *a* 1627 HAYWARD *Edw. VI* (1630) 32 The charge was giuen with so well gouerned fury, that the left corner of the Scots battalion was enforced to giue in. 1648 JENKYN *Blind Guide* iii. 57 You give in..and shew your self..a founder'd disputant. 1805 *Sporting Mag.* XXVI. 56 According to the boxing phrase, [he] shewed the white feather and gave in. 1873 MRS. OLIPHANT *Innocent* II. ii. 36 'You won't give in?' said Frederick. 'You are just like all women. You will never allow you are in the wrong.' 1877 M. COLLINS *Yng. Musgrave* I. xv. 264 The squire won't give in he owns them. 1890 DOYLE *Firm of Girdlestone* xxiii. 262 Nothing..would..bring her to give in upon that point.

b. To yield *to* (a habit, fashion, opinion, or person). [Probably originated by a false analysis of *give into* (see 51) = F. *donner dans*. (Most of our examples of *give into* appear in later edd. as *give in to*.)]

1793 T. JEFFERSON *Writ.* (1830) IV. 483 So far from giving in to this opinion..he was clear the debt was growing on us. 1845–6 TRENCH *Huls. Lect.* Ser. II. i. 160 No doubt there is a temptation to give in to this. 1873 M. COLLINS *Squire Silchester's Whim* I. x. 138 You advise me to give in to Louisa on this point? 1882 W. BLADES *Caxton* 87 Caxton never gave in to the new-fangled ideas of printers about the advantage of title-pages to books.

c. To fail, die off.

1840 *Jrnl. R. Agric. Soc.* I. III. 288 These plants 'gave in': and hardly a cane three feet high was left in the following year.

†**d.** To intervene. Also, to rush into conflict. *Obs.*

1610 HEALEY *Vives Comm. St. Aug. Citie of God* (1620) 116 In the midst of the fight the women gaue in betwixt the battells. 1640 tr. *Verdere's Rom. Rom.* I. 139 The gallant Pagan..gave in upon them with the Giants, hoping to break them. 1641 EARL MONMOUTH tr. *Biondi's Civill Warres* I. iv.-v. 159 Fearing..that, if new troopes of the enemy should come up, the enterprise would bee the more difficult, hee resolutely gave in amongst them.

e. *trans.* To hand in, to deliver (an account, return, etc.) to the person officially appointed to receive it. ***to give in one's adhesion to***: to notify formally one's acceptance of (principles, etc.). †Also, to deliver (a thrust); to prefer (an accusation).

1602 MARSTON *Ant. & Mel.* II. Wks. 1856 I. 27 Pray you give in an epithite for love. 1678 BUNYAN *Pilgr.* (1875) 57 The third..gave him a Roll with a Seal upon it, which he bid him look on as he ran, and that he should give it in at the Cœlestial Gate. 1688 BURNET *Lett. Italy* 104 Some Accusations were given in to the Inquisitors against him. 1692 SIR W. HOPE *Fencing Master* 4 The figures giving in the thrust are Paried by the figures opposite to them. 1722 DE FOE *Plague* (1884) 132 The..Officers did not give in a full Account. 1879 MISS YONGE *Cameos* Ser. IV. x. 118 The Scots gave in their adherence to the peace of Crespy. 1890 *Standard* 5 Nov. 5/1 The formula to which Mr. Gladstone bids us believe they have given in their adhesion. *Mod.* Names of competitors must be given in before the end of the month.

f. To bestow in addition.

1886 MRS. C. PRAED *Miss Jacobsen's Chance* I. viii. 157 Don't be led away by that professional manner of his. It's the regulation thing, given in gratis with the prescription.

g. Of a pugilist: To droop (the head).

1814 *Sporting Mag.* XLIV. 240 Donnelly shewed evident symptoms of weakness, and gave his head in.

60. give off.

†**a.** *trans.* To relinquish; to cease, leave off. Sometimes with *inf.* as object. *Obs.*

1595 SHAKS. *John* v. i. 27 Did not the Prophet Say, that before Ascension day at noone, My Crowne I should giue off? 1613 WITHER *Satyr. Ess.* (1615) 232 But yet I must not heere giue off to speake, To tell men wherein I haue found them weake. 1649 WOOD *Life* (O.H.S.) I. 151 A. Wood's mother..being much out of purse..she gave off house-keeping. 1697 R. PEIRCE *Bath Mem.* II. viii. 375 He was perswaded to give off Riding. 1729 STACKHOUSE *Body Divin.* (1776) II. IV. i. §2 The necessity of giving off all intercourse with him.

†**b.** *intr.* To cease; to withdraw, quit the field.

1606 SHAKS. *Ant. & Cl.* IV. iii. 23 Follow the noyse so farre as we haue quarter. Let's see how it will giue off. 1655 STANLEY *Hist. Philos.* III. (1701) 119/2 Diodorus without acting any thing memorable, gave off safe. 1692 LOCKE *Educ.* §112 It would be kept from being too much, if we gave off as soon as we perceiv'd that it reach'd the mind.

c. *trans.* To emit, throw off.

1839 *Jrnl. R. Agric. Soc.* I. II. 192 They gave off their moisture to the air. **1861** *Temple Bar* I. 260 These gases are given off very readily. **1878** HUXLEY *Physiogr.* 67 Every piece of open water..is constantly giving off vapour.

d. To send off as a branch.

1831 R. KNOX *Cloquet's Anat.* 681 Near its origin, this artery gives off several branches to the scaleni muscles. **1849** *Jrnl. R. Agric. Soc.* X. II. 580 Arteries..give off many branches. **1870** ROLLESTON *Anim. Life* 132 The paired nerves are given off very close to each other.

61. give on. † **a.** *intr.* To make an assault. *Obs.*

c **1611** CHAPMAN *Iliad* XVII. 230 The Troians first gaue on. **1646** EARL MONMOUTH tr. *Biondi's Civill Warres* II. vi.-ix. 152 With Cheerefull countenance he gave on upon the Enemy, and was as cheerefully followed by his men. **1666** WALLER *Instr. to Paint.* 12 Where he Gives on, disposing of their Fates, Terror and Death on His loud Cannon waits. **1667** DRYDEN *Ann. Mirab.* cclxxx, He saw the Town's one half in rubbish lie And eager flames give [*ed.* 2. (1688) drive] on to storm the rest.

b. = CONTANGO *v.*

1928 [see CONTANGO *v.*]. **1928** *Morning Post* 19 Nov., He will approach a fellow-member in the House, and say that he wishes to give on 50 shares.

62. give out.

a. *trans.* To utter, publish; to announce, proclaim, report. ***to give (it) out***: to profess, give it to be believed *that*. Also, ***to give (a person) out*** to be (so and so), and *absol.*

c **1340** *Cursor M.* 29518 (Cott. Galba) And þat cursyng vnlawful es..þe whilk es gifen out over tyte, with-owten ani right respite. **1481** CAXTON *Reynard* (Arb.) 113 And thenne by goddes grace I shal yeue out the sentence and Iugement. **1593** ABP. BANCROFT *Daung. Posit.* I. vi. 20 They gaue it out ..that some were licentious. **1605** SHAKS. *Macb.* v. viii. 8 Thou bloodier Villaine Then tearmes can giue thee out. *a* **1610** HEALEY *Theophrastus* (1636) 27 Hee gives himselfe out to bee Generall of the..knights of the Post. **1688** BURNET *Lett. Italy* 23 His Followers were given out to be Hereticks. **1726** *Adv. Capt. R. Boyle* 9 My Master gave out to my Mistress that he should be oblig'd to go..to look after some Goods. **1748** *Anson's Voy.* III. viii. 370 He gave out at Macao, that he was bound to Batavia. **1879** M. J. GUEST *Lect. Hist. Eng.* xxxvii. 374 Some gave themselves out as 'poor scholars'. **1884** *Manch. Exam.* 7 June 4/7 It was given out that Germany and Austria had the same policy in Europe. **1889** 'J. S. WINTER' *Mrs. Bob* II. xii. 177 Not quite so young as she gives out. **1892** *Chamb. Jrnl.* 7 May 303/2 The factory clock..gave out the hour of three.

b. To announce (a hymn) to be sung; to read out (the words) for the congregation to sing; †also (see quot. 1825).

1712 STEELE *Spect.* No. 503 ¶2 When the psalm was given out, her voice was distinguished above all the rest. **1825** DANNELEY *Encycl. Mus.*, *Give out the Psalm or Hymn Tune* is to perform upon the organ the tune once over..for the purpose of enabling the congregation to join..in the singing of the psalms and hymns. **1887** BARING-GOULD *Gaverocks* II. xxv. 51 The clerk in church..gave out the psalm.

c. To send forth, emit; to cause to be sent forth. †Also, to put forth, utter (prayers).

1450–1530 *Myrr. our Ladye* 321 O Mary flowre of vyrgyns as rose or lyly, gyue oute prayers to thy sonne for the helthe of crysten people. **1626** BACON *Sylva* §388 In Orenges..the Nipping of their Rinde giueth out their Smell more. **1799** SIR H. DAVY in T. Beddoes *Contrib. Phys. & Med. Knowledge* 153 Dr. Ingenhouz discovered that vegetables give out vital air, when exposed to the solar light in contact with water. **1861** *Temple Bar* III. 178 The gold gave out its red glow. **1884** *Illustr. Lond. News* 20 Dec. 606/2 It [the explosive apparatus] fell..making a tremendous noise, giving out a huge flash of fire. **1890** *Ibid.* 26 Apr. 530/1 The carbonic-acid gas and other waste matters you give out with each breath.

d. To issue; to distribute.

1710 STEELE *Tatler* No. 189 ¶3 Write down what you give out to your Landress, and what she brings Home again. **1724** DE FOE *Mem. Cavalier* (1840) 163 The king gave out arms to them. **1870** tr. *Erckmann-Chatrian's Waterloo* 160 At the end of twenty minutes the advance money was given out. **1887** BARING-GOULD *Gaverocks* II. xxxiii. 183 Rose had the key of the storeroom, but forgot to give out supplies.

e. *intr.* Of persons: To desist (in later use, to desist through exhaustion of strength or patience). Of an implement, a limb, a machine, etc.: To break down, get out of order, fail. Of a supply: To run short, come to an end.

1523 FITZHERB. *Husb.* §2 Those plowes gyue out to sodemly, and therfore they be the worse, to drawe. **1629** H. BURTON *Babel no Bethel* 7 [He] is willing rather to play small play, then to giue out. **1729** SWIFT *Grand Quest.*, Madam, I always believ'd you so stout, That for twenty denials you would not give out. **1740** tr. *De Mouhy's Fort. Country Maid* (1741) II. 170 When a Man is agreeably engaged, he can't always give out at Pleasure: instead of one [glass], he drank several. **1815** *Sporting Mag.* XLV. 161 The first in a lark, but the last to give out. **1856** OLMSTED *Slave States* 25 A new leader took the place of the old man, when his breath gave out. **1861** W. H. RUSSELL in *Times* 24 Sept., Tea, coffee, and clothing are nearly exhausted, or have, as the American phrase has it, 'given out'. **1875** LOWELL *Wks.* (1890) IV. 280 Even the laborious Selden, who wrote annotations on it [the 'Polyolbion']..gave out at the end of the eighteenth book. **1878** *Scribner's Mag.* XV. 635/1 His strength gave out more than once. **1882** EDNA LYALL *Donovan* xxiv, His eyes have given out, so he won't go up this term. **1890** *Lippincott's Mag.* Feb. 210 Our powder gave out. **1890** *Sat. Rev.* 9 Aug. 158/1 The Ruby's engines gave out for a time. **1893** *Surrey Gloss.* s.v., His leg gives out; he's troubled to get about. **1895** *Daily News* 9 Feb. 5/3 They are threatened with one great danger. Before spring their finances may give out.

63. give over.

a. *trans.* To leave off, finish, cease from (an action); to give up, abandon (an attempt, a habit, a mode of life). †Also with *infin.* as obj.

c **1325** *Poem times Edw. II* (Percy Soc.) xlvii, Pryde and covetise Gyveth over al jugement, And turneth lawes up and down. **1542** UDALL *Erasm. Apoph.* 344 b, Certain persones ..saiyng that Demades had now geuen ouer to bee suche an haine, as he had been in tyme past. **1550** CROWLEY *Last Trump.* 489 Geue over all thy tippillyng. **1577** HARRISON *England* II. v. (1877) I. 111 Giuing over in these daies to mainteine such pompous vanitie. **1583** STUBBES *Anat. Abus.* II. (1882) 93 This man..ought not at any hand to giue over his calling, but to perseuere in the same to the end. **1600** SHAKS. *A. Y. L.* I. ii. 190 We pray you for your owne sake to embrace your own safetie and giue ouer this attempt. **1603** KNOLLES *Hist. Turks* (1638) 23 Neither did the Turks thus oppressed, giue it ouer, but..fought it out with inuincible courage. **1636** BRATHWAIT *Lives Rom. Emp.* 161 Why then give over to be Emperour? **1645** BOATE *Ireland's Nat. Hist.* (1652) 98 Before we give over this discours of Lime, we shall adde [etc.]. **1688** BURNET *Lett. Italy* 38 It was time for people to give over going to Confession. **1708** —— *Lett.* (ed. 3) 251 Before I give over writing concerning this Place [etc.]. **1711** ADDISON *Spect.* No. 62 ¶5 When he resolves to give over his Passion, he tells us that one burnt like him for ever dreads the Fire. **1720** MRS. MANLEY *Power of Love* (1741) 135 She rested in this conceit 'till the King gave over play. **1801** A. RANKEN *Hist. France* I. 345 Their fleet being almost annihilated, they gave over their piracies. **1842** J. H. NEWMAN *Eccl. Miracles* (1843) 188 One thing then they did: they gave over the contest. **1889** MRS. OLIPHANT *Poor Gentlem.* II. xii. 218, I know your little ways. You'll have to give them over when we're married. **1892** *Black & White* Jan. 54/2 It's time she gave over that sort of pride.

b. *absol.* or *intr.* To cease; desist, leave off. †Of a factory: To stop working.

1526 *Pilgr. Perf.* (W. de W. 1531) 23 Let hym contynue his labour, and neuer gyue ouer. **1611** BIBLE *Transl. Pref.* 7 He offended the Prophet for giuing over then. **1688** in Ellis *Orig. Lett.* Ser. II. IV. 159 Last week a great Tin-work gave over, by which four hundred Tinners are out of Employ. **1741** MIDDLETON *Cicero* I. vi. 418 The assembly grew so impatient, and made such a noise and hissing, that he was forced to give over. **1746** *Exmoor Courtship* 377 (E.D.S.) Es ..wont be mullad and soulad.—Stand azide, come, gi' o'er. **1840** *Jrnl. R. Agric. Soc.* I. IV. 432 He gave over at the end of about six hours, and set to again the next morning. **1858** HAWTHORNE *Fr. & It. Jrnls.* I. 251 They ran hastily beside the carriage, but got nothing, and finally gave over.

†**c.** *trans.* To abandon, desert (a person, cause, etc.). *Obs.*

c **1477** CAXTON *Jason* 65 These knightes of grece abandonne us and gyue us ouer. **1513** DOUGLAS *Æneis* XII. xiii. 66 And now forsuyth, thy will obey sall I, And giffis owr the caus perpetualy. **1663** BUTLER *Hud.* I. ii. 506 The Cause, for which we fought and swore So boldly, shall we now give o'er?

d. To devote, resign, surrender, hand over: (*a*) with obj. a person, oneself. †Also in *pa. pple.*, 'left to oneself', abandoned by God *to* one's own evil passions.

1483 CAXTON *Gold. Leg.* 192 a/2 The chylde marcyal.. gafe hym self all ouer unto our lord Jhesu cryste. **1573** J. SANFORD *Hours Recreat.* (1576) 105, I feele yᵗ sleepe will giue me ouer to his sister. **1570–6** LAMBARDE *Peramb. Kent* (1826) 157 Men given over to beleeve illusions. *c* **1585** R. BROWNE *Answ. Cartwright* 34 The power of the word..to rebuke and giue ouer to execration. *a* **1586** SIDNEY *Arcadia* II. (1633) 113 O my Zelmane, gouerne and direct me: for I am wholly giuen ouer vnto thee. **1639** FULLER *Holy War* I. xvi. (1640) 23 Giving themselves over to pleasure. **1649** BP. HALL *Cases Consc.* (1650) 142 Should I be so farre given over, as to have my hand in blood..I should [etc.]. **1656** —— *Occas. Medit.* (1851) 6 Though I have a will of mine own; yet let me give myself over to be ruled and ordered by thy Spirit. **1701** GREW *Cosm. Sacra* III. iii. §6. 106 When the Babylonians..had given themselves over to all manner of Vice: it was time [etc.]. **1859** THACKERAY *Virgin.* xxiv, Colonel Lambert gave over the young Virginian to Mr. Wolfe's charge. **1870** ROGERS *Hist. Gleanings* Ser. II. 59 Oxford is given over to heretical depravity. **1871** R. ELLIS tr. *Catullus* xi. 17 Live on yet, still given o'er to nameless Lords. **1877** MISS YONGE *Cameos* Ser. III. x. 87 They worked up their fury against the traitor Bishop who..wanted to give them over to the Pope.

(*b*) with obj. a thing.

1481 CAXTON *Godefroy* clxxxv. 272 The turkes..were disconfyted and gaf ouer the toures. **1568** GRAFTON *Chron.* II. 107 It was of him demaunded, whether he should be slaine, or be deposed, or should voluntarily geve over the crowne? **1621** BURTON *Anat. Mel.* II. ii. IV. (1651) 272 Dioclesian..gave over his scepter, and turned gardiner. **1889** DOYLE *M. Clarke* xxi. 201 Bearing with me the small package which Sir Jacob Clancing had given over to my keeping.

e. To pronounce incurable as far as concerns the speaker. Now *rare*. (Cf. *give up*, 64 h.)

1530 PALSGR. 565/2, I geve over, as physiciens gyve over a man that they wyll no more meddle with, or as we do thynges that we have forsaken, *je habandonne*. **1619** DRAYTON *Idea* lxi, Now if thou would'st, when all haue giuen him ouer, From Death to Life, thou might'st him yet recouer. *a* **1641** SUCKLING *Fragm. Aurea* (1648) 54 Since it is lawfull for every man to practise upon them that are forsaken and given over..I will adventure to prescribe to you. *c* **1696** PRIOR *Remedy worse than Dis.*, I sent for Ratcliffe; was so ill, That other doctors gave me over. **1746** BERKELEY *2nd Let. Tar-water* §12 When patients are given over, and all known methods fail. **1820** *Examiner* No. 615 Garth being given over by an intimate medical friend. **1850** MRS. JAMESON *Leg. Monast. Ord.* (1863) 166 Who had been ill of a fever, and given over by her physician.

f. To abandon the hope of seeing, finding, overtaking, etc. Also, ***to give over for (dead, lost)***: see FOR 19 b. ? *Obs.*

1674 tr. *Martiniere's Voy. N. Countries* 66 They gave us over for lost. **1678** LADY CHAWORTH in *12th Rep. Hist. MSS. Comm.* App. v. 47 When the Doctors have given him over for dead. **1748** *Anson's Voy.* II. xiii. 274 Having seen nothing of our boat, we gave her over for lost. **1777** SHERIDAN *Sch. Scandal* v. ii, Sir Peter, you are come in good time, I promise you; for we had just given you over. **1797** COLERIDGE *Lett.* (1895) 15, I was now almost given over, the ponds, and even the river, near where I was lying, having been dragged. **1830** H. ANGELO *Remin.* I. 218 His friends.. had given him over for lost.

†**g.** To give in, yield (*to*). *Obs.*

1530 PALSGR. 565/1, I geve over, as a man dothe that is overcome, I yelde in a mate, *je succumbe*..and *je me rens*. **1568** GRAFTON *Chron.* II. 57 He..was content to geve over to the kinges request.

h. *intr.* To give way, give oneself up. *rare.*

1892 *Harper's Mag.* July 299 The big female gives over to despair.

64. give up.

a. *trans.* To resign, surrender; to hand over, part with. Const. with dat. or *to*. (*a*) with obj. a thing. †Also *ellipt.*, to yield (precedence) *to*.

1154 *O.E. Chron.* an. 1132 [He] sende efter him & dide him ȝyuen up ðe abbotrice of Burch. *a* **1400–50** *Alexander* 813 Than þai gave hym vp þe ȝerd & yolden þe realme. *a* **1533** LD. BERNERS *Huon* lix. 203 Whan Iuoryn & Galaffer saw that the towne was gyuen vp by the frenchemen they enteryd in to it. *a* **1601** ? MARSTON *Pasquil & Kath.* I. 105 But still expect and gape with hungrie lip When hee'le giue vp his gowtie stewardship. **1710** *Tatler* No. 258 ¶4, I am resolved to give up my Farm, sell my Stock and remove. **1732** BERKELEY *Alciphr.* IV. §18 This is in fact to give up the point in dispute. **1781** *Hist. Eur.* in *Ann. Reg.* 25/1 The fort was given up, and the garrison surrendered. **1800** tr. *Lagrange's Chem.* I. 214 When the nitrous gas is all decomposed, it gives up its oxygen to the pyrophorus, and burns it. **1823** *Mirror* I. 68/1 At table all gave up to Tom For handling knife or fork. **1838** LYTTON *Alice* 19 She could not give up her canaries. **1886** *Law Times Rep.* LIII. 708/1 Dr. Cox has..retired from his incumbency and given up his benefice. **1890** *Graphic* Summer No. 24/3 The moat after nine days had given up its dead.

(*b*) with obj. a person: To deliver (a fugitive, oneself) into the hands of an officer of justice, an enemy, etc.; to abandon (oneself) to a feeling, an influence. Also *refl.* to yield (to evidence, etc.).

a **1568** ASCHAM *Scholem.* I. (Arb.) 81 They geuing themselues vp to vanitie. **1599** SHAKS. *Hen. V*, IV. vi. 32 All my mother came into mine eyes, And gaue me vp to teares. **1711** ADDISON *Spect.* No. 108 ¶7 His Parents gave him up at length to his own Inventions. *Ibid.* No. 110 ¶6 Could not I give myself up to this general Testimony of Mankind, I should to the Relations of particular Persons who are now living. **1722** DE FOE *Plague* (1884) 221 They gave themselves up, and..abandon'd themselves to..Despair. **1803** *Pic Nic* No. 13 (1806) II. 210 They gave themselves up to Credulity. **1852** THACKERAY *Esmond* II. i, He went to give himself up at the prison. **1872** C. E. MAURICE *S. Langton* ii. 121 He gave himself up unhesitatingly to the guidance of Innocent.

b. To forsake, abandon, relinquish, desist from, relinquish the prospect of; to cease to have to do with (a person); to sacrifice, 'lay down' (one's life). †Also *ellipt.*, ***to give up*** (friendship) ***with***.

1558 W. TOWRSON in Hakluyt *Voy.* (1589) 129 Hauing taken out the artillerie, goods, victuals, and gold..We gaue her vp 25 degrees by north the line. **1697** COLLIER *Ess.* II. *Despair* 123 Such an Expectation..will never come to pass: Therefore I'll e'en give it up, and go and fret my self. **1712** STEELE *Spect.* No. 478 ¶2 Providence in this case makes use of the folly which we will not give up. *a* **1715** BURNET *Own Time* (1823) I. 518 He indeed pressed me to give up with Sir Robert Murray. **1748** *Anson's Voy.* III. viii. 380 They gave up the contest. **1777** SHERIDAN *Sch. Scand.* II. iii, But you say he has entirely given up Charles—never sees him, eh? **1795** *Ann. Reg.*, *Hist.* 144 They gave up all ideas of resistance. **1849** MACAULAY *Hist. Eng.* iv. I. 433 The medical attendants had given up all hope. **1851** HT. MARTINEAU *Hist. Peace* II. v. xiv. 412 Many who leaned to the Chartists before..gave them up altogether on the appearance of this symptom of the agitation. **1862** *Temple Bar* IV. 553 Match-making mammas gave him up as a bad job. **1870** ROGERS *Hist. Gleanings* Ser. II. 48 Men were ready to give up their lives rather than surrender their books. **1879** M. J. GUEST *Lect. Hist. Eng.* xliii. 435 It is very difficult to give up what we have believed from our childhood. **1885** *Law Rep.* 29 *Ch. Div.* 476 The first ground of complaint put forth in the pleadings..has been virtually given up. **1889** DOYLE *M. Clarke* xxxii. 359 It was so hopeless to clean them that I gave it up in despair. **1894** *Law Times* XCVII. 388/1 He was asked..whether he would not now be compelled to give up Sunday School work.

c. *intr.* To leave off; to cease from effort, leave off trying; to stop. Also, to succumb.

1611 SHAKS. *Cymb.* II. ii. 46 She hath bin reading late, The Tale of Tereus, heere the leaffe's turn'd downe Where Philomel gaue vp. **1714** SWIFT *Pres. St. Aff.* Wks. 1755 II. I. 209 They have been..very near giving up in despair. **1827** D. JOHNSON *Indian Field Sports* 195, I had killed about a hundred, when I thought it high time to give up, as evening was near approaching. **1852** MRS. STOWE *Uncle Tom's C.* xix, My mother gave up in despair. **1862** *Temple Bar* V. 46 Another camel gave up, and could proceed no further. **1890** *Sat. Rev.* 31 May 657/2 Unless England is so weak that she has simply to give up. **1892** *Longm. Mag.* Jan. 264 He..was engaged as accountant and collector, but lost his place because the firm gave up.

d. *trans.* To devote entirely *to*; to abandon, addict *to*. Chiefly with reflexive pron. as obj.

1604 SHAKS. *Oth.* II. iii. 322 He hath deuoted, and giuen vp himselfe to the Contemplation..of her parts and graces. **1650** JER. TAYLOR *Holy Living* iv. §1 Faith 229 To give ourselves wholly up to Christ in heart and desire. **1673** STILLINGFL. *Def. Disc. Rom. Idol.* (J.), If any be given up to believe lyes, some must be first given up to tell them. **1711** STEELE *Spect.* No. 79 ¶9, I know a Lady so given up to this sort of Devotion, that..she never misses one constant Hour of Prayer. *a* **1748** WATTS (J.), Give yourself up to some hours of leisure. **1834** T. MEDWIN *Angler in Wales* I. 36 The landlady gives herself wholly up to the promotion of his comfort. **1870** ROGERS *Hist. Gleanings* Ser. II. 149 These men gave themselves up to.. debauchery. **1883** GILMOUR *Mongols* xviii. 213 Before Buddhism came to them, they were in ignorance and darkness, given up to deeds of superstition and cruelty. **1885** MRS. LYNN LINTON *C. Kirkland* II. i. 16 Her salon was given up to table-turning. **1886** ADEL. SERGEANT *No Saint* I. xiv. 267 He gave himself up to his new faith heart and soul. **1890** *Temple Bar* Aug. 574 The forenoons.. were given up to business. **1892** *Black & White* Christm. No. 20/2 The whole ground floor was given up to the saloon.

†**e.** To deliver, render, give in (an account, etc.): to present (a petition, etc.). *Obs.*

1414 in *Rot. Parl.* IV. 22 Or the Petitions biforesaid yeven up yn writyng. **1559** SANDYS *Let. to Parker* Apr. in Strype *Ann. Ref.* (1709) I. viii. 114 They were forced.. to give up a confession of their faith. **1579** GOSSON *Sch. Abuse* (Arb.) 53 So shall you.. giue vp a good account of your stewardship. **1594** SHAKS. *Rich. III*, I. iv. 189 What lawfull Quest haue giuen their Verdict vp Vnto the frowning Iudge? **1611** BIBLE *2 Sam.* xxiv. 9 And Joab gaue vp the summe of the number of the people vnto the king. **1613** PURCHAS *Pilgrimage* (1614) 466 They.. give up these Supplications, written in the leaves of a tree. **1647** HAMMOND *Power of Keys* iv. 85 [They] have.. defamed that Christian Profession, to which they had given up their names. **1673** *Essex Papers* (Camden) I. 72 A resolution never to give up my consent to any thing that in my conscience I know to be notoriously inconvenient. **1701** SWIFT *Contests Nobles & Comm.* Miscell. (1711) 27 His Accounts were confused, and he could not then give them up. **1705** ATTERBURY *Serm.* (1726) II. 57 'Tis not hard to imagine how he may be brought to give up the clearest Evidence.

f. To emit, breathe forth; to utter (a cry). *Obs.* exc. in phr. ***to give up the ghost***: see GHOST *sb.* 1.

c **1386** CHAUCER *Knt.'s T.* 1569 It gan al the temple for to lighte; And sweete smel the ground anon vp yaf. —— *Merch. T.* 1120 Vp he yaf a roryng and a cry As dooth the mooderwhan the child shal dye. **1557** NORTH tr. *Gueuara's Diall Pr.* 231 b/2 Oftentymes they haue lost their sences, and are readye to geue vp the spirite. **1602** MARSTON *Ant. & Mel.* III. Wks. 1856 I. 37 His credit hath given up the last gaspe. **1606** —— *Sophonisba* IV. i. Ibid. 198 Now even heaven Gives up his soule amongst us. **1617** MORYSON *Itin.* I. 95 And they shew the place where the Saint gave up his last breath.

g. To divulge, reveal. †Also, to disclose the name of.

a **1625** BEAUM. & FL. *Queen Corinth* I. iii, Ile not stale them By giving up their characters. **1757** FOOTE *Author* I. Wks. 1799 I. 136, I never gave up but one author in my life, and he was dying of a consumption, so it never came to a trial. **1890** *Lippincott's Mag.* May 628 We do not give up the names of our contributors.

h. (*a*) To pronounce (a person) incurable, (a puzzle) insoluble as far as concerns the speaker. (Cf. *give over*, 63 e.) (*b*) To renounce the hope of seeing. (*c*) ***to give up for*** (*lost*), etc.: see FOR 19 b.

1589 PUTTENHAM *Eng. Poesie* III. xxiv. (Arb.) 285 The Phisitions had all giuen him vp. **1841** DICKENS *Barn. Rudge* viii, It's so late, we gave you up. **1844** J. T. HEWLETT *Parsons & W.* l, Conundrums.. invented and answered, or given up. **1861** *Temple Bar* I. 564 'When's a man not a man?'.. 'Give it up.' **1883** MRS. F. MANN *Parish Hilby* iv. 49, I wonder you troubled to come at all; we gave you up long ago. **1884** *Brit. Q. Rev.* Apr. 458 He suffered from hip-disease, and was, in fact, given up by Sir B. Brodie. **1890** *Lippincott's Mag.* Mar. 385 He.. had given himself up for lost. **1890** *Cornh. Mag.* May 469 [Their] breadwinner is at sea, 'given up' at Lloyd's.

i. With *on*: to lose one's belief or trust in (something); to forsake or abandon. *colloq.* (orig. *U.S.*).

1970 *New Yorker* 21 Nov. 48/3 When I was nineteen, I gave up on the Church. **1976** *National Observer* (U.S.) 11 Dec. 16/2 He had lost his faith, switched jobs, given up on his country's leaders. To boot, his marriage was in trouble. **1984** A. WEST *H. G. Wells* iv. 80 They were alive, but they had given up on themselves and on the possibility of a future. **1986** *Times Lit. Suppl.* 24 Jan. 76/4 It is as if he has given up on America and in so doing he has given up on grappling with the complexity of his position and allegiances.

☞ *Phrase-key.*

Give me (expressing preference), 3 c; give me myself, 39 c; give ye (= by your leave), 39 b; given *pa. pple.* (= dated) 19, (= dowered) 30, (= posited) 32; and see GIVEN *ppl. a.*; my heart gives me, it gives me, 22; the weather gives, 40 e; one would give ——, 9 c; *g* about, 52; *g* again, 53; *g* against, 50; *g* oneself airs, 37 c; *g* and bequeath, *g* and devise, 4; *g* answer, 16; *g* arms, 24; *g* one as good as he brings, 9 b; *g* at, 14 d; *g* (an) attempt, 15; *g* away, 54; *g* back, 55; *g* a back, 21; *g* (one) best, 39; *g* birth to, 44; *g* a blessing, 16; *g* a broadside, 14 c; *g* by, 56; *g* the case (for or against), 18 b; *g* one's compliments, 6 d; *g* a date (to), 41; *g* a day, 30 b; *g* down, 57; *g* (one) his due, 9 b; *g* one's ears, 9 c; *g* (an) end (to), 41; *g* (an) example, 23; *g* fire (to), 14 c, 41; *g* for (= account as), 31 b; *g* for granted, 31 c; *g* forth, 58; *g* a give, or gift, 8; *g* (one) good morning, etc., 17; *g* ground, 45; *g* a gun, 14 c; *g* one's honour, 8; *g* in, 59; *g* in charge, 7; *g* in hand, 5, 41; *g* in marriage, 5; *g* into, 43, 51; *g* into custody, into the hands of, 7; *g* it, 46; *g* it (for or against), 18 b; *g* (one) joy, 17; *g* one's kind regards, one's love, 6 d; *g* little of, 9 d; *g* one's mind to, 13; *g* a name, 30 b, 28 b; *g* nought of, 9 d; *g* off, 60; *g* on, 14 d, 43, 61; *g* on to, 43; *g* order, 16; *g* out, 62; *g* (a batsman) out, 18 b; *g* over, 63; *g* (one) his own, 9 b; *g* part, 29; *g* a period (to), 41; *g* (one) a piece of one's mind, 29; *g* place, 47; *g* the point, 14 b; *g* a price, 34; *g* rise to, 48; *g* a Roland for an Oliver, 9 b; *g* a shot, 14 c; *g* show, *g* a sign, 23; *g* a stop (to), 41; *g* the time of day, 17; *g* (one) to believe, to understand, etc., 29 c; *g* to keep, 7; *g* to lot, 30; *g* to reflect, to think, 38; *g* to the world, to the public, 29 b; *g* tribute, 10; *g* up, 64; *g* upon, 14 d, 43; *g* a volley, 14 c; *g* way, 49; *g* (oneself) wonder, 37 c; *g* one's word, 8; *g* (good or bad) words (to), 16; *g* the world, 9 c; *g* one the worse, 37.

For many other phrases, as *give* ACCOUNT (of), (the) ADVENTURE *sb.*, AIM, (the) ALARM, one's ARM, (an) ASSAULT, ATTENTION, the BAG, BATTLE, a (good, wide) BERTH *sb.* to, (a) CHARGE, the CHARGE of, CHASE, the COLD SHOULDER, CONSENT, COUNTENANCE, CREDENCE, CREDIT, the DOR, EAR, EFFECT to, (an) ENSAMPLE, EVIDENCE, an EYE to, (one's) FAITH, GATE (to), the GLEEK, the GO-BY, a GUESS, (one's) HAND(S, (one) his HEAD, HEED, LAW, LEAVE, the LIE, (a) LOOSE to, the MEETING, the MITTEN *sb.*, one's MIND to, MOUTH, NOTICE, OCCASION, OFFENCE, POINTS, PROMISE, QUARTER, the REIN(S to, the SACK, SATISFACTION, the SLIP, SUCK, THANKS, TONGUE, UTTERANCE (to), VENT, (the) VENTURE, a VISIT, the WALL, WARNING, etc., see under the different words.

give, obs. form of GYVE, IF.

giveable ('gɪvəb(ə)l), *a.* [f. GIVE *v.* + -ABLE.] Capable of yielding.

1884 *Standard* 25 Sept. 5/1 The Liberal flood which ran at that time swept away in its rush everything that was loose and givable.

give ale ('gɪveɪl). *Hist.* Also 6 **gifeale, gif ale**, 7 **gev(e)all, yev(e)all, -ale, (geavale, yeovale)**. [f. GIVE *sb.* + ALE.] An annual feast or banquet, formerly observed in some parishes in Kent, the cost being provided by money bequeathed for that purpose.

1524 *Acta Archid. Roffen.* 73 a in *Archæologia* XII. 13 Jo. Bromley, subtrahit de la gifeale xviiis. a lumine beatæ Marie apud Woldham. **16..** in Thorpe *Custumale Roffense* (1788) 41 Alsoe I will that specially my feoffees and executors see that the yeovale of St. James be kept for ever. *Ibid.* 46 Alsoe I will that the geavale of Alhallows in Hoo have one acre of land after my wifes decease to maintaine it. *Ibid.* 47 A gevall house lying at Grenehill prout wardens and the brethren of the gevall. **1796** *Archæologia* XII. 13 The giveales.. were the legacies of individuals, and from that circumstance entirely gratuitous.

give and take, *sb.* [See GIVE *v.*]

1. *Sporting.* Used *attrib.* **a.** In ***give and take plate***, a prize for a race in which the horses which exceed a standard height carry more, and those which fall short of it less, than the standard weight. **b.** In various connexions, implying the alternation of favourable and unfavourable conditions.

1769 *St. James's Chron.* 12–15 Aug. 2/3 Will be run for on Huish Downs.. A Free Plate of 50*l.* Give and Take, by any Horse, Mare, or Gelding. **1776** MRS. J. HARRIS in *Lett. 1st Earl Malmesbury* (1870) I. 348 Two races again, one as usual for the Give-and-take plate. **1814** *Sporting Mag.* XLIV. 260 Give-and-take plates were then all the vogue. **1823** 'JON BEE' *Dict. Turf, Give and take*—plates, turf-weight according to inches; the standard being 9 stone for 14 hands, but carrying 14 oz. extra for every eighth of an inch above, and allowing the same for every eighth less: thus 12 hands would carry 5 stone, 15 hands 11 stone. **1856** WHYTE MELVILLE *Kate Cov.* xv, I indulged them [the ponies] with a good strong 'give and take' pull. **1887** HISSEY *Holiday on Road* 320 Hard continuous climbing is.. more fatiguing to horses than double the distance of equally hilly but give-and-take ground. **1891** *Field* 7 Mar. 346/3 [Coursing] A give-and-take course of fair length followed.

2. The practice of mutual yielding, making allowances, or concessions; compromise, exchange of equivalents.

1778 F. BURNEY *Evelina* I. xxv. 207 Give and Take is fair in all nations. **1816** *Remarks Eng. Mann.* 62 In short we do not act in foreign countries on the system, (to use a familiar phrase), of 'give and take'. **1855** S. HERBERT in Ld. Malmesbury *Mem. Ex-Minister* (1884) II. 40 Mutual forbearance and much give-and-take. **1890** *Spectator* 25 Jan., Surely there is room here for a little give-and-take.

attrib. *a* **1817** JANE AUSTEN *Persuasion* (1818) III. xi. 232 So unlike the usual style of give-and-take invitations, and dinners of formality and display. **1844** *Fraser's Mag.* XXX. 125/1 There must be.. more of the give-and-take system in legislation. **1860** *All Year Round* No. 65. 346 A speckled thrush pulling a worm out of the lawn.. with a give and take, pull-baker pull-devil principle. **1897** *Argus* (Melbourne) 1 Mar. 5/4 Representatives.. ought to go into council in a give-and-take spirit.

3. Exchange of talk, esp. of repartee, jest, or raillery.

1870 A. W. WARD tr. *Curtius' Hist. Greece* (1873) I. II. i. 205 Men learnt the give-and-take of Spartan speech. **1885** L. STEPHEN in *Dict. Nat. Biog.* I. 125/2 Addison's sensitive modesty disqualified him for the rough give-and-take of mixed society. **1894** *Review of Rev.* Aug. 166 An amount of give and take, sharp exchange of personalities.. that [etc.].

attrib. **1837** T. HOOK *Jack Brag* xv, In the every-day give-and-take conversation of the best society. **1848** DICKENS *Dombey* ii, In their matrimonial bickerings they were.. a well-matched.. give-and-take couple. **1879** G. MEREDITH *Egoist* xix. (1889) 175 The sweetest give and take rattle he had ever enjoyed.

give-away ('gɪvəweɪ). *colloq.* (orig. *U.S.*). Also **give away, giveaway**. [f. the vbl. phr. *to give away* (see GIVE *v.* 54).] **1.** The act of giving something away; a thing or things that are given away; a free gift; *spec.* (*a*) a game in which the object is to lose points or to force one's opponent to make captures, etc.; (*b*) a price so low that the goods so sold are virtually 'given away'; (*c*) a radio or television programme or the like in which prizes are given to participants for performing some specified task. Freq. *attrib.*

1872 *Newton Kansan* 19 Dec. 2/2 We are decidely opposed to the give-away game. **1889** 'MARK TWAIN' *Yankee* xlii. 486 The stock was for sale at a giveaway. **1899** J. D. CHAMPLIN *Young Folks' Cycl. Games* (ed. 2) 181 *Give-away chess...* The Give-away game differs from the ordinary one. **1905** *Westm. Gaz.* 13 Sept. 8/1 They are advertising their stock at give-away prices. **1916** R. K. WOOD *Tourist's Northwest* xiii. 361 Alert Bay and other Indian villages of the British Columbia coast are occasionally enlivened by Potlatch or Give-away festivals, at which the Indian host bestows his worldly goods upon his invited amid formal dancing. **1934** M. H. WESEEN *Dict. Amer. Slang* (1935) XII. 167 *Give away*, free samples and prizes. **1940** *Time* 22 June 56/2 *Information Please*, opposite *Pot o' Gold*, in self-defence instituted a giveaway on its own high intellectual plane—sets of Encyclopaedia Britannica. **1948** *Ibid.* 4 Oct. 33/2 Plugged as a giveaway show.. *Split the Atom* was even endowed with a sponsor. **1948** *Tuscaloosa* (Ala.) *News* 11 Nov. 4/6 He denies that 'audience participation' shows—he dislikes the term 'giveaways'—are only nuisance programs that attract morons. **1952** *Manch. Guardian Weekly* 13 Mar. 4/4 The state pays out.. 'giveaway grants' to Negroes who.. deserve a university education. **1953** *Ibid.* 11 June 4/3 Where a considerable choice of viewing exists.. the bulk of viewers would immediately transfer their allegiance.. to a.. big 'give-away' show. **1958** *Punch* 8 Oct. 457/3 Railwaymen loading cereal packets at Stretford found a live 3·7 anti-aircraft shell in the wagon. They say this is taking give-away too far. **1960** *Guardian* 16 Mar. 8/5 They have their 'give-aways', ranging from a set of books to a motor-car. **1962** *Rep. Comm. Broadc. 1960* 58 in *Parl. Papers 1961–2* (Cmnd. 1753) IX. 259 The appeal of the 'give-away', of prizes of values quite disproportionate to the skill or knowledge involved in the contest. **1969** *Daily Tel.* 20 Oct. 1/1 The feeling among.. MPs is that the Prime Minister will wait for the electoral benefits of a 'give-away' Budget before calling an Election.

2. An inadvertent betrayal or revelation of oneself, of plans, the truth, etc.; freq. in ***dead give-away***, a complete betrayal; also, a person or thing that causes such a betrayal or revelation.

1882 W. A. BAILLIE-GROHMAN *Camps in Rockies* 14 The dead 'give away'.. removed the shadowy blemish from his character. **1882** G. W. PECK *Peck's Sunshine* 83 A piece of that dog as big as a finger would ruin a butcher. It would be a dead give away. **1897** C. M. FLANDRAU *Harvard Episodes* 224, I gave my own name, but Dilly didn't; he had one all ready that went with his initials on his underclothes, so it wouldn't be a give-away. **1901** *Westm. Gaz.* 28 Sept. 2/1 'When I was at Poona in '76—' 'My dear Colonel,' purred Reginald, 'fancy admitting such a thing! Such a give-away for one's age!' **1904** *Ibid.* 19 May 3/2 When Mr. Chamberlain went on to declare that the Government's amendment and his own had the same idea, the give-away was complete. **1924** GALSWORTHY *White Monkey* II. ix, She also realised the give-away. **1924** G. OVERTON *Cargoes for Crusoes* 156 The patient has come to the conclusion that he is a dead giveaway, that everybody sees in him what the psycho-analyst sees. **1952** [see ANALYSE *v.* 4 b]. **1959** 'P. QUENTIN' *Shadow of Guilt* xi. 96 Her expression was a dead give-away. **1970** *Daily Tel.* 11 Aug. 11/2 An ancient parquet-floored hall which even the stealthiest house breaker couldn't negotiate without a salvo of giveaway creaks.

†**'givel**, *v.* *Obs.*$^{-1}$ [ad. OF. **geveler, javeler* to heap up, f. *gevele* heap; cf. GAVEL *sb.*[2]] *trans.* To heap up. Only in pa. pple.

c **1300** *Havelok* 814 He.. cast a panier on his bac, With fish giueled als a stac.

†**giveler.** *Obs. rare*$^{-1}$. [a. OF. *givelier* (Froissart), of unknown meaning.] A term of contempt.

1399 LANGL. *Rich. Redeles* III. 130 With gyuleris Ioyfull ffor here gery Iaces, And ffor her wedis so wyde.

given (gɪv(ə)n), *ppl. a.* (and *sb.*) Forms: see GIVE *v.* Used adjectively in senses of the vb.

A. *ppl. a.* **1. a.** Bestowed as a gift.

1382 WYCLIF *Ecclus.* xx. 10 Ther is ȝouen thing, that is not profitable; and ther is ȝoue thing, whos ȝelding is double. *c* **1400** *Rom. Rose* 2380 But, in love, free yeven thing Requyrith a gret guerdoning. **1539** TAVERNER *Erasm. Prov.* 67 A giuen horse.. maye not be loked in the mouthe. **1892** *Daily News* 10 Feb. 5/1 The millionaire, like the ordinary citizen.. probably finds that given goods never prosper.

b. ***given name***: the name given at baptism, the Christian name. ? Chiefly *Sc.* and *U.S.*

1827 J. F. COOPER *Red Rover* I. 19 The youth, whose christian or 'given' name, as it is even now generally termed in New-England [etc.]. **1859** BARTLETT *Dict. Amer.*, *Given Name*, the Christian name, or name that is *given* to a person, to distinguish it from the surname, which is not given, but inherited. Cobbett calls it a Scotticism. It was probably introduced by the Puritans instead of 'Saint's name', or 'Christian name'. **1895** CROCKETT *Men of Moss Hags* i. 1 Maisie Lennox (for that was her proper given name) was my cousin. **1936** *S.P.E. Tract* XLVII. 244 Thoughtful parents often provide Smith with a second surname, usually as his second 'given' name, as John Howard Smith. **1954** *Manch. Guardian Weekly* 11 Nov. 2 His given names recall the majesty of the great judge.

2. Used predicatively: Inclined, disposed, addicted, prone. Const. *to*. Also †***well, piously***, etc. ***given***.

1375 BARBOUR *Bruce* IV. 735 Men, kyndly to i[wi]ll giffin. **1535** STEWART *Cron. Scot.* II. 692 How Duncane was crovnit King of Scotland and was weill gevin. **1589** COGAN *Haven Health* ccxviii. (1636) 253 Those things that breed rheumes, doe likewise breed the goute in such as bee given thereunto. **1601** HOLLAND *Pliny* II. 118 What man is there well giuen and honestly minded, who [etc.]. **1662** J. DAVIES tr. *Olearius' Voy. Ambass.* 285 The Chancellor, who was not given to those Excesses, would have excus'd himself. **1709** STEELE *Tatler* No. 56 ¶ 1 This ill Fortune makes most Men contemplative and given to Reading. **1747** WESLEY *Wks.* (1872) XII. 93, I fear you are somewhat enthusiastically given. **1844** WILLIS *Lady Jane* II. 9 Women given To the society of famous men. **1869** FREEMAN *Norm. Conq.* (1876) III. xi. 11 Others who were devoutly given knew well the sins of England. **1885** F. Anstey *Tinted Venus* 121 To tell you the honest truth, I'm not given that way myself.

3. Granted as a basis of calculation, reasoning, etc.; definitely stated, fixed, specified.

1570 Billingsley *Euclid* I. i, Vpon a right line geuen not beyng infinite, to describe an equilater triangle. **1726** tr. *Gregory's Astron.* I. ii. 287 The Obliquity of the Ecliptic being given, to find by Calculation, the Right Ascension and Declination of a given Point in it. **1756** C. Lucas *Ess. Waters* I. 66 No two agree in the quantity of water requisite to dissolve a given portion of any salt. **1807** T. Thomson *Chem.* (ed. 3) II. 590 The quantity of nitric acid of a given density necessary to saturate a given weight of the salt. **1840** Lardner *Geom.* 118 Since the given triangles are similar, the angles A and A′ are equal. **1860** Tyndall *Glac.* i. xxiv. 175 A better means of accomplishing a given end. **1870** Max Müller *Sci. Relig.* (1873) 349 To determine whether a given religion may be considered as the work of one man.

4. *Comb.* with advs., as ***given-away, -out, -over.***

a **1586** Sidney *Arcadia* iii. (1590) 259b, She sawe Philoclea sitting lowe vpon a cushion, in such a giuen-ouer manner, that one would haue thought silence, solitarinesse, and melancholie were come there..to [etc.]. *Ibid.* iii. (1598) 355 Is this the reward of thy giuen-away [**1629** p. 369 given-way] libertie? Hath too much yeelding bred crueltie? **1795** *Fate Sedley* I. 105 Lady Dorothy, whom I expected to have seen laid out in funeral pomp, received me in her chamber; and judge my surprise when I beheld this given over damsel, sitting with great composure. **1868** Dickens in *All Year Round* 19 Dec. 63/2 It come to her through two hands... The second hand took the risk of the given-out work. **1920** J. M. Hunter *Trail Drivers of Texas* I. 211 The Indians had just as soon have these..given-out cattle as any.

B. *absol.* as *sb.* What is given; the known facts, situation, etc.

1879 W. James *Coll. Ess. & Rev.* (1920) 132 If the philosopher fails to find a satisfactory formula of exorcism for his datum, the only thing he can do is to..assume the Given as his necessary ultimate. **1883** F. H. Bradley *Princ. Logic* I. i. 32 There is no practical interest in anything but the given, and what does not interest is not anything at all. **1965** *Case Conference* Mar. 280/2 The past cannot be seen as a fixed 'given', its meaning is imposed upon it by the stand that we take in relation to it. **1970** E. Leach *Lévi-Strauss* iii. 45 'The English language'..from the point of view of any individual speaker..is a 'given', it is not something he creates for himself.

† **'giveness.** *Obs. rare.* [f. given + -ness; cf. OE. *ȝifnes* favour, grace.]

1. = forgiveness.

c **1200** *Trin. Coll. Hom.* 107 þe giuenesse of sinne is þe beste giue. *a* **1300** *Cursor M.* 25338 We thoru tendernes of vr flexs mai giue til oþer na giuenes.

2. The act of giving.

1537 'T. Matthew' *Isa.* xliii. 21 *marg.*, To preache..the geuenes of euerlastyng lyfe by the mercy of God for Christes sake.

givenness ('gɪv(ə)nnɪs). [f. given (sense 3) + -ness.] The fact of being given or posited.

a **1866** J. Grote *Treatise* (1876) 390 But in us reflective creatures, being and thinking, fact (or *givenness*) and self-formation (or self-improvement)..are mingled together in a complicated doubleness. **1895** B. Bosanquet *Presid. Addr.* in *Proc. Aristot. Soc.* (1896) III. ii. 10 Little more inference lies from the given-ness of Time in the Absolute, to the Absolute being in Time, than from the given-ness of colour in the Absolute to the Absolute having a colour.

giver ('gɪvə(r)). Forms: α. 4 ȝyvere, 4–5 ȝever, yever(e, -our. β. 4 gifer, 4–6 gevar, -ear, -er, -our, gyver(e, giff-, gyfer, 5–6 *Sc.* giffar, 4– giver. [f. give *v.* + -er¹, = OHG. *kebari* (MHG. and G. *geber*), MDu. *gevere*, Du. *gever*, Sw. *gifvare*, Dan. *giver*.] One who gives, in senses of the vb.; a bestower, distributor, donor, grantor. Often preceded by a sb. as object, as *alms-, example-, law-, light-*, etc. *giver*.

α. **1340** *Ayenb.* 95 Þeruore is ariȝt þe holy gost propre-liche yefþe and yevere vor he him yefþ and is y yeve. **1382** Wyclif *2 Cor.* ix. 7 God loueth a glad ȝyuere. *c* **1449** Pecock *Repr.* 552 The ȝeuers trustiden that the receyuers wolden expende thilk good vertuoseli. **1483** *Act 1 Rich. III* c. i. §1 The Sellers feffours yevours or grauntours.

β. *a* **1300** *Cursor M.* 28804, I to þe was first giuer. *a* **1340** Hampole *Psalter* i. 3 God lufis wele cherid gifers. **1377** Langl. *P. Pl.* B. vii. 70 He that beggeth..but if he haue nede..he bigileth the gyuere [A. viii. 72 the ȝiuere]. *c* **1450** *St. Cuthbert* (Surtees) 4368 God loues a gyfer glade. **1552** Abp. Hamilton *Catech.* (1884) 15 The haly spreit is giffar of all halynes. **1667** Milton *P.L.* v. 317 Well we may afford Our givers thir own gifts. *c* **1704** Prior *Henry & Emma* 211 The gift still prais'd, the giver still unknown. **1809** Pinkney *Trav. France* 11 Though they cost little to the giver, are not the less valuable to the receiver. **1838** Dickens *Nich. Nick.* xiii, I returned it [a blow] to the giver, and with good interest too. **1868** W. Whitman *Chants Democr.* i. Poems 67 The fresh free giver, the flowing Missouri. **1884** *Athenæum* 25 Oct. 540 Givers of Dinners, Balls, and At Homes.

b. with adv., as ***giver-in, out.***

1885 *Instr. to Census Clerks* 68 Cotton Manufacture. Looming and Taping Room:..Giver-in. Odd Hands:..Weft Giver-out.

givete, obs. form of gift.

Givetian (ʒɪ'viːʃən, -eɪʃən), *a. Geol.* [ad. F. *Givétien* (J. Gosselet 1879, in *Ann. de la Soc. géol. du Nord* VI. 130), f. *Givet*, name of a commune in north-eastern France: see -ian. The Fr. spelling was formerly in English use.] Name of the upper one of the two stages that constitute the Middle Devonian in Europe; of or pertaining to this stage or the geological period during which it was deposited. Also *absol.*

1882 A. Geikie *Textbk. Geol.* vi. 702/1 Givetien. The great limestone of the middle Devonian series, well seen at Givet. **1902** A. J. Jukes-Browne *Student's Handbk. Stratigr. Geol.* x. 176 [In the Belgian Ardennes] the upper stage of the Middle Devonian is a massive limestone 1300 feet thick, and is well seen at Givet on the Meuse, whence it is known as the Givétien [ed. 2, Givetian]. **1931** Gregory & Barrett *Gen. Stratigr.* vi. 96 In central Russia the Eifelian is also absent, but the Givetian is represented by marls and limestones. **1967** Teichert & Yochelson *Essays in Paleont. & Stratigr.* 184, 15 genera from the Eifelian and only ten genera from the Givetian Stage. **1967** D. H. Rayner *Stratigr. Brit. Isles* v. 161 Near Padstow the Middle Devonian is represented by grey slates with Eifelian and Givetian goniatites.

'give-up. *U.S.* [f. the vbl. phr. *to give up* (see give *v.* 64).] **1.** The act of giving up; submission, relinquishment. *colloq.*

1895 *Harper's Mag.* Nov. 887/1 There was no give-up to those English. **1942** Berrey & Van den Bark *Amer. Thes. Slang* §306/2 Submission; surrender,..*give-up*.

2. *Stock Exchange.* (See quots.)

1934 Webster, *Give-up*, a [stock-exchange] transaction in which the broker reveals the name of his principal, who is under obligation to complete the transaction. **1963** B. E. Shultz *Securities Market* (ed. 2) xvi. 302 A 'floor give-up' in which specialists and two-dollar brokers give up the names of the firms for which they are acting. **1964** Hazard & Christie *Investment Business* xxiii. 368 There is no reason to countenance give-ups in the over-the-counter market. **1969** *Times* 5 May (Suppl.) p. v/5 Many of them depended for their very existence on commission-splitting, or the 'give-up' as it was known informally.

give-way sign. [Cf. give *v.* 49 b.] A traffic sign ordering the road-user to yield the right of way to traffic on the road he is joining.

1963 *Rep. Committee Traffic Signs (Min. Transport)* 12 In recommending this *Give way* sign we are deliberately departing from the Protocol not only by adding words but in advocating that the sign should be made mandatory. **1969** *Daily Tel.* 15 Aug. 17/5 Roundabouts and 'give way' signs offer a far more fluid method of traffic control than lights. **1970** *Times* 11 Mar. 14/2 He ignored a 'give way' sign and white lines on a side road.

givey, givy ('gɪvɪ), *a. dial.* or *colloq.* [f. give *v.* 40.] Inclined to yield or give way; pliable, springy, soft; moist (see also quots.).

1829 *Virginia Lit. Museum* I. 457 *Givy*, 'muggy'. The weather is said to be givy, when there is much moisture in the atmosphere. **1859** Bartlett *Dict. Amer.* (ed. 2), *Givy*, a term applied to tobacco leaves, in a certain condition of their preparation for market. **1887** Parish & Shaw *Dict. Kentish Dial.* 64 The ground is said to be *givey* when the frost breaks up and the roads become soft and rotten. **1965** 'S. Harvester' *Assassins Road* xiii. 129 He longed to sprawl on a bed. Any bed provided it was givey.

giving ('gɪvɪŋ), *vbl. sb.* [f. give *v.* + -ing¹.] The action of the vb. give.

1. a. In transitive senses. Occas. *pl.*

13.. *K. Alis.* 839 Alisaundre god los Of that gevying him aros. *c* **1374** Chaucer *Compl. Mars* 230 Rest nis ther noon in his yeving. *c* **1449** Pecock *Repr.* 400 Thes iiij maners of ȝeuyngis. **1573** J. Sanford *Hours Recreat.* (1576) 211 Promissing is the vigile of giving. **1581** T. Rogers *St. Aug. Praiers* xvii. (1597) 70 For euerie good giuing and euerie perfect gifte is from aboue. **1612** Woodall *Surg. Mate* Wks. (1653) 21 *The giving of it Glisterwise in a fume to a patient. **1732** Pope *Mor. Ess.* iii. 348 Constant at Church and 'Change; his gains were sure; His givings rare, save farthings to the poor. **1851** Robertson *Serm.* Ser. iii. xi. 137 When the spirit of giving was substituted for the spirit of mere rivalry. **1881** Duffield *Don Quix.* II. 492 We go..to hold givings and takings with giants.

b. Gerundially with †*a* (*on*) or with omission of the prep.

1583 Golding *Calvin on Deut.* lxiv. 387 Euen while Gods lawe was a giuing to them..they prouoked Gods Vengeaunce. **1707** S. Sewall *Diary* 2 July (1879) II. 190, I could not hear one word while the Degrees were giving.

2. In intransitive senses.

1710 Addison *Tatler* No. 254 ¶10 Upon the first Giving of the Weather. **1818** *Sporting Mag.* II. 189 The men closed after three distinct rallies, in which there was a considerable giving. **1867** Smyth *Sailor's Word-bk.*, *Giving*, the surging of a seizing; new rope stretching to the strain.

3. With adverbs, as ***giving back, in, over, out, up.*** Also ***giving way*** (see give *v.* B. 52).

1530 Palsgr. 225/1 Gevyng over a thyng, *resignation.* **1585** T. Washington tr. *Nicholay's Voy.* i. xix. 23 To treat of some good accord touching the giving over of the castle. **1604** Shaks. *Oth.* iv. i. 131 This is the Monkeys owne giuing out. **1606** Bryskett *Civ. Life* 18 To make me resolue the giuing ouer that place. **1611** Cotgr., *Pas d'escrevisse*, a..giuing backe. **1726** Leoni *Alberti's Archit.* I. 43 Their Platform..by the giving way of the Earth, became ruinous. **1804** *Morning Post* in *Spirit. Publ. Jrnls.* (1805) VIII. 244 The ambiguous givings out, and the unambiguous promptings that are pent within. **1831** T. Moore *Mem.* (1854) VI. 168 [He] seemed to think it very much of a giving in on the part of his brother agitators. **1852** R. S. Surtees *Sponge's Sp. Tour* (1893) 366 A giving up that had been most unhandsomely accepted by his landlord. **1884** *Law Times Rep.* LI. 229/2 The immediate cause of the subsidence was the giving way of a stratum of soft mud. **1894** *Daily News* 9 Mar. 3/7 The cruiser..having broken down through the giving out of her cylinders.

†**4.** *concr.* That which is given; a gift. *Obs.*

1382 Wyclif *Ecclus.* xxxviii. 2 Fro the king he schal take ȝyuyng [Vulg. *donationem*]. **1664** Pepys *Diary* (1879) III. 46 My aunt Wight did send my Wife a new scarfe, laced, as a token for her many givings to her. **1667** Milton *P.L.* vi. 730 Scepter and Power, thy giving, I assume, And gladlier shall resign.

5. *attrib.*, as **giving-set**, an apparatus for giving blood transfusions or the like.

1955 D. F. E. Nash *Princ. Surgical Nursing* ii. ix. 138 All giving-sets must of course be supplied in a sterile container. **1961** *Lancet* 2 Sept. 537/1 The recent appearance of new sterile-packed, disposable giving-sets. *Ibid.* 16 Sept. 662/1 Any general practitioner undertaking domiciliary midwifery should..have at hand..a transfusion giving set.

giving ('gɪvɪŋ), *ppl. a.* [f. give *v.* + -ing².] That gives, in senses of the vb.

1382 Wyclif *Ecclus.* li. 23 To the ȝyuende to me wisdam I shal ȝyue glorie. **1611** Cotgr., *Moite*,..giuing as stones in rainie weather. **1681** Flavel *Meth. Grace* xxviii. 482 O get a heart mortified to all these things, and you will bless a taking as well as a giving God. **1728** Pope *Dunc.* ii. 200 From his soft, giving palm.

‖**givre** (ʒivr). [F. *givre* hoar-frost.] (See quot.)

1888 Holmes in *Encycl. Brit.* XXIV. 66/2 s.v. *Vanilla*, The best varieties of vanilla pods..are covered with a crystalline efflorescence technically known as *givre*.

Giw(e, obs. form of Jew.

giwe (pa. pple. **giwin**), obs. Sc. f. give *v.*

†**gixy.** *Obs.* [? Connected with gig; cf. *Betsy, Nancy*, also the adjs. *tricksy*, etc.] A wench.

1611 Cotgr., *Gadrouillette*, a minx, gigle, flirt, callet, Gixie. [Again s.v. *Saffrette*.] *a* **1693** Urquhart *Rabelais* iii. xxviii, Carvel..entred into a very profound suspition that his new-married Gixy did [etc.].

gizard, obs. form of gizzard.

gizen: see gizzen *v.*

gizmo, var. gismo.

gizz (dʒɪz). *Sc.* Also 8 jiz. [Origin unknown; ? cf. jasey.] A wig.

a **1774** Fergusson *Poems* (1807) 241 Sometimes they [squibs] catch a gentle gizz..And singe, wi' hair-devouring bizz, Its curls away. **1785** Burns *Addr. to Deil* 98 Wi' reekit duds, an' reestit gizz. —— *Mauchline Wedding* 43 His Sunday's jiz Wi' powther Weel smear'd that day.

gizzard ('gɪzəd). Forms: α. 4, 6 giser, 5 gyser, -our, -owr, 6–7 gysar, (7 gesier, gizier, gizzar). β. 6 guisard, guysard, 6–7 gysard(e, 7–8 gizard, 8 ghizzard, 7, 9 *dial.* gisard, 7– gizzard. See also gizzern. [a. OF. *giser, gezier, juisier, jugier*, also *guiser*, gizzard, mod.F. *gésier*, commonly explained as:—popular Latin **gicerium* = L. *gigeria* neut. pl., the cooked entrails of a fowl.

The final *d* of the β-forms is parallel to that of 16th c. *garnerd* for *garner*, and the vulgar *scholard* for *scholar*. The pronunciation with (g) seems to come from the unexplained OF. form *guiser* (Godefr. *Compl.*).]

1. The second or muscular stomach of birds in which the food is ground, after being mixed with gastric juice in the proventriculus or first stomach.

α. [*c* **1374**: see 3.] *c* **1430** *Two Cookery-bks.* i. 9 Take fayre garbagys of chykonys, as þe hed, þe fete, þe lyuerys, an þe gysowrys. *c* **1450** *Ibid.* ii. 72 Chikenes hedes, ffete, lyvers, And gysers. **1533** Elyot *Cast. Helthe* (1541) 10a, The innermost skine of a hennes gysar. **1601** Holland *Pliny* I. 295 They haue within their throat another kind of gizzar besides their craw. *Ibid.* II. 625 In the gesiers of cocks there be found certaine stones, called..Alectoriæ.

β. **1565** Cooper *Thesaurus, Alectoria*..a stone in the mawe or gysarde of a cocke. **1577** B. Googe *Heresbach's Husb.* iii. (1586) 145 The Guysard of the Storke. **1620** Venner *Via Recta* iii. 68 The Gysard or Maw of Fowles. **1621** Jonson *Masque Gypsies* Wks. (1692) 623 To these, an overgrowne Justice of Peace, With a Clerk like a Gizzard thrust under each Arm. **1789** G. White *Selborne* (1853) 348 The gizzard was thick and strong. **1836–9** Todd *Cycl. Anat.* II. 11/2 The gizzard is of much smaller dimensions than the crop. **1872** Mivart *Elem. Anat.* xi. 444 Another complication of stomach is produced by an enormous increase of the muscular coat of the pylorus. A stomach so thickened is called a gizzard, and is found in most birds.

fig. **1647** Ward *Simp. Cobler* 26, I look at her as the very gizzard of a trifle,..the epitome of Nothing.

b. The stomach of the gillaroo trout.

1776 Pennant *Zool.* III. 262 The trouts of certain lakes of Ireland..are remarkable for the great thickness of their stomachs, which from some slight resemblance to the organs of digestion in birds, have been called gizzards. **1780** A. Young *Tour Irel.* I. 351 The Gillaroo trout with gizzards.

c. *Ent.* The proventriculus or first stomach of certain insects.

1826 Kirby & Sp. *Entomol.* xlviii. IV. 434 As to their anatomy, the Orthoptera have a ventricle or gizzard. **1868** Carpenter *Microsc.* §521 The muscular Gizzard..is often lined by several rows of strong Horny Teeth, for the reduction of the food... These are particularly developed among the Grasshoppers, Crickets, and Locusts.

d. *Zool.* The thickened muscular stomach found in certain molluscs.

1841 T. R. Jones *Anim. Kingd.* 122 In *Brachionus urceolaris*..the gizzard..exhibits through its transparent coats the peculiar dental organs placed within it. **1850** G. Johnston *Conchol.* 311 The muscular gizzard of the latter [Aplysia] is studded with numerous sharp pyramidal knobs of a semi-cartilaginous consistence. **1851–6** Woodward *Mollusca* 182 Bullidæ..Gizzard armed with calcarious plates.

2. Jocularly attributed to persons, esp. in phrases, ***to fret one's gizzard***: to worry oneself. ***to stick in one's gizzard***: to remain as something unpleasant or distasteful, to be disagreeable or unpalatable to one.

1668 PEPYS *Diary* 17 June, I find my wife hath something in her gizzard that only waits an opportunity of being provoked to bring up. **1672** R. WILD *Declar. Lib. Consc.* 11 There was some grumbling of the Gizard. **1679** *Vind. Sir T. Player* 1/2 'Tis the Matter, not the Manner that sticks in our Unworthy Respondents Gizzard. **1692** R. L'ESTRANGE *Fables* cccxlix. 305 Satisfaction and Restitution lie so Cursedly hard upon the Gizzards of our Publicans, that [etc.]. **1738** SWIFT *Pol. Conversat.* i. 93 Don't let that stick in your Gizzard. **1755** JOHNSON s.v., 2. It is proverbially used for apprehension or conception of mind: as, he *frets his gizzard*, he harrasses his imagination. *c* **1765** FLLOYD *Tartarian T.* (1785) 47/1, I was going home, grumbling in the gizzard. **1828** *Craven Gloss.* s.v., 'To grumble in the gizzard', to complain and be dissatisfied. **1833** R. H. FROUDE *Rem.* (1838) I. 322 That odious Protestantism sticks in people's gizzard. **1871** B. TAYLOR *Faust* (1875) II. II. iii. 134 That little one, she warms my gizzard. **1879** MRS. MACQUOID *Berksh. Lady* 153 Pick a quarrel and..run him through the gizzard.

¶ **3.** Used (after F. *juisier*: see Littré s.v. *gésier*) to translate L. *jecur*, liver.

c **1374** CHAUCER *Boeth.* III. metr. xii. 84 (Camb. MS.) The fowel that hihte voltor that etith the stomak or the gyser of ticius.

4. *attrib.* and *Comb.*, as **gizzard hue**; **gizzard-fallen** *a.*, **-fish**, **-shad** (see quots.); **gizzard-trout** = GILLAROO.

1765 *Treat. Dom. Pigeons* 37 Another disease to which they [Pigeons] are subject is *gizzard-fallen, that is, the gizzard falls down to the vent. **1883** SIMMONDS *Dict. Usef. Anim.*, **Gizzard fish*, a name for the white fish (*Coregonus albus*), belonging to the salmon family. *a* **1845** HOOD *Irish Schoolm.* viii, A pair of shaggy brows O'erhang as many eyes of *gizzard hue. **1889** FARMER *Americanisms*, **Gizzard-shad*, the Carolinan name for the Ale-wife. **1773** *Phil. Trans.* LXIV. 119 The Gillaroo or *Gizzard trout. **1837** M. DONOVAN *Dom. Econ.* II. 187 Gizzard-trout.

gizzen (gɪz(ə)n), *a.* *Sc.* [a. ON. *gisenn* (Sw. *gisten*, dial. *gissen*) leaky, app. from a root **gis-* to gape, cf. Icel. *gis-tenntr* (Sw. dial. *gis-tändt*) having wide-set teeth.] Of casks, etc.: Leaky (through heat, or for want of moisture). ***to gang gizzen*** (see quot.). Also *fig.*

1790 SHIRREFS *Poems* Gloss., *Gizzen, gizzen'd*, rent with heat, dry. **1804** TARRAS *Poems* 134 Nir lat's gang gizzen, fy for shame Wi' drouthy tusk! **1825–80** JAMIESON s.v., *To gang gizzen*, to break out into chinks from want of moisture; a term applied to casks.

gizzen (gɪz(ə)n), **gizen** (gaɪz(ə)n), *v. north.* and *Sc.* Forms: 8 **gysen, geyzen, guizen,** 9 **geysan, geisen, gisen, -an, gizen, gyzen,** 8–9 **gizzen.** [a. ON. *gisna* (Sw. *gistna*): see prec.] *intr.* To become dry and leaky, as an empty barrel. Also *fig.* of persons.

1721 RAMSAY *Poems* Gloss., *Gysened*, when the wood of any vessel is shrunk with dryness. *a* **1774** FERGUSSON *Poems* (1807) 225 My kirnstaff now stands gizzened at the door. *a* **1816** *Song, Handsome Katie* in *Pocket Encycl. Songs* I. 167 Now winter comes..And nips wi' frost the gizzen'd gowan. **1833** M. SCOTT *Tom Cringle* xii. 270 A wee outspoken sour crabbit gizzened anatomy of an old woman. **1863** JANET HAMILTON *Poems* 87 A wee bit drap Was a' that e'er gade owre my weasan—E'en noo my gab begins to geysan. **1871** W. ALEXANDER *Johnny Gibb* xlix. (1873) 268 Yet when one is 'gizzen't' for want of news some shift must be made. **1877** *N.W. Linc. Gloss.*, *Gyze, Gyzen*, to warp, to twist, by the sun or wind. **1893** *Northumbld. Gloss.*, *Gizen*, An empty cask lying in the sun becomes gizened—that is, dry and shrunken.

gizzern ('gɪzən). *Obs.* exc. *dial.* Forms: 4 **gisarn,** 5 **gesarne, -erne,** 5–7 **gysern(e,** 6–7 **gisern(e,** 7 **guis(s)erne, gyzerne, gyzzarn,** 8 **gizern,** 7, 9 *dial.* **gizzern,** 9 *dial.* **gizzen, -in.** [App. a variant of *giser* GIZZARD; the addition of *n* is unexplained.] = GIZZARD.

1398 TREVISA *Barth. De P.R.* v. xliv. (1495) 161 The fyrste mete of the fowles is receyuyd and kepte in the croppe to the seconde dygestyon, that shall be made in the gisarn or mawe. *c* **1440** *Promp. Parv.* 195/1 Gyserne (*P.* of fowles). **1530** PALSGR. 225/1 Gyserne of a foule, *jevsier*. *a* **1605** MONTGOMERIE *Flyting* 331 Thy gall and thy guisserne to glaids shall bee given. **1611** COTGR., *Sauce froide*, Another [sauce] made of the liuers, and giserns of chickens. **1693** SIR T. P. BLOUNT *Nat. Hist.* 10 Shaped like a split Gysern. **1707** FLOYER *Physic. Pulse Watch* xx. (1710) 149 The inward skin of Gizerns powder'd. **1878** *Cumbld. Gloss.*, *Gizzern, Gizzin*, gizzard. 'It sticks in his gizzern'—he remembers it with unpleasant feelings.

‖**gjetost** ('jɛːtəʊst). Also **gjedeost.** [Norwegian, f. *gjet, geit* goat + *ost* cheese.] A Norwegian cheese made from goat's milk.

1908 DOANE & LAWSON *Varieties of Cheese* 27 Hvid gjedeost. This is a goat's-milk cheese made in Norway.. only for local consumption. **1923** A. WARD *Encycl. Food* 92 *Gjedeost*, a sweet, rich, strong-flavored, brown, Norwegian, goat's milk cheese, moist but firm enough to slice well. **1956** A. L. SIMON *Cheeses of World* 124 *Mysost* or whey cheese was first made from goat's milk and named *Gietost* (*gjet* means goat). **1960** *House & Garden* Apr. 111/2 A cheese called Gjetost which..has been produced in Norway for over 1,000 years.

glaad, glaam, glaas, obs. forms of GLAD, GLAM[1], GLASS.

‖**glabella** (glə'bɛlə), **glabellum** (glə'bɛləm). [mod.Lat.; specific application of L. *glabella* (? sc. *pars*), *glabellum*, fem. and neut. of *glabellus* adj., dim. of *glaber* smooth, GLABROUS. Cf. F. *glabelle*.]

1. *Anat.* The small space in the human forehead between the eyebrows and immediately above a line from one to the other.

[**1598** R. HAYDOCKE tr. *Lomazzo's Artes Paintinge* I. v. 29 The space betweene the eyebrowes, the Italians call *glabella*.] **1823** CRABB *Technol. Dict.*, *Glabella*. **1861** BUMSTEAD *Ven. Dis.* (1879) 545 These tubercles are prone to appear in an irregularly triangular group, with the apex at the glabella and the base near the margin of the scalp. **1866** HUXLEY *Preh. Rem. Caithn.* 95 The nasal depression is very slight, the glabella prominent, but the supraciliary ridges little developed.

2. 'The smooth median portion of the cephalic shield of a Trilobite' (*Syd. Soc. Lex.* 1885).

1849 MURCHISON *Siluria* ix. (1867) 203 The glabella has only two pairs of furrows. **1877** HUXLEY *Anat. Inv. Anim.* vi. 259 On the occipital or lateral margin of the limb a suture commences, and passing between the eye and the glabellum, meets that of the opposite side.

glabellar (glə'bɛlə(r)), *a.* [f. GLABELL-A + -AR[1].] Pertaining to the glabella.

1814 J. H. WISHART tr. *Scarpa's Treat. Hernia* p. xv, The aspect or position of those parts near the corona are *coronal*; ..that of those near the glabella, *glabellar*. **1880** *Nature* 8 Jan. 223 Skulls possessing great projections in the glabellar and supraciliary regions.

glabello- (glə'bɛləʊ), comb. form of GLABELLA, as ***glabello-inial, -occipital***, pertaining to the glabella together with the inion, the occiput.

1863 HUXLEY *Man's Place Nat.* iii. 120 Fig. 23: the skull from the Cave of Engis... *a*, glabella; *b*, occipital protuberance; *a* to *b*, glabello-occipital line. **1866** —— *Preh. Rem. Caithn.* 119 Dr. Thurnam figures a typical skull of these long-barrow Britons, which he thus describes..The greatest length is 7·3 inches (the glabello-inial diameter 7·1 inches).

glabrate ('gleɪbrət), *ppl. a.* *Bot.* and *Zool.* [ad. L. *glabrāt-us*, pa. pple. of *glabrāre* to make bald or smooth, f. *glaber* GLABROUS.] (See quots.)

1857 A. GRAY *First Less. Bot.* Gloss. 217 *Glabrate*, becoming glabrous with age, or almost glabrous. **1870** HOOKER *Stud. Flora* 333 Humulus lupulus..branchlets glabrate. **1889** *Century Dict.*, *Glabrate*, in *Zool.*, smooth; bald; glabrous; having no hair or other appendages.

†**'glabreate,** *v.* *Obs.*$^{-0}$ Also 9 **glabriate.** [Badly for **glabrate*: cf. prec.] (See quot. 1623.)

1623 COCKERAM, *Glabreate*, to make plaine or smoothe. **1828–32** WEBSTER, *Glabriate*. And in later Dicts.

glabreity (gleɪ'briːɪtɪ). [ad. F. *glabréité*; cf. GLABRITY.] Baldness; want of hair.

1885 in *Syd. Soc. Lex.*

glabrescent (gleɪ'brɛsənt), *a.* *Bot.* [ad. L. *glabrescent-em*, pres. pple. of *glabrescĕre* to grow smooth or glabrous.] (See quot. 1857.)

1857 HENFREY *Bot.* §98 Glabrescent is used to signify that a surface, hairy when young, becomes smooth when the leaf is mature, by the hairs falling off. **1872** OLIVER *Elem. Bot.* App. 303 Common Wallflower..Stem..hoary at first with minute adpressed hairs, glabrescent.

†**glabretal.** *Obs.*$^{-0}$ [f. L. *glabrēta* pl., bare patches of soil (f. *glaber* GLABROUS) + -AL[1].] (See quot.)

1623 COCKERAM, *Glabretall*, a bare splat in the earth.

†**'glabrify,** *v.* *Obs.*$^{-1}$ [f. L. *glabri-*, comb. form of *glaber* bald + -FY.] *trans.* To make bald.

1657 TOMLINSON *Renou's Disp.* 205 Which places they much desire to depilate and glabrify.

glabrirostral (gleɪbrɪ'rɒstrəl), *a.* *Ornith.* [f. as prec. + ROSTRAL.] 'Smooth-billed; having few and slight, if any, bristles along the gape' (*Cent. Dict.* quoting P. L. Sclater).

†**'glabrity.** *Obs. rare*$^{-0}$. [ad. L. *glabritās*, f. *glaber*.] Smoothness, baldness.

1727 in BAILEY vol. II, and in later Dicts.

glabrous ('gleɪbrəs), *a.* [f. L. *glaber* without hair, smooth, bald (see GLAD) + -OUS.] Free from hair, down, or the like; having a smooth skin or surface. Now only as a scientific term.

1640 WILKINS *New Planet* viii. (1707) 224 If the Concavity of the Moon's Orb..is of so smooth and glabrous a Superficies. **1664** EVELYN *Sylva* (1679) 30 The French Elm, whose leaves are..more florid, glabrous and smooth. **1776** WITHERING *Brit. Plants* (1830) II. 387 Anthriscus. Beak shorter than the seeds, glabrous. **1828** STARK *Elem. Nat. Hist.* II. 290 The body of the insects of this genus is.. glabrous. **1854** R. G. LATHAM *Native Races Russian Emp.* 135 Whenever any nation..presents a notable amount of flattened faces, glabrous skins [etc]. **1872** OLIVER *Elem. Bot.* I. i. 5 Foliage-leaves..may be hairy, or nearly glabrous, that is, destitute of hairs. **1879** J. M. DUNCAN *Lect. Dis. Women* xxiv. (1889) 196 She was suffering from a glabrous mucous cyst.

b. Humorously used for: Smooth.

1860 O. W. HOLMES *Elsie V.* xii. (1891) 166 Two or three notabilities of Rockland, with geoponic eyes, and glabrous, bumpless foreheads.

†**glace,** *sb.*[1] *Obs. rare.* [a. F. *glace*:—popular L. **glacia* = L. *glaciēs*] Ice. ***on a glace***: frozen.

a **1400–50** *Alexander* 3002 Alexander..asperly rydis To þe grete flode of Granton and it on a glace [*Dublin MS.* as glas] fyndis. **1540** PATE in *State P. Hen. VIII* (1849) VIII. 346 That the verite cummyng in place must nedes vade away, even as the glace by the fervor of the sone. **1676** COLES, *Glace*, Ice.

†**glace,** *sb.*[2] *Obs.* Also 5 **glase.** [f. GLACE *v.* Cf. mod. dial. 'gleece, a surprise' (*Northumbld. Gloss.*).] A swift or glancing blow; a wound, graze.

c **1400** *Melayne* 1347 What! wenys thou..þat I faynte bee For a spere was in my thee, A glace thorowte my syde. *c* **1460** *Towneley Myst* xiii. 316 *Uxor.* It were a fowll blott to be hanged for the case. *Mak.* I haue skapyd..oft as hard a glase. *Ibid.* xxi. 418 *Primus tortor.* We haue gyfen hym a glase..*Secundus tortor.* Sir..with knokys he is indoost.

glace, *v.* *Obs.* exc. *dial.* Also 5 **glase,** 9 **glease, gleaze.** [ad. OF. *glacer, glacier, glacher*, to glide, slip:—pop. L. **glacicāre* to slip, slide, f. L. *glaciēs* ice.

OF. *glacer* had also a transitive sense 'to cause to glide or slip'; cf. Cotgrave's '*Glacer vn mot*, to insert, put, thrust or foist a word into a writing'. The mod. F. *glisser* to slip is by some philologists supposed to be an altered form of OF. *glier* under the influence of *glacer*.]

1. *intr.* To glance, glide; to move lightly or quickly (cf. GLANCE, GLENT). *rare.*

13.. *E.E. Allit. P.* A. 171 Suche gladande glory con to me glace, As lyttel byfore þerto watz wont. *a* **1400** *Hymns Virg.* 108 Ay let gabbynges glyde and gon A-wey wher þei wol glace [*Lamb. MS.* glase] or glent.

2. Of weapons: To glance off, to slip, to fail in giving a direct blow; also, to glide, pass easily *through*.

13.. *Sir Beues* 4177 (MS. A.) Doun of þe helm þe swerd gan glace And karf riȝt doun be-fore is face. *c* **1400** *Sowdone Bab.* 1208 It glased down by his sheelde And carfe his stedes neke a-sonder. **1412–20** LYDG. *Chron. Troy* III. xxii, The head of stele..Through plate & mayle mightly gan to glace. *c* **1450** *Guy Warw.* (C.) 5067 Hys swerde glasedde lowe And stroke vpon the sadull bowe. **1480** CAXTON *Chron. Eng.* i. (1482) 5 And as this brute shold shete unto an hert his arowe myshapped and glaced and so there Brute quelled his fader.

3. *trans.* (*dial.*) (See quot.)

1876 *Whitby Gloss*, *Glease* or *Gleaze*, to glide past. 'I just gleas'd it', as an object is nearly hit by a stone thrown at it. [So *glaze* in West Scotland (Rev. W. B. R. Wilson).]

Hence **'glacing** *vbl. sb.*

c **1440** *Promp. Parv.* 197/1 Glacynge, or wronge glydynge of boltys or arowys (*S.* glansyng, *P.* glaunsinge of shetinge), *devolatus*. **1855** ROBINSON *Whitby Gloss.*, *A Gleasing*, a hot pursuit, a sweat. 'I have had a good gleasing after him', a sharp run. And in a legal sense, 'He has had to bide a bonny gleasing', sustain the heavy charges of a law suit. Also in the general meaning of loss or deprivation.

glace, obs. form of GLASS *sb.*

‖**glacé** (glase), *a.* [Fr. pa. pple. of *glacer* to 'ice', give a gloss to, etc., f. *glace* ice.]

1. Of cloth, leather, etc.: Having a smooth surface with a high polish or lustre. Also *absol.* = glacé silk (and *attrib.* as ***glacé finish***), and = glacé leather.

1847 E. GRAY *Let.* 5 May in W. James *Order of Release* (1947) iii. 31, I see a great many cloaks of pale glacé silk. **1850** *Harper's Mag.* I. 431 Glacé or damask bareges are the most *recherchés*. *Ibid.*, Dress of glacé silk. **1851** *Illustr. Catal. Gt. Exhib.* 505 Shot glacés, woven by Spitalfields hand-loom weavers. **1859** SALA *Tw. round Clock* (1861) 117 The bevy of youthful bridesmaids—all in white tulle over pink glacé silk. **1889** *Charity Organis. Rev.* Jan. 9 Now-a-days glacé kid (the skill of the leather-dresser having discovered novel methods of imparting the glacé finish to inferior..skins) is used for boots of a low grade. **1900** *Queen* 28 Apr. (Advt.), Patent 'Lantry' shoe..in Glacé. Buckles extra. **1936** N. COWARD *To-night at 8.30* II. 38 A navy blue school dress with a glacé red leather waist belt. **1955** *Times* 11 July 13 *Glacé* kid..is also a full chrome upper leather.

2. Of fruits: Covered with icing or sugar.

1882 MISS BRADDON *Mt. Royal* I. vii. 215 Somebody said it was a theatre which looked as if it ought to be filled with glacé chestnuts, or crystallized violets.

†**'glacery.** *Obs.* ? Anglicized form of GLACIER.

1782–3 W. F. MARTYN *Geog. Mag.* II. 337 The Glaceries of Savoy may be considered as some of the natural curiosities of Italy.

†**'glaciable,** *a.* *Obs.* [f. L. *glaciā-re* to freeze + -BLE.] That may be frozen or congealed.

1658 SIR T. BROWNE *Pseud. Ep.* II. i. (ed. 4) 59 As sensible Phylosophers conceive of the generation of Diamonds, Iris, Beryls. Not making them of frozen icecle, or from meer aqueous and glaciable substances.

glacial ('gleɪʃɪəl, -ʃəl), *a.* Also 7 **glaciale.** [a. F. *glacial*, ad. L. *glaciālis* icy, f. *glaciēs* ice.]

1. Full of, or having the nature of, ice; cold, icy, freezing. *rare.*

1656 BLOUNT *Glossogr.*, *Glacial*, where ice is, freezing, cold. **1701** GREW *Cosm. Sacra* IV. v. §38. 203 Snowy or what ever else he [Spinoza] means by Glacial Air, or Clouds, may serve to darken the Day, but not at all prolong it. **1890** *Edin. Rev.* Jan. 61 Unintermittent glacial rain set in.

fig. **1852** LONGF. in *Life* (1891) II. 229 No wonder that their stricken faculties uttered themselves in such broken accents, such glacial metres! **1860** MOTLEY *Netherl.* xvii. II. 303 His frame was slight..his manner more glacial and sepulchral than ever.

b. Consisting of ice.

1794 SULLIVAN *View Nat.* I. 409 The enormous glacial masses of the poles. **1853** KANE *Grinnell Exp.* viii. (1856) 57 The gelid flow of these glacial rivers.

2. Of chemical substances: Glass-like; crystallized. (*Obs.* exc. as in b.)

1681 BOYLE *New Exper. Icy Noctiluca* 18, I thought it not amiss to call our consistent Self-shining Substance, the Icy or Glacial Noctiluca (and for variety—Phosphorus). **1693** SALMON *Bates' Dispens.* I. (1713) 358/2 From lb. iij. of the first Matter, you will have, says Rolfincius, a Glaciale Butter. **1771** WATSON *Phil. Trans.* LXI. 217 White vitriol, a few glacial spicula. **1796** KIRWAN *Elem. Min.* (ed. 2) II. 104 Phosphoric acid in a Glacial state.

b. ***glacial acetic acid***, pure acetic acid in crystals; ***glacial phosphoric acid***, metaphosphoric acid (HPO_3); ***glacial sulphuric acid***, †***glacial oil of vitriol***, pure sulphuric acid in crystals.

1786 H. CAVENDISH in *Phil. Trans.* LXXVI. 268 The oil of vitriol prepared from green vitriol, has sometimes been obtained in such a state as to remain constantly congealed.. whence it acquired its name of glacial. **1800** tr. *Lagrange's Chem.* II. 42 Glacial sulphuric acid. **1819** BRANDE *Man. Chem.* (1841) 685 When dried and fused in a crucible, a transparent glass is obtained, commonly called glacial phosphoric acid. **1843** PEREIRA *Food & Diet* 149 Glacial or Crystallisable Acetic Acid, the strongest procurable, contains one equivalent of water. **1879** *Cassell's Techn. Educ.* IV. 357/2 The acetic acid..usually employed in photography is what is termed *glacial*, and should become solid at about 40°.

3. *Geol.* Characterized by the presence of ice. ***glacial epoch, era, period***, a geological period during which it is supposed that the northern hemisphere was in great part covered by an ice-sheet. ***glacial sea***: the sea of the glacial epoch.

In America this period is also known as the *drift epoch* (see DRIFT *sb.* 10), *ice-age*, etc.

1846 PROF. E. FORBES in *Mem. Geol. Surv.* I. 363 The remarkable strata known under the names of 'Boulder clay', 'Arctic or northern drift'..including (in part) the 'Till' deposits, which for convenience I shall henceforth mention as *glacial*, or as *beds of the glacial epoch*. **1851** RICHARDSON *Geol.* viii. 211 The rhinoceros and elephant, which lived under the latitude of the glacial sea. **1853** PHILLIPS *Rivers Yorksh.* iv. 124 For all Holderness was a sea-bed in the 'glacial' period. **1862** DANA *Man. Geol.* 541 The Drift epoch is usually called the Glacial epoch, under the idea that ice either in the form of icebergs or glaciers, was concerned in the transportation of the boulders, pebbles, and earth. **1873** DAWSON *Earth & Man* xii. 283 The earlier Post-pliocene period of geology may be called the Glacial era.

b. Produced by the presence of ice in the form of glaciers, etc. or by its action upon the surface of the earth; pertaining to glaciers or ice-sheets.

1858 GEIKIE *Hist. Boulder* ii. 17 They corroborate our conclusions as to the glacial origin of the boulder-clay. **1860** G. H. K. *Vac. Tour* 120 Curious mounds of gravel, which look very like glacial moraines. **1863** LYELL *Antiq. Man* i. (ed. 3) 2, I shall give a description of the glacial formations of Europe and North America. **1872** NICHOLSON *Palæont.* 18 The glacial mud of the Polar regions. **1878** HUXLEY *Physiogr.* 164 Evidence of glacial denudation in countries which are now free from anything like glaciers or icebergs.

Hence ˌ**glacia'lation**, the condition of being covered with ice or glaciers; '**glacialism**, the theory of the action of ice upon the earth's surface; '**glacialized** *ppl. a.*, acted upon by ice.

1864 *Reader* 2 Apr. 432/2 They present characters in common with lake-basins occurring in regions which were intensely glacialized. **1881** W. B. DAWKINS in *Nature* XXIII. 309 Dr. James Geikie..pushes glacialism and interglacialism to an extreme. **1889** *Standard* 25 June 5/2 The plucky trip of Dr. Nansen has now rendered the entire glacialation of inner Greenland no longer a theory.

glacial ('gleɪʃɪəl, -ʃəl), *sb.* [f. the adj.] A glacial epoch or period.

1935 *Discovery* Nov. 317/2 Hardly one of the species present in England today could possibly have persisted here from the Tertiary Period through the glacials. **1957** G. E. HUTCHINSON *Treat. Limnol.* I. i. 49 High lake levels in equatorial Africa represent pluvial periods corresponding to the glacials.

†**glacialin(e** ('gleɪʃɪəlɪn). *Obs.* [f. GLACIAL *a.* + -IN[1].] A food preservative composed of boric acid and glycerine. In full ***glacialin(e salt***.

1876 W. F. GRIER *Brit. Pat. 3107*, My said Invention.. relates to a new or improved compound for preserving meat, fish, poultry, game, eggs, butter, milk... This liquid preservative I call 'glacialine', and its special value consists in the large proportion of hydric borate obtained in a solved or liquid state. **1883** *Encycl. Brit.* XVI. 304/2 Boracic acid and borax are also employed by dairymen, the former being known as glacialine salt. **1904** *Westm. Gaz.* 7 Jan. 7/1 Various preparations of boric acid are in use, the most common of which are glacialin salt and boro-glycerine.

glacialist ('gleɪʃɪəlɪst). [f. GLACIAL *a.* + -IST.] **a.** One who makes a special study of glacial phenomena. **b.** One who explains certain geological phenomena as due to glacial action.

1854 *Fraser's Mag.* XLIX. 249 Ice, a tolerably hard, brittle solid (notwithstanding the plasticity with which modern glacialists endow it). **1878** HUXLEY *Physiogr.* 165 Nor is it only the effects of land-ice which the glacialist sees marked upon the rocks of Britain. **1889** G. F. WRIGHT *Ice Age N. Amer.* 358 The glacialist sees indubitable evidences of a former vast expanse of water.

glacially ('gleɪʃɪəlɪ), *adv.* [f. as prec. + -LY[2].]

1. *Geol.* By means of glacial action.

1865 LYELL *Elem. Geol.* xii. (ed. 6) 158 Boulders of far-transported rocks, glacially polished and scratched on more than one side. **1880** A. R. WALLACE *Isl. Life* ix. 168 The present agencies may be said to be just beginning to carve a new line of features out of the old glacially-formed surface.

2. In an icy fashion, icily. *lit.* and *fig.*

1882 SALA *Amer. Revis.* xiii. (1883) 166 The high 'stoops' before the houses were also glacially glassy as to surface. **1883** MRS. LYNN LINTON *Ione* II. xx. 179 She asked this as calmly, almost glacially, as if she were not interested. **1889** —— *Thro' Long Night* I. I. xv. 251, 'I was looking at your room', returned Charlie, glacially polite.

‖**glaciarium** (gleɪʃɪ'ɛərɪəm). [f. L. *glaci-ēs* ice + *-arium* as in *aquarium, vivarium*.] A skating-rink with ice artificially produced.

1878 *19th Cent.* Mar. 555 The real ice at the Chelsea glaciarium. **1889** *Catholic News* 18 May 8/4 The shareholders of the Southport Glaciarium..passed a resolution to wind up the concern.

glaciate ('gleɪʃɪeɪt), *v.* [f. L. *glaciāt-* ppl. stem of *glaciāre* to freeze, f. *glaciēs* ice.]

†**1. a.** *intr.* (See quot.) **b.** *trans.* To freeze.

a. 1623 COCKERAM, *Glaciate*, to be frozen, to turne to Ice. **1755** in JOHNSON; and in later Dicts.

b. 1656 BLOUNT *Glossogr.*, *Glaciate*, to congeal or freeze, to turn to ice. **1665** [see GLACIATING]. **1721** in BAILEY.

2. *Geol.* Only in pass. pple. *glaciated*.

a. Rubbed or polished by glacial action.

1865 *Reader* 9 Sept. 297 All that we know at present..is that they have been glaciated in some form. **1876** DAVIS *Polaris Exp.* App. 661 Rocky surfaces which have once been glaciated, if I may thus express the peculiar action of ice upon rocks..can never be mistaken for anything else. **1894** *Chamb. Jrnl.* 1 Sept. 556 Some of the paving flags are basalt blocks, perhaps glaciated.

b. Covered with ice; furnished with glaciers.

1880 A. R. WALLACE *Isl. Life* vii. 108 The comparatively small Heard Island is even now glaciated down to the sea. **1887** H. HOWORTH *Mammoth* xx, I do not believe..in the possibility of tropical America being so glaciated that the valley of the Amazon was filled with ice.

3. *techn.* 'To give an ice-like or frosted appearance to' (*Cent. Dict.* 1889).

1887 *U.S. Consular Rep.* No. 73½. 215 (Cent.) [Iron] chimneys, oven, etc...not enamelled, glaciated, or tinned.

Hence '**glaciated**, '**glaciating** *ppl. adjs.*

1665 *Phil. Trans.* I. 48 What change was produced in it [water] betwixt the hottest time of Summer and first glaciating degree of Cold. **1861** H. MACMILLAN *Footnotes fr. Nature* 76 The..deep striæ or flutings peculiar to glaciated surfaces. **1875** CROLL *Climate & T.* xiv. 233 But when the glaciated hemisphere began to grow warmer [etc.]. **1881** *Nature* XXIII. 281 The glaciating agent has swept completely..over it. **1887** *Academy* 26 Nov. 355 Those fertile mountain spots met with in all glaciated countries.

glaciation (gleɪʃɪ'eɪʃən). [n. of action f. L. *glaciāre* to freeze: see prec. and -ATION.]

†**1.** The process of freezing; a result of this. *Obs.*

1646 SIR T. BROWNE *Pseud. Ep.* II. i. 54 So is it [Ice] plaine upon the surface of water, but round in hayle, (which is also a glaciacion). **1658** J. ROBINSON *A Calm Vent.* 120 A violent motion of water, is a preservative against glaciation. **1690** BOYLE *Chr. Virtuoso* I. 66 'Tis plain..that by Glaciation, Water is rather expanded.

2. *Geol.* The condition of being covered by an ice-sheet or by glaciers; glacial action or its result.

1863 LYELL *Antiq. Man* ix. (ed. 3) 165 These erratic blocks..are often polished and striated, having undergone what is called glaciation. **1875** —— *Princ. Geol.* I. I. xiii. 283 Mr. Croll's Theory of alternate glaciation. **1880** DAWKINS *Early Man* v. 117 The climate must have been arctic in its severity during this period of glaciation. **1881** *Nature* No. 626. 606 Between Reykjavik and Hafnarfjörd the glaciation is distinctly from south-east to north-west.

glacier ('glæsɪə(r), 'gleɪʃ(ɪ)ə(r)). Also 8 **glaciere**. [a. F. *glacier* (earlier *glacière*), f. *glace* ice; app. Savoyard word. Cf. GLETSCHER.]

1. A large accumulation or river of ice in a high mountain valley, formed by the gradual descent and consolidation of the snow that falls on the higher ground. The resulting mass is often many miles in length, and continues to move slowly downward until it reaches a point where the temperature is high enough to melt the ice as fast as it descends.

1744 (*title*) An Account of the Glacieres or Ice Alps in Savoy, in two Letters. **1774** PENNANT *Tour Scotl. in* 1772 327 With snowy glacieres lodged in the deep shaded apertures. **1775** C. & F. DAVY *Bourrit's Glac. Savoy* 88 The Glaciers..are beds of ice, more or less thick, which are lodged upon declivities between mountains. **1789** MRS. PIOZZI *Journ. France* II. 229 We have the pleasure of seeing Switzerland, without..climbing its glacieres. **1817** BYRON *Manfred* I. i. 68 The Glacier's cold and restless mass Moves onward day by day. **1823** SCORESBY *Whale Fishery* 229 There are two glaciers, or land icebergs. **1860** TYNDALL *Glac.* II. 422 Glaciers are derived from mountain snow, which has been consolidated to ice by pressure. **1883** OUIDA *Wanda* I. 30 The ice bastions of a thousand glaciers glow in the sunrise.

2. *attrib.* and *Comb.* **a.** attrib., as ***glacier-drift, -flea, -foot, -ice, -lake, -mass, moraine, -motion, -phenomenon, -pool, -river, -sea, -slope, -track, -valley, -water***. **b.** instrumental, as ***glacier-choked, -clad, -ploughed, -worn*** adjs. **c.** special comb., as **glacier breeze** (see quot.); **glacier burst**, the sudden release of water impounded by a glacier; **glacier-mill**, = MOULIN; **glacier-mud** (see quot.); **glacier-rope**, a rope used in traversing glaciers, to attach the members of a party together, as a precaution against accidents; **glacier-silt** = *glacier-mud*; **glacier-slow** *a.*, slow as (the movement of) a glacier; **glacier snout** = SNOUT *sb.*[1] 4 c; **glacier-snow**, the snow at the upper end of a glacier, not yet hardened into ice by pressure; **glacier-table** (see quot.); **glacier tongue** (see quot. 1956).

1930 *Meteorol. Gloss.* (ed. 2) 86 **Glacier breeze*, a cold breeze, blowing down the course of a glacier, which owes its origin to the cooling of the air in contact with the ice. **1904** *Nature* 29 Sept. 541/1 The importance of *glacier-bursts in shaping the topography of glaciated areas. **1950** T. LONGSTAFF *This my Voyage* ix. 178 We saw a 'glacier-burst' from a small hanging glacier..a crashing roar of falling stones followed by a great rush of black, muddy water down the hillside. **1897** *Pembrokesh. Antiq.* 25 Those days of ice-capped hills, *glacier-choked valleys, mammoths and cave men. **1889** G. F. WRIGHT *Ice Age N. Amer.* 76 The vast *glacier-clad interior of the country. **1876** L. AGASSIZ *Geol. Sketches* Ser. II. 89 Upon these surfaces..rests the drift, having everywhere the characteristic composition of *glacier-drift. **1884** MACMILLAN in *Sunday Mag.* Aug. 526/1 Under the stones..may be found lively colonies of the small black *glacier flea. **1856** KANE *Arct. Expl.* II. xxi. 208 The stream..tunnels its way out near the *glacier-foot. **1882** GEIKIE *Text Bk. Geol.* II. II. §6. 110 When the granular névé slowly slides down into the valleys, it acquires a more compact crystalline structure and becomes *glacier-ice. **1876** L. AGASSIZ *Geol. Sketches* Ser. II. 31 The 'parallel roads' of Glen Roy mark the ancient levels of the *glacier-lakes in that glen. **1873** J. GEIKIE *Gt. Ice Age* (1894) 243 They were doubtless formed by the same *glacier-mass. *Ibid.* 435 *Glacier-mills that gave rise to 'giant's kettles'. **1853** HERSCHEL *Pop. Lect. Sci.* vi. §34 (1873) 250 A *glacier moraine might be redistributed by tidal action over the floor of the Ocean. **1860** TYNDALL *Glac.* II. ix. 270 The fact of *glacier-motion has been known for an indefinite time to the inhabitants of the mountains. **1865** *Q. Jrnl. Geol. Soc.* XXI. 166 The Boulder-earth or *Glacier-mud. Resting on the surface of the ice-worn rocks we find a widespread accumulation of boulder-earth, an unstratified mass of coarse gritty mud, in which are imbedded pebbles, boulders, and stony particles. **1863** A. C. RAMSAY *Phys. Geog.* 73, I will describe to you..various other *glacier-phenomena affecting the scenery of the Alps. **1888** *Century Mag.* XXXVI. 791/1 New England. Its stony hills and rocky coast, its *glacier-plowed and niggardly soil. **1860** TYNDALL *Glac.* II. xxiv. 357 Figures..formed in the ice on the surface of *glacier-pools. **1914** D. H. LAWRENCE *Prussian Officer* 16 The whity-green *glacier-river twisted through its pale shoals. **1936** *Discovery* May 139/2 Another excellent river..[for fishing] is the glacier river Blandá. **1897** *Westm. Gaz.* 16 Aug. 4/2 He was tied to a rope and lowered. Three *glacier-rope lengths were necessary before he reached Sachs. *a* **1835** MRS. HEMANS *Alp-Horn Song* Poems (1875) 294 The sparkling blue of the *glacier-sea. **1895** *Funk's Stand. Dict.*, **Glacier-silt*. **1856** KANE *Arct. Expl.* I. xxv. 332 Some of its *glacier-slopes were margined with verdure. **1861** LOWELL *Lett.* (1894) I. 318 So I submitted, took to pentameters, and only hope the thoughts are good enough to be preserved in the ice of the colder and almost *glacier-slow measure. **1933** *Ibid.* Jan. 28/1 Nor is the correlation of *glacier-snout movement with Brückner cycles by any means a fact. **1883** OGILVIE *Suppl.*, **Glacier-snow*, same as *Névé*. **1860** TYNDALL *Glac.* I. vi. 44 *Glacier tables; flat masses of rock, raised high upon columns of ice. **1930** *Ibid.* Mar. 91/2 *Glacier-tongues provided the starting point. **1956** ARMSTRONG & ROBERTS *Illustr. Ice Gloss.* 6 *Glacier tongue*, an extension of a glacier, projecting seaward, and usually afloat. **1876** L. AGASSIZ *Geol. Sketches* Ser. II. 66 This western track of the glacier is crossed transversely..by two other *glacier-tracks. **1860** TYNDALL *Glac.* II. viii. 264 A succession of old lateral moraines, such as many *glacier-valleys exhibit. *Ibid.* I. xii. 86 Beer, cold as the *glacier water. **1876** L. AGASSIZ *Geol. Sketches* Ser. II. 41 The inequalities of the *glacier-worn surfaces.

Hence '**glaciered** *ppl. a.*, covered with glaciers; also (of water) proceeding from a glacier.

1824 *New Monthly Mag.* X. 16 Those sublime and glacier'd peaks. **1834** T. MEDWIN *Angler in Wales* I. 234 The glaciered water is too cold for them [fish]. **1847** DISRAELI *Tancred* III. iv, What need of..mountains of glaciered crest. **1853** KANE *Grinnell Exp.* xvii. (1856) 130 A barrier apparently as permanent as the glaciered hills with which it is united.

‖**glacière** ('glasjɛr). [Fr., = ice-house.] An ice-cave.

1865 G. F. BROWNE *Ice-Caves* iv. 46 The upper glacière of the Pré de S. Livres. **1879** *Encycl. Brit.* X. 270/1 Cases.. occur where ice forms in caverns (*glacières*) even in warm and comparatively low districts.

glacieret (glæsɪə'rɛt, 'gleɪs-, 'gleɪʃ-). [f. GLACIER + -ET.] A small glacier; applied by Leconte to a mass of ice revealed after an extended period of dry weather has caused the wastage of overlying névé in the Sierra Nevada.

1875 J. LECONTE in *Amer. Jrnl. Sci.* X. 138 The thin moving ice-fields, the glacierets which still linger among the highest peaks and shadiest hollows of the Sierra. **1904** G. K. GILBERT *Glaciers & Glaciation* i. 11 Small alpine glaciers are sometimes called *glacierets*, or, if visible high on the sides of mountain valleys, *hanging* glaciers. **1922** WRIGHT & PRIESTLEY *Glaciology* 109 A snow-drift glacier, or glacieret. **1951** G. TAYLOR *Geogr. 20th Cent.* 614 *Glacierets*, small glaciers, may develop from snow-drifts.

'**glacierist.** *rare.* [f. GLACIER + -IST.] One who studies glaciers.

1850 WHEWELL in Todhunter *Acct. W.'s Writings* (1876) II. 366 Hugi, the glacierist was there. **1862** —— *ibid.* II. 427 Have any of the recent glacierists given any observations on a large scale as to the direction which the crevasses really follow?

glacieri'zation. [f. GLACIER + -IZE + -ATION.]

1. Conversion into glacier. *nonce-wd.*

1850 *Westm. Rev.* Oct. 267 A general glacierization (*vergletscherung*) of the whole island is a thing not to be thought of.

2. The covering of land by an ice-sheet; the state of being so covered.

1922 WRIGHT & PRIESTLEY *Glaciology* v. 134 'Glacierisation'—the inundation of land by ice. **1954** W. D. THORNBURY *Princ. Geomorphol.* vi. 149 Pleistocene glacierization caused many of the valleys beyond the margins of the ice sheets..to receive quantities of glacial outwash beyond the transporting capacities of the streams in them. **1968** R. W. FAIRBRIDGE *Encycl. Geomorphol.* 472/2 The continuity of the present ice age is suggested by the continued ice coverage (glacierization) of Antarctica.

glacification (glæsɪfɪˈkeɪʃən). [f. L. *glaci-ēs* ice + -FICATION.] **a.** The action of converting into ice. **b.** The action of covering with ice.

1860 TYNDALL *Glac.* II. v. 252 The second great agent in the process of glacification, namely pressure. **1875** tr. *Schmidt's Desc. & Darw.* 63 The diluvial period..includes, both in Europe and America, a repeated glacification of countries, and vast portions of the world.

glacifluvial (gleɪʃɪ-, gleɪsɪˈfluːvɪəl), *a.* [f. L. *glaci-ēs* ice + FLUVIAL *a.*] = *fluvio-glacial* adj.

1937 *Proc. Prehist. Soc.* III. 154 The erratics found in the latter must be derived, either directly or indirectly by means of glacifluvial transport, from the deposits of the North Sea Drift. **1946** F. E. ZEUNER *Dating Past* III. v. 111 Two superimposed glacial deposits (such as boulder clays or bottom moraines; or glacifluvial or meltwater gravels).

glacio- (ˈgleɪsɪəʊ, ˈgleɪʃɪəʊ), used as the combining form of L. *glaciēs* ice, as in **ˌglacio-ˈeustasy, -ˈeustatism**, changes in the sea-level caused by the waxing and waning of ice-sheets; hence **ˌglacio-euˈstatic** adj.; **ˌglacio-ˈfluvial** *a.* = *fluvio-glacial* adj.; **ˌglaciolaˈcustrine** *a.*, of or pertaining to a lake or lakes deriving water from the melting of ice.

1962 *New Scientist* 2 Aug. 243/1 Given a few decades or millenia of warmer summers, and the glaciers melt; the hydrologic balance swings to the positive side and the ocean level rises. This is the phenomenon of 'glacio-eustasy'. **1963** D. W. & E. E. HUMPHRIES tr. *Termier's Erosion & Sedimentation* vi. 152 The glacio-eustatic retreat of the seas at the time of the first glaciation. **1935** H. BAULIG *Changing Sea Level* 4 This kind of phenomena, for which the name glacio-eustatism would seem appropriate. **1954** Glacio-eustatism [see EUSTATIC *a.*]. **1903** *Amer. Geol.* May 285 The glacio-fluvial deposits of the Wisconsin epoch. **1935** *Discovery* Mar. 78/1 Glacial and glacio-fluvial streams. **1910** *Encycl. Brit.* XII. 59/1 Professor Chamberlin and other American geologists have recognized the following stages in the glaciation of North America:.. The Glacio-lacustrine substage. **1963** D. W. & E. E. HUMPHRIES tr. *Termier's Erosion & Sedimentation* vii. 162 The attribution of ancient deposits of similar type to the same cause, thus identifying them as glacio-lacustrine in origin.

glaciological (gleɪsɪ-, gleɪʃɪəˈlɒdʒɪkəl), *a.* [f. GLACIOLOGY + -ICAL.] Concerned with glaciology.

1889 in *Cent. Dict.* **1933** *Discovery* Mar. 89/1 Glaciological observations will be made at the ice-cap station. **1955** *Times* 13 July 4/4 One of the oversea expeditions will be in northern Norway engaged on geological, glaciological, biological, and survey work. **1970** *Nature* 28 Feb. 793/1 Because of the greater depth of erosion, glaciological knowledge based on Quaternary information may be enhanced.

glaciˈologist. [f. next + -IST.] = GLACIALIST a.

1886 SIR J. W. DAWSON in *Nature* 2 Sept. 410/2 Your veteran glaciologist, Dr. Crosskey. **1937** H. W. TILMAN *Ascent of Nanda Devi* i. 2 To other learned men, glaciologists, ethnologists or geographers, the Himalaya are a fruitful source of debate. **1958** *New Scientist* 13 Nov. 1245/2 Glaciologists in all parts of the world are beginning to watch the ice [of glaciers] with much interest. **1970** *Daily Tel.* 3 Sept. 13/7 Our glaciologists, working to a depth of 10,000 feet on the Antarctic ice cap, will be able to show how that cap has been polluted during the many centuries past.

glaciology (gleɪʃɪˈɒlədʒɪ). [f. GLACIO- + -LOGY.] The science which treats of ice or glaciers.

1889 in *Cent. Dict.* **1892** *Nation* (N.Y.) 29 Dec. 497/2 Already this suggestion finds favor among some of our leaders in glaciology. **1921** H. G. PONTING *Gt. White South* 138 Taylor could tell us more in an hour about Physiography and Glaciology than we could have absorbed in months of reading on such matters. **1971** *Nature* 12 Feb. 508/3 A synoptic view of the properties of ice for those engaged in research in glaciology, cloud physics and other related fields.

glaciˈometer. [f. as prec. + Gr. μέτρον measure: see -METER.] A measure of glacial action.

1892 *Edin. Rev.* Apr. 310 They serve in Dr. Wright's phrase as glaciometers.

†**ˈglacious,** *a. Obs.*⁻¹ [ad. F. *glacieux* (obs.), f. L. *glaciēs* ice.] Resembling ice.

1646 SIR T. BROWNE *Pseud. Ep.* II. i. 50 *Aqua fortis*.. exhaled and placed in cold conservatories will Crystallise and shoot into white and glacious bodyes.

glacis (ˈgleɪsɪs, glasi). [a. F. *glacis* (first recorded in the 16th c.), orig. 'a place made slipperie by wet lately fallen and frozen on' (Cotgr.), and related to OF. *glacier* to slip, slide (see GLACE *v.*). In med.L. (*c* 1270) *glatia* is found with the meaning of *glacis* (in fortification).]

1. A gently sloping bank (see quot. 1712).

In mod. use probably *transf.* from sense 2.

1672 *Phil. Trans.* VII. 4081 That so the water..spreading it self upon the glacis or slope..may not spoil the Causey. **1712** J. JAMES tr. *Le Blond's Gardening* 37 A Slope that lies under the Diagonal of a Square, or less than 45 Degrees, they [the French] term Glacis. **1787** M. CUTLER in *Life*, etc. (1888) I. 275 We were walking on the northern side of the Garden, upon a beautiful glacis. **1830** LYELL *Princ. Geol.* I. 245 When nothing appears above water but the higher part of that sloping glacis which we before described. **1892** STEVENSON *Across the Plains* ii. 79 The foam..mounts in an instant to the ridge of the sand glacis.

2. a. *Fortif.* 'The parapet of the covered way extended in a long slope to meet the natural surface of the ground, so that every part of it shall be swept by the fire of the ramparts' (Voyle *Mil. Dict.*). Also *fig.*

1688 CAPT. J. S. *Fortif.* 27 The Glacis or Esplanade, a kind of Parapet which loseth itself insensibly, level with the Earth. **1692** LUTTRELL *Brief Rel.* (1857) II. 486 The enemy ..made 4 attacks on the glacis of the counterscarp. **1755** T. FORBES in C. Gist *Jrnls.* (1893) 151 The Soldiers Barracks.. are built between the Stockadoes and the Glacis of the Fort. **1782** P. H. BRUCE *Mem.* I. 15 Upon our breaking ground on the glacis, or covered way, I was with the pioneers. **1823** BYRON *Juan* VIII. xxxiv, The rest, who kept their valiant faces And levell'd weapons still against the glacis. [*c* **1870** HAY *Banty Tim* 32, I sprawled on that cursed glacee.] **1879** HOWELLS *L. Aroostook* iv. 40 The black guns looked out over the neatly shaven glacis. **1955** *Times* 3 Aug. 9/2 This view of east Germany as part of Russia's defensive glacis has never been dropped. **1960** *Observer* 7 Feb. 7/6 The countries of Eastern Europe..form the glacis between the Soviet Union and the West.

b. In full *glacis plate*. A sloping armour-plate protecting an opening, etc., in a ship.

1889 J. J. WELCH *Text Bk. Naval Archit.* xiv. 149 These openings are generally further protected by working sloped armour plates—called *glacis plates*—around them about 3" thick. **1933** *Jane's Fighting Ships* 520 Armour (Krupp): 2" deck (amidships), ¾" deck (ends), 3½" glacis to engine room hatches.

†**3.** *Build.* (See quot.)

1727–41 CHAMBERS *Cycl.*, The glacis of the cornich is an easy imperceptible slope in the cymatium of the cornich, to promote the descent and draining off of the rain-water.

4. *attrib.*, as *glacis-form*; *glacis-shaped* adj.

1844 *Hull Dock Act* 65 The Company shall slope off the eastern side of the said wharf..in an oblique or glacis form. **1884** *Milit. Engin.* I. II. 35 When made glacis-shaped these screens are more difficult to cut through than when shaped like an ordinary parapet.

†**ˈglacitate,** *v. Obs.*⁻⁰ [ad. late L. *glacitāre*.]

1623 COCKERAM, *Glacitate*, to cry like a gander.

glack (glak). *Sc.* Also 6 **glak**. [a. Gael *glac* valley, hollow, etc.]

1. A deep and narrow mountain-valley.

1535 STEWART *Cron. Scot.* II. 147 Herbis that in the mont than grew, And glak and glen in hole and mony hirne. *a* **1800** *Water-kelpie* ix. in Scott *Minstr. Scott. Bord.* (1810) III. 389 Frae yon deep glack at Catla's back. **1826** G. BEATTIE *John o' Arnha'* in *Life & Poems* 229 Deep i the glack, and round the well. **1888** D. BEVERIDGE *Betw. the Ochils & Forth* vii. 98 A beautiful defile or glack, as it is called in that part of the country.

2. a. The fork of a tree. **b.** A spot where roads diverge.

18.. *Donald & Flora* 155 (Jam.) That is the spreading branch that used to shade us, And that's the braid wide glack we used to sit on. **1871** W. ALEXANDER *Johnny Gibb* xxv. (1873) 145 Yon was him't we met at the glack o' the roads.

‖**glaçon** (glasɔ̃). Also **glacon**. [Fr.] A medium-sized ice-floe (see quots.).

1933 *Geogr. Jrnl.* LXXXI. 60 Drift-ice was pretty thick and we were constantly under helm to avoid the 'pans', as the seamen and fishermen call them, or 'glacons', which, I believe is the scientific term. **1963** D. W. & E. E. HUMPHRIES tr. *Termier's Erosion & Sedimentation* iv. 85 '*Glacons*', smaller than 650 feet [in diameter].

glacyer, obs. form of GLAZIER.

glad, *sb.*[1] Also 4 **glath**(e. [f. the adj.]

†**1.** Gladness, joy. *Obs.*

With quot. *a* 1300 compare FOR- *pref.*[1] 10. In quot. 1608 prob. pseudo-arch.

c **1000** *Be Manna Wyrdum* (Gr.-Wülk.) 68 Dryhten.. dæleþ sumum earfeþa dæl, Sumum ȝeoȝoþe glæd. *a* **1300** *Cursor M.* 17873 þei seide for glad [*Gött.* wid gladnes] wiþ gretyng gle 'þis ilke liȝt forsoþe is he, þat maker is of lastyng liȝt'. *c* **1330** R. BRUNNE *Chron. Wace* (Rolls) 3260 Al þus þen ended þe breþere wrathe, þer tene turned to game & glathe. *c* **1440** *Generydes* 1255 When he was come and knewe that it was she, For very glad he wist not what to saye. **1608** SHAKS. *Per.* II. Prol. 38 All perishen of man, of pelfe, Ne ought escapend but himselfe; Till Fortune tir'd with doing bad, Threw him a shore, to giue him glad.

2. *ellipt.* for *glad eye* (see GLAD *a.* 4 d).

1927 W. E. COLLINSON *Contemp. Eng.* 93 To give the glad-eye.., often abbreviated to the glad. **1956** A. WILSON *Anglo-Saxon Attitudes* I. iii. 46 Like a lot of old birds giving the glad in the Circus, or the York Road, Waterloo, more likely.

glad (glæd), *sb.*[2] Colloq. abbrev. of GLADIOLUS. Usu. *pl.*

1923 *Bull. Canad. Gladiolus Soc.* I. 3 We shall have a membership of at least five hundred (500) active 'Glad' enthusiasts. *Ibid.* 43 Cutting of Glads calls for a little discrimination. *Ibid.* 44 The wonderful Shows..have placed the 'Glad' in the very forefront of flower culture. **1934** S. ROBERTSON *Devel. Mod. Eng.* (1936) v. 120 Sometimes the problem of rival plural forms is resolved by retaining both..so it is with foci and focuses, gladioli and gladioluses. The last instance is further complicated by varying accentuation..hence some who have occasion to use the word dodge the issue altogether and say *glads*. **1949** [see CUKE]. **1969** 'J. FRASER' *Cockpit of Roses* xx. 151, I think them's my irises..and I'm certain those are my glads because that's my knot on the raffia.

glad (glæd), *a.* Forms: 1, 3 **glæd**, 3 **gled, glead, glað**, 3–4 **gladd**(e, 4–5 **glade**, (5 **glaad**), 4–6 *Sc.* **glaid**, 3– **glad**. [OE. *glæd* = OS. *glad* (only in comb. *glad-môd*), ON. *glaðr* (Sw. *glad*, Da. *glad*), bright, joyous. The orig. sense of the word is app. found in OHG. *glat* smooth, and is retained in G. *glatt*, Du. *glad*, *glat* (MDu. also *gelad*, *gelat*), Fris. *gled* (also Da. *glat*, Sw. *glatt*, from German). The OTeut. type **glaðo-* is cognate with OSl. *gladŭkŭ* (Russ. *gladkiĭ*) and L. *glaber* smooth (:—**ghladhro-*; cf. *ruber*, *uber* with *red*, *udder*).]

†**1.** Bright, shining, beautiful. (Cf. 5.) *Obs.*

a **1000** *Cædmon's Gen.* 2719 (Gr.) [He] sealde him to bote ..gangende feoh and glæd seolfor. *a* **1000** *Phœnix* 289 in *Exeter Bk.*, þonne sweȝles leoht ȝimma gladost..eastan lixeð. *a* **1000** *Sal. & Sat.* (Kemble) 975 Oðer biþ golde glæ dra, oðer biþ grundum sweartra. **1412–20** LYDG. *Chron. Troy* I. iii, Under theise braunches & theis bowes glade. *c* **1450** *Cov. Myst.* (Shaks. Soc.) 168 Heylle, I cum to the with gold glade. *a* **1500** *Flower & Leaf* 35 Leves new..Som very rede, and som a glad light grene.

2. a. Of persons: †Cheerful, joyous, or merry in disposition (*obs.*); joyful, happy (*arch.*). †*to make glad*: = 'to make merry'.

The sense in the first quot. is uncertain; it is prob. a vague figurative use of 1, and may have meant 'noble', 'glorious', rather than 'cheerful'; cf. BRIGHT *a.* 6.

Beowulf (Z.) 58 [He] heold þenden lifde gamol & guðreouw glæde Scyldingas. *c* **897** K. ÆLFRED *Gregory's Past.* xliv. 322 Sanctus Paulus..cwæð þætte ðone gladan ȝiefan [L. *hilarem datorem*] God lufode. *c* **1205** LAY. 7013 Æuer wes þe king glad & æuere he gomen luueden [*v.r.* louede]. *c* **1250** *Gen. & Ex.* 2297 In fulsumhed he wurðen glaðe. *c* **1290** *S. Eng. Leg.* I. 366/2 Faire man and noble he was, and glad and of swete mode. **13..** *Minor Poems fr. Vernon MS.* xxxvii. 705 While þou miȝt, make þe glad and muri! Lengor liueþ a glad mon þen a sori. **1375** BARBOUR *Bruce* I. 332 To Parys can he ga And levyt thar full sympyllly, The quhethir he glaid was and Ioly. *c* **1400** *Gamelyn* 470, I sitte fasting & oþer men make glade. **1500–20** DUNBAR *Poems* xxiii. 1 Be mirry and glaid, honest and vertewous. **1702** STEELE *Funeral* I. i, Did I not give..twenty shillings a week, to be sorrowful? and the more I give you, I think, the gladder you are. **1780** COWPER *Progr. Err.* 165 A day of luxury..When the glad soul is made heaven's welcome guest. **1799** WORDSW. *Fountain* xii, Often, glad no more, We wear a face of joy, because We have been glad of yore. **1865** R. BUCHANAN *Sutherland's Pansies* v, There grew a.. sadness in his tone When he was gladdest.

†**b.** Borne with cheerfulness. *Obs.* [Cf. L. *læta paupertas*.]

c **1386** CHAUCER *Wife's T.* 327 Glad pouerte is an honeste thyng certeyn.

†**c.** *glad with*: pleasant, kindly, affable to (a person). *Obs.*

Beowulf (Z.) 1173 Beo wið ȝeatas glæd, ȝeofena ȝemyndiȝ *c* **1000** ÆLFRIC *Gen.* xliii. 14 Min drihten hine ȝedo glædne [L. *placabilem*] wið eow, þæt he aȝife eow eowerne broðor. *c* **1305** *11,000 Virgins* 121 in *E.E.P.* (1862) 69 Gladdest he was wiþ his soster..þat heo scholde so ȝung & so clene suffrie deþes pyne.

3. Rejoiced, affected with pleasure by some particular cause; = FAIN *a.* Now only *predicative*.

In mod. Eng. (at least in prose use) the sense is much weaker than that which the word had in the older language, and which appears in the derivatives *gladly*, *gladness*. In general 'pleased' would now be an adequate synonym, while 'delighted' or 'rejoiced' suggest a much stronger feeling.

a. *simply.* (With the cause indicated contextually).

c **950** *Lindisf. Gosp.* John viii. 56 Abraham fæder iuer ȝefeade þætte ȝeseȝe dæȝe minne & ȝesæh & ȝegladade *vel* glæd uæs. *a* **1100** *O.E. Chron.* (Laud MS.) an. 656 Ða þa kyning heorda þæt ȝe secgon, þa wærð he swiðe glæd. *a* **1225** *Juliana* 70 Ha herede godd in heouene, & warð swiðe gled [*Bodl. MS.* glead]. **1297** R. GLOUC. (Rolls) 3817 þe [*v.r.* þo] king arthure hurde þis no gladdore mon nas. *c* **1350** *Will. Palerne* 67 A gladere wommon under god no miȝt go on erþe þan was þe wif wiþ þe child. **1388** WYCLIF *Prov.* x. 1 A wijs sone makith glad the fadir [**1535** COVERDALE and **1611** maketh a glad father]. *c* **1450** *St. Cuthbert* (Surtees) 476 þan þai ware bathe glad and blithe. **1617** MORYSON *Itin.* I. 185 One thing in this miserie made me glad. **1633** EARL MANCH. *Al Mondo* (1636) 192 As a wearied traveller..is then gladdest when he comes within kenning of his Country. **1842** TENNYSON *Audley Court* 87 We were glad at heart. *Mod.* 'Your friend has won his case.' 'Yes; I am very glad.'

b. with *prep. glad of*: †(*a*) made happy or joyful, delighted or pleased with (an object possessed) (*obs.*); (*b*) = 'glad to have or get' (see 3 d); (*c*) joyful on account of, delighted or pleased by (an event, a state of things). Also const. *at* (an event, usually one affecting another person, esp. unfavourably), *for* (*arch.*), †*in*, †*with*.

c **950** *Lindisf. Gosp.* Luke i. 14 And bið gifea ðe & glædnise & monigo in accennisse his biðon glæde. *c* **1200** ORMIN 3179 Elysabæþ Wass gladd inoh & bliþe Off hire dere child Johan. *c* **1205** LAY. 3962 þe king wes gled for his kime & for þen cnihtes bet come mid hine. *c* **1250** *Gen. & Ex.* 3671 Moyses was bliðe and glað of ðis. **1388** WYCLIF *Prov.* xvii. 5 He that is glad in the fallyng of another man [**1611** He that is glad at calamities] schal not be vnpunyschid. **1480** CAXTON *Chron. Eng.* liv. (1482) 38 He wepte ful tenderly..and netheles he was somdele glad of his deth. **1548** HALL *Chron.*, *Edw. IV*,

204 b, The kyng, glad of this victory, commaunded [etc.]. **1585** SIDNEY *Let.* 22 Nov., Misc. Wks. (1829) 307, I fynd the people very glad of me. **1592** SHAKS. *Rom. & Jul.* IV. ii. 28 Why, I am glad on't. **1611** —— *Cymb.* I. i. 15 Not a Courtier ..hath a heart that is not Glad at the thing they scowle at. **1617** MORYSON *Itin.* I. 178 They gave us flesh to eat, whereof I was glad as of a dainty I could not get in Italy. **1625–6** PURCHAS *Pilgrims* II. 1165 And he sent me word that he was very glad with my safe arrival. **1648** GAGE *West Ind.* xii. (1655) 49 Garcia Holguin being a glad man of such a prisoner. **1697** DRYDEN *Æneid* x. 1118 The Trojan, glad with sight of hostile Blood. **1738** SWIFT *Pol. Conversat.* 119 Madam, Dinner's upon the Table.—Faith, I'm glad of it. **1784** MISS BURNEY *Diary* 22 Apr. II. 310, I am so glad of seeing your sentiments, when I cannot hear them, that your letters are only less valuable to me than yourself. **1807** SOUTHEY *Espriella's Lett.* III. 320 The Westminster boys were working an engine in the cloisters..D... said they were glad at the fire. **1842** TENNYSON *Dora* 66 When his heart is glad Of the full harvest. **1870** MORRIS *Earthly Par.* II. III. 229 For life and love that has been, I am glad. **1874** DASENT *Half a Life* II. 201, I was glad at the sport.

c. With clause as complement: *glad that*, etc. In later usage chiefly with omission of *that*.

c **1200** ORMIN 2812 He wass gladd, Laffdiȝ, forr þatt tu come. *c* **1205** LAY. 9374 An oðer halue he wes glæd þat his ifon weoren dæd. **1375** BARBOUR *Bruce* III. 724 Blyth, and glaid, that thai war sua Eschapyt the hidwyss wawys fra. *a* **1450** *Knt. de la Tour* (1868) 15 And she saide that she was gladder that she had do it [her hood] of to hym thanne to a lorde. **1559** W. CUNNINGHAM *Cosmogr. Glasse* 71, I am glad you understand the reason of it. *a* **1605** POLWART *Flyting w. Montgomerie* 37, I am right glaide Thou art begun in write to flyte. **1632** J. HAYWARD tr. *Biondi's Eromena* 58 Perseus, now a glad man, that the business had so succeeded according as he desired. **1683** TEMPLE *Mem.* Introd. Wks. 1731 I. 374, I am the gladder..that my publick Imployment should contribute something to your Entertainment. **1855** LORD HOUGHTON in *Life* (1891) I. xi. 527, I am glad I came, as Lord E. is very low. **1884** MRS. EWING *Mary's Meadow* (1886) 37, I am very glad you like it.

d. With infinitive: Happy, delighted, pleased *to* (do, be, etc.); also, well content *to* (do, have, etc. something in default of better). In mod. use freq. in the phrases ***I am glad to hear, see*** (etc.); also, ***I should be glad to*** (***hear, know***, etc.) with sarcastic force.

c **1340** *Cursor M.* 19396 (Trin.) Oþes þenne to hem þei made To do hit were þei wondir glade. *c* **1386** CHAUCER *Clerk's T.* 320 Thise ladyes were nat right glad To handle hir clothes wher Inne she was clad. *c* **1450** *St. Cuthbert* (Surtees) 6372 To wyn away he was full glad. **1526** *Pilgr. Perf.* (W. de W. 1531) 5 Euery chrysten man or woman.. sholde be the gladder to fulfyll his blessed wyll. **1572** *Satir. Poems Reform.* xxxiii. 261 Now [they are] glaid to get Peis breid and watter Caill. **1670** LADY MARY BERTIE in *12th Rep. Hist. MSS. Comm.* App. v. 21, I received yours and am very glad to heare you are so merry with the musicke and danceing. **1711** STEELE *Spect.* No. 52 ¶3 We shall be heartily glad to see your short face in Oxford. **1767** *Junius Lett.* iii. 19, I should be glad to know where you have received your intelligence? **1814** D. H. O'BRIAN *Captiv. & Escape* 16 And told us that we ought to have been glad to have got any thing. **1849** MACAULAY *Hist. Eng.* vii. II. 164 He was glad to turn away from the stage and to talk about publick affairs. **1897** MARY KINGSLEY *W. Africa* 298, I was glad to see the mangrove-belt.

4. a. Of feelings, looks, actions, etc.: Filled with, marked by, or expressive of joy or delight.

a **900** CYNEWULF *Christ* 315 in *Exeter Bk.*, Him godes engel þurh glædne ȝeþonc þa wisan onwrah. *c* **1000** *Ags. Ps.* (Th.) lii. 8 þonne Iacob byð on glædum sælum, and Israelas ealle bliðe. *a* **1225** *Ancr. R.* 70 Heo schal habben leaue to.. makien signes touward hire of one glede chere. *a* **1240** *Sawles Warde* in *Cott. Hom.* 257 [He] þonkeð god ȝeorne wið swiðe glead heorte. *c* **1340** *Cursor M.* 2535 (Trin.) Melchisedech wiþ wille glade Offryng of wyn & breed made. *c* **1385** CHAUCER *L.G.W.* 1038 *Dido*, So yong so lusty with hire eyen glade. *c* **1475** *Rauf Coilȝear* 178 Doun he sat the King neir And maid him glaid & gude cheir. **1483** CAXTON *Gold. Leg.* 217/1 She aroos up peasibly with a glad visage. **1567** *Satir. Poems Reform.* iii. 33 In gamis glaid he was rycht weill asswetit. **1667** MILTON *P.L.* VII. 291 Thither they Hasted with glad precipitance. **1696** TATE & BRADY *Ps.* cxlix. 1 O praise ye the Lord, prepare your glad Voice. **1769** SIR W. JONES *Palace Fortune* Poems (1777) 27 The damsel rose; and, lost in glad surprize, Cast round the gay expanse her opening eyes. **1847** LYTTON *Lucretia* 416 Surely the discovery of your son should create gladder emotions. **1852** M. ARNOLD *Poems, Youth of Nature*, Cold the elation of joy In his gladdest airiest song. **1860** TYNDALL *Glac.* I. xxii. 159, I was soon at the bottom..fairly out of danger, and full of glad vigour.

b. Of tidings, news, etc.: Full of, or bringing, joy.

a **1240** *Sawles Warde* in *Cott. Hom.* 257 Let him in..he bringeð us gleade tidinges. *c* **1470** HENRY *Wallace* II. 344 With glaid bodword, thar myrthis till amend. **1597** J. PAYNE *Royal Exch.* 13 Wch ys the gladdest news and ioy-fullest tydings. **1611** BIBLE *Luke* viii. 1 Shewing the glad tidings of the kingdome of God. **1833** HT. MARTINEAU *Tale of Tyne* vii. 131 It was a glad day for him and Effie when leave was got to sell coal in London by weight. **1872** C. GIBBON *For the King* xxi, You have given me the gladdest tidings, Johnstone, that I have heard for many days.

†**c.** Welcome, acceptable. *Obs. rare.*

a **1586** SIDNEY *Arcadia* I. (1590) 87 Her conuersation More gladde to me, then to a miser monie is. **1690** EVELYN in *Pepys' Diary* (1879) VI. 170 Which, though it make a gap in my poor Collection, to which it was glad, I most cheerfully bestow it upon you.

d. *the glad eye*: a look or movement of the eyes designed to attract a person of the opposite sex; hence **glad-eye** *v. trans.*, to give (someone) the glad eye. *colloq.*

1911 *Punch* 22 Nov. 382/2 The lover, the elderly philanderer, the girl with the glad eye. **1913** 'I. HAY' *Happy-go-Lucky* ii, Miss Welwyn..from the safe harbourage of her mother's arms, was endeavouring to administer to him what is technically known, I believe, as The Glad Eye. **1923** W. L. GEORGE *Hail, Columbia!* iv. 119, I have never seen an American girl give to a man in the street what the English call the 'glad eye'. **1935** A. J. CRONIN *Stars look Down* I. xvi. 150 Purves..'glad-eyeing' Hetty, trying 'to get off with her'. **1939** A. HUXLEY *After Many a Summer* II. i. 189, I *do* see her giving the glad eye to Pete.

e. *glad hand* (freq. used somewhat ironically): (the) hand of welcome; a cordial handshake or greeting; a welcome; esp. in phr. *to give* (someone) *the glad hand*; also *attrib.*; hence **glad-hand** *v. trans.*, to greet cordially, to welcome, to please; also *intr.*; **glad-handed** *ppl. a.*; **glad-hander**, one who gives people the glad hand; one who acts cordially towards everybody; **glad-handing** *vbl. sb.* and *ppl. a. colloq.* (orig. *U.S.*).

1895 W. C. GORE in *Inlander* Dec. 116 *Give the glad hand*, to welcome. **1896** ADE *Artie* i. 4 She meets me at the door, puts out the glad hand and says: 'Hang up your lid and come into the game.' **1903** —— *People You Know* 175 Every time he started down town he would have to zigzag so as to cover both sides of the street and glad-hand all his Acquaintances. **1908** J. M. SULLIVAN *Criminal Slang* 11 *Glad hand*, handshake without any real friendship behind it. **1911** H. S. HARRISON *Queed* ii. 14 Mr. Bylash didn't go out to give her the glad hand, and welcome her into our humble *coturee*. **1929** C. E. MERRIAM *Chicago* 275 One type is the good fellow,..the glad hander, whose chief reliance is the cultivation of the personal friendship of individuals and the acquaintance with all sorts of groups and societies. **1930** *Time & Tide* 11 Oct. 1256 He makes a habit of cutting out glad-hand phrases and smooth generalities. **1939** MICHIE & RYHLICK *Dixie Demagogues* x. 207 Happy was stumping the hinterlands, glad-handing, back-slapping, and singing. **1945** AUDEN *Sea & Mirror* ii. 55 Such are the alternative routes, the facile glad-handed highway or the virtuous averted track. **1957** M. GAIR *Sapphires on Wednesday* ix. 114 He was probably quite a kindly old geezer..but a professional glad-hander. **1958** *Economist* 8 Nov. 492/2 General de Gaulle has stood aloof from the backslapping and glad handing. **1959** *New Statesman* 17 Jan. 62/2 Crude economic reasons do not explain why Mikoyan should have been given the glad hand. **1960** *Guardian* 8 Dec. 9/7 The glad-handing undertaker loves his job because 'it makes you feel closer to people'.

f. *glad rags* (occas. *glad clothes*): (one's) best clothes; very smart or fancy clothes; *spec.* formal evening dress. *colloq.* (orig. *U.S.*).

1902 'D. DIX' *Fables of Elite* 72 All the Females Assembled in their Glad Rags and proceeded to go through their particular Stunts for his Benefit. **1905** *Daily Chron.* 11 Jan. 4/5 Only when starvation stares him in the face will he relinquish his 'glad clothes', as the cowboys call them. **1907** N. MUNRO *Daft Days* vii. 60 'There's a big garden-party to be at it—' 'My! I guess I'll put on my best glad rags.' **1916** J. FARNOL *Definite Object* iii, 'Are you comin' wi' me, sir?' inquired Spike... 'I surely am.' 'But—but not in them glad rags?' and Spike pointed to Mr. Ravenslee's exquisitely tailored garments. **1922** H. B. HERMON-HODGE *Up against it in Nigeria* v. 76 We all turned out in our glad rags to join in the procession. **1931** E. LINKLATER *Juan in Amer.* II. xii. 143 All dolled up in glad rags,..They call you Glad Rag Doll!

5. a. Of inanimate nature or its conditions: Full of brightness or beauty; suggesting feelings of cheerfulness and delight.

1667 MILTON *P.L.* VII. 386 Glad Evening and glad Morn crownd the fourth day. **1697** DRYDEN *Virg. Georg.* IV. 813 Mighty Cæsar..On the glad Earth the Golden Age renews, And his great Father's Path to Heav'n pursues. **1700** PRIOR *Carmen Seculare* 355 Let her glad valleys smile with wavy corn. **1712** TICKELL *Spect.* No. 410 ¶6 It wants no Glad Perfume Arabia yields In all her Citron Groves, and spicy Fields. *a* **1790** COWPER *Morning Dream* 1 'Twas in the glad season of spring. **1835** LYTTON *Rienzi* VIII. iii, The glad sun rising gorgeously from the hills revived his wearied spirit. **1853** C. BRONTE *Villette* iv. (1876) 34 What a living spring! What a warm, glad summer! **1865** SWINBURNE *Ballad of Life* 2 Full of sweet trees and colour of glad grass.

†**b.** Fertile, flourishing (= L. *lætus*). *Obs. rare.*

c **1420** *Pallad. on Husb.* II. 8 In placis glade [and lene], in placis drie The medis clensid tyme is now to make. *Ibid.* 186 They [lettuces] that thynnest stondith beth gladdest.

6. *dial.* (See quots.)

Cf. Sw. dial. *glad* 'open', said e.g. of a door which does not shut closely. In some Eng. dialects *glid* and *gleg* are found in the same sense.

1674–91 RAY *N.C. Words* 31 *Glad*, is spoken of Doors, Bolts &c., that go smoothly and loosely. **1883** *Almondb. Gloss.*, *Glad*, smooth, easy. A screw turns too glad when the hole is too large.

7. quasi-*adv.* = GLADLY *adv. poet.*

c **1340** *Cursor M.* 13697 (Fairf.) To þe temple he ȝode for to teyche..þe men atte glad walde him here. *c* **1475** *Rauf Coilȝear* 601 He saw the king was engreuit, and gat furth glaid. **1500–20** DUNBAR *Poems* lxix. 45 How glaid that ever I dyne or sowp. **1727–46** THOMSON *Summer* 477 The heart beats glad. *c* **1790** COWPER *Needless Alarm* 62 He..knows.. How glad they catch the largess of the skies.

8. *Comb.*, as *glad-cheered, -eyed, -flowing, -hearted, -sad, -surviving* adjs.; †**glad-milch** *adj.*, giving milk freely (of cows; cf. quot. 1883).

c **1330** R. BRUNNE *Chron. Wace* (Rolls) 9752 Doughtiest knyght at alle nedes..*Glad-chered, louely, & lordlyest of alle. **1878** J. G. WHITTIER *Vision of Echard* 59 The freedom of the unshamed wind Among the *glad-eyed flowers. **1818** L. HUNT *Epist. B. Field* 76 And then taking our food, 'Tis exercise turns it to *glad-flowing blood. **1869** W. P. MACKAY *Grace & Truth* 243 The loving constant service of the *glad-hearted girl. **1601** HOLLAND *Pliny* XXVIII. ix, The bigger bodied beasts be more *glad-milch. [**1883** *Almondb. Gloss.*, *Gladmelshed*, said of a cow which loses her milk even as she lies down.] **1614** SYLVESTER *Bethulia's Rescue* 354 This Hymn shee sings with *glad-sad warbling voice. *a* **1618** —— *Paradox agst. Libertie* 630 Whose glad-sad crosse conflicts afflict him day and night. **1630** DRAYTON *Moses* I. 107 The glad-sad parents full of joy and care Faine would reserue their Infant if they could. **1603** B. JONSON *Sejanus* III. i, Out only *glad-suruiuing hopes, The noble issue of Germanicus.

glad (glæd), *v.* Pa. t. and pa. pple. **gladded**. Forms: 1 (ȝe-)gladian, *Mercian* gleadian, 2–3 **gladien**, 3 **gleadien**, 3–4 **gledien**, 4–5 **gladie**, **gladye**, **gladen**, **gladd**(e, 4–6 **glade**, 6 *Sc.* **gled**, 4– **glad**. [OE. *gladian* (also *ȝegladian*):—OTeut. **glaðôjan*, f. **glaðo-* GLAD. The *intr.* sense 'to be glad' is the orig. one; the *trans.* use 'to make glad' is found in ON. *glaða* of similiar formation. ON. had also *gleðja* (:—**glaðjan*) 'to be glad, to make glad'.]

†**1.** *intr.* To become or to be glad; to rejoice. Const. *on, in, of, for. Obs.*

c **950** *Lindisf. Gosp.* John viii. 56 Abraham..ȝegladade [*Rushw.* gladade] *vel* glæd wæs. *c* **1000** *Sax. Leechd.* III. 442 Ne gladiȝe on þæt noþer ne cyning ne worul(d)rica. *c* **1205** LAY. 4410 Þa Brennes hauede ihirde his hirde-manne lare, þa gladede is mod. *a* **1225** *Ancr. R.* 358 Blescieð ou & gledieð. *a* **1340** HAMPOLE *Psalter* ix. 2, I sall be fayn & i sall glade in þe. **1382** WYCLIF *Ecclus.* xxx. 5 In his lif he saȝ, and gladide in hym [**1388** and was glad in hym]. *c* **1460** *Towneley Myst.* vii. 111 Myrth I make till all men And warn theym that thay glad. **1496** *Dives & Paup.* (W. de W.) I. xxviii. 66/1 Man byrde & beste begynne to gladde for Joye of the lyght. *a* **1586** SIDNEY *Arcadia* III. (1598) 334 Absence shall not take thee from mine eyes, nor afflictions shall barre me from gladding in thy good. **1621** LADY M. WROTH *Urania* 520 The one as a friend glading in his presence. **1622** MASSINGER *Virg. Mart.* II. ii, Gladst thou in such scorne? I call my wish backe.

2. *trans.* To make glad, to cause to rejoice. *arch.*

c **825** *Vesp. Psalter* ciii. 15 Win ȝeblissað heortan monnes þæt he gleadie onsiene in ele. *c* **1000** ÆLFRIC *Lev.* i. 3 Bringe he..an unwemme oxancelf..drihten mid to gladienne [Vulg. *ad placandum sibi dominum*]. *c* **1200** *Trin. Coll. Hom.* 97 He us fette ut of helle wowe and þermide us gledede. *c* **1230** *Hali Meid.* 27 Streon of feire children þat gladien muchel þe ealdren. *a* **1300** *Cursor M.* 3795 Wel was he gladed o þis sight. **1352** MINOT *Poems* v. 53 Þe gude Erle of Glowceter, God mot him glade. **1377** LANGL. *P. Pl.* B. xx. 170 And gaf hym golde..that gladded his herte. *c* **1450** *Mirour Saluacioun* 3089 Now last herd ȝe how crist gladide oure faders in helle. **1526** *Pilgr. Perf.* (W. de W. 1531) 36 Care not for dremes, for they gladdeth none but foles. **1595** SPENSER *Col. Clout* 266 At length we land far off descryde: Which sight much gladed me. **1602** *Thomas Ld. Cromwell* II. ii. B 2 b, It glads my hart to thinke vpon the slaue. **1663** F. HAWKINS *Youth's Behav.* I. 7 When thou shalt hear the misfortunes of another, shew not thy self gladded for it. **1682** BUNYAN *Holy War* 261 They were greatly gladded thereat. **1749** SMOLLETT *Regicide* II. i, By heav'n it glads me, that my sword shall find An ample field to-day. **1816** BYRON *Ch. Har.* III. i, The hour's gone by When Albion's lessening shores could grieve or glad mine eye. **1867** *Sat. Rev.* 6 July 23/2 Here the Chorus..trills a downright English song that glads the heart. **1870** MORRIS *Earthly Par.* II. III. 326 Yet shame of me, That I should dull the joy that gladdeth thee.

b. *transf.*

1596 SPENSER *F. Q.* VI. x. 44 Like to a flowre that feeles no heate of sunne Which may her feeble leaves with comfort glade. **1622** WITHER *Philarete* (1633) 623 'Tis as when a flash of light Breakes from heaven to glad the night. **1646** CRASHAW *Sospetto d' Herode* I. xiv, Green vigour Gladding the Scythian rocks and Libian sands. **1671** F. PHILIPPS *Reg. Necess.* 412 Those causes which have fertilized and gladded the Vallies of our Israel. **1704–9** POPE *Autumn* 72 Now bright Arcturus glads the teeming grain.

3. *refl.* To rejoice. *Obs.* exc. *arch.*

1340 *Ayenb.* 238 Þe dyeulen ham gledieþ huanne hi moȝe ouercome..ane guodne man. *Ibid.* 258 Ne glede þe naȝt ine uayr ssroud. *c* **1386** CHAUCER *Sqr.'s T.* 601 Alle thyng repeirynge to his kynde Gladeth hym self. *c* **1500** *Plumpton Corr.* 110, I recomend me unto your mastership..ever me glad to here of your prosperytie. **1686** GOAD *Celest. Bodies* III. ii. 401 All men gladded themselves with this conclusion. **1871** BROWNING *Balaust.* 461, I glad me in my honours too!

Hence †'**gladded** *ppl. a.*, gladdened, delighted.

1568 GRAFTON *Chron.* II. 3 Then the joyfull Kentishe men did conduct the gladded Normanes. **1627–77** FELTHAM *Resolves* I. i. 1 When a rich Crown has newly kiss'd the Temples of a gladded king. **1659** C. NOBLE *Answ. Immod. Queries* 5 A thousand gladded mouthes will speak the contrary.

glad(d, obs. pa. t. of GLIDE *v.*

gladden ('glæd(ə)n), *v.* [f. GLAD *a.*; see -EN *suffix*⁵ and cf. mod. Icel. *glaðna* to become bright. It seems doubtful whether the word was ever common in colloquial language.]

1. *intr.* To be glad; to rejoice. ? *Obs.*

The modern instances are not a continuation of the older use, but are derived from the *trans.* sense.

a **1300** *E.E. Psalter* xcvi. 8 Herd and fained es Syon, And gladeneden doghtres of Iude. **1801** BLOOMFIELD *Rural T.* (1802) 49 As we climb Hills and gladden as we climb. **1809** WORDSW. '*Advance—come forth*', That all the Alps may gladden in thy might. **1839** BAILEY *Festus* viii. (1848) 96 Purer powers Which do unseen surround us aye and gladden In human good.

2. *trans.* To make glad; to render joyous or bright.

1558–62 PHAER *Æneid* VIII. Ccj, Lyke Lucifer,.al darknes he resolues, and gladneth skyes wᵗ face deuyne. **1712** STEELE *Spect.* No. 270 ¶1 Such beautiful Prospects gladden our Minds. **1791** MRS. RADCLIFFE *Rom. Forest* i, Her heart was gladdened with complacent delight. **1820** W. IRVING *Sketch Bk.* II. 105 A small pleasantry frankly uttered by a patron, gladdens the heart of the dependant. **1860** TYNDALL *Glac.* I. xxvii. 204 The sight of the little mansion has gladdened me. **1887** RUSKIN *Præterita* II. 265 [An orchard] which was gladdened..by flushes of almond and double peach blossom.

Hence **'gladdened, 'gladdening** *ppl. adjs.* Also **'gladdener**, one who makes glad.

1728 POPE *Dunc.* III. 79 Thence to the south extend thy gladden'd eyes. **1729** T. COOKE *Tales, &c.* 61 Welsted, envy'd Bard divine, And Hammond, glad'ning as the Day. **1815** BYRON *'The Harp the Monarch Minstrel swept'* ii, It made our gladden'd valleys ring. **1837** HT. MARTINEAU *Soc. Amer.* III. 168 He and many others have done this with gladdening success. **1856** KANE *Arct. Expl.* II. xviii. 188 Crawl out and breathe in the gladdening air. **1879** BUTCHER & LANG *Odyss.* 200 Circe..who charged me very straitly to shun the isle of Helios, the gladdener of the world. **1885** *Athenæum* 20 June 790/2 O for the Spring, the pale, pure, gladdening Spring.

gladden, var. GLADDON.

† **gladder**. *Obs.* [f. GLAD *v.* + -ER¹.]

1. One who rejoices. *rare*⁻¹.

1382 WYCLIF *Isa.* lxiv. 5 Thou aȝen came to the gladere. [**1388** Thou mettist him that is glad. L. *lætanti.*]

2. One who cheers or makes glad.

c **1386** CHAUCER *Knt.'s T.* 1365 O lady myn Venus..Thow gladere of the Mount of Citheron. **1508** DUNBAR *Gold. Targe* 124 Thare was Bacus the gladder of the table. **1528** LYNDESAY *Dreme* 423 Lanterne of the hevin And glader of the sterris, with his lycht. [**1700** DRYDEN *Palamon & Arc.* 1421 Thou gladder of the mount of Cytheron.]

† **'gladding**, *vbl. sb. Obs.* [f. GLAD *v.* + -ING¹.] The action of the verb GLAD; delight, joy, rejoicing.

c **1000** *Be Muneca Cynne* in Grein *Bibl. Ags. Prosa* II. 137 Swylce hy heora ȝeswinc mid godcundre gladunge ȝefremmen. *a* **1225** *St. Marher.* 3 Mi gleo ant mi gledunde [? gledunge]. *a* **1225** *Ancr. R.* 94 Holi men wuteð wel.. þet euerich worldlich gledunge is unwurð her aȝeines. *c* **1320** *Cast. Love* 841 Hire gostliche gladynge Destruyed sleuþe þorw alle þinge. **1382** WYCLIF *1 Kings* iv. 8 Woo to us! forsothe ther was not so mych gladynge ȝisterday. *c* **1450** *Mirour Saluacioun* 4955 Thi sawle aldere graciouseste in godde thi salutere gladyng. ? *a* **1500** *Chester Pl.* (E.E.T.S.) ii. 696 To god did I so amisse That I shall never haue gladinge. **1607** HIERON *Wks.* I. 213 This was that which was Dauids delight, the ioy of his heart, and gladding of his soule.

† **'gladding**, *ppl. a. Obs.* [f. as prec. + -ING².] That makes glad.

13.. *E.E. Allit. P.* A. 171 Suche gladande glory con to me glace. *c* **1394** *P. Pl. Crede* 515 But now the glose is so greit In gladding tales..þat þei bene cursed of Crist. **1568** T. HOWELL *Arb. Amitie* (1879) 53 She was..at home a glasse, to viewe in gladding chere. **1616** B. JONSON *Irish Masque at Court*, Come vp and view The gladding [*printed* glad, ding] face of that great king, in whom So many prophecies to thine are knit. **1635** A. STAFFORD *Fem. Glory* (1869) 13 Of whose all gladding Shine, the first man participated.

gladdon (glæd(ə)n). Now chiefly *dial.* Forms: 1 gladinæ, glædene, 3-5 gladene, 5 gladyne, (-yyn), -one, 6 gladin, -yn, -on, 7-8 gladwin(e, (9 -wyn), 8 glader, 6- gladen, gladdon, 8- gladden. [Of obscure etymology; Pogatscher regards it as prob. a. popular L. **gladīna*, altered form of L. *gladiolus* 'sword-lily' (Lewis & Sh.), dim. of *gladius* sword, from the shape of the leaves.

The form *glader* which appears in various dicts. of the 18th c. (Phillips, Johnson, etc.) may have been originally due to a misprint.]

1. A popular name of the iris (*Iris Pseudacorus* and *Iris fœtidissima*; the latter is sometimes distinguished as 'stinking gladdon'). ***corn-gladdon*** (quot. 1666) = CORN-FLAG.

a **700** *Epinal Gloss.* 920 *Scilla*, gladinae. *a* **800** *Corpus Gloss.* 1815 *Scilla*, glædine. *c* **1000** *Sax. Leechd.* I. 144 Wið wæter seocnysse ȝenim þas wyrte þe man bulbi scillitici & oðrum naman glædene nemneð. *c* **1265** *Voc. Plants* in Wr.-Wülcker 556/15 *Gladiolum*, flamine, gladene. *a* **1400-50** *Alexander* 4094 A dryi meere Was full of gladen & of gale & of grete redis. *c* **1450** *M.E. Med. Bk.* (Heinrich) 155 Take þe rote of gladene & make pouder þer of. **1533** ELYOT *Cast. Helthe* (1541) 11 Thinges good for a colde head..Galingale ..Gladen. **1562** TURNER *Herbal* II. 23 Iris..hath leaues like vnto the herbe called Gladiolus, that is to saye, the gladdon or swerdlynge. **1657** W. COLES *Adam in Eden* xxxiii. 67 Gladwin which is a kind hereof [Flower de Luce]. **1666** J. DAVIES *Hist. Caribby Isl.* 58 Leaves..pointed at the extremity, as those of Corn-Gladen. **1747** WESLEY *Prim. Physic* (1762) 69 Thirty grains of powder'd Root of Gladwin. **1800** SIR J. E. SMITH *Flora Brit.* I. 42 *Iris fœtidissima*..Stinking Iris, or Gladwyn. **1829** GLOVER *Hist. Derby* I. 106 *Iris fœtidissima*, stinking gladdon. **1897** WILLIS *Flower. Pl.* II. 201 *Iris Pseudacorus* L. the yellow flag, and *Iris foetidissima* L., the gladdon.

2. (See quots.)

1787 W. MARSHALL *Norfolk* (1795) II. 380 Gladdon, or Gladen, *Typha latifolia* and *angustifolia*, large and small cats-tail. **1895** *E. Angl. Gloss.*, *Gladden*, or gladden bushes, bulrushes.

3. *attrib.*, as ***gladdon-bed, leaf***.

1601 HOLLAND *Pliny* II. 99 The Gladen leafe is like a sword blade indeed, and keen-edged according to the name. **1889** P. H. EMERSON *Eng. Idyls* 5 Ellen, lulled by the melodies in the gladen-beds, sat staring at her float.

gladdy ('glædɪ). *dial.* A name given (in Devon and Cornwall) to the yellow-hammer.

1859 CAPERN *Ball. & Songs* 127 The gladdie on an hawthorn twig His golden vest displayed. **1891** *Hartland Gloss.*, *Gladdy*, the yellow ammer. **1893** Q. [COUCH] *Delectable Duchy* 215 Lookin' as peart as a gladdy.

† **glade**, *sb.*¹ *Obs.* [Perh. of Scandinavian origin: cf. Sw. dial. (Rietz) *gladas*, *gla(d)na*, to set (of the sun); also *sola ä gladder* the sun has just set), Norw. dial. *gla* to set (of sun and moon); Sw. *sol-gla(d)ning*, Norw. *solaglad* sunset = ON. *sólarglaðan*, found only in *Hervarar Saga* (ed. 1847) p. 15, where *nær sólarglaðan* of the prose corresponds to *við sólarsetri* in the verses. Etymological connexion with GLAD *a.* is possible.] ***to go to glade***: to set, sink to rest (said of the sun).

c **1200** *Winteney Rule St. Benet* (1888) 25 Ær sunne go to glade. **1387** TREVISA *Higden* (Rolls) V. 189 In the Ester eve whanne þe sonne ȝede to glade [L. *sole occidente*]. *c* **1475** *Partenay* 992 Thys Joustes dured till sonne went to glad. After to euessong went euery wyght. **1548** UDALL, etc. *Erasm. Par. Matt.* viii. 18 Now the sunne was gone to glade. **1589** PUTTENHAM *Eng. Poesie* II. xi. (Arb.) 116 Likening her Majestie to the Sunne for his brightnesse, but not to him for his passion, which is ordinarily to go to glade, and sometime to suffer eclypse. **1614** J. DAVIES (Heref.) *Eclogue* 255 Phoebus now goes to glade. *a* **1788** *A Yola Zong* (Wexford Dialect) in Ellis *E.E. Pronunc.* v. 26 Tel ee zin [= till the sun] go t'glade.

transf. **1581** T. HOWELL *Deuises* (1879) 258 As now by me appeares, whose ioyes doe vade, Whose griefe doth grow, whose comfort glides to glade.

glade (gleɪd), *sb.*² Also 6 gleade. [Of obscure origin.

If the primary sense be 'sunny place', the word may be connected with GLAD *a.* (sense 1); cf. Sw. dial. *glänna* '1. sunny spot; 2. open place in a wood' (Rietz). But difficulties are created by the occurrence of the form GLODE, which seems to be equivalent (cf. the place-name *Cockglode* in Notts. with sense 1 b below). Conceivably *glade, glode* might represent respectively northern and midland forms of an OE. **gláda* wk. masc.,:—**glaidon-*, f. root **glai-*: see GLEAM. There is, however, no indication that the word is specially northern.]

1. a. A clear open space or passage in a wood or forest, whether natural or produced by the cutting down of trees.

The earlier examples often explain the word as meaning a light or sunny place. From the latter part of the 17th c., when the word had perh. become merely literary, many writers have associated it with *shade*.

1529 MORE *Comf. agst. Trib.* III. Wks. 1233/1 His folke grubbe vppe these..busshes of our earthlye substaunce and carye them quyte awaye from vs, that the woorde of God sowen in oure hartes maye haue roume therein, and a glade rounde aboute, for the warme sunne of grace, to come to it. **1538** LELAND *Itin.* IV. 126, I came by 2 fayre woodes on the Hill Sides, and passed in a Glade or Bottome betwixt them. **1573-80** BARET *Alv.* G 262 To make a glade in the middest of the wood; to loppe or cut away boughes where they let the light. **1589** GREENE *Menaphon* (Arb.) 19 Yet never viewd I such a pleasant Greene As this, whose garnisht gleades, compare denies. **1615** G. SANDYS *Trav.* 203 Thorow a large glade betweene two hils, we leisurely descended for the space of two houres. **1697** DRYDEN *Virg. Georg.* III. 516 Or solitary Grove, or gloomy Glade, To shield 'em with its venerable Shade. **1730-46** THOMSON *Autumn* 435 He bursts the thickets, glances thro' the glades. **1788** J. MAY *Jrnl. & Lett.* (1873) 103 This morning very cold, and considerable frost in the glades. **1836** KINGSLEY *Lett.* (1878) I. 33 The bright glades of the forest pleased her not. **1874** GREEN *Short Hist.* ii. §6. 87 The Red King was found dead by peasants in a glade of the New Forest.

transf. **1586** WARNER *Alb. Eng.* II. vii. (1612) 28 Resolving or to win the Spurres, or lose himselfe therefore, He makes a bloudie glade, vntill the Thebane he espide.

b. An opening in a wood, etc. utilized for snaring birds. (See quot. 1617.)

1617 MORYSON *Itin.* III. 111 Italian Gentlemen much delight in the art to catch birds, and in gardens fitted to that purpose, with nets, bushes and glades. [**1621** : see GLODE.] **1678** RAY *Willughby's Ornith.* I. Addit. iii. 33 We in England are wont to make great Glades through thick Woods, and hang Nets across them; And so the Wood-cocks shooting through these Glades..strike against the Nets, and are entangled in them. [**1691** BLOUNT *Law Dict.*, *Gallivolatium*, a cockshoot or cockglade.]

2. *U.S.* **a.** (See quot. 1859 and cf. EVERGLADE.)

1796 MORSE *Amer. Geog.* I. 649 Interspersed through the other parts, are glades of rich swamp. **1859** BARTLETT *Dict. Amer.*, *Glades*, everglades; tracts of land at the South covered with water and grass. So called in Maryland, where they are divided into wet and dry glades.

b. (See quots.)

1828-32 WEBSTER, *Glade*..2. In *New England*, an opening in the ice of rivers or lakes, or a place left unfrozen. *Ibid.*, *Glade*, smooth ice. (*New England.*) [In recent American Dicts. stated to be *Local, U.S.*]

† **3. a.** A clear or bright space in the sky; a flash (of light or lightning). *Obs.*

1555-8 PHAER *Æneid* II. F j, Down from heauen by shade A streaming star descends, and long wᵗ great light makes a glade. **1706** *Phil. Trans.* XXV. 2220 This Glade of Light.. was much like the Tail of a Comet, but pointed at the upper End. **1734** EAMES *ibid.* XXXVIII. 248 The white Pyramidal Glade, which is now entitled by the Name of the Aurora Borealis. **1741** SHORT *ibid.* XLI. 628 It went all over this Country..pretty sharply, but nothing near so quick as a Glade of Lightning.

† **b.** *fig.* ? A gleam of hope. *Obs.*

1522 MORE *De quat. Noviss.* Wks. 79/1 Than geueth he some false glade of escapyng that sickenes.

4. *attrib.* and *Comb.*, as ***glade-broken, -like*** adjs.; **glade mallow** *U.S.*, a tall herb, *Napæa dioica*, of the family Malvaceæ; **glade-net** (see quot. 1678 in 1 b).

1842 J. WILSON *Chr. North* I. 367 Thence to Calgarth is all one forest—yet glade-broken, and enlivened by open uplands. **1849** SPRAGUE & GRAY *Genera Plants U.S.* II. 55 Glade Mallow. Flowers diœcious. **1880** DISRAELI *Endym.* ii. 42 Glade-like terraces of yew trees. **1882** OGILVIE, *Glade-net.* **1963** H. A. GLEASON *Illustr. Flora Northeastern U.S.* II. 529 Napaea L. Glade Mallow... A monotypic genus.

† **glade**, *v. Obs. rare*⁻¹. [f. GLADE *sb.*²] *trans.* To make a glade or clearing in (a forest).

1621 T. WILLIAMSON tr. *Goulart's Wise Vieillard* 100 Fountaines without water, forrests grubd up and gladed, trees without fruit.

glade, dial. var. GLEDE, kite.

glade, obs. f. GLAD; obs. pa. t. of GLIDE.

† **'gladen**. *Obs. rare*⁻¹. [? Connected with GLADE *sb.*²; cf. dial. '*Gladden*, a glade' (J. H. *Tour to Caves*, 1781), '*Gladden*, a void place free from incumbrances' (Halliwell).] ? A space left unguarded.

a **1400-50** *Alexander* 131 When he was grabed with his gere a gladen he waytis, And passis furþe at a Posterne preualy alane.

gladen(e, var. GLADDON.

glader, obs. form of GLADDER, GLADDON.

gladful ('glædfʊl), *a.* Also 3 gledful, 6 *Sc.* glaidful. [f. GLAD *sb.*¹ + -FUL.] Full of gladness or joy. Now only *arch.*

a **1225** *Ancr. R.* 286 Gostlich gledschipe, & froure of gledful hope. *Ibid.* 394 ȝet her is gledfulure wunder. *a* **1300** *E.E. Psalter* xlvi. 2 Alle genge..Miries to god in gladful steuen. **1549** *Compl. Scot.* vi. 37 In this glaidful recreatione I conteneuit quhil Phebus was discendit. **1596** SPENSER *F. Q.* IV. vi. 34 Desiring of his Amoret to heare Some glad-full newes. **1880** W. WATSON *Prince's Quest* (1892) 50 Then came the gladful morn.

Hence **'gladfully** *adv.*; **'gladfulness**.

c **1450** *St. Cuthbert* (Surtees) 2389 Cuthbert toke it glad-fully. **1591** SPENSER *Muiopot* 208 He..there him rests in riotous suffisaunce Of all his gladfulnes, and kingly ioyaunce. **1893** A. L. HADDON *What ails the House?* III. 43 Why had she not gone forth gladfully to meet him?

† **'gladhead**. *Obs. rare*⁻¹. [f. GLAD *a.* + -HEAD.] Gladness.

1303 R. BRUNNE *Handl. Synne* 12461 Gode forȝyveþ alle wyþ gladehede.

gladiate ('gleɪdɪət), *a. Bot.* [f. L. *gladi-us* sword + -ATE².] Sword-shaped (see quots.).

1793 MARTYN *Lang. Bot.*, *Gladiata siliqua*. *Gladiatum legumen*. A gladiate or sword-shaped silique or legume. **1836** *Penny Cycl.* V. 252 *Gladiate*, the same as ensiform, but broader and shorter. **1856** HENSLOW *Dict. Bot. Terms*, *Gladiate*, flat, straight or slightly curved, with the edges parallel and apex acute; as the leaves of an Iris. Also a synonyme for 'ancipital'.

gladiator ('glædɪeɪtə(r)). [a. L. *gladiātor*, f. *gladiaus* sword.]

1. *Hist.* Among the ancient Romans, one who fought with a sword or other weapon at public shows; usually a slave or captive trained for the purpose.

Gladiator is employed by Cicero as a term of abuse; cf. quot. 1541.

1541 PAYNEL *Catiline* xviii. 31 b, If I had demed it best.. to put Catiline to deth, I wolde not haue giuen this gladiatour one houre space to liue. **1598** BARCKLEY *Felic. Man* v. 447 This man dreamed..that when the Gladiators or Fencers exercised their arte at Syracusa..he should be slaine by one Retiarius. **1608** D. T. *Ess. Pol. & Mor.* 72 The Gladiator thinkes it a disgrace, to see himselfe compos'd with one..inferiour to himselfe. **1621** BURTON *Anat. Mel.* II. ii. IV. (1676) 172/1 Amphitheatres..wherein they [Romans] had several delightsome shews to exhilarate the people; Gladiators, combats of men with themselves, etc. **1741** MIDDLETON *Cicero* I. VI. 452 The Tribun Cato was perpetually inveighing against keeping Gladiators. **1772** PRIESTLEY *Inst. Relig.* (1782) I. 219 The barbarous exhibition of gladiators. **1816** KEATINGE *Trav.* (1817) I. 12 *note*, Something is requisite beyond the skill of the mere gladiator, to conduct war itself. **1818** BYRON *Ch. Harold* IV. cxl. **1869** LECKY *Europ. Mor.* II. i. 39 The Christians steadily refused to admit any professional gladiator to baptism.

fig. *a* **1668** DENHAM *Progr. Learning* 193 Then whilst his Foe each Gladiator foyls, The Atheist, looking on, enjoys the spoyls. **1751** EARL ORRERY *Remarks Swift* (1752) 40 Not so Dr. Swift; he appears like a masterly gladiator. He wields the sword of party with ease, justness and dexterity. **1841-4** EMERSON *Ess.*, *Politics* Wks. (Bohn) I. 244 The gladiators in the lists of power feel..the presence of worth. **1864** BURTON *Scot Abr.* I. v. 265 Intellectual gladiators, each trying his strength against the rest. **1884** *Chr. World* 23 Oct. 805/2 Mr. Chamberlain has..figured..prominently as a Ministerial gladiator.

† **2.** A professional swordsman or fencer. *Obs.*

1621 BURTON *Anat. Mel.* II. ii. IV. (1676) 174/1 For that cause, Playes..Gladiators, Tumblers, Jugglers, etc., and all that crew is admitted. **1712** STEELE *Spect.* No. 449 ¶7 [cf. No. 436] There is a Mystery among the Gladiators which has escaped your Spectatorial Penetration. **1733** *Epitaph in St. Michael's churchyard, Coventry*, John Parkes..a Gladiator by Profession, who after Having fought 359 battles in the principal parts of Europe..at length quitted the stage [etc.]. **1769** *Junius Lett.* (1772) I. xxiii. 166 His own honour would have forbidden him from mixing his private pleasures or conversation with jockeys, gamesters, blasphemers, gladiators, or buffoons.

3. *attrib.* and *Comb.*, as ***gladiator fight***; ***gladiator-like*** adv.

1818 BYRON *Ch. Har.* IV. xciv, The new race of unborn slaves, who..rather than be free, Bleed gladiator-like. **1846** H. TORRENS *Mil. Lit. & Hist.* I. 109 Their gladiator fights ..offer sufficient proof of the sanguinary nature of the people.

gladiatorial (ˌglædɪəˈtɔərɪəl), *a.* [f. L. *gladiātōri-us* (f. *gladiātor*) + -AL[1].]

1. Of or pertaining to gladiators.

1751-67 JORTIN *Eccl. Hist.* II. 290 He [Constantine] made a law against Gladiatorial shews, which however continued till Honorius put an end to that wicked diversion, A.D. 403. **1773** MELMOTH *Cato* (1820) 140 'You were disappointed', said he, 'of being present at the gladiatorial combats in Rome'. **1811** BYRON *Hints fr. Horace* 273 The gladiatorial gore we teach to flow In tragic scene disgusts. **1857** BIRCH *Anc. Pottery* (1858) II. 279 The games of the circus, the incidents of gladiatorial life. **1875** POSTE *Gaius* III. Comm. (ed. 2) 422 The first gladiatorial show at Rome was exhibited B.C. 264. **1890** G. A. SMITH *Isaiah* II. xii. 202 We do not vivisect our murderers nor kill them off by gladiatorial combats.

2. *fig.* Of debate or controversy which is merely contentious.

1813 A. BRUCE *Life A. Morus* vi. 148 This contentious and gladiatorial manner of speaking. **1851** ROBERTSON *Serm.* Ser. IV. (1863) I. Introd. 6 They spent their days in tournaments of speeches, and exulted in gladiatorial oratory. **1886** EARL SELBORNE *Def. Ch. Eng.* III. xvii. 294, I have dealt with the more substantial accusations brought against the Church of England. The rest are gladiatorial.

†**gladiaˈtorian**, *a. Obs.* [f. as prec. + -AN.]

a. = prec. b. Resembling a gladiator.

1647 A. ROSS *Myst. Poet.* vi. (1675) 126 And such gladiatorian women..have shaken off all modesty. **1710** SHAFTESB. *Adv. Author* II. §3. 113 The Gladiatorian, and other sanguinary Sports which we allow our People, sufficiently discover what our National Taste is. **1711** —— *Charac.* Misc. I. ii. III. 12 A kind of Amphitheatrical Entertainment exhibited to the Multitude, by these Gladiatorean Pen-men. **1732** BERKELEY *Alciphr.* I. 181 Their insolent treatment of Captives..their Bloody Gladiatorian Spectacles.

gladiatorism (ˈglædɪeɪtərɪz(ə)m). [f. GLADIATOR + -ISM.] The practice of fighting after the fashion of gladiators. Also *fig.*

1860 in WORCESTER (citing *Ch. Ob.*). **1862** MILMAN in *Gibbon's Decl. & F.* Mem. 92 *note*, Two Christian prelates engaged in this fierce intellectual gladiatorism. **1884** R. F. BURTON *Bk. Sword* 283 Gladiatorism lasted in England after a fashion till the days of Addison.

gladiatorship (ˈglædɪeɪtəʃɪp). [f. as prec. + -SHIP.] The occupation of a gladiator; display of gladiatorial skill. Also *fig.*

1830 CROLY *George IV*, 378 They saw nothing in the most gallant successes, but a waste of national blood..a vulgar gladiatorship. **1849** *Tait's Mag.* XVI. 788 There was no contention of mind with mind..no brilliant gladiatorship. **1883** *Contemp. Rev.* Nov. 707 Browning seems positively to revel, as though for the mere mental gladiatorship..in these labyrinthine convolutions of juggling sophistry.

†ˈ**gladiatory**, *a.* and *sb. Obs.* [ad. L. *gladiātōri-us.*] A. *adj.* = GLADIATORIAL.

1602 SEGAR *Hon. Mil. & Civ.* IV. iii. §3. 213 The first vse of wearing Crownes was in Tragedies and gladiatory combats. **1652** URQUHART *Jewel* Wks. (1834) 220 In the gladiatory art so superlatively expert and dextrous. **1716** M. DAVIES *Athen. Brit.* III. *Crit. Hist.* 7 The Gladiatory Tribe of the Independants. **1730** A. GORDON *Maffei's Amphith.* 3 Gladiatory combats..were long in Use at Rome.

B. *sb.* Gladiatorial art or practice. In quot. *fig.*

1653 SIR W. DENNY *Pelican.* III. 223 How comes..such a Gladiatory in the Schools..such Challenges of the Pen, such Animosities in Discourse?

gladiatrix (glædɪˈeɪtrɪks). *rare.* [f. GLADIATOR: see -TRIX.] A female gladiator.

1802 W. GIFFORD tr. *Juvenal* I. 34 *note*, Her profligacy, however, may have tempted Juvenal to transfer her name to this noble gladiatrix.

†ˈ**gladiatry.** *Obs. rare*[−1]. [app. f. GLADIATOR, after sbs. in -RY.] Gladiators collectively.

1658 W. SANDERSON *Graphice* 74 So Ruben in his affected Colouring..and Cornelius of Harlem in his loose & untrussed figures, like old and beaten Gladiatry; seem..to abuse that gentle and modest licence, which [etc.].

†ˈ**gladiature.** *Obs. rare.* [ad. L. *gladiātūra*, f. *gladius*: cf. GLADIATOR.] = GLADIATORSHIP.

1654 GAYTON *Pleas. Notes* IV. xxi. 271 Nay in their Amphitheatricall gladiatures, the lives of captives lay at the mercy of the Vulgar. **1656-81** BLOUNT *Glossogr.*, *Gladiature*, the feat of fighting with sword.

gladin, obs. form of GLADDON.

gladiole (ˈglædɪəʊl). Also 5, 7 gladiol, 6 gladioll. [ad. L. *gladiol-us*: see next.] = GLADIOLUS.

c **1420** *Pallad. on Husb.* I. 1016 And curiage, and gladiol the longe; Eek amarak, and other fresshest flouris. **1578** LYTE *Dodoens* II. xxxviii. 196 Corne flagge, or Gladioll. **1605** SYLVESTER *Du Bartas* II. iii. I. *Vocation* 562 The yellow Night-shade and blew Gladiol's juyce, Where-with her sleep-swoln heavy lids she glews. **1803** *J. Abercrombie's Ev. Man Own Gard.* (ed. 17) 603 Narcissuses and jonquils.. gladioles, bulbous-iris..may now be planted. **1863** *Denise* I. 169 Tall pink gladioles in the patches of green corn.

‖**gladiolus** (glæˈdaɪələs, glædɪˈəʊləs). Pl. gladioli, -oluses. [L. (dim. of *gladius* sword); used as a plant-name by Pliny. Cf. F. *glaieul.*]

1. †a. The wild iris or GLADDON. b. Any plant of the iridaceous genus *Gladiolus*, having sword-shaped leaves and spikes of brilliant flowers; the commonly cultivated species are South African.

Sometimes, instead of the pl. *gladioli*, the sing. is used with a collective force; see quots. 1664, 1866.

c **1000** *Sax. Leechd.* I. 182 Wið blædran sare..ʒenim þysse wyrte wyrttruman uteweardne ðe man gladiolum, & oþrum naman glædene nemneþ. **1567** MAPLET *Gr. Forest* 45 Gladiolus, his form and proportion of leafe is like to Sedge, his flower yealow in a maner like to the flower Deluce. **1664** EVELYN *Kal. Hort.* (1679) 21 Take up your Gladiolus now yearly, the Blades being dry. **1775** MASSON in *Phil. Trans.* LXVI. 279 We collected a great number of beautiful plants, particularly ixiæ, irides, and gladioli. **1796** tr. *Thunberg's Cape G. Hope* in Pinkerton *Voy.* (1814) XVI. 65 It [a mole] feeds on several sorts of bulbous roots..especially Gladioluses, Ixias, Antholyzas, and Irises. **1864** B'NESS BUNSEN in Hare *Life* (1879) II. vii. 346 A clump of the large scarlet gladiolus is my daily delight at present. **1866** *Cornh. Mag.* Nov. 538 White arums, orchises, and pink gladiolus. **1873** OUIDA *Pascarel* II. 162 The millet filled with crimson gladioli and great scarlet poppies.

2. *Anat.* 'A term for the second piece or body of the sternum' (*Syd. Soc. Lex.* 1885).

†ˈ**gladish**, *v. Obs. rare*[−1]. [ad. F. *glatiss-*, lengthened stem of OF. *glatir* to bark = It. *ghiattire*, Sp. Pg. *latir*, med.L. *glattīre*, prob. of imitative origin.] *intr.* To bark.

1584 HUDSON *Du Bartas' Judith* III. 104 As doth the hounds..Com gladishing at hearing of his horne.

‖**gladius** (ˈgleɪdɪəs). [L. *gladius.*]

1. A sword. *nonce-use.*

1873 BURTON *Hist. Scot.* I. i. 6 Charge them with the gladius.

2. The sword-fish (so called by Pliny).

c **1520** ANDREWE *Noble Lyfe* xv. in *Babees Bk.* 234 Gladius is a fisshe so named because he is mouthed after the fascyon of a sworde poynt.

3. *Anat.* 'The horny endoskeleton or pen of cuttle-fishes' (*Syd. Soc. Lex.* 1885).

1872 NICHOLSON *Palæont.* 295 Dibranchiate Cephalopods.—Fam. 3. Teuthidæ.—Shell consisting of an internal horny 'pen' or 'gladius', composed of a central shaft and two lateral wings.

gladless (ˈglædlɪs), *a. rare.* [f. GLAD *sb.*[1] + -LESS.] Devoid of gladness or joy.

c **1590** T. WATSON *On death Sir F. Walsingham* Poems (Arb.) 163 Now in the woods let night-rauns croak by daie, and gladles Owles shrike out. **1894** R. H. DAVIS *Eng. Cousins* 221 There are no such faces anywhere else in the world. They are brutal, sullen, and gladless.

gladly (ˈglædlɪ), *a. Obs.* exc. *arch.* [f. GLAD *sb.*[1] + -LY[1].] †a. Bright, beautiful, splendid, precious (*obs.*). b. Glad, joyous, joyful.

a. *a* **1000** *Widsith* 66 (Gr.) Me þær Guðhere forʒeaf glædlicne maþþum songes to leane.

b. *c* **1000** *Ags. Ps.* (Th.) cxxxii. 1 Efne hu glædlic bið and god swylce [L. *quam bonum et quam jucundum*] þætte broður on an beʒen hicgen. *a* **1310** in Wright *Lyric P.* 36 Heo glystnede ase gold when hit glemede, Nes ner gome so gladly on gere. **1387** TREVISA *Higden* (Rolls) V. 115 Þe ilondes of þe world, þat beeþ alwey gladliche for to hire new þinges. **1842** PUSEY *Crisis Eng. Ch.* 132, I trust that 'the burden and heat of the day' will be gladlier to us. **1864** —— *Lect. Daniel* vi. 306 At the Feast of Tabernacles..when hearts would be gladliest.

gladly (ˈglædlɪ), *adv.* Forms: 1 glædlīce, 3 glad(d)like, gladluche, -liȝ, -li(e, 3-4 gledliche, 3-5 gladliche, (4 -lik, -lygh), 5 gladdely, 5-6 *Sc.* glaidlie, 6 gladlye, 3- gladly. *Comp.* 3 gledluker, gladliker, 4 gladloker, -laker, -liere, 5-6 gladlyer, (5 gladlyur), 6- gladlier. *Sup.* 4 gladlyest, 6- gladliest. (Now commonly *more, most gladly.*) [f. GLAD *a.* + -LY[2].]

1. In a glad fashion; with gladness or joy. Also, in weaker sense, willingly, with alacrity, esp. in phr. ***I (you, he*****, etc.) *would gladly*** (do something).

c **900** tr. *Bæda's Hist.* II. vii. (1890) 116 He glædlice all eorðlic þing wæs oferhleapende. *a* **1100** *O.E. Chron.* (Laud MS.) an. 1014 Ða com Æðelred cyning..ham to his aʒenre ðeode, & he glædlice fram heom eallum onfangen wæs. *c* **1200** ORMIN 12384 Þeȝȝ..didenn gladdliȝ þatt he badd Onnȝæn Drihhtiness wille. *a* **1225** *Ancr. R.* 188 Goð nu þeonne gledluker..touward þe muchele feste of heouene. *c* **1300** *Havelok* 906 Gladlike wile ich feden þe. *c* **1400** MAUNDEV. (1839) xviii. 195 Thei drynken gladlyest mannes Blood. *c* **1460** *Towneley Myst.* viii. 144 Gladly thay Wold me greyf, if I sych bodworde broght. **1552** *Bk. Com. Prayer, Ordering Deacons*, Will you doe this gladly and willingly? **1591** SPENSER *M. Hubberd* 289 Gladliest I of your fleecie sheepe..would take on me the keep. **1617** MORYSON *Itin.* I. 237 They would gladly have taken this occasion to extort much money from the Friers. **1667** MILTON *P.L.* VI. 731 Scepter and Power, thy giving, I assume, And gladlier shall resign. **1709** BERKELEY *Theory Vision* §112, I should gladly be informed whether it be not true. **1831** LAMB *Elia* II. *To Shade Elliston*, Or art thou enacting Rover (as we would gladlier think) by wandering Elysian streams? **1875** JOWETT *Plato* (ed. 2) I. 80, I applaud your purpose, and will gladly assist you.

†b. *do gladly*: a polite phrase used when offering food to a person. *Obs.*

15.. *Friar & Boy* 75 in Ritson *Anc. Pop. P.* 38 The boye drewe forth suche as he had, And sayd, do gladly.

†2. a. Aptly, with evident reason. b. *to do* or *be ...gladly*: to be accustomed or 'apt' to. (Cf. Gr. φιλεῖν to love, to be accustomed.) *Obs.*

c **1385** CHAUCER *L.G.W.* 770 *Thisbe*, And this was gladly in the eue tyde Or wondyr erly, lest men it espiede. *c* **1386** —— *Pars. T.* ¶813 Auowtrie is set gladly in the ten comandementz bitwixe thefte and manslaughter, for it is the grettest thefte that may be. **1398** TREVISA *Barth. De P.R.* VIII. xvii. (Tollem. MS.), A scorpion is a beste þat styngeþ gladly with þe tayle. **1430-40** LYDG. *Bochas* I. ix. (1544) 18 b, The wrong partie gladly hath a fall. **1483** CAXTON *Gold. Leg.* 140/2 Where as ben corners there is gladly filth.

gladness (ˈglædnɪs). [f. GLAD *a.* + -NESS.] The state of being glad; joy, rejoicing. †Also, cheerfulness, alacrity (in action).

c **900** tr. *Bæda's Hist.* v. xvii. [xix.] (1891) 454 Þa ongan se bysceop lustfullian þæs iungan snytro..& glædnesse his dæda. *a* **1225** *Ancr. R.* 126 Al þet hurt & al þet sore were uorȝiten & forȝiuen uor glednesse. *a* **1240** *Ureisun* in *Cott. Hom.* 199 Ich þe biseche..þat þu bringe þene Munuch to þire glednesse. *a* **1300** *Cursor M.* 5249 Quen ioseph wit his fader mett..þai gret for gladnes. **1382** WYCLIF *1 Esdras* iv. 63 Thei ioȝeden ful out with musikis and gladnessys seuene daȝes. **1413** *Pilgr. Sowle* (Caxton 1483) IV. xx. 64, I had ioye entier and eke gladnesse. **1548** HALL *Chron., Hen. V*, 75 The greate gladnes, the hertie rejoysyng and the greate delight that the comen people had at this concorde. **1606** SHAKS. *Tr. & Cr.* I. i. 39 Sorrow, that is couch'd in seeming gladnesse, Is like that mirth, Fate turnes to sudden sadnesse. **1751** JOHNSON *Rambler* No. 141 ¶4 My company gave alacrity to a frolick, and gladness to a holiday. **1814** S. ROGERS *Jacquel.* I. 74 Her every gesture said 'rejoice', Her coming was a gladness. **1874** GREEN *Short Hist.* v. §1. 213 It is this new gladness of a great people which utters itself in the verse of Geoffrey Chaucer.

gladon, obs. form of GLADDON.

†ˈ**gladship.** *Obs.* [f. GLAD *a.* + -SHIP.] = GLADNESS.

c **975** *Rushw. Gosp.* John iii. 29 ʒifea *vel* glædscip min ʒifylled is. *c* **1000** *Sax. Leechd.* III. 436 Drihten crist is.. mid ealles modes gledscype to herienne. *c* **1200** ORMIN 783 Annd tu shallt off þatt child Habbenn gladdshipe & blisse. *a* **1240** *Ureisun* in *Cott. Hom.* 191 Alle cristene men owen.. singen ðe lofsong mid swuðe muchele gledschipe. *a* **1300** *Cursor M.* 23603 Þair ioi, þair gladdscip, qua can tell? **1375** BARBOUR *Bruce* XII. 209 In hert gret gladschip can he ta. *c* **1430** *Pilgr. Lyf Manhode* I. ii. (1869) 1 Ther was al gladshipe, ioye with oute sorwe. *c* **1500** *Lancelot* 2761 Yow may bewail the day As of his deith, and gladschip aucht to ses. *a* **1597** *Way to Thrift* in *Certain MS. Poems* F 6 b, When gladdshippe growes into grame.

gladsome (ˈglædsəm), *a.* Also 4-5 gladsum, 4, 6 gladsom, 6 *Sc.* glaidsum. [f. GLAD *sb.*[1] + -SOME.]

1. Of things, events, places, etc.: Productive of gladness; cheering, pleasant.

c **1386** CHAUCER *Nun's Pr. Prol.* 12 Swich thyng is gladsom as it thynketh me And of swich thyng were goodly for to telle. **1480** CAXTON *Chron. Eng.* ccxxvi. 232 All thynges and wethers fallen to me joyfull and lykyng and gladsum as I wold haue hem. **1597** T. PAYNE *Royal Exch.* 17 A greater confidens of that gladsome resurrection. **1611** SPEED *Hist. Gt. Brit.* IX. viii. §8 The Kings Gouernour after the victory rode..with the gladsome tidings..to the King and Legate. **1633** EARL MANCH. *Al Mondo* (1636) 60 Noah when hee had been tossed but a yeare upon the waters, then Mount Ararat was to him a gladsome place. **1728** POPE *Odyss.* XXIV. 453 On chairs and beds in order seated round They share the gladsome board. **1775** ADAIR *Amer. Ind.* 298 He flattered himself that the scalps..would prove a gladsome sight to our people. **1853** DE QUINCEY *Autobiog. Sk.* Wks. I. 202 The day on which a Roman triumphed was the most gladsome day of his existence. **1877** MRS. OLIPHANT *Makers Flor.* vi. 163 We have the gladsome and joyful sight of fruitful slopes.

2. Of looks and feelings: Expressive of, or characterized by, gladness.

1375 BARBOUR *Bruce* XI. 256 He welcummyt thame vith gladsum fair. *a* **1420** HOCCLEVE *De Reg. Princ.* 1365 Hir gladsome looke made me truste hir wele. **1582** N. LICHEFIELD tr. *Castanheda's Conq. E. Ind.* iv. 11 Clapping their hands for ioy thereof, which manner of gladsome reioysing, they vsed three or foure times. **1605** CAMDEN *Rem.* 3 Whereas the saide Panegyrist falleth into a gladsome admiration. **1729** T. COOKE *Tales, &c.* 81 The Sailor so, with gladsome Eye, Th' unruffel'd Main..Views. **1832** LANDER *Adv. Niger* I. iii. 113 Countenances more gladsome and animated than can be conceived.

b. *transf.* said of inanimate nature and its aspects.

1513 DOUGLAS *Æneis* XII. Prol. 78 The cornis croppis and the beris new brerd Wyth glaidsum garmond revesting the erd. **1633** G. HERBERT *Temple, Pilgrimage* iv, At length I got unto the gladsome hill. **1710** PHILIPS *Pastorals* ii. 6 Their Notes soft-warbling to the gladsome Spring. **1816** J. WILSON *City of Plague* III. i, When the silent stars Stole out so gladsome through the dark-blue heavens. **1868** HAWTHORNE *Amer. Note-Bks.* (1879) II. 75 The gladsome sunshine.

3. Of persons, the mind, heart, etc.: Having a glad or joyous nature or mood; filled with gladness. Also of birds. †*gladsome of*: glad of (cf. GLAD *a.* 3 b).

c **1410** *Sir Cleges* 30 Sche was full good sekyrly, And gladsum both day and nyghte. **1482** *Monk of Evesham* (Arb.) 89 The monke schewyd hym selfe to the abbot..ful gracyous of syghte and gladsum of chere. **1530** PALSGR. 314/1 Gladsome, cherefull, *alaigre*. **1570-6** LAMBARDE *Peramb. Kent* (1826) 390 Queen Elizabeth..our most gratious and gladsome Gove[r]nour. **1606** J. CARPENTER *Solomon's Solace* ii. 8 He vsed to be gladsome and merily conceited. **1624** MILTON *Ps.* cxxxvi. 1 Let us with a gladsome mind Praise the Lord. **1635** J. HAYWARD tr.

Biondi's Banish'd Virg. 61 So gladsome was the Knight of this gift, that [etc.]. **1793-4** WORDSW. *Guilt & Sorrow* xxviii, We two had sung, like gladsome birds in May. **1804** J. GRAHAME *Sabbath* 13 From the sky the gladsome lark warbles his heaven-tuned song. **1837** HAWTHORNE *Twice-Told T.* (1851) II. xii. 184 Peter smiled like a gladsome man. **1867** G. MACDONALD *Poems* 143 Carried it about the land, Gladsome as a boy.

4. quasi-*adv.* Gladly.

1540 PALSGRAVE *Acolastus* IV. ii. S iij, I have done it gladsome .i. with a good wyll.

gladsomely ('glædsəmlɪ), *adv.* [f. prec. + -LY².] In a gladsome fashion.

1375 BARBOUR *Bruce* XVI. 20 He resauit hym gladsumly. *c* **1550** U. L. *Pleasant Pathwaye*, etc. A j b (T.), I.. behelde the sunne shyne so gladsomely. **1635** J. HAYWARD tr. *Biondi's Banish'd Virg.* 175 Whom hee findes gladsomely enjoying the sweete company of [etc.]. **1663** *Flagellum, or O. Cromwell* (1672) 29 Those who had lodg'd their private hopes in the Common Ruine, did most gladsomely salute the Designs of Oliver. **1830** *Blackw. Mag.* XXVII. 80 Which meets us soothingly, be we in sadness, or gladsomely, be we in joy. **1890** C. DIXON *Stray Feathers* vii. 81 The birds singing gladsomely.

gladsomeness ('glædsəmnɪs). [f. as prec. + -NESS.] The state or condition of being gladsome; gladness, joy.

1413 *Pilgr. Sowle* (Caxton 1483) v. xiii. 104 Ryal robes of ioye and of gladsomnesse. **1549** CHALONER tr. *Erasm. on Folly* I iij a, The same not seeldome disavaileth to the gladsomenesse and pleasure of the lyfe. *a* **1651** CALDERWOOD *Hist. Kirk* (1843) II. 132, I.. declared unto her your Majestie's gladsomnesse of her recoverie of her late sickenesse. **1816** J. WILSON *City of Plague* III. i. 246 Childhood lost Its bounding gladsomeness. **1849** ROCK *Ch. of Fathers* III. ix. 294 The bells from every church steeple swung forth their peals of gladsomeness.

Gladstone ('glædstən). [f. the name of William E. *Gladstone* (1808–98).] Used *attrib.* or *ellipt.* to designate certain articles. **a.** ***Gladstone (claret)***: a jocular name given to the cheap French wines, the importation of which greatly increased in consequence of the reduction in Customs duty made by Gladstone while Chancellor of the Exchequer in 1860.

1864 *Athenæum* 558/3 The word 'Gladstone' will probably continue to indicate those French wines which his Act cheapened for the general market. **1871** TROLLOPE *Ralph the Heir* iii, Yes, we've got sherry, and port wine, and Gladstone. **1884** A. BIRRELL *Obiter Dicta* Ser. I. 86 To make him unbosom himself over a bottle of Gladstone claret.

b. ***Gladstone (bag)***: a light kind of portmanteau or travelling-bag.

1882 MISS BRADDON *Mt. Royal* III. i. 11 Hamleigh's servant sitting behind, walled in by a portmanteau and a Gladstone-bag. **1887** E. J. GOODMAN *Too Curious* vi, With his Gladstone-bag in his hand. **1889** J. K. JEROME *3 Men in Boat* iv. 54 We got a big Gladstone for the clothes.

c. 'A roomy four-wheeled pleasure carriage with two inside seats, calash top, and seats for driver and footman' (Webster 1864).

Gladstonian (glæd'stəʊnɪən), *a.* and *sb.* [f. prec. + -IAN.] **A.** *adj.* Belonging to or characteristic of W. E. Gladstone; after 1886 used *spec.* (chiefly by opponents) as the designation of the party which supported Gladstone's proposals for establishing Home Rule in Ireland.

1861 *Illustr. Lond. News* 27 Apr. 392/1 Another gigantic Gladstonian oration. **1865** *Sat. Rev.* 5 Aug. 177 Anything.. more Gladstonian than the written book it is impossible to lay hands upon. **1886** *Times* 9 June 9/1 Where can the Gladstonian Liberals hope to win seats? Against the Conservatives, supported as the latter will be by the Unionist Liberals, Gladstonian candidates will fight at a far greater disadvantage than in November last.

B. *sb.* **1.** A supporter of Gladstone; *spec.* a member of the 'Gladstonian' party (see A).

1847 MOZLEY *Lett.* 6 Aug. (1885) 183 Rogers described the melancholy meeting of three or four Gladstonians [i.e. supporters of Gladstone in the Oxford University election]. **1886** *Times* 26 May 9/2 Mr. Fenwick.. encouraged Ministers, in a speech much applauded by the Gladstonians and Parnellites, to stand firm and adhere to the [Home Rule] Bill.

2. = GLADSTONE a.

1864 *Daily Tel.* 3 May, The finest Chateau Lafitte was introduced alongside the most rasping Gladstonian.

Hence **Glad'stonianism**.

1886 *Pall Mall G.* 9 Mar. 10/2 He.. thought that what the House of Lords was really out of sympathy with was Gladstonianism. **1888** *Sat. Rev.* 22 Sept. 345/2 The whole political capital of Gladstonianism.

Gladstonism ('glædstənɪz(ə)m). [f. the name of W. E. *Gladstone* + -ISM.] The principles or policies of Gladstone. So **'Gladstonite** = GLADSTONIAN *sb.* 1.

1873 CARLYLE *Let.* 15 Nov. (1904) II. 300 Stephen has evidently got intertwisted with Gladstonism. **1887** SWINBURNE *Let.* Apr. (1962) V. 184 Feeling deeply that the cause of Gladstonism can only be served by truth. *Ibid.* 186 A convinced and conscientious Gladstonite. *c* **1890** J. GOTT *Lett.* (1918) 110 My host is a lawyer—M. P. Gladstonite.

gladsum, obs. form of GLADSOME.

gladwin(e, -wyn, var. GLADDON.

glady ('gleɪdɪ), *a. rare.* [f. GLADE *sb.*² + -Y¹.] Glade-like; abounding in glades.

1837 ARNOLD *Let.* clvi. in Stanley *Life* (1858) II. 72 The snugness of that delicious glady field. **1851** MRS. MARSH *Ravenscliffe* III. ii. 22 As the door opened, giving a view of the copsy and glady wood beyond. **1854** *Tait's Mag.* XXI. 138 A magnificent banyan tree, that stood in the glady openings of the forest.

gladye, obs. inf. of GLAD *v.*

gladyn(e, -yyn, vars. GLADDON.

glæd, obs. f. GLAD *a.*; obs. pa. t. of GLIDE *v.*

glæu, var. GLEW *a. Obs.*

glafe, obs. form of GLAIVE.

† **glagol**¹. *Obs. rare*⁻¹. [a. OF. *glagol*, *glagel*, mod.F. *glaïeul*.] = GLADIOLUS 1 a.

1480 CAXTON *Ovid's Met.* XIII. iv, The flour is of glagol, and smellett only of complaynte.

Glagol² ('glægəl). [app. a back-formation from next.] The Glagolitic alphabet. (In recent Dicts.)

Glagolitic (glægə'lɪtɪk), *a.* [ad. mod.L. *glagolitic-us* (cf. Ger. *glagolitisch*), f. Serbo-Croat. *glagolica* (*c* = ts), the Glagolitic alphabet, f. the Common Slavonic *glagol*, word.

The reason for the name is uncertain; it is conjectured (Miklosich *Glagolitisches Alphabet* in Ersch & Gruber *Encycl.*) that *glagol* may in some dialect have had the sense of 'letter'; similarly *slovo*, which in Slavonic generally means 'word', has also the sense of 'letter' in Croatian.]

The distinctive epithet of the ancient Slavonic alphabet (called also 'Hieronymian', 'Illyrian', and 'Slovenish') still retained in the service-books of the Roman Catholics of the Slavonic rite in Dalmatia, etc.; also used as a designation of the Roman Catholics of the Slavonic rite.

1861 NEALE *Notes on Dalmatia*, etc. 98 In the case of mixed marriages between a Glagolitic and Latin Catholic, the children follow the rite of the father. **1861** MAX MÜLLER *Sci. Lang.* v. 187 *note*, Oldest dated MS. of 1056, written for Prince Ostromir. Some older written with Glagolitic letters. **1881** *Academy* 26 Mar. 226 The Slaves, when they became converts to Christianity, framed two alphabets, the Cyrillic and the Glagolitic.

glaid, obs. Sc. f. GLAD *a.*, GLEDE.

glaid, obs. Sc. pa. t. and pa. pple. of GLIDE *v.*

glaif, obs. Sc. form of GLAIVE.

glaik (gleːk), *sb. Sc.* [Of obscure origin; connexion with GLEEK is suggested by the sense, but its phonological possibility is not evident.

Possibly sense 4, though recorded late, may be the original; the notion of 'deceit' has often developed from that of 'dazzling'. Otherwise sense 4 must be regarded as a distinct word.]

1. *pl.* Mocking deception; chiefly in the phrases ***to give*** (†***play***) ***one the glaiks***, to cheat, swindle one; ***to get the glaik***(*s*, to be cheated or deceived. Cf. GLEEK *sb.*²

1508 KENNEDIE *Flyting w. Dunbar* 497 Greit in the glaykis, gude Maister Gilliam gukkis. **1535** LYNDESAY *Satyre* 1871, I se they haue playit me the glaiks. **1571** *Satir. Poems Reform.* xxv. 110 This sylit, begylit, They will bot get þe glaikis. **1596** DALRYMPLE tr. *Leslie's Hist. Scot.* x. 471 Another writeng sensles, ful of Gukis and Glaikis. **1681** COLVIL *Whigs Supplic.* (1751) 59 We did nothing but hunt the glaiks. *Note. Hunt the glaiks*, go of a fool's errand. **17..** in *Herd's Coll. Anc. Sc. Songs* (1776) II. 230 She gave me the glaiks when a' was done. **1755** R. FORBES *Ajax's Sp.* 7 Yet routh o' honour he has got, Ev'n tho' he gets the glaik. **1805** A. SCOTT *Poems* (1808) 121 Lads the glaiks did gie ye.. when ye were young.

2. A contemptuous epithet applied to a person.

[*a* **1550** *Christis Kirke Gr.* xxiii, His wyf bad him ga hame, Gib Glaiks.] **1814** *Saxon & Gael* I. 20 Och sorrow be on the glaik, my own heart will never warm to her.

3. 'A child's toy or puzzle' (Jam.).

[**1638**: perh. quot. for *glaxe* should come here; see GLAIKS.] **1890** W. GREGOR *Notes to Dunbar's Poems* (S.T.S.) 62, I have seen a toy called 'the glaykis', which was composed of several pieces of notched wood fitted into each other in such a manner that they can be separated only in one way. **1896** CROCKETT *Grey Man* iii, Why should a grown man.. care about the glaiks and puppet plays of a lassie of sixteen?

4. A flash of light. Also *fig.*

1818 SCOTT *Hrt. Midl.* xii, Gazing, glancing-glasses they are, fit only to fling the glaiks in folk's een. **1819** W. TENNANT *Papistry Storm'd* (1827) 175 His een.. Ae single styme afore his nose, They couldna see for glaiks. **1823** GALT *Entail* II. 186 He has glaiks and gleams o' sense about him, that [etc.]. **1830** —— *Laurie T.* III. v. (1849) 100 The rising sun was.. sprinkling the floor of the forest aisles with glaiks and gleams.

† **glaik**, *v. Sc. Obs.* Also 6 glak. [f. GLAIK *sb.*]

1. *intr.* To gaze wantonly or idly.

c **1560** A. SCOTT *Poems* (S.T.S.) xx. 42 The blenkyne of ane E Ay gart the goif and glaik. *c* **1590** BUREL *Pass. Pilgr.* in J. Watson *Collect.* (1706) II. 29 On sick consaits to glaik.

2. *trans.* **a.** To befool, delude. **b.** ? To pervert, sophisticate.

1500-20 [see below]. *c* **1560** A. SCOTT *Poems* (S.T.S.) xi. 33 Get ȝe ane goldin hour to glak thame [women]. **1567** *Gude & G. Ballatis* (1897) 178 Thocht thow be of Religioun ..ȝit and thow glaik or gagioun The treuth, thow sall cum downe.

3. To dazzle (the eyes).

1819 W. TENNANT *Papistry Storm'd* (1827) 3 Thou at his elbuck stood unseen, And wi' thy glamour glaik'd his een.

Hence † **'glaiking** *vbl. sb.* Also † **'glaiker**, one who 'glaiks'.

1500-20 DUNBAR *Poems* xvii. 4 Sum takkis our littill awtoritie, And sum our mekle, and that is glaiking; In taking sowld discretioun be. *a* **1605** POLWART *Flyting w. Montgomerie* 751 Gleyd glaiker, roome raiker.

'glaikery. *Sc.* Also 6 glaikrie. [f. GLAIK *sb.* + -ERY.] Foolish, wanton, or giddy conduct.

c **1580** *Satir. Poems Reform.* xliii. 203 Young men for glaikrie can not agrie with age. **1816** J. DUFF *Poems* 81 Ye'd quite yere glaikery, an' at last be wise.

glaikit ('gleːkɪt), *a. Sc.* and *north.* Also 5 **glakyt**, 6 **glaykit**, **-yt**, 8 **glakit**, 6- **glaiket**. [Related to GLAIK *sb.* and *v.*, but recorded earlier than these.] Senseless, foolish. In later use: Thoughtless, flighty, giddy (said esp. of women).

c **1450** HENRYSON *Sum Practysis Med.* i. Poems (1865) 43 Your saying I haif sene, and on syd set it, As geir of all gaddering, glaikit, nocht gude. *c* **1470** HENRY *Wallace* x. 845 Ȝon glakyt Scottis can ws nocht wndyrstand; Fulys thai ar. **1549** *Compl. Scot.* xv. 136 It vas beleuit be al the Romans that he [Brutus] vas becum frenetic and glaykit. *a* **1605** MONTGOMERIE *Poems* x. 18 Some we sie, in evry age, Lyk glaikit fools, gang gooked gaits. **1786** BURNS *To Unco Guid* 12 Poor mortals, That frequent pass douce Wisdom's door, For glaikit Folly's portals. **1824** SCOTT *Redgauntlet* ii, A glaiket ne'er-do-weel. **1862** HISLOP *Prov. Scot.* 67 Glib i' the tongue is aye glaiket at the heart. **1893** in *Northumbld. Gloss.*

Hence **'glaikitly** *adv.*, foolishly, thoughtlessly; **'glaikitness**, flightiness.

a **1500** *Ratis Raving* 342 Al thar disport and thar blychtnes Is al in foly and glaikitness. **1823** LOCKHART *Reg. Dalton* III. 171 Bid her have done wi' her glaiketness for a wee, and let's hear plain sense for ance. **1837** R. NICOLL *Poems* (1843) 299 If glaikitly we yokit, We wad be toilin' sair. **1893** *Northumbld. Gloss.*, *Glaikedness*, giddiness.

glaiks. *Sc.* (? *Obs.*) and *Anglo-Irish.* Also 7 **glaxe**. (See quot. 1880; but the sense in the other passages is doubtful; quot. 1638 may belong to GLAIK *sb.* 3.)

1638 ADAMSON *Muses Threnodie, Invent. Gabions* 96 In one nooke stood Loquhabrian axes, And in another nooke the glaxe is. **1814** TRAIN *Mountain Muse* 144 With platter, glaiks and quern mill. **1880** *Antrim & Down Gloss.*, *Glaiks*, a lever attached to a churn-staff, by use of which the churning is less laborious.

glair (glɛə(r)), *sb.*¹ Forms: 4-6 **glayre**, **gleyre**, (5 **gleyere**, **gleyȝy(e)r**, 6 **gleyr**), 4-7 **gleire**, (6 **gleir**, **gle(e)re**, 6-7 **gleare**), 7-9 **glare**, 5- **glaire**, 8- **glair**. [a. F. *glaire*, found in 13th c. The forms in the other Rom. languages (Pr. *glara*, *clara*, It. *chiara*, Sp. *clara*) indicate L. *clāra*, fem. of *clārus* bright, clear, as the source of the Fr. word.

The change of initial from *c* to *g* must have been early, as Ælfric's Gloss. (*c* 1000) has '*Glara*, æȝ-lim'; some scholars have ascribed it to confusion with *glārea* gravel, but this is unlikely, as there is no evidence that this word had the sense of 'clay' or adhesive soil. Med.L. *glaria*, applied to the viscid juice of grapes in Barth. *De Propr. Rerum*, is prob. a latinization of F. *glaire*.]

1. The white of an egg; freq. in full ***the glair of an egg***, ***of eggs***. Also, a technical term for preparations made from the whites of eggs and used in various trade-processes, esp. book-binding (see quot. 1893).

13.. *E.E. Allit. P.* A. 1025 Þe wal of Iasper þat glent as glayre. *c* **1386** CHAUCER *Can. Yeom. Prol. & T.* 253 Vnslekked lym Chalk and gleyre of an ey. **1430-40** LYDG. *Bochas* I. xx. 36 b, They have strictories to make their skin to shine Wrought subtilly of gommes and of glaire. *c* **1440** *Promp. Parv.* 198/2 Gleyre of eyryne, or whyte lyke (*K.* gleyere, *H.* gleyȝyre, *P.* gleyȝyer' of eyr'), *glarea*. *c* **1485** *E.E. Misc.* (Warton Club) 72 Grynde vermelone one a stone with newe glayre, and put a lytylle of the ȝolke of an ay thereto, and so write therewith. **1573** *Art of Limming* 3 To make glaire take the whyte of newe laide egges [etc.]. **1634** PEACHAM *Gent. Exerc.* I. xxi. 67 Gumme lake is made with the glaire of egs, strained often and very short. **1761** *Brit. Mag.* II. 45 Instead of the glair of eggs, gum-water is frequently used. **1811** *Self Instructor* 560 To make the glare of eggs. **1883** *St. James's Gaz.* 30 Nov. 5/1 The yelk is compounded with phosphorus, the glair with albumen, and the shell is made with lime. **1893** *Q. Rev.* July 185 The 'glaire' or adhesive substance with which those portions of the cover are to be coated which are intended for gold ornamentation.

Comb. **1858** SIMMONDS *Dict. Trade*, *Glaire-dealer*, a vender of broken eggs, albumen, &c.

2. *transf.* Any similar viscid or slimy substance.

a **1529** SKELTON *E. Rummyng* 25 Her lewde lyppes twayne They slauer, men sayne, Lyke a ropy rayne, A gummy glayre. **1574** *Mirr. Mag.*, *Morindus* xv, Rammishe stenche, bloud, poyson, slymy glere That in his body, so aboundaunt were. **1665** HOOKE *Microgr.* 51 Any glutinous Liquor, as.. Oyl of Turpentine, Glare of Snails, &c. **1790** SIR W. FORDYCE *Muriatic Acid* 11, I found the tongue black and dry, with a black glare on the teeth. **1860** GOSSE *Rom. Nat. Hist.* 160 The mass, which seems a mere drop of thin glaire, almost or quite homogeneous [etc.]. **1865** T. R. JONES in

Intell. Observ. Mar. 122 The transparent glair produced from decomposing vegetables.

†**glair**, *sb.*^{2} *Obs. rare*$^{-1}$. In 5 glayre. [a. OF. *glaire, glayre*:—L. *glārea*.] Gravel.

1481 CAXTON *Myrr.* II. xxi. 111 By Acres the Cyte is founden a maner of sande and there is founden also of the glayre of the see whiche ben medled to gydre, And of thyse two myxtyons is made good glasse and clere.

glair (glɛə(r)), *v.* Forms: 6 gleer, glare, 8 glaire, 9 glair. [f. GLAIR *sb.*^{1}] *trans.* To smear with glair; †also *gen.* to paint, daub.

1563–87 FOXE *A. & M.* (1684) I. 754/2 Lewd Wrights of Stocks hew and form such Crosses and Images, and after that, lewd Painters gleer them with Colours. **1598** J. MARSTON *Metam. Pigmalion*, etc. Sat. iii. (1598) 52 His clothes perfum'd, his fustie mouth is ayred, His chinne new swept, his very cheekes are glared [*printed* glazed; *but note the rime*]. **1755** JOHNSON, *To Glaire*, to smear with the white of an egg. This word is still used by the book-binders. **1885** LOCK *Workshop Rec.* Ser. IV. 245 The edge [of the book] is now glaired evenly, and the gold..is then gently laid on the edge which has been glaired.

fig. **1563** *Mirr. Mag.*, *Rivers* ix, Well saust with lyes, and glared all with glee.

glair, var. GLAR *sb.*, GLARE *a.*

glaireous ('glɛəri:əs), *a.* Also 8–9 glareous, glairous. [f. GLAIR *sb.*^{1} + -(E)OUS. Cf. F. *glaireux*.] Having the nature or appearance of glair.

1755 JOHNSON, *Glareous*. **1765** *Univ. Mag.* XXXVII. 146/2 There is a glareous liquor. **1806** KNIGHT in *Phil. Trans.* XCVII. 104 A glareous fluid, as Du Hamel has stated, exudes from the surface of the alburnum. **1819** H. BUSK *Vestriad* I. 219 These glareous eyes Death's fingers glue. **1848** MAUNDER *Treas. Nat. Hist.* 787 *Glareous*. **1882** OGILVIE, *Glaireous, Glairous*. [As distinct words.] So in later Dicts.

glairigenous (glɛə'rɪdʒɪnəs), *a.* [f. GLAIR *sb.*^{1} + -GEN^1 + -OUS.] Producing slime, or mucus, or glairin. (*Syd. Soc. Lex.* 1885.)

glairin ('glɛərɪn). Also glairine. [f. GLAIR *sb.*^{1} + -IN.] (See quots. and cf. *barégin(e)*.)

1838 T. THOMSON *Chem. Org. Bodies* 693 Of Glairin. This name has been given to a peculiar substance which has been observed in the sulphureous mineral waters of the Pyrenees. **1869** E. A. PARKES *Pract. Hygiene* (ed. 3) 20 Other nitrogenous substances are found—the so-called Glairine or the Zoogene. **1893** *Brit. Med. Jrnl.* 22 Apr. 866/2 Many mineral waters on evaporation leave an organic residuum which goes by the name of glairine.

glairy ('glɛərɪ), *a.* Also 7 gleary, 8 gliry, 8–9 glary. [f. GLAIR *sb.*^{1} + -Y^1.] Of the nature of glair; viscid, slimy. Chiefly *Path.*

1662 J. CHANDLER *Van Helmont's Oriat.* 196 The venal bloud being resolved by other poysons into a liquor Sunovie or Gleary water, poyson, jaundous excrement, &c. doth flow forth. **1737** BRACKEN *Farriery Impr.* (1743) II. 216 The Quantity of brownish gliry Matter that ran out. **1741** MONRO *Anat. Nerves* (ed. 3) 26 A wounded Nerve yields a *glairy Sanies*. **1809** HOME in *Phil. Trans.* XCIX. 185 By *mucus of animals*, I mean a glary fluid. **1827** W. KENNEDY *Poems* 123 Two glairy eyes Masked by foul putrefaction were unveiled. **1848** CARPENTER *Anim. Phys.* i. (1872) 31 When a considerable quantity of it exists in a fluid (as in the white of the egg) it gives to it a glairy tenacious character. **1853** *Zoologist* II. 3823 On raising the skin, a glairy appearance of the muscles and flesh (which was much wasted) presented itself. **1880** GRAY *Struct. Bot.* 115 A glairy secretion is poured out from numerous immersed glands.

Comb. **1883** J. E. ADY in *Knowledge* 15 June 354/1 Threads..coated over with a glairy-looking deposit [protoplasm].

Hence **'glairiness**, viscidity.

1866–7 LIVINGSTONE *Last Jrnls.* (1873) I. ii. 45 A little glariness seemed to be present on the foreleg.

glaise^1. *Sc.* ? *Obs.* [Possibly a var. of GLACE *sb.*^{2}; cf. *glaze*, mod. Sc. var. of GLACE *v.*] A touch of fire, a scorch. Also *fig.*

a **1572** KNOX *Reform. Scotl.* Wks. 1846 I. 17 Being bound to the staik in the myddest of some coallis [etc.] a trane of powder was maid and sett a fyre, quhilk gaue to the blessed martyre of God a glaise, skrimpled his left hand, and that syd of his face. **1825** JAMIESON s.v., *A glaise o' the ingle*, the act of warming one's self hastily at a strong fire.

†**glaise**^{2}. *Sc. Obs.* [Origin and sense uncertain; perh. a OF. *glais, glas*, resounding noise (see GLASS *sb.*^{2}); perh. var. of GLACE *sb.*^{2}, used *fig.*]

1585 JAS. I. *Ess. Poesie* (Arb.) 23 Whyles in that toung I gaue a lusty glaise For to descryue the Troian Kings of olde.

glaise, obs. form of GLAZE.

glaistig ('glastɪk). Also glaishrig, glaisrig, glastick, -ig. [Gael.] A supposed she-devil or hag in the shape of a goat; also, a beautiful female fairy, usu. seen at the bank of a stream.

1903 *Q. Rev.* July 24 Fairies, brownies, kelpies and glasticks. **1925** *Contemp. Rev.* Oct. 537 The water-kelpies, the water-bulls, the mermaids, the glastigs. **1926** T. HANNAN *Beautiful Isle of Mull* xiii. 83 The green glaistig is always represented with masses of long yellow hair. **1959** K. M. BRIGGS *Anat. Puck* 189 The Glaistig is a female fairy, generally half-woman, half-goat, but sometimes described as a little, stout woman, clothed in green.

glaive (gleɪv), *sb.* Also 3–6 gleyve, (6 gleive, glieve), 4–6, 9 *dial.* gleve, 6–7, 9 *dial.* gleave, 9 *dial.* gleeve; 4 gla(y)fe, 4–6 glayve, (6 *Sc.* glaif), 5–7 glave. [a. OF. *glaive, gleive* lance (mod.F. *glaive* poet. = sword).

Hatz-Darm. regard OF. *glaive* as an adapted form of L. *gladius* (through the stages *gladie, glaie, glavie*). Ascoli supposes it to represent a Celtic **cladivo-* (OIr. *claideb* sword, Gael. *claidheamh*). Neither view, however, accounts for the earliest meaning of the word in OF., which is also that of MHG. *glavie, glævîn*, MDu. *glavie, glaye*, Sw. *glaven*.]

A name given at different periods to three distinct kinds of weapons, viz. lance, bill, and sword.

The second of these senses seems to be peculiar to English, the others are derived from French; in a large number of passages it is impossible to determine from the context which weapon is intended, esp. in the case of later writers.

†**1.** A lance or spear. *Obs.*

1297 R. GLOUC. (Rolls) 4165 He hem ssende Mid gleyue oþer mid roches, and vewe aliue he let. *a* **1300** *Cursor M.* 7745 Nou her I leue þe kynges glaiue. *c* **1380** *Sir Ferumb.* 4690 Hure ȝeate [þay] gunne defende, Wyþ launces & gleues kene. *c* **1450** LONELICH *Grail* xiii. 786 Togederis they weren Met The lengthe of A Gleyve with-outen let. **1592** WYRLEY *Armorie, Ld. Chandos* 50 Sir Eustace..Did baisse his gleaue and well imbrace his shield.

†**b.** A lance set up as winning-post in a race, and given as a prize to the successful competitor; hence, a prize. *Obs.*

c **1380** WYCLIF *Serm.* Sel. Wks. II. 258 'Certis þei rennen all, but oon of hem takiþ þe gleyve..' Men usen ofte þis gamen, þat two men..rennen a space for a priis, and he þat comeþ first to his ende shal have þe gamen þat is sett, wheþer it be spere or gloves [*v.r.* gleyves] or oþir þing þat is putt. **1483** *Cath. Angl.* 157/2 A Glayfe, *brauium*. **1500** *Ortus Vocab.* Eiij, *Brauium* est primum [**1518** premium] vel victoria: the pryce of a game, or a glayue. *a* **1555** BRADFORD in Coverdale *Lett. Mart.* (1564) 282 Caste your eies on the gleue ye runne at, or els ye wil loose the game.

Comb. **1483** *Cath. Angl.* 157/2 A Glayfe wynner, *braueta*.

c. *dial.* A fish-spear.

1639 HORN & ROB. *Gate Lang. Unl.* xxxviii, There are some that glave small fishes with a three-tined fish-spear (glave). **1854** MISS BAKER *Northamptonsh. Gloss.*, *Gleeve*, a pole about four yards long, with serrated prongs, used for catching eels. **1879** W. G. WATERS in *Norfolk Archæology* viii. 170 *Gleave*, an eel spear. **1893** BARING-GOULD *Cheap Jack Z.* II. 102 He..produced a singular weapon or tool, locally termed a gleve.

†**2.** A weapon consisting of a blade fastened to a long handle; a kind of halbert. *Obs.*

c **1450** *Cov. Myst.* (Shaks. Soc.) 270 Ordeyn eche man..to be ther redy, With exys, gleyvis, and swerdys bryth. **1523** LD. BERNERS *Froiss.* I. lix. 80 He had in his hond a great glaue, sharpe and well stelyd, and aboue the blade, ther was a sharpe hoke of stele. **1542** UDALL *Erasm. Apoph.* 276 Yᵉ senates..stood in feare of his billes & glieues. **1596** SPENSER *F.Q.* v. xi. 58 [They] over all the fields themselves did muster, With bils and glayves making a dreadfull luster. **1629** MAXWELL tr. *Herodian* II. VII. 49 Suddenly the Country Clownes came in with their Clubs and Glaiues [orig. τά τε ξύλα καὶ τοὺς πελέκεις: on p. 48 the same words are rendered 'Clubs and Bills']. **1678** BUTLER *Hud.* III. ii. 543 Zeal, with aged clubs and gleaves Gave chase to rochets and white sleeves.

†**b.** A soldier armed with a glaive. *Obs.*

1577 HOLINSHED *Chron. Eng.* II. 954/1 There be in that towne more than iij C. glaiues, and iij C. yeomen.

3. A sword; *esp.* a broadsword. *arch.* and *poet.*

In early quots. possibly repr. Gael. *claidheamh*; cf. *glaymore* = CLAYMORE.

c **1470** HENRY *Wallace* x. 367 Awkwart he straik with his scharp groundyn glawe [= 358 his gud suerd of steill]. **1513** DOUGLAS *Æneis* III. viii. 23 The feirs Orion with his goldin glaif. **1670** MILTON *Hist. Eng.* II. Wks. 1851 V. 70 The Britans had a certain skill with their broad swashing Swords and short Bucklers..Agricola discerning that those little Targets and unweildie Glaves ill pointed, would soon become ridiculous against the thrust and close, commanded [etc.]. **1786** BURNS *When Guilford good* iv, But Clintons glaive frae rust to save, He hung it to the wa', man. **1812** BYRON *Ch. Har.* II. lviii, The Delhi with his cap of terror on, And crooked glaive. **1820** SCOTT *Ivanhoe* xviii, To maintain the..honour of his English ancestry with the glaive and brown-bill, the good old weapons of his country. **1887** BOWEN *Virg. Æneid* II. 393 [He] girds on the Achæan's glittering glaive.

fig. **1502** *Ord. Crysten Men.* (W. de W. 1506) II. xii. 119 And therfore sayth the psalmyst, that the tonges of synners is the glayues of yᵉ deuyll.

Hence **glaive** *v.*, † (*a*) to spear (a fish) (*obs.*); (*b*) to arm with a glaive (*nonce-use*). **glaived** *ppl. a.*, armed with a glaive.

1639 [see 1 c above]. **1821** JOANNA BAILLIE *Metr. Leg.*, *Wallace* vii. 9 Which helmed his brow, and glaved his hand. **1869** LOWELL *Cathedr.* Poet. Wks. 1890 IV. 61 Of the glaived tyrant and long-memoried priest.

glaizie, obs. form of GLAZY.

glak, obs. form of GLACK; var. GLAIK *v. Obs.*

glakit, -yt, obs. forms of GLAIKIT.

glam^1. *Obs.* exc. *dial.* [a. ON. *glam(m* noise, din (Sw. *glam* merriment, loud mirth, Da. *glam* barking of dogs), prob. echoic in origin.] Any loud noise, as shouting, loud or merry talk, barking of dogs, etc.; also, a shout, cry.

13.. *E.E. Allit. P.* B. 830 þenne seten þay at þe soper..þe gestes gay & ful glad, of glam debonere. **13..** *Gaw. & Gr. Knt.* 1426 Such a glauerande glam of gedered rachchez Ros, þat þe rocherez rungen aboute. *Ibid.* 1652 Much glam & gle glente vp þer-inne, Aboute þe fyre vpon flet. *a* **1400–50** *Alexander* 5504 He heres A grete glauir & a glaam of grekin tongis. **1886** ELWORTHY *W. Somerset Word-bk.* s.v., Hold your glam, anybody can't year theirzel spake.

glam^2. *Sc.* Also glaum. [var. of CLAM *sb.*^{1}; cf. GLAN and GLAND *sb.*^{3}] *pl.* **a.** The iron jaws of a vice (cf. CLAM *sb.*^{1} 2 b). **b.** Pincers, nippers (so *clams* in dial.). **c.** Hands (cf. CLAM *sb.*^{1} 3).

1580 *Inv. R. Wardr.* (1815) 302 Item, in the smiddie ane irne studie ane licht hammer ane littill pair of glammis but the vys. **1824** MACTAGGART *Gallovid. Encycl.*, *Glaums*, instruments used by horse-gelders, when gelding. **1847–78** HALLIWELL, *Glams*, the hands. *Northumb.*

glam^3. Var. of CLAM *sb.*^{2} 1.

1797 POLWHELE *Hist. Devon.* I. 123 The Glam, a shell-fish of the muscle kind, is found above Totnes wear.

glam (glæm). Colloq. abbrev. of *glamorous*, *glamorize*, and *glamour*; also **glam-rock**, a style of rock music (typically of the early to mid-1970s) characterized by male performers dressed in glamorous clothes, with the suggestion of androgeny or sexual ambiguity; cf. *glitter rock* s.v. GLITTER *sb.*^{1} 3. Hence **glammed-up** *a.*, glamorized, 'tarted up'; **glammy** *a.*, glamorous.

1936 in *Amer. Speech* XI. 192/2 The glammiest of the glamour girls—Tallulah Bankhead. **1937** *Motion Picture* June 17/1 Loretta Young—does that girl know how to glam! **1957** J. OSBORNE *Look Back in Anger* III. i. 85 Get yourself glammed up, and we'll hit the town. **1961** PARTRIDGE *Dict. Slang* Suppl. 1109/1 *Glam*, glamour: film-world hangers-on: since ca. 1940. **1963** 'M. CORRIGAN' *Why do Women..?* iv. 28 Have you any 'glam' night spots near by? **1964** C. DALE *Other People* v. 107 She was..wearing eye-shadow and a great deal of lipstick. 'You're looking very glam,' he said. **1966** J. CAIRD *Perturbing Spirit* vii. 72 We dress up for our dinner. We're not usually so glam. **1968** L. BERG *Risinghill* 45 In Risinghill Street itself..there are no glammed-up places. [**1974** *Music Scene* Jan. 47/1 There was also nothing to say that he was the 'King of Glamour Rock'.] *Ibid.* Mar. 10/4 Many bands started resorting to gimmicks in their acts... Thus was born the age of 'glam rock'. **1984** *Melody Maker* 6 Oct. 5/4 Robin..recently produced the stunning Wrathchild glam rock album.

glam, var. GLAUM *v. Sc.*, to snatch.

glama, obs. form of LLAMA.

†'**glamer**, *sb. Sc. Obs.* [? Alteration of CLAMOUR; but cf. GLAM^1 and Icel. *glamra* to rattle.

Gael. *clambar* wrangling, evil report, scandal, and *glambar* noise, outcry, are prob. from Eng. or Scottish.]

A loud noise or tumult; public outcry, scandal.

1500–20 DUNBAR *Poems* lvii. 20 Sum [seekers after office] hes thair advocattis in chamer And takis thame selffe thairof na glamer. **1570** *Satir. Poems Reform.* x. 182 Than come ȝour king and sum Lords with ane glamer, And reft him [Riccio] from hir. **1584** *Ibid.* xlv. 393 Without respect of warldlie glamer He past into the witchis chalmer.

Hence †'**glamer** *v. trans.*, to raise a clamour against, defame. †'**glamerous** *a.*, noisy, clamorous.

c **1470** HENRY *Wallace* VIII. 302 At the reskew thar was a glamrous rerd. **1490** *Extracts Aberd. Reg.* (1844) I. 46 Openly glammerand him, saiand scho sald ger banys the said Schir John out of this toune.

glamer, glammar, glamor, obs. ff. GLAMOUR.

glammerie, obs. form of GLAMOURY.

glamorize, glamourize ('glæməraɪz), *v.* orig. *U.S.* Also -ise. [f. GLAMOUR *sb.* + -IZE.] *trans.* To make glamorous or attractive. Hence **glamo(u)ri'zation**; '**glamo(u)rized** *ppl. a.*

1936 *Silver Screen* Dec. 5 They [*sc.* film stars] are so glamorized and vaporized and made to appear in print as somebody they aren't at all. **1938** *News of World* 12 June 7/2 Is this the way to glamorise 'a godsend'..? Shouldn't your advisers be aware that..his employers are..mightily concerned in finding him tough, he-man roles? **1941** *Amer. Speech* XVI. 98 Although the advertising writer does a creditable job of glamourizing colors and fabrics, he reserves his best efforts for the finished products. **1942** 'M. INNES' *Daffodil Affair* I. ii. 13 The glamorized advertisements, the pulsing sexy music. **1952** *Scrutiny* XIX. I. 39 A startling and quite unacceptable palliation, indeed glamorization, of acts which are by the book's own canons grievous sins. **1953** A. W. FIELDING *Stronghold* 28 An outlaw whom the passage of time has glamourized into a figure..improbably noble. **1966** *Listener* 1 Sept. 300/2 What about the glamorization of crime as it is alleged to take place on certain mass media, particularly television? **1967** W. SOYINKA *Kongi's Harvest* 24 The State will adopt towards him and to all similar institutions the policy of glamourised fossilism.

glamorous ('glæmərəs), *a.* Also glamourous. [f. GLAMOUR + -OUS.] Full of glamour. Cf. next.

1882 *Ch. Q. Rev.* Apr. 139 The eagle flight of Plato..has always the effect of making the plain world..seem to reel and spin..it grows faint and glamorous. **1885** C. E. CRADDOCK in *Harper's Mag.* Dec. 136/1 The mountains..wore a glamourous purple. **1938** D. SMITH *Dear Octopus* I. 22 *Cynthia*. I work for her. *Belle*. As a mannequin? *Cynthia*. Nothing so youthful and glamorous. **1942** PARTRIDGE *Usage & Abusage* 144/2 *Glamorous* for *romantic* or (of a scene, a night, etc.) *lovely* or (of a woman) *beautiful and attractive* or (of a way of life) *exciting* or *adventurous* or (of a love-affair or a flirtation) *sex-filled* or *amorous* belongs to the advertising of films—and should be treated as the dubious privilege of boss-driven copywriters. **1946** F. WAKEMAN *Hucksters* (1947) xiv. 195 Her innocence was wonderful. In his world of hep, glamorous dames, he'd forgotten about the jeune fille. **1967** *Times* 8 July 11/4 Recently I visited a West End store and told the glamorous lady assistant that I wanted a bottle of scent.

Hence **'glamorously** *adv.*

1891 E. CASTLE *Consequences* I. I. ii. 34 The whole scene ..became as it were glamorously illuminated.

glamour ('glæmə(r)), *sb.* Also 8 **glamer, glamor, glammar,** 9 *Sc.* **glaumour.** [Originally *Sc.*, introduced into the literary language by Scott. A corrupt form of GRAMMAR; for the sense cf. GRAMARYE (and F. *grimoire*), and for the form GLOMERY.]

1. Magic, enchantment, spell; esp. in the phrase *to cast the glamour over one* (see quot. 1721).

?**17..** *Johnny Faa* in Ritson *Sc. Songs* (1794) II. 177 As soon as they saw her well far'd face, They coost the glamer o'er her. **1720** RAMSAY *Rise & Fall Stocks* 152 Like Belzie when he nicks a witch, He..Casts o'er her een his cheating glamour. **1721** —— *Gloss. to Poems* s.v., When devils, wizards or jugglers deceive the sight, they are said to cast *glamour* o'er the eyes of the spectator. **1789** BURNS *Capt. Grose's Peregrin.* iv, Ye gipsy-gang that deal in glamor, And you deep read in hell's black grammar, Warlocks and witches. **1830** SCOTT *Demonol.* iii, This species of Witchcraft is well known in Scotland as the glamour, or *deceptio visus*, and was supposed to be a special attribute of the race of Gipsies. **1859** TENNYSON *Enid* 743 That maiden in the tale, Whom Gwydion made by glamour out of flowers. **1860** READE *Cloister & H.* I. 98 He knows father and daughter both. They cast their glamour on him. **1894** D. C. MURRAY *Making of Novelist* 199 The man had a glamour for me and drew me with the attraction of a magnet.

2. a. A magical or fictitious beauty attaching to any person or object; a delusive or alluring charm.

1840 HOOD *Kilmansegg, Fancy Ball* xxxvi, For to paint that scene of glamour It would need the Great Enchanter's charm. **1863** OUIDA *Held in Bondage* 97, I know how quickly the glamour fades in the test of constant intercourse. **1874** GREEN *Short Hist.* v. §1. 213 A sudden burst of military glory threw its glamour over the age of Cressy and Poitiers.

b. Charm; attractiveness; physical allure, esp. feminine beauty; freq. *attrib.* (see sense 3). *colloq.* (orig. *U.S.*).

1937 *Daily Tel.* 26 Oct. 8/5 His hero is just another Glamour Guy. **1947** PARTRIDGE *Usage & Abusage* 353/1 A girl or a gigolo may possess glamour: and it makes no matter whether the girl is glamorous in her own right or by the catch-guinea arts of her dressmaker or her cinematographic producer. **1951** M. MCLUHAN *Mech. Bride* 94/1 The trade motto 'Bodies by Fisher'..insists on the close relation of motorcar glamour to sex. **1958** *Woman* 22 Feb. 8/2 Kitchen needs glamour badly; looks too antiseptic due to all-over white painted walls.

3. *attrib.* and *Comb.*, as ***glamour gift, might***; ***glamour-learned*** ppl. a.; **glamour boy,** a young man who possesses glamour; *spec.* (*slang*) a member of the R.A.F.; **glamour girl,** a glamorous young woman; a 'pin-up girl'; **glamour puss** *slang*, a glamorous person.

1939 M. BRINIG *Anne Minton's Life* (1940) 91 People do him a great injustice by calling him a glamour boy. **1941** *New Statesman* 30 Aug. 218/3 *Glamour boys*, R.A.F., especially flying crews. **1942** T. RATTIGAN *Flare Path* I. 105 I'm going to pour it on with a bucket. If I can't look like the screen's great lover, I can at least smell like a glamour boy. **1954** M. CROFT *Spare Rod* I. v. 36 Those are your two glamour boys. You can't afford to leave them alone in the classroom or you'll have half the girls in as well. **1813** PICKEN *Pastoral Eulogy* 129 May be some wily lass has had the airt, Wi' spells, an' charms, to win our Robin's heart; An' hauds him, wi' her Glaumour-gift, sae fell. **1935** *Mademoiselle* Dec. 66/1 Horrible grimacing pictures of the Glamour Girl. **1936** [see GLAM]. **1940** *Illustr. London News* CXCVI. 464/2 There emerged the new glamour-girl, as one must call her nowadays, as thin and slender as a flake of silver leaf, as blanched as an almond, as 'platinum' as a wedding-ring. **1956** Glamour girl [see ANSWER *sb.* 6 b]. **1819** G. S. FABER *Dispensations* (1823) II. 94 During the reign of our glamour-learned first James. **1805** SCOTT *Last Minstr.* III. ix, It had much of glamour might, Could make a ladye seem a knight. **1952** N. STREATFEILD *Aunt Clara* 95 Though Aunt Bess is an angel, nobody could say she was a glamour-puss. **1959** C. MACINNES *Absolute Beginners* 54 'Now listen, glamour puss,' I said, flicking his bottom with my towel. **1968** *Times* 6 Jan. 17/6 As every good Butterfly must, she develops visibly and vocally from glamourpuss to grand tragic heroine.

glamour ('glæmə(r)), *v.* [f. prec. sb.] **a.** *trans.* To affect with glamour; to charm, enchant.

1832-52 W. FERGUSSON in *Whistle-Binkie* (Scot. Songs) Ser. III. 109 For ither scenes, and ither charms, Hae glamour'd Willie's een. **1835** J. P. KENNEDY *Horse Shoe R.* xxxiv. (1860) 382 He was wrought upon, bewildered, glamoured (to use a most expressive Scotch phrase) by the remembrance of a sickly dream. **1889** *Times* 28 Oct. 5/6 The Greeks..glamoured with the prospect of an addition to their European consequence and greatness.

b. To glamorize. Const. *up. colloq.* (orig. *U.S.*).

1951 L. HOBSON *Celebrity* (1953) xv. 243 It's lost some of the subtlety of the book..and they've glamoured it up a little too much. **1958** B. RUCK *Third Love Lucky* ix. 58 Where was his sweet, sporting, glowing, skating partner with such pretty natural ways? All glamoured up and spoiled.

Hence **'glamouring** *ppl. a.*

1871 B. TAYLOR *Faust* (1875) I. xxi. 182 The mountain's side along Sweeps an infuriate glamouring Song.

glamoured ('glæməd), *ppl. a.* [f. GLAMOUR *sb.* + -ED[2].] Affected with glamour.

1724 RAMSAY *Vision* xiv. in *Evergreen* (1761) I. 220 All this and mair maun cum to pass, To cleir zour glamourit Sicht. **1889** RIDER HAGGARD *Cleopatra* iii, The place, to their glamoured sight, was a seething sea of snakes.

glamoury ('glæmərı). Also **glaumerie, glammerie, glamourie.** [Var. GLAMOUR *sb.*; for the termination cf. GRAMARYE.] Glamour, magic.

1821 *Edin. Mag.* Apr. 352 It maun surly be the pithiness o' the style or sum bewitching glaumerie that gars fowk glaum at them whare eir they can get a claucht. **1822** PRAED *Lillian* Poems 1866 I. 80 The shades of glamoury depart. **1847** J. WILSON *Chr. North* (1857) I. 249 Glad as if we had escaped from glamoury. **1882** *Contemp. Rev.* July 24 Ballads ..all more or less touched with glamourie.

glamp (glamp), *v. Sc.* [Of obscure origin; cf. GLAUM *v.* and GLAM[2].] *intr.* To grope, as in the dark. ***to glamp at***: to make snatches at.

1768 ROSS *Helenore* I. 38 An' sae I wakn'd glamping here an' there. **1813** D. ANDERSON *Poems* 79 (Jam.) He glampin' raise An' tremblin', pat his claise on. **1826** G. BEATTIE *John O'Arnha'* in *Life* (1863) 234 [Some] glampit at the vacant air.

†**glan.** *Obs. rare*[−1]. [var. GLAM[2], CLAM; cf. GLAND[3].] A comb-maker's vice (cf. quot.).

1688 R. HOLME *Armoury* III. 383/2 A pair of Glans, which belong to the Trade of a Comb maker..The Glans..is two pieces of Wood, square at top, and rounded off below, with an Iron Pin through both yet so as they may widen a little.

glan, obs. form of GLEN.

glance (glɑːns, -æ-), *sb.*[1] [f. GLANCE *v.*]

1. a. A swift oblique movement or impact. † ***by glance***: obliquely. Also *fig.* ? *Obs.*

1570 LEVINS *Manip.* 21/10 A Glance, *transitus.* **1599** HAKLUYT *Voy.* II. I. 134 For they saile away, being not once touched with the glaunce of a shot, and are quickly out of the Turkish canons reach. **1654** H. L'ESTRANGE *Chas. I* (1655) 55 And though these speeches did not take their aime directly at his Majesty, yet did they by glance and obliquely deeply wound him. **1735** SOMERVILLE *Chase* III. 332 The watchful angry Beast Th' Advantage spies; and at one sidelong Glance Rips up his Groin.

b. *Cricket.* (See quot. 1897.)

1883 *Cricket* 19 Apr. 39/1 Leg glances being his favourite stroke. **1892** *Daily News* 1 July 2/2 A remarkable ability to play the stroke, which can be best described as the leg glance. **1897** RANJITSINHJI *Jubilee Bk. Cricket* 172 There is another stroke by which good-length balls on the leg-side can be played—the glide or glance... The face of the bat is turned slantwise to meet the ball, which should glance off towards fine-long-leg... In these days, with perfect wickets, the glance-stroke is very useful.

†**2.** *fig.* **a.** A satirical hit or allusion, a jest *at* (or *upon*) something. **b.** Allusion, reference. *Obs.*

a. 1602 FULBECKE *2nd Pt. Parall.* 36 This was but the glaunce of Diogenes, who made more accompt of his scoffe then his state. **1605** BACON *Adv. Learn.* I. vii. §8 (1873) 57 Silenus was gravelled..not knowing where to carp at him; save at the last he gave a glance at his patience towards his wife. **1639** HORN & ROB. *Gate Lang. Unl.* §842 Pleasant jests, conceits, and witty glances [L. *allusiones*] beseem men of civility, but not bitter tart girds. **1697** POTTER *Antiq. Greece* IV. xiii. (1715) 317 In these Songs they now and then gave a Satyrical Glance upon those who had misbehav'd themselves in the Wars.

b. 1665 SIR T. HERBERT *Trav.* (1677) 349 Albeit in that brief discourse I made..there are some glances at it; I shall here..speak a little further upon that subject. **1702** ECHARD *Eccl. Hist.* (1710) 5 Every part of it [the temple-ministration] had a glance at a future and better state of things.

3. A sudden movement producing a flash or gleam of light; also, the flash or gleam itself.

1503 DUNBAR *Thistle & Rose* 96 Reid of his cullour, as is the ruby glance. *a* **1547** SURREY *Æneid* II. 223 Yea thrise.. In glaunces bright she glittered from the ground [L. *terque ipsa solo..Emicuit*]. **1637** EARL STIRLING *Jonathan* I. lxxxi, Each swords bright glance, seem'd summons from their fate. **1665** SIR T. HERBERT *Trav.* (1677) 387 The Sun.. shines with utmost ardour upon those parts..whether his glances be oblique or perpendicular. **1667** MILTON *P.L.* VII. 405 Fish..sporting with quick glance, Show to the Sun thir wav'd coats. **1796** MORSE *Amer. Geog.* I. 132 The famous Ice-glance... It is a large high field of ice, whose glance in the air may be seen for many leagues at sea. **1810** SCOTT *Lady of L.* I. xxxv, The silver light, with quivering glance, Played on the water's still expanse. **1849** T. WOOLNER *My Beautiful Lady* (1863) 21 As knight led captive, in romance Through postern and dark passage, past grim glance Of arms.

fig. **1814** *Apostate* v. ii, How awful is this silence Which has succeeded to that glance of sound! **1827** HOOD *Plea of Mids. Fairies* xxiii, So do we flutter in the glance of youth.

4. A brief or hurried look. Also ***a glance at, into, of, over, upon***, etc. (the object looked at).

1591 GREENE *Disc. Coosnage* (1592) 4 The verser cuts off some four cards, and..geueth the cony a glance of the bottom card. **1592** DAVIES *Immort. Soul* Introd. xli. (1742) 11 The Glance of this Dame's angry Eyes. **1606** SHAKS. *Tr. & Cr.* III. ii. 126, I was won my Lord With the first glance. **1667** MILTON *P.L.* IX. 1034 So said he, and forbore not glance or toy Of amorous intent. **1718** LADY M. W. MONTAGU *Let. to C'tess Mar* 10 Mar., In most courts..the glance of the monarch is watched, and every smile is waited for with impatience. **1796** H. HUNTER tr. *St.-Pierre's Stud. Nat.* (1799) II. 532 This arrangement pleases at first glance, but soon fatigues the eye by it's uniformity. **1828** SCOTT *F.M. Perth* xxxiii, He passed the papers through his hands, turning some over with a hasty glance. **1860** TYNDALL *Glac.* I. xvi. 113 Casting a glance over the glorious scene beneath us [etc.]. **1874** GREEN *Short Hist.* iii. §7. 154 A glance satisfied him of the hopelessness of the struggle.

fig. **1781-3** COWPER *Verses A. Selkirk* 41 How fleet is a glance of the Mind! **1805** FOSTER *Ess.* IV. i. 105 A decisive glance of thought. **1849** E. B. EASTWICK *Dry Leaves* 200 It is idle hypocrisy now to pretend that our design..included the slightest glance at their advantage.

5. *Comb.* **glance-pitch** (see quot. 1897); **glance-wood,** a hard wood grown in Cuba, and used for gauging-instruments, carpenter's rules, etc.

1871 MCELRATH *Dict. Words Comm.* (Webster 1890) *Glance-wood.* **1897** *Birm. Weekly Post* 18 Sept. 5/1 Barbadoes is commencing to export 'manjak or glance-pitch', of the nature of petroleum in a bituminous form.

glance (glɑːns, -æ-), *sb.*[2] Also **glanz.** [ad. G. *glanz* (Du. *glans*) brightness, lustre, also glance-ore.] A variety of ore having a lustre which indicates its metallic nature. *Obs.* exc. in *antimony-, bismuth-, copper-, iron-, lead-, silver-glance*, q.v.

[**1457-8, 1747**: see GLANCE-ORE.] **1828** STARK *Elem. Nat. Hist.* II. 488 Order XI.—Glance. Lustre metallic. Gray black. **1847** in CRAIG. **1858** WHEWELL *Hist. Sci. Ideas* II. 141 The Orders Pyrites, Glance, and Blende, are common to Naumann and Mohs.

b. *Comb.* **glance-coal,** a variety of anthracite (G. *glanzkohle*, Du. *glanskool*).

1805 *Edin. Rev.* VI. 230 With respect to glance-coal..it is surely far from being new under its vulgar name of blind-coal. **1848** SIR J. G. WILKINSON *Dalmatia*, etc. I. 198 It is a variety of glanz coal. *c* **1865** LETHEBY in *Circ. Sci.* I. 117/1 Glance-coal, or anthracite, is not rich enough in hydrogen to be of any use to the gas manufacturer.

glance (glɑːns, -æ-), *v.*[1] Forms: 5 **glench, glens, gla(u)nche,** 5-6 **glence,** 6 **gla(u)nse, glawnse,** *Sc.* **glanss,** 6-7 **glaunce,** 6- **glance.** [Of obscure origin. As the earliest sense is the same with that of GLACE *v.*, it seems possible that the word may be a nasalized form of OF. *glaichier* to slip, slide, perhaps influenced by OF. *guenchir, guencir* to turn aside, or by GLENT *v.*

The word has been commonly explained as f. GLANCE *sb.*[1], a. Du. or Sw. *glans*, but these are only adoptions of MHG. *glanz* brightness, lustre (related to GLENT, GLINT).]

1. a. *intr.* Of a weapon: To glide off an object struck, without delivering the full effect of the blow. Also ***to glance aside, off. to glance on***: to strike obliquely upon and turn aside.

c **1450** *Merlin* 198 The stroke of the ax glenched, and smote the horse bak asunder. *c* **1500** *Melusine* xxxvi. 250 The helmet was hard and þe swerd glenced asyde & dommaged hym nought. **1590** SIR J. SMYTH *Disc. Weapons* 30 Most of their volees of arrowes should have..glaunced or lighted upon the piques. **1725** POPE *Odyss.* XXII. 309 And from Ctesippus' arm the spear elanc'd On good Eumæus' shield and shoulder glanc'd. **1828** SCOTT *F.M. Perth* ii, The blow only glanced on the bone, and scarce drew blood. **1882** LECKY *Eng. in 18th C.* IV. 245 The heaviest shot glanced harmlessly from the sides of the assailing vessels.

transf. and *fig.* **1596** SHAKS. *Tam. Shr.* V. ii. 61 As the Iest did glaunce awaie from me, 'Tis ten to one it maim'd you too out right. **1626** JACKSON *Creed* VIII. xxi. §4 Their projects.. doe often glance or fall upon some other object then they thought of. **1846** TRENCH *Mirac.* xx. (1862) 329 He..means that rebuke to glance off on Him who has put forth on this day his power to help and to save.

†**b.** To pass *by* without touching.

c **1540** tr. *Pol. Verg. Eng. Hist.* (Camden) I. 246 The river Nadder..glawnceth bie the village Wersminster. *a* **1682** SIR T. BROWNE *Christ. Mor.* II. iii. (1716) 49 Some have digged deep, yet glanced by the Royal Vein.

†**2.** To move rapidly, esp. in an oblique or transverse direction; to dart, shoot; to spring *aside.*

1489 CAXTON *Faytes of A.* I. ix. 23 The manere how they shall glaunche or with-drawe themself from y[e] strokes. *c* **1500** *Melusine* xix. 67 He glanched asyde, and so the kyngis nevew, for he recountred ayenst nothing, fell doun to the grounde. *c* **1600** SHAKS. *Sonn.* lxxvi. 3 Why with the time do I not glance aside To new found methods? **1618** BOLTON *Florus* IV. ii. (1636) 264 The warre..glanced into Asia, and lay heavy upon Africke. **1647** H. MORE *Song of Soul* II. ii. II. xxiv, If that, the object gone, away those forms do glance. **1786** tr. *Beckford's Vathek* (1868) 20 Glancing from the precipice with the rapidity of lightning, [he] was lost in the gulf below.

fig. **1604** T. WRIGHT *Passions* III. i. 79 If thou see..one eate very greedily..such actions glaunce out of gluttony.

3. With reference to discourse: To pass quickly *over*, glide *from, off* (a subject). ***to glance at*** (***upon,*** †***against***): to allude or refer to obliquely or in passing, usually by way of censure or satire; to hit at, reflect upon.

1570 DEE *Math. Pref.* 33 Yet will I glanse ouer it, with wordes very few. **1591** GREENE *Disc. Coosnage* Pref. (1592) 3 Thus Gentlemen I haue glaunst at the Barnards lawe. **1603** SHAKS. *Meas. for M.* V. i. 311 To call him villaine: and then to glance from him To th' Duke himselfe, to taxe him with Iniustice. **1621** T. WILLIAMSON tr. *Goulart's Wise Vieillard* To Rdr. A iv, The wise Old Man..seemes to glance at our English Proverb: No foole to the old foole. **1672-3** MARVELL *Reh. Transp.* I. 40 Whatsoever may have glanced upon him, was directed only to our Author. **1720** SWIFT *Fates of Clergymen* Wks. 1755 II. II. 29 Verses.. wherein he glanced at a certain reverend doctor. **1819** W. TAYLOR in *Monthly Mag.* XLVII. 119 The discourse mostly glanced upon the corruption of Manners and Morals among the Romans. **1872** O. W. HOLMES *Poet Breakf.-t.* vi. 174, I glanced off, as one often does in talk. **1893** STEVENSON *Catriona* 39 Words which glance upon the purity of justice.

4. To cause a flash of light by rapid movement; †*Sc.* to shine. Of light: To dart, flash, gleam.
1568 *Satir. Poems Reform.* xlviii. 76 To..mak it [cloth] weill hewit And gar it glanss lyk Dunmygrane. **1617** MORYSON *Itin.* I. 19 The Sunne beames glancing on my face, as I lay in bed. **1648** MILTON *Psalm* lxxxvii. 27 In thee [Sion] fresh brooks and soft streams glance. **1727** P. WALKER *Life Peden* (1827) 49 He broke out in a Rapture about our Martyrs, saying..now they are all Glancing in Glory. **17..** RAMSAY *Ode Mem. Mrs. Forbes* 13 Her soul glanc'd with each heavenly ray. **1781** COWPER *Truth* 242 Now flashing wide, now glancing as in play, Swift beyond thought the lightnings dart away. **1822** SCOTT *Pirate* xxiii, These pretty feet and ancles, that glance so white in the moonbeam. **1852** MRS. STOWE *Uncle Tom's C.* xxxiv, An insane light glanced in her heavy black eyes. **1859** TENNYSON *Marr. Geraint* 172 He..glancing like a dragon-fly In summer suit and silks of holiday.
fig. **1824** MISS FERRIER *Inher.* xcvi, The thought glanced upon her, that L. would be glad to see her so protected. **1884** W. C. SMITH *Kildrostan* I. i. 242 The ripples that glimmer and glance Where the sun flashes.

5. Of the eye: To move quickly, to cast a momentary look, to flash. Also said of the person looking; esp. ***to glance at***, to give a brief look at; ***to glance over***, to look quickly over, to read hurriedly (also ***to glance through***); and with various preps. and advs., as ***to glance down, up***, etc.
1583 STANYHURST *Æneis* II. (Arb.) 61 In this wise musing myn eye glaunst to my coompanye fensiue. **1586** T. B. *La Primaud. Fr. Acad.* I. xxiii. 233 They that glaunce at honor [Fr. *qui iettent legerement les yeux à l'honneur*], as if that were vertue it selfe. **1590** SHAKS. *Mids. N.* v. i. 13. **1638** F. JUNIUS *Paint. Ancients* 293 The eyes..loosly swimming in pleasure, glancing and (to speake so) venereall. **1816** SCOTT *Old Mort.* xxxv, A horseman..gave a letter. Claverhouse glanced it over. **1820** W. IRVING *Sketch Bk.* I. 51 A beautiful face glanced out at the window and vanished. **1823** SCORESBY *Whale Fishery* 396 Some of those who glance over these pages, may have been the 'sons and daughters of affliction'. **1831** T. L. PEACOCK *Crotchet Castle* xvi. 252 Her eye glanced on something which made her change colour. **1843** W. H. AINSWORTH *Windsor Castle* I. iii, The duke..was glancing rather wistfully at them. **1862** G. MACDONALD *D. Elginbrod* II. xviii, Every now and then glancing up at her from her work. **1865** M. C. HARRIS *Christine* (1866) xxx. 181 Mrs Sherman and the party..glanced off their cards and chatted. *Ibid.* 187 She glanced up at the clock. *Ibid.* xxxiii. 208 He would..open her books, and glance through them for some trace of her in them. **1871** L. STEPHEN *Playgr. Europe* iii. (1894) 81 We crept..cautiously along..glancing down the mighty cliffs beneath us. **1881** C. E. L. RIDDELL *Sen. Partner* I. v. 96 He did not glance round as the manager entered. *Ibid.* III. vi. 139 'No,' she agreed, glancing nervously around her. **1881** J. FOTHERGILL *Kith & Kin* I. ii. 22 She..glanced for a moment into his face. **1894** A. CONAN DOYLE *Mem. Sherlock Holmes* 147 Glancing very keenly across at me. **1902** R. MACHRAY *Night Side of London* v. 93 You indulge in pleasant little dreams, or glance away from what may become a tragedy. **1907** *Smart Set* Jan. 54 Her brother-in-law glanced after her. *a* **1953** E. O'NEILL *Long Day's Journey* (1956) II. i. 57 As she talks, she glances everywhere except at any of their faces. *Ibid.* ii. 70 He glances away, ignoring her question. *Ibid.* IV. 132 He glances up at the chandelier disapprovingly. *Ibid.* 152 She glances around vaguely.
fig. **1861** GEO. ELIOT *Silas M.* 37 His thoughts glanced at all the neighbours who had made any remarks.

6. *trans.* **a.** ***to glance one's eye, look***: †(*a*) to turn aside one's gaze as when dazzled (cf. sense 2); (*b*) to give a quick or momentary look; also, to look quickly *at* or *upon* an object.
1590 GREENE *Never too late* (1600) F, Finding the sunne too glorious for my sight, I glaunst my looke. *c* **1600** SHAKS. *Sonn.* cxxxix. 6 Deare heart, forbeare to glance thine eye aside. **1632** BROME *North. Lasse* I. vii. Wks. 1873 III. 16 Now glaunce your eye on this side, on the yoke, You bring your neck to. **1642** *Life, etc. J. Puffe* 4 in Hazl. *E.P.P.* IV. 315 His downcast eyes upon his boots are glanct. **1716** ADDISON tr. *Ovid* Wks. 1753 I. 194 Fire broke in flashes when he glance'd his eyes. *a* **1794** GIBBON *Misc. Wks.* (1814) I. 177 After glancing my eye over Addison's agreeable dialogues, I more seriously read the great work of Ezekiel Spanheim. **1826** DISRAELI *Viv. Grey* II. xiii, Vivian glanced a look of annihilation. **1837** HAWTHORNE *Twice-Told T.* (1851) I. i. 21 He..glancing his severe eye around the group ..at last bent it sternly on Sir Edmund Andros.

b. To survey with a glance; to catch a glimpse of.
1635–56 COWLEY *Davideis* II. 182 Still does he glance the fortune of that day. **1765** J. BROWN *Chr. Jrnl.* (1814) 163 With enrapturing joy shall we glance the countless facts of redeeming love. **1797** MRS. A. M. BENNETT *Beggar Girl* (1813) V. 302 Lady Gauntlet just glanced the hind wheels of two carriages, which drove round to the back of the house. **1828** MONTGOMERY *Vision Heaven* 28 Who ever glanced the Heavens, nor dream'd of God..and things divine? *Ibid.* 39 Those burning mysteries that mortals glance With wonder.

c. To express or convey with a glance (of the eye).
1717 PRIOR *Alma* II. 185 There his eyes took distant aim, and glanc'd respect to that bright dame. **1843** E. JONES *Sens. & Event* 109 Glancing sublime devotion. **1845** BROWNING *Luria* Poet. Wks. (1868) 105 As if there were no glowing eye i' the world, To glance straight inspiration to my brain.

†**7.** To touch obliquely; to graze, barely touch; *fig.* to glance at, allude to. *Obs.*
1590 SHAKS. *Com. Err.* v. i. 66 Alone, it was the subiect of my Theame: In company I often glanced it. **1651** EVELYN *Diary* 15 Sept., I observ'd that the mall gos the whole square thereof next yᵉ wall, and bends with an angle so made as to glance yᵉ wall.

8. a. To direct obliquely. *lit.* and *fig.*
a **1656** BP. HALL *Rem. Wks.* (1660) 22 One morning as I lay in my bed, a strong motion was suddenly glanced into my thoughts of going to London. **1685** *Gracian's Courtier's Orac.* 32 Seeing they [words or hints] are cunningly glanced, so also are they to be cautiously received. **1697** DAMPIER *Voy.* I i. 10 They will purposely strike their Harpoons.. aside, or so glance them as to kill nothing. **1704** SWIFT *T. Tub* x. 191, I will here take Leave to glance a few Innuendo's. *a* **1800** COWPER *Wks.* (1835–7) I. 120 Formerly, in my happiest hours, I had never been able to glance a single thought that way. **1806** R. CUMBERLAND *Mem.* (1807) I. 404 He came home..to refute some malicious imputations that had been glanced at his character. **1825** CARLYLE *Schiller* III. (1845) 165 He narrowly escapes killing or ducking for having ventured to glance a censure at the General.

b. To emit with a flash or gleam. ***to glance back***: to flash back, reflect.
1746–7 HERVEY *Medit.* II. 7 The curling Waves, glowing with purple in one place..in another, glancing a cast of undulating Green. **1824** SCOTT *Redgauntlet* Let. iv, The bink, with its usual arrangement of pewter and earthenware ..glanced back the flame of the lamp merrily.

c. *Cricket.* To deflect (the ball) with the glance-stroke (see GLANCE *sb.*[1] 1 b). Also *absol.*, and with the bowler as obj.
1898 K. S. RANJITSINHJI *With Stoddart's Team* (ed. 4) iii. 50 He seemed able to 'drive',..or 'glance'..with equal skill and success. **1899** *Captain* I. 593/1 You had better practise slipping and glancing the ball. **1899** *Daily News* 22 July 4/2 Men were then less apt to 'glance and glide', like The Brook, and K. S. Ranjitsinhji. **1928** *Daily Express* 19 Dec. 3/2 White..glancing Ironmonger for three. **1963** A. ROSS *Australia 63* vii. 129 Simpson glanced Statham's fourth ball and Smith, diving, caught it.

glance, *v.*[2] *U.S.* [? ad. Du. *glanzen* to polish, planish (metals), f. *glans* lustre: see GLANCE *sb.*[2] Cf. G. *glänzen*, Sw. *glansa*.] *trans.* To planish.
1894 *Times* 16 Aug. 6/3 Sheet steel, polished, planished, or glanced,..one and three-fourths cents per pound.

†**glance-ore.** *Obs.* [A half adoption, half translation of Du. *glanserts* (a. G. *glanzerz*), f. *glans* lustre + *erts* ORE.] (See quot. 1747.)
1457–8 in Plowden *Rep.* (1571) 320, cxliiij Bolles de Glaunce ore domini Regis valoris xv li. vj s'. viij d. **1747** HOOSON *Miner's Dict.* O j, Lead Ore we distinguish into three kinds which we Miners observe, the first is Potters Ore, which is the same with that we call Glance Ore; the second is Steel Ore; and the last is that called White Ore.

glancer (ˈglɑːnsə(r), -æ-). *nonce-wd.* [f. GLANCE *v.*[1] + -ER[1].] One who glances.
1567 HARMAN *Caveat* (E.E.T.S.) 61 Be holdinge with ardante eyes thys glymmeringe glauncer. **1782** MAD. D'ARBLAY *Diary* 28 Oct., Every glance I met was followed by a whisper from the glancer to his or her party. **1882** *Athenæum* 4 Mar. 279/3 The pregnant meaning of this curious glance has never been equalled since Lord Burghley's nod. The glancer or smiler is a certain Lady Ridgeway.

glanche, obs. form of GLANCE *v.*[1]

glancing (ˈglɑːnsɪŋ, -æ-), *vbl. sb.* [f. GLANCE *v.*[1] + -ING[1].] The action of the vb. GLANCE, in various senses.
1494 FABYAN *Chron.* VII. ccxxv. 252 This Kynge Wyllyam ..by glaunsynge of an arowe..was wounded to yᵉ deth. **1523** LD. BERNERS *Froiss.* I. ccclxxiii. 617 Sir Wylliam Fermyntone excused hymselfe and sayde..howe he coulde nat amende it [his stroke], bycause of glaunsynge of his fote. **1642** MILTON *Apol. Smect.* Wks. 1738 I. 110 By this upbraiding to me the Bordello's, as by other suspicious glancings in his Book, he would seem privily to point me out ..as one whose custom of Life were not honest. **1701** BEVERLEY *Apoc. Quest.* 42 All which speak the Openings, and Glancings [*printed* Glaneings] out of the Kingdom of Christ. **1832** HT. MARTINEAU *Ireland* v. 82 She saw a glancing and gleaming on the extreme point of the track..It was the glittering of the arms of a strong party of soldiers. **1843** PRESCOTT *Mexico* (1850) I. 257 The glancing of their weapons, and the shrill cry of the trumpet, all filled the spectators with astonishment.

b. *Comb.*, as **glancing-glass** *Sc.*, 'a glass used by children for reflecting the rays of the sun on any object' (Jam.). In quots. *fig.*
1728 WALKER *Life Peden* (ed. 3) 95 A glazing Glancing-glass, who loves to hear himself speak, and the World to notice him. **1818** [see GLAIK *sb.*[4]].

ˈ**glancing,** *ppl. a.* [f. GLANCE *v.*[1] + -ING[2].] That glances (in various senses of the verb).
1596 SPENSER *F.Q.* v. vi. 38 The glauncing sparkles through her bever glared, And from her eies did flash out fiery light. **1692** R. L'ESTRANGE *Josephus, Antiq.* XVII. xiv. (1733) 477 He insinuated, by this glancing Way, some remote Pretension that he might have to the Crown. **1725** POPE *Odyss.* XIX. 464 This [scar] on Parnassus combating the boar, With glancing rage the tusky savage tore. **1814** SOUTHEY *Roderick* XVII. 49 The stream—with its shadows and its glancing lights. **1876** GEO. ELIOT *Dan. Der.* VI. xlviii, She had a glancing forethought of what she would do in that case.

†**b.** ***a glancing view***, a cursory look or survey.
1691 T. H[ALE] *Acc. New Invent.* p. xii, This glancing View of these two great Inventions. **1707** NORRIS *Treat. Humility* iii. 102 To take a short glancing view of the imperfections of our nature.

c. *Comb.*, as †*glancing-wise*.
1548 PATTEN *Exped. Scotl.* H iiij, Syr Thomas Darcy vpon hys approch to the enemies, was strooken glauncing wyse on the ryght syde, with a bullet. **1580** NORTH *Plutarch* (1676) 18 He had never opened it to them but in dark speeches, and glaunsing wise, and so much as sufficed to put them in some hope.

Hence ˈ**glancingly** *adv.*, in a glancing fashion.
1556 J. HEYWOOD *Spider & F.* xxxv. 47 Tharbiters glaunsingly, Ere the flies ought saide..Had betweene them selues these woords. **1577–87** HOLINSHED *Chron.* (1807–8) III. 125 Others glansinglie passe by it, as a matter of no great observation. **1668** H. MORE *Div. Dial.* III. xxix. (1713) 253 These six..I distinctly remember, but had cursorily and glancingly cast mine Eye on all twelve. **1827** *Blackw. Mag.* XXI. 502 My feet shall bear me glancingly along to the merry music of streams. **1855** *Tait's Mag.* XXII. 119 There are plenty of witty men..whose faculties play glancingly upon the surface of things.

glancy (ˈglɑːnsɪ, -æ-), *a. rare*⁻¹. [f. GLANCE *sb.*[1] + -Y[1].] Bright; quick in movement.
1733 RAMSAY *Tea-t. Misc.* (1775) I. 108 Her glancy een like comets sheen, The morning sun outshining.

gland[1] (glænd). [ad. L. *gland-em*, *glans* acorn, perh. through F. *gland*.]
1. An acorn. *Obs.* exc. (occas.) *Bot.* = GLANS 2.
1631 R. H. *Arraignm. Whole Creature* x. §1. 76 Many Countries lived of Pulse, and Gland, and Dates. **1721** BRADLEY *Philos. Acc. Wks. Nat.* 45 A hundred Bushels, which may probably contain in Number 384000 Acorns; for reckoning sixty Glands to the Pint, which is 3840 to the Bushel, in a hundred Bushels there will be the aforesaid Number. **1836** *Penny Cycl.* V. 252/3 *Gland*,..the fruit of the oak, the hazel, &c. **1880** [see GLANS 2].
†**2.** (See quot.; so Gr. *βάλανος*.) *Obs.*
1684 tr. *Bonet's Merc. Compit.* XIX. 745 Glands, or Suppositories.
3. = GLANS 1. (Mayne *Expos. Lex.* 1854.)
4. *Hist.* An acorn-shaped ball of lead, used as a missile.
1852 BURN *Naval & Milit. Dict.* 183 *Gland*,..leaden ball for a sling, in the form of an acorn, having frequently devices engraved upon it. **1927** J. MOTHERSOLE *In Roman Scot.* xviii. 252 These leaden sling-bullets (called 'glandes' because they were shaped like acorns) were only used up to the close of the first century.

gland[2] (glænd). [ad. F. *glande* gland, tumour, altered form of OF. *glandre* (see GLANDER), **glandle*, ad. L. **glandula* GLANDULE.]
1. *Phys.* An organ, composed of nucleated cells and either simple or complex in structure, which separates from the blood certain constituents for use in the body, or for ejection from it.
Simple and compound glands are also distinguished as CONGLOBATE (cf. LYMPHATIC) and CONGLOMERATE, q.v. Certain organs, such as the spleen, thymus, thyroid, and adrenals, which perform the function of glands but have no excretory duct, are known as DUCTLESS (also *aporic*) glands. Individual glands, or groups of glands, are chiefly named from their position, as *cervical*, *cœliac*, *iliac*, etc., or from their discoverer, as *Blandin's*, *Bowman's*, etc.
1692 RAY *Dissol. World* 132 Shells found in Animal Bodies, in whose Glands they were originally formed. *a* **1711** KEN *Hymnotheo* Poet. Wks. 1721 III. 109 Soft Love compress'd the Gland in either Eye, And Tears flow'd down. **1718** J. CHAMBERLAYNE *Relig. Philos.* (1730) I. iii. §4 There are in the Mouth so many Glands or Fountains of Spittle. **1781** E. DARWIN *Bot. Gard.* I. (1791) 155 The Chyle's white trunk..Winds into glands, inextricable clues. **1830** R. KNOX *Béclard's Anat.* 75 The cellular tissue is more abundant in the muscles than in the glands. **1851** CARPENTER *Man. Phys.* (ed. 2) 298 In Mammalia, the Absorbent system presents itself in its most developed and concentrated state..the glands are much more numerous. **1872** MIVART *Elem. Anat.* x. (1873) 430 Each gland consists essentially of a net-work of finely divided lymphatic vessels on and amongst which capillary blood vessels ramify.
2. *Bot.* A secreting cell or group of cells on the surface of a plant-structure (cf. quots. 1845–78).
1785 MARTYN *Rousseau's Bot.* xii. 131 At one end of these [filaments] is a gland, at the other an anther. **1805** *Med. Jrnl.* XIV. 543 Leaves circular..with two glands running one into another on the inner side above the base. **1845** LINDLEY *Sch. Bot.* i. (1858) 19 Glands are either hairs with a head or secreting organ..or internal nuclei..or little tubercles upon various organs. **1878** MCNAB *Bot.* (1879) 59 Glands are cells or aggregations of cells distinguished..by containing resinous, oily, sugary, or fragrant substances.
3. *attrib.* and *Comb.*, as ***gland-alveolus, -cell, -cyst, -duct, -fever, -follicle, -lesion, -lobule, -mass, -nerve, -orifice, -patch, -pit, -salts, -secretion, -structure, -tissue, -tube, -tumour, -vesicle***; also ***gland-bearing, -ciliate(d, -dotted, -like, -tipped*** adjs.
1897 *Allbutt's Syst. Med.* II. 809 Numerous small *gland alveoli open along its course. **1860** DARWIN in *Life & Lett.* (1887) III. 319 One of the *gland-bearing hairs of Drosera. **1875** —— *Insectiv. Pl.* iii. 56 The fluid within the *gland cells passes outwards. **1880** BEALE *Slight Ailm.* 110 As age advances the gland-cells become more feeble. **1870** HOOKER *Stud. Flora* 465 *Nephrodium rigidum*..involucre, *gland-ciliate. *Ibid.* 124 *Rosa canina*..densely *gland-ciliated bracts. **1885** *Syd. Soc. Lex.*, **Gland-cyst*, a cyst developed in a gland from obstruction of a duct or distension of a follicle. **1870** HOOKER *Stud. Flora* p. xi, *Hypericineæ*..leaves opposite often *gland-dotted. **1860** SIR H. THOMPSON *Dis. Prostate* (1868) 62 Pus is, in such cases, often found filling the sinus pocularis and the *gland-ducts around. **1885** *Syd. Soc. Lex.*, **Gland-fever*, a fever having connection with a disordered condition of the glands. **1878** T. BRYANT *Pract. Surg.* I. 138 The kind of tissue which is found between the *gland-follicles. **1897** *Allbutt's Syst. Med.* III. 659 The *gland-lesion was essentially primary. **1849–52** TODD *Cycl. Anat.* IV. 1214/1 The whitish *gland-like mass. *Ibid.* 829/1 The *gland-lobules have the same relation to the efferent renal veins. **1897** HUTCHINSON *Archives Surg.* VIII. 205 A very considerable *gland-mass had now appeared on the left iliac fossa. **1897** *Allbutt's Syst. Med.* III. 307 *Gland-nerves are..held to contain at least two sets of fibres. **1878** T. BRYANT *Pract. Surg.* I. 102 The dilatation of occluded ducts or natural *gland-orifices. **1849–52** TODD *Cycl. Anat.* IV. 839/1 In many Mammalia certain Peyerian *gland-patches

show a constant..size at all periods. **1906** *Academy* 6 Jan. 8/2 The pre-orbital *gland-pit which has been traced in the skulls of Hipparion. **1873** T. H. GREEN *Introd. Pathol.* (ed. 2) 79 In those cases in which calcification is associated with retained *gland-secretions, the calcareous matters will consist of the specific *gland salts. *Ibid.* 154 The adenomata always originate from pre-existing *gland-strucures. **1870** HOOKER *Stud. Flora* 110 Quite glabrous, i.e. without bristles or *gland-tipped hairs. **1860** SIR H. THOMPSON *Dis. Prostate* (1868) 62 More fluid than natural is found in the *gland-tissue, and freely issues on being pressed. **1881** *Trans. Obstetr. Soc. Lond.* XXII. 48 The lumen of the *gland-tubes. **1902** *Encycl. Brit.* XXV. 394/1 The forms of the several kinds of glands depend on the degree of branching of these gland tubes. **1897** HUTCHINSON *Archives Surg.* VIII. 201 The following notes describe a case in which a *gland tumour..continued to grow steadily for many years. **1849–52** TODD *Cycl. Anat.* IV. 831/2 A microscopic examination of the expressed contents of the *gland-vesicles reveals nuclei.

gland[3] (glænd). *Mech.* [? var. of GLAN, GLAM[2]; cf. Sc. *glaun(d* 'a clamp of iron or wood' (Jam.).]

1. A sleeve employed to press a packing tight on a piston-rod (cf. FOLLOWER 5 d, and *clam* 'a movable collaring for a pump' (*Eng. Dial. Dict.*).

1839 R. S. ROBINSON *Naut. Steam Eng.* 53, *bb* is the cover of the casing, furnished with a stuffing box, gland, &c. **1871** *Daily News* 6 Nov., The glands were leaking, and I thought every minute the steampipe would go. **1890** W. J. GORDON *Foundry* 23 The glands on the top of each low-pressure cylinder..will be enclosed in a steam-tight casing.

2. A cross-piece or clutch made fast to a shaft, and communicating motion to a machine by engaging with part of the gearing.

1825 J. NICHOLSON *Operat. Mechanic* 31 Clutches or glands may be used with much advantage as a coupling for double bearings. Fig. 57 represents a coupling of this kind; it consists of two crosses..one fixed to each shaft.

3. *Founding.* **a.** 'A hooked bar by which the parts of a molder's flask are clamped together.' **b.** 'A plate through which the ends of a band or tightening clevis pass. A clip-plate.'

1875 in KNIGHT *Dict. Mech.* 971/2.

4. *Comb.*, as ***gland-packer***; **gland-cock** (see quot.).

1884 KNIGHT *Dict. Mech.* IV. 400/1 *Gland-cock*, a faucet held in place by a gland. **1885** *Instr. Census Clerks* 42 *Engine, Machine maker*..Gland Packer (Loco.).

glandaceous (glæn'deɪʃəs), *a.* [f. L. *gland-, glans* GLAND[1] + -ACEOUS.] Acorn-coloured.

1885 in *Syd. Soc. Lex.* **1886** J. THOMAS *Med. Dict.*, *Glandaceous*, yellowish brown; the color of an acorn.

†**'glandage.** *Obs.*[−0] [a. OF. *glandage* (med.L. *glandagium, glandāticum*), f. *gland* acorn: see -AGE.] (See quot.)

1656–81 BLOUNT *Glossogr.*, *Glandage* (Fr.) Mast, also Mastage, the season of turning hogs into the woods; the feeding of hogs by Mast.

glan'darious, *a.* [f. L. *gland-*, GLAND[1] + -ARIOUS.] Acorn-like in shape; glandiform (*Cent. Dict.*).

glandele, obs. form of GLANDULE.

glandenous, var. GLANDINOUS, *Obs.*

glander ('glændə(r)). Forms: 5 glaundre, 6–7 glaunder, 7– glander(s. [a. OF. *glandre*, *glandle GLAND[2], ad. L. *glandula* GLANDULE.]

†**1.** A glandular swelling about the neck. *Obs.*

1483 CAXTON *Gold. Leg.* 372/2 She had..aboute her necke & throte a twenty botches called glaundres. **1523** FITZHERB. *Husb.* §86 A glaunder, whan it breaketh, is lyke matter.

2. *pl.* (const. as *sing.*) (*the*) ***glanders***: a contagious disease in horses, the chief symptoms of which are swellings beneath the jaw and discharge of mucous matter from the nostrils.

1523 FITZHERB. *Husb.* §86 Glaunders is a disease, that.. appereth at his nosethrylles, and betwene his chall bones. **1530** PALSGR. 183 *Les glandres*..a disease of a horse called the glaunders. *a* **1637** DEKKER, etc. *Witch Edmonton* IV. i. Wks. 1873 IV. 397 My Horse this morning runs most pitiously of the glaunders. **1774** GOLDSM. *Nat. Hist.* I. 437 *note*, A consumption of the ethmoid bones of the nose called the glanders, is with us the most infectious and fatal [disease of the horse]. **1809** WELLINGTON in Gurw. *Desp.* (1837) IV. 416 Some of the stables at Lisbon are infected by Glanders. **1875** ZIEMSSEN *Cycl. Med.* III. 320 Glanders and farcy are perfectly identical affections, both equally contagious, and differing only in their local manifestations.

fig. **1602** *2nd Pt. Return fr. Parnass.* I. ii. 327 They haue some of them beene the old hedgstakes of the presse, and some of them are at this instant the botts and glanders of the printing house.

b. The same disease communicated to man.

1871 DARWIN *Desc. Man* I. i. 11 Man is liable to receive from the lower animals, and to communicate to them, certain diseases, as hydrophobia, variola, the glanders, &c. **1878** T. BRYANT *Pract. Surg.* I. 76 Glanders is a specific disease given to man by inoculation from the horse.

3. *attrib.* and *Comb.*, as ***glander-pest, -pustule.***

1764 GRAINGER *Sugar Cane* I. 616 No glander-pest his airy stables thinn'd. **1884** MACKENZIE *Dis. Throat & Nose* II. 420 The characteristic glander-pustules appear in crops on the face.

glandered ('glændəd), *ppl. a.* [f. prec. + -ED[2].] Affected with glanders.

1667 J. LACY *Sauny the Scot* III. Dram. Wks. (1875) 345 Petruchio is coming..upon an old, lean, lame, spavined, glandered [cf. SHAKS. *Tam. Shr.* III. ii. 51 possest with the glanders] broken-winded jade. **1752** BERKELEY *Farther Th. on Tar-water* Wks. III. 501 It hath recovered even a glandered horse that was thought incurable. **1835–6** TODD *Cycl. Anat.* I. 429/1 The blood of a glandered horse will impart glanders. **1870** HOLMES *Syst. Surg.* I. (ed. 2) 700 The discharge may continue for many months..unattended by any other symptom, and yet the horse be decidedly glandered.

glanderous ('glændərəs), *a.* [f. as prec. + -OUS.] Affected with, or of the nature of, glanders.

1727 BRADLEY *Fam. Dict.* s.v. *Glanders*, Several have observed that when a Horse has had the Farcin, he will easily become glanderous. **1753** J. BARTLET *Gentl. Farriery* 328 Another hole..should be made..to give issue to the glanderous matter washed away by the injection. **1880** BLACKMORE *Mary Anerley* III. v. 72 He left an oozy channel drying, (like a glanderous sponge) in August; and virulent fever came into his tent. **1897** *Allbutt's Syst. Med.* II. 514 Evidence of the presence of the glanderous condition.

glandiferous (glæn'dɪfərəs), *a.* [f. L. *glandifer* acorn-bearing (f. *gland-, glans* acorn + *-fer* bearing) + -OUS.] Bearing acorns or similar fruit.

1647 A. ROSS *Myst. Poet.* iv. (1675) 103 Virgil calls Acorns *Chaonias glandes*, and all glandiferous woods by the name of Dodona. **1664** EVELYN *Sylva* (1679) 10 Into these Furrows ..throw..all the Glandiferous Seeds, Mast, and Key-bearing kinds. **1707** MORTIMER *Husb.* 338 The Beech is of two sorts and numbred amongst the Glandiferous Trees. **1865** *Pall Mall G.* 13 July 11/1 Many [trees] which are divided by Pliny into glandiferous and pitch-bearing cannot be included in either division.

Hence **glan'diferousness.**

1727 in BAILEY vol. II.

glandiform ('glændɪfɔːm), *a.* [ad. L. type **glandiformis*, f. *glandi-, glans* acorn: see -FORM.]

a. Acorn-shaped. **b.** Resembling a gland.

1822–34 *Good's Study Med.* (ed. 4) I. 84 In a few instances half the length of the œsophagus has been completely gorged by a single fleshy or glandiform excrescence. **1836–9** TODD *Cycl. Anat.* II. 990/2 The penis..is terminated by a soft and glandiform structure. **1857** DUNGLISON *Med. Lex.* 413 Glandiform ganglions.

†**'glandinous,** *a. Obs. rare.* Also 6 glandenous, -ynous. [app. f. late L. *glandin-, glandō* = L. *gland-em* GLAND[1]: see -OUS.] = GLANDULOUS.

1541 R. COPLAND *Guydon's Quest. Chirurg.* G iij b, They [the pappes] be composed of whyte glandenous flesshe, and with veynes, arteres, & synewes. **1725** BRADLEY *Fam. Dict.*, *King's Evil*, tumours that usually arise about the Neck and sometimes in some other glandinous parts.

†**'glandi-'similar,** *a. Obs.* [f. mod.L. *glandī similis* (after SIMILAR).] Resembling a gland.

1753 N. TORRIANO *Midwifry* 38 Womb..Its substance is somewhat glandi-similar.

glandle, obs. form of GLANDULE.

glandless ('glændlɪs), *a. Bot.* [f. GLAND[2] + -LESS.] Destitute of glands.

1830 LINDLEY *Nat. Syst. Bot.* 150 Polypetalous dicotyledons, with..exstipulate glandless leaves. **1870** HOOKER *Stud. Flora* 221 *Hieracium murorum*..almost glandless.

glandular ('glændjʊlə(r)), *a.* [ad. F. *glandulaire*, f. *glandule* GLANDULE: see -AR[1].] Of or pertaining to a gland or glandule; resembling, or of the nature of, a gland; containing, bearing, or consisting of, a gland or glands. **a.** *Phys.* **b.** *Bot.*

a. 1740 CHEYNE *Regimen* 188 The nervous membranous Tubuli, and the glandular Machinulæ. **1789** W. BUCHAN *Dom. Med.* (1790) 83 Glandular obstructions..generally proceed from inactivity. **1836–9** TODD *Cycl. Anat.* II. 481/2 The prevailing ideas respecting the essential characters of the glandular organization are..vague and indefinite. **1856–8** W. CLARK *Van der Hoeven's Zool.* I. 15 We cannot admit a proper Glandular Tissue, as most authors do. **1872** HUXLEY *Phys.* v. 117 The liver is the largest glandular organ in the body.

b. 1793 MARTYN *Lang. Bot.* s.v. *Glandulosum*, A glandular leaf, is that which has glands either on the surface or on the serratures. *a* **1794** SIR W. JONES *Sel. Indian Plants* Wks. 1799 II. 99 Germ awled; pointed, furrowed, with prominent seedlets, sitting on a glandular pedicel. **1859** FAIRHOLT *Tobacco* (1876) 2 The leaves..are covered with glandular hairs. **1870** HOOKER *Stud. Flora* 121 *Rosa villosa*..sepals more or less persistent densely glandular.

Hence **'glandularly** *adv.*

1840 PAXTON *Bot. Dict.*, *Glandularly-crenated, Glandularly-serrated*, having crenatures or serratures tipped with glands. [And other examples.]

glandulation (glændjʊ'leɪʃən). *Bot.* [f. as prec. + -ATION.] 'The mode of occurrence or presence of glands in plants' (*Syd. Soc. Lex.* 1885).

1760 J. LEE *Introd. Bot.* III. xix. 210 Glandulation respects the secretory Vessels; which are either Glandules, Follicles, or Utricles. **1791** E. DARWIN *Bot. Gard.* I. *Note at end*, On Vegetable Glandulation.

glandule ('glændjuːl). Chiefly *pl.* Also 5 glandele, 7 glandul, (glandle). [a. F. *glandule*, ad. L. *glandula* (in pl. glands of the throat, tonsils), dim. of *gland-, glans* acorn: cf. GLAND *sb.*[1]]

†**1.** A gland. *Obs.*

The word is chiefly current in the 17th cent. and is then applied esp. to the glands of the throat and neck, or to the tonsils, though also used as a general term.

c **1400** *Lanfranc's Cirurg.* 84 Glandeles þat ben kirnelis þat ben in þe ground [= groin]. **1601** HOLLAND *Pliny* I. 339 The spungeous kernels, which in men be called Tonsillæ, or the Almands, are in swine named the Glandules. **1634** T. JOHNSON *Parey's Chirurg.* XVII. xv. (1678) 382 At the greater corner of the eye there is a glandule, made for containing and receiving the moisture. **1676** J. COOKE *Marrow Surg.* 424 The rest of the Glanduls of the Body do serve either to Excretion, as those of the Testicles, Prostates [etc.]; or for reduction as *Glandulæ Renales.* **1713** DERHAM *Phys. Theol.* IV. viii. 162 For the affording this oily or muciliginous Matter, there are Glandules very Commodiously placed near the Joynts. **1748** tr. *Vegetius' Distemp. Anim.* 161 The glandules also are sometimes troublesome to animals.

b. A small gland.

1751 in CHAMBERS *Cycl.* **1870** ROLLESTON *Anim. Life* Introd. 63 Oral salivary glands are represented only by small glandules impacted in the mucous membrane of the mouth.

†**2.** *pl.* A swelling of the glands in the throat or neck (so L. *glandulæ*). *Obs. rare.*

[*c* **1400** *Lanfranc's Cirurg.* 207 Also blood is medlid wiþ greet fleume & malancolie, & engendriþ glandulas & Scrophulas.] *c* **1550** LLOYD *Treas. Health* lxiiii. (? 1560) V vi, To take away the glandules, incorporate brimstone and whete bran w[t] Terpentine. **1616** SURFL. & MARKH. *Country Farme* 98 For the strangles or glandules which happen vnder the Oxe his throat..plucke away their glandules, and after couer his head with some couering.

3. A morbid swelling or growth in the body.

1656 R. WHITLEY in *Nicholas Papers* (Camden) III. 263 His distemper was a great swelling on his brest below his clauis. Phisitians..found..y[t] he had there a glandule by wearing of armes or something else. **1670** G. H. *Hist. Cardinals* III. III. 296 They found his Reins to be wasted, and two Callous Glandules (which the Physicians call *Tuberculi*) obstructing the passage of his Urine. **1822–34** *Good's Study Med.* (ed. 4) I. 377 Sometimes [the diseased omentum has been] loaded with many thousand glandules.

Hence **glandu'laceous** *a.* [see -ACEOUS], 'like to a gland' (*Syd. Soc. Lex.* 1885).

glanduliferous (glændjʊ'lɪfərəs), *a.* [f. GLANDULE + -(I)FEROUS.] Bearing glands or glandules.

1702 DRAKE in *Phil. Trans.* XXIII. 1236 It wou'd be a weak objection, to alledge that the Observation and Experiment being made on the Uterus of a Cow, the inference wou'd not hold from thence to a Woman, the one being Glanduliferous, and the other Placentiferous. **1811** A. T. THOMSON *Lond. Disp.* (1818) 222 The petals are..longer than the filaments, which are in ternaries..and the three innermost glanduliferous at the base. **1882** *Nature* XXV. 327 One may sometimes examine all the leaves without detecting a single glanduliferous one.

So **glandu'ligerous** *a.* [f. L. *-ger*, f. *gerĕre* to bear.] = prec.

1857 GOSSE *Creation* 229 A protrusion and eversion of the glanduligerous edge of the mantle.

'glanduliform, *a.* [f. L. *glandula* GLANDULE + -(I)FORM.] 'Having the appearance of a gland or glandule' (*Syd. Soc. Lex.* 1885).

'glandulite. *Min.* ? *Obs.* [a. F. *glandulite*, f. *glandule*: see GLANDULE and -ITE.] Pudding-stone, an agglomeration of gland-like pebbles.

1811 PINKERTON *Petral.* II. 119 The stones called glandulites by Saussure.

glandulose ('glændjʊləʊs), *a. Bot.* [ad. L. *glandulōs-us*: see GLANDULOUS.] Full of glands or gland-like formations; having the nature of a gland.

1847 W. E. STEELE *Field Bot.* 52 Leaves glandulose. **1881** BAKER in *Jrnl. Linn. Soc.* XVIII. 275 Panicle with spreading, few-flowered, secund, glandulose, slender branches.

†**glandu'losity.** *Obs. rare*[−1]. [f. as prec. + -ITY.] A gland-like formation.

1646 SIR T. BROWNE *Pseud. Ep.* III. xxv. 176 In the upper parts of wormes, there are likewise found certaine white and ovall glandulosities which Authors terme egs.

glandulous ('glændjʊləs), *a. Phys.* ? *Obs.* Also 5 glandelous, -ose. [ad. F. *glanduleux*, ad. L. *glandulōs-us*, f. *glandula* GLAND, GLANDULE.] Of or pertaining to a gland or glandule; having the nature of a gland; containing, or consisting of, glands.

c **1400** *Lanfranc's Cirurg.* 28 Anoþer maner fleisch þer is þat is glandelose, þat is as it were accornis. *Ibid.* 267 Al þe fleisch of þe tetis is glandelous. **1541** R. COPLAND *Guydon's Quest. Chirurg.* C iij, The other is glandulouster, odenose [? *read* glandulous or adenose], or cruddy and kyrnele, as is the flesshe of the ballockes, of the dugges and the flesshe of the emuntores. **1575** TURBERV. *Faulconrie* 272 Then must you fall to giuing hir of those glandulous kirnels of the Weather. **1657** W. COLES *Adam in Eden* lxviii. 129 The tuberous and glandulous Cloggs being not much unlike those hard swellings. **1760–72** tr. *Juan & Ulloa's Voy.* (ed. 3) I. 57 It [the gallinazo] has a wrinkled, glandulous and rough skin. **1801** *Phil. Trans.* XCI. 251 Its substance is glandulous and compact. **1846** BUCHANAN *Technol. Dict.*, *Glandular, Glandulous.*

b. *Bot.* = GLANDULOSE.

1794 MARTYN *Rousseau's Bot.* xxix. 454 Having the lower serratures glandulous.

Hence **'glandulousness.**
1727 in Bailey vol. II.

glandynous, var. GLANDINOUS, *Obs.*

glaneing, obs. form of GLEANING.

glangore, var. GLENGORE, *Obs.*

† **'glannen, 'glanen**, *sb. Obs. rare.* [a. Welsh *gwlanen* woollen, f. *gwlân* wool: see FLANNEL.] Woollen cloth, FLANNEL. Also *attrib.*
1596 *Lanc. Wills* (Chetham Soc.) III. 2 A glanen waste coate. 1688 R. Holme *Armoury* III. 348/2 Flannel, or Glannen..is one of several sorts of Cloth made of Wool.

‖ **glans** (glænz). [L. *glans* acorn, cognate with the synonymous Gr. βάλανος; cf. GLAND.]
1. *Anat.* The *glans penis.*
So Gr. βάλανος (Aristotle); L. *glans penis* is in Celsus.
1650 Bulwer *Anthropomet.* 202 Buttoning up the Prepuce with a Brasse or Silver-button on both sides of the Glans. 1789 W. Buchan *Dom. Med.* (1790) 509 The prepuce must be..divided, in order to..set the imprisoned glans at liberty. 1831 R. Knox *Cloquet's Anat.* 818 The Glans (*Balanus*) of the penis. 1881 Mivart *Cat* 241 The distal end of the organ is called the glans.
2. *Bot.* (See quots.)
1704 in Harris *Lex. Techn.* 1866 *Treas. Bot.* 533/1 *Glans*, an inferior fruit, one-celled by abortion, not dehiscing, containing one or two seeds, and seated in a cupule; as in the acorn. 1880 Gray *Struct. Bot.* 296 The nut is often enclosed or surrounded by a kind of involucre, termed a Cupule; such as the cup at the base of the acorn, the bur of the chestnut, and the leaf-like covering of the hazel-nut. The name Glans (sometimes Gland in English) is technically applied to such nuts.

glanse, glanss, obs. ff. GLANCE *v.*[1]

glanz, var. GLANCE *sb.*[2]

glar, glaur (glɑːr, glɔːr), *sb. Sc.* and *north. dial.* Also **glair, gloar.** [Of unknown origin; cf. next vb. and ON. *leir* mud.] Slime, mud.
1500-20 Dunbar *Poems* xxxiii. 108 He..in a myre, vp to the ene, Amang the glar did glyd. 1596 Dalrymple tr. *Leslie's Hist. Scotl.* I. 45 Five myles of this loch of Spynie.. is now maid glare and myre. 1715 Ramsay *Christ's Kirk Gr.* II. iii, Then took his bonnet to the bent And daddit aff the glar Fou clean that day. 1843 Carlyle *Let.* Jan. in Froude *Life in Lond.* (1884) I. xi. 285 Like building a dry brick house out of a quagmire of clay and glar! 1867 Sir W. Elliott in *Proc. Berw. Nat. Field Club* 310 Holes full of black glaur. 1893 *Northumbld. Gloss.*, *Glair, glaur, gloar, glar*, liquid mud of the filthiest sort.
Hence **glaury** *a.*, muddy. *rare.*
1788 Picken *Poems* 38 Through glaury holes an' dybes nae mair Ye'll ward my pettles frae the lair. 1879 R. Adamson *Lays Leisure Hours* 85 Frae gilded throne to glaury sheuch.

glar, glaur (glɑːr, glɔːr), *v. Sc.* Also 9 **glawr.** [cf. prec. sb. and GLORY *v.*[2]] *trans.* To make muddy.
*c*1450 Henryson *Wolf & Lamb* iii. Poems (1865) 211 That suld presume, with thy foull lippis vyle, To glar my drink, and this fair watter fyle. 1809 Skinner *Misc. Poet.* 132 Just whare their feet the dubs had glawr'd, And barken'd them like bryne.

glare (glɛə(r)), *sb.*[1] Also 5 **glayre.** [f. GLARE *v.*]
1. Dazzling brilliance (of a light, fire, sun, etc.); a strong fierce light. Also *absol.*, dazzling or oppressive sunshine, esp. when falling upon reflecting surfaces and not relieved by shadow or verdure.
*c*1400 *Destr. Troy* 5926 All shone his shilde & his shene armur, Glissenond of gold with a glayre hoge. 1697 Dampier *Voy.* (1729) I. 4 Betwixt 10 and 11 it cleared up.. The glare did not continue long before it rained again. 1700 Dryden *Pal. & Arc.* II. 546 The frame of burnished steel, that cast a glare From far. 1716 Addison *Ovid, Met.* II. 131 The seat with party-colour'd gems was bright; Apollo shin'd amid the glare of light. 1748 *Anson's Voy.* III. iii. 320 The frequent glare of the lightning had prevented the explosions from being observed. 1764 Goldsm. *Trav.* 71 The naked negro, panting at the line..Basks in the glare. 1832 W. Irving *Alhambra* II. 45 The owl, who hated the glare and bustle of crowded streets [etc.]. 1869 Freeman *Norm. Conq.* (1876) III. xi. 71 The comet..shone over the land with a fearful glare. 1877 A. B. Edwards *Up Nile* ii. 36 At a little before midday, when the heat and glare were becoming intolerable.
fig. 1809-10 Coleridge *Friend* (1865) 29 Books..looked at through the thick mists of ignorance, or amid the glare of prejudice and passion. 1850 Carlyle *Latter-d. Pamph.* viii. (1872) 258 There rose this..glare of hope upon Ignatius. 1878 Browning *Poets Croisic* 66 Who knows if this our René's quick Subsidence from as sudden noise and glare Into oblivion was impolitic.
b. The glistening or shining of some surface.
1658 W. Sanderson *Graphice* 86 Wash it over with.. Gum-dragon, steeped or dissolved in water, which will set a glare or freshnesse upon the Picture. *a*1700 B. E. *Dict. Cant. Crew*, *Glare*, a Glister; also the weak Light of a Comet, Candle, or Glow-worm. 1702 C. Mather *Magn. Chr.* IV. vii. (1852) 128 What would it avail if a man could make a glare on his face, by smearing it with some of the noctilucas invented by the modern chymistry? 1811 *Self Instructor* 550 Take the glare off the copper.
2. *fig.* Dazzling or showy appearance; gaudiness; tawdry brilliance.
1706 Estcourt *Fair Examp.* IV. i. 49, I find, that Virtue was but a Glare to blind my Jealousie. 1790 Mad. D'Arblay *Diary* 6 May, She is a very fine woman..but with rather too much glare, both without and within. 1812 Byron *Ch. Har.* I. ix, Maidens, like moths, are ever caught by glare. 1856 H. Rogers *Ess.* II. viii. 361 The imagery is too profuse, the diction too ornate; in a word, there is too much of the pomp and glare of rhetoric.
3. A fierce or piercing look.
1667 Milton *P.L.* IV. 402 About them round A Lion now he [Satan] stalkes with fierie glare. 1774 Goldsm. *Nat. Hist.* (1776) VII. 156 Winged serpents..destroying mankind by a single glare. 1792 S. Rogers *Pleas. Mem.* II. 48 Mark the fixed gaze, the wild and frenzied glare. 1834 Lytton *Pompeii* I. vi, His eyes were hollow, and shone with a brilliant and feverish glare. 1849 Macaulay *Hist. Eng.* iv. I. 450 The glare of his eyes had a fascination for the unhappy victim on whom they were fixed.

glare (glɛə(r)), *sb.*[2] [Of obscure origin: cf. GLARE *sb.*[1] 1 b.] †**a.** Frost, icy condition (*obs.*). **b.** *U.S.* A sheet of ice.
1567 Turbervile *Epit.*, etc. 81 b, How may Glare and Frost intise a feruent sweate. 1569 *Ibid.* (1587) 186 b, Eight monthes the Winter dures, The glare it is so great. 1854 M. S. Cummins *Lamplighter* xiii, You noticed how everything was covered with ice, this morning..the pavement was..a perfect glare.

glare (glɛə(r)), *a. U.S.* Also **glair.** [? attrib. use of GLARE *sb.*[2]] Smooth and bright or translucent, glassy. Chiefly of ice.
1856 Olmsted *Slave States* 345 A congealed pool of rosin ..firm and glair; varying in color, and glistening like polished porphyry. 1859 F. A. Griffiths *Artil. Man.* (1862) 63 *note*, The recoil of guns on Sleighs varies from four or five feet when on rough ground..to twenty or thirty yards when on glare ice. 1872 C. King *Mountain. Sierra Nev.* iv. 89 Looking down the glare front of ice. 1890 W. P. Lett in Shields *Big Game N. Amer.* 85 It [the Caribou] then suddenly squats upon its haunches, and slides along the glare-ice.

glare (glɛə(r)), *v.* [ME. *glaren* = MDu., MLG. *glaren* (mod. dial. Du. *glarien*) to gleam, glare. Kilian explains *glaerende ooghen* as 'gray eyes' (*oculi cæsii, glauci*), and *glaer-oogigh* as 'gray-eyed'. To the same set of words may perh. be referred MHG. (*ver*)*glarren*, LG. *gleren, glerren*; and connexion with GLASS seems probable.]
1. *intr.* To shine with a brilliant or dazzling light. Also of light itself.
*c*1250 *Kent. Serm.* in *O.E. Misc.* 27 þet Gold þet is bricht and glareth ine þo brichtnesse of þo sunne [etc.]. *c*1384 Chaucer *H. Fame* I. 272 Hyt is not al golde that glareth. *c*1440 *Promp. Parv.* 198/1 Glaryn, or bryghtly shynyn ..*rutilo.* 1530 Palsgr. 568/1, I glare or glystre, as golde dothe, *je reluys.* 1658 W. Sanderson *Graphice* 4 Light..It twinckles in a Star; Blazes and glares out in a Comet. 1764 Goldsm. *Trav.* 174 No zephyr fondly sues the mountain's breast, But meteors glare, and stormy glooms invest. 1795-1814 Wordsw. *Excurs.* I. 2 Southward the landscape indistinctly glared, Through a pale steam. 1839 Longf. *Hyperion* I. vii, The setting sun glared wildly from the summit of the hills. 1860 Tyndall *Glac.* I. xiv. 93 Through the fissures..the morning light glared strangely. 1885 *Athenæum* 23 May 667/1 The whitish dust which glares in the brilliant sunlight of the Dorsetshire coast.
b. *fig.* To display oneself ostentatiously; to be obtrusively evident or conspicuous.
1712 Pope *1st Ep. to Miss Blount* 53 She glares in Balls, front Boxes, and the Ring, A vain, unquiet, glitt'ring, wretched Thing! *a*1748 Watts *Improv. Mind* II. iii. §9 Though the demonstration glare in their faces. 1791 Boswell *Johnson* (1816) III. 298 A writer [Pennant].. whose ungenerous prejudice against the house of Stuart glares in misrepresentation. 1816 Keatinge *Trav.* (1817) I. 128 It is insufficient to say French influence prevails..The fact is—it glares—it is too ostensible and obtrusive. 1856 Emerson *Eng. Traits, Aristocr.* Wks. (Bohn) II. 76 The feudal character of the English state..glares a little, in contrast with the democratic tendencies.
2. To look fixedly and fiercely. Const. *at, on, upon.*
1609 W. M. *Man in Moone* F 2 b, Mo-ckso..glared vpon me, as if he would haue looked through me. 1659 D. Pell *Impr. Sea* 110 *note*, The Hebrews call anger Aph, because therein..the whole man swells like a Toad, and glares like the Devil. 1740 Somerville *Hobbinol* III. 375 She haunts him still, And glares upon him with her haggard Eyes. 1810 Scott *Lady of L.* II. xxxiv, And each upon his rival glared. 1859 F. Paget *Curate*, etc. 313 You actually glared on his daughters with a most morose aspect. 1871 B. Taylor *Faust* (1875) I. xxi. 183, I peeped at the owl in her nest alone: How she stared and glared.
fig. 1717 Prior *Alma* II. 41 When arguments too fiercely glare, You calm them with a milder air. 1871 L. Stephen *Playgr. Europe* iii. (1894) 83 The black ribs of the mountains glaring at you through rents in the clouds.
3. *trans.* To send forth or express with a glare.
1667 Milton *P.L.* VI. 849 Every eye Glar'd lightning, and shot forth pernicious fire. 1758 L. Temple *Sketches* (ed. 2) 83 One of the most insipid Fellows that ever glared weary Stupidity from a large dead Eye. 1791 Cowper *Iliad* IX. 294 Hector glares revenge. 1845 Browning *Soul's Trag.* I. 87 If I could not say it, I glared it at him. 1855 Milman *Lat. Chr.* VI. iii. (1864) III. 460 Two popes glaring defiance at each other from opposite quarters of the city.
4. To reflect with a glare. Also *to glare back.*
1694 Southerne *Fatal Marriage* V. i. Dram. Wks. 1721 II. 162 All the images Of a long mis-spent life were rising still To glare a sad reflection of my crimes. 1820 Byron *Mar. Faliero* IV. i. 70 Worlds mirror'd in the ocean, goodlier sight Than torches glared back by a gaudy glass.
5. The vb. stem in *Comb.*, as †**glare-eye**; **glare-eyed** *a.*, with glaring eyes; **glare-worm**, a glow-worm (cf. *glaze-worm, glass-worm*).
1607 Topsell *Four-f. Beasts* (1658) 420 Nitedula..I rather take that word to signifie a glare-worm. 1683 Chalkhill *Thealma & Cl.* 138, I spy'd A Lion running after him glare-eyed, And full of rage. 1711 *Lond. Gaz.* No. 4875/4 Lost..a Strawberry Mare..two glare Eyes. 1847-78 Halliwell, *Glare-worm*, a glow-worm. *I. Wight.*

glare, var. GLAIR *sb.*[1]; obs. form of GLAIR *v.*

glareal ('glɛərɪəl), *a. Bot.* [f. L. *glarea* gravel + -AL.] Growing on dry exposed soils. (Cf. GLAREOUS *a.*[1] b.)
1847 H. C. Watson *Cybele Britannica* I. 66 *Glareal*, plants of dry exposed ground, chiefly on gravel or sand. 1930 G. C. Druce *Flora Northants.* 278 *Brachypodium pinnatum*... Native. Glareal.

glareless ('glɛəlɪs), *a.* [f. GLARE *sb.*[1] + -LESS.] Free from glare.
*c*1815 Fuseli in *Lect. Paint.* vi. (1848) 480 The glareless evenness of plain daylight. 1881 W. Wilkins *Songs of Study* 40 Be thy slumber unfevered, And thornless and glareless thy bed. 1941 R. A. Heinlein *Menace from Earth* (1966) 58 A steady glareless light filled the room from no apparent source. 1962 H. C. Weston *Sight, Light & Work* (ed. 2) v. 149 This 'indirect' method of artificial lighting is sometimes claimed to be the best on the grounds that it is 'glareless and shadowless'.

glareose (glɛərɪ'əʊs), *a.* [ad. L. *glārēōs-us*: see next.] = GLAREOUS b.
1866 *Treas. Bot.* 533/1 *Glareose*, growing in gravelly places.

glareous ('glɛərɪəs), *a.*[1] [ad. L. *glārēōs-us*, f. *glārea* gravel; cf. OF. *glaireux.*] †**a.** Of soil: Gravelly (*obs.*). **b.** *Bot.* (See quot. 1880.)
*c*1420 *Pallad. on Husb.* IV. 497 With stonys mixt hit stont in argillous Lond, and with grauel mixt in glareous. 1610 W. Folkingham *Art of Survey* I. xi. 43 Their Vines are best fitted with a glareous soyle, viz. dry, leane and creachy. 1675 Evelyn *Terra* (1676) 43 Be the Stones or Rock Glareous, Metallic, Testaceous, Salts or any other Concretes whatsoever. 1880 Gray *Struct. Bot.* 413/2 *Glareous*, growing in gravel.

glareous, *a.*[2]: see GLAIREOUS.

glariness: see GLARY *a.*[1]

glaring ('glɛərɪŋ), *vbl. sb.* [See -ING[1].] The action of the verb GLARE, in various senses.
1563 Man *Musculus' Commonpl.* 149 b, They which..are oftentimes trained oute of the waie of truth, by the likely glarings [L. *spectris*] of reason. 1667 Pepys *Diary* (1877) V. 455 A chimney-piece of Dancre's doing, in distemper, with egg to keep off the glaring of the light. 1706 *Refl. Ridic.* 51 Those perpetual discourses..are but counterfeit glarings to dazzle a too credulous husband. 1786 tr. *Beckford's Vathek* (1868) 46 The glaring of eyes which could belong only to devils or tigers.

'glaring, *ppl. a.* [See -ING[2].] That glares.
1. Of the eyes: Staring fiercely or wildly.
*c*1386 Chaucer *Prol.* 684 Swiche glarynge eyen hadde he as an hare. *a*1600 Hayes in Hakluyt *Voy.* III. 158 He passed along..yawning and gaping wide, with ougly demonstration of long teeth and glaring eies. 1697 Dryden *Virg. Georg.* III. 658 He leaves the Fens, and leaps upon the Ground; And hissing, rowls his glaring Eyes around. 1827 Pollok *Course T.* IX, Trying whiles to send his glaring eye Beyond the wide circumference of his woe.
†**b.** Bright, sparkling. *Obs. rare*$^{-1}$.
1622 Drayton *Poly-olb.* xxi. 72 And looke my manly face, in thy sweet glaring eyes.
2. That gives out or reflects a dazzling light. Also of light, colours, etc.: Vivid, dazzling, excessively bright.
1515 *Scot. Field* 61 in *Chetham Misc.* (1856) II, He durst not counter with our king..For all the glaring [*Percy MS.* gloring] goulde, under god of heaven! 1638 F. Junius *Paint. Ancients* 339 A phlegmaticke eye..abhorreth all manner of bright and glaring colours. 1693 Dryden *Persius, Sat.* III. 1 The glaring Sun Breaks in at ev'ry Chink. 1739 J. Trapp *Righteous Over-m.* (1758) 64 These *Ignes Fatui*, these glaring Meteors. 1833 Ht. Martineau *Vanderput & S.* i. 2 Reflected in gleams upon the glaring white fronts of the houses. 1850 Kingsley *Alt. Locke* i, As the midnight brightened into dawn and the glaring lamps grew pale. 1879 Farrar *St. Paul* (1883) 139 They had been traversing a bare, bleak, glaring, undulating plain.
*fig. a*1653 G. Daniel *Idyll* iii. 35 Kings Suffer, when they give Inhærent Light, long-fixt Prærogative, To fill a glareing Office. 1749 J. Edwards *Life Brainerd* App. 294 The glistering Appearance and glaring Show of false Religion dazzles their eyes. 1766 Fordyce *Serm. Yng. Wom.* (1767) I. ii. 73 Distinguish between what is glaring and what is genteel.
3. That displays itself openly; obtrusively evident or conspicuous. Now chiefly with sbs. which have a bad sense, as *fault, falsehood*, etc.
1706 *Refl. Ridic.* 42 A man ought not to descend to a slavish and glaring complaisance. 1718 Atterbury *Serm.* (1737) III. 186 Such a glaring proof of his resurrection. 1748 *Anson's Voy.* II. vii. 209 There were some few.. incapable of discerning the force of equity, however glaring. 1812 H. & J. Smith *Rej. Addr.* x. (1873) 94 To elude this glaring absurdity. 1850 McCosh *Div. Govt.* II. ii. 193 Let us notice some of the more glaring defects of the work. 1869 Freeman *Norm. Conq.* (1876) III. xii. 245 These glaring contradictions do not indeed affect the belief that there is some groundwork of fact for the story.

glaringly ('glɛərɪŋlɪ), *adv.* [f. prec. + -LY[2].] In a glaring fashion.
*a*1586 Sidney *Arcadia* III. (1590) 278 But the colours for the grounde were so well chosen, neither sullenly darke nor glaringly lightsome. 1709 Steele *Tatler* No. 92 ¶1 The Satyrist never falls upon Persons who are not glaringly faulty. 1746 Wesley *Princ. Methodist* 64 This is glaringly self-evident. 1831 Mackintosh *Hist. Eng.* II. 15 Few

pretensions can be more glaringly absurd. **1845** DARWIN *Voy. Nat.* xii. (1879) 261 The day was truly Chilian: glaringly bright. **1881** SEELEY in *Macm. Mag.* XLV. 47, I ask why Macaulay is so glaringly unlike Grote.

glaringness (ˈglɛərɪŋnɪs). [f. as prec. + -NESS.] The quality of being glaring.

1664 PEPYS *Diary* (1879) III. 57 [Mr. Cocker came] to show me the manner of his gaining light to grave by, and to lessen the glaringnesse of it at pleasure by an oyled paper. **1742** JARVIS *Quix.* I. I. i. (1749) 2 The glaringness of his prose, and the intricacy of his style, seemed to him so many pearls. **1763** C. JOHNSTON *Reverie* II. 58 A dress whose glaringness and singularity must attract the notice of every one who saw it. **1885** G. MEREDITH *Diana Crossways* II. vi. 132 The likeness..became striking to glaringness.

glarney (ˈglɑːnɪ). [? Corruption of GLASSY.] A glass marble.

1953 *Eng. Digest* June 93 The girls play skipping... The boys favour..'glarneys'. **1961** PARTRIDGE *Dict. Slang Suppl.* 1109/1 *Glarney*.., a corruption of *glassy*. **1969** E. WILKINS *Rose-Garden Game* 15 Seeing my bowls of taws and glarnies, some people would ask what they were *for*.

glary (ˈglɛərɪ), *a.*^{1} [f. GLARE *sb.*^{1} + -Y^{1}.] Full of glare; dazzling, glaring. Hence ˈ**glariness**.

1632 VICARS *Æneid* VIII. 241 Chopt from the neck, whose gogling glarie eyes, Rouling in rage, beholders stupifies. **1659** BEALE in *Boyle's Wks.* (1772) VI. 135, I know, that bright crystal glass is glary; and to avoid that glariness, our artificers run into the other extreme. **1816** L. HUNT *Rimini* I. 186 Purple smearings, with a velvet light, Rich from the glary yellow, thickening bright. **1866** [see FLARY *a*]. **1883** BURTON & CAMERON *To Gold Coast* I. iv. 113 A garden, formerly dusty, glary, and dreary.

glary (ˈglɛərɪ), *a.*^{2} [f. GLARE *sb.*^{2} + -Y^{1}; cf. GLARE *a.*] †**a.** Icy, frozen (*obs.*). **b.** *U.S.* Smooth and slippery.

1569 TURBERV. *Epit.*, etc. (1587) 186 b, For in the winter time, so glarie is the ground: As neither grasse nor other graine in pastures may be found. **1854** LOWELL *Jrnl. in Italy* Prose Wks. 1890 I. 137 Behind, a glary slope invited me constantly to slide over the horse's tail.

glas, glasce, glase, obs. forms of GLASS *sb.*

glase, var. GLACE *sb.*^{2}, *Obs.*

glase, obs. form of GLACE *v.*, GLAZE *v.*^{1}

glase(e)r, obs. ff. GLAZER, GLAZIER.

glasen, obs. form of GLASSEN *a.*

Glaserian (gleɪˈzɪərɪən). Also **Glasserian**. [f. *Glaser*, the name of a Swiss anatomist (died 1675).] In ***Glas(s)erian fissure*** (see quot. 1854).

1840 G. ELLIS *Anat.* 282 Above the membrana tympani, and rather in front of it, is the Glasserian or glenoid fissure. **1849-52** TODD *Cycl. Anat.* IV. 937/2 That part which is anterior to the glasserian fissure is lined with cartilage. **1854** MAYNE *Expos. Lex.*, *Glasserian Fissure*, term for the fissure which is situated between the squamous and petrous portions of the temporal bone, and in the glenoid cavity.

glaserite (ˈgleɪzəraɪt). *Min.* [From 'sal polychrestum *Glaseri*' the pharmaceutical name of potassium sulphate, discovered by Christoph *Glaser*, a Swiss chemist of the 17th c.] = APHTHITALITE.

1852 *Amer. Jrnl. Sci.* Ser. II. XIV. 266 Sulphate of Potash (Glaserite). **1882** DANA *Man. Min. & Lith.* Index, Glaserite v. Arcanite.

glasery(e, var. GLASSERY, *Obs.*

†**glash,** *v. Sc. Obs.* [? onomatopœic: cf. FLASH *v.*] *intr.* To come like a flash of light.

17.. *Young Andrew* xxxvi. in Child *Ballads* II. xlviii. (1884) 434/2 Soe they ffought together like two lyons, And fire betweene them two glashet out.

glashan, var. GLOSSAN *Anglo-Irish*, coal-fish.

glasier, -ior, obs. forms of GLAZIER.

‖**glasnost** (ˈglæznɒst, ˈglɑːznɒst, -snɒst; ‖ˈglasnəstj). [Russ. *glasnost'*, lit. 'the fact of being public; openness to public scrutiny or discussion'.] In relation to the affairs of the Soviet Union: a declared party policy since 1985 of greater openness and frankness in public statements, including the publication of news reflecting adversely on the government and political system; greater freedom of speech and information arising from this policy. Also applied *transf.* to similar developments in other countries.

The Russ. word is recorded in dictionaries from the eighteenth century, but in the more general sense of 'publicity'. It was used in the context of freedom of information in the Soviet State by V. I. Lenin, and called for in an open letter to the Soviet Writers' Union by Aleksandr Solzhenitsyn in 1969, but did not become a subject of serious public debate in the Soviet Union until an *Izvestiya* editorial requested letters on the subject on 19 Jan. 1985. Its use by Mikhail Gorbachev on 11 Mar. 1985 in a speech accepting the post of General Secretary of the CPSU has subsequently led to its being associated particularly with his policies.

[**1972** BURG & FEIFER *Solzhenitsyn* xxxii. 288 Solzhenitsyn [in an]..open letter to the Writers' Union dated November 12 [1969]..used the word *glasnost*, roughly 'openness and candor in public affairs', to evoke the rallying call of Russian liberals a century before. **1981** *N.Y. Times* 13 Mar. A7/1 The Russians, it seems, have rediscovered the value of Lenin's dictum that '*glasnost*', the Russian word for openness or publicity, is a desirable form of conduct. **1985** *Summary World Broadcasts: Soviet Union* (B.B.C.) 1 Apr. B1 This [*sc.* popular consciousness of Party work] cannot be achieved without consistent observance of the principle of publicity (Russian: glasnost).] **1986** *N.Y. Times* 22 Feb. I. 2/1 Exposes of corruption, shortages and economic problems appear virtually daily in the [Soviet] press. It is a change that became evident after Mikhail S. Gorbachev came to office last March and called for more 'glasnost', or openness, in covering domestic affairs. **1986** *Guardian* 1 May 19/7 There are more than 50 million Soviet citizens in much more contaminated areas... If they are not told soon ..it will no longer be a question of media policy of 'Glasnost'. **1986** *Scotsman* 9 May 10/1 What seemed to be at risk was Mr. Gorbachev's 'glasnost' policy, the essence of which is more openness. **1986** *Daily Tel.* 10 Oct. 6/6 What about Mr Gorbachev's exciting campaign for greater 'glasnost', meaning frankness, in tackling defects in the Soviet system? **1987** *Los Angeles Times* 30 May I. 4/1 (*heading*) Life is still hard under glasnost, Vietnamese style. **1987** *Jerusalem Post Mag.* 19 June 6/5 On the emigration front,..the era of *glasnost* has seen decidedly mixed results.

glason, glaspe, obs. ff. GLASSEN *a.*, CLASP *sb.*

glass (glɑːs, -æ-), *sb.*^{1} Forms: 1, 3 **glæs**, 2-4 **gles(e**, 4-7 **glas**, (4-5 **glase**), **glasse**, (5 **glaas**, **glasce**, 6 **glace**, **glasshe**, 9 *Sc.* **glaas**), 6- **glass**. [OE. *glæs* str. neut. (? *erron.* masc. in *Bæda's Eccl. Hist.* v. v.) = OS. *glas*, *gles* (Du. *glas*), OHG. *glas* (MHG. and mod.G. *glas*):—OTeut. **gláso*^{m}; a variant with consonant-ablaut, *glazó*^{m}, is represented by ON. *gler*, Da., MSw. *glar*; the mod. Scandinavian langs. have *glas* from Ger. (already in MSw. and MDa.).

A related word is prob. OE. *glǽr* (masc., if the pl. *glæsas* 'succina' be miswritten for **glǽras*) amber, representing the OTeut. word (? **glǣzo-*, ? **glǣzi-*) adopted in Latin as *glēs(s)um*, *glæsum*. The OHG. *glas* occurs as a gloss to *electrum* amber. The ultimate root may be OTeut. *glă-*, *glǣ-* ablaut-variant of *glô-* to shine: see GLOW *v.*]

I. As a substance.

1. A substance, in its ordinary forms transparent, lustrous, hard, and brittle, produced by fusing sand (silica) with soda or potash (or both), usually with the addition of one or more other ingredients, esp. lime, alumina, lead oxide.

For the different kinds see CROWN-, FLINT-, PLATE-, WATER-GLASS, etc.; also *bottle-*, *crystal-*, *cut-glass*, etc. under the different words.

c **888** K. ÆLFRED *Boeth.* v. §1 Ne me nane lyst mid glase ȝeworhtra waȝa. *a* **900** CYNEWULF *Crist* 1282 in *Exeter Bk.*, þæt scire glæs. *c* **1175** *Lamb. Hom.* 83 þet gles ne brekeð ne chineð. *a* **1225** *Ancr. R.* 164 Vor gles ne to-brekeð nout bute sum þinc hit arine. **13..** *K. Alis.* 7665 Theo wyndowes weoren of riche glas. **1382** WYCLIF *Rev.* iv. 6 As a se of glas, lijk to cristal. **14..** *Lat. Eng. Voc.* in Wr.-Wülcker 619/41 *Vitrum*, glaas. *c* **1425** *Eng. Voc.*, ibid. 648/39 *Hoc uitrum*, glasse. **1502** *Ord. Crysten Men* (W. de W. 1506) I. vii. 79 Of ferne brente and put in to asshes man maketh by crafte these vesselles of glasshe. **1541** *Extracts Aberdeen Reg.* (1844) I. 174 Ane futt of glace. **1590** SPENSER *F.Q.* I. i. 35 That olde man..well could file his tongue as smooth as glas. *a* **1633** G. HERBERT *Jac. Prud.* (1651) §196 Whose house is of glasse, must not throw stones at another. **1715** PRIOR *Down-Hall* 53 One window was canvas, the other was glass. **1784** COWPER *Tiroc.* 463 Though the jewel be but glass. **1839** URE *Dict. Arts* 589 They next try whether the glass be ready for casting. **1851** *Illustr. Catal. Gt. Exhib.* 700 Many of the specimens..are of 'cased glass'. This term is applied to glass which has received one or more layers of coloured glass. **1875** FORTNUM *Majolica* i. 8 The paste of which these examples are formed is to all appearance an ordinary potter's clay glazed with a true glass.

transf. **1877** BRYANT *Poems, Little People of Snow* 65 And ..touched the pool, And turned its face to glass.

2. Applied in a wider sense to various other substances, artificial and natural, which have similar properties or analogous chemical composition.

glass of antimony, a vitreous oxy-sulphide fused; ***glass of borax***, a vitreous transparent substance obtained by exposing to heat the crystals of sodium biborate; ***glass of lead*** (see quot. 1753); ***glass of phosphorus*** (see quot. 1819).

1579 LYLY *Euphues* (Arb.) 120 There is..a great distinction to be put betweene Vitrum and the Christall, yet both glasse. **1594** PLAT *Jewell-ho.* II. 45, I cannot here omit that..infinite extention of the glasse of Antimony. **1753** CHAMBERS *Cycl. Supp.*, *Glass of lead*, a glass made with the addition of a large quantity of lead, of great use in the art of making counterfeit gems. **1811** PINKERTON *Petral.* II. 443 The volcanic glass called obsidian, appears in such quantities as to constitute rocks. **1816** ACCUM *Chem. Tests* (1818) 222 These substances..yield readily to glass of borax. **1819** BRANDE *Chem.* (1841) 484 A transparent substance is thus obtained, consisting of phosphoric acid, with phosphate, and a little sulphate of lime, commonly known under the name of glass of phosphorus. **1826** HENRY *Elem. Chem.* II. 613 A large quantity of glass of lead was lately introduced into the London market, as glass of antimony.

3. a. The substance considered as made into articles of use or ornament (for which see II). Hence as collect. sing. = things made of glass: e.g. vessels or ornaments of glass, window-panes or lights.

1625 BACON *Ess.*, *Building* (Arb.) 551 You shall haue sometimes Faire Houses, so full of Glasse, that one cannot tell, where to become, to be out of the Sunne, or Cold. **1833** TENNYSON *Goose* xiii, The glass blew in, the fire blew out. **1850** *Gloss. Archit.* (ed. 5) I. 236 A splendid collection of elaborate stained glass..exists at Gilling castle, Yorkshire. *Ibid.*, *note*, Such has been..the destruction of old glass in this country, that few churches retain more than fragments of their original glazing. **1855** THACKERAY *Newcomes* I. xix. 176 A waggon full of fenders, fire-irons, and glass, and crockery. *Mod.* The glass is kept in one cupboard and the silver in another.

b. *esp.* as used in horticulture for greenhouses, frames. etc. Hence, greenhouses, etc., collectively.

1838 *Penny Cycl.* XII. 319 The potato..will not thrive under glass unless placed very near it. **1873** D. THOMSON (*title*) Handy Book of Fruit Culture under glass. **1885** SIR L. W. CAVE in *Law Times Rep.* LII. 627/1 There is..that amount of conservatory and glass which one would expect. **1897** *Gardener's Chron.* XXIII. 295/3 [The plaintiffs] were told their glass would be measured and assessed at the rate of £100 per acre.

II. Something made of glass.

4. a. A glass vessel or receptacle. Also, the contents of the vessel.

The specific application as in 5 is now so predominant that the word is now commonly applied only to vessels more or less resembling a drinking glass; a glass bottle or jar, for instance, is no longer called 'a glass'. But the wider use survives in the collective plurals.

a **1225** *Ancr. R.* 164 Healewi in one bruchele glese. *c* **1380** WYCLIF *Last Age Ch.* p. xxxv, Wiþ his blood he anoyntide þe glas, þe glass to barst and þe brid fleye his wey. *c* **1386** CHAUCER *Prol.* 700 In a glas he hadde pigges bones. *c* **1422** HOCCLEVE *Min. Poems* (1892) 232 He had a lytil glas, Which, with þat watir anoon filled he. **1484** CAXTON *Fables of Æsop* II. xiii, Only he lycked the glas by cause he cowde not reche to the mete with his mouthe. **1530** *Privy Purse Exp. Hen. VIII* (1827) 67 For bringing a glasse of Relike water fro Wyndeso^{r}. **1535** COVERDALE *1 Sam.* x. 1 Then toke Samuel a glasse of oyle, and poured it vpon his heade. **1549-62** STERNHOLD & H. *Ps.* lvi. (1566) 134 Reserue them [my teares] in a glasse by thee and write them in thy booke. **1596** SHAKS. *Tam. Shr.* Induct. i. 7 You will not pay for the glasses you haue burst? **1606** *Vestry Bks.* (Surtees) 287 A glasse of sallett oyle for the clock, viij*d.* **1608** CHAPMAN *Byrons Trag.* Q iv b, A glasse of ayre, broken with lesse then breath. **1728** E. SMITH *Compl. Housew.* (ed. 2) 165 When the Juice boils, put in your Currants and boil them till your Syrup jellies..then put it in your Glasses. **1738** SWIFT *Pol. Conversat.* 153 Miss, will you reach me that Glass of Jelly? **1803** *Med. Jrnl.* IX. 375 He shall be happy to furnish them with recent virus..if they will send their lancets or glasses to his house. **1870** *Mrs. Loudon's Amateur Gardener* (1880) 141 Those who grow hyacinths..in glasses. **1884** WALLACE-DUNLOP in *Mag. of Art* VII. 154/2 No illustrations can do justice to the endless diversities of Venetian glasses.

b. = *musical glasses* (see MUSICAL).

1762 FRANKLIN *Let.* 13 July in *Mem.* (1818) III. 357 The glasses being thus tuned, you [etc.]. *Ibid.* 358 My largest glass is G, a little below the reach of a common voice.

5. *spec.* A drinking-vessel made of glass; hence, the liquor contained, and *fig.* drink.

1392-3 *Earl Derby's Exped.* (Camden) 235/31 Pro glases et verres. *c* **1400** *Destr. Troy* 804 Sho gafe hym a glasse with a good lycour. **1535** COVERDALE *Prov.* xxiii. 31 Loke not thou vpon the wyne..what a coloure it geueth in the glasse. **1596** SHAKS. *Merch. V.* I. ii. 104, I pray thee set a deepe glass of Reinish wine on the contrary Casket. **1633** G. HERBERT *Temple, Ch. Porch* v, Drink not the third glasse, which thou canst not tame, When once it is within thee. **1653** WALTON *Angler* xiii. 239 So Master, here is a full glass to you of that liquor. **1744** BERKELEY *Siris* §219 On taking a glass of tar-water. **1757** tr. *Hentzner's Itin.* 89 It is common for a number of them, that have got a glass in their heads, to [etc.]. **1777** SHERIDAN *Sch. Scandal* III. ii. (*Song*), Let the toast pass, Drink to the lass, I warrant she'll prove an excuse for the glass. **1789** WOLCOT (P. Pindar) *Ep. to falling Minist.* Wks. 1812 II. 116 A jolly fellow o'er his glass. **1833** TENNYSON *Miller's Dau.* 17 Yet fill my glass: give me one kiss. **1847** MARRYAT *Childr. N. Forest* xi, This bargain concluded, they took a glass with the landlord.

6. a. A SAND-GLASS for the measurement of time; *esp.* an HOUR-GLASS, and *Naut.* the half-hour glass, the half-minute and quarter-minute glasses. ***to flog the glass***: see FLOG *v.* 1 d.

[*c* **1515**: cf. HOUR-GLASS.] **1557** *Tottel's Misc.* (Arb.) 138, I saw, my tyme how it did runne, as sand out of the glasse. **1582** N. LICHEFIELD tr. *Castanheda's Conq. E. Ind.* xlvi. 102 To bring him a running glasse of an houre. **1601** SHAKS. *All's Well* II. i. 168 Or foure and twenty times the Pylots glasse Hath told the theeuish minutes, how they passe. **1670** EACHARD *Cont. Clergy* 21 He is counted dull to purpose, that is not able..to fasten upon any text of scripture; and to tear and tumble it till the glass be out. **1711** *Milit. & Sea Dict.* (ed. 4) 11, *Glasses*, are the Hour, Four Hour, and Minute Glasses, us'd at Sea. **1726** SHELVOCKE *Voy. round World* (1757) 142 At the turning of every glass, during the night, we beat three ruffs on the drums. **1780** COWPER *Table T.* 41 The glass that bids man mark the fleeting hour. **1831** TRELAWNY *Adv. Younger Son* xcv. (1890) 387 Every hour the ship's glass was turned. **1867** SMYTH *Sailor's Word-bk.*, *Glass clear?* Is the sand out of the uppper part? asked previously to turning it, on throwing the log. **1871** JOAQUIN MILLER *Songs Italy* (1878) 71, I will wait in the pass Of death, until Time he shall break his glass.

b. The time taken by the sand of such a glass to run out. *Naut.* Usually said of the half-hour glass; hence, a glass = half an hour.

1599 HAKLUYT *Voy.* II. II. 126 The 28. we lay sixe glasses a hull tarying for the pinesse. **1610** SHAKS. *Temp.* v. i. 223 Our Ship, Which but three glasses since, we gaue out split Is tyte. **1627** CAPT. SMITH *Seaman's Gram.* ii. 12 Glasses (which are but halfe houres). **1677** *Lond. Gaz.* No. 1215/4 They engaged, and fought very briskly, during six Glasses. **1694** *Acc. Sev. Late Voy.* I. 186 So standing in North-east, sometimes two Glasses, that is one hour. **1758** JOHNSON *Idler* No. 7 ¶14 The *Bulldog* engaged the *Friseur*..three glasses and a half. **1814** *Sailor's Return* I. vii, There, my hearty, keep that but so half a glass, and Ise warrant you'll be sound as a roach.

c. *fig.*

1638 SIR T. HERBERT *Trav.* (ed. 2) 303, 200 yeares agoe, the Towne was rich.. But now, whither her glasse is runne ..or [etc.]. **1663** BP. GRIFFITH *Serm. on 4 Admir. Beasts* 17 When their race is run, and their glass is out. **1756** C. LUCAS *Ess. Waters* I. 196 They are rendered..decrepid and old before half their glass is run. **1847** GROTE *Greece* II. xxvii. (1862) III. 42 The glass of this worthless dynasty is run out.

7. A pane of glass, *esp.* the window of a coach, etc.; the plate of glass covering a picture; a glazed frame or case (e.g. for the protection of plants).

1439 *E.E. Wills* (1882) 117 The tabelet with the Image of oure lady with a glasse to-fore hit. *c* **1566** J. ALDAY tr. *Boaystuau's Theat. World* R v b, There faire eyes that are the windowes of all the bodie, and glasses of the soule. **1581** PETTIE tr. *Guazzo's Civ. Conv.* III. (1586) 159 As Goldsmithes sometime cover their ware and Jewells with a Glasse, to make them shew the better. **1642** *Rates Merchandize* 28 Glasses for windows. **1664** EVELYN *Kal. Hort.* (1679) 25 Cover them [Plants] with glasses, having cloath'd them first with sweet, and dry Moss. **1670** LASSELS *Voy. Italy* II. 163 The stone upon which the gridiron stood, upon which S. Laurence was broiled. Its covered with a great glass through which you see it. **1697** tr. *C'tess D'Aunoy's Trav.* (1706) 131 It had Glasses twice as big as my hand, made fast to each end of the coach, for the conveniency of calling to the Footmen. *c* **1710** C. FIENNES *Diary* (1888) 249 On Each side are Rowes of posts on w[ch] are Glasses—Cases for Lamps w[ch] are Lighted in ye Evening. **1717** PRIOR *Alma* III. 234 He..Breaks watchmen's heads, and chairmen's glasses. *a* **1718** MOTTEUX *Epil. Vanbrugh's Mistake* 18 We dare not..with a friend at night..With glass drawn up, drive about Covent-garden. **1782** COWPER *Pineapples & Bee* 20 While Cynthio ogles, as she passes The nymph between two chariot glasses. **1796** C. MARSHALL *Garden.* xiv. (1813) 212 When the plants cannot be contained under the glasses, let them be carefully trained out. **1816** KEATINGE *Trav.* (1817) II. 116 He lowers the front glass, and bids the..coachman drive him to his surgeon's. **1833** T. HOOK *Widow & Marquess* i, Bang went the door, up went the glass.

8. a. A glass mirror, a LOOKING-GLASS.

13.. *K. Alis.* 4108 Theo maydenes lokyn in the glas, For to tyffen heore fas. **14..** *Metr. Voc.* in Wr.-Wülcker 623 *Speculum*, glasse. **1484** CAXTON *Fables of Æsop* II. xvii, Men sayen comynly who that beholdeth in the glas well he seeth hym self. **1545** *Rates Custom-ho.* B iij b, Glasses called lokyng glasses the groce .iiiis. **1593** SHAKS. *Lucr.* 1758 Poore broken glasse, I often did behold In thy sweet semblance, my old age new borne. *a* **1637** B. JONSON *Celebr. Charis* v. 40 The glass hangs by her side, And the girdle 'bout her waist. **1712** ADDISON *Spect.* No. 311 ¶4 A Fop who admires his Person in a Glass. **1868** DICKENS *Lett.* 25 Feb. (1880) II. 363 It is actually swelling his head as I glance at him in the glass while writing.

†**b.** applied to a mirror of other material.

1530 *Privy Purse Exp. Hen. VIII* (1827) 81 A payer of tabulls and chesses, A stele glasse [etc.]. **1571** DIGGES *Pantom.* I. xxi. F iv b, The best kinde of glasse for this purpose is of steele finely pullished. **1576** GASCOIGNE (*title*) The Steele Glas. **1615** G. SANDYS *Trav.* 114 Hauing placed a magical glasse of steele on the top. **1861** *Our Eng. Home* 116 The mirror..was made of beryl, or high polished steel, but called a glass.

c. *poet.* applied to water as a mirror.

1605 SYLVESTER *Du Bartas* II. iii. III. *Law* 954 Proud that his glass Gliding so swift, so soon re-youngs the grass. **1667** MILTON *P.L.* XI. 844 The cleer Sun on his wide watrie Glass Gaz'd hot. **1716** ADDISON *Salmacis & Herm.* 37 In the limpid streams she views her face, And drest her image in the floating glass.

d. *fig.*

1548 HALL *Chron., Hen. V.* 81 b, He was the floure of kynges passed, and a glasse to them that should succede. **1570** DEE *Math. Pref.* 3 To behold in the Glas of Creation, the Forme of Formes. **1579** LYLY *Euphues* (Arb.) 107 Louers that haue bene deceiued by fancy, the glasse of pestilence. **1607** TOURNEUR *Rev. Trag.* IV. iii. Wks. 1878 II. 128 Be thou a glasse for maides. **1673** TEMPLE *Obs. United Prov.* Wks. 1731 I. 25 He began to see, in the Glass of Time and Experience, the true Shapes of all human Greatness and Designs. **1714** FORTESCUE-ALAND *Pref. to Fortescue's Abs. & Lim. Mon.* 72 History and Antiquity is the Glass of Time. **1771** WESLEY *Wks.* (1872) V. 283 We are to see the Creator in the glass of every creature. **18..** LOWELL *Poet. Wks.* (1879) 387 Man, Woman, Nature, each is but a glass Where the soul sees the image of herself.

e. A magic mirror, a crystal, etc., used in magic art. Also *glass of skill*.

c **1566** J. ALDAY tr. *Boaystuau's Theat. World* S vi b, A childe, who after he had looked in a glasse shewed him of hys destruction. **1584** R. SCOT *Discov. Witchcr.* XIII. xix. 316 The regular, the irregular, the coloured and cleare glasses. **1589** R. ROBINSON *Gold. Mirr.* (Chetham Soc.) 53 He stept into his cave And brought a glass of skill exceeding brave. **1605** SHAKS. *Macb.* IV. i. 119 Yet the eight appeares, who beares a glasse, Which shewes me many more.

9. a. A piece of glass shaped for a special purpose, e.g. one of the glasses of a pair of spectacles, a lens, a watch-glass.

1545 *Rates Custom-ho.* B iij b, Glasses for spectacles. **1657** R. LIGON *Barbadoes* (1673) 29 Not unlike the mould that the Spectacle-makers grinde their glasses on. **1665** HOOKE *Microgr.* 73, I provided me with a Prismatical Glass, made hollow, just in the form of a Wedge. **1802** PALEY *Nat. Theol.* iii. 24 Our artist..produced a correction of the defect by imitating, in glasses made from different materials, the effects of the different humours through which the rays of light pass before they reach the bottom of the eye. **1815** SCOTT *Guy M.* lvi, Pleydell wiped the glasses of his spectacles. **1820** SCORESBY *Acc. Arctic Reg.* I. 390 Having cleaned the glasses of a good telescope, I hastened to the mast-head. **1833** N. ARNOTT *Physics* (ed. 5) II. 208 Equally whether the lens be of water inclosed between glasses like watch-glasses, or of solid glass. *Ibid.* 211 The image or picture of the sun formed by that glass or lens. **1884** F. J. BRITTEN *Watch & Clockm.* 112 [A] Glass Height Guage.. is especially useful in fitting glasses to hunting watches where there is but little spare room.

b. A burning-glass.

a **1631** DONNE *To Mr. R. Woodward* 21 Wks. (Grosart) II. 76 As Men force the sun with much more force to passe, By gathering his beams with a christall glasse. **1670** DRYDEN *2nd Pt. Conq. Granada* v. ii, For if that heat your glances cast were strong, Your eyes, like glasses, fire, when held so long.

10. An optical instrument used as an aid to sight.

a. *gen.*

1700 T. BROWN tr. *Fresny's Amusem. Ser. & Com.* 90 They view a single Shilling in a Multiplying Glass, which makes it appear a Thousand. **1736** BUTLER *Anal.* I. i. 29 How sight is assisted by glasses.

fig. **1768–74** TUCKER *Lt. Nat.* (1852) I. 563 It is only the half-reasoner, who..uses a glass full of flaws, that hunts for it in vain. **1788** GIBBON *Decl. & F.* xlvii. IV. 553 *note*, In the contemplation of a minute or remote object, I am not ashamed to borrow the aid of the strongest glasses. **1847** L. HUNT *Men, Women & B.* I. i. 6 The strong glass of science has put an end to the assumptions of fiction.

b. A telescope or other instrument for distant vision. More explicitly SPY-GLASS, FIELD-GLASS, OPERA-GLASS, etc.

1613–16 W. BROWNE *Brit. Past.* II. i, As a man..Taketh a glasse prospective good and true, By which things most remote are full in view. **1638** WILKINS *New World* iii. (1707) 26 By the help of Galileus's Glass..the Heavens are made more present to us than they were before. **1677** PLOT *Oxfordsh.* 215 He used these glasses in Celestial Observations. **1724** DE FOE *Mem. Cavalier* (1840) 97 We could see him..by our glasses. **1779** G. KEATE *Sk. fr. Nat.* (ed. 2) II. 87 Three or four ladies..were come up with their glasses in their hands, to take a view of the new-arrived Indiamen. **1840** MARRYAT *Poor Jack* xxi, A first-rate glass, Jack. **1873** TRISTRAM *Moab* vi. 99 Even without a glass we could distinctly make out Jerusalem.

c. A microscope. More explicitly ***magnifying-glass***.

1646 J. HALL *Horæ Vac.* 185 Small peeces best commend themselves through a Magnifying Glasse. **1664** POWER *Exp. Philos.* 4 If you divide the Bee..you shall without help of the glasse, see the heart beat most lively. **1665** HOOKE *Microgr.* 162 Through an ordinary single Magnifying Glass. **1721** BRADLEY *Philos. Acc. Wks. Nat.* 47 Every one knows (who has been conversant with Microscopes) that we have some Glasses which will magnify a simple Point..so as to [etc.]. **1780** HARRIS *Philol. Enq.* Wks. (1841) 425 Those beings which, without the aid of glasses, even escape our perception. **1884** F. J. BRITTEN *Watch & Clockm.* (1892) 290 If the finger is..looked at through the stone with a watchmaker's glass, the grain of the skin will be plainly visible if the stone is not a diamond.

d. An EYE-GLASS; also in *pl.* spectacles.

1660 F. BROOKE tr. *Le Blanc's Trav.* III. 314 Well mounted, and glasses before his eyes to preserve them from the wind. **1746** COLLINS *Odes, Manners* (1771) 78 While ever varying as they pass To some Contempt applies her glass. **1784** COWPER *Task* VI. 288 Stationed there..With glass at eye, and catalogue in hand. **1790** WESLEY *Wks.* (1872) IV. 490 My eyes were so dim, that no glasses would help me. **1813** MAR. EDGEWORTH *Patron.* II. xxiii. 57 Looking through her glass at the man who was lighting the argand lamps. **1864** TENNYSON *Grandmother* xxvii, Get me my glasses, Annie. **1866** MRS. GASKELL *Wives & Dau.* xi. (1867) 117 My lady took off her glasses.

†**11.** *transf.* The eye-ball, the eye. *poet.*

1593 SHAKS. *Rich. II*, I. iii. 208 Euen in the glasses of thine eyes I see thy greeued heart. **1607** —— *Cor.* III. ii. 117 The smiles of Knaues Tent in my cheekes, and Schoole-boyes Teares take vp The Glasses of my sight! **1608** *Yorksh. Trag.* I. x, O, were it lawfull that your pretty souls Might look from heaven into your father's eyes, Then should you see the penitent glasses melt. *a* **1621** BEAUM. & FL. *Thierry & Theod.* v. ii, Love, I must die, I faint, close up my glasses.

12. a. A WEATHER-GLASS, a barometer. **b.** A thermometer.

a. **1688** J. SMITH *Baroscope* 66 Such times as the Wind sets ..contrary in Nature to that Weather which the Glass predicts. **1710** STEELE *Tatler* No. 214 ¶4 A state weather-glass, that..presages all changes and revolutions in government, as the common glass does those of the weather. **1781** W. BLANE *Ess. Hunting* (1788) 9 When he..finds the air moist..the quick-silver in his glass moderately high. **1843** LADY GRANVILLE *Lett.* (1894) II. 370 South-west wind, not sunny, glass at fair. **1867** DICKENS *Lett.* 13 Nov. (1880) II. 304 The glass is rising high to-day.

b. **1775** T. HUTCHINSON *Diary* 21 July I. 493 Warm like a New England day—the glasses in the shade about 75.

†**III. 13.** [Perh. another word; cf. GLASS *v.*, GLAZE *v.*] = GLOSS *sb.*[2] 1, 1 b.

1552 [see *glass-worm* in 16]. *a* **1569** KYNGESMILL *Confl. w. Satan* (1576) A vij b, The more shamefull facts he leadeth vs vnto, the more goodly glasse he setteth on them. **1579** TOMSON *Calvin's Serm. Tim.* 89/1 By this meanes, he giueth greater glasse [orig. *plus grand lustre*] to y[e] grace which he vseth. **1594** HOOKER *Eccl. Pol.* Pref. vii. § 1 It is no part of my secret meaning..to set upon the face of this cause any fairer glass than the naked truth doth afford. **1598** FLORIO, *Accauigliare*, to stringe silke or giue it a glasse. **1605** BRETON *Old Man's Less.* (Grosart) 10/2 Sattens..with such a glasse, that you may almost see your face in it. **1622** MABBE tr. *Aleman's Guzman d' Alf.* II. 220 To take away the dust from them, or to giue them a better glasse.

IV. *attrib.* and *Comb.*

14. *simple attrib.*, passing into quasi-*adj.*

a. Made of glass.

Formerly often united with a hyphen.

c **900** tr. *Bæda's Hist.* v. v. (MS. B; E.E.T.S. II. 494), He ..him onsende an glæs-fæt mid wine ȝefylled. *c* **1205** LAY. 17724 He nom his glæs-fat [*c* **1275** vrinal] anan & þe king mæh þer on. **1600** SURFLET *Countrie Farme* II. lxx. 419 Put them all together in a glasse vessell, or earthen one well glassed. **1641** FRENCH *Distill.* i. (1651) 36 That..Oyle may be better..if it be drawn in Balneo, with a gourd, and glasse-head. **1642** *Rates Merchandize* 29, Glasse pipes. **1657** W. COLES *Adam in Eden* cviii. 154 The distilled water hereof, that is drawn forth with a Glasse-Still. **1664** POWER *Exp. Philos.* 88 Several Glass-Trunks, or Cylindrical Glass-Tubes. **1665** HOOKE *Microgr.* 36 Take a small Glass-Cane about a foot long, seal up one end. **1676** tr. *Guillatiere's Voy. Athens* 269 A kind of Glass-bottles that hold each of them three or four pints. *c* **1678** *Hatton Corr.* (1878) I. 169 Neither the glass penns nor any other sorts are neare soe good [as steel pens]. **1722** DE FOE *Col. Jack* (1840) 6, I was a dirty glass-bottle-house boy, sleeping in the ashes. **1743** *Lond. & Country Brew.* III. (ed. 2) 245 Some..use the Glass Stopple instead of the Cork. **1800** tr. *Lagrange's Chem.* I. 439 If care be taken..to break the largest lumps with a glass-pestle or spatula. **1839** URE *Dict. Arts* 574 By boiling concentrated sulphuric acid in a glass vessel. **1853** *Househ. Words* 11 June 353/2 There is (or was) a famous glass-bead factory at Murano. **1853** W. GREGORY *Inorg. Chem.* (ed. 3) 101 Small bottles..closely fitted with glass stoppers. **1865** TYNDALL *Fragm. Sci.* viii. (1871) 185 Glass lenses were employed to concentrate the rays.

b. Glazed, having pieces or panes of glass set in a frame. Cf. GLASS-CASE, -COACH, -HOUSE, etc.

1599 HAKLUYT *Voy.* II. I. 308 A turret of stone..hauing a great glasse-lanthorne in the toppe..with a great copper pan in the midst to holde oile, with twenty lights in it. *a* **1631** DONNE in *Select.* (1840) 128 The bees have made it their first work to line that glass-hive, with a crust of wax, that they might work and not be discerned. **1664** EVELYN *Kal. Hort.* (1729) 193 You may..have early Sallets on the Hot-Bed, and under Glass Frames and Bells. **1700** T. BROWN tr. *Fresny's Amusem. Ser. & Com.* 116 Every Coffee-House is Illuminated..without by a fine Glass-Lanthorn. **1834** *Gentl. Mag.* CIV. I. 208 He can look through a glass-door at the German Curiosity-chamber within. **1838** *Penny Cycl.* XI. 75 Peas or beans..such as are forced and require glass frames to protect them. **1845** JAMES *Smuggler* III. 129 Sir Robert Croyland they found looking out of the glass-door. **1886** TUPPER *My Life as Author* 240 Our glass-porch entrance at Albury. **1895** *Daily News* 23 Feb. 5/2 'We work in a glass hive', said the late Lord Russell many years ago.

15. General comb.: **a.** attributive, as ***glass business, -line, -shop, trade***.

1799 *Spirit Publ. Jrnls.* (1800) III. 330, I am 32 years of age, a widow, in the *glass line, in London. **1823** *Ibid.* (1824) 211 He..is himself in the glass line..but is, at present, out of business. **1639** CARTWRIGHT *Royall Slave* I. iii, Would doe as much harme in a Kingdome, as a monkey in a *Glasse-shop.

b. objective, as ***glass-beveller, -embosser, -engraver, -grinder, -maker, -mender, -painter, -polisher, -seller, -silverer, -stainer; glass-annealing*** (in quot. *attrib.*), ***-bevelling, -colouring, -embossing, -engraving, -gilding, -grinding, -making, -painting, -silvering, -soldering, -spinning, -staining*** vbl. sbs. Also GLASS-CUTTER, -CUTTING.

1842 FRANCIS *Dict. Arts*, *Glass annealing furnace. **1891** *Daily News* 16 June 6/6 Delegates..representing the *glass-bevellers of the London and provincial branches. *Ibid.* 3 Nov. 3/6 Employers who are interested in *glass-bevelling. **1875** KNIGHT *Dict. Mech.*, *Glass-coloring*, tinting glass by incorporating metallic oxides in its substance. **1858** SIMMONDS *Dict. Trade*, **Glass-embosser*, an ornamenter of glass. **1894** *Westm. Gaz.* 17 July 3/1 The girls and women working in the..*glass-embossing room. **1858** SIMMONDS *Dict. Trade*, **Glass-engraver*, a workman who cuts figures on glass. **1875** KNIGHT *Dict. Mech.*, **Glass-engraving*. **1811** *Self Instructor* 529 The most important secret in *glass-gilding. *a* **1691** BOYLE *Wks.* (1744) I. 255/2 The *glass grinders often complain of the trouble they meet with in separating such bodies. **1768** *Chron.* in *Ann. Reg.* 113/1 The glass grinders assembled in a body to petition parliament for an augmentation of their wages. **1795** ASH, Suppl., **Glass-grinding*. **1576** GASCOIGNE *Steel Gl.* (Arb.) 55 One that was, a *Glassemaker in deede. **1750** tr. *Leonardus's Mirr. Stones* 44 A certain stone, with which our glass-makers whiten their vessels. **1611** COTGR., *Vitrerie*, a glasing or *Glasse-making. **1872** YEATS *Techn. Hist. Comm.* 44 Glass-making was certainly known to the Egyptians. **1644** DIGBY *Nat. Bodies* iii. 21 When the smith and the *glassemender driue theire white and fury fires. **1762** H. WALPOLE *Vertue's Anecd. Paint.* I. vi. 126 He [Marc Willems] made designs for most of the painters, *glass-painters, and arras-makers of his time. **1847** LD. LINDSAY *Chr. Art* I. 110 Miniature and *glass-painting..and similar..graceful branches of art. **1897** *Daily News* 13 May 8/5 T. A., *glass-polisher, pleaded guilty to [etc.]. **1720** STRYPE *Stow's Surv. Lond.* II. v. xv. 240/2 The *Glass-Sellers in London were much aggrieved at this. **1858** SIMMONDS *Dict. Trade*, **Glass-silverer*, one who coats glass with quicksilver for mirrors, &c. **1875** KNIGHT *Dict. Mech.*, **Glass-silvering*, glass for mirrors or ornamentation is silvered by one of two methods. *Ibid.*, **Glass-soldering*. *Ibid.*, **Glass-spinning*. **1858** SIMMONDS *Dict. Trade*, **Glass-stainer*. See *Glass-painter*. *Ibid.*, **Glass-staining*, the process of colouring or painting glass.

c. similative, as ***glass-clear*** (cf. OE. *glæs-hluttor*), ***-coloured, -green, -grey, hard*** adjs.; also ***glass-like*** adj. and adv.

1890 *Dominion Illustr.* Christm. No., A lakelet whose water was waveless and *glass-clear. *a* **1661** HOLYDAY *Juvenal* 174 It was sprinkled over with hyaline or *glass-colour'd dust. **1790** A. WILSON *Hardyknute* Poet. Wks. (1846) 136 Loose from his side a *glass-green horn he drew. **1912** E. POUND *Ripostes* 16 Out through the glass-green fields. **1939** T. S. ELIOT *Old Possum's Pract. Cats* 40 He gives one flash of his glass-green eyes. **1910** W. DE LA MARE *Three Mulla-Mulgars* vi. 81 Whose eyes were pink, rather than *glass-grey. **1920** A. HUXLEY *Leda* 74 The glass-grey silver of rivers. **1882** NARES *Seamanship* (ed. 6) 243 Round bars of *glass-hard steel. **1889** *Nature* 7 Nov. 12 If steel has to be made glass-hard..mercury is used. **1616–61** HOLYDAY *Persius* 309 How he swells, And breaks with *glass-like choller. **1621** LADY M. WROTH *Urania* 180 Sometimes would hee..cast a glasse of comfort on him, but glasse-like was it brittle. **1662** DRYDEN *Astræa Redux* 208 For by example most we sinn'd before, And glass-like clearness mix'd with frailty bore. **1889** HISSEY *Tour in Phaeton* 190 The Mirror Broad..may not be always so smooth and glass-like as when we saw it.

d. parasynthetic and instrumental, as ***glass-bowled, -built, -cased*** (cf. GLASS CASE), ***-clad, -covered, -distilled, -doored, -fronted, -jewelled, -legged, -lidded, -lined, -panelled, -sided, -topped, -walled*** adjs.

1891 *Daily News* 28 May 6/1 That was with a *glass-bowled lamp, whereas this was a brass and copper one. **1781** E. DARWIN *Bot. Gard., Econ. Veg.* IV, In *glass-built fanes. **1901** *Westm. Gaz.* 30 Dec. 2/1 The black marble *glass-cased clock. **1902** *Ibid.* 8 Feb. 2/1 The glass-cased eatables. **1961** *Listener* 28 Sept. 464/1 He would say that his *glass-clad buildings bring man in contact with nature. **1898** *Westm. Gaz.* 11 Mar. 1/1 There is a spacious balcony, which opens into a *glass-covered gallery. **1956** *Nature* 10 Mar. 471/2 Dissolved in *glass-distilled water. **1924** H. CRANE *Let.* 23 Sept. (1965) 190 Books..in the *glass-doored bookcase. **1902** *Westm. Gaz.* 11 Aug. 9/1 The great *glass-fronted, gilded coach. **1960** C. DAY LEWIS *Buried Day* v. 90 Theological works in glass-fronted bookcases. **1916** H. G. WELLS *Mr. Britling* I. ii. 55 Fastened with a large green *glass-jewelled brooch. **1824** *Body & Soul* (ed. 4) I. 42 The *glass-legged stool of an electrifying apparatus. **1947** C. MORGAN *Judge's Story* xxx. 199 The girl sitting..at a *glass-lidded table. *a* **1877** KNIGHT *Dict. Mech.* II. 980/2 **Glass-lined pipe*, one in which the metal of the outer pipe is protected from corrosion by any liquids. **1960** *Farmer & Stockbreeder* 16 Feb. 72/1 There was the bottom unloading mechanism as with the glass-lined silo. **1895** *Westm. Gaz.* 28 Jan. 5/1 A *glass-panelled hearse drawn by four horses. **1901** 'L. MALET' *Hist. R. Calmady* v. viii. 443 The *glass-sided hearse. **1905** *Westm. Gaz.* 15 May 10/2 One of the compartments of the *glass-topped case. **1966** A. LA BERN *Goodbye Piccadilly* i. 10 Glass-topped tables furnished with ashtrays too heavy to steal. **1959** N. MAILER *Advts. for Myself* (1961) 397 The institutional world, the monumental world, the world of skyscrapers and *glass-walled banks. **1963** B. FOZARD *Instrumentation Nucl. Reactors* v. 57 In the latter the envelope is most commonly of glass (glass-walled tube).

16. Special comb.: **glass-artist**, one who designs coloured or stained glass windows; **glass-ball**, a ball made of glass, used as an ornament or toy, a mark for shooting at, etc.; †**glass-band**, one of the strips of lead for securing the panes of glass in a window; **glass-bell** = BELL-GLASS; †**glass-belly**, a bellied glass flask, serving the purpose of a retort; **glass-blower**, one who blows and fashions glass; so **glass-blowing** *vbl. sb.*; **glass-breaker** *Sc.*, ? a tippler; **glass brick** (see quot. 1909); **glass-calm**, a calm when the sea is smooth as glass; **glass-cavity**, a cavity in a mineral filled with a glassy substance; **glass-chalcedony, -chord** (see quots.); **glass-crab**, the larva of a palinuroid or scyllaroid shrimp; **glass-culture**, culture of fruit, etc., under glass; **glass-cupboard**, a glazed book-case; **glass disease** (see quot. 1937); **glass-drop** = DROP *sb.* 10 h; **glass-dust**, powdered glass, used for grinding and polishing; **glass-eel, -enamel** (see quots.); **glass-faced** *a.*, reflecting, like a mirror, the looks of another; **glass-furnace**, a furnace in which the materials of glass are fused; **glass-gall**, a whitish salt scum cast up from glass in a state of fusion; **glass-gazing** *a.*, given to contemplating oneself in a mirror; †**glass-gilt** *a.*, thinly coated with a glassy surface; **glass-glazed** *a.*, (of pottery) having a glaze of substantial thickness; **glass-grenade**, a grenade with case made of glass instead of metal; **glass-height-gauge**, an instrument for measuring the height of watch-glasses; †**glass-helmet**, a glass covering used by early chemists as a protection for the head; **glass-metal**, glass in a state of fusion; **glass-mosaic, -mould, nautilus** (see quots.); †**glass-ore**, a rich kind of silver ore; **glass-organist**, ? a performer on the musical glasses; **glass-oven** (see quot.); **glass-paper**, paper covered with finely-powdered glass for polishing or smoothing wood, bone, etc.; so **glass-paper** *v.*, to rub or polish with glass-paper; **glass-plate**, †(*a*) (see quot. 1642); (*b*) a sheet of glass; **glass-pock, -pox**, an eruptive disease, *Varicella coniformis*; **glass-porcelain** (see quot.); **glass-pot**, a pot or crucible used for fusing the materials of glass in a glass-furnace; **glass-press, -proof** (see quots.); **glass-rope (sponge)**, the genus HYALONEMA; †**glass-salt** = *glass-gall*; **glass-sand**, sand used in the manufacture of glass; †**glass-set** *a.*, put into shape before a mirror; **glass-shaped** *a.*, shaped like a drinking-glass, cyathiform; **glass-shell**, a name given to certain molluscs (see quots.); **glass-shrimp**, a larval form of certain stomatopodous crustaceans; **glass silk** (see quot. *a* 1884); **glass silkworm**, the cylinder on which glass silk is spun; **glass-slag**, the refuse of glass-manufacture; **glass slipper** [mistranslation of Fr. *pantoufle en vair* fur slipper, mistaken for *verre* glass], a slipper made of glass, esp. the one lost by Cinderella in the fairy-tale; **glass-snail**, a snail of the genus *Vitrina*, having a thin translucent shell; **glass-snake**, (*a*) a large limbless lizard, *Ophiosaurus ventralis*, with a very brittle tail, common in the southern U.S.; (*b*) a lizard of the genus *Pseudopus*; **glass-soap**, a name given, in glass-making, to peroxide of manganese (see quot.); **glass-sponge** = *glass-rope sponge* (above); †**glass-stone**, a kind of transparent stone, ? mica; also ? Brazilian pebble; **glass-tinner**, the workman who applies tin-foil to mirror-plates; **glass-ware**, articles made of glass; †**glass-weed** = GLASS-WORT; **glass wool** (see quot.); **glass-worm**, the glow-worm (cf. *glare-, glaze-worm*); †**glass-wright** = GLAZIER. Also GLASS FIBRE.

1889 H. A. DODDS *Rep. Paris Exhib.* 7 The *glass-artist.. when he designs a window, frankly recognizes these restrictions. **1687** A. LOVELL tr. *Thevenot's Trav.* I. 22 It is full of Lamps, and curiosities in *glass balls, of which one, for instance, contains a little galley. **1753** CHAMBERS *Cycl. Supp., Glass-balls*,..circular or otherwise shaped hollow vessels of glass coloured within so as to imitate the semi-pellucid gems. **1880** *New Virginians* II. 223 There are also hunting and fishing clubs, and glass-ball matches. **1577** in *Burgh Rec. Glasgow* (1876) 67 The said erle furnesand *glasbandis, soilburdis, lyme, and sand. **1641** FRENCH *Distill.* iii. (1651) 68 Over it hang a *Glasse-bell. **1719** LONDON & WISE *Compl. Gard.* 309 We must sow upon it, under Glass-Bells, some good bright Curled Lettuce. **1831** CARLYLE *Sart. Res.* III. vii, Wert thou..covered up within the largest imaginable Glass-bell. **1681** tr. *Willis' Rem. Med. Wks.* Vocab., *Balneum Mariæ*, is a way of distilling with a *glass-belly, holding the ingredients put into a vessel of water. *c* **1515** *Cocke Lorell's B.* 10 Broche makers, *glas blowers. **1872** RUSKIN *Eagle's N.* §139 A Venetian glass-blower swept you a curve of crystal from the end of his pipe. ? **1829** *Lond. Encycl.* X. 230/2 *Glass-blowing is the art of forming vessels of glass. **1815** SCOTT *Guy M.* xlv, I think we had better lie down, Captain, if ye're no agreeable to another cheerer. But troth, ye're nae *glass-breaker; and neither am I. **1909** *Chem. Abstr.* III. 1210 *Glass Brick: A New Building Material... Description of a hollow glass brick. In use the brick is laid up in the usual way and the inside filled with concrete, forming a monolithic concrete wall with a glass surface. **1938** *Archit. Rev.* LXXXIII. 205/2 (*caption*) The office counter, showing the glass-brick wall which is used as a display background. **1893** *Times* 3 July 11/1 There was a *glass calm down the Renfrew and Ayrshire shores. **1896** *Daily News* 12 June 6/7 A glass calm set in which stayed the cutter. **1857** SORBY in *Q. Jrnl. Geol. Soc.* XIV. 466 It appears to me that we cannot do better than adopt a term analogous to that so generally adopted for fluid-filled cavities, and call these glass-filled cavities *glass-cavities. **1874** WARD *ibid.* XXXI. 397 The augite crystals present many glass-cavities. **1753** CHAMBERS *Cycl. Supp.*, **Glass-Chalcedony*, a mixture of several ingredients, with the common matter of glass, will make it represent the semi-opake gems, the jaspers, agates, chalcedonies, &c. **1825** DANNELEY *Encycl. Mus.*, **Glass chord*, a clavier instrument, mounted with glass bars instead of strings. **1855** OGILVIE, Suppl., **Glass-crab*, the name given to species of the genus Phyllosoma which are as transparent nearly as glass. **1877** HUXLEY *Anat. Inv. Anim.* 356 The Glass-crabs, or Phyllosomata are singular marine pelagic crustacea. **1884–5** *Riverside Nat. Hist.* (1888) II. 55 *Loricata*..the young forming the 'glass crabs', which formerly, under the name *Phyllosoma*, were regarded as adults. **1886** *Pall Mall G.* 19 June 14/1 *Glass culture is also now so cheap. **1711** SHAFTESB. *Charac.* (1737) III. 328 Folio's and other volumes..on the advanc'd shelves or *glass-cupboards of the lady's closets. **1902** *Lancet* 25 Oct. 1143/1 Lately it has been found that a peculiar '*glass disease' has broken out amongst the windows of York Cathedral. **1937** *Burlington Mag.* Nov. 218/1 There is..[a] sort of decay, proceeding from within, which is due to too large a proportion of alkali in the composition of the glass itself. This 'glass disease' (as it is often called) may, and generally does, show itself within a short time after making, and takes the form at first of an interior network of very fine cracks. **1662** *Glass Drops [see DROP *sb.* 10 b]. **1710** J. CLARKE *Rohault's Nat. Phil.* (1729) I. 137 The scattering about of the Particles of the Glass-drop, is owing to [etc.]. **1598** SYLVESTER *Du Bartas* II. ii. II. *Babylon* 264 We..in *glasse-dust did commence To draw the round Earth's fair circumference. **1840** F. D. BENNETT *Whaling Voy.* II. 267 The *Glass-Eel, or Small-Head. (*Leptocephalus*, Sp.). This is one of the most extraordinary and paradoxical fishes the ocean affords. **1875** KNIGHT *Dict. Mech.*, **Glass-enamel*, a semi-lucid or an opaque glass, which owes its milkiness to the addition of binoxide of tin. **1607** SHAKS. *Timon* I. i. 58 The *glasse-fac'd Flatterer. **1632** SHERWOOD, A *Glasse-furnace, *verriere*. **1671** LOCKE *Hum. Und.* (*MS. draft*) (1931) xxxix. 93 The glowing heat of a glass furnace. **1880** *Harper's Mag.* Dec. 63 Since.. Pittsburgh's first glass furnace in 1796 this industry has found in that city..congenial soil. **1599** A. M. tr. *Gabelhouer's Bk. Physicke* 69/1 Take *glassegaule, or Cristalle. **1683** PETTUS *Fleta Min.* I. (1686) 246 Mingle it with fluss, and a little Glass-galls. **1832** G. R. PORTER *Porcelain & Gl.* 166 A white porous scum, known by the name of sandiver or glass-gall, rises through the mass. **1605** SHAKS. *Lear* II. ii. 19 A..whoreson *glasse-gazing super-seruiceable finicall Rogue. *c* **1684** *Frost of 1683–4* (Percy Soc.) 28 Whilst on its *glass gilt face strange buildings stand. **1883** MOLLETT *Dict. Art & Archæol.*, **Glass-glazed wares.* **1664** EVELYN *Mem.* 4 Feb., I had discourse with the King about an invention of *glass-grenades. **1884** *Glass-height gauge* [see sense 9]. **1660** BOYLE *New Exp. Phys. Mech.* viii. 64 The wide Orifice (which in common *Glass-Helmets is the only one). *a* **1626** BACON *Phys. Rem.* Wks. 1827 VII. 191 Let proof be made of the incorporating of copper or brass with *glass-metal. **1854** FAIRHOLT *Dict. Art*, **Glass-mosaic*, a modern Italian work in imitation of the antique.. formed of small squares of coloured glass..and used for brooches [etc.]. **1879** SIR G. G. SCOTT *Lect. Archit.* I. 178 The introduction of..glass mosaic on the tombs of the builder and rebuilder of the Abbey. **1875** KNIGHT *Dict. Mech.*, **Glass-mold*, a metallic shaping-box in which glass is pressed or blown to form. **1836** *Penny Cycl.* VI. 294/1 The shells of this genus [Carinaria] were formerly known to collectors under the name of..'*Glass Nautilus'. **1683** PETTUS *Fleta Min.* I. ii. 5 *Glass-Oars (as the cheifest of the leaden Coloured Oars) almost to be compared to the best digested Silver. **1759** GRAY *Lett.* Wks. 1884 III. 22 The fire is said to have begun in the chamber of that poor *glass-organist who lodged at a coffee-house in Swithin's Alley. **1875** KNIGHT *Dict. Mech.*, **Glass-oven*, a heated chamber in which just-made glass in sheets or ware is placed to cool gradually. **1815** *Niles' Weekly Reg.* IX. 94/2 *Glass paper [was manufactured]. **1847** SMEATON *Builder's Man.* 97 This being done, the work may be cleaned off with a piece of glass-paper. **1873** SPON *Workshop Rec.* Ser. I. 84/1 Take a sheet of the finest glass-paper, and when the first coating of varnish is perfectly dry, glass-paper the whole surface, and make it smooth as before. **1642** *Rates Merchandize* 29 *Glasse plates or sights for looking glasses unfyled. **1839** URE *Dict. Arts* 579 In forming glass-plates by the extension of a cylinder into a plane, the workman first [etc.]. **1858** B. RIDGE *Health & Dis.* 118 The superfluity of the acid and acrid materials in children will beget *glass-pock. **1879** *St. George's Hosp. Rep.* IX. 603 The patient had in his youth suffered from scarlatina and 'glass-pox'. **1753** CHAMBERS *Cycl. Supp.*, **Glass porcelain*, the name given by many to a modern invention of imitating the china ware with glass. *Ibid.*, **Glass Pots.* **1819** BRANDE *Chem.* (1841) 1039 The glass-pots are placed round a dome-shaped furnace..there are generally six in each furnace. **1875** KNIGHT *Dict. Mech.*, **Glass-press*, a device to apply pressure to glass in a mold while in a plastic state. **1842** FRANCIS *Dict. Arts*, **Glass proofs*, see *Bologna Phials. Bologna Phials* or *Proofs* are small round bottles of unannealed glass, which fly to pieces directly anything angular is dropped into them. **1855** KINGSLEY *Glaucus* (1878) 86 Hyalonemas, or *glass-rope sponges. **1712** tr. *Pomet's Hist. Drugs* I. v. §21 Of Sandiver, or *Glass Salt. **1863** A. C. RAMSAY *Phys. Geog.* 139 The *glass-sand used in this country is chiefly derived from the Eocene beds of the Isle of Wight, and from the sand-dunes on the borders of the Bristol Channel. **1599** MARSTON *Sco. Villanie* ii. vi. 201 Then Mato comes with his new *glasse-set face. **1776–96** WITHERING *Brit. Plants* (ed. 3) II. 201 Male, nectary in the centre; *glass-shaped. **1854** MAYNE *Expos. Lex., Glass-shaped.* See *Cyathiformis.* **1851** GOSSE *Zool.* 220 *Glass shells (a. *Hyalea tridentata*; b. *Cleodora pyramidata*). **1855** OGILVIE, Suppl., *Glass-shell*, species of Hyalea, whose shells look as if they had been blown out of the thinnest glass. **1879** ROSSITER *Dict. Sci. Terms* s.v., Glass shell = *Carinaria*, belongs to Gasteropoda. *Ibid.*, **Glass shrimp* = Erichthus. *a* **1884** KNIGHT *Dict. Mech.* Suppl. 405/1 **Glass silk*, a product obtained by winding fine threads of glass in fusion on rapidly rotating and heated cylinders. **1937** *Archit. Rev.* LXXXII. 120 Glass silk has been used for the sound insulation of internal partitions. **1899** *Jrnl. Soc. Arts* XLVIII. 64/1 Should they [*sc.* bubbles] pass into the *glass silk-worms, the continuity of the thread would be broken. **1612** STURTEVANT *Metallica* (1854) 113 *Glasse-slage is a liquid materiall of a glassie substance. **1878** *Ure's Dict. Arts* (ed. 7) IV. 408 *Glass-slag.* **1729** tr. *Perrault's Histories* 73 (*title*) Cinderilla: or, The little *Glass Slipper. **1819** M. WILMOT *Let.* 21 Dec. (1935) 46 *Cinderella* in her glass slippers and Fairy gifted finery was *dull* to the brilliancy of every creature. **1969** 'J. MUNRO' *Innocent Bystanders* iv. 64 If Cinderella had lost her glass slipper in New York, Loomis had said, her foot would have been in it all the time. **1851–6** WOODWARD *Mollusca* 163 *Glass-snail. **1736** MORTIMER *Nat. Hist. Carolina* in *Phil. Trans.* XXXIX. 258 *Cæcilia maculata*: The *Glass-Snake. **1796** MORSE *Amer. Geog.* I. 221 The glass snake..A small blow with a stick will separate the body, not only at the place struck, but at two or three other places, the muscles being articulated in a singular manner, quite through to the vertebra. **1884–5** *Riverside Nat. Hist.* (1888) III. 434 *Pseudopus gracilis*, the Khasya glass-snake..inhabiting the Khasya Hills of India. **1832** G. R. PORTER *Porcelain & Gl.* 148 Black oxide of manganese has long been used for clearing glass from any foul colour which it might accidentally possess through the impurity of the alkali employed..This property..occasioned it to be anciently known as *glass soap. **1875** *Scribner's Mag.* Nov. 42 *Glass-sponges. **1884** tr. *J. J. Rein's Japan* 486 The well-known glass-sponge (Hyalonema Sieboldi). **1601** HOLLAND *Pliny* I. 54 The hither part [of Spain] aboundeth besides with stone glasses, or *glasse stones [orig. *specularibus lapidibus*]. *Ibid.* II. 595 The best plastre..is..made of the Talc or the glasse stone aforesaid. **1642** *Rates Merchandize* 29 Glasse stone, plates, for spectacles rough the dozen 00. 13. 04. **1839** URE *Dict. Arts* 592 The *glass-tinner..taking a sheet of tinfoil adapted to his purpose..spreads it on the table, and applies it closely with a brush. **1745** *De Foe's Eng. Tradesman* xxvi. (1841) I. 267 *Glass ware from Sturbridge. *c* **1850** *Arab. Nts.* (Rtldg.) 225 He was a poor man, who had laid out the little money he possessed in a basket of glassware. **1568** TURNER *Herbal* III. 37 It maye be called also *Glasswede, because the ashe of it serve to make glas with. **1712** tr. *Pomet's Hist. Drugs* I. 101 A Plant..which the Botanists call Kali..and we..Glass-weed. **1879** *English Mechanic* 30 May 282/3 The patentee, therefore, proposes to employ..*glass wool. **1885** *Syd. Soc. Lex., Glass-wool*, glass spun out to a very fine fibre. Used in the filtration of acids. **1962** A. NISBETT *Technique of Sound Studio* 239 Soft absorbers (glass wool, fibre board, etc.)..are poor absorbers at low frequencies. **1552** HULOET, *Glasse worme or grene worme, whiche shyneth in the nyghte wyth a glasse lyke golde, *cantharis, cantharida.* **1658** ROWLAND *Moufet's Theat. Ins.* 976 In English, Glow-worm, Shine-worm, Glass-worm. *c* **1440** *Promp. Parv.* 198/1 *Glasse wryte..*vitrarius.* **1627** *Dumbarton Burgh Rec.* in J. Irving *Hist. Dumbartonsh.* (1860) 478 Thay ordanit the glasswryt mak up a new glas to the Tolbooth in the loist windo.

†**glass**, *sb.*[2] *Obs. rare.* [a. OF. *glas, glais.*] A resounding noise.

1483 *Cath. Angl.* 158/1 A Glasse of ringynge or trumpynge, *classicum.*

†**glass**, *a. Obs. rare.* Also **glase**. [perh. f. GLASS *sb.*[1]; but cf. Welsh *glas*, grey.]

1547 BOORDE *Brev. Health* xiii. 11 b, The thyrde is of a glasse or a greenyshe colour. *Ibid.* xciv. 37 Some [men] hath glase and dankyshe skynnes.

glass (glɑːs, -æ-), *v.* [f. GLASS *sb.*[1]; cf. GLAZE *v.*[1], which represents an equivalent older formation.]

1. *trans.* To fit or fill in with glass; = GLAZE *v.*[1] Now *rare.*

1540 *Ludlow Churchw. Acc.* (Camden) 1 To master glasier for glassynge the wyndous. **1599** MINSHEU, To Glasse or glaze. *a* **1661** FULLER *Worthies, Devonshire* I. (1662) 257 The Lady glassing the Window in her husbands absence.. caused one child more then she then had, to be set up. **1665** BP. COSIN *Corresp.* (Surtees) II. 114 Are the windows well and fairly glassed, the floor..well and even layd? **18..** CLOUGH *Poems & Rem.* (1869) II. 97 [The sun] Southwestering now, thro' windows plainly glassed. **1886** *Chesh. Gloss., Glass v.* to glaze. Glassing the windows is to put the panes into their frames.

2. a. To protect by a covering of glass, to enclose or case in glass (*rare*). Also (*nonce-use*), to keep *away* (from the air) by enclosing in glass.

1588 SHAKS. *L.L.L.* II. i. 244 As Iewels in Christall for some Prince to buy. Who tendring their own worth from whence they were glast, Did point out to buy them along as you past. **1799–1805** WORDSW. *Prelude* IX. 88 Tranquil almost and careless as a flower Glassed in a green-house. **1886** *Century Mag.* XXXII. 863/1 As if a boy were an orchid or other frail exotic to be glassed away from the rough air of manhood.

†**b.** To put into a glass vessel for the purpose of storing or keeping, to bottle. Also *to glass up.*

1728 E. SMITH *Compl. Housew.* (ed. 2) 155 When your Quinces are clear..glass them up, and when they are cold, paper them and keep them in a Stove. *Ibid.* 182 When the Syrup will jelly and the Oranges look clear, they are enough; then glass them with the holes uppermost, and pour the Syrup upon them.

c. To put (bees) into a glass hive.

1791 *Trans Soc. Arts* IX. 108, I endeavoured to prevent such an increase by glassing them; but many of the stocks warmed before the glasses or small hives were full.

†**3. a.** To cover with a vitreous or glass-like surface; = GLAZE *v.*[1] 2. *Obs.*

1577 FRAMPTON *Joyful Newes* I. (1596) 8 In siluer, Glasse or Tinne [vessels], or any other things glassed. **1657** TOMLINSON *Renou's Disp.* 80 In an earthen [vessel] well glassed. **1658** tr. *Porta's Nat. Magick* V. v. 170 Make a vessel of potters earth..glassed within with glass. **1661** BOYLE *Scept. Chem.* I. 58, I have observ'd little Grains of Silver to lie hid in the small Cavities (perhaps glass'd over by a vitrifying heat) in Crucibles, wherein Silver has been long kept in Fusion.

b. said of frost. *rare.*

1880 *Echo* 11 Dec. 2/6 Streams..glassed with ice. **1890** *Boy's Own Paper* 11 Jan. 230/1 The hedgerows..were glassed with most amazing traceries in diamond arabesque.

c. To make (the eye) glassy. (Cf. GLAZE *v.*[1] 6.)

1841 EMERSON *Ess.* Ser. I. iv. *Spiritual Laws,* What he is engraves itself on his face..His vice glasses his eye, demeans his cheek.

4. a. To set (an object, oneself) before a mirror or other reflecting surface, so as to cause an image to be reflected; also to view the reflection of, see as in a mirror. Often *refl.* Also *transf.* and *fig.*

a **1586** SIDNEY *Arcadia* II. (1629) 147 Me-thinkes I am partaker of thy passion, And in thy case doe glasse mine owne debilitie. *Ibid.* III. 358 He had lifted vp his face to glasse himselfe in her faire eyes. *c* **1595** SOUTHWELL *St. Peter's Compl.* 17 O pooles..Where Saints rejoyce to glasse their glorious face. **1651** *Raleigh's Ghost* 38 Whose infinite puissance..we are partly able to glass and see (as it were by reflection). **1818** BYRON *Ch. Har.* IV. clxxxiii, Thou glorious mirror, where the Almighty's form Glasses itself in tempests. **1837** *Fraser's Mag.* XVI. 559 Many of his contemporaries aimed at glassing themselves in his mirror, and becoming his echoes. **1852** M. ARNOLD *Youth Nat.* 38 Helicon glassed in the lake Its firs. **1856** MRS. BROWNING *Aur. Leigh* I. 7 All which images Concentred in the picture, glassed themselves Before my meditative childhood. **1887** GISSING *Thyrza* I. i. 7 The opposite slopes glassed themselves in the deep dark water.

b. Of a mirror or reflecting surface: To reflect, give back an image of.

a **1628** F. GREVILLE BROOKE *Cœlica* Poems (1633) 220 Let my present thoughts be glassed In the thoughts which you have passed. **1817** BYRON *Manfred* II. ii. 26 Thy calm clear brow, Wherein is glass'd serenity of soul. **1849** C. BRONTE *Shirley* II. iii. 92 His serene mind could glass a fair image without feeling its depths troubled by the reflection. **1853** M. ARNOLD *Sohrab & Rustum* 573 Never more Shall the lake glass her, flying over it. **1887** T. HARDY *Woodlanders* I. viii. 152 Both looked attractive as glassed back by the faithful reflector.

c. To view or look for (something) with the aid of field-glasses.

1935 E. HEMINGWAY *Green Hills Africa* (1936) II. vii. 166 We glassed the country. **1952** *Blackw. Mag.* Feb. 100/1 It was going to be a fine day with adequate light to 'glass' birds at a distance. **1964** F. O'ROURKE *Mule for Marquesa* (1967) iv. 53 Fardan glassed the south, then the north where pursuit would come first, if it came.

5. *techn.* To dress (leather) with a glassing-jack or glassing-machine. Also *to glass out.*

1885 *Harper's Mag.* Jan. 278/1 The hides are..again 'glassed'. They are 'filled' with paste, glassed in the paste. **1897** C. T. DAVIS *Manuf. Leather* (ed. 2) 268 For the morocco or lining finisher it [a machine] will glaze, roll, pebble and glass out.

6. *intr.* To glisten like glass. *nonce-use.*

1896 *Atlantic Monthly* May 607/1 Below them the river glassed and gleamed in its crooked bed.

7. *to glass off* (*Surfing*). Of the sea: to become smooth and transparent.

1967 J. SEVERSON *Great Surfing* Gloss., *Glass-off*—when the wind dies (usually in the afternoon), causing the water to become very smooth or glassy slick. **1968** W. WARWICK *Surfriding in N.Z.* 22/1 When the waves glass off in this way ..surfriding takes on a truly aesthetic appearance not often seen.

glass case.

1. (as two words). A case with the upper part made chiefly of glass, so that the objects contained may be seen but not handled. (The first quot. may belong to 2.)

1649 *Bury Wills* (Camden) 220, I give vnto my daughter Mary Chapman..a glascase, a leafe table [etc.]. **1709** STEELE *Tatler* No. 34 ¶5 The China Figure of a Lady in the Glass-Case. **1788** H. WALPOLE *Remin.* ix. 74 She..decorated waxen dolls of him and of herself to be exhibited in glass-cases in Westminster-Abbey. **1834** T. MEDWIN *Angler in Wales* II. 103 [A temple] that deserves to be carved in ivory, and put into a glass case. **1857** HAWTHORNE *Eng. Note-Bks.* (1870) II. 357 His veritable cardinal's hat, in a richly ornamented glass case.

†**b.** *Gardening.* A garden frame. *Obs.*

1819 REES *Cycl.*, *Glass-case.*

c. *jocosely.* A place partitioned off with glass or glazed panels.

1776 FOOTE *Capuchin* I. Wks. 1799 II. 388, I saw him in one of the glass-cases at church;..his majesty looked at me very hard. **1855** DICKENS *Dorrit* I. x, Having on previous occasions awaited that gentleman successively in a hall, a glass case, a waiting-room [etc.].

2. **'glass-case.** A case to hold glass-ware.

1734 *Hope's Minor Practicks* 540 App., A Glass-case for Drinking-glasses.

'glass-cloth.

1. A linen cloth used for drying glass-ware; also as a background for embroidery (see quot. 1882).

1851 *Illustr. Catal. Gt. Exhib.* 512 Plain and checked glass-cloths. **1882** CAULFEILD & SAWARD *Dict. Needlework. Glass cloths*..have been..much adopted for the purpose of embroidery, as well as for aprons and chair covers. **1891** *Times* 5 Oct. 4/3 Narrow width towellings, glass cloths, and the like.

2. A woven fabric made of fine-spun glass thread. (Only as two words.)

1875 in KNIGHT *Dict. Mech.* **1882** CAULFEILD & SAWARD *Dict. Needlework, Glass cloth*..manufactories for the production of ecclesiastical decorative fabrics composed of glass fibre are in operation in Austria, France and Italy.

3. Cloth covered with powdered glass, used like sand-paper for smoothing or polishing.

1873 SPON *Workshop Rec.* Ser. I. 407/1 Polishing Bullocks' Horns. Well scrape with glass or steel scraper, afterwards with finest glass-cloth.

†**glass-coach.** *Obs.* The name originally given to a coach with glass windows, as distinguished from those which were unglazed (cf. e.g. *curtain-coach*); esp. applied to a 'private' coach let out for hire, as distinguished from those on public stands.

1667 PEPYS *Diary* 23 Aug., Abroad to White Hall in a hackney-coach with Sir W. Pen..we were forced to leap out ..Query, whether a glass-coach would have permitted us to have made the escape. **1689** *Lond. Gaz.* No. 2487/4 A Glass Coach, Lin'd within with rich Figur'd Velvet..is to be sold. **1706** *Ibid.* No. 4224/3 Three Hackney Glass Coaches..are to be sold. **1721** *Ibid.* No. 5942/3 Gentlemen..may have a Glass-Coach or Chariot, instead of a Curtain Coach. **1831** MACAULAY in Trevelyan *Life* I. 243 At seven, the glass coach which I had ordered for myself and some of my friends came to the door. **1839** *Sat. Mag.* Aug. Supp. 87/1 Glass-coaches are a kind of private coach kept by persons who let them out generally for the day or half-day; and they are considered a grade higher in rank than hackney-coaches. **1844** J. F. COOPER *M. Wallingford* x, Hackney-coaches..are not admitted into the English parks. Glass-coaches are; meaning by this term..hired carriages that do not go on stands. **1844** J. T. HEWLETT *Parsons & W.* xxxiv, Glass-coach after glass-coach deposited its burden of ladies. **1882** SERJT. BALLANTINE *Exper.* (1890) 17 When middle-class people went to the play..they performed the operation in what was called a glass coach.

'glass-,cutter.

1. One whose occupation it is to cut glass (e.g. to sizes for glazing), or to ornament glass-ware by grinding.

1703 T. N. *City & C. Purchaser* 156 The London Glass-cutters..have their Rules Centesimally divided. **1832** G. R. PORTER *Porcelain & Gl.* 309 The grinding of glass, or frosting it..forms a branch of the glass-cutter's art. **1890** W. J. GORDON *Foundry* 140 The glass-cutter works at a frame, in which a thin iron wheel..derives its cutting grittiness from a mixture of sand and water..As the wheel spins the glass is held against its edge and slowly cut into.

2. A tool for cutting glass; a glazier's diamond.

1881 YOUNG *Every Man his own Mechanic* §1692. 751 On examining the glass-cutter it will be noticed that there are notches of different widths in it. **1892** *Daily News* 13 July 7/3 Stealing therein 37 glaziers' diamond glass-cutters.

So **glass-cutting** *vbl. sb.*

1839 URE *Dict. Arts* 595 Glass cutting and grinding.

glassed (glɑːst, -æ-), *ppl. a.* [f. GLASS *sb.*[1] and *v.* + -ED.]

1. †**a.** Glazed, covered with a glaze. *Obs.*

1577 FRAMPTON *Joyful Newes* I. (1596) 8 It is not conuenient..to bee kept in any other vessel then in siluer, Glasse or Tinne, or any other thing glassed. *Ibid.* 16 When it is cold, let it be strained into a glassed vessel.

b. *glassed-in*: fitted with glass, glazed.

1894 C. N. ROBINSON *Brit. Fleet* III. iii. 250 These [stern] galleries began to be discarded..for closed glassed-in stern-lights. **1955** E. BOWEN *World of Love* xi. 222 A glassed-in bar. **1969** J. ROSS *Dead at First Hand* xvi. 152 Above the main doors a glassed-in bulb pushed out a sickly nimbus of light.

2. Poured into glasses.

1820 KEATS *Cup & Bells* xl. Poems (1889) 533 Sherry in silver, hock in gold, or glass'd champagne?

'glassen, 'glazen, *a. Obs.* exc. *dial.* and *arch.* Forms: α. 1 **glæsen,** 2 **glesen,** 4–7 **glasen,** 4–6 **glasyn(e,** (4 **glasun,** 6 **glasin(g, glason),** 7– **glazen.** β. 5–6 **glassin,** (6 **-yn),** 6–7, 9 *dial.* **glassen.** [OE. *glæsen,* f. *glæs* GLASS *sb.*[1] + -EN; OHG. had *glesîn*:—**glasîno-*, but the absence of umlaut in the OE. word shows that it was a new formation or refashioned after the sb. The β-forms represent a second new formation in the 15th c.]

1. Made of glass. Also *fig.*

α. **971** *Blickl. Hom.* 209 þonne wæs onȝean ðyssum wæter-scipe glæsen fæt on seolfrenre racenteaȝe ahangen. *c* **1175** *Lamb. Hom.* 83 þe sunne scineð þurh þe glesne ehþurl. **1377** LANGL. *P. Pl.* B. xx. 171 Thei gyuen hym agayne a glasen houve. **1382** WYCLIF *Rev.* xv. 2, I siȝe as a glasen se mengid with fijr. *c* **1400** *Lanfranc's Cirurg.* 190 In a glasen vessel. **1471** RIPLEY *Comp. Alch.* Ep. in Ashm. (1652) 115 A little glasen Toune. **16..** SEMPILL *Picktooth for Pope* in *Harp of Renfrewsh.* Ser. II. (1873) 17 Such glazen arguments will bide no hammer. **1641** FRENCH *Distill.* v. (1651) 119 Closed up..in a glazen womb sealed with Hermes seales. **1765** J. BROWN *Chr. Jrnl.* (1814) 207 To prepare the glazen sea of his righteousness.

β. **1516** *Pilton Churchw. Acc.* (Som. Rec. Soc.) 73 Item for yᵉ mendyng off yᵉ glassyn wyndowys..ijˢ. viᵈ. **1559** MORWYNG *Evonym.* 20 Some use..glassen limbeckes. **1600** HAKLUYT *Voy.* (1810) III. 270 Who for a recompence gaue them kniues and glassen Beades. **1642** *Remonstr. Ch. Irel.* 49 The King..rode disguised, and had glassen eyes, because he would not be knowne. **1662** J. CHANDLER tr. *Van Helmont's Oriat.* 75 Fill a glassen and great Bottle with pieces of Ice. **1669** WORLIDGE *Syst. Agric.* (1681) 185 We have also an Experiment of Glassen-Hives, published by Mr. Hartlib in his Common-wealth of Bees. **1866** WH. STOKES in *Voy. Bran* (1895) 220 A glassen veil between them. *Ibid.* 221 The City, and seven glassen walls around it. **1886** ELWORTHY *W. Somerset Word-bk., Glassen.*

†**b.** *Sc. glassen-work*: window-glazing. Also *glassen-, glazen-wright,* a glazier. *Obs.*

[**1379** *Nottingham Bor. Rec.* I. 204 John Glasenwryghte.] **1473** in *Ld. Treas. Acc. Scotl.* (1877) I. 46 To ane glasyn wricht in the Abbay, for a wyndow to the Qwenis chalmire. **1497** *Ibid.* 364 In payment of the glassin werk. **1500–20** DUNBAR *Poems* lxiii. 15 Glasing wrichtis, goldsmythis, and lapidaris. **1577** in *Burgh Rec. Glasgow* (1876) 67 George Elphinstoun glasin-wricht, burges of Glasgow. **1641** *Sc. Acts Chas. I* (1817) V. 540/2 Cowperis, glassinwrichtis.

2. Resembling glass. Of eyes: Glassy, glazed.

α. *c* **1380** WYCLIF *Last Age Ch.* p. xxxv, So oure Lord þe Fadir of heuene hadde Mankynde in helle, þat was glasyne, þat is to seye, britil as glas. **1401** *Pol. Poems* (Rolls) II. 100 Thou approvest ȝour capped maistres with a glasen glose. **1590** P. BURROUGH *Meth. Phisick* 241 Glasen fleume is the coldest of all other fleumes [cf. GLASSY 1]. **1605** B. JONSON *Volpone* V. i, Old glazen eyes, He hath not reach'd his despair yet. **1607** TOPSELL *Four-f. Beasts* (1658) 371 Gray Horses, with glasen eyes, which are most swift, and which dare only meet Lions, when other Horses dare not abide the sight of Lions. **1609** C. BUTLER *Fem. Mon.* (1634) 14 They [bees] take such pains at the door in rubbing and wiping their glazen eyes, that they might the better discern their way forth and back. **1848** J. A. CARLYLE tr. *Dante's Inf.* XXXIII, That thou more willingly mayest rid the glazen tears from off my face.

β. *a* **1637** B. JONSON *Underwoods* xxxii. *Ep. to Friend* 135 [The palsied gamester] pursues The Dice with glassen eyes.

†**'glassen, 'glazen,** *v. Obs.* [Extension of GLASS *v.*, GLAZE *v.*[1]; cf. -EN[5].]

1. *trans.* To fit with glass, to glaze.

1566 *Eng. Ch. Furniture* (1866) 171 The churche was glassened. **1664** in Grant *Burgh Sch. Scotl.* II. xv. (1876) 513 [In 1664 the council of Jedburgh employ a glazier for] 'glassening' [the school windows].

2. = GLAZE *v.*[1] 2.

1657 TOMLINSON *Renou's Disp.* 648 Oyl..is..imposed in a glass, or earthen vessel well glazened. **1709** T. ROBINSON *Nat. Hist. Westmoreld.* 76 Wadd or Black-Lead..it's now made use of to glazen and harden Crucibles. **1828** *Craven Gloss., Glazzen,* to glaze. **1849** *Teesdale Gloss., Glazen,* to glaze. **1877** in *N.W. Linc. Gloss.*

Hence **'glassened, 'glazened** *ppl. a.* Also **'glassener, 'glaz(e)ner,** a glazier. *Obs.* exc. *dial.*

1585 *Vestry Bks.* (Surtees) 20 Given to William Shadforth for servinge the glasner that day which he mended the windowes. **1593** *Rites & Mon. Ch. Durh.* (Surtees) 40 Foure faire coulered and sumptuous glasened wyndowes. **1596** *Vestry Bks.* (Surtees) 271 Given to the glaysner for repairing of the glas windowes. **1678** *Anct. Trades decayed* 16 Instead of Perpetuana or a Shalloon to Lyne Mens Coats with, is used sometimes a Glazened Calico. **1728** JOHN HOBSON *Diary* 13 Aug. (Surtees 1877) 281 John Guest, glazener, of Barnsly. **1825** SCOTT *Talism.* xviii, It seemed as if a tear.. were gathering in his dry and glazened eye. **1883** *Almondbury Gloss., Glassener* (pronounced glazzener), a glazier. **1888** *Sheffield Gloss., Glazener,* a glazier.

glassen, var. GLOSSAN, coal-fish.

†**'glassery.** *Obs.* Also **glasery(e.** [f. GLASS *sb.*[1] + -ERY.] Glazier's work and materials.

1663 GERBIER *Counsel* 83 Glassery. The best French Glasse wrought with good lead, well simmoned, is worth sixteen Pence a foot. **1667** PRIMATT *City & C. Build.* 70 Glasery. *Ibid.* 147 For Glassery, at Sixpence a Foot.

glass eye.

†**1.** An eye-glass; usually *pl.*, spectacles, 'glasses'. (Cf. Sw. *glasögon.*) *Obs.*

1605 SHAKS. *Lear* IV. vi. 174 Get thee glasse-eyes, and like a scuruy Politician, seeme to see the things thou dost not. **1639** DAVENPORT *New Trick* IV. i, Enter the Divell like a Gentleman, with glasse eyes. **1642** *Remonstr. Ch. Irel.* 5 His Highness was..riding up and down disguised, and with glasse-eyes, desiring not to be discovered. **1719** D'URFEY *Pills* III. 18 With a pair of Glass Eyes to clap on my Nose. **1721** *Lond. Gaz.* No. 5925/3 He..wears a Glass Eye.

b. (See quot.)

1796 *Grose's Dict. Vulg. Tongue* (ed. 3), *Glass Eyes*, a nick name for one wearing spectacles.

2. A false eye made of glass (see also EYE *sb.*[1] 26).

1687 SETTLE *Refl. Dryden* 24, I have heard of *glass* Eyes being taken out of peoples heads, and put in agen, but never of *natural* Eyes before. **1895** *Westm. Gaz.* 17 Sept. 3/2 When a glass eye fits the socket nicely, it moves with it.

3. *Farriery.* A species of blindness in horses.

1831 YOUATT *Horse* (1843) 167 Another species of blindness..is Gutta Serena, commonly called *glass eye*. The pupil is more than usually dilated: it is immovable, and bright, and glassy.

4. A name given to: **a.** a Jamaican thrush (*Turdus jamaicensis*), so called from its bluish-white glass-like iris; **b.** (See quot. 1884–5.)

1847 GOSSE *Birds Jamaica* 143 My lad shot a male Glass-eye by the roadside at Cave. **1884–5** *Riverside Nat. Hist.* (1888) III. 228 Wall-eyed pike..glass-eye, and dory are names in which the largest of the American pike-perches (*Stizostedion vitreum*) rejoices.

Hence **glass-eyed** *ppl. a.*

1889 *Century Dict.*, *Glass-eyed*, having a white eye, or one which in some other respect, as texture or fixedness, is likened to glass or to a glass eye; wall-eyed; goggle-eyed. **1895** *Westm. Gaz.* 17 Sept. 3/2 Are glass-eyed people fairly cheerful?

glass fibre. **a.** An individual filament of glass, of any length.

1824 *Edin. Philos. Jrnl.* X. 39, I brought to within half an inch of each other, two conductors, and I united them by a very fine glass thread. One..was connected with an electrical machine, and the other communicated with the ground. In this manner, the light appeared to pass continuously along the glass fibre, which..formed a fine and brilliant line of light. **1949** R. N. HAWARD *Strength of Plastics & Glass* vii. 228 Many of the outstanding mechanical properties of the fibre-glass laminates appear to be largely determined by the properties of the glass fibres. **1954** R. H. SONNEBORN *Fiberglas Reinforced Plastics* p. v, *Fiberglas is the trademark..of Owens-Corning Fiberglas Corporation for a variety of products made of or with glass fibers. **1963** H. R. CLAUSER *Encycl. Engin. Materials* 569/1 Glass fibers for reinforcement are available in several forms. Individual fibers have a diameter of from 0·00025 to 0·0006 in.

b. (Also **glass-fibre, glassfibre.**) Collectively, glass in the form of such filaments, as used for manufacturing purposes or the like; any material made from such filaments, as a textile woven from them or a plastic containing them as reinforcement: = FIBREGLASS.

1882 CAULFEILD & SAWARD *Dict. Needlework* 223/1 Ecclesiastical decorative fabrics composed of glass fibre. **1913** *Chem. Abstr.* VII. 3212 Porous articles of glass fiber. **1947** W. J. BROWN *Fabric Reinforced Plastics* ii. 23 Glass fibre cloth is not suitable for high-pressure laminating processes because of a tendency to crush the fibres. **1955** *Times* 6 July 13/1 Structural plastics consist of a reinforcing agent, such as glass fibre, bonded with a synthetic resin. **1958** C. A. REDFARN *Guide to Plastics* (ed. 2) iii. 51 Glass fibre is of great interest as the reinforcing agent in plastics designed for use under highly stressed conditions. **1959** *Listener* 5 Mar. 435/1 For curtains, glass fibre has several advantages. **1961** *Times* 7 Aug. 2/2 A remarkable performance was given by the small glass-fibre boat Winkle. **1967** *New Scientist* 25 May 448/3 The glassfibre has been tried on other parts like the compressor casing. **1968** *Daily Tel.* 30 Oct. 25/6 The glass-fibre tanks will have an initial storage capacity of 400,000 gallons. **1970** *Commercial Motor* 25 Sept. 121 The roof is of translucent glass fibre.

glassful ('glɑːsfʊl, -æ-), *sb.* Pl. **glassfuls.** [f. GLASS *sb.*[1] + -FUL 2.] As much as fills a glass (sense 5).

[*c* **900** tr. *Bæda's Hist.* v. v. (1891) 398 (*MS. Ca.*: see GLASS *sb.* 14) He..sende him glæs fulne wines.] **1663** SIR T. HERBERT *Mem. Chas. I* (1702) 133 The King..drank a small Glassful of Claret-Wine. **1683** SALMON *Doron Med.* I. 258 Put into a Glass-full of Water. **1747** MRS. GLASSE *Cookery* iii. 54 Then boil a Glass full of Milk. **1823** BYRON *Juan* XIII. xxxvii, About a liquid glassful will remain. **1840** DICKENS *Old C. Shop* xxi, Quilp..drank three small glass-fulls of the raw spirit.

†'**glassful**, *a. Obs. rare*[−1]. [f. GLASS *sb.*[1] + -FUL 1.] ? Mirror-like.

1606 MARSTON *Fawne* Epil., Mineruas glassefull shield.

glasshe, obs. form of GLASS *sb.*[1]

glass-house.

1. The building or works where glass is made.

1385 [see GLAZIER 1]. **1580** HOLLYBAND *Treas. Fr. Tong.*, *Vne voarriére*, a glasse house where glasses be made. *a* **1598** G. LONGE in Ellis *Orig. Lett.* Ser. II. III. 158 Other men erected..divers Glasshouses in sundry parts of the Realm. **1660** BOYLE *New Exp. Phys. Mech.* Proem. 8 We caus'd several such Glasses, to be blown at the Glass-house. **1711** *Vind. Sacheverell* 98 Thou art as hot as a Glass-house. **1726** *Adv. Capt. R. Boyle* 158 We could perceive the Volcano burning like the Flame of a Glass-house. **1779–81** JOHNSON *L.P.*, *Savage* Wks. III. 325 [Savage]..lay down..in the winter..among the ashes of a glass-house. **1839** URE *Dict. Arts* 577 The glass-houses are usually built in the form of a cone..The furnace is constructed in the centre of the area.

2. a. A building with walls and roof made chiefly of glass, *esp.* a greenhouse or conservatory.

1838 *Penny Cycl.* XI. 72/1 Glasshouses, in which plants might be grown in an artificial climate. **1880** DISRAELI *Endym.* xxxiv, 'Is not this lovely? How superior to anything in our glass-houses.' **1885** *Law Times* LXXIX. 345/2 This exhibition..will be held..in the spacious glasshouse erected in the gardens for the purpose.

Proverb. [*a* **1633** (see GLASS *sb.*[1] 1); cf. GLASS-WINDOW, quot. 1670.] **1869** HAZLITT *Proverbs* 400 They who live in glass houses should not throw stones.

b. A photographer's room with a glass roof.

1864 J. TOWLER *Silver Sunbeam* iii. 27 In many instances the artist has the privilege of superintending the construction of his glass house. *Ibid.* v. 43 The camera, which is situated in the darkest part of the glass-house.

c. A military prison or guard-room (see quot. 1925). Also *attrib. slang.*

1925 FRASER & GIBBONS *Soldier & Sailor Words* 105 *Glass house*, detention barracks. An old Army expression, originally particularly applied to the detention barracks for the Aldershot Command at Woking. Later used of any place of military detention. Guard-room, Cells, etc. **1945** *Penguin New Writing* XXVI. 49 But surely they didn't give you the glasshouse for going to Dunkirk? *Ibid.*, The glasshouse man continued to recount his experiences in detention. **1946** *News Chron.* 2 Mar. 4/4 Glasshouse rioters' final stand... Some of the men at Northallerton barracks..holding out on the roof. **1947** J. BERTRAM *Shadow of War* 202 Someone with a lengthy 'crime sheet'—perhaps..a notorious frequenter of the glasshouse.

3. *attrib.* and *Comb.* (sense 1), as ***glass-house fire, furnace, man***; **glass-house pot** = *glass-pot* (in GLASS *sb.*[1] 16).

1711 ADDISON *Spect.* No. 72 ¶7 The Fire burns from Generation to Generation, and has seen the *Glass-house Fires in and out above an Hundred times. **1799** G. SMITH *Laboratory* I. 121 Place it in a *glass-house furnace to digest and purify. **1764** *Low Life* 68 Stone-Sawyers, *Glass-House-Men and Men belonging to the Publick Lay-Stalls. **1807** T. THOMSON *Chem.* (ed. 3) II. 490 The *glass-house pots are formed of the purest kinds of clay that can be procured. **1839** URE *Dict. Arts* 577 Glass-house pots have the figure of a truncated cone, with the narrow end undermost.

'**glassichord.** *U.S. Obs.* exc. *Hist.* Also **glassy-chord.** [f. GLASS *sb.*[1] 4 + ***-chord*** as in *harpsichord*.] = HARMONICA 1 a.

1835 J. H. INGRAHAM *South-West* I. ii. 24 The musical rippling of the eddies—like a glassichord, rapidly run over by light fingers. **1886** *Harper's Mag.* July 286/1 Turning upon his perch, he [*sc.* the cricket] brings to view his 'glassichord', or shrilling organ. **1954** *Grove's Dict. Mus.* (ed. 5) I. 205/2 Franklin's invention..was also popularly known as the 'glassy-chord'.

glassier, obs. form of GLAZIER.

glassily, glassiness: see after GLASSY.

glassin, var. GLOSSAN, coal-fish.

glassine ('glɑːsiːn, -æ-). [GLASS *sb.*[1] + -INE[5].] A glossy transparent paper. Also *attrib.* or as *adj.*

1916 W. W. YOUNG *Story of Cigarette* vi. 98 Each carton is wrapped by hand in moisture-proof and germ-proof glassine paper and firmly sealed. **1925** *Pulp & Paper Mag.* 6 Aug. 881 The manufacture of glassine paper requires great care, exceptionally clean raw materials, experienced labor, and specially designed machinery... Glassine is a paper which is made from very clean pulps, and which must be highly transparent. **1931** F. HURST *Back St.* lviii. 507 Her dry mouth open, with a bubble, as if of glassine paper, spanning it. **1957** P. MANSFIELD *Final Exposure* xvi. 242 Enclosed in a glassine sheath, there lay a negative. *Ibid.* 244 The negative had been carefully released from the glassine envelope. **1970** S. ELLIN *Man from Nowhere* xxxii. 155 He had stored Thoren's envelope and scrap paper in glassine packets.

glassing ('glɑːsɪŋ, -æ-), *vbl. sb.* [See -ING[1].] The action of the vb. GLASS, in various senses.

1617 *Extracts Aberd. Reg.* (1848) II. 349 The repairing, and glassin of the wyndoes, of the said kirk. *a* **1652** J. SMITH *Sel. Disc.* vi. 195 This glassing of divine things by hieroglyphics and emblems in the fancy. **1656** H. PHILLIPS *Purch. Patt.* (1676) A v b, The Tyling, Plaistering, Lead, and Glassing. **1875** KNIGHT *Dict. Mech.*, *Glassing*..The operation of dressing leather on the grain side by a tool consisting of a glass slip set in a wooden handle. **1897** C. T. DAVIS *Manuf. Leather* (ed. 2) 263 Machines for rolling, pebbling, glassing or polishing.

b. *attrib.* and *Comb.*, as ***glassing effect***; †**glassing board**, ? a board or table used by a glazier for his work; **glassing-jack, -machine**, machines used in dressing leather.

1544 *Ludlow Churchw. Acc.* (Camden) 18 To mr. glasyer for a *glassynge borde..xvjd. **1861** L. L. NOBLE *Icebergs* 170 Along the lower portion [of the Iceberg] where you see the *glassing effects of the waves, there it resembles the rarest Sèvres vase..so exquisitely fine is the polish. **1884** KNIGHT *Dict. Mech.* Suppl., **Glassing Jack*,..a machine in which is fitted a plate glass slicker for polishing and smoothing leather. **1885** *Harper's Mag.* Jan. 278/1 To further prepare the surface each one is held under a 'glassing-jack', a kind of bar or arm moving swiftly to and fro above a solid bed. **1885** C. T. DAVIS *Manuf. Leather* xxvi. 458 The *glassing machine..is adapted for work on all kinds of upper leather, sheep, goat, and Morocco.

Glassite ('glɑːsaɪt, -æ-). [f. the name *Glass* + -ITE.] A member of the religious sect founded by the Rev. John Glass, a minister of the Established Church of Scotland (deposed in 1728). The Glassites are also called *Sandemanians*.

1772 J. WESLEY *Jrnl.* 29 Apr. (1827) III. 447 Seceders, Glassites, Nonjurors, and what not! **1876** C. M. DAVIES *Unorth. Lond.* (ed. 2) 173 Their twofold title of Glassites or Sandemanians is derived from their founder, John Glass.. and Robert Sandeman, his son-in-law, who developed Glass's doctrine. **1879** FARRAR *St. Paul* (1883) 730 The Sandemanians or Glassites are a Christian body in London.

attrib. or *adj.* **1862** *Chambers's Encycl.* IV. 784/2 A number of small churches were soon formed on Glassite principles.

glassless ('glɑːslɪs, -æ-), *a.* [f. GLASS *sb.*[1] + -LESS.] Having no glass, without glass.

1824 MISS MITFORD *Village* Ser. I. (1863) 87 The Great House..whose glassless windows and dilapidated doors form [etc.]. **1884** J. PAYN *Canon's Ward* II. 84 A..man, whose eyes shone..in the flaring glassless gas.

'**glass-man.**

1. A dealer in glass-ware.

In 16–17th c. the hawking of glass was often a pretext for begging; see quots.

1597–8 *Act 39 Eliz.* c. 4 §15 This Statute..shall [not] extend..to any such Glassemen as shalbe of good Behaviour, and do travaile in or through any Cuntry without begging, having lycense for their travayling. **1619** DALTON *Countr. Just.* xlvii. (1630) 123 All Pedlers, pettie Chapmen, Tinkers and Glassemen wandering abroad. **1667** BOYLE in *Phil. Trans.* II. 592 Glass-mens Shops are not near so well furnisht as the Stationers. **1712** ADDISON *Spect.* No. 535 ¶¶6, 7. *a* **1745** SWIFT *Direct. Serv.* i. (1745) 35 The Profit of Glasses..consists only in a small Present made by the Glass-man. **1818** COBBETT *Pol. Reg.* XXXIII. 7 Mr. Samuel Brooks, glass-man, in the Strand. **1848** WHARTON *Law Lex.*, *Glass-men*, wandering rogues or vagrants. 1 Jac. I. c. 7.

2. A man engaged in the making of glass.

1610 B. JONSON *Alch.* III. i. F 3 b, Where haue you greater Atheists then your Cookes? Or more prophane, or cholerick, then your Glasse-men? **1626** BACON *Sylva* §399 Fire doth it not [*sc.* doth not make men black], as wee see in Glassemen, that are continually about the Fire. **1703** T. S. *Art's Improv.* p. xiii, In the Glassmans Trade, and Looking-glass makers. **1765** DELAVAL in *Phil. Trans.* LV. 20 The glass-men tinge their glass green therewith. **1866** TATE *Brit. Mollusks* iv. 116 The glass-men of Newcastle once a year have a snail feast.

glassock ('glɑːsək, -æ-). *Sc. local.* [Cf. GLOSSAN.] The Coal-fish, *Merlangus carbonarius.*

1793 *Statist. Acc. Scotl.* VI. 290 In summer, glassocks, or says, are got in great plenty. **1810** NEILL *List Fishes* 7 (Jam.), When a year old, the coal-fish begins to blacken over the gills ..and we have then a new series of names..in Sutherland glassocks. **1864** COUCH *Brit. Fishes* III. 84 Moulrush and Black Pollack are other names [of the Coalfish], with Glassock.

glass window. A window filled with glass.

1526 *Pilgr. Perf.* (W. de W. 1531) 252 b, Yf thou se ony crucifix..or suche other lyke picture in ony glaswyndowe. **1532** MORE *Confut. Tindale* Wks. 597/2 He..therby willingly suffred the deathe of sinne to entre into hys heart by the glasse windowes of hys eyen. **1664** POWER *Exp. Philos.* 43 The very Stancheons and Panes in the Glass-windows. **1667** DRYDEN *Wild Gallant* Prol. 10 He grows to break glass-windows in the end. **1670** RAY *Prov.* 11 Who hath glass-windows of his own must take heed how he throws stones at his house. **1726** AMHERST *Terræ Fil.* xliv. 235 Walk in and see..are not these fine new painted altar-pieces and glass-windows! **1838** DICKENS *O. Twist* xxvii, A light shining through the glass-window of the little parlour.

So †**glass-windowed** *a.*

1647 R. STAPYLTON *Juvenal* 55 Borne in her close and large glasse-window'd chaire.

'**glass-work.**

1. *pl.* (rarely *sing.*) The works or factory where glass is made.

1626 BACON *Sylva* §770 They crush the Ashes into Lumps,..And so sell them to the Venetians for their Glasse-workes. **1634–5** BRERETON *Trav.* (Chetham Soc.) 89 Here at Newcastle, is the finest quay in England..from Tine-bridge all along Towere-wall, and almost to the glass-works, where is made window-glass. **1751** CHAMBERS *Cycl.* s.v. *Glass*, He..set up a glass-work. **1778** *Eng. Gazetteer* (ed. 2) s.v. *Sturbridge*, A well-built town, much enriched by iron and glass works. **1861** W. F. COLLIER *Hist. Eng. Lit.* 175 Travelling on the Continent—as agent for a glass-work.

2. The manufacture of glass and glass-ware. Also, the fitting of glass, glazing.

1611 COTGR., *Vitrage*, Glasse, Glasse-worke or Glasing worke. **1662** MERRET tr. *Neri's Art of Glass* 1 The foundation of the Art of Glass-work. **1883** *B'ham Daily Post* 11 Oct., Plumbers.—Wanted, few good men, used to Glass-work.

3. Vessels, utensils, and other articles made of glass; glass as a manufactured article.

1725 DE FOE *Voy. round World* (1840) 94 Glass-work, looking-glasses, and drinking-glasses. **1819** REES *Cycl.* s.v. *Glass-case*, The front, top, and both ends being of glass-work. **1897** *Worc. County Express* 3 Apr., A particular class of work of a certain size, called small glass work.

4. *slang.* A method of cheating at cards by means of a small convex mirror concealed in the palm of the hand (Farmer *Slang* 1893).

So '**glass-,worker**, one who works in glass or is engaged in the manufacture of glass.

1842 FRANCIS *Dict. Arts*, *Glass-worker's table*, a table fitted up with double bellows, blow-pipe, jet, lamp, &c. for the use of those who manufacture small articles in glass. **1878** *Ure's Dict. Arts* (ed. 7) IV. 91 It must be left to practical glass-workers to determine whether [etc.].

glasswort ('glɑːswɜːt, -æ-). A name for certain plants containing a large amount of alkali, and on that account formerly used in the manufacture of glass. **a.** A plant of the genus *Salicornia*, esp. *S. herbacea*; called also ***jointed glasswort.*** **b.** *Salsola Kali*; called also ***prickly glasswort.***

1597 GERARDE *Herbal* II. cxlvii. 429 *Salicornia*, Glassewoort, or Saltwoort.. The herbe is also called of diuers *Kali articulatum*, or iointed Glassewoort. **1640** PARKINSON *Theat. Bot.* 1284 *Kali spinosum*, Prickly Glassewort. **1646** SIR T. BROWNE *Pseud. Ep.* II. v. 84 Fine sand, and the ashes of glassewort or fearne [the ingredients of glass]. **1742** *Phil. Trans.* XLII. 71 The Salt of Glass-wort (called in England Barillia). **1775** R. TWISS *Trav. Port. & Sp.* 216 Ships loading wines, salt and glass-wort. **1854** H. MILLER *Sch. & Schm.* (1858) 397 The fleshy, jointed stems of the glass-wort. **1861** S. THOMSON *Wild Fl.* III. (ed. 4) 213 The much-branched but leafless glasswort (*Salicornia herbacea*). **1862** ANSTED *Channel Isl.* II. viii. (ed. 2) 177 The salt-wort or glass-wort (*salsola kali*), grows freely on most of the shores.

glassy ('glɑːsɪ, -æ-), *a.* and *sb.*[1] In 4–6 glasy; 6–7 glassie. [f. GLASS *sb.*[1] + -Y[1].

Glassy is not phonetically identical with the earlier *glasy* (cf. GLAZY *a.* 1), but a distinct new formation.]

A. *adj.* **1. a.** Having the nature or properties of glass, vitreous; resembling glass in any of its conspicuous properties; appearing as if made of glass.

†*glassy phlegm*: (= med.L. *fleuma vitreum*, see quot. 1398).

1398 TREVISA *Barth. De P.R.* IV. ix. (1495) 94 Some flewmes ben glasy and ben soo callyd for liknesse of colour of glasse. **1530** PALSGR. 314/1 Glasye of the nature of glasse, *voierreux*. **1593** SHAKS. *Lucr.* 102. **1612** WOODALL *Surg. Mate* Wks. (1653) 64 They help the collick proceeding from a glassie tough flegme. **1796** KIRWAN *Elem. Min.* (ed. 2) I. 168 Glassy actinolite. **1811** PINKERTON *Petral.* II. 627 The glassy quartz retains its natural consistence. **1821** *Examiner* 172/1 Her singing.. used.. to be occasionally too hard and glassy. **1823** F. CLISSOLD *Ascent Mt. Blanc* 23 The glassy pinnacles of the surrounding Alps. **1830** LYELL *Princ. Geol.* I. 333 This lava.. is remarkable for the glassy felspars which it contains. **1853** KANE *Grinnell Exp.* xxx. (1856) 258 We had to quarry out the blocks [ice] in flinty, glassy lumps. **1854** GOSSE *Nat. Hist., Mollusca* 71 The shell is glassy and colourless.

b. ***glassy humour*** (of the eye): now usually called the VITREOUS *humour* (see quot. 1727–41). ***glassy membrane*** (see quot. 1885).

1541 R. COPLAND *Guydon's Quest. Chirurg.* E iij b, Ye glasy humour that susteyneth & compryseth all the hyndre party of ye humour crystallyne. **1607** [see GLAZY *a*]. **1633** P. FLETCHER *Purple Isl.* v. 54 *note*, The third.. is called the glassie humour. **1665** HOOKE *Microgr.* 178 Resembling the watry or glassie humours of the eye. **1727–41** CHAMBERS *Cycl.* s.v. *Humour*, The vitreous, or glassy humour, fills the posterior part of the eye; and is denominated from its resemblance of melted glass. **1885** *Syd. Soc. Lex.*, *Glassy membrane*, a hyaline membrane immediately outside the outer root-sheath of the hair-follicle.

c. *Path.* Of a surface: Hard and lustrous.

1822–34 *Good's Study Med.* (ed. 4) II. 480 The surface [of a wound] continues glassy with a display of pale and flabby granulations. **1835–6** TODD *Cycl. Anat.* I. 462/2 The skin is pale and glassy and stretched.

d. Of properties, etc.: Resembling what pertains to glass.

1634 PEACHAM *Gentl. Exerc.* I. xxiv. 84 A Glassie Gray. *c* **1790** IMISON *Sch. Art* II. 150 The composition will.. appear of a most beautiful bright, and glassy nature. **1840** E. E. NAPIER *Scenes & Sports For. Lands* II. App. 273 The cool glassy look a snake always has. **1882** B. HARTE *Flip* i, The glassy tinkle of water. **1884** *Congregationalist* June 493 The green glassy tints of the Viescher glacier.

†**e.** *fig.* Brittle or frail as glass. *Obs.*

[**1561** DAUS tr. *Bullinger on Apoc.* 473 It is called glassy because of the frailetie and bricklenes.] *a* **1591** R. GREENHAM *Wks.* (1599) 44 It is to be feared, that.. mens teaching will become glassie, bright and brittle. **1637** RUTHERFORD *Lett.* lxxxii. (1862) I. 209 Let them beware of glassy and slippery youth. **1642** R. CARPENTER *Experience* II. vii. 181 Come let us.. tell him of what weake and glassie matter he hath made us. **1649** T. FORD *Lusus Fort.* 43 Pleasures.. fitly are they compared to a Sea of glasse.. but alas! how soon is that glassie glory crack't! **1785** COWPER *Task* IV. 306 Snapping short The glassy threads with which the Fancy weaves Her brittle toils.

2. Of the eye, etc.: Having a fixed unintelligent look, lacking fire or life, dull.

1412–20 LYDG. *Chron. Troy* II. xvii, Yet they be as Iargaunt as a pye Right pale cheared with a glasye eye. **1815** BYRON *Hebrew Mel., Saul*, Death stood all glassy in his fixed eye. **1824** W. IRVING *T. Trav.* I. 28 Casting a glassy look about the apartment. **1831** MACAULAY in *Life & Lett.* (1880) I. 237 His eyes have an odd glassy stare. **1857** LIVINGSTONE *Trav.* vii. 144 Their fixed glassy eyes glare as if in anger.

3. Of water, etc.: **a.** Lustrous and transparent as glass. **b.** Having a surface like glass, smooth, unruffled. Hence also ***glassy calm, quiet.***

1535 COVERDALE *Rev.* xv. 2 And I sawe as it were a glassye see [**1382** WYCLIF a glasen see, **1611** a sea of glasse], mingled with fyre. **1589** GREENE *Menaphon* (Arb.) 41 Her tresses gold, her eyes like glassie streames. **1667** MILTON *P.L.* VII. 619 The clear hyaline, the glassy sea. **1781** COWPER *Truth* 259 His conscience, like a glassy lake before, Lashed into foaming waves, begins to roar. **1852** MRS. STOWE *Uncle Tom's C.* xxi, Pointing to the glassy water, which, as it rose and fell, reflected the golden glow of the sky. **1871** MACDUFF *Mem. Patmos* xix. 267 Stilled into a glassy calm. **1871** R. ELLIS *Catullus* iv. 24 All the weary way From outer ocean unto glassy quiet here.

†**4.** Of glass; made of or consisting of glass.

c **1440** *Promp. Parv.* 198/1 Glasy, or glasyne, or made of glas,.. *vitreus*. **1548** tr. *Papius conc. Apoth.* in Recorde *Urin. Physick* (1651) 234 That the matter.. bee poured forth into a glassie dish or platter. **1590** SPENSER *F.Q.* III. ii. 21 The glassy globe that Merlin made. **1611** COTGR., *Monstre*,.. the glassie box that stands on the stalls of Gold-smiths, Cutlers, &c. **1669** BOYLE *Contn. New Exp.* I. xi. 33 The Glassie part of this compounded Syphon. **1739** R. BULL tr. *Dedekind's Grobianus* 199 Of painted Earth a Vessel quickly take.. Or else a glassy Bowl, the brittler Ware. **1807** CRABBE *Par. Reg.* III. 363 A glassy globe, in frame of ivory, prest.

5. *Comb.*, as ***glassy-eyed, -headed, -smooth*** adjs.

1725 POPE *Odyss.* v. 500 Glassy smooth lay all the liquid plain. **1859** TENNYSON *Vivien* 618 A little glassy-headed hairless man. **1895** K. GRAHAME *Gold. Age* 183 A glassy-eyed, and stiff-kneed circle.

B. *sb.* *Surfing.* (See quot. 1967.)

1962 T. MASTERS *Surfing made Easy* 64 *Glassy*, smooth water, no wind, if the surf is up then the best of surfing conditions. **1965** J. POLLARD *Surfrider* ii. 20 Last week the surf was a 'glassy', no wind and the waves smooth. **1967** J. SEVERSON *Great Surfing* Gloss., *Glassy*, an extremely smooth surface or wave, usually giving off a glasslike reflection.

Hence **'glassily** *adv.*; **'glassiness.**

1611 COTGR., *Vitrification*, Glassinesse or the making of Glasse. **16..** PETTY in *Sprat's Hist. Roy. Soc.* (1667) 294 So Gum may give the Silk a glassiness, that is, may make it seem finer, as also stiffer. **1766** SMOLLETT *Trav.* xxxi. 230 The glassiness (if I may be allowed the expression) of the surface throws, in my opinion, a false light on some parts of the picture. *a* **1788** POTT *Chirurg. Wks.* II. 92 The eyes have now a languor and glassiness. **1811** *Self Instructor* 525 The frequent workings over of the crayons would cause glassiness. **1827** MOORE *Epicur.* viii. (1839) 67 Waters.. rolled glassily over the edge. **1851** D. JERROLD *St. Giles* xxiv. 251 He.. did nothing but slightly bow, and look glassily about him. **1871** PALGRAVE *Lyr. Poems* 5 Glassily lisping, lisping low, lisping amorously. **1884** A. T. WISE in *Q. Jrnl. R. Meteorol. Soc.* Oct. 214 In contrast with the glassiness of its tranquil waters. **1891** S. J. DUNCAN *Amer. Girl in Lond.* 108 The brassiness of the crowns, and the glassiness of the jewels.

glassy ('glɑːsɪ, -æ-), *sb.*[2] Also **glassey, glassie.** [f. GLASS *sb.*[1] + -Y[6].] A glass marble.

1887 T. DARLINGTON *Folk-Speech S. Cheshire* 203 *Glassey*, a marble or 'taw' made of glass of various colours. **1915** D. H. LAWRENCE *Rainbow* viii. 200 Then suddenly she ceased to hear, having caught sight of a glassie rolled into a corner. **1933** J. THORPE *Happy Days* i. 29 The owner of a 'glassy', which was decorated internally with beautifully twisted colours, placed it in the centre of the road. **1952** [see AGATE *sb.* 1 b].

†**'glaster,** *v.*[1] *Obs. rare.* [? Altered form of GLISTER, suggested by GLASS.] *intr.* To glitter.

1447 BOKENHAM *Seyntys* (Roxb.) 21 An huge dragon glasteryng as glas. *Ibid.*, His eyne glastryd as sterrys be nyht.

†**glaster,** *v.*[2] *Sc. Obs.* Also **glaister.** [Cf. GALSTRE.] *intr.* To bawl, hence to brag or boast.

1513 DOUGLAS *Æneis* VIII. Prol. 47 Sum glasteris, and thai gang at all for gayt woll. **1721** RAMSAY *Poems* I. Gloss., *Glaister*, to bawl or bark.

glastick, -ig, varr. GLAISTIG.

Glastonbury ('glɑːstənbərɪ, -æ-). [A town in Somersetshire, famed for its abbey.] Used *attrib.* in **Glastonbury chair**, a kind of arm-chair, designed in imitation of 'the Abbot of Glastonbury's chair' preserved in the Bishop's Palace at Wells (see drawing in Litchfield *Hist. Furniture* 78); **Glastonbury thorn**, a variety of hawthorn (see quot. 1879).

a **1691** AUBREY *Nat. Hist. Wilts* (1847) 57 Mr. Anthony Hinton.. did inoculate.. a bud of Glastonbury Thorne, on a thorne at his farm-house at Wilton, which blossomes at Christmas as the other did. **1733** MILLER *Gard. Dict.*, *Mespilus*.. The Glastenbury Thorn. **1853** *Cox & Sons' Acc. Ch. Ornaments*, etc. (1858) 17 Carved Glastonbury Chairs of the annexed design are manufactured at a very moderate price. **1868** EASTLAKE *Househ. Taste* ii. 57 As a rule, the 'Glastonbury' chairs and 'antique' bookcases sold in that venerable thoroughfare [Wardour St.] will prove.. to be nothing but gross libels on the style of art which they are supposed to represent. **1873** MISS BRADDON *Str. & Pilgr.* III. vi. 288 Seated in a Glastonbury chair within the shelter of the porch. **1879** BRITTEN & HOLLAND *Plant-n.*, *Glastonbury Thorn*, an early-flowering variety of *Cratægus Oxyacantha*, popularly supposed to have sprung up at Glastonbury from the staff of Joseph of Arimathea, and to produce its blossoms on Christmas-day.

‖**'glastum.** [L., a. OCeltic *glaston*, represented by Ir. Gael. *glas*, Welsh *glas*, bluish or greenish grey.] The plant woad (*Isatis*).

c **1540** tr. *Pol. Verg. Eng. Hist.* (Camden) I. I. 49 They smeered their face with an herbe called glastum.. This glastum being like unto plantaine.. is thought to bee that which is.. called.. vulgarlie in Englishe wode. **1670** W. SIMPSON *Hydrol. Ess.* 140 Dyers Woad or Glastum.

Glaswegian (glæ'swiːdʒ(ɪ)ən, glæz-), *sb.* and *a.* [f. *Glasgow*, after GALWEGIAN, NORWEGIAN.]

A. *sb.* A native or inhabitant of Glasgow. **B.** *adj.* Belonging to or characteristic of Glasgow or its inhabitants.

1818 SCOTT *Rob Roy* xxii, The Glaswegian took him by the hand. **1884** *Illustr. Lond. News* 12 Jan. 27/1 Any of the ten words.. in addition to the Glaswegian four. **1923** *Glasgow Herald* 15 Nov. 8 'Glaswegian' is both ugly and absurd... Let us in the name of etymology and common sense be Glasgovians. **1945** *Archit. Rev.* XCVII. 122/1 The fertility of these people will not be maintained when they become Glaswegians or Londoners. **1971** *Times* 26 Nov. 12/8 One of the tarts becomes Glaswegian. **1971** T. J. HONEYMAN *Art & Audacity* 247 In Pollok House there will be an abundance of riches for the art lover and scholar, and a magnetic attraction for Glaswegians and their visitors.

glasy, -are, -er(e, obs. ff. GLASSY, GLAZIER.

glasyn(e, var. GLASSEN *a.*

†**glat,** *a. Obs. rare*[−1]. [a. MDu. *glat* smooth (see GLAD).] Smooth.

1481 CAXTON *Reynard* (Arb.) 103 Thenne was his body also glat and slyper, that the wulf sholde haue none holde on hym.

glat, glath(e, obs. ff. GLEET *sb.*, GLAD.

†**'glattering,** *ppl. a. Obs.*[−1] = CLATTERING.

1638 F. JUNIUS *Paint. Ancients* 135 The Persians did not onely use their horses to the tingling sound of glattering armour,.. but they [etc.].

'glauber. Also 9 globar. Short for GLAUBER'S SALT(S.

1799 KIRWAN *Geol. Ess.* 374 Whether the bitterness proceeds from glauber, or muriated lime.. is not known. **1830** *Fraser's Mag.* I. 354, I hold in utter execration your sennas and globars.

glauberite ('glɔː-, 'glaʊbəraɪt). *Min.* [f. *Glauber* (see next) + -ITE.] Sulphate of calcium and sodium, found in white, grey, or reddish crystals, in association with salt rock.

1809 NICHOLSON *Jrnl.* XXIV. 65 The form of glauberite is that of an oblique prism. **1811** PINKERTON *Petral.* II. 50 *Glauberite*,.. A diamictonic rock, composed of quartz, impregnated with slate. **1884** DANA *Min.* 627.

Glauber's salt, -s. Also **Glauber salt, -s.** [Named after Johann Rudolf *Glauber*, a German chemist (1604–1668).] Sulphate of sodium. (It was first artificially made by Glauber in 1656.)

1736 BAILEY *Housh. Dict.* 503 If drink become thick.. put in a little fix'd nitre or Glaubers salt. **1761** STERNE *Let.* 28 July, Lett. 1894 I. 52 If you had not [etc.].. the glauber-salts could not have hurt. **1789** W. BUCHAN *Dom. Med.* (1790) 499 A dose or two of Glauber's salts, or some other cooling purge, may be taken. **1812** SIR H. DAVY *Chem. Philos.* 31 Glauber's salt, which consists of sulphuric acid and fossil alkali. **1856** *Farmer's Mag.* Jan. 29, I have.. tried Glauber salts in small doses of three ounces, with very great success. **1871** TYNDALL *Fragm. Sci.* (1879) I. xii. 357 A solution of common sulphate of soda or Glauber salt.

glaucescence (glɔː'sɛsəns). [f. next: see -ENCE. Cf. F. *glaucescence.*] The condition of being glaucescent.

1874 COUES *Birds N.W.* 639 The green of the bill with a peculiar hoary glaucescence. **18..** *Gardener's Assistant* (Ogilvie), Destitute of glaucescence or bloom.

glaucescent (glɔː'sɛsənt), *a. Bot.* [f. L. *glauc-us* (see GLAUCOUS) + -ESCENT. Cf. F. *glaucescent, -ente.*] Somewhat glaucous.

1829 LOUDON *Encycl. Plants* 1099 *Glaucescent* or *Glaucine*, having something of a bluish, hoary appearance. **1880** GRAY *Struct. Bot.* 413/2 *Glaucescent*, verging upon or becoming glaucous.

glaucic ('glɔːsɪk), *a. Chem.* [f. mod.L. *Glaucium* name of a genus of papaveraceous plants (L. *glaucion* celandine) + -IC.] ***glaucic acid***, 'an acid obtained from *Glaucium luteum*, identical with *Fumaric acid*' (*Syd. Soc. Lex.* 1885).

1844 HOBLYN *Dict. Med.*, *Glaucic acid*, an acid procured from the teazle and scabious plants.

glaucine ('glɔːsɪn), *a. Bot.* [f. L. *glauc-us* (see GLAUCOUS) + -INE.] = GLAUCESCENT.

1829 [see GLAUCESCENT]. Hence **1860** in WORCESTER; and in later Dicts.

†**'glaucitate,** *v. Obs. rare*[−0]. [f. L. *glaucitāre* to yelp: see -ATE.] (See quot.)

1623 COCKERAM, *Glaucitate*, to cry like a whelpe. **1681** in BLOUNT *Glossogr.*

glaucodot ('glɔːkədɒt). *Min.* Also **glaucodote, glaukodot.** [Named by Breithaupt 1849 in Ger. form *glaukodot*; said to be f. Gr. γλαυκός (see GLAUCOUS) + δοτήρ giver, the mineral being used in making smalt.] A sulph-arsenide of cobalt and iron, occurring in tin-white, orthorhombic crystals.

1850 DANA *Min.* 474 Glaucodot.. is essentially a cobaltic mispickel. **1861** BRISTOW *Gloss. Min.* 154 Glaucodot or glaucodote.

glaucolite ('glɔːkəlaɪt). *Min.* [f. Gr. γλαυκός (see GLAUCOUS) + -LITE.] A massive variety of wernerite of a bluish or greenish colour.

1827 in *Philos. Mag.* Ser. II. II. 463 *Glaucolite.* A new Mineral Species. **1868** DANA *Min.* (ed. 5) 320.

glaucoma (glɔː'kəʊmə). Also 7 **glaucome.** [a. Gr. γλαύκωμα, f. γλαυκός: see GLAUCOUS.] A disease of the eye, characterized by increased tension of the globe and gradual impairment or loss of vision. The word was formerly used to denote cataract (*Syd. Soc. Lex.* 1885).

1643 HERLE *Answ. Ferne* 2 Physicians tels us of a disease in the eye, called a Glaucome, whereby it sees every thing coloured, as the distemper of the aqueous humour. **1705** *Lond. Gaz.* No. 4185/3 An Obstruction in the Optick Nerves, and a Glaucoma. **1739** SHARP *Surg.* xxviii. 159 Since..the Glaucoma is no other Disease than the Cataract. **1879** P. SMITH *Glaucoma* 1 Primary glaucoma, though not rare, is one of the less common maladies of the eye. **1885** *Syd. Soc. Lex.* s.v., Brisseau, in 1705, established by his dissections the distinction between true glaucoma..and ordinary cataract, showing that the former was a disease of the vitreous body, and the latter of the crystalline lens.

fig. **1886** MORGAN DIX *Gospel & Philos.* 113 The moral confusion and intellectual glaucoma of the day.

attrib. **1879** *St. George's Hosp. Rep.* IX. 489 In the fifth glaucoma patient the affection was combined with old iritic and corneal trouble.

glaucomatic (glɔːkəʊˈmætɪk), *a.* [f. as next + -IC.] Of or pertaining to glaucoma.

1852 *Fraser's Mag.* XLVI. 91 Who..can ever know how much of grey and how much of green went to make up the glaucomatic hue of Minerva's iris. **1885** in *Syd. Soc. Lex.*

glaucomatous (glɔːˈkəʊmətəs, glɔːˈkɒmətəs), **glaucomatose** (-ətəʊs), *a.* [f. mod.L. *glaucōmat-* (stem of GLAUCOMA) + -OUS, -OSE.] Of, pertaining to, or affected with glaucoma.

1822–34 *Good's Study Med.* (ed. 4) III. 161 A glaucomatous eye. **1847** *Blackw. Mag.* LXII. 299 A glaucomatous state of the eye always precedes by some days the moult. **1854** MAYNE *Expos. Lex.*, *Glaucomatosus*,.. glaucomatose, or glaucomatous. **1879** *St. George's Hosp. Rep.* IX. 488 Symptoms indicative of recurring glaucomatous mischief.

glauco'niferous. [f. as next + -(I)FEROUS.] = GLAUCONITIC.

1852 *Q. Jrnl. Geol. Soc.* VIII. 290 The glauconiferous crag, or the dark green shelly sand of Antwerp.

glauconite (ˈglɔːkənaɪt). *Min.* [Named by Keferstein 1828 (in Ger. form *glaukonit*), f. Gr. γλαυκόν, neut. of γλαυκός adj. (see GLAUCOUS) + -ITE.] Hydrous silicate of iron, potassium, and other bases, commonly called green earth.

1836 T. THOMSON *Min.* I. 387 Glauconite is employed as a colour by painters. **1851** RICHARDSON *Geol.* (1855) 179 The glauconite, or fire-stone of the chalk formation. **1865** LYELL *Elem. Geol.* xvii. (ed. 6) 311 Marls and sands, often containing much green earth, called glauconite.

Hence **glauco'nitic** *a.*, containing or resembling glauconite.

1864 *Q. Jrnl. Geol. Soc.* XXI. 20 The Glauconitic sands—These sands are of a dark-green colour, and consist of glauconitic and arenaceous grains in a slightly argillaceous paste. **1879** RUTLEY *Study Rocks* xiv. 289 The lower portion, termed the grey chalk..is generally slightly glauconitic at the base.

glaucophane (ˈglɔːkəfeɪn). *Min.* [Named by Haussmann 1845 (in Ger. form *glaukophan*); f. Gr. γλαυκό-ς (see GLAUCOUS) + -φανής shining, f. root of φαίνειν to show.] A mineral closely resembling Amphibole.

1849 *Amer. Jrnl. Sci.* Ser. II. VIII. 123 Glaucophane comes from the island of the Cyclades. **1882** [see GASTALDITE].

glaucophyllous (glɔːkəʊˈfɪləs), *a.* [f. Gr. γλαυκός sea-green + φύλλον leaf + -OUS.] 'Having leaves of a sea-green or azure colour' (*Syd. Soc. Lex.* 1885).

glaucopicrine (ˌglɔːkəʊˈpɪkraɪn). *Chem.* [f. Gr. γλαυκό-ς (whence the botanical name *Glaucium*) + πικρός bitter + -INE.] A bitter alkaloid obtained from the root of alkaloid *Glaucium luteum*.

1847 in CRAIG.

† **glaucose**, *a. Obs.* [f. L. *glauc-us* + -OSE.] = GLAUCOUS.

1713 PETIVER in *Phil Trans.* XXVIII. 183 The Peculiarity in this Plant is its glaucose or frosty Heads. *Ibid.* 191 Its Leaves long, narrow, smooth and glaucose.

glaucosis (glɔːˈkəʊsɪs). [a. Gr. γλαύκωσις, f. γλαυκός: see next + -OSIS.] 'The origination of *Glaucoma*. Also, blindness from *Glaucoma*' (*Syd. Soc. Lex.* 1885).

1706 PHILLIPS (ed. Kersey), *Glaucoma*, or *Glaucosis*, a Fault in the Eye, when the Crystalline Humour is chang'd into a Gray, or Sky-colour. **1847** in CRAIG; and in mod. Dicts.

glaucous (ˈglɔːkəs), *a.* Chiefly *Nat. Hist.* [f. L. *glauc-us* (a. Gr. γλαυκός) bluish-green or grey + -OUS.] Of a dull or pale green colour passing into greyish blue; *spec.* in *Bot.* covered with 'bloom'.

1671 RAY in *Rem.* (1760) 182 The Leaves are small, of a Glaucous Colour. **1750** G. HUGHES *Barbadoes* 118 A reddish stalk, generally clouded over with a glaucous mealiness. **1816** SOUTHEY *Poets's Pilgr.* III. 26 The vigorous olive.. Tower'd high, and spread its glaucous foliage wide. **1820** SHELLEY *Prom. Unbd.* II. i. 44 Under the glaucous caverns of old ocean. **1862** SYMONDS in *Biog.* (1895) I. 202 The eyes are small, and very glaucous grey. **1863** BERKELEY *Brit. Mosses* iii. 17 The leaves vary from bright or glaucous green to.. brown, red or purple. **1864** THOREAU *Maine W.* iii. 270 The dark mountains..were seen through a glaucous mist. **1874** COUES *Birds N.W.* 420 Eggs of both these birds sometimes show a peculiar glaucous cast, something like the 'bloom' on a grape. **1880** GRAY *Struct. Bot.* 413/2 *Glaucous*, covered or whitened with a bloom, like that on a Cabbage leaf.

b. *glaucous gull*: a name for *Larus glaucus*, from the colour of its plumage.

1828 STARK *Elem. Nat. Hist.* I. 310 *Glaucous Gull.* The Burgomaster of the Dutch. Back, shoulders, and wing-coverts, bluish cinereous. **1878** A. H. MARKHAM *Gt. Frozen Sea* iv. 58 The glaucous gull and the pretty kittiwake soared above our heads.

‖**glaucus** (ˈglɔːkəs). [mod.L.; sense 1 echoes Pliny's use of L. *glaucus*, a. Gr. γλαῦκος, prob. a subst. use of γλαυκός adj. (see prec.); the other senses are direct applications of the L. adj.]

† **1.** Some kind of fish. *Obs.*

c **1520** ANDREW *Noble Lyfe* xv. in *Babees Bk.* 234 Glaucus is a whyte fissh that is but selden sene except in darke rayne weder. *a* **1529** SKELTON *Bk. 3 Foles* Wks. 1843 I. 203 More bytterer thenne the gall of the fyshe glauca. **1598** *Epulario* G j, To dresse a glaucus or *corbo grosso* fish. **1607** TOPSELL *Four-f. Beasts* (1658) 16 A fish called Glaucus, whereof the male swalloweth up all the young ones when they are endangered..and afterwards yeeldeth them forth again. **1706** PHILLIPS (ed. Kersey), *Glaucus*, the Sea-stickling, a sort of Fish; also the Sea-Blewling.

2. The burgomaster gull (*Larus glaucus*).

1785 LATHAM *Gen. Synopsis Birds* III. II. 374 Glaucus Gull. *Larus glaucus.* **1848** LYTTON *K. Arthur* IX. xxxvii, The ravening glaucus [*foot-note* The *Larus Glaucus*, the great bird of prey in the Polar regions]. **1862** —— *Str. Story* I. ii. 18 Rows of gigantic birds—ibis and vulture, and huge sea glaucus—glared at me.

3. 'A genus of nudibranchiate molluscs, found in the warmer latitudes, floating in the open sea, beautifully colored with blue' (Webster).

1847 in CRAIG. **1851–6** WOODWARD *Mollusca* 195 Glaucus. **1854** BUSHNAN in *Circ. Sci.* (*c.* 1865) II. 29/1 The Glaucus, a beautiful little mollusc, of the Indian Seas and Mediterranean, painted in blue and silver. **1883** *Harper's Mag.* Dec. 107/1 The fantastic glaucus and luminous salpa.

† **'glaucy**, *a. Obs. poet.* [irregularly f. L. *glaucus* (see GLAUCOUS) + -Y[1].] Of a glaucous hue; sea-green.

1593 B. BARNES *Parthenophil* Madrigal xvi. in Arb. *Garner* V. 398 Sleep Phœbus still, in glaucy Thetis' lap. **1596** FITZ-GEFFRAY *Sir F. Drake* (1881) 42 Their gallies..Made glaucie Nereus groane, and seeme to shrinke.

† **'glaudkin.** *Obs.* In 6 glaudkyn. [The word might be read as *glandkyn*, but the etymology is unknown.] Some kind of cloak or gown.

1518 *Househ. Accts. Hen. VIII* in Harl. MS. 2284 lf. 16 Delyuerd..xvii yerdes of yelowe cloth of gold for lynyng of a glaudkyn of purpull veluete opon veluete purled, for the kinges grace. *Ibid.*, Delyuerd..xxj yerdes quarter of white cloth of siluer, cutt and poynted opon cloth of gold, with a border of gold Richely enbrauded, for a glaudkyn with wyde slyves for the kinges grace. *Ibid.* lf. 25, lf. 33 b. ? **1527** in Harl. MS. 4217 leaves 2–4 (*headings*).

glaum (glɔːm), *v. Sc.* Also **glam.** *intr.* To snatch *at* (a thing). Also, to make threatening movements.

1715 *Sherrifmuir* in *Jacobite Songs* (1887) 96 The cluds O'clans frae woods in tartan duds Wha glaum'd at kingdoms three, man. **1819** W. TENNANT *Papistry Storm'd* (1827) 39 He beheld ilk bishop's claw Glaum at his fish and cleik them a'. **1823** GALT *R. Gilhaize* II. iii. 26 He had fearful visions of bloody hands and glimmering daggers glaming over him from behind his curtains. **1823** ELIZA LOGAN *St. Johnstoun* III. vi. 145 He might hae glammed at our royal crown itsel'.

glaum, glaumerie: see GLAM[2], GLAMOURY.

glaunce, glaunse, obs. forms of GLANCE *v.*

glaur, glave, vars. GLAR, GLAIVE.

† **'glaver**, *sb. Obs. rare.* Also **glavir.** [Cf. CLAVER.] Chatter; loud noise.

13.. *Gaw. & Gr. Knt.* 1426 þenne such a glauerande [? *read* glaver and; *cf. next quot.*] glam of gedered rachchez Ros. *a* **1400–50** *Alexander* 5504 And þar in an Ilee he heres A grete glauir & a glaam of grekin tongis.

† **'glaver**, *v. Obs.* [Of obscure origin; Ray *North-country Words* has an adj. '*glave* or *glafe*, smooth', of which this may be a derivative; see -ER[5]. This is plausible with regard to the sense, but the genuineness of the adj. requires confirmation, and it has no obvious etymology, unless it be an altered adoption of ON. *glað-r* GLAD. Cf. the synonymous vb. GLOTHER. The Welsh *glafru* to flatter is prob. from English.]

1. *trans.* To flatter, deceive with flattery.

13.. *E.E. Allit. P.* A. 688 þat takez not her lyfe in vayne Ne glauerez her nieȝbor wyth no gyle. **1594** BARNFIELD *Affect. Sheph.* (Arb.) 23 Beare not a flattring tongue to glauer anie.

2. *intr.* To talk plausibly and deceitfully; to flatter. ***to glaver on*** or ***upon***: to lavish blandishments upon.

1380 WYCLIF *Wks.* (1880) 330 Hou-euer antecrist glauer, he letteþ not god to do his wille. **1508** FISHER 7 *Penit. Ps.* xxxviii. Wks. (1876) 75 They glauer and prayse it so moche that anone we synne in vaynglory. **1579** J. STUBBES *Gaping Gulf* E vj, It is a very french popish woeng, to sende hyther smooth tongued Simiers to glose and glauer & hold talk of mariage. **1609** HOLLAND *Amm. Marcell.* XXVII. xi. 322 He [Probus] was..smiling also after a bitter sort; yea and glavering [L. *blandiens*] otherwhiles upon a man to do him harme. **1643** BURROUGHES *Exp. Hosea* xix. (1652) 468 Those who will glaver upon you, and seem as if their hearts were with you. **1681** H. MORE *Exp. Dan.* Pref. 37 Partly to glaver and curry favour with the Pontifician party.

Hence † **'glavering** *vbl. sb.* Also † **'glaverer.**

c **1425** *St. Mary of Oignies* II. v. in *Anglia* VIII. 165/26 Made proude wiþ glauerynge of prosperite. *Ibid.* 168/36 Pryde gaf me comforte..wiþ brighte beemes of glauerynge. **1544** BALE *Chron. Sir J. Oldcastle* in *Harl. Misc.* (Malh.) I. 256 He had bene falsely informed by his hired spyes, and other glosing glauerers. **1545** JOYE *Exp. Dan.* iv. G iv b, Princes eyres corrupt with the gloriouse glavering of flatterers. **1598** MARSTON *Satyre* I. 137 For shame..Leaue glauering on him in the peopled presse. **1689** J. SCOTT *Serm.* Wks. 1718 II. 87 To carry ourselves at an equal distance from contempt and haughtiness on the one hand and sneaking and glavering on the other. **1706** E. WARD *Hud. Rediv.* (1707) II. xi. 7 The hypocritick Cant And pious Glav'rings of a Saint.

'glavering, *ppl. a. Obs.* exc. *arch.* [f. GLAVER *v.* + -ING[2].] That 'glavers'; deceitful, flattering.

c **1394** *P. Pl. Crede* 51 þat wicked folke..bigileþ hem of her good wiþ glauerynge wordes. ? *a* **1400** *Morte Arth.* 2538 Siche glauerande gomes greues me bot lyttille. **1563–87** FOXE *A. & M.* (1596) 1423/1 The Chauncellor with a glauering and smiling countenance, called to the Bishop. **1601** B. JONSON *Poetaster* III. iv. (1602) F 3 b, Giue him warning, Admonition, to forsake his sawcy glauering Grace. **1670** STUCLEY *Gospel-Glass* xxv. 242 A glavering tongue and seeming affection to our Neighbours good. **1694** R. L'ESTRANGE *Fables* 90 A glavering Council is as dangerous on the one hand, as a wheedling Priest..is on the other. *a* **1716** SOUTH *Serm.* (1717) VI. 121 Some slavish, glavering, flattering Parasite. **17..** FIELDING *Ess. Char. Men* Wks. 1771 VIII. 164 A constant, settled, glavering, sneering smile in the countenance, is so far from indicating goodness, that [etc.]. **1753** *Gray's Inn Jrnl.* (1756) II. 10 Drawn in by false Allurements and a glavering Smile. **1866** *Athenæum* 7 July 23/3 The doorkeeper is a wily, elderly Italian..He..holds his face forwards, and looks down, with a steady glavering smile, or simper, in the corners of his mouth.

b. *fig.* of things.

1581 J. BELL *Haddon's Answ. Osor.* 466 b, Such as in tymes past did persequute the Gospell of Christ..being seduced by glauering conceipt of colorable error. **1609** BP. W. BARLOW *Answ. Namless Cath.* 363 Whom this Censurer heere vouchsafeth to besmeare with his glauering balme.

† **'glavery.** *Obs. rare*[−1]. [f. GLAVER *v.* + -Y[3].] Flattery.

1584 BABINGTON *Frailty & Faith* (1596) 37 In all orations ..honest plainenesse was euer an argument of fauour and succour, and hollow smoothing glauerie a note of reproch.

glavir, var. GLAVER, *sb.*, *Obs.*

† **glawke**, *a. Obs. rare*[−1]. [ad. L. *glauc-us.* See GLAUCOUS *a.*] Blue or grey.

1412–20 LYDG. *Chron. Troy* II. xv, With eyen glawke, large, stepe, and great.

glawnse, obs. form of GLANCE *v.*[1]

glaxe: see GLAIKS.

† **glay.** *Obs.* ? Altered form of GLAIVE.

1568 T. HOWELL *Arb. Amitie* 31 b, I see full plaine, that some whose paine, haue hoorded riches great: By sodaine glay, are whipt away, for paines no fruite they get.

† **glaye**, pseudo-dial. form of CLAY.

1575 *Gammer Gurton* I. ii, Gogs bones thys vylthy glaye has drest mee to bad.

glaye, obs. form of GLEE *v.*

glayfe, glayk(it, obs. ff. GLAIVE, GLAIK(IT.

glaym, var. GLEIM *v.*, *Obs.*, to smear.

glaymore, obs. form of CLAYMORE.

glaymous, glaymy, var. GLEIMOUS, -Y.

glayre, glayve, obs. ff. GLAIR, GLARE, GLAIVE.

glaze (gleɪz), *sb.* [f. GLAZE *v.*[1]; the sb. is not in Johnson.]

1. The vitreous composition used for glazing pottery, etc.

1807 T. THOMSON *Chem.* (ed. 3) II. 493 The glaze employed to cover vessels of stoneware may be distinguished into three kinds. **1839** URE *Dict. Arts* 1016 When it reaches the melting point of the glaze. **1881** *Porcelain Works, Worcester* 15 The materials for the Glaze of English porcelain are ground flint, Cornish stone, borax, lead, &c.

2. *gen.* A transparent substance used for coating anything, so as to produce a glazed or lustrous surface. *spec.* in *Cookery* (see quot. 1877); also ***of a glaze***, of the consistency of glaze.

1784 MRS. GLASSE *Cookery* ii. 74 (*Fowl à la Braise*) Strain the sauce, and after you have skimmed off the fat, boil it down till it is of a glaze. **1877** *Cassell's Dict. Cookery*, *Glaze* is made from clear stock, boiled down until it forms a sort of meat varnish or strong jelly; it is used to improve the appearance of many dishes. **1880** *Print. Trades Jrnl.* No. 30. 39 Mix with glaze slightly diluted.

3. A smooth and glossy surface, a bright polished appearance.

1791 COWPER *Iliad* XVIII. 741 Glossy as the glaze of oil. **1845** MISS ACTON *Mod. Cookery* xvi. 335 The fine yellow glaze appropriate to meat pies is given with beaten yolk of egg. **1879** *Cassell's Techn. Educ.* IV. 223/1 The result is a beautiful transparent glaze. **1881** GREENER *Gun* 313 Dense hard powder will take a higher glaze than the softer kinds.

4. *U.S.* A coating or covering of ice; also, a stretch of ice.

1752 J. MACSPARRAN *Amer. Dissected* (1753) 39, I rode 30 Miles upon one continued Glaze of Ice upon the Land. **1796** MORSE *Amer. Geog.* I. 215 Whenever the winter..sets in with rain, so as to cover the branches and leaves of trees with a glaze of ice. **1853** KANE *Grinnell Exp.* xxviii. (1856) 229 Old seasoned hummock, covered with a slippery glaze. **1858** THOREAU *Maine W.* (1894) 187 They [moose] cannot run on a 'glaze', though they can run in snow four feet deep; but the caribou can run on ice.

5. *Painting.* A thin coat of transparent colour laid over another colour so as to modify the tone.

1860 RUSKIN *Mod. Paint.* V. VIII. iv. 193 *note*, In cleaning the 'Hero and Leander'..these upper glazes were taken off and only the black ground left. **1885** *Mag. Art* Sept. 471/2 The employment..of glazes which are dull and have little more reflective power than paint.

6. *slang.* A window. *on, upon the glaze*: robbing jewellers' shops after smashing the windows.

a **1700** B. E. *Dict. Cant. Crew, Glaze*, the Window. **1719** ALEX. SMITH *Lives Highwaymen* II. 43 At Dublin, he [Jack Waldron] went upon the Glaze, which is robbing Goldsmiths Shew-Glasses on their Stalls, by cutting them ..with a Glazier's Diamond; or else waiting for a Coach coming by, breaking 'em with the hand. **1743** *Discov. J. Poulter* (ed. 2) 39 Undub the Jeger, and jump the Glaze. **1823** MONCRIEFF *Tom & Jerry* III. ii, *Jerry.* What are you about, Tom? *Tom.* I'm going to mill the glaze—I'll —— (Is about to break the Glass, when [etc.]).

7. *attrib.* and *Comb.*, as *glaze liquor*; **glaze-ice** *U.S.*, thin surface ice; **glaze-kiln**, a kiln in which glazed ware is placed for firing; **glaze-wheel**, a wooden wheel used by cutlers for polishing knives, etc.; **glaze-work** = GLAZING *vbl. sb.*; **glaze-worm** [? f. GLAZE *v.*[1]], a glow-worm: cf. *glassworm*.

1896 *N.Y. Weekly Witness* 23 Dec. 4/1 Much of the ice was *glaze-ice. **1839** URE *Dict. Arts* 1015 **Glaze-kiln.* This is usually smaller than the biscuit kiln. *Ibid.* 1017 The piece of ware..is immersed in the *glaze liquor. **1853** O. BYRNE *Handbk. Artizan* 451 The cutlers' wood or *glaze wheels are mostly fed with emery cake. **1799** G. SMITH *Laboratory* I. 190 Colours for potters' *glaze-work. **1579** LYLY *Euphues* (Arb.) 91 Dost thou not know yat a perfect friend should be like the *Glaze-worme, which shineth most bright in the Dark? **1895** *E. Angl. Gloss., Glaze-worm*, glow-worm.

glaze (gleɪz), *v.*[1] Forms: 4-5 glase-n, (5 glacyn, glaysse), 4-7 glase, 6- glaze. [ME. *glasen*, f. *glas* GLASS *sb.*[1] Cf. MHG. *glasen*, and GLASS *v.*]

1. *trans.* To fit or fill in (a window, etc.) with glass, to furnish (a building) with windows of glass, to cover (a picture, etc.) with glass. *to glaze in*: to enclose with glass. †*to glaze one's houve*: to provide with a head-covering of glass, hence app. to mock, delude, befool (see HOUVE).

1362 LANGL. *P. Pl.* A. III. 50 Woldustow glase the gable and graue therinne thi nome, Siker schulde thi soule ben for to dwellen in heuene. *c* **1369** CHAUCER *Dethe Blaunche* 323 With glas Were all the wyndowes well yglased. *c* **1374** —— *Troylus* v. 469 Fortune his howve entended bet to glase [cf. II. 867]. *c* **1440** *Promp. Parv.* 198/1 Glasyn' wythe glasse, *vitro, vel vitrio.* **1509** HAWES *Past. Pleas.* XVII. x, The rofe was wrought, curyously and well; The wyndowes glased marvaylously to tell. **1577** HARRISON *England* II. xii. (1877) I. 237 The houses of our princes..were often glased with Berill. **1601** CORNWALLYES *Ess.* II. xxxvi. (1631) 123 The soule hath nothing, no not her windowes glased. **1631** WEEVER *Anc. Funeral Mon.* 406 Raph Astrie..new roofed this Church..and beautifully glased it. **1667** PRIMATT *City & C. Build.* 83 For glasing the two windows. **1756-7** tr. *Keysler's Trav.* (1760) II. 162 This instrument is subscribed by John Codurz..and some others. It is glased for its better preservation, it being certainly a piece which should by all means be transmitted to posterity. **1774** GOLDSM. *Nat. Hist.* (1776) VIII. 53 The windows are so well glazed, as not to admit the least air. **1837** HT. MARTINEAU *Soc. Amer.* ii. 204 Persons..have baskets of glass of various sizes sent to them from the towns, and glaze their own windows. **1851** *Illustr. Catal. Gt. Exhib.* 668 Greater facility for repairing or glazing than those [lamps] of the ordinary sort. **1878** BROWNING *Poets Croisic* li, Somebody saw a portrait framed and glazed At Croisic. **1885** *Times* (weekly ed.) 11 Dec. 17/2 The back wall on either side of the central door is glazed in and forms a case in which is arranged a vast collection of ancient arms and armour.

2. To cover (the surface of pottery, etc.) with a vitreous substance which is fixed by fusion. Also, to vitrify the surface of.

c **1400** *Lanfranc's Cirurg.* 187 Sette hem..in a vessel of erþe glasid wiþinne. **1460-70** *Bk. Quintessence* 5 Take what vessel of glas þat ȝe wole, or of erþe strongly glasid. **1563** HYLL *Art Garden.* (1593) 97 A newe earthen pot not glased. *a* **1691** BOYLE *Wks.* (1744) I. 207/2 An ore, which for its aptness to vitrify, and serve the potters to glaze their earthern vessels, the miners call pottern-ore. **1719** DE FOE *Crusoe* (1840) I. ix. 143, I had no notion..of glazing them [pots] with lead. **1764** HARMER *Observ.* IX. iii. 100 Green and blue bricks which are glazed, so that when the sun shines, the eye is perfectly dazzled. **1825** J. NICHOLSON *Operat. Mechanic* 483 The bamboo, or cane-coloured pottery..is never glazed outside. **1845** DARWIN *Voy. Nat.* xvii. 373 A few fragments of granite, curiously glazed and altered by the heat. **1881** *Porcelain Works, Worcester* 27 The process of glazing is simple, but requires a practised hand so that every piece may be equally glazed.

b. *fig.* To cover as with a glaze, to gloss *over*.

1605 CHAPMAN *All Fooles* II. i. D 1 b, The fond world Like to a doting Mother glases ouer Her childrens imperfections with fine tearmes. **1712** STEELE *Spect.* No. 443 ¶4 By putting forth base Methods in a good Light, and glazing them over with improper Terms.

c. To fix (paint) *on* pottery by this process. Similarly (*nonce-use*), to throw (light) like a glaze *on*

1807 T. THOMSON *Chem.* II. 503 The vessel being now baked, the paint is glazed on. *a* **1861** T. WOOLNER *My Beautiful Lady* (1863) 35 Her window now is darkness, save the sheen Glazed on it by the moon.

3. To overlay or cover with a smooth and lustrous coating. Also, to cover (the eyes) with a film.

1593 SHAKS. *Rich. II*, II. ii. 16 For sorrowes eye, glazed with blinding teares, Diuides one thing intire, to many obiects. **1613** HEYWOOD *Silver Age* I. Wks. 1874 III. 92 That I may glaze my harpe in the bloud Of Tyrant Pretus. **1632** —— *1st Pt. Iron Age* II. ibid. 293 A field glazd with swords. **1653** *Cloria & Narcissus* I. 90 Thus he continued glasing his sight, all the while, with the troubled water of sorrowfull teares. **1666** J. DAVIES *Hist. Caribby Isl.* 121 The delightful smoothness wherewith they [Venus-shells] are glaz'd both within and without. **1687** A. LOVELL *Thevenot's Trav.* II. 63 A great Plain of very smooth whitish ground, glazed over with Salt. **1773** COOK *Voy.* (1777) I. II. iii. 219 As they have a method of glazing it [cloth], it is more durable, and will resist rain for some time, which Otaheite cloth will not. **1798** COLERIDGE *Anc. Mar.* III. i, Each throat was parched, and glazed each eye. **1810** SCOTT *Lady of L.* III. viii, Till darkness glazed his eyeballs dim. **1842** TENNYSON *Locksley Hall* 51 His eyes are heavy: think not they are glazed with wine. **1845** MISS ACTON *Mod. Cookery* xvi. 335 To glaze or ice pastry. **1885** *Manch. Exam.* 5 June 5/6 Messrs. Farmer's apparatus..for chasing, glazing, and embossing cloth. **1897** C. T. DAVIS *Manuf. Leather* (ed. 2) 613 Tawed leather..is glazed in the same manner..with the exception that the glazing fluid is applied twice.

fig. **1879** GEO. ELIOT *Theo. Such* 137 Some minds seem well glazed by nature against the admission of knowledge.

b. *esp.* of frost, etc. Also with *over, up.*

1627 MAY *Lucan* I. 20 Where winter..With lasting cold doth glaze the Scythian seas. **1638** COWLEY *Love's Riddle* IV. Wks. 1711 III. 118 Where a perpetual Winter binds the Ground And glazeth up the Floods? **1725** POPE *Odyss.* XIV. 537 Snow whitening all the fields Froze with the blast, and gath'ring glaz'd our shields. **1746-7** HERVEY *Medit.* (1818) 182 Cold, whose icy breath glazed yearly the Russian seas. **1853** KANE *Grinnell Exp.* xxii. (1856) 179 The sound presented a novel spectacle to us; the young ice glazing it over. **1883** E. PENNELL-ELMHIRST *Cream Leicestersh.* 337 A sharp wind-frost had..glazed the fallows.

4. *Painting.* To cover (a painted surface) with a thin coat of a different transparent colour, so as to modify the tone without mixing. Also, to lay (a transparent colour) *over* another.

1622 PEACHAM *Compl. Gentl.* xiii. (1634) 133 When it is dry glaze it over with a little Lake. **1658** W. SANDERSON *Graphice* 83 All Stones..must be glazed upon silver, with their proper colours, with a varnish. **1672** BEALE in H. Walpole *Vertue's Anecd. Paint.* (1782) III. 128 He glazed the whole place, where the face and haire were drawn in a colour over thin. **1695** DRYDEN tr. *Du Fresnoy's Art Paint.* Observ. ¶382 White with other strong Colours, with which we paint at once that which we intend to glaze, are as it were the Life, the Spirit, and the Lustre of it. **1798** *Trans. Soc. Arts* XVI. 298, I glazed the proper colours over it. **1846** RUSKIN *Mod. Paint.* (1848) I. II. II. ii. §17. 166 Red..mixed with the pure blue, or glazed over it.

5. To make to shine like glass; to give a smooth glassy surface to (anything), *esp.* by rubbing; to polish, to render brilliant.

c **1440** *Promp. Parv.* 197/1 Glacyn or make a þy(n)ge to shyne, *pernitido.* **1515** BARCLAY *Egloges* II. (1570) B i/1 For lacke of vsing, a sworde earst glased bright With rust is eaten. **1599** MARSTON *Sco. Villanie* III. viii. 211 He..Lyes streaking brawny limmes in weakning bed, Perfum'd, smooth kemb'd, new glaz'd. **1599** B. JONSON *Cynthia's Rev.* III. ii, There stands a neophyte glazing of his face, Pruning his clothes, perfuming of his hair, Against his idol enters. **1639** in *Proc. Soc. Antiq.* Ser. II. XIV. 373 Blacke Marble ritchly glaszd. **1648** BOYLE *Seraph. Love* (1660) 155 Like polish'd Silver, or well glaz'd Arms. **1715** LEONI *Palladio's Archit.* (1742) I. 10 Polishing and glazing even to the very Channelling or Flutes of the Columns. **1760** STERNE *Tr. Shandy* III. xlii, So worn, so glazed..was it with fingers. **1846** GREENER *Sci. Gunnery* 240 You may glaze powder and make it so smooth that it would be very difficult to ignite. **1881** —— *Gun* 313 The next process is to glaze or polish the individual grains [of gunpowder].

b. *Cutlery manufacture.* (See quot.)

1888 *Sheffield Gloss., Glaze*, to roughly polish a knife. This is an intermediate process between grinding and polishing.

6. *intr.* To become glazed, assume a glassy appearance.

1747 MRS. GLASSE *Cookery* i. 30 Put in a Ladleful of Gravy, boil it and strain it..and then put in the Sweet-breads to glaze. **1883** H. GEORGE *Soc. Probl.* ix. (1884) 119 What shall it matter, when eyeballs glaze and ears grow dull, if [etc.]. **1889** *Opelousas* (Louisiana) *Democrat* Dec., The crop is usually cut for ensilage purposes when the ears are commencing to 'glaze'. **1895** *Ramshorn* (Chicago) 8 June 3 Gradually his eyes glazed and closed.

glaze, *v.*[2] *Obs.* exc. *dial.* [Cf. GAZE, GLARE.] *intr.* To stare.

1601 SHAKS. *Jul. C.* I. iii. 21 Against the Capitoll I met a Lyon Who glaz'd vpon me, and went surly by. *a* **1816** WOLCOT (P. Pindar) *Middlesex Election* i. Wks. 1816 IV. 172 O Lord, my lord, I'm in a maze, I do so look about and glaze. **1880** *E. Cornw. Gloss., Glaze*, to stare.

glazed ('gleɪzd), *ppl. a.* [f. GLAZE *v.*[1] + -ED[1].]

1. Furnished or filled in with glass; fitted with windows of glass; covered with a piece of glass.

1591 PERCIVALL *Sp. Dict.*, *Vidriado*, glased. **1630** *R. Johnson's Kingd. & Commw.* 291 A faire glazed window. **1638** PENKETHMAN *Artach.* L iij b, My Studie or glazed Shop against the Rolls. **1664** EVELYN *Kal. Hort.* (1729) 207 Covering the Head and the rest of the Tree above, with a glaz'd Frame. **1667** MILTON *P.L.* III. 590 A spot like which perhaps Astronomer..Through his glaz'd Optic Tube yet never saw. **1849** JAMES *Woodman* iv, Two larger houses.. had glazed windows. **1883** GILMOUR *Mongols* xxxii. 368 A framed and glazed table, hung up conspicuously, where every traveller may see the exact amount payable.

2. Coated with a vitreous or glassy surface.

1662 MERRETT tr. *Neri's Art of Glass* xviii, Glased pans. **1663** GERBIER *Counsel* 90 Black glased Holland pan tiles. **1747** MRS. GLASSE *Cookery* xvi. 146 A glazed Jug with a long Neck. **1824** W. IRVING *T. Trav.* I. 58 A great fireplace, with the whole Bible history in glazed tiles. **1842** PARNELL *Chem. Anal.* (1845) 404 The mass..is..carefully powdered in a glazed mortar.

3. a. Having a smooth shining surface, produced either by a coating substance or by friction, etc.; made glassy in appearance. Also, in *Painting*, of colours: Covered with a 'glaze' of another colour. (See GLAZE *v.* 2, 3, 4, 5.)

1530 [see GLAZEDNESS]. **1608** MIDDLETON *Fam. Love* II. ii. B 4 a, The iocund morne lookes more liuely and fresh, then an oulde gentlewomans glaz'd face in a new perriwigge. **1695** DRYDEN tr. *Dufresnoy's Art Paint.* Observ. ¶382 Glaz'd Colours have a Vivacity which can never be imitated by the..most brilliant Colours. **1719** DE FOE *Crusoe* I. xiii, Two pounds of glazed powder. **1726** LEONI *Alberti's Archit.* I. 35 Sea-sand..the blackest and most glazed is not wholly to be despis'd. **1747** MRS. GLASSE *Art of Cookery* iii. 54 Glazed Fish. **1800** tr. *Lagrange's Chem.* I. 235 There are two kinds of gunpowder: that used in war, and that used for shooting game; the former is coarser, and not glazed; the latter is glazed, and much finer. **1814** CARY *Dante's Inf.* XXXIII. 125 The glazed tear-drops that o'erlay mine eyes. **1824** BYRON *Juan* XV. lxv, They also set a glazed Westphalian ham on. **1832** BABBAGE *Econ. Manuf.* xi. (ed. 3) 90 The glazed calico is now passed between the rollers. **1840** DICKENS *Old C. Shop* iv, Men in glazed hats and round jackets. **1845** MRS. CARLYLE *Lett.* I. 352 Written on glazed paper. **1875** KNIGHT *Dict. Mech., Glazed Board*, a kind of mill-board having a hard, smooth surface, to give a smooth face to the paper or fabric pressed between such boards.

b. Of the eye (see GLAZE *v.*[1] 3). Also *Path.* of the tongue, of the surface of a wound, etc.

1735 SOMERVILLE *Chase* I. 375 With heavy Eyes Glaz'd, lifeless, dull. **1822** B. CORNWALL *Sicilian Story* xix. 6 Settled Madness in her glazed eye Told of a young heart wronged. **1822-34** *Good's Study Med.* (ed. 4) I. 554 In some examples of fully developed typhus, where the tongue was glazed, dry and brown. **1840** LISTON *Elem. Surg.* II. 766 Farther dressing is delayed for six or eight hours, when the oozing has entirely ceased, and the visible cut surface becomes glazed. **1889** JESSOPP *Coming of Friars* iv. 197 A subordinate..finishing the work which his master's glazed eye perhaps never rested on.

c. *glazed frost* (see quot.).

1889 *Daily News* 25 Dec. 2/4 In the year 1808 the phenomenon of 'glazed frost' was observed, the rain freezing as it touched the ground.

d. *Metallurgy.* Having a smooth shining surface or fracture owing to a high silicon content (in the case of pig-iron) or fusion of the surface (in the case of blister steel).

1874 W. H. GREENWOOD *Man. Metallurgy* I. ix. 160 Aired and glazed bars are unfit for melting into best cast-steel, and require reconverting. **1884** —— *Steel & Iron* iv. 55 The excess of fuel employed when first blowing in a furnace often results in the metal first tapped being more highly siliceous than that produced in subsequent workings, and..the siliceous pig known as glazed or blazed pig often results. **1923** HARBORD & HALL *Metall. Steel* (ed. 7) I. x. 245 Sometimes..the pots become too highly heated, with the result that the surface of the bars is slightly fused, and these are known as 'glazed bars'. **1967** A. K. OSBORNE *Encycl. Iron & Steel Industry* (ed. 2) 182 *Glazed pig*, pig iron containing a very high silicon content, e.g. 5%, which gives a very fine grained lustrous fracture.

†**4.** ? *fig.* Brilliant, splendid. *Obs.*

a **1550** *Treat. Galaunt* 69 in Hazl. *E.P.P.* III. 154 Thy glased lyfe and glotony be glewed so in fere That Englande may wayle that euer it came here.

Hence **'glazedness.**

1530 PALSGR. 225/2 Glasednesse, *uoyroyseté.*

glazen, var. GLASSEN *a.* and *v.*

glazer ('gleɪzə(r)), *sb.* Also 5 gla(u)ser, 9 glazor. [f. GLAZE *v.*[1] + -ER[1].] One who or that which glazes.

†**1.** = GLAZIER. *Obs.*

1408 *Mem. Ripon* (Surtees) III. 138 Pro plumbar et glauser. **1466** *Paston Lett.* No. 549 II. 268 To the glaser for takyn owte of ii. panys of the wyndows of the schyrche for to late owte the reke of the torches.

2. a. A polisher or burnisher. **b.** A workman who applies the glaze to pottery, etc.

1586 T. B. *La Primaud. Fr. Acad.* I. (1594) 698 Armorers, glazers, sadlers, spur-makers, smithes, and such like. **1839** URE *Dict. Arts* 1016 The glazer provides himself at each round with a stock of these ball watches. **1858** SIMMONDS *Dict. Trade, Glazer*..a workman who applies the vitreous incrustation to the surface of earthenware.

3. An implement for glazing; *esp.* a wheel used in roughly polishing knives, etc.

1812-16 J. SMITH *Panorama Sci. & Art* I. 35 Some glazors are covered with strong leather. **1831** J. HOLLAND *Manuf. Metal* I. 291 The glazer, composed of cuneiform radii of wood firmly glued together. **1875** KNIGHT *Dict. Mech., Glazer*..2, a calendering or calico-smoothing wheel.

Hence †**'glazery**, glazier's work.

1723 CHAMBERS tr. *Le Clerc's Treat. Archit.* I. 2 The Masonry, Carpentry..Glazery, Roofing, &c.

† **'glazer**, *v. Obs.* [f. GLAZER *sb.*] *trans.* To polish, burnish.

1743 SIR J. PASTON in *P. Lett.* No. 727 III. 95 As ffor my byll that is gylt, I wolde it weer taken head too; ther is one in the town, that can glaser weel i nowe.

glazier ('gleɪzɪə(r), 'gleɪʒ(ɪ)ə(r)). Forms: 4–6 glasyer(e, (5 glasyare), 4–7 glasier, (5 glacyer, 6 glasior, glassier, -yer, 7 glaseer), 9 *dial.* glassiver, 7– glazier. [f. GLASS *sb.* + -ER[1], with assimilation to Rom. words in -IER, q.v.]

† **1.** One engaged in the manufacture of glass, a glass-maker. *Obs.*

1385 *Grant by R. Suzonne, Bailiff of Atheringlow* (MS. in private hands), Feare en le boys auauntdit vn Glashous et le despendre come office de Glasiere apent. **1398** TREVISA *Barth. De P.R.* XVI. xcix. (1495) 587 Glasse is so plyaunt that it takith anone dyuers and contrary shapis by blast of the Glasier. *Ibid.* XVII. lxiii. (1495) 639 Beche..is moost nedefull to Glasyers craft for of asshen therof..glas is craftly arayed. **1477** NORTON *Ord. Alch.* vi. in Ashm. (1652) 96 Tincture with anealing of Glasiers.

2. a. One whose trade it is to glaze windows, etc.

1408 *Nottingham Rec.* II. 56 Hugo Hopwell, de Lenton, glasyer. **1418** in C. WELCH *Tower Bridge* (1894) 72 [A payment for mending broken windows was made in 1418 to Hugh Wyse] Ducheman Glasyere. *c* **1481** CAXTON *Dialogues* (E.E.T.S.) 34/25 Steven the glasyer. **1487** *Churchw. Acc. Wigtoft, Linc.* (Nichols 1797) 83 To 2 glasyers for mendyng of divers glasse wyndowes rounde aboute ye chirch. **1540** *Ludlow Churchw. Acc.* (Camden) 1 To master glasier for glassynge the wyndous in the vestrie. **1563** SHUTE *Archit.* A ii b, Caruers, Ioynars, Glassyers, Grauers. **1600** *Chester Pl.* (E.E.T.S.) Banes 99 You painters and glasiors. **1666** PEPYS *Diary* 28 Sept., By and by the glazier comes to finish the windows of my house. **1774** *Westm. Mag.* II. 374 Reputation, like glass, if once broken the pane, No art of the Glazier can heal it again. **1814** BYRON *Diary* 9 Apr., This.. diamond..is..hardly fit to stick in a glazier's pencil. **1823** P. NICHOLSON *Pract. Build.* 421 Glaziers value their work by feet, inches, and parts.

b. In colloq. phrases addressed to a person who is obstructing one's view, etc. (see quots.).

1738 SWIFT *Pol. Conversat.* I. 13 *Lady Smart*... You stand in your own Light... *Ld. Sparkish.* I'm sure he sits in mine: Prythee, *Tom*, sit a little farther: I believe your Father was no Glasier. **1891** J. M. DIXON *Dict. Idiomatic Eng. Phrases* 132 *Is your father a glazier?*—a vulgar expression, signifying, 'Do you suppose that I can see through you?' It is used when a person in front of you obstructs your view. **1910** P. W. JOYCE *English as we speak it in Ireland* viii. 113 'Your father was a bad glazier': said to a person who is standing in one's light.

3. = GLAZER 2 b.

In recent Dicts.

† **4.** = GLAZER 3. *Obs.*

1688 R. HOLME *Armoury* III. 91/1 He beareth Argent, A Cutler at his Glassier or Polishing Wheel, polishing a Knife.

† **5.** *old slang. pl.* The eyes. *Obs.*

1567 HARMAN *Caveat* (1869) 82 Glasyers, eyes. **1611** MIDDLETON & DEKKER *Roaring Girle* K iij b, The balles of these glasiers of mine (mine eyes). **1641** BROME *Joviall Crew* II. Wks. 1873 III. 389 Toure out with your Glasiers. **1673** R. HEAD *Canting Acad.* 19 Thy Glaziers shine As Glymmar by the Salomon. **1785** in GROSE *Dict. Vulg. Tongue.*

† **6.** *slang.* (See quots. 1676, 1785.) *Obs.*

1673 R. HEAD *Canting Acad.* 191 The fifth is a Glazier, who when he creeps in: To pinch all the Lurry, he thinks it no sin. **1676** *Warn. Housekeepers* 4 Glasiers, thieves who enter houses, thro' windows, first remouing a pane of glass. *a* **1700** in B. E. *Dict. Cant. Crew.* **1785** GROSE *Dict. Vulg. Tongue, Glazier*, one who breaks windows and shew glasses to steal goods exposed for sale.

glaziery ('gleɪʒ(ɪ)ərɪ). [f. prec. + -Y[1].] Glazier's work; also *attrib.*

1841 J. T. HEWLETT *Parish Clerk* I. 100 The little accounts for glaziery and crockery. **1883** *Standard* 6 Apr. 4/8 A snug business in the glaziery line. **1893** *Westm. Gaz.* 13 Apr. 4/3 Mr. M.'s glaziery warehouse.

glazily, glaziness: see after GLAZY.

glazing ('gleɪzɪŋ), *vbl. sb.* [f. GLAZE *v.* + -ING[1].] The action of the vb. GLAZE.

1. The action of furnishing a building with windows or filling windows with glass; the trade or business of a glazier.

1427 in Heath *Grocers' Comp.* (1869) 5 Of diverse persones ikallyd Bacheleris to the glazyng of the parlore, £9 13*s.* 4*d.* **1494** FABYAN *Chron.* v. cxxxiv. 120 This Benet was the firste that broughte the crafte of glasynge into this lande. **1531** *Privy Purse Exp. Hen. VIII* (1827) 111 Paied to galien the glasier for glasing at yorke Place. **1533** in Weaver *Wells Wills* (1890) 91 The glasynge of a wyndowe in the new yeld. **1703** T. N. *City & C. Purchaser* 157 Of taking Dimensions, &c. In..this Profession of Glazing, it is generally taken to parts of Inches. **1709** HEARNE *Collect.* 6 Nov. (O.H.S.) II. 301 Nevill contributed either to ye Building or Glazing of it. **1807** HUTTON *Course Math.* II. 88 What will the glazing a triangular sky-light come to, at 10*d.* per foot? **1855** MACAULAY *Hist. Eng.* xii. III. 174 In spite of constant glazing and tiling, the rain perpetually drenched the apartments.

b. *concr.* Glazier's work; glass fixed in windows or frames.

c **1369** CHAUCER *Dethe Blaunche* 327 Al the storie of Troye Was in the glasing y-wroght thus. *c* **1500** in Arnolde *Chron.* (1811) 277 The chirche and the chauncel is nat repaired in glasinge in dyuers placis. **1618** in Picton *L'pool Munic. Rec.* (1883) I. 213 He shall maintayne the Church windowes wth sufficient glasinge, wyer and leade. **1631** WEEVER *Anc. Funeral Mon.* 421 As appeareth by his Armes both in the stone-worke..and glasing. **1735** BERKELEY *Querist* §377 Walls of rough stone, without plaster, ceiling, or glazing. **1868** M. C. LEA *Photogr.* vi. 152 The light on the side away from the glazing shall be maintained as subsidiary.

2. The action of polishing or burnishing.

c **1440** *Promp. Parv.* 197/1 Glacynge or scowrynge of harneys, *pernitidacio.* **1570–6** LAMBARDE *Peramb. Kent* (1826) 486 Some Corne milles, and one for the glasing of Armour. **1842** FRANCIS *Dict. Arts, Glazing*..the polishing of a metallic, wooden or stone surface, by the friction against it of a polishing powder. **1881** GREENER *Gun* 314 The glazing [of gunpowder] takes from five to eight hours, in wooden barrels revolving thirty-four times per minute.

3. The operation of coating with a glaze, or of giving (a substance) a smooth shiny surface.

1677 PLOT *Oxfordsh.* 251 The skill that hath been wanting to set up a manufacture of this transparent Earthen-ware in England, like that of China, is the glazing of the white Earth. **1789** *Trans. Soc. Arts* VII. 190 Very useful for driving of calendars for glazing of cloth, &c. **1872** YEATS *Techn. Hist. Comm.* 43 The glazing of bricks was practised at least 800 years before the Christian era. **1897** C. T. DAVIS *Manuf. Leather* (ed. 2) 612 Glazing and glossing of leather. Glazing —This operation is executed in various ways, but best with the use of a decoction of flaxseed mixed with solution of white soap.

b. *concr.* The material used for producing a glaze or glassy surface; also, the glassy surface thus produced: = GLAZE *sb.* 4.

1694 SALMON *Bates' Disp.* (1713) 132/2 Earthen Vessels, if unglas'd, would suck most of the Matter into them; and if glas'd, they would prey upon the Lead or Glasing. **1726** LEONI *Alberti's Archit.* I. 32 The Glazing, when it is melted over it, makes an even Surface. **1753** HANWAY *Trav.* (1762) I. III. xxxvii. 167 The Persians use a certain glazing in their cotton tents, which..prevents their being penetrated by water. **1841** CATLIN *N. Amer. Ind.* (1844) II. liv. 165 The rock..polished, as if a liquid glazing had been poured over its surface. **1845** MISS ACTON *Mod. Cookery* xvi. 335 This glazing..takes a slight colour, if used before the pastry is baked. **1852** MORFIT *Tanning & Currying* (1853) 77 Artificial coloring matter, which is probably the same for both kinds of tea, and consists of a mixture of Prussian blue, gypsum, and turmeric. This colouring matter is called the glazing. **1859** R. F. BURTON *Centr. Afr.* in *Jrnl. Geog. Soc.* XXIX. 78 Paper—soft and soppy by the loss of glazing.

4. *Painting.* The application of a thin coat of transparent colour over another in order to modify the tone without mixing; the colour thus laid on.

1706 *Art of Painting* (1744) 169 Sometimes with glazing in the shadows. **1807** OPIE in *Lect. Paint.* iv. (1848) 321 Richness and transparency may be obtained by glazing, and passing the colours one over another without suffering them to mix. **1859** GULLICK & TIMBS *Paint.* 261 Seldom repeating his colours, and using few glazings. **1880** W. SEVERN in *Macm. Mag.* No. 245. 375, I will now say a few words about 'glazing', or putting one colour over another instead of mixing them.

5. *attrib.* and *Comb.*, as ***glazing colour, compound, fluid, knife, machine, room***; **glazing-barrel**, a rotatory barrel in which gunpowder is glazed; **glazing-wheel** (see quot.).

1878 *Engineering* 22 Feb. 138/2 A set of *glazing barrels consists of four. **1825** J. NICHOLSON *Operat. Mechanic* 727 The plate is to be varnished..the varnish being tinted with any *glazing colour. **1859** GULLICK & TIMBS *Paint.* 227 All colours which, when mixed with suitable vehicle, are transparent, are termed glazing colours. **1832** G. R. PORTER *Porcelain & Gl.* 72 A *glazing compound, which is sufficiently fusible without containing a particle of lead. **1897** C. T. DAVIS *Manuf. Leather* (ed. 2) 612 The *glazing fluid is prepared as follows. **1825** J. NICHOLSON *Operat. Mechanic* 636 The *glazing-knife is used for laying in the putty in the rebates of the sash [etc.]. **1871** *Amer. Encycl. Print.* (ed. Ringwalt), **Glazing machine*, a machine used for putting a polished surface on printed papers, or for burnishing gold and color work. **1897** C. T. DAVIS *Manuf. Leather* (ed. 2) 263 The glazing machine was one of the first steam-driven tools introduced into the trade. **1881** GREENER *Gun* 315 In..the *glazing-room and stoves, the floors are laid with leather. **1873** *Weale's Dict. Terms* (ed. 4), *Glazers* or **Glazing-wheels*, wooden wheels charged with emery and used for polishing are called by this name.

glazing ('gleɪzɪŋ), *ppl. a.* [f. as prec. + -ING[2].] That glazes: said chiefly of the eye.

1808 SCOTT *Marm.* VI. xxxii, A light on Marmion's visage spread, And fir'd his glazing eye. **1813** BYRON *Giaour* xlii, I ..thank thee for the generous tear This glazing eye could never shed. **1835** LYTTON *Rienzi* VII. v, It was the face of a woman that looked upward through passionate and glazing tears.

glazor, var. GLAZER.

glazy ('gleɪzɪ), *a.* [f. GLAZE *sb.* or *v.* + -Y[1]; in part perh. a survival of *glasy*: see GLASSY.]

† **1.** = GLASSY *a.* 1 b. *Obs.*

1607 TOPSELL *Four-f. Beasts* (1658) 284 The eies of a horsse..see perfectly in the night; yet their colour varieth as it doth in men, according to the caprine and glazie humour.

2. a. Glass-like, glassy, glittering like glass. **b.** Resembling a glaze; having the smooth shiny appearance of a glaze or glazed surface.

1724 RAMSAY *Tea-t. Misc.* (1733) II. 129 The finny squadrons are content, To leave their wat'ry element, In glazie numbers down they bent. **1768** W. DONALDSON *Sir Bart. Sapskull* I. 132 Divine miracles, beautifully and ingeniously delineated in those glazy ornaments [Dutch tiles]. **1786** BURNS *To Auld Mare* ii, I've seen thee dappl't, sleek, an' glaizie. **1811** *Self Instructor* 527 Your paper is to be perfectly dry, otherwise the work will appear glazy. **1870** MISS BRIDGMAN *Ro. Lynne* II. xiv. 291 The hat so glazy and knowing. **1873** SPON *Workshop Rec.* Ser. I. 360 A better [india-rubber] solution is obtained..by not shaking, but drawing off the clear glazy liquid.

c. *glazy iron* (see quot.).

1881 RAYMOND *Mining Gloss.* s.v. *Iron*, So-called silver-gray, glazy, or carbonized iron is usually an iron rendered brittle by excess of silicon.

3. Of the eye or its gaze: = GLASSY *a.* 2.

1838 ELIZA COOK *Melaia* xxi. 10 His eyeballs had a glazy beam. **1880** J. HATTON *3 Recruits* I. I. iii. 61 They had something of the serpent in their glazy stare.

Hence **'glazily** *adv.*; **'glaziness.**

1708 *Phil. Trans.* XXVI. 130 Which in the evaporating of the Water, were coagulated upon the first mentioned clear Salts, and so eclipsed the shining or glaziness of those Salts. **1825** *Ann. Reg.* 239* The pupils of his eyes are large..but.. there is a glaziness in the sight. **1858** FABER *Spir. Confer.* (1870) 412 The wild enquiring eye so glazily fixed upon us.

gle, gleab(e, gleaby, obs. ff. GLEE, GLEBE, GLEBY.

glead(e, obs. form of GLAD, GLEDE, GLEED *sb.*

gleake, obs. form of GLEEK.

gleam (gli:m), *sb.* Forms: 1 **glǽm**, 3–4 **glem**, 4–6 **gleme**, 6–7 **gleame**, 3, 7– **gleam.** [OE. *glǽm* (:—**glaimi-z*) is related by ablaut to OHG. *glîmen* to glow, shine, OS. *glîmo* brightness, OHG. *glîmo* (MHG. *glîme*) glow-worm, in which sense OHG. had also *gleimo* (MHG. *gleime*), agreeing in root-grade with the ME. word. The lowest grade of the root, **glim-*, appears in several forms in MHG. and ME.: see GLIM, GLIMMER, GLIMPSE.]

1. In early use, a brilliant light (e.g. of the sun). In mod. use, a subdued or transient appearance of light, emitted or reflected.

In ME. both sb. and vb. are rare except in alliterative verse.

a **1000** *Guthlac* 1278 in *Exeter Bk.*, þa se æþela glæm setl-gong sohte. *a* **1225** *St. Marher.* 12 Semde as þah ha sehe iþe glistinde glem þe deore rode areachen to þe heouene. *c* **1300** *Havelok* 2122 So stod ut of his mouth a glem Rith al swilk so the sunnebem. **13..** *Gaw. & Gr. Knt.* 604 þat al [the harness] glytered & glent as glem of þe sunne. *c* **1400** *Destr. Troy* 3067 A necke..glissonand as the glemes þat glenttes of þe snaw. *c* **1440** *York Myst.* xxxii. 20 And myne eyne þei glittir like þe gleme in þe glasse. **1508** DUNBAR *Gold. Targe* 31 All the lake as lamp did leme of licht, Quhilk schadovit all about wyth twynkling glemis. **1602** MARSTON *Ant. & Mel.* III. Wks. 1856 I. 30 Is not yon gleame, the shuddering morne that flakes, With silver tinctur, the east vierge of heaven? **1665** SIR T. HERBERT *Trav.* (1677) 30 A gleam of light, so bright that he could easily read by it. **1762** GOLDSM. *Cit. W.* cxvii, The dying lamp feebly emits a yellow gleam. **1805** WORDSW. *Peele Castle* iv, If mine had been the Painter's hand, To express what then I saw: and add the gleam, The light that never was, on sea or land. **1838** LYTTON *Leila* IV. i, See you not a gleam of spears, yonder, over the mountain? **1860** TYNDALL *Glac.* I. xxiii. 162 When the staff was dug into the snow and withdrawn, the blue gleam appeared. **186.** BRET HARTE *John Burns* 99 The gleam of his old white hat from afar.

Comb. **1804** J. GRAHAME *Sabbath* (1808) 39 Forward the gleam-girt castle coastwise glides.

b. *fig.* A bright or vivid manifestation (of some quality, etc.); in mod. use chiefly with the notion of limitation, a faint, transient, or intermittent appearance.

a **1225** *Ancr. R.* 50 þat te soðe sunne, þat is Jesu Crist, haueð wiðuten..unseauliche imaked ou þurh gleames of his grace. *a* **1547** SURREY *Prisoned in Windsor* in *Tottel's Misc.* (Arb.) 13 The palme play, where..With dazed eies oft we by gleames of loue Haue mist the ball. **1576** GASCOIGNE *Philomene* (Arb.) 96 He..still behelde her gestures all, And all her gleames of grace. *a* **1711** KEN *Psyche* Poet. Wks. 1721 IV. 250 When first my Heart, thou Lord, didst melt, And of thy Love one Gleam I felt. **1793** HOLCROFT *Lavater's Physiog.* xxvi. 127 A gleam of sympathy and resemblance may easily deceive thee. **1840** F. D. BENNETT *Whaling Voy.* I. 75 Her smile..casts at once a gleam of beauty over otherwise but ordinary features. **1855** MACAULAY *Hist. Eng.* xii. III. 228 On the fifteenth of June a gleam of hope appeared. **1874** L. STEPHEN *Hours in Library* (1892) II. ii. 36 One temporary gleam of good fortune cheered him for a time. **1885** *Spectator* 30 May 716/1 Now and then..we get an occasional gleam of humour.

† **c.** ***hot gleam*** (also *gleam* simply), a warm ray (of the sun); a bright warm interval between rain-showers. Also, a hot wind (cf. GLOOM *sb.*[1]). *Obs.*

1601 HOLLAND *Pliny* I. 33 The middle of the earth, whereas the Sun hath his way..is euen parched and fried againe with the hot gleames thereof. **1669** WORLIDGE *Syst. Agric.* (1681) 188 If the weather be warm and calm, the Bees delight to rise, but especially in a hot Gleam, after a Showre or Gloomy Cloud hath sent them home. **1697** DAMPIER *Voy.* (1729) I. 530 We felt a brisk Gale..so violent hot, that we thought it came from some burning Mountain..Just such another Gleam I felt one afternoon also.

† **2.** *transf.* Brightness, radiance; radiant beauty.

a **1000** *Cædmon's Gen.* 1017 (Gr.) Heo þe hroðra oftihð, glæmes grene folde. *a* **1000** *Juliana* 167 in *Exeter Bk.*, Min se swetesta sunnan scima, Iuliana, hwæt þu glæm hafast.. geoguðhades blæd. *c* **1250** *Meid Maregrete* xxxii, On þe holi meidan he sende litt ant glem. **13..** *E.E. Allit. P.* B. 218 þaȝ þe feloun [Lucifer] were so fers for his fayre wedeȝ & his glorious glem þat glent so bryȝt. **1591** SPENSER *Vision Bellay* v, Then was the faire Dodonian tree far seene, Upon seaven hills to spred his gladsome gleame. **1683** TRYON *Way to Health* 36 The white clear bright Gleam in every Creature.. does arise and proceed from the divine Principle.

b. A bright or joyous look.

1769 SIR W. JONES *Poems & Ess., Pal. Fort.* (1777) 15 O'er his smooth cheeks diffus'd a lively gleam. **1852** MRS. STOWE

Uncle Tom's C. vi, His black visage lighted up with a curious, mischievous gleam.

gleam (gliːm), *v.*[1] Also 4–6 **gleme**. [f. prec.]

1. *intr.* To emit gleams, to shine either with emitted or reflected light; in mod. use chiefly, to shine with a brightness subdued by distance or an intervening medium.

a **1225** *Leg. Kath.* 1653 Al þat terin is glistinde & gleaminde, as hit were seoluer oðer gold smeate. **13..** *Gaw. & Gr. Knt.* 597 A sadel þat glemed ful gayly with mony golde frenges. *c* **1400** *Destr. Troy* 3943 Faire Ene hade þe freike.. Glemyt as þe glasse and gliet a little. **1508** DUNBAR *Tua mariit wemen* 20 So glitterit as the gold wer thair glorius gilt tressis, Quhill all the gressis did gleme of the glaid hewis. *c* **1570** *Satir. Poems Reform.* xxxvii. 20 Forcit fyris with gritter gleidis out glemis. **1700** DRYDEN *Cymon & Iph.* 588 The palace gleams with shining swords. **1792** S. ROGERS *Pleas. Mem.* I. 316 When not a distant taper's twinkling ray Gleamed o'er the furze to light him on his way. **1813** SCOTT *Rokeby* VI. x, Torches and cressets gleam'd around. **1842** LYTTON *Zanoni* 28 There gleam the columns of Capua. **1859** KINGSLEY *Misc.* (1860) II. 247 Keen, honest eyes gleamed out from his brown, scarred weather-beaten face. **1878** BROWNING *La Saisiaz* 10 What will be the morning glory, when at dusk thus gleams the lake?

fig. **1815** *Hortensia* II. iii, A forc'd smile gleam'd faintly o'er her visage. **1867** TROLLOPE *Chron. Barset* I. xiii. 109 Standing upright.. with something of a noble anger gleaming over his poor wan face. **1874** GREEN *Short Hist.* vii. §2. 358 Even the commonest lives gleamed for a moment into poetry at the stake. **1878** C. STANFORD *Symb. Christ* i. 10 Some hints of the reasons for the deep veneration in which he was held gleam in almost every line.

b. quasi-*trans.*, esp. with advs.

1593 SHAKS. *Lucr.* 1378 Dying eyes gleem'd forth their ashie lights. **1796** MRS. M. ROBINSON *Angelina* III. 28 Tapers, faintly pale, gleaming blue light upon the altar, then suddenly disappearing! **1818** MILMAN *Samor.* 52 The northern clouds.. Stream in their restless wavings to and fro, While the sea billows gleam them mellower back.

fig. **1802** H. MARTIN *Helen of Glenross* IV. 259 She lies still, except in the movements of convulsions, that recur as often as thought gleams a recollection of her miseries.

†**2.** To glance, look. *Obs. rare.*

1340–70 *Alisaunder* 505 Nectanabus.. nyed hym tyll And gleming gainelich too þe gome saide. **1508** DUNBAR *Tua mariit wemen* 228, I cast on him a crabbit E.. And lettis it is a luf-blenk, quhene he about glemys.

gleam, *v.*[2] *Falconry.* ? *Obs.* [Later form of GLEIM *v.*] (See quot. 1704.)

1575 TURBERV. *Faulconrie* 103 And when shee hath caste, then hoode hir agayne gyving hir nothing to feede on untill she gleame after hir casting. **1704** WORLIDGE *Dict. Rust.* s.v., When a Hawk casteth, she gleams; that is throws up Filth from her Gorge.

So **gleam** *sb.* (see quot.).

1891 HARTING *Bibl. Accipitr.* 223 *Gleam*, the substance thrown up after casting gorge.

gleame, obs. form of GLEAN *v.*

gleaming (ˈgliːmɪŋ), *vbl. sb.* [f. GLEAM *v.*[1] + -ING[1].] The action of the vb. GLEAM; a gleam.

c **1400** *Destr. Troy* 11777 There is no greuaunce so grete vndur god one, As the glemyng of gold, þat glottes þere hertis. *c* **1440** *Promp. Parv.* 198/2 Glemynge or lemynge of lyghte, *conflagracio, flammacio.* **1508** DUNBAR *Tua mariit wemen* 202 He had the glemyng of gold, and wes bot glase fundin. **1720** WELTON *Suffer. Son of God* II. xv. 409 For my sake it is.. that Thou wast so exposed to the Gleamings of the Sun. **1771** *Ann. Reg., Hist. Eur.* 79*/2 Some gleamings of peace.. appeared thro' all the horrors of war.

gleaming (ˈgliːmɪŋ), *ppl. a.* [f. as prec. + -ING[2].] That gleams, in senses of the verb.

13.. *E.E. Allit. P.* A. 70 Þe glemande glory þat of hem glent. **1450–70** *Golagros & Gaw.* 557 Gaudifeir and Galiot in glemand steil wedis.. grymly thai ride. **1508** DUNBAR *Tua mariit wemen* 108 Sa heklis he my chekis That as a glemand gleyd glowis my chaftis. **1671** MILTON *P.R.* III. 326 The field all iron cast a gleaming brown. **1769** SIR W. JONES *Poems & Ess., Pal. Fort.* (1777) 21 There hung enamour'd o'er the gleaming spoil. **1828** SCOTT *F.M. Perth* iv, A ring that sparkles like a gleaming candle. **1871** L. STEPHEN *Playgr. Europe* ix. (1894) 211 To watch the gleaming snow-line against the cloudless sky.

Comb. **1860** G. H. K. *Vac. Tour.* 135 Fringing many a sparkling loch and wild hill-side, may the sweet-scented gleaming-leaved birch be found.

Hence **ˈgleamingly** *adv.*

1847 *Tait's Mag.* XIV. 156 Full gleamingly her flashing eye lit up her smile of scorn. **1897** *Westm. Gaz.* 4 Feb. 3/1 Tunis seems sleeping in the sun down below, gleamingly white.

gleamless (ˈgliːmlɪs), *a.* [f. GLEAM *sb.* + -LESS.] Destitute of a gleam (of light).

1891 *Blackw. Mag.* CL. 579/1 The gleamless dogmas of fatalism.

gleamy (ˈgliːmɪ), *a.* [f. GLEAM *sb.* + -Y[1].]

1. That gleams or sends forth gleams (of light).

1593 NASHE *Christ's T.* (1613) 145 So beset they their fore-heads.. with glorious borrowed gleamy bushes. **1745** COLLINS *Ode Death Col. Foss* vi, Again they snatch the gleamy steel. **1821** JOANNA BAILLIE *Metr. Leg., Wallace* xcv. 13 Her gleamy lakes and torrents clear. **1826** DISRAELI *Viv. Grey* V. xv, Fish, gleamy with prismatic hues. **1842** FABER *Styrian Lake*, etc. 269 His eye surfeited with blaze of gems And gleamy metals.

2. That is lighted up by gleams; esp. of weather: marked by intermittent sunshine. Now *rare*.

1681 CHETHAM *Angler's Vade-m.* xli. §7 (1689) 313 Sultry or gleamy day. **1688** CLAYTON in *Phil. Trans.* XVII. 947 If gleamy Weather happen at that time, it [the tobacco-plant] breeds a small Flie. **1792** WORDSW. *Descrip. Sketches* 214 And antique castles seen through gleamy showers. **1880** DISRAELI *Endym.* xii, They caught enticing vistas of the gleamy glades, and the abounding light and shade softened and adorned everything. **1880** BLACKIE in *Scotsman* 2 Sept., 'Twas a cold gleamy day all hueless and gray. **1889** *N.W. Linc. Gloss.* (ed. 2), *Gleamy*, weather that is fitful and uncertain. Rain-clouds and sunshine blended is called 'gleamy' weather.

b. Of sunshine: Intermittent, coming in gleams.

1883 HOLME LEE *Loving & Serving* I. xiv. 261 A gleamy, wild sunshine burst forth. **1892** *Field* 14 May 718/2 The shafts of sunlight are rare and gleamy.

3. Of light or colour: Having the nature of a gleam.

1700 DRYDEN *Wife of Bath's T.* 214 The moon was up and shot a gleamy light. **1776** MICKLE tr. *Camoens' Lusiad* 201 Soon as the gleamy streaks of purple morn The lofty forest's topmost boughs adorn. **1857** BIRCH *Anc. Pottery* (1858) II. 333 Sometimes the paste is intermingled with micaceous particles.. which gives it a gleamy colour when broken. **1867** JEAN INGELOW *Dreams that came true* lxxi, Stands by his fire, and dulls its gleamy light.

Hence **ˈgleaminess**.

1830 *Fraser's Mag.* II. 58 Of.. the gleaminess which seemeth to fall like an angel's raiment about the form of poetry, the author of the *Rambler* knew nothing.

gleamy, var. GLEIMY, *Obs.*

glean (gliːn), *sb.*[1] *Obs.* exc. *dial.* Also 5 **glene**. [a. OF. *glene, glane* = med.L. *glena, glana*, sb. related to OF. *glener*, late L. *glenāre* to GLEAN.] Something gleaned or gathered.

1. (See quots.)

c **1430** LYDG. *Min. Poems* (Percy Soc.) 98 A braunche of vynes.. hym thought he dide se, And therwithe al a gracious gleene [*printed* gleeve] of whete. *c* **1490** *Promp. Parv.* 199/1 (MS. *K*) Glene, *spicatum.* **1602** *Withals' Dict.* 87 A gleane or heape of Corne, commonly gathered and bound by handfuls together, *spicilegium.* *a* **1728** KENNETT *Gloss.* in *Lansdowne MS.* 1033 (Promp. Parv. 199 *note*) A glean, a handfull of corne gleaned and tied up by the gleaner or reaper. Kent. **1887** in *Kent Gloss.* s.v.

transf. and *fig.* **1654** FULLER *Comm. Ruth* ii. 153 Abraham gleaned a great gleane of Faith. **1697** DRYDEN *Virg., Georg.* IV. 267 The Gleans of yellow Thime distend his Thighs.

2. A sheaf of hemp; a bundle of teasels (see quots.).

1664 *Instr. Jury-men on Comm. Sewers* 41 in *N.W. Linc. Gloss., Glean*, a sheaf of hemp. **1794** GRIGGS *Agric. Essex* 19 These heads [of teasel] are.. bound up in small bunches, or gleans, of five and twenty heads each. **1799** A. YOUNG *Agric. Linc.* 157 For which purpose they tie it in gleans single. **1849** *Jrnl. R. Agric. Soc.* X. I. 177 The price of pulling 100 gleans [of hemp] (as they were termed) was 1*s*... Set it up in stooks of five or six gleans.

†**glean**, *sb.*[2] *Obs.* [A variant of *clean* (? f. CLEAN *v.*), which has the same sense in some mod. dialects; also called *cleaning* and *cleansing*.] The placenta or after-birth, esp. of a cow.

1601 HOLLAND *Pliny* II. 327 The gleane of a Cow hauing newly calued.. is good for any vlcers of the visage. *Ibid.* 341 The pellicle or glean wherein a kid was infolded within the dams wombe. **1750** W. ELLIS *Mod. Husbandm.* IV. I. 150 To bring away her [a cow's] glean.

Hence †**glean** *v.*, to cast the placenta.

1750 W. ELLIS *Mod. Husbandm.* III. I. 107 To make a Cow glean well, and keep her in Health.

glean (gliːn), *v.* Forms: 4–5 **glene**, 6–7 **gleane**, (5–6 **gleyne**, 6 **glayne, gleme, gleame, gleime**), 7– **glean**. [a. OF. *glener, glainer* (F. *glaner*) to glean = Prov. *glenar, grenar*, late L. (6th c.) *glenare*, of unknown origin. The commonly assumed connexion with med.L. *gelima*, OE. *ȝielm*, sheaf, is inadmissible; the forms with *m* are prob. due to association with *gleam*.]

1. *intr.* To gather or pick up ears of corn which have been left by the reapers.

In the southern and western counties the popular word is LEASE (cf. quot. 1393).

c **1385** CHAUCER *L.G.W.* Prol. 75 Ye han her beforne Of makynge ropen and lad awey the Corne; And I come after, glening here and there. **1393** LANGL. *P. Pl.* C. IX. 67 Alle þat helpen me to erye other elles to weden, Shal haue leue.. to go and glene after [*B.* to lese here in heruest]. **1483** *Cath. Angl.* 158/2 To Glene, *aristare.* **1530** PALSGR. 568/1 Put nat your horses in to the corne felde yet, for my folkes have nat gleaned there yet. *a* **1541** WYATT *Of mean Estate* in *Tottel's Misc.* (Arb.) 85 In haruest tyme while she might go and gleane. **1611** BIBLE *Ruth* ii. 7, I pray you, let mee gleane and gather after the reapers amongst the sheaues. **1768** BLACKSTONE *Comm.* III. 212 The poor are allowed to enter and glean upon another's ground after the harvest, without being guilty of trespass. **1796** H. HUNTER tr. *St. Pierre's Stud. Nat.* (1799) III. 424 They reap, and I glean. I carry then to the common heap a few ears picked behind their steps [etc.]. **1898** *Contemp. Rev.* Sept. 397 Mary was gleaning in a field of corn.

2. *trans.* To gather or pick up (ears of corn or other produce) after the reapers, etc.

1387–8 T. USK *Test. Love* I. Prol. (Skeat) l. 112 Yet also haue I leue.. to come after.. these great workmen, and glene my handfuls of the shedynge after their handes. **1552** HULOET, Gleme corne, *spicilegium facere.* **1570** LEVINS *Manip.* 208/20 To Gleame corne, *spiciligere.* **1600** SHAKS. *A.Y.L.* III. v. 102, I shall thinke it a most plenteous crop To gleane the broken eares after the man That the maine haruest reapes. **1611** BIBLE *Ruth* ii. 2 Let me now goe to the field, and gleane eares of corne. **1832** HT. MARTINEAU *Ireland* ii. 31 They might glean potatoes enough among the ridges, after the digging, to keep them for a few days. **1862** BURTON *Bk. Hunter* (1863) 402 How much has yet to be gleaned off this stony field. **1870** MORRIS *Earthly Par.* I. 536 After his harvesting, the men must glean What he had left.

b. To strip (a field, vineyard, etc.) of the produce left by the regular gatherers.

a **1533** LD. BERNERS *Gold. Bk. M. Aurel.* xvi. (1566) M v b, Other gathered the grapes & thou gleynedest the vyne. **1611** BIBLE *Lev.* xix. 10 Thou shalt not gleane thy vineyard, neither shalt thou gather euery grape of thy vineyard. **1730–46** THOMSON *Autumn* 217 She went To glean Palemon's fields. ['Very common in Suffolk' (F. Hall).]

fig. **1581** MULCASTER *Positions* xxxix. (1887) 206 The pillage of the poore people? which are to sore gleaned: by the needle and neuer contented professours? **1860** PUSEY *Min. Proph.* 73 God.. will not, as it were, glean Ephraim, going over it again, as man doth, in order to leave nothing over.

3. *transf.* and *fig.* To gather or pick up in small quantities; to scrape together. Now chiefly with immaterial object, esp. ***to glean information, experience***, etc.

13.. *E.E. Allit. P.* A. 954 In þat oþer [Jerusalem] is noȝt bot pes to glene. *c* **1350** *Wynnere & Wastoure* 231 in Gollancz *Parl. 3 Ages*, Alle þat I wynn thurgh witt he wastes thurgh pryde; I geder, I glene, and hee lattys goo sone. *a* **1420** HOCCLEVE *De Reg. Princ.* 495 For alle the good that men may rippe and glene Wasted is in outrageous aray. *c* **1420** *Pallad. on Husb.* I. 362 In flood, or lene Cley lond, or nigh the see, grauel let glene. **1601** R. JOHNSON *Kingd. & Commw.* (1603) 151 He gleaneth whatsoever is good or ought woorth through his whole kingdome. **1604** E. G. *D'Acosta's Hist. W. Indies* To Sir R. Cecill A 3, The advantage I have gleaned from idle hours.. is commended to your Honors Patronage. **1634** SIR T. HERBERT *Trav.* 224 A hundred others haue since that gleaned severall additions of Titles and new names their distributed. **1673** LD. F. AUNGIER in *Essex Papers* (Camden) I. 60 Calling upon S[r] Arthur Forbes, I have glean'd from him what I am now to tell y[r] Ex[cye]. **1759** ROBERTSON *Hist. Scot.* I. I. 4 From them [he] gleaned materials which he formed into a regular history. **1812** BYRON *Ch. Har.* II. lxx, For many a joy he could from Night's soft presence glean. **1869** LECKY *Europ. Mor.* II. i. 56 A few examples have been gleaned from mediæval Chronicles.

†**b.** To gather or collect *into* (one receptacle, one mass). *Obs.*

1540 HEN. VIII in *State P.* (1834) III. 228 Where the sayde Sir Anthony shall fynde the Kynges Majestes landes be otherwise surveyed, or otherwise glayned in to oon hande. **1613** SHAKS. *Hen. VIII*, III. ii. 284 Yes, that goodnesse Of gleaning all the Lands wealth into one, Into your owne hands (Card'nall) by Extortion. **1646** J. HALL *Horæ Vac.* 154 Oppressed factions when they seeme utterly extinct, gleaning themselves into a head [etc.].

c. With advs.; esp. ***to glean up***, to gather up, collect. † Also ***to glean away***, to carry off; ***to glean out***, to ascertain by investigation of details. *Obs.*

1601 R. JOHNSON *Kingd. & Commw.* 131 The plague.. which gleaned away many thousand people. **1613–18** DANIEL *Coll. Hist. Eng.* (1626) 105 His stay in England was ..spent in gleaning out what possible this kingdome could yeeld. **1659** D. PELL *Impr. Sea* 501 By which means you have been enabled.. to glean up your præinformations how the sands have lain. **1697** COLLIER *Ess. Mor. Subj.* II. 105 They Glean up Custom from their Neighbours; and so what one gets, the other loses. **1704** ADDISON *Italy* 375 The several little Springs and Rills, that break out of the Sides of the Mountain, are glean'd up, and conveyed.. into the main Hollow of the Aqueduct. **1730** FIELDING *Author's Farce* III. Wks. 1882 VIII. 234 He does not only glean up all the bad words of other authors, but makes new bad words of his own. **1844** LOWELL *Pres. Crisis* Poet. Wks. (1890) I. 183 While the hooting mob of yesterday in silent awe return To glean up the scattered ashes into History's golden urn.

†**d.** To cut off (a remnant or stragglers) in warfare. Also ***to glean up***. *Obs.*

1611 BIBLE *Judges* xx. 45 And they gleaned of them in the high wayes fiue thousand men. *c* **1665** MRS. HUTCHINSON *Mem. Col. Hutchinson* (1848) 217 Those horse that were in the garrison following their rear gleaned up two lieutenants and two or three other officers. *a* **1711** KEN *Edmund* Poet. Wks. 1721 II. 306 Bowmen.. on the Danish camp discharge a Show'r To glean the Danes the Wolves should not devour. **1726** CAVALLIER *Mem.* I. 77 When we perceived the general rout, we.. pursu'd them as Hounds do Stags, gleaning now and then some of them.

Hence **gleaned**, **ˈgleaning** *ppl. adjs.*; **ˈgleanable** *a.*, that may be gleaned.

1599 SHAKS. *Hen. V*, I. ii. 151 The Scot.. Came pouring like the Tyde.. Galling the gleaned Land with hot Assayes. **1611** FLORIO, *Spicardino ingegno*, a.. loose gadding, skipping or gleaning wit. **1693** G. STEPNY in *Dryden's Juvenal* VIII. (1697) 201 Your Cruel Guilt will little Booty find, Since gleaning Marius has already seiz'd All that from Sun-burnt Africk can be squees'd. **1830** TENNYSON *Ode to Memory* iii, Showering thy gleaned wealth into my open breast. **1851** *Jrnl. R. Agric. Soc.* XII. II. 410 Few families make their own bread, except from the flour of their 'gleant corn'. **1876** G. MACDONALD *T. Wingfold* xx. 175 Fields.. gleanable for generations.

glean, var. GLEEN, *Obs.*

gleaner (ˈgliːnə(r)). Also 5 **glenar, -er**, 6 **gleamer**. [f. GLEAN *v.* + -ER[1]; cf. OF. *glenere*, F. *glaneur*.] One that gleans.

c **1440** *Promp. Parv.* 199/1 Glenar of corne, *spicator.* **1530** PALSGR. 225/2 Glenar of corne, *glaneur.* **1552** HULOET, Gleamer of corne, *spicilegus.* **1582** BENTLEY *Mon. Matrones* Pref. B ij, I have laboured as you see (good reder) like a poore gleaner or grape gatherer. **1642** FULLER *Holy & Prof. St.* II. xix. 121 It is difficult for gleaners, without stealing whole sheaves, to fill a barn. **1713** BENTLEY *Freethinking* II. §46 Wks. 1838 III. 410 O wretched gleaner of weeds! Has he read that noble work, *The Intellectual System*, to no better purpose? **1730–46** THOMSON *Autumn* 165 The gleaners spread around, and here and there, Spike after spike, their scanty harvest pick. **1878** J. E. JENKINS *Haverholme* 39 Such figures..may be picked out day by day by the careful gleaner in the throng.

Comb. **1814** CARY *Dante, Par.* XXXII. 7 [Ruth] the gleaner-maid.

Hence †'**gleaneress**, a female gleaner.

1611 COTGR. *Grappeuse*, a grape-gleaneresse. **1632** SHERWOOD, A gleaneresse of grapes.

gleaning ('gli:nɪŋ), *vbl. sb.* [f. GLEAN *v.* + -ING¹.] The action of the vb. GLEAN; also (chiefly *pl.*) that which is or may be gleaned.

c **1440** *Promp. Parv.* 199/1 Glenynge, *conspicacio.* **1535** COVERDALE *Micah* vii. 1 Wo is me: I am become as one, that goeth a gleenynge in the haruest. **1552** HULOET, Glemynge of corne, *spicilegium.* **1565** COOPER *Thesaurus, Racematio*.. the gleiminge of grapes. **1576** FLEMING *Panopl. Epist.* 303 Not the whole and perfect harvest, yet some gleanings of pleasure. **1611** BIBLE *Judges* viii. 2 Is not the gleaning of the grapes of Ephraim better then the vintage of Abiezer? **1633** HEYWOOD *Eng. Trav.* III. Wks. 1874 IV. 45 In full fields, The gleanings are allowed. *a* **1637** B. JONSON *Underwoods, Execr. Vulcan* (1640) B 3, Twice twelve years Stor'd-up-Humanity And humble gleanings in Divinity, After the Fathers. **1702** J. LOGAN in *Pa. Hist. Soc. Mem.* IX. 101, I must still crave leave to add the following gleanings. **1777** ROBERTSON *Hist. Amer.* (1778) II. VI. 207 The victorious troops..found there a considerable booty, consisting..of the gleanings of the Indian treasures. **1844** H. H. WILSON *Brit. India* II. 373 They are tenanted by various barbarous races..subsisting on the produce of their cattle, the gleanings of the chase [etc.]. **1881** FREEMAN *Subj. Venice* 320 The second Mahomet..brought under his power, as a gleaning after the vintage, the Frank lordship of Attica [etc.].

Proverb. **1546** HEYWOOD *Prov.* (1867) 28 Thou goest a glenyng er the cart haue caried.

Comb. **1579** TOMSON *Calvin's Serm. Tim.* 965/1 It is saide in the Prophete Michah, that the Jewes in those dayes would needs have had glening and haruest preachers, for they would bring them nothing but pleasant newes. **1826** POLWHELE *Trad. & Recoll.* I. 47 The merry maidens cross the brook Each in her hand a gleaning-hook To reap the ripen'd good.

gleare, gleary, obs. ff. GLAIR *sb.*, GLAIRY.

glear-eyed, ? var. *glare-eyed* (GLARE *v.* 5); but see GLEERING.

1600 *Look About You* F 4 b, O would I were a Basiliske, to kill These gleare ey'd villaines.

glearing, var. GLEERING, *Obs.*

glease, dial. var. GLACE *v.*

gleat, obs. form of GLEET *v.*

gleave, obs. or dial. form of GLAIVE.

gleaze, dial. var. GLACE *v.*

gleb, obs. form of GLIB *sb.*¹

gleba ('gli:bə). *Bot.* [mod.L. use of *glēba, glæba* clod, lump, GLEBE.] The fleshy, spore-bearing tissue of certain kinds of fungi, the Gasteromycetes and the Tuberales.

1847 J. LINDLEY *Elem. Bot.* (ed. 5) p. xliii/1 Gleba, Glebula.—The peridium or the fleshy part of certain Fungals. **1887** H. E. F. GARNSEY tr. *De Bary's Compar. Morphol. & Biol. Fungi* v. 309 They form together a mass of tissue which is distinguished from the adjoining tissue by its chambered structure and by the formation of spores and is known as the *gleba.* **1950** E. A. BESSEY *Morphol. & Taxon. Fungi* xv. 531 The gleba consists of a more or less fleshy mycelial growth containing usually numerous hymenium-lined cavities (hymenial cavities) but only one in a few cases. **1968** J. H. BURNETT *Fund. Mycol.* v. 119 One or more hymenium-lined cavities develop from potentially sporogenous tissue, the gleba.

glebe (gli:b), *sb.* Forms: 6–7 gleabe, 6–8 *Sc.* gleib, (7 glieb), 7 gleab, gleebe, gleb, 4– glebe. [ad. L. *glēba, glæba* clod, lump; land, soil. Hence also Pr., It., Sp. *gleba*, F. *glèbe.*]

1. The soil of the earth, regarded as the source of vegetable products; earth, land. Occas. *soil and glebe*. Now only *poet.* or *rhet.*

1387 TREVISA *Higden* (Rolls) I. 397 Þey þat this londe [Wales] Be wel lasse þan Engelonde, As good glebe is oon as other [L. *par glebæ gloria*]. **1398** —— *Barth. De P.R.* XIV. xliv. (Tollem. MS.) The glebe [**1535** soile] of þat mounte [Thabor] bereþ vynes, olyues, and oþer tren with frute. **1513** BRADSHAW *St. Werburge* I. 222 The soyle and glebe is set plentuous and commendable. **1598** T. BASTARD *Chrestoleros* (1880) 37 Howses by three, and seauen, and ten he raseth, To make the common gleabe, his priuate land. **1635–56** COWLEY *Davideis* IV. 969 The fertile Glebe requires no time to breed; It quickens and receives at once the Seed. **1747** HERVEY *Medit.* II. 30 The frosts mellow the soil..the Rains impregnate the Glebe and fit it to become a magazine of plenty. **1800–24** CAMPBELL *Power Russia* v, The glebe of fifty kingdoms shall be till'd To feed his dazzling, desolating train. **1841** CATLIN *N. Amer. Ind.* (1844) II. lviii. 224 The great family of North American Indians..are dying at our hands and rendering their glebe to our possession. **1866** FELTON *Anc. & Mod. Greece* I. II. iii. 321 A troop of boys.. pile upon the golden glebe the triumphs of the day.

†**b.** Crop. *Obs. rare*⁻¹.

1661 J. CHILDREY *Brit. Bacon.* 99 The Soil is..in som parts so fruitful, that after three years Gleab of Saffron..the Land..wil yeeld plenty.

2. A piece of cultivated land, a field. Now *poet.*

1387 TREVISA *Higden* (Rolls) VIII. 335 Þe nynþe scheef [of] everich glebe [L. *de omni gleba*] of Engelond he ordeyned for his owne iourneys. **1712** ADDISON *Ps.* xxiii, When in the sultry Glebe I faint, Or on the thirsty Mountains pant. **1764** *Oxford Sausage* 195 To see his Brethren [horses]..Smoak through the Glebe, or trace the destin'd Road. **1792** BURNS '*O, for ane and twenty*', A gleib o' lan', a claut o' gear, Was left me by my auntie, Tam. **1833** TENNYSON *Poems* 57 Many an..upland glebe wealthy in oil and wine.

b. *spec.* A portion of land assigned to a clergyman as part of his benefice.

[**1302–3** *Year-bk. Edw. I* (Rolls) 207 Chose qe est une feez glebe ne poet estre jammes fraunche aumoyne.] *c* **1380** WYCLIF *Wks.* (1880) 449 Ȝif persouns hadden no glebe & no propre hous as eritage, þey sueden more Crist & his apostlis. **1502** ARNOLDE *Chron.* 70 b, Prouided alwey that this acte extende not to cherches beyng in spiritual mennys handis ne to gleuis [*so printed*; ? *read* glebis] off the same. **1574** tr. *Littleton's Tenures* 107 a, If a parson of a church charge the glebe of hys church by his dede [etc.]. **1654** GATAKER *Disc. Apol.* 48, I let out my whole Tithe and Gleab for One hundred pounds by the year. **1704** NELSON *Fest. & Fasts* x. (1739) 598 The Laws of the Land assign to the Clergy..the Manse, or House and Glebe. **1825** COBBETT *Rur. Rides* 427 This parish is a rectory; it has a glebe, and a good solid house. **1859** THACKERAY *Virgin.* v, Virginia was a Church of England colony: the clergymen were paid by the State and glebes allotted to them. **1873** DIXON *Two Queens* III. i. I. 118 Investing every yard and inn, and when their wants were pressing every glebe and hall.

†**3. a.** A clod or mass of earth, ore, etc. (cf. quot. 1727–51). Also *fig. Obs.*

1513 BRADSHAW *St. Werburge* I. 3470 Than this vitall glebe [the body of St. Werburge] by diuine ordinaunce Voluntary permytted naturall resolution. **1583** *Leg. Bp. St. Androis* Pref. 53 Judas Iscariot, for a gleib of geir, Betrayed his Maister lyk a traytour tod. **1625** JACKSON *Creed* v. I. §6 Gold being severed from drosse or gleibs of earth often intermingled with it. **1727–51** CHAMBERS *Cycl., Glebe, Gleba*, in natural history, chemistry, etc., a clod or piece of stone or earth, frequently containing some metal or mineral. The glebes are carried to the forges to be washed, purified, melted, etc. **1756–66** AMORY *J. Buncle* (1825) III. 26 The glittering glebes of a gold colour found here, can be nothing else than glebes gilt with copper. *Ibid.* 239 It is found sometimes in glebes or clods.

†**b.** A small grain or speck of a mineral or chemical substance. *Obs.*

a **1735** ARBUTHNOT *Aliments, Expl. Chym. Terms*, The Chymists define Salt..to be a Body fusible in the Fire, congealable again by Cold into brittle Glebes, or Crystals. **1756** C. LUCAS *Ess. Waters* III. 124 Sulphur, intermixed with glebes of galæna or lead ore. **1765** DELAVAL in *Phil. Trans.* LV. 36 *note*, Iron examined with a microscope when it first becomes rusty, shews it's surface covered with a number of pellucid vitriolic lamellæ, or glebes.

†**4.** An earth, earthy mineral. *Obs.*

1577 HARRISON *England* III. x. (1878) II. 68 The sulphurous glebe called bitumen. **1657** TOMLINSON *Renou's Disp.* 408 Which [Cinnabar] seems to be a purpureous glebe. **1675** E. W[ILSON] *Spadacrene Dunelm.* 42 The Ore or Glebe of Vitriol. **1712** OLDISWORTH *Horace's Odes* VII. 22/2 The old Latins gave Chalk the name of Creta, because that sort of Glebe was imported from Crete. **1701** J. H[AMMOND] *Scelera Aquarum* 25 London is situated on a Wicked Bottom of Earth, called Blue clay..This Blue Kind of Glebe.. maleficates equally Air and Water. *a* **1723** QUINCY *Dispens.* II. xiv. 231 We must consider that Clay is a mineral Glebe.

5. *attrib.* (sense 2 b), as **glebe-house**, a parsonage, manse (now only in Ireland); also †*glebe-land house*; **glebe-land(s** = 2 b above.

1536 *Act 28 Hen. VIII*, c. 11 §4 All the profites of the corne growyng uppon the same glebe landes so manured and sowen. **1625** MASSINGER *New Way* II. iii, You may, with the lease of glebe land call'd knaues-acre, A place I would manure, requite your vassall. **1642** tr. *Perkins' Prof. Bk.* xi. §709. 309 If a parson of a Church be seised of Glebe Land in the right of his Parsonage or Vicarage. *c* **1645** HOWELL *Lett.* I. v. xvi. (1650) 153 It lies upon the Thames, and the Glebe-land house is very large and fair. *a* **1825** T. JEFFERSON *Autobiog.* Wks. 1859 I. 38 A glebe house and land with the other necessary appendages. **1867** TROLLOPE *Chron. Barset* I. xxxiii. 284 The archdeacon..had purchased a property.. contiguous to the glebe-land. **1870** *Daily News* 11 Feb., His promised Bill for affording facilities for the acquisition of glebes and glebe-houses by the different religious denominations in Ireland.

Hence **glebe** *v. rare. trans.* (*a*) To furnish (clergyman or church) with a glebe. (*b*) To set apart as a glebe. (*c*) (See quot. 1611.)

1611 FLORIO, *Glebáre*, to gleebe or breake clods of earth. **1641** SIR B. RUDYARD *Sp. Ho. Comm.* 15 June, Landlords.. gleabed them [parish Churches] with some portion of land. **1797** *Statist. Acc. Scotl.* XIX. 329 A great part of the common was subdivided or glebed.

glebeless ('gli:blɪs), *a.* [f. GLEBE *sb.* + -LESS.] Having no glebe.

1846 in WORCESTER, citing *Gentl. Mag.*

glebie, obs. form of GLEBY.

†**glebose,** *a. Obs.*⁻⁰ [ad. L. *glēbōs-us.*] = GLEBOUS. (Bailey vol. II. 1727.)

†**gle'bosity.** *Obs.*⁻⁰ [f. L. *glebōs-us* full of clods + -ITY.]

1656 BLOUNT *Glossogr., Glebosity*, fulness or clods, or turfs. **1775** in ASH; and in mod. Dicts.

glebous ('gli:bəs), *a. rare.* [ad. L. *glēbōs-us* full of clods, f. *glēba* GLEBE.] Clod-like, earthy; abounding in clods.

1671 J. WEBSTER *Metallogr.* xiii. 216 White silver Ore that was glebous, or cloddy, found at Sneberg. **1721–90** BAILEY, *Glebous*, full of Clods, Cloddy. **1822** T. TAYLOR *Apuleius* 2 The dewy turf and the glebous plains. *Ibid.* 300 Flame-coloured animals are generated in fire..and such as are glebous [L. *glebulenta*] in earth.

†'**glebulent,** *a. Obs.*⁻⁰ [ad. L. *glēbulent-us* (in Apuleius; see GLEBOUS, quot. 1822).]

1721–90 BAILEY, *Glebulent*, cloddy, &c. **1775** in ASH.

glebulose ('gli:bjʊləʊs), *a.* [f. L. *glēbul-a* (dim. of *glēba* clod) + -OSE.] Having glebulæ or small roundish elevations, as the thalli of some lichens.

1866 in *Treas. Bot.* s.v. *Glebulæ*.

gleby ('gli:bɪ), *a.* ? *Obs.* Also 6 glebie, -ye, 7 gleaby. [f. GLEBE *sb.* + -Y¹.] Of soil: Full of clods; rich, fertile.

1566 DRANT *Horace's Sat.* I. ii. A viij b, A landed man.. Whose medowes fayre, and glebye groundes Revenues ample yeeldes. *c* **1611** CHAPMAN *Iliad* III. 81 You dwelling safe in gleby Troy, the Greeks retire their force, T' Achaia. **1622** DRAYTON *Poly-olb.* xxvi. 156 Her Banks, which all her course on both sides do abound With Heath and Finny olds, and often gleaby ground. **1718** PRIOR *Solomon* I. 696 Pernicious flatt'ry! Thy malignant Seeds..Sadly diffus'd o'er Virtue's Gleby Land, With rising Pride amidst the Corn appear. **1794** *Gentl. Mag.* II. 1132 Summer's gleby covert breaks. **1833** O'BRIEN tr. *Villanueva's Phoenic. Irel.* xv. (1837) 161 In that language bolun means a glebe or gleby land.

†**gled,** *ppl. a. Obs.* [Variant of *cled*, see CLEAD *v.*] Clothed, dressed.

c **1375** *Sc. Leg. Saints, Seven Sleepers* 191 He in sorow led his lyf, Sytand in askis & gled in hare. *a* **1450** *Le Morte Arth.* 3172 Hym thowht he satte, in gold Alle gledde,..vpon A whele, that fulle wyde spredd.

gled, obs. form of GLAD, GLEED.

gled, gledful, obs. ff. GLAD, GLADFUL.

glede, gled (gli:d, glɛd). Forms: α. 1 glida, glioda, 4– glede, (6 gleede, gleyd, 7, 9 gleed, 9 *dial.* gleid), 6– glead, (6 gleade). β. *Sc.* 5– gled, (7–8 glaid, 9 glade). [OE. *glida* wk. masc. corresponds to Icel. *gleða*, MSw. *gladha*, Sw. *glada* wk. fem.; the OTeut. form was prob. **glidon-* and with *o-* umlaut *gleđon-*, f. *gliđ-* weak grade of the root of **glīdan* to GLIDE. For the radical sense cf. Da. *glente*, Sw. dial. *glänta* kite, glede, which seem to be related to GLENT *v.*] The kite (*Milvus regalis*). Now chiefly *north.* and *Sc.* (in form *gled*).

The name is also locally applied to other birds of prey, as the buzzard, osprey, and peregrine falcon. The kite is sometimes distinguished as the ***fork-tail(ed)***, ***red***, or ***salmon-tailed gled***, while the names of ***blue***, ***brown*** and ***white-aboon gled*** are given to the hen-harrier.

α. *c* **725** *Corpus Gloss.* 1313 *Milvus*, glioda. *c* **1000** ÆLFRIC *Hom.* I. 586 Se ðe þurh reaflac ȝewilnað ða ðing þe he mid his eaȝum wiðutan sceawað, se is glida, na culfre. **13..** *E.E. Allit. P.* B. 1696 Holȝe were his yȝen & vnder campe hores, & al watz gray as þe glede. *a* **1340** HAMPOLE *Psalter* lxii. 8, I am þi bridde, and if þou hill me not þe glede will ravishe me. **1398** TREVISA *Barth. De P.R.* v. xl. (1495) 156 Some fowles haue a grete galle on the lyuer..as in a goshawke and in a kyte or glede. **1523** FITZHERB. *Husb.* §146 To se that they [chickens] be well kepte from the gleyd, crowes, fullymartes & other vermin. **1609** HOLLAND *Amm. Marcell.* XIV. iii. 7 The Saracens..spoyled and destroyed, like unto ravenous Gledes and Kites [L. *milvi*]. **1688** CLAYTON in *Phil. Trans.* XVII. 989 The largest I take to be that they call the Grey Eagle, being much of the colour of our Kite or Glead. **1766** *Chron.* in *Ann. Reg.* 63/1 One James Haxup of Tadcaster shot a glead or kite that measured six feet between wing end and wing end. **1829** SOUTHEY *Inscrip. Caledon. Canal* 2 The glede Wheeling between the mountains in mid air. **1881** *Standard* 2 Mar. 5 The kite, or glead, or puttock is almost extinct.

β. *c* **1450** HENRYSON *Tale of Dog* 30 The Gled, the Graip at the bar couth stand, As Advocatis expert in to the lawis. **1457** *Sc. Acts, Jas. II*, c. 32 (1814) II. 51/2 Ruks crawys and vþer foulys of reif as ernys, bussards gledds and myttalls. **1535** STEWART *Cron. Scot.* (1858) I. 108 All that tyme with falsheid he thame fed, As quha wald set ane girne befoir ane gled. *a* **1605** MONTGOMERIE *Flyting w. Polwart* 331 Thy gall and thy guisserne to glaids shall bee given. **1768** ROSS *Helenore* I. 58 As..hen upo' the midden head Wad tent her chuckens frae the greedy glaid. *a* **1774** FERGUSSON *Leith Races* Poems (1845) 33 Then dinna gape like gleds, for greed, To sweel hale bickers down. **1814** SCOTT *Wav.* xlii, I am as hungry as a gled. **1884** W. C. SMITH *Kildrostan* 64 My old heart Goes pit-a-pat to hear it; like the merle That sees a gled o'erhead.

b. *Comb.*, as †*glede-coloured* adj.; also **gled wing**, the name of an artificial fly.

1564 *Richmond. Wills* (Surtees) 171 A yonge black horsse, xlˢ. A yonge gled-coloured, price xlˢ. **1680** *Lond. Gaz.* No. 1478/4 Stolen..a Dun glaid coloured Nag, with some white hairs. **1693** *Ibid.* No. 2867/4 Stolen..a Sandy grey or Glead coloured Horse. **1867** F. FRANCIS *Angling* x. (1880) 359 The Gled Wing or Red Wing.

glede, obs. form of GLEED.

gledge (glɛdʒ), *v. Sc.* [Of obscure origin; cf. GLEE, GLEG *vbs.*] *intr.* 'To look asquint, to take a side view; to look cunningly and slily on one side' (Jam.).

1805 A. SCOTT *Poems* 56 (Jam.) Here cautious love maun gledge a-squint, And stounlins feast the ee. **1813** HOGG *Queen's Wake* I. 71 The corby craw cam gledgin near, The ern gede veeryng bye. **1818** SCOTT *Br. Lamm.* xxvi, Let them be gentles allenarly, without ony fremd servants..to be gledging and gleeing about.

Hence **gledge** *sb.*, a side-glance; a sly look.

1816 SCOTT *Old Mort.* xxxviii, He gae a gledge wi' his ee, that I kenn'd he took up what I said.

gleditschia (glɛˈdɪtʃ(ɪ)ə). *Bot.* Also **gleditsia**, **gleditzia**. [mod.L. (C. Linnæus *Genera Plantarum* (ed. 2, 1742) 480), f. the name of J. G. *Gleditsch* (1714–1786), a German botanist + -IA[1].] An ornamental tree of the genus so called, belonging to the family Leguminosæ, and including the honey locust tree of North America.

1770 R. WESTON *Univ. Botanist* I. 116 Gleditsia of Java. **1838** J. C. LOUDON *Arboretum et Fruticetum Britannicum* II. 650 The three-thorned gleditschia, or honey locust, in favourable situations in its native country, attains the height of 70 ft. or 80 ft. **1855** A. M. MURRAY *Let.* 7 May (1856) II. xxv. 157 A stream..bordered by..gleditzias, cedars, sweet and black gum-trees. **1905** C. S. SARGENT *Man. Trees N. Amer.* 556 Gleditsia is confined to eastern North America.. south-western Asia, China, Japan, and west tropical Africa. **1914** W. J. BEAN *Trees & Shrubs Hardy in Brit. Isles* I. 594 No Gleditschia has any beauty of blossom, the flowers being small, green, and borne in racemes a few inches long. **1957** M. HADFIELD *Brit. Trees* 360 Locust is a name given in North America both to trees of the genus *Robinia* and to the rather similar *Gleditsia*.

gledliche, gledluker: see GLADLY.

glednesse, -schipe, -scype, obs. ff. GLADNESS, -SHIP.

gledunge, var. GLADDING *vbl. sb.*, *Obs.*

†ˈ**gledy**, *a. Obs. rare*⁻¹. [f. *glede* GLEED + -Y[1].] Glowing hot.

c **1385** CHAUCER *L.G.W.* Prol. 105 Constreyned me with so gledy desire.

glee (gliː), *sb.* Forms: α. 1 **glíu, glíw, gléow-**, 3 **gleow, gleu, (gleaw)**, 3, 5 **glu**, 3–4 (*Sc.* 6) **glew**, 4–5 **glewe**. β. 1 **glío, (glíȝ-)**, 1–2 **gléo**, 4 **gleo**, 3–6 **gle**, 3, 6 *Sc.* **glie**, 6 **glye**, 4– **glee**. [OE. *glíw, gléo* neut. = ON. *glý* (rare); the word is wanting in the other Teutonic languages. The orig. stem **gliujo-* was variously treated in OE., yielding the forms *glieȝ-*, *glíȝ-* (in compounds and oblique cases), *glíw* (the nom. is found only in glosses, but *glíwes*, etc. are common in poetry, more rarely *gléow-*), and *gléo* (poetic). From the two latter forms came ME. *glew* and *gle*, of which *glew* became obs. in the 16th c., surviving longest in the northern dialects. (Cf. HUE from orig. **hiujo-*.)

In OE. and ME. the word is chiefly poetic. After the 15th c. it seems to have been rarely used, and in the 17th c. is almost entirely absent from literature. Phillips (1706) marks it as obsolete, and Johnson considered it a merely comic word (see 3, quot. 1755). It again became common towards the end of the 18th c., but the cause of its revival is not apparent.]

†**1. a.** Entertainment, play, sport; *occas.* scornful jesting, mockery. Also ***chamber-glew*** = CHAMBERING 2. *Obs.*

α. *a* **700** *Epinal Gloss.* 398 *Facitiæ* [sic], gliu. *Ibid.* 550 *In mimo*, in gliuuæ. *a* **1000** *Phœnix* 139 in *Exeter Bk.*, Ǽniȝ þara dreama þe dryhten ȝescop gumum to gliwe in þas ȝeomran woruld. *c* **1300** *Havelok* 2332 þo mouthe men se eueril gleu. *a* **1310** in Wright *Lyric P.* 114 Mury hit ys..in hyre bour, With gomenes ant with gleowes. *c* **1450** HENRYSON *Mor. Fab.* 19 Of chalmer-glew..Wasted hee was, of nature colde and dry. **1535** STEWART *Cron. Scot.* III. 256 The bemand buglis all of bras that blew, Quhilk for to heir it wes ane glorius glew.

β. *c* **725** *Corpus Gloss.* 354 *Cabillatio*, glio. *c* **1000** tr. *Basil's Admon.* ix. (1849) 54 Hi hæfdon him to gliȝe his halwendan myneȝunge. *a* **1225** *Ancr. R.* 210 Summe iuglurs beoð þet ne kunne seruen of non oðer gleo, buten makien cheres, & wrenchen mis hore muð, & schulen mid hore eien. *a* **1300** *Floriz & Bl.* 793 Þer was alle kunnes gleo þat miȝte at eni briddale beo. **13..** *E.E. Allit. P.* A. 95 So grac[i]os gle couþe no mon gete As here & se her adubbement. *c* **1386** [see GAME *sb.* 1]. **1542** UDALL *Erasm. Apoph.* 297 b, Wherupon wer made plaies for a triumphe almoste in euery cornere through out the citee..And euen emiddes all this glye, the report goeth, that [etc.]. **1567** *Gude & Godlie B.* (S.T.S.) 206 O Jesu! gif thay thocht greit glie To se Goddis word downe smorit. **1579** LYLY *Euphues* (Arb.) 109, I shall be..flowted and reflowted with intolerable glee.

†**b.** In phrases. ***to have glee, to make oneself glee***: to make sport. ***to make one's glee of*** or ***on***: to make sport of (a person or thing). *Obs.*

a **1300** *Floriz & Bl.* 477 Þis oþere loȝen and hadde gleo, And goþ aȝen and leteþ beo. **13..** *Guy Warw.* (A.) 3648 Of mi wounde þou madest þi gle. *a* **1450** *Le Morte Arth.* 1164 Now thou on knyghtis makeste thy glewe to lye vppon hem for envye. **1602** CAREW *Cornwall* (1723) 108 b, Many wayfarers make themselues glee, by putting the Inhabitants in mind of this priuiledge [etc.]. **1607** *Schol. Disc. agst. Antichr.* II. vi. 62 Doth not the papist make himselfe glee, to see the preachers..throwne downe into the depth of miserie?

†**c.** *north.* Affair, business (cf. GAME *sb.* 5). *Obs.*

α. *a* **1300** *Cursor M.* 12933 It was sene he noght him kneu, quen he be-gan do suilk a gleu. **1375** BARBOUR *Bruce* VI. 558 The kyng said, as the glew is gane, Bettir than thou I mycht It do. *c* **1425** WYNTOUN *Cron.* VIII. v. 142 Gyve Brws beis kyng of Scotland,..yhe sall sare rew Ðat ewyre of þis begouth þe Glewe.

β. **1375** BARBOUR *Bruce* I. 90 Thai trowyt that he..Wald hawe iugyt in lawte; Bot other wayis all ȝheid the gle. *c* **1475** *Rauf Coilȝear* 98 The gude wyf glaid with the gle to begin.. To the dure went our Dame [etc.].

†**2. a.** Musical entertainment, playing; music, melody. Also *fig.* of other sounds. *Obs.*

α. *c* **1000** *Versus Gnom.* 172 (Gr.) Ðy læs ðe him con leoða worn, oððe mid hondum con hearpan gretan, hafað him his gliwes ȝiefe. *c* **1000** *Ags. Ps.* (Th.) lxvii. 24 Ealdormenn.. gleowe sungon. *c* **1250** *Gen. & Ex.* 459 Iobal is broðer song and glew, Wit of musike, wel he knew. *a* **1300** *Cursor M.* 7433 Quil wit gleu, and quil wit sang..þus he serued saul lang. *c* **1320** *Sir Tristr.* 290 He tauȝt him ich alede Of ich maner of glewe And euerich playing þede. *c* **1440** *Promp. Parv.* 200/1 Glu or mynstralcye, *musica, armonia*.

β. *Beowulf* (Z.) 2105 Þær wæs ȝidd and gleo..; hwilum hildedeor hearpan wynne, gomenwudu grette. *c* **897** K. ÆLFRED *Gregory's Past.* xxvi. 183 Ðonne ȝefeng Dauid his hearpan, & ȝestillde his wodðraȝa mid ðæm gliȝe [*Cott. MS.* gliȝȝe.] *c* **1205** LAY. 7006 He cuðen [*v.r.* cuþe] al þeos songes & þat gleo of ilche londe. *c* **1275** *Serving Christ* 28 in *O.E. Misc.* 91 Þer is gronynge and grure and gryslich gle. **1297** R. GLOUC. (Rolls) 5515 Þere he harpede so wel þat he payde al þe route Hii ȝeue him siluer uor is gle & lete him go is wey. *c* **1366** CHAUCER *A.B.C.* 100 We han none other melody ne glee Us to rejoyce in our adversitee. *c* **1400** *Rowland & O.* 34 Burdours in to þe haulle þay brynge, þat gayly with þaire gle gan synge. **1508** DUNBAR *Tua mariit wemen* 518 Thai [the birds] maid a glorius gle amang the grene bewis. **1523** SKELTON *Garl. Laurel* 278 That in the forest was non so great a tree But that he daunced for joye of that gle.

†**b.** An instrument of music. *Obs.*

a **1225** *Leg. Kath.* 145 Ha iherde..ludinge of þe men, gleowinge of euch gleo [L. *multimodum genus organorum*]. *a* **1300** *Cursor M.* 1521 (Gött.) Tobal first vnderfang Musyk ..Organis, harpe, and oþer gleu, He drou þaim vt of music neu. **13..** *K. Alis.* 191 Orgles, tymbres, al maner gleo Was dryuen ageyn that lady freo. *c* **1320** *Sir Tristr.* 1224 His gles weren so sellike þat wonder þouȝt hem þare. His harp, his croude was rike. **1387** TREVISA *Higden* (Rolls) VI. 179 He hadde and used instrumentis of musik, pipes and strenges, and oþere manere of glee.

c. A musical composition, of English origin, for three or more voices (one voice to each part), set to words of any character, grave or gay, often consisting of two or more contrasted movements, and (in strict use) without accompaniment.

The glee differs from the *madrigal* in involving little or no contrapuntal imitation, and from the *part-song* in the independence of its parts, which form 'a series of interwoven melodies' (Stainer & Barrett).

1659 PLAYFORD *Sel. Ayres & Dial.* 84 A glee to Bacchus with chorus. **1767** PERCY *Reliq.*, *Notes on Ess. Anc. Minstr.* 57 As for the word Glees, it is to this day used in a musical sense, and applied to a peculiar piece of composition. **1775** SHERIDAN *Rivals* II. i, 'Sdeath, to make her self the pipe and ballad monger of a circle, to soothe her light heart with catches and glees. **1835** HOOD *Poetry, Prose, & Worse* xxvi, Suppose that..They were all set as glees for four voices. **1886** W. A. BARRETT *Eng. Glees & Part-songs*, Pref. vi.

3. a. Mirth, joy, rejoicing; in modern use, a lively feeling of delight caused by special circumstances and finding expression in appropriate gestures and looks. In early quots. frequently in phrase ***game and glee***.

α. *a* **1250** *Prov. Ælfred* 47 in *O.E. Misc.* 104 He is one god ouer alle godnesse. He is one gleaw [*v.r.* gleu] ouer alle glednesse. He is one blisse ouer alle blissen. *a* **1300** *Cursor M.* 23359 Of alkin gladnes es þar [in heaven] gleu And þat es euer ilike neu. *c* **1375** *Sc. Leg. Saints, George* 666 To þe tempil..al ȝed with grete glew for to se George sacryfy. *c* **1430** *Hymns Virg.* 29 His moornynge schulde turne into ioie briȝt, His longynge into glewe. **1560** ROLLAND *Crt. Venus* I. 90 In Venus Bowr [*printed* Bowe] to eik baith game and glew. *a* **1568** in *Bannatyne MS.* (Hunter. Club.) 653/20 And I may nych hir neir Than gon wer neuir my glew.

β. *a* **1200**, *c* **1250** [see GAME 1]. *c* **1275** *Long Life* 40 in *O.E. Misc.* 158 Ine deð schal þi lif endi, And ine wop al þi gleo. *a* **1300** *Cursor M.* 3370 Rebecca and ysaac er samen Mette wit mikel gle [*later MSS.* ioye] and gammen. *c* **1375** *Sc. Leg. Saints, Thomas* 328 Gyfe ȝe wil parcenaris be Of his grete blys & lestand gle. *c* **1410** *Chron. Eng.* 456 in Ritson *Metr. Rom.* II, Muche he lovede gle ant gome. *c* **1460** *Towneley Myst.* i. 84, I am so fare and bright, Of me commys alle this light, This gam & all this gle. **1598** MARSTON *Pygmal.* IV. 156 Laugh and sport with me At strangers follies with a merry glee. *c* **1600** *Timon* II. iv. (1842) 35 By Iove, my hearte is full of glee That I haue founde out such a one as hee. **1714** GAY *Sheph. Week* v. 27 Is Blouzelinda dead? farewel my Glee! No Happiness is now reserv'd for me. **1755** JOHNSON, *Glee*, joy; merriment; gayety..It is not now used, except in ludicrous writing, or with some mixture of irony and contempt. **1770** GOLDSM. *Des. Vill.* 201 Full well they laugh'd with counterfeited glee. **1787** MAD. D'ARBLAY *Diary* 18 Jan., A person..spoke to me by my name; I never heard the sound with more glee. **1802** WORDSWORTH *Sonn. Liberty* xii. 1, There came a Tyrant, and with holy glee Thou fought'st against him. **1814** D. H. O'BRIAN *Captiv. & Escape* 124 My feet were healing very fast, and I advanced with great glee. **1828** *Life Planter, Jamaica* 288 Attired in their best and gayest apparel, they seemed all life and glee. *a* **1859** MACAULAY *Hist. Eng.* xxiii. V. 117 William felt all the glee of a schoolboy who is leaving harsh masters and quarrelsome comrades to pass the Christmas holidays at a happy home. **1884** J. COLBORNE *Hicks Pasha* 165 They displayed all the childish glee of semi-savage natures.

†**b.** In phrases. ***to make glee***: to be glad or merry, to rejoice. ***(there) glads (gains, games) him no glee***: nothing gives him pleasure. ***to have glee of***: to find pleasure in. ***to make one good glee***: to welcome or entertain heartily. *Obs.*

α. *a* **1300** *Cursor M.* 11031 [The child] Again him mad gladnes an glu [*Gött. MS.* ioi and gleu; *Trin. MS.* murþes newe]. *c* **1330** R. BRUNNE *Chron.* (1810) 295 Whan þei þe trumpe herd, þat he to bataile blewe, & saw þe ȝates sperd, þan gamened þam no glewe. *c* **1430** *Syr Tryam.* 462 There dwellyd that lady longe Moche myrthe was them amonge, But ther gamyd hur no glewe.

β. *c* **1300** *Maximon* in *Rel. Ant.* I. 123 Of nothing that y se Ne gladieth me no gle. *a* **1352** MINOT *Poems* (ed. Hall) iv. 57 When sir Philip of France herd tell þat king Edward in feld wald dwell þan gayned him no gle. *c* **1375** *Sc. Leg. Saints, Baptist* 404 He [John] in his modir wambe mad gle. *c* **1475** *Rauf Coilȝear* 717 Dame, of thy glitterand gyde haue I na gle. **1579** SPENSER *Sheph. Cal.* May 282 Being within, the Kidde made him [the fox] good glee.

†**c.** A state of exaltation or prosperity. *Obs.*

1579 SPENSER *Sheph. Cal.* Feb. 224 Now stands the Brere like a Lord alone, Puffed vp with pryde and vaine pleasaunce; But all this glee had no continuance. **1588** GREENE *Perimedes* 28 Alexander the great..amidst his most glee and greatest glorye, was cowardlye poysoned.

†**d.** Applied to a person (cf. JOY). *Obs.*

c **1610** MIDDLETON, etc. *Widow* I. ii, Thou art my glee, Martino.

†**4. a.** Bright colour, beauty. *Obs.*

c **1440** *York Myst.* i. 82 What I am worthely wroght with wyrschip, i-wys! For in a glorius gle my gleteryng it glemes. ? *a* **1500** *Chester Pl.* vii. 343 It semes..a bright star for to bee ..from it we may not flee but aye glow [2 *MSS.* glye] on the glee, till it downe glide. **1567** FENTON *Trag. Disc.* vii. 141 Conuerting the naturall coollour [of her haire] in to a glistering glee suborned by arte. **1573–80** *Baret's Alv.* To Rdr. A vj a/1 Large wide feelds..Adornde with floures most beautifull in glee.

†**b.** Phr. ***gold and glee***: cf. prec. and quot. 1567.

1563 *Mirr. Mag.*, *Buckingham* xli, Agaynst whose feare no heapes of golde and glie [*rime-wd.* skye]..His cruell hart of safetie could assure. [**1567** FENTON *Trag. Disc.* vii. 139 To encrease the glee of his golden coffers.] **1590** SPENSER *F.Q.* I. ix. 32 Not for gold nor glee will I abyde By you.

5. *attrib.* and *Comb.*, as ***glee-book, -god, -maiden, -singer, -singing, -woman***; **glee-club**, a society formed for the practice and performance of glees and part-songs; also *transf.* †Also (OE. and early ME.) **glee-beam**, a poetical term for the harp; **glee-craft**, minstrelsy; **glee-dream**, delight of minstrelsy. Also GLEEMAN.

Beowulf (Z.) 2263 Næs hearpan wyn, gomen *gleobeames. *a* **1240** *Ureisun* in *Cott. Hom.* 193 Mid ham is muruhðe moniuold wið-ute teone and treie Gleobeames and gome inouh. **1862** O. W. NORTON *Army Lett.* (1903) 124, I would rather see two or three pretty girls and a *glee-book ..than the whole of them. **1814** R. CLARK (*title*) The words of the most favourite pieces, performed at the *Glee Club, the Catch Club, and other public Societies. **1879** J. R. PLANCHÉ *Extrav.* I. 46 Come to the Glee-club, at the Cat and Swallow. **1879** *Encycl. Brit.* X. 677/1 The most famous amongst these—The Glee Club—was founded in 1783, and at first used to meet at the house of Mr R. Smith, in St Paul's Churchyard. **1934** H. NICOLSON *Let.* 7 Nov. (1966) 187 He would ask the glee-club to sing that song. **1971** *Times* 30 Jan. 13/1 Labour members will neither win back the confidence of the country nor prevent the passage of the Industrial Relations Bill by turning themselves into a political glee club. *a* **900** tr. *Gregory's Dial.* I. ix. (Lye) *Gliȝ-cræft. *c* **1205** LAY. 7012 Al þis mon-cun þat of him iherden tellen seiden þat he wes god of alle gleo-cræften. *Beowulf* (Z.) 3021 Nu se here-wisa hleahtor aleȝde gamen ond *gleo-dream. *c* **1205** LAY. 1823 Brutus & his duȝeðe makeden halinesse..mid murie gleo-dreme. **1586** WARNER *Alb. Eng.* III. xvii, Whom Brutons did their *Glee-god for his skill in Musicke call. *c* **1000** *Ags. Ps.* (Spelm.) lxvii. 27 Madena glywiendra *vel* *gliew meden. **1810** SCOTT *Lady of L.* VI. vi, Thou now hast glee-maiden and harp. **1811** JANE AUSTEN *Let.* 18 Apr. (1952) 269 There is to be some very good Music, 5 professionals, 3 of them *Glee singers. **1838** DICKENS *Nich. Nick.* ii, Itinerant glee-singers. **1854** E. TWISLETON *Let.* 29 June (1928) xi. 213 Mrs. Adderley's concert was all *glee-singing, English music and very pretty. **1912** W. OWEN *Let.* 22 Sept. (1967) 162 Putting together..a Glee-Singing Band. **1828** SCOTT *F.M. Perth* x, Here is a strolling *glee-woman with her viol, preparing to sing beneath the royal windows.

Hence †**glee** *v.* (*a*) *intr.* to make merry, to rejoice; (*b*) *trans.* to delight, gladden. Also ˈ**gleeing** *vbl. sb.*, playing. *rare.*

The vb. corresponding to *glee* sb. was properly GLEW (q.v.), and the following instances of *glee* vb. are of doubtful value.

a **1300** *K. Horn* 1490 (Ritson) Hue gonne murie synge And makeden huere gleynge [*v.r.* gleowinge]. *a* **1400** *Pistill of Susan* 84 On grapes þe goldfinch þei gladen and glees [*v.r.* gladyn in her glees]. *Ibid.* 354 Alle þe gomus..gladen and glees [*v.r.* gladid in her glees]. *a* **1400** *Sir Beues* (MS. C.) 189, I wolde, þow it hadde The for to glee.

glee, gley (gliː, glaɪ), *v. Obs.* exc. *north.* and *Sc.* Forms: α. 3 **glei, glaye**, 3–4, 9 **gley**. β. 4–6 **gle**, 5–7, 9 **glee**. γ. 4 **gliȝe**, 5 **gly-**, 6, 8 **glye, glie**, 7 **gly**. [Of obscure origin. The northern forms (α and β) are normal variants from an orig. ME. *glēȝen*; in the midland dialects this was narrowed to *glīȝen*, whence later *gly* (cf. DIE, EYE, FLY, etc.). The vbs. GLEDGE, GLEG are related as FLEG *v.*[1] to FLEY *v.*] *intr.* To look asquint; to have a cast in one or both eyes. Also, to look with one eye (see quot. 1866).

α, β. *a* **1300** *Cursor M.* 3862 Þe eilder sister [Leah] he forsok For sco gleied [*Gött. MS.* gleyed], als sais þe bok. [*Fairf. MS.* gleand ho was for-soþ of loke.] *c* **1400** *Destr. Troy* 3772 With grete Ene & gray, gleyit a litill. **1483** *Cath. Angl.* 158/2 To Glee, *limare*. **1526** SKELTON *Magnyf.* 2093, I daunsed the darlynge on my kne; I garde her gaspe, I garde her gle. **1552** HULOET, Glaye, or loke a skope, *transuertere hirquos*. **1570** LEVINS *Manip.* 46/28 To Glee, *lippire*. **1691** RAY *Collect. Words* 63 To look a squint, to glee. **1808–80** JAMIESON, *Gley, glee, glye*, to squint, to look obliquely. **1818** [see GLEDGE]. **1824–7** MOIR *Mansie Wauch* xii. (1828) 189 But I could scarcely keepe from laughing when I glee'd round over my shoulder, and saw [etc.]. **1866** GREGOR *Banffsh. Gloss.*, *Gley*, to take aim; to look with one eye. **1876** *Mid. Yorksh. Gloss.*, *Glee*, to squint.

γ. *c* **1340** *Cursor M.* 3862 (Trin.) Þe elder sister [Leah] he forsoke For she gliȝed seiþ þe boke. *c* **1400** *Destr. Troy* 3943 Faire Ene hade þe freike, & of fyn colour, Glemyt as þe glasse and gliet a little. ? *a* **1500** Glye [see GLEE *sb.* 4]. **1570** LEVINS *Manip.* 99/13 To Glye, *lippire.* **1573-80** BARET *Alv.* G 274 To glie, or looke askue, ouerthwart. **1673** WEDDERBURN *Voc.* (Jam.) *Laborat strabismo*, he glieth. **1674** RAY *N.C. Words* 21 *To Gly* (Lincoln), to look a-squint. **1721** KELLY *Scot. Prov.* 339 There's a time to Glye and a time to look even.

Hence **'gleeing** *vbl. sb.* and *ppl. a.*; **'gleer, 'gleyer, 'glyer**, one that squints; **glee, gley** *sb.*, a squint, a glance or side-look. Also *Comb.*, as ***glyhalter*** (see quot. 1825).

c **1440** *Promp. Parv.* 199/1 Glyare, or goguleye (*S.* gloyere), *limus, strabo. Ibid.*, Glyynge, *strabositas.* **14..** *Nom.* in Wr.-Wülcker 709/23 *Hec stroba* [sic], a woman glyande. *Ibid.* 709/33 *Hic strabo*, a glyere. **1483** *Cath. Angl.* 158/2 A Gleer, *limus.* *a* **1605** POLWART *Flyting w. Montgomerie* 788 Feard flyar, loud lyar, gooked gleyar on the gallows. **1824-7** MOIR *Mansie Wauch* xii. (1828) 191 Giving first a glee eastward. *a* **1825** FORBY *Voc. E. Anglia*, *Gly-halter*, a halter or bridle with blinkers, as those of draught-horses. **1857** J. SCHOLES *Jaunt to see th' Queen* 6 (Lanc. Gloss.) Iv yoan tay notis yoan see ut aw've o sooart ov o gley wi mi een. **1897** *Blackw. Mag.* Nov. 610 A servant lass with one eye on the pot and the other up the lum as we say of a glee or cast.

gleece, dial. var. GLACE *sb.*

gleed (gliːd), *sb.* Forms: 1 glœ́d, gléd, 2-6 glede, 4-6 gleede, 5-6 *Sc.* gleid, 6-7 glead(e, 7- gleed. [Common Teut.: OE. *glœ́d, gléd* str. f. = OFris. *glêd*, OS. *glôd-* (MDu. *gloet, gloed-*, Du. *gloed*), OHG. *gluot* (mod.G. *glut*), ON. *glóð* (Sw., Da. *glöd*):—OTeut. **glôđi-z*, related to GLOW *v.*]

1. A live coal; an ember. Now only *arch.* or *dial.*

c **950** *Lindisf. Gosp.* John xviii. 18 Woeron stondende ðа esnæs & embeht-menn æt gloedum forðon cald uæs. *c* **1000** *Ags. Ps.* (Th.) cxl[i]. 2 Swa ricels byð, þonne hit ȝifre gleda bærnað. *c* **1175** *Lamb. Hom.* 43 Summe þer wepeð, and all heore teres beoð berninde gleden. *a* **1225** *Ancr. R.* 122 Seint Lorens also iðolede þet te gredil hef him upwardes mid berninde gleden. *c* **1386** CHAUCER *Pars. T.* ¶474 Looke how that fir of smal gleedes that been almoost dede vnder asshen wollen quike agayn whan they been touched with brymstoon. *c* **1450** HENRYSON *Mor. Fab.* 15 Thine owne fire (friend) so it bee but a gleid, It warmeth well, and is worth gold to thee. **1563** SACKVILLE *Induct. Mirr. Mag.* lxviii, I can no more but tell howe there is seene Fayre Ilium fal in burning red gledes downe. *a* **1656** BP. HALL *Occas. Medit.* §37 Yet, when I stir up these embers to the bottom, there are found some living gleeds, which do both contain fire, and are apt to propagate it. **1814** CARY *Dante, Parad.* xiv. 47 As the gleed Which gives out flame. **1847** LONGF. *Ev.* I. v. 98 The wind seized the gleeds and the burning thatch.

fig. *c* **1386** CHAUCER *Reeve's T.* Prol. 29 Foure gleedes han we whiche I shal deuyse Avauntyng lyng Anger Coueitise Thise foure sparkles longen vn to eelde. **1412-20** LYDG. *Chron. Troy* I. ii, So of enuy hotter brent the glede. **1589** R. ROBINSON *Gold. Mirr.* (1851) 35 My name is Mars that am the bloody God The gleids that glow within my breast breed mischief al abrode. **1612-15** BP. HALL *Contempl. O.T.* xx. ix, Yet even now out of the gleeds of Judah doth God raise up a glorious light to his forlorne Church. *a* **1656** —— *Occas. Medit.* §22 Those few weak gleeds of grace, that are in me, might soon go out, if they were not thus refreshed. **1678** BUNYAN *Come & Welc.* 57 The sweet and warm gleads of the promise are like the comfortable beams of the Sun, which liven and refresh.

†**b.** Frequent in similes, as ***red*** (***hot, fierce***) ***as a gleed***; ***to burn*** (***glow, glister, glitter***) ***as a gleed***; ***to spring as gleed*** or ***as spark of gleed***. *Obs.*

c **1300** *Havelok* 91 That he ne sprong forth so sparke of glede. *c* **1330** R. BRUNNE *Chron.* (1810) 295 Was no cheyne so hie, þat he ne sprong ouer als glede. *c* **1386** CHAUCER *Knt.'s T.* 1139 The crueel Ire reed as any gleede. ? *a* **1400** *Morte Arth.* 116 His brode eghne That fulle brymly for breth brynte as the gledys. *c* **1430** *Pilgr. Lyf Manhode* I. (1869) 23 She hadde hire handes vnder hire sides, and hire eyen glowynge as gleedes. **1513** DOUGLAS *Æneis* XI. x. I Turnus hym self, als fers as ony gleid, Ful bissely addressit on his weid. **1535** STEWART *Cron. Scot.* II. 67 Tha fled als fast as spark gois out of gleid. **1566** DRANT *Horace's Sat.* II. vi. H viij b, Where scarlet vestures reade, On Iuery beddes, did glose with gleames, as it were glowing gleade. *a* **1650** *Arth. & King Cornw.* 113 in Furniv. *Percy Folio* I. 63 The eyes that beene in his head, they glister as doth the gleed.

†**2.** A fire. *Obs.*

13.. *Gaw. & Gr. Knt.* 1609 Braydez out þe boweles, brennez hom on glede. *c* **1375** *Sc. Leg. Saints, George* 682 þane com a fyre.. fra of þe hewine.. & brynt þe temple in a glede. *c* **1386** CHAUCER *Miller's T.* 193 He.. sente hire.. wafres pipyng hoot out of the gleede. *c* **1470** HENRY *Wallace* IV. 751, I haiff seruit to be brynt in a gleid. *c* **1500** *New Notbroune Mayd* 353 in Hazl. *E.P.P.* III. 15 Though he deserue To brynne and sterue In the infernall glede. **1567** TURBERV. *Epit.* etc. 42 And when you see the Pellet pierce the Skyes And Powder make a proufe of hidden gleede. **1755** R. FORBES *Ajax's Sp.* 5, I.. stood the brunt An' slocken'd out that gleed.

†**3.** A beam (of light). *Obs. rare.*

1566 ADLINGTON *Apuleius* II. (1596) 20, I thought that.. I should see and heare some Oracle from heauen, and from the gleede of the Sunne. **1566** STUDLEY tr. *Seneca's Medea* IV. 41 The bygger beare with golden gleede the greekish fleete doth guyde.

4. *local. pl.* Cinders, coke used as fuel, esp. by nail-makers.

1853 *Ann. Reg.* 89 She went to work at Pelsall, washing 'gledes' at a shilling a day. **1870** *Gd. Words* 1 Apr. 253/2 A little girl.. blows the 'gleeds' (refuse fuel from the puddling-furnaces of the Black Country) into blue interlambent flames. **1882** *Standard* 26 Dec. 2 In the centre of the shed.. there is a 'hearth', fed by 'gledes' or breezes. **1891** T. ANDERTON *Lett. fr. Country Ho.* 237 They poke out the gleeds at the bottom with the tickler, and put them at the top with the tongs.

5. *Comb.*, as ***gleed-like, -red*** (cf. ON. *glóðrauðr*) adjs.

a **1240** *Sawles Warde* in *Cott. Hom.* 249 Euch an bereð.. an unrude raketehe gled read of fure. *Ibid.* 253 Eawles gled reade. **1839** BAILEY *Festus* (1848) 75/1 The grave was gone, And in the stead there stood a gleedlike throne.

Hence **gleed** *v. pseudo-arch.*, (*a*) *intr.* to burn, glow; (*b*) *trans.* to light up. *rare.*

1567 TURBERV. *Ovid's Ep.* R ij, The nearer I approche, the more my flame dooth gleede. *a* **1823** *Baronne o' Gairtly* vi. in A. Laing *Thistle* 13 The fyre flaucht gleeds the skie, Ye're welcome, quo' the baul Baronne, To licht me on my wye.

gleed, gleyd (gliːd, glaɪd), *ppl. a. Obs.* exc. *north.* and *Sc.* Forms: 5 gleyit, 5-7 gleid, 6 glyed, 7 glide, 6, 8-9 gleyd, 9 gleyed, 8-9 gleed. [f. GLEE *v.* + -ED[1].]

1. Of persons: Having a cast in one or both eyes; squint-eyed. Also, one-eyed (see quots. *c* 1470 and 1866).

c **1470** HENRY *Wallace* VI. 469 [He] couth weyll luk and wynk with the ta E; Sum scornyt him, sum gleid carll cald him thar. **1482** *Acta Dom. Audit.* (1839) 101/1 The sade gleyit andro being oft tymes callit & nocht comperit. **1535** COVERDALE *Lev.* xxi. 20 For who so euer hath a blemysh vpon him shal not come nere whether he be blynde.. or hath eny blemysh in the eye or is gleyd. *c* **1565** LINDESAY (Pitscottie) *Chron. Scot.* (1728) p. xvi, The crooked Hume and the glyed Hepburn. *a* **1605** POLWART *Flyting w. Montgomerie* 751 Gleyd glaiker. **1724** RAMSAY *Tea-t. Misc.* (1733) I. 90 There will be gleed Geordy Janners. **1812** MACNEILL *Poems* (ed. 3) II. 117 Gleyed Sawnie, the haivrel, he met me yestreen. **1866** GREGOR *Banffsh. Gloss.*, *Gleyt*, blind of an eye. Rarely used in the sense of squint-eyed. **1893** *Northumbld. Gloss.*, *Gleed*,.. squinting. 'Gleed Will' —squinting Will.

b. Of the eyes: Squint-.

a **1613** OVERBURY *Crumms* Wks. (1856) 256, I think such speech becomes a King noe more than glide-eyes does his face, when I think he looks on me, he sees me not.

2. Not straight, crooked, twisted. Also *transf.* of character. ***to gang gleed***: to go wrong.

c **1565** LINDESAY (Pitscottie) *Chron. Scot.* (1728) 115 And there to jeopardy a rose-noble on a cast, against a gleed half-peny. **1808-80** JAMIESON, *Gleyd*,.. oblique, not direct.. *That wa's gleyd*, that wall stands obliquely. **1818** SCOTT *Rob Roy* vi, 'What is Miss Vernon, Andrew?'.. 'Other than a gude ane, I'm fearing', said Andrew.. 'something glee'd —your honour understands me?' **1822** —— *Nigel* xxxii, Did you ever hear of the umquhile Lady Huntinglen.. ganging a wee bit gleed in her walk through the world. **1893** *Northumbld. Gloss.*, *Gleed, Glide*, crooked, or twisted, not straight.

Hence †**'gleedness.**

1673 WEDDERBURN *Voc.* (Jam.), *Strabismus*, gleidness.

gleed(e, var. GLEDE.

gleeful ('gliːfʊl), *a.* [f. GLEE *sb.* + -FUL.] Full of glee; possessed by or manifesting a feeling of glee.

1586 WARNER *Alb. Eng.* IV. xx. (1589) L 3 a, Nor lackes he gleeful tales to tell, whil'st that the Bole doth trot. **1588** SHAKS. *Tit. A.* II. iii. 11 Wherefore look'st thou sad, When euery thing doth make a Gleefull boast? **1594** CAREW *Tasso* (1881) 96 The wylie wench them makes her gleefull game. **1736** W. THOMPSON *Epithal. Roy. Nupt.* viii, Deign to receive the Nation's publick Voice.. who gleeful stand.. and thus express their Joys: In Peals of loud Acclaim, and Mirth's confused Noise. **1863** GEO. ELIOT *Romola* III. xxiii, [Her] ardour.. was doubly strengthened by the gleeful triumph she saw in hard and coarse faces. **1886** J. K. JEROME *Idle Thoughts* 25 The Chinee, gleeful at the length of his pigtail.

Hence **'gleefully** *adv.*, in a gleeful manner; with glee.

1862 LYTTON *Str. Story* II. 8 He would be led on to boast gleefully of thoughts which the most cynical of criminals.. would shrink from owning. **1873** OUIDA *Pascarèl* I. 9 They wore it.. grinning gleefully from ear to ear. **1890** 'L. FALCONER' *Mlle. Ixe* (1891) 130 The children plunged gleefully into the copse.

gleeishly ('gliːɪʃlɪ), *adv. rare.* [f. GLEE *sb.* + -ISH + -LY[2].] = GLEEFULLY.

1828 BANIM *Anglo-Irish* III. 7 His humoursome message.. which had made the young beauty laugh so gleeishly. *Ibid.* III. 47. **1838** *Tait's Mag.* V. 276 Saunders now tittered gleeishly.

gleek (gliːk), *sb.*[1] Forms: 6 gleke, 6-7 gleeke, (7 glick), 7- gleek. [a. OF. *glic*, in 1464 written *ghelicque*, perh. ad. MDu. *ghelic* (Du. *gelijk*, Ger. *gleich*) LIKE, the possession of three cards of the same kind (see sense 2) being one of the points in the game; but the word has not been found in Du. as the name of a game.]

1. A game at cards, played by three persons; forty-four cards were used, twelve being dealt to each player, while the remaining eight formed a common 'stock'. Also ***penny*** (***halfpenny, two-penny***, etc.) ***gleek***. Now only *Hist.*

1533 ELYOT *Knowledge* Pref., It is.. lerned sooner.. thanne Primero or Gleeke. **1577** NORTHBROOKE *Dicing* (1843) 9 What is a man now a dayes if he know not.. to play.. at cards, dice, &c. post, cente, gleke, or such other games? **1616** B. JONSON *Devil an Ass* v. ii, When you please, Sir, I am For three peny Gleeke, your man. **1630** BRATHWAIT *Eng. Gentlem.* (1641) 126 As in games at cards the Man requires a quicke conceit, the gleeke (because of variety) requires a retentive memory. *a* **1680** BUTLER *Rem.* (1759) II. 160 Yet you've an Imposition laid on Brick, For all you then laid out, at Beast, or Gleek. **1680** SHADWELL *Woman-Capt.* IV, The rogue bids for his liberty, as if it were a Stock at 12[d] Gleek. **1762** GOLDSM. *Nash* 56 The games of Gleek, Primero, In and In, and several others now exploded, employed our sharping ancestors. **1822** SCOTT *Nigel* xxi, Would win ten times as much at gleek and primero as I used to do at put and beggar-my-neighbour. **1855** W. SARGENT *Braddock's Exp.* 113 It was at some place of lower resort that he.. staked his little means at gleek [etc.].

†**2.** A set of three court cards of the same rank in one hand, in the game of gleek. *Obs.*

1614 J. COOKE *Greene's Tu Quoque* D 2 b, *Sta.* Give me a mournaval of aces, and a gleeke of queens. *Long.* And me a gleeke of knaves. *Scat.* Vdslid, I am gleek't this time. **1615** TOMKIS *Albumazar* III. v, *Tri.* At gleeke? content. A morneuall of Ases, gleeke of Knaues, Iust nine apeece. [A mournival of aces counted for 8 points, and a gleek of knaves for 1 (Cotton).] **1670** COTTON *Gamester* vi. 68 A Mournival is either all the Aces, the four Kings, Queens, or Knaves, and a Gleek is three of any of the aforesaid.

†**b.** *transf.* A set of three; a trio. *Obs.*

1615 TOMKIS *Albumazar* IV. x, For this day wee'l celebrate A gleeke of Marriages. **1625** B. JONSON *Staple of N.* IV, *Cen.* Let a protest goe out against him. *Mir.* A mournivell of protests; or a gleeke at least! **1662** *Rump Songs* (1874) I. 160 From a gleek of Lord Keepers of one poor Seal, *Libera nos* [etc.]. *c* **1671** MARVELL *On 3 Dukes killing the Beadle* in *Roxb. Ball.* (1883) IV. 526 'Twas there a Gleek of Dukes [etc.]. **1710** *Brit. Apollo* III. No. 25. 3/2 Like Paris with his Gleek of Wagtails on Ida.

†**3.** ***Dutch gleek*** (see quot.). *Obs.*

1654 GAYTON *Pleas. Notes* III. v. 96 He was not able to stirre his jawes, nor could be partaker of any of the good cheer, except it were the liquid part of it, which they call Dutch gleek, where he plaied his cards so well, and vied and revied so often that he had scarce an eye to see withall.

Hence †**'gleeker**, a player at the game of gleek. *rare.*

1676 ETHEREDGE *Man of Mode* II. i, There never was so unsatiable a Carder, an old Gleeker never lov'd to sit To't like her.

†**gleek**, *sb.*[2] *Obs.* Forms: 6 glike, glyke, (? glyeke), (glyg), gleke, (gleake), 6-7 glick(e, gleeke, 7, 9 gleek. [Of obscure origin; possibly a diminutive of GLEE: cf. GLAIK.]

1. A gibe, jest, gird.

c **1550** *Image Hypocr.* 732 They durst not fight ne strike They feared of a gleke. **1564** HARDING *Answ. Jewel's Challenge* Pref. 5 Glykes, nyppes and scoffes, bittes, cuttes and gyrdes, become not that stage. **1566** DRANT *Horace's Sat.* VII. D vj b, With gybes, and glickes, and taunting stryfe. **1580** LYLY *Euphues* (Arb.) 291 What greater discurtesie.. then with so many nips, such bitter girdes, such disdainful glickes to answere him that honoured hir. **1589** *Pappe w. Hatchet* E ij b, If thy vain be so pleasant, and thy wit so nimble, that all consists in glicks and girds; pen some playe for the Theater. **1617** COLLINS *Def. Bp. Ely* I. iv. 175, I meane to take downe the confident and the ouerweener with a sober gleeke. **1819** W. TENNANT *Papistry Storm'd* (1827) 22 Blasphemin' wi' a valiant zeal Twa ne'er-do-weels, the Paip and deil, Wi' gleeks at Guise and Mary.

b. ***to give one a*** (or ***the***) ***gleek***: to make a jest at his expense; to mock, make sport of, play a trick upon him.

1567 TURBERV. *Ovid's Ep.* X vj, Now wholly she delights Anchises eye to leake: To him alone she closely clinges, and giues the rest the gleake. *c* **1580** JEFFERIE *Bugbears* IV. v. in *Archiv Stud. d. neueren Spr.* (1897) If they thinke to beguyle or geve me such a gleke, they must aryse earlye. **1587** GOLDING *De Mornay* xiii. (1617) 203 A wise man to giue a glike to another wise man, ciphereth a letter grossely for the nonce. **1599** *Life More* in Wordsw. *Eccl. Biog.* (1853) II. 101 Sir Thomas, seeing the exceeding vanitie of the man, thought he needed modestie, and gave him this gentle gleeke. **1607** *Peele's Jests* (*c* 1620) 15, I vow by Iove, if I can see him weare it, Ile giue him a glyg.

2. A coquettish glance. *rare.*

1599 B. JONSON *Cynthia's Rev.* Palinode 10 Coy glances, glickes, cringes, and all such simpring humours. **1623** FLETCHER & ROWLEY *Maid of Mill* II. ii, A pretty gleek coming from Pallas' eye.

gleek, *v. Obs.* Forms: see GLEEK *sb.*[2] [f. prec.]

1. *trans.* To trick, circumvent. (In quot. 1614 with allusion to GLEEK *sb.*[1])

1577 G. HARVEY *Letter-bk.* (Camden) 56 Methinkes thou gleekiste many a lorde. **1598** *Tom Tyler & Wife* (1661) 3 The more that I get her, the more she doth glike me. **1614** J. COOKE *Greene's Tu Quoque* D 2 b, *Scat.* Come Gentlemen, what's your game? *Sta.* Why Gleeke, that's your onely game. Gleeke let it be, for I am perswaded I shall gleeke some of you; cut sir. **1653** URQUHART *Rabelais* I. xii. 59 He hath gleeked us to some purpose, bobbed we are now for ever.

2. *intr.* To make a jest or gibe (*at* a person).

1590 SHAKS. *Mids. N.* III. i. 150 Nay, I can gleeke vpon occasion. **1599** —— *Hen. V*, v. i. 78, I haue seene you gleeking & galling at this Gentleman twice or thrice. **1593** NASHE *Strange Newes* Wks. (Grosart) II. 197 Not mee alone did hee reuile.. but glickt at Pap-hatchet once more. *a* **1687** COTTON *Poet. Wks.* (1765) 150 Besides, you must not take a Picque, If he sometimes speak plain and gleek.

3. (See quot.)

1611 COTGR., *Limer*,.. to gleeke, or looke askew at.

Hence **'gleeking** *vbl. sb.* and *ppl. a.*

c **1534** BYGOD *Treat. conc. Impropriat.* in *Lever's Serm.* (Arb.) Introd. 13 By the glykynge and gleynyng.. scrapinge and rakynge togyther of almost all the fatte benefyces within this realme. **1592** G. HARVEY *New Letter* I The sly Information of the fine French [historian], a glicking Remembrancer. **1641** MILTON *Animadv.* Wks. (1851) 246 Bacchanalia's good store in every Bishops family, and good gleeking. *a* **1859** L. HUNT *Shewe of Faire Seeming* xxix, Well wotting such be gullery all, and gleeking.

gleeless (ˈgliːlɪs), *a. rare*⁻¹. [f. GLEE *sb.* + -LESS.] Devoid of glee.

1850 BLACKIE *Æschylus* I. 202 The gleeless song, and the lyreless strain.

gleeman (ˈgliːmən). *Obs.* exc. *Hist.* Forms: 1 **glīʒ-**, **glii(ʒ)-**, 1–4 **gléo-**, 3 **gley-**, 4–6 **gle-**, 4, 8- **gleeman**. *β.* 2, 5 **glew-**, 3 **gleu-**, 5 **glu-**, **glwman**. [f. GLEE *sb.* + MAN.] A professional entertainer at social gatherings; esp. a singer, musician, or minstrel.

a. *Beowulf* (Z.) 1160 Leoð wæs asungen, Gleomannes gyd. *c***897** K. ÆLFRED *Gregory's Past.* xliv. 327 Moniʒe weliʒe menn..lætað cuelan hungre Cristes ðearfan & fedað yfle gliiʒmenn mid oferwiste. *c***1000** ÆLFRIC *Gloss.* in Wr.-Wülcker 150/18 *Mimus, jocista, scurra*, gliʒmon. *c***1205** LAY. 18856 Al him scal abuʒe þat wuneð inne Bruttene; of him scullen gleomen godliche singen. *c***1300** *Havelok* 2329 Ther mouthe men here the gestes singe, The gleymen on the tabour dinge. **1362** LANGL. *P. Pl.* A. XI. 110 Thenne was I ..Gladdore then the gleo-mon is of his grete ʒiftes. **1387** TREVISA *Higden* (Rolls) IV. 31 Bledgaret passede alle his predecessoures in musik and in melodie, so þat he was i-cleped god of glee men [L. *deus joculatorum*]. **1500–20** DUNBAR *Poems* xxvi. 104 Na menstrallis playit to thame but dowt, For gle-men thair wer haldin out. **1794** PERCY *Reliq.*, *Notes on Ess. Anc. Minstr.* 66 *note*, Gleeman continued to be the name given to a Minstrel both in England and Scotland almost as long as this order of men continued. **1876** FREEMAN *Norm. Conq.* V. xxv. 587 We had, beyond all doubt, our own history, alike mythical and real, sung by our own gleemen in our own tongue.

β. *c***1200** *Trin. Coll. Hom.* 29 Gef þu..best rum-handed to glewmen and to hores þu shalt ben lef and wurð and liken alle men. *a***1300** *Cursor M.* 28382, I..to gleumen cald and to ioglere. *a***1400** *Isumbras* 19 He luffede glewmene wele in haulle. *c***1440** *Promp. Parv.* 200/2 Gluman, or mynstral, *musicus*.

gleen (gliːn), *sb. Obs.* exc. *arch. rare.* Also 7 **glean**. [Prob. a dialect word, of Scandinavian origin: cf. Sw. (dial.) *glena*, Da. (dial.) *glene* a clear strip or patch of sky. The ON. mythologic name *Glenr*, the husband of the sun, is perhaps connected.] A gleam of light; a warm blaze of sunlight.

1656 W. D. tr. *Comenius' Gate Lat. Unl.* §35. 17 Fiery Meteors; namely, falling Stars, flying Dragons, fals Fiers; also Gleans, Flashings, openings of the skie, suddenly disappearing. **1686** GOAD *Celest. Bodies* I. xvi. 104 Another time I remember suffocating Gleans of the Sun, πνῖγος the Ancients call it. **1825** HOGG in *Blackw. Mag.* XVII. 111 All glitter'd with a glowing gleen.

†**gleen**, *v. Obs. rare.* Also 6 **glene**. [See prec. and cf. Sw. (dial.) *glena* to shine.] = GLEAM *v.* Hence †ˈ**gleening** *vbl. sb.* and *ppl. a.*

1547–64 BAULDWIN *Mor. Philos.* (Palfr.) 145 Those.. being led by their owne blind iudgements..are oftentimes trained out of the way of truth by likely glenings of reason. **1662** J. CHANDLER *Van Helmont's Oriat.* Proph. conc. Auth., If thou belov'd Narcissus hadst not seen Thy proper figure in a well to gleen [etc.]. *c***1709** PRIOR *1st Hymn Callim.* 86 Those who..Bend stubborn steel, and harden gleening armour.

gleer: see GLEE *v.*²

gleer(e, obs. form of GLAIR *sb.*¹ and *v.*

†ˈ**gleering**, *ppl. a. Obs.* Also 6 **glyering**, **gleryng**, 7 **glearing**. [? f. *gly*, GLEE *v.* + -ER⁵ + -ING².] ? Looking askance, casting covetous or cunning glances, sly.

*a***1536** TINDALE *Exp. Matt.* vi. 19–21 Couetousnes blynded the eyes of that gleryngе fox [Sir Thomas More] more and more. **1548** CRANMER *Catech.* 101 b, Lykewyse God, euen nowe a dayes doth punyshe these glyeryngе keytes, that seke their pray in euery place. **1602** *2nd Pt. Return fr. Parnass.* IV. ii. (Arb.) 57 How like thy snout is to great Lucifers. Such tallants had he, such a gleering [*v.r.* glaring] eye. **1611** COTGR., *Saluta-libenter*, a cogging, flattering, or gleering mate.

¶ ? Misused for *glaring*.

1631 P. FLETCHER *Sicelides* IV. vi. Wks. (Grosart) III. 102 O those gleering eyes that dart the beames, The beames that drownd my heart with fierie streames. **1634** SIR T. HERBERT *Trav.* 188 From his head issue foure great hornes..his eyes gleering, mouth like a port Cullis.

gleesome (ˈgliːsəm), *a.* [f. GLEE *sb.* + -SOME.] = GLEEFUL.

1603 CHETTLE *Eng. Mourn. Garm.* in *Harl. Misc.* (Malh.) II. 505 It adds another cause of gleesome mirth. **1613–16** W. BROWNE *Brit. Past.* II. iv, Gleesome hunters, pleased with their sport. **1630** *Tinker of Turvey* 41 This smith was ..As merry as bird on brier, Jocund and gleesome. *a***1774** FERGUSSON *Ode to Gowdspink*, The gowdspink chatters joyous here, And courts wi' gleesome sangs his peer. **1816** SCOTT *Antiq.* xxvii, Lawyers were talking, with gleesome anticipation, of the probability of a 'great Glenallan cause'. **1842** DICKENS *Amer. Notes* (1850) 21/1 Those who were at play, were gleesome and noisy as other children. **1870** MORRIS *Earthly Par.* II. III. 434 These wandering churls are full Of meat and drink, and need no rope to pull Wild words and gleesome from them.

Hence ˈ**gleesomely** *adv.*, ˈ**gleesomeness**.

1847 *Fraser's Mag.* XXXVI. 16 Youth, with all its gleesomeness and innocent wildness. **1850** J. B. JOHNSTONE *Mem. R. Shirra* iv. 36 Mr. Shirra..gleesomely talked of the circumstance. **1889** J. MASTERMAN *Scotts of Bestminster* III. xiv. 2 The gleesomeness of youth had passed from him.

gleet (gliːt), *sb.* Forms: 4 **glette**, 4–5 (9 *Sc.*) **glet**, (4 **glat**), 5 **glett**, 6 **glit(te**, (7 **glyte**), 9 *Sc.* **glit(t**, 7- **gleet**. Cf. GLUT *sb.*⁴ [a. OF. *glette* slime, filth, purulent matter, 'frothe of an egge', 'gelly of any thyng that congeleth' (Palsgr.); mod.F. *glette* litharge, whence app. G. *glätte*, Du. *glit*, Sw. *glitte*. The development of the English forms is obscure; with its present form and meaning the word first becomes common in the 18th c.]

1. Slimy matter; sticky or greasy filth. Also *fig. Obs.* exc. *Sc.*

1340 HAMPOLE *Pr. Consc.* 459 Thar [in the womb] duellid man in a myrk dungeon..Whar he had na other fode Bot wlatsom glet, and loper blode, And stynk and fylthe. **13..** *E.E. Allit. P.* A. 1059 þat foysoun flode..swange þurȝ vch a strete, With-outen fylþe oþer galle oþer glet. *Ibid.* C. 269 He [Jonah] glydez in by þe giles, þurȝ glaymande [? *read* glaym and] glette. *a***1400–50** *Alexander* 4516 þus ilk cantell of ȝour cors ȝe call þam driȝtins..Of ilk gobet of þat glett ȝe a god make. **1483** *Cath. Angl.* 158/2 Glett, *viscositas.* **1824** MACTAGGART *Gallovid. Encycl.*, *Glitt*, oily matter, which makes the stones of brooks slippery in summer. **1856** AIRD *Poet. Wks.* 123 The stream is almost shrunk Down to the green gleet of its slippery stones. **1894** CROCKETT *Raiders* (ed. 3) 100 The night dew had left a sticky 'glet' on the face and hands.

2. Phlegm collected in the stomach, esp. of a hawk. (So OF. *glette*.) *Obs.* exc. *Sc.*

*a***1340** HAMPOLE *Psalter, Cant.* 512 Haly mennys affecciouns ere as of hertis [L. *quasi cervorum*] þat..kastis out of þaire hert all glet [in *Wyclif's Sel. Wks.* III. 32 al vile glat (*v.r.* glet) þat stoppiþ her breeþ]. **1486** *Bk. St. Albans* C vb, If she [a hawk] holde not her mete bot cast it that is tokyn of the foule glet. **1575** TURBERV. *Faulconrie* Commend. Hawking, By cunning skill to cause hir cast such glit, as breedes hir skath. **1688** R. HOLME *Armoury* II. 239/1 Glyte or Glut is a slimy substance in the Pannel or Belly of the Hawk. **1808–80** JAMIESON, *Glit*, tough phlegm, that especially which gathers in the stomach when it is foul.

3. A morbid discharge of thin liquid from a wound, ulcer, etc. Now *rare*.

1535 STEWART *Cron. Scot.* I. 444 The oftar ay that plastrit be the wound, With greedie glit far mair it dois abound. **1699** *Phil. Trans.* XXI. 154, I found the applications on the Wound very wet with a serous Humor, commonly called a Gleet. **1706** PHILLIPS (ed. Kersey), *Glitt* or *Gleet*, a thin matter issuing out of Wounds and Ulcers; especially when the nervous or sinewy Parts are bruis'd and hurt. **1713** R. RUSSELL in *Phil. Trans.* XXVIII. 276 But upon having a Discharge from..her Breast, of a thin Gleet, all Symptoms vanished. **1767** GOOCH *Treat. Wounds* I. 320 A discharge of a fetid gleet from the membranes or brain. **1836** *Penny Cycl.* V. 261 Some strange..stories have been told of gleet from the nose, giddiness, and inflammation of the brain having been produced by them [bots in sheep]. **1855** SINGLETON *Virgil* I. 176 When The fiery fever..Hath shrivelled up their wretched limbs, again O'erflowed a liquid gleet.

b. *spec.* A morbid discharge from the urethra.

1718 QUINCY *Compl Disp.* 125 Old Gleets, that proceed more from Debility than any Malignity. **1813** J. THOMSON *Lect. Inflam.* 425, I imagine..that the internal surface of a fistulous ulcer is in some degree similar to the inner surface of the urethra, when it is forming the discharge commonly called a gleet. **1878** T. BRYANT *Pract. Surg.* (1879) II. 171 Gleet may be the result of some stricture or local urethral disease, such as an ulcer.

gleet, *v.* Also 6 **glyt**, 7 **gleat**. [f. prec. sb.]

†**1.** *intr.* Of a morbid discharge, also of water: To ooze, flow slowly. *Obs.*

1527 [see GLEETING]. **1612** WOODALL *Surg. Mate* Wks. (1653) 54 Very good to cure wounds in joynts, where the joynt-water gleeteth out. **1687** *Phil. Trans.* XVI. 471 The Water presently precipitates, gleeting down by the Crannies of the Stone. **1697** *Ibid.* XIX. 584 The Cavities of the Rocks are filled up with the Rills that gleet from the Hills. **1725** HUXHAM *Ibid.* XXXIII. 389 The Desquammation was very slow, the black Crust adhering several Days, nay Weeks.. while abundance of purulent Matter gleeted from under them.

2. Of the body or its parts: To discharge a thin purulent matter. Also quasi-*trans*.

1676 WISEMAN *Surg.* I. xi. 57 His Thumb being inflamed ..I made Incision into it to the Bone: this not onely bled, but gleeted a few drops. **1705** OLIVER in *Phil. Trans.* XXV. 2180 It made his Nose run and gleet. **1753** J. BARTLET *Gentl. Farriery* viii. 74 He [a horse] gleets often at the nose. **1785** POTT *Chirurg. Wks.* II. 510 A prodigious fungus, which.. gleeted largely, and at times bled profusely. **1812** *Examiner* 4 May 287/1 Making the sleeper's nose run and gleet.

Hence ˈ**gleeting** *vbl. sb.* and *ppl. a.*

1527 ANDREW *Brunswyke's Distyll. Waters* Q j b, The same water with cotton warme layd in the woundes stoppeth the glyttynge water betwene the joyntes. **1677** PLOT *Oxfordsh.* 60 Used by Chirurgians to dry gleeting sores. **1684** tr. *Bonet's Merc. Compit.* I. 5 This gleeting or dripping continues so long as till the hole in the coat be cured. **1741** *Compl. Fam.-Piece* III. 440 Running at the Eyes, and gleeting at the Nostrils, are Signs of a Cold.

†ˈ**gleetous**, ˈ**glittous**, *a. Obs. rare.* [ad. OF. *gleteus*, *gletteux*, *glettous* affected with gleet or phlegm, filthy, f. *glette* GLEET *sb.*] **a.** Of a hawk: Affected with phlegm. **b.** Of persons: Filthy (in conduct). **c.** *fig.* ? Sticky, ensnaring.

1486 *Bk. St. Albans* C vj a, The hawke will be very eegre and gleetous of the sekenes. **1535** STEWART *Cron. Scot.* I. 102 In word and work this king he wox rycht vile; Gredie and glittus in gulositie. *Ibid.* II. 521 Gold is so glittis, as ȝe knaw and ken, Quhilk of befoir hes causit mony men To tak on hand..The thing efter that maid thame for to rew. *Ibid.* 534 This Culenus..So glittous was than into chalmer glew [etc.].

gleety (ˈgliːtɪ), *a.* Also 5 (9 *dial.*) **gletty**, 9 *Sc.* **glittie**. [f. GLEET *sb.* + -Y¹.]

1. Slimy. *Obs.* exc. *Sc.* and *north.*

1483 *Cath. Angl.* 159/1 Gletty, *viscosus.* **1820** *Edin. Mag.* May VI. 423/2 The water-asks, sae cauld and saft, Crawl'd ower the glittie flure. **1820** HOGG *Wint. Even. T.* II. 71 The sei-mawe couris on his glittye stene, For it's greine withe the dewe of the jaupyng maine. **1856** AIRD *Poet. Wks.* 22 The outer wheel still black Though sleek with gleety green—Is doing duty. **1893** *Northumbld. Gloss.*, *Gleety*, green and slimy, applied to the appearance of stagnant water.

2. Of the nature of gleet.

1822–34 *Good's Study Med.* (ed. 4) II. 484 The frequent and involuntary secretion of a gleety matter. **1861** BUMSTEAD *Ven. Dis.* (1879) 273 One of the earliest symptoms of organic stricture is generally a gleety discharge from the urethra. **1876** GROSS *Dis. Bladder* 82 In inveterate cases, there is a discharge of thin gleety matter from the bladder.

gleff, obs. form of GLIFF *v.*

gleg (glɛg), *sb. Obs.* exc. *north.* [f. GLEG *v.*] A side-glance, sly look; also simply, a look.

*a***1650** *In a May morning* 15 in Furniv. *Percy Folio* (1867) IV. 74 Euerye one that comes by shall haue a glegge ont. **1821** CLARE *Vill. Minstr.* II. 65 Searching with minutest gleg, Oft I've seen [etc.]. **1877** *Holderness Gloss.*, *Gleg*, a sly glance.

gleg (glɛg), *a. north.* and *Sc.* [a. ON. *glegg-r*, *gloggr*, *gløggr* clear, clear-sighted = Goth. **glaggwu-s* (cf. the adv. *glaggwuba* carefully):—OTeut. **glawwu-*, whence also OHG. *glau*, *klau*, OS. *glau*, OE. *gléaw* wise, clever, GLEW *a.* (cf. ON. *døgg* = DEW *sb.*, *høggva* = HEW *v.*).]

1. Quick in perception by any of the senses; esp. quick-eyed, sharp-sighted. Chiefly with defining phrase, as ***gleg of the eye***, ***of touch***.

*a***1300** *Cursor M.* 13448 Es na foȝl [*MS.* foxl] sa gleg of ei [as the eagle]. *a***1449** W. BOWER in *Fordun's Scotichron.* (1759) II. 376 Wyth prik ȝoukand eris, as the awsk gleg. **1536** BELLENDEN *Cron. Scot.* (1821) I. p. xlv, Thir mussillis ar sa doyn gleg of twiche and hering that [etc.]. **1808–80** JAMIESON, *Gleg of the ee*, sharp-sighted. 'Gleg o' the glour,' Loth. **1858** M. PORTEOUS *Souter Johnny* 11 He was..As gleg's a hawk.

b. Of the eye: Quick, sharp.

1755 R. FORBES *Ajax's Sp.* 17 The gods tho look on mortal men, Wi' eyn baith just and gleg. **1795** BURNS *'I see a form'* 15 Gleg as light are lover's een. **1837** R. NICOLL *Poems* (1842) 138 I've glour'd at her aft wi' a gleg e'e.

2. Quick in action or movement; sharp, smart. ***gleg at***, quick or clever at (doing something); ***gleg at (of) the uptake***, quick in understanding a thing; ***gleg at*** or ***with***, quick or clever in using.

1755 RAMSAY *Let. to Jas. Clerk.* 46 When interest points, he's gleg and gare, And will at naithing stop or stand. *a***1774** FERGUSSON *Wks.* (1807) 227 He's a man weel versed in a' the laws..And ay right gleg..At sattlin' o' a nice or kittle point. **1814** SCOTT *Wav.* xlii, He's gleg aneuch at the broadsword and target. **1816** —— *Old Mort.* vii, Everybody's no sae gleg at the uptake as ye are yoursell, mither. **1821** GALT *Ayrsh. Legatees* x. 286 The drivers were so gleg and impudent, that it was worse than martyrdom to come with them. **1844** W. H. MAXWELL *Sports & Adv. Scotl.* ix. (1855) 94 He was ower gleg in the tongue for ye. **1876** *Whitby Gloss.* s.v., 'Quite gleg at it', quick at comprehending it. 'Gleg at walking'. 'Gleg at eating'. **1886** STEVENSON *Kidnapped* xx, Ye're no very gleg at the jumping. **1894** CROCKETT *Raiders* (ed. 3) 72 Gleg wi' the knife as a souter wi' his elshin.

3. Sprightly, lively, cheery.

1818 SCOTT *Ht. Midl.* ix, The body..looking unco gleg and canty, she didna ken what he might be coming out wi' next. **1823** CORBETT *Petticoat T.* I. 226 Ye look as gleg as if ye had got a prize in the lottery. **1881** *N. Linc. Gloss.*, *Gleg*, ..pleased, happy.

4. *transf.* Of things: †**a.** Bright, clear. *rare*⁻¹.

1533 BELLENDEN *Livy* v. (1822) 441 Bot the mone wes sa gleg, schinand al nicht, that the batall wes fochtin to the uter end, als weil as it had bene day licht.

b. Sharp, keen.

1728 RAMSAY *Fables, Monk & Miller's Wife* 214 A Sage.. Whase Wit was gleg as ony Razor. **1787** BURNS *Tam Samson's Elegy* 99 For yet unskaith'd by death's gleg gullie, Tam Samson's livin. **1805** J. NICOL *Poems* I. 107 (Jam.) Death snaps the thread Wi' his gleg shears.

c. Smooth (see quots.).

1808–80 JAMIESON s.v., *Gleg ice*, ice that is very smooth. **1851** *Cumbld. Gloss.*, *Gleg*, smooth; slippery. **1893** *Northumbld. Gloss.*, *Gleg*, worn smooth; hence loose fitting. A tap that turns too easily and leaks from wear is said to be getting gleg.

5. quasi-*adv.* = GLEGLY.

1720 RAMSAY *Rise & fall of Stocks* 27 The lad wha gleggest waits upon it, Receives the Bubble on his Bonnet. **1789** BURNS *On Grose's Peregrin.* 43 Forbye, he'll shape you aff, fu' gleg, The cut of Adam's philibeg.

6. *Comb.*, as ***gleg-eyed***, ***-lugged***, ***-tongued*** adjs.

1721 RAMSAY *Addr. Town Counc. Edin.* 15 Yet Gleg-eyed Friends throw the Disguise Receiv'd it as a dainty Prize. **1804** TARRAS *Poems* 2 He tunes his lay, Till gleg-lug'd echo tak her dinsome rout. **1818** SCOTT *Hrt. Midl.* xii, I haud a' your gleg-tongued advocates..as legalists and formalists.

Hence ˈ**glegly** *adv.*, quickly, cleverly, readily; also, brightly, clearly; ˈ**glegness**, acuteness (of perception), quickness.

1768 ROSS *Helenore* III. 122 To this auld Colen glegly 'gan to hark. **1814** *Watchman* I. ii, If ye look glegly after thieves and randies, folk can put up wi' the want of being wakened. **1818** SCOTT *Rob Roy* xiv, A kail-blaid, or a colliflour, glances sae glegly by moonlight, it's like a leddy in her diamonds. **1835** MRS. CARLYLE *Lett.* I. 37, I heard with my wonted glegness..a couple of handsome smacks! **1843** R. PAUL *Let.* in *Mem.* xiv. (1872) 181, I don't recollect things so glegly. **1895** CROCKETT *Men of Moss Hags* 42 The Lord..did not stint me as to glegness of eye.

gleg (glɛg), *v. dial.* [cf. GLEDGE *v.* and GLEE *v.*] (See quots.) Also **'glegging** *ppl. a.*

a **1796** PEGGE *Derbicisms* Ser. II. 102 (E.D.S.), *Glegg*, to squint a little, to have a cast of the eye. **1821** CLARE *Vill. Minstr.* II. 78 The simple rustics try their arts the while With glegging smiles, and hopes and fears between, Snatching a kiss to open what they mean. **1877** *Holderness Gloss.*, *Gleg*, to give a sidelong glance. **1887** *S. Chesh. Gloss.*, *Gleg*, to look furtively or askance.

gleg, var. CLEG.

1851 STEPHENS *Bk. Farm* (ed. 2) II. 188/1 The cleg or gleg .. Hæmatopola pluvialis .. is so well known, that [etc.].

glei, obs. form of GLEE *v.*[2]

glei, var. GLEY.

gleib, obs. form of GLEBE.

‖**Gleichenia** (glaɪ'kiːnɪə). *Bot.* [mod.L. from the name of F. W. *Gleichen*, a German naturalist (1717–1783).] A genus of ferns, chiefly natives of the southern hemisphere; a plant of this genus.

1865 GOSSE *Land & Sea* (1874) 352 Out of the rough bark of the tall trees .. spring several kinds of Gleichenia, a genus of Ferns .. possessing wide-spread fronds of very lax habit, and of very minute segments, but so peculiarly elegant and delicate, that [etc.]. **1882** *Garden* 27 May 375/3 The finest plants in the group .. were two excellent Gleichenias.

‖**Gleichschaltung** ('glaɪxʃaltʊŋ). Also with lower-case initial. [G.] The standardization in authoritarian states of political, economic, and cultural institutions. Also *transf.*

Other parts of speech related to the G. word (e.g. *gleichschalten* v. trans., to impose *Gleichschaltung* upon; *gleichgeschaltet* ppl. a.) are also occas. found in English contexts.

1933 *Week-End Rev.* 12 Aug. 149/2 The only test can be whether or not the efforts to *Gleichschalten* Austria continue. **1934** *Surv. Internat. Affairs 1933* II. i. 140 The new masters of the Reich had succeeded in carrying out their revolutionary programme of *Gleichschaltung* far enough to have changed the whole face of German life. **1935** S. LEWIS *It can't happen Here* xv. 150 His ripe experience in the *Gleichschaltung* of Mississippi. **1937** AUDEN in Auden & MacNeice *Lett. fr. Iceland* v. 57 You would, hearing honest Oswald's call, Be gleichgeschaltet in the Albert Hall. **1940** *Economist* 31 Aug. 280/2 Holland under German control... Slowly the *Gleichschaltung* takes place. Many trade unions and similar organizations are unified. **1941** KOESTLER *Scum* 209 It looked as if France were already *gleichgeschaltet* before we even knew the armistice terms. **1950** *Ann. Reg. 1949* 264 The heavy hand of Soviet *gleichschaltung* descended on art, literature, and even music. **1964** D. DAICHES *Crit. Hist. Eng. Lit.* iv. 85 One cannot but welcome this failure of critical *Gleichschaltung*. **1969** J. MANDER *Static Soc.* viii. 254 There was no effective resistance .. to Peron's gleichschaltung of the CGT.

gleid, dial. f. GLEDE; obs. f. GLEED.

†**gleim**, *sb. Obs.* In 4–5 gleyme, 6 gleme. [Connected with GLEIM *v.*]

1. Any sticky or slimy substance, as bird-lime or glue; also, rheum or phlegm.

c **1440** *Promp. Parv.* 198/1 Gleyme or rewme, *reuma.* Gleyme of knyttynge or byyndynge to-gedyrs, *limus, gluten, glucium.* **1516** *Ortus Vocab.*, *Viscus*, gleme [*edd.* **1500**, **1509** *have* glewe] or lyme.

2. *fig.* **a.** Infection. **b.** Attachment, affection.

c **1394** *P. Pl. Crede* 479, I trowe þat some wikked wyȝt wrouȝte þis ordres [of friars] þoruȝ [*v.r.* Trow ye] þat gleym of þat gest þat Golias is y-calde. *c* **1449** PECOCK *Repr.* III. xv. 377 [He] lackith wijf and children, and al the gleyme, loue, and delectacions whiche violentli comen anentis his wijf and hise children.

Hence †**gleimed** *a.*, affected with phlegm.

14.. *Med. MS.* in *Promp. Parv.* 198 *note*, For a.. gleymede stomak, þat may noȝt kepe mete.

†**gleim**, *v. Obs.* In 4 glaym, 4–5 gleym(yn; see also GLEAM *v.*[2] [Of obscure origin.] *trans.* To smear with a sticky substance. Also *fig.* in pass.: To be infected (as with a disease); to be attached *to* something (cf. ENGLEIM).

1387 TREVISA *Higden* (Rolls) V. 197 [He] sente hem bisshoppes of þe Arrians, and þerfore alle the Gothes were infecte and i-gleymed [L. *infecta fuit*]. *c* **1440** *Promp. Parv.* 198/2 Gleymyn or yngleymyn, *visco, invisco.* *c* **1449** PECOCK *Repr.* III. xv. 376 A preest forto haue in possessioun movable godis .. (so that he be not gleymed with ouer myche loue to it).

Hence †**'gleiming** *vbl. sb.*, (*a*) the act of sticking; (*b*) infection. Also †**'gleiming** *ppl. a.*, sticky; †**'gleimingness**, stickiness.

13.. *E.E. Allit. P.* C 269 He glydez in by þe giles, þurȝ glaymande [? *read* glaym ande] glette. **1387** TREVISA *Higden* (Rolls) VII. 337 And þey covetise be a special vice to Lombardes, he put þat gleymynge [L. *contagium*] fer from his persone. **1398** —— *Barth. De P.R.* VII. lxx. (1495) 290 Some medycynes laxen with gleymyngnesse and makyth slypper as Mercurii and Hockes and other suche. *Ibid.* XVI. ii. (Tollem. MS.) For unctuouse þinge is mene bitwene gleymynge [**1535** gleymie] and vaporatyf þinge. *Ibid.* XVII. i. (1495) 592 In some trees the leues abyde in wynter tyme for plente of humour: other for gleymynge or for sadnesse and soundnesse of the tree.

gleime, obs. f. GLEAN *v.*

†**'gleimous**, *a. Obs. rare.* In 4 gleymouse. 5 -ows(e, glaymous. [f. GLEIM *sb.* + -OUS.] Sticky, slimy; full of rheum or phlegm. (Cf. ENGLEIMOUS.)

1398 TREVISA *Barth. De P.R.* XVII. clxxxv. (1495) 725 Redde wyne clensyth and wypyth and puttyth awaye vnclenenesse and gleymouse humours. *c* **1440** *Promp. Parv.* 198/2 Gleymowse, or full of rewme, *reumaticus.* Gleymows, or lymows, *limosus, viscosus, glutinosus.* **1486** *Bk. St. Albans* A iij b, For sum gobbit will be yolow and sum grene and sum glaymous and sum cleere .. It [this euell] wil arise in the hede and make the hede to swell & the iyen all glaymous and dyrke. **1676–1732** COLES, *Glaymous*, muddy and clammy. **1730–90** in BAILEY.

Hence †**'gleimousness**, stickiness.

c **1440** *Promp. Parv.* 198/2 Gleymowsenesse, or lymowsnesse, *limositas, viscositas.* **1727** BAILEY vol. II, *Glaymousness*, Muddiness, Clamminess.

†**'gleimy**, *a. Obs.* Forms: 4, 6 gleymy, (4 glymye), 6 glaymy, glemy, 6–8 gleamy. [f. GLEIM *sb.* + -Y[1].] Sticky, slimy.

1398 TREVISA *Barth. De P.R.* V. xxi. (1495) 128 Another postume of the tongue is full of blode, and speche and taste is lette by gleymy humours. *Ibid.* VI. i. (Tollem. MS.), The firste childhode .. is ȝit tender and nesche, quavy and gleymy [**1495** claymy, **1535** clammy; L. *limosa*]. *a* **1529** SKELTON *Agst. Garnesche* iii. 168 Thou gresly gargone glaymy, Thou swety slouen seymy. **1541** R. COPLAND *Guydon's Quest. Chirurg.* N ij, The blode flewmatyke is thycke and gleymy and whyte in colour, and swete in sauour. **1704** F. FULLER *Med. Gymn.* (1711) 93 The Cynogloss .. seems to have something of a like Gleamy Substance in it.

Hence †**'gleiminess**, stickiness.

1398 TREVISA *Barth. De P.R.* XVIII. i. (1495) 745 Beestys that ben nighe the aege of suckynge ben of grete moysture and gleymynesse and sledernesse.

gleir(e, obs. form of GLAIR *sb.*[1]

†**gleit**, *v. Sc. Obs. rare.* Also glete. [? var. GLIT *v.*] *intr.* To glitter, shine.

1501 DOUGLAS *Pal. Hon.* II. viii, Causand gros leid all of maist gudnes gleit. **1508** DUNBAR *Gold. Targe* 66 All the feldis wyth thai lilies quhite Depaynt war brycht, quhilk to the hevyn did glete. **1597** MONTGOMERIE *Cherrie & Slae* 1288, I now deny now That all is gold that gleits. *a* **1605** —— *Misc. Poems* v. 42 All is not gold that gleitis.

gleive, gleiwye, obs. ff. GLAIVE, GLUEY.

gleke, obs. f. GLEEK, *sb.*[1]; var. GLEEK *sb.*[2], *Obs.*

glem, gleman, obs. ff. GLEAM, GLEEMAN.

gleme, obs. f. GLEAM, GLEAN; var. GLEIM, *Obs.*

glemer, -yr, obs. ff. GLIMMER.

†**glemish.** *Obs. rare*[−1]. [? var. of GLIMPSE *sb.*] A glimpse.

1576 BP. WOOLTON *Chr. Man.* H ij, I haue indeauowred before to shadow (as it were) and geue a glemish thereof.

glemy, var. GLEIMY, *Obs.*

glen[1] (glɛn). Forms: α. 6, 8 glenne, 8 glenn, 6– glen. β. 6 glan. γ. 6–7 *pl.* glynnes; 7 glin, 7–8 glyn, 8 glynn. [a. Gael. *gleann*, earlier *glenn*, mountain-valley = Welsh *glyn*. The α-forms are of Scottish origin, having been adopted from Gael. before the vowel of *glenn* was broken into *ea*. The form *glan* represents the Irish pronunciation of *gleann*, while *glin* is derived from the pl. *glinn*, and was at first employed only in the pl. *glins*; some examples of *glyn*, *glin* in 17–18th c. represent the Welsh or the Cornish form.

Until the middle of the 18th c. the form *glen* occurs in English writers only as an echo of Spenser; the 'Glosse' to the *Shepherd's Calendar* by E. K. wrongly explains the word as 'a country hamlet or borough'.]

a. A mountain-valley, usually narrow and forming the course of a stream.

At first applied to the narrow valleys of the mountainous districts in Scotland and Ireland, but now extended to similar places in other countries.

α. **1489** *Barbour's Bruce* IV. 372 (Edinb. MS.) In A glen [*Camb. MS.* vnder ane bra]. **1508** DUNBAR *Flyting w. Kennedie* 153 In till ane glen thow hes .. Ane laithly luge. **1533** BELLENDEN *Livy* II. (1822) 185 Thir Veanis laid ane strang garnisoun of armit men in secrete glennis to recountir the Fabis. **1579** SPENSER *Sheph. Cal.* Apr. 26 But now from me hys madding mynd is starte, And woes the Widdowes daughter of the glenne. **1596** DALRYMPLE tr. *Leslie's Hist. Scot.* I. 102 Be thir places of wildernes, bygates, kraigs and glenis. **1748** PHILIPS *Pastorals* i. 79 Now left heiress of the glen she'll deem Me, landless lad, unworthy her esteem. *a* **1756** COLLINS *Superstit. Highlands* 213, I, perhaps, may tread Your lowly glens o'erhung with spreading broom. **1773** JOHNSON *Lett. to Mrs. Thrale* 21 Sept., About noon we came to a small glen, so they call a valley. **1784** COWPER *Task* VI. 403 The wilderness is theirs with all its caves, Its hollow glenns. **1796** JANE AUSTEN *Pride & Prej.* x. (1813) 219 The valley, here contracted into a glen. **1838** THIRLWALL *Greece* II. xvi. 337 The Oeroe .. flows through a narrow glen at the western foot of Cithaeron. **1843** PRESCOTT *Mexico* (1850) I. 362 The Spaniards .. suffering the wily enemy to draw them into a narrow glen or defile, intersected by a little stream of water.

β. **1586** J. HOOKER *Girald. Irel.* II. vi. 180 They came to the side of a mounteine, where there was a glan, and in it a little groue of wood.

γ. **1596** SPENSER *State Irel.* Wks. (Globe) 615/1 He did shutt them up within those narrow corners and glinnes under the mountaynes foote. **1600** HOLLAND *Livy* VII. xiv. 258 All these hee chargeth .. to get .. into the hils, and among the glins and woods, to bestow themselves close. **1611** SPEED *Hist. Gt. Brit.* IX. xxiv. 316 In the midst of Winter hee entred the Glinnes, that is, the Vallies of Leinster, a secure receptacle of the Rebels. **1685** BOYLE *Salub. Air* 10 Another great scope of land, which was divided from it but by a glin. **17..** C. LITTLETON in C. A. Johns *Week at Lizard* (1848) 81 Another rotten moor brings you to a *Glyn* or narrow Valley. **1753** *Phil. Trans.* XLVIII. 1 This stream of wind .. arose from a glin called Allgolan. **1756** HOME *Douglas* III. i, We found him lurking in the hollow glynn. **1767** BUSH *Hibernia Cur.* (1769) 72 The glyns, or dark vallies .. of this country, are many of them remarkably beautiful.

b. *Comb.*, as *glen-boy*, *-full*, *-head*, *-man.*

1841 S. C. HALL *Ireland* I. 186 We reached the pleasant and improving inn at Kenmare, and dismissed the *glen-boy. **1859** M. NAPIER *Mem. Visc. Dundee* I. i. 45 That *glen-full [Glencoe] of murdered Scotchmen! **1799** J. ROBERTSON *Agric. Perth* 423 Sheep .. ought to be allowed as much of the *glenheads, breas, and foot of the hills, as will support them during the severity of the winter and spring months. **1880** BREWER *Reader's Hand-bk.*, s.v. *Glencoe*, The massacre of M'Ian and thirty-eight of his *glenmen.

c. Also *attrib.*, designating check fabrics, esp. GLENURQUHART check.

1923 *Daily Mail* 13 Feb. 1 (Advt.), Smartly tailor made Glen Check Tweed. *Ibid.*, The new glen and plumage checks. **1967** 'T. WELLS' *What should you know of Dying?* x. 115 A double-breasted glen plaid suit was his uniform of the day. **1968** J. IRONSIDE *Fashion Alphabet* 218 *Glen check.* 'Glen' describes many check fabrics originally Scottish in design. It is similar to Shepherd's check but can be in any combination of colours and has a large overcheck.

Hence **'glenikin, 'glenlet**, a little glen. *nonce-wds.*

1835 *Blackw. Mag.* XXXVIII. 120 Every glen and glenikin had its river, or its stream, or its burn, or its rill. **1892** *Gd. Words* Apr. 239/1 A prettily wooded glenlet.

glen[2]. *Sc.* 'A daffodil' (Jam.).

1864 A. MCKAY *Hist. Kilmarnock* 297 The wild lilies, or glens, of Craufurdland Castle. **1880** *Jubilee W. O. Fenwick* 3 The children .. were .. supplied each one with a large bouquet of glens.

glenar, obs. form of GLEANER.

glence, glench, obs. forms of GLANCE *v.*[1]

glendoveer (glɛndəʊ'vɪə(r)). [Avowedly an alteration of *grandouver* in Sonnerat *Voy. aux Indes* (1782); from the context in which the word occurs in that work (I. 185 ff.), it appears to represent Skr. *gandharva*, a kind of semi-divine spiritual being.] One of a race of beautiful sprites in Southey's artificial quasi-Hindu mythology.

1810 SOUTHEY *Kehama* VI. ii, The Glendoveers, The loveliest race of all of heavenly birth. **1812** H. & J. SMITH *Rej. Addr.* ('Rebuilding by R. S.'), I am a blessed Glendoveer. **1835** *Tait's Mag.* II. 228, I looked carefully to his shoulders, in hopes that I had discovered a glendoveer. **1842** LYTTON *Zanoni* IV. xi, Glendoveers and sylphs.

‖**glene** ('gliːniː). *Anat.* [mod.L., a. Gr. γλήνη the ball or pupil of the eye; used by Galen to denote a shallow joint-socket, distinguished from κοτύλη COTYLE.] **a.** The ball or socket of the eye. **b.** A glenoid cavity.

1706 in PHILLIPS (ed. Kersey); and in later Dicts.

glene, -er, obs. forms of GLEAN, -ER.

glengarry (glɛn'gærɪ). [f. *Glengarry* in Inverness-shire.] A kind of man's cap, higher in front than at back, of Highland origin, now chiefly worn by persons dressed in Highland costume, and till lately by soldiers of certain regiments when in undress uniform.

1841 in *Hist. Rec. Queen's Own Cameron Highlanders* (1909) II. 280 When the glengarry bonnet is used for evening dress, it is to be made of fine cloth, [etc.]. **1858** SIMMONDS *Dict. Trade*, *Glengarry*, a Scotch bonnet; a man's cap. **1870** *Illustr. Lond. News* 24 Sept. 327 The *Globe* states that a slight change is about to be made in the uniform of her Majesty's brigade of Guards. The present undress cap is to be replaced by a Scotch glengarry. **1891** BARRIE *Little Minister* (1892) 13 Margaret was at home making a glengarry for him out of a piece of carpet.

glengore, -goir, corrupt var. GRANDGORE, *Obs.*, venereal disease.

Glenlivet (glɛn'lɪvɪt, *Sc.* -'liːvɪt). Also **Glenlivit, -at.** [f. *Glenlivet* in Banffshire, the place of manufacture.] A variety of Scotch whisky.

1822 J. WILSON *Noct. Ambr.* vi. in *Blackw. Mag.* XII. 371, I never drank better Glenlivit. **1824** SCOTT *St. Ronan's* xxxix, The Captain offered a bet to Jekyl of a mutchkin of Glenlivat, that both would fall by the first fire. **1841** LEVER *C. O'Malley* xxx. 160 Glenlivat and guava jelly. **1854** AYTOUN *Bon Gaultier Ball.*, *Massacre Macpherson* viii, Which he would have done, I at least believe it, Had ta mixture peen Only half Glenlivet.

gleno- ('gliːnəʊ), mod. comb. form of GLENE in anatomical terms, as *gleno-humeral*, belonging to the glenoid cavity together with the humerus; so also *gleno-vertebral.*

1847–9 TODD *Cycl. Anat.* IV. 575 A second band, 'the gleno-humeral ligament' described by the late Dr. V. Flood, is thrown across the head of the humerus. **1889** A. MACALISTER *Human Anat.* 146 A projecting superior gleno-humeral fold (Flood's ligament) lies above the sub-scapular tendon. **1889** in *Century Dict.*

glenoid ('gliːnɔɪd), *a. Anat.* [ad. Gr. γληνοειδής, f. γλήνη a shallow joint-socket (see GLENE) + εἶδος form, appearance: cf. F. *glénoïde.*] ***glenoid cavity, fossa, surface***, a shallow cavity on a bone (esp. the scapula and temporal bone) which receives a projection of another bone to form a joint. ***glenoid ligament*** (see quot. 1831). ***glenoid fissure***, see GLASERIAN.

1709 BLAIR in *Phil. Trans.* XXVII. 108 The length of the Sinus, called in Human Subjects the Glenoid Cavity. **1769** WHITE *Ibid.* LIX. 43 This osseous matter could not proceed from the scapula, the glenoid cavity of that bone not being divested of its Cartilage. **1831** R. KNOX *Cloquet's Anat.* 203 *Glenoid Ligament*.. This is a sort of fibro-cartilaginous rim, which seems intended to increase the depth of the glenoid cavity. **1872** MIVART *Elem. Anat.* 77 A shallow cavity placed on each side in front of the external auditory opening, and termed the glenoid surface. **1876** C. S. TOMES *Dental Anat.* 31 The glenoid fossæ of the temporal bone, formed partly by the squamous and partly by the vaginal portions of the bone. **1879** *St. George's Hosp. Rep.* IX. 728 By.. pressing the arm downwards with my leg, the head of the bone slipped into the glenoid cavity.. with unusual ease.

So **gle'noidal** *a. Anat.* [cf. F. *glénoïdal*].

1847 in CRAIG. **1871** HUXLEY *Anat. Vert.* vi. 290 In the Carinatæ, the glenoidal end of the scapula is divided into two portions; a glenoidal process, which expands to form the upper part of the glenoidal cavity.. and an acromial process. **1883** MARTIN & MOALE *Vertebr. Dissect.* II. 119 The distal or glenoidal end of the coracoid.

glens, obs. form of GLANCE *v.*[1]

glent (glɛnt), *sb.* Now only *dial.*: see also GLINT. [f. GLENT *v.*]

1. A look, a glance; = GLINT 2.

13.. *E.E. Allit. P.* A. 1143 So wern his glentez gloryous glade. **13..** *Gaw. & Gr. Knt.* 1290 Þenne ho gef hym god-day, & wyth a glent laȝed. *c* **1746** J. COLLIER (Tim Bobbin) *View Lanc. Dial.* Wks. (1862) 46, I.. ran o mile.. ofore eh ga one glent behund meh. *a* **1866** in Harland *Lanc. Lyrics* 134 He.. just gi'es a glent wi' his ee, his ee.

2. A passing view, a glimpse; = GLINT 3.

c **1570** *Pride & Lowl.* (1841) 18, I looked up and had a glent Of one that came toward us leasurely. *a* **1796** PEGGE *Derbicisms* Ser. I. 27 (E.D.S.), *A glent*, a glimpse or transient sight of anything. *a* **1825** FORBY *Voc. E. Anglia, Glemth, Glent, Glint*, a glimpse, a short and slight view. **1887** *S. Cheshire Gloss., Glint*, a glimpse.. Also *Glent*, equally common.

3. a. A slip, a fall. **b.** A quick movement, a spring.

1526 SKELTON *Magnyf.* 1688 For all that he is lyke to have a glent. **18..** *Lady Margery* xix. in Child *Ballads* III. lxv. (1885) 119 When he came to the bale-fire, He lighted wi a glent.

4. A gleam, flash (of light).

1728 RAMSAY *Fables, Monk & Miller's Wife* 79 An Opening.. Throw whilk he saw a Glent of Light.

5. *in a glent*: in a moment.

1768 ROSS *Helenore* II. 89 Syn in a glent they were out o' my sight.

†**glent**, *a. Obs.* [? from attrib. use of prec.] Glowing, lustrous.

1526 SKELTON *Magnyf.* 993 It is.. A byrde full swete.. Her browys bent, Her eyen glent.

glent (glɛnt), *v. Obs.* exc. *dial.* Forms: *Pres. t.* 4–6 **glente**, 5 **glentte**, 4– **glent**. *Pa. t.* 3–6 **glent(e**, 5 **glented**. *Pa. pple.* **glente**. [Prob. of Scandinavian origin; cf. Sw. (dial.) *glänta, glinta, glätta* to slip, slide; to open slightly; to shine, gleam. The root (OTeut. **glint-, glant-*) appears also in OHG. *glanz* adj., bright, clear, whence OHG. *glęnzen* (G. *glänzen*) to shine, glitter; and perh. in ON. *glettr, gletta* banter, railing, *glettask* to banter, taunt; Sw. (dial.) *glänta*, Da. *glente* a kite (cf. GLEDE). The orig. sense is prob. that of quick motion, the application to light being secondary; for a similar development cf. GLANCE *v.*]

†**1.** *intr.* To move quickly or with a gliding motion, esp. in an oblique direction. Also *to glent aside*: to start aside. *Obs.*

13.. *Coer de L.* 1076 Kyng Rychard thenne besyde he glente. *c* **1330** R. BRUNNE *Chron.* (1810) 322 For þe quene he sent.. Fro Cawod scho glent, to Donnefermelyn to fare. ? *a* **1400** *Morte Arth.* 2563 Þe gome.. gyrdis at syr Gawayne, as he by glentis. *c* **1430** LYDG. *Min. Poems* (Percy Soc.) 114 In at a gape as he glent By the medylle he was hent. *c* **1430** *Syr. Gener.* (Roxb.) 7081 She knew his voice, and glent a-side As she from him wold hir hide. *c* **1465** *Chevy Chase* 25 Grea hondes thorowe the grevis glent, For to kyll thear dear. ? *a* **1500** *Chester Pl.* viii. 114 Our light from vs away is glent. *a* **1650** *Scot. Feilde* 71 in Furniv. *Percy Folio* I. 215 They glenten to Callice; with great shipps of warre. *a* **1796** PEGGE *Derbicisms* Ser. I. 27 (E.D.S.), *Glent*, to move hastily by. *fig.* **13..** *E.E. Allit. P.* A. 671 Bot he to gyle þat neuer glente, At inoscente is saf & ryȝte. **13..** *Gaw. & Gr. Knt.* 1652 Much glam & gle glent vp þer-inne. *c* **1430** *Hymns Virg.* 109 Lete euere gabbing glide & goon Away, wheþer it wole glase or glent.

b. Of a weapon, missile, etc.: To glance, strike obliquely (cf. GLACE *v.* and GLANCE *v.*).

14.. *Sir Beues* 4205 (MS. M.) The poynte on the pawment glente. *a* **1440** *Sir Degrev.* 279 Gleves gleteryng glent Opone geldene scheldus. *c* **1440** HYLTON *Scala Perf.* (W. de W. 1494) II. xxxvii, It hurteth not: but glenteth awaye & passeth forth. *c* **1530** LD. BERNERS *Arth. Lyt. Bryt.* (1814) 34 The stroke glented downe on the lifte syde. *a* **1533** —— *Huon* xxxiv. 108 Yᵉ stroke glent & the fauchon lyght upon a pyller. **1867** SMYTH *Sailor's Word-bk., Glent*, to turn aside or quit the original direction, as a shot does from accidentally impinging on a hard substance.

†**c.** *trans.* To cause to glide; to hurl. Also *fig.* To thrust aside; to conceal. *Obs.*

13.. *Coer de L.* 5295 Out off hys sadyl he hym glente. *c* **1430** *Pol. Rel. & L. Poems* 170 Þis wickid lijf þat y lyue ynne Y may it not from þi knowynge gleynt.

†**2.** To look askance: to glance. Also *to glent aside*: to give a side-look. (Cf. GLINT *v.* 3.) *Obs.*

c **1250** *Gen. & Ex.* 1029 Ȝhe glente and ðhoȝte, miȝte it noȝt ben. **1303** R. BRUNNE *Handl. Synne* 6184 Þe frere ȝaf gode tente Whyderward hys yȝen glente. **13..** *Gaw. & Gr. Knt.* 82 Þe comlokest to discrye Þer glent with yȝen gray. *c* **1374** CHAUCER *Troylus* IV. 1195 (1223) As þat here eyen glente A-syde a-noon she gan his swerd aspye.

†**b.** *trans.* = GLINT 3 b. *Obs.*[−1]

c **1380** *Sir Ferumb.* 354 Fyrumbras on him glent his eye scornfuly & low.

3. Of light, etc.: To be reflected, flash, gleam, etc. Of luminous or reflecting objects: To shine. (Cf. GLINT *v.* 1.) Now only *dial.*

13.. *E.E. Allit. P.* A. 1025 Þe wal of Iasper þat glent as glayre. *c* **1400** *Destr. Troy* 3067 Glissonand as the glemes þat glenttes of þe snaw. ? *a* **1500** *Chester Pl.* (E.E.T.S.) 398 Leat and fyre.. from the sonne to the firmament Vp and downe shall stryke and glent. **1555** ABP. PARKER *Ps.* cxxxvi, Who made.. The moone and starres: on night to glent. **1724** RAMSAY *On Royal Archers* 4 Phœbus well pleas'd, shines from the blew Serene, Glents on the Stream [etc.]. *a* **1774** FERGUSSON *Wks.* (1807) 340 Whan flowers and gowans wont to glent In bonny blinks upo' the bent.

b. quasi-*trans.* Of the eyes: To flash (fire).

1819 W. TENNANT *Papistry Storm'd* (1827) 154 Ae Lollard man got ere he wist A lounder frae a Papish fist, That garr'd his een glent fire.

Hence '**glenting** *vbl. sb.* and *ppl. a.*

c **1440** HYLTON *Scala Perf.* (W. de W. 1494) II. xxiv, For though thou fele & perceyue glentynges & proferynges of vayne thoughtes. **1807** STAGG *Poems* 7 Wi' glentin' spurs an' weel clean'd buits.

Glenurquhart, Glen Urquhart (glɛ'nɜːkət). [f. *Glenurquhart* in Inverness-shire.] A Scottish district check (see quot. 1956). Also *attrib.*

1923 *Daily Mail* 23 Apr. 8 Checked materials are not in fashion, with perhaps the exception of brown Glenurquharts—of which the nicest carry a red line or overcheck. **1944** C. MACKENZIE *North Wind of Love* I. 10 This remark came from a lanky young man.. in plus-fours of a modest Glen Urquhart tweed. **1956** M. B PICKEN *Fashion Dict.* 255/1 (*caption*) Glenurquhart Plaid. Squares of small woven checks alternated with squares of larger checks, in one or two muted colors with white. **1959** M. STEEN *Tower* I. vii. 93 A dapper little character in Glenurquhart tweed. **1967** R. WILKINSON *Pressure Men* x. 95 She wore a green glenurquhart check two-piece suit.

glenynge, obs. form of GLEANING.

gleo(w, obs. form of GLEE *sb.*

gleowian, obs. form of GLEE *v.*[1]

glere, obs. form of GLAIR *sb.*[1]

gles(e, gles(s)en, obs. ff. GLASS(EN, GLISTEN.

glet, obs. form of GLEET *sb.*

gletcher, var. GLETSCHER.

glete, var. GLEIT *v.*, *Obs.*

gleter, -tre, obs. forms of GLITTER.

glethurly, *adv.*: see GLIDDER *a.*

‖'**gletscher**. *rare.* Also **gletcher**. [G. *gletscher*, adopted in 16th c. from Swiss dialect = F. *glacier*.] A glacier.

1762 tr. *Busching's Syst. Geog.* III. 578 Vast fragments of ice called Gletschers. **1796** *Duncan's Ann. Med.* I. 23 In those very countries nearest to the gletschern [etc.]. **1825** *Blackw. Mag.* XVII. 308 Ev'n at th' eternal Gletscher's ice-clad foot I sought and found cabins inhabited. **1932** AUDEN *Orators* III. 104 Or be ducked in a gletcher, as they ought to be. **1938** L. MACNEICE *Earth Compels* 32 Riding the sullen landscape far from friends Through the jungle of lava.. Fording the gletcher.

glett(e, gletty, obs. ff. GLEET, GLEETY *a.*

gleu, var. GLEW *a.* and *v.*, *Obs.*

gleu, gleuman, obs. ff. GLEE *sb.*, GLEEMAN.

gleve, obs. or dial. form of GLAIVE.

†**glew**, *a. Obs.* Forms: 1 **glēaw**, 1, 3 **gleu**, 3 **glæu**, **gleuȝ**. [Comm. Teut.: OE. *glēaw*:—OTeut. *glawwu-*; see GLEG *a.*] Wise, prudent, clever. Only OE. and early ME.

c **725** *Corpus Gloss.* 1768 *Sagax*, gleu. *c* **825** *Vesp. Psalter* cxviii[i]. 98 Ofer feond mine gleawne mec dydes. *c* **1000** *Ags. Gosp.* Matt. x. 16 Beoð.. gleawe swa næddran. *c* **1205** LAY. 16237 Þer wes þe aðele eorl.. cnihten alre glæuest. *a* **1250** *Prov. Ælfred* 362 in *O.E. Misc.* 124 Þvrh sawe mon is wis And þurh hiselþe [*v.r.* þurrh selþe] mon is glev. *a* **1250** *Owl & Night.* 193 He is wis and war of worde; He is of worde swiþe gleu. *c* **1290** *S. Eng. Leg.* I. 261/13 Þare nas man in no mester so gleu ne so quoynte.

†**glew**, *v.*[1] *Obs.* Forms: 1 **glēowian**, **glīwian**, 3 **gleowian**, **gleu**, 4 **glew**, 5 **glewe**. [f. *gleow, glew* GLEE *sb.*]

1. *intr.* To make merry; to jest; to play on musical instruments.

c **900** tr. *Bæda's Hist.* IV. xxv. [xxiv.] (1891) 346 He.. sumu þing mid his sprecende ætgædere and gleowiende wæs þe þær ær inne wæron. *c* **1000** *Canons of Edgar* c. 58 in Thorpe *Laws* II. 256 Þæt ænig preost ne gliwiᵹe. *c* **1205** LAY. 20315 Mid his harpe he ferde to þas kinges hirede, and gon þær to gleowien [*c* **1275** pleoye] and muche gome to makien. *a* **1225** *Ancr. R.* 368 Me seide him þet heo gleowede and gomede.. and liuede in delices. *a* **1300** *Cursor M.* 7426 Bot do we litel dauid cum, Wit his harp.. We sal him do bath gleu and sing. *a* **1310** in Wright *Lyric P.* xi. 38 Hire gladshipe nes never gon, Whil y may glewe.

2. To call loudly *on*.

13.. *E.E. Allit. P.* C. 164 Bot vchon glewed on his god þat gayned hym beste.

3. *trans.* To afford entertainment or pleasure to; to make happy. (Cf. phrase under GAME *v.* 2.)

a **1300** *Cursor M.* 7254 (Cott.) Bi a piler was he [Samson] þar sett To gleu [*Gött.* mirth] þaa gomes at þair mete. **1303** R. BRUNNE *Handl. Synne* 1910 Þere ys no solas undyr heuene.. þat shulde a man so moche glew As a good woman þat loveþ trew. *c* **1430** *Syr Tryam.* 108 No game schulde the glewe! *a* **1510** DOUGLAS *K. Hart* II. xviii, Thay never cum the for to glew.

Hence †'**glewing** *vbl. sb.*, playing, music.

a **1300** *K. Horn* 1468 Hi.. gunne murie singe, And makede here gleowinge. *a* **1300** *Cursor M.* 7411 His scepe þam-self war sembel samen Of his suete gleuing [*other MSS.* melody, minstralcy] for to here.

†**glew**, *v.*[2] *Obs. rare.* [Perh. pseudo-archaic = GLOW *v.*[2]] *intr.* To gaze, stare. Hence '**glewing** *ppl. a.*

1587 TURBERV. *Trag. T.* I. 17 Uplifted he his head, and glewde aboute To see what wooful wight it was. *Ibid.* I. 17 b, Who gallopt on, and glewde with fell regarde. *Ibid.* IV. Lenvoy vi. 70 b, The glewing grome that fyghts before he commes Is eyther voyded, or by sleight subdued.

glew(e, obs. form of GLEE, GLUE, GLOW *v.*

glewie, glewy, obs. forms of GLUEY.

glewish(e, obs. form of GLUISH.

glewman, obs. form of GLEEMAN.

gley (gleɪ). *Soil Science.* Also **glei**. [Ukrainian, = sticky bluish clay (see quot. 1963); cogn. w. CLAY *sb.*] A blue-grey soil or soil layer in which iron and manganese compounds are reduced through being waterlogged; also, such a soil mottled with brownish oxidized patches as a result of periods of relative dryness. Also ***gley horizon, soil***, etc.

1927 C. F. MARBUT tr. *Glinka's Great Soil Groups* 36 In the last two groups the 'Glei' horizon, developed under the influence of ascending moisture, is often present. **1953** H. L. EDLIN *Forester's Handbk.* v. 77 Gleys.. are soils that develop where drainage is impeded, so that there is a fluctuating water-table or saturated layer in the soil structure. **1963** BIRRON & COLE tr. *Vilenskii's Soil Sci.* xxi. 308 The words 'glei' and 'gleification' were derived from the popular Ukrainian and introduced into scientific terminology in 1905 by G. N. Visotskii. **1969** *Jrnl. Soil Sci.* XX. 207 Failure to distinguish between sulphide-containing and sulphide-free gley soils causes considerable confusion.

Hence '**gleyed** *ppl. a.*, turned into a gley; '**gleying, gleiing** *vbl. sb.*, **glei'zation** (gleɪ-), the formation of a gley.

1934 *Forestry* VIII. 30 The gleyed horizon is usually of a greenish or bluish colour. **1938** H. G. BYERS et al. in *Yearbk. Agric.* (U.S.) IV. 975 The bluish or greenish waterlogged horizons are sometimes called glei or gley, and the process by which they are formed is sometimes called gleization. **1949** *Jrnl. Soil Sci.* I. 205 It is not clear when it was first realized that gleying is caused by a microbial reduction of ferric compounds. *Ibid.*, A laboratory study of the gleying process. **1949** J. S. JOFFE *Pedology* (ed. 2) xi. 430 Morphologically, the B horizon has also been affected by the gleiing process. **1956** C. D. PIGOTT in D. L. Linton *Sheffield* 80 Where water-logging occurs.. the soils are gleyed and in many places the ground flora is almost exclusively dominated by *Allium ursinum*. **1971** *Nature* 1 Jan. 45/1 Marked peatiness of the soil and gleying are only found toward the upper limit of lower Montane forest.

gley, var. GLEE *v.*[2], GLOY *v.*, *Sc.*

†**gleyd.** *Sc. Obs.* Also 6, 8 **glyde**, **gloyd**. An old worn-out horse.

a **1568** *Bannatyne MS., Wowing of Jok & Jenny* 45 Ane crukit gloyd fell our ane huch. *a* **1586** *Satire* 56 in *Maitland P.* (1786) 183 In it may be sene Tuelf gait glydis deir of a priene. **1724** RAMSAY *Tea-t. Misc.* (1733) II. 182 Ane auld gawd gloyd fell owre a heugh [cf. quot. *a* 1568]. **1787** W. TAYLOR *Scots Poems* 42 Seldom hae I felt the loss O' Gloyd or Cow, Ouse, Goat or Yowe. **1787** BURNS *Let. to W. Nicol* 1 June, My auld, ga'd gleyde o' a meere.

gleyd, obs. form of GLEDE.

gleyd, gleyed, vars. GLEED *ppl. a.*

gleyer, var. GLEER; see under GLEE *v.*[2]

gleyere, gleyȝy(e)r, obs. forms of GLAIR *sb.*[1]

gleyit, obs. form of GLEED *ppl. a.*

gleym, var. GLIME *v. dial.*, to squint; GLEIM.

gleyman, obs. form of GLEEMAN.

gleyme, var. GLEIM *sb.* and *v.*, *Obs.*

gleymouse, -owse, var. GLEIMOUS *a.*, *Obs.*

gleymy, var. GLEIMY *a. Obs.*, sticky.

gleyr(e, gleyve, obs. ff. GLAIR *sb.*[1], GLAIVE.

glia ('glaɪə). *Phys.* [a. Gr. γλία glue.] = NEUROGLIA; freq. *attrib.*, as ***glia-tissue***; **glia cell**, any of the different kinds of cell in neuroglia.

1886 W. R. GOWERS *Man. Dis. Nerv. Syst.* I. III. 107 Fine fibres..form a network. At their intersections are peculiar cells consisting of a nucleus and small cell body ('glia-cells', 'cells of Deiters'). **1890** BILLINGS *Nat. Med. Dict.* I. 586/1 *Glia*, neuroglia. *G.-cells*,..small flattened cells found in the spinal cord. **1891** *Quain's Anat.* (ed. 10) I. II. 323 The neuroglia is, in fact, composed of greatly ramified cells (glia-cells). **1899** *Allbutt's Syst. Med.* VII. 172 Investigations of Weigert..seem to establish that new formations of glia may be either cellular or fibrous in structure. *Ibid.* 171 A subsequent proliferation of the embryonal epiblastic elements, or a thickening of the normal glia tissue. **1908** *Practitioner* Oct. 562 By a new staining method, which stains the neuro-fibril networks but leaves the glia totally unstained, [they] have demonstrated..that the Golgi pericellular nets are glial and not nervous in origin. **1964** J. Z. YOUNG *Model of Brain* iv. 60 Glia cells are said to show electrical phenomena when suitably stimulated. **1964** *Jrnl. Neurophysiol.* XXVII. 291 No special mechanism providing for electrical interaction between neurons and glia could be detected.

gliadin ('glaɪədɪn). *Chem.* [a. F. *gliadine*, f. Gr. γλία glue.] The viscid portion of gluten. Called also *glutin*.

1830 LINDLEY *Nat. Syst. Bot.* 303 The gluten of Wheat yields the two chemical principles called gliadine and zimome. **1859** FOWNES *Man. Chem.* 570 The gliadin may be extracted by boiling alcohol. **1892** G. L. GOODALE *Physiol. Bot.* II. §958.

glial ('glaɪəl), *a.* [f. GLIA + -AL.] Of or pertaining to glia.

1888 B. BRAMWELL *Intracranial Tumours* ix. 224 The tumour is found to be composed of small round or oval cells, and of extremely delicate fibres (glial threads). **1908** [see prec.]. **1910** ALLBUTT & ROLLESTON *Syst. Med.* (ed. 2) VII. 856 The normal glial structure of the spinal cord. **1954** S. DUKE-ELDER *Parsons' Dis. Eye* (ed. 12) xxiii. 321 These sheaths are separated by glial tissue and a neurilemma is absent. **1966** *New Statesman* 9 Sept. 349/1 The so-called glial cells, for example, which greatly outnumber the nerve cells, turn out to be more than the mere padding they were thought to be.

glib (glɪb), *sb.*[1] *Hist.* Also 6 **glibe**, 6, 9 **glyb(be**, 7 **gleb**, 6, 7, 9 **glib(b(e**. [a. Irish *glib*.] A thick mass of matted hair on the forehead and over the eyes, formerly worn by the Irish.

1537 *Act 28 Hen. VIII*, c. 15 Stat. Irel. (1678) 92 No person..shall..use the wearing of haire upon their heads, like unto long lockes, called glibbes. **1570** PERROTT in O'Flanagan *Munster Circuit* (1880) 3, I have caused all the Irishry in this province to forego their glybbes. **1577** STANYHURST *Descr. Irel.* viii. 28 in *Holinshed*, For default of other stuffe, they paune theyr glibs, the nailes of their fingers and toes [etc.]. **1610** HOLLAND *Camden's Brit.* (1637) 123 The lappets of their eares hidden under the curled glibbes and lockes of haire lying all over them. **1812** SOUTHEY *Lett.* (1856) II. 304 My hair has escaped cutting..and..shall be reserved for a *glib* till the spring. **1842** S. C. HALL *Ireland* II. 384 A sort of covering, resembling a monk's cowl, or the glibbe of the ancient Irish.

attrib. **1861** WILDE *Catal. Antiq. in Roy. Ir. Acad.* 325 The glibb-fashion of wearing the hair.

b. A man who wears a glib.

1618 GAINSFORD *Glory Eng.* xvii. 151 In Tyrconnell the haire of their head grows so long and curled, that they goe bareheaded, and are called Glibs, the women Glibbins.

Hence **glibbed** *ppl. a.*, wearing a glib.

1581 DERRICKE *Image Irel.* (1883) 38 With glibbed heddes like Mars hym self. **1812** J. NOTT *Dekker's Gulls Horn-bk.* 88 *note*, These wood-karne went with glibbed heads, or wearing long bushy hair over their eyes.

†**glib**, *sb.*[2] *slang. Obs.* In 8 **glibb**. A ribbon.

1753 *Discov. of J. Poulter* 39 A Lobb full of Glibbs; a Box full of Ribbons.

glib (glɪb), *a.* and *adv.* Also 6–7 **glibb(e**. [See GLIBBERY *a.*] **A.** *adj.*

1. Smooth and slippery in surface or consistency; moving easily; offering no resistance to motion. Of movement: Easy, unimpeded. Now *rare* exc. *dial.*

1599 PLAT *Jewell-ho.* III. 12 White and glib worms, which the anglers call Gentils. **1600** SURFLET *Countrie Farme* v. ii. 664 Arable groundes..bring forth..more in one place then in another, according as the ground shall be moist and glib [etc.]. **1615** CROOKE *Body of Man* 144 His superficies or face is like the Liuer smooth and glib. **1627** CAPT. SMITH *Seaman's Gram.* ii. 13 A white mixture of Tallow, Sope and Brimstone..is the best to..make her glib or slippery to passe the water. **1681** GLANVILL *Sadducismus* I. (1682) 158 This easiness of the sliding of bodies perfectly smooth and glib. **1683** A. SNAPE *Anat. Horse* I. x. (1686) 20 Covered with a slimy or snotty substance, for the more free and glib passage of the Dung. *c* **1720** W. GIBSON *Farrier's Dispens.* VII. iii. (1734) 193 A small quantity of Oil and Flour..would ..render them more glib to swallow. **1772** FLETCHER *Logica Genev.* 108 Why should those who can swallow five or six camels as a glib morsel, strain at three or four gnats. **1789** DAVIDSON *Seasons* 161 Wi' channel-stanes, baith glib an' strong, His army did advance. **1796** E. MILLER *Diary* in C. A. Markham *Hist. Buildings of Northamptonsh.* (1885) 20 The Alleys in the Gaol yard were as glib as Glass. **1818** L. HUNT *Nymphs* I. 256 With..coral, and the glib sea flowers, They furnish their faint bowers. **1827** CLARE *Sheph. Cal.* 3 Seeking bright glib ice, to play And slide the wintry hours away. **1853** KANE *Grinnell Exp.* xxxiv. (1856) 310 A fine bare surface of fresh ice, extremely glib and durable. **1879** BROWNING *Ivan Ivanovitch* 101 The snow lies glib as glass and hard as steel. **1888** *Sheffield Gloss.*, *Glib*, soft, smooth.

transf. and *fig.* **1607** SHAKS. *Timon* I. i. 53 All Mindes, As well of glib and slipp'ry Creatures, as Of Graue and austere qualitie, tender downe Their seruices to Lord Timon. **1678** MARVELL *Growth Popery* 27 That this House might appear still necessary to the People, and to make the money more glib.

2. Of an action, method, procedure: Easy, meeting no obstruction; off-hand.

1598 MARSTON *Pygmal.* v. 157 He's a God that can doe villany With a good grace, and glib facility. **1643** MILTON *Divorce* Wks. 1738 I. 162 The method is so glib and easy. **1668** H. MORE *Div. Dial.* IV. xii. (1713) 313 How glib, how easie and how natural would it have been upon this Hypothesis? **1852** D. G. MITCHELL *Dream Life* 124 The glib, easy way of one student, and his perfect *sang-froid* completely charm you.

3. Of a speaker or writer, of the tongue, etc.: 'Well-oiled', ready and fluent in utterance. Of language: Characterized by fluency and readiness. Chiefly in contemptuous use, implying lack of thought or of sincerity.

1602 MARSTON *Antonio's Rev.* I. ii. Wks. 1856 I. 77 Is glib rumor growne a parasite? **1605** SHAKS. *Lear* I. i. 227, I want that glib and oylie Art, To speak and purpose not. **1606** —— *Tr. & Cr.* IV. v. 58 These encounterers so glib of tongue. **1605** BRETON *Old Man's Lesson* F, Take heede of a Leering Eye and a Glibbe tongue. **1606** DEKKER *Sev. Sinnes* I. (Arb.) 12 A hye sound and glib deliuery. **1639** FULLER *Holy War* v. xix. (1640) 261 Their glib pennes making no more reckoning of men then of pins. **1669** W. SIMPSON *Hydrol. Chym.* 234 Familiarity..begets a current glib language. **1705** BERKELEY *Commonpl. Bk.* Wks. 1871 IV. 429 Glib, coherent, methodical discourses, which nevertheless amount to just nothing. **1792** D. LLOYD *Voy. Life* 79 Prompt Deception glib with flatt'ring lies! **1820** COLERIDGE *Lett., Convers., etc.* I. 137 A contemptible democratical oligarchy of glib economists. **1827** LADY GRANVILLE *Lett.* Oct. (1894) I. 435 The..husband talks very good glib French and is intelligent. **1848** LYTTON *Harold* I. i, Thou art too glib of tongue for a subject. **1884** G. ALLEN *Philistia* II. 87 The ordinary glib commonplaces of obituary notices. **1892** STEVENSON *Across the Plains* 255 His glib, random criticism took a wider range. **1893** VIZETELLY *Glances Back* II. xxix. 152 [He] was..a glib and ready speaker.

†**b.** Of words: Easy to pronounce. Also of a statement: Easily 'swallowed', plausible. *Obs.*

1603 H. CROSSE *Vertues Commonw.* (1878) 103 O how will they diue into the bottome of their braine! for fluant termes ..to varnish theyr lyes and fables to make them glib. **1608** MIDDLETON *Mad World* v. i. 74 The Slip! by my troth a pretty name, and a glib one.

4. *Comb.*, as ***glib-tongued*** adj.; †**glib-board** (see quot. 1894); **glib-gabbet** *a. Sc.*, voluble, loquacious.

1682 J. COLLINS *Salt & Fishery* 29 Men walking on them [Brine Pans] with Boards tyed to their Feet called *Glib-Boards. **1894** HARRIS *Techn. Fire Insur. Comment.*, *Glib boards*, in salt-works, the boards tied to the men's feet to enable them to walk in the salt-pans. **1786** BURNS *Earnest Cry* xiii, That *glib-gabbet Highland Baron The Laird o' Graham. **1605** *Laugh & lie downe* in Collier *Bibl. Acc.* (1865) I. 452 The next was a nimble witted and *glib-toung'd fellow. **1837** CARLYLE *Fr. Rev.* II. III. ii, Fauchet approves himself a glib-tongued, strong-lunged, whole-hearted human individual. **1895** *Educat. Rev.* 223, I have not said that a liberal education includes of necessity the prolonged scholastic study of many languages, much less the glib-tongued use of many languages.

B. *adv.*

1. Smoothly; easily. Now *rare*.

1594 NASHE *Unfort. Trav.* 5 After I had moistned my lippes, to make my lie run glibbe. **1600** BRETON *Pasquils Fooles-cap* (Grosart) 19/2 An idle Mate, Whose tongue goes all too glibbe vpon the seare. **1627** DRAYTON *Agincourt*, etc. 189 Let your numbers run Glib as the former, so shall it liue long. **1696** W. MOUNTAGUE *Delights Holland* 223 Having a little Tub of Water upon the Sledge, which they often spill on the Ground, to make it go the glibber. **1712** ARBUTHNOT *John Bull* III. iii, A noose that slipt as glib as a bird-catcher's gin. *a* **1734** NORTH *Exam.* I. iii. §39 (1740) 145 The Bill did not pass glib. **1775** FLETCHER *Script. Scales* II. xx. Wks. 1795 V. 303 *note*, To make it go down glib with all the rigid bound-willers in Christendom. **1830** SCOTT *Doom Devorgoil* III. ii, Father's razor slips as glib As from courtly tongue a fib. **1867** J. M. SEWALL *Laughing* in *Bk. Humor. Poet.* 103 It makes the wheels of nature glibber play.

2. Volubly; fluently.

1628 W. PEMBLE *Rec. Lord's Supper* 62 If the tongue goe glibbe. **1682** DRYDEN *Dk. of Guise* IV. iii, Love has oiled your tongue to run so glib. **1778** FOOTE *Trip Calais* I. Wks. 1799 II. 339 Mere infants..sputter French, more freer and glibber than your daughter. **1813** E. S. BARRETT *Heroine* (1815) III. 27 You talked so glib of your great estates. **1887** BESANT *The World went* i. 7 The words drop out glib, and seem to mean nothing.

3. *Comb.*, as ***glib-gliding*** adj.

1591 SYLVESTER *Du Bartas* I. vii. 90 How th' Airs glib-gliding firmness body bears Such store of Fowls, Hail-storms, and Floods of tears.

glib (glɪb), *v.*[1] Also 6 **glibe**. [f. the adj.]

†**1.** *trans.* To render glib, smooth, or slippery. Also *fig. Obs.*

1599 MARSTON *Sco. Villanie* I. iv. 188 Retayling others wit, long barrelled, To glib some great mans eares, till panch be fed. **1602** —— *Antonio's Rev.* II. ii. Wks. 1856 I. 93 The clapper of my mouth's not glibd With court oyle. **1678** *Lively Orac.* 223 Each commission [of villany] smoothing and glibbing the way to the next.

2. To render glib or fluent.

1628 BP. HALL *Rem. Wks.* (1660) 20 There is a drunken liberty of the Tongue, which being once glibbed with intoxicating liquor runs wilde. **1671** MILTON *P.R.* I. 371, I undertook that office, and the tongues Of all his flattering prophets glibbed with lies. **1683–4** *Whole Duty Man* xiii. §17. 101 Men have so glibbed their tongues to lying, that they do it familiarly upon any or no occasion. **1863** ROBSON *Bards Tyne* 310 They glibb'd their jaws at Lunnin. **1890** *Daily News* 15 Oct. 5/4 Those false prophets whom Mr. Bright once denounced, the prophets whose mouths were glibbed with lies.

3. *intr.* To talk volubly. *Obs.* exc. *dial.*

1602 WARNER *Alb. Eng.* XI. lxv. (1612) 279 Least perhaps he should haue glib'd. **1890** *Gloucestersh. Gloss.*, *Glib*, to talk rapidly or glibly. 'He glibbed it over, I'll be bound.'

†**4.** (See quot.) *Obs.*

1598 FLORIO, *Guizzare*..to slide, or glide, or slip, glibe away sodainely as an eele doth out of ones hand.

Hence **glibbed** *ppl. a.*, '**glibbing** *vbl. sb.*

1598 FLORIO, *Guizzo*, a sliding, a gliding, a slipping, a glibbing away sodainely. **1654** GAYTON *Pleas. Notes* IV. ix. 234 Their moistned braines gave leave for their glibb'd tongues to chat liberally. **1821** CLARE *Vill. Minstr.* II. 22 Smooth as glass the glibbed pool is froze.

†**glib**, *v.*[2] *Obs. rare.* [app. a corruption of LIB *v.*] *trans.* To castrate; to geld.

1611 SHAKS. *Wint. T.* II. i. 149, I had rather glib my selfe, then they Should not produce faire issue. **1640** SHIRLEY *St. Patrick for Irel.* v, If I come back, let me be glib'd.

glibber ('glɪbə(r)), *a. dial.* [See GLIBBERY *a.*] (See quot.)

1847–78 HALLIWELL, *Glibber*, worn smooth. *North.*

†'**glibber**, *v. Obs.*$^{-1}$ [See GLIBBERY *a.*] *intr.* To slip; to slide.

1599 A. M. tr. *Guillemeau's Fr. Chirurg.* Aiv b, This bullet-drawer is dentified, becaus the bullet being therin, it should not glibber therout.

†'**glibbery**, *a. Obs.* [Corresponds to Du. *glibberig* (not found in MDu.), late MLG. *glibberich* (mod. LG. *glibbrig*). Cognate forms are Eng. GLIB *a.*; Du. (dial.) *glib* curds; Eng. GLIBBER *a.* and *v.* = Du. *glibber* adj., *glibberen* vb.; cf. also Du. *glippen*, *glipperen* to slip, slide, *glipperig* slippery. It is possible that the words may stand in ablaut-relation to OHG. *gleif* sloping, oblique, or that they may be onomatopœic formations suggested by the wk. grade *glid* of Du. *glijden*, Eng. GLIDE *v.*; cf. GLIDDER.] Slippery; *fig.* shifty, untrustworthy.

1601 ? MARSTON *Pasquil & Kath.* I. 127 Let who will climbe ambitions glibbery rounds, And leane vpon the vulgars rotten loue. **1601** B. JONSON *Poetaster* v. i, What, shall thy Lubricall and glibbery Muse Liue, as she were defunct, like Punque in Stewes! **1602** MARSTON *Ant. & Mel.* I. Wks. 1856 I. 13 His love is glibbery; there's no hold ont, wench. *Ibid.* IV. Wks. 1856 I. 46 The glibbery ice Of vulgar favour. **1630** BRATHWAIT *Eng. Gentlem.* (1641) 7 The tongue..is a small member, but very glibbery and prone to ruine. *a* **1634** RANDOLPH *Muses' Looking-Gl.* II. iv. (1638) 33 No, feed on Widdowes, have each meale an Orphan Serv'd to your Table, or a glibbery heire With all his lands melted into a morgage. **1646** FULLER *Wounded Consc.* (1841) 321 Anointed with oil to make them sleek and glibbery.

†'**glibbin.** *Obs.*$^{-1}$ [f. GLIB *sb.*[1] Of doubtful genuineness: Irish *glibin* means 'a rag'.] A woman who wears a glib.

1618 [see GLIB *sb.*[1] b].

glibe, obs. form of GLIB *sb.*[1] and *v.*[1]

glibly ('glɪblɪ), *adv.* [f. GLIB *a.* + -LY[2].] In a glib manner.

1. Smoothly; easily; without impediment.

1605 B. JONSON *Volpone* I. i, You shall ha' some will swallow A melting heire, as glibly as your Dutch Will pills of butter. **1632** MASSINGER *City Madam* I. i. (1658) 4 *Tradewell.* Here's no grosse flattery: Will she swallow this? *Goldwire.* You see she does, and glibly. **1686** J. DUNTON *Lett. fr. New Eng.* (1867) 13 Nor was there wanting to all this good chear, plenty of Wines to make it go down glibly. **1744** ARMSTRONG *Preserv. Health* II. 498 The sapless habit daily to bedew, And give the hesitating wheels of life Gliblier to play. **1787** BEST *Angling* (ed. 2) 84 These..lines..have no knots to prevent their running glibly through the rings of the rod. **1807** *Sporting Mag.* XXIX. 70 Every thing went on glibly. **1818** M. G. LEWIS *Journ. W. Ind.* (1834) 258 The old lady..seemed to swallow the lie very glibly. **1844** THACKERAY *Wand. Fat Contrib.* ii. Wks. 1886 XXIV. 78[It] was slipping down his throat as glibly as an oyster. **1864** LOWELL *Fireside Trav.* 196 His broken fragments will reunite more glibly than the head and neck of Orrilo.

2. Fluently, with ready utterance.

1669 W. SIMPSON *Hydrol. Chym.* 232 Let them come to make a familiar discourse in Latine..they do it not glibly, in a current Style. **1792** MARY WOLLSTONECR. *Rights Wom.* Introd. 8 These caricatures of the real beauty of sensibility, dropping glibly from the tongue, vitiate the taste. **1801** MAR. EDGEWORTH *Angelina* iv. (1832) 76 Mrs. Puffit, having glibly run off this speech, left the room. **1853** KANE *Grinnell Exp.* xxxi. (1856) 269 None knew their parts, and the prompter could not read glibly enough to do his office. **1885** *Manch. Exam.* 4 Feb. 3/5 We talk glibly of 'Dutch painting'.

glibness ('glɪbnɪs). Also 7 **glibbe-, glibbiness.** [f. GLIB *a.* + -NESS.] The quality of being glib.

1. Smoothness; slipperiness.

1611 COTGR., *Glissade*, a slip, or slipping..; also, glibnesse. **1615** CHAPMAN *Odyss.* XII. 130 A polisht ice-like glibnesse doth enfold The rocke so round. **1631** SANDERSON *Serm.* (1664) II. 9 A kind of gentle softnesse, and smoothnesse, and supple glibbinesse: wherewith the touch is much delighted. **1644** DIGBY *Nat. Bodies* xiv. 125 The glibbenesse of Mercury and of melted mettalls. **1733**

CHEYNE *Eng. Malady* I. x. §4 (1734) 98 The Fluids [are].. only intended to preserve them [solids] in due Plight, Glibness [etc.]. **1768–74** TUCKER *Lt. Nat.* (1852) I. 97 Our organs.. continue the motions we put them into, after they have gone out of our sight, thereby working themselves to a glibness and smoothness.

2. Facility, readiness.

1631 MASSINGER *Believe as you List* III. iii. (1849) 55 With what glibnesse My flatteries, oyl'd with hopes of future greatnesse, Are swallow'd by this dull pate.

3. Fluency, volubility.

1633 T. ADAMS *Exp. 2 Peter* i. 10 Physicians judge of the body's health, not.. by the glibness of the tongue.. but by the pulse of the arm. **1669** W. SIMPSON *Hydrol. Chym.* 232 A current glibness in the utterance of any language. **1848** THACKERAY *Bk. Snobs* xxiv, The word slips out of their lips with.. glibness. **1865** *Sat. Rev.* 11 Mar. 284 He.. said what he had to say with the usual glibness.

† **'gliciride.** *Obs.*$^{-1}$ [ad. late L. *gliciriza*, L. *glycyrrhiza, -on*, Gr. γλυκύρριζα, -ον LIQUORICE.] = LIQUORICE.

c **1420** *Pallad. on Husb.* XI. 358 An vnce of melion, of gliciride Thre vnce.

glick(e, obs. f. GLEEK *sb.*[1]; var. GLEEK *sb.*[2] and *v.*, *Obs.*

† **glid**, *v. Obs.*$^{-0}$ [Cf. GLY.] *intr.* To look awry, squint.

1648–60 HEXHAM *Dutch Dict.*, To Glid, looke awry, sidewaies, or asquint, *scheel, ofte van ter zijden sien.*

glidder ('glɪdə(r)), *sb. dial.* [related to GLIDDER *a.* and OE. *gliddrian*: see GLIDDER *v.*] A loose stone on a hillside.

1799 SCOTT *Shepherd's T.* 190 Beneath the cavern dread Among the glidders grey A shapeless stone with lichens spread Marks where the wanderer lay. **1863** GREENWELL in *Trans. Tyneside Nat. Field Club* VI. 18 A very steep descent, covered with loose rolling stones, here called *glidders* or *glitters*.

glidder ('glɪdə(r)), *a. Obs.* exc. *dial.* Also 4 glethur. [OE. *glidder*, f. *glid-* wk. root of *glīdan* GLIDE *v.*] 'Slippery' (Halliwell). Hence **'glidderly** *adv.* (in 4 glethurly), with smooth unimpeded motion.

c **825** *Vesp. Hymns* xi. 6 *Lubricam*, glidder. *c* **1000** WULFSTAN *Hom.* 239/14 Ofer þone glideran weȝ hellewites brogan. **13..** *Sir Beues* (MS. C.) 4313 + 161 So glethurly the swyrde went, That the frye owt of the pawment sprent.

glidder ('glɪdə(r)), *v. Obs.* exc. *dial.* [f. prec. (OE. had *gliddrian* intr., to totter).] *trans.* To glaze over; to cover with ice.

1616 B. JONSON *Devil an Ass* IV. iv, Keepe it in your galley-pot well glidder'd. **1778** W. PRYCE *Min. Cornub.* II. i. 78 Those Fissures are commonly gliddered or coated over with a hard.. earthy substance. **1867** ROCK *Jim & Nell* xxix. (E.D.S. 76) The plaunching's lick a gliddered pond.

gliddery ('glɪdərɪ), *a. dial.* [f. GLIDDER *v.* + -Y[1]; cf. MDu. *gliderich*, LG. *glidderig*] Slippery; *fig.* treacherous.

1869 BLACKMORE *Lorna D.* iv, Two men led my mother down a steep and gliddery stair-way. *Ibid.* vii, The world was green and gliddery. **1880** —— *Mary Anerley* I. x. 131 Up that gravelly and gliddery ascent.. the heavy boats must clamber somehow.

glide (glaɪd), *sb.* [f. next.]

1. a. The action of gliding, in various senses.

1596 FITZ-GEFFRAY *Sir F. Drake* (1881) 57 The waters glide should still record the same. **1600** SHAKS. *A. Y. L.* IV. iii. 113 [The snake] with indented glides, did slip away Into a bush. **1647** FARINGDON *Serm.* iv. 70 A kind of Majesty.. which makes a.. pleasing glide into the minds of men. **1781** COWPER *Charity* 186 The ruffian.. with the ghostly glide.. steals close to your bedside. **1795** PAINE *Age Reason* II. (1819) 83 The glide of the smallest fish.. exceeds us in motion. **1812** J. WILSON *Isle of Palms* I. 269 With a winged glide this maiden would rove. **1818** L. HUNT *Sonn. to Keats*, Surely as I feel.. Overhead the glide of a dove's wings. **1841** WHITTIER *Exiles* 176 To hear the dip of Indian oars, The glide of birch canoes.

b. *spec.* in *Cricket.* A stroke by which the ball is deflected towards long leg by the turned blade of the bat; = GLANCE *sb.*[1] 1 b. In full *glide stroke.*

1888 STEEL & LYTTELTON *Cricket* ii. 67 Fig. 10 shows W. G. Grace attempting the glide... This is a stroke in which W. G. Grace excels. **1897** K. S. RANJITSINHJI in *Encycl. Sport* I. 228/1 There is no more effective stroke on the leg side than the 'glide' or 'glance'. **1911** C. B. FRY in P. F. Warner *Bk. Cricket* xiii. 227 His [*sc.* Ranjitsinhji's] so-called 'glide' strokes. **1955** *Times* 9 July 4/7 Neame was beautifully caught at the wicket off a thin leg glide.

c. A step in certain ballroom dances; a gliding type of dance.

1889 *Cent. Dict.*, *Glide*,.. in *dancing*, a peculiar waltz-step performed in a smooth and sliding manner. **1926** WHITEMAN & MCBRIDE *Jazz* xi. 224 'Avalon'.. was one of the greatest fox trots of the late 'glide' period. *Ibid.* 230 The original 'glide two step' fox trot of the 'Japanese Sandman' period. **1939** *Britannica Bk. of Year* 197/1 The 'Palais Glide', another group ballroom dance from England, made some headway in America.

d. *Aeronaut.* The act of gliding; a flight accomplished by gliding.

1902 *Encycl. Brit.* XXV. 103/1 He made over 2000 glides safely, using gravity as a motive power. **1909** A. BERGET *Conquest of Air* II. iii. 175 This descending glide. **1916** H. BARBER *Aeroplane Speaks* iv. 43 The Pilot is satisfied that he is now sufficiently high to secure.. a long enough glide to earth to enable him to choose and reach a good landing-place. **1940** L. B. BARRINGER *Flight without Power* v. 87 On windy days.. the two ropes can be joined to make an 800-foot line enabling the pilot to get high enough to make a much longer glide. **1955** WELCH & IRVING *Soaring Pilot* viii. 135 The sort of approach which is often seen on aerodromes—a good deal of air-braking early on followed by a long flat glide—is useless for getting into small fields. **1971** *Sailplane & Gliding* XXII. 364/1 Many hours later Barrie pulled off a 'fingernail-biting' final glide to receive a tumultuous welcome.

2. *concr.* A stream (*obs.*); also, the gliding portion of a stream, a shallow.

1590 GREENE *Never too late* II. (1600) Q4 He that in Eurotas siluer glide Doth baine his tresse. **1591** —— *Maiden's Dreame* 4 Wks. (Grosart) XIV. 301 A silent spring.. The glide whereof gainst weeping flints did beat. **1746** BOWLKER *Angling* (1833) 40 The chief haunts of the smaller Greyling are in glides. **1882** *Gd. Words* 604 Both times as he [a fish] reaches the glide he leaves it.

† **3.** A passage; an avenue (of trees). *Obs.*

c **1710** C. FIENNES *Diary* (1888) 21 A good hall wth 2 parlours and has a glide through the house into the gardens. *Ibid.* 143 Through a fine Visto or Glide of trees w[ch] runs along ye parke.

4. *Mus.* and *Phonetics.* (See quots.)

1835 WILSON *Dict. Mus.*, *Glide*, the slur, to join two successive sounds without articulation, also the unaccented notes or anticipations in a *portamento* passage. **1856** A. J. ELLIS *Univ. Writing & Printing* 6 The Glide and Syllable. When the bow is drawn, while a finger is slid down a violin string, a succession of sounds is heard, called a Glide. When the voice or whisper is continued, while the position of the organs of speech changes from that due to one sound to that due to another, a Vocal Glide is heard. **1867** A. MELVILLE BELL *Visible Speech* 69 A series of semi-consonant, semi-vowel sounds.. which we call 'Glides'. **1888** SWEET *Hist. Eng. Sounds* §23 The 'glide', or sound produced in passing from the one position [of the organs of speech] to the other.

5. *Cryst.* Plastic deformation of a crystal in which there is a movement of one atomic plane over another, resulting in the lateral displacement of part of the lattice.

1934 *Nature* 16 June 912/1 Glide commences in a single crystal when the shear stress on the glide plane, and in the glide direction, reaches a certain value. **1952** *Jrnl. Iron & Steel Inst.* CLXXI. 225/2 Lead.. in single crystal form is, after a few per cent. glide, harder than cadmium. **1954** E. O. HALL *Twinning* ii. 31 The areas where glide occurs then appear as steps on the surface of the crystal. **1960** *Metallurgia* Mar. 125/1 He demonstrates glide, partial dislocations.. and a number of other imperfections in structure. **1970** KELLY & HENDRICKS *Crystallogr.* vi. 169 At low temperature crystals yield plastically by a process called glide.

6. *Comb.*, as **glide bomb**, a bomb fitted with aerofoils that enable it to glide towards its target when released from an aircraft; hence as *v. intr.*, to drop glide bombs; **glide-consonant** (see quot.); **glide-direction**, a direction in a glide-plane in which glide can occur; **glide path**, the line of descent followed by a landing aircraft; *spec.* one indicated to the pilot by radar, etc., from the ground; **glide-plane** *Cryst.*, a plane in a crystal in which glide occurs; also, a symmetry element of a space-lattice such that reflection in the plane followed by a translation parallel to it produces a lattice congruent with the original; **glide-sound**, in *Phonetics*, the sound of a glide; **glide-twinning** *Cryst.*, the formation of a twin by the gliding of adjacent layers of a crystal lattice over one another; so **glide-twin**; **glide-vowel**, a vowel which cannot form a syllable by itself; † **glide-worm**, some kind of worm or snake.

1943 *Newsweek* 8 Mar. 24 A divebomber pilot must be able to glide bomb in certain circumstances. **1943** *Time* 25 Oct. 23/1 The airmen knew that 1,800 fighters equipped with cannon, machine guns, some with glide bombs.. are concentrated between Denmark and Belgium. **1954** K. W. GATLAND *Devel. Guided Missile* (ed. 2) v. 135 The Petrel.. rocket-propelled 'glide bomb'.. was capable of a short undersurface run, the wings and rocket motors breaking off as the missile entered the water close to the target. **1888** SWEET *Hist. Eng. Sounds* §33 Glide-consonants in the special sense of the word are consonants formed without any fixed configuration. **1933** W. H. & W. L. BRAGG *Crystalline State* I. viii. 198 The relative movement occurs along a definite crystallographic axis lying in the plane, the 'glide direction'. **1934** Glide direction [see 5 above]. **1936** *Electr. Commun.* XV. 196/1 The experimentally tested glide path (Gleitweg) process.. can be utilized as, for example, in Switzerland, where the glide path is followed down within a few meters from the ground. **1938** *Jrnl. R. Aeronaut Soc.* XLII. 747 Such essential elements as runway localisers, glide path and markers are analysed. *Ibid.* 490 There is a vertical glide path indicator. **1968** *Guardian* 28 Dec. 1/5 Apollo 8 had to aim at a 'keyhole' entrance to the earth, an imaginary corridor only 35 miles wide. This is the so-called 'glidepath' they had to shoot at as they entered the upper atmosphere. **1970** *Times* 8 Apr. 10/3 A lower approach, much more like coming down the glide path of an airport, should create fewer troubles from a dust storm raised by the rocket motors. **1895** N. S. MASKELYNE *Crystallogr.* i. 7 The glide-planes, in the case of deformed crystals, are.. planes along which disruption can be easily effected. **1946** *Nature* 21 Sept. 395/1 Space-groups, rotation-axes, glide-planes. **1963** E. S. HILLS *Elem. Struct. Geol.* 117 The relatively high ductility of metals is due to the non-directional nature of the metallic bond.., which permits ready re-establishment of cohesion across glide planes and crystal boundaries. **1911** *Encycl. Brit.* XXI. 465/2 Acoustically speaking.. voiceless stops are pure glide-sounds, the stop itself being inaudible. **1933** BLOOMFIELD *Lang.* vi. 96 The intervening non-distinctive glide-sounds that are produced while the vocal organs change their position. **1938** W. A. WOOSTER *Text-bk. Crystal Physics* ii. 52 The indices of the crystallographic twin.. and those of the glide-twin. **1951** N. F. M. HENRY et al. *Interpr. X-Ray Diffraction Photogr.* i. 17/2 In certain substances showing the special type of homogeneous deformation called glide twinning the amount of relative displacement is absolutely fixed for a particular glide in a given substance. *Ibid.*, In order to define a glide twin completely, it is necessary to specify (i) the glide plane, (ii) the glide direction, and (iii) the amount of glide. **1957** *Encycl. Brit.* VI. 828I/2 Plasticity [of a crystal] is sometimes associated with glide-twinning, a process in which there is a sudden switching of the atoms to a second stable position related in a definite geometrical way to the first. **1888** SWEET *Hist. Eng. Sounds* §22 These diphthongic or 'glide-' vowels are written consonant size. *c* **1425** *Voc.* in Wr.-Wülcker 643/6 *Hec incedula*, glyde-worme.

glide (glaɪd), *v.* Pa. t. and pa. pple. glided. Forms: *Infin.* 1 glīdan, 3 gliden, 4–6 glyde, (5 glyede, 6 glyd), 3– glide, *3rd pers. pres. ind.* 4 glit, glyt. *Pa. t.* 1–2 glād (*pl.* glidon), 3–5 glad, (3 glæd, 4 gladd), 4–5 glade, 5–6 *Sc.* glaid, 3–5 glod, (3 gload), 4–5 glood(e, 4–6, 9 glode, 5, 7, 9 glid, 7– glided. *Pa. pple.* 1– 4 gliden, 6 glaid, 9 glid, (glode), 7– glided. [A common WGer. str. vb.: OE. *glīdan, glād, glidon, gliden* corresponds to OFris. *glīda*, OS. *glīdan* (Du. *glijden*; now usually *glijen*), OHG. *glîtan* (MHG. *glîten*, mod.G. *gleiten*); not found in Goth. or ON., but (prob. by adoption from LG.) in MSw. *gliidha* (mod.Sw. *glida*), Da. *glide*. The OTeut. type is **glîdan, glaid-, glidum, glidono-*; outside Teut. no cognates are known.

The affinity of sense with OTeut. **glado-*, smooth, slippery (see GLAD *a.*) is remarkable, but etymological affinity is hardly possible, unless indeed the Teut. root **glid-* was evolved from **slid-* SLIDE *v.* through the influence of the adj. or its root. The Eng. vb. remained strong until the present century; the usual inflexion is now *glided*, though *glid* might be used in the past tense without causing surprise. All other str. forms occurring in recent writings are distinctly archaistic.]

1. *intr.* To pass from one place to another by a smooth and continuous movement, without effort or difficulty.

a. along the surface of, or through, a liquid.

Beowulf (Z) 515 ȝit.. glidon ofer garsecg. *a* **1000** *Andreas* 498 (Gr.) þes bat.. glideð on ȝeofone. *c* **1290** *S. Eng. Leg.* I. 324/69 þat schip bi-gan to glide. **13..** *K. Alis.* 6194 So wyght undur the water they rideth, So ony schip above glideth. **1513** DOUGLAS *Æneis* x. v. 81 And throu the wallis on the tother part [the ship] Glydis away vndir the fomy seis. **1583** STANYHURST *Æneis* III. (Arb.) 72 From shoare we be glyding. **1632** J. HAYWARD tr. *Biondi's Eromena* VI. 163 Whilest then the Galleyes.. glided on a maine speede. **1649** STANLEY *Europa* 9 Down leaps he, Dolphinlike glides through the seas. **1820** W. IRVING *Sketch Bk.* I. 13 A distant sail, gliding along the edge of the ocean. **1834** *W. India Sk. Bk.* I. 245 We glided gradually past a great number of shipping to the landing-place. **1863** DASENT *Jest & Earnest* (1873) II. 183 Harold's own vessel stood the proof, and glode safely over the obstacle. **1871** B. TAYLOR *Faust* I. ii. 43 One at the window sits.. And sees all sorts of ships go down the river gliding.

b. of a liquid, a stream, etc. † In early use often of tears or blood, where *flow* would now be used.

c **1175** *Lamb. Hom.* 43 Alle heore teres beoð berninde gleden glidende ouer heore aȝene nebbe. *c* **1205** LAY. 12773 Him gunnen glide teores. *c* **1300** *Havelok* 1851 The blod ran of his sides So water that fro the welle glides. *a* **1400** *Sir Perc.* 537 The teres oute of his eghne glade. *c* **1430** *Hymns Virg.* 28 Al he suffride þat was wisest, His blood to lete doun glide. **1500–20** DUNBAR *Poems* lxxii. 92 Quhill blude and wattir did furth glyde. **1526** *Pilgr. Perf.* (W. de W. 1531) 234 b, As water glydeth on the erth so our lyfe vanyssheth & passeth. **1597** DRAYTON *Heroic Ep.* v. 41, I.. aske the gentle flood as it did glide If thou didst passe or perish by the tide? **1699** GARTH *Dispens.* I. 15 A while his curdling Blood forgot to glide. **1707** *Curios. in Husb. & Gard.* 68 The Waters that glide in the Sinuosities of the Earth, meet with Sulphur or Lime. **1707** E. SMITH *Phædra & Hipp.* III. 31 Soft Cydonian Oyl, Whose balmy Juice glides o'er th' untasting Tongue. **1764** GOLDSM. *Trav.* 320 Where.. brighter streams than fam'd Hydaspes glide. **1802** WORDSW. *Sonn.*, '*Earth has not anything to show*,' The river glideth at his own sweet will. **1848** W. H. BARTLETT *Egypt to Pal.* xi. (1879) 246 The little stream glided and rippled by.. over its rocky bed. **1885** BIBLE (R.V.) *Song Sol.* vii. 9 Gliding through the lips of those that are asleep.

fig. **1691–1701** NORRIS *Ideal World* I. ii. 110 Truth.. whose.. streams.. glide through the barren regions of our.. sensible world. **1764** GOLDSM. *Trav.* 434 With secret course.. Glides the smooth current of domestic joy. **1820** HAZLITT *Lect. Dram. Lit.* 50 The dialogue glides and sparkles like a clear stream from the Muses' spring.

c. of motion through the air. *spec.* of an aeroplane: to fly without engine power; also *trans.*, to traverse in a glider.

Beowulf (Z.) 2073 Heofones ȝim glad ofer grundas. *a* **1000** *Andreas* 1304 (Gr.) Sunne ȝewat to sete glidan under niflan næs. *c* **1175** *Lamb. Hom.* 91 Swa reðe swa his sceada heom on glad heo weren iheled. *a* **1300** *Cursor M.* 11428 þe stern alwais þam forwit glade. *c* **1386** CHAUCER *Merch. T.* 643 The moone.. was in to Cancre glyden. —— *Sqr.'s T.* 385 The vapour which þat fro the erthe glood Made the sonne to seme rody and brood. ? *a* **1400** *Morte Arth.* 799 þe worme.. Comes glydande fro þe clowddez. *c* **1440** *York Myst.* xxx. 76 þe sonne.. glydis to þe grounde with his glitterand glemys. *c* **1450** *St. Cuthbert* (Surtees) 1239 When he saw aungels fra heuen glyde. **1557** *Tottel's Misc.* (Arb.) 116 Whyle, through his signes, fiue tymes great Titan glode. **1615** CHAPMAN *Odyss.* XII. 585 And through, and through the ship, his lightning glid. **1667** MILTON *P.L.* XII. 629 The Cherubim descended.. Gliding Meteorous, as Ev'ning Mist. **1827** JAS. MONTGOMERY *Pelican Island* III. 113 Where glid the sunbeams through the latticed boughs. **1850** MRS.

Browning *Poems* I. 152 On the back of the quick-winged bird I glode. 1865 Livingstone *Zambesi* xxi. 426 One glides with quivering pinions to the centre of the open space. 1910 C. C. Turner *Aerial Navig.* xx. 252 The best means of becoming proficient in flying is first to learn to glide. 1916 H. Barber *Aeroplane Speaks* iv. 53 The Aeroplane with noiseless engine glides over the boundary of the Aerodrome. 1931 *Times* 23 June 17/4 The claim that he was the first man to 'glide' the Channel. 1940 L. B. Barringer *Flight without Power* ii. 15 The very efficient high performance gliders can glide a long way without losing much height. 1958 D. Piggott *Gliding* ii. 12 Launching signals and procedure are more or less standard..wherever you glide in England.

d. in general. Now often applied to the progression of a person walking or riding, of a carriage, etc., to express extreme smoothness of movement and the absence of perceptible motion of the limbs, wheels, etc.

*a*1275 in *Hist. Holy Rood-tree* (1894) 79 So gleam glidis þurt þe glas..þurt þe hoale þurch he gload. *c*1290 *S. Eng. Leg.* I. 443/375 Þat wedur bi-gan to glide, in þe oþur half of þe churche. 1494 Fabyan *Chron.* vii. 337 An hyll remouyd from his propre place and glode by many a myle. *c*1611 Chapman *Iliad* xxiii. 655 All rankt, Achilles show'd The race-scope. From the start, they glid. 1697 Dryden *Virg. Georg.* iv. 679 Th' Infernal Troops like passing Shadows glide. 1805 Wordsw. *Waggoner* i. 43 The Horses have worked with right good-will..And now they smoothly glide along. 1812 J. Wilson *Isle of Palms* i. 35 She glides away like a lambent flame. 1816 L. Hunt *Rimini* iv. 79 Looking round about, As he glode by. 1835 W. Irving *Tour Prairies* 289 The two horsemen glided down from the profile of the hill. *a*1839 Praed *Poems* (1864) I. 127 In through the lattice did my chariot glide. 1877 G. Macdonald *Marq. Lossie* xlv, Before him glode the shape of Clementina. 1888 R. Buchanan *City of Dream* ii. 40 Mighty priests Glode by on steeds bridled with glittering gold.

2. Said of the mode of progression of reptiles.

*c*1250 *Gen. & Ex.* 370 Niðful neddre,..sal gliden on hise brest neðer. *a*1300 *Cursor M.* 11608 Vte o þis coue þan sagh þai glide Mani dragons. *c*1315 Shoreham 161 Opone thy wombe thou schalt glyde. 1390 Gower *Conf.* II. 260 She [Medea] glode forth, as an adder doth. 1398 Trevisa *Barth. De P.R.* xvii. i. (1495) 735 Some beestes crepith and glydeth on the grounde. *c*1440 *Promp. Parv.* 199/1 Glydyn, *serpo*. 1547 Surrey *Æneid* ii. (1557) Bj b, The serpentes twine with hasted traile they glide To Pallas temple. 1697 Dryden *Virg. Georg.* iii. 645 [The Snake] in some secret Cranny slowly glides. 1819 Crabbe *T. of the Hall* vii. I. 138 There the birds of darkness loved to hide, The loathed toad to lodge, and speckled snake to glide. 1842 Mrs. Browning *Grk. Chr. Poets* 24 Oh, would the serpent had not glide along To Eden's garden-land.

3. To go unperceived, quietly, or stealthily; to insinuate oneself, steal, 'slip' *into, out of* a place.

*a*1300 *Cursor M.* 16492 Judas..kest þe penis on þe flore, and son a-wai he glad. 1393 Langl. *P. Pl.* C xxi 479 May no grysliche gost glyde þer hit shadeweþ. *a*1400–50 *Alexander* 358 Þis grete god full of grace sall glide to þi chambre. *c*1485 *Inscription Carlisle Cathedral* in *St. Cuthbert* (Surtees) [11] Her by prayers fendys ovt farn [*i.e.* out of Farne] glad. 1634 A. Huish *Hymn*, O holy Spirit..Vouchsafe into our soules to glide. 1736 Earl Orrery *Let.* 18 Mar. in *Swift's Lett.* (1766) II. 247 You see, Curll, like his friend the Devil, glides through all key-holes. 1847 Mary Howitt *Ballads*, etc. 393 And the Holy Mother of Jesus Glid in with footsteps light. 1850 D. G. Mitchell *Reveries Bachelor* 47 He takes up his hat and glides out stealthful as a cat. 1859 Kingsley *Misc.* (1860) I. 148 A great dog-fox as red as the fir-stems through which he glides.

†**4. a.** Used in poetry for: To pass from one place to another, to go or come. Also with advs. *forth, up, down*, etc. *Obs.*

*c*1205 Lay. 19517 Muche folc him after glæd. *a*1275 *Prov. Ælfred* 618 in *O.E. Misc.* 136 Drunken mon..Gef him þe weie reme and let him ford gliden. *a*1300 *Cursor M.* 20830 (Gött.) Fourti dais in erd he badd, Ar he vp till his fadir glad. 13.. *E.E. Allit. P.* B. 677 Þen glydez forth god, þe god-mon hym folȝez. *c*1386 Chaucer *Sir Thopas* 193 Forth vp on his wey he glood [*v.r.* rood], As spark out of the bronde. *a*1400 *Sir Perc.* 466 Forthirmore ganne he glyde Tille a chambir. *c*1400 *Destr. Troy* 2996 The lady..glod on fyll gayly. *c*1450 *St. Cuthbert* (Surtees) 7442 At morne besyde þe way we glade To þe next kirke, messe to here. *c*1460 *Towneley Myst.* xii. 68 So galy in gere As he glydys. *c*1475 *Rauf Coilȝear* 484 He is the gayest in geir, that euer on ground glaid. 1513 Douglas *Æneis* vii. iv. 12 With swyft pays thai on thare message glaid. 1596 Spenser *F.Q.* iv. iv. 23 Like sparke of fire that from the andvile glode.

†**b.** of a weapon, a blow. (Perh. with the notion of swift or unresisted movement.) *Obs.*

*c*1205 Lay. 1750 Heo letten to gliden gares swiþe scarpe. 13.. *K. Alis.* 1355 A brod gavelock he lette glide. *c*1330 *Arth. & Merl.* 5160 On his helme he him smot, þe ax glod, god it wot. *c*1380 *Sir Ferumb.* 848 Þorw scheld, haberke, & aketoun þat sper him gan to glyde. *c*1386 Chaucer *Knt.'s T.* 717. *c*1400 *Sowdone Bab.* 1183 The stroke glode down by his bake. *c*1450 *Guy Warw.* (C.) 4914 Hys spere thorow the body glode. 1513 Douglas *Æneis* ix. vii. 156 The swerd, wyghtly stokit, or than was glaid Throu owt hys cost. [1699 Dryden *Pal. & Arc.* ii. 124 He trembl'd ev'ry Limb, and felt a Smart, As if cold Steel had glided through his Heart. (Echoing Chaucer *Knt.'s T.* 717.)]

†**c.** To fall. *Obs.*

*c*1205 Lay. 800 Leteð the Grickisca gliden to grunde. 13.. *Coer de L.* 5306 Eyther stede to grounde glode, And brake her nekkes. ?1370 *Robt. Cicyle* 60 Y felle in pryde, As the aungelle that can of hevyn glyde. *a*1400 *Sir Perc.* 2116 Righte there appone the faire molde The ryng owte glade. *c*1460 *Launfal* 575 Another cours togedere they rod, That syr Launfal helm of glod.

†**d.** Of the eye: To glance, turn aside *upon*.

*c*1425 *Seven Sag.* (P.) 2099 The childe lette hys [eyen] glyede Oppon hys maystyr al asyde.

5. a. To slide, move unobstructedly over a polished surface. Also, †to slip, lose one's footing on ice or muddy ground (*obs.*); to slide on ice as a sport (*dial.*).

*c*1290 *S. Eng. Leg.* I. 212/430 For heo [the bridge] was narovȝ, and slider, and heiȝ, þat he ne scholde him so bitelle, ȝif þat he glufte [*v.r.* glide] in ani half, þat he ne fulle in-to helle. 1674 J. Scheffer tr. *Hist. Lapl.* 4 The Laplanders gliding upon the ice. 1835–6 Todd *Cycl. Anat.* I. 255/2 One surface glides over the other limited by the ligaments. 1881 *Leicestersh. Gloss., Glide*, to slide on the ice.

b. To slip *away*, elude one's grasp, like something greasy.

*c*1510 More *Picus* Wks. 25 The pleasure, whiche thine euill worke doth contayne, Glideth his way, thou maist him not restraine. 1712 Addison *Spect.* No. 281 ¶7. It glided through the Fingers like a smooth Piece of Ice. 1823 Lamb *Elia* Ser. ii. *Pop. Fallacies* ii, They do not find..that all gold glides, like thawing snow, from the thief's hand.

6. To pass lightly and without interruption *along* or *over* a surface. Also *transf.* of the eye, the mind, etc.

1822 Lamb *Elia* Ser. ii. *Detached Th. on Bks.*, Books of quick interest, that hurry on for incidents, are for the eye to glide over only. *a*1834 —— *Let. to Wordsw.* Lett. xvii. 162 The light paragraphs must be glid over by the proper eye. 1851 Ruskin *Stones Ven.* (1874) I. xxv. 284 The eye..ought to glide along the basic rolls to take measurement of their length. 1863 Geo. Eliot *Romola* i. vi, His hand glided from the face and rested on the young man's shoulder.

7. In various immaterial applications.

a. Of time, one's life, etc.: To pass gently and imperceptibly. Also with *along, away*, †*forth, on*, etc.

*c*1250 *Gen. & Ex.* 3460 Quiles ðis daiȝes forð ben gliden. 1500–20 Dunbar *Poems* xi. 6 Hyne glydis all thy tyme that heir is. 1779 J. Moore *View Soc. Fr.* (1789) I. xviii. 143 The hours glide along very smoothly. 1835 Marryat *Jac. Faithf.* xxxvi, My life glided on as did my wherry—silently and rapidly. 1837 Disraeli *Venetia* i. iii, Two serene and innocent years had glided away. 1887 Bowen *Virg. Eclog.* x. 43 Here life ever should glide..beside thee gently away.

†**b.** Of the Holy Ghost: = proceed. *Obs.*

*a*1225 *Juliana* 2 Ant o þes haligastes þat glideð of ham baðen. *c*1320 *Cast. Love* 1454 Þe Holy Gost þat glit of hem bo.

c. *to glide into*: to pass by imperceptible degrees into (a condition or state); to fall insensibly into (doing something). Said also of a species, etc.: To shade off insensibly into, have no clear demarcation from (something else).

1800 Hatchett in *Phil. Trans.* XC. 391 Muscle, ligament, and tendon, seem to glide almost imperceptibly into each other. 1825 Lytton *Falkland* 22, I suffer one moment to glide into another. 1842 Alison *Hist. Europe* (1849–50) X. lxvi. §77. 190 All feelings of hostility..glide into those of peculiar courtesy. 1865 Dickens *Mut. Fr.* iii. v, I have glided into telling you the secret. 1869 Lecky *Europ. Mor.* I. ii. 282 The peasant proprietor soon glided hopelessly into debt.

d. *Phonetics. to glide on to*: (of a consonant or vowel) to be uttered continuously with (the following sound).

[1774: cf. 8.] 1867 A. J. Ellis *E.E. Pronunc.* i. iii. 57 A short accented vowel is in English always followed by a consonant on to which it glides.

8. *trans.* = to cause to glide (in different senses). Also † *to glide away*.

1650 Trapp *Comm. Gen.* iv. 17 Silly are they that think to glide away their groans with games, and their cares with cards, &c. 1774 W. Mitford *Harmony Lang.* 48 They sound *i*, but glide it so imperceptibly into the following vowel that it cannot form a distinct syllable. 1834 *W. India Sk. Bk.* I. 299 Enjoying the..light airs which began to play on the surface of the water, and to glide the vessel quietly on her course. 1893 Gunter *Miss Dividends* 128 Ferdie glides the graceful Louise through the room in poetic motion. 1897 W. Anderson *Surg. Treat. Lupus* 14 The raw surface may be covered in by gliding portions of detached integument from an adjacent part.

9. *Cryst. intr.* Of particles in a crystal: to move, be displaced. Also of a crystal: to undergo glide. Cf. glide *sb.* 5.

1895 N. S. Maskelyne *Crystallogr.* i. 7 The particles..aligned on all lines parallel to the edge *e* have..glided into new positions in the crystal-block. 1924 A. E. H. Tutton *Nat. Hist. Crystals* xviii. 215 Many of the softer crystallised substances develop the property of permitting one layer to glide over another by gentle side pressure with a knife blade. 1938 W. A. Wooster *Text-bk. Crystal Physics* ii. 49 The crystal glides on the (0112) plane in the [0111] direction. 1970 Kelly & Hendricks *Crystallogr.* vi. 169 Sapphire crystals can be made to glide at room temperature under a pressure of 25,000 atm.

10. *Cricket. intr.* To make the glide stroke (see prec. 1 b).

1899 *Daily News* 22 July 4/2 Men were then less apt to 'glance and glide', like The Brook, and K. S. Ranjitsinhji. 1927 T. E. Casson *Century of Roundels* 17 Ranjitsinhji, when he glides, Stands at the crease in posture cringy.

glideless ('glaɪdlɪs), *a. Phonetics.* [-less.] Unaccompanied by a glide (glide *sb.* 4).

1902 Sweet *Primer Phon.* 63 Combinations of stops and vowel like consonants..are glideless in English.

glider ('glaɪdə(r)). Also 5–6 glydar(e, -er. [f. glide *v.* + -er¹.] **1. a.** One who, or that which glides; also, that which aids in gliding. Also with *up*.

*c*1440 *Promp. Parv.* 199/1 Glydare, *serptor*. 1530 Palsgr. 225/2 Glydar a slyder, *glancevr*. 1579 Spenser *Sheph. Cal.* Aug. 94 *Per.* The glaunce into my heart did glide, *Will.* hey ho the glyder. 1597 A. M. tr. *Guillemeau's Fr. Chirurg.* A v b, The little Glysorye, or Glidere vp and downe. 1850 H. H. Wilson tr. *Rig-veda* I. 219 The Maruts..are gliders (through the air).

b. An appendage that aids in gliding.

1873 J. Pettigrew *Anim. Loco.* (1874) 170 The elytra or anterior wings are frequently employed as sustainers or gliders in flight.

c. (See quot. 1940.)

1926–7 *Army & Navy Stores Catal.* 192/3 Unbreakable glass gliders... Makes furniture easily movable. 1940 *Chambers's Techn. Dict.* 379/1 *Gliders*, dome-shaped metal pieces fastened to the feet of chairs, settees, etc., in place of casters.

d. A runner (runner 13 b) for a curtain.

1957 *Archit. Rev.* CXXII. 356/3 A concealed curtain track called 'Silent Gliss' and manufactured by Silent Gliss Ltd. will be shown; nylon gliders to which curtain may be attached direct or by means of hooks, runners or eyes, run in aluminium runners. 1961 *Lancet* 5 Aug. 297/2 Typical cubicle equipment, comprising aluminium tube and curtain-rail with nylon gliders.

2. *Aeronaut.* **a.** An engineless aeroplane.

1897 *Aeronaut. Ann.* 144, I made my first trials with a soaring machine in the summer of '95... It is exceedingly difficult to make a glider with one surface only which will sail properly. 1903 *Daily Chron.* 29 Oct. 6/7 The longitudinal stability of aerial gliders. 1909 H. G. Wells *Tono-Bungay* iii. i. 208, I was developing a glider into a flyer. 1931 *Daily Tel.* 6 Jan. 12/4 [He] had a leg and an arm broken when his glider crashed. 1950 *Engineering* 10 Feb. 158/1 The glider had the advantage of being able to land with great accuracy. 1965 'Sergeant' & Watson *Gliding Bk.* iv. 50 The upward flow is called an 'anabatic' wind and it is occasionally strong enough to support a glider in flight.

b. One who glides or is an expert in gliding.

1910 C. C. Turner *Aerial Navig.* xx. 253 It will be well to take the experiences of the great gliders in proper order, beginning with Lilienthal. 1960 C. H. Gibbs-Smith *Aeroplane* 197 As to the 'tower-jumpers' of history,..there is happily no telling who was the first to deflect himself from the vertical sufficiently to earn the title of first 'flier' or 'glider' in history.

3. (See quot. 1939.) *U.S.*

1932 *Hadley Co., Springfield, Mass., Advt.* July, Junior Gliders! 1939 Webster Add., *Glider*, a porch swing with cushioned seat or couch suspended by links from an upright framework. 1969 P. Highsmith *Tremor of Forgery* xxiv. 225 Adams's terrace faced the gulf and had a glider, table and chairs.

4. *attrib.* and *Comb.*, as **glider air-train** (see quot.); **glider bomb** = *glide bomb* (s.v. glide *sb.* 6); **glider-borne** *a.*, of troops, etc.: carried by glider; **glider train** = *glider air-train*; **glider-tug**, a powered aircraft that tows gliders.

1935 C. G. Burge *Compl. Bk. Aviation* 377/1 *Glider 'air train'*, an 'air train' consists of an aeroplane attached to which are one or more gliders in tow. 1944 *Times* 24 Jan. 2/4 The enemy pressed home determined attacks on the convoy with glider bombs. 1945 W. Ley *Rockets* 272 There is no technological similarity between the radio-controlled glider bomb and the jet-propelled flying bomb V-1. 1942 *Air News* Oct. 27/2 Existing equipment could drop glider-borne troops. 1946 G. Gibson *Enemy Coast Ahead* xii. 157 Combined use of parachute troops, glider-borne troops, anti-flak fighters and bombers. 1940 *Aeronautics* Nov. 44/3 Flight tests have shown that more than one glider can be towed by an aeroplane, so that a glider train is not out of question. 1944 *Jane's All World's Aircraft 1943–44* 43a/2 The principal glider-tug..is capable of towing up to three gliders at a time.

'**glidewort.** [a half-adoption, half-translation of MDu. *glidcruijt* (Du. *glidkruid*) = Ger. *glidkraut*; the first element seems to mean 'limb', the reference being to the use of the herb as a remedy for gout.] †**a.** An old name for species of *Sideritis*. **b.** (See quot. 1866.)

1640 Parkinson *Theat. Bot.* 588 The Germans [call it] Glidkraut, the Dutch Glidcruijt, and wee in English after the Dutch name, Glidewort of some, and Ironwort of most. 1866 *Treas. Bot.*, Glidewort, *Galeopsis Tetrahit*. 1879 Britten & Holland *Plant-n.* 207.

gliding ('glaɪdɪŋ), *vbl. sb.* [See -ing¹.] **1. a.** The action of the vb. glide in various senses.

1398 Trevisa *Barth. De P.R.* xviii. xcv. (1495) 841 The serpent..crepyth wyth preuy paces and glydynges. *c*1440 *Promp. Parv.* 199/1 Glydynge, *serpcio*. 1576 Turberv. *Venerie* 122 Making great glydings and hitting his dewclawes upon the grounde. 1600 S. Nicholson *Acolastus* (1876) 48 With a silent gliding, A Christall brooke ran. 1644 Digby *Nat. Bodies* viii. 63 It [light] will follow the nature of grosser bodies, and haue glidinges like them. 1794 Sir W. Jones *Inst. Hindu Law* vi. §63 The glidings of this vital spirit through ten thousand millions of uterine passages. 1817 Byron *Beppo* xiv, The loveliness at times we see In momentary gliding. 1842 E. Wilson *Anat. Vade M.* (ed. 2) 93 Gliding is the simple movement of one articular surface upon another. 1856 Grindon *Life* ii. (1875) 14 The gliding of the clouds before the wind. *a*1859 Macaulay *Hist. Eng.* xxiv. (1861) V. 208 A rapid yet easy gliding before the trade winds.

b. *Cryst.* = glide *sb.* 5; also, the lateral movement of particles that occurs in glide. So ***gliding-plane*** = *glide-plane*.

1886 *Mineral. Mag.* Dec. 82 In every crystal, in addition to..the planes along which slipping accompanied by a rotation of certain of the molecules occurs (gliding-planes), there is a..set of 'structure-planes'. 1938 W. A. Wooster *Text-bk. Crystal Physics* ii. 42 Gliding in crystals is restricted to certain crystallographically defined planes and directions. 1942 M. P. Billings *Struct. Geol.* ii. 26 Gliding is of two types, translation-gliding and twin-gliding. 1959 *Chambers's Encycl.* X. 775/1 Plastic deformation occurs as a result of the mutual gliding of these planes over one another.

2. *Aeronaut.* Flight which is not dependent on engine power; the action of flying in this way.

Freq. *attrib.*, as **gliding angle, contest, flight, school**; **gliding-boat**, a hydroplane; **gliding machine** = GLIDER 2 a; **gliding path** = *glide path.*

1896 O. CHANUTE *Diary* 23 June in *Wright Papers* (1953) I. 641 It is a gliding but not a soaring mach[in]e and little is to be expected from it. **1898** *Sci. Amer. Suppl.* 22 Jan. 18390/2 It was a great deal more difficult to control any gliding machine on the ground than when the operator was in the air. **1902** *Encycl. Brit.* XXV. 103/1 Reducing gliding flight to regular practice. **1904** *Trans. Inst. Naval Archit.* XLVI. 245 Mr. Wilbur Wright found that if the hollowness [of the plane] was seriously increased, the centre of effort, instead of continuing to move forward as the gliding angle was diminished, actually moved backwards again. **1906** *Sci. Amer.* 22 Sept. 211/1 The term gliding machine (meaning soaring machine) should..be dropped from the nomenclature of aeronautics, as it is liable to be confused with the hydroplane or gliding boat, which is also a gliding machine. **1910** *Daily Chron.* 12 Mar. 3/3 To establish a gliding school at Hockley, in Essex. **1922** *Daily Mail* (Continental ed.) 19 Oct., The third day of the gliding contest at Itford Hill, near Lewes, Sussex. **1922** *Westm. Gaz.* 23 Oct., 'Gliding' is no longer an adequate name for the new form of flight which has been discovered. **1930** *Proc. Inst. Radio Engin.* May 833 A special radiobeam..is so oriented..as to define the proper gliding path which..will permit..landings. **1950** *Gloss. Aeronaut. Terms (B.S.I.)* I. 8 *Gliding angle*, the angle between the flight path in a glide and the horizontal. **1960** C. H. GIBBS-SMITH *Aeroplane* 197 The historical assessment of true gliding.

gliding ('glaɪdɪŋ), *ppl. a.* [See -ING^{2}.] **1.** That glides (in various senses of the vb.).

c **1420** LYDG. *Assembly Gods* 613 On a glydyng serpent rydyng a gret pas. **1603** FLORIO *Montaigne* (1634) 576, I commend a gliding, an obscure and reposed life. **1645** MILTON *Colast.* (1851) 378, I may bee driv'n to curle up this gliding prose into a rough Sotadic. **1649** T. FORD *Lusus Fort.* 107 Transitory things which are as gliding as the stream of a swift current. **1718** ROWE tr. *Lucan* 195 The rolling Flood the gliding Navy bore. **1764** GOLDSM. *Trav.* 294 The willow-tufted bank, the gliding sails. **1881** C. A. EDWARDS *Organs* 112 These drawbacks have been overcome by the 'gliding' coupler. **1885** *Syd. Soc. Lex.*, *Gliding joint*, a form of diarthrosis in which the articular surfaces of the bones are nearly flat, and have only a sliding motion between each other. **1888** SWEET *Eng. Sounds* §23 It is often difficult to draw the line between gliding and fixed configuration.

b. *spec.* in *Her.* (See quot.)

1765–87 in PORNY *Heraldry* Gloss. **1868** CUSSANS *Her.* (1893) 129 Gliding, or *Glissant*, used to describe serpents when moving forwards in Fess.

†**2.** = GLIB *a.* 1. *Obs.*$^{-1}$

1594 T. B. *La Primaud. Fr. Acad.* II. 401 Both the childs body, and the way also is thereby made more gliding and slippery.

glidingly ('glaɪdɪŋlɪ), *adv.* [f. GLIDING *ppl. a.* + -LY^{2}.] In a gliding manner.

1797 HOLCROFT *Stolberg's Trav.* (ed. 2) IV. xci. 181 Archimedes..drew it..over the ground as glidingly as if it had been in the sea. *a* **1839** GALT *Demon Dest.* v. (1840) 33 He then beheld a matron glidingly approach. **1881** *Daily News* 14 Dec. 5/6 Clouds of smoke..sailed glidingly in the still air.

glie, glieb, obs. forms of GLEE, GLEBE.

gliff (glɪf), *sb.* Now only *Sc.* or *north.* [f. GLIFF *v.*]

1. A passing view; a glance, glimpse.

1570 LEVINS *Manip.* 117/29 A Glyffe, *respectus.* **1730** T. BOSTON *Mem.* App. 45 But the first gliff as we call it is the worst. *a* **1743** RELPH in *Songs & Ballads Cumberld.* (1866) 16 Here it was..That first I gat a gliff o' Betty's feace. **1802** R. ANDERSON *Cumberld. Ball.* 52 My fadder he just gat a gliff on't. **1845** G. MURRAY *Islaford* 108 'Twas a smothering gliff and a thought on thee. **1882** *Lanc. Gloss.*, *Gliff* (N. Lanc.), a glimpse, a transient sight.

b. A look or appearance that reminds one (of a person).

1886 STEVENSON *Kidnapped* vi. 50 And yet ye have a kind of gliff of Mr. Alexander.

2. A short space of time; a moment.

1816 SCOTT *Old Mort.* xix, Where is Edith? Gone to her room..and laid down in her bed for a gliff. **1820** —— *Monast.* xxvi, I gaed a gliff up the burn. **1824** —— *Redgauntlet* ch. xi, Bide a gliff.

b. A quick movement; a whiff.

1820 *Edin. Mag.* May 423 The mirk came in gliffs—in gliffs the mirk gade.

3. A sudden fright; a scare.

1732 RAMSAY *Sc. Prov.* (1797) 82 There came never sic a gliff to a daw's heart. **18..** *Rhymes* in *Proc. Berw. Nat. Club* I. No. 5. 149 The browster gied us a' a gliff Wi' his barley bree. **1816** SCOTT *Antiq.* xxvii, I, like a fule, gat a gliff wi' seeing the lights and the riders. **1825** *Blackw. Mag.* XVII. 669/2 Oh, I was in a terrible gliff! **1855** ROBINSON *Whitby Gloss.* s.v., I gat a sare gliff.

gliff (glɪf), *v.* Now only *Sc.* or *north.* Also 3 **gluffe (y)**, 4 **gleffe**, 4, 6 **glyff(e**. [Of obscure origin. Sense 1 is akin to that of Du. *glippen* and its cognates (see GLIBBERY *a.*), but the form presents difficulty. Sense 3 may be a distinct word, perh. cogn. with GLOPPEN. The pa. t. *glyfte* may belong to GLIFT *v.*]

†**1.** To slip, glance aside; *fig.* to make a slip in reading.

a **1225** *Ancr. R.* 46 ȝif ȝe þurh ȝemeleaste gluffeð [*v.r.* gliffen] of wordes. *c* **1290** [see GLIDE *v.* 5]. *c* **1330** *Arth. & Merl.* (Kölbing) 8990 He wold his nek smiten eft, & þe dint a litel gleft.

†**2. a.** To look quickly, to give a glance; also quasi-*trans.*, *to gliff one's eyes.* **b.** To shine suddenly; to make a flash. *Obs.*

a. *c* **1330** R. BRUNNE *Chron. Wace* (Rolls) 3399 Atte passage glyfte þey þer eyene [*v.r.* þei glift Ine]. **13..** *E.E. Allit. P.* B. 849 Þe god man glyfte with þat glam & gloped for noyse. **13..** *Gaw. & Gr. Knt.* 2265 Bot Gawayn on þat giserne glyfte hym bysyde. *c* **1420** *Anturs of Arth.* xxviii, He gliffed [*Thornton MS.* glyfte] vp with his eighen on þat burde bright. *c* **1430** *Syr Gener.* (Roxb.) 7310 That saw [Clarionas] and glift, The blade she perceiued bright. **1570** LEVINS *Manip.* 117/31 To Glyffe, *respicere.*

b. *a* **1400–50** *Alexander* 4599 Garlands ne no gay gere to glyffe in ȝour eȝen.

3. *trans.* To frighten. Cf. AGLIFF and GLOFF.

1823 ELIZA LOGAN *St. Johnstoun* III. 144 Ye hae gliffed us amaist out o' our very senses. **1863** *Tynside Songs, Clock Fyece* 2 Noo lisen me, An' thou shall hear what's gliffed me see. **1891** *Newcastle Daily Jrnl.* 13 Mar. 5/5, I only meant to gliff him.

†**'gliffen**, *v. Obs.* [f. GLIFF *v.* + -EN^{5}.] *intr.* To look, take a glance. In quots. with *up.*

1375 BARBOUR *Bruce* VII. 184 The kyng..slepit nocht full ynkurly Bot gliffnyt vp oft suddandly. *a* **1510** DOUGLAS *K. Hart* I. xlviii, The Quene is walknit with ane felloun fray, Vp glifnit, and beheld scho wes betraysit.

'gliffing, *vbl. sb. Sc.* [f. GLIFF *v.* + -ING^{1}.]

1. The time required to give a glance; an instant.

1815 SCOTT *Guy M.* xxii, Tib Mumps will be out wi' the stirrup-dram in a gliffing. **1819** W. TENNANT *Papistry Storm'd* (1827) 38 In a gliffin' ilka bishop Ramm'd in his hand and cleik'd his fish up.

2. A surprise, fright.

1813 PICKEN *Misc. Poems* II. 47 It was an unco gliffin.

gliffy ('glɪfɪ). [f. GLIFF *sb.* + -Y^{4}.] = GLIFF *sb.* 2.

1820 *Blackw. Mag.* Nov. 203 My mother had..thrown hersel' back just for a gliffy, to tak' a nap, in the easy chair. **1838** J. STRUTHERS *Poetic T.* 79 Ae gliffy brings a dart severe Whilk breeds us wae. **1871** P. H. WADDELL *Psalms* vi. 10 Scham't sal they be, in a gliffie.

†**glift**, *v. Obs.* Also 5 **glyfft**. [var. of GLIFF *v.*] *intr.* To look, gaze. Hence †**'glifting** *vbl. sb.*

? *a* **1400** *Morte Arth.* 2525 Sir Gawayne glyftes on the gome with a glade wille! *Ibid.* 3949 Than gliftis the gud kynge, and glopyns in herte. *c* **1440** *York Myst.* xxvi. 158 Thy glyfftyng is so grymly þou gars my harte growe.

glike, var. GLEEK *sb.*^{2} and *v.*, *Obs.*

glim (glɪm) *sb.* Also 4 **glymme**. [Ultimately f. the weak-grade of the Teut. root **glīm-, glaim-* (see GLEAM); but the history is obscure. Possibly the word in sense 2 may be a modification of *glims* GLIMPSE, and in sense 3 a shortening of GLIMMER, its earlier synonym. It is not certain that the sb. existed in OE. or ON., though some of the continental Teut. langs. have a word of coincident form and meaning: cf. MHG. *glim* (mod.G. *glimm*) masc., spark, Sw. dial. *glim* flash, Du. (obs.), Flem. *glim*, also *glimp*, glow, glance, passing appearance.]

†**1.** ? Brightness. *Obs. rare*$^{-1}$.

So commonly explained on etymological grounds; the context by itself would rather suggest 'delight'.

13.. *E.E. Allit. P.* A. 1087 So watz I rauyste wyth glymme pure.

2. *Sc.* †A passing look, a glimpse (*obs.*). Hence, as much as is seen at a glance; a scrap.

c **1620** A. HUME *Brit. Tongue* (1865) 2 If the way might be found to draue your eie, set on high materes of state, to take a glim of a thing of so mean contemplation. **1818** SCOTT *Hrt. Midl.* xxx, Now, old Meg, d—n me, if I can understand a glim of this story of yours.

3. *slang.* **a.** A light of any kind; a candle, a lantern. ***douse the glim*** (see DOUSE *v.* 4).

a **1700** B. E. *Dict. Cant. Crew*, *Glim*, a Dark-Lanthorn used in Robbing Houses. *c* **1742** in Hone *Every-day Bk.* II. 526 Glim, and Leather-dresser, viz. the Utensils of a Link and Black-shoe Boy. **1798** in J. H. Vaux *Mem.* (1819) I. viii. 75 When in the Cockpit all was dim And not a Mid dar'd shew his glim. **1815** SCOTT *Guy M.* xxxiv, Are you in the dark?.. Where should I have a glim? **1838** DICKENS *O. Twist* xxii, Show a glim, Toby. **1840** MARRYAT *Poor Jack* xxiii, Do top that glim, Bill! **1845** ALB. SMITH *Fort. Scatterg. Fam.* xviii. (1887) 61 She's always got that little glim alight at her stern. **1852** E. Z. C. JUDSON *Myst. N.Y.* I. iv. 37 Old Jack bade Harriet trim the glim. **1883** STEVENSON *Treas. Isl.* I. v, Sure enough, they left their glim here.

b. An eye.

1820 in Egan *Grose's Dict. Vulg. Tongue* (1823) s.v., His glims I've made look like a couple of rainbows. **1830** LYTTON *P. Clifford* vii, Queer my glims, if that ben't little Paul. *a* **1845** BARHAM *Ingol. Leg.*, *Housewarming* 43 Harold escaped with a loss of a glim.

4. *Comb.* (*slang*), as ***glim lamp, light***; **glim-fenders**, andirons; also punningly, handcuffs; **glim-glibber**, a lingo or jargon; **glim-jack**, a link-boy; **glim-stick**, a candlestick.

a **1700** B. E. *Dict. Cant. Crew*, **Glimfenders*, Andirons. **1750** [MRS. R. GOADBY] *Apol. Life B. M. Carew* (ed. 2) 338 *Glimfenders*, hand irons. **1823** J. BEE *Dict. Turf*, *Glim-fendors*, hand-cuffs, or wrist manacles. **1844** LD. BROUGHAM *A. Lunel* III. vi. 180 All of the same caste (or, as he jocosely termed it, of the same cant) had a *glimglibber of their own, and quite understood one another, like freemasons. *a* **1700** B. E. *Dict. Cant. Crew*, **Glimjack*, a Link-boy. **1942** W. SIMPSON *One of our Pilots is Safe* ii. 40 At dusk the control officer for the night arrived and arranged a path of small electric *glim lamps in the form of a capital L. **1943** *Glim light [see BAT *sb.*^{2} 3 f]. *a* **1700** B. E. *Dict. Cant. Crew*, **Glimstick*, a Candlestick. **1812** in J. H. VAUX *Flash Dict.*

glim (glɪm), *v.* Also 5 **glymm**. [In sense 1, ad. Du. *glimmen* to glow = MHG., Ger. *glimmen*, Sw. *glimma*, Da. *glimme*, f. the root *glim-* (see GLIM *sb.*). In sense 2, f. GLIM *sb.*]

†**1.** *intr.* To shine, gleam. *Obs.*$^{-1}$

1481 CAXTON *Reynard* (Arb.) 98 Ther laye in a grete ape with tweyne grete wyde eyen, and they glymmed as a fyre.

2. *trans.* To brand or burn in the hand. *slang.*

a **1700** B. E. *Dict. Cant. Crew* s.v., As the cull was Glimm'd, he gangs to the Nubb, if the Fellow has been Burnt in the Hand, he'll be Hang'd now. **1708** *Mem. J. Hall* 33 Profligate Women..are glimm'd for that Villany. **1785** in GROSE *Dict. Vulg. Tongue.*

†**'glimble.** *Obs.* [f. GLIM *v.* + dim. ending *-le* with inserted *b.*] A glimmer, a glimpse.

1658 A. FOX *Wurtz' Surg.* v. 352, I found it by experience how hurtful hot glimbles of shines are to eyes.

glimce, obs. form of GLIMPSE *sb.*

glime (glaɪm), *sb. north.* [f. the vb.] A side look or glance.

1887 HALL CAINE *Deemster* x. 69 'Aw, ye wouldn't think it's true, would ye, now?' said Ned, with a wink at Dan, and a 'glime' at Davy. 'And what's that?' said Dan, with another 'glime' at the lad.

glime (glaɪm), *v. dial.* Also 9 **gleym, glyme.** [Of obscure origin: the localities would suggest derivation from ON., but no similar form occurs in that lang. Cf. GLEE *v.*]

†**1.** *intr.* To squint. *Obs.*$^{-0}$, implied in GLIMER.

2. To look askance or shyly.

1684 *Yorksh. Dial.* 481 (E.D.S. No. 76) Thou Glincks and glimes seay, I'd misken'd thy Face, If thou had wont at onny other place. *a* **1743** RELPH *Miscell. Poems* (1747) 2 Heedless I glim'd, nor cou'd my een command, Till gash the sickle went into my hand. **1803** R. ANDERSON *Cumberld. Ball.* 65 Aye he owre his shou'der glym'd. **1886** HALL CAINE *Son of Hagar* I. vii, All the lasses wad be glyming at him. **1894** —— *Manxman* 187 Pete grunted and glimed, smoked up the chimney, and [etc.].

Hence †**'glimer**, one who squints.

1483 *Cath. Angl.* 159/1 A Glymyr, *luscus, limus.*

glimery, obs. f. GLIMMERY *a.*^{1}; var. GLIMMERY *a.*^{2}, *Obs.*

glimflashy ('glɪm,flæʃɪ), *a. slang.* Also 7 **glimflashly**, 9 **glimflashey**. [f. GLIM *sb.* + FLASHY *a.*] Angry.

a **1700** B. E. *Dict. Cant. Crew*, *Glimflashy*, angry or in a Passion. **1725** in *New Cant. Dict.* **1830** LYTTON *P. Clifford* xxxi, 'And this is what you call well!' said Clifford angrily. 'No, captain, don't be glimflashey! you have not heard all yet!'

glimmer ('glɪmə(r)), *sb.*^{1} Also 5 **glymyr**, 6–7 **glymmar**, 7 **glymmer**. [f. the vb.]

1. A feeble or wavering light; a tremulous play of reflected light, a sheen, shimmer.

1590 SHAKS. *Com. Err.* v. i. 315 My wasting lampes [have yet] some fading glimmer left. **1800** *Phil. Trans.* XC. 176 The liquid seemed to have lost its luminous quality except a little glimmer floating at the top. **1818** MRS. SHELLEY *Frankenst.* iv. (1865) 65 By the glimmer of the half-extinguished light, I saw the dull yellow eye of the creature open. **1855** TENNYSON *Maud* I. xxii. ix, In gloss of satin and glimmer of pearls, Queen lily and rose in one. **1861** T. A. TROLLOPE *La Beata* I. viii. 196 This glimmer proceeded from a lamp of silver. **1873** BLACK *Pr. Thule* (1874) 64 Both the young men at once recognized the glimmer of the small white feather. **1884** *Bazaar* 17 Dec. 647/3 The painting was remarkable for the actuality of brilliant moonlight, and the marvellous imitation of its glimmer on the leaves of the laurels. **1888** W. H. H. ROGERS *Mem. West* i. 3 The white glimmer in the far distance is Axminster.

2. *fig.* **a.** Showiness of manner (? *obs.*). **b.** A faint gleam (of knowledge, hope, etc.); a faint perception; a glimpse.

a. 1827 SCOTT *Jrnl.* 22 Jan., No dash, or glimmer, or shine about him, but great simplicity of manners and behaviour.

b. 1837–9 HALLAM *Hist. Lit.* i. §7 (1847) 5 As early as the sixth century a little glimmer of light was perceptible in the Irish monasteries. **1859** BRIGHT *Sp. India* 1 Aug., He has not a glimmer of the grammar. **1868** FREEMAN *Norm. Conq.* (1876) II. vii. 86 Here we get the first glimmer of Austin canons. **1871** R. ELLIS tr. *Catullus* lxiv. 186 Nowhere flight, no glimmer of hope. **1885** TENNYSON *Despair* xix, I have had some glimmer, at times, in my gloomiest woe, Of a God behind all.

3. *slang.* †**a.** Fire. *Obs.*

1567 HARMAN *Caveat* (Shaks. Soc.) 61 A Demaunder for Glymmar... These Demaunders for glymmar be for the most parte women; for glymmar in their language, is fyre. **1665** R. HEAD *Eng. Rogue* I. iv. (1680) 45 *Glymmer*, fire.

b. *pl.* The eyes.

1814 *Sailor's Return* I. vi, Get out of my way, you booby, or I'll darken your glimmers for you. *Ibid.* I. vii, Come, my lad, close your glimmers, and I'll apply a plaster.

Hence **'glimmerless** *a.*, without a glimmer.

1889 *Chamb. Jrnl.* Jan. 10/1 The liquid dusk that hung glimmerless above the horizon.

glimmer ('glɪmə(r)), *sb.*^{2} *Min.* [a. Ger. *glimmer*, f. *glimmen*, GLIM *v.*] Mica (see quot. 1859).

1683 PETTUS *Fleta Min.* I. 7 Silver Oars..free from Flint..Mispickle, Glimmer [*ibid.* I. 201 *spelt* Glimer], Wolferan [etc.]. **1686** PLOT *Staffordsh.* 118 *Mica arenosa*..which the

Germans call Catsilver or Glimmer. **1778** WOULFE in *Phil. Trans.* LXIX. 30 May not the green and yellow glimmers from Johngeorgenstadt be of this kind? **1804** C. B. BROWN tr. *Volney's View Soil U.S.* 55 The interior boundary of this sand is a ridge or bank of granitic talc,..called, by the Swedish traveller Kalm, glimmer. **1859** PAGE *Handbk. Geol. Terms, Glimmer*, the term applied by Werner to the several varieties of mica; occasionally used to designate talcose and micaceous compounds.

glimmer ('glɪmə(r)), *v.* Forms: 4-5 **glemer,** 5 **glym(m)er,** 6- **glimmer.** [OE. **glimorian*, a frequentative f. the root *glim-*: see GLIM *sb.*, GLEAM. Cf. Du., MHG., Ger. *glimmer(e)n*, Da. *glimre*, Sw. *glimra*.]

†**1.** *intr.* To shine brightly; to glitter. Of the eyes: To flash. *Obs.*

13.. *Gaw. & Gr. Knt.* 172 His arsounz..þat euer glemered & glent al of grene stones. *c* **1440** *Promp. Parv.* 199/1 Glymeryn, *radio.* *c* **1450** LONELICH *Grail* xxxi. 158 Cler Schynenge As the sonne vppon the water whanne it is Glemerynge. **1481** CAXTON *Reynard* (Arb.) 56 He was so ferdful to loke on that his eyen glymmerd as fyre. *c* **1530** LD. BERNERS *Arth. Lyt. Bryt.* (1814) 394 He sawe yᵉ bryght sonne glimmering on yᵉ faire chirches & hye steples.

2. a. In weaker sense: To give a faint or intermittent light; to shine faintly. Also with *away*, *out*, and quasi-*trans.* with cognate obj.

1483 *Cath. Angl.* 159/1 To Glymer, *sublucere.* **1605** SHAKS. *Macb.* III. iii. 5 The West yet glimmers with some streakes of Day. **1639** T. BRUGIS tr. *Camus' Moral Relat.* 207 The smallest starres, which the obscurity of night causeth to glimmer in the skye. **1718** PRIOR *Solomon* II. 928 The rising motion of an infant ray Shot glimmering thro' the cloud, and promis'd day. **1794** MRS. RADCLIFFE *Myst. Udolpho* xxv, A light glimmered through the grates of the lower chamber. **1797** MRS. MARY ROBINSON *Walsingham* III. 73 The festoons of coloured lamps glimmered their last rays. **1832** HT. MARTINEAU *Irel.* iv. 65 They had..felt themselves secure while the beacon glimmered south-east of them. **1862** BURTON *Bk. Hunter* (1863) 404 There are many who will remember the white house glimmering through the trees. **1871** L. STEPHEN *Playgr. Europe* iii. (1894) 83 Enormous spaces of hill and plain..glimmering away to the indistinct horizon.

b. *transf.* and *fig.*

1561 T. NORTON *Calvin's Inst.* IV. xix. (1634) 719 In the Sacraments, that which is of God, scarcely glimmereth in at holes, among the rout of the inventions of men. **1618** BOLTON *Florus* (1636) 307 So soone..as any occasion glimmered out, they stuck not to break in upon us. **1758** JOHNSON *Idler* No. 66 ¶2 We should have..travelled upward to the original of things by the light of History, till in remoter times it had glimmered in fable, and at last sunk into darkness. **1809-10** COLERIDGE *Friend* (1865) 1 Antecedent to all history, and long glimmering through it as a holy tradition. **1844** *Mem. Babylonian P'cess* II. 265 A name which will be honoured and revered, as long as one spark of virtue glimmers on the face of the earth. **1858** HAWTHORNE *Fr. & It. Jrnls.* I. 101 The voice came glimmering and bubbling up a flight of stone steps. **1860** GEO. ELIOT *Mill on Fl.* VII. ii, The idea of ever recovering happiness never glimmered in her mind for a moment.

c. *to glimmer into*: to pass *into* with a glimmer.

1858 HAWTHORNE *Fr. & It. Jrnls.* I. 216 The figures sadly glimmered into something like visibility.

d. *to go glimmering*: to die away, die out, vanish, 'peter out'. *U.S. slang.*

1891 *Memphis Appeal-Avalanche* 8 May 4/1 The union depot project appears to have gone glimmering down the vale of things that were. **1910** W. M. RAINE *B. O'Connor* 28 My reputation has gone glimmering. **1945** *La Junta* (Colo.) *Tribune-Democrat* 1 June 1/8 Plans for a new building.. went glimmering today as School District 11 was turned down on its application for Lenham funds for this purpose.

3. a. To look or glance with half-closed eyes; to see indistinctly. *rare.* †**b.** *trans. causatively.* (See quot. 1580.) *Obs. rare.*

1579 TOMSON *Calvin's Serm. Tim.* 56/1 If we doe not looke with full open eyes, but onely glimmer in passing by, we shall se such gret villaneis, that they are inough to put out our eyes. **1580** HOLLYBAND *Treas. Fr. Tong, Esblouir les yeux*, to glimmer the eies, to dazell. **1896** *N.Y. Weekly Witness* 30 Dec. 13/2 The little fellow had one eye closed entirely, and the other was glimmering.

4. *Comb.*, as **glimmer-gowk** *dial.*, an owl.

1877 *N.W. Linc. Gloss., Glimmer-gowk*, an owl. 'A glimmer-gowk's afore ony cat for mice.' **1880** TENNYSON *Village Wife* vii. 6 'E sit like a greät glimmer-gowk wi' 'is glasses athurt 'is noäse.

†'**glimmerer.** *slang. Obs.* [f. GLIMMER *sb.*¹ (sense 3 a) + -ER¹.] (See quots.)

[**1567**: cf. GLIMMERING *ppl. a.* 2.] **1605** DEKKER & WILKINS *Iests* (1607) 33 Another sort of these shee morts, or monsters ..& they are the Glimerers. Your Glimerer, shees vp in the morning, [enters a house on the pretext of procuring a light for her fire, and steals what she can lay hands on]. **1673** R. HEAD *Cant. Acad.* 84 The Glymmerers are such as travel up and down with Licenses to beg, under the pretence that they have lost all by fire. **1688** R. HOLME *Armoury* II. iii. §68 Glymmerers, Firers of Houses, thereby to steal in Confusions. **1785** GROSE *Dict. Vulg. Tongue, Glimmerers*, persons begging with sham licences, pretending losses by fire.

glimmering ('glɪmərɪŋ), *vbl. sb.* [See -ING¹.]

1. The action of the vb. GLIMMER; the shining of a faint or wavering light; a twinkle.

c **1440** *Promp. Parv.* 199/1 Glymerynge of lyghte ..*lucubrum.* **1529** MORE *Comf. agst. Trib.* II. Wks. 1181/2 By the glymeringe of the moone, he had espied..them himself. **1628** GAULE *Pract. Theor.* (1629) 90 Can a Light be shrouded vnder a Bushel, and yeald no glimmering? **1738** GRAY tr. *Tasso* 45 Wks. 1836 I. 171 The watery glimmerings of a fainter day Discover'd half, and half conceal'd their way. **1803** WORDSW. *Green Linnet* iv, Shadows and sunny glimmerings, That cover him all over. **1843** PRESCOTT *Mexico* (1850) I. 240 At the first glimmering of light he mustered his army. **1868** LOCKYER *Guillemin's Heavens* (ed. 3) 4 Milky Ways..so distant that the most powerful instruments were able only to distinguish a confused glimmering.

fig. *c* **1440** HYLTON *Scala Perf.* (W. de W. 1494) I. xlviii, Yf thou maye in clennes of conscyence fele þe homely and the peesful presence of that blessed man Jhesu Cryste as a shadowe or a glemeryng of hym. **1642** R. CARPENTER *Experience* II. xi. 228 Look upon the Transfiguration and admire the beautifull glimmerings of his Godhead. **1711** ADDISON *Spect.* No. 120 ¶15 Without the least Glimmerings of Thought or common Sense. *a* **1745** SWIFT *Let. fr. Grand Mistr. Free-Masons* Wks. 1765 XII. 267 For our guardian will have it so, that the pagan priesthood was always in the druids or masons, and that there was a perceivable glimmering of the jewish rites in it, though much corrupted. **1758** J. S. *Le Dran's Observ. Surg.* (1771) 60 The Patient had a Glimmering of Sense. **1856** MAX MÜLLER *Chips* (1867) II. xvi. 104 A strange glimmering of the old mythe in the mind of the poet. **1871** L. STEPHEN *Playgr. Europe* ii. (1894) 36 It is quite possible for a scoffer at the Alps..to have glimmerings of good taste [etc.].

†**b.** A glance, a look. *Obs.*⁻¹

1759 *Compl. Let. Writer* (ed. 6) 225 His odious smiles and glimmerings..were thrown away upon her.

2. A partial view, of either a material or immaterial object; a glimpse, an inkling; a faint notion.

c **1380** WYCLIF *Wks.* (1880) 339 þis kunne we not knowe ful certeyne, but han glymeryng & supposyng. **1470-85** MALORY *Arthur* XI. xiv, Syre Percyuale hadde a glemerynge of the vessel and of the mayden that bare hit. **1549** LATIMER *5th Serm. bef. Edw. VI* (Arb.) 133, I haue but a glymmeringe of it Yet in generally, I remember the scope of it. *a* **1639** WOTTON *Dk. Buckingham* (1642) 6 On the way..the baggage post boy, who had been at Court, got (I know not how) a glimmering who they were; But his mouth was easily shut. **1851-9** AIRY *Astron.* vi. (1868) 236 It is only possible to give a glimmering of what I desire to convey. **1871** FREEMAN *Norm. Conq.* (1876) IV. xviii. 176 We get glimmerings of fighting on the borders of these shires.

glimmering ('glɪmərɪŋ), *ppl. a.* [See -ING².]

1. That glimmers (see the vb.).

c **1350** *Will. Palerne* 1427 þe messageres..were arayde.. al in glimerand gold. *c* **1435** *Torr. Portugal* 427 Yt ys ase glimyrryng ase the glase. **1590** SHAKS. *Mids. N.* II. i. 77 Didst thou not leade him through the glimmering night. **1649** J. H. *Motion to Parl.* 12 Their glimmering notions were but lighted at our candle. **1682** H. MORE *Glanvil's Sad. Triumph., Contn. Remark. Stor.* 60 A glimmering light appeared all about the Room. **1750** GRAY *Elegy* ii, Now fades the glimmering landscape on the sight. **1800** *Asiat. Ann. Reg.* 104/1 By a faint glimmering light it was difficult for the Killedar to recognize the features. **1847** TENNYSON *Princ.* Concl. 117 Little Lilia, rising quietly, Disrobed the glimmering statue of Sir Ralph From those rich silks. **1879** TRENCH *Poems* 3 Some lone fisher, that has stood For days beside the glimmering flood.

†**2.** ***glimmering mort*** [see GLIMMER *sb.*¹ 3 a]: a woman who travels the country begging, saying that she has lost her all by fire: = GLIMMERER. *Obs. slang.*

1567 HARMAN *Caveat* (E.E.T.S.) 61 This glimmering Morte..Thys glymmeringe glauncer.

Hence '**glimmeringly** *adv.*

1561 T. NORTON *Calvin's Inst.* I. 5 The darke myste of malice dooth choke..those sparkes, that glimmeringly shined to make them see the glorie of God. **1665** WITHER *Lord's Prayer* 41, I have such a strong desire to express what I glimmeringly apprehend of it. **1820** *Blackw. Mag.* VI. 529 The more faintly and glimmeringly one object, as it were, melted into another. **1868** BROWNING *Ring & Bk.* I. 611 Glimmeringly did a pack of were-wolves pad the snow.

glimmerous ('glɪmərəs), *a. rare.* [f. GLIMMER *sb.* + -OUS.] **a.** Lighted by a glimmer, or fitful light. **b.** Shining unsteadily.

1792 BURNS *Let. to W. Nicol* 20 Feb., When shall the elfine lamp of my glimmerous understanding..shine like the constellation of thy intellectual powers. **1793** —— *Let. to Ainslie* 26 Apr., My elfine, lambent, glimmerous wanderings have misled his stupid steps.

glimmery ('glɪmərɪ), *a.*¹ Also 6 **glimrye,** 7 **glimery.** [f. GLIMMER *sb.*¹ + -Y¹.] †**a.** Of fire: Burning dimly (*obs.*). **b.** *Theat. slang.* Of an actor: Wanting in definite conception of his part.

1583 STANYHURST *Æneis* IV. (Arb.) 102 When fiers glimrye be listed In clowds grim gloomming with bounce doo terrifye worldlings. **1892** *Athenæum* 9 Apr. 466/3 'Mr. Edgar' is too vague and 'glimmery' for the part he has to play.

c. Glimmering. Also advb.

1906 KIPLING *Puck of Pook's Hill* 36 A loose glimmery gown of chain-mail. **1907** *Daily Chron.* 4 Mar. 6/4 The marble bust..glimmery white. **1927** *Blackw. Mag.* Mar. 308/2 A great white wall of snow and rock, all glimmery in the rising sun, rose above us. **1953** H. H. PRICE *Thinking & Exper.* ii. 47 When I see the ice, I..do not infer the coldness from the glimmery look.

†'**glimmery,** *a.*² In 7 **glimery.** [f. GLIMMER *sb.*² + -Y¹.] Micaceous.

1683 PETTUS *Fleta Min.* I. 230 There appertains to the harsh flowing copper Oars, the harsh copper Flint, and what is splendy mispickly glimery or spady.

glimpse (glɪmps), *sb.* Forms: 6 **glymse,** 6-7 **glimce, -s(e, glimps, glymps(e,** 7 **glinse,** 7- **glimpse.** [f. the vb.]

1. A momentary shining, a flash. *lit.* and *fig.* Now somewhat *arch.* and with mixture of sense 3. ***the glimpses of the moon*** (Shaks.): the earth by night; often quoted in wider sense, sublunary scenes.

1602 SHAKS. *Ham.* I. iv. 53 What may this meane? That thou..Revisits thus the glimpses of the Moone? **1610** G. FLETCHER *Christ's Vict.* II. xxvi, His staring eyes did glow.. their glimpse did showe Like Cockatrices eyes. **1635-56** COWLEY *Davideis* I. 85 No dear Glimpse of the Sun's lovely Face, Strikes through the solid Darkness of the Place. **1658** SIR T. BROWNE *Gard. Cyrus* iv. 66 They that held the Stars of heaven were but rayes and flashing glimpses of the Empyreal light, through holes and perforation of the upper heaven. **1700** DRYDEN *Ilias* I. Fables 214 One glimpse of Glory to my Issue give. **1828** SCOTT *F.M. Perth* xxx, A glimpse of the moon showed the dark and huge tower. **1833** HT. MARTINEAU *Briery Creek* i. 1 There had been glimpses of starlight in the intervals of the shifting spring storms. **1840** DE QUINCEY *Rhet.* Wks. 1862 X. 25 English Crackenthorpius..though buried for two centuries, will revisit the glimpses of the moon. **1844** WHITTIER *Bridal of Pennacook* 62 Sweet human faces, white clouds of the noon, Slant starlight glimpses through the dewy leaves. **1847** TENNYSON *Princ.* Concl. 46 We climb'd The slope to Vivian-place, and turning saw..The shimmering glimpses of a stream.

b. A moment. *rare.*

1812 BYRON *Ch. Har.* I. xiii (Orig. Draft) Pleased for a glimpse appear'd the woeful childe.

2. A faint and transient appearance. †Also, an occasionally perceptible resemblance; a tinge or trace (of a quality). *Obs.*

c **1540** SURREY *Descr. Fickle Affect. Panges* 46 in *Tottel's Misc.* (Arb.) 7 Reuiued with a glimse of grace olde sorowes to let fall. *a* **1602** W. PERKINS *Cases Consc.* (1619) 147 God would manifest his glory vnto him..by a glympse or imperfect representation. **1606** SHAKS. *Tr. & Cr.* I. ii. 25 There is no man hath a vertue, that he hath not a glimpse of. **1643** SIR T. BROWNE *Relig. Med.* I. §33 There is not any creature that hath so neere a glympse of their [spirits'] nature, as light in the Sunne and Elements. **1671** MILTON *P.R.* I. 93 In his face The glimpses of his Father's glory shine. *a* **1704** T. BROWN *Persius' Sat.* I. Wks. 1730 I. 53 A glimpse of human stamp it has. **1836** EMERSON *Nature, Prospects* Wks. (Bohn) II. 170 Imperfect theories and sentences which contain glimpses of truth. **1842** TENNYSON *Will Waterproof* viii, If old things, there are new; Ten thousand broken lights and shapes, Yet glimpses of the true.

†**b.** Mere appearance. *Obs.*

1579 TOMSON *Calvin's Serm. Tim.* 603/2 Men, yᵗ neuer did any thing worth in their life, but only in a glimce & shew.

3. A momentary and imperfect view (*of*), a passing glance. (The current sense.)

1579 LYLY *Euphues* (Arb.) 363 The Basilike, whose eyes procure delight to the looker at the first glymse, and death at the second glaunce. **1682** BUNYAN *Holy War* 208 Here and there one or other had a glimpse of him as he did make his escape out of Mansoul. **1726** POPE *Let.* 3 Sept. in *Swift's Wks.* 1841 II. 589/2, I had a glimpse of a letter of yours lately. **1797** MRS. RADCLIFFE *Italian* i. (1826) 6 He hoped to obtain a glimpse of Ellena at a lattice. **1820** W. IRVING *Sketch Bk.* I. 16, I had a glimpse of two or three half-naked wretches, rushing from her cabin. **1872** JENKINSON *Guide Eng. Lakes* (1879) 13 At one point a glimpse is caught of the whole of Coniston Lake.

b. *fig.*

1570 DEE *Math. Pref.* 26 To wynne a glyms (as it were) or shaddow of perceiuerance. **1596** SPENSER *Hymn Heavenly Beauty* 221 Seene but a glims of this which I pretend. **1633** EARL MANCH. *Al Mondo* (1636) 193 Of this joy thy dazeled eyes might have some glimps. **1681** R. WITTIE *Surv. Heavens* 36 From the Contemplation of the Heavens..we have some glimpse of God's Infinity. **1729** BUTLER *Serm.* Wks. 1874 II. 190 Those..cannot have the least glimpse of the subject before us. **1822** HAZLITT *Table-t.* Ser. II. v. (1869) 121 Not a glimpse can you get of the merits or defects of the performers. **1874** GREEN *Short Hist.* IV. §4. 188 Whenever we get a glimpse of the inner history of an English town.

glimpse (glɪmps), *v.* Forms: 3 **glymsen,** 6 **glynce, glym(p)se,** 6-7 **glimse,** 6- **glimpse.** [ME. *glymse-n* (?:—OE. **glimsian* :—WGer. **glimmisôjan*) = MHG. *glimsen*, f. root of GLIM *sb.* and *v.*]

1. *intr.* To shine faintly or intermittently; to glimmer, glitter. *lit.* and *fig.*

c **1400** *R. Gloucester's Chron.* (Rolls) App. xx. 252 Hure fon were loþ to loke on snou þat was so whit þat glymsede on hare eyȝen. *c* **1540** SURREY *Forsaken Louer* in *Tottel's Misc.* (Arb.) 23 In my hert her eye Hath made her thought appere, By glimsing with such grace. **1592** *Conspir. Pretended Ref.* Pref. 2 No sooner did the beames of his Gospell beginne to glimpse and breake foorth. **1601** MUNDAY *Downf. Earl Huntington* II. i. in Hazl. *Dodsley* VIII. 255 Little glow-worms glimpsing in the dark. **1635** PAGITT *Christianogr.* 181 The Law of God, which glimpsed in their hearts. **1657** W. MORICE *Coena quasi Κοινή* Def. xxxiii. 307 Some discern some light thereof glimpsing from the precedent verses. **1843** LD. HOUGHTON *Mem. Many Scenes, Moon of South* 69, I have watched the shapes thy glory made, Glimpsing like starlight through the massive pine.

b. To come into view; to appear faintly; to dawn. Now only *poet.* or *arch.*

1603 DRAYTON *Bar. Wars* v. xlv, Deformed shadowes glimpsing in his sight, As darknes for it would more darkned be, Through those poore crannies forc'd it selfe to see. **1633** P. FLETCHER *Purple Isl.* XII. xlvi, Then glimpst the hopefull morrow. **1851** WHITTIER *Chapel Hermits* 41 Yet sometimes glimpses on my sight, Through present wrong, the eternal right. **1856** AIRD *Poet. Wks.* 90 Come dusky masses glimpsing through the night. **1862** B. TAYLOR *Home & Abr.* Ser. II. 103 The intervening plain glimpsed nearer.

†**2.** To have a glimmering of vision. *Obs.*

c **1386** [see GLIMPSING *vbl. sb.*] **1519** HORMAN *Vulg.* 30 b, I se but half glyncynge at myddyl noone [*cæcutio*].

†**3.** *trans.* (See quot.) *Obs.*⁻⁰

1598 FLORIO, *Abbacinare*.. to glimpse or blinde the sight.

4. To give a glimpse of. Also with *out*. *rare*.

1663 SIR G. MACKENZIE *Relig. Stoici* i. (1685) 6 The twilight of darkened reason glimsing to man that impressa of the divine Image. **1671** FLAVEL *Fount. Life* ii. 4 Now, to glimpse out the unspeakable felicity of that State of Christ. **1888** *Science* XI. 257/1 The psychology of the developing child, glimpsing as it does.. the microcosm of the race and an epitome of the struggle for civilization.

5. To catch a glimpse of (either a material or immaterial object); to see by glimpses.

1779 FORREST *Voy. N. Guinea* 292 Sometimes Rajah Moodo would ask the Spanish envoy and me to talk about religion; glimpsing in some things the difference between Romish and Protestant. **1823** *New Monthly Mag.* VIII. 503 She glimpsed the peak of my mitre in the waters. **1851** J. HAMILTON *Royal Preacher* xx. (1854) 257 His penetrating eye can glimpse the tokens of a bright Epiphany. **1870** J. R. LOWELL *My Study Wind.* I. 5, I seem to glimpse something of this familiar weakness in Mr. White. **1879** LOCKYER in *Nature* 6 Nov. 8/1 It will.. be granted that an inorganic evolution is already glimpsed. **1885** HOWELLS *Silas Lapham* (1891) I. 235 Her face, glimpsed now and then in the moonlight.. had a fascination which kept his eye.

6. *intr.* To cast a passing glance. Const. *at*, *upon*; also with advs.

1833 WHITTIER *Ex. New Eng. Leg.* 13 No more the unquiet churchyard dead Glimpse upward from their turfy bed. *a* **1834** LAMB *Let. to Moxon* in *Final Mem.* viii. 277 When I came home I read your letter, and glimpsed at your beautiful sonnet. **1854** HAWTHORNE *Eng. Note-Bks.* (1883) II. 70 Glimpsing in, you see that a cottager's life must be the very plainest and homeliest that ever was lived by men and women. **1878** B. TAYLOR *Deukalion* III. vi. 130 Here glimpse upon the soul-imagined shores.

Hence **glimpsed** *ppl. a.* Also **'glimpser**, one who glimpses.

1649 R. DINGLEY (*title*) Messiah's Splendor; or, the Glimpsed Glory of a Beauteous Christ. *c* **1800** K. WHITE *Time* 245 By indistinct and half-glimpsed images. **1841** *Blackw. Mag.* L. 77 Hear it ye glimpsers into Almacks!

'glimpsing, *vbl. sb.* [f. GLIMPSE *v.* + -ING[1].] The action of the vb. GLIMPSE.

c **1386** CHAUCER *Merch. T.* 1139 Ye han som glimsing and no parfit sighte. **1563** *Homilies* II. *Almsdeed* III. (1859) 398 The fear of children and fools, which when they see the bright glimpsing of a glass, they do imagine straightway that it is the lightning. **1602** BEAUMONT *Hermaphrodite* Poems (1640) D 2 He sent Aurora from him to the skye To give a glimpsing to each mortall eye. **1814** *Witness* II. ii, She hath a look so witchlike and so wild, That I would shun the glimpsing of her eyes.

glimpsing ('glɪmpsɪŋ), *ppl. a.* [See -ING[2].] That glimpses; glimmering; shining faintly; appearing by glimpses, affording glimpses.

1551 RECORDE *Pathw. Knowl.* To Rdr., That finer wittes maie fashion them selues with such glimsinge dull light. **1577** STANYHURST *Descr. Irel.* iv. 16 in *Holinshed*, S. Patrike .. besought God.. to giue out some euident or glimsing token of the matter. **1583** T. WATSON *Centurie of Loue* xlvi. Poems (Arb.) 82 The Sunne may sooner shine by night, And twinckling starres giue glimsinge sparkes by day: Then I can cease to serue my Sweete delight. **1602** *Metamorphosis Tabacco* 25 Lik'ning her eyes vnto the glimsing light That guides poore heardsmen to their home at night. **1803** LEYDEN *Scenes Infancy* III. (1819) 374 The spectre-ship, in livid glimpsing light, Glares baleful on the shuddering watch at night. **1835** AIRD *Chr. Bride* I. vii, A nymph.. walking on the checkered floors of woods.. Chasing the shadows with her glimpsing feet. **1835** —— *Arthur* III. iii. in *Blackw. Mag.* XXXVIII. 92 I've seen the time I joyed to wander in these glimpsing woods. **1874** D. GRAY *Poet. Wks.* 9 Like ghosts in glimpsing moonshine, wildly run The children.

glimrye, obs. form of GLIMMERY *a.*[1]

glims(e, obs. form of GLIMPSE *sb.* and *v.*

†**'glimster**, *v. Obs.* [app. f. GLIM after Du. *glinsteren* to glimmer.] *intr.* To glimmer feebly.

1565 T. STAPLETON *Fortr. Faith* 65 Glimstering but neuer shining. *Ibid.* 88 All these ix. C. yeares it hath glimstered a litle in preuy congregations.

glinkite ('glɪŋkaɪt). *Min.* [Named by Romanofski in 1847 after Gen. Glinka, governor of the Ural Mines.] A pale-green variety of chrysolite.

1849 *Amer. Jrnl. Sci.* Ser. II. VIII. 121 Chemical Analysis of Glinkite. **1892** in *Dana's Min.* 452.

glinse, obs. form of GLIMPSE *sb.*

glint (glɪnt), *sb.*[1] See also GLENT. [f. the vb.

The text of the first quot. is insecure, and the existence of the word before 19th c. is therefore doubtful.]

1. A gleam; a faint or momentary appearance of light or of some lustrous object.

a **1541** WYATT *Ps.* cxliii. Prol. 13 The glint of light, that in the air doth lome, Man redeemeth. **1826** J. WILSON *Noct. Ambr.* Wks. 1855 I. 163 Their daughters.. who have been singing at their domestic toils, frae the earliest glint o' morn. **1861** *Court Life Naples* II. 255 The last glint of the lamp as we drove off showed me the face of my husband. **1865** *Pall Mall G.* 19 June 4 Glints of blue sky come through the tall open windows. **1885** A. J. C. HARE *Russia* iii. 128 The detached groups of.. birches and firs, and the lovely glints of sea between them.

fig. **1871** C. GIBBON *Lack of Gold* x, Can you not give a poor soul one glint of consolation?

b. Shining appearance; shine.

1844 LOWELL *Ghost-seer* Poet. Wks. (1879) 84 But it has the cold, hard glint Of new dollars from the mint.

2. A passing look, a glance; a momentary view, glimpse. Chiefly *Sc.* or *north.*

1832-53 *Whistle-Binkie* (Scot. Songs) Ser. I. 43 When ilka glint, conveys a hint To tak a smack—before folk. **1877** *N.W. Linc. Gloss.*, *Glint*, a glimpse. 'I nobbut just got a glint o' my lady as she was walkin' doon to th' chech.' **1883** BLACK *Shandon Bells* xxx, I.. was having a glint at the newspaper. **1889** BARRIE *Window in Thrums* 86 They gie ye a glint o' their een.

b. = GLIFF *sb.* 1 b.

1853 MRS. GASKELL *Ruth* I. iv. 101 She's a pretty creature, with a glint of her mother about her.

glint (glɪnt), *sb.*[2] *Geol.* [ad. Sw. *klint* cliff, Norw. *klint* cliff by the sea: cogn. w. CLINT *sb.*] An escarpment of almost horizontal strata formed as a result of denudation of the adjacent lower rocks. Also *attrib.*, as **glint lake**, a lake formed by glacial excavation at a glint; **glint line**, the line followed by a glint, esp. that on the edge of the Baltic shield.

1906 H. SOLLAS tr. *Suess's Face of Earth* II. 65 In Russia the feature formed by these basset edges is known as the *glint*, and we shall in future employ this term for long lines of escarpment formed of flat-lying beds, when they are due, not to fracture, but to denudation. The glint of each of the two shields is marked by a long series of freshwater lakes. *Ibid.*, The glint line of the Baltic shield runs.. through the gulf of Finland, which also has the position of a glint lake. **1939** *Geogr. Jrnl.* XCIII. 234 The large glint lakes bordering the Canadian Shield. **1959** WOOLDRIDGE & MORGAN *Outl. Geomorphol.* (ed. 2) vi. 81 The south-eastern limit in Scandinavia [of the Caledonian ranges] is the famous 'glint-line', along which the folded terrain adjoins the Baltic or Fenno-Scandian block, which functioned as the hinterland in the original folding.

†**glint**, *a. Obs.* [Cf. Sw. (dial.) *glinta* to slip on ice: see GLINT *v.*] Slippery.

c **1475** *Partenay* 4934 Fro that place glint þat full hy tho was, Don vppon the Roch A fall gan purchas. **1523** SKELTON *Garl. Laurell* 572 Go softly, she sayd, the stones be full glint.

glint (glɪnt), *v.* [Rare in the 15th c.; subsequently first in Sc. writers of the 18th c.; it has been adopted into English literary use in the present century. Prob. an altered form of the earlier GLENT *v.*, which the rime shows to have been the original reading in two of the 15th c. passages; cf. *hint* as the northern form of HENT *v.*]

1. *intr.* To move quickly, esp. obliquely; to glance aside; = GLENT *v.* 1, 1 b.

c **1440** *Partonope* 1036 Suche a dynt That thurgh his hede hit glynt. *c* **1440** *Generydes* 2481 With his swerd when that his stroke glynt Owt of ther sadill full redely they went. **1794** BURNS '*How Long and dreary*', How slow ye move, ye heavy hours!.. It was na sae ye glinted by, When I was wi' my dearie. *a* **1800** in SCOTT *Minstr. Scott. Bord.* (1803) III. 338 Ae fire-flaught darted through the rain.. and glinted o'er the raging main. **1848** LYTTON *Harold* IV. iii, From the mirth of sunny Leofwine sorrow glints aside.

2. To shine with a flashing light; to glance, gleam, glitter. Also with *forth*.

c **1440** *Generydes* 6088 The fyre sparkelid and fro the harneys glynt [*rime-word* went]. **1787** BURNS *Holy Fair* i, The risin' sun owre Galston muirs Wi' glorious light was glintin. **1801** MACNEILL *Poems* (1844) 114 The sun-beams glint sae cheerfu'. **1828** [AIRD] *Buy a Broom* i, in *Blackw. Mag.* XXIV. 712/1 Sickles were seen glinting on the far yellow uplands. **1839** BAILEY *Festus* vi. (1848) 57 Leaves Between which the light glints. **1859** DICKENS *T. Two Cities* I. iv, The specks of sail that glinted in the sunlight far at sea. **1860** WHYTE MELVILLE *Holmby House* 269 As the sun glinted back from a dozen of carbines. **1863** M. TAYLOR *Tara* xiii, The sun's gleams.. glinting from spear-head, morion, and steel armour.. lighted up faces of varied character. **1877** *N.W. Linc. Gloss.*, Th' sun glinted upo' th' glass winders that bad that I was omust blind wi' it. **1879** G. MACDONALD *P. Faber* III. iii. 38 A few silvery threads glinted in his hair. **1879** J. LONG *Æneid* VIII. 29 As when the sunshine or the moonlight clear, Dancing on water in a brazen vat, Glints everywhere. **1888** RIDER HAGGARD *Col. Quaritch* vii, His face working with passion and his grey eyes glinting.

fig. **1865** *Reader* Feb. 158/2 The magic effects that glint forth from his quaint words and phrases.

b. *trans.* (causatively).

1844 LOWELL *Poet. Wks.* (1879) 373 The willow.. glints his steely aglets in the sun. **1872** BLACK *Adv. Phaeton* ii. 15 The window of some.. tavern glints back the light. **1889** *19th Cent.* Oct. 684 The morning sun.. is glinted back, as from a hundred heliographs from the golden domes on your left. **1893** BURRELL & CUTHELL *Indian Memories* 174 The sun glinted the boughs overhead.

3. *intr.* To peep, take a glance. Cf. GLENT *v.* 2.

1888 *Century Mag.* XXXV. 448 Glinting around, [he] asked for the tenth time if [etc.]. **1891** *Hartland Gloss.* s.v., Doan' ee stan' there glintin' roun' the cornder.

b. quasi-*trans.* To glance (the eye).

1832-53 W. CROSS in *Whistle-binkie* (Scot. Songs) Ser. III. 18 She glintit her e'e at him slyly.

Hence **'glinted, 'glinting** *ppl. adjs.*

1868 SILL *Serenity* i. Poems 100 Shimmering and trembling, Doth the glinted star-shine Sparkle and cease. **1883** *Daily News* 22 Sept. 3/4 Those glinting blue-green feathers which originate on the drake's neck and breast. **1884** *St. James's Gaz.* 10 May 6/2 The glinting silver of the statuette. **1889** BARRIE *Window in Thrums* 178 But let Kitty, or any other maid, cast a glinting eye on Jamie.

glinter ('glɪntə(r)), *v. rare*[−1]. [f. GLINT *v.* + -ER[5].] = GLINT *v.* 2.

1851 D. G. MITCHELL *Fresh Gleanings* 261 Then it would glinter out in feeble rays into the deep darkness.

glioblastoma (glaɪəʊblæ'stəʊmə). *Path.* [f. GLIO(MA + -BLAST + -OMA.]

= SPONGIOBLASTOMA. ***glioblastoma multi'forme***, a fast-growing malignant glioma of the cerebrum in which there are cells of many kinds, most of them resembling spongioblasts.

1926 BAILEY & CUSHING *Class. Tumors of Glioma Group* v. 95 One might.. designate the.. [bipolar and unipolar spongioblasts] as bipolar and unipolar glioblasts... One would then employ *glioblastoma* multiforme and unipolare in the place of *spongioblastoma* multiforme and unipolare. **1953** *Brit. Jrnl. Psychol.* Feb. 59 Twenty months after the patient's first admission to hospital a cystic glioblastoma multiforme was demonstrated at operation. **1970** PASSMORE & ROBSON *Compan. Med. Studies* II. xxviii. 4/2 The more rapidly growing and pleomorphic of these tumours [*sc.* gliomata] are often called glioblastomata.

glioma (glaɪ'əʊmə). *Path.* Pl. gli'omata. [mod.L. *gliōma* (Virchow), f. Gr. γλί-α glue.] 'A tumour originating from, and largely consisting of, the neuroglia cells of the central nervous system, esp. of the brain' (*Syd. Soc. Lex.* 1885).

1870 PAGET *Lect. Surg. Path.* (ed. 3) 471 A group of tumours to which Virchow has given the name Glioma. **1873** T. H. GREEN *Introd. Pathol.* (ed. 2) 121. **1876** T. BRYANT *Pract. Surg.* I. 109.

gliomatosis (ˌglaɪəʊmə'təʊsɪs). *Path.* [ad. G. *gliomatose* (F. Schultze 1882, in *Arch. f. path. Anat. und Physiol. und f. klin. Med.* LXXXVII. 535), f. mod.L. *gliōmat-*, GLIOMA + -OSIS.] A diffuse proliferation of glia cells associated with or arising from a glioma; gliosis.

1886 W. R. GOWERS *Man. Dis. Nerv. Syst.* I. 436 The neuroglia may be regarded as a persistent, slightly modified, embryonal tissue, and these exuberant masses of tissue bear considerable resemblance in structure to glioma, so that the condition has been called 'gliomatosis'. **1899** *Allbutt's Syst. Med.* VII. 48 From syringomyelia and central gliomatosis it may be impossible to distinguish the later results of hæmatomyelia. **1924** R. MUIR *Text-bk. Path.* xvii. 624 Intermediate varieties are met with, between a distinct tumour and a more diffuse overgrowth which may be called gliomatosis... Gliomatosis occurs also in relation to the central canal of the spinal cord in connection with syringomyelia. **1947** W. R. BRAIN *Dis. Nerv. Syst.* (ed. 3) iii. 225 Sometimes a glioma seems to arise diffusely, as in so-called 'gliomatosis cerebri', or from multible centres at the same time. **1959** RUSSELL & RUBINSTEIN *Path. Tumours Nerv. Syst.* ii. 33 Diffuse gliomatosis of the pia-arachnoid of the spinal cord was recorded by Harbitz (1932, case 1), the glioma apparently being of astrocytic character.

gliomatous (glaɪ'əʊmətəs), *a.* [f. mod.L. *gliōmat-* GLIOMA + -OUS.] Of the nature of glioma.

1870 PAGET *Lect. Surg. Path.* (ed. 3) 471 In some cases the gliomatous tumour has a firm consistence. **1879** *St. George's Hosp. Rep.* IX. 429 The medulla oblongata was the seat of a hard gliomatous growth.

gliosarcoma (ˌglaɪəʊsɑː'kəʊmə). *Path.* Pl. gliosar'comata. [f. GLIO-MA + SARCOMA.] 'A term applied to those tumours which resemble both a glioma and a sarcoma' (*Syd. Soc. Lex.* 1885).

1869 *New Syd. Soc. Retrosp. Med.* 1867-8. 278 The tumour.. is described as a 'gliosarcoma'. **1881** tr. *Rosenthal's Dis. Nerv. Syst.* I. 96 Gliosarcomata.

gliosis (glaɪ'əʊsɪs). *Path.* [ad. G. *gliose* (F. Schultze 1882, in *Arch. f. path. Anat. und Physiol. und f. klin. Med.* LXXXVII. 535), f. GLI(A: see -OSIS.] Proliferation of glia cells, esp. of the fibrillar processes of astrocytes.

[**1890** *Brain* XIII. 299 Inflammation confined to a special tissue, as the neuroglia, has then its particular characteristics of gliomatous proliferation... Schültze [*sic*] would naturally call this special kind of inflammation *gliose* or *gliomatose*.] **1892** W. OSLER *Princ. Med.* 849 The condition is now regarded as a gliosis, a development of embryonal neurogliar tissue in which hæmorrhage or degeneration takes place with the formation of cavities. **1899** *Allbutt's Syst. Med.* VII. 172 He [*sc.* Weigert] wholly discards the hypothesis of syringomyelia to which the name spinal gliosis has been applied. **1934** H. W. C. VINES *Green's Man. Path.* (ed. 15) xxxvi. 809 If any destructive lesion of the brain tissue should occur, the astrocytes proliferate, and repair of the lesion occurs by gliosis comparable to the reparative fibrosis in other tissues. **1964** S. DUKE-ELDER *Parsons' Dis. Eye* (ed. 14) xxxiv. 545 In syringomyelia cavities form around which secondary gliosis develops in the cervical and upper dorsal cord. **1966** WRIGHT & SYMMERS *Systemic Path.* II. xxxiv. 1143/1 Gliosis is not always pathological. It may be found to some extent in normal brains in such places as the olivary nuclei.. and the central canal of the spinal cord.

gliotoxin (glaɪəʊ'tɒksɪn). *Biochem.* [f. mod.L. *Glio-cladium*, name of a genus of fungi (f. Gr. γλία glue + κλάδ-ος shoot, branch) + TOXIN.] An indole derivative, $C_{13}H_{14}N_2O_4S_2$, which has antibiotic activity against many fungi and bacteria and is produced by the growth of some fungi, esp. various species of *Penicillium* and *Aspergillus*.

1941 R. WEINDLING in *Phytopathology* XXXI. 991 The principal purpose of this article is to present data on factors determining production, stability, and activity of the crystalline *Gliocladium* toxin (gliotoxin)... The term 'gliotoxin' has been suggested by J. R. Johnson. **1944** *Nature* 25 Nov. 667/2 Strains of *Trichoderma viride* produce gliotoxin, and.. it is extremely probable that the fungus used by Weindling was not *G[liocladium] fimbriatum*, but was a *Trichoderma* as he originally supposed. **1953** PRATT & DUFRENOY *Antibiotics* (ed. 2) xiv. 286 Some antibiotics (actidione and gliotoxin, for example)..are too toxic for systemic chemotherapy in man. **1970** *Nature* 18 July 300/2 *T. viride* may retard the development of other fungi by producing the antibiotic gliotoxin or viridin.

gliriform (ˈglaɪərɪfɔːm), *a. Nat. Hist.* [f. L. *glīr-*, *glīs* dormouse + -(I)FORM.] Resembling the *Glires* or *Rodentia* in form or character.

1839–47 TODD *Cycl. Anat.* III. 298/1 The masseter in this gliriform Marsupial is single.

glirine (ˈglaɪərɪn), *a.* [f. L. *glīr-*, *glīs* dormouse + -INE.] Pertaining to the order *Glires* of mammals.

1836 J. F. DAVIS *Chinese* II. 342 Mr. Reeves discovered a glirine animal, nearly allied to the bamboo-rat of Sumatra. **1848** MAUNDER *Treas. Nat. Hist.* 787 *Glirine*, belonging to that order of Mammals, which includes such animals as have two fore teeth, a cutting one in each jaw, no tusks, and feet with claws; comprehending guinea-pigs, rabbits, hares, squirrels, mice, beavers, &c. **1860** in WORCESTER.

†**ˈgliscent**, *a. Obs.*⁻¹ In 7 glyssent. [ad. L. *gliscent-em*, pres. pple. of *gliscĕre* to increase.] Increasing.

1669 W. SIMPSON *Hydrol. Chym.* 55 A redintegration of the glyssent ferments of the blood.

†**glise**, *v. Obs.* Forms: 1 glisian, (? 3 clise-n), 3–5 glisien, glisen. [OE. *glisian* = OFris. *glisa*, MLG. *glisen*, MDa. *glise*; f. OTeut. root **glīs-*, prob. extended from **glī-*:—pre-Teut. **ghlei-ghli-*.] *intr.* To glitter, shine. Hence **ˈglising** *ppl. a.* (ME. *glisiand*, *-ing*), shining.

c **1000** ÆLFRIC *Gloss.* in Wr.-Wülcker 121/25 *Cicindela*, se glisiȝenda wibba. *c* **1205** LAY. 21725 Sceldes þer cliseden. *c* **1275** *Serving Christ* 21 in *O.E. Misc.* 91 For gold ne for seoluer ne for glysyinde wede. **1320–30** *Horn Ch.* in Ritson *Metr. Rom.* III. 288 Everiche strete and everi sty Glised.. Of her brinis bright. **1340–70** *Alisaunder* 180 With large forhed & long loueliche tresses, Glisiande as goldwire. *Ibid.* 697 Hee hath hye on his hed hornes of syluer, With golde gailye begonne glisiing bright.

glish (glɪʃ), *v. Obs.* exc. *dial.* [? Southern variant of GLISK *v.*] *intr.* = GLISK *v.*

1570 LEVINS *Manip.* 143/46 To Glish, *corruscare.* **1869** *Lonsdale Gloss.*, *Glish*, to glitter, or shine.

Hence **glish** *sb.* = GLISK *sb.* 2.

1570 in LEVINS *Manip.* 143/41.

glisk (glɪsk), *sb. Sc.* [f. the vb.]

1. A slight look; a glimpse.

c **1692** A. PITCAIRNE *Assembly* (1722) 18 The Malignants, whom they knew by the first Glisk of their Face. **1716** *Wodrow Corr.* (1843) II. 164, I was much pleased with the glisk I took of it [a book]. **1814** SCOTT *Wav.* lxiv, They just got a glisk o' his Honour as he gaed into the wood. **1922** J. BUCHAN *Huntingtower* vii. 138, I took a walk and got a glisk of the House and I liked the look of it.

2. A glance (of the eye); a gleam, glimmer, flash (of light).

1824 MISS FERRIER *Inher.* xviii, I wauld na gi'e a glisk of thae bonny een of yours for aw the eyes o' the world put thegither. **1870** A. WANLESS in Crockett *Minstr. Merse* (1893) 231 The glisks o' heaven will never fade. **1898** *Blackw. Mag.* Mar. 341 The rapture of her eye infected me like a glisk of the sun.

fig. **1883** W. C. SMITH *N. Country Folk* 105 And you need a glisk of religion to glamour the days that are past. **1893** STEVENSON *Catriona* 209, I had a glisk of pleasure.

glisk (glɪsk), *v. Obs.* exc. *dial.* [? perh. f. root *glis-* or *glit-* (see GLISE, GLITTER *vbs.*) + suffix *-k*, as in *walk*, *talk*, etc.]

†**1.** *intr.* To glance *over*. *Obs.*

1720 *Wodrow Corr.* (1843) II. 490, I have only got time to glisk it over cursorily.

2. *dial.* To glitter, shine.

1855 ROBINSON *Whitby Gloss.* s.v., It glisk'd like a piece of glass.

glisnen, obs. form of GLISTEN.

†**glisory**. *Obs.*⁻¹ [a. F. *glissoire*, f. *glisser* to slide.] A slider on a trepanning instrument.

1597 A. M. tr. *Guillemeau's Fr. Chirurg.* 15 b/2 The little Glysorye, or Glidere vp and downe [orig. *glissoire*].

gliss., gliss (glɪs), abbrev. of GLISSANDO.

1926 *Melody Maker* Mar. 31 The aforementioned mute modifier..is used to get the necessary 'gliss' which I have marked by means of slurs. **1931** G. JACOB *Orchestral Technique* viii. 76 A straight line joining the two notes with the word 'gliss.' added is all that is required. **1966** *Crescendo* Jan. 6/2 After a trombone gliss there's a comic Eastern bit.

glissade (glɪˈsɑːd, -ˈseɪd), *sb.* [a. F. *glissade*, f. *glisser* to slip, slide; a mountaineering term.]

1. The action of sliding down a steep slope (esp. of ice or snow).

1862 TYNDALL *Mountaineer.* vii. 61 In some places the rocks are worn to a powder, along which we shoot by glissades. **1871** L. STEPHEN *Playgr. Europe* v. (1894) 133 He appeared..none the worse for his involuntary glissade. **1895** A. F. MUMMERY *Climbs Alps & Caucasus* iii. (ed. 3) 62 Burgener suggested a standing glissade..We trusted to luck and a sitting glissade.

transf. and *fig.* **1870** SPURGEON *Treas. Dav.* Ps. xxxvi. 2 The descent to eternal ruin is easy enough, without making a glissade of it. **1882** A. EDWARDES *Ballroom Repent.* I. 74 The hundred thousand miles glissade of some shooting meteor. **1883** STEVENSON *Silverado Sq.* 88 Here and there dwarf thicket clinging in the general glissade.

2. *Dancing.* A step consisting of a glide or slide to the right or left.

1843 MARY HOWITT *F. Bremer's Home* I. x. 120 'Our Louise in time will dance very well', remarked the Judge to his wife, as he noticed with great pleasure the little *glissades* and *chassées* of his daughter.

glissade (glɪˈsɑːd, -ˈseɪd), *v.* [f. prec.] *intr.* To perform a glissade. **a.** *Dancing.* (See GLISSADE *sb.* 2.) Also *to glissade it*. **b.** *Mountaineering.* To slide down a steep slope.

1837 *Lett. fr. Madras* (1843) 57 Glissading up to me, waving her pretty little hands, and making a number of graceful, unmeaning antics. **1845** *Blackw. Mag.* LVIII. 628 He comes 'glissarding [*sic*] it' into the drawing-room, and bowing like a dancing-master. **1859** FARRAR *J. Home* 213 Kennedy and Cyril..glissaded gallantly over the slopes of snow. **1877** A. B. EDWARDS *Up Nile* xiii. 347 Driving our heels well into the sand, we half ran, half glissaded, and soon reached the bottom.

Hence **gliˈssading** *vbl. sb.* and *ppl. a.* Also **gliˈssader**, one who glissades.

1832 FR. A. KEMBLE *Rec. Girlhood* (1878) III. 189 Gibbering, glissading women greeting one another with the rapid music of the original scene. **1861** F. W. JACOMB in *Peaks, Passes, & Glac.* Ser. II. I. 315 That undignified attitude peculiar to the inexperienced glissader. **1865** *Reader* No. 143. 348/2 Talking of glissading. **1892** C. T. DENT *Mountain.* vi. 194 Snow slopes..on which patches of ice intervene, are unfit for glissading. *Ibid.* 195 A good glissader can go fast and stop quickly.

glissando (glɪˈsændəʊ). *Mus.* Pl. glissandi, -dos. [Italianized form of Fr. *glissant*, gerund and pres. pple. of *glisser* to slide.] A slurring or sliding effect produced by a musical instrument; = PORTAMENTO.

1873 H. C. BANISTER *Music* 240 *Glissando*, gliding; applied to the playing of several notes successively, on the Pianoforte, by the same finger, sliding from one to the other. **1876** STAINER & BARRETT *Dict. Mus. Terms* (1898) 202/2 *Glissando*.., (1) playing a rapid passage in pianoforte music, by sliding the tips of the fingers along the keys instead of striking each note with a separate finger. (2) A rapid slur in violin playing. **1924** *Living Age* 18 Oct. 170/1 The trombone whose glissandos are becoming a favorite. *Ibid.*, A whole special technique of the violin..employing..the very slowest of glissandos. *Ibid.* 172/2 A combination of glissando and vibrato techniques. **1926** WHITEMAN & MCBRIDE *Jazz* ix. 202 The glissando is one of the chief embellishments of jazz. **1931** G. JACOB *Orchestral Technique* viii. 76 Harp glissandos are frequently used. **1939** *Scrutiny* VII. IV. 398 The vocal descriptions (by means of leaps of major sevenths, quarter tones, shouts, croaks and glissandi) of hail and lightning in *Soliloquy* are open to the same criticism. **1958** J. ALDAM in P. Gammond *Duke Ellington* III. 200 One of the greatest New Orleans clarinettists..he [*sc.* Barney Bigard] plays with a warm, vocalized tone, full of inflections and long glissandi. **1970** R. SMITH BRINDLE *Contemp. Percussion* vi. 32 Sometimes glissandos are written out in full, but it is much more usual to indicate the first and last notes played, and connect them by a straight or wavy line.

glissant (ˈglɪsənt), *a. Her.* [a. F. *glissant*, pr. pple of *glisser* to glide.] = GLIDING *ppl. a.* 1 b.

1868 [see GLIDING *ppl. a.*].

‖**glissé** (glise). *Ballet.* [F., pa. pple. of *glisser* to slide.] A sliding step in which the flat of the foot is often used; also *pas glissé*. Cf. GLISSADE 2.

1913 C. D'ALBERT *Dancing* 78 *Glissades Glissés.* These steps are used both in stage and ballroom movements. The foot can glide in any direction. By the term *pas glissé* is understood a step sideways and a gliding of the other foot. Temps glissé is made by raising on both feet, fall back on one foot and glide the other in any direction. **1953** E. TAYLOR *Sleeping Beauty* vi. 116 She then did a little glissé.

glissen, obs. form of GLISTEN *v.*

glissette (glɪˈsɛt). *Math.* [as if a. F. **glissette* (after *roulette*), f. *glisser* to slide.] (See quot. 1870.)

1870 W. H. BESANT *Notes on Roulettes & Glissettes* Pref., I have ventured to introduce, and employ, the word Glissette, as being co-expressive with Roulette. *Ibid.* 33 Glissettes are the curves traced out by points, or enveloped by curves, carried by a curve, which is made to slide between given points or given curves. **1882** MINCHIN *Unipl. Kinemat.* 104 The locus of a point *P* carried in this way is properly called a Glissette.

glisson, obs. form of GLISTEN *v.*

glist (glɪst), *sb. rare* (? *dial.*) [f. the vb.]

1. A gleam, glistening.

1864 J. MILLER *Songs Sierras* (1872) 196 Shadows that shroud the to-morrow, Glists from the life that's within. **1894** HALL CAINE *Manxman* v. xxii. 351 The scars of the turf were still unhealed and the glist of the spade was on the grass.

2. An old name for MICA.

1715 THORESBY *Leeds* 467 A red Daze or small Glist. **1728** NICHOLLS in *Phil. Trans.* XXXV. 407 A pseudometallick Substance, by the Miners term'd Glist. **1776** PRYCE *Min. Cornub.* 321 *Glist*, a shining black or brown Mineral of an iron cast, somewhat like Cockle.

glist (glɪst), *v.* Now only *Sc.* [Early ME. in pr. pple. *glistinde*, perh. reduced from *glistninde*: see GLISTEN *v.*] *intr.* To glisten. Hence **ˈglisting** *ppl. a.*

a **1225** *St. Marher.* 9 Wið þæt ha sehen þæt unselhðe glistinde as hit ouerguld were. *a* **1225** *Leg. Kath.* 838 þe glistinde wordes þæt beoð in ower bokes (þe beoð wiðuten godleic & empti wiðinnen). **1719** *Hardy Knute* in Maidment *Scot. Ballads & Songs* (1868) I. 13 Her girdle shawed her Middle gimp, And gowden glist her Hair.

glisten (ˈglɪs(ə)n), *sb.* [f. the vb.] Glitter; sparkle.

1840 S. BAMFORD *Life of Radical* xx. 133 Away it went i' th' glizzen an' th' thunner-din, o'er th' moor. **1853** C. BRONTË *Villette* xiv, The sight of a piece of gold would bring into her eyes a green glisten, singular to witness. **1855** TENNYSON *Daisy* 35 Oft we saw the glisten Of ice, far up on a mountain head. **1880** HOWELLS *Undisc. Country* xx. 309 His vision was full of the sunny glisten of meadows. **1897** *Westm. Gaz.* 30 Dec. 3/1 The lace skirt..softens..the glisten of the satin.

Hence **ˈglistenless** *a.*, without glisten.

1854 MARION HARLAND *Alone* xi, The golden trumpet was glistenless as the rest, and the stars only kept guard over the slumbering city.

glisten (ˈglɪs(ə)n), *v.* Forms: 1 glis-, glysnian, 3 glisnien, glistnen, 4 glis-, glysnen, -ien, glystnen, 4–5 gles(s)en, glisson, 5–8 glissen, (5 glyssen, -on, -yn), 9 *dial.* glizzen, 4– glisten. [OE. *glisnian*, f. the root of GLISE *v.*: see -EN⁵.] *intr.* To shine with a fitful twinkling light; to glitter; to sparkle with light. *lit.* and *fig.*

c **1000** *Runic Poem* 30 (Gr.) He glisnað glæshluttur. *c* **1000** in Cockayne *Shrine* 149 Se engel hæfde tweȝen beaȝas on hys handa ða glysnodon hwylum swa rosan blosman. *a* **1225** *St. Marher.* 9 Glistnede as gleam deð. *c* **1275** LAY. 21725 Scealdes þar glissenede. **13..** *E.E. Allit. P.* A. 1017 Masporye as glas þat glysnande schon. *c* **1400** *Rowland & O.* 1365 His armours glyssenede full bryhte. *a* **1660** HAMMOND *Serm.* xiv. Wks. 1683 IV. 660 How unpolish't soever this Diamond be, yet if it do but glissen, 'tis too pretious to be cast away. **1741–2** RICHARDSON *Pamela* (J.), The ladies eyes glistened with pleasure. **1770** GOLDSM. *Des. Vill.* 236 While broken tea-cups..Ranged o'er the chimney, glisten'd in a row. **1802** PALEY *Nat. Theol.* xxi. (ed. 2) 400 These masses would shine, indeed, and glisten, but it would be in the dark. **1840** BAMFORD *Life of Radical* xx. 133 It wur as fair a gowden yallo as ever glizzent. **1865** GEIKIE *Scen. & Geol. Scot.* viii. 214 Here and there a mass glistens white as if it were snow. **1870** YEATS *Nat. Hist. Comm.* 58 The Irish rivers glisten with salmon.

fig. **1763** C. JOHNSTON *Reverie* II. 179 Vanity glissened through her grief. **1815** *Apollo's Choice* II. ii, Ah, gentle swain, I prythee listen, Let pity in thine eye-balls glisten. **1866** G. MACDONALD *Ann. Q. Neighb.* x, Very tall and very stately, he was talking now to this old man, now to that young woman, and every face glistened towards which he turned.

Hence **ˈglistener** *slang*, a gold coin (cf. *shiner*).

1818 MOORE *Fudge Fam. Paris* vi. 45 Gemmen, who touched the Treasury glisteners, Like us, for being trusty listeners.

glistening (ˈglɪs(ə)nɪŋ), *vbl. sb.* [See -ING¹.]

1. The action of the vb. GLISTEN; glitter, sparkle.

1398 TREVISA *Barth. De P.R.* II. ix. (1495) 37 He callyth the shynyng the illumynacion and glisnynge. **1753** J. BARTLET *Gentl. Farriery* xv. 143 Rub the quicksilver till no glistening appears. **1791** MAD. D'ARBLAY *Diary* July, The Princess spoke feelings I could not expect, by the immediate glistening of her soft eyes. **1822–34** *Good's Study Med.* (ed. 4) II. 417 There was a muddy glistening in her eyes which I had seen described. **1860** TYNDALL *Glac.* I. v. 40 On the walls a glistening was here and there observable. **1873** T. W. HIGGINSON *Oldport Days* iv. 91 Jelly-fishes..shot through and through in the sun-light with all manner of blue and golden glistenings.

2. Something that causes to glisten.

1631 *Celestina* VI. 78 Clothing them [their faces] with divers colours, glissenings, paintings, unctions. *a* **1641** SUCKLING *Farewell to Love* vii. (1648) 48 The Gum and glistning, which with art And studi'd method, in each part Hangs down the heart, Looks (just) as if, that day Snailes there had crawl'd the Hay.

glistening (ˈglɪs(ə)nɪŋ), *ppl. a.* [f. GLISTEN *v.* + -ING².] That glistens. *lit.* and *fig.*

1388 WYCLIF *Hab.* iii. 11 In the liȝt of thin arrowis thei schulen go, in the schynyng of thi spere glisnynge. *a* **1400–50** *Alexander* 3015 His ginge & all his garysons in glyssynand wedis, Gaes him on to granton & graithes þare his tentis. **1549** COVERDALE, etc. *Erasm. Par. Acts* x. 30 A certayne man..stoode visible before me, in a glystenyng garment. **1726–46** THOMSON *Winter* 262 The bleating kind Eye the bleak heaven, and next the glistening earth, With looks of dumb despair. **1789** E. DARWIN *Bot. Gard.* II. (1791) 133 The tuneful Goddess on the glowing sky Fix'd in mute extacy her glistening eye. **1849** RUSKIN *Sev. Lamps* ii. §1. 28 But it is the glistening and softly spoken lie..that [etc.]. **1870** BRYANT *Iliad* II. XIV. 63 A bright golden cloud Gathered, and shed its drops of glistening dew.

Hence **ˈglisteningly** *adv.*, in a glistening manner.

1611 COTGR., *Luisantemente*,..glisteningly. **1873** BROWNING *Red Cott. Nt.-cap* 1060 Glisteningly beneath the Maynight moon. Herbage and floral coverture bedeck Yon splintered mass.

glister (ˈglɪstə(r)), *sb.* [f. the vb.]

1. A glistering; a bright light, brilliance, lustre.

1535 COVERDALE *Ezek.* i. 10 The fyre gaue a glistre, and out off the fyre there wente lighteninge. *c* **1590** GREENE *Fr. Bacon* xi. 33 Ere the morning starre Sends out his glorious glister on the North. **1647** H. MORE *Insomn. Philos.* ix. *Philos. Poems* 325 Half therefore just of this dark Orb was dight With goodly glistre and fair golden rayes. **1841**

THACKERAY *Men & Pictures* 99 Fair was the sight..and bright the river's glister. **1884** C. E. CRADDOCK *In Tennessee Mts.* viii. 315 She caught a glimpse of..the glister of a great lucent, tremulous star.

fig. a **1572** KNOX *Hist. Ref.* I. Wks. 1846 I. 292 The glister of the proffeit, that was judged heirof to have ensewed to Scotishmen at the first sight blynded mony menis eyis. a **1659** BP. BROWNRIG *Serm.* (1674) I. iv. 48 Outward Glister and Pomp. **1718** *Entertainer* xxii. 146 'Tis a World of Glister that we live in. **1759** HUME *Hist. Eng.* (1806) III. App. 814 The false glister catches the eye, and leaves no room..for the durable beauties of solid sense and lively passion.

2. *Min.* = GLIST *sb.* 2.

1722 *Phil. Trans.* (Lowe's Abridgem.) 568 *Glister*, blood red and black.

Hence **'glistery** *a. rare* [-Y[1]], full of glister.

1806 STRUTHERS *House Mourning* I. Wks. 1850 I. 77 His hope, the self-deceiver's transient gleam That, glistery, glimmers on the dazzled eye.

glister ('glɪstə(r)), *v. arch.* and *dial.* Forms: 4 **glystre**, 4–6 **glistre**, (5 **glistere**), 4–7 **glyster**, 4– **glister**. [Corresponds to MLG. *glistern*, MDu., Du. *glisteren*; f. root *glis- (see GLISE *v.*) + suffixes *-t-* and -ER[5].] *intr.* To sparkle; to glitter; to be brilliant.

The word is obsolete in ordinary colloq. use (though preserved in dialects); by recent writers employed with reminiscence of Shaks. or the Bible in the literal sense only.

c **1380** *Sir Ferumb.* 4438 Ys browes were boþe rowe and grete..ys eȝene depe, & glystryd as þe glede. **1390** GOWER *Conf.* II. 252 The water glistred over all. a **1420** HOCCLEVE *De Reg. Princ.* (Roxb.) 150 A croked hors never the better is entecchede Althoughe his bridelle glistre of golde & shyne. **1514** BARCLAY *Cyt. & Uplondyshm.* (Percy Soc.) p. lxx, All the walles within of fynest golde..Glistering as bright as Phoebus orient. **1535** COVERDALE 4 (2) *Esdras* x. 25 Hir face dyd shyne & glyster. **1542** BECON *Potation Lent* B iij b, The vnfruytfull fygge tree glystereth it neuer so pleasantly with grene leaues, shall be cursed & commytted vnto hell fyre. **1670–98** LASSELS *Voy. Italy* II. 159 When the sun shines upon it, you may see it glister two miles off. **1725** SWIFT *Wood's Petition* Wks. 1755 IV. I. 284 Buy up my half-pence so fine..Observe how they glister and shine. **1775** ADAIR *Amer. Ind.* 236 On the tops of several of these mountains, I have observed tufts of grass deeply tinctured by the mineral exhalations from the earth; and on the sides, they glistered from the same cause. **1808** SCOTT *Marm.* II. xxi, It did a ghastly contrast bear To those bright ringlets glistering fair. **1857–8** SEARS *Athan.* vi. 52 Sandy plains which burn and glister under an orient sun. **1870–74** J. THOMSON *City of Dreadf. Nt.* I. iv, Waste marshes shine and glister to the moon. **1877** *N.W. Linc. Gloss.*, *Glister*, to glisten.

fig. **1535** COVERDALE *Dan.* xii. 3 The wyse..shal glister as the shyninge of heauen. **1560** BECON *Catech.* Wks. 1564 I. 294 The godles and heathenishe people..outwardly glistered wyth goodly vertues. **1579** GOSSON *Sch. Abuse* (Arb.) 53 Thunder in words and glister in works. **1611** SHAKS. *Wint. T.* III. ii. 171 How he glisters Through my Rust? a **1661** FULLER *Worthies* (1840) II. 45 He went to Oxford where for some years he glistered in the oratoric and poetic sphere. **1685** *Gracian's Courtiers Orac.* 37 That Superiority glisters in all sorts of people, but much more in great men.

b. *Proverb.* (Cf. GLITTER *v.* 1 b.)

(In mod. use 'glitters' is commonly substituted for *glisters.*)

1553 BECON *Reliques of Rome* (1563) 207 All is not golde that glistereth. **1596** SHAKS. *Merch. V.* II. vii. 65. **1649** MILTON *Eikon.* viii. (1851) 395 They think all is gold of pietie that doth but glister with a shew of Zeale. **1650** HUBBERT *Pill Formality* 36 Seriously trie before we choose, lest we take all for gold that glisters. a **1771** GRAY *Death Fav. Cat.* vii, Not all that tempts your wand'ring eyes..is lawful prize..Nor all that glisters, gold. **1802** CANNING *Poet. Wks.* (1827) 44.

†**c.** quasi-*trans.* To send *forth* with glitter.

a **1586** SIDNEY *Arcadia* III. (1590) 281 With eies which glistered forth beames of disdaine.

Hence †**'glisterer**, one who glisters, a showy person.

1628 EARLE *Microcosm., Downe-right Scholler* (Arb.) 42 Hee shall out ballance those glisterers as far as a solid substance do's a feather, or Gold Gold-lace.

glister, obs. or dial. f. CLYSTER.

glistering ('glɪstərɪŋ), *vbl. sb.* [See -ING[1].] The action of the vb. GLISTER; brilliance, glitter.

c **1460** *Emare* 100 For glysteryng of the ryche ston Redy syght had he non. **1579–80** NORTH *Plutarch* (1656) 395 The glistering of their..Harnesse, so richly trimmed and set forth with Gold and Silver. **1603** DEKKER *Wonderfull Yeare* A iij, That worship Glow-wormes (instead of the Sun) because of a little false glistering. **1706** STANHOPE *Paraphr.* III. 375 There is indeed a Glistering but no Intrinsick Value in them.

'glistering, *ppl. a.* [See -ING[2].] That glisters.

1398 TREVISA *Barth. De P.R.* VIII. xxix. (1495) 342 Shynynge comyth to the vtter partyes of a glysteryng body. c **1460** *Emare* 350 A boot he fond by the brym, And a glysteryng, thyng theryn. **1535** COVERDALE *Job* xx. 25 A glisteringe [so also **1611**] swearde. **1597** A. M. tr. *Guillemeau's Fr. Chirurg.* 31 b/2 Venomous [horse-leeches] have ther bodye shininge like vnto glistering wormes. **1611** BIBLE *Luke* ix. 29 His raiment was white and glistering. a **1716** SOUTH *Serm.* (1737) IV. ii. 80 This glistring person so much admired by them is now a preparing for his ruin, and fatting for the slaughters of eternity. **1718** LADY M. W. MONTAGU *Verses Chiosk Brit. Pal., Pera* 19 The barren Meads no longer yield Delight, By glistring Snows made painful to the Sight. **1849** M. ARNOLD *Poems, New Sirens* 107 If the glistering wings of morning On the noon shook their dew. **1854** HAWTHORNE *Eng. Note-Bks.* (1879) II. 120 A wide waste of glistering sands.

Hence **'glisteringly** *adv.*, in a glistering manner.

1587 TURBERV. *Trag. T.* etc. (1837) 323 All is not gold that glistringly appeere. **1649** J. H. *Motion to Parl. Adv. Learn.* 22 This light that breaks so brightly and glistringly in. **1814** CARY *Dante, Parad.* xvii. 118 The brightness..first shone glisteringly.

fig. **1843** E. JONES *Sens. & Event* 4 He stops, and glisteringly rides His laughter forth again.

glit(te, obs. form of GLEET *sb.*

glitch (glɪtʃ). *slang.* [Etym. unknown.] **a.** A surge of current or a spurious electrical signal (see quots.); also, in extended use, a sudden short-lived irregularity in behaviour. **b.** *Astronauts' slang.* A hitch or snag; a malfunction.

1962 J. GLENN in *Into Orbit* 86 Another term we adopted to describe some of our problems was 'glitch'. Literally, a glitch is a spike or change in voltage in an electrical circuit which takes place when the circuit suddenly has a new load put on it... A glitch..is such a minute change in voltage that no fuse could protect against it. *Ibid.* 245 *Glitch*, a momentary change in voltage in an electrical circuit; (*slang* —a hitch). **1962** R. F. GRAF *Mod. Dict. Electronics* (1963) 124 *Glitch*, low-frequency interference in a television picture. It is seen as a narrow bar moving vertically. **1969** *Product Engineering* 27 Jan. 15/3 It generated digital transients that caused the abort guidance to send false signals. Phillips said it took an inordinately long time to find this glitch. **1969** *Funk & Wagnalls Dict. Electronics* 70 *Glitch*, a stray current or signal, usually one that interferes in some way with the functioning of a system. **1969** *Daily Tel.* 15 Nov. 1/3 [Apollo moon flight] Thinking back to when we had our big glitch, I remember seeing it get light outside the window after we were in the clouds, and I'm pretty sure we got hit by lightning. **1971** *Nature: Physical Sci.* 14 June 146/2 Two pulsars have exhibited a sudden increase in frequency (glitch), after which the usual slowing down has been resumed.

glitter ('glɪtə(r)), *sb.*[1] [f. the vb.]

1. Glittering or sparkling light; brightness, brilliance, lustre, splendour. See also AGLITTER *adv.*

1602 MARSTON *Antonio's Rev.* I. ii, Tinsill glitter, or rich purfled robes..Are not the true adornements of a wife. **1667** MILTON *P.L.* x. 452 With what permissive glory since his fall Was left him, or false glitter. **1788** V. KNOX *Wint. Even.* (1790) II. ii. 15 A boldness of utterance and assertion, which often sets off base metal with the glitter of gold. **1852** MRS. STOWE *Uncle Tom's C.* xxxix, Cassy, with a keen, sneering glitter in her eyes, stood looking at him. **1856** KANE *Arct. Expl.* I. xv. 169 A water-pool, in which my lantern made the glitter. **1882** MISS BRADDON *Mt. Royal* III. vi. 104 Louis Quinze coat, all a glitter with cut-steel. **1898** *Daily News* 22 Jan. 6/5 Glitter is the key-note of smart outdoor dress at the moment.

fig. **1863** W. PHILLIPS *Speech* xi. 255 The glitter of whose fame makes doubtful acts look heroic. **1868** MILMAN *St. Paul's* vii. 152 The glitter of miracles which attested his [S. Erkenwald's] virtues. **1874** L. STEPHEN *Hours in Library* (1892) II. iii. 91 He seems to have tired of the glitter of Junius.

2. App. a mistake for GUTTER.

1727–51 CHAMBERS *Cycl.* s.v. *Head*, The part that bears the antlers, royals, and tops, is called the *beam*, and the little streaks therein are *glitters.* **1774** GOLDSM. *Nat. Hist.* III. v. 114.

3. Special Comb. **glitter rock**, a variety of rock music played by performers dressed flamboyantly in glittering costumes and make-up; cf. *glam rock* s.v. GLAM.

1972 *New Musical Express* 14 Oct. 12 (*heading*) Carly Simon: This Jaggeresque lady antidote to glitter rock. **1973** *Newsweek* 28 May 65/2 Alice [Cooper] has come a long way —from star of his high-school cross-country team to star of that garish division of the rock world known variously as glitter-rock, deca- (for decadent) rock or punk rock. Its hallmarks are chaos and confusion—chaotic sounds, confusion of logic and sexual identity. **1980** J. COLLIS *Rock Primer* 300 Rock's social dimension has been reduced to grotesques and parodies:..the flirting with sexual doubts which 'glitter-rock' exploited.

glitter, *sb.*[2] *dial.* = GLIDDER *sb.*

1863 [see GLIDDER *sb.*]. **1882** J. HARDY in *Proc. Berw. Nat. Club* IX. 480 A craggy and glitter-faced hill.

Hence **'glitterless** *a.*, devoid of glitter; †**'glitterous** *a.* = next; **'glittery** *a.*, full of glitter.

1596 R. L[INCHE] *Diella* (1877) 50 Her hayre of such corruscant glitterous shine, as are the smallest streames of hottest sunne. **1757** tr. *Henckel's Pyritol.* vii. 113 The white metals..usually..acquire a glittery..form. **1880** BIRDWOOD *Ind. Art* II. 10 If Indian jewelry should become mechanical, and hard, and glittery, it will at once cease to be artistic. **1882** SHARP *Rossetti* ii. 55 The sea is a white blank, waveless, glitterless.

glitter ('glɪtə(r)), *v.* Forms: 4–5 **gliter**, 4–6 **gleter**, **glyter**, 6 **glittre**, 4– **glitter**. [Not recorded in OE.; ME. *gliteren* is prob. a. ON. *glitra* = MHG., mod.Ger. *glitzern*; a frequentative formation (see -ER[5]) from the Teut. root **glīt-* in OS. *glîtan* str. vb., OHG. *glîzan* (mod.Ger. *gleiszen*) to shine, ON. *glit* brightness, *glita* to shine, Goth. *glitmunjan* to shine; the pre-Teut. root **ghleid-*, *ghlid-* seems to occur in Gr. χλιδή luxury.]

1. *intr.* To shine with a brilliant but broken and tremulous light; to emit bright fitful flashes of light; to gleam, sparkle.

13.. *Gaw. & Gr. Knt.* 604 Golde naylez, þat al glytered & glent as glem of þe sunne. a **1400–50** *Alexander* 4957 Al glitered þe ground for glori of his wedis. c **1475** *Rauf Coilȝear* 669 Gowlis glitterand full gay, glemand in grene. a **1533** LD. BERNERS *Huon* liii. 181 Many helmes gletred agaynst the sonne. **1596** SPENSER *F.Q.* IV. xi. 27 The waves glittering like Christal glas. **1675** TRAHERNE *Chr. Ethics* xi. 162 The stars..glitter in their motions only to serve us. **1755** GRAY *Progr. Poesy* III. iii, Before his infant eyes would run Such forms, as glitter in the muse's ray. **1781** COWPER *Hope* 42 Earth glitters with the drops the night distils. **1817** MOORE *Lalla R.* (ed. 2) 220 A gem from Persia's plunder'd mines, Shall glitter on thy Shrine of Shrines. **1860** KINGSLEY *Misc.* II. 17 As their wings glittered in the light they looked like flakes of snow. **1863** GEO. ELIOT *Romola* I. xx, She looked up at him with trusting eyes, that still glittered with tears.

b. *Proverb.* (Cf. GLISTER *v.* b.)

1638 DRUMM. OF HAWTH. *Biblioth. Edinb. Lectori* Wks. (1711) 222 All is not Gold which glittereth. **1784** JOHNSON 2 Oct. in *Boswell* (ed. 2), All is not gold that glitters, as we have been often told.

2. *fig.*; esp. of persons: To make a brilliant appearance or display; to be showy or splendid (in dress, etc.).

1548 UDALL, etc. *Erasm. Par. Luke* ii. 48–52 She perceiued and founde a certain power of the godhed to glittre and shewe foorth in hym. **1683** KENNETT tr. *Erasm. on Folly* 48 Nature glitters most in her own plain homely garb. **1728** T. SHERIDAN *Persius* Prol. 5 If the Hope of Money does but once glitter in their Thoughts. **1751** JOHNSON *Rambler* No. 109 ¶4 They had both..glittered in playhouses. **1766** FORDYCE *Serm. Yng. Wom.* (1767) I. ii. 75 Our gay assemblies..would glitter less. **1790** BURKE *Fr. Rev.* (ed. 2) 112, I saw her [the queen of France]..glittering like the morning star. **1841–4** EMERSON *Ess., Prudence* Wks. (Bohn) I. 97 Talent which..glitters to-day, that it may dine and sleep well to-morrow. **1879** MCCARTHY *Own Times* II. xxix. 362 Every chapter glittered with vivid and highly coloured description.

glitterance ('glɪtərəns). *rare.* [f. GLITTER *v.* + -ANCE.] Glittering appearance.

1801 SOUTHEY *Thalaba* XII. ii, Till from the glitterance of the sunny main He turn'd his aching eyes. **1814** CARY *Dante, Purgat.* xxix. 136 A sword, whose glitterance and keen edge..Appall'd me. **1831** *Blackw. Mag.* XXX. 984 The glitterance of the frost-woven snows.

glitterati (glɪtə'rɑːtiː), *sb. pl. slang* (orig. *U.S.*). [Punningly f. GLITTER *sb.*[1] (GLITTERING *ppl. a.*, etc.) + *-ati*, as in LITERATI *sb. pl.*] The celebrities or 'glittering' stars of fashionable society, or of the literary and show-business world. Also *transf.*

1956 *Time* 12 Mar. 124/3 Bobbing and weaving about the premises are a passel of New York glitterati. There is a highbrow editor of a popular magazine who is keen on starting a new literary journal [etc.]. **1978** *N.Y. Times Mag.* 23 July 23/2 So say the formerly beautiful people, once the jet set, now called the glitterati, which appears to be a combination of literati, or illuminati, with a glittering generality. **1982** *Radio Three Mag.* Dec. 47/1 But they too appeared apprehensive about the impact on the generous but clear warmth of the empty hall of those 2,812 black tie, bejewelled glitterati. **1984** *Times* 14 Mar. 14/5 One member of the glitterati..offered to send her own hairdresser to Billie's hotel.

glitterer ('glɪtərə(r)). [f. GLITTER *v.* + -ER[1].] One who or that which glitters.

1823 BYRON *Juan* XIV. lvii, Fondly the wheeling fire-flies flew around her, Those little glitterers of the London night. **1945** G. MILLAR *Maquis* i. 2 At the Berkeley, among the glitterers that were so unlike the major.

glittering ('glɪtərɪŋ), *vbl. sb.* [f. GLITTER *v.* + -ING[1].] The action of the vb. GLITTER.

1567 MAPLET *Gr. Forest* 3 b, To the intent that..this maner might shew some glittring. **1607** J. DAVIES *Summa Totalis* E iv, Which nought comes nere for Clouds and Glitterings. **1635–56** COWLEY *Davideis* II. 12 So near a storm wise David would not stay, Nor trust the glittering of a faithless Day. **1678** DRYDEN *All for Love* Pref. b 3 If a little glittering in discourse has pass'd them on us for witty men, where was the necessity of undeceiving the World?

†**b.** *concr.* Something that glitters. *Obs.*

1670 EACHARD *Cont. Clergy* 46 They count all discourses empty, dull, and cloudy, unless bespangl'd with these glitterings. c **1698** LOCKE *Cond. Underst.* Introd. §3 Every Man carries about with him a Touchstone, if he will make use of it to distinguish substantial Gold from superficial Glitterings.

'glittering, *ppl. a.* [f. GLITTER *v.* + -ING[2].]

1. That glitters. *lit.* and *fig.*

13.. *Seuyn Sages* (W.) 3335 With gerlandes & with gleterand thing Was sho made out of knawing. a **1400–50** *Alexander* 3346 Þe sext of gletirand gold gayle was forgid. a **1550** *Christis Kirk Gr.* xviii, Her glitterand hair that wes full gowdin, Sa hard in lufe him laist. a **1586** SIDNEY *Arcadia* I. (1598) 81 O glittring miseries of man. **1601** HOLLAND *Pliny* II. 534 Glorious and glittering painters. **1617** F. MORYSON *Itin.* III. 171 It is proverbially said, that the..Neopolitans are glittering and sumptuous. a **1700** SOAME & DRYDEN *Boileau's Art Poetry* I. 44 Let Italians be Vain Authors of false glitt'ring Poetry. **1764** GOLDSM. *Trav.* 45 Ye glittering towns, with wealth and splendour crown'd. **1818** HAZLITT *Eng. Poets* vii. (1870) 185 The thistle's glittering down. **1826** DISRAELI *Viv. Grey* IV. v, His glittering youth was gone and wasted. **1874** L. STEPHEN *Hours in Library* (1892) II. iv. 110 The satire is..more distantly allied to poetical unction than to glittering rhetoric.

2. *glittering generality* (orig. *U.S.*), a platitude or cliché; used (esp. in *pl.*) of superficially convincing but empty phrases characteristic of the language of politicians, advertisements, etc.

1849 *Providence* (Rhode Island) *Jrnl.* 14 Dec. 2/6 We fear that the glittering generalities of the speaker have left an impression more delightful than permanent. **1892** W. S. Walsh *Handy-bk. Lit. Curiosities* 416 *Glittering generalities*, ..the sounding but uncompromising resolutions which make up the greater part of the platforms of political parties in the United States. **1958** R. Brown *Words & Things* ix. 339 The works of Christ, Buddha, Kierkegaard, and Laotse are filled with emotional expressions and glittering generalities. **1981** *N.Y. Times* 12 Mar. A22/6 It is to be hoped that Mrs. Shriver's book will avoid glittering generalities and describe concretely how families' participation in their children's lives can be made into a positive force. **1986** *Summary World Broadcasts: Soviet Union* (B.B.C.) 4 Sept. A1/2 National interest is a slogan, a ..glittering generality, a cliche, behind which a whole lot of bad designs..have hidden themselves throughout history.

Hence **'glitteringly** *adv.*, in a glittering manner.

1611 Cotgr., *Luisantement*,..glitteringly. **1647** H. More *Song of Soul* II. ii. II. xvi, The nimble phantasie..more glitteringly Displayes her spreaden forms. **1820** Moir in *Blackw. Mag.* VII. 627 Pendant and twining glitteringly, Like amethysts of purple dye. **1887** *Pall Mall G.* 12 Nov. 1/2 Briskly and glitteringly carriage after carriage rolls by.

glitterwax ('glɪtəwæks). [f. glitter *v.* + wax *sb.*[1]] A kind of coloured modelling-wax.

1944 *Horizon* May 307 They give their children glitter-wax or plasticine to play with. **1967** M. Drabble *Jerusalem the Golden* vi. 149 Clelia, who used as a child to have a passion for modelling things out of an obsolete substance known as Glitterwax.

glittie, Sc. var. gleety *a.*

glittous, (-is, -us): see gleetous.

glitzy ('glɪtsɪ), *a. slang* (orig. and chiefly *N. Amer.*). [Prob. f. G. *glitzern* to glitter (perh. via Yiddish); cf. G. *glitzerig* glittering: see -y[1].] Characterized by glitter or extravagant show; ostentatious, glamorous; hence, tawdry, gaudy; glitteringly spectacular, but in poor taste. Cf. glittering *ppl. a.* 2, glitterati *sb. pl.*

1966 *N.Y. Times* 31 Aug. 66/4 Advertising will stress that Devil Shake is 'glitzy'. This claim will be hard to deny, at least until someone defines the word. **1968** *Britannica Bk. of Year* 745/1 John Kander's music,..Patricia Zipprodt's glitzy-tawdry costumes, and Ronald Field's wittily obscene choreography were fused..into a corrosively brilliant symbol of human depravity. **1975** *New Yorker* 5 May 138/2 This number, like the ballet as a whole, is much too restless and glitzy. **1976** *Globe & Mail* (Toronto) 22 Nov. 1/4 The restaurants of the future..will..be big gala places with entertainment and booze-ups and big bills...The Cossacks has gone glitzy. **1977** *Sounds* 1 Jan. 5/3 The five man band play havoc-wreaking rock 'n' roll, much in the tacky, glitzy style of lamented British Bands such as Spearhead and the Heavy Metal Kids. **1979** *Maclean's Mag.* 28 May 51/1 But in a forum ringing with the clack of easy typewriters and the back-thumping of glitzy cynics, words like style, art, commitment are booed offstage. **1983** E. Leonard *LaBrava* (1985) i. 7 But look at the dressing room, all the glitzy crap, the tinfoil cheapness. **1985** *Listener* 21 Mar. 27/1 The Oscars are the high point of the Western film industry's year —a glitzy, vulgar affirmation that they're getting things right.

Hence [as back-formation] **glitz**, an extravagant but superficial display; showiness, ostentation, esp. show-business glamour or sparkle.

1977 *New Republic* 19 Feb. 21/2 Stoppard's plays have been marked by undergraduate cleverness and glitz and ultimate sterility. **1977** *Time* 4 July 52/2 Her style is often derivative of Tom Wolfe and Joan Didion, but Babitz has the one indispensable quality for her kind of work: true glitz. **1983** *Times Lit. Suppl.* 25 Feb. 200/1 One American reviewer swooned over *Mistral's Daughter*, Judith Krantz's latest bundle of glitz. **1985** *Toronto Life* Sept. 41/3 There was too much Third-World esoterica and not enough Hollywood glitz.

gload, obs. pa. t. of glide.

†**gloak**. *slang. Obs.* Also gloach. [Of unknown origin; cf. bloke.] A man, fellow, 'cove'. (See also buzz-gloak.)

1795 Potter *Dict. Cant.*, *Gloak*, a man. *High Tober gloak*, a highwayman well dressed and mounted. **1812** J. H. Vaux *Flash Dict.*, *Gloak*, synonymous with Gill. **1821** Haggart *Life* 48, I said 'I will punsh outsides with your nibs, but not with that gloach'. **1834** W. H. Ainsworth *Rookwood* III. v, The prince of the high-toby gloaks.

gloam (gləʊm), *sb. rare.* [Back-formation from gloaming.] Twilight, gloaming.

a **1821** Keats *La Belle Dame sans merci* x, I saw their starved lips in the gloam, With horrid warning gaped wide. **1881** Rossetti *Ball. & Sonnets* 85 And blithe is Honfleur's echoing gloam When mothers call the children home.

gloam (gləʊm), *v.* Chiefly *Sc.* [f. as prec.] *intr.* To darken, become dusk. Also *to be gloamed*: to have grown dusk.

1819 Rennie *St. Patrick* I. xi. 166 By this time, it was turn't gayan gloam't. **1825–80** Jamieson, *It glooms*, twilight comes on, Aberd. **1847** *Tait's Mag.* XIV. 176 When purple evening gloameth. **1871** W. Alexander *Johnny Gibb* xl. (1873) 223 An' ye cudna expeck fowk hame fae a mairriage afore it wer weel gloam't. **1876** *Mid Yorksh. Gloss.* s.v., I must be going homewards before it glooms.

gloaming ('gləʊmɪŋ). Forms: 1 glómung, (æfen-)glommung, 5 glomyng, 5–7 gloming, 8– gloaming. [repr. OE. *glómung* str. fem., f. (on the analogy of *æfning* evening) *glóm* twilight, prob. f. the Teut. root **glô-* (see glow); the etymological sense would thus seem to be the 'glow' of sunset or sunrise (cf. gloom *sb.*[2]), whence the passage to the recorded sense is not difficult.

The vowel of the mod. *gloaming* is anomalous, as OE. *glómung* should normally become *glooming*. The explanation probably is that the *ó* was shortened in the compound *æfen-glommung* (as the spelling seems to show was actually the case), and that from this compound there was evolved a new sb. *glŏmung*, which by normal phonetic development became ME. *glǭming*, mod.E. *gloaming*. In the literary language the word is a comparatively recent adoption from Scottish writers; but it is found in the dialect of Mid. Yorks.]

1. a. Evening twilight.

c **1000** Ælfric *Gloss.* in Wr.-Wülcker 117/7 *Crepusculum*, glomung. *c* **1000** *Latin Hymns Ags. Ch.* (Surtees 1851) 16 *Crepusculum mens nesciat*, æfen glommunge mod nyte. *c* **1425** Wyntoun *Cron.* IV. vii. 827 Fra the glomyng off the nycht. **1536** Bellenden *Cron. Scot.* (1821) II. 115 He.. efter supper, past furth in the gloming. *c* **1610** in Pitcairn *Crim. Trials* III. 3 This fell furth in the gloming. **1786** Burns *Twa Dogs* 232 By this, the sun was out of sight, An' darker gloaming brought the night. *c* **1800** Hogg *Song.* 'Tween the gloaming and the mirk, When the kye comes hame. **1807** Byron *Elegy Newstead Abbey* ix, Soon as the gloaming spreads her waving shade. **1830** Tennyson *Leonine Elegiacs*, Lowflowing breezes are roaming the broad valley dimmed in the gloaming. **1866** Geo. Eliot *F. Holt* 2 The happy outside passenger seated on the box from the dawn to the gloaming [etc.].

fig. **1785** Burns *Ep. to James Smith* 79 When ance life's day draws near the gloamin. **1889** Barrie *Window in Thrums* 144 The help she and Hendry needed in the gloaming of their lives.

b. Said occas. of morning twilight.

1873 Tristram *Moab* iii. 38 The sun had scarcely cast the gloaming of approaching dawn over the eastern peaks. **1894** Crockett *Raiders* 21, I rowed home in the gloaming of the morning.

c. Shade, dusky light.

1832 Motherwell *Jeanie Morrison* vii, And in the gloamin o' the wood, The throssil whusslit sweet.

2. *attrib.* (in some instances passing into *adj.*), as *gloaming-fall, -hour, -sight, -sky, starlight*; also **gloaming-shot**, (*a*) a shot in the twilight (in quot. *fig.*); (*b*) the beginning of twilight; **gloaming sight**, a front sight specially adapted for evening shooting.

1788 Picken *Poems* 176 Gin gloamin hours reek't Eben's haun. **1793** Burns *Let. to G. Thomson* Aug., I once more roved out yesterday for a gloamin-shot at the muses. **1795** —— *'Had I the wyte'* 29 At gloamin-shot it was, I wot, I lighted on the Monday. *a* **1810** Tannahill *'The Midges dances aboon the burn'* Poems (1846) 114 Beneath the golden gloaming sky, The mavis mends her lay. **1818** Scott *Rob Roy* xxi, He has a gloaming sight o' what's reasonable..a glisk and nae mair. **1821** *Blackw. Mag.* VIII. 401 A cannie hour at gloaming-fa' under the hazel bower birks. **1843** Lytton *Last Bar.* IV. v, Even I grow hungered in these cool gloaming hours. **1856** Mrs. Stowe *Dred* II. xii. 125 The gloaming starlight was just sufficient to show him that all was desolate. **1895** *Army & Navy Co-op. Soc. Price List* 15 Sept. 925/1 New gloaming sight for guns and rifles. **1907** *Yesterday's Shopping* (1969) 639 Gloaming sights for rifles. .. Specially adapted for evening sport.

gloar, var. glore to stare; dial. var. glower.

gloase, obs. form of gloze *sb.*

gloat, *sb.*[1] [f. gloat *v.*] †**1.** A side-glance; ? a furtive or sullen look. *Obs. rare.*

1645 Featly *Dippers Dipt* Ep. Ded. B, Satans watchful eye is upon it [the Gospel], and he casts an envious gloate at it. **1654** Gayton *Pleas. Notes* II. vi. 61 The Frowne, the Gloat, the Hung-lip, the Neglect, the Go-by.

2. An act of gloating; a look, feeling, or expression of triumphant satisfaction.

1899 Kipling *Stalky & Co.* 13 They spun wildly on their heels, jodelling after the accepted manner of a 'gloat'. **1921** Galsworthy *To Let* II. iii, To watch the gloat in his eye. **1927** *Bulletin* 7 Oct. 17/2 Preparing to enjoy a satisfying gloat over some of his critics. **1930** 'Hay' & King-Hall *Middle Watch* xx, She now stood regarding the Admiral's wife with a certain deliberate..insolence of expression. One might almost call it a gloat. **1970** A. Hunter *Gently with Innocents* viii. 106 He was having a gloat over his gold.. picking it up, gloating over it.

gloat, *sb.*[2] *dial.* Also 8 glout, 8–9 glut, 9 glot. [Etymology unknown.] A species of eel (see quots.). Also *gloat-eel*.

1747 Mrs. Glasse *Cookery* xxi. 163 Grigs, Shafflins and Glout. **1769** Pennant *Zool.* III. 114 There is another variety of this fish [the eel] known in the Thames by the name of Grigs, and about Oxford by that of Grigs or Gluts. **1776** Twiss *Tour Irel.* 97 Perch, salmon, pike, trout, glut-eels, silver-eels. **1883** G. C. Davies *Norfolk Broads* xxxi. 243 The 'hooking' eel or 'gloat,'—the blackish medium-sized eel taken by anglers, babbers, and on night-lines. **1895** in *E. Angl. Gloss.*, *Gloat* or *Glot*.

gloat (gləʊt), *v.* Forms: 6–7 gloate, gloit, gloyt, 7 glott, 7–9 glote, 7– gloat. [Of obscure origin, but apparently = MHG. and mod.G *glotzen* to stare, Sw. (dial.) *glotta* to peep, ON. *glotta* to grin. Prob. taken up in the 16th c. from some dialect, in which it may have been an adoption from ON.

Although common in the 17th and 18th c., the word is not in Phillips and was unknown to Johnson, who quotes the lines from Rowe (see 2 below) with the remark, 'This word I conceive to be ignorantly written for *gloar*'.

The development of sense 3 has prob. been more or less influenced by association with glut *v.*]

†**1.** *intr.* To look or gaze askance; to look with a furtive or sidelong glance. Also *to gloat it*. *Obs.*

1575 Laneham *Let.* (1871) 60 With myne eyz, az I can amorously gloit it. **1576** Gascoigne *Compl. Philomene* (Arb.) 96 Ne could he loke a side, But like the cruel catte Which gloating casteth many a glance Vpon the selly ratte. **1590** Nashe *Pasquil's Apol.* I. A iij b, Though in silence I gloate through the fingers at other matters, yet am I not carelesse of the quarrell nowe in hand. **1615** Chapman *Odyss.* XII. 150 She [Scylla]..streakes From out a ghastly whirle-poole, all her necks; Where (gloting round her rocke) to fish she falles. **1619** R. Weste *Bk. Demeanor* 33 in *Babees Bk.*, Nor let thine eyes be gloting downe, cast with a hanging looke. **1650–3** G. Daniel *Idylls* iii. 8 (Grosart) IV. 219 Purblind in Ethicks, as yᵉ Running Hare Gloats either way. **1668** R. L'Estrange *Vis. Quev.* (1708) 240 Come hither Sirrah, cryes Lucifer; and so the poor Cur went wrigling and glotting up towards his Prince. **1684** Creech *Ovid's Eleg.* II. vii. in *Dryden's Miscell.* I. 129 If at the Play I in Fop-corner sit, And with a squinting Eye glote o'er the pit. **1727** Gay *Fables* xxxiii. 29 Like you [a snake], they..With malice hiss, with envy glote, And for convenience change their coat. [**1881** *Isle of Wight Gloss.*, *Gloat*, to look sulky, to swell. 'He gloats like a tooad.']

†**b.** In *pa. pple.* Of the eyes: Turned *up* or *upward*. *Obs.*

1624 Bp. R. Mountagu *Immed. Address* 31 So sighs, and groanes, as many as you will; and eyes gloyted vpward, God knoweth why, or whether. *a* **1641** —— *Acts & Mon.* vii. (1642) 396 Their gloited-up eyes, their groning bellies.

c. Of light: ? To glance aside. *rare.*

1644 [see gloating *ppl. a.* b]. **1866** Thornbury *Greatheart* III. 224 The light gloated on some strange-shaped glasses, and on a retort that stood on a side-table.

†**2.** To cast amorous or admiring glances. Const. *on*, *upon*. *Obs.*

1676 Wycherley *Pl. Dealer* II. i. 16 In short, I cou'd not glote upon a man when he comes into a Room, and laugh at him when he goes out. **1678** Otway *Friendship in F.* III. 32 My revenge shall be to love you still; gloat on and loll after you where ere I see you [etc.]. **1680** Dryden *Limberham* I. 8 (Aside) Are you gloting already? then there's hopes, i' faith. **1710** Rowe *Jane Shore* IV. i, Teach every Grace to smile, in your Behalf, And her deluding Eyes to gloat for you. **1727** Gay *Fables* xiv. 27 Some praise his sleeve and others glote Upon his rich embroider'd coat [etc.].

quasi-*trans.* **1676** Wycherley *Pl. Dealer* IV. i, Her tongue, I confess, was silent; but her speaking Eyes gloted such things.

3. To gaze with intense or passionate satisfaction (usually implying a lustful, avaricious or malignant pleasure). Now almost exclusively *to gloat on, upon,* or *over*: to feast one's eyes upon, to contemplate, think of, or dwell upon with fierce or unholy joy.

1748 Richardson *Clarissa* III. xiii. 89 [The spider] suspends it [the fly], as if for a spectacle to be exulted over: Then stalking to the door of his cell, turns about, glotes over it at a distance. **1764** Churchill *Ep. W. Hogarth* 339 Hogarth, a guilty pleasure in his eyes, The place of Executioner supplies. See how he glotes, enjoys the sacred feast, And proves himself by cruelty a priest. **1794** Godwin *Cal. Williams* (1796) III. x. 182 Mr. Spurrel perfectly gloted, with eyes that seemed to devour everything that passed. **1801** Wolcot (P. Pindar) *Tears & Smiles* Wks. 1812 V. 69 The youth upon her tuneful lips Did full of rapture glote. **1815** Scott *Guy M.* xx, Over such [books] the eye of Dominie Sampson gloated with rapture. **1839–40** W. Irving *Wolfert's R.* (1855) 217 Never did miser gloat on his money with more delight. **1855** Macaulay *Hist. Eng.* III. 510 He had caught the scent of carnage, and came to gloat on the butchery in which he could no longer take an active part. **1861** Reade *Cloister & H.* IV. 7 Her sweet eyes turned and gloated on the little face..in silence. **1868** E. Edwards *Raleigh* I. xxiv. 557 Circumstances..which are gloated over in the vile letters of..Northampton. **1874** L. Stephen *Hours in Library* (1892) I. vi. 235 He..rejoiced greatly in gloating over the mysteries of iniquity. **1884** Sir S. St. John *Hayti* iii. 93 Soulouque went with his staff to inspect their mangled bodies..and gloat over the scene. **1885** [see ghoul].

Hence **'gloating** *vbl. sb.* Also **'gloater**, one who gloats.

1593 *Tell-Troth's N.Y. Gift* 29 The eye receivinge kinde glaunces for amorous glotinges. **1659** Torriano, *Sguaraguardatóre*, a starer, a gloter. **1850** Browning *Christmas Eve* xxii. 89 His Bourbon bully's gloatings In the bloody orgies of drunk poltroonery.

'gloating, *ppl. a.* [f. gloat *v.* + -ing[2].] That gloats (in the different senses of the vb.).

1602 Marston *Antonio's Rev.* v. iii, From beneath swoln brows Appeares a gloting eye of much mislike. **1625** Bp. R. Mountagu *Appello Cæs.* 253 He is in that case as jealous of Gods honour, as any gloyting Puritan in the Pack. **1682** Mrs. Behn *City Heiress* 33, I saw you playing with my Rival, Sigh'd, and lookt Babies in his gloating Eyes. **1817** J. Scott *Paris Revisit.* (ed. 4) 36 Changing the cast of his look from one of gloating satisfaction to one of doleful regret. **1837** Disraeli *Venetia* IV. xiv, The coarse wonder of the gloating multitude. **1877** L. Morris *Epic Hades* I. 7 But as I looked There came a hunger in the gloating eyes.

†**b.** Of light: ? Glancing aside, refracted. *rare.*

1644 Digby *Nat. Bodies* xiii. 116 Colours may be made by reflexion, as also, gloating light.

Hence **'gloatingly** *adv.*

1681 Otway *Soldier's Fort.* II. i, How glotingly they look upon me! **1830** J. Wilson in *Blackw. Mag.* XXVII. 662 Your face has..been fixed as gloatingly as that of a Satyr. **1885** Stevenson *Dynamiter* 192 His eyes lingered gloatingly on his dear boxes.

glob (glɒb). *slang.* [? Blend of BLOB *sb.* and GOB *sb.*^{1}] A mass or lump of some liquid or semi-liquid substance.

1900 H. LAWSON *Over Sliprails* 44 The pup curled like a glob of mud on the sand in the moonlight. **1957** J. MASTERS *Far, Far the Mountain Peak* 96 Very large, mysterious snowflakes, wet and solid, drifted like globs of ice cream into their eyes. **1962** *New Scientist* 5 Apr. 807/2 Throughout the long coasting time, the fuel has been free of the pull of gravity. It is probably floating around the half-empty fuel tank in globs. **1965** E. TUNIS *Colonial Craftsmen* vi. 138 The blower gathered a parison, a 'glob' of hot glass, from the pot by dipping the tip of a six-foot blowing iron (tube) into the mass.

glob, obs. form of GLOBE.

global ('gləʊbəl), *a.* [f. GLOBE *sb.* + -AL^{1}.]

1. Spherical, globular. *rare.*

1676 R. DIXON *Nat. 2 Test.* 2, I could challenge the best Mathematician..to demonstrate..that they can so much as ..frame a Global Circle without the least gibbosity or concavity therein. **1848** *Lond. Mag.* 119 According to the modern System..there is no Upper nor Under, the Earth being global.

2. [After Fr. *global.*] Pertaining to or embracing the totality of a number of items, categories, etc.; comprehensive, all-inclusive, unified; total; *spec.* pertaining to or involving the whole world; world-wide; universal.

1892 *Harper's Mag.* Sept. 492/2 M. de Vogüé loves travel; he goes to the East and to the West for colors and ideas; his interests are as wide as the universe; his ambition, to use a word of his own, is to be 'global'. **1927** *Contemp. Rev.* Aug. 241 The essence of the American proposal therefore was its 'global' criterion. **1928** *Times* 1 Oct. 14/1 The proposal for a readjustment of tonnage proportions within the global limits originally proposed by the United States. *Ibid.*, The original French proposal was for global tonnage. **1928** *John o' London's* 24 Nov. 252/1 Adding figures of commerce and foreign investments..so as to show to-day's global contacts. **1943** *Air Force* Feb. 22 (*title*) Guides for global war. *Ibid.*, In this global war they [*sc.* maps] are vital to airmen. **1943** *Ann. Reg. 1942* 283 The hard lesson of modern global warfare. **1944** *Amer. Speech* XIX. 137 Its extremely healthy global attitude ('Linguistic isolationism..will be regarded as..outmoded and ridiculous..'). **1946** J. S. HUXLEY *Unesco* i. 8 A scientific world humanism, global in extent and evolutionary in background. **1948** *Ann. Reg. 1947* 14 The global sum of £300 million looked like the result of bargaining with the Treasury. **1951** *Sun* (Baltimore) 7 Jan. 2/6 American 'global bombers'—giant B-36's which can carry an atom bomb 10,000 miles. **1952** *Brit. Jrnl. Psychol.* May 101 There are..other and more satisfactory objective methods for investigating..the temperamental and general behavioural traits... A 'global' picture can be obtained from the use of such techniques as Rorschach or T.A.T. **1957** *Economist* 12 Oct. (Suppl.) 17, 10 days of global cruising. **1959** P. H. SPAAK *Why Nato?* iv. 30 The allies could only meet the global challenge of the Soviet Union with a global retort. **1970** *Sci. Jrnl.* Apr. 52/3 The meteorological global telecommunications system required poses a second major problem in the development of an effective system of global numerical weather prediction.

b. *global village*, a term popularized by M. McLuhan (1911–80) for the world in the age of high technology and international communications, through which events throughout the world may be experienced simultaneously by everyone, so apparently 'shrinking' world societies to the level of a single village or tribe; also in extended use.

1960 CARPENTER & MCLUHAN *Explorations in Communication* p. xi, Postliterate man's electronic media contract the world to a village or tribe where everything happens to everyone at the same time: everyone knows about, and therefore participates in, everything that is happening the minute it happens. Television gives this quality of simultaneity to events in the global village. **1962** M. MCLUHAN *Gutenberg Galaxy* 31 The new electronic interdependence recreates the world in the image of a global village. **1967** *Punch* 4 Oct. 520/1 Howdy neighbour, how're things over in your corner of the global village? Wife and audio-tactile kids okay? **1968** MCLUHAN & FIORE (*title*) War and peace in the global village. **1970** *Sat. Rev.* 24 Oct. 19/2 There are no boundaries in a global village. All problems will become so intimate as to be one's own. **1980** *Jrnl. R. Soc. Arts* June 437/1 In the 'global village' which..the mass media in particular have made of the world there is a temptation to see everything in global terms. **1986** R. FORD *Sportswriter* vi. 152 She told me about..her theories of Abstract Expressionism, the global village, and a Great Books course.

Hence **'globalism**, internationalism; **globali'zation**, the act of globalizing; **'globalize** *v. trans.*, to render global; so **globalized** *ppl. adj.*

1959 *Economist* 4 Apr. 65/1 Italy's 'globalised quota' for imports of cars has been increased. **1961** WEBSTER, Globalism... Globalization. **1962** *Spectator* 5 Oct. 495 Globalisation is, indeed, a staggering concept. **1962** *Sunday Times* 28 Jan. 12/2 Our own comparatively timid intentions towards globalising the Common Market. **1965** *Economist* 23 Jan. 316/1 Between globalism and isolationism there is extensive middle ground.

globally ('gləʊbəlɪ), *adv.* [f. prec. + -LY^{2}.] In a global manner; to a global extent; comprehensively; universally; throughout the world.

1930 *N.Y. Times* 9 Nov. 1 The 'minor technical question' of whether to limit naval officers and men globally or by categories. **1957** *Economist* 5 Oct. 31 To-day, more than ever before, exporters must plan *globally*, especially in view of the growing economic importance of the world's new markets. **1958** *Engineering* 21 Feb. 236/2 Globally, 50 to 100 times this amount may be produced annually by the end of the century. **1958** *New Biol.* XXVII. 53 Two world wars and facilities for increasingly rapid travel and communication have induced the more perceptive to think globally—that is to say to consider the total situation whether in politics or science. **1971** *Nature* 7 May 17/1 There is some evidence that lead from car exhausts is building up globally.

†**'globar**, *a. Obs.* [f. GLOBE *sb.* + -AR.] = GLOBAL *a.*

1699 *Phil. Trans.* XXI. 298 The French call this Shell the Purse, because there is joyn'd to it's long and narrow Mouth ..a Globar [*printed* Glolar] puff, like a full Bag, or Purse. *a* **1711** KEN *Hymnotheo* Poet. Wks. 1721 III. 49 He..flew.. Down to the dusky Air, to gather Cloud, Which in its Globar Form should them enshroud.

globard, var. GLOWBARD, *Obs.*

globate ('gləʊbeɪt, -ət), *a. rare.* [ad. L. *globāt-us*, pa. pple. of *glob-āre* to form into a mass or globe, f. *glob-us* GLOBE *sb.*] **a.** Having the form of a globe. **b.** (See quot. 1854.)

1847 in CRAIG. **1854** MAYNE *Expos. Lex.*, *Globate.* Applied to glands that are formed of lymphatic vessels connected together by cellular membrane, and which pass out again, having no excretory duct. **1860** GOSSE *Brit. Sea-Anem. & Corals* p. xxxiv, Globate Cnidæ. *Ibid.* p. xxxvi, The *cnidæ* of the spiral and globate kinds.

globated ('gləʊbeɪtɪd), *a. rare.* [f. as prec. + -ED^{1}.] Formed into a globe. Also *fig.*

1727–36 in BAILEY. **1755** JOHNSON, *Globated*, formed in shape of a globe; spherical; spheroidical. **1869** G. MACDONALD *R. Falconer* I. xxi. 143 What a full globated symbolism lay then around the heart of the boy in his book, his violin, his kite! **1888** tr. *Renan's Hist. People Israel* I. 239 He [Jahveh] was the universal *rouah* under a globated form, a kind of condensed electric mass.

†**globbe, glubbe**, *v. Obs. rare*$^{-1}$. [Onomatopœic: cf. GLOFF, GLOP, GULP.] *trans.* To gulp down (liquor); to eat gluttonously. Hence **'globber**, a glutton.

1377 LANGL. *P. Pl.* B. v. 346 [They] seten so til euensonge ..Tyl Glotoun had y-globbed [*v.rr.* (y-)glubbed, globed] a galoun an[d] a Iille. *Ibid.* IX. 60 Moche wo worth that man that mysreuleth his Inwitte, And that be glotouns globbares [*v.rr.* glubberes, clobberis], her god is her wombe.

globe (gləʊb), *sb.* Also 7 **glob.** [a. F. *globe*, ad. L. *globus* a round body or mass; a ball, sphere, etc. The ME. *glob(be, glub(be*, GLUB, used by Wyclif to render L. *globus* in the sense 'body of men', etc. is prob. etymologically distinct.]

1. a. A body having (accurately or approximately) the form of a SPHERE.

1551 RECORDE *Pathw. Knowl.* I. *Defin.*, But in a Globe, (whiche is a bodie rounde as a bowle) there is but one platte forme, and one bounde. **1559** W. CUNNINGHAM *Cosmogr. Glasse* 15 A diameter of a sphere, or globe, is any lyne drawen thorowe the same, goyng by the center of the sphere, or globe. **1595** SPENSER *Col. Clout* 613 The fume..mounts ..In rolling globes vp to the vauted skies. **1617** MORYSON *Itin.* I. 79 The outward roofe is divided into foure globes, covered with leade. **1662** STILLINGFL. *Orig. Sacr.* III. ii. §18 All those particles were not at first Sphærical, because many such little Globes joyned together will not fill up a continued space. **1783** FRANKLIN in Ellis *Orig. Lett.* (1843) 424 The experiment of a vast Globe [a balloon] sent up into the air, much talk'd of here at present. **1784** COWPER *Task* VI. 155 The other tall [*foot-note* The Guelder Rose], and throwing up into the darkest gloom Of neighbouring Cypress..Her silver globes. **1812–16** J. SMITH *Panorama Sci. & Art.* I. 277 The earth is not a perfect globe. **1821** SHELLEY *Prometh. Unb.* III. iii. 139 Bright golden globes Of fruit, suspended in their own green heaven. **1854** TOMLINSON *Arago's Astron.* 55 The sun is an immense globe, 1,300,000 times greater than the earth. **1875** JOWETT *Plato* (ed. 2) III. 616 In the form of a globe, round as from a lathe.

b. *fig.* A complete or perfect body, a 'full-orbed' combination.

1607–12 BACON *Ess.*, *Gt. Place* (Arb.) 284/1 In the discharge of thie place, sett before thee the best Exemples; For Imitacion is a Globe of Preceptes. **1642** MILTON *Apol. Smect.* (1851) 300 No sooner did the force of so much united excellence meet in one globe of brightnesse and efficacy, but [etc.].

†**c.** A fire-ball (see quot.). *Obs.*

1563 W. FULKE *Meteors* (1640) 9 b, Of Shields, Globes or bowles. These Meteors also have their name of their fashion, because they..appeare to be round.

†**d.** The SPHERE of a planet. *Obs. rare.*

1559 W. CUNNINGHAM *Cosmogr. Glasse* 41 The Fyre.. shal ascend above them, and be next the Globe of the Mone.

2. a. *the* (or *this*) *globe*, the earth. †Formerly often ***the globe of*** (***the***) ***earth***, ***of the world***; ***the earthly*** or ***terrestrial globe*** (cf. BALL *sb.* 2).

1553 EDEN *Treat. Newe Ind.* (Arb.) 9 The hole globe of the world hath been sayled aboute. **1575** *App. & Virg.* in Hazl. *Dodsley* IV. 113 Gods that rule the skies, The Globe, and eke the Element. **1590** SHAKS. *Mids. N.* IV. i. 102 We the Globe can compasse soone, Swifter then the wandring Moone. *c* **1630** RISDON *Surv. Devon* §192 (1810) 204 He was the second that circumpassed the earthly globe. *a* **1649** DRUMM. OF HAWTH. *Poems* 23 The sun, from east to west who all doth see, On this low glob sees nothing like to thee. **1717** LADY M. W. MONTAGU *Let. to C'tess Mar* 1 Apr., I wish..you were..regular in letting me know what passes on your side of the globe. **1752** HUME *Ess. & Treat.* (1777) I. 219 The same set of manners will follow a nation..over the whole globe. **1769** WESLEY *Jrnl.* 8 Sept. (1827) III. 369 The globe of earth..can hardly afford a more pleasing scene. **1842** TENNYSON *Locksley Hall* 183 Thro' the shadow of the globe we sweep into the younger day. **1891** *Speaker* 2 May 534/1 The harnessing of electricity to the commerce of the globe.

b. One of the planetary or celestial bodies.

c **1566** J. ALDAY tr. *Boaystuau's Theat. World* S iv b, If thou art minded to surpasse al ye globes of the firmament, and see what is there contained. **1651** DAVENANT *Gondibert* II. v. xx, Those vaste bright Globes..Were made but to attend our little Ball. **1840** J. H. NEWMAN *Par. Serm.* (1842) V. iv. 56 Supposing a man told that he should suddenly be carried off to some unknown globe in the heavens.

3. A spherical structure on whose surface is depicted the geographical configuration of the earth (***terrestrial globe***), or the arrangement of the constellations (***celestial globe***).

The terrestrial and celestial globes were formerly included under the name of ***the globes***, esp. in the phrase (***to learn, teach***) ***the use of the globes***.

1553 EDEN *Treat. Newe Ind.* (Arb.) 8 In the moste parte of Globes and Mappes they see the continente or fyrme land. **1559** W. CUNNINGHAM *Cosmogr. Glasse* 114 *note*, An objection against the terestriall Globe. **1592** DEE *Comp. Rehears.* (Chetham) 28 Two globes of Gerardus Mercators best making on which were my divers reformations both geographicall, and celestiall. **1625** N. CARPENTER *Geog. Del.* (1635) I. vii. 166 A Mappe differs from a Globe, in that the Globe is a round solide body, more neerely representing the true figure of the Earth. **1665** HOOKE *Microgr.* 218, I have observ'd..several magnitudes of Stars less then those of the six magnitudes commonly recounted in the Globes. **1701** WALLIS in *Collect.* (O.H.S.) I. 329 With arithmetick, and the use of the globes. **1762–71** H. WALPOLE *Vertue's Anecd. Paint.* (1786) III. 25 The celestial and terrestrial globes, the largest that had then ever been printed. **1866** MRS. GASKELL *Wives & Dau.* I. xi. 131, I suppose you've been taught music, and the use of globes, and French, and all the usual accomplishments.

4. The golden ball or orb borne along with the sceptre as an emblem of sovereignty (cf. BALL *sb.* 3).

1614 SELDEN *Titles Hon.* 158 In Christianitie there is now appropriated to supreme Princes a Globe, and an infixt Crosse. **1636** MASSINGER *Gt. Dk. Florence* I. i, If I had beene the heire Of all the Globes and Scepters mankind bowes to, At my best you had deserv'd me. **1688** *Lond. Gaz.* No. 2309/3 At the reading of the Gospel the Emperor stood up, holding his Scepter in one Hand, and the Globe in the other. **1753** *Scots Mag.* Mar. 156/1 The globe and cross..shew him to have been a..King. **1780** COWPER *Table T.* 39 The globe and sceptre in such hands misplaced, Those ensigns of dominion, how disgraced! **1813** SCOTT *Trierm.* III. xxxv, With crown, with sceptre, and with globe, Emblems of empery.

5. *Anat.* ***globe of the eye***, ***ocular globe***, the eyeball (see quot. 1885).

1774 GOLDSM. *Nat. Hist.* (1776) VI. 162 The globe [of a fish's eye]..is furnished behind with a muscle, which serves to lengthen or flatten it according to the necessities of the animal. **1835–6** TODD *Cycl. Anat.* I. 510/2 It [the tissue] abounds..around the globe of the eye. **1870** ROLLESTON *Anim. Life* Introd. 54 The globe of the eye consists of two segments, the anterior of which is more or less conical. **1879** *St. George's Hosp. Rep.* IX. 468 Three females and one male ..were admitted for enucleation of wasted globes. **1885** *Syd. Soc. Lex.*, *Ocular globe*, the eyeball after the separation of its muscles and outer connections.

6. A glass vessel of approximately spherical form; esp. **a.** a glass lamp-shade; **b.** a vessel filled with water, used for exhibiting ornamental fish, or as a lens.

1665 HOOKE *Microgr.* Pref. E, A pretty large Globe of Glass, fill'd with exceeding clear Brine. **1776** G. SEMPLE *Building in Water* 142 The Globes..must be made of very thick white Glass. **1796** *Hist. Ned Evans* I. 10, I met a post chaise and four on the turnpike road: it had globes with lights in them. **1800** *Med. Jrnl.* IV. 179 This instrument consists of a very strong glass tube..and ends in a globe of 1.2 or 1.3 inch in diameter. **1839** CHATTO *Wood Engraving* viii. 652 Filling a large transparent glass-globe with clear water, and placing it in such a manner..that the light after passing through the globe, may fall directly on the block. **1873** STEWART *Conserv. Force* i. 8 A glass globe containing numerous gold-fish. **1874** MICKLETHWAITE *Mod. Par. Churches* 194 Globes are seldom used in churches. **1885** *Harper's Mag.* Mar. 592/2 It was a new lamp, with a.. figured globe.

7. *Mil.* †**a.** A kind of grenade. *Obs.*

1672 W. T. *Mil. & Mar. Discipline* III. *Compl. Gunner* III. ix. 7 There is given to these sort of Globes the names of Granadoes. *Ibid.* III. xiii. 10 Stinking Globes are made to annoy the Enemy.

b. ***globe of compression*** (= F. *globe de compression*): an overcharged mine, the explosion of which produces a crater of greater radius than depth.

1838 *Penny Cycl.* XI. 263/2 *Globe of Compression*, a name given by Belidor to mines in which the highest charges of powder are employed... They were first employed by the King of Prussia, in 1762, at the siege of Schweidnitz. **1876** in VOYLE *Milit. Dict.* s.v. *Compression.*

8. In imitation of a Latin use: A compact body (of persons).

1610 G. FLETCHER *Christ's Triumph* xiii, Out there flies A globe of winged Angels, swift as thought. **1667** MILTON *P.L.* II. 512 Him round A Globe of fierie Seraphim inclos'd. **1837** *Blackw. Mag.* XLII. 113 The Bashkirs collected into 'globes' and 'turms', as their only means of meeting the long lines of descending Chinese cavalry.

†**9.** *Path.* = GLOBUS. *Obs.*

1758 R. BROOKES *Gen. Pract. Physic* II. 122 Then they feel a sort of a Globe arise from the lower Part of the Belly to the *Hyphochondria* and Diaphragm.

10. *attrib.* and *Comb.* **a.** General combinations, as *globe-maker*; *globe-making* vbl. sb.; *globe-billed*, *-cheeked*, *-engirdling*,

-girding, -girdling ppl. adjs.; ***globe-like*** adj.; ***globe-wise*** adv.

1847 CRAIG, **Globe-billed curassow*, in Ornithology, the *Crax globicera* of Linnæus, a native of Guiana. **1819** W. TENNANT *Papistry Storm'd* (1827) 18 Around the altar prance and pace *Globe-cheekit Fun. **1622** DRAYTON *Poly-olb.* xix. 307 *Globe-engirdling Drake, the Nauall Palme that wonne. **1847** EMERSON *Poems, Monadnoc* Wks. (Bohn) I. 433 The alps' *globe-girding chain. **1875** *Temple Bar* June 255 A somewhat old-fashioned house, not working any of your *globe-girdling speculative gigantic operations. **1943** *Amer. Mag.* Mar. 98/1 A network of globe-girdling airways. **1597** DRAYTON *Heroic. Ep.* iii. 29 Whilst I behold thy *Globe-like rouling eye, Thy louely cheeke (mee thinks) stands smiling by. **1620–55** I. JONES *Stone-Heng* (1725) 67 Unto Vesta..they built Temples of a round Form Globelike. **1657** W. COLES *Adam in Eden* lxi. 117 The Globe-like Throat-worts..grow naturally in divers places beyond the Seas. **1740** HARRIS in *Phil. Trans.* XLI. 324 The *Globe-makers might save us the Trouble and Expence of having these graduated Slips of Brass, by dividing some Meridian. **1878** C. H. COOTE in *Trans. New Shaks. Soc.* 98 It was a 'new map' on a new projection made by one of the most eminent globe-makers of his time. **1875** KNIGHT *Dict. Mech.* 986/2 In the history of *globe-making, the name of Ferguson, the mathematician, has an honourable place. **1599** H. BUTTES *Dyets drie Dinner* F vij, [Artichokes] somewhat resemble Pine-apples, consisting of many skales, compacted *Globe-wise. **1698** LISTER *Journ. Paris* (1699) 192 In the Orangerie were..two pair of Mirtles in Cases, cut Globe-wise.

b. Special combinations: **globe-amaranth(us** (see AMARANTH 3); †**globe-animal, -animalcule**, a minute globular locomotive organism (*Volvox globator*); **globe-artichoke** = ARTICHOKE 1; **globe-cock** (see quot.); **globe-crowfoot** = *globe-flower*; **globe-daisy**, *Globularia vulgaris*; †**globe-dial**, a sun-dial in the form of a globe; †**globe-fennel**, some variety of fennel; **globe-fish**, a fish of globular form, esp. one of the *Tetrodontidæ* or *Diodontidæ*, which assume this shape by inflation; **globe-flower**, *Trollius europæus*, a ranunculaceous plant with yellow flowers; **globe-lamp**, a lamp in which the light is protected by a globe; **globe-lightning** = FIRE-BALL 1; **globe-loadstone**, a spherical magnet; **globe-ranunculus** = *globe-flower*; **globe-sight**, a front sight for a rifle, etc., consisting of a ball or disk; **globe-slater**, a sessile-eyed crustacean of the genus *Sphæroma*; **globe-thistle**, a name for species of *Echinops*; **globe-trot** *v. intr.* [back-formation from *globe-trotter, -trotting*], to go globe-trotting; also *trans.*; **globe-trotter**, one who goes globe-trotting; **globe-trotting**, extensive and hurried travelling over the world for the sake of sight-seeing; **globe-valve** (see quot.).

1733 MILLER *Gardener's Dict.* (ed. 2) I, *Amarantoides*, *Globe Amaranthus or Everlasting Flower. **1755** JOHNSON (citing MILLER), *Globe amaranth*. **1806** PRISCILLA WAKEFIELD *Dom. Recreat.* vi. 92 The *globe animal, so named on account of its form, which is like a round ball without any appearance of head, tail, or fins. **1867** J. HOGG *Microsc.* II. i. 275 This little cell, so well known to the older observers as the *globe-animalcule or revolving-cell. **1858** GLENNY *Gard. Every-day Bk.* 219/1 **Globe Artichoke*. **1882** *Garden* 11 Mar. 169/3 Now is a good time to make plantations of Globe Artichokes. **1875** KNIGHT *Dict. Mech.*, **Globe-cock*, formerly a sphere with a stem by which it was moved..now a circular disk of similar use, and retaining the name. **1597** GERARDE *Herbal* II. cccli. 810 The globe flower is called..in English *Globe Crowfoote, Troll flowers, and Lockron gowlons. *Ibid.* II. cxciii. §7. 512 The blewe Daisie is called..in English blew Daisies and *Globe Daisie. **1625** in Willis & Clark *Cambridge* (1886) I. 183 For gilding and working y^e *globe dialls £3. **1688** R. HOLME *Armoury* III. 372/2 A Ball, or Globe Dial, to shew the Hour without a Gnomon. **1713** PETIVER in *Phil. Trans.* XXVIII. 190 Smooth *Globe-Fennel. **1668** WILKINS *Real Char.* II. 142 Fishes of a hard crustaceous skin..Sphærical..[as] *Orbis Scutatus*, *Globe-fish. **1735** MORTIMER in *Phil. Trans.* XXXIX. 113 *Orbis lævis variegatus*: The Glob-Fish. **1884–5** *Riverside Nat. Hist.* (1888) III. 289 *Tetrodontidæ*..have received numerous popular names, such as swell-fish, bottle-fish, bellows-fish, globe-fish..etc. **1597** *Globe flower [see *globe-crowfoot*]. **1854** S. THOMSON *Wild Fl.* II. 97 The..globe-flower. **1788** B. FRANKLIN *Autobiogr.* (1905) 381 The *globe lamps we were at first supply'd with from London. **1825** H. WILSON *Mem.* IV. 67 This room..was lighted by large, ground-glass, French globe-lamps, suspended from the cieling. **1897** *Daily News* 7 Jan. 6/7 The boatswain was taking a globe lamp into the forepeak. **1888** TAIT in *Encycl. Brit.* XXIII. 330/1 '*Globe-lightning' or 'fireball'. **1664** POWER *Exp. Philos.* 170 Not to mention how hard a thing it is; first, to find the two Polary points in a *Globe-Loadstone [etc.]. **1733** MILLER *Gardener's Dict.* (ed. 2) I, *Helleboro-Ranunculus*, *Globe Ranunculus *vulgo*. **1884** *Harper's Mag.* Aug. 367/1 At this short distance you don't care for the peep and *globe sights. **1879** ROSSITER *Dict. Sci. Terms* s.v. *Globe*, *Globe-slaters = *Sphæroma*. **1597** GERARDE *Herbal* II. cccclxii. 990 *Carduus Globosus*..is called in English, *Globe Thistle, and Ball-Thistle. **1658** SIR T. BROWNE *Gard. Cyrus* iii. 47 And he that inquireth into the little bottom of the globe-thistle, may finde that gallant bush arise from a scalpe of like disposure. **1794** MARTYN *Rousseau's Bot.* xxvi. 404 Common Globe-thistle is so called from the flowers growing in globular heads. **1883** *Manch. Guardian* 6 June 6/1 He drives from London to York..and is amusing; he *globetrots and is not amusing. **1883** LD. R. GOWER *My Reminisc.* II. 180 Nothing nowadays is easier and safer than to 'globe-trot' round the world. **1928** *Observer* 8 Apr. 5/7 You are never instructed, never globe-trotted. **1929** C. DAY LEWIS *Transitional Poem* I. 16 To..globe-trot with the wind. **1970** *Oxf. Univ. Press Record* xv. 3 Bill Waterfield..globe-trotted for several years after reading Botany at University College. **1875** E. K. LAIRD (*title*) Rambles of a *globe-trotter in Australia, Japan, China, Java, India and Cashmere. **1883** STEVENSON *Silverado Sq.* I It is no place of pilgrimage for the summary globe-trotter. **1880** *Daily News* 6 May 4/8 The season for *globe-trotting..has seriously set in. **1875** KNIGHT *Dict. Mech.*, **Globe-valve*, 1. A ball-valve, one of a spherical shape... 2. A valve inclosed in a globular chamber.

globe (gləʊb), *v.* Also 7 **glob**. [f. prec.; cf. L. *globāre*.]

1. *trans.* To form into a globe. Also *refl.*

1641 MILTON *Ch. Govt.* II. iii, Yet is it [Self-respect, previously designated as 'the radical moisture' of 'every worthy enterprize'] not incontinent to bound it self, as humid things are, but hath in it a most restraining and powerfull abstinence to start back, and glob it self upward from..any soile wherewith it may peril to stain itself. **1838** EMERSON *Addr. Cambridge, Mass.* Wks. (Bohn) II. 191 The moral traits which are all globed into every virtuous act and thought. **1864** TENNYSON *En. Ard.* 598 The great stars that globed themselves in Heaven. **1876** G. MEREDITH *Beauch. Career* I. vii. 101 A small round brilliant moon hung almost globed in the depths of heaven.

2. *intr.* To assume or have the form of a globe.

1856 MRS. BROWNING *Aur. Leigh* III. 275 My eyes globed luminous Through orbits of blue shadow. **1889** E. ARNOLD *Lt. World* v. (1891) 223 So the dew Globes on a grass-blade.

Hence **'globing** *ppl. a.*

1861 THORNBURY *Turner* (1862) I. 30 The myriads of houses over which the black globing dome dominates.

globed (gləʊbd), *ppl. a.* [f. GLOBE *sb.* and *v.* + -ED.]

1. Having the form of a globe.

1820 KEATS *Melanch.* ii, Then glut thy sorrow on a morning rose..Or on the wealth of globed peonies. **1850** MRS. BROWNING *Poems* I. 26 As twilight drifted Through the cedar masses, The globed sun we lifted. **1863** T. WOOLNER *My Beautiful Lady* 86 Their [birds'] fluttering bursts the globèd seeds.

2. Furnished with a globe.

1832 L. HUNT *Poems* 172 Of the old kings with high exacting looks, Sceptred and globed. **1867** G. MUSGRAVE *Nooks Old France* II. 136 The garden walks were illuminated by about sixty very large globed gas-lamps.

globelet ('gləʊblɪt). *nonce-wd.* [f. GLOBE *sb.* + -LET.] A small globe or globule; a drop.

1839 BAILEY *Festus* xviii. (1848) 185 Like a phosphor globelet in the sea. **1885** RODEN NOEL in *Harper's Mag.* Apr. 815/2 Where a rainbow globelet crosses.

globerd(e, var. GLOWBARD, glow-worm.

globical ('glɒbɪkəl, 'gləʊbɪkəl), *a.* [f. GLOBE *sb.* + -IC + -AL¹.]

†**1.** Globular, spherical. *Obs.*

1612 DEKKER *London Triumphing* A 4 b, The earth: whose Globicall Rotundity is Hieroglifically represented by the wheele of the Chariot. **1658** R. FRANCK *North. Mem.* (1821) p. xv, For God through wisdom hung up aloft these bright, shining, and globical bodies, whereby to illuminate this stupendous creation. **1698** A. VAN LEEUWENHOEK in *Phil. Trans.* XX. 170 A Globical Roundness.

2. *Her.* Having the general outline circular.

1688 R. HOLME *Armoury* I. 44/2 It is also Blazoned a Cross Patee Globicall (and Patee Circulated or Circuled). **1828–40** BERRY *Encycl. Herald.* I, *Globical*, or *Convex*, circular on the outside. **1847** *Gloss. Herald.* s.v. *Cross*, The *Cross pattée alisée* or *globical* is a circle in general outline instead of a square.

Hence †**'globically** *adv.*

1672 W. T. *Mil. & Marit. Discipline* III. *Compl. Gunner* III. ix. 7 The Hand Granadoes..are Globically or perfectly round and hollow in their interior part in manner of a Sphere.

globiferous (gləʊ'bɪfərəs), *a.* *Ent.* [f. L. *globi-* GLOBE *sb.* + -FEROUS.] Having a globe or bulb at the end of the antennæ.

1826 KIRBY & SP. *Entomol.* IV. 323 *Globiferous*, when the setigerous joint [of the antennæ] is larger than the preceding one, and globose.

‖**globigerina** (gləʊbɪdʒə'raɪnə). Pl. **globigerinæ**. [mod.L., f. L. *globi-*, *globus* GLOBE *sb.* + *-ger* carrying + *-ina* -INE; named by D'Orbigny in 1826.] A foraminiferous rhizopod, found in immense numbers in deep parts of the ocean.

1847 in CRAIG. **1863** LYELL *Antiq. Man* xiv. 268 Their stomachs were full of globigerina, of which foraminiferous creatures..the oozy bed of the ocean at that vast depth was found to be exclusively composed. **1875** DAWSON *Dawn of Life* iv. 89 In the Globigerinæ..only eight or ten segments are ordinarily produced by continuous gemmation. **1880** A. R. WALLACE *Isl. Life* vi. 89 The Globigerinæ have been shown by the Challenger explorations to abound in all moderately warm seas.

b. *attrib.*, as ***globigerina-shell***; also **globigerina-mud, -ooze**, deep-sea mud or chalky ooze, consisting of decayed globigerinæ.

1872 DANA *Corals* ii. 143 A mud full of foraminifers, Globigerina mud, as it is called from the species characterizing it. **1878** HUXLEY *Physiogr.* xvi. 270 There is no sufficient evidence that pure and clean Globigerina shells contain any appreciable proportion of such mineral matter. **1880** A. R. WALLACE *Isl. Life* vi. 87 The white oceanic mud, or Globigerina-ooze, found in all the great oceans at depths varying from 250 to nearly 3,000 fathoms.

globigerine (gləʊ'bɪdʒərɪn), *a.* [See prec. and -INE.] Belonging to the *Globigerinæ*.

1869 *Student's Mag.* Feb. 33 Globigerine deposits. **1880** *Nature* XXI. 219 The areas occupied by the globigerine, or calcareous 'ooze'.

globin ('gləʊbɪn). [f. L. *glob-us* GLOBE *sb.* + -IN.] (See quot. 1877.) Now more widely: any of various colourless basic polypeptides that are the protein components of hæmoglobin, myoglobin, and related molecules (the non-protein part in each case being hæm).

1877 FOSTER *Physiol.* II. ii. 241 The proteid which is precipitated when a solution of hæmoglobin is exposed to the air, though belonging to the globulin family has characters of its own. It has been named by Preyer *globin*. **1898** *Jrnl. Chem. Soc.* LXXIV. I. 719 Nearly pure globin is obtained. This..must be distinguished from Preyer's 'globin' obtained from methæmoglobin. *Ibid.* 720 The blood of the goose, however, yields a globin which possesses different properties. **1925** [see HÆM]. **1930** *Jrnl. Gen. Physiol.* XIII. 475 The denatured globin may be largely converted into a soluble, apparently native form which can combine with heme to form hemoglobin. **1957** FOX & FOSTER *Introd. Protein Chem.* xviii. 348 The isoelectric points of the globins, which are very rich in histidine, are usually on the alkaline side of 7·0. **1962** E. G. YOUNG in Florkin & Stotz *Comprehensive Biochem.* VII. i. 5 Globin has been the most carefully studied of the histones. It was first prepared from crystalline hæmoglobin by Preyer in 1868. **1970** R. W. MCGILVERY *Biochem.* ii. 13 Each peptide chain of globin has a sequence of amino acids that makes certain three-dimensional arrangements more likely than others, and the most likely of all is one that, in the presence of heme, causes it to fold around the heme.

†**'globiness.** *Obs. rare*⁻⁰. [f. GLOBY + -NESS.]

1611 COTGR., *Rondeur*, roundnesse, globinesse.

globird, var. GLOWBARD, *Obs.*, glow-worm.

†**'globist.** *Obs. rare*⁻¹. [f. GLOBE *sb.* + -IST.] One versed in the use of the globes.

1642 HOWELL *For. Trav.* (Arb.) 87 Being a good Globist, hee will quickly find the Zenith, the distances, the climes and the Parallells, and distances of Regions.

globoid ('gləʊbɔɪd), *a.* and *sb.* [f. GLOBE *sb.* + -OID.]

A. *adj.* Of approximately globular form.

1887 *Pop. Sci. Monthly* XXX. 324 These bush-retreats of the mice were all distinctly globular, or globoid.

B. *sb.* *Bot.* (See quots.)

1875 BENNETT & DYER *Sachs' Bot.* 52 Non-crystalline, roundish, or clustered granules, known as Globoids. These are a double calcium and magnesium phosphate, in which the latter base is greatly in excess. **1885** G. L. GOODALE *Physiol. Bot.* (1892) 47 Amorphous or globular concretions..known as globoids.

globose (gləʊ'bəʊs), *a.* [ad. L. *globōs-us*, f. *globus* GLOBE; cf. OF. *globeux*, GLOBOUS.] Having the form of a globe; completely or approximately spherical. Now only in scientific use.

c **1475** in *11th Rep. Hist. MSS. Comm.* App. III. (1887) 15 In the begynnynge when thow made all of nowght, A globose mater, and derke undur confusion. **1667** MILTON *P.L.* VII. 357 First the Sun..he framd..then formd the Moon Globose. **1707** *Phil. Trans.* XXV. 2389 Two great Globose Tumors. **1757** PULTNEY *ibid.* L. 61 The fruit is a globose berry. **1807** CRABBE *Par. Reg.* I. 140 The leek, with crown globose and reedy stem. **1822–34** *Good's Study Med.* (ed. 4) IV. 74 It is then that the breasts assume a globose plumpness. **1874** COUES *Birds N.W.* 133 The egg is usually rather globose.

absol. (quasi-*sb.*) **1667** MILTON *P.L.* v. 753 All the Earth, And all the Sea, from one entire globose Stretcht into Longitude.

Hence **glo'bosely** *adv.*, **glo'boseness**.

1727 BAILEY, *Globoseness*. **1840** PAXTON *Bot. Dict.*, *Globosely-elliptical*, between spherical and oval. **1854** WOODWARD *Mollusca* II. 162 *Helix Pomatia*..Shell..globosely depressed or conoidal. **1880** WATSON in *Jrnl. Linn. Soc.* XV. No. 82. 98 Shell—globosely conical.

globosite ('gləʊbəʊsaɪt). *Min.* [ad. G. *globosit* (Breithaupt 1865, in *Berg- und hüttenmännische Zeitung* XXIV. 321/2), f. L. *globōs-us* GLOBOSE: see -ITE¹.] An ill-defined phosphate of ferric iron found in small globular concretions.

1868 J. D. DANA *Syst. Min.* (ed. 5) v. 584 Globosite. This name is given by Breithaupt..to a mineral occurring at the Arme Hilfe mine near Hirschberg. **1925** *Proc. Acad. Nat. Sci. Philadelphia* LXXVII. 8 Globosite was described by Breithaupt from the Arme Hilfe mine Hirschberg, where it occurred as wax-yellow to yellowish-gray globular concretions... No reliance can be placed in the analysis... It is probably identical with strengite.

globosity (gləʊ'bɒsɪtɪ). [ad. late L. *globōsitāt-em*: see GLOBOSE and -ITY.] The condition of being globose; roundness, rotundity. Also, a globose or rounded part.

a **1657** BALFOUR *Ann. Scotl.* (1824–5) II. 74 In the globositie therof, to admire his wisdoome. **1662** H. MORE *Philos. Writ.* Pref. Gen. 20 At which Timidity of mine none can justly wonder that considers how shie the ancient Fathers were of the Globosity of the Earth. **1811** PINKERTON *Petral.* I. 199 When..the figures..are more turgid, and each part disfigured with some globosity, it is probable that they were formed with a little auger or trepan. **1830** *Examiner* 53/1 The Johnsonian globosity of his periods. **1847–8** H. MILLER *First Impr.* xvi. (1857) 265 The trunk..wearing all its huger globosities behind.

†**glo'bosous**, *a. Obs. rare*⁻¹. [f. L. *globōs-us* GLOBOSE + -OUS.] = GLOBOSE.
1681 WHARTON *Eclipses* Wks. (1683) 103 The earth is not cubical, nor pyramidal.. but on every side perfectly Round, or terminated by a Globosous Figure.

globous ('gləʊbəs), *a.* [ad. F. *globeux* (obs.) or L. *globōs-us* GLOBOSE.] = GLOBOSE. Now *rare*.
The form is frequent in the 17th and early 18th c. Johnson distinguishes *globous* and *globose* on metrical grounds. 'When the accent is intended to be on the last syllable, the word should be written *globose*, when on the first *globous*.'
1610 HEALEY *St. Aug. City God* 300 The ayre thickning it selfe into a globous body, produceth a world. **1615** CROOKE *Body of Man* 433 Though the figure of the head be round, yet is it not exquisitely and to a haire globous, but somewhat long. **1667** MILTON *P.L.* v. 649 Wider farr Then all this globous Earth in Plain outspred. **1712** BLACKMORE *Creation* 22 That they [atoms] Should muster there.. And draw together in a globous form. **1790** E. SIBLY *Astrol.* (1792) I. 15 The earth is a wheel or globe of sea and land, circumscribed by the atmosphere, which is globous too. **1865** GIDLEY *Aletes* 136 The azure sky Which vaults the globous earth.
Hence '**globously** *adv.*, '**globousness**.
1653 R. SANDERS *Physiogn.* etc. 276, I shall define the cheeks to be those parts of the face which from the mouth arise globously and most eminent. **1683** *Phil. Trans.* XIII. 207 These Globules then changed into the form of couls.. and then they retook their former globousness.

globular ('glɒbjʊlə(r)), *a.* [a. L. type **globulāris*, f. *globulus* GLOBULE; cf. F. *globulaire*.
Although etymologically related to GLOBULE, the word is commonly employed in senses corresponding to those of GLOBE, in place of GLOBOSE; for other examples of the same phenomenon see -ULAR.]
1. a. Having the form of a globe: spherical, round.
1656 BLOUNT *Glossogr.*, *Globular*, Round, like a Globe. *Bac[on]*. **1662** STILLINGFL. *Orig. Sacr.* III. ii. §18 Globular particles. **1664** POWER *Exp. Philos.* 8 Her eye is large and globular. **1691–1701** NORRIS *Ideal World* I. ii. 51 At the presence of a globular body I have naturally excited in me the idea of a perfect globe or sphere. **1772–84** COOK *Voy.* (1790) IV. 1239 In this station two globular hills appeared near its N.E. part. **1800** VINCE *Hydrostat.* x. (1806) 97 It is better to make the bulb flat than globular. **1866** G. MACDONALD *Ann. Q. Neighb.* ix. (1878) 140 From the centre of the ceiling.. hung a globular lamp. **1868** E. P. WRIGHT *Ocean World* i. 15 Minute globular creatures, called Noctilucæ.
b. Of protein: having a relatively compact molecular structure showing considerable folding.
1935 *Biochem. Jrnl.* XXIX. 2353 Edestin is thus a typical 'globular' protein. **1954, 1968** [see FIBROUS *a.* 1 d]. **1970** R. W. MCGILVERY *Biochem.* ii. 9 Hemoglobin is a representative of the globular proteins—those with a compact structure that are usually quite soluble in the water phase of tissues.
2. Composed of globules.
1733 CHEYNE *Eng. Malady* II. i. §5 (1734) 118 The Blood .. separates into two Parts, one of a more glutinous and solid Texture, call'd the Globular. **1830** KNOX *Anat.* 61 There is at first no determinate texture in the organs; there are not even globules at the commencement. At a later period, the entire mass of the body appears globular or granulated. **1885** *Syd. Soc. Lex.*, *Globular dentine*, a layer of dentine, presenting rounded masses, lying immediately beneath the enamel.
3. ***globular projection***, that method of map-making in which the sphere is represented as it would appear if viewed from a distance = half the chord of 90°. ***globular chart***, a chart on this projection. ***globular sailing*** (see quot. 1838). ***globular cluster***, a spherical cluster (see CLUSTER *sb.* 3 c) of stars; also ellipt. *globular*. ***globular lightning*** = FIRE-BALL 1.
1727–41 CHAMBERS *Cycl.*, *Globular chart*.. *Globular sailing*. **1756** R. ROLT *Dict. Trade & Com.* s.v. *Chart*, Globular Chart, is a projection so called, from the conformity it bears to the globe itself. **1859, 1928** Globular cluster [see CLUSTER *sb.* 3 c]. **1959** *Listener* 2 July 14/2 Altogether, about 100 globulars are known. **1961** *Ibid.* 7 Dec. 973/1 Globular clusters are of particular importance in modern astronomy, since studies of them have provided a great deal of information about the shape and structure of the Galaxy. *Ibid.*, From Britain only the great globular in Hercules—Messier 13—is distinctly visible to the naked eye. **1904** GOODCHILD & TWENEY *Technol. & Sci. Dict.* 259/1 *Globular lightning*, an electrical phenomenon whose nature is not understood: an appearance resembling a globe of fire, sometimes visible for a number of seconds, is produced. **1937** *Jrnl. R. Aeronaut. Soc.* XLI. 739 A Junkers Ju. 86.. was struck by globular lightning. **1838** *Penny Cycl.* XI. 263/2 *Globular projection*. **1727–41** Globular sailing [see *globular chart* above.] **1838** *Penny Cycl.* XI. 263/2, *Globular sailing*, a term of navigation, employed to denote the sailing from one place to another over an arc of a great circle, or the shortest distance between the two places.
Hence **globu'larity**, '**globularness**, the property of being globular; '**globularly** *adv.*
1727 BAILEY vol. II, *Globularness*, the same as *Globoseness*. **1809** PEARSON in *Phil. Trans.* XCIX. 344 The globularity of expectorated matter. **1812** SIR H. DAVY *Chem. Philos.* 68 It is the same force (cohesion), which.. gives globularity to fluids. **1826–34** *Good's Bk. Nat.* (ed. 3) II. 73 The globularity of the head, and the flatness or sharpness of the face. **1856** *Rogue's Life* ii. in *Household Wds.* 8 Mar. XIII. 181/1 When a man has no perceptible eyelids and when his eyes globularly project so far out of his head, that [etc.].

globule ('glɒbjuːl). Also 7 globul, 8 globle. [a. F. *globule*, ad. L. *globulus* (dim. of *globus* GLOBE), round lump, ball, pill.]
1. A spherical body of small size; a round drop (of water, etc.). *Biol.* Applied to many minute spherical structures, e.g. the corpuscles of the blood.
1664 POWER *Exp. Philos.* 44 In that Meal-like Powder of *Mercurius Cosmeticus*, were globules of ☿ plainly discernable. **1682** T. GIBSON *Anat.* 100 It seems to be compacted out of many Globules or knots included in a common membrane. **1702** E. BAYNARD *Cold Baths* II. (1709) 322 The constituent Parts of that Fluid [the Blood], viz. the Globles, being broken and destroy'd. **1812** SIR H. DAVY *Chem. Philos.* 68 When two particles of quicksilver are brought into apparent contact they may be made to unite and form one globule. **1831** BREWSTER *Nat. Magic* vi. (1833) 155 A vertical stratum of vapour, consisting of exceedingly minute globules of water. **1860** TYNDALL *Glac.* II. v. 251 The saturation.. of the snow.. enables the air to form itself into globules.
Comb. **1835–6** TODD *Cycl. Anat.* I. 693/1 The yolk is.. marked with two rows of small spots, globule-like.
2. *Bot.* The antheridium or male reproductive organ of *Characeæ* (see quots.).
1830 LINDLEY *Nat. Syst. Bot.* 326 In the axillæ of the uppermost whorls.. the organs of reproduction take their origin; they are of two kinds, one called the nucule, the other the globule. **1858** CARPENTER *Veg. Phys.* §776 The fructification of the Characeae is of two kinds, nucules, and globules, both of them seated in the axils of the branchlets.
3. A small pill or pilule, such as is used in homœopathy.
1849 LYTTON *Caxtons* III. v, My father had not as much pride as a homœopathist could have put into a globule. **1874** SPURGEON *Treas. Dav.* Ps. xci. 3 Too many among us.. place more reliance in a phial or a globule than in the Lord and giver of life. **1876** B'NESS BUNSEN in Hare *Life* (1879) II. viii. 467 Prescribe sometimes for myself the globules.
Hence '**globuled** *ppl. a.*, formed into a globule.
1806 J. GRAHAME *Birds Scot.* 4 The dew that globuled lies upon her mottled plumes.

globulet ('glɒbjʊlɪt). *rare.* [f. GLOBULE + -ET¹.] A small or minute globule.
1671 *Phil. Trans.* VI. 3040 To this Chapter also he makes an Appendix of Thorns, Hairs, and Globulets, explaining both their Constitution and Use. **1671** GREW *Anat. Plants* I. v. §21 All Flowers have their Powders or Globulets. **1802** BINGLEY *Anim. Biog.* (1813) III. 494 Under the microscope, their bodies seem to be covered with numerous globulets of different sizes.

globuliferous (ˌglɒbjʊ'lɪfərəs), *a.* [f. GLOBULE + -(I)FEROUS.] That bears or produces globules.
1796 WITHERING *Brit. Plants* (ed. 3) III. 428 Calyx 5-cleft, segments oval, covered with short globuliferous hairs. **1862** DANA *Man. Geol.* 71 Some varieties are also called globuliferous when the concretions are isolated globules and evenly distributed through the texture of a rock. **1878** LAWRENCE tr. *Cotta's Rocks Class.* 86 Spherulitic or Globuliferous.

globuliform ('glɒbjʊlɪfɔːm), *a. rare*⁻¹. [f. as prec. + -(I)FORM.] Shaped like a globule.
1834 MᶜMURTRIE *Cuvier's Anim. Kingd.* 382 The.. genus .. Monotama, is distinguished.. by the.. globuliform club .. of the antennæ.

globu'limeter. [f. L. *globul-us* GLOBULE + Gr. μέτρον measure, -METER.] = HÆMATOMETER b.
1885 in *Syd. Soc. Lex.*

globulin ('glɒbjʊlɪn). Also -ine. [f. GLOBULE + -IN, -INE.]
1. *Bot.* A name for starch-granules and chlorophyll-granules. ? *Obs.*
1835 LINDLEY *Introd. Bot.* (1848) I. 112 The starch-like granules called Globuline by Turpin.
2. A proteid found in blood, the crystalline lens, and other structures; one of the two constituents of hæmoglobin, the other being hæmatin; called also CRYSTALLIN.
1845 G. E. DAY tr. *Simon's Anim. Chem.* I. 88 In the analysis of the blood, the principal component parts, the water, albumen, hæmatin, globulin and fibrin, are usually determined. **1859** *Fownes' Chem.* 548 Globulin exists in concentrated solution in the crystalline lens, and in the blood-globules. **1875** DARWIN *Insectiv. Pl.* vi. 134 How far globulin would be nutritious to animals is not known.
b. *pl.* General name of a class of proteids insoluble in water, of which globulin is the type.
1873 RALFE *Phys. Chem.* 27 All the albuminoids are remarkable for their instability.. the globulins are the least .. stable of the whole group.

globulism ('glɒbjʊlɪz(ə)m). [f. as prec. + -ISM.] A term sometimes applied to homœopathy (see GLOBULE 3). So '**globulist**, a homœopathist.
1857 DUNGLISON *Med. Lex.*, *Globulism*, Homœopathy. **1865** *Daily Tel.* 15 July, I would rather be killed by a legitimate practitioner than get well under the hands of a globulist. *Ibid.* 24 Nov. 5/1 We shall hear the glories of globulism sounded throughout Europe.

globulite ('glɒbjʊlaɪt). *Min.* [f. GLOBULE + -ITE.] *pl.* Minute rounded bodies developed in the process of devitrification.
1879 RUTLEY *Study Rocks* x. 161 The globulites represent the most embryonic stage of crystallogenesis.
Hence **globu'litic** *a.*, belonging to, or containing, globulites.
1884 *Amer. Jrnl. Sci.* Ser. III. XXVIII. 256 Between these microlites.. could be detected a trace of pyroxene.. with.. dark globulitic base.

globuloid ('glɒbjʊlɔɪd), *a.* [f. as prec. + -OID.] 'Resembling a globule or globules' (*Cent. Dict.*).

globulose ('glɒbjʊləʊs), *a.* [f. as prec. + -OSE.] = GLOBULOUS.
1840 in PAXTON *Bot. Dict.*

globulous ('glɒbjʊləs), *a.* Now *rare.* [a. F. *globuleux*.] Having the form of a globule or globules; consisting of globules. †Also *rarely* = GLOBULAR 1.
1668 H. MORE *Div. Dial.* III. xxviii. (1713) 251 In each of these Circles was there also a small Globulous Speck. **1679** M. RUSDEN *Disc. Bees* 33 Where they [bees] make one entire globulous body neer the upper parts of the Hive. **1703** MOXON *Mech. Exerc.* 5 Small Globulous Work, as the Heads of Pins that round off towards the Edges. **1786–7** BONNYCASTLE *Astron.* xix. 310 Des Cartes defines it to be a globulous matter, diffused through the universe. **1868** DUNCAN *Figuier's Insect World* iii. 113 The antennæ are short, with a second globulous articulation, and a small terminal hair.
Hence † '**globulousness**.
1665 BOYLE *Exper. Cold* 715 The same drops.. will readily adhere to Gold, and lose their Globulousness upon it.

‖**globus** ('gləʊbəs). *Path.* [L. *globus* GLOBE.] Short for ***globus hystericus***, the medical term for a choking sensation, as of a lump in the throat, to which hysterical persons are subject.
1794–6 E. DARWIN *Zoon.* (1802) II. 530 The *globus hystericus* consists in the retrograde motion of the œsophagus. **1822–34** *Good's Study Med.* (ed. 4) III. 405 *note*, The epileptic patient does not laugh or shed tears.. neither is globus a sensation known to him. **1853** KANE *Grinnell Exp.* xxxiii. 293, I looked at him [the sun] thankfully with a great globus in my throat. **1897** *Allbutt's Syst. Med.* II. 803 He commonly suffers from globus.

globy ('gləʊbɪ), *a.* [f. GLOBE *sb.* + -Y¹.] Globular, spherical.
1600 ROWLANDS *Letting Humours Blood* vii. 83 The worlds whole globy round. **1643** MILTON *Divorce* I. vi, One of the highest Arcs that human Contemplation.. can make from the globy Sea whereon she stands. **1844** L. HUNT *Blue-stocking Revels* III. 59 Thus, talks he of roses? They come, thick and globy.

gloce, obs. form of GLOSS, GLOZE.

glochideous (gləʊ'kɪdɪəs), *a. Bot.* [f. as next + -(E)OUS.] = next.
1880 GRAY *Struct. Bot.* 413/2 *Glochideous*, *Glochidiate*, when bristles and the like are barbed at the tip.

glochidiate (gləʊ'kɪdɪət), *a. Bot.* Also **glochidate**. [f. mod.L. *glōchidi-um* barbed hair of a plant (a. Gr. *γλωχίδιον, dim. of γλωχίς point of an arrow) + -ATE. Cf. F. *glochidé*.] Barbed at the tip (see quots.).
1829 LOUDON *Encycl. Plants* 1100 *Glochidate*, having hairs, the ends of which are split and hooked back, so that the hook is double. **1845** LINDLEY *Sch. Bot.* vi. (1858) 86 Involucre globose, glochidate (covered with scales terminating in a sharp hard hook, and finally constituting a bur). **1861** BENTLEY *Man. Bot.* 46 If presenting two or more hooks at their apex, they are glochidiate or barbed. **1870** HOOKER *Stud. Flora* 297 Utricularia.. seeds.. pitted or covered with capitate or glochidiate hairs. **1880** [see GLOCHIDEOUS].

glochidium (gləʊ'kɪdɪəm). Pl. -idia (-'ɪdɪə). [mod.L.: see GLOCHIDIATE.] **1.** The larva of a pond-mussel of the family Unionidæ. Also *attrib.*
1875 HUXLEY & MARTIN *Elem. Biol.* 110 There is a single adductor muscle and a rudimentary foot, from which one or two long structureless filaments, representing the *byssus* of the sea-mussel, proceed. These byssal filaments become entangled with one another and tend to keep the 'Glochidia' in their places. **1888** ROLLESTON & JACKSON *Forms Anim. Life* 137 This *Glochidium* is eventually set free from the parent. **1930** G. R. DE BEER *Embryol. & Evol.* 44 The Glochidium larva of Unio. **1961** P. STREET *Shell Life on Seashore* v. 78 Many fresh-water fish serve as hosts to these fresh-water glochidia.
2. *Bot.* (See quot. 1900.) (Also '**glochid.**)
1882 S. H. VINES tr. *Sach's Text-bk. Bot.* (ed. 2) II. 454 In some species [of *Azolla*] these massulæ have their surfaces covered with hair-like appendages, barbed at their free ends (*Glochidia*). **1889** BENNETT & MURRAY *Handbk. Cryptogamic Bot.* I. 30 In some species.. the surface of these massulæ is covered with hair-like appendages, barbed at the apex, the *glochids*. **1900** B. D. JACKSON *Gloss. Bot. Terms*, *Glochid*, *glochidium*.., (1) a barbed hair or bristle; (2) a similar structure on the massulae of certain Cryptogams which act as organs of attachment to a macrospore. **1905** D. H. CAMPBELL *Struct. & Devel. Mosses & Ferns* (ed. 2) xi. 417 Upon the outside of the massulæ are formed the curious anchor-like 'glochidia'. **1938** G. M. SMITH *Cryptogamic Bot.* II. ix. 360 Massulae of species belonging to the section *Rhizosperma* lack glochidia. **1965** BELL & COOMBE tr. *Strasburger's Textbk. Bot.* III. 582 Arising from the surface of each massula are a number of small, barbed hooks or glochidia.

glochinate ('gləʊkɪnət), *a.* [f. Gr. γλωχῖν-, stem of γλωχίς (see GLOCHIDIATE *a.*) + -ATE.] = GLOCHIDIATE.
1854 in MAYNE *Expos. Lex.*

†**glocidate**, *v. Obs. rare*$^{-0}$. [f. L. *glocid-āre* to cluck (in Festus) + -ATE.] *intr.* (See quot.)

1623 COCKERAM, *Glocidate*, to clocke like a Hen.

glockenspiel ('glɒkənʃpiːl, -spiːl). [G., lit. 'bell-play'.] **1.** (See quots.)

1825 J. F. DANNELEY *Dict. Music* s.v. *Carillon*, *Glockenspiel*, in Italian, *campanetta*, an organ-stop, composed of bells, comprising the upper half of the clavier. **1898** STAINER & BARRETT *Dict. Mus. Terms* (ed. 2) 202/2 *Glockenspiel*,.. an organ stop of two ranks.

2. A musical instrument consisting of a series of small bells or metal bars which are struck with a hammer, or by levers acted upon by a keyboard.

1833-4 CARLYLE *Sart. Res.* (1836) I. vii. 46 Some few, of musical turn, have a whole chime of bells (*Glockenspiel*) fastened there [*sc.* on their girdles]. **1880** GROVE *Dict. Mus.* II. 7/1 The instruments of percussion which give definite notes.. are the Kettle Drums.., Glockenspiel (bells used in military bands and occasionally with orchestra), and the Harmonica. **1889** G. B. SHAW *London Music 1888-89* (1937) 193 In the waltz from Die Meistersinger I heard no glockenspiel. **1892** *Work* 2 July 253/3 The glockenspiel proper consists of a set of eight or more clock bells, mounted on a central spindle, which is inserted in a wooden handle. **1957** AUDEN & KALLMAN *Magic Flute* 59 Though Papageno, one is sad to feel, Prefers the juke-box to the glockenspiel. **1970** R. SMITH BRINDLE *Contemp. Percussion* vii. 53 By reason of the brief duration, limited volume and relative indefiniteness of its sounds, the glockenspiel is rarely used to contribute in a decisive way to harmonic structures.

glockerite ('glɒkəraɪt). *Min.* [See quot. Named by Nauman in 1855.] A ferric sulphate of a yellow-brown or black colour and a resinous lustre.

1868 DANA *Min.* (ed. 5) 662 Glockerite was named after the mineralogist, E. F. Glocker.

glod, glode, obs. str. pa. t. GLIDE.

†**glode.** *Obs. rare.* [See GLADE *sb.*²]

1. ? A place free from brushwood. (Cf. GLADE² I.)

13.. *Gaw. & Gr. Knt.* 2181 Hit [a hill] hade a hole on þe ende, & on ayþer syde, & ouer-growen with gresse in glodes ay where.

b. = GLADE *sb.*² 1 b. (Cf. the place-name *Cockglode* = *cockglade*.)

1621 FLETCHER *Wildgoose Chase* v. iv, 'Bless me: what Thing is this? two Pinacles Upon her pate! Is't not a glode to catch Wood-cocks?

2. ? A bright place in the sky; a flash of light; = GLADE *sb.*² 2.

13.. *E.E. Allit. P.* A. 79 Quen glem of glodez agaynz hem [the leaves] glydez, Wyth schymeryng schene ful schrylle þay schynde.

3. (Meaning uncertain: perh. a misreading.)

a **1400-50** *Alexander* 1334 þan bowes he to þe baistall & brymly it semblis, Gedirs of ilk glode grettir & smallire, And prekis furth with his pray.

gloebard(e, -beard(e, var. GLOWBARD, *Obs.*

glœocapsoid (gliːəʊ'kæpsɔɪd), *a. Bot.* [f. mod.L. *Glœocapsa* a genus of bluish-green algæ (f. Gr. γλοία glue + L. *capsa* box, case) + -OID.] Belonging to or resembling the genus *Glœocapsa*.

1857 BERKELEY *Cryptog. Bot.* §139. 165 The singularity consists in the repeated division of the endochrome, till we have a tube constricted at regular intervals, each division containing a glœocapsoid mass.

gloet, obs. pa. t. of GLOW.

gloe-worm, obs. form of GLOW-WORM.

glof(e, obs. form of GLOVE.

gloff (glɒf), *sb. Sc.* [cf. GLIFF *sb.*] A sudden fright, scare, start.

1721 KELLY *Scot. Prov.* 337 There came never such a Gloff to a Daw's Heart. **1768** ROSS *Helenore* (1789) 42, I sanna tell yow, what a gloff I got.

gloff (glɒf), *v. Sc.* [cf. GLIFF *v.*] *intr.* To be startled or scared; to give a scared look.

1755 R. FORBES *Jrnl. fr. Lond.* 30 I'm seer you wou'd hae laughin sair, gin ye had seen how the auld hag gloffed fan she fell down. **1768** ROSS *Helenore* (1789) 64, I gard a witch fa' headlins in a stank.. The carling gloff'd and cry'd out will-awae.

†'**gloffer.** *Obs.* [Echoic: cf. GLOBBE, GLOP, GULP; also Da. (dial.) *gluffe*, Sw. (dial.) *gluffa*, to eat hastily or noisily (said e.g. of pigs), *gluffi* a glutton.] A gluttonous eater. So also '**gloffing** *vbl. sb.*, gluttonous eating.

c **1440** *Promp. Parv.* 199/2 Gloffare, or devowrare, *devorator*.. *vorator*.. Gloffynge, or devowrynge, *devoracio, voracio*. [Cf. 16th c. quots. s.v. GLOSSER².]

glogh, obs. form of GLOW *v.*²

gloiocarp ('glɔɪəkɑːp). *Bot.* [f. Gr. γλοία glue, or γλοιός glutinous substance + καρπός fruit. (The analogical form would be *glœocarp.)] The quadruple spore of some algals.

1866 in *Treas. Bot.* 535/1.

gloir(e, obs. Sc. form of GLORY.

‖**gloire** (glwar). [Fr.] In full *la gloire*. Glory; *spec.* the national glory and prestige of France.

1854 E. TWISLETON *Let.* 28 Nov. (1928) xiii. 252 If *la gloire* forsakes the French eagles, they will say.. that he [*sc.* Louis Napoleon] has driven away all their best generals. **1861** MRS. BEETON *Bk. Househ. Managem.* 302 M. Curmer .. tells us.. that French beef is far superior to that of England. This is mere vaunting on the part of our neighbours, who seem to want *la gloire* in everything. **1867** 'OUIDA' *Under Two Flags* II. i. 11 She had.. but two deities, 'la Gloire' and 'la France'. **1963** *Times* 7 Feb. 9/1 After the debacle with the High Military Tribunal, the present spectacle, both in and out of the court-room, hardly adds to the *gloire* of French justice. **1965** A. HORNE *Fall of Paris* ii. 31 Had Louis-Napoleon succeeded in his pursuit of '*la gloire*', the dynasty might have been assured a much longer life in France. **1969** *Listener* 16 Oct. 518/2 They [*sc.* the French] care only.. for a slightly fake sense of their own importance, as Frenchmen, for that umbrella concept, *la gloire*.

Gloire de Dijon (glwar də diʒɔ̃). *Bot.* [Fr., lit. 'glory of Dijon'.] A yellow hybrid tea rose. Also *attrib.*

1854 T. RIVERS *Rose Amateur's Guide* (ed. 5) 119 A new variety exhibited last year in Paris, raised at Dijon, and called Gloire de Dijon, is a great acquisition. **1864** G. MEREDITH *Let.* 6 Sept. (1970) I. 280, I want you to see my Marie blooming. She is a full and perfect rose. You know the Gloire de Dijon? **1869** S. R. HOLE *Book about Roses* ix. 132 All the Roses in this list, except Gloire de Bordeaux, Gloire de Dijon, and Jaune Desprez, are of the Hybrid Perpetual family. **1885** C. M. YONGE *Two Sides of Shield* I. v. 72 The verandah.. was hung with.. a Gloire de Dijon rose. **1928** GALSWORTHY *Swan Song* I. xiii. 102 He took up a rose and sniffed at it deeply. So many different kinds now —he had lost track! In his young days one could tell them —La France, Maréchal Niel, and Gloire de Dijon—nothing else to speak of. **1928** D. H. LAWRENCE *Lady Chatterley* xiv. 255 She still lay naked and faintly golden like a Gloire de Dijon rose in the bed. **1969** *Jrnl. R. Hort. Soc.* XCIV. 241 'Gloire de Dijon' over a century old, is also of the tea rose persuasion.

gloit, obs. form of GLOAT *v.*

glom (glɒm), *v. U.S. slang.* Also **glahm**. [Var. GLAUM *v.*] *trans.* To steal; to grab, snatch. Also *intr.*, usu. const. *on to*. Hence '**glomming** *vbl. sb.*

1907 J. LONDON *Road* (1914) 182 We.. discovered that our hands were gloved. 'Where'd ye glahm 'em?' I asked. 'Out of an engine-cab,' he answered. **1914** JACKSON & HELLYER *Vocab. Criminal Slang* 38 *Glom*, to grab; to snatch; to take; implying violence. Example: 'Glom this short and drop off two blocks below.' **1925** G. H. MULLIN *Adv. Scholar Tramp* xii. 180, I learnt that stealing clothes from a clothes-line is expressed in Hoboland by the hilarious phrase, 'Glomming the grape-vine'. **1926** *Flynn's* 16 Jan. 638/1 'Course, th' rule is, glom while th' glomin's good. **1930** *Ibid.* 25 Jan. 524/1 In his hip-pocket, where even the lowest kind of lush-worker would have no difficulty in glomming it. **1960** J. PHILIPS *Whisper Town* (1965) II. v. 105 You think we ought to go out to the school and glom on to that gun? **1962** —— *Dead Ending* (1963) I. i. 7 In the process of glomming onto that property in Venezuela some people got killed. **1969** C. ARMSTRONG *Seven Seats to Moon* xiii. 126 Trust Lily Eden, though, to glom on to a customer.

glome (gləʊm). [ad. L. *glomus* ball, clue.]

†**1.** A ball or clue of yarn, etc. In quot. *fig.*

1643 SIR T. BROWNE *Relig. Med.* I. §43 There is therefore a secret glome or bottome of our days. **1656** BLOUNT *Glossogr.*, *Glome*, a clue, or bottom of thread.

2. *Bot.* = GLOMERULE 1.

1793 MARTYN *Lang. Bot.*, *Glomus*, a glome, or roundish head of flowers. **1890** *Lippincott's Mag.* Jan. 99 The flood Doth sometimes stain the marsh-flowers' moon-white glomes.

3. '*Glome of frog*: Bracey Clark's name for the two rounded, elastic eminences, separated by a cleft, which form the posterior extremity or base of the frog of the horse's foot' (*Syd. Soc. Lex.* 1885).

glome, var. GLOOM *v.*², *Obs.*

glomerate ('glɒmərət), *a.* [ad. L. *glomerātus*, pa. pple. of *glomerāre*: see next.] Compactly clustered, having the form of a rounded mass or cluster. Chiefly *Bot.*; also *Anat.* (see quot. 1854).

1793 MARTYN *Lang. Bot.*, *Glomerata spica-panicula*. A glomerate spike.. The glomerate panicle is exemplified in *Poa ciliaris*. **1806** GALPINE *Brit. Bot.* 35 Pan. 1-rowed, superdecompound, glomerate. **1846** DANA *Zooph.* iv. §69 (1848) 68 These zoophytes have generally a form irregularly glomerate, rather than symmetrically globular. **1854** MAYNE *Expos. Lex.*, *Glomerate, Anat.* Applied to glands that are formed of a clue, as it were, of sanguineous vessels having an excretory duct but no cavity. **1870** HOOKER *Stud. Flora* 147 Cymes glomerate. **1880** GRAY *Struct. Bot.* 413/2 *Glomerate*, compactly clustered.

†'**glomerate**, *v. Obs.* [f. L. *glomerāt-*, ppl. stem of *glomerāre* to form into a ball or mass, to collect, f. *glomer-*, *glomus* ball, etc.: see GLOME.]

a. *trans.* To roll or wind up into a ball; to gather into a rounded mass. **b.** *intr.* To wind or twist about.

1638 SIR T. HERBERT *Trav.* (ed. 2) 313 They glomerate and wind in dances. **1655** FULLER *Hist. Camb.* 24 Gathering their votes, commonly written, and.. glomerated, i.e., rolled and rounded up in a piece of paper. **1656** BLOUNT *Glossogr.*, *Glomerate*, to wind round, to assemble, to gather, or heap round together. **1755-73** JOHNSON, *Glomerate*, to gather into a ball or sphere. A filamentous substance gathered into a ball is said to be *glomerated*, but discontinuous particles are *conglobated*.

Hence '**glomerated** *ppl. a.* = GLOMERATE; '**glomerating** *ppl. a.*, winding about.

1634 SIR T. HERBERT *Trav.* 92 We rode over, and about hils so high and glomerating, as if Olympus had beene cut into Dedalian Labyrinths. **1638** *Ibid.* (ed. 2) 66 A river, which from Caucasus after many glomerating dances increases Indus. *a* **1798** PENNANT *Zool.* (1812) IV. 359 S. with a round spiral shell, glomerated, and having three raised ridges on the upper side.

glomeration (glɒmə'reɪʃən). *rare.* [ad. L. *glomerātiōn-em*, n. of action f. *glomerāre*: see prec.] The process of forming into a ball or rounded mass; in wider sense, a heaping together, agglomeration, aggregation; also quasi-*concr.*, a cluster of things compactly gathered together.

1626 BACON *Sylva* §832 The Raine-Bow consisteth of a Glomeration of Small Drops. **1812** *Chron.* in *Ann. Reg.* 68 The eyes were struck with momentary blindness, and the ears stunned with the glomeration of sounds. **1822-34** *Good's Study Med.* (ed. 4) IV. 226 The term glomeration or 'heaping into a ball', in the generic definition is preferred to the more common terms protuberance or extuberance. *Ibid.* 238 The cyst, or rather the glomeration of cysts, weighed nine pounds. **1839-40** DE QUINCEY *Casuistry* Wks. VIII. 298 Like the glomeration of moonbeams upon moonbeams.

glomerel ('glɒmərəl). *Obs.* exc. *Hist.* [ad. med.L. *glomerellus*, ad. OF. *glomerel* ('les clers d'Orliens glomeriaus', *La Bataille des vii Ars* in *Œuvres.. Rutebeuf* 1839 II. 415), f. *glomerie GLOMERY.] A term formerly in use in the University of Cambridge, apparently denoting a pupil of a grammar-school.

1276 [see GLOMERY]. **1841** G. PEACOCK *Stat. Camb.* App. p. xxxv, The master of glomery.. would continue.. the exercise of the same jurisdiction over his scholars or glomerells which he had possessed and exercised before the appearance of a new and more highly privileged body. **1873** MULLINGER *Univ. Camb.* I. 226 The Glomerels.. constituted a body distinct from the Scholars of the University. [**1895** RASHDALL *Univ. Europe* II. II. 555 *note*, The word 'Glomerellus' is used of the Grammar-boys in the School founded by Abbot Samson at Bury S. Edmund's. British Museum Add. 14,848 f. 136.]

¶The following explanation of the term rests upon a misunderstanding of the early statutes.

[**1626** SPELMAN *Gloss.* 316 *Glomerarii, Glomerelli*. In Statutis Accademiæ Cantabrig... asseruntur fuisse q. Commissarii dati ad lites inter Scholares & ministros suos audiendas.] **1729** G. JACOB *Law Dict.*, *Glomerells*, Commissaries appointed to determine differences between Scholars of a School or University, and the Townsmen of the Place. **1848** in WHARTON *Law Lex.*; and in some mod. Dicts.

†'**glomerous**, *a. Obs. rare*$^{-0}$. [f. L. *glomer-*, *glomus* ball + -OUS.] (See quots.)

1656 BLOUNT *Glossogr.*, *Glomerous*, round as a bottom, swarmed together. **1727** BAILEY vol. II, *Glomerous*, round like a Bottom of Thread, Yarn, &c. **1755-73** JOHNSON, *Glomerous*, gathered into a ball or sphere, as a ball of thread.

glomerular (glɒ'mɛrələ(r)), *a.* [f. next + -AR.] Of or pertaining to the glomeruli (of the kidneys). ***glomerular nephritis***, disease in the glomerules of the kidneys, occurring in connexion with scarlet fever; also called ***glo'merulo-ne'phritis***.

1885 *Jrnl. Physiol.* VI. 385 To determine that.. circulation through the glomeruli and glomerular activity are wholly stopped Nussbaum employed two methods. **1886** FAGGE *Princ. & Pract. Med.* II. 460 Glomerulo-nephritis. **1897** *Allbutt's Syst. Med.* II. 168 Dr. Klein has described the presence of definite glomerular nephritis in twenty-three consecutive cases of scarlet fever. **1917** A. R. CUSHNY *Secretion of Urine* iv. 44 The blood pressure in the glomerular capillaries suffices for filtration. **1962** *Gray's Anat.* (ed. 33) 1501 The glomerular capsule is the blind, expanded end of the renal tubule, indented for the reception of the glomerulus. **1966** WRIGHT & SYMMERS *Systemic Path.* I. xxiv. 733/2 The glomerular changes in the chronic stage of type 1 glomerulonephritis. **1970** PASSMORE & ROBSON *Compan. Med. Stud.* II. xi. 2/1 The rate of glomerular filtration is raised by agents which increase renal blood flow, cardiac output or blood volume.

glomerule ('glɒməruːl). Also in mod.L. form **glomerulus** (gləʊ'mɛr(j)ʊləs), pl. **glomeruli**. [a. F. *glomérule*, ad. mod.L. *glomerulus*, dim. of *glomer-*, *glomus* ball, clue.]

1. *Bot.* **a.** A cluster or head of flowers (cf. quot. 1880).

1793 MARTYN *Lang. Bot.*, *Glomerulus*, a Glomerule, or small glome. **1806** GALPINE *Brit. Bot.* 397 *Amaranthus*. Glomerules lateral. **1861** BENTLEY *Bot.* 212 The Glomerule ..is a cyme which consists of a number of sessile flowers. **1880** GRAY *Struct. Bot.* v. 152 One form of the regular cyme, on account of its compactness, is named the *Glomerule*. This is merely a cymose inflorescence, of any sort, which is condensed into the form of a head, or approaching it.

b. A soredium.

1855 OGILVIE, Suppl. *s.v.*, Glomerules are also the heaps of powdery bodies which lie upon the surface of the thallus of lichens; these are also called soredia. **1866** *Treas. Bot.* 535/1 *Glomeruli*.

2. A compact cluster of small organisms, animal tissues, etc.; esp. a group or plexus of capillary blood-vessels, as those in the Malpighian corpuscles of the kidney.

1856 *Quain's Elem. Anat.* (ed. 6) III. 325 The Malpighian corpuscles.—These small red bodies or *glomeruli*, discovered by Malpighi. **1857** DUNGLISON *Med. Lex.* 245 A convoluted mass of blood-vessels, which constitutes the true glandule, corpuscle, or glomerule of Malpighi. **1872** HUXLEY *Phys.* v. 108 A bunch of looped Capillaries, called a *glomerulus.* **1874** JONES & SIEV. *Pathol. Anat.* 102 What are called glomeruli or granule-cells. **1885** C. S. DOLLEY *Technol. Bacteria Invest.* 220 The Spirilla gradually gather upon the surface of the clot, often in large groups of twenty or more twisted up in a glomerule.

Hence **glo͵meru'litis** (see quot. 1885); **glo'merulose** *a.*, gathered in small clusters.

1882 CROMBIE in *Encycl. Brit.* XIV. 556/2 *Haplogonidia*.. of a protococcoid form, or sometimes glomerulose. **1885** *Syd. Soc. Lex.*, *Glomerulitis*, inflammation of the glomeruli of Malpighi and their capsule. **1897** *Allbutt's Syst. Med.* II. 983 In the more chronic cases [of lead poisoning in rabbits] there was a glomerulitis followed by thickening of the vessels and interstitial nephritis.

glo͵merulo͵scle'rosis. *Path.* [f. GLOMERULAR *a.* + -O + SCLEROSIS.] Fibrosis or hyalinization of the glomeruli of the kidneys.

1936 KIMMELSTIEL & WILSON in *Amer. Jrnl. Path.* XII. 85 We have..contrasted the features of this special group [of cases] with those of true intracapillary and extracapillary glomerulonephritis... The term intercapillary glomerulosclerosis has been applied to the group of cases under discussion. **1964** S. DUKE-ELDER *Parsons' Dis. Eye* (ed. 14) xxii. 328 The fully developed ocular picture with micro-aneurysms is often associated with evidences of glomerulosclerosis in the kidney. **1966** R. H. HEPTINSTALL *Path. Kidney* iii. 59 Congenital glomerulosclerosis is almost always a purely incidental finding.

glomery ('glɒmərɪ). *Obs.* exc. *Hist.* [ad. med.L. *glomeria*, prob. ad. AF. **glomerie* = **gramarie* GRAMMAR; for the form cf. GLAMOUR.]

Master of Glomery (= L. *Magister Glomeriæ*), the title of an official formerly recognized by the University of Cambridge, apparently the head of the grammar-school or schools (see quot. 1873). (Cf. GLOMEREL.)

[**1276** BP. BALSHAM in Fuller *Hist. Camb.* (1655) 22 Inprimis volumus & ordinamus quod magister Glomeriæ Cant. qui pro tempore fuerit, audiat & decidat universas [? *a word missing*] glomerellorum ex parte rea existentium. ?**1500** *Stat. Camb.* (1785) 33 Quod nullus sit simul magister glomeriæ et procurator universitatis. *Ibid.* 57 Tunc demum per magistrum grammaticæ..vel per magistrum glomeriæ in ejus defectu procuratoribus præsentetur.] *a* **1591** STOKYS in G. Peacock *Stat. Camb.* (1841) App. p. xxxii, The Master of Grammar shall be browght by the Bedyll to the Place where the Master of Glomerye dwellyth, at iij of the Clocke, and the Master of Glomerye shall go before, and his eldyst son nexte him. [**1655** FULLER *Hist. Camb.* 24 But what should be the sense of Glomerelli and Magister Glomeriæ.. we must confess our selves Seekers therein..let it suffice us to know, that the original of this word seems barbarous, his office narrow and topical (confin'd to Cambridge) and his certain use at this day antiquated and forgotten.] **1841** G. PEACOCK *Stat. Camb.* App. p. xxxv, When..the university was regularly established, and the schools of glomery in some respect associated with it. [**1873** MULLINGER *Univ. Camb.* I. 140 It was customary in the earliest times to delegate to a non-academic functionary the instruction of youth in the elements of the [Latin] language. Such, if we adopt the best supported conjecture, was the function of the *Magister Glomeriæ.*]

gloming, -yng, obs. ff. GLOAMING, GLOOMING.

glom(m)ing, var. GLUMMING, *Obs.*

glomus ('gləʊməs). Pl. 'glomera, (erron.) glomi. [L., = ball of thread.]

†**1.** *Bot.* = GLOMERULE 1 a. *Obs.*

1832 J. LINDLEY *Introd. Bot.* 111 Suppose the flowers of a simple umbel to be deprived of their pedicels, and to be seated on a receptacle or enlarged axis, and we have a *capitulum* or head, named *glomus* by some, *glomerulus* by others. **1856** J. S. HENSLOW *Dict. Bot. Terms* 81 *Glomus*, synonyme for capitulum.

2. *Anat.* A small body consisting of a plexus of blood-vessels and associated tissue. **a.** Applied, chiefly in mod.L. phrases, to various specific structures in the body.

1839–47 R. B. TODD *Cycl. Anat.* III. 635/2 The former are most numerous at that part which was called by the Wenzels glomus, where the choroid plexus turns up from the inferior cornu into the horizontal portion of the lateral ventricle [of the brain]. **1897** W. N. PARKER tr. *Wiedersheim's Compar. Anat. Vertebr.* (ed. 2) IX. 341 These vessels become coiled to form a rete mirabile known as the *glomus.* **1905** J. S. FERGUSON *Normal Histol.* xxii. 458 The Carotid Gland. This body.., from its intimate relation to the blood vessels and nerves, is also known as the glomus caroticum. *Ibid.* 459 The Coccygeal Gland... It is richly supplied with broad capillaries or sinusoids and hence is also known as the glomus coccygeum. **1928** G. R. DE BEER *Vertebr. Zool.* xii. 189 Capillaries grow out from the dorsal aorta forming the glomus. **1949** A. S. ROMER *Vertebr. Body* xiii. 435 The tails of many mammals (such as dog, cat, rat) show small tissue masses, termed caudal glomeruli, which contain retia mirabilia. **1956** W. J. HAMILTON *Textbk. Human Anat.* 315 A chemo-receptor is also present in this region [*sc.* the aortic arch] and constitutes the aortic body, or glomus aorticum. **1962** W. H. HOLLINSHEAD *Textbk. Anat.* xxiii. 823/2 Behind the upper end of the common carotid.. is a flattened, somewhat ovoid body, the carotid body (glomus caroticum). This is a highly vascular epithelial body that also contains special nerve fibers. **1964** J. MAHON tr. *Baer's Compar. Anat. Vertebr.* 153 This knot of blood vessels forms the glomus or glomerulus, where filtration of the blood occurs. **1965** R. P. MOREHEAD *Human Path.* xxxiv. 1381/2 Tumors of the glomus tympanicum may arise in the middle ear.

b. [named by P. Masson 1924, in *Lyon chirurgical* XXI. 257.] One of the large number of structures in the skin of the digits in which a special arrangement of muscle and nerve tissue encloses an arterio-venous anastomosis by-passing the capillaries.

1938 *Physiol. Rev.* XVIII. 234 Masson was dissatisfied with the name 'arteriovenous anastomosis' because of the confusion with the traumatic and other unusual connections which have received the same name. Since those in the finger often occur in the form of a group which makes a sort of ball, or skein, and since they have a morphology similar to those found in the glomus coccygeum..he adopted the term 'glomus'... Tumors involving them he termed 'glomus tumors' or 'glomic tumors'. **1950** A. W. HAM *Histology* xxii. 383/1 In the skin of the fingers and toes, and in certain other sites, arteriovenous anastomoses are present in little bodies called glomi that are disposed deep in the dermis. **1962** *Gray's Anat.* (ed. 33) 727 The glomera play an important part in regulating body temperature. **1965** R. P. MOREHEAD *Human Path.* xxii. 580 A glomus tumor is a benign mass of the cutaneous glomus consisting of epithelium-lined spaces surrounded by glomus cells.

glonoin(e ('glɒnəʊɪn). [app. suggested by the two first letters of *glycerine* and the chemical symbols O (oxygen) and NO_3 (nitric anhydride). See -IN.] A name given to nitro-glycerine, esp. as used in medicine.

1860 *N. Syd. Soc. Year-bk.* 1859. 182 Glonoine. **1878** *Ure's Dict. Arts* (ed. 7) IV. 409 *Oil of Glonoin*, a name occasionally given to nitro-glycerine. **1883–4** *Med. Ann.* 40/2 Dr. Hering..gave it [nitro-glycerine] the name of Glonoine.

gloar, dial. var. GLOWER.

glood(e, obs. pa. t. of GLIDE.

gloom (gluːm), *sb.*[1] Also 6–7 *Sc.* gloume, glowme, 7 gloome. [In sense 1 f. GLOOM *v.*; in senses 2–3 perh. back-formation from GLOOMY; app. unconnected with OE. *glóm* twilight (see GLOAMING).

In the sense of 'darkness' the word may possibly be a new formation by Milton; it occurs 9 times in his poems, but our material contains no other examples earlier than the 18th c.]

1. (Only *Sc.*) A sullen look, frown, scowl. ?*Obs.*

1596 DALRYMPLE tr. *Leslie's Hist. Scot.* x. 462 Bosting the pane confirmet be the edict with a gloume inttollerable. **1629** Z. BOYD *Last Battell* i. 4 Nowe Gods glowmes..make heart and soule to melt. **1636** RUTHERFORD *Lett.* (1862) I. 184, I trust in God not to call His glooms unkind again. **1720** RAMSAY *Rise & Fall of Stocks* 75 The miser hears him with a gloom, Girns like a brock and bites his thumb. *a* **1800** in Scott *Minstr. Scot. Bord.* (1803) III. 16 But sick a gloom, on ae brow-head, Grant I ne'er see agane!

2. An indefinite degree of darkness or obscurity, the result of night, clouds, deep shadow, etc. Sometimes *pl.*

Originally *poet.*, and still somewhat rhetorical in use. By association with the fig. sense 3, the word has latterly tended to denote a painful or depressing darkness, though instances of the wider (Miltonic) use are not wanting in recent poetry.

1629 MILTON *Christ's Nativity* 77 Though the shady gloom Had given day her room, The Sun himself withheld his wonted speed. **1667** —— *P.L.* I. 244 Is..this the seat That we must change for Heav'n, this mournful gloom For that celestial light? **1717** POPE *Eloisa* 38 Now warm in love, now with'ring in my bloom, Lost in a convent's solitary gloom! **1726–46** THOMSON *Winter* 58 Thus Winter falls A heavy gloom oppressive o'er the world. **1784** COWPER *Task* IV. 278 An hour..spent in parlour twilight; such a gloom Well suits the thoughtful..mind. **1832** W. IRVING *Alhambra* II. 258 He heard the tramp of hoofs, and, through the gloom of the overshadowing trees, imperfectly beheld a steed descending the avenue. **1855** BROWNING *Childe Roland* xix, A sudden little river crossed my path..No sluggish tide congenial to the glooms. **1863** GEO. ELIOT *Romola* II. xxvi, A gloom unbroken except by a lamp burning feebly here and there. **1882** FROUDE *Short Stud.* (1883) IV. I. x. 124 With a few steps he would have been lost in the gloom of the cathedral.

b. A deeply shaded or darkened place.

1706 ADDISON *Rosamond* I. ii, Your Highness..Has chose the most convenient Gloom; There's not a Place in all the Park Has Trees so thick, and Shades so dark. **1747** COLLINS *Passions* 64 Through glades and glooms the mingled measure stole. **1832** TENNYSON *Pal. Art* xiv, Full of long sounding corridors it was That overvaulted grateful glooms. **1871** R. ELLIS *Catullus* lxiii. 32 Cometh on Taborine behind him, Attis, thoro' leafy glooms a guide.

†**c.** Twilight. [Possibly another word, connected with GLOAMING.] *Obs.*$^{-1}$

a **1699** LADY HALKETT *Autobiog.* (1875) 10 He..had rod up and downe that part of the country only till itt was y^{e} gloome of y^{e} evening to have the more privacy in coming to see mee.

3. A state of melancholy or depression; a sad or despondent look. Also in *pl.* fits of melancholy.

1744 HARRIS *Three Treat.* III. (1765) 183 The Face of Nature, said he, will perhaps dispel these Glooms. **1773** N. FROWDE *Life*, etc. 139, I recovered, and grew calm; but bore a settled Gloom in my Mind and Countenance. **1786** W. THOMSON *Watson's Philip III*, VI. (1839) 349 A comet.. aggravated the general gloom; and the minds of men were agitated at once by the alarms of war, and a superstitious terror. *c* **1808** MARY LAMB *to Mrs. Hazlitt* in Talfourd *Final Mem. Lamb* v. (1848) I. 160 Hazlitt..was a more useful one ..when he dropt in after a fit of the glooms. **1838** DICKENS *Nich. Nick.* xxii, The uncertainty of the morrow cast a gloom upon him. **1842** BARHAM *Ingol. Leg.*, *Misadv. Margate*, The gloom upon your youthful cheek speaks anything but joy. **1874** GREEN *Short Hist.* vii. §8. 445 No outer triumph could break the gloom which gathered round the dying Queen. **1879** GEO. ELIOT *Coll. Breakf. P.* 598 The sick morning glooms of debauchees.

4. *attrib.* and *Comb.*, as ***gloom-bird***, ***-gladdener***; ***gloom-bound***, ***-buried***, ***-enamoured***, ***-laden***, ***-roaming*** ppl. adjs.

1820 KEATS *Hyperion* I. 171 Or *gloom-bird's hated screech. **1863** P. S. WORSLEY *Poems & Transl.* 18 Some *gloom-bound cell Under the level of a stormy lake. **1853** M. ARNOLD *Mod. Sappho* vii, [He] Looks languidly round on a *gloom-buried world. *a* **1784** JOHNSON *Parody Medea* Wks. (1816) I. 353 Where *gloom-enamour'd Mischief loves to dwell. **1833** *Blackw. Mag.* XXXIV. 961 Delicate thy harp-touch, our own Dora, the *gloom-gladdener. *a* **1847** ELIZA COOK *Song Old Year* iii, Ye have murmur'd of late at my *gloom-laden hours. **1848** *Secret Soc., Tribunals* 373 Like the Nemesis, or the '*gloom-roaming' Erinnys, of antiquity.

gloom, *sb.*[2] Also 6 glome. [Possibly, in spite of the chronological gap, repr. OE. *glóm*, in its unrecorded primary sense: see GLOAMING.]

†**1.** ***hot gloom***, excessive heat (of the sun). (Cf. GLEAM *sb.* 1 c.) *Obs.*

1577 HELLOWES *Gueuara's Chron.* 289 The sunne did shine with as hote a glome as in ye heate of summer. **1633** T. JAMES *Voy.* 77 We haue such hot gloomes, that we cannot endure in the Sunne. **1759** tr. *Duhamel's Husb.* I. xiv. (1762) 74 Hot glooms which mildew the corn.

2. *Comb.* in **gloom-stove** (also **gloom** simply), a variety of drying-oven used in the manufacture of gunpowder.

1839 URE *Dict. Arts* 629 Gunpowder..dried..by radiation from red-hot iron, as in the gloom stove. **1867** SMYTH *Sailor's Word-bk.*, *Gloom-stove*, Formerly for drying powder..steam-pipes are now substituted.

gloom (gluːm), *v.*[1] Forms: 4 gloumbe, glowmbe, 5–6 gloum, 6 glowm(e, 6–7 gloome, 6– gloom. See also GLUM *v.* [ME. *gloum(b)e* (**glūme-n*:—OE. **glúmian*) = MG. (13th c.) *glūmen*, ? to be savage (in *ein glûmender hunt* a savage dog); cf. MG. (14th c.) *beglûmen*, ? to defraud, LG. *glûm* muddiness, fraudulent conduct, *glum* muddy, turbid (adopted by Luther, Ezek. xxxii. 2), *glummen*, *gläumen* to make turbid, MDu. *gloom* (*gloym*) adj. foggy, whence *glomich* foggy. The OE. *glóm*, twilight (whence GLOAMING), is app. not etymologically cognate, as it belongs to a different ablaut-series.

With the representation of ME. *gloum(b)e* by mod.Eng. *gloom*, cf. ME. *roum* (OE. *rúm*), mod.Eng. *room.* The variant GLUM *v.* is parallel with mod.Eng. *thumb* from OE. *þúma*, ME. *thoum(b)e.*]

1. *intr.* To look sullen or displeased; to frown, scowl, lower; also ***to gloom on*** or ***at*** (a person). In recent use also (through influence of GLOOMY): To look dismal or dejected, to wear an air of sombre melancholy; to be gloomy.

α. **13..** *E.E. Allit. P.* C. 94 'Our syre syttes', he [Jonah] says, 'on sege so hyȝe..& gloumbes ful lyttel, þaȝ I be nummen in Niniuie & naked dispoyled. *c* **1400** *Rom. Rose* 4356 Fortune..whilom wole on folk smyle, And glowmbe on hem another while. **1515** BARCLAY *Egloges* IV. (1570) C v/1 Assoone as clerkes begin to talke and chat, Some other glowmes and hath envy thereat. **1535** STEWART *Cron. Scot.* I. 415 O fekill Fortune..With busteous browis glowmand on hir brie. *a* **1572** KNOX *Hist. Ref.* IV. Wks. (1848) II. 358 Sche glowmed boyth at the messenger and at the requeast, and skarselie wold geve a goode worde or blyth countenance to any [etc.]. **1628** RUTHERFORD *Let. to Chr. Gentlewoman* 23 Apr., That long loan..deserveth more thanks..then that ye should gloom and murmure when He craveth but his own. **1697** CONGREVE *Mourn. Bride* I. vi, What's he, who with contracted Brow, And sullen Port, glooms downward with his Eyes? **1720** MRS. MANLEY *Power Love* (1741) I. 76 He gloomed from beneath his Eyes, bit his Lips [etc.]. **1724** RAMSAY *Tea-t. Misc.* (1729) 16, I wat on him she did na gloom, But blinkit bonnilie. **1831** *Fraser's Mag.* II. 699 Some gloomed upon him; others pitied the tall and gallant fellow. **1848** THACKERAY *Van. Fair* l, Her father, sitting glooming in his place at the other end of the table. **1860** FROUDE *Hist. Eng.* VI. 94 The Stanleys, Howards, Talbots, and Nevilles were glooming apart, indignant at the neglect of their own claims. **1870** MORRIS *Earthly Par.* II. III. 390 But whoso gloomed at tidings men might show, It was not Kiartan. **1881** MRS. LYNN LINTON *My Love* III. 36 She was glooming over her daughter's prolonged absence, and fearing she scarcely knew what. **1883** *Century Mag.* XXV. 891/2, I hate myself for glooming about the house in secret. **1967** 'A. GARVE' *Very Quiet Place* I. iv. 59 'What did you do?' 'Gloomed for a week—then started to write it again.' **1968** H. FRANKLIN *Crash* vi. 77, I sat and gloomed in the hotel lounge.

quasi-*trans.* **1858** CARLYLE *Fredk. Gt.* III. v. I. 171 They.. gloomed unutterable things on George and his Speech. **1865** *Ibid.* XIV. vi. V. 226 'What interloping fellow is this?' gloomed Valori.

2. a. Of the weather, the sky, etc.: To lower, look dark or threatening; to be or to become dull and cloudy. Also *fig.*

a **1400–50** *Alexander* 4142 Þe wedire gloumes. **1535** COVERDALE *Matt.* xvi. 3 It wil be foule wedder to daye for the szkye is reed & gloometh. **1639** R. BAILLIE *Lett.* (1775) I. 91 Storms are likely to arise in that flat air of England, which long has been glooming. **1780** BURKE *Sp. at Bristol* Wks. 1842 I. 265 You remember the cloud that gloomed over us all. **1795** *Cicely* I. 114 The day gloomed, the wind whistled cold thro' the almost leafless trees. **1846** HAWTHORNE *Mosses* I. i. 16 The sky gloomed through the dusty garret windows. *a* **1861** T. WOOLNER *My Beautiful Lady* (1863) 135 Long toil-devoted years have gloomed and shone Since these events closed up my doors of life.

b. = GLOAM *v.*

1595 SPENSER *Epithal.* xvi, Ah when will this long weary day have end. Long though it be, at last I see it gloome. **1819** J. HODGSON in J. Raine *Mem.* (1857) I. 232 We left Bromley ..as the evening began to gloom. **1858** G. MACDONALD *Phantastes* iii. (1878) 28 In the midst of the forest it gloomed earlier than in the open country.

3. To have a dark or sombre appearance; to appear as a dark object.

1770 GOLDSM. *Des. Vill.* 318 The black gibbet glooms beside the way. **1790** WOLCOT (P. Pindar) *Rowland for Oliver* Wks. 1812 II. 307 Alas! what dangers gloom'd of late around. **1813** BYRON *Br. Abydos* II. xxviii, While dark above The sad but living cypress glooms. **1836** LYTTON *Athens* (1837) I. 470 Mount Parthenius amidst whose wild recesses gloomed the antique grove dedicated to Telephus. **1850** MRS. BROWNING *Sonnets Portuguese* xix, The dim purpureal tresses gloomed athwart The nine white Muse-brows. **1879** DOWDEN *Southey* vi. 188 Skiddaw gloomed solemnly overhead.

4. a. *trans.* To make dark or sombre; to cover with gloom; †to give a scowling or sullen look to (the countenance).

1576 STANYHURST *Descr. Irel.* iii. 10 in *Holinshed*, You should neuer marck him or his bedfellowe..bende their browes, or gloome their countenaunces, or make a sower face at anie guest. *a* **1592** GREENE *Philomela* (1615) C 3 b, Frosty Winter thus had gloomed Each fayre thing that sommer bloomed. **1742** YOUNG *Nt.-Th.* ii. 358 A night, that glooms us in the noon-tide ray, And wraps our thought, at banquets, in the shroud. **1753** H. WALPOLE *Lett. H. Mann* ccxlvii. (1834) III. 44 A bow-window..gloomed with limes that shade half each window. **1842** TENNYSON *Letters* 2 A black yew gloom'd the stagnant air. **1851** MRS. BROWNING *Casa Guidi W.* 65 One temple, with its floors Of shining jasper, gloom'd at morn and eve By countless knees of earnest auditors.

b. *fig.* To make dark, dismal, or melancholy.

1745 THOMSON *Tancred & Sigis.* II. i, We meet to-day with open hearts and looks, Not gloomed by party, scowling on each other. **1795** *Char.* in *Ann. Reg.* 23* The neighbouring territory..is impoverished and gloomed by the dominion of ecclesiastics. **1841** CATLIN *N. Amer. Ind.* (1844) II. xxxvi. 33 Her swamps and everglades gloom the thoughts of the wary traveller. **1859** TENNYSON *Vivien* 323 Such a mood as that, which lately gloom'd Your fancy when you saw me following you. **1873** SYMONDS in *Biog.* (1895) II. 83 The boredom of this delay at Trapani has, I dare say, gloomed my views of the outer world.

Hence **gloomed** *ppl. a.*, rendered dark or dismal.

1830 TENNYSON *Poems* 36 Would that my gloomed fancy were As thine, my mother [etc.].

†**gloom**, *v.*[2] *Obs.* Also 5 **glome**. [cf. GLOOM *sb.*[2]] *intr.* To glow.

c **1420** *Anturs of Arth.* xxxi. (Thornton MS.), His gambesouns glomede [*v.r.* glowed] als gledys. **1579–1881** [see GLOOMING *ppl. a.*[2]].

gloomful ('glu:mfʊl), *a. rare.* [f. GLOOM *sb.*[1] + -FUL.] Full of gloom or darkness; dark.

a **1849** J. C. MANGAN *Poems* (1859) 263 In her gloomful dome. **1862** MISS THACKERAY *Elizabeth* I. in *Cornh. Mag.* VI. 332 Looking intently into her own dark, gloomful eyes. **1870** R. R. COVERDALE *Poems* 25 Adieu! thou gloomful vale profound.

gloomily ('glu:mɪlɪ), *adv.* [f. GLOOMY + -LY[2].] In a gloomy or sombre manner.

1727–46 THOMSON *Summer* 268 The window..where gloomily retir'd, The villain spider lives, cunning and fierce. **1794** MRS. RADCLIFFE *Myst. Udolpho* vi, 'My dear Sir, do not think so gloomily', said Emily. **1849** MACAULAY *Hist. Eng.* vi. II. 149 When he had found opposition vain, he had gloomily submitted. **1871** L. STEPHEN *Playgr. Europe* iv. (1894) 96 We parted with him with great regret, and proceeded gloomily on our way.

gloominess ('glu:mɪnɪs). [f. as prec. + -NESS.]

1. The condition of being gloomy; absence of clear light.

1611 BIBLE *Joel* ii. 2 A day of darkenesse and of gloominesse. —— *Zeph.* i. 15. **1618** BOLTON *Florus* III. iv. 177 Curio pierced as farre as Dracia: but the gloominesse of the Woods coold his courage. **1686** AGLIONBY *Painting Illustr.* 236 The reflexion and warmth of the other Lights being painted with such a proper Gloominess. **1711** ADDISON *Spect.* No. 26 ¶1 The Gloominess of the Place.. is apt to fill the Mind with a kind of Melancholy. **1791** MRS. RADCLIFFE *Rom. Forest* viii, She now perceived that the gloominess of evening was deepened by the coming storm. **1844** *P. Parley's Ann.* V. 2 The gloominess of the season is given to us that we may brighten it by deeds of benevolence.

fig. **1691** BEVERLEY *Thous. Years Kingd. Christ* 10 Besides the yet continuing Darkness, and Gloomyness cast upon us from the Apostasie in the Atmosphere or Black Air of which, we yet continue. **1730** A. GORDON *Maffei's Amphith.* 315 That kind of Merchandise is current everywhere, spreading its Gloominess over the Globe. **1876** BANCROFT *Hist. U.S.* III. vi. 93 It was a matter fixed in his mind, that this trade of importing slaves, and way of life in keeping them, were dark gloominess hanging over the land.

2. Depression of spirits; melancholy look.

1607 BEAUM. & FL. *Woman Hater* II. i, I haue me thinkes a kind of feauer vpon me, A certaine gloominesse within me. **1712** ADDISON *Spect.* No. 419 ¶5 That gloominess and melancholy of temper, which is so frequent in our nation. **1844** J. T. HEWLETT *Parsons & W.* xiii, A serious gloominess pervaded..the countenances of the domestics. **1881** LADY HERBERT *Edith* ii. 49 Her grave and taciturn father, whose gloominess seemed to increase day by day.

glooming ('glu:mɪŋ), *vbl. sb.* [f. GLOOM *v.*[1] + -ING[1].]

1. The action of frowning, etc.; a frown, scowl; a fit of sullenness.

13.. *Peter & Paul* 74 in Horstm. *Altengl. Leg.* (1881) 77 Hetheli glowminge & wordes grete. *a* **1572** KNOX *Hist. Ref.* Wks. 1846 I. 146 From glowmyng thei come to schouldering; frome schouldering, thei go to buffettis. **1645** RUTHERFORD *Tryal & Tri. Faith* (1845) 259 Christ's gloomings..have much of heaven in them. **1854** CARLYLE *Fredk. Gt.* IV. 383 A great deal of trouble with his gloomings.

2. *poet.* Twilight, gloaming; also, early dawn, morning twilight.

[Perh. an artificial adaptation for GLOAMING or OE. *glômung.*]

1842 TENNYSON *Gard. Dau.* 258 Or while the balmy glooming, crescent-lit, Spread the light haze along the river-shores. **1877** MORRIS *Sigurd* 315 Good tidings with the daybreak, fair fame with the glooming is born. **1879** TRENCH *Poems* 23 For where the watcher, who..could ever say When the faint glooming in the sky First lightened into day?

glooming, *ppl. a.*[1] [f. as prec. + -ING[2].]

1. Sullen, frowning, scowling, melancholy.

c **1440** *Gesta Rom.* liii. 233 (Harl. MS.) But she Reprevide him moche, & shewid to him much glowmynge cher. *c* **1450** HENRYSON *Mor. Fab.* 10 What pleasure is in feastes delicate, The which are given with a glouming brow. **1725** RAMSAY *Gentle Sheph.* I. ii, With glooman brow the laird seeks in his rent. **1889** STEVENSON *Master of B.* (1896) 77 There is altogether some excuse if Ballantrae showed something of a glooming disposition.

2. That grows or appears dark.

1535 COVERDALE *Joel* ii. 1 A darcke daye, a gloomynge daye, a cloudy daye. **1595** SPENSER *Col. Clout* 954 The glooming skies Warnd them to draw their bleating flocks to rest. **1822** 'B. CORNWALL' (Proctor) *Flood of Thessaly* I. 191 Towards the glooming shore The tempest sailed direct. **1839** LONGF. *Hyperion* III. iii, For a long time they gazed at the glooming landscape, and spake not. **1896** HOWELLS *Impressions & Exp.* 203 The glooming reaches and expanses of the corridors.

fig. **1592** SHAKS. *Rom. & Jul.* v. iii. 305 A glooming peace this morning with it brings, The sunne for sorrow will not shew his head.

Hence **'gloomingly** *adv.*, in a glooming fashion.

1598 FLORIO, *Foltamente*..throngingly, pressingly, gloomingly. **1831** J. WILSON in *Blackw. Mag.* XXX. 550 You look too gloomingly at every thing.

'glooming, *ppl. a.*[2] *Obs.* exc. *dial.* Also 6 **gloming**. [f. GLOOM *v.*[2] + -ING[2].] †**a.** Gleaming, shining (*obs.*). **b.** *dial.* (See quot. 1881.)

In quot. 1579 perh. a forced use of GLOOMING *ppl. a.*[1] With quot. 1601 cf. GLOAMING 1 b.

1579 *Remedy Lawlesse Loue* (Roxb.) C ij b, The Cormorant That makes his God of earthly gloming Golde. **1590** SPENSER *F.Q.* I. i. 14 His glistering armor made A litle glooming light, much like a shade. **1601** ? MARSTON *Pasquil & Kath.* II. 93 The glooming morne with shining armes hath chaste The siluer Ensigne of the grimme-cheekt night. **1881** *Leicester Gloss., Glooming*, glowing, burning hot.

gloomless ('glu:mlɪs), *a. rare*[−1]. [f. GLOOM *sb.*[1] + -LESS.] Free from gloom.

1820 KEATS *Hyperion* III. 80 Apollo then, With sudden scrutiny and gloomless eyes, Thus answer'd.

gloommish, var. GLUMMISH *a.*, *Obs.*

†**gloomth.** (App. peculiar to Walpole.) [f. GLOOM *v.*[1] or *sb.*[1] + -TH[1].] Gloom.

1753 H. WALPOLE *Lett. to Mann* 27 Apr. (1833) III. 40 One has a satisfaction in imprinting the gloomth of Abbeys and Cathedrals on one's house. **1754** —— *Let. to G. Montagu* 8 June, Priv. Corr. (1820) I. 347 [Strawberry] is now in the height of its greenth, blueth, gloomth, honeysuckle, and seringahood. **1770** —— *Let.* 11 June Ibid. III. 331 Strawberry, with all its painted glass and gloomth.

gloomy ('glu:mɪ), *a.* [f. GLOOM *sb.*[1] (or perh. originally f. GLOOM *v.*[1], as the sb. is not recorded so early) + -Y[1].]

1. Full of gloom; dark, shaded, obscure.

1588 SHAKS. *Tit. A.* IV. i. 53 The ruthlesse, vast, and gloomy woods. **1602** MARSTON *Ant. & Mel.* IV. F 4 a, Roul'd vp in gloomie clouds as black as ayer. **1635** J. HAYWARD tr. *Biondi's Banish'd Virg.* 1 The obscure sable night.. surrendred up the field unto a gloomy morning. **1697** DRYDEN *Virg. Georg.* II. 614 Narycian Woods of Pitch, whose gloomy Shade Seems for Retreat of heav'nly Muses made. **1784** COWPER *Task* V. 140 The gloomy clouds find weapons, arrowy sleet. **1822** BYRON *Werner* I. i, Have a care, The staircase is a little gloomy. **1860** TYNDALL *Glac.* I. xvi. 110 At a little distance below me, a gloomy fissure opened its jaws.

†**b.** Of colours: Dark, blackish. *Obs.*

1632 J. HAYWARD tr. *Biondi's Eromena* 187 And the hew of the inhabitants countenances which in Arabia..are gloomie and swarffee.

2. Of persons and their attributes: Affected with gloom or depression of spirits; having dark or sullen looks.

1590 MARLOWE *Edw. II*, IV. vi. (1598) G 3 b, I suspect A gloomie fellow in a meade belowe; A gaue a long looke after vs. **1602** MARSTON *Ant. & Mel.* I. B 4 b, What gloomy soule in strange accustrements Walkes on the pauement. *a* **1639** SIR H. WOTTON *Life Dk. Buckingham* (1642) 22 John Felton, by nature of a deep melancholy, silent, and glomy constitution. **1725** POPE *Odyss.* x. 637 Grisly Pluto and his gloomy bride. **1735** SOMERVILLE *Chase* IV. 202 The glouting Hound..Retiring to some close, obscure Retreat, Gloomy, disconsolate. **1751** EARL ORRERY *Remarks Swift* (1752) 174 His countenance being dark, bilious, and gloomy. **1833** HT. MARTINEAU *Brooke Farm* xi. 127 But there stood Norton with a gloomy brow. **1861** WRIGHT *Ess. Archæol.* II. xxiii. 230 There are people of that gloomy character who never laugh. **1882** OUIDA *Maremma* I. 13 In a gloomy silence, broken only by gloomier mutterings of the crowd, the carabiniers drew rein before the prison.

3. Causing gloom or depression of spirits; dismal, disheartening.

1710 SHAFTESB. *Adv. Author* III. ii. 156 The gloomy Prospect of Death. **1722** *Wodrow Corr.* (1843) II. 643 Things look very gloomy in public affairs abroad and in England. **1781** GIBBON *Decl. & F.* III. 183 The intelligence of the massacre of Pavia filled the mind of Stilicho with just and gloomy apprehensions. **1838** THIRLWALL *Greece* IV. xxxiv. 328 He had spent a part of the night in gloomy reflections. **1848** W. H. KELLY tr. *L. Blanc's Hist. Ten Y.* I. 187 At some leagues distance from tumultuous Paris, St. Cloud presented a gloomy and afflicting spectacle. **1873** MISS BRADDON *L. Davoren* I. iv. Prol. 47 The stranger took the gloomiest view of the position.

4. *Comb.*, as ***gloomy-browed***, ***-faced***, ***-looking***, ***-minded***, ***-sluggish*** adjs.

1727 THOMSON *Sir I. Newton* 157 Ye hopeless gloomy-minded tribe. *c* **1727** *Gulliver decypher'd* 39 An over-grown gloomy-looking Fellow. **1803** J. KENNY *Society* 165 The gloomy-faced fiends that the breast of slumbering innocence load. **1849** J. A. CARLYLE tr. *Dante's Inferno* p. xliv, The Sullen-sour, or Gloomy-sluggish..have their appropriate punishment. **1863** JEAN INGELOW *Poems* 178 Demeter seeks her far and wide, And gloomy browed doth ceaseless roam.

gloomyish ('glu:mɪɪʃ), *a.* [f. GLOOMY + -ISH.] Somewhat gloomy.

1821 *Blackw. Mag.* X. 570 It is somewhat darkish—at least gloomyish, dampish, rawish.

gloose, gloove, obs. ff. GLOZE, GLOVE.

glop (glɒp), *v.*[1] *Obs.* exc. *dial.* [? Shortening of GLOPPEN *v.*]

1. *intr.* To stare, to gaze in alarm or wonder.

13.. *E.E. Allit. P.* B. 849 Þe god man glyfte with þat glam & gloped for noyse. *a* **1743** RELPH *Misc. Poems* (1747) 4 The lads began to glop. **1875** in *Whitby Gloss.* **1878** *Cumbld. Gloss., Glop*, to stare, look wildly.

2. *trans.* To startle, cause to stare.

1807 STAGG *Poems* (1808) 37 The people glop'd wi' deep surprise, Away their wark-gear threw.

Hence †**glop** *sb.*[1], a start, surprise. *Obs. rare*[−1].

c **1460** *Towneley Myst.* xvi. 264 O my hart is rysand now in a glope. [Cf. '*Glopping*, a palpitation' (*Leicester Gloss.*).]

†**glop**, *v.*[2] *Obs. rare*[−1]. [Echoic; cf. GLOBBE, GLOFF, GLOUP, GULP; Sw. (dial.) *glåpa* to gulp down.] *trans.* To swallow greedily. Also **'glopping** *vbl. sb.*

1362 Ygloppid [see GLOUP *v.*]. *c* **1394** *P. Pl. Crede* 92 Glotony is her God · wiþ gloppynge [*v.rr.* goppyng, golping] of drynk.

glop, *sb.*[1]: see GLOP *v.*[1]

glop (glɒp), *sb.*[2] *U.S. slang.* [Cf. GLOP *v.*[2]] A liquid or viscous substance or mixture; *spec.* inferior or unappetising food.

1945 *N.Y. Times Mag.* 4 Nov. 12/3 The somewhat pleasanter words, mostly referring to food, such as 'glop', meaning any food mixture. **1952** BERREY & VAN DEN BARK *Amer. Thes. Slang* (ed. 2) §91/2 Inferior food..*glob* [index has 'glop'] **1962** J. POTTS *Evil Wish* vi. 88 A cheap, soiled cosmetic case crammed with little bottles of glop. **1965** *New Yorker* 15 May 21 (Advt.), This glop can choke an Army whirlybird... The blobs on the left are drops of helicopter fuel—after it has been contaminated by dust, grit and dirt.

gloppen ('glɒp(ə)n), *v. Obs.* exc. *dial.* Forms: 3 **glopnen, glopen** (also 8 *dial.*), **glopin**, 4–5 **glopn-**, 5 **glopyne, gloppyn(e, -un**, 3, 5, 8–9 **gloppen**). Cf. also AGLOPENED, FORGLOPPENED (FOR- *pref.*[1] 6). [a. ON. *glúpna* to be downcast. A root of identical form appears in OFris. *glûpa*, MLG. *glûpen* to lie in wait for, Du. *gluipen* to watch slily, to sneak, OSw. *glupa* to gape, swallow, Sw. *glupande*, Da. *glubende* ravenous, fierce; whether there is any etymological connexion is uncertain.]

Synonymous forms in various Eng. dialects are *glocken*, *glopper*, *glotten*.

†**1.** *intr.* **a.** To be distressed or downcast. **b.** To stare in amazement, to be startled or frightened.

? *a* **1400** *Morte Arth.* 1074 Thane glopnede þe glotone and glorede un-faire. *Ibid.* 2854 Gloppyns noghte, gud mene, for gleterand scheldes. *c* **1420** *Anturs of Arth.* vii, Now kindeles my care, I gloppen and I grete.

2. *trans.* To startle, frighten, astound. Chiefly in pass. pple. *gloppened*.

a **1225** *Ancr. R.* 212 Þeos bodieð biuoren hwu þe ateliche deouel schal ȝet agesten [*T.* glopnen] ham. *a* **1300** *Cursor M.* 1288 (Cott.) Quen [he] þar-of son had a sight, Al was he gloppend for [*Gött.* dredand of] þat light. *Ibid.* 12622 (Gött.) Leue sun, qui has þu glopened vs? ? *a* **1400** *Morte Arth.* 2580 'ȝa', quod syr Gawayne..'Thowe wenys to glopyne me with thy gret wordez!' **1740** in *Gentl. Mag.* X. 460/2 Bounce gus her hart, an hoo wur so glopen, That out o' th' windo hoo'd like fort lopen. *c* **1746** J. COLLIER (Tim Bobbin) *View Lanc. Dial.* Wks. (1862) 55 I'r weawnedly glopp'nt, for the Dule o hawpunny had eh! **1848** MRS. GASKELL *M. Barton* ix, Don't look so gloppened because thou'st fallen asleep. **1865** B. BRIERLEY *Irkdale* II. 97 Come, let's goo i' th' heawse an gloppen her. **1887** *S. Chesh. Gloss., Glockent*, astounded, startled. Also pronounced *gloppent*.

Hence **'gloppenedly** *adv.*, in a state of alarm; **'gloppening** *vbl. sb.*, alarm; **'gloppening** *ppl. a.*, distressed, sorrowful.

a **1300** *Cursor M.* 19634 Saulus þan quok, sa was he radd, For gloppning in his mod al madd. **13..** *E.E. Allit. P.* B. 896 Ful erly þose aungelez þis haþel þay ruþen & glopnedly on godez halue gart hym vpryse. ? *a* **1400** *Morte Arth.* 3863 For glent of gloppynyng glade be they never! *Ibid.* 4330 The baronage of Bretayne..Graythes theme to Glaschenbery with gloppynnande hertes, To bery thare the bolde kynge.

glor(e, obs. Sc. f. GLORY.

glore (glɔə(r)), *sb. dial.* Also 7 glorre, 9 glur, glor. [Of obscure origin.] Loose fat; excessive quantity of fat. Commonly *attrib.* or quasi-*adj.* in *glore-fat.*

a **1661** FULLER *Worthies, Hantsh.* II. (1662) 2 Their flesh.. though not all Glorre (where no bancks of lean can be seen for the Deluge of fat) is no less delicious to the taste. **1684** *Yorksh. Dial.* 165 (E.D.S. No. 76) Here's fine Backon, Sister, its glore Fat. **1796** W. MARSHALL *Yorksh.* (ed. 2) Gloss. (E.D.S.), *Glor-fat*, very fat. **1855** ROBINSON *Whitby Gloss.*, *Glor fat*, loose fat. 'All of a glor and a jelly', tremulous with adiposity. **1876** *Mid-Yorksh. Gloss.* s.v., Of a very fat person whose flesh shakes upon her, it will be said, 'She's fair glor fat', quite loose fat. **1887** *S. Chesh. Gloss.* s.v. *Glur*, Hey's brought this Christmas beif wom; an' it's aw of a glur.

glore, *v. Obs.* exc. *dial.* Also 8–9 gloar, glooar, 9 gloor. [ME. *glōren* = Du. *gloren*, LG. *glôren* to glow (of embers), WFris. *gloarje*, Sw. and Norw. dial. *glora* to glow, stare, Icel. *glóra* to gleam, glare (as the eyes of a cat); app. f. the root *glō-*: see GLOW *v.*[1] A form *gluren* of like meaning is found in Du. and LG., but may be of different origin.

Sense 2 is identical with that of GLOWER *v.*, but the words cannot be immediately related to each other. Recent dialect glossaries show that *gloar* or *gloor* (*glooar*) is still in common use in Yorkshire, Lancashire, and Lincolnshire; for the variation in the vowel compare *floor* (:—OE. *flór*) and *moor* (:—OE. *mór*).]

†**1.** *intr.* To shine, glitter, glisten. (= GLARE *v.* 1.) *Obs.*

13.. *St. Bernard* 356 in Horstmann *Altengl. Leg.* (1878) 47 Ne hit nas parseyued no more Till þat his lippes þerof deede glore. *c* **1350** *Barlaam & Josaphat* 347 Feyr it gloriþ wᵗ oute, wit inne it is nouȝt. **1540** PALSGR. *Acolastus* Prol. Biv, Why glore thyn eyes..in thy heade [*quid ardent lumina?*]?

2. To look fixedly, gaze intently; to stare open-eyed. (= GLARE *v.* 2, GLOWER *v.*) *Obs.* exc. *dial.*

Explained in Bailey 1728 'To look a-skew'.

? *a* **1400** *Morte Arth.* 1074 Thane glopnede þe glotone and glorede un-faire. *c* **1450** *St. Cuthbert* (Surtees) 4859 With blody eyne he gloryd. **1570** LEVINS *Manip.* 174 To Glore, gase, *patulis oculis spectare.* **1703** THORESBY *Let. to Ray* (E.D.S.), *Glore*, to look staringly. **1708** T. WARD *Eng. Ref.* II. (1716) 222 Sometimes..a greedy Gull Would get his Gullet cram'd so full Ast' make him glore, and gasp for Wind. *c* **1746** J. COLLIER (Tim Bobbin) *View Lanc. Dial.* Wks. (1862) 38 He glooart at't a good while. **1821** J. CLARE *Village Minstr.* I. 159 Under the wenches' bonnets he'd glower [*rimes with* sore]. **1833** *York Minster Screen* 152 (E.D.S. 76) Oa'd Jamie..Glooaring at t' fire. *a* **1861** T. WOOLNER *My Beautiful Lady* (1863) 135 Like a foe, whose settled leering eye In silence gloared with hope to mark his fall.

3. *Comb.* †**glore-eye** (cf. *glare-eye*, GLARE *v.* 5), a staring eye.

1640 J. GOWER *Ovid's Fest.* VI. 127 Great heads; glore eyes; hook-beaks upon their jaws.

Hence **'gloring** *vbl. sb.*, gleaming, glittering.

1632 BROME *Novella* II. i. (1653) I. 5 b, A man may spie An old whore-master in the darkest night Like an old Cat, by th' gloring of his eyes.

‖**Gloria** ('glɔərɪə). Also gloria. Pl. *occas.* glorias. [L. *glōria* GLORY.]

1. a. A name for each of several formulæ in Christian liturgical worship. (*a*) ***Gloria Patri***, the doxology beginning 'Glory be to the Father', which follows the recitation of the psalms and certain canticles, and occurs in other places. (*b*) ***Gloria tibi***, the response 'Glory be to Thee, O Lord', which follows the announcement of the gospel in the communion service or mass. (*c*) ***Gloria in excelsis***, the hymn 'Glory be to God on high' (beginning with the words of *Luke* ii. 14), forming part of the communion service or mass. **b.** The music to which the last-mentioned is set.

a. *c* **1420** WYNTOUN *Orig. Cron.* v. xciii. (St. Andrews MS.), This cheptour tellis trewly Quha maid fyrst Gloria patri. *c* **1430** *Freemasonry* 632 And blesse the fayre, ȝef that thou conne, When gloria tibi is begonne. **1514** BARCLAY *Cyt. & Uplondyshm.* (Percy Soc.) 19 The blessyd aungelles.. songe that gloria flyenge in the skye. **1563** PILKINGTON *Confut.* C viii b, On good friday there is neyther Epistle, nor Gospel, Gloria in exelsis [sic], nor Crede. *c* **1661** *Papers on Alter. Prayer Bk.* 77 The Gloria patri..according to the common opinion was formed in the council of Nice. **1706** A. BEDFORD *Temple Mus.* iv. 91 Sometimes in a lowder Voice, as at the Gloria Patri. **1745** R. POCOCKE *Descr. East* II. I. 18 The Latins celebrated the mass of the resurrection, and at Gloria in excelsis, a cover was let down [etc.].

b. **1597** MORLEY *Introd. Mus.* 21 They had it in the Tenor part of the Gloria of his Masse *Ave Maris stella.* **1853** ROCK *Ch. of Fathers* III. II. 212 In it [the Graduale] might be found..the Kyries, Glorias [etc.]. **1884** R. BUCHANAN *Foxglove Manor* I. iv. 72 She then turned to another of the vicar's favourites, a Gloria of Mozart's.

2. An aureole or nimbus. (= GLORY *sb.* 9.) Also, a head-ornament in imitation of this.

1784 *Europ. Mag.* Mar. 233 And over the windows,.. Glory is represented by a Saint George with a superb gloria. **1866** HOWELLS *Venet. Life* xvi. 243 Little girls..with wings and glorias, walked scattering flowers.

3. The French name for coffee with brandy or rum.

1845 E. ACTON *Mod. Cookery* xxvii. 547 Burnt coffee. (In France vulgarly called Gloria.) Make some coffee..sweeten it..pour brandy on the top..set fire to it..and drink the gloria quite hot. **1934** S. BECKETT *More Pricks than Kicks* 119 Reader, a gloria is a coffee laced with brandy.

4. A closely-woven fabric of silk and wool or cotton, etc., used for dresses, the covering of umbrellas, etc.; also, a dress of this fabric.

1895 *Montgomery Ward Catal.* 4/2 Black Silk Warp Sublime or Gloria Cloth..much used for dresses, blouse waists and underskirts. **1897** *Sears, Roebuck Catal.* 248/1 Men's Fine Black Gloria Silk Umbrella. **1908** *Daily Chron.* 3 Aug. 4/5 Men abroad carry a grey or tan gloria sunshade. **1908** L. M. MONTGOMERY *Anne of Green Gables* xxv. 280 Anne took the dress and looked at it in reverent silence. Oh, how pretty it was—a lovely brown gloria with all the gloss of silk. **1917** —— *Anne's House of Dreams* (1926) i. 8, I remember the first pretty dress I ever had—the brown gloria Matthew gave me. **1921** *Daily Colonist* (Victoria, B.C.) 18 Oct. 19/6 (Advt.), Umbrellas at All Prices... Strong durable covers in mercerized cotton, gloria and laventine. **1970** T. S. CRAWFORD *Hist. Umbrella* vii. 142 [In the 1860s] the silk mixture known as Gloria was also introduced as a covering.

†**'gloriable**, *a. Obs.*[−1] [ad. med.L. *glōriābil-is*, f. *glōriārī* to GLORY.] That may be gloried in or boasted of.

c **1640** FELTHAM *Lusoria*, etc. (1661) 89 Job, of all we read, was the most confident of his own Integrity (which, indeed, was rare and gloriable).

gloriation (glɔərɪ'eɪʃən). Now *rare* or *Obs.* Also 6 gloriacion. [ad. L. *glōriātiōn-em*, n. of action f. *glōriārī* to boast, f. *glōria* GLORY. Cf. OF. *gloriacion.*] The action of glorying; boasting; triumphant exultation.

1504 ATKINSON tr. *De Imitatione* III. xv. 210 And what may clay or erthe haue any gloriacion or pryde agaynste his maker? **1543** G. JOYE *Confuteth Win. false Articles* 14 b, Lo here is all gloriacion of works blown down. **1611** SPEED *Hist. Gt. Brit.* IX. xii. (1632) 706 Though theire owne selues make no mention of any defeat of the English which afforded them matter for the shadow of such gloriations. **1669** GALE *Crt. Gentiles* I. III. ix. 90 But al this gloriation is vain. **1734** E. ERSKINE *Serm.* Wks. 1871 II. 269 God is manifested to us in Christ as matter of joy and gloriation. **1837** J. HALLEY in Arnot *Life* (1842) 101, I am impelled to test the sincerity of your gloriation by the speedy infliction of a postage.

gloriette (glɔərɪ'ɛt). *Hist.* Also gloriet. [a. F. *gloriette.* Cf. Sp. *glorieta.*] A highly decorated chamber in a castle or other building. Also *attrib.*

[**1280–1** in T. Bond *Corfe Castle* 85 (A chamber called 'La Gloriet' is mentioned in the Corfe records of this date). ? *a* **1500** *Obituary* in Willis *Monastery Christ Ch. Canterb.* (1869) 107 *note*, Edificavit turrim quandam, cameræ Prioris vocatæ La gloriet contiguam.] **1839** LONGF. *Hyperion* I. vi. (1865) 30 Rodolph's ancient castle, with its Gothic gloriette and fantastic gables. **1884** *Athenæum* 13 Sept. 330/3 Besides an Oriel or a 'Gloriet' Tower, a mediæval castle contained many a 'cruel habitation'.

glorifiable ('glɔərɪˌfaɪəb(ə)l), *a.* [f. GLORIFY *v.* + -ABLE.] That may be glorified.

a **1656** BP. HALL *Solil.* 68 How justly glorifiable is Thy name in the gracious..preservation of thy children. **1857** H. H. WILSON tr. *Rig-veda* III. 105 Offer with fire the acceptable libation to that most glorifiable Mitra. **1869** BUSHNELL *Wom. Suffrage* iii. 58 A finer and more glorifiable humanity.

†**glo'rificate**, *pa. pple. Obs.*[−1] [ad. late L. *glōrificāt-us*, pa. pple. of *glōrificāre* to GLORIFY.] Glorified.

c **1460** in *Pol. Rel. & L. Poems* 82 O lemyng lawmpe, in light passyng nature! How greately is thy name glorificate! **1508** KENNEDIE *Flyting w. Dunbar* 528 Deuill, dampnit dog, sodomyte insatiable, With Gog and Magog grete glorificate.

glorification (ˌglɔərɪfɪ'keɪʃən). [ad. late L. *glōrificātiōn-em*, n. of action f. *glōrificāre* to GLORIFY.]

†**1.** *Alch.* The action of refining; the state of being refined. *Obs.*

1460–70 *Bk. Quintessence* 4 By contynuel ascendynge and descendynge..it is sublymed to so myche hiȝnes of glorificacioun.

2. The action of glorifying or investing with glory; the condition or state of being glorified.

1549 COVERDALE, etc. *Erasm. Par. Rev.* xix. 6–10 In heauen it is the immortal glorificacion of body & soule. **1660** JER. TAYLOR *Duct. Dubit.* I. v. §8 (1676) 151 They whose sins accidentally thus serv'd the glorification of God. **1860** PUSEY *Min. Proph.* 390 The enormous mass of human strength, which its [Thebes'] victorious kings had gathered from all nations to toil for its and their glorification. **1885** *Manch. Exam.* 30 Mar. 5/2 Her trial and the glorification which she is likely to receive at the hands of the French public.

b. *esp.* The exaltation (of Christ) to the glory of heaven; the admission (of human souls) to the bliss of heaven.

1502 *Ord. Crysten Men* (W. de W. 1506) I. vi. 50 Creacyon, redempcyon, and gloryfycacyon..apperteyneth all onely to the blessyd trynyte. **1643** SIR T. BROWNE *Relig. Med.* II. §8 An accessary of our glorification. **1681–6** J. SCOTT *Chr. Life* II. vii. §10 The good Angels..are ready enough to congratulate their [sinners'] Glorification. **1685** BAXTER *Paraphr. N.T.*, *Mark* xvi. 19 His Ascension they beheld, and his Glorification they believed by the Spirit's revelation. **1871** MACDUFF *Mem. Patmos* xvii. 230 Until the spirits of the just are 'made perfect'—until they are ushered into their state of glorification.

c. Transformation into a more magnificent form; *colloq.* a 'glorified' variety *of* something which is naturally humble or inferior.

1885 *Century Mag.* XXXII. 424/2 Sometimes..these houses..are..glorifications of the humble, early, shingled New-England farm-house.

d. *jocularly.* A time of 'glorious' enjoyment, a festive occasion.

1843 BETHUNE *Sc. Fireside Stor.* 41 Glad to see you able to stir at all after your last night's glorification.

3. The ascription of glory or praise to (a person or thing).

1850 L. HUNT *Autobiog.* v. 100 The glorifications of their masters with which they entertain the kitchen. **1862** MERIVALE *Rom. Emp.* (1865) V. xli. 102 [The Georgics]..we must regard..as the glorification of Labour. **1863** *Boston Commonwealth* (U.S.) 23 Oct., Captain Swift, in his peripatetic glorifications of Gen. Banks, omits [etc.]. **1892** *Speaker* 3 Sept. 292/2 Mr. Huxley's..prologue is..a glorification of 'science'.

b. A set form of praise; a doxology.

1660 JER. TAYLOR *Duct. Dubit.* II. ii. (1676) 277 They offered sacrifice and sang..glorifications of God. **1730** WATERLAND *Rem. Clarke's Expos. Catech.* 15 The Glorification in the Close was in common to Father, Son, and Holy Ghost. **1873** WHITNEY *Orient. Stud.* 6 The songs are for the most part simple invocations and glorifications of the divinity.

glorified ('glɔərɪfaɪd), *ppl. a.* [f. GLORIFY *v.* + -ED[1].]

1. In senses of the vb.: Invested with glory, rendered glorious; beautified; †refined.

a **1340** HAMPOLE *Psalter* cxlvi. 3 When we ryse glorifyde in body and saule. ? *a* **1500** *Wycket* (1828) p. viii, Whether make they the gloryfyed bodye ether make they agayne the spirituall bodye. **1608** W. SCLATER *Malachy* (1650) 196 It repugnes the nature of a glorified body. **1655** EARL ORRERY *Parthen.* (1676) 7 He drew out the Copy of so glorified an Original. **1657** G. STARKEY *Helmont's Vind.* Ep. to Rdr., Thus also may be made.. the glorified Sulphur of Antimony. **1681–6** J. SCOTT *Chr. Life* (1747) III. 510 Other unknown Purposes peculiar to his glorified State. **1726** AYLIFFE *Parergon* 172 The..Soul..will resume its Body again in a glorify'd Manner. **1841** W. SPALDING *Italy & It. Isl.* II. 345 Angels and glorified saints adore the Mother and her Son. **1862** TYNDALL *Mountaineer.* vi. 47 Long stretches of crimson light drawn over the higher snow-fields linked the glorified summits together. **1878** BROWNING *Poets Croisic* li, Who may be this glorified Mortal unheard-of hitherto?

absol. **1871** B. TAYLOR *Faust* I. xx. 214 They turn their faces, The glorified, from thee.

2. *colloq.* That has undergone transformation into something glorious. (Often used sarcastically, e.g. to imply that a person of distinguished position has essentially the ideas or type of mind characteristic of some inferior rank or class.) Also, gorgeously attired or adorned.

1821 LAMB *Elia* Ser. I. *My first Play*, I judged it to be sugar-candy—yet to my raised imagination..it appeared.. a glorified candy! **1846** THACKERAY *Snob Papers* Wks. (1886) XXIV. 318 A glorified flunkey, in lace, plush, and aiguillettes. **1887** MAHAFFY *Greek Life & Thought* x. 201 We feel ourselves in a sort of glorified *Holborn Restaurant*, where the resources of art are lavished on the walls of an eating-room. **1894** SALA *Lond. up to Date* ii. 21 A glorified.. gentleman..takes from you your second card. **1896** *Daily News* 1 Oct. 4/6 There was a great deal of what has been called a glorified school-boy about Lord Randolph. **1897** MARY KINGSLEY *W. Africa* 163 It is a real island of a rocky nature, and not a glorified sandbank that has [etc.]. *Mod.* He sneered at the head of his college as 'a sort of glorified board-schoolmaster'.

glorifier ('glɔərɪfaɪə(r)). [f. GLORIFY + -ER.] One who glorifies (in various senses of the vb.).

1579 J. JONES *Preserv. Bodie & Soule* I. xviii. 33 The glorifyer of God, tryer of tastes, and Ambassadour betweene man and man. *a* **1677** MANTON in Spurgeon *Treas. Dav.* Ps. cxix. 97 Preserver, Deliverer, and Glorifier of Mankind. **1846** TRENCH *Mirac.* xix. (1862) 323 Not..the destroyer of the law..but its transformer and glorifier. **1880** KINGLAKE *Crimea* VI. ix. 265 By the help of his salaried glorifiers.

glorify ('glɔərɪfaɪ), *v.* [ad. F. *glorifier*, ad. late L. *glōrificāre*, f. *glōrificus*, adj. f. *glōria* GLORY + *fac-ĕre* to make.]

1. *trans.* To render glorious; to invest with glory, procure glory for. In early quots. *esp.* to exalt to the glory of heaven.

a **1340** HAMPOLE *Psalter* xiv. 5 þaim þat dredis god he glorifys. þat is he haldis þaim gloriouse and worthi to rest in godis hill. **1382** WYCLIF *John* vii. 39 Ihesus was not ȝit glorified. [So also **1551** and **1611**.] *c* **1400** MAUNDEV. (Roxb.) xv. 67 þe gude he sall drawe on his party and glorify þam in ioy withouten end. *c* **1440** *Gesta Rom.* xxviii. 107 (Harl. MS.) When a man shalle be glorifiede in body and in soule, in the day of dome. **1520** *Caxton's Chron. Eng.* III. 27/1 That the temporall peas myght gloryfye the natyvyte of our Savyour. **1603** S. DANIEL *Panegyr. to King's Majesty* lviii, Those righteous issues, which shall glorifie And comfort many Nations with their worth. *a* **1625** BEAUM. & FL. *Laws of Candy* III. ii, Nothing More glorifies the noble, and the valiant, Than to despise contempt.

b. In physical sense: To throw a glorious light upon, to invest with radiance. †Formerly also, to beautify or embellish, deck with splendid ornament.

1503 Hawes *Examp. Virt.* vi. 9 Vp came dame fortune so gayly gloryfyed. **1592** Shaks. *Ven. & Ad.* 485 As the bright sunne glorifies the skie. **1595** —— *John* II. i. 442. **1648** Jos. Beaumont *Psyche* II. liv. (1702) 18 To glorify a Wall With Tapestry feats is womanish, say I. **1880** Miss Braddon *Just as I am* xli, The harvest moon glorified the dinginess of Milton Street. **1882** *Harper's Mag.* Dec. 13/2 The cliffs and crags..are glorified by the beams of the departing orb.

c. To transform into something more glorious or splendid; to invest (something common or inferior) with charm or beauty.

1867 Miss Braddon *R. Godwin* I. i. 5 The sunshine.. transforms and glorifies the commonest objects, until the earth seems unfamiliar and beautiful as fairyland. **1880** J. F. Clarke *Self-Culture* viii. 187 Burns, Wordsworth, Whittier ..have known how to glorify common life and every-day people with the charm of romance.

2. a. To advance the glory of (God, His name) by faithful action or suffering. (Cf. glory *sb.* 2 b.) **b.** To ascribe glory and praise in adoration to (God).

1340 *Ayenb.* 196 Þet we maki oure guode dedes to-uore þe uolkerede þeruore þet god by y-hered and y-glorefied. **1388** Wyclif *John* xxi. 19 Signfiyinge bi what deth he schuld glorifie God. *a* **1400** *Prymer* (1891) 50 Make sauf alle men þ^t^ glorefiȝeth the. *c* **1460** *Towneley Myst.* iv. 245 Thi will, Thi name, to glorifye Ouer all this warld so wide. **1526** *Pilgr. Perf.* (W. de W. 1531) 181 b, Glorifyed be thy holy name. **1650** Jer. Taylor *Holy Living* iv. ad §10 (1727) 331, I bless and glorifie thy name. **1715** De Foe *Fam. Instruct.* I. i. (1841) I. 33 The goodness..of God..which has given me.. so many ways to glorify him.

3. To describe or represent as glorious; to extol, honour, magnify with praise (a person or thing).

1557 North tr. *Gueuara's Diall Pr.* 69 a/1 Prayse and gloryfye thy beautye asmuche as thou thinckest good, yet [etc.]. **1596** Spenser *State Irel.* Wks. (Globe) 641/1 Whomsoever they find to be most licentious of life..him they sett up and glorifye in theyr rimes. **1602** Marston *Antonio's Rev.* v. v. K 2 b, He weepes: now doe I glorifie my hands, I had no vengeance, if I had no teares. *a* **1631** Donne *Poems* (1633) 229 No chymique yet th' Elixar got, But glorifies his pregnant pot, If [etc.]. **1834** Mrs. Boddington *Remin. Rhine* I. 30 There is bad taste in thus seeking to glorify *one* particular wound amidst so many instances of devotedness even to death. **1879** Froude *Cæsar* xx. 341 Cæsar, who was being so much praised and glorified.

4. *refl.* (†and *intr.* for *refl.*) To boast or vaunt oneself, to make one's boast, exult. Now *rare*. Const. *in*, *of*, *to* with infin., or *that*.

1340 *Ayenb.* 25 Þus him ioisseþ and him glorifieþ þe wreche ine his herte. *Ibid.* 270 Naȝt of oþre þinge ne glorefye þe. *c* **1374** Chaucer *Troylus* III. 137 (186) 'Immortal God!'.. Cupide I mene, of this mayst glorifye. *c* **1384** —— *H. Fame* III. 44 He ought him lytel glorifye That her on bilt. *c* **1400** *Rom. Rose* 5450 They maken foolis glorifye Of hir wordis [greet] speking. **1474** Caxton *Chesse* 30 And they glorefye them in theyr connyng. **1484** —— *Curiall* 3 b, Arystotle the phylosophre gloryfyed in him self that he had lefte the hye palays of kyng Alysaundre. **1523** Ld. Berners *Froiss.* I. ccccxviii. 732 Philyppe glorifyed so in his fayre fortune and victory..that [etc.]. **1539** Tonstall *Serm. Palm Sund.* (1823) 17 Men in erth do glorifie in hym. **1548** Hall *Chron., Hen IV*, 16 b, Owen Glendor glorifying hymself in these twoo victories, invaded the Marches of Wales. **1655** tr. *De Parc's Francion* VII. 15 Some senselesse Courtiers..glorifie that they have feathers as great as the Mules in the Kings stable. **1836** E. Howard *R. Reefer* xxvi, For the which he glorified himself exceedingly.

5. *Alch.* To refine, sublime.

1657 [see glorified *ppl. a.* 1].

glorifying ('glɔːrɪfaɪɪŋ), *vbl. sb.* [f. glorify *v.* + -ing[1].] The action of the verb glorify.

a **1340** Hampole *Psalter* xvi. 3 In glorifiynge of me and myn. **1561** Daus *Bullinger on Apoc.* (1573) 314 b, The spirite ..crieth busily to the Lord for our..glorifieng. **1709** Addison *Tatler* No. 108 ¶7 Religion..does not only promise the entire Refinement of the Mind, but the glorifying of the Body. **1746–7** Hervey *Medit.* (1818) 194 Devote..the chief of your strength to the glorifying of His name.

¶ As an alleged term for a company (of liars).

c **1470** in *Hors, Shepe, & G.* etc. (Roxb. Club) 32 A glorifieing of lyers.

†**'gloring,** *ppl. a. Obs.* [f. glore *v.* + -ing[2].] **a.** Shining, glittering. **b.** Staring.

a. *a* **1400–50** *Alexander* 3627 [He] mas to beete all of bras as bernes it ware, And full of glorand gledis þaim to þe gorge fillis. **1503** *Test. Ebor.* (Surtees) IV. 217 One par scherys, with xx glorynge nayles. **1602** *2nd Pt. Return fr. Parnass.* I. i. (Arb.) 8 Vnlesse it dare out-face the gloring [*Macray* glaring] light. **1647** H. More *Poems* 136 Gilded clouds Arching an eye-lid for the gloring Morn. *a* **1650** *Scot. ffeilde* 103 in Furniv. *Percy Folio* I. 217 He durst not venter with our King..For all the gloring gold.

b. *a* **1400–50** *Alexander* 4552 To be grindand gluttis & glorand dronkin. *c* **1440** *York Myst.* xxvi. 157 Go hense, þou glorand gedlyng.

gloriole ('glɔːrɪəʊl). [a. F. *gloriole*, ad. L. *glōriola*, dim. of *glōria* glory.] †**a.** A scrap of glory (*obs.*). **b.** An aureole; a halo.

1813 Wellington in Gurw. *Desp.* (1838) XI. 181 It is unworthy of one of his reputation to get his brigade into scrapes, for the sake of the little *gloriole* of driving in a few picquets. **1844** Mrs. Browning *Vision of Poets* Poems 1850 I. 235 The broad gloriole round his brow Did vibrate with the light below. **1863** Jean Ingelow *Brothers* 113 As a gloriole sign o' grace. **1874** W. Tay tr. *Hebra's Dis. Skin* III. xxxiv. 70 Several years ago, another athlete..exhibited himself, who could elevate his extraordinarily abundant and long hair as a gloreole around his head.

†**glori'oso.** *Obs.* [a. It. *glorioso*, ad. L. *glōriōsus* boastful.] A boaster, a braggart. Hence †**glori'oser** in the same sense.

1589 Greene *Menaphon* (Arb.) 82 Emptie vessells haue the highest sounds..and pratling gloriosers, the smallest performaunce of courage. **1599** *Life More* in Wordsw. *Eccl. Biog.* (1853) II. 102 This glorioso..knew not so much as the meaning of the terms. **1600** Abp. Abbot *Exp. Jonah* 215 The Magnificoes of the world and great-mouthed Gloriosoes. *a* **1661** Fuller *Worthies, Devonsh.* I. (1662) 259 His Holinesse did forfeit a parcel of his infallibility, in giving credit to such a Glorioso.

glorious ('glɔːrɪəs), *a.* Forms: 4–6 glorio(u)se, -ius, gloryous, (5 gloryowse, 6 *Sc.* glori-, gloryuss, glorous), 3– glorious. [a. AF. *glorious* = OF. *glorieus*, *-os*, Pr. *glorios*, Sp., Pg., It. *glorioso*, ad. L. *glōriōsus*, f. *glōria* glory: see -ous.]

† **1.** Boastful; ostentatious, fond of splendour; proud, haughty; vainglorious. *Obs.*

1382 Wyclif *Prov.* xxv. 14 A man glorious and the behestes not fulfillende. *c* **1440** *York Myst.* xvi. 19, I am fairer of face þan glorius gulles þat [etc.]. *c* **1530** Tindale *Prol. to Jonas* (1863) A vj b, Ande one y^t^ cast out deuels in Christes name they [the apostles] forbade because he wayted not on them, so glorious were they yet. **1577** J. Brooke *Guido's Staffe Chr. Faith* Pref., A soil and heape of glorious deceiuers, which hyde and boast themselues. **1612** Bacon *Ess., Vaine-glory* (Arb.) 462 They that are glorious, must needs be factious; for all brauery stands vpon comparisons. **1654** tr. *Scudery's Curia Pol.* 25 If they [Princes] are..gay and glorious, they are reviled as incompassionate. **1692** Dryden *St. Euremont's Ess.* 13 Whether..Posterity, glorious throughout, were desirous that their Ancestors should be Masters of Vertues, when they were not of Greatness. *a* **1734** North *Exam.* I. ii. §32. 46 After he was possessed of the Great Seal, he was in Appearance the gloriousest Man alive.

†**2.** Eager for glory. *Obs.*

1608 Shaks. *Per.* I. Prol. 9 The purchase is to make men glorious. **1621** Fletcher *Pilgrim* IV. ii, I am not watchfull to do ill, Nor glorious to pursue it still. **1704** Hearne *Duct. Hist.* (1714) I. 392 He always left such to Heroes as were purely Glorious.

3. a. Of persons and things: Possessing glory; entitled to brilliant and lofty renown, illustrious. *spec.* As an epithet of: (*a*) the 'First of June', the date of a sea battle between the British and French in 1794, ending in victory for the British; (*b*) the 'Twelfth' of August [twelfth 1 c]; (*c*) (*U.S.*) the 'Fourth' (of July).

Now somewhat *rare*; the mod. use as applied to persons (e.g. in 'Glorious John' as a designation of Dryden) belongs to sense 5. (The AF. Coronation Oath of 1307 speaks of 'le glorious Rei Seynt Edward'.)

13.. *K. Alis.* 7441 Now is ded kyng Porus, Alisaunder is kyng glorious. ? *a* **1400** *Morte Arth.* 1 Grett glorious Godd, thurgh grace of hym selvene..Schelde us ffro schamesdede and synfulle werkes. *c* **1460** *Towneley Myst.* iii. 166 My name is of dignyte, and also full glorius. **1483** Caxton *Gold. Leg.* 174/1 Saynt austyn preched a glorious sermone & declared there to the kynge the crysten feythe openlye. **1500–20** Dunbar *Poems* xxv. 91 Quhilk grant the glorius Trinitie! **1604** E. G. tr. *D'Acosta's Hist. Indies* I. i. 2 The glorious Crysostome (a man better seene in the studie of holy Scriptures, then in the knowledge of Philosophie). **1660** Blount *Boscobel* 1 Charles the Second undoubted heir of Charles the First of Glorious Memory. **1720–21** Swift *Let. to Pope* 10 Jan., Wks. 1824 XVI. 352, I will tell you what my political principles were in the time of her late glorious majesty. **1794** (*title*) Songs, Duetts, Choruses, &c. In a New and Appropriate Entertainment. Called *The Glorious First of June*. **1827** [see fourth *a.* 2 b]. **1841** Lane *Arab. Nts.* I. 88 He answered, O glorious King, it hath been said, by the ancients [etc.]. **1854** W. G. Simms *Southward Ho!* xiii. 253 Our dinner on the glorious Fourth was worthy of the occasion. **1871** R. Ellis tr. *Catullus* xxxiv. 23 Still keep safely the glorious Race of Romulus olden. **1879** M. Arnold *Poems of Wordsw.* Pref. (near end), He is one of the very chief glories of English Poetry; and by nothing is England so glorious as by her poetry. **1895** E. G. Mackenzie *In Grouseland* xvii. 125 The glorious twelfth! Despite critical politics, the continuous fine weather and the certainty of sport has again filled all the saloon carriages bound northward. **1899** W. L. Clowes *Royal Navy* IV. xxxv. 230 (*heading*) The Glorious first of June. **1948** *Miami* (Okla.) *Daily News-Record* 4 July 1/5 Where are Miami's glorious fourths of yesteryear? **1966** *Chambers's Encycl.* V. 660/2 The Glorious First of June..the name given to a sea battle of the French revolutionary war. **1971** D. Ayerst *Guardian* xxx. 468 With the 'glorious twelfth' only three days off politicians were deserting Westminster for the grouse moors.

b. Of an achievement, action, circumstance, state of things, etc.: Conferring glory; entitling to brilliant and lofty renown; conspicuously honourable. Const. *to*.

1548 Hall *Chron., Hen. V*, 49 For this day by famous death or glorious victory I wyl wynne honor. **1577** Northbrooke *Dicing* (1843) 36 It is glorious when the preachers are certaine of their doctrine which they teache. **1659** D. Pell *Impr. Sea* 56 It is one of the gloriousest works in the world, to have an hand in..the saving of a soul. **1659** B. Harris *Parival's Iron Age* 16 Which followed close upon the glorious Battel (but with small fruit) of Lepanto. **1709** Steele & Swift *Tatler* No. 66 ¶8 The great and glorious Victory obtained over the Enemy on the 11th Instant. **1774** Chesterf. *Lett.* (1792) I. ii. 5 As it is more difficult to express one's thoughts in verse than in prose, the being capable of doing it is more glorious. **1789** in *Sir J. Sinclair's Corr.* (1831) II. 282 The surrender of Oczakow, an event so remarkable in the history of Russia, and so glorious to the hero. **1849** Macaulay *Hist. Eng.* vi. II. 147 He..declared that..he should think it glorious to die in his sovereign's cause.

†**c.** In non-laudatory sense: Conducive to reputation. *Obs.*

1665 Boyle *Occas. Refl.* v. iv. (1848) 309 And though a needless Ostentation of ones Excellencies may be more glorious, a modest Concealment of them is usually more safe.

4. Splendid in beauty or richness of adornment. Now only with emotional connotation as in 5. †Formerly also in a weaker sense, of textures, colours, etc.: Brilliant, shining, lustrous.

13.. *E.E. Allit. P.* A. 914 As þou art gloryous withouten galle. *c* **1315** Shoreham 128 The glorious beerde [*sc.* our levedy], Out of thyse world the gloriouse ferde Wyth greate melodye. **1390** Gower *Conf.* III. 114 Mars the planet bataillous Next to the sonne glorious. *a* **1396** Chaucer *Rosemounde* 3 For as the crystal glorious ye shyne, And lyke ruby ben your chekes rounde. *c* **1420** *Anturs of Arth.* 366 Here gide was glorious and gay, of a gresse grene. **1509** Fisher *Funeral Serm. C'tess Richmond* Wks. (1876) 304 It [the body] shall ryse bryght and gloryous. **1535** Coverdale *2 Macc.* viii. 35 He put of his glorious rayment, fled by see, and came alone to Antioche. **1596** Spenser *F.Q.* Ded. to Lady Carew, Those glorious ornaments of hevenly grace. **1606** Shaks. *Tr. & Cr.* I. iii. 89 The glorious Planet Sol. **1664** Power *Exp. Philos.* I. 1 The Iris (as vibrissant and glorious as a Cat's eye) most admirable to behold. *Ibid.* 43 So clear and glorious a body as glass. **1665** R. Hooke *Microgr.* 169 The colours..must necessarily be very glorious, vivid and cleer, like those of Silk and Feathers. *a* **1687** Petty *Pol. Arith.* (1690) Pref., Notwithstanding all this..the Buildings of London grow great and glorious. **1732** Berkeley *Alciphr.* v. §12 The glorious light of the gospel. **1792** *Munchausen's Trav.* xxiv. 108 The sun shone glorious on the water. **1803** Wordsw. *Intim. Immort.* ii, The sunshine is a glorious birth. **1860** Tyndall *Glac.* I. ix. 62 All conspired to render the scene glorious. **1866** G. Macdonald *Ann. Q. Neighb.* xxvii. (1878) 470 The heavens were glorious with stars.

5. a. Used vaguely as a rapturous expression of admiration or delight: Splendid, magnificent, intensely delightful. Now often with jocular hyperbole.

1623 Mabbe tr. *Aleman's Guzman d'Alf.* II. 216 As a good Chine of Bacon, makes glorious porrige. **1772** Nugent *Grosley's Lond.* I. 44 Which casual appearance [of the sun] procures the Londoners a few of what they call *glorious days*. **1816** 'Quiz' *Grand Master* VII. 24 They call a servant, and require, Immediately, a *glorious* fire. **1822** Scott *Pirate* II. i. 14 'You forget glorious John', said Mordaunt. 'Ay, glorious you may well call him'. **1853** Kane *Grinnell Exp.* xli. (1856) 375 What a glorious feed for the scurvy-stricken ships. **1863** Mary Howitt *F. Bremer's Greece* I. viii. 263 What glorious afternoons and evenings have I spent at Phalerus! **1875** W. S. Hayward *Love agst. World* 11 'What glorious fun' said Florence.

b. *ironical phrase.*

According to *Gentl. Mag.* (1830) Aug. 98/1, the phrase was first used at a dinner of the Judges and Counsel about 1756, when after the toast of 'the glorious memory of King William' had been drunk, a Mr. Wilbraham proposed 'the glorious uncertainty of the law', in sarcastic allusion to Ld. Chief Justice Mansfield's bold overruling of former decisions.

1759–93 Macklin *Love à la mode* II. i. (1793) 27 The law is a sort of hocus-pocus science..and the glorious uncertainty of it is of mair use to the professors than the justice of it. **1803** Sheridan in *Parl. Hist.* (1820) XXXVI. 1204 The glorious uncertainty of the law, was a thing well known and complained of, by all ignorant people, but all learned gentlemen considered it as its greatest excellency. **1811** J. Adams *Wks.* (1854) IX. 630 When I applied the epithet 'glorious' to the uncertainty of politics, I meant it ironically, as we say the 'glorious uncertainty of the law'. *Mod.* The glorious uncertainty of cricket.

6. *jocularly.* Ecstatically happy from drink.

1790 Burns *Tam o' Shanter* 57 Kings may be blessed, but Tam was glorious, O'er a' the ills of life victorious. **1836** E. Howard *R. Reefer* lii, As fast as one man could be..flogged into sobriety, another would become glorious. **1861** Thackeray *B. Lyndon* xviii. (1869) 254, I was taken up 'glorious', as the phrase is, by my servants, and put to bed.

7. *Comb.* (quasi-*adv.*), as ***glorious-doing***, ***-sounding***, ***-talking*** adjs.

1670 Brooks *Wks.* (1867) VI. 324 The most *glorious-doing Christian. **1768** Boswell *Corsica* iii. (ed. 2) 214 Fame's *glorious-sounding trumpet breath. **1662** Cokain *Ovid* IV. i. (1669) 78 My *glorious talking Captain, I shall not Be won with empty words.

gloriously ('glɔːrɪəslɪ), *adv.* [f. glorious *a.* + -ly[2].] In a glorious manner.

†**1.** Boastfully, proudly, vaingloriously. *Obs.*

1566 Adlington *Apuleius, Life* (1596) A 3 b, He gloriously calleth himself the nourice of Carthage. **1599** B. Jonson *Ev. Man out Hum.* II. i, I speake it not gloriously, nor out of affectation. **1602** J. Clapham *Hist. Eng.* 59 Such as before the Battell were so wary and wise in aduenturing ..after the euent..grew to speake gloriously of themselues. **1660** tr. *Amyraldus' Treat. conc. Relig.* I. v. 73 How gloriously they vaunt of their inventions.

2. With an accompaniment of glory or renown; illustriously.

a **1340** Hampole *Psalter* Cant. 503 Gloriously he is worshipid. **1382** Wyclif *Luke* xiii. 17 Al the peple ioyede in al thingis, that weren don gloriously of him. **1494** Fabyan *Chron.* III. liii. 35 Whenne that this Kymbalyne had reygned gloryously ouer the Brytons [etc.]. **1500–20** Dunbar *Poems* lxxvii. 38 The nobill Stewarts syne, of great renoun, Thow gart upspring, with branches new and greine, Sa gloriouslie, quhill glaided all the toun. **1711** Addison *Spect.* No. 165 ¶1 Our Warriors..are so gloriously successful in beating down their Power. **1781** Gibbon *Decl. & F.* III. 137 This narrow pass of Thermopylae, where Leonidas and the three hundred Spartans had gloriously devoted their lives. **1841**

JAMES *Brigand* xiv, The purpose may..pass away, war be continued gloriously and long, and France be ruined.

3. Brilliantly, splendidly; †brightly, lustrously. Now only with emotional connotation; cf. GLORIOUS *a.* 4, 5.

1393 LANGL. *P. Pl.* C. xx. 15 The glose gloryousliche was wryte wyth a gylt penne. *c* **1400** *Three Kings Cologne* 5 Gloriously propheciede of þe Incarnacioun of oure lorde Ihesu Crist. *c* **1420** LYDG. *Assemb. Gods* 823 Gloryously besene, as he had come from heuyn. **1529** FRITH *Antithesis* Wks. (1572) 101 Tombes well gilt with many a torch and great solemnitie, with angels gloriously portered. **1586** SPENSER *Death Sidney* 94 Those beames Of vertue kindled in his noble brest, Which after did so gloriously forth shine. **1644** EVELYN *Diary* 17 Oct. (1879) I. 98 The house is most magnificently built without, nor less gloriously furnish'd within. **1697** DAMPIER *Voy.* I. 427 These Rings when first polished look very gloriously, but time makes them fade, and turn to a pale yellow. **1717** LADY M. W. MONTAGU *Let. to C'tess Mar* 18 Apr., I never saw anything so gloriously beautiful. **1868** HOLME LEE *B. Godfrey* xxxvi. 197 The children enjoyed it gloriously. **1870** SPURGEON *Treas. Dav.* xxxii. *title*, David wrote this gloriously evangelic Psalm. **1885** *Manch. Exam.* 10 Sept. 5/5 This morning the weather opened gloriously fine.

ironical. **1834** DARWIN in *Life & Lett.* (1887) I. 249, I draw my own conclusions, and most gloriously ridiculous ones they are, I sometimes fancy.

4. *colloq.* With reference to intoxication. (Cf. GLORIOUS *a.* 6.)

1784 COWPER *Task* IV. 510 Drink, and be mad then; 'tis your country bids! Gloriously drunk obey th' important call! **1843** BETHUNE *Sc. Fireside Stor.* 50 Dr. Bridges was in a state which may be described as gloriously drunk.

gloriousness ('glɔːrɪəsnɪs). [f. GLORIOUS *a.* + -NESS.] The attribute of being glorious. †**a.** Boastfulness (*obs.*). **b.** Splendour, magnificence.

c **1440** *Promp. Parv.* 199/2 Gloryowsnesse, *gloriositas.* **1526** TINDALE *1 Cor.* ii. 1, I..cam not in gloriousnes of wordes or of wisdom. **1552** T. BARNABE in Strype *Eccl. Mem.* II. App. E. 154, I do se the gloriousnes of the Frenchmen and how they do rejoyce of their roberies. **1651** HOBBES *Leviath.* III. xxxv. 219 The gloriousnesse, and admirable height of that throne. **1681** H. MORE *Exp. Dan.* vi. 211 It may also signify a solid greatness and gloriousness. *a* **1849** J. C. MANGAN *Poems* (1859) 410 You'll witness my gloriousness. **1877** MORLEY *Crit. Misc.* Ser. II. 239 The gift of intellectual fatherhood is..surrounded by such singular gloriousness.

glory ('glɔːrɪ), *sb.* Forms: 4-7 glori(e, -ye, 5-7 (chiefly *Sc.*) gloir(e, glor(e, 4- glory. [a. OF. *glorie* (also in semi-popular form *glo(i)re*), ad. L. *glōria.*]

†**1.** *subjectively.* **a.** The disposition to claim honour for oneself; boastful spirit. *Obs.* exc. in the combination VAINGLORY.

1362 LANGL. *P. Pl.* A. XI. 70 Suche motyues þei meuen þei maistres in heor glorie. *c* **1386-1520** [see VAINGLORY]. **1624** MASSINGER *Parl. Love* v. i, A little glory in a soldier's mouth Is not uncomely. **1650** HOBBES *Hum. Nat.* ix. §1. 91 Glory, or internal gloriation or triumph of the Minde. **1656** EVELYN *Mem.* (1857) III. 73 My animadversions..will I hope..totally acquit me either of glory or impiety. **1753** SMOLLETT *Ct. Fathom* (1813) I. 119 The disappointment of the ladies my glory will not permit me to overlook.

†**b.** Desire for fame; ambition. *Obs.*

1594 MARLOWE & NASHE *Dido* v. i, All glory hath forsaken thee.

2. *objectively.* **a.** Exalted (and, in mod. use, merited) praise, honour, or admiration accorded by common consent to a person or thing; honourable fame, renown.

c **1385** CHAUCER *L.G.W.* 2531 *Phillis*, It oughte be to yow but lyte glorye. **1387-8** T. USK *Test. Love* II. viii. (Skeat) l. 68 O glorye, glorye, thou art none other thinge to thousandes of folke, but a great sweller of eares. *c* **1460** FORTESCUE *Abs. & Lim. Mon.* v. (1885) 119 What dishonour is this, and abatynge of the glorie of a kynge. **1513** DOUGLAS *Æneis* v. iv. 58 ȝe vailȝeand feris of worthy Hector..think on ȝour glor. **1582-8** *Hist. James VI* (1804) 158 Quhat gloir and renowne he obtenit of thir twa victories, was all cassin doun by the infamy of the next attempt. **1618** LITHGOW *Pilgr. Farew.* Ej, The Noblest striue for State, ambitious Glore. **1663** GERBIER *Counsel* F viij a, Letters, which the Ægiptians did attribute unto them, though the Assyrians would have the glory thereof. **1730-46** THOMSON *Autumn* 1278 Let such as deem it glory to destroy Rush into blood. **1752** HUME *Ess. & Treat.* (1777) II. 5 The glory of Malebranche is confined to his own nation and his own age. **1821** J. S. ADAMS in C. Davies *Metr. Syst.* III. (1871) 295 The glory of the first attempt belongs to France. **1823** BYRON *Juan* VIII. xiv, Yet I love Glory;—glory's a great thing.

b. *the glory of God*: the honour of God, considered as the final cause of creation, and as the highest moral aim of intelligent creatures.

1382 WYCLIF *1 Cor.* x. 31 Do ȝe alle thingis in to glorie of God. **1558** *Extracts Aberd. Reg.* (1844) I. 313 In the meinteining and uphalding of Goddis seruice in our saide p[a]roche kirk, to the honor and gloir of God. *c* **1680** BEVERIDGE *Serm.* (1729) I. 408 No man can do any thing for God's glory but what will tend also to his own. **1715** DE FOE *Fam. Instruct.* I. i, You are to live here to the glory of Him that made you.

3. Something that brings honour and renown; a subject for boasting; a distinguished ornament; a special distinction; a 'boast and pride'. Also *pl.*

1382 WYCLIF *Prov.* xvii. 6 The glorie of sones the fadris of hem. **1597** HOOKER *Eccl. Pol.* v. xlii. §7 The glory of all things is that wherein their highest perfection doth consist. **1601** SHAKS. *Jul. C.* III. i. 149 Are all thy Conquests, Glories, Triumphes, Spoiles, Shrunke to this little Measure? *a* **1680** BUTLER *Rem.* (1759) II. 1 A Learn'd Society of late, The Glory of a foreign State, Agreed [etc.]. **1715** DE FOE *Fam. Instruct.* I. iii, That which was the glory of a Christian, viz. to worship and call upon him that made him. **1776** BURKE *Corr.* (1844) II. 107 It is the glory of the tories that they always flourish in the decay..of the glory of their country. **1790** —— *Fr. Rev.* 61 Leading advocates, the glory of the bar. **1792** *Anecd. W. Pitt* IV. App. 263 The glories of Mr. Pitt's administration are the successes of the war. **1836** J. GILBERT *Chr. Atonem.* viii. (1852) 245 It is the glory of the Christian Sacrifice that it was made by God as well as to him. **1870** F. R. WILSON *Ch. Lindisf.* 33 The chief glory of the district..is the grand old castle. **1874** GREEN *Short Hist.* vii. §7. 413 Literature had hardly found a place in the glories of the time.

4. a. Praise, honour, and thanksgiving offered in adoration.

1382 WYCLIF *Luke* ii. 14 Glorie be in the hiȝeste thingis to God. **1530** *Mirr. Our Ladyes* 41 b in Maskell *Mon. Rit.* II. 3 *note*, When ye bydde glory to the father, and to the sone, and to the holy goste. *c* **1560** A. SCOTT *Poems* (S.T.S.) xxxv. 29 To Fader gloir be evirmoir, To Sone and Haly Spreit. **1603** *Philotus* clx, Giue gloir to God that in this thrang, Hes bene all our relief. **179.** COLERIDGE *Sibyl. Leaves* (1862) 271 Glory to Thee, Father of Earth and Heaven!

†**b.** *nonce-use. Obs.*

1627-77 FELTHAM *Resolves* I. xiii. 21 How unmovedly did he take his poyson? as if he had been drinking off a Glory to the Deity. [Similarly **1718** *Entertainer* xxi. ¶3. 139.]

c. Used as a devout ejaculation (short for ***Glory be to God***) in the worship of various religious sects. Hence *vulgarly* as a mere exclamation expressive of delight. Also in form ***glory be!***

1816 *Sporting Mag.* XLVIII. 29 One of the poachers said 'glory!' and a line was formed in the wood. **1853** F. HALL in *Ledlie's Miscell.* II. 174 To *get religion*, as he words it, periodically, costs him nothing more than a few spasmodic *amens* and epigastric *glorys*. **1893** Q. [COUCH] *Delectable Duchy* 109 Was it only you?.. O, glory be! **1954** KOESTLER *Invis. Writing* xxxvi. 392 For, glory be, man is a stubborn creature. **1968** B. TURNER *Sex Trap* xiii. 120 'Your hours are numbered.' Grange's eyes sparkled... 'Glory be!'

5. In Biblical phraseology: ***the glory of God***: the majesty and splendour attendant upon a manifestation of God.

1382 WYCLIF *Rom.* i. 23 Thei chaungiden the glorie of God vncorruptible..in to the lyknesse of an ymage of corruptible man. **1526** *Pilgr. Perf.* (W. de W. 1531) 3 Moyses..made supplicacyon to god..that he wolde shewe hym his glory. **1611** BIBLE *Ezek.* ix. 3 The glory of the God of Israel was gone vp from the Cherub whereupon hee was. **1689-90** TEMPLE *Ess. Learning* Wks. 1731 I. 299 Moses was ..admitted both to see his Glory, and to learn his name, Jehovah.

6. Resplendent beauty or magnificence. Now often with suggestion of sense 5 or 7: An effulgence of light such as is associated with our conceptions of heaven; *fig.* an unearthly beauty attributed by imagination. Also *pl.*, features of resplendent beauty or magnificence, splendours.

13.. *E.E. Allit. P.* A. 933 Loke on þe glory of þys gracious gote. **1390** GOWER *Conf.* III. 166 To themperour in all his gloire He said: Take [etc.]. **1509** FISHER *Funeral Serm. C'tess Richmond* Wks. (1876) 306 The kynge..was crowned in..grete tryumphe and glorye. **1585** M. W. in Jas. I *Ess. Poesie* (Arb.) 10 O Phœbus then reioyce with glauncing glore. **1602** T. A[CHERLEY] *Massacre Money* B ij, Whilst that my glory midst the clouds was hid. *a* **1693** AUBREY *Lives, Barrow* (1898) I. 91 As he lay expiring..the standers-by could heare him say softly, I have seen The glories of the world. **1726** C. D'ANVERS *Craftsm.* xvi. (1727) 134 The Roll appeared encompassed with rays of glory. **1738** WESLEY *Psalms* v. ii, None without Holiness shall see The Glories of thy Face. **1791** MRS. RADCLIFFE *Rom. Forest* ii, Which, quickly expanding, the sun appeared in all his glory. **1803-6** WORDSW. *Intim. Immort.* ii, There hath past away a glory from the earth. **1826** DISRAELI *Viv. Grey* II. iv, The scarlet glories of the *pyrus japonica.* **1836** EMERSON *Nature, Beauty* Wks. (Bohn) II. 146 The heavens..reflect their glory or gloom on the plains beneath. **1878** BROWNING *La Saisiaz* 10 What will be the morning glory, when at dusk thus gleams the lake?

7. a. The splendour and bliss of heaven. (Cf. F. *la gloire éternelle.*)

c **1375** *Sc. Leg. Saints, Placidas* 264 Quhare euir-lestand glore sal be, & eschewine of al payne. *a* **1533** LD. BERNERS *Huon* lvi. 190 It semed to them that they were in the glory of paradyce. **1552** ABP. HAMILTON *Catech.* (1884) 42 The glore quhilk is promissit to the sonnis of God. **1631** MILTON *Epit. Marchioness Winchester* 61 Thou, bright Saint, high sitt'st in glory. **1648** *Shorter Catech. Westm. Assemb.* Answ. 37 The souls of Beleevers are at their death made perfect in holiness, & do immediately pass into glory. **1732** LAW *Serious C.* (ed. 2) 9 And strive to enter through the Strait Gate into a life of eternal Glory. **1848** MRS. JAMESON *Sacr. & Leg. Art* (1850) 34 The crown is placed on the head of the maternal Virgin in glory.

b. *colloq. to go to glory*: to go to heaven; to die.

1814 *Sailor's Return* I. i, Adimar was in the act of boarding, with several others, when the Dasher went to glory. Thus was he saved. **1852** MRS. STOWE *Uncle Tom's C.* xli, Tell her ye found me going into glory. **1884** CRADDOCK *In Tennessee Mts.* i. 9 He hev been in glory twenty year. **1897** MARY KINGSLEY *W. Africa* 179 Had we got caught in this, we should have..gone to glory.

8. A state of exaltation and splendour. ***in one's glory***: in one's highest state of magnificence or prosperity; also *colloq.*, in a state of unbounded gratification or enjoyment.

1613 PURCHAS *Pilgrimage* I. xvii. 90 Tyrus, now called Sur, (whose glorie is sufficiently blazed by the Prophets Esay, and Ezechiel). **1816** KEATINGE *Trav.* (1817) II. 62 The real Spanish beau..at midnight and at the billiard-table, he appears in his glory. **1829** W. IRVING *Granada* I. xiii. 132 They thought that the days of their ancient glory were about to return. **1879** MISS BRADDON *Clov. Foot* xiv, Mr. Smolendo was in his glory. **1893** G. E. MATHESON *About Holland* 14 The commerce of Holland was at its full glory. *a* **1895** LD. C. E. PAGET *Autobiog.* vii. (1896) 209, I think, too, the fleet liked my coming and living on board and taking an interest in everybody and everything; in truth, I was in my glory.

9. a. The circle of light represented as surrounding the head, or the whole figure, of the Saviour, the Virgin, or one of the Saints; an AUREOLE *sb.* or NIMBUS.

1646 SIR T. BROWNE *Pseud. Ep.* v. ix. 247 Radiant Halo's ..which after the French expression are usually tearmed, the Glory. **1745** *Gentl. Mag.* 197 A glory, which is..that border of light which adorns the pictures of saints. **1862** H. KINGSLEY *Ravenshoe* I. xxi. 246 Her own glorious golden hair, which hung round her lovely face like a glory. **1864** SKEAT *Uhland's Poems* 19 On Thy clear eyes she [Mary] fixed her view, And thence celestial lustre drew Till o'er her glowed a glory bright.

b. A representation of the heavens opening and revealing celestial beings. ? *Obs.* (Cf. F. *gloire.*)

1708 *New View Lond.* II. 488/1 Painted on Glass under a Glory between 2 Cherubims. **1782** R. CUMBERLAND *Anecd.* (1787) II. 136 The Holy Virgin is displayed in the center of the piece, above is a glory of Angels.

c. *transf.* Any circle or ring of light; a halo, corona. Also, † a name for the star of an order of knighthood (*obs.*), and *spec.* an anthelion or fog-bow.

1693 *Lond. Gaz.* No. 2845/2 They presented to his Electoral Highness..the Two Stars or Glories, and Two Pieces of Ribbon of the Order [of the Garter]. **1697** DRYDEN *Virg. Georg.* I. 504 Seeming Stars fall headlong..And..gild the Night With sweeping Glories, and long Trails of Light. **1725** *Lond. Gaz.* No. 6382/1 With a Glory or Rays issuing from the Center. **1766** ENTICK *London* IV. 88 An altar piece gilt and carved, with a glory and the king's arms above the commandments. **1811** PINKERTON *Petral.* I. 559 Anthracite ..consumes slowly without any flame; but only encircled with a little glory, or irradiation. **1823** W. SCORESBY *Whale Fish.* 275 The interior circle..forms a brilliant anthelion, or glory, round the spectrum of the observer. **1842** W. HOWITT *Rur. & Dom. Life Germany* 452 If the fog is dry, you see not only yourself, but your neighbour; if very damp, only yourself, surrounded by a rainbow-coloured glory. **1871** tr. *Schellen's Spectr. Anal.* xlix. 207 This crown of rays is usually designated the glory. **1884** W. C. SMITH *Kildrostan* 43 A broad beam of the garish light Smote with a glory her golden hair. **1884** P. G. TAIT *Light* §167 It seems possible that glories may be due to a cause somewhat analogous to that which produces the spurious rainbows. **1888** *Encycl. Brit.* XXIV. 435/1 (*margin*) Coronas or glories. **1910** C. C. TURNER *Aerial Navig.* 141 Halos round the sun and moon, rainbows, 'glories', or 'aureoles'—the coloured rings seen round the shadow cast by the balloon on the clouds. **1925** C. F. BROOKS *Why Weather?* x. 122 Sometimes there is a double glory, that of larger diameter containing the full range of colors of the rainbow, from violet to red. **1963** G. C. BOWDEN tr. *Schöpfer's Young Specialist looks at Weather* vi. 95 The airman is also familiar with the 'glory', as he often sees the system of coloured rings surrounding the shadow of his aircraft cast by the sun on a layer of cloud below.

†**d.** *Bot.* = CORONA 7 b. *Obs.*

1785 MARTYN *Rousseau's Bot.* xxvii. 427 The petals of the corol are white, with a double purple fringe, star, or glory. *Ibid.* 428 The glory or crown is violet.

10. In names of insects and plants. (See quots.)

1819 G. SAMOUELLE *Entomol. Compend.* 247 *Endromis versicolor* (Kentish glory). **1866** *Treas. Bot.* 757/1 Morning Glory, a name applied to certain species of *Ipomœa* and *Pharbitis*, e.g. *P. hispidus* the Convolvulus major of gardens. **1897** WILLIS *Flower. Pl.* II. 86 *Chionodoxa Luciliae* (glory of the snow) is a favourite border plant.

11. *attrib.* and *Comb.* **a.** simple attrib., as ***glory-bath, -crown, -days, -mist, -robe, -seat, -throne.*** **b.** instrumental, as ***glory-cinctured, -circled, -crowned, -laden, -smitten, -stricken, -tinged*** adjs. Also **glory-box** *Austral.* and *N.Z.*, a box in which a woman stores clothes, etc., in preparation for marriage; cf. GLORY-HOLE 1 b; **glory-pea**, a name for the Australasian genus *Clianthus*; **glory-tree**, a shrub of the genus *Clerodendron.*

1875 BROWNING *Inn Album* I. 50 He leans into a living *glory-bath Of air and light. **1949** D. M. DAVIN *Roads from Home* II. iv. 129 Seeing the neatly folded linen there, the carefully worked doilies and table spreads, the unworn silk nightdress, she knew she had blundered on Moira's hoard, her *glory-box. **1963** *Wanganui Herald* (N.Z.) 9 July 16/2 Sideboard (as new), 2 wardrobes, 4 fireside chairs, tin trunk, light oak glory-box. **1971** *Sunday Australian* 8 Aug. 46/8 The traditional work used on all the linen items in a girl's glory box. **1853** TALFOURD *Castilian* IV. ii, These *glory-cinctured towers. *a* **1711** KEN *Hymns Evang.* Poet. Wks. 1721 I. 66 The *Glory-circled Infant. **1895** MRS. HINKSON *Miracle Plays* 13 On his head a *glory crown Fine as the evening star. **1603** J. DAVIES (Heref.) *Microcosmos* (Grosart) 16/2 Such Kings should be obaid, and *glory-cround, Because their Vertues al men's else exceede. **1850** TENNYSON *In Mem.* xcvii, He finds on misty mountain-ground His own vast shadow glory-crown'd. **1956** R. ANDREWS (*title*) *Glory days of logging. **1984** *Economist* 20 Oct. 73/3 In Opec's glory days in the mid and late 1970s, the spot markets accounted for only 5–10% of internationally-traded oil. **1825** D. L. RICHARDSON *Sonn.* 19 Her radiant smile Illumines now this *glory-haunted Isle. **1866** J. H. NEWMAN *Let. Pusey* (ed. 2) 91 That pure Virgin..So weak yet so strong; so delicate yet so *glory-laden. **1875** E. WHITE *Life in Christ* III. xvii. (1878) 210 If it be urged that Christ hid much of His truth in a *glory-mist of metaphors [etc.]. **1848** *Rural Cycl.* II. 458 *Glory-pea or Glory-flower—botanically *Clianthus*..The crimson glory-pea, *Clianthus puniceus*, is a native of the northern island of New Zealand. **1827** KEBLE *Chr. Y., St. Michael* vii, Brighter and brighter streams his *glory-robe. **1838** ELIZA COOK *Poems, Melaia* lxxxi, The *glory-seat of arts and power. **1817** COLERIDGE *Biog. Lit.* 156 The two *glory-smitten summits of the poetic mountain. **1871** G. MACDONALD *Manchester Poem* 210 *Glory-stricken birds. **1827** KEBLE *Chr. Y., Palm Sunday* iii, Angels round His *Glory-throne. **1839** TALFOURD *Glencoe* III. ii, To wander on the bank Of *glory-tinged Loch-Leven. **1848** *Rural Cycl.* II. 458 *Glory-tree: see *Clerodendron.*

glory ('glɔərɪ), *v.*[1] Also 6 *Sc.* glore, gloir. [ad. L. *glōri-ārī*, f. *glōri-a* GLORY.]

1. *intr.* To exult with triumph, rejoice proudly. Const. *in*, †*on*, *to* with *inf.*, and *that.*

13.. *E.E. Allit. P.* B. 1522 þise lordes..gloryed on her falce goddes & her grace calles. **1548** UDALL, etc. *Erasm. Par. Mark* xii. 13–17 Thou gloryest in the name and tytle of a Chrystian manne. *Ibid. Luke* ii. 25–32 Nowe from hensforth the gostly Israel..shall glory on thy sonne. **1552** ABP. HAMILTON *Catech.* (1884) 42 We glore & ar blyth throw the hoip quhilk we haif. *a* **1586** SIDNEY *Arcadia* II. (1633) 129 With like iudgement glorying, when he had happened to do a thing well, as when he had performed some notable mischiefe. **1596** DALRYMPLE tr. *Leslie's Hist. Scot.* x. 406 Quha tuik to thame the title gloireng in the name. **1613** SHAKS. *Hen. VIII*, II. i. 66 Let 'em looke they glory not in mischiefe. **1667** MILTON *P.L.* I. 238 Both glorying to have scaped the Stygian flood As Gods. **1795** *Gentl. Mag.* 542/1 Licentiousness, prophaning the sacred name of liberty, has gloried in the destruction of order. **1832** HT. MARTINEAU *Ella of Gar.* iii. 36 Cries that would have dismayed a stranger but which Archie always gloried in provoking. **1863** FR. K. KEMBLE *Resid. in Georgia* 17, I have heard it..repeatedly asserted—and, what is more, much gloried in. **1868** J. T. NETTLESHIP *Ess. Browning's Poetry* i. 59 Would I not glory to go into your very tomb?

†**2.** To boast. Const. *of*, *to* with *inf.*, or *that.* Also *refl.* and quasi-*trans.* with *complement* in *indirect passive. Obs.*

1382 WYCLIF *Judith* viii. 17 As oure herte is disturbid in the pride of hem, so also of oure mecnesse wee glorien. **1549** COVERDALE, etc. *Erasm. Par. 2 Cor.* 51 Albeit we maye glory our selfes of the stocke of Jewes [etc.]. **1635** PAGITT *Christianogr.* 47 The Romanists glory much of the conversion of these Indians. **1640** tr. *Verdere's Rom. Rom.* I. 114 That which I require of you, replied she, is, that..I may one day glory, that I have seen a number of good knights unhorsed upon the quarrell of my beauty. **1648** SYMMONS *Vind. Chas. I* 138 We have seen a glimpse of that perspicuity and modesty which is gloried to be in these annotations. **1673** *Vain Insolency Rome* 25, I think the same might now be said in several instances, to those of Rome, in reference to St. Peter, of whom she glorieth.

†**3.** *trans.* **a.** To give glory to; to honour. **b.** To make glorious; to adorn. *Obs.*

c **1400** *Apol. Loll.* 37 Glory þe bischop, wan he haþ chosun wise prestis, for þe cause of ruyn of þo peple are iuil prestis. **1501** DOUGLAS *Pal. Hon.* Prol. 88 Quha that constranit ar in luifis rage Weill auchtis the till gloir and magnifie. **1563–76** FOXE *A. & M.* To Rdr. ¶ii b, Let vs yelde thus much vnto their commemoration, to glory the Lord in hys saintes. **1594** GREENE & LODGE *Looking Glasse* Wks. (Rtldg.) 118 The troop That gloried Venus at her wedding-day. *a* **1639** WOTTON *Ps.* civ. in *Reliq. W.* (1651) 527 Be ever gloried here Thy Soveraign Name. **1661** DAVENPORT *City Night-cap* I. 4 See How he that glories Heaven with no Honour, Covets to glorifie himself with Honesty.

†**4.** *intr.* Of light: To spread like a 'glory'.

1651 N. BACON *Disc. Govt. Eng.* II. vi. (1739) 36 It is a good sign of a clear morning, when the Sun-rising glorieth upon the top of the Mountains.

Hence †'**gloried** *ppl. a.*

1671 MILTON *Samson* 334 If old respect..towards your once gloried friend, My son, now captive, hither hath informed Your younger feet.

†'**glory**, *v.*[2] *Obs.* [? cf. GLAR *v.*] (See quot.)

c **1440** *Promp. Parv.* 199/2 Gloryyn, or wythe onclene þynge defoylyn, *maculo, deturpo.*

'**glory-hole.** [In sense 1, perh. related to GLORY *v.*[2] (cf. Sc. *glaury* adj. s.v. GLAR); if so, sense 2 is prob. later in origin, and suggested by the formal coincidence of the first element with GLORY *sb.*]

1. a. *slang.* (See quot. 1845). **b.** *dial.* A receptacle (as a drawer, room, etc.) in which things are heaped together without any attempt at order or tidiness.

1825 M. WILMOT *Let.* 20 Nov. (1935) 227 A sort of play room or glory hole for poor Wilmot to keep his rubbish. **1845** T. COOPER *Purg. Suicides* (1877) p. vi, A filthy, stifling cell to which prisoners are brought from the gaol on the day of trial, and which in the language of the degraded beings who usually occupy it, is called the 'glory hole'. **1871** MRS. WHITNEY *We Girls* iii. 62 You can bring out your old ribbon-box..It's a charity to clear out your glory-holes once in a while. **1893** *Wiltsh. Gloss., Glory-hole*, a place for rubbish or odds and ends, as a housemaid's cupboard, or a lumber room.

c. *Naut. colloq.* Any of various compartments of a ship, as: (*a*) the lazaretto; (*b*) one or more rooms between or below decks used as sleeping-quarters for stewards. Also *fig.*

1839 W. H. LEIGH *Reconnoitering Voy.* ii. 16 The other one was of the dog-fish species, and had nothing in his 'glory hole' worth notice. **1897** E. G. CONSTANTINE *Marine Engin.* ix. 108 In the 'glory-hole', which had to be descended to tighten up the inner trunk gland near the crank pit. **1898** *Pearson's Mag.* V. 213/2 They went through every part of her, from the sodden shaft-tunnel, to the glory-hole where the stewards live. **1927** G. BRADFORD *Gloss. Sea Terms* 74/2 *Glory hole*, a term sometimes given to the firemen's quarters of a steamer; sometimes applied to the lazarette. *a* **1941** R. BEDFORD in *Austral. Short Stories* (1951) 95 I'm..waitin' till I can sneak out on the boat deck to sleep—the glory hole being so hot.

2. *Glass-making.* (See quots.)

1849 PELLATT *Curios. Glass Making* 65 The large goods receive a final reheating at the mouth of a pot heated by beech-wood, and called the Glory Hole. **1889** *Harper's Mag.* July 250 The working furnaces..are small blast-furnaces..each providing a number of openings directly into the flames. A spectator sees at once the appropriateness of their name—'glory-holes'.

3. A large cavernous opening or pit into a mine; an open quarry. Hence as *v. intr.*, to carry on surface mining. *N. Amer.*

1902 *Geol. Survey Canada Summary Report 1901* 64A, The larger properties..are now mining by large quarries or 'Glory holes', from which the material will be loaded directly into ore cars. **1916** *Daily Colonist* (Victoria, B.C.) 21 July 3/3 The Mother Lode mine has been working for some sixteen years, partly as a glory hole and partly by shaft and drift. **1926** *Ibid.* 13 July 3/2 The strike..was made in the glory hole of the property..and there is considerable of the high-grade free milling quartz. **1927** W. N. BURNS *Tombstone* 381 In this tunnel beneath the town the Grand Central mine 'gloryholed', taking out $840,000. **1943** *Copper Camp* 29 Parks' 'glory hole'..turned out over a million dollars' worth of high grade copper. **1966** *McGraw-Hill Encycl. Sci. & Technol.* VIII. 481/1 Glory-holing is an underhand stoping method occasionally used to develop funnel-shaped excavations in large ore bodies.

4. *Army slang.* (See quots.)

1925 FRASER & GIBBONS *Soldier & Sailor Words* 105 *Glory hole*, a colloquial expression for any small billet or dug-out. **1950** PARTRIDGE *Here, There & Everywhere* 67 The small dug-outs are *cubby-holes*..and the smallish are *glory-holes.*

glorying ('glɔərɪɪŋ), *vbl. sb.* [f. GLORY *v.* + -ING[1].] The action of the vb. GLORY.

1382 WYCLIF *1 Cor.* v. 6 ȝoure gloriynge is not good. **1588** A. KING tr. *Canisius' Catech.* 128 Of defense of sin [proceeds] gloiring thairin, of gloiring dreedfull damnation. **1651** HOBBES *Leviath.* I. vi. 27 Joy, arising from imagination of a man's own power and ability..is called Glorying. **1756** BURKE *Subl. & B.* I. xvii, Hence proceeds what Longinus has observed of that glorying and sense of inward greatness, that always fills the reader of such passages in poets and orators as are sublime. **1836** MRS. BROWNING *Poet's Vow* III. ii, The self-poised God may dwell alone With inward glorying.

glorying ('glɔərɪɪŋ), *ppl. a.* [f. GLORY *v.* + -ING[2].] That glories. Hence '**gloryingly** *adv.*, in a glorying manner.

1851 E. B. ELLIOTT *Horæ Apocal.* (1862) IV. 33 Sustaining his Church upon the seven hills..and gloryingly up-bearing and exhibiting her. **1865** G. MEREDITH *Rhoda Fleming* xvii. (1890) 122 No posterity of his would point them out gloryingly.

'**gloryless**, *a.* [See -LESS.] Without glory.

1540 PALSGRAVE *Acolastus* Prol. B iij b, We our selfe being glorylesse .i. without gloryous fame or renome. **1594** PEELE *Battle Alcazar* II. iii, He on whose glorie all thy ioy should stay, Is souleless, glorylesse, and desperate. **1861** MISS PRATT *Flower. Pl.* III. 91 It [*Adoxa moschatellina*] has several rustic names, as Glory-less, Bulbous Fumitory, etc.

glos(e, glos-: see GLOZE, GLOZ-.

glosarye, obs. form of GLOSSARY[1].

†'**glose-worm.** *Obs. rare.* Also glouse-. [? app. an alteration of GLOW-WORM. Cf. GLOZE *v.*[3], GLOSS *sb.*[2]; also *glass-worm*, *glaze-worm.*] = GLOW-WORM.

1519 HORMAN *Vulg.* 108 A flye or a worme called a glouberde, or a glouse worme. **1589** R. HARVEY *Pl. Perc.* (1860) 21 Changeable coloured vrchins, which can glisten like a glose worme neare gold.

gloss (glɒs), *sb.*[1] Also 6–7 glosse, 7–8 glos. [var. of *glose*, GLOZE *sb.*, refashioned in 16th c. after L. *glōssa*, Gr. γλῶσσα in the same sense. (In the 15th c. the spelling *glosse* appears occas. for *glos(e* GLOZE *sb.* and *v.*; see those words.)]

1. A word inserted between the lines or in the margin as an explanatory equivalent of a foreign or otherwise difficult word in the text; hence applied to a simliar explanatory rendering of a word given in a glossary or dictionary. Also, in a wider sense, a comment, explanation, interpretation. Often used in a sinister sense: A sophistical or disingenuous interpretation. (Cf. GLOZE *sb.* I.)

1548 UDALL, etc. *Erasm. Par. Matt.* xxiii. 108 Like as by a glosse ye subuerte the commaundement. **1598** DRAYTON *Heroic. Ep.* vi. 109 The Canon Text shall have a common Glosse. **1608** BP. HALL *Vert. & Vices* I. 15 Neither doth his tongue..make good a lie with the secret glosses of double or reserved senses. **1622** SPARROW *Bk. Com. Prayer* (1661) 66 The Church rather uses this..then any other Glosse or Paraphrase. **1647** CLARENDON *Hist. Reb.* I. §49 Malicious Glosses made upon all he had said. **1647** N. BACON *Disc. Govt. Eng.* I. ii. (1739) 2 The ways of future providence may be looked upon as a gloss of those Prophecies. **1667** MILTON *P.L.* V. 435. **1695** KENNETT *Par. Antiq.* ix. 641 The gloss indeed destroys the text, by pretending the word [etc.]. *a* **1708** BEVERIDGE *Priv. Th.* II. (1730) 41 Nothing being more needful than to rescue the Words of our blessed Saviour from those false Glosses. **1767** BLACKSTONE *Comm.* II. 495 A gloss of pope Innocent IV, written about the year 1250. *a* **1834** COLERIDGE *Shaks. Notes* (1875) 134 A parenthesis or gloss slipt into the text. **1837–9** HALLAM *Hist. Lit.* I. i. I. §68. 63 Irnerius began the practice of making glosses, or short marginal explanations, on the law books. **1868** KIRK *Chas. Bold* III. v. ii. 363 Secret glosses.. intended to make that part of the contract a nullity. **1875** WHITNEY *Life Lang.* x. 183 The Cymric includes the Welsh, with 'glosses' from the ninth century.

b. A collection of such explanations, a glossary; also, an interlinear translation of, or series of verbal explanations upon, a continuous text.

1579 E. K. in *Spenser's Sheph. Cal.* Ep. Ded. §4 A.. Glosse or scholion, for the exposition of old wordes. **1756–7** tr. *Keysler's Trav.* (1760) II. 55 A manuscript Homer, with a gloss interlined, said to be five hundred years old. **1774** WARTON *Hist. Eng. Poetry* Diss. II. I. sig. E3b, A manuscript of Ovid's Art of Love, in very antient Saxon characters, accompanied with a British gloss. **1841** D'ISRAELI *Amen. Lit.* (1859) II. 95 E. K...whose gloss has preserved much curious knowledge of ancient English terms and phrases. **1894** CLARKE HALL *Ags. Dict.* Pref., Mostly obscure words only found in glosses.

¶ **c.** In the sense of Gr. γλῶσσα: A foreign or other obscure word, requiring explanation. *Obs.*[−1] (Hardly an Eng. sense, though given in some recent Dicts., app. on the ground of quot. 1837–9).

1603 HOLLAND *Plutarch's Mor.* 28 The interpretations of obscure termes, which we call *Glosses.* **1837–9** HALLAM *Hist. Lit.* I. i. I. (1847) 62 A gloss, γλῶσσα, properly meant a word from a foreign language, or an obsolete or poetical word, or whatever requires interpretation.

2. A poetical composition in which a stanza of some well-known poem is treated as a text for amplification, each of the successive stanzas of the 'gloss' being made to end with one of the lines or couplets of the text.

1598 YONG *Diana* 437 He sung a glosse vpon this Dittie. **1823** ROSCOE *Sismondi's Lit. Eur.* (1846) II. xxxix. 538 Each verse is intended to form the subject of a strophe, in the gloss, or comment.

3. *attrib.* and *Comb.*

1624 BEDELL *Lett.* iii. 64 Although the Glosse writer were no excellent Calculator. **1648** JENKYN *Blind Guide* iv. 87 According to G. the glossmaker. **1888** G. W. PROTHERO *Life Bradshaw* 237 A gloss-hunt was a genuine relaxation to him.

gloss (glɒs), *sb.*[2] Also 6–7 glosse; and see GLASS *sb.*[3] [First recorded in 16th c.; cf. Du. (obs.) *gloos* a glowing, gleaming = MHG. *glos, glose* (still extant in Swiss dialects); Sw. (dial.) *glossa, glåsa* to gleam, glow (of coals), to shine (of cloth), Icel. *glossi* a blaze (see GLOZE *v.*[3]). A variant *glass* (see GLASS *sb.* 13) appears about the same date, perh. as a substitute for the less familiar word.]

1. a. Superficial lustre. Also *pl.*

1538 ELYOT *Dict.*, *Cantharis uel Cantharida*..a greene worme shynynge with a glosse of golde. **1553** T. WILSON *Rhet.* 65 Beinge in the rayne,..[he] standeth naked himself, for savynge the glosse of his gaye coate. **1594** PLAT *Jewell-ho.* III. 72 Some maintaine the glosse of this leather with a peece of black veluet onely. **1607** TOPSELL *Four-f. Beasts* (1658) 486 The glosse of the wool was..beautiful, for the purity of the black. **1610** SHAKS. *Temp.* II. i. 63 Our Garments being..drencht in the Sea, hold notwithstanding their freshnesse and glosses. **1680** MOXON *Mech. Exerc.* I. 221 They set a Gloss on it [Hard Wood] with a very dry Woollen Rag, lightly smear'd with Sallad Oyl. **1686** PLOT *Staffordsh.* 157 Which [pebbles] all took so specious and elegant a gloss, that [etc.]. **1774** GOLDSM. *Nat. Hist.* (1776) II. IV. iii. 396 Its [the Carcajou's] fur is held in the highest estimation, for its..beautiful gloss. **1828** STARK *Elem. Nat. Hist.* I. 249 Upper parts of the body brilliant copper-colour, with a golden gloss. **1855** TENNYSON *Maud* I. XXII. ix, In gloss of satin and glimmer of pearls. **1874** T. HARDY *Far fr. Mad. Crowd* II. i. 15 Amaranthine glosses came over them [clouds].

b. In obvious figurative uses. Also (sometimes perh. confused with GLOSS *sb.*[1]), a deceptive appearance, fair semblance, plausible pretext.

1548 UDALL, etc. *Erasm. Par. Luke* xii. 1–7 Beware ye that all your life bee void of all cloking or countrefaicte glosse [L. *ut omnis uita uestra fuco careat*]. **1576** FLEMING *Panopl. Ep.* 401 (*margin*) In the glosse of their glorie..that is, when they were most famous. **1596** SPENSER *F.Q.* IV. v. 15 He much more goodly glosse thereon doth shed, To hide his falshood, then if it were trew. **1599** NASHE *Lenten Stuffe* (1871) 17 King John..in furthering of this new waterwork..set a fresh gloss upon it [Yarmouth]. **1606** SHAKS. *Tr. & Cr.* II. iii. 128 Yet all his vertues..Doe in our eyes, begin to loose their glosse. **1640** YORKE *Union Hon.* 1 The first Glosse that William Duke of Normandy had for this Crowne and Diadem of England, was thus. **1652** CULPEPPER *Eng. Physic.* (1809) 19 To put a gloss upon their practice, the physicians call an herb..Archangel. **1660** T. M. *Hist. Independ.* IV. 28 The better to cast a seeming gloss of legality upon his usurpation, he summons another Parliament. *a* **1680** BUTLER *Rem.* (1759) I. 249 Art, That sets a Gloss on what's amiss. **1726** SWIFT *Poems, To a Lady*, You, like some acute philosopher, Ev'ry fault have drawn a gloss over. **1756** BURKE *Vind. Nat. Soc.* Pref., There is a sort of gloss upon ingenious falsehoods, that dazzles the imagination. **1760–2** GOLDSM. *Cit. W.* iii, The most trifling occurrences give pleasure till the gloss of novelty is worn away. **1761–2** HUME *Hist. Eng.* (1806) III. xxxix. 278 A woman thus..provides only thin glosses to cover her exceptionable conduct. **1834** J. H. NEWMAN *Par. Serm.* (1837) I. iii. 45 The false gloss of a mere worldly refinement makes us decent and amiable. **1852** MRS. STOWE *Uncle Tom's C.* xv, As the glosses and civilities of the honeymoon wore away, he discovered that [etc.]. **1872** BLACKIE *Lays Highl.* 24, I have used no gloss, no varnish To make fair things fairer look.

2. A layer of glowing matter. *rare.* Also *dial.* of a fire: A bright glow.

1762 *Gentl. Mag.* 338 The earth being all on a fiery gloss for four inches deep. *c* **1817** HOGG *Tales & Sk.* IV. 54 The smith..covered the gloss neatly up with a mixture of small coals, culm, and cinders. **1893** *Northumbld. Gloss.* s.v., Ye can bake the cyek noo; the fire hes a fine gloss.

3. †**a.** = GLAZE *sb.* 1. *Obs.*

1825 J. NICHOLSON *Operat. Mechanic* 470 The earthenware is now ready to receive the smooth coating called glaze or gloss.

b. *Comb.*: **gloss-fireman, -oven** (now *glost-fireman, -oven*: see GLOST); **gloss-meter**, a photometric device for measuring the gloss of surfaces; **gloss paint**, paint that contains varnish and gives a glossy finish; also **gloss enamel**.

1908 *Sears, Roebuck Catal.* 74/1 Seroco gloss enamel—a high gloss interior paint. **1926–7** *Army & Navy Stores Catal.* 297 Jackson's gloss black enamel. **1825** J. NICHOLSON *Operat. Mechanic* 474 The gloss-fireman raises the temperature as quickly as possible to a height sufficient to fuse the glaze. **1930** *Jrnl. Optical Soc. Amer.* XX. 24 The entire range of objective gloss..may be covered. The essentials of the gloss-meter are shown in Fig. 1. **1961** J. H. GOODIER *Dict. Painting & Decorating* 118 The gloss meter works on the principle of directing a beam of light on to a painted panel and allowing the reflected beam to excite a galvanometer. **1962** *New Scientist* 10 May 299/3 Though the instrument has been developed specifically for pearls, the principle of the glossmeter can be adapted for measurements of the gloss of ball bearings and other industrial items with curved surfaces whose gloss may be a criterion of their excellence. **1825** J. NICHOLSON *Operat. Mechanic* 474, The gloss-oven is sometimes fired to a greater degree of heat than some colours will bear. [**1875**, **1882** see GLOST.] **1926–7** *Army & Navy Stores Catal.* 299/1 Hard gloss finishing paint. **1933** *Drugs, Oils & Paints* Apr. 135/1 Portions of both the one and two-coat finishes are then given a final coat of gloss paint. **1960** *House & Garden* June 72/2 Gloss paints seem to get better and better in quality.

gloss (glɒs), *v.*[1] [f. GLOSS *sb.*[1]]

1. *trans.* To insert glosses or comments on; to comment upon, explain, interpret; = GLOZE *v.*[1] 1.

1603 FLORIO *Montaigne* I. xii. (1632) 21 Some that studie, plod, and glosse their Almanackes. **1615** T. ADAMS *Two Sonnes* 88 For all his big words, his stomach comes downe, if I may take leave to glosse it. **1641** J. JACKSON *True Evang. T.* II. 144 'My beloved is white, and ruddy'.. is thus glossed, 'white' in his life, 'ruddy' in his death. **1643** MILTON *Divorce* 39 Kimchi, and the two other Rabbies who glosse the text are in the same opinion. **1809** SOUTHEY in *Q. Rev.* I. 219 This accursed custom was not known when the Institutes of Menu were written, nor when they were glossed by Calidas. **1864** PUSEY *Lect. Daniel* vi. 377 He manifoldly glossed the text. **1866** *Reader* 16 June 580 Sir F. Madden can hardly have been the first editor who glossed the word.

b. *intr.* To introduce a gloss, comment, or explanation upon a word or passage in a text. Also in wider sense, to make comments or remarks (esp. unfavourable ones) *upon* a person's words or actions. Const. *on*, *upon*, †*at*. (Cf. GLOZE *v.*[1] 1 b.)

1579 E. K. in *Spenser's Sheph. Cal.* Ep. Ded. §4 Which maner of glossing and commenting. **1639** T. BRUGIS tr. *Camus' Moral Relat.* 301 He was so jealous of Eleusipe, that he glossed on all her words..and on the smallest of her actions. *a* **1652** J. SMITH *Sel. Disc.* VII. v. (1660) 327, I may fairly thus gloss at his whole Discourse upon this Argument. **1657** TRAPP *Comm. Ps.* lxxxvi. 1 So Basil glosseth here. **1671** MILTON *Samson* 948 Bearing my words and doings to the lords To gloss upon, and censuring, frown or smile. **1678** CUDWORTH *Intell. Syst.* I. iv. §16. 293 Psellus thus glossing upon that Oracle. **1718** PRIOR *Pleasure* 758 Some gloss'd, how love and wisdom were at strife. **1727** SWIFT *Gulliver* II. vi. 151 In penning those laws, which they assumed the liberty of interpreting and glossing upon at their pleasure. **1875** MAINE *Hist. Inst.* i. 15 The Celts seem to have had a special habit of glossing.

2. *trans.* To veil with glosses; to explain away; to read a different sense into. Also with *away*, *over* (the latter perh. influenced by GLOSS *v.*[2]). (Cf. GLOZE *v.*[1] 2.)

1638 CHILLINGW. *Relig. Prot.* I. vii. §7. 390 If you may glosse the Text so farre..why should you not glosse it a little farther? **1715** BENTLEY *Serm.* x. 360 Who have gloss'd and warp'd all the severe Rules of the Gospel about Chastity. **1764** CHURCHILL *Candidate* Wks. II. 35 With nice distinctions glossing o'er the text. **1852** H. ROGERS *Ecl. Faith* 226 The Pharisees, who were sunk in formalism, and who had glossed away every moral and spiritual precept of the Law. **1865** MERIVALE *Rom. Emp.* VIII. lxiv. 99 He could hardly resist the temptation to pervert or gloss the truth. **1879** *Q. Rev.* Apr. 325 Difficulties which their school has been in the habit of glossing over with conventional but inadequate explanations.

gloss (glɒs), *v.*[2] [f. GLOSS *sb.*[2]] *trans.* To put a gloss upon. **a.** In immaterial sense: To give a fair appearance to; to veil in specious language. Also with *over*, and in indirect passive.

The earlier quots. may be a development of GLOSS *v.*[1] 1 influenced by GLOSS *sb.*[2]

a **1656** USSHER *Ann.* VI. (1658) 511 His expedition was glossed with the specious pretence of settling Ariobarzanes the new Elect in his kingdom. **1658** SIR T. BROWNE *Hydriot.* iv. 19 Christians have handsomely glossed the deformity of death, by careful consideration of the body. **1659** HAMMOND *On Ps.* lxii. 4 And this traiterous designe they glosse and varnish over with fair flattering language. **1729** BUTLER *Serm.* Wks. 1874 II. 87 He glosses over that same wickedness, dresses it up in a new form. *a* **1743** LD. HERVEY *Flora to Pompey* in Dodsley *Coll. Poems* (1782) IV. 96 Urge not, to gloss thy crime, the name of friend. **1761** FOOTE *Liar* II. Wks. 1799 I. 293 His friends, who are tender of his fame, gloss over his foible, by calling him an agreeable novelist. **1856** MISS MULOCK *J. Halifax* xxii, Such transactions.. were yet generally glossed over, as if a certain discredit attached to them. **1886** *Pall Mall G.* 30 Sept., Mr. Chalmers ..would fain gloss over the hardships he has suffered.

b. In material sense: To render bright and glossy; to glaze.

1762 tr. *Busching's Syst. Geog.* II. 347 Black armozins are glossed by a decoction of beer and Seville oranges. **1796** J. OWEN *Trav. Eur.* I. 227 We entered upon the Glacier, but found great difficulty in keeping our feet. The sun had glossed the surface. **1797–1804** BEWICK *Brit. Birds* I. 305 Back black, glossed with blue. **1801** SOUTHEY *Thalaba* V. xxii, The moonlight fell, glossing the sable tide That gush'd tumultuous out. **1828** STARK *Elem. Nat. Hist.* I. 249 The head red, glossed with bronze.

Hence **'glossing** *vbl. sb.*; also *attrib.*

1875 KNIGHT *Dict. Mech.*, *Glossing*, an operation upon silk thread by which it is moistened with steam and stretched to develop a gloss. **1893** *Queen* 4 Feb. 197/3 Pressing them pretty heavily with the glossing iron. **1897** C. T. DAVIS *Manuf. Leather* (ed. 2) 614 Glossing of ordinary leather is very frequently effected by brushing the leather over with a rind of bacon and rubbing [etc.]. For finer qualities of leather a glossing mass consisting of a fat-emulsion..may be advantageously used.

gloss (glɒs), *adv. Ceramics.* [f. GLOSS *sb.*[2]] Glossily; so as to have a gloss.

1825 J. NICHOLSON *Operat. Mechanic* 476 The pottery.. for gold lustre is made of the red clay of the district, and when fired gloss, has just a sufficient tint left to give to the articles that peculiar colour on them.

glossal ('glɒsəl), *a.* [f. Gr. γλῶσσα tongue + -AL[1].] Of or pertaining to the tongue.

1860 in FOWLER *Med. Voc.* **1878** FOSTER *Phys.* III. i. 393 If any real union took place it must have been between the lingual fibres and the end-plates of the glossal muscular fibres. **1885** LANDOIS & STIRLING *Physiol.* II. 813 The glossal branches [of the glossopharyngeal nerve].

glossalgia (glɒ'sældʒɪə). *Path.* [mod.L., a. Gr. γλωσσαλγία, in class. Gr. only in sense 'talking till one's tongue aches', f. γλῶσσα tongue + ἄλγος pain; cf. F. *glossalgie*.] Pain in the tongue, neuralgia of the tongue.

1847 in CRAIG.

glossalgy (glɒ'sældʒɪ). [Anglicized form of prec.] **a.** = prec. **b.** (*nonce-use*) Talkativeness.

1854 in MAYNE *Expos. Lex.* **1873** W. CORY *Let. & Jrnls.* (1897) 330 So I who bore no one with questions, suffered for the glossalgy of others.

'glossan. *Anglo-Irish.* Also 8 **glassen**, 9 **glassin**, **glashan**. [The form *glashan* represents Gael. *glaisean* 'a coal-fish in its second or third year', f. *glas* grey; the other forms seem to represent a local Irish *_glasán_ f. the same stem. Cf. GLASSOCK.] The coal-fish, *Merlangus carbonarius*.

1780 A. YOUNG *Tour Irel.* I. 251 Some wherries come for cod, ling, glassen [etc.]. **1825** HONE *Every-day Bk.* I. 83 In this pond [at Port Nessock, Wigtonshire]..there are also blochin or glassin. **1864** COUCH *Brit. Fishes* III. 84 In Ireland..when of full size they [Coalfish] are Glashan, or Glossan or Glassin. **1880** *Antrim & Down Gloss.*, *Glashan*, the coal fish..Called also Blockan.

glossanthrax (glɒs'ænθræks). [f. Gr. γλῶσσα tongue + ANTHRAX.] A disease of the tongue and mouth in horses and cattle (cf. quot.).

1849–52 TODD *Cycl. Anat.* IV. II. 1156 The tongue is liable to a peculiar gangrenous ulceration, called 'Glossanthrax' or 'Malignant pustule'. (In mod. Dicts.)

glossarial (glɒ'sɛərɪəl), *a.* [f. GLOSSARY *sb.* + -AL[1].] Of or pertaining to a glossary; of the nature of a glossary.

1821 BOSWELL *Advt. Shaks.* I. p. xxiii, In the glossarial index of former editions, the reader has merely been presented with a long list of words. **1824** DIBDIN *Libr. Comp.* 248 The labours..of the latter are paleological or glossarial. **1864** HAZLITT *E.P.P.* I. Introd. 11 A few notes of a glossarial and miscellaneous kind have been given. **1878** GROSART in *H. More's Poems* 208 *note*, The labour spent on this Glossarial Index.

glossarian (glɒ'sɛərɪən). [f. L. *glossāri-um* + -AN.] = next.

1887 *Q. Rev.* CLXIV. 145 These are the qualifications of the ideal glossarian.

glossarist ('glɒsərɪst). [f. GLOSSARY + -IST.]

1. One who writes a gloss or commentary.

1774 WARTON *Hist. Eng. Poetry* (1778) II. 169 The glossarist I take to be Philip de Pergamo, a prior at Padua; who wrote a most elaborate Moralisation on Cato. **1810** D. STEWART *Philos. Ess.* V. iii. 188 When the speculations of the mere scholar, or glossarist, presume to usurp..the honours of Philosophy. **1841** D'ISRAELI *Amen. Lit.* (1867) 149 All the counties in England seemed to rise against the luckless glossarist. **1880** MUIRHEAD *Gaius* IV. §16 *note* 7, Says the glossarist—'it was fifty'.

2. One who compiles a glossary.

1782 TYRWHITT *Vind.* 162 The interpretations assigned to them by those two Glossarists [Speght and Skinner]. **1801** W. TAYLOR in *Monthly Mag.* XI. 289 The glossarist should everywhere refer to, or record, the true spelling. **1862** *Sat. Rev.* 8 Feb. 159 The play [of the Sacrament] contains..a number of words and forms interesting to the English glossarist.

glossary[1] ('glɒsərɪ). Also 5 **glosarye**. [ad. L. *glossārium*, f. *glōssa* GLOSS *sb.*[1]: see -ARY. Cf. F. *glossaire*.] A collection of glosses; a list with explanations of abstruse, antiquated, dialectal, or technical terms; a partial dictionary.

a **1380** *S. Paula* 36 in Horstm. *Altengl. Leg.* (1878) 8 As seiþ þe bok, iclept Glosarie. **1483** CAXTON *Gold. Leg.* (1892) 1084 It is sayd in the glosarye that clemente is sayd rightwys, swete, rype and meke. **1610** HOLLAND *Camden's Brit.* I. 364 Whence it is that an Old Glossary interpreteth *Alpes Italie* The Woulds of Italie. **1696** *Phil. Trans.* XIX. 264 The Glossary, at the end, is not only an Account of Words and Phrases, but also an explication of ancient Customs, Laws, and Manners. **1785** COWPER *Needless Alarm* 70 He..needs no glossary to set him right. **1797** W. TURTON (*title*) A Medical Glossary. **1894** J. T. FOWLER *Adamnan* Pref. 8 A glossary is appended.

fig. **1838** DICKENS *Nich. Nick.* iii, The expression of a man's face is commonly a help to his thoughts, or glossary on his speech. **1859** I. TAYLOR *Logic in Theol.* 49 Having no participation of the elements of the animal and moral nature, it would want the glossary of mundane life.

b. *attrib.* or *adj.*

1715 M. DAVIES *Athen. Brit.* I. 311 Whether J. Perkins made those Glossary Contexts, or no.

†**'glossary**[2]. *Obs.*[−1] [as if a. L. *_glōssārius_, f. *glōssa* GLOSS *sb.*[1]] = GLOSSATOR.

1705 HICKERINGILL *Priest-cr.* II. i. 11 The Glossaries have the Confidence to say..That the Pope can change the nature of things, can make (or create) Something out of Nothing.

glossate (glɒ'seɪt), *v.* [f. med.L. *glōssāt-*, ppl. stem of *glōssāre* to gloss, f. *glōssa* GLOSS *sb.*[1]] *trans.* To write glosses or a commentary upon.

1884 *Cape Law Jrnl.* I. 219 Much of their time was devoted to expounding and 'glossating' the ancient writings.

glossator (glɒ'seɪtə(r)). Also 4 **glosatour**, 7, 9 **glossater**. [a. med.L. *glōssātor* (cf. F. *glossateur*), agent-n. f. *glōssāre* to gloss, f. *glōssa* GLOSS *sb.*[1]] A writer of glosses; a commentator; *spec.* one of the mediæval commentators on the texts of Civil and Canon Law.

c **1380** WYCLIF *Sel. Wks.* III. 258 þe wordis of þes glosatouris passiþ Goddis lawe. **1550** HOOPER *Jonas* v. 122 b, The glossator interpreteth these wordes in ye Canon of the Masse (*Jube hec perferri*). **1593** BELL *Motives Romish Faith* Pref. (1605) 4 The Popish parasites, the glossators of the Canons, ascribe more magnificall..titles unto the Pope. **1619** BRENT tr. *Sarpi's Counc. Trent* VIII. (1629) 816 Hee forbade all Glossators, and Commentators to expound it. **1726** AYLIFFE *Parergon* 29 In this Respect the Glossators Opinion must be false and erroneous in Point of Law. **1822** T. TAYLOR *Apuleius* VII. 164 *note*, These words were written by some glossator. **1886** I. M. RIGG in *Dict. Nat. Biog.* VI. 145 The Summa or Manual of the civil law compiled by the celebrated glossator, Azo of Bologna.

Hence **glossa'torial** *a.*, of the nature of glosses.

1899 STRACHAN in *Philol. Soc. Trans.* Jan., From the rest of the glossatorial literature [*sc.* besides the Würzburg Glosses] have been given only instances which [etc.].

glossecollite (glɒsiː'kɒlaɪt). *Min.* [irreg. f. Gr. γλῶσσα tongue (dative γλώσσῃ) + κολλ(ᾶσθαι) to adhere + -ITE. So called by Shepard 1857 from its property of adhering to the tongue.] A white earthy variety of halloysite.

1857 C. U. SHEPARD *Min.* (ed. 3) Suppl. p. iii, Glossecollite..Adheres strongly to the tongue. **1892** DANA *Min.* 688 Glossecollite is milk-white and earthy.

glossed (glɒst), *ppl. a.*[1] [f. GLOSS *v.*[1] + -ED[1].] Furnished with glosses.

1605 CAMDEN *Rem.* 15 The antientist that I can finde, was ..found in an antient Saxon, glossed Evangelists. **1628** JACKSON *Worthy Man* Title-p., Glossed and scholied. **1845** GRAVES *Rom. Law* in *Encycl. Metrop.* 779/1 The old glossed editions consist of five volumes. **1886** STUBBS *Lect. Med. & Mod. Hist.* xiii. 308 The Constitutions of Othobon..with those of Otho..were the first codified and glossed portions of the national church law.

glossed (glɒst), *ppl. a.*[2] [f. GLOSS *v.*[2] + -ED[1].] †**a.** Invested with a gloss, or bright appearance. Of the eyes: Glazed (*obs.*). **b.** Of immaterial things: Wearing an outside show, made to look specious.

a. 1602 MARSTON *Antonio's Rev.* I. ii. Wks. 1856 I. 77 Poore Maria must appeare ungrac't Of the bright fulgor of gloss'd majestee. *Ibid.* I. v. 86 Lies thy cold father dead, his glossed eyes New closed up by thy sad mothers hands?

b. 1631 MASSINGER *Believe as You List* II. ii, My truth, thowgh yet conceal'd, the mountaines of Thy glossed fictions in her strength remov'd, Shall in a glorious shape appeare. **1664** H. POWER *Exp. Philos.* Pref. 18 Their profoundest Speculations herein [are] but gloss'd outside Fallacies. **1853** BRIGHT *Sp. on India* 3 June, 11 The glossed and burnished statement. **1892** BARING-GOULD *Trag. Cæsars* I. 276 He began his complaints in words of glossed resentment.

†**'glossem.** *Obs. rare*[−1]. [ad. Gr. γλώσσημα, f. γλῶσσα GLOSS *sb.*[1]] A gloss, comment.

1609 BP. HALL *Pharis. & Chr.* Wks. (1627) 414 The Church of Rome shall vie strange glossems and ceremonious obseruations with them. [*a* **1641** BP. R. MOUNTAGU *Acts & Mon.* (1642) 420 They are..but a meere glossema, as we call it, a note by some Reader put downe in the margine..for some memoriall and observation.]

glossematic (glɒsiː'mætɪk), *sb. pl.* and *a. Linguistics.* [f. GLOSSEM(E + -*atics*, after Gr. words like φώνημα, φωνηματικ- and θέμα, θεματικ- and the names of sciences like *mathematics* (see -IC 2); perh. influenced by med.L. *glōssēmaticus* adj., though its sense is not related.] **A.** *sb. pl.* const. as *sing.* A theory of structural linguistics introduced by the Danish scholar Louis Hjelmslev (born 1899) in 1936, and concerned esp. with developing an abstract theory of the distribution of minimal forms (glossemes) and their mutual relationships.

1936 HJELMSLEV & ULDALL in *Humanistisk Samfund Skrifter* (Aarhus) I, (*title*) Synopsis of an outline of Glossematics. **1939** L. HJELMSLEV in *Proc. Third Internat. Congr. Phonetic Sci.* 272 This whole deductive theory of plerematics and cenematics, established by Mr. Uldall and myself under the common name of *glossematics*, bases the definitions of forms on their function among themselves. **1956** J. WHATMOUGH *Language* vii. 115 Accordingly, a theory of the *system* (the pattern of mutual relationships of linguistic elements); of the *norm* (i.e. a set of rules based on the system and describing the limits of variation for each element); and of *usage* (a set of rules based on the norm and describing the limit of variation tolerated in a given speech-community at a given time)—this comprehensive theory is designated *glossematics*. **1964** *Language* XL. 231 'Form' and 'substance' is a basic dichotomy which glossematics makes in both expression and content. **1965** M. HEPPELL tr. *Ivić's Trends in Linguistics* xv. 178 Glossematics is concerned with the systematic comparison of the structures of existing languages with the basic structures of all semiotic systems.

B. *adj.* Of, relating to, or characteristic of glossematics.

1952 A. COHEN *Phonemes of English* 6 The glossematic approach..aims at investigating various codes of communication, not merely speech, from the structural point of view. **1962** *Amer. Speech* XXXVII. 63 Application of glossematic phonological analysis to the Åsele dialect of Swedish. **1965** M. HEPPELL tr. *Ivić's Trends in Linguistics* xv. 183 The beginner in glossematic studies is held up at every step by terminological difficulties.

Hence **glossema'tician**, **glo'ssematist**, an expert in, or student of, glossematics.

1937 *Trans. Philol. Soc.* 137 Phoneticians, phonologists, and the very recent glossematicians were prone to emphasize their differences. **1950** *Archivum Linguisticum* II. II. 180 Here Lotz is in agreement with the glossematists. **1953** C. E. BAZELL *Linguistic Form* 9 Glossematists would distinguish two morphemes (not mere components). **1963** J. LYONS *Structural Semantics* iii. 48 The Glossematicians' dependence on *translation* is especially clear in Uldall.

†**glosse'matical**, *a.* *Obs.*$^{-0}$ [f. med.L. *glōssēmatic-us* (f. *glōssēmat-* GLOSSEM) + -AL[1].]

1656 BLOUNT *Glossogr.*, *Glossematical*, that makes a Comment or Gloss upon a book or text. [Edd. **1670–81** *Glossomatical*; so **1678** PHILLIPS (ed. 4), List Barbarous Words, *Glossomatical*, belonging to a Gloss or short Comment.]

glosseme ('glɒsiːm). *Linguistics.* [ad. Gr. γλώσσημα, f. γλῶσσα GLOSS *sb.*[1]] Any feature in a language (whether of form, stress, order, or the like) that carries meaning and cannot be analysed into smaller meaningful units.

1926 BLOOMFIELD in *Language* II. 161 Whatever has meaning is a glosseme. **1956** J. WHATMOUGH *Language* 114 Just as a *phoneme* is the smallest unit of structural analysis, being a bundle of *distinctive* features, so a term is required for the smallest unit of *significance*; for this the term *glosseme* ..has been introduced.

glosser[1] ('glɒsə(r)). [f. GLOSS *v.*[1] + -ER[1].] One who glosses a text; = GLOSSATOR.

1603 SIR C. HEYDON *Jud. Astrol.* xviii. 365 The Glossers are besides their text. **1643** CARYL *Sacr. Covt.* 29 Woe be unto those glossers that corrupt the Text. **1708** HEARNE *Collect.* 24 Dec. (O.H.S.) II. 159 Fermannus the Glosser and Interpreter of Rushworth's MS. of the Gospels. **1747** WARBURTON *Shaks. Wks.* 1778 VII. 284 The late Roman writers and their glossers agree to give this sense to it [a word]. **1886** STUBBS *Lect. Med. & Mod. Hist.* xiii. 307 The opinions of the glossers are often cited as of equal authority with the letter of the law.

glosser[2] ('glɒsə(r)). [f. GLOSS *v.*[2] + -ER[1].] One who puts on a gloss (in either a material or immaterial sense).

1828–32 in WEBSTER. **1835** URE *Philos. Manuf.* 204 Croppers, singers, glossers, pressers, brushers, and steamers. **1889** B. WHITBY *Awakening M. Fenwick* III. ii. 58 A poet was..an exaggerator of trifles..a glosser of facts.

†'**glosser**[3]. *Obs.* Also 6 gloser. [Of unknown origin; possibly a misprint for GLOFFER (the genuineness of which is attested by the alphabetical position of *gloffare*, *gloffynge* in the Winchester MS. of *Promp. Parv.*); but in the 3 quots. below the reading of the original editions is clearly *glo(s)ser*, *glossyng*. Cf. GLOWSING *vbl. sb.*] A glutton. So also '**glossing** *vbl. sb.*, gluttonous eating.

1549 LATIMER *Serm. bef. Edw. VI*, iii. E vij b, Some sayed ..that he had a Deuyll wythin him, a gloser, a drincker, a pot-companion. *Ibid.* vi. T iiij, They were wonte to goo a brode in the fyeldes a shootynge, but nowe it is turned in to glossing, gullyng, and whoringe wythin the housse. **1560** BECON *Jewel of Joy* Wks. II. 27 They..fall to banketynge, drynkyng, gullyng and glossyng, to hunting..and al the dayes of their life they liue dissolutely.

†'**glossful**, *a.* *Obs. rare*$^{-1}$. [f. GLOSS *sb.*[2] + -FUL.] Full of gloss, glossy.

1606 MARSTON *Sophonisba* I. ii, Instead of my soft armes Clasping his well strong lims with glossfull steele.

glossic ('glɒsɪk), *a.* and *sb.* [f. Gr. γλῶσσα tongue, language + -IC.] Applied by A. J. Ellis to a phonetic system of spelling invented by him in which each letter or digraph represents the sound which it most commonly expresses in English. Usually *absol.* as *sb.*

1871 ELLIS *E.E. Pronunc.* III. p. v, For the purpose of writing all English dialects in one alphabet on an English basis, I have improved the Glossotype of Chapter vi., and append its new form under the name of *Glossic*. **1879** *Sat. Rev.* 13 Sept. 322 The glossic alphabet. **1880** *Athenæum* 4 Sept. 302/3 Mr. Ellis's glossic, although admirably contrived for its purpose, is hideous to look at.

glossily, glossiness: see after GLOSSY.

glossing ('glɒsɪŋ), *ppl. a.* [f. GLOSS *v.*[2] + -ING[2].] That glosses (in senses of the vb.).

1581 T. HOWELL *Deuises* (1879) 175 Glossing shewes clokt vnder friendships vayle. **1701** ROWE *Amb. Step-moth.* v. ii. 2500, I am not lucky at the glossing Art Of catching Girls with Words. **1855** COSTELLO *Stor. Screen* 8 Rudenz..had the gift of a glossing tongue.

glossist ('glɒsɪst). [f. GLOSS *sb.*[1] + -IST.] A writer of glosses; a commentator.

1641 BAKER *Apol. Laymen* 91 The Scribes and Pharises were no Priests; yet who greater Glossists. **1652** COLLINGES *Caveat for Prof.* ix. (1653) 49 All which savour of a Glossist, or a Casuist. **1880** *Libr. Univ. Knowl.* II. 74 [Azo, Univ. Bologna, 13th cent.] was one of the most eminent of the glossists, or commentators of his time.

glossitis (glɒ'saɪtɪs). *Path.* Also GLOTTITIS. [f. Gr. γλῶσσα tongue + -ITIS.] Inflammation of the tongue.

1822–34 *Good's Study Med.* (ed. 4) I. 93 They are widely different from the instances more commonly recorded, which are specimens of glossitis. **1878** HABERSHON *Dis. Abdomen* (ed. 3) 25 Inflammation of the tongue or glossitis is also a disease which varies greatly in severity.

Hence **glo'ssitic** *a.*, pertaining to, or affected with glossitis.

1854 in MAYNE *Expos. Lex.*

glossless ('glɒslɪs), *a.* [f. GLOSS *sb.*[2] + -LESS.] Without gloss or lustre.

1849 A. J. SYMINGTON *Harebell Chimes* 186 Ripening sloes Of glossless downy purple. **1885** MIDDLETON in *Encycl. Brit.* XIX. 612/1 The glossless vases painted in dull ochre browns and reds.

glossly ('glɒslɪ), *a. rare*$^{-0}$. [f. GLOSS *sb.*[2] + -LY[1].] 'Appearing specious; bright.'

1847 in CRAIG. Hence in mod. Dicts.

glosso- ('glɒsəʊ), rarely **glotto-** ('glɒtəʊ), before vowels sometimes **gloss-**, combining form of Gr. γλῶσσα, γλῶττα, tongue, in some mod. anatomical terms. **ˌgloss(o)-epi'glottic** *a.* (also **ˌglotto-**), **ˌglosso-epi'glottid** *a.*, **ˌglosso-epiglo'ttidean** *a.*, pertaining to the tongue and to the epiglottis; **ˌglosso'hyal** [HY(OID) + -AL], *a.* pertaining to the tongue and to the hyoid bone; *sb.* a bone or cartilage extending forwards from the basihyal, and constituting the hard basis of the tongue; **ˌglosso-kinæs'thetic** *a.*, relating to control of the movement of the tongue and speech organs; **ˌglosso-labio-la'ryngeal** *a.*, relating to the tongue, lip, and larynx; **ˌglosso-la'ryngeal** *a.*, pertaining to the tongue and to the larynx; **ˌglosso-'palatine** *a.* = PALATO-GLOSSAL *a.*; **ˌglossopha'ryngeal** *sb.*, the glosso-pharyngeal nerve; *a.*, pertaining to the tongue and to the pharynx or gullet.

1847 CRAIG, **Glossoepiglottic*. **1857** DUNGLISON *Med. Lex.*, *Glossepiglottic*. **1872** COHEN *Dis. Throat* 10 The *glotto-epiglottic fold. *Ibid.* 51 The glosso-epiglottic ligament, the bridle rein forcing the epiglottis to participate in the movements of the tongue. **1849–52** TODD *Cycl. Anat.* IV. II. 1121 Three folds..passing from the base of the tongue to the epiglottis, called the *glosso-epiglottid folds. **1881** MIVART *Cat* 230 The *glosso-epiglottidean muscles pass from the back of the tongue downwards, to the base of the front of the epiglottis. **1854** OWEN in *Circ. Sci.*, *Organ. Nat.* I. 177 A bone directed forwards, entering the substance of the tongue, called '*glossohyal'. **1872** MIVART *Elem. Anat.* 124 A long, median, projecting process, termed a glosso-hyal. **1939** L. H. GRAY *Found. Lang.* 89 The *glossokinaesthetic area, which governs speech-utterance. **1941** Glossokinaesthetic [see CHEIROKINÆSTHESIA]. **1908** *Practitioner* June 758 All the usual phenomena of a *glosso-labio-laryngeal paralysis. **1872** W. AITKIN *Sci. & Pract. Med.* (ed. 6) II. 283 In *glosso-laryngeal paralysis the lower part of the face alone remains motionless. **1888** *Encycl. Brit.* XXIII. 79/2 The *glosso-palatine arch. **1823** CRABB *Technol. Dict.*, **Glosso-pharyngeal nerves*, the ninth pair of nerves. **1875** HUXLEY & MARTIN *Elem. Biol.* 182 The trunk of the glossopharyngeal. **1881** MIVART *Cat* 274 The 9th, or Glosso-Pharyngeal nerve..has its deep origin in the grey matter of the posterior part of the medulla oblongata.

glossocele ('glɒsəʊsiːl). *Path.* [f. GLOSSO- + Gr. κήλη tumour. Cf. F. *glossocèle*.] 'Protrusion of the tongue from the mouth in consequence of inflammatory swelling, hypertrophy, salivation, or other cause'(*Syd. Soc. Lex.* 1885).

1823 in CRABB *Technol. Dict.* **1857** DUNGLISON *Med. Lex.* 426 A chronic glossocele.

†'**glossocome**. *Obs.*$^{-1}$ In 6 glossocombe. [a. F. *glossocome*, ad. Gr. γλωσσόκομον, var. of γλωσσοκομεῖον: see next.] = next.

1597 A. M. tr. *Guillemeau's Fr. Chirurg.* C iij b/1 The extended Arme, on the Glossocombe or Ambi (Hippocrates).

‖**ˌglosso'comium**. *Obs.* [mod.L., ad. Gr. γλωσσοκομεῖον, lit. a case to keep the reeds or tongues of musical instruments, f. γλῶσσα tongue + κομέειν to take care of.] A case or frame for reducing a fractured or dislocated limb.

1676 [see COMMANDER 7]. **1704** in HARRIS *Lex. Tech.*

glossograph ('glɒsəgrɑːf, -græf). [(1) f. GLOSSO- + -GRAPH; (2) ad. Gr. γλωσσογράφ-ος: see next.]

1. A contrivance for reproducing speech automatically by electrical action.

1883 *Pall Mall G.* 27 Sept. 11/2 A new Electrical Miracle. Gentilli's glossograph.

2. = next.

1885 *Amer. Jrnl. Philol.* VI. 158 A glance at this scholium is enough to show that its author, like so many other editors and glossographs..made up a good part of his note directly from his text.

glossographer (glɒ'sɒgrəfə(r)). Also GLOTTOGRAPHER. [f. Gr. γλωσσογράφος (f. γλωσσο- GLOSSO- + -γραφος, f. γράφειν to write) + -ER[1]. Cf. F. *glossographe*.] A writer of glosses or commentaries.

1607 TOPSELL *Four-f. Beasts* (1658) 457 Avicen and his glossographer. **1679** BLOUNT *Anc. Tenures* Pref. 3 Some [words] I believe may pose the ablest Glossographer now living. **1771** RAPER in *Phil. Trans.* LXI. 516 The Glossographer last quoted makes 9 Nummi equal to ⅜ of a Siliqua. **1818** REBECCA WARNER *Epist. Curios.* Ser. I. 171 *note*, Abel Boyer, a well-known glossographer. **1846** GROTE *Greece* I. xxi. II. 275 *note*, In the verbal criticism of Homer the Alexandrine literati seem to have made a very great advance, as compared with the glossographers who preceded them.

glossography (glɒ'sɒgrəfɪ). [ad. F. *glossographie*, f. *glosso-* GLOSSO- + -γραφία writing.]

1. The writing of glosses or commentaries; the compiling of glossaries.

1623 COCKERAM, *Glossographie*, an expounding of strange words. **1721–1800** BAILEY, *Glossography*, the art of writing a glossary. **1827** POLLOK *Course T.* VIII. (1860) 216 Glossography itself..scarce more Of folly raved.

2. A description of the tongue.

1842 in DUNGLISON *Med. Dict.*: and in some later Dicts.

3. A description or grouping of languages.

1889 in *Century Dict.*

Hence **ˌglosso'graphical** *a.*, pertaining to, or of the nature of, glossography.

1727 in BAILEY vol. II. **1846** in WORCESTER.

‖**glossolalia** (ˌglɒsəʊ'læliə). Also in anglicized form **glo'ssolaly**. [f. Gr. γλωσσο- GLOSSO- + -λαλία speaking, f. λαλέειν to speak.] The faculty or practice of speaking with 'tongues'.

1879 FARRAR *St. Paul* I. 52 Those soliloquies of ecstatic spiritual emotion which were known as Glossolalia, or, 'the Gift of Tongues'. **1882** —— *Early Chr.* II. 446 In Corinth the terrible abuses of glossolaly had led to outbreaks which entirely ruined the order of worship. **1898** W. S. LILLY in *19th Cent.* Sept. 503 Those of the disciples who possessed that singular gift of glossolaly, or speaking with tongues.

Hence **glo'ssolalist** [-IST], one who speaks with 'tongues'.

1879 FARRAR *St. Paul* II. 81 The rivalry of unmeaning sounds among the glossolalists.

glossological (glɒsəʊ'lɒdʒɪkəl), *a.* [f. GLOSSOLOG-Y + -IC + -AL[1].] Of or pertaining to glossology.

1716 M. DAVIES *Athen. Brit.* I. 103 Revivers of the Hebrew and Oriental Tongues in England were Robert Wakefield and Robert Sherwood, who writ several little Essays of their Glossological Faculties in that Oriental Commerce. **1807** W. TAYLOR in *Ann. Rev.* V. 535 Long critical and glossological comments, are provided. **1868** LOWELL *Shaks.* Pr. Wks. 1890 III. 27 We should demand.. a thorough glossological knowledge of the English contemporary with Shakespeare.

glossologist (glɒ'sɒlədʒɪst). [f. next + -IST.]

1. a. 'One who defines and explains terms' (W. 1864). **b.** One versed in the science of language.

1817 W. TAYLOR in *Monthly Rev.* LXXXIII. 91 Adelung ..the greatest glossologist of the present age. **1845** WHEWELL *Indic. Creator* 164 But what glossologist will venture to declare that the efficacy of such causes has been uniform? **1887** *Q. Rev.* CLXIV. 144 Colonel Yule represents the ideal glossologist.

2. One versed in the pathology of the tongue. *rare.*

1844 RIDGE *Glossology* 58 This fur is not a moveable deposit, capable of being scraped off; if it were so, a patient might scrape his tongue to deceive his doctor; but the Glossologist is not to be deceived by any scrapings.

glossology (glɒ'sɒlədʒɪ). [f. GLOSSO- + Gr. -λογία discourse: see -LOGY.]

1. †**a.** The study of a language or languages; linguistic learning (*obs.*). **b.** The science of language (= GLOTTOLOGY).

1716 M. DAVIES *Athen. Brit.* III. *Critic. Hist.* 2 They pitch upon one of the ablest in the Oriental Glossology..to hold forth a little Lecture out of the Hebrew to the Junior Divines. **1808** W. TAYLOR in *Ann. Rev.* VI. 660 We appeal to every lover of glossology in general, and of English literature in particular, for assistance to promulgate and to preserve a supplement to Johnson's Dictionary, which [etc.]. **1847** WHEWELL *Hist. Induct. Sci.* (ed. 2) I. 21 Ethnology and Glossology. **1857** STODDART (*title*) Glossology, or the Historical relations of Languages. **1874** BLACKIE *Self-Cult.* 35 Study the theory of language, the organism of speech, and what is called comparative philology or Glossology.

2. The definition and explanation of terms in use in any science; also, the assemblage or stock of such terms (= TERMINOLOGY).

1832 LINDLEY *Introd. Bot.* 369 Book IV, Glossology; or, of the terms used in Botany. **1880** GRAY *Struct. Bot.* Introd. 3 Glossology or Terminology is a necessary part of Phytography or Descriptive Botany.

3. The study of the tongue, in medicine. *rare.*

1844 B. RIDGE (*title*) Glossology: or the additional means of diagnosis of disease to be derived from indications and appearances of the tongue.

† **glossomachicall**, *a. Obs. nonce-wd.* [as if f. Gr. *γλωσσομάχος (f. γλῶσσα tongue + -μάχος fighting) + -IC + -AL[1].] Given to wordy strife.

1597 G. HARVEY *Trimming T. Nashe* Wks. (Grosart) III. 13 God saue you (right glossomachicall Thomas).

‖ **glosso'petra.** *Obs.* [mod.Lat. use of L. *glŏssopetra* (Pliny), a stone said to have the shape of the human tongue, a. Gr. γλωσσοπέτρα, f. γλῶσσα tongue + πέτρα rock.] ? Some kind of fossil tooth.

1668 EVELYN *Diary* 23 July, At the Royal Society, were presented divers *glossa petra's.* **1794** SULLIVAN *View Nat.* I. 488 Why are the glossopetra and the relics of other fishes so universally found in the deepest, as well as the most elevated, strata of the earth? **1795–8** T. MAURICE *Hindostan* (1820) I. I. xiii. 474 The glossopetræ, or sharks' teeth, found so plentifully in the island of Malta.

glossophagine (glɒ'sɒfədʒaɪn), *a.* [f. mod.L. *Glossophaga* (f. Gr. γλῶσσα tongue + φαγεῖν to eat) + -INE[1].] Belonging to or characteristic of the Glossophaginæ, a subfamily of South American bats which have long tongues used for obtaining food. Also as *sb.*

1884 T. GILL in J. S. Kingsley *Stand. Nat. Hist.* V. 173 Glossophagines have the muzzle long and narrow..and the tongue is much more elongated. **1899** *Cent. Dict.*, Glossophagine, adj. **1913** *Ann. & Mag. Nat. Hist.* 8th Ser. XII. 271 Other Glossophagine bats have light bases to the fur. **1964** E. P. WALKER et al. *Mammals of World* I. 283/1 *Glossophaga* is one of the long-snouted, extensible-tongued glossophagine group of bats.

glossophorous (glɒ'sɒfərəs), *a.* [f. GLOSSO- + Gr. -φόρ-ος bearing + -OUS.] Having a tongue: said of certain *Mollusca.*

1885 *Science* IV. 143 (Cent.) The very general presence of jaws in the Glossophorous mollusca.

‖ **glossoplegia** (glɒsəʊ'pliːdʒɪə). *Path.* Rarely in anglicized form **glossoplegy.** [mod.L., f. Gr. γλωσσο-, γλῶσσα tongue + πληγή stroke; cf. *hemiplegia.*] Paralysis of the tongue.

1854 MAYNE *Expos. Lex.*, *Glossoplegia*, glossoplegy. **1863** *N. Syd. Soc. Year-bk. 1862* 79 (*title*) On Laloplegia, or Glossoplegia. **1885** LANDOIS & STIRLING *Text-bk. Human Phys.* II. 824 Paralysis of the hypoglossal (*glossoplegia*) which is usually central in its origin, causes disturbance of speech.

glossopteris (glɒ'sɒptərɪs). [a. F. *Glossopteris* (A. Brongniart 1822, in *Mém. Mus. d'Hist. Nat. Paris* VIII. 232), f. Gr. γλωσσο-, γλῶσσα tongue + πτερίς fern.] A fossil fern belonging to the genus so named. Also *attrib.*

1883 *Encycl. Brit.* XX. 173/1 The northern coal-fields [in Queensland] display the *Glossopteris*, [etc.]. **1897** A. C. SEWARD in *Science Progress* VI. 178 The Glossopteris Flora; an extinct flora of a Southern Hemisphere Continent. **1905** E. A. N. ARBER *Catal. Fossil Plants Glossopteris Flora Brit. Mus.—N.H.* p. xviii, This flora is especially characterised by the frequent occurrence of *Glossopteris*, a fern-like plant not only of wide distribution but often found in..extreme abundance. **1912** J. W. GREGORY *Making of Earth* III. x. 184 Glossopteris was a fern or fern-like plant with large blunt leaves, each of which has a prominent midrib. **1956** *Nature* 11 Feb. 337/2 The sorus-like body borne by a *Glossopteris.*

glossoscopy (glɒ'sɒskəpɪ). [ad. Gr. *γλωσσοσκοπία, f. γλωσσο-, γλῶσσα tongue + -σκοπία inspection.] 'The inspection or observation of the tongue for the purposes of the diagnosis and the treatment of disease' (*Syd. Soc. Lex.* 1885).

1854 in MAYNE *Expos. Lex.*

glossotheca (glɒsəʊ'θiːkə). *Ent.* [mod.L. *glossothēca*, f. Gr. γλωσσο-, γλῶσσα tongue + θήκη case.] The tongue-case, or that part of the integument of a pupa which encloses the haustellum.

1826 KIRBY & SP. *Entomol.* (1828) III. xxx. 250 The glossotheca covers both the legs and tongue in some of the sphinxes.

glossotomy (glɒ'sɒtəmɪ). *Surg.* [f. GLOSSO- + -τομία cutting.] **a.** Dissection of the tongue. **b.** Amputation or excision of the tongue.

1842 in DUNGLISON *Med. Dict.*: and in later Dicts.

glossotype ('glɒsəʊtaɪp). [f. GLOSSO- + TYPE.] One of the systems of phonetic symbols invented by A. J. Ellis (afterwards improved into GLOSSIC).

1867 ELLIS *E.E. Pronunc.* I. 13. **1871** [see GLOSSIC].

glossy ('glɒsɪ), *a.* [f. GLOSS *sb.*[2] + -Y[1].] **a.** Having a gloss; smooth and shining; highly polished; lustrous. *spec.* in *Path.*, designating morbid symptoms, as ***glossy skin, glossy tongue.*** Also designating photographic or printing paper that is smooth and shiny; hence denoting a magazine, etc., printed on such paper, or something that is characteristic of the type of material which is published in such magazines.

1556 J. HEYWOOD *Spider & F.* xxxviii. 141 Yet hath that glossy web estimacion more. **1635–56** COWLEY *Davideis* III. 675 Merabs long hair was glossy chestnut brown. **1667** MILTON *P.L.* I. 672. **1697** DRYDEN *Virg. Past.* II. 72 Myself will search..For downy Peaches and the glossie Plum. **1702** POPE *Sappho* 44 Glossy jett is pair'd with shining white. **1766** W. GORDON *Gen. Counting-ho.* 430, 10½ yards striped glossy silk. **1796** KIRWAN *Elem. Min.* (ed. 2) I. 183 Its streak somewhat glossy. **1808** *Med. Jrnl.* XIX. 224 His eyes were of a glossy white, and his tongue furred. **1861** HUGHES *Tom Brown at Oxf.* iv, He comes..in a very glossy hat, the only man in the room not in cap and gown. **1870** J. PAGET *Surg. Path.* (ed. 3) ii. 32 The American army surgeons..have confirmed my description [in 1864] of this 'glossy skin'. **1877** BLACK *Green Past.* xxxi, The sharp contrast between the dazzling white of the tables and the glossy black faces and heads of the waiters. **1897** *Allbutt's Syst. Med.* III. 345 If general it [i.e. glossitis] is often called glossy tongue. **1897** C. M. HEPWORTH *Animated Photogr.* p. xv (Advt.), Citos glossy P.O.P. Citos matte P.O.P. **1930** *Post Office Electr. Engin. Jrnl.* July 101/1 The stock of printing papers, which all are 'Glossy'. **1934** R. MACAULAY *Going Abroad* xii. 88 One of those smart, glossy, illustrated magazines. **1936** *Archit. Rev.* LXXX. 135/1 Salzburg, full of Americans in green corduroy shorts reading their glossy magazines. **1955** M. GILBERT *Sky High* viii. 117 She had made a pile of the glossy weeklies, and was looking at the latest copy of *Country Life.* **1958** *Times Lit. Suppl.* 7 Nov. 636/4 Like *Harper's* it is 'semi-glossy' and determinedly middle-brow, half way between the stringently intellectual and specialized *Kenyon, Sewanee, Hudson* and *Partisan Reviews* and the glossy and sophisticated *Ladies' Home Journal, Harper's Bazaar* and *Vogue.* **1967** *Observer* 1 Oct. 9/1 The ignorant and the downright stupid, whose only idea of what to expect is derived from glossy travel brochures.

b. *fig.* Having a specious appearance or fair outward show.

1698 FRYER *Acc. E. India & P.* 269 The adulterate and glossy Customs in esteem among the Persians. **1724** R. WELTON *Subst. Chr. Faith* 359 They appear varnish'd, fair, and glossy to the world. **1791** BOSWELL *Johnson* an. 1754 I. 143 He [Ld. Chesterfield], however, with that glossy duplicity which was his constant study, affected to be quite unconcerned. **1796** *Mod. Gulliver's Trav.* 154 Protect chicane with rhet'ric's glossy shew. **1857** H. S. RANDALL *T. Jefferson* I. xv. 616 To a pure mind, there is something at first revolting in the smooth, glossy pretences of diplomacy!

c. *Comb.*, as ***glossy-black, -leaved, -rinded, -white*** adjs.

1806 R. CUMBERLAND *Mem.* (1807) II. 107 Dishevelled locks, *glossy black as the plumage of the raven. **1784** COWPER *Task* I. 314 Some *glossy-leav'd, and shining in the sun. **1880** C. R. MARKHAM *Peruv. Bark* 251 A large proportion were of the glossy-leaved myrtle family and composites. **1757** DYER *Fleece* I. 35 The tall growth of *glossy-rinded beech. **1806** R. CUMBERLAND *Mem.* (1807) II. 83 Streaming with blood down his *glossy-white sides from the shoulder to the flank.

Hence **'glossily** *adv.*, **'glossiness.**

1680 BOYLE *Producible. Chym. Princ.* I. 50 Their Surfaces had a smoothness and glosiness much surpassing whatever I had observed in Marine or Common Salt. **1727** BAILEY vol. II, *Glossily*, with a Lustre or Brightness; also by way of Shew or Appearance. **1781** MAD. D'ARBLAY *Diary* May, She was struck with the beautiful glossiness of the paper of a letter. **1834** *Brit. Husb.* I. 147 The sleekness and glossiness of their coats. **1848** C. BRONTË *J. Eyre* xvii. 173 Her dark hair shone glossily under the shade of an azure plume. **1871** NAPHEYS *Prev. & Cur. Dis.* II. i. 364 Glossiness of the skin.

glossy ('glɒsɪ), *sb. colloq.* (orig. *U.S.*). [f. the adj.] **a.** A photograph with a glossy surface. Also *fig.*

1931 J. E. BAKELESS *Mag. Making* 303 Photographs for half-tone reproduction should be 'glossies', that is, prints with a high gloss finish. **1946** T. GODSEY *Free Lance Photogr.* iii. 45 Most of the photos produced by a free lance are glossies. **1967** *Boston* (Mass.) *Herald* 8 May 25/1 Poor Robert, I thought, it is still true what another critic once wrote of him: he is 'an eight by 10 glossy'.

b. A 'glossy' magazine or the like (see GLOSSY *a.*); also, a copy of such a magazine; material printed in such magazines.

1945 G. ENDORE *Methinks the Lady* (1947) ii. 25 She wrote most everything: pulp, glossy, copy, one-act plays. **1952** A. WILSON *Hemlock & After* I. iii. 55 The slightly too smart appearance, which the world of women's glossies had imposed upon her. **1955** J. CANNAN *Long Shadows* iv. 65 Running your scissors through the poor girl's picture and then leaving the damned glossy about for anyone to see. **1960** *Punch* 17 Feb. 267/2 Give me the glossiest glossy and I mightn't glance at it. **1970** *Daily Tel.* 31 Mar. 13/2 The smart new decoration colours for the Seventies as decreed by the American glossies.

c. *Cinemat.* A film depicting fashionable life.

1960 *Guardian* 19 Nov. 4/7 One of those large-scale Hollywood 'glossies'. **1961** *Ibid.* 18 Mar. 5/3 Both [films] are large-scale glossies.

glost (glɒst). *Ceramics.* [app. a dialectal alteration of GLOSS *sb.*[2] (sense 3).] The lead glaze used for pottery. In **glost-fireman**, the man who attends to a glost-oven (= †*gloss-fireman*); **glost-oven**, the oven in which glazed ware is fired (= *glaze-oven*, †*gloss-oven*); **glost-placer**, the operative who applies the glost.

1875 KNIGHT *Dict. Mech.*, *Glost-Oven.* **1882** *W. Worc. Gloss.*, *Glost-oven.* **1885** *Instr. to Census Clerks* xxi. §4 (China, Porcelain Manufacture) Glost Placer, Fireman. **1899** *Rep. Commission* in *Westm. Gaz.* 27 Mar. 6/2 That young persons and women should be excluded from employment as..glost placers in factories where lead glaze is used.

glot(e, gloten, obs. ff. GLOAT *v.*, GLUTTON.

glotani, -any, obs. forms of GLUTTONY.

gloten-, gloter-: see GLUTTON-, GLUTTER-.

† **'glother,** *v. Obs.* Also 4 **gloþer, gluter, gluther,** 6 *Sc.* **gluder.** [Cf. GLAVER *v.*] **a.** *trans.* To flatter; to cajole. **b.** *intr.* To use flattering terms; to gloze.

a **1300** *Cursor M.* 8401 (Cott.) Ne Noþier i kepe þe gab ne gloþer [*Gött.* to gabb ne glose]. *c* **1375** *Sc. Leg. Saints, Baptista* 495 Scho gluterit hyme rycht ofte With wysing fare & wordis softe. *Ibid.*, *Agnes* 118 þane þe prefet newit his spek & gluthryt hir with wordis mek. ? *a* **1550** *Freiris Berwick* 34 in *Dunbar's Poems* (1893) 286 Thir silly Freiris with wyffis weill cowld gluder.

Hence † **'glothering** *vbl. sb.*, flattery. Also † **'glotherer**, a flatterer.

c **1325** *Metr. Hom.* 37 Thir glotherers That in thair an hand fir beres, In the tother water ber thai. *Ibid.*, Thai kindel baret wit bacbiting, And slokenes it wit thair glothering. *c* **1375** *Sc. Troy-bk.* II. 1257 He our-commys.. Ine glutherynges And thrught arte fallas of spekynges.

glotor-, gloto(u)n-: see GLUTTER-, GLUTTON-.

glotri, -rie, -ry, var. ff. GLUTTERY, *Obs.*

glottal ('glɒtəl), *a.* [f. GLOTT-IS + -AL[1].] Pertaining to, or produced in, the glottis. ***glottal catch*** or ***stop***, a sound produced by the sudden opening or shutting of the glottis with an emission of breath or voice.

1846 in WORCESTER (who cites *Ch. Obs.*). **1860** HALDEMAN *Anal. Orthogr.* iv. 30 Neither Latin, Greek, nor English takes the Hebrew..Q, which represents a glottal K. *Ibid.* vii. 37 The larynx is reduced within to a narrow opening, extending back and front, named the glottal fissure. **1877** SWEET *Handbk. Phonetics* II. 6 The most familiar example of this 'glottal catch' is an ordinary cough. **1888** —— *Hist. Eng. Sounds* I The Glottal stop is produced by a sudden shutting or opening of the glottis, as in a cough. **1911** W. H. VAN DER SMISSEN *Harrap's Mod. German Gram.* p. xiii, The utterance of every German initial vowel, unless wholly unstressed, begins with the 'glottal stop'. **1964** R. A. HALL *Introd. Ling.* I. viii. 42 A complete stoppage of the breath-stream by the vocal cords is called a *glottal stop* or *glottal catch* (such as we make between the two *oh*'s of 'Oh-oh!' when said in surprise or reproof).

glottalic (glɒ'tælɪk), *a. Phonetics.* [f. GLOTTAL *a.* + -IC.] Relating to the glottis and its total or partial closure.

1942 BLOCH & TRAGER *Outl. Ling. Analysis* 31 [Stops] with inner closure at the glottis, glottalic. **1959** *Archivum Linguisticum* XI. I. 6 The source and direction of the air-stream: pulmonic, glottalic, velaric. **1964** R. H. ROBINS *Gen. Ling.* iii. 103 Sharpness when the glottalic pressure is released.

glottalite ('glɒtəlaɪt). *Min.* [f. *Glotta*, an alleged ancient name of the river Clyde (for *Clōta*, Tacitus) + -LITE.] = EDINGTONITE.

1836 T. THOMSON *Min.* I. 328 Glottalite..coats one side of a fragment of greenstone. **1868** DANA *Min.* (ed. 5) 417 Glottalite..is probably edingtonite, mixed with harmotome.

glottalize ('glɒtəlaɪz), *v. Phonetics.* [f. GLOTTAL *a.* + -IZE.] *trans.* To articulate with total or partial closure of the glottis. So **,glottali'zation; 'glottalized** *ppl. a.*; **'glottalizing** *ppl. a.*

1916 E. SAPIR in *Geol. Survey Canada Mem.* 90 83 One of the most striking American examples of phonetic accord.. is the occurrence in a considerable number of West Coast linguistic groups..of..glottalized ('fortis') stops. **1921** —— *Lang.* ix. 199 A 'glottalized' series of stopped consonants. **1933** BLOOMFIELD *Lang.* vi. 101 Some languages have glottalized spirants (preceded, accompanied, or followed by a glottal stop). *Ibid.* 102 Some American languages have a whole series of laterals, with differences of position, glottalization, or nasalization. **1949** E. A. NIDA *Morphology* (ed. 2) iii. 63 The final vowel..in turn glottalizes the preceding vowel. **1953** W. J. ENTWISTLE *Aspects of Lang.* iv. 136 The original *p t k* series is amplified in some languages, such as Quechua, by aspiration and glottalization. **1965** *Canad. Jrnl. Linguistics* Spring 179 A glottalizing form. *Ibid.* Fall 35 The laryngeal pair of aspiration or breathiness and glottalization.

'glotten, *v. Sc. local.* (See quot.)

1825–80 JAMIESON, *Glotten* (1) to thaw gently; (2) a river is said to be *glottenit*, when it is a very little swelled, its colour being somewhat changed, and the froth floating on its surface.

Hence † **'glotnit** *ppl. a.*, clotted. Of the eyes: ? Bloodshot.

1513 DOUGLAS *Æneis* II. vii. 77 Reuthfully in vane behaldand hevin, alaik! With glotnyt ene. *Ibid.* v. vi. 74 Nisus fallis, vnhappely, Apon the glottnit blud.

glottenie, obs. form of GLUTTONY.

†**'glotter**, *v. Obs.* [? echoic.] *intr.* To chatter.
1656 W. D. tr. *Comenius' Gate Lat. Unl.* §252. 69 The Snake hisseth, the Eagle clangeth, the Stork glottereth, the Chough caweth. **1688** R. HOLME *Armoury* II. 310/2 The Stork glottereth, this is a kind of fictitious term from the sound, chattereth.

glottery, var. GLUTTERY, *Obs.*

glottic ('glɒtɪk), *a.*[1] [ad. Gr. γλωττικός, f. γλῶττα, Attic form of γλῶσσα tongue.] Of or pertaining to language or 'tongues'; linguistic.
1802 W. TAYLOR in *Monthly Mag.* XIII. 10 That vanquisher of glottic difficulties, Joshua Sylvester.
So †**'glottical** *a.*, concerned with the study of languages.
1660 EVELYN *Mem.* (1857) III. 132 Dr. Petty..had a main design to erect a Glottical College.

glottic ('glɒtɪk), *a.*[2] [f. GLOTT-IS + -IC.] Of or pertaining to the glottis.
1839–47 TODD *Cycl. Anat.* III. 573 The usual operation for urgent glottic dyspnœa. **1885** *Syd. Soc. Lex., Glottic souffle*, the sound heard through the stethoscope over the neck produced by the passage of the air through the glottis in respiration. **1896** *Allbutt's Syst. Med.* I. 746 Hoarseness is the commonest form [of paraphonia] being a lesion of the simple glottic sound and not of the articulated voice.

glottid ('glɒtɪd). [a. Gr. γλωττιδ-, γλωττίς GLOTTIS.] A vocal sound produced by the glottis.
1880 SWEET in *9th President's Address to Philol. Soc.* 45 No consonants are more liable to be absorbed into the preceding vowels than these 'glottids'. **1888** A. J. ELLIS *Pronunc. for Singers* vii. 56 'Glottids' are actions of the glottis and the parts connected with it.

glottidean (glɒ'tɪdɪən), *a.* [f. as if L. *glŏttide-us (f. *glŏttid-* GLOTTIS) + -AN.] Of or pertaining to the glottis.
1859 TODD *Cycl. Anat.* V. 283/2 The glottidean chink is embraced by two minute semilunar pieces of cartilages.

glottis ('glɒtɪs). [a. mod.L. *glōttis*, a. Gr. γλωττίς, f. γλῶττα var. of γλῶσσα tongue.] The opening at the upper part of the trachea, or windpipe, and between the vocal chords, which, by its dilatation and contraction, contributes to the modulation of the voice.
1578 BANISTER *Hist. Man* IV. 50 Glottis is a long rift placed in the middest of Larinx. **1615** CROOKE *Body Man* 636 The Larynx and the whistle or pipe thereof which we call Glottis. **1692** RAY *Creation* II. 105, I believe the Beaver hath the like Epiglottis exactly closing the Larynx or Glottis, and hindring all Influx of Water. **1767** GOOCH *Treat. Wounds* I. 111 When more air passes out through the aperture, than enters them through the glottis, or rimula of the larynx. **1859** DARWIN *Orig. Spec.* xxvii. (1878) 148 The beautiful contrivance by which the glottis is closed.

glottiscope ('glɒtɪskəʊp). [f. GLOTTI-S + Gr. -σκόπος looker.] = LARYNGOSCOPE.
1878 T. BRYANT *Pract. Surg.* (1879) II. 26 The first laryngoscope was introduced to the profession in 1829 by the late Dr. B. G. Babington, under the term 'glottiscope'.

glottitis (glɒ'taɪtɪs). *Path.* [f. Gr. γλῶττα tongue (see GLOTTIS) + -ITIS.] = GLOSSITIS.

glotto-: see GLOSSO-.

glottochronology (ˌglɒtəʊkrə'nɒlədʒɪ). *Linguistics.* [f. GLOTTO- (see GLOSSO-) + CHRONOLOGY.] The application of statistics to vocabulary to determine the degree of relationship between two or more languages and the chronology of their splitting off from a common ancestor. Hence also ˌ**glottochrono'logic(al** *adjs.*
1953 J. B. CARROLL *Study of Lang.* ii. 62 Glottochronology, a technique for inferring, from statistical comparisons of language systems, estimates not only of their probable familial relationships but also of the dates when the branches of a language family broke off from one another and from the parent language. **1955** *Internat. Jrnl. Amer. Ling.* XXI. 116 There has been considerable interest in the application of statistical techniques to the study of language vocabulary, variously called glottochronology and lexico-statistical dating. *Ibid.* 118 An entirely different glottochronologic study. **1957** J. H. GREENBERG *Ess. in Linguistics* iv. 54 Recently glottochronological methods have been used. **1961** *New Scientist* 13 July 77/3 The application of lexicostatistics (glottochronology) to African languages. **1964** R. A. HALL *Introd. Ling.* lxvi. 381 The glottochronological method is based on a count, not of structural, but of lexical items.

glottogonic (glɒtəʊ'gɒnɪk), *a.* [f. GLOTTO- (see GLOSSO-) + Gr. γονικ-ός pertaining to production.] Relating to the origin of language or languages.
1885 *Encycl. Brit.* XVIII. 782/1 The general interest still clung to Bopp's old glottogonic problems. **1895** M. BLOOMFIELD in *Amer. Jrnl. Philol.* XVI. 412 Reduplication, in early glottogonic periods of language, cannot have represented anything more than an attempt to make an idea tarry.

†**glo'ttographer.** *Obs.*[−1] [f. as prec. + Gr. -γραφος, f. γράφειν to write.] = GLOSSOGRAPHER.
1659 HOWELL *Lex. Tetragl.* To Tru Philol., Touching Europe, Glottographers tell us..that she hath eleven Originall, Independent, and Mother Toungs.

glottology (glɒ'tɒlədʒɪ). [f. as prec. + Gr. -λογία discourse: see -LOGY.] The science of language: comparative philology; = GLOSSOLOGY 1 b.
1841 PRICHARD *Nat. Hist. Man* (1845) 132 Glottology, or the history of languages, founded on an accurate analysis of their relations, is almost a new field of inquiry. **1849–52** TODD *Cycl. Anat.* IV. II. 1345 There is no department of ethnology in which progress is at present so rapid, as it is in the study of glottology. **1868** MAX MÜLLER in *Sel. Ess.* (1881) I. 29 The conception of a science of language, of Glottology, was reserved for the nineteenth century.
Hence **glotto'logic, glotto'logical** *adjs.* = GLOSSOLOGICAL; **glo'ttologist** = GLOSSOLOGIST 1 b.
1848 *Edin. Rev.* LXXXVIII. 478 Thus it appears that glottological considerations afford a strong presumption in favour of the origin of the nations of Asia, Europe, America, and Polynesia, from one common stock. **1874** SAYCE *Compar. Philol.* vi. 236 As glottologists, we have to begin with roots. **1879** CAYLEY in *Trans. Philol. Soc.* 588 A wide scope for glottologic observation and research. **1883** *St. James's Gaz.* 26 Jan. 6 The glottological aspect of the question. **1893** *Athenæum* 23 Dec. 883/1 A general glottologist of the rarest attainments.

glotton, -ous, obs. ff GLUTTON, GLUTTONOUS.

glotun-, glotyn-: see GLUTTON-.

glouberd(e, var. GLOWBARD, *Obs.*, glow-worm.

Gloucester ('glɒstə(r)). The name of an English county; hence ellipt., with prefixes *single-*, *double-*, the name of a cheese made there, seldom in full ***Gloucester cheese***.
1802 LAMB *Let. to Coleridge* 4 Nov., If you find the Miltons in certain parts..soiled with a crumb of right Gloucester..look to that passage more especially. **1816** *Times* 25 Jan., Distinguish between..Gloucester and Double Gloucester. **1836** E. HOWARD *R. Reefer* viii, An oblong..yellow substance..known among the initiated as single Gloucester. **1838** DICKENS *O. Twist* xxxix, Pound of best fresh; piece of double Glo'ster. **1871** M. COLLINS *Mrq. & Merch.* I. ii. 57 Home-made bread and double Gloucester cheese.

gloue, obs. var. GLOW *v.*[1]

‖**glou-morceau** (glumɔrso). Also glout-. [A provincial Fr. name (Godefr. s.v. *glout*), lit. 'tit-bit'.] A kind of pear.
1859 THOMPSON *Gardener's Assist.* 483 Glou Morceau.. a dessert pear of the highest excellence. **1860** THOREAU *Autumn* (1892) 95 Their excellence is in their flavor, which speaks to a grosser sense, they are *glout-morceaux*. **1897–8** RIVERS *Catal. Fruit-trees* 8 Glou Morceau, a well-known and excellent melting pear.

gloup, *v. Obs.* exc. *dial.* [Cf. GLOBBE, GLOFF, GLOP, GULP] *trans.* To gulp, swallow greedily.
1362 LANGL. *P. Pl.* A. v. 191 Til Gloten hedde I-gloupet [*v.rr.* y-gloppid, y-gulpid, y-golped] A Galoun and a gille. **1893** *Northumb. Gloss.*, *Gloup*, to gulp, to swallow.

glour, obs. form of GLOWER.

glouse worme, var. GLOSE-WORM, *Obs.*

glout (glaʊt), *sb. rare.* [f. the vb.] A frown; a sullen look. ***in the glout***: in the sulks.
1641 *Copie of Let.* etc. (N.), Ben Johnson cast a glout, And swore a mighty oath hee'd pluck him out. **1748** RICHARDSON *Clarissa* (1811) II. xx. 140 My mamma was in the glout with her poor daughter all the way.

glout (glaʊt), *v.* Now *rare.* Also 4–8 glowt. [Perh. an ablaut variant of GLOAT *v.*] *intr.* To look sullen, frown, scowl. Const. *at*, *upon.*
13.. *Coer de L.* 4770 He gan to moorne, and held hym stylle; He glowtyd, and gan to syke. **1611** BIBLE *Transl. Pref.* 2 The same setteth himselfe vpon a stage to be glouted vpon by euery euil eye. *a* **1679** LD. ORRERY *Guzman* IV, Guzman glouts at her, sighs, and folds his Arms. **1699** GARTH *Dispens.* II. (1706) 17 Glouting with sullen Spight the Fury shook Her clotter'd Locks. **1708** *Brit. Apollo* No. 91. 3/2 He'd Glowt, She stil'd it eager Glances. **1750** COVENTRY *Pompey Little* I. x. (1785) 27/1 They had glouted at one another for several days. **1884** BARING-GOULD *Mehalah* xx. 279, I will not have you glouting in there any longer.
b. *transf.* Of the clouds, weather, etc.
1739 H. WALPOLE *Corr.* (1820) I. 35 Heavy clouds that hung glouting. **1831** FR. A. KEMBLE in *Rec. Girlhood* (1878) III. 9 As sulky a day as ever glouted in an English sky.
Hence '**glouting** *vbl. sb.* and *ppl. a.*
c **1460** J. RUSSELL *Bk. Nurture* 281 Glowtynge ne twynkelynge with youre yȝe ne to heuy of chere. **1641** MILTON *Ch. Govt.* I. (1851) 4 Even that Feast of love and heavenly-admitted fellowship..became the Subject of horror, and glouting adoration, pageanted about, like a dreadfull Idol. **1673** R. HEAD *Canting Acad.* 63 They saw a blackish thing with a broad glouting Countenance. **1735** SOMERVILLE *Chase* IV. 200 If, in dark sullen Mood, The glouting Hound refuse his wonted meal [etc.]. **1749** FIELDING *Tom Jones* VIII. viii, Mrs. Western..had been in what is vulgarly called a glouting humour ever since. **1754** RICHARDSON *Grandison* IV. xx. 150 If I find his aspect very solemn—Come, come, no glouting, friend, I will say. *a* **1763** SHENSTONE *Ess.* (1765) 212 There are some people who find a gloomy kind of pleasure in glouting.

glout, var. GLOAT *sb.*[2], GLUT *sb.*[2]

glouttonnous, obs. form of GLUTTONOUS.

gloutynge, var. GLUTTING *vbl. sb.*[1]

glovar(e, obs. form of GLOVER.

glove (glʌv), *sb.* Forms: 1 glóf, 4–5 glofe, (4 *Sc.* gluwe), 5 glowe, gluff, 5–7 gloove, 5–7 *Sc.* gluif, glufe, 6 *Sc.* gluve, 3– glove. [OE. *glóf* str. fem. (also wk. pl. *glófan*) = ON. *glófe* wk. masc.
By some scholars considered to represent an OTeut. **galôfâ, -on-*, f. *ga-* prefix (see Y-) + *lôf-* root of Goth. *lôfa*, ON. *lófe*, hand (see LOOF *Sc.*).]
1. a. A covering for the whole of the hand, usually one with a separate sheath for each finger. ***hawks' glove*** = ***hawking glove*** (see HAWKING *vbl. sb.*). ***glove of mail***, a gauntlet.
Beowulf (Z.) 2085 Glof hangode..Sio wæs orðoncum eall ȝegyrwed deofles cræftum ond dracan fellum. *a* **1000** *Prose Life Guthlac* xi. (1848) 54 Wilfrið..cwæð þæt he forlete his twa glofan on þam scipe. *c* **1205** LAY. 28581 Mon mihte i þare lasten twa glouen iþraste. *c* **1470** HENRY *Wallace* IX. 169 The Rede Reiffar..Held out a gluff, in takyn off the trew. **1530** PALSGR. 225/2 Glove of mayle, *mitaigne de fer.* **1594** BARNFIELD *Affect. Sheph.* II. xvii, New Gloues to put vpon thy milk-white hand Ile giue thee. **1642** FULLER *Holy & Prof. St.* IV. v. 262 Never saw I glove that would serve both hands. **1711** STEELE *Spect.* No. 109 ¶5 He would sign a Deed that passed away half his Estate with his Gloves on. **1715** DE FOE *Fam. Instruct.* I. i, Another Sunday, for want of a pair of gloves you stayed at home. **1801** STRUTT *Sports & Past.* I. ii. §9 At Hampton Court, in the jewel house, were seven hawkes' gloves embroidered. **1813** SCOTT *Trierm.* I. xii, From beneath his glove of mail, Scann'd at his ease the lovely vale. **1849** ROCK *Ch. of Fathers* II. 162 *note*, This form of the episcopal glove, with its tassel, or tuft of silk, is well seen on Archbishop Chicheley's effigy, in Canterbury Cathedral.
b. ***a pair of gloves*** given as a present or claimed as a forfeit (see quots. 1714 and 1828); †mentioned as a pretext for making a present in money (cf. *glove-money*). ***white gloves*** (see quot. 1851).
1563–7 BUCHANAN *Reform. St. Andros* Wks. (1892) 14 Sa mony of the assistandis to thys act as be graduat in divinite ..sal haif for their presens and decoryng of the act, ane pair of gluvis. **1631** SHIRLEY *Love's Cruelty* V. ii, *Mi.* [a servant] Pray excuse me sir! *Hi.* Twill purchase but a pair of Gloves. **1714** GAY *Sheph. Week* Sat. 38 Cic'ly, brisk maid, steps forth before the rout, And kiss'd with smacking lip the snoring lout. For custom says, Whoe'er this venture proves, For such a kiss demands a pair of gloves. **1741** RICHARDSON *Pamela* II. 346 You'll accept of that for a Pair of Gloves, on this happy Occasion; and I gave him ten Guineas. **1755** *Mem. Capt. P. Drake* II. iii. 148 He squeezed a Louis d'Or into my Hand for a Pair of Gloves. **1828** SCOTT *F.M. Perth* v, Thou knowest the maiden who ventures to kiss a sleeping man, wins of him a pair of gloves. **1851** *Offic. Catal. Gt. Exhib.* 576 White gloves are..presented to the Judges on occasion of a maiden-assize.
†**c.** A symbol of investiture; in ***to grant and assign by a glove***. *Sc. Obs.*
1493 *Extracts Aberd. Reg.* (1844) I. 51 Alexander Iruyne ..gaff, grantit and assignit be ane gluff to David Irwyne, his sone, all and hale his gudis beand within the landis of Coule. [**1727–41** CHAMBERS *Cycl.* s.v., The custom..of blessing gloves, in the coronation of the kings of France, is a remain of the eastern practice of giving possession with the glove.]
d. as token of a pledge or of a challenge to battle. Also to ***†cast, take up, throw (down) the glove.*** *lit.* and *fig.*
13.. *Sir Beues* (A.) 4137 Here glouen þai gonne vp holde In þat forward. *a* **1440** *Sir Degrev.* 183 Be he squiere othere knyght Here my glove one to ffyght. **1481** CAXTON *Reynard* (Arb.) 102 And therto I caste to the my gloue and take thou it vp I shal haue right of the or deye therfore. **1535** STEWART *Cron. Scot.* II. 691 Syne kest his gluif to preif that all wes trew. **1579** GOSSON *Apol. Sch. Abuse* (Arb.) 64 But if they take vp my gloue, and enter the Lyste..I will..teach them to know the weyght of my clubbe. **1599** SHAKS. *Hen. V*, IV. i. 226 Heere's my Gloue: Giue mee another of thine. **1606** —— *Tr. & Cr.* IV. iv. 65. **1607** —— *Timon* V. iv. 49. **1896** FROUDE *Counc. Trent* ii. 44 Luther..was throwing down the glove to the whole system of ecclesiastical domination.
†**e.** ? set up on a post to indicate the goal of a race. *Obs.* (Cf. GLAIVE 1 b.)
c **1380** [see GLAIVE 1 b]. **1555** LATIMER *Let.* in Strype *Eccl. Mem.* (1721) III. II. 101 He that runnythe at the Merk, doth not loke on other that stands by,..but lokyth altogether on the Glove or Merk. **1632** W. LITHGOW *Trav.* IV. 156 The custome of the great Turke is, euery Friday..to run at the Gloue in a open place before all the people, with some Hagars, or yong striplings that accompany him, who haue the Gloue hanging as high on a sticke, as we haue the ring with vs.
f. Phrases: ***to fit like a glove***: to fit or suit perfectly. ***to handle without gloves***: to treat severely or without mercy; so ***to handle with gloves off***, etc. † ***not to set at a glove***: to contemn utterly. ***to go for the gloves*** (*Racing*): to bet recklessly. ***to take the gloves off***: to 'set to' in earnest; to use no mercy (cf. sense 2). Also HAND AND GLOVE.
c **1430** *Pilgr. Lyf Manhode* IV. ix. (1869) 180, I hatte jolyfnesse þe lyghte..þat sette nouht alle daungeres at a glooue. **1771** SMOLLETT *Humph. Cl.* 10 June Let. i, The boots..fitted me like a glove. **1827** A. SHERWOOD *Gaz. Georgia* 94 Marion County has been handled without gloves. **1828** *Richmond Enquirer* 20 May 3/4 (Th.), The Baltimore Republican handles Mr. C[lay] with gloves off. **1838** J. C. NEAL *Charcoal Sks.* 217 I'll give you a touch of natur' without no gloves on. **1861** WHYTE MELVILLE *Mkt. Harb.* 74 It won't be my fault to-morrow if I don't 'go for the gloves', as we used to say in the Old Country. **1876** E. FITZGERALD *Lett.* (1889) I. 389 Boccaccio must be read in

his Italian, as Cervantes in his Spanish: the Language fitting either 'like a Glove' as we say. **1886** EARL SUFFOLK etc. *Racing* (Badm.) 77 The whole legion of stable-followers is 'going for the gloves'. *Ibid.* 255 Hardly worth mentioning are the backers who come in for a hit-or-miss dash at the ring—'to go for the gloves', as it is called in Turf parlance. **1892** *Nation* (N.Y.) 5 May 345/2 The prophets and practitioners of the naturalistic school..are here handled without gloves. **1922** *S.P.E. Tract* XI. 15 Dead metaphors lately noticed:..The flower of our manhood. Taking off the gloves. **1928** *Daily Express* 21 Mar. 1/1 It is time, Mr. Mayor, that we took the gloves off and showed the County of London Electric Supply Company that we will fight. **1931** *Times Lit. Suppl.* 10 Sept. 669/4 Like Lewis Carroll, who was too polite to 'take the gloves off' in his assault on 'Hiawatha'. **1934** J. E. NEALE *Queen Eliz.* xii. 199 At still greater length, in caustic tones, and with many shrewd hits, Mary answered. The gloves were off.

2. = *boxing-glove* [see BOXING *vbl. sb.*]. *glove of death* = CESTUS².

1725 POPE *Odyss.* VIII. 140 Laodame whirls high, with dreadful sway, The gloves of death. **1847** ALB. SMITH *Chr. Tadpole* xl. (1879) 345, I..put on the gloves with the Brummagem Clinker, and knocked him about. **1890** BESANT *Demoniac* vi. 65 They are capital fellows: they..put on the gloves with good temper.

†**3.** *slang.* Some kind of drinking vessel. *Obs.*

1609 DEKKER *Gulls Horn-bk.* Proem. 4 The Englishmans healthes, his hoopes, cans, half-cans, Gloues, Frolicks, and flap-dragons.

4. In *Hat-making*, a smooth piece of wood, fastened to the hand by a string, employed in rubbing the sheets of felt at the 'battery'.

1875 in KNIGHT *Dict. Mech.*

5. *attrib.* and *Comb.* **a.** simple attrib., as *glove-case, -factory, -kid, -leather, -shop, -trade*; **b.** objective, as *glove-cleaner, -maker, -making, -manufacturer, -sewer, -washer*; **c.** instrumental (sense 1), as *glove-guarded* adj.; (sense 2), as *glove-fight, -fighter, -fighting*; **d.** similative, as *glove-shaped* adj.; also *glove-like* adj.

1874 'S. COOLIDGE' *What Katy did at School* xi. 206 *Glove-cases, of quilted silk, delicately scented. **1926–7** *Army & Navy Stores Catal.* 814/1 Glove case. Pigskin. **1858** SIMMONDS *Dict. Trade*, **Glove-cleaner*. **1895** *Westm. Gaz.* 20 Dec. 8/1 At Worcester alone nearly five miles are covered by *glove factories. **1890** *Guardian* 24 Sept. 1478/1 A *glove-fight between F. Slavin and J. M'Auliffe. **1889** *Standard* 28 Oct., We must insist on a stop being put to the revival of the evils of the Prize Ring under the flimsy pretext of *glove-fighting. **1796** COLERIDGE *To Friend writing no more Poetry* 35 These [henbane and nightshade] with stopped nostril and *glove-guarded hand Knit in nice intertexture. **1895** *Daily News* 21 Mar. 5/1 Messrs. P——..export very largely, sending thousands of pairs of *glove-kid boots to Australia. **1721** HALLEY in *Phil. Trans.* XXXI. 178 These Wires we coated with thin *Glove-leather. *c* **1790** IMISON *Sch. Art* II. 29 A piece of paper or glove-leather, rolled hard and cut almost to a point, like a pencil, is useful ..to blend the shades. **1568** *Hist. Jacob & Esau* IV. viii, I haue brought sleues of kid next to thy skin to weare. They be made *glouelike, and for eche finger a stall. **1609** SKENE *Reg. Maj.* 146 It is statute, that na Skinner nor *Gluifmaker ..sall make wooll of skinnes, from the feast of Whitsonday, vntill Michaelmes. **1830** GEN. P. THOMPSON *Exerc., Free Trade* (1842) I. 192 But if the glove-maker procures a law that gloves shall not be bought from France, it is plain that Sheffield goods must stop. **1744** HALLETT in *Phil. Trans.* XLIII. 155 He would..work at his Trade of *Glove-making. **1884** *Pall Mall G.* 16 May 4/2 The *glove-sewers of the district assemble at a fixed place..and receive their work. **1839** URE *Dict. Arts* 599 *Glove-sewing. **1885** *Syd. Soc. Lex.*, **Glove-shaped*, having the appearance of the finger of a glove, as the corolla of the fox-glove, *Digitalis purpurea*. **1813** JANE AUSTEN *Let.* 20 May (1932) II. 78, I went into it rather because it was near than because it looked at all like a *glove shop. **1859** G. A. SALA *Tw. round Clock* 157 Jewellers, French glove shops, perfumery, and point lace shops. **1891** *Pall Mall G.* 14 Dec. 3/1 Miss Ada Heather-Bigg..goes thoroughly and with much research into the English *glove-trade past and present. **1723** *Lond. Gaz.* No. 6195/10 Elizabeth Brown..*Glove-washer.

6. Special comb.: **glove-band**, 'a strap or ribbon formerly used to confine the glove round the wrist or arm' (*Cent. Dict.*); **glove box**, (*a*) a box for holding gloves; (*b*) = *glove compartment*; (*c*) a closed chamber into which a pair of gloves project from openings in the side, enabling radioactive or other material to be handled while isolated from the operator; **glove-buttoner**, a small button-hook used for buttoning gloves; **glove-calf** (see quot.); **glove-clasp**, (*a*) = *glove-band*, (*b*) = *glove-buttoner*; **glove compartment**, a recess in the dashboard of a motor car for small articles such as gloves, etc.; †**glove-dog** (sense obscure); **glove-finger** (see FINGER *sb.* 6); **glove-fit**, something that fits like a glove; **glove-fitting** *a.*, that 'fits like a glove' (cf. sense 1 f); **glove-hand**, an operative employed in making gloves; **glove-hook** = *glove-buttoner*; **glove-money**, (*a*) a gratuity given to servants ostensibly to buy them gloves; (*b*) *Law*, extraordinary rewards formerly given to officers of English courts, etc.; *esp.* money given by the sheriff of a county, in which no offenders were left for execution, to the clerk of assize and the judges' officers; **glove puppet**, a puppet consisting of a dress, a head and hands, made to fit on the hand like a glove; **glove-sheep** (see quot. for *glove-calf*); **glove-silver** = *glove-money*; **glove-sponge**, a kind of sponge in the shape of a glove; **glove stitch** (see quot. 1964); **glove-stretcher**, an instrument in the shape of a pair of scissors for stretching the fingers of gloves.

1858 SIMMONDS *Dict. Trade*, **Glove-band*, a protection for the glove round the wrist. **1852** *Harper's Mag.* July 185/2 We..beheld our *glove-box enriched with half-a-dozen pair of snowy French sevens! **1858** SIMMONDS *Dict. Trade*, *Glove-box*, a long paper-box for holding gloves. **1897** *Sears, Roebuck Catal.* 351/1 Silk Plush Glove Box, lined with fine puffed satin, silvered catch and hinges. **1946** 'P. QUENTIN' *Puzzle for Fiends* xxv. 239, I sat for a minute in the front seat,..I looked in the glove box. **1950** GLASSTONE *Sourcebk. Atomic Energy* xviii. 521/2 Glove boxes are also often used for experimental work with emitters of soft, i.e., low energy and short range, beta particles. **1959** *New Scientist* 23 Apr. 919/1 The glove box..is in essence a sealed plastic-windowed container kept at a pressure slightly below atmospheric. Manipulations are carried out through plastic gloves. **1971** *Daily Tel.* (Colour Suppl.) 4 June 39/1 This little hole..which they actually call a glove-box. **1885** C. T. DAVIS *Manuf. Leather* xxxii. 525 *Glove-calf and glove-sheep are also sub-names for Morocco leather, and are used principally for toppings. **1858** SIMMONDS *Dict. Trade*, **Glove-clasp*, a kind of hook-and-eye, or stud, for fastening gloves at the wrist; a contrivance for buttoning gloves. **1939** R. CHANDLER *Big Sleep* xvii. 138, I went to the car and got a pair of handcuffs out of the *glove compartment. **1959** I. FLEMING *Goldfinger* xii. 173 He took a small pair of binoculars out of the glove compartment. **1659** *Lond. Chanticleers* vi. 15 I'l kick you into *glove-dogs, you mungrells, hell-hounds, whelps. **1864** H. SPENCER *Biol.* I. 227 A cavity..like that which results in a *glove-finger when the finger is partially withdrawn and the glove sticks to its end. **1910** C. E. MONTAGUE *Hind let Loose* viii. 145 The putting of *glove-fits on Brumby and Pinn was too near the craftsman's heart to be quite given up. **1967** *Listener* 8 June 760/1 The rather odd and amateur scansion of the lyrics is a glove-fit to the melody. **1868** *Englishwoman's Dom. Mag.* Jan. 17 (*heading*) Thomson's *Glove-fitting Corset. *Ibid.* 18/1 The name Glove-Fitting is certainly well chosen. **1920** D. H. LAWRENCE *Lost Girl* i. 17 The slim, glove-fitting Princess Robe. **1872** T. COOPER *Life* 165 He was what is called a '*glove-hand' and therefore earned better wages than a stockinger. **1729** JACOB *Law Dict.* s.v. *Glove-silver*, *Glove-Money has been also applied to extraordinary Rewards given to Officers of Courts, &c. **1881** T. F. T. DYER *Dom. Folk Lore* vii. 93 The gift of a pair of gloves was at one time the ordinary perquisite of those who performed some small service; and in process of time, to make the reward of greater value, the glove was 'lined' with money; hence the term 'glove-money'. **1937** W. S. LANCHESTER *Hand Puppets & String Puppets* 10 *Glove Puppets. This is the simplest form of puppetry. *Ibid.* 15 Some glove puppet workers use spring clothes pegs for hands. **1969** E. H. PINTO *Treen* 213 Hand or glove puppets are the simplest type and, for the travelling showman, have the great advantage of taking up little space. **1701** *Cowel's Interpr.*, **Glove-silver*, Money given to some Servants by custom to buy them Gloves as a reward and encouragement of their Labours. **1885** LADY BRASSEY *The Trades* 311 There were..bright scarlet *glove-sponges branching up like huge hands. **1886** H. A. BLAKE in *Fortn. Rev.* Feb. 179 The sponges are sorted..into glove, reef, lamb's-wool, grass, &c. **1964** *McCall's Sewing* ii. 29/1 **Glove stitch*, decorative top-stitching made by taking the same size stitch on both sides of the work. **1858** SIMMONDS *Dict. Trade*, **Glove-stretchers*.

glove (glʌv), *v.* [f. prec. sb.] *trans.* To cover with, or as with a glove; to provide with gloves. Of a thing: To serve as a glove for.

1597 SHAKS. *2 Hen. IV*, I. i. 147 A scalie gauntlet now, with ioynts of steele Must gloue this hand. **1606** HOLLAND *Sueton.* 156 They were wont likewise to glove his hands.. with his shoes, that as he suddenly awaked hee might rub his face and eyes therewith. **1628** EARLE *Microcosm., Vpstart Countrey Knt.* (Arb.) 38 Hee..is exceeding ambitious to..haue his fist Glou'd with his Iesses. **1853** G. JOHNSTON *Nat. Hist. E. Bord.* I. 158 Our little girls glove their fingers with them. **1887** BOWEN *Virg. Æneid* v. 379 Who dares challenge him now? Who gloves in defiance his hands? **1890** ANNIE THOMAS (Mrs. Pender Cudlip) *Love of a Lady* II. v. 39 Miss Daubeny 'boots' and 'gloves' herself fairly well.

Hence **gloved** *ppl. a.*

1573 J. SANDFORD *Hours of Recr.* (1576) 212 A gloved catte can catche no myse. **1623** MASSINGER *Bondman* II. ii, Lady, I would descend to kisse your hand, But that 'tis glou'd, and Ciuit makes me sicke. *a* **1658** CLEVELAND *Fuscara* 22 The next he preys on is her Palms..Tender as 'twere a Jelly glov'd. **1822** *Blackw. Mag.* XII. 70 Shawl'd, fur-tippeted and gloved. **1864** H. SPENCER *Biol.* I. 227 If a gloved-finger be taken to represent a growing shoot.

gloveless (ˈglʌvlɪs), *a.* [f. GLOVE *sb.* + -LESS.] Having or wearing no glove or gloves.

1812 H. & J. SMITH *Rej. Addr.* xiii. (1873) 122 Tender Beauty..Protrudes her gloveless hand. **1858** *Chamb. Jrnl.* X. 191 Draggled, dirty, gloveless as I was.

fig. **1852** FORD in *Q. Rev.* Mar. 422 Charles the Bold..put down these turbulent townsmen with a gloveless hand.

glover¹ (ˈglʌvə(r)). Also 5 **glovare, -ere, glower(e, gloyfer, glufer, 6 glovar.** [f. GLOVE *sb.* + -ER¹.] One who makes or sells gloves.

c **1400** *Destr. Troy* v. 1584 Goldsmythes, Glouers, Girdillers noble. **1464** *Ripon Ch. Acts*, Joh. Bryggede Skelgatt, glower. **1558** W. FORREST *Grisylde* II. 81 After this Prouerbe..The Glouer (craftelye) brought this reason ynne. **1598** SHAKS. *Merry W.* I. iv. 21 Do's he not weare a great round Beard, like a Glouers pairing-knife? **1600** *Chester Pl.* Banes 124 You, of glovers the wholl occupation. **1720** STRYPE *Stow's Surv.* (1754) II. v. xv. 323/1 The Company of Glovers were incorporated the 10th day of September 1639. **1786** H. WATSON in *Med. Commun.* II. 110 With a glover's needle and thread. **1864** A. MCKAY *Hist. Kilmarnock* 111 The pouch represented the tailors; the breeches, the glovers.

†**b.** *wet glover*: a maker of leather gloves.

1688 R. HOLME *Armoury* III. 86/2 The Wett-Glover. **1724** *Lond. Gaz.* No. 6249/7 Humphry Topping..Wet Glover.

c. *Comb.*, as **glover's shreds**, shreds of glove-leather used to make size; **glover's stitch**, (*a*) the stitch used in sewing the seams of gloves; (*b*) (see quot. 1721); **glover's suture**, a suture made with the *glover's stitch*.

1542 *MS. Acc. St. John's Hosp., Canterb.*, Payd for halfe a busshell of glovers schredis jd ob. **1672** WISEMAN *Treat. Wounds* 15 In great fluxes of bloud the Glovers stitch is best. **1703** T. S. *Art's Improv.* I. 44 Take Vermilion and grind it very fine with size, made of Glovers-shreds. **1721** BAILEY, *Glovers stitch* (in Surgery), is when the Lips of a Wound are sewed upwards, after the manner of Glovers. **1767** GOOCH *Treat. Wounds* I. 158 The glover's, spiral, or continued suture, is now only used in wounds of the intestines or stomach. **1886** *Treves' Man. Surg.* III. 167 An incised wound must be stitched up with the Glover's or spiral suture.

Glover² (ˈglʌvə(r)). [The name of John *Glover* (1817–1902), English plumber and chemical engineer.] *Glover* (†*Glover's*) *tower*: in the chamber process for the manufacture of sulphuric acid, the tower in which 'nitrous vitriol' from the Gay-Lussac tower is denitrated and sulphuric acid from the chambers is concentrated by being passed down through packing against an upward flow of hot sulphur dioxide and air, which undergo cooling on the way to the chambers; also *ellipt.*; *Glover acid*: the sulphuric acid formed at the bottom of the Glover tower, of a higher concentration than the chamber acid.

1871 *Jrnl. Chem. Soc.* XXIV. 1100 A detailed description, with drawings, of 'Glover's towers', as used on the Tyne. **1873** *Chem. News* 21 Mar. 135/2 There are two methods at present in use on the Tyne for the denitration of the nitro-sulphuric acid; the Glover towers, and denitration by steam. **1873** J. GLOVER in *Ibid.* 28 Mar. 152/2 With a properly proportioned and worked Glover's tower none of the drawbacks..mentioned by him exists. **1896** BLOUNT & BLOXAM *Chem. for Engineers & Manuf.* II. i. 13 The saturated acid ('nitrous vitriol') running out at the foot of the Gay-Lussac is pumped..to the top of the Glover. *Ibid.* 15 For alkali making by the Leblanc process, Glover acid is suitable. **1902** *Times* 6 May 10/3 Though the first one was not built till 1859, and the system not adopted in Lancashire till nearly ten years later, the Glover towers are now almost universal in sulphuric acid manufactories. **1936** A. M. FAIRLIE *Sulfuric Acid Manuf.* viii. 159 Most lead Glover towers of modern design have brick walls laid up in 'acid-proof' cement. **1962** J. A. KENT *Riegel's Industr. Chem.* (ed. 6) iv. 71 It is the modern practice to pass all the chamber acid through the Glover and thus concentrate it to 60° Bé without expense for heat. The Glover acid is cooled in double-walled lead receiving tanks.

gloveress (ˈglʌvərɪs). [f. GLOVER + -ESS.] A female glove-maker.

1712 *Lond. Gaz.* No. 5009/4 Sarah Lewis..a Gloveress by Imployment. **1837** THACKERAY *Ravenswing* iv, A gloveress ..lets me have dem. **1862** MRS. H. WOOD *Mrs. Hallib.* (1864) I. xviii. 99 Quite a colony of workwomen—gloveresses as they are termed in the local phraseology.

†**ˈglovery.** *Obs.* [f. GLOVER + -Y².] A place in which gloves are made or sold.

1483 *Cath. Angl.* 160/1 A Glufery; *cirothecarium*.

gloving (ˈglʌvɪŋ), *vbl. sb.* [f. GLOVE *sb.* and *v.* + -ING¹.] **a.** The action of putting on gloves. **b.** The action or practice of making gloves; the work done by a glove-maker.

1795 ASH, Suppl., *Gloving*, the trade of a glover. **1826** MISS MITFORD *Village* Ser. II. (1863) 277 Oh the bracing, the lacing, the bonneting, the veiling, the gloving. **1883** *Gd. Words* 240 The women earn a few weekly pence by gloving. **1891** MISS A. HEATHER-BIGG in *19th Cent.* Dec. 940 The young woman, in lively chat with a neighbour who had brought in her gloving.

attrib. **1807** VANCOUVER *Agric. Devon* (1813) 386 The gloving business..has furnished means of employment to many.

glow (gləʊ), *sb.* [f. GLOW *v.*]

1. The state or condition of glowing with heat.

a. Shining heat. Phr. *in a glow* (cf. AGLOW).

1827 KEBLE *Chr. Y.* 4th Sund. aft. Easter vii, The struggling spark of good within..They quicken to a timely glow. **1847** EMERSON *Poems, Woodnotes*, Drifting sand-heaps feed my stock In summer's scorching glow. **1850** D. G. MITCHELL *Reveries Bachelor* 82 But my fire is in a glow. **1878** HUXLEY *Physiogr.* 77 The merest point remains in a state of glow. **1881** MAXWELL *Electr. & Magn.* I. 56 The electrical glow is therefore produced by the constant passage of electricity through a small portion of air in which the tension is very high.

b. A lively sensation of animal heat. Phr. *in a glow, colloq.* (*all*) *of a glow.*

1793 BEDDOES *Calculus* 194 The glow experienced in coming out of a cold bath. **1820** W. SCORESBY *Arct. Reg.* II. 353 In chasing each other round the decks, they had excited a genial glow of heat in their bodies. **1831** J. DAVIES *Manual Mat. Med.* 59 In a few minutes a comfortable glow succeeded. **1865** DICKENS *Mut. Fr.* I. vi, 'Sit close to the fire ..You must be frozen.' 'Well Lizzie, I ain't of a glow, that's certain.'

2. Brightness and warmth of colour; a state of glowing brightness, a flush. Applied esp. to the warm red of the cheeks indicating youth or health.

1600 SHAKS. *A.Y.L.* III. iv. 57 A pageant truely plaid Betweene the pale complexion of true Loue, And the red glowe of scorne. **1727–46** Thomson *Summer* 147 At thee the ruby lights its deepening glow. **1775** Sheridan *Duenna* II. i, Then the roses on those cheeks are shaded with a sort of velvet down, that gives a delicacy to the glow of health. **1795** *Gentl. Mag.* 540/1 The glow of ripe fruits and declining leaves mark the Autumn. **1813** Scott *Rokeby* I. i, The moon is in her summer glow. **1835** W. Irving *Tour Prairies* 77 We perceived..a ruddy glow flushing up the sky. **1855** Macaulay *Hist. Eng.* xix. IV. 534 Mary was gone, cut off in the prime of life, in the glow of beauty. **1860** Tyndall *Glac.* I. i. 228 The red glow of the mountains at sunset. **1867** Lady Herbert *Cradle L.* iv. 125 Her face seemed lighted up with an unearthly glow. **1878** Browning *La Saisiaz* 85, I.. Saw proceed the transmutation—Jura's black to one gold glow.

3. Warmth of feeling or passion; ardour.

1748 J. Mason *Elocut.* 35 Cicero observes that there must be a Glow in our Stile if we would warm our Hearers. **1815** Byron '*There's not a joy the world can give*' i, When the glow of early thought declines in feeling's dull decay. **1853** J. H. Newman *Hist. Sk.* (1873) II. II. iii. 253 On this occasion he felt the glow of self-approbation. **1863** Geo. Eliot *Romola* II. viii, Romola felt herself surrounded and possessed by the glow of his passionate faith. **1865** Dickens *Mut. Fr.* III. vi, 'And you come, brother', said Mr. Wegg in a hospitable glow. **1867** Stanley *Westm. Abb.* vi. (1868) 454 In the glow of a religious revival.

4. *Comb.*, some of which may be combs. of vb. glow: **glow-beetle**, †**glow-bug** = glow-worm; **glow-discharge**, 'the luminous discharge of electricity from the pointed conductor of an electric machine in vigorous action where the electrified particles of air stream away' (*Syd. Soc. Lex.* 1885); also, the luminous electrical discharge in a gas-filled tube; **glow-fly** = fire-fly; **glow-lamp**, a lamp in which the light results from the incandescence of a resisting substance, e.g. carbon, produced by the passage of an electric current; **glow-light**, a glowing light; *spec.* a glow-lamp; **glow-lighting**, lighting by glow-lamps; **glow plug**, an electrically heated plug used to ignite the gas in a gas turbine or rocket engine.

1860 Piesse *Lab. Chem. Wonders* 2 Glow-worm, more correctly *glow-beetle. **1781** S. Peters *Hist. Connecticut* 259 The *Glow-bug both crawls and flies, and is about half an inch long. **1844** H. M. Noad *Lect. Electr.* (ed. 2) ii. 45 **Glow discharge*, when a fine point is used to produce disruptive discharge from a positively charged conductor, the brush gives place to a quiet phosphorescent continuous glow. **1871** tr. *Schellen's Spectr. Anal.* lxx. 423 The glow-discharge is perfectly noiseless. **1937** *Discovery* Feb. 54/1 The glow discharge from the first electrode. **1963** B. Fozard *Instrumentation Nucl. Reactors* ii. 25 Any further increase in applied voltage is likely to initiate a continuous glow discharge which may cause irreparable damage to the tube. **1789** E. Darwin *Bot. Gard.* II. 137 So shines the *glow-fly, when the sun retires. **1851** P. H. Gosse *Naturalist's Soj. Jamaica* 106, I will now speak of our other luminous insect, the Glow-fly (*Pyrophorus noctilucus*). **1884** *Daily News* 6 Mar. 5/1 For general domestic illumination he thought the *glow-lamp, as made by Swan and Edison, was the proper one. **1891** *Cassell's Family Mag.* Oct. 700/2 Ten shillings is paid for an equivalent *glow-light in the same time. **1913** *Pop. Mag.* 1 May 85/2 The *Potomac's* captain ordered even the tiny glow light illuminating the compass..to be covered. **1934** T. S. Eliot *Rock* ii. 84 Glow-worm glow-light on a grassblade. **1894** *Daily News* 2 Oct. 6/6 For *glow-lighting there is one 200 kwt. steam alternator for supplying 5,700 eight candle-power lamps. **1947** *Jrnl. Brit. Interplanetary Soc.* VI. 106 A spark or *glow plug projecting directly into the chamber can be used. **1961** *Guardian* 3 Apr. 4/1 When you press the switch, an electric glow-plug heats up and ignites the oil vapour in the burner.

glow (gləʊ), *v.*[1] Pa. t. and pa. pple. **glowed**. Forms: OE. **glówan**, 4, 6 **glowe(n**, 5 **glowyn**, **glewe**, (7 **gloue**), 4– **glow**. *Pa. pple.* 8 *rare* **glown**. [OE. *glówan*, recorded only in pr. pple. *glówende* and pa. t. *gléow*, was a redupl. str. vb., but the corresponding vbs. in the other Teut. langs. are weak: OS. *glôjan* in Oxf. glosses (Du. *gloeien*), OHG. *gluoen* (MHG. *glüen*, *glüejen*, mod.Ger. *glühen*), ON. (**glówa*) *glóa*, also *glǿja* (MSw. ?*gloa*, *glöia*, Sw. dial., Da. *glo*; for Sw., Da. *glo* to stare, see glow *v.*[2]). As the vb. is wk. after OE., it is possible that the existing word may not be the descendant of OE. *glówan*, but an adoption from ON. The Teut. root **glô-* appears also in gleed, and perh. in OE. *glóm* (see gloaming), though the latter may possibly contain the ablaut-variant **glǣ-*; the weak-grade of the root, **glă-*, is found in glass, perh. also in glade.]

1. a. *intr.* To be heated to the point of incandescence; to emit bright light and heat without flame. Said also of a fire. † *to glow out*, to go out with a glow, subside from its glow.

c **1000** Ælfric *Hom.* (1844) I. 424 Lecȝað ða isenan clutas hate glowende to his sidan. —— *Saints' Lives* vii. 240 þæt fyr wearð þa acwenced þæt þær an col ne gleow. *c* **1050** *Aldhelm Glosses* (Bodl.) in Napier *O.E. Glosses* I. 4409 Fulminauit, *pro claruit*, gleow, scan. *c* **1290** *Michael* 531 in *S.E. Leg.* I. 315 Ase ȝif a man nome a sclabbe of Ire þat glowynde were a-fuyre. **1340** Hampole *Pr. Consc.* 7221 With brynand bandes hate glowand. *a* **1400** *Isumbras* 394 Smethymene thore herde he blawe, And fyres thore bryne and glewe [*rime* ploghe]. *c* **1440** *Promp. Parv.* 200/1 Glowyn, as hoote yryne, *candeo*. **1623** Cockeram, *Glow*, to be hot or red. **1780** Johnson *Let. to Mrs. Thrale* 9 June, I..found it [Newgate] in ruins, with the fire yet glowing. **1799** G. Smith *Laboratory* I. 146 When it is nearly all glown out, add such another quantity to it, and let it glow for an hour.

fig. **1393** Langl. *P. Pl.* C. xx. 188 Til the holy gost bygynne to glowen and blase.

b. quasi-*trans.* with cognate obj.

1742 Young *Nt. Th.* iv. 192 Shall pagan pages glow celestial flame, And christian languish?

c. Of the eyes: *to glow into*, to penetrate as by burning. *nonce-use.*

1842 Lytton *Zanoni* vii. xiii, Mine eyes shall glow into thy brain.

2. a. To shine, emit light, appear suffused with radiance, like something intensely heated.

13.. *E.E. Allit. P.* A. 114 Glas þat glowed & glyȝt. *a* **1400–50** *Alexander* 3368 The fourte was a granate þat glowys all þar fynest. *c* **1420** *Anturs of Arth.* xxxi, His gloues and his gamesuns gloet [*v.rr* glowed, glomede] as the gledes. **1667** Milton *P.L.* iv. 604 Now glow'd the Firmament With living Saphirs. **1711** Pope *Temp. Fame* 143 As heav'n with stars, the roof with jewels glows. **1802** Campbell *Hohenlinden* v, But redder yet that light shall glow On Linden's hills of stainèd snow. **1827** Scott *Let. to Lockhart* in *Life* v, The eye [of Burns]..glowed (I say literally glowed) when he spoke with feeling or interest. **1860** Tyndall *Glac.* I. xvi. 106 One peak of snow in particular glowed like fire.

b. To gaze with 'glowing' eyes. *rare*$^{-1}$. Cf. glow *v.*[2] (quot. *c* 1374).

1856 Mrs. Browning *Aur. Leigh* II. 343 There he glowed on me With all his face and eyes.

c. To pass *to* or *into* a glowing colour.

1888 Mrs. H. Ward *R. Elsmere* xi, The stretches of purple heather, glowing into scarlet under the touch of the sun. **1906** E. Phillpotts *Portreeve* II. i, The breath of ocean made visible..glowed into red gold as the sun descended.

3. To be brilliant and 'warm' in colouring.

c **1386** Chaucer *Knt.'s T.* 1274 The cercles of hise eyen in his heed They gloweden bitwyxen yelow and reed. **1667** Milton *P.L.* viii. 618 A smile that glow'd Celestial rosie red, Loves proper hue. *a* **1700** Dryden (J.), Clad in a gown that glows with Tyrian rays. **1703** Pope *Vertumnus* 100 The fair fruit that on yon' branches glows. **1727–46** Thomson *Summer* 1327 Or as the rose..Fresh from Aurora's hand, more sweetly glows. **1792** S. Rogers *Pleas. Mem.* II. 65 Quaff the palm's rich nectar as it glows. **1834** Lytton *Pompeii* I. i, His tunic glowed in the richest hues of the Tyrian dye. **1867** Deutsch in *Rem.* (1874) 2 Pictures teeming with life, glowing with colour.

4. To be excessively hot; to be on fire, to burn. *lit.* and *fig.*

1393 Langl. *P. Pl.* C. iv. 103 And þenne falleþ þer fur on false menne houses, And good menne for here gultes gloweþ on fuyr after. **1697** Dryden *Virg. Georg.* I. 323 The torrid Zone Glows with the passing and repassing Sun. **1709** E. Smith *To Mem. J. Philips* 150 Yawning Gulphs with flaming Vengeance glow. **1716** Addison *Ovid's Met.* II. *Phaeton* 105 From their nostrils flows The scorching fire, that in their entrails glows. **1789** E. Darwin *Botanic Garden* II. ii. 103 Then fly the spoles, the rapid axles glow.

5. To burn with bodily heat; usually with the accompaniment of heightened colour. Also const. with predic. adj.

c **1386** Chaucer *Can. Yoem. Prol. & T.* 1096 For shame of him my chekes wexen rede; Algates, they biginnen for to glowe. **1535** Joye *Apol. Tindale* 42 Myne eares glowed for shame to here him. **1601** Holland *Pliny* xxviii. ii. 297 c, Moreover, is not this an opinion generally received, That when our ears do glow and tingle, some there be that in our absence doe talke of us? **1693** Dryden *Ovid's Met.* I. 650 She glows with blushes, and she hangs her head. **1708** Hearne *Collect.* 3 Feb. (O.H.S.) II. 92 A..Sermon, which would have made ye Ears of ye Whiggs glow. **1830** Cunningham *Brit. Paint.* II. 66 His brow glowed, he burst into tears and hurried out of the room. **1838** Lytton *Alice* 126 Her cheek glowed while she spoke. **1855** Kingsley *Westw. Ho!* i, Turning first deadly pale, and then glowing red. **1884** W. C. Smith *Kildrostan* 95 Girls, all glowing with the flush of life. **1907** *Smart Set* Jan. 126/2 With cheeks glowing red.

6. To burn with the fervour of emotion or passion. Said of persons and their feelings.

a **1649** Drumm. of Hawth. *Hymn Fairest Fair* 1, I feele my Bosome glow with wontlesse Fires. **1706** Prior *Ode on Success Her Majesty's Arms* 141 While with fiercest ire Bellona glows. **1732** Berkeley *Alciphr.* iii. §1 A certain ardour or enthusiasm that glowed in the breast of a gallant man. **1741** Richardson *Pamela* (1824) I. 131, I glowed between shame and delight. **1787** Mad. D'Arblay *Diary* 27 Jan., I trembled and glowed alternately with surprise and pleasure at this recital. **1788** Gibbon *Decl. & F.* V. lii. 440 The courage of the first ages of the republic glowed in his breast. **1855** Macaulay *Hist. Eng.* xv. III. 521 The Tories, glowing with resentment which was but too just, were resolved [etc.]. **1878** R. W. Dale *Lect. Preach.* ix. 270 Some of them glowing with the heat of early enthusiasm.

†**7.** *trans. causatively.* To make hot; to heat.

1599 A. M. tr. *Gabelhouer's Bk. Physicke* 125/1 Glowe them [Wallenuttes] in the fyere, then proiecte them in a gobblet with oulde wine. **1606** Shaks. *Ant. & Cl.* II. ii. 209 Fannes whose winde did seeme, To gloue the delicate cheekes which they did coole. **1683** Pettus *Fleta Min.* I. 140 Glow it often that it may not be shivery.

glow, *v.*[2] *Obs.* exc. *dial.* Also 5 **glogh**; cf. glew *v.*[2] [Cf. Sw., Da. *glo* to stare, look sullen; it may possibly be a use of glow *v.*[1]] *intr.* To stare.

c **1374** Chaucer *Boeth.* I. pr. i. 2 (Camb. MS.) She was a lytel amoued and glowede with cruwel eyen. *c* **1400** *Destr. Troy* 2922 To glogh vppon gomes at gedering of folke. *c* **1420** [see gaw *v.*]. **1611** Cotgr., *Borgnoyer*, to glow, glote, or loure. **1678** Dryden & Lee *Œdipus* iv. i, A thousand frantick Spirits..Peep'd from the watry Brink, and glow'd upon me. **1843** *John's Acc. Trip to Bristol* in Halliwell *Dict.* Introd. 27/2 Tha 'osses did glowy, an' tha sheep glowied too. **1863** in Barnes *Dorset Gloss.* **1880** *W. Cornwall Gloss.*, *Glow*, to stare; to look cross.

glow(e, obs. form of clove *sb.*[2]

1398 Trevisa *Barth. De P.R.* xvii. lxxix. (1495) 652 Glowes highte Gariophili.

†**glowbard.** *Obs.* Forms: 5–6 **glo(u)berd(e**, 6 **glo(e)bard(e**, **glowberde**, **gloebeard(e**, 7 **glo(w)bard**, **-bird**. [f. glow *v.* + bird *sb.*; cf. *lady-bird.*] A glow-worm.

c **1475** *Pict. Voc.* in Wr.-Wülcker 766/19 *Hec nocticula*, a glouberd. **1519** Horman *Vulg.* 108 A flye or a worme called a glouberde. **1572** R. H. tr. *Lavaturus' Ghostes* I. xi. 51 A Gloewoorme, or gloebearde [*ed.* **1596** Globard]. **1601** Holland *Pliny* I. 326 These Glowbards neuer appeare before hay is ripe. **1607** Topsell *Four-f. Beasts* 566 The worme which is called a gloworme, or a Globird.

glowe, obs. form of glove, glue *sb.*

glower (ˈglaʊə(r)), *sb.* Chiefly *Sc.* For forms see the vb. [f. glower *v.*] The action of glowering; a fixed and intent look; an open-eyed gaze or stare. Also, *a glower of* (something).

1715 Pennecuik *Poems* 22 Every Glour they give would fright a Coward. **1786** Burns *Interv. with Ld. Daer* iv, To show Sir Bardy's willyart glowr. —— *Winter Night* i, When Phœbus gies a short-liv'd glow'r Far south the lift. **1826** J. Wilson *Noct. Ambr.* Wks. 1855 I. 240 Let me hae anither glower o' my galloping goddess. **1859** J. Brown *Rab & F.* (1862) 20 James..gave him [the mastiff] a glower from time to time, and an intimation of a possible kick.

glower (ˈglaʊə(r)), *v.* Forms: 6 **glowir**, 6–8 **glowr**, 6, 8–9 **glour**, 8 **glowre**, **glow'r**, 9– **glower**. [Of obscure etymology: in sense the word agrees with glore *v.* 2, but the difference in vowel is against its immediate identity with this. It may possibly be f. glow *v.*[2] + -er[5].]

1. *intr. Sc.* To stare with wide-open eyes; to gaze intently or with an air of surprise. Also *to glower at, over.*

1500–20 Dunbar *Poems* xlix. 24 On gallow treis ȝitt dois he glowir. *Ibid.* lxxv. 19 As ane gaist I glour and grane, I trymble sa, ȝe will not trow. **1535** Lyndesay *Satyre* 136 He glowris, euin as he war agast, Or fleyit of ane gaist. ? *a* **1550** *Freiris Berwik* 350 in *Dunbar's Poems* (1893) 297 He granit, and he glowrit, as he wer woid. *a* **1605** Montgomerie *Flyting w. Polwart* 399 Some glowring to the ground; some grieuouslie gaipe. **1711** Ramsay *Elegy M. Johnston* 32 Fou closs we us'd to drink and rant Until we did baith glow'r and gaunt. **1724** —— *Tea-t. Misc.*, *Katy's Answer* i, My mither's ay glowran o'er me Tho' she did the same before me. **1725** —— *Gentle Sheph.* I. i. sang i, Upon a dyke I lean'd, glowring about. **1785** Burns *Holy Fair* ii, As lightsomely I glowr'd abroad, To see a scene so gay. **1818** Scott *Hrt. Midl.* x, I never ask what brings the Laird of Dumbiedikes glowering here like a wull-cat. **1869** Gibbon *Robin Gray* ix, 'What are ye glowering at, laddie', said his mother. **1885** R. Buchanan *Annan Water* xiv, Why do you glower at me like that.

quasi-*trans.* ? *a* **1665** W. Guthrie *Serm.* (1709) 7 (Jam.) There the poor men stood gazing and glowring out their eyne, to behold the place where he ascended.

transf. **1785** Burns *Death & Dr. Hornb.* iv, The rising moon began to glowr The distant Cumnock hills out-owre.

2. To look angrily or crossly; to scowl. Also *dial.* of the weather: To be gloomy.

This sense is perh. partly due to misapprehension of the meaning of *glower* in Scottish writers, but may also be based on the English dialect use, which appears to be genuine.

1775 Mad. D'Arblay *Early Diary* 4 Mar. 'But', added he, drily, 'I did not. Well, Bell, what do you glow'r at?' *a* **1791** Pegge *Derbicisms* 102 Glowres, is dull or lowering. **1822** T. L. Peacock *Maid Marian* 177 The baron glowered about him with an expression of countenance that shewed he was mortally wroth with somebody. **1841** Lever *C. O'Malley* lxxxviii, The M'Nab and the Englishman.. sat glowering at each other like twa tigers. **1857** Trollope *Barchester T.* (1861) 315 Mr. Slope saw it, and glowered with jealousy. **1861** Hughes *Tom Brown at Oxf.* xv. (1889) 146 Don't sit glowering as if you had swallowed a furze bush. **1885** *Pall Mall G.* 2 Jan. 2/1 They had nothing to show but..Europe glowering upon us with hate. **1886** *Chester Gloss.*, *Glour* or *Glower*, to have a cross look. 'When the clouds threaten bad weather we call them glowering.' W.

Hence ˈ**glowering** *vbl. sb.* Also ˈ**glowerer**, one who glowers, an idle gazer.

1715 Sir. J. Clerk *Mem.* (1895) 86 He called to a friend ..next his bed, that if hee pleased the Glourers might come in, meaning the Gasers, and such who rather out of curiosity than sympathy..attend the sick till their breath go out. **1826** J. Wilson *Noct. Ambr.* Wks. 1855 I. 132 A' thae things.. justifies the leddies to a certain extent o' their glowerin.

glower(e, obs. form of glover.

glowering (ˈglaʊərɪŋ), *ppl. a.* [f. glower *v.* + -ing[2].] That glowers.

1508 Dunbar *Flyting w. Kennedie* 98 Na, glowrand, gaipand fule, thow art begyld. **1535** Stewart *Cron. Scot.* II. 493 With atrie visage and with glowrand ene. *a* **1791** Pegge *Derbicisms* 102 Glowring, gloomy. **1826** J. Wilson *Noct. Ambr.* Wks. 1855 I. 128 Only see Mullion's een—how gleg and glowrin in perfect greed and glory. **1865** Dickens *Mut. Fr.* III. i, Sitting down..to stare at his glowering friend with his back to the fire.

Comb. **1877** Black *Green Past.* xx, An invitation to dine with this thick-headed and glowering-eyed Scotchman.

Hence ˈ**gloweringly** *adv.*

1859 F. Francis *Newton Dogvane* II. xi. 287 The ladies.. looked rather gloweringly upon the wretched Chilli. **1859** Dickens *T. Two Cities* I. v, The people..croaked over their scanty measures of thin wine and beer, and were gloweringly confidential together.

glowgelofre, obs. form of CLOVE-GILLYFLOWER.

glowing (ˈgləʊɪŋ), *vbl. sb.* [f. GLOW *v.* + -ING[1].] The action of the vb. GLOW, in its various senses.

c **1440** *Promp. Parv.* 200/1 Glowynge of hoote fyre, or yryn, or oþer lyke, *candor.* **1562** TURNER *Baths* 11 b, They are good for..the glowyng or sounde of the eares. **1579** LYLY *Euphues* (Arb.) 171 And God grant thee that glowing and sting in conscience. **1704** ADDISON *Italy* (1733) 52 You have no Concern in..the Glowings of Summer. **1733** CHEYNE *Eng. Malady* II. xi. §2 (1734) 229 Uncertain Fits of Coldness and Rigour, with succeeding Glowings. **1862** W. BRANKS *Life in Heaven* iv. (1865) 58 Their Souls are warmed with the glowings of divine love. **1866** ODLING *Anim. Chem.* 63 The glowing is soon succeeded by a brilliant combustion. **1891** *Athenæum* 22 Aug. 245/3 The luminosity..is due to a simple glowing.

†**b.** In transitive sense: The action of causing to glow. *Obs.*

1683 PETTUS *Fleta Min.* I. 140 The glowing must be done in a golden little half Pipkin.

glowing (ˈgləʊɪŋ), *ppl. a.* [f. GLOW *v.* + -ING[2].] That glows, in senses of the vb.

1. That is in a glow from the action of heat; burning, incandescent.

c **1000** *Sax. Leechd.* II. 216 Gemeng togædere mid glowende isene. *c* **1200** ORMIN 1067 O þatt allterr haffdenn þeȝȝ Glowennde gledess ȝarrkedd. *c* **1290** *S. Eng. Leg.* I. 187/81 He let nime platus of Ire..þo heo glowinde were. *a* **1300** *Cursor M.* 23438 If it war scoit into þi hefd, A glouand iren þar in beleued, and [etc.]. *c* **1450** *ME. Med. Bk.* (Heinrich) 70 Ley hem on a glowynge tylston. **1535** STEWART *Cron. Scot.* II. 512 Richt oft he fell into ane glowand heit. **1597** A. M. tr. *Guillemeau's Fr. Chirurg.* 24 b/2 A glowinge or redde-hotte Cauterium. **1621** T. WILLIAMSON tr. *Goulart's Wise Vieillard* 52 But old men are like..a small gloing fire, which dyes and goes out of it selfe. **1704** ADDISON *Italy* 240 Like a vast Caldron fill'd with glowing and melted Matter. **1848** LYTTON *Harold* VIII. vi, The Vala paused..gazing in awe on the glowing stone. **1879** PROCTOR *Pleas. Ways Sci.* i. 3 The glowing vapour of the familiar metal, iron.

2. Brilliantly luminous; brilliant, rich, and warm in colouring; also, having the glow or exuberant colouring of excitement or health.

13.. *E.E. Allit. P.* C. 94 Our syre syttes..on sege so hyȝe In his glwande glorye. **1637** MILTON *Lycidas* 145 The glowing violet. **1697** DRYDEN *Alexander's Feast* 70 The master saw the madness rise; His glowing cheeks, his ardent eyes. **1712** ADDISON *Spect.* No. 477 ¶1 The glowing redness of the berries. **1727–46** THOMSON *Summer* 1315 Her naked limbs of glowing white. **1794** MRS. RADCLIFFE *Myst. Udolpho* i, Nor was it in the soft and glowing landscape that she most delighted. **1800** *Asiat. Ann. Reg., Misc. Tr.* 231/1 Female musicians, with glowing cheeks and faces like the sun. **1833** TENNYSON *Lady Clara Vere de V.* viii, In glowing health, with boundless wealth, But sickening of a vague disease. **1860** TYNDALL *Glac.* I. iii. 24 As he stood in the glowing light of the fire. **1879** G. A. SALA in *Daily Tel.* 8 May, Sir John's glowing canvas might be mistaken for a moment for some Bacchanalian triumph.

b. *fig.*

1827 STEUART *Planter's G.* (1828) 32 The glowing colours of the historian. **1851–5** BRIMLEY *Ess., Tennyson* 50 The dramatic colouring throughout is maintained at a glowing tone. **1871** FREEMAN *Norm. Conq.* (1876) IV. xvii. 80 A glowing description of the wealth of England.

3. That glows with passion; ardent, impassioned, fervid.

a **1577** GASCOIGNE *Absent Dame Complaineth* Wks. Herbs (1587) 138 The priuie coales, of glowing ielousie. **1747** COLLINS *Passions* 7 By turns they felt the glowing mind. **1805** N. NICHOLLS *Let.* in *Corr. w. Gray* (1843) 45 He was much struck with the glowing eloquence..of Rousseau. **1835** URE *Philos. Manuf.* 15 Arkwright..had the..boldness to predict in glowing language, how [etc.]. **1869** RUSKIN *Q. of Air* §53 Athena, spiritually, is the queen of all glowing virtue. **1883** SIR T. MARTIN *Ld. Lyndhurst* iv. 120 It was not without cause that the fond mother wrote of her son in such glowing terms.

4. quasi-*adv.* in phr. ***glowing hot.***

c **1450** *ME. Med. Bk.* (Heinrich) 115 Take an hoot tile, þat is glowynge hoot. **1523** FITZHERB. *Husb.* §62 Take a culture ..or suche an other yren, & take it glowing hote. **1664** POWER *Exp. Philos.* I. 54 A parcel of the Flint or Steel.. which..is made so glowing hot, that 'tis melted into glass. **1784** COWPER *Tiroc.* 304 The little ones, unbuttoned, glowing hot, Playing our games, and on the very spot. **1848** J. A. CARLYLE tr. *Dante's Inferno* IX, All over so glowing-hot, that iron more hot no craft requires.

Hence ˈ**glowingly** *adv.*, in a glowing manner, with brightness, high colour, or warmth; ardently, enthusiastically.

a **1616** BEAUM. & FL. *Wit without M.* IV. i, Out hee must breake, glowingly againe, And with a greater luster. *c* **1815** MOORE *Irish Melodies, When cold in the earth* 15 If happiness ..glowingly smil'd On his ev'ning horizon. **1822** *Examiner* 428/2 We do not look at this group coldly but glowingly. **1871** L. STEPHEN *Playgr. Europe* II. v. 305 The tremendous cliffs..have been glowingly described in..many Alpine books. **1883** *Harper's Mag.* Mar. 533/2 She was glowingly proud of her kitchen. *a* **1887** JEFFERIES *Field & Hedgerow* (1889) 20 Some [apples]..more glowingly beautiful than the rest.

glowir, obs. Sc. form of GLOWER.

glowr, obs. form of GLOWER.

†**glowsing**, *vbl. sb. Obs.* [Cf. GLOSSER[3].] Carousing.

1622 T. STOUGHTON *Chr. Sacrif.* viii. 106 Belshazzar's drinking and glowsing in the cups of the Lord..cost him both his life and his kingdome.

glowt, obs. form of GLOUT *v.*

glowton, obs. Sc. form of GLUTTON.

glow-worm (ˈgləʊwɜːm). Forms: 4 glou-, 5 gloo-, 6–7 glo-, gloe-, glowe-, 6– glow-worm (etc.: see WORM). See also GLOSE-WORM. [f. GLOW *v.* + WORM.] A coleopterous insect (*Lampyris noctiluca*, Linn.), the female of which emits a shining green light from the extremity of the abdomen. The female is wingless; the male is winged, but non-luminous.

a. *c* **1320** N. BOZON *Contes Moralisés* §76. 95 Un autre nature de ceo verm qe est appelle en Latyn eruke et en Engleiz glouworm. **1444** LYDG. in *Pol. Poems* (Rolls) II. 216 A fowle gloowerm in dirknesse shewith a lyght. **1530** PALSGR. 225/2 Glowe worme that shyneth by night. **1555** EDEN *Decades* 212 In this Iland are certeyne glo woormes that shyne in the nyght as doo owres. **1602** SHAKS. *Ham.* I. v. 89 The Glowworme..gins to pale his vneffectuall Fire. **1626** BACON *Sylva* §224 A great Light drowneth a smaller, that it cannot be seene; As the Sunne that of a Gloworme. *c* **1750** SHENSTONE *Elegies* vi. 30 No lover bless'd the glow-worm's pallid ray. **1789** G. WHITE *Selborne* (1853) 382 Male glow-worms attracted by the light..come into the parlour. **1847** TENNYSON *Princess* IV. 7 Where below No bigger than a glow-worm shone the tent.

b. *fig.* (In 17th c. often applied contemptuously to persons.)

1624 BURTON *Anat. Mel.* II. iii. II. 260 A Nobleman therefore in some likelyhood..[is] an outside, a gloworme, a proud foole, an arrant asse. **1628** TIMME *Silver Watch Bell* ix. §7 (ed. 10) 164 Reason (which the Fathers call *Noctilucam cerebri*, the brains Glo-worme). **1634** FORD *P. Warbeck* IV. iv, A slave! A vagabond! A glow-worm! **1652** BP. HALL *Rem. Wks.* (1660) 152 The world is full of such glow-wormes, that make some show of Sprirituall Light from God.

c. *attrib.* and *Comb.*

1621 LADY M. WROTH *Urania, Pamph. to Amphil.* 47 How Glowworme-like the Sun doth now appeare. **1623** B. JONSON *Time Vindic.*, He works by glow-worme light, the Moone's too open. **1630** J. TAYLOR (Water P.) *Wks.* II. 341/1 Though I know my selfe vnworthy farre, With my poore Glow-worme Muse, t'attend this starre. *a* **1649** DRUMM. OF HAWTH. *Poems* Wks. (1711) 44 How oft have we.. Condemn'd earths glow-worm greatness. **1664** BUTLER *Hud.* II. iii. 450 He..rais'd it [his engine] till it levell'd right Against the glow-worm tail of kite. **1670** DRYDEN *2nd Pt. Conq. Granada* II. iii, For, glow-worm-like, you shine, and do not see. **1686** HORNECK *Crucif. Jesus* iv. 60 Meer glowworm light, that shines, but warms not.

†ˈ**glowy**, *a. Obs.*[−1] [f. GLOW *sb.* + -Y[1].] Glowing; bright.

1670–98 LASSELS *Voy. Italy* I. 102 This fire..appear'd to me..to be..of the same glowy colour.

glowyn, obs. form of GLOW *v.*[1]

gloxinia (glɒkˈsɪnɪə). [mod.L.; named by L'Héritier after B. P. *Gloxin*, who described the plant in 1785.] An American tropical plant (N.O. *Gesneraceæ*) with large bell-shaped flowers.

1816–20 T. GREEN *Univ. Herbal* I. 621 *Gloxinia Maculata*; Spotted Gloxinia. **1863** *Sir Rohan's Ghost* 129 Vases of the..violet-coloured gloxinia. **1882** *Garden* 18 Mar. 186/1 Some of the old bulbs of Gloxinias should now be potted.

†**gloy.** *Obs.* [a. F. *glui*; cf. Du. *glui* (supposed to be an adoption from Fr.] Straw.

c **1336** *Durham MS. Burs. Roll*, In factura nattarum de Gloy pro Refectorio, ijs. vjd. **1483** *Cath. Angl.* 159/1 Gloy, *spicamentum.* **1513** DOUGLAS *Æneis* VIII. xi. 31 Quhais rufis laitly full rouch thykyt war Wyth stra or gloy by Romulus the wycht.

gloyd, var. GLEYD, *Obs.*, a worn-out horse.

gloyfer, gloyse, obs. ff. GLOVER, GLOZE.

gloyt, obs. form of GLOAT *v.*

gloze (gləʊz), *sb.* Forms: 3–7, 9 glose, (4 glos, 5 gloce, gloyse, *Sc.* glois, gloss, 6 gloase, gloose), 6– gloze. Also GLOSS *sb.*[1] [a. OF. *glose*, ad. med.L. *glōsa*, L. *glōssa*, a word needing explanation, hence later the explanation itself, a Gr. γλῶσσα, orig. tongue, hence language, foreign language, a foreign or obscure word.]

1. A comment, or marginal note; an exposition; = GLOSS *sb.*[1] 1. *arch.*

1340 HAMPOLE *Pr. Consc.* 4479 þe glose of þe buke says alswa þat [etc.]. **1377** LANGL. *P. Pl.* B. XVII. 13 þe glose was gloriously writen with a gilte penne. *c* **1430** *Pilgr. Lyf Manhode* III. xxi. (1869) 147 Now vnderstonde it wel, and expownde it as þou wolt, both þe texte and þe glose. **1548** HALL *Chron., Hen. V*, 36 See nowe howe an euell glose confoundeth the text. **1579** FENTON *Guicciard.* v. (1599) 212 Making gloses vpon the capitulations past, rather like a Lawyer, then as a king. **1602** WARNER *Alb. Eng.* IX. lii. (1612) 234 That with new Glozes tainte the Text. **1834–43** SOUTHEY *Doctor* Interch. xvii. (1862) 427 It is proper in this glose, commentary or exposition to [etc.]. **1855** BROWNING *Master Hugues of Saxe-Gotha* Prol., Not a glimpse of the far land Gets through our comments and glozes.

2. Flattery, deceit; an instance of this, a flattering speech, etc. †***to make glose*** (const. *dat.*), to talk smoothly or flatteringly to. Now *rare.*

c **1290** *S. Eng. Leg.* I. 194/12 Heo, and hire douȝtren also maden hire þe glose. **1297** R. GLOUC. (Rolls) 2381 Me it ortrowede & ne leuede noȝt is glose. *c* **1386** CHAUCER *Sqr.'s T.* 158 This is a verray sooth with outen glose. *c* **1450** *Bk. Curtasye* 312 in *Babees Bk.*, Yf any thurgh sturnes þe oppose, Onswere hym mekely and make hym glose. *c* **1460** *Towneley Myst.* xxii. 225 Thou has made many glose with thy fals talkyng. **1580** LYLY *Euphues* (Arb.) 368 Women.. giue more credit to their own glasses, than mens gloses. **1601** B. JONSON *Poetaster* III. v, He..Spurns back the gloses of a fawning spirit. **1674** BLOUNT *Glossogr.* (ed. 4), *Glose*, flattery or dissimulation. **1874** J. G. HOLLAND *Mistr. Manse* II. iii. 92 No..dainty gloze Could give him pleasure half so fine As that which tingled to her blows.

b. A pretence, false show, specious appearance; also, a disguise. Now *rare.*

a **1300** *Cursor M.* 26774 þai com to scrift a glos to make. **1340–70** *Alex. & Dind.* 1016 ȝoure fingrus..ȝe fullen wiþ ryngus As is wommenus wone for wordliche glose. **1581** SAVILE *Tacitus' Hist.* I. lxxi (1591) 39 This glose of vertues [L. *falsæ virtutes*] increased men's feare. *a* **1586** SIDNEY *Arcadia* I. (1598) 81 If then a bodily euill in a bodily gloze be not hidden, Shall [etc.]. **1600** HOLLAND *Livy* I. xxiii. (1609) 16 Gloses, and goodly shews of words. **1649** BP. HALL *Cases Consc.* i. (1654) 11 We are naturally too apt..to flatter ourselves with fair glozes of bad intentions. **1846** RUSKIN *Mod. Paint.* (1848) I. II. I. ii. §8. 55 A gloze, whether purposely worn or unconsciously assumed.

3. = GLOSS *sb.*[1] 2 [ad. It. *glosa*].

1823 ROSCOE *Sismondi's Lit. Eur.* (1846) II. xxxvi. 460 We also meet with several gloses or voltas upon a variety of devices or canzonets.

4. *Comb.*, as ***gloze-giver.***

c **1449** PECOCK *Repr.* I. xii. 65 Expowners and gloze ȝeuers.

gloze (gləʊz), *v.*[1] Forms: 4–6 glose(n, 5 glosin, -yn, 5–6 *Sc.* glois(s, gloss, 6 gloase, 6– gloze. [a. F. *gloser* (12th c.), f. *glose* GLOZE *sb.*[1] (OE. had *glésan* to gloss, interpret, f. **glóse*, ad. L. *glōssa*).]

†**1.** *trans.* To make glozes or glosses upon; to discourse upon, expound, interpret. Also, to interpret (a thing) *to be* (so and so). *Obs.*

1362 LANGL. *P. Pl.* A. Prol. 57, I font þere Freres.. Glosynge þe Gospel as hem good likeþ. *c* **1425** *Hampole's Psalter* Metr. Pref. 23 Rychard Hampole Glosed the sauter that sues here. *c* **1449** PECOCK *Repr.* I. vi. 31 Hise writingis ouȝten be glosid and be expowned. *c* **1450** HOLLAND *Howlat* 35, I haue mekle matir in metre to Glos Of ane nothir sentence. **1453** *Test. Ebor.* (Surtees) II. 190 Ane English boke of ye Pater Noster, glosid, with Matynes of ye Passion. **1513** DOUGLAS *Æneis* VIII. vii. 54 Quhairfor, myne awin hart deyr, Sa far about thou glosis thi mater? **1563** WINȜET *Four Scoir Thre Quest.* To Rdr., Wks. 1888 I. 56 A werk.. cunninglie gloissit be sum weill leirnit and discrete man. **1559** SHAKS. *Hen. V*, I. ii. 40 Which Salike land, the French vniustly gloze To be the Realme of France. **1762** *Crazy Tales* 76 You may gloze any word. **1820** SCOTT *Monast.* v, The church hath her ministers to gloze and to expound the same [the Word].

b. *absol.* or *intr.* To interpose a gloss or explanation; to comment. Const. *on*, *upon*; also in indirect passive.

c **1380** WYCLIF *Wks.* (1880) 384 Clerkis..willen glose here and say [etc.]. *c* **1385** CHAUCER *L.G.W.* Prol. 254 For in pleyn text it nedyth nat to glose. **1413** *Pilgr. Sowle* (Caxton 1483) IV. xxxvii. 85 No more men maye glosen withouten text than bylde materles. **1566** T. STAPLETON *Ret. Untr. Jewel* III. 64 He saieth not, Not so rightly, as M. Jewell gloseth. **1581** T. WATSON *Centurie of Loue* xvii. (Arb.) 53 Yf Poets haue done weell..To gloze on trifling toyes. **1614** BP. HALL *Recoll. Treat.* 821 Let your Authors glose as they list, Popery is but a yong faction. **1813** SCOTT *Rokeby* I. xi, A while he glozed upon the cause, Of Commons, Covenant, and Laws. **1821** SHELLEY *Prometh. Unb.* III. iv. 167 Tomes Of reasoned wrong, glozed on by ignorance. **1872** BROWNING *Fifine* xxxi, Gloze No whit on your premiss.

c. (See quot. and cf. GLOZE *sb.*[1] 2.)

1837–9 HALLAM *Hist. Lit.* I. ii. §43 In this [the Spanish *glosa*] a few lines..were glosed, or paraphrased..in a succession of stanzas, so that the leading sentiment should be preserved in each, as the subject of an air runs through its variations.

2. *trans.* To veil with specious comments; to palliate; to explain away, extenuate. Frequently with *over*; †also with *out.*

1390 GOWER *Conf.* I. 84 Telle out and let it nought be glosed. *c* **1394** *P. Pl. Crede* 345 Lere me to som man..þat ..gloseþ nouȝt þe godspell. **1509** BARCLAY *Shyp of Folys* p iv b, A ryche mannys dede may no man hyde nor glose. *a* **1536** TINDALE *Exp. Matt.* v–vii. Wks. (1573) 187/2 They that..seeke liberties..to sinne vnpunished, and glose out the lawe of God. *a* **1541** WYATT in *Tottel's Misc.* (Arb.) 56 Nor I can not endure the truth to glose. **1548** HALL *Chron., Edw. IV*, 242 Thus is the league made with Lewes the French kyng, fraudulently glosed and dissimuled. **1586** T. B. *La Primaud. Fr. Acad.* I. (1594) 380 With what impudencie soever the wicked outwardlie gloze their corrupt dealings. **1665** MANLEY *Grotius' Low C. Warres* 31 Least he should..give Credit, to a thing so profane and detestable, however glosed over by those malitious People. **1827** HOOD *Mids. Fairies* xcii, Beshrew those sad interpreters of nature, Who gloze her lively universal law. **1845** WHITTIER *Lines Washington* vi, With the tongue of flattery glozing deeds which God and Truth condemn. **1878** in *N. Amer. Rev.* CXXVI. 469 The facts of human iniquity are not disputed, glozed over, or extenuated. **1884** R. GLOVER in *Chr. World* 9 Oct. 767/1 It is not charity to gloze over the sins and sorrows of men.

3. *intr.* To talk smoothly and speciously; to use fair words or flattering language; to fawn. Sometimes coupled with *flatter*; also *to gloze it.* Now *rare.*

a **1300** *Cursor M.* 8401 (Gött.) Neyder i kepe to gabb ne glose. *c* **1386** CHAUCER *Merch. T.* 1107, I kan nat glose, I am a rude man. *c* **1400** *Destr. Troy* 11468 Glose hit not lengur. **1519** *Interl. Four Elem.* (Percy Soc.) 4 Some to opteyn favour wyll flatter and glose. **1567** R. EDWARDS *Damon & Pithias* (1571) H iij b, Painted speache, that gloseth for gayne. **1603** KNOLLES *Hist. Turks* (1621) 704 Rogendorff..

made as if he would have used only the Hungarians, and glosed with Revalius. **1632** SANDERSON *12 Serm.* (1637) 606 Let us take heed we doe not gloze with him, as we doe one with another. **1783** WHITEHEAD *Ode New Year* 11 Ye Nations hear! nor fondly deem Britannia's ancient spirit fled; Or glosing weep her setting beam. **1833** CARLYLE *Misc.* (1857) III. 202 The dog glozed with professions of life-weariness. **1848** LYTTON *Harold* IX. iii, We would not that thou shouldest learn too early how men's tongues can gloze and flatter. **1858** W. JOHNSON *Ionica, Reparabo* ii, While my comrades pass away To bow and smirk and gloze.

†**b.** quasi-*trans.* To tell speciously. *Obs.*$^{-1}$

1608 ROWLANDS *Humors Looking Gl.* 15 Vnto the Man he goes, And vnto him this fayned tale doth gloze.

†**c.** *trans.* To clothe (words, etc.) with specious adornment.

1430-40 LYDG. *Bochas* III. xviii. 90 This sentence is not glosed. **1509**, *c* **1520**, **1630** [see GLOZED *ppl. a.*].

4. *trans.* To flatter, deceive with smooth talk; to coax, wheedle. Rarely const. *to*. *Obs.* exc. *arch.*

c **1330** R. BRUNNE *Chron.* (1810) 34 Pes forto haue þei glosed him fulle mykelle. *c* **1386** CHAUCER *Manciple's Prol.* 34 Of me certeyn thou shalt nat been yglosed. *c* **1420** *Pallad. on Husb.* IV. 758 [778] Now glose hem feire. *c* **1440** *Jacob's Well* (E.E.T.S.) 96 His eem . . glosyd him to hym wyth fayre woordys. **1480** CAXTON *Chron. Eng.* xiii. 16 My two doughters glosed me tho and now of me they sette lytel prys. **1540-54** CROKE *13 Ps.* (Percy Soc.) 21 They that me with tales wold glose, Agaynst me worke the worst they maye. **1555** ABP. PARKER *Ps.* xxxvi. 93 For he himselfe doth glose In hys bewitched eyes. **1829** CARLYLE *Misc.* (1857) II. 61 The parasite glozes his master with sweet speeches.

gloze (gləʊz), *v.*^{2} *rare.* [Of obscure origin; cf. GLOW *v.*^{2}] *intr.* To look earnestly and fixedly; to gaze with pleasure; to peer.

1853 JERDAN *Autobiog.* IV. vii. 120 The pleasure of seeing oneself in print, [is] only to be estimated by those who have glozed over the type. **1864** MRS. LLOYD *Ladies Polc.* 103 That little Preventative fellow up on the cliff, that's al'ays a-glozing out to sea.

Hence †**gloze** *sb.*, an eager look, a gaze.

1654 GAYTON *Pleas. Notes* II. v. 56 Give a good glose from thy strain'd goggle eye.

gloze (gləʊz), *v.*^{3} *rare.* [Cf. GLOSS *sb.*^{2}] **a.** *intr.* To shine brightly, to blaze; also, to gleam. **b.** *trans.* To cause to shine. Hence **'glozing** *vbl. sb.* and *ppl. a.*

1820 A. SUTHERLAND *St. Kathleen* III. 167 Gudewife, carry up a glozin' peat, an' kennel a spunk o' fire in them baith. **1880** L. WALLACE *Ben-Hur* 396 An illusory glozing of the light glimmering dismally. *Ibid.* 398 The scanty light glosed them with the glory of day.

†**glozed**, *ppl. a. Obs.* [f. GLOZE *v.*^{1} + -ED^1.] In senses of the vb.: Provided with glosses, commented on; speciously adorned; specious.

1393 LANGL. *P. Pl.* C. VII. 303 What lede leyueþ þat ich lye loke in þe sauter glosed. **1483** CAXTON *Cato* 2 b, He sayd that he helde Cathon glosed for the best boke of his lyberarye. **1509** BARCLAY *Shyp of Folys* (1570) 168 It is not peased . . With cunning of Retorike, ne glosed eloquence. *c* **1520** —— *Jugurth* l. 70 b, My vertue sheweth it selfe playnelie ynough without glosedde or payntedde wordes. **1563** *Homilies* II. *Agst. Peril Idol.* III. K kij, Suche glorious glosed fables. **1630** LORD *Banians* Introd., Smiling out a glosed and bashfull familiarity.

†**'glozer.** *Obs.* Forms: 4 glosour, 4-5 glosar(e, 4-7 gloser, (6 glosier), 7- glozer. [f. GLOZE *v.*^{1} + -ER^1; after OF. *gloseor.*]

1. One who writes glosses; a commentator.

1380 WYCLIF *Wks.* (1880) 284 Falce gloseris maken goddis lawe derk. *c* **1440** *Promp. Parv.* 199/2 Glosare of textys, *glosator*. **1565** JEWEL *Def. Apol.* (1567) 226 But that these woordes . . touche . . onely the Priestes and the Ministers, the very Gloser [*ed.* **1611** glosser] him selfe was neuer . . so impudent, so to saie. **15..** FULKE in Marbeck *Bk. of Notes* (1581) 55 These words (saith the Romish gloser) are the Ciuill and Ecclesiasticall power.

2. A flatterer, sycophant.

c **1400** *Apol. Loll.* 105 Simplist glosars, & warst willid traytoris. *a* **1420** HOCCLEVE *De Reg. Princ.* 3088 A gloser also kepethe his silence Often, where he his lorde seethe hym mystake. **1456** *Pol. Poems* (Rolls) II. 235 Now gloserys fulle gayly they go. **1575** *Gammer Gurton* IV. i Yet must I talke so sage and smothe, as though I were a glosier [*rime-wd.* loser]. **1604** MIDDLETON *Father Hubbards T.* Wks. (Bullen) VIII. 61 Else would not glosers oil the son, Who, while his father liv'd, his acts did hate. **1659** HAMMOND *On Ps.* cxxxix. 14 God would at length discover and bring out such glozers. **1783** *Ainsworth's Lat. Dict.* (Morell) I, A glozer, *adulator*.

glozing ('gləʊzɪŋ), *vbl. sb.* [f. GLOZE *v.*^{1} + -ING^1.] The action of the vb. GLOZE.

1. a. The action of glossing or commenting; exposition, interpretation. Also *concr.* a gloss, a comment. **b.** The action of glossing or explaining away; extenuation, palliation.

c **1340** *Cursor M.* 26095 (Fairf.) To make to prest our synnis couþ . . wiþ-out glosing. **1377** LANGL. *P. Pl.* B. XIII. 74, I wist neuere freke that as a frere ȝede . . Taken it for her teme and telle it with-outen glosynge. *c* **1380** WYCLIF *Sel. Wks.* III. 439 He [antichrist] groundiþ . . þe deds þat he doiþ . . in . . glosyng of freris. **1413** *Pilgr. Sowle* (Caxton) II. xliii. (1859) 49 They peruertyn holy Scripture by fals vnderstandynge, glosynge [etc.]. **1562** WINȜET *Cert. Tractatis* ii. Wks. 1888 I. 20 But wrysting, wrying, gloissing, or cloking. **1575** G. HARVEY *Letter-bk.* (Camden) 96 Terming . . all others mere counterfayte glozings. **1587** GOLDING *De Mornay* xvi. (1617) 280 The glosing of some wrong. **1642** MILTON *Apol. Smect.* viii, Immediately he falls to glozing. **1829** *Q. Rev.* XLI. 344 This gentleman . . has made several marginal glosings. **1859** I. TAYLOR *Logic in Theol.* 28 This doctrine, whatever may be the softening or the glozings that are attached to it.

2. Flattery, cajolery, deceitful blandishment, specious talk or representation.

1297 R. GLOUC. (Rolls) 2319 Her of he let hem segge soþ as it were in glosinge. *c* **1330** R. BRUNNE *Chron. Wace* (Rolls) 2319 Scheo seyd nought glosyng til his wille. **1377** LANGL. *P. Pl.* B. XX. 124 With glosynges and with gabbynges he gyled þe peple. *c* **1450** *Mirour Saluacioun* 355 O man be warre in this of wikkid womans glosing. **1526** *Pilgr. Perf.* (W. de W. 1531) 57 Flee . . glosynge, pleasures & vayne gloryes. **1640** YORKE *Union Hon.* Battles 49 Perkin using all his glosings, could not prevaile with the Citizens to open their Gates. *a* **1677** BARROW *Serm.* v. Wks. 1687 I. 65 Flattering colloguings and glozings. **1765** H. WALPOLE *Otranto* iv. (1798) 65 Discompose not yourself for the glosing of a peasant's son. **1820** W. IRVING *Sketch Bk.* II. 164 His sturdy nature would break through all their glozings.

†**3.** An alleged name for a 'company' (of taverners). *Obs.*$^{-1}$

1486 *Bk. St. Albans* F vi b, A Glosyng of Tauerneris.

glozing ('gləʊzɪŋ), *ppl. a.* [f. GLOZE *v.*^{1} + -ING^2.] That glozes; flattering, coaxing, cajoling.

1297 R. GLOUC. (Rolls) 10218 Hii nadde of him bote is old wone Glosinde wordes & false. *c* **1400** *Apol. Loll.* 105 Glosandist flaterars, & bitandist bacbitars. **1528** ROY *Rede Me* (Arb.) 43 In his glosynge pistles before tyme. **1562-3** *Jack Jugler* (Roxb.) 33, I woll nat be deludyd with such a glosing lye. **1597** HOOKER *Eccl. Pol.* v. iv. §2 Where the snares of glosing speech doe lye to intangle them. **1686** HORNECK *Crucif. Jesus* xiv. 336 A glozing pleasure invites them to consent. **1766** FORDYCE *Serm. Yng. Wom.* (1767) III. viii. 42 A grave face and glozing accent. **1791** COWPER *Iliad* IX. 668 Henceforth his glozing arts Are lost on me. **1832-4** DE QUINCEY *Cæsars* Wks. 1862 IX. 154 A glozing tempter in search of accomplices. **1871** W. H. DIXON *Tower* III. v. 43 Whose . . glozing tongue had won him favour.

Hence **'glozingly** *adv.*, in a glozing manner.

a **1420** HOCCLEVE *De. Reg. Princ.* 1918 They that . . glosyngly unto her frendes talke, Spreden a nette before hem where they walke. **1607** R. WILKINSON *Merchant Royall* 1 A Scripture written in praise of women, yet not glosingly to make them better than they be. **1661** *Sir H. Vane's Politicks* 14 Without self-assentation (which even I glozingly declined).

glu, obs. var. GLEE *sb.*, GLUE *sb.*

†**glub**^{1}. *Obs. rare.* In 4 glob, glub(be. [Perh. cognate with *glubbe* GLOBBE *v.*; used to render L. *globus*, prob. from the similarity of sound.]

1. A mass or heap. *rare*$^{-1}$.

1382 WYCLIF *Josh.* iii. 13 The watres . . that camen fro aboue shulen stoond togidre in o glob [**1388** gobet; L. *in una mole*].

2. A band, company, troop, esp. of warriors in close array.

1382 WYCLIF *Num.* xvi. 11 To hym silf he hath maad thee to comyn nyȝ . . that . . al thi glubbe [**1388** gaderyng; L. *globus*] stoonde aȝens the Lord? —— *2 Kings* ix. 17 Thanne the wayte . . see the glub of Hieu commynge, and seith, I see a glub [**1388** multitude; L. *globum*].

†**glub**^{2}. *Obs.*$^{-1}$ [echoic: cf. GLUCK, GLUG.] An inarticulate sound rendered by this spelling.

1794 G. ADAMS *Nat. & Exp. Philos.* I. ii. 58 An adequate quantity of air will enter through the neck with a kind of glub.

glubbe, var. GLOBBE *v.*, GLUB^1, *Obs.*

glucagon ('gl(j)u:kəgɒn). *Physiol.* [f. GLUC(O- + Gr. ἀγών AGON or ἀγῶν, pres. pple. of ἄγειν to lead, bring.] A crystalline polypeptide hormone formed in the pancreas which stimulates glycogenolysis.

1923 KIMBALL & MURLIN in *Jrnl. Biol. Chem.* LVIII. 342 This hyperglycemic substance has been given the name glucagon and its properties will be described more fully in a later paper. **1961** *Times* 22 Dec. 5/7 Insulin reduces the blood-sugar level and glucagon raises it. **1967** *Martindale's Extra Pharmacopœia* (ed. 25) 673/1 Glucagon has also been employed in terminating insulin coma. **1968** *New Scientist* 29 Feb. 481/1 Glucagon, a hormone produced in and excreted by the pancreas together with insulin, was recently successfully synthesized.

glucase ('gl(j)u:keɪz, -s). *Biochem.* [ad. G. *glukase* (R. Géduld 1892, in *Jahresber. Fortschr. Lehre Gährungs-Organismen 1891* II. 250), f. GLUCO- + -ASE.] = MALTASE.

1894 *Jrnl. Chem. Soc.* LXVI. I. 258 Glucase which occurs in maize slowly hydrolyses dextrin. **1910** [see AMYLASE]. **1950** A. GOTTSCHALK in Sumner & Myrbäck *Enzymes* I. I. xv. 553 He [*sc.* Géduld] found the enzyme in the grains of many cereals and called it 'glucase'.

glucate ('gl(j)u:kət). *Chem.* [f. GLUC-IC + -ATE^4.] A salt of glucic acid.

1840 [see GLUCIC].

glucic ('gl(j)u:sɪk), *a. Chem.* [a. F. *glucique*, f. Gr. γλυκ-ύς sweet: see -IC.

In this word, as in *glucina, glucinum, glucose*, etc., terms of chemistry chiefly formed in Fr. in the 19th and the latter part of the 18th c., the Gr. υ is abnormally represented by *u*, instead of by *y*. Littré in his Dict. substitutes *glyc-* for *gluc-* in these words (cf. also GLUCINA, quot. 1819); but the proposed correction has not found acceptance among either French or English chemists.]

In *glucic acid*, an acid obtained by the action of alkalis or acids on glucose.

1840 *Turner's Elem. Chem.* (ed. 6) III. 981 By the formation of glucic acid, 1 eq. of sugar disappears for each eq. of lime, and the molasses then contain glucate of lime. **1859** *Fownes' Man. Chem.* 354 Glucic acid is very soluble and deliquescent, has a sour taste, and acid reaction.

glucina (gl(j)u:'saɪnə). *Chem.* Formerly also **glucine, glycine.** [Latinized form of F. *glucine*, (Vauquelin, 1798), f. Gr. γλυκ-ύς sweet (some of the salts of glucina having a sweet taste): see note s.v. GLUCIC. For the ending *-a*, cf. *magnesia, soda*, etc.] The oxide of glucinum or beryllium, otherwise called BERYLLIA.

1800 tr. *Lagrange's Chem.* I. 157 Glucine. **1807** T. THOMSON *Chem.* II. 72 The discovery of a new earth, to which Vauquelin and his associates gave the name of glucina. **1819** REES *Cycl.*, *Glycine, Glucine.* **1831** T. P. JONES *Convers. Chem.* xvii. 172 Glucina or glucine. **1884** F. J. BRITTEN *Watch & Clockm.* 215 The Crystoberyl is an aluminate of glucina.

glucinum (gl(j)u:'saɪnəm). *Chem.* Also **glucinium.** [quasi-L., f. GLUCINA; q.v.

In 1808 Davy suggested *glucium* as the name for the still hypothetical metal: see quot. s.v. ALUMIUM.]

A white metal obtained from beryl. Also called BERYLLIUM. Symbol Be or Gl.

1812 SIR. H. DAVY *Chem. Philos.* 358 Glucina is a compound of a peculiar metallic substance, which may be called glucinum, and oxygene. **1838** *Penny Cycl.* XI. 277/1 *Glucinium*, the metallic base of an earth or oxide (Glucina) discovered by Vauquelin. **1883** A. H. CHURCH *Prec. Stones* v. 42 The fluorides of aluminium and glucinum have been made to yield distinct chrystals of chrysoberyl.

gluck (glʌk), *sb.* [echoic: cf. GLUG *sb.*^{2}] An inarticulate sound supposed to be expressed by this spelling. So with reduplication **gluck-gluck.**

1880 *Chamb. Jrnl.* No. 202. 635 It is as when we pour liquid from a full bottle; at first it runs intermittently, with a 'gluk-gluk'. **1892** *Sportsman* 9 July 8/1 A clatter of knives and forks on plates . . a 'gluck-gluck' of poured out drinks, and the merry laughter of the lunchers. **1894** HALL CAINE *Manxman* 113 The swish of the scythe . . the gluck of the wheels of the cart.

gluck (glʌk), *v.* [echoic: cf. GLUG *v.*] *intr.* To make a sound rendered by 'gluck'.

1898 *Blackw. Mag.* Jan. 19 The blood glucked at the thrapple.

Hence **'glucking** *vbl. sb.* and *ppl. a.*

1847 LEICHHARDT *Overland Exped.* ii. 29 The glucking bird—by which name, in consequence of its note, the bird may be distinguished—was heard through the night. **1860** TYNDALL *Glac.* I. xvii. 120 A mellow glucking sound . . continued long afterwards.

gluco- ('gl(j)u:kəʊ), before a vowel also **gluc-**, used as comb. form of Gr. γλυκ-ύς sweet (see GLYCO- and note s.v. GLUCIC *a.*), and of GLUCOSE in the designation of: (*a*) substances containing, related to, obtained from, or producing glucose, or affecting its metabolism; (*b*) processes affecting the metabolism of glucose. Also, in some terms not now widely used, = GLYCO-. **,gluco-a'scorbic** *a.*, in *gluco-ascorbic acid*, a compound, $C_7H_{10}O_7$, related to ascorbic acid; **gluco'corticoid** *Biochem.*, any of the steroid hormones produced in the adrenal cortex which are esp. concerned in carbohydrate metabolism; **gluco'heptose** [a. G. *glucoheptose* (E. Fischer 1890, in *Ber. d. Deut. Chem. Ges.* XXIII. 934)], any heptose derived from glucose; **glu'colysis** *Biochem.*, the metabolic breakdown of glucose to pyruvic acid or lactic acid; glycolysis in which glucose is the starting point; **,gluconeo'genesis** *Biochem.*, the metabolic formation of glucose from non-carbohydrate precursors, esp. from proteins; hence **,gluconeoge'netic, -'genic** *adjs.*; †**gluco'proteid**, = *glycoprotein*; **gluco'protein** [ad. F. *glucoprotéine* (P. Schutzenburger 1879, in *Ann. de Chim. et de Phys.* 5th Ser. XVI. 365)], †(*a*) any of various amino acids or mixtures of amino acids to which were ascribed the empirical formula $C_nH_{2n}N_2O_4$, where *n* is between 6 and 12 (*obs.*); (*b*) = *glycoprotein*; **,glucosa'ccharic** *a.*, in *glucosaccharic acid*, the saccharic acid obtained by the oxidation of glucose; **glu'cosazone** [see OSAZONE], the osazone derived from glucose, as well as from fructose and mannose; **'glucosone** [ad. G. *glucoson* (E. Fischer 1889, in *Ber. d. Deut. Chem. Ges.* XXII. 87): see OSONE], the osone derived from glucose, as well as from fructose and mannose; **glucova'nillin** [a. G. *glucovanillin* (Haarmann & Reimer 1883, in *Deutsches Reich Pat.* 279,992)], a glucoside, $C_{14}H_{18}O_8$, of vanillin which has been isolated from several plants.

1934 D. K. BAIRD et al. in *Jrnl. Chem. Soc.* 62 We have also described improved methods for the preparation of gluco-ascorbic acid (3-keto-*d*-glucoheptonofurano-lactone). **1967** CANTARON & SCHEPARTZ *Biochem.* (ed. 4) xxv. 667 Although scurvy-like manifestations are produced in mice and rats . . by glucoascorbic acid, this condition is not cured by administration of ascorbic acid. **1950** E. H. VENNING in E. S. Gordon *Symposium Steroid Hormones* 98 Certain compounds . . will cause an increase in liver glycogen. These substances will be referred to as glucocorticoids, as they appear to be intimately associated with the regulation of carbohydrate metabolism. **1970** R. W. McGILVERY *Biochem.* xxiii. 565 The most active of the glucocorticoids in humans is cortisol, or hydrocortisone. **1890** *Jrnl. Chem. Soc.* LVIII. I. 599 Glucoheptose.. crystallises from water in beautiful tables which melt at about 190° with decomposition. **1963** K. MAYER tr. *Staněk's Monosaccharides* ii. 47 Fischer defined the heptose obtained from D-glucose by the cyanohydrin synthesis as D-glucoheptose. **1932** Glucolysis [see FRUCTOLYSIS]. **1943** *Thorpe's Dict. Appl. Chem.* (ed. 4) VI. 74/1 'Glucolysis' has been the name given to the phenomenon of glucose breakdown to lactic acid. **1912** *Jrnl. Biol. Chem.* XII. 511 (*heading*) The chemistry of gluconeogenesis. I. The quantitative conversion of propionic acid into glucose. **1968** PASSMORE & ROBSON *Compan. Med. Studies* I. xxxi. 4/2 If the dietary carbohydrate intake is insufficient, gluconeogenesis helps to replenish the stores of liver glycogen. **1961** WEBSTER, Gluconeogenetic. **1969** PONTREMOLI & GRAZI in Florkin & Stotz *Comprehensive Biochem.* XVII. iv. 184 At one time, the reductive carboxylation of pyruvic acid.. had been assigned a key role in the gluconeogenetic process. **1954** A. WHITE et al. *Princ. Biochem.* xvii. 441 Gluconeogenic materials include many of the amino acids. **1894** *Jrnl. Chem. Soc.* LXVI. I. 310 A knowledge of glucoproteïds (proteïds from which sugar is obtainable by hydrolytic agents) is therefore of practical importance. **1900** *Ibid.* LXXVIII. I. 478 Galactosamine.. was obtained as a decomposition product of the glucoproteid of the albuminous gland of the frog. **1879** *Ibid.* XXXVI. 545 For these latter bodies, the name glucoproteins has been adopted, on account of their sweet taste. **1906** *Ibid.* XC. I. 776 His [*sc.* Lepierre's] so-called 'α-glucoproteins' are mixtures of monoamino-acids. **1911** J. A. MANDEL tr. *Hammarsten's Text-bk. Physiol. Chem.* (ed. 6) iii. 163 (*heading*) Glycoproteins (glucoproteins). **1963** E. G. YOUNG in Florkin & Stotz *Comprehensive Biochem.* VII. i. 10 The class was initially known as the gluco- or glycoproteins. **1941** *Brit. Chem. Abstr.* A. II. 350 (*heading*) Grignard synthesis of glucosaccharic acid from *l*-arabinose. **1964** N. G. CLARK *Mod. Org. Chem.* xvi. 316 Somewhat more vigorous oxidation employing aqueous nitric acid brings about the additional oxidation of the primary alcohol group, resulting in a tetrahydroxy-dicarboxylic acid, or saccharic acid; glucose gives glucosaccharic acid. **1886** *Jrnl. Chem. Soc.* L. 934 Isoglucosamine.. is obtained by treating.. phenylglucosazone.. with.. zinc-dust and.. acetic acid. It is kept at a temperature of 50°, and vigorously shaken until the glucosazone is entirely dissolved. **1964** N. G. CLARK *Mod. Org. Chem.* xvi. 319 Additional reactions gave rise to glucosazone. **1889** *Jrnl. Chem. Soc.* LVI. 484 The author [*sc.* E. Fischer] proposes 'osone' as a general term for compounds of the type of oxyglucose, and throughout the paper refers to this compound as glucosone. **1956** *Science* 27 July 171/3 Crude extracts of *Iridophycus* were also capable of forming glucosone and galactosone from the corresponding sugars. **1884** *Jrnl. Chem. Soc.* XLVI. 1343 When coniferin is oxidised with aqueous chromic acid, it is converted into glucovanillin. **1966** *McGraw-Hill Encycl. Sci. & Technol.* VI. 224/2 Vanillin is the aromatic principle of commercial vanilla extract, and is released from the glucoside (glucovanillin) by enzymatic hydrolysis during curing of vanilla beans.

glucogene, -genic: see GLYCOGEN, -GENIC.

gluconate ('gl(j)uːkəneɪt). *Chem.* [f. GLUCONIC (ACID + -ATE[4].] A salt or ester of gluconic acid; ***calcium gluconate***, an odourless, tasteless, water-soluble, crystalline or granular substance, used therapeutically as a source of calcium for the body.

1884 *Jrnl. Chem. Soc.* XLVI. 424 Calcium gluconate, $(C_6H_{11}O_7)_2Ca + H_2O$, crystallises in microscopic needles. **1915** *Jrnl. Amer. Chem. Soc.* XXXVII. 355 The new, normal β-lactone has been obtained both from free *d*-gluconic acid and from ethyl *d*-gluconate. **1938** *Thorpe's Dict. Appl. Chem.* (ed. 4) II. 297/1 Calcium gluconate, being soluble, practically tasteless, and non-irritating to tissues, is being increasingly used in medicine. **1963** FLORKIN & STOTZ *Comprehensive Biochem.* V. ii. 73 Ferrous gluconate.. is used in the treatment of iron-deficiency anaemia, and calcium gluconate can be given in cases of calcium deficiency.

gluconic acid (gl(j)uː'kɒnɪk). *Chem.* [tr. G. *gluconsäure* gluconic acid (Hlasiwetz & Habermann 1870, in *Ann. d. Chem. und Pharm.* CLV. 125), f. GLUC(O + -ONIC.] The acid derived from glucose by oxidation of the aldehyde group to a carboxyl group.

1871 *Jrnl. Chem. Soc.* XXIV. 547 Hlasiwetz.. considers gluconic acid to be bibasic. **1929** *Industr. & Engin. Chem.* XXI. 1198 (*heading*) Semi-plant production of gluconic acid by mold fermentation. **1963** E. PERCIVAL in Florkin & Stotz *Comprehensive Biochem.* V. ii. 73 Gluconic acid is important in the pharmaceutical, food, animal feeding stuffs and general chemical industries. **1970** J. F. R. KUCK in C. N. Graymore *Biochem. Eye* iii. 213 The role of gluconic acid, found in the human lens by van Heyningen (1958), is unknown.

glucosamine (gl(j)uː'kəʊzəmiːn, -səmiːn). *Chem.* [f. GLUCO- after GLYCOSAMINE.] Any amino-sugar derived from glucose by substitution of an amino group for a hydroxyl group; *spec.* 2-amino-2-deoxy-D-glucose. Cf. GLYCOSAMINE.

1884 *Jrnl. Chem. Soc.* XLVI. 724 G. Ledderhose gave the name glucosamine hydrochloride to a crystalline substance, $C_6H_{13}NO_5$, HCl, obtained by boiling chitin with concentrated hydrochloric acid. **1956** [see GALACTOSAMINE]. **1957** W. PIGMAN *Carbohydrates* viii. 465 The *N*-methyl derivative of L-glucosamine (the enantiomorph of the common D-glucosamine) has been isolated from the degradation product of streptomycin. **1959** H. S. GOLDBERG *Antibiotics* ii. 140 The third moiety in the hydrolyzates of kanamycin B yields a ninhydrin-positive reducing test, but it is not 6-glucosamine present in kanamycin itself. **1967** CANTAROW & SCHEPARTZ *Biochem.* (ed. 4) ii. 21 Glucosamine, also called 'chitosamine', is the basic unit in the polysaccharide, chitin, which forms part of the integument of arthropods. **1969** [see GALACTOSAMINE].

glucosan ('gl(j)uːkəsæn). *Chem.* [ad. F. *glucosane* (A. Gélis 1860, in *Compt. Rend.* LI. 333), f. GLUCOSE.] **a.** Any of several isomeric anhydrides, $C_6H_{10}O_5$, of glucose.

1862 H. WATTS tr. *Gmelin's Hand-bk. Chem.* XV. 329 Glucose, dried between 100° and 110°, gives off water at 170°, becoming coloured at the same time, and is converted into glucosan. **1950** G. M. DYSON *Man. Org. Chem.* x. 805 An enquiry into.. the structure of the remaining product led to the recognition of a number of isomeric glucosans, for it appears that glucose can lose one molecule of water in almost every conceivable way. **1963** E. PERCIVAL in Florkin & Stotz *Comprehensive Biochem.* V. i. 54 The constitution of β-glucosan.. was established by reaction with periodate.

b. Any polysaccharide composed chiefly of glucose residues.

1925 *Jrnl. Chem. Soc.* CXXVIII. I. 233 Brigl's observation.. that Pictet's supposed method of preparation of unimolecular α-glucosan.. yields polymeric glucosans is confirmed. **1948** R. J. McILROY *Chem. Polysaccharides* iv. 37 In addition to the above mannan, a glucosan has been isolated from bakers' yeast. It has molecular weight 6,500, and consists of glucopyranose units. **1966** P. McDONALD et al. *Anim. Nutrition* ii. 17 Cellulose is a glucosan and is the most abundant plant constituent.

glucose ('gl(j)uːkəʊs). *Chem.* Also **glycose**. [First formed as F. *glucose* (Dumas 1838, in *Compt. Rend.* VII. 109); cf. Gr. γλυκ-ύς sweet and -OSE[2].] **1. a.** One of the aldo-hexoses, $CHO(CHOH)_4CH_2OH$, obtainable as dextro- and lævo-rotatory enantiomorphs and as a racemic mixture; *spec.* the dextro-rotatory form (D-*glucose*, *dextrose*, *grape-sugar*), a white or colourless sweet-tasting crystalline solid which is the commonest sugar in nature; it is important in the metabolism of almost all organisms and occurs naturally in the free state, as in sweet fruit juices and in the blood, and in combination, as in glucosides, in some oligosaccharides (such as sucrose), and in some polysaccharides (such as cellulose, starch, and glycogen, all of which are composed wholly of glucose residues).

In chemical terms glucose is the aldo-hexose in which the hydroxyl groups attached to the second, fourth, and fifth carbon atoms can be regarded as being on the same side of the molecule when this is represented as a linear structure.

1840 *Turner's Elem. Chem.* (ed. 6) III. 969 Although the identity of the different kinds of sugar classed under the name of grape sugar or glucose be generally admitted. **1844** HOBLYN *Dict. Med.*, *Glucose*, another name for starch sugar, diabetic sugar, or the sugar of fruits. **1847** LEWES *Hist. Philos.* (1867) II. 361 The crystals of sugar have to be decomposed and the sugar transformed into glucose. **1880** *Times* 5 Oct. 4/6 Brewers do not disdain the use of glucose. **1938** M. L. WOLFROM in H. Gilman *Org. Chem.* II. xvi. 1400 The central compound of the carbohydrates is *d*-glucose. **1951** A. GROLLMAN *Pharmacol. & Therapeutics* xxvi. 572 In diabetic animals and patients, the injection of insulin is followed by.. the disappearance of glucose and acetone bodies from the urine. **1959** *Chambers's Encycl.* III. 92/2 Although fructose is laevorotatory, it is configurationally related to dextrorotatory and not to laevorotatory glucose. **1965** BELL & COOMBE tr. *Strasburger's Textbk. Bot.* (new ed.) I. 19 Soluble carbohydrates, especially the disaccharides sucrose and maltose and the monosaccharides glucose and fructose, are the most frequent components of the cell sap. **1968** PASSMORE & ROBSON *Compan. Med. Stud.* I. ix. 13/1 There is a continual uptake of glucose from the blood by many organs, notably the brain, which probably cannot utilize other sources of energy.

†**b.** Any of the hexoses, $C_6H_{12}O_6$, (or more broadly, any monosaccharide), including dextrose along with fructose, galactose, etc. *Obs.*

[**1859** M. BERTHELOT in *Ann. de Chim. et de Phys.* 3me Sér. LV. 270 Le nom de *glucose*, appliqué jadis au sucre de raisin seulement, désigne aujourd'hui toute une série de sucres distincts;.. séchés à 110 degrés, ils sont isomères et répondent à la formule $C^{12}H^{12}O^{12}$. Tels sont le glucose de raisin, le glucose de malt, le glucose de fruits lévogyre, le glucose lactique.] **1866** H. E. ROSCOE *Less. Elem. Chem.* xxxvii. 325 Dilute acids convert lactose into a peculiar glucose, called galactose. **1887** *Encycl. Brit.* XXII. 623/1 'Sugar' is now a collective term for two chemical genera named saccharoses (all $C_{12}H_{22}O_{11}$) and glucoses (all $C_6H_{12}O_6$). **1889** G. M'GOWAN tr. *Bernthsen's Org. Chem.* 285 The glucoses result.. from the carbohydrates of the cane sugar and starch groups by the taking up of water. **1911** *Encycl. Brit.* XXVI. 33/1 It is convenient to divide the sugars into two main groups: monosaccharoses (formerly glucoses) and disaccharoses (formerly saccharoses).

2. A non-crystallizable colourless or yellowish brown syrup containing glucose (dextrose), maltose, dextrin, and water and obtained by the incomplete hydrolysis of starch. Also called ***glucose syrup, starch syrup***, etc.

1852 T. R. BETTON tr. *Regnault's Elem. Chem.* II. IV. 488 Glucose is found in commerce under three different forms: syrup of fecula, glucose in mass, and granulated glucose... Glucose, in syrup or in bulk, is used in the manufacture of beer and alcohol. **1885** E. R. SOUTHBY *Syst. Handbk. Pract. Brewing* (ed. 2) xv. 222 There is a liquid form of glucose known amongst other names as glucose syrup, which when well refined is a very good brewing material. **1891** *B'ham. Instit. Mag.* Nov. 163 Glucose syrups. **1906** THRESH & PORTER *Preservatives in Food* xxxi. 396 It was proved at Quarter Sessions that glucose was composed of 40 per cent. destrose, 40 per cent. dextrine, and 20 per cent. water,.. and that glucose was not injurious to health, but was used to prevent the marmalade crystallizing. **1950** G. H. RAUCH *Jam Manuf.* iii. 50 The addition of glucose gives jam a brighter appearance. **1963** TRIEBOLD & AURAND *Food Composition & Anal.* v. 211 Some of the syrup sold as commercial glucose is colored by the addition of other syrups and materials.

3. *attrib.* and *Comb.*, as ***glucose ferment, syrup*** (see 2), ***tablet***; **glucose phosphate**, any of the phosphoric acid esters of glucose; esp. either of two monophosphates, $C_6H_{11}O_5(O{\cdot}PO_3H_2)$, important in carbohydrate metabolism in animals and plants: (*a*) ***glucose-6-phosphate***, the compound formed by the reaction of glucose with adenosine triphosphate in the first stage in the metabolism of glucose; (*b*) ***glucose-1-phosphate***, the compound formed from glucose-6-phosphate in the synthesis of polysaccharides; **glucose tolerance test**, a test for abnormalities in carbohydrate metabolism, esp. diabetes, in which glucose is given orally after a period of fasting and the blood sugar measured at intervals afterwards, the results being depicted graphically as a ***glucose tolerance curve***.

1885 *Syd. Soc. Lex.*, *Glucose ferment*, the ferment in the animal body which is instrumental in the conversion of glycogen into glucose. **1912** E. F. ARMSTRONG *Simple Carbohydrates & Glucosides* (ed. 2) 145 (*heading*) References to glucose phosphates. **1938** A. L. RAYMOND in H. Gilman *Org. Chem.* II. xvii. 1479 In this manner there have been synthesized the Robison ester.. as well as glucose-1-, 3-, 4-, and 5-phosphates, leaving only the 2-phosphate unknown in the glucose series. **1963** H. BURN *Drugs, Med. & Man* (ed. 2) xiv. 146 One of the first steps in using glucose within the cell is its conversion into a glucose-phosphate combination. **1964** A. WHITE et al. *Princ. Biochem.* (ed. 3) xx. 366 In the cells of liver, intestine, and kidney only, glucose 6-phosphate may be hydrolyzed, releasing glucose to the environment. **1965** BELL & COOMBE tr. *Strasburger's Textbk. Bot.* (new ed.) II. 266 The formation of.. starch in the living cell appears to begin not from α-glucose itself but from the energy-rich glucose-1-phosphate, which.. is probably the actual substance produced in photosynthesis. **1959** J. BRAINE *Vodi* xiii. 172 He started carrying digestive tablets and glucose tablets. **1923** *Arch. Internal Med.* XXXI. 248 It would be interesting to hear from someone doing frequent glucose tolerance curves how low the reaction may be. *Ibid.* 258 Ohler has reported several cases in which glucose tolerance tests were done three times at intervals of about one year. **1966** *Lancet* 24 Dec. 1377/2 The findings depended on.. the reliability of the glucose-tolerance test in athero-sclerotic patients.

Hence **glu'cosic** *a.* [-IC], of or pertaining to glucose.

1860 *Illustr. Lond. News* 23 June 614/1 On the glucosic fermentation of cane-sugar. **1861** BENTLEY *Man. Bot.* 766 A nitrogenous body playing the part of a glucosic ferment.

glucoside ('gl(j)uːkəsaɪd). *Chem.* Formerly also **glycoside** (now distinguished in sense). [f. GLUCOSE + -IDE.] One of a class of vegetable substances which being treated with dilute acids or alkalis, or subjected to the action of ferments, are resolved into a sugar and some other substance. Now usu. restricted to mean: a GLYCOSIDE which on hydrolysis gives glucose.

The earliest known example is as G. *glucosid* (W. Mayer 1854, in *Ann. d. Chem. u. Pharm.* XCII. 125), but it is not clear whether he was the first to use the word; the F. word *glucosamide* was coined in 1852 with the same meaning (A. Laurent in *Ann. de Chim. et de Phys.* XXXVI. 333). For examples of the form *glycoside* see GLYCOSIDE.

1855 W. MAYER in *Chem. Gaz.* 15 Mar. 113 It appeared probable that this resin might consist essentially of a glucoside. **1857** W. A. MILLER *Elem. Chem.* III. vii. 511 (*heading*) Glucosides, or compounds which contain glucose. **1866** ODLING *Anim. Chem.* 94 Tannin is a glucoside of gallic acid. **1878** KINGZETT *Anim. Chem.* 32 All glucosides yield sugar, and many starches also yield sugar. **1889** G. M'GOWAN tr. *Bernthsen's Org. Chem.* 512 As glucosides are designated a series of vegetable substances which are so broken up by alkalies, acids, or ferments, that one of the products of this decomposition is a glucose, usually grape sugar. **1895** *Naturalist* 23 Amygdalin, which is the glucoside of the oil of bitter almonds. **1910** *Encycl. Brit.* XII. 142/1 Although glucose is the commonest sugar present in glucosides, many are known which yield rhamnose or iso-dulcite; these may be termed pentosides. **1930** [see GLYCOSIDE 2]. **1932** I. D. GARARD *Introd. Org. Chem.* x. 150 The most important glucosides are natural products. The sugar is generally but not always glucose. **1957** *Encycl. Brit.* X. 444/1 The complex sugars (polysaccharides) may.. be regarded as glucosides since they consist of ethers formed from two or more simple sugars. **1967** I. L. FINAR *Org. Chem.* (ed. 5) I. xviii. 486 The hemiacetol form (lactol) of a sugar [can] react with a molecule of an alcohol to form the acetal derivative, which is known under the generic name of glycoside; those of glucose are known as glucosides; of fructose, fructosides, etc.

Hence **gluco'sidal, -ic** *adjs.*, characteristic of a glucoside or glucosides; also, glycosidic; ***glucosidic bond*** or ***linkage*** = ***glycosidic linkage***.

1924 *Chem. Abstr.* 10 Apr. XVIII. 973 Acid hydrolysis removed the glucosidic Me group in addn. to the oleyl group. **1927** *Jrnl. Biol. Chem.* LXXIV. 787 Certain substances of glucosidic nature.. exhibit a characteristic cardiac or so called digitalis action. **1929** R. A. GORTNER *Outl. Biochem.* xxiii. 513 The linkage between the glucuronic acid and the benzoic acid is not a glucosidal linkage, for the aldehyde group is still free. **1954** A. WHITE et al. *Princ. Biochem.* xvii. 393 Amylose is a linear polysaccharide comprising glucose units linked to each other in a repeating fashion by an α-1, 4-glucosidic bond. **1963** R. R. A. HIGHAM *Handbk. Papermaking* ii. 33 The glucosidic chain linkages constituting the cellulose formation.

glucupicron: see GLYCYPICRON.

glucuronate (gl(j)uːˈkjʊərəʊneɪt). *Chem.* [f. next + -ATE⁴.] A salt or ester of glucuronic acid.

1904 J. A. MANDEL tr. *Hammarsten's Text-bk. Physiol. Chem.* (ed. 4) xv. 522 According to the body with which they are conjugated, the glucuronates show different behavior. **1966** G. J. DUTTON *Glucuronic Acid* iii. 261 A growing weight of evidence..suggests that administration of glucuronate..assists the excretion, or decreases the toxicity, of certain compounds.

glucuronic (gl(j)uːkjʊˈrɒnɪk), *a.* *Chem.* [f. GLUCO- after GLYCURONIC *a.*] ***glucuronic acid***: the uronic acid derived from glucose; cf. GLYCURONIC *a.*

1909 *Cent. Dict.* Suppl., *Glucuronic*, same as glycuronic. **1911** *Encycl. Brit.* XXIII. 969/2 Sodium amalgam reduces it [*sc.* saccharic acid] to glucuronic acid, $C_6H_{10}O_7$ or $OHC[CH{\cdot}OH]_4CO_2H$. **1955** *Sci. News Let.* 2 July 6/3 The aspirin apparently acts by combining, or conjugating, with glucuronic acid. **1966** G. J. DUTTON *Glucuronic Acid* p. xv, The compound now known as glucuronic acid was first described as a curious sugar acid occurring in the urine conjugated with certain drugs. This led to it being christened 'glykuronsaüre' by Schmiedeberg & Meyer.

glucuronide (gl(j)uːˈkjʊərəʊnaɪd). *Chem.* [f. prec. + -IDE.] Any glycosidic compound formed by glucuronic acid.

1934 *Chem. Abstr.* XXVIII. 184 A specific enzyme may.. be assumed for the cleavage of glucuronides. **1948** W. PIGMAN *Chem. Carbohydrates* xi. 509 Many phenols and alcohols when injected into animals are detoxified by conjugation as glucuronides. **1967** CANTAROW & SCHEPARTZ *Biochem.* (ed. 4) ii. 21 Glucuronic acid is found in the urine, conjugated (as a glucuronide) to foreign substances.

glucuronoside (gl(j)uːkjʊˈrɒnəʊsaɪd). *Chem.* [f. as prec. + -OSIDE.] = prec.

1934 E. F. & K. F. ARMSTRONG *Carbohydrates* (ed. 5) vi. 67 Menthol glucuronate is hydrolysed by emulsin, and therefore is a β-glucuronoside. **1963** E. PERCIVAL in Florkin & Stotz *Comprehensive Biochem.* V. ii. 74 A molecule of water is eliminated in the glucuronoside formation.

gluder, Sc. var. of GLOTHER *v.*, *Obs.*, to flatter.

glue (gl(j)uː), *sb.* Forms: 4–5 glu, 4–8 glew(e, (4 glyu, 5 glowe, gluwe, glewȝ, 6 gleu), 4– glue. [ad. OF. *glu* (sense 1), Pr. *glut*:—late L. *glūt-em*, *glūs* glue.]

†**1.** Bird-lime. Also *fig. Obs.*

c **1380** WYCLIF *Serm.* Sel. Wks. I. 223 Flee we her sentence as heresie or fendis glewe. *c* **1440** *Promp. Parv.* 200/1 Glu, of festynge, *viscus*. **1480** CAXTON *Chron. Eng.* xcv. (1482) 75 They made engyns with glew of nettes. **1704** *Collect. Voy.* (Churchill) III. 26/1 Who..take so many [birds] with Glue or Nets.

2. A hard, brittle, brownish gelatin, obtained by boiling the hides and hoofs of animals to a jelly; when gently heated with water, it is used as a cement for uniting substances. ***fish-glue*** (see FISH *sb.*¹ 7). ***Dutch*** or ***Flanders glue***: a very fine kind of glue. ***lip*** or ***mouth-glue***: a compound of glue and sugar, which can be used by moistening with the tongue.

c **1400** *Lanfranc's Cirurg.* 135 As it were two bordis weren ioyned togidere with cole or with glu. **1456** *Tintinhull Churchw. Acc.* (Som. Rec. Soc.) 187 It. in gluwe ad idem opus [bookbinding]..iiijᵈ. *c* **1520** *Mem. Ripon* (Surtees) III. 206 Item pro j lib. le glew, 3*d.* **1594** PLAT *Jewell-ho.* I. 30 Dippe your hande in molten glewe. **1658** A. FOX *Wurtz' Surg.* II. xxvi. 175 Just as glue is betwixt two boards to hold them fast together. **1712** tr. *Pomet's Hist. Drugs* I. 180 Leaving it to dry..to the Consistence of Flanders Glue. **1768–74** TUCKER *Lt. Nat.* (1852) II. 86 Awkward joinings by seams, tenons, nails, and glues, betraying the imperfections of their workman to the eye. **1800** tr. *Lagrange's Chem.* II. 293 Every substance..an infusion of which can precipitate animal glue, possesses a tanning property. **1846** G. E. DAY tr. *Simon's Anim. Chem.* II. 377 An odour of burned horn or glue.

3. a. Used loosely for any substance that serves as a cement. ***marine glue*** (see quot. 1876).

1382 WYCLIF *Isa.* xli. 7 Seiende to the glyu, It is good. *c* **1425** *Seven Sag.* (P.) 1232 He sette a deppe caudron of bras, A manere of glowe he dyde thare-inne. *c* **1477** CAXTON *Jason* 81 And wyth this glue thou shalt enoynte the mosels of these two meruayllous booles. **1617** MARKHAM *Caval.* VI. Ded., Whilest the glew of Lime and Simant shall knit stones together, so long in our house will be held their memories. **1731** ARBUTHNOT *Aliments* (1735) 192 The Flowers of Grains, mix'd with Water, will make a sort of Glue. **1876** PREECE & SIVEWRIGHT *Telegraphy* 15 *note*, The marine glue, patented by Jeffrey in 1842, is formed by dissolving one pound of caoutchouc in four gallons of naphtha... Two parts of shellac are then added to one part of this mixture.

†**b.** = GUM. Also ***cherry-tree***, ***plum-tree glue***.

1683 SALMON *Doron Med.* I. 233 Cherry-tree, or Plum-tree Glew. **1802** PALEY *Nat. Theol.* xix. (ed. 2) 357 The glue or gum, being passed through these minute apertures, forms hairs of almost imperceptible fineness.

†**c.** Bitumen, pitch. *Obs.*

1382 WYCLIF *Gen.* vi. 14 With ynne and with oute thow shalt diȝten it [the ark] with glew. **1398** TREVISA *Barth. De P.R.* xv. xxii. (Tollem. MS.), Also þere [in Babylon] was a toure, þe mater þerof was brent tyll made of glewe. *Ibid.* XVI. xix. (1495) 559 Glewe is slymy gleue of the erth [*Bitumen est terra a gleba limosa*].

†**d.** = *bee-glue* (see BEE 7): tr. L. *gluten*. *Obs.*

1694 ADDISON *Virgil* Misc. Wks. 1726 I. 16 For this they hoard up glew. **1697** DRYDEN *Virg. Georg.* IV. 55 Th' industrious Kind..with their Stores of gather'd Glue, contrive To stop the Vents and Crannies of their Hive.

e. *fig.*

1340 *Ayenb.* 246 He him ioineþ to god be a glu of loue. **1547–64** BAULDWIN *Mor. Philos.* (Palfr.) 48 Life is nothing else but as it were a glue, which in man fastneth the soule and body together. **1589** R. BRUCE *Serm.* (1843) 154 Love is that celestial glue that conjoins all the faithful members in the unity of one mysticall body. **1608** HIERON *Wks.* I. 717/2 Dissolue this glue, by which my affections are so close fastned vnto those earthly things. *a* **1659** BP. BROWNRIG *Serm.* (1674) II. xvi. 205 Charity..'tis the glew and cement of the World. **1858** LOWELL *Amer. Tract Soc.* Prose Wks. 1890 V. 9 We Americans are very fond of this glue of compromise.

4. *Soap-making.* A name for the condition of soap at an early stage of its manufacture (see quot.).

1885 W. L. CARPENTER *Soap & Candles* 167 Practice alone will enable the operator to judge of the completion of this first operation, called 'pasting' (French *empâtage*)..the soap is then said to be..in a 'hitch' or 'glue'.

5. *attrib.* and *Comb.* **a.** simple attributive, as ***glue-bandage***, ***-brush***, ***-can***, ***-cliché***, ***-kettle***, ***-paper***, ***-size***; **b.** objective, as ***glue-boiler***, ***-factor***, ***-maker***. Also ***glue-like*** adj.

1894 *Westm. Gaz.* 29 Jan. 6/2 Wood splints were placed across the bandages and firmly wrapped in lint, the whole being covered by a *glue bandage. **1755** JOHNSON, **Glue-boiler*, one whose trade is to make glue. **1847** SMEATON *Builder's Man.* 85 The glue..does not drop from the *glue-brush as water or oil. **1889** *Anthony's Photogr. Bull.* II. 367 The manufacture of the *glue clichés is now an easy matter. **1880** *Pl. Hints Exam. Needlework* 67 Nets are used by the *glue factors in Bermondsey and Southwark, for drying the glue. **1895** G. M. TUCKER *Com. Speech* 2 A rusty stove surmounted by a *glue-kettle. **1897** *Allbutt's Syst. Med.* II. 514 A thin watery discharge which gradually becomes thick, viscid and *glue-like. **1885** *Syd. Soc. Lex.* s.v., Diseases of *glue-makers. **1825** J. NICHOLSON *Operat. Mechanic* 475 He ..forcibly presses the *glue-paper against it.

6. Special comb.: **glue-plant**, a sea-weed, *Plocaria tenax* (*Syd. Soc. Lex.* 1885); **glue-sniffer**, a person who inhales the fumes of plastic cement for their narcotic effects; so **glue-sniff** *v. intr.*, **glue-sniffing** *vbl. sb.*; **glue-stock**, hides used as material for glue; **glue-water**, water in which glue has been dissolved. Also GLUE-POT.

1963 *New Society* 20 June 14/1 A new threat to teen-age stability..is glue-sniffing, the deliberate inhaling of the fumes from plastic cement. *Ibid.* 14/2 The glue sniffers.. frequently fall asleep in class. **1968** *Daily Colonist* (Victoria, B.C.) 6 Oct. 21/1 That particular glue-sniffer told police his story in Los Angeles, but it could just as easily have been in any police department in Greater Victoria. **1971** E. E. LANDY *Underground Dict.* 90 *Glue sniff* v., inhale model-airplane glue... Glue sniffing is regarded as an adolescent type of drug abuse, but it causes organic brain damage, and it can cause liver, kidney and bone-marrow damage. Eventually most glue sniffers outgrow glue and go to more adult-type drugs such as marijuana, [etc.]. **1971** J. DRUMMOND *Farewell Party* xxv. 131 One of those red brick boxes..with a nice view of the glue factory... A glue-sniffer could get high there..just by holding his breath. **1885** C. T. DAVIS *Leather* i. 55 All stag, tainted, and badly scored.. hides..must go at two-thirds price, unless they are badly damaged, when they are classed as *glue stock. **1683** PETTUS *Fleta Min.* I. (1686) 20 Moisten them [the Ashes] with strong-Beer..or with a *Glew-water.

glue (gl(j)uː), *v.* Forms: 3 glywe-n, 4 gluwe, 4–8 glew(e, 5 glu-yn, glw-yn, glyewe, 6– glue. Also *pa. pple.* 4 i-glewed, y-glywed. [f. the sb. Cf. F. *gluer* (from 13th c.).]

1. a. *trans.* To join or fasten (together) with glue, or some similar viscous substance. Const. *on* or *upon*, *to* or *unto*. Also with advs., as *on*, *together*, *up*.

13.. *K. Alis.* 6180 A clay they haveth..Therof they makith bour and halle..And wyndowes y-glywed by gynne Never more water no comuth therynne. *c* **1386** CHAUCER *Sqr.'s T.* 174 The hors of bras, þat may nat be remewed, It stant as it were to the ground yglewed. **1412–20** LYDG. *Chron. Troy* I. vi, Theyr iawes togither it shall glyewe. **1535** COVERDALE *Ecclus.* xxii. 7 Who so teacheth a foole, is euen as one that gleweth a potsherde together. **1588** SHAKS. *Tit. A.* II. i. 41 Goe too: haue your Lath glued within your sheath, Till you know better how to handle it. **1680** MORDEN *Geog. Rect.* (1685) 62 Rolls of paper, Cut into long scrowles, and glu'd..together. **1702** W. J. *Bruyn's Voy. Levant* xxxvii. 146 Several Linnen Clothes glew'd upon each other. **1741** MONRO *Anat. Bones* (ed. 3) 290 The Cartilage seems to glew the two Bones together. **1781** COWPER *Charity* 50 The hand ..Was glued to the sword-hilt with Indian gore. **1850** *Ann. Nat. Hist.* Ser. II. V. 284 These globules are probably composed of some tenacious mucus with which to glue the egg to any substance on which it may happen to settle. **1842–59** GWILT *Archit.* (ed. 4) 579 The way in which bodies are glued up together for different purposes..Two boards glued up edge to edge. **1889** J. M. DUNCAN *Lect. Dis. Women* xxviii. (ed. 4) 228 The ovaries and intestines and broad ligaments and parietal pelvic peritoneum became glued together.

†**b.** To involve or entangle in some sticky substance (such as bird-lime), so as to impede or clog free motion (*lit.* and *fig.*). Also, to constipate (the bowels); = GLUTINATE 1 b. *Obs.*

1387 TREVISA *Higden* (Rolls) VI. 301 Þe kynge [Louis] wiste nouȝt how faste he hadde i-glewed hym self. *c* **1440** *Gesta Rom.* xxxi. 117 (Add. MS.) Wherfore his tethe of the oynement were so glewed [L. (ed. Oesterley) *gummo pleni erant*]. **1562** TURNER *Herbal* II. 33 Duckes meat..gleweth or bindeth or maketh fast the bowelles of yong childer. **1603** FLORIO *Montaigne* (1634) 492 Those silly harmlesse beasts indiscreetly..ensnared, glewed..and shackled themselves. **1691** DRYDEN *K. Arthur* III. ii, Heaven's birdlime wraps me round, and glues my wings.

c. ***to glue up***: to seal up as with glue; to shut up tightly. †Also without *up*.

1658 W. SANDERSON *Graphice* 82 Put into a gallon pot certain plaits of clean fine lead..glewing the pot with clean Lome. **1817** COBBETT *Wks.* XXXII. 3 The approaching Session of Parliament will open millions of pairs of eyes, which have been glued up by false alarms for the last twenty-five years. **1853** KANE *Grinnell Exp.* xxx. (1856) 258 We were glued up.

2. *transf.* and *fig.* To cause to adhere closely or firmly; to fix or attach firmly (as if by gluing). Formerly often without explicit reference to the lit. use, esp. in sense: To attach in sympathy or affection. Const. as in 1. Also with *up*.

c **1384** CHAUCER *H. Fame* III. 671 Let men glewe on us the name. **1547** *Homilies* I. *Contention* (1859) 135 We cannot be joined to Christ our Head, except we be glued with concord and charity one to another. **1593** SHAKS. *3 Hen. VI*, II. vi. 5 My Loue and Feare, glew'd many Friends to thee, And now I fall. *a* **1659** BP. BROWNRIG *Serm.* (1674) II. xxv. 314 Prosperity glues us to this life, Afflictions loosen us. **1700** DRYDEN *Fables, Sigism. & Guisc.* 641 She..Then to the heart ador'd devoutly glew'd Her lips. **1758** RUTTY *Spirit. Diary* (ed. 2) 114 Why then so glued to this life? **1770** FOOTE *Lame Lover* II. Wks. 1799 II. 79 With your eyes glew'd close to the key-hole. **1771** SMOLLETT *Humph. Cl.* 13 July, She now began to glue herself to his favour with the grossest adulation. **1821–30** LD. COCKBURN *Mem.* vi. (1874) 336 This single fact glued the whole Tories together. **1826** SCOTT *Woodst.* ix, He glued the huge flagon to his lips. **1853** C. BRONTE *Villette* xiii. (1855) 121 Her ear having been glued to the key-hole. **1884** *World* 20 Aug. 15/2 Our men are taught to pound along automatically, with their left hand glued to their trousers' seams.

3. *intr.* **a.** To stick together in virtue of some inherent property; to adhere. Also *fig.* **b.** To admit of being fastened by glue.

c **1420** *Pallad. on Husb.* I. 66 A roten swerd..tough to glewe ayeyn though hit me delue. **1607** MIDDLETON *Five Gallants* IV. viii, Here be five on's; let's but glue together, why now the world shall not come between us. **1664** EVELYN *Sylva* (1679) 27 It is observ'd that Oak will not easily glue to other Wood. **1701** GREW *Cosm. Sacra* III. ii. 97 The Flesh will glew together, with its own Native Balm. **1885** *Spons' Mechanics' Own Bk.* 131 The wood glues well.

†**4.** *trans.* To daub or smear with glue or other viscous substance. Also with *over*. ? *Obs.*

1382 WYCLIF *Exod.* ii. 3 He tok a ionket of resshen, and glewide it with glewishe cley, and with picche. **1398** TREVISA *Barth. De P.R.* XIX. cxxviii. (1495) 934 The vessell in the whyche Moyses was in was glewed or pytched. **1726** LEONI tr. *Alberti's Archit.* I. 49/2 Swallows..when they build their Nests, first dawb or glue over the beams which are to be the foundation. **1808** J. BARLOW *Columb.* VII. 532 All the tar-beat floor Is clogg'd with spatter'd brains and glued with gore.

glued (gl(j)uːd), *ppl. a.* [f. GLUE *v.* + -ED¹.] **1.** Fastened with or as with glue; also, smeared with glue.

1705 ELSTOB in Hearne *Collect.* 30 Nov. (O.H.S.) I. 108 Were..his glew'd tongue let loose. **1858** *Skyring's Builder's Prices* 59 Glued and mitred slips. **1890** *Anthony's Photogr. Bull.* III. 74 Glued thread is pasted on a piece of heavy cardboard.

2. glued-on, affixed by means of glue; *fig.* of literary devices, effects, etc.: carelessly superimposed and not integrated with the body of the work; **glued-up** *fig.*, applied to a medley of scenes or incidents with little apparent connection or unity.

1906 *Westm. Gaz.* 15 Feb. 2/3 What the Americans call a 'glued-up' or nailed-up drama. *Ibid.* 16 Sept. 3/2 To avoid auxiliary complications and eschew 'glued-on' comic relief. **1969** *Jane's Freight Containers 1968–69* 482/2 Covered on both sides with glued-on aluminium alloy panels.

glueily (ˈgl(j)uːɪlɪ), *adv.* Also **gluily**. [f. GLUEY *a.* + -LY².] In a gluey manner.

1925 F. M. FORD *No More Parades* i. 37 His very thick soles moved gluily and came up after suction. **1928** A. HUXLEY *Point Counter Point* ii. 31 The great Pongileoni glueily kissed his flute.

ˈ**glue-pot. 1.** A pot in which glue is melted by the heat of water in an outer vessel.

1483 *Cath. Angl.* 160/1 A Glew pott, *glutinarium*. **1599** B. JONSON *Ev. Man out of Hum.* V. iv, I thinke thou dost Varnish thy face with the fat on't, it lookes so like a Glew-pot. *a* **1634** RANDOLPH *Muse's Looking-gl.* III. ii, He, with the pegs of amity and concord, (As with the glue-pot of good government) Joints 'em together. **1678** MOXON *Mech. Exerc.* I. 102 Pour it into your Glew-pot to use, but let your Glew-pot be very clean. *Mod.* Put the glue-pot on the fire at once.

2. A patch of wet or muddy ground in which one 'sticks'. *colloq.*

1892 *Daily News* (Morris), The Bishop of Manchester.. assures us that no one can possibly understand the difficulties and the troubles of a Colonial..clergyman until he has..struggled through what they used to call 'glue-pots'. **1907** *Daily Chron.* 18 July 7/2 The veriest 'glue-pot' of a wicket. **1916** J. B. COOPER *Coo-oo-ee* x. 137 Was it surprising that in a short time the 'glue pot' no longer bogged the jinker? **1963** *Times* 14 Jan. 3/2 If Cardiff is not a gluepot these two should be able to launch some fine attacks.

gluer ('gl(j)uːə(r)). [f. GLUE *v.* + -ER[1].] One who glues.

1483 *Cath. Angl.* 160/1 A Glewer, *glutinarius.* **1573–80** BARET *Alv.* G 288 A gluer, *glutinator.* **1837** WALSH tr. *Aristoph. Clouds* I. v. 446 A blackguard, a gluer-together of lies.

gluey ('gl(j)uːɪ), *a.* Forms: 4–5 **gluwy**, 6–7 **glewey**, **glewie**, **gluie**, 6–8 **gluy**, (7 **gleiwye**, 8 **gleuwy**), 5–9 **glewy**, 8– **gluey**. [f. GLUE *sb.* + -Y[1].] Resembling glue; having the properties of glue; full of, or smeared with, glue; viscous, glutinous, sticky. In early use: †Bituminous.

1382 WYCLIF *Gen.* xiv. 10 The wodi valei forsothe had manye pyttis of gluwy [*v.r.* glewyche] cley. **1398** TREVISA *Barth. De P.R.* v. lvii. (1495) 172 In the fyrste joynynge of the bones is a maner of glewy and glemy moysture. *c* **1420** *Pallad. on Husb.* I. 75 And loke yf hit [a clod] be glewy, tough to trete. **1587** HARRISON *England* II. xxi. (1877) I. 333 There is a kind of glewie matter which holdeth birds so fast as birdlime. **1695** BLACKMORE *Pr. Arth.* IV. 104 Part is spun in silken Threads, and Clings Entangled in the Grass in glewy Strings. **1774** GOLDSM. *Nat. Hist.* (1776) VIII. 99 Letting fall upon them a few drops of gluey matter with which their bodies are provided. **1884** J. COLBORNE *Hicks Pasha* 180 A crass, gluey substance filled his throat.

Comb. **1866–7** LIVINGSTONE *Last Jrnls.* (1873) I. viii. 196 Gluey-looking gum.

transf. and *fig.* *c* **1430** *Pilgr. Lyf Manhode* IV. xiii. (1869) 183 Ful of cley and arestinge, and glewy is þilke, of wordlich richesse of wurshipe, of strengthe of idel fairnesse. **1649** G. DANIEL *Trinarch.* To Rdr. 18 Till waken'd by the Clangor of fresh Quarts It breake the Gleiwye Prison, and vp-starts A fresh. **1663** COWLEY *Cutter Coleman St.* I. Wks. 1710 II. 813, I will not have one Penny of the Principal pass through such glewy Fingers. **1768–74** TUCKER *Lt. Nat.* (1852) II. 446 It is possible to gain the art of grasping our ideas without letting them grasp upon the mind, or take such gluey hold as that we cannot wipe off at pleasure.

Hence **'glueyness**, the quality, condition, or state of being gluey.

1611 COTGR., *Glueur*, glewinesse, clamminesse. **1659** tr. *Comenius' Gate Lang. Unl.* x. *marg.*, Which..ropeth out by reason of its clamminess or gluiness. **1727** in BAILEY vol. II, *Gluiness.* **1733** CHEYNE *Eng. Malady* I. iii. §2 (1734) 16 This Class of nervous Disorders seems..to arise from a.. Glewyness or Viscidity of the Animal Juices.

glufe, glufer, obs. ff. GLOVE, GLOVER.

gluff, gluffe, obs. ff. GLOVE, GLIFF *v.*

†**glug**, *sb.*[1] *Obs.*[−1] [cf. GLUB[1].] A clod.

1382 WYCLIF *Job* xxviii. 6 Place of a safyr is stones, and the gluggis [1388 clottis; L. *glebæ*] of hym gold.

glug (glʌg), *sb.*[2] [echoic: cf. GLUCK *sb.*] A word formed to imitate an inarticulate sound (see quots.). Also redupl. **glug-glug**.

1768–74 TUCKER *Lt. Nat.* (1852) I. 55 Pretty bottle, says Sganarelle, how sweet are thy little glug glugs. **1843** LEVER *J. Hinton* vi. (1878) 38 Glug, glug, glug, flowed the bubbling liquor. **1882** G. MACDONALD *Castle Warlock* xv. (1883) 83 Lord Mergwain listened to the glug-glug in the long neck of the decanter. **1897** MARY KINGSLEY *W. Africa* 275 While hesitating as to where was the next safe place to plant their feet, the place that they were standing on went in with a glug.

glug (glʌg), *v.* [echoic: cf. GLUCK *v.*] *intr.* To make the sound rendered by 'glug'. Hence **'glugging** *vbl. sb.* and *ppl. a.*

1895 W. WRIGHT *Palmyra & Zen.* xxviii. 343 Their voices, a kind of glugging bark, seemed borrowed from the camel. **1897** *Westm. Gaz.* 6 Mar. 2/1 The..'glugging' of the liquor as it trickled down his throat.

‖**glühwein** ('glyːvaɪn). Also **gluhwein**. [G.] Mulled wine.

1898 *Elizabeth & her German Garden* (1900) 158 Waiting for the New Year, and sipping *Glühwein*... It was hot, and sweet, and rather nasty. **1929** E. HEMINGWAY *Farewell to Arms* xxxix. 232 We..drank hot red wine with spices and lemon in it. They called it *glühwein.* **1959** *Listener* 15 Jan. 134/3 The hot bath and the *Glühwein.* **1967** 'G. CARR' *Lewker in Tirol* vi. 82 A glass of *gluhwein*, red wine sugared and heated.

gluif, obs. Sc. f. GLOVE.

gluing ('gl(j)uːɪŋ), *vbl. sb.* [f. GLUE *v.* + -ING[1].] The action of the vb. GLUE; also *concr.*

1395 TREVISA *Barth. De P.R.* VII. lxx. (1495) 290 Some medycynes percen humours with..glewynge and thurstynge..as Mirabolianis. *c* **1440** *Promp. Parv.* 200/1 Gluynge to-gedyr, *conglutinacio, conviscacio.* **1573–80** in BARET *Alv.* G 292. **1628** EARLE *Microcosm., Plodding Stud.* (Arb.) 72 His disposition of them is as iust as the Bookbinders, a setting or glewing of them together. **1703** T. N. *City & C. Purchaser* 29 They first Joint, and Glue the Boards..which Gluing being dry, they..Plane. **1890** *Athenæum* 25 Oct. 547/3 When this gluing has been carefully done, it is impossible to separate the layers.

b. *attrib.*, as ***gluing-matter***, ***-shed***.

c **1440** *Promp. Parv.* 200/1 Gluynge matere, as paste ..*gluten.* **1898** B. REDWOOD *Rep. Schibaieff's Petrol. Refinery* 13 One wooden building used as a cooperage and gluing shed, provided with the usual fittings.

†**'gluing**, *ppl. a. Obs.* [f. GLUE *v.* + -ING[2].] Adhesive.

1572 HULOET (ed. Higins), Glewyng, or glewy ..*glutinosus.* **1587** GOLDING *De Mornay* xxiv. (1617) 413 The glewing vanities that sticke so fast to vs. **1635** SWAN *Spec. M.* vi. §4 (1643) 262 Comfrey is..of a clammie and gluing moisture. **1657** W. COLES *Adam in Eden* cccxxvi. 602 The Leaves and Bark of the Elme..being also of a certain clammy and glewing quality.

gluish ('gl(j)uːɪʃ), *a.* [f. GLUE *sb.* + -ISH.] Somewhat resembling glue; having some of the properties of glue.

1382 WYCLIF *Exod.* ii. 3 He..glewide it with glewishe cley. **1519** HORMAN *Vulg.* 178 b, If it [earth] be gluishe..it is a token of a fatte grounde. **1574** NEWTON *Health Mag.* 46 They loose muche of their toughe clamminesse and glewish humoure. **1601** HOLLAND *Pliny* II. 438 A fish there is named Icthyocolla, which hath a glewish skin. **1763** *Nat. Hist.* in *Ann. Reg.* 91/2 The floor..was thick smeared with a glueish moisture. **1847** in CRAIG; and in mod. Dicts.

fig. *a* **1653** GOUGE *Comm. Heb.* III. (1655) 59 This world hath..a gluish quality to hold them close to it.

Comb. *a* **1722** LISLE *Husb.* (1752) 177 A very thick-rinded, and cold glewish-floured barley.

Hence **'gluishness**, the quality of being gluish.

1608 TOPSELL *Serpents* (1658) 655 Some part of amends made by the rare clammy glewishnesse of the same.

glulam ('gl(j)uːlæm). [f. GLU(E *sb.* + LAM(INATION.] A building material consisting of laminations of timber glued together.

1953 *Civil Engineering* Feb. 87 (Advt.), The glulam girders which carry the load are formed of kiln dried timber, bonded together with waterproof glue which is as strong and permanent as the wood. **1961** *Engineering* 29 Sept. 411/3 Rectangular glulam sections.

glum (glʌm), *sb. rare.* Also 6 **glome**, **glumme**. [f. GLUM *v.* or *a.*; cf. GLOOM *sb.*]

†**1.** A sullen look. *Obs.*

1523 SKELTON *Garl. Laurel* 1118 She loked hawtly, and gave on me a glum, There was amonge them no worde then but mum. *a* **1529** —— *Bowge of Courte* 80 On me she gaue a glome [*rimes with* come *vb.*] With browes bente. **1530** PALSGR. 225/2 Glumme, a sower loke, *rechigne.*

2. Glumness, sullenness. *nonce-use.*

1825 LOCKHART in *Scott's Fam. Lett.* (1894) II. 323 It is much that the seven members have gone through it all without anything even like a single flash of glum.

glum (glʌm), *a.* Also 6 **glumme**, **glomme**. [Related to GLUM *v.* and GLOOM *v.*; cf. LG. *glum* turbid, muddy.]

1. Of persons: Sullen, frowning; having an air of dejection or displeasure, esp. in phr. ***to look glum***; also ***to look glum on*** (a person, action, etc.).

1547 SALESBURY *Welsh Dict.*, *Gwg*, glumme, lowring. **1556–8** PHAER *Æneid* IV. K ij b, She hym beheld wt loking glomme, With rollyng here and there her eyes, and still in sylens domme. **1567** DRANT *Horace's Ep.* To Rdr., If..they will by worde of mouthe be answered, then wellfayre my laste shootanchor, glum silence. **1674** RAY *N.C. Words* 21 *To be Glum*, to look sadly or sowrly, to frown..A word common to the vulgar both in North and South. **1676** ETHEREDGE *Man of Mode* II. i. (1684) 16 You need not look so glum, Sir. **1678** RYMER *Tragedies* 3 And not Athens only, but..so austere and glum a generation as those of Sparta.. agreed the same honour to these Athenian Poets. **1755** JOHNSON, *Glum*, a low cant word formed by corrupting *gloom.* **1771** FOOTE *Maid of B.* III. Wks. 1799 II. 229 You all sit as silent and glum—why, can't you speak out? **1786** MAD. D'ARBLAY *Diary* 6 Oct., The moment he sees any one that he..dislikes, he assumes a look of glum distance and sullenness. **1807–8** W. IRVING *Salmag.* (1824) 123 [He] is as glum and grim and cynical as his master. **1849** THACKERAY *Lett.* 4 Sept., I ought not to show you my glum face or my dismal feelings. **1887** BESANT *The World went* xiii. 108 [He] sat glum, and presently grew impatient and went out.

quasi-*adv.* **1796** R. BAGE *Hermsprong* xii, I suppose at that time I might answer rather glum.

2. Of things: Gloomy, dark; dismal. Now only *fig.* from sense 1.

1557–8 PHAER *Æneid* VI. Q j, Thou Chaos, and you firy boyling pittes and places glumme. **1593** *Tell-Troth's N.Y. Gift* 31 The glomest daye maye darken the sunne, but not abate his pride. **1648** EARL WESTMORELAND *Otia Sacra* (1879) 6 The Glum And horrid beat of Thunders Drum We hear or see. **1848** THACKERAY *Lett.* 1 Nov., We walked in the park..surveying..the glum old bridge.

3. *Comb.*, as ***glum-like***, ***-looking*** adjs.

1756 MRS. CALDERWOOD *Jrnl.* viii. (1884) 219 Mr. Burrage was a glum-like carle. **1866** *Sat. Rev.* 26 May 617/1 The air of the glum-looking Englishman..surveying mankind at a ball in Paris. **1888** ANNA K. GREEN *Behind Closed Doors* vi, She was afraid to risk herself with such a glum-looking customer..I suppose.

glum, *v. Obs.* exc. *dial.* Also 5 **glom**, 5–6 **glome**, 6 **glumme**. [var. of *glo(u)mbe*, GLOOM *v.*] *intr.* To look sullen; to frown, scowl.

c **1460** *Towneley Myst.* xxx. 596 Sir, I trow thai be dom somtyme were full melland; Will ye se how thai glom. **1509** HAWES *Past. Pleas.* (Percy Soc.) 166 Upon me he gan to loure and glum. **1530** PALSGR. 568/2 It is a sower wyfe, she is ever glomyng. *a* **1547** SURREY in *Tottel's Misc.* (Arb.) 27 [He] hath his home Not..as a den vncleane: Nor palacelyke, wherat disdayn may glome. **1598** *Tom Tyler & Wife* (1661) 5 He shall be soon appeased, If either he gaspeth or glometh. **1876** *Whitby Gloss.* s.v., If thou doesn't want it, say thou doesn't': thou need not go and glum over it.

glumaceous (gl(j)uː'meɪʃəs). *a.* [f. GLUME + -ACEOUS.] Of the nature of glumes; bearing glumes. Also, belonging to the N.O. *Glumaceæ* of plants, which includes the grasses and sedges.

1828–32 in WEBSTER (citing BARTON). **1830** LINDLEY *Nat. Syst. Bot.* 255 [Of Xyrideæ] Calyx glumaceous, 3-leaved. **1846** MCCULLOCH *Acc. Brit. Empire* (1854) I. 103 Several alpine grasses and other glumaceous plants. **1854** S. THOMSON *Wild Fl.* I. (ed. 4) 60 The perianth, composed of six glumaceous pieces. **1872** OLIVER *Elem. Bot.* I. v. 58 *Monocotyledons*..with chaffy glumes or scale-like bracts enclosing the flower, hence called Glumaceous.

glumal ('gl(j)uːməl), *a.* [f. GLUME + -AL[1].] = prec.: Lindley's name for an 'alliance' of glume-bearing endogens (see ALLIANCE *sb.* 6). Also **'glumal** *sb.*, a member of this alliance.

1846 LINDLEY *Veg. Kingd.* 105 *Glumales*, the Glumal Alliance... Natural orders of Glumals.

gluman, obs. form of GLEEMAN.

glume (gl(j)uːm). *Bot.* [ad. L. *glūma* (rare) hull, husk (of grain); cf. F. *glume.*] One of the chaff-like bracts which form the calyx or outer envelope in the inflorescence of grasses and sedges; the husk of corn or other grain.

[**1577** B. GOOGE *Heresbach's Husb.* (1586) 26 b, Gluma is the huske of the corne whose top is the aane. **1699** *Phil. Trans.* XXI. 300 Each gluma or husk terminates in three Awns, two of which are even, the other somewhat longer.] **1789** E. DARWIN *Bot. Gard.* II. (1791) 9 *note*, The chaffy scales of the calyx..and the glume in some Alpine grasses.. grow into leaves. **1831** LOUDON *Encycl. Agric.* (ed. 2) 888 Rye-grass..is now cut..when it is just coming into flower; and therefore to collect the glumes or empty husks can be of no use as seed. **1880** A. R. WALLACE *Isl. Life* 472 Their seeds, often enveloped in chaffy glumes. **1896** EDMONDS *Bot. for Beginners* 85 Each flower [of wheat] is contained within a flowering glume and a pale.

‖**glumella** (gl(j)uː'mɛlə). *Bot.* [mod.L. dim. of *glūma* GLUME.] An inner glume or palea.

1861 MISS PRATT *Flower. Pl.* VI. 43 Each flower usually consists of two dissimilar valvelets called glumellas.

glu'melle. *Bot. rare.* [cf. F. *glumelle.*] = prec.

1836 GRAY *Elem. Bot.* iv. §1. 158 [Grasses] Each flower is provided with a pair of bracts of a second order, or bracteoles, much resembling the glumes..which may be termed *glumelles* or *paleæ.*

glumellule (gl(j)uː'mɛljuːl). *Bot.* [ad. mod.L. *glūmellula*, dim. of GLUMELLA; cf. F. *glumellule.*] One of the scales frequently found at the base of the ovary in grasses; a lodicule.

1861 BENTLEY *Bot.* 193 Each flower has..frequently at the base of the ovary..two or more little scales, also of the nature of bracts, which are generally termed *squamulæ*, *glumellules*, or *lodiculæ.*

glumly ('glʌmlɪ), *adv.* [f. GLUM *a.* + -LY[2].] In a glum manner.

1805 *Morn. Chron.* in *Spirit Publ. Jrnls.* (1806) IX. 308 His thumbs thus glumly twirling. **1851** D. JERROLD *St. Giles* xx. 206 'Walk!' echoed Tangle, looking glumly. **1886** CHURCH *Let.* 11 Nov. in *Life & Lett.* (1894) 321 We sat glumly at our breakfasts every morning.

glumme, obs. form of GLUM.

†**glum-metal**. *local. Obs.*

1686 PLOT *Staffordsh.* iv. 152 The stone..call'd Glum-metall, about Bradwall..which..though as hard to digg as any rock; yet the Air, rains, and frosts, will mollify it so, that it will run as if it were a natural Lime.

†**'glumming**, *vbl. sb. Obs.* [f. GLUM *v.* + -ING[1].] The action of the vb. GLUM.

a **1450** *Knt. de la Tour* (1868) 35 And so there was never pees betwene hem, but ever glomyng, louring, and chiding. *a* **1529** SKELTON *Col. Cloute* 83 And as for theyr connynge, A glommynge, and a mummynge, And make thereof a jape. *a* **1553** UDALL *Royster D.* I. i. (Arb.) 12, I haue yond espied hym sadly comming, And in loue for twentie pounde, by hys glommyng. **1575** *Gamm. Gurton* III. iii, What deuill woman, plucke vp your hart, & leue of al this gloming.

†**'glumming**, *ppl. a. Obs.* [f. GLUM *v.* + -ING[2].] That looks glum or sullen.

1526 *Pilgr. Perf.* (W. de W. 1531) 94 But declyne from his company, with glummynge or froward manner. **1549** CHALONER *Erasm. on Folly* C j, Who would..serche the maner of living of those soure and glommyng gods? **1572** tr. *Buchanan's Detect. Mary* N ij, There was all the way a sad glumming silence. **1573–80** BARET *Alv.* G 296.

†**'glummish**, *a. Obs. rare.* Also **gloommish**. [f. GLUM *a.* + -ISH.] Somewhat gloomy.

1573 TWYNE *Æneid* XI. Kk ij b, An Ilex tree with glummish darkish shade bespreddes the same, that none may see. **1583** STANYHURST *Æneis* III. (Arb.) 91 His one light, That stood in his lowring front gloommish malleted onlye, Like Greekish tergat glistring. **1589** R. ROBINSON *Gold Mirr.* (Chetham Soc.) 1 And Boreas breth was blacke, and glummish chill.

glummy ('glʌmɪ), *a.* [f. GLUM *a.* + -Y[1].]

†**a.** Gloomy (*obs.*). **b.** Glum.

1580 E. KNIGHT *Tryal Truth* 27 It can not be denyed, but that such casual blastes may happen, as are most too be feared, when the wether waxeth darke and glummy. **1884** L. L. ALCOTT in *Chr. Treasury* Jan. 21/1 A smile..touching the glummiest face like a streak of sunshine.

glumness ('glʌmnɪs). [f. GLUM *a.* + -NESS.] The condition of being glum.

1727 BAILEY vol. II, *Glumness* [printed *Gluinness*], Sullenness in Looks. **1786** MAD. D'ARBLAY *Diary* 11 Nov., He made us amends for the glumness of Colonel Goldsworthy. **1874** *Daily News* 2 June 5/5 He was continually on the look-out for boon companions who could enliven the glumness of his official mansion.

glumose (gl(j)uː'məʊs), *a.* [ad. mod.L. *glūmōsus*, f. *glūma* GLUME.] Furnished with a glume or husk.

1793 MARTYN *Lang. Bot.*, *Glumosus flos*..a glumose flower, is a kind of aggregate flower, having a filiform receptacle, with a common glume at the base. **1806** GALPINE *Brit. Bot.* C 1 b, Fl[owers] inferior..glumose.

So †**glu'mosity.** *Obs. rare*⁻¹.
1657 Tomlinson *Renou's Disp.* 164* That the exterior shell and all glumosity may be excussed.

glumous ('gl(j)uːməs), *a.* [f. glume + -ous.] = glumose.
1828–32 in Webster (citing Martyn); and in later Dicts.

glump (glʌmp), *sb. dial.* [f. glump *v.*]
a. A sulky person. b. *pl.* (See quots.)
a. **1804** Tarras *Poems* 131 A peevish girnin glump. **1825** Jamieson, *Glump, Glumph*, a sour or morose person.
b. **1825** Jamieson s.v., *In the glumps*, in a gloomy state, out of humour. **1855** Robinson *Whitby Gloss.*, *Glumps*, sulks. 'Down in the glumps', sulky, 'glumpy'. **1893** *Northumbld. Gloss.*, *Glumps*, the sulks.

glump (glʌmp), *v. dial.* [Of obscure formation; cf. glum, glop, dump, grumpy, etc.] *intr.* To sulk, be glum or sullen. Also '**glumping** *vbl. sb.* and *ppl. a.*
c **1746** *Exmoor Scolding* (E.D.S.) 39 Ya gurt chounting, grumbling, glumping.. Trash. *Wilmot.* Don't tell me o' glumping. **1802** R. Anderson *Cumberld. Ball.* 37 Neist time we met, he glump'd and gloom'd, And turn'd his head anither way. **1804** Tarras *Poems* 52* Glumpin wi' a sour disdain.. She wi' a youl began to mourn. **1876** *Whitby Gloss.*, s.v., 'Pray thee, what's thou glumping at.'

glumpish ('glʌmpɪʃ), *a.* Chiefly *dial.* [f. glump *sb.* or *v.* + -ish.] = glumpy.
1800 Helena Wells *Constantia Neville* II. 139 Jerry said he was glumpish, and in his airs. **1802** Mrs. Jane West *Infidel Father* I. 26 Her father and mother.. were.. glumpish awkward beings. **1860** Geo. Eliot *Mill on Fl.* vi. iv, "An it worrets me as Mr. Tom 'ull sit by himself so glumpish, a-knittin' his brow, an' a lookin' at the fire of a night.' **1869** E. Farmer *Scrap Bk.* (ed. 6) 46 He sits glumpish and moody.

glumpy ('glʌmpɪ), *a.* [f. as prec. + -y¹. Cf. grumpy.] Glum, sullen, sulky.
1780 Mad. D'Arblay *Diary* June, I began to be monstrous glumpy upon this last speech, which indeed was impertinent enough. **1800** A. Carlyle *Autobiog.* 347 Armstrong was naturally glumpy. **1853** Miss Sewell *Experience Life* xix. 189 You are not used, Sally, to look glumpy because your head aches. **1881** E. J. Worboise *Sissie* xlvii, Mr. Brooke was certainly glumpy, and inclined to snap and snarl at everything his wife presumed to say.
Hence '**glumpily** *adv.*
1864 M. Eyre *Lady's Walks in S. France* v. (1865) 64, 'I knew that before', said I, rather glumpily. **1884** *Punch* 19 July 35/1 "Ave told you afore', he said, glumpily, to Mr. T.

glunch (glʌnʃ), *v. Sc.* Also **glunsh.** [Cf. glum *a.* and clunch *a* 2.] *intr.* To look sour or glum; esp. in phrase ***to glunch and gloom.***
1719 Ramsay *Ep. to Jas. Arbuckle* v, But when ane's of his merit conscious, He's in the wrang, when prais'd, that glunshes. **1786** Burns *Earnest Cry* 25 Does ony great man glunch and gloom? Speak out, an' never fash your thoom! **1890** 'P. Cushing' *Bull i' th' Thorn* I. ix. 204 This failed to satisfy Crump. He glunched and gloomed and spat out some hot oaths.
Hence **glunch** *sb.*, a sour look; **glunch** *a.*, sulky.
1786 Burns *Sc. Drink* xvii, Wha twists his gruntle wi' a glunch O' sour disdain. **1816** Scott *Antiq.* ix, 'But what's the use o' looking sae glum and glunch about a pickle banes?'

†**glunimie.** *Sc. Obs.* Also **glune-amie, glunyieman.** [Prob. a corruption of some Gaelic phrase often heard from Highlanders.] A Lowland name for a Highlander.
a **1745** Meston *Poet. Wks.* (1767) 115 Upon a time.. Some Glunimies met at a fair, As deft and tight as ever wore A durk, a targe and a claymore. **1825** Jamieson, *Glunyieman*, a rough unpolished boorish-looking man, a term generally applied to a Highlander. *Banffs.* **1828** Scott *F.M. Perth* iii, And he is but half a Highlander neither, and wants a thought of the dour spirit of a Glune-amie.

gluon ('gluːɒn). *Particle Physics.* [f. glu(e *sb.* + -on¹.] Any of a group of massless bosons possessing colour that are postulated as carriers of the colour force that binds quarks together in a hadron.
1971 *Physics Bull.* Dec. 710/3 Gell-Mann and Fritsch prefer to talk of 'current quarks',.. whose properties they 'abstract' from a field theory of quarks interacting with vector 'gluons'. **1975** *Sci. Amer.* Oct. 45/1 The color gauge theory postulates the existence of eight massless particles, sometimes called gluons, that are the carriers of the strong force, just as the photon is the carrier of the electromagnetic force. **1981** D. Wilkinson in J. H. Mulvey *Nature of Matter* i. 25 When you look into the force that is generated between quarks by gluon exchange you find that.. it *increases* as the separation between the particles increases. **1985** *Sci. Amer.* Apr. 70/2 Within this polarized vacuum, however, the quark itself continuously emits and reabsorbs gluons, thereby changing its color.
Hence **glu'onic** *a.*
1976 *Physics Lett.* B. LX. 183 The identification of the gluonic widths with the widths for decay into ordinary hadrons of the new particles. **1984** *Nature* 24 Nov. 313/1 With psi decays we have an unparalleled opportunity to study gluonic excitations.

glur, var. glore *sb.*

†**glusk,** *v. Obs.*⁻⁰ [Derivation obscure.] *intr.* To squint; implied in †'**glusker**, one who squints; †'**glusking** *vbl. sb.*, squinting. (Cf. East Anglian *glusky* sulky, in Forby *Voc. E. Anglia.*)
c **1440** *Promp. Parv.* 200/2 Gluscare, *idem quod*, glyare. *Ibid.*, Gluskynge, *idem quod* Glyenge (*K. P.*) *strabositas.*

gluster, obs. form of cluster *sb.*

†**glut,** *sb.*¹ *Obs. rare.* [a. OF. *glut, glout* greedy, gluttonous.] = glutton.
c **1394** *P. Pl. Crede* 67 What glut of þo gomes may any good kachen, He will kepen it hymself. *a* **1400–50** *Alexander* 4552 Ane [of the gods] leris ȝow to be licherus.. Ane, to be grindand gluttis & glorand dronkin.

glut, *sb.*² *Obs.* exc. *dial.* Also 6 **gloute.** [a. OF. *glout* gulp, sb. related to *gloutir*, glut *v.*²] A gulp or full draught; the amount (of liquid) swallowed at a gulp.
1533 Elyot *Cast. Helth* (1541) 41 b, Let him drinke a lytel smal biere or ale, so that he drinke not a great glut, but in a lytel quantite. **1555** W. Watreman *Fardle Facions* II. x. 223 Many of the Tartarres when the bodies lie fresshe bliedinge on the grounde, laye them downe alonge, and suck of yᵉ bloud a full gloute. **1658** R. White tr. *Digby's Powd. Symp.* (1660) 31 Moving sands, which covered and buried heretofore at one glut the puissant army of King Cambyses. *c* **1785** *J. Thompson's Man* 23 And for a continual Diet-Drink, take five great Gluts of the Decoction of Mother Wit three Times a Day. **1844** Stephens *Bk. Farm.* II. 217 Should the horse have to undertake a longer journey.. a stinted allowance of water before starting.. is requisite, say to 10 gluts. **1893** *Northumbld. Gloss.*, *Glut*, a drink. 'Tyek a glut or twee an' ye'll be bettor.'

glut (glʌt), *sb.*³ Also 6 **glutte.** [f. glut *v.*¹]
1. The act of glutting or condition of being glutted with food, etc.; full indulgence in some pleasure, ending in satiety or disgust; one's 'fill' of something which finally cloys the appetite; a surfeit.
1594 Plat *Jewell-ho.* iii. 3 Use the first water againe for the vehiculum.. because the same hath alreadie receyved his glutte of the oyles. **1602** Marston *Antonio's Rev.* v. iv. Wks. 1856 I. 137 Even I have glut of blood. **1607** Topsell *Four-f. Beasts* (1658) 295 The glut of provender or other meat not digested, doth cause a Horse to have great pain in his body. **1631** R. H. *Arraignm. Whole Creature* vi. 41 They cannot have alwayes their glut, their fill, and their will in Sinne. *a* **1659** Bp. Brownrig *Serm.* (1674) I. xxvi. 346 This glut of wealth, and a full satiety of all pleasure, is sinful. **1667** Milton *P.L.* x. 989 So Death Shall be deceiv'd his glut, and with us two Be forc'd to satisfy his ravenous maw. **1723** Pope *Let. to Swift* 12 Jan., A Glut of study and retirement in the first part of my life, cast me into this [dissipation]. **1815** Col. Hawker *Diary* (1893) I. 138 We got two hours' glut at their pheasants. **1868** Bain *Ment. & Mor. Sci.* iii. viii. §5 If the chief fact be the glut of sensuality and of power, the feeling is one of great and acute pleasure.
transf. **1667** Milton *P.L.* vi. 589 Those deep-throated Engins.. disgorging foule Thir devillish glut, chain Thunderbolts and Hail Of Iron Globes.
†**b.** *pl. Obs.*
1599 B. Jonson *Ev. Man out of Hum.* ii. iv, Husbands must take heed They giue no gluts of kindness to their Wiues. **1628** Jackson *Creed* vi. i. vi. §2 The gluts or gushes of pleasure may at one time be much greater than another, yet still transient, never consistent. **1692** R. L'Estrange *Josephus* (ed. 5) 892 But the Gluts and the Loathings of an irregular Love are unaccountable.
2. A supply of any mercantile commodity which is greatly in excess of the demand; freq. ***a glut in the market.***
1594 Plat *Jewell-ho.* iii. 31 Buying store of Roses when you finde a glut of them in the market. **1662** Petty *Taxes* 47 We should have no such gluts of wool upon our hand. **1735** Berkeley *Querist* App. §215 By a glut of paper, the prices of things must rise. **1787** T. Jefferson *Writ.* (1859) II. 261 The present glut is occasioned by their importing too much. **1848** Mill *Pol. Econ.* iii. xiv. §1 (1876) 337 Dearth, or scarcity, on the one hand, and over-supply, or, in mercantile language, glut, on the other, are incident to all commodities. **1868** Rogers *Pol. Econ.* (ed. 3) viii. 79 As a rule, the phenomenon of a glut in the labour market attends any great exaltation in the price of food.
attrib. **1829** *Blackw. Mag.* XXVI. 115 Low, glut prices are highly injurious to them.
3. An excessive quantity or number. Now *rare.*
[**1639** Fuller *Holy War* i. xvii. (1640) 27 Seeing the world in that age had rather a glut, then famine of Saints.] **1653** A. Wilson *Jas. I*, 76 At our Kings first accesse to the Crown, there was a glut of Knights made. **1742** Richardson *Pamela* IV. 114 To.. patch up a Drama in Italian, in order to throw in a Glut of minuitish Airs. **1824** Byron *Juan* xv. xxxiii, They have at hand a blooming glut of brides.
4. An excessive influx of water, rain, etc. Now *rare.*
1636 B. Jonson *Discov.* (1640) 116 If you powre a glut of water upon a Bottle, it receives little of it. **1661** J. Childrey *Brit. Baconica* 47 Extream gluts of rain, or lasting wet weather. **1727** Thomson *Summer* (1st vers.) 494 Collected all In one big glut.. Th' impetuous torrent, tumbling down the steep Thunders. **1852** T. Thompson *Ann. Influenza* (1863) 82 There were some great gluts of rain after the long drought. **1862** H. Spencer *First Princ.* ii. x. §87 (1875) 268 These currents from all sides lead to a wave of accumulation where they meet—a glut.
fig. **1748** Chesterf. *Lett.* (1792) I. cxxxvii. 369 The thaw has, I suppose, by this time, set them [letters] at liberty.. and you will receive a glut of them at once.
†**b.** An excessive flow of saliva, bile, etc. *Obs.*
1579 Langham *Gard. Health* (1633) 108 Put it in a linen bag, and hold it to thy teeth, and shut thy mouth while one may say three Pater nosters, then open thy mouth, and let out the glutt. **1719** *Acct. Sickness & Death Dr. W—dw—d* in *Arbuthnot's Misc. Wks.* (1751) I. 179 Throughout the whole Tract of the Intestines there was nothing remarkable, besides an exceeding Flatulency, and great Gluts of vitiated Bile.
†**5.** That which gluts or chokes up (a channel).
1695 Woodward *Nat. Hist. Earth* i. (1723) 44 The Shells were by some Glut, Stop, or other Means arrested in their Passage. **1704** Addison *Italy* (1705) 113 He gathers in his tedious Course Ten Thousand Streams, and swelling as he flows, In Scythian Seas the Glut of Rivers throws.

†**glut,** *sb.*⁴ *Obs.* [Alteration of *glit* gleet *sb.*, associated with glut *sb.*³ (sense 1).] = gleet *sb.* 2.
1611 Markham *Country Content.* (1649) 38 To enseame your hawke, which is, to cleanse her from grease, fat, and glut. **1615** Latham *Falconry* (1633) 7 She gathers no glut to decay her stomacke.

†**glut,** *sb.*⁵ *Obs. rare*⁻¹. [? ad. Gr. γλῶττις landrail (?), given in quot. as the equivalent term.] A kind of bird; ? the muff or whitethroat.
1661 Lovell *Hist. Anim. & Min.* 181 Gluts. Muff. *Glottides*.. They feed in the fennes upon red seedes, bents and wormes.

glut (glʌt), *sb.*⁶ *techn.* or *dial.* [Perhaps an altered form of *clut*, dial. var. of cleat, assimilated to glut *v.*¹; related to glut *v.*³, where 'choked or glutted' in the quot. suggests glut *v.*¹ 4.]
1. A wedge of wood or iron (see quots.).
1790 Marshall *Midl. Cties.* II. 437 *Glut*, a large wooden wedge. **1825** Jamieson, *Gluts*, two wedges used in tempering the plough. The end of the beam being movable in the stilt into which it was inserted, these wedges were anciently employed in raising or depressing it. **1846** Young *Naut. Dict.*, *Glut*, a piece of wood inserted as a fulcrum to get a better lever-power on any thing, or inserted beneath the thing prized in order to prevent its recoil when freshening the nip of the lever. **1852** *Newcastle Mining Gloss.* (Northumbld. Gloss.), *Glut*, a piece of wood to fill up behind cribbing or tubbing. **1852** Seidel *Organ* 140 Wood pipes which produce a tremulous tone are remedied by a small wooden glut being driven into the wedge of the mouth. **1869** Sir E. J. Reed *Shipbuild.* viii. 145 The edges which are to be welded are introduced into the grooves of an H-shaped piece of iron, which the patentee calls a 'glut'.
2. (See quots.)
1875 Knight *Dict. Mech.* *Glut*, a small brick or block introduced into a course to complete it. **1889** C. T. Davis *Bricks & Tiles* (ed. 2) 285 The plunger is then at or about its lowest point, and a 'glut', or green brick is placed in the mould [etc.].
3. *Naut.* (See quot.)
1841 Dana *Seaman's Man.* 107 *Glut*, a piece of canvas sewed into the centre of a sail, near the head. It has an eyelet-hole in the middle for the bunt-jigger or becket to go through.

glut, *sb.*⁷ A kind of eel. (See gloat *sb.*²)

glut (glʌt), *v.*¹ Also 4 (*vbl. sb.* **gloutynge**), **glotye, glotte.** [Prob. f. glut *sb.*¹ or its OF. source.]
1. *trans.* To feed to repletion; to indulge (appetite) to the utmost. Chiefly *refl.* or *pass.* Const. *with.* †Also *to glut up* (hunger).
c **1315** [see glutting *vbl. sb.*¹]. **1393** Langl. *P. Pl.* C. x. 76 To a-glotye [*Ilchester MS.* glotye] with here gurles. [See aglut.] **1526** *Pilgr. Perf.* (W. de W. 1531) 99 That they fele theyr stomackes partly hungry, and not vtterly saciate or glutted. **1549** Cheke *Hurt Sedit.* (1569) E iv, Ye haue waxed greedye now vpon Cities, and haue attempted mightie spoyles, to glut vppe and ye coulde your.. hunger. **1632** tr. *Bruel's Praxis Med.* 407 As they are forbidden to glut themselues, so they must not be altogether fasting. **1735** Somerville *Chase* ii. 497 Grim Slaughter strides along Glutting her greedy Jaws. **1822–34** *Good's Study Med.* (ed. 4) I. 116 There are other persons who have had a taste for harder substances, and have glutted themselves with stones, glass, and even leaden bullets. **1852** Hawthorne *Tanglewood T., Minotaur* (1879) 33 Destined to glut the ravenous maw of that detestable man-brute.
transf. **1667** Milton *P.L.* iii. 259 Thou.. shalt look down and smile, While.. I ruin all my Foes, Death last, and with his Carcass glut the Grave. **1715–20** Pope *Iliad* xxi. 337 Stay, and the furious flood shall cease to rave: 'Tis not thy fate to glut his angry wave. **1808** J. Barlow *Columb.* i. 626 Crew and cargo glut the watery grave. *a* **1878** Bryant *Freeman's Hymn* (Cent.), Where famine never blasts the year, Nor plagues, nor earthquakes glut the grave.
b. *intr.* for *refl.*
1632 Lithgow *Trav.* ii. 74 Her babes were brought forth for the sword to glut upon. **1847** Tennyson *Princ.* ii. 365 Like three horses that have broken fence, And glutted all night long breast-deep in corn, We issued gorged with knowledge.
2. *fig.* To gratify to the full (in earlier use, a sense or appetite of any kind, now, esp., a ferocious or lustful desire). Also ***to glut a person, his eyes,*** etc. *with*, †*in* something.
1549 Sir J. Cheke *Hurt of Sedition* (1569) C ij b, You.. are better contented to suffer famine.. to glutte your lustes, than [etc.]. **1621** Burton *Anat. Mel.* ii. iii. iii. (1651) 323 A country man may travel from kingdome to kingdome.. and glut his eyes with delightful objects. **1632** E. Reynolds *Expl. 110th Psalm* 287 To glut themselves with the bloud of his people. **1633** P. Fletcher *Poet. Misc.* 82 Where idle boyes may glut their lustfull taste. **1639** J. S. *Clodamas* 31 Not content to glut himselfe in such sins as might have some excuse. **1662** Pepys *Diary* 23 Aug., My Lady Castlemaine stood over against us upon a piece of White Hall, where I glutted myself with looking on her. **1696** tr. *Duquesne's Voy. E. Ind.* 124 Those who admire shell-work, may glut their fancy here. **1743** J. Davidson *Æneid* ix. 289 We have glutted ourselves with Vengeance to the full. **1835** Lytton *Rienzi* iv. v, My employers are enough to glut your rage an' you were a tiger. **1853** Kingsley *Hypatia* Pref., The realms of nature and of art were ransacked to glut the wonder, lust,

and ferocity of a degraded populace. **1874** GREEN *Short Hist.* vi. §5. 317 His ambition was glutted at last with the rank of Cardinal.

b. *intr.* (and †*refl.*) To take one's fill of thinking, gazing, etc. *on* something; to gloat *on*. Also to long greedily *for*. *rare.*

1632 E. REYNOLDS *Expl. 110th Psalm* 310 By gazing and glutting themselves on the objects of the world. *a* **1639** T. CAREW *Poems* (1651) 81 Love doth with an hungry eye Glut on Beauty. *Ibid.* 87 Let others glut on the extorted praise Of vulgar breath. **1814** *Spaniards* IV. i, Yes, Boabdil, seize on the royal power; Thy hand gluts for it. **1870** E. H. PEMBER *Trag. Lesbos* x. 139 Dost think she wants To see thy dog's eyes glutting on her? Off!

3. To overload or surfeit with food; hence, to surfeit, cloy, or sicken with excess of anything.

Used *occas.* for: To exhaust the power of gratifying desire; opposed to *sate*, which implies the extinction of the desire itself.

c **1400** *Destr. Troy* 11777 There is no greuaunce so grete vndur god one, As the glemyng of gold, þat glottes þere hertis. **1530** PALSGR. 568/2, I glut with meate, *Je engloutte.* I glut one with to moche aboundance of any thynge, *je assouuys.* There is no carnall pleasure but a man may be glutted in it. *Ibid.*, I glut with slepe, *je assopis.* **1577** VAUTROUILLIER *Luther on Ep. Gal.* 286 When the Gospell is diligently and daily preached, many being glutted therwith begin to loth it. **1589** PUTTENHAM *Eng. Poesie* II. ix. (Arb.) 96 The ouer busie and too speedy returne of one maner of tune, [doth] too much annoy and as it were glut the eare. **1618** LATHAM *2nd Bk. Falconry* (1633) 22 Francke food with rest breeds imperfection, and glots the stomacke. **1621** T. WILLIAMSON tr. *Goulart's Wise Vieillard* 103 This life hath many commodities: so it is that wee may be full gorged, satiated, and glutted with them. **1642** FULLER *Holy & Prof. St.* IV. I. 241 He leaveth his Prince alwayes with an appetite, and never gluts him with his company. **1718** PRIOR *Solomon* II. 95, I found The fickle ear soon glutted with the sound. **1774** GOLDSM. *Nat. Hist.* (1776) III. 237 Swallowing their blood at large draughts, and seeming rather glutted than satiated with its abundance. **1803** JANE PORTER *Thaddeus* ix. (1831) 84 Some straggling Cossacks from the town.. glutted, but not sated, with blood. **1822** HAZLITT *Table-t.* Ser. II. xv. (1869) 304 The ear is cloyed and glutted with warbled ecstasies or agonies.

4. To fill (a receptacle, channel, pipe, etc.) to excess; to choke up; to saturate, impregnate thoroughly *with* some substance. Now *rare.*

1471 RIPLEY *Comp. Alch.* VII. in Ashm. (1652) 169 But geve yt not so much that thou hyt glut. **1570–6** LAMBARDE *Peramb. Kent* (1826) 118 The abundance of the light sand (wherewith the Sea hath of latter yeeres glutted the haven). **1594** PLAT *Jewell-ho.* I. 46 Ground..which..hath been glutted with salt water. **1680** BOYLE *Scept. Chym.* II. 126 Sal Tartari dulcify'd by Distilling from it Spirit of Wine till the Salt be sufficiently glutted with its Sulphur. **1796** C. MARSHALL *Garden.* iv. (1813) 47 When manure is applied, the ground is not to be glutted with dung. **1840** HOOD *Miss Kilmansegg, Her Fancy Ball* vii, With light all the square is glutted. **1878** BROWNING *Poets Croisic* xi, Crystals grown where ocean gluts Their promontory's breadth with salt.

5. To overstock with mercantile goods. Chiefly ***to glut the market.***

1624 CAPT. SMITH *Virginia* VI. 236 Some of the rest..so glutted the market, that the price was abated. **1687** A. LOVELL *Thevenot's Trav.* III. 111 The Dutch carry to Japan ..Cloves, but in a small quantity..that the Japanese may not be glutted with them. **1757** JOS. HARRIS *Coins* 63 The European markets are never glutted with either..gold or silver. **1768** GRAY *Let.* Poems (1775) 333 Dodsley has contrived to glut the town already with two editions beforehand. **1825** MᶜCULLOCH *Pol. Econ.* II. iv. 173 We should ere long glut the market of the world with our commodities.

glut (glʌt), *v.*[2] [ad. F. *glotir, gloutir* (obs.) to swallow:—L. *gluttīre.*] *trans.* To swallow greedily, gulp down; also *to glut down, in* (cf. ENGLUT, used earlier in this sense). Now *rare.*

1600 J. LANE *Tom Tel-troth* 128, I pray thee stirre my jawes that I may glut it. **1610** SHAKS. *Temp.* I. i. 63 Hee'l be hang'd yet, Though euery drop of water sweare against it, And gape at widst to glut him. **1666** G. HARVEY *Morb. Angl.* xii. 138 Those that glut down such immeasurable proportions of flesh. **1773** J. ROSS *Fratricide* VI. 320 (MS.) O that thou [Earth] would'st Gape and..glut the Murd'rer's in! **1790** A. WILSON *1st Ep. to J. Dobie* Poet. Wks. (1846) 18 Tell them a plan o' cent. per cent., They'll glut yer words like hinee. **1861** LYTTON & FANE *Tannhäuser* 23 A throbbing light that grows and glows From glare to greater glare, until it gluts And gulfs him in.

glut (glʌt), *v.*[3] *Naut.* [cf. GLUT *sb.*[6]] (See quot.)

1867 SMYTH *Sailor's Word-bk.* s.v., Glut used [? *read* is used for] to prevent slipping, as sand and nippers glut the messenger; the fall of a tackle across the sheaves, by which it is choked or glutted.

glut-, abbreviated combining form of GLUTEN used in the formation of chemical terms, as **gluta'conic** *a.*, derived from gluten and aconitine; ***glutaconic acid***, $C_5H_6O_4$. **gluta'minic** *a.*, derived from gluten and amidogen: ***glutaminic acid***, $C_5H_9NO_4$. **glu'tamine** = *glutamic amide.* **glu'tanic** *a.*, in *glutanic acid*, $C_5H_5O_5$ (see quot.). **glutaric** *a.*, derived from gluten and tartaric acid $(CO_2H)_2(CH_2)_3$. **'glutazine**, $C_5H_6N_2O_2$, a white crystalline compound derived from pyridine.

1889 MUIR & MORLEY *Watts' Dict. Chem.* II. 613 **Glutaconic acid*..isomeric with citraconic acid. **1885** *Syd. Soc. Lex.*, **Glutamin*, an amide of asparagin existing in beet root, in the shoots of the vetch, and the pumpkin. *Ibid.*, **Glutanic acid*, a substance obtained by acting on a watery solution of glutaminic acid with a current of nitrous acid gas ..Also called oxyglutaric acid. *Ibid.*, **Glutaric acid*, a crystalline substance obtained by heating glutanic acid with hydriodic acid. **1889** MUIR & MORLEY *Watts' Dict. Chem.* II. 614 *Glutaric acid*, normal pyrotartaric acid. *Ibid.* **Glutazine* = di-oxy-amido-pyridine.

glutæal, gluteal (gl(j)uːˈtiːəl), *a.* [f. GLUTÆ-US + -AL[1].] Of or belonging to the glutæi.

1804 ABERNETHY *Surg. Obs.* 98 Cysts..originally formed in the..great gluteal muscle. **1831** R. KNOX *Cloquet's Anat.* 197 The glutæal vessels and nerve. **1842** E. WILSON *Anat. Vade M.* (ed. 2) 315 The Gluteal Artery is the continuation of the posterior trunk of the internal iliac. **1878** T. BRYANT *Pract. Surg.* I. 20 It may..appear in the buttock as a 'gluteal abscess'.

So **glu'tean** *a.*

1888 *Portfolio* Nov. 222/1 The glutean muscles.

glutæo-, gluteo- (gl(j)uːˈtiːəʊ), combining form of GLUTÆUS, = pertaining to the GLUTÆAL region (and some other part of the body), as ***glutæo-femoral*** adj.

1890 BILLINGS *Med. Dict.*, *Gluteo-femoral crease*, gluteal fold. **1900** DORLAND *Med. Dict.*, *Gluteofemoral*, pertaining to the buttock and thigh. **1962** *Gray's Anat.* (ed. 33) 690 A second [bursa] is found between the tendon of the muscle and that of the vastus lateralis (gluteofemoral bursa).

‖**glutæus, gluteus** (gl(j)uːˈtiːəs). Pl. glutæi, -tei (-ˈtiːaɪ). [mod.L. *glūtæus, glūtēus*, f. Gr. γλουτός rump, buttock.] One of the three large muscles (distinguished as ***glutæus maximus, medius, minimus***) which form the buttock, and serve to move the thigh in man; sometimes applied to their analogues in the lower animals. Also in *attrib.* or *adj.* use, ***glutæus muscle, glutæi muscles.***

1681 tr. *Willis' Rem. Med. Wks.* Vocab., *Glutæi*, muscles of the thigh. **1706** PHILLIPS (ed. Kersey), *Glutæi.* **1816** A. C. HUTCHISON *Pract. Obs. Surg.* (1826) 116 From the ankle to the trochanter, and over the glutæi muscles. **1840** G. ELLIS *Anat.* 454 Other small branches of the sciatic come from beneath the border of the gluteus. **1855** RAMSBOTHAM *Obstetr. Med.* 2 The attachment of the three powerful glutæi muscles. **1893** A. S. ECCLES *Sciatica* 53 Muscular rheumatism of the gluteus.

glutamate (ˈgl(j)uːtəmeɪt). *Chem.* [f. next. + -ATE[4].] A salt or ester of glutamic acid; *esp.* the monosodium salt, widely used to flavour food.

1876 *Jrnl. Chem. Soc.* I. 906 Glutimide..obtained by heating ammonium glutamate. **1929** *Industr. & Engin. Chem.* Oct. 984/2 In China and Japan monosodium glutamate is manufactured on a commercial scale and consumed as a condiment. **1943** *Thorpe's Dict. Appl. Chem.* (ed. 4) VI. 34/1 The glutamates..have a characteristic meat-like flavour. **1960** *Spectator* 16 Sept. 417 That curious prickly after-taste which appears to be characteristic of every foodstuff in which monosodium glutamate figures. **1970** C. N. GRAYMORE *Biochem. Eye* x. 670 This work immediately suggested that glutamate might play some special role in nervous tissue. **1971** *Times Lit. Suppl.* 12 Feb. 189/2 Flour..was said to be adulterated by things that make our ubiquitous monosodium glutamate sound positively delicious.

glutamic (gl(j)uːˈtæmɪk), *a. Biochem.* [tr. G. *glutaminsäure* glutamic acid (H. Ritthausen 1866, in *Jrnl. f. prakt. Chem.* XCIX. 6), f. GLUT- + AMIC *a.*] ***glutamic acid***: an amino-acid, $HOOC{\cdot}CH_2CH_2CH(NH_2){\cdot}COOH$, widely distributed in nature and a normal constituent of proteins.

1871 *Jrnl. Chem. Soc.* XXIV. 721 Aspartic acid, $C_4H_7NO_4$, and glutamic acid, $C_5H_9NO_4$. **1878** KINGZETT *Anim. Chem.* 364 Coaglutin yields glutamic acid. **1888** MUIR & MORLEY *Watts' Dict. Chem.* I. 164 *Amidoglutaric acid* = Glutamic acid. **1897** *Allbutt's Syst. Med.* II. 788 Lactic, succinic, glutamic, and aspartic acids. **1921** [see GLUTATHIONE]. **1946** *Nature* 9 Nov. 676/1 (*heading*) Action of penicillin in preventing the assimilation of glutamic acid by *Staphylococcus aureus.* **1970** C. N. GRAYMORE *Biochem. Eye* x. 670 The role of glutamic acid in the transport of potassium in nervous tissues.

glutamyl (ˈgl(j)uːtəmaɪl, -ɪl). *Chem.* [f. prec. + -YL.] Either of the univalent radicals derived from glutamic acid by the loss of one or other of the hydroxyl groups.

1909 *Jrnl. Chem. Soc.* XCVI. I. 369 The latter substance is converted by aqueous ammonia into glycylglutamyldiglycine, $C_{11}H_{18}O_7N_4$. **1956** *Nature* 25 Feb. 377/1 Secondary non-enzymic breakdown of γ-glutamyl peptides. **1965** *Nomencl. Org. Chem.* (*I.U.P.A.C.*) C. 120 α-Glutamyl: $HOOC-CH_2-CH_2-CH(NH_2)-CO-$. γ-Glutamyl: $-CO-CH_2-CH_2-CH(NH_2)-COOH$. **1968** A. WHITE et al. *Princ. Biochem.* (ed. 4) v. 108 Glutamyl derivatives may be of the γ type as well as the α variety.

glutathione (gl(j)uːtəˈθaɪəʊn). *Biochem.* [f. GLUTA(MIC *a.* (see quot. 1921).] A tripeptide of glutamic acid, cysteine, and glycine, metabolically important, esp. as a coenzyme, and perhaps present in all cells.

1921 F. G. HOPKINS in *Biochem. Jrnl.* XV. 297 Provisionally, for easy reference, the name *Glutathione* will perhaps be admissible. It leaves a link with the historic *Philothion*, has the same termination as *Peptone*, which has long served as a name for the simpler peptides, and is a sufficient reminder that the dipeptide contains glutamic acid linked to a sulphur compound. **1925** *Glasgow Herald* 5 Dec. 4 The oxygen-transporting and oxygen-liberating power of glutathione. **1949** H. W. FLOREY et al. *Antibiotics* II. xxi. 812 Glutathione and thiothreonine antagonized the anti-bacterial action of penicillin. **1969** *Nature* 11 Oct. 117/1 The tripeptide glutathione is an almost universal constituent of functioning biological systems.

glutelin (ˈgl(j)uːtəlɪn). *Biochem.* [f. GLUTE(N + *-lin*, perh. after GLOBULIN.] Any of a group of simple proteins all characteristically soluble in dilute acids and alkalis but insoluble in neutral saline solutions and found esp. in seeds.

1908 *Jrnl. Biol. Chem.* IV. p. xlix, *Glutelins*, simple proteins insoluble in all neutral solvents but readily soluble in very dilute acids and alkalies. **1963** E. G. YOUNG in Florkin & Stotz *Comprehensive Biochem.* VII. i. 7 By modern criteria of purity the glutelins are heterogeneous and poorly characterized.

gluten (ˈgl(j)uːtɛn). Also 8 glutton. [a. L. *glūten* glue, perh. through F. *gluten* (16th c.).]

1. Any sticky substance; a gum or glue. *rare.*

1639 DU VERGER tr. *Camus' Admir. Events* 98 The love of vertue (which was the cement, or gluten of their friendship). **1821** CRAIG *Lect. Drawing* ii. 110 The use of some kind of gum, or gluten, by way of size. **1870** EMERSON *Soc. & Solit., Civiliz.* Wks. (Bohn) III. 8 The power of a wafer or a drop of wax or gluten to guard a letter.

b. A viscid animal secretion.

1802 BINGLEY *Anim. Biog.* (1813) III. 456 The gluten supplied by a gland [in the mussel]. **1834** R. MUDIE *Brit. Birds* I. 224 Those swallows which construct their nests of humid mud (they too may secrete less or more of a similar gluten) never build so high..as the swift.

†**2.** The albuminous element of animal tissues, now called FIBRIN. Sometimes ***animal gluten.***

1597 LOWE *Chirurg.* I. vi. (1634) 21 The fourth [humour] is called Gluten, and is the proper humiditie of the similar parts. **1658** A. FOX tr. *Wurtz' Surg.* I. vi. 22 With that poaking and searching they break and destroy that natural Gluten or Balsom (which settleth for the healing, and is the healing it self). **1746** R. JAMES in Moufet & Bennet *Health's Improv.* Introd. 65 The much smaller Quantity of the oleaginous Liquor that is found in fresh Vegetables, in Comparison of what is found in Flesh..prevents the Formation of a too tenacious Glutton. **1800** HENRY *Epit. Chem.* (1808) 306 Gluten forms the basis of the muscular or fleshy parts of animals. **1822–34** *Good's Study Med.* (ed. 4) I. 547 Fibrin or fibrous matter, frequently also called coagulable lymph, and gluten.

3. The nitrogenous part of the flour of wheat or other grain, which remains behind as a viscid substance when the starch is removed by kneading the flour in a current of water.

1803 *Med. Jrnl.* X. 45 The eighth part of these 45, seems to be resin, intimately mixed with gluten. **1822** IMISON *Sci. & Art* II. 128 Gluten is insoluble in water and is elastic like elastic gum. **1837** M. DONOVAN *Dom. Econ.* II. 301 Wheat contains pure vegetable matter along with..gluten, which very much approximates to the character of animal matter. **1845** TODD & BOWMAN *Phys. Anat.* I. 40 Gluten..yields a principle which is called vegetable fibrine. **1876** HARLEY *Mat. Med.* (ed. 6) 371 Oats contain a larger proportion of gluten than any of the other cereals in use.

4. *Geol.* A tenacious mass (as of clay, bitumen, etc.). So F. *gluten.* ? *Obs.*

1811 PINKERTON *Petral.* I. 530 A pudding-stone of fragments of black hornstein in a gluten of clay, iron, and lime.

5. *Comb.*, as **gluten-bread**, bread containing a large proportion of gluten, prescribed in the diet of patients suffering from diabetes; **gluten-casein, -fibrin**, the vegetable casein and fibrin which form constituents of gluten.

1846 G. E. DAY tr. *Simon's Anim. Chem.* II. 296 Gluten-bread containing only one-half the amount of starch, but three times the amount of nitrogenous matter, was given in its place. **1876** *Trans. Clinical Soc.* IX. 148 A partially restricted dietary was commenced, gluten bread being substituted for the ordinary loaf. **1885** GOODALE *Physiol. Bot.* 363 Casein of plants comprises the following substances: legumin, gluten-casein, conglutin. *Ibid.* 364 Gelatin of plants. The associated matters are (1) Gliadin, (2) Mucedin, (3) Gluten-fibrin.

glutenerie: see GLUTTONRY.

glutenin (ˈgl(j)uːtənɪn). *Biochem.* [f. GLUTEN + -IN[1].] A glutelin found esp. in wheat.

1893 OSBORNE & VORHEES in *Amer. Chem. Jrnl.* XV. 457 It would be desirable to return to Taddei's original name and in future call this proteid zymon. Unfortunately this name is derived from the Greek word ζύμη, a ferment, and.. this name is undesirable. As this proteid is especially characteristic of gluten, it seems appropriate to call it *glutenin*, a name suggested to us by Professor S. W. Johnson. **1963** E. G. YOUNG in Florkin & Stotz *Comprehensive Biochem.* VII. i. 8 Those proteins of the group which have been isolated and studied are glutenin of wheat..and avenin of oats.

†**ˈglutenite.** *Geol. Obs. rare*[−1]. [f. GLUTEN + -ITE.] A conglomerate rock (cf. GLUTEN 4).

1811 PINKERTON *Petral.* I. 138 Glutenite, consisting of fragments of granite, cemented by trap. Siderous glutenite, or pudding-stone of the most modern formation.

gluter, var. GLOTHER, *Obs.*, to flatter.

†**ˈgluterness.** *Obs.* [? ad. OF. *glouternie* gluttony; but cf. ON. *glutr* wasteful luxury.] Gluttony.

c **1200** ORMIN 11650 Forrþi birrþ uss allre firrst Offtredenn gluterrnesse..Forr gluterrnesse waccneþþ all Galnessess laþe strenncþe..& alle fule lusstess Biginnenn þære & springenn ut Off gluterrnessess rote. [Very frequent in Ormin.]

gluterous, -ery, var. GLUTTEROUS, -ERY, *Obs.*

glutethimide (gl(j)uːˈtɛθɪmaɪd). *Pharm.* [f. *α-ethyl-α-phenylglutarimide*, the systematic chemical name for glutethimide, by rearrangement of some of its elements.] A colourless, odourless crystalline compound with hypnotic properties.

1955 *Unlisted Drugs* Jan. 4/2 Doriden (C-11, 511, glutethimide). **1966** *New Scientist* 1 Dec. 530/2 Glutethimide, a widely-sold sleeping tablet. **1967** *Martindale's Extra Pharmacopoeia* (ed. 25) 304/1 It has been suggested that, since glutethimide is chemically related to thalidomide, it may also have teratogenic effects.

†glut-glut, *v. Obs. rare*⁻¹. [echoic: see quot.] *trans.* To swallow or gulp down.

1650 TRAPP *Comm. Prov.* xxx. 15 Whiles he glutgluts their blood, as the young Eaglets are said to do (Iob 39. 30) by a word made from the sound.

gluther, Sc. var. GLOTHER, *Obs.*, to flatter.

glut-herring. 'The blueback, *Clupea æstivalis*, an American clupeoid fish closely related to the alewife' (*Cent. Dict.*).

glutin (ˈgl(j)uːtɪn). *Chem.* Also **glutine**. [a. F. *glutine* (obs.) vegetable albumen, prob. f. L. *glūt(en)* + *-ine*: see -IN.]

†**1.** = GLUTEN 1 and 3. *Obs.*

1825 J. NICHOLSON *Operat. Mechanic* 407 He..wets the fibres [of flax or hemp] and rubs them together, which, by the glutine remaining in them will cause them to adhere. **1866** ROSCOE *Elem. Chem.* xli. 354 Glutin, or the sticky, elastic substance contained with starch in wheaten flour, is vegetable fibrin.

2. 'Vegetable albumen, as distinguished from gluten' (Mayne *Expos. Lex.* 1854); = GLIADIN.

1838 T. THOMSON *Chem. Org. Bodies* 684 Of Glutin. This name has been given by M. de Saussure to the substance.. described by Einhoff, under the name of *kleber*. It may be obtained by boiling alcohol upon the gluten of wheat, and freeing the solution from mucin..If the alcohol be evaporated, the glutin is left in the state of a yellowish translucent matter. **1844** HOBLYN *Dict. Med., Glutine*, a principle resembling gluten, but differing from it in not being soluble in alcohol.

3. 'A distinct form of gelatin obtained from skin, hoof, bone, etc.' (Mayne *Expos. Lex.* 1854).

1845 G. E. DAY tr. *Simon's Anim. Chem.* I. 26 By long continued boiling, glutin loses its power of gelatinizing. **1852** MORFIT *Tanning & Currying* (1853) 142 Glutin is the principal component of glue.

†ˈglutinant, *ppl. a. Obs. rare*⁻¹. [ad. L. *glūtinant-em*, pres. pple. of *glūtināre* to GLUTINATE.] = GLUTINATIVE *a.*

1684 tr. *Bonet's Merc. Compit.* VII. 252 Which dressing may be kept on by a defensative and glutinant Plaster.

†ˈglutinate, *v. Obs.* [f. ppl. stem of L. *glūtināre*, f. *glūtin-*, *glūten* glue.]

1. *trans. Med.* **a.** To close up, heal (a wound). **b.** To cure relaxation in (the bowels, veins, etc.); to constipate. Also *absol.*

1564 P. MOORE *Hope Health* II. ix. 37 Comferie.. glutinateth and ioyneth together freshe woundes. **1610** BARROUGH *Meth. Physick* II. xii. (1639) 91 You must minister those medicines which will glutinate and heale up the ulcer. **1641** FRENCH *Distill.* v. (1651) 165 The inward use of these bath-waters is..by reason of the sulphur to dry, mollifie, discusse, and glutinate, and to help all uterine effects. **1684** tr. *Bonet's Merc. Compit.* III. 79 It may, by the power of Nature, be glutinated with a kind of bony cicatrice. **1748** tr. *Vegetius' Distemp. Horses* 344 It is thought that this will glutinate any of the inward Parts or Vessels.

2. (See quots.)

1604 R. CAWDREY *Table Alph., Glutinate*, to glue, or ioyne together. **1698** [see *Glutinated*]. **1721–1800** BAILEY, *Glutinate*, to glue or stick together. Hence in TODD, etc.

Hence **†ˈglutinated**, **†ˈglutinating** *ppl. adjs.*

1634 T. JOHNSON *Parey's Chirurg.* 1033 Drinesse and astriction produce a glutinating and cicatrizing faculty. **1655** CULPEPPER *Riverius* II. xiii. 88 You must use Astringent and Glutinating Medicines. **1698** FRYER *Acc. E. India & P.* 356 Their Bows..not made of Wood, but glutinated Horn.

†glutiˈnation. *Obs.* [ad. L. *glūtinātiōn-em*, n. of action f. *glūtināre*: see prec.]

1. *Med.* The process of closing or healing (wounds, etc.); also *pl.*, appliances for this purpose.

1607 TOPSELL *Four-f. Beasts* (1658) 546 The wounds made of them are dangerous, because..it is..impossible to bring them to a glutination with medicines. **1657** *Physical Dict., Glutinations*, such things that (like glue) are used to joyn and close up broken bones, veins, &c. **1684** tr. *Bonet's Merc. Compit.* III. 53 Asses milk..cures the Ulcer by cleansing.. and by glutination.

2. Gluing.

1676 in COLES. **1706** PHILLIPS (ed. Kersey), *Glutination*, a gluing together, or joyning together with Glue. **1721–1800** in BAILEY. Hence in TODD and mod. Dicts.

†ˈglutinative, *a.* and *sb. Med. Obs.* [ad. late L. *glūtinātīv-us*, f. *glūtināre*: see GLUTINATE.]

A. *adj.* Having the property of joining together or closing up (wounds, etc.); constrictive.

1578 LYTE *Dodoens* I. ciii. 146 The same [rootes of Comferie] are so glutinatiue that if [etc.]. **1585** BANISTER tr. *Wecker's Chyrurg.* 336 Such a one is to be ioyned..by stitching and glutinatiue medicines. **1657** TOMLINSON *Renou's Disp.* 452 It [Isinglass] is rightly mixed with glutinative Salves. **1706** PHILLIPS (ed. Kersey), *Glutinative*, proper to glue, that has a gluing Quality. **1721–1800** in BAILEY; hence in TODD and mod. Dicts.

B. *sb. pl.* Medical preparations which serve to close up (wounds, etc.) or bind together.

[*c* **1400** *Lanfranc's Cirurg.* 6 Cap. v of glutinatiuis & consolidatiuis, þat buþ closeres & consouderes, & þe difference of hem.] **1656** RIDGLEY *Pract. Physick* 67 If the bone be broken withal, common glutinatives restrain the venome. **1684** tr. *Bonet's Merc. Compit.* XVIII. 600 The place must be cicatrized by astringents and glutinatives.

Hence **†ˈglutinativeness**, 'gluey quality'.

1727–36 in BAILEY.

†glutinatory, *a. Med. Obs. rare*⁻¹. [ad. late L. (medical) *glūtinātōri-us*.] = GLUTINATIVE *a.*

1657 TOMLINSON *Renou's Disp.* 31 That medicament is called..glutinatory which conjoynes..parts disjoyned.

†ˈglutining, *ppl. a. Obs. rare*⁻¹. [f. L. *glutin-*, *glūten* glue + -ING².] Sticky, gluey.

1658 R. WHITE tr. *Digby's Powd. Symp.* (ed. 2) 43 These [the beames from the Moon] clean contrary do refresh and moysten in a notable manner, leaving an aquatick, and viscous glutining kind of sweat upon the glasse.

glutinize (ˈgl(j)uːtɪnaɪz), *v.* [f. as prec. + -IZE.] *trans.* To render viscous or gluey. Hence **ˈglutinizing** *ppl. a.*

1750 G. HUGHES *Barbadoes* 153 This gluey substance may be of further use if gathered by butterflies or other flying insects..to glutinize their bags or webs, before they enter into the Aurelia state. **1814** *Last Act* II. i, Thinking about him..freezes my soul and glutinizes my blood. **1883** *Hardwich's Photogr. Chem.* (ed. Taylor) 203 Iodide of Cadmium..would have superseded the other Iodides, had it not been for its glutinizing action on Pyroxyline.

glutinoid (ˈgl(j)uːtɪnɔɪd), *a.* [f. as prec. + -OID.] Resembling gluten.

1876 HARLEY *Mat. Med.* (ed. 6) 729 Grape-juice also contains gum,..colouring matter, and a glutinoid substance.

glutinose (ˈgl(j)uːtɪnəʊs), *a.* [See -OSE.] = GLUTINOUS.

1840 in PAXTON *Bot. Dict.* **1882** in OGILVIE.

glutinosity (gl(j)uːtɪˈnɒsɪtɪ). [f. L. *glūtinōs-us* GLUTINOUS + -ITY.] The quality or condition of being glutinous.

c **1400** *Lanfranc's Cirurg.* 45 Þe stipticite of þe rosis..& glutinosite of þe wormes..remeuen þe akþe of þe senewis. **1608** TOPSELL *Serpents* (1658) 782 The Spider..new strengthneth them afresh..with another new glutinosity, or fast-binding clamminesse. **1684** tr. *Bonet's Merc. Compit.* III. 51 Austere things..give glutinosity and toughness to Fluids. **1876** tr. *Wagner's Gen. Pathol.* (ed. 6) 246 The cause of the glutinosity lies in the fine processes, which the cells invariably have also during their onward flow.

glutinous (ˈgl(j)uːtɪnəs), *a.* Also 7 **gluttinous**. [ad. L. *glūtinōs-us*, f. *glutin-* GLUTEN. Cf. F. *glutineux*.] Of the nature of glue or gluten; viscid, sticky, gluey.

1576 BAKER *Jewell of Health* 237 Masticke..gum, or any other matter, that being wrought and made glutynous or glewishe [etc.]. **1603** B. JONSON *Sejanus* I. i, We haue..No soft, and glutinous bodies, that can stick, Like Snailes on painted walls. **1620** VENNER *Via Recta* iii. 52 The nourishment thereof is too moist, grosse, glutinous, and obstructiue. **1727** SWIFT *Gulliver* III. v. 209 Gums, oils, and other glutinous matter. **1779** FORREST *Voy. N. Guinea* 188 As I went in barefooted, I found the miry stuff stick to my feet. Being very glutinous, it was not easily washed off. **1820** KEATS *Lamia* I. 210 God Bacchus..Stretch'd out, at ease, beneath a glutinous pine. **1851–6** WOODWARD *Mollusca* 113 Some of the gasteropoda can suspend themselves by glutinous threads. **1875** JOWETT *Plato* (ed. 2) III. 658 The sinews have a firmer and more glutinous nature than flesh.

fig. **1638** ROUSE *Heav. Univ.* (1702) 157, I may be able to hold thee fast with the glutinous bond of true love. **1655** FULLER *Ch. Hist.* IX. xvi. §38 Besides the glutenous nature of all aspersions to stick where they light. **1721** R. KEITH tr. *T. à Kempis' Solil. Soul* ix. 170, I am fettered with the glutinous Affection of fading slippery Things. **1883** A. FORBES in *19th Cent.* Oct. 722 The accent of the lower classes, which is a glutinous Cockney.

Hence **ˈglutinously** *adv.*, **ˈglutinousness**.

1620 DEKKER *Dreame* (1860) 29 The Ægyptian Caliginous black vapor..glutinously thick. *a* **1661** FULLER *Worthies Dorset.* I. (1662) 277 His [the tench's] Natural unctuous glutinousness, which quickly consolidateth any green gash in any fish. **1685** BOYLE *Enq. Notion Nat.* 192 Spirit of Wine, whose Tenacity and Glutinousness is far less than that of Water. **1851** RUSKIN *Stones Ven.* I. xxvii. §16 As if one had dipped it [the shaft] into a mass of melted ornament..and brought up a quantity adhering glutinously to its extremity. **1872** GEO. ELIOT *Middlem.*, The most glutinously indefinite minds enclose some hard grains of habit.

glutiry, var. GLUTTERY, *Obs.*

glutition (gl(j)uːˈtɪʃən). [n. of action f. L. *glūtīre* to swallow.] The action of swallowing, deglutition.

1888 *Med. News* LIII. 508 (Cent.) This..does not, as a rule, prevent glutition.

ˈglutless, *a. nonce-wd.* [f. GLUT *sb.*³ or GLUT *v.*¹ + -LESS.] Insatiable.

1787 BEST *Angling* 8 The greedy Trout and glutless Eel.

†ˈglutman. *Obs.* [f. GLUT *sb.*³ + MAN.] (See quot.)

1796 COLQUHOUN *Police Metrop.* 64 Inferior Officers of the Customs, and particularly that class of supernumerary tides-men who are employed, *pro tempore*, when there is hurry of business, and who, from that circumstance, are called glutmen.

glutrie, -y, varr. GLUTTERY, *Obs.*

glutt(e, obs. form of GLUT *sb.* and *v.*

glutted (ˈglʌtɪd), *ppl. a.*¹ [f. GLUT *v.*¹ + -ED¹.] In senses of the vb.

a **1586** SIDNEY *Arcadia* III. (1633) 296 But those valiant couples..gave new appetites to the almost glutted eyes of the beholders. **1635** QUARLES *Embl.* II. ii. (1718) 69 She sucks and draws her brother's golden store Until her glutted orb can suck no more. **1702** POPE *Wife of Bath* 262 A glutted market makes provision cheap. **1718** PRIOR *Solomon* I. 219 The faithful hound..Takes what the glutted child denies to eat. **1856** EMERSON *Eng. Traits, Lit.* Wks. (Bohn) II. 113 Glutted markets and low prices.

glutted (ˈglʌtɪd), *ppl. a.*² *rare*⁻¹. [f. GLUT *v.*² + -ED¹.] That is swallowed greedily.

1667 MILTON *P.L.* x. 633 My Hell-hounds..cramm'd and gorg'd nigh burst With suckt and glutted offal.

glutteny, obs. form of GLUTTONY.

glutter (ˈglʌtə(r)). *rare.* [echoic.] Splutter.

1826 J. WILSON *Noct. Ambr.* Wks. 1855 I. 240 What a glutter of gutturals. **1884** R. BUCHANAN *Foxglove Manor* II. xxvi. 244 Here and there..ran a weazel..in one eternal glutter and hurry of bloodthirsty emotion.

†ˈglutterous, *a. Obs. rare.* In 4 **gloterous(e, glotorous**, 5 **gluterus**. [ad. OF. *gloutereux; cf. next.] = GLUTTONOUS.

1382 WYCLIF *Lev.* xi. 30 A mygal, that is a beeste born trecherows to bigile, and moost gloterous [**1388** *margin* a gileful and most gloterouse mous]. **1483** *Cath. Angl.* 160/1 Gluterus..*edax, gulosus, ingluuiosus.*

†ˈgluttery. *Obs.* Forms: 3 **glot(e)ri, glotory, glutry, -rie**, 3–4 **glotery, -ori**, 4 **glot(te)ry, gluttery, -eri(e, -erye, glutiry, -urry**, 4–5 **glotorye**, 5 **gluterye, glutery, gluttre**. [a. OF. *glotirie, glouterie*, f. *glot* glutton: see GLUT *sb.*¹ and -ERY.] Gluttony.

The word is chiefly northern, occurring frequently in the *Cursor Mundi* and in Hampole.

a **1300** *Cursor M.* 10114 Þe fleche has redili him bi, Foli liking, and gloteri. *a* **1340** HAMPOLE *Psalter* lxviii. 19 Þe wickid delites of glutiry and lichery. **1382** WYCLIF *Deut.* xxi. 20 This oure sone..to glotryes [**1388** glotonyes] takith hede, and to leccherye, and to feestis. *c* **1400** MAUNDEV. (Roxb.) xv. 69 Þai..occupiez all þe day..in drinkyng and in glotry. *c* **1450** *St. Cuthbert* (Surtees) 7172 Þai turned to glutery and confusioun. *c* **1470** HENRY *Wallace* VII. 349 Throuch full gluttre in swarff swappyt lik swyn.

glutting (ˈglʌtɪŋ), *vbl. sb.*¹ [f. GLUT *v.*¹ + -ING¹.] The action of the verb GLUT¹; feeding to repletion, cramming, or cloying. Also *concr.*, an amount (of food) that gluts.

c **1315** SHOREHAM 97 And that thou ne werche nauȝt, Ac gest to þyne gloutynge..Thou halst..wel wors thane masse-day Thane manne myd hys workynge. **1549** CHEKE *Hurt Sedit.* (1569) G iv b, By vsing of..glutting of meates which weakeneth the body. **1598** FLORIO, *Corpacciata*, a panchfull, a glutting. **1626** BACON *Sylva* §300 Some Food we may vse long and much, without Glutting. **1649** JER. TAYLOR *Gt. Exemp.* III. xiv. 26 Nothing but gluttings of the sence. **1653** ROUSE *Myst. Marr.* 303 So temperate a moderation between glutting and starving, that the soul be neither too fat nor too lean.

glutting (ˈglʌtɪŋ), *vbl. sb.*² *rare.* [f. GLUT *v.*² + -ING¹.] **a.** The action of the verb GLUT²; greedy swallowing, gulping. Also ***glutting down***. **b.** A sound as of swallowing.

1632 LITHGOW *Trav.* III. 127 He swimmes, and sinkes, and in that glutting downe, The angry Fates, did kind Leander drowne. **1733** CHEYNE *Eng. Malady* II. xi. §2 (1734) 229 The Breathing difficult, with Glutting, Gulping, or Choaking.

ˈglutting, *ppl. a.*¹ [f. GLUT *v.*¹ + -ING².] That gluts, sates, or cloys.

1574 T. NEWTON *Dir. Health Mag.* 52 A great gluttinge draught drowneth the meate. **1634** RAINBOW *Labour* (1635) 15 Glutting morsels spread..upon..purples. **1681** FLAVEL *Meth. Grace* xii. 252 The loveliness of every creature is of a cloying and glutting nature.

Hence **ˈgluttingly** *adv.*, so as to glut.

1611 FLORIO, *A satietà*, with saciety, hold-belly-hold, gluttingly.

ˈglutting, *ppl. a.*² [f. GLUT *v.*² + -ING².] That gluts or swallows greedily.

1555 HARPSFIELD *Divorce* (1878) 287 This insatiable, glutting Charibdis and Sylla.

gluttinous, obs. form of GLUTINOUS.

†gluttish, *a. Obs. rare.* [f. GLUT *sb.*² + -ISH.] Cloying, satiating.

1655 MOUFET & BENNET *Health's Improv.* (1746) 113 If they be over sweet and gluttish, they soon turn into Choler, stop the Liver [etc.]. *Ibid.* 272 No Eel is free from a venomous Malignity and a kind of gluttish suffocating Juice.

glutton (ˈglʌt(ə)n), *sb.* and *a.* Forms: 3 **glutun, glotun**, 3–4 **glotoun**, (4 **glotoune, -owne, -en**), 4–6 **gloton**, (5 **glotone, gluton**), 5–6 **glotton**, (6 **glutten**,

Sc. **glowton, glouttoun**), 6- **glutton.** [a. OF. *glutun, gluton* (mod.F. *glouton* = Sp. *gloton*, Pg. *glotão*, It. *ghiottone*):—L. *glūtōn-em, gluttōn-em*, sb. related to *glūtire* to gulp down, swallow. The L. nom. *glūto* is represented by shorter forms in some of the Romanic languages, as OF. *gloz, gluz, glous*, etc. (later *glout* masc., *gloute* fem.), Prov. *glotz*, It. *ghiotto*; cf. GLUT *sb.*[1]]

A. *sb.* **1. a.** One who eats to excess, or who takes pleasure in immoderate eating; a gormandizer.

a **1225** *Ancr. R.* 214 Þe ȝiure glutun is þes feondes manciple. *a* **1300** *K. Horn* 1122 Hue..fulde him of the broune A bolle of a galoun, Hue wende he were a glotoun. **1387** TREVISA *Higden* II. 171 In berynge þey beeþ menstralles and heraudes, in talkynge grete spekeres, in etynge and in drynkynge glotouns. *c* **1450** *Mirour Saluacioun* 658 The Gloton knawes erthlinesse and vnknawes hevenly thing. **1526** *Pilgr. Perf.* (W. de W. 1531) 233 The couetous person..hath his meditacion on his goodes, the gloton on his inordynat appetytes, and so of other. *c* **1586** C'TESS PEMBROKE *Ps.* LXXVIII. xiii, Gods wrathfull rage upon these gluttons sent, Of all their troupes the principallest slew. **1725** POPE *Odyss.* XI. 149 There foul adulterers to thy bride resort, And lordly gluttons riot in thy court. **1774** GOLDSM. *Retal.* 18 At a dinner so various, at such a repast Who'd not be a glutton, and stick to the last? **1821** SYD. SMITH *Wks.* (1867) I. 329 But you will never separate the wealthy glutton from his pheasant. **1880** MRS. FORRESTER *Roy & V.* I. 38 Fancy her wanting to marry a lovely girl to a disgusting old glutton like the Baron.

fig. **1548** HALL *Chron., Hen. VI*, 137 Suche a strong percer is money, and suche a gredie glotton is avarice.

Prov. *c* **1530** R. HILLES *Common-Pl. Bk.* (1858) 140 Non sygheth so sore as the gloton that may no more.

†**b.** ***the* (*rich*) *glutton***, the rich man of the parable (Luke xvi. 19), who 'fared sumptuously every day'.

= L. *dives epulo*, in the Vulgate heading of the chapter. [*c* **1380** WYCLIF *Serm.* Sel. Wks. I. 1 Þere was a riche man þat disuside his richesse in pride and in glotonye.] **1413** *Pilgr. Sowle* (Caxton 1483) III. ix. 56 The riche gloton lacketh water to kele with his tonge. **1568** LAUDER *Prettie Mirrour* 101 The Gluttoun, quha fed delicius..That petiit nocht the pure Lazarus. *a* **1592** H. SMITH *Serm.* (1622) 351 That fiery lake, where the Glutton begges but a drop of water to coole the tip of his tongue. **1722** DE FOE *Relig. Courtsh.* I. ii. (1840) 66 Would you change your condition with me that am the rich glutton?

c. applied to animals. (Cf. 4, 5.)

1398 TREVISA *Barth. De P.R.* XVIII. i. (1495) 738 Some bestes ben grete glotons and grete deuourers of meete. **1697** DRYDEN *Virg. Georg.* IV. 166 Sweet Gardens, full of Saffron Flow'rs, invite The wand'ring Gluttons, and retard their Flight. *c* **1750** SHENSTONE *Elegies* xv. 67 From their own streams their choicer fare they drew; To lure the scaly glutton to the shore.

2. *fig.* **a.** One who is inordinately fond of some specified object or pursuit, esp. ***a glutton of books***, after L. *helluo librorum*. Also const. *for*.

a **1704** T. BROWN *Sat. Fr. King* Wks. 1730 I. 60 Since 'tis no sin of books to be a glutton, I truck'd St. Austin for a leg of mutton. **1706** GRANVILLE *Brit. Enchanters* I. i. 4 Foes alike to Good, Gluttons in Murder, wanton to destroy. **1768–74** TUCKER *Lt. Nat.* (1852) II. 484 We talk of a thirst of knowledge, a glutton of books. **1860** MARSH *Eng. Lang.* xxi. 464 The elder Pliny..the most voracious literary glutton of ancient times. **1895** KIPLING *Day's Work* (1898) 197 He's honest, and a glutton for work. **1971** C. EGLETON *Last Post for Partisan* iii. 29 This bug may not look up to much but the Volks is a glutton for punishment. **1971** E. LEMARCHAND *Death on Doomsday* ix. 131 Glutton for work, aren't you?

b. *Sporting slang.* (See quots.)

1809 *European Mag.* LV. 22 The term *glutton* whether at a fight or a feast is now indiscriminately applied to every man of true bottom. **1819** MOORE *Tom Crib* (ed. 3) p. xvi, A 'glutton'..the classical phrase at Moulsey-Hurst, for one who..takes a deal of punishment before he is satisfied.

†**3.** As a general term of reproach or contempt: A vile wretch; 'a knaue, rascall, filthie fellow' (Cotgr.). (The earliest sense recorded in OF.) *Obs.*

c **1300** *Havelok* 2104 None but wicke men, Glotuns, reu[e]res, or wicke theues. *c* **1380** *Sir Ferumb.* 164 'A, glotoun', saide þe Emperer, ' entempre þou beter þy tonge'. **1432–50** tr. *Higden* (Rolls) VII. 327 Sease, gloton [L. *nebulo*], y am kynge of Ynglonde. *c* **1489** CAXTON *Sonnes of Aymon* iii. 83 'Go forth, glotton, goddis curse haue thou' sayd Aymon to his sone Reynawde. **1523** LD. BERNERS *Froiss.* I. ccclxxxii. 626 Watte Tyler, Jacke Strawe, and Johan Ball..founde the archebysshoppe of Caunterbury..these glottons [F. *ces gloutons*] toke hym and strake of his heed.

4. A voracious animal, *Gulo luscus* or *arcticus*, belonging to the *Mustelidæ* or weasels and martens, but much larger than other members of that family. It is a native of the northern parts of Europe, Asia, and America; the American variety is commonly called WOLVERENE or CARCAJOU.

1674 tr. *Scheffer's Lapland* 134 The Gluttons..have a round head, strong and sharp teeth, like a Wolfs..some compare it to the Otter, but it is far greedier than he, for thence it gets its name. **1774** GOLDSM. *Nat. Hist.* (1776) III. 395 The Glutton..for several reasons, seems to belong to this tribe [the weasels], and this only. **1834** MCMURTRIE *Cuvier's Anim. Kingd.* 61 Linnæus..placed the Gluttons among the bears, but they approximate much nearer to the weasels in their teeth as well as in their habits. **1865** LUBBOCK *Preh. Times* ix. (1869) 295 The glutton or wolverine..has been found in three of the English bone-caves.

5. A species of the genus *Volvox* of Infusoria. ? *Obs.*

1769 ELLIS in *Phil. Trans.* LIX. 150 Fig. 6. is the *volvox vorax*, or the glutton.

6. *Comb.*, as ***glutton-like*** adj. and adv.

1592 SHAKS. *Ven. & Ad.* xci, Gluttonlike she feeds, yet neuer filleth. **1599** T. M[OUFET] *Silkwormes* 43 And glutton-like to vomit vp their meate. **1697** CONGREVE *Mourning Bride* I. i. 3 Some unsuspected hoard of darling Grief, Which they unseen, may wail and weep and mourn, And Glutton-like alone devour.

B. *adj.* = GLUTTONOUS; also (see A 3) †villainous. (Cf. F. *glouton* adj.)

1387–8 T. USK *Test. Love* III. ix. (Skeat) 65 Right as I was sorowed thorow the gloton cloud of manifolde sickly sorow. *a* **1547** SURREY *Ps.* lxxiii. 26 in Park *Nugæ Antiq.* (1804) II. 365 Whose glutten chekes slouth feads so fatt, as scant their eyes be sene. **1682** DRYDEN *Religio Laici* 33 In Pleasure some their glutton souls would steep. **1712** CONGREVE *Ovid's Art Love* III. Wks. 1730 III. 324 No Glutton Nymph, however Fair, can wound, Tho' more than Helen she in Charms abound. **1725** POPE *Odyss.* XIX. 645 The geese (a glutton race) by thee deplor'd, Portend the Suitors fated to my sword. **1805** in *Spirit Publ. Jrnls.* (1806) IX. 244 His glutton stomach would have gorged the world. **1856** J. H. NEWMAN *Callista* xv. 136 The small patches of ground belonging to the poor peasants..are the prey of these glutton invaders [*sc.* locusts].

†**'glutton**, *v. Obs.* [f. the sb.; cf. OF. *gloutonner*.] *intr.* To feed voraciously or excessively.

c **1600** SHAKS. *Sonn.* lxxv, Thus do I pine and surfet day by day, Or gluttoning on all, or all away. **1602** MARSTON *Antonio's Rev.* I. iii. Wks. 1856 I. 82 Sing one of Signior Renaldo's ayres, To rouse the slumbring bride from gluttoning, In surfet of superfluous sleepe. **1747** tr. *Mem. Nutrebian Court* II. 23 Fierce dogs were sitting, to gorge and glutton on their bowels. **1781** W. BLANE *Ess. Hunting* (1788) 83 Hares never..glutton on their food, like the wise Heads that hunt them.

Hence †**'gluttoned** *ppl. a.*, surfeited, gorged; †**'gluttoning** *vbl. sb.* (also ***gluttoning-in***). Also †**'gluttoner**, a glutton.

1482 *Monk of Evesham* (Arb.) 82 Y leue oute and pas by..lyers and forswerers glotyners..and a thousand mo of this wyse. **1607** TOPSELL *Four-f. Beasts* 435 It resembleth a Wolfe..in voracity and gluttoning in of flesh. **1641** MARMION *Antiquary* H ii b, Come, honest cook, let me see how thy imagination has wrought, as well as thy fingers..for gluttoning delights to be ingenious. *a* **1658** LOVELACE *Lucasta Posth.* (1659) 81 Then after all your fooling, fat, and wine, Glutton'd at last, [you] return at home to pine. **1721** STRYPE *Eccl. Mem.* III. I. 324 They were not deprived for gluttoning, nor swearing, nor dicing.

glutton, obs. form of GLUTEN.

'gluttoness. *rare.* [f. GLUTTON *sb.* + -ESS.] A female glutton.

1611 COTGR., *Gourmanderesse*, a gluttonnesse. **1835** *Blackw. Mag.* XXXVIII. 547 We might be otherwise were we too purveyors for that gluttonness [the reading public] to whom the grave is an epicure.

gluttonish ('glʌtənɪʃ), *a. rare.* [f. GLUTTON *sb.* + -ISH.] Glutton-like, voracious.

a **1586** SIDNEY *Arcadia* IV. (1633) 426 Having now framed their gluttonish stomackes to have for food the wild benefits of nature. **1886** SHELDON tr. *Flaubert's Salammbô* 5 They swallowed, in gluttonish mouthfuls, all the Greek wine.

Hence †**'gluttonishness.**

1598 FLORIO, *Leccatura*, a licking. Also gluttonishnes, lickrishnes.

'gluttonism. *nonce-wd.* [f. as prec. + -ISM.] The practice of being a glutton (in quot. *fig.*, cf. GLUTTON *sb.* 2).

1823 DE QUINCEY *Lett. Yng. Man* Wks. 1860 XIV. 46 One of the chief symptoms is an enormous 'gluttonism' for books, and for adding language to language.

gluttonize ('glʌtənaɪz), *v.* [f. as prec. + -IZE.] *intr.* To feast gluttonously. Const. *on*, †*in*. Also † *to gluttonize it.*

1656–81 BLOUNT *Glossogr.*, *Gormandize*, to ravine, devoure, glut, or gluttonize it. **1659** *Gentl. Calling* i. §5 (1660) 78 For how else can it become possible, that one rank of men should gluttonize, and another starve? **1678** CUDWORTH *Intell. Syst.* I. v. 810 That conceit that evil demons..were..delighted with the blood and nidours of sacrifices,..which they did, as it were, luxuriate and gluttonize in. **1748** RICHARDSON *Clarissa* (1811) IV. xxv. 136 The palliating consolation of an Hottentot heart, determined rather to gluttonize on the garbage of other foul feeders than to reform. **1804** C. B. BROWN tr. *Volney's View Soil U.S.* 368 When game is plenty..they revel and gluttonize.

b. *trans.* To feast gluttonously on.

1795 COLERIDGE *Lett.* (1895) 136 Mine eye gluttonizes the sea.

Hence **'gluttonizing** *vbl. sb.* and *ppl. a.*

1827 *Mirror* II. 435/2 Greet this gluttonizing day, And hail the new Lord Mayor. **1887** *Pall Mall G.* 21 Dec. 4/1 The Christmas gluttonizing of the well-to-do.

†**'gluttonly,** *adv. Obs. rare*[−1]. In 4 glotounliche. [f. as prec. + -LY[2]; cf. OF. *gloutement*, F. *gloutonnement*.] Greedily.

1340 *Ayenb.* 111 Þet is þet bread and þe mete þet þou..sselt ete zuyþe and glotounliche.

gluttonous ('glʌtənəs), *a.* Forms: 4 **glotounius, -onous, -enous,** 5 **glotenose, -ynous, glouttonnous,** 6 **glottonous,** (7 **glutenous, -inous,**) 6- **gluttonous.** [f. GLUTTON *sb.* + -OUS; no corresponding form is recorded in OF.]

1. Given to excess in eating; characterized by, or of the nature of, gluttony.

1340–70 *Alex. & Dind.* 790 Ȝe ben glotounius gle glad for to haunte, & han no mesure on molde of mete ne of drynke. *c* **1374** CHAUCER *Boeth.* I. met. vi. 16 (Camb. MS.) Ne seke thow nat, with a glotonous hond to stryne and presse the stalkes of the vyne in the ferst somer sesoun. *c* **1449** PECOCK *Repr.* I. iii. 13 A man ouȝte be temperat in eting and drinking and not be glotenose. *c* **1586** C'TESS PEMBROKE *Ps.* CVI. vi, Gluttonous they flesh in desert crave. **1610** HEALEY *St. Aug. Citie of God* XVI. xxxvii. (1620) 576 It is not the kinde of meate but the gluttonous affect that hurts. **1733** CHEYNE *Eng. Malady* II. vii. §2 (1734) 185 Gluttonous..Animals..have always overgrown Livers. **1802** BINGLEY *Anim. Biog.* (1813) I. 210 Although the Wolf is the most gluttonous of quadrupeds,..yet his rapacity does not exceed his cunning. **1848** LYTTON *Harold* II. i, Though a Norman was not gluttonous, he was epicurean. **1875** FARRAR *Seekers* I. v. 72 After one of his gluttonous suppers.

fig. *a* **1631** DONNE *Holy Sonn.* iii. Poems (1633) 33 Gluttonous death will instantly unjoynt My body, and my soule, and I shall sleepe a space.

2. *transf.* Excessively greedy or insatiable *of* (or †*after*) something. Also *absol.*

1669 WOODHEAD *St. Teresa* I. xviii. 112 My intention is no other than to make Soules, as it were, gluttonous, after the obtaining of so high a good. **1754** RICHARDSON *Grandison* V. xxi. 125 O my dear! you must be gluttonous of grief in your solitary hours. **1829** I. TAYLOR *Enthus.* iii. (1867) 61 Extravagance becomes gluttonous of marvels. **1860** MOTLEY *Netherl.* (1868) I. i. 4 Philip the Prudent, as he grew older and feebler in mind and body seemed to become more gluttonous of work. **1870** EMERSON *Soc. & Solit.*, *Bks.* Wks. (Bohn) III. 87 That scribatiousness which grew to be the habit of the gluttonous readers of his time.

†**3.** Of food: ? Fit for gluttons. *Obs.*

1600 W. VAUGHAN *Dir. Health* (1633) 19 Pastery..is rather gluttonous then healthy, not easie to digest.

Hence **'gluttonously** *adv.*

1398 TREVISA *Barth. De P.R.* XVIII. xcix. (1495) 845 A sowe etyth and deuouryth glotenously all maner stynkynge thynges and vnclene. **1484** CAXTON *Curiall* 3 b, And we ete so gredyly and gloutonnously that otherwhyle we caste it up agayn and make vomytes. **1612** DEKKER *If it be not good*, etc. Wks. 1873 III. 282 Thou saist (vile yongman) they haue arguments To proue it lawfull gluttonously to feede. **1666** J. DAVIES *Hist. Caribby Isl.* 331 So insatiable an appetite to mans flesh, that they gluttonously eat it raw. **1856** KANE *Arct. Expl.* I. xxx. 418 The Esquimaux, however gluttonously they may eat [etc.].

†**'gluttonry.** *Obs. rare*[−1]. In 2 glutenerie. [a. OF. *glutunerie* (P. de Thaun *c* 1150), F. *gloutonnerie*, f. *glouton* GLUTTON: see -ERY.] Gluttony.

c **1175** *Lamb. Hom.* 49 We stondeð in þe putte..also þeos men doð þe liggeð inne eubruche and ine glutenerie.

†**'gluttonsly,** *adv. Obs. rare*[−1]. [f. GLUTTON + -LY[2]; cf. *felonsli, vilainsly*, etc.] Gluttonously.

1475 CAXTON *Chesse* III. vi. (1481) H 3 b, Therfore ought euery man..not lyue to ete glotonsly, & for to drynke dronk.

gluttony ('glʌtənɪ). Forms: 3 **glutunie,** 3–6 **glotonie, -ye,** (4 **glotoni, -ani, -any, -(o)unye, -owny, -enie, -yne),** 4–5 **gloteny(e,** 4–6 **glotony,** 6 **glottenie, gluttenie, -eny,** (*Sc.* **glwtone),** 7 **gluttonie,** 6- **gluttony.** [a. OF. *glutunie, glotonie, glo(u)tenie*, etc. (also *glouternie*, etc.), abstract sb. related to GLUTTON, in mod.F. replaced by *gloutonnerie* (see GLUTTONRY).] The vice of excessive eating. (One of the seven deadly sins.) Also *rarely* an instance of this.

a **1225** *Ancr. R.* 194 Þe inre uondunge is twouold..flesliche ase of lecherie & of glutunie, & of slouhðe. *Ibid.* 204 Þe Suwe of ȝiuernesse, þet is, Glutunie. *c* **1380** WYCLIF *Serm.* Sel. Wks. I. 109 Þe fend bigan to tempte first Crist at pryde and glotonye. *c* **1440** *Jacob's Well* (E.E.T.S.) 141 Glotonye is, þat þe bely louyth, & it wastyth bothe body & soule, & a mannys good. **1541** ELYOT *Image Gov.* 7 This monstruouse Emperour, whiche consumed daies and nightes in lechery and glotony. **1604** JAS. I. *Counterbl.* (Arb.) 102 The cleering of his conscience from that deadly sinne of gluttonie. **1671** MILTON *P.R.* IV. 114 Their sumptuous gluttonies and gorgeous feasts. **1681** PRIDEAUX *Lett.* (Camden) 117, I attribute it to his gluttony, he being yᵉ greatest eater that ever I knew. **1752** HUME *Pol. Disc.* ii. 28 The Tartars are oftener guilty of beastly gluttony, when they feast on their dead horses, than European courtiers with all their refinements of cookery. **1803** SYD. SMITH *Wks.* (1859) I. 39/2 He lives only to digest, and, while the organs of gluttony perform their office, he has not a wish beyond. **1876** HUMPHREY *Coin-Coll. Man.* xxiv. 325 This monster of gluttony [Vitellius].

personified. *a* **1310** in Wright *Lyric P.* 49 Whil mi lif was luther ant lees, Glotonie mi glemon wes. **14..** LYDG. *Assemb. Gods* 628 Aftyr whom rood Glotony, with hys fat berde. **1500–20** DUNBAR *Poems* xxvi. 91 Than the fowll monstir Glutteny, Off wame vnsasiable and gredy, To dance he did him dress. **1590** SPENSER *F.Q.* I. iv. 21. **1634** MILTON *Comus* 776 Swinish gluttony Ne'er looks to heav'n amidst his gorgeous feast, But..Crams, and blasphemes his feeder.

†**b.** *fig. rare*[−1].

1704 STEELE *Lying Lover* II. (1747) 29 No, he has a Gluttony, an Hunger for me.

glutun, glutunie, obs. ff. GLUTTON, GLUTTONY.

gluturry, var. GLUTTERY, *Obs.*

gluve, gluwe, obs. forms of GLOVE *sb.*, GLUE.

gluwy, gluyn, obs. forms of GLUEY, GLUE *v.*

glwyn, obs. form of GLUE *v.*

gly, obs. form of GLEE *v.*, to look asquint.

glycæmia (glaɪˈsiːmɪə). *Physiol.* Also **glycemia**. [f. GLYC(O- + Gr. αἷμα blood: see -IA[1].] The presence of sugar in the blood; the blood-sugar level. (Rare, except in translations.) Cf. *glycohaemia* (s.v. GLYCO-). Hence **glyˈcaemic** *a.*
1901 *Index-Catal. Surg.-Gen. U.S.* 2nd Ser. VI. 266/1 (*heading*) Glycaemia. *See* Blood (Sugar in); Diabetes (Blood in). **1913** *Jrnl. Chem. Soc.* CIV. I. 923 The injection of adrenaline can induce perturbations in the glycæmia of an animal. **1923** *Archives Internal Med.* XXXI. 242 The term blood sugar curve is here applied to any glycemic reaction obtained in a tolerance test. **1936** Glycæmic [see *glycotropic* s.v. GLYCO-]. **1946** *Nature* 26 Oct. 589/1 Both groups of dogs show the known glycæmic response to the alloxan. **1966** *Canad. Jrnl. Physiol. & Pharmacol.* XLIV. 615 (*heading*) Glycemia and consecutive passive transfers of an anaphylactoid reaction inducing factor in rats.

glyceral (ˈglɪsərəl). *Chem.* [f. GLYCER-INE + AL(DEHYDE).] A compound obtained by heating glycerine with an aldehyde.
1872 WATTS *Dict. Chem.* 1st Suppl. 637 *Glycerals.*

glyceraldehyde (ˌglɪsəˈrældɪhaɪd). *Chem.* Also †**-aldehyd.** [f. GLYCER(IC *a.* + ALDEHYDE.] A colourless, sweet-tasting, crystalline compound, CHO·CHOH·CH_2OH, which is the simplest optically active sugar.
1882 *Jrnl. Chem. Soc.* XLII. 1308 The oxidation of the glyceraldehyd to tartronic acid. **1899** *Ibid.* LXXVI. I. 110 It [*sc.* acraldehyde dibromide] apparently gives rise to glyceraldehyde when left in contact with water. **1951** I. L. FINAR *Org. Chem.* I. xviii. 358 Glyceraldehyde has now been chosen as the standard configuration in sugar chemistry. **1965** *New Scientist* 17 June 761/2 The patients.. were also given glyceraldehyde, a normal intermediate product of glucose metabolism.

glycerate (ˈglɪsərət). [f. GLYCER-IC + -ATE[4].]
1. *Chem.* A salt of glyceric acid.
1864 WATTS *Dict. Chem.* II. 876 The glycerates are soluble in water and crystallise well.
2. 'A solution of some substance in glycerin' (*Syd. Soc. Lex.* 1885).

glyceria (glɪˈsɪərɪə). [mod.L. (R. Brown *Prodromus Floræ Novæ Hollandiæ* (1810) 179), f. Gr. γλυκερός sweet, in reference to the leaves and roots of some species.] A plant belonging to a widespread genus of aquatic grasses so named, of the family Gramineæ. Cf. SWEET-GRASS.
1829 J. C. LOUDON *Encycl. Plants* 62 *Glyceria*.. is found in stagnant water, and its long narrow leaves float on the surface. **1847** [see MANNA[1] 9]. **1934** A. ARBER *Gramineae* xvi. 376 At the periphery of the circular tufts of *Spartina*, the turf of *Glyceria* is, little by little, raised up and forced outwards. **1964** D. H. N. SPENCE in J. H. Burnett *Veget. Scotl.* ix. 352 *Glyceria* is a typical fen dominant in East Anglia.

glyceric (glɪˈsɛrɪk, ˈglɪsərɪk), *a.* *Chem.* [f. GLYCER-INE + -IC.] Of, derived from, or relating to glycerine. ***glyceric acid***, an acid obtained by the action of nitric acid on glycerine.
1864 WATTS *Dict. Chem.* II. 876 Glyceric acid is isomeric with pyruvic acid. **1873** *Fownes' Chem.* (ed. 11) 627 Glyceric monochlorhydrin. **1880** CLEMINSHAW *Wurtz' Atom. Theory* 200 The several series of glyceric ethers are comparable to the several series of ordinary phosphates. **1885** REMSEN *Org. Chem.* (1888) 166 Glyceric acid is a thick syrup which mixes with water and alcohol.

glyceride (ˈglɪsəraɪd). *Chem.* [f. GLYCER-INE + -IDE.] A compound ether of glycerine.
1864 WATTS *Dict. Chem.* II. 877 *Glycerides, Glycerin-ethers, Glyceryl-ethers, Saponifiable Fats*.. These bodies are the compound ethers of the triatomic alcohol, glycerin. **1866** ODLING *Anim. Chem.* 93 Caproic acid is met with as a glyceride in goat's butter. **1866** ROSCOE *Elem. Chem.* xxxv. 318 The drying oils are generally glycerides of acids.. nearly related to the fatty acid series.

glycerinate (ˈglɪsərɪneɪt), *v.* [f. GLYCERINE + -ATE.] To treat with glycerine. Chiefly in ppl. a. **ˈglycerinated**, said esp. of vaccine lymph.
1897 *Allbutt's Syst. Med.* II. 654 No growths arise in any of the ordinary culture media inoculated with such glycerinated lymph. **1898** *Westm. Gaz.* 24 Mar. 3/3 This new-fangled glycerinated lymph.

glycerine, glycerin (ˈglɪsərɪn, -iːn). [mod. f. Gr. γλυκερός sweet + -IN, -INE (see quot. 1842).]
1. A colourless, sweet, syrupy liquid obtained from animal and vegetable oils and fats by saponification. Largely used in *Med.* as an ointment and emollient dressing, as a vehicle for medicaments, etc. Chemically it is a triatomic alcohol, the hydrate of glyceryl. The name GLYCEROL is now preferred in systematic chemical nomenclature.
1838 T. THOMSON *Chem. Org. Bodies* 436 Glycerin is evolved, and a fatty acid, which combines with the alkali, and forms the soap. **1842** *Penny Cycl.* XXII. 169/1 He [Chevreul] also discovered that stearin is composed of stearic acid and a peculiar principle which on account of its sweet taste he named *glycerin*. **1868** *Q. Rev.* No. 248. 347 Another material which was for a long time considered a noxious refuse.. is glycerine. **1874** ROSCOE *Elem. Chem.* xxxvi. 387 The natural oils and fats are all compounds of glycerin, chiefly with palmitic, oleic, or stearic acids. **1875** H. C. WOOD *Therap.* (1879) 584 In man no symptoms of poisoning have ever been produced by glycerine.
2. Formerly used as a general name for the group of alcohols of which glycerine is a member.
1866 ROSCOE *Elem. Chem.* xxxvi. 315 The glycerines [*in later eds.* glycerins] of the mono- and dicarbon series have not been prepared; that of the tri-carbon series is best known; amyl glycerine has also been prepared.
3. *Pharmacy.* Applied to preparations consisting of a specified substance dissolved or suspended in glycerine.
1879 *St. George's Hosp. Rep.* IX. 565 Glycerine of tannin.
4. *attrib.* and *Comb.* **glycerine tear**, a drop of glycerine used in theatrical make-up to simulate a tear (TEAR *sb.*[1]).
1864 Glycerin ether [see GLYCERIDE]. **1876** tr. *Wagner's Gen. Pathol.* 579 Lactic acid (isomeric with glycerin-aldehyde). **1898** *Daily News* 20 July 9/4 Glycerine makers. [**1926** MAINES & GRANT *Wise-Crack Dict.* 7/1 *Cork the glycerine*, stop the movie tears.] **1934** C. LAMBERT *Music Ho!* IV. 270 Even synthetic sentiment, the musical equivalent of glycerine tears, is harder to achieve than abstraction. **1969** *Listener* 13 Nov. 669/1 In a scene where Genevieve Page is producing the required tears with frightening realism, Wilder instructs the make-up man to add to them. 'Glycerine tears.. great big Hollywood false tears...'

glycerined (ˈglɪsərɪnd), *ppl. a.* [f. GLYCERINE + -ED[2].] Treated with glycerine.
1866 J. M. SIMS *Notes Uterine Surg.* I. 161 This glycerined cotton is to be removed and renewed daily.

glycerinized (ˈglɪsərɪnaɪzd), *a.* [f. GLYCERINE + -IZE + -ED[1].] = GLYCERINATED.
1897 *Daily News* 9 Feb. 3/2 Glycerinised calf-lymph.

glycerite (ˈglɪsəraɪt). *Pharmacy.* [f. GLYCER-INE + -ITE.] A preparation consisting of a medicinal substance dissolved or suspended in glycerine.
1875 H. C. WOOD *Therap.* (1879) 18 Glycerites are preparations in which glycerine is the solvent.

glycerized (ˈglɪsəraɪzd), *a.* [f. GLYCER-INE + -IZE + -ED[1].] Compounded with glycerine.
1886 in *Syd. Soc. Lex.* **1888** *Med. News* LIII. 216 (Cent.) Pasteur's vials containing glycerized broth.

glycerizine, bad form of GLYCYRRHIZIN.

glycero- (ˈglɪsərəʊ). Used as a comb. form of GLYCERINE. **ˌglyceroˈkinase** *Biochem.*, an enzyme found chiefly in the liver and adipose tissue which catalyses the reaction of glycerol and adenosine triphosphate to glycerophosphate and adenosine diphosphate; **ˌglyceroˈphosphate**, a salt of glycerophosphoric acid; **ˌglyceropho'sphoric acid** (see quot.). (Watts *Dict. Chem.* 1864 has other similar names of acids, as *glycero-citric, -oxalic, -tartaric*, which do not appear in recent authorities.)
1864 WATTS *Dict. Chem.* II. 891 *Glycerophosphoric acid*.. This acid exists in the yolk of eggs and in the brain.. and is produced by the action of phosphoric acid or phosphoric anhydride on glycerin. *Ibid.* 892 The glycerophosphates are for the most part soluble in water. **1873** RALFE *Phys. Chem.* 125 Glycerophosphoric acid is never found in a free state in fresh and healthy brain. **1954** BUBLITZ & KENNEDY in *Jrnl. Biol. Chem.* CCXI. 951 The name *glycerokinase* seems to be appropriate and convenient for this enzyme, although the purified enzyme also phosphorylates dihydroxyacetone and glyceraldehyde. **1956** *Nature* 7 Jan. 22/1 The isolation and partial purification of a rat liver enzyme, glycerokinase. **1962** A. PIRIE *Lens Metabolism Rel. Cataract* 433 The relative activities of glycerokinase and α-glycerophosphate dehydrogenase in rabbit tissues.

glycerol (ˈglɪsərɒl). *Chem.* [f. GLYCER-INE + -OL (the characteristic suffix of the names of alcohols).] = GLYCERINE I.
1884 ROSCOE & SCHORLEMMER *Treat. Chem.* III. II. 344 Glycerine, or, as we now prefer to term it, glycerol. **1889** in MUIR & MORLEY *Watts' Dict. Chem.*

glycerole (ˈglɪsərəʊl). *Pharmacy.* [f. GLYCER-INE + *-ole* (used arbitrarily).] A preparation in which glycerine is used as a vehicle. Also *attrib.*
1861 *N. Syd. Soc. Year-bk.* 1860. 262 Glycerole of lead. **1866** J. M. SIMS *Notes Uterine Surg.* I. 71 Glycerole cotton. **1880** M. MACKENZIE *Dis. Throat & Nose* I. 100 Glycerole of morphia.

glycerose (ˈglɪsərəʊz, -əʊs). *Chem.* [a. G. *glycerose* (Fischer & Tafel 1888, in *Ber. d. Deut. Chem. Ges.* XXI. 2636), f. GLYCER(INE, -OL + -OSE[2].] **a.** A mixture of glyceraldehyde and dihydroxyacetone, two isomers obtained by the oxidation of glycerol. **b.** = GLYCERALDEHYDE.
1888 *Jrnl. Chem. Soc.* LIV. 1264 For the preparation of glycerose, the lead glyceroxide is spread in thin layers [etc.]. **1937** M. STEEL *Biol. & Clin. Chem.* ii. 27 The simplest carbohydrate to possess an asymmetric carbon atom is glycerose. **1967** I. L. FINAR *Org. Chem.* (ed. 5) I. xi. 287 Bromine water, sodium hypobromite and Fenton's reagent ..oxidise glycerol to a mixture of glyceraldehyde (predominantly) and dihydroxyacetone; this mixture is known as glycerose.

†**ˈglycerule.** *Chem. Obs.* [f. GLYCER-INE + -ULE.] = next.
1840 *Turner's Elem. Chem.* (ed. 6) III. 1034 When dry, the hydrated oxide of glycerule forms a syrupy liquid.

glyceryl (ˈglɪsərɪl). *Chem.* Also -yle. [f. GLYCER-INE + -YL.] (See quot. 1864.) ***glyceryl trinitrate*** = NITROGLYCERINE.
1845 G. E. DAY tr. *Simon's Anim. Chem.* I. 70 The glycerin, prepared in this manner.. is considered as the hydrate of an oxide of a radical, glyceryl (C_6H_7), which has not yet been isolated. **1850** DAUBENY *Atom. Theory* vii. (ed. 2) 214 The radicals of bases are cacodyle, methyle, ethyle, glyceryle [etc.]. **1864** WATTS *Dict. Chem.* II. 893 *Glyceryl*, C^3H^5. The triatomic radicle of glycerin and the glycerides. **1892** *Jrnl. Chem. Soc.* LXII. 692 Glyceryl trinitrate reduces alkaline copper tartrate. **1963** *Brit. Pharm. Codex 1963* 342 Glyceryl trinitrate solution causes the relaxation of involuntary muscle. **1968** J. H. BURN *Lect. Notes Pharmacol.* (ed. 9) 34 Glyceryl trinitrate.. is used by those who suffer from 'effort angina'.
attrib. **1864** Glyceryl ether [see GLYCERIDE]. **1873** RALFE *Phys. Chem.* p. xix, Glyceryl alcohol. **1885** REMSEN *Org. Chem.* (1888) 220 Oleïn, or glyceryl trioleate.. is the chief constituent of the fatty oils, such as olive oil, whale oil, etc.

glycic (ˈglɪsɪk), *a.* *Chem.* Corrected form of GLUCIC (acid).
1889 MUIR & MORLEY *Watts' Dict. Chem.*, *Glucic acid*, glycic acid.

glycicoll: see GLYCOCOLL.

glycide (ˈglɪsaɪd). *Chem.* [f. GLYC-ERINE + -IDE.] (See quot. 1864.)
1864 WATTS *Dict. Chem.* II. 895 *Glycide*, $C^3H^6O^2$. The hypothetical alcohol corresponding to the glycidic ethers.
Hence **glyˈcidic** *a.*, pertaining to, or derived from glycide. ***glycidic ethers*** (see quot. 1864).
1864 WATTS *Dict. Chem.* II. 896 *Glycidic ethers*, a class of diatomic ethers, closely related to the glycerides, and produced from them by the action of alkalis. **1889** MUIR & MORLEY *Watts' Dict. Chem.*, *Glycidic acid.*

glycidyl (ˈglɪsɪdɪl). *Chem.* [f. GLYCIDE + -YL.]
1864 WATTS *Dict. Chem.* II. 899 *Glycidyl*, C^3H^4. The diatomic radicle which may be supposed to exist in the glycidic ethers.

glycin (ˈglaɪsɪn). *Photogr.* [f. GLYCIN(E.] A crystalline derivative of glycine, used as a developer; *p*-hydroxyphenylaminoacetic acid.
1893 *Brit. Jrnl. Photogr.* XL. 804 Glycin is a special developer for lantern plates. **1961** A. L. M. SOWERBY *Dict. Photogr.* (ed. 19) 355 In buying glycin from a pharmacist, make sure he is not supplying glycine (aminoacetic acid) which.. has no developing properties at all. **1963** JOHN & FIELD *Textbk. Photogr. Chem.* v. 67 Glycin finds some use in fine-grain developers for negatives.

glycine (ˈglaɪsiːn). *Biochem.* [ad. G. *glycin* (J. Berzelius 1848, in *Jahres-Ber. über d. Fortschritte d. Chem. und Min.* XXVII. 654), f. Gr. γλυκ-ύς sweet + -INE[5].] A colourless sweet-tasting crystalline compound, NH_2CH_2COOH, which is the simplest amino-acid and a general constituent of proteins; = GLYCOCOLL, *amino-acetic acid.*
1851 G. E. DAY tr. *Lehmann's Physiol. Chem.* I. 152 Glycine has not yet been found in an isolated state in the animal body. **1885** REMSEN *Org. Chem.* (1888) 291 Hippuric acid can be made by heating glycine with benzoic acid to 160°. **1957** *New Biol.* XXIII. 79 In one experiment, radioactive glycine, valine and lysine were injected simultaneously into a lactating goat, and casein, a milk protein, was isolated from milk collected 4 hours later. **1965** A. MEISTER *Biochem. Amino Acids* (ed. 2) I. i. 11 In 1820, Braconnot obtained glycine from a sulfuric acid hydrolyzate of gelatin... Subsequently Braconnot's 'sugar of gelatin' was named glycocoll and later glycine. **1969** *Times* 25 Aug. 4/8 In the genetic code three guanylic acid units are.. the code for glycine.

glycine, obs. form of GLUCINA.

glyco- (glaɪkəʊ, glɪkəʊ), irregularly used (instead of *glycy-*) as a combining form of Gr. γλυκ-ύς sweet, and in names of chemical compounds to indicate the presence of *glycerol* or some other substance with a name beginning with *glyc-*. In mod. chemical nomenclature, usu. used to refer to sugars generally, in contradistinction to GLUCO-: so *glycose*, *glycoside*, etc. (cf. *glucose, glucoside*). **ˌglycobenˈzoic, -cyˈamidine, -ˈcyamine** (see quots.); **glyco-ˈgelatin**, a combination of glycerine and gelatin used in the making of lozenges and pastilles; **glycoˈhæmia** (see quot.); **glycoˈlipid** *Biochem.*, any substance which is a combination of both a carbohydrate (or carbohydrate derivative), esp. a sugar, and a lipid; **ˈglycophyte** *Ecology*, a plant whose growth is inhibited by saline soil (cf. *halophyte* s.v. HALO-); hence **glycoˈphytic** *a.*; **glycoˈprotein** (also †**-proteid**) *Biochem.*, any of a group of proteins with one or more usually relatively short side chains composed generally of a mixture of carbohydrates or carbohydrate derivatives; **glycoˈtropic** *a. Biochem.*, antagonistic to insulin.
1852 *Fownes' Man. Chem.* (ed. 4) 481 *Glycobenzoic acid is a crystalline substance, slightly soluble in water. **1864** WATTS *Dict. Chem.* II. 906 *Glyco-cyamidine, an organic base homologous with creatinine, and related to glycocyamine in the same manner as creatinine to creatine. *Ibid.*, *Glyco-cyamine, a compound homologous with creatine, produced by the union of cyanamide with glycocine. **1884** M. MACKENZIE *Dis. Throat & Nose* II. 551

The basis of the preparation [of pastils] is *glyco-gelatine, a compound much employed in the manufacture of pessaries and soluble bougies. **1866** A. Flint *Princ. Med.* (1880) 73 *Glycohaemia signifies the presence of sugar in the blood. **1940** *Jrnl. Biol. Chem.* CXXXII. 178 The cerebroside.. belongs to a new class of *glycolipids which probably differ from previously described cerebrosides only because they contain glucose in place of galactose. **1970** C. N. Graymore *Biochem. Eye* vii. 507 Cerebrosides and gangliosides may also be classified as glycolipids, both containing hexoses. **1947** R. F. Daubenmire *Plants & Environment* ii. 61 Because salts so evidently interfere with the absorption of water by *glykophytes, saline soils have long been considered 'physiologically dry'.. for these plants. **1964** V. J. Chapman *Coastal Veget.* 96 Glycophytes such as White clover. **1969** Salisbury & Ross *Plant Physiol.* xxix. 692/1 Ecologists further classify those plants that are sensitive to relatively high concentrations of salt in the surrounding liquid medium.. as glycophytes. **1964** V. J. Chapman *Coastal Veget.* iv. 89 Other evidence of elevation is the existence of obvious invasion by glycophytic species. **1898** *Jrnl. Physiol.* XXIII. 177 It is probable that every tissue containing proteids will be found to contain some admixture of *glycoproteids. **1902** *Encycl. Brit.* XXXI. 724/1 Glycoproteids—a number of proteids, on treatment with acid, yield various sugar-like bodies. **1908** *Jrnl. Biol. Chem.* IV. p. l, **Glycoproteins*. Compounds of the protein molecule with a substance or substances containing a carbohydrate group other than a nucleic acid. **1945** *Adv. Protein Chem.* II. 250 The group of proteins which contain less than 4 per cent hexosamine, classified as glycoproteins, embraces many proteins listed as albumins and globulins in the accepted classification of proteins. **1968** A. White et al. *Princ. Biochem.* (ed. 4) vi. 118 The distinction between glyco- and mucoproteins is arbitrary, and intermediate types exist. **1970** R. W. McGilvery *Biochem.* xxiv. 585 The carbohydrate chains on glycoproteins are oligosaccharides. **1936** F. G. Young in *Lancet* 8 Aug. 301/2 The pituitary substance responsible for the rapid development of an exaggerated glycæmic response to hypoglycæmia will be called the '*glycotropic factor' without prejudice to the question of its existence as a separate entity. *Ibid.*, Glycotropic extracts. **1955** E. B. Astwood in Pincus & Thimann *Hormones* III. vii. 256 A prolactin preparation had some glycotropic activity in the dog.

glycocholate (glaɪkəʊˈkɒlət, glɪk-). *Chem.* [f. as next + -ate¹.] A salt of glycocholic acid.

1872 Huxley *Phys.* v. 122 The taurocholate and glycocholate of soda, or bile salts as they are sometimes called. **1889** Muir & Morley *Watts' Dict. Chem.* II. 626/2 All the glycocholates are soluble in alcohol.

glycocholic (glaɪkəʊˈkɒlɪk, glɪkəʊ-), *a. Chem.* [f. glyco- + cholic *a.*] ***glycocholic acid***, the principal acid in ox-gall.

1864 Watts *Dict. Chem.* II. 899 *Glycocholic acid*, this acid, discovered by L. Gmelin.. constitutes, in the form of a sodium-salt, the essential part of ox-bile. **1878** Kingzett *Anim. Chem.* 84 Glycocholic acid.. is only present in small quantity in human bile.

glycocin (ˈglaɪkəsɪn, ˈglɪkəsɪn). *Chem.* Now little used. [app. suggested by prec.: see -in.] = glycocoll.

1852 *Fownes' Man. Chem.* (ed. 4) 481 Glycocine. **1873** Ralfe *Phys. Chem.* 136 The taurin and glycocin united to the cholic acid form the conjugated bile acids.

glycocoll (ˈglaɪkəkɒl, ˈglɪkəkɒl). *Chem.* Also glycicol(l, glykokoll. [f. glyco- + Gr. κόλλα glue; perh. suggested by the sound of glycocholic.] A crystalline substance contained in bile and formed when glycocholic acid and hydrochloric acid are boiled together. Also called *gelatin-sugar*.

1840–2 *Turner's Elem. Chem.* (ed. 7) iii. 1193 Gelatine sugar or glycicoll. **1848** Fownes *Man. Chem.* (ed. 2) 542 Glycocoll. **1872** Thudichum *Chem. Phys.* 18 Glykokoll appears in an excretion as hippuric acid.

glycogen (ˈglaɪkədʒɛn, ˈglɪkə-). *Chem.* Also glu-, **glycogene.** [f. glyco- + -gen; the name refers to the fact that the substance is the source of the sugar in animal tissues.] A white, amorphous, tasteless, inodorous, starch-like substance found in animal tissues, esp. the liver; it is easily convertible into dextrose by boiling in dilute acid.

1860 *N. Syd. Soc. Year-bk.* 1859. 86 The liver possesses the power of forming glucogene. **1864** Watts *Dict. Chem.* II. 906 *Glycogen, Animal starch, Animal dextrin, Hepatin.* **1872** Huxley *Phys.* v. 117 The liver.. elaborates from the blood passing through it a substance called glycogen.

glycogenic (glaɪkəʊˈdʒɛnɪk, glɪkəʊ-), *a.* Also glu-. [f. as glycogen + -ic.] Of or pertaining to the formation of sugar (or of glycogen from sugar), as in the animal body. ***glycogenic acid*** (see quot. 1889). ***glycogenic matter***: glycogen.

1859 *Fownes' Man. Chem.* 566 The glycogenic matter passes through a state corresponding to dextrin into sugar. **1860** *N. Syd. Soc. Year-bk.* 1859. 86 Glucogenic matter. **1864** W. B. Carpenter *Princ. Human Physiol.* (ed. 6) ix. 387 It appears that another purpose is fulfilled by the Liver—the production of an amyloid substance termed Glycogen; and we shall now proceed to consider the chief facts.. in reference to this so-called 'Glycogenic function of the Liver'. **1873** A. Flint Jr. *Phys. Man, Nerv. Syst.* viii. 243 The view which we have advanced with regard to the glycogenic function is that the liver is constantly producing sugar during life. **1889** Muir & Morley *Watts' Dict. Chem.*, *Glycogenic acid.* Formed by treating an aqueous solution of glycogen at 100° with bromine, and then adding Ag_2O... Very acid syrup. Is perhaps identical with gluconic acid. **1900** Dorland *Med. Dict.* 282/1, *Glycogenic*, pertaining to glycogenesis or to glycogen. **1913** *Proc. Roy. Soc.* B. LXXXVI. 560 The liver will be found to contain only traces of glycogen. This effect is due to an inhibition of the glycogenic function of the liver. **1926** J. J. R. Macleod *Carbohydrate Metabolism & Insulin* xi. 159 In the strict sense, the term glycogenic should be restricted to the formation of glycogen from protein (and fat) and its breakdown to sugar, rather than to the polymerisation of sugar itself into that substance.

So **glycoˈgenesis**, the production or formation of sugar (or of glycogen from sugar), as in the animal body; **glycogeˈnetic, glyˈcogenous** *adjs.*, ? = glycogenic; **glyˈcogeny** = *glycogenesis* (above).

1869 E. A. Parkes *Pract. Hygiene* (ed. 3) 161 A glycogenous substance may also be derived from albuminates. **1872** Thudichum *Chem. Phys.* 8 The glycogenetic function of the liver. **1886** *Syd. Soc. Lex.*, *Glycogenesis.* **1888** Huxley & Martin *Elem. Biol.* 311 *note*, Similar glycogenous cells are met with in the walls of the lacunar spaces and on the 'mesenteries' of the Snail. **1889** *Webster's Dict.*, *Glycogeny.* **1897** *Lippincott's Med. Dict.* 434/2 *Glycogenesis*, the formation of sugar, or of glycogen. **1900** Dorland *Med. Dict.* 282/1, *Glycogenesis*, the production of sugar or of glycogen. **1970** W. V. Thorpe et al. *Biochem.* (ed. 9) xix. 251 The reactions involved in muscle glycogenesis are the same as those in liver glycogenesis.

glycogenolysis (ˌglaɪkəʊdʒəˈnɒlɪsɪs). *Phys.* [f. glycogen + -o + lysis.] The hydrolytic breakdown of glycogen to glucose. Hence **ˌglycogenoˈlytic** *a.*, of, pertaining to, or causing glycogenolysis.

1909 *Jrnl. Biol. Chem.* VI. p. xl, It was found that glycogenolysis is quite slow immediately after death but afterwards becomes very rapid. It therefore takes some time after death for the glycogenolytic process to become active. **1929** *Proc. Soc. Exper. Biol. & Med.* XXVI. 490 The glycogenolytic properties of insulin. **1968** A. White et al. *Princ. Biochem.* (ed. 4) xix. 443 Glycogenolysis (glycogen breakdown) is hydrolytic in the intestine.

glycol (ˈglaɪkɒl, ˈglɪkɒl). *Chem.* [f. glyc(erine) + -ol; the original intention of the name being to designate a substance intermediate in composition between 'glycerine' and 'alcohol'.]

a. Formerly applied to the compound now called *ethyl glycol* or *ethylene alcohol* $C_2H_4(OH)_2$, a sweetish, colourless, inodorous viscid liquid obtained from the decomposition of ethylene dibromide. **b.** In wider sense, a general name for the group of fatty diatomic alcohols of which this is the type, having the general structure $C_nH_{2n}(OH)_2$.

1858 *Fownes' Man. Chem.* (ed. 7) 466 An alcoholic body being formed, to which the name ethylene-alcohol, or glycol, has been given. **1864** Watts *Dict. Chem.* II. 574. **1866** Roscoe *Elem. Chem.* xxxiii. 294 Glycol is obtained by the action of ethylene dibromide upon silver acetate. **1873** *Fownes' Chem.* (ed. 11) 614 The diatomic alcohols of the fatty group are called glycols. **1881** W. Spottiswoode in *Nature* xxv. 141 It was.. Professor Karl Adolph Wurtz.. who first made those remarkable alcohols called glycols.

glycollate (glaɪˈkɒlət, glɪk-). *Chem.* [f. glycol + -ate.] A salt of glycollic acid.

1864 Watts *Dict. Chem.* II. 908 *Glycollates.* **1873** *Fownes' Chem.* (ed. 11) 706 All the glycollates are more or less soluble and crystallisable.

glycollic, glycolic (glaɪˈkɒlɪk, glɪ-), *a. Chem.* [f. glycol + -ic.] Of or containing glycol. ***glycollic acid***, an acid obtained by the oxidation of glycol.

1852 *Fownes' Man. Chem.* (ed. 4) 481 Glycobenzoic acid.. may be viewed as a conjugate acid, containing benzoic and glycolic acids. **1864** Watts *Dict. Chem.* II. 910 Glycollic acid appears to exist in two, if not in a greater number of isomeric modifications. **1869** Roscoe *Elem. Chem.* 341 Glycollic [*ed.* 1 **1866** Glycolic] Acid, $C_2H_4O_3$.

glycollide. *Chem.* [f. glycol + -ide.] (See quot.)

1864 Watts *Dict. Chem.* II. 919 *Glycollide*, $C^2H^2O^2$. *Glycollic anhydride.*—A compound isomeric with glyoxal, and differing from glycollic acid by 1 at. water.

glycolysis (glaɪˈkɒlɪsɪs). *Biochem.* [f. glyco- + lysis.] An important metabolic process, the initial pathway in cell respiration, in which sugar, sugar phosphates, or precursors of these are broken down by enzymic reactions releasing energy and yielding esp. pyruvic acid or lactic acid in animal tissues; by extension, used of similar processes in other organisms yielding different products, such as ethyl alcohol in fermentation. (Orig. used of the disappearance of sugar from drawn blood.)

1892 *Jrnl. Chem. Soc.* LXII. i. 89 (*heading*) Hematic glycolysis. Estimation of glycogen in the blood. **1895** *Ibid.* LXVIII. ii. 361 Glycolysis.. is not a vital process, but the blood corpuscles contain substances which possess the power in question. **1937** Halliburton & McDowall *Handbk. Physiol. & Biochem.* (ed. 35) xl. 591 The blood is kept under oil to prevent loss of CO_2. Oxalate is added to prevent clotting and fluoride to prevent glycolysis. **1959** *New Scientist* 29 Jan. 218/1 On death the blood supply stops and the tissues become depleted in oxygen and fermentation (or anærobic glycolysis) sets in. **1968** A. White et al. *Princ. Biochem.* (ed. 4) xviii. 395 Meyerhof prepared soluble extracts of muscle that catalyzed glycolysis and later demonstrated that, except for the final steps, glycolysis and alcoholic fermentation are essentially similar. **1968** Miall & Sharp *New Dict. Chem.* (ed. 4) 270/1 The metabolic breakdown of carbohydrates.. may occur in the presence of oxygen ('aerobic glycolysis') or in its absence ('anaerobic glycolysis').

Hence (as a back-formation) **ˈglycolyse** *v. trans.*, to metabolize (a substance) in glycolysis.

1938 *Biochem. Jrnl.* XXXII. 337 The tumour slices had been permitted to glycolyse anaerobically normally for 45 min. **1951** F. Dickens in Sumner & Myrbäck *Enzymes* II. i. lxiii. 625 Allowing the somewhat vague expression 'glycolysis' to be replaced by the more specific indications of the sugar glycolyzed, if this is known. **1962** R. van Heyningen in A. Pirie *Lens Metabolism Rel. Cataract* 399 Most of the glucose used by the lens is glycolysed.

glycolytic (glaɪkəʊˈlɪtɪk, glɪkəʊ-), *a.* [f. glyco- + Gr. λυτικός resolvent, f. λύειν to loose, resolve.] Having the property of decomposing sugar.

1897 *Allbutt's Syst. Med.* III. 229 Lépine.. has produced, however, from malt diastase, a glycolytic ferment.

glycoˈnean, glyˈconian, *a. rare.* [f. L. *Glycōnīus, -ēus*, Gr. Γλυκώνειος (f. Γλύκων: see next) + -an.] = next.

1727–41 Chambers *Cycl.*, *Glyconian.* **1730–6** Bailey (folio), *Glyconian Verse*, a verse consisting of.. a spondee and two dactyls, or rather a spondee, choriambus and a Pyrrhic. **1850** *Smith's Dict. Gr. & Rom. Biogr.* II. 278/1 *Glycon*.. A lyric poet, from whom the Glyconean metre took its name.

glyconic (glaɪˈkɒnɪk), *a.* and *sb.* [f. Γλύκων the name of a Greek lyric poet + -ic.]

A. *adj.* Epithet of a lyric metre or verse, essentially a logaœdic tetrapody consisting of three trochees and a dactyl (see quot. 1885); also (of a poem, stanza, etc.), composed or consisting of such verses. **B.** *sb.* A glyconic verse.

The type of verse with which the name is in modern use most generally associated is the catalectic form used by Latin poets, esp. Catullus and Horace: -ᴗ-ᴗᴗ-ᴗ

1670–81 Blount *Glossogr.*, *Glyconick*, a kind of verse consisting of a Spondey and two Dactyles. **1779–81** Johnson *L.P.*, *Watts*, His verses to his brother, in the Glyconick measure.. are remarkably easy and elegant. **1821** *Blackw. Mag.* X. 386 The lines are glyconics. **1878** Munro *Crit. Catullus* 135 The observance of this law by Catullus gives to his glyconics much of their charm and spirit. *Ibid.* 138 One of the essential properties of these glyconic odes is that the stanzas end with a completed sentence. **1885** Jebb *Sophocles, Oed. Col.* p. lviii, A dactyl comes first; then three chorees.. But the dactyl might also stand *second*.. or *third*. .. According to the place of the dactyl, the verse was called a *First, Second*, or *Third* Glyconic.

glycosamine (glaɪˈkəʊzəmiːn, -səmiːn). *Chem.* [ad. G. *glycosamin* (G. Ledderhose 1876, in *Ber. d. Deut. Chem. Ges.* IX. 1200), f. glycos(e + amine.] **a.** = glucosamine. **b.** Any amino-sugar in which the amino group replaces a hydroxyl group other than that attached to the first carbon atom.

1877 *Jrnl. Chem. Soc.* i. 64 (*heading*) Glycosamine hydrochloride... When purified chitin is heated.. with pure strong hydrochloric acid, it dissolves.. forming a blackish-brown solution. **1948** W. Pigman *Chem. Carbohydrates* ix. 375 An important additional group of nitrogenous derivatives [of the carbohydrates] is the amino sugars, among which are the glycosamines. **1963** *Biol. Abstr.* XLII. i. 720/2 A method of colorimetric determination of d-glycosamine has been developed by the authors. **1967** Cantarow & Schepartz *Biochem.* (ed. 4) ii. 21 The second type of amino sugar is the glycamine or glycosamine, in which alcoholic hydroxyl groups in the sugar molecule are replaced by amino groups.

glycose (ˈglaɪkəʊs, -z).

1. Obs. var. glucose.

2. [cf. glyco-.] Any of the monosaccharides.

1938 M. L. Wolfrom in H. Gilman *Org. Chem.* II. xvi. 1418 The methylglycosides (glycose referring to any sugar) and their acetates. **1957** W. Pigman *Carbohydrates* i. 3 A glycose is any monosaccharide.

glycoside (ˈglaɪkəʊsaɪd). *Chem.* [f. glyco- after glucoside.] †**1.** Used as a variant spelling of *glucoside* before the two words were distinguished in sense (see sense 2 and glucoside). *Obs.*

1878 *Chem. News* 2 Aug. 60/1 The glycosides and colouring matters of quercitron and of Persian berries are very near to each other. **1890** Billings *Med. Dict.* I. 592/1 *Glycoside*, glucoside.

2. Any of a class of compounds, many of which are present in plants, which on hydrolysis give a sugar and one or more other compounds, one of which is usu. an alcohol or a phenol.

1930 *Jrnl. Amer. Chem. Soc.* LII. 1681 The word glycoside is used in the generic sense to include glucoside-like derivatives of any of the aldoses or ketoses; the term glucoside is limited to the glycosides of the particular sugar glucose. **1951** R. J. McIlroy *Plant Glycosides* i. 1 Glycosides are derivatives of the cyclic forms of sugars in which the reducing or potential aldehyde group of the sugar is substituted by condensation with an alcohol or a phenol to form a hemi-acetal. **1960** S. F. Dyke *Carbohydrates* vii. 112 Many plant pigments responsible for the color of flowers are glycosides. **1961** *New Scientist* 7 Dec. 639/3 The active principles of digitalis are glycosides (such as Digitoxin and Digoxin). **1965** Bell & Coombe tr. *Strasburger's Textbk. Bot.* (new ed.) i. 21 The enzyme emulsin decomposes amygdalin, the glycoside of bitter almonds, into glucose, benzaldehyde and hydrocyanic acid. **1968** A. White et al. *Princ. Biochem.* (ed. 4) iii. 41 All glycosides, including oligo-

and polysaccharides, can be hydrolyzed with varying degree of difficulty.

Hence **glyco'sidal, -ic** *adjs.*, of the nature of or characteristic of a glycoside or glycosides; ***glycosidic bond*** or ***linkage***, a bond between the hydroxyl group attached to the first carbon atom of a cyclic monosaccharide and a hydroxyl group of another compound; **glyco'sidically** *adv.*

1925 *Jrnl. Amer. Chem. Soc.* XLVII. 269 He adopted Tollens' suggestion that the union between the monosaccharides in the structures of the compound sugars is of the semi-acetal ring form and this idea of the 'glycosidic union' has proved to be correct. **1931** E. F. & K. F. ARMSTRONG *Glycosides* ii. 10 Glycosidic compounds. **1938** R. A. GORTNER *Outl. Biochem.* (ed. 2) xxiv. 619 The linkage between the glucuronic acid and the benzoic acid is not a glycosidal [ed. 1 (1929), glucosidal] linkage, for the aldehyde group is still free. **1943** *Thorpe's Dict. Appl. Chem.* (ed. 4) VI. 83/1 The majority of polysaccharides have linkages of the glycosidic type. **1948** W. PIGMAN *Chem. Carbohydrates* i. 13 The uronic acid components of the polyuronides are likewise joined glycosidically by 1,4'-linkages. **1953** FRUTON & SIMMONDS *Gen. Biochem.* xvii. 380 The glycosidic linkage occupies a place in carbohydrate chemistry analogous to the role of the peptide bond in protein chemistry. **1964** N. G. CLARK *Mod. Org. Chem.* xvi. 331 This sugar comprises two D-glucose units linked glycosidically. **1965** BELL & COOMBES tr. *Strasburger's Textbk. Bot.* (new ed.) I. 21 Tannins are mixtures of quite different aromatic substances, partly glycosidic in nature.

‖**glycosuria** (ˌglaɪkəʊ's(j)ʊərɪə, ˌglɪkəʊ-). *Path.* [quasi-Latin, f. F. *glycose* GLUCOSE + Gr. οὖρ-ον urine + L. suffix *-ia*.] (See quot. 1866.)

1860 *N. Syd. Soc. Year-bk.* 1859. 384 On the Glycosuria of Lying-in Women. **1866** A. FLINT *Princ. Med.* (1880) 73 If the quantity of sugar in the blood exceed a certain amount .. sugar apears in the urine, constituting the condition called glycosuria.

Hence **glyco'suric** *a.*, relating to or affected with glycosuria.

1883 *Brit. Q. Rev.* July 25 Claude Bernard discovered the 'glycosuric centre' in the brain. **1889** MUIR & MORLEY *Watts' Dict. Chem.*, *Glycosuric acid* occurs in urine in disease. **1897** *Allbutt's Syst. Med.* III. 184 As gouty persons advance in life, they sometimes become glycosuric.

glycuronic (glaɪkjʊ'rɒnɪk), *a. Chem.* [tr. G. *glykuronsäure* glycuronic (glucuronic) acid (Schmiedeberg & Meyer 1879, in *Zeitschr. f. physiol. Chem.* III. 433), f. GLYC(O- + URONIC *a.*] ***glycuronic acid***: = *glucuronic acid*.

1882 *Jrnl. Chem. Soc.* XLII. 952 Urochloralic acid .. is decomposed, on boiling with dilute acids, into trichlorethyl alcohol and glycuronic acid. **1949** H. W. FLOREY et al. *Antibiotics* II. xxxvii. 1219 There was a marked increase in the excretion of glycuronic acid in rabbits given penicillin. **1968** J. H. BURN *Lect. Notes Pharmacol.* (ed. 9) 53 In the body it [*sc.* chloral] is first reduced to an alcohol, and then combined with glycuronic acid, to be excreted in the urine as urochloralic acid.

glycyl ('glaɪsɪl, 'glaɪsaɪl). *Chem.* [a. G. *glycyl* (Fischer & Fourneau 1901, in *Ber. d. Deut. Chem. Ges.* XXXIV. 2869), f. GLYC(INE + -YL.] The univalent radical $NH_2{\cdot}CH_2{\cdot}CO-$ derived from glycine.

1901 *Jrnl. Chem. Soc.* LXXX. I. 675 This paper [of Fischer & Fourneau] deals with molecular anhydrides of amino-acids .., and in it the name glycyl is used for the radicle $NH_2{\cdot}CH_2{\cdot}CO$. *Ibid.*, Glycylglycine hydrochloride. **1924** T. B. ROBERTSON *Princ. Biochem.* (ed. 2) vii. 155 Chloracetyl chloride for the introduction of glycyl. **1968** A. WHITE et al. *Princ. Biochem.* (ed. 4) v. 108 The synthesis of a dipeptide, glycyl-L-proline.

glycyphyllin (glaɪ-, glɪsɪ'fɪlɪn). *Chem.* [f. mod.L. *glycyphyll-a*, epithet of a species of *Smilax*, f. Gr. γλυκύ-ς sweet + φύλλ-ον leaf + -IN[1].] A rhamnoside, known only from *Smilax glycyphylla*, having phloretin as the aglycone.

1881 WRIGHT & RENNIE in *Jrnl. Chem. Soc.* XXXIX. 240 Were its identity and distinctiveness established, the term glycyphyllin might perhaps be applied to it. **1966** A. H. WILLIAMS in T. Swain *Comp. Phytochem.* xvii. 304 In the monocotyledons we have the isolated example of glycyphyllin in some samples of one species of *Smilax* in the Liliaceae.

‖**glycy'picron.** ? *Obs.* Also 7 glucu-. [a. Gr. γλυκυπικρόν, neut. of γλυκυπικρός adj., f. γλυκύς sweet + πικρός bitter.] Something composed of sweet and bitter.

1599 H. BUTTES *Dyets Drie Din.* C viij, Embleme of Love .. A bitter sweete, an Oxymel or Glycypicron. **1621** BURTON *Anat.* II. iii. I. i, He saith our whole life is a Glucupicron, a bitter sweet passion.

†'**glycyrize.** *Obs.* Also 6 glicyris. [ad. L. *glycyrrhiza*, Gr. γλυκύρριζα LIQUORICE.] Liquorice.

1599 H. BUTTES *Dyets drie Din.* D b, Eate Penidice, Saccarum Violarum, Sugar Candid, Glicyris, or such other pectorals after them. *a* **1661** FULLER *Worthies, Nottinghamsh.* II. (1662) 315 *Glycyrize* or *Liquoris*.

glycyrrhetic (glɪsɪ'ri:tɪk, -'retɪk), *a. Chem.* [f. next + -IC.] ***glycyrrhetic acid***: a triterpene, the aglycone of glycyrrhizic acid.

1907 *Jrnl. Chem. Soc.* XCII. I. 545 When it [*sc.* glycyrrhizic acid] is boiled for five hours with 3% sulphuric acid, air being excluded, glycyrrhetic acid, $C_{32}H_{48}O_7$.., m.p. 210° (hitherto known as 'glycyrrhetin'), is precipitated. **1966** *McGraw-Hill Encycl. Sci. & Technol.* XIV. 112/1 The ammonium salt of glycyrrhetic acid is the taste principle of licorice. Therapeutically, glycyrrhetic acid is reported to be the active ingredient of licorice having desoxycortone-like activity.

glycyrrhetin (glɪsɪ'ri:tɪn, -'retɪn). *Chem.* Also glycyrretin. [ad. F. *glycyrretin* (E. von Gorup-Besanez 1861, in *Ann. d. Chem. und Pharm.* CXVIII. 242), f. GLYCYRRH(IZIN + -ETIN.] = GLYCYRRHETIC *a.*

1864 H. WATTS *Dict. Chem.* II. 919 *Gycyrretin*, .. a substance obtained, together with glucose, by boiling glycyrrhizin with dilute acids. **1907** [see GLYCYRRHETIC *a.*]. **1943** *Thorpe's Dict. Appl. Chem.* (ed. 4) VI. 98/1 Glycyrrhetin, glycyrrhetic acid, $C_{32}H_{48}O_7$.

glycyrrhizic (glɪsɪ'raɪzɪk), *a. Chem.* [f. GLYCYRRHIZ(IN + -IC.] ***glycyrrhizic acid***: a glycoside obtained from liquorice root.

1879 *Jrnl. Chem. Soc.* XXXVI. 1040 Glycyrrhizic acid prepared by the action of sulphuretted hydrogen on the lead salt, resembles dried albumin in appearance. **1907** *Ibid.* XCII. I. 545 Glycyrrhizin consists of the potassium and calcium salts of glycyrrhizic acid and was isolated from liquorice. **1969** J. H. THOMPSON in J. A. Bevan *Essent. Pharmacol.* xxix. 303 Carbenoxolene sodium .. is a pentacyclic triterpene prepared from glycyrrhizic acid and licorice glycoside.

glycyrrhizin (glɪsɪ'raɪzɪn). *Chem.* Also glycyrhizin, glycyrrhidzin. [f. Gr. γλυκύρριζα LIQUORICE + -IN.] The glucoside contained in the root of liquorice (*Glycyrrhiza glabra*).

1838 *Penny Cycl.* XI. 278 Robiquet found it [*Glycyrhiza glabra*] to contain a peculiar sugar, which is uncrystallizable, called *glycion* or *glycyrhizin*, and other matters. **1841** BRANDE *Chem.* 1083 Liquorice Sugar. Glycyrhizin. **1875** H. C. WOOD *Therap.* (1879) 579 Liquorice root... In the form of glycyrrhizin it is said to conceal almost entirely the bitter taste of quinine and similar substances. **1877** *Blackie's Encycl.* III. 705/2 Glycyrrhidzin does not ferment.

glyde, var. GLEYD, an old horse.

glye, glyed, obs. ff. GLEE *v.*, GLEED *ppl. a.*

glyede, obs. form of GLIDE *v.*

glyer, var. GLEER; see under GLEE *v.*

glyering, var. GLEERING *ppl. a.*, *Obs.*

glyewe, obs. form of GLUE *v.*

glyg, glyke, varr. GLEEK *sb.*[2], *Obs.*

glymbe, obs. var. of CLIMB *v.*

c **1320** R. BRUNNE *Medit.* 630 (Harl. MS.) Twey enmyes on hem smartly gun glymbe [*Bodl. MS.* climbe].

glymse, obs. form of GLIMPSE.

glymye, var. GLEIMY *a.*, *Obs.*, sticky.

glymyr, glynce, glyn(n, obs. ff. GLIMMER, GLIMPSE, GLEN.

glyoxal (glaɪ'ɒksəl). *Chem.* [f. GLY-COL + OX-ALIC + *-al* (in CHLORAL, etc.).] A white amorphous solid, called also *oxalic aldehyde*. Hence **glyo'xalic** *a.*, in ***glyoxalic acid*** (see quot.).

1857 H. DEBUS in *Phil. Mag.* 4th Ser. XIII. 40 This residue consisted almost entirely of the aldehyde of glyoxylic acid; I propose to call it Glyoxal, $C_2H_4O_3$. **1858** *Fownes' Man. Chem.* (ed. 7) 467 By treating ethylic alcohol with nitric acid, M. Debus has obtained two compounds —an aldehyde-like body, glyoxal, and an acid, glyoxalic acid, which obviously belong to the same series. **1869** ROSCOE *Elem. Chem.* xxxiii. 335 Glyoxal stands in the relation of an aldehyde to Glycol.

glyoxalase (glaɪ'ɒksəleɪz, -s). *Biochem.* [f. prec. + -ASE.] Either of two enzymes which together convert methylglyoxal to lactic acid in the presence of glutathione; orig. considered a single enzyme.

1913 DAKIN & DUDLEY in *Jrnl. Biol. Chem.* XIV. 423 The catalyst .. effects the rapid conversion of methyl glyoxal into lactic acid... We propose that it be named 'glyoxalase'. **1951** *Ibid.* CXC. 685 The first step consists in a condensation reaction between methylglyoxal and glutathione catalyzed by an enzyme referred to in this paper as glyoxalase I. This condensation product, in a second step which is catalyzed by glyoxalase II, is then broken down into glutathione and lactic acid. **1961** *Biochem. Jrnl.* LXXIX. 481/1 Ophthalmic acid .. was a competitive inhibitor in the reaction catalysed by glyoxalase I.

glyoxaline (glaɪ'ɒksəli:n). *Chem.* [f. GLYOXAL + -INE[5].] = IMIDAZOLE.

1858 H. DEBUS in *Chem. Gaz.* XVI. 353 The other [organic base] in solution, to which in this paper the name of glyoxaline will be applied. **1943** *Thorpe's Dict. Appl. Chem.* (ed. 4) VI. 99/1 Glyoxalines are weak bases. **1946** A. A. MORTON *Chem. Heterocyclic Compounds* xiii. 363 Glyoxaline is an empirical name, used sometimes for imidazoles, because the parent member of the series was first derived from glyoxal and ammonia. **1968** I. L. FINAR *Org. Chem.* (ed. 4) II. xii. 532 Imidazole (iminazole, glyoxaline) is isomeric with pyrazole.

glyoxilin (glaɪ'ɒksɪlɪn). Also -yline. [? after *glyoxylic* (see GLYOXAL).] The name of an explosive (see quots.).

1875 *Ure's Dict. Arts*, etc. (ed. 7) II. 321 Glyoxiline consists of a mixture of gun-cotton pulp and saltpetre converted into porous pellets, which are saturated with nitro-glycerine. **1883** MAJENDIE in *Fortn. Rev.* May 645 Sir Frederick Abel's 'glyoxilin' (gun-cotton saturated with nitro-glycerine).

glyoxime (glaɪ'ɒksi:m, -ɪm). *Chem.* Also glyoxim. [Blend of GLYOXAL and OXIME.] **a.** The dioxime, HON:CH·CH:NOH, of glyoxal. **b.** Any of the dioximes of the α-diketones.

1895 *Jrnl. Chem. Soc.* LXVIII. I. 36 Configuration of certain glyoximes. **1906** MUIR & MORLEY *Watts' Dict. Chem.* II. 642/2 *Glyoxim*... Formed by the action of hydroxylamine on glyoxal. **1951** A. W. JOHNSON et al. in E. H. Rodd *Chem. Carbon Compounds* IA. xi. 728 When glyoxal, of which the monoxime is not known, pyruvic aldehyde and the α-diketones are treated with hydroxylamine, the α-dioximes or glyoximes are formed. *Ibid.*, Glyoxime, CH(:NOH)·CH(:NOH), m.p. 178°, is readily soluble in hot water.

glyoxylate (glaɪ'ɒksɪleɪt). *Chem.* [f. next + -ATE[4].] A salt or ester of glyoxylic acid.

1856 H. DEBUS in *Phil. Mag.* 4th Ser. XII. 362 The filtrate yields .. a crystallization of a new compound of lime, which I propose to call glyoxylate of lime. **1969** M. F. UTTER in J. M. Lowenstein *Citric Acid Cycle* v. 254 These two reactions form the basis of the glyoxylate cycle .. which can convert acetyl-CoA to oxalacetate.

glyoxylic (glaɪɒk'sɪlɪk), *a. Chem.* [f. GLYOX(AL + -YL + -IC.] ***glyoxylic acid***: the simplest aldehydic acid, obtained as a thick syrupy liquid, CHO·COOH, with a suffocating smell or as a hydrated crystalline solid, $CH(OH)_2{\cdot}COOH$; it is an important metabolic intermediate and occurs in animal and plant tissues and fluids, esp. in unripe fruit. Also called *glyoxalic acid*.

1856 H. DEBUS in *Phil. Mag.* 4th Ser. XII. 363 Oxalic acid separates the lime completely as oxalate of lime, and liberates the glyoxylic acid. **1903** WALKER & MOTT tr. *Holleman's Text-bk. Org. Chem.* 290 Glyoxylic acid contains one molecule of water, which cannot be separated from the acid or its salts without their undergoing decomposition. **1966** *McGraw-Hill Encycl. Sci. & Technol.* VI. 222/1 During metabolic degradation, glycine is deaminated to glyoxylic acid, which is oxidized to formate and carbon dioxide.

glyph (glɪf). [ad. Gr. γλυφή carving, carved work, f. γλύφ-ειν to cut out, carve. Cf. F. *glyphe* (1701 in Hatz.-Darm.).]

1. A sculptured mark or symbol. *rare.* (Cf. HIEROGLYPH.)

1825 COLERIDGE *Aids Refl.* (1848) I. 204 They were originally symbolical glyphs or sculptures, and afterwards translated into words. **1861** G. MOORE *Lost Tribes* 196 The sacred law is named 'Tára', and .. is represented by ten upright glyphs, rolls or pillars. **1895** HOFFMANN *Begin. Writing* ii. 19 The glyphs, made in intaglio, relievo, and intaglio-relievo, were divided into two classes, pure and linear.

2. *Arch.* A groove or channel, usually vertical, used as an ornament, esp. in the Doric frieze. Cf. TRIGLYPH.

[**1727-41** CHAMBERS *Cycl.*, *Glyphe*, or *Glyphis*, in sculpture and architecture, a general name for any cavity, or canal, whether round, or terminating in an angle; used as an ornament, in any part.] **1775** ASH, *Glyph*. **1818** in TODD. **1837** *Penny Cycl.* VII. 281/2 The triglyphs .. are upright, slightly projecting tablets .. channelled with two grooves or glyphs (γλυφαί), and with a half groove chamfering off each of its outer edges. **1842-59** GWILT *Archit.* I. ii. (ed. 4) 58 In the Doric order, the ends of these joists were called triglyphs, from their being sculptured with two whole and two half glyphs or channels.

glyphic ('glɪfɪk), *a.* and *sb.* [ad. Gr. γλυφικ-ός of or pertaining to carving: see -IC.]

A. *adj.* Carved, sculptured.

1857 H. MILLER *Test. Rocks* vii. 283 Glyphic representatives of the tradition.

B. *sb.* = GLYPH I.

1716 M. DAVIES *Athen. Brit.* III. 111 The Virgil was to be enrich'd with the Miniature Glyphicks of the Virgil in MS. in the Vatican Library. *a* **1818** *Hist. Peru* 43 (T.) Glyphicks. **1818** in TODD; and in later Dicts.

glyphograph ('glɪfəgrɑ:f, -græf), *sb.* [Back-formation from next.] A plate made by glyphography, or an impression taken from such a plate.

1855 in OGILVIE, Suppl. **1871** G. W. REID (*title*) A Descriptive Catalogue of the Works of George Cruikshank, Etchings, Woodcuts, Lithographs, and Glyphographs.

So '**glyphograph** *v.*, to form plates by glyphography (Ogilvie, *Suppl.* 1855); **gly'phographer**, one who practises glyphography; **glypho'graphic** *a.*, relating to or produced by glyphography.

1843 E. PALMER *Glyphography* (ed. 2) 3 Plates of all sizes, properly prepared for Glyphographic Drawing.. Glyphographic Plates. *Ibid.* 11 The kind of point that has been found to answer best .. by every successful glyphographer. **1846** H. L. JONES in *Archæol. Cambrensis* I. 68 The font .. of which a glyphographic view, by an amateur, is given below. **1851** *Illustr. Lond. News* 5 July 26/3 Gazetteer with glyphographic maps.

glyphography (glɪ'fɒgrəfɪ). [f. Gr. γλυφο-, γλυφή carving, sculpture + -γραφία writing, painting, f. γράφειν to write.] An electrotype process by which a copy of an engraved plate is obtained with a raised surface, suited for letter-press printing.

1843 E. PALMER (*title*) Glyphography; or Engraved Drawing, for printing at the type press after the manner of woodcuts. **1844** *Art Union Jrnl.* Feb. 38 Glyphography is the name given by the patentee, Mr. Palmer,..to a process ..for the formation of blocks with designs in relief, to be used with type. **1845** *Penny Cycl.* Suppl. I. 520/2 The terms *Electrotint* and *Glyphography* have been applied to two methods of etching by galvanism. **1851** R. HUNT *Sci. Exhib.* in *Art Jrnl. Illustr. Catal.* IV. p. xvi*/1 'Stylography'—a process bearing much analogy to our glyphography.

glyptal ('glɪptəl). Also † **glyptol**. [Proprietary name, perh. f. GLY(CEROL, -YL + *phthalic*, -ate.] Any of the alkyd resins, esp. those formed from glycerol and phthalic anhydride or phthalic acid. Also *glyptal resin*.

1915 *Bull. U.S. Bureau Standards* XI. 385 The glyptol is an artificial resin furnished by the research department of the General Electric Co. *Ibid.* 406 Glyptol is a synthetic compound which has the appearance and many of the properties of amber. **1923** C. ELLIS *Synthetic Resins* xvii. 293 Thus far the commercial applications of glyptal resins are of a minor character. **1926** *Trade Marks Jrnl.* 5 May 1033 *Glyptal.* Varnishes and Lacquers, included in Class 1. British Thomson-Houston Company. **1937** R. S. MORRELL et al. *Synthetic Resins* ix. 205 The glyptal resins are formed by condensation of polybasic acids with polyhydric alcohols. **1943** [see ALKYD]. **1967** I. L. FINAR *Org. Chem.* (ed. 5) I. xi. 286 With dibasic acids, glycerol forms condensation polymers known as alkyd resins, the commonest of which is glyptal, formed by heating glycerol with phthalic anhydride.

glyptic ('glɪptɪk), *a.* and *sb.* [ad. Gr. γλυπτικ-ός, f. γλύφειν to carve, engrave. Cf. F. *glyptique.*]

A. *adj.* **1.** Of or pertaining to carving or engraving, esp. on precious stones.

1847 in CRAIG. **1850** LEITCH tr. *C.O. Müller's Anc. Art* (ed. 2) §85 The glyptic art (in precious stones). **1853** C. T. NEWTON *Ess. Archæol.* 50 It will be convenient after noticing sculpture in marble to take next in order Bronzes and Terracottas; we thus pass by a natural transition from Glyptic to Plastic Art. **1877** W. JONES *Finger-ring* 216 During the Middle Ages the glyptic art had declined very much.

2. '*Min.* Figured' (Webster 1864).

B. *sb.* The art of carving or engraving, esp. on precious stones. Also *pl.*

1818 TODD, *Glyptick.* **1855** tr. *Labarte's Arts Mid. Ages* i. 51 The Egyptians are supposed first to have cultivated glyptics.

Hence '**glyptical** *a.* = sense A. 1.

1887 SIR S. FERGUSON *Ogham Inscript.* 138 If the mind be ..prepared to recognize familiar forms, though in glyptical masquerade.

glyptician (glɪp'tɪʃən). *rare*$^{-1}$. [f. GLYPTIC + -IAN.] A lapidary.

1883 *Times* 20 July 4 The famous Koh-i-noor was re-cut by a great Dutch glyptician after it came into the possession of the Queen.

glyptodon ('glɪptədɒn). Also **-dont**. [mod.L., f. Gr. γλυπτός sculptured + ὀδοντ-, ὀδούς tooth.

According to ordinary rules for the formation and latinization of Gr. compounds, the mod.Lat. nominative should be **glyptodūs* (cf. πολυόδους many-toothed). The ending *-odon* (cf. *mastodon*, etc.) was inferred from the oblique cases.]

An extinct South American quadruped allied to the armadillos, of the size of an ox, covered with a solid carapace, and having fluted teeth. Hence **glypto'dontoid** *a.*, resembling (that of) a glyptodon.

1838 OWEN in Sir W. Parish *Buenos Ayres* 178 e, From the regularly fluted or sculptured form of the tooth, I would propose to name the genus typified by this animal, 'glyptodon' (γλυφω, *sculpo*, οδους, *dens*). **1872** MIVART *Elem. Anat.* 37 Vertebræ..anchylosed together into a solid bone, as in the extinct Glyptodon. **1889** *Century Dict.*, *Glyptodont.* **1895** E. BONAVIA *Stud. Evol. Anim.* 121, I do not say that the Jaguar is descended from a Glyptodon, but I do say that this mammal descended from some extinct animal with a glyptodontoid carapace.

glyptography (glɪp'tɒgrəfɪ). [f. Gr. γλυπτός carved + -γραφία writing; cf. F. *glyptographie.*] **a.** The art of engraving upon gems. **b.** The descriptive science of engraved gems.

1797 *Brit. Critic* X. 455 These general prolegomena are followed by the author's Introduction to Glyptography (*l'étude des pierres gravées*). **1850** LEITCH tr. *C. O. Müller's Anc. Art* (ed. 2) §315 The Literature of glyptography is given by Millin..and Murr. **1855** tr. *Labarte's Arts Mid. Ages* i. 55 Glyptography requires such general knowledge and such profound study, as to render it sufficient of itself to occupy the whole leisure of an amateur.

So '**glyptograph** [cf. GLYPHOGRAPH], 'an engraving on a precious stone'; **glyp'tographer**, 'an engraver on precious stones' (Ogilvie); **glypto'graphic** *a.*, pertaining to glyptography.

1797 *Brit. Critic* X. 455 A particularly valuable part of this introduction is the Glyptographic Lithology.

glysen, glysnian, -n(i)en, obs. ff. GLISTEN.

glyssen, -on, -yn, obs. ff. GLISS *v.*, GLISTEN.

glyster(e, glystery: see CLYSTER, CLYSTERY.

glyt(e, obs. form of GLEET.

glyter, obs. form of GLITTER.

glyu, glywe(n, obs. ff. GLUE *sb.* and *v.*

gm. Abbrev. of GRAM².

1875 J. D. EVERETT *Illustr. C.G.S. Syst. Units* p. ix, The abbreviation *gm.* is used for *gramme* or *grammes.* **1885** [see *g* (s.v. G III. f)]. **1962** A. R. W. HAYES *Revision Physics* 12 Density of hydrogen = 0·09 gm/litre.

G-man ('dʒiːmæn). Also **G man**. [Probably f. the initial letter of *government* but perh. in Ireland an arbitrary use of the letter 'G'.] **a.** A political detective in Ireland. **b.** In the U.S., a special agent of the American Federal Bureau of Investigation.

1917 M. SKINNIDER *Doing Bit for Ireland* 177 One morning I was informed there was a 'G-man', as we call government detectives, waiting down-stairs to see me. **1922** JOYCE *Ulysses* 160 Jack Power could a tale unfold: father a G man. *Ibid.* 294 The bloody old lunatic is gone round to Green street to look for a G. man. **1926** P. BÉASLAÍ *Michael Collins* I. v. 107 The political detectives of the 'G' division of the Dublin Police came like a flock of carrion crows to pick out 'suspects'... Anyone who had seen that sight may be pardoned if he felt little compunction at the subsequent shooting of these same 'G' men. **1930** F. D. PASLEY *Al Capone* (1931) i. 33 He offered a G man (Government agent) ten gran' to forget it. **1935** *Punch* 3 July 6/2 For G-men, as they are called.., form the new licensed killers organised by the Federal Government to override all State laws in the suppression of gangster crime and the capture of every Public Enemy. **1946** WODEHOUSE *Joy in Morning* iii. 24 He was still giving me that searching look, like a G-man hobnobbing with a suspect. **1958** *Spectator* 3 Oct. 447/1 Mr. Hoover has built up..an immense personal reputation..by creating a legend of the G-man that has largely transferred the romantic interest from the robbers to the cops.

gmelinite ('gmɛlɪnaɪt). *Min.* [Named by Brewster in 1825 after Prof. C. A. *Gmelin*: see -ITE.] Hydrous silicate of aluminium, calcium, and sodium, found in colourless, yellow, and flesh-coloured crystals.

1825 *Edin. Jrnl. Sci.* II. 262 Gmelinite, a New Mineral Species. **1868** DANA *Min.* (ed. 5) 437.

gmina ('miːnə). Pl. **gminy**. [Polish.] A local division of the Polish administrative organization.

1885 *Encycl. Brit.* XIX. 311/1 The 'primary cell' of the administrative organization of Poland is the *gmina*. *Ibid.* 311/2 Justice is represented by the *gmina* tribunals. **1905** *Daily Chron.* 19 Sept. 5/4 Voters are divided into three classes. 1.—Landed proprietors. 2.—Members of gmina or cantons who own three to twenty acres. 3.—Urban electors. **1959** *Chambers's Encycl.* XI. 8 For purposes of local government the provinces are divided into districts..which are sub-divided in turn into sub-districts (*gminy*).

gnab(b)le, var. KNABBLE, *Obs.*, to nibble.

† '**gnacche,** *v.* *Obs. rare.* [Prob. an onomatopœia suggested by GNAW; cf. *snatch*.] *intr.* = GNASH *v.* 1. Hence † '**gnacching** *vbl. sb.* Also † '**gnaccher**, one who gnashes.

13.. *Sat. Blacksmiths* in *Rel. Ant.* I. 240 Thei gnauen and gnacchen, thei gronys to-gydere, And holdyn hem hote with here hard hamers. *c* **1490** *Promp. Parv.* 200/2 (MS. K.) Gnastere (*K.* gnachar), *fremitor.* Gnastyn (*K.* gnachyn), *fremo.* Gnastynge (*K.* gnachynge), *fremitus.*

gnack, obs. var. KNACK, trick.

gnagged, var. KNAGGED, *Obs.*, knotted.

gnaghe, obs. form of GNAW *v.*

gnaist(e, var. GNAST *v.*, *Obs.*

gnamma hole ('næmə həʊl). *Austral.* Also **namma hole**. [Aboriginal.] A natural hole in rock, containing water; a native well.

1893 *Australasian* 5 Aug. 252/4 (Morris), The route all the way from York to Coolgardie is amply watered, either 'namma holes' (native wells) or Government wells being plentiful on the road. **1903** J. MARSHALL *Battling for Gold* 14 The gnamma holes were full of water. **1927** M. TERRY *Through Land of Promise* xii. 154 He found two gnamma holes (or rock holes) each holding about 40 gallons of water. **1928** K. S. PRICHARD *Coonardoo* iv. 52 His eyes, namma holes in viscid orbits, glittered at her, as he swung his naked feet. **1950** C. GOOD *Yarns of Yilgarn* 9 A native well (or gnamma hole) in the rocks.

gnap (næp), *sb. Sc.* [f. the vb.] A bite, morsel.

1768 ROSS *Helenore* (1789) 69, I was sent to them with their small disjune:..And whan I saw their piece was but a gnap, Thought with mysell of mending their mishap. **1866** GREGOR *Banffsh. Gloss.*, *Gnap*, a morsel of anything eatable. **1871** W. ALEXANDER *Johnny Gibb* (1873) 15 'That's to lat 'imsel' get a gnap too!'

gnap, *v.* *Obs.* exc. *Sc.* See also KNAP *v.*² [Onomatopœic; cf. GNIP, SNAP, etc.] To bite in a snapping fashion. Usually *intr.* or *absol.*

The sense in quot. 1501 is doubtful: it may be 'chirped'.

1303 R. BRUNNE *Handl. Synne* 10208 Sum gnappede here fete and handes As dogges doun þat gnawe here bandes. **1501** DOUGLAS *Pal. Hon.* Prol. 44 The greshoppers amangis the vergers gnappit. **1523** FITZHERB. *Husb.* (1534) G 6, As manye horses as do playe with him, that is sore, and gnappe of the matter that renneth out of the sore, shall haue the same sorance within a moneth after. **1587** FRAUNCE *C'tess Pembroke's Ivychurch* II. ii, Noebody giues them [Goates] Thyme and other flowers to be gnapping. **16..** MELVILL *MS.* 55 (Jam.) In the nethermost [window] the Earle of Morton was standing gnapping on his staffe end. **1810** COCK *Simple Strains* 119 (Jam.) She..disna spare her cheese an cakes To had our teeth a gnappin, Fu' crump, that night.

b. *fig.* **to gnap at**, to snap at, find fault with; also, to clip (words) in speaking.

1533 ELYOT *Knowledge* Pref., [They] be alwaye gnappynge and kyckynge at suche examples. **1789** SHIRREFS *Poems* (1790) 293 Keep me frae your travel'd birds, Wha.. only ken to gnap at words. **1866** GREGOR *Banffsh. Gloss.*, *Gnap at*, to taunt and find fault with; as, 'He's a nyatterin' bodie: he's eye gnappin' at something'.

gnapweed, gnar, var. ff. KNAPWEED, KNAR.

gnar (nɑː(r)), *v.* Also 5 **gnare**, 6 **gnarr(e**, 9 **gnarr**; see also NAR. [Onomatopœic: cf. MLG. *gnarren*, MDu. *gnerren*, *gnorren* to grunt; G. *knarren*, *knirren* to creak, *knurren* (Da. *knurre*, Sw. *knorra*) to grumble, snarl; also OE. *gnyrran* (Wulfstan 138/29; cf. *gnyrende*, rendering L. *stridens*, *Sax. Leechd.* III. 210).] *intr.* To snarl, growl. (Cf. GNARL *v.*¹)

1496 *Dives & Paup.* (W. de W.) I. lviii. 100 He shall gnasche or gnare with his teeth. **1522** SKELTON *Why not to Court* 297 For and this curre do gnar, They must stande all a far, To holde vp their hande at the bar. **1583** GOLDING *Calvin on Deut.* li. 305 Let those mastife dogs barke and gnarre as much as they list. **1630** J. TAYLOR (Water P.) *Taylor's Motto* Wks. II. 44/2 Those will in their kennels lye And gnar and snarle, and grumble secretly. **1737** *Albania* 196 No lion here the traveller assails With midnight roar, nor ruthless panther gnars. **1868** ATKINSON *Cleveland Gloss.*, *Gnarr*, to growl, as a dog.

transf. and *fig.* **1850** TENNYSON *In Mem.* xcviii, A thousand wants Gnarr at the heels of men. **1880** WEBB *Goethe's Faust* IV. xvi, When the storm in the forest roars and gnarrs.

Hence '**gnarring** *vbl. sb.*

1652 URQUHART *Jewel* Wks. (1834) 238 Like a snarling curr that in his gnarring snatcheth at the taile. *a* **1693** —— *Rabelais* III. xiii, He..was..surrounded..with the barking of Currs..gnarring of Puppies. **1843** CARLYLE *Past & Pr.* III. iv, With preternatural gnarring, growling and screeching..there began..this song.

† **gnare,** *sb.* *Obs.* Also 5 **gnarre**. [Of obscure origin; the coincidence in sense with *snare* is remarkable, but the sb. cannot have originated in a scribal error, as the following vb. is derived from it.] A snare.

a **1325** *Prose Psalter* xxiv. [xxv.] 16 He shal drawe out myn feet of þe gnare. *c* **1380** WYCLIF *Serm.* Sel. Wks. II. 363 Blyndenes in þis point makiþ men to be taken in his [þe fendis] gnaris. **1382** —— *2 Sam.* xxii. 6 There wenten before me the gnaris [**1388** snaris] of deeth. *c* **1440** N. LOVE *Bonaventura's Mirror* xxvi. lf. 56 (Gibbs MS.) þat worchyp is one of þe most perylouse gnarre [**1530** *W. de W.* snare] of þe enemy to cacche and bygyle mannes soule. *c* **1450** tr. *De Imitatione* III. lix, Nature..drawiþ many men & holdiþ hem as in a gnare.

† **gnare,** *v.* *Obs.* Also 6 **gnarre**. [f. prec.] *trans.* To choke, strangle. Also, to snare, entrap.

c **1380** WYCLIF *Wks.* (1880) 437 þes two lawis ben granes [*printed* graues] to þe fend to gnare men in his net. *c* **1380** —— *Serm.* Sel. Wks. I. 96 þes double mannis lawes..gnaren þe Chirche, as tares gnaren corn. **1382** —— *Prov.* vi. 2 Thou art gnarid [Vulg. *illaqueatus*] with the woordis of thi mouth. **1412-20** LYDG. *Chron. Troy* v. xxxvi, Erygona..toke a rope ..and ther-withall gan her selfe to gnare. **1530** PALSGR. 569/1, I gnarre in a halter or corde, I stoppe ones breathe or snarle one, *je estrangle.* He pulled the towel so strayte about my necke that he had almoste gnarred me.

† '**gnarity.** *Obs. rare*$^{-0}$. [ad. L. *gnāritās*, f. *gnārus* knowing.] (See quot.)

1623 COCKERAM, *Gnaritie*, experience, knowledge.

gnarl (nɑːl), *sb.*¹ [Back-formation from GNARLED. A sb. *knarle* knot (of hair), occurs early in 17th c.] A contorted knotty protuberance, esp. on a tree.

1824 MISS MITFORD *Village* Ser. I. (1863) 184 The knots and gnarls of the exterior coat [of a tree]. **1866** LOWELL *Carlyle* in *Study Wind.* (1886) 171 It is always the knots and gnarls of the oak that he admires. **1871** B. TAYLOR *Faust* (1875) I. xxi. 180 Living knots and gnarls uncanny Feel with polypus antennæ For the wanderer.

gnarl, *sb.*² *rare*$^{-1}$. [f. GNARL *v.*¹] A snarl.

1847 E. BRONTE *Wuthering Heights* (1885) 4 My caress provoked [from the dog] a long guttural gnarl.

† **gnarl** (nɑːl), *v.*¹ *Obs.* [frequentative f. GNAR *v.*]

1. *intr.* To snarl.

1593 SHAKS. *2 Hen. VI*, III. i. 192 Thus is the Shepheard beaten from thy side, And Wolues are gnarling, who shall gnaw thee first. **1596** NASHE *Saffron Walden* 103 What will not a dogge doo that is angerd, bite and gnarle at anie bone or stone that is neere him. **1814** CARY *Dante Inf.* XXI. 129 Dost not mark How they do gnarl upon us.

2. *slang.* (See quot.)

1812 J. H. VAUX *Flash Dict.*, *Gnarl*, to gnarl upon a person is the same as splitting or nosing upon him; a man guilty of this treachery is called a gnarling scoundrel.

Hence † '**gnarling** *ppl. a.*, † '**gnarler** (see quot.).

1597 SHAKS. *Rich. II*, I. iii. 292 (Qo. 1) For gnarling sorrow hath lesse power to bite, The man that mocks at it and sets it light. **1811** *Lex. Balatron.*, *Gnarler*, a little dog that by his barking alarms the family when any person is breaking into the house. **1812** [see sense 2 above].

gnarl (nɑːl), *v.*² Chiefly in pa. pple. [Back-formation from GNARLED.] *trans.* To contort, twist, make knotted and rugged like an old tree. Also *transf.* and *fig.*

1814 *Mermaid* I. ii, Her lean large hands, So gnarl'd with bone, and shrivell'd without veins. **1844** *Mem. Babylonian P'cess* II. 74 Their roots being gnarled and distorted into extraordinary forms. **1853** KANE *Grinnell Exp.* xxii. (1856)

175 Limestone cliffs..forming stupendous piers gnarled by frost degradation. **1891** C. JAMES *Rom. Rigmarole* ii. 11 Time had gnarled him a good deal, and seemed half inclined to tie him into a knot.

Hence **'gnarling** *vbl. sb.*

1885 *Atlantic Monthly* Apr. 443 Some grotesque gnarling of limbs..of the great trees that stretched above.

gnarl (nɑːl), *v.*[3] *dial. trans.* To gnaw.

1821 CLARE *Vill. Minstr.* I. 202 The little chumbling mouse Gnarls the dead leaves for her house. **1855** ROBINSON *Whitby Gloss.*, *To Gnarl*, to gnaw as a mouse.

gnarled (nɑːld), *ppl. a.* Also 9 **knarled**. [var. of KNURLED; the form occurs in one passage of Shaks. (for which the sole authority is the folio of 1623), whence it came into general use in the nineteenth century.] Of a tree: Covered with protuberances; distorted, twisted; rugged, knotted.

1603 SHAKS. *Meas. for M.* II. ii. 116 Thy sharpe and sulpherous bolt Splits the vn-wedgable and gnarled Oke. **1803** LEYDEN *Scenes of Infancy* I. 224 Bare are the boughs, the knarled roots uptorn. **1816** SHELLEY *Alastor* 382 The gnarled roots Of mighty trees. **1839–40** W. IRVING *Wolfert's R.* (1855) 15 Its orchard of gnarled and sprawling apple-trees. **1847–8** H. MILLER *First Impr.* ix. (1857) 145 Old gnarled stems of ivy wind, snake-like round the..trunks. **1871** R. ELLIS tr. *Catullus* lxiv. 107 When as his huge gnarled trunk in furious eddies a whirlwind Riving wresteth amain.

transf. and *fig.* **1821–30** LD. COCKBURN *Mem.* vi. (1874) 293 His drawn bayonet in his large gnarled hand. **1851** CARLYLE *Sterling* I. ii. (1872) 7 That wild-wooded rocky coast, with its gnarled mountains. **1871** SMILES *Charac.* viii. (1876) 219 The great gnarled man [Luther] had a heart as tender as a woman's.

gnarly ('nɑːlɪ), *a.* [f. GNARL *sb.*[1] + -Y[1]. Cf. KNURLY.] = GNARLED.

1829 LANDOR *Imag. Conv.* Wks. 1846 II. 180 Like a dry and gnarly log of mountain-ash. **1877** *Fraser's Mag.* XV. 110 From a gnarly branch a delicate blossom issues.

Comb. **1877** LANIER *Hard Times in Elfland* 70 An aged Ram, flapp'd, gnarly-horn'd.

b. *transf.* Of a person.

1863 KINGSLEY *Water-Bab.* vii. (1878) 323 A dogged gnarly foursquare brick of an English boy. **1865** *Q. Rev.* July 85 He [Browning] loves a gnarly character, or a knotty problem. **1876** LANIER *Poems, Waving Corn* 1 Ploughman, whose gnarly hand yet kindly wheeled Thy plough.

gnarring ('nɑːrɪŋ), *ppl. a.* [f. GNAR *v.* + -ING[2].]

†**a.** Of an animal or person: Growling, snarling. *Obs.*

1592 G. HARVEY *Four Lett.* etc. 65, I seldom call a snarling curr, a curr, But wish the gnarring dog, as sweete a mouth As bravest horse, that feeleth golden spurr. **1600** FAIRFAX *Tasso* IV. viii. 56 The gnarring porter durst not whine.

b. Of sound: Strident. *rare.*

a **1849** J. C. MANGAN *Poems* (1859) 114 The portal oped with a gnarring sound.

gnash (næʃ), *sb. rare.* [f. GNASH *v.*] A gnashing or snap of the teeth.

1804 J. GRAHAME *Sabbath* (1839) 24/1 The scowl and gnash malign Of Superstition, stopping both her ears.. dismays him not. **1882** G. MACDONALD *Castle Warlock* xix. (1883) 117 A beast in the hills that went biting every living thing..he appeared..made his gnash, and was gone.

†**gnash**, *a. Obs.*−[1] [f. GNASH *v.*] Gnashing.

1583 STANYHURST *Æneis* I. (Arb.) 27 Lyke bandog grinning, with gnash tusk greedelye snarring.

gnash (næʃ), *v.* Forms: 5 **gnasche**, 6 **gnasshe**, **gnasz(s)he**, 6- **gnash**. [First recorded at the end of the 15th c.; app. a modification of the older verb GNAST.

Perh. the mod. word originated in the pa. t. *gnaist* (see GNAST *v.*), which may have undergone a change of pronunciation parallel to that of *abaist* into *abascht*. But cf. GNACCHE *v.*]

1. *intr.* To strike together or 'grind' the teeth, esp. from rage or anguish. Also with *against*, *on*, *upon*. Said also of the teeth.

1496 [see GNAR *v.*]. **1530** PALSGR. 569/1, I gnasshe with the tethe. Loke in 'I gnast'. **1535** COVERDALE *Ps.* xxxiv. (xxxv. 16) They gnaszshed vpon me with their teth. **1539** TAVERNER *Erasm. Prov.* (1552) 6 The Lion..gnassheth wt his teeth against her. **1557** GRIMALD *Death Zoroas* in *Tottel's Misc.* (Arb.) 122 The Macedon, perceyuing hurt, gan gnash. **1646** CRASHAW *Sospetto d'Herode* viii, His Teeth for Torment gnash. **1667** MILTON *P.L.* VI. 341 There they him laid, Gnashing for anguish and despite and shame. **1808** HELEN ST. VICTOR *Ruins of Rigonda* I. 157 His teeth gnashed against each other, and each limb shook with the violence of his emotions. **1870** BRYANT *Iliad* I. v. 136 He fell, and in the fall Gnashed with his teeth upon the cold bright blade.

transf. **1897** T. H. WARREN *By Severn Sea* xvii, Jagged floes That gnashed and justled as they downward bore.

2. *trans.* To strike (the teeth) together, as in rage or anguish.

1590 SPENSER *F.Q.* II. vii. 21 And both did gnash their teeth. **1697** DRYDEN *Virg. Georg.* IV. 653 The Seer..Rowl'd his green Eyes..And gnash'd his Teeth. **1720** GAY *Poems* (1745) I. 178 Two boars..Gnash their sharp tusks, and.. Dispute the reign of some luxurious mire. **1812** BYRON *Ch. Har.* II. xl, What gallant warhounds..gnash their fangs, loud yelling for the prey! **1843** BETHUNE *Sc. Fireside Stor.* 102 He almost gnashed his teeth with rage. **1871** B. TAYLOR *Faust* (1875) I. xxiii. 204 Gnash not thus thy devouring teeth at me!

3. To bite upon, grind the teeth upon; to bite *in twain* with champing teeth.

1812 H. & J. SMITH *Rej. Addr.* xii. (1873) 112 Hot spice gingerbread, Which black from the oven he gnashes. **1816** BYRON *Prisoner Chillon* ix, I strove..To rend and gnash my bonds in twain. **1829** LANDOR *Imag. Conv.* Wks. 1846 II. 48 The tiger gnashed the fox, the ermine and the sloth.

Hence **'gnashing** *ppl. a.*

1700 DRYDEN tr. *Iliad* I. 361 With boiling Rage Atrides burn'd; And Foam betwixt his gnashing Grinders churn'd. **1705** STANHOPE *Paraphr.* I. 73 Trembling Knees, Wringing Hand and Gnashing Teeth. **1848** LYTTON *Harold* IX. i, The beast twisted in vain, to and fro, with gnashing jaws. **1860** TRENCH *Serm. Westm. Abb.* viii. 90 The gnashing teeth and the fierce faces of foes.

gnash, incorrect spelling of NESH *a.*

gnashing ('næʃɪŋ), *vbl. sb.* [f. GNASH *v.* + -ING[1].] The action of the vb. GNASH.

1495 *Trevisa's Barth. De P.R.* (W. de W.) VII. vii. 228 Gnasshyng of teeth. **1535** COVERDALE *Matt.* viii. 12 There shal be wepinge, & gnaszhing of teeth. **1621–3** MIDDLETON & ROWLEY *Changeling* V. iii, Howls and gnashings shall be music to you. **1791** COWPER *Iliad* XI. 508 And from beneath Loud gnashings hear. **1803** *Med. Jrnl.* X. 576 The masticatories opened and closed the jaws with gnashing of the teeth.

†**gnasp**, *v. Obs. rare*−[0]. [Cf. GNAP, GRASP.] *intr.* to snap (*at*).

1530 PALSGR. 568/2, I gnaspe at a thyng to catche it with my tethe, *je hanche*. **1611** COTGR., *Hancher*, to gnaspe, or snatch at with the teeth.

†**gnast**, *sb. Obs.* Also 5 **gnaste**. [OE. *-gnást* (in *fýr-gnást*) str. masc., spark, cognate with OHG. *gneista* wk. fem., *gneisto* wk. masc., also *ganeheista* (MHG. *ganeist(e*, *gneist(e*), ON. *gneiste* wk. masc. The OHG. *ganeheista* suggests formation from OTeut. **ga-* + *ana* prep. (= ON) + **hait* (see HOT); some scholars refer the word to the Teut. root **aið-* to burn (as in OE. *ád* funeral pyre).] A spark; the snuff of a candle.

c **1175** *Lamb. Hom.* 81 þe oðer [brond] is aquenched al buten a gnast. **1382** WYCLIF *Isa.* xxix. 5 And shal be..as a gnast thurgh passende, the multitude of hem that aȝen thee hadden maistri. **1412–20** LYDG. *Troy-bk.* I. iv. (1513) Bij, And as a gnast firste of lytell hate Encauseth flawme of contek and debate. *c* **1440** *Promp. Parv.* 277/2 Knast, or gnaste of a kandel (*K.* knast of candelle), *emunctura*. **14..** *Voc.* in Wr.-Wülcker 592/31 *Lichinus*, gnast of candele.

†**gnast**, *v. Obs.* Forms: 3–6 **gnaist(e**, **gnayste**, 4–6 **gnaste**, 3–6 **gnast**. [The early form *gnaiste* would seem to point to adoption of an ON. **gneista*, an ablaut-var. of *gnísta* to gnash the teeth. ON. had also *gnastan*, *gnastran* (beside *gnístan*, *gnístran*) gnashing of teeth, and a str. vb. *gnesta* to crack, clatter. The ultimate origin is prob. onomatopœic, which may account for the anomalous variation in the root-vowel.]

1. *intr.* = GNASH *v.* 1.

a **1300** *Cursor M.* 19434 þai bigan to gnast with toth. *a* **1300** *E.E. Psalter* ii. 1 (Horstm.) Wharfore gnaisted gomes swo. **1340** HAMPOLE *Ps.* xxxiv. 19 þai gnaystid on me wiþ þaire tethe. **1382** WYCLIF *Isa.* v. 29 He shal gnasten [L. *frendet*], and holden the prei. *c* **1450** *Mirour Saluacioun* 1756 This hors..gnaisting and neeing hym vndere his fete he keste. **1470–85** MALORY *Arthur* VI. xv, All tho greued and gnasted at syre launcelot. **1508** FISHER 7 *Penit. Ps.* vi. Wks. (1876) 22 They gnaste with theyr tethe. **1530** PALSGR. 569/1, I gnast with the tethe. I make a noyse by reason I thruste one tothe upon another.

2. *trans.* = GNASH *v.* 2.

a **1300** *Cursor M.* 19354 þen be-gan þai for tene þair tethe to gnast. *a* **1300** *E.E. Psalter* cxi[i]. 10 (Horstm.) Sinful sal se..And gnaiste his tethe he sal with-al. *c* **1460** J. RUSSELL *Bk. Nurture* 301 Good son þy tethe be not pikynge, grisynge, ne gnastynge.

Hence †**'gnaster**, one who gnashes.

c **1440** *Promp. Parv.* 200/2 Gnastere,..*fremitor*.

†**'gnasting**, *vbl. sb. Obs.* [f. GNAST *v.* + -ING[1].] The action of the vb. GNAST; gnashing.

a **1300** *Cursor M.* 26760 þar endles gnasting es to toth. *c* **1380** WYCLIF *Serm.* Sel. Wks. I. 49 þere shal be wepyng and gnastinge of teeþ. **1382** —— *Prov.* xix. 12 As the gnasting [Vulg. *fremitus*] of a leoun, so and the wrathe of the king. **1387** TREVISA *Higden* (Rolls) VII. 81 þe voyces of gnastynge. **1388** WYCLIF *Jer.* viii. 16 Gnastyng [**1382** fnesting; Vulg. *fremitus*] of horsis therof is herd fro Dan. *c* **1440** *Promp. Parv.* 200/2 Gnastynge (*K.* gnachynge), *fremitus*. **1508** FISHER 7 *Penit. Ps.* vi. Wks. (1876) 41 Gnastynge of tethe.

gnat[1] (næt). Forms: 1 **gnæt**, 2–3 **gnet**, 3–6 **gnatte**, (6 **ganatte**), 4–6 **knatt(e**, (5, 8 **knat**), 4- **gnat**. [OE. *gnæt(t* str. masc., cogn. with Ger. dial. *gnatze* wk. fem.]

1. a. A small two-winged fly of the genus *Culex*, esp. *Culex pipiens*, the female of which has a sharp pointed proboscis, by means of which it punctures the skins of animals and sucks their blood. In U.S., the common mosquito, *Culex mosquito*.

c **893** K. ÆLFRED *Oros.* I. vii. §1 þæt gnættas comon ofer eall þæt land. *c* **1000** *Sax. Leechd.* I. 267 Ðeos wyrt [fleabane] gnættas & micgeas & flean acwelleþ. *c* **1250** *Gen. & Ex.* 2988 Gnattes..smale to sen, and sarp on bite. *c* **1350** *Parl. Three Ages* 50 Gnattes gretely me greuede and gnewen myn eghne. **1398** TREVISA *Barth. De P.R.* XII. xiii. (1495) 422 A gnatte is a lytill flye and highte Culex. **1471** *Paston Lett.* No. 674 III. 12, I wold fayne my gray horse wer kept in mew for gnattys. **1529** MORE *Comf. agst. Trib.* III. Wks. 1226/2 Lawes..lyke vnto cobwebbes, in whych the lyttle Knattes, and Flyes stycke styll and hange fast. **1562** TURNER *Herbal* II. 169 Ye same moysture [of the Elm Tree] after yt is dried vp, is resolued into litle flies like Ganattes. **1592** SHAKS. *Rom. & Jul.* I. iv. 64 Her Waggoner, a small gray-coated Gnat. **1617** HIERON *Wks.* II. 75 Let not our sermons be as the spiders web, thorow which doe breake the greater flies, while onely the lesser gnats are taken. **1789** MRS. PIOZZI *Journ. France* I. 278 One is bit to death by animals, gnats in particular. **1816** KIRBY & SP. *Entomol.* (1843) I. 88 Species..whose bite is severe, but none to be compared to the common Gnat (*culex pipiens*). *c* **1850** *Arab. Nts.* (Rtldg.) 363 He perceived two persons sleeping..their heads covered with linen to protect them from the gnats.

fig. **1669** WOODHEAD *St. Teresa* I. xviii. 115 This importunate little Gnat of the Memory hath her wings burnt here.

b. Used as a type of something insignificant; freq. in allusion to Matt. xxiii. 24. Cf. CAMEL *sb.* 1 c.

c **1000** *Ags. Gosp.* Matt. xxiii. 24 La blindan latteowas ȝe drehnigeað þone gnætt [*c* **1160** *Hatton Gosp.* gnet] aweȝ & drincað þone olfend. *a* **1225** *Ancr. R.* 10 Ase moni þet isihð þene gnet & swoluweð þe vliȝe, þet is, makeð muchel strencðe þer as is lutel. *c* **1386** CHAUCER *Manciple's T.* 151 Noght worth to thee, in comparison, The mountance of a gnat. **1526** SKELTON *Magnyf.* 1732 But, and I were as ye, I wolde not set a gnat By Magnyfycence. **1535** COVERDALE *Matt.* xxiii. 24 O ye blynde gydes, which strayne out [**1611** straine at] a gnat, but swalowe vp a Camell. **1562** J. HEYWOOD *Prov. & Epigr.* (1867) 101 Thou neuer durst abyde to fyght with a gnat. **1611** SHAKS. *Cymb.* I. iii. 21 Till the diminution Of space, had pointed him sharpe as my Needle: Nay..till he had melted from The smalnesse of a Gnat, to ayre. **1692** BENTLEY *Boyle Lect.* iii. 86 To discern the smallest Hair upon the leg of a Gnat. **1889** *Spectator* 14 Dec. 842 We find it a little amusing that he..should so summarily avenge himself upon the little gnat of a writer who has punctured his own cuticle.

2. Applied to other insects resembling this; in U.S., to a small stinging fly of the genus *Simulium*.

1787 BEST *Angling* (ed. 2) 99 The Little black Gnat. *Ibid.* 116 The Blue-Gnat. **1799** G. SMITH *Laboratory* II. 290 The white-gnat. This is composed of a black head, and a pale wing. **1867** F. FRANCIS *Angling* vi. (1880) 217 The Black Gnat..has been called 'the fisherman's curse'.

3. *attrib.* and *Comb.*, as **gnat-like** adj. and adv.; **gnat-catcher**, an American bird of the genus *Polioptila*, esp. *P. cærulea*; **gnat-flower**, a name for *Ophrys apifera*; †**gnat-gnapper** = *gnat-snapper*; **gnat-hawk**, a provincial name of the Nightjar; **gnat-net**, a net to protect one from the attacks of gnats; **gnat's** (or **gnats'**) **piss** *slang*, a very weak beverage; a drink of poor quality; **gnat satyrion** ? = *gnat-flower*; **gnat-sin** *nonce-wd.*, a trivial sin (in reference to Matt. xxiii. 24); **gnat-snap**, **-snapper**, a name given to various small birds; in 17th c. used to translate L. *ficedula*; see also GNAT[2]; also *fig.*, as a term of contempt; **gnat-strainer** (see quot.; after Matt. xxiii. 24); so ***gnat-straining***; **gnat-worm**, the larva of a gnat.

1883 *Century Mag.* Sept. 685/1 The nest of..the little gray *gnat-catcher. **1688** R. HOLME *Armoury* II. 109/1 The *Gnat Flower, that is yellow and brown. **1755** JOHNSON, *Gnat-flower*, a flower otherwise called the beeflower. **1627** HAKEWILL *Apologie* IV. vii. §8. 364 In the morning fasting, he dispatched..an hundred *gnat-gnappers [tr. L. *ficedulas*] & forty oysters. [*Marg.*] A bird like a nightingall, feeding on figges. **1885** SWAINSON *Prov. Names Birds* 97 Nightjar (*Caprimulgus europæus*)..From its fondness for moths and beetles it has also the names of..Moth hawk (Forfar). *Gnat hawk (Hants). **1905** *Westm. Gaz.* 1 Feb. 2/3 Drifts *gnat-like to the flame. **1915** E. R. LANKESTER *Divers. Naturalist* 216 In early September, golf links..swarm with a large gnat-like fly of reddish-brown body. **1950** W. DE LA MARE *Inward Compan.* 37 A gnatlike wail. **1658** SIR T. BROWNE *Gard. Cyrus* ii. 42 The ancient Conopeion or *gnatnet of the Ægyptians. **1597** GERARDE *Herbal* I. ci. 163 *Gnat Satirion..The stalke groweth to the height of an hand, whereon are placed verie orderly small flowers like in shape to Gnats and of the same colour. **1646** FULLER *Wounded Consc.* (1841) 332 That those should be choked with a *gnat-sin, who have swallowed many camel-sins. **1591** SYLVESTER *Du Bartas* I. v. 714 The little *Gnat-snap (worthy Princes Boords). **1610** W. FOLKINGHAM *Art Survey* IV. iii. 83 The Godwit, Gnat-snap, Knot. **1885** [see GNAT[2]]. **1598** FLORIO, *Culobianco*, a birde called a *gnat-snapper. **1633** HART *Diet Diseased* I. xxiii. 104 [He] had them [Parrats]..served in at table as though they had beene but ordinary Gnat-snappers. **1653** URQUHART *Rabelais* I. xxv. 116 Calling them..grouthead gnat-snappers. **1731** MEDLEY *Kolben's Cape G. Hope* II. 154 Gnat-snappers, which are much seen at the Cape (where they are likewise call'd Honey- or Bee-Eaters) some reckon a sort of Tit-mouses. **1959** I. & P. OPIE *Lore & Lang. Schoolch.* ix. 164 Weak tea may be '*gnat's piss'. **1963** B. S. JOHNSON *Travelling People* v. 110 Where'd you get this gnatspiss from, Maurie?.. I can get you gnatspiss as good as this gnatspiss for sixteen bob a bottle. **1966** 'L. LANE' *ABZ of Scouse* 41 Gnats' piss, cider, near beer, weak tea or any drink. **1846** WORCESTER, **Gnat-strainer*, one who places too much importance on little things. **1858** DICKENS *Lett.* (1880) II. 82 Whereof comes all manner of camel-swallowing and of *gnat-straining. **1858** SIR T. BROWNE *Gard. Cyrus* iii. 59 He that would behold a very anomalous motion, may observe it in the Tortile and tiring stroaks of *Gnat-worms. **1806** PRISCILLA WAKEFIELD *Dom. Recreat.* x. 150 Before the gnat-worms have attained their full growth.

gnat[2] (næt). *Obs.* exc. *dial.* Also **knat**. [Corruption of KNOT *sb.*[2], prob. influenced by the synonyms *gnat-snap*, *-snapper* (see prec.).] A kind of Sandpiper (*Tringa canutus*); see also quot. 1864.

a **1616** B. JONSON *Epigr.* I. ci. 20 (1616) 799 Partrich, pheasant, woodcock..godwit..knat, raile, and ruffe too.

1672 SHADWELL *Miser* III. Wks. 1720 III. 57 *Goldingham.* Peace, Sirrah, and tell me what we must have [*sc.* for supper] ..*James.* Partridges, Gnats, Godwits. *a* **1682** SIR T. BROWNE *Norf. Birds* Wks. 1835 IV. 319 Gnats or knots, a small bird, which, taken with nets, grow excessively fat, being mewed and fed with corn. **1864** ATKINSON *Prov. Names Birds, Gnat* or *Knat,* prov. name (Kent) for Lesser Tern. *Sterna minuta.* **1885** SWAINSON *Prov. Names Birds* 194 Knot (*Tringa canutus*). So called, according to Camden, in honour of King Canute.. Whence also Gnat; Knat; Knet ..Gnat snap.

gnathal ('neɪθəl), *a.* [f. Gr. γνάθ-ος jaw + -AL[1].] = GNATHIC *a.*

1888 *Amer. Naturalist* Oct. 941 Of these three primary segments (macrosomites) of the primitive body, the first corresponds to the sum of the jaw-bearing (gnathophorous) metameres—gnathal macrosomites. **1935** R. E. SNODGRASS *Princ. Insect Morphol.* vi. 100 The embryonic gnathal segments constitute a distinct gnathal section of the trunk. **1964** R. W. & J. M. FOX *Introd. Compar. Ent.* v. 138 It is interesting to find that the Diplopoda, despite the difficulty in homologizing their gnathal segments, also have four pairs of glands.

gnathic ('næθɪk, 'neɪθɪk), *a.* [f. Gr. γνάθ-ος jaw + -IC.] Of or pertaining to the jaws; *spec.,* pertaining to the alveolus of the jaws, alveolar.

1882 *Quain's Elem. Anat.* (ed. 9) I. 83 Skulls with a gnathic index below 98 are orthognathous. **1892** R. L. GARNER *Sp. Monkeys* xiii. 134 The vocal powers were correctly measured by the gnathic index.

gnathion ('neɪθɪɒn). *Anat.* [f. Gr. γνάθ-ος jaw + -ION[2].] In the cranium, the lowest point of the inferior border of the mandible in the mid-line; the menton.

1888 *Catal. Marsupialia Brit. Mus.* p. viii, Basal length. —From the 'basion', or lower front edge of the *foramen magnum,* to the 'gnathion'. **1920** H. H. WILDER *Lab. Man. Anthropometry* I. 44 *Gnathion* (gn). The lowest median point on the lower border of the mandible. **1951** *N. & Q. Anthrop.* (ed. 6) I. 12 The distance between the nasion and the gnathion, which is the lowest and most anterior point on the lower border of the lower jaw. **1968** D. H. ENLOW *Human Face* xii. 281/1 The subjective location of gonion and menton (or gnathion), another method of forming the mandibular plane, tends to be just that.

gnathite ('neɪθaɪt). *Zool.* [f. Gr. γνάθ-ος jaw + -ITE.] One of the mouth-appendages of the Arthropoda.

1870 NICHOLSON *Zool.* 191 There is always a complicated set of 'gnathites', or appendages modified for masticatory purposes, surrounding the mouth. **1877** HUXLEY *Anat. Inv. Anim.* vi. 256 There is a stage in which the gnathites are completely converted into jaws.

‖**gnathitis** (neɪ'θaɪtɪs). *Med.* [mod.L., f. Gr. γνάθ-ος jaw + -ITIS.] (See quot. 1853.)

1847 in CRAIG. **1853** DUNGLISON *Med. Dict.* (ed. 9), *Gnathitis*..inflammation of the cheek or upper jaw. **1882** OGILVIE, *Gnathitis;* and in other mod. Dicts.

†'**gnatho.** *Obs.* Also 6–7 **gnato.** [a. L. *Gnathō,* ad. Gr. γνάθων, used as the proper name of a parasite (f. γνάθος jaw).] A person resembling the Gnatho of Terence; a parasite, sycophant.

1533 ELYOT *Knowledge* Pref. A 5, For there be Gnathos in Spayne as wel as in Grece. **1549** LATIMER *2nd Serm. bef. Edw. VI* (Arb.) 68 Take hede of these claubacks..that wyll folowe lyke gnatoes and Parasites. **1624** BURTON *Anat. Mel.* I. ii. I. ii. (ed. 2) 45 Vndeseruing Gnatoes & vitious parasites. **1704** N. N. tr. *Boccalini's Lett. fr. Apollo* I. 141 Parasites and Gnatho's.

gnatho- ('neɪθəʊ). Combining form of Gr. γνάθος jaw, as in **gnatho'cephalon** (see quot. 1935); hence **gnathoce'phalic** *a.*; **gnathochi'larium,** a mouth-part found in Diplopoda; **gnathodyna'mometer** (see quot. 1969); **gnatho'soma, 'gnathosome** (see quot. 1964); hence **gnatho'somal** *a.*; **gnatho'theca,** the horny covering of the lower beak of a bird.

1935 R. E. SNODGRASS *Princ. Insect Morphol.* vi. 102 The gnathocephalon is the region of the insect head that supports the mandibles, the maxillae, and the labium. **1964** R. M. & J. W. FOX *Introd. Compar. Ent.* ii. 42 The gnathocephalon bears the mouthparts. *Ibid.,* The gnathocephalic ganglia frequently are fused into a single mass. **1887** *Ann. New York Acad. Sci.* June 39 This genus [sc. *Nannolene*]..approaches *Julomorpha,* especially in the construction of the gnathochilarium. **1964** R. M. & J. W. FOX *Introd. Compar. Ent.* iii. 85 Diplopods have an accessory feeding structure located behind and between the mandibles, a highly modified affair called the gnathochilarium. **1959** *New Scientist* 2 Apr. 736/1 Many devices [for measuring biting power] have been produced.., with the titles of oral force-meters or gnathodynamometers. **1969** *Gloss. Terms Dentistry* (*B.S.I.*) 75 *Gnathodynamometer,* an instrument for measuring the force exerted in closing the jaws. **1948** *Smithsonian Misc. Coll.* CX. x. 61 The distinctive feature relating to the feeding apparatus of the Acarina is the presence of a discrete head structure carrying the mouth parts, known as the *capitulum, capitellum,* or *gnathosoma.* **1959** T. E. HUGHES *Mites* x. 135 The gnathosoma is movable on the rest of the body and is well sclerotized... The gnathosomal roof consists of the fused tergites of the segments concerned. **1964** R. M. & J. W. FOX *Introd. Compar. Ent.* iii. 81 The large, complex order Acarida is characterized by the presence of a gnathosome (capitulum) formed from anterior segments and having the appearance of a little head bearing the mouthparts. **1870** BAIRD & COOPER *Ornithol.* I. 567 *Gnathotheca,* the covering of the lower jaw. **1889** *Cent. Dict.,* Gnathotheca. **1890** E. COUES *Handbk. Field & Gen. Ornithol.* II. iii. 151 The entire covering of both jaws together is called *rhamphotheca*..of the under, *gnathotheca*..but these terms are not much used. **1959** VAN TYNE & BERGER *Fund. Ornith.* ii. 31 The oral cavity is bounded by the horny coverings of the upper (*rhinotheca*) and lower (*gnathotheca*) mandibles.

gnathobase ('neɪθəʊbeɪs). *Zool.* [f. GNATHO- + BASE *sb.*[1]] A process developed from the lower part of a segmented limb in certain arthropods, modified to bite or crush food. Hence **gnatho'basic** *a.*

1881 E. R. LANKESTER in *Q. Jrnl. Micr. Sci.* Apr. 348 Of the six endites the proximal is somewhat isolated and pushed towards the middle line... It is a jaw process, and may be spoken of as the 'gnathobase'. **1902** —— in *Encycl. Brit.* XXV. 695/1 The five pairs of appendages of the post-oral somites of the head or prosoma thus constituted all primitively carry gnathobasic projections on their coxal joints, which act as hemignaths; in the more specialized forms the mandibular gnathobases cease to develop. **1904** W. T. CALMAN in *Ann. & Mag. Nat. Hist.* Feb. 155 The double series of epipodial lamellæ, the segmentation of the thoracic limbs, the double gnathobasic lobes of the first pair. **1932** BORRADAILE & POTTS *Invertebrata* x. 274 Some of the evidence suggests an archetype [arthropod] with a nine-segmented axis bearing on the median side of the first segment a biting process (gnathobase). **1964** *New Scientist* 13 Aug. 365/2 The mandibles themselves may either derive from the basal part of a segmented limb (the gnathobase) or from a whole jointed limb.

gnathonic (neɪ'θɒnɪk), *a.* Also 7 **gnatonick.** [ad. L. *Gnathōnicus,* f. *Gnathōn-em* GNATHO.] = GNATHONICAL *a.*

1637 GILLESPIE *Eng. Pop. Cerem.* Ep. A ij b, The gnathonick Parasite sweareth to all that this benefactor holdeth. **1652** URQUHART *Jewel* Wks. (1834) 276 Thinks no better of adulatory assentations then of a gnatonick sycophantizing, or parasitical cogging. **1855** KINGSLEY *Westw. Ho!* viii, That Jack's is somewhat of a gnathonic and parasitic soul, or stomach, all Bideford apple-women know.

†**gna'thonical,** *a. Obs.* Also 6–7 **-all, gnatonical(l.** [f. as prec. + -AL[1].] Resembling Gnatho or his proceedings; parasitical, toad-eating.

1540 PALSGR. tr. *Acolastus* IV. ii. S ij, The chiefe or principal honour of the gnathonical sect. **1590** GREENE *Orl. Fur.* (1599) 13 Knowing him to be a Thrasonicall mad-cap, they haue sent mee a Gnathonicall companion, to giue him lettice fit for his lips. **1603** BP. W. BARLOW *Conf. Hampton Crt.* To Rdr., Whome it might haue pleased, without his Gnathonical appeale to haue rested in his Maiesties determination. **1631** R. H. *Arraignm. Whole Creature* vii. 52 Bee not uncased, out of your lands, your livings..by such gnatonicall Conny- (money) catchers. **1721–1800** BAILEY, *Gnathonical,* flattering, deceitful in Words, soothing a Person's Humour to get by him.

Hence †**gna'thonically** *adv.*

1596 NASHE *Saffron Walden* Wks. (Grosart) III. 206, I hope there be some Bishops..doo disdaine their high calling should be so Gnathonically compar'd. **1623** COCKERAM, *Gnathonically,* flatteringly.

gnathonism ('neɪθənɪz(ə)m). *nonce-wd.* [See next and -ISM.] Sycophancy.

1838 COLERIDGE *Lit. Rem.* III. 187 And yet Hacket must have lived to see the practical confutation of this shallow Gnathonism in the result of the marriage with the Papist Henrietta of France!

†'**gnathonize,** *v. Obs. rare*[−1]. [f. L. *Gnathōn-em* GNATHO + -IZE.] *intr.* To behave as a 'Gnatho' or sycophant, to flatter.

1619 H. HUTTON *Follie's Anat.* A vij a, Note..this Timist ..See how he squares it, takes a priuate stand, To Gnathonize, to act it with his hand. Behold his gesture..Lo how he whispers in his Master's eare. **1656** BLOUNT *Glossogr.,* To *Gnathonize,* to play the smell-feast, to flatter. **1727** BAILEY vol. II, *Gnathonizing,* flattering, soothing the Humour of a Person.

gnathophorous (neɪ'θɒfərəs). *rare.* [f. Gr. γνάθο-ς jaw + -φόρ-ος bearing + -OUS.]

1888 [see GNATHAL].

gnathopod ('neɪθəpɒd). [f. as prec. + ποδ-, πούς foot.] = next.

1887 NICHOLSON *Man. Zool.* (ed. 7) 891 *Gnathopods,* the foot-jaws of Crustaceans.

gnathopodite (neɪ'θɒpədaɪt). *Zool.* [f. as prec. + -ITE.] 'One of those limbs which, in crustaceans, have been modified into accessory organs of mastication' (Ogilvie 1882).

18.. *Nature* (Ogilvie), If the Trilobites have true walking legs instead of mouth-feet (*gnathopodites*) only, they would be more closely related to the Isopoda.

gnathostegite (neɪ'θɒstɪdʒaɪt). *Zool.* [f. Gr. γνάθο-ς + στέγ-ειν to cover + -ITE.] (See quot.)

1877 HUXLEY *Anat. Inv. Anim.* vi. 345 A broad plate, which, with its fellow, covers over the other organs, and hence receives the name of the gnathostegite.

gnathostome ('neɪθəʊstəʊm). [a. G. *gnathostome* (E. Haeckel *Anthropogenie* (1874) xviii. 432), f. GNATHO- + STOMA.] A member of the Gnathostomata, a superclass of vertebrates with fully developed upper and lower jaws. Also as *adj.,* of or pertaining to this group. Also **gnatho'stom(at)ous** *a.*

1889 *Cent. Dict.,* Gnathostomatous. **1905** J. MCCABE tr. *Haeckel's Evol. Man* II. xxi. 560 All the vertebrates or gnathostomes, from the fishes to man, descend from a common, extinct, fish-like ancestor. **1908** W. H. GASKELL *Orig. Vertebr.* i. 60 From such gnathostomatous fishes the cyclostomes were supposed to have descended. **1909** E. S. GOODRICH in R. Lankester *Treat. Zool.* IX. 92 The Gnathostomes might be divided into the Ichthyomorpha (Pisces) and the Tetrapoda (Amphibia, Reptilia, Aves, Mammalia). **1933** A. S. ROMER *Vertebr. Paleont.* iii. 35 All possess jaws, structures indicating so great and significant an advance that these forms..are often spoken of as gnathostomes ('jaw-mouthed'). **1936** NEAL & RAND *Compar. Anat.* viii. 305 Gnathostome fishes have an immovable tongue. **1954** G. C. KENT *Compar. Anat. Vertebr.* iii. 48 Agnathons lack true jaws..; all other vertebrates, because they exhibit jaws, are gnathostomes. **1968** R. ZANGERL tr. *Peyer's Compar. Odontology* 30 The placoderms are all more or less clearly gnathostomous.

gnatling ('nætlɪŋ). [See -LING.] A small gnat. Also *fig.,* an insignificant person or thing.

1614 SYLVESTER *Tobacco battered* 198 They Who swallow Camels, swallow Gnatlings may. **1761** CHURCHILL *Rosciad* Poems I. 24 If some man..Should dare attack these gnatlings in their nest; At once they rise..Whet their small stings, and buzz about the stage. **1805** FESSENDEN *Democr. Unveild* v. 156 Lest the reader think the topic..too microscopic We'll..show Our gnat-ling in a note below.

‖**gnatoo** (nə'tuː; properly 'ŋatu). [Polynesian (Tonga); now spelt *gatu* (g = ŋ).] (See quot. 1817.)

1817 J. MARTIN *Mariner's Acc. Tonga Isls.* II, Tonga Voc., *Gnátoo,* the substance used for clothing, prepared from the bark of the Chinese paper mulberry tree, and imprinted; before it is imprinted it is called *tápa.* **1823** BYRON *Island* vii, A pine torch, strongly girded with gnatoo. *Ibid.* viii, The mat for rest; for dress the fresh gnatoo.

gnatter ('nætə(r)), *v. Obs.* exc. *dial.*

1. a. *trans.* To nibble. Also with *away.* **b.** *intr.* To nibble *at.*

1747 MASON *Musæus* 65 Tityrus [i.e. Chaucer]..thus in antique guise short talk did hold..Old Time..Gnawen with rusty tooth continually, Gnattrid my lines, that they all cancrid ben. **1757** E. DARWIN *Let.* 24 Dec. in *Life* (1879) 22 Here Time with his long Teeth had gnattered away the remainder of this Leaf. **1882** *Lanc. Gloss.* s.v., 'He's olus gnatterin' at his finger-nails.'

2. *intr.* **a.** To 'rattle on' in talk; to talk fretfully, grumble. **b.** (See quot. 1888.)

1806–7 J. BERESFORD *Miseries Hum. Life* (1826) *Post. Groans* xxxv, Gnattering and chattering with all his might, by way of treble to the running bass of my horse-laugh. **1888** *Sheffield Gloss., Gnatter,* to grumble, to complain, to be peevish or querulous. *Ibid., Gnatter,* to rattle.

gnatty ('nætɪ), *a.* [f. GNAT[1] + -Y[1].] Resembling a gnat; infested with gnats.

1846 J. J. HOOPER *Adv. Simon Suggs* ii. 28 You..gnatty, flop-eared varmint! **1909** *Amat. Photographer* 14 Sept. 252/2 They can venture into the 'gnattiest' woods without suffering any assault.

gnaur, var. KNAR.

†'**gnavity.** *Obs.*[−0] [ad. L. *gnāvitās,* f. *gnāvus* diligent.] (See quots.)

1623 COCKERAM II, *Actiuity,* Gnauity, Strenuity, Dexterity. **1656** BLOUNT *Glossogr., Gnavity*..(*gnavitas*), activity, lustiness, quickness. **1721–90** in BAILEY.

†**gnaw,** *sb. Obs. rare*[−1]. [f. GNAW *v.*] = GNAWING *vbl. sb.*

1735 BOYSE *Written in Pal. Falkland* 44 Nine days I struggled—think the cruel strife! The gnaw of anguish, and the waste of life!

gnaw (nɔː), *v.* Pa. t. **gnawed.** Pa. pple. **gnawed, gnawn.** Forms: 1 **gnaȝan,** (2 **gneȝeð,** *3rd sg.*), 3–6 **gnawe,** (4 **gnaȝ-, gnaghe,** 5 **gnawyn,** 6 *Sc.* **gnau**), 4, 7– **gnaw;** also 5 **knawyn,** 6 **knaw-, knawe,** 7–8 **knaw.** *Pa. t.* (*strong*) 3 **gneu,** 3–5 **gnow(e,** (4 **gnogh, gnowȝe, gnouȝ**), 4–8 **gnew,** (5–6 **gnewe**); (*weak*) 4 **gnawid-,** 5 **knawed,** 8 **knaw'd,** 8– **gnawed.** *Pa. pple.* (*strong*) 3 **ignahen,** 4, 6 **gnawen,** 4–5 **gnawe,** 6 **knaw(e)n,** *Sc.* **gnawin,** (**gnaw**), 6–7 **gnawne,** 7– **gnawn;** (*weak*) 7 **knaw'd,** 7– **gnawed.** [OE. *gnaȝan,* pa. t. **gnóȝ, gnóȝon* (in *forgnóȝon,* see FORGNAW), pa. pple. *gnaȝen* (in *forgnaȝen*); corresponding to OHG. *gnagan, nagen* (MHG. and mod.G. *nagen*), ON. *gnaga* (Sw. *gnaga,* Da. *gnave,* also *nage* from LG.; mod.Icel. *naga*). Forms with initial *k* instead of *g* appear in OHG. *chnagen,* MDu. *cnaghen,* mod.Du. (and G. dial.) *knagen.* In English the spelling *knaw* is found occas. in 15th c., and is quite common during 16–17th c.; but this only implies that *kn-* and *gn-* were already identical in sound.

In the romance of *Sir Amadas* 247 a form *gnave* is found riming with *grave, have,* but this may be a case of assonance; compare, however, the mod. *wave* from ME. *wawe.*]

1. *trans.* To bite (something) persistently so as to injure it or remove portions of it; to wear away by a continued biting or nibbling.

a **1000** *Be Domes Dæge* (Lumby) 211 Hy wæl-grimme wyrmas slitað and heora ban gnaȝað bryniȝum tuxlum. *c* **1000** ÆLFRIC *Gram.* (Z.) 171/1 *Rodo,* ic gnaȝe. **1023** in Thorpe *Dipl. Angl. Aevi Sax.* (1865) 318/29 Ðæt gewrit beo geworpen musen to gnaȝene. *c* **1175** *Lamb. Hom.* 43 Summe þer graninde sikeð, summe þer reowliche gneȝeð his aȝene tunge. *c* **1290** *S.E. Leg.* I. 206/230 Some [of the adders] heo gnowen, and some heo stounge; and some with scharpe tieth heom bite. **1297** R. GLOUC. (Rolls) 8632 To þe rode he sturte, & bigan to frete & gnawe þe armes vaste & þis, & mid is teþ to drawe. *c* **1350** *Parl. Three Ages* 50 Gnattes gretely me greuede and gnewen myn eghne. *c* **1440** *Gesta Rom.* xxxii. 124 (Add. MS.) The maiden..gnewe [*Harl. MS.* bote] the Girdell with her tethe, and brake it on iii.

peces. **1484** CAXTON *Fables of Æsop* I. xviii, The ratte beganne thenne to byte the lace or cord, and so long he knawed it that the lace brake. **1526** TINDALE *Rev.* xvi. 10 They gnewe [so **1535** COVERDALE; **1611** gnawed] their tonges for sorowe. **1555** EDEN *Decades* 122 Howe these woormes knawe and corrode the shyppes we haue declared before. **1628** *World Encomp. by Sir F. Drake* 24 The remnants of Seales.. which they had gnawne with their teeth like dogs. **1728** POPE *Dunc.* I. 117 [He] gnaw'd his pen, then dash'd it on the ground, Sinking from thought to thought. **1739** 'R. BULL' tr. *Dedekindus' Grobianus* 33 Press'd with both Hands by wholesale Knaw your Meat. **1768** ROSS *Helenore* (1789) 43 At last in twa the dowie raips he gnew. **1794** MARTYN *Rousseau's Bot.* xix. 257, I could scarcely find any but what had been gnawn by insects. **1855** MACAULAY *Hist. Eng.* xii. III. 233 The stock of salted hides was considerable, and by gnawing them the garrison appeased the rage of hunger. **1881** JEFFERIES *Wood Magic* I. ii. 35 In the night she meant to have gnawn your throat.

b. With adverbial or other complement, expressing the result of the action, as *to gnaw away, off, out, up; asunder, in two.*

a **1300** *Cursor M.* 6043 Þat beist þan gneu [*other MSS.* gnow(ȝe] vp al bidene þat þe thoner left. **1340** HAMPOLE *Pr. Consc.* 863 Wormes þan sal it al to-gnaw Til þe flesshe be gnawen oway and byten. **1535** COVERDALE *Baruch* vi. 19 The serpentes and wormes.. gnawe out their hertes. **1590** SHAKS. *Com. Err.* v. i. 249. *Ibid.* 289 He.. gnaw'd in two my cords. **1620** SHELTON *Quix.* III. xii. I. 243 After he had gnawn off almost the Half of one of his Nails. **1631** GOUGE *God's Arrows* iii. §52. 282 A lion may stand in need of the helpe of a mouse to gnaw asunder the cord wherewith he is hampered. *a* **1839** PRAED *Poems* (1864) I. 204 He hath gnawed in twain my choicest line. **1873** BROWNING *Red Cott. Nt.-cap* 1041 Some work of art gnawn hollow by Time's tooth.

c. *absol.* or *intr.*, often with preps. *at*, †*on*, *upon.*

13.. *Coer de L.* 5074 Many of the hethene houndes With her teeth gnow on the groundes. **1382** WYCLIF *Job* xxx. 3 That gnowen [**1388** gnawiden; L. *rodebant*] in wildernesse, waxende foul with wreechidnesse and sorewe. *c* **1440** *Gesta Rom.* xxx. 110 (Harl. MS.) Twoo bestes.. gnowe at the Rote of the tree with alle theire myght. **1484** CAXTON *Fables of Æsop* II. xviii, He that is wonte and acustomed to robbe and gnawe, with grete payne he may absteyne him self fro hit. **1513** MORE *Rich. III*, Wks. 54/1 He returned.. frowning and froting and knawing on hys lippes. **1594** SHAKS. *Rich. III*, I. iv. 25, I saw.. A thousand men that Fishes gnaw'd vpon. **1647** COWLEY *Mistr., Dialogue* vii, That Worm which now the Core does wast, When long 't has gnaw'd within will break the skin at last. **1648** JENKYN *Blind Guide* i. 8 As an hungry dog that teareth and gnaweth upon a dry bone, and can suck nothing out of it.. by long gnawing upon it. **1843** BORROW *Bible in Spain* 322 Gaunt dogs were busy here, growling, tearing, and gnawing. **1877** FARRAR *Days of Youth* xv. 145 The worm of sin gnaws deepest into the idle heart.

2. Of destructive agents: To corrode, waste away, consume. (Cf. FRET *v.* 3.) Said also of internal pains.

1530 PALSGR. 569/1, I gnawe, as wynde or the colyke gnaweth one in the belly, *je trenchaysonne.* **1561** HOLLYBUSH *Hom. Apoth.* 31 b, For them whose guttes are gnawen or wounded.. caused by a salte Flegma. **1599** H. BUTTES *Dyets drie Dinner* D 6 b, Pine-Nuts.. much eaten, gnaw the stomach and belly. **1611** CORYAT *Crudities* 58 In certaine places it [the Rhone] doth continually gnawe and eate his bankes. **1633** P. FLETCHER *Purple Isl.* I. xv, But last when eating Time shal gnaw the proudest towers. **1655** CULPEPPER *Riverius* III. i. 97 And for the breaking or corroding of the Tympane,.. if there were formerly any vehement Causes that could break or gnaw the same [etc.].

3. *fig.* Said esp. of passion, remorse, etc. (cf. FRET 3 b). †Also, to carp at.

c **1230** *Hali Meid.* 29 Al þe este & al þe eise is her as þe oðre beoð godlese & ignahene. *a* **1340** HAMPOLE *Psalter* cxviii. 40 Enuy, that supposis reprofe in men when it may noght gnaghe þe life. **1526** *Pilgr. Perf.* (W. de W. 1531) 115 So done these irefull thoughtes frette and gnawe the mynde of man or woman. *c* **1680** BEVERIDGE *Serm.* (1729) I. 353 Their consciences are always gnaw'd and tormented. **1749** SMOLLETT *Regicide* II. vii, Thy fears that I may 'scape, Like vultures gnaw thee! **1801** SOUTHEY *Thalaba* x. xxiv, The years that it has gnawn me! and the load Of sin that it has laid upon my soul! **1832** LYTTON *Eugene A.* I. ix, Silently, he had gnawed his heart. **1860** RUSKIN *Mod. Paint.* V. IX. xii. §10 As the flower is gnawed by frost, so every human heart is gnawed by faithlessness.

b. *absol.* and *intr.*; esp. with preps. *to gnaw at* (†*on*), *into* (cf. 1 c); also in indirect passive.

1598 SHAKS. *Merry W.* II. ii. 207 My Coffers ransack'd, my reputation gnawne at. **1651** HOBBES *Leviath.* I. xii. 52 So that man.. hath his heart all the day long, gnawed on by feare of death. **1727** DE FOE *Syst. Magic* I. i. (1840) 30 The eager desire after the knowledge of them gnawed into his very vitals. **1845** S. AUSTIN *Ranke's Hist. Ref.* I. 237 The rage which had long gnawed at his heart might burst forth. **1850** HAWTHORNE *Scarlet L.* xvii. (1879) 224 Torments that have so gnawed into thy life! **1859** —— *Fr. & It. Jrnls.* II. 227 Something gnawed within him, and kept him forever restless and miserable. **1880** G. MEREDITH *Tragic Com.* (1881) 303 The terrible mournfulness.. of the truth gnawed within her.

4. *Comb.*: †**gnaw-bone**, †**gnaw-crust**, terms of derision for one abjectly poor.

1607 A. BREWER *Lingua* v. ii, Begon ye gnawe-bone, rawbone, rascal. **1611** COTGR. *Masche-crouste*, a gnaw-crust, hungrie companion, snatch-crust.

Hence **gnawed** *ppl. a.*; *spec.* in *Bot.* (see quot. 1832).

1820 *Lond. Mag.* June 631/2 Fragments of gnawed gingerbread. **1832** LINDLEY *Introd. Bot.* 387 Gnawed (*erosus*) having the margin irregularly toothed, as if bitten by some animal. **1888** *Daily News* 30 Nov. 3/1 His [the squirrel's] traces lie about in plenty on the ground in the shape of gnawed fir-cones.

gnawable ('nɔːəb(ə)l), *a.* [f. GNAW *v.* + -ABLE.] Capable of being gnawed.

1885 H. O. FORBES *Nat. in E. Archipel.* VI. v. 484 The rats.. in the night gnawed everything gnawable. **1891** *Illustr. Sport. Dram. News* Christm. No. 1/2 His fair moustache was scarcely long enough to be gnawable.

gnawer ('nɔːə(r)). [f. GNAW *v.* + -ER[1].] One that gnaws; a rodent. Now chiefly *Zool.*

1607 TOPSELL *Four-f. Beasts* (1658) 292 The little Mouse.. is justly tearmed.. *rosor omnium rerum*.. a gnawer of all things. **1691** TRYON *Wisd. Dictates* 51 These Gnawers of other Mens harmless Papers. **1828** STARK *Elem. Nat. Hist.* II. 245 *Thysanoura*.. The insects of this order are gnawers. **1845** DARWIN *Voy. Nat.* v. (1879) 82 Among them were the teeth of a gnawer, equalling in size.. those of the Capybara. **1892** *Pall Mall G.* 1 Mar. 2/1 Caverns made by these infinitely little gnawers [microbes].

gnawing ('nɔːɪŋ), *vbl. sb.* [f. as prec. + -ING[1].]

1. The action of the verb GNAW, in various senses.

1340 HAMPOLE *Pr. Consc.* 6873 Þe tend payne es gnawyng with-in Of conscience þat bites als vermyn. **1388** WYCLIF *Isa.* xiii. 8 Gnawyngis and sorewis schulen holde Babiloyns. *c* **1440** *Promp. Parv.* 200/2 Gnawynge, or fowle bytynge, *corrosio.* **1580** HOLLYBAND *Treas. Fr. Tong, Corrosion*, a gnawing, biting, or consumyng as rust, plaisters and poyson. **1622** MALYNES *Anc. Law-Merch.* 336 For this is a biting, nay a verie gnawing to the bones of your Christian brother. **1768–74** TUCKER *Lt. Nat.* (1852) I. 641 The scorchings of unextinguishable flames and gnawings of the never dying worm. **1801** SOUTHEY *Thalaba* IX. xxxviii, At dawn the Worm Will wake, and this poor flesh must grow to meet The gnawing of his hundred poison-mouths! **1894** HALL CAINE *Manxman* III. xix. 190 He.. calmed the gnawings of his love with dreams of ambition.

2. A persistent fretting pain (in the bowels); now only of such pain caused by want of food; *pl.* pangs (of hunger).

1398 TREVISA *Barth. De P.R.* IV. x. (1495) 94 Yf the waye is stoppyd that is bytwene the galle and the bowelles, thereof fallyth gnawynge and passio colica. *c* **1450** *ME. Med. Bk.* (Heinrich) 184 Hyt destryeþ gnawyng & wynd in mannes body. **1578** LYTE *Dodoens* II. xciv. 275 It is singular against the griping torment and knawings or frettings of the belly. **1605** TIMME *Quersit.* I. xv. 77 From them [salts] doe arise inward gnawings, impostums,.. the hemoroides, and such like. **1850** PRESCOTT *Peru* II. 319 To appease the gnawings of hunger, they were fain to eat the leather of their saddles and belts. **1876** BESANT & RICE *Gold. Butterfly* Prol. i, This pilgrim has tightened his belt to stave off the gnawing at his stomach.

gnawing ('nɔːɪŋ), *ppl. a.* [f. as prec. + -ING[2].] That gnaws, in senses of the verb.

1567 DRANT *Horace's Epist.* I. xviii. F iv, Greedie thrist, and knawinge pyne of siluer and of goulde. **1583** STUBBES *Anat. Abus.* II. 52 Monie wanting, they applie bitter potions, nipping medicines, gnawing corrosiues. **1588** SHAKS. *Tit. A.* v. ii. 31, I am Reuenge, sent.. To ease the gnawing Vulture of the mind. **1797** GODWIN *Enquirer* II. ii. 170 It fixes on him an ever gnawing anxiety. **1822–34** *Good's Study Med.* (ed. 4) I. 57 The incisor teeth of the gnawing animals. **1842** H. E. MANNING *Serm.* (1848) I. 44 Memory, like a gnawing stream, gathers its tinge from the soil through which it winds its sullen way.

Hence **'gnawingly** *adv.*

1841 HOR. SMITH *Moneyed Man* III. x. 278 A feeling of indignation still lurked gnawingly at my heart.

gnawn (nɔːn), *ppl. a.* [pa. pple. of GNAW *v.*] Bitten away, corroded.

1583 STANYHURST *Æneis* I. (Arb.) 21 The southwynd merciles ager Three gallant vessels on rocks gnawne craggye reposed. **1610** BARROUGH *Meth. Physick* II. x. (1639) 88 You must restore the gnawne parts with meates of good juice. **1784** M. MADAN *Perseus* (1795) 37 Nor does he beat his desk, nor taste his gnawn nails.

†**gnede**, *a. Obs.* [Of difficult etymology. The ordinary OE. forms *gnéað, gníeðe* (*gnéðe*), are not represented in later Eng.; the type **gníede* (**gnéde*), whence the ME. form, appears to be authenticated by the MS. forms *gnedra* (gen. pl.), *ungnyde*, though these are usually regarded as scribal errors.

The three Eng. types seem to represent OTeut. **ga-nauþo-*, **ga-nauþjo-*, **ga-naudjo* (f. **ga-* = Y- *prefix* + **nauþ-*, *naud-*: see NEED *sb.*); the last of these occurs in OHG. *ginôti, gnôte* (MHG. *genœte*) close, narrow, eager for. The fluctuation between the *-o-* and *-jo-* declension may perh. indicate (as in many other adjs.) an original *u* stem.]

1. Of persons: Sparing, niggardly, miserly. Also *gnede of* (gifts, etc.).

Beowulf (Z.) 1930 Næs hio hnah.. ne to gneað ȝifa ȝeata leodum. *c* **900** tr. *Bæda's Hist.* v. xvii. [xix.] (1891) 452 He.. on þam mæȝenum eaðmodnesse & hyrsumnesse nohte þon læssa ne gneðra [*v.r.* gnedra] wæs. *a* **1300** *Body & Soul* 20 in *Map's Poems*, Me thinketh God is the to gnede [*printed* guede], That alle thine frend beon fro the fledde. *a* **1300** *Cursor M.* 17218 Ask me þi will.. for am i noght of giuetes gnede. *c* **1300** *Havelok* 97 He was large, and no wicth gnede. *a* **1400** *Sir Perc.* 1689 The childe was of gamene gnede. *a* **1440** *Sir Degrev.* 1159 Off gyffte was he never gnede.

2. Of things: Scarce, scanty; small. Also in stronger sense, altogether lacking or wanting. *to make the gates gnede*: to go straight to one's destination.

c **1000** in Cockayne *Shrine* 110 He self lifde on gneaðum worold life; an tunece wæs his ȝeȝerela.. & beren hlaf wæs his ȝereorde. *c* **1050** *Cott. Gloss.* in Wr.-Wülcker 441/30 *Mediocri*, gneþre. *c* **1275** *Serving Christ* 48 in *O.E. Misc.* 92 In heþene helle þer hirdsype is gnede. *a* **1300** *Cursor M.* 5392 Sua lang has þir tua boght þair sede Þat þair mone wex al gnede. *Ibid.* 8599 Þair clathes was sa gnede and fa, þat þai moght nan part þam fra. *c* **1320** *Sir Tristr.* 2838 It [a castle] nas to large no gnede. *a* **1400** *Sir Perc.* 607 He made thame gammene fulle gnede. *Ibid.* 724 Tille his fete he ganne hym too, The gates that he scholde goo Made he fulle gnede. *Ibid.* 752 Now es me fyre gnede! *c* **1400** *Rowland & O.* 1392 Sir Barlot loste his lyfe.. His lyfe was hym full gnede. *Ibid.* 1422, 1509. *c* **1450** MYRC 319 Þat day þat þow syst goddes body.. Mete & drynke at thy nede Non schal þe þat day be gnede.

b. Barely so much.

a **1300** *Cursor M.* 15424 Þai asked Iudas quat he wald ask þam for his mede. And he þat traitur fell, þam said, 'bot thritti penis gnede'.

Hence †**'gnedely** *adv.*, sparingly, frugally; †**'gnedeship**, miserliness; †**'gnedy** *a.*, miserly.

c **1000** *Gregory's Dial.* I. vii. 15 He.. heom be bead þæt hy namon þone ele.. & hine to dældon swiðe gneðelice ȝeotende ȝeond ealle þæs mynstræs fatu. *a* **1225** *Ancr. R.* 202 Al þet mon oðer wummon wilneð more þen heo mei gnedeliche leden hire lif bi.. al is ȝiscunge & rote of deadlich sunne. *Ibid.* 350, 414. *c* **1375** *Sc. Leg. Saints, Margarete* 52 Na slawnes, na lychery Na wreth, na gnedschepe, na glutony. **1393** LANGL. *P. Pl.* C. XVI. 86 Ac this doctor and diuinour and decretistre of canon, And al-so a gnedy gloton with to grete chekes, Hath no pite on vs poure.

gneeve (gniːv). *Anglo-Irish.* Also 8 **gineve**. [a. Ir. *gniomh* work, act. The term is said to be still in use in the S. of Ireland.] The twelfth part of a ploughland.

1638 EARL CORK *Diary* in *Lismore Papers* Ser. I. (1886) V. 50 Paid.. for the purchace of 4 gneeves of land. **1672** PETTY *Pol. Anat.* 372 As to their town-lands, plough-lands, colps, gneeves.. they are all at this day become unequal both in quantity and value, having been made upon grounds which are now obsolete and antiquated. **1780** A. YOUNG *Tour Irel.* II. 85 Land is let by the plough land and gineve, 12 gineves to the plough land.

gneiss (naɪs, gnaɪs). *Geol.* Also 8 **kneiss**. [a. Ger. *gneiss, kneis.*] A metamorphic rock, composed, like granite, of quartz, feldspar or orthoclase, and mica, but distinguished from it by its foliated or laminated structure.

1757 tr. *Henckel's Pyritol.* 44 Shiver, kneiss [*Note.* A black, fatty sort of vein stone or rock], ochre, jasper. **1777** R. E. RASPE tr. *Born's Trav. Temeswar* viii. 42 Gneiss.. covered the whole country. **1851** RICHARDSON *Geol.* (1855) 127 Gneiss may be termed stratified, or slaty granite... When the gneiss is associated with granite, it approaches to the character of that substance; and when the two come in contact, it is scarcely possible to distinguish between them. **1873** BLACK *Pr. Thule* i. (1875) 3 Great grey boulders of gneiss fixed fast into the black peat-moss.

attrib. **1845** DARWIN *Voy. Nat.* ii. (1890) 30 The formation which Humboldt designates as gneiss-granite. **1854** H. MILLER *Sch. & Schm.* v. 95 The tract though a primary one forms one of the tamer gneiss districts of Scotland.

gneissic ('naɪsɪk, 'gnaɪsɪk), *a.* [f. prec. + -IC.] Of the nature of gneiss.

1859 R. F. BURTON *Centr. Afr.* in *Jrnl. Geog. Soc.* XXIX. 205 The sides of these hills, composed of hornblende and gneissic rock.. are steep, rugged and thickly wooded. **1880** RAMSAY in *Times* 26 Aug. 5/2 In the Highlands of Scotland.. there are gneissic rocks of pre-Cambrian age.

So **gnei'ssitic** *a. rare.*

1856 RUSKIN *Mod. Paint.* IV. v. xv. §16 Dependent on the junction of the gneissitic beds with, or their transition into, the harder protogine of the aiguilles.

gneissoid ('naɪsɔɪd, 'gnaɪsɔɪd), *a.* [f. GNEISS + -OID.] Resembling gneiss; imperfectly gneissic.

1849 DANA *Geol.* xiii. (1850) 561 The granite of the coast near Valparaiso is, to a great extent, gneissoid, and in some places passes to a perfect gneiss. **1882** *Rep. Ho. Repr. Prec. Met. U.S.* 458 The western belt is gneissoid in structure, verging into hornblendic and mica schist.

gneissose ('naɪsəʊs, 'gnaɪsəʊs), *a.* [f. as prec. + -OSE.] = GNEISSIC; also quasi-*sb.* = gneissic rock.

1843 PORTLOCK *Geol.* 171 They are much more extensively developed in the lower or gneissose portion than in the upper or slaty portion. **1875** DAWSON *Dawn of Life* ii. 21 The limestone.. is traversed by many gray layers of gneissose. **1880** *19th Cent.* Nov. 850 The venerable gneissose rocks of the north-west of Scotland.

gneissy ('naɪsɪ, 'gnaɪsɪ), *a.* [f. as prec. + -Y[1].] = GNEISSIC *a.*

1757 tr. *Henckel's Pyritol.* 224 Accompanying shivery, loamy, and kneissy minerals. **1799** W. TOOKE *View Russian Emp.* I. 114 On the gneissy country.. appears a coarse serpentine. **1854** HOOKER *Himal. Jrnls.* II. xxii. 136 Angular blocks of white gneissy granite.

gnet, obs. form of GNAT[1].

gnetaceous (niː'teɪʃəs), *a. Bot.* [f. mod.L. *Gnetace-æ* (f. *Gnetum*, the name of the typical genus) + -OUS.] Belonging to, or resembling, the Gnetaceæ, an order of gymnospermous shrubs or small trees, having jointed stems or branches.

1886 VINES in *Encycl. Brit.* XX. 429/2 In the Gnetaceous *Ephedra altissima*, a process of cell-formation goes on in the oospore.

gneu, gnew(e, obs. pa. t. of GNAW *v.*

gnib (nɪb), *a. Sc.* Sharp, smart, eager.

1755 R. FORBES *Ajax's Sp.* 15 Wi' mischief he was sae gnib, To get his ill intent. **1768** ROSS *Helenore* (1789) 64 Says a gnib elf, 'As an auld carle' [etc.]. **1813** W. BEATTIE *Fruits Time Parings* (1873) 39 The mair we drank, we grew the gnibber.

gnibble, obs. form of NIBBLE.

†**gnide**, *v. Obs.* Forms: 1 gnídan, 3 gnide(n, gnyde. *Pa. t., sing.* 3 gnade; *pl.* 1 gnidon, 3 gniden; also 4 (weak) gnidded. [OE. *gnídan* (*gnád, gnidon, gniden*) = OHG. *gnítan, knítan*, OSw. *gnidha* (Sw. *gnida*, Da. *gnide*); also ON. *gniða* (wk. verb).] *trans.* To rub with or between the hands; to bruise, crush; to rub *out*. Also *intr.* to crumble away. (Cf. GNODDE *v.*)

c **1000** *Ags. Gosp.* Luke vi. 1 Hys leorning-cnihtas þa ear pluccedon & mid hyra handum gnidon & æton. *a* **1225** *Ancr. R.* 238 þeo hwule þet ȝichinge ilest, hit þuncheð god for to gniden [*Titus MS.* gnudden]. *Ibid.* 260 Heo breken þe eares bi þe weie, & gniden [*Titus MS.* gnuddeden] þe cornes ut bitweonen hore honden. *a* **1250** *Prov. Ælfred* 201 in *O.E. Misc.* 114 If þu hafst..gold and seoluer, hit schal gnyde [*later text* wurþen] to nouht, to duste hit schal dryuen. *a* **1300** *E.E. Psalter* xvii[i]. 43 [42], I sal gnide als duste bifor wind likam. *Ibid.* lxxxviii[i]. 45 [44] His sete in land þou gnade bidene. *c* **1330** *Arth. & Merl.* 2514 Herbes he souȝt and fond And gnidded hem bituix his hond.

gnidge (nɪdʒ), *v. Sc.* [? connected with prec.] *trans.* To rub, squeeze, press. Also ***to gnidge aff.***

1755 R. FORBES *Ajax's Sp.* 8 In hell..Fare a fun-stane does Sisyphus Down to the yerd sair gnidge. **1768** Ross *Helenore* (1789) 135 And then frae our fingers to gnidge aff the hide, With the wearisome wark of the rubbing o't.

†**gnip**, *v. Sc. Obs.* [? onomatopœic; cf. NIP, KNIP.]

trans. To nip, bite. Of a horse: To champ (the bit).

c **1425** WYNTOUN *Cron.* v. iv. 605 Syne in his body gnyp and gnaw. **1513** DOUGLAS *Æneis* III. viii. 64 Heir..I saw.. four horsis quhite as snaw Gnyppand gersis the large feildis on raw. *Ibid.* IV. iv. 11 Hir fers steid stude..Rungeand [*v.r.* gnyppand] the fomy goldin bitt.

†**gnit**. *Obs. rare*⁻¹. In 5 gnyt. [? a. ON. *gnit* (Sw. *gnet*, Da. *gnid*) a nit; cf. G. *gnitze* a midge.] ? A nit.

a **1483** in *Rel. Ant.* I. 86 Gnyttus and snayllus cam routtyng in schyppus.

gnocchi (ˈnɒkɪ, ‖ˈɲɔkki), *sb. pl.* [It., pl. of *gnocco*, f. *nocchio* a knot in wood.] Small dumplings made with flour, semolina, potato, etc., cooked and served with cheese or seasoning.

1891 A. B. MARSHALL *Larger Cook. Bk. of Extra Recipes* 541 Gnocchi à la Française. *Ibid.* 542 Stand the tin containing the Gnocchi in a tin with boiling water. **1927** M. DIVER *But Yesterday* xii. 142 He no longer damned lunch when he found himself eating gnocchi flavoured and fried to perfection. **1963** *Punch* 12 June 869/3 People gave me spaghetti and gnocchi and pannini.

†**gnodde**, *v. Obs.* Also 3 gnudden. [Cf. Icel. *nudda* (? = **gnudda*) to rub.] *trans.* To rub, bruise, crush. (Cf. GNIDE.)

a **1225** [see GNIDE]. **13..** *K. Alis.* 2373 Mony knyght, with dethes wounde, Gnodded [*printed* guodded] gras on the grounde. **1398** TREVISA *Barth. De P.R.* XVII. xcvii. (1495) 663 Flexe is bounde in bundels and afterward knockyd: beten and brayd and carflyd: rodded and gnodded: ribbyd and herkelyd: and at the laste sponne. **14..** *MS. Sloane* 73. lf. 214 (Halliw.) And after gnodde and wasche wel thi saflour bagge in thilke lyȝe with bothe thyn hondis.

†**gnoff**. *Obs.* Also gnof, gnoffe, gnuffe, gnooffe, (knuffe). [Cf. East Fris. *knufe* lump, *gnuffig* thick, rough, coarse, ill-mannered.] A churl, boor, lout.

c **1386** CHAUCER *Miller's T.* 2 A riche gnof, that gestes heeld to bord, And of his craft he was a Carpenter. **1566** DRANT *Horace, Sat.* I. i. A i b, The chubbyshe gnof that toyles and moyles and delueth in the downe. **1567** TURBERV. *Epit.*, etc. 4 If Vulcan durst presume That was a Gnuffe to see..Dame Venus to assaile. **1575** A. NEVILLE *De furor. Norf.* 141 The cuntry gnooffes, Hob, Dick, & Hick, with clubs, and clouted shoon [so *a* **1627** in Hayward *Edw. VI*, 76 (but spelt *knuffes*)]. **1581** J. STUDLEY *Seneca's Hercules Œtæus* 198 The covetous charle, the greedy gnoffe in deede ..In plenty pines the wreatch. **1610** HEALEY *St. Aug. Citie of God* XIV. iv. 501 The Pagans wisdome and vertues were scorned of the ritch gnoffes [L. *crassis diuitibus*] that held shades for substances, and vertues for meere vanities.

gnogh, obs. pa. t. of GNAW *v.*

gnome¹ (nəʊm, ˈnəʊmiː). [a. Gr. γνώμη thought, judgement, opinion; pl. γνῶμαι sayings, maxims (L. *sententiæ*), f. γνω- root of γιγνώσκειν to KNOW.] A short pithy statement of a general truth; a proverb, maxim, aphorism, or apophthegm. Also *spec.* with reference to Old English verse.

1577 H. PEACHAM *Gard. Eloquence* V iij, Gnome, a saying pertaining to the maners and common practises of men, which declareth, by an apte breuity, what in this our lyfe ought to be done, or not done. **1846** GROTE *Greece* II. iii. II. 363 The rudiments of that which afterwards ripened into moral philosophy as manifested in gnomes or aphorisms. **1873** SYMONDS *Grk. Poets* i. 16 Many of the sublimer flights of meditation in Sophocles are expansions of early Gnomes. **1914** B. C. WILLIAMS *Gnomic Poetry Anglo-Saxon* 66 The *dol bið* gnome and its analogues have been noticed as occurring in Christian passages. **1935** A. C. BARTLETT *Larger Rhet. Patterns Anglo-Saxon Poetry* 73 One..does find..most gnomes in *Beowulf, Wanderer, Widsith*, and most homiletic passages in the 'Christian' poems. **1948** S. O. ANDREW *Postscript on Beowulf* viii. 93 The gnome serves to connect the idea of evil endured in the sentence preceding it with that of deliverance..in the sentence following it.

gnome² (nəʊm). [a. F. *gnome*, ad. mod.L. *gnomus*, used by Paracelsus.

Paracelsus (*De Nymphis* etc. Wks. 1658 II. 391, and elsewhere) uses *Gnomi* as a synonym of *Pygmæi*, and says that the beings so called have earth as their element (or, as he calls it, their *chaos*: cf. etymological note on GAS), through which they move unobstructed as fish do through water, or birds and land animals through air. The context in the passage above referred to suggests that the name was *not* invented by Paracelsus himself, and that it means 'earth-dweller'; possibly it may be a blunder for **gēnomus*, representing a Gr. type *γηνόμος (for which cf. θαλασσονόμος dwelling in the sea). The term, however, may possibly be a mere arbitrary invention, like many others found in Paracelsus. The connexion commonly assumed with Gr. γνώμη (see prec.) or γνώμων (cf. GNOMON) seems unlikely.]

1. a. One of a race of diminutive spirits fabled to inhabit the interior of the earth and to be the guardians of its treasures; a goblin, dwarf.

1712–14 POPE *Rape Lock* Ded., According to these Gentlemen [the Rosicrucians], the four elements are inhabited by Spirits, which they call Sylphs, Gnomes, Nymphs, and Salamanders. The Gnomes or Dæmons of Earth delight in mischief. *Ibid.* I. 63 The graver Prude sinks downward to a Gnome, In search of mischief still on Earth to roam. **1816** *Gentl. Mag.* LXXXI. I. 46 To festive songs my Gnomes attune the lyre. **1837** HAWTHORNE *Twice-Told T.* (1851) I. viii. 154 Small enough to be king of the fairies, and ugly enough to be king of the gnomes. **1877** BRYANT *Little People of Snow* 12 No, let us have a tale of elves that ride By night, with jingling reins, or gnomes of the mine. *fig.* **1809–10** COLERIDGE *Friend* (1818) III. 173 A scientific method, that dissipating with its earliest rays the gnomes of hypothesis and the mists of theory, may [etc.].

b. A statue or figure of a gnome, esp. one placed in a garden. Cf. *garden gnome* (GARDEN *sb.* 6).

1938 D. KINCAID *Brit. Social Life in India* xii. 288 An imitation pergola and a coloured plaster gnome or two. **1955** E. COXHEAD *Figure in Mist* ii. 65 'She sculpts too, did you know?' Agnes said. 'No, how unspeakable. You mean those gnomes one sees about?' **1969** V. C. CLINTON-BADDELEY *Only Matter of Time* 18 In the centre of the grass was a lily pond. On the edge a gnome sat fishing. **1971** J. BETJEMAN in Betjeman & Vaisey *Vict. & Edw. Oxford* p. vii, They are now acres of detached and semi-detached houses, blocks of flats and housing estates, gnomes, birdbaths and shopping arcades.

c. *colloq.* An international financier or banker, *spec.* one who is Swiss; esp. in phr. ***the gnomes of Zurich***.

1964 *New Statesman* 27 Nov. 822/3 The gnomes of Zurich and their related goblins in the more politically involved capitals. **1968** P. EINZIG *Leads & Lags* p. vii, Sterling was devalued in 1949 and again in 1967, not because of speculation by the 'gnomes' of Zurich. **1969** *Listener* 12 June 828/2 One doesn't have to posit gnome couriers flying in from Zurich with weekly instructions.

2. *U.S.* A name of various humming-birds, as the Giant Gnome (*Patagona gigas*).

1889 in *Cent. Dict.*

3. *attrib.* and *Comb.*, as ***gnome-like*** adj.; **gnome-owl** *U.S.*, a small owl of the genus *Glaucidium*.

1801 MAR. EDGEWORTH *Good Fr. Governess* (1832) 175 Things went on much better after the gnome-like influence of Mrs. Grace had ceased. **1843** LYTTON *Last Bar.* I. ii, Upon a mound formed by the gnarled roots of the dwarfed and gnome-like oak, she sat down and wept. **1884–5** *Riverside Nat. Hist.* (1888) IV. 330 The pigmy, or gnome-owls, as they are frequently called. **1897** S. L. HINDE *Congo Arabs* 85 The seemingly magical appearance of these gnome-like beings within 3 or 4 yards of us.

Hence **gnomed** *ppl. a.*, inhabited by gnomes.

1820 KEATS *Lamia* II. 236 Philosophy will..Conquer all mysteries by rule and line, Empty the haunted air, and gnomed mine.

gnomic (ˈnəʊmɪk), *a.* and *sb.* [ad. Gr. γνωμικός dealing in maxims, sententious, f. γνώμη GNOME¹; cf. F. *gnomique*.] **A.** *adj.* **a.** Of the nature of, or consisting of, gnomes or general maxims. Also *spec.* with reference to Old English verse. ***gnomic poet***, a composer of gnomic verses.

1815 J. JEBB *Corr.* (1834) II. 257 Some gnomic verses from Bishop Ken. **1826** W. D. CONYBEARE in J. J. Conybeare *Illustr. Anglo-Saxon Poetry* 205 Another gnomic poem..concludes by tracing the origin of discord to the homicide of Cain. **1838** *Fraser's Mag.* XVIII. 130 In Aeschylus, the poetical faculty developed itself in grandeur; ..in Euripides, in gnomic wisdom, sententious philosophy. **1842** B. THORPE *Codex Exoniensis* p. viii, The 'Gnomic Verses' are, as their title imports, a string of proverbial sentences. **1847** GROTE *Greece* II. xxix. IV. 110 Amidst the multifarious veins in which Archilochus displayed his genius, moralising or gnomic poetry is not wanting. **1871** H. SWEET in W. C. Hazlitt *Warton's Hist. Eng. Poetry* II. 18 The curious poem, *Salomon and Saturn*, consists also of a variety of gnomic sentences, mixed..with a variety of other matter. **1873** SYMONDS *Grk. Poets* iii. 65 Gnomic poets are simply those who embody γνῶμαι or sententious maxims on life and morals in their verse. **1882** A. W. WARD *Dickens* ii. 25 The fashion of Sam's gnomic philosophy is at least as old as Theocritus. **1914** B. C. WILLIAMS *Gnomic Poetry Anglo-Saxon* 6 Anglo-Saxon verse is gnomic so far as the presence of gnomic lines here and there adds sententiousness. **1948** K. MALONE in A. C. Baugh *Lit. Hist. Eng.* I. I. iii. 26 One might have expected to find end-stopping used a good deal in the gnomic verses.

b. *Gram.* ***gnomic aorist*** (see quots.).

1867 FARRAR *Grk. Syntax* §154 The aorist is used in proverbs, &c. (gnomic aorist) to express what *once happened*, and has thereby established a precedent for all time. **1884** HADLEY *Grk. Gram.* §840 Gnomic Aorist.—General truths are often expressed by the aorist indicative, as having proved true in past instances.

B. *sb. pl.* ***the gnomics*** (= F. *les gnomiques*), the older Greek gnomic poets.

1821 CAMPBELL in *New Monthly Mag.* II. 238 In the days of Solon and Theognis, we find the observations of the gnomics on the oeconomy of life pretty various.

gnomical (ˈnəʊmɪkəl), *a.*¹ [f. as prec. + -AL¹.] = GNOMIC. Of a person: Given to uttering gnomes.

1603 BP. W. BARLOW *Conf. Hampton Crt.* (1604) 44 His Maiesty..adding this excellent, gnomical, and Canon-like Conclusion, that [etc.]. **1641** J. JACKSON *True Evang. T.* II. 133 A speech..so gnomicall and waighty, that St. Augustin highly commends it. **1650** H. MORE in *Enthus. Triumph.* (1656) 134 In this whole page Anthroposophus is very Gnomicall, and speaks Aphorisms very gracefully. **1887** J. KNIGHT in *Dict. Nat. Biog.* IX. 356/2 Her gnomical utterances are often thoughtful and pregnant.

†ˈ**gnomical**, *a.*² *Obs. rare.* [Irreg. f. GNOM-ON + -IC + -AL¹.] = GNOMONIC *a.*

1611 COTGR. s.v. *Avantagé, Bien avantagé en nez*, Nosed with aduantage, well nose-growne, hauing a Gnomicall, or goodly long, nose. **1744** [see quot. 1688 s.v. GNOMONIC].

gnomide (ˈnəʊmɪd). *rare.* [a. F. *gnomide*, f. *gnome*: see GNOME² and -IDE.] A female gnome.

1727–51 CHAMBERS *Cycl.* s.v. *Gnomes*, The females of this species are called gnomides.

gnomish (ˈnəʊmɪʃ), *a.* [f. GNOME² + -ISH.] Resembling a gnome; gnome-like.

1822 *New Monthly Mag.* V. 542 A gloomy, perverse, gnomish sprite. **1897** *Daily News* 18 June 5/4 Their excited gesticulations, their gnomish faces full of disgust.

gnomist (ˈnəʊmɪst). *rare.* [f. GNOME¹ + -IST.] A gnomic poet or writer.

1874 MAHAFFY *Soc. Life Greece* iv. 83 The high moral standing of the earlier gnomists made it impossible to keep their works pure and undefiled.

†ˈ**gnomograph**. *Obs.* [ad. Gr. type *γνωμογράφος, f. γνώμη GNOME¹ + γράφειν to write.] = prec.

1560 BECON *Catech.* VI. Wks. 1564 I. 542 b, Idlenes as yᵉ Gnomagraph [*sic*] saith bringeth much euil.

So †**gnoˈmographer**.

a **1619** FOTHERBY *Atheom.* Pref. (1622) 4 There could none haue any cause to insult ouer another: not the Hymnographer ouer the Historiographer, nor the Gnomographer ouer either.

gnomologic (nəʊməʊˈlɒdʒɪk), *a. rare.* [ad. Gr. γνωμολογικός, f. *γνωμολόγος, f. γνώμη GNOME¹ + -λόγος speaker.] Of the nature of general maxims; sententious.

1751 HARRIS *Hermes* I. vii. (1786) 125 Gnomologic Sentences after the same manner make likewise Aorists of the Future. **1780** —— *Philol. Enq.* II. ix. (1781) 179 That other, and more limited species of it [Sentiment], which I call the Gnomologic, or Preceptive. **1841** W. SPALDING *Italy & It. Isl.* I. 124 Lucretius, however, who had only the gnomologic verses of the Greeks as his models.

gnomoˈlogical, *a. rare*⁻⁰. [f. as prec. + -AL¹.] = prec.

1775 in ASH. **1818** TODD, *Gnomological*, pertaining to gnomology. [Blount *Glossogr.* 1670–81 and Coles 1676 have '*Gnomological*, pertaining to the art of dialling': see GNOMONOLOGICAL.]

gnomologist (nəʊˈmɒlədʒɪst). *rare.* [f. Gr. type *γνωμολόγ-ος (see GNOMOLOGIC) + -IST.] A gnomic writer.

1813 W. TAYLOR in *Monthly Rev.* LXXII. 520 The gnomologists, or versifiers of short moral apophthegms. **1882** FARRAR *Early Chr.* II. 22 The style of St. James is formed on the Hebrew prophets, as his thoughts are influenced by the Hebrew gnomologists.

gnomology (nəʊˈmɒlədʒɪ). [ad. Gr. γνωμολογία the uttering or collecting of gnomes, f. γνώμη GNOME¹ + -λογία discoursing, collection, f. λογ-, λεγ- to say, to collect: see -LOGY.]

1. A collection of general maxims or precepts.

1645 MILTON *Tetrach.* Wks. (1847) 204/2 Which art of powerful reclaiming, wisest men have also taught in their ethical precepts and Gnomologies. **1651** BIGGS *New Disp.* ⁋ 234 These Hæmatognomists..in their Gnomologies may be compared to [etc.]. **1736** BAILEY (folio) Pref., *Gnomologies*.. Adagies or Proverbs. **1837–9** HALLAM *Hist. Lit.* II. I. II. §21, 22 Several of the publications of Neander are gnomologies, or collections of moral sentences from the poets.

2. Gnomic discourse; the sententious element in writing.

1806 W. TAYLOR in Robberds *Mem.* II. 143 There is sound sense in the thinking, selection in the gnomology, condensation in the style [etc.]. **1889** *Edin. Rev.* No. 345. 74 Ben Sira expanded the gnomology of preceding writers by opening up the larger vistas of human relations.

gnomometry (nəʊˈmɒmɪtrɪ). *rare.* [ad. Gr. type *γνωμομετρία, f. γνώμη GNOME¹ + -μετρία measurement.] (See quot.)

1882 *Athenæum* 8 July 43/1 The intricate question of stichometry as opposed to gnomometry..whether the ancient writers divided their books according to subject or according to some standard measure of lines or στίχοι.

gnomon ('nəʊmən). Also 6–7 (Florio, *pseudo-etymologically*) **gnow-, know-man,** 7, 9 *erron.* **gnomen.** [a. Gr. γνώμων inspector, indicator (*spec.* the gnomon of a dial, a carpenter's square), f. γνω-, γιγνώσκειν to perceive, judge, KNOW. The proximate source may have been L. or F. *gnomon.*]

1. A pillar, rod, or other object which serves to indicate the time of day by casting its shadow upon a marked surface; esp. the pin or triangular plate used for this purpose in an ordinary sun-dial.

1546 LANGLEY *Pol. Verg. De Invent.* II. v. 42b, Anaximenes..founde..the first dial that declareth the houres by the Shadowe of the Gnomon. **1598** FLORIO, *Gnomone*, the know-man or gnow-man of a diall. **1601** HOLLAND *Pliny* I. 150 In all the circumference of this climat and parellele, at noon tide vpon an Equinoctiall day, the stile in the diall which they call Gnomon 7 foot long, casteth a shadow not aboue 4 foot. **1646** SIR T. BROWNE *Pseud. Ep.* IV. ii. 181 We usually say a Gnomon or needle is in the middle of a Diall. **1742** YOUNG *Nt. Th.* II. 427 Warnings point out our danger; Gnomons, time. **1834** H. MILLER *Scenes & Leg.* xxix. (1857) 431 On the western gable there was fixed a huge gnomon of bronze. **1860** TYNDALL *Glac.* I. xxv. 177 Like gnomons of a vast sundial, the Aiguilles cast their fanlike shadows, [etc.].

b. A column or other apparatus employed in observing the meridian altitude of the sun.

1625 N. CARPENTER *Geog. Del.* I. vi. (1635) 138 In the time of either Equinoctiall in some Horizontall plaine in the Sunne-shine, let there bee erected a Gnomon. **1727–41** CHAMBERS *Cycl.*, *Gnomon*, Those conversant in observation prefer the gnomon, by some called the astronomical gnomon, to the smaller quadrants. **1837–9** HALLAM *Hist. Lit.* I. iii. I. §70. 189 The gnomon erected by Toscanelli in the cathedral at Florence..is by much the loftiest in Europe. **1854** TOMLINSON *Arago's Astron.* 17 Anaximander.. constructed at Sparta the gnomon that enabled him to observe the equinoxes and the solstices.

†**c.** *jocularly.* The nose. *Obs.*

1583 STANYHURST *Æneis*, etc. (Arb.) 145 Syth mye nose owtpeaking, good syr, your lip-labor hindreth, Hardlye ye may kisse mee, where no such gnomon apeereth. [**1599** B. JONSON *Cynthia's Rev.* v. iv, Her nose [is] the gnomon of Loues diall, that tells you how the clocke of your heart goes.] **1781** COWPER *Convers.* 271 The emphatic speaker dearly loves to oppose, In contact inconvenient, nose to nose, As if the gnomon on his neighbour's phiz, Touched with the magnet had attracted his. *a* **1803** C. L. LEWES *Mem.* (1805) I. 92 Giving him at the same time, a blow that demolished the gnomen of poor Roger's face.

†**2.** Occasionally applied to other instruments serving as 'indicators' (see quots.). Also *fig. Obs.*

1599 *Broughton's Lett.* viii. 28 S. Austen [is] your Index and gnomon for S. Peters place of preaching to the spirits. **1600** R. CAWDRAY *Treas. Similies* (1609) 114 The Saylers Gnomon, or rule, which is commonly called the Marriners Needle. **1755** B. MARTIN *Mag. Arts & Sci.* III. vii. 325 Professor Richman..lost his Life by an electrical Stroke.. as he was observing..the Effects of Electricity upon his Gnomon, or Electrometer.

†**3.** *pl.* The teeth which indicate the age of a horse, etc. (= Gr. οἱ γνώμονες). *Obs. rare*$^{-1}$.

1607 TOPSELL *Four-f. Beasts* (1658) 18 An Asse and a Mule have 36 teeth..Their third and fourth teeth are called 'gnomons', that is 'regulars', because by them there is a tryed rule to know their age.

†**4.** A rule, canon of belief or action. *Obs.*

[So Gr. γνώμων; a transferred use of the sense 'carpenter's square'. (In quot. 1698 perh. an error for GNOME.)]

1626 W. SCLATER *Expos. 2 Thess.* (1629) 203 Making Scripture my gnomon and canon. **1651** BIGGS *New Disp.* ¶ 180 A nimiety of redundance of bloud is the only Gnomon in the table of directions for phlebotomy. **1660** JER. TAYLOR *Duct. Dubit.* II. III. rule xiv. §10 Eunomius..affirm'd tradition of the Fathers to be the Gnomon or Canon of faith, and yet said [etc.]. **1698** [R. FERGUSON] *View of an Ecclesiastic* 67 To spare Mens Persons when we speak of their Faults, according to the common Gnomon, *Mea & Tua Persona pro Ego & Tu.*

5. *Geom.* The part of a parallelogram which remains after a similar parallelogram is taken away from one of its corners.

[So Gr. γνώμων, from the resemblance of the shape to a carpenter's square.]

1570 BILLINGSLEY *Euclid* II. def. ii. 61 In euery parallelogramme, one of those parallelogrammes, which soeuer it be, which are about the diameter, together with the two supplementes, is called a Gnomon. *a* **1696** SCARBURGH *Euclid* (1705) 121 Therefore the Gnomon KLM, and the square CF are equal to the Rectangle. **1838** YOUNG *Euclid* II. Def. ii. 57.

†**b.** An odd number. (So called by the Pythagoreans.) *Obs.*

The difference between two squares being geometrically a gnomon, the name was applied in arithmetic to the differences between the squares of successive integers, i.e. to the odd numbers 3, 5, 7, 9, 11, etc.

1660 STANLEY *Hist. Philos.* IX. (1701) 379/1 Odd Numbers they called Gnomons, because being added to Squares, they keep the same Figures; so Gnomons do in Geometry.

†**c.** Each of the successive subtrahends (after the first) in the process of finding the square root.

1674 JEAKE *Arith.* (1696) 194 The second number to be substracted, called a Gnomon.

†**6.** Something shaped like a carpenter's square; an L-shaped bar, etc. *Obs.*

1669 BOYLE *Contn. New Exp.* II. (1682) 8 GGG is the Gnomon fastened to the plate BB. *Ibid.* 16 H is the Gnomon affixed to the Globe AA making fast the spring G. **1777** DARWIN in *Phil. Trans.* LXVIII. 89 A gnomon of thin brass was made to stand over his nose.

Hence **'gnomonless** *a.*

1832 WILSON in *Blackw. Mag.* XXXII. 133 The dial-stone..stands gnomenless.

gnomonic (nəʊ'mɒnɪk), *a.* and *sb.* Also 7 **gnomonicke, -ique.** [ad. L. *gnōmonic-us* (F. *gnomonique*), a. Gr. γνωμονικός, f. γνώμων GNOMON.]

A. *adj.*

1. Pertaining to the gnomon or sun-dial, or to the measuring of time, etc. by means of this. ***gnomonic column*** (see quot. 1727–41).

1601 HOLLAND *Pliny* I. 35 The Gnomonicke art. **1672** *Phil. Trans.* VII. 5151 The whole Science Gnomonique. **1688** BOYLE *Final Causes Nat. Things* iv. 154 [He] may have given him a Dial furnish'd with a Magnetic Needle, rather than an Ordinary Gnomonic [Wks. 1744 IV. 539/1 gnomical] Dial. **1727–41** CHAMBERS *Cycl.* s.v. *Column*, *Gnomonic Column*, a cylinder, whereon the hour of the day is represented by the shadow of a style. **1837** *Fraser's Mag.* XVI. 632 The gnomonic phenomena of the year of complete days recurred at the interval of this cycle.

b. ***gnomonic projection.*** (See quot. 1866.)

The principle of gnomonic projection is especially used in the construction of star maps.

1706 W. JONES *Syn. Palmar. Matheseos* A iv b, With the Laws of the..Gnomonic Projection of the Sphere. **1858** (*title*) Stanford's Maps of the Paths of Comets..drawn by J. Breen on six maps on the gnomonic projection. **1866** PROCTOR *Handbk. Stars* 16 The first point we meet with suitable for a centre of projection is the centre of the sphere. A projection having this point as centre is called gnomonic from its relation to the art of dialling.

2. *transf.* in *nonce-uses.* **a.** That indicates like a gnomon. **b.** Resembling a gnomon (cf. GNOMON 1 c).

1809–10 COLERIDGE *Friend* (1818) III. 79 Spurzheim's Cranioscopy (a scheme, the indicative or gnomonic parts of which have a stronger support in facts than the theory in reason or common sense). **1859** L. F. SIMPSON *Handbk. Dining* xi. (1865) 111 M. H. R. turned his gnomonic nose to the west.

¶ **3.** ? Misused for GNOMIC *a.* (But cf. GNOMON 4.)

1706 PHILLIPS (ed. Kersey) *Gnomonick*, full of Sentences, as the *Gnomonick Poets*, Writers of Sententious Verses. **1874** H. R. REYNOLDS *John Bapt.* I. §1. 6 The Jewish sages..made use of apologues, and uttered gnomonic sayings. **1884** *Ch. Times* 569/1 It is easy to fish a gnomonic saying out of the voluminous writings of the Fathers.

B. *sb.*

1. Pl. ***gnomonics*** (rarely sing. *gnomonic* = L. *gnōmonica, -icē,* Gr. γνωμονική): the art of dialling. *Obs.* exc. *Hist.*

1656–81 BLOUNT *Glossogr.*, *Gnomonick*, the art of Dyalling; consisting in the knowledge of the scituation, lying or measure of any place or Country. **1677** PLOT *Oxfordsh.* 269 The Cylindrical Dyal in Corpus Christi College Quadrangle..is a fine old piece of Gnomonicks. **1727–41** CHAMBERS *Cycl.*, *Gnomonica*..or *Gnomonicks*, the art of dialling; or of drawing sun and moon dials, etc., on any given plane. **1792** T. TAYLOR *Proclus* I. 79 One part of this [astrology] is gnomonics, which is exercised in settling the dimension of the horary gnomons. **1837** [see DIALLING 1]. **1876** FOX BOURNE *Locke* I. ii. 56 He lectured..also on optics and gnomonics.

¶ †**2.** A gnomic verse. *Obs. rare*$^{-1}$. (Cf. A. 3.)

1688 OGILBY tr. *Magaillan's Hist. China* 96 There are also several Gnomonics or Verses containing Precepts, which are sung at their Funerals.

gnomonical (nəʊ'mɒnɪkəl), *a.* ? *Obs.* [f. as prec. + -AL[1].] = GNOMONIC.

1570 DEE *Math. Pref.* 41 Who also, left to theyr posteritie, many Engines and Gnomonicall workes. **1603** SIR C. HEYDON *Jud. Astrol.* iii. 128, I expected..mathematicall demonstrations and reasons, either out of Gnomonicall obseruation, or out of the Perspectiues. **1688** R. HOLME *Armoury* III. 373/1 A Gnomonical Semi-Circle, a semi-circle set in a declining reclining Dial Plate, whereby to make the Stile its true height. **1761** J. J. KIRBY *Perspect. Archit.* II. 3 When placed at the center, the projection is named gnomonical. **1790** WILDBORE in *Phil. Trans.* LXXX. 536 The gnomonical projection of the track on a plane touching the sphere at C.

b. *Bot.* (See quot.)

1862 M. C. COOKE *Man. Bot. Terms*, *Gnomonical*, when a stalk is bent at right angles. **1866** in *Treas. Bot.*

Hence **gno'monically** *adv.*, in the manner of a gnomonic projection.

1706 W. JONES *Syn. Palmar. Matheseos* 277 The method of projecting the Hour Circles Gnomonically..is hence also evident. **1838** *Penny Cycl.* XI. 281/1 The most convenient method of projecting the whole sphere gnomonically is to imagine a cube inscribed about it, on each face of which one-sixth part of the sphere is projected. **1866** PROCTOR *Handbk. Stars* 8 *note*, Now these circles are gnomonically projected on the polar tangent plane as two straight lines.

†**'gnomonist.** *Obs. rare*$^{-1}$. [f. GNOMON + -IST.] One interested or skilled in gnomonics.

1688 BOYLE *Final Causes Nat. Things* iii. 97 The sun..do [*sic*]..enable the Gnomonist to make accurate Dials, to know exactly how the Time passes.

gnomo'nology. *rare*$^{-0}$. [f. GNOMON + -(O)LOGY.] A treatise on dialling.

1775 in ASH; and in later Dicts.

So **gnomono'logical** *a.*, 'belonging to the Art of Dialling' (Bailey 1721–90).

gnooffe, var. GNOFF, churl.

gnoscopine ('nɒskəpiːn, -ɪn). *Chem.* [irreg. f. Gr. γι-γνώσκ-ειν to know + OP(IUM + -INE[5].] Either of two isomeric alkaloids, $C_{22}H_{23}NO_7$, designated α- and β-gnoscopine, of which α-gnoscopine is found in opium and β-gnoscopine obtained synthetically.

1878 T. & H. SMITH in *Pharm. Jrnl. & Trans.* 3rd Ser. IX. 82/1 In the mother liquors from the purification of narceine we have now repeatedly met with a crystalline body, which ..was..ascertained to be a hitherto unknown alkaloid, and which we have named Gnoscopine. **1914** HOPE & ROBINSON in *Jrnl. Chem. Soc.* CV. II. 2087 It is proposed to call the substance melting at 180° β-gnoscopine, reserving the name α-gnoscopine for the compound previously known as gnoscopine or *r*-narcotine, which melts at 229°. **1951** A. GROLLMAN *Pharmacol. & Therapeutics* iv. 88 The remaining [opium] alkaloids (laudanosine,..codamine, gnoscopine, etc.) occur in too small quantity to have any influence on the action of the crude drug. **1954** STANEK & MANSKE in Manske & Holmes *Alkaloids* IV. xxxii. 181 Both of the gnoscopines were convertible into narceine, indicating that the only differences were stereochemical ones, and β-gnoscopine was partly isomerized to α-gnoscopine.

gnosiological (nəʊzɪə'lɒdʒɪkəl), *a.* Also **gnoseological.** [f. GNOSIOLOGY + -ICAL.] Of or pertaining to gnosiology.

1928 in *Funk's Stand. Dict.* **1938** G. REAVEY tr. *Berdyaev's Solitude & Society* II. i. 38 We have also to elucidate the relationship between the pure subject of cognition, the *gnosiological* subject, and the Ego, the knowing subject. **1963** V. NABOKOV *Gift* iv. 235 In eliminating metaphysical dualism he fell into gnoseological dualism.

gnosiology (nəʊzɪ'ɒlədʒɪ). Also **gnoseology.** Cf. GNOSTOLOGY. [f. Gr. γνῶσι-ς, γνώσεως knowledge + -(O)LOGY.] The philosophy of cognition or the cognitive faculties.

[**1836–7** SIR W. HAMILTON *Metaph.* vii. (1859) I. 122 Some older treatises..afford a name not unsuitable for a nomology of the cognitions,—viz. Gnoseologia or Gnostologia.] **1899** M. P. W. BOLTON *Inquis. Philos.* 142 It is impossible to understand his [Hamilton's] doctrine about knowledge (or Gnosiology) unless we understand his views concerning the Conditioned and the Unconditioned.

‖**gnosis** ('nəʊsɪs). *pl.* (*rare*) **gnoses** ('nəʊsiːz). [a. Gr. γνῶσις investigation, knowledge (in Christian writers *esp.* a higher knowledge of spiritual things), f. γνω- root of γιγνώσκειν to KNOW.] A special knowledge of spiritual mysteries. Often with reference to the claim to such knowledge made by the Gnostics: Gnostic philosophy, Gnosticism.

1703 S. PARKER tr. *Eusebius* 19 Peter and John..had.. receiv'd the *Gnosis*, or *Gift of Knowledge*, from him after his Resurrection. **1727–41** CHAMBERS *Cycl.* s.v. *Gnosimachi*, They were perfectly averse to all the gnoses of christianity, i.e. to all the science, or technical knowledge thereof. **1854** MAURICE *Mor. & Met. Philos.* (ed. 2) II. 28 The Gnosis would take its colour from every different locality, from every different thinker. There must be a Syrian Gnosis and an Alexandrian Gnosis [etc.]. **1856** R. A. VAUGHAN *Mystics* VIII. vii. (1860) II. 76 Behmen and the mystics..essay to pass the ordinary bounds of knowledge and to attain a priviledged gnosis. **1871** J. F. CLARKE *Ten Gt. Relig.* (1888) I. vi. §7. 255 The common Christian lives by faith, but the more advanced believer has gnosis, or philosophic insight of Christianity as the eternal law of the soul. **1884** D. HUNTER tr. *Reuss's Hist. Canon* iv. 65 Another struck by the mystical and speculative spirit of the Fourth Gospel and recognizing ..some colouring of his own gnosis [etc.].

gnostic ('nɒstɪk), *a.* and *sb.* Also 7 **gnostick, gnostique.** [ad. Gr. γνωστικ-ός pertaining to knowledge, f. the root γνω-: see prec.]

A. *adj.*

1. Relating to knowledge; cognitive; intellectual.

1656 STANLEY *Hist. Philos.* v. (1701) 191/1 The Souls of the Gods have a dijudicative Faculty, called Gnostic. **1792** T. TAYLOR *Proclus* I. *Dissert.* xiv, They [the numbers] exist in a vital, gnostic, and speculative, but not in an operative manner. **1836–7** SIR W. HAMILTON *Metaph.* xli. (1859) II. 415 The distinction taken in the Peripatetic School by which the mental modifications were divided into Gnostic or Cognitive, and Orectic or Appetent. **1884** *Nonconf. & Indep.* 10 Oct. 975/1 Gnostic pride will continue to feed itself on doctrine that leads to no action.

b. *nonce-use.* Believing in the reality of transcendental knowledge; opposed to *agnostic.*

1888 R. FLINT in *Mind* XIII. 596 Idealism is not necessarily either gnostic or agnostic, but is more apt to be the former than the latter.

c. Possessing esoteric spiritual knowledge.

1800 W. TAYLOR in *Monthly Mag.* VIII. 797 Their disciples..have formed in the different churches an interior gnostic or illuminated order, rather than independent congregations.

d. In humorous or slang use: Clever, knowing.

1819 *Blackw. Mag.* V. 681 Mr. Seward..threw over to us a letter written in a large gnostic sprauling hand. **1824** SCOTT *St. Ronan's* v, I said you were a d——d gnostic fellow, and I laid a bet you have not been always professional. **1859** TROLLOPE *W. Indies* v. (1860) 76 It [punch] should partake duly of the..spirit and..the saccharine according to the skill and will of the gnostic fabricator, who in mixing knows his own purposes.

2. (With capital initial.) Pertaining to the Gnostics; having an occult or mystic character.

1838 *Penny Cycl.* XI. 281/1 The origin of the Gnostic system has been traced to various sources. **1851** D. WILSON *Preh. Ann.* (1863) II. IV. ii. 223 A Gnostic gem of agate, on which a z-formed symbol is twice repeated. *Ibid.* 224 The early phases of Gnostic philosophy. **1885** *Catholic Dict.* (ed. 3) 375/1 In Alexandria, the Gnostic tendencies gathered life and strength.

B. *sb.*

1. *Hist.* (With capital initial.) Chiefly *pl.* The designation given to certain heretical sects among the early Christians who claimed to have superior knowledge of things spiritual, and interpreted the sacred writings by a mystic philosophy (cf. GNOSIS).

[**1563** WINȜET *Wks.* (1890) II. 51 Iowis, Gentilis, and thai callit Gnostici. *Marg.* Sua nameit for ostentatioun of thare science.] **1585–7** T. ROGERS *39 Art.* (1607) 44 Some, as the Gnostics.. affirm there be more Gods than one. **1641** WILKINS *Mercury* x. (1707) 43 From such idle Collections as these, many Heresies of the.. Gnosticks had their first Beginnings. **1744** BERKELEY *Siris* §187 The Gnostics, Basilidians, and other ancient heretics. **1841** TRENCH *Parables* ii. (1877) 18 The ghastly dream of Gnostic and Manichæan. **1877** C. GEIKIE *Christ* xxviii. (1879) 315 The Christian Gnostics began to make likenesses of him.

transf. **1645** MILTON *Tetrach.* Introd. (1851) 136 Thought new and dangerous by some of our severe Gnostics, whose little reading.. holds ever with hardest obstinacy that which it took up with easiest credulity.

b. *Comb.*, as *Gnostic-like* adj.

1664 H. MORE *Expos. 7 Epist.* 71 The Balaamites.. were of a more Gnostick-like temper, too much leaning towards the Flesh.

2. In general sense: †One skilled or learned in any subject (*obs.*). Also *slang*, 'a knowing one', an adept in dishonest acts.

1641 R. BROOKE *Eng. Episc.* 9 He that is a Gnostique in one, cannot be a meere Tyrunculus in the other. **1819** MOORE *Tom Crib* (ed. 2) p. xxvii, Many of the words used by the Canting Beggars in Beaumont and Fletcher.. are still to be heard among the gnostics of Dyot-street and Tothill-fields.

gnostical (ˈnɒstɪkəl), *a.* [f. prec. + -AL[1].] = GNOSTIC *a.*

1828 E. B. PUSEY *Hist. Enquiry* 163 The old error of the Gnostical interpreters in the early Church was thus revived. **1854** MAURICE *Mor. & Met. Philos.* (ed. 2) II. 26 Saturninus is memorable in history as the author of one of the so-called gnostical heresies. **1881** *Athenæum* 2 Apr. 460/1 Dr. Joel in his monograph.. has advanced the knowledge.. of mystical and Gnostical passages in this book [the Talmud].

Hence **ˈgnostically** *adv.* (In quots. used humorously; cf. GNOSTIC A. 1 d.)

1824 SCOTT *St. Ronan's* iv, This is the very fellow that we saw down at the Willow-slack on Saturday—he was tog'd gnostically enough, and cast twelve yards of line with one hand. **1826** WILSON in *Blackw. Mag.* XX. 782 Smoking and leering, with tongue-lolling cheek, finger-tip and nose-tip gnostically brought together.

Gnosticism (ˈnɒstɪsɪz(ə)m). [f. GNOSTIC *sb.* + -ISM.] The system or principles professed by the Gnostics.

1664 H. MORE *Antid. agst. Idol.* To Rdr. O 2 a, Though it be indeed but a spice of the old abhorred Gnosticism. **1713** R. NELSON *Life Bull* §69. 394 Till Platonism and Gnosticism crept into the Church. **1838** *Penny Cycl.* XI. 281/2 Gnosticism is merely a generic term, and.. included many sects that differed considerably from each other. **1865** LECKY *Ration.* I. iii. 224 Gnosticism exercised a very great influence over Christian art.

gnosticity (nɒˈstɪsɪtɪ). *nonce-wd.* [f. as prec. + -ITY.] Knowingness; pretensions to knowledge.

1830 *Blackw. Mag.* XXVIII. 581 The philosophy of a Bacon,.. the wisdom of a Wordsworth, the genius of a Byron, the gnosticity of a John Bee.

gnosticize (ˈnɒstɪsaɪz), *v.* [f. as prec. + -IZE.] **a.** *intr.* To adopt or expound Gnostic views. **b.** *trans.* To interpret on Gnostic principles; to give or impute a Gnostic character to.

1664 H. MORE *Expos. 7 Epist.* 37 Too many began to Gnosticize, as it is called, in that point, and think it a small thing to deny the Faith in the time of Persecution. **1840** G. S. FABER *Regenerat.* xviii, Let all the Fathers.. gnosticize ever so copiously on Fasting and Celibacy. **1842** —— *Provinc. Lett.* (1844) II. 31 Clement would gnosticise his words as spiritually and covertly importing: *I cultivate* [etc.]. **1851** BUNSEN *Hippolytus* (1854) I. 108 The writers of those Ophite books were acquainted with the Gospel [of St. John] and attempted to Gnosticize it. **1880** *Encycl. Brit.* XI. 854/2 Attempts to Christianize paganism, to conciliate Judaism, or to gnosticize Christianity.

Hence **ˈgnosticizing** *vbl. sb.* and *ppl. a.*; also **ˈgnosticizer**, one who gnosticizes.

1840 G. S. FABER *Regenerat.* xvi, They.. occupied themselves, not very profitably, in gnosticising upon the virtues of Celibacy. **1842** —— *Provinc. Lett.* (1844) II. 49 Under the new and gnosticising aspect of its being inherently a State of greater Moral Purity and Perfection than [etc.]. **1875** LIGHTFOOT *Comm. Col.* (ed. 2) 170 The doctrine.. taught by the Gnosticizers at Colossae.

gnostology (nɒˈstɒlədʒɪ). *rare.* [f. Gr. γνωστός known, knowable + -LOGY.] = GNOSIOLOGY.

1846 SIR W. HAMILTON *Dissert.* in *Reid's Wks.* 770 Gnostology, the Philosophy of Knowledge.

gnotobiology (ˌnəʊtəʊbaɪˈɒlədʒɪ). *Biol.* [f. as next + BIOLOGY.] = GNOTOBIOTICS.

1963 T. D. LUCKEY *Germfree Life & Gnotobiology* i. 29 Many quantitative biological relationships.. need simple and exact description... A system which describes the quantitative relationships presently known in gnotobiology.. is recommended. **1970** *Sci. Jrnl.* Apr. 46/2 A highly specialized segment of the ultraclean technology is gnotobiology, the raising of germ free animals, largely for research purposes.

gnotobiotic (ˌnəʊtəʊbaɪˈɒtɪk), *a.* *Biol.* [f. Gr. γνωτ-ός known (f. γιγνώσκειν to know) + -O + βιωτικ-ός pertaining to life, f. βιωτός worth living, f. βιοῦν to live (βίος life).] Of an organism (esp. a higher animal) or its environment: artificially rendered devoid of bacteria and other organisms which would normally be present as parasites, commensals, symbionts, etc., or having only a few known organisms of this kind present.

1949 J. A. REYNIERS et al. in *Lobund Rep.* Feb. 160 [After] the process of freeing an organism from its contaminants.. the organism becomes gnotobiotic. **1964** F. POHL in *Galaxy* Oct. 176/2 They had a gnotobiotic atmosphere, a little rich in oxygen, a little more humid than the ambient air. **1969** *Nature* 29 Nov. 846/1 Bacterial interactions.. in gnotobiotic flies (grown from germ free eggs and fed a known mixture of bacteria). **1970** *New Scientist* 15 Jan. 103/1 Gnotobiotic animals.. provide a highly sensitive system for detecting small numbers of micro-organisms.

Also **gnotobiˈosis** [Gr. βίωσις way of life], the state of being gnotobiotic; **gnotobiˈotics** [-IC 2], the field of study concerned with rearing and using gnotobiotic organisms.

1949 J. A. REYNIERS et al. in *Lobund Rep.* Feb. 160 Gnotobiotics.. would be the field of investigation concerned with growing living things by themselves or in an association with other completely known kinds of organisms. *Ibid.*, The state of 'germ-freeness' or being without contaminants is gnotobiosis. **1953** *Parasitology* XLII. 260/1 As defined by Reyniers et al., *gnotobiosis* is synonymous with *axenity* only, even though *gnotobiotics* is proposed for the science of *both* axenic and synxenic cultivation; this seems inconsistent, and I feel that the term *gnotobiosis* should be used in the broader sense. *Ibid.*, The literature on gnotobiotics of animal organisms. **1970** *New Scientist* 15 Jan. 101/1 Gnotobiotics includes the study of both 'germ-free' animals and animals whose microbial flora can be completely specified.

gnouȝ, gnow(ȝ)e, obs. pa. t. of GNAW *v.*

gnu (nuː). Also 8 **gnoo.** [Hottentot word.] A South African quadruped (*Catoblepas gnu*), belonging to the antelope family, but resembling an ox or buffalo in shape; also known by its Dutch name *wildebeest*. The brindled gnu (*Catoblepas gorgon*) is a distinct species.

1777 G. FORSTER *Voy. round World* I. 83 There is another species of wild ox, called by the natives gnoo. **1786** SPARRMANN *Voy. Cape G.H.* II. 132 The gnu resembles the antilopes and capræ in its hair, inasmuch as this is short. **1834** PRINGLE *Afr. Sk.* viii. 273 The gnu, which is now become rare. **1857** LIVINGSTONE *Trav.* iii. 56 The presence of the.. gnu is always a certain indication of water. **1884–5** *Riverside Nat. Hist.* (1888) V. 341 The Brindled gnu or Blue Wildebeest.. (*Catoblephas gorgon*) is still found in Zululand, and abundant in Damaraland.

gnuffe, var. GNOFF, churl.

go (gəʊ), *sb.*[1] Pl. **goes.** [f. the vb.]

1. The action of going, in various senses. Also, manner of going, gait. *rare* (chiefly in *nonce-uses*). For *come and go* see COME *sb.*[1] 2.

1727 BOYER *Fr. Dict.* s.v., This Horse has a good Go with him, (he goes well, or paces well). **1842** LADY GRANVILLE *Lett.* (1894) II. 333 A most distinguished-looking blowen, such a *maintien* and walk, like Dino and Orleans in her go. **1865** G. MACDONALD *A. Forbes* II. xxix. 267 All night Tibbie Dyster had lain awake in her lonely cottage, listening to the quiet heavy *go* of the water. **1893** *Chamb. Jrnl.* 28 Jan. 56/1 Rolling with the come and go of small waves.

2. *colloq.* **a.** Orig. of a horse: Power of going, mettle, spirit. Hence of persons, etc.: Dash, energy, vigour. Also of musical compositions, etc.: Brightness, animation, 'swing'.

1825 C. M. WESTMACOTT *Eng. Spy* I. 178 She's only fit to carry a dean or a bishop.—No go in her. **1830** A. FONBLANQUE *Eng. under 7 Administ.* (1837) II. 50 Ellenborough [spoken of as a horse],.. all action, and no go. **1843** J. H. NEWMAN in J. Ornsby *Mem. J. R. Hope-Scott* (1884) II. 31 Its integrity, vigour—in a word, its go. **1864** J. BROWN *Pl. Words on Health* Pref. 9 A queer man.. always scheming—full of 'go', but never getting on. **1872** BAGEHOT *Physics & Pol.* (1876) 201 Oh, he has plenty of go in him. **1882** *Daily Tel.* 9 Oct. 2/7 Mr. Grossmith's music is.. full of humour and 'go'. **1884** *Congregationalist* Feb. 109 Numbers of people who like the 'swing' and 'go'.. of these popular religious ballads. **1887** *Daily Tel.* 10 Sept. 2/5 She.. looked like a boat with a great deal of 'go' in her. **1892** LESLIE *Lett. to Marco* (1893) 223 Physically, he is a wonderful man.. very wiry, and full of energy and go.

b. Vigorous activity; hard work; esp. in phr. *it's all go*. *colloq.*

1965 *New Statesman* 14 May 777/1 Believe me, it's all go with these tycoons, mate. Life's just one frenetic whirl of soigné secretaries and sex-mad air 'ostesses. **1967** *Boston Sunday Herald* 14 May II. 16/6 All the time it's go in Florida.

3. *colloq.* or *vulgar.* A proceeding; a turn of affairs, unexpected course of things; now chiefly one that causes embarrassment. Usually with adj., as ***a pretty, queer, rum go.***

1796 MRS. MARY ROBINSON *Angelina* II. 168 'You may take off the four horses; the gentlewoman goes in the stage.' 'This a good go enough!' cried one of the post-boys. **1797** MRS. A. N. BENNETT *Beggar Girl* (1813) III. 61 'There's a go now!' cried Miss, with a hoyden laugh. **1803** KENNEY *Raising Wind* I. iii. 17 Ha! ha! ha! Capital go! isn't it? **1820** *Jack Randall's Diary* (Farmer), It's what I call the primest go. **1833** MARRYAT *P. Simple* I, It might have been a *pretty go.* **1841** *Punch* I. 169 Stating his conviction that 'this was rayther a rummy go'. **1849** MRS. CARLYLE *Lett.* II. 43 'Kept at sea double the time', and 'short of provisions';—that would have been a go! **1869** MRS. H. WOOD *R. Yorke* III. xli. 240 And leave us to old Brown! that *will* be a nice go! **1869** BRET HARTE *Return Belisarius* 14 You knew that he's got the consumption? You didn't! Well, come, that's a go. **1876** GEO. ELIOT *Dan. Der.* I. vii, I see a man with his eye pushed out once—that was a rum go as ever I see.

4. *colloq.* **a.** A turn (at doing something); a single spell of doing something, esp. in phr. ***at one go***; an attack or attempt *at*, freq. as ***to have a go at.*** Also (without const.) ***to have a go***: to make an attempt; to act resourcefully or with initiative; *spec.* (*a*) in *Cricket*, to hit out recklessly in an attempt to make runs; (*b*) to take independent or single-handed action against criminals.

1825 J. NEAL *Bro. Jonathan* I. 8 He would rivet his large eyes, for half an hour at a 'go', upon some part of the wall. **1835** R. H. FROUDE *Rem.* (1838) I. 417 And now I will have another go at you, about your rule of faith in fundamentals. **1846** SIR R. OWEN *Let.* 5 Nov. in *Life* (1894) I. 304 As men spread they.. killed the hyænas off at one go in Yorkshire, for example. **1877** *5 Yrs' Penal Servit.* iii. 221 I've twelve this go. I did a lagging of seven, and [etc.]. **1889** J. K. JEROME *3 Men in Boat* 58, I agreed and sat down, and they had a go. **1894** N. GALE *Cricket Songs* 25 Toss him down a slow, you see, He's sure to have a go, you see! **1895** *Cornh. Mag.* Aug. 176 We'll have another go at this game next Thanksgiving. **1898** JOS. ARCH *Story of his Life* xvi. 381, I wrote it in 2 goes of 6 hours each. **1912** W. ELMHIRST *Freshman's Diary* 28 Apr. (1969) 67 We paddled most of the way up.. & then Beach had a go at punting. Coming back I had a go for some time. **1933** *Punch* 1 Feb. 126/1 Whether my voice would work the charm, Frankly, I didn't know; But as it couldn't do much harm I thought I'd have a go. **1963** *Times* 28 Feb. 3/6 After several overs, during which he seemed to command the bowling, he announced to Reid, who was his partner, that he had 'had it' and was going to have a go. **1965** *Times* 1 Jan. 4/6 Mr. Bacon was asked what advice he would give to members of the public who saw a gunman carrying out a raid. '..if you can have a go then have a go,' he replied. *Ibid.*, It is completely wrong to encourage people to 'have a go'.. particularly when the criminals they are.. having a go at are trigger-happy hooligans. **1966** *Economist* 6 Aug. 534/1 There is a cryptic passage about legal protection for citizens who fight against crime (Russians who 'have a go'?). **1971** *Daily Tel.* 4 Mar. 15/4 A cashier who tried to 'have a go' was hit on the head with a gun butt.

b. A contest or battle; a fight, esp. a prize-fight or boxing-match; an argument. *colloq.*

1890 *Texas Siftings* 1 Nov. 7/3 Cost me five dollars the other day to see the tamest kind of a go. There wasn't a knockdown in ten rounds. **1893** K. MACKAY *Out Back* (ed. 2) II. i. 153 Douglas and Wrixon dearly loved a 'go' between horses. **1902** W. SATCHELL *Land of Lost* xxvi. 243 There was the little go we 'ad on the gumfield—'e 'ad all the best of that. **1959** I. & P. OPIE *Lore & Lang. Schoolch.* x. 197 The Liverpudlian says 'Come on I'll 'ave you a go'.. or 'I'll have you a scrap'.

c. An attack or bout of some sickness or ailment.

1890 LD. LUGARD *Diary* 3 Jan. (1959) I. 62 Afraid shall have a go of fever, for which this place is notorious. **1920** *Blackw. Mag.* May 614/2 A bad go of snow-blindness had driven me in to Leh. **1928** GALSWORTHY *Swan Song* v. 45 No second go of measles, Jon.

d. (*a*) ***fair go***: equitable treatment; a fair chance, a 'square deal'; *spec.* a fair fight; also without *fair*; also *int.* and as an expression of enquiry; ***to give it a go***: to give it a try; to make an attempt. Chiefly *Austral.* and *N.Z. colloq.*

1911 L. STONE *Jonah* II. vi. 215 The spinner handed his stake of five shillings to the boxer, who cried 'Fair go!' The spinner placed the two pennies face down.. and then.. the coins flew twenty feet into the air. **1918** *Chrons. N.Z.E.F.* 11 Oct. 130/1 An interesting competition. Give it a go! *Ibid.* 22 Nov. 264/2 It's a bit tight, but we'll give it a go. **1919** W. H. DOWNING *Digger Dial.* 22 *Fair go*, equitable treatment; a fair field and no favor. **1937** J. A. LEE *Civilian into Soldier* I. 25 'I'm not getting a fair go.' Guy tried to explain the injustice. **1941** BAKER *Dict. Austral. Slang* 27 *A fair go*, a fight. *Ibid.* 28 *Fair go!*, be reasonable! Give him (it, etc.) a chance! **1944** W. E. HARNEY *Taboo* (ed. 3) 125 So he said, 'All right, old man, you sing rain and that boy can have Rosie. Fair go.' **1947** 'A. P. GASKELL' *Big Game* 22 No, fair go, Bomb. The Adjutant wants you. **1959** H. P. TRITTON *Time means Tucker* vii. 55/1 Dutchy.. asked him to give us a fair go. **1961** B. CRUMP *Hang on a Minute Mate* xiii. 149 Fair go? asked Jack, scenting a yarn in Sam's tone. **1961** P. WHITE *Riders in Chariot* xi. 346 A man stands a better chance of a fair go if he's got a mate. **1963** *Times* 31 Jan. 4/1 Had England been left to score 300 or more at something like 70 an hour as was possible and 'given it a go', the odds would have been heavily against them. **1969** *Advertiser* (Adelaide) 12 May 5/4 Stop whingeing and give a bloke a go, mates. **1969** *Coast to Coast 1967–68* 23 He braced himself, but staggered under their onslaught and came down on his knees. 'Fair go!' 'Poor Daddy,' she murmured, settling down beside him. **1971** *N.Z. Listener* 22 Mar. 13/1 Finger's out, honest. I'm giving it a go, Dad.

5. A quantity of anything supplied at one time. Cf. GANG *sb.*[1] 7. **a.** of yarn for weaving. ? *Obs.*

1805 *Trans. Soc. Arts* XXIII. 249 Beaming webs of any number of half gangs, goes, runners, or equal quantities of warps or chains of yarn.

b. *colloq.* of liquor; *rarely* of food.

1799 in *Spirit Publ. Jrnls.* (1800) III. 352 [I] drank four *goes* of brandy and water. **1821** COBBETT in *19th Cent.* (1886) Feb. 254 Now he must live on plates of beef and goes of gin for the next seven years. **1836** DICKENS *Sk. Boz* (1892) 52 Oysters, stout, cigars, and 'goes' innumerable, are served up. **1855** THACKERAY *Newcomes* I. i. 6 The goes of stout.. passed round merrily. **1865** *Daily Tel.* 26 Dec. 3/3 Two or three 'goes' of roast mutton. **1883** STEVENSON *Treas. Isl.* II. viii, Three goes o' rum!

c. *colloq.* The vessel containing this quantity.

1796 *Grose's Dict. Vulg. Tongue* (ed. 3), *Go-shop*, the Queen's Head in Duke's-court.. where gin and water is sold in three-halfpenny bowls, called Goes. **1861** A. SMITH *Med. Student* 33 A pewter 'go' which, if everybody had their own, would in all probability belong to Mr. Green.

6. In certain games. **a.** *Skittles.* A delivery of the ball; also, any one of the recognized varieties of effect which this can produce.

1773 A. JONES (*title*) The Art of Playing at Skittles.. Shewing both the Old and New Methods of forming General Goes and Tips. **1884** *Sat. Rev.* 18 Oct. 494/1 The best players always attempted their goes in diagonals of the frame, or from corner to corner. **1884** *Brit. Stand. Handbks. Sports & Pastimes* II. II. 16 *Skittles*, That all pins be knocked down, but should one remain standing it shall be considered an extra 'go'... That the number of 'goes' be limited to five.

b. *Cribbage.* A 'cry' uttered by the player if he cannot play a card in his turn; the position thus indicated (for which the adversary scores one point).

1821 LAMB *Elia* Ser. I. *Mrs. Battle*, She could never heartily bring her mouth to pronounce 'Go'—or 'That's a go'. She called it an ungrammatical game. **1830** HARDIE *Hoyle made familiar* 54 [*Cribbage*], [At 30] if B can play an ace, he says thirty-one, and takes two points; if not, he says go, and A scores one point for the go.

7. *colloq.* **a.** Something that 'goes' or has a 'run'; a 'success'; esp. in phr. ***to make a go of it.***

1876 SOTHERN in J. F. Daly *Life A. Daly* (1917) 222, I learn yr. new piece is a 'great go'—so it's quite on the cards you can do as well without me. **1877** BARTLETT *Dict. Amer.* s.v., 'Make a go of it', i.e. make it succeed. **1888** *Harper's Mag.* Oct. 689/1 Determination to make the venture a go. **1896** [see B.P. (a) s.v. B III]. **1898** *Daily News* 23 June 6/1 'The Miscellany' seems to have been a 'go'. *a* **1911** D. G. PHILLIPS *Susan Lenox* (1917) I. xv. 254 He had told the company that Susan was sure to make a go; and after she had made a go, he announced the beginning of a season of triumph. **1933** *Punch* 19 Apr. 442/3 There seemed every reason for Tilly and Stevan to make a go of it. **1942** E. PAUL *Narrow St.* xxix. 261 The Amances had been unable to make a go of the hotel, and Monsieur Henri had been obliged to take it over. **1959** G. FREEMAN *Jack would be Gent.* viii. 168 You have to make a go of marriage, you have to work to make a marriage a success.

b. A bargain, an agreement, a 'deal'; usu. in phr. ***it's a go.*** *colloq.*

1878 B. HARTE *Man on Beach* 61 'Then it's a go?'.. 'It's a go.' **1908** *Magnet* I. 1, The Remove don't like you now, but we'll stick together, and bring them round. Is it a go? **1936** WODEHOUSE *Laughing Gas* i. 15 'Then say no more,' I said. 'It's a go.'

8. Phrases.

a. (***it's***) ***no go*** (colloq.): the attempt is hopeless. Also applied to a person: no good; not a success. See also NO-GO.

1825 C. M. WESTMACOTT *Eng. Spy* I. 178 It won't do, *no go* Dick. **1829** T. CREEVEY *Let.* 20 Oct. in J. Gore *Creevey's Life & Times* (1934) xiv. 311 According to the Earl and myself, Fanny Kemble is *no go*. **1833** MARRYAT *P. Simple* xxxi, That's *no go*. **1837** DICKENS *Pickw.* ii, Dog stopped —whistled again—Ponto—no go.. wouldn't move. **1848** MRS. CARLYLE *Lett.* II. 26 Amusement after a certain age is no go.. merely distraction. **1848** THACKERAY *Van. Fair* xxxiv, You want to trot me out, but it's no go. **1888** LOWELL *Heartsease & Rue* 207 'You must rise', says the leaven. 'I can't', says the dough; 'Just examine my bumps, and you'll see it's no go'. **1912** J. LONDON *Let.* 19 Nov. (1966) 368 No; I told Eliza, George is no go.

attrib. **1829** *Sporting Mag.* XIII. 242 Stating the names of the constantly 'no go' coverts.

b. ***the go*** (now only, ***all*** or ***quite the go***): said predicatively of persons and things; The height of fashion; the 'correct thing'; the 'rage'. *colloq.*

1793 COLERIDGE *Lett.* (1895) 50 Have you read Mr. Fox's letter to the Westminster electors? It is quite the political go at Cambridge, and has converted many souls to the Foxite faith. **1800** MRS. HERVEY *Mourtray Fam.* I. 183 He is quite the thing; the *go* in every respect. **1810** *Splendid Follies* I. 69 But kittens, you must recollect, are all the go. **1819** MOORE *Ep. fr. Tom Cribb* 2 Is this the new go?—kick a man when he's down! **1821** EGAN *Tom & Jerry* vi. (1870) 116 In the Parks, Tom was the go among the 'goes'. **1840** BARHAM *Ingol. Leg., Lay St. Nicholas*. But who doth not know it [a costume] was rather the go With Pilgrims and Saints in the second Crusade? **1841** *Fraser's Mag.* XXIII. 15 He becomes all the go in the university. **1852** R. S. SURTEES *Sponge's Sp. Tour* vi. (1865) 25 Elegant shawls labelled..' Quite the Go'. **1880** G. R. SIMS *Ball. Babylon* 82 Her *carte* is hung in the West-end shops,.. And all day long there's a big crowd stops To look at the lady who's 'all the go'.

c. ***near go*** (colloq.): a going near (to a danger or the like); a 'close shave'.

1827 *Sporting Mag.* XXI. 47 Some Christchurch men remember that go, and how near a go it was! **1841** *Fraser's Mag.* XXIII. 15 Which.. would have been a near go for his neck.

d. ***on*** or ***upon the go*** (colloq.): †(*a*) on the verge of destruction (*obs.*); (*b*) in a state of decline (? *obs.*); (*c*) in constant motion, in a restless state; (*d*) *slang*, slightly intoxicated.

(*a*) *c* **1680** HICKERINGILL *Hist. Whiggism* Wks. 1716 I. 133 They did so many Irrational, Senseless, and Destructive Acts, that almost all lay at Stake.. and was just upon the go. (*b*) **1727** MRS. M. ROBINSON *Walsingham* IV. 318 The good fellow is upon the go; his life's not worth six weeks' purchase. *a* **1800** T. BELLAMY *Beggar Boy* (1801) I. 6 No longer could she pay attention to the larder, and there daily examine that part of its stores which was somewhat—another saying of her's—'On the go'. **1842** E. FITZGERALD *Lett.* (1889) I. 99 As to poor old England, I never see a paper, but I think with you that she is on the go.

(*c*) **1843** BETHUNE *Sc. Fireside Stor.* 26 But if you can only afford to wait till you get us on the go. **1874** ALDRICH *Prud. Palfrey* xiii. (1885) 203 Ever since the day we said good-bye .. I have been on the go. **1898** *Daily News* 14 May 5/7 He might keep them on the go for a long time.

(*d*) **1821** EGAN *Tom & Jerry* ix. (1870) 210 The fine old wines of the Corinthian had made him a little bit 'on the go'.

e. ***great, little go***, see the adjs.

go (gəʊ), *sb.*² Also Go, Goh, I-go. [Jap. *go* small stone.] A Japanese board game of territorial possession.

1890 B. H. CHAMBERLAIN *Things Japanese* 136 *Go*, sometimes, but with little appropriateness, termed 'checkers' by European writers, is the most popular of the in-door pastimes of the Japanese. **1911** H. F. CHESHIRE *Goh or Wei Chi* 15 In the East proficiency in Goh is one of the best recommendations to high places. **1958** *Listener* 13 Nov. 786/2 The game that does seem to me to be superior to chess, in that it has both depth and simplicity, is the Japanese game of Go. **1960** R. C. BELL *Board & Table Games* iii. 96 This Japanese game [*sc.* Gobang].. is a poor relation of the intellectual I-go.

go (gəʊ), *v.* Pa. t. **went** (wɛnt); pa. pple. **gone** (gɒn, -ɔ:-). Forms: see below. [A Com. Teut. defective vb., perh. originally existing only in the pres.-stem, though a str. pa. pple. occurs in some of the Teut. langs. The forms in the WGer. langs. are as follows: OE. inf. *gán*, pr. t. *gá*, etc. (see below), pa. pple. *ȝegán*; OFris. pr. t. 3rd pers. sing. *gâth*, *geith*, pa. pple. *gên*; OS. inf. *-gân* in *fulgân* to accomplish; OLow Frankish *gân* (MDu. *gaen*, Du. *gaan*, pr. t. *ga*, *gaast*, etc.); OHG. (Alemannic) inf. *gân*, pr. t. *gâm*, *gâs*, *gât*, *gâmês*, etc., (Bavarian) inf. *gên*, pr. t. *gêm*, *gês*, etc. (MHG. *gân*, *gên*, mod.Ger. *gehen*, pr. t. *gehe*, *gehst*, etc.); the MHG. pa. pple. *gegân* is not found in OHG. The Scandinavian langs. have forms which appear to belong to this vb.: ON. inf. *gá* (late and rare), Sw. *gå* (pr. t. *går*, etc.), Da. *gaa(e* (pr. t. *gaar*, pa. pple. *gaaet*); but it is possible that these may have been evolved from the pa. t. *gekk* of *ganga* (GANG *v.*), on the analogy of *fá*, *fekk* (see FANG *v.*). The vb. does not occur in Wulfila's Gothic, but the Crim-Gothic of the 16th c. had, according to Busbeck, the inf. *geen*.

As is shown by the evidence of OHG., the vb. belongs to the class of 'verbs in *-mi*'. The forms in the various langs. point to a twofold OTeut. stem, *gǣ-*, *gai-*, which seems to have been apprehended as having the same relation to the stem *gaŋg-* (see GANG *v.*) as *stǣ-*, *stai-*, to the extended stem *stand-* (see STAND *v.*); thus in OHG. *gên*, *stên* (which are strictly parallel in conjugation) are functionally mere variants of *gangan*, *stantan*. It is probable that the words expressing the contrasted notions 'go' and 'stand' have exercised some analogical influence on each other. Whether there is any etymological connexion between *gǣ-* (*gai-*) and *gaŋg-* is uncertain. Three suppositions are conceivable: (1) that the two are unrelated, and have been associated owing to their similarity in sense and sound; (2) that *gaŋg-* (:—OAryan *ghongh-) is a nasalized reduplication of the root preserved in Teut. *gǣ-* (*gai-*), (3) that the shorter vb. was evolved from the proportion *stand-* : *stǣ-* (*stai-*) :: *gang-* : *gǣ-* (*gai-*). The first two of these views leave the etymology undetermined. Kluge proposes an OTeut. type **ga-îm(i*, f. *ga-* prefix + the root *ī* (Aryan *ei-*, *i-*) of Gr. ἰέναι (εἶμι), L. *īre*, but this has not been generally accepted. Other scholars have suggested affinity with Skr. *hā* to leave, forsake, with Gr. κιχάνειν, κιχῆναι to attain, reach, or with Lettish *gaju* 'I went'.

The place of the missing pa. t. was supplied in OE. by *éode* (*-dest*, *-de*, *-don*), believed to be an extension, with the suffix *-de* of weak preterites, of a lost form equivalent to the synonymous Goth. *iddja*:—OTeut. **ijjôm*, an imperfect or aorist of the Indogermanic vb. *yā-* to go, an extended form of *ei-*, *i-* (see above); there are, however, some unsolved difficulties (see Sievers *Ags. Gr.*³ §114, Brugmann *Grdriss.* II. 861). The OE. *éode* became in ME. *ȝede*, *yede*, *yode*, etc.; in the south these forms died out in the 15th c., and were superseded by the pa. t. of WEND, as this vb. had become synonymous with *go*, and its inf. and pr. tense had ceased to be in frequent use. The use of *went* as a pa. pple. is sometimes heard in illiterate speech. In Sc. and northern dialects *yede* was superseded, not by *went*, but by a new formation on the present-stem, *gaed* (see A. 3b). In the archaistic language of Sackville and Spenser, YEDE was used as a present-stem, and *yode* as the corresponding pa. t.

The perfect tenses were originally formed with *be*; this is still used where the tense expresses a state, *have* being substituted where it expresses an action; in many cases either auxiliary may be used without perceptible difference of meaning.]

A. Inflexional Forms.

1. *Infinitive.*

a. *Simple Infinitive*, go (gəʊ). Forms: 1–2 **gán**, *Northumb.* **gáa**, ? **gáe**, **gǽ**, 3 *Orm.* **gan**, 3–4 **gon**, 4 *Kent.* **guo**, 4–5 **ga(a**, (**gay**), **gan(e**, **goo(n**, (5 **gwon**), 4–7 **gon(e**, (6 **goen**, *Sc.* **gea**), 6–7 **goe**, 9 *Sc.* **gae**, 4– **go**.

Beowulf (Z.) 1163 þa cwom Wealhþeo forð gan under gyldnum beaȝe. *c* **950** *Lindisf. Gosp.* Matt. viii. 18 Ðe hælend.. geheht.. gaa ofer.. stream. *Ibid.* 28 Gae. *c* **1000** ÆLFRIC *Deut.* xiii. 2 Uton gan and feliȝean fremdum godum. *c* **1200** ORMIN 913 þe preost wass shridd tærwiþþ To gan till Godess allterr. *c* **1290** *S. Eng. Leg.* I. 195/69 Ase heo in prisone al one was, an old man þare cam gon. *a* **1300** *Cursor M.* 15034 þe childer þat war waike To ga þat pres a-mang. *Ibid.* 20135 Ne wald he neuer fra hir gan. **13..** *Guy Warw.* (A.) 1219 Gon, fader, quod he, ich-ille. **1340** *Ayenb.* 60 Uor þet þe zeneȝere hine ssolde guo þe hardylaker. *c* **1340** *Cursor M.* 1436 (Fairf.) Quen [adam] was dede sone an-nane his saule forþ to hel con gane. *c* **1375** *Sc. Leg. Saints, Paulus* 315 [Paule] lewit nero in sic effray, He of wit ner can gay. *a* **1400** *Isumbras* 719 His mene awaye gane gaa. *c* **1400** *Sowdone Bab.* 50 Shope him to grene woode to goon. *c* **1400** MAUNDEV. (1839) v. 56 This Weye is most schort, for to go streyghte unto Babiloyne. *c* **1420** *Chron. Vilod.* st. 616 In hast to Wylton he byth ȝow gon. *c* **1420** *Sir Amadas* (Weber) 670 With me then schall thei gwon. **1423** JAS. I *Kingis Q.* cvii, Bothe to cum and gone. *c* **1450** HENRYSON *Mor. Fab.* 296 in *Anglia* IX. 351 On to ga quha that mycht formest win. *c* **1511** *1st Eng. Bk. Amer.* (Arb.) Introd. 27 They can goen vnder the water. **1583** *Satir. Poems Reform.* xlv. 1054 Fand out some vther gait to gea. **1608** TOPSELL *Hist. Serpents* (1658) 705 There was not one But forced forth the venomd-bloud, along his sides to gone. **1683** *Col. Rec. Pennsylv.* I. 74 Ralph Withers desires Leave to goe home. **1838** JAS. GRANT *Sk. Lond.* 39 Do you think, man, that ye can gae like a cripple?

b. *Dative Infinitive* (with *to*) **to go**, in OE. **tó gánne**, ME. **to ganne, guonne, gonde**.

c **1000** ÆLFRIC *Hom.* II. 32 ȝearo to ganne. *a* **1225** *St. Marher.* 4 þe weie þæt ich am in begunnen to ganne. *a* **1300** *Floriz & Bl.* 612 (Hausknecht), And Babiloine ihc understonde Dureþ sixti mile to gonde. **1340** *Ayenb.* 226 Bysye to guonne an to comene ganglinde.

2. *Indicative Present.*

a. *1st pers. sing.* **go**. Forms: 1 **gá, gáa**, *Northumb.* **gǽ** (? **gáe**), **gáæ**, 3–4 **ga**, 5–6 **goo**, 6–7 **goe**, 9 *Sc.* **gae**, 4– **go**.

[*c* **825** *Vesp. Psalter* xli. 10 Forhwon unrot ic ingaa.] *c* **950** *Lindisf. Gosp.* John xvi. 5 Nu ic gææ to him. *c* **1000** *Ags. Gosp.* Matt. xxi. 30 Ic ga [*c* **950** *Lindisf.* gae]. *a* **1225** *Juliana* 73 Ne ga i neauer mare þrefter o grene. *c* **1305** *Edmund Conf.* 63 in *E.E.P.* (1862) 72 Wiþ þe ic go in eche stede. *c* **1340** *Cursor M.* 25459 (Fairf.) þusgatis on erþ I ga. *c* **1500** *Melusine* xxiv. 174 'I goo'.. 'putte my peple in aray'. **1794** BURNS '*Out over the Forth*', I look to the west, when I gae to rest.

b. *2nd pers. sing.* **goest** ('gəʊɪst). Forms: 1 **gǽst**, *Northumb.* **gǽs** (? **gáes**), **gáæs**, **gást**, 2–3 **gast**, 2–4 **gest**, 3 **gæst**, 4 *Sc.* **gays**, 4–5 **gas(e**, **gost**, **goost**, 5 **gose**, 6 *Sc.* **gais**, 6– **goest**.

c **950** *Lindisf. Gosp.* Matt. viii. 19 Ic fylgo ðe sua huider ðu gaes. *Ibid.* Luke xii. 58 Mið-ðy ðu gast mið wiðerworde ðinum. *Ibid.* John xiii. 36 Drihten huidir gaæs ðu. **971** *Blickl. Hom.* 249 For hwan gæst þu swa buton wæstme þines ȝewinnes. *c* **1200** ORMIN 4666 Hu ferr þu gast Ut off þe rihhte weȝȝe. *c* **1205** LAY. 26437 ȝif [þu] gæst him a leoð. *a* **1300** *Cursor M.* 27482 If þou man gas þin offrand to mak. **1340** *Ayenb.* 129 Huannes comst þou. Huyder gest þou. *c* **1375** *Sc. Leg. Saints, Machor* 465 Quhare þu gays, wil I ga. *c* **1386** CHAUCER *Sec. Nun's T.* 56 Thou goost biforn. *c* **1430** *Freemasonry* 677 Uche fote that thou gost then. *c* **1460** *Towneley Myst.* ix. 114 If thou here any saghes sere.. Of that lad where that thou gase. *Ibid.* x. 186 Who owe this child thou gose with all? **1508** DUNBAR *Flyting* 216 We sall gar scale our sculis all the to scorne, And stane the vp the calsay quhair thow gais. **1535** COVERDALE *Gen.* xxviii. 15, I.. wyll kepe the where so euer thou goest.

c. *3rd pers. sing.* **goes** (gəʊz); *arch.* **goeth** ('gəʊɪθ). Forms: α. 1 **gǽþ**, *Northumb.* **gá(a)ð**, (? **gáeð**), 2 **gæþ**, 2–4 **geð**, 3 **gaþ**, **geað**, 4–5 **geth(e**, **goþ(e**, 4–6 **goth(e**, **gooth**, (4 **goith**), 5– (9 *arch.*) **goeth**. β. 1 *Northumb.* **gaas**, **gáæs**, **gǽs** (? **gáes**), 4–7 **gas**, **gays**, 4–5 **gas(e**, **gos(e**, 4 **gez**, (**gotz**), 5 **gaes**, **goys(e**, 6 *Sc.* **geas**, **gois**, 7 **go's**, 7– **goes**.

α. *Beowulf* (Z.) 455 Gæð a wyrd swa hio scel! *c* **950** *Lindisf. Gosp.* Matt. xxvi. 24 Sunu.. monnes gaeð sua awritten is of him. *c* **1000** *Ags. Gosp.* John iii. 8 þu nast.. hwyder he gæþ [*c* **950** *Lindisf.* gaað, *c* **1160** *Hatton* geð]. *c* **1175** *Lamb. Hom.* 29 þeo sunnen, þe he geð to scrifte fore. *c* **1200** ORMIN 1224 Oxe gaþ o clofenn fot. *a* **1225** *Juliana* 57 Ah hwa se obote ne geað ne schal he beon i borhen. *c* **1315** SHOREHAM 109 Ase al that hys here By sove daȝes geth. **1340** *Ayenb.* 56 In þise manere geþ þe tyme. *c* **1340** *Cursor M.* 3051 (Trin.) Now goþ þat wrecche wille of wone. *c* **1386** CHAUCER *Sqr.'s T.* 269 On the daunce he gooth with Canacee [*var.* goth *MS. Camb.*, goþ *Corp.*, *Petw.*, goþe *Lansd.*]. **1388** WYCLIF *John* x. 4 He goith bifor hem. **1390** GOWER *Conf.* III. 104 So it geth Out of the see. *c* **1435** *Torr. Portugal* 2042 Se, where the kyng gethe. **1508** FISHER 7 *Penit. Ps.* xxxii. Wks. (1876) 23 This holy prophete gooth shortly on all these. **1523** FITZHERB. *Surv.* iii. (1539) 7 The pasture.. that he gothe in. **1535** COVERDALE *Luke* vii. 8, I saye vnto one: Go, and he goeth. **1839** LANE *Arab. Nts.* I. 107 He knoweth not.. whither she goeth, nor what she doth.

β. *c* **950** *Lindisf. Gosp.* Matt. Pref. 7 Swa hwidir gaas[t] gaæs hea gæð. *Ibid.* viii. 9 Ic cueðo ðissum gaæ & gaes. *Ibid.* xv. 17 Eghuelc þæt in muð inngaas in womb gaas. *a* **1300**

Cursor M. 1970 þar gas [*Fairf.* gase] na ransun bot liue for lijf. *Ibid.* 12914 Als bedel gais be-for iustis. *a* 1300 *Floriz. & Bl.* 63 Floriz gez to his rest. 13.. *E.E. Allit. P.* B. 325 Alle þat glydez & gotz, & gost of lyf habbez. *c* 1330 R. Brunne *Chron.* (1810) 147 He gos to S. Deny. *c* 1386 Chaucer *Reeve's T.* 117 Right by the hopur wil I stande..and se how that the corn gas In. *a* 1400-50 *Alexander* 3016 [Darius] Gaes him on to granton, & graithes þare his tentis. *c* 1420 *Sir Amadace* (Camden) ix, Sone a-gayn gose he. *a* 1440 *Sir Eglam.* 98 Mornyng to hys hedd he gays. 1486 *Bk. St. Albans* E vj b, At huntyng..when he goys. 1500-20 Dunbar *Poems* xiii. 23 Sum super expendit gois to his bed. 1513 Douglas *Æneis* I. iv. 11 Within the watter in ane bosum gais. 1583 *Leg. Bp. St. Androis* 781 in *Satir. Poems Reform.* xlv, To that bischop in he geas. 1602 Marston *Ant. & Mel.* Wks. 1856 I. 33 How goes the time? 1640 *Wits Recreat.* Epigr. 369 Alwaies to the wall the weakest go's.

d. *plural* **go.** Forms: α. 1 **gáð**, *Northumb.* **gaað, gæð,** 2, 3 **gað, goð,** 4 **guoþ,** 4–6 **gooþ, -th,** 6 **goth.** β. 1 *Northumb.* **gáas, -es, gǽs,** 4 *north.* **gas, gaas, gos,** 6 *Sc.* **gois.** γ. 3 *Orm.* **gan,** 3–5 **ga,** 4–7 **gon(e,** 4–6 **goon(e,** 5 **goo,** 6–7 **goe,** 4– **go.**

α. *c* 825 *Vesp. Hymns* vi. 23 In lehte scotunge ðine gað. *c* 950 *Lindisf. Gosp.* Luke ii. 3 Gaað alle..syndrio In his ceastra. *a* 1200 *Moral Ode* 347 þos goð [*printed* god] unieþe toȝeanes þe clive. *a* 1225 *St. Marher.* 15 Swa ich habbe ablend ham þæt ha blindlunge gað. 1340 *Ayenb.* 34 Alle guoþ þrin, uor to lyerni. 1387 Trevisa *Higden* (Rolls) I. 403 They fiȝteþ better..Whan þey gooþ þan whan þei rideþ. *c* 1500 *God Speed Plough* 73 in *P. Pl. Crede* 71 Prestis that goth to rome. 1526 *Pilgr. Perf.* (W. de W. 1531) 1 All christians gooth this pilgrymage.

β. *c* 950 *Lindisf. Gosp.* Matt. Pref. 5 Wæ ðæm..ða ðe gaes æfter gaast hiora. *Ibid.* xiii. 49 In endung worldes gæs englas & [etc.]. *Ibid.* Mark vi. 10 Suahuælc ȝie gaas in hus ðer wunað. *a* 1300 *Cursor M.* 6822 þam..þat til wikcud dedes gaas [*Trin.* gos]. *Ibid.* 13106 Messels er hale, cripels gas [*Trin.* go] right. 1508 Dunbar *Poems* iv. 17 Onto the ded gois all Estatis.

γ. *c* 1200 Ormin 11945 Godess þeowwess gan onn himm. *a* 1240 *Sawles Warde* in *Cott. Hom.* 255 ȝef we hire haldeð þenne ga we sikerliche. *c* 1350 *Will. Palerne* 1687 þe beres ..þe gon most gresli to eche gomes siȝt. *c* 1386 Chaucer *Prol.* 771 As ye goon by the weye, Ye shapen yow to talen. *a* 1400-50 *Alexander* 459 How þat ȝe ga sa grete gud dame? *Ibid.* 3456 þai gone agrayther vp þaire gods. *c* 1485 *Digby Myst.* (1882) v. 380 In ony place wher ye goo or Ryde. 1529 More *Dyaloge* B v b/1 They yt goone on pylgrymage. 1611 Tourneur *Ath. Trag.* C 2 b, If you goe to buffets among the Boyes, they'l giue you one. 1627 Bp. Hall *Ps. Metaphrased* ix, All that gone Through daughter Sions beauteous gate.

3. *Indicative Past.* †**a. yede, yode.** *Obs.* Forms: *sing.* 1–3 **éode,** (*2nd sing.* **-est**), *Northumb.* **éade,** 2–4 **ȝeode,** 3–5 **ȝodd, ȝod(e,** 4–5 **yodd, yod(e,** 2–5 **ȝede,** *north.* and *Sc.* **ȝeid(e,** 4 **ȝedd,** 4–5 **yedd, yed(e,** *Sc.* **yeid,** 3–5 **ede,** (3 **ȝied(e, hiede, yhode, yoede,** 4 **giede, ȝide, ȝood, ȝud(e, yeid(e, yhed,** 5 **ude, youd, yude**), 6 *arch.* **yede,** 6, 7, 9 *arch.* **yod(e** (*2nd sing.* **-est**); *pl.* 1 **éodon, -un, -an,** *Northumb.* **éada, -e, -o, -un,** 2–4 **eode(n,** (2 **oden**), 3–4 **ȝeode(n,** 4 **ȝod(e,** (4 **yoede**), 4–6 **yod(e, ȝud(e,** (5 **yhude**), 2 **ieden,** 3–5 **ȝed(e(n, ede(n,** 3 *Orm.* **ȝedenn,** (3 **hiden,** 5 **hedon**), 4–5 **yed(e(n,** (4 **ȝiden**), 4–6 *Sc.* **ȝeid.**

sing. *Beowulf* (Z.) 1232 Eode þa to setle. *c* 950 *Lindisf. Gosp.* John ix. 11 Ic eade & ic aðuog & ic ȝesæh. *c* 1200 *Trin. Coll. Hom.* 135 þe child þe hie mide hiede. *Ibid.* 175 Ure helende ȝiede bi þe se. *a* 1225 *Juliana* 6 Euch deis dei [heo] eode to chirche. *c* 1250 *Gen. & Ex.* 2030 ȝhe ȝod him bitterlike a-gen. *c* 1275 *Orison* 15 in *O.E. Misc.* 139 As oþer childre þu eodest and speke. *a* 1300 *Cursor M.* 3353 (Cott.) He yode þar walkand be þe strete. *Ibid.* 4567 (Cott.) þas oþer seuen yede i to see. *c* 1300 *Ibid.* 21601 (Edin.) To mete hir giede mani barune. *c* 1300 *Beket* 76 [He] ȝeode aboute as a best. 1375 Barbour *Bruce* III. 302 His cause ȝeid fra ill to wer. *Ibid.* VII. 36 Bot othir wayis the gammyn ȝude. *c* 1420 *Chron. Vilod.* st. 649 As hole, as fayre, as hit upon urthe ude. 1424 *Paston Lett.* No. 4. I. 15 The seyd Walter yede at large owt of warde. *c* 1449 Pecock *Repr.* 225 The Lord sie that Moyses ȝede to se. *c* 1460 J. Russell *Bk. Nurture* 35 Where euer y ede day by day. 1494 Fabyan *Chron.* v. lxxxiii. 61 The Bysshop..yode vnto the house. ? *a* 1500 *Chester Pl.* (Shaks. Soc.) II. 60 He toulde over all ther as he yeide That [etc.]. 1555 Phaer *Æneid* I. B ij, Venus..Her self by skye to Paphos yede wher stonds her honor seates [etc.]. 1591 *Eclog. Death Sir P. Sidney* in Arb. *Garner* I. 276 Along the banks of many silver streams, Thou with him yodest. 1613 W. Browne *Brit. Past.* I. iv, Then forth she yode. *a* 1650 *Glasgerion* 46 in Furniv. *Percy Folio* I. 250 He did not kisse that Lady gay when he came nor when he youd. 1808 Scott *Marm.* III. xxxi, In other pace than forth he yode.

plural. *c* 825 *Vesp. Hymns* v. 37 Bearn soðlice [Israhel] eodun ðorh dryȝe ðorh midne se. *c* 950 *Lindisf. Gosp.* Luke xxiv. 13 Tuoeȝe from him eado ðe ilca dæȝe in..emmaus. 971 *Blickl. Hom.* 67 þonne eodan hie him toȝeanes. 1154 *O.E. Chron.* an. 1137 Sume ieden on ælmes þe wæron sum wile rice men. *c* 1175 *Lamb. Hom.* 155 Heo oden wepende. *c* 1200 Ormin 3396 þeȝȝ ȝedenn forþ Till Beþþleæmess chesstre. *a* 1300 *E.E. Psalter* xvii[i]. 46 þai halted þare þai yhode. *a* 1300 *Cursor M.* 11010 (Cott.) þair modres..Yoede at ans wit þair child. *c* 1340 *Ibid.* 19038 (Trin.) [He] wiþ þe apostlis ȝood. 1340 *Ayenb.* 233 þe wyse maydines..yeden in mid þe bredgome. 1362 Langl. *P. Pl.* A. Prol. 41 Beggers faste a-boute eoden [1377 ȝede]. *a* 1400 *Pistel Susan* 228 To þe ȝate ȝaply þei ȝeoden wel ȝare. *c* 1420 *Chron. Vilod.* st. 758 For ever where ever þey hedoun þey wentoun dauncyng. 1450-70 *Golagros & Gaw.* 577 Gaudifeir and Galiot baith to grund yhude. 1535 W. Stewart *Cron. Scot.* II. 217 In till array syne neir the Saxonis ȝude. *c* 1560 A. Scott *Poems* (S.T.S.) v. 16 In May quhen men ȝeid everich one,..To bring in bowis.

b. *north. dial.* **gaed.** Forms: 5–6 **gaid,** 6 **geid,** 8 **gade,** 8–9 **gaed,** 9 **gede, geed.**

c 1400 *Destr. Troy* 369 He..Gaid vp by a grese all of gray marbill. 1596 Dalrymple tr. *Leslie's Hist. Scot.* IX. 173 [He] led her with him quhair euer he gaid. *Ibid.* 185 Of this the nobilitie geid til a counsell. 1725 Ramsay *Gentle Sheph.* II. iv, When first thou gade wi' shepherds to the hill. 1785 Burns *Holy Fair* ii, The third..gaed a-wee a-back. 1813 Hogg *Queen's Wake* 167 Bonnye Kilmeny gede up the glen. 1855 Robinson *Whitby Gloss.* s.v. *Geed,* 'I geed to market o' foot'. 1864 *Fraser's Mag.* Nov. 629 He used to tak me along with him when he gaed to the hills.

c. went. Forms: 3–5 **wente,** 3– **went;** *2nd sing.* 6– **wentest, went'st.** For earlier quots. see wend *v.*

1484 Caxton *Fables of Alfonce* iii, A good man labourer wente fro lyf to deth. 1535 Coverdale *2 Sam.* vii. 9 Whither so euer thou wentest. 1590 Shaks. *Com. Err.* IV. iv. 90 Wentst not thou to her? 1592 Nashe *P. Pennilesse* Wks. 1883-4 II. 25 They went a Boot-haling one night. 1670 Lady Chaworth in *12th Rep. Hist. MSS. Comm.* App. v. 19 Heere is talke as if the Duke of M[onmouth] went Deputy into Ireland. 1705 Arbuthnot *Anc. Coins,* etc. (1727) 273 Trajan..descended to the Mouths of the Tigris and Euphrates, and went upon the Ocean.

4. *Subjunctive Present* **go.** Forms: *sing.* 1 **gá, gáe,** (? **gǽ**), 2–3 **ga,** 6 *Sc.* **ga,** 3– **go.** *plural.* 1–2 **gán, gá,** *Northumb.* **gáe,** (? **gǽ**), 3 *Orm.* **ga,** 4– **go.**

sing. *Beowulf* (Z.) 1394 Ga þær he wille! [*c* 825 *Vesp. Psalter* lxxii. 17 Oððæt ic ingae in godes haliȝ portic. 835 *Charter* in *O.E. Texts* 447 Wið ðan ðe he..hire ðearfa bega.] *c* 1175 *Lamb. Hom.* 21 þet he ne ga to bote. *a* 1300 *E.E. Psalter* xvi. 2[3] Fra þi lickam mi dome forthga. *c* 1300 *Beket* 1316 This cas ȝe mote amendi, how so hit evere go. 1393 Langl. *P. Pl.* C. XII. 200 Go ich to helle, go ich to heuene, ich shal nouht go myn one! 1596 Dalrymple tr. *Leslie's Hist. Scot.* x. 373 Quhat gait that euir it ga. 1796 *Plain Sense* III. 10, I shall desire that she go to bed. 1847 Tennyson *Princess* vi. 190 All good go with thee!

plural. *c* 950 *Lindisf. Gosp.* Matt. xiv. 15 þæt hia ȝegaæ in ceastra. *Ibid.* Mark i. 38 Gæ we..in ða neesto lond. *Ibid.* xiv. 12 Hwidder wællesðu þæt we gae. *c* 1175 *Lamb. Hom.* 33 þah ȝe gan of sunne ower sunne to bote. *c* 1200 Ormin 3390 Ga we nu till þatt illke tun. *c* 1350 *Will. Palerne* 804 Go we to þe gardyn.

5. *Subjunctive Past.* †**a. yede.** Forms: 1 *Northumb.* **éade, éode,** 6 **yede.**

[*c* 950 *Lindisf. Gosp.* Matt. viii. 34 [Hi] ȝebedon þæt eferade from ȝemærum hiora. *Ibid.* Mark vi. 45 þætte hia foreeode hine ofer luh.] *c* 1500 *Nutbrowne Mayde* in Arnolde *Chron.* (1811) 202 Bettyr were, the power squyer, alone to forest yede.

b. *dial.* **gaid.**

1500-20 Dunbar *Poems* xxx. 25 Ga bring to me ane bischopis weid, Gife evir thow wald my saule gaid vnto Hevin.

c. went. Forms: see 3 c.

1611 Shaks. *Cymb.* II. i. 46 Is it fit I went to looke vpon him?

6. *Imperative* **go.** Forms: *sing.* 1 **gá, gáa,** *Northumb.* **gáæ, gáe** (? **gǽ**), 2–5 **ga,** 3– **go.** *plural.* 1 **gáð,** *Northumb.* **gáað, gáeð,** 2–3 **gað,** 3–4 **goð,** 5 **goythe;** also 1 *Northumb.* **gaas, gáes,** 5 **gase;** 4 *north.* **ga;** 4– **go.**

sing. *c* 825 *Vesp. Psalter* vii. 8 In heanisse gaa eft. *Ibid.* cxlii[i]. 2 Ne ga ðu inn in dome mid ðiowe ðinum. *c* 950 *Lindisf. Gosp.* Matt. ii. 20 Gae In eorðo israheles. *Ibid.* viii. 9 Gaæ. *c* 1175 *Lamb. Hom.* 35 Ga to þine feder burinesse. *c* 1205 Lay. 26107 Ga..and hefd him binim her. *a* 1225 *Juliana* 190 Go swiþe..and bring me of is bende. 1382 Wyclif *1 Kings* xviii. 11 Now thou seist to me, Go. *a* 1400-50 *Alexander* 5406 Ga lawere & be-hald.

plural. [*c* 825 *Vesp. Psalter* xcv. 8 Ingað in ceafurtunas his.] *c* 950 *Lindisf. Gosp.* Matt. ii. 8 Gaes & ȝefraignes innueardlice of ðæm cnæht. *Ibid.* viii. 32, & cueð to him gaeð. *Ibid.* xx. 4 Gaað. *Ibid.* Mark xvi. 15 Gaas on middanȝeard allne. *a* 1000 *Andreas* 1334 Gað fromlice. *c* 1175 *Lamb. Hom.* 33 Gað to scriffte. *c* 1200 *Trin. Coll. Hom.* 71 Goð and scheweð ȝiu ȝiuwer prest. *c* 1200 Ormin 9269 Gaþ alle, & takeþþ upponn ȝuw Rihht shrifft off ȝure sinness. *a* 1225 *Leg. Kath.* 349 Gað ȝet. *a* 1375 *Joseph Arim.* 373 Gos to oure Maumetes, and proues heore mihtes. 1382 Wyclif *Matt.* xx. 4 Go and ȝee in to my vyne ȝerd. *c* 1386 Chaucer *Monk's T.* 204 'Gooth, bryngeth forth the vessels' [tho] quod he. *a* 1400-50 *Alexander* 3522 Gase quen ȝow likis. *c* 1460 *Towneley Myst.* ii. 204 Fy on yow! goyth hence Out of my presence.

7. *Present Participle* **going** ('gəʊɪŋ). Forms: 1 **gánde,** 4 **gaande, goand(e, -ende, -inde, -onde, gonde (guoinde),** 4, 6 **goinge, -yng(e,** 5 **gooing,** 8–9 *Sc.* **gaun,** 9 *north.* **gawn,** 6– **going.**

c 825 *Vesp. Psalter* xviii[i]. 6 Swe swe brydguma forð gande of brydbure his. 13.. *Gaw. & Gr. Knt.* 2214 For now is gode Gawayn goande ryȝt here. *c* 1340 *Cursor M.* 401 (Fairf.) Al gaande [*Trin.* goynge] bestes, þe sext day. *Ibid.* 2005 (Trin.) þe world was goonde In elde of þe þridde þousonde. 1340 *Ayenb.* 120 Guodes..þet by chonginde and guoinde. *c* 1380 *Sir Ferumb.* 1890 'þow semest bet', quaþ Amerel, 'a deuel gonde in dale, þan' [etc.]. *c* 1430 *Syr Gener.* (Roxb.) 4424 Here gooing wel perceiued was. 1500-20 Dunbar *Poems* lxix. 30 A journay going everie day. 1583 Stubbes *Anat. Abus.* II. (1882) 73 This..discourageth not a fewe from goyng to their bookes. 1785 Burns *Holy Fair* v, I'm gaun to Mauchline holy fair. 1802 R. Anderson *Cumberld. Ball.* 29, I pass'd her gawn owre the lang meedow. 1823 *Blackw. Mag.* Mar. 313/2 Ye had the gaun days o' prosperity for twenty years!

8. *Past Participle.* **a. gone** (gɒn, -ɔː-). Forms: 1 **ȝegán,** 3–6 **gan(e,** 3–6, 8 **gon,** 4 **goon(e,** *Sc.* **gayn(e,** (**gain, geen(e,** 5 **gonne, goyn,** 6 **goen,** *Sc.* **gaine,** 7 **gaene**), 4–6 **go,** (5 **goe, goo**), 9 *Sc.* **gaen,** 4– **gone.** Also 3 **i-gon, (h)i-go,** 4–5 **i-, y-gan, -gon, -goon,** 6 **i-goen,** 3, 6–7 **y-go(e.** (Cf. ago.)

c 1000 *Judith* 140 Oð hie glædmode ȝegan hæfdon to ðam weall gate. *c* 1200 Ormin 14226 þurrh þatt teȝȝre win wass gan. *c* 1200 *Trin. Coll. Hom.* 3 þe fireste tocume of ure louerd is gon. *c* 1205 Lay. 2064 þus is þis eit-lond i-gon [*c* 1275 hi-go] from honde to hond. *a* 1300 *Cursor M.* 5171 (Cott.) Thriti yere es siþen gain. *Ibid.* 17288 + 436 (Cott.) Intil a strang plas..all þe apostels wore goone. *Ibid.* 23833 (Gött.) It es gane mani rath. *c* 1300 *Harrow. Hell* 4 Jhesu wes to helle y-gan. *c* 1305 *Pilate* 116 in *E.E.P.* (1862) 114 If þu haddest hider igon. *c* 1340 *Cursor M.* 1917 (Fairf.) A twelfmonþe was go by this. *Ibid.* 5275 A dreme lange siþen I-gan. 1375 Barbour *Bruce* II. 80 Lettres ar gayn To the byschop. *c* 1375 *Sc. Leg. Saints, Margaret* 639 Mychty god, makare of al warldis, þat gayne are or cum sal. 1382 Wyclif *Rom.* Prol., Goende to Jerusalem. *c* 1386 Chaucer *Prol.* 286 A Clerk..That vn to logyk hadde longe ygo. —— *Reeve's T.* 158 [A northern speaker asks:] Whilk way is he geen. —— *Shipman's T.* 212 Vp to hir housbonde is this wyf ygon. 1399 Langl. *Rich. Redeles* II. 11 The gayes han y-gon. *c* 1400 A. Davy *Dreams* 38 It is more þan twelue moneþ gon. *c* 1440 *Partonope* 337 She was goo. *c* 1440 *Generydes* 55 The day was gonne. *c* 1450 *Cov. Myst.* (Shaks. Soc.) 206 Alle oure gode days than xulde sone be goe. *c* 1460 *Towneley Myst.* xviii. 218 This day is goyn nere ilka deyll. *a* 1529 Skelton *Epit. Dk. Bedford* 33 Wo, alas..for he is go. 1548 Udall *Erasm. Par.* Pref. 18 Where not many yeares goen. 1552 Abp. Hamilton *Catech.* (1884) 23, I haif nocht gaine efter Baalim. 1559 *Mirr. Mag., Jas. I* (Scot.) xiii. 7 So was he suer I goen to haue his pray. *c* 1560 A. Scott *Poems* (S.T.S.) x. 59 Evirilk greif is gane. 1579 Spenser *Sheph. Cal.* Nov. 76 The..floure..Is faded quite and into dust ygoe. 1601 J. Manningham in *Shaks. C. Praise* 45 A Citizen gaene soe farr in liking with him. 1647 H. More *Song of Soul* IV. v, If that one substance also were ygo. 1710 Prideaux *Orig. Tithes* ii. 65 *margin,* They will have Phineas to have gon this Expedition. 1869 Gibbon *R. Gray* v, She's gaen out to the grass.

†**b. went.** *Obs.* exc. *dial.* (See also etym. note s.v. wend *v.*)

1642 W. Sedgwicke *Zions Deliv.* (1643) Ep. Ded., A Judge that would have went right, if [etc.]. 1729 Switzer *Hydrost. & Hydraul.* 319 The Length of Time it [an engine] has went. 1749 Bp. Lavington *Enthusiasm* i. (1754) I. 25 Whether Mr. Wesley has not went to Bed since that time, others may know as well as himself. 1883 'Mark Twain' *Life on Mississippi* xliv. 450 The unpolished [Southerners] often use 'went' for 'gone'... 'He had n't ought to have went.' 1884 —— *Huck. Finn* xxviii. 287 I'll tell Miss Susan to..say you've went away for a few hours. 1886 F. T. Elworthy *W. Somerset Word-Bk.* 825 You never didn ought to a-went; for—You ought not to have gone. 1890 *Dialect Notes* I. 7 Mr. Emerson mentioned the principal parts *go, went, went* (*have went* for *have gone*).

B. Signification.

gen. An intransitive verb of motion, serving as the most general expression (I) for a movement viewed without regard to its point of departure or destination; (II) for a movement *away from* the speaker, or from the point at which he mentally places himself; and (III) for a movement *to* or *towards* a place which is neither in fact nor in thought that occupied by the speaker. The verb is thus on the whole co-extensive in meaning with the Latin *ire*; in the branches II and III it admits of being contrasted with come (= L. *venire*). Besides this general sense, it had formerly a special application to *walking* as distinguished from other modes of progression; possibly this may be the primitive sense, but only faint traces of it remain in current English. Like *come*, it is applied both to self-originated and to impressed movement, but the former application is felt to be the primary one.

I. Of movement, irrespective of the point of departure or destination.

†**1. a.** = To walk; to move or travel on one's feet (opposed to *creep, fly, ride, swim,* etc.); to move on foot at an ordinary pace (opposed to *run,* etc.). *to go alone*: to walk without support. *Obs.*

c 1000 *Ags. Gosp.* Matt. xi. 5 Blinde ȝeseoþ, healte gað. *c* 1200 [see A 3 a]. *a* 1300 *Cursor M.* 14370 Do crepels gan, þe blind haf sight. *Ibid.* 15392 Fra þan he ran him ilk fote, ne yode he noght þe [*Gött.* a] pas Til [etc.]. *c* 1386 Chaucer *Knt.'s T.* 493 That other wher him list may ryde or go. 1387 [see A 2 d α]. 1412-20 Lydg. *Chron. Troy* I. i, Men..Which on their fete upright gan to gon. *c* 1450 *St. Cuthbert* (Surtees) 1076 He was halt and myght not go. 1523 Fitzherb. *Husb.* §166 He..made..the lame to go. 1523 [see A 2 c α]. 1587 *Wills & Inv. N.C.* (Surtees 1860) 288 One stud mare..going now in Langshawes. *a* 1592 Greene *Jas. IV,* III. iii, Tut, go me thus, your cloake before your face. 1605 Shaks. *Lear* I. iv. 134 Ride more then thou goest. 1611 Beaum. & Fl. *Knt. Burn. Pestle* II. ii, Though I can scarcely go, I needs must run. 1628 Coke *On Litt.* 70 It may be that he..is languishing, so as he can neither goe nor ride. 1633 P. Fletcher *Purple Isl.* IX. xiii, But when he could not go, yet forward would he creep. 1661 Lovell *Hist. Anim. & Min.* Introd., These only amongst crustates swimme not, but goe. 1684 Bunyan *Pilgr.* II. (1862) 313, I have resolved to run when I can, to go when I cannot run, and to creep when I cannot go. 1751 R. Paltock *P. Wilkins* I. xviii. 179 A charming Child, able to go in his twelfth Month. 1768 Goldsm. *Good-n. Man* IV. Wks. (Globe) 632/1 I'm so frightened, I scarce know whether I sit, stand, or go. 1836 [see creep 1 b].

fig. 1707 Watts *Hymn,* 'Come Holy Spirit', Our souls can neither fly nor go To reach eternal joys.

b. *to go on, upon, the earth, the ground* (also simply): to live and move.

c 1385 Chaucer *L.G.W.* 1669 *Medea,* In his [Jason's] dayes nas ther noon y-founde So fals a lover going on the grounde. *c* 1420 *Chron. Vilod.* st. 598 As saffe as hole as he upoun urthe ȝede. 1500-20 Dunbar *Poems* xxviii. 22 Ȝe tailȝouris, with weilmaid clais Can mend the werst maid man that gais. 1579 Spenser *Sheph. Cal.* Nov. 39 The fayrest May she was that euer went.

c. With *adj., pres. pple.* or *adv.* indicating the manner of stepping or walking; *esp.* of a horse: *to*

go narrow, wide (see the adjs.); ***to go the wrong end before*** (see quot. 1737); ***to go above his ground*** = to step high.

a 1200 [see A 2 d α]. **a 1300** [see A 2 d β]. **1382** WYCLIF *Prov.* xxx. 29 Thre thingus ben, that weel gon, and the ferthe that goth welsumely. **1577** B. GOOGE *Heresbach's Husb.* II. (1586) 115 b, If he [a horse]..goeth wide, his pace will be the surer. **1681** *Lond. Gaz.* No. 1638/8 Stolen or strayed..a young Black Gelding..goes narrow behind. **1724** DE FOE *Mem. Cavalier* (1840) 73 My horse went very awkwardly and uneasy. **a 1732** T. BOSTON *Crook in Lot* (1805) 8 A slip of the foot may soon be made, which will make a man go halting all along after. **1735** *New Jersey Archives* (1894) XI. 422 Ran away..a Servant Man..He goes crooked. **1737** BRACKEN *Farriery Impr.* (1739) II. 40, I don't think our saying, such a Horse goes the wrong End before, altogether improper, when we speak it of a Horse that goes wide before, and near behind. **1791** 'G. GAMBADO' *Ann. Horsem.* (1809) 109 That a horse could not go too much above his ground. **1838** [see A 1 a].

2. a. To move or pass along, proceed, journey, travel (irrespective of the mode of progression). Said of persons and things.

c 825 [see A 3 a *pl.*]. **c 1000** ÆLFRIC *Gen.* iii. 14 God cwæð to þære næddran..þu gæst on þinum breoste. **13..** *E.E. Allit. P.* B. 931 And ay goande on your gate. **a 1300** *Cursor M.* 4803 Gas warli thoru vncuth land. **c 1400** MAUNDEV. (Roxb.) i. 4 Thurgh þe land of Hungary men gase to a cytee þat es called Chippron. **1426** AUDELAY *Poems* 7 The pore that goth be the way. **1483** *Cath. Angl.* 149 To Ga on mowntayns; *tran[s]alpinare.* **1577** B. GOOGE *Heresbach's Husb.* I. (1586) 21 b, The weedes..so thicke, as you can scarse see where the Coulter hath gone. **a 1586** SIDNEY *Arcadia* II. (1633) 154 And so she went, and she went, and never rested the evening, where she went in the morning, till [etc.]. **1608** [see A 1 a]. **1664** PEPYS *Diary* 31 Oct., The Duke of York..being now resolved to go in the Charles. **1667** *Ibid.* 13 June, At two hours' warning they did go by the coach into the country. **1837** DICKENS *Pickw.* v, Winkle, will you go on horseback? **1842** L. S. COSTELLO *Pilgr. Auvergne* I. 319 A boulevard too tempting to allow us to go through the arch. **1847** MARRYAT *Childr. N. Forest* v, We shan't have far to go ..the animal is done up.

b. with *adj.* or *adv.* indicating the speed or amount of vigour put forth: *lit.* and *fig.* ***go bet*** (see BET *adv.*[2]). ***to go like blazes*** (see BLAZE *sb.* 2 b). ***to go even*** (see EVEN *adv.* I. 2). ***to go full drive, full tilt*** (see the sbs.).

c 1340 *Cursor M.* 5191 (Trin.) Childer he seide go we stronge Into egipte þinke me longe. **c 1440** *Promp. Parv.* 202/2 Goo slowly, *lento.* **1583** HOLLYBAND *Campo di Fior* 307 How well that barke goeth with the saile. **1609** BIBLE (Douay) *2 Kings* ix. 20 It is the pace as it were the pace of Jehu the sonne of Namsi, for he goeth amayne. **a 1610** HEALEY *Theophrastus* (1636) 66 He goes strong with his witnesses. **1688** MIEGE *Gt. Fr. Dict.* II. s.v., To go fast or softly.. *aller vite ou bellement.* **1856** RUSKIN *Mod. Paint.* III. IV. xvii. §35 It does..a man..no harm to go slow. **1885** *Illustr. Lond. News* 23 May 539/2 You take my advice, go easy for a bit. **1893** *Sketch* 15 Feb. 178/1 The Government ..are going very strong, as the rowing-man says. **1897** FL. MARRYAT *Blood Vampire* xviii, We have been going a little too fast.

c. with adverbial accusative of the way pursued, the distance traversed, or the rate of speed. For ***to go the pace*** fig. (*colloq.* or *slang*), see PACE *sb.*

a 1300 *Cursor M.* 15392 (Cott.) Fra þan he ran him ilk fote, ne yode he noght þe pas. **c 1300** *Ibid.* 19076 (Laud) A grete pas to the tempyll he gos. **c 1340** *Ibid.* 14195 (Fairf.) Qua has to ga any way gode is to ga on liȝt of day. **c 1380** WYCLIF *Wks.* (1880) 32 No weddid man owiþ to leue his wife..& goo many hundred myles in drede of þeues and enemyes. **1430** [see A 2 b]. **1430–40** LYDG. *Bochas* I. (1554) 31 b, Toward him a great pace gan she goe. **c 1550** *Peebles to Play* vii, They had nocht gane half of the gait Quhen the madinis come upon thame. **1568** GRAFTON *Chron.* II. 250 Who had horses so charged with baggage, that they might scant go any great pace. **1607** TOPSELL *Four-f. Beasts* (1658) 210 The Hare.. having gone so much ground as she did before..betaketh her to rest the second time. **1677** MIEGE *Eng.-Fr. Dict.* s.v., To go three miles in an hour. **1688** BUNYAN *Heavenly Footman* (1886) 155 Usually those by-paths are most beaten, most travellers go those ways. **1841** *Fraser's Mag.* XXIII. 15 After 'going the pace' for some years. **1887** G. R. SIMS *Mary Jane's Mem.* 49 Oh, the nice cakes she made..I'd go miles for one now.

d. with cognate obj., as ***to go (the) circuit, a cruise, errand, journey, pilgrimage, progress, a voyage.*** Occas. in *indirect pass.*

1526 [see A 2 d α]. **1638** SIR T. HERBERT *Trav.* (ed. 2) 38 Little boyes..who are ready..to runne, go arrands or the like. **1642** W. PRICE *Serm.* 4 Men use to goe (saith Seneca) not the way that should be gone, but that way which is most gone. **1669** LADY CHAWORTH in *12th Rep. Hist. MSS. Comm.* App. v. 12 They talk heere as if the King would goe a northerne progresse this summer. **1671** CHARENTE *Let. Customs* 15 This Voyage is only gone in the night time. **c 1710** C. FIENNES *Diary* (1888) 216 Had I known yᵉ Danger before, I should not have been very willing to have gone it [the passage]. **1727** DE FOE *Syst. Magic* I. iii. (1840) 82 As Elijah said to the priests of Baal, he might be busy, or asleep, or gone a journey. **1825** *New Monthly Mag.* XVI. 130 Pomposo still goes the circuit. **1880** FOWLER *Locke* vii. 110 Locke..entreats him not to go circuit. **1883** BLACK *Yolande* III. x. 190 He wants me to go a cruise with him.

†**e.** Hence *occas.* in distinctly *transitive* use: To go through (a tract of country); to go over (a river). Also *fig.*, to go through (a course of study).

1483 CAXTON *Gold. Leg.* 47 b/1 With my staf I have goon this ryver of Jordan. **1579** SPENSER *Sheph. Cal.* Dec. 23, I went the wastefull woodes and forest wyde. **1683** WOOD *Life* 28 Sept. (O.H.S.), When the elaboratorie was quite finisht certaine scholars went a course of chimistrie.

3. *spec.* In *Hunting* language, the technical term for 'to ride' (to hounds).

1841 *Fraser's Mag.* XXIII. 16 A first-flight Meltonian is not said to ride well, but to go well, after hounds. **1884** H. SMART *Post to finish* xxx. 219 There would be far too many there who had seen Gerald Rockingham 'go' with the York and Ainstey.

4. a. To take a specified course (in either a physical or a moral sense), which is often expressed by an advb. acc. Said of persons and things.

Beowulf [see A 2 c α]. **a 1225** [see A 1 b]. **a 1300** *Cursor M.* 11736 We wil þe wai ga be þe se. **c 1380** *Antecrist* in Todd *Three Treat. Wyclif* (1851) 152 þei gon not þe streiȝt weie. **1555** in Strype *Eccl. Mem.* III. App. xliv. 125 Alas! how should the people of God go the right way. **1599** PORTER *Angry Wom. Abingt.* (Percy Soc.) 21 Nay, turne it this way, then the bowle goes true. **1611** SHAKS. *Wint. T.* III. ii. 218 How ere the businesse goes, you haue made fault I' the boldnesse of your speech. **1660** *Trial Regic.* 23 If you go otherwise..it will be, as if you pleaded not at all. **1662** STILLINGFL. *Orig. Sacr.* I. iii. §10 Vossius goes another way to work. **1727** BOYER *Fr. Dict.* s.v., You go the wrong way to work, *Vous vous y prenez mal.* **1816** SCOTT *Antiq.* vi, They didna gang the road by the turnpike,..they gaed by the sands. **1818** CRUISE *Digest* (ed. 2) V. 498 Now if the use would have gone this way before the statute, it would still go the same way since the statute. **1861** HUGHES *Tom Brown at Oxf.* ii, An exhortation to..go outside of the barge which was coming up. **1880** M. MACKENZIE *Dis. Throat & Nose* I. 386 It is from food 'going the wrong way'. **1888** *Sat. Rev.* 5 Aug. 136/1 The man who goes straight in spite of temptation. **1895** MARIE CORELLI *Sorrows Satan* xxix. (1897) 353 She will never go my way,—nor, I fear, shall I ever go hers.

b. *Naut.* ***as you go! as she goes*** = on the same course.

1692 *Capt. Smith's Seaman's Gram.* I. xvi. 76 To keep her upon the *same Point,* they use, *Steddy,* or *as you go.* **1898** *Pall Mall Mag.* Jan. 122 'Keep her [the ship] as she goes', I said. 'As she goes, sir', the man at the wheel..said.

c. Of a line, etc.: To have its course, 'run' (in a certain direction).

1889 *Eng. Illustr. Mag.* Dec. 258 On either side went a range of berths. *Mod.* The boundary here goes parallel with the river.

d. in connexion with various adverbs, as *acrook, afield, agly, amiss, aside, astern, astray, at large, contrary, counter, evil, ill,* †*miss, right, well, wrong*: see the advs.

1393 LANGL. *P. Pl.* C. XXIII. 192 And gyuede me with goutes, ich may nat go at large. **c 1440** *Promp. Parv.* 202/2 Goo wronge, *devio, deliro.* **1871** FREEMAN *Norm. Conq.* (1876) IV. xviii. 113 Most likely the reckonings of the men of Kent did not go so far afield. **1873** H. SPENCER *Stud. Sociol.* xiv. 337 There are more ways of going wrong than of going right. **1879** M. J. GUEST *Lect. Eng. Hist.* xlvii. 470 James continued to go contrary to the wishes of his people. **1880** MRS. LYNN LINTON *Rebel of Family* II. ix, All the well-laid schemes had gone agley.

5. a. Of persons: To be guided *by*; to act in dependence *on* or *upon, according to,* in accordance or harmony *with.* Also in *indirect pass.* Frequent in phrases, ***to go with the tide*** or ***the times.***

1485 CAXTON *Chas. Gt.* (1881) 230 The whyche..went by hys commaundement holyly. **a 1631** DONNE *Lett.* (1651) 50, I had the same desires, when I went with the tyde. **1662** STILLINGFL. *Orig. Sacr.* III. i. §17 When we go according to them [our imaginations], it is impossible to apprehend things as our reason tells us they are. **1672** VILLIERS (Dk. Buckhm.) *Rehearsal* III. i. (Arb.) 73 That's the measure I go by. **1688** MIEGE *Gt. Fr. Dict.* II. s.v., To go according to the Times. **1692** BENTLEY *Boyle Lect.* viii. (1724) 320 The reasons that they went upon were very specious and probable. **1815** W. H. IRELAND *Scribbleomania* 190 The Somerset-house society..is perhaps the best criterion to go by. **1840** CARLYLE *Heroes* ii. (1858) 233 The Koran..is admitted everywhere as the standard of all law and all practice; the thing to be gone-upon in speculation and life. **1841** *Fraser's Mag.* XXIII. 15 The politician goes with his party, whether he approves of the measure or not. **1879** 'CAVENDISH' *Card Ess.*, etc. 109 Had he gone on the chances, he would have won. *Ibid.* 167 Refer the case to the best judge in the room, and go by his decision. **1885** DORA RUSSELL *Gold. Hinges* II. xiii. 194 It's the turn the world's taken, and we must go with the times. **1889** DOYLE *Micah Clarke* xxii. 218 It is a good rule to go upon. **1891** *Athenæum* 14 Mar. 342/2 The British Government had only vague information on which to go.

b. Of things: To be apportioned, determined, or regulated *by*; †to be arranged *according to*; to proceed *upon* (an idea, supposition).

1590 H. SMITH *Serm.* (1866) I. 289 Neither virtue nor vice goeth by age. **1594** HOOKER *Eccl. Pol.* I. x. §9 Laws..must make common smaller offices to go by lot. **1599** SHAKS. *Much Ado* III. i. 105 Louing goes by haps. **1627** W. BEDELL in *Lett. Lit. Men* (Camden) 136 Album Registrum Vestiarii, which went according to the letters of the alphabet. **1729** BUTLER *Serm., Hum. Nat.* ii, Now all this licentious talk entirely goes upon a supposition. **1777** PRIESTLEY *Matt. & Spir.* (1782) I. VII. 82 The Cartesian hypothesis..goes upon the idea that the essence of mind is thought. **1879** MISS YONGE *Cameos* Ser. IV. viii. 96 Nothing in this strange reign ever went by ordinary rules of justice or probability. **1881** MRS. C. PRAED *Policy & P.* I. ix. 188 Things go by contraries out here. **1890** *Leisure Hour* Jan. 165/2 A vivid picture is drawn of a world where all went by chance. **1892** *Eng. Illustr. Mag.* IX. 908 Promotion goes solely by length of service.

6. With complementary adj. or equivalent phrase: To be habitually in a specified condition, esp. with regard to attire or circumstances affecting personal comfort. Now chiefly with reference to conditions implying neglect, privation, or disadvantage; cf. *to go without* (sense 69). *to go short* (see SHORT).

c 1000 *Ags. Gosp.* Luke xx. 46 Warniað wið þa boceras ða þe wyllað on ȝeȝyrlum gan. **1398** TREVISA *Barth. De P.R.* XVII. liii. (1495) 634 They yede crownyd wyth iuy that serued in the temple of Bachus. **c 1460** *Towneley Myst.* ii. 141 Then myght I go with a ryffen hood. **1509** [see GAY *a.* 4]. **c 1511** *1st Eng. Bk. Amer.* (Arb.) Introd. 27 This people goeth all naked. **1535** COVERDALE *Gen.* xv. 2, I go childles [so **1611**]. **1604** [see GAY *a.* 4]. **1616** R. C. *Times' Whistle* II. 749, I see..How basely in apparrell he doth goe. **1618** MYNSHUL *Ess. Prison, Creditors* 12 If another weare thy coate, and thou goest cold, thou maist plucke it from his shoulders. **1634** SIR T. HERBERT *Trav.* 19 Both sexe goe naked. **1668** DRYDEN *Even. Love* IV. i. Wks. 1883 III. 322 Piquing at each other, who shall go the best dressed. **1688** MIEGE *Gt. Fr. Dict.* II. s.v., He has gone a great while under an ill Report. **1738** SWIFT *Pol. Conversat.* 146 Why, he us'd to go very fine, when he was here in Town. **1845** STEPHEN *Comm. Laws Eng.* (1874) I. 150 There is an antient enactment against going armed. **1878** *Scribner's Mag.* XV. 788/2 The men drink; the children go in rags. **1888** G. MACDONALD *Elect Lady* xvi. 144 Some girls miser their clothes, and never go decent. **1890** *Temple Bar* June 192 Twenty pounds could be saved by going on short commons. **1891** *Ibid.* Dec. 481 Protestants went in mortal fear. **1897** J. C. LEES *Hist. Inverness* xvi. 265 It [the land] was allowed to go waste till [etc.].

7. Of a female: To pass (a specified period) in gestation: to be pregnant. More fully, ***to go with calf, child*** (see CHILD *sb.* 17), ***foal, young.*** Now usu. in phr. (***to be***) (a specified period) ***gone***: to have been pregnant for that amount of time.

c 1200 [see A 3 a *sing.*]. **c 1460** [see A 2 b]. **1577** B. GOOGE *Heresbach's Husb.* II. 117 They [Mares] go with foale aleuen monthes, and fole in the twelfth. **1601** HOLLAND *Pliny.* II. 220 Bitches..goe with young threescore daies. **c 1645** HOWELL *Lett.* (1650) I. §3. xxiv. 76 The Queen is big, and hath not many days to go. **1661** LOVELL *Hist. Anim. & Min.* Introd., The woolf goeth a month or forty daies. **1684** OTWAY *Atheist* IV. (1735) 79 The Drab is full gone with Bastard. **1747** *Gentl. Mag.* 106 The queen is pray'd for in the churches, being several months gone with child. **1748** SMOLLETT *Rod. Rand.* II. xlvi. 107, I am now four months gone with child by him. **1795** *Nat. Hist.* in *Ann. Reg.* 84* The female goes two months, and then brings forth two young ones. **1841** *Fraser's Mag.* XXIII. 15 The mother of man is said to *go* nine months in producing him. **1845** *Jrnl. R. Agric. Soc.* V. II. 518 A mare goes somewhere about eleven months with young. **1900** *Daily Express* 19 June 4/5 Vincent was turned out into Commissioner-street with Mrs. Vincent seven months gone. **1931** W. HOLTBY *Poor Caroline* iv. 133 Brought her to the Home, four months gone, and won't be fifteen till next March. **1935** N. MITCHISON *We have been Warned* IV. 407 My mother found she was six months gone. **1955** [see CATCH *v.* 9 b].

8. To be moving.

a. Of persons, *esp.* in the sentry's challenge ***who goes? who goes there?***

1593 SHAKS. *3 Hen. VI,* IV. iii. 26 Who goes there? **1611** B. JONSON *Catiline* IV. vii, Stand, who goes there? **1805** T. DIBDIN *Eng. Fleet* III. ii. Duet, 'Who goes there? stranger —quickly tell.' **1847** TENNYSON *Princess* v. 3 'Stand, who goes?' 'Two from the palace.' **1883** STEVENSON *Treas. Isl.* IV. xx, Who goes? Stand, or we fire.

b. Of the sea (with defining word): To have or be in a specified kind of motion. Cf. RUN *v.*

a 1611 BEAUM. & FL. *Maid's Trag.* I. ii, The sea goes hie, Boreas has rais'd a storme. **1627** CAPT. SMITH *Seaman's Gram.* xiii. 60 The Sea goes too high to boord her. **1633** T. JAMES *Voy.* 36 There went a..great Surfe. The Sea still went very loftie. **1719** DE FOE *Crusoe* I. i. (1840) 7 The sea went very high.

c. Of a piece of mechanism: To be set or kept in motion; to act, work. †Const. *with.* See also GOING *vbl. sb.* 8.

1680 MOXON *Mech. Exerc.* I. 235 The Common Lathe that goes either with the Treddle Wheel, or the great Wheel. **1686** J. SMITH *Nat. Time* 33 A short Pendulum that goes well when clean, shall go faster than the mean time when foul. **1712** J. JAMES tr. *Le Blond's Gardening* 81 A Knee-Joint..having a Screw to it, which makes the Joint go stiffer, or slacker, at Pleasure. *Ibid.* 192 Mills that go with the Help of the Wind or Water. **1739** ELLICOTT in *Phil. Trans.* XLI. 132 In a few Minutes it described an Arch of two Degrees, and the Clock went. **1823** *New Monthly Mag.* IX. 314/1 A church clock may be made to go eight days without winding. **1878** *Scribner's Mag.* XV. 868/1 Everything will have to go like clockwork. **1890** *Chamb. Jrnl.* 12 July 439/2 [The] church clock has not gone for twenty years.

transf. and *fig.* **1565** COOPER *Thesaurus, Arteriæ micant,* the pulses beate or goe. **1599** [see GNOMON 1 c]. **1887** LOWELL *Democr.* 55 Those who believe that democracy.. will go of itself. **1889** *Cornh. Mag.* Dec. 581 She felt her heart 'go' in a most unusual manner. *Mod. colloq.* Her tongue goes nineteen to the dozen.

d. *esp.* Of a watch or clock (with defining word or phr.): To maintain a (specified) action, to keep (good or bad) time. Also *transf.*

1588 SHAKS. *L.L.L.* III. i. 194 Neuer going a right, being a Watch: But being watcht, that it may still goe right. **1639** FULLER *Holy War* II. xlvi. (1640) 107 These curious observations (like over-small watches) not one of a hundred goeth true. **1710** STEELE *Tatler* No. 181 ¶1 When we wind up a Clock that is out of Order, to make it go well for the future. **1819** BYRON *Juan* I xvii, Even her minutest motions went as well As those of the best time-piece made by Harrison.

9. With reference to sound.

a. Of a musical instrument (esp. an organ), a bell: To sound. Of a gun: To be fired.

1503 HAWES *Examp. Virt.* xiii. st. 16 The organs went and the bellys dyd rynge. **1584** R. SCOT *Discov. Witchcr.* XV. xxiv. 439 To sing when the organs go. **1622** BACON *Holy War* Wks. 1827 VII. 129 This pope is decrepit, and the bell goeth for him. **1667–8** PEPYS *Diary* 20 Jan., To advise about the making of a flageolet to go low and soft. **1825** *New*

Monthly Mag. XIV. 495 A bell shall go for hours telling us that Mr. Ching is dead. **1841** *Fraser's Mag.* XXIII. 16 The bell goes for church, as also for dinner. **1880** *Daily Tel.* 7 Sept., First gun goes to the boat ahead.

b. Of a clock (with numeral as cognate obj.): To strike (the hour). Said also of the hour.

1709 PRIOR *Hans Carvel* 113 The Chimes went Twelve: the Guests withdrew. **1721** D'URFEY *New Opera's* 241 The Clock, said I, just Twelve has gone. **1793** MRS. PARSONS *Castle Wolfenbach* I. 1 The clock from the old castle had just gone eight. **1859** GEO. ELIOT *A. Bede* II. xviii, Don't you know church begins at two, and it's gone half after one a'ready? **1887** WESTALL *Capt. Trafalgar* i. 15 The clock on the mantel-piece went eight. **1889** STEVENSON *Master of B.* v. 133 Twelve was already gone some time upon the clock.

10. In senses 8 and 9, with imitative interjections or verb-stems used adverbially, e.g. ***to go bang, clatter, cluck, crack, crash, patter, smash, snap, tang, whirr***, etc.

1791 COWPER *Retired Cat* 79 His noble heart went pit-a-pat. **1812** H. & J. SMITH *Rej. Addr., Theatre* 25 Tang goes the harpsichord. **1818** MOORE *Fudge Fam. Paris* viii. 2 My stays..I knew would go smash with me one of these days. **1887** BARING-GOULD *Gaverocks* II. xxxiv. 200 Clatter, clatter, went the horses' hoofs. **1889** MRS. E. KENNARD *Landing a Prize* II. xii. 211 Something seemed to go snap within me. *Ibid.* III. ii. 30 Whirr went the reel. **1890** MRS. HUNGERFORD *Life's Remorse* III. xi. 127 Patter, patter, goes the rain. **1891** *Daily News* 24 Oct. 5/3 A tyre..that will [not] go pop all of a sudden. **1892** *Sat. Rev.* 2 July 10/2 Crack went the mast.

11. a. Of time, a space of time: To pass, elapse. (For special uses of *going* and *gone* in this sense, see V.)

a **1300** *Cursor M.* 11281 Ten dais on þe monet was gan. *c* **1385** CHAUCER *L.G.W.* 427 He made also, goon ys a grete while, Origenes upon the Maadeleyne. *c* **1400** MAUNDEV. (Roxb.) xxiv. 110 It es noȝt ȝit gane viii^xx ȝere sen [etc.]. *c* **1470** HENRY *Wallace* I. 271 This passit our, quhill diuers dayis war gane. **1548** HALL *Chron., Edw. IV*, 240 b, Which yere with foure more were passed and gone. **1602** MARSTON *Ant. & Mel.* III. Wks. 1856 I. 33 How goes the time? **1782** COWPER *Convers.* 382 'Yes Ma'am', and 'No Ma'am', uttered softly, show Every five minutes how the minutes go. **1835** MRS. CARLYLE *Lett.* I. 20 One week and half of another is already gone. **1889** MRS. E. KENNARD *Landing a Prize* I. viii. 147 The afternoon went pleasantly enough.

†**b.** Of an event, etc.: To pass, happen, take place. *Obs.*

c **1200**, *c* **1340** [see A 8 a]. **1609** in *Digby Myst.* (1882) p. xxiii, When ye whitson playes weare played, then ye showe at midsomer wente not.

12. a. Of coin, banknotes: To pass from hand to hand, to circulate; to be accepted or pass current *at* a certain value (cf. 24). ***to go (for) current*** (see CURRENT *a.* 8).

c **1400** MAUNDEV. (Roxb.) xxv. 117 Þis monee..gase thurgh all þe Grete Caan landes. **1503** *Act 19 Hen. VII*, c. 5 The Coins of a Sovereign [etc.]..shall go and be current in Payment, through all this his Realm. **1547** BOORDE *Introd. Knowl.* xviii. (1870) 169 All maner of gold goth there. **1663** PEPYS *Diary* 19 May, Groats..as good and better than those that commonly go. **1669** DRYDEN *Tyrannic Love* v. i. Wks. 1883 III. 460 Love is the only coin in heaven will go. **1688** MIEGE *Gt. Fr. Dict.* II. s.v., This half Crown will never go, 'tis brass. **1696** G. HARRIS in *Blackmore's Hist. Conspiracy* (1723) 122, Guineas then going at thirty Shillings apiece. **1813** *Sporting Mag.* XLI. 242 One of the shillings he was afraid, would not go. **1872** *Punch* 7 Sept. 101/2 Bank-notes, she supposes, will go everywhere.

†**b.** Of a ransom: To be accepted. *Obs.*

c **1175** *Lamb. Hom.* 9 Nouþer gold ne seoluer ne moste gan for þe. *a* **1300** *Cursor M.* 4494 Bot sal it wit-in thre dais be, It sal na raunsun ga for þe.

13. a. Of a report, tale, etc.: To pass from mouth to mouth, be current. Const. *of*, †*on*, †*upon*. Phr. ***the report (tale, story), goes that*** etc.; ***as the story goes***.

1542 [see GLEE *sb.* 1 β]. **1548** HALL *Chron., Hen. VII*, 5 b, The fame went and many menne surely supposed kyng Edwardes chyldren not to be dead. **1623** LISLE *Ælfric on O. & N. Test.* Ded., He of whom that ancient tale hath gon. *a* **1633** AUSTIN *Medit.* (1635) 192 Something it is to haue a Fame goe on a Man. **1665** BOYLE *Occas. Refl.* v. vi. (1842) 317, I wonder not at the story that goes of a Grand Signior. *a* **1715** BURNET *Own Time* (1823) I. 428 To try the truth of these scandalous reports that went upon the clergy. **1745** W. HARRIS in *Priv. Lett. Ld. Malmesbury* I. 4 Now the story goes that he [the young Pretender] is in the Highlands. **1868** FREEMAN *Norm. Conq.* (1876) II. viii. 187 As the story goes.

†**b.** Of a health, toast: To be passed round.

1698 WANLEY in *Lett. Lit. Men* (Camden) 257 Having dined with Madame Isted to day, where your health went over and over.

14. a. To be known *by* (a name or title). ***to go by*** or ***under the name*** or ***title of***: to be known as; also (of a literary composition), to be ascribed to.

1599 SHAKS. *Much Ado* II. i. 211 The Princes foole!.. It may be I goe vnder that title, because I am merrie. **1630** W. T. *Justif. Relig. now Professed* iii. 28 The Liturgies that go vnder the name of Basil. **1662** STILLINGFL. *Orig. Sacr.* I. iv. §3 He that goes under the name of Orpheus. **1687** BURNET *Contin. Reply Varillas* 12 That Book that goes by the name of P. Martyr's Common Places. **1711** ADDISON *Spect.* No. 169 ¶2 That Disposition of Mind which in our Language goes under the Title of Good-nature. **1756** P. BROWNE *Jamaica* 254 Wax, which..goes by the name of Terra Orellana. **1849** MACAULAY *Hist. Eng.* ii. I. 244 *note*, The 'Character of a Trimmer'..went under the name of his kinsman, Sir William Coventry. *a* **1859** *Ibid.* xxiii. (1861) V. 92 The monk who..sometimes went by the alias of Johnson. **1879** M. J. GUEST *Lect. Hist. Eng.* xxxv. 356 Shakespeare did not write that play, though it generally goes under his name.

†**b.** with *adj.* as complement: To pass for, to be currently accounted. *Obs.*

1663 *Flagellum, or O. Cromwell* (ed. 2) 3 A Gentleman who went no lesse in esteem..then any of his Ancestors. **1670** COTTON *Espernon* I. III. 130 Had he apply'd himself wholly to his Book, [he] might have gone equal to the most famous Church-men of this latter age.

15. To have ordinarily a certain degree or range of value, amount, excellence, etc. ***as men, things***, etc. ***go***: judging by the standard commonly attained.

1545 BRINKLOW *Compl.* 15 b, Whan rentys went at a moch lower pryce. **1552** *Act 5 & 6 Edw. VI*, c. 14 §8 As the Price of Corn then goeth in the said Market or Fair. *a* **1604** CHURCHYARD in *Chips* (1817) 19 Some friends I found, as friends do go. **1639** CHAPMAN & SHIRLEY *Ball* IV. iii, *Col.* And are you sure he's honest? *Lac.* As lords go now a-days that are in fashion. **1719** DE FOE *Crusoe* II. xiv. (1840) 295 They call it fortified, and so it is, as fortifications go there. *a* **1735** ARBUTHNOT (J.), I think, as the world goes, he was a good sort of man enough. **1841** *Fraser's Mag.* XXIII. 16 'How goes it, Joe?' 'Pretty well, as times go.' **1872** BLACK *Adv. Phaeton* xxii. 314 It was a good enough luncheon, as hotels go. **1880** G. R. SIMS *Dagonet Ball., Sal Grogan* iii, A decent chap was her father, as folks in alleys go.

16. Of a document, language, etc.: To have a specified tenor, to run.

1605 SHAKS. *Macb.* I. iii. 87 You shall be King. And Thane of Cawdor too: went it not so? **1631** WEEVER *Anc. Funeral Mon.* 288 Thus goes the Bull. **1682** N.O. *Boileau's Lutrin* IV. 314 The General cry went still, Ay! one and all! Let the Proud Pulpit, Let the Pulpit fall! **1685** BAXTER *Paraphr. N.T., Matt.* i. 10 In a very ancient Hebrew Copy of the Gospel, this verse goeth (and Eliakim begat Abner [etc.]). **1852** DICKENS *Bleak Ho.* xlv, Those who are put in authority over me (as the catechism goes).

17. Of verses: To glide along rhythmically. Cf. FLOW *v.* 4. Of a song: To admit of being sung; also, to follow the measure of, to adapt itself *to* (a tune).

1589 PUTTENHAM *Eng. Poesie* I. vii. (Arb.) 28 When they could make their verses goe all in ryme. **1599** SHAKS. *Much Ado* III. iv. 44 Claps into Light a loue, (that goes without a burden). **1611** —— *Wint. T.* IV. iv. 295 This is a passing merry one, and goes to the tune of two maids wooing a man. **1702** STEELE *Funeral* II. iii, I con'd this Song before I came in, and find t'will go to an excellent Air of Old Mr. Laws's. **1879** 'ANNIE THOMAS' *Lond. Season* II. 79 They [verses] 'go' easily enough. **1882** STEVENSON *Fam. Stud.* 289 The lines go with a lilt. **1892** *Harper's Mag.* June 78/1 The verses seem to go of themselves.

18. a. Of a series of events, etc.: To have a specified (favourable or unfavourable) course or issue; to turn out (well or ill). Const. *with*, (†*for*). Often with subject *it* or *things*. See also HARD *adv.* 2 c.

c **1489** CAXTON *Blanchardyn* xxvii. 102 He vnderstode.. that the thynge wente euyll for hym. *a* **1533** LD. BERNERS *Huon* lxvi. 229 Gerames..parceyued anone that the mater was lyke to go euyll. **1535** COVERDALE *Deut.* v. 16 That it maye go well with the in the londe, which the Lorde thy God shall geue the. **1594** SHAKS. *Rich. III*, III. ii. 98 How goes the World with thee? **1625** BURGES *Pers. Tithes* 36 We know how it went with Israel when there was no King among them. **1663-4** PEPYS *Diary* 2 Mar., He believes that things will go very high against the Chancellor. **1711** STEELE *Spect.* No. 49 ¶6 When Eubulus seems to intimate that Things go well. **1764** REID *Let.* Wks. I. 40/2 After I have given you so full an account of my own state, spiritual and temporal, how goes it with you? **1820** *Examiner* No. 627. 249/2 His partizans seeing how things were going. **1872** S. BUTLER *Erewhon* ix. 73 It would have gone hardly with him. **1885** MRS. LYNN LINTON *C. Kirkland* III. vii. 241 All went merry as a wedding-bell. **1889** 'B. W. D.' & 'CAVENDISH' *Whist w. & without Perception* 46 The hand went so strangely that I couldn't possibly tell.

b. Of a contest, war, also a vote, an election: To issue, or result in some specified manner. Said also of a constituency in respect of its vote, or of a politician in respect of his decision to support one side or the other; *colloq.* often with an adjectival complement.

1597 SHAKS. *Lover's Compl.* 113 On this side the verdict went. **1597** BACON *Col. Good & Evil* (Arb.) 140 So in many Armies, if the matter should be tryed by duell betweene two Champions, the victory should go on one side, and yet if it be tried by the grosse, it would go of the other side. **1610** in *Crt. & Times Jas. I* (1848) I. 120 The greatest voice goeth for my Lord of Southampton. **1682** DRYDEN *Medal* Ep. Whigs A 3 b, When a Vote of the House of Commons goes on your side. **1712** ARBUTHNOT *John Bull* IV. vii. (Arb.) 653 Sometimes they were like to pull John over: then it went, all of a sudden, again on John's side. **1781** *Hist. Eur.* in *Ann. Reg.* 142/1 The elections went much in favour of the court. **1849** *Tait's Mag.* XVI. 94/1 The war..went favourably to the Cavaliers. **1887** PROCTOR *Americanisms* in *Knowledge* Dec. 28 s.v., A State is said to *go* Democratic, or to *go* Republican, when it votes for one or the other cause after being for a time doubtful, or on the other side. **1889** *Sat. Rev.* 23 Nov. 589/2 Marlborough was by no means unlikely to have gone Jacobite after all. **1890** *Ibid.* 22 Feb. 213/2 The constituency has alternately 'gone' Gladstonian and Tory. **1890** T. F. TOUT *Hist. Eng.* 52 A general election went decidedly against him.

c. To take its course; esp. in phrase ***to let (judgement***, etc.) ***go by default***.

1820 *Examiner* No. 622. 171/1 The defendant had let judgement go by default. **1890** *Sat. Rev.* 18 Oct. 444/1 The corn-porters' case has practically gone by default. **1892** *Boston* (Mass.) *Jrnl.* 5 Nov. 12/7 The Tillmanites will..let the election go by default.

d. ***what has gone of* —— *?, what is gone with* —— *?*** = 'What has become of —— ?' or 'What is the matter with —— ?' (Cf. COME *v.* 43 b.)

1771 MRS. J. HARRIS in *Lett. 1st Earl Malmesbury* (1870) I. 235 He started and asked what was gone of all the company, and begged to be conducted to them. **1803** S. PEGGE *Anecd. Eng. Lang.* 239 The London expression of enquiry after any body is 'What is gone with such a one?' **1814** LAMB *Lett.* (1837) I. 332 What has gone of..M—— and his gos-lettuces? **1865** DICKENS *Mut. Fr.* I. vi, What's gone with that boy? **1875** WHYTE MELVILLE *Katerfelto* xxx. (1876) 339 Nobody in Porlock ever knew what was gone with him. **1882** B. HARTE *Flip* v, What's gone with ye?

19. a. Of a performance, ceremony, etc.: To proceed in a specified manner with regard to degree of success; to be gone through *well*, *badly*, etc.

1665-6 PEPYS *Diary* 23 Feb., Teaching her my song of 'Beauty retire', which she sings and makes go most rarely. **1745** CHESTERF. *Lett.* (1792) I. ciii. 284 He tells me that your Greek grammar goes pretty well. **1890** *Sat. Rev.* 20 Dec. 709/2 The *Adelphi* never seems to us to go quite so well as the *Andria*. **1892** *Eng. Illustr. Mag.* IX. 449 The annual dinner..never goes better than when he is in the chair.

b. To be successful, meet with applause or support. (Cf. *go down*, 80 g.) ***to go big***: to be a big success, have a large sale (cf. 89 h); *slang* (orig. *U.S.*).

1742 FIELDING *J. Andrews* II. xvii, You must not tip us the Traveller; it won't go here. **1866** *Public Opinion* 13 Jan. 51/1 His London street-railway scheme didn't go. **1891** E. PHILLPOTTS *Folly & Fresh Air* xii. 192 He..always found a banjo to 'go' better than anything. **1892** H. LE CARON 25 *Y. Secret Service* (1893) 132 The paper..caught the public fancy and 'went' amazingly. **1893** *Sketch* 15 Feb. 170/1 It became evident from an early point in the play that it would 'go'. **1893** *Daily News* 26 June 2/5 If only the manufactured iron trade can be got to 'go', then there is every probability of the revival being sustained. **1903** ADE *People you Know* 88, I done that with a Piece called 'A Boiled Dinner', and it always went big. **1930** *Publishers' Circular* 22 Feb. 186 We have reason to believe that *The Miracle of Peille*..will go big. **1936** WODEHOUSE *Laughing Gas* xxi. 231 The nosegay didn't seem to go very big. I was not feeling strong enough to pick it up, but I shoved it forward with my foot.

c. *spec.* Of a route, etc., in Mountaineering: to be usable.

1883 W. S. GREEN *High Alps of N.Z.* xiv. 232 The route to the northern ridges of the peak..would not 'go'. **1937** H. W. TILMAN *Ascent of Nanda Devi* vi. 52, I wanted to have a look at the difficult part of the gorge to see if the route would still 'go'. **1956** C. EVANS *On Climbing* vii. 112 It is important, as on rocks, to cultivate an eye for what will 'go' and what will not, so that no time is wasted.

d. To be acceptable or permitted; esp. in phr. ***anything*** (or ***everything***) ***goes***. *colloq.*

1879 G. MEREDITH *Egoist* II. i. 17 Everything goes on the stage, since it's only the laugh we want on the brink of the action. **1887** *Lantern* (New Orleans) 19 Feb. 5/1 As everything goes..I'll pass it by with never a word to say. **1891** *Harper's Mag.* Dec. 104/2 Any other night goes, but not this night. **1892** KIPLING *Many Invent.* (1893) 168 Remember, everything goes in the States, from a trouser-button to a double-eagle. **1921** *Ladies' Home Jrnl.* June 80/3 One of the few real 'movie' fortunes has been made by a man who..has constantly exploited the vicious theory that 'anything goes in fun'. **1934** COLE PORTER (*show- and song-title*) Anything goes. **1958** M. ALLINGHAM *Hide my Eyes* 191 Anything goes if it's done by someone you're fond of. **1959** *Listener* 15 Jan. 113/1 In a brawl, they're deadly. Anything goes—spurs, hobble chains, the lot. **1960** *Sunday Express* 12 June 14/3 In the evening anything goes..from Baby Doll frills to matador pants and a billowing overskirt.

e. To be accepted or carried into effect; to have authority or effectiveness; to be valid; to be obeyed without question; esp. in phr. ***what I say goes***. *colloq.* (orig. *U.S.*).

1891 *Century Mag.* Dec. 190/1 'Can you fix it?'.. 'I guess what I say to Jim goes,' she said. **1901** MERWIN & WEBSTER *Calumet 'K'* 62 My only order was, 'Clear the road—and be damn quick about it.' What I said went. **1931** *Punch* 18 Mar. 286/3 An emergency Cabinet of five..with supreme emergency powers..subject of course to full democratic control. But what I say goes. **1949** G. B. SHAW *Buoyant Billions* III. 31 He makes so much money that whatever he says, goes.

¶**20.** ***that goes without saying*** = 'that is a matter of course'; transl. of F. *cela va sans dire*.

1878 *Scribner's Mag.* XVI. 397/2 That goes without saying. **1897** *Literature* 27 Nov. 185/2 It goes without saying that the books are not ordinary ones.

II. Uses in which movement *from* a place is the primary notion.

21. a. To move away, depart, leave a place. Const. *from*, †*of*. See also *go away* (75 below).

c **1000** *Ags. Gosp.* John xiv. 31 Arisað, uton gan heonon. *a* **1225** [see A 2 a]. *a* **1300** [see A 1 a]. *c* **1300** *Beket* 1114 in *S.E. Leg.* (1887) 138 Fram Norehamptone þar he eode for holi churche to fiȝte. *c* **1320** *Sir Tristr.* 331 Rohand toke leue to ga His sones he cleped oway. *c* **1325** *Cursor M.* App. II. 730 Off fyue þousand was þer none, that myȝt of þat stede gone. *a* **1400-50** *Alexander* 4008 Quen þe gouernoure is gane þan is þe gomes wastid. *c* **1450** *Merlin* 142 Lete vs gon. **1535** STEWART *Cron. Scot.* (1858) I. 3 Now tell me or ȝe ga. **1535** COVERDALE *1 Sam.* xxx. 22 Let euery man take his wife & his children and be goynge. **1610** SHAKS. *Temp.* II. i. 122 No, no, hee's gone. **1671** MILTON *Samson* 1237 Go, baffled coward, lest I run upon thee. **1894** S. J. WEYMAN *Under Red Robe* iv, Turning sharply to the right, [she] was in an instant gone from sight. **1897** FL. MARRYAT *Blood Vampire* xii, I couldn't let you go without saying how grieved..I am.

b. with cognate acc. ***to go one's way***, etc.

c **1400** MAUNDEV. (Roxb.) v. 14 He..ȝode his way. **1481** CAXTON *Reynard* xi. (Arb.) 25 The vytayller..was goon his way. **1535** COVERDALE *Judith* viii. 34 Go thy waye in peace. **1641** MILTON *Ch. Govt.* I. vi. Wks. (1847) 39/2, I willingly depart, I go my ways. **1801** SOUTHEY *Thalaba* II. xxviii, Now go thy way, Abdaldar!

c. *fig.*, esp. in ***to go from one's word***, etc. (Cf. *go back*, 76 c.)

1530 PALSGR. 571/2, I go from a thynge, I denye a thing that I have ones sayd, *je desauoue*. **1611** BIBLE *1 Macc.* ii. 22 We will not hearken to the kings words, to goe from our religion, either on the right hand, or the left. **1726–31** TINDAL *Rapin's Hist. Eng.* (1743) II. XVII. 114 To give her a pretence to go from her word. **1888** F. BARRETT *Lady Biddy Fane* III. liv. 104 They had given their promise to do so, and would not go from their word.

†**d.** Used in *imp.* as a rebuke or remonstrance. (Cf. COME *v.* 34 b; also *go along*, 73 a, *go on*, 86 j.)

1592 SHAKS. *Rom. & Jul.* I. v. 88 You are a Princox, goe. **1599** —— *Hen. V*, v. i. 73 Go, go, you are a counterfeit cowardly Knaue.

e. *to let go* (see LET *v.*). In fig. phr. ***let it go at that***: let that account, estimate, conclusion, etc., be accepted; let us say no more about it.

1881 J. C. HARRIS *Uncle Remus* xxx. 111 Hit wuz Miss Molly Cottontail, en I speck we better let it go at dat. **1898** E. N. WESTCOTT *David Harum* 306 'Very well,' said John, 'we will let it go at that.' **1917** J. FARNOL *Definite Object* ii. 19 Eleven will do as well as any other time; let it go at that. *Ibid.* xxxvi. 312 Somebody tried to kill me, but somebody didn't kill me; here I am, getting stronger every day, so we'll let it go at that. **1955** J. D. SALINGER *Franny & Zooey* (1962) 13 I'm no Freudian Man or anything like that, but certain things you can't just pass over as capital-F Freudian and let them go at that.

f. ***go well.*** A form of address, of African vernacular origin, used at parting.

1948 A. PATON *Cry, Beloved Country* I. ii. 14 That was good of you. Go well, small one. **1951** P. ABRAHAMS *Wild Conquest* II. ii. 298 'Where do you journey?' 'To the land of the Basuto.' 'Go well, my friend.' 'Go well, white man.' **1961** H. STANTON *Go Well stay Well* 5 'Go well.' 'Stay well.' Sesuto: 'Tsamea pila.' 'Sala pila.' These words constitute the customary expressions of good-will when African friends are parting. The friend who stays says to the friend who goes, 'Go well', conveying the thought, 'May God protect you on your journey.'

22. a. To begin to move from a given point or state, to begin any action; esp. in imperative *go!*, said by the starter in a race, etc. Of an explosive = *to go off* (see 85 c); also *fig.* HERE *goes*, THERE *goes*, TOUCH *and go*: see these words. ***from the word go***: from the start, from the very beginning (*colloq.*, orig. *U.S.*).

c **1386** [see A 2 c a]. **1577** B. GOOGE *Heresbach's Husb.* IV. (1586) 181 That when they [bees] are ready to flie, or going, they make a great humming. **1820** *Examiner* No. 641. 473/2 The Revolution in Spain has been succeeded by a Revolution in Naples. We thought that Prussia would go next. **1834** D. CROCKETT *Narr. Life* 59, I was plaguy well pleased with her from the word go. **1837** DICKENS *Pickw.* ii, Hear the company—fiddles tuning—now the harp—there they go! **1867** SMYTH *Sailor's Word-bk.*, *Go!* A word sometimes given when all is ready for a launch of a vessel from the stocks. **1885** HOWELLS *Silas Lapham* (1891) I. 82 He was a drag and a brake on me from the word Go. **1892** *Field* 2 Apr. 479/3 On the word 'to go' being given Oxford started well. *Ibid.*, Opposite there Mr. D. H. McLean gave the word go. **1934** H. G. WELLS *Exper. Autobiogr.* I. v. 211, I lost him from the word Go. **1937** —— *Star Begotten* vii. 135 People will hate them from the word Go! **1963** *Times* 24 Jan. 6/6 It was wrong from the word 'go' to put in a limitation such as 60.

b. To play jazz or similar music excitingly or uninhibitedly; to 'swing'. Freq. *imp.*

1926 *Melody Maker* Jan. 19 Atta-boy, let's go! **1935** *Vanity Fair* Nov. 71 Hot artists or bands that can put across their licks successfully..can 'go'. **1958** *Punch* 27 Aug. 270/1 In a kind of trance I began to cry rhythmically 'Go man go!'

23. In conjunction with adjs. having a negative sense, as *quit*, *unpunished*, *unrewarded*, etc. where the original sense is that of leaving a court of justice or the like, but passing now into that of continuing in a specified state (cf. sense 7). ***to go free*** (see FREE *a.* 5).

a **1225** *St. Marher.* 18 Hit were þi gein þet tu þe gest unblescet. *a* **1300** *Cursor M.* 6713 (Gött.) Þe bestis lauerd sal ga [*Trin.* go] quite Of alkines chalange and wite. **1484** CAXTON *Fables of Alfonce* iii, The trouthe was knowen wherfore the poure man went quyte. **1610** SHAKS. *Temp.* IV. i. 242 Wit shall not goe vn-rewarded while I am King of this Country. **1820** *Examiner* No. 655. 699/2 The only method..is to let all opinions go free. **1877** MISS YONGE *Cameos* Ser. III. i. 4 Such forays usually went unpunished. **1888** G. GISSING *Life's Morning* I. ii. 72 Her worldly tastes did not go altogether ungratified.

24. a. To pass or be disposed of by sale. Const. *at*, *for* (so much); also ***to go cheap.*** In auctioneers' phraseology ***going!*** = on the point of being sold! ***gone!*** = sold!

c **1430** *Freemasonry* 92 Pay thy felows after the coste, As vytaylys goth thenne. **1549** LATIMER *1st Serm. bef. Edw. VI* (Arb.) 39 For that herebefore went for .xx. or .xl. pound by yere..now is it let for .l. or a .C. pound by yeare. **1677** YARRANTON *Engl. Improv.* 21 Twenty years purchase, which they will go at, and much more. **1754** H. WALPOLE *Lett.* (1857) II. 412, I can't conclude my letter without telling you what an escape I had at the sale of Dr. Mead's library, which goes extremely dear. **1764** H. WALPOLE *Let.* 10 May (1904) VI. 62 There was a whole-length of Sir Henry Sidney, which I should have liked, but it went for fifteen guineas. **1777** SHERIDAN *Sch. Scand.* IV. i. (1782 Dublin) 41 I'll knock 'em down at forty pounds. Going—going—gone. **1803** *Pic Nic* No. 13 (1806) II. 227 When any article under sale was going for less than its appointed value. **1814** MOORE *Sale of Tools* ii, Once, twice, going, going, thrice, gone!—it is yours, sir. **1862** *Temple Bar* VI. 414 Going at four pounds fifteen, if there is no advance. **1881** A. LANG *Library* i. 19 The bidders are professionals, in a league to let the volumes go cheap. **1968** M. TORRIE *Your Secret Friend* v. 54 What did Little Monkshood go for? Do you know? **1971** *Radio Times* 30 Oct.–5 Nov. 36/3 Sunday tv..Going for a Song. Customers and connoisseurs explore the world of *Antiques*.

†**b.** Phrase. ***he goes for my money*** = 'he's the man for me'. *Obs.*

1549 LATIMER *Ploughers* (Arb.) 38 Amonge al the packe of them that haue cure the Deuil shall go for my money. **1589** R. HARVEY *Pl. Perc.* 15 He goes for my money.

25. a. Of money: To be parted with, to disappear, be expended or spent. Const. *in.*

1393 LANGL. *P. Pl.* C. xx. 75 And that goth mor for hus medicine ich make the good aȝenwarde. **1879** M. J. GUEST *Lect. Hist. Eng.* xxx. 299 Whatever money he got..it all went in books. **1889** MRS. OLIPHANT *Poor Gentleman* II. ix. 163, I should make the money go.

†**b.** To be paid *out of* the revenues of. *Obs.*

1487 *Paston Lett.* No. 893 III. 331 [It] was the will of her husbonde that the annuyte schulde go oute of the seide maner of Swaynesthorpe. **1512** *Act 4 Hen. VIII*, c. 11 The seid annuell rentes appoynted to be goyng out of the seid Maners.

26. To be given up, relinquished, or sacrificed. †Also, to be forfeited.

a **1715** BURNET *Own Time* II. 55 If any person suffered in England on the account of the letters betrayed by him, his head should go for it. **1832** FR. A. KEMBLE in *Rec. Girlhood* (1878) III. 196 The house must go, the carriage must go, the horses must go, and yet [etc.]. **1850** *Tait's Mag.* XVII. 659/2, I have parted with..everything except my marriage-ring, and it must go next. **1890** *Jrnl. Educ.* 1 June 297/2 Greek, not being a primary subject, must go, except for the classical specialist.

27. a. To cease to exist or to be present; to be taken away, lost, or consumed; to come to an end, be abolished.

c **1200** [see A. 8 a]. *a* **1310** in Wright *Lyric P.* xx. 61 Al goth bote Godes wille. *c* **1375** *Lay-folks' Mass-bk.* 137 Til his parchemyn was al gon. *c* **1450** *Golagros & Gaw.* 36 All thair vittalis was gone. **1610** SHAKS. *Temp.* III. ii. 73 Take his bottle from him; When that's gone, He [etc.]. **1772** *Junius Lett.* lxviii. 335 The reputation you pretend to is gone for ever. **1857** BUCKLE *Civiliz.* I. xiii. 717 All its independence was gone. **1883** BLACK *Yolande* II. xiv. 255 One of the results of using those..drugs is, that the will entirely goes. **1885** MRS. LYNN LINTON *C. Kirkland* I. vi. 168 Sometimes the eyesight goes for ever. **1892** *Sat. Rev.* 5 Nov. 527/2 The Bishop's veto, of course, is to go..The Ecclesiastical Courts are to go too.

b. *Cricket.* Of a wicket: To be 'lost'. Also, of a batsman: to be 'out'.

1862 *Baily's Mag.* Aug. 90 Hornby..was the first to go. **1890** *Field* 10 May 672/3 The next three wickets went before anything had been added to the score. **1904** P. F. WARNER *How we recovered Ashes* vii. 105 Three of the greatest batsmen in the world gone for nine runs on a perfect wicket!

28. a. To 'depart this life', die.

1390 GOWER *Conf.* I. 44 Wherof the worlde ensample fette May after this, whan I am go. **1426** AUDELAY *Poems* 9 Do for ȝoure self ore ȝe gone. **1535** COVERDALE *Job* xxxvi. 12 They shall go thorow the swearde, & perish or euer they be awarre. *a* **1610** HEALEY *Epictetus' Man.* (1636) 46 Thy neighbours wife..dyeth. Every one can say, Why! wee are all mortall;..but when his owne goes, then [etc.]. **1708** PRIOR *Turtle & Sp.* 375 We're here to-day and gone to-morrow. **1830** FR. A. KEMBLE in *Rec. Girlhood* (1878) II. iii. 89 Have I lived to see him go before me! **1850** *Tait's Mag.* XVII. 722/2 Your brother's gone—died half-an-hour ago.

b. In many phrases signifying 'to die', some of which are of Biblical or religious origin, as ***to go the way of all the earth*** (*1 Kings* ii 2, *Josh.* xxii. 14, often misquoted ***to go the way of all flesh, of all living***), ***to go to a better world, to one's account, to one's own place***, etc.; while others are jocular or slang, as *to go aloft, off the hooks, off the stocks, to* (*the*) *pot*, etc. (see the accompanying words).

29. To fail, give way; to succumb to pressure, strain, or any deteriorating influence.

a. Of a material object: To break, also to break with noise, to crack; to wear (*in* or *into holes*).

1798 NELSON in Nicolas *Disp.* (1845) III. 20 About half-past three the foremast went in three places. **1840** R. H. DANA *Bef. Mast* xxxiii. 125 We looked every moment to see something go. **1867** *Judy* 1 May 5/2 It [a window] wasn't cracked..that morning, and she thought she heard it go when she was over the way. **1883** FENN *Middy & Ensign* xiii. 74 Your major split some stitches somewhere, for I heard them go. **1892** *Cassell's Mag.* July 469/2 His jerseys go into holes, and his flannels shrink. **1892** *Field* 15 Oct. 579/3 Sacks split or go in holes.

b. To faint, become unconscious. (Perh. with mixed notion of *go off*, *go to sleep*.)

1768 GOLDSM. *Good-n. Man* v. Wks. (Globe) 637/2 Help, she's going, give her air.

c. Of a crop, etc.: To be attacked by disease or decay.

1735–40 DYCHE & PARDON *Dict.*, *Going*..also a term applied to liquor, meat, &c. when it is perishing or spoiling. **1855** LD. HOUGHTON in *Life* (1891) I. xi. 516 The crop good, but the potatoes..going everywhere.

d. Of living beings, their organs or faculties: To fail, decline, give way, break down.

1809 MALKIN *Gil Blas* VII. iv. ¶3 You see that my lord archbishop is going very fast. **1890** *Daily News* 17 Nov. 7/2 His [a pugilist's] legs had gone, and he had been over-trained. **1892** *Sat. Rev.* 9 Jan. 41/1 Omnibus-horses generally go first in the loins. **1892** *Chamb. Jrnl.* 6 Aug. 509/2 I could feel my brain going.

III. Uses in which the prominent notion is that of the destination or direction. Here the verb is distinguished from COME by the implication that the movement is *not* towards the speaker, or the person whose point of view he for the moment assumes.

* *of self-originated movement or action.*

30. a. To move, take one's way, pass, or proceed to or towards a place, into the presence of a person, or in a specified direction. Const. *to*, *towards*, *into*, or with any prep. or adv. indicative of motion whither.

971 [see A 3 a *pl.*] *c* **1000** *Ags. Gosp.* Matt. xxiv. 38 Oð þone dæg þe noe on þa earce eode. *a* **1175** *Cott. Hom.* 229 Heo ȝede to þan iudeiscan folce. *c* **1175** *Lamb. Hom.* 3 Goð [*printed* God] in þane castel þet is onȝein eou. *a* **1225** *Ancr. R.* 128 Þeos eoden into ancre huse ase dude Saul into hole. *a* **1300** [see A 3 a]. *a* **1300** *Cursor M.* 4537 'Ga to þe prisun', said þe king. *c* **1380** WYCLIF *Wks.* (1880) 45 Who euere of freris..wilen goon among sarasyns. **1393** LANGL. *P. Pl.* C. III. 168 Mede..graunteth to go with a good wille To Londoun. *a* **1400–50** *Alexander* 2111 [He] to þe place goys. *a* **1450** *Knt. de la Tour* (1868) 120 She went vnto the kinge and..made pees betwene the kinge and her husbonde. **1591** SHAKS. *Two Gent.* III. i. 388 Must I goe to him? **1598–9** E. FORDE *Parismus* II. (1636) 229 And the Judges gone to the Dungeon to bring forth the Prisoner. **1600** FAIRFAX *Tasso* I. lxxvii, To the Christian Duke by heapes they gone. **1665** PEPYS *Diary* 17 Apr., That he do appoint a fleet to go to the Northward. **1897** FL. MARRYAT *Blood Vampire* xv, The Baron..turned round to go downstairs.

b. ***to go to Jericho, Bath, Hong Kong, Putney***, etc.: used imperatively or optatively to imply that one desires to see no more of a person, or does not care what becomes of him. Similarly ***to go to Halifax*** (for which see GIBBET).

1648 *Mercurius Aulicus* Nos. 7–9. 5 Let them all goe to Jericho, And n'ere be seen againe. **1669** *Depos. Cast. York* (Surtees) 165 Sirrah! goe to Hallifax. **1758** A. MURPHY *Upholsterer* II. (1763) 33 He may go to Jericho for what I cares. **1857** TROLLOPE *Three Clerks* xxvii, 'She may go to Hong-Kong for me'. **1859** THACKERAY *Virgin.* xvi, 'She may go to Tunbridge, or she may go to Bath, or she may go to Jericho for me'.

c. *transf.* Of a road, passage, door, etc.: To 'lead' *to*, *into*, etc.

13.. *K. Alis.* 6250 He..dude perforce stoppe the pas, That goth fro Taracounte to Capias. *a* **1533** LD. BERNERS *Huon* lxvi. 228 This other way goeth to Rome. **1583** HOLLYBAND *Campo di Fior* 89 Can you set vs in the waye, that goeth to Philopons schoole? *a* **1586** SIDNEY *Arcadia* III. (1633) 245 Follow him through the door that goes into the garden. **1719** DE FOE *Crusoe* I. xviii, Their Men..secur'd..the Scuttle which went down into the Cook-Room. **1749** FIELDING *Tom Jones* VII. x, Which way goes to Bristol.

d. Colloq. phr. ***where do we go from here*** (or ***there***)? = what shall we do next? what happens next?

1922 WODEHOUSE *Clicking of Cuthbert* ix. 222 'I've had three ginger ales,' observed the boy. 'Where do we go from here?' **1937** A. CHRISTIE *Death on Nile* II. xxvi. 255 Well, sir, where do we go from here? **1952** R. VICKERS *Sole Survivor* 45 He was as bewildered as I was myself... I asked: 'Where do we go from *here*, Gramshaw?' **1954** M. HUTTON in *Best One-Act Plays of 1952–53* 57 Right. We've got her name. Where do we go from there?

31. With implication of an additional meaning.

a. The place mentioned as the destination is often intended to include, or simply stand for, what is done there; as in *to go to the* BALL, *to* BED (also *to go into*, *to bed to*), *to* CHURCH, *to* COURT, *to* GRASS, *to* MARKET, *to* PRESS, *to* SCHOOL, *to* STOOL, etc. (see these words).

b. Of female animals (occas. of male): ***to go to*** (*the*) ***bull, cow, horse***, etc. = to copulate with.

1577 B. GOOGE *Heresbach's Husb.* II. (1586) 117 What age doe you thinke best for the Mare to go to the horse. *Ibid.* III. 129 The time for going to Bull, some take to be best in the midst of the spring. *Ibid.* 129 b, If you suffer him immediately..to go to the Cowe, it is certayne hee may get a Calfe. **1616** B. JONSON *Epigr.*, *On Mill, My Lady's Woman* 3 When Mill first came to Court, the vnprofiting foole..Was dull, and long, ere shee would goe to man.

c. In some contexts, *to go to* a place is used to imply the additional notion of entering on a mode of life, employment, or the like, which is associated with it; e.g. in ***to go to college, to the university, to prison***, etc. ***to go to the bar***: to become a barrister. ***to go †on the highway*** (or ***†the road***), ***on the stage, on the streets***: to become a highwayman, an actor, a prostitute.

1727 BOYER *Fr. Dict.* s.v., To go upon the Highway (to be a High-way man). *a* **1745** SWIFT *Direct. Servants* Wks. (1869) 569/2, I..advise you to go upon the road..the only post of honour left you. **1849** *Tait's Mag.* XVI. 37/1, I should have bid adieu to the Muses, and gone to the bar. **1883** D. C. MURRAY *Gate of Sea* I. v. 138 She had gone upon the stage..to make bread for herself. **1891** *Review of Rev.* 15 Sept. 299/1 Few of the working women proper go upon the streets. **1897** HALL CAINE *Christian* xi, Drake had gone to Harrow and thence to Oxford.

d. ***to go to sea***: to go a voyage; also (more usually) to become a sailor. Of rigging: To be carried adrift.

1599 MASSINGER, etc. *Old Law* v. i, She's going to sea—your grace knows whither better than I do. **1664–5** PEPYS *Diary* 8 Mar., He was to go to sea in her. **1770** NELSON in Southey *Life* (1813) I. 4, I should like to go to sea with uncle Maurice. **1857** S. P. HALL in *Merc. Marine Mag.* (1858) V. 12 The spare lower yard started from its lashings..and went to sea.

e. ***to go places***: to go to various places; to travel; *spec.* (*fig.*) to be successful, to 'make the grade'; to make progress. *colloq.* (orig. *U.S.*).

1925 S. LEWIS *M. Arrowsmith* xx. 232 The habit of social ease, of dressing, of going places without nervous anticipation. **1932** *Lit. Digest* 30 Jan. 36/2 All Russians love to 'go places'. **1933** A. WAUGH *Wheels within Wheels* xi. 222

You want to be able to go places and do things. *Ibid.* vii. 137 He hasn't been places yet. **1934** M. WESEEN *Dict. Amer. Slang* x. 142 *Go places*, to be successful; to get ahead. **1944** L. A. G. STRONG *Director* 254 They were jealous because she'd made the grade... She was going places. **1947** N. CARDUS *Autobiogr.* 250 This for me, is to live and to 'go places'. **1958** 'A. GILBERT' *Death against Clock* 85 We're going places right away.

f. To urinate or defecate; to go to the lavatory; freq. ***to go somewhere***. *colloq.*

1926 E. BOWEN *Ann Lee's* 71 Do you want to go somewhere? Have you got a pain? **1935** *Time* 24 June 45/1, I took off all my clothes but my drawers and—well—I had to go. **1959** W. GOLDING *Free Fall* ii. 61 But I been three times. .. I can't pee any more! **1962** J. WAIN *Strike Father Dead* 138 He's in the men's room. He's been wanting to go all evening, but as long as you were playing he didn't want to miss a note. **1967** F. MULLALLY *Prizewinner* i. 19 Excuse me .. I've got to go somewhere.

32. Instead of, or in addition to, the place of destination, the purpose or motive of going is often indicated. This may be expressed in various ways:

a. by the simple *inf.* ***to go get***: to go and get; to reach; to work hard or ambitiously (cf. GO-GETTER). Now *colloq.* and *U.S.*

go look! used to convey a contemptuous refusal to answer a question (*obs.* exc. *dial.*; common in Derbyshire).

Beowulf [see A 3 a]. **1375** BARBOUR *Bruce* I. 433 Ga purches land quhar euir he may. *c* **1386** CHAUCER *Shipman's T.* 223 Lat vs heere a messe and go we dyne. *a* **1400–50** [see A 2 d γ]. *c* **1475** *Rauf Coilȝear* 157 Ga tak him be the hand. **1542–5** BRINKLOW *Lament.* (1874) 111 That I shulde go pour out my vyces in the eare of an vnlearned buzarde. **1591** SPENSER *Teares Muses* 398 Now thou maist go pack. **1602** *Narcissus* (1893) 87 Come, daunce vs a morrice, or els goe sell fishe. *a* **1625** FLETCHER *Mad Lover* II. i, There's the old signe of Memnon: where the soule is You may go look. **1668** HOWE *Bless. Righteous* (1825) 199 We mighte as well go preach to devils. **1724** DE FOE *Mem. Cavalier* (1840) 71, I bid him go take care of his .. things. **1795** *Ann. Agric.* XXIII. 315 Nor does the drilled corn .. go lie (as the farmer calls it) so readily as the broad-cast. **1813** JANE AUSTEN *Lett.* (1884) II. 216 Your Streatham and my Bookham may go hang. **1831** S. LOVER *Paddy the Piper, Leg. & Stor. Irel.* 151 There's an iligant lock o' straw, that you may go sleep in. **1849** *Tait's Mag.* XVI. 170/1 Go hire the needful workmen. **1849** *Eng. Illustr. Mag.* Sept. 888 As to a hauberk I must needs go lack; for I could not come by it. **1893** [see CHASE *v.*[1] 7 c]. **1912** *Pedagogical Seminary* XIX. 96 A rebuke to pride with the notion of 'get out',..'Go jump in the lake.' **1922** JOYCE *Ulysses* 750, I dont like a man you have to climb up to go get at. **1928** F. HURST *President is Born* viii. 113 They're the go-getters without your brains to go-get! **1929** GALSWORTHY *Roof* iii. 45 *Froba.* Heu! You are go-getters. *Bryn.* What is a go-getter? *Froba.* Kind of an early bird—go gets the worm. **1968** *Globe & Mail* (Toronto) 17 Feb. 35 (Advt.), Now there is polish as well as boyish personal appeal. Go see. **1968** *Encounter* Sept. 22/1 Go hit your head against the wall. **1969** A. GLYN *Dragon Variation* vii. 216 Let's go get ourselves a drink.

b. by the *inf.* with *to.*

For weakened senses of this construction in which the notion of movement in space is lost, see 34 b, c.

a **1225** *Ancr. R.* 10 þet beoð, alse he seide, þe goð to helpen widewen. *a* **1300** [see A 2 b]. *c* **1470** HARDING *Chron.* IX. ii, He bidden was to ga To helpe the kyng Euandre. **1590** SHAKS. *Com. Err.* v. i. 225 Our dinner done, and he not comming thither I went to seek him. **1817** BYRON *Beppo* xl, Coach, servants, gondola, he goes to call. **1879** EDNA LYALL *Won by Waiting* xiv, Esperance .. went to dress for dinner.

c. by *and* with a co-ordinated verb. In the modern colloquial use of this combination the force of *go* is very much weakened or disappears altogether. In the positive imperative *go* is often nearly redundant (cf. L. *i nunc, et*...); otherwise, ***to go and*** (do something) = 'to be so foolish, unreasonable, or unlucky as to ——'. So in the vulgar phrase (***I have, he has,*** etc.) ***been and gone and*** (done so and so).

c **1000** *Ags. Gosp.* Matt. ix. 13 Gað soðlice and leorniȝeaþ [Vulg. *euntes autem discite*] hwæt is [etc.]. *a* **1300** *Cursor M.* 7519 Gaes and fottes me in hij Mine aun armur. *c* **1380** WYCLIF *Sel. Wks.* III. 385 Men schulen fle to heven wiþoutin peyne if þei wolden goo and slee .. Cristen men. *c* **1430** LYDG. *Chichev. & Byc.* in Dodsl. *O. Pl.* XII. 335, I ful longe may gon and seeke Or I can fynde a goode repast. **1558** SIR T. GRESHAM in H. H. Gibbs *Colloquy on Currency* App. 6 Againste all wisdome the seyd bishoppe went and vallewid the French crowne at vjs. ivd. **1600** SHAKS. *A. Y. L.* II. iii. 31 Would'st thou haue me go & beg my food. *a* **1631** DONNE *Poems* (1650) 3 Goe and catch a falling starre. **1755** H. WALPOLE *Corr.* cclxvii. (ed. 3) III. 105 Don't go and imagine that £1,200,000 was all Sunk in the gulph of Madame Pompadour. **1815** *Houlston Juvenile Tracts* vi. *Cork Jacket* 6 He might go and hang himself for all they cared. **1878** *Scribner's Mag.* XVI. 87/1 The fool has gone and got married. **1891** *Temple Bar* Aug. 470 That I should actually have been and gone and told him so!

d. by a sb. (governed by *to*, and often without article) denoting an action that is to be performed, a ceremony at which one is to be present, etc.

Also with weakened sense in *to go to* SLEEP.

c **1175** [see A 2 c α]. *c* **1330** [see A 2 c β]. *c* **1430** *Hymns Virg.* (1867) 56 Seynt iohun .. for ihesus loue to deep gan goon. *c* **1485** *Digby Myst.* (1882) III. 578 Tyme drayt ny to go to dyner. **1548** HALL *Chron., Rich. III*, 33 To morow we wyl common more: let us go to supper. *a* **1586** SIDNEY *Arcadia* III. (1633) 232 When they were all gone one day to dinner. *a* **1745** SWIFT *Mem. Creichton* Wks. 1841 I. 589 As soon as he was gone to rest. **1794** [see A 2 a]. **1879** EDNA LYALL *Won by Waiting* xxix, He took a fancy for going to the afternoon service at the abbey.

e. by the vbl. sb. governed by *a* (= *on*; in mod. use frequently omitted); also by ordinary sbs. denoting an action, governed by †*in, on,* rarely *upon.* ***go a begging*** (see BEGGING *vbl. sb.* 2 b).

1388 WYCLIF *Matt.* xxv. 14 A man that goith in pilgrimage, clepide hise seruauntis [etc.]. *a* **1440** *Sir Eglam.* 409 The kyng of Sydon an-huntyng ys gon. **1530** PALSGR. 570/1, I go a foragyng .. I go a grasyng, as a horse or beest dothe. **1562** VERON *Invoc. Saints* 83 Why .. dydde they goe a gaddynge to our Ladye of Wilsdone. **1604** EDMONDS *Observ. Cæsar's Comm.* 65 Such an inconuenience, as might make him repent for going a birding. **1684** BUNYAN *Pilgr.* II. (1879) 192/9 The Women .. that called at his House as they were going on Pilgrimage. **1766** GOLDSM. *Vic. W.* xx, I was resolved not to go sneaking to the lower professors. *Ibid.* xxx, That you will permit .. two of your servants to go upon a message. **1802–12** BENTHAM *Rationale Judic. Evid.* v. (1827) 214 The plaintiff .. is obliged to go upon the hunt for other witnesses. **1855** MACAULAY *Hist. Eng.* xxi. IV. 665 The King was certainly going a hunting. **1888** MISS F. WARDEN *Witch of Hills* I. iv. 76, I said that I was going boar-hunting. **1897** FL. MARRYAT *Blood Vampire* iii, Do let me keep her [the baby], whilst nurse goes on her errand.

f. by a complementary sb., denoting the function or capacity in which the subject is to be employed. *Obs.* exc. in ***to go apprentice*** (now *rare*), and ***to go bail***, now chiefly *fig*, as ***I will go bail*** (colloq.) = 'I will be bound', I am certain.

1665 PEPYS *Diary* 6 Dec., My Lord Sandwich goes Embassador to Spayne speedily. **1670** MARVELL *Corr.* cxli. Wks. 1872–5 II. 314 The King .. ordered the Lord Barclay to go Lord Lieutenant. **1707** HEARNE *Collect.* 24 Jan. (O.H.S.) I. 321 He went Chaplain to the Factory. **1768** GOLDSM. *Good-n. Man* I, It was but last week he went security for a fellow whose face he scarce knew. **1852** THACKERAY *Esmond* II. iv, One of the boys 'listed; the other had gone apprentice. **1884** RIDER HAGGARD *Dawn* lxxv, He won't marry her now, I'll go bail. **1890** *Cassell's Mag.* July 470/2, I will go bail for your character.

33. To have recourse, refer, appeal *to* (an authority, source of information, etc.); to carry one's case *to* or *before* (a tribunal, etc.). †Sometimes in *imp.* with *me* as ethical dative. ***to go to the country*** (see COUNTRY 6 b).

1377 LANGL. *P. Pl.* B. x. 192 Who so gloseth as gylours don go me to the same. *c* **1400** *Apol. Loll.* 93 Goþ more to þe lawe & to þe witnes. **1532** MORE *Confut. Tindale* Wks. 376/2 Go me to the newe lawe and to those sacramentes which Tyndall agreeth for sacramentes. **1825** *New Monthly Mag.* XIV. 193 Mr. Salmon .. is determined to go to a jury. **1874** BLACKIE *Self-Cult.* 76 You must go to Aristotle for that. **1878** *Scribner's Mag.* XV. 737/1 Why does not this artist go to nature? **1881** *Philad. Rec.* No. 3463. 4 When the bar-tender goes before a jury the above statement evidently will be his defence. **1892** *Sat. Rev.* 8 Oct. 419/2 She need not go to others for her *bons mots.*

34. a. To turn *to*, betake oneself *to* (an employment or occupation); to proceed to some specified course of action; to resort to some specified means of attaining one's object. ***to go to blows, cuffs, law, war, work,*** etc. (see the sbs.).

a **1250** *Owl & Night.* 873 ȝif þu gest herof to disputinge. *a* **1300** [see A 2 d β]. **1467** *Eng. Gilds* (1870) 409 And þe electo^rs^ to go to a new eleccioun. **1535** COVERDALE *Prov.* xxix. 9 Yf a wyse man go to lawe with a foole .. he getteth no rest. **1577** B. GOOGE *Heresbach's Husb.* I. (1586) 3 b, I goe to writing or reading, or suche other businesse as I have. **1596** SHAKS. *1 Hen. IV*, II. iii. 35 O, I could diuide my selfe, and go to buffets, for mouing such a dish of skim'd Milk with so honourable an Action. **1611** [see A 2 d γ]. **1678** BUTLER *Hud.* III. iii. 530 He that .. goes to Law to be Reliev'd Is sillier than a sottish Chews. **1790** *By-stander* 79 *note*, Two of these different professions having disagreed, they went to boxing. **1891** MARY WILKINS *Humble Rom.*, etc. 277 He had rented a pretty little tenement over in Rye, and gone to housekeeping.

†**b.** To set oneself, attempt *to* (do something).

1662 STILLINGFL. *Orig. Sacr.* I. ii. §2 Nay, he goes to prove the truth of Sanchoniathons History by [etc.]. **1776** *Maiden Aunt* I. 55 But mind me, Emma, if you go to slip out of the room, I'll send old Harley to plague you.

c. In negative or hypothetical contexts, *to go (for) to* (do something) is vulgarly used for: 'To do anything so improper as to ——', 'to be so foolish, bold, or severe as to ——'.

1752 FOOTE *Taste* II. Wks. 1799 I. 22 Indeed I did not go to do it. **1798** T. MORTON *Secr. worth Knowing* I. i. 6 Sure nobody wou'd go to kill so handsome and good a creature. **1803** MARY CHARLTON *Wife & Mistress* II. 59 A non-natural woman, to go to leave her children. *Ibid.* II. 151 Who would go for to take him for a Lord's son? **1824** MRS. CAMERON *Pink Tippet* III. 16, I am sure she would not go to tell a lie of any body. **1847** C. M. YONGE *Scenes & Characters* vi. 57, I told my brother I did not think Mr. Devereux would go for to say such a thing. **1886** H. BAUMANN *Londinismen* 65/1 Don't you go for to think that 'cos my 'air is grey, I ain't got any strength left me. **1890** MRS. H. WOOD *House of Halliwell* II. xi. 293 'Dear ma'am', uttered Nurse Gill, 'you'd never go to suspect her!' **1895** 'M. E. FRANCIS' *Daughter of Soil* iii. 29 O' course, I wouldn't go for to say sich a thing o' th' Squire.

35. a. To carry one's action to a specified point of progress or completeness. Const. *to*; also with adv. or adverbial phrase, and with cognate or adverbial accusative, as in *to go the* LENGTH *of*. For many phrases, see FAR, NEAR, NIGH.

† *if you go to that* = 'if you come to that.' (*he*) *will go far*: in recent journalistic use, said of an author, statesman, etc., to imply that he is likely to achieve great things (= F. *il ira loin*).

1577 B. GOOGE *Heresbach's Husb.* I. (1586) 21 In Syria, where they cannot goe very deepe, they use .. very little Plowes. **1631** SHIRLEY *Love's Cruelty* II. ii. (1640) D i b, *En.* Meere trifles. *Hi.* And you go to that, Lady, that which you part withall for All these pleasures, is but a trifle. **1681** FLAVEL *Meth. Grace* xxviii. 483 Death need not pull and hale; such a man goes halfway to meet it. **1689** T. R. *View Govt. Europe* 3 We are not to stick at the Letter, but go to the foundation, to the inside and essence of things. **1690** LOCKE *Hum. Und.* IV. vi §7 (1825) 446 Unless we can discover their natural dependence, which, in their primary qualities, we can go but a very little way in. **1695** CONGREVE *Love for Love* II. ii. (ed. 2) 27 Well, if you go to that, where did you find this Bodkin? **1697** COLLIER *Ess.* I. (1703) 187 The generality .. want either force or inclination to go to the bottom, and try the merits. **1757** FOOTE *Author* Epil., Wks. 1799 I. 129 When she's quite in voice, she'll go to C! **1776** G. SEMPLE *Building in Water* 59 Even at the Depth we went to at the North End. **1849** MACAULAY *Hist. Eng.* ii. I. 182 Having gone all lengths with a faction while it was uppermost. **1879** M. J. GUEST *Lect. Hist. Eng.* xlvii. 476 Strafford really went some way towards bringing his scheme to pass.

b. *esp.* with regard to the amount of an offer or a concession in mercantile or other negotiations. † ***to go less***: to offer or accept a lower price or less onerous conditions, take less extreme measures, etc.

1626 SHIRLEY *Maid's Rev.* III. ii. (1639) E iv, We can prolong life. *Ans.* And kill too, can you not? *Sh.* Oh any that will goe to the price. **1632** MASSINGER *Maid of Hon.* III. i, It is too little; yet, Since you haue said the word, I am content, But will not goe a gazet lesse. *c* **1645** HOWELL *Lett.* (1650) III. xv. 27 The Parlement persists in their first Propositions, and will go nothing less. *a* **1648** LD. HERBERT *Hen. VIII* (1683) 418 It was objected .. that the Law having made the Offence to be Death, it was not safe to go less. **1659** J. ARROWSMITH *Chain Princ.* 101 The Sybils books .. two whereof .. were purposely cast into the fire .. because Tarquin would not go to the price of them. **1704** N. N. tr. *Boccalini's Advts. fr. Parnassus* I. 92 Poor *Literati* .. could not afford to go the Price of Better Meat. **1721** PERRY *Daggenh. Breach* 30 Having made it sure that no Man else would go below him. **1849** MACAULAY *Hist. Eng.* vi. II. 65 Lewis consented to go as high as twenty-five thousand crowns. **1892** *Strand Mag.* IV. 294/2 The price was higher than she cared to go to.

c. In various phrases with the general sense 'to share equally in something', chiefly with adverbial accusative, as ***to go halves (with)***, formerly also † ***to go (another person's) halves, to go shares, snacks, snips***; or (cf. 32 f) with complementary sb. as ***to go sharer, mates, partners***. (See the various sbs.).

d. To put or subject oneself *to* (trouble, expense).

1842 *Jrnl. R. Agric. Soc.* III. I. 18 The tenant .. went to very needless expense. **1890** *Temple Bar* Aug. 576 Arden has gone to the ridiculous cost of engaging Ridge. **1895** MARIE CORELLI *Sorrows of Satan* ix. (1897) 98 Few publishers .. go to the trouble of .. giving the number of copies for an Edition.

e. *trans.* (on the analogy of cognate accusatives). To go to the extent of; to venture as far as. ***to go the whole hog*** (see HOG 11 b). *spec.* To eat or drink (something specified); esp. in phr. ***I, you,*** etc., ***could go*** (a drink, etc.). (Cf. quot. *c* 1882.) *colloq.*

1855 H. GREELEY 1 Dec. in *Greeley on Lincoln* 89 He .. tells everybody he is connected with the Tribune, but doesn't go its isms. *c* **1882** *Comic Song 'West End Boys'* iii. (Farmer), Another bitter I really can't go. **1883** 'MARK TWAIN' *Life on Mississ.* xliii. 390 There's one thing .. which a person won't take in pine if he can go walnut; and won't take in walnut if he can go mahogany .. That's a coffin. **1929** F. BOWEN *Sea Slang* 58 *To go*, to eat. **1944** F. I. COOZE *Kiwis in Pacific* 12 God, how I could go a nice, long cool beer. **1948** D. BALLANTYNE *Cunninghams* (1963) I. iv. 25, I could go a good feed of eels just now.

f. To yield, produce (a certain amount). *U.S.*

1816 U. BROWN *Jrnl.* 23 July in *Maryland Hist. Mag.* (1915) X. 369 None [of the fields] that I saw will go 15 Bushels to the Acre. **1868** *Iowa State Agric. Soc. Rep. 1867* 160 Corn.—On well-manured land .. will go seventy-five bushels. **1869** 'MARK TWAIN' *Innoc. Abr.* 57 An altar with facings of solid silver—at least they call it so and I think myself it would go a couple of hundred to the ton (to speak after the fashion of the silver miners).

36. *trans.* **a.** To risk, adventure (a certain sum), to stake, wager. Also *absol.*; sometimes with indirect object. ***to go better***, in certain card games, to offer a higher stake than is named in the adversary's challenge; so ***to go one better***: hence often *fig.* to outbid or outdo somebody else. Similarly (*U.S.*) ***to go*** (an amount) ***better***: to raise the bet by (so much); ***to go*** (a person) (***one***) ***better***: to outbid or outdo (someone).

1605 B. JONSON *Volpone* III. v, Like your wanton gam'ster at primero, Whose thought had Whisper'd to him, not goe lesse. **1672** MARVELL *Reh. Transp.* I. 283 This Gentleman would always go half a Crown with me. **1768** GOLDSM. *Good-n. Man* III. i, Men that would go forty guineas on a game of cribbage. **1845** S. F. SMITH *Theatr. Apprent.* 148 My adversary went the dollar, and five better. **1855** DICKENS *Dorrit* vi, And I'll go another seven and sixpence to name which is the helplessest, the unborn babe or you. **1864** W. B. DICK *Amer. Hoyle* (1866) 174 B. puts down a dime. C. says, 'I'll go a dime better,' and he puts down two dimes. **1874** *Congress. Rec.* 17 Feb. 1556/1 The Senator from North Carolina .. proposes an increase of 46 millions of banking circulation. The Senator from Pennsylvania .. goes him better, and proposes an unlimited increase. **1878** *Scribner's Mag.* XV. 660/2 I'll do better than the church. I'll see 'em that and go one better. **1879** 'CAVENDISH' *Card Ess.*, etc. 59 Each that stood might pass or make the *renvi*, that is go better again. **1886** MCCARTHY & MRS. C. PRAED *Right Honourable* I. vii. 142 Our fellows wanted to be popular. These fellows .. want to go one better. **1889** K. MUNROE *Golden Days* 66 [I was] going him one better every time for a fifty vara lot. 1890 *Temple Bar* June 199 You ought to go on the zero. 1890 [see SEE *v.* 13—second *transf.* example]. 1953 W. STEVENS *Let.* 21 Dec. (1967) 805 The weather was constantly going me one better. 1960 W. H. WHYTE *Organization Man* 34 Some European critics of America have gone them one better.

b. With personal object: to take on (a person) in a wager, game, or offer. *U.S. colloq.*

a 1846 W. T. PORTER *Quarter Race Kentucky* 179, I knows Bill well, and I'll go you an independent on his beating yon feller bad. 1876 BESANT & RICE *Gold. Butterfly* Prol. ii. 11 The very dice on the counter with which the bar-keeper used to 'go' the miners for drinks. *a* 1889 *Spirit of Times* (Farmer), I goes you five dollars, this time. 1902 S. E. WHITE *Blazed Trail* xxiv. 161 'Surely you won't refuse to be my guest here..!' 'Wallace,' said Thorpe, 'I'll go you.' 1909 'O. HENRY' *Options* (1916) 38 'Believe I'll go you,' he said, brightening. 'I'll accept the invitation gladly.'

c. *Cards.* To make a call or declaration of; to accept (a specified number of cards).

1876 [see NAPOLEON 4]. *c* 1884, 1898 [see NAP *sb.*[5] 2b]. 1932 *Sunday Express* 6 Mar. 13/2 Cries of 'I'll stick' and 'I'll go four' heard by police.. led to.. a summons for permitting gaming. 1964 N. SQUIRE *Bidding at Bridge* ii. 25 The principle of the rebid of 1 NT.. may cause you to go a trick too high. *Ibid.* iii. 30 Four No-trumps over an opening bid of One No-trump means: 'Go six if you are maximum!'

** *of passive movement, change of state*, etc.

37. a. To be carried, moved, impelled, etc. *to, towards* a place or person, *into* a place, etc. *lit.* and *fig.* ***to go to the bottom*** (see BOTTOM *sb.* 2).

c 1050 *Byrhtferth's Handboc* in *Anglia* (1885) VIII. 305 & on þissum monðe gæð seo sunne on þæt tacn. *a* 1300 *Metr. Eng. Psalter* xvii[i]. 7 Mi crie in his sighte in eres yhode euen. 1340 *Ayenb.* 206 Zuo longe geþ þet pot to þe wetere, þet hit comþ to-broke hom. *a* 1586 SIDNEY *Arcadia* II. (1633) 162 His old blood going to his heart. 1591 SHAKS. *Two Gent.* II. i. 116 Being ignorant to whom it goes, I writ at randome. 1749 SMOLLETT *Gil Blas* (1782) I. 156 This very day I met two of them going to their long home. 1895 LORD SHAND in *Law Times Rep.* LXXIII. 637/2, I am further of opinion.. that there was evidence of negligence to go to the jury.

b. fig. ***to go to one's heart***: to cause one great sorrow, pity, or the like.

1481 CAXTON *Reynard* (Arb.) 88, I trowe hit shold not moche goo to my herte so that another dyde it. 1687 BURNET *Reply to Varillas* 126 This it seems went to his heart. 1694 F. BRAGGE *Disc. Parables* IX. 314 How does every rub and hindrance go to their very heart. 1844 *Fraser's Mag.* XXX 587/2 It goes to my heart to be disunited from them. 1859 THACKERAY *Virgin.* xviii, It went to my heart to say no to her. 1890 *Murray's Mag.* VII. 96 The look of sorrow.. went to his heart.

38. a. (Chiefly *will go*, but also in indefinite present tense.) To be capable of passing, to find room to pass *into, through*, etc., a place. Hence, of a number, to be contained (so many times) *in* another number; also *impers.* ('won't go') in division or subtraction (cf. quots. 1856, 1890).

1686 J. SMITH *Of Nat. Time* 39 Let two plain and flat plates or boards.. be joyned so close together that a Six-pence may but just go between. 1825 J. NICHOLSON *Operat. Mechanic* 18 Five will go twelve times in sixty. 1856 *Titan Mag.* Dec. 498/1 Twelves in two—won't go! *Ibid.* 499/1 Twelve will go once in fourteen, and leave two over. 1879 M. J. GUEST *Lect. Hist. Eng.* xx. 198 All the good we can find about him will go into a very few words. 1881 A. LANG *Library* ii. 62 Elzevirs.. go readily into the pocket. 1890 *Universal Rev.* 15 July 445 Four from three won't go—borrow one.

b. To be usually or properly put into, to have its proper position in a certain place.

1729 SWITZER *Hydrost. & Hydraul.* 97 A Brass Pillar.. having a Ball at the Bottom of it, that goes into a Socket. *Mod.* This box goes on the third shelf from the top.

39. a. To pass *to* a person; to fall to his lot; to be allotted or awarded to him; to pass into his hands, into his pocket, under his control, etc.

1607 SHAKS. *Cor.* II. iii. 129 Let the high Office and the Honor go To one that would doe thus. 1807 CRABBE *Par. Reg.* (1812) I. 122 Nor has he care to whom his wealth shall go. 1849 *Tait's Mag.* XVI. 288/1 American ships.. divide the freights which formerly went to the British.. shipowner. 1850 *Ibid.* XVII. 675/1 One might have known the estate would go to creditors. 1869 HUGHES *Alfred Gt.* xiv. 168 A fine of 120 shillings (half to go to the king). 1878 *Scribner's Mag.* XV. 638/2 The money I had saved went to the doctors. 1890 *Field* 10 May 687/1 The first and second prizes went to colts. 1890 T. F. TOUT *Hist. Eng.* 100 The newly enclosed land nearly all went to the big landlords. 1891 *Field* 19 Dec. 949/3 Both games going to Courtney.

b. Of a dignity, an estate, office, property, etc.: To pass by inheritance, succession, or otherwise.

1818 CRUISE *Digest* (ed. 2) VI. 120 Where an estate was devised specifically, and was afterwards sold by the testator by a contract executory, the estate went from the devisee. 1831 *Society* I. 34 It was proved it [a large estate] should not have gone in the female line. 1877 MISS YONGE *Cameos* Ser. III. vi. 55 The dukedom went to his brother. 1879 M. J. GUEST *Lect. Hist. Eng.* xliii. 432 The crown was then to go to the descendants of Henry's younger sister.

40. To be applied or appropriated to a purpose. Const. *to, towards*; also *to* with *inf.*

c 1420 *Pallad. on Husb.* I. 375 The fistulose & softer [stone] let hit goon To cover with. 1688 BURNET *Lett. State Italy* 162 All the Revenue goes to the keeping up of the Magnificence of the Court. 1850 *Tait's Mag.* XVII. 718/1 An increase of yield goes all to the amount of produce sold. 1867 *Jrnl. R. Agric. Soc.* Ser. II. III. II. 549 Fees.. do not go towards the sustentation of the school. 1889 *Macm. Mag.* Dec. 126/1 The capital.. goes to swell the profits of the original possessors of the soil.

41. a. To contribute to a result; to be amongst the conditions requisite for a purpose; to be one of the constituent elements of something. Const. *to, towards*; also, *to* with *inf.*

1607 DONNE *Lett.* (1651) 141 Here also you have true businesse and many *quasi negotia*, which go two and two to a businesse. 1626 BACON *Sylva* §903 The Medicines which goe to the Ointments are so strong, that [etc.]. 1663 GERBIER *Counsel* 52 There goeth four load of Sand, which.. cost two shillings six pence. 17.. SWIFT *To Pope* (J.), Something better and greater than high birth and quality must go toward acquiring those demonstrations of public esteem and love. 1755 *Man* No. 26. 3 With a single glance we view an army, without attending to every separate soldier that goes to compose it. 1789 COWPER *Lett.* 8 Aug., There goes more to the composition of a volume than many critics imagine. 1851 MRS. BROWNING *Casa Guidi* 62 Count what goes To making up a Pope. 1870 NICHOLSON *Man. Zool.* (1880) 447 The bones which go to form the head and trunk. 1882 J. C. MORISON *Macaulay* 1 With a good eye for the influences which go to the formation of character. 1890 *Harper's Mag.* May 961/2 Whole gardens of roses go to one drop of the attar.

†**b.** To be allotted as proportionate *to*. *Obs.*

1672 PETTY *Pol. Anat.* (1691) 58 One Horse plows 10 acres, and there goes 1 Man to 3 Horses.

c. To amount *to*, be equivalent *to*.

1841 *Fraser's Mag.* XXIII. 17 Sixteen ounces go to the avoirdupoise pound. 1879 MISS YONGE *Cameos* Ser. IV. xvii. 177 How many loaves go to a bushel of wheat. 1889 PHILIPS & WILLS *Fatal Phryne* I. iii. 54 Twenty-five francs go to the pound. 1890 *Chamb. Jrnl.* 21 June 389/1 'How many.. go to a crew with you, captain?' 1890 *Graphic* 11 Oct. 407/2, 150 glasses go to the keg.

42. To conduce, tend *to*; with *sb.* or *v.* in *inf.* †Formerly also, to have an object or result amounting *to*. Esp. in phr. ***to go to show***: to tend to show; to indicate; to serve as evidence *that*. Freq. *absol.*, to indicate or prove something implied.

1781 *Hist. Europe* in *Ann. Reg.* 46/1 An attempt.. which in its success would have gone to the destruction of himself, his party, and friends. 1804 TENNANT *Indian Recr.* I. 47 Fastidious ideas regarding rank.. went nearly to the exclusion of this useful set of men from the society of.. grandees. 1818 JAS. MILL *Brit. India* III. VI. i. 50 The bill, therefore, went to the confiscation of the whole of the Company's property. 1820 *Examiner* No. 634. 361/2 [They] would also go to account for much of the personal violence. 1823 T. JEFFERSON *Writ.* (1830) IV. 385 Those geographical schisms which go immediately to a separation. 1823 *New Monthly Mag.* IX. 244/1 It [the amendment] went to a half approval of the conduct of ministers. 1842 EMERSON *Jrnl.* May in *Sel. Writings* (1965) 111 Then this new molecular philosophy goes to show that there are astronomical interspaces betwixt atom and atom. 1850 *Tait's Mag.* XVII. 375/1 Two things go to render this statement.. worthless. 1889 *Advent Rev. & Sabbath Herald* 16 July 450/3 Events.. which go to show, with peculiar eloquence, to what extent the Romish policy has succeeded. 1889 *Sat. Rev.* 14 Dec. 684/2 It goes to show that the Dutch are not the equals of the English. 1925 *New Yorker* 25 July (Advt. inside front cover), Which just goes to show. Wherever you go in Paris you will find The New Yorker. 1937 D. L. SAYERS *Busman's Honeymoon* 17 It does rather go to show, doesn't it, that there is something not quite right about the Wimseys. 1962 *Listener* 7 June 1000/1 Dramatic cases of child neglect only go to show, and wild generalizations are based upon them. 1966 A. THOMAS *Judge* i. 16 It seemed unlikely that our paths would cross... Which, as they say, only goes to show. 1969 'A. GILBERT' *Missing from Home* viii. 134 'It just goes to show, doesn't it, you can't be too careful.' 'Yes,' agreed Mr. Crook hollowly, 'it just goes to show.'

43. a. To attain, reach, extend; with advb. phrase indicating the point aimed at or attained. Cf. 35.

a 1586 SIDNEY *Arcadia* I. (1633) 19 His love was not so superficiall, as to goe no further than the skin. 1690 LOCKE *Hum. Und.* II. i. §19 No man's knowledge here can go beyond his experience. 1707 FREIND *Peterborow's Cond. Sp.* 149, I think it is hardly possible that Modesty could go a greater length. 1825 *New Monthly Mag.* XIII. 233 The history.. goes very far back. 1864 J. H. NEWMAN *Apologia* 182 My memory goes to this,—that I had asked a friend [etc.]. 1873 P. V. SMITH *Hist. Eng. Instit.* I. ii. 48 These proceedings did not go to the length of treason. 1874 DEUTSCH *Rem.* 362 But the difference goes still further. 1885 MRS. LYNN LINTON *Chr. Kirkland* I. ii 43 His mathematics did not go very deep. 1892 *Black & White* 19 Nov. 580/1 The horns go to great lengths, but are not very thick at base.

b. ***as*** (or ***so***) ***far as it goes***: a phrase used to limit the applicability of a statement, etc., or the extent or efficiency of what is referred to.

[1420 *Searchers Verdicts* in *Surtees Misc.* (1888) 16 Als farre als thayre syde house gas.] 1789 TWINING *Aristotle on Poetry* (1812) I. 10 The resemblance is, indeed, real, as far as it goes. 1818 CRUISE *Digest* (ed. 2) V. 598 The case of Martin v. Strachan decided this case, as far as it went. 1820 *Examiner* No. 651,632/1 He has a real notion of pleasantry, as far as mere pleasantry goes. 1862 H. SPENCER *First Princ.* II. i. §37 (1875) 132 We make a statement, true as far as it goes. 1885 *Law Times* LXXIX. 130/1 The poor law system .. is, so far as it goes, Socialism pure and simple.

c. ***to go a good, great, long, short way*** (***to*** or ***towards***): to have a great, little effect; also, to have great influence *with* (a person).

1697 COLLIER *Immor. Stage* i. (1730) 18 A very indifferent Religion well Believed, will go a great way. 1749 CHESTERF. *Lett.* (1792) II. ccxi. 308 Your stay at Rome will go a great way towards answering all my views. 1820 *Examiner* No. 612. 1/2 A mode of testimony which ought to go a good way with the Laureat. 1841 MACAULAY in Trevelyan *Life* (1876) II. ix. 123 Where people look for no merit, a little merit goes a long way. 1849 *Tait's Mag.* XVI. 233/2 Every walk a man takes.. is as good as a course of lectures.. and goes far more toward his spiritual fashioning and culture. 1885 *Times* (weekly ed.) 25 Sept. 15/1 The farm produce goes a short way to filling the mouths.

d. With *far, as* or *so far, further, a long way*, etc. Of a stock of provisions, etc.: To hold out, suffice for distribution. Of clothing: To last, wear. Of money: To have purchasing power.

1419 *E.E. Wills* (1882) 40 ȝefe euere man and woman a Love and a galon of ale, als fer als it will go. 1667 DRYDEN *Prol. Secret Love*, Now old pantaloons Will go as far as formerly new gowns. *a* 1672 WILKINS (J.), Considering the cheapness, so much money might go farther than a sum ten times greater could do now. 1693 TATE *Juvenal, Sat.* xv. 105 Whose Flesh, torn off by Lumps, the rav'nous Foe In Morsels cut, to make it farther go. 1840 *Jrnl. R. Agric. Soc.* I. IV. 410 Turnips, if consumed under sheds, go so much further. 1879 M. J. GUEST *Lect. Hist. Eng.* xlii. 430 £4 a year .. in those days would go as far as forty would do now. 1889 MRS. E. KENNARD *Landing a Prize* III. i. 15 Money goes a long way in Norway.

44. To pass into a certain condition. Chiefly implying deterioration.

a. With adj. complement: To become, get to be (in some condition). (Cf. COME 25 a.) †***to go less***: to be abated or diminished. Also with *sb.* complement: to become, use, or adopt the characteristics of (something specified); ***to go all*** ——: see ALL C. 2 c; ***to go bush***: see BUSH *sb.*[1] 9 e; ***to go missing***: to get lost; ***to go native***: to turn to or relapse into savagery or heathenism; also *transf.* (cf. FANTI b); ***to go —— on*** (someone): to adopt a particular mode of behaviour towards or affecting (that person); ***to go public***: to become a public company.

1583 T. STOCKER tr. *Civ. Warres Lowe C.* I. 117 The siege of Leyden continued, & their victuals went very low. 1654 EARL MONM. *Bentivoglio's Warrs Flanders* II. 32 The Regent went every day less in her authority. 1688 R. HOLME *Armoury* II. 173/1 Boniclatter [is] Cream gone thick. 1769 MRS. RAFFALD *Eng. Housekpr.* (1778) 231 Let them [apricots] go cold betwixt every time. 1803 S. PEGGE *Anecd. Eng. Lang.* 243 He went dead about three months ago. 1845 HOOD *Love* iii, A poet gone unreasonably mad. 1861 *Temple Bar* III. 23 He went bankrupt. *Ibid.* 248 Fright and.. anxiety have.. made strong men go gray in a single night. 1881 J. P. SHELDON *Dairy Farm.* 56/1 If it [the milk] is not taken proper care of it soon goes sour in hot weather. 1884 R. BUCHANAN *Foxglove Manor* III. xxxiii. 122 Her cheeks went scarlet. 1888 LADY D. HARDY *Dang. Exper.* III. iv. 84, I trembled and went hot and cold. 1890 BOLDREWOOD *Col. Reformer* (1891) 419 Suppose he goes lame all of a sudden! 1891 *Sat. Rev.* 24 Jan. 101/2 Any bishopric or benchship that has just gone vacant. 1891 *Harper's Mag.* Oct. 720/2 Before us lay a sea of fern, gone a russet brown from decay. 1901 KIPLING *Kim* vii. 177 Kim did not sweep the board with his reminiscences; for St. Xavier's looks down on boys who 'go native altogether'. 1928 L. P. GREENE *Red Idol* 253, I do all the heavy work... That's the only thing that's saved me from going native altogether. 1929 J. P. MCEVOY *Hollywood Girl* (1930) vii. 102, I thought he was the one who had gone Hollywood. Pictures in the paper, guest of this and that. It's a wonder you notice me, I told him. 1930 *Times Lit. Suppl.* 4 Sept. 694 Religious ceremonies which suggest to him that the new religion of Christianity [in S. America] has, after the fashion of new religions, gone native. 1953 *Economist* 24 Oct. 273/2 (*headline*) BBC goes VHF. 1958 F. NORMAN *Bang to Rights* 56 The snout had gone missing. 1960 E. W. HILDICK *Boy at Window* iii. 29 The best white mouse I ever had! Nearly human! And now it's gone native! 1963 *Times* 28 Jan. 2/7 Tentative plans are that on reaching a total of 3,000 acres a private limited company should be formed, and that at 5,000 acres it should 'go public'. 1963 *Sat. Even. Post* 15 June 4/2 Don't go too 'arty' on us. 1965 *Listener* 16 Dec. 983/1 Within twelve years 2,500,000—one in seven—had gone missing. 1966 [see *city page* s.v. CITY 9]. 1966 *New Society* 17 Mar. 25/3 (*headline*) Amis goes serious on us. 1966 *New Yorker* 1 Oct. 183 (Advt.), Then I write my letter accusing them of going establishment. 1970 *Sci. Jrnl.* Aug. 3/3 It is not the fact that we are going nuclear that should give us pause. 1971 *Guardian* 6 July 7/6 A warning about the affairs of V and G was given as early as 1962, the year after the company went public.

b. To turn, be transformed *to*. Also *rarely*, to be reduced *to*.

1591 SPENSER *Teares Muses* 596 Eftsoones such store of teares shee forth did powre, As if shee all to water would haue gone. 1796 MRS. GLASSE *Cookery* iii. 28 If you boil pickled pork too long, it will go to a jelly. 1858 CARLYLE *Fredk. Gt.* II. v. (1872) I. 72 The Vohburg Family.. was now gone to this one girl. 1859 *Jrnl. R. Agric. Soc.* XX. II. 431 The more the produce is Graminaceous, the more it goes to flower and seed. 1889 MRS. BARR *Feet of Clay* xii. 236 The devil's corn all goes to bran. 1891 C. DUNSTAN *Quita* II. I. xv. 17 She has lost all her colour, and has gone to skin and bone.

c. Const. *to* with sb. indicating some ruined condition; in many phrases, as ***to go to pieces, to rack, ruin, smash***, etc., for which see the sbs.

IV. Quasi-*trans.* with pronoun as obj.

45. With pleonastic refl. pron. in various foregoing senses. Now only *arch.* [Cf. F. *s'en aller.*]

c 1175 *Lamb. Hom.* 27 Þe unclene gast þe geð him of þan sunfulle mon and geð him of þan stude to stude. *a* 1300 *Fall & Passion* 53 in *E.E.P.* (1862) 14 God him ȝed an erþ here xxxti winter an somdel mo. *a* 1300 *Cursor M.* 13191 Efter quen þe dai es gan, þai [Wod men] haf þair wijt and gas þam ham. 1400-50 *Alexander* 535 Gais him vp at þe grece. 1892 *Cosmopolitan* XIII. 727/2 So I may go me to mass, mamma, Along with my coal man lover.

46. go it.

†**a.** To direct one's course. *Obs.*

1689 H. PITMAN *Relation* in Arb. *Garner* VII. 365 When these had shared her cargo, they parted company: the

French with their shares went it for Petty Guavas, in the Grand Gustaphus.

†**b.** *imp.* = Be off! away with you! *Obs.*

1797 Mrs. M. Robinson *Walsingham* III. 306 So you had better be moving..take yourself off—go it—budge.

c. *colloq.* and *slang.* To go along at great speed; to pursue one's action with furious vigour; to engage recklessly in dissipation. ***to go it blind***: to plunge into a course of action without regarding the consequences. ***to go it alone***: to act by oneself, without support or assistance; hence ***go-it-alone*** adj., characterized by independent action. See also bald-headed *a.* b, strong *adv.* 1 c.

1821 Egan *Tom & Jerry* (1870) 236 Logic, under the domino, had been 'going it' on a few of his friends with much humour. **1830** *Chron.* in *Ann. Reg.* 191/1 A gentleman ..presented himself at the balcony..declaring that he would fire upon the first man that attempted to enter the house..A cry of 'Go it! go it!' was raised by the mob. **1840** Marryat *Olla Podr.* (Rtldg.) 301 That's going it rather strong. **1842** *Spirit of Times* 9 Apr. 67/1 George pulled..to the head of the next quarter stretch, where his jockey looking at what he had in 'hand', determined to 'go it alone'. **1848** Lowell *Biglow P.* Poet. Wks. 1890 II. 126 Honest folks that mean to go it blind. **1855** *Knickerbocker* Apr. 335 A ball through his frontal bone Laid him flat on his back on the hard-fought ground, And left Captain Davis to go it alone. **1856** *Titan Mag.* Aug. 101/1 'Go it, governor; smash, dash, and crash!' **1907** J. London *Iron Heel* xv. 193 He broached a scheme to have the Locomotive Engineers make terms with the railroads and to 'go it alone' so far as the rest of the labour unions were concerned. **1956** A. L. Rowse *Early Churchills* 225 Holland could not 'go it alone'. **1961** *Daily Tel.* 27 Apr. 19/5 A 'go-it-alone' British space programme would be a waste of scarce scientific manpower and resources. **1964** M. Gowing *Britain & Atomic Energy* vi. 196 In England..a 'go it alone' programme was being drawn up. **1966** *Rep. Comm. Inquiry Univ. Oxf.* I. 28 The appropriate question must be posed: not 'how far can any college go it alone?' but 'how far can the colleges..co-operate to form the policies of Oxford?'

V. Special uses of the pples.

47. Uses of the pr. pple. *going*.

a. ***going in*** or ***of*** ——: about to attain (a specified age) on one's next birthday; also without prep. Cf. *going on* ——, 61 b, *going upon*, 67 e, *going on for* ——, 86 k.

1700 Congreve *Way of World* v. v, Till she was going in her fifteen. **1785** Trusler *Mod. Times* I. 47 She knew she was as much a woman as herself, and that she was going in eighteen. **1877** *Gd. Words* XVIII. 5/2 Doris is goin' fifteen. **1886** *Chesh. Gloss.* 144 'How old is your daughter?' 'Oo 's goin' of eighteen.' **1888** G. Allen *Devil's Die* I. ix. 124 She would have given her age, if asked, as 'going thirteen'.

b. ***going to*** (with active or pass. inf.): on the way to, preparing or tending to. Now used as a more colloquial synonym of *about to*, in the auxiliaries of idiomatic compound tenses expressing immediate or near futurity. Cf. F. *je vais*. ***(to be) just going to***: (to be) on the point of (doing so and so).

1482 *Monk of Evesham* (Arb.) 43 Thys onhappy sowle.. was goyng to be broughte into helle for the synne and onleful lustys of her body. **1672** Lady Mary Bertie in *12th Rep. Hist. MSS. Comm.* App. v. 26, I believe next news I heare will be that you are going to be married. **1703** Locke *Let.* 23 July (*On Dr. Pococke*), As I was going to say. **1752** Mrs. Lennox *Fem. Quix.* i. xii, Glanville..saw himself going to be discarded a second time. **1789** T. Twining *Aristotle on Poetry* (1812) I. 153 At the instant that he is going to be sacrified, the discovery is made. *Ibid.* II. 129 When a brother kills, or is going to kill. **1826** in Cobbett *Rur. Rides* (1885) II. 61 Lambs..to be sold..to those who are going to keep them. **1861** Geo. Eliot *Silas M.* vi. 103, 'I aren't a-going to try and 'bate your price'. **1890** *Chamb. Jrnl.* 14 June 370/2 It seems as if it were going to rain.

48. Uses of the pa. pple. *gone*.

a. By a development from the ordinary use of *gone* in the perfect tense conjugated with *be* (esp. in sense 21), the phrase ***to be gone*** has assumed the sense: To depart (promptly or finally), to take oneself off. See also begone. Similarly ***to get oneself gone***, for which see get *v.* 28 c.

1577 B. Googe *Heresbach's Husb.* iv. (1586) 181 To shewe by their comming out, a greate desire to bee gone. **1599** H. Buttes *Dyets drie Dinner* P iv, Its safest we be gone, Lest [etc.]. **1628** Gaule *Pract. Theories* (1629) 384 He thrust in among some, and faine would haue bin gone from others. **1653** Walton *Angler* ii. 41 Come honest Viator, lets be gone. **1727** Boyer *Fr. Dict.* s.v. *Gone*, If you will not be gone presently. **1791** Mrs. Radcliffe *Rom. Forest* i, In the morning La Motte rose at an early hour impatient to be gone.

b. In *Archery*, said of an arrow when from its flight it is seen to have been shot beyond the mark. Similarly in *Bowls*, of a bowl which runs beyond the jack (hence *transf.* of the player).

1545 Ascham *Toxoph.* (Arb.) 36 Escheweing shorte, or gone, or eithersyde wide. **1611** Cotgr. s.v. *Passé*, *Ie suis passé*, I am gone, or ouercast, I haue throwne ouer, at Bowles, &c.

c. Dead; departed from life. See 28. Also ***dead and gone*** (see dead).

1595 Shaks. *John* iii. iv. 163 If that yong Arthur be not gone alreadie, Euen at that newes he dies. **1705** Addison *Italy* 230 A Dog, that has his Nose held in the Vapour, dies in a very little time; but if carry'd into the open Air.. recovers, if he is not quite gone. **1852** Mrs. Stowe *Uncle Tom's C.* xxviii, Strange that..one should be living, warm and beautiful..one day, and the next be gone, utterly gone, and for ever!

†**d.** In a state of swoon, unconscious (cf. 29 b). Also (very freq. in 17th c.), Dead drunk (more fully, ***gone in drink***).

1641 Hinde *Life Bruen* lxvi. 219 Hee could take no food.. but he was ready to faint and to be gone upon it. **1657** in *Burton's Diary* (1828) II. 70 The Speaker..said, I am a yea, a no, I should say. This caused an alternate laughter all the House over, and some said he was gone. **1661** Pepys *Diary* 9 Sept., Sir W. Penn..had been drinking to-day, and so is almost gone, that we could not make him understand it. **1681** H. More *Expos. Dan.* Pref. p. vii, Men so much gone in drink..would not be able to make any thing of it. **1691** tr. *G. d'Emilianne's Observ.* 249 The Singing-men [having drunk freely]..were quite gon, and knew no longer what they sung.

e. Infatuated (*in* love, wickedness, etc.). ***gone on***: (in recent colloq. or vulgar use) enamoured of, infatuated about.

1698 J. Collier *Short View* i. 12 Silenium is much gone in Love, but modest withal. **1858** Guthrie *Christ Inherit. Saints* (1860) 38 Gone in iniquity they boast..of the victims whom they have seduced. **1885** *Illustr. Lond. News* Xmas No. 7/1 Iris was gone on you yesterday. **1885** F. Anstey *Tinted Venus* 59, I saw directly that I'd mashed her—she was gone, dead gone, sir. **1888** *Lady* 25 Oct. 374/1 They seem to be quite gone on the culture and elevation of the people by the eye.

f. ***far gone***: in an advanced stage of a disease; deeply engaged or entangled; greatly fatigued or exhausted, etc. Usu. const. *in*; *spec.* extremely insane, drunk, or evil. See also far *adv.* 3 b.

1593 Shaks. *Rich. II*, ii. i. 184 Yorke is too farre gone with greefe. **1616** T. Roe *Jrnl.* 25 Oct. (1899) II. 303 The king returned at Euening, hauing beene ouer night farr gone in wyne. **1656** Baxter *Ref. Pastor* iv. §2 Wks. 1707 IV. 369 Some Men are so far gone in Pride, that [etc.]. **1713** Steele *Guardian* No. 106 ¶3, I am myself very far gone in this Passion for Aurelia. **1741** Mrs. Manley *Power Love* II. 152 Caton was far gone in Impudence. **1771** Smollett *Humph. Cl.* II. 49, I will follow you to the world's end, if you don't think me too far gone to be out of confinement. **1793** Beddoes *Let. to Darwin* 31 Far gone in a Consumption of the lungs. **1804** Eugenia de Acton *Tale without a Title* II. 187 She is far gone in the fashionable heroism of the English day. **1815** H. C. Robinson *Diary* 26 Feb. (1967) 39 Charles Lamb..[took] too much wine. He was not so far gone as to be outrageous..but he was flurried in his manner. **1822** *Osmond* II. 2 Osmond being a great deal too far gone in the tender passion. **1849** C. M. Yonge in *Magazine for Young* June 188 Poor Ned, he must have been far gone, indeed, to let his children go without Baptism! **1850** *Tait's Mag.* XVII. 681/2 Agenor was now too far gone in guilt to recede. **1872** Earl Pembroke & G. H. Kingsley *S. Sea Bubbles* i. 21 Two horses too far gone to be able to gallop. **1878** *Scribner's Mag.* XV. 363/2 The captain was..by no means so far gone in his infatuation. **1887** J. Ball *Nat. in S. Amer.* 253 Two ladies ..both far gone in intoxication. **1939** F. Thompson *Lark Rise* i. 8 They were not too far gone in poverty to neglect such means as they had to that end. **1947** J. Harvey *Gothic England* ii. 62 The latter [*sc.* painting] is now too far gone for detailed stylistic analysis.

g. Lost, ruined, undone. Of a battle, game, etc.: Lost. †***to give for gone***: to regard as hopeless.

1596 Shaks. *Merch. V.* iii. v. 20 Well, you are gone both waies. **1603** —— *Meas. for M.* v. i. 302 Is the Duke gone? Then is your cause gone too. **1621** Fletcher *Custom Country* v. i, I am gon. **1625** in *Virginia Mag. Hist. & Biog.* I. 162 The terror whereof..so dismaide the whole Colony, as they allmost gave themselves for gone. **1709** Mrs. Manley *Secret Mem.* (1736) II. 248 That would be giving the Matter for gone. **1798** *Invasion* I. 226 Waterford, at the first sight of a person by whom he was known, gave himself up for gone. **1858** Carlyle *Fredk. Gt.* iii. v. (1865) I. 166 Seeing the Battle gone..Ludwig too had to fly. **1889** 'B. W. D.' & 'Cavendish' *Whist with & without Perception* 71 If he leads the usual ace, king, the game is distinctly gone.

†**h.** In the absolute construction with a designation of an interval of time: = ago, since.

a **1300** *Cursor M.* 17331 (Cott.) For godd had said gan siþen lang 'Mi-self [etc.]'. *c* **1340** *Ibid.* 14188 (Trin.) Was þou not but litil gone Almest þere wiþ iewes slone. *c* **1386** Chaucer *Sqr.'s T.* 528 But sooth is seyd goon sithen many a day. **1549** Coverdale, etc. *Erasm. Par. Rom.* 29 Christe so many hundred yeares gone was in prophecies promysed. **1657** Cromwell *Sp.* 21 Apr. in *Carlyle*, Now six years gone.

i. Used to indicate that an interval is reckoned backward from a specified past date. (Cf. come *v.* 36 b.)

1837 Carlyle *Fr. Rev.* I. i. ii, It is twenty years, gone Christmas-day, since Lord Chesterfield [etc.]. *Ibid.* III. iii. i, On Monday gone five weeks..we saw Paris beheading its King, stand silent.

j. Preceding or following a statement of age: Over, more than the age mentioned. Cf. 47 a.

1858 Carlyle *Fredk. Gt.* vii. ii. II. 241 No hurry about Fritz's marriage; he is but eighteen gone. **1893** *Temple Bar* XCVII. 216 A man 'gone ninety years of age'.

VI. With prepositions, in specialized uses.

49. go about——.

†**a.** To encompass. Also in *indirect pass.*

1297 R. Glouc. (Rolls) 3 Þe see geþ him al aboute, he stond as in an yle. *c* **1300** *St. Brandan* 2 The see of occian.. goth the worlde aboute. *c* **1420** *Pallad. on Husb.* i. 788 Another with a diche aboute ygoon is. *c* **1440** *Promp. Parv.* 202/2 Goon a-bowtyn.., *circino*.

b. To busy oneself about; to set to work upon, take in hand; in early use, †to seek after. (Cf. *to be* about.) Also in *indirect pass.*

c **1532** Du Wes *Introd. Fr.* in *Palsgr.* 905 To go about rychesse, *ambicion*. **1577** B. Googe *Heresbach's Husb.* (1586) iv. 187 If they [bees] go about their businesse chere-fully. **1650** Trapp *Comm., Numbers* xi. 13 Lust is un-satisfiable; to go about it is to go about an endless piece of work. **1687** Burnet *Reply to Varillas* 33 Those who write upon true Information, know what they go about. **1739** Wesley *Wks.* (1872) XII. 108 Let the leaden cistern be gone about. **1885** Mary Linskill *A Lost Son*, etc. 247 She went about her work in a cold, impassive way.

50. go after——. To go in pursuit of; to visit as a wooer or a disciple.

The expression 'to go after other gods' in all Eng. versions of the Bible, is a literal rendering of Vulg. *ambulare post deos alienos* and its Heb. original, which expresses rather the sense 'to walk in the train of', 'follow the guidance of'.

c **1440** *Promp. Parv.* 202/2 Goon aftyr, *succedo*. **1847** Marryat *Childr. N. Forest* iv, Now, Edward, we are going after a fine stag. **1889** *Cornh. Mag.* Dec. 659 Don't you go after that Frenchwoman. They're not to be trusted.

51. go against, †**again**——.

†**a.** To go to meet. *Obs.*

c **1290** *Beket* 2058 in *S. Eng. Leg.* I. 165 Þare-with wel baldeliche: he eode a-3ein is fon. *c* **1350** *Will. Palerne* 4954 Gladli wiþ grete lordes sche goþ him a3ens. *c* **1477** Caxton *Jason* 62 She wente agaynst him and toke him by the hande. **1530** Palsgr. 570/1, I go agaynst one, I go to mete hym.. We be ynowe to go against hym.

b. Of a contest, an enterprise: To result unfavourably to.

a **1533** Ld. Berners *Huon* xv. 40 Ye mater was lykely to go yll agaynst the erle. **1568** Grafton *Chron.* II. 112 Never thing prospered with me, but it hath gone against me. **1816** Scott *Old Mort.* xxxviii, The law gaed again the leddies at last. **1862** *Temple Bar* V. 25 The case had gone dead against them from the beginning.

c. To run counter to, oppose, militate against.

1530 [see against *prep.* 10]. **1688** Burnet *Lett. State Italy* 111 The smallest thing, that seems..to go against their Interest, is lookt after with a very watchful care. **1878** *Scribner's Mag.* XVI. 82/2 How will he ever expect to get the money if he goes against my wishes? **1885** Mrs. Lynn Linton *Chr. Kirkland* I. viii. 224 Literature..was a thing which went dead against our family traditions.

d. ***to go against the*** grain, hair, †***heart*** (also simply *against me* = against my feelings): (of an action) to be uncongenial, excite repugnance (see against 9 b, 10).

c **1460** *Towneley Myst.* ii. 221 It goyse agans myn hart full sore. *a* **1586** Sidney *Arcadia* i. (1633) 49 As it went against my heart to breake any way from you. **1749** Fielding *Tom Jones* xi. ii, It would go horribly against me to have her come to any harm. **1888** McCarthy & Mrs. C. Praed *Ladies' Gallery* I. ii. 57 It went against me not to give the poor fellow some sort of burial.

52. go at——. To make an attack upon; to take in hand vigorously. ***to go at it***: to enter upon an action, contest, etc. with energy. ***to go at the collar*** (said of a horse: see collar *sb.* 6).

1820 *Examiner* No. 637. 403/1 Our..Orator went at it again, like a Titan refreshed. **1863** Kingsley *Water-bab.* 324 At his legs the little dog went. **1881** Mrs. C. Praed *Policy & Passion* I. x. 204 I'm a plain-spoken man, and I go at a thing straight, without beating through the bush. **1887** P. Fendall *Sex to Last* I. i. x. 248 Selina went at her again for further information. **1888** *Berksh. Gloss.* s.v., A labourer enquired in the morning, 'What be I to go at to-daay?' **1888** *Harper's Mag.* July 183 In front..stretched a mighty crevasse..He went at it with a bound. **1890** Boldrewood *Col. Reformer* (1891) 291 The highly-conditioned horses went at their collars..and..rattled along.

53. go before——.

a. To precede in time or serial order, be anterior to.

1382 Wyclif *Ecclus.* i. 3 The wisdam of God goende beforn alle thingus, who enserchede? **1521** Fisher *Serm. agst. Luther* Wks. (1876) 328 The workes that gothe before faythe. **1629** H. Burton *Babel no Bethel* 6 The Councell.. surpasseth..all that went before it. **1837-8** Sir W. Hamilton *Logic* xv. (1866) I. 276 The other two [propositions], as naturally going before the conclusion, they have styled the premisses. **1849** *Tait's Mag.* XVI. 81/2 Pity 'tis these should pay for the bad men who have gone before them.

†**b.** To take precedence of, be superior to. *Obs.*

1611 Shaks. *Cymb.* i. iv. 78 If she went before others I haue seene as that Diamond of yours out-lusters many I haue beheld.

54. go behind——. (See behind *prep.* 3 and 8 c.) Also, in recent use, to reopen a question settled by (a previous decision or agreement).

1888 R. A. King *Leal Lass* II. iv. 63 Marry May he must —this was a postulate he would not go behind. **1890** *Spectator* 8 Feb., It was a piece of sharp practice, an attempt to go behind the settlement made by Cardinal Manning [etc.]. **1892** *Law Reports* 2 Q. Bench 544 In such a case the Court will go behind the compromise in order to see the nature of the original debt.

†**55. go beside**——. To pass over, miss. *Obs.*

c **1375**, **1382** [see beside B4]. **1530** Palsgr. 571/1, I go besydes my purpose, *je faulx a mon esme*. **1798** *Geraldina* I. 39 He cannot bear to see the loaves and fishes go beside his family.

†**56. go between**——. To act as a mediator between; to reconcile. *Obs.*

1549 Latimer *2nd Serm. bef. Edw. VI* (Arb.) 63 The regent of France was fain to be sent for from beyond the seas, to set them at one, and go between them. **1601** Shaks. *All's Well* v. iii. 256, I did goe betweene them as I said, but more then that he loued her.

57. go by——.

†**a.** To neglect, pass without notice; to pass unheeded. *Obs.* (Cf. go-by *sb.*)

c **1450** *St. Cuthbert* (Surtees) 7167 Þair ordure reule þai went bathe by And leuyd our dishonestly. **1513** Douglas *Æneis* vii. viii. 66 The messinger is nocht gone by myne eris [L. *non..meas effugit nuntius aures*]. **1549** *Compl. Scot.* viii. 72 O ignorant..pepil, gone by the pathvaye of verteouse Knaulage. *a* **1592** H. Smith *Wks.* (1866-7) I. 234 When you can go by an offence, and..suffer trouble quietly, you have a kind of peace and joy in your heart.

†**b.** *to go by one's day*: to pass one's prime. **1818** *Sporting Mag.* I. 295 Rainer..was considered rather gone by his day.

†**c.** *to go by the worse, worst*: to be worsted. **1563** GOLDING *Cæsar* I. (1565) 23 To whom the Heduanes .. had..gyuen battell: wherin going by the wors, they had receyued great domage. **1639** F. ROBARTS *God's Holy Ho.* ix. 63 As he [Moses] lifted up his hands to God, Amalek went by the worst. **1671** MILTON *Samson* 903 In argument with men a woman ever Goes by the worse. **1727** BOYER *Fr. Dict.* s.v., To go by the worst, *avoir du pire.*

58. go for——.

†**a.** To set out, leave, start for (a destination). **1616** in *Crt. & Times Jas. I* (1848) I. 428 The Lord Roos is gone for Spain. **1595, 1660–1** [see FOR *prep.* 12a]. **1704** MARLBOROUGH *Lett. & Disp.* (1845) I. 244, I may have the satisfaction of embracing you before I go for Holland. **1807** MILNER *Martyrs* III. ii. 124 At length having left Rome, we went for Bavaria. **1883** 'MARK TWAIN' *Life on Mississippi* xxiv. 269 They break camp and go for the woods.

b. To go to fetch; to fetch. **1594** MARLOWE & NASHE *Dido* III. i, Anna, good sister Anna, go for him. **1923** [see *bird dog* s.v. BIRD *sb.* 9]. **1937** D. L. SAYERS *Busman's Honeymoon* vi. 110 Leave everything as it is. Crutchley, you'd better go for the police.

c. To pass as or as equivalent to; to be accounted or valued as. Now only in *to go for nothing, little, something*, or the like. **1556** *Chron. Gr. Friars* (Camden) 68 Item the v. day of December [1550] was proclamyd that the French crownes shuld goo but for vjs. iiijd. **1577** *St. Aug. Manual* (Longman) 13 He that cares not to lyve for thee Lord, is nothing and goeth for nought. *a***1586** SIDNEY *Arcadia* I. (1590) 12b, Since she goes for a woman. **1623** LISLE *Ælfric on O. & N. Test.* 17 Which for likenesse of stile and profitable vse haue gone for his. **1655** GURNALL *Chr. in Arm.* verse 11. II. ix. §3 (1656) 150 Faith before temptation hath much heterogeneal stuffe that cleaves to it, and goes for faith. **1688** BURNET *Lett. State Italy* 186 The oaths..went for nothing, but matters of form. **1691** LOCKE *Consid. Lower. Int.* (1692) 21 Many who go for English Merchants, are but Dutch Factors, and Trade for others in their own Names. *Ibid.* 137 A Crown with us goes for 60 Pence. **1820** *Examiner* No. 655. 690/1 His testimony would go for nothing. **1867** FREEMAN *Norm. Conq.* (1876) I. iv. 193 His plighted faith went for as little as the plighted faith of a deliberate perjurer. **1885** MRS. LYNN LINTON *Chr. Kirkland* III. vii. 240 She was pretty too; and that went for something.

d. To have for one's aim; to aim at securing; †also = the later *go in for* (see 83). In recent use also with stronger sense (cf. e), to concentrate effort on the attainment of (an object). Also, to be enamoured of or enthusiastic about; to care for, like, or prefer; to choose, accept, or support. *c***1560** A. SCOTT *Poems* (S.T.S.) xvi. 30 Quha suld my dullit spreitis raiss, Sen for no lufe my lady gaiss? **1641** H. PEACHAM *Worth of a Peny* 32 Some go for recreations which trouble..the mind more then the hardest study, as Chesse. **1790** *By-stander* 288 It is a pity Captain Parslowe did not go for twenty thousand pounds, for through such a judge and such a jury he would have received every halfpenny of it. **1800** ADDISON *Amer. Law Rep.* 23 The present form of action..goes only for the money supposed to have been actually received. **1830** W. L. GARRISON in *Life W. L. Garrison* (1885) I. 201 In politics..I go for the people—the whole people. **1835** P. HONE *Diary* 13 Nov. (1889) I. 172 Daniel Webster's claim is incomparably stronger than that of either of the other candidates. He is entitled to the people's votes... I go, therefore, for Webster. **1839** *Congress. Globe* 6 Dec. 25 No, sir, I go for the laws and the Constitution, whether they define the qualifications of the voter, or prescribe the manner in which this right shall be exercised. **1864** *Jrnl. R. Agric. Soc.* XXV. II. 445 Their breeders go for open wool as much as possible. **1877** *Scribner's Mag.* XV. 7/1 Each dog selected his bird, and went for it steadily. **1882** MISS BRADDON *Mt. Royal* III. viii. 155 Miss Vandeleur had made up her mind not to 'go for' any marriageable man in too distinct a manner. **1930** *Amer. Mercury* Dec. 456/1, I go for that gee. He's a righto. **1936** *Studies in Eng.* (Univ. Texas) XVI. 44 *Go for*..signifies..to become enthusiastic over something or somebody. **1940** HARRISSON & MADGE *War begins at Home* ix. 241 Comedy songs that are anti-Hitler the public are at first inclined to go for. **1950** A. BARON *There's no Home* 65, I could go for you in a big way, kid. **1952** M. R. RINEHART *Pool* xxi. 196 She doesn't go for whiskers. **1962** *Listener* 8 Nov. 759/1, I myself don't go at all for that heartiness, that matey stuff..which figures so largely in mountaineering books. **1962** K. ORVIS *Damned & Destroyed* i. 12 The people will never go for that guff.

e. *colloq.* To assail, attack; whether with physical force or violent language. **1880** *Sat. Rev.* 18 Sept. 369/2 Every now and then Mr. Mercer goes for the citizens with a bowie. **1890** *Illustr. Lond. News* 16 Aug. 194/2 A couple of novelists..have 'gone for' the critics. **1890** BOLDREWOOD *Col. Reformer* (1891) 243 The black cow..immediately went for him.

f. To go for the purpose of becoming; to become; to act as. **1741**, etc. [see FOR *prep.* 8b]. **1957** A. WILSON *Bit off Map* 1 I'm well made all right. I could go for a model if I wanted.

g. To be valid or applicable for (a person); usu. in phr. *that goes for me*, etc. = that applies to me; that is my opinion. orig. *U.S.* **1923** C. E. MULFORD *Black Buttes* iii. 36 In case nobody ever told you to go to hell before, I'm tellin' you now. That goes for the town an' everybody in it. **1925** T. DREISER *Amer. Trag.* (1926) I. II. xxx. 360 She thinks I don't like her, and that's right, I don't... And that goes for that little Cranston show-off, too. **1936** WODEHOUSE *Laughing Gas* v. 63, I don't care if Pittsburgh chokes. And that goes for Cincinnati, too. **1941** *Punch* 2 July p. v/2 (Advt.), If you require *anything* that can possibly be connected with wire or wire-ropes (and this goes for manila and hemp ropes and canvas, too), British Ropes Ltd. can supply you. **1959** *Listener* 5 Mar. 431/2 That goes for all his music written.. in the last twenty years and it applies to his lighter style of writing as well.

h. *to go for broke*: to make strenuous efforts; to go 'all out'. *U.S. slang.* **1951** *Amer. Speech* XXVI. 26 *Go for broke* means to bend every effort, to 'shoot the works'. **1963** *Guardian* 5 June 6 If he were to go for broke on behalf of the Negroes..the President would endanger the moral reform cause. **1968** *Ibid.* 19 Feb. 1/7 The enemy is 'going all out—..he is going for broke'.

i. To be in one's favour; to be favourable or advantageous to; esp. in phr. *to have* (something) *going for one. colloq.* **1967** *Melody Maker* 29 July 6/7 But his swing is ridiculous. He's got everything going for him. **1968** *Listener* 5 Dec. 749/2 Mr and Mrs White Rhodesia have quite enough going for them to make do with a few minor self-denials. **1970** *New Yorker* 10 Oct. 174/2 She has a lot going for her. Her serve..comes in hard and fast.

59. go into——.

a. See simple senses and INTO. †*to go into the field*: i.e. for the purpose of fighting a duel. *to go into (a Cabinet, Parliament)*: to become a member of. *to go into society*: to appear habitually at private or public entertainments. **1616** in *Crt. & Times Jas. I* (1848) I. 433, I heard yesternight that Sir Henry Rich was gone into the field with Sir Ralph Sheldon. **1831** WELLINGTON in *Blackw. Mag.* CXXXV. 267/2, I should be very sorry to go into any Cabinet of which he is not a member. **1855** DICKENS *Dorrit* II. v, Miss Fanny..had become the victim of an insatiate mania for what she called 'going into society'. **1888** McCARTHY & MRS. C. PRAED *Ladies' Gallery* I. iii. 62 He wanted to go into Parliament. *Ibid.* II. iii. 34, I don't go into society much.

b. To join or take part in; to undertake. **1688** BURNET *Lett. State Italy* 11 Those who are discontented do naturally go into every new thing that.. promises relief. *a***1715** —— *Own Time* (1823) I. 61 When the war broke out in England, the Scots had a great mind to go into it. **1861** *Temple Bar* I. 270 He had gone largely into government contracts. **1877** MISS YONGE *Cameos* Ser. III. xxvi. 253 He went eagerly into the compact. **1889** F. PIGOT *Strangest Journ. Life* 213 He went into a railway, and no dividend was declared.

†**c.** To agree, accede to. *Obs.* **1713** ADDISON *Cato* II. iii, Cato, we all go into your opinion. *a***1715** BURNET *Own Time* (1823) I. 456 All these schemes settled in a proposition into which the King went. **1741** MIDDLETON *Cicero* I. iii. 211 Cicero's friends were going forwardly into it, as likely to create the least trouble to Cicero himself. **1762** *Gentl. Mag.* 10/2 Cuchullin, of himself willing to fight, went into the opinion of Calmar.

d. To enter upon a specified state, condition, or process; to take up a specified attitude. Also in *indirect pass.* **1776** FOOTE *Capuchin* I. Wks. 1799 II. 386, I might have gone into keeping. **1781** *Hist. Eur.* in *Ann. Reg.* 191*/2 If the enquiry was seriously gone into. **1845** *Jrnl. R. Agric. Soc.* VI. II. 301 Expensive improvements have been already gone into. **1845** LD. HOUGHTON in T. W. Reid *Life* (1891) I. 356 The *Times* has gone into open opposition to the Government on all points except foreign policy. **1898** *Athenæum* 23 Apr. 537/2 'The Marchioness against the County', is just going into its third edition.

e. To pass or allow oneself to pass *into* (ecstasies, hysterics, passion, etc.). **1677** LADY CHAWORTH in *12th Rep. Hist. MSS. Comm.* App. v. 41 Lord Worcester's lady is gone almost into a mopishnesse with malancolly. **1831** FR. A. KEMBLE in *Rec. Girlhood* (1878) III. 71, I..nearly went into hysterics. **1849** MACAULAY *Hist. Eng.* vi. II. 41 The King..went into a rage with Saxton. **1889** *Temple Bar* Dec. 533 The man..who went into ecstasies at discovering that Cape Breton was an island. **1889** F. BARRETT *Under Str. Mask* I. vi. 93 An artist would have gone into raptures over the scene.

f. To enter as a profession or occupation. **1820** *Examiner* No. 616. 65/1 His Royal Highness then went into the army. **1825** *New Monthly Mag.* XIV. 328 Since he went into orders, he is very anxious not to swear. **1841** *Fraser's Mag.* XXIII. 15 The young divine goes into the church. **1850** *Tait's Mag.* XVII. 340/1 He was skilful in many ways, but never went into regular service. **1878** *Scribner's Mag.* XVI. 860/2 Hicks naturally went into law. **1888** GOODMAN *Paid in his own Coin* I. xiii. 245 He went into practice for himself. **1890** *Field* 8 Mar. 347/1 [He] went keenly into dairying. **1890** *Sat. Rev.* 13 Sept. 320/1 The American gentleman seldom or never goes into politics.

g. To adopt as a style of dress, to dress oneself or be dressed in (*esp.* mourning). **1666** PEPYS *Diary* 15 Oct., Lady Carteret tells me ladies are to go into a new fashion shortly. **1671** LADY MARY BERTIE in *12th Rep. Hist. MSS. Comm.* App. v. 23 We are all goeing into mourning for the Dutchesse of York. **1711** ADDISON *Spect.* No. 64 ¶1 When it is the Fashion to go into Mourning. **1862** *Temple Bar* IV. 554 She..shocked Mrs. Grundy by refusing to go into full mourning. *Mod.* To go into frocks, long dresses, trousers, etc.

h. *to go into* (†*a*, †*the*) *committee* (see COMMITTEE 3). Said also of a bill. **1820** *Examiner* No. 620. 136/1 The House then went into the Committee. **1823** *New Monthly Mag.* IX. 290/1 The.. Bill went into a committee. *Ibid.* 293 The House went into a Committee on the..Bill.

i. To examine or discuss minutely. *to go into detail(s* (see DETAIL *sb.* 3). **1820** *Examiner* No. 616. 71/2 It was not necessary for him to go into the character, public and private, of the great statesman. **1855** MACAULAY *Hist. Eng.* xv. III. 499 It is not easy to believe that any tribunal would have gone into such a question. **1879** M. J. GUEST *Lect. Hist. Eng.* xvii. 161 We cannot of course go into the history of these wars.

j. *Pugilism.* To assail vigorously. **1811** *Sporting Mag.* XXXVII. 100 Molineux..went into Crib pell mell.

60. go off——.

a. See simple senses and OFF. †*to go off the tool*: to leave the workman's hands (*obs.*). *to go off one's head* or *chump* (see HEAD *sb.* 34, CHUMP *sb.* 2b). *to go off milk*: (of a cow) to leave off yielding milk. **1665** J. WEBB *Stone-Heng* (1725) 44 The outward Course of Stones..appear not so smooth, and neat, as when first they went off the Tool. **1884** *Times* (weekly ed.) 5 Sept. 14/4 Or the cows go off milk for a time, and then they [the owners of the cows] must be content to drink water.

b. To shirk; to fail to fulfil. **1749** FIELDING *Tom Jones* XVII. iii, Did I ever go off any bargain when I had promised?

c. To cease to like; to begin to dislike. **1934** E. BOWEN *Cat Jumps* 232 That's where I went right off him. In fact, he's not a nice man. **1965** M. SPARK *Mandelbaum Gate* iii. 76, I simply don't feel anything for him any more. In fact, I've gone off him. **1969** *Listener* 24 July 127/1 Then word came down that the editor had gone off the idea and was averse to naming individual pubs.

61. go on——.

a. See simple senses and ON. *to go on a wind*: to avail oneself of it for sailing. *to go on board* (see BOARD *sb.* 14b). *to go on one's knees* (see KNEE). **1844** KINGLAKE *Eothen* (1847) 66 They rarely go on a wind if it blows at all fresh.

b. To approach (a point of time) usu. in *pres. pple.*; freq., to approach (a specified age). Cf. senses 47a and 86k. **1577** HANMER *Anc. Eccl. Hist.* (1585) 377 When the Emperour Theodosius went on the eight yeare of his age. **1670** W. WALKER *Idiomat. Anglo-Lat.* 226, I am going on my fourscore and four. *Quartum annum ago & octogesimum.* **1798** CHARLOTTE SMITH *Yng. Philos.* III. 160 Scarce any body have come to see her here, though she have been here going on three weeks. **1876** T. E. BROWN *Doctor* 17 The only child,..And just about goin' on twenty-one. **1880** 'MARK TWAIN' *Tramp Abroad* xx. 193 Been here going on two years. **1924** C. C. O'CONNOR *Case of Galileo* viii. 45 He.. appealed to his judges to consider his age (he was going on seventy). **1959** O. HAMMERSTEIN II (*song-title*) Sixteen going on seventeen.

†**c.** To enter on, take up (a subject) for discussion; to begin, undertake (an action). **1508** FISHER *7 Penit. Ps.* xxxii. Wks. (1876) 23 This holy prophete gooth shortly on all these in the same ordres as we haue rehersed to you. **1611** SHAKS. *Wint. T.* II. i. 121 This Action I now goe on, Is for my better grace.

†**d.** To consider the case of, examine judicially. (Cf. *go upon*, 67c.) **1662** GURNALL *Chr. in Arm.* verse 17 xiv. §2. 106 When the Jury shall go on thy murdered soul,..thou wilt be found guilty of thine own damnation.

e. To care for, concern oneself about; usu. in negative contexts, esp. in phr. *not to go much on* (something). *colloq.* (orig. *U.S.*). **1824** in N. E. Eliason *Tarheel Talk* (1956) 274 The people goes more on making nice cloth hear than they did thare. **1882** B. HARTE *Flip* ii, We don't go much on that kind of cattle here. **1892** *Eng. Illustr. Mag.* IX. 460 She didn't go much on me, but the boy was everything to her. **1940** F. SARGESON *Man & Wife* (1944) 80, I don't go much on putting people away, I said. **1941** *Coast to Coast 1941* 197 They didn't go much on any of the chaps. **1958** *Daily Express* 17 Feb. 3/6 Waterloo was fascinating. But I didn't go much on the old armour. **1960** 'N. SHUTE' *Trustee from Toolroom* 12 Jo says she wants to live in Tahiti, but I don't go much on that, myself. **1963** P. WILLMOTT *Evolution of Community* vii. 73 This estate is low class. I don't go on the other people here myself.

f. To become chargeable to (the PARISH, the funds of a friendly society, etc.). (Cf. *go upon*, 67b.)

g. To use (something) as evidence or as a starting-point. *colloq.* **1947** K. TENNANT *Lost Haven* xix. 318 'Course I've got nothing to go on, but I wouldn't be a bit surprised if the johns wasn't on to us.

62. go over——.

a. To cross, pass to the other side of. *to go over the top*: see TOP *sb.*[1] 3d. **1535** COVERDALE *Deut.* iv. 21 And the Lorde was angrie with me for your sakes, so that he sware, yt I shulde not go ouer Iordane.

b. To visit and inspect the various parts of (a building, an estate, etc.). **1830** FR. A. KEMBLE in *Rec. Girlhood* (1878) II. vi. 183, I have been gratified and interested..by going over one of the largest manufactories of this place. **1885** *Law Times* LXXIX. 74/2 The defendants had gone over the house before taking it.

c. To admit of being placed or laid over. **1841** *Jrnl. R. Agric. Soc.* II. II. 181 Sufficient dung is made on the farm to go over the fallow. **1890** *Eng. Illustr. Mag.* Sept. 891 Fox gave him a vizard to go over his face.

d. To pass in review; to consider seriatim. *a***1586** SIDNEY *Arcadia* II. (1633) 170 So in this jolly-scoffing bravery he went over us all, saying he left one, because she was over-wayward; another, because [etc.]. **1644** DIGBY *Two Treat.* Ded. 6, I should haue kept it by me, till I had once againe gone ouer it. **1687** BURNET *Contin. Reply to Varillas* 66 Thus I have gone over his third Tome. **1695** LOCKE *Further Consid. Value Money* 91 And thus I have gone over all Mr. Lowndes's Reasons for raising our Coin. **1781** E. RUTLEDGE in Sparks *Corr. Amer. Rev.* (1853) III. 389, I really believe we shall have the whole business of civil government to go over. **1873** BLACK *Pr. Thule* xxi. 337 One after the other she went over the acquaintances she had made. **1881** Miss G. M. Craik *Sydney* III. i. 13 Horace and I have been going over old letters.

e. To read over; to rehearse.

1779 Sheridan *Critic* III. i, *Whisk.* I wish, Sir—you would practise this without me.. *Puff.* Very well; we'll go over it by and bye. **1841** *Fraser's Mag.* XXIII. 16 The school-boy goes over his lesson, before going up before the master.

f. To repeat, tell over.

1690 Locke *Hum. Und.* II. xvi. §7 And some, through the default of their memories.. are not able all their life-time to reckon, or regularly go over any moderate series of numbers. For he that will count twenty [etc.]. **1878** *Scribner's Mag.* XVI. 228/1 He went over the explanation two or three times.

g. To examine in detail and operate on as is found necessary; to revise or retouch throughout (a piece of work). Often with *again*.

1897 *Garden* 1 May 318/2 It is necessary to go over the beds daily. *Mod.* Is the picture finished, or must you go over it again?

h. *slang.* To search and rob (a person). (Cf. *go through*, 63 f.)

1889 *Referee* 2 June 1/2 A few who had.. gone over the landlord, left him skinned.

63. go through——.

a. †To execute (a design) (*obs.*); to deal in succession with all the stages of (a business, a course of study, etc.).

a **1586** Sidney *Arcadia* I. (1633) 18 The world sooner wanted occasions, than hee valour to goe through them. **1598** Grenewey *Tacitus' Ann.* VI. viii. (1622) 133 Barbarous people count temporizing and delay, as base and seruile; and to goe through presently their deseignments, a royall point. **1700** Wallis in *Collect.* (O.H.S.) I. 316 He did with them go through a whole course of chymistry. **1707** Addison *Pres. State War* (1708) 38 The greatest Powers in Germany are borrowing Mony, in order to.. go thorough their part of the Expence. **1813** Southey *Life Nelson* II. vi. 37 When he discovered that the judge's orders were to go through the business in a summary manner [etc.].

b. To examine and discuss seriatim; to scrutinize thoroughly.

1668 Marvell *Corr.* xcix. Wks. 1872–5 II. 252 The Committee of the whole House hath now gon through that Bill. **1711** Addison *Spect.* No. 44 ¶8, I have now gone through the several dramatick Inventions which are made use of by the ignorant Poets. **1861** *Temple Bar* I. 405 It took the party some time to go through the contents of the casket. **1887** L. Carroll *Game of Logic* i. §1. 14 It would take far too long to go through all the Propositions.

c. To declaim, recite, sing, etc. at full length; to perform in detail, to enact the several points of.

1766 Goldsm. *Vic. W.* xvii, He has taught that song to our Dick.. and I think he goes through it very prettily. **1815** Chalmers *Let.* in *Life* (1851) II. 21 They must have four [Ministers] to every funeral, or they do not think that it has been genteelly gone through. **1869** A. W. Ward *Curtius' Hist. Greece* II. II. iv. 33 The youths went through their exercises under the superintendence of the law. **1877** Miss Yonge *Cameos* Ser. III. xvii. 154 A form of trial was gone through.

d. To experience, submit to, suffer, undergo.

1712 Arbuthnot *John Bull* III. App. ii, I tell thee, it is absolutely necessary for the common good, that thou shouldst go through this operation. **1820** *Examiner* No. 619. 113/1 He has already gone through unutterable agonies. **1847** Helps *Friend in C.* (1851) I. 19 All that men go through may be absolutely the best for them. **1889** *Repent. P. Wentworth* I. viii. 158 Wentworth had gone through a process of moral hardening.

e. Of a book: To have all the copies sold of (an edition); now only, to be published successively in (so many editions). (Cf. *pass, run through.*)

1820 *Examiner* No. 629. 278/1 The *Cenci*.. had nearly gone through the first edition. **1889** J. M. Robertson *Ess. Critical Meth.* 18 The 'Elements'.. went through seven editions.

f. *slang.* To search and rob. Also, to search (a person). (Cf. *go over*, 62 h.)

1861 *Calif. Police Gaz.* (San Francisco) 31 Mar. 2/4 Upon 'going through him', over $2,000 was found upon his person. **1865** T. W. Knox *Camp-fire & Cotton-field* 421 Not being privileged to 'go through' me as they had anticipated, the gentlemanly guerrillas went through the overseer. They took his money, his hat, his pantaloons, and his saddle. **1887** F. Francis Jr. *Saddle & Mocassin* iv. 71 These gentlemen [cow-boys] had lately 'gone through' the coaches with great regularity. **1896** *Westm. Gaz.* 20 Apr. 2/3 Two men were charged in the police-courts on Saturday with attempting to 'go through' the pockets of an elderly gentleman. **1931** 'D. Stiff' *Milk & Honey Route* 205 Train crews also *go through* the hobos. **1945** R. W. Service *Ploughman* 194 The girls were 'going through' a drunken sailor.

g. To wear out, make holes in; to use up.

1959 H. Pinter *Birthday Party* I. 2 He goes through his socks terrible. **1966** *Which?* Jan. 25/1 No fewer than 80 (of 118) reported water pump failure, and these members have between them gone through 103 pumps.

64. go to ——. Colloq. phr. *to go to it*: to go ahead; to get to work; to 'get cracking'; freq. *imp.*

1735–6 S. Legge *Alphabet of Kenticisms* (1876) 30 *Going to 't*, i.e. going to do it; as, 'do this or that;' the answer is—'I am going to 't.' **1917** Megrue & Hackett *It pays to Advertise* I. 40 Go to it. **1932** Wodehouse *Louder & Funnier* 12 Stoke up and go to it. **1952** C. Day Lewis tr. *Virgil's Aeneid* IX. 188 How they went to it then!

65. go under——.

To submit to, undergo. *Obs.* exc. *dial.*

c **1449** Pecock *Repr.* II. x. 204 Which with thi fre wil hast goon vndir for us the lawis of deeth [L. *ultro qui mortis pro nobis jura subisti*]. **1881** *Lanc. Gloss.*, *Go-under*, to undergo; to suffer, as in the case of a surgical operation.

66. go up ——. See simple senses and up. *to go up King Street*: to become bankrupt (Australian). *to go up the form* (see quot. 1683).

1683 Moxon *Mech. Exerc.* II. 318 Thus Beating from the hither towards the farther side, is in Press-mens phrase called Going up the Form. *Ibid.*, Then in like manner he again skips the Balls from the second and fourth Row to the first and third Row, and again Goes up the Form with the Balls. **1890** Boldrewood *Col. Reformer* (1891) 368 That stuck-up beggar.. may marry his cousin, and go up King Street the next week for all we care.

67. go upon——. (See simple senses and upon.)

†a. To attack, proceed against. *Obs.*

1430–40 Lydg. *Bochas* I. xiv. (1554) 27a, Meleager.. Pulled out a sweord and upon them he goeth. *c* **1500** *Melusine* lix. 348 Go we vpon our enemyes to helpe & socoure our frendes. **1530** Palsgr. 570/2, I go upon a mannes enemye, or assayle hym.

†b. To be chargeable to. *Obs.* (Cf. *go on*, 61 f.)

1660 Marvell *Corr.* iii. Wks. 1872–5 II. 18 All things are to go upon his Majestye's own purse.

†c. Of a judicial authority: To consider the case of. (Cf. *go on*, 61 d.) *Obs.*

[**1215** *Magna Carta* §39 Nec super eum ibimus, nec super eum mittemus. **1817** J. Evans *Excurs. Windsor* 283 The expressions, we will not go upon him, we will not send upon him, signify, that the king would not sit in judgment, or pronounce sentence on any freeman.]

a **1586** Sidney *Arcadia* III. (1633) 313 He needed no Judge to goe upon him: for no man could ever thinke any other worthy of greater punishment, than hee thought himselfe. **1706** S. Sewall *Diary* 6 June (1879) II. 163 The Govr. bundled up the papers and sent them into the House of Deputies, without asking the Council whether they would first go upon them, with whom the Petition was entered. *a* **1715** Burnet *Own Time* (1823) II. 38 They next went upon the duke of Buckingham.

d. To take in hand. Also in *indirect pass.*

1607 Shaks. *Cor.* I. i. 282 Let's hence, and heare.. in what fashion.. he goes Vpon this present Action. **1743** Johnson *Let. to Cave* Aug. in *Boswell*, The Life of Savage I am ready to go upon. **1751** R. Paltock *P. Wilkins* I. xxv. 242 The first Thing I went upon was a Table; which.. I intended to make big enough for us all. **1896** *Pall Mall Mag.* Dec. 470, I.. cannot bear to see things botched or gone upon with ignorance.

†e. = *go on*, 61 b. *Obs.*

1622 Mabbe tr. *Aleman's Guzman d'Alf.* II. III. ii. 231 In all the time that I haue serued his Maiesty.. which is now going vpon the three and twentieth yeare.

f. = *go on*, 61 g.

1909 F. Barclay *Rosary* xv. 154 You see, this gave me something to go upon.

68. go with——.

a. To accompany, attend as a companion; in vulgar use, to 'keep company with' as a lover.

1523 Ld. Berners *Froiss.* I. ccxcvi. 439 Ye shall be souerayne and gouernour.. of all theym that gothe with you. **1603** *Philotus* xcv, 3e sall ga with me hame. **1849** Macaulay *Hist. Eng.* v. I. 544 It was determined that.. Fletcher should go with Monmouth to England. **1892** *Harper's Mag.* May 932/1 The 'young ladies' he had 'gone with' and 'had feelin's about' were now staid matrons.

b. To be associated with, be a concomitant of.

1601 Shaks. *All's Well* I. i. 49 For where an vncleane mind carries vertuous qualities, the commendations go with pitty. **1751** Jortin *Serm.* (1771) IV. i. 6 Poverty and riches are of themselves things indifferent; and the blessing of God may go with them both. **1873** H. Spencer *Stud. Sociol.* xv. 361 Criminality habitually went with poverty.

c. To side with. (Cf. B. 5 a.)

c **1460** Fortescue *Abs. & Lim. Mon.* ix. (1885) 129 The peple will go with hym þat best mey susteyne and rewarde ham. **1611** Shaks. *Cymb.* v. 76 The day Was yours by accident: had it gone with vs, We should not [etc.]. **1886** *Athenæum* 7 Aug. 169/3 We cannot go with him in defending the MS. 'tibi'.. as an ethical dative. **1892** *Cornh. Mag.* July 47 My sympathies went strongly with the lady.

d. To match; to harmonize with.

1710 *Tatler* No. 157 ¶12 A Dulcimer.. goes very well with the Flute. **1852** Dickens *Bleak Ho.* xl, The innocence which would go extremely well with a sash and tucker is a little out of keeping with the rouge and pearl necklace. **1888** F. Barrett *Lady Biddy Fane* III. lxii. 199, I made a hat for my lady; not so much like a woman's as a boy's, that it might go fairly with her habit. **1890** *Murray's Mag.* Nov. 629 Pride is a luxury which goes ill with poverty. **1893** *Cornh. Mag.* July 93 A delightful baritone, which 'went' beautifully with her own soprano.

e. To understand; to follow intelligently.

a **1873** Lytton *Ken. Chillingly* xiii, 'Do you go with me?' 'Partly, Sir, but I'm puzzled a little still.' **1891** *Law Times* XC. 462/1 The Court declared the deed a nullity on the ground that the mind of the mortgagee did not go with the deed she signed.

69. go without——. Not to have; to dispense with, put up with the want of.

1596 Shaks. *Merch. V.* I. ii. 97, I hope I shall make shift to goe without him. **1647** Trapp *Comm. Titus* i. 16 Faint chapmen that go without the bargain, as he did that came kneeling to our Saviour, and saying, What shall I do to inherit eternall life? **1650** Arnold Boate in *Abp. Ussher's Lett.* (1686) 558 Rather than he should go without it, I would bestow mine own Copy upon him, if I had it still. **1825** *New Monthly Mag.* XIII. 139 We had rather eat the same dinner two days following than go without one. **1872** S. Butler *Erewhon* ii. 10, I had to go without my own grog. **1889** Mona Caird *Wing of Azrael* I. ii. 10 Viola had to go almost without education.

absol. or *ellipt.* **1458** in *Turner's Dom. Archit.* III. 43 Of the pore penyles the hiereward wold habbe A hood or a girdel, and let hem goo without. **1589** Puttenham *Eng. Poesie* III. xix. (Arb.) 218 That one man should haue many at once, and a great number goe without that were as able men. **1695** Locke *Further Consid. Value Money* 58 Silver which every Goldsmith.. was content to pay high for, rather than go without. **1889** Gissing *Nether World* III. xii. 253 You'll eat this or go without.

VII. Combined with adverbs.

70. go about.

a. To go to and fro, move hither and thither, travel in divers places; (of a report, money) to circulate, have currency; also, †to move round in a circle, to complete a cycle.

a **1300** *Cursor M.* 12611 Sua lang a-bute þan had mari gan þat weri was sco bath lith and ban. *c* **1435** *Torr. Portugal* 2041 As Seynt Antony about yede, Byddyng his orysoun. **1529** More *Comf. agst. Trib.* III. Wks. 1214/1 As I go more aboute than you, so muste I nedes more here.. the maner of men in thys matter. **1530** Palsgr. 569/2, I go aboute, as a whele dothe, *je rotis.* **1594** Bp. J. King *Jonas* (1599) ii. 36 The moneths of the year haue not yet gone about, wherin the Lorde hath bowed the heavens, and come downe amongst vs. **1605** Shaks. *Macb.* I. iii. 34 The weird sisters, hand in hand.. Thus do go about, about. **1664** *Waller's Poems* Printer to Rdr., For we see clipt and washt Money go about when the entire and weighty lies hoarded up. **1749** Fielding *Tom Jones* VIII. ii, I think it is great Pity that such a pretty young Gentleman should undervalue himself so, as to go about with these Soldier Fellows. **1849** Thackeray *Pendennis* xlvii, An attorney's clerk, indeed, that went about with a bag. **1877** Miss Yonge *Cameos* Ser. III. xxi. 198 A report went about that Henry had murdered him.

b. *Mil.* To turn round.

1796–7 *Instr. & Reg. Cavalry* (1813) 65 Should it be required again to form in line on the same ground, the divisions will go about, ranks by three's.

†c. To use circumlocution. *Obs.*

1815 *Woman's Will* II. i, Why do you go about with me thus—why not speak to be understood?

d. *Naut.* (See about A 6 b.)

e. *to go about to* (see about A 10).

c **1380–1690** [see about A 10]. **1697** Collier *Ess. Mor. Subj.* II. (1703) 14 But because they [Diseases] are natural, it seems we must not go about to cure them. **1875** E. White *Life in Christ* IV. xxiv. (1878) 371 It is no sufficient answer to our argument to go about to prove that life carries with it an association of moral ideas.

71. go abroad. (See simple senses and abroad.)

a. Of a report, etc.: To circulate, have currency, be widely diffused. (Somewhat *arch.*) **†b.** To tear, come to pieces (*obs.*). **c.** To go out of doors or away from home (*obs.* exc. *dial.*). **d.** To go to a foreign country.

a. 1513 More in Grafton *Chron.* (1568) II. 768 That thereby shall be ceassed the slaunderous rumour and obloquy nowe going abrode. **1535** Coverdale *Micah* iv. 3 The tyme wil come, that thy gappes shal be made vp, and the lawe shal go abrode. *a* **1719** Addison *Evid. Chr. Relig.* (1733) 3 The report which had gone abroad concerning a life so full of miracles. **1888** McCarthy & Mrs. C. Praed *Ladies' Gallery* II. viii. 125 My fame had gone abroad in London.

b. 1568 *Satir. Poems Reform.* xlviii. 40 It tuggis in hoilis, and gais abbreid.

c. 1530 Palsgr. 569/2, I go abrode, as one dothe that gothe out of his chambre after a sickenesse, or gothe out of his house to be sene. **1725** Pope *Let. to Swift* 15 Oct in *S.'s Wks.* (1841) II. 580 Here is Arbuthnot recovered from the jaws of death.. He goes abroad again, and is more cheerful than even health can make a man. *c* **1785** Cowper *Ep. to J. Hill* 23 Horatio's servant.. begg'd to go abroad.. 'Tis but a step, sir, just at the street's end. **1815** Jane Austen *Emma* I. xiii, The going abroad in such weather.

d. 1719 [see abroad A 4]. **1786** Mrs. Piozzi *Anecd. of Johnson* 168 His desire to go abroad, particularly to see Italy, was very great. **1871** Geo. Eliot *Middlemarch* I. ix, And now he wants to go abroad again.

72. go ahead. (See ahead.) To make one's way to the front in a race, etc. Also (until recently chiefly U.S.), to go forward, or to proceed with one's work, etc., without pause or hesitation; to make rapid progress.

1831 *American* (Harrodsburg, Ky.) 25 Mar. 2/5 We say to our Clay friends, 'go ahead.' **1839** Mill in *Westm. Rev.* XXXII. 508 The man.. who 'goes a-head' with a policy adapted for uniting the Reformers, will find all things prepared for him. **1840** [see ahead *adv.* 5]. **1845** *Punch* 8 Mar. 116/1 We should still go a-head, as this moment we do. **1868** *Nat. Encycl.* I. 618/2 *Go-ahead* is of American origin, and is used.. where the British would say 'all right'. **1870** R. Brough *Marston Lynch* xii. 110 Go a-head! in whatever you feel to be your vocation. **1877** C. Loftus *My Life* I. ii. 45 My brother.. quickly passing him, went ahead, and won the match easily. **1883** *Harper's Mag.* Nov. 871/1, 'I will show the way.'.. 'Oh, then go ahead.' **1898** *Pall Mall Mag.* Jan. 82 'Don't interrupt me when I am explaining problems to you'.. 'All right—go ahead'. **1966** *Listener* 23 June 904/2 In the meantime Sixtus was authorized to go ahead.

73. go along.

a. See simple senses and along *adv.* In *imp. go along! go along with you!* = 'Be off'; also as an expression of impatience or derision, = *go on.*

1535 Coverdale *Deut.* ii. 27, I wil go a longe by the hye waye, I wil nether turne to the righte hande ner to ye lefte. **1688** Miege *Gt. Fr. Dict.* II. s.v., To meditate as one goes along. **1840** *P. Parley's Ann.* I. 29, I asked her for a half-penny twelfth-cake just now, and she said, 'Go along; go along'. **1897** Fl. Marryat *Blood Vampire* vi, 'Go along with you, you bad boy', chuckled the Baroness.

b. *to go along with*: to proceed or travel in company with; †to follow intelligently (an exposition); to agree with or approve of (up to a specified point); to accompany, attend upon; to be the regular concomitant of; †to be classed together with.

1602 SHAKS. *Ham.* I. ii. 15 Nor haue we heerein barr'd Your better Wisedomes, which haue freely gone With this affair along. **1695** LOCKE *Further Consid. Value Money* 8 If this Security goes not along with the publick Stamp, Coining is labour to no purpose. *a* **1698** TEMPLE *Of Her. Virtue* Wks. 1720 I. 196 Whatever remains in Story of Atlas ..is so obscured with Age or Fables, that it may go along with those of the Atlantick Islands. **1727** BOYER *Fr. Dict.* s.v., I go so far along with you. **1866** *Lond. Rev.* 17 Feb. 188/1 So far we go along with M. Deak and his friends. **1883** H. SPENCER in *Contemp. Rev.* XLIII. 14 It may..result that diminished happiness goes along with increased prosperity.

74. go around. a. = *go round* (sense 90 g). *U.S.*

1883 [see AROUND *adv.* 4]. **1965** *Word Study* Feb. 4/1 There are simply not enough words to go around for things.

b. To go here and there; to wander about; *spec.* to be regularly in company *with* (someone, esp. a sweetheart) (= *go with*, sense 68 a).

[**1896** in *Eng. Dial. Dict.* s.v. *around*, A seed em gangen aroond.] **1959** J. BRAINE *Vodi* xii. 162 Once he started going around with her there were more withdrawals than deposits in his Post Office savings book.

75. go away. (See simple senses and AWAY.)

a. To depart, go *from* a place or person. †Of time: To pass.

c **1200** *Vices & Virtues* (1888) 11 Ga awei fram me, ðu ȝewereȝede, forð mid te dieule! *c* **1400** *Apol. Loll.* 89 Wan þe pope goþ a wey fro Crist, & doþ þe contrari..þan is not he Cristis vicar. *c* **1450** *St. Cuthbert* (Surtees) 4675 þe schip sayland away ȝode. **1577** B. GOOGE *Heresbach's Husb.* IV. (1586) 181 After which hours, they [Bees] commonly goe not away. **1610** SHAKS. *Temp.* v. i. 304 This one night, which part of it, Ile waste With such discourse, as I not doubt, shall make it Goe quicke away. **1711** HEARNE *Collect.* (O.H.S.) III. 163 'Tis pretended that this Smith must have went away that Morning. **1841** LANE *Arab. Nts.* I. 102 He went away as he had come. **1869** C. GIBBON *R. Gray* xix, I saw her gaeing awa' in a gig wi' a man.

b. *to go away with*: to carry off as one's own. †*to go away with it*: to get the best of it, to win the advantage.

1597–8 BACON *Ess., Faction* (Arb.) 80 The Traitor in Factions lightly goeth away with it. **1611** BIBLE *Transl. Pref.* 4 The Edition of the Seuentie went away with the credit. **1633** BP. HALL *Hard Texts, N.T.* 561 Thou maiest goe away with the glory of a perfect and irreprehensible justice. **1688** MIEGE *Gt. Fr. Dict.* II. s.v., They shall not go away with it so. *Ils me la payeront, ou je m'en vengerai.*

†**c.** To pass away, die. (Cf. *go off*, 85 d.)

1611 in *Crt. & Times Jas. I* (1848) I. 148 He was reasonably well recovered in show, but went away in his sleep, when it was least looked for.

†**d.** To faint. (Cf. *go off*, 85 h.)

1740 RICHARDSON *Pamela* (1741) I. 31, I was two Hours before I came to myself; and just as I got a little up on my Feet, he coming in, I went away again with the Terror.

e. To go freely or with speed.

a **1732** T. BOSTON *Crook in Lot* (1805) 115 Mariners spread out their sails when the wind begins to blow, that they may go away before it.

76. go back. (See simple senses and BACK *adv.*)

a. To retrace one's steps; to return; *fig.* to revert to a former state or mode of action; †also, to lose ground.

1530 PALSGR. 571/1, I go backe, I go backwarde, *je recule.* **1570** *Satir. Poems Reform.* x. 357 He wald not lat the Papists cause ga bak, Gif it wer Just, bot wald be for him frak. **1583** HOLLYBAND *Campo di Fior* 285 Let us goe backe, lest they take awaye our clothes. **1631** WIDDOWES *Nat. Philos.* 9 Plannets are said to goe backe, when removing themselves, they goe not forward their course, but returne backe the way they came, in some part. **1647** CHAS. I *Let.* in *Antiquary* (1880) I. 97, I will be content that yᵉ come to some convenient Place to dyne, & goe back at night. **1782** COWPER *Gilpin* 199 'Twas for your pleasure you came here, You shall go back for mine. **1811** *Minutes Evidence, Berkeley Peerage* 218, I was going back to Gloucester. **1849** *Tait's Mag.* XVI. 141/1 The attempts of English proprietors in the Highlands to go back to the exploded middle-age plan. **1883** *Stubbs' Mercantile Circular* 8 Nov. 982/2 The people in Nagasaki are fast going back to their old practice of spinning this class of fabric for themselves.

b. To carry one's view backward in time.

1662 STILLINGFL. *Orig. Sacr.* III. i. §12 The further we go back in history, the fuller the world was of Deities. **1701** DE FOE *True-born Eng.* 3 Go back to Elder Times, and Ages past.

c. *to go back from* (now also colloq. *of*, *on*, *upon*): to withdraw from (an engagement, promise, or undertaking).

1530 PALSGR. 571/1, I go backe from my worde that I have sayd, *je me desdis.* **1704** MARLBOROUGH *Lett. & Disp.* (1845) I. 244 Her Majesty can't go back from what she has promised. **1862** MRS. CARLYLE *Lett.* III. 106 He could not well go back upon his implied assent. **1882** B. HARTE *Flip* iv, Don't go back on your promise. **1886** MISS TYTLER *Buried Diamonds* xxxii, I will never go back from my word. **1888** R. A. KING *Leal Lass* II iv. 79 If Gower went back of his promise.

d. *to go back on*: to prove faithless or disloyal to; to betray. *colloq.* (orig. *U.S.*).

1859 G. W. MATSELL *Vocabulum* 38 He won't go back on the cove; he is staunch. **1868** *Putnam's Mag.* Jan. 21 Are these Dobbs' Ferry villagers A going back on Dobbs! 'Twould n't be more anom'lous If Rome went back on Rom'lus. **1883** *L'pool Daily Post* 22 Jan., Some member of the secret organisation has gone back on his comrades. **1893** GUNTER *Miss Dividends* 122 Godby has gone back on them, and the Walkers are no more to be relied upon for Church dues.

e. *to go back of* (U.S.): = *go behind*, 54.

1890 E. H. GRIFFIN in *Science* 14 Feb. 104 The public.. ought not to be compelled to go back of academic titles to find out what they mean. **1891** *N.Y. Tribune* 14 Nov. 6/3 (Funk) They cannot go back of the returns. It is their business simply officially to announce the result.

f. To extend backwards (in space or time); to have a history extending back *to*.

1789 A. YOUNG *Jrnl.* 17 Aug. in *Travels* (1792) I. 165 The family of Polignac claim an origin of great antiquity; they have pretensions that go back, I forget whether to Hector or Achilles. **1873** H. SPENCER *Stud. Sociol.* ix. 227 English Geology goes back to Ray. **1892** *Eng. Illustr. Mag.* X. 45 The cavity goes back some fourteen inches.

†**g.** *Bridge.* To redouble. *U.S. Obs.*

1907 R. F. FOSTER *Bridge* 16 If either the eldest hand or the pone doubles, it is the privilege of the player who named the trump to double him again, the usual expression being; 'I go back'. *Ibid.* 60 When you go over, never forget the possibility of their going back. **1920** —— *Auction made Easy* 111 *Going back*, redoubling.

77. go backward(s.

a. See simple senses and BACKWARD, BACKWARDS. †**b.** To change for the worse, take an unfavourable turn, decline in prosperity.

1483 *Cath. Angl.* 147/1 To Ga bakwarde, *retrogradi.* **1530** PALSGR. 571/1, I go backwarde, I fall in dette or behynde hande. **1607–12** BACON *Ess., Ambit.* (Arb.) 222 They..looke vpponn Men and matters with an evill Eye, and are best pleased when thinges goe backward. **1691** LOCKE *Consid. Lower. Int.* (1692) 120 Landed Men..accommodating their Expences to their Income, keep themselves from going backwards in the World.

78. go before. (See simple senses and BEFORE.)

a. *lit.* To go in advance. **b.** To precede in time or serial order.

1548 HALL *Chron., Edw. IV* (1550) 18b, The Erle of warwicke determined..to go before with parte of the nauie. **1585** ABP. SANDYS *Serm.* xii. 188 We learne in the text that goeth before in this chapter, that [etc.]. **1590** SHAKS. *Com. Err.* I. i. 96 Gather the sequell by that went before. **1616** B. JONSON *Epigr.* xxxiii, Thou art but gone before, Whither the world must follow. **1819** S. ROGERS *Human Life* 751 Those that he loved so long and sees no more, Loved and still loves —not dead..but gone before.

79. go by.

a. To go past, pass (see BY *adv.* 3).

1508 DUNBAR *Ball. Kynd Kittok* 38 Drink with my Guddame, as ȝe ga by, Anys for my saik. **1601** SHAKS. *Twel. N.* III. iv. 398 The time goes by: Away. **1634** SIR T. HERBERT *Trav.* 66 They tooke no notice of us, but let us goe by without any ceremonie. **1857** BUCKLE *Civiliz.* I. ix. 586 They see in those good old times which are now gone by, many sources of consolation. **1877** MISS YONGE *Cameos* Ser. III. xxxiv. 359 No Italian could see such a chance..go by without trying to profit by it. **1885** W. M. CONWAY in *Mag. Art* Sept. 463/2 They..let no day go by without its jest.

†**b.** To go unregarded, etc. *Obs.*

1450–70 *Golagros & Gaw.* 1225 Quhan on-fortone quhelmys the quheil, thair gais grace by. **1596** SHAKS. *Tam. Shr.* I. ii. 256 Sir, sir, the first's for me, let her go by. **1603** —— *Meas. for M.* II. ii. 41 Mine were the verie Cipher of a Function To fine the faults, whose fine stands in record, And let go by the actor.

80. go down. (See simple senses and DOWN *adv.*)

a. To proceed, move, or change to a lower place or condition; to descend (*from*, †*of*); also *transf.* (of a road, passage, etc.) to lead downwards. Of a vessel: To go to the bottom, sink. *to go down on one's knees* (see KNEE).

a **1300** [see DOWN *adv.* 8]. *c* **1340** *Cursor M.* 11612 (Trin.) He went doun of his modir kne. **1388** WYCLIF *Ps.* cvi. 23 Thei that gon doun in to the see in schippis. *a* **1400–50** *Alexander* 5050 And he gose doun be grece, a-gayn to his tentis. *c* **1440** *Gesta Rom.* xvii. 328 (Add. MS.) Whan the Emperour vndirstode that, he went downe of his horse. **1548** HALL *Chron., Hen. VI*, 105 b, His father..whiche was gone downe to dinner. **1659** D. PELL *Impr. Sea* 604 Reproof unto those that go down into the Seas, and forget all their mercies. **1700** S. L. tr. *Fryke's Voy. E. Ind.* 75, I went down into the Boat with the other Surgeons. **1768** J. BYRON *Narr. Wager* (1778) 90 There ran such a sea, that we expected, every instant, the boat would go down. **1883** *Cambridge Staircase* ii. 21 They would probably go down to posterity with more than an ordinary share of glory. **1890** *Temple Bar* June 156, I do not think he cares a straw whether your temperature goes up or down.

b. To extend, be continued down *to* a certain point.

1890 *Sat. Rev.* 5 Apr. 422/2 Mr. Thornton's..sketch.. goes down to the death of James II.

c. To be overthrown; to fall *before* a conqueror.

1599 SHAKS. *Hen. V*, III. Chor. 34 The nimble Gunner With Lynstock now the diuellish Cannon touches, And downe goes all before them. **1749** in H. T. Waghorn *Cricket Scores* (1899) 42 They..had two wickets to go down. **1788** *World* 25 Aug. 3/2 Hampshire won, with 5 Wickets to go down. **1857** HUGHES *Tom Brown* II. viii, There are only twenty-four runs to make, and four wickets to go down. **1874** GREEN *Short Hist.* ii. §4. 71 Horse and man went down before his lance at Val-ès-dunes. **1878** *Scribner's Mag.* XV. 143/1 Fanaticism, though brilliant in its first efforts, went down before discipline. **1892** *Blackw. Mag.* CLI. 98/1 Five of the best bats in England went down before Spofforth's bowling.

d. To be set down in writing.

1887 G. MACDONALD *Home Again* v. 32 Down it must go in her book. **1888** FARJEON *Miser Farebrother* II. vii. 84 All this..went down on the account..and was debited against them.

e. Of waves, wind, etc.: To subside.

1670 DRYDEN *1st Pt. Conq. Granada* II. i, My boiling passions settle, and go down. **1840** MARRYAT *Poor Jack* x, The sea had gone down. **1873** BLACK *Pr. Thule* iv, The wind had altogether gone down.

f. To be swallowed. (Cf. DOWN *adv.* 11.)

1579 GOSSON *Sch. Abuse* (Arb.) 20 The deceitfull Phisition giueth sweete Syrropes to make his poyson goe downe the smoother. **1665** BOYLE *Occas. Refl.* (1848) 340 A belief that the toothsome would make the nutritive part go smoothly down. **1747** *Gentl. Mag.* XVII. 24 His hunger makes his bread go downe Altho' it be both stale and brown. **1890** *Illustr. Sport. & Dram. News* 31 May 372/1, I..want no extra inducement in the shape of sauce or pickle to make it go down.

g. *fig.* To find acceptance (*with* a person).

1608 DEKKER *Lanthorne & Candle-L.* H 3, The woorst hors-flesh..does best goe downe with him. **1679** DRYDEN *Troil. & Cr.* Prol., The fulsome clench, that nauseates the town, Would from a judge or alderman go down. **1690** LOCKE *Hum. Und.* IV. xx. §10 The grossest absurdities.. being but agreeable to such principles, go down glibly, and are easily digested. **1733** FIELDING *Intrig. Chambermaid* Epil., English is now below this learned town, None but Italian warblers will go down. **1821** LAMB *Elia* Ser. I. *Mackery End*, Nothing goes down with her, that is quaint, irregular, or out of the road of common sympathy. **1822** HAZLITT *Table-t.* II. iv. 64 A poet who would not go down among readers of the present day. **1885** W. E. NORRIS *A. Vidal* I. vii. 121 In fashion or out of fashion, they [sensational novels] always pay and always go down with the public.

h. To deteriorate; to decline in health or prosperity; to collapse or die. Also, to be subject to or suffer *with* (a specified illness or disease).

1857 [see DOWN *adv.* 17 a]. **1892** M. E. FREEMAN *Jane Field* 10 Well, I hope Lois ain't goin' down. I heard she looked dreadful. **1911** A. BENNETT *Hilda Lessways* II. ii. 153 Calder Street's going down—it's getting more and more of a slum. **1934** W. SAROYAN *Daring Young Man* (1935) 11 Hope he hasn't gone down; he deserved to live. **1953** 'N. SHUTE' *In Wet* 4, I went down with a severe attack of malaria. **1968** K. WEATHERLY *Roo Shooter* 41 The air remained as dry as ever. On some of the stations the cattle were going down; all the earth tanks were dry.

i. To go away from a university or college; *spec.* to leave it permanently.

1861 J. A. SYMONDS *Let.* 4 Mar. (1967) I. 279 Another plan..is that I should go down myself next Term—take a Grace Term. **1883** [see DOWN *adv.* 2]. **1914** C. MACKENZIE *Sinister St.* II. III. xii. 738 Guy Hazlewood had gone down and was away in Macedonia, trying to fulfil a Balliol precept to mix yourself up in the affairs of other nations or your own as much as possible. **1955** *Times* 12 May 14/3 From the time he went down from Cambridge until war broke out in 1914. **1965** J. FLEMING *Nothing is Number* II. iii. 67 'I haven't seen him since the summer term. He's gone down.' 'Gone down?' 'Left Oxford.'

j. To be sent to prison. *slang.*

1906 RUSSELL & RIGBY *Making of Criminal* vi. 76 'Going down', as it is termed, for seven or fourteen days. *Ibid.*, The same youth will 'go down' time after time, and become more reckless and indifferent with every repetition. **1920** E. WALLACE *Daffodil Mystery* iii. 29 Twice Sam had gone down for a short term, and once for a long term of imprisonment. **1945** M. ALLINGHAM *Coroner's Pidgin* xvii. 142 He went down for eighteen months and is now in Italy pulling his weight, I believe. He's a crook, but not a traitor.

k. *Bridge.* To fail to fulfil one's contract.

1918 E. BERGHOLT *Royal Auction Bridge* (ed. 2) 57 If he calls Four Hearts, as is probable, Z. and A. pass, but Y. doubles; and AB. are bound to go down. **1933** A. G. MACDONELL *England, their England* vi. 78 [He] had gone down 650 points above the line whereas he ought to have made two no-trumps. **1964** N. SQUIRE *Bidding at Bridge* ii. 24 You may go down quite often in game contracts.

l. In a card-game: to put one's cards on the table; to reveal one's cards.

1934 *Neuphilologische Mitteilungen* XXXV. 131 *To go down* 'to put one's hand down (as dummy)'. **1964** A. WYKES *Gambling* vii. 176 A player may declare his hand ('go down') when the unmatched cards in his hand count 10 or less.

m. To happen. *slang* (orig. *U.S.*).

1946 MEZZROW & WOLFE *Really Blues* 374 *Go down*, happen. **1956** 'B. HOLIDAY' *Lady sings Blues* (1958) xxi. 171 If they'd known about that they might never have let him off. Or they might have. In view of what went down later, who can say? **1970** *It* 12–25 Feb. 4/4 If everyone was aware of what went down in these organisations perhaps there would be enough response to keep them from petrifying and dying.

n. Usu. with *on*: to perform fellatio or cunnilingus on (a person). *slang* (orig. *U.S.*).

1916 H. N. CARY *Slang of Venery* I. 112 *Going down*, to tongue a woman, or suck a man. **1941** G. LEGMAN in G. W. Henry *Sex Variants* II. 1167 *Go down* (*on*), to fellate or cunnilingue. The object of this verb phrase is the person and not his or her genitalia. **1959** N. MAILER *Advts. for Myself* (1961) 96 They're still in love... He goes down on her and everything, and she loves him. **1974** K. MILLETT *Flying* (1975) I. 53, I do not want her body. Do not want to see it, caress it, go down on it. **1978** K. J. DOVER *Gr. Homosexuality* II. 101 Against the absence of scenes of human homosexual fellation, we must set scenes in which a youth is cramming his penis into a woman's mouth..or a man threatening a woman with a stick and forcing her to 'go down on' him.

81. go forth. (Now *arch.* or *rhetorical.*)

a. See simple senses and FORTH. (Cf. FORTHGO.)

c **1200** [see A 3 *a pl.*]. *c* **1300** *Cursor M.* 28725 (Cott. Galba) Go now furth and sin nomare. **1393** LANGL. *P. Pl.* C. I. 4 Ich wente forth in þe worlde, wonders to hure. **1549** LATIMER *Ploughers* (Arb.) 17 The ploughman went furth to sowe his seede. **1607** SHAKS. *Cor.* IV. vi. 35 If he had gone forth Consull. **1610** —— *Temp.* I. ii. 448 O, if a Virgin, And your affection not gone forth, Ile make you The Queene of Naples. **1845** S. AUSTIN *Ranke's Hist. Ref.* VI. ix. 603 As soon as the king should go forth with his mighty banner. **1886** A. SERGEANT *No Saint* II. xvii. 336 He wanted to go forth like the Apostles.

†**b.** To continue. Const. *in*, *to* with *inf. Obs.*

1513 MORE in Grafton *Chron.* (1568) II. 777 That where he had repented the way that he had entred, yet would he go forth in the same. **1535** COVERDALE *Job* xxix. 1 So Iob proceaded and wente forth in his communicacion. **1542**

BECON *Pathw. Prayer* xxxix. P v, Let vs also desyre hym that he wyll go forth to be a beneficial father vnto vs.

c. Of a decree, etc.: To be issued.

1535 COVERDALE *Hab.* i. 4 For the lawe is torne in peces, and there can no right iudgment go forth. **1593** SHAKS. *2 Hen. VI*, v. iii. 26 Let vs pursue him ere the Writs go forth. **1611** BIBLE *Isa.* ii. 3 For out of Zion shall goe forth the lawe. **1834** J. H. NEWMAN *Par. Serm.* (1837) I. xvii. 257 The decree goes forth to build or destroy. **1888** B. W. RICHARDSON *Son of a Star* II. iii. 30 The order goes forth that all the encampment is to pass before Caesar.

go forward: see FORWARD *adv.*

82. go in.

a. See simple senses and IN.

to go in and out: in quasi-Biblical lang., to conduct oneself, 'to do the business of life' (J.). The Heb. phrase on which this is founded appears in the Eng. Bible as *to go out and to come in*; but cf. *John* x. 9.

*c*975 *Rushw. Gosp.* Matt. vii. 13 Gaþ inn þurh naarwe ʒeate. *c*1000, *a*1225 [see IN *adv.* 1]. *c*1340 *Cursor M.* 13789 (Trin.), I ne may to þat watir wynne For oþere goon bifore me Inne. *c*1440 *Promp. Parv.* 202/2 Goon yn to a place, *introio, ingredior.* **1598** SHAKS. *Merry W.* III. iii. 142 He 's too big to go in there: what shall I do? *a*1631 DONNE *Lett.* (1651) 61 In that life one is ever in the porch or postern, going in or out, never within his house himself. **1878** *Scribner's Mag.* XVI. 149/1 The men allowed the matter to go in at one ear and out at the other. **1889** MONA CAIRD *Wing Azrael* II. xix. 72 You are cold.. Would you like to go in? **1890** *Lippincott's Mag.* Apr. 477 This tunnel goes in a hundred and fifty feet.

b. To enter as a competitor in a contest or game. Phr. *go in and win.* In *Poker* (see quot.).

1837 DICKENS *Pickw.* ii, This advice was very like that which bystanders.. give to the smallest boy in a street fight; namely 'Go in and win'. **1882** *Poker: how to play it* 49 After the cards have been dealt.. each player.. determines whether he will *go in* or not. And the player who decides to go in, that is, to play for the pool, must put into the pool double the amount of the ante, except [etc.]. **1889** PHILIPS & WILLS *Fatal Phryne* II. iii. 78 Sit down well in your saddle, and go in and win.

c. *Cricket.* To take the batting. Also, *to go in to bat.* Said either of an individual player or of the whole 'side'.

1718 *Weekly-Jrnl.* 6 Sept. 543/1 Three of their Men made an Elopement, and got off the Ground without going in. **1770** J. LOVE *Cricket* 16 Equal in Numbers, bravely they begin The dire Dispute.—The Foes of Kent go in. **1849** in 'Bat' *Cricket Man.* (1850) 57 If the striker be hurt, some other person may stand out for him, but not go in. **1890** *Field* 31 May 790/2 Lancashire went in to bat at five minutes to six.

d. Of the sun, etc.: To be obscured by a cloud.

1884 R. BUCHANAN *Foxglove Manor* III. xxxiv. 132 The sun had gone in, and the air was full of a heavy lowering sadness. **1889** MARY E. CARTER *Mrs. Severn* III. III. ix. 221 The moon had gone in, and it was too dark to see him.

e. *to go in to* or *unto*: used in all Eng. versions of the Old Testament (after the Heb.) for: To have carnal knowledge of (a woman).

f. *to go in at*: to assail vigorously. *colloq.*

1812 *Sporting Mag.* XXXIX. 138 Dogherty went in at his antagonist's head. **1849** DICKENS *Dav. Copp.* xviii, Sometimes I go in at the butcher madly and cut my knuckles open against his face. **1887** *Pall Mall G.* 19 Feb. 2/2 Napoleon's pet soldiers were far more eager to go in at their fellow-citizens than at the German enemy.

83. go in *for*. (Recent and *colloq.*; see 82 b.)

a. To make one's avowed object; to select as one's speciality or 'line of things', or as one's usual style or fashion; to commit oneself to the advocacy of (a principle or measure); to venture on acquiring or wearing (something); to indulge in, permit oneself (some action).

1849 *N.Y. Tribune* 25 Dec. (Bartlett), We go in for all the postage reduction President Taylor recommends. **1862** *Temple Bar* V. 331, I do not 'go in' with great heart for the education of the masses. **1863** KINGSLEY *Water-Bab.* 316 My mamma says that my intellect is not adapted for methodic science, and says that I must go in for general information. **1872** EARL PEMBROKE & G. H. KINGSLEY *S. Sea Bubbles* x. 293 He had run through seven helps-meet for him, and was about to go in for the eighth. **1873** MRS. OLIPHANT *Innocent* III. x. 167 Not elegant—the judge had never gone in for elegance—but forcible and clear. **1875** M. PATTISON *Casaubon* 94 Lect.. had gone in for council business. **1876** *Tinsley's Mag.* XVIII. 149 Why has no interesting heretic gone in for Polydiabolism? **1885** *Manch. Exam.* 28 Sept. 5/1 An overwhelming majority of the Liberal candidates have gone in for Disestablishment. **1889** *Sat. Rev.* 30 Mar. 388/1 Thomas [Becket] deliberately 'went in' for saintship and martyrdom. **1891** A. J. FOSTER *Ouse* 136 Cyclists who go in for road-racing. **1897** MARIE CORELLI *Ziska* xii, Why in Cairo should not a lady go in for a Theban dance without being considered improper? **1897** MARY KINGSLEY *W. Africa* 223 They do not go in for hats.

b. To offer oneself for examination in; to enter one's name as a candidate *for.* (Cf. *to be* IN *for.*)

1845 *Punch* 6 Sept. 108/2 Having heard that there was a better thing than the Newfoundland Judgeship to be had in the neighbourhood, he determined to 'go in for it'. **1879** LUBBOCK *Addr. Pol. & Educ.* iii. 56, 1061 candidates went in for mathematics. **1889** *Eng. Illustr. Mag.* Dec. 178 Our girls like to test the thoroughness of their mental achievements by going in for examinations. **1894** WILKINS & VIVIAN *Green Bay Tree* I. 127 You are going in for the History Tripos, like myself, I suppose.

84. go in *with*.

†**a.** To agree with; to concur with. **b.** To join.

1725 *Wodrow Corr.* (1843) III. 232, I heartily go in with your Lordship's observations upon the subject, which are very just. **1886** MCCARTHY & MRS. C. PRAED *Right Honourable* II. xxiv. 214 Do you want to get up a republican party? And are you going in with that unfortunate Masterton and men like that? **1889** BOLDREWOOD *Robb. under Arms* iii, If you like to go in with me, we'll go share and share.

85. go off. (See simple senses and OFF.)

a. To depart (often implying suddenness or haste); to start, set out. Of an actor: To leave the stage. At cards: to lead. *to go off at score* (see SCORE). *to go off at a tangent* (see TANGENT).

1606 SHAKS. *Ant. & Cl.* IV. xiii. 6 The Soule and Body riue not more in parting, Then greatnesse going off. **1660** PEPYS *Diary* 20 May, Commissioner Pett.. caused the boats to go off. **1665** SIR T. HERBERT *Trav.* (1677) 121 The Mahometans.. on their thumb commonly wear a ring of horn, which makes the Arrow go off both strongly and easily. **1711** STEELE *Spect.* No. 51 ¶5 His Turkish Majesty went off with a good Air. **1749** FIELDING *Tom Jones* XV. viii, His daughter had taken the opportunity of almost the first moment of his absence, and gone off with a neighbouring young clergyman. **1861** *Temple Bar* I. 406 Ethelind went off to bed. **1879** 'CAVENDISH' *Card Ess.* etc. 165 If he had only gone off with that suit the game was over. **1889** *Repent. P. Wentworth* I. xv. 302 My last proofs went off to the publisher's to day.

b. To be taken off (esp. quickly or suddenly).

*c*1440 *Anc. Cookery* in *Househ. Ord.* (1790) 425 Take clene qwete and bray hit wele in a morter that the holles gone alle of. **1594** SHAKS. *Rich. III*, IV. v. 4 If I reuolt, off goes yong Georges head. **1601** —— *All's Well* v. iii. 279 This womans an easie gloue my Lord, she goes off and on at pleasure. **1662** J. DAVIES tr. *Olearius' Voy. Ambass.* 397 Protesting that if he had him, his head should go off for it. **1792** A. WILSON *Watty & Meg*, Aff gaed bonnet, aff gaed shoon.

c. Of firearms, explosives: To be discharged, explode.

1579 GOSSON *Sch. Abuse* (Arb.) 21 When they haue sounded Allarme, off go the peeces to encounter a shadow. **1670** CLARKE *Nat. Hist. Nitre* 30 Gun-powder.. with greater force and noise going off. **1815** SCOTT *Guy M.* xxx, The piece went off in the awkward hands of the poor parson. **1890** BOLDREWOOD *Col. Reformer* (1891) 298 A pocket Derringer, which.. had a trick of going off unexpectedly.

d. To pass away, die.

1605 SHAKS. *Macb.* v. viii. 36 *Mal.* I would the Friends we misse, were safe arriu'd. *Sey.* Some must go off. **1709** *Tatler* No. 86 ¶7 In this manner.. he [Cæsar] went off, not like a Man that departed out of Life, but a Deity that returned to his Abode. **1779** *Phil. Trans.* LXIX. 56 She.. was better a few hours before her death, and went off pretty easy. **1888** RIDER HAGGARD *Col. Quaritch* xxv. (1889) 188 The doctors told me that he might go off any day.

e. Of a sensation: To pass away, cease to be felt.

1825 *New Monthly Mag.* XVI. 591 This feeling.. gradually goes off.

f. To deteriorate; to lose brightness, quality, or vigour.

1695 WOODWARD *Nat. Hist. Earth* (1702) 211 The Sun being now gone off, and ceasing any longer to operate upon it, the Vapour stagnates. **1731** SWIFT *Let. to Pope* 12 June, Women who live by their beauty, and men by their wit, are seldom provident enough to consider that both wit and beauty will go off with years. **1768** STERNE *Sent. Journ.* (1778) II. 130 (*Fragment*) [A manuscript] so faded and gone off by damps and length of time. **1832** FR. A. KEMBLE in *Rec. Girlhood* (1878) III. 216, I never played this part well, and am now gone off in it, and play it worse than not well. **1842** *Jrnl. R. Agric. Soc.* III. II. 298 My wheat-crops.. went off in the spring so as to be very bad at harvest. **1851** MACAULAY *Life & Lett.* (1883) II. 299 His style had then gone off. **1881** WHITEHEAD *Hops* ii. 14 It is necessary to pick Jones hops just as soon as they are ripe.. as they soon 'go off'. **1888** MISS TYTLER *Blackhall Ghosts* II. xvii. 72 Her good looks.. were unmistakably going off.

g. To start into sudden action; to break *into* a fit of laughter, extravagance of language, irrelevant or unintelligible discourse, etc.

1825 *New Monthly Mag.* XVI. 342 The patriarch and fifty monks.. go off into praises of her beauty. **1844** *Fraser's Mag.* XXX. 467/1 In the intervals of the most lugubrious chants.. the organ went off with some extremely cheerful.. air. **1879** J. C. SHAIRP *Burns* v. 115 The rest of the letter goes off in a wild rollicking strain.

h. To pass into unconsciousness; more explicitly, *to go off to sleep, in* or *into a faint, a fit*, etc.

1844 *Fraser's Mag.* XXX. 65/2 She went off in a fit. **1887** *Mohammed Benani* xxii. 225 She will go off in hysterics. **1887** G. M. FENN *Devon Boys* xxxi. 266 His regular breathing told that he had gone off. **1891** F. W. ROBINSON *Her Love & His Life* III. VII. v. 281 Satisfied with this surmise, he went off to sleep. **1896** *Daily News* 2 Oct. 5/2 He ..began inhaling, and soon 'went off' to his entire satisfaction.

i. To fail to be carried out, fall through.

1749 GRAY *Let.* 8 Aug. (1935) I. 324, I know not how, it has gone off again, & we have heard no more lately about it. **1813** JANE AUSTEN *Pride & Prej.* II. ii. 18 It seems likely to have been a desirable match... I am sorry it went off. **1884** LD. SELBORNE in *Law Rep.* 25 Ch. Div. 493 The marriage may go off. **1890** *Sat. Rev.* 20 Dec. 714/1 If he died the bargain must go off.

j. To be disposed of by sale. Also, of daughters, to be married. *colloq.*

1641 BEST *Farm. Bks.* (Surtees) 112 Fatte horses, and especially geldinges, goe allsoe well of. **1687** BURNET *Reply to Varillas* 5 In this the Printer did wisely: for he was sure his Book would go off the better. **1691** LOCKE *Consid. Lower. Int.* Ess. (1883) 596 So trade flourishes, and his commodities go off well, he will be able to pay his rent on. **1749** FIELDING *Tom Jones* XIV. vii, Her reputation might have been otherwise safe.. and the girl might have gone off never the worse. **1819** *Metropolis* I. 74 Such second-hand furniture as a Perlet or a Fusil.. would go off no where else but with the fanciful of London. **1884** MRS. HOUSTOUN *Caught in Snare* I. xii. 131 Plain girls.. did sometimes 'go off' when pretty ones hung on hand. **1890** *Temple Bar* Nov. 437 The tickets will go off at the end with a rush.

k. Of a performance, etc.: To be (more or less) successful.

1775 E. A LINLEY *Let.* 9 Mar. in T. Moore *Life of R. B. Sheridan* (1825) 102 In my life, I never saw any thing go off with such uncommon applause. **1804** MAR. EDGEWORTH *Pop. Tales, Lame Jervas* 18 The whole thing, as the carpenter said, went off pretty well. **1878** *Scribner's Mag.* XV. 868/2 We tried to sing and have games, but they wouldn't go off.

†**l.** To become bankrupt.

1688 MIEGE *Gt. Fr. Dict.* s.v., He is gone off, he is broke, *il a fait banqueroute.* **1703** LUTTRELL *Brief Rel.* (1857) V. 328 Mr. C——, a great exchange broker, who dealt mostly in stocks, went off, as said, for about 100,000*£.*

m. To experience a sexual orgasm. *slang.*

1928 D. H. LAWRENCE *Lady Chatterley* v. 62 You couldn't go off at the same time as a man, could you? *Ibid.* xiv. 244 They always make you go off when you're *not* in the only place you should be, when you go off. **1949** H. MILLER *Sexus* (1969) ii. 59 Bango! I went off like a whale.

n. *to go off at* (a person): to reprimand angrily; to abuse. *colloq.*

1941 BAKER *Dict. Austral. Slang* 31 *Go off at*, to reprove, express anger towards someone. **1948** D. W. BALLANTYNE *Cunninghams* (1963) II. xi. 175 He had to get away home else his father would go off at him.

86. go on. (See simple senses and ON.)

a. To continue a journey.

*c*1440 *Generydes* 6484 Goth on in Goddis name. **1610** SHAKS. *Temp.* II. i. 327 Goe safely on to seeke thy Son. **1817** W. SELWYN *Law Nisi Prius* (ed. 4) II. 953 The ship having touched at C. for orders and gone on to S. **1888** W. ROGERS *Remin.* 119 We were told that we should have to go on next day in a caboose.

b. To continue, advance, persevere, persist, in a course of action, in making, dealing with or using something; to continue in speech. Const. *in, with,* †*to* with *inf.*; also *simply.* Also with pr. pple. as complement. *to be going on with*: to start with; for the present; usu. in phr. ***enough to be going on with.***

1583 HOLLYBAND *Campo di Fior* 235 Marke how well shee singeth.. And goeth on alwayes continuing her songe. *a*1586 SIDNEY *Arcadia* II. (1590) 148 Therefore now (said she) Dorus go on. **1634** SIR T. HERBERT *Trav.* 156, I.. will here goe on with the description. **1662** PEPYS *Diary* 31 Dec., The Bishops.. go on without any diffidence in pressing uniformity. **1725** N. ROBINSON *Th. Physick* 306 Let him go on with the following Prescription. **1737** WHISTON *Josephus' Hist.* IV. v. §2 They esteemed it needless to go on with killing them. **1739** CHESTERF. *Lett.* (1792) I. xxv. 92 If you go on to learn at this rate, you will soon puzzle me, in Greek especially. *a*1822 LAMB *Elia* Ser. I. *Dream Childr.*, They looked up, and prayed me not to go on about their uncle, but to tell them some stories about their pretty dead mother. **1871** EARLE *Philol. Eng. Tongue* 65 This fashion, like all fashions, went on spreading. **1873** H. SPENCER *Stud. Sociol.* xv. 362 They go on perversely in bad habits. **1884** R. BUCHANAN *Foxglove Manor* III. xxxii 81 Go on with your preparations. **1890** *Jrnl. Educ.* 1 Sept. 478/2 We begin work at 12 and go on till half-past one. **1967** *Listener* 19 Jan. 105/2 There are other semi-concealed social problems.., but to be going on with Cathy is quite enough to prove [etc.]. **1968** *Ibid.* 29 Aug. 260/3 Milton seems to have thought the English climate was a punishment for sin. In which case we have surely been punished enough to be going on with.

c. To proceed *to* (do something) as the next step.

1666 MARVELL *Corr.* lv. Wks. 1872–5 II. 192 However, I shall go on to continue from my last Letter. **1687** BURNET *Contin. Reply to Varillas* 39 He goes on to make a Parallel between the late Protector and King Henry's Minister. **1824** R. STUART *Hist. Steam Engine* 186 They then go on to name a number of individuals on whom 'the eternal gratitude of all Spaniards is invoked'. **1891** *Sat. Rev.* 11 July 61/2 He goes on to quote two passages from Seneca.

d. To fare; to carry on or get on; to 'manage'.

1719 DE FOE *Crusoe* I. iii. (1840) 40 We went on very sociable together. **1803** *Med. Jrnl.* X. 356 For the first two days he went on very well. **1820** SOUTHEY *Life Wesley* II. 164 Still it [the school] went on badly. **1820** *Examiner* No. 631. 314/1 Affairs in Spain go on swimmingly. **1879** M. J. GUEST *Lect. Hist. Eng.* xlvii. 475 The king now determined to go on without parliament at all.

e. Of an action, work, process, state of things: To proceed, continue further; also, to be in progress; to happen, occur. Of time: To pass, proceed.

1711 SWIFT *Jrnl. Stella* 18 Nov., [The business] had it gone on, would have cost three times as much. **1735** J. PRICE *Stone-Br. Thames* 6 Two Piers.. at proper Distances,.. both to go on at the same time. **1844** *Fraser's Mag.* XXX. 119/1 This state of things cannot possibly go on. **1851** RUSKIN *Stones Ven.* (1874) I. xvii. 188 The idle and curious, who care only about what is going on upon the earth. **1861** M. PATTISON *Ess.* (1889) I. 38 As time went on, the English court grew impatient. **1864** LOWELL *Biglow P.* Poet. Wks. (1879) 247 A thunderstorm was going on. **1873** C. M. YONGE *Pillars of House* I. iii. 55 How long has this been going on? **1879** M. J. GUEST *Lect. Hist. Eng.* lvi. 574 The struggle is still going on. **1886** F. R. STOCKTON *Hundredth Man* v, People would stop to look into Vatoldi's to see what was going on. **1955** *Times* 30 June 8/3 The governing council has in a sense admitted that it did not know all that went on.

f. To conduct oneself, act, behave (in some reprehensible manner).

1777 SHERIDAN *Sch. Scand.* I. i, Sad comfort whenever he returns, to hear how your brother has gone on! **1819** BYRON *Juan.* I. cxlvi, How dare you think your lady would go on so? **1890** F. BARRETT *Betw. Life & Death* II. xvii. 12 She is playing the fool to go on in this style.

g. *colloq.* To talk volubly; to rail, storm *at*. Also, to talk excessively or tiresomely *about* (a subject); to discuss *ad nauseam*.

1863 MRS. C. CLARKE *Shaks. Char.* vi. 162 Her first scene with Fenton is inimitable, where she goes on about a wart on his face. **1873** *Argosy* XVI. 361 He would go on at Fred for making himself common. **1878** *Scribner's Mag.* XVI. 415/2 He went on dreadful because he couldn't get at his ladder. **1884** G. ALLEN *Philistia* II. xii. 9, I wish you could only see the way father goes on at me about chapel. **1921** M. ARLEN *Romantic Lady* 235 For God's sake don't go on about it, Iris, else I won't be able to bear it at all. **1921** H. CRANE *Let.* 21 Nov. (1965) 70, I don't need to go on about it, as you have probably seen it. **1960** L. COOPER *Certain Compass* 61 She doesn't go on about things, one of the many reasons why I like her. **1969** *Listener* 24 July 114/2 How much of what I have been so tediously going on about here is reflected in the programme itself?

h. Of an article of dress: To admit of being put on.

1847 in CRAIG. **1861** *Temple Bar* I. 270 Shoes that wouldn't go on, and muskets that wouldn't go off.

i. *Cricket*. To take up the bowling, begin to bowl. *Theatr.* To appear in a part.

1769 S. BARRY *Let.* 27 Oct. in *Corr. Garrick* (1831) I. 370 The managers..expected she would continue to go on in the pageant as long as she was able. **1839** DICKENS *Nich. Nick.* xiv. 123 The daughter of a theatrical fireman, who 'went on' in the pantomime. **1861** *Times* 25 May 9/4 A change of bowling was tried, Atkinson going on at Hodgson's end. **1883** *Daily Tel.* 15 May 2/7 Bates went on. **1888** MISS F. WARDEN *Witch of Hills* I. vii. 157, I only got small parts, and it's dreadful to have to go on with nothing to say. **1890** *Field* 24 May 752/1 A double change of bowling was tried, Sharpe and Abel going on.

j. *imp.* Expressing impatience or derision: = Go your ways; go along with you. Also expressing surprise or incredulity. *colloq.*

In representations of cockney speech often written *garn*.

1886 F. T. ELWORTHY *W. Somerset Word-Bk.* 295 In a quarrel either of the parties themselves, or a third, who wishes to stop it, says '*go on*'! and means 'be quiet'. **1894** SOMERVILLE & 'ROSS' *Real Charlotte* II. xix. 67 Ah, go on, Mr. Dysart Why, I see the white water, and the black rocks, and all! **1940** L. A. G. STRONG *Sun on Water* 59 'Ah, go on.' 'Well, we added it up and..it came out incontrovertibly.. two years, one month, and five days.' 'Eighteen months, if it's a day.' **1960** [see GET *v.* 61 b].

k. *going on for*: approaching (a certain age or period). Also in absolute use, = 'nearly' (so long ago).

1848 J. H. NEWMAN *Loss & Gain* 195, I was very uncomfortable about the Articles, going on for two years since. **1887** MRS. H. MARTIN *Amor Vincit* II. xiii. 265, I shall be twenty-three, going on for twenty-four. **1891** MISS DOWIE *Girl in Karp.* xiii. 174 It was going on for eight o'clock.

†**l.** To make an attack. *Obs.*

1611 B. JONSON *Catiline* I. i, Bold Cethegus, Whose valour I haue..prais'd so into daring, as he would Goe on vpon the gods. **1617** F. MORYSON *Itin.* II. 165 They attempted another Trench..the Serjeant in going on was shot through the body. **1802** JAMES *Milit. Dict.*, *To go on*, to make an attack.

m. To go on to another engagement.

1903 MRS. H. WARD *Lady Rose's Daughter* i. 17 'Now, you are going on,' said Lady Henry... 'Freddie says I must,' said the other. **1934** P. BOTTOME *Private Worlds* iii. 29 Charles noticed that Myra was elaborately dressed... She must be going on somewhere else afterwards. **1961** F. & R. LOCKRIDGE *Murder has Points* (1962) ix. 98 Faith Constable had had to 'go on' from the party and had, presumably, gone on. **1969** D. RUTHERFORD *Gilt-Edged Cockpit* v. 79 'Would you like to go on somewhere else?' Patrick had asked when coffee and a Calvados had been disposed of.

87. go out.

a. *lit.* To go from within (a place, a house, anything which contains); *esp.* to go from one's house. (See simple senses and OUT.)

a **1225** *Ancr. R.* 54 A meiden..Jacobes douhter..eode vt uor to biholden uncuðe wummen. *c* **1250** *Meid Maregrete* xxxiv, Al þet blod..out it ede þo. *c* **1340** *Cursor M.* 10951 (Laud) He bad the folk go out echone While he praide in the chirch allone. **1388** WYCLIF *Matt.* viii. 32 Thei ȝeden out, and wenten into the swyne. **1480** CAXTON *Chron. Eng.* iii, That Coryn priuely sholde gone oute and bussh hym in a wode til amorne. **1711** STEELE *Spect.* No. 137 ¶3 She calls for her Coach, then commands it in again, and then she will not go out at all. **1727** DE FOE *Hist. Appar.* IV. (1840) 31 He can appear though the doors be shut; and go out, though bolted and barred in. **1863** KINGSLEY *Water-Bab.* 10 Instead of going out to dinner at half-past eight.

†**b.** With adj. complement: To turn out, prove.

a **1240** *Lofsong* in *Cott. Hom.* 213 For to schewen hu þis hope to þin ones help schal gon me betere ut þen dude er þe oðres.

c. To march as a soldier; to take the field (now chiefly *Hist.* with reference to the Jacobite risings of 1715 and 1745); also to take part, as principal, in a duel. Also in full. *to go out to fight*. Also, to leave one's country for the battle front.

1387 TREVISA *Higden* (Rolls) I. 251 þey [the *proletarii*] were i-constreyned for to goo out [orig. *exire*] of skarsnesse of knyȝtes. **1597** SHAKS. *2 Hen. IV*, III. ii. 126 There are other men fitter to goe out than I. **1802** JAMES *Milit. Dict.* s.v., He went out with a brother officer, and was slightly wounded. **1841** *Fraser's Mag.* XXIII. 15 The quarrelsome man goes out to fight. **1870** RAMSAY *Remin.* vi. (ed. 18) 228 One of the lairds..proposed to go out, on the occasion of one of the risings for the Stuarts. **1890** *Cornh. Mag.* Dec. 626 He must go out or be under a social ban. Out they go accordingly, and the trained pistol-shot kills his civilian opponent. **1917** S. MCKENNA *Sonia* viii, 'Is David going out?..What's he in?' 'The Midland Fusiliers.' **1928** BLUNDEN *Undertones of War* i. 1, I read the notice that I was under orders for France... Berry, a subaltern of my set,.. might pipe to me, 'Hi, Blunden, we're going out: have a drink;' I could not dance. **1936** S. SASSOON *Sherston's Progress* II. i. 98 She had hoped and prayed that I might get a home-service job; but now she just accepted the fact that I'd got to go out again.

d. Of a fire, light, a luminary, etc.: To be extinguished. Also *transf.* and *fig.*

c **1400** MAUNDEV. (Roxb.) viii. 31 His lawmpe gase oute. **1599** SHAKS. *Hen. V*, IV. i. 270 Thinks thou the fierie Feuer will goe out With Titles blowne from Adulation? **1683** *Apol. Prot. France* v. 59 The Sun goes not out when it is Eclipsed. **1742** POPE *Dunc.* IV. 640 And at her felt approach and secret might, Art after art goes out, and all is night. **1819** BYRON *Juan.* I. clxxxiv, Out went the light. **1843** MRS. CARLYLE *Lett.* I. 189, I heard Helen lighting the fire, which had gone out. **1879** MORLEY *Burke* ix. 206 A life went out which..had made great tides in human destiny very luminous. **1889** *Eng. Illustr. Mag.* Dec. 259 My cigar went out.

e. In University use. †(*a*) With complement: To take the degree of (doctor, master, bachelor) (*obs.*). (*b*) At Cambridge: To take the degree of B.A. *in* a specified subject or *in* honours.

1646 FANSHAWE tr. *Guarini's Faithf. Sheph.* IV. ix. 157 Thy bow Th' hast pli'd so well about these words, that now Th' art gone out thy Arts-master. **1688** MIEGE *Gt. Fr. Dict.* II. s.v., To go out Doctor, or to take the Degree of a Doctor. **1705** HEARNE *Collect.* 7 Dec. (O.H.S.) I. 119 Who went out A.M. June 27, 1684, and B.D. Feb. 4, 1695. **1880** TROLLOPE *Duke's Childr.* I. iii. 33 He had gone out in honours, having been a second class man. **1890** *Guardian* 18 June 1000/1 She went out in natural science, but her place in the class is not recorded.

transf. **1690** W. WALKER *Idiomat. Anglo-Lat.* 209 That I should so suddenly go out poet.

f. To die. In early use, *to go out of the world*.

1697 COLLIER *Ess. Mor. Subj.* II. (1703) 31 There are some Opportunities of going out of the World, which are very well worth ones while to come in for. **1703** PRIOR *Ode to G. Villiers* 38 The ancient sage, who did so long maintain, That bodies die, but souls return again, With all the births and deaths he had in store, Went out Pythagoras, and came no more. **1891** S. C. SCRIVENER *Our Fields & Cities* 10 [Said of a dying man] He will go out with the tide, may be.

g. Of the tide: To recede.

1869 W. LONGMAN *Hist. Edw. III*, I. xiv. 252 Waiting for the tide to go out.

h. To retire from office.

1820 *Examiner* No. 664. 846/2 The burthen of all our speeches should be, Ministers must go out. **1881** MRS. C. PRAED *Policy & Passion* I. ix. 186 It is an absolute certainty that the Government will go out. **1890** T. F. TOUT *Hist. Eng.* 173 Stanley..went out for fear of the Appropriation Clause.

i. *ellipt.* for *to go out of date, fashion, use*, etc.

1840 CARLYLE *Heroes* i, Hero-worship, professes to have gone out, and finally ceased. **1841** *Punch* I. 113/1 To use the flippant idiom of the day, they [pockets] are going out! **1879** MCCARTHY *Own Times* II. xxv. 217 The practice of the duel in England had utterly gone out. **1890** *Harper's Mag.* Jan. 315/1 Has tolerance gone out with astrology? **1895** *Westm. Gaz.* 22 Apr. 1/2 Very little yellow is worn—it seems to have quite gone out.

j. Of a year: To terminate.

1877 MISS YONGE *Cameos* Ser. III. xv. 134 The year 1470 went out with Henry on the throne. **1896** *Daily News* 7 Dec. 3/7 The year will go out upon a much better state of things all round in the manufacturing industries.

k. *Thieves' slang.* (See quot. 1812.)

1812 J. H. VAUX *Flash Dict.*, *Go out*, to follow the profession of thieving; two or more persons who usually rob in company, are said to go out together. **1819** —— *Mem.* I. xii. 141 We continued to go out with one or other of the gentlemen frequenting the Swan.

l. To go *to* another country as a colonist, ambassador, missionary, agent, etc.

1850 *Tait's Mag.* XVII. 466/1 An offer being made to him to go out to Australia.

m. Chiefly of girls or women: To leave home, to find employment away from home. Const. *to*.

1816 JANE AUSTEN *Emma* III. ix. 154 He had long made up his mind to Jane Fairfax's going out as a governess. **1837** DICKENS *Pickw.* xxxiii, Betsy Martin..Goes out charing and washing, by the day. **1849** MACAULAY *Hist. Eng.* ii. I. 330 His boys followed the plough; and his girls went out to service. **1871** MRS. STOWE *Oldtown Fireside Stor.* 80 When she went out to tailorin', she was allers be-spoke six months ahead. **1886** MISS SERGEANT *No Saint* II. ii. 46 You may go out and earn your own living. **1889** MRS. H. L. CAMERON *Lost Wife* II. v. 61 'Something to do' meant in my case going out as a governess, or as a companion.

n. To mix in general society.

1768 FOOTE *Devil on two Sticks* III. (1778) 67 My father, Sir, as we seldom went out, established a domestic kind of drama. **1880** MCCARTHY & MRS. C. PRAED *Right Honourable* I. iii. 46 Betty liked society, and was made for it. She went out incessantly. **1890** *Temple Bar* Jan. 24 We do not intend to go out at all in Florence—I mean into society.

o. To be issued, published; to be broadcast.

1892 SIR N. LINDLEY in *Law Times Rep.* LXVII. 143/1 They allowed this prospectus to go out with statements in it which were false. **1968** *Listener* 26 Sept. 420/1 Yorkshire's *Gazette*, a drama series about the lives and hard times on a weekly paper, goes out in London at 11 p.m. and cannot therefore hope for an audience. **1969** *Ibid.* 20 Feb. 241/2 In the discussion of abortion that went out on 13 January.. Philippa Foot raised the essential question: when does a human being begin? **1971** R. BUSBY *Deadlock* xiv. 210 'Cut —for Christ's sake, cut. This is all bloody going out.'.. The screens went blank.

p. To abandon work. In full, *to go out on strike*. (Cf. COME *v.* 67 c.)

1889 *Sat. Rev.* 14 Dec. 672/1 The gas-workers who had gone out on strike have found their places filled. **1892** *Nation* (N.Y.) 25 Aug. 135/1 The New York Central switchmen 'went out'..because the others went out.

q. *Cricket*, etc. Of a batsman: To retire from batting, end one's innings; of a side: to be dismissed from batting.

1735 in H. T. Waghorn *Cricket Scores* (1899) 10 London headed the county 42 notches before they went out. **1854** J. PYCROFT *Cricket Field* (ed. 2) xi. 247 Had not an easy catch been missed, The Eleven of All England would have gone out for a run apiece. **1888** STEEL & LYTTLETON *Cricket* (Badm.) v. 232 Nothing would induce the injured batsman to remain..he had been given out and was going out. **1891** *Strand Mag.* II. 518/2 [In Tipcat] If either of the cats fall to the ground, both batters go out and the feeders get their turn.

r. To be drawn or impelled *to* (a person) by affection or sympathy. Esp. in phr. *my heart goes out*. Also of the feeling itself: To go forth *to*.

[**1779** F. BURNEY *Diary* Feb. (1842) I. 184 [Johnson *loq.*] I love Burney: my heart goes out to meet him!] **1842** E. B. BROWNING *Eliz. Barrett to Miss Mitford* 22 Aug. (1854) 130 My heart goes out to you in full devotion. **1860** GEO. ELIOT *Let.* 27 Aug. in J. W. Cross *Life* (1886) II. 228 My heart goes out with venerating gratitude to that mild face. **1881** *Atlantic Monthly* May 594/2 His own sympathy went out fully to cases of individual suffering. **1884** EDNA LYALL *We Two* i, His heart went out more and more to the beautiful girl. **1887** MRS. PERKS *Fr. Heather Hills* I. x. 162 Her whole heart went out in greeting. **1890** *Review of Rev.* Nov. 428/1 His whole soul goes out in sympathy to Edmund Burke. **1891** *Pictorial World* 19 Dec. 239/1 The love of a nation goes out to its great men.

†**s.** *imp.* in contracted form *gout* = go about your business. (Cf. *go on*, 86 j).

1600 *Look About You* xviii. E 3, Gout I haue curtall'd what I could not borrow. *Ibid.* xix. E 3 b, *Glo.* Gods mother doe you scorne me? *Io.* Gout, what then?

t. To go hunting.

1877 TROLLOPE *American Senator* I. i. 7 He..is not much thought of..except by those who go out with the hounds. **1932** R. LEHMANN *Invitation to Waltz* III. v. 209 'Were you out today?' 'Oh yes.'.. 'Um. Going out on Saturday—?'.. 'Oh, I thought you meant... I misunderstood. I don't—as a matter of fact, I don't really hunt.' **1967** R. RENDELL *New Lease of Death* ii. 24 He's very conscious of his status..since he bought Forby Hall. Goes out with the Pomfret hounds and all that.

u. To faint, lose consciousness, collapse; esp. in phr. *to go out like a light*. *U.S. colloq.*

1934 J. M. CAIN *Postman always rings Twice* ix. 81 A doctor was working on my arm. I went out again as soon as I saw it. It was running blood. **1934** R. CHANDLER in *Black Mask* Oct. 15/1 Something swished and I went out like a light.

88. go out of.

a. See simple senses and OUT. *to go out of the stable*: (of a horse) to be entered for a race. *to go out of hand* (see HAND 33 b).

c **975** *Rushw. Gosp.* John iv. 30 And ut eodun of ðær byric. *c* **1200** [see A 2 b]. *a* **1300** *Cursor M.* 17704 (Gött.) Ga noght vte of þi hus a step. **1483** *Cath. Angl.* 149/1 To Ga owte of way, *deuiare, exhorbitare*. **1583** HOLLYBAND *Campo di Fior* 29 Before thou goest out of thy chamber. **1665** PEPYS *Diary* 21 June, I find all the town almost going out of town [on account of the plague]. **1711** ADDISON *Spect.* No. 112 ¶5 No body presumes to stir till Sir Roger is gone out of the Church. **1882** *Daily Tel.* 30 Jan., Mr. Linde allowed Seaman, Lord Chancellor, and Woodbrook to go out of the stable one after the other. **1884** M. MACKENZIE *Dis. Throat & Nose* II. 311 If..a patient is obliged to go out of doors he should plug his nostrils with cotton wool. **1888** MCCARTHY & MRS. C. PRAED *Ladies' Gallery* II. v. 86 It has quite gone out of my head. **1892** *Chamb. Jrnl.* 3 Sept. 563/2 The estates went out of the family.

b. *to go out of cultivation, fashion, use*, etc.: to cease to be cultivated, fashionable, or used. *to go out of print*: said of a book, etc., when all the printed copies are sold off. *to go out of gear* or *order*: to become disarranged. *to go out of one's mind* or *senses*: to become deranged.

1483 *Cath. Angl.* 149/1 To Ga owte of mynde, *dementare*. **1818** HALLAM *Mid. Ages* (1872) I. 277 Much land had gone out of cultivation in Gaul. **1825** *New Monthly Mag.* XIV. 558 The May-pole is almost gone out of fashion. **1883** BLACK *Yolande* I. xviii. 344 He will go out of his senses. **1886** WALSINGHAM & PAYNE-GALLWEY *Shooting* (1895) 93 Hammerless guns..are..very apt to go out of order. **1890** *Murray's Mag.* VII. 60 The first edition went out of print. **1890** *Blackw. Mag.* CXLVIII. 855/2 Our military machinery had rusted and gone out of gear. **1892** *Monthly Packet* Oct. 430 The name..had in some way gone out of use.

89. go over.

a. See simple senses and OVER; often, to cross a piece of water, a hill, etc. *spec.* To go 'over the top' (see TOP *sb.*[1] 3 d).

1481 CAXTON *Reynard* (Arb.) 12 Ther bysyde was an hie montayne..and there muste brune in the myddel goon ouer for to goo to maleperduys. **1605** SHAKS. *Macb.* III. iv. 138, I am in blood Stept in so farre, that should I wade no more, Returning were as tedious as go ore. **1648** *Hamilton Papers* (Camden) 202 He will goe over wheather and when you aduisse. **1737** SWIFT *Let. to Pope* 23 July, It will be time enough when his lordship goes over [i.e. crosses from Ireland to England]. **1919** GALSWORTHY *Saint's Progress* II. i. §3 Calculating exactly where he meant to put foot and hand for the going over. **1931** W. V. TILSLEY *Other Ranks* 49 His only comment on 'going over' had been: 'Well, Dick, Brettle's going to have his chance.'

b. To pay a visit to a place at some distance.

1847 MARRYAT *Childr. N. Forest* xxi, I fear that you cannot go over to the cottage.

c. To pass, be transferred *to* another owner.

1818 Cruise *Digest* (ed. 2) II. 19 The estate must go over to the next in remainder.

d. To change one's party; to secede from one side *to* another. *to go over* (*to Rome*): to become Roman Catholic. *to go over to the majority* (= L. *abire ad plures*): to die (see majority).

1687 Burnet *Contin. Reply to Varillas* 123 Some went over to the Queen with flying Colours. **1704** Addison *Italy* (1705) 516 In the Change of Religion, Men.. don't so much consider the Principles as the Practice of those to whom they go over. **1823** *New Monthly Mag.* IX. 341/1 Morillo.. has gone over to the French with a part of his force. **1860–1** Thackeray *Lovel* ii, Pye of Maudlin, just before he 'went over', was perpetually in Mrs. Prior's back parlour with little books, pictures [etc.]. **1878** Miss Braddon *Open Verd.* I. vi. 103 After this, I shouldn't be at all surprised at his going over to Rome. **1885** Mrs. Lynn Linton *Chr. Kirkland* II. v. 154 You will at once adopt [his views] and go over to his side. **1892** *Standard* 26 Apr. 4/7 When a large section, headed by the old Leader, had gone over, it was hopeless to prolong the struggle.

e. Of a vehicle: To be overturned or upset. Said also of the driver or passengers.

1890 Boldrewood *Col. Reformer* (1891) 127 It took all.. Ned could do.. to keep from going over in some of the waggon tracks.

f. Of a bill, motion, etc.: to be postponed for consideration. *U.S.*

1894 'Mark Twain' in *Century Mag.* Feb. 556 According to the by-laws it must go over to the next regular meeting for action. **1900** *Congress. Rec.* 3 Jan. 632/2, I ask that it may go over until to-morrow, so that we can have an opportunity to see it. *Ibid.*, The resolution goes over under the rule.

†**g.** *Bridge.* To double. *U.S. Obs.*

1902 J. B. Elwell *Bridge* 111 *Going over* ... The effect of 'over', 'over', etc., is that the value of each trick point is doubled, quadrupled, etc. **1907** R. F. Foster *Bridge* 60 If you are reasonably certain of the odd trick, you should go over in order to make it more valuable. *Ibid.* [see 76 g]. **1920** —— *Auction made Easy* 111 *Going over*, obsolete for doubling.

h. Of a play, speech, etc.: to be successful in its appeal to the audience; to 'get across', 'get over'. Also *gen.* to have a vogue or success; to be well received; esp. in phr. *to go over big* (cf. 19 b). orig. *U.S. slang.*

1923 H. C. Witwer *Fighting Blood* ix. 281 These synthetic actors.. are going over big with their parents. **1923** H. Crane *Let.* 18 Feb. (1965) 126 One of my campaigns that not only 'went over big' but is theoretically a good piece of work. **1924** *Ibid.* 3 Feb. 174 My copy on the cheese book went over without any changes. **1927** *Daily Express* 29 Aug. 5 'Little Bits of Love' went over with its accustomed success. *Ibid.* 23 Nov. 13 'Escape' has gone over with a great bang. **1930** *New Statesman* 1 Nov. 115/2 Experienced novelists know that a good trial always goes over big. **1936** D. Powell *Turn, Magic Wheel* i. 39 As this went over big he forgave Dennis. **1961** J. B. Priestley *Saturn over Water* xiv. 193 Dr Magorious had rated a whole column report, and clearly was going over big in Melbourne.

90. go round.

a. To revolve, rotate. Of the head: To 'swim'.

1606 Shaks. *Ant. & Cl.* ii. vii. 124 Cup vs till the world go round. **1611** —— *Cymb.* v. v. 232. **1782** Cowper *Gilpin* 41 Smack went the whip, round went the wheels. **1875** Jowett *Plato* (ed. 2) III. 579 The earth goes round. **1897** Fl. Marryat *Blood Vampire* x, Better now, Mamma, thank you! only my head keeps going round.

b. To complete a revolution.

1603 Shaks. *Meas. for M.* i. ii. 172 So long, that ninteene Zodiacks haue gone round.

c. To make a circuit or tour; to visit various places in succession.

1849 *Tait's Mag.* XVI. 80/2 They went round into the markets, and bought up all the corn. **1861** Hughes *Tom Brown at Oxf.* i, I spent a day or two in.. going round and seeing the other colleges.

d. To circulate, pass from one person to another in a company.

1500–20 Dunbar *Poems* lvi. 14 Lat anis the cop ga round about, And wyn the covanis banesoun. **1613** Shaks. *Hen. VIII*, i. iv. 97 A health Gentlemen, Let it goe round. **1779** Cowper *Yearly Distress* xii, The punch goes round, and they are dull And lumpish still as ever. **1801** Miss Aikin *Begg. Man, Poetr. Childr.* (1826) 1 Jokes went round and careless chat. **1890** *Cornh. Mag.* July 11 The frequent laugh goes round.

e. To make a detour. Also *colloq.* to pay a visit in an incidental or informal way. (Cf. come 71 a.)

1664 Pepys *Diary* 5 Nov., The coach being forced to go round by London Wall home, because of the bonfires. **1873** Black *Pr. Thule* xvi. 264 Her husband was going round for an hour to a ball that Mrs. Kavanagh was giving. **1885** G. Allen *Babylon* viii, He went round to see Cicolari.

f. To be long enough to encompass.

g. Of food, or anything to be distributed or apportioned: To be sufficient in number or quantity to supply every member of the party. Also, in *Card-playing*, said of a suit led, when all the players are able to follow.

1869 P. T. Barnum *Struggles & Triumphs* xvi. 259 When it [*sc.* a turkey] was carved, there was not enough of it to 'go round'. **1878** *Scribner's Mag.* XV. 334/2 We have barely enough to go round. **1879** 'Cavendish' *Card Ess.* etc. 230 Its policy lies chiefly in the hope that spades may go round three times. **1889** Miss Sergeant *E. Denison* I. i. iii. 28 To see.. that the cups and saucers would go round. **1891** *Sat. Rev.* 18 July 84/1 The haunch of venison was in such demand that Jacob Tonson learnt with horror that it would never 'go round'.

h. *Theatr.* Of a member of an audience: to go behind the scenes at a theatre; esp. to visit an actor, etc., backstage after a performance; (in quot. 1866, to go into the audience from backstage).

1866 'Old Stager' *Stage Reminisc.* i. 7 The scene-shifters.. had thought it would be worth while seeing Kean's reception from the front, and had gone round for that purpose. **1900** T. E. Pemberton *Kendals* xi. 326 After the piece was over, I went 'round' to offer her my congratulations. **1952** A. Christie *Mrs. McGinty's Dead* xvii. 128 The play itself she had enjoyed, but the ordeal of 'going round afterwards' was fraught with.. terrors. **1966** D. Blakelock *Eleanor* iii. 29 I'm not fond of 'going round' to see people.

91. go through.

a. See simple senses and through. †**b.** To complete what is entered upon or undertaken. *Obs.*

1513 More in Grafton *Chron.* (1568) 777 And sithence he had once begonne, he would stoutly go thorowe. **1631** Shirley *Traitor* iv. i, You chang'd Your purpose, why did you not go through, And murder him? *a* **1715** Burnet *Own Time* (1823) II. 300 They promised these witnesses a large share of the confiscated estates, if they went through in the business. **1716** Jer. Collier tr. *G. Nazianzen's Paneg.* 9, I have seen you all go nobly through, and come off with Conquest about you.

c. Of a proposition: To be carried. Of a deal: to be completed.

1889 *Kansas Times & Star* 8 Apr., Kump intimates the deal won't go through. **1895** *Boston* (Mass.) *Jrnl.* 14 Jan. 7/7 Confirmation of Secretary Francis considered, but does not go through.

d. To desert, decamp, abscond; also, to desist, give up. *Austral. slang.*

1943 Baker *Dict. Austral. Slang* 35 *Go through*, to desert from a northern base to the south. War slang. **1944** J. Devanny *By Tropic Sea & Jungle* xi. 89 'Cutting cane's not living: it's death in life... You're going through,' I told myself. 'You're going through!' **1949** J. Cleary *You can't see round Corners* i. viii. 63 The corporal looked up and there was a faint stirring in the ranks... 'He's gone through. Went last night.'

92. go through *with.*

a. To complete, carry to completion, perform thoroughly, get to the end of.

1568 Grafton *Chron.* II. 32 He seazed upon his goods.. whereby he became the stronger, and better able to go thorowe with this enterprise. *a* **1586** Sidney *Arcadia* ii. (1633) 123 Finding Pyrocles able euery way to goe thorow with that kinde of life. **1677** Temple *Ess. Gout* Wks. 1731 I. 145 The Gout is commonly the Disease of aged Men, who cannot go through with these strong Remedies. **1748** *Anson's Voy.* iii. iii. 323 They were prepared for going through with this undertaking. **1787** Cowper *Let.* 27 Aug., It is the only one [romance], indeed, of an old date that I ever had the patience to go through with. **1820** *Examiner* No. 629. 287/1 He would have gone through with it to the very bottom, or else have perished in the attempt. **1890** *New Review* Jan. 85 He is only going through with it as a duty.

†**b.** To complete an enumeration or description of. *Obs.*

1726 Leoni *Alberti's Archit.* II. 73/2, I think I have now gone thro' with all the ornaments that relate to public Edifices.

93. go to, †go till.

†**a.** To go about one's work, to get to work. Chiefly in *imp.* as an exhortation = Come on! L. *age. Obs.*

c **1200** Ormin 9199 Gaþ till, & ȝarrkeþþ Godess weȝȝe. *Ibid.* 14038 Ant teȝȝ ȝedenn till, & didenn þatt he seȝȝde. *a* **1250** *Owl & Night.* 836 Thu gest al to mid swikelede. *c* **1420** *Pallad. on Husb.* iii. 668 In ver let sowe, in October go to And transplaunte hit. *c* **1460** *Towneley Myst.* iii. 236 Here shal no man tary the, I pray the go to! **1513** Douglas *Æneis* ix. ii. 12 Hay, hay, go to! than cry thai with ane schout. **1573** *Satir. Poems Reform.* xxxix. 112 Our Cronall als, quha is ane freik bot feir, With all his Capitanes reddie to ga to. **1583** Hollyband *Campo di Fior* 9 Go to now bring me a doublet. **1611** Bible *Gen.* xi. 3 And they sayd one to another; Goe to, let vs make bricke. **1645** Ussher *Body Div.* (1647) 56 Go to then, shew first how many ways sinne is to be considered. **1690** W. Walker *Idiomat. Anglo-Lat.* 208 Go to! let it be done.

b. Used in *imp.* to express disapprobation, remonstrance, protest, or derisive incredulity; = Come, come! †Also used to introduce a contemptuous concession.

1513 More in Grafton *Chron.* (1568) II. 769 But go to, suppose that she feareth (as who may let her to feare her awne shadowe). **1589** R. Harvey *Pl. Perc.* (1860) 4 Go to, Martin, go to: I know a man is a man though he haue but a hose on his head. **1602** Marston *Ant. & Mel.* iii. Wks. 1856 I. 31 Goe to, goe to; thou liest, Philosophy. **1741** Richardson *Pamela* I. 190 Go to, go to, naughty mistrustful Mrs. Pamela. **1798** T. Twining *Recr. & Studies* (1882) 232 Go to with your doubts and your wisdom. **1822** Byron *Werner* ii. i. 429 Go to! you are a wag. **1861** Hughes *Tom Brown at Oxf.* i, Go to, why should we not make the public pay for the great benefits we confer upon them? **1886** J. Payne *Decameron* I. 50 'Go to, son', rejoined the friar; 'what is this thou sayest?'

†**c.** *Sc.* Of the sun: To go down, set. *Obs.*

1588 A. King tr. *Canisius' Catech.* 152 Thou sall pay him the price of his labour befoir the sunne ga to. **1622** [see going *vbl. sb.* 5 b].

d. To shut, close.

1481 Caxton *Reynard* (Arb.) 92 The grynne wente to.

94. go together.

a. See simple senses and together. *to go together by the ears* (see ear *sb.*[1] I. i. d).

b. To be mutually concomitant or compatible.

1606 Shaks. *Ant. & Cl.* iv. xv. 47, *Ant.* Of Cæsar seeke your Honour, with your safety. *Cleo.* They do not go together. **1620** *Examiner* No. 651. 631/1 Vixenishness and virtue go together. **1889** Philips & Wills *Fatal Phryne* I. v. 104 Baldness, science, and snuff-taking go together.

†**c.** To collapse. *Obs.*

1387 Trevisa *Higden* (Rolls) VII. 7 þat tyme was so greet tempest.. þat it semede þat al þe worlde schulde goo to giders.

d. To keep company as lovers; to 'go steady'; to be courting or engaged.

1899 M. E. Wilkins *Jamesons* iii. 77 People began to say that Harry Liscom and the eldest Jameson girl were going together. **1958** E. Dundy *Dud Avocado* i. ix. 154 Now that Jim and I were seen around.. in public, it became obvious.. that we were 'going together'.

95. go under. Of persons: To fail; to succumb in the struggle for life; to go to ruin; to disappear from society; in *U.S. slang*, to die. Of a literary work: To drop out of sight.

1849 Ruxton *Life Far West* 13 Five of our boys got rubbed out that time.. How s'ever, five of us went under. **1879** J. Payn *Finding His Level, High Spirits* I. 234 Poor John Weybridge, Esq., became as friendless as penniless, and eventually 'went under', and was heard of no more. **1885** B. Harte *Maruja* vii, What with old Doc. West going under so suddent. **1890** *Sat. Rev.* 15 Mar. 330/2 Intended for publication a considerable time ago.. they 'went under'.. and only recently turned up again. **1891** H. C. Halliday *Someone must suffer* III. xvi. 264 He had 'gone under' in the struggle, as the terribly expressive phrase runs.

96. go up.

a. To go, pass, or change to a place or position which is, or is viewed as, higher; to ascend, rise. †Of a sword: To be put *up* (into the sheath), to be sheathed. *spec.* To go to a university or college; also, to enter *for* an examination.

c **1386** Chaucer *Shipman's T.* 212 Vp to hir housbonde is this wyf ygon. *c* **1400** *Destr. Troy* 4978 Goand vp by degrees þurgh mony gay Alys. **1535** Coverdale *Gen.* xlvi. 29 Ioseph bended his charett fast, and went vp to mete Israel his father. **1601** Shaks. *Jul. C.* v. i. 52, I draw a Sword against Conspirators, When thinke you that the Sword goes vp againe? **1719** De Foe *Crusoe* ii. xi. (1840) 233 The great.. gulf which goes up to Siam. **1793** Smeaton *Edystone L.* §289 The moveable shears, that had gone up with us, from the top of the first room. **1820** *Examiner* No. 615. 57/2 Pope.. resolved to go up to London. **1844** *Fraser's Mag.* XXX. 504 The writ went up to the Lords. **1861** Hughes *Tom Brown at Oxf.* Introd., He.. did not go up to reside at Oxford till the end of the following January. **1861** *Temple Bar* III. 515 A certain number.. go up for examination to be ruthlessly plucked. **1875** L. Troubridge in *Life amongst Troubridges* (1966) 23 'Ernest has passed *first of all*!'... Fancy, first of all the sixty-eight boys who went up. **1879** C. M. Yonge *Magnum Bonum* I. xxi. 426, I mean to go up for a scholarship next year. **1885** A. Edwardes *Girton Girl* III. xiii. 230 Very likely I may go up to Girton as a bye-term man in January. **1890** *Gd. Words* Aug. 520/2 The barometer.. is going up at a tremendous rate. **1895** Suffling *Land of Broads* 70 There is no such thing as a level street in the city: those which do not go up, go down. **1955** *Times* 9 May 13/1 He was educated at Sywell House School, Llandudno, whence he went up to Oxford.

b. Chiefly *U.S.* To go to ruin; to be destroyed; to become bankrupt. Also, to be killed (or †hanged); to die; to be done for; esp. in phr. *to be gone up. colloq.*

1825 J. Neal *Bro. Jonathan* III. 233 Whose narrow escape, when his brother spy 'went up', he said, was quite a 'muricle'. **1864** *Index* June (Farmer), Soon after the blockade, many thought we should go up on the salt question. **1867** W. H. Dixon *New America* I. xi. 132 Gone up, in the slang of Denver, means gone up a tree—that is to say, a cotton tree... In plain English, the man is said to have been *hung*. **1878** *Scribner's Mag.* XVI. 864/2 Oh, they are all going to pieces.. I should not be surprised to hear of their going up at any moment. **1888** P. H. Sheridan *Mem.* I. 86 He remarked, 'Well, I fear that they are gone up,' a phrase used.. to mean that they had been killed. **1892** Stevenson & L. Osbourne *Wrecker* xvi. 248 We've rather bad news for you.. your firm's gone up. **1907** J. Masefield *Tarpaulin Muster* 101 To your prayers, boys. We're gone up. *Ibid.* 209 You're gone up, my son.

c. Of a cry, etc. = ascend I c.

1535 Coverdale *1 Sam.* v. 12 The noyse of the cite wente up into heauen. **1611** Bible *ibid.* **1869** Hughes *Alfred the Gt.* i. 8 This cry.. has been going up from all sections of English society. **1890** *Murray's Mag.* Oct. 556 A shriek has gone up as to the wickedness of carrying cattle upon deck.

d. To be put or lifted up; to be raised or reared.

1882 *Daily Tel.* 19 May, After some slow play, the 50 went up. **1887** Mrs. Perks *Fr. Heather Hills* I. vi. 114 Eliza's hands went up in horror. **1892** *Harper's Mag.* May 959/2 Already barricades were going up in the larger streets.

e. To increase in number, price, or value.

1883 Mrs. C. Praed *Moloch* I. i. iv. 79 Wool would go up a penny a pound. **1890** T. F. Tout *Hist. Eng.* 95 Norwich.. went up from 30,000 to 60,000 inhabitants. **1892** *Standard* 9 Feb. 5/3 Beef and mutton will 'go up' for a time.

f. *to go up and down* (see up).

g. To 'ascend' (see ascend *v.* 9) in ancestry.

1872 A. de Vere *Leg. St. Patrick* p. xiii, Her genealogies went up to the first parent. **1930** J. L. Myres *Who were the Greeks?* 308 Hecataeus' genealogy went back sixteen generations, and then 'went up to a god'.

h. To explode, burn, be consumed. Also *fig.*

1932 A. J. Worrall *Eng. Idioms* 77 A bomb is dropped on a model house which goes up in flames. **1933** *Punch* 3 May 498/1 Civilisation Would probably go up in smoke If unsophisticated folk like you and me.. Employed companionation. **1940** 'N. Blake' *Malice in Wonderland* i. vii. 96 He fairly went up in smoke about the camp. **1950** A. P. Herbert *Independent Member* 167 The shattered 'skid' astern of a mine-sweeper that meant a mine gone up. **1971** *Daily Tel.* (Colour Suppl.) 5 Nov. 29/2 He left the sea, having had what amounted to a nervous breakdown, 'always thinking of the other ships that went up, the bombings and suchlike'.

VIII. The vb.-stem occas. forms phraseological combs. (chiefly *colloq.* or *techn.*) having the function either of sb. or adj.; as **go-about** (see quot.); † **go-alone plough**, ? one that requires little guidance from the ploughman; **go-anywhere** *a.*, that can go anywhere; **go-ashore** (*a*) *adj.*, characteristic of a sailor when ashore; also, designating clothes worn or articles used by sailors when ashore; (*b*) *sb. pl.*, clothes worn by a sailor when ashore, 'the seaman's best dress' (Smyth *Sailor's Word-bk.* 1867); (*c*) *New Zealand*, an iron cauldron with three feet, and attachments for hanging it over a fire [said to be a corruption of Maori *kohua*] (see Morris *Austral-Eng.*); **go-as-you-please** *a.*, (of a race, hence *gen.* of proceedings likened to this) unfettered by regulations; **go-as-you-please(ness** *sb.*, want of regularity or order; freedom; **go-at-it** *a.*, full of dash; **go-back**, a going back, a return; also *attrib.* in ***go-back game*** (see quot.); † **go-before**, a harbinger, an usher; † **go-by-(the)-ground**, (*a*) *adj.*, cringing, low; (*b*) *sb.*, something that creeps along the ground; a dwarf; a low carriage; **go-fever**, a feverish restlessness or longing for movement; † **go-free** (see quot.); **go-no-further**, a variety of apple; **go-out** (see quot.; cf. GOUT *sb.*[2]); **gae-through-land** *Sc.* a vagabond; **go-stop** *a.*, designating an economic system or situation characterized by alternating periods of inflation and deflation; cf. STOP-GO *a.*; **go-to-bed**, one who is ready to go to bed, sleepy; **go-to-bed-at-noon**, a dial. name for GOAT'S-BEARD 2; **go-up-able** *a.*, that may be ascended; † **go-well**, a prosperous journey outward; **go-within-each-other** *a.*, of boxes, when each will go into the next larger. Also GO-BETWEEN, GO-BY, GO-CART, GO-DOWN.

1611 COTGR., *Entourure*, a compasse..any thing that compasseth, and incloseth another; a *goe-about. **1806–7** A. YOUNG *Agric. Essex* (1813) I. 143 Mr. Newman uses the skim coulter constantly... I saw it working well on his farm, attached to his *Go-alone plough. **1963** BIRD & HUTTON-STOTT *Veteran Motor Car* 27 The sturdy, no-nonsense, *go-anywhere machine. **1966** G. N. LEECH *Eng. in Advertising* xv. 139 The go-anywhere Electrolux 16 refrigerator. **1862** MARSH *Eng. Lang.* xi. 164 A sailor will not be likely to interlard his *go-ashore talk with clew-lines [etc.]. [**1834** E. MARKHAM *N.Z. or Recollections of It* 39 The Natives now begin to use Iron pots, known to them by the name of 'Go on Shores' from the circumstance of Boats going up and down the Rivers, coming to an Anchor and going on Shore to Cook.] **1839** J. D. LANG *N.Z. in 1839* ii. 34 Bought a large tract of eligible land..for two check shirts and an iron-pot, or *go-ashore, as it is called by the natives. **1840** R. H. DANA *Bef. Mast* xvi. 140 Go-ashore jackets and trousers [were] got out and brushed. **1849** W. T. POWER *Sketches in N.Z.* xviii. 160 Engaged in the superintendence of a Maori oven, or a huge gipsy-looking cauldron, called a 'go-ashore'. **1879** C. L. INNES *Canterbury Sketches* iii. 23 There was another pot used, called by the euphonious name of a 'Go ashore', which used to hang by a chain over the fire, this was used for boiling. **1885** RUNCIMAN *Skippers & Sh.* 98 Burnage looked very well in his go-ashores. **1933** J. MASEFIELD *Bird of Dawning* 246 All his go-ashore things were there, laid up with camphor in tissue paper, including his tall hat. **1953** *Landfall* Sept. 173 Edwards had a whare, ..A Brown Bess, a go-ashore. **1885** *Pall Mall G.* 13 Jan. 1/2 Governments entering into a *go-as-you-please competition in annexation. **1889** *Judge* 20 Apr. 21/2 A Western Go-As-You-Please. **1890** *Century Mag.* June 207/1 Most of these long distance matches are now of the go-as-you-please class. **1920** H. G. WELLS *Mr. Britling* I. iv. §6. 117 Explaining.. to this American..how excellent was the backwardness of Essex and English go-as-you-please. **1935** B. RUSSELL *In Praise of Idleness* 120 An element of free growth, of go-as-you-please and untrained natural living, is essential if men are not to become misshapen monsters. **1971** R. ROBERTS *Classic Slum* viii. 117 In later years, after cinema had begun to outstrip live entertainment..our theatre, like many others, tried 'go as you please' competitions on Friday evenings when local amateurs..trod the boards. **1927** *Observer* 1 May 15/3 The impromptu quality of the entertainment—its untidy *go-as-you-please-ness. **1904** *Daily Chron.* 27 June 7/2 They are a versatile, well-balanced, *go-at-it side, and they field as if they like it. **1873** 'CAVENDISH' & BENNETT *Billiards* 11 He played the best amateurs the *go-back game, fifty-up.. It seems only to have been played by screwing back and by crossing; and not by returning from the slow list cushion. **1896** MRS. CAFFYN *Quaker Grandmother* 320 It's a sort of go-back into the old life. **1625** MASSINGER *New Way* I. ii, You thinke you haue spoke wisely goodman Amble, My ladie's *go-before. **1659** GAUDEN *Tears Ch. Eng.* IV. xvii. 521 Would any thing..be more..despicable in the eyes of the people..than..such *Go-by-ground Governours. **1581** J. BELL *Haddon's Answ. Osor.* 384 b, Creeping yet lyke a seely goebyground. **1595** COPLEY *Wits, Fits, & Fancies* 202 Indeed sir..I had need haue two eyes, to discerne so pettie a goe by ground as you. **1797** MARY ROBINSON *Walsingham* III. 176 A go-by-the-ground, with two wheels, just for all the world like a cart. **1809** MALKIN *Gil Blas* IV. ix, He was a little go-by-the-ground, scarcely up to my shoulders. **1891** KIPLING *Light that Failed* 125 He's as restless as a swallow in autumn... He has the beginnings of the *go-fever upon him. **1900** J. BUCHAN *Half-hearted* vi. 78 There comes a thing called the go-fever, which is not amenable to reason. **1907** N. MUNRO *Daft Days* xxiv, I'd not been twenty minutes in her society before I found out she had the go-fever pretty bad. **1966** *Word Study* Dec. 2/1 'Everyone I think sort of gets go-fever,' Colonel Glenn was heard to remark at his news conference. **1885** EDWARDS in *Encycl. Brit.* XIX. 585/1 Stamped wrappers for newspapers were made experimentally in London by Mr. Charles Whiting under the name of '*go-frees', in 1830. **1664** EVELYN *Kal. Hort.* 80 Apples. Rousetting,..the *Go-no-further, or Cats-head. **1855** MISS MANNING *Old Chelsea Bun-House* xiv. 228 The large Cat's-head Apples that some call 'Go-no-farther'. **1875** KNIGHT *Dict. Mech.*, **Go out* (Hydraulic engineering), a sluice in an embankment for allowing water to escape from tidal lands when the tide is out. **1964** *Punch* 21 Oct. 591/2 The damage done by '*go-stop' economics. **1965** *New Statesman* 5 Nov. 680/2 The natural 'go-stop' cycle of the capitalist economy. **17..** *Clerk Tamas* xiii. in Child *Ballads* VIII. cclx. (1892) 428 Woud I forsake my ain gude lord And follow you, a *gae-through-land? **1759** *Compl. Let.-writer* (ed. 6) 221 The crowd of *Go-to-beds had taken themselves away. **1578** LYTE *Dodoens* I. xvii. 167 This hearbe is now called..in English Goates bearde..and *Go to bedde at Noone. **1597** GERARDE *Herbal* II. cclii. 73 It shutteth it selfe at twelve of the clocke..wherefore it was called Go to bed at noon. **1852** SMEDLEY *L. Arundel* xxxiii. 249 Starting for the Rhine, which..it was their intention to go up as far as it was *go-up-able. **1641** BROME *Joviall Crew* II. Wks. 1873 III. 388 Now bowse a round health to the *Go-well and Com-well Of Cisley Bumtrincket that lies in the Strummel. **1889** *Anthony's Photogr. Bull.* II. 2 The *go-within-each-other boxes, my camera.

☛*Phrase-key.*

Go! imper. 21 d, 22; from the word go, 22; as far as it goes, 43 b; as men, things (etc.) go, 15; as you go, as she goes (*Naut.*), 4 b; if you go to that, 35; (as) the story goes, 13; he goes for my money, 24 b; here goes, there goes, 22; that goes without saying, 20; touch and go, 22; what has gone of, is gone with —— ? 18 d; who goes (there)? 8 a; —— will *or* won't go, 38 a; going, 47; gone, 48; going! gone! 24; (see also GOING, GONE); *g* a-begging, a-hunting, etc., 32 e; *g* about (*prep.*) 49, (*adv.*) 70; *g* abroad, 71; *g* according to, 5; *g* after, 50; *g* against, 51, 18 b; *g* ahead, 72; *g* along, 73; *g* and——, 32 c; *g* apprentice, 32 f; *g* at, 52; *g* at a price, etc, 12, 24; *g* away, 75; *g* back, 76; *g* back from, 76 c; *g* back upon, 76 c, d; *g* backward(s, 77; *g* bail, 32 f; *g* bang, etc., 10; *g* before, (*prep.*) 53, (*adv.*) 78; *g* before a jury, 33; *g* behind, 54; *g* beside, 55; *g* better, 36; *g* between, 56; *g* by, (*prep.*) 57, (*adv.*) 79; *g* by (= be guided or determined by), 5; *g* by default, 18 c; *g* by a name, 14; *g* cheap, 24; *g* current, 12; *g* down, 80; *g* far, 35, 43; *g* for, 58, 18 b; *g* for a price, 24; *g* for current, 12; *g* for to do, 34 c; *g* forth, 81; *g* free, 23; *g* from one's word, 21 c; *g* halves (with), 35 c; *g* hard, 18; *g* high, 8 b; *g* ill (with), 18; *g* in, 82; *g* in (= be spent in), 25; *g* in and out, 82 a; *g* in at, 82 f; *g* in for, 83; *g* in to *or* unto, 82 e; *g* in with, 84; *g* in favour of, 18 b; *g* in *or* into holes, 29 a; *g* into, 59, 38; *g* it, 46; *g* (great) lengths, 35; *g* less, 35 b, 44; *g* near, nigh, 35; *g* off, (*prep.*) 60, (*adv.*) 85; *g* on, (*prep.*) 61, (*adv.*) 86; *g* on (= act or depend on), 5; *g* on (= be reported concerning), 13; *g* on the highway, road, streets, 31 c; *g* on one's side, 18 b; *g* out, 87; *g* out of, 88; *g* out of (= be paid out of), 25 b; *g* over, (*prep.*) 62, (*adv.*) 88; *g* the pace, 2 c; *g* quit, 23; *g* round, 90 l; *g* shares (with), 35 c; *g* short, 6; *g* through, (*prep.*) 63, (*adv.*) 91; *g* through with, 92; *g* to (*adv.*), 93; *g* to the bad, 43 b; *g* to the bar, 31 c; *g* to Bath, Jericho, etc., 30 b; *g* to blows, cuffs, etc., 34; *g* to the bull, etc. (= copulate with), 31 b; *g* to do (= attempt or venture to do), 34 b, c; *g* to expense, trouble, etc., 35 d; *g* to one's heart, 37 b; *g* to law, 34; *g* to pieces, to rack and ruin, 44 c; *g* to sea, 31 d; *g* to sleep, 30 d; *g* to war, 32; *g* to work, 34; *g* together, 94; *g* under, (*prep.*) 64, (*adv.*) 95; *g* under a name, 14; *g* unpunished, unrewarded, etc., 23; *g* up, (*prep.*) 65, (*adv.*) 96; *g* upon, 67; *g* upon (= act or proceed upon, 5; *g* upon (= be reported concerning), 13; *g* (a great, long, some) way (towards), 35, 43 c, d; *g* one's way, 21 b; *g* well (with), 18, 19; *g* with, 68; *g* with (= act in harmony with), 5 a; *g* with child, 7; *g* without, 69.

go (gəʊ), *a. colloq.* (orig. *U.S.*). [f. the vb.]

1. Functioning properly; ready and prepared; esp. of devices in space-craft. So **go-no-go** *a.* (see quot. 1959).

A 'go' gauge (quot. 1951) is one which must pass through (or be passed through by) the piece, a 'no(t)-go' gauge one which must not, thus ensuring that the dimensions are within acceptable limits.

1910 *Engineering* 22 July 118/2 There are 'go' and 'no go' gauges in use for holes, diameters, screw-threads, slots, [etc.]. **1959** W. A. HEFLIN *Aerospace Gloss.* 43/2 *Go-no-go a.*, of a rocket missile launch: so controlled at the end of the countdown as to permit an instantaneous change in decision on whether to launch or not to launch. **1961** *Words of Space Age* (*Newsweek*) 12 The fuel system is go. **1962** *Guardian* 22 Feb. 8/6 Colonel Glenn reported..'I am Go; all systems are Go.' **1962** *Flight International* LXXXII. 164/2 One of the biggest single contributions which could be made on jet aircraft is a Go-No Go indicator. **1962** A. SHEPARD in *Into Orbit* 102 Inside the Mercury Control Centre itself, all the lights were green. All conditions were 'Go'. **1962** *Sunday Times* 4 Mar. 31/8 A..better University..creatively responding to the new challenges, and good luck indeed to them, their system too is no doubt Go. **1963** [see ABORT *v.* 1 c]. **1969** J. GARDNER *Founder Member* ii. 26 Fuel is go... Oxygen is go.

2. Fashionable, modern, progressive, 'go-ahead', 'with it'. Cf. GO-GO *a.*

1962 in *Amer. Speech* XXXVII. 286 What is a Junior?.. A size, of course, not a matter of age! It stands for 'Go' in the fashion world. **1963** *Time* 4 Jan. 36/3 Beatniks, whose heavy black turtleneck sweaters had never looked particularly go with white tennis socks. **1964** *Punch* 8 July 43/1, I am not a go person.

Goa[1] ('gəʊə). The name of a city in west central India (the capital of the former Portuguese dominion in that country), used *attrib.* in the names of certain articles, as ***Goa bean***, the seed of *Psophocarpus tetragonolobus* (J. Smith *Dict. Names Pl.* 1882); ***Goa plum***, the fruit of *Parinarium excelsum* (Yule); ***Goa powder***, a medicament used for Bombay eczema, derived from the Brazilian araroba-tree (Yule); ***Goa stone*** (also ***Goa ball***), a fever medicine at one time greatly in vogue, consisting of various drugs made up in the form of a hard ball, from which a portion was scraped as required (see quots.).

1696 OVINGTON *Voy. Suratt* 262 The Snake Stone.. much excels the deservedly fam'd *Gasper Antoni*, or Goa Stone. **1698** FRYER *Acc. E. India & P.* 149 Gasper Antonio, a Florentine, a Lay-Brother of the Order [of Paulistines], the Author of the Goa Stones, brings them in 50,000 Xerephins, by that invention Annually. **1710** T. FULLER *Pharm. Extemp.* 30 Take..Goa Stone..half a scruple. **1719** D'URFEY *Pills* V. 347 Perfum'd with fragrant Goar Stone. **1757** BROOKE in *Phil. Trans.* LI. 79, I seemed to find great relief by drinking punch, into which Goa stone had been plentifully grated. **1865** C. W. KING *Nat. Hist. Gems* (1867) 256 The Goa-stone..is of the shape and size of a duck's egg, has a greyish metallic lustre, and, though hard, is friable. **1874** FAYRER in *Med. Times & Gaz.* 24 Oct. 471/1 Goa powder..is a fine yellowish powder without smell or taste. .. It is sold by the chemists in Calcutta and Bombay in small phials.

goa[2] ('gəʊə). [Corruptly a. Tibetan *dgoba* (Jäschke *Tib. Dict.*).] A Tibetan antelope, *Procapra picticauda* (Hodgson).

1846 B. H. HODGSON *A New Species Tibetan Antelope* in *Jrnl. Asiatic Soc. Bengal* XV. 335 This exceedingly graceful little animal..is called by the Tibetans Rágóa or Góá simply. **1888** *Blackw. Mag.* Aug. 242 We intended to try our luck after the goa. **1893** LYDEKKER *Horns & Hoofs* 183 The pretty little goa, or Tibetan gazelle (*Gazella picticaudata*).

goa[3] ('gəʊə) A name of the marsh crocodile.

1863 WOOD *Nat. Hist.* III. 31 The Marsh Crocodile (*Crocodilus palustris*), sometimes known by the names of Mugger, or Goa.

goad (gəʊd), *sb.*[1] Forms: 1 **gád**, (**gaad**), 4–6 **gode**, (**gohode**), 5 **goode**, 6 **goade**, 7– **goad**. [OE. *gád* str. fem. corresponds to Lombard *gaida* arrow-head:—OTeut. type **gaidâ*; for possible cognates see GARE *sb.*[1] The northern form is GAID (q.v.), but in ME. both northern and southern forms are less common than the synonymous, though unrelated, GAD *sb.*[1]]

1. A rod or stick, pointed at one end or fitted with a sharp spike and employed for driving cattle, esp. oxen used in ploughing (cf. GAD *sb.*[1] 4).

c **725** *Corpus Gloss.* 1937 *Stiga* [sic], gaad. *a* **1000** *Sal. & Sat.* 91 (Gr.) Hafað gudmæcga ʒierde lanʒe, gyldene gade. **1388** WYCLIF *Ecclus.* xxxviii. 26 He that holdith the plow, and he that hath glorie in a gohode [L. *in jaculo*], dryueth oxis with a pricke. *c* **1394** *P. Pl. Creed* 433 His wijf walked him wiþ [at the plough] with a longe gode. **14..** *Voc* in Wr.-Wülcker 586/23 *Gerusa*, a goode. *c* **1440** *Promp. Parv.* 184/1 Gad or gode, *gerusa.* **1539** TAVERNER *Erasm. Prov.* (1552) 15 It is harde kyckynge agaynst the gode. **1627** DRAYTON *Sheph. Sirena* 361 They their Holly whips haue brac'd, And tough Hazell goades haue gott. **1635–56** COWLEY *Davideis* IV. 166 With the same Goad Samgar his Oxen drives Which took..six hundred lives. **1703** MAUNDRELL *Journ. Jerus.* (1732) 110 In ploughing they us'd Goads..about eight foot long. **1783** HOOLE *Orl. Fur.* xxxvii. 804 A hind..A rustic weapon for her rage supply'd, A pointed goad he brought. **1816** SCOTT *Old Mort.* xv, Countrymen armed with scythes ..hay-forks..goads. **1875** HELPS *Ess., Organiz. in Daily Life* 109, I had a thought that drove me like a goad.

2. *fig.* Something that pricks or wounds like a goad. **a.** A torment, 'thorn', 'sting'.

1561 tr. *Calvin's 4 Serm. agst. Idolatries* i. C ij b, Those same goads and prickes wherwith their consciences are prikt and wounded. **1641** J. JACKSON *True Evang. T.* II. 138 These pointed and diamonded speeches, which doe indeed leave a sting, and goad in the mind of the pious Auditor. **1689** SHADWELL *Bury F.* III. 181 Where is my Goad' my damned for better or worse. **1759** FRANKLIN *Ess.* Wks. 1840 III. 255 French forts and French armies so near us will be everlasting goads in our sides. **1861** TRENCH *Comm. Ep. to Ch. Asia* 80 There are ever goads in the memory of a better and a nobler past. **1879** FARRAR *St. Paul* (1883) 140 The wounding goad of a reproachful conscience.

b. A strong incitement or instigation, 'spur', stimulus.

1600 HOLLAND *Livy* XXXIX. xv. (1609) 1032 These..who pricke and provoke (as it were) with goads [L. *stimulis*] of furies your spirits and minds. **1608** ARMIN *Nest Ninn.* (1842) 4 That's the way to spoyle all, but with your goad pricke me on the true tract. **1615** CROOKE *Body of Man* 284 Those Females which are castrated or gelt..the goads of lust are in them vtterly extinguished. **1798** MALTHUS *Popul.* III. i. (1806) II. 82 The labour..will not be performed without the goad of necessity. *a* **1859** MACAULAY *Biog.* (1867) 110 He no longer felt the daily goad urging him to the daily toil. **1876** MOZLEY *Univ. Serm.* iv. (1877) 94 Knowledge is a goad to those who have it.

3. A measure of length. † **a.** A cloth-measure = $4\frac{1}{2}$ feet. *Obs.*

1481 *Howard Househ. Bks.* (Roxb.) 17 My Lord schal haue of hym iiij.^c goodes off white..and my Lord schal pay him for euery goode, ix.*d.* **1552** *Act 5 & 6 Edw VI*, c. 6 § 1 Cottonnes called Manchester..and Chesshire Cottonnes.. shalbe in lenghe twentie two goades and conteyne in bredith thre quarters of a yarde in the water. **1674** JEAKE *Arith.* (1696) 65 In 1 Goad..$4\frac{1}{2}$ Feet, a Measure in some places for Land and Cloth received by Custom. **1721** C. KING *Brit. Merch.* I. 181, 1200 C. Goads of Cotton. **1727** W. MATHER *Yng. Man's Comp.* 399 In London, the Yard is used for Silks, Woollen Cloth, &c. The Ell for Linnen Cloth, &c., and the Goad for Frizes, Cotton, and the like.

b. A land-measure (see quots. and cf. GAD 6).

1587 FLEMING *Contn. Holinshed* III. 1353/1 The space of fortie goad (euerie goad conteining fifteene foot). **1880** *E. Cornw. Gloss.* s.v., It represents nine feet, and two goads square is called a yard of ground.

4. A spike = GAD *sb.*[1] 1.

1855 J. Hewitt *Anc. Armour* I. 81 The spur of this period consisted of a single goad, sometimes of a lozenge form, sometimes a plain spike.

5. *Comb.*, as **goad-groom**, **-prick**; also **goad(s)-man** = GADMAN; **goad-spur**, a spur without a rowel and with one point (cf. *prickspur*).

1614 Sylvester *Little Bartas* 877 Thou.. by one man, one *Goad-groom (silly Sangar), Destroy'dst six hundred in religious anger. **1605** —— *Du Bartas* II. iii. IV. *Captaines* 710 And *Goad-man Sangar. **1765** A. Dickson *Treat. Agric.* (ed. 2) 248 The goadman or driver. **1816** Scott *Old Mort.* vi, Ye may be goadsman.. and tak tent ye dinna o'erdrive the owsen. *c* **1826** Hogg in *Wilson's Wks.* (1855) I. 176 The goadman whistles sparely. **1609** Bible (Douay) *1 Sam.* xiii. 21 Even to the *godeprick, which was to be mended. **1889** *Century Dict.*, *Goad-spur.*

goad (gəʊd), *sb.*[2] *slang.* (See quots.)

a **1700** B. E. *Dict. Cant. Crew*, *Goads*, those that Wheedle in Chapmen for Horse-coursers. **1889** *Century Dict.*, *Goad* ..a decoy at an auction; a Peter Funk.

goad (gəʊd), *v.* [f. GOAD *sb.*[1]]

1. *trans.* To prick with a goad or other pointed instrument; to drive or urge on *to* something by such means. Also with *on* or *onwards*.

1619 Fletcher & Massinger *False One* v. iii, Goad him on with thy sword. **1697** Dryden *Virg. Georg.* I. 70 Produce the Plough, and yoke the sturdy Steer, And goad him till he groans beneath his Toil. **1704** Addison *Italy* (1733) 44 His angry Keeper goads him to the Fight. **1841** James *Brigand* xxii, No hand tames me and goads me on. **1855** Kingsley *Heroes* ii. IV. (1856) 110 Jason bound them to the plough, and goaded them onward with his lance. **1875** Jowett *Plato* (ed. 2) III. 457 They are driven to it by the stings of the drones goading them. **1879** Stevenson *Trav. Cevennes* (1892) 42, I was goading Modestine down the steep descent.

2. *fig.* To assail or prick as with a goad; to irritate; to instigate or impel by some form of mental pain or annoyance; to drive by continued irritation *into* or *to* some desperate action or uncontrolled state of mind. Also with advs. *on*, *onward*, *along*, etc.

1579 Tomson *Calvin's Serm. Tim.* 530/1 It is verie hard for vs not to be greeued, when we heare ourselues so euil spoken off, and men goade vs. **1603** Shaks. *Meas. for M.* II. ii. 182 Most dangerous Is that temptation, that doth goad vs on To sinne, in louing vertue. **1607** —— *Cor.* II. iii. 271 This [mutiny] shall seeme.. their owne, Which we haue goaded on-ward. **1696** Tate & Brady *Ps.* xxxv. 6 Thy vengeful Ministers of Wrath Shall goad them as they run. **1789** T. Jefferson *Writ.* (1859) II. 555 He was continually goaded forward by the public clamors. **1790** Wolcot (P. Pindar) *Compl. Ep. J. Bruce* Wks. 1812 II. 356 Tis famine goads him, like an Ox, along. **1790** Burke *Fr. Rev.* Wks. V. 264 Goaded on with the ambition of intellectual sovereignty. **1801** Southey *Thalaba* II. xxix, That rankling hope within him, that by day Goaded his steps, still stinging him in sleep. **1817** Coleridge *Lay Serm.* 401 They might goad ignorance into riot, and fanaticism into rebellion. **1849** Macaulay *Hist. Eng.* v. I. 575 Many of them.. had been goaded by petty persecution into a temper fit for desperate enterprise. **1858** Froude *Hist. Eng.* IV. xviii. 80 The deputy, goaded by opposition and unreason, had dashed into toleration of the rebels. **1865** Livingstone *Zambesi* xviii. 363 The Ajawa was evidently goaded on by Portuguese agents. **1874** Green *Short Hist.* iv. §5. 201 Taunts and defiances goaded the proud Baronage to fury.

Hence **'goaded** *ppl. a.*, **'goading** *vbl. sb.* and *ppl. a.*

1718 Rowe tr. *Lucan* IV. 1203 By swords and goading Darts compell'd, Dronish he drags his Load across the Field. **1815** W. H. Ireland *Scribbleomania* 259 Morality's rules planted deep in the breast, Where goading of turpitude ne'er was impress'd. **1841** Dickens *Barn. Rudge* xix, 'I don't want to say more', rejoined the goaded locksmith. **1851** Gallenga *Italy* 91 What prudent considerations could prevail on the trampled, goaded Milanese, to endure any longer? **1867** Parkman *Jesuits N. Amer.* xxxi. (1875) 413 Still the goadings of famine were relentless and irresistible.

†**'goadloup.** *Sc. Obs.* Var. GANTLOPE.

1721 R. Wodrow *Hist. Ch. Scot.* I. App. 102 They threatned.. that whosoever gave me a Drink of Water should get the Goadloup.

'goadster. *rare*⁻¹. [f. GOAD *v.* + -STER.] A driver who uses a goad.

1837 Carlyle *Fr. Rev.* II. III. vii, Cars drawn by eight white horses, goadsters in classical costume.

goaf[1] (gəʊf). *E. Angl. dial.* Forms: 5 golf(e, 6 goulfe, goef, 6, 8 goff, 6, 9 gofe, 7–9 goffe (7–8 geoff(e), 8 gulph, 9 goof, goaf. Also *pl.* 9 goaves. [a. ON. *gólf* floor, apartment; Sw. *golf*, Da. *gulv* floor, bay (of a house or barn). Cf. GOAVE *v.*

Where houses or barns were constructed with a wooden framework, the upright posts were placed at regular intervals along each side, the space between two posts forming a 'bay' (see BAY *sb.*[3] 2), and the size of the building was frequently given by stating the number of bays it contained. Each of these divisions is in the Scandinavian languages called a 'floor' (see above, and cf. Icel. *stafgólf* f. *stafr* a post). See *goaf-stead* below.]

The quantity of grain stacked in one bay of a barn.

14.. *Addit. MS.* 12195 in *Promp. Parv.* 202 *note*, *Ingelimum*, golfe. *c* **1440** *Promp. Parv.* 428/1 Reek or golf (*Pynson* golfe or stak), *arconius*. **1530** Palsgr. 226/1 Goulfe of corne, so moche as may lye bytwene two postes, otherwyse a baye. **1573** Tusser *Husb.* lvi. (1878) 125 Let shock take sweate, least gofe take heate. **1669** Worlidge *Syst. Agric.* (1681) 326 A Geoff or Goffe, a Mow or Reek. **1787** W. Marshall *E. Norfolk* II. 380 (E.D.S.) *Gulph*, a mow, or bay-full, in a barn. **1800** Larwood *Norfolk Dial.* (E.D.S. No. 76) 122 The stra that the throsher had hull'd down from the gofe in the barn. **1823** Moor *Suffolk Words*, *Goof* or *Goaf*, the mass of corn in the straw in a barn. 'Riding the goof', is the work of a boy on horse-back, to compress the corn as thrown on the goof. *a* **1825** Forby *Voc. E. Anglia*, *Goaf*, a rick of corn in the straw laid up in a barn; if in the open air it is a *stack*. Pl. goaves.

b. *attrib.* and *Comb.*, as **goaf-flap** (see quots.); **goaf-horse** (see quot. and cf. quot. 1823 above); **goaf-ladder**, a ladder for use in a barn; **goaf-stead** (see quots.); also **goaf-burned** *ppl. a.* (see quot.; cf. Da. *gulv-brændt*).

1573 Tusser *Husb.* xvii. (1878) 35 Gofe ladder, short pitchforke and long, flaile, strawforke and rake. **1787** W. Marshall *E. Norfolk* II. 380 (E.D.S.) *Gulph-stead*, *Goafstead*, *Gostead*, a bay or division of a barn. *a* **1825** Forby *Voc. E. Anglia*, *Goaf-flap*, a wooden beater to knock the ends of the sheaves, and make the goaf or stack more compact and flat. *Ibid.*, *Goaf-stead*, every division of a barn in which a goaf is placed. A large barn has four or more. **1840** Spurdens *Suppl. to Forby*, *Goaf-horse*, the horse ridden upon the corn deposited in a barn, in order to compress it. **1863** Morton *Cycl. Agric.* II. Gloss. (E.D.S.), *Goaf-burned*, corn heated in a barn.

goaf[2] (gəʊf). *Coal-mining.* Also **goave.** [Of obscure origin; the difference in locality and remoteness in sense are unfavourable to identification with prec. Cf. the synonymous GOB *sb.*[4]] (See quots.)

1839 Ure *Dict. Arts* 978 Before proceeding to take away another set of pillars, it is necessary to allow the last-made goaff to fall. **1851** Greenwell *Coal-trade Terms Northumb. & Durh.* 29 *Goaf*, a space from which the coal pillars have been extracted. **1854** F. C. Bakewell *Geol.* 39 These reservoirs of gas, called by the miners 'goafs'. **1871** Hartwig *Subterr. W.* xxiii. 279 The fire-damp is very liable to accumulate in old workings, or goaves. **1881** H. C. Merivale in *19th Cent.* No. 48. 238 The empty area left by the extraction of the coal, which, however, is soon filled up by falls of stone from the strata overlying the bed, is called the 'goaf'. **1893** *Northumbld. Gloss.*, *Goave*, space cleared of coal. Usually printed, but inaccurately, as *goaf*.

goafing ('gəʊfɪŋ). *Coal-mining.* [f. prec. + -ING[1].] **a.** = prec. **b.** (See quot. 1875.)

1875 *Ure's Dict. Arts* II. 686 *Gobbin* or *Goaffin*, the refuse left behind in working coal, and thrown into the goaf. **1881** *Standard* 15 Sept. 5/7 The fire was attributed to the spontaneous combustion of the coal dust or the small coal in the goafings.

go-ahead ('gəʊə,hɛd), *a. colloq.* (orig. *U.S.*) [f. the phr. *go ahead*: see GO *v.* and AHEAD 5.] Forward and energetic in undertaking; 'pushing', enterprising.

1840 Gen. P. Thompson *Exerc.* v. (1842) 147 The active, the wide-awake, or as the Americans would call it the 'go ahead' portion of the Established Sect. **1846** H. Beckely *Hist. Vermont* 132 They were men.. of a bold, go-ahead character. **1858** *Philadelphia Press* 24 July (Bartlett), America is a dashing, go-ahead, and highly progressive country. **1859** J. S. Mill *Dissert. & Discuss.*, *Democr. Amer.* II. 64 Do we find in Canada that go-ahead spirit—that restless, impatient eagerness for improvement in circumstances? **1864** C. Kingsley *Let.* in *Life* (1879) II. 167 What a go-a-head place France is! **1886** *All Year Round* 14 Aug. 34 Hence our go-ahead farmers are taking to machines.

b. Occas. used for: Proceeding straight forward without pause, forthright.

1879 Dana *Man. Geol.* (ed. 3) 116 An animal, as its ordinary movements manifest, is preëminently a go-ahead thing. **1884** G. Allen *Philistia* III. 196 Straight off without a break, in her go-ahead, breathless, voluble fashion.

Hence **go-a'headative**, **-itive** *a.*, **go-a'headativeness** (*U.S.*); **go-a'headedness**; **go-a'headishness**; **go-a'headism**; **go-a'headity**; **'go-aheadness**, etc.

1846 C. Kingsley in *Life* (1877) I. 143 It is the new commercial aristocracy, it is the scientific go-a-head-ism of the day, which must save us. **1847** G. W. Kendall *Texan Santa Fé Exped.* 153 The indefatigable go-a-headity which characterizes the Anglo-Saxon race. **1855** *N.Y. Times* 17 May (Bartlett), The natural activity and go-aheadativeness of our American business men. **1864** *Reader* 17 Sept. 343 In North American.. you see in railway-literature.. an almost exact counterpart of our English system, carried out.. with somewhat more go-aheadness. **1869** H. Deedes *Ten Months Amer.* 60 The go-aheaditiveness of the inhabitants [of Chicago] is only equalled by the go-aheaditiveness of the buildings. **1881** *Daily News* 28 Dec. 3/1 The go-aheadedness of the United States. **1882** Miss Braddon *Mt. Royal* I. v. 136 The young ladies of the present day have a certain Yankee go-a-headishness which very much lightens the chaperon's responsibility. **1890** *Murray's Mag.* Apr. 459 Passing from Kimberley with its money-making.. and smart shops, and 'go-aheadness'.

go-ahead ('gəʊəhɛd), *sb.* [f. GO *v.* 72 and GO-AHEAD *a.*] **1.** The action or the spirit of going forward; progress; ambition, energy, or initiative. *U.S. colloq.*

1840 C. F. Hoffman *Greyslaer* I. iii. 32 Sarting! he does make a clean go-ahead of it. But when did he come up here to mix in our doings? **1844** G. W. Kendall *Narr. Santa Fé Exped.* II. xix. 362 There is a little 'go-ahead' in a spirited, showy, well-trained Mexican horse. *a* **1861** T. Winthrop *Canoe & Saddle* (1883) xii. 251 It racks my heart to know that I must still demand much go-ahead from you. **1885** W. D. Howells *Rise Silas Lapham* xi, Some of the fellows that had the most go-ahead were fellows that hadn't ever had much more to do than girls before the war broke out. **1942** Berrey & Van den Bark *Amer. Thes. Slang* §240/3 Initiative; enterprise; 'push',.. go-ahead.

†**2.** An advance agent of a touring theatrical company, circus, etc. *Obs.*

1861 *All Year Round* 16 Nov. 184/2 'The agent in advance', or *go-ahead*, as he is now called,.. accompanied by a bill-sticker, starts off in advance of the troupe.

3. A signal, order, or permission to proceed. Also *attrib. colloq.*

1941 *B.B.C. Gloss. Broadcasting Terms* 13 *Go-ahead signal*, spoken instruction from a control room to the personnel at a programme source, indicating that all is ready for a programme to begin. **1942** Berrey & Van den Bark *Amer. Thes. Slang* §226/2 *The go-ahead*, the command or permission to do. **1948** *Sierra Club Bull.* (San Francisco) May 2/2 It must receive Congressional approval.. for its go-ahead on construction. **1953** *Encounter* Oct. 14/1 The party had given the go-ahead signal after months of discreet silence. **1958** *Times* 6 June 12/3 Given the go-ahead, the system is likely to be in operation within two years. **1967** *Listener* 30 Mar. 429/1 B.E.A., which now has the backing of four major airlines for its project, is very confident that it will get the go-ahead.

goal (gəʊl), *sb.* Forms: 4 gol, 6 gowle, 6–7 go(a)le, 7– goal. [Of difficult etymology.

After the solitary (but app. unquestionable) occurrence in Shoreham's Poems *c* 1315) the word first appears in 1531, and soon afterwards is very common; prob. it had survived only as a technical term of some rustic sport, and so failed to be recorded in literature.

Shoreham's form *gol*, riming with *y-hol*, suggests (though it does not necessarily imply) descent from an OE. **gál*. (This would be quite certain if the word could be positively identified with the *gale* found in *Cursor M.* 8710 (Cott.): 'O þis quick þai bath wald be Moder.. And aither wald þai haf it hale, Bot þai mai neuer com to þat gale'. But it is not unlikely that in this passage *gale*, obviously chosen for the sake of rime, is merely a forced use of GALE *sb.*[2] in the sense of 'joy'.) Of the existence of an OE. sb. **gál*, with the sense 'obstacle, barrier', some indirect evidence is afforded by the apparent derivatives *gǽlan*, *ágǽlan*, to hinder, delay. The transition from the sense of 'barrier' to that of 'boundary' (sense 1) is easy, and the further sense-development is parallel to that of L. *mēta*, and of DOOL *sb.*[2]; in view of the history of the latter word, Halliwell's alleged '*Goale*, a barrow or tumulus', might be compared, if there were any ground for believing it to be genuine. But the absence of any record of OE. **gál* or of its equivalent in any Teut. lang. (ON. *geil*, narrow passage, being too remote in sense) renders this etymology very insecure.

The suggestion of Henshaw (in *Skinner's Etymologicon* 1671), accepted by all subsequent etymologists, that the word is an adoption of F. *gaule*, pole, stick, switch, has nothing to recommend it. There is no evidence that F. *gaule* ever meant 'goal', or that Eng. *goal* ever meant 'pole' or 'switch'. Besides, for the form in Shoreham, the Fr. derivation appears to be phonologically inadmissible.

A Welsh *gâl* is given by Davies *Antiq. Ling. Brit. Dict.* I. (1632) with Latin renderings (*stadium*, *meta*, *statio*) which would make it equivalent to Eng. *goal*. If this word be genuine (which seems to be doubtful) it must apparently be an early adoption from English; the suggestion in Fick *Idg. Wb.*[2] II., that it represents an OCeltic **gaslâ* stone, being phonologically untenable (Prof. Rhys). The current word in most parts of Wales for 'goal' with reference to games is *col*, mutated *gol* (gɒl), which prob. has obtained this meaning through its similarity of sound to the Eng. word. The Windhill dialect has a word pronounced (gɒl), explained as meaning 'goal', used in a certain game played with brass buttons (cf. GOG[4]); but its identity with this word is doubtful.]

†**1.** A boundary, limit. *Obs. rare*⁻¹.

c **1315** Shoreham 145 God nys nauȝt in þer worldle a-closed, Ac hy hys ine hym. Þaȝ hy nabbe ende ne forþe gol, Ȝet over al he hys y-hol.

2. a. The terminal point of a race: any object (as a pillar, mound, etc.) by which this is marked; a winning-post, or the like.

1531 Elyot *Gov.* III. xx. (1534) 224 a, As in rennynge, passynge the gole, is accounted but rasshenesse, so rennynge halfe waye is reproued for slownesse. **1538** —— *Dict.*, *Meta*, a but, or pricke to shote at, somtyme a marke or gowle in the felde, wherevnto men or horses do runne. **1561** T. Norton *Calvin's Inst.* III. 222 Let that be appointed the gole for vs to run and trauaill vnto. **1612** Dekker *If it be not good* Wks. 1873 III. 276 The winning of the gole crownes each mans race. *a* **1628** Preston *Breastpl. Love* (1631) 163 A childe may runne, and another man may walke.. the child should have it [the prize], though he that walkes come to the goale before him. **1728** Young *Love Fame* I. (1757) 80 Congreve, who, crown'd with laurels, fairly won, Sits smiling at the goal, while others run. **1781** Cowper *Charity* 566 So self starts nothing, but what tends apace, Home to the goal, where it began the race. **1875** Jowett *Plato* (ed. 3) III. 510 Runners, who run well from the starting-place to the goal.

b. *fig.* The object to which effort or ambition is directed; the destination of a (more or less laborious) journey. *spec.* in *Psychol.* An end or result towards which behaviour is consciously or unconsciously directed; freq. *attrib.* and *Comb.*

[**1548–1573**: see 3.] **1608** Shaks. *Per.* II. i. 171 Then Honour be but a Goale to my Will, This day Ile rise, or else adde ill to ill. **1732** Pope *Ess. Man* II. 237 Each individual seeks a sev'ral goal; But Heav'n's great view is One, and that the Whole. **1788** H. Walpole *Corr.* III. 87 Having.. strolled into a narrow path that led to no goal.. I see the idleness of my journey. **1839** G. Bird *Nat. Phil.* Introd. 27 In many cases we exhaust every variety of error before we attain the desired goal [truth]. **1856** Kane *Arct. Expl.* II. xxiv. 239, I.. beheld the open water, so long the goal of our struggles. **1888** Bryce *Amer. Commw.* II. lxx. 550 The presidency is the great prize of politics, the goal of every statesman's ambition. **1917** Glueck & Lind tr. *Adler's Neurotic Constitution* (1921) p. viii, The entire picture of the neurosis as well as all its symptoms are influenced by.. an imaginary fictitious goal... The potency of this 'goal idea' is revealed to us by the trend and evaluation of the pathological phenomena. **1934** *Mind* XLIII. 111 Not all action is due to goal-seeking propensities. **1940** R. S. Woodworth *Psychol.* (ed. 12) ii. 42 The reader becomes set or adjusted for the situation portrayed in the story and for the 'goal', the outcome of the story. **1945** E. S. Russell *Directiveness of Organic Activities* i. 8, I shall use, with due caution, and without any implication of conscious purpose on the part of the organism or other organic agent, the concepts of goal or completion and of biological end. *Ibid.* iv. 81 It is not implied by the use of the word 'goal' that the agents concerned are conscious of it before it is reached; their action is directive, but not purposive. *Ibid.* v. 110 Goal-directed activity is limited by conditions, but is not determined by them. **1949** Koestler *Insight & Outlook* xv. 214 All cultural achievements appear as ersatz formations for goal-inhibited sexuality. **1951** R. Firth *Elem. Social Organiz.* vii. 220 This action is goal-oriented. **1952** T. Parsons *Social System* 8 The goal-directedness of action. **1953** *Brit. Jrnl. Psychol.* Aug. 203 When this state is absent or disturbed the system becomes active and..continues to be active until that state is established or restored. We may say of such a system that its activity is goal directed. **1956** J. Klein *Study of Groups* 141 'Instrumental', 'conative', 'goal-oriented' behaviour is concerned with decision-making. **1964** Gould & Kolb *Dict. Soc. Sci.* 290/1 *Goal* in psychology and in some social psychology has come increasingly to denote an end result of an act or series of acts whether or not it can be said to be intended by the organism acting. **1965** P. Caws *Philos. Sci.* xl. 310 The deliberate and conscious production of novelty, that is,..what we ordinarily call purposive or goal-seeking behaviour. **1965** *Philos.* XL. 348 Central-state behaviourism..hopes to account for intentionality in terms of neuro-physiology and goal-directed systems. **1968** *Canad. Jrnl. Linguistics* XIII. 126 He found..that a tendency towards hypercorrect forms in the lower middle class seems rooted in a profound linguistic insecurity—evidence that linguistic behaviour is highly normative or goal-directed.

†**c.** Used for 'contest, race'. *Obs.*$^{-1}$

[*a* **1555**: cf. *gole-end* in 6.] **1617** F. Moryson *Itin.* ii. 145, I am glad, even in this great goale of honour, to runne equally with him.

3. a. In football, hockey, lacrosse, and similar games, the posts between which the ball is driven to win a point in the game. Also in phrases (often *fig.*) *to* †*carry, get, take, win a goal*: to drive the ball through the goal. Hence the sb. has acquired the sense: The winning of a goal, the point in the game scored for this; so *to make, score a goal*. *to drop a goal*: see drop *v.* 24. † *to play a goal*: to play at a game till a goal is won by one side.

The early quots. (1548, 1553, 1573) may belong to 2b. **1548** Hall *Chron., Rich. III* (1809) 388 There was no person..could nor should haue wone the ring or got the gole before me. **1553** Wilson *Rhet.* 11 David, beyng wonderfully over-matched, made his partie good, and gotte the gole of a monster. **1573** Tusser *Husb.* cxiv. (1878) 216 Thy vsage thus in time shall win the gole, Though doughtful haps, dame fortune sendes betweene. **1577** Stanyhurst *Descr. Irel.* ii. 5 a/2 in *Holinshed*, I purpose..before he beare the ball to the goale, to trippe him, if I may. **1594** *2nd Pt. Contention* (1843) 127 The goale is lost thou house of Lancaster. **1596** Drayton *Leg.* ii. 108 The most Judiciall Eyes Did give the Goale impartially to me. *c* **1600** Day *Begg. Bednall Gr.* v. (1881) 110 I'll play a gole at Camp-ball. **1602** Carew *Surv. Cornw.* 73 b, For hurling to goales, there are [etc.]... They pitch two bushes in the ground..which they terme their Goales, where some indifferent person throweth vp a ball, the which whosoeuer can catch and cary through his aduersaries goale, hath wonne the game. **1612** Drayton *Poly-olb.* i. 7 Or when the Ball to throw And driue it to the Gole. **1658** Cromwell *Sp.* 25 Jan., Some of these..care not who carry the goal, [so they but get their ends]. **1672** R. Wild *Declar. Lib. Consc.* 12 Let our Ministers stand by and keep our Gole, and strike never a stroke..and let any point ..be the Foot-ball. **1808** Pike *Sources Mississ.* (1810) 100 One catches the ball in his racket, and..endeavors to carry it to the goal [in Lacrosse]. **1857** Hughes *Tom Brown* i. v, But how do you keep the ball between the goals? **1886** *Laws Lacrosse* ix. §2 A match shall be decided by a majority of goals taken within a specified time. **1887** Shearman *Athletics & Football* (Badm.) 304 A goal counting as three, and a try as one point. *Ibid.* 342 In front of the opponents' goal. *Ibid.*, A player..must not only know how to score a goal with a swift low shot from his toes, but [etc.]. **1895** Wolseley *Decl. & Fall Napoleon* ii. 74 The ball was at his [Napoleon's] foot; but he turned back instead of making a goal.

b. Used (also *pl.*) as the name of certain games.

1884 *Harper's Mag.* Jan. 304/1 A sort of shinney..or what we used to call, when we were boys, 'gool'. I suppose we meant goal, or golf. **1884** *Eng. Illustr. Mag.* Nov. 79/2 Perhaps a primitive sort of football, 'goals' as it seems to have been called at Eton in the last century, was the game.

†**4.** In archery, the mark aimed at. *Obs. rare*$^{-1}$.

1678 *Noble Birth*, etc. *Robin Hood* C j, And now the Kings Archers had shot three Goles, and were three for none.

5. a. *Roman Antiq.* Used as transl. of L. *mēta*, the conical column marking each of the two turning points in a chariot race.

1667 Milton *P.L.* ii. 531 Part curb thir fierie Steeds, or shun the Goal With rapid wheels. **1756** Nugent *Gr. Tour* III. 277 The Circi or Circus's..where the Romans used to run races in chariots, or on horseback, round a goal which stood in the middle. **1781** Gibbon *Decl. & F.* II. 16 The space between the two *metæ* or goals was filled with statues and obelisks. **1857** Willmott *Pleas. Lit.* xi. 42 Their fiercest struggles only carry the chariot nearer to the goal. *fig.* **1634** Milton *Comus* 100 The..sun..Pacing toward the other goal Of his chamber in the east. **1817** Coleridge *Sibyll. Leaves* (1862) 234 The Angel of the Earth..while he guides His chariot-planet round the goal of day.

¶**b.** Used for: The starting-point of a race (= L. *carcer*). Also *fig. rare*.

1697 Dryden *Virg. Georg.* iii. 165 Hast thou beheld, when from the Goal they start, The Youthful Charioteers.. Rush to the Race? **1852** Conybeare & H. *St. Paul* (1862) I. viii. 257 From this goal he started to overthrow the august dynasties of the East.

6. *attrib.* and *Comb.*, as ***goal-bar, -dropper,*** †***-end, -getter, -getting, -post, -scorer, -shooter; goal-ward*** adj.; **goal average**, the sum of the goals scored by a team divided by the goals scored against it, used to rank teams in a football league, etc., which are equal on points; **goal-crease** (see quot.); **goal difference**, the difference between the number of goals scored by a team in a competition and the number of goals scored against it, used as an alternative to *goal average* in calculating league positions, etc.; **goal-keeper**, a player whose special duty is to protect the goal; so ***goal-keeping*** vbl. sb.; **goal-kick**, (*a*) in association football (see quot. 1960[1]); (*b*) in rugby football, an attempt to kick a goal; (*c*) = *goal-kicker*; **goal-kicker**, one who scores a goal or makes a goal-kick; so ***goal-kicking***; **goal-line**, the line which bounds each end of the field of play, and in the centre of which the goal is placed; **goal-mouth**, the space between the goal-posts and under the cross-bar in association football, hockey, etc.; also, the area near the goal; **goal-net**, the net behind the goal-mouth; **goal-tender** *N. Amer.*, a goal-keeper in ice-hockey; so ***goal-tending*** vbl. sb.

1892 *Football News* 20 Feb. 1/7 The Ilkeston players say their *goal average is 120 against 20. **1920** *Ibid.* 6 Nov. 1/3 The barest decimal in goal average. **1951** *Sport* 27 Apr.–3 May 3/2 A goal-average miracle..will have to take place if Chesterfield are to avoid the 'drop' at the expense of Luton. **1976** *Eastern Even. News* (Norwich) 22 Dec. 14/5 League leaders Ipswich, just above Liverpool on goal-average, are working desperately to have £200,000 striker Paul Mariner fit. **1886** *Football: Laws*, etc. 7 The ball hitting the..*goal-bar, and rebounding into play, is considered in play. **1886** *Laws Lacrosse* xiii, *Goal Crease shall be a ground-space six feet square in front of the goal-posts. **1970** F. C. Avis *Soccer Dict.* (ed. 3) 44 **Goal difference*, that method of deciding league positions, where clubs have equal points, by deducting goals scored against the team from the total they have scored. **1976** *Scotsman* 27 Dec. 12/3 Celtic stay ahead of the pack by virtue of goal difference and share the leading total of 20 points from 14 games with Aberdeen. **1892** *Pall Mall G.* 15 Feb. 1/3 [The club] is fortunate in possessing a fine *goal-dropper. *a* **1555** Philpot in Coverdale *Lett. Mart.* (1564) 242 There is none crowned but suche as holde out to the *gole end. **1887** M. Shearman *Athletics & Football* ii. iv. 345 The doctor had the reputation of being the best centre and *goal-getter in Scotland. **1910** *Westm. Gaz.* 21 Jan. 12/1 The goal-getters for the winners were [etc.]. **1932** Auden *Orators* iii. 102 Goal-getter, holer-in-one. **1904** *Daily Chron.* 29 July 4/5 His *goal-getting stroke. **1904** *Ibid.* 21 Nov. 8/3 Goal-getting did not..enter largely into the argument. **1658** Osborn *Adv. Son* (1673) 92 Mr. John Hambden..made himself still the *Goal-keeper of his Party. **1877** *Football Annual* 15 The goal-keeper may be changed during the game, but [etc.]. **1886** *Laws Lacrosse* ix. §7 The goal-keeper..may put away with his hand or foot, or block the ball in any manner with his crosse or body. **1893** L. H. Gay in *Association Football Handbk.* 19 The most important rule in *goalkeeping is never to use your feet when you have time to use your hands. **1891** *Football: its Laws, Rules, & Definition of Terms* 15 Two linesmen shall.. decide when the ball is out of play, and which side is entitled to the corner flag-kick, *goal-kick, or throw in. **1897** *Encycl. Sport* i. 429/1 *Goal-kick.* (R.) The attempt to kick a goal from a try. (A.) The kick-out when the ball has gone behind. It must be made from a spot within 6 yards of the nearest goal-post. **1960** J. R. Witty in Fabian & Green *Assoc. Football* I. ii. iii. 169 The ball may have gone over the goal-line, but not into goal. If it were last played by an attacking player, the re-start is a *goal kick*. Here the ball is placed somewhere within the goal area (the 6 yards area) on that side where it passed out of play, and it must be kicked directly, by a defender, somewhere into the field of play beyond the penalty area (18 yards) marking, and it is not in play until then. **1960** T. McLean *Kings of Rugby* xi. 160 Henderson..was a goalkick of excellence. **1965** D. Law *Tackle Soccer this Way* v. 44 In most league games today.. modern goalkeepers prefer the short goal-kick just out of the box to a defender,..to the long goal-kick downfield. **1909** *Bendigonian* 24 Aug. 21/2 The *goal-kickers were: [etc.]. **1961** *Times* 5 Jan. 3/5 Du Preez probably owes his selection to his recent success as a goal-kicker. **1963** *Times* 29 May 3/7 Hosen..had a singularly unhappy day in both *goalkicking, in which he failed with half a dozen attempts, and also in fielding. **1867** *Rugby School Football Laws* 9 He makes a mark with his heel outside the *goal-line. **1882** in Charles-Edwards & Richardson *They saw It Happen* (1958) 300 The ball..was headed back from the *goal mouth by Suter. **1908** *Westm. Gaz.* 7 Oct. 4/2 The yawning goal-mouth was not fed with that elusive leather sphere. **1970** *Times* 8 June 5/3 Charlton looking younger than ever swept into the Brazilian goalmouth. **1897** *Windsor Mag.* Dec. 22/1 *Goal-nets.. would have had to be pretty strong. **1857** Hughes *Tom Brown* i. v, The sixth-form boy who has the charge of goal, has spread his force (the goal-keepers) so as to occupy the whole space behind the *goal-posts. **1886** *Laws Lacrosse* ix. §4 In the event of a goal-post being knocked down during a match. **1909** *Daily Chron.* 20 Mar. 8/5 He heads the list of West Ham *goal scorers. **1929** *Evening News* 18 Nov. 13/4 The League's leading goalscorer. **1961** *Times* 20 Jan. 17/4 The embracing and mobbing of the goal-scorer is entirely unnecessary. **1959** J. Fingleton *Four Chukkas to Australia* 155 The soccer field where the players fall upon the neck of the *goal-shooter. **1909** Webster *Goal tender. **1926** T. K. Fisher *Ice Hockey* ii. 12 A good goal-tender should be an alert and agile athlete. **1967** *Boston Sunday Herald* 26 Mar. 18/4 Charlie Driscoll, whose son Charlie Jr., was a great hockey goal-tender at Boys' High. **1968** *Globe & Mail* (Toronto) 5 Feb. 17/2 Ed Giacomin's shutout *goaltending ..ended Montreal's National Hockey League winning streak. **1852** *Meanderings of Mem.* I. 131 With a giddy foot and *goal-ward rush.

goal (gəʊl), *v. Rugby Football.* [f. the sb.] *trans.* To convert (a try) into a goal.

1922 *Weekly Dispatch* 29 Oct. 10 Bennett..intercepted a pass and scored a try, which Tebbutt goaled. **1954** J. B. G. Thomas *On Tour* 138 Saxton made a magnificent blind-side burst which put Sherratt over for a second try, which Cook goaled.

goal(e, -er, obs. ff. *gaol, -er*: see jail, jailer.

goalie ('gəʊlı). Also **-ee**. *colloq.* [f. goal *sb.* + -ie.] A goal-keeper.

1921 *Oxf. Mag.* 28 Jan. 158/2 C. V. Hill..journeyed to Henley..much to the discomfiture of the opposing goalee. **1926** *Spectator* 24 Apr. 753/1 One can imagine an indignant Cockney ejaculating as he regarded the rotundity of the Red goalee. **1957** *Encycl. Brit.* XII. 42A/1 The positions on a six-man [ice] hockey team are goal tender (more commonly called goalies in the United States and goaler in Canada), [etc.]. **1966** *Reader's Digest* Mar. 64/2 The players [at ice hockey] (three forwards, two defencemen, one goalie)..are chosen for their ability to skate swiftly, [etc.]. **1967** J. Potter *Foul Play* vii. 84 Most English goalies were prize examples of British phlegm, but Basil outdid the continental keepers in panache.

goalless ('gəʊllıs), *a.* [See -less.]

1. Purposeless; having no destination.

a **1886** E. Dickinson *Compl. Poems* (1960) 230 A goalless Road. **1906** *Daily Chron.* 23 Oct. 4/4 He has never taken a solitary, goalless walk. **1923** W. de la Mare *Riddle* 277 One late afternoon, in my goal-less wandering.

2. *Association Football.* Without a goal scored by either side.

1904 *Daily Chron.* 18 Nov. 1/7 At Southall Oxford City played a goalless draw with the local team. **1928** *Daily Tel.* 28 Aug. 9/5 The game..ended in a goalless draw. **1971** *New Society* 1 July 24/3 Pools companies had to re-appraise their points system because of the number of goal-less draws.

goam, obs. form of gaum *v.*[1]

goan, dial. var. of gawn, gallon.

1674 Ray *N.C. Words* 20 A Gawn or Goan, Chesh.: a Gallon, by contraction of the word. **1726** in *Dict. Rust.* (ed. 3) *s.v.* **1877** in Egerton Leigh *Gloss. Chesh.*

Goan ('gəʊən), *a.* and *sb.* [See -an.] = next.

1927 J. Furtado (*title*) A Goan Fiddler. **1927** E. Gosse *Ibid.* Pref. p. vi, He was..not happy among the Goans. **1961** *Daily Tel.* 8 Dec. 1 There is no solution to the Goan problem except the Portuguese walking out. **1966** C. Sweeney *Scurrying Bush* viii. 119 An Indian or Goan at the other end began asking me seemingly irrelevant questions. **1971** *Illustr. Weekly India* 25 Apr. 9/1 Goans and Parsis were the pioneers but now the [modelling] profession has full representation.

Goanese (gəʊə'ni:z), *a.* and *sb.* [f. Goa[1] + -ese, after *Japanese*, etc.] **A.** *adj.* Of or belonging to Goa. **B.** *sb.* A native of Goa; the Goanese people.

1851 R. F. Burton *Goa* v. 91 The Goanese smoke all day, ladies as well as gentlemen. *Ibid.* 93 A Goanese noble. **1909** *Chambers's Jrnl.* Aug. 523/1 A batch of Goanese tailors' shops. **1920** *Ibid.* May 299/2, I was obliged to read the burial service in Latin out of a prayer-book lent me by a Goanese cook. **1961** *Daily Tel.* 20 Dec. 8 Did the Goanese really yearn for 'liberation'? **1970** *Times* 10 Feb. 17/2 (Advt.), A rare late 17th century Goanese cabinet.

goanna (gəʊ'ænə). *Austral.* Also formerly **gohanna**. [Corruption of iguana; cf. guana.] Any of various large monitor lizards of the genus *Varanus*.

1891 'Rolf Boldrewood' *Sydney-side Saxon* vi. 99 A goanna startled him [a horse]. **1898** Morris *Austral Eng.* s.v. *Goanna*, In New Zealand, the word Guano is applied to the lizard-like reptile *Sphenodon punctatum*... In Tasmania, the name is given to *Tiliqua scincoides*, White, and throughout Australia any lizard of a large size is popularly called a Guana, or in the bush, more commonly, a Goanna. **1900** H. Lawson *Over Sliprails* 108 The four little Australians..ate underdone kangaroo..with an occasional treat of oak grubs and gohanna. **1903** *Blackw. Mag.* Apr. 468/2 My tongue was like a gohanna's back. **1923** *Chambers's Jrnl.* Aug. 527/1 Snakes, goannas (guanas), scorpions, and centipedes are numerous. **1946** I. L. Idriess *In Crocodile Land* ix. 60 The goanna burrows into the nest. **1965** A. Keast *Window to Bushland* 102 Goannas are the giants of the lizard tribe.

goapen, var. gowpen.

goar, -y, goard, obs. ff. gore, gory, gourd *sb.*[1]

goat (gəʊt). Pl. goats. Forms: *α.* 1–3 **gát**, 4–5 **gayte**, (5 **gatt**), 5–6 **gaytt**, 6 **gate**, 6– *north.* **gait**; *pl.* 3 **gaten**, 4 **gaytes**, 6 **gates**, *Sc.* **gaitis**. *β. pl.* 1– 3 **gǽt**, 1–4 **gét**, 3 **geat**, 4 **geete**, **geyte**, *north.* **gaite**, **gayte**, 4–5 **geet**, **gete**, 5 **gheet**, *north.* **gate**, 6 (**gheate**), *north.* **gait**. *γ.* 4 **geet**, **geit**, **geyt**, (**gehet**, 5 **get(t**, 6 **geat**); *pl.* 4 **geetis**. *δ.* 3–5 **got**, 4 **goote**, **goet**, 4–5 **goot**, (5 **gothe**), 4–6 **gote**, 6–7 **goate**, **gott(e**, 6– **goat**; *pl.* 3 **gotes**, 4 **gootes**, 6–7 **goates**, 7– **goats**. [Com. Teut.: OE. *gát* fem. = MDu. *geit, geet(e*, Du. *geit* (obs. *geite, geyte*), OHG. *geiz, keiz* (MHG. *geiz*, mod.G. *geisz*, ON. *geit* (Sw. *get*, Da. *ged*), Goth. *gait-s*:—OTeut. **gait-* cogn. w. L. *hædus* kid:—OAr. **ghaid-*.

In OE. the vowel of the nom. sing. remained in the gen. *gáte*, gen. pl. *gáta*, dat. pl. *gátum*, but was mutated in the dat. sing. and nom. pl. *gǽt*. In ME. the northern dialects show the normal *gāt*, *gait*, the southern *goot*, *goat*. The pl. *gǽt* is represented in southern and midland dialects by *gēt*, *geet*, *geat*; the northern dialects show an unmutated form *gait* (? influenced by ON. *geitr*). A sing. *geet* in 14th c. is prob. the result of assimilation to the plural.]

OE. *gát* being fem. denoted only the female goat; the male was called *bucca* BUCK *sb.*[1], also *gátbucca* GOAT-BUCK. The extended sense seems to occur in early ME., and is frequent in the 14th c. The distinctive terms *he-goat* and *she-goat* appear about the end of that century, and are now the recognized terms for the two sexes (colloquially also *billy-goat* and *nanny-goat*). The young animal is called a KID.

1. a. A ruminant quadruped of the genus *Capra*.

The goat is indigenous to the Eastern Hemisphere, but by domestication naturalized in all parts of the world. It is especially noted for its hardy, lively and wanton nature, and its strong odour. Most of the species have hollow horns, curving backwards, and the male is usually bearded.

Occas. used with allusion to the mention of 'sheep' and 'goats' in *Matt.* xxv. 32, 33, as symbolical respectively of the righteous and the wicked at the Day of Judgement.

α. *a* **700** *Epinal Gloss.* 1028 *Titule* [? read *caulæ*] gata loc. *a* **1000** *Riddles* xxv. 2 (Gr.) Ic..blæte swa gat. *c* **1000** *Sax. Leechd.* I. 352 Ȝenim þæt wæter þe innan gæt byþ. *c* **1200** ORMIN 1200 For gat iss..Gal deor & stinnkeþþ fule. *c* **1205** LAY 21310 Þeh..þer weoren in ane loken fif hundred gaten. *Ibid.* 21315 Ich am wulf & he is gat. *a* **1225** *Ancr. R.* 100 Wend ut & go efter gate herden. [*Ibid.*, Foluwe heorden of geat.] *a* **1340** HAMPOLE *Psalter* xlix. 14 [l. 13] Whether i sall ete fleysse of bulles, or i sall drynke blode of gaytes. *c* **1400** MAUNDEV. (Roxb.) vii. 24 It had..fra þeine vpward þe schappe of a gayte. *a* **1550** *Christis Kirke Gr.* ii, Thay squelit lyke ony gaitis. **1579** SPENSER *Sheph. Cal.* May 177 The Gate her dame..Yode forth abroad [*gloss.* the Gote: Northernely spoken, to turne O into A]. **1609** SKENE *Reg. Maj.* 155 Swyne, hens, geese, gaites. **1737** RAMSAY *Scot. Prov.* (1797) 94 Ye come to the gait's house to thigg woo. **1893** *Northumbld. Gloss.*, *Gait*, a goat.

β. *a* **900** CYNEWULF *Christ* 1230 in *Exeter Bk.*, Hy..reotað and beofiað fore frean forhte swa fule swa gæt. *c* **1000** *Sax. Leechd.* III. 214 Ȝif þu ʒesihst maneʒa get, ydel ʒetacnað. *c* **1200** ORMIN 1206 Forrþi sinndenn alle þa..Effnedd wiþþ gæt & nemmnedd gæt. *c* **1205** LAY. 25682 He makeþ him to mete..ruðeren hors & þa scep, gæt [*c* **1275** geat] and þa swin eke. *a* **1225** *Ancr. R.* 100 Hwat beoð heorden of geat? **1340** HAMPOLE *Pr. Consc.* 6134 Hys angels..Sal first departe þe gude fra þe ille, Als þe hird þe shepe dus fra þe gayte. *c* **1350** *Eng. Gilds* (1870) 354 Alle marchauntes of Get, Shep, oþer swyn. **1382** WYCLIF *Gen.* xxxii. 14 She geyte two hundrid, hee geyte twenty [**1388** geet..buckis of geet]. **1387** TREVISA *Higden* (Rolls) I. 311 In þat londe beeþ many scheep and geet and fewe roos and hertes. *c* **1440** *Gesta Rom.* liv. 373 (Add. MS.) Lyouns be pride, Foxes be fraude..Gete be stynke of lechery. *c* **1480** HENRYSON *Mor. Fab.* 27 Under ane tree hee saw an trip of Gate. **1481** CAXTON *Reynard* (Arb.) 34 After that I wente to the gheet in to the wode, there herde I the kyddes blete. **1513** DOUGLAS *Æneis* III. iv. 24 Flockis and hirdis of oxin..And trippis eik of gait. **1596** DALRYMPLE tr. *Leslie's Hist. Scot.* I. 7 Verie conuenient to feid horse or nout, or flockis of scheip or gait.

¶ In the following quots. the plural forms *geat(s* and *goats* are distinguished as fem. and masc. respectively.

1567 THOMAS *Ital. Dict.*, *Zebe*, gheate, the femalles of the ghoates. **1576** TURBERV. *Venerie* 147 The female (which are called Geats and the buckes Goates).

γ. **1382** WYCLIF *Gen.* xv. 9 Take..to thee a kow of thre ȝeer, and a she gehet [**1388** a geet] of thre ȝeer. —— *Lev.* iv. 24 An hee geit of the geetis. **14..** *Songs & Carols 15th C.* (Percy Soc.) 65 An adamant stone it is not frange-byll Wyth no thyng but with mylke of a gett.

δ. *a* **1225** *Ancr. R.* 100 As of a ticchen..kumeð a stinkinde got oðer a bucke [etc.]. *c* **1275** LAY. 21310 Þeh þar were on flockes two hundred gotes. **1382** WYCLIF *Lev.* xvi. 5 He shal take..two gootes. *Ibid.* 8 The goot that shal be sent out. *c* **1475** *Pict. Voc.* in Wr.-Wülcker 758/27 *Hec capra*, a gothe. **1484** CAXTON *Fables of Æsop* II. vi, Of a wulf whiche sawe a lambe among a grete herd of gootes. **1535** COVERDALE *Lev.* xvii. 2 What so euer he be..y^{t} kylleth an oxe, or lambe, or goate in the hoost [etc.]. **1584** R. SCOT *Discov. Witchcr.* v. i. 89 The diuell..dooth most properlie and commonlie transforme himselfe into a gote. **1611** SHAKS. *Cymb.* IV. iv. 37, I scarse euer look'd on blood, But that of Coward Hares, hot Goats, and Venison. **1628** SIR W. MURE *Spirituall Hymne* 326 The damned goates hee doth despise; Poynts out his lambes, whose sinfull dyes hee purgde with bloody streame. **1725** POPE *Odyss.* XIV. 59 He..A shaggy goat's soft hyde beneath him spread. **1817** COLERIDGE *Sibyll. Leaves* (1862) 184 Ye wild goats sporting round the eagle's nest! **1833** TENNYSON *Œnone* 50 Leading a jet-black goat white-horned, white-hooved.

Phrase. **1611** COTGR., *Paillard comme vn Moine*,..as lecherous as a Goat (say we).

b. Used *Zool.* in *plural* as a rendering of mod.L. *Caprinæ*, the name of the sub-family to which the genus *Capra* belongs. Also, with distinctive prefix, applied to certain antelopes, as †**blue goat** = BLAUWBOK; **Rocky Mountain goat**, *Haplocerus montanus*; **yellow goat** = DZEREN.

1731 MEDLEY *Kolben's Cape G. Hope* II. 114 The Blew goats are shaped like the tame, but are as large as an European hart. **1884–5** *Riverside Nat. Hist.* (1888) V. 343 The Rocky Mountain goat (*Haplocerus americanus*).

2. *transf.* **a.** The zodiacal sign CAPRICORN.

1387 TREVISA *Higden* (Rolls) II. 207 Capricornus þe goot. **1594** BLUNDEVIL *Exerc.* III. I. xxiv. (1636) 330 The tenth Signe called Capricornus, that is to say, the Goat. *a* **1631** DONNE *Progr. Soul* I. 336 The Sun hath twenty tymes both Crabb and Goate Parchèd, since first launch'd forth this livinge boat. **1868** LOCKYER *Guillemin's Heavens* (ed. 6) 330 To the west of this constellation we again find the Waterbearer and the Goat.

†**b.** The star Capella (Alpha Aurigæ). *Obs.*

1551 RECORDE *Cast. Knowl.* (1556) 264 Then foloweth Erichthonius, with the Goate and the 2 Kyddes. **1674** MOXON *Tutor Astron.* II. (ed. 3) 63, I take Capella, alias Hircus, the Goat on Auriga's shoulder.

†**c.** [transl. of Gr. αἴξ.] A fiery meteor. *Obs.*

1656 STANLEY *Hist. Philos.* VI. 63 Hence come those [fiery exhalations] they call firebrands, goates, falling-starres [etc.].

d. Short for GOATSKIN.

1895 *Montgomery Ward Catal.* 290/2 Men's goat driving gloves. **1927** J. S. HEWITT-BATES *Bookbinding for Schools* 13 Goat or Morocco. *Ibid.* 14 Persians..may be made either from goat or sheep. **1927** *Longman's Class. Cat. Educ. Works* 12 Hand grained goat, gilt edges.

3. *fig.* **a.** A licentious man.

1675 TRAHERNE *Chr. Ethics* vii. 90 When a covetous man doteth on his bags of gold..the drunkard on his wine, the lustful goat on his women..they banish all other objects. *a* **1700** B. E. *Dict. Cant. Crew*, *Goat*, a Lecher, or very Lascivious Person. **1863** HOLLAND *Lett. Joneses* iii. 51, I think this devotion of your life to music has had the tendency..to make you intellectually an ass and morally a goat.

b. ***to play the*** (***giddy***) ***goat***: to frolic foolishly; to play the fool; to behave in an irresponsible manner. Also, ***to act the goat***. *colloq.*

1879 H. HARTIGAN *Stray Leaves from Mil. Man's Note Bk.* i, Don't be actin' the goat. **1887** KIPLING *From Sea to Sea* (1900) I. xiv. 162 You'll find some o' the youngsters play the goat a good deal when they come out o' stable. **1888** —— *Under Deodars* (1890) 91 Generally, as he explained, 'playing the giddy garden goat all round'. **1927** GALSWORTHY *White Monkey* I. v, It's playing the goat for no earthly reason. **1929** W. P. RIDGE *Affect. Regards* 61 Haven't I got enough trouble without you acting the goat in this fashion?

c. ***to get*** (a person's) ***goat***: to make (him) angry; to annoy or irritate. *slang* (orig. *U.S.*).

1910 J. LONDON *Let.* 2 Aug. (1966) 316 Honestly, I believe I've got Samuels' *goat*! He's afraid to come back. **1912** C. MATHEWSON *Pitching in a Pinch* ii. 28 Lobert..stopped at third with a mocking smile on his face which would have gotten the late Job's goat. **1914** *Sat. Even. Post* 4 Apr. 10/3 It got my goat—that and the cold and that light in all the dark. **1919** H. JENKINS *John Dene of Toronto* (1920) iv. 70 There are some things in this country that get my goat. **1922** *Weekly Westm. Gaz.* 27 May 8/1 What gets my goat is the assumption that the misty subject is necessarily more artistic than the sharp and regular one. **1924** GALSWORTHY *White Monkey* II. i, That had got the chairman's goat!—Got his goat? What expressions they used nowadays! **1929** J. B. PRIESTLEY *Good Companions* III. i. 474 Now this is what gets my goat, and you can't blame me. **1960** B. KEATON *Wonderf. World of Slapstick* (1967) i. 22 What got my goat was that when I finally did get knocked off..it was due to an accident outside the theatre.

d. A fool; a dupe. *colloq.*

1916 C. J. DENNIS *Songs of Sentimental Bloke* 39 The drarmer's writ be Shakespeare, years ago, About a barmy goat called Romeo. **1947** K. TENNANT *Lost Haven* i. 20 You old goat! Shut up and get out before I slam you out. *Ibid.* xxi. 365 'Don't be a goat.' Silly young fools, all three of them. **1949** PARTRIDGE *Dict. Underworld* 296/1 Goat,..a dupe; swindler's victim. **1971** *Inside Kenya Today* Mar. 37/2 'I must discipline these idiots,' Omolo said to himself. .. 'I must beat them today, goats!'

4. *attrib.* and *Comb.* **a.** General combs., as ***goat-beard***, ***-bell***, ***-carriage***, ***-cheese***, ***-feet*** (also *attrib.* or *adj.*), ***-fell***, ***-fold***, ***-horn***, ***-house***, ***-kid***, ***-kind***, ***land***, ***-milk*** (also *attrib.*), ***-pen***, ***-shed***, ***-stand***, ***-thigh***; ***goat-like*** adj. and adv.; ***goat-bearded***, ***-eyed***, ***-fed***, ***-footed***, ***-headed***, ***-horned***, ***-nursed*** ppl. adjs.

14.. *Nom.* in Wr.-Wülcker 703/14 *Hoc stirillum*, a *gaytt berde. **1604** MIDDLETON *Father Hubburd's T.* Wks. (Bullen) VIII. 105 A *goat-bearded usurer. **1876** LONGF. *Dutch Picture* 29 Old sea-faring men come in, goat-bearded gray, and with double chin. **1884** *Macm. Mag.* Oct. 434/1 Turkish *goat-bells and Albanian goat-bells are quite different. **1897** *Blackw. Mag.* Dec. 779/2 He used to come in his *goat-carriage to see me. **1893** E. H. BARKER *Wand. South. Waters* 311 She gave me some excellent *goat-cheese. **1656** W. D. tr. *Comenius' Gate Lat. Unl.* §290 Hee..that looketh with his eyes drawn together, *goat-eyed. **1824** SWAN tr. *Gesta Rom.* lxxvi. I. 267 The goat-eyed man of physic acquiesced. *c* **1616** CHAPMAN *Odyss.* IX. 384 We Cyclops care not for your *Goat-fed Ioue. **1590** MARLOWE *Edw. II*, I. i. 60 My men, like satyrs grazing on the lawns, Shall with their *goat-feet dance the antic hay. *a* **1649** DRUMM. OF HAWTH. *Poems* Wks. (1711) 8 Nymphs of the forrests..shewing your beauty's treasure To goat-feet sylvans. **1436** *Pol. Poems* (Rolls) II. 160 Commodytes..commynge out of Spayne.. Iren, wolle, wadmole, *gotefel, kydefel also. **1630** J. TAYLOR (Water P.) *Sculler* Wks. III. 17/2 He..to Hels *Goat-fold aye doth millions bring, Of soules. **1776** R. CHANDLER *Trav. Greece* (1825) II. 74 The *goat-footed god quitted his habitation on the mountain. **1896** A. LILLIE *Worship Satan Mod. France* Pref. 17 Where was the logic of the pact in blood with a *goat-headed monstrosity? **1549** *Compl. Scotl.* vi. 65 Ane pipe maid of ane *gait horne. **1863** LYELL *Antiq. Man* 26 The small race of *goat-horned sheep still lingers in some Alpine valleys of the Upper Rhine. *c* **1550** CHEKE *Matt.* xxvi. 71 As he was going forth into y^{e} *goathous. **1675** HOBBES *Odyss.* (1677) 207 [To] lead my goats afield..& my goat-houses sweep. **1752** in *Scots Mag.* (1753) Oct. 510/2 The goat-house in the moor. **153.** *Wills & Inv. N.C.* (Surtees 1860) 76, xxiij ould gaytt 38/4. iiij *gaytt keedes 4/. **1774** GOLDSM. *Nat. Hist.* (1776) III. 35 Of Animals of the Sheep and *Goat Kind. **1621** FLETCHER *Pilgrim* IV. iii, He is a mountaineere, a man of *Goteland. **1583** STANYHURST *Æneis* III. (Arb.) 89 A meigre leane rake with a long berd *goatlyke. **1594** CAREW *Huarte's Exam. Wits* v. (1596) 68 It behoueth that in humane learning there be some Goat-like wits. **1653** R. SANDERS *Physiogn.* 249 The forehead round, or Goat-like wrinkled. **1862** MARG. GOODMAN *Exper. Sister of Mercy* 87 A goat-like descent from rock to rock. **1897** HUGHES *Mediterr. Fever* iv. 156 A characteristic goat-like odour. *c* **1400** MAUNDEV. (Roxb.) vii. 27 Putte þerto *gayte mylke. **1726** *Wodrow Corr.* (1843) III. 266 In June most of the ministers of Glasgow were out of town at the goat-milk. **1771** SMOLLETT *Humph. Cl.* 8 Aug., Dr. Gregory..advises the Highland air, and the use of goat-milk whey. **1725** POPE *Odyss.* IX. 330 We Cyclops are, a race above Those air-bred people, and their *goat-nursed Jove. **1601** HOLLAND *Pliny* II. 322 *Goat-pens and stals where they [goats] be kept. **1851** *Zoologist* IX. 2978 Our guide at length conducted us to a *goat-shed. **1775** R. CHANDLER *Trav. Asia M.* (1825) I. 340, I discovered a *goat-stand in a dale. **1879** BROWNING *Pheidippides* 68 Under the human trunk the *goat-thighs grand I saw.

b. Special combs., as **goat and bee**, used *attrib.* to designate a type of Chelsea porcelain; also, applied to silverware bearing the same pattern; **goat-antelope**, an antelope of the genus *Nemorhædus*; †**goat-beetle** = *goat-chafer*; **goat-chafer**, a capricorn beetle (cf. quots.); †**goat-doe**, a female goat; **goat-drunk** *a.*, lascivious from drink; **goat-fig** = L. *caprificus* see quot.); **goat-fish**, a name given to several species of fish, as the *Balistes capriscus* and *Phycis furcatus* of Europe, and the *Upeneus maculatus* of America; **goat-foot** [after Gr. *αἰγιπόδης*, *αἰγίπους*], a faun or satyr; the god Pan (cf. also *goat-feet*); also *attrib.*; **goat-god**, the god Pan; **goat hair**, the hair or skin of the goat; †**goat-hart** (see quot.); **goat-leap** = *goat's leap*; †**goat-marjoram** (see quot. and cf. *goat's-marjoram*); †**goat-milker** = GOAT-SUCKER; **goat-moth** (see quot. 1859); **goat-owl** = GOAT-SUCKER; **goat-path**, a narrow mountain track, such as is made by goats; †**goat-peach** (see quot.); **goat-pepper** (see quot.); **goat-root**, the plant *Ononis Natrix*; **goat-rue** = *goat's rue* (see 4 c); †**goat-sea**, the Ægean Sea; **goat-singing**, **-song**, renderings of Gr. τραγῳδία TRAGEDY; †**goat-speech** = ECLOGUE (q.v.); **goat-star** = GOAT 2 b; **goat-stones** = *goat's-stones*; **goat-track** = *goat-path*; **goat-weed**, a name for the W. Indian plants *Capraria biflora* and *Stemodia durantifolia*; ? also for *Ægopodium Podagraria* (Goutweed); **goat-willow**, *Salix caprea*; †**goat-wool** = *goat's-wool* (a). See also GOAT-BUCK, -HERD, -SKIN, -SUCKER.

1931 E. WENHAM *Domestic Silver* v. 98 Various curious shapes were adapted to these small jugs, one being the so-called '*goat and bee'. This is supposed to have been designed by Nicholas Sprimont, a silversmith, and.. examples in silver are extremely rare. **1957** MANKOWICZ & HAGGAR *Encycl. Eng. Pott. & Porc.* 97/1 '*Goat and Bee' jug*, a jug decorated with goats and a bee, incised in the base with the word Chelsea, a triangle, and a date, generally 1745. **1847** CRAIG, *Goat or goral antelopes. **1658** SIR T. BROWNE *Gard. Cyrus* iii. ¶ 28 Since..we find so noble a scent in the tulip-fly and *goat-beetle. *Note*, The long and tender green *capricornus*, rarely found. **1658** ROWLAND *Moufet's Theat. Ins.* 1006 *Capricornus*; the Germans call it Holtzback; the English, *Goat-chafer. **1792** BELKNAP *Hist. New Hampsh.* III. 181 Goat Chaffer, *Cerambyx coriarius*. **1837** M. DONOVAN *Dom. Econ.* II. 207 The silk-cotton tree worm.. is..the caterpillar of a large capricorn beetle, or goat-chafer. **14..** *Voc.* in Wr.-Wülcker 570/22 *Capra*, a *gootdoo [*ibid.* 30 a gotdo]. **1592** NASHE *Pierce Penilesse* 24 The seuenth is *Goate drunke, when in his drunkennes he hath no minde but on Lecherie. **1601** ? MARSTON *Pasquil & Kath.* III. 7 Mounsieur's Goat drunke, and he shrugs, and skrubs, and hee's it for a wench. *a* **1640** DAY *Peregr. Schol.* (1881) 52 In theise two..the goates blood is predominante; and such we call Goate-Drunk. **1835** BOOTH *Analyt. Dict.* 106 The common Figtree..when in its wild state is called *Caprificus* or *Goat-fig. *a* **1639** T. CAREW *Cæl. Brit.* Wks. (1824) 160 The centaure, the horn'd *goatfish capricorne. **1864** COUCH *Brit. Fishes* III. 125 Goatfish. The Greater Fork-beard, *Phycis furcatus*. **1885** LADY BRASSEY *The Trades* 302 There were..bright, scarlet fish, known locally as 'red-mullet', although they are really, I believe, goat-fish, with a little tuft under their lower jaw. **1878** WILDE *Ravenna* v. 10 Some *goat-foot Pan. **1898** G. MEREDITH *Odes Fr. Hist.* 6 To veil an evil leer, And bid a goatfoot trip it like a fay. **1906** *Daily Chron.* 13 Aug. 4/4 It was the hour of Pan. I could almost think I saw the goat-foot playing his pipes by the brook. **1912** R. BROOKE *Poems* (1918) 54 To glimpse a Naiad's reedy head, Or hear the Goat-foot piping low. **1925** E. SITWELL *Troy Park* 9 The goat-foot satyr waves. **1879** BROWNING *Pheidippides* 76 Go, say to Athens, 'The *Goat-God saith: When Persia..is cast in the sea, Then praise Pan'. **1896** F. B. JEVONS *Introd. Hist. Relig.* xxiii. 351 The Satiric chorus.. wore goat skins..to mark their intimate relation with the goat-god. **1895** *Montgomery Ward Catal.* 102/3 Infants' white *goat hair brushes, fine and soft. **1960** *Farmer & Stockbreeder* (Suppl.) 29 Mar. 4/1 A multilayer goat-hair fleece. **1967** J. RATHBONE *Diamonds Bid* iii. 27, I have plenty of kilims and goat-hair rugs. **1706** PHILLIPS (ed. Kersey), **Goat-hart*, or Stone-buck, a wild Beast. **1726** *Dict. Rust.* (ed. 3) s.v. *Capriole*, The *Goat-leap, when a horse at the full height of his Leap, yerks or strikes out his hind legs. **1755** JOHNSON, **Goat marjoram*, the same with Goatsbeard. [Hence in later Dicts.] **1611** COTGR., *Caprimulge*, a *Goat-milker. **1706** PHILLIPS (ed. Kersey), *Goat-milker* or *Goat-sucker*, a kind of Owl. **1802** BINGLEY *Anim. Biog.* (1813) III. 221 The *goat moth. **1859** THOMPSON *Gardener's Assist.* 533 The caterpillars of the goat-moth (*Cossus ligniperda*). **1768** PENNANT *Zool.* II. 246 *Goat Owl. **1897** *Daily News* 13 Apr. 5/7 Here..the only roads are *goat-paths in the mountains. **1693** EVELYN *De la Quint. Compl. Gard.* Gloss., **Goat-Peaches* are Peaches that are very hairy. **1836** *Penny Cycl.* VI. 274/1 A much hotter species is the *Capsicum fruticosum* or *goat-pepper, a native of the East Indies. **1840** PAXTON *Bot. Dict.*, **Goat-root*, see *Ononis Natrix*. **1756** P. BROWNE *Jamaica* 289 Galega..The shrubby *Goat-rue. **1565** GOLDING *Ovid's Met.* IX. (1593) 223 Miletas swiftly past The *gote-sea. **1789** T. TWINING *Aristotle on Poetry* (1812) I. 111 note 7 *Tragedy*, i.e., according to the most usual derivation of the word, *the *goat-singing*. **1822** SHELLEY *Hellas* Pref., The only *goat-song which I have yet attempted. **1483** *Cath. Angl.* 148/2 A *Gayte speche *egloga*. **1894** GLADSTONE *Horace's Odes* III. vii. 6 Him wild *Goat-

stars vexed. **1657** W. COLES *Adam in Eden* cclxxviii, It is called..in English Satyrion, Orchis, Doggestones, *Goatestones, Foolestones [etc.]. **1889** C. EDWARDES *Sardinia* 153 We at length..hit upon the *goat-track. **1756** P. BROWNE *Jamaica* 268 *Goat weed. This plant..grows about most houses in the lower Savannas. **1864** GRISEBACH *Flora W. Ind.* 784 Goat-weed, *Capraria biflora* and *Stemodia durantifolia*. **1861** MISS PRATT *Flower. Pl.* V. 99 Great Round-leaved Sallow, or *Goat-Willow. **1894** *Jrnl. R. Agric. Soc.* June 240 For coppice, probably *Salix caprea*, the Goat Willow or English Palm, would be best. **1513** DOUGLAS *Æneis* VIII. Prol. 48 Sum glasteris, and thai gang at all for *gayt woll.

c. Comb. with gen. *goat's*, as ***goat's horn, -milk***, etc.; also **goat's-bane** (see quot.); †**goat's-cullions** = *goat's-stones*; **goat's-foot**, †(*a*) (see quot. 1786; = F. *pied de chèvre*); also *attrib.*; (*b*) a name for the South African plant *Oxalis caprina*; **goat's hair** (see quot.); †**goat's-jump** = *goat's-leap*; **goat's-leaf** (see quots.); †**goat's-leap** = CAPRIOLE; †**goat's-marjoram**, ? wild marjoram (*Origanum vulgare*); †**goat's-orchis** = *goat's stones*; †**goat's-organy** = *goat's-marjoram*; **goat's-rue**, *Galega officinalis*; †**goat's-stones**, the name of several orchids, esp. *Orchis mascula* or *hircina*; **goat's-thorn**, a name for *Astragalus Tragacanthus* and other species; **goat's-wheat**, a rendering of mod.L. *Tragopyrum*, a Siberian genus of plants allied to the buckwheat; **goat's-wool**, (*a*) something non-existent (= L. *lana caprina*); (*b*) the fine wool mingled with the hair of some species of goats. See also GOAT'S-BEARD.

1840 PAXTON *Bot. Dict.*, *Goat's-bane, see *Aconitum tragoctonum*. **1578** LYTE *Dodoens* II. lvi. 222 The third kinde [of Orchis]..is called..in English Hares Balloxe and *Goates Cullions. **1672** W. T. *Mil. & Mar. Disc.* III. *Compl. Gunner* I. xxviii. 47 An Iron *Goats-foot with a Crow. **1786** GROSE *Treat. Anc. Armour* 59 The smaller cross bows were bent with the hand by means of a small steel lever, called the goat's foot, from its being forked on the side that rested on the cross bow and the cord. **1829** LOUDON *Encycl. Plants* 384 *Oxalis caprina*, Goat's-foot. **1869** BOUTELL *Arms & Arm.* viii. 141 The hind's foot (called also the goat's foot) cross-bow. **1895** *Edin. Rev.* Apr. 531 It is the cloud known to seamen..as '*goats' hair' or 'mares' tails'. **1589** *Pasquil's Counter-C.* 3 O how my Palfrey fetcht me uppe the Curuetto, and daunced the *Goats jumpe. **1861** MISS PRATT *Flower. Pl.* III. 139 The foliage of our Woodbine is very agreeable to goats, hence our plant is sometimes called *Goat's-leaf. **1861** MRS. LANKESTER *Wild Flowers* 71 The Perfoliate Honeysuckle, or Goat's-leaf. **1598** FLORIO, *Capriola*, a capriole, a sault or *goates leape that cunning riders teach their horses. **1623** COCKERAM, *Capriole*, the leaping of a horse aboue ground, called by horsemen the goats leape. **1530** PALSGR. 226/2 *Gottesmylke, *laict de chieure*. **1848** BUCKLEY *Iliad* 207 The woman grated over it a goat's-milk cheese. **1597** GERARDE *Herbal* II. ccix. §2. 543 Goates Organie is called..in English *goates Organie, and *goates Marierome. **1578** LYTE *Dodoens* II. lvi, 222 Rootes of Standergrasses (but especially of Hares Balloxe, or *Goates Orchis) eaten..doth, [etc.]. *Ibid.* IV. xxxi. 490 Galega..is called in English Italian Fetche and *Goates Rue. **1897** WILLIS *Flower. Pl.* II. 170 Galega officinalis L., is sometimes cultivated as a fodder-plant (goat's rue). **1597** GERARDE *Herbal* I. c. §1. 159 There be three sorts or kinds of *Goates stones. *Ibid.* III. xxiii. 1148 Tragacantha..in English for want of a better name, *Goates Thorne. **1611** COTGR., *Barbe regnard*, Goats-thorne; the shrub whose root yeeldeth Gumme dragogant. **1829** LOUDON *Encycl. Plants* 638 *Astragalus Tragacantha*, gt. Goat's Thorn. *Astragalus Poterium*, sm. Goat's Thorn. **1840** PAXTON *Bot. Dict.*, *Goat's-wheat, see *Tragopyrum*. **1588** J. UDALL *Demonstr. Discipl.* (Arb.) 11 The controuersie is not about *goats woolle (as the prouerbe saeth) neither light and trifling maters. **1704** *Lond. Gaz.* No. 3983/4 The Cargo of the Ship Hamstead Galley..consisting of..Goats-wooll, Cotton-yarn, Cotton-wooll, &c. will be exposed to..Sale. **1812** J. SMYTH *Pract. Customs* (1821) 314 Turkey Goat's Wool.

goat, var. GOTE, stream, sluice.

†**'goat-buck.** *Obs.* [f. GOAT + BUCK *sb.*[1]; cf. Du. *geitebok* (earlier *geytenbok*), G. *geiszbock* (MHG. *geizboc*).] A he-goat.

c **1000** ÆLFRIC *Gloss.* in Wr.-Wülcker 119/29 *Capra ægida*, gatbuccan hyrde. **1388** WYCLIF *Gen.* xxx. 35 And he departide..the geet and scheep, geet buckis and rammes. **1398** TREVISA *Barth. De P.R.* VIII. x. (1495) 313 A gote bucke is a beest wyth hornes stondynge vpwarde. *c* **1475** *Pict. Voc.* in Wr.-Wülcker 758/26 *Hic caper*, a get buk. **1535** COVERDALE *Ezek.* xliii. 22 Take a gootbuck without blemish for a synoffringe. **1567** MAPLET *Gr. Forest* 88 The Gote-bucke is verie wanton or lasciuious. **1607** TOPSELL *Four-f. Beasts* (1658) 181 Of the Goat, Male and Female. The male or great Goat-Buck [etc.].

goatee (gəʊ'tiː). orig. *U.S.* Also **goaty.** [f. GOAT: see -EE[2].] A beard trimmed in the form of a tuft hanging from the chin, resembling that of a he-goat.

1844 LEE & FROST *Ten Yrs. Oregon* viii. 102 A few individuals..leave what is called, by some of their politer neighbors, a 'goaty' under the chin. **1847** J. K. PAULDING *Noble Exile* 107 A queer little amber-colored goatee. **1856** MISS BIRD *Englishw. Amer.* 366 They [Americans] also indulge in eccentricities of appearance in the shape of beards and imperials, not to speak of the 'goatee'. **1884** *St. James's Gaz.* 10 May 6/1 A large 'goatee' beard. **1886** MRS. PHELPS *Burglars in Par.* vii. 133 The man with the goatee arose and shuffled to the..door.

goat-herd, goatherd ('gəʊthəd). [f. GOAT + HERD *sb.*[2]; cf. Du. *geitenherder*, G. *geiszhirt* (MHG. *geizhirte*), Sw. *getherde*, Da. *gedehyrde*.] One who tends goats.

c **1000** *Rect. Sing. Pers.* §15 in Schmid *Gesetze* 380 Gat-hyrde ȝebyreð his heorde meolc ofer Martinus mæssedæiȝ [etc.]. *c* **1050** *Voc.* in Wr.-Wülcker 379/12 *Caprarius*, gat-hiorde. *c* **1440** *Promp. Parv.* 206/1 Goot herde, *capercus*. *c* **1475** *Pict. Voc.* in Wr.-Wülcker 814/13 *Hic capriarius*, a gateheyrd. **1579** SPENSER *Sheph. Cal.* July 1 Is not thilke same a goteheard prowde, That sittes on yonder bancke. *c* **1580** *Satir. Poems Reform.* xliii. 67 Gyges the gait-hird, ane michtie conquerour. **1607** TOPSELL *Four-f. Beasts* (1658) 183 The Goatherds of the Countrey do give thereof to their Cattel. **1791** COWPER *Odyss.* XVII. 298 To whom the goat-herd answer thus return'd. **1814** SCOTT *Ld. of Isles* V. i, The goat-herd drove his kids to steep Ben-Ghoil. **1882** OUIDA *Maremma* I. 188 Yet he was only a young goatherd about 10 years of age.

quasi-*adj.* *a* **1586** SIDNEY *Arcadia* II. (1598) 219 Ye Gote-heard Gods, that loue the grassie mountaines.

Hence **'goat-herdess**, a female goat-herd.

1773 MRS. A. GRANT *Lett. fr. Mts.* (1807) I. vi. 51, I will not be a shepherdess, but a goatherdess. **1830** *Blackw. Mag.* XXVIII. 2 He is flirting with a red-headed Highland goatherdess. **1891** *Pall Mall G.* 4 Dec. 6/1 Mdme. T...in her early days, was a shepherdess, or, to be quite accurate, a 'goatherdess' in rural France.

goatish ('gəʊtɪʃ), *a.* Also 6–7 **gotish(e.** [f. GOAT + -ISH.] Characteristic of, or resembling, a goat in some feature or quality.

a **1529** SKELTON *Bouge of Court* 237 He gased on me with his gotyshe berde. **1567** DRANT *Horace's Ep.* I. xviii. F iij, An other vseth brablarie for very gotish wol [L. *de lana caprina*]. **1633** P. FLETCHER *Purple Isl.* VII. lxxvi, The goatish Satyres dance around. **1638** SIR T. HERBERT *Trav.* 316 Carving Gods to worship, after the shapes of Pan, Priapus, and other gotish fancies. **1794** MARTYN *Rousseau's Bot.* xxvii. 418 The flower has a strong goatish smell. **1806** W. TAYLOR in *Ann. Rev.* IV. 773 We have tasted the coarse-grained mutton of Lincolnshire..and the rank and goatish muskiness of the South-downs.

b. *spec.* Lascivious, lustful.

1598 E. GILPIN *Skial.* (1878) 11 Iudge if this gull deserued his mistris fauour, Who thus his goatish humours did relate. **1605** SHAKS. *Lear* I. ii. 138. **1624** HEYWOOD *Gunaik.* IV. 167 Shee did not only admit but allure and compell into her goatish embraces many of her souldiers. **1751** SMOLLETT *Per. Pic.* (1779) I. xxix. 266 A goatish, ram-faced rascal.

Hence **'goatishly** *adv.*, **'goatishness.**

1835 BOOTH *Analyt. Dict.* 104 He behaves Goatishly, or, is inclined to Goatishness. **1870** *Pall Mall G.* 23 Aug. 11 There are times when the goat will preach against goatishness, the frail will testify against frailty.

goatling ('gəʊtlɪŋ). [f. GOAT + -LING dim. suffix.] A young goat (cf. quot. 1883).

1870 *Daily News* 17 May, An old goat is dozing in the sun glare, while the goatling tumbles gleefully on the sward. **1883** *Times* 6 Dec. 7 [At] the half-yearly meeting of the British Goat Society..held yesterday..the newly-coined word 'goatling' was adopted, to distinguish goats above 12 months and under 2 years old. **1886** *Bazaar*, etc. 8 Oct. 1068 The goatlings, though few, were a beautiful lot.

'goatly, *a. nonce-wd.* [f. GOAT + -LY[1].] Goat-like; goatish.

1850 MRS. BROWNING *Poems* I. 338, I started first, as some Arcadian, Amazed by goatly God in twilight grove.

†**'goatress.** *Obs. rare*[−1]. [arbitrarily f. GOAT.] A goat-herdess.

1607 *Barley Breake* (1877) 21 What haughtie Shepheard, what neat spangled Goatresse, Shall not plucke downe and strike to thee the sayle?

†**'goatrill.** *Obs.*[−1] [f. GOAT after COCKEREL.] A young goat.

1688 R. HOLME *Armoury* II. 132/1 A Goat, 1 yeare a Kid, or Goatrill, and alway after a Goat.

'goat's-,beard. The name of various plants.

1. *Spiræa Ulmaria*, meadow-sweet.

1578 LYTE *Dodoens* I. xxix. 41 This herbe is called in Latine *Barba Capri*..in English Medewurte and Medesweete, and of some after the Latine name Goates bearde. **1605** TIMME *Quersit.* III. 177 Goates beard otherwise called meed-wort. **1616** SURFL. & MARKH. *Country Farme* 207 Goats-beard groweth verie well in a moist ground..The Latines call it Vlmaria, because the leaues are like to the leaues of Elme. **1882** *Garden* 27 May 376/3 *Spiræa Aruncus astilboides*, a plant similar to the Goat's Beard.

2. *Tragopogon pratensis*; also *T. porrifolius*, salsify.

1548 TURNER *Names of Herbes* (1881) 19 Barba Hirci named in greeke Tragopogon..It maye be called in englishe gotes bearde. **1597** GERARDE *Herbal* II. ccxli. §1. 594 Goates beard or Go to bedde at noone hath hollow stalkes, smooth, and of a whitish greene colour. **1640** PARKINSON *Theat. Bot.* 411 The Sommer Goates beard..is a small plant rising up with one stalke little above a foote high. **1699** EVELYN *Acetaria* 28 Goats-beard..is excellent even in Sallet, and very Nutritive. **1732** ARBUTHNOT *Rules of Diet* I. 250 Goat's beard, an alimentary Root, has most of the qualities of Scorzonera. **1796** C. MARSHALL *Garden.* xix. (1813) 353 *Goats beard*, the young shoots are eat (as those of salsafy) like asparagus at spring. *a* **1806** CHARLOTTE SMITH *Beachy Head* etc. (1807) 113 The Goatsbeard spreads its golden rays. **1854** S. THOMSON *Wild Fl.* II. (ed. 4) 122 The purple goat's-beard, the leopard's-bane..are well-favoured plants.

3. Some species of mushroom. ? *Obs.*

1688 R. HOLME *Armoury* II. 55/2 There are several kinds of these Mushrooms, as..the Goat's Beard, of which there are the reddish one and the spongy one and the Pepper tasted one. **1854** MAYNE *Expos. Lex.*, *Goat's-Beard Mushroom*, common name for the *Clavaria coralloides*.

goatskin ('gəʊtskɪn). Also 4 **geet skin**, 6 **goats skin.** The skin of a goat, esp. one used for a garment, a wine-bottle, etc.

1388 WYCLIF *I Sam.* xix. 13 An heeri skyn of geet [*v.r.* a rouȝ geet skin]. *a* **1586** SIDNEY *Arcadia* II. (1590) 102 b, Where..she found Dorus, apparelled in flanen, with a goats skin cast vpon him. **1611** BIBLE *Heb.* xi. 37 They wandered about in sheepskinnes, and goat skins. **1725** POPE *Odyss.* IX. 229 A goat-skin filled with precious wine. **1842** TENNYSON *St. Simeon S.* 114, I wear an undress'd goatskin on my back. **1883** STEVENSON *Treas. Isl.* III. xv, The marooned man in his goatskins trotted easily and lightly.

attrib. **1725** POPE *Odyss.* XXIV. 264 His head..Fenc'd with a double cap of goatskin hair. **1814** SCOTT *Wav.* xvi, The goat-skin purse, flanked by the usual defences, a dirk and steel-wrought pistol, hung before him.

'goat,sucker. [A rendering of L. *caprimulgus* (f. *capra* goat + *mulgēre* to milk), tr. Gr. αἰγοθήλας (f. αἰγο-, αἴξ goat + θηλάζειν to suck); cf. *goat-milker*, GOAT 4 b.] A name given to the bird *Caprimulgus europæus*, from a belief that it sucks the udders of goats. Also applied to other birds of the same genus, or of the family *Caprimulgidæ*.

1611 COTGR., *Grand merle*, a Goat-sucker; a mountaine bird. **1676** WILLUGHBY *Ornith.* 70 *Caprimulgus*..The Goat-sucker. **1678** RAY *Willughby's Ornith.* II. iii. 108 The American Goat-sucker, called Ibijau by the Brasilians, Noitibo by the Portugues. **1834** MCMURTRIE *Cuvier's Anim. Kingd.* 129 Goatsuckers live solitarily, and never venture abroad, except at twilight, and in the night during fine weather. **1884** J. G. WOOD in *Sunday Mag.* Apr. 246/2 It is the Nightjar..absurdly..called the Goatsucker.

goaty ('gəʊtɪ), *a.* Also 7 **goatie.** [f. GOAT + -Y[1].] Goat-like; goatish.

1600 SURFLET *Country Farme* I. xxvi. 164 It is no shame for a man to call another, goatie, if he be found mutable and full of changes in his manners and cariage. **1611** COTGR., *Caprin*, goatie; of a Goat. **1845** FORD *Handbk. Spain* II. 576 A goaty, shirtless..unshod Capuchin. **1882** *Garden* 10 June 417/2 Fresh and myriad-blossomed, but with a slightly goaty smell. **1893** LYDEKKER *Horns & Hoofs* 92 The very characteristic 'goaty' odour of that sex.

goava, obs. form of GUAVA.

goave (gəʊv), *v. E. Angl. dial.* Forms: 4–5 **golve**, 5 **golvon, -vyn**, 6 **golfe**, 6–7 **gove**, 9 **goave.** [Corresponds to GOAF[1]; cf. Da. *gulve*, in same sense.] *trans.* To stack (grain) in a goaf.

c **1325** *Gloss. W. de Biblesw.* in Wright *Voc.* 154 En la graunge vos blées muez; *glossed* golue [*printed* golne] thi corn. **14..** *Addit. MS.* 12195 in *Promp. Parv.* 202 *note*, *Gelimo*, to golue. *c* **1440** *Promp. Parv.* 202/1 Golvyn, or golvon, *arconiso*. **1573** TUSSER *Husb.* lvii. (1878) 131 In gouing at haruest, learne skilfully how ech graine for to laie, by it selfe on a mow: Seede barlie the purest, goue out of the way, all other nigh hand goue as just as ye may. *a* **1825** FORBY *Voc. E. Anglia*, *Goave*, to stow corn in a barn. 'Do you intend to stack this wheat, or to goave it?'

goave, var. GOVE, to stare.

go-away (gəʊəweɪ). (Stress variable) Also **go-way.** [Imitative of its cry *kway-kway* (cf. Bechuana *maquaai*).] In full *go-away bird.* A South African touraco of the genus *Corythaixoides*.

1881 E. E. FREWER tr. *Holub's Seven Yrs. S. Afr.* I. 289 A great grey lory, that from its cry is called the 'go-away' by the English, whilst by the Boers it is known as the 'grote Mausevogel'. **1896** H. L. TANGYE *In New S. Afr.* II. vii. 401, I continue my walk along the kopje top, succeeding in obtaining specimens of the 'Go away' bird. **1897** J. P. FITZPATRICK *Outspan* 55 There is a sort of bastard cockatoo in those parts which is commonly known as the 'Go way' bird, on account of its cry, which closely resembles these words. **1906** *Chambers's Jrnl.* Mar. 214/2 A pair of gray crested parrots, or 'go-away birds', as they are called. **1940** [see *alarm-bird* s.v. ALARM *sb.* 13]. **1951** R. CAMPBELL *Light on Dark Horse* v. 93 The 'Go 'way Bird' or grey lory. **1958** M. SPARK *Go-away Bird* 74 All over the Colony it was possible to hear the subtle voice of the grey-crested lourie, commonly known as the go-away bird by its call, 'go 'way, go 'way'. **1964** A. L. THOMSON *New Dict. Birds* 843/2 The characteristic call of *Corythaixoides* spp. is a nasal 'gwaaa', hence the name of 'go-away-bird'.

gob (gɒb), *sb.*[1] Also 4, 6 **gobbe**, 6 **gobb, gubbe, goubbe.** [App. a. OF. *gobe, goube* (mod.F. *gobbe*), a mouthful, lump, etc. (in mod.F. only in the special senses of a food-ball for poisoning dogs, feeding poultry, etc., and a concretion found in the stomachs of sheep), related to the vb. *gober* to swallow: see GOBBET.]

1. a. A mass or lump (cf. GOBBET 3). Now *dial.*

1382 WYCLIF *Isa.* xl. 12 Who heeng vp with thre fingris the heuynesse [*Douce MS.* gobbe; L. *molem*] of the erthe. **1892** JANE BARLOW *Irish Idylls* iii. 47 He was a rael gob o good nature.

b. A lump, clot of some slimy substance. (Cf. GOBBET 2 b, GOBBON 2.) Now *dial.* or *vulgar.*

1555–8 PHAER *Æneid* II. H iij b, Belching out the gubbes of blood. **1753** J. BARTLET *Gentl. Farriery* vi. 59 He [a horse]..throws out of his nose and mouth great gobs of white phlegm. **1872** 'MARK TWAIN' *Innoc. Abr.* vii. 45 Suggestive of a 'gob' of mud on the end of a shingle. **1877** *N.W. Linc. Gloss.*, *Gob*, a large thick expectoration. **1886** ELWORTHY *W. Somerset Word-bk.*, *Gob*, a piece, a mass or lump; usually applied to some soft substance. **1893** CROCKETT *Stickit Minister* 197 Cleg took a 'gob' of hard mud in his hand.

c. *Glass-making.* A lump of molten glass that is used to make a single bottle, jar, etc.

1925 Hodkin & Cousen *Textbk. Glass Technol.* xxxii. 427 This plunger, moving vertically with a reciprocating motion, serves to form and deliver gobs of suitable size and shape. **1941** C. J. Phillips *Glass* ix. 191 As each section passes a feeding station served by a gob feeder, a gob of glass is dropped into the press mold and pressed into a parison. **1967** *Times Rev. Industry* July 47/2 (Advt.), The shear blades cut off a lump of this molten glass (bottlemakers call it a 'gob') from which each bottle is made.

†**2.** A large sum of money. Also *gob* (*gubbe*) *of gold.* Obs.

1542 Udall *Erasm. Apoph., Socrates* §31. I. 14 A bodye.. to whom hath happened some good goubbe of money. **1566** Drant *Horace, Sat.* vi. H vj, He to whome God Hercules did bringe A gubbe of goulde. **1574** Studley tr. *Bale's Pageant Popes* 104 a, That she might heape vppon thee many gubs of goulde. **1593** Nashe *Choise Valentines* (1899) 8/70 And tenne good gobbs I will unto thee tell, Of golde or siluer. **1598** Barret *Theor. Warres* v. v. 167 The gobbes of gold by heapes in their studies. **1655** *Nicholas Papers* (Camden) II. 352 My..grandsonne whoe..only knowes where my poore recruites are, of which if I heare nothing this next weeke nor can haue poore gubb from his Matie, I must of necessity slip out of the [world?] or be disgraced for euer. **1692** R. L'Estrange *Fables* (1694) 265 Dost think I have so little wit as to part with such a Gob of money for God-a-mercy?

3. a. A lump or large mouthful of food, esp. of raw, coarse, or fat meat. (Cf. gobbet 3.) Now *dial.* or *vulgar.*

1557–8 Phaer *Æneid* vi. Q 3 b, He [Cerberus] gaping wyde his threfold iawes, All hungry caught that gubbe [L. *offam*]. **1602** Marston *Ant. & Mel.* ii. C 4 b, O that the stomack of this queasie age Digestes, or brookes such raw vnseasoned gobs, And vomits not them forth! **1613** F. Robarts *Revenue Gospel* Title-p., The eagle spies, A gob [L. *offam*] she lurch'd, and to her young she flies. **1711** E. Ward *Quix.* I. 369 Than for your worship's Eyes to follow Each Gob or Morsel that I swallow. **1774** Foote *Cozeners* i, The venison was over-roasted, and stunk, but Doctor Dewlap twisted down such gobs of fat. **1828** J. Wilson *Noct. Ambr.* in *Blackw. Mag.* XXIII. 124 A father that gaed aff at a city-feast wi' a gob o' green fat o' turtle half way down his gullet. **1871** Mrs. Stowe *Oldtown Fireside Stor.* 8 Ye tell 'em one story, and they jest swallows it as a dog does a gob o' meat.

†**b.** *at a* (or *one*) *gob*, at one mouthful. *Obs.*

Perhaps a different (though cognate) word; cf. Fr. (obs.) *avaler tout de gob*, whence the mod.Fr. phrase *tout de go* easily, without trouble or ceremony.

1599 Nashe *Lenten Stuffe* (1871) 65 And flead him, and thrust him down his pudding-house at a gobb. **1611** L. Barrey *Ram Alley* i. i. A 3 b, That little land a gaue Throte the Lawyer swallowed at one gob For lesse then halfe the worth.

gob (gɒb), *sb.*² *north. dial.* and *slang.* [Of obscure origin; possibly a. Gael. and Irish *gob* beak, mouth, but cf. gab *sb.*³] **a.** The mouth.

a **1550** *Christis Kirke Gr.* xx, Quhair thair gobbis wer ungeird, Thay gat upon the gammis. *a* **1605** Polwart *Flyting w. Montgomerie* 754 Misly kyt! and thou flyt, Ile dryt in thy gob. **1674–91** Ray *N.C. Words* 134 A *Gob*, an open or wide mouth. **1693** *Scot. Presbyt. Eloq.* (1738) 112 Beware of the Drunkenness of the Goose, for it never rests, but constantly dips the Gob of it in the Water. **1788** W. Marshall *Yorksh.* II. 332 *Gob*, a vulgar name for the mouth. **18..** R. Burrowes in *Father Prout's Rem.* ix. 267 Just to..moisten his gob 'fore he died. **1833** M. Scott *Tom Cringle* i. (1859) 3, I thrust half a doubled up muffin into my gob. **1851** Mayhew *Lond. Labour* I. 421 He tied my hands and feet so that I could hardly move, but I managed somehow to turn my gob (mouth) round and gnawed it away. **1893** *Northumbld. Gloss.*, *Gob*, the mouth..The form *gab* is quite unknown in Northumberland.

b. *Comb.*, as **gob-mouthed** *a. dial.*, gaping; **gob-stick**, (*a*) *dial.*, a spoon; (*b*) *Fisheries* (see quot. 1883); (*c*) *slang* a clarinet; **gob-stopper** *slang*, a large, hard, freq. spherical sweet for sucking; **gob-string**, a bridle.

1894 Hall Caine *Manxman* 27 Hould your dirty tongue, you *gobmouthed omathaun! **1674–91** Ray *N.C. Words* 142 A *Gobstick. Cochleare. **1788** W. Marshall *Yorksh.* II. 332 *Gobstick*, a wooden spoon. **1876** *Whitby Gloss.*, *Gobstick*, a wooden spoon or other implement for conveying food to the mouth. **1883** *Fisheries Exhib. Catal.* 195 Halibut-killer and gob-stick for killing the fish and disgorging the hook. **1936** *Amer. Mercury* May x/2 *Gob stick*, a clarinet. **1938** Dylan Thomas *Let.* 16 May (1966) 195 The double-bed is a swing-band with coffin, oompah, slush-pump, gob-stick. **1959** 'F. Newton' *Jazz Scene* 292 The player as such calls his instrument a clarinet..; *qua* hipster he may call it..the obs. *gobstick.* **1928** W. de la Mare *Come Hither* (ed. 2) 769 **Gob-stoppers* and *toffee*—are these not 'good' names for goodies? **1959** D. Barton *Loving Cup* 89 The sky looks like one of those orange gobstoppers we used to buy in the tuckshop. **1971** *Times* 6 Jan. 12/5 A large ball of green leaves is formed in the cheek which makes *qat* chewers looks [*sic*] as though they are perpetually sucking gobstoppers. **1785** Grose *Dict. Vulg. Tongue*, *Gab* or **gob string*, a bridle. **1855** in Robinson *Whitby Gloss.*

gob (gɒb), *sb.*³ *dial.* [= gab *sb.*², but prob. apprehended by speakers as a fig. sense of prec.] Talk, conversation, language. ***gift of the gob*** (see gab *sb.*² 1 b). ***to give gob*** (see quot. 1855).

1695 Colvil *Whigs Supplic.* To Rdr. A v, [Pretended quot. from Z. Boyd] There was a Man called Job, Dwelt in the land of Uz, He had a good gift of the Gob. [*a* **1700** B. E. *Dict. Cant. Crew* s.v., *Gift of the Gob*, a wide, open Mouth; also a good Songster, or Singing-master.] **1855** Robinson *Whitby Gloss.* s.v., 'To gie gob', to mouth, or give word, to abuse. **1893** *Northumbld. Gloss.* s.v., 'It's a grand thing the gift o' the gob'.

gob (gɒb), *sb.*⁴ *Coal-mining.* Also **gobb.** [Perh. an alteration of goaf², influenced by gob *sb.*¹] The empty space from which the coal has been extracted in the 'long-wall' system of mining (cf. goaf); also, the material used for packing such a space (= *gobbing*).

1839 Ure *Dict. Arts* 979 The place where the coal is removed is named the gobb or [*printed* or gobb] waste; and gobbin or gobb-stuff is stones or rubbish taken..to fill up that excavation as much as possible. *Ibid.* 980 The roads are carried either progressively through the gobb, or the gobb is entirely shut up. **1871** *Trans. Amer. Inst. Mining Eng.* I. 304 The roof being allowed to come down on to the packings of the gob behind the miners. **1883** *Standard* 23 Oct. 3/6 A large quantity of the 'gob' was on fire in the Bullhurst seam. **1884** *Times* 29 Jan. 10/4 After driving 10 yards through the gob the body of Mr. Thomas was found.

b. *attrib.*, as **gob-fire, road, -stuff** (see quots.).

1839 Gob stuff [see above]. **1860** *Weale's Mining Gloss.* (ed. 2) *S. Staff. terms*, *Gob-road*, a road..through that part of the mine which has been previously worked. **1881** Raymond *Mining Gloss.*, *Gob-fire*, fire produced by the heat of decomposing *gob.* **1898** *Daily News* 20 Apr. 8/5 A 'gob' fire, caused by a heap of fire-clay, duct, and coal slack.

gob (gɒb), *sb.*⁵ *slang* (orig. *U.S.*). [Cf. gobby.] An American sailor or ordinary seaman. Also *attrib.*

1915 *Recruiters' Bulletin* (U.S.) Dec. 34/2 Even though us 'gobs' were on the 'Conny' standing by, Why, we all had a finger in the pie. **1923** R. D. Paine *Comrades of Rolling Ocean* iii. 44, I was feeding the coal to her when most of those..amateur gobs were seasick and useless. *Ibid.* xiv. 241 Here is one Yankee gob..that will be there on the first call. **1925** J. Gregory *Bab of Backwoods* xvi. 193 Step lively, you gobs! **1944** T. Rattigan *While Sun Shines* i. 187 Can you beat that—an earl being a gob. **1951** *Landfall* V. iii. 193 He wore..a little white gob hat.

gob (gɒb), *v.*¹ *techn.* [? f. gob *sb.*¹] **a.** *trans.* To choke up or obstruct (a furnace). **b.** *intr.* Of a furnace: To become choked or obstructed (see quots.).

1863 *Rep. Brit. Assoc.* 738 Frequent interruption..led at length to the furnace being 'gobbed' and ultimately abandoned. ? **1877** in Davies *Suppl. Gloss.* s.v., If you put into your furnaces a quantity of stuff in which..silica preponderates, your furnaces will not flux, but they gob. **1881** Raymond *Mining Gloss.*, *Gob-up*, of a blast furnace, to become obstructed in working by reason of a scaffold or a salamander.

gob (gɒb), *v.*² *dial.* [f. gob *sb.*³ Cf. gab *v.*²] *intr.* To prate, brag. Hence **'gobbing** *vbl. sb.* and *ppl. a.*

a **1810** Tannahill *Poems* (1846) 88 Quoth gobbin Tom of Lancashire, To northern Jock. **1832** W. Stephenson *Gateshead Poems* 99 It's worth your while..To hear their jaw and gobbins. **1893** *Northumbld. Gloss.*, *Gob*, to talk impudently, to brag.

gob (gɒb), *v.*³ [f. gob *sb.*¹] *trans.* and *intr.* To spit. Also with *up.*

1881 A. B. & S. Evans *Leicestershire Words* 161 *Gob*, to spit out; expectorate. **1933** L. A. G. Strong *Sea Wall* ii. xvi. 223 Come on, man, gob it up. **1953** Dylan Thomas *Under Milk Wood* (1954) 50 And they thank God, and gob at a gull for luck.

gobang (gəʊ'bæŋ). [Corruptly a. Japanese *goban*, said to be ad. Chinese *k'i pan* chess-board.] A game of Japanese origin, played on a chequer-board, each player endeavouring to get five pieces into line before his opponent.

1886 Guillemard *Cruise 'Marchesa'* I. 267 Some of the games are purely Japanese..as *go-ban. Note*, This game is the one lately introduced into England under the misspelt name of Go Bang. **1888** *Pall Mall G.* 1. Nov. 3/1 These young persons..played go-bang and cat's cradle.

†**gobard, gobart.** *Obs.* Vars. of cobbard, gawberd.

1403 *Nottingham Rec.* II. 20 Unius gobart de ferro. **1411** *Ibid.* 86, j. gobard, iijd. *c* **1475** *Pict. Voc.* in Wr.-Wülcker 770/3 *Hec ipepurgium* [printed *ipegurgium*], a gobard.

†**gobbed,** *ppl. a. Obs. rare*⁻¹. [f. OF. *gobe*, proud, vain + -ed¹.] Proud.

? *a* **1400** *Morte Arth.* 1346 Thane answers sir Gayous full gobbede wordes.

gobbelett, obs. form of goblet.

†**gobber-tooth.** *Obs. rare.* [Of obscure formation; cf. gab *v.*³ and gag-tooth, gubbertush.] A projecting front tooth.

1646 Gaule *Cases Consc.* 5 Every old woman with a wrinkled face..a gobber tooth..is pronounced for a witch. **1685** H. More *Para. Prophet.* 412 Two gobber teeth were set in, one on this side, the other on the inner side.

Hence †**gobber-toothed** *ppl. a.*

1655 Fuller *Ch. Hist.* v. iv. §20 Lean-visaged long-sided, gobber-toothed, yellow-complexioned.

gobbet ('gɒbɪt), *sb.* Now *rare* exc. *arch.* Forms: 4–6 gobet(t, 5–6 gobbet(t, (6 *Sc.* gobbat, -it), 5– gobbet. [a. OF. *gobet* (pl. *gobez, gobès*), dim. of *gobe* gob *sb.*¹; cf. gobbon.

For the development of sense cf. morsel. In French the etymological sense seems always to have been the prevailing one, whereas in English the more general meaning 'portion', 'lump', is earlier and commoner than that of 'mouthful'.]

†**1. a.** A part, portion, piece, fragment of anything which is divided, cut, or broken. *Obs.*

c **1320** R. Brunne *Medit.* 85 Alle yn smale gobettes he hyt kytte. **1382** Wyclif *Matt.* xiv. 20 And thei token the relifis of broken gobetis twelue cofyns ful. [So Tyndale and Bible of **1551**.] *c* **1386** Chaucer *Prol.* 696 He seyde he hadde a gobet of the seyl That seint Peter hadde. *c* **1420** *Chron. Vilod.* 4508 For by help of þat mayde so fulle of grace His fedrys [= fetters] weron alle to gobetus y-broke. **1483** Caxton *Gold. Leg.* 66 b/2 And he wente to Saul and cutte of a gobet of his mantel. **1532** More *Confut. Tindale* Wks. 614/1 Ther is nothing but a memorial of his passion in a cup of wyne & a gobbet of cake bread. **1538** Bp. Shaxton *Injunct.* A iv, Suche thinges as be set forth..vnder the name of holy relyques..Namely..gobbettes of wodde vnder ye name of percelles of the holy crosse [etc.]. **1562** Bulleyn *Dial. Soarnes & Chir.* 22 a, Looke seriously, that no shiuer nor gobet of bone be lefte in the wounde. **1577** B. Googe *Heresbach's Husb.* iv. (1586) 160 b, Others againe doe cut Garlike in gobbettes. **1610** [see gobonated]. **1684** T. Burnet *Th. Earth* i. 291 If a rock or mountain cannot.. divide it self, either into great gobbets, or into small powder [etc.]. **1847–78** Halliwell s.v., A large block of stone is called a gobbet by workmen.

b. *spec.* A piece of raw flesh; mostly pl. in phrases ***to cut*** (***chop, hack,*** etc.) ***in*** or ***into gobbets.***

c **1320** R. Brunne *Medit.* 85 Thys lomb toke vp cryst Ihesus..Alle yn smale gobettes he hyt kytte. *c* **1400** Maundev. (1839) xxvi. 309 The Prestes..smyten alle the Body of the dede man in peces..And then the Preestes casten the gobbets of the Flesche [etc.]. *c* **1450** *Mirour Saluacioun* 181 When he his fadirs body efter deth vnherthid And made it in gobbets kitt. **1513** Douglas *Æneis* iv. xi. 32 Mycht I nocht caucht and rent in pecis his cors, Syne swak the gobbatis in the sey. **1544** Phaer *Regim. Lyfe* (1546) L vj, Two or thre yonge cattes, wel chopped in smal gobbettes. **1615** Markham *Eng. Housew.* ii. ii. (1668) 64 Put in good thick gobbets of well fed Beef..also like gobbets of the best Mutton. **1849** Thoreau *Week Concord Riv.* 235 Small red bodies, little bundles of red tissue—mere gobbets of venison. **1862** Sir H. Taylor *St. Clement's Eve* i. ii. Wks. 1864 III. 114 We'd slice them into gobbets And fling their flesh to the dogs.

c. *fig.*

1393 Langl. *P. Pl.* C. vi. 100 So hope ich to haue of hym þat is al-myghty A gobet of hus grace. *c* **1440** *Jacob's Well* (E.E.T.S.) 181 And loke, þi schryfte be hole to oo preest, & noȝt to manye; on gobet told to oon preest, an-oþer gobet told to an-oþer preest, is noȝt goodly. **1550** Bale *Apol.* 73 Now wil I English..your ragged gobbettes taken out of Ambrose glose. **1659** *No Sacril. to purchase Ch. Lands* 79 Found it most seasonable to cut large gobbets out of their estates.

d. A piece of a literary or musical work removed from its context; *spec.* an extract from a text set for translation or comment.

1912 *Punch* 6 Mar. 173/1 He'll gorge you with gobbets of Homer. **1930** D. L. Sayers *Strong Poison* 160 Playing the most ghastly tripe, sandwiched in with snacks of Mendelssohn and torn-off gobbets of the 'Unfinished'.

†**2.** A lump or mass. **a.** In general; chiefly, a lump of metal, esp. gold (cf. gob *sb.*¹ 1). *Obs.*

c **1374** Chaucer *Boeth.* ii. metr. v. 51 Allas what was he þat first dalf vp þe gobets or þe weyȝtys of gold couered vnder erþe. **1382** Wyclif *Ecclus.* xxii. 18 Grauel, and salt, and a gobet of iren. *c* **1430** *Pilgr. Lyf. Manhode* ii. xc. (1869) 108 Annoye of lyf that..dulleth the folk, riht as a gobet of led. *c* **1550** *Disc. Common Weal Eng.* (1893) 124 Everye tenaunte had his landes, not all in one gobbet in everye feilde. *c* **1580** Jefferie *Bugbears* i. iii. in *Archiv Stud. d. neu. Spr.* (1897) XCVIII. 313 For your daughters dowry you must save and spare: it is a good round gobett.

†**b.** Of coagulated or solidified substances, as clay, mud, ice, fat, blood, etc. *Obs.*

1382 Wyclif *Rom.* ix. 21 Wher a pottere of clay hath not power of the same gobet [L. *massa*] for to make sothli o vessel into honour [etc.]. **1388** —— *Josh.* iii. 13 The watris that comen fro aboue schulen stonde togidere in o gobet [**1382** glob]. **1481** Caxton *Reynard* (Arb.) 100 She was lyke the deuyls doughter, and on her chyldren hynge moche fylth cloterd in gobettis. **1576** Baker *Jewell of Health* 181 a, This powder then set in the sunne, untyll it cleaveth together in gobbettes or bygge pieces. *c* **1586** C'tess Pembroke *Ps.* cxlvii. v, Gross icy gobbetts from his hand he flings. **1602** Plat *Delightes for Ladies* (1605) 54 Keepe your sugar alwaies in good temper in the bason, that it burne not into lumpes or gobbets. **1625** Hart *Anat. Ur.* ii. iv. 73 He sent me a little ..dish almost halfe full of gobbets of..clotted bloud. **1662** J. Chandler *Van Helmont's Oriat.* 195 After what manner ..*Aqua vitæ* may be truly changed into a yellow gobbet or lump. **1712** tr. *Pomet's Hist. Drugs* I. 105 Green glass Fritt ..is a Composition made of..common Ashes..or else of Gobbets ground to a fine Powder.

†**3. a.** A portion to be swallowed; a large lump or mouthful of food; *spec.* a ball of flour, etc. used in feeding poultry [= F. *gobbe*]. *Obs.*

1382 Wyclif *Dan.* xiv. 26 Danyel toke picche, and fatnesse, and heris, and seethide to gydre; and he made gobettis, and ȝaue into mouthe of the dragoun. *c* **1420** *Pallad. on Husb.* i. 732 Of figis grounde and watir temprid, sclendir Gobbettis yef thy gees. **1600** Holland *Livy* (1609) Index ii. 1424 When they [chickens] pecked either corne, or gobbets called *offæ.* **1657** Trapp *Comm. Job* xx. 15 Like as Camels are fed by casting gobbets into their mouth. **1739** 'R. Bull' tr. *Dedekindus' Grobianus* 130 Large Gobbets choak the tender Fowls. **1814** Lamb *Let. to Coleridge* 26 Aug., May it burst his pericranium, as the gobbets of fat and turpentine ..did that old dragon in the Apocrypha!

fig. **1634** Sanderson *Serm.* II. 291 These gobbets are but Satans baits: which when we swallow, we swallow a hook with them. **1849** Lowell *Biglow P.* Poet. Wks. (1879) 189/1 Doubtless that they might be hereafter incapacitated for swallowing the filthy gobbets of Mahound. **1862** *Sat. Rev.* 6 Sept. 275 One dwells with lingering delight on these unctuous and mouth-filling gobbets.

†**b.** *attrib.* quasi-*adj.*

1714 *Orig. Canto Spencer* xxi, For this their Office good, the Sorcerer Forth from a Wallet which beside him hung, Threw many gobbet Offals of good Cheer.

c. A lump of half-digested food. Also *fig.*
1553 T. Wilson *Rhet.* 67 b, If a gentleman..should vomite..and..caste oute gobbets. 1590 Spenser *F.Q.* i. i. 20. 1594 J. Dickenson *Arisbas* (1878) 75 From depth of poisnous mawe the monster fierce Did belch foule gobbets. *c* 1645 Howell *Lett.* I. i. xxvii, They would make us believe..that Ætna in times pass'd hath eructated such huge gobbets of fire, that [etc.]. 1700 Addison *3rd Æneid* Misc. Wks. 1726 I. 61 Belching raw gobbets from his maw, o'rcharged. 1866 Conington tr. *Æneid* iii. 96 Ejecting from his monstrous maw Wine mixed with gore and gobbets raw.

†**gobbet**, *v.* *Obs.* Also 4–5 **gobete**, 5 **gobette**. [a. OF. *gobeter* to swallow as a morsel or gobbet (mod.F. *gobeter* to point a wall), but in some examples prob. f. GOBBET *sb.*]

1. *trans.* To swallow as a gobbet or in gobbets. Also with *down*, *up*.
1607 C. Lever *Crucifix* cix. (Grosart) 51 To gobbet up a supper at a bit. 1647 R. Stapylton *Juvenal* 275 They gobbet downe his flesh, his bones they gnaw, And are most highly pleas'd to eate him raw. 1692 R. L'Estrange *Fables* iv. (1714) 4 Down comes a Kite Powdering upon them in the Interim, and Gobbets up both together.

2. To divide into portions or gobbets; given by some writers (following the Book of St. Albans) as the correct term for cutting up a trout.
c 1450 *Two Cookery-bks.* ii. 112 Nym lings, turbot, and elys, & gobete hem in mosselys. 1486 *Bk. St. Albans* F vij b, A Trought gobettid. 1670 Covel *Diary* (Hakluyt Soc.) 262 Minc't meat, gobbeted in vine leaves. 1726 *Gentl. Angler* 149 To Gobbet a Trout, *i.e.* To cut it up.

†**'gobbetly**, *adv.* *Obs. rare.* [f. GOBBET *sb.* + -LY².] In gobbets or pieces, piecemeal.
1552 Huloet, Gobetly or in pieces, *frustratim, incisim.*

†**'gobbetmeal**, *adv.* *Obs.* In 4 **gobetmele**, 5 **gobettmale**, 5–6 **gob(b)et-meale**. [f. GOBBET *sb.* + -MEAL.] In gobbets; piecemeal.
1382 Wyclif *2 Macc.* xv. 33 He comaundide the tunge of vnpitous Nychanore kitt off, for to be ȝouen to briddis gobetmele. 1387 Trevisa *Higden* (Rolls) IV. 103 His fader was i-slawe..and i-þrowe out gobetmele [L. *membratim*] traytoursliche by preostes. *c* 1425 *Found. St. Bartholomew's* (E.E.T.S.) 22 Yn that the schippe with the rochis schulde be gobettemele be mynusid. 1494 Fabyan *Chron.* iii. lv. 36 Armager..slewe the forenamed Hamo..and hym, so slayne, threwe gobetmeale into the same see. 1540 Palsgr. *Acolastus* ii. iv. M iv, The praye..shall be toren in pieces with our nayles gobbet meale.

†**'gobbet-royal**. *Obs.* In 4 **gobetreall, reale, ryal**. [app. a. F. **gobet reial* royal tit-bit: see GOBBET and ROYAL *a.*] Some kind of sweetmeat.
1361–2 *Durham Acct. Rolls* (Surtees) 126 Cofyns de anys confyt et gobetes reale. 1390–1 *Earl Derby's Exped.* (Camden) 19 Pro ij lb. gobete real, ij. s. 1399–1400 *Durham MS. Burs. Roll*, Anis comfeth, et gobet ryal.

gobbin ('gɒbɪn). *Coal-mining.* [dialectal pronunc. of GOBBING *vbl. sb.* But cf. GUBBINS.] (See quot. *a* 1843 and cf. GOB *sb.*⁴)
1839 Ure *Dict. Arts* 980 In such powerful beds the Shropshire method is impracticable from want of gobbin. *a* 1843 Southey *Comm.-pl. Bk.* IV. 407 The refuse of Collieries called Gobbins in some districts. 1867 W. W. Smyth *Coal & Coal-mining* 143 Others will bend gently down to the refuse or gobbin.

gobbin, var. GOBBON *sb.*, *Obs.*

gobbing ('gɒbɪŋ), *vbl. sb.*¹ *Coal-mining.* [f. GOB *sb.*⁴] The action of packing an excavated space with waste rock; the material used for this.
1839 Ure *Dict. Arts* 979 The miners secure the waste by gobbing. 1881 Raymond *Mining Gloss.*, *Gobbing*, packing with waste rock. See *Stowing*.

gobbing, *vbl. sb.*² and *ppl. a.*: see GOB *v.*²

gobbit, obs. Sc. f. GOBBET *sb.*

gobble ('gɒb(ə)l), *sb.* *Golf.* [Prob. f. next vb.] A rapid straight 'putt' into the hole.
1878 'Capt. Crawley' *Football*, etc. 83 (Golf) *Gobble*, a straight quick put at the hole. 1890 Hutchinson *Golf* (Badm. Libr.) 241 The other may play, with a free hand, for a 'gobble'.

gobble ('gɒb(ə)l), *v.*¹ Not now in dignified use. Also 7 **goble, gobbel**. [Of obscure origin; prob. a vague formation on GOB *sb.*¹ or *sb.*², with suggestion of the sound made by noisy swallowing.]

1. *trans.* To swallow hurriedly in large mouthfuls, esp. in a noisy fashion. Often with adv., esp. ***to gobble up, down***, formerly †*in*. Also *fig.*
1601 Holland *Pliny* I. 516 Birds being hungrie, haue greedily gobled vp seed and fruit whole and sound. 1608 Topsell *Serpents* (1658) 602 Then they suddenly goble in the beast or meat before them, without any great ado. 1611 Coryat (*title*), Crudities hastily gobled vp in five Moneths trauells in France [etc.]. 1621 Burton *Anat. Mel.* ii. ii. i. ii, That which he doth eat, must be well chewed, and not hastily gobbeled. 1729 Swift *Lady's Jrnl.* 276 The Supper gobbled up in haste, Again afresh to Cards they run. 1742 Blair *Grave* 646 And thousands at each hour thou gobblest up. 1791 Wolcot (P. Pindar) *Rights Kings* Wks. 1812 II. 393 How he gobbles down the broth and meal. 1826 T. Jefferson *Writ.* (1830) IV. 437 To sell it..not to have it gobbled up by speculators. 1845 Hood *Fairy Tale* ii, A stray horse came, and gobbled up his bower. 1865 G. Macdonald *A. Forbes* 21 They gobbled down their breakfasts with all noises except articulate ones. 1882 A. Clark in *Med. Temp. Jrnl.* No. 51. 132, I get home and gobble a hurried dinner.

2. *U.S. slang.* To seize upon graspingly or greedily; to snatch up, lay hold of, 'collar'.
1825 J. Neal *Bro. Jonathan* III. 144 He thought of poor Olive; sprang up—gobbled on the clothes..and set off. 1851 B. H. Hall *College Wds.*, *Gobble*, at Yale College, to seize; to lay hold of; to appropriate; nearly the same as to *collar* q.v. 1861 *Chicago Evening Post* July (Cent.), Nearly four hundred prisoners were gobbled up after the fight, and any quantity of ammunition and provisions. 1888 H. James in *Harper's Mag.* Feb. 344, I happen to know..that the moment Mr. Pringle should propose to my daughter she would gobble him down.

3. *Comb.*, as **gobble-gut** (*obs.* or *vulgar*), a glutton; **gobble-stitch**, a stitch made too long through haste or carelessness.
1632 Sherwood, A *goble-gut, *gobequinaut, goulard.* *a* 1845 Hood *A blow-up*, Miss M. the milliner—her fright so strong—Made a great *gobble-stitch, six inches long. 1859 F. E. Paget *Cur. Cumberworth* 47 A dilapidated green silk parasol..darned in divers places with a sort of gobble-stitch of the same scarlet worsted which adorned her frill.

Hence **'gobbling** *vbl. sb.* Also **'gobbler**.
1632 Sherwood, A gobling, *goulardise.* 1755 Johnson *Gobbler*, one that devours in haste; a gormand; a greedy eater. 1852 *Q. Rev.* Mar. 431 An alderman and a greedy gossiping gobbler. 1873 Helps *Anim. & Mast.* iii. (1875) 63 Sir Arthur and Milverton are gobblers of books. 1883 *Harper's Mag.* Dec. 4/2 Christmas..was all guzzling and gobbling.

gobble ('gɒb(ə)l), *v.*² [Imitative, but perh. suggested by prec.] *intr.* Of a turkey-cock: To make its characteristic noise in the throat; also rarely *transf.* Also quasi-*trans.* with *out*, *over*.
Imitative variations (nonce-wds.) are *gob-gobble* vb. (Southey *Doctor* I. 119) and *goblobling* vbl. sb. (Bage *Barham Downs* I. 126).
1680 Morden *Geog. Rect.* (1685) 495 When they speak they gobble like Turkie Cocks. 1709 Prior *Ladle* 74 Fat Turkeys gobbling at the Door. 1774 Goldsm. *Nat. Hist.* V. ii. iv. 181 He..struts about the yard, and gobbles out a note of self-approbation. 1820 W. Irving *Sketch Bk.* II. 365 Regiments of turkeys were gobbling through the farm yard. 1862 Sala *Seven Sons* I. ix. 210 The turkeys that gobbled over the scandal of the poultry-yard. 1892 R. Kipling in *Pall Mall G.* 24 Mar. 3/1 A tiny geyser gobbled.

Hence **'gobbling** *vbl. sb.* and *ppl. a.*; **'gobble** *sb.*, the noise made by a turkey-cock; **'gobbler**, a turkey-cock; also **'gobblery**, turkey-cocks collectively.
1737 Bailey vol. II. *Canting Words*, *Gobbler*, a Turkey-Cock. 1774 Goldsm. *Nat. Hist.* V. ii. iv. 180 The turkey cock..with his peculiar gobbling sound, flies to attack it. 1781 Pennant in *Phil. Trans.* LXXI. 69 On being interrupted they fly into great rages, and change their notes into a loud and guttural gobble. 1784 Wesley *Wks.* (1872) XIII. 502 He heard as it were the gobbling of a turkey-cock close to the bed-side. 1798 Sotheby tr. *Wieland's Oberon* (1826) I. 50 When cocks at dayspring crow, Then all the goblery..Soon as they [etc.]. 1835 Marryat *Jac. Faith.* xlvi, The poultry, who would now and then raise a gobble. 1843 Haliburton *Attaché* I. xi. 197, I never see an old gobbler, with his gorget, that I don't think of a kernel of a marchin' regiment. 1871 Darwin *Desc. Man.* II. xiii. 60 When the female of the wild turkey utters her call in the morning, the male answers by a different note from the gobbling noise which he makes. 1885 *Harper's Mag.* Apr. 706/1 The..turkey-tail fan..she had had made from one of her own..gobblers. 1898 *Speaker* 3 Sept. 286/2 Scratching hens and gobbling turkeys.

gobbledygook ('gɒb(ə)ldɪˌgʊk, -ˌguːk). orig. *U.S.* Also **gobbledegook**. [Prob. repr. a turkey-cock's gobble.] Official, professional, or pretentious verbiage or jargon.
1944 *Amer. N. & Q.* Apr. 9/1 Gobbledygook talk: Maury Maverick's name for the long high-sounding words of Washington's red-tape language. 1944 M. Maverick in *N.Y. Times Mag.* 21 May 11/1 Just before Pearl Harbor, I ..got my baptism under 'gobbledygook'..its definition: talk or writing which is long, pompous, vague, involved, usually with Latinized words. It is also talk or writing which is merely long. 1945 *Tuscaloosa* (Ala.) *News* 7 Aug. 4/3 The explanations sound like gobbledegook to me. 1947 *Time* 7 July 7/1 The Veterans Administration translated its bureaucratic gobbledygook. 1950 'S. Ransome' *Deadly Miss Ashley* ii. 16 It now seemed a tricked-up system of gobbledegook wherein justice had foundered. 1951 Wodehouse *Old Reliable* vii. 94 You insult my intelligence by trying to put gobbledy-gook like that over me. 1959 M. Dolinsky *There is no Silence* i. 5, I had been subjected to too much psychiatric gobbledygook. 1968 M. Black *Labyrinth of Lang.* vi. 124 Jargon (or 'gobbledygook', to use the more expressive term).

gobblin(g, obs. form of GOBLIN¹.

gobbock, var. GABBOCK.

†**gobbon**, *sb.* *Obs.* Forms: 4–5 **goboun**, 5 **gobyn**, (? **gobene**), 5–6 **gobone**, 6 **gobbon**, (**-in**), **gowbin**, **gubbon**. See also GUBBINS. [Presumably a. OF. **gobon*, an unrecorded form related to *gobbe* and *gobet*: see GOB *sb.*¹ and GOBBET, and cf. GOBONATED, GOBONY.]

1. A portion, slice, gobbet.
1387 Trevisa *Higden* (Rolls) IV. 155 Gobouns of chayers, of formes, and of stooles [L. *fragmentis subselliorum*]. 14.. *Noble Bk. Cookry* (1882) 34 Chope the pik when he is slit out and let the gebenes [? *read* gobenes] hong eche by othere. *c* 1460 J. Russell *Bk. Nurture* 580 þey must be takyn of as þey in þe dische lowt, bely & bak by gobyn þe boon to pike owt. 1513 *Bk. Keruynge* in *Babees Bk.* (1868) 281 Than cut a gobone of the lampraye, & mynce the gobone thynne. 1555 W. Watreman *Fardle Facions* ii. viii. 178 Leauing no element vnransaked to gette a gowbin for their glotenous gorge. 1578 Lyte *Dodoens* iii. xxiv. 348 The same [roote] cut into gobbins or slices, and put into fistulas, taketh away the hardnesse of them. 1583 T. Stocker *Civ. Warres Lowe C.* i. 130 Rootes and skinnes cut in small gobbins, and sodden in butter mylke.

2. = GOB *sb.*¹ 1 b.
1548 Thomas *Ital. Dict.* (1567), *Farfalloni*, gubbons of fleame that olde men vse to spitte. 1598 Florio, *Farfallone*, the filthie snot of ones nose or gubbon of fleame.

†**gobbon**, *v.* *Obs.* [f. prec.] *trans.* To cut into gobbets.
? *a* 1400 *Morte Arth.* 4165 þay gobone of þe gretteste with growndone swerdes. 1513 *Bk. Keruynge* in *Babees Bk.* (1868) 280 A salte lampraye, gobone it flatte in .vii. or .viii. peces.

gobby ('gɒbɪ). *slang.* [Said to be f. dial. and vulgar *gob* expectoration + -Y⁶.] (See quot. 1929.)
1890 in Farmer & Henley *Slang* III. 168/1 When a meeting takes place the men indulge in a protracted yarn and a draw of the pipe. The session involves a considerable amount of expectoration all round, whereby our friends come to be known as gobbies. 1904 Kipling *Traffics & Discoveries* 126 Think o' her Number One chasin' the mobilised gobbies round the lower deck flats. 1929 F. Bowen *Sea Slang* 58 *Gobby*, in the British Navy, a coastguard, or in the old days a quarterdeckman. In the American, any bluejacket.

Gobelin (‖gɔblɛ̃, 'gɒbəlɪn). Also **Gobelins**. [f. *Gobelins*, the state-factory of tapestry in Paris, so named after its founders.]

1. Used *attrib.*, as in ***Gobelin tapestry***, the tapestry made at the Gobelins, and imitations of this; also *ellipt.*; ***Gobelin blue***, a blue like that used in Gobelin tapestry; ***Gobelin stitch*** (see quot. 1882).
1788 A. Young *Travels* 10 Oct. (1792) 98 Four fine tablets of the Gobelin tapestry. 1802 C. Wilmot *Let.* 31 Jan. (1920) 44, I tell you of the 'Gobelins tapestry' which we went to see. *Ibid.* 19 June 72 The apartments were hung over with fine Gobelins. 1817 M. Edgeworth *Harrington* I. xv. 399 The gobelin tapestry of the back drawing-room. 1823 W. Irving *Life & Lett.* (1864) II. 134 Dinner served up in room where there is very good Gobelin tapestry. 1864 Sala *Quite Alone* I. xiv. 218 You saw the beautiful Gobelins tapestry, marvellous in the minute finish of its work. 1882 Caulfeild & Saward *Dict. Needlework* s.v. *Embroidery*, *Gobelin Stitch*, a short upright stitch, also called Tapestry.

2. *absol.* 'A variety of damask used for upholstery, made of silk and wool or silk and cotton' (*Cent. Dict.*).

gobelin, obs. form of GOBLIN¹.

‖**gobemouche** (gɔbəmuʃ). [a. F. *gobe-mouches* (f. *gober* to swallow + *mouche* fly) flycatcher (bird and plant), credulous person.
In F. *gobe-mouches* is the form employed for both sing. and pl., though Littré points out that *gobe-mouche* might be written, on the analogy of *chasse-mouche*. English writers treat the Fr. form as a pl. and use *gobemouche* for the sing.]

One who credulously accepts all news, however improbable or absurd. Also *attrib.*
1818 E. Blaquiere tr. *Sig. Panänti* 52 Such a representation the *gobes mouches* [*sic* incorrectly] of Florence might have readily magnified into a change of religion. 1837 Thackeray *Ravenswing* vii, 'You don't say so!' says gobemouche Fitz-Urse. 1844 Kinglake *Eöthen* (1847) 49 The gobemouche expression of countenance with which he is swallowing an article in the National. 1845 Ford *Handbk. Spain* i. 43 Their idle stories are often believed by the gobemouche class of book-making travellers. 1884 *Pall Mall G.* 19 Aug. 3 Those Continental gobemouches whose gift for believing the incredible almost approaches to genius.

gobet, gobett, obs. forms of GOBBET.

'go-beˌtween. [f. GO *v.* + BETWEEN *adv.*]

1. One who passes to and fro between parties, with messages, proposals, etc.; an intermediary.
In the second quot. *between* serves as a prep.
1598 Shaks. *Merry W.* ii. ii. 273 Euen as you came in to me, her assistant or goe-betweene, parted from me. 1631 Massinger *Emperor East* i. ii, You are The Squire of Dames, deuoted to the seruice Of gamesome Ladies..the Goe-between This female, and that wanton Sir. 1641 Milton *Animadv.* 63 They onely are the internuntio's, or the go-betweens of this trim devis'd mummery. 1710 Steele *Tatler* No. 225 ⁋1 The Broker..as a Go-between.. shall find his Account in being in the good Graces of a Man of Wealth. 1836–48 B. D. Walsh *Aristoph.* 281 *note*, Certain convenient old women, who officiated as go-betweens. 1887 Jessopp *Arcady* viii. 227 The clerk was..a sort of go between when parson and people were a little out of gear.

2. Anything that goes between or connects two other things. Also *attrib.*
1862 H. Marryat *Year in Sweden* II. 371 Each double window vies with its neighbour in the taste of its go-betweens. 1853 Herschel *Pop. Lect. Sci.* vii. §7 (1873) 305 If they are exactly equal, the go-between ball will carry off all the motion of the ball which strikes it. 1886 C. Scott *Sheep Farming* 13 Altogether they form a sort of go-between sheep, dividing the Lowlands from the Highlands. 1895 *Pop. Sci. Monthly* Apr. 768 This is the limpkin..a most perfect go-between connecting the rails and the cranes.

gobiid (ˈgəʊbɪɪd), *a.* and *sb.* [f. L. *gōbi-us* GOBY + -ID.] **A.** *adj.* Belonging to the *Gobiidæ* or gobies proper. **B.** *sb.* One of the *Gobiidæ*; a goby.
1884–5 *Riverside Nat. Hist.* (1888) III. 257 On the Californian coast is a Gobiid (*Gillichthys mirabilis*) remarkable for the great extension backward of the jaws.

gobiiform (ˈgəʊbɪɪfɔːm), *a.* [f. mod.L. *gōbi-us* GOBY + -(I)FORM.] Having the characteristics of the gobiids; gobioid (*Cent. Dict.*).

gobioid (ˈgəʊbɪɔɪd), *a.* (*sb.*) *Ichthyol.* [f. L. *gōbi-us* GOBY + -OID.] **A.** *adj.* Belonging to the family *Gobioides* of Cuvier or to the superfamily *Gobioidea* of more recent systems, comprising fishes allied to the Goby. **B.** *sb.* A fish of this kind.
1854 OWEN *Circ. Sci., Organ. Nat.* I. 273 Sciænoids, cottoids, gobioids. **1880** GÜNTHER *Fishes* 111 In some Gobioids..the eyes..can be elevated and depressed at the will of the fish.

goblet[1] (ˈgɒblɪt). Forms: 4 gobelet, goblot, 5–6 goblett, 6 gublett-, gobbelett-, 7 gobblet, 5– goblet. [a. OF. *gobelet* (in 13th c. *gubulet*), f. *gobel*, *gobeau* cup, of uncertain origin.]
1. A drinking-cup of metal or glass, properly bowl-shaped and without handles, sometimes mounted on a foot and fitted with a cover. In later use, a general term for a wine-cup. Now only *arch.*
13.. *E.E. Allit. P.* B. 1277 Þe gredirne & þe goblotes garnyst of syluer. ?*a* **1400** *Morte Arth.* 207 The kyngez cope-borde was closed in silver, In grete gobilettez overgylte. **1481–90** *Howard Househ. Bks.* (Roxb.) 422 Item, for sawdyring and gyltyng of a goblett, with the kever, price iiij.*s.* **1552** *Bury Wills* (Camden) 144 Thre gilt goblettes wᵗ the cover. **1600** SHAKS. *A.Y.L.* III. iv. 26, I doe thinke him as concaue as a couered goblet, or a Worme-eaten nut. **1682** MILTON *Hist. Mosc.* Wks. 1738 II. 143 A Cupboard of huge and massy goblets, and other Vessels of gold and silver. **1703** POPE *Thebais* 634 The banquet done, the monarch gives the sign To fill the goblet high with sparkling wine. **1756–7** tr. *Keysler's Trav.* (1760) III. 366 A large round porphyry vessel..It consists of one piece, and resembles a shallow goblet. **1814** SCOTT *Wav.* xi, The Baron..produced a golden goblet of a singular and antique appearance, moulded into the shape of a rampant bear. **1849** MACAULAY *Hist. Eng.* iv. I. 449 He..filled a goblet to the brim with wine. **1871** B. TAYLOR *Faust* (1875) I. vi. 108 Give us a goblet of the well known juice!
†**b.** (See quot.) *Obs.*
1688 R. HOLME *Armoury* III. 271/2 A kind of a Drinking Cup..made of the small top of a Bull or Cows Horn, the Tip end Reversed..It is by some Gentlemens Buttlers termed a Souce, or Gogles, or Goblet.
c. A glass with a foot and stem, as distinguished from a tumbler.
Marked 'U.S.' in the *Century Dict.*; but current in England in tradesmen's price lists.
d. *transf.* A goblet-shaped part of a flower.
1851 *Beck's Florist* July 163 The Cephalote, from the Australian bogs, whose delicate goblets reared their richly-carved and many-tinted crests above their bed of moss.
†**2.** A conical cup or thimble used by conjurers. (So F. *gobelet.*) *Obs.*
1519 HORMAN *Vulg.* 280 The iugler carieth clenly vnder his gublettis. **1529** MORE *Dyaloge* I. Wks. 153/1 Excepte ye thinke the iugler blow his galles through the gobletes bottom. **1552** HULOET, Goblet or boxe for a iugler, *acetabulum.* **1692** QUICK *Synodicon* I. 194 To that Article of Players and Mummers, shall be added Juglers, Players of Hocus-pocus, Tricks of Goblets, Puppet-playing [etc.].
3. *Sc.* A kind of deep saucepan with bulging sides and a straight handle.
†**4.** Some kind of embossed ornament on a gauntlet. *Obs.*⁻¹
?*a* **1400** *Morte Arth.* 913 His gloues..grauene at þe hemmez, With graynez and gobelets, glorious of hewe.
5. *attrib.* and *Comb.*, as ***goblet-boy***, ***-glass***, ***-pledge***; ***goblet-shaped*** adj.; **goblet-cell**, 'an epithelial cell of crateriform shape' (*Cent. Dict.*); **goblet-office** *nonce-wd.* [= F. *le gobelet*] (see quot.).
1800 MOORE *Anacreon* xxxii. 6 Young Love shall be my *goblet-boy. **1878** BELL tr. *Gegenbaur's Comp. Anat.* 525 These structures which are also known as gustatory *goblet-cells. **1851** MRS. BROWNING *Casa Guidi W.* 125 Here's *goblet-glass, to take in with your wine The very sun its grapes were ripened under. **1653** URQUHART *Rabelais* I. xviii, Bring them to the *goblet-office, which is the Buttery, and there make them drink. **1850** MRS. BROWNING *Wine of Cyprus* 6 The Cyprus..I am sipping..At the hour of *goblet-pledge. **1854** MAYNE *Expos. Lex.*, *Goblet-shaped. See *Scyphiform.* **1866** *Treas. Bot.*, *Goblet-shaped*, the same as Crateriform. **1878** BELL tr. *Gegenbaur's Comp. Anat.* 524 A number of goblet-shaped organs.
Hence **ˈgobleted** *a.* = *goblet-shaped*; †**ˈgobleter**, a cup-bearer; **ˈgobletful**, the quantity required to fill a goblet.
1541 R. COPLAND *Guydon's Formul.* Y iij, Admynyste a gobletful when he goth to bed, and he shal slepe. **1623** tr. *Favine's Theat. Hon.* II. xiii. 237 Gobletters and Butlers to Apollo. **1869** BLACKMORE *Lorna D.* xix. (ed. 12) 110 Moss was in abundant life, some feathering, and some gobleted. **1883** C. F. HOLDER in *Harper's Mag.* Jan. 182/2 A goblet-ful of the noctilucæ produces light sufficient to read by at a distance of two feet.

†**goblet**[2]. *Obs.* = GOBBET *sb.* (possibly a misprint).
1530 PALSGR. 225/2 Goblet, a lumpe or a pece, *monceau.* **1654** GAYTON *Pleas. Notes* III. v. 101 Sighing often betwixt the goblets, for the inability of his Mandibles. **1688** R. HOLME *Armoury* III. 293/2 The Goblet or Country Pye, is made of large pieces of Flesh..which large or square pieces, are termed Goblets. **1742** PERRY in *Phil. Trans.* XLII. 48 It ..seem'd as if Goblets of Fat were fluctuating in it.

goblin[1] (ˈgɒblɪn). Forms: 4 gobelin, -olyn, 4–5 -elyn, 7 gobling, gobblin(g, 6– goblin. [a. F. *gobelin* (obs., recorded only from the 16th c.; but in the 12th c. Ordericus Vitalis mentions *Gobelinus* as the popular name of a spirit which haunted the neighbourhood of Évreux). Perh. f. med.L. *cobalus, covalus*, a. Gr. κόβαλος a rogue, knave, κόβαλοι wicked sprites invoked by rogues.]
1. A mischievous and ugly demon.
a **1327** *Pol. Songs* (Camden) 238 Sathanas..Seyde on is sawe Gobelyn made is gerner Of gromene mawe. **1388** WYCLIF *Ps.* xc. 6 Of an arowe fliynge in the dai, of a gobelyn goynge in derknessis. *a* **1400–50** *Alexander* 5492 Gamarody þe goblyn, anothire grym sire. *c* **1500** *Melusine* i. 4 Many manyeres of thinges, the whiche somme called Gobelyns, the other ffayrees, and the other 'bonnes dames' or good ladyes. **1574** STUDLEY tr. *Bale's Pageant Popes* 73 b, They stirred vp walking spirits, bugs, goblins, fierye sightes, & diuers terrible goasts & shapes of thinges. **1600** FAIRFAX *Tasso* IX. xv. 162 The shriking gobblings each where howling flew, The Furies roare, the ghosts and Fairies yell. **1667** MILTON *P.L.* II. 688 To whom the Goblin [Death] full of wrath replied. **1742** COLLINS *Ode to Fear* 2 And goblins haunt from fire or fen, Or mine or flood, the walks of men. **1841** ELPHINSTONE *Hist. India* I. 179 Bhutas are evil spirits of the lowest order, corresponding to our ghosts and other goblins of the nursery. **1871** B. TAYLOR *Faust* (1875) II. I. iii. 37 From goblins that deceive you, I'm unable to relieve you.
fig. **1703** S. PARKER tr. *Eusebius* VI. 111 But this Goblin [a heresy] disappear'd in an instant. **1856** EMERSON *Eng. Traits, Wealth* Wks. (Bohn) II. 71 When to this labour and trade..was added this goblin of steam.
2. *attrib.* and *Comb.* **a.** attributive, passing into an adj. (of, pertaining to, or suitable for goblins), as ***goblin appearance***, ***cave***, ***cheek***, ***sport***, ***story***, ***word***; **b.** appositive, as ***goblin man***; **c.** instrumental, as ***goblin-haunted***, ***-peopled*** adjs.
1827 in Hone *Every-day Bk.* II. 551 The *goblin appearance of the 'Barguest'. **1810** SCOTT *Lady of L.* III. x, Coir-Kriskin, thy *goblin Cave! **1827** POLLOK *Course T.* IV. 178 Observe his *goblin cheek; his wretched eye. **1874** GREEN *Short Hist.* i. §2.12 The heap of *goblin-haunted stones. **1856** EMERSON *Eng. Traits, Ability* Wks. (Bohn) II. 34 Trolls—a kind of *goblin men. **1861** E. WAUGH *Goblin's Grave* 32 The *goblin-peopled-gloom. **1842** LYTTON *Zanoni* 22 That spirit-like life of sound which night after night threw itself in airy and *goblin sport over the starry seas. **1726–46** THOMSON *Winter* 619 Heard solemn, goes the *goblin story round, Till superstitious horror creeps o'er all. **1649** MILTON *Eikon.* 36 Setting aside the affrightment of this *Goblin word, *Demagogue.*
Hence **ˈgoblin** *v. trans.*, to convert into a goblin (*rare*); **ˈgoblinish** *a.*, goblin-like; **ˈgoblinism**, belief in goblins; **ˈgoblinize** *v.* = GOBLIN *v.* (above); **ˈgoblinry**, the acts or practices of goblins.
1829 SCOTT *Doom Devorgoil* III. i, My nether parts Are goblinized. *Ibid.*, Is there nothing, then, save rank imposture, In all these tales of goblinry. **1870** LOWELL *Among my Bks.* Ser. I. (1873) 118 Once goblinized, Herodias joins them. **1873** *Contemp. Rev.* XXII. 453 The nursery goblinism, grotesquerie, and allegoric wire-drawing, which are present in the *Divine Comedy.* **1883** P. S. ROBINSON *Sinners & Saints* 358 If the sunset was weird, the moonlight was positively goblinish. **1893** LELAND *Mem.* I. 53 Even deer and doves seemed uncanny and goblined.

†**goblin**[2] (ˈgɒblɪn). *Obs. slang.* Also o'goblin. [Shortened form of JEMMY O'GOBLIN.] A sovereign; twenty shillings.
1887 W. E. HENLEY *Poems* (1908) II. 231 Your merry goblins soon stravag. **1909** WODEHOUSE *Swoop* II. ii. 68 Come now, your Grand Grace, is it a deal? Four hundred and fifty chinking o'Goblins a week for one hall a night. **1925** —— *Carry on, Jeeves* iv. 99 Five hundred o'goblins a year.

gob-line: see GAUB[1].

goblinesque (ˌgɒblɪˈnɛsk), *a.* [f. GOBLIN + -ESQUE.] = GOBLINISH *a.*
1916 *Proc. Mus. Assoc.* 1915–16 106 The weird, goblinesque effect of the bass-clarinet accompanied by the celesta will be remembered. **1934** *Times Lit. Suppl.* 1 Feb. 65/3 The goblinesque figure of 'old Wicked-shifts', Henry Brougham.

goblot, gobolyn, obs. ff. GOBLET, GOBLIN[1].

gobo (ˈgəʊbəʊ). orig. *U.S.* [Origin unknown.] (See quots.)
1930 *Sel. Gloss. Motion Pict. Techn.* (*Acad. Motion Pict., Hollywood*) 15/2 *Gobo*, portable wall covered with sound-absorbing material. **1936** *Words* Oct. 6/2 A 'gobo' is a small black screen used to deflect light. **1970** *T.V. Times* (Austral.) 1 Apr. 8/3 A gobo is anything that goes between, e.g., the light and the set.

gobonated (ˈgɒbəʊneɪtɪd), *ppl. a. Her.* [f. med.L. **gobonāt-us* (f. *gobon* GOBBON) + -ED.] = GOBONY.
1486 *Bk. St. Albans, Her.* E iij b, Ther is an other bordure that is calde a bordure gobonatit..for hit is made of ij. coluris quadratli ioynyt, yᵗ is to say of blacke & white. **1610** GUILLIM *Heraldry* I. v. (1611) 21 Sometimes you shall finde Bordures gobonated of two colours..and such a bearing is so termed, because it is divided in such sort, as if it were cut into small Gobbets. **1661** MORGAN *Sph. Gentry* I. i. 7 So that while the four Elements were blended (as it were) it was checkered, and while they were divided from each other, they were Gobonated. **1718** NISBET *Ess. Armories* iii. 40 Within a Border Gobonated Argent and Gules. **1722–42** —— *Her.* II. 26 The Border Gobonated or Componee is now a Mark of Bastardy in Britain, by our late Practices. **1860** *Handbk. Ludlow* (1865) 77 Gobonated pearl and sapphire within a garter.

gobone, var. GOBBON *sb.*, *Obs.*

†**ˈgoboned**, *ppl. a. Obs. rare*⁻¹. [f. *gobon* GOBBON + -ED.] = GOBONY.
1572 BOSSEWELL *Armorie* II. 37 As this border is dented, so it maie be borne engraled, enuecked, goboned, vaire, etc. **1611** FLORIO, *Scaccáto*, checkie, gobonit, or counter componie in Armorie.

gobony (gəˈbəʊnɪ), *a. Her.* [f. as prec. + -Y.] = COMPONÉ. (Cf. quot. 1882 and GOBONATED.)
1611 FLORIO, *Scácchi*,..also checkie, gobony or counter-compony in armory. **1694** *Lond. Gaz.* No. 2986/4 The College Arms, which are France and England, quarterly with a Border Gobony [*printed* Gobong]. **1763** COLE *Coll. Top. & Gen.* (1837) IV. 48 A border gobony. **1838** *Family Crest Bk.* II. 54 Gobony, divided into squares by different colours. **1882** CUSSANS *Handbk. Her.* iv. (ed. 3) 67 A Bordure or other Ordinary composed of Metal and Colour alternately is termed Compony or Gobony.
Hence †**goˈbony** *v. trans.*, to make gobony.
1611 FLORIO, *Scaccheggiáre*,..to checkie to gobonie or counter-compony any coate of armes.

goboun, var. GOBBON *sb.*, *Obs.*

goburra (gəˈbʌrə). *Austral.* [See KOOKABURRA.] The bird Laughing-jackass, *Dacelo gigas.*
1862 H. C. KENDALL *Poems* 123 And wild goburras laughed aloud Their merry morning songs. **1870** F. S. WILSON *Austral. Songs* 167 The rude rough rhyme of the wild 'go-burra's' song.

goby (ˈgəʊbɪ). [ad. L. *gōbius, cōbius* (also *gōbio, cōbio*), a. Gr. κωβιός some small fish (usually rendered by its etymological equivalent GUDGEON). As modern scientific terms, the forms *Gobius* and *Gobio* denote quite unrelated fishes; for the latter see GUDGEON.] One of a genus (*Gobius*) of small acanthopterygian fishes having the ventral fins joined into a disk or sucker. Also more widely, a member of the family *Gobiidæ*.
1769 PENNANT *Zool.* III. 175 (*heading*), The Black Goby. **1770** *Phil. Trans.* LX. p. xiv, The spotted Goby. **1803** SHAW *Zool.* IV. 242 Arabian Goby. **1838** JOHNSTON in *Proc. Berw. Nat. Club* I. No. 6. 172 The Doubly-spotted Goby. **1854** BADHAM *Halieut.* 249 The gobies..possess a singular disk, formed by the union of the two thoracic ventrals. **1876** SMILES *Sc. Natur.* xiv. (ed. 4) 290 She sent home a specimen of the Black Goby or Rock-fish (Gobius niger). **1884** *Longm. Mag.* Mar. 523 There are several species of tropical gobies found very abundantly on the Indo-Pacific coasts.

go-by (ˈgəʊbaɪ). [f. GO *v.* + BY *adv.*]
1. The action of going by in various senses; the passing of a river, of time, or of a body from place to place. *Obs.* exc. in *nonce-uses.*
1673 EVELYN *Mem.* (1857) II. 92 Now growing into years, yet thinking little of this go-by. **1674** N. FAIRFAX *Bulk & Selv.* 100 All stirrings one and other are nothing but go-byes or shiftings of bodies. **1869** BLACKMORE *Lorna D.* vii, In the go-by of the river he is gone as a shadow goes.
b. *Coursing* and *Racing.* The action of getting in front of another dog or horse. (See also 3 a.)
1611 MARKHAM *Countr. Content.* I. vii. (1615) 105 If a coate shall be more than two turnes and a goe by, or the bearing of the Hare equall with two turnes. **1816** *Sporting Mag.* XLVII. 43 The other horse..determined not to be again surprised by a go-by. **1875** 'STONEHENGE' *Brit. Sports* I. III. viii. §3. 269 The Go-bye is where a greyhound starts a clear length behind his opponent, and yet passes him in a straight run, and gets a clear length before him.
2. *concr.* Something that 'goes by', or is superior to (something else). *rare.*
1823 *Examiner* 710/1 The Cataract of the Ganges amounts to a go-by to every thing that has preceded it.
3. Phr. ***to give*** (slang, †***to tip***) ***the go-by to***:
a. To outstrip, leave behind. (Cf. sense 1 b.) †Also, to leave.
1642 FULLER *Holy & Prof. St.* IV. xvii. 328 Who had rather others should make a ladder of his dead corps to scale a city by it, than a bridge of it whilest alive for his punies to give him the Goe-by, and passe over him to preferment. **1688** MIEGE *Gt. Fr. Dict.* II. *s.v.*, To give one the go-by in a Race. **1797** MARY ROBINSON *Walsingham* III. 260 What business have you in this lady's chamber?..Tip us the go-by, or I shall be apt to shew you the way. **1798** in *Spirit Publ. Jrnls.* (1799) II. 386 Does a man of fashion drive his curricle ..passing his competitors?..He is then said to 'Tip them the go-by'. **1825** *Sporting Mag.* XVI. 340 One dog gives another the go-by. **1833** *Blackw. Mag.* XXXIII. 846/2 We have given the go-by to our excellent friend Mitchelson's beautiful woods. **1835** SIR G. STEPHEN *Adv. Search Horse* xiv. (1841) 203 Eager to 'give it the go by', they put the horse to his speed.
b. To give the slip to, elude, escape from by artifice. †Also, to pass a deception on. *Obs.*
1659 B. HARRIS *Parival's Iron Age* 211 But the King, understanding of this division, gave Waller the go-by, returned towards Oxford [etc.] **1697** COLLIER *Ess. Mor.*

Subj. I. (1709) 70 Except an Apprentice is fully instructed how to Adulterate, and Vernish, and give you the Go-by upon occasion, his Master may be charged with Neglect. **1720** WELTON *Suffer. Son of God* I. ix. 211 He..found that they had not made for Jerusalem in their way Back, but had Given him the Go-by. **1836** MARRYAT *Midsh. Easy* xxxviii, We may give him the go-by by running through the Needles. **1886** STEVENSON *Kidnapped* ix. (1888) 74 A French ship..gave us the go-by in the fog.

c. To pass without notice, to disregard, slight; to 'cut' (a person); to evade (a difficulty). Also in *indirect pass.*

1654 [see GLOAT *sb.*[1]]. **1658–9** *Burton's Diary* (1828) III. 398 If they can give you the go-by in it, the issue is obvious. **1712** S. SEWALL *Diary* 22 Aug. (1879) II. 361 The Govr. speaks with some earnestness that we should not give the Ordinary Court the go-by, in taking off Entails. **1805** *Edin. Rev.* VI. 136 He gave the go-by to a multitude of toasts. **1833** *Blackw. Mag.* XXXIV. 987 In two of the Latin versions the difficulty is grappled with but not overcome; and in two it is given the go-by. **1848** THACKERAY *Van. Fair* xlviii, Becky..gave Mrs. Washington White the go-by in the Ring. **1862** BURTON *Bk. Hunter* II. 115 Successive licensers had given the work a sort of go-by. **1880** McCARTHY *Own Times* III. xlv. 382 It gave the go-by to such inconvenient questions. **1892** *Law Times* XCII. 156/2 A junior judge..sitting in another division, practically gives that order the go-by.

gobyn, var. GOBBON *sb.*, *Obs.*

'go-cart. [f. GO *v.* + CART.]

1. A light frame-work, without bottom, moving on castors or rollers, in which a child may learn to walk without danger of falling.

1689 PRIOR *Ep. to Shephard* 86 As young children, who are try'd in Go-carts, to keep their steps from sliding. **1711** STEELE *Spect.* No. 109 ¶4 The Ladies now walk as if they were in a Go-cart. **1800** MAR. EDGEWORTH *Belinda* (1832) I. v. 99 Put her into a hoop, and she looks as pitiful a figure.. as much a prisoner, as a child in a go-cart.
fig. **1710** MRS. MANLEY *Mem. Europe* I. 243 They.. Petitioned Cæsar, That he would be pleas'd to Reign alone. They ask'd that his Go Carts might be dismissed. **1847** EMERSON *Repr. Men, Napoleon* Wks. (Bohn) I. 377 All men know..that the institutions we so volubly commend are go-carts and baubles. **1879** E. GARRETT *House by Works* II. 11 The rest of us must be thankful for the little go-carts which help us to totter on the right way.

b. A child's carriage drawn by hand.

1854 THACKERAY *Newcomes* I. ii. 18 Upsetting his two little brothers in a go-cart. **1887** *Religious Herald* 24 Mar. (Cent.), I used to draw her to school on a go-cart nearly half a century ago.

2. Applied to a litter, palankeen, or the like.

1676 *Character Quack Doctor* in Strutt *Sports & Past.* (1876) 317 The Sultan Gilgal, being violently afflicted with a spasmus, came six hundred leagues to meet me in a go-cart. **1897** MARY KINGSLEY *W. Africa* 31, I got into a 'rickshaw, locally called a go-cart.

3. A hand-cart.

1759 GOLDSM. *Bee* No. 2 ¶12 She [Mrs. Roundabout] put me in mind of my Lord Bantam's sheep, which are obliged to have their monstrous tails trundled along in a go-cart. **1803** R. EDINGTON *Plan Penitentiary Ho.* 78 The waggons now used..are not much above the construction of go-carts, they have neither brakes to retard their motion down hill, nor aids to propel them up hill. **1838** F. W. SIMMS *Public Works Gt. Brit.* 65 The hand barrow or go-cart is used for the purpose of conveying earth.

4. A kind of light open carriage.

1828 *Sporting Mag.* XXI. 240 He started in a go-cart for Bracknell. **1837** W. B. ADAMS *Eng. Pleas. Carriages* xvii. 278 They all more or less bear a strong resemblance to the vehicles called 'go-carts', which ply for hire..in the neighbourhood of Lambeth. **1858** HUGHES *Scouring White Horse* vi. (1859) 122 A dozen parties, in all sorts of odd go-carts and other vehicles.

Hence †**go-carted** *ppl. a.*

1748 RICHARDSON *Clarissa* (1811) VIII. 246 The hanging-sleeved, go-carted property of hired slaves.

Goclenian (gəʊ'kliːnɪən), *a. Logic.* [f. *Goclenius* (see below) + -AN.] Epithet of a variety of the Sorites first formulated by Rudolf Goclenius (1547–1628), otherwise called the *descending sorites*, opposed to the *Aristotelian* or *ascending sorites.* (See SORITES.)

god (gɒd). Also 3–4 godd. [Com. Teut.: OE. *god* (masc. in sing.; pl. *godu*, *godo* neut., *godas* masc.) corresponds to OFris., OS., Du. *god* masc., OHG. *got*, *cot* (MHG. *got*, mod.Ger. *gott*) masc., ON. *goð*, *guð* neut. and masc., pl. *goð*, *guð* neut. (later Icel. pl. *guðir* masc.; Sw., Da. *gud*), Goth. *guþ* (masc. in sing.; pl. *guþa*, *guda* neut.). The Goth. and ON. words always follow the neuter declension, though when used in the Christian sense they are syntactically masc. The OTeut. type is therefore **guðom* neut., the adoption of the masculine concord being presumably due to the Christian use of the word. The neuter sb., in its original heathen use, would answer rather to L. *numen* than to L. *deus.* Another approximate equivalent of *deus* in OTeut. was **ansu-z* (Goth. in latinized pl. form *anses*, ON. *óss*, OE. *Ós-* in personal names, *ésa* genit. pl.); but this seems to have been applied only to the higher deities of the native pantheon, never to foreign gods; and it never came into Christian use.

The ulterior etymology is disputed. Apart from the unlikely hypothesis of adoption from some foreign tongue, the OTeut. **guðom* implies as its pre-Teut. type either **ghudho-m* or **ghutó-m.* The former does not appear to admit of explanation; but the latter would represent the neut. of the passive pple. of a root **gheu-*. There are two Aryan roots of the required form (both **g,heu*, with palatal aspirate): one meaning 'to invoke' (Skr. *hū*), the other 'to pour, to offer sacrifice' (Skr. *hu*, Gr. χέειν, OE. *ȝéotan* YETE *v.*). Hence **g,hutó-m* has been variously interpreted as 'what is invoked' (cf. Skr. *puru-hūta* 'much-invoked', an epithet of Indra) and as 'what is worshipped by sacrifice' (cf. Skr. *hutá*, which occurs in the sense 'sacrificed to' as well as in that of 'offered in sacrifice'). Either of these conjectures is fairly plausible, as they both yield a sense practically coincident with the most obvious definition deducible from the actual use of the word, 'an object of worship'. Some scholars, accepting the derivation from the root **g,heu-* to pour, have supposed the etymological sense to be 'molten image' (= Gr. χυτόν), but the assumed development of meaning seems very unlikely.

From a desire to utter the name of God more deliberately than the short vowel naturally allows, the pronunciation is often (gɔːd) or even (gɑːd), and an affected form (gʌd) is not uncommon: see GUD. (For the variations in oaths see 10 and 11.) In Sc. the usual pron. is (god), but *Gude* (gød), i.e. GOOD *a.*, is frequently substituted in such expressions as *Gudesake*, *Gude keep's*, etc.]

I. In the original pre-Christian sense, and uses thence derived.

1. A superhuman person (regarded as masculine: see GODDESS) who is worshipped as having power over nature and the fortunes of mankind; a deity. (Chiefly of heathen divinities; when applied to the One Supreme Being, this sense becomes more or less modified: see 6 b).

Even when applied to the objects of polytheistic worship, the word has often a colouring derived from Christian associations. As the use of *God* as a proper name has throughout the literary period of English been the predominant one, it is natural that the original heathen sense should be sometimes apprehended as a transferred use of this; 'a *god*', in this view, is a supposed being put in the place of *God*, or an imperfect conception of *God* in some of His attributes or relations.

Besides having been thus modified by the influence of the Christian use, this sense as expressed in the definition has been affected by the pagan uses of L. *deus* and Gr. θεός, of which *god* is the accepted rendering. Thus, in speaking of Greek mythology, we distinguish the *gods* from the *dæmons* or supernatural powers of inferior rank, and from the *heroes* or *demigods*, who, though objects of worship, and considered as immortal, were not regarded as having ceased to be men; and the analogy of this nomenclature is often followed in speaking of modern polytheistic religions.

When the word is applied to heathen deities disparagingly, it is now written with a small initial; when the point of view of the worshipper is to any extent adopted, a capital may be used.

c **825** *Vesp. Psalter* xcv. 5 Alle godas ðioda [sind] ðioful. *a* **1000** *Juliana* 121 ðif..þu fremdu godu forð bigongest. *a* **1175** *Cott. Hom.* 227 And com se deofel to har anlicnesse and þer an wnede and to mannen sprece swice hi godes were. *c* **1205** LAY. 5405 Æðes we sulleð þe swerien..uppen ure godd..þe is icliped Dagon. *a* **1300** *Cursor M.* 780 Als godds suld ȝee seluen be. **1387** TREVISA *Higden* (Rolls) II. 299 Fogous..ordeyned temples to worschip þe false goddes ynne; þerfore he was acounted a god amonge hem þat worschipped suche goddes. *c* **1400** *Destr. Troy* 8145 Our hegh goddes, Wold be wrothe at our werkes. **1577** NORTHBROOKE *Dicing* (1843) 99 They conteyne the wicked actes and whoredomes of the goddes. **1610** SHAKS. *Temp.* II. ii. 122 That's a braue God, and beares Celestiall liquor. **1671** MILTON *Samson* 1176 By combat to decide whose God is God, Thine or whom I with Israel's Sons adore. **1697** DRYDEN *Virg. Georg.* IV. 643 Audacious Youth, what Madness cou'd provoke A Mortal Man t' invade a sleeping God? **1752** YOUNG *Brothers* I. i. Wks. 1757 II. 212, I do not think at all; The gods impose, the gods inflict, my thoughts. **1841** ELPHINSTONE *Hist. Ind.* I. 205 Some changes are made by the Jáins in the rank and circumstances of the Hindú gods. **1842** MACAULAY *Lays, Horatius* i, Lars Porsena of Clusium By the Nine Gods he swore That [etc.]. **1870** MORRIS *Earthly Par.* I. I. 300 Surely no man this is, But some god weary of the heavenly bliss.

†**b.** *occas.* prefixed (without article) to the name of a deity (or of a person likened to one). *Obs.*

1508 KENNEDIE *Flyting w. Dunbar* 490 A monstir maid be god Mercurius. **1599** SHAKS. *Much Ado* III. iii. 143 Like god Bels priests in the old Church window. **1606** —— *Tr. & Cr.* I. iii. 169 Yet god Achilles still cries excellent.

c. Used with defining addition, chiefly referring to the department of nature or human activity or passion, over which a particular god was supposed to rule. In this use the reference, unless there is indication to the contrary, is usually to Græco-Roman mythology, the deities of which are often mentioned rhetorically or humorously as mere personifications of qualities or influences. ***the god of day***: the Sun. ***the god of war***: Mars (Ares). ***the god of love, the blind god***: Amor (Eros), or Cupid. ***the god of wine***: Bacchus.

1483 *Cath. Angl.* 161/1 A God of batylle, *mars.* **1545** ASCHAM *Toxoph.* I. (Arb.) 39 Apollo god of learninge. **1808** J. BARLOW *Columb.* II. 616 Hail us children of the God of day. **1816** J. WILSON in J. Hamilton *Mem.* ii. (1859) 53 The last beams of the God of day.

d. ***the god of this world***: the Devil, Satan.

1382 WYCLIF *2 Cor.* iv. 4 In whiche the God of this world hath blyndid the soules of men out of the bileue.

e. Phrases. ***ye gods*** (***and little fishes***)! used to express mock-heroic indignation. ***a feast, sight,*** etc. (***fit***) ***for the gods***: said of something delightful or amazing.

1601 SHAKS. *Jul. C.* II. i. 173 Let's carue him, as a Dish fit for the Gods. **1761** BOSWELL *Let.* (1857) 17 Dec. 383 It is Captain Andrew! it is! it is! Ye gods, he seizes! he opens! he reads! **1807** C. WILMOT *Let.* 15 May *Russ. Jrnls.* (1934) II. 243 Oh! ye Gods! How you are to be envied & every Mortal alive. **1871** L. M. ALCOTT *Little Men* ii. 27 But out of school,—Ye gods and little fishes! how Tommy did carouse! *a* **1900** *Mod.* The fierce scrimmage that ensued was a sight for the gods. **1909** H. G. WELLS *Ann Veronica* i. 9 'Ye gods!' she said at last. '*What* a place!' **1927** W. E. COLLINSON *Contemp. Eng.* 26 We used harmless expletives like..Ye Gods and little fishes. **1964** W. MARKFIELD *To Early Grave* (1965) xi. 187 He cried to himself 'Ye Gods!' and 'Whoosh!'

f. ***god from*** (or ***out of***) ***the*** (or ***a***) ***machine*** = DEUS EX MACHINA.

1868 TROLLOPE *Phineas Finn* (1869) I. xxxi. 257 A gallant young member of that House..had appeared upon the spot at the nick of time;—'As a god out of a machine,' said Mr. Daubeny, interrupting him. **1888** KIPLING *Soldiers Three* 1 (*title of story*) The god from the machine. **1910** CHESTERTON *G. B. Shaw* 116 Shaw..disliked the god from the machine —because he was from a machine. **1959** *Listener* 26 Nov. 911/2 The heads of government of the Great Powers are not gods from the machine. **1970** N. FISHER *Walk at Steady Pace* III. 157 If the God from the Machine was to solve my troubles he was by far the most convincing candidate.

2. An image or other artificial or natural object (as a pillar, a tree, a brute animal) which is worshipped, either as the symbol of an unseen divinity, as supposed to be animated by his indwelling presence, or as itself possessing some kind of divine consciousness and supernatural powers; an idol.

c **1000** *Laws of Ælfred* c. 10 in Schmid *Gesetze* 58 Ne wyrc þu þe gyldne godas oððe seolfrene. *c* **1000** ÆLFRIC *Exod.* xx. 4 Ne wirc þu þe agrafene godas. *c* **1250** *Gen. & Ex.* 3541 He seiden to aaraon 'Mac vs godes foren us to gon'. **1382** WYCLIF *Gen.* xxxi. 30 Why hast thow stoln my goddis? **1535** COVERDALE *Exod.* xxxiv. 17 Thou shalt make ye no goddes of metall. **1697** POTTER *Antiq. Greece* I. xix. (1715) 105 The Consecration of new Gods. **1731** POPE *Ep. Burlington* 8, Statues, dirty Gods, and Coins. **1838** ARNOLD *Hist. Rome* I. i. 1 They remembered to carry their gods with them, who were to receive their worship in a happier land.

3. *transf.* **a.** of persons, as objects of adoration, or as possessed of absolute power.

c **1000** ÆLFRIC *Exod.* vii. 1 And drihten cwæð to Moise, Nu ic ȝesette þe Pharaone to gode. **1577** B. GOOGE *Heresbach's Husb.* I. (1586) 1 Yf these goddes of the Earth would suffer me to enjoy suche happinesse. **1579** GOSSON *Sch. Abuse* (Arb.) 49 Some there are that make gods of soldiers in open warrs. **1592** SHAKS. *Rom. & Jul.* II. ii. 114 Sweare by thy gratious selfe, Which is the God of my Idolatry. **1692** S. JOHNSON *Abrog. Jas. I* 29 Such an Usurper is a God upon Earth, which it is easie for some sort of Men to make. **1864** TENNYSON *Aylmer's F.* 14 Sir Aylmer Aylmer, that almighty man, The county god. **1883** SIR F. POLLOCK in *Fortn. Rev.* 1 Oct. 537 The ruling gods of the circulating libraries.

b. of things.

a **1586** SIDNEY *Arcadia* III. (1633) 282 Like a man whose will was his God, and his hand his law. **1625** FLETCHER *Nt. Walker* I. i, The old mans god, his gold, has wonne upon her. **1852** ROBERTSON *Lect. Ep. Cor.* xlvii. (1859) 430 A man's god is that which has his whole soul and worship, that which he obeys and reverences as his highest. **1896** in *Daily News* 30 Dec. 6/2 [He] is convinced there is no God so omnipotent as that of the full purse.

4. *Theat.* [So called because seated on high.] *pl.* The occupants of the gallery. Also ***gallery-gods.*** Also *rarely* in *sing.*

1752 *Adventurer* No. 3 The servant whose business it is, as Homer says, 'To shake the regions of the gods with laughter'. **1806** SURR *Winter in Lond.* (ed. 3) II. 108 The high regions assigned to that part of the audience called the 'gods', namely, the galleries. **1812** H. & J. SMITH *Rej. Addr.*, *Drury Lane Hustings* v, Each one shilling God within reach of a nod is, And plain are the charms of each Gallery Goddess. **1843** THACKERAY *Irish Sk.-bk.* xxvii, One young god between the acts favoured the public with a song. **1851** —— *Eng. Hum.* vi. 301 Does he..appeal to the gallery gods with claptraps and vulgar baits to catch applause. **1885** *Manch. Exam.* 4 May 5/3 The wrath of the pittites and the gods was appeased.

II. In the specific Christian and monotheistic sense. The One object of supreme adoration; the Creator and Ruler of the Universe. (Now always with initial capital.)

5. As a proper name.

c **825** *Vesp. Psalter* xlvi. 3 God [is]..cyning micel ofer alle godas. *c* **1175** *Lamb. Hom.* 15 þis beoð godes word þe god seolf idihte. *c* **1200** ORMIN 623 Godess enngell Gabriæl Comm dun o Godess hallfe I Godess hus wiþþ Godess word. *a* **1300** *Cursor M.* 1061 Rightwis he was, and godds freind. **1523** LD. BERNERS *Froiss.* I. clxii. 199 The lorde Chandos sayd to the prince..this iourney is yours: God is this day in your handes. **1616** R. C. *Times' Whistle* I. 129 God is an Essence intellectuall, A perfect Substance incorporeall. **1651** HOBBES *Leviath.* II. xxxi. 191 God; in which is contained Father, King, and Lord. **1741** RICHARDSON *Pamela* (1824) I. 227 God, the all-gracious, the all-good, the all-bountiful, the all-mighty, the all-merciful God. **1877** E. R. CONDER *Bas. Faith* iii. 95 For by this name God we understand an Infinite Mind, everywhere present, the source and foundation of all other existence, possessed of all possible power, wisdom, and excellence.

b. *Proverbs.* (See also DISPOSE *v.* 7.)

c **1450** *Merlin* 524 Ther-fore is seide a proverbe, that god will haue saued, no man may distroye. *a* **1533** LD. BERNERS *Huon* cxxx. 480 It is a comune prouerbe sayde, 'whome that god wyll ayde, no man can hurt'. **1545** ASCHAM *Toxoph.* II. (Arb.) 132 He maye..haue cause to saye so of his Fletcher, as ..is communelye spoken of Cookes:..that God sendeth vs good fethers, but the deuyll noughtie Fletchers. **1546** J.

HEYWOOD *Prov.* (1867) 54 Spend, and god shall send saith tholde ballet. **1562** —— *Prov. & Epigr.* 165 God is where he was. **1599** SHAKS. *Much Ado* II. i. 25 It is said, God sends a curst Cow short hornes. **1721** BAILEY s.v., As sure as God's in Gloucestershire. **1768** STERNE *Sent. Journ.* II. 175 God tempers the wind, said Maria, to the shorn lamb. **1822** SCOTT *Nigel* xxvii, That homely proverb that men taunt my calling with,—'God sends good meat, but the devil sends cooks'.

c. Phrases. ***to depart to God***, to die and go to heaven. ***with God***, in heaven. ***out of God's blessing into the warm sun***, from a better to a worse situation. Also in legal use, ***act of God*** (see ACT *sb.* 4); †***to go to God***, of a cause, to be adjourned *sine die*.

1548 HALL *Chron., Hen. VI*, 104 Thomas duke of Excester, late departed to God. **1562** [see BLESSING *vbl. sb.* 3]. *a* **1612** SIR J. HARINGTON *Epigr.* II. lvi, Pray God they bring vs not, when all is done, Out of Gods blessing into this warme sunne. **1612** in *Crt. & Times Jas. I* (1848) I. 186 That which you have done about my transplantation doth very well agree with my desire; and I account it to be out of the warm sun into God's blessing. **1617** *Ibid.* II. 51 As due to his memory, who is with God. **1651** FULLER *Abel Rediv.* Ep. A 3 b, Doctor Featly, now at rest with God.

d. With additional title or epithet: ***The Lord God, Almighty God***, GOD-ALMIGHTY. Also prefixed to the designations of the persons of the Trinity, ***God the Father, God the Son, God the Holy Ghost.*** (For further examples, see the accompanying words.)

c **900** tr. *Bæda's Hist.* IV. xvii. (1891) 312 Wuldriende God Fæder butan fruman. *c* **1000** ÆLFRIC *Saints' Lives* (1890) II. 40 Sy þu ȝebletsod drihten god. *Ibid.* 78 Se ælmihtiȝa god. **1340** *Ayenb.* 99 Godes sone hit made. To god þe uader ine worde. God þe holy gost þet is þet me acseþ. *c* **1420** *Prymer* (E.E.T.S.) 47 God, fadir of heuene.. God þe sone.. God þe holi gost, haue merci of us!

†**e.** In ME. often used without addition for Christ. Similarly, in 16th c., ***in the year of God*** = Anno Domini. *Obs.* (Cf. *Mother of God*: see MOTHER.)

c **1380** WYCLIF *Sel. Wks.* III. 500 And þan he receyves God gostly. *c* **1386** CHAUCER *Clerk's T.* 1006 By god that for us deyde. *c* **1565** LINDESAY (Pitscottie) *Chron.* (1728) 43 This Battle was stricken upon the Ascension-Day, in the Year of God, One thousand four hundred and fifty three Years.

f. The possessive is sometimes rhetorically introduced before certain sbs. ***God's poor***, †***God's poverty***: the poor regarded as entrusted by God to the care of the devout. ***God's truth***: the absolute truth. ***on God's earth***: now often used as a mere emphatic synonym for 'on earth'.

c **1400** *Plowman's T.* 531 Of goddes pore they haten gestes. *c* **1440** *Jacob's Well* (E.E.T.S.) 124 A gouelere is a turmentour of goddys pore peple. **1563** *Homilies, Keeping Clean Ch.* II. 86 Not forgettyng to bestowe our almes vppon Goddes pouertie [**1623** poore]. **1583** T. STOCKER *Ciuile Warres Lowe C.* I. 138 b, There were but 200 Spaniardes laid on Gods deare earth. **1847–78** HALLIWELL, *God's-truth*, an absolute truth. (So **1886** ELWORTHY *W. Somerset Word-bk.*) **1898** *Daily News* 31 May 6/6 We talked of work-houses .. and then for the first time I heard colloquially the phrase, 'God's poor.'

6. As an appellative.

a. A Being such as is understood by the proper name *God*; a sole Divine Creator and Ruler of the Universe; that which God is represented to be according to some particular conception (as ***the God of philosophy, of pantheism, of Judaism***), or is manifested to be in some special department of His action (as the ***God of nature, of revelation, of providence***); God as contemplated in some special attribute or relation (as ***the God of love, of mercy, of vengeance***, etc., ***the God who made us***, etc., ***my*** or ***our God***, etc.).

[**1382** WYCLIF *2 Cor.* xiii. 11 Haue ȝe pees, and God of pees and loue schal be with ȝou.] **1535** COVERDALE *Rom.* xv. 5 The God of pacience and consolacion. **1563** B. GOOGE *Eglogs* viii. (Arb.) 63 A God there is, that guyds the Globe, and framde the fyckle Spheare. **1678** CUDWORTH *Intell. Syst.* I. v. 889 To Believe a God, is to Believe the Existence of all Possible Good and Perfection in the Universe. **1784** COWPER *Task* II. 161 Happy the man, who sees a God employ'd In all the good and ill that checker life! **1813** HURN *Ps. & Hymns* 283 The God of truth his church has bless'd. **1817** COLERIDGE *Sibyll. Leaves* (1862) 187 The God who framed Mankind to be one mighty family. **1827** KEBLE *Chr. Y., Communion*, O God of Mercy, God of Might. **1877** E. R. CONDER *Bas. Faith* Pref. 12 Is there a God? Is there an Infinite, All-wise, All-powerful Spirit? *Mod.* An unjust God would be no God at all.

b. With partial reversion to the general sense (see 1), in contexts where the One True God is contrasted with the false gods of heathenism.

c **1000** *Ags. Ps.* (Th.) cxxxv. 2 Þam þe ece is ealra godena god. *c* **1000** ÆLFRIC *Deut.* x. 17 Drihten sylf ys goda god, mære god and mihtiȝ. *c* **1400** MAUNDEV. (1839) xii. 142 There is no God but on & Machomete his Messager.

c. ***God of the gaps***, God adduced as an explanation for phenomena not yet explained by science; God thought of as acting only in those spheres not otherwise accounted for.

[**1894** H. DRUMMOND *Ascent of Man* x. 426 There are reverent minds who ceaselessly scan the fields of Nature and the books of Science in search of gaps—gaps which they will fill up with God. As if God lived in gaps? **1927** C. E. RAVEN *Creator Spirit* iv. 113 Only disaster awaits the religion which .. tries to fit God into the gaps left by scientific study.] **1955** C. A. COULSON *Science & Christian Belief* i. 20 There is no 'God of the gaps' to take over at those strategic places where science fails. **1966** I. G. BARBOUR *Issues in Sci. & Relig.* ii. 43 God the Cosmic Plumber, mending the leaks in his system... This was 'the God of the gaps', introduced to explain areas of scientific ignorance. **1970** J. A. BAKER *Foolishness of God* x. 250 There is a phrase which has had some currency as a taunt against Christians on the run in a scientific age. They are said to believe in a 'God of the gaps', the gaps in question being the ever-closing gaps in our scientific knowledge. **1979** A. R. PEACOCKE *Creation & World of Sci.* I. i. 24 The two-realm ontologies lead to a God-of-the-gaps concept of God's relation to the world.

III. Phraseological uses of sense 5.

* *Exclamatory and parenthetic phrases expressing feeling or desire.*

7. The vocative, as ***ah God, oh God, my God, good God***, etc., is used to express strong feeling or excitement.

1340 *Ayenb.* 92 A god hou hi byeþ foles [etc.]. **1573** *New Custom* II. iii, Preciouse God, it frettes mee to the very gall. *c* **1586** C'TESS PEMBROKE *Ps.* LXXVIII. xvi, And yet (good God) how ofte this crooked kind, Incenst him in the desert every where? **1593** SHAKS. *3 Hen. VI*, II. v. 61 Who's this? Oh God! It is my Father's face. *a* **1603** HEYWOOD *Woman killed w. Kindn.* (1617) B 3, *Sus.* O God: a Surgeon there. **1812** T. AMYOT *Speeches Windham* I. 134 In which the words, 'My God!' had been made use of on a light occasion. **1855** TENNYSON *Maud* I. 60 Ah God, as he used to rave.

†**b.** Followed by a wish. Chiefly *Sc.* in the phrases ***God gif, God nor*** = would to God that...

A verb may have been dropped in these expressions.

c **1475** *Rauf Coilȝear* 734 Greit God gif I war now .. Vpon the mure. **1500–20** DUNBAR *Poems* lxii. 4 God gif ȝe war Johne Thomsounis man. **1535** LYNDSAY *Satyre* 1325 God nor my trewker mence ane ledder. **1570** *Satir. Poems Reform.* xxii. 50 O monstrous bird! God nor ye gleddis ȝe [= thee] get. **1599** SHAKS. *Much Ado* IV. i. 308 O God that I were a man.

8. In phrases expressive of a strong wish, chiefly for the benefit or injury of some person, as ***God bless, damn, help, preserve, save,*** †***shield,*** †***speed,*** †***yield*** (you, him, etc.); also ***God forbid, grant*** (that); ***God give*** (something): for these see the various verbs. Hence occasionally used in participial expressions.

Some of these phrases assumed abbreviated or corrupted forms through frequent use, as ***God eyld*** (***ild, dild***) ***you, goddilge yee*** = God yield you (see YIELD); ***God b'wy*** (***buy***) ***ye*** = God be with you (see GOOD-BYE); ***God*** (***Godge***) ***you good even*** = God give you, etc. (also ***God dig-you-den, God(g)igoden***: see GOOD-EVEN). In such phrases as have remained current, *God* is often omitted, as *bless you, damn you, preserve us.*

1579 G. HARVEY *Let. to Spenser* Wks. (Grosart) I. 24 Youre Latine Farewell is a goodly braue yonkerly peece of work, and goddilge yee, I am alwayes maruellously beholding vnto you, for your bountifull Titles. **1599** MARSTON *Sco. Villanie* III. xi. 226 This bumbast foile-button.. after the God-sauing ceremony, For want of talke-stuffe, fals to foinery. **1600** NASHE *Summers Last Will* Wks. (Grosart) VI. 89 God giue you good night in Watling Street. **1604** SHAKS. *Oth.* I. iii. 189 God be with you [*Qq.* God bu'y]: I haue done. **1612** in *Crt. & Times Jas. I* (1848) I. 194 God keep them from base courses! **1809** MALKIN *Gil Blas* IV. viii. ¶8 A profusion of farewells and God-be-with-you's. **1814** WELLINGTON in Gurw. *Desp.* (1838) XII. 6 God send that I may be in time to prevent mischief! **1840** DICKENS *Barn. Rudge* xl, To be.. God-blessed.. by one who carried 'Sir' before his name.. was something for a porter. **1894** H. GARDENER *Unoff. Patriot* 236 I'll burn every God-damned house I come to.

God bless is also used *ellipt.* for 'God bless you' as a wish for God's blessing on a person or as an expression of goodwill, esp. at parting.

1964 P. M. HUBBARD *Picture of Millie* iv. 42 She took the drink... 'I don't know what to say,' she said. 'Would "God bless" do?' **1964** 'J. ROFFMAN' *Likely to Die* vi. 69 'That would mean that I'd arrive here soon after half-past five.' She smiled. 'That will be fine. God bless, Albert.' **1966** 'E. PETERS' *Piper on Mountain* i. 20 Now good night, and God bless! Don't stay up too late! **1967** 'M. HUNTER' *Cambridgeshire Disaster* xvi. 109 Try and forget me, David, God bless.

b. Many of these combinations, as ***God bless me*** (***my soul***, etc.), ***God save me***, etc. are used (profanely) as mere exclamations of surprise (see the vbs.). †So in the shortened form ***Gods*** (= God save) ***me, my life, my soul***, etc.

1590 SHAKS. *Mids. N.* IV. i. 209 Gods my life! Stolne hence and left me asleepe. **1598** B. JONSON *Ev. Man in Hum.* III. iv, Gods my life; did you euer hear the like? *a* **1603** HEYWOOD *Woman killed w. Kindn.* (1617) F 4, Gods me no such dispatch. **1605** CHAPMAN *All Fooles* III. i. E 3 b, Gods my deare soule, what sudden change is here! **1640** tr. *Verdere's Rom. Rom.* II. 191 Gods me, said Trasiclea.

†**c.** ***God's forbot*** (see FORBODE) = God forbid. Hence corruptly ***God sware-bot, Godsworbet.*** *Obs.*

c **1460** *Towneley Myst.* ii. 38, I fend, godis forbot, that euer thou thrife. *c* **1530** *Int. Beauty & Properties Women* A v b, Ells godds forbod She hath equall power of my lyff vnder god. **1611** COTGR. s.v. *Dieu, A dieu ne plaise*, God forbid, God shield, God sware-bot. **1641** *Witts Recreat.* Epigr. 526 One tels strange newes, tother Godsworbet cries, The third shakes head, alack replies.

d. God forbid, *Rhyming slang* (see quots.). Cf. *Gawd-forbid.*

1909 J. R. WARE *Passing Eng.* 144/2 *God-forbids*, kids—a cynical mode of describing children by poor men who dread a long family. **1960** J. FRANKLYN *Dict. Rhyming Slang* 70/1 *God forbid(s)*, (1) Kids (child or children), (2) Yids (Jews), (3) *lid* (hat).

9. In phrases which express dependence upon or grateful recognition of divine providence.

a. ***if*** (or †***and***) ***God will*** (also dial. ***an Gothill, a Goddil***); ***God willing***, †***will God***. (***and God will*** was formerly sometimes used ironically, = 'save the mark'.)

c **1400** *Rom. Rose* 4561 Love shal never, if god wil, Here of me,.. Offence or complaynt. *c* **1470** HENRY *Wallace* IV. 766 Will God, I sall eschape this tresoune fals. **1526** WOLSEY in *St. Papers Hen. VIII* (1830) I. 184 The said realme may yet, God willing, be preserved and releved. **1542** BECON *Pathw. Prayer* xlvi. R ij b, Monstures, Monckes I would haue sayd, & other religious parsons, and God wyll, as they desyre to be called. **1588** *Marprel. Epist.* (Arb.) 28 Naye (quoth Penrie) neuer so long as I liue god-willing. **1602** SHAKS. *Ham.* I. v. 187. *c* **1688** H. HERBERT in Reb. Warner *Epist. Curios.* Ser. I. 72 We both intend, God willing, to set forward for London on Munday next. **1706** WYCHERLEY *Let. to Pope* in *P.'s Lett.* (1735) 25 Afterwards to spend two Months (God willing) with you, at Binfield. **1790** MRS. WHEELER *Westmld. Dial.* (1821) 43 Ise find tea a maister, a goddil! **1825–80** JAMIESON s.v. *Gothill, An Gothill*, if God will... 'In Gothill I'll be there'. **1835** MRS. CARLYLE *Lett.* I. 25 Next year, God willing, I shall see you all again.

b. ***by*** (†***with***) ***God's grace; by*** (***with***) ***God's help, assistance, blessing***, etc.

832 *Kentish Charter* in *O.E. Texts* 40/11 Ic ceolnoð mid godes gefe ercebiscop. **13..** *Sir Beues* (A.) 412 Y nam no truant, be godes grace. **1500–20** DUNBAR *Poems* xviii. 51, I sall, with Goddis grace, Keip his command. **1619** SANDERSON *Serm. ad Cler.* i. (1689) 3, I shall by Gods assistance proceed.. to inquire how [etc.]. **1662** *Bk. Com. Prayer, Catechism*, Yes verily; and by Gods help so I will. **1859** TENNYSON *Enid* 344 Here, by God's grace, is the one voice for me.

†**c.** (***and***) ***God before*** (or ***to fore***), under God's guidance. ***with God to friend***: with God's help or protection. *Obs.*

c **1374** CHAUCER *Troylus* I. 1049 And dredelees, if that my lyf may laste, And god to-forn, lo, som of hem shal smarte. *c* **1400** *Rom. Rose* 7198 They shal neuere haue that myght And god to forne for strif to fight That [etc.]. *a* **1450** *Knt. de la Tour* (1868) 14 Diuerse exsaumples, the whiche, and God before, ye shalle take hede of. *c* **1500** *Melusine* xxi. 127 For god before we tende & purpose to gyue bataylle to the Sawdan. **1533** J. HEYWOOD *Pard. & Friar* B iv, I wyll neuer come hether more, Whyle I lyue and god before. **1590** SPENSER *F.Q.* I. i. 28 So forward on his way (with God to frend) He passed forth. **1594** KYD *Cornelia* III. E 4 b, Els (god to fore) my selfe may liue to see His tired corse lye toyling in his blood. **1599** SHAKS. *Hen. V*, I. ii. 307 For God before, Wee'le chide this Dolphin at his fathers doore. **1609** DRAYTON *Cromwell* 36 For in my skill his sound recouerie lies, Doubt not thereof if setting God before.

d. ***under God***: as a secondary cause or mediate object of gratitude.

1607 *Peele's Jests* B 1 a, Yet, quoth he, vnder God, I wil doe him some good. **1619** in *Crt. & Times Jas. I* (1848) II. 170 The blessedness of this good work, under God, is to be attributed to the king alone.

e. ***thank God; God be thanked, praised***, etc. †Earlier ***Gode þonc***. Also ***praised*** (†***loved***) ***be God.***

c **1200** *Trin. Coll. Hom.* 11 Unbileue is aiware aleid and rihte leue arered godeðonc. **1352** MINOT *Poems* (Hall) i. 53 Bot, loued be God, þe pride es slaked Of þam [etc.]. **1599** SHAKS. *Much Ado* V. i. 190 You breake iests as braggards do their blades, which God be thanked hurt not. **1607** *Peele's Jests* B 1 b, The fellow told him God be praised, his good Landlord was well recouered. **1753** *Scots Mag.* July 320/2 Most of the landholders have now, thank God! abandoned that.. religion. **1842** TENNYSON *Lady Clare* 17 'O God be thank'd!.. That all comes round so just and fair.'

10. ***God*** (†***it***) ***wot*** (*arch.*; see GODDOT), ***God knows.*** **a.** Used to emphasize the truth of a statement.

a **1300** *Cursor M.* 4473 (Gött.) God wat.. I sal vndo þe wele þi sueuen. *c* **1300** *Havelok* 2527 Þer-of held he wel his oth, For he it [a priory] made, god it woth. *a* **1529** SKELTON *Col. Cloute* 234 Than renne they in euery stede, God wot, with dronken nolles. ? *a* **1550** *Freiris Berwik* 61 in *Dunbar's Poems* (1893) 287 He went fra hame, God wait, on Weddinsday. **1564** COVERDALE *Lett. Martyrs* 77 It is impossible to set forth.. al yᵗ was (God knoweth) tumultuously spoken. **1590** SHAKS. *Com. Err.* V. i. 229 The Chaine, Which God he knowes, I saw not. **1594** —— *Rich. III*, II. iii. 18 Stood the State so? No, no, good friends, God wot. *a* **1617** BAYNE *On Eph.* i. (1643) 214 Commonly the most Christians are counted good men godwot, but simple soules, of no parts. **1859** TENNYSON *Elaine* 197 God wot, his shield is blank enough.

b. Used with indirect question to imply that something is unknown to the speaker, and probably to every other human being.

1568 GRAFTON *Chron.* II. 98 The sayd John was had after in great suspicion, whether justly or unjustly God knoweth. **1646** BUCK *Rich. III*, III. 85 Their bodies were bestowed God wot where. **1822** BYRON *Werner* IV. i. 51 The country.. Is over-run with—God knows who. **1823** —— *Juan* IX. lxvii, They fell in love;—she with his face, His grace, his God-knows-what.

11. In earnest appeals or exhortations, as ***for God's sake; for God's love; in*** (also †***a, o'***) ***God's name***; †***on*** or ***a God's half*** (see HALF *sb.* 2 d). For the use of adjuratory forms to the same effect, see 14.

1297 R. GLOUC. (Rolls) 8968 Madame he sede uor godes loue is þis wel ido þat þou þes vnclene limes handlest. *a* **1300** *Cursor M.* 4798 (Cott.) Ga we alle, in gods name. *Ibid.* 4800 (Gött.), I ȝou pray for goddes sake [etc.]. *c* **1386** CHAUCER *Prol.* 854 What, welcome be the cut, a goddes name. **1548** W. PATTEN *Exped. Scotl.* K viij, These a Gods name wear their targettes again the shot of our small artillerie. **1583**

HOLLYBAND Campo di Fior 15 For God sake let not my tutor know it. 1593 SHAKS. Rich. II, II. i. 251 But what o' Gods name doth become of this? 1610 B. JONSON Alch. V. iii, For Gods sake, when will her Grace be at leasure? 1735 POPE Prol. Sat. 101 Hold! for God's sake—you'll offend. 1859 TENNYSON Elaine 504 For God's love, a little air! 1864 —— En. Ard. 505 For God's sake..let it be at once.

†**12.** ***God pays***: a proverbial expression of indifference to the consequences of one's action. _Obs._

1605 Lond. Prodigal C1b, There be some that bares a souldiers forme, That..Goes swaggering vp and downe from house to house, crying God payes. 1616 B. JONSON Epigr. I. xii. Lieut. Shift, His onely answere is to all, god payes. 1626 —— Masque of Owls, Whom since they have shipt away, And left him God to pay.

** _In oaths._

13. ***by God***, †***before*** (or ***fore***) ***God***; also ***by God above***, etc. (cf. BY A 2).

From a desire to avoid actual use of the sacred name come various distorted or minced pronunciations of the word; see COCK, DOD, GAD, GAR, GED, GOG, GOLES, GOLLY, GOM, GOSH, GOS(SE, GUD, GUM; also ADAD, ADOD, BEDAD, BEGAD, BEGAR, ECOD, EGAD, ICOD, IGAD. Of these forms only Cock and Gog are common before 1600; the others occur mainly in the 17th and 18th c. Gar is by the dramatists chiefly put in the mouths of foreigners (cf. 14).

1297 R. GLOUC. (Rolls) 7000 Vor gode [v.r. By god] þe nexte king..ne ȝef hom noȝt folliche so muche. a1300 Cursor M. 7934 'Bi godd o-liue', he suor his ath. 13.. Sir Beues (A.) 1098 'For gode', queþ Beues, 'þat ich do nelle'. c1400 Gamelyn 469 It is nought wel served, by god that al made. 1460 Lybeaus Disc. 219 Be god þat bouȝte me dere. c1500 Melusine xxxvi. 293 By god, my lord, shame is therof to you. 1519 Interl. Four Elem. (Percy Soc.) 48 That is well sayd, be God Almyght! c1540 HEYWOOD Four P.P. (Copland) C iv, Pardoner. I thought ye lyed. Poticary. And so thought I by god that dyed. 1557 Interl. Youth B j b, I sweare by God in Trinitie I wyll go fetche him vnto the. Ibid. B ij b, A wyfe nay nay for God auowe He shall haue fleshe inoughe. 1599 PORTER Angry Wom. Abingt. (Percy Soc.) 22 Fran. Are they so? Comes. I, before God, are they. 1610 B. JONSON Alch. I. iii, 'Fore God, my intelligence Costs me more money, then my share oft comes too. 1617 MORYSON Itin. II. 157 By God, Sir, I will doe for Queene Elizabeth that which I will not doe for my selfe. 1841–4 EMERSON Ess., Poet Wks. (Bohn) I. 170 He says with the old painter, 'By God, it is in me, and must go forth of me'. 1885 ORMSBY Don Quix. II. xxxiv. III. 384 'By God and upon my conscience', said the devil, 'I never observed it'.

14. In possessive combinations serving as asseverative or adjuratory formulæ. Preceded by _by_ or (in adjuratory use: cf. 11) by _for_; also with omission of prep. (Cf. GAD sb.[5] 3.)

Corrupt or minced forms of these oaths are also common, God's being altered or abbreviated to Ads, Cocks, Cods, Cuds, Gads, Gogs, Guds, His, 'Ods, 'S, 'Uds, 'Z (in Zooks, Zounds); of these only Cocks and Gogs are old, the others coming into use about 1600 or later; the full forms are rarely found after that date except as archaisms. The form Gars is assigned to foreigners, as gars blur, garzowne in Doctor Dodypoll (Bullen O. Pl. III. 129), garzoon in Farquhar (Beaux Strat. III. iii, etc.).

a. With ordinary sbs., sometimes preceded by an adj.; also with the adj. used elliptically, as ***God's blest, precious***, etc.

In some of these oaths the sb. denotes an attribute of Deity; more usually, God's = Christ's, as in God's arms, body, blood, etc. In some jocular oaths, as in God's brother, fish, hat, malt, the sb. has no meaning in its connexion, being substituted for some word of solemn import.

1611 BEAUM. & FL. Knt. Burn. Pestle I. iv, Bid the plaiers send Rafe, or by *Gods—, and they do not [etc.]. 1608 Merry Devil Edmonton (1617) C 2 b, By *Gods blessed Angell, Thou shalt well know it. c1386 CHAUCER Pard. T. 326 By *goddes Armes if thou falsly pleye [etc.]. c1530 Hickscorner (c1550) E ij, I forsake thy company. Imagynacyon. Goddes armes my company and why. 1575 Gamm. Gurton V. ii, A great deale more (by *Gods blest,) than cheuer by the got. 1549 LATIMER 7th Serm. bef. Edw. VI (Arb.) 200 To sweare by *goddes bloude. 1562–3 Jack Jugler (Roxb.) 21 *Godes body horeson thefe who tolde thee that same. 1596 SHAKS. 1 Hen. IV, II. i. 29 (Qo.) Gods bodie. The Turkies in my Panier are quite starued. c1386 CHAUCER Shipm. Prol. 4 For *godis bonys Telle vs a tale. 1573 New Custom III. i, Else I will smite thee..by goddes bones. 1622 MABBE tr. Aleman's Guzman d'Alf. II. 142 *Gods-bores [cf. BORE sb. and GOG], what a deale of doe is here about nothing? 1535 LYNDESAY Satyre 932 That sall wee do, be *Gods breid. 1592 SHAKS. Rom. & Jul. III. v. 177 Gods bread, it makes me mad. c1537 Thersites (Roxb.) 64 Ye that I wyll, by *goddes deare brother. Ibid. 70 By goddes blessed brother Yf [etc.]. c1386 CHAUCER Miller's T. 557 By *goddes corpus this goth faire and weel. 1535 LYNDESAY Satyre 1943 Be *Gods croun..I sall slay thee. ?a1550 Freiris Berwik 234 in Dunbar's Poems (1893) 293 Awalk for *Goddis deid. 1859 TENNYSON Elaine 676 Yea, by *God's death..ye love him well. 1564–78 *Gods dentie [see DENTIE]. c1386 CHAUCER Reeve's T. 350 Thow shalt be deed by *goddes dignitee. ?a1550 Freiris Berwik 295 in Dunbar's Poems (1893) 295, I will thame haif be Goddis dignite. 1599, 1605 *God's dines [see DINES]. 14.. Sir Beues (Pynson) 2013, 'I graunt', sayde Beuys, 'by *goddys dome'. c1460 Towneley Myst. xii. 305, A, *godys dere dominus, what was that sang? 1340 Ayenb. 45 A knyȝt wes þet zuor be *godes eȝen. c1530 Hickscorner (c1550) E ij b, By *goddes fast I was ten yere in Newgate. c1570 Marr. Wit & Science v. E j b, *Gods fishe hostes and knowe you not mee. 1675 MARVELL Corr. Wks. 1872–5 II. 431, I have a passable good estate, I confess, but, God's-fish, I have a great charge upon't. 1716 C'TESS COWPER Diary (1864) 95 To which he replied, God's Fish! (that was his common Oath) I don't believe a Word of all this. c1550 WEVER Lusty Juventus D j, Yea by *gods foote that I wyl be busye. 1599 PORTER Angry Wom. Abingt. (Percy Soc.) 58 Gods foote—I crye God hartely mercy! 1748 SMOLLETT Rod. Rand. xi, *God's fury! there shall no passangers come here. 1535 LYNDESAY Satyre 393 Or ȝe tuik skaith, be *Gods goun [etc.]. 1573 New Custom II. iii, Nowe by *goddes guttes I will neuer staye Tyll [etc.]. 1569 T. PRESTON Cambyses D iv b, *Gods hat neighbour come away. c1386 CHAUCER Pard. T. 323 By *goddes precious herte and by his nayles. —— Miller's T. 629 Help for goddes herte. 1573 New Custom II. iii, Nay by Goddes harte, if I might doe what I list [etc.]. 1548 HALL Chron., Edw. V, 19 By *god his blessed lady, I am a bacheler. 1589 PUTTENHAM Eng. Poesie III. xix. (Arb.) 238 Gods lady I reckon my selfe as good a man as he. 1598 B. JONSON Ev. Man in Hum. II. iii, By *Gods lid, and you had not confest it ——. 1609 Ev. Wom. in Hum. II. i. in Bullen O. Pl. IV, By Gods-lid, if I had knowne [etc.]. 1604 DEKKER Honest Wh. (1635) G 3 b, *Gods life, I was ne'r so thrumbed since I was a Gentleman. 1596 SHAKS. 1 Hen. IV, III. iii. 71 (Qo.) *Gods light I was neuer cald so in mine owne house before. a1603 HEYWOOD Woman killed w. Kindn. (1617) D 4, Gods light, harke within there. 1519 Interl. Four Elem. (Percy Soc.) 36 *Goddis Lorde! seist not who is here now? 1600 DEKKER Shoemaker's Holiday (1618) D 4, Gods Lord tis late, to Guild Hall I must hie. 1575 Gamm. Gurton v. ii, *Gods malt, Gammer gurton. c1386 CHAUCER Sqr.'s Prol. 1 Ey *goddes mercy seyde our Hoost tho. c1540 HEYWOOD Four P.P. (Copland) D j b, No stone left standyng by *goddes mother. 1613 SHAKS. Hen. VIII, v. i. 153 Gods blest Mother, I sweare he is true-hearted. c1460 Towneley Myst. xvi. 116 By *gottys dere nalys I wyll peasse no langer. 1600 DEKKER Shoemaker's Holiday (1610) H 2 b, Gods nailes do you thinke I am so base to Gull you? 13.. Sir Beues (A) 2191 Be *godes name, Ichaue for þe sofred meche shame. c1460 Towneley Myst. ii. 400 Peasse, man, for *godis payn. c1386 CHAUCER Shipm. Prol. 13 A-bide for *godis digne passion. 1535 LYNDESAY Satyre 1438 That sall we do..be Gods passioun. 1589 PUTTENHAM Eng. Poesie III. xvii. (Arb.) 194 Gods passion.. said she, would thou haue me beare mo children yet? 14.. Sir Beues (Pynson) 2090, I the tel by *goddys pyne. c1386 CHAUCER Melib. Prol. 18 Gladly..by goddes swete pyne. c1460 Towneley Myst. iii. 227, I swere bi godis pyne. 1569 T. PRESTON Cambyses B j b, Yea *Gods pittie, begin ye to intreat me? 1592 GREENE Upst. Courtier Wks. (Grosart) XI. 219 There were sweete Lillies, *Gods plenty, which shewed faire Virgins neede not weepe for wooers. 1562–3 Jack Jugler (Roxb.) 23 Hens or by *gods precious I shall breake thy necke. 1602 How a man may choose Good Wife K 3, Gods pretious call me dotard. 1599 PORTER Angry Wom. Abingt. (Percy Soc.) 59 Go to, mistris; by *Gods pretious deere, If [etc.]. 1859 TENNYSON Enid 368 Here by *God's rood is the one maid for me. 1575 Gamm. Gurton v. ii, *Gods sacrament the villain knaue hath drest vs round about. 1577 Misogonus II. iv. 157 (Brandl Quellen 448) *Gods sacringe, I haue lost a noble at two settes. c1460 Towneley Myst. ii. 458 Bi *Godis sydis, if thou do, I shall [etc.]. c1530 Hickscorner (c1550) E ij, By goddes sydes I had leuer be hanged. c1386 CHAUCER Miller's Prol. 24 By *goddes soul..that wol nat I. 1573 New Custom I. ii, I can not by goddes sowle. 1598 B. JONSON Ev. Man in Hum. IV. i, Draw, or by *Gods will ile thresh you. 1599 PORTER Angry Wom. Abingt. (Percy Soc.) 96 Gods will, tis sir Ralph Smith. c1550 WEVER Lusty Juventus D ij, This is an ernest fellow of *gods worde. 1535 LYNDESAY Satyre 991 That sall I nocht, be *Gods wounds. 1573 New Custom II. iii, By goddes glorious woundes hee was worthy of none.

†**b.** With sbs. not found in other contexts, and prob. in most instances corrupt or fabricated, as (***by***) ***God's bodykins, pittikins*** (= body, pity); ***by God's diggers***; ***God's ludd***; ***by God's me*** (? from 8 b); ***God's nigs***; (***by***) ***God's santy, sonties*** (? = sanctity); ***God's sokinges***. See also GODSOOKERS and GAD sb.[5] 3. _Obs._

1602 SHAKS. Ham. II. ii. 254 *Gods bodykins man, better. 1651 CLEVELAND Poems 21 By *Gods-diggers, Hee'l swear in words at large. 1577 Misogonus IV. i. 144 (Brandl Quellen 481) *Gods ludd. 1599 PORTER Angry Wom. Abingt. (Percy Soc.) 104 Yet, by *Gods me, Ile take no wrong. 1622 MABBE tr. Aleman's Guzman d'Alf. II. 142 *Gods nigs (my masters) you need not find such fault with it. a1643 W. CARTWRIGHT Ordinary IV. i. (1651) 59 Godsnigs the Farme is mine, and must be so. 1600 DEKKER Shoemaker's Holiday (1618) C 3, *Gods pittikins, hands off, sir, heres my Lord. 1604 —— Honest Wh. (1635) K 2, *Gods santy, yonder come Friers. 1596 SHAKS. Merch. V. II. ii. 47 Be *God sonties, 'twill be a hard waie to hit. 1577 Misogonus II. ii. 1 (Brandl Quellen 437), *Gods sokinges, houlde your handes.

†**c.** ***God's my arms, passion, pity***, etc. (by confusion with 14 a and 8 b). _Obs._

1577 Misogonus I. iii. 74 (Brandl Quellen 432) Godes my armes. 1599 CHAPMAN Hum. Dayes Myrth Plays 1873 I. 58 Gods my passion what haue I done? 1604 DEKKER Honest Wh. (1635) C 4 b, Gods my pittikins, some foole or other knocks. Ibid. D, Nay, Gods my pitty, what an Asse is that Citizen to lend monie to a Lord!

15. In solemn asseverations, as †***so God me bless, save***, etc.; ***so help me God*** (see HELP); ***as God's my judge***, etc. Also with omission of _so_ or _as_, and occasional corruption of the verb.

c1386 CHAUCER Melib. Prol. 4 Also wisly god my soule blesse, Myn eres aken [etc.]. c1460 Towneley Myst. xiii. 550 No, so god me blys. 1589 Tri. Love & Fortune IV. (Roxb.) 120 As god juggle me, when I came neere them [etc.]. 1598 B. JONSON Ev. Man in Hum. II. ii, I am asham'd of this base course of life, (God's my comfort) but [etc.]. Ibid. IV. i, As Gods my judge, they should haue kild me first. a1611 BEAUM. & FL. Philaster IV. iii, God uds me, I understand you not. 1842 TENNYSON Lady Clare 23 'As God's above..I speak the truth.'

IV. _attrib._ and _Comb._

16. Substantive combs. **a.** attributive and appositive, as ***god-belly, -clan, -crocodile***, etc., and in pl. ***gods-avengers***, †***-guardians***; †**god-bote** (see quot. 1674); **God-box**, (_a_) _slang_, a church or other place of worship; (_b_) (with lower-case initial) (see quot. 1923); **god-home**, _nonce-wd._, the home of God, heaven; also used by W. Morris as transl. of ON. _Goðheimr_, the abode of the gods; **god-shelf**, a shelf-like shrine of white wood holding the sacred images in a Shinto household; **God slot** [SLOT sb.[2] 6], a period in a broadcasting schedule regularly reserved for religious programmes; **God squad** _slang_ (orig. _U.S. Colleges'_), (the members of) a religious organization, esp. an evangelical Christian group; those representing the religious interest; **god-tree** (a tree worshipped as a god; also see quot. 1866).

1868 GLADSTONE Juv. Mundi xv. §3 (1869) 527 That under-ground region, in which dwelt the *Gods-Avengers, and which was the realm of Aïdes and Persephone. 1540 R. WISDOME in Strype Eccl. Mem. I. App. cxv. 322 This article [disbelief in masses for the dead] they take for my greatest Heresie. For indede this wringeth their *God-belly, that his eyes water for pain. 1675 J. SMITH Chr. Relig. Appeal II. 20 That devouring God-belly-gulph Heliogabalus. c1000 Laws of Æthelred VI. c. 51 in Thorpe Laws I. 328 And ȝif for *god-botan feoh-bot ariseð. 1674 BLOUNT Glossogr. (ed. 4), God-bote (Sax.), a Fine or amerciament for crimes and offences against God; also an Ecclesiastical or Church fine. [Hence in PHILLIPS, BAILEY, and mod. Dicts.] 1923 OGDEN & RICHARDS Meaning of Meaning ii. 37 The priests in whom gods were supposed to dwell (a belief which induced the Cantonese to apply the term '*god-boxes' to such favoured personages)—are amongst the victims of this logophobia. 1928 GALSWORTHY Swan Song III. xii. 305 This great box —God-box the Americans would call it—had been made centuries before the world became industrialised. 1962 New Statesman 25 May 768/2 A ring-a-ding God-box that will go over big with the flat-bottomed latitudinarians. 1889 R. B. ANDERSON tr. Rydberg's Teut. Myth. 142 One of the *god-clans has committed the murder. a1661 HOLYDAY Juvenal 272 Whiles..the *god-crocodile seem'd tame, all was well. 1665 SIR T. HERBERT Trav. (1677) 56 This their *Godfire is not composed of common combustibles. 1876 MORRIS Sigurd III. 217 The kin of the *God-folk. 1844 MRS. BROWNING Dead Pan xiii, Shall..no hero take inspiring From the *God-Greek of her lips? 1610 HEALEY St. Aug. Citie of God 125 For all the helpe of these *gods-guardians, there was not one king of them that continued his raigne in peace. 1839 BAILEY Festus xiii. (1848) 120 *God-home and glory-land. 1876 MORRIS Sigurd III. 216 A burg of people builded for the lords of God-home meet. Ibid. IV. 379 Round the fettered and bound they throng As men in the bitter battle round the *God-kin over-strong. 1862 H. SPENCER First Princ. II. xv. §122 (1875) 344 All titles of honour are originally the names of the *god-king. 18.. MRS. BROWNING Island xxvii, Or Poet Plato, had the undim Unsetting *God-light broke on him. a1711 KEN Hymnotheo Poet. Wks. 1721 III. 109 The holy Jesus..Co-effluent *God-Love on his Spirit shed. 1634 MASSINGER Very Woman III. i, They have new creators, *God-tailor, and *God-mercer. 18.. MRS. BROWNING Seraph & Poet, The seraph sings before the manifest *God-One. 1772 NUGENT tr. Hist. Fr. Gerund I. 522 Building to the *God-Ram the first temple. 1876 F. V. DICKINS tr. Chikamatsu's Chiushingura 171 One of these O-harai ought to find a place upon every domestic Kami-dana, or *god-shelf—a small model of a Shinto temple to be found in almost every house, labelled with the names of various deities. 1903 S. L. GULICK Evol. Japanese xxv. 292 There is hardly a house in Japan but has some..of these charms, either nailed on the front door or placed on the god-shelf. 1905 D. SLADEN Playing Game xii, They are never too poor to have a little light burning on the god-shelf. 1972 Times 12 Oct. 17/6 Of course there is a balance on TV. Peter Hain and Jimmy Reid get their chance on the *God slot on Sunday, or Late Night Line-up when everybody is in bed. 1985 Sunday Tel. 17 Feb. 3/2 This latest move cuts by half the religious programming on ITV on Sunday afternoon and evening, and could lead to the disappearance of the 'God slot', the so-called 'closed period' for religious programmes on television. 1697 DRYDEN Æneid Ded. b 4, Æneas..had the same *God-Smith to Forge his Arms as had Achilles. 1969 Current Slang (Univ. S. Dakota) III. 57 *God squad, Crusade for Christ on Campus.—University of Kentucky. The God Squad will not meet tonight. 1977 Time 26 Dec. 42/3 Cleaver was later converted by a prison 'God squad'. 1983 Observer 29 May 3/5 BBC executives..said: 'Beware the unexpected—and keep tabs on the God squad.' 1839 BAILEY Festus (1854) 412 He in the *God-state first..passed away. 1866 Treas. Bot., *Godtree, Eriodendron anfractuosum. 1896 F. B. JEVONS Introd. Hist. Relig. xix. 252 A branch of the god-tree, some actual ears of wheat or maize, are worshipped as Very God.

b. objective, as ***God-*** (or ***god-***) ***consciousness, -foe, -hater, -idea, -maker, -monger***, etc.; ***God-dreading, -making*** vbl. sbs.

1894 G. M. GRANT Relig. World ii. 29 The *God-consciousness of Israel expanded under the leadership of a long succession of prophets and psalmists. 1914 F. B. WILSON (title) The man of to-morrow. Human evolution impelling man onward to God-consciousness. a1300 Cursor M. 29205 þe gift o wijt..o *gode dreding. 1615 CHAPMAN Odyss. I. 118 The *God-foe Polypheme. 1643 VICARS (title) A Looking-Glasse for Malignants: or God's hand against *God-haters. 1898 W. JAMES Coll. Ess. & Rev. (1920) 429, I am now using the *God-idea merely as an example, not to discuss as to its truth or error. 1910 E. S. AMES Psychol. Relig. Experience 319 The God-idea is a teleological idea. 1924 W. B. SELBIE Psychol. Relig. 119 The origin of the god-idea varies with different peoples. 1949 Horizon Mar. 225 However primary and archetypical the God-idea may be. 1541 BARNES Wks. (1573) 340/1 Now woulde I knowe of these new *Godmakers, by whose power and helpe that the first Sainte came into heauen. 1875 M. ARNOLD Isa. xl–lxvi. Notes 122 This God-maker is hungry and faint, even at the very time that he is at his God-making. 1613 PURCHAS Pilgrimage (1614) 652 Art..in this matter of *God-making, commonly gets the upper hand. 1883 J. PARKER Apost. Life II. 206 You will be but jostling a whole crowd of *god-mongers. 1647 TRAPP Comm. John iii. 15 By like reason we may say that sin is *God-murther. —— Comm. Rom. i. 30 Haters of God. And so *God-murtherers. —— Comm. Coloss. i. 21 Haters of God..and so *God-slaiers. —— Mellif. Theol. in Comm. Ep. 730 This is Deicidium, *God-slaughter. 1681 DRYDEN Abs. & Achit. 50 Gods they had tried of every shape and size That *god-smiths could produce, or priests devise. 1895 SPURGEON in Daily News 7 Oct. 6/4 When I was at Pompeii I saw a God-smith's shop. He had several statues finished up to the face.

c. possessive (see also 5 f), as † **God's band,** the bond of marriage; † **God's board** (see BOARD *sb.* 6); † **God's body,** the sacramental bread; **God's book,** the Bible; † **God's chest,** the temple-treasury; † **God's cope** (see COPE *sb.*³ 2); **God's (own) country** (see COUNTRY 2 b); **God's-daughter,** † **day** (see quots.); † **God's eye** [= med.L. *Oculus Christi*], CLARY; also (see quot. 1880); **God's-eye-view,** a view as seen by God; † **God's flower,** *Helichrysum Stœchas* (*Treas. Bot.* 1866); **God's (own) gift,** a godsend; † **God's guests,** strangers, chance comers; † **God's house,** (*a*) ? a pyx, (*b*) an almshouse [cf. F. *maison Dieu*]; **God's image,** the human body (after *Genesis* i. 27); † **God's kichel** (see quot.); † **God's marks** (see quot. 1558); **God's quantity** *colloq.*, a large amount; an abundance; **God's service,** †in Coverdale [after Ger. *gottesdienst*] = worship, an act of worship; † **God's sond, send,** what is sent by God; hence, worldly possessions (cf. GOD'S GOOD); **God's Sunday** (see quots.); † **God's tokens** = *God's marks.* See also GOD'S ACRE, GOD'S GOOD, GOD'S-PENNY.

In OE. and ME. the possessive was also employed in such phrases as *God's church, house, lamb, man, mother, son, word,* etc. where the modern expression commonly is *the church, house,* etc. *of God*; see the various sbs.

1375 BARBOUR *Bruce* IV. 41 Hyr dochtir.. Was coupillyt in-to *goddis band, With Walter, stewart off Scotland. **1387** TREVISA *Higden* (Rolls) VI. 313 A wenche.. fenge *Goddes body an Ester day. **1549** PONET *Def. Marr. Priests* 45 He hadde the same day sayde masse (which he called the makynge of Gods body). **971, 1548** *God's book [see BOOK *sb.* 14]. **1635** D. DICKSON *Hebr.* vi. 28 As manie Plagues as are written in God's Booke. **1535** COVERDALE *Mark* xii. 41 Iesus sat ouer agaynst the *Gods chest & behelde how the people put money in to the Gods chest. **1520–53** *God's cope [see COPE *sb.*³ 2]. **1598** FLORIO, *Montemari*, impossibilities, gods cope, heauen and earth, seas and mountaines. *c* **1440** *Jacob's Well* (E.E.T.S.) 292 He mordryth *goddys dowȝter, þat is, his owen soule. **14..** *Exortacio in die Pasche* in Hampson *Medii Ævi Kal.* I. 186 [The Paschal Day] in some place is callede Esterne Day, and in sum place *Goddes Day. **14..** *MS. Sloane* No. 5 in HALLIWELL s.v., *Godeseie, *gallitritum.* **1880** BRITTEN & HOLLAND *Plant.-n.*, God's Eye *Veronica Chamædrys.* **1920** *God's-eye view [see EYE VIEW]. **1936** A. HUXLEY *Eyeless in Gaza* vii. 85 One has made a habit of not feeling anything very strongly; it's easy, therefore, to take the God's-eye view of things. **1970** *Guardian* 14 May 9/6 Frank Tuohy's.. short stories.. are mostly studies in suburban isolation,.. the God's-eye-view with God on the stage. **1597** GERARDE *Herball* II. cxcvii. § 5. 522 Golden Flower is called in Latine *Coma aurea* .. in English Golde Flower, *Gods Flower, and Golden Stœcados. **1393** LANGL. *P. Pl.* C. xvi. 199 Mynstralcie can ich nat muche bote make men murye.. and welcome *godes gistes. *c* **1400** *Plowman's T.* 747 On the pore they woll nought spend Ne no good give to goddes gest. **1938** 'E. QUEEN' *Four of Hearts* (1939) I. i. 9 (*heading*) *God's gift to Hollywood. **1941** M. ALLINGHAM *Traitor's Purse* xx. 228 Amanda was God's own gift to anyone in a hole. **1953** H. CLEVELY *Public Enemy* xxi. 151 It may do him a bit of good to find out he isn't God's gift to women walking the earth. **1377–8** *Durham Acct. Rolls* 387 Item in uno Chaliskays et uno *Godeshous pro rotulis officii, vjd. **1425** in Entick *London* (1766) IV. 354 The same house to be called for ever *God's-house*, or almes-house. **1610** HOLLAND *Camden's Brit.* I. 284 Sir Richard de Abberbury.. founded for poore people a Gods-house [*Note,* Almeshouse]. **1837** COL. THOMPSON *Sp. Ho. Com.* 19 May, Many in that House were old enough to have seen *God's image sorely mangled .. for what were termed political offences. **1598** SPEGHT *Chaucer's Wks.* B bbb, A cake.. called a *Gods kichell, because godfathers and god-mothers vsed commonly to giue one of them to their god-children, when they asked blessing. **1531** in W. H. Turner *Select. Rec. Oxford* (1880) 105 He.. also was full of *Godys markys. **1558** WARDE tr. *Alexis' Secr.* (1568) 39 A very good remedye agaynst the markes of the plague, commonly called Goddes markes. **1630** J. TAYLOR (Water P.) *Wks.* I. 59/2 Some with Gods markes or Tokens doe espie, Those Marks or Tokens, shew them they must die. **1911** C. E. W. BEAN *'Dreadnought' of Darling* xxviii. 242 There was *God's quantity of fish. **1922** JOYCE *Ulysses* 287 Big foxy thief.. lifted any God's quantity of tea and sugar. **1679** J. BROWN *Life Faith* (1716) II. xv. 127 We should make the Cross of Christ wel-come, because it is *God's Send. **1535** COVERDALE *2 Sam.* xv. 8, I shal do a *Goddes seruyce vnto the Lorde. —— *Acts* xvii. 23, I haue gone thorow & sene youre gods seruyce. **1306** in *Pol. Songs* (Camden) 223 Alle þe oþer pouraille.. mihten be ful blyþ e ant thonke *godes sonde. *c* **1386** CHAUCER *Shipman's T.* 219 Ye have ynough pardee of goddes sonde. *c* **1440** *York Myst.* xiii. 217 With synne was I never filid, Goddis sande is on me sene. **14..** *Exortacio in die Pasche* in Hampson *Medii Ævi Kal.* II. 184 þis is callede in some place Astur Day; & in sum place Pasche Day, & in summe place *Godeis Sunday. **1483** *Festival* d iiij, This day also is callyd goddes sonday. For crist goddes sone thys day rose from deth to lyf. **1582** HESTER *Secr. Phiorav.* III. xxix. 45 *Gods tokens, the whiche commonly come vnto those that haue the Pestilent Feuer.

17. Participial combinations. **a.** With active pples. (chiefly objective), as ***God-adoring, -affronting,*** etc.

a **1711** KEN *Hymnotheo* Poet. Wks. 1721 III. 326 A *God-adoring Race. **1671** M. BRUCE *Good News Evil Times* (1708) 10 The most *God-affronting Perjury. **1885** W. DE GRAY BIRCH *Life Harold* Prol. 105 The glorious and *God-bearing Cross. *a* **1649** DRUMM. OF HAWTH. *Poems* Wks. (1711) 33 Men awless, lawless live.. a *God-contemning race. *Ibid.* 34 *God-despising wights. *a* **1711** KEN *Hymnarium* Poet. Wks. 1721 II. 111 The Sin, which.. from the *God-detesting Spirit streams. **1895** J. SMITH *Message Exod.* xv. 250 This *God-disowning, good-defying spirit. **1718** ROWE tr. *Lucan* 180 The wily, fearful, *God-dissembling Maid. **1673** JANEWAY *Heaven on E.* (1847) 294 *God-estranging sins. **1850** CARLYLE *Latter-d. Pamph.* iv. 39 Putrid unveracities and *godforgetting greedinesses. **1603** HARSNET *Pop. Impost.* 73 The *God-gastring Giants, whom Jupiter overwhelmed with Pelion and Ossa. **1607** R. C. tr. *Estienne's World of Wonders* I. i. 20 They tell vs strange tales of god-gastering Giants, who heaped mightie mountains one vpon another. *a* **1711** KEN *Urania* Poet. Wks. 1721 IV. 448 *God-hymning Saints. —— *Blandina* ibid. 519 *God-intenerating Pray'rs. **1678** GALE *Crt. Gentiles* III. 65 Christ's crucifixion .. was a sin.. containing.. *God-killing bloud-guiltinesse. **1838** S. BELLAMY *Betrayal* 64 Example fair Thou wast, of *God-loving humility. **1639** FULLER *Holy War* II. xxxvii. (1640) 93 A *God-mocking equivocation. **1860** PUSEY *Min. Proph.* 306 Amaziah and the *God-opposing party. **1612** DRAYTON *Poly-olb.* v. 76 Her *God-resembling sonne [Achilles]. **1892** J. HUTCHISON *Our Lord's Signs* i. 25 A believing *God-seeing heart.

b. With passive pple. (chiefly instrumental), as ***God-begotten, -built, -created,*** etc.

1929 W. B. YEATS *Winding Stair* 11 And *God-appointed Berkeley that proved all things a dream. **1894** C. L. JOHNSTONE *Canada* 56 Carrying on the *God-assigned task of conquering the earth. *a* **1602** DRAYTON *Heroic. Ep.* xi. 80 That horse of fame, that *God-begotten steed. **1839** BAILEY *Festus* i. (1848) 3 All souls, impregned with spirit, God-begot. **1838** J. STEVENSON tr. *Beda's Eccl. Hist.* (1853) 577 That.. the sanctity of the *God-beloved further might be manifested to the faithful. **1715–20** POPE *Iliad* XIII. 1030 Your boasted city, and your *god-built wall. **1735** THOMSON *Liberty* IV. 297 The seeming God-built City. **1956** C. S. LEWIS *Let.* (1966) 269 The test of music or religion.. is always the same—do they make one.. more *God-centred.. and *less self-centred*? **1841** MIALL in *Nonconf.* I. 97 An image .. not *God-created, but made by the hands of man. **1715–20** POPE *Iliad* VI. 236 The.. *god-descended chief. **1862** H. SPENCER *First Princ.* II. xv. §122 (1875) 344 Presently others of the god-descended race were similarly saluted. **1845** WHITTIER in *Amer. Liberty Almanac 1846* 26 And the solemn priest to Moloch, on each *God-deserted shrine. **1895** W. M. RAMSAY *St. Paul* x. ii. 216 The usual type of *God-driven devotees. **1868** LD. HOUGHTON *Select. fr. Wks.* 105 The greatest of all possible gifts, Which *God-empowered man can give to man. *a* **1711** KEN *Hymns Evang.* Poet. Wks. 1721 I. 129 Food to ev'ry *God-enamour'd Mind. **1860** PUSEY *Min. Proph.* 562 Let the *God-enlightened soul go on [etc.]. **1864** —— *Lect. Daniel* ii. 61 Human power.. has a majesty, lent it by God, even when it abuses the *God-entrusted gift. **1675** HOBBES *Odyss.* (1677) 34 Choisest meat, Which none but *god-fed kings eat. **1643** MILTON *Divorce* I. ii. 6 If the woman be naturally so of disposition, as will not help to remove.. that same *God-forbidd'n loneliness, which [etc.]. **1889** R. BUCHANAN *Heir of Linne* vi, 'A *God-forgotten place', he said at last, as the dog-cart stopped. **1888** A. J. BUTLER *Dante, Par.* II. 17 The *God-formed realm. **1863** TENNYSON *Milton* in *Cornh. Mag.* Dec. 707 *God-gifted organ-voice of England. **1907** 'D. DONOVAN' *Gold-spinner* I. i 'God-gifted and beautiful' was Helga Arnold! **1800** *Asiat. Ann. Reg., Chron. India* 31/2 This *God-given victory. **1865** SEELEY *Ecce Homo* ii. (ed. 8) 14 The Messiah was.. to crush all opposition by God-given might. **1711** SHAFTESB. *Charac.* (1737) II. 337 In this case 'tis not a self-govern'd but a *God-govern'd machine. **1927** W. B. YEATS *October Blast* 22 These *God-hated children. **1860** PUSEY *Min. Proph.* 287 The natural *God-implanted feeling is the germ of the spiritual. **1865** MILL *Comte* 30 Hippocrates.. could say with impunity, speaking of what were called the *god-inflicted diseases, that to his mind they were neither more nor less god-inflicted than all others. **1936** L. MACNEICE tr. *Aeschylus' Agamemnon* 52 From whence these rushing and God-inflicted Profitless pains? **1622** DRAYTON *Poly-olb.* xxiv. 505 That *God inspired man, with heauenly goodnesse fild. **1839** BAILEY *Festus* xx. (1848) 265 God-inspired To utter truth. **1839** LONGF. *Hyperion* II. vi. (1853) 103 He is what the Transcendentalists call a *God-intoxicated man. **1877** E. CAIRD *Philos. Kant* iii. 43 Spinoza is more truly described by Novalis as a God-intoxicated man. **1870** MORRIS *Earthly Par.* III. IV. 246 Grief must he hide.. If he would be *god-loved and conquering still. **1598** DRAYTON *Heroic. Ep.* xii. 69 Nor do I boast my *God-made Grandsires skars. **1860** PUSEY *Min. Proph.* 336 The *God-opposed world. **1831** CARLYLE *Sart. Res.* III. vii, New Churches, where the true *God-ordained.. may find audience, and minister. **1884** 'RITA' *Vivienne* VI. i, One of those *God-sent chances which sometimes befriend us in our hours of peril. **1838** S. BELLAMY *Betrayal* 61 Nor longer tarrieth, *God-sped, and fain His course to finish. **1886** RUSKIN *Time & Tide* 20 The wisely sharp methods of Godsped courage. **1871** R. ELLIS tr. *Catullus* lxii. 30 When shone an happier hour than thy *god-speeded arriving? **1676** CUDWORTH *Serm. 1 John* ii. 3, 4 (ed. 3) 40 He is a true Christian indeed.. that is *God-taught. **1839** BAILEY *Festus* viii. (1848) 91 His *God-vouched inheritance of Heaven. **1870** MORRIS *Earthly Par.* III. IV. 24 Some *god-wrought eagle-wings.

18. Adjective combinations, as † ***God-full, †-unlike.*** Also GODFUL, GODLIKE.

1609 J. DAVIES *Holy Roode* F 3 b, Wilt be so God vnlike, to see thy God Embrace the Whip, and thou abhorre the Rod? **1648** HERRICK *Farewell vnto Poetrie* 22 in *Hesper.* (1869) 440 Those god-full prophets.

god (gɒd), *v.* Now *rare.* [f. the sb.]

1. a. *trans.* To make into a god, to deify; to worship as a god. **b.** quasi-*trans. to god it*: to play the god.

1595 SPENSER *Col. Clout* 810 Ioue.. taking [Cupid] up to heaven, him godded new. **1606** SYLVESTER *Du Bartas* II. iv. III. *Schisme* Argt. 3 Hee, Godding Calves, makes Israel to Sin. **1607** SHAKS. *Cor.* V. iii. 11 This last old man.. Lou'd me aboue the measure of a Father, Nay godded me indeed. **1668** GLANVILL *Plus Ultra* (1688) 93 In those days.. men Godded their Benefactors. **1871** H. N. HUDSON *Shaks., Jul. C.* Introd., We have Caesar.. godding it in the loftiest style .. The passage where Cassius mockingly gods Caesar. **1884** TENNYSON *Becket* v. iii, How the good priest gods himself! **1896** F. H. TRENCH in *Daily News* 21 Dec. 6/5 Who, by the silent Greeks' immortal main, Gods it on earth against the human cause.

2. In passive pple. *godded with God*, made partaker of the Divine nature, a phrase used by the Familists in the 16–17th c. (cf. CHRISTED).

1576 J. KNEWSTUB *Serm.* in *Confutation* (1579) S 1 b, For H.N. his Christe was.. first man, and after, by his suffering, was Godded with God. **1647** PAGITT *Heresiogr.* (ed. 4) 95 All illuminated Elders are godded with God, or deified. **1656** [see CHRISTED]. **1661** PAGITT *Heresiogr.* (ed. 6) 215 There was one Richard Lane, a young man.. said.. that he was changed into the Divine nature, that he was Christed with Christ and Godded with God and consequently perfect God and perfect man. **1739** J. TRAPP *Righteous over-m.* (1758) 62 Ridiculous jargon of being Godded with God.

Hence **'godded** *ppl. a.*

a **1616** BEAUMONT *Marr. Yng. Gentlewoman w. Ancient Man* Poems (1640) I 1 a, Smooth, as the godded Swan, or Venus Dove. **1675** J. SMITH *Chr. Relig. Appeal* I. 18 While impious Cæsar and his Godded rout spurn [etc.].

god, obs. form of GOOD.

God-almighty (gɒdɔːl'maɪtɪ), *sb.* and *adv.* Also 7– (*colloq.* and *dial.*) **God-a-mighty.**

A. *sb.* **1. a.** = GOD *sb.* 5. (See also ALMIGHTY, ALMIGHT, ALMIGHTIN.)

c **870** *Codex Aureus Inscr.* 15 in *O.E. Texts* 175 On Godes almaehtiȝes noman. *a* **1000** *Dream of Rood* 39 Onȝyrede hine þa ȝeong hæleð, þæt wæs god ælmihtiȝ. *c* **1175** *Lamb. Hom.* 5 In swa muchele edmodnesse godal-mihti hine dude for us. *a* **1300** *Cursor M.* 179 (Gött.) Godd all-mightin Turnd water into win. **1594** HOOKER *Eccl. Pol.* III. i. §10 Our hartie prayer vnto God almightie is, that [etc.]. **1604** DEKKER *1st Pt. Honest Wh.* (1635) I 3 b, Tell me, whither is he gone? *Tow.* Why to God a mighty. **1643** DIGBY *Observ. Relig. Med.* 29 Steered and levelled by God Almighty. **1864** TENNYSON *North. Farmer* 45 Do godamoighty knaw what a's doing?

b. In derisive use (with *a* and in *pl.*): One who poses, or is regarded by others, as omnipotent.

[**1609** C. BUTLER *Fem. Mon.* i. (1623) C 4, I haue read.. How there were Bees so wise and skilful, as.. to descrie a certain little God-a mightie, though he came among them in likeness of a Wafer-Cake.] **1682** DRYDEN *Medal* 110 This side to day, and that to morrow burns; So all are God-a'mighties in their turns. **1795** WOLCOT (P. Pindar) *Ode to French* Wks. 1812 III. 354, I, in life's more early day, Deem'd Kings young God-almighties, form'd for sway.

2. *dial.* (See quots.)

1847–78 HALLIWELL, *God-Almighty's-Cow*, the lady bird. **1886** ELWORTHY *W. Somerset Word-bk.*, *God Almighty's bread and cheese*, wood sorrel, *Oxalis Acetosella*. *God Almighty's cock and hen* [the robin and wren]. **1893** G. D. LESLIE *Lett. to Marco* xiv. 95 *note*, An Oxford friend tells me of a curious name for woodlice current in Oxfordshire, namely 'God Almighty's pigs'.

B. *adv.* Extremely, excessively. *colloq.*

1906 E. DYSON *Fact'ry 'Ands* vii. 85 It's that go'lmighty funny I can't laugh.. 'n' I'm dyin' to. **1923** D. H. LAWRENCE *Kangaroo* viii. 164 Why should people.. be so God-Almighty puffed up?

† **God-a-'mercy,** *int. phr. Obs.* Also 6 **godamarsey, gathamercy,** 7 **god-a-massy.** [= *God have mercy* (sometimes so written; see 2, quot. *a* 1617), used in the sense 'God reward you' (see MERCY), and hence as a mere expression of thanks.]

1. Used as an exclamation of applause or thanks. Const. *of*.

(In the latest examples app. used as a mere exclamation.)

a **1440** *Sir Eglam.* 96 'Nay, syr.. Ye are a nobylle knyght .. God a mercy, syr!' seyde hee. *c* **1485** *Digby Myst.* (1882) III. 619 God a mercy, symont, þat þou wylt me knowe. *c* **1520** *King & Barker* 116 in Hazlitt *E.P.P.* 9 Godamarsey, sayd our kyng, of they serueyse to daye. **1568** *Like Will to Like* A iv, By masse god a marsy my vreend nickol. **1631** CHETTLE *Trag. Hoffman* D 3 b, Well god-a-mercy friend, thou got'st me grace: But more of that at leasure. **1658** FORD, etc. *Witch Edmonton* I. ii, *Warb.* Wilt be angry, Wasp? *O. Cart.* God-a-mercy, Sue, She'll firk him on my life, if he [etc.]. **1790** *By-stander* 213 God a mercy.. what a happy thing for old Corin. **1828** SCOTT *F.M. Perth* v, Nay, God-a-mercy, wench, it were hard to deny thee time to busk thy body-clothes.

Prov. phr. **1597** J. PAYNE *Royal Exch.* 5 As the hostes reckonyng with her gest less willinge to lodge in her hows, then his tyred horse, made low curtesy.. to the beaste, and seyd gathamercy horse. **1710** *Brit. Apollo* III. No. 118. 3/1, I find I'm whole, *God a Mercy Horse.*

b. *ironically*; = 'Many thanks (to).'

1598 T. BASTARD *Chrest.* (1880) 26 But our Eliza liues, and keepes her crown, Godamercy Pope, for he would pull her downe. **1603** FLORIO *Montaigne* III. ix. (1632) 547 Theeves and stealers (godamersie their kindnesse) have in particular nothing to say to me.

2. quasi-*sb.* An expression of thanks, a 'thank-you'. ***worth god-a-mercy,*** worth giving thanks for, of some value or importance (similarly ***not worth g.***). ***no god-a-mercy,*** no special merit.

1563–87 FOXE *A. & M.* (1596) 103/2 As it is trulie said of Tullie: out of Asia (saith he to liue a good life, is no god-amercie; but in Asia.. that is praise woorthie. **1600** HOLLAND *Livy* XXIX. iv. (1609) 712 He would be readie to assist him with such a power of foote and horse as were worth god amercy [L. *haud contemnendis*]. *a* **1617** BAYNE *On Eph.* (1643) 130 For to choose one out of grace to have this or that hee shall well pay for, is grace not worth God have mercy. **1626** MEADE in Ellis *Orig. Lett.* Ser. I. iii. No. 328 If we stayed to expect the event in Parliament, it would not be worth God-ha-mercy. **1655** BRAMHALL *Def. True Lib.* 103 All this is most true, of a just Law justly executed. But this is no god-a-mercy to T. H. [*i.e.* Thomas Hobbes] his opinion of absolute necessity. **1692** [see GOB *sb.*¹ 2].

† **godard.** Corrupt form of *godere*, GUTTER.

c **1400** *Destr. Troy* 1607 The water.. Gosshet through Godardys & other grete vautes.

godard, obs. form of GODDARD.

godas, obs. form of GODDESS.

†**God-a-thank.** *Obs. rare*$^{-1}$. [= *God have thank(s)*; cf. GOD-A-MERCY.]

1657 TRAPP *Ps.* cvi. 3 Those that say God a thank only, and no more, are not only contumelious, but injurious.

God-awful (ˌgɒdˈɔːfʊl), *a. slang* (orig. *U.S.*). Also **God awful, Godawful.** [f. GOD *sb.* + AWFUL *a.*] Terrible; extremely unpleasant. (In quot. 1878 the sense is 'impressively large'.)

1878 J. H. BEADLE *Western Wilds* xxxvii. 611 Put thirty acres..into wheat, and went to work with a hurrah in 1874 to make a God-awful crop. **1897** C. M. FLANDRAU *Harvard Episodes* 88 Ellis is such a God awful fool. **1930** W. S. MAUGHAM *Breadwinner* II. 124 Your affairs are in a god-awful mess. **1946** 'S. RUSSELL' *To Bed with Grand Music* i. 14 Listen to the most godawful programmes on the radio. **1958** R. GRAVES in *Times Lit. Suppl.* 15 Aug. p. x/4 The credible and vivid story that any context (red-brick, yellow-brick, or otherwise God-awful) offers. **1959** P. MCCUTCHAN *Storm South* iv. 63, I heard the most God-awful racket above my head.

†ˈ**god-ˌbairn.** *Obs. rare.* [Cf. OSw. *gudhbarn*, mod.Sw. *gudabarn.*] = GOD-CHILD.

1014 WULFSTAN *Serm. ad Anglos* in *Hom.* (1883) 160 Godsibbas and godbearn to fela man forspilde. **1558** *Richmond. Wills* (Surtees) 113 Item I gyue to euery godbayrne I haue iiij^{d}., and to euery scoller I haue ij^{d}.

b. *god-bairn gift*: a present made to a god-child.

1535 LYNDESAY *Satyre* 788 Quhat salbe my Godbairne gift. **1579** *Sc. Acts Jas. VI* (1814) III. 164 The samyne landis beand gevin in godbairne gift to the erle of huntly be þe cardinall. *a* **1605** MONTGOMERIE *Misc. Poems* iv. 24 Quhy did the gods for godbarne-gift me geive Ambrosian bread..?

†ˈ**god-ˌbrother.** *Obs. rare*$^{-1}$. A male person who has the same godfather as another.

1571 CAMPION *Hist. Irel.* II. viii. (1633) 102 For which cause the Earle of Desmond remained many yeares Deputy to George Duke of Clarence his god-brother.

ˈ**godbush.** (Also **gad-**.) A Jamaican name for several plants of the mistletoe family, Loranthaceæ.

1851 P. H. GOSSE *Nat. Sojourn Jamaica* 131 But what interests me most in this place is a flourishing Misseltoe, or God-bush, as the negroes call it. **1864** A. H. F. GRISEBACH *Flora of Brit. West Indian Islands* 784/1 Gad-bush: *Arcenthobium gracile.* **1914** FAWCETT & RENDLE *Flora Jamaica* III. 88 The members of this family [*sc.* Loranthaceæ] are generally known by the popular names, Godbush and Mistletoe. **1961** F. G. CASSIDY *Jamaica Talk* xvi. 380 There is *god-bush* too, the mistletoe.

godcept, obs. form of GOSSIP *sb.*

ˈ**god-ˌchild.** [f. GOD *sb.* + CHILD (see GODFATHER).] A person considered in relation to his or her god-parent or god-parents; a godson or god-daughter.

a **1225** *Ancr. R.* 210 To longe abiden vorte techen god-childe pater noster and credo. **1417** *E.E. Wills* (1882) 39 Euere god-chyld þat y haue. *c* **1450** MYRC 152 Godfader and godmoder þou moste preche That they here godchyldere to gode teche. **1546** J. HEYWOOD *Prov.* (1867) 69 Ye haue many god children. **1791** BOSWELL *Johnson* an. 1784, His gentleness..to a young lady his god-child. **1834** COLERIDGE *Let.* 13 July in *Lit. Rem.* (1838) III. 420 My dear Godchild.

†**godcund**, *a. Obs.* [f. GOD *sb.* + *-cund* related to, of the nature of; cf. OS. *godkund*, OHG. *gotkund.*] Divine, spiritual. (Only OE. and ME.)

a **900** *O.E. Chron.* an. 601 Wel moniȝe godcunde lareowas. *a* **1000** *Cædmon's Gen.* 2612 Us ȝewritu secȝeað, godcunde bec, þæt [etc.]. *c* **1200** ORMIN 14257 Crist..turrnde waterr inntill win þurrh hiss goddcunnde mahhte. *c* **1205** LAY. 10139 Þet he sende [*MS.* senden] him anan sumne godcundne man.

†Hence **godcunde** (i.e. *-cünde* = OS., OHG. *godkundi*), **godcundhede, -leȝc, godcun(d)ness**, divinity, divine nature or power.

c **1000** ÆLFRIC *Hom.* i. 24 (Gr.) Seo haliȝe þrynnys..on anre godcundnysse æfre wuniȝende. *c* **1000** *Sax. Leechd.* I. 152 Ðeos wyrt hæfð mid hyre sume wundorlice godcundnesse. *a* **1200** *Moral Ode* 389 God is so mere & swa muchel in his godcunnesse þat [etc.]. *c* **1200** ORMIN 1357 Jesu Crist iss..Soþ Godd i Goddcunndnesse. *Ibid.* 1388 All swa comm Cristess Goddcunndleȝȝc All cwicc upp intill heoffne. *c* **1205** LAY. 24960 Godd sulf hit makede þurh his godd-cunde. *c* **1220** *Bestiary* 592 He speken godcundhede And wikke is here dede.

God-ˈdamn(-me). Forms: 7 **God-damn(e)-me(e, -dam-me, -damme(e, -dame,** 9 **God-dam, Goddem.** [See GOD *sb.* 8 and DAMN *v.*]

1. The utterance of this phrase as a profane oath. Also *attrib.* and as quasi-*adj.*, accursed, damnable. So **God-damned** *a.*

1640 *Wits Recreat.* No. 380 I 4 b, Swears from Believe me, & Good-faith & troth, Up to God-damn-me. **1647** WARD *Simp. Cobler* 61, I would pray hard to his Maker..to save his soule, notwithstanding all his God-damne mee's. **1652** PEYTON *Catastr. Ho. Stuarts* (1731) 28 The Courtiers garnished their mouths with God-dammes, as if they desired Damnation rather than Salvation. **1663** BUTLER *Hud.* I. ii. 510 The Solemn League and Covenant Will seem a meer God-dam me Rant. **1689** PHILOPOLITES *Grumbletonian Crew* 3 Unless their Throats be so furred with God Dame's, that no other Oath will slip. **1851** MAYNE REID *Scalp Hunt.* ix. 72 The 'sacre' and the English 'God-dam', were hurled at everything Mexican. **1869** *St. James's Mag.* IV. 226 It was the fashion in France, on the stage..to represent the Englishman as habitually saying, 'Godam'. **1898** W. P. DRURY *Tadpole of Archangel* 149 Before I could say 'Goddam', ..they would be fired. **1918** *Wine, Women & War* (1926) 29 If and when I do get home, I'll be the same God damned crab I was when I went away. **1921** J. DOS PASSOS *Three Soldiers* (1922) i. 10 Yer right not to go with any of the girls in this goddam town. **1928** *Queen* 7 Nov. 6/3 Mr. Frederick Leister was as usual convincing in the usual Leister 'God-damn-me!' type of part, though here the godamns were tempered with strong emotion. **1929** ABU NADAAR in *Mercury Story Bk.* 99 It was the utter goddam monotony that was the worst. **1929** D. H. LAWRENCE *Pansies* 82 My mother was..cut out to play a superior rôle In the god-damn bourgeoisie. **1939** N. COWARD *This Year of Grace* in *2nd Play Parade* II. 90 I'm so sick of their God-damned faces. **1952** S. KAUFFMANN *Philanderer* (1953) ii. 32 What a God-damned fool I am, he thought. *Ibid.* iv. 57 Perry leaped from his seat and came across the room enthusiastically. 'Jesus, the God-damnedest thing just happened.' **1958** *New Statesman* 6 Sept. 330/3 And I'll ponder upon the son-of-a-don Who turned my goddamed thesis down. **1970** W. C. WOODS *Killing Zone* (1971) ii. 23 Now you men knock off the goddam chatter in there and listen up.

†**2.** One who is addicted to swearing (applied by the Puritans to the Cavaliers). Also *attrib. Obs.*

1640 *Wits Recreat.* No. 233 F 6 a, What is the reason of God-dam-me's band, Inch-deep?.. God-dam-me saves a labor, understand, In pulling't off when he puts on the halter. **1643** S. MARSHALL *Let. Spir. Advice* 15 If their long conversing with God-dammee's, hath not drawn such a Kawl over the hearts, that to them damnation is ridiculous. **1643** PRYNNE *Sov. Power Parl.* I. (ed. 2) 17 The God-dam-me Cavaliers. **1679** *Essex's Excel.* 5 Such words as only befitted a railing parson in his Pulpit, or a drunken God-damme. **1713** *Gentl. Instr.* III. vii. (ed. 5) 430 Others were of the Town-cut, Young God-damme's that spoke ill, and liv'd worse.

‖**3.** (After F. *goddam* = OF. *godon.*) An Englishman.

1431 [see DAMN *v.* 5]. **1830** J. P. COBBETT *Tour in Italy* 8 It seems the 'Goddems' are having some fun. **1865** *Dublin Univ. Mag.* I. 3 The Norman era was the true era of the 'Goddems'. **1893** *Athenæum* 25 Nov. 728/1 The English..confiscated..even the small possessions of farmers and burgesses in order to people their new colonies with fresh-imported 'God-dams', red-bearded..foreign-tongued, as Eustache Deschamps depicts them.

ˈ**goddard.** *Obs.* exc. *dial.* Also 5 **godard,** 6 **god(d)erd.** [a. OF. *godart* (in a document of 1397 quoted by Godefroy; 'Item iiii pos de cuivre et le grant godart de la cuisine'), app. related to F. *godet* GODET.] A drinking-cup or goblet.

1432–50 tr. *Higden* (Rolls) I. 309 That londe bryngethe furthe white clay and redde, of whom pottes or godardes be made. **1444** in Cripps *O.E. Plate* (1878) 216, ij litil masers called Godardes, covered. **1512** *Nottingham Rec.* III. 116, iiij. goderdes et ij. pychers. **1555** EDEN *Decades* 117 Sundry kindes of iugges, godderdes, drynkyng cuppes, pottes. **1630** J. TAYLOR (Water P.) *Navy Land Ships* Wks. I. 82/2 Her Ordnance are Gallons, Pottles..Kannes, Goddards. **1654** GAYTON *Pleas. Notes* III. vi. 102 A Goddard, or Rummer, or lusty Bowle. **1882** *Antiquarian & Bibliogr.* Dec. 293 Drinking-cups are called in some parts of North Wales, and especially in Anglesey, goddards to the present day.

Hence †ˈ**goddardine**, in *pot goddardine.*

1508 *Will of Stury* (Somerset Ho.), A couple of pottes godardyne..a pott godardyne nyghe a potell.

ˈ**god-ˌdaughter.** [See GODFATHER.] A female considered in relation to her sponsors.

1002 *Will of Wulfric* in Kemble *Cod. Dipl.* VI. 149 Ic ȝeann minre goddohtor..ðæt lande æt Strættune [etc.]. *a* **1300** *Cursor M.* 28480 Mi godd doghter i gafe ne grith. **1340** *Ayenb.* 48 To his godmoder oþer to his goddoȝter. *c* **1440** *Promp. Parv.* 201/2 Goddowter, *filiola.* **1597** SHAKS. *2 Hen. IV*, III. ii. 8 How doth..your fairest daughter, and mine, my God-Daughter Ellen. **1641** BAKER *Chron., Hen. I*, an. 1104 (1660) 43 To do a favour to the Queen, that was his God-daughter, he [etc.]. **1776** MRS. DELANY *Lett.* Ser. II. II. 203 Mrs. Anne Foley called on me yesterday with my little god-daughter. **1880** MISS BROUGHTON *Sec. Th.* II. III. viii. 251 'Sophia is your god-daughter', she says abruptly.

godden (good evening): see GOOD EVEN.

godder-hail(e, -hale, vars. GODER-HEAL, *Obs.*

ˈ**goddery.** *nonce-wd.* [f. GOD *sb.* + -ERY 2.] An assemblage of gods.

1819 W. LAWRENCE *Physiol.*, etc. (1822) 17 The appropriation of a mutilated statue to its rightful owner in some heathen goddery.

goddess (ˈgɒdɪs). Forms: 4 **goodesse,** 4–5 **godesse, (godes, godas),** 4–6 **goddes,** (5 **goddis),** 4–7 **goddesse,** (6 *Sc.* **goddace),** 7– **goddess.** [f. GOD *sb.* + -ESS; cf. Du. *godes.*]

1. A female deity in polytheistic systems of religion. Freq. with phrase denoting the sphere of influence or power, as *goddess of love, night*, etc. (Cf. GOD I.)

1340–70 *Alex. & Dind.* 561 Proserpine þat ȝe..holden godesse god to gien ȝou here. *Ibid.* 690 Ȝe sain þat Ceres..is a goodesse god. *c* **1386** CHAUCER *Knt.'s T.* 243, I noot wher she be womman or goddesse. *c* **1400** MAUNDEV. (1839) iv. 23 A Goddesse that was clept Deane. **1490** CAXTON *Eneydos* xxii. 83 Proserpine of hell, the gret goddesse. **1548** HALL *Chron., Edw. IV*, 192 Such an unstable and blind goddes is fortune. **1606** SHAKS. *Ant. & Cl.* III. vi. 17 She In th' abiliments of the Goddesse Isis That day appeer'd. **1667** MILTON *P.L.* v. 78 Taste this, and be henceforth among the Gods Thy self a Goddess. **1710** STEELE *Tatler* No. 194 ¶2 This Temple..bore the Name of the Goddess Venus. **1835** THIRLWALL *Greece* (1839) I. v. 153 Theseus..is said to have found her dancing in the temple of the goddess. **1847** TENNYSON *Princ.* I. 194 Remembering how we three presented Maid Or Nymph, or Goddess [etc.].

2. Applied to a woman. *one's goddess*: the woman whom one 'worships' or devotedly admires.

1579 E. K. *Gloss. Spenser's Sheph. Cal.* Apr. 26 Lauretta the diuine Petrarches Goddesse. **1729** H. CAREY *Poems* (ed. 3) 205 He call'd her his Goddess, she call'd him an Ass. **1877** MRS. OLIPHANT *Makers Flor.* i. 18 Only looks had passed between the lad and his goddess.

3. A female spectator in a theatre-gallery (cf. GOD 4).

1812 [see GOD *sb.* 4]. **1824** CAPT. B. HALL *Jrnl. Voy. Chili*, etc. (1825) I. iii. 133 The gallery aloft, where the goddesses keep up an increasing fire during the whole evening.

4. *attrib.* and *Comb.*, as *goddess-mother, -train, -worker*; *goddess-like* adj. and adv.; *goddess-born* ppl. a.

1697 DRYDEN *Æneid* III. 402 Are you alive, O *Goddess born! she said, Or if a Ghost, then where is Hector's Shade? **1870** BRYANT *Iliad* I. VI. 186 Achilles the great leader whom they call The goddess-born. *a* **1586** SIDNEY *Arcadia* I. (1633) 51 Or that she (*goddess-like) would worke this miracle with her selfe. **1611** SHAKS. *Cymb.* III. ii. 8 She..vndergoes More Goddesse-like, then Wife-like, such Assaults [etc.]. **1667** MILTON *P.L.* VIII. 59 With Goddess-like demeanour forth she went. **1758** CHARLOTTE LENNOX *Henrietta* (1761) II. 208 What signifies attributing such goddess-like perfections to an obscure girl? **1662** R. D. *Ternary Eng. Plays* To Rdr. *3 b, I thought it best to get them [the Graces] to stand *goddess-mothers jointly for all three [plays]. **1715–20** POPE *Iliad* I. 746 Thou, Goddess-Mother, with our Sire comply. **1855** KINGSLEY *Heroes* III. 104 The voice which my goddess mother gave me. **1725** POPE *Odyss.* VIII. 364 Modesty withheld the *Goddess-train. **1587** GOLDING *De Mornay* iii. 37 It is the Wisedome whereby God worketh, which is the *Goddesse-worker.

ˈ**goddesshood.** *rare.* [f. prec. + -HOOD.] The nature, character, or position belonging to a goddess; divine personality.

1748 RICHARDSON *Clarissa* (1811) IV. 360 And should not my beloved, for her own sake, descend, by degrees from goddess-hood into humanity. **1851** SARA COLERIDGE in *Mem. & Lett.* II. 437 With an expectation of going back into her original state of goddesshood the day after. **1888** A. NUTT *Holy Grail* 241 *note*, Who might woo without forfeiting womanly modesty, in virtue of her goddesshood.

ˈ**goddess-ship.** [f. as prec. + -SHIP.] = prec. Chiefly in *her (your*, etc.) *Goddess-ship*, as a jocular title.

1610 HEALEY *St. Aug. Citie of God* 58 To please her goddesse-shippe. **1675** CROWNE *Calisto* v. Dram. Wks. 1873 I. 310 Go exercise your goddess-ship above. *a* **1704** T. BROWN *Praise of Wealth* Wks. 1730 I. 84 Zeal for your Goddessship's honour. **1818** BYRON *Ch. Har.* IV. li, In all thy perfect goddess-ship, when lies Before thee thy own vanquish'd Lord of War? **1831** MOORE *Summer Fête* 323 And, lo, how pleased..Her Goddess-ship approves the air. **1833** *New Monthly Mag.* XXXVIII. 179 Her Goddess-ship's qualities and attributes.

goddet, var. GODET, *Obs.*

†ˈ**goddikin.** *Obs.* = GODKIN.

1675 COTTON *Burlesque upon B.* 180 A little Goddikin, No bigger than a Skittle-pin.

goddis, obs. form of GODDESS.

†ˈ**goddish**, *a. Obs. rare*$^{-1}$. [f. GOD *sb.* + -ISH.] Godlike; divine.

a **1547** SURREY *Æneid* IV. 17 Of Goddish race some ofspring shold he be.

goddize (ˈgɒdaɪz), *v. rare.* [f. GOD *sb.* + -IZE.] *trans.* To make into a god; to deify.

1592 WARNER *Alb. Eng.* VII. xxxv, He (whose Sowles Soule goddiz'd her). **1602** *Ibid.* IX. xliv. 212 And faire, lou'd, feard, Elizabeth, heere Goddiz'd euer sence. **1874** PUSEY *Lent. Serm.* 246 A little created likeness of Thy perfections; ..a little god upon earth, goddized by the presence of God.

†**goˈddot.** Also **god(d)ote, goddoth,** (**-ut**). [Corruption of *God wot* (see GOD 10).] God knows.

a **1300** *Cursor M.* 870 [God speaks] Goddot, adam! þis said I are. *Ibid.* 11891 'Nai goddut', þai said, 'sir king'. *c* **1300** *Havelok* 2543 Goddoth! i shal do slou hem baþe.

goddspel(l, obs. form of GOSPEL.

gode, obs. form of GOAD *sb.*^{1}, GOOD.

Gödel (ˈgøːdəl). The name of Kurt *Gödel* (born 1906), Austrian mathematician, used *attrib.* and in the possessive to designate his metamathematical theorems and related techniques and constituents; as *Gödel number, numbering*; *Gödel's proof*; **Gödel('s) theorem**, the demonstration (first published in *Monatshefte f. Math. u. Physik* (1931) XXXVIII) that in logic and in mathematics there must be true formulas which are neither provable nor disprovable, thus making mathematics essentially incomplete, and also the corollary that the consistency of such a system as arithmetic cannot be proved within that system. Also **Gödelian** (gœˈdiːlɪən), *a.*

1933 M. BLACK *Nature of Math.* 167 (*heading*) Note on Gödel's Theorem. **1942** *Mind* LI. 259 (*title*) Goedelian sentences: a non-numerical approach. **1952** S. C. KLEENE *Introd. Metamath.* viii. 204 We designate the first of these theorems, which entails the other as corollary, as 'Gödel's theorem'. *Ibid.* 206 We call this a Gödel numbering, and the correlated number of a formal object its Gödel number. **1956** E. H. HUTTEN *Lang. Mod. Physics* ii. 34 Gödel's theorem, when first published in 1930, plunged many logicians and mathematicians into the pit of despair. **1959** NAGEL & NEWMAN (*title*) Gödel's proof. **1962** W. & M. KNEALE *Devel. Logic* vii. 476 This discovery is closely akin to Gödel's theorem on the incompletability of formal arithmetic. **1964** *Philos.* XXXIX. 196 Machines could never be selfconscious in the way that human minds are, and.. Gödel's theorem illustrates this. **1965** R. L. WILDER *Introd. Found. Math.* (ed. 2) xi. 275 In some of these systems, analogues of the Gödel theorems have been shown to hold.

godele(n, -y, vars. GOTHELE *v., Obs.*

godelich, godely, obs. ff. GODLY, GOODLY.

‖**godemiche** (gɔdəmiʃ). [Fr.] = DILDO[1].

1879–80 *Pearl* (1970) 265 'A godemiche? What's that for?' ..'Oh! Oh! We ladies use it to excite ourselves.' **1886** R. F. BURTON *Arab. Nts.* X. 239 Of the penis succedaneus, that imitation of the Arbor vitæ,..which..the French [call] godemiché. **1887** L. C. SMITHERS tr. *Forberg's Man. Class. Erotol.* vi. 148 There are expounders..who..have imagined that Bassa misused women by introducing into their vagina a leathern contrivance, an olisbos, a godemiche. **1966** L. COHEN *Beautiful Losers* II. 168, I also have in this trunk a number of artificial phalli (used by women), Vaginal Vibrators, the Rin-No-Tam and Godemiche or Dildo.

godere, obs. form of GUTTER.

†**'goder-heal.** *adv.* and *sb. Obs.* Forms: 2–3 goder(e-hele, 3 -hæle, -heale, goddre heale, 3–4 goder-, godder-hail(e, -hale, 5 goder-hayll(e. [= OE. *(*tó*) *gódre hǽle*: see HEAL *sb.* 2 b.]

A. *adv.* (more fully *to goderheal*) With good fortune, fortunately, profitably. **B.** *sb.* Welfare, prosperity. Also as *int.* = good-luck!

c **1175** [see HEAL *sb.* 2 b]. *c* **1175** *Lamb. Hom.* 65 Gif we þos bode þus bileggeð, ful goderhele we hit seggeð. *c* **1205** [see HEAL *sb.* 2 b]. *c* **1230** *Hali Meid.* 29 To goderheale þin he hit þoleð to fonde þe hweðer þu beo treowe. **1297** [see HEAL *sb.* 2 b]. *a* **1300** *Cursor M.* 15415 And godder-hail þan sal þou se, For luue of þis teching. *Ibid.* 23527 'Ful godderhail', coth þou, 'mai fall, If þai als i wald, sua wald all'. *c* **1460** *Towneley Myst.* xii. 226 Ha, ha, goder-hayll! I let for no cost.

godet (gəʊdeɪ, gəʊ'dɛt). Also 6 goddet. [a. F. *godet.*]

†**1.** A drinking-cup (cf. GODDARD). *Obs.*

[**1383** *Durh. Acct. Rolls* 420 Item unum Godet cum treacle. **1384–5** *Ibid.* 264 In capella unus calix, unum godettum de cupro, etc.] **1580** HOLLYBAND *Treas. Fr. Tong, Vn Godet,*..a Goddet, a stone cup. **1601** HOLLAND *Pliny* II. 482 C. Marius after he had defeited the Cimbrians, contented himselfe to drinke in a woodden godet and tankerd. **1629** —— *Cyrupædia* (1632) 4 He hath an earthen pot [Margin] Or Godet.

2. A triangular piece of stuff inserted in a dress, glove, etc. Also *attrib.*, as ***godet pleat, skirt.***

1872 *Young Englishwoman* Dec. 646/1 A basque disposed behind in three godet pleats. **1896** *Strand Mag.* July Advt. p. xiv, Costume..consisting of wide Godet Skirt. **1923** *Daily Mail* 10 Apr. 14 Black 'godets' in white kid (or white in black). **1925** *Brit. Weekly* 15 Oct. 59/1 Some of the smartest models have a full centre-piece instead of side godets. **1926** *Queen* 17 Feb Advt. p. vii, The simple bodice has the new long sleeves and the full godet skirt is finished self binds. **1928** *Daily Mail* 31 July 1/2 The skirt has full godet of lace each side. **1960** CUNNINGTON & BEARD *Dict. Eng. Costume* 96/1 *Godet pleat,* a hollow tubular pleat, narrow above and expanding downwards to give a fluted effect to the skirt. *Godet skirt,* a day skirt with godet pleats at the back and sides.

3. A driven roller or wheel around which filaments of certain man-made fibres are drawn during their manufacture. Also *attrib.*

1927 T. WOODHOUSE *Artificial Silk* 41 The group [of filaments] is then passed behind a guide-wire, partly round a roller, usually termed a godet, and often made of glass, [etc.]. **1950** R. W. MONCRIEFF *Artificial Fibres* viii. 100 As the filaments emerge from the jet..they are led to an eye at the surface of the bath, and thence guided round the bottom godet rollers. **1957** *Textile Terms & Defs.* (ed. 3) 52 *Godet,* a pulley, usually having one flange, round which threads pass in order to regulate their speed during the extrusion of certain man-made fibres. **1960** J. G. COOK *Handbk. Textile Fibres* (ed. 2) 174 On leaving the Godet wheel, the fibres pass around a second wheel which is moving faster than the first.

godetia (gə'diːʃɪə). [Named after M. *Godet* a Swiss botanist.] A genus of free-flowering hardy annuals, with large heads of cup-shaped flowers; any plant of this genus.

1840 PAXTON *Bot. Dict., Godetia,*..Very pretty annuals, well worthy of a place in every garden. **1885** *Bazaar* 30 Mar. 334/3 Godetias are remarkably showy plants.

go-devil ('gəʊdɛv(ə)l, 'gəʊdɛvɪl). orig. and chiefly *U.S.* [f. GO *v.* + DEVIL *sb.*] A name for various contrivances used in farming, logging, drilling for oil, etc. (see quots.).

1835 *Knickerbocker* Apr. 273 Led on by what they call in school-sports, a go-devil, prancing about in high horns, and a spear on the end of his tail. **1852** C. L. FLEISCHMANN *Wegweiser* 173 In Indiana und Illinois bedient man sich zum Zudecken der Maiskörner einer Art Hacke, welche unter dem Namen *Goe-Devil* bekannt ist. **1885** *Harper's Mag.* June 14/2 The graceful 'go-devil' rake,..gathering up the hay with all the ease of a lady's carpet-sweeper. **1886** *St. Nicholas* Nov. 48/1 A queer-looking, pointed piece of iron, called the 'go-devil', is dropped down the well, and [strikes] ..a cap on the top of the torpedo. **1889** *Cent. Dict., Go-devil,* ..a movable-jointed contractible apparatus..introduced into a pipe-line for the purpose of freeing it from obstructions... A rough sled used for holding one end of a log in hauling it out of the woods, etc. **1896** B. REDWOOD *Petroleum* I. 275 To explode the charge, an iron weight, known as a *go-devil*, was dropped into the well, and, striking the disc, exploded the cap and fired the torpedo. Now, however, a miniature torpedo known as a *go-devil squib*..is almost invariably employed. *Ibid.* II. 473 To remove obstructions in the pipes..an automatic rotary scraper is forced through... The scraper is known as a 'go-devil'. **1931** *Walters* (Okla.) *Herald* 19 Feb. 6/4 Farm Implements (Advt.), 1 2-row go-devil. **1931** *Randolph Enterprise* (Elkins, W.Va.) 1 Jan. 1/1 We had to [open the roads]..with.. sleighs, 'Yankee Jumpers' and 'Go Devils'. **1937** D. LUTES *Home Grown* 64 Old Man Covell came over to borrow a go-devil with which to split a stubborn log. **1958** *Publ. Amer. Dial. Soc.* xxx. 13 *Go-devil*.., a U-shaped rig for skidding logs. **1959** *Times* 13 Apr. 14/2 A piece of equipment called a 'go devil' is inserted every 24 hours at one end of the pipe and it emerges some hours later at the other end. **1959** *New Scientist* 30 Apr. 963/2 'Go-devils' have been used to scour and clean out oil, gas and water pipes... The go-devil, a sort of torpedo with rubber washers, scraper vanes or wire brushes mounted on it, is forced through the pipe under air or water pressure. **1960** *Publ. Amer. Dial. Soc.* xxxiv. 42 *Go-devil,* V-shaped ditch-cleaner. **1961** *Amer. Speech* XXXVI. 268 A rather confusing situation exists with regard to *go-devil* in Colorado. One Colorado informant even explains the word as a generic term for 'all kinds of contraptions'... It may, in eastern Colorado, refer to a cultivator, but several times it clearly means 'buck rake'. In central and western Colorado it is much more likely to refer to a Y-shaped ditch cleaner. **1962** *Lebende Sprachen* VII. 8/1 Pipelines are regularly cleaned by a bristling metal contraption known as a 'go-devil'. This device scrapes out the coating of sludge which collects inside the pipe.

'god,father, *sb.* [f. GOD *sb.* + FATHER *sb.*: see below.]

1. A male sponsor considered in relation to his god-child.

According to the practice of the Roman, Greek, Anglican, and some other churches, certain persons (commonly two at least, a man and woman) assist at the administration of baptism, make profession of the Christian faith on behalf of the person baptized, and guarantee his or her religious education. In accordance with the view that these persons enter into a spiritual relationship with the baptized person and with each other, they were in OE. denoted by designations formed by prefixing *god-* to the words expressing natural relationship, as *godsib, godfæder, godmódor, godbearn,* etc. The same terms are employed in the Scandinavian languages (ON. *guðdóttir, -faðir, -móðir,* etc., and corresponding forms in Sw. and Da.), prob. as adoptions from OE. The Du. *godmoeder, godvader* (also *goed-*), recorded in Kilian, are obsolete (if they were ever used) in Holland, but are still current in certain parts of Belgium.

c **1000** *Laws of Ine* c. 76 in Schmid *Gesetze* 56 Gif hwa oðres..slea..god-fæder. **1002** *Will of Wulfric* in Kemble *Cod. Dipl.* VI. 148 Hit wæs mines godfæder ʒyfu. *c* **1175** *Lamb. Hom.* 73 þet mon scule childre fulhten and heore godfaderes and heore godmoderes scullen onswerie for hem [etc.]. **1303** R. BRUNNE *Handl. Synne* 1691 þou shalt not.. Wedde þy godfadrys wyfe. *c* **1350** *Will. Palerne* 4085 Alphouns his gode godfaderes dede him þan calle at kyrke for his kinde name. *c* **1386** CHAUCER *Pars. T.* ¶835 Right so as he that engendreth a child is his flesshly fader right so is his godfather his fadere spiritueel. **1426** AUDELAY *Poems* (Percy Soc.) 11 Oure godfars, oure godmoders. **1479** *Surtees Misc.* (1888) 38 Whose godfadre was John Elwalde. **1548** HALL *Chron., Edw. IV*, 226 Whome for a farther affinitie, he had made Godfather to hys sonne Charles the Doulphyn. **1650** B. *Discolliminium* 44, I am glad God-fathers are cashiered for his sake. **1661** *Except. agst. Liturgy* 25 The far greater number of persons baptized within these twenty years last past, had no Godfathers nor God-Mothers at their Baptism. **1662** *Bk. Com. Prayer, Publick Baptism,* There shall be for every male child to be baptized..two Godfathers and one Godmother: and for every female, one Godfather and two Godmothers. **1732** LAW *Serious C.* x. (ed. 2) 140 He refused to be Godfather to his Nephew because he will have no trust of any kind to answer for. **1839** DICKENS *Lett.* (1880) I. 24, I must solicit you to become godfather.

b. A male sponsor at Confirmation.

In the Roman Catholic church new sponsors are appointed for confirmation.

1549 *Bk. Com. Prayer* S ij b, Then shall they bee brought to the Bushop by one that shalbee his godfather or godmother, that euery childe maye haue a wittenesse of his confirmacion. **1721** STRYPE *Eccl. Mem.* II. i. 4 The Archbishop of Canterbury, the Duke of Norfolk, Godfathers at the Font, and the Duke of Suffolk, Godfather at the Confirmation, were served with like Spices, Wafers and Wine.

c. A 'sponsor' at the consecration of a bell.

1498–9 in Kerry *St. Lawrence, Reading* (1883) 84 Godfaders and godmoder at the consecracyon of the same bell. **1756–7** tr. *Keysler's Trav.* (1760) I. 8 In the middle ages, the baptising of bells was attended with much festivity ..The godfathers who were unlimited,..gave grand entertainments. **1844** DICKENS *Chimes* i, They had had their Godfathers and Godmothers, these Bells (for my own part ..I would rather incur the responsibility of being Godfather to a Bell than a Boy). **1851** LONGF. *Gold. Leg.* IV. *Cloisters,* Conrad..who stood Godfather to our bells.

2. *transf.* and *fig.* (Often with reference to the godfather's naming the child at baptism).

The equivalent words in various continental languages (F. *parrain,* etc.) have certain recognized transferred senses, which the Eng. word has sometimes been used to render: e.g. 'a name anciently given to a kind of seconds, who attended and assisted the knights in tournaments or single combats' (Chambers *Cycl.* 1751, s.v.); also, under the rule of the Inquisition, one who attended a condemned person at an auto-da-fé (cf. Littré s.v. *Parrain*).

1588 SHAKS. *L.L.L.* I. i. 88 These earthly Godfathers of heauens lights, That giue a name to euery fixed Starre. **1592** —— *Ven. & Ad.* Ded., If the first heire of my inuention proue deformed, I shall be sorie it had so noble a god-father. **1617** MORYSON *Itin.* I. 37 After they had fined me some cannes of wine, and..had made me free, it remained that he whom they had chosen to be my God-father,..should instruct me with some precepts. *c* **1626** *Dick of Devon.* I. ii. in Bullen *O. Pl.* II. 16 The Popes Holynes would needes be Godfather To this most mighty big limbd Child, and call it Th' Invincible Armado. **1645** MILTON *Tetrach.* Wks. (1851) 220 When law contracts a kindred and hospitality with transgression, becomes the godfather of sinne and names it Lawfull [etc.]. **1674** JOSSELYN *Voy. New Eng.* 219 America so named from Americus Vespucius,..although Columbus and Cabota deserved rather the honour of being Godfathers to it. **1815** *Sporting Mag.* XLVI. 117 The author has acknowledged but one godfather throughout his work. **1839** MARRYAT *Phant. Ship* (Rtldg.) 335 The culprits who had been spared were led back to the Inquisition by their godfathers.

†**b.** *pl.* In jocular use: Jurymen whose verdict brings a man to the gallows. Also ***godfathers-in-law.*** *Obs.*

1596 SHAKS. *Merch. V.* IV. i. 398 In christning thou shalt haue two godfathers, Had I been iudge, thou shouldst haue had ten more, To bring thee to the gallowes, not to the font. **1616** B. JONSON *Devil an Ass* v. iii, Not I, If you be such a one Sir, I will leaue you, To your God-fathers in Law. Let twelue men worke. *a* **1634** RANDOLPH *Muses Looking-gl.* IV. iv. (1638) 79, I had rather zee him remitted to the jayle, and haue his twelue God-vathers, good men and true, contemne him to the Gallowes.

c. (Freq. with capital initial.) One of the leaders of the American Mafia; the head of a 'family', a 'don'; *spec.* [after the film *The Godfather* by Francis Ford Coppola (1972), based on the novel by Mario Puzo (1969)], the leader of the American Mafia, the 'boss of all bosses'. Also *transf. slang* (orig. *U.S.*).

1963 *Illicit Narcotics Traffic: Hearings Comm. Govt. Operations* (88th U.S. Congress, 1 Sess.) 184 Are you the godfather of any other member 'made' since then? **1972** *N.Y. Times Mag.* 4 June VI. 91/1 Just to run down the names of the nearly dozen capos—all subordinate to the family boss, or godfather, as he is also called—heading the different regimes within the family..illustrates what this investigator means when he says the Colombo combine is deep into 'everything'. **1974** *Times* 15 Jan. 2/5 [The] London restaurant owner..said to have been known as 'The Godfather' in a drug smuggling ring, was jailed. **1978** *N.Y. Times* 13 Feb. A12/1 Some critics say the I.R.A. has become a children's army... The youngsters, they say, are manipulated by a little band of experienced 'godfathers' who make the plans but never risk their own lives. **1984** *Sunday Times* (Colour Suppl.) 4 Nov. 38/3 In America one can catch the same faces on trade union leaders, corporate executives, mafia godfathers, mafia lieutenants, some congressmen and..some of President Reagan's close advisers.

Hence **'godfatherhood,** the fact of being a godfather; **'godfatherless** *a.*, without a godfather; **godfatherly** *a.*, befitting a godfather; also *transf.*; **'godfathership,** the position of a godfather.

15.. *Colkelbie Sow* in *Bannatyne MS.* (Hunter. Club) 1047 Colkelby..bocht Xxiiij hen heggis, and with thame socht To his gud sone, for godfadirly reward. **1677** Godfathership [see GODMOTHERSHIP]. **1807** SOUTHEY *Let. to Miss Barker* Lett. II. 37 Danvers is one of those dissenters who..look upon godfathership as a relic of Popish superstition. **1859** MRS. GASKELL *Round the Sofa* 328 These poor last folks must just be content to be godfatherless orphans and Dissenters, all their lives. **1896** DU MAURIER in *Critic* (U.S.) 31 Oct. 270/1 The kind thought which prompted you to let me know of my godfatherhood. **1928** *Observer* 29 Jan. 17/2 That 'brighter cricket' which Lord Hawke, on behalf of Yorkshire, promises for the coming season. This taking of godfatherly vows for a county team is a picturesque departure, which, we may hope, will have no anti-climax. **1958** WODEHOUSE *Cocktail Time* xv. 128 Lord Ickenham patted his arm in a godfatherly manner.

'godfather, *v.* [f. prec.] *trans.* To act as godfather to; to take under one's care, make oneself responsible for; to give a name to.

1780 BURKE *Sp. Œcon. Reform.* Wks. III. 327 The colonies which have had the fortune of not being godfathered by the board of trade, never cost the nation a shilling. **1879** GEO. ELIOT *Theo. Such* 69 All which views were godfathered by names quite fit to be ranked with that of Grampus. *a* **1884** M. PATTISON *Mem.* i. (1885) 50 Belfield godfathered me, introduced me into his set. **1890** *Temple Bar* Jan. 19 Via Garibaldi, street of palaces that deserves an antiquer name than that of the..recent hero who has godfathered it.

'God-,fearing, *ppl. a.* That fears God, deeply religious.

1835 in *Gentl. Mag.* Nov. 492 A good, God-fearing man was he. **1855** MACAULAY *Hist. Eng.* xi. III. 87 Those honest, diligent, and godfearing yeomen and artisans, who are the true strength of a nation. **1864** TENNYSON *En. Ard.* 112 A grave and staid God-fearing man.

Hence **'godfearingness.** *nonce-wd.*

1894 STOPF. BROOKE *Tennyson* xi. 386 Arden's godfearingness is not uncommon.

'God,fearingly, *adv.* In a God-fearing way.

1899 J. H. RIGG *Oxford High Anglicanism* (ed. 2) 404 If, from point to point, the wise and equitable thing is Godfearingly carried out.

'God-for,saken, *ppl. a.* Of persons: depraved, profligate, abandoned. Of places: desolate, dismal, dreary. Hence **,God-for'sakenly** *adv.*, **,God-for'sakenness.**

1856 EMERSON *Eng. Traits, Aristocr.* Wks. (Bohn) II. 77 Knowing..what a crew of God-forsaken robbers they are. **1860** G. DU MAURIER *Lett.* (1951) 25 Tom, nurse & foster thine aversion towards the Godforsaken city in which thy lines are cast now. **1886** T. HENEY *Fortunate Days* 85 The God-forsakenest spot that ever mine eyes were set on. **1903** *Westm. Gaz.* 11 Feb. 12/1 Of course, it is not of the same date as Brive. But it has the God-forsakenness, the *misère*, the penetrating sadness, its essentially French charm. **1913** D. H. LAWRENCE *Let.* 13 May (1932) 123 Some of the reviews have been so God-forsakenly stupid. **1923** W. P. KER *Art of Poetry* 60 You come with Milton..to the Paradise of Fools in a dry, parched, and god-forsaken land on the outside of the fixed stars. **1959** 'M. CRONIN' *Dead & Done With* iv. 61 You wouldn't know any place in this God-forsaken spot?

Godfrey[1] ('gɒdfrɪ). *Med.* [f. the name of Thomas *Godfrey* of Hunsdon, Hertfordshire, fl. early 18th c.] In full, *Godfrey's cordial.* (See quot. 1961.)

[**1722** *Applebee's Original Weekly Jrnl.* 17 Feb. 2298/1 To all Retailers and Others. The General Cordial formerly sold by Mr. Thomas Godfrey of Hunsdown in Hertfordshire, deceased, is now prepared, according to a Receipt written by his own Hand, and..is now sold by me Thomas Humphreys of Ware in the said County, Surgeon.] **1785** *Act 25 Geo. III* c. 79 Schedule..Containing the names by which many medicinal preparations..are known and distinguished... Godfrey's Cordial. **1845** L. PLAYFAIR *Rep. Large Towns Lancs.* 115 We want more of your Godfrey, for it does not produce convulsions in our children, like some of the other Godfreys. **1856** C. M. YONGE *Daisy Chain* II. xx. 563 'What have you nearest?' 'Godfrey's Cordial, sir,' quickly suggested the nurse. **1875** A. S. TAYLOR *Poisons* (ed. 3) lvi. 563 *Godfrey's cordial.* This is chiefly a mixture of infusion of sassafras, treacle, and tincture of opium... In 1837–38, twelve children were killed by this mixture. **1927** C. H. LA WALL *Four Thousand Years Pharmacy* ix. 418 Godfrey's Cordial..was a popular household remedy in Great Britain in 1722, when an advertisement of it appeared, announcing the transfer of the formula to John Humphreys, Apothecary, by the estate of Thomas Godfrey, deceased. **1961** *Brit. Med. Dict.* 622/2 *Godfrey's cordiale*, a sweetened and flavoured tincture of opium, a preparation rarely prescribed in modern medicine.

Godfrey[2] ('gɒdfrɪ). *U.S. slang.* A euphemistic assimilation of *God* to the name *Godfrey*, used as an exclamation of strong feeling or surprise (cf. GOD *sb.* 7 a); also in phr. ***by guess and by Godfrey***: see GUESS *sb.* 1.

1904 *Dialect Notes* II. 425 *Godfrey!* An ejaculation. Also *godfrey mighty*, and *godfrey Lijah*. **1906** W. CHURCHILL *Coniston* 274 'Godfrey!' exclaimed Ephraim. **1907** *Dialect Notes* III. 188 *Godfrey mighty*, softened form of God Almighty. **1909** *Dialect Notes* 411 *Godfrey*, used as a mild oath in the phrase *by Godfrey*. **1909** J. C. LINCOLN *Keziah Coffin* vii. 104 If ever a craft was steered by guess and by godfrey, 'twas that old hooker of Zach's t'other night. *Ibid.* viii. 124 Oh, my godfreys mighty! **1916** 'B. M. BOWER' *Phantom Herd* v. 71 Why my godfrey, man, the stuff's all punch. **1930** S. HENRY *Conquering Plains* 136 And there are the Government troops at Riley and Harker—by Godfrey! —if it comes to that. **1942** W. FAULKNER *Go Down, Moses* 15 They hadn't even cast the dogs yet when Uncle Buck roared, 'Gone away! I godfrey, he broke cover then!'

† **Godfright,** *a. Obs.* Forms: 1 godfyrht, -ferht, 2 godfurht, -fruct, -friht. [f. OE. *god* GOD *sb.* + *fyrht* afraid of:—OTeut. **furhtjo-*; cf. OE. *forht* afraid:—OTeut. **furhto-* (see FRIGHT *sb.*).] God-fearing; devout, pious.

a **1000** *Andreas* 1516 (Gr.) Godfyrhte guman, Iosua & Tobias. *a* **1100** *O.E. Chron.* an. 656 Ic haue here godefrihte muneces. *c* **1175** *Lamb. Hom.* 7 Ʒef we beod under sod scrifte and godfructe. *Ibid.* 27 Wel iscrifen and godfurht. *c* **1200** *Trin. Coll. Hom.* 187 Iob was ofeald man and rihtwis and Godfriht.

Hence † **godfrightihead,** devotion, piety.

c **1250** *Gen. & Ex.* 495 Enos..gan ali wune Of bedes, and of godefrigtihed, for liues helpe and soules red.

† **'Godful,** *a. Obs. rare.* [See -FUL 1.] Full of God, godly. (Cf. *God-full*, GOD *sb.* 18.)

1593 G. HARVEY *Not. Contents* Wks. (Grosart) I. 273 One of the most sacred and godfull arguments, that the holyest deuotion could admire. **1593** —— *Pierces Supererog.* ibid. II. 202 They knew his mercifull, and Godfull meaning, that [etc.].

godhead ('gɒdhɛd). Forms: 3 godd(e)hed, 3–4 goddhede, 3–6 godhed, 4–6 godhede, (4 -ede, -heede, 5 -heed, 6 *Sc.* -heid), 6– godhead. [f. GOD *sb.* See -HEAD; cf. MDu. *godheit* (Du. *godheid*), MHG. *got(e)heit* (G. *gottheit*).]

1. The character or quality of being God or a god; divine nature or essence; deity.

a **1225** *Ancr. R.* 390 Þis scheld þet wreih his Godhed was his leoue licome þet was ispred on rode. *a* **1300** *Cursor M.* 561 His godhed es in trinite. *c* **1320** *Cast. Love* 81 Þat bi-falleþ to Godes godhede As wel as to his monhede. *a* **1400–50** *Alexander* 5622 Sum grayne of godhede, I gesse, was growen ʒow within. *c* **1460** *Towneley Myst.* xx. 46 That fatoure says that three shuld euer dwell in oone godhede. **1513** DOUGLAS *Æneis* x. Prol. 27 Set our natur God hes to hym vnyte, Hys Godhed incommixt remanis perfyte. **1579** FULKE *Confut. Sanders* 616 Some of the Gentiles thought some priuie godhead or power to be contained in their images. **1667** MILTON *P.L.* III. 207 Man..sinns Against the high Supremacie of Heav'n, Affecting God-head. **1698** CROWNE *Caligula* III. Dram. Wks. 1874 IV. 396 If Caesar be a god, as he pretends, His godhead in creation was display'd. **1794** COLERIDGE *Relig. Musings* 31 He [Christ] on the thought-benighted sceptic beamed Manifest Godhead. **1856** R. A. VAUGHAN *Mystics* (1860) I. 191 Then hath the created spirit lost itself in the spirit of God, yea, is drowned in the bottomless sea of Godhead. **1875** JOWETT *Plato* (ed. 2) I. 359 Do you mean that I do not believe in the godhead of the sun or moon?

† **b.** As a title: Divine personality. *Obs.*

c **1386** CHAUCER *Knt.'s T.* 1523 If so be..þat my myght be worthy for to serue Thy godhede [etc.]. **1587** GOLDING *De Mornay* xxxii. 599 As for Caligula, Domitian, Heliogabalus, and others..they were not so soone dead, but their God-heads were dragged in the myre lyke doggs. **1607** SHAKS. *Timon* III. vi. 84 Were your Godheads to borrow of men, men would forsake the Gods. **1664** DRYDEN *Ind. Queen* III. ii, Summon their godheads quickly to your aid. **1718** POPE *Iliad* XV. 117 Supreme he sits: and sees..Your vassal god-heads grudgingly obey.

2. a. ***the Godhead***: the Supreme Being; the Deity; = GOD *sb.* 5. (Also *rarely* without article.)

1357 *Lay Folks' Catech.* 83 The first poynt that we sal trowe of the godhede Is to trowe stedefastly in a trew god. *c* **1380** WYCLIF *Wks.* (1880) 362 Þis state or power [the secular lords] is þe vicar of þe god-heede. *c* **1485** *Digby Myst.* (1882) II. 182 Saule faulyth down of hys horse: that done,.. godhed spekyth in heuyn. *c* **1532** DU WES *Introd. Fr.* in *Palsgr.* 1020 Wolde to God that the Godheed full of goodnesse had graunted to me [etc.]. **1588** A. KING tr. *Canisius' Catech.* 5 The first personne in godheid is the father cœlestiall. **1622** AILESBURY *Serm.* (1623) 13 The Godhead neuer was distracted either from soule or body. **1672** DRYDEN *Marr. à la Mode* III. i, 'Tis true I am alone; So was the Godhead, ere he made the world. *a* **1711** KEN *Hymnotheo* Poet. Wks. 1721 III. 354 Great Godhead.. Thou art eternal, pure Activity. **1742** YOUNG *Nt. Th.* IV. 693 In glory's terrors all the godhead burns. **1879** KEANE tr. *Lefèvre's Philos.* ii. 181 The god-head, whether one or many, has no place in the system of Epicurus.

b. A deity or divinity. = GOD *sb.* 1. Now *rare.*

a **1586** SIDNEY *Arcadia* II. (1622) 149 Esteeming that could bee no Godhead, which could breede wickednesse. *c* **1611** CHAPMAN *Iliad* VII. 21 At Jove's broad beech these godheads met. **1647** R. STAPYLTON *Juvenal* 272 Th' huge long-taild monkey is a godhead there [at Thebes]. **1725** POPE *Odyss.* IV. 632 What Godhead interdicts the wat'ry way? **1808** J. BARLOW *Columb.* II. 551 These eyes must see ..yon bright Godhead circle thrice the year [etc.]. **1876** MORRIS *Sigurd* III. 222 Lest e'en as a Godhead banished he dwell in the world apart.

godhood ('gɒdhʊd). [f. GOD *sb.*: see -HOOD.]

1. In early use: = GODHEAD 1. Now chiefly, the state or rank of being a god.

a **1225** *Ancr. R.* 112 [Christ's flesh] euer was iliche cwic of þe cwike godhod þet wunede þerinne. **1563** *Homilies* II. *Nativity* (1859) 405 Christ consisteth of two several natures; of his manhood..and of his Godhood. **1579** FULKE *Heskins' Parl.* 105 Wee must know to contemper the perfect man-hoode and the perfect Godhood. **1613** HEYWOOD *Silver Age* II. i. Wks. 1874 III. 106 He by his power and God-hood will contract Both births in one. **1624** —— *Gunaik.* I. 3 The same Philosophers attributed a God-hood to the Starres. **1837** CARLYLE *Fr. Rev.* III. VII. iv, Shorter godhood had no divine man. **1850** HARE *Mission Comf.* 65 When He vouch-safes to come forth out of His absolute Godhood, in the Person of His Son and Spirit. **1876** H. SPENCER *Princ. Sociol.* (1877) I. 416 This elevation to godhood of a living member of the tribe.

† **b.** = GODHEAD 1 b. *Obs.*

1683 E. HOOKER *Pref. Ep. Pordage's Mystic Div.* 11 Momus..who wold be ever carping (such was the snarl of his godli godhood).

† **2.** = GODHEAD 2 b. *Obs.*

1602 WARNER *Alb. Eng. Æneidos* 336 So farre off from a Godhoode, as thou shewest thy selfe lesse than a man, and worser than a Diuell.

† **'godify,** *v. rare.* [See -FY.] *trans.* To make into a god, deify; also, to make partaker of God's nature (cf. GOD *v.* 2). Hence † **'godified** *pa. pple.*

1621 BP. R. MOUNTAGU *Diatribæ* III. 435 Here is mention of Tithes to be payed vnto Hercules..to be giuen after his death and goddefying. **1645** [see DEVILIFIED].

Godism ('gɒdɪz(ə)m). [See -ISM.] A derisive term for belief in God. Also **Godite** ('gɒdaɪt), one who believes in God.

1891 J. M. ROBERTSON *Mod. Humanists* 18 Call his [*sc.* Carlyle's] creed 'Godism', and you limit the confusion of words by separately labelling his confusion of thought. *Ibid.* 37 At the mere sound of that word [*sc.* atheism], the Godite always became rabid. **1909** *Lit. Guide* 1 Aug. 124/1 The *Contemporary Review* permits Mr. G. K. Chesterton to make faces over Meredith's grave, and claim him as a believer in godism.

† **'godivoe.** *Obs.* [a. F. *godiveau*, of uncertain origin.] A kind of forcemeat (see quots.), a pie made from this; also ***godivoe-pie.***

1706 PHILLIPS (ed. Kersey), *Godivoe* (*Fr.* in *Cookery*), a sort of Pie fill'd with a delicious Farce made of Veal, and several other kinds of Meat; or else of Carps, Pikes, and other Fish, for Days of Abstinence. **1725** BRADLEY *Fam. Dict.* s.v., To have a Godivoe-pye, you are to prepare it with a Fillet of Veal, some Marrow [etc.]. **1727** *Ibid.* s.v. *Eel*, A good Godivoe is to be made with the Flesh of the Eel, which must be pounded in a Mortar. [**1846** FRANCATELLI *Mod. Cook* 57 Godiveaux in general.]

godkin ('gɒdkɪn). Also GODDIKIN. [f. GOD *sb.* + -KIN; cf. Du. *godeken* (obs.).] = GODLING.

1802 COLERIDGE *Lett.* 405 There was a Godkin or Goddessling included in each. **1819** W. TENNANT *Papistry Storm'd* (1827) 19 Aloft the godkin sits in pride, Exultin' in the jokes o' men. **1856** MASSON *Ess.* iii. 74 The little godkin, Man, is quite as odd as on the day he was made. **1865** *Macm. Mag.* July 282 Who bathed in the baths?.. Who worshipped the godkins?

godless ('gɒdlɪs), *a.* [f. GOD *sb.* + -LESS; cf. Du. *goddeloos*, G. *gottlos*, ON. *guðlauss* (Sw., Da. *gudlös*), Goth. *gudalaus.*] **a.** Of persons, systems of thought, etc.: Without a god; not recognizing or worshipping God; irreligious, ungodly. **b.** Of actions, etc.: Done without regard to God; impious, wicked. ***godless florin*** (see quot. 1897).

1528 TINDALE *Obed. Chr. Man* Pref. 7 [He] disceaveth him selfe and maketh a mocke of him selfe vnto the godlesse ypocrites and infidels. **1549** COVERDALE, etc. *Erasm. Par. Heb.* Argt., Yᵉ heathen, whome the Jewes aborred as vnreligious and godles. *c* **1586** C'TESS PEMBROKE *Ps.* LXXIII. iii, See here the godlesse crew..all happiness possesse. **1623** BINGHAM *Xenophon* 38 Tissaphernes a most godlesse and faithlesse man. **1632** MASSINGER & FIELD *Fatal Dowry* II. ii, When I think of..The godless wrong, done to my general dead, I rave indeed. **1667** MILTON *P.L.* VI. 811 Behold Gods indignation on these Godless pourd. **1725** POPE *Odyss.* IX. 579 What boots the godless giant to provoke, Whose arm may sink us at a single stroke? **1858** SEARS *Athan.* II. xii. 249 The bat-like fallacies Of our godless metaphysics. **1861** THACKERAY *Four Georges* i. 9, Military men..rushed thither ..to.. partake of all sorts of godless delights. **1870** [see GRACELESS *a.* 1 a]. **1873** SYMONDS *Grk. Poets* vii. 192 The glory of godless Asia vanished like a dream. **1897** *N. & Q.* Ser. VIII. XII. 13 Nov. 387/2 The florin which came from the Mint in 1849 without the words 'Dei gratia' is now called both godless and graceless. **1966** P. A. RAYNER *Coin Collecting for Amateurs* v. 84 The florins of 1849 are known as 'godless' florins, because they omitted the Queen's titles '*Dei Gratia*'.

c. ***the Godless*** [Russ. *bezbózhnik*]: the title of a union (and its press organs) in Soviet Russia, having for its primary object the suppression of religion.

1927 OLESHCHUK in *The Anti-Religious* No. 10, The Union of the Godless makes every effort in order to transform the International Union of the Godless into an active staff of class conflict,..and to make the fight with religion in the West a factor in the class struggle of the proletariat with the bourgeoisie. **1930** *Slavonic Rev.* Mar. 518 The Union of the Godless is a semi-State institution... The Union organises special 'cells of the Godless' in factories, villages and units of the Red Army. **1967** G. VON STACKELBERG in Fletcher & Strover *Relig. & Search for New Ideals in U.S.S.R.* 95 Publication of atheist propaganda was ..revived in 1947 when the Association of Militant Godless was dissolved and the Society for Dissemination of Political and Scientific Knowledge established.

Hence **'godlessness,** the fact or state of being godless; an impious act.

1553 *Short Catech.* 66 a, The principal point of godlines is ..to know God only..To thys godlynesse is directly contrary godlessnesse. **1587** GOLDING *De Mornay* iii. 29 *marg.*, Many gods, saith Proclus, is godlesnesse. **1612–15** BP. HALL *Contempl.*, *O.T.* XII. iv, It is an unmannerly godlesseness to take Gods creatures without the leave of their maker. **1866** LIDDON *Bampt. Lect.* iii. 187 The literal godlessness of the Positive Philosophy. **1870** *Athenæum* 19 Nov. 653 That they should pass their lives in utter.. Godlessness.

godlet ('gɒdlɪt). [f. GOD *sb.* + -LET.] A petty god or deity.

1877 PATMORE *Unknown Eros* (1890) 127 Lest he devour her and her Godlets both. **1884** *Academy* 28 June 450/1 He might always be baffled by the incalculable caprice of those innumerable godlets who..are regarded as the creatures of His hand. **1894** *Daily News* 27 Oct. 6/2 Many a local godlet came off badly during the terrible floods in the Valley of the Yangtze some years ago.

godliche, obs. form of GODLY, GOODLY.

godlike ('gɒdlaɪk), *a.* [f. GOD *sb.* + -LIKE.]

1. Of persons: Resembling God (or a god) in some quality, esp. in nature or disposition; divine.

1513 DOUGLAS *Æneis* I. v. 45 Is this the honour done to thame bene godlik? **1535** STEWART *Cron. Scot.* II. 707 This ilk Dauid,..Godlike he wes, full of deuotioun. **1596** SPENSER *F.Q.* IV. ii. 1 A god or godlike man..Such as was Orpheus. **1667** MILTON *P.L.* VII. 110 Thus the Godlike Angel answerd milde. **1711** STEELE *Spect.* No. 139 ¶3 By such Measures this Godlike Prince learned to conquer. **1725** POPE *Odyss.* V. 256 Thus spoke Calypso to her god-like guest. **1800** LAMB *Lett.* (1888) I. 156, I think that a more god-like honest soul exists not in the world. **1852** TENNYSON *Death Wellington* 266 On God and Godlike men we build our trust.

b. quasi-*adv.* After the fashion of a god.

1667 MILTON *P.L.* IV. 289 Two of far nobler shape erect and tall, Godlike erect. **1674** DRYDEN *State Innoc.* IV. Wks. 1883 V. 152 Praise Him alone, who god-like formed thee free, With will unbounded as a deity.

2. Of qualities, actions, appearance, etc.: Appropriate to a god; resembling (that of) God or a god.

c **1555** HARPSFIELD in *Bonner's Hom.* 3 Endued with most heuenly & godlike qualities. **1596** SHAKS. *Merch. V.* III. iv. 3 Madam,..You haue a noble and a true conceit Of god-like amity. **1697** DRYDEN *Virg. Georg.* IV. 139 Godlike to behold, His Royal Body shines with Specks of Gold. **1713** ADDISON *Cato* I. iv, To what a godlike height The Roman virtues lift up mortal man. **1725** BERKELEY *Proposal*, etc. Wks. III. 230 An excellent and godlike temper of mind. **1809–10** COLERIDGE *Friend* (1865) 32 The God-like faculty of reason. **1830** MACKINTOSH *Eth. Philos.* Wks. 1846 I. 130 He was compelled..to forego his work of heroic, or rather godlike benevolence. **1870** BRYANT *Iliad* I. III. 81 Paris of the godlike form Appeared in sight.

b. *absol.* (quasi-*sb.*)

1831 CARLYLE *Sart. Res.* (1858) 136 Is not a Symbol ever, to him who has eyes for it, some dimmer or clearer revelation of the Godlike!

Hence **'godlikeness**, godlike quality; likeness to God.

1649 J. CARDELL *Morbus Epidem.* (1650) 35 Godliness is God-likeness. **1825** COLERIDGE *Aids Refl.* Wks. 1848 I. 216 Godliness, that is, godlikeness. **1839** LONGF. *Hyperion* I. ii. (1853) 9 The expiring God-likeness of Jesus of Nazareth. **1875** E. WHITE *Life in Christ* II. xi. (1878) 117 The Holy Spirit..communicating to good men of every age and generation God-likeness and immortality.

'godlily, *adv.* Now *rare.* Cf. GODLY *adv.* [f. GODLY *a.* + -LY².] In a godly fashion.

1548 UDALL, etc. *Erasm. Par. Mark* ii, 27, 28 He breaketh the Sabboth daye godlily, who..breaketh it onely for the good zeale he hath to helpe his euen Christen. **1561** tr. *Calvin's 4 Godly Serm. agst. Idol.* A iv b, Albeit God doeth geue vs at this time liberty to serue him purely and godlilye. **1652** COLLINGES *Caveat for Prof.* xii. (1653) 66 Feast-dayes ..holily and godlily celebrated. **1691** NORRIS *Pract. Disc.* 319 Teaching us, that..we should live Soberly, Righteously and Godlily. **1798** COLERIDGE *Let.* 20 Oct. *Lett.* (1895) I. 264 This invaluable and infallible Medicine has been godlily extracted therefrom by the slow processes of the Sun.

godliness ('gɒdlɪnɪs). [f. GODLY *a.* + -NESS.]

1. The quality of being godly; devout observance of the law of God; piety.

1531 TINDALE *Exp. 2 John* (1537) 91 Charite conteyneth al exercyse of godlynesse. **1591** SPENSER *M. Hubberd* 844 But what car'd he for God or godliness? **1597** HOOKER *Eccl. Pol.* v. i. §2 Godlinesse being the chiefest top and welspring of all true vertues. *a* **1656** BP. HALL *Rem. Wks.* (1660) 122 Making a shew of Godliness and denying the power of it in their lives. *a* **1708** BEVERIDGE *Thes. Theol.* (1710) I. 249 This worship of God in Scripture is called Godliness. **1781** COWPER *Hope* 661 Bigotry..Pretends a zeal for godliness and grace. **1802** WORDSW. *London*, So didst thou travel on life's common way, In cheerful godliness. **1878** MORLEY *Carlyle* 191 The same principle which revealed the valour and godliness of Puritanism.

†**2.** Used as a title (*your Godliness*). *Obs.*

a **1656** USSHER *Power Princes* II. (1683) 231 We beseech your Clemency..that..if it so please your Godliness, you command us to return to our Churches.

godling ('gɒdlɪŋ). [f. GOD *sb.* + -LING; cf. GODDIKIN, GODKIN, GODLET.]

1. A little god; an inferior deity, one imagined as possessing little power or of diminutive size. (Chiefly in jocular use; common in the 17th c.)

In the first quot. perh. a misreading for GADLING².

?*a* **1500** *Chester Pl.* (Shaks. Soc.) I. 157 Suche doterdes never shall..make my righte title seace! But I shall knightlye kepe it..Againste that yonge godlynge [*Harl. MS.* 2124, gedling]. **1570–6** LAMBARDE *Peramb. Kent* (1826) 394 What remaineth..but that altars should be raised..to this our newe found Godlyng? *a* **1638** MEDE *Disc. 2 Peter* ii. 1 Wks. (1672) I. 242 Under-gods, or, if you will, Godlings, which the Greeks call Dæmon-gods. **1693** DRYDEN *Persius* Sat. ii. (1697) 430 Thy puny Godlings of inferiour Race, Whose humble Statues are content with Brass. **1794** WOLCOT (P. Pindar) *Pathetic Odes* Wks. 1812 III. 232 Gods of the Earth are Emperors, Popes, and Kings; Godlings, our Dukes and Earls, and such fine folk. **1855** BAILEY *Mystic* 39 Isis twin godlings, silence and the light. **1892** *Edin. Rev.* Apr. 471 Gods, godlings and demons.

attrib. **1629** DRUMM. OF HAWTH. in *Sir W. Moore's True Crucifixe*, Every painted wall Grac't with some antik face, some Godling make.

2. An image of a 'godling'.

1762 BEATTIE *Pigm. & Cranes* 34 He finds the puny mansion fallen to earth, Its godlings mouldering on the abandon'd hearth. **1792** WOLCOT (P. Pindar) *Ep. to Sir W. Hamilton* Wks. 1812 III. 189 Send the Gods and Godlings back again.

godly ('gɒdlɪ), *a.* [f. GOD *sb.* + -LY¹; parallel forms are found in the cognate languages much earlier than in English, as OHG. *gotelîh* (MHG. *got(e)lich*, *göt(e)lich*, G. *göttlich*); MDu. *god(d)elijc*, *godlijc* (Du. *goddelijk*) divine; ON. *guðligr* (Sw. *gudlig*, Da. *gudelig*) divine, pious. (The early identity in spelling of GODLY and GOODLY renders some quotations ambiguous.)]

1. Of or pertaining to God; coming from God; divine; spiritual. *Obs.* exc. *arch.*

In first quot. = THEOLOGICAL, q.v.

c **1380** WYCLIF *De Eccl.* ii. Sel. Wks. III. 340 þes two godliche virtues [faith and hope]. **1450–1530** *Myrr. our Ladye* 4 In the syghte of hys Godly forknowynge. **1553** EDEN *Treat. Newe Ind.* (Arb.) 24 Yet haue they no knowledge of dyuine or godly thinges. **1567** *Gude & Godlie Ball.* (S.T.S.) 146 Thow onlie Maker of all thing..From end to end all rewling Be thy awin godly mycht. **1583** STANYHURST *Æneis* II. (Arb.) 66 Uow'd to the godly Ceres. **1599** B. JONSON *Cynthia's Rev.* v. i, The grace diuinest Mercurie hath done me..Binds my obseruance..to his godly will. **1849** SAXE *Times* 120 Daring the dangers of the angry main For civil freedom and for godly gain.

2. Devoutly observant of the laws of God; religious, pious. **a.** Of conduct, speech, etc. *arch.*

godly sorrow, Tindale's rendering (followed in later versions) of ἡ κατὰ Θεὸν λύπη.

1526 TINDALE *2 Cor.* vii. 9 For godly sorowe causeth repentaunce. *c* **1530** H. RHODES *Bk. Nurture* 789 in *Babees Bk.*, Delight to reade good Godly bookes, and marke the meaning well. *a* **1533** FRITH *Disput. Purg.* (1829) 137 These works God would have us do, that the unfaithful might see the godly and virtuous conversation of his faithful. **1548** HALL *Chron., Rich. III*, 58 He..rendred to almightie God his harty thankes wᵗ devoute and Godly orisons. **1641** HINDE *J. Bruen* xviii. 55, I hold him worthy great commendation..for his godly care in chusing [servants]. **1691** HARTCLIFFE *Virtues* 343 The fear and love of God, and godly Sorrow, and true Repentance [etc.].

b. Of persons; also *absol.* as pl. *the godly.*

1529 MORE *Dyaloge* I. Wks. 116/1 The good godly man Moyses. **1564** *Brief Exam.* A iij b, Godly men may vse them Godly, and to the glory of God. **1597** HOOKER *Eccl. Pol.* v. xliv, The godly should be alwayes prepared to dye. **1612** DRAYTON *Poly-olb.* xi. 178 What age a godlier Prince then Ethelred could bring? **1631** GOUGE *God's Arrows* I. §12. 17 Of the godliest exemption from the ungodlies destruction. **1663** DRYDEN *Wild Gallant* v. i, I am somewhat godly at present. **1680** OTWAY *Orphan* Epil. 7 Should I the Godly seek, And go a conventickling twice a Week? **1715** DE FOE *Fam. Instruct.* I. viii, What, are you grown godly too, Pin? **1849** MACAULAY *Hist. Eng.* ii. I. 165 Soon the world begins to find out that the godly are not better than other men. *a* **1862** BUCKLE *Civiliz.* (1869) III. ii. 84 They were the godly men; and it was the business of the ruling classes to endow them with benefices.

†**3.** *godly mother*, a rendering of L. *pia mater*, the inner membrane inclosing the brain. *Obs.*

1594 T.B. *La Primaud. Fr. Acad.* II. 149 Besides this skinne, there is another named the godly mother, which is fine and very slender.

4. *Comb.*, as *godly-hearted*, *-minded* ppl. adjs.

1679 KID in G. Hickes *Spirit of Popery* (1680) 15 Many Godly-hearted men in this Island. **1856** R. A. VAUGHAN *Mystics* (1860) I. 190 These are they whom St. Dionysius calls godly-minded men.

godly ('gɒdlɪ), *adv.* Now *rare.* [See prec. and -LY²; cf. GODLILY.] In a godly fashion.

1530 TINDALE *Gen.* Table exp. Words s.v. *Curse*, That.. true purgatorye of oure flesh, thorow which all must go that will lyue godly and be saued. **1535** COVERDALE *Prov.* xix. 1 Better is the poore that lyueth godly, then the blasphemer that is but a foole. **1547** *Act 1 Edw. VI*, c. 1 Preamble, Many Things well and godly instituted. **1631** WEEVER *Anc. Funeral Mon.* 69 To have liued godly, and died Christianly. **1871** HAWTHORNE *Septimius* (1879) 143 Now she tried to.. talk reasonably and godly.

b. *Comb.*, as *godly-disposed* adj.; †**godly-learned** *a.*, learned in divinity; †**godly-wise** *a.*, wise in divine things.

1532 MORE *Confut. Tindale* Wks. 502/2 Is not this wene ye a Godly-wise waye? **1545** BRINKLOW *Compl.* xi. (1874) 26 Make no iudgys therfore (I say) but such as be godly-lernyd, and able to iudge between man and man. **1564** *Decrees Counsel of Trent* (title-p.), Written for those godlye disposed persons sakes, whych [etc.]. **1611** BIBLE *Transl. Pref.* 5 For all that the godly-learned were not content to haue the Scriptures in the Language which themselues vnderstood. **1633** BP. HALL *Medit. & Vows* xxiii. (1851) 29 O God, let me rather die..than justly offend thy godly-wise, judicious, conscionable servants.

'god-ma,mma. Used in childish or familiar speech for GODMOTHER.

1828 MISS MITFORD *Village* Ser. III. 278 Cordially welcomed by all its members except my godmamma. **1837** PRAED *Verses in Child's Bk.* iii. 4 A God-mamma, who proves..that she loves Her God-child very dearly. **1856** LEVER *Martins of Cro' M.* viii, So good-by, God-mamma.

'God-'man. [tr. Gr. θεάνδρος, θεάνθρωπος; cf. Du. *Godmensch*, G. *Gottmensch*, F. *Homme-Dieu.*] One who is both God and man; said of Christ. Also *transf.*

1559 in Neal *Hist. Puritans* (1754) I. 93 After the consecration [of the host] there remains not..any other substance but God-Man. **1597** J. PAYNE *Royal Exch.* 45 Yt ys God-man that hathe fought and suffred in his humanitie: and yt ys the Man-god wch hathe conquered by his Devinitie. **1654** WARREN *Unbelievers* 39 All this constituted Christ God-man. **1666** SPURSTOWE *Spir. Chym.* (1668) 239 He who is the Saviour of Believers is God-man manifested in the Flesh. *a* **1711** KEN *Hymnotheo* Poet. Wks. 1721 III. 356 Mary..for the Mother of God-man design'd. **1853** KINGSLEY *Hypatia* xxiv, Then clear and fair arose before him the vision of the God-man, as He lay at meat in the Pharisee's house. **1866** G. MACDONALD *Ann. Q. Neighb.* viii. (1878) 128 Jesus Christ, the living, loving God-man. **1899** C. J. C. HYNE *Further Adv. Capt. Kettle* ii. 34 'He God-man. Lib for here on gin-palaver.' 'Trading missionary, is he?' **1924** E. WALLACE *Room 13* 56 You couldn't undo what that old God-man did this morning.

Comb. **1861** W. L. ALEXANDER tr. *Dorner's Pers. Christ* (1872) I. I. 1 It will ever remain the ideal of human life, that it is God-manlike.

Hence **'God-'manhood**, the state or condition of being at once God and man.

1877 C. GEIKIE *Christ* (1879) 4 Nothing loftier offers itself to humanity than the God-manhood realized in Jesus Christ. **1893** J. ORR *God & World* vi. 289 The God-manhood is the wonder of all wonders.

'god,mother. [Cf. GODFATHER.] A female sponsor considered in relation to her god-child.

c **1000** *Martyrol.* in Cockayne *Shrine* 140 Heo slep æt þære godmodor huse. *c* **1175** [see GODFATHER]. **1303** R. BRUNNE *Handl. Synne* 1693 Also shal þe womman wonde To take here godmodrys husbonde. **1340** [see GOD-DAUGHTER]. *c* **1420** *Chron. Vilod.* st. 553 Hurre godfather and hurre godmores. **1494** FABYAN *Chron.* VII. 435 They founde yᵗ Mawde..was godmother vnto yᵉ Kyng Charlys hir husbonde. **1548** HALL *Chron., Edw. IV*, 210 Christened and Baptised, the Godfathers beyng the Abbot and Pryor of Westmynster, and the godmother the lady Scrope. *a* **1649** DRUMM. OF HAWTH. *Hist. Jas. V*, Wks. (1711) 105 The arch-bishop of St. Andrew's & earl of Arran being his godfathers, & the old queen, the king's mother, his godmother. **1710–11** SWIFT *Lett.* (1767) III. 87 A girl..and was poor Stella forced to stand for godmother? **1849** LYTTON *Caxtons* 12 When the question of godmother and godfather was fairly put to him, he [etc.]. *a* **1878** PRINCESS ALICE in *Mem.* (1884) 78 Louis's mother is to be god-mother.

b. A female 'sponsor' of a bell.

1844 DICKENS *Chimes* i, They had had their Godfathers and Godmothers, these Bells.

Hence **'godmother** *v.*, to provide with a godmother. Also **'god,motherhood**, **'god-,mothership**, the office of a godmother.

1677 W. HUGHES *Man of Sin.* II. x. 175 Urbanus holds it lawfull that Sons and Daughters of Godfathers and Godmothers born before or after such their Godfather or Godmothership, should marry. **1741** RICHARDSON *Pamela* (1824) I. xlviii. 376 My Lord Davers, and the Earl of C——, shall be godfathers; and it must be doubly godmothered too. **1848** DICKENS *Dombey* v, Elevated thus to the godmothership of little Paul..Miss Tox was [etc.]. **1863** MRS. CARLYLE *Lett.* III. 190 But the Godmotherhood?..I don't belong to the English Church.

'godness. *rare.* [f. GOD *sb.* + -NESS; cf. OHG. *gotnissa*, *-nissi.*]

†**1.** = GODHEAD. *Obs.*

c **1175** *Lamb. Hom.* 99 God is icundeliche on þreom hadan, feder & sune..& þe halȝe gast..Heore cunde is..efer wuniende on ane godnesse. *Ibid.* 101 þere halȝan þremnesse is an godnesse.

2. Divine element or nature. *nonce-wd.*

1883 G. MACDONALD *D. Grant* III. ii. 10 It rests with him to cultivate either the godness or the selfness in him.

godown¹ (gəʊ'daʊn). *Anglo-Indian.* Also 6 **godon**, 7 **gadonge**, **gedong**, **goedown.** [ad. Malay *gadong*, *godong*, supposed to be a. Telugu *giḍaṅgi*, Tamil *kiḍaṅgu* 'a place where goods lie', f. *kiḍu* 'to lie' (Yule). Some early writers state that these stores were subterranean, which may partly account for the form which the word has assumed in English.] A warehouse or store for goods, in India and other parts of Eastern Asia.

1588 T. HICKOCK tr. *C. Frederick's Voy.* 27 a, The merchants haue all one house or Magason, which house they call Godon. **1615** R. COCKS *Diary* (Hakl. Soc.) I. 15 We delivered 500 sackes of wheat..440 out of our gedong. *Ibid.* 89 In full payment of the fee symple of the gadonge over the way. **1632** R. FITCHE in *St. Papers, Col. E. Ind.* 309 His bottles..will be safe in the godown. **1788** *Ann. Reg.* 239 The godowns mostly carried away. **1816** 'QUIZ' *Grand Master* IV. 83 Which some parsee had brought from town, And lodg'd it safe in a godown. **1861** BP. G. SMITH *Ten Weeks Japan* xviii. 254 The streets of Yokuhama are wide..containing on either side merchants' godowns and offices. **1878** J. H. GRAY *China* II. xix. 69 There are khans which are depots or godowns for the goods of travelling merchants.

attrib. **1804** W. TENNANT *Ind. Recreat.* (ed. 2) I. 45 The innumerable items of godown, and house rent.

go-'down². Also 9 *Sc.* **gae-down.** [f. phrase *go down*: see GO *v.* 80.]

1. A draught, gulp (of liquor). ? *Obs.*

The phrase *six go-downs on reputation* in quots. 1690 and *a* 1705 app. refers to some customary rule among drinkers that each one must take off his liquor in so many draughts, if he wished to maintain his reputation as a drinker.

1641 *Wits Recreat.* Epigr. 364 At three go downes Dick doffs me off a pot. *Ibid.* Fancies Y 7 b, We have frolick rounds, we have merry goe downs. **1690** D'URFEY *Collin's Walk* IV. 162 Many more whose quality Forbids their toping openly, Will privately, on good occasion, Take six go-downs on Reputation. *a* **1705** SHIPPERY in Hearne *Collect.* 13 Dec. an. 1709 (O.H.S.) II. 327 Then in true English Liquor, my Masters begin Six Godowns upon Rep. to our true English King. **1708** MOTTEUX *Rabelais* v. Prol. (1737) 57 Take me off your Bumpers, nine go-downs. **1755** *Mem. Capt. P. Drake* I. xvii. 189 He held it [a flask] up to me himself, and I took three or four go-downs. **1827** *Sporting Mag.* XX. 12 A bottle of wine a-piece, kept down by large go-downs of brandy, is each man's allowance. **1848** *Rural Cycl.* II. 472 *Go-down*, a single gulp of water, allowed to a heated or fatigued horse while journeying or working.

†**b.** *fig.* A spell of sleep. *Obs.*

1687 T. BROWN *Saints in Uproar* Wks. 1730 I. 73 A pack of drowsy sleepy sots, who..fancied they slept several scores of years at one go-down. **1688** CROWNE *City Politicks* I. i. Dram. Wks. 1873 II. 112 Constantly after supper my eyes us'd to call for their evening's draught, and I was no sooner in bed, but they wou'd tope off fourteen hours at one go-down.

2. *Sc.* 'A guzzling or drinking match' (Jam.).

1815 SCOTT *Guy M.* ii, Sicken a blithe gae-down as we had again e'en.

†**3.** A welcome, acceptance (see GO *v.* 80 g).

1753 A. MURPHY *Gray's-Inn Jrnl.* No. 52 ¶3 A Touch now and then upon the Ministry, and a Stricture upon the Constitution would have a pretty go down with us in the Country.

4. *U.S.* (Western). 'A cutting in the bank of a stream for enabling animals to cross or to get to the water' (*Cent. Dict.*).

'god-pa,pa. Used in childish or familiar speech for GODFATHER.

1826 MISS MITFORD *Village* Ser. II. (1863) 310 My dear and venerable godpapa, for whom, although we had never met since the christening, I entertained the most lively affection. **1858** *Athenæum* 25 Dec. 829 Godpapa has a list of a hundred places to spend his future summers in.

'god-,parent. A sponsor; a godfather or godmother.

1865 PUSEY *Eiren.* 38 The exhortation to Godparents in the Baptismal service. **1879** EDNA LYALL *Won by Waiting* xxxvii, Frances..and Gaspard were to be the god-parents. **1885** *Catholic Dict.* (ed. 3) 210/2 Those to be confirmed are brought to the sacrament by their god-parents.

†**'god-phere.** *Obs. rare*⁻¹. [App. f. *phere* FERE *sb.*¹ 'companion'; but perh. a misunderstanding

of the rustic *godfer*, *godfar* = GODFATHER 1 (see quot. 1426).] A godfather.

1633 B. JONSON *Tale Tub* IV. ii, My God-phere was a Rabian, or a Iew,.. They call'd 'un Doctor Rasi. *Scr.* One Rasis was a great Arabick Doctor. *Cle.* Hee was King Harry's Doctor, and my God-phere.

godroon, mod. var. of GADROON.

God's acre. [ad. G. *Gottesacker*, Du. *Godsakker*.]

Properly, 'God's seed-field', in which the bodies of the departed are 'sown' (1 Cor. xv. 36-44) in hope of the resurrection.

A churchyard.

1617 MORYSON *Itin.* I. 7 They have (as many Cities in Germany have) a beautiful place to bury their dead, called Gods-aker, vulgarly Gotts-aker. **1646** TRAPP *Comm. John* xi. 11 The Greeks call their Church-yards dormitoryes, sleeping-places. The Germans call them Godsacre. [**1668** R. STEELE *Husbandman's Calling* x. (1672) 251 Remember that the heart is God's acre, a place prepared for the Lord.] **1841** LONGF. *God's-acre*, I like that ancient Saxon phrase which calls The burial-ground God's-acre. **1862** SALA *Accepted Addr.* 219 That God's Acre looks, with its white and grey tombstones, so peaceful and so tranquil.

godsend ('gɒdsɛnd). [Altered form of *God's send*, *sond* in GOD *sb.* 16c; see also SOND.]

1. Some desirable thing received unexpectedly and as it were from the hand of God, esp. something of which the recipient is greatly in want.

1820 LADY GRANVILLE *Let.* 20 Aug. (1894) I. 159 Even a bore was a godsend. **1834** SOUTHEY *Lett.* (1856) IV. 391 Mr. Telford..has left me £500..This is truly a Godsend. **1844** MRS. CARLYLE *Lett.* I. 291 If you will still send me some books..they will be a godsend. **1848** MILL *Pol. Econ.* v. vii. §2 (1872) 529 Any casual gain or godsend, is naturally devoted to the same purpose. **1892** G. S. LAYARD *C. Keene* iii. 45 Louis Napoleon was little less than a godsend to the journalistic enterprise of those days.

b. *spec.* A wreck. *dial.*

1814 PEGGE *Suppl. to Grose*, *God-send*, the wreck of a ship. Kentish coast. [**1821** MAD. D'ARBLAY *Let. to Mrs. Piozzi* 15 Mar., The inhospitable shore, where shipwreck is.. considered as a godsend.] **1822** SCOTT *Pirate* viii, It's seldom sic rich Godsends come on our coast.

2. A welcome event; a happy chance.

1831 SIR J. SINCLAIR *Corr.* II. 295 The peace was reckoned a God-send, both by the fleet and army. **1845** J. W. CROKER in *C. Papers* 30 Dec. (1884), Potatoe famine was a godsend which enabled him to open a long conceived design. *a* **1859** DE QUINCEY *Ceylon* Wks. XII. 27 By a mere god-send, more troops happened to arrive from the Indian continent. **1885** *Truth* 11 June 924/1 So far as the Government are concerned, the defeat is a perfect godsend.

godsep, godsepte, obs. forms of GOSSIP *sb.*

'God's ˌgood. *Obs.* exc. *dial.* [See GOD *sb.* 16c.]

†**1.** Property or possessions belonging to God (applied esp. to Church property); also, worldly possessions, food, etc., viewed as the good gift of God. *Obs.*

c **1400** *Plowman's T.* 762 What think these men to say That thus dispenden goddis good? *c* **1460** *Towneley Myst.* xxvii. 284 Forto sowpe we make vs bowne, Now of oure fode; we haue enogh, sir, bi my crowne, Of godys goode. ?*c* **1550** *Freiris Berwik* 315 in *Dunbar's Poems* (1893) 295 Heir is now annwch of Godis gud.

†**2.** Applied to what is considered to be without human owner, and therefore open to be appropriated by any one; *spec.* in Cornwall = GODSEND 1 b.

1553 *Respublica* IV. iii. 28 (Brandl *Quellen* 323) Now vor lacke of a sallet, whan my lyege hath neade, Cham vaine to take an hatte of godsgood on my heade. **1693** ROKEBY *Diary* (1887) 28 The cause of ye Orange Merchts agt ye Cornish Wreckers for God's goods, soe (wickedly) called.

3. Barm, yeast.

1468-9 *Brewers' Bk. Norwich* in *Norf. & Norw. Archæol. Soc.* V. 324 Wheras berme, otherwise clepid goddis good.. hath frely be goven or delyvered for brede, whete [etc.],.. and noon warned, bicause it cometh of the grete grace of God [etc.]. **1542** BOORDE *Dyetary* x. (1870) 256 Yest, barme or godesgood. **1674** RAY *S. & E.C. Words* 67 *Gods good*, Yeast, Barm. Kent, Norf., Suff. **1887** in *Kent. Gloss.*

†**4.** ? Grace after meat. [? = God is good.]

1580 LYLY *Euphues* (Arb.) 230 He that for euery qualme will take a Receipt, and can-not make two meales, vnlesse Galen be his Gods good: shall be sure to make the Phisition rich, and himselfe a begger.

godship ('gɒdʃɪp). [f. GOD *sb.* + -SHIP.] The position or personality of a god: esp. as a jocular title (***his, your***, etc. ***godship***).

a **1553** UDALL *Royster D.* IV. i. (Arb.) 59, I thinke verily Neptunes mightie godshyp, Was angry with some that was in our shyp. **1649** MILTON *Eikon.* xxvii. 220 It is..beneath the honour of a..free Nation, to begg and supplicate the Godship of one Fraile Man. **1652-62** HEYLYN *Cosmogr.* IV. (1682) 5 It seemeth that his Godship was not so much respected by strangers. **1690** DRYDEN *Amphitryon* I. i, *Mercury*. Your name and mine were used with less reverence than became our godships. **1705** HICKERINGILL *Priest-cr.* I. (1721) 60 He accepted the *Godship* and *Adoration*, with as much Devotion, as *Herod*. **1792** WOLCOT (P. Pindar) *Ep. to Ld. Macartney* Wks. 1812 III. 136 The Man of Straw Flew up and put their Godships in a fright. **1823** BYRON *Juan* XIV. lxxv, I..beg his British godship's humble pardon. **1829** T. HOOK *Bank to Barnes* 118 Their godships dead drunk must sleep under the table. **1862** MERIVALE *Rom. Emp.* (1865) VII. lv. 4 Lucan..challenged him to choose what godship he would assume in heaven. **1896** E. ARNOLD *Bk. Good Counsels* 92, I am an ambassador from his Godship the Moon.

godsib, -sip, obs. forms of GOSSIP *sb.*

†**'god-sister.** *Obs. rare*⁻¹. A female who has the same god-parents as another.

1496 in *Surtees Misc.* (1888) 50 God suster unto þe said William Robynson.

†**God-so.** *int. Obs.* [? var. of GADSO, after oaths beginning with *God's*.]

1604 DEKKER *Honest Wh.* (1635) I 3 b, God so, here's Father Anselmo. **1606** *Sir G. Goosecappe* I. i. in Bullen *O. Pl.* III. 13 God so Jack, I thinke they have supt.

godson ('gɒdsʌn). Also 5 gosson. [f. GOD *sb.* + SON: cf. GODFATHER.] A male god-child.

a **900** *O.E. Chron.* an. 890 Æþelstan, se wæs Ælfredes cyninges godsunu. *c* **900** tr. *Bæda's Hist.* III. v. [vii.] (1890) 168 þa onfeng he him & nom æt fulwihte bæðe..him to godsuna. *c* **1050** *Martyrol.* in Cockayne *Shrine* 74 He [St. Mark] was..Petres godsunu on fulwihte. *c* **1315** *Shoreham* 69 Godfader wedded godsones child Fol wel. **1420** *E.E. Wills* (1882) 45 Iohn Forster my godsonne. *c* **1440** *Promp. Parv.* 201/2 Godson, or gosson..*filiolus*. **1501** *Bury Wills* (Camden) 83 To sr Nycholas Kyng my godson vj *s.* viij *d.* and to eche othyr of my godsonys xij *d.* **1776** MRS. DELANY *Life & Corr.* Ser. II. II. 208 He desires his love to you and blessing to his godson. *a* **1839** PRAED *Poems* (1864) II. 216 Your godson..Was entered at Eton last May. **1868** FREEMAN *Norm. Conq.* (1876) II. ix. 426 Earl Ralph had left a son, a namesake, probably a godson of the great Earl.

†**Godsookers, -sokers.** For other forms see GAD *sb.*⁵ 3. [a comb. of *God's*; the second element is unmeaning or corrupt; see GOD 14 b.]

1672 VILLIERS (Dk. Buckhm.) *Rehearsal* III. ii. (Arb.) 75 God sookers, you'l spoil all my Play. **1687** MONTAGUE & PRIOR *Hind. & P. Transv.* 15 Godsokers! Why no more she does not yet, fear either Man or Beast. **1688** SHADWELL *Sqr. Alsatia* I. Wks. 1720 IV. 15 Godsookers, Cousin! I always thought they had been wittiest in the universities.

'God-'speed. [See GOD *sb.* 8 and SPEED *v.*]

1. ***to bid (wish) one God-speed***, to utter the words 'God speed (you)'; *esp.* to express a wish for the success of one who is setting out on some journey or enterprise.

c **1470** HENRYSON *Mor. Fab.* II (*Town & C. Mouse*) xv, This burges brocht thame sone quhair thay suld be; Without god speid thair herberie was tane. *Ibid.* xxiv, Quhen in come gib hunter..And bad god speid. **1526** TINDALE *2 John* 10 Yf ther come eny vnto you and bringe not this learninge him receave not to housse: neither bid him God spede. **1593** SHAKS. *Rich. II*, I. iv. 32 A brace of Draymen bid God speed him well. **1776** WESLEY *Wks.* (1872) IV. 76 Every one seems to bid us God-speed! **1865** LOWELL *Polit. Ess.* (1888) 229 Every humane and generous heart..has wished us God-speed. **1878** BOSW. SMITH *Carthage* 300 Fulvius..marching by inner lines, amidst a population who bade him God-speed, managed to reach Rome [etc.].

2. In substantival use, ***a God-speed***, a parting wish for one's success.

1856 KANE *Arct. Expl.* I. viii. 90 Three hearty cheers from all hands followed us,—a God-speed as we pushed off. **1887** R. BUCHANAN *Heir of Linne* vi, Old Sampson bade the stranger a God-speed on his journey.

b. *attrib.* in ***God-speed dinner, party***. (Cf. FAREWELL *sb.* 4.)

1867 *Athenæum* 26 Oct. 539/1 Lord Lytton will preside at a Godspeed dinner to be given to Mr. Charles Dickens, on Saturday, next week, November 2. **1887** T. A. TROLLOPE *What I remember* II. vii. 127, I went, and the God-speed party was a very pleasant one.

3. *fig.* †**a.** ***the Godspeed*** (of a thing), the conclusion, finish. Also, ***in the Godspeed***, in the nick of time. *Obs.*

1606 DAY *Ile of Guls* IV. G 4, But and I come to the god-speed ont, ile tel em ont soundly. **1668** R. L'ESTRANGE *Vis. Quev.* (1708) 201 A Devil came in just in the God-speed, and told them [etc.]. **1740** tr. *De Mouhy's Fort. Country Maid* (1741) II. 61 Had not the Curate interposed in the Godspeed, the Inn-keeper had certainly crippled him. **1803** MARY CHARLTON *Wife & Mistress* II. 248 So the old housekeeper, she comes in, in the God's speed [*sic*].

b. ***at the back of God-speed*** = at the back of beyond (BEYOND C b).

1858 TROLLOPE *Dr. Thorne* v. (1859) 63, If I don't leave you at the back of God-speed before long, I'll give you the mare and the horse too.

godspel(l, -le, obs. form of GOSPEL.

'God's-ˌpenny. [See GOD *sb.* 5 f; so called from being originally devoted to some religious or charitable purpose. Cf. Du. *godspenning*, G. *gottespfennig*, OSw. *gudspäning*; F. *denier à Dieu*.]

1. A small sum paid as earnest-money on striking a bargain, esp. on concluding a purchase or the hiring of a servant (cf. ARLES-PENNY, EARNEST-PENNY). Now only *dial.*

1340 *Ayenb.* 91 þe loue of herte, þet is þe godes peny huermide me bayþ alle þe guodes of þe wordle. **1490** *Burgh Recs. Edinb.* (1869) 59 That the thesaurer of the towne.. proffer a goddis penny and bye the same [vittaillis or tymmer] vpoun a competent pryce. **1530** PALSGR. 586/2 Holde forthe thy hande, take an ernest penny or a Goddes penny [F. *vng denier en arres* or *vng denier a Dieu*]. **1603** OWEN *Pembrokesh.* (1891) 190 Savinge onelie in earnest peny at the bargaine makinge wch the plaine men called a gods penie. **1609** SKENE *Reg. Maj.*, *Stat. Gild* 144 Gif any man buyes Hering..and hes given Gods pennie, or silver in arles [etc.]. **1625** *N. Riding Rec.* (1885) III. II. 254 His wife had formerly hired the said woman and given her a Godes penny. **1662** PEPYS *Diary* 23 Sept., In both which places at the making all contracts and bargains they give so much, which they call God's penny. **1832** *Yorksh. Dial.*, Ah'd a godspenny at Stowsley market. **1855** ROBINSON *Whitby Gloss.*, *Godspenny*, earnest money, generally half-a-crown given to a servant when hired. **1887** in *Mid. Yorks. Gloss.* *fig.* **1602** R. T. *Five Godlie Serm.* 26 Admitting them his tenants by giuing them the Gods penny or earnest pennie of his spirit.

b. A rebate given on making a payment.

1885 *Law Jrnl. Rep.* LIV. 136/1 The legal effect was to be as if the whole was paid down and a portion thrown back as a God's-penny.

†**2.** A penny given in charity. *Obs.*

1550 CROWLEY *Epigr.*, *Beggers* Wks. (1872) 16 Go fyll me thys quarte pot, full to the brynke. The tonge muste haue bastynge, it wyll the better wagge, To pull a Goddes penye out of a churles bagge.

†**3.** *nonce-use.* A broker's commission. *Obs.*

?**1483** CAXTON *Dialogues* (E.E.T.S.) Olyuer the brocour wynneth by brocorage, with one goddes peny [F. *a vng denier a dieu*] twenty pound or thirty.

godsyb(be, godsypp, obs. forms of GOSSIP *sb.*

Godward ('gɒdwəd), *adv.* and *a.* [f. GOD *sb.* + -WARD.]

A. *adv.* In early use ***to Godward*** (see TOWARD).

1. Of progress, tendency, etc.: Towards God; in the direction of God. †Also of love, affection, etc.: Directed towards God.

1401 *Pol. Poems* (Rolls) II. 83 To tille folk to God-ward, I holde it no theft. *c* **1420** LYDG. *Assemb. Gods* 917 Louers of Cryst, confounders of yll, And all that to godward yeue her good wyll. *c* **1510** MORE *Picus* Wks. 7/1 The litle affection of an olde man or an olde woman to godwarde [etc.]. *a* **1592** H. SMITH *Wks.* (1867) II. 489 Christ is the sole commander, To lead to God-ward. **1597** HOOKER *Eccl. Pol.* v. lxxix. §2 Their colde affection to Godward made their presents to bee little woorth. *a* **1711** KEN *Sion* Poet. Wks. 1721 IV. 410 My soul..Godward springs for God alone. **1842** MRS. BROWNING *Grk. Chr. Poets* Poems 1890 V. 153 As if, being in the world, their tendency was Godward. **1884** *Congregational Year Bk.* 82 Anticipations of a nature struggling Godward.

2. In relation to God; with respect or reference to God.

1390 GOWER *Conf.* I. 71 She, which was all honeste To godward..At night vnto the temple wente. *c* **1440** *Jacob's Well* (E.E.T.S.) 168 A-forn alle oþere sorwys, þi sorwe muste be al opyn to god-ward. **1531** TINDALE *Exp. 1 John* (1537) 3 But to Godwarde is ther no satisfaction saue fayth in Christes bloude. **1612** T. TAYLOR *Comm. Titus* ii. 12 They hope they may haue as good hearts as the best to god-ward. **1676** ALLEN *Address Nonconf.* 91 So far as there is any ground to hope well of them in reference to their state Godward. **1728** SWIFT *Let. to Pope* 26 July, Wks. 1841 II. 617 You are the most temperate man Godward, and the most intemperate yourselfward of most I have known. **1824** SCOTT *Redgauntlet* Let. xi, His was a sudden call,..no time to set his house in order: weel prepared Godward, no doubt, which is the root of the matter. **1868** GLADSTONE *Juv. Mundi* ix. (1869) 376 All other functions of our nature, outside the domain of the life to god-ward.

B. *adj.* Tending or directed towards God.

1861 *Westm. Rev.* Apr. 533 Had he [Cromwell] been merely religious,—had the Godward tendency absorbed his being, and [etc.]. **1867** MONSELL *Our New Vicar* 84 'Priest' and 'Altar' speak of his God-ward office: 'Minister' and 'Lord's Table' refer to his man-ward ministrations. **1883** H. DRUMMOND *Nat. Law in Spir. W.* (ed. 8) 117 Every Godward aspiration of the soul.

Godwards ('gɒdwədz), *adv.* [f. as prec.: see -WARDS.] = GODWARD *adv.* (Orig. ***to Godwards***: see TOWARDS.)

c **1560** R. MORICE in *Lett. Lit. Men* (Camden) 25 Manifest blasphemy to Godwards. *c* **1645** HOWELL *Lett.* (1650) II. xi. 22 What the Eye of a Bat is to the Sun, the same is all human understanding to Godwards. **1758** S. HAYWARD *Serm.* I But they never enquire into their state God-wards. **1839** BAILEY *Festus* (1848) 25/1 Any heart, turned Godwards, feels more joy In one short hour of prayer [etc.]. **1850** ROBERTSON *Serm.* Ser. III. ii. (1872) 20 When we speak of the Church we generally mean a society to aid men in their progress God-wards.

Godwinian (gɒd'wɪnɪən), *a.* and *sb.* [f. the name of William *Godwin* (1756-1836) + -IAN.]

A. *adj.* Pertaining to or characteristic of Godwin's views on politics, social reform, etc. **B.** *sb.* An adherent of Godwin's views. So **'Godwinism**, Godwin's doctrine or ideas; **'Godwinist**, an adherent of Godwinism.

1801 C. WILMOT *Let.* 13 Dec. (1920) 15 But I begin to smoke a little of the Visionary on the Godwinean System of living beyond the term of Man. **1811** SHELLEY *Let.* *c* 16 Nov. (1964) I. 184 Jealousy has no place in my bosom; I am indeed at times very much inclined to think the Godwinian plan is best. **1892** L. STEPHEN *Hours in Library* (new ed.) III. 79 The Godwinism, indeed, is strongest in the crude poetry of 'Queen Mab'. **1913** H. N. BRAILSFORD *Shelley, Godwin* 216 The ideal man of the Godwinian conception, who lives by reason. **1937** 'C. CAUDWELL' *Illusion & Reality* 97 A Godwinist, Shelley believed that man is naturally good. **1946** BLUNDEN *Shelley* 123 She was a child, a Godwinian. **1951** *Essays in Criticism* I. I. 17 The Godwinian Urging the gallows for the mildest crimes. *Ibid.* 28 The aftermath of Godwinism. *Ibid.* 31 *Guilt and Sorrow*, that Godwinian plaint Of man's inhumanity to man.

godwit ('gɒdwɪt). Also 6 godwitte, -wipe, 7 -witt, -wike, gotwit, 8-9 goodwit, 9 godwyn. [Origin obscure.] A marsh-bird (genus *Limosa*) resembling a curlew, but having the bill slightly curved upwards. The black-tailed godwit (*L. ægocephala* or *melanura*) and the bar-tailed godwit (*L. lapponica* or *rufa*) are British species; others are natives of northern Europe and America. Formerly in great repute, when fattened, for the table.

In 16–17th c. often used to render L. *attagen*, Sp. *francolin*.

[**1544** TURNER *Avium Præcip. Hist.* C 3 b, Erasmus.. attagenam auem palustrem facit & uarijs maculis distinctam, quod si satis exploratum mihi esset Anglorum godwittam sive fedoam attagenam esse..auderem adfirmare.] **1552** ELYOT *Dict.*, *Attagen* and *Attagena*, a byrde, which is found in Ionia.. Thei are deceiued that take him for a wood-cocke, it is moost lyke a byrde called amonge vs a godwitte. **1579** J. JONES *Preserv. Bodie & Soule* I. xiv. 26 Dottrel, Snipe, Godwipe, Dicken [etc.]. **1591** PERCIVALL *Sp. Dict.*, *Francolin*, a godwit, *Attagen*. **1609** B. JONSON *Sil. Wom.* I. iv. 38 Halfe a dozen of phesants, a dozen or two of godwits. **1612** *Naworth Househ. Bks.* (Surtees) 25 A godwike and a redshanke, iij*d*. **1620** SHELTON *Quix.* IV. viii. 56 A God-wit of Milan, or a Pheasant of Rome. *a* **1637** B. JONSON *Horace, Praises Country Life* 53 Th' Ionian God-wit, nor the Ginny hen Could not goe downe my belly then More sweet than Olives. **1678** RAY *Willughby's Ornith.* 292 The Godwit, called in some places the Yarwhelp, or Yarwip, in others, the Stone-Plover. *a* **1682** SIR T. BROWNE *Norf. Birds* Wks. 1835 IV. 319 Godwyts..accounted the daintiest dish in England; and, I think, for the bigness, of the biggest price. **1766** PENNANT *Zool.* (1768) II. 353 The red godwit is superior in size to the common kind. **1853** KINGSLEY *Hypatia* xi. 129 The whistle of the godwit and curlew, came ringing up the windings of the glen. **1863** BARING-GOULD *Iceland* 412 The black tailed godwit arrives the last week in April.

God-wottery, Godwottery (gɒd'wɒtərı). Also with lower-case initial. [f. *God wot* (cf. GOD *sb.* 10) in the line 'A garden is a lovesome thing, God wot!' in T. E. Brown's poem *My Garden* (1876) + -ERY.] An affected or over-elaborate style of gardening or attitude towards gardens (see quots.); also (in quot. 1939), archaic language.

1939 N. LOFTS *Colin Lowrie* (Author's note), I have written this so-called historical novel in so-called modern language... I am foolish enough to believe that people..will appreciate this lack of 'God-wottery'. **1952** *Archit. Rev.* CXI. 59/2 The God-wottery..in that anaemic kind of 'Trajan' which societies concerned with what they generally call 'amenities' seem to think particularly refined. *Ibid.* CXII. 235 He plays fast and loose with the average Englishman's sentimental leanings towards God-wottery, drawing his clichés from the Cotswolds where, it is widely believed, lie the typical English villages and the homeland of the picturesque. **1960** 'A. BURGESS' *Right to Answer* i. 7 Who shall describe..those semi-detacheds with the pebble-dash .., the tiny gates which you could step over, the god-wottery in the toy gardens? **1969** *Guardian* 18 Aug. 7/1 'Godwottery', the sentimental preconception of what a garden should be, results in a very strange collection of elements... Cotswold stone retaining walls; vaguely Spanish wrought iron gates; 'crazy' paving, nowadays often coloured yellow, green, and pink; plainly irregular ponds, now usually of pale blue fibre-glass, fed by streams of impossible source; gnomes, fairies, and animals, usually plastic.

godzyb(be, obs. form of GOSSIP *sb.*

goe, var. GEO, gully, creek; obs. f. GO *v.*

go-easy, *a.* [f. the vbl. phr. *to go easy*: see GO *v.* 2 b and EASY *adv.* 4 a.] Easy-going; characterized by leisurely behaviour.

1877 *Rep. Vermont Dairym. Assoc.* VIII. 22 The many serious drawbacks which the 'go easy' dairymen of Vermont are compelled to encounter. **1936** R. C. K. ENSOR *England 1870–1914* i. 12 The purchase system kept officering as an occupation for gentlemen, and not a trade for professional men. If it became the latter, it might menace our go-easy oligarchic liberties. **1940** S. O'CASEY *Star turns Red* I. 8 The workers..with their lightning strikes, stay-in strikes, stay-out strikes, sit-down strikes, and go-easy strikes.

goed, goef, obs. forms of GOOD, GOAF[1].

goel, var. of GOLE *a.*, *Obs.*

goen, obs. form of *gone*: see GO *v.*

goer ('gəʊə(r)). [f. GO *v.* + -ER[1].]

1. a. One who or that which goes (see the vb.).

1377 LANGL. *P. Pl.* B. ix. 104 A gedelynge, a goer to tauernes! **1387–8** T. USK *Test. Love* II. i. (Skeat) l. 63 The envyous people, whiche alway ben redy, both ryder and goer, to scorne and to jape this leude book. **1548** UDALL, etc. *Erasm. Par. Matt.* i. 20, 21 The Angel brought the message beyng as a goer betwene God and her. **1577–87** HARRISON *England* II. x. (1877) I. 217 They mooue the harts of the goers by such places where they lie, to yerne at their miserie. *a* **1639** WOTTON *Parallel* Reliq. W. (1651) 16 The Earl..was so far from being a good dancer, that he was no gracefull goer. **1734** SWIFT *Corr.* Wks. 1841 II. 725 The intervening officious impertinence of those goers between us. **1862** LATHAM *Channel Isl.* III. xiv. (ed. 2) 329 He was named Rolf Ganger; i.e. Rolf the Goer on foot, or Rolf Walker.

†**b.** with adverbs, *about, back, between, by*, etc.

1546 in Turner *Select. Rec. Oxford* 182 The procurars therof and goars about theryn to be punysshed. **1548** UDALL, etc. *Erasm. Par. John* 28 b, I haue doen the office of a goer before. **1601** SHAKS. *All's Well* I. ii. 48 Goers backward. **1606** —— *Tr. & Cr.* III. ii. 208 Goers betweene. **1611** —— *Cymb.* I. i. 169, The goer backe. *a* **1616** BEAUM. & FL. *Little Fr. Lawyer* II. iii, These two long houres I have trotted here, and curiously Survei'd all goers by. **1668** R. L'ESTRANGE *Vis. Quev.* (1708) 108 Some such Reverend Goer-between, that's a Well-willer to the Mathematicks. *a* **1774** GOLDSM. tr. *Scarron's Com. Romance* (1775) II. 6 All the neighbours and goers-by came into the inn. **1800** BENTHAM *Wks.* (1838–43) X. 356 Comers-in by birth;.. goers-out by death.

c. Of a horse, rider, coach, clock, etc.; preceded by some adjective, indicating the manner or speed of going. Also *simply*, one that goes fast. *transf.* One who behaves in a lively, persevering, or profligate manner; also, a successful man; an expert.

a **1586** SIDNEY *Apol.* (Arb.) 19 Hee sayde, they [horsemen] were..speedy goers, and strong abiders. **1613** BEAUM. & FL. *Cupid's Rev.* II. vi, Is the rough French horse brought to the dore? They say he is a high goer; I shall soone try his mettall. **1697** *Lond. Gaz.* No. 3281/4 Stolen or strayed..a light grey Nag..about 8 years old, a very good Goer. **1710** *Ibid.* No. 4689/4 She is hard mouthed but a very pleasant Goer. *c* **1810** W. HICKEY *Mem.* (1960) v. 78 The whole party, male and female, were of the description yclept 'hard goers'. This did not alarm me, for..I could keep way with the best of them at fair drinking. **1811** [see ARTICLE *sb.* 14 b]. **1830** H. ANGELO *Remin.* I. 205 Hence all his clocks were 'good goers'. **1835** SIR G. STEPHEN *Adv. Search Horse* i. (1841) 6 A charming goer: so docile that a lady might drive him with a pack-thread. **1843** HALIBURTON *Attaché* I. ii. 41 'He looks..as if he'd trot a considerable good stick..I guess he is a goer.' **1857** HUGHES *Tom Brown* I. iv, The Tally-ho was a tip-top goer, ten miles an hour including stoppages. **1857** G. A. LAWRENCE *Guy Livingstone* xx. 185 She was always deeply engaged, and generally to the best goers in the room. **1859** F. E. PAGET *Curate of Cumberworth* 81 My watch is a perfect goer. **1883** E. PENNELL-ELMHIRST *Cream Leicestersh.* 48 Several of the best and hardest goers of the hunt got off badly. **1886** *Century Mag.* Jan. 371/2 A dog with a broad, bull-dog chest is never a good goer. **1908** MRS. A. GUNN *We of Never-Never* i. 5 By George!..she *is* a regular goer. **1946** F. SARGESON *That Summer* 38 Miss Briggs is a goer anyhow. You want to see her on a wet day. **1959** *Observer* 1 Mar. 10/2 Princie is a 'goer', nerveless and brave, say the other members of the team. **1966** P. WILLMOTT *Adolescent Boys E. London* iii. 51 'She was a right banger,' said a 17 year old of one girl. 'A banger's a goer—a girl who'll do anything with anyone.'

d. One who frequently or regularly attends a specified place, type of entertainment, etc.; usu. with defining word prefixed: see CHURCH-GOER, *cinema-goer, concert-goer, film-goer, theatre-goer*.

2. Phr. ***goers and comers*** (more usually ***comers and goers***): travellers or guests arriving and departing.

c **1400** MAUNDEV. (1839) xxvii. 277 And so thei eten every day in his Court, mo than 30000 persones, with outen goeres and comeres. **1526** [see COMER 1]. **1648** GAGE *West Ind.* xviii. (1655) 136 Which never shut gate against any goer or comer. **1694** ECHARD *Plautus* 173, I shall have a fine time on't, if I must be bound to draw water for all comers and goers. **1885** *Manch. Exam.* 17 June 5/3 All the comers and goers appear to be fairly well pleased.

†**3.** A foot. *Obs.*[−1]

1615 CHAPMAN *Odyss.* XIII. 329 His fair goers graced With fitted shoes.

Goethian ('gœtɪən), *a.* and *sb.* Also **Goethean**. [f. the name of the German poet Johann Wolfgang von Goethe (1749–1832) + -IAN.]

A. *adj.* Of, pertaining to, or characteristic of Goethe, his writings, opinions, etc.

1840 MILL *Diss. & Disc.* (1875) I. 428 Such views are.. the characteristic feature of the Goethian period. **1856** *Mem. F. Perthes* I. ix. 133, I find in these letters the Goethean paganism. **1884** J. R. SEELEY in *Contemp. Rev.* Oct. 496 What may be the value of this fundamental Goethian maxim I do not inquire.

B. *sb.* An admirer or follower of Goethe.

1850 MARG. FULLER *Life without & L. within* (1860) 51, I am inclined..to look upon myself for thinking them, with as much contempt as Mr. Carlyle or Mrs. Austin..might do, to say nothing of the German Goetheans.

Hence **'Goethianism**, the opinions or views of Goethe or his followers.

1880 VERN. LEE *Belcaro* ix. 233 You believe in Art for Art's own sake—Goethianism—that sort of thing, I know.

goethite, göthite ('gœtaɪt). *Min.* [Named after the poet Goethe (Göthe) by Lenz in 1806: see -ITE.] A hydrous oxide of iron, of reddish or dark-brown colour, occurring in orthorhombic crystals, also massive.

1823 BROOKE *Crystallogr.* 468 Gothite. **1837** ALLAN *Phillip's Min.* 221 Goethite. **1869** PHILLIPS *Vesuv.* x. 282 Göthite—Hydrous Oxide of Iron—is mentioned in ejected blocks and dykes. **1878** LAWRENCE tr. *Cotta's Rocks Class.* 58 Göthite or stilpnosiderite is a mineral very closely allied to limonite.

†**goetian.** *Obs.*[−1] In 6 *erron.* geocian. [f. GOETY + -AN.] One who practises 'goety'.

1569 J. SANFORD tr. *Agrippa's Van. Artes* 57 b, It is no maruaile if the Geocians [*L. goetici*]..doo binde sprites with the inuocation of the name of God.

goetic (gəʊ'ɛtɪk), *a.* and *sb. Obs.* exc. *arch.* Also 7 goetick(e, -ique, (8 *erron.* geotick). [ad. Gr. γοητικός pertaining to witchcraft (ἡ γοητικὴ μαγεία, μαντεία = γοητεία GOETY) through med.L. *goēticus* or F. *goétique*.]

A. *adj.* Of or pertaining to 'goety'.

1610 HEALEY *St. Aug. Citie of God* (1620) 353 Those that go about any such mischiefe with magical enchantments.. think they can hurt others, and that others by art Goetique may hurt them. **1635** HEYWOOD *Hierarch.* VII. Comm. 471 This Goeticke and Necromanticke Majicke. **1834** LYTTON *Pompeii* II. viii, The theurgic, or benevolent magic—the goetic, or dark and evil necromancy—were alike in preeminent repute.

B. *sb.* **1.** One who practises 'goety'; a magician, wizard, sorcerer.

1652 GAULE *Magastrom.* xxvi, This is the reason why these Goeticks onely make use of evill spirits.

2. = GOETY.

1727 BAILEY vol. II, *Geotick*..a sort of Magick, performed by the Assistance of a Dæmon, the same as Geomancy.

†**go'etical**, *a. Obs.* Also 6 *erron.* geoticall. [f. as prec. + -AL[1].] = GOETIC *a.*

1569 J. SANFORD tr. *Agrippa's Van. Artes* 62 b, By Geoticall inchauntmentes, and praiers and deceites of the Deuill. **1652** GAULE *Magastrom.* 110 Whether their distinguishing betwixt Magick Theurgicall and Goeticall.

goety ('gəʊɪtɪ). *Obs.* exc. *arch.* Also 7 **goetie**, (6 *erron.* **geocie**, 8 **geoty**). [ad. Gr. γοητεία (f. γοητ-, γόης sorcerer, wizard, app. f. γοάειν to wail, cry, cf. quot. 1610), through med.L. *goetia* or F. *goétie*.] Witchcraft or magic performed by the invocation and employment of evil spirits; necromancy.

The erroneous forms *geocie, geoticke*, etc. in this word and its cognates either proceeded from or suggested a mistaken etymological association with GEO-.

1569 J. SANFORD tr. *Agrippa's Van. Artes* 57 b, The partes of ceremoniall Magicke be Geocie, and Theurgie. **1610** HEALEY *St. Aug. Citie of God* (1620) 353 Goety worketh vpon the dead by inuocation, so called of the noyse that the practisers hereof make about graues. **1681** HALLYWELL *Melampron.* vii. 51 Porphyry and some others did distinguish these two sorts [of Magic], so as to condemn indeed the grosser, which they called Magic, or Goety. **1730–6** BAILEY (folio), *Geoty*, geotick magick. **1751** BP. LAVINGTON *Enthus. Methodists & Papists* (1754) II. iii. 190 In the Academy of Salamanca they taught both Theurgy and Goety in the Publick Schools. **1855** E. SMEDLEY *Occult Sci.* 237 All that is properly called 'goety' or the 'black magic' of the middle ages.

†**gofe.** *Sc. Obs.* Also 5–6 goyf(f, 5–6 goif, gof, gouchf, gowcht, gowff, gowife. *Pl.* 6 govis. [Of obscure origin; it is difficult to see what original form the diverse spellings can represent.] *sing.* and *pl.* The pillory.

1489 *Extracts Aberd. Reg.* (1844) I. 417 The said William sall offer and present his crag to the goyfs..thar to stand at the will of the said Thomas. **1498** *Burgh Rec. Edin.* (1869) I. 73 To be set on the goif, and thair haldin thrie dayis. **1520** *Ibid.* 201 The mercat for the selling of aitis and hors corne be halden at the govis aboue the Tolbuith stair. **1530** *Extracts Aberd. Reg.* (1844) I. 129 To cause, big, and mak an goif againe on the towne sid. **1538** *Aberd. Reg.* XV. 141 (Jam.) His crag & hands to stand in the gofe. **1594** *Extracts Aberd. Reg.* (1848) II. 93 Hir craig to be put in the govis. **1608** *Stirling Kirk Sess. Reg.* in *Maitland Misc.* (1833) I. 450 They salbe brankit thrugh the toun, put in the govis, and banesit the toun.

b. *Comb.*, as *gofe-stair, -stocks*.

1538 *Extracts Aberd. Reg.* (1844) I. 155 Thai ordane the said Besse..to stand in the Gowistair. **1558** *Ibid.* 309 Thair feit to be fetterit..in the goif stoikis xxiiij houris.

Hence †**gofe** *v.*, to put in the pillory; only in †**'goving** *vbl. sb.*

1498 *Burgh Rec. Edin.* (1869) I. 73 The caus of his goving.

gofe, var. of GOAF[1]; obs. form of GOVE.

gofer[1] ('gəʊfə(r)). *dial.* Forms: 8–9 gofer, 9 gopher, gaufer, gaufre. [a. F. *gaufre* (earlier also *goffre, gofre*) honeycomb, thin cake; ultimately of LG. origin: see WAFER and WAFFLE.]

a. A thin batter-cake on which a honeycomb pattern is stamped by the iron plates (see b) between which it is baked.

1769 MRS. RAFFALD *Eng. Housekpr.* (1778) 165 To make Gofers. Beat three eggs well, with three spoonfuls of flour, and a little salt. *c* **1845** C. BRONTË *Professor* (1857) II. xxi. 109 Having eaten an unlimited quantity of 'gaufres'. **1847–78** HALLIWELL, *Gofer*, a species of tea-cake of an oblong form, made of flour, milk, eggs, and currants, baked on an iron made expressly for the purpose, called a *gofering iron*, and divided into square compartments. *Linc.* **1853** C. BRONTË *Villette* I. viii. 142 Regaled with *gaufres* and *vin blanc*. **1876** *Whitby Gloss.*, *Gaufers*, tea-cakes of the muffin sort, square, and stamped like net-work with the 'gaufering-irons'. **1883** P. ROBINSON *Sinners & Saints* i. 14 Here, too, in Chicago, I found a man selling 'gophers'... I do not know the American name for this vanish-into-nothing sort of pastry.

b. *Comb.*: **gofer-irons, -tongs**, also **gofering-iron** (see quots. 1847–78 and 1876 above): the implement in which 'gofers' are baked.

1877 *Holderness Gloss.*, **Gaufre-irons*, a bivalved iron mould with long handles, in which gaufres are baked on the fire. **1769** MRS. RAFFALD *Eng. Housekpr.* (1778) 165 Make your *gofer tongs hot, rub them with fresh butter, fill the bottom part of your tongs, and clap the top upon, then turn them, and when a fine brown on both sides, put them in a dish.

gofer[2] ('gəʊfə(r)). *slang* (orig. and chiefly *N. Amer.*). Also go-fer, gopher. [f. vbl. phr. *to go for* (GO *v.* 58), influenced by GOPHER *sb.*[1]; cf. TWOFER.] Someone who runs errands, esp. one employed for such duties on a film set or in an office (see quot. 1972); a general dogsbody.

1967 J. O'HARA *The Instrument* I. 65 'Teddy's used to being my gofer.' 'Your what?' said Ellis Walton. 'You never worked in radio. A gofer goes for coffee.' **1968** W. SAFIRE *New Lang. Politics* 167/1 Just after John Lindsay took office as New York's Mayor in 1966, a minor controversy arose when it was charged that policemen were being used as 'gophers'—to bring coffee into the Lindsay offices. **1972** *Telegraph* (Brisbane) 8 Mar. 30/4 It has got to be *charm* all the way for the high-powered diplomats at the U.S. State Department, should their secretaries courteously offer to fetch them cups of coffee. For..a secretary is not a 'go-fer', as Americans term those who 'go for' coffee, cigarettes or sandwiches at the behest of the boss. **1975** *Weekend Mag.* (Montreal) 8 Nov. 12/1 He finally gave the job to Geary, the team go-fer,..the man who..had never been given a chance to show his stuff. **1978** J. KRANTZ *Scruples* x. 285 A producer was somebody on a studio payroll who was used chiefly as liaison between the studio heads and the director, a glorified gofer. **1978** M. PUZO *Fools Die* xlvi. 488 His assistant..was really a gopher for Simon but tried to give us some of his own ideas on what should be in the script. **1981** *Listener* 22 Jan. 124/1 Burt Lancaster plays Lou, an ex-bodyguard and gofer for the mob, still running the bedraggled tail of the numbers racket. **1982** *Underground Grammarian* Nov. 8/2 The typesetter, the printer, a few untitled gofers, and even the assistant circulation manager, were led into ineptitude and disorder a couple of months ago.

gofer, var. of GOFFER.

†**goff**[1] *Obs. rare.* [? Abbreviation of *goffer, godfa'r = GODFATHER. Cf. GOM.]

a. A godfather. **b.** = GAFFER 1 and 2.

1483 *Cath. Angl.* 161/2 A Goffe, a godefader. **1532** MORE *Confut. Tindale* Wks. 711/1 A very cold conseeit of my goffe that he found. **1577** *Misogonus* II. iii. (Brandl *Quellen* 443), Cha bene sadlinge my gofe cuccolds cowe. **1683** *Yorksh. Dial.* 33 See if Goff Hyldroth be gaen hand. *Ibid.* 49 God ya god moarne, Goff.

goff[2] (gɒf). *Obs.* exc. *dial.* Also 9 guff. [App. a. F. *goffe* awkward, stupid, ad. It. *goffo* (Sp. *gofo*), of uncertain origin.] (See quots.)

1570 LEVINS *Manip.* 156/37 A Goffe, foole, *morio, bardus*. **1678** *Pol. Ballads* (1860) I. 205 He calls the bishop Greybeard Goff, And makes his power a mere scoff. **1790** GROSE *Prov. Gloss.* (ed. 2), *Goff*, a foolish clown. North. **1801** R. ANDERSON *Cumbld. Ball.* 18 My mudder caws me peer deyl'd guff. **1818** HOGG *Brownie of Bodsbeck*, etc. II. 186 Weel I wat ye'll never get the like o' her, great muckle hallanshaker-like guff. **1869** *Lonsdale Gloss.*, *Goff*, a foolish clown, a silly fellow, an oaf. **1878** *Cumbld. Gloss.*, *Goff*, *Guff*, a fool.

goff, obs. form of GOAF[1]; var. of GOLF.

goffan, goffen. *Min.* = COFFIN *sb.* 11 a.

1880 *W. Cornw. Gloss.*, *Goffans*, *Coffans*, old surface excavations in a mine. **1881** RAYMOND *Mining Gloss.*, *Goffan* or *Goffen* (Corn.), a long narrow surface-working.

goffer ('gɒfə(r)), *sb.* [ad. F. *gaufre*: see the vb. In sense 1 the mod.Fr. term is *gaufrier*.]

1. A goffering-tool.

1865 *Daily Tel.* 27 Sept., The thumb and finger get sore and blistered from working the goffers.

2. 'An ornamental plaiting used for the frills and borders of women's caps, etc.' (Ogilvie).

goffer ('gɒfə(r), 'gəʊfə(r)), **gauffer** ('gɔːfə(r)), *v.* Also gopher, gofer, gauf(f)re, (8 *Sc.* gowpher). [ad. F. *gaufrer* to stamp or impress figures on cloth, paper, etc. with tools on which the required pattern is cut, f. *gaufre* honeycomb (see GOFER[1]). The usual sense of the English word is in French expressed by *gauffrer à la paille*.] *trans.* To make wavy by means of heated goffering-irons; to flute or crimp (the edge of lace, a frill, or trimming of any kind).

1706 [see GOFFERED *ppl. a.*]. **1824** MISS FERRIER *Inher.* xxi. (D.), I'll have to get it [my ruff] all goffered over again. **186.** B. P. BRENT in Tegetmeier *Pigeons* xxiii. (1868) 178 A small conical hollow, which gives the plumage the appearance of having been goffered or raised by a fine pair of curling tongs. **1879** MRS. A. E. JAMES *Ind. Househ. Managem.* 15 Flounces and frills a *dhobie* [= washerman] will get up and gauffre beautifully. **1895** CROCKETT '*Men of Moss Hags*' 233 Her cap ..was fairly and daintily goffered at the edges.

fig. **1856** AIRD *Poet. Wks.* 230 No plaited folds of favour, crimped and goffered by ceremony.

Hence '**gofferer** (cf. F. *gaufreur*).

1885 *Instr. to Census Clerks* 75 Milliner, etc... Gofferer or Gopherer.

goffered ('gɒfəd), *ppl. a.* Also 8 *Sc.* gowphered, 9 gauffered. [f. GOFFER *v.* + -ED[1].]

1. Of frills, etc.: Fluted, crimped.

[**1578** *Inv. R. Househ.* (1815) 223 A lows gowne of quheite satene gowfre [= F. *satin gaufré*] crispit alower with thre small cordonis of gold togidder.] **1706** *J. Watson's Collect. Poems* I. 29 Ev'n his whole shirt his skin doth hide. Gowpherd, Gratnizied, Cloaks rare pointed, Embroider'd, lac'd [etc.]. **1860** B. P. BRENT *Pigeon Bk.* 54 Having the peculiar curled, or as if it were goffered plumage. **1880** *Cassell's Mag.* June 441 The petticoats worn with short dresses should have a ruche, or frill, or goffered border.. showing beneath the dress. **1885** *Instr. to Census Clerks* 73 Goffered Rouche Manufacturer. **1888** *Daily News* 26 Dec. 2/1 A little gophered mob cap with strings tied under the chin.

2. *Bookbinding* and *Printing*. Embossed or impressed with ornamental figures, esp. *goffered edges*. (Also in Fr. form *gaufré*.)

1866 *Bookseller's Catal.*, Sternhold's Psalms, 1649..in contemporary embroidered binding..gauffered edges. **1879** *Print. Trades Jrnl.* XXVI. 13 The tops of each card are shaped and goffered. **1894** BRASSINGTON *Bookbinding* xii. 166 Henry VIII of England had many of his books adorned with gilt and gauffered edges. [**1895** ZAEHNSDORF *Short Hist. Bookbinding* 24 *Gaufre Edges*, impressions made with the tools of the finishers on the gilt edges of a book.]

3. *Ent.* Of the elytra of certain beetles: Having very prominent longitudinal lines or carinæ, which in many cases diverge from the base and converge towards the tip (*Cent. Dict.*).

goffering ('gɒfərɪŋ), *vbl. sb.* [f. GOFFER *v.* + -ING[1].] The action of the vb. GOFFER; also, the result of this; goffered lace, frills, etc.

1848 WEBSTER, *Gauffering*, a mode of plaiting or fluting frills, etc. **1885** FAIRHOLT *Costume* Gloss., *Goffering*, an ornamental pleating, used for the frills and borders of women's caps, etc. **1889** *Century Dict.*, *Goffering*, flutes, plaits, or crimps collectively. **1894** BRASSINGTON *Bookbinding* xii. 166 Accordingly we find in the sixteenth century.. much pains bestowed upon gilding, tooling or gauffering, and painting of the edges of books.

b. *attrib.* and *Comb.*, as ***goffering-frame, hand, machine, process, work***; **goffering-iron, -tongs**, an iron tool used for goffering lace, frills, etc.; **goffering-press**, a press for crimping the material used in the manufacture of artificial flowers.

1893 *Northumbld. Gloss.*, **Gofferin-frame*, a frame made for holding a series of sticks or canes between which a frill is worked in and out in waving form. The whole is clamped by a screw. **1885** *Instr. to Census Clerks* 70 Lace Finishing ..*Gophering Hand. **1863** MRS. BEETON *Househ. Managem.* 1013 *Gauffering-tongs or irons must be placed in a clear fire for a minute. **1801** *Morning Post* in *Spirit Pub. Jrnls.* (1802) V. 180 The skin might be found useful in mending the instep of a Hessian boot, or a *goffreeing machine. **1851** MAYHEW *Lond. Labour* I. 335 Crimping and goffering-machines. **1875** KNIGHT *Dict. Mech.*, **Gauffering-press*. **1857** J. G. WILKINSON *Egyptians in Time Pharaohs* 41 The waving lines purposely impressed upon it [linen] by the **goeffreying* [sic] process. **1847-78** HALLIWELL, **Gofering-work*, a sort of crimping performed on frills, caps, etc.

[**gofysshe**, *a.* Error for *gosysshe* GOOSISH *a.*, silly, stupid, occurring in Thynne's ed. (1532) of Chaucer's *Troylus* (III. 584) and perpetuated in some modern editions. Hence the following dictionary entries:

1658-1706 PHILLIPS, *Gofish* (old word), sottish. **1864** WEBSTER, Goffish [citing *Chaucer*]; so in **1890** *Century Dict.*]

†**Gog**[1]. *Obs.* A corrupt form of GOD employed in oaths. (See GOD *sb.* 13, 14.)

1. ***by Gog, Gog of heaven, Gog give***, etc.

13.. *Gaw. & Gr. Knt.* 390 'Bi gog', quoth þe grene knyȝt. *c***1460** *Towneley Myst.* ii. 172 Gog of heuen, take it to good. *a***1553** UDALL *Royster D.* IV. viii. (Arb.) 78 Slee else whom she will, by gog she shall not slee mee.

2. Possessive combs., as ***(by) Gog's arms, blood, body***, etc. (cf. GOD *sb.* 14).

*a***1553** UDALL *Royster D.* I. iii. (Arb.) 27 *Gogs armes knaue, art thou madde? **1575** *Gamm. Gurton* v. ii, By *gogs blest..I know the blowes he bare away. **1560** *Nice Wanton* B j a, Bi *gogs bloud, I wene god & the deuyl be agenst me. **1519** *Interl. Four Elem.* (Percy Soc.) 18 By *goggys body I tell you trew! **1575** *Gamm. Gurton* IV. ii, By *gogs bones.. he shal sure [etc.]. **1595** PEELE *Old Wives' T.* Wks. (1829) I. 239 By gogs-bones, thou art a flouting knave. **1602** *Content. Liberality & Prodigality* I. iv. in Hazl. *Dodsley* VIII. 338 By *Gog's bores, these old stumps are stark tired. **1619** FLETCHER *M. Thomas* III. i, Gogs bores, I am well. **1575** *Gamm. Gurton* II. ii, *Gogs bread, that will I doo. *Ibid.* I. v, *Gogs crosse Gammer if ye will laugh looke in but at the doore. *Ibid.* I. iv, *Gogs deth how shall my breches be sewid. **1569** T. PRESTON *Cambyses* B j, *Gogs flesh and his wounds these warres reioyce my hart. **1567** *Trial Treas.* B ij b, By *gogs precious harte, euen so doe I. **1575** *Gamm. Gurton* I. v, Gogs harte, help and come vp. *Ibid.* II. i, Well done be *Gogs malt. *a***1553** UDALL *Royster D.* IV. vii. (Arb.) 72 By *gogs deare mother, I woulde not leaue one stone vpon an other. **1519** *Interl. Four Elem.* (Percy Soc.) 42 *Gogges naylys, I have payed som of them, I tro. **1568** *Like will to Like* C ij b, By *gogs nowns chad thought iche had been in my bed. **1616** B. JONSON *Devil an Ass* I. i, To sweare by Gogs-nownes. **1519** *Interl. Four Elem.* (Percy Soc.) 24 *Gogges Passyon! sayd ye not thus. **1575** *Gamm. Gurton* I. iii, *Gogs Sacrament, I would she had lost tharte out of her bellie. **1569** T. PRESTON *Cambyses* B 3 *Gogs sides Maister Ruf are ye so crusty? **1519** *Interl. Four Elem.* (Percy Soc.) 38 Why, *Goggis soule! wyll ye..Breke poyntment. **1567** *Trial Treas.* E ij, *Gogs woundes these panges encrease euer more. **1602** *How to choose Good Wife* D 3 b, He that with greatest grace can sweare *gogs zounds..Hee's a braue man.

†**gog**[2]. *Obs.* Also 7 gogge. [App. formed by substitution of *on gog* for earlier AGOG (q.v.), *gog* being subsequently employed as an independent sb.] ***to set on gog***, to stir up, excite, make eager; also ***to set (put) in such a gog for*** (or ***of***). ***to be upon the gog of***, to be eager for.

1560 PHAER *Æneid* x, What wrath what feare sets these or those on gog not suffring rest to shield nor speare. **1575** [see AGOG]. **1587** HUGHES *Misfort. Arthur* III. i. (1828) 47 The selfsame cause which first Set them on gog, even fortunes favours quail'd. **1602** BRETON *Wonders worth hearing* (Grosart) 11/2, I set her in such a gogge for a husband..that [etc.]. *a***1616** BEAUM. & FL. *Wit without M.* III. i, You have put me into such a gogge of going I would not stay for all the world. **1672** LACY *Old Troop* II. (1698) 11 You have put me in such a gog of marriage, that it will not out of my head. **1673** O. WALKER *Educ.* (1677) 43 When all Europe was upon the gog of fighting.

gog[3] (gɒg). *Obs.* exc. *dial.* Also gogg. [Of obscure origin; possibly f. the onomatopœic **gog* to shake (see GOGGLE *sb.* 5 and *v.*[1]); for the sense cf. QUAGMIRE.] A bog, swamp.

1583 [see b]. **1625** N. CARPENTER *Geog. Del.* II. iii. (1635) 46 Waters..bursting out of secret..concauities, doe produce infinite Fennes, Gogges, Lakes, and Marishes. *a***1691** AUBREY *Nat. Hist. Wilts* (1847) 25 In Minety Common in Bradon forest..is a boggy place called the Gogges, where is a spring or springs, rising up out of fuller's earth. **1847-78** HALLIWELL, *Gog*, a bog. *Oxon.* **1854** MISS BAKER *Northamptonsh. Gloss.*, *Gog*, a bog. 'The land's full of gogs', or 'all of a gog'.

b. *Comb.*, as **gog-mire**, a quagmire.

1583 FULKE *Defence* i. §47. 61 Though it be tedious for vs to rake in such a gogmyre of your forgeries, and false accusations, yet [etc.]. **1862** *Aubrey's Topogr. Collect.* 271 *note*, 'I be all in a gogg-mire' is a North Wilts phrase for being in what appears an inextricable difficulty.

Hence '**goggy** *a.*, *dial.*, boggy.

1854 MISS BAKER *Northamptonsh. Gloss.*, *Goggy*, boggy, soppy; as heavy, deep land. 'It's very goggy'. In very general use among our agricultural labourers.

gog[4]. *Sc.* [Origin obscure.] 'The object set up as a mark in playing at Quoits, Pitch and Toss, etc.' (Jam.).

1821 *Blackw. Mag.* Aug. 35/2 The parties stand at a little distance and pitch the halfpenny to a mark or gog. **1893** *Northumbld. Gloss.*, *Gog*, a boy's marble, or taw in ring in the game of boorey.

†'**gogar.** *Sc. Obs. rare.* Only in *gogar-gown*, some kind of long gown.

1494 in *Ld. Treas. Acc. Scotl.* (1877) I. 223 Item..xv ellis of velvous to be the King a gogar goune. **1495** *Ibid.* 225 Item ..v ellis of Rissillis blak, to be a gogare gowne.

gogathes, var. of GAGATE, *Obs.*, jet.

gogel, obs. form of GOGGLE *v.*[1]

gogement, obs. form of JUDGEMENT.

goge(o)n, obs. form of GUDGEON.

'**goget.** *rare*⁻⁰. [Formation obscure.] (See quot.)

1835 BOOTH *Analyt. Dict.* 224 The *Gobius niger*, a smaller fish, is the Black Goby, Goget, or Sea Gudgeon.

go-getter ('gəʊ,gɛtə(r)). *colloq.* (orig. *U.S.*). [f. *to go get* (see GO *v.* 32 a) + -ER[1].] An active, enterprising, pushing person. Also *attrib.*

1921 S. FORD *Inez & Trilby May* xii. 216 Think you're one of these go-getters, do you? **1922** P. B. KYNE (*title*) The Go-Getter. A story that tells you how to be one. **1926** F. SWINNERTON *Summer Storm* v. i. 197 The go-getter despises the non-go-getter; but never as much as the non-go-getter despises the go-getter. **1928, 1929** [see GO *v.* 32 a]. **1932** J. CARY *Aissa Saved* 159 MacEwen did not write in the vein of a go-getter business expert seeking out inefficiency. **1959** M. CUMBERLAND *Murmurs in Rue Morgue* vii. 48 He was a go-getter, an *arriviste*,..a bull charging at competitive life.

So '**go-,getting** *ppl. a.*, enterprising, pushing; also as *sb.*, the behaviour of a go-getter; enterprise, ambition. Hence **go-'gettingness**.

1921 J. G. FREDERICK *Great Game of Business* p. v, The true forward-looking 'go-getting' American business point of view. **1924** R. CUMMINS *Sky-High Corral* 25 He was one of them flyin' son-of-a-guns an' they say he was a go-gettin' fool. **1928** *Daily Express* 27 June 10/7 Such jobs generally call for..a 'go-getting' attitude to life that the public school boy does not possess. *Ibid.* 5 July 13/7 All of which has somewhat shattered my faith in the 'pep' and 'go-gettingness' of the American reporters. **1931** F. F. BOND *Mr. Miller* 170 The students herded to hear breezy young instructors exhale the new gospel of 'go-getting'. **1946** R. KNOX *Epistles & Gospels* 97 There are some critics who maintain that when St Paul uses this particular word (it is really 'go-getting' rather than 'covetousness'), he is thinking of the ninth commandment, not of the tenth. **1959** *Punch* 21 Oct. 340/2 My future as a go-getting reporter was bleak indeed.

‖**gogga** ('xɔxa). *S. Afr.* Also †gogo (dim. *gogotje*, now *goggatjie*). [ad. Hott. *χόχόn* insects collectively.] An insect (of any type).

[**1905** J. DU PLESSIS *Thousand Miles in Heart of Africa* iii. 54 This country ought to be called *Gogoland*: it simply swarms with insects.] **1909** *East London Dispatch* 8 Jan. 5 We have heard South Africa described as a land of *goggas*. **1911** *Ibid.* 27 Nov. 6 Another old, well-grown tree..is infested with those abominable *gogotjes* which have already done considerable damage to it. **1926** E. LEWIS *Mantis* II. vi. 103 He said he'd find me lots of beautiful goggas to make pictures of much better than that. **1927** W. PLOMER *I speak of Africa* 243 *Mrs. White.* Another huge black beast! What is it? *White.* It looks like a gogga. **1956** A. G. MCRAE *Hill called Grazing* vii. 62 There were other *goggas* in Italy.

goggan ('gɒgən). *dial.* Also 6 goggon, -en, (?-ey). [Origin obscure.

Gael. *gogan* is explained as 'a small wooden dish made up of staves, and without handles', but this, with *cogan* of similar meaning (cf. COGUE), is perh. not a native word.]

A wooden or metal dish.

1586 *Inv. of Atkinson* (Somerset Ho.), ij bassons ij goggons & dishes. **1590** *Wills & Inv. N.C.* (Surtees 1860) 180, iiij drinckinge potts, of tynne 2s. 8d. One goggen 4d. **1593** *Ibid.* 230, xij tyne spoynes, a putter goggey, and ij tyne ladelles. **1894** HALL CAINE *Manxman* 60 According to the goggans they lay hands on, so will be the trades of their husbands.

goggle ('gɒg(ə)l), *sb.* Also 7 gogle. [f. GOGGLE *v.*[1]]

I. 1. One who goggles. *rare.*

a **1616** BEAUM. & FL. *Knt. Malta* II. i, I am in sowce I thank ye; thanke your beauty Your most sweet beauty: pox upon those goggles. *Ibid.* v. ii, Do ye stare, gogles, I hope to make winter bootes o' thy hide yet. *a* **1859** L. HUNT *Sonn., Fish, Man & Spirit* ii, O scaly..wights, What is't ye do? what life lead? eh, dull goggles?

†**2.** A goggling look; a squint, leer, stare. *Obs.*

1651 RANDOLPH, etc. *Hey for Honesty* I. i, *Chr.* But others, such as your demure Cheaters. *Car.* That have the true gogle of Amsterdam. *a* **1659** CLEVELAND *Gen. Poems*, etc. (1677) 127 Such a Goggle of the Eye, such a melodious Twang of the Nose [etc.]. **1688** MARQ. HALIFAX *Advice to Dau.* (ed. 2) 9 Others will have such a Divided Face between a Devout Goggle and an Inviting Glance, that [etc.].

3. *slang.* In *pl.*: The eyes. †Also in *sing.*: The white of the eye.

1705 HICKERINGILL *Priest-cr.* IV. (1721) 227 If..I should turn up my Eyes, 'till the black Pupil be lost under the Upper Eye-lid, and nothing but the *pious Goggle*, and *innocent White* appears, (*that's a precious Man*, say the Women). **1710** *Brit. Apollo* III. No. 96. 2/1 Whose dim Goggles cou'd not bear the Rays of the Sun. *a* **1763** BYROM *Dissect. Beau's Head* viii, Those Muscles..wherewith a Man ogles, When on a fair Lady he fixes his Goggles. **1815** W. H. IRELAND *Scribbleomania* 141 Villains so often assume diff'rent scowls, And glare with their goggles.

4. a. *pl.* (rarely *sing.*) A kind of spectacles, having glasses (usually coloured) or fine wire-netting, fixed in short tubes, and worn to protect the eyes from dust, excess of light, etc.; formerly also so constructed as to correct squinting. Esp. used by motor-cyclists (and formerly motorists) and underwater divers.

(Applied *colloq.* or *jocularly* to spectacles with round glasses.)

1715 tr. *C'tess D'Aunoy's Wks.* 406 A pair of blue Goggles, hedg'd in with long black Eyebrows. **1806–7** J. BERESFORD *Miseries Hum. Life* (1826) Post. Groans xxxv, Pinking and blinking, with his up-and-down-goggles, full at me. **1820** *Sporting Mag.* VII. 96 Just call in St. Martin's-le-Grand For some goggles for Mary (who squints). **1853** KANE *Grinnell Exp.* xli. (1856) 380 A disk of hard wood, with a simple slit..we found a better protection than the goggle or colored lens. **1868** DICKENS *Uncomm. Trav.* xxii, A little spare man who sat breaking stones..regarding me mysteriously through his dark goggles of wire. **1879** T. HARDY *Return Native* IV. ii, The goggles he was obliged to wear over his eyes. **1899** J. K. JEROME *Three Men on Bummel* xiii, Their goggle-covered eyes, their necks tied up in comforters. **1903** G. B. SHAW *Man & Superman* II. 55 He cares for nothing but tearing along in a leather coat and goggles..at sixty miles an hour. **1904** A. B. F. YOUNG *Compl. Motorist* (ed. 2) xi. 260 Goggles are, unhappily, almost a necessity when travelling at any but the lowest speeds. **1908** *Motor Cycle* 12 Feb. 132 A new goggle constructed after the principle of the four-glass goggle. **1908** E. J. BANFIELD *Confessions of Beachcomber* I. iv. 152 All were wearing swimming goggles which enable them when diving to distinguish objects at a considerable range. **1957** T. GUNN *Sense of Movement* 11 In goggles, donned impersonality.

Comb. **1810** W. TAYLOR in *Monthly Rev.* LXII. 502 But place..goggle spectacles over this focus of expression, and a slight change of dress will deceive us as to the person.

b. (See quot.)

1808 JAMIESON, *Goggles*, blinds for horses that are apt to take fright, to prevent their seeing objects from behind, S. **1818** in TODD. **1828** in WEBSTER; and in later Dicts.

II. 5. *pl. the goggles*, a disease of sheep; the staggers or sturdy.

With the sense cf. the dialect (Hants, Wilts, Glouc.) phrase '*all of a goggle*', all shaking, giddy.

1793 J. CLARIDGE *Agric. Dorset* 11 A disorder peculiar to sheep,..called the Goggles;..the first symptoms is a violent itching, which is soon succeeded by a dizziness in the head, staggering of gait [etc.]. **1807** VANCOUVER *Agric. Devon* (1813) 343 The goggles is a disease sometimes, though rarely, experienced on the confines of Somerset and Dorset. **1825** LOUDON *Encycl. Agric.* §6524 Staggers, gid, turnsick, goggles [etc.]..are all popular terms for hydatids, or an animal..which..finds its way to the brain. **1893** in *Northumbld. Gloss., Goggles*, a disease in sheep.

6. *attrib.* and *Comb.*, as **goggle-box** *slang*, a television set; **goggle-dive**, an underwater dive made by a person wearing goggles; hence as *v. intr.*; also ***goggle-diver, -diving.***

1959 *Guardian* 9 Nov. 5/5 Switch the goggle-box on at 10 a.m. **1967** *Times* 2 Oct. 1/1 Mr. Wilson was..so good at television appearances, that he had convinced himself that he, single-handed, could win elections 'with the help of the goggle box'. **1953** J. Y. COUSTEAU *Silent World* 5 Two years of goggle-dives passed before I met Dumas. *Ibid.* 7 In the goggle-diving era Dumas made a light-hearted bet at Le Brusq that he could spear two hundred and twenty pounds of fish in two hours. *Ibid.* 16 The merou, virtually unknown in the Provençal markets until goggle divers went down and speared them. **1958** *Sunday Times* 19 Oct. 17/3 It was impossible to goggle dive without seeing a fish.

goggle ('gɒg(ə)l), *a.* Also 6 gogle, gogyll, google. [Properly the vbl. stem GOGGLE in comb., the purely adjectival use being a modern development.] Of the eye: Protuberant, prominent, full and rolling; also, †squinting.

1540 RAYNOLD *Byrth Mankynde* II. 78 b, Yf the chylde haue google eyes [L. *strabos oculos*]. **1544** PHAER *Regim. Lyfe* (1546) Cc ij b, Of gogle eyes. **1563** *Mirr. Mag., Hastings* lxxi, Lowryng on me with the goggle eye. **1667** COTTON *Virg. Travest.* IV. 106 The Queen in wrathful wise, Rowling about her goggle eyes. **1680** BAXTER *Cath. Commun.* §11 (1684) 28 If goggle Eyes judge each line to be a yard distant from another, I cannot cure them. **1774** GOLDSM. *Hist. Earth* VI. 239 He [a shark] is furnished with great goggle eyes. **1840** THACKERAY *Paris Sk. Bk.* (1869) 177 His goggle eyes were always rolling about wildly. **1885** G. S. FORBES *Wild Life in Canara* 105 The face was broad, the mouth wide, the eyes goggle.

goggle ('gɒg(ə)l), *v.*[1] Forms: 4 gogel, 5–7 gogle, 6 google, 6– goggle. [Perh. a frequentative of an onomatopœic *gog, expressive of oscillating movement (cf. *jog, joggle*); cf. GOG [2] and [3]; also GOGGLE *sb.* 5. It may be noticed that mod. Welsh and Gaelic have several words of similar form and sense: Welsh *gogi* to shake, Gael. *gog* a nodding or tossing of the head, *gogshùil* (? from Eng.) a goggle-eye. The verb, like the combinations *goggle-eye, -eyed*, first becomes common in the 16th c., and is, with the few exceptions given under II, always used of movement of the eye, though in later use its meaning has been somewhat altered.

The Gaelic forms *gogaid, gogaild, gogaill, gogag*, 'a light-headed woman, giddy female, coquette', are prob. not related to *gog* and its derivatives, but merely adaptations of earlier English *cocket* = COQUETTE.]

I. 1. a. *intr.* Of persons: To turn the eyes to one side or other, to look obliquely, to squint; also ***to goggle with the eyes*** and ***to goggle at*** (a thing). In later use, to look with widely-opened, unsteady eyes; to roll the eyes about.

c **1380** WYCLIF *Wks.* (1880) 341 Pharesees alargen her browes & gogelen fer fro goddis lawe. **1544** PHAER *Regim. Lyfe* (1560) X iiij a, Lay the chylde so..that he may..not..turne hys eyes on ether of both sides. If yet he begin to gogle, than set y[e] cradell after such a fourme, that the light may be on y[e] contrary syde. **1563–87** FOXE *A. & M.* (1684) II. 431 An old rotten stock..wherein a man should stand inclosed with an hundred wyers..to make the image goggle with the eyes. **1616** R. C. *Times' Whistle* vii. 3099 He squints, and she doth goggle wondrous faire. **1664** BUTLER *Hud.* II. i. 120 Which made him hang the Head and scoul And wink and goggle like an Owl. **1671** CROWNE *Juliana* I. 9 'Tis true, he doth not goggle at it so plain, as Mr. Mumpsimus o' Curland doth; but..he squints at it fearfully. **1742** RICHARDSON *Pamela* IV. 319 The poor little Thing lies on the Nurses Lap..goggling and staring with its Eyes. **1757** FOOTE *Author* Epil., Wks. 1799 I. 129 Look, my Lord!—She goggles! **1830** GALT *Lawrie T.* VI. ii. (1849) 256 A sum that I thought would make the old man goggle. **1880** *W. Cornw. Gloss.* s.v., Stand goggling for gapes like an owl at an eagle. **1938** G. GREENE *Brighton Rock* II. i. 67 She goggled hopelessly at the Boy. **1960** I. CROSS *Backward Sex* 105 It was not unreasonable of her to have expected that I would be well past goggling at her body now that we were such friends. **1965** *Listener* 24 June 949/1 The contemporary reader..has better things to do than goggle into the dim past.

b. Of the eyes: To turn to one side, to squint. In modern use, to project from the head and move unsteadily, to roll.

1540 RAYNOLD *Byrth Mankynde* II. 79 Marke on whiche syde that the eyes do gogle. **1584** R. SCOT *Discov. Witchcr.* VII. vi. 138 The wiers that made their eies gogle. **1683** DRYDEN *Plutarch* 42 She came out foaming at the mouth, her eyes gogling, her breast heaving [etc.]. **1850** W. IRVING *Goldsm.* xxxix. (1851) 334 His eyes goggled with eagerness. **1855** THACKERAY *Newcomes* I. 1 The frog's hideous large eyes were goggling out of his head. **1879** EARL DESART *Kelverdale* I. iv. 45 His large eyes goggled and watered as he kept them fixed upon the piece of sugar.

2. *trans.* To turn (one's eye) to one side, or (in modern use) from side to side with an unsteady motion. Also with *about.*

1583 STANYHURST *Æneis* I. (Arb.) 32 Whilst in temple corners he gogled his eyesight Wayting for Dido. **1616** J. LANE *Cont. Sqr.'s T.* vii. 572 So with a crooked curtchie, wried aright, goglinge bothe eies. **1713** STEELE *Englishm.* No. 8. 50 The Wagg..goggled his Eyes, and then fixing them dreadfully upon the Fellow. **1829** T. L. PEACOCK *Misfort. Elphin* xi. 147 The stranger goggled about his eyes in an attempt to fix them steadily on Taliesin. **1884** *Harper's Mag.* Oct. 695/1 He could..goggle his eyes at Agnes.

II. 3. *intr.* To sway or roll about; move loosely and unsteadily. Also ***to goggle with the head***, to shake or wag the head. *Obs.* exc. *dial.*

c **1400** *Beryn* 163 Then passed they forth boystly, goglyng with hir hedis. **1519** HORMAN *Vulg.* 149 Maydens: that cary geere vpon theyr heed putte a wrethe of haye betwene the vessell and theyr heed to stay it from goglynge. *a* **1650** *Robin Hood* 26 in Furniv. *Percy Folio MS.* I. 16 But Robin did on this old mans hood, itt gogled on his crowne. **1893** *Wilts. Gloss., Goggle*, to shake or tremble, as a table with one leg shorter than the others.

†**4.** *trans.* To cause to shake. *fig.*

1576 NEWTON *Lemnie's Complex.* II. 97 b, Y[e] lack wherof googleth [**1581** gogleth] theyr vnstayed heades, and caryeth them into many inordinate pranckes of childishe insolencie.

goggle ('gɒg(ə)l), *v.*[2] [Onomatopœic: an occasional substitute for GOBBLE, as suggesting a similar sound, but made more in the throat.]

1. *trans.* = GOBBLE *v.*[1] I.

1611 COTGR., *Goulardé*,..gulped, or goggled downe. *Ibid., Goularder*,..to rauine, goggle, glut vp, swallow downe, huge morsells, or mouthfulls. **1888** [see 2].

2. *intr.* = GOBBLE *v.*[2]

1831 MRS. CARLYLE *Lett.* (1889) 186 The Bubbly goggeling neither sweetly nor profitably. **1888** *Sheffield Gloss., Goggle*, to swallow, to make a gurgling noise in the throat.

'goggled, *ppl. a.*[1] Now *rare.* [f. GOGGLE *v.*[1] + -ED[1].] Of the eyes = GOGGLE *a.*

1503 *Kalender Sheph.* (1656) xlii, A person that is Blear-eyed, gogled & squint. **1589** *Hay any Work* 7 Vnnatural squint gogled eies. **1664** POWER *Exp. Philos.* I. 9 A Louse, her two eyes were like two black beads, gogled and protuberant. **1872** DASENT *Three to One* II. 30 One eye..was bigger and more goggled than the other.

'goggled, *ppl. a.*[2] [f. GOGGLE *sb.* + -ED[2].] Equipped with or wearing goggles.

1903 *Westm. Gaz.* 20 July 2/3 These ghastly goggled motor guys. **1908** *Ibid.* 22 Aug. 10/1 The swimmer's head, goggled and capped, emerging from the water. **1909** H. G. WELLS *Tono-Bungay* III. ii. 237 A short figure,..hugely goggled,..and surmounted by a table-land of motoring cap. **1919** *N.Y. Times* 9 Feb., A goggled aviator making ready for a flight. **1945** J. R. ULLMAN *White Tower* 425 He brought the watch closer to his goggled eyes.

goggle-eye ('gɒg(ə)l,aɪ). [See GOGGLE *a.* and *v.*] †**a.** One who squints (*obs.*). †**b.** Obliquity of vision; squinting (*obs.*). **c.** *U.S.* = GOGGLER 2. **d.** (See quot. 1897.)

c **1440** *Promp. Parv.* 199/1 Glyare or goguleye.., *limus, strabo.* **1822–34** *Good's Study Med.* (ed. 4) III. 183 This disease, in colloquial language now called *squinting*, was formerly denominated *goggle-eye.* **1883** *Fisheries Exhib. Catal.* (ed. 4) 160 Two Kegs of Pickled Goggle-eyes. **1897** WEBSTER, *Goggle-eye*, one of two or more species of American fresh-water fishes of the family *Centrarchidæ.*

goggle-eyed ('gɒg(ə)laɪd), *a.* [f. *goggle eye* (see GOGGLE *a.*) + -ED[2].] **a.** Having prominent, staring or rolling eyes; also, †squint-eyed. Also *fig.*

1382 WYCLIF *Mark* ix. 46 It is good to thee for to entre gogil y3ed in to rewme of God, than [etc.]. **1484** CAXTON *Fables of Alfonce* (1889) 7 Whan the porter byheld hym he perceyued that he was goglyed..And the goglyed wold paye nought. *c* **1515** *Cocke Lorell's B.* 5 Gogle eyed tomson shepster of lyn. **1530** PALSGR. 226/1 Goggleyed man, *lovche.* **1635** QUARLES *Embl.* V. xiv. (1718) 302 Giddy doubt, and goggle-ey'd suspicion. **1711** SWIFT *Jrnl. to Stella* 12 July, Young Manley's wife is..goggle-eyed, and looks like a fool. **1844** DICKENS *Mart. Chuz.* ix, He's the most hideous, goggle-eyed creature. **1919** W. H. DOWNING *Digger Dial.* 26 *Goggle-eyed*, dazed. **1942** E. PAUL *Narrow St.* xvii. 128 The way in which the American male seemed to be pushed around by his womenfolk left Parisians goggle-eyed. **1957** *Times Lit. Suppl.* 20 Dec. 765/4 Modern society need not stand goggle-eyed before it [*sc.* the automated production line].

b. ***goggle-eyed Jack*** = GOGGLER 2.

1884–5 [see GOGGLER].

goggler ('gɒglə(r)). [f. GOGGLE *v.*[1] + -ER[1].]

1. *slang.* An eye.

1821 *Sporting Mag.* VIII. 234 Every goggler had the combatants within its focus. **1822** *Blackw. Mag.* XI. 163 How plain folks roll'd their gogglers. **1840** THACKERAY *Bedford-Row Conspir.* iii, Her ladyship..turning her own grey gogglers up to heaven.

2. *U.S.* (See quot.)

1884–5 *Riverside Nat. Hist.* (1888) III. 187 The big-eyed scad, also more generally known as the goggler, and goggle-eyed Jack—the *Trachurops crumenopthalmus* of naturalists. The very large prominent eyes are the most striking feature of the fish.

goggling ('gɒglɪŋ), *vbl. sb.* [f. GOGGLE *v.*[1] + -ING[1].] The action of the vb. GOGGLE.

1540 RAYNOLD *Byrth Mankynde* II. 79 By this meane, the goglynge of the eyes maye bee retorned to the ryghte place. **1651** RANDOLPH, etc. *Hey for Honesty* II. iii, Thy eyes Unconstant gogling, call thee guilty.

goggling ('gɒglɪŋ), *ppl. a.* [f. GOGGLE *v.*[1] + -ING[2].] That goggles, in senses of the vb.

a **1586** SIDNEY *Arcadia* II. (1598) 226 They that see with goggling eyes. **1599** HARSNET *Fraud. Pract. J. Darrel* III. 216 His eyes were somewhat gogling out, but otherwise no more than ordinary. **1611** CORYAT *Crudities* 180 Medusaes head ..with..great gogling eyes. **1618** WITHER *Motto, Nec Curo* Wks. (1633) 550 Places..from whose ever-gogling station, all May at the pleasure of another fall. **1825** HOGG *Q. Hynde* 77 The stars were sprinkled o'er the night, With goggling and uncertain light. **1875–7** RUSKIN *Morn. in Florence* (1881) 51 Faces with goggling eyes and rigid lips.

goggly ('gɒglɪ), *a.* [f. GOGGLE *sb.* + -Y[1].]

1. Of eyes: Goggle, goggling.

a **1693** AUBREY *Lives, Birkenhead* (1898) I. 105 He was of midling stature, great goggli eies. **1923** WODEHOUSE *Inimitable Jeeves* ix. 93 He was a thin, tall chappie with..pale-blue goggly eyes which made him look like one of the rarer kinds of fish. **1969** *Daily Tel.* 2 Oct. 22/3 The great goggly eyes are unforgettable and endearing.

2. Of sheep: Affected with the 'goggles'. (Cf. Glouc. dialect *goggly* giddy.)

1840 *Jrnl. R. Agric. Soc.* I. III. 297, I once knew a flock of 200 sheep, 64 of which died goggly.

gogin, obs. form of GUDGEON.

†**'gogingstool.** *Obs.* Also goginstole. [Var. CUCKING-STOOL.]

1679 BLOUNT *Anc. Tenures* 151 This Gogingstool is the same which in our Law-Books is written Cuckingstool. **1797** TOMLINS *Jacob's Law Dict.* s.v. *Castigatory*, It is also termed goginstole and cokestole.

gogion, gogle, obs. ff. GUDGEON, GOGGLE.

goglet[1] ('gɒglɪt), **gugglet** ('gʌglɪt). *Anglo-Indian.* Also 7 gurgulet, 9 guglet, gurglet. [ad. Pg. *gorgoleta*, 'an earthen and narrow-mouthed vessel, out of which the water runs and guggles' (Lacerda *Pg. Dict.*); cf. F. *gargoulette* of similar meaning. The English forms may be due to association with GOGGLE *v.*[2], GUGGLE *v.*] A long-necked vessel for holding water, usually made of porous earthenware, so that the contents are kept cool by evaporation.

1698 FRYER *Acc. E. India & P.* 47 Gurgulets and Jars, which are Vessels made of a porous kind of Earth. **1766** CLIVE in Long *Govt. Rec.* (1869) 406 (Y.) To have a man with a Goglet of water ready to pour on his head. **1855** R. F. BURTON *Pilgr. El Medinah & Meccah* II. xix. 196 The earth is sweet and makes excellent gugglets. **1879** *Blackw. Mag.* Jan. 55 They trusted to the porous goglets for cooling the water. **1880** L. WALLACE *Ben-Hur* 10 A sponge and a small gurglet of water.

†**'goglet**[2]. *Obs. rare*⁻¹. (See quot.)

1688 R. HOLME *Armoury* III. 271/2 A kind of a Drinking Cup or Vessel made off the higher end, or the small top of a Bull or Cows Horn.. It is by some Gentlemens Buttlers termed a Souce, or Goglet, or Goblet.

†**'Gogma,gog.** *Obs.* [f. *Goemagot*, the greatest of the British giants, according to Geoffrey of Monmouth; altered after the biblical names *Gog* and *Magog* (Ezek. xxxviii–xxxix).] A giant, a man of immense stature and strength.

[*c* **1205** LAY. 1806 Geomagog.. Godes wiðer-saka. **1297** R. GLOUC. (Rolls) 508 Gogmagog was a geant, suiþe gret & strong. *c* **1330** R. BRUNNE *Chron. Wace* (Rolls) 1763 Gogmagog.. was strong, gret, & bold. **1559** *Mirr. Mag., Owen Glendour* xxiii, Affirming Henry to be Gogmagog.] *c* **1580** JEFFERIE *Bugbears* III. iii. in *Archiv Stud. d. neu. Spr.* (1897), Harpyes, Gogmagogs, lemures. **1605** *Tryall Chev.* II. i. in Bullen *O. Pl.* III. 289 And thou hast under thy charge any other then Pigmies I am a Gogmagog. **1630** J. TAYLOR (Water P.) *Laugh & be Fat* Wks. II. 73/1 Thy booke he titles Gogmogog the huge.

Hence †**Gogma'gotical** *a.*, as huge as Gogmagog (*Gogmagot*).

1630 J. TAYLOR (Water P.) *Laugh & be Fat* Wks. II. 69 In a huge volume Gogmagoticall.

go-go ('gəʊgəʊ), *a.* [Reduplication of GO *sb.* (sense 2) or *v.* (cf. sense 22 b), influenced perh. by GO *a.*] **a.** Fashionable, 'swinging', 'fabulous', unrestrained; (of funds on the stock exchange) speculative. Cf. GO *a.* 2. **b.** *spec.* Of a dancer or a dance, the music, etc., at a discothèque, strip club, etc.: full of verve, excitement, and movement (often deliberately erotic). Also as *v. intr.*, to dance in this manner. Also **go-go(-go)** *sb.*, continual movement, hustle and bustle.

1962 V. PACKARD *Pyramid Climbers* (1963) xiii. 156 Most executives of promise have a built-in go-go-go. **1964** *Punch* 8 July 38/1 It's fab.. and withitly gogo. **1965** *N.Y. Times Book Rev.* 31 Jan. 42/4 (Advt.), The gorgeous Go-Go girls are your escorts to the discotheque that swings with the latest in dance crazes. **1966** H. NIELSEN *After Midnight* (1967) xii. 149 The room exploded into a wild go-go beat. **1966** *T.V. Times* (Austral.) 4 May 6/4 In clubs they Go-Go in cages on elevated platforms, under red lights. **1967** *Boston Herald* 1 Apr. 17/6 Brash, young Gypsy Joe Harris, squirming and twisting like a go-go dancer. *Ibid.* 8 May 21/4 Spring has come and it will be 'Go-Go' at the Cambridge Boat Club's annual spring regatta. *Ibid.*, Five girls.. have volunteered to be Go-Go Regatta Girls. **1968** *Economist* 3 Aug. 69/2 Tesco.. became an early favourite for London's equivalent of New York's go-go funds. **1968** *Guardian* 23 Dec. 1/3 The main point is that it [*sc.* journey of spacecraft to the moon] is all go-go-go. **1968** 'O. MILLS' *Sundry Fell Designs* ii. 24 It'd take someone with a bit of go-go-go to take on swarming up one of those pylons with a banner. **1968** O. WYND *Sumatra Seven Zero* ii. 18 He.. stared out.. at a Post Office Tower erected by the go-go Britain boys. **1969** *Sunday Times* 9 Feb. 32/4 Only seven of the big 'go-go' funds managed to out-perform the market as a whole. **1969** *Winnipeg Free Press Weekly* 2 Aug. 18/3 Everybody is 'on the go' in this go-go generation. **1970** *Daily Tel.* 14 Feb. 12 Lurid invitations to see the topless go-go girls.. and the pornographic peep-shows.

gogo: see À GOGO *phr.*

gogon, gogram, obs. ff. GUDGEON, GROGRAM.

gogul, var. of GOOGUL.

gogyll, gogyn(e, obs. ff. GOGGLE *a.*, GUDGEON.

gohanna, var. GOANNA.

gohode, obs. form of GOAD *sb.*[1]

†**'goibert.** *Obs. rare*⁻¹. An alleged name for the hare.

a **1325** *Names Hare* in *Rel. Ant.* I. 133 The gras-bitere, the goibert.

Goidel ('gɔɪdɪl). *Hist.* [a. OIr. *Góidel* (pl. *Góidil*), a GAEL. See GADHELIC.] A GAEL in the widest sense; i.e. a person belonging to that branch of the Celtic people represented by the Irish and the Highlanders of Scotland, in contradistinction to the Brythonic or Cymric branch represented by the Welsh, Cornish, and Bretons.

1882 RHYS *Celtic Britain* 3 As there is a tendency in this country now to understand by the word Gael the Gael of the North alone, we shall speak of the group generally as Goidels and Goidelic. **1889** I. TAYLOR *Orig. Aryans* 80 The second invasion was that of the Brittones.. driving the Goidels before them to the West and North.

Goidelic (gɔɪ'dɛlɪk), *a.* and *sb.* [f. prec. + -IC.] **A.** *adj.* Of or pertaining to the Goidels. **B.** *sb.* The language of the Goidels. (Cf. GADHELIC.)

1882 RHYS *Celtic Britain* 196 This could only happen through the medium of men who spoke Goidelic. **1896** SIR H. MAXWELL *Hist. Dumfries* etc. ii. 32 Novantia, however, remained Pictish,—i.e. Goidelic—in speech and race. **1897** ANWYL *Welsh Gram.* §2 The Celtic branch falls into two groups:—1. The Goidelic, consisting of Erse or Irish Gaelic, Scottish Gaelic, and Manx Gaelic. 2. The Brythonic.

goien, obs. form of GUDGEON.

goif, obs. form of GOVE *v.*[1]

goile, var. of GOYLE *dial.*, trench, ravine.

goilk, obs. form of GOWK.

'go-'in. *colloq.* [f. vbl. phrase *go in*: see GO *v.* 82.] With *at*: An attack or onslaught upon; also, a spell of work upon.

1858 HUGHES *Scouring White Horse* 27 We used to have a regular go in about once a quarter at the unpaid magistracy. **1890** BOLDREWOOD *Col. Reformer* (1891) 321, I was having a go-in at the garden here.

‖**'goinfre.** *Obs. rare*⁻¹. [F. *goinfre* gourmand, of unknown origin.] An epicure, a gourmand.

1643 SIR K. DIGBY *Observ. Sir T. Browne's Relig. Med.* 107 A well experienced Goinfre that can criticise upon the several tasts of liquors.

going ('gəʊɪŋ), *vbl. sb.* [f. GO *v.* + -ING[1].]

I. In ordinary substantival use.

1. a. The action of the vb. GO, in various senses.

a **1300** *E.E. Psalter* xvi. 5 Fulmake mi steppes in sties þine, þat noght be stired gainges mine. *c* **1440** *Gesta Rom.* v. 12 (Harl. MS.) Ouer our hedis ys passage and goyng of peple. **1523** LD. BERNERS *Froiss.* I. ccclxxxvi. 657 It is no goynge thyder, without ye wyll lose all. **1605** SHAKS. *Macb.* III. iv. 119 Stand not vpon the order of your going, But go at once. **1611** BEAUM. & FL. *King & No K.* v. iv, Prayers were made For her safe going, and deliverie. **1776** PAINE *Com. Sense* (1791) 75 No going to law with nations. **1867** G. MACDONALD *Poems* 120 That moment through the branches overhead, Sounds of a going went. **1889** *Spectator* 16 Nov., Made happy by six thousand miles of continuous going.

b. *esp.* Departure. † *long going*: departure on a long journey, i.e. death.

c **1340** *Cursor M.* 3245 (Trin.) þis mon made him redy soone Faste he hyȝed to his goyng. **1399** LANGL. *Rich. Redeles* III. 136 They lepith als lyghtly at the longe goyinge, Out of the domes cart. ? *c* **1475** *Sqr. lowe Degre* 273 Ye shall not want at your goyng Golde, nor sylver, nor other thyng. **1667** MILTON *P.L.* XI. 290 Thy going is not lonely; with thee goes Thy husband. **1792** COWPER *Let.* 30 July, Pray for us, my friend, that we may have a safe going and return. **1807** WORDSW. *White Doe* I. 148 The day is placid in its going.

†**c.** The faculty of walking. *Obs.*

c **1430** *Life St. Kath.* (1884) 37 By whos myghty vertu goynge is restored to þe lame. **1480** CAXTON *Chron. Eng.* cci. 182 God hath yeuen.. to crepels hir goyng. **1594** R. ASHLEY tr. *Le Roy's Variety of Things* 77 a, He gaue.. straight going to the lame. **1635** PAGITT *Christianogr.* III. (1636) 54 Life was given to the dead.. going to the lame.

†**2.** Manner or style of going; gait. In *pl.* of a horse: Paces. (Cf. GO *v.* 1 d.) *Obs.*

1382 WYCLIF *2 Kings* ix. 20 The goynge is as the goynge of Hieu, the sone of Nampsy. **1393** LANGL. *P. Pl.* C. XXI. 328 In goynge of an addre. *a* **1674** CLARENDON *Hist. Reb.* XI. §223 And the king all the morning found fault with the going of his horse. **1701** *Lond. Gaz.* No. 3703/4 A.. cropt Gelding .. full aged.. and all his Goings. **1805** WORDSW. *Waggoner* IV. 148 Erect his port, and firm his going.

†**3. a.** Means of access; a path, road; a passage, gangway (in a church). *Obs.*

1382 WYCLIF *Isa.* lxii. 10 Pleyn maketh the going. **1516** *Test. Ebor.* (Surtees) V. 73 To be buried.. in the myddes of the loweste goyng, even enens my stall. **1715** LEONI *Palladio's Archit.* (1742) I. 94 The going to the galleries.. should have been by some few steps.

b. *Building.* Width of passage (of a stair).

1712 J. JONES *Gardening* 125 A.. Rest of two Paces broad, and as long as the Going of the Stairs. **1842–59** GWILT *Archit.* §2179 Want of space.. often obliges the architect to submit to less [width] in what is called the going of the stair.

4. a. Condition of the ground for walking, driving, hunting or racing. Also, a line or route, considered as difficult or easy to follow; advance or progress as helped or hindered by the nature of the ground; *heavy going*: something difficult to negotiate; slow or difficult progress; freq. *fig.*

1848 BARTLETT *Dict. Amer.* 159 The going is good since the road was repaired. **1859** *Ibid.* (ed. 2), *Going*, travelling; as 'The going is bad, owing to the deep snow in the roads'. **1884** BADDELEY & WARD *North Wales* 191 The going consists of stones and ruts concealed by heather to such an extent that almost every step is a matter of careful consideration. **1887** SIR R. H. ROBERTS *In the Shires* ii. 27 The fences are fair and the going pretty good, although the late rains have made it somewhat heavy. **1901** 'LINESMAN' *Words by Eyewitness* v. 101 A narrow path just above the water-line, overhung with bushes in parts, formed the 'going'. **1925** E. F. NORTON *Fight for Everest, 1924* 114 We made very poor going, descending at a very much slower pace than we had made two years before. **1930** J. B. PRIESTLEY *Angel Pavement* iii. 124 He found such books too heavy going and preferred a detective story. **1935** *Economist* 5 Oct. 647/1 The 'going' was then still good. For the immediate future during the last quarter of the year, the 'going' in the new capital market seems likely to be heavy and uneven. **1936** *Discovery* May 142/1 The next stage, up the North Ridge, is not very difficult technically but is, nevertheless, heavy going. **1958** *Listener* 18 Sept. 433/3 A book that is not only full of interest but is completely without heavy going.

b. Colloq. phr. ***while the going is good***: while the conditions are favourable; freq. ***to go while the going is good.***

1916 H. L. MENCKEN *Let.* 10 July (1961) 85 You would be a maniac not to go out for all that money while the going is good. **1927** H. WADDELL *Wandering Scholars* ii. 48 Warned in time, the two.. had gone while the going was good. **1958** HAYWARD & HARARI tr. *Pasternak's Dr. Zhivago* I. vii. 199 She.. made off with her, home to their village while the going was good.

5. a. With adverbs, expressing the action of the vbl. combinations under GO *v.* VI. Also *attrib.* ***going-away***: used *attrib.* to designate: (*a*) clothes worn by a bride when she departs for her honeymoon; (*b*) a savings club in which members build up holiday funds by small part-payments.

1388 WYCLIF *Ps.* cxx. 8 The Lorde kepe thi goyng in and thi goyng out. *c* **1440** *Jacob's Well* (E.E.T.S.) 264 His fadyr & modyr, for his goyng awey, sowȝtyn hym in dyuerse londys. **1583** STUBBES *Anat. Abuses* 51 All other goynges together and coitions are damnable. **1599** H. BUTTES *Dyets drie Dinner* F iij, The fourth day of her going abroad. **1641** BEST *Farm. Bks.* (Surtees) 29 After a longe declininge and goinge backe. **1659** HAMMOND *On Ps.* lix. 12 Their continual going on, and obstinate impersuasiblenesse therein. **1824** MISS FERRIER *Inher.* xxviii, The nuptials, which they merely thought of as Bell's going off. **1850** 'BAT' *Cricketer's Man.* 46 Place the order of going in, on the left-hand side of the striker's name. **1884** *Pall Mall G.* 27 Aug. 7/2 Mrs. H—'s going-away gown being a dark brown cashmere. **1910** H. G. WELLS *Mr. Polly* vi. 175 The heroine had stood at the altar in 'a modest going-away dress'. **1912** A. BENNETT *Matador* 135 William Henry began grimly to pay his subscriptions to the next year's Going Away Club. **1928** *Observer* 1 July 21/4 The amount of money which has been disbursed by the 'Going-away clubs' is as large as ever. **1959** D. EDEN *Sleeping Bride* iv. 30 This is my going-away suit.

b. *going down*: setting (of the sun), sunset. †Also *going to, under.*

a **1325** *Prose Psalter* xlix. [l.] 2 Fram þe sonne arisyng vn-to þe going a-doune. **1490** CAXTON *Eneydos* xxii. 80 Atte euen, about yᵉ gooyng vnder of yᵉ sonne. **1582** N. LICHEFIELD tr. *Castanheda's Conq. E. Ind.* ix. 22 Vpon the Saterday.. about the going doune of the Sunne. **1622** SIR R. HAWKINS *Observ. Voy. S. Sea A.D. 1593* xxvii. 60 The twenty two of this moneth, at the going too of the Sunne, we descryed a Portingall ship, and gaue her chase. **1866** A. D. WHITNEY *L. Goldthwaite* iv, They watched the long, golden going-down of the sun. **1917** W. B. YEATS *Wild Swans at Coole* 15 From going-down of the sun.

fig. **1837** DICKENS *Pickw.* ii, Mr. Winkle looked up at the declining orb, and painfully thought of the probability of his 'going-down' himself, before long.

c. **goings-on** (see *go on*, GO *v.* 86 d and f.): Proceedings, actions, doings. Usually with implied censure: Questionable proceedings, extravagances, frolics.

1775 JOHNSON *Let.* 26 July, Then I shall see what have been my master's goings on. **1777** ELIZ. RYVES *Poems* 153 See if he will release you, when he hears of your pretty goings-on. **1842** MANNING *Serm.* (1848) I. 67 The warm and clinging fondness which they still have for the goings on of their worldly life. **1888** J. PAYN *Myst. Mirbridge* II. xx. 61 Suspicions of his young master's goings-on with her ladyship's *protegée*.

†**d.** *goings-out*: expenses, outgoings. *Obs.*

a **1704** T. BROWN *Two Oxf. Scholars* Wks. 1730 I. 7, I shall quickly feel my goings-out. *a* **1745** SWIFT *Riddle* iv. 35 Computing what I get and spend My Goings out and Comings in. **1807** SOUTHEY in *Life & Corr.* (1850) III. 113, I cannot afford the expense of the journey; for I have had extraordinary goings-out, this year, in settling myself.

6. *attrib.* and *Comb.*, as **going-barrel** (see quot.), also *attrib.*; **going-board** *Coal-mining* (see quot.); **going-fusee** (see quot.); **in going order** (primarily of a clock, hence often *transf.*), in a condition for 'going' properly, cf. *in working order*; **going-to-press** *a.*, designating the latest items of news in a newspaper or the like; **going-train**, a train of wheels in a clock, answering the same purpose as the going-barrel in a watch; **going-wheel**, an arrangement for keeping a clock in motion while it is being wound up.

1884 F. J. BRITTEN *Watch & Clockm.* (1892) **Going Barrel*, the barrel of a watch or clock round which are teeth for driving the train direct without the intervention of a fusee. *Ibid.* (1884) 131 The keyless mechanism most generally adopted in English going-barrel watches. **1851** GREENWELL *Coal-trade Terms Northumb. & Durh.* 29 The coals are brought down a board for one, two, or more pillars .. to the crane. This board is called the *going (or 'gannen') board. **1838** *Penny Cycl.* XII. 301/1 When this principle [maintaining power] is applied to a fusee, it is termed a *going fusee. **1887** LADY BELLAIRS *Gossips with Girls* II. 92 To keep her eyes in '*going order'.. without being obliged to resort to glasses. **1906** *Westm. Gaz.* 24 Apr. 7/3 The following are *going-to-press Stock Exchange prices. **1838** *Penny Cycl.* XII. 299/2 That part of it [a clock] which is called the *going or watch train.

II. In the combination *a-going* (see A *prep.*[1] 13), whence, in later use, the simple form *going*, treated as a present participle, in agreement with the sb.

7. *a-going* (also †*in going*), in senses of the vb. GO. Now only *vulgar*.

1526 *Pilgr. Perf.* (W. de W. 1531) 9 The iourney.. towarde the hye Jerusalem in heuen, to yᵉ whiche we be in goynge. **1658–9** ELIZ. BODVILE in *Hatton Corr.* (1878) 17 My Lord Chisterfild hoe is agoeing into Francs himselfe. **1662**

GLANVILLE *Lux Orient.* ii. (1682) 10 Before they consider whither they are a-going. **1861** [see GO *v.* 47 b].

8. *to set* (*keep*, etc.) *a-going* or *going*: to set (keep, etc.) in motion; to start (or maintain) in any activity.

1583 A. CONHAM in *Babington's Commandm.* Ded. to Godly Rdrs. (1637) a vj, With lesse paines to keepe agoing that which he had moved, and set a going. **1726** CAVALLIER *Mem.* IV. 310 All the Water Works were set a going. **1809** MALKIN *Gil Blas* v. i. ¶62 My savings were .. wanted to set us going in a genteel style among our country neighbours. **1837** WHITTOCK, etc. *Bk. Trades* (1842) 384 The means of keeping it [machinery] 'a going'. **1850** *Tait's Mag.* XVII. 146/2 He set them [watches] all going. **1865** MOZLEY *Mirac.* vii. 159 Influences, which were originally set agoing by that agency. **1888** W. J. KNOX-LITTLE *Child of Stafferton* xv. 205 She kept the conversation going.

9. Used either as simple predicate, or added after the sb., esp. when preceded by a superlative: Existing, in existence (so as to be accessible or within reach); current or prevalent; to be had.

1720 WODROW *Corr.* (1843) II. 510 That you may have any thing that is agoing, please to receive [etc.]. **1790** *Bystander* 392, I says we beggars be the cleverest fellows going. **1849** RUSKIN *Sev. Lamps* vii. §4. 187 A man who has the gift, will take up any style that is going. **1857** HUGHES *Tom Brown* I. viii, Brandy punch going, I'll bet. **1865** M. ARNOLD *Ess. Crit.* ii. (1875) 76 If you have genius and powerful ideas, you are apt not to have the best style going. **1871** RUSKIN *Fors Clav.* iv. 8 Mr. Mill does not know, nor any other Political Economist going.

going (ˈgəʊɪŋ), *ppl. a.* [f. GO *v.* + -ING².] That goes (in various senses); departing; current; working. A ***going concern***: one in actual operation; a flourishing business; a profitable enterprise. †***going gear***: working machinery. †***going money***: current coin. Often with some limiting sb., as ***church-***, ***theatre-***, etc.; or adv., as ***high-***, ***low-going***.

c **1340** *Cursor M.* 401 (Trin.) Alle goynge beestis .. he made. **1523** The goyng geyre [see GEAR *sb.* 6 a]. **1591** G. FLETCHER *Russe Commw.* (Hakluyt Soc.) 67 One hundred rubbles of going money of Mosko. **1665** COTTON *Poet. Wks.* (1765) 108 I'll haunt thee like a going Fire. **1713** STEELE *Englishm.* No. 3. 20 The Weaver .. has not so many Looms going as he had a few Months ago. **1724** RAMSAY *Tea-t. Misc.* (1733) I. 8 Twa good ga'en yads. **1839** *Penny Cycl.* XIII. 25/2 The sheriffs are generally nominated by the going judges. **1881** *Daily News* 21 June 6/8 The business being a going concern. **1883** *Athenæum* 8 Dec. 744/1 Ladies on a pier, watching the going ship. **1930** *Economist* 26 Apr. 938/2 It is .. unlikely that Europe will recover her pre-war economic position unless and until Russia becomes a 'going concern' again. **1932** N. HODGINS *Some Canadian Essays* 111 If a religion is a going concern, in the sense of helping a man to face life and death honestly, it has already proved its substantial truth. **1939** *Brit. Jrnl. Psychol.* Jan. 221 Stragglers will return once they see the church is a 'going concern'. **1955** T. WILLIAMS *Orpheus Descending* II. i. 62, I got a going concern in this mercantile store.

Hence †ˈ**goingly** *adv.*, at a walking pace. ? *nonce-use.*

1651 BEDELL in *Fuller's Abel Rediv.*, *Erasmus* 73 He can run but goingly, who ties himselfe to another mans footsteps.

going over, going-over (ˌgəʊɪŋˈəʊvə(r)). [See GOING *vbl. sb.* 5 a and cf. GO *v.* 62.]

†**1.** A passage over a stream. *U.S. Obs.*

1662 in *Early Records of Providence, R.I.* (1893) III. 17 The high way which Leadeth from the goeing over att the River. **1782** *Southampton* (N.Y.) *Records* (1878) III. 292 The path from the going over at the River head up to the Great Pond.

2. A scolding, a talking-to, a dressing-down. *U.S. colloq.*

1872 *Chicago Tribune* 23 Oct. 4/2 The Cincinnati *Commercial* gives these male Mrs. Grundys a 'going over' in an article well worth reading. **1884** 'MARK TWAIN' *Huck. Finn* iii, I got a good going-over in the morning from old Miss Watson on account of my clothes. **1937** D. RUNYON *More than Somewhat* viii. 155 Many a time I hear Bookie Bob giving her a going-over about something or other, and generally it is about the price of something she orders to eat. **1969** E. BLISHEN *This Right Soft Lot* II. i. 130 Sir, don't give me a going over—but this desk's too small for me. Honest!

b. An inspection or examination; an overhaul; attention to or work on something. *colloq.* (orig. *U.S.*).

1919 H. L. WILSON *Ma Pettengill* x. 286 She wanted to give these here accounts a thorough going-over while the sensation lasted. **1931** *Kansas City Star* 18 July, The lawn mower could profit by a complete 'going over'. **1950** 'J. TEY' *To love & be Wise* ix. 108 Having given the room a quick going-over, he now went over it in detail. **1958** B. HAMILTON *Too Much of Water* i. 9 His first serious going-over of the scores of the .. Bruckner symphonies. **1960** H. PINTER *Caretaker* II. 48 How do you think the place is looking? I gave it a good going over.

c. A beating; a thrashing. *slang* (orig. *U.S.*).

1942 BERREY & VAN DEN BARK *Amer. Thes. Slang* §510/2 'Third degree' .. *going-over*. **1948** W. G. SMITH *Last of Conquerors* (1949) IV. 193 'Let's give him a little going over,' one of the M.P.s suggested. **1963** T. & P. MORRIS *Pentonville* xi. 240 Most serious of all are the premeditated 'goings over' of individuals by small groups of men who are the bodyguard of a gang leader. **1970** A. ROSS *Manchester Thing* 81 'Got a going over, did you?' 'Not much, I got a going over. Want to see the bruises?'

†**3.** *Bridge.* Doubling. *U.S. Obs.*

1902, etc. [see GO *v.* 89 g]. **1904** *To-Day* 5 Oct. 286/2 If any player double out of turn here, there is no penalty, but over the water the declaring player has the right to say whether the doubling, or 'going over', shall stand or not.

gointer, goion(e, obs. ff. JOINTURE, GUDGEON.

gois(s)halk, goist, obs. ff. GOSHAWK, GHOST.

goit, variant of GOTE.

goitre (ˈgɔɪtə(r)). Forms: 7 gouitre, goytre, 7–8 goistre, 8 goter, 8, 9 *U.S.* goiter, 9 goiture (goto), 8– goître, 7– goitre. [a. F. *goitre, goître*, back-formation from *goitreux*, ad. Prov. *goitros*:—popular L. **gutturiōsum*, f. *guttur* throat.]

1. *Path.* A morbid (often enormously developed) enlargement of the thyroid gland of the neck; bronchocele.

1625 PURCHAS *Pilgrims* IV. 1624 The Gouitres of Sauoye. *c* **1645** HOWELL *Lett.* I. I. xliii. (1650) 76 The people who dwell in the Valleys .. are subject to a strange swelling in the Throat, called Goytre. **1670** LASSELS *Voy. Italy* I. 5 The Goistre of Piedmont. **1683** BOYLE in *Phil. Trans.* XVII. 638 Persons .. troubled with these disfiguring Goitres. **1752** J. SPENCE *Crito* 49 That sort of Swellings in the Neck, which they call Goters. **1838** SOUTHEY in C. Southey *Life & Corr.* VI. 379 Those inhabitants of the Alps who suffer with goitres. **1871** SMILES *Charac.* vi. (1876) 175 There is a village in South America where gotos or goitres are so common that to be without one is regarded as a deformity.

transf. and *fig.* **1854** LOWELL *Jrnl. Italy* Prose Wks. 1890 I. 206 In Rome they [domes] are so much the fashion that I felt as if they were the goitre of architecture. **1860** EMERSON *Cond. Life* Wks. (Bohn) II. 364 This goitre of egotism is so frequent among notable persons that [etc.].

2. A swelling of the neck in certain lizards.

1834 tr. *Cuvier's Anim. Kingd.* II. 31 The greater proportion of them [*Anolis*] have a dewlap or goitre under the throat. **1835** [see ANOLI].

3. *Comb.*, as ***goitre-like*** adj.; **goitre-stick**, the stems of the *Sargassum bacciferum* (see quot.).

1849 tr. *Cuvier's Anim. Kingd.* 277 The greater number have a goitre-like appendage under the throat. **1860** FOWLER *Med. Voc.*, *Goitre-sticks*, the stems of a sea-weed, chewed in South America as a remedy for goitre.

Hence ˈ**goitral** *a.* [-AL], ˈ**goitred** *a.* [-ED²] = GOITROUS *a.*

1836–9 TODD *Cycl. Anat.* II. 471/2 The goitral .. affections .. are striking examples of the effect of hereditary influence. **1851** E. RUSKIN *Let.* 24 Aug. in M. Lutyens *Effie in Venice* (1965) II. 183 The number of Cretins and Goitred persons is perfectly dreadful. **1923** *Blackw. Mag.* Aug. 152/1 A gentle frog-like croak proceeded from the goitred throat.

goitrigenous (gɔɪˈtrɪdʒɪnəs), *a. Med.* Also **goiˈtrogenous.** [f. GOITR(E + -I-, -O + -GENOUS.] = GOITROGENIC *a.*

1917 R. MCCARRISON *Thyroid Gland* III. i. 88 When children are subjected to goitrigenous influences for the first time they are considerably more susceptible to the disease than are adults. **1928** *Bull. Johns Hopkins Hosp.* XLIII. 281 Exposure to goitrogenous influences. **1937** J. H. MEANS *Thyroid & its Diseases* iv. 104 It seems likely .. that certain so-called goitrigenous principles .. depend for their action upon a reduction in the responsiveness of tissue cells to thyroid hormone. *Ibid.* viii. 175 The goitrigenous properties of cabbage.

goitrogenic (gɔɪtrəʊˈdʒɛnɪk), *a. Med.* Also **goiteroˈgenic.** [f. GOITR(E (or the variant *goiter*) + -O + -GENIC.] Causing goitre. Hence ˈ**goitrogen**, a goitrogenic substance; **goitroˈgenesis**, the production or development of goitre.

1929 *Proc. Soc. Exper. Biol. & Med.* XXVI. 823 Although cabbage is an excellent food for rabbits it is evident that it contains a powerful goiterogenic agent. **1931** *Indian Jrnl. Med. Res.* XVIII. 1311 It is now definitely known that a *positive* goitrogenic agent exists in cabbage. **1947** *Endocrinology* XL. 348 The ability of a solution containing elemental iodine .. to prevent the formation of a goiter is not due to a decreased intake of goiterogen. **1950** R. H. WILLIAMS *Textbk. Endocrinol.* iii. 103 Goitrogenesis due to cabbage apparently is related to its cyanide content. **1961** *Lancet* 30 Sept. 742/1 The spontaneous regression of iodide goitres when the goitrogen is recognised and withdrawn makes surgery unnecessary. **1966** WRIGHT & SYMMERS *Systemic Path.* II. xxxi. 1099/1 Goitres can also be caused by the administration of chemical goitrogens, or antithyroid drugs. *Ibid.*, The goitrogenic effect of thiocyanates and perchlorates.

goitrous (ˈgɔɪtrəs), *a.* [ad. F. *goitreux, -euse*: see GOITRE and -OUS.] Affected with, of the nature of, or pertaining to, goitre. Of a locality: Characterized by the prevalence of goitre.

1796 J. OWEN *Trav. Europe* I. 241 Nor did I see any goitrous persons here. **1830** T. ROSCOE *Tourist Switz. & Italy* 101 Frightfully deformed with the goitrous swelling. **1836–9** TODD *Cycl. Anat.* II. 471/2 The union of goitrous persons .. leads to the production of Cretins. **1869** E. A. PARKES *Pract. Hygiene* (ed. 3) 80 The evidence that the water of goitrous places is derived from limestone and dolomitic rocks .. is very strong. **1872** COHEN *Dis. Throat* 221 Goitrous tumors. **1882** E. C. BABER in *R. Geogr. Soc. Suppl. Papers* I. I. 86 With .. goitrous neck, and long finger nails. **1887** *Q. Rev.* Jan. 196 The whole goitrous region of the New World.

gojon, obs. form of GUDGEON.

go-kart (ˈgəʊkɑːt). [Commercial adaptation of GO-CART.] (See quot. 1963.) Also *attrib.* Cf. KART.

1959 *Times* 17 Sept. 5/7 The R.A.C. are prepared in principle to accept the control in Britain of go-kart racing—the new miniature car racing popular in the United States. **1959** *Daily Tel.* 26 Oct. 15/4 (*caption*) Drivers negotiating straw-bale obstacles while competing .. yesterday in a Go-Kart meeting, the first in England. **1960** *Sunday Express* 11 Sept. 5/3 The Go-karts, which were bought for Prince Charles and Princess Anne .. are capable of about 15 miles an hour. **1963** *Times* 12 Feb. 15/3 The name 'go-kart' was given to a miniature racing car, which consisted of a bare skeleton or chassis of small size mounted on four wheels and powered by a light two-stroke internal combustion engine, with the driver's seat a few inches from ground level. **1971** *Flying* Apr. 47/2 Tallman has a wooden leg, but he got it in a freak accident on a go-kart.

goke (gəʊk). *Naut.* [Var. of *coke*, COLK¹. The forms *goak* and *gowk* also occur in northern dialects.] The core or heart (of a rope): see quot.

1800 S. STANDIDGE in *Naval Chron.* III. 474 The .. rope .. has generally about one-eighth part of the weight and substance in the middle of the rope, called a goke, in order to make it round.

goke, obs. form of GOWK.

gok't, variant of GUCKED, foolish.

†ˈ**goky.** *Obs. rare*⁻¹. [? f. *goke* GOWK; but cf. mod. GAWKY.] A fool, simpleton.

1377 LANGL. *P. Pl.* B. XI. 299 The gome that gloseth so chartres, for a goky is holden. So is it a goky, by god, that in his gospel failleth.

gol, obs. form of GOAL: var. of GOLL, *Obs.*

‖**gola, gula** (ˈgola, ˈgjuːlə). *Arch.* [It. *gola* (*lit.* throat):—L. *gula*, whence the second form above.] = CYMA I.

1664 EVELYN tr. *Freart's Archit.* xxviii. 68 The Gula or Ogee which composes the Crown of the Cornice. **1728** R. MORRIS *Ess. Anc. Archit.* 51 Cymatium, or, as some call it, Gola. **1842–59** GWILT *Archit.* Gloss., *Gola* or *Gula* (It.). The same as Cyma, which see.

‖**golah.** *Indian.* [Hindustani *golā*, f. *gol* round.] A store-house for grain, salt, etc.

1771 *Gentl. Mag.* XLI. 402 Seapoys were stationed at their Golahs, to prevent the delivering any rice without a permit. **1772** *Ann. Reg.* 205/2 The golahs or granaries about Calcutta. **1860** *Illustr. Times* 3 Mar. 138 The 'golahs' in which indigo-seed is stored up. **1878** *Life in Mofussil* II. 77 He had large rice golahs in the village.

Golconda (gɒlˈkɒndə). The old name of Hyderabad, formerly celebrated for its diamonds, used as a synonym for a 'mine of wealth'.

[**1780** H. WALPOLE *Lett.* (1858) VII. 438, I .. would not for the mines of Golconda find myself ..] **1884** F. BOYLE *Borderld. Fact & Fancy* 400 If stray diamonds were found sticking in the house-wall, there must be a new Golconda in the soil beneath. **1890** W. SHARP *Browning* iii. 66 To the lover of poetry 'Paracelsus' will always be a Golconda.

gold¹ (gəʊld). Also 3 **guold**, 5–6 **golde**, (5 **gowlde**), 8–9 *Sc.* and *north. dial.* **gowd.** [Common Teut.: OE *gold* str. neut. = OFris. *gold*, OS. *gold* (MDu. *goud-, gout, golt*, Du. *goud*), OHG. *gold, golt, colt* (MHG. *gold-, golt*, G. *gold*), ON. *goll, gull* (Sw., Da. *guld*), Goth. *gulþ*:—OTeut. **gulþo*ᵐ:—pre-Teut. **ghḷto-*, app. formed, with suffix *-to-*, from the wk. grade of the root **ghel-* yellow (see GALL *sb.*¹); cf. OSl. *zlato*, Russ. *zoloto*, of similar origin. (Finnish *kulta* is an early adoption from Teutonic.)]

I. 1. The most precious metal: characterized by a beautiful yellow colour, non-liability to rust, high specific gravity, and great malleability and ductility. Chemical symbol Au.

Its relative purity is expressed in carats, see CARAT 3.

c **725** *Corpus Gloss.* 1401 *Obrizum*, smaete gold. *c* **1200** ORMIN 8168 Bætenn gold & sillferr. *c* **1290** *S. Eng. Leg.* I. 85 A croune of guold heo bar a-doun. **1382** WYCLIF *Exod.* xxxvii. 17 A candilstik, forgid of moost clene gold. **1548** HALL *Chron.*, *Rich. III*, 55 b, His heare yelow lyke the burnished golde. **1667** MILTON *P.L.* I. 717 The roof was fretted gold. **1725** WATTS *Logic* I. ii. §3 So yellow color and ductility are properties of gold. **1800** tr. *Lagrange's Chem.* II. 136 Gold, next to platina, is the heaviest of metals. **1860** PIESSE *Lab. Chem. Wonders* 81 Gold is the only metal which is found in a metallic state.

2. a. The metal regarded as a valuable possession or employed as a medium of exchange; hence, gold coin; also, in rhetorical use, money in large sums, wealth.

c **870** *Codex Aureus Inscr.* 5 in *O.E. Texts* 175 Mid uncre clæne feo, ðæt ðonne wæs mid clæne golde. *c* **1000** ÆLFRIC *Gen.* xliv. 8 Wenst þu, þæt we þines hlafordes gold oððe his seolfor stælon? *a* **1123** *O.E. Chron.* an. 1102 Mycel .. on golde and on seolfre. *c* **1205** LAY. 4779 And he him wolde ȝeuen al þat gold þe he haueden i Denemark lond. *c* **1386** CHAUCER *Shipman's T.* 368 This Marchant .. Creanced hath, and payd .. To certeyn lumbardes .. The somme of gold. **1478** W. PASTON, Jun. in *P. Lett.* No. 824 III. 237 A nobyll in gowlde. **1565** *Child-Marriages* 66 Gold and siluer was put on the boke and a ringe put on her finger bie the priest. **1604** SHAKS. *Oth.* III. i. 26 Ther's a poore peece of Gold for thee. **1616** R. C. *Times' Whistle* VI. 2549 Where gold makes way Ther is no interruption. **1734** POPE *Ess. Man.* iv. 187 Judges and Senates have been bought for gold. **1796** H. HUNTER tr. *St. Pierre's Stud. Nat.* (1799) II. 506 Gold is a powerful commander of respect with the commonalty. **1832** W. IRVING *Alhambra* I. 142 The poorest beggar, if he begged in rhyme, would often be rewarded with a piece of gold. **1858** HOMANS *Cycl. Commerce* 97/1 Sending notes..to be exchanged for gold.

Phrase. **1708** MRS. CENTLIVRE *Busie Body* III. iv. 46 If wearing Pearls and Jewels, or eating Gold, as the old Saying is, can make thee happy, thou shalt be so.

†**b.** In *pl.* = gold coins. *Obs. rare.*

1588 J. MELLIS *Briefe Instr.* G j, You may expresse diuers and sundry goldes, as ducates..crowns, and such other.

3. a. *fig.* With allusion to the brilliancy, beauty, and transcendent preciousness of gold. Often in phr. ***of gold*** = GOLDEN *a.* ***heart of gold***: a noble-hearted person (= F. *un cœur d'or*); a kind or noble heart.

a **1553** [see HEART 14]. **1596** COLSE *Penelope* (1880) 169 Yet (Heart a gold) restraine thy heat. **1599** SHAKS. *Hen. V*, IV. i. 44 The King's a Bawcock, and a Heart of Gold. *a* **1628** PRESTON *Breastpl. Love* (1631) 187 The good man..there is silver and golde in his speeches and actions, that is, they are likewise precious. **1629** MILTON *Ode Nativity* 135 Time will run back and fetch the Age of Gold. **1642** FULLER *Holy & Prof. St.* IV. xvii. 329 He makes his flying enemy a bridge of gold. **1693** DRYDEN *Juvenal's Sat.* (1697) Ded. 9 In the same Paper, written by divers Hands..I cou'd separate your Gold from their Copper:..tho' I cou'd not give back to every Author his own Brass. **1831** SCOTT *Jrnl.* 10 Jan., A fine fellow, and what I call a heart of gold. **1858** LYTTON *What will he do with It?* VII. i. 208 If, with gentle blood, youth, good looks, and a heart of gold, that fortune does not allow him to aspire to any girl whose hand he covets, I can double it. **1863** LONGF. *Wayside Inn, Q. Sigrid* xv, If in his gifts he can faithless be, There will be no gold in his love to me. **1877** BARING-GOULD *Myst. Suffering* 51 What a glorious world.. what gold of gladness, what sunshine of felicity it affords. **1896** *Westm. Gaz.* 1 July 1/1 The smiling generosity that has done almost as much to charm her public as has her voice of gold. **1923** WODEHOUSE *Inimitable Jeeves* xi. 123 While she may have had a heart of gold, the thing you noticed about her first was that she had a tooth of gold. **1936** G. GREENE *Journey without Maps* III. iii. 244 He had a heart of gold under that repressive exterior. **1971** *Times* 12 Dec. 19/4 Tarts invariably turn out to have a heart of gold.

b. *Proverbs.* (See also GLISTER, GLITTER *vbs.*)

c **1386** CHAUCER *Can. Yeom. Prol. & T.* 409 But al thyng which þat schineth as the gold Nis nat gold, as þat I haue herd told. *c* **1530** R. HILLES *Common-Pl. Bk.* (1858) 140 Yt ys not all gold that glowyth. **1546** J. HEYWOOD *Prov.* (1867) 66 A man may by gold to deere. *a* **1665** J. GOODWIN *Filled w. the Spirit* (1867) 124 Men will not, as our common proverb is, buy gold too dear.

c. The metal as employed for coating a surface, or as a pigment; gilding.

1596 SHAKS. *Merch. V.* II. vii. 36 Let's see once more the saying grau'd in gold.

d. *pl.* Kinds of gold. *rare.* [Cf. *Or* 2 in Littré.]

1683 PETTUS *Fleta Min.* II. xv. 142 After this manner and method are to be proved all other Golds. **1765** H. WALPOLE in *Lett. C'tess Suffolk* (1824) II. 314 Huge hunting-pieces in frames of all-coloured golds.

†**4.** The metal as used for the ornamentation of textile fabrics; gold thread (see 10); in early use often with the place of manufacture specified, as ***gold of Bruges***, ***of Genoa***, ***of Venice***. Hence, textile materials embroidered with or partly consisting of this.

c **1340** *Cursor M.* 23452 (Trin.) Wymmen..in cloþing als of riche golde [*other MSS.* of riche falde]. **1465** *Paston Lett.* No. 978 III. 436 An unce of golde of Venyse. **1516** *St. Papers Dom. Hen. VIII*, II. II. 1565 The sayd ladyes heeds imparylled with loos golld of damask, as well as with wovyn flat goold of damaske [etc.]. **1545** *Rates Custom ho.* b iij b, Golde of bruges the maste viii. *s.* **1566** in Hay Fleming *Mary Q. of Scots* (1897) 499 Ten hankis off gold and ten hankis of silver the fynest that can be gottin. **1596** SHAKS. *Tam. Shr.* II. i. 356 Vallens of Venice gold, in needle worke. *a* **1800** in Scott *Minstr. Scott. Bord.* (1802) II. 78, I sall learn your turtle dow To lay gowd wi' her hand.

5. Used with defining words in the names of various kinds of gold, alloys, counterfeit imitations of gold, etc.

ANGEL, CROWN, DUCAT, DUTCH, FOOL'S, FULMINATING, GERMAN, GIPSY, GRAPHIC, LEAF, MOSAIC, ROMAN, STANDARD, VIRGIN GOLD: see these words.

argental gold, native gold containing a percentage of silver; ***coloured gold***, gold that has had its lustre destroyed by nitric acid; ***dead gold***, unburnished gold or gold without lustre; ***dentist gold*** (see quot. 1858); ***duke gold?*** = ducat gold; ***Etruscan gold*** = ***coloured gold***; ***fairy gold*** = fairy money (see FAIRY C 2); ***green gold***, gold alloyed with silver; ***jeweller's gold***, 'an alloy containing three parts of gold to one of copper' (Webster 1864); †***leprous gold*** (see quot.); ***Mannheim gold***, a brass alloy of copper, zinc, and tin used in making cheap jewellery; ***mock gold***, an alloy of copper, zinc, and platinum; ***red gold***, gold alloyed with copper; ***shell gold*** (see quot. 1727–41); ***spangle gold*** (see quot. 1611); ***white gold***, 'an alloy of about five parts of silver to one of gold' (Funk).

1839 URE *Dict. Arts* 603 Another ore of gold is the alloy with silver, or *argental gold, the electrum of Pliny, so called from its amber shade. **1858** HOMANS *Cycl. Commerce* 835/2 *Dentist Gold is gold leaf carried no further in the process than that of the cutch, and should be perfectly pure gold. **1683** PETTUS *Fleta Min.* II. i. 100 All Goldish oars..have good *Duke gold. **1611** SHAKS. *Wint. T.* III. iii. 127 This is *Faiery Gold boy..vp with 't, keepe it close. **1430–40** LYDG. *Bochas* VII. viii. (1554) 172 b, Lede (of philosophers) is called *gold leprus. **1825** J. NICHOLSON *Operat. Mechanic* 714 *Manheim-gold, or Similor. **1727–41** CHAMBERS *Cycl.* s.v. *Gold*, *Shell Gold is that used by the illuminers..they put it in shells, where it sticks. **1611** COTGR., *Or en paille*, *Spangle Gold, or Gold beaten thinne for Spangles.

6. The colour of the metal: a bright golden yellow. Ordinarily an absol. use of the adj. (see 8 b); but in poetic and rhetorical lang. directly *transf.* from 1.

c **1400** tr. *Secreta Secret., Gov. Lordsh.* (E.E.T.S.) 80 Whos colour ys gold, lyk þat ys meen bytwen reed and ȝalwe. **1667** MILTON *P.L.* III. 642 Many a colourd plume sprinkl'd with Gold. **1704** POPE *Windsor For.* 118 His painted wings, and breast that flames with gold. **1866** G. MACDONALD *Ann Q. Neighb.* i. (1878) 15 Gazing at the red and gold and green of the sunset sky. **1895** C. ROPER *Zigzag Trav.* I. 5 Across this blue shot long rays of the most clear pinks and whites and golds.

7. *Archery.* The gilt centre or bull's-eye of a target. ***to make a gold***: to hit the bull's-eye.

1876 GEO. ELIOT *Dan. Der.* I. I. x. 189 Three hits running in the gold. **1882** *Standard* 31 Aug. 6/4 The prize given..for the lady making the greatest number of golds and reds at archery.

II. *attrib.* and *Comb.*

8. *simple attrib.*, passing into *adj.* **a.** Made (wholly or partly) of gold; consisting of gold. †Also, gilded.

c **1205** LAY. 7048 His hæð wes swulc swa beoð gold wir. **13..** *Sir Beues* 2299 (S.) He may see in his goldryng, What any man dooth. **1483** *Cath. Angl.* 161/2 Golde wyre, *filum Aureum.* **1592** SHAKS. *Rom. & Jul.* I. iii. 92 That Booke.. That in Gold claspes, Lockes in the Golden storie. **1617** MORYSON *Itin.* I. 10 Hangings of gold lether. **1727** SOMERVILLE *Fable* xiv, *Fortune Hunter* II. 146 A cobler bidding fair For the gold-chain and next lord-mayor. **1837** MRS. SHERWOOD *H. Milner* III. xxii. 464 Two young [Oxford] men, one of whom had a gold tassel. **1884** F. J. BRITTEN *Watch & Clockm.* 58 The gold spring is hammer-hardened.

b. Gold-coloured, golden yellow. Also, ***old gold***, having the colour of old gold, of a dulled golden yellow with a brownish tinge; also as *sb.*

1590 SHAKS. *Mids. N.* II. i. 11 The Cowslips tall, her pensioners bee, In their gold coats, spots you see, Those be Rubies. **1732** POPE *Hor. Sat.* II. ii. 20 Yet hens of Guinea full as good I hold [as pheasant] Except you eat the feathers green and gold. **1776** MICKLE tr. *Camoens' Lusiad* 77 The purple blazes, and the gold-stripes shine. **1808** SCOTT *Marm.* I. xv, His skin was fair, his ringlets gold. **1879** M. E. BRADDON *Vixen* III. xi. 313 Curtains..in dirty yellow, or, in upholsterer's language, 'old gold'. **1880** *Drapers' Jrnl.* 27 May 5/2 Edged with a narrow plissé of old gold. **1882** MISS BRADDON *Mt. Royal* II. x. 206 Loose flowing tea-gowns of old gold sateen. **1935** N. L. MCCLUNG *Clearing in West* xxix. 227 Mother had a silk eiderdown on her bed, old gold on one side and flowered with red geraniums on the other. **1966** J. B. PRIESTLEY *Salt is Leaving* ii. 25 The general effect suggested a palace made of milk chocolate. The old-gold lighting did nothing to spoil this effect.

c. With reference to the use of gold for coinage and as a standard of value, as ***gold currency***, ***standard***, ***value***. Also designating a money of account: reckoned at its full undepreciated value according to a gold standard.

1776 ADAM SMITH *W.N.* II. ii, The..nominal sum of the gold and silver currency of the country. **1831** *Deb. Congress U.S.* 22 Feb. p. cl/2 The present rate (of our gold standard) was the result of information clearly incorrect. **1832** *Mechanics' Mag.* 11 Feb. 344/1 Notwithstanding 'the gold standard' is not the United States the modern *El Dorado*? **1857** GEO. ELIOT *Let.* 23 Dec. (1954) II. 414 The opponents of the 'gold standard' do not make it sufficiently clear.. that they presuppose..some guarantee such as government security, as a basis for confidence. **1868** J. LAING *Theory of Business* (ed. 2) iv. 65 Had India possessed a gold currency. **1898** T. H. FARRER *Stud. Currency* p. xviii, The relation between the Gold value of the legal Rupee and the Gold value of Silver. **1911** *Encycl. Brit.* XVIII. 704/2 The 'gold-exchange standard' system, in which the ordinary currency is of a metal coined only by the state, and so limited as to keep it in a prescribed value ratio to another metal (gold) which..acts as the standard of value. **1914** *Rep. R. Comm. Indian Finance* 14 in *Parl. Papers* (Cd. 7236) XX. 709 The system adumbrated by the Committee of 1898, viz., a gold standard based on a gold currency in active circulation such as the system in the United Kingdom is commonly held to be. *Ibid.* 15 The Indian currency system based on what is now known as the gold exchange standard. **1917** W. F. SPALDING *East. Exch. Currency* ii. 13 The exchange value of the Rupee was satisfactorily maintained between the gold points. **1923** *Westm. Gaz.* 22 Aug., If we take the franc of to-day as having one-quarter of the purchasing power of the pre-war gold franc. **1926** *Encycl. Brit.* Suppl. I. 776/2 In the final phase people reckoned in gold marks and stipulated for payment in paper marks at the exchange of the day... This competition of the gold mark as a money of account was the final undoing of the paper mark. **1933** B. ELLINGER *This Money Business* i. 9 This state of affairs lasted until September 18th of 1931, when we went off the gold standard. **1948** G. CROWTHER *Outl. Money* (ed. 2) ix. 279 Nowadays, virtually every currency in the world consists (apart from subsidiary..coins) entirely of paper. When this paper money is made by law freely interchangeable with gold at a fixed ratio the currency is on the gold standard. **1970** *Encycl. Brit.* X. 547/2 Gold standard, a monetary system in which the standard unit is a fixed weight of gold or is kept at the value of a fixed weight of gold.

d. ***gold medal***: a golden medal, usu. awarded as the first prize in a contest, esp. in the Olympic Games. Also *ellipt.* as *gold.*

1908 T. A. COOK *Olympic Games* i. 16 For all these gold, silver, and bronze prize medals have been allotted. **1960** *Times* 5 Sept. 4/6 Hill..was representing a Germany united for Olympic purposes, which won three gold and a silver. **1968** *Guardian* 22 Oct. 1/1 In the equestrian event, the gold was taken by the team.

e. Designating a framed gold gramophone record presented to a recording artist or group for a record whose popularity is marked by sales of a predefined level (orig. in the U.S., for a single with sales of $1 million: now also determined by copies sold). Applied chiefly *attrib.*, as ***gold disc***, etc., and as *adv.* (***to go gold***) to a record with such sales. Cf. PLATINUM 2 d. orig. *U.S.*

1957 *Variety* 9 Jan. 237/2 In 1940 Shaw's classic 'Stardust' and Miller's 'Tuxedo Junction' won each of them an additional gold record. **1958** *Ibid.* 26 Feb. 43/1 The gold disk awards will continue to be made by the individual manufacturer. **1969** *New Yorker* 1 Mar. 38/3 His records sell extremely well—since 1964 he has had three gold albums ..and three gold singles. **1976** *National Observer* (U.S.) 7 Aug. 16/3 *The Outlaws*..climbed high on the popular music charts..and then went 'gold', earning more than $1 million in sales. **1977** *Maclean's Mag.* 5 Sept. 31/1 Her last six singles all shot to number one on the national country music charts, and the first album she recorded for RCA..went 'gold' (it sold more than 50,000 copies in Canada). **1977** *Music Week* 18 June 39 Top 60 Albums... Gold LP (£300,000 on or after 1st Jan. '77). *Ibid.* 41 Top 50 Singles. .. ½ million (gold). **1984** [see PLATINUM 3].

9. General comb.: **a.** attributive, as ***gold-balance***, ***-coast***, ***-country***, ***-lode***, ***-ore***, ***-scales***, ***-vein***, ***-yield***.

1530 PALSGR. 226/1 *Golde balance, *poix, trebuchet.* **1877** RAYMOND *Statist. Mines & Mining* 66 The *gold-coast of Klamath and Del Norte. **1831** CARLYLE *Sart. Res.* (1858) 127 We are to guide our British Friends into the new *Gold-country, and show them the mines. **1877** RAYMOND *Statist. Mines & Mining* 352 Some promising *gold-lodes have also been found. **1340–70** *Alex. & Dind.* 525 þe grauel of the ground was of *gold ore. **1587** FLEMING *Contn. Holinshed* III. 1270/1 The blacke stone, which the goldfiners had said to hold gold, and therefore called the same Gold ore. **1638** SANDERSON *Serm.* (1681) II. 98 The poor Indians..parting with a massie lump of gold-ore for a three-halfpeny knife. **1638** A. TOUNSHEND in Cary *Romulus & T.* To Author, A vj b, In their *Gold-scales to weigh both him and you. **1565** COOPER *Thesaurus* s.v. *Aurum*, *Venæ auri*, *golde veynes. **1683** PETTUS *Fleta Min.* II. ii. 109 There also Flinty and Horn-stony Gold Veins. **1877** RAYMOND *Statist. Mines & Mining* 234 The *gold-yield was not less than $150,000.

b. objective, as ***gold-bearing***, †***-breathing***, ***-containing***, ***-producing***, ***-promising***, ***-seeking***, ***-staining*** adjs.: ***gold-finding***, ***-gathering***, ***-milling***, ***-mining***, ***-seeking***; ***gold-broker***, ***-diviner***, ***-falsifier***, ***-hunter***, ***-layer***, ***-miner***, ***-prospector***, ***-refiner***, ***-seeker***. Also GOLD-BEATER, GOLD-FINER, GOLD-WASHER, etc.

1799 M. PARK *Trav.* (ed. 2) 304 Were the *gold-bearing streams to be traced to their fountains. **1879** *Encycl. Brit.* X. 742/2 Gold-bearing deposits. **1894** *Pop. Sci. Monthly* June 174 The northern rivers and creeks have gold-bearing sand. **1600** NASHE *Summers Last Will* 1493 Wks. (Grosart) VI. 145 *Golde-breathing Alcumists. **1882** *Rep. to Ho. Repr. Prec. Met. U.S.* 539 A broad *gold-containing zone. **1871** B. TAYLOR *Faust* (1875) II. I. ii. 18 Along what shafts and mines corroded, The *gold-diviner's steps are goaded. **1593** NASHE *Strange News* To Gentlm. Rdrs., Wks. (Grosart) II. 184 Our forenamed *Gold-falsifiers. **1852** EARP *Gold Col. Australia* 5 Many poor men make fortunes..by the lottery of *gold-finding. **1877** RAYMOND *Statist. Mines & Mining* 19 During the early days of *gold-gathering. **1852** G. S. RUTTER (title), Hints to *Gold-hunters. **1890** BOLDREWOOD *Miner's Right* v. 48 One of the reckless gold-hunters. **1565** COOPER *Thesaurus, Bractearius*,..a *golde layer: a gilter. **1853** *Visit to Australia* iii. 82 Unless the great body of *gold miners should themselves be seized with a fit of reflection, we can see but little hope. **1860** H. GREELEY *Overland Journey* 142 Experienced gold-miners from Georgia, California, and even Australia. **1934** *Times Lit. Suppl.* 4 Jan. 2/3 The Lydenburg gold-miners (mostly British), and the Boers of that district also, were contemptuous of Pretoria. **1960** G. BLAINEY *Mines in Spinifex* viii. 70 He wrote a letter ..to an uncle who was a gold miner in Victoria. **1852** J. A. PHILLIPS (title), *Gold-mining and Assaying: a Scientific Guide for Australian Emigrants. **1852** MILL *Pol. Econ.* (ed. 3) II. III. ix. §2. 26 A pound weight of gold will, in the *gold-producing countries, ultimately tend to exchange for as much of every other commodity, as is produced at a cost equal to its own. **1943** WYNDHAM LEWIS *Let.* 26 Jan. (1963) 343 This [*sc.* Canada] is after Africa the second largest gold-producing centre on the planet. **1970** *Encycl. Brit.* X. 536A/1 The major gold-producing areas are in British Columbia, Ontario..and the Northwest Territories. **1894** H. NESBIT *Bush Girl's Rom.* 197 The *gold-promising quartz predominated. **1893** *Month* Feb. 205 He had been found alive by a party of *gold-prospectors. **1891** *Pall Mall G.* 10 Dec. 7/2 A *gold-refiner of Clerkenwell, proved buying a quantity of silver from Clapham. **1852** EARP *Gold Col. Australia* 130 A system which should give encouragement to *gold seekers. **1887** *Pall Mall G.* 28 Oct. 11/2 The prosecution of..*gold-seeking in the Kimberley district. **1890** BOLDREWOOD *Miner's Right* xv. 150 The great gold-seeking multitude had swelled..to the population of a province. **1603** J. DAVIES *Microcosmos, Extasie* Wks. (Grosart) I. 91/1 Vpon the verge of whose *gold-stayning haire, Illustrious Saphires ev'nly ranked were.

c. instrumental (with pres. or pa. pple.) as ***gold-bound***, ***-broidered***, ***-ceiled***, ***-daubed***, ***decked***, ***-embroidered***, ***-enwoven***, †***-flourished***, ***-graved***, †***-imbased***, ***-inlaid***, ***-lit***, ***-made***, ***-mounted***, ***-rolling***, ***-strung***, ***-studded***, ***-wrought***, etc., adjs.

1605 SHAKS. *Macb.* IV. i. 114 Thy haire Thou other *Gold-bound-brow, is like the first. **1823** MRS. HEMANS *Siege Valencia* ix. Poems (1875) 291 The *gold-broider'd mantle. *a* **1649** DRUMM. OF HAWTH. *Poems* Wks. (1711) 39/1 Nero's sky-resembling *gold-ceil'd halls. **1598** E. GILPIN *Skial.* (1878) 56 All in *gold-dawbed sutes. **1627** MAY *Lucan* III. E ij b, Arimaspians With *gold deck'd lockes. **1647** R. STAPYLTON *Juvenal* VI. 506 Her faire *gold-embroyder'd garment. **1954** L. MACNEICE *Autumn Sequel* 61 Gold-embroidered brocade. **1867** MORRIS *Jason* XVII. 660

The *gold-enwoven crown. **1593** NASHE *Christ's T.* Wks. (Grosart) IV. 214 Though we glister it neuer so in our ..*golde-florisht garments. **1875** BROWNING *Aristoph. Apol.* 365 A *gold-graved writing. **1602** WARNER *Alb. Eng.* IX. xlvi. 218 Our *gold-imbased World. **1863** LONGF. *Wayside Inn, Saga K. Olaf* ii. 77 Harness *gold-inlaid and burnished. **1855** *Woman's Devotion* II. 154 Her lovely *gold-lit ringlets. **1630** DRAYTON *Moses* III. 302 A *gold-made god how durst you euer name? **1828** SCOTT *Jrnl.* 26 May, A *gold-mounted pair of glasses. *a* **1649** DRUMM. OF HAWTH. *Poems* Wks. (1711) 4/1 *Gold-rolling Tagus. **1607** *Lingua* III. vii. G 3 b, The *gold strung harpe of Apollo. **1870** BRYANT *Iliad* I. I. 14 Pelides to the ground Flung the *gold-studded wand. **1625** K. LONG tr. *Barclay's Argenis* V. xvii. 392 A garland of *Gold-wrought Purple.

d. similative, as ***gold-bright, -bronze, -brown,*** †***-burned, -green*** (sb. and adj.), ***-like, -red, -yellow*** adjs.

1839 BAILEY *Festus* xix. (1848) 225 *Gold-bright stars. **1909** *Westm. Gaz.* 23 Oct. 7 Her *gold-bronze hair was dressed low on her neck. *a* **1930** D. H. LAWRENCE *Last Poems* (1932) 204 Gold-bronze flutters beat through the thick upper air. **1881** WILDE *Poems* 154 Dame Jeannette had not that *gold-brown hair. **1944** BLUNDEN *Shells by Stream* 39 And coloured, like a country grange, Gold-browns and bluebell grays. *c* **1430** LYDG. *Compl. Bl. Knt.* v, The sonne, *gold-burned in his spere. **1830** TENNYSON *Recoll. Arab. Nts.* 82 Flush'd all the leaves with rich *gold-green. **1863** KINGSLEY *Water-Bab.* i. 11 The great elm-trees in the gold-green meadows. **1589** WARNER *Alb. Eng.* IV. xx. 86 A Globe-like head, a *Gold-like haire. **1839** BAILEY *Festus* xiv. (1848) 147 Hands..Whose gold-like touch makes kings of men. **1871** PALGRAVE *Lyr. Poems* 75 The *gold-red apples. **1597** A. M. tr. *Guillemeau's Fr. Chirurg.* 31 b/2 With *gouldeyellow strokes. **1887** *Pall Mall G.* 5 Nov. 4/2 Gold-yellow silk stockings.

e. parasynthetic, as ***gold-backed, -banded, -capped, -chained, -clasped, -crested, -fringed, -haired, -headed, -hilted, -rimmed, -robed, -sanded, -stopped, -striped, -walled, -winged*** adjs.

1874 HOTTEN *Slang Dict.* 179 **Goldbacked uns*, body lice. **1963** C. R. COWELL et al. *Inlays, Crowns & Bridges* vii. 66 A very close bite may necessitate a gold-backed crown. **1860** DICKENS *Let.* 24 Sept., [Sydney] stood waving the *gold-banded cap. **1742** POPE *Dunc.* IV. 117 Three hundred *gold-capt youths. **1905** *Daily Chron.* 27 Feb. 4/7 This first of Count Benckendorff's predecessors..was received..by eighty *goldchained City merchants. **1861** MISS YONGE *Stokesley Secret* iii. (1862) 44 A *gold-clasped Prayer Book. **1880** G. MEREDITH *Tragic Com.* (1881) 37 Lucretia the gold-haired; the *gold-crested serpent. **1685** *Lond. Gaz.* No. 2094/4 He has a pair of *Gold-fringed Gloves. **1621** G. SANDYS *Ovid's Met.* VI. 131 The *gold-haird mother. **1725** CONGREVE *Will & Test.* (1730) 7 Item, To Col. Charles Churchill..my *Gold-headed Cane. **1895** A. NUTT in K. Meyer's *Voy. Bran* I. 180 A *gold-hilted sword. **1900** 'S. GRAND' *Babs* (1901) xxxix, Mr. Jellybond Tinney adjusted his *gold-rimmed pince-nez. **1965** A. NICOL *Truly Married Woman* 17 He unfolded his gold-rimmed spectacles. **1855** BROWNING *Men & Wom.* II. *Popularity* ix, When *gold-robed he took the throne. **1591** SYLVESTER *Du Bartas* I. iii. 122 *Gold-sanded Tagus. **1915** E. CORRI *30 Yrs. Boxing Ref.* vii. 149 The good-natured black giant..smiled and laughed all the time, revealing his rows of glittering, *gold-stopped teeth. **1948** C. DAY LEWIS *Otterbury Incident* 5 He grinned a lot, showing his bad teeth and a gold-stopped one. **1833** *Penny Cycl.* I. 78/2 The Red or *Gold-striped [variety of maple]. **1655** STANLEY *Hist. Philos.* I. (1701) 53/2 Crœsus..Who to his Gods did *Gold-wall'd Temples build. **1598** SYLVESTER *Du Bartas* II. ii. II. *Babylon* 536 *Gold-winged Morpheus.

10. a. Special comb.: **gold-amalgam**, gold combined with mercury in a soft or plastic state (applied by Schneider in 1848 to a native form found in small white grains); **gold-bank** (see quot.); †**gold-beat**, †**-beaten** *ppl. adjs.*, adorned with beaten gold; **gold-beating**, the act or process of beating out gold into leaf; **gold beetle** *U.S.*, a name for various beetles of the families Chrysomelidæ and Cassididæ; **gold beryl** = CHRYSOBERYL; **gold bloc**, the bloc of countries having a gold standard; **gold blocking** (see quot. 1960); **gold-bob**, a gold ornament (see BOB *sb.*[1]); **gold-book** = BOOK *sb.* 13; **gold braid**, a collective slang name for naval officers or senior prison warders; **gold-bug** *U.S.*, (*a*) = *gold-beetle* (Funk); (*b*) a plutocrat, millionaire; also 'a political nickname for an advocate of a single (gold) standard'(Funk); **gold bullion standard** *Economics* (see quots. and cf. sense 8 c above); **gold-carp** = GOLDFISH; **gold certificate** *U.S.*, a certificate or note certifying that gold to the amount stated on the face of the certificate has been deposited and is available for redeeming it; **gold clause** *U.S.* (see quots.); **gold-cloth**, cloth of gold (see CLOTH *sb.* 9 c); **gold-copper ore**, ore yielding both gold and copper; **gold-digging**, (*a*) the action or occupation of digging for gold; also *fig.* (cf. GOLD-DIGGER 2) and as *ppl. adj.*; (*b*) *pl.* the place where gold-digging is carried on; †**gold-drawer**, one who draws gold wire; **gold-dredge(r**, a dredger by means of which gold is dug up from river-beds, etc.; so *gold-dredging*; **gold-driver** = GOLD-BEATER 1; **gold-drop** *slang*, a gold coin; **gold-dropper** (see quot. 1785); †**gold-end-man**, one who buys up broken pieces of gold; **gold-fever**, the rage for going in search of gold; **gold-film (glass)** (see quot. 1958); †**gold-finger**, the third or ring-finger; **goldfinny**, a fish of the wrasse family (see quot.); **gold flat** (see FLAT *sb.*[3] 8 f); †**gold-flint**, flint containing gold; **gold-flux**, = AVENTURINE 1; **gold-fringe**, a moth (see quot.); †**gold-ground** *a.*, having a ground of gold; **gold-hammer**, a gold-beater's hammer; **gold-head**, *a.*, gold-headed; **gold-heart** *a.*, gold-hearted; †**gold-hewn** = *gold-beaten*; †**gold-house**, a treasury; **gold-hunger**, keen desire for gold; **gold-lip**, a yellow-edged oyster shell, used as money in parts of Melanesia; †**gold-mestling**, brass; **gold-mill**, a mill in which gold ore is crushed; also *fig.*; †**gold-mint**, a place where gold is coined; **gold-mouthed** *a.*, whose speech is golden; **gold-note** (*U.S.*), a bank-note payable only in gold; **gold-pan** = PAN *sb.*[1] 2 e; †**gold-paper** = *gold-foil*; **gold plate**, vessels made of gold; **gold-plating**, gold in thin sheets; **gold point** (see quot. 1925); **gold-powder**, gold in the form of or reduced to powder; †also, in 18th c., ? the name of some quack medicine; †**gold-proof** *a.*, proof against being bribed or tempted by gold; **gold-purple** (see quot.); †**gold-quarrel**, a gold-mine; **gold-quartz**, quartz containing gold; freq. *attrib.*; **gold-rain** = *golden rain* (see quot. and GOLDEN *a.* 10); **gold reserve**, the reserve [RESERVE *sb.* 1 b] of gold coin or bullion held by a central authority, bank, etc.; **gold-rush**, a rush to goldfields in search of gold; **gold salt**, a salt of gold; in *Pharm.*, esp. any of several compounds containing gold and sulphur that have been used in the treatment of rheumatoid arthritis and lupus erythematosus; **gold-sand**, sand containing particles of gold; also *fig.*; **gold-shell**, a shell on which powdered gold mixed with gum water is spread for painters' use; **goldsinny** = *goldfinny*; **gold-size**, a size laid on as a surface on which to apply gold-leaf; **gold-skin**, ? goldbeater's skin; **gold-solder**, †(*a*) = CHRYSOCOLLA 1; (*b*) an alloy for soldering gold; **gold-spangle, gold-spot**, names of moths (see quots.); **gold-stone**, †(*a*) (see quot. 1626); (*b*) a piece of gold ore; (*c*) (see quot. 1850); (*d*) = AVENTURINE 1 (in some mod. Dicts.); †**gold-stroke**, the rubbing of gold on a touchstone in order to test it; **gold swift**, a moth (see quot.); **gold-tail (moth)**, the moth *Porthesia chrysorrhæa*; **gold therapy**, treatment with sodium aurothiomalate or other compounds containing gold (see *gold salt*); **gold-thirst**, intense desire for gold; so ***gold-thirsty*** adj.; **gold-thread** (see quot. 1727–41); **gold-tipped** *a.*, having a gold tip; *spec.* of a cigarette having a band of gilded paper at one end; **gold-washed** *a.*, thinly plated with gold; **gold-web**, †(*a*) cloth of gold; (*b*) (see quot. 1769); †**gold-worm**, a glow-worm.

1850 DANA *Min.* 555 *Gold Amalgam..In small white grains as large as a pea. **1889** *Century Dict.*, **Gold-bank*, a national banking association of a class organized under United States Revised Statutes to issue notes payable in gold coin. *c* **1374** CHAUCER *Anel. & Arc.* 24 Theseus with the laurer corovned, in his chare *gold bete. *c* **1386** —— *Knt.'s T.* 1642 (Harl. MS.) *Gold-beten [*other MSS.* gold-hewen] helmes. *c* **1394** *P. Pl. Crede* 188 And louely ladies y-wrouȝt..In many gay garmentes þat weren gold-beten. **1763–6** W. LEWIS *Comm. Phil.-Techn.* 50 The process of *gold-beating is considerably influenced by the weather. **1807** A. AIKIN *Dict. Chem. & Min.* I. 539 *Gold Beryl. **1935** *Economist* 12 Jan. 57/2 The figures for the *gold *bloc* countries reveal a noticeable contrast between the movement of French wholesale prices on the one hand and of Italian and German prices on the other. **1970** *Encycl. Brit.* X. 548/2 A small group of continental countries led by France continued the struggle to maintain convertibility at the old price until 1936. This gold bloc collapsed because the depreciation of sterling and the dollar meant that the exports of the gold bloc countries were at a competitive disadvantage in world markets. **1902** *Ibid.* XXVI. 302/2 In the matter of *gold blocking there must be great care exercised in the matter of the heat of the block. **1960** G. A. GLAISTER *Gloss. Bk.* 155 *Gold blocking*, the stamping of a design on a book cover, using a heated die or block in a press, and gold leaf. **1694** ECHARD *Plautus* 95 Top-knots, Fingle Fangles, and *Gold-Bobs. **1933** G. INGRAM *Stir* (ed. 2) iii. 52 The chief warder... All the screws get their orders through him. The other *gold braid you 'ave to be careful of are the principals, those blokes with the gold braid on the peaks of their caps. **1945** 'TACKLINE' *Holiday Sailor* xi. 113 There'd be more gold-braid than that, buzzing around like a fly in a strange gash-basket. **1933** B. ELLINGER *This Money Business* i. 6 After the Act of 1925 it was only gold bullion which could be obtained in exchange for notes, and therefore it was known as the '*gold bullion standard' instead of the vaguer term 'gold standard'. **1948** G. CROWTHER *Outl. Money* (ed. 2) ix. 280 When gold coins do not circulate, but the Central Bank is nevertheless under legal obligation to buy and sell gold in exchange for currency at a fixed price..it is known as the 'gold bullion standard'. **1883** *Fisheries Exhib. Catal.* (ed. 4) 107 Crucian Carp, *Gold Carp. **1864** *Santa Fe Weekly New Mexican* 27 May 2/3 The boys in New York..join[ed] in the procession of *gold certificate buyers. **1935** *Economist* 23 Feb. 415/1 The changes in the item 'gold certificates' have given some suggestion that the fund has been used in greater volume than has been expressed in gold movements to date. **1935** *Ibid.* 19 Jan. 116/1 The clause..was quite definite, calling for payment in United States gold coin of the weight and fineness existing at the time of the issue of the bond. The holding, and..receipt, of gold coin was made illegal last year and Congress passed a resolution invalidating all '*gold clause' contracts. **1965** J. L. HANSON *Dict. Econ.* 201/1 A 'gold clause', which offers lenders the security of repayment in terms of the gold equivalent of the currency at the time the loan was floated. **1868** MORRIS *Earthly Par.* (1870) I. I. 287 *Gold cloth so wrought that nought of gold seemed there. **1906** *Daily Chron.* 26 Jan. 4/5 A large deposit of *gold-copper ore. **1908** *Westm. Gaz.* 1 July 6/3 There are piles of gold-copper ore. **1802** *Monthly Mag.* XIV. 93/1 (*title*) *Gold-digging ants, and the griffins of the ancients. **1831** *Boston Transcript* 27 May 2/3 Gold digging, combined with slave holding, may always keep those states a whole century behind their neighbors. **1927** *Cleveland Press* 29 Jan., The charge of gold-digging is one of the major counts in Browning's [divorce] case. **1928** *Daily Tel.* 18 Sept. 6/5 She feels the consequences of a 'gold-digging' mother's love affairs without entirely understanding them. *Ibid.* 16 Oct. 10/7 She will go to his house, and (in the American phrase) do a little gold-digging—without, you understand, giving anything in return. **1936** I. L. IDRIESS *Cattle King* xiii. 121 So started the first ration store on the gold-diggings at Tibooburra. **1958** *Times* 2 Oct. 3/1 To his gold-digging mistress the publisher..is an ageing man foolishly pretending to be younger than he is. **1852** EARP *Gold Col. Australia* 160 A case of extraordinary success at the *gold-diggings has been related to us. **1869** BLACKMORE *Lorna D.* lxi, Because of my refusal to become a slave to the gold-digging. **1536–7** *P.P. Exp. P'cess Mary* (1831) 12 Payed to the *goldedrawer for Pypes and pyrles for a gowne to my ladys grace vij*li.* xviij*s.* [**1945** *Jefferson Co. Republican* (Golden, Colo.) 31 Oct. 2/1 The troops visited a large gold mining dredge.] **1948** P. JOHNSTON *Lost & Living Cities Calif. Gold Rush* 25/1 Land that has once been mined by a *gold dredge is utterly ruined for all time. **1901** *Daily Colonist* (Victoria, B.C.) 1 Oct. 10/4 The new North Thompson River *gold dredger, in a fraction over four days' actual gold dredging operations, secured 32 ounces of gold. **1909** *Daily Chron.* 23 Jan. 1/1 Houses have been swept away [in the Transvaal] and a gold-dredger has been sunk. **1892** W. E. SWANTON *Notes on N.Z.* iii. 159 The Gillespie Beach *Gold Dredging Company['s]..object is to dredge the sea at the mouth of the Grey River and bring up the sand and mud, which contain large quantities of gold-dust washed down by the stream. **1959** A. MCLINTOCK *Descr. Atlas N.Z.* p. xvi, The unsightly piles of gravel or 'tailings'..a legacy from the gold-dredging boom of 60 years ago. **1662** *Elegy on Cleveland* 21 in *C.'s Wks.* (1687) 284 As *Gold-drivers that make Spangles rare, Do beat the yielding Metal into Air. **1797** MARY ROBINSON *Walsingham* II. 176 So touch the *gold drops..divide them among you. *a* **1700** B. E. *Dict. Cant. Crew*, **Gold-droppers*, Sweetners, Cheats, Sharpers. **1785** GROSE *Dict. Vulg. Tongue*, *Gold-droppers*, sharpers who drop a piece of gold, which they pick up in the presence of some unexperienced person for whom the trap is laid; this they pretend to have found [etc.]. **1605** MARSTON, etc. *Eastward Hoe* v. i. G 3 b, His daughter that he has married a sciruy *gold-end man & his Prentise. **1610** B. JONSON *Alch.* II. i, He looks like a gold-end-man. **1847** *Californian* (San Francisco) 22 May 4/1 After the *gold fever was over, these ships were very successful in taking oil in the bay. **1888** BARBOUR *Clara* ix. 13 The gold fever coursed through every vein. **1958** *Chambers's Techn. Dict.* (ed. 2) 983/1 **Gold-film glass*, glass incorporating a thin gold film which can be electrically heated for demisting and de-icing. **1962** *Engineering* 2 Feb. 179/1 Heated gold-film windows for the flight deck of the de Havilland Trident aircraft. *c* **1000** ÆLFRIC *Gloss.* in Wr.-Wülcker 158/36 *Medicus, uel annularis*, *goldfinger. **1836** YARRELL *Brit. Fishes* I. 296 The *Goldfinny, or Goldsinny, *Crenilabrus Cornubicus*. **1683** PETTUS *Fleta Min.* II. i. 101 *Gold flints which have not only Gold but silver also. **1694** SALMON *Bate's Disp.* (1715) 536/2 This Tincture if it be made out of Gold-Flints, Pebles, or Sand, is none of the least Medicines. **1884** *Cassell's Encycl. Dict.*, **Gold-flux*, avanturine. **1819** G. SAMOUELLE *Entomol. Compend.* 427 *Pyralis costalis*, the *gold Fringe. **1591** SYLVESTER *Du Bartas* I. iii. 1144 His Wardrobe..With *gold-ground Velvets. **1763–6** W. LEWIS *Comm. Phil.-Techn.* 48 The *gold hammer, or finishing hammer weighs ten or eleven pounds. **1606** SYLVESTER *Du Bartas* II. iv. II. *Magnificence* 722 *Gold-head darts. **1869** MORRIS *Earthly Par.* (1870) III. IV. 6 Maidens' feet Brushing the *gold-heart lilies. *c* **1386** *Gold hewen [see *gold-beaten*]. *c* **1400** *Sege Jerus.* 755 Þe gold-hewen helme haspeþ he blyue. **14..** *MS. Cantab.* Ff. 2. 38, lf. 133 (Halliw.) The kyng to hys *golde-hows toke hys way. **1652** H. L'ESTRANGE *Americans no Jewes* 64 And being still whetted and sharpned on with *Gold-hunger, their sword devoured many Myriades of the Americans. **1908** E. J. BANFIELD *Confessions of Beachcomber* II. i. 267 When such a prize as a *gold-lip shell was found, it was used to the last possible fragment. **1929** A. B. LEWIS *Melanesian Shell Money* 11 In south-western New Britain a [pearl] shell of the golden yellow variety ('gold-lip') was specially valued. **1957** M. WEST *Kundu* ii. 29 Time was when a man's wealth was measured by the number of his pigs or by his store of gold-lip shell. *a* **1100** *Ags. Voc.* in Wr.-Wülcker 334 *Auricalcum*, *goldmæslinc. *a* **1200** *Ibid.* 550 *Auricalcum*, goldmestling. *a* **1400** *Plowman's T.* I. 187 Styroppes gay of gold-mastling. **1683** PETTUS *Fleta Min.* II. iv. 118 The building up of the *Gold-Mill. **1881** STEVENSON *Virg. Puerisque* 127 Hours..dedicated to furious moiling in the gold-mill. **1530** PALSGR. 226/1 *Goldemynt. **1593** DONNE *Sat.* vi. 9 Poems (Grosart) I. 51 *Gold-mouth'd Spencer. **1873** J. MILLER *Life amongst Modocs* 57 [The miners]..washed their hands and faces in the *gold-pan that stood by the door. **1901** *Daily Colonist* (Victoria, B.C.) 22 Oct. 1/5 The party of six men had but one gold pan. **1463** *Bury Wills* (Camden) 34 An ymage of oure lady in *gold papyr. **1545** *Rates Custom ho.* b iij b, Golde papers the groce ii*s.* **1864** PUSEY *Lect. Daniel* ii. 91 A magnificent temple..its whole walls covered with *gold-plating. **1882** *Peel City Guardian* 2 Dec., The New York exchange has kept hovering at only a little above the *gold point. **1925** S. E. THOMAS *Elem. Econ.* xxix. 461 We find that the rates at which one currency will exchange for another fluctuate between two limits on each side of the Mint Par, marking the points at which it becomes more profitable to send or to receive gold rather than to send or receive a credit instrument. These theoretical limits are known as the *gold points*. **1930** J. M. KEYNES *Treat. Money* II. 320 The degree of separation of the gold points is a vital factor in the problem of managing a country's currency. **1743–4** MRS. DELANY *Life & Corr.* (1861) II. 250 Your letter.. I believe drove away my headache..: every testimony of your love and friendship is better to me than *gold-powder or sal volatile. **1839** URE *Dict. Arts* 612 The mechanical mode [of gilding] is the application of gold leaf or gold powder to various surfaces. *a* **1611** BEAUM. & FL. *Maid's Trag.* v. iv, Art thou *gold-proof? There's for thee. **1849–50** WEALE *Dict. Terms*, **Gold purple*, or *Cassius's purple precipitate*, the compound oxide which is precipitated upon mixing the solutions of gold and tin. *c* **1475** *Pict. Voc.* in Wr.-Wülcker 798/11 *Aurifodina*, a *goldquarelle. **1850** *Calif. Courier* (San Francisco) 18 July 2/3 If *gold quartz rock comes in, in this way, we will begin to believe that.. we are wrong. **1908** *Chambers's Jrnl.* Sept. 637/1 The discovery of some very rich gold-quartz veins. **1672** VENN *Compleat Gunner* III. x. 19 *Gold-rain. **1875** KNIGHT *Dict. Mech.*, *Gold-rain*, (Pyrotechnics), small cubes ¼ inch square, used instead of stars for rockets, etc. **1870** *N.Y. Herald* 8 July 4/3 [The national banks'] interests.. lie in a paper circulation only, and in not being compelled to hold a *gold reserve. **1879** A. J. WILSON *Banking Reform* vii. 189 More stringent provisions for maintaining an adequate gold reserve would be required here than seems to have been thought necessary in the American Union. **1967** *Times* 5 July 1/8 Britain's gold and convertible currency reserves fell by £43m. last month. **1893** G. TREGARTHEN *Austral. Commw.* 158 The *gold-rush had introduced many unruly spirits. **1849** *Q. Jrnl. Chem. Soc. Lond.* I. 169 The crystals are a mixture of the *gold salts of cyaniline and aniline. **1907** G. S. NEWTH *Text-bk. Inorg. Chem.* (ed. 12) III. v. 568 Most metals, when placed in a solution of a gold salt, precipitate the gold. **1937** *Lancet* 9 Oct. 840/1 The cause of the jaundice is the temporary toxic effect of the gold salts upon the liver cells. **1970** *Guardian* 20 Feb. 6/7 People being treated with gold salt for rheumatoid arthritis have no cause for concern. **1683** PETTUS *Fleta Min.* II. i. 101 [A river] too small to inrich so many Gold-Mines with *Gold-sand. **1873** E. BRENNAN *Witch of Nemi*, etc. 258 As the gold-sand of life disappears. *a* **1705** RAY *Syn. Pisc.* (1713) 163 *Gold-sinny, *Cornubiensium*. **1769** PENNANT *Zool.* III. 209 The tail.. of the Goldsinny is even at the end. **1611** COTGR., *Assiette à dorer*, size to gild with, *gold size. **1842** BRANDE *Dict. Sci.*, etc., *Gold size*.. is drying oil mixed with calcined red ochre. **1545** *Rates Custom ho.* b iij b, *Golde skinnes the kyppe xiii.s. iiiid. **1601** HOLLAND *Pliny* II. 454 *marg.*, *Chrysocolla*, *i.* *Gold-soder. **1842** FRANCIS *Dict. Arts*, Gold Solder, the alloy used for soldering gold articles is [etc.]. **1819** G. SAMOUELLE *Entomol. Compend.* 403 *Noctua bractea*, the *gold Spangle. *Ibid.* 422 *Noctua Festucæ*, the *gold Spot. **1626** BACON *Sylva* §960 The *Gold-Stone, which is the Yellow Topaze. **1683** PETTUS *Fleta Min.* II. ii. 112 If there be a great quantity of the Gold-stones, then there may be made more Ovens. **1850** AINSWORTH *Ovingdean Grange* VI. iv. (1860) 196 An enormous mass of breccia, or goldstone, as the common folk call it. **1683** PETTUS *Fleta Min.* II. x. 128 That every Assayer may.. so well order his *Gold stroak, that he may not be esteem'd as one without understanding. **1819** G. SAMOUELLE *Entomol. Compend.* 397 *Hepialus hectus*, the *gold Swift. **1816** KIRBY & SP. *Entomol.* (1817) II. 21 The *gold-tail-moth. **1937** *Lancet* 9 Oct. 840/2 Nervous complications are perhaps the rarest seen in *gold therapy. **1970** A. & E. F. GROLLMAN *Pharmacol. & Therapeutics* (ed. 7) xlii. 926/1 It would thus appear that [for rheumatoid arthritis] conservative therapy.. is the preferred method of treatment and that the hazards of gold therapy do not support its use. *a* **1618** SYLVESTER *St. Lewis* 423 A heart whose *Gold-Thirst never *sat* is. **1568** BIBLE (Bishops') *Isa.* xiv. 4 How hath the oppressour ceased? and the *gold thirstie Babel rested? *c* **1386** CHAUCER *Monk's T.* 485 Nettes of *gold threed hadde he greet plentee. **1623** MASSINGER *Bondman* II. iii, Cheating heirs With your new counterfeit gold thread and gummed velvets. **1727–41** CHAMBERS *Cycl.*, *Gold Thread*, or spun Gold, is a flatted gold wrapped, or laid over a thread of silk, by twisting it with a wheel, and iron bobins. **1882** 'SHWAY YOE' *Burman* I. xxiv. 311 The *gold-tipped ox-goad.. is covered with jewels. **1904** A. E. W. MASON *Truants* x. 92 Lighting a gold-tipped cigarette he.. began to talk. **1951** R. SENHOUSE tr. *Colette's Chéri* 174 Stub-ends of gold-tipped cigarettes. **1872** E. EGGLESTON *End of World* ix. 65 Pewter watch-seals, *gold-washed. *c* **1420** *Sir Amadace* (Camden) xlv, Thenne Sir Amadace he him cladde, And that was in a *gold webbe. **1769** MRS. RAFFALD *Eng. Housekpr.* (1778) 189 To spin a Gold Web for covering Sweet-Meats.. when your sugar is melted it will be of a gold colour, take your ladle off the fire, and begin to spin it with a knife. **1483** *Cath. Angl.* 161/2 A *Golde worme, *noctiluca*.

b. in names of plants, as **gold-balls** = *gold-cups*; **gold basket**, *Alyssum saxatile*; **gold-bloom**, the marigold; **gold-chain**, (*a*) the stonecrop, *Sedum acre*; (*b*) the laburnum; †**gold-crap**, **-cups**, names of a species of *Ranunculus*; **gold-flower**, †(*a*) *Helichrysum Stœchas*; (*b*) the South African genus *Gorteria*; **gold-knap**, **-knop(s** = *gold-cups*; **gold-lily**, ?*Amaryllis aurea*; **gold-moh(u)r**, also **gul mohur**, the Indian name for *Poinciana regia* (or *Delonix regia*), an ornamental tree bearing scarlet flowers, which has been introduced into several tropical countries from Madagascar; cf. FLAMBOYANT *sb.*, *peacock-flower*; **gold of pleasure**, *Camelina sativa*; **gold-seed** (see quot.); **gold-shrub**, *Palicourea speciosa* (*Treas. Bot.* 1866); **gold-thread**, *Coptis trifolia*, so called from its fibrous yellow roots.

1854 MISS PRATT *Flower. Pl.* (1857) I. 33 The Buttercup has several old English names.. Gold Cups and *Gold Balls are names now almost forgotten. **1857** WRIGHT *Dict. Obs. & Provinc. Eng.*, *Gold-bloom, the marigold. **1857** MISS PRATT *Flower. Pl.* II. 331 Country people call it [*Sedum acre*] ..*Gold Chain. **1580** HOLLYBAND *Treas. Fr. Tong.*, *Des Bassinets*, an herbe called crowfoote, *golde crap, or yellow crawe. **1578** LYTE *Dodoens* III. lxxiv. 421 Golde knoppe.. yᵉ single and double, or els the garden *Golde-cuppe, and the wilde. **1849** *Reverberations* II. 45 Goldcups in the meadows. **1578** LYTE *Dodoens* I. lxi. 89 *Golde floure, Motheworte, or Golden Stechados. **1812** A. PLUMTRE *Lichtenstein's S. Africa* II. 166 The abundance of *gorteria*, gold-flowers, which grow upon its banks. **1552** HULOET, **Gold-knappe*, or yelow craye herbe,.. *batrachium*, *Chrisanthemum*. **1736** AINSWORTH *Lat. Dic.* II, *Polyanthemon*,.. An herb called crowfoot, goldcup, or gold-knap. **1567** MAPLET *Gr. Forest* 39 b, Crowfoote.. It beareth yelowe flowers called *Goldknops. **1842** TENNYSON *E. Morris* 146 While the *gold-lily blows. **1874** E. LEAR *Indian Jrnl.* June (1953) viii. 147 The wonderful orange blossomed *gold-mohr tree is now a sight here as every compound has one or two in it, besides lots of other flowers. **1901** A. PERRIN *East of Suez* 83 The clambering bougainvillea and gold-mohur blossoms. **1953** N. L. BOR *Man. Indian Forest Bot.* 71 The flowers of the *Gul Mohur* are described as having four scarlet petals, while the fifth, or standard, is variously variegated with gold and vermilion. **1597** GERARDE *Herbal* II. xxii. 214 *Golde of pleasure.. is called properly Myagrum. **1882** G. ALLEN *Colours Flowers* ii. 43 The most primitive and simple forms have yellow flowers, as in the case of.. the gold-of-pleasure (*Camelina sativa*). **1855** MORTON *Cycl. Agric.* I. 596/2 These grains [of *Cynosurus Cristatus*] commonly called seeds, being yellow, give rise to the provincial name of **gold seed* applied to the species. **1806** MOORE *Epist.* ix. 90 Where the *gold-thread loves to creep. **1830** LINDLEY *Nat. Syst. Bot.* 7 The root of Coptis trifolia, or Gold-thread, is a pure and powerful bitter.

c. in the names of birds, as **gold-breasted trumpeter**, *Psophia crepitans*; **gold-capped weaver bird**, *Ploceus icterocephalus*; **goldcrest** = *golden-crested wren* (see WREN); **gold-hammer**, the yellow-hammer; **gold-head**, the pochard, *Fuligula ferina*; **gold robin**, the Baltimore oriole.

1783 LATHAM *Gen. Synopsis Birds* II. II. 793 *Gold-breasted Trumpeter. **1868** WOOD *Homes without H.* xi. 205 The beautiful nest of the *Gold-capped Weaver bird. **1824** T. FORSTER *Peren. Cal.* in Hone *Every-day Bk.* II. 119 The king Of birds the *goldcrest. **1706** PHILLIPS (ed. Kersey), **Gold-hammer*, a Bird. **1744** *State Co. Down* xviii. 230 Called the Pochard, or red-headed Widgeon, and in this County.. commonly the *Gold Head. **1872** WHITTIER *Pennsylv. Pilgrim* 436 The *gold-robin cried A-swing upon his elm.

gold² (gəʊld). *Obs.* exc. *dial.* Forms; α. 1, 4–6 golde, 5 goolde, 6 goold, gowl(e, 4– gold, 6– gould (9 *dial.* goode, goud). β. *Sc.* (and *north.*) 6 guld, guilde, 6, 8 guild, 8 guil(l, gule, gool, 8–9 gull. [OE. *golde* wk. fem., app. related to GOLD¹: the marigold is called 'gold-flower' in several of the cognate languages, as Du. *goudbloem*, *goudsbloem* (MDu. *goutbloeme*), G. *goldblume*, Sw. *guldblomma*.

In many dialects there is a difference in pronunciation between this sb. and GOLD¹. In the name of the plant, as also in *mould*:—OE. *molde*, the northern dialects have generally the vowel ordinarily corresponding to OE. *ó*, ME. close *ō*, while in GOLD¹ the pronunciation descends normally from OE. *gŏld*, ME. *gōld*. (Cf. esp. Sc. *guil(d*, corn-marigold, with *gowd*, the metal.) The difference is doubtless due to the fact that the one word was disyllabic, the other monosyllabic, in OE. and early ME.]

1. †**a.** The marigold (*Calendula officinalis*). *Obs.* **b.** The corn-marigold (*Chrysanthemum segetum*). Freq. in *pl.* **c.** (see quot. 1882). ¶ Sometimes used by early writers to render L. *intuba* or *cichorea* (endive or chicory).

The mediæval L. names *solsequium*, *heliotropium*, &c. denote the marigold (*Calendula*), the sunflower (*Helianthus annuus*) being then unknown in Europe. In mod. dialect use the name of 'white gold' is sometimes given to the ox-eye daisy (*Chrysanthemum Leucanthemum*), the corn-marigold being then distinguished as the 'yellow gold' (Britten and Holland 1879).

α. *c* **1000** *Ags. Voc.* in Wr.-Wülcker 301/6 *Solsequia*, golde. [? **13..** *Beauchief Abbey Charter* in *Monast. Anglic.* (1661) II. 610 De terris suis.. à goldis mundandis. **1373** *Durham Halmote Rolls* (Surtees) 118 Injunctum est omnibus tenentibus villæ quod evacuent quandam herbam vocatam gold.] *c* **1386** CHAUCER *Knt.'s T.* 1071 Ialousye, That wered of yelewe gooldes a gerland. **1390** GOWER *Conf.* II. 356 She sprong up out of the molde Into a flour, was named golde, Which stant governed of the sonne. *c* **1420** *Pallad. on Husb.* v. 97 Oynouns, myntes, goordes, & goldys [L. *intubæ*]. *c* **1440** *Promp. Parv.* 202/1 Goolde, herbe, *solsequium* ..*calendula*. **1523** FITZHERB. *Husb.* §20 There be diuers maner of wedes, as thistyls.. darnolde, gouldes. *Ibid.* Golds ..is an yll wede, and groweth commenlye in barleye and pees. **1527** ANDREW *Brunswyke's Distyll. Waters* cclxxxii. Tiva, Water of the herbe of gowles or ruddes. *Cicorea*, *sponsa solis Sol sequium* in latyn. **1595** SPENSER *Col. Clout* 341 With Roses dight and Goolds. **1612** DRAYTON *Poly-olb.* xv. 166 The crimsin Darnell Flower, the Blew-bottle, and Gold. **1629** PARKINSON *Paradisi* lxiii. 298 We call them in English generally, either Golds or Marigolds. **1633** *Gerarde's Herbal* Suppl., *White Golds* is great Daisy. **1790** W. MARSHALL *Midl. Co.* II. 437 Gloss., Golds, *chrysanthemum segetum*;—corn marigolds. **1882** *Lanc. Gloss.*, *Goode* (N. Lanc.) the ox-eye daisy. **1886** *S.W. Linc. Gloss.*, *Goud* or *Gold*, the yellow Corn Marigold.

β. **1536** BELLENDEN *Cron. Scot.* (1821) II. 164 He that sufferis his land to be fild with guld, or siclik unproffitabil wedis [etc.]. **1563** WINȜET *Wks.* (1890) II. 59 Fra hand spring wp guild and humlokis. **1609** SKENE *Reg. Maj.* Table 81 Guilde (quhilk is ane pernicious herbe, or rather ane wide). ? **17..** *Scottish Saying* in JAMIESON s.v., The Gool, and the Gordon, and the Hudy Craw Are the greatest curses ever Moray saw. **1794** *Statist. Acc. Scotl.* XIII. 537 A weed with a yellow flower that grows among the corns, especially in wet seasons, called Gool. **1794** HUTCHINSON *Hist. Cumb.* I. 220 *note*, *Gulls*, a weed which infested the cornland, totally rooted out. **1878** *Cumbld. Gloss.*, *Gull*, the corn-marigold.

2. *Comb.*, as **gold flower**; also **goldweed**, **-wort** = sense 1. Also †**gool-riding** *Sc.*, the custom of searching fields for 'golds', a fine being imposed on the farmer for each plant found; so **gool-rider**.

c **1325** *Gloss. W. de Biblesw.* in Wright *Voc.* 162 Cy crest la flur de surcye [*glossed* golde-flurs (solicle)]. *a* **1400** *Med. MS.* in *Archæol.* XXX. 367 Yᵉ golde flour is good to sene. *c* **1400** *Med. Wks. 14th C.* (1899) 45 Take mat-felon and flouris of gold-wort. *c* **1450** *Alphita* (Anecd. Oxon.) 86/1 *Incuba*, *sponsa solis*.. goldwort. *Ibid.* 88/1 *Kalendula*, *sponsa solis*.. golduurt uel rodes. **1744–50** W. ELLIS *Mod. Husbandm.* II. I. 19, I saw a Field of Barley.. full of this Gould-weed. **1794** *Statist. Acc. Scotl.* XIII. 537 An old custom takes place in this parish [Cargill], called Gool-riding.. Certain persons stiled gool-riders, were appointed to ride through the fields, search for gool, and [etc.].

goldarn (ˌgɒlˈdɑːn), *v.*, *a.*, and *adv.* *U.S. slang.* Also gol darn, goldurn, etc. [Euphemistic substitute for GOD-DAMN.] = DAMN *v.*, DAMN *a.* and *adv.* Cf. DARN, DARNATION, DARNED. So ˌ**golˈdarned** *ppl. a.*, damned.

1832 *New England Mag.* III. 380 We have..'*Gaul darn you*' for G—— D—— you. **1849** *Picayune* (New Orleans) 6 May 2/6 I'll be gaul-durned ef I deu. **1856** F. L. OLMSTED *Journey Slave States* 312 Seems to me them gol-darned lazy niggers aint a goin' to come over arter you now. **1870** B. HARTE *Sensation Novels* iv. 87 Dog-gone. *Note*, A euphemism common with the men of the West, and equal to the English 'O drat it', or 'Gol darn'. **1885** *Harper's Mag.* Aug. 397/2 Hannah-Maria-Jemimy! goldarn an' blue blazes! *Ibid.* 400/2 You're a goldarn liar, Balaam. **1907** N. MUNRO *Daft Days* xxxii, Every gol-darned idiot in England. **1910** R. W. SERVICE *Ballads of Cheechako* 50 Goldarn his eyes. **1920** S. LEWIS *Main St.* 431 Cy Bogart had the 'flu, but of course he was too gol-darn mean to die of it. **1948** *Reader's Digest* Mar. 128 Another great story ruined by a goldurned eyewitness. **1964** MRS. L. B. JOHNSON *White House Diary* 17 July (1970) 183 Well, I'll be gol-durned—the salesman that sold it to me said it was Harry Truman.

Goldbach's conjecture. *Math.* The hypothesis put forward by the German mathematician C. Goldbach (1690–1764) in 1742 (in a letter to a fellow mathematician, Euler) that every even number greater than 2 can be represented as the sum of two primes. Also *Goldbach's hypothesis*, *theorem*, etc.

1919 L. E. DICKSON *Hist. Theory of Numbers* I. xviii. 422 G. Cantor verified Goldbach's theorem up to 1000. **1941** COURANT & ROBBINS *What is Math.?* 31 Until recently, a proof of Goldbach's conjecture seemed completely inaccessible. **1949** W. KNEALE *Probability* §18. 79 The attitude of mathematicians.. can.. be expressed by ..'Goldbach's conjecture looks like a theorem, but it may conceivably be false'. **1960** P. SUPPES *Axiomatic Set Theory* vii. 217 Goldbach's Hypothesis.. is false for ordinal numbers. **1965** PHILLIPS & WILLIAMS *Inorg. Chem.* I. i. 25 There still exist a number of very simple problems which have yet to find solutions. These include the four-colour problem, Goldbach's conjecture, and Fermat's last theorem.

ˈ**gold-ˌbeater.**

1. One who beats out gold metal into thin plates or gold-leaf.

1415 in *York Myst.* Introd. 21 Goldbeters. **1483** *Act 1 Rich. III*, c. 12 §1 The Artificers.. that is to say Goldebeters [etc.]. *c* **1515** *Cocke Lorell's B.* (Percy) 9 Bokell smythes, horse leches, and gold beters. **1671** BOYLE *Consid. Usef. Exper. Philos.* II. x. §4. 36 Some of our Gold-beaters in London. *a* **1800** COWPER *Flatting Mill* iii, It is doomed to sustain The thump after thump of a gold-beater's mallet. **1868** GLADSTONE *Juv. Mundi* xv. (1870) 522 The gold-beater and.. smith, are known to Homer.

b. *goldbeater's skin*, a prepared animal membrane employed to separate the leaves of gold-foil during the operation of beating; sometimes used to cover wounds.

1710 STEELE *Tatler* No. 266 ⁋3 Gold-beaters Skin applied to stop the Blood. **1796** WITHERING *Brit. Plants* (ed. 3) IV. 94 Leaves.. thin as gold beaters skin. **1852** MORFIT *Tanning & Currying* (1853) 540 Goldbeater's skin is prepared from the external or peritoneal coat of the coecum, or blind gut of neat cattle.

2. (See quot.)

1847 CRAIG, *Goldbeaters*.. a genus of Coleopterous insects, remarkable for their beautiful golden-green and copper colours.

gold brick, gold-brick, *sb.* [f. GOLD¹ + BRICK *sb.*¹ 4.] **1.** A brick-shaped piece of gold.

1853 *San Francisco Sun* 7 June 2/2 (*heading*) Gold brick. **1877** R. W. RAYMOND *Statistics of Mining* VIII. 354 Individuals are constantly carrying out bags of gold and gold bricks and some silver bricks. **1899** *Monthly South Dakotan* I. 196 [He] found in a water hole a gunny sack in which was a gold brick.

2. A brick that appears to be made of gold; hence, something having only a surface appearance of value; a fraud; esp. in phr. *to sell* (someone) *a gold brick*, to swindle. Also *attrib.* *slang* (orig. *U.S.*).

1881 *National Police Gaz.* (U.S.) 24 Dec. 10/2 (*heading*) The Gold Brick Trick. *Ibid.*, The gold brick swindle is an old one but it crops up constantly... The bar, or brick as it is called,.. is really of base metal. One corner, however, is of gold. **1887** *Chambers's Jrnl.* 1 Oct. 637/1 A 'gold-brick swindler'. **1889** *Kansas Times & Star* 30 Nov., What's new down at the old union depot shack? Any eruptions, gold bricks being sold or important arrivals? **1901** S. E. WHITE *Westerners* xiii. 94 Bunco men can clean him out in a gambling joint, but who ever heard of their selling him a gold brick? **1911** B. WASHINGTON *My Larger Educ.* 292 In many cases, the diploma that the student carries home at the conclusion of his course is nothing less than a gold brick. **1915** WODEHOUSE *Something Fresh* vi, Preventing Fate from working off on us any of those gold bricks, coins with strings attached, and unhatched chickens at which Ardent Youth snatches. **1923** H. C. BAILEY *Mr. Fortune's Practice* iii. 82 'He is said to be negotiating deals in Russian mining properties.' 'Sounds like a gold brick.' **1947** *Chicago Daily News* 16 May 18/5 It used to be the city slicker who sold gold bricks to the hick from the country.

3. A shirker; a lazy person (see also quots.). *U.S. slang.*

1914 *Dialect Notes* IV. 107 *Gold-brick, n.*, applied to army lieutenants appointed from civil life. 'The gold-bricks are overbearing.' **1926** L. NASON *Chevrons* viii. 275, I think you're a goldbrick... You don't look as if you were wounded the slightest bit. **1929** *Papers Mich. Acad. Sci.* X. 296/2 *Gold brick* (Am.), I, an unattractive girl; II, a shirker; one who tries to avoid work, or to get an easy job. **1943** *Reader's Digest* Oct. 97 The wise guy always complains when there is work to do. Sometimes [in the army] he is called a Gold Brick. **1958** J. STEINBECK *Once there was War* (1959) p. xviii, In the ranks, billeted with the stinking, cheating, foul-mouthed goldbricks, there were true heroes.

Hence **gold-brick** *v.*, (*a*) *trans.* to cheat, swindle, defraud; (*b*) *intr.* to shirk, to have an easy time; **gold-bricker**, (*a*) a shirker; (*b*) a swindler; **gold-bricking** *vbl. sb.* and *ppl. a. slang* (orig. and chiefly *U.S.*).

1902 H. L. WILSON *Spenders* xxviii. 328 He'll be gold-bricked if he wears 'em [*sc.* his whiskers] scrambled that way around this place. **1914** *Munsey's Mag.* Jan. 738/1 Well, look out they don't gold-brick you, sonny. **1926** L. NASON *Chevrons* ii. 39 You were somewhere in hospital goldbricking your time away. **1928** J. B. WHARTON *Squad* vi. 208 If there's any one here sick enough to stay, I'll see the Lieutenant... But no gold brickin' now, mind! **1932** *Blue Valley Farmer* (Okla. City) 4 Feb. 8/4 No country worth fighting for was ever built on slacker's devotion or gold-bricker's patriotism. **1937** *Amer. Speech* XII. 74/2 *Gold bricker*, duty-shunner, lazy soldier or enrollee. **1952** M. MCCARTHY *Groves of Academe* (1953) iv. 67 Students with applied art or science majors tended to gold-brick on their reading courses. **1958** J. K. GALBRAITH *Affluent Society* vii. 63 The typical business executive..would endanger his chance for advancement if he were suspected of goldbricking because of his resentment over his taxes. *Ibid.* viii. 91 We have feather-bedding unions and gold-bricking workmen and slothful supernumeraries everywhere. **1968** *Courier-Mail* (Brisbane) 18 May 3/7 As in any large outfit, there is obvious goldbricking.

'gold-ˌcolour. The colour of gold; a deep yellow. Also *attrib.*

1678 RAY *Willughby's Ornith.* 368 A lovely yellow or gold-colour. **1791** HAMILTON *Berthollet's Dyeing* II. II. III. vii, The wax is coloured..for aventurine or gold-colour with orpiment. **1854** MRS. GASKELL *North & S.* xlvi, It's not a dead gold-colour, ma'am. It's a straw-colour. **1887** *Lady* 20 Jan. 38/3 A broad stripe of gold-colour plush.

So **'gold-ˌcoloured** *a.*

1687 *Lond. Gaz.* No. 2214/4 A black Hat, with a gold coloured Hatband. **1728** ? ARBUTHNOT *Congr. Bees* Misc. Wks. (1751) II. 149 A gold-colour'd Flie. **1854** MRS. GASKELL *North & S.* xlvi, Oh, Dixon! not those horrid blue flowers to that dead gold-coloured gown. What taste!

'gold-ˌdig, *v. slang* (orig. *U.S.*). [Back-formation f. GOLD-DIGGER 2.] *trans.* To behave as a gold-digger (GOLD-DIGGER 2) towards (a man); to extract money from.

1926 S. LEWIS *Mantrap* xii. 148, I gold-dig you for all the money I can get. **1931** A. POWELL *Afternoon Men* xiii. 141 Of course he was intended by nature to be gold-dug and as a compensation given a temperament that enjoys the process. **1947** J. STEINBECK *Wayward Bus* 206 I'll bet she just gold-dug Eddie.

'gold-ˌdigger. [GOLD[1].] **1.** One who digs for gold. Also *fig.*

1830 *Cherokee Phoenix* (New Echota, Ga.) 24 Mar. 3/3 There are tippling shops on every hill where these gold diggers are collected. **1850** MRS. BROWNING *Poems* II. 305 We cheer the pale gold-diggers. **1855** R. HENNING *Let.* 29 Mar. (1966) 25 Dressed-up in a blue gold-digger's shirt over his clothes. **1948** O. WESTON *Mother Lode Album* 28 Savage and his party of Indian gold diggers encamped under a big oak. **1954** KOESTLER *Invis. Writing* xix. 218, I had been done in..as thoroughly and completely as a choir-boy in a gold-digger town.

2. A girl or woman who attaches herself to a man merely for gain. *slang* (orig. *U.S.*).

1920 B. MANTLE in *Best Plays of 1919–20* 360 'Jerry' Lamar is one of a band of pretty little salamanders known to Broadway as 'gold diggers', because they 'dig' for the gold of their gentlemen friends and spend it being good to their mothers and their pet dogs. **1928** *Sunday Dispatch* 19 Aug. 20 The professional gold-digger is generally a girl of good family who finds she can supplement her allowance by going out with, say, half-a-dozen men. **1934** G. B. SHAW *On Rocks* II. 263 All I can get out of her is that she is not a gold digger, and wouldnt be seen at a wedding with a lousy viscount. **1959** J. BRAINE *Vodi* xii. 162 It was expensive; that appealed to Lois. Not that she was a gold-digger; but once he started going around with her there were more withdrawals than deposits in his Post Office savings book.

gold dust, 'gold-dust.

1. Gold in extremely fine particles, the form in which it is commonly obtained in a natural state.

1703 *Lond. Gaz.* No. 3886/2, 80 Pound weight of Gold Dust. **1705** BOSMAN *Guinea* 81 Dust-Gold, or Gold-Dust.. almost as fine as Flower. **1879** H. GEORGE *Progr. & Pov.* I. iii. (1881) 55 Gold dust passed as currency by weight.

fig. **1837** HT. MARTINEAU *Soc. Amer.* II. 368 The day will come when their eyes will be cleansed from the gold-dust which blinds them.

2. *Bot.* A popular name of *Alyssum saxatile*, which bears a profusion of small yellow flowers. Also of *Sedum acre* (Britten & Holland 1879).

1866 in *Treas. Bot.* 539/2.

'gold-ˌdusty, *a.* [f. GOLD DUST + -Y[1].] Resembling or covered with gold dust.

a **1907** F. THOMPSON *Shelley* in *Dublin Rev.* (1908) July 37 He is gold-dusty with tumbling amidst the stars. **1931** R. LEHMANN *Let. to Sister* 12 The infinitesimal flicks of gold-dusty midge-swarms.

†'golded, *ppl. a. Obs.* [f. GOLD[1] + -ED[2].]

1. Made of gold, golden.

1382 WYCLIF *Baruch* vi. 69 So ben the treenen goddis, and sylueren, and goldid. **1447** BOKENHAM *Seyntys* (Roxb.) 57 At the goldede gates she sey Hyr dere spouse comyn. **1647** WARD *Simp. Cobler* 40 Evangelicall policies should be framed..by a golded Reed.

2. Possessed of gold, wealthy.

c **1450** *Pol. Poems* (Rolls) II. 227 The grete and the goldede they made but a jape. **1610** *Histrio-mastix* I. i, Vnmaske thy face thou minister of Time..let thy golded hand, Ride (with distinctlesse motion) on the eyes Of this fayre *Chorus*, till the Raigne of *Peace*, Hath propagated *Plenty*.

golden ('gəʊld(ə)n), *a.* Forms: 3– **golden**; also 4, 6 *Sc.* **goldin, -yn,** (4 **goldein, -un, coldin,** 5 **goldene, -on,** 6 **-ing**), 6 **goulden,** 8–9 *Sc.* **gowden,** 9 *dial.* **goolden** (*superl.*, 6 **goldnest,** 7 **-enst**). [f. GOLD[1] + -EN[4], taking the place of the earlier GILDEN (q.v.). Cf. Du. *gouden*, G. *golden.*]

1. a. Made of gold, consisting of gold.

the golden fleece, the fabulous fleece of gold in search of which Jason went to Colchis; (***Order of the***) ***Golden Fleece*** (see FLEECE *sb.* 1 b). ***golden ball***, the apple of discord (see APPLE *sb.* 5). ***golden gates***, the gates of Heaven.

c **1275** LAY. 4251 þe goldene [*c* **1205** guldene] croune. *Ibid.* 14298 Ane goldene [*c* **1205** guldene] bolle. *a* **1300** *Cursor M.* 6503 A goldin calf þar-of þai blu. **1398** TREVISA *Barth. De P.R.* XVI. iv. (1495) 553 A thynne plate of golde of the whyche golden threde is made. *c* **1400** *Destr. Troy* 667 The wethir was wonen, & away borne, The grete goldyn flese with a greke noble. **1548** HALL *Chron., Rich. III*, 38 b, To promes to the duke..golden hilles and sylver ryvers. **1595** CHAPMAN *Ovid's Banquet Sence* (1639) 18 With the goldnest arrow in his Quiver. *a* **1671** LD. FAIRFAX *Mem.* (1699) 118 The King was the golden ball cast between the two parties, the Parliament and the army. **1676** W. ROW *Contn. Blair's Autobiog.* xi. (1848) 352 A large Bible with golden clasps. **1794** BURNS *My lord a-hunting*, My lady's gown there's gairs upon't, And gowden flowers sae rare upon't. **1833** HT. MARTINEAU *Berkeley the Banker* I. ii. 30 Golden guineas are rare things now. **1887** RUSKIN *Præterita* II. 422 The higher religious souls, hoping to lead me to the golden gates.

b. In *fig.* expressions, referring to gold coin or money. ***to kill the goose that lays the golden eggs***: see GOOSE *sb.* 1 d.

1597 BRETON *Wits Trenchmour* (Grosart) 8/1 Fishing with the golden hooke, which rich men onely layde in the deepe consciences of the covetous. *a* **1618** SYLVESTER *Hymn Alms* 334 While Great-ones..Had oft their Fingers in the Golden Py; For private Profit [etc.]. **1626** BRETON *Pasquils Mad-cap* (Grosart) 8/1 If she haue the golden hony-bees, She shall [etc.]. **1629** *Leather* 12 What cannot golden hookes plucke away from vs. **1636** MASSINGER *Gt. Dk. Florence* III. i, That petition lined too With golden birds, that sing to the tune of profit. **1842** TENNYSON *Locksley H.* 100 Every door is barr'd with gold, and opens but to golden keys.

2. Containing or yielding gold; auriferous. Of a country or district: Abounding in gold. ***the Golden State***, California.

1398 TREVISA *Barth. De P.R.* XV. cviii. (1495) 527 Ophir ..was in olde tyme callyd the golden londe. *a* **1618** SYLVESTER *Hymn Alms* 417 Pactolus, Ganges, and the golden Tay. **1666** DRYDEN *Ann. Mirab.* ccvi, Some, bound for Guinea, golden Sand to find. **1701** DE FOE *True-born Eng.* 6 The golden mines of Mexico. **1819** HEBER *Hymn 'From Greenland's icy Mountains'* i, Where Afric's sunny fountains Roll down their golden sand. **1847** *Congress. Rec.* 7 May, App. 246/2 From the hills of the Golden State we will send..cattle of every breed. **1893** GUNTER *Miss Dividends* 238, I thought a tour of 'the Golden State' would please me. **1967** *Boston Sunday Globe* 21 May A5/2 If Mayor Yorty gets the Senate nomination, Lyndon Johnson may have to write off the Golden State in 1968.

3. a. Of the colour of gold; that shines like gold.

c **1300** *Cursor M.* 17865 (Arundel MS.) To vs þer brast a goldein leme. **1552** HULOET, Golden heere, *chrysocoma.* **1624** HEYWOOD *Captives* I. i, The blackest serpents weare the goldenst scales. **1725** POPE *Odyss.* XV. 444 Her rich vallies wave with golden corn. **1838** LYTTON *Leila* I. ii, The hair and curling beard were of a deep golden colour. **1852** MRS. STOWE *Uncle Tom's C.* xii. 107 She saw sunshine sparkling on the water, in golden ripples.

fig. **1548** HALL *Chron., Hen. VII*, 32 Belevinge no fraude nor deceate to be hid or cloked undre this golden tale. **1588** SHAKS. *Tit. A.* IV. iv. 97 For I can smooth and fill his aged eare, With golden promises. **1795** MACNEILL *Will & Jean* II. xxv, A' his gowden prospects vanish'd.

b. In the names of several kinds of tobacco, e.g. 'Golden Cloud', 'Golden Flake', etc.

4. a. Resembling gold in value; most excellent, important, or precious. †***golden vein*** [= med.L. *vena aurea*, Ger. *goldader*]: the hæmorrhoidal vein.

c **1400** *Rom. Rose* 5650 Pictagoras himsilf reherses In a book that the Golden Verses Is clepid. **1498** W. DE WORDE (*title*), Here begynneth the legende named in Latyn Legenda Aurea that is to saye in Englysshe the Golden Legende. For lyke as passeth golde in valewe all other metallys, so this legende excelleth all other bookes. **1526** *Pilgr. Perf.* (W. de W. 1531) 144 b, Men & women, bothe rude & vnlerned that haue spoken golden wordes. **1527** ANDREW *Brunswyke's Distyll. Waters* D ij a/1 The same [great plantayn water] is good agaynste the flode & bledynge of the golden vayne. **1559** MORWYNG *Evonym.* 155 Of waters of vertues or golden waters. **1605** SHAKS. *Macb.* I. vii. 33, I haue bought Golden Opinions from all sorts of people. **1607** TOPSELL *Four-f. Beasts* (1658) 197 It hath been proved for a golden remedy, to take and anoint it with Goats-grease. **1739** CIBBER *Apol.* (1756) II. 35 He was a golden actor. **1838** ARNOLD *Hist. Rome* (1846) I. vii. 102 He had a golden wit within.

b. Of time, an opportunity: Of inestimable value; exceedingly favourable or propitious.

1601 SHAKS. *Twel. N.* V. i. 391 When that is knowne, and golden time conuents. **1646** J. HALL *Horæ Vac.* 20 'Tis.. unsufferable..to let the Golden houres of the morning passe without advantage. **1703** ROWE *Fair Penit.* I. i. 156, I snatch'd the glorious, golden opportunity. **1806–7** J. BERESFORD *Miseries Hum. Life* (1826) II. xviii, At such a golden moment as this. **1884** EARL GREY in *19th Cent.* Mar. 514 The golden opportunity was thrown away.

5. a. Of rules, precepts, etc.: Of inestimable utility; often *spec.* with reference to the precept, 'whatsoever ye would that men should do to you, do ye even so to them' (*Matt.* vii. 12).

1674 R. GODFREY *Inj. & Ab. Physic* 54 Whilst forgetting that Golden Law *do as you would be done by*, they make self the center of their actions. **1741** WATTS *Improv. Mind* I. xiv. §8 Such is that golden principle of morality which our blessed Lord has given us. **1807** *Med. Jrnl.* XVII. 242 The best rule in this respect is..the golden rule of Dr. Jenner; not to take matter after the areola begins to spread. **1885** HOWELLS *Silas Lapham* II. xxv, In our dealings with each other we should be guided by the Golden Rule. **1887** RUSKIN *Præterita* II. 13 'When you have got too much to do, don't do it',—a golden saying.

†b. *Math.* ***the golden rule***, the rule of three.

1542 RECORDE *Gr. Artes* (1575) 240 The rule of Proportions, whiche for his excellencie is called the Golden rule. **1571** DIGGES *Pantom.* I. xiv. E j, By the rule (called the golden precept). **1636** FEATLY *Clavis Myst.* xxi. 279 The rule of three, or golden rule, as it is called in sacred algebray. **1806** HUTTON *Course Math.* I. 44 The Rule of Three..is often called the Golden Rule.

c. (*a*) ***golden mean***, (*a*) the avoidance of excess in either direction [tr. L. *aurea mediocritas*, Hor. *Odes* II. x. 5]; (*b*) = *golden section* (see sense d).

1587 *Mirr. Mag.* (1815) I. 52 The golden meane is best. **1590** SPENSER *F.Q.* II. ii. Argt., The face of golden Meane: Her sisters, two Extremities, Strive her to banish cleane. **1636** MASSINGER *Gt. Dk. Florence* I. i, We, whom for our high births, they conclude The onely free men, are the onely slaves: Happy the golden meane! **1725** POPE *Odyss.* XV. 80 Both the golden mean alike condemn. *a* **1817** T. DWIGHT *Trav. New Eng.* etc. (1821) II. 269 That middle state of poverty, which so long, and so often, has been termed Golden. **1821–2** WORDSW. *Sacheverel*, As if a Church.. must owe To opposites and fierce extremes her life,—Not to the golden mean. **1917** D. W. THOMPSON *On Growth & Form* xiv. 643 This celebrated series, which..is closely connected with the *Sectio aurea* or Golden Mean, is commonly called the Fibonacci series. **1929** [see FIBONACCI]. **1945** *Burlington Mag.* Jan. 7/1 Various people have tried to prove..that the 'golden mean', in which Italian artists believed, was applied here by Franciscus Florentinus.

d. ***golden section***, (the proportion resulting from) the division of a straight line into two parts so that the ratio of the whole to the larger part is the same as the ratio of the larger part to the smaller, viz. $\frac{1}{2}(\sqrt{5} + 1)$, or 1·61803...; 'extreme and mean ratio'.

This celebrated proportion has been known since the 4th century B.C., and occurs in Euclid (II. 11, VI. 30). Of the several names it has received, *golden section* (or its equivalent in other languages) is now the usual one, but it seems not to have been used before the 19th century.

[**1835** M. OHM *Die reine Elementar-Mathematik* (ed. 2) II. 194 Diese Zertheilung einer beliebigen Linie *r* in 2 solche Theile, nennt man wohl auch den goldenen Schnitt. **1844** J. HELMES in *Arch. Math. und Physik* IV. 15 (*heading*) Eine.. Auflösung der sectio aurea. **1849** A. WIGAND (*title*) Der allgemeine goldene Schnitt und sein Zusammenhang mit der harmonischen Teilung.] **1875** *Encycl. Brit.* I. 220/1 Zeising..asserts that the most pleasing division of a line, say in a cross, is the golden section. **1898** [see SECTION *sb.* 3 e]. **1914** T. A. COOK *Curves of Life* xx. 426 In Sandro Botticelli's Venus..the line containing the figure from the top of the head to the soles of the feet is divided, at the navel, into the exact proportions given by that ancient formula the 'Golden Section'. **1931** T. L. HEATH *Man. Gr. Math.* viii. 181 Proclus speaks of theorems which Plato 'originated regarding the "section"', and, if this 'section' was what came to be called the 'golden section',..Plato may well have had this case in mind. **1951** G. SARTON in *Isis* XLII. 47/2 As far as we know now, the expression divine proportion was introduced by Pacioli in 1509 [in his treatise, *Divina proportione*], and the expression golden section by Martin Ohm in 1835. It is almost certain that they had predecessors [*printed* predecessors]. Who were they? **1953** 'M. INNES' *Christmas at Candleshoe* i. 5 It so happens that in the picture-space we are contemplating, the one line cuts the other in a ratio which artists call golden section. **1955** T. DANTZIG *Bequest of Greeks* v. 59 Just as specious are the contentions that certain proportions in human anatomy conform to the golden-section rule. **1963** H. READ *Contrary Experience* IV. viii. 345 Certain correspondences are easily established—the prevalence, for example, in art and in both organic and inorganic matter of the proportion known as the Golden Section. **1970** [see FIBONACCI]. **1970** *Oxf. Compan. Art* 489/1 Statistical experiments are said to have shown that people involuntarily give preference to proportions that approximate to the Golden Section.

Similarly ***golden rectangle***, a rectangle in which the ratio of the longer side to the shorter is the golden section.

1953 *Scripta Math.* XIX. 136 Since the diagonal of a pentagon is τ times its side, this rectangle is a golden rectangle, whose sides are in the ratio τ:1. *Ibid.* 138 The golden rectangle can be dissected into two pieces: a square and a smaller golden rectangle. **1967** W. J. REICHMANN *Spell of Math.* v. 90 The sides of the rectangle are thus in golden section, and the rectangle may therefore be called a golden rectangle... If we draw the largest square possible within this rectangle..then the next remaining rectangle will also be golden.

6. ***golden number*** [tr. med.L. *aureus numerus*; so called from its importance in calculating the date of Easter]: the number of any year in the Metonic lunar cycle of nineteen years.

This number for a year *n* of the Christian era is (*a*) the remainder of $(n + 1) \div 19$, or (*b*) if there be no remainder, 19. Hence these numbers are retained in the ecclesiastical calendar in connexion with the computation of the time of Easter. The golden number is found by adding 1 to the remainder left after dividing the number of the year by 19.

1552 *Bk. Com. Prayer, Almanack*, The Golden Number. **1561** EDEN *Arte Nauig.* II. vi. 30b, This present yeare of 1545, we haue .7. of the golden number. **1594** BLUNDEVIL *Exerc.* VII. i. (1636) 654 The Golden number is the number of 19, proceeding from 1 to 19, and so to begin againe at 1. **1686** PLOT *Staffordsh.* 431 They scrupled not to set them in the margins of their Calendars in characters of gold, whence they are stiled to this day, also the golden number.

7. Of a time or epoch: Characterized by great prosperity and happiness; flourishing, joyous. †*golden world* = GOLDEN AGE.

1530 TINDALE *Pract. Prelates* Bij b, Then they called a parliament (as though the golden worlde shuld come agayne). **1548** HALL *Chron., Hen. VII*, 20b, That golden worlde of Tully. **1597** SHAKS. *2 Hen. IV*, v. iii. 100 Tydings do I bring, and luckie ioyes, and golden Times. **1600** —— *A.Y.L.* I. i. 125 [They] fleet the time carelesly as they did in the golden world. **1661** COWLEY *Disc. Govt. O. Cromwell* Ess. (1669) 72 The golden times of our late Princes. **1775** BURKE *Corr.* (1844) II. 90 Your gentleman does well to call the days of Lord Clare *golden*. **1855** MACAULAY *Hist. Eng.* xviii. IV. 174 In the golden days of the Plot he had been allowed three times as much. **1877** TENNYSON *Harold* IV. iii, Our day..will not shine Less than a star among the goldenest hours Of Alfred.

†**8.** Pertaining to gold (as the object of desire, pursuit, etc.). *Obs.*

1613 PURCHAS *Pilgrimage* (1614) 817 He would carry them where their Golden thirst should be satisfied. **1623** R. JOBSON (*title*), The Golden Trade, or a discovery of the River Gambia and the golden Track of the Ethiopians. **1720** DE FOE *Capt. Singleton* vii. (1840) 120 Thus ended our first golden adventure.

9. *Comb.* **a.** with adjs. of colour, as ***golden-brown***, ***-chestnut***, ***-green***, ***-olive***, ***-red***, ***-yellow***.

1796 WITHERING *Brit. Plants* (ed. 3) IV. 172 Juice golden yellow. **1845** E. ACTON *Mod. Cookery* (ed. 2) ii. 60 Fry them a clear golden brown in plenty of boiling lard. **1863–5** THOMSON *Sunday at Hampstead* viii, The great dusk emerald golden-green. **1865** EARL DERBY *Iliad* XI. 777 Golden-chesnut mares. **1891** *Leeds Mercury* 27 Apr. 4/7 A dress of golden brown silk.

b. quasi-adverbial 'with or like gold', as ***golden-gleaming***, ***-glowing***, ***-wrought***.

1777 POTTER *Æschylus, Agamem.* 231 Golden-gleaming rays. **1796** T. TOWNSHEND *Poems* 34 And in her pearly hand a lyre She held of golden-glowing wire. **1870** MORRIS *Earthly Par.* III. IV. 49 Her array all golden-wrought.

c. parasynthetic, as †***golden-aged***, ***-coloured***, ***-fettered***, ***-fleeced***, ***-footed***, ***-fruited***, ***-girdled***, ***-haired***, ***-hearted***, ***-hilted***, ***-locked***, ***-railed***, †***-slopt***, ***-tongued***, ***-trapped***, ***-winged***, ***-wired***, etc.

1568 T. HOWELL *Arb. Amitie* (1879) 101 To runne the race of Nestors yeeres, a *golden aged man. *c* **1610** SIR J. MELVIL *Mem.* (1735) 98 She [Queen Elizabeth] delighted to show her *golden-coloured Hair wearing a Caul and Bonnet. **1824** J. BOWRING *Batavian Anthol.* 46 Many a *golden-fetter'd fool. **1591** SYLVESTER *Du Bartas* I. vi. 118 The *golden-fleeced Sheep. **1757** DYER *Fleece* III. 405 Around the globe, The *golden footed sciences their path Mark, like the sun. *a* **1835** MRS. HEMANS *Dreams Heaven* Poems (1875) 518 In..*golden-fruited grove. **1848** J. R. LOWELL *New Year's Eve, 1844* in *Uncoll. Poems* (1950) 52 Blithely as the *golden-girdled bee Sinks into the sleepy poppy's cup of flame. **1552** HULOET, *Golden heered, or hauynge golden heere or lockes, *chrysocomus*. **1850** MRS. BROWNING *Poems* II. 273 Thou golden-haired, and silver-voicèd child. **1646** CRASHAW *Music's Duel* Poems 89 A *golden-headed harvest. **1907** *Dublin Rev.* Jan. 30 She is the *golden-hearted rose that held our perfect joy. **1960** *Times* 30 Jan. 11/2 We have..never until now seen him in other than golden-hearted parts. **1859** TENNYSON *Enid* 166 Nor weapon, save a *golden-hilted brand. **1871** EARLE *Philol. Eng. Tongue* §660c, A brave, bold, *golden-locked boy. **1833** TENNYSON *Pal. Art* xii, The light aërial gallery, *golden-rail'd, Burnt like a fringe of fire. **1599** MARSTON *Sco. Villanie* I. iii. 107 When some slie, *golden-slopt Castilio Can cut a manors strings at Primero. **1645** HOWELL *Dodona's Grove* 101 That flexanimous and *golden toungd Orator. **1648–99** JOS. BEAUMONT *Psyche* IX. cliii, The Sun.. had from the east Prick'd forth his *Golden-trapped Steeds. *c* **1625** MILTON *Death Fair Infant* 57 Or wert thou of the *golden-wingèd host. **1596** FITZ-GEFFRAY *Sir F. Drake* (1881) 25 Her silver-feathered turtle-doves, Which in their *golden-wired cage remaine.

10. a. Specialized combinations and phrases, as **golden balls** (see BALL *sb.* 20); **golden book**, a register of the nobility of the state of Venice; **golden boy**, a popular or successful boy or man; similarly *golden girl*; **golden-bull** (see BULL *sb.*[2] 3); **golden cat**, either of two honey-coloured wild cats, *Felis aurata* or *F. temmincki*, found in west Africa and south-east Asia; **Golden Chersonese** [tr. Gr. Χρυσῆ Χερσόνησος], the Malay Peninsula; **golden-comb**, some kind of shellfish; **golden ear**, a moth, *Hydrœcia nictitans*; **golden earth**, yellow arsenic or orpiment; **golden-fly** = *golden-wasp*; **golden girl** (see *golden boy*); **golden handcuffs** orig. *U.S.*, benefits provided by an employer, esp. a corporation, to make it difficult or unattractive for an employee to leave and work elsewhere; **golden handshake**, a gratuity given as compensation for dismissal or compulsory retirement; also *transf.*; **golden hello** [after *golden handshake*], a substantial sum offered to a senior executive, etc., as an inducement to change employers, and paid in advance when the new post is accepted; **golden hoof**, said of the action of sheep or other animals trampling the ground beneath them, consolidating and improving its texture; **golden-knop**, a lady-bird; **golden maid**, the fish *Crenilabrus melops* or *tinca*; **golden-mouth**, used to render the name *Chrysostom* (see GILDEN *a.* 1b); **golden-mouthed** *a.*, whose speech is golden (used chiefly as prec.); **golden perch**, 'a fresh-water fish of Australia, *Ctenolates ambiguus*' (Morris); †**golden-poll** (see quots. and GILT-HEAD); **golden rain**, a kind of firework forming a shower of golden sparks; **golden retriever**, a retriever with a thick golden-coloured coat; **golden-ring** (see quot.); **golden sherry**, a type of sweet sherry; **golden shower** = *golden rain*; **golden spur**, a papal order, the order of St. Sylvester; **golden star**, 'a kind of monstrance or ciborium used at Rome in the Papal High Mass on Easter-day' (Lee *Gloss. Eccl. Terms* 1877); **golden sulphide**, **sulphuret**, persulphide of antimony or antimony pentasulphide, Sb_2S_5 (Watts *Dict. Chem.* I. 334); **golden syrup** (see SYRUP); **golden-wasp**, a brightly-coloured hymenopterous insect of the family *Chrysididæ*, esp. *Chrysis ignita*; **golden wedding** (see WEDDING); **golden wrasse** = *golden maid*; †**golden yard**, the belt of Orion (see quot.).

1712 *Lond. Gaz.* No. 5022/6 The Senate..designs to open the *Golden Book, to enter such Persons as will buy the Nobility of Venice for themselves or Families. **1937** C. ODETS (*title*) The *golden boy. *Ibid.* III. i. 196 He walks down the street respected—the golden boy! **1964** 'J. WELCOME' *Hard to Handle* viii. 91 Poor dear Richard... What a change from being the golden boy of English racing. **1965** P. MOYES *Johnny under Ground* xx. 250 *That* would have been the end of Beau Guest, the young chevalier, the golden boy. **1971** *Sunday Times* (Johannesburg) 28 Mar. 24/1 Ever since he assumed the 'golden boy' mantle, Richards has studiously avoided local opposition. [**1867** *Proc. Zool. Soc.* 815 An adult specimen of the Golden Tiger-cat of Sumatra (*Felis aurata*, Temm.) received June 19th.] **1883** D. G. ELLIOT *Monogr. Felidæ* tab. xvi. (*caption*) Temminck's *Golden Cat. **1954** G. DURRELL *Bafut Beagles* ix. 154 The Golden Cat, one of the smaller, but one of the most beautiful, members of the cat family. **1667** *Golden Chersonese [see CHERSONESE]. **1883** I. L. BIRD (*title*) The Golden Chersonese and the way thither. **1863** KINGSLEY *Water-Bab.* v. 192 Live cockles and whelks and razor shells and sea-cucumbers and *golden-combs. **1819** G. SAMOUELLE *Entomol. Compend.* 433 *Noctua auricula*. The *golden Ear. **1567** MAPLET *Gr. Forest* 10 The stone Arsenick..which also they call the *golden earth. **1823** CRABB *Technol. Dict.*, **Golden-fly*, an insect so called from its gilt body, which is generally found in the holes of old walls, the *Chrysis* of Linnæus. **1896** R. LE GALLIENNE (*title*) The quest of the *golden girl. **1966** 'W. COOPER' *Mem. New Man* III. iv. 245 Alice liked him, but I'm bound to admit that she didn't see him as such a golden boy as I did. Nor..did she see Roz as such a golden girl. **1976** D. W. MOFFAT *Econ. Dict.* 130/2 **Golden handcuffs*, benefits provided by employers in such a manner as to make it costly for employees to change jobs, thereby removing the competitive advantage an individual would otherwise have in selling his labor. **1982** *Wall St. Jrnl.* 9 Feb. 16/3 Getty Oil is trying to lock 'golden handcuffs' on explorationists by offering them four-year loans 'up front' equal to 80% of an employee's salary. **1985** *Times* 4 Apr. 30/1 Managers..have private health insurance, a better than average pension scheme, a car, and perhaps help with independent school fees from the company. These 'golden handcuffs' are a hangover from the days of labour shortages and income policies and higher tax rates. **1960** *Economist* 9 Apr. 179/2 There is little public sympathy for the tycoon who retires with a *golden handshake to the hobby farm. **1960** *Times* 8 July 13/2 On the financial side, Cyprus receives its golden handshake of over £14 m. **1969** 'B. GRAEME' *Blind Date* i. 13, I knew there would be no future in the Forces... So I came out, and have been living on the golden handshake ever since. **1983** *Observer* 15 May 15/8 Following the 'golden handshake', the '*golden hello' is taking root in British industry. Being paid a handsome lump sum before you even start a new job may sound too good to be true. But, last year alone, 50 top directors got such 'golden hellos'. **1985** *Listener* 6 June 8/3 They're often tempted away to a rival by a 'golden hallo': a sort of transfer fee on top of a sizeable salary increase. **1927** *Daily Tel.* 15 Nov. 11/7 Much of the country [*sc.* Denmark] has land of the typical sheep and barley class, but it is successfully farmed without the aid of the *golden hoof. **1941** M. GRAHAM *Soil & Sense* iii. 47 It is presumably this essential difference between crumb structure and floury structure that has made the 'golden hoof' of the sheep important in consolidating land in which there is too little clay. **1946** L. D. STAMP *Britain's Struct.* xi. 99 On light soils..they [*sc.* cattle] pack together the particles of soil by the treading action of the 'golden hoof'. **1957** E. J. RUSSELL *World of Soil* vii. 171 So great was the benefit to the succeeding crop and to the condition of the soil that farmers regularly spoke of the 'golden hoof' as the best amendment for light soils. **1691** RAY *S. & E.C. Words, Bishop*, the.. lady-bird. I have heard this insect in other places called a *golden-knop. *a* **1825** FORBY *Voc. E. Anglia*, Golden-knop. **1827** HONE *Every-day Bk.* II. 108 The fish called *golden maids, were picked up on Brighton beach. *c* **1340** *Cursor M.* 11393 (Fairf.) Iohn tellyth vs als *goldyn- [*other MSS.* gilden-] mowthe. **1542** T. BECON *Pathw. Prayer* xxxiii. Oj a, S. John golden mouth. **1887** T. W. ALLIES *Throne of Fisherman* 320 This is borne witness to already by the Goldenmouth himself. **1577** tr. *Bullinger's Decades* (1592) 773 Chrysostome that *golden-mouthed man. **1596** FITZ-GEFFREY *Sir F. Drake* (1881) 21 Golden-mouthed Drayton musicall. **1655** MOUFET & BENNET *Health's Improv.* (1746) 243 *Lucernæ.* Gilt-heads or *Golden-poles, are very little unlike the Gournard, save that it seems about the Noddle of the Head as tho' it were all besprinkled with Gold-filings. **1672** VENN *Compleat Gunner* III. x. 19 *Golden rain. **1892** *Pall Mall G.* 1 Nov. 5/2 The 'Golden Rain'.. is a mixture of charcoal, saltpetre, and sulphur charged into a small yellow case. **1919** T. MARPLES *Show Dogs* (ed. 2) xv. 73 The following is the *Golden Retriever Club's standard of points for Golden Retrievers. **1959** R. COLLIER *City that wouldn't Die* v. 66 Then he set off on patrol like a country squire inspecting his coverts—tweeds, walking-stick, golden retriever Punch trotting at his side. **1727** BAILEY vol. II, **Golden-ring*, a Worm that gnaws the Vine, and wraps it self up in its Leaves. **1840** THACKERAY in *Fraser's Mag.* July 93/1 A bottle of fine old *golden sherry..for 1*s.* 9*d.* **1854** Golden sherry [see *brown sherry* s.v. BROWN *a.* 7]. **1957** *Encycl. Brit.* XX. 500/2 A 'sweet', 'cream' or 'golden' sherry [contains] not over 7% [grape sugar]. **1839** URE *Dict. Arts* 480 Stars for *golden showers, nitre 16; sulphur, 10 [etc.]. **1817** KIRBY & SP. *Entomol.* II. 234 The *golden-wasp tribe also (*Chrysis* and *Parnopes*)..roll themselves up..into a little ball when alarmed. **1551** RECORDE *Cast. Knowl.* (1556) 268 Other thre stande as bullions set in his gyrdle, and are called by manye englyshe men the *Golden yarde.

b. in the names of plants, as †**golden apple**, the tomato; **golden-ball** *dial.*, (*a*) the globe flower, *Trollius europæus*; (*b*) the guelder-rose, *Viburnum Opulus* (Britten & Holland *Plant-n.* 1879); **golden bell** = FORSYTHIA; **golden-chain** *dial.*, the laburnum; **golden-club**, the American plant *Orontium aquaticum*; **golden-crown**, the American genus *Chrysostemma* (*Treas. Bot.* 1866); **golden cudweed**, *Helichrysum orientale*; also *Pterocaulon virgatum* (Grisebach *Flora W. Ind.* 1864); **golden-cup**, a popular name of various species of *Ranunculus*, *Caltha*, *Trollius*; **golden-cup oak** = *golden oak* (b); **golden dust** = GOLD-DUST 2; **golden feather**, the common golden-leaved *Pyrethrum*; **golden flower**, the corn marigold; **golden flower of Peru**, the sunflower; **golden-hair**, *Chrysocoma comaurea* (Paxton *Bot. Dict.* 1840); **golden herb**, the orach; **golden-knob** = *golden-cup*; **golden-locks**, a name for various plants, now esp. the fern *Polypodium vulgare*; also *Pterocaulon virgatum* (Grisebach *Flora W. Ind.* 1864); †**golden-lungwort**, Ray's name for the Wall Hawkweed, *Hieracium murorum*; †**golden Mary**, ? the marigold; **golden moss**, †(*a*) the moss *Polytrichum commune*; (*b*) the stonecrop, *Sedum acre*; **golden mothwort** = *golden cudweed*; **golden nugget** (see quot.); **golden oak** *U.S.* (*a*) the false foxglove, *Aureolaria virginica*; (*b*) the canyon live-oak, *Quercus chrysolepis*; (*c*) a light-coloured finish used on furniture; **golden oat**, the yellow oat-grass; **golden osier**, (*a*) *Salix vitellina*; (*b*) *Myrica Gale*; **golden pert**, *Gratiola aurea* (*Treas. Bot.* 1866); **golden-rayed lily**, *Lilium auratum*; **golden samphire**, *Inula crithmoides*; **golden saxifrage**, the genus *Chrysosplenium*; **golden-seal**, *Hydrastis Canadensis* of N. America; **golden shower** = *pudding-pipe tree* (PUDDING *sb.* 11c); **golden-spoon**, the West Indian plant *Byrsonima cinerea*; **golden spur**, a variety of daffodil; **golden thistle**, the composite genus *Scolymus*, esp. *S. hispanicus*; **golden-top** *U.S.*, a grass, *Lamarckia aurea*; **golden trefoil**, *Hepatica triloba*; **golden tuft**, *Pterocaulon virgatum*; formerly also applied to other plants; **golden willow** = *golden osier*; **golden-withy**, *Myrica Gale*. Also GOLDEN-ROD.

1578 LYTE *Dodoens* III. lxxxvi. 439 Of Amorus Apples or *Golden Apples. **1893** W. ROBINSON *Eng. Flower Garden* (ed. 3) II. 417/1 Forsythia (*Golden Bell). **1968** N. TAYLOR *Guide to Garden Shrubs & Trees* v. 341 The golden bells are of the easiest culture in any ordinary garden soil. **1860** WORCESTER, **Golden-club*, a perennial aquatic plant, bearing yellow flowers. **1597** GERARDE *Herbal* II. cxcvi. §2. 520 Golden Motherwort is called in English..*Golden Cudweed; being doubtlesse a kinde of *Gnaphalium*, or Cudweede. **1736** AINSWORTH *Lat. Dict.* *Golden cup [herb]. *Polyanthemon.* **1879** BRITTEN & HOLLAND *Plant-n.*, Golden cup. *Ranunculus acris, R. bulbosus, R. Ficaria*, and *R. repens.* **1886** ELWORTHY *W. Somerset Word-bk.*, *Golden cup.* 1. Marsh marigold. The usual name. *Caltha Palustris* ..2. *Ranunculus globosa.* **1897** B. B. SUDWORTH *Nomencl. Arborescent Flora U.S.* 164 *Quercus chrysolepis*,..*Golden-cup Oak (Cal.). **1878** *R. Thompson's Gardener's Assist.* 795 *Pyrethrum Parthenium aureum*, one of the very finest and hardiest of all golden-leaved plants used in carpet bedding, is well known..under the name of *golden feather. **1551** TURNER *Herbal* I. Kj b, Chrysanthemom or calchas..hath floures wonderfully shynynge yellowe..The herbe may be called in Englysh *goldenfloure. **1866** *Treas. Bot.*, Golden-flower, *Chrysanthemum.* **1578** LYTE *Dodoens* II. xxxiv. 191 The Indian Sunne, or *golden floure of Perrowe.. groweth to the length of thirtene or fouretenne foote. **1736** AINSWORTH *Lat. Dict.*, *Atriplex*.. An herb called orage, or orach; *golden herb. **1820** T. MITCHELL *Aristoph.* I. 218 They love a tale of scandal to their hearts, And his had been as quick in birth as golden-herb. **1835** W. BAXTER *Brit. Phænog. Bot.* II. 153 *Caltha palustris*..*Golden-knobs. **1882** *Hardwicke's Science Gossip* XVIII. 165 Local Names extant in rural Oxfordshire..'golden knobs', buttercups. **1736** BAILEY *Housh. Dict.* 305 **Golden-Locks* call'd also Golden tufts. **1844** E. NEWMAN *Brit. Ferns* (ed. 2) 112 It [*Polypodium vulgare*].. is called by these gatherers Golden Locks, and Golden Maiden-hair. **1670** RAY *Catal. Plant. Angl.* 255 *Pulmonaria Gallica sive aurea*, ..French or *Golden Lungwort. **1649** LOVELACE *Poems* (1864) 62 So opens loyall *golden Mary. **1597** GERARDE *Herbal* III. clvii, This is called in English Goldilockes Polytrichon.. It might also be termed *Golden Mosse, or Hairie Mosse. **1863** BERKELEY *Brit. Mosses* i. 1 *Sedum acre*,..the Golden Moss of every cottager. **1597** GERARDE *Herbal* II. cxcvi. 519 Of *Golden Mothwoort, or Cudweede. **1882** *Garden* 19 Aug. 156/2 *Balsamita grandiflora*..or *Golden Nugget..a good and effective hardy plant. **1830** C. S. RAFINESQUE *Med. Flora U.S.* II. 223 *Gerardia Quercifolia*, Mx. **Golden Oak.* Specific of the Sioux for the bite of rattle snakes, used also for the tooth ache. **1899** *Chicago Daily News* 30 May 14/3 Solid golden oak finish handsome dressers. **1909** *Cent. Dict.* Suppl. s.v. *Live-oak*, An evergreen oak of the Pacific coast, ..also called golden oak, maul oak, and Valparaiso oak. **1913** BRITTON & BROWN *Illustr. Flora Northern U.S.* (ed. 2) III. 208 *Dasystoma virginica*... In dry or moist woods, Maine to Minnesota, south to Florida and Illinois. Golden-oak. July–Sept. **1921** A. F. HALL *Handbk. Yosemite Nat. Park* 127 The Transition Zone..is characterized by the yellow pine, Douglas spruce, golden oak, black oak, and incense cedar. **1928** F. N. HART *Bellamy Trial* i. 2 Nine rows of the golden-oak seats packed with grimly triumphant humanity. **1969** *New Yorker* 25 Oct. 58/1 His wife was black and blue as a new stovepipe, but their children and grandchildren are best described as 'golden oak'. **1842** C. W. JOHNSON *Farmer's Encycl.* 150/2 *Avena flavescens*, *Golden oat or yellow oat-grass. **1838** LOUDON *Arboretum Brit.* III. 1528 *Salix vitellina* L. The..yellow Willow, or *Golden Osier. **1856** W. A. BROMFIELD *Flora Vectensis* 466 Golden Withy.. Golden Osier. **1784** CUTLER in *Mem. Amer. Acad. Arts & Sci.* (1785) I. 403 *Veronica*..*Goldenpert. **1821** W. P. C. BARTON *Flora N. Amer.* I. 71 *Gratiola aurea.* Golden pert. [**1862** *Curtis's Bot. Mag.* LXXXVIII. 5338 (*caption*) Golden-striped Lily.] **1870** W. ROBINSON *Wild Garden* II. 118 *Golden-rayed Lily. *Lilium auratum.* **1880** H. J. ELWES *Monogr. Genus Lilium* Pl. 15, I believe the Golden-rayed Lily can be grown to greater perfection in pots than in the open ground. **1908** *Pall Mall Gaz.* 20 Apr. 3/2 The golden-rayed lily, be it never so gorgeous. **1970** M. TEMPLETON tr. *Feldmaier's Lilies* i. 7 Japan is the home of some of the finest lilies of all, such as *L[ilium] auratum*, the Golden-Rayed Lily of Japan. **1776** WITHERING *Brit. Plants* II. 515 Elecampane ..*Golden Samphire. **1578** LYTE *Dodoens* II. cii. 288 The *golden Saxifrage groweth in certayne moyst and waterie places. **1855** *Trans. Mich. Agric. Soc.* VI. 179 We have the sarsaparilla, ginsing, *goldenseal, sweet cicily. **1881** S. P. MCLEAN *Cape Cod Folks* ii. 38 The golden seal..was served in a diluted state with milk and sugar and taken as a beverage. **1897** WILLIS *Flower. Pl.* II. 198 Golden-seal..is used as a tonic. **1914** L. H. BAILEY *Standard Cycl. Hort.* II. 680/2 [*Cassia*] *Fistula*, Linn. Pudding-Pipe Tree. *Golden Shower. **1934** R. CAMPBELL *Broken Record* 82 Palms, golden shower, grenadillas. **1953** D. LESSING *Five* i. 14 The other neighbour was a house whose walls were invisible under a mass of golden shower—thick yellow clusters, like smoky honey, dripped from roof to ground. **1893** *Daily News* 28 Mar. 2/2 *Golden spur..a magnificent trumpet daffodil of brilliant colour and noble form. **1597** GERARDE *Herbal* II. cccclxiv. 993 *Carduus Chrysanthemus.* The *golden Thistle. **1909** *Cent. Dict.* Suppl., **Goldentop*, an ornamental grass.. introduced from the Mediterranean region into southern California. **1934** A. ARBER *Gramineae* ix. 186 In Goldentop, however, the tendency to reduced fertility is stronger than in Dog's-tail-grass. **1959** P. A. MUNZ *California Flora* 1495 *Lamarckia* Moench. Goldentop. **1597** GERARDE *Herbal* II. cccclxxxvii. 1031 Of noble Lyuerwoort, or *golden Trefoile. *Ibid.* II. cxcvi. 520 *Coma aurea.* Golden tuft. **1686** RAY *Hist. Plant.* I. VI. x. 280 *Stœchas citrina*..Oriental Goldy-locks or Golden-tufts. **1864** GRISEBACH *Flora W. Ind.* 784/1 Golden-tuft, *Pterocaulon virgatum.* **1861** *Trans. Ill. Agric. Soc.* IV. 447 The *Golden Willow has been a favorite with me. **1866** [see WILLOW *sb.* 2 b]. **1847–78** HALLIWELL, **Golden-withy*, bog myrtle.

c. in the names of varieties of fruit, esp. apples, as †**golden-doucet, -drop,** †**ducat-doucet,** †**munday, -pippin, -rennet,** †**russet,** †**russeting.** Also **golden berry** (see quot. 1951).

1951 *Good Housek. Home Encycl.* 385/1 Tinned cape gooseberries are imported from South Africa (usually under the name of *golden berries). **1958** *Times* 6 Dec. 1/4 (Advt.), One tin each:—..Goldenberries,..Strawberries. **1664** EVELYN *Kal. Hort.* (1729) 191 Apples..*Golden Doucet. *a* **1825** FORBY *Voc. E. Anglia*, **Golden-drop*, the variety of plum, called in our catalogues of fruits..*drap d'or.* **1882** *Garden* 21 Jan. 48/2 That king of dessert Plums—the old Golden Drop. **1883** [see DROP *sb.* 10 f]. **1747** MRS. GLASSE *Cookery* xxi. 164 The *golden Ducket Dauset..Apples. **1725** BRADLEY *Fam. Dict.* s.v. *Apple*, *Golden Munday. **1718** LADY M. W. MONTAGU *Let. to Abbé Conti* 31 Oct., The honest English squire..who verily believes..that the African fruits have not so fine a flavour as *golden pippins. **1823** J. BADCOCK *Dom. Amusem.* 47 The golden pippin has gradually become a shy grower in this country. **1778** *Eng. Gazetteer* (ed. 2) s.v. *Tenham*, [Tenham] being the place where Richard Harris, fruiterer to Henry VIII. first planted cherries, pippins, and *golden-renates. **1824** MISS MITFORD *Village* Ser. I. (1863) 47 That great tree, bending with the weight of its golden-rennets. **1664** EVELYN *Kal. Hort.* (1729) 232 *Golden Russet. **1707** MORTIMER *Husb.* 535 The Aromatick or *Golden Russeting.

d. in the names of birds, as **golden back**, 'the American golden plover, *Charadrius dominicus*' (*Cent. Dict.*); **golden cuckoo**, an African cuckoo belonging to one of the races of *Chrysococcyx cupreus*; cf. *emerald cuckoo* (s.v. EMERALD 5 d); **golden-head** (see quot.); **golden-wing**, the golden-winged woodpecker (*Colaptes auratus*). Also *golden-breasted vulture, golden-cheeked warbler; golden-crested kinglet, regulus, wren; golden-crowned kinglet, sparrow, thrush, wren; golden eagle, manakin, oriole, pheasant, plover, robin, warbler; golden-winged warbler, woodpecker*: see the sbs. Also GOLDEN-EYE.

[**1811** W. J. BURCHELL *Jrnl.* 29 Dec. in *Trav. S. Afr.* (1822) I. xix. 502 The Green-and-gold Cuckoo was found in abundance.] **1827** G. THOMPSON *Trav. & Adv. S. Afr.* I. i. 6 His chief occupation was the stuffing of birds for sale, especially that very beautiful and much-prized species called the *Golden Cuckoo. **1876** H. BROOKS *Natal* iv. 136 It [*sc.* the emerald cuckoo] is in all probability nearly allied, if not identical, with the golden cuckoo..of the Cape. **1937** *Discovery* XVIII. 265/2 Two more new races—a new Scops owl and a new golden cuckoo—have been added to the Arabian list. **1953** BANNERMAN *Birds W. & Equat. Afr.* I. 583 This bird [*sc.* the yellow-throated cuckoo] is about the size of Klaas' Cuckoo but has not the brilliance in the plumage of the other Golden Cuckoos. **1753** CHAMBERS *Cycl. Supp.*, **Golden-head*, a name by which some have called the *anas artica clusii*, a web footed fowl, common on our shores. **1885** SWAINSON *Prov. Names Birds* 154 Wigeon (*Mareca penelope*)..Golden head, or Yellow poll. The male is so called on the east coast of Ireland. **1895** *Atlantic Monthly* July 61, I had a call from a family of flickers or *goldenwings.

golden ('gəʊld(ə)n), *v. rare.* [f. the adj.]

a. *trans.* To cover or tinge with a golden hue. **b.** *intr.* To assume a golden colour.

1850 MRS. BROWNING *Poems* II. 307 The sun strikes, through the farthest mist, The city's spire to golden. **1866** NEALE *Sequences & Hymns* 187 The pumpkin ripened and goldened. **18..** LOWELL *Endymion* IV. Poet. Wks. 1890 IV. 152 Like loose mists that blow Across her crescent, goldening as they go.

Hence '**goldened,** '**goldening** *ppl. adjs.*

1863 A. B. GROSART *Small Sins* (ed. 2) 102 The goldening sunlight. **1876** SMILES *Sc. Natur.* xii. (ed. 4) 237 Sails showing brightly in the goldened light.

golden age. [tr. L. *aurea ætas*; see GOLDEN *a.* 7 and AGE *sb.* 11.] The first and best age of the world, in which, according to the Greek and Roman poets, mankind lived in a state of ideal prosperity and happiness, free from all trouble or crime. (Cf. Hesiod *Wks. & Days* 108, Ovid *Met.* I. 89.) Hence, the period in which a nation, etc., is at its highest state of prosperity, or in which some department of human activity is at its acme of excellence.

Often applied to the finest period of Lat. literature (Cicero to Ovid), in contrast to the 'silver age' which succeeded.

1555 EDEN *Decades* III. viii. 134 As wee reade of them whiche in oulde tyme lyued in the golden age. **1610** SHAKS. *Temp.* II. i. 168, I would with such perfection gouerne Sir: T' Excell the Golden Age. **1685** DRYDEN *Albion & Albanus* Pref., Those first times, which Poets call the Golden Age. **1700** —— *Fables* Pref., With Ovid ended the golden age of the Roman tongue. **1732** BERKELEY *Alciphr.* v. §25 In the golden age (as the Italians call it) of Leo the Tenth. **1869** LECKY *Europ. Mor.* II. i. 44 The golden age of Roman law was..Pagan. **1875** STUBBS *Const. Hist.* II. xv. 299 The thirteenth century is the golden age of English churchmanship.

Hence euphemistically **golden-'ager** *U.S.*, an old person.

1961 *Front Page Detective* 25 June 68 A discriminating clientele of golden-agers. **1963** in *Post & Times-Star* (Cincinnati) 9 Oct. 23. **1970** *New Yorker* 15 Aug. 57/1 There are no euphemisms in Dutch for being old—no 'senior citizen', no 'golden-ager'. **1970** H. WAUGH *Finish me Off* (1971) 135 Frank bought himself a drink in the bar..while watching the golden agers gossip in the lounge area.

†'**goldeney.** *Obs.* Also 6–7 goldn(e)y, gold(e)nie, golden-eye. [? f. GOLDEN *a.* + -Y[4]; cf. BLACKY, BROWNIE[1], etc. The form *golden-eye* is prob. due to a misunderstanding.] The name of some fish, perhaps the golden wrasse, but commonly used (like GILT-HEAD) to render L. *aurata* or *scarus.*

1552 HULOET s.v., Gilt hed or goldney fishe which cheweth like a beast, *aurata marina.* **1589** COGAN *Haven Health* clxxxiv. (1636) 167 Among which he [Galen] reckoneth the whiting, the perch, the gilthead or goldnie. **1591** SYLVESTER *Du Bartas* I. v. 314 (*margin*) The Golden-eye or Guilt-head. **1661** LOVELL *Hist. Anim. & Min.* Introd., Fishes, which are..saxatile, living neer stones, and are squammose; as the Golden eye.

'**golden-eye.**

1. a. A sea-duck of the genus *Clangula*, esp. *C. glaucion.* **b.** 'The bird *Melithreptus lunulatus*' (Morris *Austral Eng.* 1898). **c.** The Tufted Duck, *Fuligula cristata* (Newton *Dict. Birds* 368).

a. **1678** RAY *Willughby's Ornith.* 368 The Golden-eye.. The Irides of the Eyes are of a lovely yellow or gold-colour. **1709** DERHAM in *Phil. Trans.* XXVI. 466 *Anas Platyrhynchosmas Aldrov.* The Golden-Eye. **1766** PENNANT *Zool.* (1768) II. 460 *Golden eye*..These birds frequent fresh water, as well as the sea. **1810** CRABBE *Borough*, *P. Grimes*, Or sadly listen to the tuneless cry Of fishing gull, or clanging golden-eye. **1870** *Athenæum* 20 Aug. 232/3 Widgeon, teal, golden-eye, and other duck, abound in the neighbourhood of Quickjock.

b. **1827** VIGORS & HORSFIELD in *Trans. Linn. Soc.* XV. 315 *Lunulata*..'This bird', Mr. Caley says, 'is called Golden-Eye by the settlers'.

2. 'A fish, *Hyodon chrysopsis*, having a large eye with yellow iris' (*Cent. Dict.*).

3. A neuropterous insect of the genus *Chrysopa.*

1753 CHAMBERS *Cycl. Supp.*, *Chrysopis*, the golden eye,.. a species of fly, so called from the beautiful gold colour of its eyes. **1862** *Chambers's Cycl.*, Golden-eye Fly (*Hemerobius perla* or *Chrysopa perla*).

goldenly ('gəʊld(ə)nlɪ), *adv.* [f. GOLDEN *a.* + -LY[2].]

1. In a golden manner; excellently, splendidly.

1600 SHAKS. *A.Y.L.* I. i. 6 My brother Iaques he keepes at schoole, and report speakes goldenly of his profit. **1840** HOOD *Kilmansegg, Fancy Ball* xxxi, So the courtly dance was goldenly done, And golden opinions, of course, it won. **1889** LOWELL *Latest Lit. Ess.* (1892) 137 A style..so parsimonious in the number of its words, so goldenly sufficient in the value of them.

2. With a golden hue or lustre; like gold. (Said of both material and immaterial things.)

1827–35 WILLIS *To Stolen Ring* 21 The dreams Of her high heart came goldenly and soft. **1864** LOWELL *Fireside Trav.* 313 The sunlight..hovered under the dome like the holy dove goldenly descending.

3. As with gold.

c **1825** BEDDOES *2nd Brother* III. i, Dropping with starry sparks, goldenly honied. **1859** MISS MULOCK *Romant. T.* 1 Both are..written goldenly on this happy heart of mine.

goldenness ('gəʊld(ə)nnɪs). [f. GOLDEN *a.* + -NESS.] The condition of being golden.

1829 CUNNINGHAM *Brit. Paint.* I. 342 A richness of colouring, a sort of brown and glossy goldenness. **1840** LOWELL *Irene* Poet. Wks. (1879) 4 The full goldenness of fruitful prime.

'**golden-,rod.** A plant of the genus *Solidago*, esp. *S. Virgaurea*, having a rod-like stem and a spike of bright yellow flowers.

1568 TURNER *Herbal* III. 78 *Virga aurea*..may be called in English Golden-rod. **1616** SURFL. & MARKH. *Country Farme* 200 Golden-rod would be sowne in a fat ground. **1718** QUINCY *Compl. Disp.* 116 Golden-rod..flowers in July and August. **18..** BRYANT *Death of the Flowers* 15 But on the hill the golden-rod, and the aster in the wood..in autumn beauty stood.

b. goldenrod-tree, a shrub (*Bosea Yervamora*), a native of the Canary Isles.

1829 in LOUDON *Encycl. Plants.* **1866** in *Treas. Bot.*

†**gold faw,** *a. Obs.* Forms: 1 **goldfáȝ, -fáh,** 3 **goldfaw.** [OE. *goldfáh*, f. GOLD[1] + *fáh* FAW *a.*] Adorned with gold.

Beowulf (Z.) 995 Gold-faȝ scinon web æfter waȝum. *c* **1205** LAY. 26706 Leien ȝeond þan ueldes gold-faȝe [*c* **1275** goldfawe] sceldes. *Ibid.* 31406 Nim gold-fah i-wede.

'**gold-field.** A district or region in which gold is found. Also *attrib.*

1852 EARP *Gold Col. Australia* viii. 129 The gold fields of New South Wales. **1858** T. MCCOMBIE *Hist. Victoria* xv. 215 All were anxious to get away for the gold fields. **1890** BOLDREWOOD *Col. Reformer* (1891) 272 The goldfield town near which was the station.

fig. **1854** MACAULAY *Biog.*, *Bunyan* (1860) 44 He continued to work the Gold-field which he had discovered and to draw from it new treasures.

goldfielder ('gəʊldfiːldə(r)). [f. GOLD-FIELD + -ER[1].] One who works in a gold-field; a gold-miner.

1903 *Westm. Gaz.* 28 Jan. 9/1 All the goldfielders were not mere adventurers. **1933** *Bulletin* (Sydney) 20 Sept. 9/2 Goldfielders swept Westralia into the Commonwealth.

goldfinch ('gəʊldfɪnʃ). Also 1 goldfinc, 6 golde finche. [f. GOLD[1] + FINCH. Cf. Du. *goudvink*, G. *goldfink.*]

1. A well-known bright-coloured singing-bird (*Carduelis elegans*) of the family *Fringillidæ*, with a patch of yellow on its wings.

c **1000** ÆLFRIC *Gloss.* in Wr.-Wülcker 131 *Auricinctus*, goldfinc. *a* **1250** *Owl & Night.* 1130 Pinnuc goldfinch rok ne crowe Ne dar þar never cumen ihende. *c* **1386** CHAUCER *Cook's T.* 3 Gaillard he was as Goldfynch in the shawe. **1486** *Bk. St. Albans* F vj, A Cherme of Goldefynches. *a* **1529** SKELTON *P. Sparowe* 392 Euery byrde in his laye. The goldfynche, the wagtayle [etc.]. **1601** HOLLAND *Pliny* I. 308 The Gold-finch liueth among bushes and thorns. *a* **1800** COWPER *Faithful Bird* 4 Two goldfinches, whose sprightly song Had been their mutual solace long. **1876** SMILES *Sc. Natur.* xiii. (ed. 4) 270 The goldfinch is also a good singing bird.

b. *U.S.* Applied to several small yellow finches, esp. *Spinus tristis*, the thistle-bird.

1858 THOREAU *Winter* 22 Dec. (1888) 6 There may be thirty goldfinches, very brisk and pretty tame. They hang, head downwards, on the weeds.

c. *dial.* The yellow-hammer.

1848 in EVANS *Leicestersh. Words.*

2. A kind of artificial salmon-fly.

1867 F. FRANCIS *Angling* x. (1880) 349 The Goldfinch. A very showy, striking fly.

3. *slang.* †**a.** One who has plenty of gold. *Obs.*

1603 DEKKER *Wonderfull Yeare* Wks. (Grosart) I. 112 Lazarus lay groning at euery mans doore: mary no Diues was within to send him a crum, (for all your Gold-finches were fled to the woods). **1609** —— *Lanthorne & Candle-L.*

Wks. (Grosart) III. 222. *a* **1700** B. E. *Dict. Cant. Crew*, *Gold-finch*, he that has alwaies a Purse or Cod of Gold in his Fob.

b. A gold coin; a guinea or sovereign.

1602 MIDDLETON *Blurt* IV. i. F 2 a, If this Gold-finch, that with sweet notes flyes..Can worke. **1639** SHIRLEY *Gentl. Venice* III. i, Marcello, whom I employed..To my most costive uncle, for some goldfinches. **1780** STEEVENS *Shaks. Plays*. Suppl. II. 279 *note*, The vulgar still call our gold coins, gold-finches. **1828** *Sporting Mag.* XXI. 367 He was backed by a number of individuals not overburthened with goldfinches. **1842** *Punch* II. 168 Two Canaries = one Goldfinch. **1896** *Pall Mall Mag.* May 10 You've not a crown in your pocket, and ours a-bulging out with goldfinches.

'gold-,finder.

1. One whose occupation it is to find gold.

1631 WEEVER *Anc. Funeral Mon.* 51 The graue-rakers, these gold-finders are called theeues. **1749** FIELDING *Tom Jones* VI. i, The truth-finder and the gold-finder. **1852** EARP *Gold Col. Australia* viii. 130 The camp of the goldfinders was called the city of Ophir.

†**2.** A scavenger. *Obs.*

1611 COTGR., *Guigneron*, a Gold-finder, a Dung-farmer. **1685** CROWNE *Sir Courtly Nice* II. 10 A gold-finder, Madam? look into jakes for bits o' money? I had a spirit above it. **1724** SWIFT *Wood's Execution*, *Gold-finder*. I'll make him stink. **1755** *Man* No. 13. 6 My cart..might, in imitation of..the gold-finders, wait at the doors of persons of fashion, to take in a loading privately..when the prying vulgar are asleep. [**1896** *Warwicksh. Gloss.* s.v. *Gold-dust*, The name gold-finder or gold-farmer..still lingers in Shrewsbury.]

†**'gold-,finer.** *Obs.* A refiner of gold.

1483 *Cath. Angl.* 161/2 Golde Fynere. **1530** PALSGR. 226/1 Goldefynor, *affineur*. **1555** EDEN *Decades* 335 Dysshe of wod lyke vnto those which the golde finers vse. **1668** ST. SERFE *Tarugo's Wiles* III. i, Two Houses of Pleasure..one belongs to the Gold-finer of the Seraglio.

'gold-fish, goldfish. †**a.** A fish with golden markings found in the South Seas (*obs.*). **b.** A small golden-red fish (*Cyprinus auratus*) of the carp family, a native of China, commonly bred and kept for ornament in tanks, glass globes, etc. (see quot. 1802). **gold-fish bowl**, (*a*) a bowl, usually a glass globe, in which gold-fish are kept (cf. GLOBE *sb.* 6 b); (*b*) something resembling such a bowl; *spec.* a place or situation affording no privacy (see also quot. 1942). **c.** = GARIBALDI 2.

1698 FROGER *Voy.* 45 The Gold-Fish and the Bonite continually make War with them in the Water. **1712** E. COOKE *Voy. S. Sea* 342 The Gold Fish is very beautiful. **1731** MEDLEY *Kolben's Cape G. Hope* II. 192 The Cape-Gold-Fish is about a Foot and a Half long. **1791** W. BARTRAM *Carolina* 44 The gold-fish is about the size of the anchovy. **1802** BINGLEY *Anim. Biog.* (1813) III. 86 Gold Fish are natives of China..They were first introduced into England about the year 1691. **1873** B. STEWART *Conserv. Force* i. 8 A glass globe containing numerous goldfish. [**1904** 'SAKI' *Reginald* 115, I might have been a gold-fish in a glass bowl for all the privacy I got.] **1935** M. SULLIVAN *Our Times* VI. viii. 150 The situation was the more trying because it was as plain to the newspapers as to Harding and Daugherty —their relations for several months were carried on in a goldfish bowl. **1941** J. P. MARQUAND *H. M. Pulham, Esq.* xxxi. 304 She was..telling Mrs. Jones.. not to let the maid pick up the broken pieces of the goldfish bowl. **1942** BERREY & VAN DEN BARK *Amer. Thes. Slang* §466/11 *Gold-fish bowl*, the room in which the third degree is administered. **1951** *Sat. Even. Post* 22 Dec. 44/4 The towermen in their elevated air-conditioned goldfish bowls. **1958** R. STOW *To Islands* viii. 158 It's certainly not going to be easy for us, the white people. Living in a goldfish bowl is the last thing we'd do for fun. **1965** *Listener* 20 May 730/1 The White House has always been a goldfish bowl, but under Presidents Kennedy and Johnson it has become an educational theatre as well. **1966** J. DOS PASSOS *Best Times* (1968) iv. 148 They served excellent beer in glasses the size of goldfish bowls. **1969** *Guardian* 26 Mar. 2/2 President Nixon..disclosed his belief that progress towards a Vietnam settlement would come only through private talks... Serious negotiations could not take place in a goldfish bowl, he said.

'gold-foil. Gold beaten out into a thin sheet.

As a mod. technical term, *gold-foil* denotes a thicker sheet than *gold-leaf*.

1398 [see FOIL *sb.*[1] 4]. *c* **1440** *Promp. Parv.* 202/1 Gooldfuyle. **1499** *Acc.* in T. Sharp *Dissert. Cov. Myst.* (1825) 35 For colours and gold foyle & sylver foyle for iiij capps. **1587** GOLDING *De Mornay* x. 137 Such cloath, wire, or gold-foile, as no man would deeme to haue come of so grosse a matter. **1601** HOLLAND *Pliny* II. 529 A kind of gum or size to lay vnder gold-foile for to guild timber. **1892** W. S. GILBERT *Foggerty's Fairy* 273 A spacious apartment blazing with gas and gold-foil.

†**'gold-hoard.** *Obs.* A hoard of gold; treasure.

c **825** *Vesp. Psalter* cxxxiv. 7 Se forðlædeð windas of goldhordum his. *a* **1000** *Elene* 790 (Gr) þæt goldhord..þæt yldum wæs lange behyded. *c* **1175** *Lamb. Hom.* 109 þe bihut his gold hord on heouene riche. *a* **1225** *Ancr. R.* 150 Golhord is god dede, þet is to heouene iefned. **13..** *Seuyn Sag.* (W.) 2004 Undir the pyler..Ther hys a golde hord bygunne.

goldilocks ('gəʊldɪlɒks). Also 6–9 **goldylocks**, (6 **goldilocx**, 9 *north.* **goudy-locks**). [f. GOLDY *a.* + LOCK *sb.*]

†**1.** Golden hair; app. vaguely used for a woman's hair in general. *Obs.*

1566 STUDLEY *Seneca's Agamemnon* III. Fj, The soft and gentle goldilocks starte vp of her affright. **1589** FLEMING *Virg. Georg.* IV. 68 Their gay and gallant goldilockes Spred all about their necks so white. **1589** RIDER *Eng.-Lat. Dict.*, Goldilockes, or womans haire, which lieth out before over their fore heades, *capronæ*. **1593** B. BARNES *Parthenophil* Sonn. xix, She matcheth..In goldie-lockes bright Tytan. **1596** LODGE *Marg. Amer.* G, Hauing her goldilocks tied vp with loose chaines of gold, and Diamondes.

2. One who has golden hair. Also as a person's name.

c **1550** *Pryde & Abuse Wom.* 117 in Hazl. *E.P.P.* IV. 239 Huffa! goldylocx, joly lusty goldylocx; A wanton tricker is come to towne. **1591** SYLVESTER *Du Bartas* I. iv. 400 Pure goldy-locks, Sol, States'-friend, etc. **1615** SIR E. HOBY *Curry-combe* i. 49 To set out the picture like a Goldylocks, with Rebatoes, red Sattin Petticotes, and loose Gownes. *a* **1687** COTTON *Poet. Wks.* (1765) 55 My Goldy Locks (quoth she) my Joy, My pretty little tyny Boy. **1889** M. WRIGHT in A. Lang *Blue Fairy Bk.* 193 The Story of Pretty Goldilocks. **1930** *Observer* 25 May 15 But why is Mr. Max Montesole in Cassio such a quaint goldilocks?

3. A name given to various plants, esp. **a.** *Ranunculus auricomus*, a species of the buttercup; **b.** 'A modern (translated) book-name for *Chrysocoma Linosyris*' (Britten & Holland 1879); **c.** *Helichrysum Stœchas*; †**d.** (in Lyte) *Polytrichum commune*; **e.** *Trollius europæus*.

1578 LYTE *Dodoens* III. lxxi. 414 We may cal it in English Goldylockes Polytrichon. **1597** GERARDE *Herbal* II. ccvii. (1633) 647 Golden Floure gentle or goldilockes also called God's floure. **1625** B. JONSON *Pan's Anniv.*, Bring..Fair ox-eye, goldy-locks, and columbine. **1650** W. How *Phytologia Brit.* 102 *Ranunculus auricomus*..Goldylocks. **1658** ROWLAND *Moufet's Theat. Ins.* 902 Others yet advise to sow Goldilocks near where they [bees] are. **1832** J. HODGSON *Northumbld.* II. II. 459 The plant which, as a boy, I was taught to call Locken Gowen, or Goudy Locks, is the *Trolius europea* of Botanists. **1880** W. LEIGHTON *Shaks. Dream* 52 Blue hyacinths..And goldilocks.

†**'golding**[1]. *Obs.* [f. GOLD[1] + -ING[3].

The form still occurs in north midland dialects as a name of the marigold, in Kent of the ladybird.]

1. A gold coin.

c **1580** JEFFERIE *Bugbears* I. i. 77 in *Archiv Stud. d. neu. Spr.* (1897) XCVIII. 306 His goldinges that he kepes in prison.

2. A kind of apple. (See GOLDLING.)

1589 RIDER *Eng.-Lat. Dict.* s.v. *Apple*, Summer Goldings ..Winter Goldings. **1648–60** HEXHAM *Dutch Dict.*, *Guldelingh*, A Golding, an apple so called.

'golding[2]. [f. the surname: see quot. 1798.] A kind of hop. Also ***golding hop, vine***.

1798 W. MARSHALL *Rur. Econ. S. Counties* I. III. xxvi. 183 The 'golding' has, of late years, been in high repute. It is a sub-variety..of the Canterbury; which was raised by a man still living (1790) Mr. Golding, of the Malling quarter of the district [of Maidstone]. **1810** —— *Review W. Eng.* 378 There are two [varieties of hops]..in more particular esteem, both with the planter and merchant; the Golding Vine..and the Mathon White. **1900** C. SALTER tr. *Gross's Hops* 39 The Goldings are the best class of English red hops. **1902** *Times* 5 Sept. 2/5 The golding hops are reported to be developing slowly. **1959** A. CRONK *Eng. Hops Gloss.* 15 *Golding's*,..the name given to a category embracing the choicest English varieties. *Ibid.*, *Golding variety*, one of a category of varieties, having affinity to Golding's, but somewhat inferior.

goldish ('gəʊldɪʃ), *a.* [f. GOLD[1] + -ISH.] Somewhat golden.

1398 TREVISA *Barth. De P.R.* XVI. lxviii. (1495) 574 A nother kynde of marbyl..is sprongen wyth goldyssh speckes. *c* **1430** LYDG. *Chorle & Byrde* (Roxb.) 15 All is not golde that sheweth goldish hewe. **1577** DEE *Relat. Spir.* I. (1659) 174 There remaineth on the Table a goldish shine. **1683** PETTUS *Fleta Min.* II. i. 100 Further, all Goldish oars (which are commonly sandy) have good Dube gold. **1703** MOXON *Mech. Exerc.* 61 You will see the Colour change by degrees, coming to a light goldish Colour, then to a dark goldish Colour. **1774** MRS. DELANY *Lett.* Ser. II. II. 47 A little brassish, coperish, goldish thread-like stuff.

Hence †**'goldishness**.

1671 J. WEBSTER *Metallogr.* xiii. 203 Silver metalline Ore is wrought many times in a red goldishness.

goldite ('gəʊldaɪt). *U.S.* [f. GOLD[1] + -ITE[1]. Cf. SILVERITE.] An advocate of a gold standard.

1878 *Nation* 21 Feb. 126/1 They were 'goldites'. **1886** *Congress. Rec.* 24 June 6090/2 It does not frighten me to see Goldites voting to preserve greenbacks. **1904** *Westm. Gaz.* 27 Oct. 2/3 In some States there were only two sets of electors, these being practically Silverites and Goldites.

gold lace: see LACE *sb.*

'gold-laced, *a.* Ornamented with gold lace.

1630 J. TAYLOR (Water P.) *Wks.* II. 145/2 Amidst the guarded troope Of gold-lac'd Actors. **1686** *Lond. Gaz.* No. 2126/4 A gold-lac'd Coat. **1787** SIR J. HAWKINS *Life Johnson* 199 Johnson..appeared in a gold-laced waistcoat. **1838** DICKENS *O. Twist* ii, Oliver, firmly grasping his [Mr. Bumble's] gold-laced cuff, trotted beside him.

fig. **1850** CARLYLE *Latter-d. Pamph.* v. (1872) 180 In these shabby gold-laced days. **1871** PALGRAVE *Lyr. Poems* 50 E'en in the palace recesses The gold-laced conscience was stirr'd.

b. Applied to a variety of Polyanthus, the blossoms of which have a yellow border.

1878 *R. Thompson's Gardener's Assist.* 758 The gold-laced varieties [of Polyanthus].

gold leaf. (Often *hyphened.*)

a. (with pl. *gold leaves.*) A minute quantity of gold, beaten out into an extremely thin sheet, averaging from 3 to 3½ inches square. **b.** (sing. only.) Gold in this form used in gilding, etc.

1727–41 CHAMBERS *Cycl.*, *Gold-leaf*, or beaten Gold, is gold beaten with a hammer into exceedingly thin leaves... Each book ordinarily contains twenty-five gold leaves. **1799** G. SMITH *Laboratory* I. 195 You may lay on gold leaves with brandy. **1811** A. T. THOMSON *Lond. Disp.* (1818) 44 The finest silver leaf being only one-third thicker than gold leaf. **1839** URE *Dict. Arts* 611 Skins prepared from ox-gut are now interposed between each gold leaf. **1884** *Chamb. Jrnl.* 10 May 294/1 A mandarin..is graciously allowed to choke himself by swallowing gold-leaf.

c. ***gold leaf electrometer, electroscope, galvanoscope***, appliances in which gold leaf is used as a detector.

1812 SIR H. DAVY *Chem. Philos.* 168 An insulated gold leaf electrometer. **1870** R. M. FERGUSON *Electr.* 53 A gold leaf electroscope.

goldless ('gəʊldlɪs), *a.* [f. GOLD[1] + -LESS.] Without gold.

c **1386** CHAUCER *Shipman's T.* 290 But goldlees for to be, it is no game. **1823** BYRON *Island* I. x, The goldless age, where gold disturbs no dreams. **1896** W. RALEIGH *Some Authors* (1923) 146 He belongs, by right of kinship, to the 'threadbare, goldless genealogy' of those who indulge themselves with that most costly dish—speech for its own sake. **1900** *The King* 4 Aug. 135 A goldless gold region.

†**'goldling.** *Obs.*[−1] [f. GOLD[1] + -LING; cf. Du. *guldelingh* in Hexham.] = GOLDING[1] 2.

1655 MOUFFET & BENNETT *Health's Impr.* xxii. 196 Winter-goldlings [are] *Scandiana Plinii*.

†**'goldly,** *a.* *Obs. rare*[−1]. [f. GOLD[1] + -LY[1].] Resembling gold, golden.

c **1430** *Life St. Kath.* (1884) 48 A crowne shynynge al in goldly colour.

gold-mine. Also **gold mine**. A mine from which gold is obtained. Also *fig.* a source of wealth; esp. a source of abundant income or profit.

1483 *Cath. Angl.* 161/2 A Goldemyne. **1530** PALSGR. 226/1 Goldemyne, *miniere a or*. **1627** MAY *Lucan* III. Ej b, The land, that from gold-mines letts Hermus goe, And rich Pactolus. **1732** LEDIARD *Sethos* II. VII. 19 Mines of iron.. were much scarcer in these climates than gold-mines. **1833** TENNYSON *Dream Fair Wom.* 274 From the deep Gold-mines of thought to lift the hidden ore That glimpses. **1856** EMERSON *Eng. Traits*, *Ability* Wks. (Bohn) II. 42 There is no gold mine of any importance, but there is more gold in England than in all other countries. **1882** 'THORMANBY' *Famous Racing Men* 81 Mendicant..was destined to prove a 'gold mine', for ten years afterwards she brought her owner £80,000 through her famous son. **1888** J. A. FROUDE *Eng. in W. Indies* v. 56 The island was a gold mine to the Attorney-General. **1894** *Vermont Agric. Rep.* XIV. 101 We have a gold mine in our Morgan stock if we only continue to breed and develop them. **1943** E. O'NEILL *Moon for Misbegotten* (1952) 65 This farm has suddenly become a gold mine. **1967** *Listener* 22 June 829/2 These two volumes will certainly be a gold mine for future unofficial biographers. **1971** *Sunday Times* 28 Nov. 40/8 Even as he was hailing the 'gold-mine' he had struck in starting the Mail he was venting anxiety lest advertising should threaten his position as 'sole possessor'.

goldney, -nie, -ny: see GOLDENEY.

goldsmith ('gəʊldsmɪθ).

1. A worker in gold; one who fashions gold into jewels, ornaments, articles of plate, etc.

c **1000** ÆLFRIC *Gen.* iv. 22 Tubalcain, se wæs egðer ʒe goldsmið ʒe isensmið. *a* **1225** *Ancr. R.* 236 Al so alse þe goldsmið clenseð þet gold iðe fure. **1387** TREVISA *Higden* (Rolls) VII. 53 He telleþ þat Donston..made in a tyme a chalys by goldsmethes craft. **1464** *Mann. & Househ. Exp.* (Roxb.) 253 Item, payd to the goldsmythe that made the bokelys..x. s. iiij. d. **1526** *Pilgr. Perf.* (W. de W. 1531) 108 b, There was neuer yet goldsmyth that onely with betynges of the hammer coude make a fayre ymage. **1681** PRIDEAUX *Lett.* (Camden) 98 The Alderman would not vouch for payment, and thereon the goldsmith would not prepare the plate. **1857** RUSKIN *Pol. Econ. Art* i. (1868) 62 True goldsmith's work, when it exists, is generally the means of education of the greatest painters and sculptors of the day.

¶ Down to the 18th c. these tradesmen acted as bankers.

a **1674** CLARENDON *Contin. Life* (1759) 314 They [Bankers] were for the most Part Goldsmiths. **1690** CHILD *Disc. Trade* (1694) 33 His Majesty..has been enforced to give above the usual rates to goldsmiths. **1713** STEELE *Guardian* No. 2 ⁋1 He gave me a Bill upon his Goldsmith in London. **1719** W. WOOD *Surv. Trade* 340 All our large Payments are made generally in Exchequer Bills, Bank or Goldsmith notes. **1822** SCOTT *Nigel* iv, I am a goldsmith, and live by lending money as well as by selling plate.

2. Short for *goldsmith-beetle*.

1863 *Rep. U.S. Commiss. Agric.* 298 (Cent.) Large beetles, such as the common Cetonias or goldsmiths.

3. *attrib.* and *Comb.*, as †*goldsmith-craft*, †*-work*; **goldsmith-beetle**, a large scarabæid beetle (*Cotalpa lanigera*) having wing-covers of golden lustre; also, *Cetonia aurata* or other species.

1881 *Cassell's Nat. Hist.* V. 328 The *Rutelinæ*, or *Goldsmith Beetles. *c* **1449** PECOCK *Repr.* I. x. 50 The sporier and the cuteler be leerned in thilk point of *goldsmyth craft which is gilding. **1506** *Paston Lett.* No. 953 III. 404 A hatt of *goldsmyth worke. *c* **1530** *Let.* in *Ld. Berners' Froiss.* Editor's Pref. (1812) 18 The king..well apparelled in coots and clokes of gould, and gouldsmythe worke.

Hence **'goldsmithess** *nonce-wd.*, a female goldsmith. †**'goldsmithy, 'gold,smith(e)ry**, the art or trade of a goldsmith; goldsmith's work; articles made by the goldsmith.

c **1386** CHAUCER *Knt.'s T.* 1640 Harneys..so riche, and wroght so weel Of goldsmythrye, of browdynge, and of steel. *c* **1430** *Pilgr. Lyf Manhode* IV. xvi. (1869) 183, I am, quod she, þe goldsmithesse and þe forgeresse of heuene. *c* **1449** PECOCK *Repressor* I. x. 50 As if oon man had lernid the al hool craft of goldsmythi and the al hool craft of cutleri. **1483** CAXTON *Gold. Leg.* 189/2 He knew wel the crafte & arte of goldsmytherye. **1647** LILLY *Chr. Astrol.* cxlix. 632 Professions conversant in fire, whether it be in Smithery or working in Goldsmithery. **1873** BROWNING *Red Cott. Nt.-cap* 132 Their actual lord By dint of diamond dealing, goldsmithry. **1883** *Athenæum* 2 June 707 Works in iron, pewter, and bronze, as well as goldsmithery.

ˈgoldspink. *Sc.* and *dial.* Also **gowdspink.** [f. GOLD[1] + SPINK. Cf. *goldfinch* and Sw. dial *gulspink* (*gul* yellow), the yellow-hammer and titmouse.]

1. The goldfinch. Chiefly *Sc.*

1513 DOUGLAS *Æneis* XII. Prol. 240 Goldspynk and lyntquhyte fordynnand the lyft. **1549** *Compl. Scot.* VI. 39 The grene serene sang sueit, quhen the gold spynk chantit. **1724** RAMSAY *Tea-t. Misc.* (1775) I. 21 Nansy's to the Green-wood gane, To hear the gowdspink chatt'ring. **1787** BURNS *Humble Petit. Bruar Water* vi, The gowdspink, music's gayest child. **1882** *Lanc. Gloss.*, *Goldspink*, *gowdspink*, a goldfinch.

2. *dial.* The yellow-hammer.

1788 W. MARSHALL *Yorksh.* Gloss., *Goldspink*, the bird, yellowhammer. **1864** ATKINSON *Prov. Names Birds.*

gold stick, ˈgold-stick.

a. The gilt rod carried on state occasions by the colonel of the Life-Guards or the captain of the Gentlemen-at-arms. **b.** The bearer of the gilt rod; also *gold-stick in waiting*.

1804 G. ROSE *Diaries* (1860) II. 152 Lord Pelham..came out from his Majesty with the Gold stick, as Captain of the Band of Yeomen of the Guards. **1812** *Ann. Reg.* 147 The Earl of Harrington, gold-stick in waiting. **1844** *Regul. & Ord. Army* 28 The Gold Stick will continue to perform the Duty of that Office. **1863** THACKERAY *Wks.* (1872) X. 262 Goldstick in waiting is even more splendid. **1882** *Harper's Mag.* LXV. 163 Gold-sticks have resigned because of difference of opinion with her Majesty's government.

ˈgold-ˌwasher.

†**a.** One who 'sweats' gold coins (*obs.*). **b.** One who washes auriferous soil to separate the gold. **c.** An appliance for obtaining gold by washing.

c **1515** *Cocke Lorell's B.* (Percy Soc.) 11 Money baterers, Golde washers, tomblers, fogelers. **1683** PETTUS *Fleta Min.* II. ii. 102 Gold-Washers who go abroad in the Country for Gold-washing, and get their Livelihood by it. **1875** KNIGHT *Dict. Mech.* s.v., Gold-washers are of various kinds.. The pan, the rocking-cradle [etc.].

So **ˈgold-wash**, a place where gold-washing is carried on; **ˈgold-washing**, (*a*) the process of obtaining gold by washing; (*b*) = *gold-wash* (chiefly in *pl.*).

1683 Gold-washing [see above]. **1796** MORSE *Amer. Geog.* II. 241 The gold-wash of the Bannat yields upwards of 1000 ducats. **1799** W. TOOKE *View Russian Emp.* I. 98 The gold-works or gold-washes of Ekaterinenburg. **1875** KNIGHT *Dict. Mech.* s.v. *Gold-washers*, Edrisi..speaks of the employment of quicksilver in the gold-washings made by the negroes of Sofala as a long-known practice.

‖**goldwasser** (ˈgɔldvasər). [G., lit. 'gold water'.] A liqueur originally made at Danzig (see quot. 1958).

[**1848** MRS. GASKELL *Mary Barton* II. xiv. 180 He produced a square bottle of smuggled spirits, labelled 'Golden Wasser', from a corner cupboard.] **1920** G. SAINTSBURY *Notes on Cellar-Bk.* ix. 140, I hope that the rather unsettled fate of Dantzic will not dry up the fount of Goldwasser, which pleased sight and smell and taste alike. **1945** C. S. FORESTER *Commodore* xviii. 198 Bavarian beer, Swedish schnapps, Danzig goldwasser—he had drunk of them all. **1958** A. L. SIMON *Dict. Wines* 83/2 *Goldwasser*.. is a highly rectified spirit, flavoured with aniseed, cinnamon, and a number of herbs and spices... Its outstanding feature is that it contains a large number of very small pieces of gold leaf or yellow and gold-like pieces.

ˈgoldwater. = prec.

1877 E. S. DALLAS *Kettner's Bk. of Table* 152 Dantzic.. has produced the liqueur which is the most beautiful of all to look at—gold-water, a bright colourless liquid like water, with chips of gold-leaf floating in it. **1965** R. MANHEIM tr. *Grass's Dog Years* I. 52 A little glass of goldwater.

Goldwaterism (ˈgəʊldwɔːtərɪz(ə)m). [f. the name *Goldwater* + -ISM.] Rigid conservatism as represented by the views and policies of the American Republican politician Barry Morris *Goldwater* (b. 1909); adherence to or support for such conservatism. Hence **ˈGoldwaterite**, an adherent of Goldwater or Goldwaterism. Also *transf.*

1960 *Nation* 18 June 531/3 How deep is Goldwaterism? **1963** *Sunday Times* 24 Nov. 3/3 He [*sc.* Kennedy] planned to take sharp aim at Goldwaterism. **1964** *Listener* 25 June 1018/1 He..tried in public to belittle the difference between the moderates and the Goldwaterites. **1964** *Ibid.* 24 Sept. 471/3 Mr. Calder-Marshall seems to be a Goldwaterite where modern art is concerned. His 'vulgar economic realities' are the cloak for a conspiracy-theory, and he is disappointed that I don't subscribe to it. **1965** *Spectator* 22 Jan. 102/1 Goldwaterism—that is to say, far-out conservatism in general—has been the butt of Broadway humour for so long. **1970** *Times* 9 May 2/1 Let me suggest ..that we solve our..British problems in a British way, not by the importation of Goldwaterism.

†**gold-weight.** *Obs.*

a. *pl.* Scales for weighing gold. **b.** *sing.* Exact weight, such as is aimed at in weighing gold.

to the gold weight(s, with the greatest exactitude; *to be (put) gold-weight*, to be (put) in equipoise.

c **1500** *Inventory* in *Paston Lett.* No. 954. III. 408 Item, a payre of gold weghtes in a case, ijs. **1530** PALSGR. 226/1 Goldeweightes, *trebuchet*. **1621** FLETCHER *Wild Goose Chase* I. iii, To one that weighs her words and her behaviours In the gold weights of discretion! *a* **1625** —— *Love's Pilgr.* I. i, A Master of Ceremonies; But a man, beleeve it, That knew his place to the gold weight. **1630** B. JONSON *New Inn* II. ii, An host, Who should be King at Armes, and ceremonies, In his owne house! know all, to the goldweights. **1683** R. BATTELL *Vulg. Errors* 91 If Nature alone could turn the Scale without being put gold-weight by Grace, it were true, but seeing it could not raise the Scale to this equipoize without the assistance of Grace, it is false. **1727** BOYER *Fr.-Eng. Dict.* s.v., That prejudice is sufficient to turn the Scale, where it was Gold-weight before [F. *qui auparavant étoit comme en Equilibre*].

ˈgold-work, -works.

a. *sing.* The art or process of working in gold. **b.** Work done in gold; goldsmith's work. **c.** *pl.* A place where the washing, mining, or smelting of gold is carried on.

1683 PETTUS *Fleta Min.* II. ii. 102 Gold-Washers..have for the Gold-works a special proving. *Ibid.* 109 The Floor is driven over the plain Hearth with Woollen..stuff (as above, where the Gold-work hath been taught). **1722** WOLLASTON *Relig. Nat.* ix. 201 The gold-works in the confines of Egypt. **1838** THIRLWALL *Greece* V. xlii. 201 Datus was proverbial.. for the richness of its gold-works. **1844** LD. HOUGHTON *Palm Leaves* 140 Such gold-work as fairies fabricate. **1883** A. H. CHURCH *Precious Stones* iii. 23 It is employed for covering fine gold-work and miniatures.

So **ˈgold-worker**, one engaged in the obtaining or working of gold; **ˈgold-workings**, a place or places where gold-mining or -washing is carried on.

1683 PETTUS *Fleta Min.* xlvi. 216 Goldsmiths and other Gold-workers. **1852** A. RYLAND *Assay Gold & S.* 142 A Petition was brought into Parliament, by the Goldworkers of London. **1872** R. B. SMYTH *Mining Statist.* 41 Profitable gold-workings have been opened. **1882** H. DE WINDT *Equator* ii. 29 An attack was to be made by the gold-workers on Kuching. **1892** G. LAMBERT *Gold & Silversmith's Art* 49 To study with a goldsmith..as a goldworker and chaser.

Goldwynism (ˈgəʊldwɪnɪz(ə)m). [f. the name *Goldwyn* + -ISM.] A witticism uttered by or typical of Samuel G. Goldwyn, American film producer (1882–1974), esp. one that revolves round a contradiction, a colourful image, etc.

1937 *Sat. Evening Post* 8 May 82/2 'It sounds like Sam Goldwyn.' Chaplin said, 'We'll pin it on Sam,' and he repeated it until it became a world-famous Goldwynism. *Ibid.*, A kind of Goldwyn scholarship has grown up; there are specialists who can detect fake Goldwynisms as an archeologist can spot a phony Greek vase. **1938** I. GOLDBERG *Wonder of Words* xii. 245 In a phrase that has become humorously popular, and that has been attributed to the moving-picture producer Sam Goldwyn, renowned for his so-called Goldwynisms, the ideas of exclusion and inclusion have been telescoped. 'Include me out!' he is said to have exclaimed. **1959** *Globe & Mail* (Toronto) 24 Sept. 34/1 A Goldwynism..is a slight twisting of a word or a slight misstatement that makes an ordinary remark sound wittily off-beat. **1967** *Sunday Mail* (Brisbane) 13 Aug. 30 He [*sc.* S. Goldwyn] gave a new word to the English language: Goldwynism, meaning those delightful malapropisms such as: 'in two words—impossible', 'verbal contracts are not worth the paper they're written on', and 'I'll give you a definite maybe'. **1969** *Daily Tel.* 5 Nov. 17/3 He will be remembered as the master of innumerable Goldwynisms, many of which, he says, were invented by comedians and pinned on him.

ˈgoldy, *sb. dial.* Also **go(o)ldie, gouldie.** [f. GOLD[1] + -Y[4].] **a.** The goldfinch. **b.** The yellow-hammer.

1802 G. MONTAGU *Ornith. Dict.* (1833) 214 Goldfinch.. Gold-Spink..Gooldie. **1864** ATKINSON *Prov. Names Birds*, *Goldie*, *Golder*, Yellow Hammer. **1877** *Holderness Gloss.*, *Goldey*, a goldfinch, a yellow-hammer. **1893** *Northumbld. Gloss.*, *Gooldy*..The goldfinch.

goldy (ˈgəʊldɪ), *a.* Also **gowdy.** [f. GOLD[1] + -Y[1].]

a. Golden. Also, gold-like; resembling gold in colour or sheen.

c **1450** *MS. Cantab.* Ff. I. 6, lf. 12 (Halliw.) Goldy gravel in the stremys rich. **1593** [see GOLDILOCKS 1]. **1594** *Zepheria* xxxiii. Fj, There, in her goldie leaues my loue is writ. *a* **1861** T. WINTHROP *John Brent* (1883) iii. 27 'I don't think that quartz looks quite so goldy as it did at a distance' said he. **1893** *Northumbld. Gloss.*, *Goldy*, golden. **1904** R. BRIDGES *Demeter* 81 Now maids playfully dance o'er enamel'd meadows, And with goldy blossom deck forehead and bosom. **1920** GALSWORTHY *Awakening* 35 There were silver threads in her dark goldy hair. **1969** 'J. MORRIS' *Fever Grass* v. 57 The room was illuminated with a soft, goldy-bronze glow.

b. *Comb.*, as **goldy-brown, -locked** (see also GOLDILOCKS); also **goldy-stone** (see quot. 1861).

1605 B. JONSON *Volpone* I. i, It [the soul]..made quick transmigration To goldy-lock't Euphorbvs. **1861** C. W. KING *Ant. Gems* i. 63 The true Aventurine, or Goldie-stone, is a brownish semi-transparent quartz, full of specks of yellow mica. **1874** MRS. WHITNEY *We Girls* viii. 161 That piece of goldy-brown damask.

goldylocks: see GOLDILOCKS.

†**gole,** *sb.*[1] *Obs.*[−1] [? = OE. *gál* wantonness, etc.] ? = GOLENESS.

? *a* **1500** *Chester Pl.* (Shaks. Soc.) I. 229 This frecke [Dives] begines to reme and yole That makes greate dole for gole That he loved wel before.

†**gole,** *sb.*[2] *Obs. rare.* [? Var. of GOOL, GULL.] A stream, channel, ditch.

? *a* **1400** *Morte Arth.* 3725 Than sir Gawane the gude a galaye he takys, And glides vp at a gole. **1601** HOLLAND *Pliny* I. 66 Although it [the River Po] be deriued and drawne into other riuers and goles, betweene Rauenna and Atium.. yet [etc.].

†**gole,** *a. Obs.* Forms: 1 **gál,** 3 **gal,** 3 **gol,** 6 **goel,** 6–7 **gole.** [OE. *gál* = OS. *gêl* (MDu., Du. *geil*, popularly also *gail*, *geel*), OHG. (MHG., G.) *geil*, Goth. **gail-s* (whence *gailjan* to cheer, make glad), perh. cognate with L. *hilaris*, from a root **ghil*.]

1. Merry, wanton, lascivious, lustful.

c **888** K. ÆLFRED *Boeth.* xxxvii. §4 þam unᵹestæþþeᵹan & ðam hælᵹan [*v.r.* galan]. *c* **900** tr. *Bæda's Hist.* v. xiv. [xiii.] (1891) 440 þurh ða godan gastas oðþe þurh ða galan. *c* **1200** ORMIN 1201 Gat iss..Gal deor & stinnkeþþ fule. *c* **1200** *Trin. Coll. Hom.* 31 þe gole me. *c* **1275** *XI Pains Hell* 56 in *O.E. Misc.* 148 Swich pyne heo þolie schal, þat wes of his fleysse to gal.

2. Of rank or luxuriant growth (cf. quot. 1674–91).

Hilman's statement, in his *Tusser Redivivus* (1710), that 'The goeler is the yellower, which are the best setts, old roots being red', is prob. a mere guess. Grose's '*Goel* or *Gole*, yellow. Essex and Suff.' is not otherwise authenticated, and is perh. derived from this very passage.

1573 TUSSER *Husb.* xlvi. (1878) 98 Hop rootes..The goeler and yonger the better I loue; well gutted and pared, the better they proue. **1674–91** RAY *S. & E.C. Words* 100 *Gole*, big, large, full and florid. It is said of rank Corn or Grass, that the Leaf, Blade, or Ear is *goal*: so of a young Cockrel.

3. As *adv.* in comparative: More copiously.

1606 WARNER *Alb. Eng.* XVI. cv. 413 Nor goler blead his wounde but that her shee teares as fast.

Hence †**golelich** *a.* [*-lich*, -LY[1]], lustful; †**golehead** [-HEAD; cf. MDu., Du. *geilheid*, MHG., G. *geilheit*], lust.

c **1000** ÆLFRIC *Hom.* II. 156 Ælc gallic ontendnys wearð.. adwæsced. *c* **1175** *Lamb. Hom.* 145 Summe men luuieð.. galiche lectres and luðere lastes. *Ibid.* 149 Hwenne þe mon him biþenchþ þet he haueð on galiche dede to muche god iwreþed. *c* **1200** *Trin. Coll. Hom.* 13 þat man þe spuse haueð, his golliche deden wið-teo. *c* **1250** *Gen. & Ex.* 534 Golhed hunkinde he gunnen don.

gole, obs. f. GOAL; var. GOLEE, GOLES, GOLL.

†**golee.** *Obs. rare.* Also 4–5 **gole,** *Sc.* **gule,** 5 **golye.** [a. OF. *golee*, *gulee*, etc. (F. *gueulée*) = Prov. *golada*, f. Rom. *gola* (OF. *gole*, *gule*, F. *gueule*):—L. *gula* mouth, throat + *-ata*: see -ADE.] A mouthful, throatful (of words).

Hoccleve's monosyllabic *gole* is perh. due to a misunderstanding of Chaucer's form.

c **1375** *Sc. Leg. Saints*, *Georgis* 638 And gret scilence be mad, til he Had sad þat wes ine his gule. *c* **1375** *Sc. Troy-bk.* II. 1478 He One þis wyse schewede hys gule. *c* **1381** CHAUCER *Parl. Foules* 556 (MS. Gg. 4. 27) Whan euerryche hadde his large gole [*v.rr.* golee, gule, *Caxton* golye] seyd. *c* **1422** HOCCLEVE *Jereslaus' Wife* 545 Anoon to me telle out al thy gole, For treewe and trusty be to thee y wole.

golem (ˈgəʊləm, ˈgɔɪləm). Also **Golem.** [ad. Yiddish *goylem*, f. Heb. *gōlem* shapeless mass.] In Jewish legend, a human figure made of clay, etc., and supernaturally brought to life; in extended use, an automaton, a robot.

1897 H. ILIOWIZI *In Pale* 171 The Baal-Shem smiled when he was told that the official version of the *Golem's* work proclaimed, that 'the accident was caused by a red bolt of lightning, which killed the people and destroyed the building'. **1925** H. SCHNEIDERMAN tr. *Bloch's Golem* 67 They formed out of clay the figure of a person,.. And the Golem lay before them. **1928** *Funk's Stand. Dict.*, *Golem*, a homunculus or figure made to represent a man: said to have been made and endowed with life by Reb Löw of Prague in the middle ages; hence, any one who acts like an automaton. **1942** B. BERENSON *One Year's Reading* 12 Feb. (1960) 24 What a belief that the great masses are pails into which you can pour any kind of slop.., and make them act like your golems! **1958** *Times* 5 Dec. 16/6 The ungainly bronze golems that stand around the Hanover Gallery. **1964** N. WIENER *God & Golem* (1965) (front jacket-flap), The ability of machines to learn, and their potential ability to reproduce themselves, lead to the question: 'Can we say that God is to Golem as man is to machine?' (In Jewish legend *Golem* is an embryo Adam, shapeless and not fully created, hence an automaton). *Ibid.* v. 55 Rabbi Löw of Prague, who claimed that his incantations blew breath of life into the Golem of clay. **1969** *Listener* 10 July 33/1 So let us forget about robots as serfs, which is the way they were originally proposed in Capek's *RUR* (*robotnik*, in Czech, means a serf). Such robots are essentially in the 'Golem' image and have no further interest except as ingenious dolls for grown-ups.

†**ˈgoleness.** *Obs.* [f. OE. *gálnys*, f. *gál* GOLE *a.* + -NESS.] Wantonness, lasciviousness.

a **1050** *Liber Scintill.* xxi. 89 Onᵹean galnysse..na framað onᵹeanwinnan ac fleon. *c* **1175** *Lamb. Hom.* 19 þe licome luuað..muchele etinge and drunkunge, and glanesse [? galnesse], and prude. *c* **1200** *Trin. Coll. Hom.* 37 Ðis oref stincð fule for his golnesse. *c* **1200** ORMIN 8015 Off galnesse skir and fre. *a* **1250** *Owl & Night.* 492 Al his thoȝt is of golnesse.

So †'**goleship** = GOLENESS.

c **1000** ÆLFRIC *Deut.* xx. 21 He begæþ unætas and oferdrincas and galscipe. *c* **1220** *Bestiary* 610 He arn so kolde of kinde ðat no golsipe is hem minde.

goles. ? *Obs.* Also 8 gole. [Deformation of GOD; cf. GOLLY and the U.S. forms *goldam, -darn, -dasted.*] Only in the exclamation **(by) goles** = (by) God (see GOD 13).

1734 FIELDING *Virgin unmasked* (1777) 3 Why then, by goles, I will tell you—I hate you. **1742** —— *Miss Lucy in Town* 9 By Gole, I believe I shall never be a fine Lady. **1788** *Poetry* in *Ann. Reg.* 185 Lord how the Beaux do stare! Goles, what a heap! **1837** LYTTON *E. Maltrav.* IV. vii, 'By goles, but you're a clever fellow.'

golet(te, obs. form of GULLET.

golf (gɒlf, gɒf), *sb.* Forms: 5 gouff, 6 goif(f, (golfe), 6–9 goff, 8–9 gowff, (8 golff, 9 golph), 5– golf. [Of obscure origin.

Commonly supposed to be an adoption of Du. *kolf, kolv-* (= G. *kolbe*, ON. *kólfr*, etc.), ' club', the name of the stick, club, or bat, used in several games of the nature of tennis, croquet, hockey, etc. But none of the Dutch games have been convincingly identified with golf, nor is it certain that *kolf* was ever used to denote the game as well as the implement, though the game was and is called *kolven* (the infinitive of the derived vb.). Additional difficulty is caused by the absence of any Scottish forms with initial *c* or *k*, and by the fact that golf is mentioned much earlier than any of the Dutch sports. Some mod. Sc. dialects have *gowf* 'a blow with the open hand', also vb. to strike.

The Sc. pronunciation is (gəʊf); the pronunciation (gɒf), somewhat fashionable in England, is an attempt to imitate this.]

a. A game, of considerable antiquity in Scotland, in which a small hard ball is struck with various clubs into a series of small cylindrical holes made at intervals, usually of a hundred yards or more, on a golf-course. The aim is to drive the ball into any one hole, or into all the holes successively, with the fewest possible strokes; commonly two persons, or two couples (a 'foursome'), play against each other.

1457 *Sc. Acts Jas. II* (1814) II. 48/2 And at þe fut bal ande þe golf be vtterly cryt downe and nocht vsyt. **1491** *Sc. Acts Jas. IV* (1814) II. 226/2 Fut bawis gouff or vthir sic vnproffitable sportis. **1538** *Aberdeen Reg.* V. 16 (Jam.) At the goiff. *a* **1575** *Diurn. Occurr.* (Bannatyne Club) 285 Certane horsmen of Edinburgh..past to the links of Leith, and.. tuck nyne burgessis of Edinburgh playand at the golf. *c* **1615** SIR S. D'EWES *Autobiog.* (1845) I. 48 Goff, tennis, or other boys' play. **1669** SHADWELL *R. Shepherdess* III. Wks. 1720 I. 260 We merrily play At Trap, and at Reels..At Goff, and at Stool-ball. **1711** RAMSAY *Elegy M. Johnston* 37 Whan we were weary'd at the gowff, Then Maggy Johnston's was our howff. **1771** SMOLLETT *Humph. Cl.* 8 Aug., Hard by, in the fields called the Links, the citizens of Edinburgh divert themselves at a game called Golf. **1806** MAR. EDGEWORTH *Mor. T., Gardener*, Colin's favourite holiday's diversion was playing at goff. **1815** SCOTT *Antiq.* ii, Rather than go to the golf or the change-house. **1867** KINGSLEY *Lett.* (1878) II. 251 Golf is the queen of games, if cricket is the king.

b. *attrib.* and *Comb.*, as ***golf bag, cap, -course, match, -player, -stick.*** Also **golf ball,** *(a)* a ball used in playing golf; *(b)* a colloquial name given to a spherical ball in certain kinds of electric typewriter on which all the type is mounted and which is caused to move to present the required symbol to the paper; **golf cart,** *(a)* a trolley for carrying golf clubs; *(b)* a motorized cart for transporting golfers and their equipment; **golf-club** (see CLUB I. 2 and II. 14); **golf-croquet** (see quot. 1960); **golf-drive,** a drive (DRIVE *sb.* 1 d) in golf; also, a similar stroke in Cricket; **golf-links,** the ground on which golf is played; **golf shot,** a shot in golf; **golf-widow,** a woman whose husband spends much of his spare time playing golf.

1895 *Army & Navy Co-op. Soc. Price List* 1446 The New *Golf Bag. Made same style as a cricket bag and large enough to take clubs, sling, balls, etc. **1921** *Daily Colonist* (Victoria, B.C.) 12 Oct. 16/3 (Advt.), English golf bag and clubs, also violin, for sale. **1545** *Aberdeen Reg.* V. 19 (Jam.) Thre dossoun and thre *goif bawis. **1637** in Cramond *Ann. Banff* (1891) I. 78 He sauld twa of the golf ballis to Thomas Urquhart. **1824** SCOTT *Redgauntlet* ch. i, I'll get him off on the instant, like a gowff ba'. **1966** *Gloss. Automated Typesetting* (ed. 2) 87 The IBM 72 electric typewriter characterized by its stationary platen and the concentration of all type characters on a single, interchangeable globe-shaped unit called a typing element..; sometimes referred to as the '*golf ball' typewriter. **1969** *Computers & Humanities* Sept. IV. I. 76 This arrangement allows more flexibility than a line printer, since one can change the type 'golfball' but it is very, very slow. **1970** *British Printer* Dec. 73/2 Hard copy is produced by the IBM 'golfball'. **1970** A. CAMERON et al. *Computers & O.E. Concordances* 32 There is a machine which will read the product of a selectric typewriter with a special golfball. **1897** *Sears, Roebuck Catal.* 235/3 Men's Fancy *Golf Caps at 21c. **1938** Golf cap [see BALDING *a.*]. **1951** *Golfers' Year* II. 136 (Advt.), No other *golf cart has the following unique features. **1963** *Golf World* Jan. 42/2 An American-style golf cart designed to carry both you and your clubs might seem of little use on Britain's courses. **1964** MRS. L. B. JOHNSON *White House Diary* 17 July (1970) 183 We had two swift and pleasant hours—and then..into the hangar where the white golf cart waited for us. **1971** 'D. HALLIDAY' *Dolly & Doctor Bird* iii. 28 He had already hired an electric golf-cart, a sorry sight. **1508** *Reg. Privy Seal Scot.* in Pitcairn *Crim. Trials* I. 108* Slaughter committed 'on suddantie', by the stroke of a '*golf-club'. **1753** *Scots Mag.* Aug. 421/2 The city of Edinburgh's silver goff-club was played for Aug. 4. **1800** A. CARLYLE *Autobiog.* 343 Garrick..had told us to bring golf clubs and balls. **1834** in R. Clark *Golf* (1875) 79 The Royal and Ancient Golf Club of St. Andrews. **1890** H. G. HUTCHINSON *Golf* 325 The Royal Liverpool Golf Club. **1931** T. S. ELIOT *Triumphal March*, Those are the golf club Captains, these the Scouts. **1965** A. S. GRAHAM *Golf Club* x. 64 Every golf club has its distinct golfing types. **1890** *Spectator* 4 Oct. 438/1 Long stretches of turf..are indispensable for the formation of *golf-courses. **1920** W. DEEPING *Second Youth* xv, To play them at *golf-croquet. **1960** E. P. C. COTTER *Tackle Croquet This Way* i. 13 A game of Golf Croquet. This is a game in which the hoops are treated as 'holes', as in Golf. The balls play in sequence.. and the first ball to run the hoop wins the hole and then all proceed to the next hoop. **1909** *Westm. Gaz.* 16 Feb. 12/2 In such a stroke as a *golf-drive the arm that reaches its fullest extension first is almost certain to be the dominating factor in regulating impact. **1913** *Daily Mail* 7 July 9/1 A plucky forcing batsman, rather partial to the on 'golf drive'. **1801** STRUTT *Sports & Past.* II. iii. 95 *Goff-lengths, or the spaces between the first and last holes, are sometimes extended to the distance of two or three miles. [**1877** J. BLACKWOOD *Let.* 27 Mar. in Geo. Eliot *Lett.* (1956) VI. 357, I am going..to North Berwick... It is a pretty country and there is a *Golfing Links.*] **1891** H. G. HUTCHINSON (*title*) Famous *golf links. **1919** WODEHOUSE *Damsel in Distress* xv. 174 He seemed to spend all his spare time frolicking with the man on the golf-links. **1857** J. BLACKWOOD *Let.* 30 Apr. in Geo. Eliot *Lett.* (1954) II. 324 If you saw me starting for a *Golf match you would think my tastes..simple, if not even childish. **1926** WODEHOUSE *Heart of Goof* ii. 60, I am playing a very important golf-match this morning. **1971** 'H. HOWARD' *Murder One* xiii. 157 He wanted to get away..because he had a golf match at two. **1881** *Sportsman's Year-bk.* 256 Prince Henry, the elder brother of Charles I, was a zealous *golf player. **1903** H. D. G. LEVESON-GOWER in H. G. Hutchinson *Cricket* xi. 352 'You want the *golf shot?'.. He went to the wicket and made ninety. **1839** LANE *Arab. Nts.* I. 85 He..made a *goff-stick with a hollow handle. **1856** KANE *Arct. Expl.* II. xxi. 206 Each of them had a walrus-rib for a golph or shinny stick. **1928** M. H. WESEEN *Crowell's Dict. Eng. Gram.* 274 *Golf widow*, humorous colloquial name for a woman whose husband spends much time playing golf and little time at home. **1965** *Punch* 19 May 725/1 At the last census, there were more stamp-widows than golf-widows.

golf (gɒlf), *v.*[1] [f. the sb.] *intr.* To play golf.

1800 [see vbl. sb. below]. **1883** *Standard* 16 Nov. 5/2 A General Officer who Golfed. **1888** STEVENSON in *Scribner's Mag.* Feb. 271/2 You might golf if you wanted.

Hence '**golfing** *vbl. sb.*; also *attrib.*

1800 A. CARLYLE *Autobiog.* 343 We crossed the river to the golfing-ground. **1866** MISS MULOCK *Noble Life* xvii. 299 Coming in from a long golfing match. **1867** *Cornh. Mag.* Apr. 490 When the golfing day is done. **1880** *Daily Tel.* 4 Oct., Statutes were promulgated..against golfing. **1891** SIR D. WILSON *Right Hand* 139 Sets of golfing drivers and clubs.

†**golf,** *v.*[2] *Sc. Obs.* [Imitative.] *intr.* Of a pig: To grunt or snort, as in rage. Only in *pres. pple.* and *vbl. sb.*

a **1500** *Colkelbie Sow* 224 Thay come golfand full grim; Mony long tuthit bore [etc.]. *Ibid.* 740 Thay war ourthrawin ..For sory swyne for thair golfing affraid.

golf, obs. form of GULF.

golf(e, obs. form of GOAF[1], GOAVE *v.*

'**golfdom.** [f. GOLF *sb.* + -DOM.] The realm of golf.

1902 in W. W. Tulloch *Tom Morris* (1907) 290 Tom Morris, King of Golfdom. **1926** *Contemp. Rev.* Nov. 679 Mr. Wodehouse..pictures..type after type of the creatures that have beset golfdom. **1946** *Time* 24 June 51 In the U.S. Open, the steadiest wrists in golfdom get to shaking. **1971** *N.Y. Times* 17 June 51 This 71-year-old championship, most prestigious in golfdom.

golfer ('gɒlfə(r)), Also *Sc.* gowfer. [f. GOLF *v.*[1] + -ER[1].] **1.** One who plays golf.

1721 RAMSAY *Ode to the Ph—*, Driving their baws frae whins or tee, There's no nae gowfer to be seen. **1771** SMOLLETT *Humph. Cl.* 8 Aug., I was shown one particular set of golfers, the youngest of whom was turned of fourscore. **1864** *Bookseller* 31 Oct. 662 St. Andrews is the golfers' head quarters.

2. A cardigan.

1911 *Alfred Weeks' Sales Catal.*, Our Stock of Golfers will be disposed of at one price only..2/11½. **1965** *Punch* 6 Jan. p. xii/1 Lambswool golfers. **1969** *Vogue* Nov. 56/1 A cashmere golfer with an interesting reversed rib texture.

Golgi ('gɒldʒı). *Anat.* The name of Camillo Golgi (1844–1926), Italian anatomist, used *attrib.* and in the possessive to designate various microscopical methods introduced by him, and various types of cell, cell organelle, etc., discovered by or named after him.

a. ***Golgi('s) method, technique,*** any of various staining methods employing silver salts or osmium tetroxide; so ***Golgi stain.***

1885 *Jrnl. R. Microsc. Soc.* 2nd Ser. V. 904 Golgi's methods for staining nerve-elements black are based on the action of nitrate of silver and perchloride of mercury following the use of bichromate of potash. **1891** *Jrnl. Anat. & Physiol.* XXV. 448 By the Golgi method all the cells are rarely stained. **1892** *Bull. Johns Hopkins Hosp.* III. 26 (*heading*) The Golgi silver stain with the central nervous system, and its results. **1910** ALLBUTT & ROLLESTON *Syst. Med.* (ed. 2) VII. 853 The cavity is usually surrounded by a zone of thick neuroglial tissue which..is deeply stained by the Weigert haematoxylin stain, and by the Golgi stains. **1968** G. C. HIRSCH in McGee-Russell & Ross *Cell Struct. & Interpret.* xxxi. 396 This method revealed the same cell-constituents as those blackened by the classical Golgi techniques.

b. ***Golgi('s) cell,*** any of various nerve cells, esp. ***Golgi('s) type I*** and ***type II cell,*** respectively nerve cells with long and with short axons.

1892 *Bull. Johns Hopkins Hosp.* III. 28/2 Cells of the posterior horns, whose nerve processes become richly branched and correspond to Golgi's II type. **1932** W. PENFIELD *Cytol. Cell. Path. Nerv. Syst.* II. ix. 433 Golgi's epithelial cells (Bergmann cells). *Ibid.* 435 These feathered cells are probably of the same order as Golgi's epithelial cells and if completely stained would prove to have subpial expansions like the Golgi cells. **1961** T. L. PEELE *Neuroanat. Basis Clin. Neurol.* (ed. 2) i. 4/1 Structurally, nerve cells have been classed according to the length of their axons, as Golgi type I (long) and Golgi type II (short).

c. ***Golgi corpuscle, (tendon) organ, tendon spindle; Golgi-Mazzoni corpuscle, organ*** (see quots.).

1897 *Proc. R. Soc.* LXI. 248 The terminal arborisation which the nerve-fibres finally make is as a rule small as compared with the end-arborisations of ordinary Kühne-Ruffini 'spindles' or the Golgi 'tendon-organs'. **1900** *Jrnl. Compar. Neurol.* X. 165 The Golgi tendon spindles were found by him in the tendons of the eye-muscles of cattle, swine, dogs, cats, rabbits and men. *Ibid.* 174 Where a single branched nerve or several independent nerves enter the granular substance..the resemblance to the Pacinian corpuscles is lost and it is to these especially that the name 'Golgi-Mazzoni organs' is sometimes applied. **1950** R. WYBURN-MASON *Trophic Nerves* viii. 105 The sensory endings in deep tissues are of four main types:—... (2) The Golgi corpuscles found in tendons and supplied by myelinated afferent nerves. They are stimulated by tension. **1964** E. G. WALSH *Physiol. Nerv. Syst.* (ed. 2) ii. 54 Golgi tendon organs seem to bear a special relationship to the cerebellum.

d. ***Golgi apparatus, body, complex, net, network,*** etc., a cytoplasmic cell organelle of complex structure that is now believed to be involved in secretion. Also used to designate components of this structure, as ***Golgi element, material, region, rod, sac, substance, vesicle,*** etc.

1916 A. M. PAPPENHEIMER in *Anat. Rec.* XI. 110 None of these terms appear to be entirely satisfactory. I shall, therefore, refer to the structures simply as the Golgi apparatus. **1924** HOGBEN & WINTON *Introd. Rec. Adv. Compar. Physiol.* 197 In the cytoplasm are present granular bodies, of which two sorts are commonly distinguished, namely, the mitochondria and Golgi rods. **1925** E. B. WILSON *Cell* (ed. 3) 50 In many cases the Golgi 'net' is built up from originally separate bodies—lamelliform, rod-like, banana-shaped or the like... These bodies are variously designated as 'batonettes', 'dictyosomes', or Golgi-bodies. **1926** L. W. SHARP *Introd. Cytol.* (ed. 2) vii. 126 For many years the Golgi material has been chiefly the concern of students of animal tissues. **1946** *Nature* 24 Aug. 274/1 It has come to be realized that the Golgi bodies are to be found in most, if not all, living animal cells. **1949** *Q. Jrnl. Micros. Sci.* XC. 293 (*title*) Further remarks on the Golgi element. **1952** *Sci. News* XXIV. 23 The much debated reticular structure known as the Golgi apparatus. **1967** L. T. THREADGOLD *Ultrastruct. Anim. Cell* v. 164 The Golgi complex, which was such a controversial structure when it could only be observed with the light microscope, has emerged from electron microscopy with a distinct and characteristic fine structure which makes it readily recognizable in all cells. **1970** AMBROSE & EASTY *Cell Biol.* v. 164 The Golgi region was first observed in certain nerve cells.

golgotha ('gɒlgəθə). [a. L. (Vulg.) *golgotha*, Gr. γολγοθά, ad. *gogolþā*, Aramaic form of Heb. *gulgōleþ* skull: see CALVARY.]

1. A place of interment; a graveyard, charnel-house.

[**1593** SHAKS. *Rich. II*, IV. i. 144 This Land [shall] be call'd The field of Golgotha, and dead mens Sculls.] **1604** MARSTON & WEBSTER *Malcontent* IV. v, This earth is only the grave and golgotha wherein all things that live must rot. *a* **1649** DRUMM. OF HAWTH. *Skiamachia* Wks. (1711) 204 These have..dy'd the white fields in blood, turned them into a Golgotha. **1749** J. GWYN *Ess. on Design* Pref. 6 Westminster-abbey..was by no Means intended as a mere Golgotha for the Remains of the..Dead. **1878** H. M. STANLEY *Dark Cont.* I. i. 35 From time immemorial this old beach has been the depository of the dead, and unless the Prince prosecutes his good work for the reclamation of this golgotha [etc.].

†**2.** *University slang.* (See quots.) *Obs.*

1726 AMHERST *Terræ Fil.* ii. 53 Here is that famous apartment, by idle wits and buffoons nick-named Golgotha, that is, the place of sculls or heads of colleges and halls, where they meet and debate upon all extraordinary affairs. *a* **1742** LLOYD *Charity*, The Golgotha of learned fools. **1791** *2nd Heroic Ep. to J. Priestley* in *Poet. Reg.* (1808) 415 Dragg'd down to Oxford, at its stern command, Before dread Golgotha I see thee stand, Arraign'd, condemn'd. **1803** *Gradus ad Cantab.* 66 Golgotha, the place where the heads of Houses sit at St. Mary's in awful array.

goliard ('gəʊlıɑːd). *Obs.* exc. *Hist.* In 5 **goliarde.** [a. OF. *goliard, -art, -ar* glutton, f. *gole* (F. *gueule*):—L. *gula* gluttony.

In 12–13th c. the goliards were supposed to take their name from a certain *Golias*, dignified with the titles of *episcopus* and *archipoeta*, in whose name some of the poems are written. Giraldus (*Spec. Eccl.*) app. regarded him as a real person. See Wright, *Poems W. Mapes* (Camden Soc. 1841) Introd. p. x, and his *Hist. Caricature* 163.]

One of the class of educated jesters, buffoons, and authors of loose or satirical Latin verse, who flourished chiefly in the 12th and 13th c. in Germany, France, and England.

1483 CAXTON *Gold. Leg.* 35 b/2 They goon every day as goliardes in habyte shynyng and ryall apparayll. **1865** WRIGHT *Hist. Caricature* x. 163 But above all he was the father of the Goliards, the 'ribald clerks', as they are called.

Hence **goliardic** *a.* [-IC], of or pertaining to the (poetry of the) goliards; **goliardy** (in 4 *gulyardy*) [-Y^3], also **goliardery**, the practices of a goliard; the composition of goliardic verse; † **goliardous** (in 4 *gulardous*) [? subst. use of OF. *gouliardeus* adj.] = GOLIARD.

1303 R. BRUNNE *Handl. Synne* 4704 A mynstralle, a gulardous, Come onys to a bysshopes hous. *a* **1400** *Relig. Pieces fr. Thornton MS.* (1867) 35 It es a foule lychery for to delyte þe in rymes and slyke gulyardy. **1855** MILMAN *Lat. Chr.* XIV. iv. (1864) IX. 189 Goliardery was a recognised kind of mediaeval poetry. **1865** WRIGHT *Hist. Caricature* x. 163 In ecclesiastical statutes, published in the year 1289,.. a heavy penalty [is proclaimed] against those clerici 'who persist in the practice of goliardy' [etc.]. *Ibid.* 165 At a later date the goliardic poetry was almost all ascribed to..Walter Mapes. **1884** SYMONDS in *Biog.* (1895) II. 230 It seems ridiculous to translate loose Goliardic verses at this time.

† **goliardeys.** *Obs.* Also 7 *arch.* golierdis. [ad. OF. *goliardois*, f. *goliard.*] = GOLIARD.

1377 LANGL. *P. Pl.* B. Prol. 139 Thanne greued hym a goliardeys, a glotoun of wordes. *c* **1386** CHAUCER *Prol.* 560 He was a Ianglere and a goliardeys. [*a* **1643** W. CARTWRIGHT *Ordinary* II. ii. (1651) 25 Sans fail I wene you bin A Jangler, and a golierdis.]

Goliath (gəʊˈlaɪəθ). Often incorrectly Goliah; also 4, 6 golias. [a. L. (Vulg.) *Goliath*, Heb. *golyath* the giant slain by David, 1 Sam. xvii. In Wyclif's Bible the MSS. have the forms *Goliath* and *Golie*; Coverdale has only *Goliath*. The form *Golias* in Shaks. occurs also in Chaucer, and seems to have been used in med.Lat.]

1. A giant; often with allusion to details in the Scripture narrative.

1591 SHAKS. *1 Hen. VI*, I. ii. 33 None but Samsons and Goliasses It sendeth forth to skirmish. **1607** HIERON *Wks.* I. 429, I haue..chosen this clause, as a smooth stone, by which I may..smite this Goliah in the forehead. **1686** PLOT *Staffordsh.* 331 The world still affording us a Goliah now and then, as well as of old. **1830** J. G. STRUTT *Sylva Brit.* 4 These Goliahs of the forest. **1846** J. HAMILTON *Mt. Olives* iv. 105 The Goliath of English literature felt that he had studied successfully when he had prayed earnestly.

Comb. **1718** *Entertainer* xxxiv. ⁋3 He..Goliah-like defies the whole Body of the Clergy. **1847** LD. LINDSAY *Chr. Art* I. 137 The Goliath-like stature and the Herculean chest of Charlemagne himself.

2. a. A very large lamellicorn beetle, of the genus *Goliathus* or the family *Goliathidæ*.

1826 KIRBY & SP. *Entomol.* IV. 494 The vast African Goliaths. *Ibid.* 628 (Index) Goliath beetles.

b. The African giant heron, *Ardea goliath*. In full *Goliath heron*.

1860 *Ibis* II. 220 *Ardea goliath*, Temm. Goliath Heron. **1906** W. L. SCLATER *Birds S. Afr.* IV. 55 Goliath Heron. *Ibid.* 56 The Goliath is found throughout the greater part of Africa. **1970** *Animals* July 127/1 Huge goliath herons stand like statues, suddenly darting to life to spear a fish or a frog.

c. A giant frog, *Cyclorana goliath*, found in S. Cameroon. In full *Goliath frog*.

[**1914** E. G. BOULENGER *Reptiles & Batrachians* II. 208 The Giant Frog, *Rana goliath*, of Cameroon..was discovered only quite recently.] **1931** H. W. PARKER in W. P. Pycraft *Standard Nat. Hist.* XII. 501 We may mention the ..largest of all frogs, the giant Goliath-frog (*R[ana] goliath*) of the Cameroons, which is as big as a medium-sized terrier and can eat a full-grown rat. **1961** D. M. COCHRAN *Living Amphibians of World* 159/1 It seems very unlikely that a successful cross could ever be made between the goliath frog and any frog from the northern hemisphere.

3. A kind of powerful travelling crane. Also *attrib.*

1888 *Lockwood's Dict. Mech. Engin.* s.v., Goliaths, like travellers, are worked both by hand and by steam power. **1892** E. MARKS *Notes Constr. Cranes* 107 A Goliath supplied to the Government of New South Wales. *Ibid.* 108 The Goliath crane, known also as the Wellington crane. **1892** F. COLYER *Lifting & Pressing Machinery* (ed. 2) 164 'Goliath' Travellers. **1928** *Daily Express* 5 Dec. 13 Floating cranes and land cranes, goliaths and derricks. **1970** *Railway Modeller* May 155/1 Three closely spaced sidings are spanned with a Goliath crane.

† ˈ**golik,** *a. Obs.*$^{-1}$ [a. ON. *gólig-r.*] Gay, joyful.

c **1200** ORMIN 15662 Cafarrnaum bitacneþþ Golike tun.

† **goˈlilla, goˈlille.** *Obs.* Also 7–8 golilia, 8 golila, golillio. [a. Sp. *golilla* (F. *golille*) dim. of *gola* throat:—L. *gula*.] A kind of starched collar worn in Spain.

1673 WYCHERLEY *Gentl. Dancing-Master* IV. i, I had rather put on the English Pillory than this Spanish Golilia. *a* **1704** T. BROWN *Wks.* (1720) IV. 318 He wore about his Neck..a small Ruff, which had serv'd him formerly instead of a Golille, when he liv'd at Madrid. **1713** ADDISON *Count Tariff* Wks. 1721 IV. 326 A plume of feathers on his head, a Golillio about his neck. **1718** *Freethinker* No. 94. 278 A Circle of Gallant Elfins, strutting up and down in short Cloaks and Golila's.

¶ ? Mistaken for the name of a fabric.

1782 CUMBERLAND *Anecd.* (1787) II. 49 Apparelled in a vest of golilla, with rich silver lace of Milan.

golinyie, var. of GILENYIE *Sc.*, *Obs.*

† ˈ**golion.** *Obs.* Also 3 golioun, 4 golione, gulion, 4–5 golyon(e. [Of obscure origin; Roquefort has an unauthenticated OF. *goleon* 'sorte d'habit de guerre'.] A kind of gown or tunic.

c **1290** *S. Eng. Leg.* I. 368/67 In a ȝwiȝt Golioun he geth. *c* **1350** *Parlt. Three Ages* 138 A renke..In a golyone of graye, girde in the middes. **1390** GOWER *Conf.* II. 359 He..cast on her his gulion, Which of the skin of a leon Was made. *c* **1440** *Promp. Parv.* 202/1 Golyon, garment, *gunella, gunellus*.

golit, golk, obs. forms of GULLET, GOWK *sb.*

† **goll.** *Obs.* Also 6–7 gol(e. Cf. GOLLY *sb.* [Of obscure origin. Freq. in 17th c. dramatists.] A hand.

a **1586** SIDNEY *Arcadia* II. (1622) 154 But Pamela pleasantly persisting to haue Fortune their iudge, they set hands, and Mopsa..put to her golden gols among them, and Fortune (that saw not the colour of them) gaue her the preheminence. **1601** B. JONSON *Poetaster* V. iii, Make 'em hold up their Spread Golls [in taking an oath]. **1632** MASSINGER *City Madam* IV. i, All the gamsters are Ambitious to shake the golden golls Of worshipfull Mr. Luke. **1650** BULWER *Anthropomet.* 165 The Egyptian women love golden Gols. **1651** RANDOLPH, etc. *Hey for Honesty* I. ii. Wks. (1875) 391 God of wealth!..O, let me kiss thy silver golls. **1675** C. COTTON *Scoffer Scoft* 58 He [Vulcan] comes with his dirty golls [*rime-wd.* coals]. **1690** DRYDEN *Amphitryon* II. i, What an Arm and Fist he has.. and Gols and Knuckle-bones of a very Butcher.

goll, var. of GULL, throat.

gollan(d (ˈgɒlən(d). *Obs.* exc. *dial.* Forms: 4, 9 gollan, 6–9 gollande, (6 gallande, 9 gollin), 7 goulan(d, 6- golland. See also GOWAN. [Prob. related in some way to GOLD *sb.*^{2}]

A name given to various species of *Ranunculus*, *Caltha*, and *Trollius*. Also in combs. *lucken-*, *water-golland* (q.v.).

a **1387** *Sinon. Barthol.* (Anecd. Oxon.) 30 *Mentula*, an. gollan, apium emoroidarum idem. **1538** TURNER *Libellus*, Golland, *Ranunculus*. **1548** —— *Names of Herbes* 67 Ranunculus is called in greeke Batrachion, in englishe Crowfote or a Gallande. **1625** B. JONSON *Paris Anniversary*, Bring..Pinks, goulands, king-cups. **1691** RAY *N.C. Words* 32 Goulans, q.d. Goldins, Corn Marigolds. **1842** HARDY in *Proc. Berw. Nat. Club* II. No. 10. 20 The various species of crowfoot, which, in the border counties of England and Scotland, are named the yellow gowan, gowlon, or gollande. **1881** *Cumbld. Gloss.* 2nd Suppl., *Gollin*, the globe flower (*Trollius Europæus*). **1882** *Lanc. Gloss.*, *Gollin*, the marsh marigold. **1893** *Northumbld. Gloss.*, *Gollan, Golland, Gowlan*, a flower of a golden hue. 'As yalla as a gollan'.

gollar, goller (ˈgɒlə(r)), *v. Sc.* Also guller. [Echoic; cf. GOLLY.]

1. *intr.* 'To emit a guggling sound' (Jam.).

1801 HOGG *Scots Pastorals* 21. **1826** G. BEATTIE *John o' Arnha'* Life (1863) 222 I'll gar ye gape, an' glowr, an' gollar.

2. To utter loud but thick and scarcely articulate sounds; to shout. Also *trans.*, *to gollar out.*

1826 J. WILSON *Noct. Ambr.* Wks. 1855 I. 185 Gangs to.. gollaring out geggery. **1856** MRS. CARLYLE *Lett.* II. 270, I.. heard him gollaring at something. **1863** ROBSON *Bards Tyne* 107 She gollers and flays the lass oot ov her wits. **1895** CROCKETT *Men of Moss Hags* 69 Westerha' rode for-ward ..'gollering' and roaring at the bit things.

Hence ˈ**gollaring** *vbl. sb.* Also ˈ**gollar** *sb.*

1638–84 R. LAW *Mem.* (1818) 192 *note*, Their voices were changed in their groanings and gollerings with pain of hunger. **1808** *Edin. Even. Courant* 16 June (Jam.), She heard three screams and a guller..The guller was a sound as if a person was choaking.

gollet, obs. form of GULLET.

† ˈ**gollin.** *Obs.* Some kind of fish.

1747 MRS. GLASSE *Cookery* xxi. 163 Fish in Season.. Christmas Quarter..Dorey, Brile, Gudgeons, Gollin, Smelts [etc.].

gollin, variant of GOLLAND.

golliwog (ˈgɒlɪwɒg). Also gollywog, Golliwogg. [perh. suggested by GOLLY *int.* (= God) and POLLIWOG, POLLYWOG (*dial.* and *U.S.*, = tadpole).] A name invented for a black-faced grotesquely dressed (male) doll with a shock of fuzzy hair. Also shortened ˈ**golly, Golly**. Also *attrib.* and *Comb.*

1895 B. UPTON (*title*) The adventures of two Dutch Dolls —*and* a 'Golliwogg'. **1904** *Woman's Life* 7 May 227/1 One of her hobbies is the collecting of those quaint, but unbeautiful, dolls known as Gollywogs. **1907** *Westm. Gaz.* 28 May 10/2 A clever golliwogg dance received the enthusiastic applause it deserved. **1922** JOYCE *Ulysses* 347 Madcap Ciss with her golliwog curls. **1925** E. F. NORTON *Fight for Everest, 1924* 104 Every now and then I was struck afresh with the absurdly 'gollywog' appearance of the party. **1934** *Neuphilologische Mitteilungen* XXXV. 130 Abbreviated forms such as *golly* 'gollywog'. **1956** G. DURRELL *Drunken Forest* vi. 126 We came to the police-station,..shaded by a large, golliwog-headed palm tree. **1969** I. KEMP *Brit. G.I. in Vietnam* viii. 161 A short, slightly-built negro whose appearance reminded me of one of those golliwogs that decorate the labels of Robertson's marmalade jars.

gollop (ˈgɒləp), *v. dial.* and *colloq.* Also gollup. [Perhaps an extended form of GULP *v.*, influenced by GOBBLE *v.*^{1} Cf. next.] *trans.* To swallow greedily or hastily. Freq. with *down* or *up*. Also *fig.* Hence ˈ**golloping** *vbl. sb.*

1823 EGAN *Grose's Dict. Vulg. T.*, *Gollup up*, to drink down quickly. **1851** T. STERNBERG *Dial. & Folk-lore Northants* 42 Gollop (southern), to swallow greedily. **1854** A. E. BAKER *Gloss. Northants Words* 283 Gollop it down. **1927** *Brit. Weekly* 14 July 326/4 The Ancient Order of Frothblowers. The 1st Qualification for Membership is that he or she 'should gollop their beer with a zest', three gulps to the pint and 14 to the gallon. **1928** WODEHOUSE in *Strand Mag.* July 10/1 He was aware that the golloping noises [of two boys eating oysters] at his side had ceased. *Ibid.* Dec. 532/1 'Don't gollup your food, Harold,' said the second burglar. **1930** A. KENNEDY *Orra Boughs* i. 4 His conclusion, his attempt at constructive criticism, had been almost an afterthought. 'All things considered' (Ah, how he had golloped Chesterton) 'Burns does have a claim to immortality.' **1941** L. A. G. STRONG *Bay* 14 'In sips, now.' .. 'Don't go gollop it down.' **1960** *Spectator* 21 Oct. 595 The licentious Allied soldiery golloped them up. **1969** C. GEESON *Northumberland & Durham Word Bk.* 96 *Gollop.* In general dialectal use in Scotland and England. To gulp one's food. 'Dinna gollop your broth like that!' **1970** D. M. DAVIN *Not Here, Not Now* III. vii. 210 Mind if I have one before Martin gollops the lot?

gollop (ˈgɒləp), *sb. dial.* and *colloq.* [Cf. prec.] A greedy or hasty gulp (in quot. 1912, a gulping sound). Also *fig.*

1912 W. DEEPING *Sincerity* v. 43 Wolfe uncorked it, and turned it upside down. The water went 'gollop, gollop', and splashed the stones at Mr. Turrell's feet. **1933** F. E. BAUME *Half Caste* 76 They washed down the lot with great gollops of tea. **1933** J. MASEFIELD *Bird of Dawning* 152 We've all had a good gollop of fortune, being alive now. **1941** L. A. G. STRONG *Bay* 14 If I took it all in a gollop, I never had to give it another thought. **1946** B. FERGUSSON *Wild Green Earth* I. ii. 45 The mule rolled over and over down the hillside until he lay, breathing great gollops of air, helpless until his load was taken off him.

goll-sheaf, var. *gale-sheaf* (cf. quot. 1597 in GALE *sb.*^{1} b).

a **1670** HACKET *Abp. Williams* II. (1692) 92 The rest of the Articles were goll-sheaves that went out in a suddain blaze. —— *Serm. on Incarnation* v. Cent. Serm. (1675) 48 Like a gol-sheave all of a flame and out again suddenly.

† ˈ**golly,** *sb. Obs.*$^{-1}$ [Cf. GOLL.] (See quot.)

1656 W. D. tr. *Comenius' Gate Lat. Unl.* §213. 59 The hand held hollow is the Golly; stretched out, the Palm.

golly (ˈgɒlɪ), *v. Sc.* [Echoic; cf. GOLLAR *v.*] *intr.* To shout with a thick voice. Hence ˈ**gollying** *vbl. sb.*

1838 CARLYLE *Let.* in Froude *Life in Lond.* (1884) I. v. 141 The Annandale Voice gollying at them. **1894** CROCKETT *Raiders* (ed. 3) 165 We heard..the wrathful gollying of the great voice.

golly (ˈgɒlɪ), *int.* [Substituted for GOD in oaths or exclamations; cf. GOLES.] In (*by*) *golly* = (*by*) *God.*

1775 G. WHITE *Jrnls.* 21 Dec. (1931) 117 *Gouleins* (Gothic) salutatio: hence perhaps our word Golly, a sort of jolly kind of oath, or asseveration much in use among our carters, & lowest people. **1848** LOWELL *Biglow P.* Ser. I. ii. 25 My folks to hum air full ez good ez his'n be, by golly! **1883** *Harper's Mag.* July 847/2 Golly! I'd do it as quick as wink. **1888** CHURCHWARD *Blackbirding* 125 Look sharp, or by golly, they will have us for breakfast.

gollymoffry, obs. form of GALLIMAUFRY.

1772 NUGENT tr. *Hist. Friar Gerund* II. 135 Without having understood a single word of all this gollymoffry.

gollywog, var. GOLLIWOG.

golnes, variant of GULLNESS, *Obs.*, paleness.

† **golofer.** *Obs.* Also 6 goulafre, golopher. [OF. *goulafre* (F. *gouliafre*), derivative of OF. *goule* mouth, throat.] ? A glutton. Also *blood-golofer.*

1529 S. FISH *Supplic. Beggars* 10 All the substaunce of your Realme..rynneth hedlong ynto the insaciabill whyrlepole of these gredi goulafres. *a* **1535** MORE *Suppl. Soules* Wks. 295 Gredie golophers he calleth them & insaciable whyrle-poles. **1609** BP. W. BARLOW *Answ. Nameless Cath.* 300 To satiate the thirst of a blood-golofer.

goloke, obs. form of COLLOCK, a tub.

golore, dial. form of GALORE.

† **goˈlose.** *Obs.* ? = GUILLOCHE. (Cf. GALACE.)

1663 GERBIER *Counsel* 81 The Fret having a dubble golose in the bottome.

golosh, goloshoe, etc.: see GALOSH.

golpe (gɒlp). *Her.* Also 7 gulp, 8 golp. [? a. Sp. *golpe* wound. Cf. HURT *sb.*^{2}] A roundel of a purple colour.

1562 LEIGH *Armorie* (1597) 88 The field is Or, v. Golpes ..These are in signification woundes. **1610** GUILLIM *Heraldry* IV. xix. (1660) 352 If they [Roundles] be Purpure then we call them Golpes. **1666** MORGAN *Armilogia* 112 *marg.*, Gulps are purple Balls. **1727–51** CHAMBERS *Cycl.*, Golps. **1868** in CUSSANS *Her.* iv. (1882) 74.

† ˈ**golpol.** *Obs.*$^{-1}$ [? for *gold-poll*; cf. GOLDILOCKS.] A term of endearment.

1568 *Hist. Jacob & Esau* V. x. G iij, It is your deinty dearlyng, your princkoxe, your golpoll.

gols, obs. form of GULES.

golt, variant of GAULT *sb.*

goluptious (gəʊˈlʌpʃəs), *a. slang* or *humorous.* Also galoptious, galopshus, galumptious, goloptious. [Arbitrarily formed, perhaps with suggestion of VOLUPTUOUS.] Delightful, luscious.

1856 STRANG *Glasgow* 429 Raising the galoptious draught to his lips. **1862** CALVERLEY *Verses & Tr.* 79 Cooking for a genteel fam'ly, John, it's a goluptious life. **1888** J. PAYN *Myst. Mirbridge* II. xx. 63 A little scandal..is the most goluptious talk of all. **1903** J. VAIZEY *Pixie O'Shaughnessy* vi. 64 She gives you the most galumptious teas, and..you can eat as much as you like. **1926** FOWLER *Mod. Eng. Usage* 164/1 Goloptious. **1935** W. DE LA MARE *Early One Morning* 79 'Dreams' so galumptious and prolonged.

golve, golvon, -vyn, obs. forms of GOAVE *v.*

golyon(e, variant of GOLION, *Obs.*

†**gom**[1]. *Obs.* Also 5 gome, 7 gomme. [? Abbreviation of **gommer* (cf. GAMMER) = god-mother. Cf. GOFF.] = CUMMER.

1483 *Cath. Angl.* 161/2 A Gome; *vbi* a godmoder. *c* **1610** MIDDLETON etc. *Widow* I. ii, *Ric.* Lady, well met. *Fra.* I doe not think so Sir. *Ric.* A scornfull Gom..my Widow never gave me such an answer. **1611** COTGR., *Commere*,.. a gomme. **1673** *Yorksh. Dial.* 5 (E.D.S. No. 76) Wyah, Gom, I'se gea. *Ibid.* 70 Wyah, Gom Green.

†**gom**[2]. *Obs. rare*[−1]. [? var. of GONG *sb.*] ? = GONG *sb.* I.

1694 NARBOROUGH *Voy.* I. 133 The play..was much like that of a Jews-Trump, or little Gom.

gom[3] (gɒm). *dial.* Also goms. [Deformation of GOD. Cf. *by* GUM.] In phr. ***by gom(s*** = *by God.*

1806 BLOOMFIELD *Wild Flowers* 39 By gom we women fell a clacking. **1839** C. CLARK *J. Noakes & Mary Styles* 50 (E.D.S. No. 76), But oft, by gom! when we've bin there, It seem'd amos' to drizzle. **1840** SPURDEN *Suppl. to Forby's Voc. E. Anglia* 63 Goms! By Goms.

gom[4] (gɒm). *Ireland.* Also gaum. [Cf. Ir. *gamal* stupid-looking person.] A poor silly fellow.

1834 S. LOVER *Leg. Irel.* 2nd Ser. 241 Do you think me sitch a *gom*, all out, as to put me off wid four pence ha'pny. *a* **1849** J. KEEGAN *Leg. & Poems* (1907) 114 'By gor, you are no gom,' said Biddy. **1870** P. KENNEDY *Fireside Stories Ireland* 29 (E.D.D.), You were a gaum before you went to travel, and you are a gaum after it. **1894** E. MCNULTY *Misther O'Ryan* xiv. 150 But, shure, I cudn't kape quiet an' see him standin' there purtindin' to be a gaum. **1928** D. BYRNE *Destiny Bay* i. §2. 11 You big, thick-footed, herring-fed Southern gom! **1970** M. KENYON *100,000 Welcomes* iv. 24 Corrigan's a gom. This one has breeding.

Gomarist ('gəʊmərɪst). *Eccl. Hist.* Also 8 gommarist. [f. *Gomar* (see below) + -IST.] A follower of Francis Gomar (1563–1641), Professor of Divinity at Leyden, who zealously defended orthodox Calvinism in opposition to the doctrines of his colleague Arminius (see ARMINIAN).

1674 HICKMAN *Quinquart. Hist.* (ed. 2) 156 No Gomarist would refuse to subscribe the saying. **1725** tr. *Dupin's Eccl. Hist. 17th C.* I. VII. i. 291 This Contest was afterwards renew'd..betwixt the Arminians and Gommarists. **1876** BANCROFT *Hist. U.S.* II. xxii. 36 The Gomarists who satisfied the natural passion for equality by denying personal merit.

So **Gomarian** (gəʊ'mɛərɪən).

1617 SIR H. BOURGCHIER in *Abp. Ussher's Lett.* (1686) 61 The opposite Faction to the Arminian, by them termed vulgarly Gomarians. **1847** PRANDI tr. *C. Cantù's Reform. in Europe* I. 347 Arminians and Gomarians.

‖**go'mashta.** *Indian.* Also 8–9 gomastah. [Hindustani, a. Pers. *gamāshtah* 'appointed, delegated'.] A native agent or factor, a clerk for native correspondence.

1747 *MS.* in Yule & Burnell *Hobson-Jobson* s.v., Goa Masters. **1758** in VANSITTART *Narr. Trans. in Bengal* (1766) I. 26 There is a complaint lodged against an English gomastah. **1776** *Trial of Nundocomar* 77/1, I was his chief gomastah: I used to superintend his other gomastahs. **1837** *Lett. fr. Madras* (1843) 136 The Rajah's Gomashta stood by, to order her about.

gomb(e, obs. form of GUM.

gombeen (gɒm'biːn). *Anglo-Irish.* [a. mod. Irish *gaimbín*; according to Stokes (in Fick *Vergl. Wb.* II. 79) repr. a derivative of OCeltic **kṃbion*, whence med.L. *cambium*: see CHANGE.] Usury. Chiefly *attrib.*, as **gombeen-man,** a money-lender, usurer; so also **gombeen-woman.** Hence **gom'beenism,** the practice of borrowing or lending at usury.

1862 H. COULTER *West Irel.* 197 Shop keepers, Gombeen men, and others to whom they have become indebted. *Ibid.* 201 Possessed of some hundreds of pounds each, which they lend out at Gombeen. **1882** *Times* 20 July 9/3 The bank.. in Ireland, is often little more than a glorified gombeen-man. **1886** *Contemp. Rev.* Apr. 504 The evil of 'gombeenism' which has always been so prevalent in the poorer districts of Ireland. **1894** HALL CAINE *Manxman* 320 She was a gombeen woman.

gombo, var. of GUMBO.

Gombroon, Gomroon (gɒm'bruːn, gɒm'ruːn). Also 7 Gomron. [Name of a town on the Persian Gulf. Cf. GAMBROON.] A kind of Persian pottery, imitated in Chelsea ware.

1698 FRYER *E. Ind. & Persia* 331 Gombroon Ware, made of Earth, the best, next China. **1699** M. LISTER *Journ. to Paris* 139 The Gomron Ware. **1880** *Daily News* 13 Apr. 5/1 The year 1695 is authoritatively given for the appearance of the Chelsea pottery known as Gomroon. **1885** MIDDLETON in *Encycl. Brit.* XIX. 621/2 The main varieties of this Perso-Chinese ware are the following. (1) A sort of semi-porcelain, called by English dealers, quite without reason, 'Gombroon ware', which is pure white and semi-transparent.

†**gome**[1]. *Obs.* Forms: 1 **guma,** 3–4 **gum(e,** 3–5 **gom,** (5 **gomme, goom,** *Sc.* **goym),** 3–6 **gome.** [Com. Teut.; OE. *guma* = OS. *gumo*, OHG. *gumo, gomo* (MHG. *gome*), ON. *gume* (poet.), Goth. *guma*:—pre-Teut. **ghəmon-* cognate with L. *homō, homin-is*. In poetic use from OE. times to 16th c., also in *bridegome* now BRIDEGROOM, q.v.] A man.

Beowulf (Z.) 652 Grette þa guma oþerne. *c* **1205** LAY. 17295 He hæhte Gillomaurus, gomenen he wes lauerd. *a* **1225** *Juliana* 26 Te luuien godd alre gume lauerd. *a* **1300** *K. Horn* 22 Twelf feren he hadde..And alle hi were faire gomes. *c* **1380** *Sir Ferumb.* 402 'Christene knyȝt', quaþ Fyrumbras; 'þou art a wonder gome'. *c* **1400** *Destr. Troy* 10149 Philmen..Gird to Agamynon, & the gome hit. *c* **1450** HOLLAND *Howlat* 540 Mony galiard gome was on the ground levit. **1515** *Scot. Field* 108 The King was glade of that golde, that the gome brought.

b. applied to God.

c **1320** *Cast. Love* 1512 To whom joye and honour bi-come Wiþ-outen ende, þe holy Gome.

2. *Comb.*, as **gome-graith,** armour.

c **1420** *Anturs of Arth.* xxxiv, We ar in our gamene, we haue no gome [*v.r.* gude] graiþe.

†**gome**[2]. *Obs.* exc. *dial.* Also 3 gom, 9 gawm. [a. ON. *gaum-r* masc., *gaum* fem. (OSw. *göm*) care, heed, etc. = OS. *gôma* (MDu. *gome, goom*), OHG. *gouma*, etc. (MHG. *goume, goum*), Goth. **gauma* (whence *gaumjan* to take notice of, see YEME *v.*). Ulterior etymology uncertain.]

a. Heed, attention, notice, care; esp. in phrase ***to nimen*** (or ***take***) ***gome*** = to give heed. **b.** (See quot. 1877, and cf. GAUM-LIKE *a.*, GORMLESS *a.*)

c **1200** ORMIN 5086 Nu birrþ þe nimenn mikell gom Off þiss þatt I þe shæwe. *c* **1290** *S.E. Leg.* I. 209/308 Of tormens þat he þare isaiȝ, gret gome with-alle he nam. *Ibid.* 443/440 þar-of he tok luyte gome. **1297** R. GLOUC. (Rolls) 9320 Nimeþ..gome here Aȝen wat men ȝe ssolle fiȝte. *c* **1380** *Sir Ferumb.* 1745 þer-of nemaþ gome. *c* **1410** *Chron. Eng.* 97 in Ritson *Metr. Rom.* II. 274 Londone he made furst with gome, Ant yef hit his oune nome. **1877** *Holderness Gloss.*, *Gawm*, sense, wit, tact.

gome[3]. = COOM *sb.*[1] 4.

1611 COTGR., *Camboy*, the blacke, and oylie grease, of a wrought cart-wheele; some call it, the Gome.

gome, var. GOM[1], *Obs.*; obs. form of GUM.

gome(n, obs. form of GAME.

†**gomer**[1]. *Obs.* Also 4 goomor, 4–5 gomor. [a. L. *gomor*, Gr. γομόρ, transliteration of Heb. *ʿōmer*: see OMER.] A Hebrew measure = OMER; sometimes confused with HOMER[2].

c **1000** ÆLFRIC *Exod.* xvi. 16 An ȝemetfæt full, þe hiȝ gomor heton. **1382** WYCLIF *Exod.* xvi. 22 Thei gadreden.. two gomors bi eche man. **1398** TREVISA *Barth. De P.R.* XIX. cxxviii. (1495) 933 Gomor [= HOMER] is a mesure of xl modius (as Isider sayth). *c* **1450** *Mirour Saluacioun* 1832 And ilk one b[r]ot o Gomor of manna home. **1579** FULKE *Heskins' Parl.* 353 They had two gomers full. *a* **1631** DONNE *Serm.* xxxi. (1640) 308 Nor satisfied with his Gomer of Manna.

Gomer[2] ('gəʊmə(r)). [f. the name of the inventor, a French officer under Napoleon I.] ***Gomer chamber,*** a conical chamber with spherical bottom used in smooth-bore guns and mortars. Hence ***Gomer-chambered, Gomer mortar,*** etc.

1828 J. M. SPEARMAN *Brit. Gunner* (ed. 2) 135 To find the Content of a Gomer, or other Conical Chamber. **1858** GREENER *Gunnery* 211 The use of the Gomer form of chamber, is nearly universal in brass guns. **1859** F. A. GRIFFITHS *Artil. Man.* (1862) 88 Cartridges for 'Gomer' Chambered Guns. *Ibid.* 92, 8-inch Gomer mortars. **1876** in VOYLE *Milit. Dict.*

gomerel ('gɒmərəl), *sb. Sc.* and *north.* Also 9 gomeral, -il, -ill, gommarel, -eril, gomral, -rell, gaumerill. [Of obscure formation: see -REL.] A fool, simpleton, silly fellow.

1814 *Saxon & Gael* III. 73 Ye was right to refuse that clavering gomerel, Sir John. **1818** SCOTT *Rob Roy* xiv, Our auld daft laird here and his gomerils o' sons. **1843** MRS. CARLYLE *Lett.* I. 224 Ready to beat me for a distracted Gomeril. **1886** STEVENSON *Kidnapped* xx. 193, I have proved myself a gomeral this night.

gomfaynoun, obs. form of GONFANON.

gom-gom: see GUM-GUM.

gomme, var. GOM[1], GOME[1], *Obs.*; obs. f. GUM.

gomor, variant of GOMER[1], *Obs.*

gomoria, -ry, obs. forms of GONORRHŒA.

†**Gomorr(h)ean,** *a.* and *sb. Obs.* [f. *Gomorrah, Gomorrha*, on analogy of other names in *-ean.*

According to the system used in the Bible of 1611, the normal transliteration of Heb. *ʿămōrā* would be **Amorah*. The Gr. form, however, was Γόμοῤῥα; in the N.T. this was adopted as *Gomorrha*, while in the O.T. the translators employed the hybrid spelling *Gomorrah*.]

A. *adj.* Of or pertaining to Gomorrah (see *Gen.* xviii, xix).

1581 J. BELL *Haddon's Answ. Osor.* 37 b, Gomorrhean and Sodomiticall brimstone. **1593** NASHE *Strange News* Wks. (Grosart) II. 277 The tedious wildernesse of this Gomorian Epistle.

B. *sb.* An inhabitant of Gomorrah; hence, one who follows the practices of its inhabitants.

1522 SKELTON *Why not to Court* 469 The Gommoryans also Were brought to deedly wo As Scrypture recordis. **1550** BALE *Eng. Votaries* II. M iij, Hys diabolical rable of sorcerouse Gomorreanes. **1583** STUBBES *Anat. Abus.* II. (1882) 3 When the Sodomits and Gomorreans had filled vp the measures of their iniquitie. **1613** DEKKER *Strange Horse-Race* etc. Wks. (Gosart) III. 369 The Cimerians, the Sodomites, and the Gomorrhæans.

So †**Gomorreal** *a.*

1550 BALE *Apol.* 59 But where are thy scriptures, to prove a perpetuyte in thy Gomorreal vowes?

‖**gompa** ('gɒmpə). [a. Tibetan *gön-pa, göm-pa* (Jäschke *dgón-pa*), a solitary place, a hermitage.] A Tibetan temple or monastery.

[**1863** E. SCHLAGINTWEIT *Buddhism in Tibet* xiii. 179 The monasteries, in Tibetan Gonpa, 'a solitary place', are mostly at some little distance from the villages. **1895** L. A. WADDELL *Buddhism of Tibet* xi. 255 The monastery is named in Tibetan *Gön-pa*, vulgarly *Göm-pa*, or 'a solitary place' or hermitage; and most monasteries are situated..at least some distance off from villages.] **1902** [see CHORTEN]. **1933** *Times Lit. Suppl.* 28 Sept. 644/3 Vivid descriptions of the..Lamas ..of their *gompa* temples. **1939** M. PALLIS *Peaks & Lamas* xiii. 147 Time enough to sort out the remaining stores and attend a service at the *Gompa* (monastery) to which we had been specially bidden. **1960** 'S. HARVESTER' *Chinese Hammer* iv. 46 A *gompá*, one of those religious establishments whose walls housed more than a fifth of Tibetan males.

gompaauw, gompauw ('gɒmpɑːuː, ‖'xɔmpəʊ). *S. Afr.* [f. Afrikaans and Du. *gom* gum + Du. *paauw, pauw* peacock (cf. POU(w)).] The giant or kori bustard, *Ardeotis kori.*

1838 J. E. ALEXANDER *Exped. Disc. Int. Africa* II. viii. 141 Here a gum pauw, or bustard, which subsists partly on gum, was shot. **1905** W. L. SCLATER in *Science in S. Afr.* 143 The Bustards (*Otidæ*) are represented by no less than twelve species, ranging from the large *Gom Paauw* (*Otis kori*), the male of which sometimes weighs as much as 40 lbs. to the smaller Knorhaan (*Otis afra*) about the same size as a partridge. **1936** *Blackw. Mag.* Mar. 296/2 An occasional gom-paauw, the great bustard of South Africa, largest of all the family. **1948** L. G. GREEN *To River's End* iv. 40 Both the gom paauw and the smaller duin paauw feed on the gum from the kameeldoorn trees. **1962** MACKWORTH-PRAED & GRANT *Birds S. Third Afr.* 262 Kori bustard or gom paauw: *Ardeotis kori.*

gomphiasis (gɒm'faɪəsɪs). *Path.* [a. Gr. γομφίασις toothache, f. γομφίος molar tooth.] Disease of the teeth (esp. the molars) causing them to become loose in their sockets.

1706 in PHILLIPS (ed. Kersey); and in mod. Dicts.

gomphodont ('gɒmfədɒnt), *a. Zool.* [f. Gr. γόμφ-ος bolt + ὀδοντ- (ὀδούς) tooth.] Having the teeth inserted by gomphosis; socketed.

1889 in *Century Dict.*

gompholite ('gɒmfəlaɪt). *Geol.* [f. Gr. γόμφος bolt, nail: see -LITE. (Named by Brongniart.)] (See quot. 1839.)

1838 *Penny Cycl.* XI. 296/2. **1839** G. ROBERTS *Dict. Geol.*, *Gompholite*, a conglomerate of the tertiary formation, in which the imbedded pebbles appear like nails in a baronial door. **1859** in PAGE *Handbk. Geol. Terms.*

‖**gomphosis** (gɒm'fəʊsɪs). *Anat.* [mod.L., a. Gr. γόμφωσις, f. γομφόειν to bolt together, f. γόμφος bolt.] A form of immovable articulation, in which one hard part (e.g. a tooth) is received into the cavity of another, as a peg or nail into its socket.

1578 BANISTER *Hist. Man* I. 13 The manner of their [teeth] situation in the iawes is named Gomphosis. **1658** ROWLAND *Moufet's Theat. Ins.* Ep. Ded., Toothed bars, that answer one the other with a thorny gomphosis. **1658** SIR T. BROWNE *Gard. Cyrus* iii. 57 The seeds of many pappous or downy flowers lockt up in sockets after a gomphosis or mortis-articulation. **1741** A. MONRO *Anat. Bones* (ed. 3) 157 The teeth are joined to the Sockets by *Gomphosis*. **1854** R. OWEN in *Circ. Sci., Organ. Nat.* I. 216 The..plates are.. articulated by gomphosis to the..ribs.

gomral, -rell, variants of GOMEREL, fool.

gomro(o)n, variant of GOMBROON.

goms: see GOM[3].

gomuti (gəʊ'muːtɪ). Also gomuta. [ad. Mal. *gĕmuti* sugar-palm fibre.] A palm tree, *Arenga pinnata*, native to Malaya and the East Indies, and cultivated elsewhere, particularly in India; also, the fibre obtained from this tree.

1811 W. MARSDEN *Hist. Sumatra* (ed. 3) 88 This palm, named in Sumatra *anau*, and by the eastern Malays *gomuto*, is the borassus gomutus of Loureiro. *Ibid.*, The *anau* palm produces also (besides a little sago) the remarkable substance called *iju* or *gomuto*, exactly resembling coarse black horse-hair. **1836** LOUDON *Encycl. Plants* (ed. 2) Suppl. 1290 *Gomutus*,..a palm, growing to the height of 40 ft. **1886** YULE & BURNELL *Hobson-Jobson* 295/1 *Gomuti*, a substance resembling horsehair, and forming excellent cordage.., sometimes improperly called coir, which is produced by a palm growing in the Archipelago, *Arenga saccharifera.* **1889**

G. S. Boulger *Uses of Plants* vi. 168 *Arenga saccharifera*, Labill., Gomuti Palm. Ramenta, or Vegetable bristles, suggested as a covering for telegraph cables. 1908 G. Watt *Commercial Prod. India* 91 At the base of the petiole is found a beautiful black horsehair-like fibre known as the *Ejú* or *Gomuta* Fibre. 1926 E. Blatter *Palms Brit. India* iv. 357 Like the true Sago Palm.. the Gomuti Palm affords a medullary substance, from which a meal is prepared. 1953 N. L. Bor *Man. Indian Forest Bot.* 351 At the base of the petioles is found a beautiful black fibre, exactly like horsehair, known as Gomuta fibre, which is very strong and can be used under water.

gon, var. of *gan*, pa. t. of gin *v.*, to begin; obs. inf. (etc.) of go *v.*

-gon (gɒn), *suffix*. The second element (repr. Gr. -γων-ος, -ον, -angled) of heptagon, hexagon, etc., sometimes used with algebraic symbols (as *m*-gon, *n*-gon) which take the place of a Greek numeral; also with numeral prefixed, as *16-gon*.

[1652 *News fr. Lowe-Countr.* 2 For 'tis not.. Trigonall, or Pentagonall, Or any of the Gones at all.] 1867–78 J. Wolstenholme *Math. Probl.* (ed. 2) Prob. 1853 In the moving circle is described a regular *m*-gon.. The same epicycloid may also be generated by the corners of a regular *n*-gon. 1898 T. J. McCormack tr. *Schubert's Math. Ess.* 125 He constructed an inscribed 16-gon. 1964 L. F. Tóth *Regular Figures* vi. 205 The vertices of a regular 12-gon.

gonad ('gɒnæd, gəʊnæd). *Biol.* [f. Gr. γονή, γόνος generation, seed, etc. + -ad, after mod.L. *gonas*, pl. *gonades*.] Any organ in an animal (as a testis or an ovary) that produces gametes.

1880 Lankester in *Nature* XXII. 147 Having its genital sacs or gonads placed in the course of the radial canals. 1887 *Athenæum* 29 Oct. 572/1 Groups.. having the nephridia functioning as efferent ducts for the gonads. 1900 J. S. Kingsley *Text Bk. Vertebr. Zool.* 125 The ovaries are those gonads which are to give rise to the eggs or ova. 1927 Haldane & Huxley *Animal Biol.* ix. 191 The changes which take place in body and mind at puberty are also under the control of the endocrine system. The immediate control is exerted by the gonad itself. 1957 Richards & Dawes *Imms's Textbk. Ent.* (ed. 9) i. 193 The hermaphrodite reproductive system is not unlike the usual female condition but the gonad.. produces both spermatozoa and eggs. 1957 *Times* 3 Sept. 9/2 The report of a study group on the effect of radiation on human heredity says that in every exposure the X-ray beam should.. be so directed that a minimum of radiation reaches the gonads. 1962 D. J. B. Ashley *Human Intersex* iii. 34 The gonads, testes and ovaries, are the primary sex organs which house the definitive male and female germ cells which differentiate to form the gametes. 1964 Parker & Haswell *Text-bk. Zool.* (ed. 7) II. 318 The gonads are of great size in the sexually mature fish.

Hence **gonadal, gonadial** (gəʊ'neɪdəl, -dɪəl), **gonadic** (gəʊ'nædɪk) *adjs.*, of or relating to the gonads; **gona'dectomy** [-ectomy], excision of a gonad; **'gonaduct** (for *gonad-duct*: cf. quot. 1887 above).

1888 Lankester in *Encycl. Brit.* XXIV. 183/1 Nephridia (modified in some as gonaducts). 1902 A. Sedgwick in *Encycl. Brit.* XXVIII. 138/1 Formation.. of gonadial sacs. 1914 Geddes & Thomson *Sex* iv. 88 The gonadial glands of internal secretion. 1925 F. A. E. Crew *Animal Genetics* 194 The operation of gonadectomy (extirpation of the sex-gland). *Ibid.* 198 The animals which were merely castrated failed to develop the secondary gonadic characters which they would presumably have shown otherwise. 1934 Webster, Gonadal. 1946 *Nature* 20 July 95/2 Trichloracetic acid filtrates of serum were prepared during an investigation of the effects of gonadal hormones on the mineral metabolism of the immature pullet. 1963 *Lancet* 5 Jan. 3/2 There is no evidence in favour of transplants of gonadal tissue rejuvenating the senescent human.

gonadotrophic (ˌgəʊnədəʊ'trəʊfɪk), **-tropic** (-'trəʊpɪk, -'trɒpɪk), *a. Physiol.* [f. gonad + -o + -trophic, -tropic.] Regulating the activity of the gonads; of or pertaining to gonadotrophins.

1931 Wiesner & Marshall in *Q. Jrnl. Exper. Physiol.* XXI. 147 (*title*) The Gonadotropic Hormones (ρ-Factors). *Ibid.* 148 It has been shown that the gonadotropic substances can produce haemorrhagic follicles and *corpora atretica*. 1936 *Lancet* 8 Aug. 309/2 It has afforded an opportunity of investigating the gonadotropic hormone production under the exceptional circumstances of pituitary hypofunction during gestation. 1938 *Encycl. Brit. Bk. of Yr.* 227/2 The adrenotrophic, thyrotrophic, and gonadotrophic hormones. 1957 *Science News* XLIV. 85 The gonadotrophic hormones secreted by the pituitary gland stimulate equally both testis and ovary. 1968 R. H. Williams *Textbk. Endocrinol.* (ed. 4) ii. 32/1 A provisional separation of two types of gonadotropic cells has been made in the mouse by Barnes. 1970 *Sci. Jrnl.* June 46/3 The pituitary produces at least two gonadotrophic principles which in their turn stimulate the secretion of two quite separate hormones from the ovary—oestrogen and progesterone.

So ˌ**gonado'trophin, -'tropin**, any of several gonadotrophic hormones (as follicle-stimulating hormone) that originate in the pituitary or the placenta.

1937 *Endocrinology* July 489 (*title*) Excretion of gonadotropin by normal human males after the ingestion and injection of extracts of pregnancy urine. *Ibid.* 493 Biological and chemical differences may be presented as evidence for the existence of two or more gonadotropins, representing distinct products of internal secretion. 1957 *Encycl. Brit.* VIII. 434/1 Two gonadotrophins are secreted by the anterior pituitary, follicle-stimulating hormone (FSH) and luteinizing, or interstitial cell-stimulating, hormone (LH). 1964 H. H. Cole *Gonadotropins* p. iii, Until the mode of action of gonadotropins becomes known, it is unlikely that uniformity of spelling will be achieved. Arguments based on etymology are persuasive for the use of either suffix. In this volume, the 'h' has been dropped, arbitrarily. 1966 *New Scientist* 15 Dec. 618/3 Gonadotrophins are the pituitary hormones which regulate the activity of the sex glands—the ovaries in the female, and the testicles in the male. 1968 *Daily Tel.* 12 Nov. 1/6 Mrs. Pennington.. has been taking the fertility drug gonadotrophin. 1970 *Sci. Jrnl.* June 48/2 Demonstration of the presence of chorionic gonadotrophin is also the basis of nearly all pregnancy tests.

‖**gonagra** (gɒ'nægrə). *Path.* Also (in irregularly anglicized form) 7 **gonagry**. [mod.L., f. Gr. γόν-υ knee (after podagra). Cf. F. *gonagre*.] Gout in the knee.

1657 Tomlinson *Renou's Disp.* 205 By its [a vesicatory] adhibition to the feet the Gonagry and Podagry are cured. 1706 Phillips (ed. Kersey), *Gonagra.* 1886 in *Syd. Soc. Lex.*

‖**gonangium** (gɒ'nændʒɪəm). *Zool.* Pl. -ia. [mod.L., f. Gr. γόν-ος generation + ἀγγεῖον vessel.] An external chitinous receptacle within which, in the calyptoblastic genera of Hydrozoa, the sporosacs or planoblasts are developed. Hence **go'nangial** *a.*

1871 Allman *Gymnoblastic Hydroids* 26 Peculiar receptacles—the gonangia—destined for the protection of the sexual buds. *Ibid.* 47 In some cases the contents of the gonangium escape. 1877 Huxley *Anat. Inv. Anim.* iii. 131 The gonophore contained in a gonangium. *Ibid.* In the genus Aglaophenia groups of gonangia are enclosed in a common receptacle.

gonapophysis (gɒnə'pɒfɪsɪs). *Ent.* [f. Gr. γόν-ος generation + apophysis.] One of the paired processes on the eighth and ninth ventral segments of the cockroach and allied species, forming the external genital organs. Hence **gonapo'physial** *a.*

1877 Huxley *Anat. Inv. Anim.* vii. 406 The most conspicuous division of the right gonapophysis is a broad plate divided at the extremity into two portions.

Gond (gɒnd), *sb.* and *a.* [Hind., f. Skr. *goṇḍa* fleshy navel, person having this, Gond.]

A. *sb.* **a.** A member of a Dravidian people, many of them jungle-dwellers, of central India. **b.** = Gondi. **B.** *adj.* Of or pertaining to this people or their language.

The native name is *koitor*.

1810 Moxon in G. Smith *S. Hislop* (1888) 38 The Gonds .. live mostly in the hills and jungles. 1854 S. Hislop *Ibid.* 167 We found the inhabitants to consist of Gonds and Dheds. 1855 *Ibid.* 169 The Gond Raja of Dewagad. 1856 R. Caldwell *Gram. Dravidian Langs.* 8 The Gōnd or Goand. *Ibid.* 9 The people by whom the Gond and the Ku are spoken. 1867 W. D. Whitney *Lang. & Study Lang.* ix. 327 The wild Gonds and Khonds of the hilly country of Gondwana. 1914 W. H. Rivers *Kinship & Soc. Organis.* 26 The earliest reference to the cross-cousin marriage which I have been able to discover is among the Gonds of Central India. 1924 *Blackw. Mag.* Apr. 545/1 Several Gond women washing clothes. 1925 *Ibid.* Jan. 64/1 The Gond nowadays is becoming civilised and Hinduised. 1936 *Times Lit. Suppl.* 4 Jan. 18/2 And so among these Gond songs there are many which seem to be quite inconsequential. 1961 P. Spear *India* vii. 89 The Chandel Rajputs are thought to be of Gond descent. *Ibid.* xiii. 157 Tribes like the Bhils, the Gonds, or the Santhals carried on their forest and hunting craft. 1971 *Illustr. Weekly India* 25 Apr. 42/1 Bastar is a land of Marias, Murias and Gonds.

Gondal ('gɒndəl), *sb.* and *a.* **A.** *sb.* The name of an imaginary island invented by Emily and Anne Brontë; also, an inhabitant of this island. Also **Gondaland**. **B.** *adj.* Of or pertaining to this island. Hence **'Gondalan, Gon'dalian** (-'deɪl-) *adjs.*

1834 E. & A. Brontë *Diary* 24 Nov. in M. Spark *Brontë Lett.* (1966) 18 The Gondals are discovering the interior of Gaaldine. 1841 E. Brontë *Diary* 30 July in C. W. Hatfield *Poems E. J. Brontë* (1941) 167 The Gondolians [*sic*] are at present in a threatening state, but there is no open rupture as yet. 1908 C. Shorter *Brontës Life & Lett.* I. x. 215 The *Gondaland Chronicles*, to which reference is made, must remain a mystery for us. 1911 J. M. Dembleby *Key to Brontë Works* i. 17 Emily Brontë.. was writing, on July 30th, 1845, that she, Emily, was.. engaged upon and intended to continue some puerile compositions called *The Gondal Chronicles*, which she spoke of as 'delighting' her and Anne. 1912 M. Sinclair *Three Brontës* 193 There are no recognisable references to the Gondal poems. 1932 C. Morgan in H. J. & H. Massingham *Great Victorians* 70 The opening of 'The Prisoner', telling how narrator and jailer visit a dungeon and speak with a female prisoner confined there, is evidently fictitious, probably Gondal. 1941 F. E. Ratchford *Brontës' Web of Childhood* xiii. 252 Gondalan Vikings. 1941 *N. & Q.* CLXXXI. 182/2 Those [*sc.* poems of Emily Brontë] which were prepared for publication had Gondalian names and references carefully expunged. 1966 M. Spark *Brontë Lett.* 17 The Gondal manuscripts were not preserved, but the love.. and excesses of the exotic people of Gondal moved in the poetry of Emily and Anne to the time of their latest compositions.

gondala, -dalo, -delay, -delo, vars. gondola.

gonder, variant of gander.

Gondi ('gɒndiː). [Hind., f. Gond.] The native (Dravidian) language of the Gonds.

The native name is *koiyán*.

1855 S. Hislop in G. Smith *S. Hislop* (1888) 168 Inquired about the Gondi. 1875 R. Caldwell *Gram. Dravidian Langs.* (ed. 2) 513 A translation of the Gospels of St. Matthew and St. Mark into Gôndi by the Rev. J. Dawson. 1888 G. Smith *S. Hislop* iii. 62 Gondi was the tongue of the aborigines in the uplands. 1967 D. S. Parlett *Short Dict. Lang.* 52 *Gondi* (Dravidian), 2 m speakers scattered over Gondwana region, now giving way to Hindi. 1970 *Encycl. Brit.* X. 568/2 The majority of Gonds speak various, and in part mutually unintelligible, dialects of Gondi, an unwritten Dravidian language.

gondola ('gɒndələ). Forms: 6 **gondala**, 6–8 **-delay**, 7 **-dalo, -delo, -dilo, -dolo, gundalo**, (8 *U.S.*) **-delo(e, -dello, -dilo(w, -dolo**, 7–9 **gondole**, (7 **gundel**, 8 **gondel**), 6– **gondola**. Also 9 *U.S.* **gondelo, gundelow, -dalow, -dola**. [ad. It. *gondola* (whence also Sp., Pg. *gondola*, F. *gondole*) of obscure origin: see Diez, Körting, etc.]

1. a. A light flat-bottomed boat or skiff in use on the Venetian canals, having a cabin amidships and rising to a sharp point at either end; it is usually propelled by one man at the stern with a single oar.

1549 Thomas *Hist. Italie* 83 b, [He kept] one man, or two at the most, to row his Gondola. *a* 1577 Gascoigne *Flowers* Wks. (1587) 52 And from their battered barks commanded to be cast Some Gondalaes wherein upon our pleasant streams they past. 1590 Spenser *F.Q.* ii. vi. 2 A litle Gondelay. 1600 Shaks. *A.Y.L.* iv. i. 38. 1605 B. Jonson *Volpone* iii. ii, Rowing vpon the water in a gondole, With the most cunning Curtizan, of Venice. 1611 W. Venner *Beam of Brightness* B 2 b, No ratling Cart or Waggon runnes in me, but gentle Gundels swimming ore the streame. 1670 *Lond. Gaz.* No. 437/2 He was.. attended by great numbers of his friends in their Pleasure-boats and Gondola's. 1697 tr. *C'tess D'Aunoy's Trav.* (1706) 169 There's a Canal.. and another square Place in which the King has little Gundoloes painted and gilt. 1739 Lady M. W. Montagu *Let. to C'tess Pomfret* 6 Nov., The greatest equipage is a gondola, that holds eight persons. 1764 *Oxford Sausage* 157 O'er Seas of bliss Peace guide her Gondelay. 1818 Byron *Beppo* xix. 1820 —— *Mar. Fal.* iv. i, The far lights of skimming gondolas. 1831 Moore *Summer Fête* 404 Light gondolas, of Venetian breed. 1886 Ruskin *Præterita* I. 281 My love of gliding about in gondolas.

b. *transf.* (See quots.)

1827 *Mayfair* i. 31 There beauty half her glory veils In cabs, those gondolas on wheels. 1870 Disraeli *Lothair* xxvii, He hailed a cruising Hansom,.. ''Tis the gondola of London', said Lothair as he sprang in.

†**2. a.** A ship's boat. **b.** Some kind of small war-vessel. *Obs.*

1626 P. Nichols *Drake Revived* (1628) 9 A ship of Spaine ..(espying our foure Pinnaces),.. sent away her Gundeloe towards the Towne, to giue warning. 1799 *Naval Chron.* I. 273 The Brest fleet, consisting or thirty-two sail, five frigates, and five gondolas, had put to sea.

3. *U.S.* A large flat-bottomed river boat of light build; a lighter; used also as a gun-boat.

1774 J. Wentworth in *N.E. Hist. & Gen. Reg.* (1869) XXIII. 276 The cannon were sent in Gondolas up the River into the country. 1777 E. Badlam *Ibid.* (1848) II. 49 Colonel Brown has taken Ticonderoga.. a number of armed gundeloes, one armed sloop [etc.]. 1805 W. Hunter in *Naval Chron.* XIII. 39 Two Gundolas came down and fired at us. 1809 Kendall *Trav.* III. lxiv. 31 Vessels are floated down to the sea, by means of flat-boats or lighters, here [northern U.S.] called gondolas. 1866 Whittier *Snow-Bound* 254 When favoring breezes deigned to blow The square sail of the gundelow. 1886 B. P. Poore *Remin.* I. iii. 51 The Potomac River.. was navigable.. in long, flat-bottomed boats, sharp at both ends, called 'gondolas'.

4. a. = *gondola car. U.S.*

1871 Schele de Vere *Americanisms* (1872) 480 *Gondola*... The use of the word for a peculiarly shaped railroad-car is not unknown in England. 1875 in Knight *Dict. Mech.* 1906 *Westm. Gaz.* 31 Dec. 7/3 The Central News New York correspondent says.. When the driver pulled up a heavy 'gondola', or low goods wagon, broke loose from the adjacent siding. 1907 *Cosmopolitan* July 390 A flat-car.. is known amongst the fraternity as a 'gondola', with the second syllable emphasized and pronounced long. 1914 *Sat. Even. Post* 4 Apr. 10/1 At the end of the stretch of wheels was the hangout, barricaded on one side by a corrugated iron windshield.. and on the other by a derelict gondola freight car. 1922 H. Titus *Timber* iii. 37 Two Indians were loading pulp wood into a gondola on the siding. 1932 E. Wilson *Devil take Hindmost* xvii. 176 They left.. on a freight-train .. travelling in a low roofless car known as a 'gondola': the gondola was about two-thirds full of gravel.

b. An elongated car attached to the under side of a dirigible balloon or airship. (G., Du. *gondel*.) Also *transf.*, applied to a structure that resembles such a car in its purpose and mode of attachment.

[1881 W. D. Hay *300 Years Hence* xi. 301 You step into an aërial gondola,.. and are at once borne upwards.] 1896 *Strand Mag.* July 78/2 The finished balloon.. is 97 ft. in all from the cap to the bottom of the basket or gondola. 1908 *World's Work* XVI. 10804/2 He suspended his gondolas close underneath the hulk. 1914 *Evening News* 15 Oct. 1/6 The distance between the gondola carrying the engines and the body of the airship has been very much reduced. 1930 G. G. Jackson *World's Aeroplanes* 17 Each ship was given four propellers.. and these were driven by exceptionally powerful motors, divided between two cars, or gondolas, as they came to be called... The gondolas resembled the Italian craft, from which they took their name, in general design, but they were, of course, much larger. 1953 J. Ramsbottom *Mushrooms & Toadstools* viii. 89 When the balloon 'Explorer II' made its ascent to 72,395 feet.. in 1935, spores of seven moulds were enclosed in small quartz tubes fastened to the outside of the gondola. 1955 M. Savill tr. *Galland's First & Last* xxiv. 202 Two additional 20-mm. cannons were mounted below the wings. These 'gondolas' or 'bath-tubs', as we called them, [etc.]. 1959 *Sunday Times* 5 Apr. 7/8 With a float containing petrol to provide buoyancy, and a pressure-proof 'gondola' underneath. **1962** J. GLENN in *Into Orbit* 70 The 'Wheel', as we called it, combined many of the control problems we would encounter in real space flight. It consists of a pill-shaped gondola.. suspended at the end of a 50-foot arm.

c. The car attached to a ski-lift. Also ***gondola lift.***

1957 in *Amer. Speech* (1963) XXXVIII. 205 *Gondola, gondola lift*, a number of smaller enclosed cabins seating two or four persons each. The gondolas are stored at the base station poma lift style and are clamped onto the moving cable after loading. **1958** M. WEST *Second Victory* vii. 97 The Gondelbahn, the long aerial cable that swung the shining gondolas up the slope to the summit of the Grauglockner. **1964** *Harper's Bazaar* Nov. 140/1 *New this season*: gondola lift. **1970** *Times* 18 Dec. 20/2 Vail offers superb skiing... A new development..adds a second gondola.

d. An island counter used in self-service shops for the display of merchandise.

1942 *Super Market* Nov. 53 End of gondola displays may be constructed by using disc-shaped cardboard in graduated sizes. One edge of the cardboard should be cut straight and even in order to rest against the gondola. **1960** *Guardian* 16 May 3/5 Enough space is left round the 'gondolas' (the movable counters) to let shoppers take short cuts. **1962** E. GODFREY *Retail Selling & Organiz.* ii. 19 Other types of counter in common use are refrigerated runs.. and gondolas —a self-service central fixture.

5. *attrib.* and *Comb.*, as ***gondola-beak, †-boat, office***; **gondola-car** *U.S.*, a railway car having a platform body with low sides; **gondola wag(g)on** = *gondola car.*

1887 RUSKIN *Præterita* II. 101 Seeing the *gondola-beak come actually inside the door at Danieli's. **1814** COL. HAWKER *Diary* (1893) I. 123 On one [canal] are many fine *gondola boats. **1884** KNIGHT *Dict. Mech.* Suppl., **Gondola-Car.* **1887** *Pall Mall G.* 10 Aug. 14/2 The other rolling-stock comprises four double-decked open cars, twenty platform cars, twenty gondola cars [etc.]. **1821** T. MOORE *Mem.* (1853) III. 252 Lord John drove me to the *gondole office. **1918** *Chambers's Jrnl.* July 459/2 The comparatively new '*gondola' wagon serves that purpose admirably.

gondole (gɒn'dəʊl), *v.* [Back-formation from GONDOLA.] *intr.* To travel in a gondola. Also *trans.*, to propel (a gondola).

1874 W. JAMES *Let.* 13 Feb. in R. B. Perry *Tht. & Char. W. James* (1935) I. 354 Three days have I gondoled and picture-gazed, under a cloudless sky. **1928** *Daily Express* 6 July 13/6 Sir Robert Witt..used to 'gondole' his own gondola when he went to Venice. **1956** R. MACAULAY *Towers of Trebizond* 281 The one who had lent us this palazzo had left his servants in it—a cook and a gondolier —so we gondoled everywhere and ate well.

gondolet (gɒndə'lɛt). Also 7 gundelet, -olet. [ad. It. *gondoletta*, dim. of *gondola* GONDOLA.] A small gondola.

1602 MARSTON *Ant. & Mel.* III. Wks. 1856 I. 42 There's my signet, take a gundelet. **1607** DEKKER *Whore Babylon* Wks. 1873 II. 211 Those whose nets, Are cast out of our Fairy gundolets. **1828** MOORE *Venetian Air* i, Come to me, When smoothly go our gondolets O'er the moonlight sea. **1856** ANNE MANNING *Tasso & Leonora* 159 Floating in a gilded gondolet with silken awning on the sweet river.

gondolier (gɒndə'lɪə(r)). Also 7 **gundelier, gondoleer,** 7–8 **gondalier.** [a. F. *gondolier*, ad. It. *gondoliere* (pl. *-ieri*), f. *gondola* GONDOLA.] One who rows a gondola. Also as *vb. trans.*, to carry in a gondola. Hence **gondo'liering** *vbl. sb.*

1603 FLORIO *Montaigne* (1632) 477 The Gondoliers or Water men of Venice. **1604** SHAKS. *Oth.* I. i. 126 A knaue of common hire, a Gundelier. **1611** CORYAT *Crudities* 168, I meane those seducing and tempting Gondoleers of the Rialto bridge. **1740** LADY M. W. MONTAGU *Let. to Wortley Montagu* 1 June, They are rowed by gondoliers dressed in rich habits. **1818** BYRON *Ch. Har.* IV. iii, In Venice Tasso's echoes are no more, And silent rows the songless gondolier. **1880** VERNON LEE *Stud. Italy* VI. ii. 266 The gondoliers seated on the slimy steps by their moored boats. **1889** W. S. GILBERT *Gondoliers* II. 32 Take it altogether, is it—Better fun than gondoliering? **1936** F. CLUNE *Roaming round Darling* xxiv. 254 Albert gondoliered us across the stream. **1965** *Listener* 15 Apr. 560/2 Gondoliering runs in families.

gondolo, obs. form of GONDOLA.

Gondwana (gɒnd'wɑːnə). *Geol.* Also **Gondwána.** [Name of a region in central north India, f. Skr. *gonḍavana*, f. *gonḍa* GOND + *vana* forest.] **a.** The name given orig. to an extensive series of rocks in India, chiefly sandstone and shales of fluviatile origin, ranging in age from the Upper Carboniferous to the Jurassic or the Cretaceous; later used to designate similar rock systems with the same characteristic fossil flora found in other countries. Also = GONDWANALAND. **b.** Hence as quasi-*adj.*: of, pertaining to, or characteristic of the Gondwana systems or the period during which they were formed. ***Gondwanaland***: see next.

1873 H. F. BLANFORD *Rud. Phys. Geogr. Indian Sch.* x. 116 An enormous series of deposits in Central India and Bengal, apparently of fresh water origin, for which the name 'Gondwána series' has been proposed by Mr. Medlicott. **1876** O. FEISTMANTEL in *Rec. Geol. Surv. India* IX. 28 The best known, because almost the only fossiliferous, rock-series in the peninsula area of India, is that usually spoken of collectively as the plant-bearing series. This is an awkward designation; and I will at once adopt instead the name Gondwána series or system, to be understood in the same wide sense as when we speak of the Jurassic or Silurian series or system. The name was proposed some years ago by Mr. Medlicott, and has since been more or less current on the survey. **1880** *Ibid.* XIII. 190 (*heading*) The correlation of the Gondwána flora with other flora. **1895** *Ibid.* XXVIII. 117 The discovery of Gondwana plants in Argentina. **1909** *Q. Jrnl. Geol. Soc.* LXV. p. ii, Expedition to the Falkland Islands... Fossils, principally leaves of *Glossopteris*, occur in many places, and it is evident that the whole southern part of East Falkland..belongs to the Gondwana System. **1936** J. C. BROWN *India's Min. Wealth* (ed. 2) i. 11 Over 98 per cent of the coal is mined from the Lower Gondwana rocks of the peninsula. **1943** M. S. KRISHNAN *Geol. India & Burma* (1949) x. 242 The name Gondwana was introduced by H. B. Medlicott in 1872 in a manuscript report. **1956** W. J. ARKELL *Jurassic Geol. World* xiv. 384 It is necessary to return to the threefold division of the Gondwana system... According to this classification the Lower Gondwanas are Upper Palaeozoic, the Middle are Triassic and the Upper are Cretaceous. **1961** L. C. KING in A. E. M. Nairn *Descr. Palaeoclimatol.* 309 By virtue of its size Gondwanaland must have extended beyond any simple climatic girdle... The huge landspread of Gondwana, indeed, does exhibit palaeoclimatic zoning appropriate to two or three of these girdles. **1965** *New Scientist* 14 Oct. 96/2 Any reconstruction of the Gondwana supercontinent results in several Texas-sized missing pieces to this jigsaw puzzle. **1968** R. W. FAIRBRIDGE *Encycl. Geomorphol.* 484/1 The Gondwana landscape was broken up by the fragmentation of Gondwanaland.

Also *absol.* or as *sb.*, short for *Gondwana bed, formation, period, rock*, etc.

1880 *Rec. Geol. Surv. India* XIII. 90 The fluviatile deposits of the upper Gondwánas. **1895** *Ibid.* XXVIII. 117 A patch of Gondwanas..contained several rather fair coal-seams. **1933** *Q. Jrnl. Geol. Soc.* LXXXIX. p. lxxxiii, These latter beds..are typical 'Gondwanas', corresponding with the upper part of the Santa Catherina system in Brazil, the Stormberg of South Africa, and the Rajmahals of India. **1953** D. N. WADIA *Geol. India* (ed. 3) ix. 188 The Middle Gondwana was also the epoch of most extensive land-conditions in India. During the Upper Gondwana, epeiric seas began to encroach on its borders from the north-west and south-east. **1956** [see above].

Gondwanaland (gɒnd'wɑːnəlænd). *Geol.* Also **Gondwana (Gondwána) land.** [a. G. *Gondwána-Land* (E. Suess *Antlitz d. Erde* (1885) I. xii. 768), f. prec. (see quot. 1904 below) + LAND *sb.*] A vast continental area or supercontinent thought to have once existed in the southern hemisphere and to have broken up in Mesozoic or late Palæozoic times forming Arabia, Africa, South America, Antarctica, Australia, and the peninsula of India. Also, these land masses collectively as they exist today.

1896 W. T. BLANFORD in *Rec. Geol. Surv. India* XXIX. 52 The southern continent, of which India formed part, and which is widely known by an Indian name, the Gondwána land of Suess. **1904** H. SOLLAS tr. *Suess's Face of Earth* I. 596 We call this mass Gondwána-Land, after the ancient Gondwána flora which is common to all its parts. **1909** *Q. Jrnl. Geol. Soc.* LXV. p. ii, Expedition to the Falkland Islands... A claystone, containing blocks, apparently of glacial origin,..undoubtedly corresponds with the moraines from other parts of Gondwanaland. **1927** PEAKE & FLEURE *Apes & Men* 18 The movement of Africa northwards is said to be a part of a general breaking up of the ancient southern continent known to science as Gondwanaland. **1936** J. C. BROWN *India's Min. Wealth* (ed. 2) i. 13 The coalfields of Bengal, Bihar and Orissa..are isolated fragments of the once continuous Gondwana land. **1965** A. HOLMES *Princ. Physical Geol.* (ed. 2) xxx. 1190 The peripheral ring of Gondwanaland is interrupted not only by the South Atlantic, but also by the Indian Ocean. **1970** *Nature* 10 Jan. 142/2 Estimates of the time of break-up of Gondwanaland range from the Permian to the Cretaceous.

gone (gɒn, -ɔː-), *ppl. a.* [pa. pple. of GO *v.*; for the predicative uses see GO *v.* 48.]

1. Of persons: Lost, ruined, undone. Also, ***a gone case***, a hopeless case; ***gone sensation (feeling)***, a feeling of faintness or utter exhaustion. ***gone coon***: *U.S.* (see COON *sb.* 3). ***gone goose*** or ***gosling***: a person or thing that is beyond all hope; a 'gone coon'; a 'dead duck' (*colloq.*, orig. *U.S.*).

1598 BERNARD *Terence in English* (1607) 303 Truly I am but a gone man [*equidem perij*]. **1637** RUTHERFORD *Lett.* (1862) I. 445 Men think Christ a gone man now and that He shall never get up His head again. **1677** I. MATHER *Preval. Prayer* (1864) 253 We were in Appearance a gone and ruined People. *a* **1747** D. BRAINERD in Bp. Lavington *Enthus.* (1754) II. 220 One Indian felt that it was a gone Case with him, and thought he must sink down to Hell. **1748** RICHARDSON *Clarissa* (1811) III. 247 Had a parson been there, I had certainly been a gone man. **1823** SCOTT *Quentin D.* xxii, Up heart, master, or we are but gone men. **1830** *Massachusetts Spy* 7 July (Th.), You are a gone goose, friend. **1852** MRS. STOWE *Uncle Tom's C.* xxiv, But don't talk so, as if it were a gone case! *a* **1865** SMYTH *Sailor's Word-Bk.* (1867) 343 *Gone-goose*, a ship deserted or given up in despair (*in extremis*). **1886** M. THOMPSON *Banker of Bankerville* (1887) xix. 285 If they do git 'im he's a gone goslin'. **1892** *Longm. Mag.* Jan. 260 That terrible 'gone' sensation produced only by prolonged abstinence from food. **1931** D. RUNYON *Guys & Dolls* (1932) 59 But I catch pneumonia, and it looks as if maybe I am a gone gosling. **1949** *Sat. Even. Post* 19 Mar. 108/3 Two minutes more of her and I'm a gone goose. **1958** J. & W. HAWKINS *Death Watch* (1959) 88 If my luck won't hold..I'm a gone goose anyway.

2. a. That has departed or passed away; also ***past and gone. dead and gone*** (see DEAD *a.*).

1820 KEATS *Isabella* xx, To honour thee, and thy gone spirit greet. **1839** MARY HOWITT *Marion's Pilgr.* VII. xiii. 3 And the gone tenderness of youth Doth to my heart return. **1849** LYTTON *Caxtons* (1856) 115 The gone ages. **1897** *Daily News* 30 July 7/1 Past and gone conditions of fighting.

b. In *Bowls*. (See quot., and cf. GO *v.* 48 b.)

1892 *Outdoor Games* xxxi, A 'gone bowl' is one that has stopped a hopeless distance beyond the jack.

3. a. With advs., as ***gone-down, -out*** (see GO *v.* 80, 87).

1855 DICKENS *Dorrit* I. xiv, In the chair before the gone-out fire..was the gentleman whom she sought. **1888** CHURCHWARD *Blackbirding* 213, I shan't get more than the gone-down price.

b. With adj. complement, as ***gone-soft, -wild.*** (Cf. GO *v.* 44 a.)

1925 A. S. M. HUTCHINSON *One Increasing Purpose* III. xv, Not a fit man..but a gone-soft and nerve-wracked man. **1960** *Times* 13 Jan. 13/6 The mammalian predators of the rabbit: fox, badger, stoat, weasel, tame and gone-wild cats.

4. Very inspired or excited; 'out of this world'; extremely satisfying; excellent; esp. in phr. ***real gone.*** *slang* (orig. *U.S. jazz musicians'*).

1946 MEZZROW & WOLFE *Really Blues* 374/1 *Gone*, out of this world, superlative. *Gone with it*, really inspired, completely in control of the situation. **1948** *Jazz Jrnl.* Aug. 2 (*heading*) Real gone gal—the history of Nellie Lutcher. **1957** J. KEROUAC *On Road* (1958) I. xi. 60, I have found the gonest little girl in the world. **1958** *Sunday Mail* (Glasgow) 10 Feb. 11 *Gone*—the best, in the top rung, the coolest. **1959** *Spectator* 1 May 613/2 Snapping his fingers in a very gone fashion to the beat. **1959** *News Chron.* 14 Oct. 8/6 The jazz-loving 'hep-cat' who claims that the music 'sends' him until he is 'gone'. **1967** L. J. BROWN *Cat who ate Danish Modern* xvi. 141 This is a real gone pad..it's what the clients expect.

5. Used *absol.* as *sb.* Those who are dead.

1908 *Daily Chron.* 13 May 3/3 Unconscious imitations of Browning and others of the great and the gone. **1914** HARDY *Satires of Circumstance* 52 The speakers, sundry phantoms of the gone.

Hence **'goner** *slang*, one who is dead or undone; something which is doomed or ended.

1850 'DOW, JR.' in *Sunday Mercury* (N.Y.) 6 Jan. 2/6 Last Monday..the old year was not quite a goner. **1854** M. J. HOLMES *Tempest & Sunshine* v. 211 I'd soon give you up as a goner. **1857** THOREAU *Maine W.* (1894) 365 He exclaimed, 'She is a goner!'.. There, to be sure, she lay perfectly dead. **1891** NAT. GOULD *Double Event* 261 Make a noise, or follow me, and you're a goner. **1930** 'E. BRAMAH' *Little Flutter* xiii. 153 If it failed he was—if one may be permitted the word in the excitement of the moment—a 'goner'. **1933** *Boys' Mag.* XLVII. 124/2 When I found the car burnt out I thought you were a 'goner'. **1945** AUDEN *For Time Being* 12 Rome will be a goner.

gone, variant of GANE *v.*, *Obs.*, to gape; variant of *gan* pa. t. of GIN *v.*, to begin; obs. form of GUN.

gone-by, *ppl. a.* and *sb.* [f. *gone* pa. pple. of GO *v.* + BY- 2 d.]

A. *ppl. adj.* = BYGONE *ppl. a.* in various senses.

1827 W. G. S. *Excurs. Village Curate* 70 Something like an old gone-by companion. **1832** MRS. F. TROLLOPE *Dom. Manners Amer.* xiv. (1839) 124 Gone-by relics of the dark ages. **1849** ROCK *Ch. of Fathers* IV. xii. 241 The belief, and ..ritual, of gone-by ages.

B. *sb.* = BYGONE *sb.*

1859 W. CHADWICK *Life De Foe* vii. 342 You cannot let gone-byes be gone-byes quietly.

†go'nel. *Obs.*$^{-1}$ [ad. OF. *gonele, gonelle*, dim. of *gone, gonne* GOWN.] A long gown, worn over armour.

c **1380** *Sir Ferumb.* 4345 Ryȝt as marchantz wille we ryde, Wel y-armed an-vnder our gonels wyde.

goneness ('gɒnnɪs, -ɔː-). [f. GONE *ppl. a.* + -NESS.] Faintness; lassitude; exhaustion.

1853 MOTLEY *Corr.* (1889) I. v. 155 His head bobbing from side to side with an expression of 'goneness'. **1871** G. H. NAPHEYS *Prevent. & Cure Dis.* III. ii. 628 Others, without actual pain, complain of a sense of 'goneness', which leaves them exhausted and almost breathless.

gonfalon ('gɒnfəlɒn). Also 6–9 **gonfalone.** [ad. It. *gonfalone*, Pg. *gonfalão*, Sp. *confalon*, F. *gonfalon*, later form of GONFANON.] A banner or ensign, frequently composed of or ending in several tails or streamers, suspended from a cross-bar instead of being directly fastened to the pole, esp. as used by various Italian republics or in ecclesiastical processions.

1595 T. BEDINGFELD tr. *Macchiavelli's Flor. Hist.* 73 For it sufficed that anie one man cried, let vs goe to such a place, or holding the Gonefalone by the hande, looked that way. **1667** MILTON *P.L.* v. 589 Ten thousand thousand Ensignes high advanc'd, Standards, and Gonfalons twixt Van and Reare Stream in the Aire. **1706** in PHILLIPS (ed. Kersey), *Gonfalon*, the Banner of the Church carry'd in the Pope's Army. **1811** SCOTT *Don Roderick* xxvi, The fiends had burst their yoke, And waved 'gainst heaven the infernal gonfalone. **1868** KINGLAKE *Crimea* (1877) IV. vi. 131 The priests with images, gonfalons, and crosses.

fig. **1887** MCCARTHY in *Gentl. Mag.* Mar. 292 Home Rule was the gonfalon of a small, compact party of Irish members in the House of Commons.

gonfalonier (,gɒnfələ'nɪə(r)). Also 6 **gonfalonner,** 7 **confalonier, gonfollinere.** Also 8–9 (in Ital. form) **gonfaloniere.** [a. F. *gonfalonier* or It. *gonfaloniere*, f. prec.] The bearer of a gonfalon, a standard-bearer; *spec.* (*a*) the title of the chief magistrate (or other official) in several Italian republics; (*b*) (see quot. 1706).

1586 T. B. *La Primaud. Fr. Acad.* I. (1589) 588 In other places they have Gonfalonners, as at Lucques. **1659** BP. WREN *Monarchy Asserted* x. 122 Had she [Florence] not.. her Magistrates Executing? Was not the Rotation too provided for by the Annual Election of her Gonfalonier? **1673** RAY *Journ. Low C.* 378, 2 Priors and a Confalonier. **1706** in PHILLIPS (ed. Kersey), *Gonfalonier*, the Pope's Standard-bearer, which Office is claim'd as Hereditary by the Dukes of Parma. **1756** NUGENT *Gr. Tour* III. 311 Here the cardinal legate, and the gonfaloniere with his counsellors, usually reside. **1802** *Brookes' Gazetteer* (ed. 12) s.v. *Lucca*, The head of this republic has the name of gonfalonier, who has the executive power. **1889** *Athenæum* 27 July 126/2 Four years after the execution of Savonarola the people of Florence.. elected Piero Soderini Gonfalonier for life.

Hence ˌ**gonfaloˈniership**, the office of a gonfalonier.

1726 LEONI *Life Alberti* in *A.'s Archit.* I The Albertis nine times possessed the Gonfaloniership. **1889** *Athenæum* 17 Aug. 214/3 A crowned Gonfaloniership of the Church, leaving the Holy Father nominally free in Rome.

†ˈ**gonfaneur.** *Obs.* In 3 **gunfaneur.** [irregularly f. GONFANON.] = GONFALONIER.

a **1225** *Ancr. R.* 300 Schrift, lo nu, is gunfaneur, & bereð her þe banere biuoren alle Godes ferde.

gonfanon (ˈgɒnfənən). *Obs.* exc. *Hist.* Forms: 4 **gom-, gonfaynoun,** 4–5 **gon-, gunfanoun,** (4 **goffanoun, goinfa(i)noun, -faynoun, gounfanoun, gunfa(i)nun, -phanun,** 5 **confanon, ganfano(u)n),** 7–8 **gonfannon, -ennon,** 5– **gonfanon.** [a. OF. *gunfanun, gonfanon*, etc., = Pr. *gonfano*, med.L. *guntfano*, ad. OHG. *gundfano, chundfano* (OE. *gúðfana*, ON. *gunnfane*), f. **gund-* (OE. *gúþ*):—OTeut. **gunþjâ* war + *fano* banner, FANON. From the later Fr. and It. forms *gonfalon, -one* comes the doublet GONFALON.]

1. = GONFALON. In the middle ages, chiefly applied to the small flag or pennon suspended immediately beneath the steel head of a knight's lance. Also *fig.*

a **1300** *Cursor M.* 21732 On cros godd boght ur saul liues, þar-on he gaf him-seluen ranscun, And of him-seluen mad gunphanun. **13..** *K. Alis.* 1963 There was mony gonfanoun, Of gold, sendel, and siclatoun. **13..** *Sir Tristr.* 173 He bad his kniȝtes.. Com.. Wiþ hors and wepenes fele And rered goinfaynoun. *c* **1400** *Rom. Rose* 2018, I bere of Love the gonfanoun, Of Curtesye the banere. **1489** CAXTON *Faytes of A.* I. xv. 45 The chyef capytaynes of the oostis had gonfanons with certeyn deuyses. **1688** R. HOLME *Armoury* III. 272/1 A Papal Gonfanon, or square Banner... This.. is ever carried before the Popes Holiness, when he goeth, or is carried in Processions. **1794** J. P. MALCOLM in *Gentl. Mag. Libr. Topog.* III. (1893) 32 On his gonfannons a bend between six escallops. **1828–40** TYTLER *Hist. Scot.* (1864) I. 320 He holds a long spear, ornamented by a gonfanon. **1876** TENNYSON *Harold* v. i, I see the gonfanon of Holy Peter Floating above their helmets.

†**2.** A lance from which a gonfanon is suspended.

1481 CAXTON *Godfrey* cxcviii. 289 And with the gonfanon that he bare Iusted ayenst hym in suche wyse that he bare hym thurgh the bodye and slewe hym.

Hence †**gonfanoner** [= OF. *gunfanunier*], the bearer of a gonfanon.

c **1450** *Merlin* 211 The kynge Boors so smote Sarmedon, the ganfanoner, that he kutte of the arme with all the sheilde, and the baner fill to the erthe.

†**gong,** *sb.*[1] *Obs.* Also 1 **gang,** 3–6 **gonge,** 5 **goonge,** 6 **goung(e, gung(e.** [A special use of OE. *gang, gǫng*: see GANG *sb.*[1] So ON. *gang-r*, OHG. *feld-gang*, MHG., MDu. *ganc.*]

1. A privy.

c **1000** ÆLFRIC *Hom.* I. 290 þaða he to gange com. *c* **1050** *Suppl. Ælfric's Gloss.* in Wr.-Wülcker 185/18 *Latrina, uel secessus*, gang. *c* **1375** *Sc. Leg. Saints, Machor* 981 þai ware .. schot in till gong stinkand. *c* **1400** *Lay Folks Mass Bk.* App. iii. 125, I knoweleche to the that ther nys no goonge more stynkynge thenne my soule is. **1401** *Pol. Poems* (Rolls) II. 72 If every hous were honest to ete fleish inne, than were it honest to ete in a gonge. **1494** FABYAN *Chron.* VII. 347 The Iewe of Tewkysbury, which fell into a gonge vpon the Satyrday. **1515** BARCLAY *Egloges* IV. (1570) C iij b/2 In a foule prison or in a stinking gonge. **1541** PAYNEL *Salernes Regim.* 34 We shulde eschewe gunges, sinkes, gutters [etc.]. **1570** LEVINS *Manip.* 167/37 A Gonge, *forica.* **1576** GASCOIGNE *Grief of Joy* Wks. (Hazlitt) II. 282 A stately Toye, a preciows peece of pellfe, A gorgeous gong, a worthles painted wall, A flower full freshe [etc.].

2. The contents of a privy; ordure.

1562 in *Stow's Surv.* (1633) 666 No man shall bury any dung, or goung, within the Liberties of this City.

3. *attrib.* and *Comb.*, as *gong-hole, -house, -man, -pit*; **gong-farmer** [FARMER[1]], **-fayer, -fower,** a scavenger; **gong-þurl,** the hole of a privy.

c **1440** *Promp. Parv.* 203/2 *Goonge fyrmar (*K., H., S.* gongefowar; *P.* feyar), *cloacarius, latrinarius.* **1480** CAXTON *Chron. Eng.* ccxxi, They made a gong-fermer smyte of his hede. **1562** in *Stow's Surv.* (1633) 666 No Goungfermour shall carry any Ordure till after nine of the Clocke in the night. **1596** HARINGTON *Metam. Ajax* (1814) 21 Met in the street a gong-farmer with his cart full laden. *a* **1485** *Gongefowar, -feyar [see *c* 1440 above]. *c* **1440** *Promp. Parv.* 203/2 *Goo[n]ge hoole, *gumphus.* *a* **1225** *Ancr. R.* 84 Heo beoð þes deofles *gongmen, & beoð wiðuten ende in his *gong huse. *c* **1000** ÆLFRIC *Interr. Sigewulfi* xlix. (MacLean) 90 On þære nyðemestan fleringe wæs heora *gangpyt & heora myxen. **13..** *Minor Poems fr. Vernon MS.* xxix. 48 In to a gonge-put fer wiþ-Inne þe child adoun þer-Inne he þrong. *a* **1225** *Ancr. R.* 84 To wrien, & te helien þet *gong þurl.

gong (gɒŋ), *sb.*[2] [a. Malay *gǒng, gǔng*, so called in imitation of the sound made by the instrument. Hence also F. and G. *gong*, Sp. *gongo.*] **1. a.** A metallic disk with upturned rim (usually made of an alloy composed of four parts copper to one of tin) which produces resonant musical notes when suspended and struck with a soft mallet. Also ***Chinese gong***, a type of gong used in orchestras to give special effects. (See TOM-TOM *sb.* 1 b.)

Of Asiatic (Malay) origin, but now very generally employed in European countries as an instrument of call, esp. to summon a household to meals.

c **1600** *Adv. A. Battel* in Purchas *Pilgrims* (1625) II. 970 In the morning before day the Generall did strike his Gongo, which is an Instrument of War that soundeth like a Bell. **1697** DAMPIER *Voy.* (1729) I. 338 A great Drum with but one Head called a Gong; which is instead of a Clock. **1779** FORREST *Voy. N. Guinea* 176 They are fond of musical gongs, which come from Cheribon on Java. **1801** SOUTHEY *Thalaba* ix. 190 (Stanf.) The heavy Gong is heard, That falls like thunder on the dizzy ear. **1806** T. BUSBY *Dict. Mus.* (ed. 2) *Gong*, a Chinese instrument of the pulsatile kind. *Ibid.*, The *Gong* is never introduced, except to give a national cast to the music in which it is employed, or to awaken surprise, and rouse the attention of the auditors. **1816** SCOTT *Antiq.* vi, I have had equally doubt concerning my dinner call; gongs, now in present use, seemed a new-fangled and heathenish invention. **1832** HT. MARTINEAU *Demerara* iii. 30 At this moment the gong sounded the hour of dinner. **1847** J. WILSON *Chr. North* (1857) I. 143 Let the breakfast-gong sound at ten o'clock. **1882** MISS BRADDON *Mt. Royal* II. x. 225 The two damsels now appeared, summoned by the gong. **1888** STAINER & BARRETT *Dict. Mus. Terms* (ed. 3) 435/2 *Tom-tom*,.. a Chinese gong. **1900** GROVE *Dict. Mus.* (ed. 2) IV. 56/2 *Tam-tam*, the French term for the gong in the orchestra. **1961** A. BAINES *Mus. Instruments* xiv. 341 The tam-tam or gong, from Eastern Asia, has been used in the orchestra to assist a climax, with its ominous note to suggest sadness or despair. **1962** *Listener* 22 Nov. 885/3 A vibraphone, a zylophone, and four Chinese gongs. **1968** *Observer* 14 Jan. 4/7 We don't make gongs very much. *Ibid.*, The traditional home of the gong is the Far East.

b. A saucer-shaped bell, struck by a hammer or tongue moved by some mechanical device; chiefly used as an alarm or call-bell.

1864 in WEBSTER. **1875** in KNIGHT *Dict. Mech.*

c. *attrib.* and *Comb.*, as ***gong-drum, -hammer, -metal, music, -peal, -stand***; ***gong-like, -tormented*** adjs.; **gong-bell** = b (Webster 1864).

1926–7 *Army & Navy Stores Catal.* 1086 Gong drum jazz outfit... Comprising:—17-in. Gong Drum, 10-in. Side Drum and Sticks, [etc.]. **1954** *Grove's Dict. Mus.* (ed. 5) II. 773/1 A single-headed type of bass drum is the 'gong drum' or 'gong bass drum'... Introduced for theatre use to save space.. it was adopted towards the end of the 19th century ..and is still in use..to-day. **1889** *Cent. Dict.*, Gong hammer. **1906** *Westm. Gaz.* 4 Sept. 8/2 The lever which governs the escapement of the alarum makes a noise sufficient almost to wake a light sleeper without the aid of the gong-hammer striking. **1924** A. D. SEDGWICK *Little French Girl* II. v. 140 Now and then she emitted a loud gong-like laugh. **1854** J. SCOFFERN in *Orr's Circ. Sci., Chem.* 492 Bell-metal contains about twice that quantity of tin; and gong-metal somewhat less. **1969** *Australian* 7 June 16/6 Indonesian gong music and singing is the most accessible Asian music for Western ears. **1811** SCOTT *Don Roderick* xix, Gong-peal and cymbal-clank the ear appal. **1932** W. B. YEATS *Words for Music* 2 That dolphin-torn, that gong-tormented sea.

2. *slang.* **a.** A medal or decoration (see quot. 1925).

1925 FRASER & GIBBONS *Soldier & Sailor Words* 106 *A gong*, a medal. (An old Army term suggested by the shape.) **1942** 'B. J. ELLAN' *Spitfire!* xv. 80 Wilf, G—— and F/Sgt. S—— had all been awarded 'Gongs' (medals to you!) after Dunkirk. **1944** *Lancet* 9 Sept. 359/1 To balance my civilian contemporaries' achievements of the past four years, I have acquired a wife and family, some expensive tastes, the '1939–43 gong'. **1954** G. SMITH *Flaw in Crystal* 144 He'd been invalided out... There he was.. unadorned among all the wings and pips and gongs. **1958** M. DICKENS *Man Overboard* iii. 35 Other people came out of the war with Mentions and worthwhile gongs that tacked letters after their names. **1959** [see CLANGER].

b. A warning bell on a police car.

1938 F. D. SHARPE *Sharpe of Flying Squad* xxvii. 277 When they spotted the police car on their trail they opened their car out and pretended that they couldn't hear the gong, ..but they..were overhauled and pinched.

3. [? A different word.] A narcotic drug. Also ˈ**gonger,** opium; an opium pipe; **gongeˈrine,** an opium pipe. *U.S. slang.*

1914 JACKSON & HELLYER *Vocab. Criminal Slang* 38 *Gonger.* Current amongst smokers and drug fiends. An opium pipe. Also used in the diminutive form 'gongerine'. **1915** G. BRONSON-HOWARD *God's Man* VII. i. 393 Come, lie 'round and join in the fun; With the aid of 'the gong'. **1933** *Amer. Speech* VIII. 27/2 *Hitting the gong*,.. kicking the gong around. **1938** *Ibid.* XIII. 185/1 *Gonger*, any opium derivatives. **1952** J. STEINBECK *East of Eden* 198 Let the gong alone for a couple of weeks. **1955** *U.S. Senate Hearings* (1956) VIII. 4162 *Beat the gong*,.. to smoke opium. *Ibid.*, *Gong beater*, one who smokes opium.

gong (gɒŋ), *v.* [f. GONG *sb.*[2]] **1.** To sound a gong; to make a gong-like sound; to summon (a person) with a gong.

1903 H. G. WELLS in *Strand Mag.* Apr. 426/1 He has just gonged, no doubt to order another buttered tea-cake! **1959** J. WAIN *Travelling Woman* 28 The vase, which was a metal one, gonged on the floor, and the flowers fell messily at his feet. **1959** D. BARTON *Loving Cup* 167, I gong them into meals on the dot.

2. Of traffic police: to call upon (a driver) to stop by ringing a powerful 'gong'. Also *intr.* (Cf. GONG *sb.*[2] 2 b.)

1934 in WEBSTER. **1935** *Times* 9 Oct. 9/3 'If Major Gwynne had passed you a little farther down the road you would not have gonged him then because that part is not restricted?'—'No.' **1936** *Times* 12 Mar. 8/5 He..was approaching a stationary car outside the Royal Oak when he gonged, slowed down at a pedestrian crossing, and [etc.]. **1966** T. WISDOM *High-Performance Driving* xvi. 137 He will then have to 'gong' you into the side on a busy trunk road.

gong, obs. form of GANG.

ˈ**gong-ˌgong.** ? *Obs.* Also 8 **gun(g)-gun(g.** [Partly a reduplication of Malay *gong, gung* (see GONG *sb.*[2]); partly an independent echoic formation: cf. GUMGUM.

The reduplicated form may have come from some Malayan dialect; cf. *gonggong* barking of dogs, *ginggong* a 'Jew's harp' or similar toy. Cf. G. *gonggong, gonggon*, Du., Sw. *gonggong*, Da. *gongon*, a gong.]

A name given to various musical instruments of percussion in use among primitive peoples.

1771 J. R. FORSTER *P. Osbeck's Trav.* I. 186 Gungung is the Chinese name of an instrument which has the greatest resemblance to a brass bason. **1772** *Ann. Reg.* 5/2 Besides these they have little drums, great and small kettle drums, gunguns or round brass basons like frying pans, flutes [etc.]. **1800** W. TAYLOR in *Monthly Mag.* VIII. 727 But hark! the gong-gong tolls the knell of day. **1817** BOWDICH *Mission to Ashantee* I. vii. (1819) 136 The gong-gongs and drums were beat all around us.

gongora (ˈgɒŋgərə). [mod.L. (Ruiz & Pavon *Floræ Peruvianæ et Chilensis Prodromus* (1794) 117), f. the name of Don Antonio Caballero y *Góngora* (fl. 1782), Viceroy of New Granada.] A plant or flower of the genus of tropical American orchids so named.

1827 W. J. HOOKER *Exotic Flora* III. tab. 178 (*heading*) Dark-flowered Gongora. **1910** C. H. CURTIS *Orchids for Everyone* 188 The Gongoras have a quaintness that is attractive, but the species are of little value except as curiosities. **1951** *Dict. Gardening* (R. Hort. Soc.) II. 907/2 Gongoras often develop numerous erect, aerial roots.

Gongorism (ˈgɒŋgərɪz(ə)m). [f. *Gongora* (see below) + -ISM.] An affected type of diction and style introduced into Spanish literature in the 16th century by the poet Gongora y Argote (1561–1627). So ˈ**Gongorist** [-IST], one who writes in this style. Also ˈ**Gongoresque** *a.* [-ESQUE]; **gongoˈristic** *a.*

1813 W. TAYLOR in *Monthly Rev.* LXX. 461 Gongorism became the name of a finical mode of writings. **1837–9** HALLAM *Hist. Lit.* (1847) III. 17 The Gongorists formed a strong party in literature, and carried with them the public voice. **1849** TICKNOR *Hist. Span. Lit.* II. xxxiii. 52 *note*, He [Corral] is Gongoresque in his style, as is Quintana. **1886** *Q. Rev.* July 39, Euphuisitc language corresponded in date and character with Gongorism in Spain. **1925** *Times Lit. Suppl.* 26 Mar. 224/3 The suggestion,.. of omitting various passages.. which are likely to be too 'gongoristic' for contemporary taste, merits favourable consideration. **1944** *Downside Rev.* 182 We may in dealing with this question of Gracián's style and his supposed condemnation of gongoristic effects draw the attention of the reader to the richness of the paragraph on Gongora himself in the *Criticon.*

Gonhelly, variant of GOONHILLY.

Goniatite (ˈgəʊnɪətaɪt). *Palæont.* [ad. mod.L. *gōniatītēs* (de Haan, 1825), f. Gr. γωνία angle: see quot. 1847.] A genus of fossil cephalopods.

1838 *Penny Cycl.* XI. 297/2. **1841** *Trans. Geol. Soc.* Ser. II. (1842) VI. 328 Goniatites are plentiful enough in the deposits.. in Westphalia. **1847** ANSTED *Anc. World* v. 96 The most important are called Goniatites (..from the angular markings made by the intersection of the walls of the chambers and outer shell). **1849** DANA *Geol.* App. i. (1850) 708 Resembles a compressed Goniatite, but has no septa. **1864** H. SPENCER *Illustr. Univ. Progr.* 341 Until some twelve years ago, Goniatites had not been found lower than the Devonian rocks.

‖**gonidium** (gəʊˈnɪdɪəm). *Bot.* Pl. **gonidia.** [mod.L., dim. on Gr. type of γόνος child, produce.]

1. One of the cells filled with chlorophyll which are formed beneath the cortical layer in the thallus of lichens; now known to be imprisoned algæ.

1845 E. TUCKERMAN *N. Amer. Lichens* 29 The gonidia exist primarily as the gonimous layer. **1856** W. L. LINDSAY *Brit. Lichens* 58 The gonidium is a cellular bud, a reproductive cell. **1877** [see GONIDIAL].

2. a. A reproductive cell produced asexually in algæ. **b.** The conidium in fungi.

1882 [see CONIDIUM]. **1889** in *Century Dict.*

Hence **goˈnidial, goˈnidic** *adjs.*, of or pertaining to gonidia; **gonidiˈogenous** *a.*, producing or having the power to produce gonidia; **goˈnidioid** *a.*, resembling the gonidia of lichens; **goˈnidiose** *a.*, containing or provided with gonidia. Also **goˈnidiophore** = CONIDIOPHORE.

1845 E. Tuckerman *N. Amer. Lichens* 29 The gonidial propagation will be first described. **1856** W. L. Lindsay *Brit. Lichens* 38 A thin, bright-green, gonidic layer. **1857** Berkeley *Cryptog. Bot.* 341 Gonidioid cells in various conditions. **1877** Bennett tr. *Thomé's Bot.* 286 At the line where they meet the gonidia almost always constitute a zone of variable thickness, the gonidial layer. **1882** Vines *Sachs' Bot.* 273 The septum bulges out and developes into a new gonidial receptacle. **1882** Crombie in *Encycl. Brit.* XIV. 556/2 Many of these forms are more or less similar to 'gonidioid' algæ. *Ibid.* 557/1 The origin of the first Cortical Gonidiogenous Cellules. *Ibid.* 558/2 Plants..in which the thallus is but sparingly gonidiose. **1887** tr. *Goebel's Outl. Classif. & Morphol. Plants* 131 Besides these large gonidiophores, the mycelia of many genera also bear [etc.].

gonimic (gəʊˈnɪmɪk), *a.* [f. mod.L. *gonimon* (a. Gr. γόνιμον neut. of γόνιμος producing offspring, f. root γεν-, γον- to produce + -ic.] In ***gonimic layer, stratum*** (= mod.L. *stratum gonimon*) orig. a synonym of 'gonidial layer'. Now in narrowed sense, the adj. being taken to mean: Relating to gonimia; containing gonimia.

1857 Berkeley *Cryptog. Bot.* §421. 380 Every Lichen consists of at least the external, gonimic, and medullary strata. **1882** Crombie in *Encycl. Brit.* XIV. 561/1 Thallus not gelatinous, with a gonidial, rarely gonimic stratum.

‖**gonimium** (gəʊˈnɪmɪəm). *Bot.* Pl. **gonimia**. [mod.L., f. *gonimon* (see prec.).] A gonidium which is not of an absolutely green (grass-green) colour.

1882 Crombie in *Encycl. Brit.* XIV. 556/1 Gonimia (or the gonidial granules already mentioned) which are naked, pale greenish, glaucous greenish or bluish.

gonimoblast (ˈgɒnɪməʊblæst). *Bot.* [f. Gr. γόνιμος productive + -blast.] In the red algæ: see quot. 1898.

1898 H. C. Porter tr. *Strasburger's Text-bk. Bot.* 337 The fertilised egg does not become converted directly into an oospore, but, as a result of fertilisation, numerous branching filaments termed gonimoblasts grow out from the sides of the ventral portion of the carpogonium. **1945** F. E. Fritsch *Struct. & Reprod. Algae* II. 413 In most Florideae, however, the gonimoblasts do not arise directly from the zygote. *Ibid.* 599 In the life-cycle of Nemalionales the zygote constitutes the only diploid stage, while there are two haploid phases, the ordinary seaweed and the gonimoblast-threads originating from the zygote.

ˈ**gonimous**, *a. Bot. rare.* [f. mod.L. *gonim-on* (see gonimic *a.*) + -ous.] = gonimic (in the older sense).

1845 [see gonidium 1].

goniodont (ˈgəʊnɪəʊdɒnt), *a.* and *sb.* [f. Gr. γωνί-α angle + ὀδούς, ὀδοντ- tooth.]

A. *adj.* Pertaining to the *Goniodontidæ*, a family of nematognathous fishes with angulated teeth. **B.** *sb.* A fish belonging to this family.

1854 Owen *Skel. & Teeth* in *Circ. Sci., Organ. Nat.* I. 270 Bent..like a tenter-hook, as in the fishes thence called *Goniodonts*.

goniometer (gəʊnɪˈɒmɪtə(r)). [ad. F. *goniomètre*, f. Gr. γωνία angle + μέτρον measure.]

1. An instrument used for measuring angles.

Two kinds of goniometers are used in measuring angles of crystals, the old ***contact-*** or ***hand-goniometer*** invented by Carangeot, and the more accurate ***reflecting goniometer*** invented by Wollaston.

1766 B. Martin (*title*), New Art of Surveying by the Goniometer. **1802** Bournon in *Phil. Trans.* XCII. 314, I have measured this angle with more than usual care,.. having taken the precaution of using several different goniometers. **1854** J. Scoffern in *Orr's Circ. Sci., Chem.* 19 Carangeot's goniometer..consists of two metal rulers fastened together at the pivot *a*. **1895** Story-Maskelyne *Crystallogr.* §373 The contract- or hand-goniometer. *Ibid.* §374 The reflection-goniometer of Wollaston.

attrib. **1867** J. Hogg *Microsc.* I. ii. 56 Schmidt's goniometer positive eye-piece is so arranged as to be easily rotated.

2. An apparatus for determining the direction from which detected radio waves are coming, without the need for a rotating aerial, consisting essentially of a rotatable detector coil coupled to two fixed primary coils at right angles to one another, each of these being in turn connected to one of a pair of directional aerials also at right angles. Also (and orig.) called a radiogoniometer.

1921 B. Leggett *Wireless Telegr.* viii. 233 The station was located by the Germans, doubtless by means of first a goniometer and then balloon observation, and for several days it was heavily shelled. **1932** F. E. Terman *Radio Engin.* xvi. 591 When it is desirable to avoid rotating a loop antenna ..it is possible to obtain the effect of rotation by using two loop antennas at right angles to each other and combining the outputs in a goniometer. **1961** H. Jasik *Antenna Engin. Handbk.* xxviii. 21 Since dipoles are usually employed at frequencies above 50 Mc, a capacity goniometer is frequently used to avoid the necessity of shielding an inductive goniometer.

goniometry (gəʊnɪˈɒmɪtrɪ). [ad. F. *goniométrie* (Lagny, 1724), f. as prec.: see -metry.] Measurement of angles.

1823 in Crabb *Technol. Dict.* **1847** Terrot (*title*), An Attempt to Elucidate and Apply the Principles of Goniometry. **1864** C. P. Smyth *Our Inher.* iii. xv. (1874) 269 There could have been no more community of feeling.. in their goniometry than in their methods of astronomical orientation.

Hence ˌ**gonioˈmetric**, ˌ**gonioˈmetrical** *adjs.*, of or pertaining to goniometry.

1837 Goring & Pritchard *Microgr.* 45 The goniometrical part, or that which measures angles as well as distances. **1854** J. Scoffern in *Orr's Circ. Sci., Chem.* 137 A circumstance..inferred from goniometric measurement.

gonion (ˈgəʊnɪɒn). *Anat.* [a. F. *gonion* (P. Broca 1875, in *Bull. de la Soc. d'Anthrop. de Paris* X. 362), f. Gr. γωνία angle + -ion².] The outermost point on the angle of the lower jaw on each side.

1878 R. Bartley tr. *Topinard's Anthrop.* ii. ii. 235 *Gonion*, the region of the angle of the lower jaw. **1968** [see gnathion].

gonioscope (ˈgəʊnɪəʊskəʊp). [f. Gr. γωνί-α angle: see -scope.] An instrument for observing the angle of the anterior chamber of the eye, usu. consisting of a contact lens to which is attached some kind of optical system. Hence **gonioˈscopic** *a.*; **goniˈoscopy**, the art or science of using the gonioscope; inspection of the angle of the anterior chamber.

1923 A. Duane *Fuchs's Text-Bk. Ophthalmol.* xviii. 372 If the observer, standing to one side, holds the ophthalmoscopic mirror almost at right angles to the patient's line of sight, he can see deposits and adhesions in the angle of the anterior chamber, which ordinarily are invisible because hidden by the limbus (Salzmann). Such an examination is called gonioscopy. **1925** M. U. Troncoso in *Amer. Jrnl. Ophthal.* VIII. 433/2 Hoping to obtain a clear, unobstructed view of the angle [of the anterior chamber of the eye] in all directions and a sufficient magnification, I have devised and perfected a new instrument, the gonioscope, which is a microscope and a periscope combined. *Ibid.*, The term 'Gonioscopy' suggested by the author in 1921, has been adopted. *Ibid.* 445/2 A second gonioscopic examination two weeks afterwards detected a total peripheral synechia all around the limbus. **1951** H. S. Sugar *Glaucomas* ii. 27 By applying a prismatic contact lens (gonioscopic lens) to the eye, we are able to see the structures of the chamber angle. **1961** *Lancet* 22 July 166/2 The implant should not be inserted until the eye has recovered from this operation and gonioscopy shows that the desired effect has been achieved. **1961** *Ibid.* 26 Aug. 467/1 Optical methods of examination [of the eye] (chiefly the slit-lamp microscope and the gonioscope).

Gonk (gɒŋk). Also **gonk**. [Arbitrary formation.] The proprietary name of an egg-shaped doll. Also *attrib.*

1964 *Trade Marks Jrnl.* 26 Feb. 322/2 Gonks 856, 736. Games (other than ordinary playing cards), toys and playthings. Daniel Buckley Enterprises Limited, 1–5, Poland Street, London, W.1; Manufacturers—19th November, 1963. **1964** *Spectator* 29 May 726/1 Those neckless dolls called—I think—gonks, which witless adults are said to give to other adults. **1964** *Daily Mail* 2 Sept. 4/3 Gonks..are those nasty, expensive, fat balls of felt and rag that are squatting all over our houses and toy shops. **1964** *Daily Tel.* 11 Sept. 17/3 The principal of a technical college said..' ..We had one with what I believe is a "gonk" cut. His ears were invisible and you could just see his eyes and nose peeping out from under shoulder-length hair.' **1968** A. Diment *Gt. Spy Race* iii. 44 The double bed..was covered by a large tribe of Gonk dolls, paperbacks and grimy LP sleeves. **1969** A. E. Lindop *Sight Unseen* xiv. 120 Her hair had degenerated into a gonk style.

gonn(e, obs. form of gun.

gonn(e(n, pa. t. (pl.) of gin *v.*, to begin.

gonna (ˈgɒnə), colloq. (esp. U.S.) or vulgar pronunciation of *going to* (see go *v.* 47 b).

[Cf. the earlier Sc. *ganna, gaunna*: see Eng. Dial. Dict. s.v. *Go*, quots. 1806, etc.]

1913 C. E. Mulford *Coming of Cassidy* ix. 149 Yo're gonna get a good lickin'. **1929** E. W. Springs *Above Bright Blue Sky* 136, 5684 has a busted cylinder. Gonna put a new motor in it. **1952** A. Baron *With Hope, Farewell* 56 Put 'em all in clover, that's what I'm gonna do. **1967** M. Shulman *Kill* 3 ii. iv. 81 I'm gonna keep on yelling tell you let me out.

gonner, obs. form of gunner.

gonnof, gonny, variants of gonoph, gony.

gono- (ˈgɒnəʊ), *prefix*, before a vowel **gon-**, repr. Gr. γονο-, comb. form of γόνος, γονή generation, offspring, semen, etc. Used in a few compounds in Greek (of which only gonorrhœa has passed into English), and now employed in various technical terms of modern Biology, Zoology, etc. ˈ**gonoblast** *Biol.* [see -blast], a cell which takes part in reproduction; hence ˌ**gonoˈblastic** *a.* ‖ˌ**gonoblaˈstidium** *Zool.* (pl. **-idia**). [f. gonoblast + Gr. -ίδιον dim. suffix] = blastostyle; hence ˌ**gonoblaˈstidial** *a.* ‖ˈ**gonocalyx** *Zool.* [see calyx 2], the bell-shaped disk forming the swimming organ of a medusiform gonophore; hence **gonoˈcalycine** *a.* **gonocheme** (ˈgɒnəʊkiːm) *Zool.* [Gr. ὄχημα vehicle] (see quot.). **gonoˈchoric**, ˌ**gonochoˈristic** *adjs.*; **gonoˈchorism** *Biol.* [ad. G. *gonochorismus* (E. Haeckel *Gen. Morphol.* (1866) II. i. 60)], = diœcism; hence **gonoˈchorist**, a diœcious organism. ˈ**gonocœl, -cœle** (-siːl) *Zool.* [Gr. κοῖλον cavity], a body cavity that contains or gives rise to gonads. **gonoˈcoccal** *a.*, of, pertaining to, or caused by gonococci. **gonoˈcoccus** *Path.* [see coccus], the micrococcus found in the discharge of gonorrhœa. ˈ**gonocyte** *Biol.* [-cyte], any cell which may potentially undergo meiosis and produce gametes; also, any of the gametes so produced. ˈ**gonoduct** *Zool.* [cf. gonaduct], in some invertebrates, a duct from a gonad to the exterior through which gametes are discharged. ˈ**gonomere** *Biol.* [a. G. *gonomer* (V. Häcker 1902, in *Jenaische Zeitschr. f. Naturwiss.* XXXVII. ii. 312): see -mere], any nucleus which, after plasmogamy, coexists with and does not fuse with another nucleus in the same cell; hence **gonoˈmeric** *a.* **goˈnomery**, a condition characterized by the presence of gonomeres. ˈ**gonoplasm** *Mycology* [see plasm], in some genera of the fungal order Peronosporales, that portion of the contents of the antheridium which passes down the fertilization tube. ˈ**gonopore** *Zool.*, a genital pore. ˈ**gonosome** *Zool.* [Gr. σῶμα body], Allman's name for the collective body of reproductive zooids of a hydrozoan; hence ˌ**gonoˈsomal** *a.* ˈ**gonosphere** *Bot.* [sphere], the irregular globule formed by the condensation of the protoplasm of the oogonium in certain fungi; also ‖**gonoˈsphærium** (pl. *-sphæria*). ‖**gonoˈtheca** *Zool.* [Gr. θήκη a case] = gonangium; hence **gonoˈthecal** *a.* ˈ**gonotome** *Zool.* [ad. G. *gonotom* (J. W. van Wijhe 1889, in *Arch. f. mikrosk. Anat.* XXXIII. 466): see -tome.], a block of tissue within a somite destined to form a gonad; also, any somite that contains a gonad. **gonoˈzooid** *Zool.* [zooid], one of the sexual zooids enclosed in certain of the gonophores of the *Hydrozoa*; also *attrib.*

1884 A. Hyatt in *Proc. Boston Soc. Nat. Hist.* (1885) XXIII. i. 61 An apparently strong objection to the *gonoblastic theory founded on the cover-cell. **1861** J. R. Greene *Man. Anim. Kingd., Cœlent.* 46 In general, *gonoblastidia arise from the sides of the cœnosarc. **1877** Huxley *Anat. Inv. Anim.* iii. 143 The groups of male and female gonophores are borne upon separate branches of the gonoblastidium. **1870** Nicholson *Man. Zool.* 74 This system of tubes constitutes what is known as the system of the '*gonocalycine canals'. *Ibid.* 73 The gonophore is now found to be composed of a bell-shaped disc, termed the '*gonocalyx'. **1871** Allman *Gymnoblastic Hydroids* p. xv, *Gonocheme..a medusiform planoblast which gives origin directly to the generative elements. *Ibid.* 76 The medusa, whether gonocheme or blastocheme, shows [etc.]. **1876** E. R. Lankester tr. *Haeckel's Hist. Creation* I. viii. 175 (*heading*) Distinction of sexes, or *gonochorism. [*Ibid.*, Every organic individual, as a non-hermaphrodite (Gonochoristus), produces within itself only one of two generative substances.] **1904** J. McCabe tr. *Haeckel's Wonders of Life* 255 When the ovum and the sperm-cell.. are formed in two different individuals (male and female), we call them monosexual, or gonochorists. *Ibid.* 258 The oyster is usually gonochoristic, but sometimes hermaphroditic. *Ibid.* 259 Such structures..have clearly been developed from gonochoristic structures in lower forms. **1950** *Biol. Abstr.* XXIV. 2706/1 Spp. with present haploid hermaphroditism might have been derived from gonoch[o]ric ancestors. **1951** *Ibid.* XXV. 3378/2 *L[ysmata] seticaudata* is a protandric hermaphrodite whose sexual periodicity places it physiologically among the gonochoric conditions found in most malacostraceous Crustacea. **1963** E. Mayr *Animal Species & Evol.* xi. 316 In many marine invertebrates certain geographic races are gonochoristic, while others are hermaphrodite. **1965** G. Bacchi *Sex Determination* i. 21 Unisexuality, dioecism or gonochorism indicate that male and female sex organs occur in different individuals, plants or animals. The three terms are almost perfectly equivalent although the last one is mostly used by zoologists. *Ibid.* iv. 64 Significant genetical work on sex in hermaphrodites and in labile gonochorists is still very scarce. *Ibid.* vii. 156 Labile gonochoric individuals of the *Bonellia* type. **1900** J. O. Symes *Bacteriol. Every-day Pract.* 39 Now and then the *gonococcal infection may run an extremely mild course, showing only a slight muco-purulent discharge. **1923** *Daily Mail* 15 June 9 Severe forms of streptococcal, staphylococcal, and gonococcal infections. **1970** *Nature* 25 July 383/1 A few gonococcal isolates have proved resistant to rabbit antiserum. **1889** J. M. Duncan *Lect. Dis. Women* xxii. (ed. 4) 181 The *gono-coccus or microbe believed to be peculiar to venereal gonorrhœa, to be indeed its exclusive cause. **1897** *Allbutt's Syst. Med.* III. 71 Many observers have sought for the gonococcus in the synovial fluid from the affected joints. **1893** *Funk's Stand. Dict.* I, *Gonocœle. **1900** E. A. Minchin in E. R. Lankester *Treat. Zool.* II. ii. 35 Each protocœlom is in its nature a gonocœl (Goodrich), that is to say a cœlomic pouch, the epithelial walls of which produce ova or sperm or both. **1940** Parker & Haswell *Text-bk. Zool.* (ed. 6) I. ix. 631 The cœlome consists of the pericardium and the gonocœle. **1967** P. A. Meglitsch *Invert. Zool.* ix. 310 The gonocoel theory visualizes the coelom as arising from the lumen of the gonads. **1900** E. A. Minchin in E. R. Lankester *Treat. Zool.* II. iii. 60 In sponges generally two classes of tokocytes can be distinguished: first, sexual cells or *gonocytes, the mother cells of ova and spermatozoa of the normal type. **1904** J. McCabe tr. *Haeckel's Wonders of Life* 254 The two copulating sexual cells (gonocyta). **1956** *Nature* 21 Jan. 142/1 The conditions which determine the differentiation of indifferent gonocytes in hermaphrodite glands..constitute a major problem in the biology of sexuality. **1893** *Funk's Stand. Dict.* I, *Gonoduct. **1900** E. A. Minchin in E. R. Lankester *Treat. Zool.* II. ii. 36 The cœlomoducts belonging to gonocœls may be called 'gonoducts' (Lankester). **1951** L. H. Hyman *Invertebrates* II. ix. 50 Coelomate animals may..

lack gonoducts and use the nephridia for the discharge of sex cells. **1903** *Bot. Gaz.* June 443 The nuclear stages in which the idiomeres (partial nuclei) and *gonomeres (double nuclei) appear are closely related. **1920** W. E. Agar *Cytol.* 78 In the germ-track..evidences of gonomery can be found at a much later stage of development than in the somatic cells. **1925** E. B. Wilson *Cell* (ed. 3) 433 Gonomeric grouping. **1969** Brown & Bertke *Textbk. Cytol.* xxii. 531 This condition of gonomery approaches the dikaryotic phase in Basidiomycetes. **1887** H. E. F. Garnsey tr. *De Bary's Fungi* 495/2 **Gonoplasm*, in Peronosporeae: portion of protoplasm of antheridium which passes through the fertilisation-tube and coalesces with the oosphere. **1952** F. L. Wynd tr. *Gäumann's Fungi* 66 Later the sexually functional cytoplasm accumulates in the central portion, forming the gonoplasm. **1897** Parker & Haswell *Textbk. Zool.* I. vi. 276 In the female [round-worm] the reproductive aperture or *gonopore is separate from the anus, and is situated on the ventral surface. **1951** L. H. Hyman *Invertebrates* II. ix. 50 Male and female gonopores in hermaphroditic species may be separate,..or there may be a common gonopore. **1870** Nicholson *Man. Zool.* I. 26 Another series of reproductive zoöids, collectively called the '*gonosome'. **1871** Allman *Gymnoblastic Hydroids* 29 The zooids which compose the gonosome may [etc.]. **1865** Cooke *Rust, Smut,* etc. 130 The large granules which are contained in the oogonium accumulate at its centre, and form an irregular, somewhat spherical mass, which is called by De Bary a *gonosphere. **1873** Mrs. Hooker tr. *Le Maout & Decaisne's Bot.* 951 *Gonospheria only differ from oogonia in the condensation of the protoplasm at the centre of the cell. **1878** Napier in Buckland *17th Rep. Salmon Fish* 13 The surface of the gonospheria. **1861** J. R. Greene *Man. Anim. Kingd., Cœlent.* 47 The lower portion of each gonoblastidium forms a sort of peduncle, above which the cuticular investment of its ectoderm becomes separated as an urn-shaped capsule, the '*gonotheca'. **1900** J. S. Kingsley *Text. Bk. Vert. Zool.* I. 103 Whether we have metamerically repeated *gonotomes, is as yet a disputed question. **1912** —— *Compar. Anat. Vert.* 319 At one time it was thought that the anlage of the gonad was segmental in character and 'gonotomes', comparable to nephrotomes and myotomes, were described. **1969** A. J. Grove et al. *Anim. Biol.* (ed. 8) xvi. 382 [Amphioxus.] For a time each gonotome remains connected to its own somite by a short stalk, but eventually the stalk is severed and in this way a series of young gonads is formed. **1841–71** T. R. Jones *Anim. Kingd.* (ed. 4) 97 The *gonozooid, though permanently attached, is furnished with a swimming-bell. **1870** Rolleston *Anim. Life* 254 Such fixed gonozooid forms as the sea fir.

go-no-go: see GO *a.*

gonoph (ˈgɒnəf). *slang.* Also **gonnof.** [a. Heb. *gannābh* thief.] A pickpocket.

1852 Dickens *Bleak Ho.* xix, He's as obstinate a young gonoph as I know. **1876** *Life Cheap Jack* (ed. Hindley) 146 [A Jew *loq.*] Oh, you teif! you cheat! you gonnof! **1884** *Pall Mall G.* 29 Dec. 4/1 The company must consist of at least three, and preferably of four, gonophs (thieves).

gonophore (ˈgɒnəfɔə(r)). [f. Gr. γόνο- GONO- + -φορ-ος bearing. Cf. F. *gonophore.*]

1. *Bot.* The short stalk which bears the stamens and carpels in *Anonaceæ*, etc., due to the elongation of the receptacle above the corolla.

1835 Lindley *Introd. Bot.* (1848) I. 390 It is called gonophore by De Candolle. **1880** Gray *Struct. Bot.* 212 Gonophore [is used] when [a stipe] elevates both stamens and pistil.

2. *Zool.* One of the medusoid buds which contain the reproductive elements in *Hydrozoa.*

1859 Huxley *Oceanic Hydrozoa* 137 The central polype-like sac of a medusiform gonophore. **1877** —— *Anat. Inv. Anim.* iii. 127 In its simplest condition the gonophore is a mere sac-like diverticulum or outward process of the body wall.

gonorrhœa (gɒnəˈriːə). Also 6 **gomoria, gomory, gonorrhey,** 7 **gonor, gonorrhea.** [med.L. *gonorrhœa*, ad. Gr. γονόῤῥοια, f. γόνος seed + ῥοία flux; so called because it was supposed to be a discharge of semen.

With the forms *gomoria, gomory*, cf. OF. *gomorree* (14th c.), It. *gomorrea*; it is doubtful whether this spelling suggested or was suggested by the etym. given in quot. 1547.]

An inflammatory discharge of mucus from the membrane of the urethra or vagina.

1547 [see b]. **1549** *Compl. Scot.* vi. 67 The vattir lille, quhilk is ane remeid contrar gomoria. **1597** Gerarde *Herbal.* I. xxxv. §8. 50 The Gonorrhey or running of the raines. **1631** Massinger *Emperor East* IV. iii. The gonorrhea, or if you will heare it In a plainer phrase, the pox. **1710** T. Fuller *Pharm. Extemp.* 29 It's prescrib'd..in a Gonorrhœa. **1794–6** E. Darwin *Zoon.* (1801) I. 425 In the urethra it has the name of gonorrhœa. **1884** M. Mackenzie *Dis. Throat & Nose* II. 294 The inflammation results..in some still rarer instances from gonorrhœa.

fig. **1598** E. Gilpin *Skial.* (1878) 31 Filthing chaste eares with theyr pens Gonorrhey.

†**b.** *attrib.*, in ***gonorrhœa passion.***

1547 Boorde *Brev. Health* clxvi. (1557) 59 b, The 166 Chapitre doth shewe of a Gomory passion..[Gomerra passio, it is named so because Gomer and Sodome dyd synke for such lyke matter]. **1579** Langham *Gard. Health* (1633) 406 [For] Gonor passion, anoynt thy yard and clothes with Camphire.

Hence **gono'rrhœal, -'eal,** †**gono'rrhœan** *adjs.*, of, pertaining to, or affected with gonorrhœa.

1607 Topsell *Four-f. Beasts* (1658) 39 A plaister against the Gonorrhœan passion. **1611** Cotgr., *Pisse-chaude*, a burnt P. also, the Venerian flux; the Gonorrhean or contagious, running. **1807** *Med. Jrnl.* XVII. 573 On the identity of gonorrhœal and chancrous virus. **1860** Sir H. Thompson *Dis. Prostate* (1868) 51 Acute inflammation of the urethra of any kind, but especially the gonorrheal.

gonosome, -sphere, -theca, -zooid: see GONO-, *prefix.*

gonotocont (gəʊˈnɒtəʊkɒnt). *Biol.* Also **gonotokont.** [ad. G. *gonotokont* (J. P. Lotsy 1904, in *Flora* XCIII. 70), f. GONO- + Gr. τοκωντ-, τοκῶν pres. pple. of τοκᾶν to be near delivery.] Any cell that may undergo meiosis; also, any organ containing such a cell.

[**1905** *Amer. Naturalist* XXXIX. 494 Lotsy..proposes the term 'Gonotokonten'..for the mother-cells which inaugurate reduction phenomena.] **1909** A. C. Seward *Darwin & Mod. Sci.* vi. 105 In the nuclei of all those cells which we may group together as gonotokonts (i.e. cells concerned in reproduction) there are fewer chromosomes than in the adjacent body-cells (somatic cells). **1928** C. W. Dodge tr. *Gäumann's Compar. Morphol. Fungi* i. 1 The product of fertilization is called a zygote as long as it remains unicellular; it develops into a diplont which forms gonotoconts (organs in which meiosis occurs). **1965** J. Wilkinson tr. *Langeron's Outl. Mycol.* (ed. 2) ix. 375 The diplont produces gonotoconts or spore mother cells.

gonral, variant of GOMEREL.

gony (ˈgəʊnɪ). Now *dial.* Also 6, 9 **gonny,** 9 **goney, gooney.** [Of obscure formation; see GAWNEY, and cf. Sc. *gonyel* a stupid fellow.]

1. A booby, a simpleton.

c **1580** Jefferie *Bugbears* III. i. in *Archiv Stud. d. neu. Spr.* (1897), & yet the gray-beard gonnie daunceth, praunceth, & skippeth friskoioly. **1804** R. Anderson *Cumberld. Ball.* 116 She dance! what she turns in her taes, thou peer gonny. **1837–40** Haliburton *Clockm.* (1862) 139 That are Sheriff was a goney—don't cut your cloth arter his pattern. **1883** *Millionaire* I. xix, I should like to go to one of those meetings, and watch the gonies, sitting with open mouths listening to Bounce.

2. A sailor's name for the albatross and some other birds resembling it.

1839 *Knickerbocker* XIII. 386 May the 'Goneys' eat me, if he [*sc.* the whale] dodges us this time. **1850** Scoresby *Cheever's Whalem. Adv.* iii. (1859) 40 Gonies, stinkards, horse-birds..had all many a good morsel of blubber. **1851** H. Melville *Whale* xlii. 210 Sometime after I learned that goney was some seaman's name for albatross. **1895** *Westm. Gaz.* 14 Jan. 2/3 A goonie (a sea-bird..second only in size to the albatross). **1957** W. L. McAtee *Folk Names Canad. Birds* 3 Black-footed Albatross. *Gony, gony bird, goony* (B.C.); goony bird (North Pacific). These names appear to have the significance of booby or dullard and probably are applied to any albatross. **1966** R. Ardrey *Territorial Imperative* (1967) iv. 148 The albatross..became known to all the American fleet as the gooney bird.

gonys (ˈgɒnɪs). *Ornith.* [App. a mistake for *genys* = Gr. γένυς under-jaw; first used by Illiger in 1811.] The 'keel' of a bird's bill; the inferior margin of the symphysis of the lower jaw. Hence **go'nydeal** *a.*, of or pertaining to the gonys.

1836 Swainson *Birds* I. ii. 21 The corresponding ridge of the lower mandible is the gonys. **1874** Coues *Birds N.-W.* 466 Bill long..Culmen and gonys broad and depressed. *Ibid.* 722 Commissure perfectly straight; gonydeal angle slight. **1893** Newton *Dict. Birds* 33 *Gonys* or more correctly *genys*, the prominent ridge formed by the united halves of the under jaw, *e.g.* in Gulls.

gonzo (ˈgɒnzəʊ), *a.* and *sb. slang* (orig. and chiefly *U.S.*). [See the adj., quot. 1972; perh. a. It. *gonzo* fool(ish), or ad. Sp. *ganso* goose, fool.]

A. *adj.* **1. a.** *spec.* Of or relating to a type of committed, subjective journalism characterized by factual distortion and exaggerated rhetorical style. **b.** Bizarre, crazy; far-fetched.

1971 H. Thompson in *Rolling Stone* 11 Nov. 38/4 But what *was* the story? Nobody had bothered to say. So we would have to drum it up on our own. Free Enterprise. The American Dream. Horatio Alger gone mad on drugs in Las Vegas. Do it *now*: pure Gonzo journalism. **1972** in R. Pollack *Stop Presses* (1975) 184, I ask Hunter to explain... Just what is Gonzo Journalism?..'Gonzo all started with Bill Cardosa,..after I wrote the Kentucky Derby piece for *Scanlan's*..the first time I realized you could write *different*. And..I got this note from Cardosa saying, 'That was pure Gonzo journalism!'.. Some Boston word for weird, bizarre.' **1974** *National Rev.* (U.S.) 21 June 707/1 Politics, in any case, has nothing to do with this gonzo record, which transcends mundane concerns and speaks, as rock henceforth *must* speak, to universal themes alone. **1978** *People Weekly* 2 Oct. 95/3 Rock's gonzo guitarist Ted Nugent..began grandstanding, chomping on Nancy's booted leg and, when she didn't kick, tussling with her on a sofa. Finally, he drew a blood-curdling yelp when he whipped out a knife and laughingly sliced her blouse up the front. **1980** *Newsweek* 16 June 38/2 'Gonzo Station', the irreverent nickname weary U.S. sailors have given the Indian Ocean. **1985** *New Yorker* 22 July 16/2 He has a small, weird triumph with his gonzo psycho docudrama.

B. *sb.* **1. a.** 'Gonzo' journalism; one who writes in this style. **b.** A crazy person, a fool.

1972 J. A. Lucas in *More* Nov. 4 (*title*) The Prince of Gonzo. **1977** *Custom Car* Nov. 43/2 To make sure I wouldn't make too big a gonzo of myself,..I was connected by intercom to the commander who was perched up in the turret. **1980** *Newsweek* 12 May 93/1 As the chief and only true gonzo, Thompson, in his famous 'Fear and Loathing' reportage for Rolling Stone magazine, wasn't just a passive observer but played his own freaked-out part as unofficial Tom O'Bedlam to the events he covered.

goo (guː). *slang* (orig. *U.S.*). [Of obscure origin but possibly a shortening of BURGOO.] A viscid or sticky substance. Also *fig.*, sickly sentiment, gush.

1903 C. H. Sewall *Wireless Telegr.* IV. 156 The ends of the wires..are smeared..with a minute quantity of a paste which the inventor [*sc.* L. DeForest] has named 'goo'. **1911** E. Ferber *Dawn O'Hara* iii. 31 You mean to tell me that you woke me..to make me drink that goo?..I'll bet it's another egg-nogg. **1922** Joyce *Ulysses* 305 Bloom putting in his old goo. **1944** J. H. Fullarton *Troop Target* 43 It's all over blood and goo. **1949** S. Gibbons *Matchmaker* xiv. 163 He..began to measure and mince vegetable scraps and scoop out grey, gritty, oily goo from a large tin. **1951** M. McLuhan *Mech. Bride* 29/2 A crude morality which puts the best-seller goo to shame. **1959** *Times Lit. Suppl.* 20 Mar. 156/3 He writes about subjects which, in less skilled hands, have so often and so embarrassingly degenerated into a mess of gush and goo. **1959** *Punch* 17 June 815/1 *Lonely-hearts*..angered me very much by finally dissolving in a bath of sweet goo after being an excellent film for three-quarters of its length. **1960** *News Chron.* 16 Feb. 6/6 Barbara goes into the dressing-room to slap on the old goo. **1969** *Daily Tel.* (Colour Suppl.) 14 Mar. 50/3 *Crêpes Suzette*..precooked in the kitchen and reheated in the buttery goo.

goo, Sc. variant of GOUT.

gooat, variant of GOTE.

goober (ˈguːbə(r)). *U.S.* Also **gouber** (*Cent. Dict.*). The peanut, *Arachis hypogæa.*

1833 *Louisville Publ. Advt.* 7 Nov., A few bags Gouber Pea, or Ground Pea [for sale]. **1834** *Cherokee Phoenix* (New Echota, Ga.) 24 May 3/4 But he so seam I frade of he, I guess he steal my goober. **1848** *Rep. U.S. Comm. Patents 1847* 190 The ground pea of the south, or as it is sometimes called, the gouber or pindar pea. **1871** Schele de Vere *Americanisms* (1872) 57 The peanuts or earth-nuts known in North Carolina and the adjoining States as Goober peas, so that during the late Civil War a conscript from the so-called 'piney woods' of that State was apt to be nick-named a Goober. **1885** *U.S. Cons. Rep.* No. liv. 382 (Cent.) From the handling of our orchard crops to raking goobers out of the ground, there is probably [etc.]. **1887** *Boston* (Mass.) *Jrnl.* 31 Dec. 2/4 Hogs that had been fed on acorns and goobers. **1888** *Century Mag.* XXXVI. 770/2 Peanuts, known in the vernacular as 'goobers'.

good (gʊd), *a.*, *adv.*, and *sb.* Forms: 1 **gód, good,** 2–6 **god,** 4–6 **gode,** 3–4 **guod(e,** 4 **godd(e, goed, (gowde),** 4–5 **goud(e,** 4–6 **good(d)e,** 4–8 *Sc.* **guid(e,** 4–9 *Sc.* and *north.* **gud(e,** (4 **gwde,** 5 **guyd,** 6 *north.* **gewd),** 4– **good.** [Com. Teut.: OE. *gód* = OFris., OS. *gôd* (MDu. *goet*, inflected *goed-*, Du. *goed*), OHG. *guot, kuot, guat, kuat*, etc. (MHG. *guot*, G. *gut*), ON. *góð-r* (Sw., Da. *god*), Goth. *gôþ-s*, gen. *gôdis*:—OTeut. **gôdo-*. The root **gôd-* is perh. an ablaut-variant of **gad-* to bring together, to unite (see GATHER *v.*), so that the original sense of 'good' would be that of 'fitting', 'suitable'; cf. OSl. *goditi* to be pleasing, *godĭnŭ* pleasing, *godŭ* time, fitting time, Russ. *godnyĭ* fit, suitable.

The adj., as in the other Teut. langs., has no regular comparative or superlative, the place of these being supplied by BETTER, BEST; the form *goodest* occurs in jocular or playful language. The corresponding adv. is WELL.]

A. *adj.*

The most general adj. of commendation, implying the existence in a high, or at least satisfactory, degree of characteristic qualities which are either admirable in themselves or useful for some purpose.

As stronger expressions of commendation than 'good' may be used, the latter sometimes has by comparison a modified sense = 'fair', 'passable', 'fairly large', etc.

In OE. (as in OS. and OHG.) the opposite of 'good' was regularly expressed by *yfel* EVIL, but in ME. this was supplemented by ILL and BAD, the latter of which is now the more general term.

I. In the widest sense, without other specialization than such as is implied by the nature of the object which the adj. is used to describe.

1. Of things: Having in adequate degree those properties which a thing of the kind ought to have.

a. of material things or substances of any kind.

In early use often employed where a word of more definite meaning would now be substituted; e.g. as an epithet of gold or silver, = 'fine, pure'; *good stones* = 'precious stones'.

Beowulf (Z.) 1562 Eald sweord eotenisc..þæt wæpna cyst..god ond ȝeatolic ȝiganta ȝe-weorc. *c* **1000** *Ags. Gosp.* Matt. vii. 17 Ælc god treow byrð gode wæstmas. *c* **1205** Lay. 26070 Ardur..up ahof his gode brond. *c* **1250** *Gen. & Ex.* 1191 A ðhusant plates of siluer god Gaf he sarra. *a* **1300** *Cursor M.* 21281 þar es god axultreis tua. *c* **1300** *Seyn Julian* 162 He let make of wode and col a strong fur and good. *c* **1400** *Destr. Troy* 1366 No hede toke Of golde ne of garmenttes, ne of goode stonys. **1484** Caxton *Fables of Poge* ii, [She] promysed to him that she shold gyue to hym a ryght good dyner. **1562** J. Heywood *Prov. & Epigr.* (1867) 143 It is a good hors, that neuer stumbleth. **1597** Shaks. *2 Hen. IV*, III. ii. 42 How a good Yoke of Bullocks at Stamford Fayre? **1599** H. Buttes *Dyets drie Dinner* H viij b, Veale..Nourisheth excellently: makes verie good blood. **1639** Du Verger tr. *Camus' Admir. Events* 8 We thinke nothing to good for them. **1698** Fryer *Acc. E. India & P.* 6 A special good Anchor of 2400 weight. **1769** Mrs. Raffald *Eng. Housekpr.* (1778) 151 Lay over it a good cold paste. **1789** Bligh *Narr. Bounty* (1790) 52 One half of us slept on shore by a good fire.

b. of food or drink. (Often with mixture of senses 11 a, 12.) (*to keep*) *good*: untainted, fit to eat.

805–31 in *O.E. Texts* 444, xxx ombra godes uuelesces aloð. **971** [see 12]. *c* **1200** ORMIN 15408 þin forrme win iss swiþe god, þin lattre win iss bettre. **1340** *Ayenb.* 51 Huet we hedde guod wyn yesteneuen and guode metes. *c* **1440** *Promp. Parv.* 201/2 Goode wyne, *temetum.* *c* **1450** *M.E. Med. Bk.* (Heinrich) 69 Boyle hem wel in good mylke. **1600** SHAKS. *A.Y.L.* Epil., To good wine they do vse good bushes. **1609** SKENE *Reg. Maj.* lxix. (1774) 243 And gif she makes gude-ail, that is sufficent. Bot gif she makes evill ail [etc.]. **1665** *Phil. Trans.* I. 49 How Meat and Drink may be kept good in very Cold Countries. **1689** LOCKE *Governmt.* II. §46 He also bart'red away Plumbs, that would have rotted in a Week, for Nuts that would last good for his eating a whole Year. **1796** MRS. GLASSE *Cookery* xviii. 288 Let your butter be good. *Mod.* In the cold chamber meat will keep good for an indefinite time.

c. of soil: Fertile.

1382 WYCLIF *Mark* iv. 20 And these it ben that ben sowun on good lond. **1732** BERKELEY *Alciphr.* VI. §18 The seed of the gospel sown in good ground. **1836** MONTGOMERY *Hymn, 'Sow in the morn thy seed'*, The good, the fruitful ground, Expect not here nor there.

d. of coin, bank-notes, etc.: Genuine, not counterfeit. In mod. use freq. as an intensive, or as an indication of adequacy, with *money*.

1573 J. SANFORD *Hours Recreat.* (1576) 178 In taking a peece of false money for good, one may have small losse. *a* **1639** W. WHATELEY *Prototypes* II. (1640) 43 Pay me what you be able, so you bring me good money, not counterfeit. **1889** *Kansas Times & Star* 22 May, Mr. Hammerslough is putting a lot of good money into it. **1896** ADE *Artie* xi. 98 They say he makes good money. **1915** CONRAD *Victory* III. iii. 193 Father was earning good money. **1928** E. WALLACE *Again Three Just Men* x. 212 But for his inherent meanness, he would have gladly paid good money to be rid of her. **1966** 'M. RENAULT' *Mask of Apollo* x. 173 We made good money, and lingered in the pleasant places.

e. of a ship, a town. Now only as a conventional epithet in the phrases 'the good ship A——'; 'the good town of B——'.

c **1340** *Cursor M.* 24862 (Fairf.) & euer-mare þai lokid doun quen þat gode ship [*Cott.* þe scip] sulde droun. **1523** LD. BERNERS *Froiss.* I. xviii. 19 Men of ye Countre a fote, sent out of good townes at their wages. **1568** GRAFTON *Chron.* II. 242 Two hundred sayle of good shyppes. *Ibid.* 304 That the Prelates and Nobles of Fraunce, and the good townes should assemble themselves. **1577** HOGAN in Hakluyt *Voy.* (1589) 156 Being imbarked in the goode shippe, called the Gallion of London. **1634** SIR T. HERBERT *Trav.* 27 Good men of warre, though ships for traffique. **1639** *Hamilton Papers* (Camden) 96 It may troubill the gud toune, if they proue not gud subjects. **1709** STEELE *Tatler* No. 144 ¶8 There are at this Time in the good Town of Edinburgh, Beaus, Fops, and Coxcombs. **1864** *Bill of Lading* in *Law Rep., E. & I. App. Cas.* (1874) VI. 288 Shipped in good order, etc...in and upon the good ship called the Java.

f. of immaterial things. Of actions: Rightly or skilfully performed. ***good opera, radio, television, theatre***: said of an entertainment that is effective, or well suited to a specified medium.

1583 HOLLYBAND *Campo di Fior* 225 Thou wilt never make good verse. **1604** E. G. *D'Acosta's Hist. Indies* I. viii. 25 S. Augustine hath confessed this to bee conformable to good Philosophie. **1735–8** BOLINGBROKE *On Parties* 108 We call This a good Government, when..the whole Administration of publick Affairs is wisely pursued. **1793** BLACKSTONE *Comm.* (ed. 12) 70 There are decisions drawn from established principles and maxims, which are good law. **1860–1** FLO. NIGHTINGALE *Nursing* 77 Good nursing consists simply in observing little things which are common to all sick, and those which are particular to each sick individual. **1861** M. PATTISON *Ess.* (1889) I. 32 A good history of our foreign policy from the earliest period would be very useful. **1868** WHYTE MELVILLE *White Rose* I. x. 121 Are you to join directly?.. Is it a good regiment? **1889** *Sat. Rev.* 6 Apr. 415/1 The fight was a good fight, with many changes of fortune. **1892** *Speaker* 3 Sept. 294/2 M. Collignon's book, though good as far as it goes, is altogether slighter than Dr. Murray's. **1926** C. MORLEY (*title*) Good theatre. *Ibid.* 216 Don't be sore on them laughs, brother. Every one o' them screams is a meal ticket. That's what I call good theayter. **1928** *Observer* 11 Mar. 15/2 This is an excellent example of what we mean when we say that a play is 'good theatre'. **1928** *Daily Tel.* 15 May 14/5 The play.. is, to use the modern phrase, 'very good theatre'. **1958** *Listener* 24 July 138/1 This was not only good television: it also made sense of getting the two men there in the first place. *Ibid.* 140/1 It made very good radio. **1962** *Ibid.* 7 June 1009/3 It may be that this sincere, searching composer has developed an abstract theory in this case into good theatre. Whether it is good opera is another matter. **1971** *Times* 18 Nov. 15/2 There is the temptation for producers to seek what they regard as 'good television', which can mean a search for drama as such and for conflict in the studio no matter how unnecessary it may be for the presentation of a case.

g. ***that's a good one*** (or ***'un***): used ironically to characterize a statement that is incredibly mendacious or absurdly exaggerated. (Cf. 'I like that'.) *slang.*

1813 J. K. PAULDING *J. Bull & Br. Jonathan* v. 26 Now this was a good one, for every body knew [etc.]. **1869** *Punch* 30 Jan. 44 Medical-Attendance, Two-an'-Six! Well, that's a good 'un! Why, I attended on 'im. **1914** *Concise Oxf. Dict.* Addenda s.v., *That's a good 'un* (slang), what a lie. **1920** C. SANDBURG *Smoke & Steel* 45 That's a good one.

h. In the colloq. U.S. phrase *to look* or *listen good* = to look or sound promising.

1911 R. D. SAUNDERS *Col. Todhunter* iii. 43 It looks good to me, suh. **1916** H. L. WILSON *Somewhere in Red Gap* vi. 252 That listens good to her till she finds she has to give fifty-two dollars for the deck first. **1923** R. D. PAINE *Comrades of Rolling Ocean* xii. 215 'Thanks, you look good to us,' yelled Judson. **1932** *Kansas City Star* 1 Mar., It listened good.

2. a. Of persons, as a term of indefinite commendation. In early use chiefly implying distinguished rank or valour. Now rare, the adj. as applied to persons having chiefly a moral signification (see II); exc. in phrase ***good men and true*** (now *arch.*), and predicatively in comparative expressions, ***as good as, good enough for, too good for.***

O.E. Chron. an. 871 þær wærþ Heahmund biscop ofslæᵹen and fela godra monna. **1154** *Ibid.* an. 1124 þes kinges stiward of France.. & fela oðer godre cnihte. *c* **1275** LAY. 56 Nu biddeþ Laweman echne godne [*c* **1205** æðele] mon þat þes boc redeþ [etc.]. **1387** [see 5 a]. ? **1483** CAXTON *Dialogues* 10 Be ye buxom..Vnto your seruaunts: Thynke that they be As good as ye. **1513** MORE in Grafton *Chron.* (1568) II. 768 That sacred Sanctuarie, that hath bene the safegarde of so many a good mans lyfe. **1548** HALL *Chron., Hen. VII*, 5 So by this politique wisdome and ingenious meanes of the good duke. **1591** SHAKS. *1 Hen. VI*, III. i. 41 But he shall know I am as good. *Glost.* As good? Thou Bastard of my Grandfather. **1607** —— *Cor.* IV. v. 193, I do not say thwacke our Generall, but he was alwayes good enough for him. *a* **1634** RANDOLPH *Muses Looking-gl.* IV. iv. (1638) 79, I had rather.. haue his twelve Godvathers, good men and true, contemne him to the Gallowes. **1825** JAMIESON s.v. *Gud*, 'You are no sae gude as me'; i.e. 'You are not so well-born.' **1897** CAPT. MAHAN *Nelson* II. xv. 43 On one occasion..Nelson took too much champagne... Such a thing has happened on isolated occasions to many a good man and true. *Mod.* His wife is far too good for him.

†**b.** As a conventional epithet prefixed to titles of high rank. So (***one's***) ***good lord*** or ***lady***, a patron or patroness (cf. GOODLORDSHIP). Also in forms of address, as ***good my lord, good your ladyship,*** etc.

11.. *O.E. Chron.* an. 1093 þa seo gode cwen Margarita þis ᵹehyrde [etc.]. **1458** *MS.* in *Turner's Dom. Archit.* III. 43 The gode lorde of Abendon left of his londe, For the breed of the brige $\frac{xx}{iiii}$ fote large. **1463** MARG. PASTON in *P. Lett.* No. 472 II. 132, I am afferd..of these materys..but if he wyl don for ȝou and be your godelord. **15..** *Adam Bel & Clym of Clough* 507 in Ritson *Anc. P.P.* 24 Then good my lord, I you beseche, These yemen graunt ye me. *c* **1530** L. COXE *Rhethoryke* (1899) A ij a, Consyderyng my specyall good lorde howe greatly..I am bounden to your lordeshippe [etc.]. **1611** SHAKS. *Wint. T.* II. ii. 220 At the good Queenes entreatie. —— *Cymb.* II. iii. 158 She's my good Lady. **1688** SIR C. LYTTELTON 6 Nov. in *Hatton Corr.* (Camden) II. 99 Good my Lord, give me free advise in this matter. **1742** RICHARDSON *Pamela* III. 83 Good your Ladyship, let not my honour'd Master see this Letter. **1819** SHELLEY *Cenci* II. ii. 41 You, my good Lord Orsino, heard those words.

c. In wider application, as an epithet of courteous address or respectful reference. Now often jocular or depreciatory. See also GOODMAN, GOODWIFE. Also ***your (his) good lady***, your (his) wife (see LADY *sb.* 7). ***your good self*** (or ***selves***), a commercial form of polite address or reference.

c **1175** *Lamb. Hom.* 11 Gode men, nu beoð icumen þa bicumeliche daᵹes [etc.]. *a* **1300** *Cursor M.* 11853 Godd men he said quat es your sight O mi fader þat þus es dight. **1340** *Ayenb.* 190 He acsede ate guode wyfman..hou moche hi hedde him y-lete. *c* **1420** *Sir Amadace* (Camden) xxx, Gode Sirs, take noȝte on greue, For ȝe most noue take ȝour leue. **1529** MORE *Dyaloge* cxix. a/2 And what hath hurt it, good father? **1601** HOLLAND *Pliny* II. 384 Some good body tell me, I pray, how he could feele the smell thereof. **1652** CULPEPPER *Eng. Physic.* 15 It is very safe, and very fit to be kept in every good bodies house. **1705** VANBRUGH *Confed.* I. ii. (1730) 23 Who is this good woman, Flippanta? **1768** GOLDSM. *Good-n. Man* III, Two of my very good friends, Mr. Twitch and Mr. Flanigan. **1796** H. HUNTER tr. *St. Pierre's Stud. Nat.* (1799) III. 146 My good friend, your sister shall remain with us. **1798** MRS. C. SMITH *Yng. Philos.* IV. 1 The good lady was in her dressing-room. **1839** DICKENS *Nich. Nick.* i, This good lady bore him two children. **1840** —— *Barn. Rudge* xix, My good soul,..you are quite mistaken. **1850** SCORESBY *Cheever's Whaleman's Adv.* ii. (1859) 23, I was here presented with a couple of rolls of white kapa by the good woman of the house. **1860** G. H. LEWES *Let.* 6 Mar. in Geo. Eliot *Lett.* (1954) III. 269 'My good lady' (style choisi!)..is reddening her eyes..over the foolish sorrows of two foolish young persons of her imaginary acquaintance. **1923** *Daily Mail* 20 Feb. 3 It is more than probable our next orders will be placed with your good-selves. **1931** *Ch. Times* 8 May 569/3 The kindness and consideration shown by your good self to me. **1957** PARTRIDGE *English gone Wrong* i. 17 Then there are such monstrosities as your good self or selves; of recent date; [etc.]. **1967** *Daily Tel.* 30 Aug. 7, I have always understood that the words 'goodself' and 'goodselves' related to credit-worthiness.

d. ***the good neighbours, people***: (euphemistically) the fairies; also occas. = witches. Cf. also GOOD NEIGHBOUR.

1588 in Pitcairn *Crim. Trials Scot.* I. III. 162 For hanting and repairing with the gude nychtbouris and Quene of Elfame. *a* **1605** MONTGOMERIE *Flyting w. Polwart* 275 On Alhallow euen, When our good nighbours doe ryd. **1810** SCOTT *Minstr. Scott. Border* (ed. 4) II. 169 Fairies [in Ireland]..are termed 'the good people'. **1854** H. MILLER *Sch. & Schm.* vi. (1860) 59/1 Walter believed in the fairies; and though psalmody was not one of the reputed accomplishments of the 'good-people' in the low country, he [etc.]. **1889** FROUDE *Two Chiefs of Dunboy* vi, Babies had been changed in the cradles by the 'good people'. **1951** C. S. LEWIS *Let.* (1966) 234 The desolate coast on which it stands is haunted by 'the good people'. There is also a ghost but.. the faeries are a more serious danger. **1959** K. M. BRIGGS *Anat. Puck* 192 *People of Peace*..is the Highland name for the fairies, corresponding to the Lowland 'Good Neighbours'. **1966** G. E. EVANS *Pattern under Plough* xiii. 128 The countryman in Ireland poured out a little of his draught as a compliment to the 'good people' or the fairies.

e. ***good Samaritan***: see SAMARITAN b.

f. ***good buddy***, a term of address among users of a Citizen's Band or similar radio system; another CB user. *slang* (chiefly *U.S.*).

1976 *N.Y. Times Mag.* 25 Apr. 64/5 'Hey, there, eastbounders. You've got a Smokey in the grass at the 93-mile marker..he's takin' pictures.' 'Aaay, we definitely thank you for that info, good buddy. We'll back 'em down a hair.' **1976** M. MACHLIN *Pipeline* xiii. 151 What's your handle, Good Buddy? **1979** *Amer. Speech* LIV. 307 A phrase like *good buddy* (the CB term for another CBer) is now used even by those who are unaware of its origin among truckers. **1981** *Times* 5 Mar. 16/8 *Good buddy*—hello.

3. Of qualities or attributes.

a. of a quality generally: Commendable, conducing to the value or merit of the subject.

1600 SHAKS. *A.Y.L.* I. i. 150 An enuious emulator of euery mans good parts. **1601** —— *All's Well* III. vi. 12 Hee's a most notable Coward,..the owner of no one good qualitie, worthy your Lordships entertainment. **1674** [see 5 a]. **1897** *Sears, Roebuck Catal.* 289/1 A Good Quality White Marseilles Bed Spread. *a* **1900** *Mod.* The author's style is not without some good qualities. **1936** *Discovery* Dec. 375/1 A good quality silk. **1956** *Nature* 11 Feb. 289/1 A common method [of improving food intake] has been to give a concentrate feed containing about 10 per cent of good-quality protein. **1962** P. STREVENS *Papers in Lang.* (1965) xii. 146 Equipment now exists for making good-quality recordings.

b. of birth, family, social station: More or less elevated; not humble or mean.

971 *Blickl. Hom.* 211 Wæs he for worlde swiðe æþelra ᵹebyrda and godra. *a* **1674** CLARENDON *Hist. Reb.* VIII. §3 A gentleman of a good family. **1719** DE FOE *Crusoe* I. i, I was born in the Year 1632..of a good Family. **1849** MACAULAY *Hist. Eng.* iii. I. 294 Many of them were of good families, and had held commissions. **1872** GEO. ELIOT *Middlem.* I. I. i. 2 The Brooke connections, though not exactly aristocratic, were unquestionably 'good'. **1892** G. & W. GROSSMITH *Diary of Nobody* xxiii. 287 Lupin..has taken furnished apartments at Bayswater... Lupin says one never loses by a good address. **1942** D. POWELL *Time to be Born* (1943) x. 227 West Thirteenth?.. Are you sure that's a good neighbourhood? **1956** J. D. CARR *P. Butler for Defence* vi. 61 Monnie wanted Jim..to be elected to a 'good' club and join a 'good' golf-club where he might find useful contacts.

c. of state or condition, health, order, etc.: Such as should be desired or approved, right, satisfactory; sound, unimpaired. Of state of mind, courage, spirits: Not depressed or dejected. ***good cheer*** (see CHEER *sb.*[1] 3 b). ***to feel good***: to feel oneself to be in good spirits or health (*U.S. colloq.*).

c **1175** etc. [see GODER-HEAL]. *c* **1384** CHAUCER *H. Fame* II. 96 So that thou take Good herte, and not for fere quake. **1398** TREVISA *Barth. De P.R.* V. i. (1495) 101 A membre that is in gode hele. **1483** CAXTON *Gold. Leg.* 197/2 Many vexyd by Spyrytes were delyuerd & remysed in to theyr good mynde. **1513** MORE in Grafton *Chron.* (1568) II. 759 Albeit that this discention..somewhat yrked him, yet in his good health he somewhat the lesse regarded it. **1548** HALL *Chron., Hen. VI*, 106 Sir Jhon Fastolfe and his companions, set all their company in good ordre of battaill. **1576** FLEMING *Panopl. Epist.* 276, I hearing this noyse, exhorted them to have good hearts. **1583** HOLLYBAND *Campo di Fior* 243 Now he is not in his good minde. **1711** STEELE *Spect.* No. 96 ¶2 Tom, Tom have a good Heart. **1839** F. MARRYAT *Diary Amer.* 1st Ser. II. 224, I have heard a lady say, 'I don't feel *at all good*, this morning.' **1854** H. C. KIMBALL *Address* 17 Sept. in *Jrnl. Discourses* (1855) II. 224/1 You will see how good we will make the transient residents feel. **1855** MACAULAY *Hist. Eng.* xviii. IV. 119 The health of the crews had..been..wonderfully good. **1865** MRS. CARLYLE *Lett.* III. 244, I don't feel in such good heart about the Devonshire visit as I did. **1883** [see FROLICKY *a.*]. **1888** *Texas Siftings* 15 Sept. (Farmer), The saloons are going Saturday afternoons, and the men feel pretty good before they come abroad. **1904** *N.Y. Even. Post* 23 June 3 The Captain himself said, 'I feel good', but he did not look well. **1958** *Times Lit. Suppl.* 1 Aug. 438/5 [In Amer. novel] Even Bunny Muldoon, the golf professional, is kept on not because he teaches anyone golf but because he makes people feel good'.

d. of fame, reputation: Honourable.

c **1470** HENRY *Wallace* I. 26 His systir fair, off gud fame and ranoune. **1484** *Surtees Misc.* (1888) 41 Forto restore hym into his gude name and fame. **1548** HALL *Chron., Hen. VIII*, 25 b, Men of good estimacion. **1604** SHAKS. *Oth.* III. iii. 155 Good name in Man, & woman..Is the immediate Iewell of their Soules. *a* **1732** GAY *Fox dying* I. 46 A lost good name is ne'er retriev'd. **1832** AUSTIN *Jurispr.* (1879) I. xv. 400 A man's right or interest in his good-name. **1847** EMERSON *Poems* (1857) 84 Estate, good-fame, Plans, credit.

e. of appearance, shape, complexion, etc.: Satisfactory with regard to beauty. Hence *occas.* of a part of the body.

1608 SHAKS. *Per.* IV. ii. 51 She has a good face. **1618** in *Crt. & Times Jas. I* (1848) II. 109 Her good face is the best part of her portion. **1848** THACKERAY *Van. Fair* vii, A handsome gentleman with a trim beard and a good leg. **1870** DICKENS *E. Drood* ii, His face and figure are good.

4. a. Of a state of things, a purpose, a proposed course of action, etc.: Commendable, desirable, right, proper. Chiefly *predicative*, with *inf.* or clause as virtual subject.

971 *Blickl. Hom.* 139 Hu good is & hu wynsum þæt [etc.] *a* **1300** *Cursor M.* 4790 þar of es god we ta consail. *c* **1460** FORTESCUE *Abs. & Lim. Mon.* xii. (1885) 138 Sythen it were god thai hade non harnes. **1513** MORE in Grafton *Chron.* (1568) II. 764 All which thinges..were done for good purposes, and necessary. **1626** BACON *Sylva* §14 For handsomnesse sake.. it were good you hang the vpper Glasse vpon a Naile. *a* **1632** HERBERT *Jacula Prudent.* 170

Hell is full of good meanings and wishings. **1849** Macaulay *Hist. Eng.* i. I. 47 It was..good that they should be respected and obeyed. **1870** Max Müller *Sci. Relig.* (1873) 62 The inhabitants of Great Britain were persuaded that it was not good to be without an ancestor.

b. In phrases *to appear, †like,* or *seem good, to think* or *†see (it) good.*

1362 Langl. *P. Pl.* A. I. 57 Glosynge the gospel as hem good liketh. **1413** *Pilgr. Sowle* (Caxton 1483) iv. v. 60 That other shalle answere as hyr semeth good. *c* **1460** *Towneley Myst.* xxiii. 642 Do with hym what thou thynk gud. *c* **1500** *Melusine* xx. 108 Madame, yf it lyke you good they doo soo, I assent gladly therto. **1548–9** (Mar.) *Bk. Com. Prayer, Offices* 9 It is thought good that none hereafter shall be confirmed, but such [etc.]. **1573** J. Sanford *Hours Recreat.* (1576) 76 Kill, if you thinke good, all the dogges that are here. **1632** J. Hayward tr. *Biondi's Eromena* 95 To charge the enemie by land..if it seemed good to her Highnesse so to doe. **1663** Butler *Hud.* I. iii. 275 Others may do as they see good. *c* **1680** Beveridge *Serm.* (1729) I. 112 Thus much I thought good to premise. **1793** Burke *Corr.* (1844) IV. 185 It has not yet appeared good to the politics of ministers here or abroad, to permit [etc.].

c. *absol.* as an exclamation, expressing satisfaction. Also (chiefly Austral. and N.Z.) *good-oh!, good-o!, goodo!,* etc., when the same words are used as *adjs.* = *good* (sense 4) and *advbs.* = 'well'.

c **1410** *Sir Cleges* 424 Good, he seyd..Thowe haddyst [etc.]. *c* **1590** Marlowe *Faust.* x. 81 But, good, are you remembered how [etc.]. **1603** Shaks. *Meas. for M.* II. i. 163 Good, then; if [etc.]. **1807–8** W. Irving *Salmag.* (1824) 246 Good, thought I..there could not be a more important subject of investigation. **1826** Disraeli *Viv. Grey* v. xii, It is a promise, good. **1829** Marryat *F. Mildmay* xxiii, Very good, my lord. **1916** 'Anzac' *On Anzac Trail* 34 The rain came down good-oh. **1917** *Chrons. N.Z.E.F.* 31 Oct. 133 Belting her about goodo. **1926** I. M. Peacocke *His Kid Brother* x. 158 'Goodo!' said Dal. **1928** A. Waugh *Last Chukka* 85 'Good-oh!' she [an Australian] said, 'that'll be bonzer!' **1930** V. Palmer *Passage* II. x. 184 This is goodo! **1934** T. Wood *Cobbers* 210 You'll be good-O there. **1944** in *Coast to Coast 1943* 122 'How's young Jim getting along?' ..'Good-o,' she said. 'I've had a letter only this morning.' **1946** F. Sargeson *That Summer* 118 Yes, good-oh, I said, and thanks very much. **1958** D. Niland *Call me when Cross turns Over* v. 136 It sounds good-o the way he tells it. **1964** *Navy News* Dec. 1/2 What I really thought were goodo were those films on Religion and Science with that chap Erwin A. Moon.

d. *good for you (him,* etc.*)!*: a colloquial expression of approval of something said or done by the person addressed or spoken of.

1861 in M. W. Disher *Cowells in Amer.* (1934) 297 Sam's share $43.33.—Good for him. **1870** L. M. Alcott *Old-fash. Girl* (1874) iii. 35 Good for you, Polly! **1896** C. M. Yonge *Release* II. xvi. 234 'Old Sukey Shrimper,..has orders to call every Friday!' 'Good for Sukey,' quietly observed Mr. Darpent. **1904** H. James *Golden Bowl* I. x. 193 'Good for *you*!' Maggie smiled. **1922** D. H. Lawrence *England, my England* 142 'And did she take it in?' he asked. 'As much as she took anything else.' He stood grinning fixedly. Then he broke into a short laugh. 'Good for *her*!' he exclaimed cryptically. **1925** 'D. Yates' *As Other Men Are* 111 'Good for you,' she said. 'You've put it uncommonly well.' **1949** E. H. W. Meyerstein *Let.* 8 Jan. (1959) 355 Typical ex-Service husband with his reiterated 'good-for-you'. **1956** A. L. Rowse *Early Churchills* 74 Good for Sir Winston, we may say.

e. *good on you (him,* etc.*)!* = prec. Chiefly *Austral.* and *N.Z.*

1914 A. N. Lyons *Simple Simon* I. v. 84 'What ho!' she exclaimed. 'You've biffed him. Good on you, my lad!' **1944** L. Glassop *We were Rats* II. xi. 65 'What a bloke believes is his own business.' 'Good on you, mate,' said somebody behind me. 'Give it to him.' **1949** H. Wadman *Life Sentence* I. i. 8 Good on you. Of course, I oughtn't to care twopence about your opinion, but it's nice to know you agree with me. **1953** K. Tennant *Joyful Condemned* xxvii. 268 Vance laughed thunderously. 'Good on you, Rose.' **1959** *N.Z. Listener* 21 Aug. 8/4 'Good on you!' said Dad, smacking my new leg approvingly, ' that's the spirit.' **1961** P. White *Riders in Chariot* xiii. 456 'Goodonya, mate!' called the heartier of the females.

f. *good man!*: an exclamation of approbation.

1887 *Murray's Mag.* Jan. 97 She held out her hand. 'Good man! that is what I call a friend!' **1913** F. L. Barclay *Broken Halo* ii. 21 Good man! The very thing! **1933** A. G. Macdonell *England, their England* vi. 82 You can keep your mouth shut. Good man. **1955** L. P. Hartley *Perfect Woman* ix. 85 Oh, so you did go?.. Good man.

II. With reference to moral character, disposition, or conduct.

5. Morally excellent or commendable.

a. of persons, with reference to their general character: Virtuous.

1387 Trevisa *Higden* (Rolls) I. 323 [The Danes] beeþ to gode men and trewe boþe esy and mylde. **1388** Wyclif *Rom.* v. 7 For a good man perauenture summan dar die. *a* **1450** *Knt. de la Tour* (1868) 91 The whiche Ama was a worthi lady and a good. **1603** Shaks. *Meas. for M.* III. i. 185 The hand that hath made you faire, hath made you good. **1667** Milton *P.L.* ix. 465. **1674** Temple *Let. to Lady Essex* Wks. 1731 I. 129 He is a good Man that is better than Men commonly are, or in whom the good Qualities are more than the bad. **1734** Pope *Ess. Man* iv. 92 And grant the bad what happiness they would, One they must want, which is, to pass for good. **1852** Mrs. Stowe *Uncle Tom's C.* xi, She is as good as she is beautiful. **1876** Mozley *Univ. Serm.* ii. (1877) 28 Particular virtues, whether they are natural virtues or virtues of imitation, do not make the being good.

b. of conduct, life, actions, words, feelings, etc. *good deed*: spec., an act of service for others. (Adapted from the Scout Law 3.)

O.E. Chron. an. 959 God him ȝeunne, þæt his gode dæda swyðran wearðan þonne misdæda. **971** *Blickl. Hom.* 97 Ælc man þara þe her wile mid godum willan Godes bebodu healdan. *c* **1270** *S. Eng. Leg.* I. 17/546 I-cristned he was sone, And gud lijf ladde. **1340** Hampole *Pr. Consc.* 2494 Our gude dedys we shuld noght prayse. *c* **1380** Wyclif *Serm.* Sel. Wks. II. 33 Alle men shulde take hede to þere wordis þat þei ben gode. *c* **1420** *Sir Amadace* (Camden) xxxix, A mon that geuees him to gode thewis. **1508** Dunbar *Poems* v. 23 Thar ȝeris sevin Scho lewit a gud life. **1631** Massinger *Beleeve as you list* III. ii, Nor shall or threates or prayers deter mee from Doeinge a good deed in it selfe rewarded. **1670** Clarendon *Ess.* Tracts (1727) 167 No man hath a good conscience, but he who leads a good life. **1766** Goldsm. *Vic. W.* xv, I have ever perceived, that where the mind was capacious, the affections were good. **1879** H. Spencer *Data of Ethics* iii. §10. 30 If we call good every kind of conduct which aids the lives of others..then [etc.]. **1928** R. Knox *Footsteps at Lock* v. 42 This..was the spot where the boy scouts were encamped;..fourteen good deeds were registered. **1951** J. G. Fennessy *Sonnet in Bottle* VIII. ii. 253 You've done your Good Deed for the Day, visiting the sick. **1965** J. Potter *Death in Office* xiii. 127 He was wearing a frank open expression, like a Boy Scout anxious to do his good deed.

6. a. Applied to God, sometimes in the wide sense, as connoting moral perfection generally, and sometimes with more restricted reference to His benevolence (cf. sense 7).

c **1000** *Ags. Gosp.* Luke xviii. 19 Þa cwæð se hælend hwi segst þu me godne, nis nan man god buton god ana. *a* **1300** *E.E. Psalter* cvi. 1 Schriues to lauerd, for gode he is, For in werld es merci his. *c* **1420** *Avow. Arth.* lxxi, Gud Gode, that is grete, Gif him sory care! **1719** Watts *Psalm* LXIII. ii, Thou Great and Good, Thou Just and Wise, Thou art my Father and my God! **1817** Coleridge *Sibyll. Leaves* 225 It was a wicked woman's curse—God's good, and what care I?

b. Hence in exclamations containing the name of God or some substituted expression, as *good God! good gracious! good hallow! good heavens! good lack! good Lord! good me!* for which see the different words. *good grief!* (see grief *sb.* 8 a); *good iron!* (chiefly *Austral.*); also as adj. phr.

c **1386** Chaucer *Clerk's T.* 852 O gode god! how gentil and how kinde Ye semed. **1566** J. Alday tr. *Boaystuau's Theat. World* M vji, But good God, the Divell hath so entred into men at this daye. **1568** North *Gueuara's Diall Pr.* iv. xviii. 163 Good lord yt is a wonder to see what sturr there is in that mans house. **1638** Cowley *Love's Riddle* v. i, Your Son! good lack. *a* **1765** *Chield Morice* x. in Child *Ballads* iv. (1886) 270/2 Good hallow, gentle sir and dame, My errand canna wait. **1782** Cowper *Gilpin* 61 'Good lack!' quoth he, 'yet bring it me'. **1798** in *Spirit Publ. Jrnls.* (1799) II. 216, I am ready to faint! Dear me! O la! Good me! **1843** Haliburton *Attaché* II. i. 8 Good Heavens, Mr. Slick, how can you talk such nonsense? **1862** Burgon *Lett. fr. Rome* 51 The impression made in a block of marble by our Saviour's feet, (and good gracious! such feet!). **1890** Besant *Demoniac* v. 60 'Good Lord! What Fools!' said the Physician. **1895** *Bulletin* (Sydney) 9 Feb. 15/4 Oh, she's good iron, is my little clinah; She's my cobber an' I'm 'er bloke. **1899** *Ibid.* 22 Apr., *Ringer* and *good iron* are both derived from the game of quoits... *Good iron* corresponds to *good ball* at cricket. **1909** J. Masefield *Tragedy of Nan* II. 41 Good iron! A old chanti-cleer. Balm in Gilead, as the saying is. **1936** M. Franklin *All that Swagger* xi. 100 Good iron! I don't rob little boys. **1965** J. S. Gunn *Terminol. Shearing Indust.*, Pt. II. s.v. *Quoits.* This term..'good iron' for the shed's best shearer.

7. Kind, benevolent; gentle, gracious; friendly, favourable. **a.** of persons. Const. *to.* Phrase, *to be good enough* (or *so good as*) *to* (do something).

1154 *O.E. Chron.* an. 1137 Þa the suikes undergæton ðet he milde man was and softe and god, and na iustise ne dide, þa diden hi alle wundor. *a* **1310** in Wright *Lyric P.* xxxvii. 105 Thench that he the nes nout god, He wolde have thyn huerte blod. **1382** Wyclif *Ps.* lxxii[i]. 1 How good the God of Irael; to hem that ben in riȝt herte. *c* **1489** Caxton *Sonnes of Aymon* xxii. 490 How meke is Reynawde, and good of kynde, to have made peas in this maner of wyse. **1548** Hall *Chron., Hen. VIII,* 102 b, Let him resorte to me and I will be secrete and good to him. **1602** Marston *Ant. & Mel.* III. Wks. 1856 I. 39 Tis even the goodest Ladie that breathes, the most amiable. **1607** Shaks. *Cor.* iv. vi. 112 If they Should say be good to Rome. **1610** B. Jonson *Alch.* II. vi, It is the gooddest soule. **1652** H. Cogan tr. *Scudery's Ibrahim* II. iii. 45 He besought her to be so good as to relate to him all that had arrived unto her. **1656** Stanley *Hist. Philos.* vi. (1701) 230/1 One to the Gods so pious, good to Men. **1694** Dryden *Love Triumph.* II. ii, The goodest old man! he drank my health to his daughter. **1701** Rowe *Amb. Step-Moth.* iv. iii, Will you be good And think with Pity on the lost Cleone? **1806** *Simple Narrative* I. 140 They say the devil is always good to his own. **1876** Trevelyan *Macaulay* I. i. 27 If she [Hannah More] would be good enough to come in, he [etc.]. **1891** E. Peacock *N. Brendon* I. 256 They were always good to me. **1895** C. Kernahan *God & Ant* Ded. (ed. 4) 8 [They] were so good as to let me associate books of mine with their names.

b. of actions, dispositions, feelings, words. Of wishes: Tending to the happiness or prosperity of a person. *good offices, turn* (see office, turn). *†good words*: used *ellipt.* (= L. *bona verba*) for 'do not speak so fiercely'.

a **1000** *Andreas* 480 (Gr.) Wolde ic freondscipe..þinne, ȝif ic mehte, beȝitan godne. *c* **1175** *Lamb. Hom.* 3 Heo urnen on-ȝein him..mid godere heorte and summe mid ufele þeonke. *c* **1205** Lay. 665 Heo hine gretten mid godene heore worden. *a* **1400** *Octouian* 62 The holy pope Seynt Clement Weddede hem with good entent. **1548** Hall *Chron., Edw. IV,* 201 Kyng Edwarde..sente good woordes to the Erle of Pembroke. **1563** *Homilies* II. *For Rogation Week* I. (1859) 218 In some testification of our good hearts for his deserts unto us. **1576** Fleming *Panopl. Epist.* 31 A multitude innumerable, whose good harts and well wishing you have wun. **1577** B. Googe *Heresbach's Husb.* I. (1586) 15 b, Let him geve them a good countenance, and encourage them with rewardes. **1586** Hunsdon in *Border Papers* (1894) I. 367 Sondrie cawses that leades me greatlie to mistrust the Kinges good meaning towards her Majesty. *c* **1592** Marlowe *Jew of Malta* v. Wks. (Rtldg.) 175/2 Governor, good words; be not so furious. **1617** Moryson *Itin.* I. 25, I remember the good offices you did towards me a stranger. *a* **1632** Herbert *Jacula Prudent.* 155 Good words are worth much and cost little. **1633** R. Hall *Ded. to Bp. H.'s Medit. & Vows,* I obtained of him good leave to send them abroad. **1719** De Foe *Crusoe* I. xvii, Being likewise assured by Friday's father, that I might depend upon good usage from their nation on his account. **1892** *Pall Mall G.* 19 Jan. 1/2 The New..University of London appears to be in that parlous state when no impartial person can be found to say a good word for it.

c. In mildly depreciative sense implying weakness or trustful simplicity.

1581 Savile *Tacitus, Hist.* III. xx. (1591) 126 Shall we not then be forced to stand like good silly fooles gazing and gaping at the height of their towers? **1613** Shaks. *Hen. VIII,* III. ii. 357 And when he thinkes, good easie man, full surely His Greatnesse is a ripening.

8. a. Pious, devout; worthy of approbation from the religious point of view.

11.. *O.E. Chron.* an. 1086 He wæs milde þam godum mannum þe God lufedon. **1530** Tindale *Answ. More* Wks. (1573) 274/1 If I be good for the offering of a Doue, and better for a shepe [etc.]. **1581** Lambarde *Eiren.* I. vi. (1588) 35 Under the word Good, it is meant also that hee loue and feare God aright, without the which he cannot be Good at all. *a* **1661** Fuller *Worthies* (1811) I. 14 He is called..a Good Man in the Church, who is pious and devout in his conversation.

b. of books, etc.: Tending to spiritual edification. *the good book*: spec. the Bible.

1876 A. Trollope *Autobiogr.* iii. (1883) I. 68 A young man should no doubt..spend the long hours of the evening in reading good books and drinking tea. **1896** J. Skelton *Summers & W. at Balmawhapple* I. 160 In spite of the Gude Book and a bit sang at times the house feels lonely.

†c. of a day or season observed as holy by the church. *good tide*: (*a*) Christmas; (*b*) Shrove Tuesday. Cf. Good Friday.

c **1420** *Liber Cocorum* 37 Fro Martyn messe to gode tyde evyne. **1547** Salesbury *Welsh Dict., Ynyd*..shrovetide, Good tyde. **1620** *Frier Rush* 10 Vpon a good night, all the whole Convent assembled together in the Quier. [**1820** Wilbraham *Chesh. Gloss., Guttit*..Shrovetide.]

9. a. Of a child: Well-behaved, quiet and obedient, not giving trouble (= F. *sage,* G. *artig*). Also of adults (converging with sense 5 a). Phr. *as good as gold.*

1695 Congreve *Love for Love* II. iii, But come, be a good Girl, don't perplex your poor Uncle. **1727** Boyer *Dict. Angl.-Fr.* s.v., A good (or sober) Boy, *un garçon sage.* *a* **1845** Hood *Lost Heir* 30 Sitting as good as gold in the gutter. **1886** Mrs. Burnett *Lit. Ld. Fauntleroy* x. (1892) 191 She was as good as gold. **1932** N. Royde-Smith *Incredible Tale* 100 Here we are as good as gold. **1951** M. McLuhan *Mech. Bride* 118/2 Coke ads concentrate on the 'good girl' image. *Ibid.*, The 'good girl' is the nineteenth-century stock model which has long been merged with the mother image. **1955** L. P. Hartley *Perfect Woman* xxiv. 219 'Good girl,' he commented. **1958** Hayward & Harari tr. *Pasternak's Dr. Zhivago* I. vii. 212 As soon as a few were bumped off by way of example, all the others became as good as gold.

b. *be good!; if you can't be good, be careful!,* as jocular exhortations to good behaviour, esp. at parting.

1908 S. E. White *Riverman* iii. 29 Well, good-bye, boys. .. Be good! **1908** 'O. Henry' *Gentle Grafter* 119 I'll drop in on you..and we'll have dinner together. Be good. **1911** *MacLean's Mag.* Mar. 96/2 Well, old man, if you can't be good, be careful. **1929** J. B. Priestley *Good Companions* I. v. 185 I'm off then! Be good! **1951** T. Rattigan *Who is Sylvia?* III. 267 Good night, ladies. Be good.

III. Gratifying, favourable, advantageous.

10. a. Corresponding to one's desires; marked by happiness or prosperity; fortunate. Of news: Welcome, pleasing.

c **825** *Vesp. Psalter* xxxiii. [xxxiv.] 13 [12] Hwelc is mon se wile lif & willað ȝesian dæȝas gode. *a* **1000** *Body & Soul* 38 Nis nu se ende to god. *a* **1310** in Wright *Lyric P.* xix. 59 Jesu Crist, heovene kyng, ȝef us alle god endyng. *c* **1470** Henry *Wallace* II. 312 Thomas ansuerd; 'Thir tithingis ar noucht gud'. **1481** Caxton *Godfrey* clxxxii. 268 Alle theyr good ewr and fortune. **1535** Coverdale *2 Sam.* xx. 18 So came it to a good ende. **1573** J. Sanford *Hours Recreat.* (1576) 23 A joyfull feaste was to bee made in Florence, for some good newes. **1600** E. Blount tr. *Conestaggio* (ed. 2) 40 Let them goe in a good hower. **1768** Boyer *Dict. Angl.-Fr.* s.v., She's so high, that she looks for the good hour every moment. **1770** Langhorne *Plutarch* (1879) II. 828/2 Ptolemy of Cyprus, as Cato's good stars would have it, took himself off by poison. **1776** Foote *Bankrupt* I. Wks. 1799 II. 102 Never fear, things are in a very good way. **1843** Dickens *Christm. Carol* iv. 140 When she asked him faintly what news..he appeared embarrassed how to answer. 'Is it good', she said, 'or bad?'

b. of a wind: Favourable.

a **1400** *Octouian* 613 Good wynd and whedyr God hem sente. *c* **1485** *Digby Myst.* (1882) III. 1744 Þe wynd is good. **1568** Grafton *Chron.* II. 280 And had so good winde, that ..she arrived before Calice [etc.]. **1625** J. Glanvill *Voy. Cadiz* 10 That every shipp might be apt to come forth with the first good winde. **1780** Falconer *Dict. Marine, Sourdre au vent,* to hold a good wind.

c. *good afternoon! good evening! †good morn! good morning! †good time of day!* elliptical forms of salutation used at meeting or parting. Hence **good-morning** *v., nonce-wd.,* to say 'good morning'. See also good day, good even, good morrow, good night.

? *a* **1400** *Morte Arth.* 3476 The gome graythely hym grette, and bade gode morwene. *c* **1460** *Towneley Myst.* xii. 82 How, gyb, goode morne, wheder goys thou. *c* **1500** *Yng.*

Childr. Bk. 20 in *Babees Bk.*, To whom þou metys come by þe weye, Curtasly 'gode morne' þou sey. **1535** STEWART *Cron. Scot.* II. 636 The Thane of Caldar, Schir, God ȝow gude morne! **1594** SHAKS. *Rich. III*, I. i. 122 Good time of day vnto my gracious Lord. **1611** —— *Cymb.* II. iii. 66 Our deere Sonne, When you haue giuen good morning to your Mistris, Attend the Queene and vs. **1802** G. COLMAN *Br. Grins, Knt. & Friar* I. xxxvi, She met them every day, Good morninging, and how d'ye doing. **1865** DICKENS *Mut. Fr.* I. vii, Wegg nods to the face, 'Good evening'.

d. ***(to have) a good time (of it)***: a period of enjoyment. See note s.v. TIME *sb.* 6.

1666 PEPYS *Diary* 7 Mar., So thither I went, and had as good a time as heart could wish. **1681** HICKERINGILL *Wks.* (1716) II. 121 The Orthodox and Protestants had a good time of it. **1845** CARLYLE *Cromwell* (1850) IV. 11 There they had a moderately good time of it. **1863** TROLLOPE *Rachel Ray* II. vi. 109 Eating cake and drinking currant wine, but not having, on the whole, what our American friends call a good time of it. **1891** STEVENSON & L. OSBOURNE *Wrecker* (1892) 14 To enrich the world with things of beauty, and have a fairly good time myself while doing so.

e. ***to have a good night***: to sleep undisturbedly and restfully. (So F. *une bonne nuit.*)

1701 W. PENN in *Pa. Hist. Soc. Mem.* IX. 47 My daughter ..has had a good night and is better.

f. ***the good news..the bad news..***: a formula based on a type of schoolchild's joke (see quot. 1972[1]), in which a piece of good news is undermined by concomitant bad news; also in extended use.

1972 F. KNEBEL *Dark Horse* (1973) xii. 186 'There are a couple of things I want to talk to you about. From your standpoint, some bad news and some good news, we might say.'.. 'Is this like that story of the school principal who calls a father and says I've got some bad news and some good news for you? The bad news is that we've discovered your son is a fag. The good news is that he's just been elected queen of May.' **1972** *N.Y. Times* 22 Oct. IV. 6 From the Mayor on down there is good news..in the fact that the concept of Federal revenue sharing without the inevitable tangle of governmental strings is now law. Now for the bad news. **1977** C. MCFADDEN *Serial* (1978) xiv. 35/1 What happened next was a particularly humiliating version of a 'good news/bad news' joke. Harvey was given a clean bill of health...the doctor on duty..of course just *had* to be a tennis friend. **1979** *New York* 9 Apr. 10 The market has already all of the bad news and..when the good news arrives in the form of a Mideast peace treaty or record corporate-earnings reports, the market shrugs or retreats. **1985** *Observer* 22 Sept. 20/7 The good news is that the state.. would ask all prostitutes to take screening tests for the AIDS virus. The bad news is that those who fail will not be banned from working.

11. Said of things which give pleasure.

a. Pleasant to the taste. †Also of odours.

971 *Blickl. Hom.* 73 Nardus & spica, seo is brunes heowes & godes stences. *c* **1000** *Ags. Ps.* cxviii. [cxix.] 103 Me is on gomum god & swete þin aȝen word. *c* **1350** *Leg. Rood* (1871) 73 So gude sauore gan þai fele, þat [etc.]. **1599** H. BUTTES *Dyets drie Dinner* C b, Drinke old wine of good savour upon them. **1653** WALTON *Angler* ii. 58 You wil find him very good [to eat]. **1670–1** NARBOROUGH *Jrnl.* in *Acc. Sev. Late Voy.* I. (1694) 124 Small Blackberries, good and well-tasted. **1684** *Yorksh. Dial.* 484, I think you heve nut din'd, here's a good smell. **1755** HAY *Martial's Epigr.* II. xlviii. 110 Wine, and good fare. **1756–82** J. WARTON *Ess. Pope* (ed. 4) I. iv. 221 His ruling passion of good-eating.

b. Agreeable, amusing, entertaining. Of a jest, speech: Smart, witty. Also in phrase ***as good as a play***. ***good company*** (see COMPANY 4 c).

1530 PALSGR. 867/1 God sende you good company, *Dieu vous doynt bon encontre.* **1660** PEPYS *Diary* 18 Sept., Here some of us fell to handicap, a sport that I never knew before, which was very good. **1667** *Ibid.* 26 June, He answered: 'That is a good one, in faith! for you know yourself to be secure'. **1694, 1775** [see GOOD THING 18 c]. **1875** JOWETT *Plato* (ed. 2) III. 304 Are they not as good as a play, trying their hand at legislation?

12. a. Conducive to well-being, health, or advantage; beneficial, profitable, salutary, wholesome. Const. *for*, †*to*.

971 *Blickl. Hom.* 57 þæt man godne mete ete. *c* **1175** *Lamb. Hom.* 71 Ne wille ic noht þet þe sunfulle beo ded, ac libbe and nime godne red. *c* **1205** LAY. 5432 Hit wes god þat he spec. *c* **1320** *Seuyn Sag.* (W.) 1676 Sire,.. Thou dost bi a god counseil. *a* **1340** HAMPOLE *Psalter* cxviii. 11 Disciplyne of silence is goed. **1384** WYCLIF *Sel. Wks.* III. 505 If I erre in þis sentense, I wil mekely be amendid, ȝhe by þo deth, if hit be skilful, for þat I hope were gude to me. **1483** CAXTON *G. de la Tour* F iv, Therfor this ensample is very good to euery woman to see. **1548** HALL *Chron., Hen. VII*, 7 Before that this evell newly planted wede should straye and wander over the good herbes of his whole realme. **1565** COOPER *Thesaurus, Cecubum*,..a kinde of wyne good to digestion. **1573** J. SANFORD *Hours Recreat.* (1576) 95 A parable shewing that Malmesey is good at all tymes of ones meale. **1573** TUSSER *Husb.* ii. (1878) 9 Ceres..with hir good lessons told me, that [etc.]. **1599** H. BUTTES *Dyets drie Dinner* E iv b, Very good for the short winded, and splenaticke. **1634** SIR T. HERBERT *Trav.* 209 It is an Ile abounding with all good things requisite for mans use. **1711** H. LAMP *Autobiog.* iii. (1895) 27 Good counsel was dead, To go home I sham'd. **1891** C. LOWE in *19th Cent.* Dec. 858 Knowing much better what is good for its children than these latter themselves.

b. Useful as a remedy. Const. *for*, † *against*.

c **1450** *ME. Med. Bk.* (Heinrich) 101 Hit is good for al maner vices of sore yen. **1577** B. GOOGE *Heresbach's Husb.* I. (1586) 12 Beside, the pargetting or seeling, is a good safetie against fyre. **1599** H. BUTTES *Dyets drie Dinner* C ij b, Their smell is wondrous good in cordiaque passions. *Ibid.* F ij b, Good against the paulsie and quivering of the joints. **1626** BACON *Sylva* §767 The Water of Nilus..is excellent Good for the Stone. **1711** STEELE *Spect.* No. 156 ¶1 A Woman's Man..is not at a loss what is good for a Cold. **1744** BERKELEY *Siris* §9 Tar was by the ancients esteemed good against poisons. **1883** GILMOUR *Mongols* xxiii. 280 A Mongol..asked in an earnest whisper if I had any medicine good for wounds.

13. a. Of an opinion, an interpretation, an account: Favourable, approving, laudatory. ***a good press***, a favourable reception in newspapers and journals.

1601 SHAKS. *Jul. C.* II. i. 145 His Siluer haires Will purchase vs a good opinion. **1617** MORYSON *Itin.* II. 57 With promise to make good construction of his actions. *Ibid.* III. 6 Our very God is in a good sence said to be jelous. **1622** WITHER *Philarete* (1633) 594 To purchase either credit to my name, Or gaine a good Opinion. **1665** BOYLE *Occas. Refl.* IV. iv. (1848) 192 As the Apostles were Fishers of men in a good sense, so their and our grand adversary is a skilful Fisher of men in a bad one. **1813** SHELLEY *Q. Mab* v. 213 Whose applause he sells..for a cold world's good word. **1908** *Times Lit. Suppl.* 99/1 Mr. Leaf..has not had a good press lately. **1915** *Truth* 25 Aug. 301/2, I suppose he knew that was the sort of thing that would ensure a good press for him when he got back to Berlin. **1928** *Observer* 22 Jan. 14/6 The new Measure has not, upon the whole, such a 'good Press' as that which the House of Commons rejected in December. **1928** *Sunday Dispatch* 8 July 22/7 A considerable time has passed since a Scotch boxer received such a good Press in the South.

b. ***to take in good part*** (see PART *sb.*). †Hence ellipt., ***to take in good*** (cf. L. *boni consulere*).

1544 in Lodge *Illust. Br. Hist.* (1791) I. xxxix. 91 His Maiestie taketh in good your diligence.

IV. With reference to a purpose or effect.

14. a. Adapted to a proposed end; efficient, useful; suitable. Const. *for*, †*to* (a purpose or function), *to* with *inf.* ***in good †hour, time***: see the sbs.

a **1000** *Juliana* 102 He is to freonde god. *c* **1000** *Sax. Leechd.* II. 92 Sio biþ god to dolhsealfe. *c* **1205** LAY. 521 He nom his kene men þa to compe weren gode. **1461** *Paston Lett.* No. 408 II. 35 He and I thought that Richard Bloumvyle were good to that occupacion. **1484** CAXTON *Fables of Poge* iv, What are thoos that folowe the & wherto ben they good. **1551** TURNER *Herbal* I. F v b, The same [birch] is good to make hoopis of. **1573** J. SANFORD *Hours Recreat.* (1576) 49 Saying proverbially, that they [advocates, etc.] were good men to draw water to his mill. **1577** B. GOOGE *Heresbach's Husb.* I. (1586) 29 b, The roote of it is good for nothing. **1590** SPENSER *F.Q.* I. i. 8 The Aspine good for staves. **1599** H. BUTTES *Dyets drie Dinner* C iv b, The juyce is good sauce to provoke appetite. **1617** MORYSON *Itin.* II. 101 Like a Quince, requiring great cost ere it be good to eat. **1700** T. BROWN tr. *Fresny's Amusem. Ser. & Com.* 70 What are they good for else but Hanging, or Starving? **1738** SWIFT *Pol. Conversat.* 88 Ah, Colonel! you'll never be good. .. Which of the Goods d'ye mean? good for something, or good for nothing? **1865** CARLYLE *Fredk. Gt.* XV. iii. (1872) V. 294 He was not now good for much; alas, it had been but little he was ever good for.

†**b.** Easy. Const. *to* with *infin.* (Cf. EVIL *a.* 4 b.)

c **1489** CAXTON *Sonnes of Aymon* iii. 95 Traitours ben good to overcom; they shall not now endure longe agaynst us. *Ibid.* ix. 224 The foure sones of Aymon were good to knowe by thother.

c. ***a good question***, one that requires careful consideration before answering; one that is very difficult or awkward to answer.

1918 F. VON HÜGEL *Let.* 11 Dec. (1927) 259 What is the precise meaning of Thekla's insistence upon religion as primarily an is-ness, not an ought-ness? A good question. **1945** C. S. LEWIS *That Hideous Strength* ix. 235 'That's a very good question,' said MacPhee. **1960** G. W. TARGET *Teachers* 64 'I'd write something right across their arse.' ..'Wouldn't do any good.' 'What would?' said Bert. 'That's a good question, Bert.'

15. Chiefly of persons: Having the characteristics or aptitudes required or becoming in a specified or implied capacity or relationship.

a. in concord with a sb. denoting function, relationship, creed, or party.

a **1000** *Cædmon's Dan.* 11 Wæs him hyrde god, heofonrices weard. *c* **1200** *Trin. Coll. Hom.* 39 þe gode herdes wakieð on faire liflode ouer here orf. *c* **1205** LAY. 25475 Cniht he wes wunder god & he hafde swiðe muchel mod. *a* **1300** *Cursor M.* 7761 Mani gode archer þan was þar. **13..** *E.E. Allit. P.* A. 1200 To pay þe prince..Hit is ful epe to þe god krystyin. **1548** HALL *Chron., Hen. VII*, 23 b, Furnished with .lxx. thousand good fightyng men. **1613** PURCHAS *Pilgrimage* (1614) 250 He had heard even good Saracens affirme with griefe, that..they could finde no Reason in it [the Koran]. **1632** J. HAYWARD tr. *Biondi's Eromena* 84 For there have we good Chirurgions. **1697** DRYDEN *Virg. Georg.* III. 680 Good Shepherds after Sheering drench their Sheep. **1738** SWIFT *Pol. Conversat.* 102 A good Wife must be bespoke, for there is none ready made. **1849** MACAULAY *Hist. Eng.* iii. I. 396 Good Latin scholars were numerous.

b. *esp.* with agent-noun: Thorough or skilful in the action indicated.

971 *Blickl. Hom.* 207 Se bisceop þa ðær ȝesette gode sangeras & mæssepreostas. **1500–20** DUNBAR *Poems* lxiii. 42 Monsouris of France, gud clarat-cunnaris. **1577** B. GOOGE *Heresbach's Husb.* I. (1586) 14 b, That the Bailiffe be a good riser, and that..he may be the fyrst up in the mornyng. **1586** A. DAY *Eng. Secretary* I. (1625) 7 Here is *the which*..a phrase never with us accustomed, nor with any good Writer. *a* **1784** [see HATER]. **1837** DICKENS *Pickwick* ii, 'The Doctor, I believe, is a very good shot', said Mr. Winkle.

c. Competent, skilful, clever *at* or *in* (formerly also †*for*, †*of*, *to*) a certain action or pursuit. Sometimes used *simply*. So of a ship: †***good under*** or ***with sail***.

1340–70 *Alex. & Dind.* 23 þe gentil genosophistiens þat goode were of witte. *c* **1400** *Sowdone Bab.* 67 The maister sende a man to londe, Of diuers langages was gode and trewe. **1548** HALL *Chron., Edw. IV*, 209 The kynges shyp was good with sayle. **1561** BECON *Sick Mans Salve* Pref. (1572) A iij, 'My dayes', saith Job..'are passed away as the ships that be good vnder saile, & as the Egle that flyeth vnto the pray'. *c* **1566** J. ALDAY tr. *Boaystuau's Theat. World* T b, Cais Cesar was so good on horsebacke that [etc.]. **1617** MORYSON *Itin.* III. 51 The Florentines..good at the needle. **1656** WOOD *Life* 22 July, He was very good for the treble violl, and also for the violin. **1700** T. BROWN tr. *Fresny's Amusem. Ser. & Com.* 71 Brave Men indeed, if they were half as good at Praying, and Fighting, as they are at Cursing and Swearing. **1712** STEELE *Spect.* No. 497 ¶1 Such whom he observed were good at a Halt, as his phrase was. **1776** FOOTE *Bankrupt* I. Wks. 1799 II. 100 Are you good at a riddle? **1782** NELSON in Nicolas *Disp.* (1845) I. 64 He does his duty exceedingly well as an Officer: indeed I am very well off. They are all good. **1808** *Sporting Mag.* XXXII. 76 He ..shewed good, but fell on his knees on one of his adversary's blows. **1813** SCOTT *Rokeby* I. xiii, Good I am called at trumpet's sound, And good when goblets dance the round. **1849** THACKERAY *Pendennis* I. xx, I am not good at descriptions of female beauty. **1855** MACAULAY *Hist. Eng.* xiii. III. 330 All comely in appearance, and good men of their hands.

16. Reliable, safe. In various specific uses, chiefly **a.** *Comm.* Of a trader: Able to fulfil his engagements; financially sound. Of a life, with reference to insurance: Likely to continue a long time, free from exceptional risks. ***good debts***: those which are expected to be paid in full.

1570 FOXE *A. & M.* (ed. 2) 1131/2 Many..passyng it ouer one to an other for good debt, as if it had bene ready money in their purses. **1596** SHAKS. *Merch. V.* I. iii. 15 My meaning in saying he is a good man, is to haue you vnderstand me that he is sufficient. **1605** MARSTON *Dutch Courtezan* III. ii. E 2 b, *Gar.* Your bill had ben sufficient, y'are a good man. **1632** MASSINGER *City Madam* III. iii, Fair household-furniture, a few good debts..I find. *a* **1661** FULLER *Worthies* (1840) I. iv. 20 He is called..a Good Man upon the exchange, who hath a responsible estate. **1755** MAGENS *Insurances* I. 403 These Contracts are sold and re-sold at Pleasure..when they are signed by good and known People. **1788** WESLEY *Wks.* (1872) VII. 219 The whole city of London uses the words *rich* and *good* as equivalent terms. **1805** *Sporting Mag.* XXV. 193, I stood firm, and upon 'Change, was universally reported to be a *good man.* **1828** D. LE MARCHANT *Rep. Claims to Barony Gardner* 78 It was a sufficiently good life within the meaning of the terms of that insurance office. **1831** T. L. PEACOCK *Crotchet Castle* iii. 34 Good and respectable, sir, I take it, means rich?

b. ***good for*** (a certain amount): (*a*) of a person, that may be relied on to pay so much; (*b*) of a promissory note, draft, etc., drawn for so much (cf. F. *bon pour*); hence in S. African use **good-for** *sb.* (see quot. 1879); (*c*) capable of producing; valid for, etc. orig. *U.S.*

1865 TROLLOPE in *Fortn. Rev.* 1 Oct. 419 The porter.. had taken his luggage eagerly, knowing that Mr. Belton was always good for sixpence. **1873** J. H. BEADLE *Undevel. West* xviii. 337 From thirty to forty tons of ore.., good for an average profit of a hundred and fifty dollars per ton. **1879** ATCHERLEY *Boerland* 232, I halted in order to cash a 'good for' I held of the owner. These 'good fors', which answer to an English IOU, are common enough in South Africa. **1882** RIDER HAGGARD *Cetywayo* 133 As there was no cash in the country this was done by issuing Government promissory notes, known as 'goodfors'. **1901** MERWIN & WEBSTER *Calumet 'K'* vi. 104 'How's it coming out?' he asked. 'Do we know how much we're good for?' **1903** *N.Y. Tribune* 20 Sept., A 50-cent combination ticket good for every amusement on the island. *a* **1916** H. JAMES *Middle Years* (1917) i. 12 In possession of a return ticket 'good', as we say, for a longer interval than I could then dream about. **1967** *Listener* 14 Sept. 326/1, I look at a person and I say well, he's good for £5 or £6 for one watch, which cost me 30 shillings.

c. ***good for*** (a period of time, an amount of exertion): safe to live or last so long, well able to accomplish so much.

1859 DASENT *Popular Tales fr. Norse* 205 The lassie said she was good to spin a pound of flax in four and twenty hours. **1893** F. M. CRAWFORD *Marion Darche* I. 140 There is nothing in the world the matter with him; he is good for another twenty years. *Mod.* Are you good for a ten miles' walk?

d. To † ***make***, † ***become, come good for***: to be surety for. *Obs.* exc. *Sc.*

1502 *Ord. Crysten Men* (W. de W. 1506) I. iv. 45 The godfader and godmoder ben pledges & maketh good for hym. **1591** PERCIVALL *Sp. Dict., Abono*, making good, or under-taking for another, *vadimonium.* **1645** RUTHERFORD *Tryal & Tri. Faith* (1845) 79 He is become good to the Father for us. **1892** W. RAMAGE *Last Words* xxxiv. 322 Having come good for the transgressor the surety could be spared no part of the punishment.

†**e.** ***Predicatively***, of a space of time: Available (for a purpose).

1711 BUDGELL *Spect.* No. 77 ¶1 Will..pulled out his Watch, and told me we had seven Minutes good. **1749** CHESTERF. *Lett.* (1792) II. ccix. 295 You have still two years good, but no more, to form your character. **1749** FIELDING *Tom Jones* XVI. x, I suppose he hath not many Hours to live. As for you, Sir, you have a Month at least good yet.

V. Adequate, effectual, valid.

17. a. Of personal actions or activities: Adequate to the purpose; sufficient in every respect; thorough. ***good heed, good speed***: see the sbs.

1154 *O.E. Chron.* an. 1153 Al folc him luuede for he dide god iustise & makede pais. *a* **1310** in Wright *Lyric P.* xxv. 75 Jesu..send mi soule god weryyng That y ne drede non eovel thing. *Ibid.* xxxvii. 103 ȝef thou nymest wel god keep [etc.]. **1548** HALL *Chron., Edw. IV*, 240 b, The which desyre, if the Flueminges had but geven good care to. **1584** R. SCOT *Discov. Witchcr.* x. i. 177 The Prophet giueth vs good warning. **1617** MORYSON *Itin.* II. 66 [He] made a very good stand. *Ibid.* 156 So that except they steale their passage (which I feare most) I make no doubt but my Lord President will giue a very good accompt of them. **1639** T. BRUGIS tr.

Camus' Mor. Relat. 356 Who did them good and speedy justice. **1726** SWIFT *Gulliver* IV. i, I drew my Hanger, and gave him a good Blow with the flat Side of it. **1820** SHELLEY *Œdipus* I. 147, I have taken good care That shall not be. **1849** MACAULAY *Hist. Eng.* ii. I. 195 He admitted that the House ..had done good service to the crown. **1878** S. WALPOLE *Hist. Eng.* I. 371 Society did not see anything either unseemly or unmanly in a man administering a good beating to his wife.

b. of a belief, conviction, feeling, will. For the phrases (*obs.* or *arch.*) ***in good earnest, faith, sadness, sooth, truth***, see the sbs.

c **1175** *Lamb. Hom.* 5 We sulen habben ure heorte and habben godne ileafe to ure drihten. *c* **1305** *St. Lucy* 43 in *E.E.P.* (1862) 102 þi bileue þat is so god: helpeþ þi moder iwis. **1530** TINDALE *Answ. More's Dial.* G j, As if a man said, the boyes will was good to haue geuen his father a blowe. **1617** MORYSON *Itin.* II. 203 Wee are in good hope they are all gone.

18. Of a right, claim, reason, plea, proposition: Valid, sound. Of a legal decision, a contract, an act of any kind: Valid, effectual, in force; not vitiated by any flaw. ***to hold, stand good***: see the vbs.

a **1000** *Azarias* 109 A þin dom sy god & genge. *c* **1230** *Hali Meid.* 13 þu of earnest meiden to beo engle euening..& wið god rihte hwen þu hare liflade..leadest. *c* **1315** SHOREHAM 129 Ich dar segge mid gode ry3te, That [etc.]. **1340** *Ayenb.* 6 Ine guode skele me may zuerie wyþ-oute zenne. *c* **1550** CHEKE *Matt.* xx. 4 Whatsoever is good reason I wil give iou. **1560** DAUS tr. *Sleidane's Comm.* 78 b, Ferdinando..affirmed the kyngdome to be his by good right. **1562** *Act 5 Eliz.* c. 12 §4 Licences..shall have Continuaunce and be good only for one Year. **1568** GRAFTON *Chron.* II. 100 Stood foorth and proved the former election to be good. **1574** tr. *Littleton's Tenures* 7 a, If..the land is geven to the sonne, and to the heire of the bodye of his father engendred, this is a good taile. **1594** HOOKER *Eccl. Pol.* I. (1676) 69 Under this fair and plausible colour, whatsoever they utter passeth for good and currant. **1596** HARINGTON *Metam. Ajax* (1814) 107 And this stands with good reason. **1599** MASSINGER, etc. *Old Law* III. i, It is good in law too. **1617** MORYSON *Itin.* III. 28 Having the Lawes..together with a good cause on his side. **1689** LOCKE *Governmt.* I. §149 Every Father of a Family..had as good a claim to Royalty as these. *a* **1732** ATTERBURY (J.), He is resolved now to shew how slight the propositions were which Luther let go for good. **1755** MAGENS *Insurances* I. 406 Goods not proved to be neutral Property might be condemned as good Prize. **1818** CRUISE *Digest* (ed. 2) V. 509 Although a recovery be a good bar to a remainder for years [etc.]. **1855** MACAULAY *Hist. Eng.* xi. III. 29 Was not a letter written by the first Prince of the Blood..at least as good a warrant as a vote of the Rump? **1871** MORLEY *Voltaire* (1886) 8 The impression that the hearer, for good reasons or bad, happens to have formed. **1885** SIR F. NORTH in *Law Rep.* 29 Ch. Div. 541 That part of the appointment being bad, did not prevent the limitation over being good. **1898** MURISON *Sir W. Wallace* v. 91 He promptly hanged such as failed to furnish a good excuse.

19. a. Satisfactory or adequate in quantity or degree; sufficiently ample or abundant; considerable, rather great. Freq. in ***a good way*** (dial. and U.S. *ways*), a considerable distance; also *transf.* of time. For *a good deal, few, many*, see those words. ***to have a good mind to*** (see MIND).

a **1000** *O.E. Chron.* an. 913 Him beaȝ god dæl þæs folces to. *a* **1000** *Rood* 70 (Gr.) We ðær reotende gode hwile stodon on staðole. *c* **1220** *Bestiary* 404 Ne stereð ȝe noȝt of ðe stede a god stund deies. *c* **1300** *Beket* 69 Heo wende forth with wel god pas. **1382** WYCLIF *Luke* vi. 38 Thei schulen ȝyue in to ȝoure bosum a good mesure, and wel fillid. *c* **1450** *ME. Med. Bk.* (Heinrich) 72 Let þe seke vse þer of..a good qwantite at ones. **1526** TINDALE *Acts* ix. 23 After a good while. **1568** GRAFTON *Chron.* II. 22 These thynges were done a good space after. **1577** B. GOOGE *Heresbach's Husb.* I. (1586) 1 b, Being nowe of good yeeres and sickely. *Ibid.* IV. 163 Beside, you must have..good plentie of duste, wherein they may bathe and proyne themselves. **1634** SIR T. HERBERT *Trav.* 81 And having obtained a good force from the relieving Turkes and Tartars, he easily advanced. **1646** SIR T. BROWNE *Pseud. Ep.* I. viii. 30 An Author of good Antiquity. **1551**, **1662** [see WAY *sb.*[1] 8]. **1588**, **1594** [WAY *sb.*[1] 23 c]. **1665** SIR T. HERBERT *Trav.* (1677) 356 Persons of such ingenuity and so good a purse as [etc.]. **1687** A. LOVELL tr. *Thevenot's Trav.* I. 34 To play and sing a good part of the day. **1759** B. MARTIN *Nat. Hist. Eng.* II. Cardigan 364 There are a good Plenty both of River and Sea-fish. **1799** G. SMITH *Laboratory* I. 20 Fill one rocket shell with a good charge, quite full. **1809** M. L. WEEMS *Life of Marion* xiii. 116 Yes, by jing, does he live a good way up!..a matter of seventy miles. **1851** DIXON *W. Penn* xvi. (1872) 138 The composition of this work kept Penn at home a good part of the year. **1862** O. W. NORTON *Army Lett.* (1903) 125 That day may be a good way off but still I do not get homesick in the least. **1864** T. L. NICHOLS *40 Yrs. Amer. Life* I. 250 It's a good way, and you will be out late. **1877** A. B. HORTON in Moloney *Forestry W. Afr.* (1887) 38 The planting must be during the rainy season, as it requires a good quantity of water. **1885** *World* 1 Sept. 11 A good number of deer have been shot during the last fortnight.

b. Preceding another adj. (expressing either large size, strength, resisting power, or the like) to which it serves as a moderate intensive. Similarly †***good pretty*** = pretty good. (Cf. B. b.)

c **1300** *Havelok* 2554 Hand-ax, syþe, gisarm, or spere, Or aunlaz, and god long knif. **1535** COVERDALE *2 Macc.* iv. 41 Some gat stones, some good stronge clubbes. **1548** UDALL etc. *Erasm. Par. Luke* 149 b, A good preatie waie of. **1565** JEWEL *Repl. Harding* (1611) 269 He hath some good prety skill in peeuish Arguments. **1586** EARL LEYCESTER in *Leycester Corresp.* (Camden 1844) 254 A good sharp warr. **1593** G. GIFFARD *Dial. Conc. Witches* (1843) 12 We have a schoolemaister that is a good pretie scholler (they say) in the Latine tongue. **1646** H. HAMMOND in *Ld. Falkland's View* 25 A good large Province. **1787** 'G. GAMBADO' *Acad. Horsem.* (1809) 35 A good smart cut over his right cheek. **1885** *Daily News* 16 July 4/7 It will take a good long time to bring them right. *Mod.* He writes a good bold hand.

20. Qualifying a definite statement of quantity, to indicate an amount not less, and usually greater, than what is stated. Often following its sb., and so approaching an adv. (Cf. FULL *a.* 8, FULL *adv.*)

c **1000** *Sax. Leechd.* II. 292 Genim giðcornes leafa gode hand fulle. **1577** B. GOOGE *Heresbach's Husb.* III. (1586) 144 Geve to every one three spoonefulles good. **1598** STOW *Surv.* 349 More than a goode flight shot towards Kings Land. **1626** BACON *Sylva* §17 Take Violets, and infuse a good Pugill of them in a Quart of Vineger. **1662** J. DAVIES tr. *Olearius' Voy. Ambass.* 17 A good quarter of an ell high. **1690** CHILD *Disc. Trade* (1694) 7 It is a good man's work all the year to be following vintners and shopkeepers for money. **1834** L. RITCHIE *Wand. by Seine* 26 We have three quarters good to a voyage of half an hour. **1842** MRS. CARLYLE *Lett.* I. 166 The Post-office, which is a good two miles off. **1876** GEO. ELIOT *Dan. Der.* I. xii. 231 He..played a good hour on the violoncello.

VI. Idiomatic phrases.

21. as good. a. Orig. in phr. such as (*me*) *were as good* = it were as good for me (etc.); where *good* is the adj. In later developments, *I were as good, I had as good* (= I might as well), *good* tends to be felt as adverbial: cf. HAVE *v.* 22. Hence occas. such uses as *I may* or *might as good*, where *as good* is purely adverbial = as well.

? *a* **1450** *Thomas & Fairy Q.* in Halliwell *Illustr. Fairy Mythol.* (1845) 66 Me had been as good to goo To the brynnyng fyre of hell. **1480** *Robt. Devyll* 343 in Hazl. *E.P.P.* I. 233 A man had ben as good to have be smytten with thonder. ? **14..** in Utterson *Sel. E.P.P.* (1817) II. 36 One were, in a maner, as good be slayne. **1523** LD. BERNERS *Froiss.* (1812) I. 754 We were as good to go towardes Flaunders as to Boloyne. **1573** G. HARVEY *Letter-bk.* (Camden) 44 Thai miht as good ether whot Coales as deni me agajn. **1591** LYLY *Endym.* III. i. 31 As good sleepe and doe no harme, as wake and doe no good. **1605** A. WOTTON *Answ. Pop. Articles* 59 Were not Christ as good have a troubled Church as none at all? **1647** TRAPP *Comm. 1 Cor.* xiv. 2 As good he may hold his tongue, for God needs him not. **1668** SHADWELL *Sullen Lovers* I. i. Wks. 1720 I. 27 She had as good have thrown her money into the dirt. **1671** FLAVEL *Fount. Life* ii. 31 As good no Law as No Penalty. **1697** COLLIER *Ess. Mor. Subj.* II. 138 His Gold might as good have stay'd at Peru, as come into his Custody. **1789** MRS. PIOZZI *Journ. France* I. 299 It were as good live at Brest or Portsmouth..as here. **1816** SCOTT *Antiq.* xv, 'I had as gude gang back to the town, and take care o' the wean'. **1843** HALIBURTON *Attaché* II. xii. 209, I do suppose we had as good make tracks, for I don't want folks to know me yet.

b. ***as good as***: advb. phr. = Practically, to all intents and purposes.

1436 *Libel Eng. Pol.* in *Pol. Songs* (Rolls) II. 187 But if Englond were nyghe as gode as gone. **1530** PALSGR. 861/1 As good as doone, *quasi.* **1535** COVERDALE *Neh.* iv. 12 The Iewes..tolde vs as good as ten tymes. **1577** HANMER *Anc. Eccl. Hist.* VIII. vii. (1585) 149 A fierce bull which tossed..and left them as good as dead. *a* **1614** DONNE *Βιαθανατος* (1644) 147 She was brought very neer the fire, and as good as thrown in. *a* **1687** PETTY *Pol. Arith.* i. (1691) 17 The Seamen have as good as 12*s.* in Wages, Victuals [etc.]. **1699** BENTLEY *Phal.* 491 Scipio..and Cicero..do both as good as declare, that [etc.]. **1711** *Lond. Gaz.* No. 4806/2 The Marriage..is look'd upon to be as good as concluded. **1817** BYRON *Beppo* xxxv, In law he was almost as good as dead. **1871** CARLYLE in *Mrs. Carlyle's Lett.* III. 19 We had intended to make no visits this year, or as good as none. **1891** L. B. WALFORD *Mischief of Monica* viii, I as good as said you would.

c. ***to be as good as*** (***one's word***): to act up to the full sense of, to carry out fully.

1577 STANYHURST *Descr. Irel.* in Holinshed (1587) II. (K.O.). **1638** CROMWELL in Carlyle *Lett. & Sp.* App. ii, I doubt not but I shall be as good as my word for your money. **1661–2** PEPYS *Diary* 28 Feb., To be as good as my word, I bade Will get me a rod. **1713** ADDISON *Guardian* No. 136 ¶3 He has been as good as his promise. **1875** JOWETT *Plato* (ed. 2) III. 305.

22. make good. a. *trans.* To make up for; to compensate for, atone for; to supply (a deficiency), to pay (an expense). †Also (rarely) *intr.*, to make up or compensate *for*.

1377 LANGL. *P. Pl.* B. XVII. 77 What he speneth more I make the good here-after. **1389** in *Eng. Gilds* 7 þat alle þe costages that be mad aboute hym be mad good of the box. **1573–80** BARET *Alv.* S 823 If anie thing was stolne awaie, I euer made it good. *a* **1704** R. L'ESTRANGE (J.), Every distinct being has somewhat peculiar to itself, to make good in one circumstance what it wants in another. **1719** DE FOE *Crusoe* II. xi, If you will make good our pay to us. **1757** in Scrafton *Indostan* (1770) 67 What has been plundered by his people [shall be] made good. **1810** *Splendid Follies* II. 7, I like to make good for the trumpeters, and blow up such a tune as would collect a gaping multitude from a mile distant. **1846** TRENCH *Mirac.* vii. (1862) 196 Making good at least a part of the error by its unreserved confession. **1884** *Manch. Exam.* 29 May 4/7 Any deficiency in repayment shall be made good out of the county cess.

b. To fulfil, perform (a promise, etc.); to carry out, succeed in effecting (a purpose).

1535 COVERDALE *2 Chron.* vi. 16 Make good vnto my father Dauid..that which thou hast promysed him. **1657** *North's Plutarch* Notes 512. 42 The ten thousand Grecians ..made good their retreat through Asia into Europe. **1701** W. WOTTON *Hist. Rome* 208 His Men would make good his Attempt. **1712** BUDGELL *Spect.* No. 404 ¶2 Nature makes good her Engagements. **1736** BUTLER *Anal.* I. v. (Tegg) 80 Keeping upon his guard in order to make good his resolution. **1793** SMEATON *Edystone L.* §129 She might.. make her course good to land us at Fowey. **1823** SCOTT *Quentin D.* xxxiii, Will you make good your promise? **1854** H. MILLER *Sch. & Schm.* (1858) 522 Making good his upward way from his original place at the compositor's frame, to the editorship of a provincial paper. **1866** J. MARTINEAU *Ess.* I. 174 A discredited prophet unable to make good his word. **1893** EARL DUNMORE *Pamirs* I. 314 The rebels managed to make good their retreat.

c. To prove to be true or valid; to demonstrate the truth of (a statement), to substantiate (a charge). ***to make it good upon any one, his person***: to enforce one's assertion by combat, or the infliction of blows.

1523 LD. BERNERS *Froiss.* I. clxi. 196, I shulde make it good on you incontynent that ye haue no right to bere my deuyce. **1592** SHAKS. *Rom. & Jul.* v. iii. 286 This letter doth make good the Friers words. **1596** HARINGTON *Metam. Ajax* 104, I..wil make it good on their persons from the pin to the pike. **1607–12** BACON *Ess., Seeming Wise* (Arb.) 216/1 Some ..take by admittance that, which they cannot make good. **1663** GERBIER *Counsel* F viij b, You will..make good..that you are not of those who content themselves with..outsides of books. **1772** *Junius Lett.* lxviii. 334, I am now to make good my charge against you. **1820** SCOTT *Ivanhoe* xii, I should like to hear how that is made good? **1875** E. WHITE *Life in Christ* III. xxi. (1878) 303 His general argument has been made good on other grounds.

d. To make sure of; to secure (prisoners); to hold, to gain and hold (one's ground, a position).

1606 G. W[OODCOCKE] tr. *Justin's Hist.* 116 b, His own kingdom..he long honorably had made good against his enemies. **1617** MORYSON *Itin.* II. 166 This Fort his Lp. and his Company made good, till he was relieved from the Lord Deputie. **1643** *Declar. Comm., Reb. Irel.* 42 But being unarmed..they could not make good their Prisoners. **1663** BUTLER *Hud.* I. i. 700 The Bear..being bound In Honour to make good his Ground. **1804** W. TENNANT *Ind. Recreat.* (ed. 2) I. 326 The invaders have hardly any opportunity of making good a livelihood in the field. **1843** ARNOLD *Hist. Rome* III. 117 The walls..of Rome were ordered to be made good against an attack.

†**e.** ***to make one's part*** or ***party good***: to make a successful resistance (see PART, PARTY). *Obs.*

f. To repair; to replace or restore (what is lost or damaged).

1568 GRAFTON *Chron.* II. 128 If any were perished by keping, then the Abbot to make them good. **1726** LEONI *Alberti's Archit.* II. 129/2 In making good this break you must not work it up quite to the rest of the building. **1793** SMEATON *Edystone L.* §121 The space which had been previously occupied by the rock so cut down must have been made good by fresh Matter. **1884** *Law Times Rep.* LI. 161/2 The appellants undertook..to make good any damage done to the property. **1889** *Yorksh. Archæol. Jrnl.* X. 556 They have been entirely removed and the place made good with plain stonework.

g. *absol.* To fill up even or level.

1793 SMEATON *Edystone L.* §38 A set of short balks were laid..upon the next step..so as to make good up to the surface of the third step.

h. *intr.* (See sense 16 d.)

i. To succeed; to achieve success; to satisfy expectations; to fulfil a promise or obligation. orig. *U.S.*

1901 MERWIN & WEBSTER *Calumet 'K'* ii. 20 It'll play the devil with us if we can't make good. **1908** G. H. LORIMER *J. Spurlock* v. 89, I need work and I need it quick. Give me a show and I'll make good. **1908** *Daily Chron.* 25 Feb. 6/7, I made good, as the Yankees say, with my songs. **1909** H. G. WELLS *Tono-Bungay* III. i. 214 They couldn't for a moment 'make good' if the quarter of what they guarantee was demanded of them. **1910** W. M. RAINE *B. O'Connor* 55 All I ask of you is to make good. **1914** G. ATHERTON *Perch of Devil* I. 58 Ability and talent make good as always. **1927** *Daily Tel.* 7 Mar. 2 The board consider that the company will now make good. **1946** E. B. THOMPSON *Amer. Daughter* 225 You go on and make good. **1958** *House & Garden* Mar. 111 (Advt.), To record certain extracts from the Schweppshire Roll, wherein are recorded the names of Schweppshire Lads who have Made Good.

j. *Poker.* (See quots.)

1882 *Poker; how to play It* 8 When all who wish to play have gone in, the person putting up the ante..can play like the others who have gone in, by 'making good',—that is putting up in addition to the ante as much more as will make him equal in stake to the rest. **1895** 'TEMPLAR' *Poker Man.* 4 If he determines to play on, he 'makes good', as the expression is; that is, he adds to his ante as much as will make his total stake equal to that of each of the other players. **1904** R. F. FOSTER *Pract. Poker* 232 *Make Good.*—Adding enough to the blind or straddle to make it equal to the ante. **1929** ARNOLD & JOHNSTON *Poker* 150 Make good. To add sufficient to an ante or bet to meet a raise. **1950** L. H. DAWSON *Hoyle's Games Modernized* I. 122 B..does not fancy his chance of improving as worth another yellow, so refuses to 'make good', and retires.

23. good old: see OLD *a.* 8 b.

24. Proverbial phr. ***too good to be true***.

[**1578** G. WHETSTONE *Promos & Cassandra* B 3, I thought thy talke was too sweete to be true.] **1580** T. LUPTON (*title*) Siuquila. Too good to be true. **1594** J. LYLY *Mother Bombie* IV. ii, in *Wks.* (1902) III. 208 It was too good to be true. *a* **1691** J. FLAVEL *Method of Grace* (1699) vii. 133 They thought it was too good to be true. **1849** GEO. ELIOT *Let.* May (1954) I. 282 There is a sort of blasphemy in that proverbial phrase 'too good to be true'. **1908** W. S. CHURCHILL *My African Journey* v. 90 It is too good to be true. One can hardly believe that such an attractive spot can be cursed with malignant attributes. **1961** NEW ENGLISH BIBLE *Lk.* xxiv. 41 They were still unconvinced, still wondering, for it seemed too good to be true.

B. *adv.*

a. qualifying a vb. In a good manner; well; properly. Now chiefly *U.S.* exc. in vulgar or slang phrases. Also in phrase †*as good as* = 'as well as'. †**b.** qualifying an adj. or adv., with intensive force: In a high degree, 'right'. *Obs.* (Cf. A. 19 b.) **c.** In the phrase *as good* (see A. 21) the adj. sometimes becomes an adv. through change of construction.

In *good cheap* the word is not originally an adverb: see CHEAP *sb.* 8, 9.

13.. *K. Alis.* 6267 Thikke and schort and gud sette. *c* **1380** WYCLIF *Sel. Wks.* III. 130 And gode marke how Crist ..bad his gostly knyghtes go into al þo world. **1422** tr. *Secreta Secret., Priv. Priv.* (E.E.T.S.) 146 Thes goodes byth comyn als good to willde bestis as to men. *a* **1655** SIR N. L'ESTRANGE in W. J. Thoms *Anecd. & Traditions* (Camden 1839) 50 Having a fellow before him good refractorie and stubborne. *Ibid.* 59 They..good fiercely began to trusse up. *Ibid.* 74 A sturdie vagrant..begged good-saucily on Sir Drue Drurie. **1834** D. CROCKETT *Narr. Life* xii. 86, I..shot him [*sc.* a bear] the third time, which killed him good. **1838** C. GILMAN *Recoll. Southern Matron* 32 We will behave. We will behave good. **1840** *Southern Lit. Messenger* VI. 386/1 She used to tap her with it on the hands, when she behaved bad, or did not say her lesson good. **1859** BARTLETT *Dict. Amer.* (ed. 2) s.v., English travellers have repeatedly noticed the adverbial use of this word. 'He cannot read good.' 'It does not shoot good.' **1865** in S. E. Morison *Oxf. Hist. U.S.* (1927) II. 318 Columbia!— pretty much all burned; and burned *good.* **1885** W. L. ALDEN *Adv. Jimmy Brown* 90 The bee..lit on Tom's hand and stung him good. **1887** F. FRANCIS, Jr. *Saddle & Mocassin* vii. 131 I'll fix them—and fix them good while I'm about it. **1901** S. E. WHITE *Westerners* xv. 113 He'd have trimmed th' little cuss good. **1904** W. N. HARBEN *Georgians* 119, I stayed all day an' looked about good before I traded. **1946** K. TENNANT *Lost Haven* (1947) vi. 89 We're doing pretty good. **1962** J. LUDWIG in R. Weaver *Canad. Short Stories* 2nd Ser. (1968) 258 She stunk up that ritzy dress shop good. **1971** *Observer* (Colour Suppl.) 21 Nov. 65/1 If he makes it [*sc.* steel] good, it rolls good. [Steelworks in Cumberland.]

d. ***good and***, as an intensive. *colloq.* (orig. *U.S.*).

[**1834** C. A. DAVIS *Lett. J. Downing* 6 Don't forgit my face, and the Gineral's face; and let the likenesses be good and natural.] **1885** W. L. ALDEN *Adv. Jimmy Brown* 88 So I got out the needle, and jammed it into his leg with both hands, so that it would go in good and deep. **1889** *Kansas Times & Star* 18 Mar., The shamrock doubtless will be wet often, and the tyrannical lion's tail twisted good and plenty. **1892** KIPLING *Barrack-r. Ballads* 43 We met them good and large. **1896** ADE *Artie* xvi. 146, I was good and sore. **1901** MERWIN & WEBSTER *Calumet 'K'* i. 14 We got the letter the same day the red-headed man came here. His hair was good and red. **1904** J. LONDON *Let.* 17 Nov. (1966) 165 The lawyers..waded into me good and hard for the cash. **1923** R. D. PAINE *Comrades of Rolling Ocean* iv. 57 I'll roll out there when I get good and ready. **1926** *Publishers' Weekly* 15 May 1593 That made me good and provoked. **1928** *Daily Express* 2 Feb. 9/2 Colonel Ernest Cassell Maxwell..said ..'She went through it..good and proper, and I am sorry for her.' **1931** GALSWORTHY *Maid in Waiting* iii. 18 Castro got it good and strong this morning. **1954** *Encounter* Nov. 16/2 The American Machiavelli is tethered good and fast to the pole of Communism. **1969** B. KNOX *Tallyman* ii. 22 [It] can wait until we're good and ready.

C. quasi-*sb.* and *sb.*

I. 1. a. The adj. used *absol.* as *plural*: Good persons. Now only in the moral sense, and always with *the* (exc. occas. in ***good and bad***).

c **1300** *Cursor M.* 25249 (Cott. Galba) On domesday..þe euill sall fra þe gude be drawn. *a* **1450** *Le Morte Arth.* 2157 Grete pyte was on eyther syde So fele goode ther were layd downe. *a* **1592** H. SMITH *Serm.* (1637) 422 The good are knowne, because none but they which are good, strive to be better. **1613** SHAKS. *Hen. VIII*, v. v. 28 All Princely Graces ..With all the Vertues that attend the good, Shall still be doubled on her. *a* **1721** PRIOR *Henry & Emma* 713 With power invested, and with pleasure cheer'd, Sought by the good, by the oppressor fear'd. **1746** SMOLLETT *Reproof* 97 Sworn foe to good and bad, to great and small. **1810** SHELLEY *Death, a Dial.* 4 Where..the good cease to tremble at Tyranny's nod.

b. *sing.*, referring to God. *rare*$^{-1}$.

1814 CARY *Dante, Par.* VIII. 103 The Good, that guides And blessed makes this realm which thou dost mount.

II. The neuter adj. used *absol.*, passing into *sb.*: That which is good.

2. a. In the widest sense: Whatever is good in itself, or beneficial in effect.

Beowulf (Z.) 955 Alwalda þec gode forȝylde! *c* **1000** *Ags. Gosp.* Matt. xii. 35 God mann soðlice of godum goldhorde, bringð god forð. *c* **1200** *Vices & Virtues* (1888) 27 Na þing ne mai ðe ȝelimpen ne to-cumen neiðer ne euel ne god..bute [etc.]. *a* **1300** *Cursor M.* 27675 Quere þe es for ill or god. **1435** MISYN *Fire of Love* II. ix. 90 Betwyx guyd and betwix euyll. **1590** SHAKS. *Two Gentl.* v. iv. 156 They are reformed, ciuill, full of good, And fit for great employment. **1623** W. CAPPS in E. D. Neill *Virginia Vetusta* (1885) 129, I thinke God hath sent him in mercie for good to us. **1688** MIEGE *Fr. Dict.* s.v. *Bring*, To bring a Child to know Good from Evil. **1748** BUTLER *Serm.* Wks. 1874 II. 304 A person may make amends for the good he has blamably omitted. **1813** SHELLEY *Q. Mab* III. 153 He who leads Invincibly a life of resolute good. **1841** LANE *Arab. Nts.* I. 117 Remote from virtue or good. **1873** W. S. TYLER *Hist. Amherst Coll.* 444 A prayer-meeting on Sunday evening which..has become a power for good in the College.

b. The good portion, side, or aspect (of anything). (Cf. sense 4.)

1670 G. H. *Hist. Cardinals* II. III. 182 Having grown to a capacity of penetrating into the good and bad of an affair. **1858** J. B. NORTON *Topics* 152 The absence of necessity for the measure, its many evils, and its little good. **1884** RUSKIN *Pleasures Eng.* 22 True knowledge of any thing or creature is only of the good of it.

3. The well-being, profit, or benefit (of a person, community, or thing).

971 *Blickl. Hom.* 75 Swylce eac on oþres gode beon swiþe ȝefeonde. *a* **1300** *Cursor M.* 25274 þe ferth bon þou askes fode, bath for lijf and saul gode. **1340** HAMPOLE *Pr. Consc.* 5210, I was hanged upon þe rode, Bytwen twa thefes for yhour gode. **1611** BIBLE *Transl. Pref.* 1 Zeale to promote the common good. **1611** B. JONSON *Catiline* IV. ii, If he had employ'd Those excellent gifts..Vnto the good, not ruin, of the State. **1677** YARRANTON *Eng. Improv.* 100, I shall..joyn in any thing that may be for all our goods. **1773** GOLDSM. *She Stoops to Conquer* IV, Were you not told to drink freely ..for the good of the house? **1773** MRS. CHAPONE *Improv. Mind* (1774) II. 34 Be thankful to the kind hand that inflicts [pain] for our good. **1786** BURNS *Twa Dogs* 148 In..some gentle Master...thrang a parliamentin, For Britain's guid his saul indentin. **1823** KEBLE *Serm.* iv. (1848) 86 Those who invent any project for the good of mankind, commonly entertain high hopes of the success of their invention. **1863** GEO. ELIOT *Romola* II. xxviii, Love does not aim simply at the conscious good of the beloved object.

4. The resulting advantage, benefit, or profit of anything. (Cf. sense 2 b.)

1701 ROWE *Amb. Step-Moth.* IV. i. 1744 What is the good of Greatness but the Power. **1737** BRACKEN *Farriery Impr.* (1756) I. 288 What is the Good of putting down a long Train of Recipes? **1826** E. IRVING *Babylon* II. VIII. 265 No one will believe, in fact, more than he can understand; and that is generally as much as he can see the good of. **1878** JEVONS *Prim. Pol. Econ.* 24 There could be no good in building docks unless there were ships to load in them. **1883** GILMOUR *Mongols* xxvi. 311, I began by asking them what good they supposed the repetition was calculated to effect. **1885** HOWELLS *Silas Lapham* (1891) I. 148 The Colonel laughed all the more. He was going to get all the good out of this.

5. Phrases. (See also AGOOD.)

a. ***to do good***: (*a*) to act rightly, fulfil the moral law; (*b*) to show kindness *to*; (*c*) to employ oneself in philanthropic work; (*d*) to improve the condition of, be beneficial to (const. *to* or *dat.*); so in ***much good may it do you*** (and shortened forms: see esp. DICH), often *ironically*. ***to do any good***: to effect any good result; also, to make progress, 'get on', improve, thrive. †***to speak, say to*** (a person) ***good***: to address kindly. ***to speak, say,*** †***think good of***: to praise, report or think well of.

c **825** *Vesp. Psalter* xiii[i]. 1 Nis se ðe doe god nis oð enne. **971**, *c* **1000** [see EVIL *sb.* 2]. **1154** *O.E. Chron.* an. 1135 Wua sua bare his byrthen gold & sylure durste nan man sei to him naht bute god. *a* **1200** *Moral Ode* 17 Erȝe we beoð to done god. *a* **1225** *Ancr. R.* 116 þe put deð muche god to moni ancre. *a* **1300** *Cursor M.* 11806 Hu had he hert to sced pair blod þat neuer did til him bot godd? *c* **1430** *Syr Gener.* 9219 Lucas him goode spake and honoured, And vnto his delieuraunce he procured. *c* **1489** CAXTON *Sonnes of Aymon* ix. 217, I cowde nother ete nor drynke ony thyng that dyde me goode. **1535** COVERDALE *Acts* x. 38 Iesus..wente aboute & dyd good. *Ibid. 1 Tim.* vi. 18 Charge them whiche are riche..That they do good. **1577** B. GOOGE *Heresbach's Husb.* I. (1586) 18 b, Some of them doo good to the grounde the yeere folowyng. *a* **1631** DONNE *Lett.* (1651) 64 Much good do it you. **1640** SHIRLEY *St. Patrick* v. i. H 3 b, I cannot doe good upon water and sallads. **1658** W. BURTON *Comm. Antoninus* 142 Whose opinion Camden at first thought good of. **1698** FRYER *Acc. E. India & P.* 314 He finding no good to be done with me, began [etc.]. **1783** *Hist. Miss Baltimores* II. 59 Well, much good may do you! *a* **1784** JOHNSON in Mrs. Piozzi *Anecd. of J.* (1786) 208 His learning does no good, and his wit..gives us no pleasure. **1842** LD. HOUGHTON in T. W. Reid *Life* (1891) I. vii. 287 His pretty, dressy wife, too, does him no good, as she does nothing to please or attach the people. **1855** *Jrnl. R. Agric. Soc.* XVI. I. 29 The animal..falls out of condition; he appears 'to do no good', to use a familiar..phrase. **1879** E. GARRETT *House by Wks.* II. 102 Sometimes I doubt if she will be as ready to begin doing good again.

b. ***to the good***: as a balance on the right side; e.g. as net profit, as excess of assets over liabilities, or the like. ***all to the good***, generally advantageous.

1882 *Spectator* 29 Apr. 552 Boasting that he..had so much heavier a balance at the bank to the good, in consequence. **1895** LD. WATSON in *Law Times Rep.* LXXIII. 37/1 They have sold their patent..for..30,000*l.*, and..allowing a reasonable deduction for those items which they have disbursed, there still remains to the good a very considerable sum of money. **1898** *Pall Mall Mag.* Christmas No. 584 He was two wins to the good. *a* **1900** *Mod.* I finished the work in time, with two days to the good. **1943** E. GLASGOW *Let.* 25 June (1958) 323 This is all to the good, I think. **1955** D. MURRAY *Species Revalued* p. xi, It is a kind of revolt against the stark materialism of the present day; this is all to the good. **1962** P. GREGORY *Like Tigress at Bay* v. 49 The fact that you're wealthy and high up in society may attract certain people, and that's all to the good.

c. ***to good***: †(*a*) gratuitously, kindly (*obs.*); (*b*) so as to secure a good result.

832 *Charter of Lufu* in *O.E. Texts* 446 For mine saule and minra frienda and meȝa ðe me to gode ȝefultemedan. *c* **1250** *Gen. & Ex.* 2890 Hemseluen he fetchden ðe chaf, ðe men ðor hem to gode ȝaf, And ðoȝ holden ðe tiȝeles tale. **1839** W. E. FORSTER in T. W. Reid *Life* (1888) I. 112, I have disposed of all my copies [of the book] but one; I hope to good.

d. ***to come to good*** (cf. COME *v.* 48 g): in early use of a dream, †to come true; in later, to yield a good produce or result. †***to turn to good*** (const. *dat.*): to prove to a person's advantage.

a **1300** *Cursor M.* 5070 Al was for i tald a drem þat cummen es now to godd, i tem. **1573** TUSSER *Husb.* xiii. (1878) 29 It is an ill wind turnes none to good. **1623** W. BALCANQUAL *Spittle Serm.* (1634) 58 The seed that came to no good in the thirteenth of Matthew. **1850** *Tait's Mag.* XVII. 708/1 The marriages of English people with foreigners seldom come to good. **1884** *Sat. Rev.* 7 June 731/2 The scheme..could not..have come to good.

†**e.** ***to can*** or ***know one's good***: to know how to behave. ***to can mikel good***: to be highly accomplished. ***to can no good***: to be untrained.

c **1369** CHAUCER *Dethe Blaunche* 390 A whelp that..coude no goode. *c* **1374** —— *Troylus* v. 106 This Diomede, as he that coude his good, Whan this was done, gan fallen forth in speche Of this and that. *c* **1385** —— *L.G.W., Dido* 252 And therewithal so mikel good he can. **1412-20** LYDG. *Troy-bk.* I. v. (1513) C i b, For who was euer yet so mad or wood That ought of reason konne a ryght his good To gyue fayth..To any woman without experyence. **1590** SPENSER *F.Q.* I. x. 7 A gentle Squyre, In word and deede that shew'd great modestee, And knew his good to all of each degree.

f. ***for good*** (***and all***): as a valid conclusion; hence, as a final act, finally.

15.. *Parl. Byrdes* A ij, Than desyred al the Byrdes great and smal to mewe the hauke for good and all. **1603** in *Crt. & Times Jas. I* (1849) I. 25 D'Auval..is gone for good and all. **1687** CONGREVE *Old Bach.* I. i, Ay, you may take him for good-and-all if you will. **1711** SWIFT *Jrnl. to Stella* 4 July, This day I left Chelsea for good, (that's a genteel phrase). *a* **1732** T. BOSTON *Crook in Lot* (1805) 37 He was obliged for good and all to leave his country. **1850** J. H. NEWMAN *Diffic. Anglic.* 324 Throw off, for good and all, the illusions of your intellect. **1882** W. E. FORSTER *Let. To Gladstone* 10 Apr. in T. W. Reid *Life* (1888) II. viii. 421 This morning we released Parnell—not for good, but on parole.

g. colloq. ***to be any, some, no good***: to be of any, some, no use. Also of persons, ***to be no good*** = 'to be a bad lot', to be worthless. Also of things, ***a bit of no good***, quite a lot of harm.

1842 J. H. NEWMAN *Lett.* (1891) II. 396 There is no good telling you all this; but it relieves me to do so. **1848** —— *Loss & Gain* 324 It's no good talking. **1868** DASENT *Jest & Earnest* (1873) II. 359 Those which follow you, what sort of things are they, and what good are they? **1874** MICKLETHWAITE *Mod. Par. Churches* 212 If they [curtains] are heavy enough to be any good at all, they are a great obstruction to the entrance. **1875** DASENT *Vikings* III. 199 Then your feeling will be some good. **1886** H. CONWAY *Living or Dead* ix, I tried to get it from Claudine, but it was no good. **1895** MARIE CORELLI *Sorrows Satan* x. (1897) 111 He is no good, I tell you. **1958** E. A. ROBERTSON *Justice of Heart* iii. 34 They've frittered the money away, and done themselves a bit of no-good, all round. **1958** L. A. G. STRONG *Treason in Egg* x. 183 The pair of them were up to quite a bit of no good.

III. A particular thing that is good.

[Cf. G. *gut* (pl. *güter*), Du. *goed* (pl. *goederen*), a good, an advantage; property, a piece of property, an estate. Sense 9 below seems to be a specially Eng. development. In the Scandinavian langs. this sb. (:—OTeut. **gôdo*^{m}, the neut. of the adj.) does not exist, but the ordinary neut. form of the adj. (ON. *gott*, Sw., Da. *godt*) is used absol. or as sb., and its genitive (ON. *gôðs*, Sw., Da. *gods*) has passed into an indeclinable sb. with the sense 'property'.]

6. a. Something, whether material or immaterial, which it is an advantage to attain or possess; a desirable end or object. Now only in *sing.*, exc. in philosophical (ethical) language.

c **1300** *Cursor M.* 27587 (Cott. Galba) Pride it es, if a man wend his gudes war noght of grace him send. **13..** *E.E. Allit. P.* C. 286 þou art god, & alle owdez ar grayþely þyn owen. *c* **1325** *Deo Gratias* 13 in *E.E.P.* (1862) 129 Whon i seo goode depart so To sum Mon god sent gret solas, And sum Mon ay to lyue in wo, þen sei i deo gracias. *c* **1374** CHAUCER *Boeth.* I. metr. i. 1 (Camb. MS.) Fortune vnfeithful fauorede me wiþ lyhte goodes. **1532** HERVET *Xenophon's Househ.* 3 Than..ye call those thinges goodes, that be profitable, and those thynges that be hurtefull be no goodes? **1583** GOLDING *Calvin on Deut.* clxxi. 1063 To enter directly into the possession of all those goods which ly hidden from vs. **1630** LENNARD tr. *Charron's Wisd.* I. v. § 1 (1670) 16 The goods of the body are Health, Beauty, Chearfulness, Strength, Vigour. **1643** SIR T. BROWNE *Relig. Med.* (1869) 27 Not to be content with the goods of mind. *a* **1677** BARROW *Serm.* xxviii. Wks. (1686) III. 313 Pleased with true goods, and displeased at real evils incident to us. **1709** STEELE *Tatler* No. 49 ¶6 Amanda's Relish of the Goods of Life, is all that makes 'em pleasing to Florio. **1785** T. BALGUY *Disc.* 22 The goods of the mind..are not less empty. **1790** BURKE *Fr. Rev.* 48 The institutions of policy, the goods of fortune, the gifts of providence, are handed down to us. **1825** BENTHAM *Ration. Rew.* 113 Reward in its own nature is a good. **1865** GEO. ELIOT in Cross *Life* (1885) II. 400 Life..is a doubtful good to many. **1875** JOWETT *Plato* (ed. 2) IV. 3 The relation of the goods to the sciences does not appear. **1883** H. SPENCER in *Contemp. Rev.* XLIII. 8 The American, eagerly pursuing a future good, almost ignores what good the passing day offers him.

b. ***highest*** (***first, chief***, etc.) ***good***: = SUMMUM BONUM.

a **1000** *Boeth. Metr.* xx. 92 (MS. B.) Eart þe selfa þæt hehste good. **1426** LYDG. *De Guil. Pilgr.* 5900, I wende trewly..That O gret Good most souereyn Sholde..Make a thyng ffor to be ful. **1587** GOLDING *De Mornay* iii. 24 The same one is called the onely good and the goodnes it selfe. *a* **1613** OVERBURY *A Wife*, etc. (1638) 168 He is the first good to himselfe, in the next file, to his French Taylor. **1668** R. STEELE *Chr. Husb. Calling* v. (1672) 110 Loss of goods is not the loss of the chief Good. **1698** NORRIS *Pract. Disc.* IV. 187 God only is the true Good, End and Centre of all Rational Natures. **1738** WESLEY *Ps.* IV. vii, Thou hast on me bestow'd ..The Taste Divine, the Sovereign Good.

†**c.** *occasionally.* A good quality, virtue, grace.

c **1380** WYCLIF *Serm.* Sel. Wks. II. 18 þis Goost anoyntide Crist wiþ goodis of grace as fulli as ony man myȝte be anoyntid. *c* **1440** *Gesta Rom.* xciii. 423 (Add. MS.) The blessid virgine asked of the deuyll, 'say me, whethere þes iij synnes, lechery, couetese, and gloteny, mow be togedre in oon herte with these goodes, contricion, wepyng, and purpose of amendyng?' **1563** *Homilies* II. *Rogation Week* I. (1859) 474 The goodes and graces wherewith they were indued in soule, came of the goodnesse of God only.

†**d.** A good action. *Obs.*

1606 G. W[ODCOCKE] tr. *Justin's Hist.* 38 a, For which (as if he would be expeditious in this good) the Maisters of such workes were straight procured by proclamation. **1700** DRYDEN *Fables, Pal. & Arcite* III. 384 He seldom does a good with good intent.

7. Property or possessions; now in more restricted sense, movable property.

a. *pl.* (See also CHATTEL 4 c.)

c **950** *Lindisf. Gosp.* Matt. xxv. 14 Monn..ᵹeceiᵹde ðeᵹnas his & ᵹesalde ðæm godo his. *c* **1000** *Ags. Gosp.* Luke xii. 18 Ic secge minre sawle eala sawel þu hæfst mycele god. *a* **1300** *Cursor M.* 4261 (Cott.) And ioseph dueld wit his meigne, And has his godes all in hand. *c* **1300** *Ibid.* 29315 (Cott. Galba) þe nighend case [of cursing] on all þa lies þat gastly gudes selles or byes. **1382** WYCLIF *Luke* xvi. 1 He hadde wastid his goodis. *c* **1400** MAUNDEV. (Roxb.) xv. 68 Him behufez gyffe hir a porcioun of his gudes. *a* **1572** KNOX *Hist. Ref.* Wks. 1846 I. 402 The inquisitioun tane of all your guidis, movable and immovabill. **1588** *Marprel. Epist.* (Arb.) 22 When Waldegraues goods was to be spoiled and defaced. **1641** *Termes de la Ley* 49 The Civilians comprehend these things, and also lands of all natures and tenures under the word Goods, which is by them divided into Moovables and Immoovables. **1685** BAXTER *Paraphr. N.T., Matt.* xxiv. 15–18 Stay not to save your Goods or Clothes. **1789** BRAND *Hist. Newcastle* II. 531 *note*, Some disorderly persons broke and entered into a house..and took away and destroyed several goods. **1817** W. SELWYN *Law Nisi Prius* (ed. 4) II. 728 Before probate and before any seizure, the law adjudges the property of the goods of the testator in the executors. **1840** DICKENS *Old C. Shop* xii, The goods being once removed, this house would be uncomfortable.

Proverbs. **1546** J. HEYWOOD *Prov.* (1867) 38 He that hath plentie of goodes shall haue more. **1862** HISLOP *Prov. Scot.* 15 A man has nae mair gudes than he gets gude o'.

¶ The plural form occurs as a sing.: Property, an amount of property. (Cf. sense 7 d.)

1542 UDALL tr. *Erasm. Apophth.* 242 a, When his goodes was preised to bee sold [etc.]. **1556** *Chron. Gr. Friars* (Camden) 77 Alle the platte, coppys, vestmenttes, wyche drewe unto a gret goodes for the behoffe of the kynges grace.

b. *sing. Obs.* exc. *arch.*

1154 *O.E. Chron.* (Laud MS.) an. 1137 Oc namen al þe god ðæt þar inne was. **1297** R. GLOUC. (Rolls) 10193 Alle þe erchebissopes god, that he vond in þis lond. **1375** BARBOUR *Bruce* XVII. 105 So gredy war thai till the gude, That [etc.]. *c* **1400** MAUNDEV. (Roxb.) xvi. 74 He knew noȝt þe thowsand part of his gude. *c* **1449** PECOCK *Repr.* III. vii. 316 No layman ..schulde haue eny good in propre lord-schip, and that whether thilk good were mouable or vn-mouable. *a* **1533** LD. BERNERS *Gold. Bk. M. Aurel.* (1546) Cc b, The more goodde I hadde, the more couetous I was. **1556** LAUDER *Tractate* 282 ȝe suld not chuse thaim for thair blude, Nor for thare ryches, nor thare gude. **1600** HOLLAND *Livy* v. vi. (1609) 1385 *note*, For feare least if they had gathered good [etc.]. **1650** TRAPP *Comm. Gen.* xlvii. 14 Misers will as easily part with their blood, as with their good. **1873** BROWNING *Red Cott. Nt.-Cap* 259 Guardianship Of earthly good for heavenly purpose.

Prov. **1546** J. HEYWOOD *Prov.* (1867) 35 Evill gotten good neuer proueth well.

†**c.** *a man of good*: a man of property, rank, and standing. Chiefly *Sc. Obs.*

1393 LANGL. *P. Pl.* C. IV. 215 Suche a maister ys mede among men of goode. **1525** *Extracts Aberd. Reg.* (1844) I. 113 The lordis and men of gud in the cuntra bout thaim. **1535** STEWART *Cron. Scot.* I. 532 The king wes tane and men of gud threttie. **1583** *Leg. Bp. St. Androis* 1000 in *Satir. Poems Reform.* xlv, Galloway was a man of gude, Discendit of a noble blude.

†**d.** *sing.* Money. (*a*) *great good*: a great sum of money. *marriage good*: a marriage portion. *Obs.*

c **1340** *Cursor M.* 19054 (Trin.) Petur & Ion þei bi him ȝode And he bad of hem som gode. *c* **1400** *Destr. Troy* 11731 Gedrit was the goode, & gon for to kepe To sure men & certen þat sowme to deliuer. *c* **1430** *Syr Tryam.* 1306 He askyd hym gode for charyte. *c* **1460** FORTESCUE *Abs. & Lim. Mon.* xii. (1885) 137 Thai haue no wepen, nor armour, nor good to bie it with all. **1519** SIR T. BOLEYN in Ellis *Orig. Lett.* Ser. I. I. 155 It hath cost hym [Charles V] a greyt good to atteyn to this Empire. **1523** LD. BERNERS *Froiss.* I. cxlv. 172 The siege..had coste hym..moche good. **1548** HALL *Chron., Edw. V*, 20 b, The thynge..that you would have geven greate good for.

e. *pl.* Live stock. Also *sing.* in *quick good* = a head of cattle. *Obs.* exc. *dial.*

1485 *Ripon Ch. Accts.* 275 My best quyke goode..in the name of my mortuary. **1508** in Pitcairn *Crim. Trials Scot.* I. 58 Of shutting up her 'gudis'..without 'pindande' them in a 'pyndfalde'. **1523** FITZHERB. *Surv.* 23 b, Euery tenaunt.. shall gyue his best quycke good in the name of a herryotte to the lorde. **1562** *Extracts Aberd. Reg.* (1844) I. 341 In casting of fewall or pasturing of guidis. **1641** BEST *Farm. Bks.* (Surtees) 34 The shortest and most leary hey is allwayes accounted the best for any goodes, and especially for sheepe and young foales and calves. **1653** *N. Riding Rec.* V. 139 A man of Gaile presented for his goods eatinge up the grasse in a close. **1796** W. MARSHALL *Yorksh.* (ed. 2) Gloss. (E.D.S.), *Goods*, live stock.

8. *spec.* **a.** (Now only as a *countable* noun, chiefly *pl.*, but occas. in *sing.*) Saleable commodities, merchandise, wares (now chiefly applied to manufactured articles). See also DRY GOODS.

c **1460** FORTESCUE *Abs. & Lim. Mon.* xi. (1714) 81 He takyth nothyng of their Graynys, Wolls, or of any other Goods that growith to them of their Lond. *a* **1533** LD. BERNERS *Huon* xlviii. 160 They..had myche good in theyr shyppe. **1617** MORYSON *Itin.* I. 32 Horsemen..which conduct the Merchants and their goods out of the Frontiers. **1631** BRADFORD *Plymouth Plantation* (1856) 293 They had much adoe to have their goods delivered, for some of them were chainged, as bread & pease. **1634** SIR. T. HERBERT *Trav.* 47 The *Whale* (of which he was Captaine) rich laden with his Masters and his owne goods. **1706** POPE *Let. to Wycherley* 10 Apr., The great Dealers in Wit, like those in Trade, take least pains to set off their Goods. **1726–31** TINDAL tr. *Rapin's Hist. Eng.* XVII. (1743) II. 138 Warlike provisions carried to one of the contending parties, were contraband goods. **1778** *Eng. Gazetteer* (ed. 2) art. *Bewdley*, Iron ware, glass, Manchester goods, &c. are put on board barges here. **1833** HT. MARTINEAU *Loom & Lugger* I. i. 10 As long as French goods were to be had better for the same money. **1842** BISCHOFF *Woollen Manuf.* II. 195, I mean by a domestic manufacturer, a man who makes his goods in his own house or shop. **1879** *Manch. Guard.* 28 Jan., The plaintiff did not complain of the goods having been sized, but of the mode in which they had been sized. **1936** *Q. Jrnl. Econ.* May 436 All that follows will hold true of any storable good, like cotton, wool, rubber, tobacco, wheat, coffee, sugar, oil, copper, or tin; but the theory will be expounded in terms of only one of these, namely cotton, because it is easier to deal with a particular case. **1958** *Times Lit. Suppl.* 15 Aug. p. xxiii/1 As a steady, cheap, business-making consumer good,..the book is out. **1964** GOULD & KOLB *Dict. Social Sci.* 533/1 Complexities arise from many sources. For example, the existence of stocks of goods which might have to be reduced in some amount before additional resources were guided to the favoured good were ignored. **1968** *Times* 2 Jan. 18/5 Knowledge of the legal definition is important, for, under the Sale of Goods Act, 1893, a special set of rules applies to agreements involving goods, which, in legal language, are 'movable and tangible pieces of property'.

¶ (U.S.) *pl.* as *sing.* Kind of dry goods.

1875 KNIGHT *Dict. Mech.*, *Grenadine*, a gauzy dress goods.

b. Phrases. *piece of goods*: humorously, a person [Cf. Du. *goedje*]. *to deliver the goods*: to supply the objects contracted for; hence, to perform the contract undertaken; to do what one has undertaken to do; to supply what has been promised or is expected; hence, to come up to requirements or expectations. *the goods*: what is supplied or provided; what is expected or required (for a purpose expressed or implied); the real thing; the genuine article.

1751 GRAY *Lett.* Wks. 1884 II. 228 That agreeable creature,..will visit you soon, with that dry piece of goods, his wife. **1776** MAD. D'ARBLAY *Early Diary* (1889) II. 145 Miss Fitzgerald, his daughter—as droll a sort of piece of goods as one might wish to know. **1809** MALKIN *Gil Blas* III. iv. ¶6 She had always two or three pieces of damaged goods in the house. **1895** [see PIECE *sb.* 3 d]. **1955** LORD CHANCELLOR in *Hansard, Lords* 8 Dec. 1241, I should ask the noble and learned Earl for his considered construction of the phrase 'a nice piece of goods'.

[**1781** J. BURGOYNE *Ld. Manor* III. iii, *Sir John.* Hussy! how came you by all that money? *Peggy.* Perfectly honestly —I sold my mistress and myself for it—it is not necessary to deliver the goods, for his honour is provided with a mistress.] **1879** *Congress. Rec.* 4 Apr. 236/1 There are men in the North who walk around..saying; 'See me,..I will take you to victory.' They cannot deliver the goods. **1901** MERWIN & WEBSTER *Calumet 'K'* xi. 198, I told him that.. when we paid blackmail it would be to some fellow who'd deliver the goods. **1904** F. LYNDE *Grafters* viii. 120 Of the three justices, one of them was elected on our ticket; another is a personal friend of Judge MacFarlane. The goods will be delivered. **1909** H. G. WELLS *War in Air* iv. §5 As yet he was only in the beginning of the adventure. He had still to deliver the goods and draw the cash. **1911** R. W. CHAMBERS *Common Law* ii. 45 'She certainly is a looker,' nodded Annan. 'She can deliver the cultivated goods, too.' **1919** *Economist* 12 July 44/1 To win a few votes at an election a Cabinet Minister declares it to be the policy of the Government to nationalise the railways. He is duly elected, and those who are in favour of nationalisation ask him and his colleagues to deliver the goods. **1922** DK. DEVONSHIRE in *Hansard, Lords* 4 Dec. 233, I am convinced that the Irish Government intend..to deliver the goods..in the true spirit of the Act. **1936** 'F. BEEDING' *Eight Crooked Trenches* vi. 93 The goods, as they said in England, would this time be delivered. **1946** W. S. MAUGHAM *Then & Now* xxxvi. 207 She knew quite well that the chain was the price he was paying her to arrange things for him, and when she didn't deliver the goods surely the least she could do would have been to return the purchase price. **1968** *Listener* 18 July 88/1 This body has sometimes offered help to coloured workers when they were on strike, but it has never delivered the goods.

1812 *Norfolk* (Va.) *Herald* 29 May 3/4 Federalists call the troops now raising 'a standing army'. They are mistaken in the goods. **1880** A. A. HAYES *New Colorado* (1881) vii. 103 When the mariner heard an expert, who was chipping away at the wall with a little hammer, remark, 'That's good goods,' this purist stopped both ears. **1904** *Cosmopolitan* May 122 'I'll agree to make it 25 [dollars] at the end of 60 days if you are the goods,' said the editor. *a* **1910** 'O. HENRY' *Rolling Stones* (1916) 200 Take it from me—he's got the goods. **1912** C. MATHEWSON *Pitching in Pinch* ii. 33 Now O'Toole is all right if he has the pitching goods. **1915** WODEHOUSE *Psmith Journalist* xv. 109 You are, if I may say so, the goods. You are, beyond a doubt, supremely the stuff. **1918** E. M. ROBERTS *Flying Fighter* 35 Some of the road pickets would want to see our identification papers as dispatch riders, and being unable to produce the goods we were often turned back. **1919** T. K. HOLMES *Man fr. Tall Timber* xvi. 196 Believe me! this Gypsy is all the goods and then some. **1931** *Times Lit. Suppl.* 28 May 426/2 But to the 'General'..President Bonilla and the Honduras were 'the goods' in 1911. **1956** A. WILSON *Anglo-Saxon Att.* II. iii. 369 He *was* the most awful old fraud himself, you know. Oh, not as an historian, you always said he was the goods.

c. (*a*) *the goods*: the stolen articles found in the possession of a thief; unmistakable evidence or proof positive of guilt; chiefly in phr., e.g. *to catch with the goods*.

1900 ADE *More Fables* 94, I insist that he is an American traveling Incog. I suspect that I have Caught him with the Goods. **1911** *N.Y. Even. Post* 15 June (Th.), 'We've got you ..now, and you're going to yield the stolen goods.' The goods in question were the office of Commissioner of Jurors, [etc.]. **1919** *Detective Story Mag.* Nov. 50 Detective Craddock had informed Thubway Tham that, sooner or later, he was going to 'catch him with the goods'. **1923** R. D. PAINE *Comrades of Rolling Ocean* xiv. 245 You have caught me with the goods, Wyman. It was my way of getting a slant on you.

(*b*) *to have* (or *have got*) *the goods on*: to have the advantage of or superiority over; to have knowledge or information giving one a hold over (another).

1913 A. BENNETT *Regent* I. v. 134 You got the goods on her. And she deserved it. **1920** WODEHOUSE *Coming of Bill* II. xiv. 239 I'd been in a ring-seat and had the goods on him same as if I'd taken a snap-shot. **1924** W. M. RAINE *Troubled Waters* xxii. 233 They had the goods on us. We were going to hang—every one of us. **1928** *Observer* 15 July 18/2 'Well, the Old Country sure has the goods on everyone else,' said one of them [*sc.* Canadian teachers]. **1933** D. L. SAYERS *Murder must Advertise* v. 90 We got the goods on that couple you helped us to arrest the other night. **1952** M. MCCARTHY *Groves of Academe* (1953) xiii. 263 He had a sudden inkling that they would have liked to get the goods on Mulcahy. **1967** *Boston Sunday Herald* 7 May (Show Guide) 17/2 The senator stubbed his toe just once, and Overbury has the goods on him. When the time comes to peddle them.. knocking off Burden Day is easy.

d. *ellipt.* = *goods train* (sense e below).

1855 *Punch* XXIX. 163/2 Each player is furnished with a small railway train, such as an 'express', a 'stopping', a 'goods'. **1868** 'JOURNEYMAN ENGINEER' *Great Unwashed* II. 198 After the ' through goods', perhaps, comes the fiery wi-sh-sh of the night mail north. **1939** *Punch* 20 Sept. 310/2, I said couldn't they go by goods. **1959** A. WOOD *Engine-driver & Signalman* iv. 35 (*caption*) Express goods braked by engine and brake-van... Branch goods.

e. The pl. is used *attrib.* in many terms which refer to the transmission of movable property by railway, as *goods agent*, *box*, *department*, *engine*, *guard*, *lift*, *manager*, *set*, *shed*, *station*, *train*, *yard*, etc.

1858 in SIMMONDS *Dict. Trade.* **1889** G. FINDLAY *Eng. Railway* 15 The 'Goods Agent' is responsible for the goods working. **1850** L. V. LOOMIS *Jrnl. Birmingham Emigr. Co.* (1928) 131 As we..made our way to the center [of Sacramento], we would see an old pork barrell, or an old goods box. **1880** 'MARK TWAIN' *Tramp Abr.* xix. 166 A little bit of a goods-box of a barn. **1897** *Daily News* 15 Nov. 2/5 Two railway servants..were killed, one a goods checker and the other a platelayer. **1897** *Daily News* 22 Feb. 3/5 The strike is wholly confined to the railway servants in the goods departments. **1890** *Chambers's Jrnl.* 21 June 385/1 Passenger guards are men of experience, and many of them have had to work as brakesmen and goods-guards many years before they are appointed to a passenger train. **1902** *Daily Chron.* 5 Feb. 3/4 Every shunter, and..every goods guard. **1959** M. TAYLOR *Railways as Career* iii. 47 The goods guard spends almost all his working time alone in his brake-van. **1909** *Westm. Gaz.* 1 Apr. 8/3 He got into the goods lift with some fifteen other men. **1889** G. FINDLAY *Eng. Railway* 13 The executive management of the line is carried on by a General Manager, a Chief Goods Manager [etc.]. **1927** W. E. COLLINSON *Contemp. Eng.* 8 Goods sets i.e. a set of goods trucks. **1878** F. S. WILLIAMS *Midl. Railw.* 170 The use of their London goods station. **1861** J. A. SYMONDS *Let.* 26 Aug. (1967) I. 308 If sent by passenger train they wd reach me by Saturday... If sent by goods train they wd take longer. **1885** *Manch. Exam.* 17 Jan. 5/4 A goods train which was backing on to a siding. **1890** W. J. GORDON *Foundry* 153 An ordinary goods waggon carries eight tons. **1891** *Leisure Hour* 194/1 The goods-yard porter is not the least important of the railway workmen. **1900** *Westm. Gaz.* 20 Jan. 8/3 The dreary goods-yard which does duty for the entraining station of war-bound troops. **1959** M. TAYLOR *Railways as Career* iv. 64 In bigger goods yards there will be several trains being made up.

†**9. a.** *pl.* (See quot.) *Obs.*

1743 *Lond. & Country Brew.* III. (ed. 2) 193 That Ale which is made only from Goods (i.e. after a first Wort is run off the Malt) must..be unpleasant and unwholesome.

b. (See quot.)

1953 *Word for Word* (Whitbread & Co.) 21/1 *Goods*, the name often used by the brewer to describe the crushed malt grains in the mash tun.

D. *Comb.*

1. a. in such collocations as *good-boy*, *-character*, *-class*, *-conduct*, *-faith*, *-length*, *-service*, which admit of being used *attrib.*

1823 SCOTT *Lett.* 16 Jan. in *N. & Q.* 9th Ser. (1898) I. 264/1 Better adapted to..soften the heart of childhood than the *good-boy stories which have been in late years composed for them. **1864** BURTON *Scot. Abr.* II. i. 32 It was all as infallible as the fates in the Minerva Press novels and the good-boy books. **1890** W. G. BARTTELOT *Life Major Barttelot* vii. 145 Stanley..had..taken all the..*good-character men and left..the incorrigible at Yambuya. **1901** *Daily Chron.* 2 Sept. 8/2 *Good-class rudd have also been secured in this river. **1909** *Westm. Gaz.* 13 Jan. 12/2 A club ..which has a number of good-class players. **1925** E. F. NORTON *Fight for Everest, 1924* 39 He must be a good-class man of some intelligence. **1960** *Farmer & Stockbreeder* 29 Mar. 81/1 (*caption*) A typical good-class female of the breed. **1853** STOCQUELER *Mil. Dict.*, *Good-conduct pay.* **1890** J. BYRNE in *19th Cent.* Nov. 836 All good-conduct soldiers now have leave till midnight when off duty. **1893** M. J. WADE in Barrows *Parl. Relig.* (1894) I. 750 It is scandalous to see a temporary residence..treated with all judicial dignity as being a *good-faith residence required by the statute. **1891** W. G. GRACE *Cricket* 231, I played forward to nearly every *good-length ball. **1876** VOYLE *Mil. Dict.* (ed. 3), **Good-service pension.*

b. parasynthetic, as *good-bodied*, *-bottomed*, *-conceited*, *-conditioned*, *-constitutioned*, *-faced*, *-hearted* (hence *good-heartedness*), *-intentioned*, *-limbed*, *-mannered*, *-minded*, *-omened*, *-plucked*, *-sized*.

Some of these combinations have parallel forms with *well*: e.g. *well-conditioned*, *-intentioned*, *-mannered*.

1666 PEPYS *Diary* 31 May, My..sister; who is a pretty *good-bodied woman, and not over thicke. **1816** *Sporting Mag.* XLVII. 296 Nelson and Blucher, two *good-bottomed dogs belonging to Thomas Bradshaw, Esq. **1611** SHAKS. *Cymb.* II. iii. 18 Come on, tune..First, a very excellent *good conceyted thing; after a wonderful sweet aire. **1722** DE FOE *Relig. Courtsh.* I. iii. (1840) 80 One of the best-humoured, *goodest-conditioned, merriest fellows in the world. **1836** J. M. Gully *Magendie's Formul.* 130 Good conditioned pus..appears..to be not more irritating than mucus. **1861** Whyte Melville *Mkt. Harb.* 160 He's a sound, *good-constitutioned beast..and never off his feed. **1575** G. Harvey *Letter-bk.* (Camden) 93 At what..markett your *goodfaced goodliness bowte upp. **1611** Shaks. *Wint. T.* iv. iii. 123 Shall I bring thee on the way? No, good fac'd sir, no sweet sir. **1552** Latimer *8th Serm. Lincolnsh.* (1562) 134b, All they that be *good hearted, that loue godlynes, they wyshe for a parliament. **1843** Bethune *Sc. Fireside Stor.* 52 But you are a good-hearted fellow, my dear Quiddit —I know you are. **1813** *Examiner* 29 Mar. 204/1 The unadulterated *good-heartedness of its principal characters. **1905** H. G. Wells *Kipps* ii. i. 165 That sinister passion for pedagogy to which the *Good-Intentioned are so fatally liable. **1907** *Daily Chron.* 6 Mar. 3/2 It is all very nice and sentimental, and good intentioned. **1597** Shaks. *2 Hen. IV*, iii. ii. 113 A *good limb'd fellow: Yong, strong, and of good friends. **1906** *Macm. Mag.* July 695 The librarian, a functionary whom he desired good-looking, good-natured, *good-mannered, and ready of speech. *a* **1611** Beaum. & Fl. *Philaster* ii. iv, Alas *good minded Prince, you know not these things. **1681** Dryden *Sp. Friar* v. ii, Damme, quoth he. And still continued Labouring me, until a good minded Colonel came by. **1870** Emerson *Soc. & Solit.* v. 95 Every good-minded reformer. **1863** I. Williams *Baptistery* ii. xxxii. (1874) 192 Like hovering near of some *good-omen'd bird Thy soothing voice is heard. **1855** Thackeray *Newcomes* II. 202 You are a *good-plucked fellow! **1837** Mrs. Carlyle *Lett.* I. 87 Hardly gold enough to make a *good-sized thimble. **1863** Buckland *Curios. Nat. Hist.* Ser. ii. (ed. 4) 255 The Regent's Park specimens were not much larger than a good-sized sprat.

c. in quasi-adverbial combination with pr. pples. used adjectivally, as ***good-going*** (suggested by *easy-going*), ***-living***, †***-meaning***, ***-milling***, ***-paying***, †***-seeming***, ***-selling***, ***-speeching*** (nonce-wd.), ***-wearing***. Also good-looking.

In none of these instances is *good* adverbial in origin; in some it represents a predicative complement, in others the neut. adj. or sb. used as object; and in yet other cases the combination arises from phrases in which *good* qualifies a virtual compound of ppl. adj. and sb.

1927 J. Adams *Errors in School* iii. 69 If we find that three metals that we have tested all expand when heated, we jump to the easy-going conclusion that all metals expand when heated—which is a *good-going error. **1903** *Westm. Gaz.* 2 Nov. 9/2 The city had a population of ten thousand, all *good-living people. **1909** *Ibid.* 1 Mar. 1/3 A most respectable and good-living man. **1682** Bunyan *Holy War* 286 Many a *good meaning man is dead, and the Diabolonians of late grow stronger and stronger. **1877** Raymond *Statist. Mines & Mining* 43 The ledge is a very wide one, all *good-milling ore. **1898** *Daily News* 25 May 5/1 She thought she was borrowing 50*l.* to enable her to execute a number of *good-paying orders. **1645** Rutherford *Tryal & Tri. Faith* (1845) 137 There is a way *good-seeming that deceiveth us; but black death is the night lodging of it. **1908** *Daily Chron.* 10 Jan. 3/3 Ordinarily 'Edwin Drood' is one of the least '*good-selling' novels of Charles Dickens. **1845** Carlyle *Cromwell* (1871) IV. 41 The *good-speeching individual. **1879** Mrs. A. E. James *Ind. Househ. Managem.* 16 It made a warm, *good-wearing costume.

†**d.** So rarely with pa. pple. (= well-), as ***good disposed***. *Obs.*

1598 R. Charnock in *Archpr. Contr.* (Camd. Soc.) I. 66 Good disposed catholickes.

e. objective (with *good* sb. or quasi-sb.), as ***good-doing*** vbl. sb.; ***good-foreboding*** ppl. adj.

1526 Tindale *2 Thess.* ii. 17 Oure lorde Jesu Christ.. comforte youre hertes and stablysshe you in all sayinge and *goode doynge. **1571** Golding *Calvin on Ps.* lxxii. 12 Nothinge maketh men more lyke untoo God, than gooddoing. **1883** *Pall Mall G.* 5 Nov. 4/2 The tone of public opinion will be more healthy when the town council engages in good-doing than when good-doing is the monopoly of individuals or of societies. **1874** Pusey *Lent. Serm.* 14 A happy *good-foreboding close of a common-place life.

2. In certain obsolete designations of relationship: **a.** denoting a grand-parent (cf. F. *bon papa*, *bonne maman*); see good-dame, good-sire; **b.** denoting a relation by marriage (cf. F. *beau-frère*, *belle-sœur*, *beau-père*, *belle-mère*): see good-father, good-mother, good-brother, good-sister, good-son, good-daughter. Still used by elderly people in Suffolk (F. Hall).

3. Special comb.: **good-bad** *a.*, of someone or something good but of an inferior class; also in appositive use = good and bad; †**good-deed** *adv.*, in very deed; **good-enough** *a.*, that has a specified quality in a sufficient amount or degree; **good-face**, one that carries a fair or smooth face; **good fairy** = *fairy godmother*; **good-for-little** *a.*, that is of little use, insignificant; **good-for-something**, one who is of some use; cf. good-for-nothing; **good-woolled** *a.*, (of a sheep) having a good fleece; (of persons) having plenty of dash and pluck (*dial.* or *slang*).

1899 *Chambers's Jrnl.* 23 Sept. 674/1 Smugglers in the *good-bad old times pursued what they euphemistically called the 'fair trade'. **1921** E. Sapir *Lang.* 99 It is difficult to get into the frame of mind that recognizes that any particular thing may be both good and bad... Still more difficult to realize that the good-bad or black-white categories may not apply at all. **1933** A. Thirkell *High Rising* ii. 41 'Good bad books?' 'Yes. Not very good books, ..but good of a second-rate kind.' **1940** G. Orwell *Inside Whale* 134 Good bad books like *Raffles*. **1949** M. Mead *Male & Female* xvii. 346 A frequent theme of modern movies is the 'good-bad' girl. **1966** J. Laver *Victoriana* i. 14 Many of the products of the age must, one fears, be consigned to the category of what has been half humorously called 'Good Bad Art'. **1611** Shaks. *Wint. T.* i. ii. 42 Yet (*good-deed) Leontes, I loue thee [etc.]. **1570** R. Bannatyne *Mem.* 33 This was a *guid aneuch obligatioune that the castle shuld be thair friend. **1647** *Stirling Chart. & Corr.* 485 The daik [= dyke] is in good aniogh order. **1856** *Congress. Globe* 53 You will have victims who can answer as 'good enough Morgans' at least until after the election. **1888** *Century Mag.* Jan. 450/1 The hunter [was]..a good-enough shot. **1591** *Troub. Raigne K. John* (1611) 50 Gray-gown'd *good face, coniure ye, Nere trust me for a groat, If [etc.]. **1807** M. Wilmot *Let.* 27 Dec. in *Russ. Jrnls.* (1934) 313, I lit upon her sentiments on religion..being pearls & rubys dropping from the *Good Fairy's lips. **1855** Mrs. Gaskell *Let.* ? 5 June (1966) 866 What will our heroine do in such a dilemma? When lo and behold the good fairy steps in. **1876** L. Troubridge *Jrnl.* 6 May in *Life amongst Troubridges* (1966) xi. 143 If only some good fairy would present us with a ten pound note each. **1920** Galsworthy *In Chancery* ii. ii. 140 Forgiving and forgetting, and becoming the good fairy of her future. **1966** *Guardian* 16 Dec. 4/7 The familiar figure of Mrs Anne Kerr, Labour MP..dressed all in white like the Good Fairy. **1748** Richardson *Clarissa* (1768) IV. 276 The trisyllables, and the rumblers of syllables more than three, are but the *good for little magnates. **1896** *Academy* 18 July 47/2 Jim Conrad..is but an idle and good-for-little hero after all. **1884** H. Spencer in *Contemp. Rev.* Apr. 461 Good-for-nothings who in some way or other live on the *good-for-somethings. **1847–89** Halliwell s.v., A *good-woolled one, i.e., a capital good fellow. *Linc.* **1869** E. Farmer *Scrap Bk.* (ed. 6) 28 Around us are living 'good woolled uns' [*sc.* farmers] by droves. **1877** *N.W. Linc. Gloss.*, *Good-woolled.* (1) Said of Sheep with good fleeces. (2) Plucky, with a good will. 'He's a good-wool'd un; one o' that sort as nivver knaws when he's bet'.

†**good**, *v.* *Obs.* Forms: 1 gódian, 2–3 goden, 6 *Sc.* gude, 8 *Sc.* guid, 5–9 good. [f. the adj.; cf. MDu. *goeden*, MHG. *güten*.]

1. *intr.* To become better, improve; to get better.

c **1000** *Sax. Leechd.* I. 80 Đonne godiað þæra lendena sar. *a* **1154** *O.E. Chron.* an. 959 On his dagum hit godode ȝeorne, & God him ȝeuðe þæt he wunode on sibbe. *c* **1200** Ormin 6014 God mann..godeþþ aȝȝ. *Ibid.* 10866.

2. *trans.* To enrich, endow (a monastery, church, etc.). (Only in OE.)

1052 *Charter of Bp. Wulfwig* in Kemble *Cod. Dipl.* IV. 290 Đæt hiȝ mostan ðæt mynster godian. *a* **1154** *O.E. Chron.* an. 963 Đa bohte se abbot Aldulf landes feola..& godede þa þæt mynstre swiðe mid ealle. *Ibid.* an. 1137.

3. To make good, to improve; chiefly *refl.* Also, to give a good appearance to (a case).

c **1200** Ormin 2117 Hiss haliȝdom Wass godedd himm & ekedd. *Ibid.* 11832 Uss birrþ sone þess te bett & tess te mare uss godenn. *a* **1225** *Ancr. R.* 428 Ȝe muwen muchel þuruh ham beon i-goded, and i-wursed on oðer halue. **1567** Turberv. *Epit.* etc. 49b, Whose filed tongue with sugred talke would good a simple case. **1636** Henshaw *Horæ Succ.* i. Ep. Ded. 2 The end of divine reading is to good our knowledge.

b. To make (land) good by manuring it. Also *absol.* Chiefly *Sc.*

1549 D. Monroe *W. Isles Scotl.* (1774) 46 After that he guidds it weill with sea ware. **1598** A. Napier (*title*), The new order of gooding and manuring of all sorts of field land with common salts. **1628** Bp. Hall *Fast Serm.* 29 God hath taken it from the barren Downes and gooded it. **1636** Henshaw *Horæ Succ.* i. 236 Where He hath dunged and gooded, to expect a crop is but reasonable. **18..** Barry *Orkney* (MS.) 447 (Jam.) They good their land with sea ware.

4. To do good to, to benefit (a person). Also *absol.*

a **1225** *Ancr. R.* 386 Ase..mon oðer wummon þat ȝe beoð of igoded. *c* **1450** *Wisdom Solomon* in *Ratis Raving* 15 To wykyt man he gevis grete pane..& na hap to good hyme with his gwde that he has. **1563** Man *Musculus' Commonpl.* 52 God is readier to loue than to hate..and to good than to avenge. **1620** Shelton *Quix.* ii. 126 The servant sleepes and the Master wakes, thinking how he may maintaine, good him, and doe him kindnesses.

good breeding. Often *hyphened.* [See breeding *vbl. sb.* 3, 4.] A polite education; courteous bearing or correct manners resulting from such an education.

1665 Boyle *Occas. Refl.* iv. xx. (1848) 287 Young Ladies, whose Parents..condemn'd that which at the Court was wont to be called good Breeding [etc.]. **1698** Fryer *Acc. E. India & P.* 93 It being accounted among them no good breeding to let their Legs or Feet be seen whilst sitting. **1711** Addison *Spect.* No. 119 ¶2 An unconstrained Carriage, and a certain Openness of Behaviour, are the Height of Good-breeding. **1768** Sterne *Sent. Journ.* (1778) I. 72 (*In Street*) Had I serv'd seven years apprenticeship to good-breeding, I could not have done as much. **1849** Macaulay *Hist. Eng.* iii. I. 397 Her authority was supreme in all matters of good breeding, from a duel to a minuet. **1863** M. L. Whately *Ragged Life Egypt* xx. 204 Eastern good-breeding always prevented any surprise from being shown at what they did not expect.

good-brother. *Sc.* [See good D 2b.] A brother-in-law.

c **1568** in H. Campbell *Love Lett. Mary, Q. Scots* App. (1825) 25, I pray you tak it in guid part, & not after the interpretation of your fals guid-brother. *c* **1610** Sir J. Melvil *Mem.* (1735) 7 The King of England his Good-brother. *a* **1670** Spalding *Troub. Chas. I* (1829) 11 The marquis made him cold welcome for his good-brother the laird of Frendraught's cause. **1715** Ramsay *Christ's Kirk on Gr.* ii. 119 He was her ain guid-brither.

good-bye (ˌgʊdˈbaɪ). Forms: 6 god be wy you, god b'uy, god boye (yee, 6–7 god buy', buy, godbwye, god bu'y(e, 7 god b'(o)y you, god buy (or buy') you (or ye), -buoy(e, -b'wy, -b'w'y(e, -b'w', -b'y(e, good-buy, -b'wy, 8 good b'w'ye, -b'w'y', bwi't'ye, 8– goodby(e. [A contraction of the phrase *God be with you* (or *ye*); see god *sb.* 8. The substitution of *good-* for *God* may have been due to association with such formulas of leave-taking as *good day*, *good night*, etc.

It has been suggested that the phrase may have originated in *God buy you* = 'God redeem you', and that association with *God be with you* is of later date. This is not supported by the earliest forms, which as a rule show that the expression was known to be a clipped one.]

1. As an exclamation: A form of address at parting; farewell. Also in ***to bid, say good bye*** (***to***).

1573–80 [see 2]. **1588** Shaks. *L.L.L.* iii. i. 151, I thanke your worship, God be wy you. **1591** —— *1 Hen. VI*, iii. ii. 73 God b'uy my Lord. **1600** Heywood *2 Edw. IV*, Wks. (1874) I. 141 Gallants, God buoye all. **1602** Shaks. *Ham.* ii. ii. 575, I so, God buy' ye [1604 Q°. 2 God buy to you]. **1607** Middleton & Dekker *Roaring Girl* D j b, Farewell. God b'y you Mistresse Gallipot. *a* **1652** Brome *City Wit* i. ii. Wks. 1873 I. 289 Heartily Godbuy, good Mr. Crasy. *a* **1659** Cleveland *Lond. Lady* 54 But mum for that, his strength will scarce supply His Back to the Balcona, so God b' wy. [**1668** Pepys *Diary* 6 Aug., To Mr. Wren, to bid him 'God be with you!'] **1694** *Acc. Sev. Late Voy.* ii. 152 He flings up his tail..and so bids us good-b'wy. **1707** E. Ward *Hud. Rediv.* II. ii. 6 So to a Feast should I invite ye You'd stuff your Guts, and cry, Good bwi't'ye. **1719** D'Urfey *Pills* III. 135 Good B' w' 'y! with all my Heart. **1811** W. R. Spencer *Poems* 141 When How-d'y-do has failed to move, Good-bye reveals the passion! **1818** Byron *Juan* i. ccxxi, And so your humble servant, and good-b'ye! **1860** Tyndall *Glac.* i. xviii. 122 We then bade Ulrich good-bye, and went forward. **1874** F. C. Burnand *My time* x. 87 Then he said good-bye to me..and so left me.

b. abbreviated; cf. bye-bye.

a **1643** W. Cartwright *Ordinary* iv. v, B'w'y' Brother. —— *Siege* ii. iv, B'w'y' Lady of the Fan. **1687** Congreve *Old Bach.* v. viii, B'w'y George! **1748** Smollett *Rod. Rand.* iii, B'wye, old gentleman, you're bound for the other world. **1768–74** Tucker *Lt. Nat.* (1852) I. 461 Taking an amorous leave with 'By'e, sweet Socrates', and 'By'e, little Searchy'.

2. *sb.* A saying 'good-bye'; a parting greeting.

1573–80 G. Harvey *Letter-bk.* (Camden) 90 To requite your gallonde of godbwyes, I regive you a pottle of how-dyes. **1634** J. Taylor (Water P.) *Gt. Eater Kent* 16 His courtesie is manifest; for he had rather haue one farewell then 20 Godbwyes. **1853** 'C. Bede' *Verdant Green* iii. (ed. 4) 19 The good-byes and write-oftens that usually accompany a departure. **1879** Edna Lyall *Won by Waiting* xxiv, He hurried through his good-byes in the drawing-room.

attrib. **1854** B. Taylor *Lands of Saracen* xxii. 288 The old Turcoman..made a sullen good-by salutation, and left us. **1870** T. W. Higginson *Army Life* 193 Her father would seize Annie for a good-bye kiss.

Hence **good'byer**, one who says 'good-bye'; **good'bying** *vbl. sb.*, saying 'good-bye'.

1811 W. R. Spencer *Poems* 143 Since time, there's no denying, One half in How-d'y-doing goes, And t'other in Good-byeing! **1839** Col. Hawker *Diary* (1893) II. 165 Baited with bills, packing, and 'good-bye-ers' till twelve at night. **1898** T. Hardy *Wessex Poems* 92 Twas time to be Good-bying Since the assembly-hour was nighing.

†**good-dame.** *Sc.* and *north.* *Obs.* [See good D 2a.] A grandmother.

c **1425** Wyntown *Cron.* iii. iii. 167 Hyr gudame lufyde Eneas; Off Affryk hale scho Lady was. **1483** *Cath. Angl.* 167/2 A Gudame (*A.* Gude Dame), *auia*. **1508** Dunbar *Poems* v. 1 My Gudame wes a gay wif, bot scho wes rycht gend. *a* **1575** *Diurn. Occurr.* (Bannatyne Club) 344 Our souerane lordis gudame of good memorie. **1609** Skene *Reg. Maj.*, *Stat. Robt. I*, 24 The complener sall haue the briefe of recognition be reason of the death of his gudschir, and gudame, as of his father, or his mother.

good-daughter. *Sc.* and *north.* [See good D 2b.] A daughter-in-law.

1513 Douglas *Æneis* ii. xii. 48, I, the nece of mychty Dardanus, And guide dochtir vnto the blissit Venus. **1815** Scott *Antiq.* xl, If ye hae business wi' my gude-daughter, or my son, they'll be in belyve. **1866** *Cornh. Mag.* Mar. 357 More especially if, as on the present occasion, she designed to visit any of her good-daughters. **1893** in *Northumbld. Gloss.*, *Good-Dowtor*, a daughter-in-law.

good day. [See good *a.* 10c.]

1. A phrase used as a salutation at meeting or parting.

†**a.** In the full forms ***have good day***, ***God*** (***give***) ***you good day***. *Obs.*

c **1205** Lay. 12529 Habbeð alle godne dæie. *a* **1300** *K. Horn* 753 Rymenhild, have wel godne day. *c* **1330** R. Brunne *Chron. Wace* (Rolls) 5259 Y parte fro þe, & haue god day. *c* **1374** Chaucer *Troylus* v. 1074 Ȝit preye I god so ȝeve ȝou god day. *a* **1400** *Isumbras* 727 Lady, hafe now gud daye. **1441** *Pol. Poems* (Rolls) II. 207 Farewelle, London, and have good day. **1484** Caxton *Fables of Æsop* v. v, My godsep god geue you good daye. **1535** Lyndesay *Satyre* 4319 Gif ȝe be King, God ȝow gude day. **1814** Scott *Ld. of Isles* iii. xx, Thanks for your proffer—have good-day.

b. *ellipt.* in the accusative.

(So F. *bon jour*, G. *guten tag*, and equivalent phrases in all the Teut. and Rom. langs. The phr. is less common in Eng. than in Fr. or Ger., 'good morning', etc. being more usual.)

c **1460** *Towneley Myst.* xii. 128 A good day, thou, and thou. **1798** Jane Austen *Northang. Abb.* xv, And to marry for money, I think the wickedest thing in existence. Good day.

2. The salutation expressed by this phrase; chiefly in phrases ***to bid, give*** (a person) ***good day***.

c 1250 *Gen. & Ex.* 1430 Eliezer.. haueð hem boden godun dai. *a* 1300 *Cursor M.* 8068 He ferd on-wai, And gaf þam godd and als god dai. 13.. *Gaw. & Gr. Knt.* 668 Gawan.. gef hem alle goud day. 1430–40 LYDG. *Bochas* III. i. (1554) 69a, She rose her vp.. Without good day! or salutation. *c* 1450 *Guy Warw.* (C.) 1271 The ermyte he yaue gode day, And to Pole he toke the way. 1579 [see BID *v.* 9]. 1627 DRAYTON *Moon-calf* 1388 The dawne.. at the windowe biddeth them goodday. 1797 MRS. RADCLIFFE *Italian* i. (1826) 5 The old lady again bade him good-day. 1885 MISS BRADDON *Wyllard's Weird* I. v. 134 They gave him good-day if they met him in the street.

†good-deed. *Obs.* [OE. *góddǽd* (f. *gód* GOOD + *dǽd* DEED); cf. MDu. *goetdaet*, MHG. *guottat*.]

1. A good action; the act of doing good.

(For examples of *good deed* as two words, see GOOD A 5 b.)

a 1000 CYNEWULF *Crist* (Gollancz) 1286 þæt hy on þa clænan seoð Hu hi fore god-dædum glade blissiað. *c* 1175 *Lamb. Hom.* 9 A hu scolde oðermonnes goddede comen him to gode. *a* 1240 *Ureison* in *Cott. Hom.* 187 A swete ihesu.. hwine cusse ich þe sweteliche ine gaste wið swote munegunge of þine god-deden. *a* 1350 *Life Jesus* (ed. Horstmann) 201 Ore louerd loueth bet a sunful man for þinchinde is misdedes, þane a man of lesse sunne þat ȝelpez of his guod hedes [? *read* guoddedes].

2. A deed of kindness; a benefit, favour.

c 1000 *Ags. Ps.* (Th.) lxxvii[i]. 13 Ealra god-dæda hi forȝiten hæfdon. *c* 1205 LAY. 21072 Nu he me ȝilt mede: for mire god dede. *c* 1230 *Hali Meid.* 19 To þonki godd of his grace & of his goddede. *c* 1275 *Sinners Beware* 291 in *O.E. Misc.* 81 þe gode seyþ þenne, Louerd, hwer and hwenne Dude we þe goddede.

good-den: see GOOD-EVEN.

ˌgood-ˈdoer. [f. GOOD *sb.* + DOER.]

1. One who does good; a benefactor. (Now commonly *a doer of good*.)

1340 *Ayenb.* 135 þe poure man.. yelt þonkes mid herte to his guod doere. 1426 AUDELAY *Poems* 17 And pray fore here gooddeers as bred i-blest And depert here almys lest hit be lest. 1478 *Will of Sir R. Verney* in *Verney Papers* (1853) 27 To pray for my soule and the soules.. of all my goode-doers. 1588 A. KING tr. *Canisius' Catech.* 18, I come to the.. to beseike the to receaue in thy protection al my gud doars. 1887 J. HUTCHISON *Lect. Philipp.* xxiv. 269 It is a proper thing to remind good-doers of their good deeds.

2. *dial.* An animal or plant which thrives well.

1877 *N.W. Linc. Gloss.*, *Good doer*, an animal that keeps in healthy and thriving condition. 1882 *Garden* 26 Aug. 184/2 This new plant.. is what is called a 'good doer'.

gooderoon, obs. form of GADROON.

1697 *Lond. Gaz.* No. 3282/4 Lost.. a Gooderoon Candlestick, weighing about 8 Ounces.

†ˈgoodesse. *Obs. rare.* [Alteration of *goods*, as if f. GOOD *a.* + -ESS[2].] = *goods* (see GOOD C. 7 a).

1523 LD. BERNERS *Froiss.* I. ccxxiv. 120 b, They caryed away no goodesse. *Ibid.* cccxxxiii. 211 b, Their lyues and goodesse saued. [Cf. I. ccxxiv. 120 Their lyues and goodes.]

good even. *Obs.* exc. *dial.* Forms: 5 gud devon, 6 god deven, god den, 6–7, 9 (*dial.*) godden, -deen, good-den, 7 gooden, 9 *arch.* god'en. Also 6 in the phrase (see a) god(g)igoden, goddiggonden, 7 goddy-godden. [See GOOD *a.* 10 c.] A form of salutation; = Good evening (but used at any time after noon: see *Rom. & Jul.* II. iv. 116 ff.).

a. In the phrase ***God give you good even*** (variously mutilated: see above in the Forms).

1481 CAXTON *Reynard* (Arb.) 20 Tybert saide, The riche god yeue you good euen reynart. 1538 [see EVEN *sb.* 1]. 1588 SHAKS. *L.L.L.* IV. i. 42 God dig-you-den all. 1591 —— *Two Gent.* II. i. 104 Oh, 'giue ye-good-ev'n. 1592 —— *Rom. & Jul.* I. ii. 57 Godgigoden, I pray sir can you read. *Ibid.* II. iv. 116 God ye gooden faire Gentlewoman. 1651 RANDOLPH, etc. *Hey for Honesty* IV. iii, Goddy-godden, good father: pray which is the house where Plutus lives?

b. *ellipt.*

c 1420 *Sir Amadas* (Weber) 110 'Gud devon, dame', seyd he. 1575 *Gamm. Gurton* IV. ii, God deuen, my friend Diccon; whether walke ye this pace? 1591 SHAKS. *Two Gent.* IV. ii. 85 Madam: good eu'n to your Ladiship. 1607 —— *Cor.* II. i. 103 Godden to your Worships. *Ibid.* IV. vi. 20 Gooden our Neighbours. *a* 1616 BEAUM. & FL. *Wit. at Sev. Weap.* IV. i, Oh good den to you. 1684 *Yorksh. Dial.* 483 (E.D.S. No. 76) Ist God Morn or God Deen, what sesta, Will? 1820 SCOTT *Abbot* xii, The.. foreboding tone in which her niece had spoken her good-even. [1855 ROBINSON *Whitby Gloss.* s.v., 'I give you godden', good day, good luck; or 'God speed you'.]

good-father. *Sc.* [See GOOD D. 2 b.] A father in-law; also, a step-father.

1533 BELLENDEN *Livy* IV. (1822) 347 Ti. Quincius.. create Aulus Posthumius, his gude fader, dictator. 1596 DALRYMPLE tr. *Leslie's Hist. Scot.* IV. 206 Sche commandet her gudfather [L. *socerum*].. to obteine the cheif roume efter her in Britannie. 1666 *Despauter's Gram.* B 5 a (Jam.) *Socer, pater mariti vel uxoris*, the good father. *c* 1680 FATHER HAY *Mem. Families* (MS.) (Jam.), The late Roslin, my goodfather (grandfather to the present Roslin).

good-fellow, *sb.* [See FELLOW *sb.* 3.

In mod. use *good fellow* is apprehended as two words, the sb. being interpreted as FELLOW *sb.* 9.]

1. An agreeable or jovial companion; *esp.* a boon companion, a convivial person, a reveller. Also in phrase ***to play the good-fellow.*** *arch.*

c 1386 [see FELLOW *sb.* 3]. *a* 1568 ASCHAM *Scholem.* I. (Arb.) 62 It was well knowen, that Syr Roger had bene a good feloe in his yougth. 1589 COGAN *Haven Health* ccxviii. (1636) 250 If you.. would faine know where the best ale is.. marke where the greatest noyse is of good fellowes, as they call them. 1606 G. W[OODCOCKE] tr. *Justin's Hist.* 135 a, A kinswoman of the kings.. being wont to play the goodfellowe with a certaine young man of the Greeks, as she imbraced him.. vtterred the matter vnto him. *a* 1617 BAYNE *On Eph.* (1658) 125 They are in company with Swearers, Gamesters, Good-fellows. 1657 RUMSEY *Org. Salutis* Ep. Ded. (1659) 19 They use now to play the Good-fellows in this wakeful and civil drink [coffee]. *a* 1674 CLARENDON *Hist. Reb.* XIV. §138 He associated himself most with the good-fellows, and eat in their company, being well provided for the expence. *a* 1677 BARROW *Serm.* xxx. (1687) I. 410 A glutton, and a good-fellow, a friend to publicans and sinners. 1755 JOHNSON *Dict.*, *Wassail*, a liquour made of apples, sugar, and ale, anciently much used by English goodfellows. 1824 MISS MITFORD *Village* Ser. I. (1863) 223 She was hearty and jovial withal, a thorough good-fellow in petticoats.

fig. *a* 1656 HALES *Gold. Rem.* (1688) 318 For sins are good-fellows, go always in Droves.

b. ***good-fellow-well-met*** (cf. FELLOW *sb.* 3 c and HAIL-FELLOW A. b). In quot. *attrib.*

1807 SIR R. WILSON *Jrnl.* 15 May in *Life* (1862) II. vii. 218 He moved up to Lord H. as if we were all members of the 'good-fellow-well-met' club.

†2. A thief or robber. *Obs.*

1600 HEYWOOD *1 Edw. IV* (1613) E 4 Good fellows be thieues. 1600 HOLLAND *Livy* XXVII. xii. (1609) 636 Those good fellowes.. who used to live by robbing and stealing. 1608 MIDDLETON *Trick to Catch*, etc. B 4 b, *Lu.* Welcome good fellow. *Host.* Hee calles me theefe at first sight. 1633 MASSINGER *Guardian* V. iv, You are fitter far To be a church-man than to have command Over good fellows.

3. *attrib.* and *Comb.*

1542 BECON *Newes out of Heauen* Prol. B vj, It is accounted no synne.. but rather a sporte, a good felowlike dalyaunce. 1608 W. SCLATER *Malachy* (1650) 201 Before this preaching came up amongst us, we had as good fellow-like a parish, and as much good neighbourhood amongst us [etc.]. 1642 FULLER *Holy & Prof. St.* III. v. 162 Those natures which, like the good-fellow planet Mercury, are most swayed by others. 1647 TRAPP *Comm. Ephes.* v. 19 Drunkards sing.. over their cups in their good-fellow-meetings.

Hence **†goodfellow** *v. rare*[−1], *trans.* to call (a person) a good fellow; **†goodfellowhood** = GOOD-FELLOWSHIP; **good-fellowish** *a.* [+ -ISH], somewhat resembling a good-fellow; **†good-fellowly** *a.*, characteristic of a good-fellow.

1580 HARVEY in Grosart *Spenser's Wks.* I. 438 Familiar and good fellowlye writinge. 1628 FELTHAM *Resolves* I. lxxxiv. 243 Let me rather be disliked for not being a Beast, then be good-fellowed with a hug, for being one. *a* 1706 E. BAYNARD *Health* (1740) 18 Makes the spirits brisk and good; After a bad Good-fellow-Hood Had left their springy parts uncurl'd. 1880 *Athenæum* 14 Aug. 210/2, I doubt if Jaques were ever capable of developing into anything so wholesome and good-fellowish.

good-ˈfellowship. [See prec. and FELLOWSHIP 5.] The spirit or habits of a 'good-fellow'; conviviality. Now also, the spirit of true friendship or companionship.

c 1380 WYCLIF *Wks.* (1880) 174 For þei colouren pride wiþ honeste.. dronkenesse bi good felaweschipe [etc.]. 1463, 1604 [see FELLOWSHIP 5]. *a* 1586 SIDNEY *Arcadia* I. (1590) 39 b, Actiuitie & good felowship being nothing in the price it was then held in. 1612 W. PARKES *Curtaine-Dr.* (1876) 23 The Drunkard likewise hath a Curtaine for his vgly, swinish, and beastly sinne, and that he tearmes good-fellowship. 1668–9 PEPYS *Diary* 8 Mar., His age and good fellowship have made him almost fit for nothing. 1762 *Learned Diss. Dumpling* (ed. 4) 22 Why, do they inveigh against Dumpling-Eating, which is the Life and Soul of Good-fellowship? 1780 F. MARION in *Harper's Mag.* (1883) Sept. 548/1 By the laws of good-fellowship no man leaves this room till all the liquor is drank. 1828 MISS MITFORD *Village* Ser. III. (1863) 41 A hale, jovial visage, a merry eye, a pleasant smile, and a general air of good-fellowship. 1863 FR. A. KEMBLE *Resid. in Georgia* 89 Their usual habits of Milesian good fellowship.

ˈgood-for-ˌnothing, *a.* and *sb.* [The phrase *good for nothing* used *attrib.* or as *sb.*, and consequently hyphened: see GOOD *a.* 14.]

A. *adj.* Of no service or use; worthless.

1711 SWIFT *Jrnl. to Stella* 6 Nov., We reckon him here a good-for-nothing fellow. 1727 OLDMIXON *Clarendon & Whitlock* v. 253 It was a sort of a good-for-nothing Place, not worth Description. 1785 WOLCOT (P. Pindar) *Ode to P. Pindar* Wks. 1812 I. 79 Young, good-for-nothing dogs. 1818 BYRON *Juan* I. xxv, A little curly-headed, good-for-nothing, And mischief-making monkey. 1841 LYTTON *Nt. & Morn.* I. i, That good-for-nothing brother of yours. 1887 SMILES *Life & Labour* 212 Lord Chief-Justice Mansfield whose.. father was a good-for-nothing man of fashion.

absol. 1873 H. SPENCER *Study Sociol.* xiv. (1877) 344 Fostering the good-for-nothing at the expense of the good is an extreme cruelty.

B. *sb.* One who is good for nothing; a worthless person (†or thing).

1751 R. PALTOCK *P. Wilkins* I. xii, After.. clearing my House of Good-for-nothings. 1847 MARRYAT *Childr. N. Forest* xii, You young good-for-nothing. 1883 BLACK *Shandon Bells* xxix, As you are a good-for-nothing, it does not matter where you are. 1887 A. BIRRELL *Obiter Dicta* Ser. II. 183 His brother.. was a good-for-nothing, with a dilapidated reputation.

Hence **good-for-nothingness**, the quality or condition of being good for nothing.

1741 RICHARDSON *Pamela* II. 55 They have not kept such elaborate Records of their good-for-nothingness. 1807 SOUTHEY in *Life* (1850) III. 68 You may stay and be smoke-dried in London for your good-for-nothingness. 1871 *Daily News* 14 Feb., The chief beauty of the custom should consist in its dainty, complimentary good-for-nothingness: a Valentine should be [etc.]. 1896 *Allbutt's Syst. Med.* I. 690 The dyspepsia, the neuralgia, the general 'good-for-nothingness' which are expressive of the severity of the illness the patient has passed through.

ˈgood-for-ˌnought, *a.* and *sb.* [The phrase *good for nought* used *attrib.* or as *sb.*] = GOOD-FOR-NOTHING *a.* and *sb.*

1804 EUGENIA DE ACTON *A Tale without a Title* I. 265 An ungrateful good-for-naught! to serve your Honour after this fashion. 1821 CLARE *Vill. Minstr.* I. 159 A good-for-nought booby, he nettled me sore. 1834 LYTTON *Pompeii* IV. ii, My master, Diomed, is not one of those expensive good-for-noughts. 1852 DICKENS *Bleak Ho.* xxxiv, I'm a harum-scarum sort of a good-for-nought.

Good Friday. [See GOOD *a.* 8 c.] The Friday before Easter-day, observed as the anniversary of the death of Christ.

c 1290 *S. Eng. Leg.* I. 403/27 A-morewe, ase on þe guode friday: ase he deide on þe rode. *a* 1300 *Cursor M.* 17288 + 81 Vse we ay after heghe ful of þe moyne to take þe next friday, And þat hald we our gode friday. *c* 1400 [see FRIDAY 1]. *c* 1450 *Mirour Saluacion* 2931 Thus myght doelfulle marye say on the gude fridaye. 1532 [see FRIDAY 1]. 1579 SPENSER *Sheph. Cal.* Feb. 30 So semest thou like good fryday to frowne. 1635 QUARLES *Embl.* V. vii, Chear up, my soul.. and bear One bad good-friday, full mouth'd easter's near. 1791 BOSWELL *Johnson* 18 Apr. an. 1783, On April 18, (being Good-Friday) I found him.. drinking tea without milk, and eating a cross-bun to prevent faintness. 1868 [see FRIDAY 1].

attrib. 1615 MARKHAM *Eng. Housew.* II. vii. (1649) 242 Of these Greets are made the good Friday pudding. 1753 *Trial W. Smith* in J. Blackburne *Reg. Ingleby* (1889) p. xxviii, Mixing Arsenick in a Good-Friday Cake.

†ˈgoodful, *a. Obs.* In 3 godful. [f. GOOD *sb.* + -FUL.] Goodly. Hence **†ˈgoodfulhead** [+ -HEAD], goodness; **†ˈgoodfully** *adv.*, joyfully; kindly.

c 1205 LAY. 17038 Bi us þe gon græten, þat is a god-ful king, Aurilian ihaten. *Ibid.* 19710 While heo weoren a þissere worlde-richen god-fulle þeines, mid goden afeolled. *c* 1250 *Gen. & Ex.* 56 Ðhre persones and on reed, On miȝt and on godfulhed. *c* 1275 in *O.E. Misc.* 90 þe martyrs þe vnderstonde, Godfullyche, in heore honde.

goodg, obs. form of GOUGE *sb.*[1]

goodhap (ˈgʊdhæp). *arch.* [See GOOD *a.* and HAP *sb.* 1; = *good hap* as two words.] Good fortune.

1557 N. T. (Geneva) *The Epistle*, By him.. sadnes [is] made glad, mishap goodhap. 1575 G. HARVEY *Common-pl. Bk.* (1884) 148, I did think it mie great goodhap that [etc.]. 1603 KNOLLES *Hist. Turkes* 1033 Except such as by their goodhap recovered the new towne. 1870 W. MORRIS *Earthly Par.* III. IV. 75 What goodhap or increase From that ill night shall ever come? *Ibid.* II. III. 488.

†ˈgoodhead. *Obs.* Forms: 3–5 godhede, (3 godede), 4 guod(e)hed(d)e. [f. GOOD *a.* + -HEAD.] = GOODNESS.

a 1250 *Owl & Night.* 582 Thu havest i-mist al of fairhede, An lutel is al thi godede. *c* 1275 LAY. 21072 Nou he me ȝelt mede for mine god hede [*c* 1205 god dede]. *c* 1330 *Amis & Amil.* 2493 For ther trewth and here guodehede The blysse of heuen thei had to mede. 1390 GOWER *Conf.* II. 133 So as he might of his godhede. *c* 1440 *Bone Flor.* 1682 Brynge me to thy bygly blys, For thy grete godhede.

Good Henry. Also **Good King Henry (Harry).** [Equivalent to G. *der gute Heinrich*, F. *bon-Henri* (1545 in Hatz.-Darm.), med. or mod.L. *Bonus Henricus*.

Cf. further the popular German names of various plants: *der böse Heinrich* (= 'bad Henry'); *der stolze H.* ('proud H.'); *der grosse H.* ('great H.'); *der wilde H.* ('wild H.'). The allusion is unexplained, and it is uncertain whether the Eng. and Fr. forms are translated from the Ger.]

The plant Mercury Goosefoot (*Chenopodium Bonus Henricus*), sometimes used as a pot-herb.

1578 LYTE *Dodoens* v. xi. 561 This herbe is called.. in English, Good Henry, and Algood. 1597 GERARDE *Herbal* II. xlviii. (1633) 329 In Cambridgeshire it is callen Good King Harry. 1861 MISS PRATT *Flower. Pl.* IV. 276 Mercury Goosefoot, or Good King Henry. 1894 *Times* 3 Sept. 10/4 The old-fashioned pot-herb, Good King Henry.

good humour. The condition of being in a cheerful and amiable mood; also, the disposition or habit of amiable cheerfulness.

1616 in *Crt. & Times Jas. I* (1848) I. 429, I found him in so good humour and so well disposed that [etc.]. 1676 [see HUMOUR *sb.* 5]. 1711 SHAFTESB. *Charac.*, *Enthusiasm* (1737) I. 33 We must not only be in ordinary good Humour, but in the best of Humours. 1718 LADY M. W. MONTAGU *Let. to C'tess Mar* 10 Mar., Her good humour made her willing to divert me. 1780 J. HARRIS *Philol. Enquiries* Wks. (1841) 538 As man is by nature a social animal, good humour seems an ingredient highly necessary to his character. 1834 *W. Ind. Sketch Bk.* II. 141 At the president's we found every thing to put one in good humour. 1849 MACAULAY *Hist. Eng.* v. I. 531 Even the stern and pensive William relaxed into good humour when his brilliant guest appeared.

good-humoured, *a.* (The stress is variable.) [f. prec. + -ED[2].] **a.** Of persons: Possessed of or characterized by good-humour; having a cheerful, amiable, and unruffled disposition. **b.** Of a look or utterance: Indicative of good humour.

1662 PEPYS *Diary* 15 June, Nan Pepys's 2nd husband.. is a very good-humoured man, an old cavalier. 1712 STEELE *Spect.* No. 474 ¶6 The justness of which we would controvert with good-humoured warmth. 1771 *Junius Lett.* lii. 266 Nature intended him only for a good-humoured fool. 1825 J. NEAL *Bro. Jonathan* III. 145 He was permitted, with.. a good-humoured laugh, to pass on. 1867 TROLLOPE

Chron. Barset II. xlv. 8 They all pronounced her.. to be very good-humoured.

Comb. **1843** MARRYAT *M. Violet* xxxvii, The slaves so good-humoured-looking, so clean. **1864** MOTLEY *Corr.* 23 Aug. II. 173 The King of Prussia.. a tall, sturdy, good-humoured-faced elderly man.

Hence **good'humouredly** *adv.*

1786 MRS. PIOZZI *Anecd. of Johnson* 205 The truth is, Mr. Johnson was often good-humouredly willing to join in childish amusements. *a* **1801** WAKEFIELD *Mem.* (1804) I. 29 To this Johnson, good-humouredly and sarcastically, replied, 'That [etc.]'. **1883** GILMOUR *Mongols* xxxi. 363 The Peking carters.. good-humouredly revile them.

goodiness: see under GOODY *a.*

gooding ('gʊdɪŋ), *vbl. sb.* [f. GOOD *v.* (but in sense 2 app. f. GOOD *sb.*) + -ING[1].]

†**1.** The action of doing good to, or of improving.

1567 TURBERV. *Ovid's Ep.* 137b, Least I be thought for gooding of my cause False matter to alledge.

b. The action of manuring (land); *concr.* manure. (Cf. GOOD *v.* 4.)

1602 *Extracts Aberd. Reg.* (1848) II. 227 Sic persones within the burgh, as sellis fulzie or guding to extranearis, for guiding and manuring of thair landis. **1701** J. BRAND *Descr. Orkney*, etc. (1703) 19 The skirts of the Isles.. do more abound with Corns, then Places at a greater distance from the Sea, where they have not such gooding at hand. **1834** *Brit. Husb.* I. 414 That he may thus preserve the seep or gooding, or his stable-manure.

2. The practice of begging; now *dial.* the custom of collecting alms on St. Thomas's day (see quot. 1818, hence locally called *Gooding Day*). Also, *to go* (†*send*) *a-gooding*.

1560 in *Stow's Surv.* (ed. Strype 1754) II. VI. iv. 638/1 That old Woman.. that might work, and went a Gooding should be Hatchilers of the Flax. **1649** BLITHE *Eng. Improv. Impr.* (1653) 93 Some cruell Lord.. could.. dispeople a whole parish, and send many soules a gooding. **1818** TODD s.v., To go a gooding, is a custom observed in several parts of England on St. Thomas's day by women only, who ask alms, and in return for them wish all that is good.. to their benefactors [etc.]. **1851** S. JUDD *Margaret* x. (1871) 50 Thanks-giving day.. has no gooding, candles, clog, carol, box, or hobby-horse. **1886** in *S.W. Linc. Gloss.* **1889** in HURST *Horsham Gloss.*

goodish ('gʊdɪʃ), *a.* [f. GOOD *a.* + -ISH.] Somewhat good: **a.** with respect to quality.

1756 MRS. DELANY *Let.* in *Life & Corr.* 451 She seems a goodish sort of woman, rather vulgar however. **1833** M. SCOTT *Tom Cringle* xix. (1859) 530 They dashed past us on goodish nags. **1880** MRS. WALFORD *Troublesome Dau.* III. xxxii. 160 Carnochan, they tell me, is a goodish estate.

b. with respect to quantity, extent, etc.

1839 C. CLARK *J. Noakes & Mary Styles* 63 (E.D.S. No. 76) From the Heath, He lived a goodish way. **1865** DICKENS *Mut. Fr.* II. xii, Ay, a goodish bit ago. **1879** F. W. ROBINSON *Coward Consc.* II. xx, We are compelled to ask a goodish many questions. **1894** MRS. H. WARD *Marcella* I. 265, I have lent them a goodish sum of money.

c. *Comb.*

1856 WHYTE MELVILLE *Kate Cov.* x, A goodish-looking man whose name I never made out.

Hence **'goodishness**, the quality of being goodish.

1891 S. J. DUNCAN *Amer. Girl Lond.* 131 The deadly monotony of goodishness and cheapishness in everything.

†**'goodity.** *Obs.*[−1] [f. GOOD *a.* + -ITY.] Goodness.

a **1641** BP. R. MONTAGU *Acts & Mon.* (1642) i. 54 Whence had they that good in them.. but from gooddity of nature?

†**'goodlaik.** *Obs.* Forms: 3 godlec, godleic(h, *Orm.* godleȝȝc, 5 godlaik. [a. ON. *góðleik-r*: see GOOD *a.* and -LAIK.] Goodness, kindness.

c **1200** ORMIN, Ded. 267 Þatt sefennfald godleȝȝc þatt Crist Uss dide þurrh hiss come. *a* **1225** *Ancr. R.* 136 His muchele godleic touward hire, ant hire defautes touward him. *a* **1300** *Siriz* 227 Of muchel godlec miȝt thou ȝelpe, If hit be so that thou me helpe. *a* **1400–50** *Wars Alexander* 4688, I se na godlaik in gold, bot grefe to þe saule.

†**'goodless,** *a. Obs.* [f. GOOD *sb.* + LESS.]

1. Devoid of good; comfortless; worthless.

c **900** tr. *Bæda's Hist.* III. i. (1890) 154 Þis ungesælige ȝear & þat godlease. *a* **1200** *Moral Ode* 344 Hi muwen lihtliche gon.. ðurh ane godliese wude, in-to ane bare felde. *a* **1225** *Leg. Kath.* 846 Wlonke wordes, þat þuncheð se greate & beð godlese þah & bare of euch blisse. **1562** TURNER *Herbal* II. 70 Like a fals lying goodlesse man, he pretendeth [etc.].

2. Without goods or property; destitute.

c **1230** *Hali Meid.* 31, & tu.. schalt greui [*printed* greni] godles inwið waste wahes. *c* **1300** *Prov. Hending* xiv, Gredy is þe godles, quoþ Hendyng. **1581** MULCASTER *Positions* 262 Both reft of goodnesse, and left goodlesse.

†**'goodlihead.** *Obs.* [f. GOODLY *a.* + -HEAD.]

1. Goodly appearance; comeliness, beauty.

c **1374** CHAUCER *Troylus* III. 1681 (1730) Þe goodliheed or beaute which þat kynd In eny other lady had y-sette. **1423** JAS. I. *Kingis Q.* xlix, To suich delyte It was to see hir ȝouth In gudlihede. **1523** SKELTON *Garl. Laurel* 907 With margerain ientyll, The flowre of goodlyhede. **1590** SPENSER *F.Q.* III. ii. 38 Pleased with that seeming goodly-hed, Unwares the hidden hooke with baite I swallowed. **1746** W. THOMPSON *Hymn to May* [Imitation of Spenser] xvii. 6 So far in virtue and in goodlihead, Above all other nymphs Ianthe bears the meed. **1867** MORRIS *Jason* IX. 4 O love, turn round, and note the goodlihead My father's palace shows beneath the stars.

2. Goodly character; excellence, goodness.

1390 GOWER *Conf.* II. 22 In her is no violence But goodly hede and innocence Withouten spot of any blame. *c* **1440** *Generydes* 6340 In grete pleasure and in all goodlyhede. **1503** HAWES *Examp. Virt.* v. 5 Dame prudence.. Imposyble it is to shewe her goodelyhed.

3. The personality of one who is goodly.

1579 SPENSER *Sheph. Cal.* Feb. 184 Craving your goodlyhead to asswage The rankorous rigour of his might. **1590** —— *F.Q.* II. iii. 33 Mote thy goodlyhed forgive it mee.

†**'goodlike,** *a. Obs.* exc. *dial.* [f. GOOD *a.* + -LIKE.] **a.** Goodly; good-looking. **b.** Resembling what is good; having the air of being good.

1572 *Satir. Poems Reform.* xxxiii. 106 Ane Douchter.. Lusty, gude lyke, to all men fauourabill. **1592** WYRLEY *Armorie, Chandos* 107 Goodlike daies passe foorth in pleasant calme. **1597** DANIEL *Civ. Wars* v. xxii, The onely fashion in request Was to be good, or good-like, as the rest. **1669** PENN *No Cross* Wks. 1782 II. 158 A good-like young man came to Christ. **1705** HICKERINGILL *Priest-cr.* I. (1721) 59 [Jesse's sons] were all jolly good-like Men. **1741** RICHARDSON *Pamela* (1883) I. 110 The farmer, a goodlike sort of man. **1855** ROBINSON *Whitby Gloss., Goodlike,* handsome.

good-liking. ? *Obs.* [Cf. *to like one good*, GOOD *a.* 4b. See also LIKING *vbl. sb.*]

1. Friendly or kindly feeling towards a person.

1586 T. B. *La Primaud. Fr. Acad.* I. (1589) 482 Nature.. hath given hir great meanes to win the good liking and love of hir husband. **1641** HINDE *J. Bruen* ii. 6 As the Oake and the Ivy grow up together, and with love and good likeing embrace one another. **1727** SWIFT *To Very Young Lady*, Yours was a match of prudence and common good-liking. **1797–1803** J. FOSTER in *Life & Corr.* (1846) I. 194 Content himself with that mere goodliking. **1818** J. C. HOBHOUSE *Journey* II. 620 This foreign interference.. has not contributed to increase the good liking between the Mussulmans and the Franks at Smyrna.

2. Approval, good-will; satisfaction.

1583 T. STOCKER *Civ. Warres Lowe C.* I. 13 Most humblie beseeching your highnesse to haue good liking of this our bounden dutie. **1636** in Picton *L'pool Munic. Rec.* (1883) I. 211 The full assente, consente, and goodlikinge of the Aldermen. **1681** *Lond. Gaz.* No. 1676/1 The said Commissioners.. Declared their Good-liking and Consent there-unto. **1740** J. CLARKE *Educ. Youth* (ed. 3) 207 They are.. disposed of in the World, much more to their Credit, Ease, and Good-liking. **1808** SYD. SMITH *Wks.* (1859) I. 125/1 Curacies are.. granted.. for the life or incumbency or good-liking of the rector.

†**3.** Personal inclination or fancy. *Obs. rare.*

1690 LOCKE *Hum. Und.* II. xxxi. (1695) 208 The Good-liking and Will of him, that first made this Combination.

†**4.** Good condition, embonpoint. *Obs.*

1611 BIBLE *Job* xxxix. 4 Their yong ones are in good liking. **1656** P. HEYLIN *Journeys* v. ii. 226 This provision together with a liberall allowance of ease, and a little of study keepeth them exceeding plump and in a good liking.

goodliness ('gʊdlɪnɪs). [f. GOODLY *a.* + -NESS.] The quality or condition of being goodly.

1. Goodly appearance, comeliness, beauty, grace.

c **1430** *Syr Gener.* (Roxb.) 828 Of goodelynes he bereth the price. **1509** HAWES *Past. Pleas.* III. iii, For the very perfect bryghtnes.. I coulde nothyng beholde the goodlines Of that palaice where as Doctrine did wonne. *a* **1586** SIDNEY *Arcadia* I. (1633) 43 A voyce no lesse beautifull to his eares, than her goodlinesse was full of harmony to his eyes. *a* **1677** BARROW *Serm.* iv. Wks. 1687 I. 49 The goodliness to the sight, the pleasantness to the taste, which is ever perceptible in those fruits which genuine Piety beareth. **1870** MORRIS *Earthly Par.* III. IV. 122 Nor was there such another in the land For strength or goodliness.

†**2.** Goodness; kindness. *Obs.*

1434 MISYN *Mending Life* 112 *Bonitatem & disciplinam & scienciam doce me*, þat is to say: 'guydlynes, disciplyn, and conynge tech me'. *c* **1450** *Mirour Saluacion* 307 God of his myght and his grete gudlynesse. **1555** W. WATREMAN *Fardle Facions* II. iv. 136 Ordres of discipline, and ciuile gouernaunce, full of all goodlines and equitie.

3. Excellence, value. *rare.*

1832 HT. MARTINEAU *Homes Abroad* vii. 106 The bride was quite of her brother's opinion respecting the goodliness of exchange.

†**'goodlisome,** *a. Obs.* [f. GOODLY *a.* + -SOME.] = GOODLY *a.*

a **1603** Q. ELIZ. in Nichols' *Progr. Q. Eliz.* I. 10, I plucke up the goodlisome herbs of sentences by pruning, eate them by reading, chawe them by musing. **1719** HEARNE *Guil. Neubrigensis Hist.* II. 789 Many were imploy'd to destroy this goodlisome nunnery.

,good-'looker. Chiefly *U.S.* [Cf. GOOD-LOOKING *a.*, GOOD LOOKS.] One who has good looks.

1894 *Harper's Mag.* Mar. 498 She's a good-looker.. although they say she's gone off a little lately. **1902** O. WISTER *Virginian* ii. 26 'She's a good-looker.' Hm! Yes, the kind of good looks I'd sooner see in another man's wife than mine. **1920** *Blackw. Mag.* June 786/2 He was a 'goodlooker', tall, blond, gentle-spoken. **1928** *Daily Tel.* 29 May 14/2 Felstead [a horse].. is quite a good looker and is well bred. **1929** W. P. RIDGE *Affect. Regards* 121 There's a lady coming along.. A good looker, if ever there was one. **1966** 'J. HACKSTON' *Father clears Out* 189 She [*sc.* a cow] was a.. good-looker, too.

good-looking, *a.* (Stress variable.) Having a good appearance; *esp.* with reference to beauty of countenance. (Cf. the older WELL-LOOKING *a.*)

1780 DAVIES *Garrick* (1781) II. 92 Holland, to speak in a familiar phrase, was what we call a good-looking man. **1806** A. HUNTER *Culina* 52 If well dressed, this is a good looking dish. **1847** JAMES *Convict* ii, He was tall, strong, and good-looking.

Hence **good'lookingness.**

1829 J. WILSON in *Blackw. Mag.* XXV. 384 Wizened jades both, without the most distant approach to good-lookingness. **1891** *Spectator* 4 July, Dignity and good-lookingness.

good looks, *pl.* [Cf. prec.; and see LOOK *sb.*] Personal beauty, handsomeness.

1800 MAR. EDGEWORTH *Castle Rackrent* 154 Poor Judy fell off greatly in her good looks after her being married a year or two. **1871** NAPHEYS *Prev. & Cure Dis.* I. iv. 120 Consider health as well as good looks. **1885** F. ANSTEY *Tinted Venus* 6 She had some claims to good looks, in spite of a slightly pasty complexion.

†**goodlordship.** *Obs. rare.* [f. *good lord*: see GOOD *a.* 2b.] The position of 'good lord' or patron; patronage.

1438–9 *Let.* in *Priory Coldingham* (Surtees) 109, I recomaund me to ȝowr gude faderhod & gude Lordship schawit to me at all tymys. **1463** *Paston Lett.* No. 472. II. 132 But if ye have my Lord of Suffolks godelorchyp.. ye kan never leven in pese with owt ye have his godelordschep. [*cf. infra.* I am afferd.. but if he wyl don for ȝou and be your godelord.]

good luck. Good fortune; success. Now freq. as a salutation or wish. †*to drink a good luck*: to drink success to one. Also *attrib.*, as in ***good luck shilling***, a shilling given by the seller to ensure good luck with the thing sold.

1481 CAXTON *Reynard* (Arb.) 14 Tho thought reynart this is good luck. *a* **1529** SKELTON *El. Rummyng* 567 Wyth that she begynnes The pot to her plucke, And dranke a good lucke. **1535** COVERDALE *1 Kings* i. 47 The kynges seruauntes are gone in to wysh good lucke vnto oure lorde kynge Dauid. **1546** J. HEYWOOD *Prov.* (1867) 17 Nowe for good lucke, caste an olde shoe after mee. **1598** SHAKS. *Merry W.* III. v. 84 As good lucke would haue it, comes in one Mist. Page. **1651** HOBBES *Leviath.* I. x. 41 The secret working of God, which men call Good Luck. **1684** E. HALLEY *Solid Probl.* in *Misc. Cur.* (1708) II. 96 'Tis my good Luck to hit upon a certain Geometrick Effection of the central Rule. **1805** E. CAVANAGH *Let.* 4 Oct. in M. Wilmot *Russ. Jrnls.* (1934) II. 187 'Well to be sure,' sais I. 'Russia! & good luck to you, you are a comical place!' **1818** COBBETT *Pol. Reg.* XXXIII. 10 There is the 'good-luck shilling'. **1829** G. GRIFFIN *Collegians* II. xvii. 33 Good *look* to them both, wherever they are. **1858** R. A. VAUGHAN *Ess. & Rev.* I. 13 The indolent.. gaze in amazement on results which they attribute to the good luck of a rival. ? **1861** MRS. GASKELL *Let.* 28 Feb. (1966) 643 Is he really 'after' Sophy? If so, good luck for her. **1898** J. D. BRAYSHAW *Slum Silhouettes* 1 'E ain't come in fer a bloomin' forchin 'ave 'e? Jolly good luck to 'im if 'e 'as! **1942** M. MCCARTHY *Company She Keeps* (1943) v. 130 He was a mascot, a good-luck piece. **1958** 'J. BELL' *Seeing Eye* x. 115 'He has kept the Bert Lewis drawing..' 'Good luck to him!' **1958** *Photoplay* Oct. 54/2 We have received some good-luck telegrams and letters. **1963** P. WILLMOTT *Evolution of Community* ix. 99 People seem to be glad if someone else gets something. They don't grudge it. They say, 'Good luck to them.'

Proverb. **1755** SMOLLETT *Quix.* (1803) IV. 35 A pound of good luck is worth a ton of merit.

goodly ('gʊdlɪ), *a.* Forms: (see GOOD and -LY[1]). [OE. *gódlic*, corresponding to OFris. *gôdilik*, OS. *gôdlîk* (MDu. *goedelijc*, Du. *goelijk*), OHG. *guotlîh* (MHG. *guotlich*, *guetlich*).]

1. Of good appearance; good-looking, well-favoured or proportioned; comely, fair, handsome.

a **1000** *Cædmon's Gen.* 281 Ic hæbbe ȝeweald micel to ȝyrwanne godlecran stol hearran on heofne. *c* **1205** LAY. 860 Þat folc com togadere gudliche cnihtes. *c* **1300** *Siriz* 5 Wis he wes of lore, And gouthlich under gore, And clothed in fair sroud. *c* **1374** CHAUCER *Troylus* II. 831 (880) Þe goodlieste mayde Of gret estat in al þe toun of Troye. *c* **1440** *Paston Lett.* No. 25 I. 39 Of colour it wolde be a godely blew. **1483** CAXTON *Gold. Leg.* 183/2 A goodly yonge man and wel lernyd. **1509** HAWES *Past. Pleas.* I. viii, This goodly picture was in altitude Nyne fote and more, of fayre marble stone. **1632** J. HAYWARD tr. *Biondi's Eromena* 12 Two children.. both so beautifull, as that the world never produced a goodlier couple. *a* **1674** CLARENDON *Hist. Reb.* XIII. §69 The Lord Withrington was one of the most goodly Persons of that Age, being near the head higher than most tall Men. **1809** T. KELLY in R. Palmer *Bk. Praise* 48 Where no goodly plant is growing, Where no verdure ever smiled. **1886** RUSKIN *Præterita* I. 354 The next goodliest part of the college buildings,—the hall.

2. Notable or considerable in respect of size, quantity, or number (freq. with mixture of sense 1).

c **1205** LAY. 6159 Þe king of þan londe.. com to-ȝeines Gurguint: mid godliche strengðe. **1568** GRAFTON *Chron.* II. 367, xx. thousand knights, and squiers, which certainly were a goodly company. **1639** FULLER *Holy War* II. vii. (1647) 51 Surely a goodly stature is most majestical. **1735** BERKELEY *Querist* §214 Seed equally scattered produceth a goodly harvest. **1798** COLERIDGE *Anc. Mar.* VII. xx, To walk together to the kirk With a goodly company. **1870** DICKENS *E. Drood* ii, One of the two men locks the door with a goodly key. **1877** BLACK *Green Past.* xix, She glanced up at a goodly row of joints and fowls. **1881** BESANT & RICE *Chapl. of Fleet* I. 149 Mrs. Deborah cut off three or four goodly slices of cold beef.

3. Of good quality, admirable, splendid, excellent. Also, well suited for some purpose, proper, convenient (often with implication of sense 1).

c **1385** CHAUCER *L.G.W.* 77 Prol., I.. am ful glad if I may fynde an er Of ony goodly word that they han laft. *c* **1386** —— *Nun's Pr. Prol.* 13 Swich thyng is gladsom.. And of swich thyng were goodly for to telle. *c* **1430** *Syr Gener.* (Roxb.) 3019 Holden he was for oon of the wise, And of spech most godeliest. **1483** *Act 1 Rich. III* c. 6. §3 Writs of Proclamation in all goodly haste [shall] be directed to every Sheriff. **1513** *Act 5 Hen. VIII* c. 4 Preamb., Worsteds.. have been one of the goodliest Merchandise and greatest Commodity of this Realm. **1577** B. GOOGE *Heresbach's Husb.* I. (1586) 44b, The grounde after his long rest, will beare goodly Corne. **1641** J. JACKSON *True Evang. T.* III. 211 Many fair and goodly Proverbs, and Apophthegmes. **1725** POPE *Odyss.* IX. 7 How goodly seems it, ever to employ Man's social days in union and in joy? **1845-6** TRENCH *Huls. Lect.* Ser. II. i. 153 The goodliest maxim is.. nothing, save in its coherence to a body of truth. **1871** FREEMAN *Norm. Conq.* (1876) IV. xvii. 80 The land which sent forth such goodly stores.

b. freq. in ironical use.

1553 BECON *Reliques of Rome* (1563) 159 This is yᵉ goodly Godlye Catholyke doctrine wherwith the vngoodly vngodly Papests infecte the mindes of such Christians as [etc.]. **1583** HOLLYBAND *Campo di Fior* 207 Do you leane on the table? Where have you learned this goodly fashion? **1604** SHAKS. *Oth.* II. iii. 160 Heere's a goodly Watch indeed. **1654** JER. TAYLOR *Real Pres.* 151 Verily a goodly argument; if a man could guesse in what mood and figure it could conclude. **1680** ALLEN *Peace & Unity* 141 More goodly and self-conceited, more proud and imperious. **1828** SCOTT *F.M. Perth* viii, Some complaint.. for playing at foot-ball on the streets of the burgh, or some such goodly matter.

†**4.** Gracious, kind, kindly-disposed. Also *goodly of*, liberal in. *Obs.*

13.. *E.E. Allit. P.* B. 753 þenne þe godlych god gef hym onsware. *c* **1350** *Will. Palerne* 355 My godelyche moder, þat so faire haþ me fed. **1398** TREVISA *Barth. De P.R.* II. ii. (1495) 29 Angels ben goodly and not tormented by the prycke of enuye. *c* **1400** *Destr. Troy* 3766 Achilles was.. Godely of giftes, grettist in expense. *c* **1440** *Promp. Parv.* 201/1 Goodly, *benignus, benevolus.*

†**5.** phr. ***goodly and gracious!*** (see GRACIOUS).

1713 BENTLEY *Remarks* II. liii. (ed. 2) 76 Goodly and gracious! What an Honour is this to Cicero's Ashes? **1744** WARBURTON *Wks.* (1811) XI. 318 Goodly and gracious! Here he shews how capable a reader he is of *The Divine Legation.*

Hence †**'goodlily** *adv.* = next.

a **1500** *Chaucer's Dreme* 824 More friendly Unto my lady, and goodlely He spake, than any that was there.

goodly ('gʊdlɪ), *adv.* Forms: (see GOOD and -LY²). [ME. *godliche*, corresponding to OHG. *guotlîcho* (MHG. *guotlîche*).]

†**1.** So as to produce a goodly appearance or effect; beautifully, elegantly, gracefully. *Obs.*

c **1205** LAY. 100 Tuenti gode scipen he guðliche fulde. *Ibid.* 18858 Of him scullen gleomen godliche singen. *c* **1350** *Leg. Rood* (1871) 71 Michaell come and by þam stode, And oþer angels gudely graid. *c* **1374** CHAUCER *Troylus* v. 578 At þat corner.. Herde I aldyr louelyest lady dere.. Synge so wel so godly, and so clere. *c* **1400** *Ywaine & Gaw.* 832 With sper and target gudely grayd. **1515** *Scot. Field* 333 Thus he graces him godly with a greate meany. **1535** COVERDALE *Ecclus.* l. 18 They sunge goodly also with their voyces. **1556** *Chron. Gr. Friars* (Camden) 81 It was goodly hangyd with clothes, banners, and stremers, and syngers, and goodly aparelde alle the way downe to Ledynhalle.

†**2.** Favourably, graciously, kindly; courteously, in a proper or becoming manner. Also, liberally.

a **1300** *Cursor M.* 23092 Quen i was will and vte o rest, Godli toke yee me to gest. **13..** *Gaw. & Gr. Knt.* 273 þow wyl grant me godly þe gomen þat I ask. **1377** LANGL. *P. Pl.* B. I. 180 But if ȝe loven.. þe poure, Such good as god ȝow sent godelich parteth. *c* **1475** *Rauf Coilȝear* 118 The Coilȝear gudlie in feir tuke him be the hand. **1523** LD. BERNERS *Froiss.* I. ccxv. 270 Ladyes, and demoselles, right goodly dyde visyte hym. **1590** SPENSER *F.Q.* I. v. 15 Running heralds humble homage made, Greeting him goodly with new victory. **1676-7** HALE *Contempl.* II. 132 How we pride our selves in it? how goodly we look upon our selves?

3. In a goodly or excellent fashion; excellently. Also in ironical use. Now *rare.*

c **1320** *Cast. Love* 1396 He is vre Fader ariht, And so goodliche vs haþ i-diht þat [etc.]. *c* **1350** *Will. Palerne* 169 God graunt hem his blis þat godly so prayen! *c* **1430** *Syr Gener.* 1554 She liked him so goodelie in hir thoght. **1535** COVERDALE *Num.* xvi. 14 How goodly well hast thou brought Vs in to a londe that [etc.]. **1535** J. MASON in Ellis *Orig. Lett.* Ser. II. II. 55 Here be many Cyties, butt nother great nor peopled, nother yett goodly buyldid. **1680** H. MORE *Apocal. Apoc.* 283 R. H. thinke so goodly well of his confutation.. that [etc.]. **1865** MRS. CARLYLE *Lett.* III. 261 You are so good about writing that you deserve to be goodly done by. **1879** *Cassell's Techn. Educ.* II. 70/1 How goodly and cleanly they and their wives and children lived.

†**4.** Conveniently, with propriety. *Obs.*

c **1386** CHAUCER *Melib.* ¶ 53 And for ther is gret peril in werre; therefore shulde a man flee and eschewe werre in as muchel as a man may goodly. **1397** *Will Thomas Earl of Kent* in *Roy. Wills* (1780) 118 My body to be buried as sone as hit goodlich may. **1422** *E.E. Wills* (1882) 49 As son as yt may be don godly after þat I have dede. **1448** *Will of Hen. VI* in Willis & Clark *Cambridge* (1886) I. 378 The most substancial and best abidyng stuffe.. that may goodly be had. *c* **1500** *Melusine* xxx. 218 She prayed hym to retourne assoone as he goodly myght. **1513** DOUGLAS *Æneis* XIII. vii. 35 Quhen that he cummyn was so neir, That athir gudly to othir speik mycht.

†**5.** In negative clauses: Easily, readily. *Obs.*

c **1400** MAUNDEV. (1839) xi. 130 No man may passe be that weye godely, but in tyme of Wyntir. *c* **1435** *Torr. Portugal* 1601 Wors tydinges.. I myght not goodly here. **1477** EARL RIVERS (Caxton) *Dictes* 80 And so may not goodely ne wele eny man directe another, but if he dyrecte him self first. *a* **1572** KNOX *Hist. Ref.* Wks. 1846 I. 385 The quhilk, becaus it is sa strange as it is.. I can not gudlie beleif it. **1652** URQUHART *Jewel* Wks. (1834) 215 Denmark, in my opinion, cannot goodly forget the magnanimous exploits of Sir Donald Mackie Lord Reay.

6. *Comb.*, as ***goodly-ordered, -propertied, -sized*** adjs.

1656 S. HOLLAND *Zara* (1719) 26 Pomgranates and luscious Dates contended which first should salute his goodly-siz'd Grinders. **1673** DRYDEN *State Innoc.* II. i, O goodly-ordered work! O Power Divine, Of Thee I am, and what I am is Thine. **1821** LAMB *Elia* Ser. I. *All Fool's Day*, A pair of so goodly-propertied and meritoriously-equal damsels.

goodman ('gʊdmən, gʊd'mæn). [GOOD *a.* + MAN; cf. MDu. *goedman* (Du. *goeman*).]

†**1.** = *good man.* Sometimes used as a vague title of dignity or a respectful form of address. *Obs.*

Perh. really two words, though written as one.

[*c* **1175** *Lamb. Hom.* 151 Job wes anfald rihtwis Mon and swa godmon; þet ure drihten him solf hine herede.] *a* **1300** *Signs bef. Judgem.* 21 in *E.E.P.* (1862) 8 Godmen takiþ nou gome of tokninges þat commiþ bi for. *a* **1400-50** *Alexander* 436 And, gudman, [on] þe gold rynge, þe thre grauen thyngis, þai ere þus mekill to mene. *Ibid.* 2407 þan takis þe gudman þe gifte, & gretly þam þankis.

†**b.** *Sc.* Applied euphemistically to the Devil.

1779 ARNOT *Hist. Edin.* (1788) 80 Farmers left a part of their lands perpetually untilled.. this spot was dedicated to the Devil, and called the Goodman's croft.

2. The master or male head of a household or other establishment; †the host (of an inn), †the keeper (of a prison). Now only *Sc.* or *arch.*

c **1340** *Cursor M.* 13507 (Fairf.) Alle was fed godemen & knauis. **1399** LANGL. *Rich. Redeles* I. 66 Ther gromes and the godmen, beth all eliche grette. **1464** *Mann. & Househ. Exp.* (Roxb.) 247 Item, to the goodman of Cardenallys Hat for horsemet the same day vijs. vjd. **1556** *Chron. Gr. Friars* (Camden) 7 Thys yere the goodman at the Cooke in Cheppe ..was morderd in hys bede by nyght. **1581** LAMBARDE *Eiren.* II. vii. (1588) 266 In like sort is it, if the goodman of the house (perceiuing that theeues are without) wil open the doores, and go out against them. **1631** RUTHERFORD *Lett.* (1862) I. 72 Wherefore doth the word say, that our Christ, the Goodman of this house, His dear kirk, hath feet like fine brass? **1722** WODROW *Hist. Ch. Scot.* II. 636 The Goodman (Jaylor) of the Tolbooth came to him in his Chamber. **1785** BURNS *Halloween* xvii, The auld guidman raught down the pock, An' out a handfu' gied him. **1842** MACAULAY *Lays Anc. Rome, Horatius* lxx, When the goodman mends his armour, And trims his helmet's plume.

vocatively. **1724** RAMSAY *Tea-t. Misc.* (1733) I. 8 Good-man, quoth he, be ye within, I'm come your doghter's love to win. **1828** SCOTT *F.M. Perth* ii, Good-even to you, goodman.

b. A householder in relation to his wife; a husband. Now only *Sc.* or *arch.*

1513 DOUGLAS *Æneis* VIII. vii. 7 To Vulcanus, hir husband and gudeman, Within his golden chalmer sche began Thus for to speik. **1529** MORE *Comf. agst. Trib.* II. Wks. 1184/2 Shee sayde it in sport to make her good man laugh. **1593** *Tell-Troth's N.Y. Gift* 37 Why is the husband called his wives good-manne? **1609** ROWLANDS *Crew of Kind Gossips* 20 Little our goodmen knowes what their wiues thinkes. **1816** SCOTT *Old Mort.* xxxvii, 'It's my gudeman, sir', said the young woman, with a smile of welcome. **1856** MRS. BROWNING *Aur. Leigh* III. 1159 One was tender for her goodman. **1881** J. GRANT *Cameronians* I. iii. 30 The next who was knocked over was your good-man, Mrs. Garth.

†**3. a.** Prefixed to designations of occupation.

1484 CAXTON *Fables of Alfonce* iii, Hit befelle somtyme that a good man labourer went fro lyf to deth. **1592** GREENE *Upst. Courtier* D b, In my time he was counted but good-man Tailor, now he is growne since veluet breeches came in, to be called a marchant or Gentleman Marchant Tailor. **1602** SHAKS. *Ham.* v. i. 13 Nay, but heare you, goodman deluer. **1638** FORD *Fancies* I. i, A nod From goodman-usher, or the formal secretary.

†**b.** Prefixed to names of persons under the rank of gentlemen, esp. yeomen or farmers (cf. sense 4). Also in ironical use. *Obs.*

a **1577** SIR T. SMITH *Commw. Eng.* xxiii. (1589) 40 These [Yeomen] be not called masters, for that (as I said) pertaineth to Gentlemen onely. But to their surnames men adde Good-man: as.. goodman White,.. goodman Browne, amongst their neighbors, I meane not in matters of importance or in lawe. **1588** SHAKS. *L.L.L.* IV. i. 37 Dictisima goodman Dull, dictisima goodman Dull. **1618** in Kerry *St. Lawrence, Reading* (1883) 87 Itm. pᵈ. to goodman Knight for casting of the 4 bell, 6*l.* 10*s.* *c* **1626** *Dick of Devon* II. IV. i. in Bullen *O. Pl.* II. 59 Pray (goodman rascall) how long have you and he bene Brothers? **1641** BEST *Farm. Bks.* (Surtees) 42 In that howse lived goodman Akam, to whom this close belonged. **1692** WASHINGTON tr. *Milton's Def. Pop.* xii, Now I come to you again, Good-man Goosecap, who scribble so finely. **1702** *Lond. Gaz.* No. 3858/4 A Watch ..was dropt the 14th past near Goodman Peacock's Farm. *a* **1732** GAY *Poems* (1745) I. 82 The sun-beams bright.. gild the thatch of goodman Hodges' barn.

4. A man of substance, not of gentle birth; a yeoman; a Scottish 'laird' (cf. quot. 1657). *Obs.* exc. *Hist.* or *poet.*

This sense is evolved from the use in 3b.

1587 HARRISON *England* II. v. (1877) I. 137 [The yeomen] be not called masters and gentlemen, but goodmen, as goodman Smith [etc.]. **1657** *Sp. Fife Laird* in J. Watson *Collect. Poems* (1706) I. 28 When I was born.. There was no word of Laird or Knight: The greatest Stiles of Honour then, Was to be titl'd the Good-man. But changing Time.. puts a Laird in th' Good-man's place. *a* **1661** FULLER *Worthies* (1811) I. 14 He is called a Good Man in common discourse, who is not dignified with Gentilitie. **1870** MORRIS *Earthly Par.* II. III. 496 There went that morn a goodman of the dale.. His herdsman with him. **1874** STUBBS *Const. Hist.* (1875) I. xi. 424 The aldermen and brethren constituted the guild, and the reeve and good-men the magistracy of the township.

†**b.** *Sc.* The laird or tenant *of* a specified estate or farm. *Obs.*

1592 *MS.* in Hunter *Biggar & House of Fleming* (1862) xxiv. 298 John and Adam Tweedie, Sons to the Guidman of Dreva. **1604** BIRREL *Diary* in Dalyell *Fragm. Sc. Hist.* II. (1798) 61 Robert Weir broken on ane cart wheel.. for murdering the guidman of Warriston. *c* **1610** SIR J. MELVIL *Mem.* (1683) 122 Alexander Hume of Manderstoun, Coildinknows, and the Good man of North Berwick. **1640-1** *Kirkcudbr. War-Comm. Min. Bk.* (1855) 143 The gudeman of Erlistone, James Tailfeir of Haircleugh [etc.]. **1824** SCOTT *Redgauntlet* let. xi, The rental-book.. open at the place where it bore evidence against the Goodman of Primrose Knowe, as behind the hand with his mails and duties.

Hence **'goodmanlike** *a. Sc.*, husbandlike; **'goodmanship** *Sc.*, a holding conferring the rank of 'goodman'.

1823 GALT *Entail* I. 306 It's your wife, my lad.. ye'll surely never refuse to carry her head in a gudemanlike manner to the kirk-yard. **1864** BURTON *Scot Abr.* II. ii. 182 When lands were held of any of the great families, they were but a gudemanship.

good morrow, good-'morrow.

1. A salutation used at meeting in the morning, equivalent to the later *good morning* (see GOOD *a.* 10 c). Also in full phr. (variously corrupted: see GOD *sb.* 8) † ***(God) give you good morrow.*** Now *arch.*

c **1386** CHAUCER *Miller's T.* 394 Hayl, maister Nicholay! Good morwe, I se thee wel, for it is day. **1481** CAXTON *Reynard* (Arb.) 46 Noble lord and lady god gyue you good morow. **1548** *Interl. John Bon* (Percy Soc.) 13 What, John Bon! good morowe to the! **1577** B. GOOGE *Heresbach's Husb.* I. (1586) 7b, God morowe maister Rigo. **1589** *Pappe w. Hatchet* E ij, Not vnlike the theefe, that in stead of God speede, sayd stand, and so tooke a purse for God morowe. **1598** SHAKS. *Merry W.* II. iii. 21 Giue you good-morrow, sir. **1611** CHAPMAN *May-Day* Plays 1873 II. 328 Godge you God morrow Sir. **1613** PURCHAS *Pilgrimage* IV. viii. (1614) 380 Ismael.. in the breake of the day, assailed Alumut his armie, little suspecting such a good morrow. **1632** MILTON *L'Allegro* 46. **1654** WARREN *Unbelievers* 145 They and their Christ will bid good-morrow.. so often as they rise. **1677** YARRANTON *Eng. Improv.* 111 Good morrow, good morrow, Gentlemen; I hope you have slept well to Night. **1810** SCOTT *Lady of L.* III. ii, The speckled thrush Good-morrow gave from brake and bush. **1847** LONGF. *Ev.* I. iv. 8 Many a glad good-morrow.. made the bright air brighter.

†**2.** Something as void of import as the 'good-morrow' of mere civility; an idle, trivial, or empty saying; a trifling or worthless matter. *Obs.*

1546 GARDINER *Declar. Art. Joye* 9b, They began to spread abrode an enuious rumour of me.. and many good morowes. **1553** T. WILSON *Rhet.* 18b, [We] worshipped hym not in spirite, but in copes.. in shaven crounes and long gounes, and many good morrowes els, devised onely by the phantasie of manne. **1597** GERARDE *Herbal* II. xcii. 341, I finde in ancient writers many good morrowes.. as that three rootes will cure one griefe, fower another disease [etc.]. *a* **1641** BEDELL *Erasm.* in *Fuller's Abel Rediv.* (1651) 61 Promise of a yeerly pension.. and many other good-morrows, which.. he never performed. *a* **1704** T. BROWN *Wks.* (1708) III. II. 79 Some might be apt to say, the Devil's in a Man that grieves for the Loss of a Wife.. and a thousand such good Morrows.

Hence †**good-morrow** *v.*, to say 'good morrow' to.

1686 F. SPENCE tr. *Varilla's Ho. Medicis* 13 The first thing he did after having good-morrowed him.

good-mother. *Sc.* [See GOOD D. 2b.] A mother-in-law; also, a step-mother.

1536 BELLENDEN *Cron. Scot.* III. xv. (1821) I. 109 This Caratak fled to his gud moder [L. *noverca*] Cartumandia Quene of Scottis. *a* **1557** *Diurn. Occurr.* (Bannatyne Club) 19 Alex. Cant burgis of Edinburgh, was slane in the nycht in his awne hous, be his seruand and his guidmoder. **1646** R. BAILLIE *Lett.* (1775) II. 187, I pity much.. his good-mother, whose grace and virtue for many years I have highly esteemed. **1816** SCOTT *Antiq.* xxxi, 'Yes, gudemither', screamed the daughter-in-law, ' it's e'en sae'.

Proverb. **1737** RAMSAY *Scot. Prov.* (1797) 14 A green turf's a good good-mither.

good nature, good-'nature.

1. Pleasant or kindly disposition; chiefly denoting a readiness (often excessive) to comply with the wishes or importunities of others, or to permit encroachment on one's rights.

a **1450** *Knt. de la Tour* (1868) 149 The scripture praisithe this good lady for her curtesye & good nature. **1567** HARMAN *Caveat* 42 A pore neighbour of mine, who for honesty and good natur surmounteth many. **1614** T. ADAMS *Gallants' Burden* Ded., In the affiance of your good natures.. I haue presumed to make you the patron of my Labours. **1667** E. CHAMBERLAYNE *St. Gt. Brit.* I. (1684) 35 Good nature.. a thing so peculiar to the English Nation.. that it cannot well be.. practised by another people. *a* **1717** BLACKALL *Wks.* (1723) I. 194, I never do drink to excess but only.. when I am hard put upon by the Company.. and I hope my Easiness and Good-nature.. will not be imputed to me as a Fault. **1751** EARL ORRERY *Remarks Swift* (1752) 53 He had that kind of good-nature, which absence of mind, indolence of body, and carelesness of fortune produce. **1827** LYTTON *Pelham* ii, I have seen him endure with a careless good-nature the most provoking affronts. **1888** BRYCE *Amer. Commw.* III. v. xciv. 322 The national easy-goingness and good-nature.

†**2.** In moral sense: Natural goodness of character; virtue. *Obs. rare.*

1627 SANDERSON *Serm., Ad Pop.* vi (1664) 351 We may talk.. of good natured men.. But.. set grace aside.. there is no more good nature in any man than there was in Cain and in Judas. **1657** JER. TAYLOR *Serm. at Funeral Sir G. Dalstone* Wks. 1828 VI. 563 A good nature, being the relicks and remains of that shipwreck which Adam made, is the proper and immediate disposition to holiness.. When good nature is heightened by the grace of God, that which was natural becomes now spiritual. *a* **1677** BARROW *Wks.* (1686) II. 199 [Virtue in Pagans] is to be imputed to.. the reliques of good nature, to the glimmerings of natural light.. or, [etc.].

good-natured. (The stress is variable.) [f. prec. + -ED^{2}.] Characterized by good nature; pleasant, kindly, or genial in disposition. Often implying undue complaisance or easiness of disposition. †Also, in early use, with reference to moral goodness of character (cf. GOOD NATURE 2).

1577 B. GOOGE *Heresbach's Husb.* I. 17 The husband.. gladly declareth his whole dealing in euery poynt: suche good natured men dooth this knowledge make. **1627** [See GOOD NATURE 2.] **1640** BP. HALL *Chr. Moder.* (Ward) 34/2 A good-natured horse will be governed by the shadow of the wand. **1657** *North's Plutarch* (1676) Add. Lives 41 He [Charlemain] was very good Natured, Temperate, Gentle, and slow in taking revenge. **1672** CAVE *Prim. Chr.* III. iii. (1673) 301 The Laws of Christianity.. produce the most gentle and good-natur'd Principles. **1716** LADY M. W. MONTAGU *Let. to Lady X——* 1 Oct., I never saw an old woman so good-natured. **1727** DE FOE ('A. Moreton') *Secr. Invis. World Discl.* xv. (1735 ed. 2) 368 Thou art the best-humour'd, goodest-natur'd Creature alive, said I. **1768** GOLDSM. (*title*) The Good-natured Man. **1779** SHERIDAN *Critic* I. i, If it is abuse,—why, one is always sure to hear of it from one damn'd good natur'd friend or another! **1849** MACAULAY *Hist. Eng.* vi. II. 97 He was too goodnatured a man to behave harshly. **1860** TYNDALL *Glac.* I. iii. 25, I having previously declined a good-natured invitation to sleep in the big black bed.

Comb. **1854** GEO. ELIOT in J. W. Cross *Life* (1885) I. 358 His brother.. was.. a bright good-natured-looking man.

Hence **good-ˈnaturedly** *adv.*; **good-ˈnaturedness**, the quality or condition of being good-natured (Worcester, citing Talfourd).

1765 C. BRIETZCKE *Diary* 18 Feb. in *N. & Q.* (1963) 109/2 He good-naturedly promised me he would. **1791** BOSWELL *Johnson* 29 Apr. an. 1776 To this, Dr. Johnson goodnaturedly agreed. **1852** H. ROGERS *Ecl. Faith* (1853) 84 Fellowes smiled good-naturedly. **1882** J. HAWTHORNE *Fort. Fool* I. xxvi, 'Well, I sha'n't put you to that trouble', replied Bryan good-naturedly.

good neighbour. [See GOOD-NEIGHBOURHOOD.] In U.S. politics, a neighbouring country, esp. in Latin America, with which the U.S. has good relations. Also (with hyphen) *attrib.* Also in extended use.

1928 H. C. HOOVER *Mem.* (1952) II. 213 We have a desire to maintain not only the cordial relations of governments with each other but the relations of good neighbors. **1933** F. D. ROOSEVELT (Inaugural Address), In the field of world policy I would dedicate this Nation to the policy of the good neighbor. **1937** *Ann. Reg. 1936* 293 The keynote of the conference was struck by Mr. Roosevelt as the policy of 'the Good Neighbour', and the President could assure the Latin-American countries that the United States.. now interpreted the role of 'Good Neighbour' as one forbidding forcible intervention in the affairs of a neighbouring State. *Ibid.*, The President visited Quebec... The visit was intended to stress the 'Good Neighbour' policy. **1944** *Ann. Reg. 1943* 346 The 'good neighbour' policy of the U.S.A. to the Latin American States. **1963** *Listener* 28 Mar. 542/2 General de Gaulle may calculate that the Soviet Union may want to become a good neighbour in Europe again. **1967** *Ibid.* 1 June 721/1 The shelving of a good neighbour policy in favour of the Dulles mania.

ˌgood-ˈneighbourhood. [f. the phrase *good neighbour* + -HOOD.] The disposition and behaviour characteristic of a good neighbour; friendly feeling and intercourse. So also **ˌgood-ˈneighbourliness, ˌgood'neighbourship.**

1817 J. BRADBURY *Trav. Amer.* 294 In no part of the world is good neighbourship found in greater perfection than in the western territory, or in America generally. **1829** SCOTT *Rob Roy* Introd. 25 MacGregor took an opportunity to conjure Stewart, by all the ties of old acquaintance and good-neighbourhood, to give him some chance of an escape from an assured doom. **1896** *Westm. Gaz.* 5 Nov. 10/1 A right good custom.. if good-neighbourliness is to count for anything in the village.

goodness (ˈgʊdnɪs). Forms: (see GOOD and -NESS). [OE. *gódnes*; cf. MHG. *guotnisse.*]

1. The quality or condition of being good.

a. Of persons: Moral excellence, virtue. Occasionally in *pl.*: Good qualities.

c **888** K. ÆLFRED *Boeth.* xxxvii. §3 Ðæs godan godnes biþ his aȝen god and his aȝen edlean, swa biþ eac þæs yfelan yfel his aȝen yfel. *c* **1175** *Lamb. Hom.* 81 þes patriarches.. gode men weren.. and al þos godnesse hom ne mihte werien, þet ho ne wenden alle in to helle. **1297** R. GLOUC. (Rolls) 739 þe king of france hurde telle of ire godnesse & bed hire fader granti him þe gode cordeile. *c* **1340** *Cursor M.* 10086 (Trin.) Ful leef was vs þat lady lele þat godenesses [*Gött.* bountes] bare in hir so fele. *c* **1410** HOCCLEVE *Mother of God* 30 Temple of our Lord and roote of al goodnesse. *c* **1450** *St. Cuthbert* (Surtees) 4783 To bryng his folk to gudnes. *c* **1500** *Melusine* xxi. 134 Goodnes & bounte is betre than fayrenes & beaulte. **1603** SHAKS. *Meas. for M.* III. i. 215 Vertue is bold, and goodnes neuer fearefull. **1672** TEMPLE *Ess. Govt.* Wks. 1731 I. 98 Goodness, is that which makes Men prefer their Duty and their Promise before their Passions, or their Interest. **1840** MILL *Diss. & Disc.* (1859) II. 69. *note*, Fewer small goodnesses, but more greatness. **1876** MOZLEY *Univ. Serm.* iv. 85 Gifts of the intellect and imagination.. do not constitute moral goodness.

b. Of things material or immaterial: Absolute or comparative excellence in respect of some specified or implied quality. Now somewhat *rare.*

1387-8 T. USK *Test. Love* Prol. 3 Of the goodnesse or of the badnesse of the sentence take they litel hede or els non. **1488-9** *Act 4 Hen. VII* c. 8 Every other Cloth.. abrode yerde.. to be sold.. after the rate of the godenesse therof. **1589** COGAN *Haven Health* cxciv. (1636) 176 The goodnesse of the pasture helpeth much to the goodnesse of the milke. **1631** GOUGE *God's Arrows* iii. §9. 202 Circumstances make much to the goodnesse or badnesse of an action. **1651** HOBBES *Leviath.* II. xxvi. 146 Depending.. on the goodnesse of a mans own naturall Reason. **1719** LONDON & WISE *Compl. Gard.* 221 The Lettuces are gather'd first, and afterwards the Endives arrive to their full Goodness. **1781** T. JEFFERSON *Corr.* Wks. 1859 I. 298 Our superiority in the goodness, though not in the number of our cavalry. **1812** WOODHOUSE *Astron.* xliii. 429 Telescopes of the same power and goodness. **1845** STEPHEN *Comm. Laws Eng.* (1874) I. 45 The goodness of a custom depends upon its having been used time out of mind. **1870** MAX MÜLLER *Sci. Relig.* (1873) 2 Such was the goodness of the cause I had then to defend.

2. Moral excellence as displayed in one's relations to others.

a. As an attribute of the Deity (†said also of Christ and the Virgin Mary): Infinite benevolence, a desire for the happiness of all created beings; also the manifestation of this; beneficence.

c **888** K. ÆLFRED *Boeth.* xxxv. §5 þu sædes þæt Godes goodnes & his ȝesæligǌes & he self þæt þæt wære eall an. *c* **1200** *Vices & Virtues* (1888) 83 Acc nu ic bidde ðe, for ðine michele godnesse. *c* **1340** *Cursor M.* 3411 (Trin.) Oure lord þat is of godenes [*other MSS.* bounte] boun To ysaac ȝaf his benesoun. *c* **1386** CHAUCER *Man of Lawes T.* 853 Til cristes mooder.. Hath shapen, thurgh hir endelees goodnesse, To make an ende of al hir heuynesse. **1413** *Pilgr. Sowle* (Caxton 1483) IV. xii. 63 We owen nought for his goodnesse to done hym vnryght. *c* **1460** *Towneley Myst.* iv. 271, I thank the, lord, well of goodnes. **1526** *Pilgr. Perf.* (W. de W. 1531) 5 The goodnes of god.. hath ordeyned that [etc.]. **1620** SANDERSON *Serm. ad Clerum* iii. (1674) 43 As Power is ascribed to the Father, and Wisdom to the Son; so is Goodness to the Holy Ghost. **1662** *Bk. Com. Prayer, Pr. for all Conditions of Men*, We commend to thy fatherly goodness all those who are any ways afflicted. **1699** BURNET *39 Art.* i. (1700) 29 The chief Act and Design of Goodness, is the making us truly good. **1738** WESLEY *Psalms* XIII. x, I sing the goodness of the Lord, The goodness I experience now. **1860** PUSEY *Min. Proph.* 562 Goodness is that attribute of God, whereby He loveth to communicate to all, who can or will receive it, all good.

b. In men: Kindly feeling; kindness, generosity, clemency; the manifestation of this. Frequent in phrase ***have the goodness to***..., as a form of polite request (? orig. a Gallicism, = F. *ayez la bonté de*).

c **1000** ÆLFRIC *Hom.* II. 508 Se halȝa hi eft alysde, and let hi forðgan for his godnysse. *a* **1300** *Cursor M.* 10426 (Gött.) Quen þat þar day was cumyn of þe fest, þan men suld bolde þaim to be blith, And ilk man his godness to kith. *c* **1386** CHAUCER *Melib.* ¶777 We preien yow and biseke yow.. that it lyke vn-to youre grete goodnesse to fulfillen in dede youre goodliche wordes. **1548** HALL *Chron., Hen. VII*, 34b, The kynge of hys goodnes remitted their offence, and restored them to their libertie. **1613** SHAKS. *Hen. VIII*, III. ii. 263 Your great Goodnesse, out of holy pitty, Absolu'd him with an Axe. **1680** BURNET *Rochester* (1692) 55 Goodness is an inclination to promote the Happiness of others. **1709** PONCET *Voy. Æthiopia* 29 He had the Goodness to give us a Person to be our Safe-guard. **1768** STERNE *Sent. Journ.* (1778) I. 75 (*Remise*) Have the goodness, madam.. to step in. **1798** FERRIAR *Illustr. Sterne* i. 20 Mary received him with goodness. **1855** MACAULAY *Hist. Eng.* xii. III. 221 The indulgence, he said, was grossly abused:.. his Majesty would soon have reason to repent his goodness.

†**3. a.** Advantage, benefit, profit. Rarely *pl. Obs.*

a **1300** *Cursor M.* 718 (Gött.) He thoght þat thing forto stint, þat godd to gret goddnes had mint. **1303** R. BRUNNE *Handl. Synne* 10599 Hys broþer had þe godenesse of hys song. *c* **1400** MAUNDEV. (Roxb.) xviii. 85 þe folk wirschepez þe ox.. for þe sympilnes and þe gudeness þat commez of him. **1502** *Ord. Crysten Men* (W. de W. 1506) I. iv. 42 All ye goodnesses of grace of benedyccyon & of glory. **1551** ROBINSON tr. *More's Utop.* I. (Arb.) 51 A matter whiche.. should be.. great commoditie and goodness to the opener and detectour of the same. **1583** STANYHURST *Æneis* III. (Arb.) 71 Too turne too goodnesse this sight and merciles omen.

†**b.** Good fortune; prosperity. *Obs. rare.*

1422 tr. *Secreta Secret., Priv. Priv.* (E.E.T.S.) 199 In this wyse he knew god ayeyne in angwysche and in myssayse, whych he had foryetene whan he was in his goodnes. **1550** COVERDALE *Spir. Perle* xviii. (? 1555) 139 After trouble and aduersite foloweth al maner of goodnes and felicite.

†**4. a.** quasi-*concr.* Something good, a good act or deed. *Obs.*

1297 R. GLOUC. (Rolls) 8936 þe godnesse, þat þe king henry & þe quene Mold Dude here to Engelond, ne may neuere be told. *c* **1300** *St. Brandan* 533 For no godnisse that ich habbe i-do bote of oure Louerdes Milce and ore. **1523** FITZHERB. *Husb.* §162 Yf thou wolde haue any goodnes done vnto y^{e}.. lykewyse sholdest thou do vnto thy neybour, yf it lye in thy power. *a* **1533** LD. BERNERS *Huon* xliii. 142 All the goodness and greate gyftes that I haue gyuen among you. **1568** GRAFTON *Chron.* II. 370 That he was right joyous to be in his presence, trusting that some goodnesse should grow thereby.

b. *the goodness*: That which is good in anything; the strength or virtue of it.

1577 B. GOOGE *Heresbach's Husb.* I. (1586) 45 Donng.. must be laide upon the toppe of the highest of the grounde, that the goodnesse may runne to the bottome. **1796** MRS. GLASSE *Cookery* xii. 180 Strain it boiling hot through a cloth till you have all the goodness out of it. **1806** A. HUNTER *Culina* (ed. 3) 21 Stew till all the goodness be got from the meat. **1871** EARLE *Philol. Eng. Tongue* 87 Even so it is with the dialects—all their goodness is gone into the King's English.

5. In various exclamatory phrases, in which the original reference was to the goodness of God (cf. sense 2 a above), as ***goodness gracious!***, ***goodness (only) knows!***, †***for goodness!***, ***for goodness' sake!***, ***in the name of goodness!***, ***(I wish) to goodness!***, ***surely to goodness!***, ***thank goodness!***, etc., or simply ***goodness!***

In the first quot. the sense of *for goodness' sake* may be merely 'in order to be kind'; in the second from the same play it is rather 'as you trust in the goodness of God' (cf. *for mercy's*, *pity's sake*, where there is a similar equivoque). The phrases are not now in dignified use.

1613 SHAKS. *Hen. VIII* Prol. 23 Therefore, for Goodnesse sake, and as you are knowne The First and Happiest Hearers of the Towne, Be sad, as we would make ye. *Ibid.* III. i. 159 For Goodnesse sake, consider what you do, How you may hurt your selfe. **1642** *View of Print. Book int. Observat.* 20 In the name of goodnesse then, what is that which the people speak of? **1650** T. BAYLY *Herba Parietis* 26 He begs, and prayes her, for goodnesse sake,.. that she would not speake a word of what had passed. **1704** SWIFT *Battle of Bks.* Misc. (1711) 246 Goodness, said Momus, can you sit idely here [etc.]? **1806** M. WILMOT *Let.* 13 Dec. in *Russ. Jrnls.* (1934) 274, I wish to Goodness all my Books were this moment in the Music Room. **1814** *Love, Honor, & Interest* II. iii, For goodness, sir, tell me what means this haste. **1819** COL. HAWKER *Diary* (1893) I. 185 Here I remained.. for goodness knows how many hours. **1840** DICKENS *Barn. Rudge* ix, Goodness gracious me! **1872** *Punch* 11 May 199/1 Thank goodness we have a House of Lords. **1875** TROLLOPE *Way we live Now* II. lxi. 68 He 'wished to goodness' that he had dined at his club. **1876** OUIDA *Winter City* xiv. 384 He thanked goodness it was the last of her caprices. **1890** 'L. FALCONER' *Mlle. Ixe* (1891) 75, I wish to goodness your people would give a dance, Evelyn!

good night. (Also *hyphened.*) [See GOOD *a.* 10 c.]

1. A customary phrase used at parting at night or going to sleep; †orig. in full form ***have good night***, ***(God) give you good night***, etc. Also in various phrases, as ***to bid (†give) good night***, ***to make one's good nights***, etc., and in *fig.* uses implying separation, leave-taking, or loss.

c **1374** CHAUCER *Troylus* III. 371 (420) Haue now good nyȝt & lat vs boþe slepe. *c* **1420** *Sir Amadas* (Weber) 187 My leve dame, haue gud nyght! *c* **1489** CAXTON *Blanchardyn* xv. 51 The captayne gaff the goode nyght to the damoyselle. *a* **1553** UDALL *Royster D.* v. vi. (Arb.) 88 Good night Roger olde knaue. **1553** *Respublica* v. ix. 32 Than goode night the laweiers gaine. **1570** B. GOOGE *Pop. Kingd.* IV. 58 a, They.. yielding up their dronken ghostes, doe bid their mates godnight. **1602** SHAKS. *Ham.* I. i. 16 Giue you good night. **1604** MARSTON *Malcontent* II. iv. D 2, When our beauty fades, godnight with vs. **1631** HEYWOOD *Eng. Eliz.* (1641) 87 And so gave them the good-night. **1652** BP. HALL *Invis. World* II. viii, O my soul.. art thou so loth to bid a cheerful good-night to this piece of myself. **1794** MRS. RADCLIFFE *Myst. Udolpho* xxviii, Good-night, lady. **1820** SCOTT *Monast.* xx, Having wished.. to all others the common good-night. **1852** MRS. CARLYLE *Lett.* II. 177 And now good-night; I am off to bed. **1881** *Scribner's Mag.* XXII. 282/1 She promptly made her good-nights and vanished.

attrib. **1816** BYRON *Ch. Har.* III. lxxxvi, Or chirps the grasshopper one good-night carol more. **1868** HOLME LEE *B. Godfrey* lxv. 377 Give me a good-night kiss. **1871** R. ELLIS tr. *Catullus* lxiv. 382 In such prelude old, such good-night ditty to Peleus.

b. *phrases.* (Of obscure origin.)

1572 J. JONES *Bathes of Bath* To Rdr. b ij a, Al men.. greedily gape after worldly gayne, whyles in the meane tyme the members and the mynde fall into such lappes as they neuer may recouer agayne, so that then good night at Algate. **1688** in Ellis *Orig. Lett.* Ser. II. IV. 121 Pray my Lord let's have justice, or good night Nicholas.

2. *dial.* Used as an exclamation of surprise.

1893 in *Surrey Gloss.*

3. *transf.* Any parting salutation at night. †Also, ? a composition improvised when going to sleep.

1597 SHAKS. *2 Hen. IV*, III. ii. 343 A.. sung those tunes to the ouer-schutcht huswiues that he heard the Car-men whistle, and sware they were his fancies or his good-nights. **184.** LONGF. *Excelsior* vi, 'Beware the awful avalanche!' This was the peasant's last Good-night.

4. In certain names of plants.

1597 GERARDE *Herbal* II. ccclxl. 791 Of Venice Mallowe, or Goodnight at noone.. The Venice Mallow.. openeth it selfe about eight of the clocke, and shutteth vp againe at nine. **1840** PAXTON *Bot. Dict.*, Good night, *Argyreia bona-nox.*

Hence **good'night** *v.* to say good-night to.

1835 BECKFORD *Recoll.* 43 After good-nighting, and being good-nighted with another round of ceremony.

good now, 'good-ˌnow. *Obs.* exc. *dial.* [See GOOD *a.* 4 c and NOW *adv.*] An interjectional expression denoting acquiescence, entreaty, expostulation, or surprise.

1579 G. HARVEY *Letter-bk.* (Camden) 72, I am not to trouble ye often: goodnowe be a little compassionate this once. **1611** SHAKS. *Wint. T.* v. i. 19 Now, good now, say so but seldome. **1681** DRYDEN *Sp. Friar* II. iii, Good-now, good now, how your Devotions jump with mine! **1754** FOOTE *Knights* I. Wks. 1799 I. 65 A treaty with.. the Pope! Wonderful! Good now, good now! how, how? *Ibid.* II. ibid. 73 Sir, M^{r}. Jenkins begs to speak with you... Good now! desire him to walk in. **1893** *Wiltsh. Gloss.*, *Go-now, Genow, Good-now*, used as an expletive, or an address to a person (S.). 'What do 'ee think o' that, genow!'

good-o, good-oh: see GOOD *a.* 4 c.

good sense. [Cf. the equivalent F. *bon sens.*] Native soundness of judgement, *esp.* in the ordinary affairs of life. (Cf. COMMON SENSE 2 b.)

1688 LD. HALIFAX *Adv. Dau.* (ed. 2) 48 Naturally good Sence hath a mixture of surly in't. **1739** MELMOTH *Fitzosb. Lett.* (1763) 240 Good-sense is something very distinct from knowledge. **1854** J. S. C. ABBOTT *Napoleon* (1855) I. xxiv. 377 'This plan', says Thiers, 'was not, on his part, the inspiration of ambition, but rather of great good sense'. **1883** F. M. CRAWFORD *Dr. Claudius* 239 Wondering how it was that a stranger should so soon have assumed the position of an adviser, and with an energy and good sense, too, which [etc.].

†**'goodship.** *Obs.* [f. GOOD *a.* + -SHIP.] Goodness. *pl.* Instances of goodness; kindnesses.

a **950** *Durham Ritual* (Surtees) 100 Bloetsa drihten .. stove ðiosse þæte sie vs in ðæm .. eðmodnisse & godscipe & bilvitnisse. *c* **1320** *Cast. Love* 16 Þat kineworþe kyng .. þorw whom beoþ Alle þe goodschipes þ^t^ we here i-seoþ. **1390** GOWER *Conf.* II. 74 And for the goodship of this dede They graunten him a lusty mede. *c* **1430** *Pilgr. Lyf Manhode* I. cxlix. (1869) 75 Sithe to grace dieu j turnede ayen, and of hire goodshipes j thankede hire.

goodsire. *Sc.* ? *Obs.* Also 5 gudsire, -syr(e, 6 gudscheir, gud-, guidschir, 7 goodsir, gudeschir, gudscher, 8 gutcher, 9 gudesire. [See GOOD D. 2 a.] A grandfather.

c **1425** WYNTOUN *Cron.* VI. xx. 102 For to pas agayne thowcht he, And arryve in þe Empyre, Quhareof þan Lord wes hys Gud-syr. **1535** STEWART *Cron. Scot.* II. 662 This Herald suld succeid Efter his guid-schir for to bruke the croun. **1596** DALRYMPLE tr. *Leslie's Hist. Scot.* II. 161 Grate and thankful rememberance of his gudshir Metellan. **1609** SKENE *Reg. Maj.* 34 The heire of the sonne gotten of his awin bodie, may craue na mair fra his father brother, of the rest of his gudeschirs heretage (then that part quhilk was assigned to his father). *a* **1670** SPALDING *Troub. Chas. I* (1829) 11 His son being put in fee of all by the old tutor his good-sir. **1785** R. FORBES *Poems Buchan Dial.* 15 For what our gutchers did for us We scarce dare ca' our ain, Unless their fitsteps we fill up, An' play their part again. **1816** SCOTT *Antiq.* ix, 'Our gudesire gaed into Edinburgh to look after his plea'.

good-sister. *Sc.* [See GOOD D. 2 b.] A sister-in-law.

1666 *Despauter's Gram.* B 12 b (Jam.), *Glos est mariti soror vel fratris uxor*, a good sister.

good-son. *Sc.* [See GOOD D. 2 b.] A son-in-law. Also *good-son-in-law*.

1513 DOUGLAS *Æneis* VII. vii. 62 Geif that thow seikis ane alienar wnknaw To be thi magh or thi gude son in law. *Ibid.* XIII. vi. 47 Merely commandis man and page .. His gude son thai suld do welcum and meit. **1588** *Extracts Aberd. Reg.* (1848) II. 63 For himselff and .. his guidsoun. *a* **1615** *Brieue Cron. Erlis Ross* (1850) 4 William, sone of the Erll of Ross, and goodsone to the Erll of Buchane.

good-tempered, *a.* (The stress is variable.) [f. *good temper* (see TEMPER *sb.*) + -ED².] Having a good temper; not easily vexed.

1768 STERNE *Sent. Journ.* (1778) II. 88 (*Character*) The French .. are a .. good-temper'd people as is under heaven. **1837** HT. MARTINEAU *Soc. Amer.* III. 54 They have been called the most good-tempered people in the world.

Comb. **1838** DICKENS *O. Twist* xxxix, A good-tempered, faced man cook.

Hence **good-'temperedly** *adv.*

a **1822** SHELLEY *Coliseum* Prose Wks. 1880 III. 38 How good-temperedly the sage acceded to her request. **1888** *Sat. Rev.* 13 Oct. 441/2 Godin defended himself good-temperedly.

Good Templar. A member of the 'Independent Order of Good Templars', an organization of total abstainers established in the U.S. in 1851, on the model of freemasonry, and introduced into England in 1868. Hence **,Good 'Templarism, ,Good 'Templary**, the principles of this organization.

1874 (*title*) The Good Templars' Magazine; a Monthly Journal of Literature devoted to the interests of the Independent Order of Good Templars. *Ibid.* 46 Good Templary is emphasizing that teaching .. The Good Templar believes that [etc.]. **1887** *Globe* 26 Aug. 1/3 As sober as a lodge full of Good Templars. **1897** *Daily News* 13 Feb. 6/7 The mortgagee of the chapel .. objected to them on the ground that they were Good Templars, and Good Templary was not 'a distinctly Christian organization'.

good thing. [See GOOD *a.* 10, 11, etc.] **1. a.** A successful act or speculation. **b.** A witty saying or remark. **c.** *pl.* Luxuries in general; *spec.* rich food, dainties. **d.** A course of action, etc., that is commendable, desirable, etc. (cf. GOOD *a.* 4).

a. 1820 *Examiner* No. 633. 351/2 You must have made a good thing of it if you have got the 1000*l*. **1883** MRS. E. KENNARD *Right Sort* v. (1884) 51 Now and again .. Jack Clinker managed to pull off some 'good thing' on the turf. **1888** H. JAMES *Reverberator* ii. 35 He had a genius for happy speculation, the quick, unerring instinct of a 'good thing'. *a* **1889** J. ALBERY *Dram. Works* (1939) I. 191 I'll put her on to a good thing. **1889** E. SAMPSON *Tales of Fancy* 31, I was so fast that I had been kept at these 'stables' until some 'good thing' should offer. **1898** J. D. BRAYSHAW *Slum Silhouettes* 100 As luck would have it, I managed to put the old man on to a good thing. **1913** *Field* 4 Jan. 26/1 Master at Arms is not a big horse, and with 12 st 7 lb in the saddle he hardly looked like a good thing for the Sunbury Steeplechase.

b. 1694 CONGREVE *Double Dealer* I. ii, The Deuce take me if there were three good things said. **1775** JOHNSON *Let. to Mrs. Thrale* 23 June, I hope you .. heard music, and said good things. **1807** W. IRVING *Salmag.* (1824) 125 He could not for the soul of him restrain a good thing. **1840** THACKERAY *Paris Sk.-bk., Fr. Fashion. Novels*, When we say a good thing, in the course of the night, we are wondrous lucky and pleased.

c. 1821 P. EGAN *Life in London* I. iv. 58 Tom was *born* to be a happy fellow, if the enjoyment of the 'good things' of this world could have made him so. **1861** M. PATTISON *Ess.* (1889) I. 46 The German relished for his breakfast the good things .. here provided. **1888** BURGON *Lives 12 Gd. Men* II. v. 29 He would partake freely of the good things before him.

d. 1897 *Sears, Roebuck Catal.* 198/2 This Shoe we have called 'A Good Thing', because the name signifies just what we believe the shoe is. **1930** SELLAR & YEATMAN *1066 & All That* i. 3 The Roman Conquest was .. a *Good Thing*, since the Britons were only natives at that time. *Ibid.* xxi. 29 Simon de Montfort, though only a Frenchman, was .. a Good Thing. *Ibid.* xlvii. 90 Fox said in the House of Commons that the French Revolution was a Good Thing. **1942** E. WAUGH *Put out More Flags* iii. 213 He .. had a liking for books; he thought them a Good Thing. **1960** *Observer* 17 Apr. 21/6 The general assumption that the French influence on England has been 'a good thing'. **1960** *Guardian* 26 Aug. 8/6 We all believe that group counselling .. [is] a 'good thing'.

2. ***too much of a good thing***: an act, behaviour, etc., spoilt by its excess.

1600 SHAKS. *As You like It* IV. i. 123 Why then, can one desire too much of a good thing. **1809** [see TOO *adv.* 5 b]. **1852** MRS. GASKELL *Let.* 4 Sept. (1966) 197 We went at ½ p. 9, & did not get out till ¼ to 4, which was too much of a good thing. **1895** S. CRANE *Red Badge of Courage* vi. 66 This is too much of a good thing! Why can't somebody send us supports? **1932** A. HUXLEY in D. H. Lawrence *Lett.* p. xvi, The great work of art and the monument more perennial than brass are, in their very perfection and everlastingness, inhuman—too much of a good thing. **1954** J. R. R. TOLKIEN *Fellowship of Ring* I. i. 29 Some .. shook their heads and thought this was too much of a good thing.

good-time, *a.* [Cf. GOOD *a.* 3 c, 10 d.] Of a person: recklessly pursuing pleasure; esp. in *a good-time girl*. Also **good-timer**, one of this character.

1928 *Publishers' Weekly* 9 June 2393 Gerry Harris was 'a good time girl', who sought men only as playmates. **1928** A. HUXLEY *Point Counter Point* xxvi. 444 The boozers, .. the business men, the Good-Timers. **1941** O. SITWELL in *Open Door* 82 The plane was crowded. A few 'good-timers' were still there .. loyal to their favourite beat: Paris for Whitsun. **1943** *John Bull* 20 Nov. 6/2 Contribution to the controversy about war-time morals came from Capt. Cunningham Reid, who told .. the pitiful story of Mary, the 'good-time girl'. **1948** 'J. TEY' *Franchise Affair* viii. 82 Bert deserved better out of life than a good-time wife. **1957** WODEHOUSE *Over Seventy* xvii. 160 Once a combination of Santa Claus and Good-Time Charlie, Hollywood has become a Scrooge. **1958** *Times Lit. Suppl.* 18 July 414/1 This is .. a most eloquent protest against the present-day values of .. casual good-timers. **1959** *Listener* 5 Mar. 428/2 The murder of a local good-time girl. **1970** *Globe & Mail* (Toronto) 25 Sept. B2/4 So much for the view, strongly fostered by the Minister of Finance, that convention-goers are good-time Charlies.

†**goodways.** *Sc. Obs.* [f. GOOD *a.* + *ways* advb. gen. of WAY.] Amicably.

c **1565** LINDESAY (Pitscottie) *Chron. Scot.* (1814) II. 537 The queine heiring this, sent away my lord Marschall and my lord Lindsay incontinent to treat guid wayes. *Ibid.* 540.

goodwife ('gʊdwaɪf). Forms: see GOOD and WIFE. Also GOODY *sb.*¹ [Cf. GOODMAN.]

1. The mistress of a house or other establishment. (Cf. GOODMAN 2.) Now chiefly *Sc.*

c **1325** *Poem times Edw. II* (Percy) xliv, He beareth away that seluer And the good wyf beswyketh. **1375** BARBOUR *Bruce* VII. 248 'Perfay', Quod the gud wif, 'I sall ȝow say'. *c* **1470** HENRY *Wallace* v. 741 The gud wyff said, till [haiff] applessyt him best; 'Four gentill men is cummyn owt off the west'. ? *a* **1500** *Mankind* (Brandl 1896) 46/191 Wher þe goode wyff ys mastur, þe goode man may be sory. **1551** ROBINSON tr. *More's Utop.* II. (Arb.) 75 Whyche be all vnder the rule and order of the good man and the good wyfe of the house. **1634** RUTHERFORD *Lett.* (1862) I. 113 Desire the good wife of Barcapple to visit her. **1706** PHILLIPS (ed. Kersey), *Hostess*, the Landlady or good Wife of an Inn or Victualling-House. **1728** [see GOSSIPING *vbl. sb.* 1]. **1765** T. HUTCHINSON *Hist. Mass.* I. v. 436 Good-man and good-wife were common appellations. *c* **1817** HOGG *Tales & Sk.* II. 320 The ambidexterity of the goodwife. **1889** BRYDALL *Art in Scot.* vii. 131 A good deal of interest was taken in him by the goodwives.

†**2.** Prefixed to surnames (= Mrs.). Also as a civil form of address. *Obs.*

1508 *Old City Acc. Bk.* in *Archaeol. Jrnl.* XLIII, William apprentice w^t^ the good wif Sweling. **1597** SHAKS. *2 Hen. IV*, II. i. 101 Goodwife Keech the Butchers wife. **1607** in Kerry *St. Lawrence, Reading* (1883) 81 Mrs. Bowden .. Goodwife Pynke, Mrs. Newport. **1691** *Case of Exeter Coll.* 18 One Goodwife Buckland. **1824** SCOTT *Redgauntlet* Let. x, 'Ay, ye might have said in braid Scotland, gudewife'.

fig. **1632** MASSINGER & FIELD *Fatal Dowry* III. i, Some curate .. in the praise of goodwife honesty, Had read an homily.

goodwill (gʊd'wɪl). [Orig. two words (still often so written exc. in sense 4 b): see GOOD *a.* 5, 7.]

†**1.** Virtuous, pious, or upright disposition or intention. *Obs.*

In the pre-Reformation versions of *Luke* ii. 14, which follow the Vulgate, the phrase *good will* has the above sense. The 16th c. versions and that of 1611, following the 'received' Gr. text, retain the phrase, but use it in sense 2. The Revised Version of 1881 adopts the Gr. text presupposed by the Vulgate, but renders 'On earth peace among men in whom he is well pleased'.

c **893** K. ÆLFRED *Oros.* VI. viii, He [Titus] wæs swa godes willan þæt [etc.]. *c* **950** *Lindisf. Gosp.* Luke ii. 14 Wuldor In heannisum gode & In eorðo sibb monnum godes willo. [So **1382–8** WYCLIF, In erthe pees be to men of good wille.] *a* **1300** *Cursor M.* 502 Angelis .. mai neuermar held til il, Namar þan þe wick mai to god will. *c* **1500** *Melusine* lxii. 371 In som cas the good wylle of a man is accepted for the dede. **1602** J. DAVIES *Mirum in modum* (Grosart) 15/1 The foe can foile .. With Pride our Piety, and our good-will.

2. The state of wishing well to a person, a cause, etc.; favourable or kindly regard; favour, benevolence. *attrib.*

c **825** *Vesp. Psalter* v. 13 Mid scelde godes willan ðines ðu ȝebeȝades usic. *a* **1225** *Ancr. R.* 282 So muchel strencðe haueð luue & god wil þet hit makeð oðres god ure god. **1484** CAXTON *Fables of Æsop* II. iii, Thow castest not this brede for no good wylle but only to the ende that I hold my pees. **1535** COVERDALE *Luke* ii. 14 Peace vpon earth, and vnto men a good wyll. **1579–80** NORTH *Plutarch* (1676) 34 To win the love and good-wils of the people. **1611** BIBLE *Luke* ii. 14. **1630** J. TAYLOR (Water P.) *Wks.* III. 15 To helpe to tugge me a shore, at the Hauen of your goodwils. **1710** SHAFTESB. *Adv. Author* I. i. 2 In all other respects to give, and to dispense, is Generosity and Good-will. **1777** ROBERTSON *Hist. Amer.* (1783) II. 227 After repeated endeavours to conciliate their good-will, he was constrained to have recourse to violence. **1828** SCOTT *F.M. Perth* xxxiv, The great event which brought peace on earth, and good-will to the children of men. **1855** MACAULAY *Hist. Eng.* xx. IV. 459 Some pious men .. spoke of him, not indeed with esteem, yet with goodwill.

attrib. **1820** SHELLEY *Hymn Merc.* xc, And I will give thee as a good-will token The beautiful wand of wealth and happiness. *a* **1832** BENTHAM *Deontol.* (1834) II. 263 Correspondent to that same good-will fund there is an ill-will fund. **1906** *Westm. Gaz.* 20 Feb. 3/2 A large number of 'goodwill' workers are .. enlisted. **1935** *Economist* 18 May 1125/2 A lesser American naval squadron is making a 'goodwill tour' in Japanese waters. **1936** *Daily Mirror* 22 Mar. 9/1 Welsh children will broadcast their 'Goodwill Day' peace message to the World on May 18th. **1947** *Ann. Reg. 1946* 222 In July the British Labour Party sent a 'goodwill' mission to Moscow. **1961** *Listener* 21 Dec. 1081/2 President Kennedy arrives in Caracas .. at start of a 'goodwill' tour of Latin America.

3. a. Cheerful acquiescence or consent. †**b.** ***of, by, with one's (own) goodwill***: voluntarily, without constraint (cf. FREEWILL 1). **c.** Heartiness, readiness, zeal.

a. *c* **1300** *Cursor M.* 25180 (Cott. Galba) Forþi what so god sendes vs till Vs aw to suffer it with gude will. *a* **1400–50** *Alexander* 804* (Dublin MS.) Þat graunt I gladly .. with a gode wille. **1513** MORE in Grafton *Chron.* (1568) II. 771 The Lorde Cardinall shoulde first assay to get him with her good wyll. **1620** SHELTON *Quix.* III. vii. I. 180 Seek not to get that with a Good-will, which thou art wont to take perforce. **1766** GOLDSM. *Hermit* 16 And, though my portion is but scant, I give it with good will. **1794** MRS. RADCLIFFE *Myst. Udolpho* xx, With my good-will, you shall build your ramparts of gold. **1845** McCULLOCH *Taxation* II. vi. (1852) 297 [They] pay such duties .. with greater good will than any other impost whatever. **1874** STUBBS *Const. Hist.* I. xiv. 142 No prises of corn .. or other goods, shall be taken without the goodwill of their owners.

b. *c* **1400** MAUNDEV. (Roxb.) xxi. 96 Fischez þat hase all þe see at will to swymme in schall with þaire awen gude will come þider. **1535** COVERDALE *2 Chron.* xxxv. 8 His prynces of their awne good wyll gaue to the Heueofferynge for the people. **1568** GRAFTON *Chron.* II. 370 Therfore he was come of his awne good will to do some good. **1668** TEMPLE *Let. to Ld. Keeper* Wks. 1731 II. 103, I .. would by my Good-will eat dry Crusts, and lie upon the Floor, rather than do it upon any other Consideration, than of his Majesty's immediate Commands. **1816** JANE AUSTEN *Emma* II. xiv. 265 Augusta, I believe, with her own good will, would never stir beyond the park paling.

c. *a* **1300** *Cursor M.* 11153 Godd will he had to fle hir fra. **1460** *Lybeaus Disc.* 1843 Lybeauus wyth goodwyll Into hys sadell gan skyll, And a launce yn hond he hent. **1486** *Bk. St. Albans* E v b, Yf ye se yowre howndes haue goode will to renne. **1805** WORDSW. *Waggoner* I. 40 The Horses have worked with right good-will. **1849** MACAULAY *Hist. Eng.* vi. II. 151 He set himself, therefore, to labour, with real good will.

4. †**a.** Permission to enjoy the use (of a tenement). *Obs.*⁻¹

1562 *Child-Marriages* 10 Andrewe Haworthes father .. did obteyne the Landlordes goodwill of the Tenement wherein the father of the said Custance did dwell.

b. *Comm.* The privilege, granted by the seller of a business to the purchaser, of trading as his recognized successor; the possession of a ready-formed 'connexion' of customers, considered as an element in the saleable value of a business, additional to the value of the plant, stock-in-trade, book-debts, etc.

1571 *Wills & Inv. N.C.* (Surtees 1835) 352, I gyue to John Stephen .. my whole interest and good will of my Quarrell [i.e. quarry]. **1766** GOLDSM. *Vic. W.* iv, Having given a hundred pounds for my predecessor's goodwill. **1786** *Lounger* No. 79 On her marriage with the knight she had sold the good-will of her shop and warehouse. **1836** MARRYAT *Japhet* vii, The shop, fixtures, stock-in-trade, and goodwill, were all the property of our ancient antagonist. **1863** FAWCETT *Pol. Econ.* IV. ii. (1876) 536 A solicitor can either sell the good-will of his business, or leave it to his children.

†**good'willer.** *Obs.* [f. GOODWILL + -ER¹.] **a.** One who has a good will; a well-wisher. **b.** One who wills or is disposed to what is good.

a. 1533 BELLENDEN *Livy* III. (1822) 244 At his owrecumming met him his thre sonnis, with mony utheris, his gude willaris and freindis. *c* **1565** LINDESAY (Pitscottie) *Chron. Scot.* (1728) 43 His Favourers and Good-willers.

b. *a* **1541** BARNES *Wks.* (1573) 272 Heere haue you also, that God moueth vs, and causeth vs to bee good willers.

†**goodwilly**, *a. Sc. Obs.* [f. GOODWILL + -Y[1]. Cf. MDu. *goetwillich* (Du. *goedwillig*), MHG. *guotwillic* (G. *gutwillig*), ON. *góðviljugr* (Sw., Da. *godvillig*). Cf. also *ill-willy*, *evil-willy*.]

a. Volunteer. **b.** Liberal. Const. *of*. **c.** Cordial.

1533 BELLENDEN *Livy* IV. (1822) 391 Now wes..ane army rasit of gude willy knichtis, quhilk wes led to Veos be thir new tribunis militare. ?*a* **1700** *D. Ferguson's Sc. Prov.* (1785) 31 They are good willy o' their horse that has nane. **1706** *J. Watson's Collect. Poems* I. 58 But had I liv'd another year, If Folks had been good willie, I had had mair. **1788** BURNS *Auld Lang Syne* iv, We'll tak a right guid-willie waught [*otherwise* guid willie-waught] For auld lang syne.

goodwit, variant of GODWIT.

Goodwood ('gʊdwʊd). A race-meeting held near *Goodwood* Park, Sussex; freq. *attrib.*, as ***Goodwood cup, races, week***.

1839 W. H. MASON *Goodwood* 182 (*heading*) Goodwood races. Were established in 1802. **1840** J. C. WHYTE *Hist. Brit. Turf* II. xi. 498 (*heading*) The Goodwood cup.—Betting: Even on Harkaway, 2 to 1 against Deception. **1875** TROLLOPE *Way we live Now* I. xxxv. 219 Mr. Melmotte had bought Pickering Park... There were rumours that it was to be made ready for the Goodwood week. **1896** J. KENT *Rec. & Reminisc. Goodwood* x. 96 Improvements have been made to meet the requirements of the most enjoyable race-meeting in England, until it has attained the greatest pre-eminence, and is justly known as 'glorious Goodwood'. **1922** E. WALLACE *Flying Fifty-Five* x. 59 Where are you going to stay during the Goodwood week? **1951** B. W. R. CURLING *Brit. Race-courses* 84 The present Duke of Richmond is more actively interested in motor-racing than in horse-racing, but Goodwood week does not suffer on that account. **1956** *Radio Times* 27 July 38/2 (*heading*) Goodwood. *Ibid.*, The Goodwood Cup. For three-year-olds and upwards over two miles and five furlongs.

good work(s: see WORK *sb.*

goody ('gʊdɪ), *sb.*[1] [Shortened from GOODWIFE, as *hussy* from *housewife*.]

1. a. A term of civility formerly applied to a woman, usually a married woman, in humble life; often prefixed as a title to the surname. Hence, a woman to whose station this title is appropriate. †*goody-madam*: a lady who has risen from a lower rank.

1559 *Will of J. Eltoftes* (Somerset Ho.), Goody Wilkes [*Ibid.*, Goodwyff Wylkes]. *a* **1625** BEAUM. & FL. *Lover's Progr.* v. iii, So goody agent? And you think there is No punishment due for your agentship. **1638** FORD *Fancies* III. ii, I doe confesse, I thinke the goodee-madame may possibly be compast. **1664** WOOD *Life* (O.H.S.) II. 15 To gooddy Gale for mending my stockings, 6*d.* **1708** F. Fox in Hearne *Collect.* 3 July (O.H.S.) II. 117 Goody Vesey my bed-maker. **1708** T. WARD *Eng. Ref.* (1716) 156 Fame, a busie tatling Guddy. **1736** *Disc. Witchcraft* 26 We now hear talk of this old Gammar, and that old Goody. **1764** O'HARA *Midas* I. ii, Pray Goody, please to moderate The rancour of your tongue. **1798** WORDSW. (*title*) Goody Blake and Harry Gill. **1801** BLOOMFIELD *Rural T.* (1802) 6 Well Goody, don't stand preaching now. **1882** MISS BRADDON *Mt. Royal* I. iv. 109 Two or three village goodies.

transf. **1591** SPENSER *M. Hubberd* 1213 Soft Gooddie Sheepe (then said the Foxe) not soe.

¶**b.** = GOODMAN 4.

1583 STANYHURST *Conceites* in *Æneis*, etc. (Arb.) 136 Wheare rowed earst mariners, theare nowe godye carman abydeth.

2. *U.S.* At Harvard College, a woman who has the care of the students' rooms (Hall *College Words*).

1827–8 *Harvard Reg.* (Hall *College Words*), His friend the Goody, who had been so attentive to him during his declining hours. **1859** O. W. HOLMES *Prof. Breakf.-t.* viii, The late Miss M., a 'Goody' so called, or sweeper. **1893** W. K. POST *Harvard Stories* 79 There are many individuals that make up the university population of Cambridge—unofficial members. There are the..goodies. **1902** J. CORBIN *American at Oxford* 12 The scout is in effect a porter, 'goody', and eating-club waiter rolled into one.

Hence †'**goodyship**, the personality of a goody.

1663 BUTLER *Hud.* I. iii. 517 The more shame for her goody-ship, To give so near a friend the slip.

goody ('gʊdɪ), *sb.*[2] [f. GOOD *a.* + -Y.] A sweetmeat. Chiefly *pl.* Also *goody-goody*.

1745 SWIFT *Direct. to Servants* Wks. 1883 XI. 375 The only remedy is to bribe them with goody-goodies, that they may not tell tales to papa and mamma. **1756** B. FRANKLIN *Lett.* Wks. 1887 II. 454 They..present their hearty respects to you for the goodies. **1853** KANE *Grinnell Exp.* xxxi. (1856) 268 'Goodies' we had galore [at Christmas]. **1853** MRS. GASKELL *Cranford* v. 75 The 'mother dear' probably answered her boy in the form of cakes and 'goody', for there were none of her letters among this set. **1877** *Holderness Gloss.*, *Goody*, sweets. 'Fetch us a hawporth o' goody.' **1882** STEVENSON *Fam. Stud.* 241 All knowledge is to be had in a goody. **1890** C. M. YONGE *More Bywords* 137 People thought they had come fresh out of Lady Bountiful's goody-box. **1896** *Daily News* 2 Apr. 7/7 She had received the goodie-goodies and was delighted. **1931** E. WILSON *Axel's Castle* vii. 253 She is an American woman of the old sort, she who cares for the handmade goodies and who scorns the factory-made foods.

goody ('gʊdɪ), *sb.*[3] *U.S.* A sciænoid fish, the spot, *Liostomus xanthurus*.

1859 BARTLETT *Dict. Amer.*, *Cape May Goody*. **1884–5** *Riverside Nat. Hist.* (1888) III. 215 A much smaller species ..otherwise known as 'Lafayette' or 'Cape May goodie'.

goody ('gʊdɪ), *a.* and *sb.*[4] [f. GOOD *a.* + -Y.]

A. *adj.* †**1.** ? Cosy, comfortable. *Obs.*

1813 T. MOORE *Mem.* (1853) I. 344 The offer of such a quiet, goody retreat as Ready's is every way convenient.

2. Good in a weak or sentimental way; addicted to or characterized by inept manifestations of good or pious sentiment. Also, *to talk goody*. *Goody-two-shoes* (see TWO *sb.* IV. 2).

[**1810**: cf. GOODINESS below.] **1830** J. WILSON in *Blackw. Mag.* Apr. 688 Characters well drawn—incidents well managed—..moral good, but not goody. **1833** COLERIDGE *Table-t.* 20 Aug., There can be no great poet who is not a good man, though not perhaps a goody man. **1837** STERLING *Let.* 16 Nov. in Carlyle *Life* II. v. (1851) 193 All this may be mere goody weakness and twaddle, on my part. **1865** G. MACDONALD *A. Forbes* 45 The only remarks made being some goody ones about the disgrace of being kept in. **1867** H. KINGSLEY *Silcote of S.* xxvii. (1876) 178 She did not talk 'goody' to them. **1871** *Monthly Packet* Christmas No. 103 Two girls who had stopped..to see if there were anything new among the..goody-books. **1890** *Sat. Rev.* 1 Feb. 150/2 A lackadaisically sentimental and commonplace ballad.. which is sure to be popular with a certain class of 'goody people'.

B. *sb.*[4] *U.S.* A goody person. Now usu. in *colloq.* use opp. BADDY.

1873 C. M. YONGE *Pillars of House* IV. xxxix. 147 She is the most thorough Goody I ever came across. **1878** J. COOK *Conscience* ii. (1879) 25 No doubt, if a Cæsar or a Napoleon comes before some man of weak will, the latter, although he be a good man,—and especially if he be a 'goody', a very different thing—will quail. **1901** *Contemp. Rev.* Mar. 436 This goody ought to moderate the rancour of his tongue. **1951**, **1958** [see BADDY].

Hence '**goodyish** *a.*, somewhat 'goody'; '**goodyism**, 'goody' principles, something characteristic of 'goody' people; '**goodyness**, '**goodiness**, the quality of being 'goody'.

1810 COLERIDGE *Ess. Own Times* (1850) 664 Whose goodness, or (if I may be allowed to coin a word, which the times, if not the language, require) whose *goodiness*, consists [etc.]. **1841** *Edin. Rev.* LXXIII. 367 Clifford's extreme goodness (to borrow a phrase from Coleridge) not unfrequently degenerates into goodiness. **1842** *Blackw. Mag.* LII. 674 Then came the days of 'Goodyism', that left childhood a blank—whipped when naughty, and more miserable when too good. **1864** *Spectator* 24 Dec. 1479/2 A goodyish story, and about as readable as that kind of thing usually is. **1872** W. CORY in *Lett. & Jrnls.* (1897) 278 The small-townish, old-maidish goodyness of *Eugénie Grandet*. **1883** *American* V. 268 He is singularly free from the cheap unction..the goodyisms, which are the temptations of the modern pulpit. **1898** *Dublin Rev.* Jan. 218 The obtrusive goodyness which has been apt to make Catholic children shy of Catholic literature.

goody ('gʊdɪ), *int.* Chiefly *U.S.* Also **goody goody**. [f. GOOD *a.* + -Y[6]. Cf. LORDY *int.*] A childish exclamation denoting delight, satisfaction, or surprise.

1796 'A. BARTON' *Disappointment* (ed. 2) II. iii, Oh! goodee, goodee, oh! we shall see presently. **1853** B. F. TAYLOR *Jan. & June* (1871) 125 Port's tongue [being] busy the while with..'may I go?' and 'goody! goody!' to a provisional affirmative. **1886** BAUMANN *Londinismen* 67/1 *My goody*, goodness gracious! **1890** *Harper's Mag.* Mar. 608/1 You're coming home with us?.. Yes? Oh, goody! You'll come? **1898** P. L. FORD *Hon. Peter Stirling* 244 'That makes five,' said Peter. 'Oh, goody!' said Leonore, 'I mean,' she said, correcting herself, 'that that is very kind of you.' **1949** *Landfall* III. I. 57 His mother was out, goody. **1953** H. MILLER *Plexus* (1963) x. 352, I see Halvah and Baklava too. Goody goody! **1959** I. & P. OPIE *Lore & Lang. Schoolch.* ix. 161 Cries of jubilation include: Wow! Whacko! Goody gumdrops! Lovely grub! and By gog jolly custard! **1960** J. GRANT *Come Again, Nurse* x. 54 'Just in time,' said the Registrar jovially. 'Goody goody gum drops.' He walked over to the coffee pot and helped himself. **1967** N. FREELING *Strike Out* 16 Buttered toast, and cherry cake, as well as Marmite. Goody, goody gumdrops.

†**goodyear**. *Obs.* Also 6–7 goodier, -yeare, -year(e)s, (6 goodere, 7 goodye(e)re); and in pseudo-etymological forms goujeres, goujeers. [GOOD *a.* + YEAR[1]. The expletive use in questions (*What the good year?*) is equivalent to, and possibly adopted from, the early mod.Du. *wat goedtjaar*. Plantijn (1573) renders *Wat goet iaer is dat?* by F. *Que bon heur est cela?* and L. *Quid hoc ominis?* The Du. lexicographers suggest that the idiom probably arose from an elliptical use of *good year* as an exclamation, = 'as I hope for a good year'. One example of *goed jaar* approximating to the later Eng. sense (b. below) is quoted in the *Wb. der Nederl. Taal* V. 311.

Sir T. Hanmer, in his edition of Shaks. (1744), suggested that in the three Shaks. passages *good yeare(s* had the sense of the French disease', and was a 'corruption' of *goujeres*, a hypothetical derivative of 'the French word *gouje*, which signifies a common Camp-Trull'. So far as the sense is concerned, this explanation is curiously plausible, as it seems to be applicable without any violence to all the examples of the word (cf. *what the pox*, etc.). But there is no evidence that the definite meaning of 'pox' was really intended by any of the writers who used the word; and the alleged etymology is utterly inadmissible. Hanmer's spurious form *goujeres* or *goujeers* has, however, found its way into many editions of Shakspere, and was adopted as the standard form in Johnson's Dict. 1755, and hence in every later Dict. which contains the word.]

a. Used as a meaningless expletive, chiefly in the interrogative phrase ***what a*** (or ***the***) ***goodyear***. **b.** App. from the equivalence of this phrase with *what the devil*, *what the plague*, *what the pox*, etc., the word came to be used in imprecatory phrases as denoting some undefined malefic power or agency.

c **1555** ROPER *Sir T. More* (1729) 88 Who [More's wife, in 1535]..with this manner of salutacion homelie saluted him, 'What a good yeer, Mr. More..I marvaile that you' [etc.]. **1589** *Marprel. Epit.* (Arb.) 55 Now what a goodyeare was that Anthonie? **1598** SHAKS. *Merry W.* I. iv. 129 We must giue folkes leaue To prate: what, the good-ier. **1599** —— *Much Ado* I. iii. 1 What the good yeere my Lord, why are you thus out of measure sad? **1623** W. SCLATER *Tythes* 29 But how a goodyeare fell Abraham and Iacob vpon tenths without iniunction? **1628** tr. *Tasso's Aminta* II. i. D 4 b, Let her a good yeere weepe, and sigh, and rayle. **1667** DRYDEN *Sir M. Mar-all* IV. i, What a Goodier is the matter, Sir?

b. 1591 FLORIO *2nd Fruites* 7 With a good-yeare to thee, why doest thou not take it. **1596** HARINGTON *Metam. Ajax, Apol.* A a 5 The good yere of al the knauery & knaues to for me. **1605** SHAKS. *Lear* V. iii. 24 The good yeares shall deuoure them, flesh and fell. **1639** T. DE GREY *Compl. Horsem.* To Rdr., Wishing their bookes burned, and the authors at the goodyere. **1710** *Brit. Apollo* III. No. 118. 2/2 A Good Year take ye.

goodyera (gʊ'djɪərə, 'gʊdjərə). [mod.L. (R. Brown in W. Aiton *Hortus Kewensis* (ed. 2, 1813) V. 197), f. the name of John *Goodyer* (1592–1664), an English botanist.] A plant or flower of the genus of small terrestrial orchids so named.

1817 *Bot. Cabinet* I. (*index*), Goodyera pubescens—Downy Goodyera. **1825** *Curtis's Bot. Mag.* LII. 2540 (*heading*) Smaller Pubescent Goodyera. **1868** B. S. WILLIAMS *Orchid-Grower's Man.* (ed. 3) 142 The dark foliage of the *Goodyeras*. **1921** *Glasgow Herald* 16 July 4 That interesting little orchid called goodyera. **1963** W. BLUNT *Of Flowers & Village* 104 The seeds of the creeping goodyera, a little British orchid, are so light that I could send you 14 million of them by post for three-pence.

'**goody-'good**, *a.* = next *adj.* Also as *sb.*

1851 CARLYLE *Sterling* II. v. (1872) 127 We found the piece monotonous..dallying on the borders of the infantile and 'goody-good'. **1904** *Daily Chron.* 12 Apr. 4/4 One is the bad; the other is the goody-good. *Ibid.*, They must be on their guard..against cultivating the goody-good. **1922** JOYCE *Ulysses* 418 Baddybad Stephen lead astray goodygood Malachi. **1929** D. H. LAWRENCE *Pansies* 128 So our goody-good men betray us.

'**goody-'goody**, *a.* (and *sb.*) [reduplicated f. GOODY *a.*] = GOODY *a.* and *sb.*[4]

1871 SMILES *Charac.* viii. (1876) 226 Goethe used to exclaim of goody-goody persons, 'Oh! if they had but the heart to commit an absurdity!' **1873** *Punch* 4 Jan. 4/2 There are goody goody books; there are also baddy baddy books. *Ibid.* 11 Jan. 17/2 The three other Goody-goodies were *Messieurs Cabanet*, [etc.]. **1881** E. J. WORBOISE in *Chr. World* XXV. 578/1, I abominate your goody-goody, circumspect, infallibly-proper young lady. **1881** *Macm. Mag.* XLIII. 389/1 The illustrations are good, but the letter-press is of the type sometimes called 'goody goody'. **1884** BP. FRASER in Hughes *Life* (1887) 323 Don't talk goody-goody to people. **1889** *Minutes Congregational Council* (U.S.) 218 Thick-headed goody-goodies, who were fit for nothing else but to hold prayer-meetings and look after Sunday Schools. **1922** C. E. MONTAGUE *Disenchantment* viii. 122 A man who did not care to use so sound a means to his ends was thought to be a goody-goody ass. **1949** R. GRAVES *Seven Days in New Crete* 12 The atmosphere..would be described as goody-goody, a word that conveys a reproach of complacency and indifference to the sufferings of the rest of the world. **1959** I. & P. OPIE *Lore & Lang. Schoolch.* x. 191 One who makes up to a teacher.. is a 'goody-goody', a 'namby-pamby'.

Hence '**goody-'goodyism**; also '**goody-'goodyness**.

1881 *Athenæum* 19 Feb. 261/3 The story of 'What Might Have Been'..is a fair example of French goody-goodyism. **1884** *Punch* 8 Mar. 119/2 [A] speech full of..ponderous wisdom and imposing goody-goodyness. **1886** *Bookseller* Jan. 19/2 That talent..of teaching deep religious lessons, without disgusting her readers by any approach to cant or goody-goodyism.

gooey, *a. slang* (orig. *U.S.*). [f. GOO + *-ey* = -Y[1].] Of a viscid or sticky nature; *fig.*, sentimental, mawkish. Also as *sb.*, sticky food; *fig.*, a man of weak character.

1906 E. DYSON *Fact'ry 'Ands* xiii. 165 Half ther 'ouses in town 'ud give er gooey iv that sort er billet rather 'n' take on er lad with er tizzy's worth iv grit in him. **1919** *Quill* Feb. 16 We may briefly state that there are three principal schools of dunking; viz., in hot liquids, in cold liquids, and in gooey substances. **1923** H. L. FOSTER *Beachcomber in Orient* i. 9 She..extracted a gooey substance from a tube of tinfoil and smeared it with a stick upon the bowls. **1928** *Papers Mich. Acad. Sci. & Arts* X. 296 *Gooey*, hash. **1930** WODEHOUSE *Very Good, Jeeves* v. 121 Plenty of chocolates with that gooey, slithery stuff in the middle. **1935** N. MITCHISON *We have been Warned* II. 208 You'd look all goo-ey and jumpy about your Dione and give the show away. **1944** L. A. G. STRONG *All fall Down* 102 You ought to see those letters. All intense and gooey and squarmy. **1948** R. KNOX *Mass in Slow Motion* i. 3 What you mean by a dance is the wireless in the hall playing revolting stuff and you lounging round in pairs and feeling all gooey. **1959** *Manch. Guardian* 24 June 6/2, I never see you without something gooey in your hands or your mouths. **1971** *News of World* 21 Nov. 4/4 'Mmmmm, lovely,' she sighed as she tucked into calorie-laden hors d'oeuvres, fattening spaghetti, and an enormous plateful of gooey chocolate gateau.

goof (gu:f), *sb. slang.* [App. a use of dial. *goof*, GOFF².] **1.** A silly, stupid, or 'daft' person.

1916 *Sat. Even. Post* 19 Feb. 37/2 It ain't the same show, you goof!.. They change the bill every day. **1918** L. E. RUGGLES *Navy Explained* 113 To cope with the situation some goof ashore made a salt water soap. **1925** C. R. COOPER *Lions 'n Tigers* iv. 99 The most idiotic, dunce-like goof that ever struggled about on four legs. **1930** 'HAY' & KING-HALL *Middle Watch* xviii, Have you stopped to think what is happening to that poor old goof in the day-cabin, right now?

b. A mistake, esp. in an entertainment; a gaffe. Also *goof-up*.

1955 *Springfield* (Mass.) *Union* 30 May 21 He was convinced there was no 'goof' by the government at all in the polio vaccine distribution program. **1955** *Britannica Bk. of Year* 490/1 *Goof*, a mistake made in a show. **1956** *TV Guide* 13–19 Oct. 4 Randolph Churchill..has told friends his embarrassment is assuaged by past goof-ups among English men of letters. **1960** *Guardian* 15 July 19/5 His teleprompter promptly went on the blink... It was the only goof in an operation contrived..with consummate mastery. **1960** M. PHILLIPS in *Analog Science Fact & Fiction* Nov. 11/2 Every one of them came up to me to prove that the goof-ups in his particular department weren't his fault. **1970** *Daily Tel.* 11 Feb. 17/5, I believe they have made a goof.

2. *attrib.* and *Comb.* **goof ball**, (*a*) (a tablet of) any of various drugs, *spec.* marijuana; a barbiturate tablet or drug; (*b*) = sense 1 a above; **goof pill** = *goof ball* (a).

1938 *Amer. Speech* XIII. 185/1 *Goof-ball*, marijuana. **1950** *Time* 28 Aug., A goof ball is a nemmie (from Nembutal, trade name for a barbiturate), Geronimo, bomber, or any other barbiturate or sleeping pill. **1957** J. KEROUAC *On Road* (1958) 148 She took tea, goofballs, benny. **1959** *Encounter* XII. II. 33 San Francisco, which 'is already a haven for wandering psychotics and goofballs of every description'. **1962** K. ORVIS *Damned & Destroyed* v. 39 You're the granddaddy of all goofball windbags. **1963** *New Scientist* 28 Nov. 534/1 The barbiturates..are known as 'goof balls'. **1966** *Ibid.* 13 Oct. 29/2 The heroin addict nowadays never knows whether his supply [of heroin] is secure, so he supplements it with the more easily available 'goof-balls'. **1948** H. L. MENCKEN *Amer. Lang.* Suppl. II. 682 A sodium pentobarbital capsule is a goof-pill. **1960** *Guardian* 21 Oct. 3/6 'Goof' pills were..sold openly. 'Goof' pills was the term he used to refer to barbiturates.

goof (gu:f), *v. slang.* [f. the sb.] **1.** *intr.* **a.** To dawdle, to spend time idly or foolishly; to 'skive'; to gawp; to let one's attention wander. Sometimes const. *off*.

1932 J. T. FARRELL *Studs Lonigan* (1936) I. i. 5 To get even with..the Hunkie janitor, because he always ran them off the grass when they goofed on their way home from school. **1940** *Times* 23 July 2/4 Among other points of advice were:—Go quickly to your shelter or refuge room; suppress your curiosity and don't 'goof'. **1952** B. ULANOV *Hist. Jazz in Amer.* 351 *Goof* or *goof off*, to wander in attention, to fail to discharge one's responsibility. **1956** F. CASTLE *Violent Hours* (1966) ii. 21 Have you been goofing off? **1958** E. DUNDY *Dud Avocado* I. vii. 117, I shouldn't have goofed off like that. Should have stayed on with you. **1959** J. WINTON *We joined Navy* 64 'It's safer to take them [*sc.* caps] off and hold them in your hands while you're goofing.' 'Goofing?' 'Watching the flying. Anyone who watches the flying is known as a goofer. Where you're standing now is a goofing position.' **1962** J. BALDWIN *Another Country* I. ii. 113, I used to like to just..go to the movies by myself or just read or just goof. **1963** C. D. SIMAK *They walked like Men* vii. 41 I'd work over the weekend, getting out the columns, to make up for goofing off. **1968** *New Yorker* 28 Dec. 25 If you ever feel like goofing off sometime, I'll be glad to keep the old ball game going and fill in for you here.

b. To blunder, to make a mistake. Occas. const. *off*.

1941 *Amer. Speech* XVI. 166/1 *Goofs off*, makes a mistake. **1954** *Time* 8 Nov. 42 *Goof*, make a mistake. **1958** J. D. MACDONALD *Executioners* (1959) iii. 37, I goofed and I've got no apologies. **1966** *Word Study* Feb. 5/2 If a student goofs and says the tone is melancholy or sadness. **1970** W. SMITH *Gold Mine* xiii. 38 'What the hell you goofing off—' The words choked off in his throat. **1971** *Daily Tel.* 2 Sept. 4/6 The Census Bureau has admitted that it 'goofed' when it wrote it off as a ghost town.

c. Const. *up*. To take a drug or drugs. Cf. GOOF *sb.* 2.

1962 K. ORVIS *Damned & Destroyed* xxi. 155, I hope they goof-up in the dispensary.

2. *trans.* To take a stupefying dose of. Also *fig.* Freq. in pa. pple., const. *up*.

1944 *Amer. Speech* XIX. 104 There is some allusion in sailors' language to the use of drugs... Gassed up..and goofed up are cognate and self-explanatory. **1957** R. A. HEINLEIN *Door into Summer* (1960) ii. 25, I was as goofed up about Belle as is possible for a man to be. **1970** *Guardian* 7 Aug. 11/8 Thousands of youths openly..'goofed' amphetamines. **1970** *Lebende Sprachen* XV. 104/1 Goofed up. Durch Barbiturate berauscht.

3. *trans.* To bungle, mess *up* (something or someone).

1960 M. PHILLIPS in *Analog Science Fact & Fiction* Nov. 22/2 What could be anybody's purpose in goofing up a bunch of calculators the way they had? **1969** *Life* 4 Apr. 65 Now, it's hard to goof up pictures.

Hence **'goofer¹**, one who goofs (in various senses).

1925 *College Humor* Aug. 97/2 They had me fixed up to loop with that terrible egg Buster Slaton who is a nephew of the two old Slaton goofers. **1941** *Daily Mail* 31 July, *Goofers* is the term applied to people who ignore orders to seek shelter during raids, but stand out in the streets gaping up at the bombers. **1959** [see sense 1 above]. **1961** E. BROWN *Wings on my Sleeve* 98 The shortness of our take-off run astonished all the goofers on the island.

goofer², **goopher** ('gu:fə(r)). [Of Afr. origin.] A witch doctor; a curse, spell, or conjuration; ***goofer dust***: a powder used in conjuration.

1887 C. W. CHESNUTT in *Atlantic Monthly* Aug. 257/1 Aun' Peggy say dat bein' ez Henry didn' know 'bout de goopher,..she reckon she mought be able fer ter take de goopher off'n him. **1926** N. N. PUCKETT *Folk Beliefs Southern Negro* iii. 215 Some hoodoos burn a kind of powder called 'goopher dust', which represents the person being hoodooed, who is perhaps miles away at the time. This causes the conjured individual to lose his personality and to become sick or insane. **1932** B. DE VOTO *Mark Twain's Amer.* iii. 69 That the residue has not vanished is attested by the appearance of goofers and hexes. **1935** Z. N. HURSTON *Mules & Men* II. v. 281 It will be noted how frequently graveyard dust is required in the practice of hoodoo, goofer dust as it is often called. **1941** *Sat. Even. Post* 20 Sept. 56/3 No goofer dust..could kill an enemy. **1957** W. C. HANDY *Father of Blues* x. 142 Goofer dust all about—I'll fix him!

ˌgo-'off. *colloq.* [f. phrase *go off*: see GO *v.* 85.] **1.** The action or time of going off; a starting, commencement. Phr. (*at*) ***first go-off***: straight away, at one's first attempt. ***at one go-off***: in one unbroken spell of effort.

1851 H. MELVILLE *Whale* iv. 31 The first go off of a bitter cold morning. **1856** DOBIE *Recoll. Visit Pt. Phillip* iii. 52 Inducing a sympathetic reader to indulge in two years oscitation at one 'go off'. **1872** GEO. ELIOT in J. W. Cross *Life* (1885) III. 156 They..then sit up to read it 'at one go-off'. **1879** F. W. ROBINSON *Coward Consc.* I. iv, 'I don't think I would have put it in that way myself, at first go-off like'. **1888** F. WARDEN *Witch of Hills* I. xii. 253 One gentleman isn't bound to fly into the arms of another gentleman first go-off. **1894** DU MAURIER *Trilby* (1895) 208 He succeeded at his first go-off.

2. *Banking.* 'The amount of loans falling due (and therefore going off the amount in the books) in a certain period' (Lord Aldenham).

Mod. 'The Governor of the Bank of England says every Thursday to the Court "The go-off this week is £——,000"'.

goofiness ('gu:finɪs). *slang.* [f. GOOFY *a.* + -NESS.] The state of being 'goofy'; stupidity.

1929 D. HAMMETT *Dain Curse* (1930) xix. 211 Evidence of goofiness is easily found: the more you dig into yourself, the more you turn up. **1934** WODEHOUSE *Thank You, Jeeves* vii. 94 It was just plain, straight goofiness, and I can quite understand now why Sir Roderick told father that you ought to be under restraint. **1939** C. MORLEY *Kitty Foyle* 22 In spite of the general goofiness of our home doings I like to think of the little backyard.

goofus ('gu:fəs). *Mus.* [Arbitrary formation?] (See quot. 1952.)

1928 *Melody Maker* Feb. 142 (Advt.), With the coming of Rollini to the Savoy Hotel, the Goofus has leapt into popularity. It is an original instrument with two chromatic octaves, and plays both melody and accompaniment at the same time. **1935** *Vanity Fair* Nov. 71/2 New effects and new instruments (the 'goofus') have been invented. **1952** *Conc. Oxf. Dict. Mus.* (1960) 239/2 *Goofus*, an instrument introduced in the 1920's, or thereabouts. It looks like a saxophone, but has 25 finger-holes, each with its own reed, and is thus capable of producing chords.

goofy ('gu:fi), *a. slang.* [f. GOOF *sb.* + -Y¹.] **1.** Stupid, silly, daft.

1921 *Collier's* 19 Feb. 6/3 'How d'ye like California?' 'Fried!' says Knockout with a goofy grin. **1923** WODEHOUSE *Inimitable Jeeves* xvii. 232 He was lying back in an arm-chair with his mouth open and a sort of goofy expression in his eyes. **1928** *Daily Express* 26 Sept. 13 'I have gone completely goofy over Mr. Robey,'..writes one Montreal critic. **1931** *Observer* 11 Oct. 15 The 'sap' gone 'goofy'. **1932** E. WILSON *Devil take Hindmost* xxi. 214 They describe it as a 'hell-hole' where you 'get goofy with the heat'. **1938** E. BOWEN *Death of Heart* I. iii. 136 Your dear little goofy face. **1951** S. KAYE-SMITH *Mrs Gailey* 25 Two women..so utterly unlike her friends—one snooty and the other goofy. **1958** [see ANIMATION 8].

2. *Surf-riding.* **goofy foot, footer, surfer**, one who rides a surfboard with the right foot forward instead of the left.

1962 *Austral. Women's Weekly* 24 Oct. Suppl. 3/2 *Goofy foot*, a very good [surf] rider who reverses the usual way of standing by putting right foot in front of left. **1965** J. POLLARD *Surfrider* ii. 19 I'm sorry, I didn't notice you were a 'goofy footer'—a board man who rides with the right instead of the left foot forward. **1966** *Surfer* VII. No. 4. 53 Fred Hemmings displayed spectacular foot work at Yokahama, riding left foot forward and then switching to goofy foot. **1967** *International Surfing* III. III. 69 Huntington's hot goofy-footer, Farrent, is a power surfer. **1968** *Surfer Mag.* Jan. 48/1, I realised goofy-footer Carroll would have an advantage. **1968** W. WARWICK *Surfriding in N.Z.* 11 This turn is performed..by right foot forward goofy surfers, when they turn to the left. **1970** *Surf '70* (N.Z.) 13/1 Allan Byrne is one of the top goofy-foots in the world.

goog (gu:g, gʊg). *Austral. slang.* [Origin unknown.] An egg. Phr. ***full as a goog***, drunk.

1941 BAKER *Dict. Austral. Slang* 32 *Goog*, an egg. **1943** —— in *Amer. Speech* XVIII. 256 We [*sc.* Australians] say *full as a goog* where Americans would say *pie-eyed, plastered* or *tanked*. **1945** —— *Austral. Lang.* iv. 82 *Googs*, an egg (a word formed perhaps on the sense of *gog*, in *goosgog*, a gooseberry; U.S. slang has *googs*, spectacles—in all these cases roundness is implied).

googe, googing, obs. ff. GOUGE, GUDGEON.

google ('gu:g(ə)l), *v. Cricket.* [Back-formation from GOOGLY *sb.*] *intr.* Of the ball: to have a 'googly' break and swerve. Of the bowler; to bowl a googly or googlies; also (*trans.*), to give a googly break to (a ball). Hence **'googler**, a googly bowler.

1907 *Badminton Mag.* Sept. 289 The googlies that do not google. **1909** *Westm. Gaz.* 5 July 7/4 Mr. Lockhart, having 'googled' to no purpose from the 'nursery' end. **1923** *Daily Mail* 9 July 11 In R. H. Bettington they have a googler who might triumph over the best of wickets. **1928** *Daily Tel.* 12 June 19/2 Constantine..was out to a semi-yorker, which also 'googled'. **1930** *Ibid.* 25 Apr. 8/5 Grimmett..can spin the ball and google it.

google, obs. form of GOGGLE *a.* and *v.*¹

googly ('gu:gli), *sb. Cricket.* Also googlie, google. [Origin unknown.] A ball which breaks from the off, though bowled with apparent leg-break action.

1903 C. B. FRY in P. F. Warner *How We recovered Ashes* (1904) ii. 29 You must persuade that Bosanquet of yours to practise..those funny 'googlies' of his. **1904** P. F. WARNER *How We recovered Ashes* 106 Bosanquet..can bowl as badly as anyone in the world, but, when he gets a length, those slow 'googlies', as the Australian papers call them, are apt to paralyse the greatest players. **1909** P. A. VAILE in *Westm. Gaz.* 17 Sept. 14/2 The 'googly' is merely the American service at lawn-tennis introduced into cricket. **1920** [see BOSIE]. **1924** N. CARDUS *Days in Sun* 48 Hirst cultivated the swerve and Bosanquet the 'googly'. **1930** [see BOSIE]. **1954** J. H. FINGLETON *Ashes crown Year* 46 Australians call it bosie after Bosanquet..Englishmen call it the google, or googly. **1955** [see CHINAMAN 4].

fig. and *transf.*

1916 *Anzac Book* 128 You could reach it in three bomb-throws, if the last of the three happened to be a 'googly' and swerved in from the off. **1941** BAKER *Dict. Austral. Slang* 32 *Googly*, an awkward question which a person would rather not answer. **1947** I. BROWN *Say Word* 60 Australian airmen called a bomb both a bosey and a googly during the war.

b. *attrib.* or as *adj.*, esp. in ***googly bowler, bowling***.

1909 *Westm. Gaz.* 12 June 16/1 The discovery of so capable a 'googlie' bowler as Mr. Lockhart. *Ibid.* 12 Aug. 3/2 Googlie bowling is very wearisome work both to the fingers and the right side. *Ibid.* 17 Sept. 14/2 One 'googly'-man does not necessarily win Tests. **1911** P. F. WARNER *Bk. Cricket* iii. 62 Mr. Bosanquet has been called the 'Googlie King'. **1921** A. W. MYERS *20 Yrs. Lawn Tennis* 9 Fifteen years ago, Brookes mainly employed a 'googly' service. **1924** N. CARDUS *Days in Sun* 80 Tyldesley..was also one of the first batsmen to master the new 'googly' bowling. **1971** *Sunday Express* (Johannesburg) 28 Mar. 22/3 Kerry O'Keefe, 21-year-old leg break and googly bowler whom the Australians regard as the new Bill O'Reilly, has agreed to join Somerset.

googly ('gu:gli), *a.* Also -ey. [Cf. GOO-GOO *a.*] **1.** Of eyes: large, round, and staring. Hence **'googly-eyed** *a.*

1901 'H. MCHUGH' *Down Line* 35 Is id to my face you go behind my back to make googley-googley eyes. **1926** *Spectator* 21 Aug. 287/2 A golliwog hugging in its hideous embrace a googley-eyed Dutch doll. **1927** *Daily Mirror* 10 Dec. 16/1 Others with movable googly eyes in a hand-painted face. **1928** *Daily Express* 20 June 13/6 Strange, googly-eyed goldfish. **1959** I. & P. OPIE *Lore & Lang. Schoolch.* xiii. 298 No more beetles in my tea Making googly eyes at me.

2. Disposed to love-making, 'spoony'.

1929 W. DEEPING *Roper's Row* x. §3. 107 She ascribed Mr. George's googly, amorous interest to fatherliness. **1932** C. WILLIAMS *Greater Trumps* v. 85 And father would say, 'Really, Sybil!' without being googly.

googol ('gu:gɒl). [Arbitrary: see quot. 1940.] A fanciful name (not in formal use) for ten raised to the hundredth power (10^{100}). Also **'googolplex** [cf. *-plex* in *multiplex, complex*], a name for ten raised to the power of a googol.

1940 KASNER & NEWMAN *Math. & Imagination* i. 23 The name 'googol' was invented by a child (Dr. Kasner's nine-year-old nephew) who was asked to think up a name for a very big number, namely, 1 with a hundred zeros after it... At the same time that he suggested 'googol' he gave a name for a still larger number: 'Googolplex'. *Ibid.* 25 A googol is 10^{100}; a googolplex is 10 to the googol power. **1945** *Astounding Science Fiction* Jan. 126/2 George Brown..was the only one who came within a googol of light-years of guessing what they were. **1953** *Time* 6 July 68/2 *Parade*..spoofed the whole practice with a circulation brochure to prove that it is headed unmistakably toward the 'googol'. **1966** OGILVY & ANDERSON *Excurs. Number Theory* ix. 111 The googol..can easily be written out in full in about two lines of print.

goo-goo ('gu:gu:), *a. slang.* [Sometimes connected with GOGGLE *v.*¹ and *a.*] Of the eyes or glances: amorous, 'spoony'. Also *sb.*, an amorous glance, a 'glad eye'.

1900 GODFREY & HILBURY *He used to play on the Oboe*, She'd make goo-goo eyes at the bandsmen above. **1901** 'H. MCHUGH' *John Henry* 13 'It is awfully nice of you to ask me to see Bernhardt,' says The Real Thing, throwing a goo-goo at me that settles everything. *Ibid.* 76 He'll turn such a warm pair of goo-goo eyes on her that somebody will have to..yell for the fire department. **1906** N. MUNRO *Daft Days* ix, They made goo-goo-eyes at me when I said the least thing. **1906** *Westm. Gaz.* 22 Sept. 5/2, I don't go round making goo-goo eyes for roses, anyway. **1924** C. HAMILTON *Prisoners of Hope* 101 The women..fling a goo-goo at the band. **1959** J. THURBER *Years with Ross* ix. 158 There was so much spooning and goo-goo eyes.

goo-goo ('gu:gu:), *int.* [Echoic.] An imitative representation of baby talk. Hence **goo-goo** *v. intr.*, to talk in the manner of a baby; also *trans.*

1863 *Harper's Mag.* Aug. 402/2 Yes, you pet, goo goo. **1884** 'MARK TWAIN' *Huck. Finn* xxix. 295 The duke..just went a goo-gooing around, happy and satisfied. **1906** E. DYSON *Fact'ry 'Ands* xiv. 184 Baby's a baddy baddy 'icky bubb-bubb to goo-goo the wicked mans! **1922** *Ladies' Home Jrnl.* Feb. 176 Goo! Goo!—is all I can say but it means I'm happy, healthy and comfy. **1925** A. CRUSE *Bk. Myths* 145 When a baby cries '*Goo, goo*' the Indians say that he is thinking how Wasis successfully resisted the great god Glooskap.

googul ('gu:gəl). Also gogul. [a. Hind. *gugal*, Skr. *guggula, guggulu*.] The aromatic gumresin of the *Balsamodendron mukul* (cf. quots.).

1813 MILBURN *Orient. Comm.* (1825) 102 Gogul is a species of bitumen much used at Bombay..for painting the bottom of ships. **1858** SIMMONDS *Dict. Trade, Googul*, a resinous substance resembling myrrh..probably the produce of *Commiphora Madagascarensis*. **1882** J. SMITH *Dict. Pop. Names Plants, Googul*, a name in India for the gum obtained from *Balsamodendron Mukul*, a tree of the Myrrh family. **1886** *Syd. Soc. Lex., Googul tree*, the *Balsamodendron mukul* and the *B. Roxburghii*.

gook (gu:k, gʊk). *slang* (orig. and chiefly *U.S.*). [Origin unknown.] Used as a term of contempt: a foreigner; *spec.* a coloured inhabitant of (south-)east Asia or elsewhere. Also *attrib.* or as *adj.*

1935 *Amer. Speech* X. 79/1 *Gook*, anyone who speaks Spanish, particularly a Filipino. **1947** *N.Y. Herald Tribune* 2 Apr. 28/6 The American troops..don't like the Koreans —whom they prefer to call 'Gooks'—and, in the main, they don't like Korea. **1951** D. CUSACK *Say no to Death* xix. 109 The fur coat she wore must have cost her black-marketeer husband the best part of a thousand. He had seen ones like it in Tokyo when the Gooks were selling them for what they could get. **1953** *New Yorker* 7 Mar. 23/1 You'll notice it's not a gook car. **1959** R. KIRKBRIDE *Tamiko* iii. 17 Ivan looked at the..Jap... 'You get back to work, gook,' he said. **1959** N. MAILER *Advts. for Myself* (1961) 132 Miguel, he said a lot, but I just can't follow that Gook talk. **1968** *Guardian* 23 Feb. 11/3 The Gooks [*sc.* Viet Cong] hit from bunkers and the Marines had to carry half the company back. **1969** *Sunday Mail Mag.* (Brisbane) 6 July 4/2 This is a gook grave.

gool. *dial.* Also 6, 9 **goole**, 6 **goule**, 8 **goal**. [a. AF. *gole, goule* (a specific use of OF. *gole, goule* throat; cf. OF. *goulet* narrow channel, trench). See also GOLE, GULL.]

1. A small stream, a ditch; an outlet for water, a sluice.

1552 HULOET, Goole, *emissarium*. **1583** *Inquisition Sewers* 4 (in *N.W. Linc. Gloss.*), Thomas Staveley shall make one sufficient stathe at the south side of his goule. **1674–91** RAY *N.C. Words, Gool*, a ditch. Lincolnshire. **1825** HEBER *Narr. Journ.* (1828) I. 606 Raising water to the 'gools' (small channels) which convey its rills to their fields.

fig. **1542** BOWES & ELLEKER *Surv.* in Hodgson *Northumbld.* III. II. 229 The..fortresses of carrowe & sewynge-shealles..stande in suche a Goole passage & common entery of all the theves..of Liddisdale [etc.].

2. (See quot. 1706, and cf. GULL *sb.* and *v.*)

1664–5 *Act 16 & 17 Car. II*, c. 11 §7 If any Goole or Gooles, Breach or Breaches, Overflowing or Overflowings of waters shall happen at any time hereafter to be in over or through any of the said Bancks. **1706** PHILLIPS (ed. Kersey), *Gool* (Statute Law-Word), a Breach in a Bank or Sea-Wall; a passage worn by the ebbing and flowing of the Tide. **1723–8** P. BLAIR *Pharmaco-Bot.* I. (1733) 20, I have collected the specimens of no less than eighteen [species] from the Goals all along the sea coast towards Wibberton. **1832** *Holderness Drainage Act* 36 If..any sudden breach or goole may be made in..the east bank. **1848** in WHARTON *Law Lex.*

goold(e, obs. form of GOLD *sb.*[2]

gooly ('gu:lı). [App. of Indian origin; cf. Hindustani (Yates) *golī*, a bullet, ball, pill, and see R. L. Turner *Compar. Dict. Indo-Aryan Lang.* s.v. *gudá-*[1] and *gōla-*[1].] **1.** Usu. *pl.* The testicles. *slang.*

1937 PARTRIDGE *Dict. Slang* 343/1 Goolies. **1966** 'L. LANE' *ABZ of Scouse* 43 'Ow'd yer like a kick in ther goolies? **1967** B. NORMAN *Matter of Mandrake* ix. 68 Strapped naked to a bottom-less chair, having his goolies whacked with a carpet-beater. **1971** *Guardian* 27 Sept. 10/4 To get a good performance out of them [*sc.* actors]..it is sometimes necessary to kick them in the goolies.

2. A stone, pebble. *Australian slang.*

1941 BAKER *Dict. Austral. Slang* 32 *Gooly*, a stone or pebble.

gooly, variant of GULLY *Sc.*, large knife.

goom, var. GOME *sb.*[1]; obs. and dial. f. GUM.

goombay (gʊm'beı). Also **goombah**, 8 **gumbay**, 9 **gumba, gumby**. [Negro patois; cf. Kongo *nkombi*, a kind of drum.] A kind of drum used by Black West Indians, made by stretching a skin across the ends of a box, or a portion of a hollow tree, or the like. Also *goombay-drum.*

1774 E. LONG *Hist. Jamaica* II. 423 The goombah, another of their musical instruments, is a hollow block of wood, covered with sheepskin stripped of its hair. **1790** J. B. MORETON *W. Ind. Cust. & Mann.* 155 An herring barrel or tub, with sheep-skins substituted for the heads, in imitation of a drum, called a gumbay. **1828** *Life Planter Jamaica* 46 The negroes..dancing..to the sound of the gumba. **1834** M. G. LEWIS *Jrnl. W. Ind.* 322 The greatest part remained quietly in the negro houses beating the gumby-drum. **1901** *United Free Ch. Mission Record* Jan. 20/2 It was surely the beating of the Goombah drum. **1960** *Harper's Bazaar* Oct. 131 The night was filled with hi-fi—no goombay calypso. **1963** *New Yorker* 15 June 19 (Advt.), Cosmopolitan Nassau. Goombay goes till the wee hours. **1968** *Globe & Mail* (Toronto) 17 Feb. 33 Buses wait at St. George dock to carry students to old Fort St. Catherine, where goombay dancers and limboists provide exciting entertainment.

goon (gu:n). *slang.* [Perhaps a shortened form of dial. *gooney* (GONY 1) 'a booby, a simpleton'; but more immediately from the name of a subhuman creature called Alice the *Goon* in a popular cartoon series by E. C. Segar (1894–1938), American cartoonist.] **1.** A stolid, dull, or stupid person. orig. *U.S.*

1921 F. L. ALLEN in *Harper's Mag.* Dec. 121/1 (*title*) The Goon and his Style. *Ibid.* 121/2 A goon is a person with a heavy touch as distinguished from a jigger, who has a light touch. While jiggers look on life with a genial eye, goons take a more stolid and literal view. **1938** *Life* 14 Nov. 6/3 The word 'Goon' was first popularized by college students who used it to mean any stupid person. Labor union lingo has given it a second meaning: a tough or thug. Rival unions and factions speak of another's 'Goon Squads'. **1938** R. CHANDLER *Trouble is my Business* (1950) 80 Some goon here plays chess. You? **1940** R. STOUT *Over My Dead Body* iv. 57 You may be a couple of goons... But I'm asking you a damn straight question. **1942** D. POWELL *Time to be Born* (1943) vii. 175 You sit there gawping at him like some little goon. **1945** PARTRIDGE *Dict. R.A.F. Slang* 30 *Goon*, a fool, very stupid fellow; a gaper. **1951** 'J. WYNDHAM' *Day of Triffids* viii. 154 The goon started to argue. **1957** R. M. WARDLE *Oliver Goldsmith* i. 3 It was Goldsmith's misfortune that he was a jigger fallen among goons. *Ibid.* 5 William Cooke was a goon. Apparently it never entered his head that a man—especially an Irishman—might have preferred, for the joke's sake, to use a word which didn't make sense. **1959** S. CLARK *Puma's Claw* xii. 135 There, you goon. You'll bump into them if you don't watch out.

2. A person hired (esp. by racketeers) to terrorize workers; a thug. orig. *U.S.*

1938 *Amer. Speech* XIII. 178 In the Pacific Northwest we hear the word *goon* on every hand. Locally a goon is a member of a labor-union's beef-squad; that is, a person of imposing physique and inferior moral and mental qualities who can be depended on to cow and frighten recalcitrant union-members. **1938** [see sense 1 above]. **1940** *Chicago Tribune* 28 Jan. 1/8 'Goon' is a term applied to hired sluggers used in labor troubles... A typical goon murder was the recent killing in Chicago of..a garage-man involved in a union dispute. **1959** [see FINK *sb.*[2]]. **1969** *New Yorker* 20 Dec. 88/3 Many so-called 'goons'—civilian terrorists, sometimes dressed in Constabulary uniforms—took over in many provinces. **1971** *Blitz* (Bombay) 6 Mar. 13/4 Attempts on his life by goons allegedly employed by the Calcutta police authorities. **1971** *It* 2–16 June 5/1 Heath orders Habershon of Barnet CID to 'turn London over'. And he does exactly that..with 500 goons and a score of specially trained dogs.

3. A nickname given by British and U.S. prisoners of war to their German guards in the war of 1939–45. Also *transf.* So ***goon-up!***, a warning cry.

1945 G. MORGAN *Only Ghosts can Live* 140, I think it was an Australian who first called the Germans 'Goons'. *Ibid.*, The cry, 'Goon up!' remained in many camps a warning of the approach of the Detaining Power. **1948** *Amer. Speech* XXIII. 218 The word for German was invariably *goon* among airmen, American and British alike... It was also used as the adjective part of a compound noun,..e.g. a *goon-box* was one of the guard towers along the fences around the camp. **1952** E. F. DAVIES *Illyrian Venture* xi. 218 At midnight the Goon *Postern* (German sentry) was astounded to see a large naked form flying three times round the courtyard in a temperature of 25 degrees of frost. **1962** V. NABOKOV *Pale Fire* 55 Morning finds us marching to the wall Under the direction of some goon Political, some uniformed baboon.

4. (With capital initial.) Any one of the members of the cast of a popular British radio comedy series, ***The Goon Show***, noted for its crazy and absurd brand of humour.

1951 *Radio Times* 25 May 18/2 (*heading*) Crazy people... Radio's Own Crazy Gang 'The Goons'. *Ibid.* 18/3 Spike Milligan..has compiled the 'Goon Show' material. **1951** [see below s.v. *goonery]. **1958** *Observer* 18 May 14/4 The department of jokes, only a shadow of its former self without the Goons. **1958** *Listener* 25 Sept. 481/2 Lovers of the Goon Shows. **1962** A. NISBETT *Technique Sound Studio* x. 173 Just about the ultimate in this line of effects was reached when in a 'Goon Show' the script demanded 'a 16-ton, 1½-horsepower, 6-litre, brassbound electric racing organ fitted with a cardboard warhead'. **1970** *Sun* 28 July 3/5 The Goons are returning to radio—after 10 years in cold storage. **1971** S. MILLIGAN in D. Nathan *Laughtermakers* ii. 49 Prisoners of war called their German guards goons but I got it from Popeye. There was a creature called the Goon which had nothing in the face at all except hair... I liked the word and we called it *The Goons*.

5. *attrib.* and *Comb.*, as (sense 2) ***goon squad, tactics***; (sense 3) ***goon-baiting*** vbl. sb.; **goon box**, a guard tower at a P.O.W. camp; (sense 4) ***goon-like, -type*** adjs. Also **goonskin** (see quot. 1943).

1962 *Times* 12 Oct. 15/4 'Goon-baiting', which was the favourite occupation of the prisoners. **1948** Goon-box [see sense 3 above]. **1956** A. CRAWLEY *Escape from Germany* 31 Watch towers..covering the interior of the camp. To the prisoners they were known as 'goon boxes'. **1963** *Times* 21 Feb. 16/7 Mr Horst Buchholz, whose mixture of American and Indian accents is given an even more goon-like quality by the over-used attempt to inject local colour with the tag-phrase 'isn't it?' **1943** C. H. WARD-JACKSON *Piece of Cake* 32 *Goonskin*, observer's flying suit and parachute harness made in one piece. **1957** RAWNSLEY & WRIGHT *Night Fighter* 37 The fur-lined leather trousers and jacket known to us as 'Goon Skins'. **1937** *Nation* 4 Sept. 239/2 The goon squad, as it is commonly called, consists of at least twenty picked thugs and ex-convicts. **1951** E. PAUL *Springtime in Paris* xi. 202 The Existentialists allege that the Communists send goon squads to the district, as a part of their anti-American, anti-tourist campaign. **1962** K. ORVIS *Damned & Destroyed* ix. 62 I'm lucky the goon-squad haven't back-handed me into a lane and kicked me to death. **1967** N. MAILER *Cannibals & Christians* I. 32 He talked of..'strong-arm and goon tactics'. **1967** *Listener* 10 Aug. 187/3 And *I'm Sorry, I'll Read That Again*, a happy reminder of happy Goon-type days.

Hence **'goonery**, a foolish or absurd kind of humour typical of a Goon (sense 4); **'goonish** *a.*, of, pertaining to, or resembling a goon (senses 1 and 4).

1921 F. L. ALLEN in *Harper's Mag.* Dec. 122/1 A goonish style is one that reads as if it were the work of a goon. It is thick and heavy. **1951** *Picture Post* 16 June 34 Four young comics—Michael Bentine, Harry Secombe, Spike Milligan and Peter Sellers—have at last got together in a radio programme. In 'Crazy People' they put across their favoured kind of humour. This they call 'goonery'... General opinion was that if you like crazy, pun-dizzy, logic-smashing comedy that doesn't despise your intelligence, you'll like the Goons. **1958** *Vogue* Jan. 49 George Devine and Joan Plowright..made this extraordinary play a startlingly moving piece of theatre and gave the dialogue.. a quality of abstract goonery. **1959** *Listener* 12 Mar. 485/2 An hour..which had some elements of Goonery. **1959** *Sunday Times* 29 Mar. 17/5 Photographs by Inge Morath that have that air of solemnity suppressing a giggle that has become known, in this country at least, as 'goonish'. **1960** *Design* July 23/1 If you can force yourself past the first few sentences the Goonish mixture is oddly funny. **1968** *Times* 27 Feb. 3/8 This is a victory for Spike Milligan and goonery.

goon, obs. form of GUN.

‖**goonda, goondah** ('gu:ndə). [a. Hind. *gunḍā* rascal.] (See quots.)

1926 *Glasgow Herald* 27 Apr. 14 A general round-up of goondahs, or roughs, took place this morning [in Calcutta]. **1931** *Daily Tel.* 21 May 11/5 They [*sc.* the Cawnpore massacres] started through the importation of 'goondas' (hired rowdies). **1960** 'S. HARVESTER' *Chinese Hammer* xxv. 202 Bloated millionaires and lean *goonda* thugs. **1969** *Times of India* 30 July 7/2 The Lt.-Governor had denied having stated that anti-social elements or goondas enjoyed the patronage of politicians. **1970** *Guardian* 14 Apr. 11/6 Since the parties let their goondas loose in the streets to plunder and terrorise, business has been redeploying itself in safer parts of India.

goondie ('gu:ndı). *Austral.* Also **gundy**. [Aboriginal.] = GUNYAH.

1890 'R. BOLDREWOOD' *Col. Reformer* xvii. 204 There were a dozen 'goondies' to be visited. **1908** MRS. A. GUNN *We of Never-Never* xiv. 186 The man..rode out of the gundy camp, and out of our lives. **1966** BAKER *Austral. Lang.* (ed. 2) vi. 80 We have taken the words..gunyah, goondie or gundie,..from the Aborigines and used them to denote huts or shelters.

gooney, variant of GONY.

goonge, variant of GONG *sb.*[1], *Obs.*

Goonhilly ('gu:nhılı). Also 7 **gunnelly**, 7– **gonhelly**, (9 **gunhillee**). [Named after Goonhilly Downs in Cornwall.] A Cornish pony.

1640 *Wits Recreat.* Epigr. 108 Tall Afer..Mounts a Gunnelly and on foot doth ride. **1674–91** RAY *S. & E.C. Words* 83 *Gonhelly*, a Cornish horse. **1715** tr. *C'tess D'Aunoy's Wks.* 374 The House that cover'd the Princess's Gonhelly, did so glitter with Precious Stones. **1797** POLWHELE *Old Eng. Gent.* 80 On his half-goonhilly he sat still. **1848** C. A. JOHNS *Week at Lizard* 158 A strong punch, and spirited horse is, with us, generally called a Goonhilly. **1880** *W. Cornw. Gloss., Goonhilly.*

goonie, variant of GONY.

goonne, obs. form of GUN.

goop (gu:p). *slang* (orig. *U.S.*). [Arbitrary formation; cf. GOOF *sb.*] A stupid or fatuous person. So **'goopy** *a.* fatuous, esp. fatuously amorous; stupid.

[**1900** G. BURGESS (*title*) Goops, and how to be them. Manual of manners for polite infants, inculcating many juvenile virtues, both by precept and example.] **1914** *Dialect Notes* IV. 107 (Kansas) *Goop*, a boor. **1918** *Story-Teller* Feb. 695/2 You rabbit-faced goop! **1925** N. VENNER *Imperfect Impostor* i, Go on, it's a bargain. I'll be the poor goop of this piece. **1926** *Chambers's Jrnl.* Dec. 770/1 The baggage always affects strangers like that... Makes 'em frightfully goopy till they discover her for the cockatrice she is. **1929** 'A. BERKELEY' *Wychford Poisoning Case* xx. 250 Oh, ass, dolt, fool, goop and *mutt*! **1946** WODEHOUSE *Joy in Morning* i. 8 My first emotion..had been a gentle pity for the unfortunate goop slated to step up the aisle with her. **1955** *Sci. Amer.* Apr. 84/1 Americans are shocked when they go abroad and discover whole groups of people behaving like goops—eating with their fingers, making noises and talking while eating. **1959** I. & P. OPIE *Lore & Lang. Schoolch.* x. 179 A person who is 'wanting in the upper storey' is:..dotty, goofy or goopy. **1966** *Punch* 21 Dec. 908/1, I am very jealous of my position as chairman of *Juke Box Jury*,..and I don't believe one can be a placid smiling goop all the time.

goopher, var. GOOFER[2].

goor (gʊə(r)). Also **ghoor, gur.** [Hindi *guṛ*, Hindustani (Deccan) *gūṛ*.] A coarse variety of sugar made in India.

1835 BURNES *Trav. Bokhara* (ed. 2) I. 241 From extensive plantations of cane, 'goor', a coarse kind of sugar is produced. **1872** E. BRADDON *Life in India* ii. 28 Combinations of sugar, ghoor (raw sugar with the molasses in it) curds and ghee. **1886** A. H. CHURCH *Food Grains Ind.* 59 It is..then mixed with water, being eaten with gur, curds, &c. **1934** M. L. DARLING *Wisdom & Waste in Punjab Village* 26 Half a dozen figures were crushing cane... I stopped, and at once they uncovered a pan and brought me a handful of the warm gur beloved of horse and peasant. **1965** E. LINTON *World in Grain of Sand* x. 173 The harvesting of sugar cane followed by its crude and simple processing into 'gur'—the round brown unrefined sugar cakes. **1969** *Femina* (Bombay) 26 Dec. 57/2 Add a pinch of camphor and if desired grated gur (jaggery).

goora, gooral, variants of GOUROU (nut), GORAL.

goord(e, goordy, obs. ff. GOURD[1], GOURDY.

goore, goorge, obs. ff. GORE *sb.*[2], GORGE.

goorie, goory (ˈgʊərɪ). *N.Z. slang.* Also goori. [Corruption of Maori *kuri*.] A (mongrel) dog. Hence as a term of abuse.

1937 in PARTRIDGE *Dict. Slang* 343/2. **1942** R. FINLAYSON *Sweet Beulah Land* 57 You can tell it's no more'n a goorie fight to him. **1959** M. GEE in C. K. Stead *N.Z. Short Stories* (1966) 272 It's over to you, you goori. **1970** *N.Z. Listener* 12 Oct. 13/1 'Are you going to marry her?' I said. 'Why should I? Let go of me, you goorie,' he said.

goormaunde, obs. form of GOURMAND.

gooroo, obs. var. GURU.

goosander (guːˈsændə(r)). Also 7 **gossander,** 8–9 **gooseander.** [Of obscure formation. If the first element is GOOSE, the word must be of some antiquity in English, to allow of the shortened vowel (*goss-*) which appears in the earliest forms; with the ending *-ander* cf. BERGANDER and ON. *ǫnd* (pl. *ander*).] The bird *Mergus merganser*, allied to the ducks but having a sharply serrated bill.

1622 DRAYTON *Poly-olb.* xxv. 65 The Gossander with them, my goodly Fennes doe show, His head as Ebon blacke, the rest as white as Snow. **1658** R. FRANCK *North. Mem.* (1821) 316 Nor would not any man think those conceptions very sordid, to prefer the goose to the gossander. **1674** RAY *Collect. Words, Water Fowl* 94 The Gossander or Bergander: Merganser, Aldr. **1766** PENNANT *Zool.* (1768) II. 438 Mr. Willoughby too suspects that its male represents some bird similar to the Goosander. **1774** GOLDSM. *Nat. Hist.* III. 270 The Gooseander feeds upon fish for which it dives. **1848** C. A. JOHNS *Week at Lizard* 334 Goosander (*Mergus Merganser*).—Often seen in the Helford river. **1863** KINGSLEY *Water-Bab.* vii. 269 Smews and goosanders, divers and loons. **1882** HARDY in *Proc. Berw. Nat. Club* IX. 552 March 2nd, Goosander on the Teviot.

goose (guːs), *sb. Pl.* geese (giːs). Forms: *Sing.* 1 gós, 3–6 gos(e, (4 guos, 5 goce), 4–7 goos, 5 ghoos, goys, (6 gosse, gouse), 6 *Sc.* guis(s, (guss, gwis), 6, 8–9 *Sc.* guse, 5– goose. *Pl.* 1 gés, gees, 3 ges, 3–4 gies, (4 gyes, 6 giese), 3–5 gees, 4–5 geys(e, 6 *Sc.* geis(s)e, 4, 6 gese, (5 gess, ghees, 7 geose ?), 5– geese. [Common Teut.: OE. *gós* (pl. *gés*) = Fris. *gôs, gôz*, MDu. (and Du.) *gans*, OHG. (MHG. and G.) *gans*, ON. *gás* (Sw. *gås*, Da. *gaas*):—OTeut. **gans-* (cons.-stem):—OAryan **ghans-*, whence L. *anser* (for **hanser*), Gr. *χήν*, Skr. *hansá* masc., *hansí* fem., Lith. *žąsis*, and OIr. *géis* swan. Connexion with GANDER is doubtful.]

1. a. A general name for the large web-footed birds of the sub-family *Anserinæ* (family *Anatidæ*), usually larger than a duck, and smaller than a swan, including *Anser* and several allied genera.

Without distinctive addition or context, the word is applied to the common tame goose (*Anser domesticus*), which is descended from the wild grey or greylag goose (*A. ferus* or *cinereus*). The other numerous species are distinguished by adjuncts expressing colour, appearance, or habits, as ***black, blue, blue-winged, laughing, pink-footed, white-fronted goose***, etc.; habitat, as ***fen, marsh-goose***, etc.; native region, as ***American (wild), Canada, Chinese goose***, etc. See also BARNACLE-, BEAN-, BRENT-GOOSE, etc.

a **1000** *Riddles* xxv. 3 (Gr.) Hwilum ic græde swa gos. *c* **1000** *Laws of Ine* c. 70 (Schmid), x gees, xx henna. *a* **1100** *Ags. Voc.* in Wr.-Wülcker 284/12 *Anser* uel *ganra*, hwit gos. *Ganta* uel *auca*, græȝ gos. *a* **1225** *Ancr. R.* 128, & te valse ancre drauhð into hire hole & fret, ase þe uox deð, boðe ges & henhen. *c* **1300** *Havelok* 702 Hors, and swin..The gees, the hennes of the yerd. **1340** *Ayenb.* 32 Þo anlikneþ..to þe childe þet ne dar naȝt guo his way uor þe guos þ et blauþ. **1362** LANGL. *P. Pl.* A. IV. 38 Bothe my gees and my grys his gadelynges fetten. *c* **1386** CHAUCER *Reeve's T.* 217 This Millere..rosted hem a goos. *c* **1420** *Liber Cocorum* (1862) 32 Gose in a Hogge pot. **1489** CAXTON *Faytes of A.* II. xxxvii. 157 Had not be the crye of the ghoos..the cite of rome shulde haue be dystroyed. **1535** STEWART *Cron. Scot.* III. 222 Quhilk brocht with thame bayth guiss [and] gryce, and hen. **1604** *Extracts Aberd. Reg.* (1848) II. 251 Puir folkis geir, sic as geisse, foullis, peittis, and vtheris vivaris. **1612** WEBSTER *White Devil* v. I 3, *Mar.* Those words Ile make thee answere With thy heart bloud. *Fla.* Doe, like the geesse in the progresse. **1728** POPE *Dunc.* I. 211 Shall I..rob Rome's ancient geese of all their glories? **1766** PENNANT *Zool.* (1768) II. 450 The White Fronted Wild Goose. **1772** FORSTER in *Phil. Trans.* LXII. 415 The blue goose is as big as the white goose; and the laughing goose is of the size of the Canada or small grey goose. **1857** LIVINGSTONE *Trav.* xiv. 253 The Barotse valley contains great numbers of large black geese. **1859** DARWIN *Orig. Spec.* i. (1873) 28 The common goose has not given rise to any marked varieties. **1870** YEATS *Nat. Hist. Comm.* 314 In the fens of Lincolnshire, geese are kept in large numbers. **1893** NEWTON *Dict. Birds* 376 The largest living Goose is that called the Chinese, Guinea, or Swan-Goose, *Cygnopsis cygnoides*.

b. *spec.* The female bird: the male being the GANDER, and the young GOSLINGS.

c **1220** *Bestiary* 392 Ȝe fecceð ofte in ðe tun and te gandre and te gos. **1577** B. GOOGE *Heresbach's Husb.* IV. (1586) 163 b, Columella would have you keepe for every Gander, three Geese. **1622** [see 8, *goose-fair*]. **1692** L'ESTRANGE *Fables* ccxxii. 194 Why do you go Nodding, and Waggling so like a Fool, as if you were Hipshot? says the Goose to her Gosselin.

c. The flesh of this bird.

1533 ELYOT *Cast. Helthe* (1539) 30 Goose, is hard of digestion. **1726** *Brit. Apollo* (ed. 3) II. 648 Who eats goose on Michael's day, Shan't money lack his debts to pay. **1786** MRS. PIOZZI *Anecd. of Johnson* 103, I was saying to a friend one day, that I did not like goose; one smells it so while it is roasting, said I.

d. In phrases and proverbial sayings. ***all (his) geese are swans***: he invariably exaggerates or over-estimates; so ***to turn geese into swans, every goose a swan. all right*** (or ***sound***) ***on the goose***: (*U.S.*) politically orthodox. ***the old woman is picking her geese***: it is snowing. ***to cook*** (rarely ***do***) ***one's goose*** (see COOK *v.* 4 b). ***to say bo to a goose*** (see BO *int.* 2). ***to shoe the goose***: to spend one's time in trifling or in unnecessary labour. ***goose without gravy***: (*Naut.*) a bloodless flogging. ***gone goose***: see GONE *ppl. a.* 1. ***to kill the goose that laid*** or ***lays the golden eggs***, to destroy a source of one's wealth by one's own heedless action; to sacrifice future advantage to the greed of the moment; also used allusively. See also GANDER 1 b.

14.. *Why I Can't be Nun* 254 in *E.E.P.* (1862) 144 He schalle be put owte of company, And scho the gose. *c* **1460** *Towneley Myst.* ii. 84 Let furth youre geyse, the fox will preche. **1476** SIR J. PASTON in *P. Lett.* No. 777 III. 163 As for the Castell of Shene, ther is no mor in it but Colle and hys mak, and a goose may get it; but in no wyse I wold not that wey. [**1484** CAXTON *Esope* (1967) 190 This fable sayth of a man whiche had a goos that leyd euery day an egge of gold.] **1562** J. HEYWOOD *Prov. & Epigr.* (1867) 153 Steale a goose, and sticke downe a fether. *Ibid.* 186 A greene goose ..is farre the swetter. **1583** STUBBES *Anat. Abus.* II. (1882) 31 Then may he go sue yᵉ goose, for house gets he none. **1589** *Pasquil's Ret.* C, Euery Goose..must goe for a Swan, and whatsoeuer he speakes, must be Canonicall. **1589** LYLY *Pappe w. Hatchet* III. 404 A man..had a goose, which euerie daie laid him a golden egge; hee..kild his goose, thinking to haue a mine of golde in her bellie, and finding nothing but dung..wisht his goose aliue. **1604** BRETON *Grinello's Fort.* (Grosart) 5/1 Yet I can doe something else, then shooe the Goose for my liuing. **1621** BURTON *Anat. Mel.* Democr. to Rdr. 39 All his Geese are swannes. **1622** MABBE tr. *Alemans' Guzman d'Alf.* 133 There is no more pitty to be taken of her then to see a goose goe bare-foote. **1624** BP. MOUNTAGU *Gagg* 90 With Catholikes euery Pismire is a Potentate; as euery Goose a Swan. **1640** *Wizard* (MS.) (N.), He hath the goose by the neck. **1649** *Woodstock Scuffle* xl. in Scott *Woodstock* App. to Introd., There's not a man..can say (Boh!)..to a goose. **1659** HOWELL *Proverbs* I To steal a Goose, and give the giblets in almes. *a* **1700** B. E. *Dict. Cant. Crew*, s.v., *Find fault with a Fat Goose*, or without a Cause. **1692** L'ESTRANGE *Fables* cccii. 264 Sauce for a Goose is Sauce for a Gander. **1845** J. R. PLANCHÉ *Golden Fleece* I. 7 To save my bacon I must cook his goose! **1849** C. K. SHARPE *Let.* 10 Sept., Corr. 1888 II. 597 [They] may be thankful that she did not 'do their goose for them', to use a vulgar phrase. **1856** MRS. S. ROBINSON *Kansas* (ed. 3) 252 All persons who could not answer 'All right on the goose', according to their definition of right, were.. threatened with death. **1857** *Providence Jrnl.* 18 June (Bartlett), To seek for political flaws is no use, His opponents will find he is 'sound on the goose'. **1860** TROLLOPE *Framley P.* xlii, Chaldicotes..is a cooked goose, as far as Sowerby is concerned. **1862** G. DODD *Where do We get It?* ii. 103 The natives adopted a reckless way of cutting down the trees in order to obtain the sap; but they are now gradually accustoming themselves to a more economical method—they preserve the 'goose that lays the golden eggs'. **1867** SMYTH *Sailor's Word-bk.*, *Goose without gravy*. **1884** *Sat. Rev.* 5 July 25/1 The besetting temptation which leads local historians to turn geese into swans. **1887** W. E. NORRIS *Major & Minor* v, If Brian had only known how immensely he had risen in her respect by the not very extraordinary display of talent and ability which he had just made, he would doubtless have hastened to kill the goose that laid the golden eggs by playing classical compositions till he wearied her. **1917** GALSWORTHY *Five Tales* (1918) 77 You're getting a thousand a year out of my fees. Mistake to kill the goose that lays the golden eggs. I'll make it twelve hundred. **1921** T. R. ST.-JOHNSTON *Islanders of Pacific* 295 Even an insouciant native hesitates to kill the goose that lays his 'golden eggs', for the tapping of the crown is generally fatal to the palm-tree. **1923** D. H. LAWRENCE *Birds, Beasts & Flowers* 207 Is that you, American Eagle? Or are you the goose that lays the golden egg? **1930** A. E. HOUSMAN *Let.* 21 Mar. (1971) 293 On the one hand I must thank and congratulate you, but on the other you have cooked your own goose. **1935** T. S. ELIOT *Murder in Cath.* i. 25 Leave well alone, Or your goose may be cooked and eaten to the bone. **1946** W. S. MAUGHAM *Then & Now* xii. 71 'I can count on your discretion, Messer Niccolo? My life would be short if it were discovered that I have told you what I have.' 'I know. But I am not one to kill the goose that lays the golden eggs.' **1965** *Melody Maker* 25 Sept. 20 Let's hope that promoters have learned from past experience and don't kill the geese that lay the golden pop eggs.

e. With allusion to the supposed stupidity of the goose.

1583 GOLDING *Calvin on Deut.* xviii. 105/2 If his father let him haue his swindge lyke a goose: hee putteth the halter about his neck. **1584** FENNER *Def. Ministers* (1587) 40 He would thinke vs more simple then a goose, which will run from the Foxe. *a* **1586** SIDNEY *Arcadia* III. (1633) 237 Where this goose (you see) puts downe his head, before there be any thing neere to touch him. **1780** MRS. COWLEY *Belle's Stratagem* v. i, I ha'n't slept to-night, for thinking of plots to plague Doricourt;—and they drove one another out of my head so quick, that I was as giddy as a goose, and could make nothing of 'em. **1818** SCOTT *Rob Roy* xxvi, 'A twa-leggit creature, wi' a goose's head and a hen's heart.'

f. Hence *fig.* A foolish person, a simpleton.

1547 *Homilies* I. *Agst. Contention* II. (1859) 138 Shall I stand still, like a goose or a fool, with my finger in my mouth? *a* **1553** UDALL *Royster D.* IV. iii. (Arb.) 64 Go to you goose. **1588** *Marprel. Epist.* (Arb.) 19, I perceiue you will prooue a goose. **1624** BP. MOUNTAGU *Gagg* 327 Can this Goose gaggle against this? **1655** MOUFET & BENNET *Health's Improv.* (1746) 170 He did play the very Goose himselfe. **1807–8** SYD. SMITH *Plymley's Lett.*, *Catholics* (ed. 11) 5, I have always told you from the time of our boyhood, that you were a bit of a goose. **1861** *Sat. Rev.* 21 Sept. 303 If he was goose enough to be seriously and permanently angry at his wife having [etc.]. **1887** R. N. CAREY *Uncle Max* xiv. 110 What a goose I was to leave my muff behind me.

g. With allusion to the hissing noise made by the goose; esp. *Theat. slang* (see quots. 1805, 1865).

1805 C. L. LEWES *Mem.* IV. 180 By some it is said the 'goose' is in the house. **1809** MALKIN *Gil Blas* II. viii. ¶ 5 [We] began hissing, to remind him of his first appearance at Madrid. The goose grated harsh upon his tympanum. **1865** *Slang Dict.* s.v., 'To get the goose'..signifies to be hissed while on the stage. **18..** TENNYSON in *Mem.* (1897) II. i. 14 [Requirements for blank verse]. A fine ear for vowel-sounds, and the kicking of the geese out of the boat (i.e. doing away with sibilations).

2. Applied with distinguishing prefix to certain other birds of the same or a related family, as **Cape Barren goose** (*Cereopsis novæ-hollandiæ*), **Egyptian** or **Nile goose** (*Chenalopex ægyptiaca*), **spur-winged goose** (the African genus *Plectropterus*), etc.; also to certain sea-birds like or likened to a true goose, as the SOLAN-GOOSE. **Mother Carey's goose** (see quot. 1772–84); **sly goose** (see quot. 1844).

1772–84 COOK *Voy.* (1790) IV. 1272 Another sort, which is the largest of the petrels, and called by seamen, Mother Carey's goose, is found in abundance. **1843** J. BACKHOUSE *Visit Austral. Col.* vi. 75 Five Pelicans and some Cape Barren Geese, were upon the beach. **1844** W. H. MAXWELL *Sports & Adv. Scotl.* xxxvii. (1855) 293 The sheldrake.. from its wide awake habits, acquiring the Orcadian sobriquet of the *sly-goose*. **1884** BOLDREWOOD *Melb. Mem.* II. 22 The pied goose..were our chief sport and sustenance.

†**3.** ***Winchester goose***: a certain venereal disorder (sometimes simply *a goose*); also, a prostitute (see quot. 1778). *Obs.*

[**1591** SHAKS. *I Hen. VI*, I. iii. 53 *Winch.* Gloster, thou wilt answere this before the Pope. *Glost.* Winchester Goose, I cry, a Rope, a Rope. **1606** —— *Tr. & Cr.* v. x. 55 My feare is this: Some galled Goose of Winchester would hisse.] **1598** FLORIO s.v. *Carolo*. **1611** COTGR., *Clapoir*, a botch in the Groyne, or yard; a winchester goose. **1630** J. TAYLOR (Water-P.) *Wks.* I. 105/2 Then ther's a Goose that breeds at Winchester, And of all Geese, my mind is least to her. **1661** WEBSTER *Cure for Cuckold* F j a, This Informer..had belike some private dealings with her, and there got a Goose..This fellow in revenge for this, informs against the Bawd that kept the house. **1727** BOYER *Eng.-Fr. Dict.*, A Winchester Goose (or swelling in the Groin) *un Poulain*. **1778** *Eng. Gazetteer* (ed. 2) s.v. *Southwark*, In the times of popery here were no less than 18 houses on the Bankside, licensed by the Bishops of Winchester..to keep whores, who were, therefore, commonly called Winchester Geese.

4. †(*game of*) ***goose***: A game played with counters on a board divided into compartments, in some of which a goose was depicted (*obs.*). [Cf. F. *jeu de l'oie*, Du. *ganzenspel*.] ***fox and geese*** (see FOX *sb.* 16 d); also one of the pieces in this game.

1597 *Stationers' Reg.* 16 June (Arb.) III. 21 John Wolfe entered..the newe and most pleasant game of the goose. **1670** G. H. *Hist. Cardinals* III. III. 294, I am like those who play at Goose. **1770** GOLDSM. *Des. Vill.* 232 The Twelve Good Rules, the Royal Game of Goose. **1801** STRUTT *Sports & Past.* IV. ii. (1876) 418 To play this game [Fox and Geese] there are seventeen pieces, called geese. *Ibid.* 438 It is called the game of the goose, because at every fourth and fifth compartment in succession a goose is depicted, and if the cast thrown by the player falls upon a goose, he moves forward double the number of his throw.

allusively. **1823** BYRON *Juan* XII. lviii, For good society is but a game, 'The royal game of Goose', as I may say.

5. a. A tailor's smoothing-iron. Pl. gooses.

[So called from the resemblance of the handle to the shape of a goose's neck.]

1605 SHAKS. *Macb.* II. iii. 17 Come in Taylor, here you may rost your Goose. **1607** DEKKER *Knt.'s Conjur.* (1842) 36 Euery man being armed with his sheeres and pressing iron, which he call's there his goose. *a* **1680** BUTLER *Rem.* (1759) II. 348 His Tongue is a kind of Taylor's Goose or hot Press, with which he sets the last Gloss upon his coarse decayed Wares. **1778** FOOTE *Trip Calais* I. Wks. 1799 II. 342 It is the first I ever heard of a tailor's goose hissing! **1841** J. T. HEWLETT *Parish Clerk* I. 281 The seam being sewed up, he required the assistance of the goose to press it. **1881** C. GIBBON *Heart's Problem* i. (1884) 5 Teddy spat on the goose to test its heat, then polished it vigorously, and began to iron the collar of a coat.

b. (See quot.)

1886 *Chester Gloss.*, *Goose*, hatting term, an implement used in the curling of hat brims.

6. dial. ***geese and goslings*** (cf. GOSLING 4).

1854 Miss Baker *Northamptonsh. Gloss.*, *Geese and Goslings*, the blossoms of the *salix*; so denominated from the fancied resemblance to a young gosling newly hatched. **1866** *Treas. Bot.* 543/1 Goose and Goslings, *Orchis Morio*. **1889** Hurst *Horsham* Gloss., *Geese and Goslins*, the fully blown and half blown flowers of the willow.

7. *attrib.* and *Comb.*

a. attrib., as ***goose-breast***, ***-down***, ***-dung***, ***-fat***, ***-feather***, ***-giblet***, ***-head***, ***-look***, ***-pond***, ***-tribe***, ***-turd*** (†also *attrib.* referring to colour; hence ***goose-turd-green***), ***-yard***; ***goose-like*** adj.

1891 W. Morris in Mackail *Life W. Morris* (1899) II. 261 *Goose-breast colour. **1904** *Daily Chron.* 19 Mar. 8/5 Smoked goose-breasts. **1963** A. Simon *Conc. Encycl. Gastron.* vii. 565 Minced Goosebreast. **1866** Howells *Venet. Life* xv. 208 A gentle snow-fall of *goose-down. **1710** T. Fuller *Pharm. Extemp.* 52 Take..*Goose-dung..2 ounces. **1815** *Sixteen & Sixty* ii. ii, Shut that damned ugly mouth instantly, or I'll stuff it with soap cerate and *goose-fat. *c* **1450** *ME. Med. Bk.* (Heinrich) 82 Take a *gose feþer, and do awey þe foom aboue. **1545** Ascham *Toxoph.* (Arb.) 130 A sely poore gouse fether could not plese him to shoote wythal. **1820** Scott *Abbot* xv, His lance is no goose-feather, as Dan's ribs can tell. **1539** *gose gyblet [see HARE *sb.* 2]. **1599** Porter *Angry Wom. Abingt.* (Percy Soc.) 40 Tis an olde prouerbe and a true, Goose giblets are good meate, olde sacke better then new. *a* **1605** Montgomerie *Misc. Poems* x. 5 They get ay a good *goosheid In recompense of all thair pane. **1552** Huloet, *Gose lyke, or pertayninge to a gose, *anserinus*. **1605** Shaks. *Macb.* v. iii. 13 Thou cream-fac'd Loone: Where got'st thou that *Goose-looke. **1824** Miss Mitford *Village* Ser. i. 197 A ducking in the *goose-pond. **1831** Bonaparte *A. Wilson's Amer. Ornith.* IV. 341 *Anas*, or *Goose tribe. **1546** J. Heywood *Prov.* (1867) 62 Bearyng no more rule, than a *goose turd in tems. **1610** B. Jonson *Alch.* iv. ii, The citizens praise her tires, And my lord's goose-turd bands. ? **15..** *Will of C. White* (Somerset Ho.), A gowne lyned of gosetourde grene. **1597** Gerarde *Herbal* i. lxviii. §2. 94 Greenish yellow, or as we terme it, a goose turde greene. **1863** Browning *Ring & Bk.* xi. 1195 A perfect *goose-yard cackle of complaint.

b. objective, as ***goose-crammer***, ***-gagger***, ***-stealer***; ***goose-eating*** vbl. sb.; ***goose-bearing***, ***-chasing*** adjs.

1802 Bingley *Anim. Biog.* (1813) III. 438 The *Goose-bearing bernacle. **1596** Harington *Metam. Ajax* (1814) 103, I love not to ride with these *goose-chasing youths. **1828** Miss Mitford *Village* Ser. iii. (1863) 119 The Penge is almost peopled with duck-rearers and *goose-crammers. **1566** *Acc.* in T. Sharp *Cov. Myst.* (1825) 214 Payd att the *gose etynge to the mynstrelles..xij *d.* **1624** Bp. R. Mountagu *Gagg* 281 Goe learn to speak and write, Sir giddy *Goose-gagger, and then vndertake to stop the Protestants mouthes. **1565–73** *Durham Depos.* (Surtees) 104, I am neyther *goossteler nor steg steiler.

c. similative, as ***goose-gaggler***; ***goose-footed***, ***-green***, ***-grey***, ***-headed*** adjs.

1735 Somerville *Chase* iv. 398 O'er yon dank rushy Marsh The sly *Goose-footed Proler bends his Course. **1624** Bp. R. Mountagu *Gagg* 190 And yet this giddy *Goose-gaggler must prate..against the Church of England. **1614** B. Jonson *Barth. Fair* ii. i. Another [ballad] of *Goose-greene-starch, and the Deuill. *a* **1693** Aubrey *Lives*, *Sir W. Petty* (1898) II. 145 His eies are a kind of *goose-grey. **1581** N. Burne *Disput.* 187 b, Daft Abbotis ..*guseheaddit Personis.

8. a. Special comb.: **goose-barnacle** = BARNACLE *sb.*[2] 2; **goose-beak**, a name given to the dolphin from the shape of its snout (*Cent. Dict.*); **goose-bone**, a bone of a goose, *esp.* one used as a weather-guide; **goose bumps** *N. Amer.* = GOOSE-FLESH 2; **goose-cart**, a special cart for taking geese to market; **goose-chase** (see WILD-GOOSE-CHASE); **goose-club**, an association formed to provide the members with geese; †**goose-cree** (see quot. and CREW *sb.*[2]); **goose dinner** (see *goose match*); **goose drownder** *U.S. dial.* (see quot. 1969); **goose-dung-ore** *Min.*, an impure iron sinter containing silver; **goose-eye**, a pattern used in weaving; **goose-fair**, a fair held in certain English towns (still at Nottingham) about Michaelmas, when geese are in season; **goose-file** = *single* or *Indian file*; **goose-fish** *U.S.*, the angler or fishing-frog (*Lophius piscatorius*); **goose game** *Cricket*, very cautious play adopted by a batsman; **goose-gamer**, one who plays the goose game (*these terms no longer current*); †**goose-gate** [GATE *sb.*[2] 8], right of pasture for a goose; **goose-gull**, a local name of the greater black-backed gull (*Larus marinus*); **goose liver** = FOIE GRAS; **goose man** *N.Z.*, one who operates a goose saw; **goose match** *Cricket* (see quots.); **goose-mouth** (see quot.); **goose-mussel** = BARNACLE *sb.*[2] 2; **goose-oven**, a stove for heating a tailor's goose; **goose-paddle** *v. trans.* (*nonce-wd.*), to propel by paddling like a goose; †**goose-pan** *Sc.*, app. a large stew-pan; †**goose-par** = *goose-pen* (*a*); **goose-pen**, (*a*) a pen or enclosure for geese; †(*b*) a quill pen; **goose-pie**, a pie made of goose, etc.; **goose pimples** = GOOSE-FLESH 2; **goose-pudding** (see quot. 1892); **goose-riding** (see quot. and cf. *gander-pulling*); **goose-rump**, in a horse, a croup or rump falling suddenly away to the tail; hence ***goose-rumped*** adj.; **goose saw** *N.Z.* (see quot. 1957); also *ellipt.*; **goose-shot**, a particular size of shot used for shooting wild geese; **goose-silver-ore** = *goose-dung-ore* (above); **goose-teal**, 'the English name for a very small goose of the genus *Nettopus*' (Morris *Austral Eng.* 1898); **goose-trap**, a trap for a 'goose', a quibble, sophism; also *U.S.*, a swindle; **goose-yoke** *U.S.*, a yoke to hamper the movements of a goose. Also GOOSE-BILL, GOOSE-FLESH, GOOSE-GRASS, etc.

1726 *Brit. Apollo* (ed. 3) II. 648 Just rose from picking of *goose-bones. **1886** Bynner *A. Surriage* xxi. 231 My father used to say..there's no chance of a clearing when the wind backs round. Mother never heeds the wind; she goes by the goose-bone. **1933** C. Miller *Lamb in Bosom* xi. 148 She rubbed down the skin of her arms and legs where *goose-bumps stood on every pore as though it were cold weather. **1968** *Publ. Amer. Dial. Soc.* XLIX. 17 *Goose bumps*..seems to be replacing both *goose flesh* and *goose pimples*. **1970** *Washington Post* 30 Sept. D3/1, I no longer get goose-bumps before a game. **1895** J. J. Raven *Hist. Suffolk* 242 To get the advantage of the later markets, a *goose-cart was invented, four stories high. **1895** *Sat. Rev.* 17 Aug. 198/1 The cackling Cust..has fresh leisure for fresh *goose-chases. **1859** Sala *Gas-light & D.* ii. 16 Turkeys from the country; *Goose Clubs in town. **1674** Ray *N.C. Words* 134 A *Geose or Goose cree [*mispr.* Grose cree], a hut to put Geese in. **1929–33** in Wentworth *Amer. Dial. Dict.*, *Goose drownder. **1969** *Daily Progress* (Charlottesville, Va.) 22 Aug. 4/6 Other two-word names for a heavy rain.. are: bresh- or brush-mover, bridge-lifter, goose drownder, gully-washer, sand-packer, toad-strangler, and trash-mover. **1858** Greg & Lettsom *Min.* 277 The mineral ..*goose-dung ore, has been shown to be an impure variety of iron sinter. **1957** Simpson & Weir *Weaver's Craft* (ed. 8) xii. 151 The patterns most generally used for tweeds are: 1. Twill... 4. Bird eye twill. 5. *Goose eye. **1960** G. Lewis *Handbk. Crafts* 121 For this purpose [*sc.* variety] twill, goose-eye and rosepath are all excellent... Goose-eye with its diamond-shaped pattern is perhaps best employed in a rug made in one colour on a different-coloured warp. **1622** Breton *Str. Newes* (Grosart) 7/1 No man must denie his neighbours Goose his Gander, for feare of wanting Goslings at *Goose Faire. **1970** *Daily Mail* 3 Oct. 7/1 In Nottingham, stalls at the famous Goose Fair were overturned by a gale. **1876** Jas. Grant *Hist. India* I. xlviii. 244/2 The old way had been the 'Indian file', following each other in succession (vulgarly called by the soldiers '*goose-file'). **1859** Bartlett *Dict. Amer.*, **Goose-fish*. See *Devil-fish*. **1884–5** *Riverside Nat. Hist.* (1888) III. 295 The most common of the American names, 'goose-fish', alludes to its capacity to master and ingest the well-known bird in its capacious maw. **1899** J. C. Snaith *Willow the King* xiv. 224 Don't play the *goose game. Hard slogging's the sort o' thing for Grace. **1928** *Daily Tel.* 26 June 17/1 Jupp took four wickets for 37 runs. The batsmen would not go to fetch him, and nearly all of them are free players by inclination and habit. They are not good *goose-gamers. **1739** *Bewholm Inclos. Act* 2 Each cottage..hath only one *goose-gate in the fallow field. **1885** Swainson *Prov. Names Birds* 208 *Goose gull (Ireland). **1860** Dickens in *All Year Round* 7 Apr. 560/1, I set him up in business in the *goose-liver line. **1958** *Catal. County Stores Taunton* June 20 Goose Liver Purée with Truffles.. a glass 3/9. **1967** L. Deighton *London Dossier* 55 Sandwiches..with unusual fillings like game pâté, rillette, and goose liver. **1943** J. A. W. Bennett in *Amer. Speech* XVIII. 85 The timber trade..has supplied a wide variety of occupational terms..**goose man* ('drag' and 'goose' are various types of saw; cf. U.S. *drag-saw*). **1957** *N.Z. Timber Jrnl.* July 49/1 *Gooseman*, the operator of a goose saw. **1885** P. M. Thornton *Harrow School* xiv. 339 The *Goose Match is the last game of cricket played in the year at Harrow. A goose dinner follows. **1905** H. A. Vachell *Hill* ii. 27 The Goose Match, the last cricket-match of the year, played between the Eleven and the Old Boys, on the nearest Saturday to Michaelmas Day. **1970** *Sunday Tel.* 27 Sept. 29/8 He refers to the rained off Goose Match at Harrow, cancelled, he believes, for the first time in 165 years. **1879** *Leeds Mercury* 9 May, The animal [a horse] had what was called a '*goose' mouth.—His Honour: What is that?—Plaintiff: Lapping over like a hare. **1863** Wood *Nat. Hist.* III. 646 The common *Goose-mussel or Duck-barnacle. **1877** *5 Yrs.' Penal Servitude* iii. 90 One man specially attends to the '*goose-oven'. **1845** Jerrold *St. Giles & St. James* (1851) xxvi. 265 Whether the thing to be seen is a lord mayor's coach..or a zany on a river, *goose-paddled in a washing-tub, the sons of Adam will throng to the sight. **1420** *Inv.* in *Lincoln Chapter Acc. Bk.* A. 2. 30. lf. 69, 1 *gose-panne. *c* **1575** Balfour *Practicks* (1754) 235 The air sall haue..ane mekle and litle pan, ane guse pan, ane frying pan [etc.]. **1552** Huloet, *Gose parre [*sic*; **1572** *gose penne], or coupe, or francke to feade gese in, *chenoboscion*. **1601** Shaks. *Twel. N.* iii. ii. 53 Let there bee gaulle enough in thy inke, though thou write with a *Goose-pen. **1712–14** Pope *Rape Lock* iv. 52 Here sighs a Jar, and there a *Goose-pie talks. **1766** Goldsm. *Vic. W.* vi, I never dispute your abilities at making a goose-pie. **1889** *Cent. Dict.*, **Goose-pimples*, the pimples of goose-flesh. **1914** *Dialect Notes* IV. 155 Don't stay in bathing so long that you're all goose-pimples when you come out. **1956** L. Sieveking in *Plays of Year* XV. 255 'E ain't arf got a wicked fyce, 'asn't 'e. Makes one come out in goose-pimples to look at 'im. **1959** *Times* 5 Nov. 14/6 A make-up man kept dodging forward to cover up goose-pimples on the bare shoulders of the two parasolled and picture-hatted belles. **1547** Boorde *Introd. Knowl.* xxx. (1870) 199 & coppyd thinges standeth vpon theyr [women's] hed, within ther kerchers, lyke a codpece or a *gose-podynge. **1892** *Encycl. Cookery* (ed. Garrett) I. 707 In some parts of England, especially in Yorkshire, the people prepare a pudding which they term..Goose Pudding, to be served with Goose. **1785** Grose *Dict. Vulg. Tongue*, **Goose-riding*, a goose being suspended by the legs..a number of men on horseback riding full speed attempt to pull off the head, which, if they effect, the goose is their prize. This has been practised in Derbyshire within the memory of persons now living. **1696** *Lond. Gaz.* No. 3202/4 Rid away with..a brown Mare..a Rose Tail, a *Goose Rump. **1799** *Sporting Mag.* XIV. 185 The Goose-rump is..another angular infringement of Hogarth's curve of beauty. **1679** *Poor Robin's Intell.* in *Sporting Mag.* XXXIX. 61 Sour headed, saddle backed, *goose rumped. **1836** *Penny Cycl.* V. 307/1 The Belgian horses have a great defect in the form of their hips and in the croup, which falls suddenly towards the tail, which is called in England being goose-rumped. **1943** J. A. W. Bennett in *Amer. Speech* XVIII. 85 [In New Zealand] 'drag' and '*goose' are various types of saw; cf. U.S. *drag-saw*. **1950** *Landfall* IV. 125 The planer..spits out faced boards for the tailer-out to stack by the goose saw. **1957** *Brit. Commonw. Forest Terminol.* II. 163 *Pendulum* [*saw*], a crosscut circular saw mounted on a swinging arm and moved down to and across the timber to be sawn. Syn. *Swing saw*, *Swinging crosscut saw*, *Goose saw* (N.Z.). *a* **1659** Cleveland *Poems* (1677) 129 So long as there is *Goose-shot to be had for Money. **1698** Wallis in *Phil. Trans.* XX. 6 A Hole about the Bigness of a Goose-shot. **1789** *Amer. Museum* V. 580 A major..received a wound in the cheek with a goose shot. **1898** P. L. Ford *Tattle-Tales Cupid* 51 It passeth human intelligence how Freddy could inspire any sort of feeling except an intense longing for a gun loaded with goose-shot. **1776** Seiferth tr. *Gellert's Metal. Chym.* 38 *Goose silver ore. **1610** Healey *St. Aug. Citie of God* v. x. Vives' Comm. 212 And what vse is there of these *goose-traps [L. *tricis illis et verborum laqueis*]? **1799** *Aurora* (Philad.) 31 Jan. (Th.), The gulls and goose-traps that have been sported for some time past all come from the shop in which the Washington Lottery wheels remain undrawn, and where a new goose-trap, the Amuskeag canal, was some time since hammered out. **1842** C. M. Kirkland *Forest Life* I. 120 A variety store, offering for sale every possible article of merchandize, from lace gloves to *goose-yokes, ox-chains, [etc.]. **1863** 'E. Kirke' *Southern Friends* iii. 48 One half of it [*sc.* a building] was sparsely occupied with..fishhooks, log chains, goose yokes, etc. **1879** B. F. Taylor *Summer-Savory* xvii. 138 And you find it, the variety store of a hundred years ago, where needles and crowbars, goose yokes and finger-rings, liquorice-stick and leather are to be had for cash or 'dicker'. **1896** J. C. Harris *Sister Jane* 2/3 Go show your grandmother how to make a goose-yoke.

b. In various plant-names, as †**goose-bane** = HENBANE; **goose-bean**, some Canadian plant; †**goose-chite**, agrimony (*Agrimonia Eupatoria*); **goose-corn**, (*a*) a kind of rush (*Juncus squarrosus*); (*b*) = GOOSE-GRASS 4; †**goose-hairif** = GOOSE-GRASS 2, HAIRIF; †**goose-nest**, ? the bird's-nest (*Neottia Nidus-avis*); †**goose-share** [? corruption of *-hairif*] = GOOSE-GRASS 2; **goose-tansy** = GOOSE-GRASS[1]; **goose-tongue**, (*a*) sneezewort (*Achillea Ptarmica*); (*b*) = GOOSE-GRASS 2; (*c*) a crowfoot (*Ranunculus Flammula*); **goose-tree**, the tree from which barnacle-geese were believed to be produced (cf. BARNACLE *sb.*[2] 1 *note*); **goose-weed** = GOOSE-GRASS 1; **goose-wheat** (see quot.).

1600 Surflet *Countrie Farme* i. xvi. 108 [He] may keepe them [geese]..from feeding of henbane, which some call the *goosebane. **1848** Selby in *Proc. Berw. Nat. Club* II. No. 6. 262 Specimens of the *Goose-bean of Canada. **1597** Gerarde *Herbal* Suppl., *Goosechite is Agrimonie. **1762** W. Hudson *Flora Angl.* 130 *Juncus culmo nudo*,..Moss-rush or *Goose-corn. **1776** Withering *Brit. Plants* I. 211 *Juncus squarrosus*..Goose Corn. **1808** Jamieson, *Goose-corn*, Field Brome-grass, Bromus secalinus, Linn. **1551** Turner *Herbal* i. D iiij, *Goosharethe called also Clyuer.. is named in Greeke, Aparine. **1579** Langham *Gard. Health* (1633) 290 Goose-heirife or Cleuer. **1578** Lyte *Dodoens* ii. lvii. 224 Some Herborists..because that the rootes be so tangled and wrapped like to a nest, have named it *Goosenest. **1605** Timme *Quersit.* i. xiii. 65 Double leafe, otherwise called goosenest. **1578** Lyte *Dodoens* iv. lxiv. 539 This herbe is called..in Englishe, Goosegrasse, Cliuer, and *Gooseshare. **1579** Langham *Gard. Health* (1633) 629 Drinke the iuyce of Tansie, and *Goosetansie. **1691** [see GOOSE-GRASS 1]. **1776** Withering *Brit. Plants* I. 307 *Potentilla Anserina*..Goose-tansey. **1738** Deering *Catal. Stirp.* 179 *Ptarmica*..Sneezewort..by some called *Goose Tongue. **1744–50** W. Ellis *Mod. Husbandm.* III. i. 114 (E.D.S.) The goose-tongue herb grows chiefly in marshy grounds. *a* **1824** Holdich *Weeds* (1825) 14 Hariff (*Galium aparine*)..Goosetongue. **1597** Gerarde *Herbal* iii. clxvii. 1391 Of the *Goose tree, Barnakle tree, or the tree bearing Geese. **1865** W. White *E. Eng.* II. 62 Broad margins of grass and *goose-weed. **1883** *Longm. Mag.* July 307 The trailing silverweed or gooseweed of our English roadsides. **1897** *Daily News* 10 Sept. 8/3 An inferior grain (used for chicken food mostly) called *goosewheat—a bearded variety, hardy and early.

Hence (*nonce-wds.*) †ˈ**goosedom**, stupidity; ˈ**goosehood**, the fact of being a goose; ˈ**gooseless** *a.*, without a goose; ˈ**gooseship**, a mock title.

1647 Ward *Simp. Cobler* 27 The gut-foundred goosdom, wherewith they are now surcingled and debauched. **1832** *Whistle-Binkie* (Scot. Songs) (1890) I. 113 Any gooseless gander. **1837** *Fraser's Mag.* XVI. 311 His Gooseship, the Right Dull of London. **1865** Carlyle *Fredk. Gt.* xviii. vii. (1872) VII. 225 Goosehood became too apparent. **1888** *Harper's Mag.* Dec. 158/1 The bestowal of turkeys upon the turkeyless and geese upon the gooseless.

goose (guːs), *v.* [f. GOOSE *sb.*]

1. *trans.* To press or iron with a tailor's 'goose'.

1808 Jamieson, To *Goose*, to iron linen cloths, *S.*, a word now nearly obsolete. **1859** Ramsay *Remin.* 189 To prepare them [her caps] for being ironed, or, as she said, to make them ready to be goosed.

2. *Theat. slang.* To hiss, to express disapproval of (a person or play) by hissing. (Cf. GOOSE *sb.* 1 g.)

1838 *Actors by Daylight* 31 Mar. 35 In every scene, O! think of me! And may they goose thee, when you die! **1853** *Househ. Words* 24 Sept. 77/1 Actors speak of..such and such a tragedy being 'damned' or 'goosed'. **1854** Dickens

Hard T. I. vi, He was goosed last night, he was goosed the night before last, he was goosed to-day. He has lately got in the way of being always goosed, and he can't stand it. **1866** *St. James's Mag.* XVI. 69, I tired of the stage, however, although I was never 'goosed' in my life.

3. *U.S.* (See quots.)

1859 BARTLETT *Dict. Amer.*, To *Goose Boots*, to repair them by putting on a new front half way up, and a new bottom. **1889** BARRÈRE & LELAND *Slang* (1897), *Goose* ..(American) to enlarge or repair boots, by a process generally known as footing, i.e. by putting in or adding pieces of leather.

4. *slang.* To make a 'goose' of, befool.

1889 in BARRÈRE & LELAND *Slang* (1897).

5. *slang.* To poke, tickle, etc., (a person) in a sensitive part, esp. the genital or anal regions; sometimes, more specifically, = FUCK *v.* I.

1879–80 *Pearl* (1970) 257, I don't like to see vulgar girls in the town Pull their clothes up, and stand to be goosed for a crown. **1881** F. GRIFFIN in J. R. Ackerley *My Father & Myself* (1968) xvii. 200 As soon as..I had learned the goose-step, I had learned to be goosed. **1906** *Dialect Notes* III. 138 *Goose*, to create nervous excitement in a person by pointing a finger at him or by touching or tickling him and making a peculiar whistle. **1932** J. FARRELL *Studs Lonigan* (1936) 106 Paulie slapped Denny's face. Denny bawled... Paulie goosed him. Denny squirmed. **1943** M. SHULMAN *Barefoot Boy with Cheek* x. 99 As she was bending over her work-table.., a playful lab assistant goosed her. **1959** W. BURROUGHS *Naked Lunch* 82 Boys..goose each other at the peep show. **1960** I. WALLACH *Absence of Cello* (1961) 109 Elliot..lightly kissed the top of her head. It would be vulgar to say that she leaped as though goosed, but truth can survive anything including vulgarity. **1965** G. MCINNES *Road to Gundagai* vi. 111 He used to..urge them up the rope with a little skilful goosing. **1967** PARTRIDGE *Dict. Slang* Suppl. 1152/2 *Goose*, the predominant post-World War II meaning is 'to jab a finger *in ano*, in order to surprise or annoy'.

6. *slang.* Only in passive: to be finished, ruined.

1928 *Sunday Dispatch* 5 Aug. 3/2 We were just about goosed with nothing to think about when our football news supply began and put new life into us. **1959** 'J. WELCOME' *Stop at Nothing* viii. 127 If I've guessed wrong and Jason has found out right, then we're goosed.

Hence **'goosing** *vbl. sb.*; also *attrib.*

1825 JAMIESON, *Gusing-irne*, a smoothing iron, a Gipsey term, South of S. **1862** *Illustr. Lond. News* 18 Jan. 75/1 'Goosing'..appears to have been the fate of lively M. Edmond About's last new play.

gooseberry ('gʊzbərɪ). Forms: 6 gose, gows-, 6–8 goos-, 7 gous-, 9 *Sc.* guse-, 6- goose-: and see BERRY. [Prob. f. GOOSE *sb.* + BERRY *sb.*

The grounds on which plants and fruits have received names associating them with animals are so commonly inexplicable, that the want of appropriateness in the meaning affords no sufficient ground for assuming that the word is an etymologizing corruption, e.g. of Du. *kruisbezie*, G. *krausbeere*, or of a hypothetical **gorseberry* or **groseberry* (see GROSER, GROSET); though the last derives some little support from the existence of the form GOZELL for **grosell.*]

1. The edible berry or fruit of any of the thorny species of the genus *Ribes*, the best known and most commonly cultivated of which is *R. Grossularia*; also the plant or shrub itself (more fully *gooseberry-bush, -tree*)

c **1532** DU WES *Introd. Fr.* in *Palsgr.* 912 Gose berrys, *groiselles.* **1573** TUSSER *Husb.* xvi. (1878) 41 The Goose-bery, Respis and Roses. **1597** SHAKS. *2 Hen. IV*, I. ii. 196 All the other gifts appertinent to man (as the malice of this Age shapes them) are not woorth a Goose berry. **1620** VENNER *Via Recta* iii. 59 It is very good..to stuffe them with sowre-grapes, or vnripe-gooseberries. **1663** PH. HENRY *Diaries* (1882) 131 Trees received from Mr. Hammond. 6 Apples. 6 Corans. 6 Goosberryes. **1669** WORLIDGE *Syst. Agric.* (1681) 116 Goosberries being through ripe, taste the most like Grapes of any of our English Fruits. **1740** SOMERVILLE *Hobbinol* III. 42 Crystal Gooseberries Are piled on Heaps; in vain the Parent-Tree Defends her luscious Fruit with pointed Spears. **1859** THOMPSON *Gardener's Assist.* 380 In the gooseberry and currant, the leaves have chiefly performed their office when the fruit is ripened off.

†**2.** Extended to the other species of *Ribes*; see CURRANT 2. *Obs.*

1578 LYTE *Dodoens* v. lxx. 635 The Ribes or beyond sea gooseberries. *Ibid.* VI. xx. 682 The blacke gooseberries growe of them selues in moyst vntoyled places. *Ibid.* 683 *Ribes rubrum*; in English Redde Gooseberries, beyond-sea Gooseberries, Bastard Corinthes. **1655** MOUFET & BENNET *Health's Improv.* (1746) 319 Red Gooseberries.

3. Applied to various shrubs resembling the gooseberry (sense 1) in some way, as **American gooseberry**, *Heterotrichum patens* or *H. niveum*; **Barbados gooseberry**, *Pereskia aculeata*; **Cape gooseberry**, *Physalis edulis* or *P. peruviana*; **Coromandel gooseberry**, *Averrhoa Carambola*; **little gooseberry** (*Austral.*), *Buchanania mangoides*; **Otaheite** or **Tahiti gooseberry**, *Phyllanthus distichus*.

1847 LEICHHARDT *Jrnl.* xiv. 497 The little gooseberry-tree (*Coniogeton Arborescens*). **1864** GRISEBACH *Flora W. Ind.* 784 Gooseberry, American... Gooseberry, Barbadoes. **1866** *Treas. Bot.* 543/1 Coromandel Gooseberry... Tahiti Gooseberry. **1882** J. SMITH *Dict. Pop. Names Plants* s.v. *Winter Cherry*, The Cape Gooseberry..a native of tropical America.

4. Short for *gooseberry-wine*. Also applied jocularly to inferior or spurious brands of champagne.

1766 GOLDSM. *Vic. W.* v, The fond mother..insisted upon her landlord's stepping in, and taking a glass of her goose-berry. **1821** LAMB *Elia* Ser. I. *All Fools' Day*, Fill us a cup of that sparkling gooseberry—we will drink no wise, melancholy, politic port on this day. **1850** THACKERAY *Pendennis* iv, Pen could not but respect Foker's connoisseurship as he pronounced the champagne to be condemned gooseberry. **1893** K. DEIGHTON *Lamb's Ess. Elia* 130 Whether used literally of gooseberry wine, or of champagne, inferior brands of which wine are often spoken of contemptuously as 'gooseberry' [etc.].

5. A chaperon or one who 'plays propriety' with a pair of lovers, esp. in ***to play gooseberry.*** (Cf. *gooseberry-picker* in 8.)

1837 J. F. PALMER *Devonsh. Gloss.*, *Gubbs*, a go-between or gooseberry. 'To play gooseberry' is to give a pretext to two young people to be together. **1870** MISS BROUGHTON *Red as Rose* I. 169 Gooseberry I may be..but, at all events, I won't be instrumental in making myself so. **1881** W. E. NORRIS *Matrim.* I. 21 Let the old woman choose between playing gooseberry or loitering behind alone. **1889** G. ALLEN *Tents of Shem* II. 118 Madame didn't know a single word of English and was, therefore, admirably adapted..for enacting with effect the part of the common or garden gooseberry.

6. a. *slang.* ***old gooseberry*** = the deuce (DEUCE[2] a); esp. ***to play*** (†***up***) ***old gooseberry***, to make havoc (†see also quot. 1796).

1796 *Grose's Dict. Vulg. Tongue* (ed. 3) s.v., He played up old gooseberry among them; said of a person who, by force or threats, suddenly puts an end to a riot or disturbance. **1827** *Sporting Mag.* XXI. 144 Several of the gentlemen rode over the dressed grounds and played old gooseberry with them. **1844** DICKENS *Mart. Chuz.* xxxviii, I'll play Old Gooseberry with the office, and make you glad to buy me out at a good high figure. **1865** H. KINGSLEY *Hillyars & Burtons* III. xiii. 149 You should have a tea-stick, and take them [dogs] by the tail..and lay on like old gooseberry. **1883** LD. R. GOWER *My Remin.* II. xxvii. 249 A great gale..played old gooseberry with the boats.

b. ***gooseberry bush***: used allusively in reference to the explanation of child-birth sometimes given in answer to a child's question.

1944 BRAHMS & SIMON *Titania has Mother* xiii. 146 Fairy Peaseblossom..had never thought she would find herself hankering after one of Simple Simon's curious questions, but now she found she simply couldn't wait for the next one —even if it should be 'but why a goose-berry bush again' ? **1952** V. WILKINS *King Reluctant* I. iii. 47 When girls come home and tell their fond relations that they have just found a baby..under a gooseberry bush, you know what the world says, don't you? **1956** B. GOOLDEN *At Foot of Hills* x. 234 Perhaps she's one of the gooseberry bush brigade and is horrified by the precocity of the modern young. Or is it just because she loathes babies? **1964** G. L. COHEN *What's Wrong with Hospitals?* iv. 69 Middle-class mothers are an anxious lot; they have no precedent on child-rearing which hasn't been kicked into limbo along with gooseberry bushes. **1969** *Guardian* 28 Oct. 11/5 Many children said they were glad to *know* what happened, and not be fobbed off with a lot of gooseberry bushes.

7. *attrib.* and *Comb.*

a. attributive, as ***gooseberry-bush, -cream, -fair, -feast, -jam, -jelly, -pudding, -sauce, -show, -tart, -tree, -wine.*** **b.** objective, as ***gooseberry-grower.*** **c.** similative, as †***goose-berry-cheek***; also **gooseberry-eye** (cf. *goose-berry-eyed* in 8); **gooseberry-orb** = prec.

1530 PALSGR. 226/2 *Goseberry busshe, *groseillier.* **1548** TURNER *Names of Herbes* 88 *Vua crispa* is also called *Grossularia*, in english a Groser bushe, a Goosebery bush. **1771** RICHARDSON in *Phil. Trans.* LXI. 183 On the goosberry-bush and currant the same Aphides may be found. *a* **1658** CLEVELAND *Poems* (1677) 86 First on her *Gooseberry Cheeks I mine eys Blasted. **1706** *Closet Rarities* (N.), To make *Gooseberry-Cream. **1789** WOLCOT (P. Pindar) *Subj. for Painters* Wks. 1812 II. 174 How sweetly roll your *Gooseberry Eyes. **1886** RUSKIN *Præterita* I. 422 A portly gentleman with gooseberry eyes. **1825** HONE *Every-day Bk.* I. 437 What are called the '*Gooseberry fairs' by the wayside, whereat heats are run upon half-killed horses, or.. donkeys. **1796** *Sporting Mag.* VIII. 274 The late Bath annual *gooseberry feast. **1834–43** SOUTHEY *Doctor* cxxxix. (1848) 348/2 He was much esteemed among the Class of *Gooseberry Growers. **1846** 'A LADY' *Jewish Man.* viii. 165 Strawberry jam... By this recipe also are made raspberry, currant, *goose-berry, apricot, and other jams. **1861** MRS. BEETON *Bk. Househ. Managem.* 778 (*heading*) Gooseberry jam. *Ibid.* 779 (*heading*) *Gooseberry jelly. **1803** JANE PORTER *Thaddeus* (1826) III. v. 102 When [she] compared.. Pembroke's dark and ever-animated eyes, with the *gooseberry orbs of Lascelles. **1769** MRS. RAFFALD *Eng. Housekpr.* (1778) 183 *Gooseberry Pudding. **1845** E. ACTON *Mod. Cookery* iv. 137 (*heading*) *Gooseberry sauce for mackerel. **1796** *Sporting Mag.* VIII. 274 The annual *gooseberry shew, held at the house of Mr. Robert Huxley. **1859** THOMPSON *Gardener's Assist.* 559 The great number of gooseberry shows held in Lancashire, Cheshire, and Yorkshire. **1785** A. ELLICOTT in *Life & Lett.* (1908) 44 Our waiters are now preparing some *Goose-Berry Tart. **1845** BUDD *Dis. Liver* 185 After imprudently eating gooseberry tart, she was seized with violent pain. *c* **1532** DU WES *Introd. Fr.* in *Palsgr.* 914 *Gowsbery tre, *groiselier.* **1707** *Curios. in Husb. & Gard.* 197 Fig-trees, Quince-Trees, Goosberry-Trees. **1707** SIR J. MORE *England's Interest* (*title-p.*), How to Make..*Gooseberry, and Mulberry Wines. **1849** Goose-berry wine [see MARIGOLD I a]. **1971** *Times* 10 Nov. (Wine Suppl.) 3/6 Skilfully made gooseberry wine can be successfully passed off as champagne to the uninitiated.

8. Special comb.: **gooseberry-caterpillar**, ?the caterpillar of the *gooseberry-moth*; **gooseberry-eyed** *a.* (see quot.); **gooseberry-louse** = HARVEST-BUG; **gooseberry-moth**, the magpie-moth (*Abraxas grossulariata*); **goose-berry-picker**, one who picks gooseberries, *colloq.* a chaperon (so *gooseberry-picking* vbl. sb.); **gooseberry-pie**, (*a*) a pie made of gooseberries, etc.; (*b*) (see quot. 1879); **goose-berry-season**, the time when gooseberries are ripe, *esp.* in ***big gooseberry season***, the time of year when the newspapers have plenty of space to record trifles; **gooseberry-wig** (see quot.).

1882 *Garden* 6 May 319/3 A sharp look out must now be kept for *Gooseberry caterpillars. **1796** *Grose's Dict. Vulg. Tongue* (ed. 3), **Gooseberry-eyed*, one with dull grey eyes, like boiled gooseberries. **1856** MRS. CARLYLE *Lett.* II. 290 The new insect called 'harvest bugs', or '*gooseberry lice'.. imported in some American plants. **1816** KIRBY & SP. *Entomol.* xxvi. (1818) II. 452 The caterpillars of the *gooseberry-moth. **1868** YATES *Rock Ahead* II. ix, In his capacity of *gooseberry-picker, Lord S. was led..into anything but pleasant pastures. **1888** J. PAYN *Myst. Mirbridge* III. xli. 128 He had a sort of 'Don't mind me' way with him that made him quite the perfection of a 'gooseberry-picker'. **1747** MRS. GLASSE *Cookery* 114 A custard is very good with the *gooseberry pie. **1766** GOLDSM. *Vic. W.* vii, Go help your mother to make the gooseberry pie. **1879** BRITTEN & HOLLAND *Plant-n.*, Gooseberry pie, *Epilobium hirsutum* L., from the smell of the leaves. **1787** 'G. GAMBADO' *Acad. Horsemen* (1809) 26 How to make up a good stout..dose of physic for your wife or servants, in the *gooseberry season. **1796** *Grose's Dict. Vulg. Tongue* (ed. 3), **Gooseberry wig*, a large frizzled wig; perhaps, from a supposed likeness to a gooseberry bush.

'gooseberry-'fool. [FOOL *sb.*[2]]

1. A dish made of gooseberries stewed or scalded and pounded with cream.

1719 D'URFEY *Pills* III. 9 A rich clouted Cream, or a Gooseberry-Fool. **1775** JEKYLL *Corr.* 30 May, I must thank you for the recipe to make gooseberry fool. **1886** J. K. JEROME *Idle Thoughts* (1889) 70 A large dish of gooseberry-fool that was standing to cool.

Comb. **1888** *Lady* 25 Oct. 378 Gooseberry-fool-green velvet.

2. As a popular plant-name: **a.** Willow-herb (*Epilobium hirsutum*), also called *gooseberry-pie*; **b.** Lungwort (*Pulmonaria officinalis*).

1794 MARTYN *Rousseau's Bot.* xix. 257 The hairy sort [of French Willow]..vulgarly known by the name of Codlins and Cream, or Goosberry Fool, from the smell of the leaves. **1858** LADY WILKINSON *Weeds & Wild Fl.* 72 Lung-wort, Cowslip of Jerusalem..Gooseberry-fool, *Pulmonaria.*

'goose-bill. Used as a name for things resembling the bill of a goose.

1. The plant *Galium Aparine*: = GOOSE-GRASS 2.

1597 GERARDE *Herbal* Suppl., Goose bill, *Aparine.* **1886** *Syd. Soc. Lex.*, *Goosebill*, the *Galium aparine*, in reference to the serrated edges of the leaves and their resemblance to the rough edges of the mandibles of the goose.

†**2.** A kind of forceps for extracting bullets, etc. (Cf. CROW-BILL 2.) *Obs.*

1676 COLES, *Goos-bill*, a Chirurgeons instrument of the same use as a Crow-bill. **1706** in PHILLIPS (ed. Kersey). **1823** in CRABB *Technol. Dict.*

3. *Naut.* (See quot.)

1735–40 DYCHE & PARDON *Dict.*, *Goose-bill*, a particular sail used at sea, when a ship goes before the wind, or with a quarter wind.

'goose-cap. ? *Obs.* [see CAP *sb.*[1] (sense 7).] A booby, noodle, numskull, simpleton, fool.

1589 NASHE *Martins Mths. Minde* 45 And so will yon Sonnes both, like a couple of goosecaps. **1604** DEKKER *Honest Wh.* Wks. 1873 II. 81 Out you Gulles, you Goose-caps, you Gudgeon-eaters! **1638** FORD *Fancies* IV. i, What a wise goose-cap hast thou shew'd thyself! **1711** SWIFT *Jrnl. to Stella* 18 Apr., Did you ever see such a blundering goosecap as Presto? **1764** FOOTE *Mayor of G.* I. Wks. 1799 I. 169 My husband is such a goose-cap, that I can't get no good out of him at home or abroad. **1820** MISS MITFORD in L'Estrange *Life* (1870) II. 121 She's a goosecap..and a romp, and a saucebox. **1828** SCOTT *F.M. Perth* v, A plague on thee for a cold down-hearted goose-cap.

Hence **goose-'capical** *a. nonce-wd.*, foolish.

c **1785** *J. Thompson's Man* 14 Nonsensical, fantastical, goose-capical, coxcomical, and idiotical.

'goose-egg. (Pl. †*geese-eggs.*) **a.** The egg of a goose; hence *U.S.* in scoring at athletic contests, the zero or 'o' showing a miss or inability to score. (Cf. DUCK'S-EGG.)

c **1394** *P. Pl. Crede* 225 His chyn wiþ a chol lollede As greet as a gos eye. **1398** TREVISA *Barth. De P.R.* XVIII. xxxiii. (1495) 795 The cocodrill layeth eggys in the londe that ben gretter than goos eggys. *Ibid.* XIX. lxxxiii. 914 Geys eggys ben grete and harde to defye. **1577** B. GOOGE *Heresbach's Husb.* IV. (1586) 164 Of Goose Egges..never set under a Henne above five. **1650** B. *Discolliminium* 30 One Mother Huggin..got all the goose-eggs, hen-eggs, and duck-eggs she could. **1774** GOLDSM. *Nat. Hist.* (1776) VI. 294 It.. grows to the size of a goose-egg. **1867** H. CHADWICK *Scrapbooks* XI, The Buckeyes in this innings were treated to a goose-egg. **1878** C. HALLOCK *Amer. Club List & Sportsman's Gloss.* p. v, *Goose-egg*, a miss, so-called, in rifle-shooting at a range. **1886** *N.Y. Times* July (Cent.), The New York players presented the Boston men with nine unpalatable goose eggs in their [baseball] contest on the Polo Grounds yesterday. **1931** *Amer. Speech* VII. 22 *Goose egg* usually means 'no tip'.

b. *attrib.* **goose-egg moth**, *Cilix compressa.*

1819 G. SAMOUELLE *Entomol. Compend.* 254.

'goose-flesh, 'gooseflesh.

1. The flesh of a goose.

c **1425** *Voc.* in Wr.-Wülcker 661 *Caro aucina*, gosflesche. *c* **1520** L. ANDREWE *Noble Lyfe* II. x. Ljb in *Babees Bk.*, The gose flessh is very grose of nature in disiestion.

2. A rough, pimply condition of the skin, resembling that of a plucked goose, produced by cold, fear, etc.; horripilation. (Cf. GOOSE-SKIN 2.)

? **1810** COLERIDGE *Lit. Rem.* (1839) IV. 342 The very term by which the German New-Birthites express it is enough to give one goose-flesh. **1868** BROWNING *Ring & Bk.* VIII. 282 This cold day!.. Guido must be all goose-flesh in his hole. **1876** DUHRING *Dis. Skin* 29 The condition known as *cutis anserina*, or goose-flesh. **1880** BROWNING *Clive* 192 The memory of that moment makes goose-flesh rise!

fig. **1864** LOWELL *Study Wind.* (1886) 123 Irritating every pore of his vanity, like a dry north-east wind, to a gooseflesh of opposition and hostility.

attrib. and *Comb.* **1851** THACKERAY in *Scribner's Mag.* II. 134/2 The Exhibition..was..a great love-inspiring, gooseflesh-bringing sight. **1859** O. W. HOLMES *Prof. Breakf.-t.* xi, Such a 'gooseflesh' shiver ran over my skin.

Hence **'goosefleshy** *a.*, of or pertaining to 'gooseflesh'; exhibiting 'gooseflesh'. Also (*nonce-wds.*) **'gooseflesh** *v. intr.*, to experience 'gooseflesh'; **'goose-fleshed** *ppl. a.* = *gooseflesh*y adj.; **'goosefleshing** *ppl. a.*, giving one 'gooseflesh'.

1894 G. S. LAYARD *Tennyson & Illustrators* ii. 16 The true goose-fleshy appearance that would be lost in the warmth of the studio. **1895** CLARK RUSSELL *Convict Ship* II. xxvi. 159 'It's a goosefleshing discipline', said Captain Barrett. **1904** *Daily Chron.* 2 Aug. 7/1 In the life of every married man comes a moment when, with a goose-fleshy shudder, he realises that the face opposite to him at the breakfast-table is the face that will always be there. **1924** L. ABERCROMBIE *Theory of Poetry* i. 18, I gooseflesh one day, but another day I do not, at the same passage. **1932** KIPLING *Limits & Renewals* 47 A Fear leaped out of the goose-fleshed streets of London between the icy shop-fronts. **1934** A. CHRISTIE *Murder on Orient Express* I. vi. 59 This is where I'm supposed to go all goose-fleshy down the back. **1955** *Times* 13 July 10/5 Bathing under regularly warm skies spoils anyone, who is not a keen swimmer, for the chilly dips in and out, with the skin blue and goose-fleshy, which the hardy English will take. **1971** O. NORTON *Corpse-Bird Cries* iv. 80 There was a lot of stuff about whether her skin was goose-fleshy or not.

'goose-foot. Used as the name of various objects resembling the foot of a goose.

1. A plant belonging to one of the various species of the genus *Chenopodium*; so called from the shape of the leaves. Pl. **goosefoots.**

The Eng. name seems to have been a translation from the Ger. A Lat. plant-name of the same etymological meaning, *Chēnopus* (Gr. χηνόπους) occurs in Pliny.

1548 TURNER *Names of Herbes* H iij b, *Pes anserinus* is called in duch gensz [*mispr.* geusz] fusz and it may be called in englishe Goose-fote. **1555** EDEN *Decades* 262 The herbe cauled *Chenopode* (which sume caule goose foote). **1607** TOPSELL *Four-f. Beasts* (1658) 528 The hearb goosefoot is venemous to swine. **1657** W. COLES *Adam in Eden* cccix. 577 Goose-foot or Sowbane. **1698** J. PETIVER in *Phil. Trans.* XX. 401 With Leaves somewhat like our Goosefoot. **1738** DEERING *Catal. Stirp.* 34 The other Goosefoot..called by some Country People Fat Hen. **1794** MARTYN *Rousseau's Bot.* xvii. 221 Such are all the Goose-foots, of which there are no less than twenty species. **1861** MISS PRATT *Flower. Pl.* IV. 38 The goose-foots..and other unattractive plants. **1872** OLIVER *Elem. Bot.* II. 224 Artificial Shagreen used to be made by pressing a piece of leather upon the seeds of White Goosefoot so as to raise a warted surface.

b. The plant *Aspalathus Chenopoda.*

1848 *Rural Cycl.* II. 480 *Goosefoot*..A beautiful, yellow-flowered, evergreen, Cape-of-Good-Hope shrub.

2. Something arranged or made in the shape of a goose's foot; *e.g.* a three-branched hinge, or a number of roads diverging from a common point. Pl. **goose-feet.** [= F. *patte d'oie.*]

1516-17 in Willis & Clark *Cambridge* (1886) I. 417 Le gosfote ad magnam portam occidentalem collegii. **1712** J. JAMES tr. *Le Blond's Gardening* 19 A Goose-foot, which leads into the great Walks. *Ibid.* 54 The Walks of these Goose-feet center every one upon the Spouts of the Water-work. **1741** STACK in *Phil. Trans.* XLI. 683 The Goose-foot formed by the Valve being much more compounded.

'goose-girl. [After G. *gänsemagd.*] A girl employed to tend geese.

1826 E. TAYLOR tr. *Grimm's German Popular Stories* II. 1 The Goose-girl. **1906** *Westm. Gaz.* 28 July 12/3 Mr. Randal Charlton has written a fairy-tale, and his heroine is called Mave. Of course she ought to be a Princess, but she is rather of the goose-girl type. *Ibid.* 24 Nov. 7/1 Like all Bohemian geese-girls, she carried a long branch, which served as a wand to drive her flock home. **1954** WILKINS & KAISER tr. *Musil's Man without Qualities* II. cv. 245 Of course, an Arnheim might permit himself to marry even a goose-girl if he wished.

goosegog ('gʊzgɒg). A widespread local form for *gooseberry*. (Cf. dial. *goose-gob, -bob.*)

1823 E. MOOR *Suffolk Words, Gusegog*, a gooseberry—also gew-gog. *a* **1825** R. FORBY *Voc. E. Anglia* (1830) *Goose-gog*, a gooseberry; particularly when ripe. **1864** MRS. H. WOOD *William Allair* iv, Green goosegogs. **1916** E. V. LUCAS *Vermilion Box* xcix, Gertie's growing goosegogs for the Ghurkas. **1945** [see GOOG]. **1959** B. KOPS *Hamlet of Stepney Green* I. 13 Redcurrants and black-currants and golden goosegogs.

'goose-grass. Forms: α. see GOOSE and GRASS. β. 6-8 *erron.* goose-grease. The popular name of various plants, most of which are or were formerly used as food for geese.

1. Silver-weed (*Potentilla Anserina*).

a **1387** *Sinon. Barthol.* (Anecd. Oxon.) 41 *Tanacetum album*, gosegresse. *c* **1400** *Med. Wks.* 15*th C.* (Henslow 1899) 99 Tak plaunteyn, gosgres, an[d] housleke. *c* **1440** *Promp. Parv.* 204/1 Gosys gres, or camoroche, or wylde tanzy. **1597** GERARDE *Herbal* Suppl., Goosegras was sometime called *Argentina.* **1691** RAY *N.C. Words* 32 Goose grass, Goose tansie, *Argentina.* **1707** MORTIMER *Husb.* 240 Goose grass or Wild Tansie is a Weed that strong Clays are very subject to. **1853** G. JOHNSTON *Nat. Hist. E. Bord.* I. 71 *Potentilla anserina*,..Goose-grass.

2. Cleavers (*Galium Aparine*).

Hence applied with distinctive epithet to other species of *Galium*, as in † *downy-stalk goosegrass*, ? some variety of *G. scabrum* (Withering *Brit. Pl.* 1796); *yellow goosegrass*, Our Lady's Bedstraw, *G. verum* (Britten & H., citing *Rural Cycl.*). Possibly quot. *c* 1400 (sense 1) belongs to this sense.

α. **1538** TURNER *Libellus*, Goosgyrs, *Apparine.* **1578** LYTE *Dodoens* IV. lxxiv. 538 Cliuer or Goosegrasse hath many smal square branches. **1657** W. COLES *Adam in Eden* clxxxvii. 292 It is called in English..Goosegrasse, Cleavers (or Clivers). **1779** MRS. DELANY *Life & Corr.* Ser. II. II. 425 The specimen of goose grass or cleavers that you enclos'd is the right sort. **1860** *All Year Round* No. 48. 508 The seeds of avens have one single hook, those of agrimony and goosegrass many. **1861** MISS PRATT *Flower. Pl.* III. 153 (Goose-grass or Cleavers)..This plant is said to have its name from the fondness of that bird for its herbage.

β. **1530** PALSGR. 226/2 *Gose grece*, an herbe. **1587** MASCALL *Govt. Cattle* I. (1600) 15 Likewise the iuice of cleuers, or goose grease. **1691** RAY *N.C. Words* 35 Hariff and Catchweed; Goose-grease, *Aparine.* **1731** BAILEY, *Hariff* and *Catchweed*, Goose Grease.

†3. purple goose-grass, field madder or spurwort (*Sherardia arvensis*). *Obs.*

1548 TURNER *Names of Herbes* 11 It [*Alysson Plinii*] had leaues lyke madder and purple floures, it maye be named in Englishe purple goosgrafe [*sic*].

4. The wild grass *Bromus mollis.*

1853 G. JOHNSTON *Nat. Hist. E. Bord.* I. 217 *Bromus mollis*..Goose-grass: Bull-grass. **1893** in *Northumbld. Gloss.*

5. *U.S.* **a.** 'The door-weed, *Polygonum aviculare*' (*Cent. Dict.*). **b.** 'Low spear-grass, *Poa annua*' (*Stand. Dict.*).

'goose-grease. The melted fat or grease of the goose. See also GOOSE-GRASS 2 β.

1398 TREVISA *Barth. De P.R.* XVII. xliii. (1495) 629 Oyneons helpyth ache of reynes wyth gose grece or wyth hony. **1523** FITZHERB. *Husb.* §43 Let thy terre be medled with oyle, gose grease, or capons grease, these three be the beste. **1657** W. COLES *Adam in Eden* l. 99 If they be anointed with it [Garden-cresse], and Goose-grease mixed together. **1846** J. BAXTER *Libr. Pract. Agric.* (ed. 4) II. 150 Some farmers place great reliance on goose-grease. **1875** H. C. WOOD *Therap.* (1879) 582 Mutton suet and goose-grease are famous in domestic medicine, but are simply valuable because, if well prepared, they are less apt than some other fats to become rancid.

'gooseherd. Also GOZZARD. [f. GOOSE *sb.* + HERD *sb.*[2]] One who tends a flock of geese.

14.., **1773** [For the form *gosherd* see GOZZARD]. **1577** HARRISON *England* III. ii. (1877) II. 15 Their geese are driuen to the field like heards of cattell by a goose heard. **1870** YEATS *Nat. Hist. Comm.* 314 A gooseherd, it is said, can distinguish every goose in the flock by the tones of its voice. **1892** SWINBURNE *Studies* (1894) 232 The democratic theatricals of Gallican geese and gooseherds.

'goose-house.

1. A small house or shed in which geese are shut up for the night.

1474-5 *Durham Acc. Rolls* (Surtees) I. 95 Pro le flaggynge de le goyshous. **1516-17** *Ibid.* 106 Laboranti ad le Gowsehouse. **1616** SURFL. & MARKH. *Country Farme* 77 They must be put into the Goose-house, and kept asunder with hurdles. **1832** MISS MITFORD *Village* Ser. V. 154 Pigsties, goose-houses, and hen-houses out of number.

2. A village lock-up.

1841 *P. Parley's Ann.* II. 241 Several others were.. dragged off to what in the country is called, the goose-house —that is, the cage. **1847-89** in HALLIWELL.

gooseling, obs. form of GOSLING.

'goose-neck. A name given to things shaped like the neck of a goose.

1. *Naut.* (See quots. 1769, 1867, and 1961.)

1688 S. SEWALL *Diary* 29 Nov., About 12 at night..the whipstaf is somehow loosed from the Gooseneck. **1756** *Gentl. Mag.* XXVI. 15 The tiller was unshipped and the goose-neck shifted. **1769** FALCONER *Dict. Marine* (1780), *Goose-neck*, a sort of iron hook fitted on the inner end of a boom, and introduced into a clamp of iron, or eye-bolt, which encircles the mast, or is fitted to some other place in the ship, so that it may be unhooked at pleasure. **1835** MARRYAT *Olla Podr.* v, He perceived the half of a maintop-sail yard..lying on the goose-necks. **1867** SMYTH *Sailor's Word-bk.*, *Goose-neck*, a curved iron, fitted outside the after-chains to receive a spare spar, properly the swinging boom, a davit. **1961** F. H. BURGESS *Dict. Sailing* 103 *Goose neck*, a ventilating cowl bent over to keep out water.

2. *Mech.* A pipe or piece of iron, etc. curved like the neck of a goose.

1843 J. A. RANSOME *Implem. Agric.* 52 A collar chain.. having what is technically termed a 'goose neck' passing through one of its links, which is made circular for its admission. *a* **1864** GESNER *Coal, Petrol.*, etc. (1865) 77 The pipe connecting the gooseneck and worm. **1870** CONE & JOHNS *Petrolia* xi. 164 A conducting tube, called a 'goose-neck', which it resembled in shape. **1875** KNIGHT *Dict. Mech.*, *Goose-neck*..a nozzle having a universal-joint connection to the stand-pipe on a fire-engine. **1888** *Lockwood's Dict. Mech. Engin.*, *Goose Neck*, the bent rod by which the tap hole in a casting ladle is opened and closed. **1929** WILSON & WEBB *Mod. Gramophones* 125 Immediately after the war a new type of tone-arm with a 'trombone goose-neck'..was introduced. **1957** *N.Z. Timber Jrnl.* July 49/1 *Gooseneck*, (1) a strong wood bar connecting two logging trucks; (2) a curved iron at the bottom of a slide to check the speed of moving logs. **1958** A. D. MERRIMAN *Dict. Metallurgy* 113/2 *Goose-neck*, a bent air-duct or penstock that is fire-brick lined and joins the bustle-pipe to the belly pipe of a blast furnace. It conveys the hot blast to the tuyères.

3. (See quot.)

1854 MISS BAKER *Northamptonsh. Gloss.*, *Goose-neck*, a twisted stick with two sharp points to run into the thatch, to prevent the wind blowing it up. **1884** in CASSELL.

4. *attrib.* and *Comb.*, as ***goose-neck binder, handle, lamp.***

1940 E. C. STUDHOLME *Te Waimate* 155 The Woods was probably the first string binder tried here. It was known as the 'goose-neck' binder because it had a long circular arm resembling the neck of a goose, which threw the sheaves away. **1957** MANKOWITZ & HAGGAR *Eng. Pott. & Porc.* 23/2 Vases with goose-neck handles were peculiar to the [Bilston] factory. **1929** M. LIEF *Hangover* iii. 31 Books and magazines lay piled up on a library table alongside his typewriter and a gooseneck lamp. **1969** J. ROSS *Dead at First Hand* ii. 20 The pool of light cast by the gooseneck lamp on his desk.

'goose-necked, *a.* Shaped like the neck of a goose.

1907 *Yesterday's Shopping* (1969) 999/2 Goose-necked Putter... Fitted with hickory shaft—each 5/3. **1910** *Westm. Gaz.* 22 Apr. 6/3 Goose-necked and other daffodils. **1968** L. DURRELL *Tunc* v. 247 The tall, goose-necked alabaster lamps with red parchment shades.

'goose-quill.

1. One of the quills or wing-feathers of a goose; hence, a pen made of such a feather.

1552 HULOET, Goose quyll, *calamus anserinus.* **1583** HOLLYBAND *Campo di Fior* 331 We write with goose quilles. **1602** SHAKS. *Ham.* II. ii. 359 Many wearing Rapiers, are affraide of Goose-quils. **1658** MANTON *Exp. Jude* verse 3. Wks. 1871 V. 98 The goose-quill hath smote antichrist under the fifth rib. **1773** HAMILTON in *Phil. Trans.* LXIII. 327 Two wires of about the size of a goose-quill. **1834** F. B. HEAD *Bubbles of Brunnen* 138 Sensations on the eye and ear which the goose-quill has not power to impart. **1864** BURTON *Scot Abr.* I. iii. 148 A fat philosopher sitting writing in a peaceful library with a goose quill.

attrib. **1594** NASHE *Unfort. Trav.* Wks. (Grosart) V. 38 These aboue named goosequil braccahadocheos. **1661** WALTON *Angler* (ed. 3) x. 172 Three..Goose-quil floats.

†b. A writer, author. *nonce-use. Obs.*

1600 NASHE *Summers Last Will* Wks. (Grosart) VI. 149 Bowles, cards and dice, you are the true liberal sciences, Ile ne're be Goose-quil, gentlemen, while I liue.

†2. *Naut.* (See quot.; cf. GOOSE-WING 2.) *Obs.*

1769 FALCONER *Dict. Marine* (1780), *Carguer le point de la voile qui est sous le vent*, to haul up the lee-clue-garnet, or goose-quill of a sail.

Hence **† goose'quillian** *a.*

1610 *Histrio-m.* III. D 4, Not while goosequillian Posthast holds his pen.

goosery ('gu:sərɪ). [f. GOOSE *sb.* + -ERY.]

1. Silliness such as is attributed to the goose. *rare.*

1642 MILTON *Apol. Smect.* viii. Wks. (1851) 310 The lofty nakednesse of your Latinizing Barbarian, and the finicall goosery of your neat Sermon-actor. **1875-9** CARLYLE in *Mem. Tennyson* (1897) II. 235 Goldie was just an Irish blackguard, with a fine brain..and a great fund of goosery.

2. A place in which geese are kept; a collection of geese.

1828 MISS MITFORD *Village* Ser. III. 293 They set up..a cackle which might rival the din of their own gooseries at feeding-time. **1831** *Blackw. Mag.* XXX. 506 On its tiptoes rose the entire Goosery—flap went every wing.

'goose-skin.

1. The skin of a goose.

1700 FLOYER *Cold Baths* I. ii. 38 Excessive Cold, which contracts the Skin like a Goose-Skin.

2. = GOOSE-FLESH 2.

[**1638** RAWLEY tr. *Bacon's Life & Death* 150 A Rugged Skin, such as they call a Goose Skin (orig. *de cute spissiori, quam vocant anserinam*), which is, as it were, Spongie.] **1785** J. TRUSLER *Mod. Times* III. 157 He draws back when they are addressing him, as if contamination was in their breath, and is all gooseskin at a low bred man. **1824** MISS FERRIER *Inher.* ii, Her skin began to rise into what is vulgarly termed goose-skin. **1836** LADY DACRE in L'Estrange *Friendships Miss Mitford* (1882) I. 319 The learning she displays..gives me, what the poor people call the 'goose-skin'—a sort of vague sensation of awe. **1872** HUXLEY *Phys.* xii. 279 'Horripilation' or 'goose-skin'. **1896** *Allbutt's Syst. Med.* I. 341 The skin is pale, and owing to the contraction of the unstriped muscle fibres, presents the appearance called 'goose-skin'.

3. A thin soft kind of leather. Also *attrib.*

1826 *Morn. Herald* in Hone *Every-day Bk.* (1859) II. 461 The ladies all wore a goose-skin underdress, in compliment to the north-easter. **1889** in *Century Dict.*

4. The impression made upon copal by the sand or gravel in which it is found.

1859 R. F. BURTON *Centr. Afr.* in *Jrnl. Geog. Soc.* XXIX. 437 The 'goose-skin', which is the impress of sand or gravel ..To clear the goose-skin of dirt.

Hence **'goose-skinned, 'goose-skinny** *adjs.*, affected with 'goose-skin'.

1844 DICKENS *Chimes* i, A breezy, goose-skinned, blue-nosed,..tooth-chattering place it was, to wait in. **1878** LADY HERBERT tr. *Hübner's Ramble* II. ii. 258 It was the terrible revolver which had already made me feel goose-skinny on leaving Yokohama.

'goose-step, *sb. Mil.* **a.** An elementary drill in which the recruit is taught to balance his body on either leg alternately, and swing the other backwards and forwards. **b.** A balance step, practised esp. by various armies in marching on ceremonial parades, in which the legs are alternately advanced without bending the knees.

1806 SIR R. WILSON *Jrnl.* 11 Feb., The balance or goose-step introduced for their practice excites a fever of disgust. **1825** D. L. RICHARDSON *Sonnets* 32 Oft with aching bones, I marched the goose-step, cursing Serjeant Jones. **1887** T. A. TROLLOPE *What I remember* II. ix. 164 You must have superintended a course of instruction in the goose-step in your day. **1916** H. G. WELLS *Mr. Britling* II. i. 204 The small boys had discovered the goose-step. *Ibid.*, They tried it them-selves, and then set out upon a goose-step propaganda. **1922** C. E. MONTAGUE *Disenchantment* xiii. 182 Doing the Prussianist goose-step by way of *pas de triomphe.* **1941** 'G. ORWELL' *Lion & Unicorn* I. ii. 21 The goose-step ..is one of the most horrible sights in the world. **1971** *Daily Tel.* 16 Oct. 3/6 As columns approached the Shah they broke into a goose-step.

Hence **'goose-step** *v. intr.*, to practise this step or drill; also occas. *trans.* Hence **'goose-stepping** *vbl. sb.* and *ppl. a.*

1879 BARING-GOULD *Germany* I. 297 He sees them [recruits] posturing, goose-stepping, tumbling [etc.]. **1935** H. R. L. SHEPPARD *We say No* viii. 97 Hitler's goose-stepping conscripts. **1938** *Reader's Digest* Jan. 110/1 Chilean citizens of German blood are already goose-stepped by Nazi missionaries. **1941** KOESTLER *Scum of Earth* 79 A helpless, bleeding prey to be stamped on by the boots of the goose-stepping conqueror. **1951** M. MCLUHAN *Mech. Bride* 122/2 The remorseless goose-stepping of the glamorous female warrior. **1964** C. CHAPLIN *Autobiogr.* xxv. 433 Greed has poisoned men's souls.., has goose-stepped us into misery and bloodshed. **1967** *Listener* 16 Mar. 370/3 The Nazi jackboot goose-stepping on the boulevards got his goat. **1970** *Daily Tel.* 16 June 11/7 Women as well as men goose-step around the stage to the tat-tat of drums. *Ibid.* 10 Dec. 4/5 President Nyerere reviewed goose-stepping troops of Tanzania's army yesterday.

'goose-,stepper. One who practises the goose-step (used contemptuously of supposed dupes of militarism).

1923 H. L. MENCKEN *Prejudices* 3rd Ser. 10 The most timorous, sniveling, poltroonish, ignominious mob of serfs and goose-steppers ever gathered under one flag. *Ibid.* 49 The first made them almost incapable of soldierly thought and conduct; the second converted them into cringing goose-steppers. **1928** *Daily Express* 15 Oct. 9 An old topical print showing 'Big Willie' and 'Little Willie' inspecting a parade of goosesteppers.

'goose-walk. *Draughts.* (See quots.)

1892 J. LEES *Compl. Guide to Draughts* 60 (*Single Corner*) 27-24 here loses, and forms what is known as the 'Old Farmer', or the 'Goose Walk'. **1929** *Encycl. Brit.* VII. 621/1 The trap which White falls into in the above game when playing 27-24 at the 12th move is of very common occurrence, and is known by the quaint designation of the 'Goose Walk'.

'goose-wing.

1. The wing of a goose. †Sometimes used as a type of what is of trifling value. In quot. 1630 with allusion to the feathers used for arrows.

1377 LANGL. *P. Pl.* B. IV. 36 Thei ne gyueth nouȝte of god one gose wynge. **1549** LATIMER *7th Serm. bef. Edw. VI* (Arb.) 113 He was not able to giue so much as a gose wynge: for they were none of hys to gyue. **1550** CROWLEY *Epigr.* 470 They invent idle othes, ..by the goose wyng. **1577** B. GOOGE *Heresbach's Husb.* IV. (1586) 188 b, If any thing remaine, not washed away, you must sweepe it out with a Goose wing. **1586** BRIGHT *Melanch.* iv. 27 Water fowle are not of melancholicke persons to be tasted, except the goose-wings. **1630** J. TAYLOR (Water P.) *Wks.* I. 107/1 Search the Chronicles, as it is most plaine, That the Goose-wing braue conquests did obtaine.

2. *Naut.* (See quots.; cf. GOOSE-QUILL 2.)

1626 CAPT. SMITH *Accid. Yng. Sea-men* 29 Put out a goose-winge, or a hullocke of a sayle. **1627** —— *Seaman's Gram.* ix. 41 For more haste vnparrell the mizen yard and lanch it, and the saile ouer her Lee quarter, and fit Giues at the further end to keepe the yard steady, and with a Boome boome it out; this we call a Goose-wing. **1769** FALCONER *Dict. Marine* (1780), *Goose-wings* of a sail, the clues or lower corners of a ship's main-sail or fore-sail, when the middle part is furled or tied up to the yard. **1836** MARRYAT *Midsh. Easy* xxvi, Those on deck were..setting the goose-wings of the mainsail, to prevent the frigate from being pooped a second time. **1867** SMYTH *Sailor's Word-bk.*, *Goose-wings of a Sail*, the situation of a course when the bunt-lines and lee-clue are hauled up, and the weather-clue down... Also applied to the fore and main sails of a schooner or other two-masted fore-and-aft vessel; when running before the wind she has these sails set on opposite sides.

Hence **'goose-winged** *a.* Also **'goose-wing** *v.*, to set the sails of a vessel in a 'goose-wing' fashion (see sb. 2, esp. quot. 1867); in fore-and-aft rig, when running before the wind, to boom out two working sails, one on either side.

1866 J. MACGREGOR *Thousand Miles in Rob Roy Canoe* (ed. 2) vi. 108 And the white sails swell towards you, goosewinged, before a flowing breeze. **1869** *Mayne Reid's Mag.* June 515 We beheld a large ship lying to under goose-winged main-top-sail and storm-stay-sails. **1883** CLARK RUSSELL *Sailors' Lang.*, *Goose-winged*—when the weather clew of a course is down and the lee clew and the buntlines hauled up. **1896** KIPLING *Seven Seas* 61 And the *Northern Light* stood out again, goose-winged to open sea. **1920** *Blackw. Mag.* Mar. 320/1 An ability to keep clear of shifting sandbanks was deemed of more value than the correct way to 'goose-wing' a tattered topsail. **1961** F. H. BURGESS *Dict. Sailing* 103 *Goose-wing*, sail with mainsail set on one side and foresail set the other side, so that one will not blanket the other.

goosey ('guːsɪ). Also **goosy, goosie.** [f. GOOSE *sb.* + -Y.] A childish or playful diminutive of GOOSE *sb.*, applied to persons. Also **goosey-goosey, goosey-gander** (from the nursery rime 'Goosey, goosey, gander, Whither did you wander?').

a **1816** WOLCOT (P. Pindar) *Elegy* Wks. 1816 IV. 368 Or where wert thou, O goddess of the fiddle? To suffer Air to join with Goosy Gander, Cock Robin, Horner, and High-diddle diddle. **1842** in Halliwell *Nursery Rhymes* 92 Goosy goosy gander! Where shall I wander? **1852** MRS. STOWE *Uncle Tom's C.* i. 8 Do you think all the world are set on him as you are, you goosie? **1862** H. KINGSLEY *Ravenshoe* xlvii, That goosey-gander Alwright. **1868** F. LOCKER *Nice Correspondent!* iv, His bride was a goosey! **1878** M. E. JACKSON *Chaperon's Cares* I. xi. 150 'Dare say you do, but I am not such a goosey-goosey.'

gooshet, obs. Sc. form of GUSSET.

'goosified, *pa. pple. nonce-wd.* Affected with 'goose-flesh'.

1837 J. H. NEWMAN *Lett.* (1891) II. 240 [He] shrunk up as if twenty thousand pins had been thrust into him; his flesh goosified, his mouth puckered up.

goosish ('guːsɪʃ), *a.* [f. GOOSE *sb.* + -ISH.] Goose-like, silly, stupid.

c **1374** CHAUCER *Troylus* III. 535 (584) Yet gan she him biseche,..For to be war of goosish peples speche, That dremen thinges whiche that never were. **1863** *Reader* 19 Dec. 726/2 The droll carvings of asinine preachers and goosish congregations.

Hence **'goosishness.**

1864 MRS. CARLYLE *Lett.* III. 220 This creature, with her goosishness, and her self-conceit.

goosling, obs. form of GOSLING.

goossy, variant of GUSSIE[1] *Sc.*, pig.

goost(e, obs. form of GHOST.

goosy ('guːsɪ), *a.* Also **goosey.** [f. GOOSE *sb.* + -Y[1].] Goose-like.

1. Resembling a goose; hence, foolish, silly.

1811 *Ora & Juliet* IV. 163, I wanted a hearth-rug..and I would have a swan in the middle of it; but..when it was done, the swan looked so goosey that I was ashamed of it. **1866** CARLYLE *Remin.* (1881) II. 201 A foolish, goosey, innocent but very vulgar kind of mortal. **1869** *Contemp. Rev.* XI. 356 Mr. Riviere's 'Fox and Geese' made us laugh, the geese in conclave over the prostrate fox were so wonderfully goosy. **1871** CARLYLE in *Mrs. C.'s Lett.* I. 113 A goosey maid-servant at Mainhill.

2. Of the skin: In the condition of 'goose-flesh'.

1857 *Chamb. Jrnl.* VIII. 191 As if an instrument of that kind would ever persuade me out of a goosey sensation in the calves. **1887** JEFFERIES *Amaryllis at Fair* 3 The skin of her arms became 'goosey' directly.

3. [Cf. GOOSE *v.* 5.] Ticklish, nervously excited, touchy.

1906 *Dialect Notes* III. 138 *Goosy*, used of a person who is susceptible to nervous excitement when a finger is pointed at him, or when he is hardly touched or tickled. **1932** J. T. FARRELL *Studs Lonigan* (1936) I. ii. 22 Davey goosed Hennessey. Hennessey was goosey anyway, and he jumped.

Hence **'goosiness.**

1888 MISS TYTLER *Blackhall Ghosts* I. xi. 241 You are the goosiest goose, Lucy. I am rather tired of your goosiness.

goot, goote, obs. forms of GOAT, GOTE.

‖**gopak** ('gəʊpæk). Also **hopak** ('həʊpæk). [Russ. *gopák*, f. Ukrainian *hopák.*] A lively Ukrainian dance in $\frac{2}{4}$ time.

1929 G. GOULD *Democritus* 80 They..see the same Ukrainians that the two men have previously seen in Moscow, dancing the gopak. **1943** K. AMBROSE *Ballet-Lover's Pocket-Bk.* 21 Turns such as these are well suited to the virility of the Russian *Gopak.* **1958** *Economist* 25 Oct. 303/1 For some time ahead he [*sc.* Mr Gaitskell] could make Mr Bevan dance the *gopak* if he wanted to. **1959** *Collins' Mus. Encycl.* 324/1 *Hopak*, a Russian folk-dance in a lively 2-4 time, occasionally used by Russian composers. **1962** *Observer* 20 May 21/4, I was brought before her and told to dance a 'gopak' and a 'lesginka'.

gopher ('gəʊfə(r)), *sb.*[1] *U.S.* Also 9 **gophir.** [? Said to be ad. colonial F. *gaufre.*

According to Webster 1848-64, *gaufre* was used by the French settlers in North America as a name for various burrowing animals, and is a transferred use of *gaufre* honeycomb (see GOFER[1], GOFFER); cf. the vb. 'to honeycomb', as expressing the action of such animals.]

1. a. A burrowing rodent of the genera *Geomys* and *Thomomys*; a pocket gopher or pouched rat.

1812 BRACKENRIDGE *Views Louisiana* (1814) 58 The Gopher..lives under ground, in the prairies, and is also found east of the Mississippi. **1841** CATLIN *N. Amer. Ind.* (1844) II. liv. 165 The subterraneous whistle of the busy gophirs that were ploughing and vaulting the earth beneath us. **1856** BRYANT *Poems, Prairies* 64 The gopher mines the ground Where stood their swarming cities. **1883** B. HARTE *Carquinez Woods* vii. 161 [She] went like a squirrel up a tree or down like a gopher in the ground.

b. A native or inhabitant of Arkansas or Minnesota.

1845 in C. Cist *Cincinnati Misc.* 240 The inhabitants of.. Arkansas [are called] Gophers. **1872** *Harper's Mag.* Jan. 317/2 The various nicknames given to the States and people of this republic..Minnesota, Gophers. **1873** J. H. BEADLE *Undevel. West* xxxiii. 706 In May, 1859, I first became a 'gopher',—practical Western title of the Minnesotians. **1949** *Amer. Speech* XXIV. 26.

2. A burrowing or ground squirrel of the sub-family *Spermophilinæ*; a spermophile.

1874 COUES *Birds N.W.* 357 *Gopher*: Frontier vernacular name for all the ground-squirrels (*Spermophili*) indiscriminately. **1883** *Leisure Hour* 475/2 Numbers of.. grey..land squirrels (gophers) scampered..over the flats.

3. a. A burrowing land-tortoise (*Testudo carolina*), of nocturnal habits, common in the southern U.S.

1791 W. BARTRAM *Carolina* 18 The dens, or caverns, dug ..in the sand hills, by the great land-tortoise, called here Gopher, present a very singular appearance. **1845** LYELL *Trav. N. Amer.* I. 161, I frequently observed the holes of the gopher, a kind of land-tortoise. **1884** *Times* 18 Apr. 8 They vary this with a fish or gopher caught in the lakes or woods, the gopher being a species of land turtle.

b. A native or inhabitant of Florida.

1869 *Overland Monthly* III. 129 On account of the great number of gophers in that State,..a Floridian is called a 'Gopher'.

4. A large burrowing snake of the southern United States; also, the bull-snake. Also *gopher-snake.* (*Cent. Dict.*)

1837 J. L. WILLIAMS *Territory of Florida* 68 The Bull Snake..is sometimes called the Gopher snake. **1853** BAIRD & GIRARD *Catal. N. Amer. Reptiles* I. 165 Gopher Snake (*Georgia Couperi*). **1884-5** *Riverside Nat. Hist.* (1888) III. 367 *Spilotes couperi*..is known by the negroes as the indigo or gopher-snake.

5. *Mining.* A *gopher-drift* q.v.

1881 [see *gopher-drift*].

6. *attrib.* and *Comb.*, as ***gopher-burrow, -hill, -pelt***; also **gopher-drift** (see quot.); **gopher-hole,** (*a*) the opening of a gopher's burrow; (*b*) (see GOPHER *v.* 2); **gopher man,** 'a safe-blower (*Thieves' slang*)' (*Cent. Dict.*); also *gopher*, ellipt.; **gopher-plum, -root** (see quots.); **Gopher State,** a nickname for Minnesota.

1850 L. H. GARRARD *Wah-To-Yah* (1927) x. 138 The animals..stumbled more than once in the numerous *gopher burrows. **1903** A. ADAMS *Log of Cowboy* iv. 42 Officer's horse suddenly struck a Gopher burrow with his front feet. **1881** RAYMOND *Mining Gloss.*, *Gopher* or **Gopher-drift*, an irregular prospecting-drift, following or seeking the ore without regard to maintenance of a regular grade or section. **1841** CATLIN *N. Amer. Ind.* (1844) II. liv. 166 Over an extended plain are seen, like *gophir hills, their excavations ancient and recent. **1865** *N.Y. Herald* in *Morn. Star* 3 Feb., Some of our troops covering themselves from the fire by resort to the *gopher holes in the vicinage. **1883** STEVENSON *Silverado Sq.* 90 The meanest boy could lead them miles out of their way to see a gopher-hole. **1901** 'J. FLYNT' *World of Graft* 220 **Gopher-men*, safe-blowers. **1926** J. BLACK *You can't Win* ii. 12 Famous 'gopher men' who tunneled under banks like gophers and carried away their plunder after months of dangerous endeavor. **1928** M. C. SHARPE *Chicago May* 287 *Gopher*, one who tunnels to steal. **1891** *Century Mag.* Nov. 62, I cannot pay for a team each year with *gopher pelts as others do. **1893** *Funk's Stand. Dict.*, **Gopher-plum*, the Ogeechee lime (*Nyssa capitata*). **1889** *Century Dict.*, **Gopher-root*, a low rosaceous shrub, *Chrysobalanus oblongifolius*, with extensively creeping underground stems, found in the sandy pine-barrens of Florida, Georgia, and Alabama. **1880** J. M. FARRAR 5 *Yrs. Minnesota* 166 Gophers are here such a pest to the farmer that Minnesota has been called the '*Gopher State'. **1963** R. I. MCDAVID in H. L. Mencken *Amer. Lang.* x. 695 Minnesota..popularly..is the *Gopher State*,..and the football representatives of its state university are known as the *Golden Gophers.*

gopher ('gəʊfə(r)), *sb.*[2] [a. Heb. *gōpher.*] The tree of the wood of which the ark was made. Chiefly in comb. **gopher-wood**: applied in U.S. to the yellow-wood (*Cladrastis tinctoria*).

1611 BIBLE *Gen.* vi. 14 Make thee an Arke of Gopher-wood. **1856** AIRD *Poet. Wks.* 101 There to a pillar of black gopher-wood Brought near, a fettered prisoner he stood. **1867** JEAN INGELOW *Story Doom* I. 20 Where the palm, The almug, and the gophir shot their heads.

gopher ('gəʊfə(r)), *v. U.S.* [f. GOPHER *sb.*[1]]

1. *intr.* To act like a gopher; to burrow.

1893 *Scribner's Mag.* Apr. 473/2 At first were those who.. gophered under the mighty walls of the temple.

2. 'In *Mining*, to begin or carry on mining operations at hap-hazard, or on a small scale; mine without any reference to the possibility of future permanent development. Such mine-openings are frequently called *gopher-holes* and *coyote-holes* (Pacific States)' (*Cent. Dict.*). So **'gophering** *vbl. sb.*

1905 R. E. BEACH *Pardners* i. 22 We kept gophering around till March, in hopes. **1910** *Sat. Even. Post* 13 Aug. 4/1 Promising mines did 'gophering' or development work by contract. **1916** *Daily Colonist* (Victoria, B.C.) 19 July 3/3 The numerous dumps along the hillside indicate how thoroughly the gulch has been gophered in the search for gold. **1927** C. M. RUSSELL *Trails plowed Under* 129 This old boy is a prospector and goes gopherin' 'round the hills, hopin' he'll find somethin'. **1966** *McGraw-Hill Encycl. Sci. & Technol.* VIII. 481/1 Gophering, or coyoting, refers to small-scale mining utilizing small, irregular excavations in ground that usually stands without support.

gopher, variant of GOFER, GOFFER.

‖**gopi** ('gəʊpɪ). *India.* Also Gopi. [Skr.] (See quot. 1962.)

1880 *Encycl. Brit.* XI. 845/2 The mystic dwelling on the amours of Krishna and the *Gopis* of Braj has been often compared to the mystical interpretation of the *Song of Solomon.* **1893** KIPLING *Day's Work* (1898) 33 The young herd [*sc.* herdsman], the darling of the Gopis,..Krishna the Well-beloved. **1933** S. SITWELL *Canons of Giant Art* 121 They are the gopis, milkmaids of the herd, Dancing-girls of paradise, the park's fine pleasures. **1962** BRAHMACHARINI

USHA *Ramakrishna-Vedanta Workbk.* 33 *Gopi*, a milkmaid of Brindavan. The gopis were companions and devotees of Sri Krishna. **1968** *Jrnl. Mus. Acad. Madras* XXXIX. 21 Krishna's sport of going on boat with the Gopis.

gopin, goping, goppen, obs. ff. GOWPEN.

goppe, variant of GUP *int.*, *Obs.*

gopura (ˈgəʊpʊrə). *India.* Also **-am.** [Skr. *gōpura* city gate, f. *gō* eye + *pura* city.] The great pyramidal tower over the entrance-gate to the precinct of a temple (in S. India).

1862 C. R. MARKHAM *Trav. Peru & India* 408 The *gopurams* or towers of the great pagoda. **1895** R. W. FRAZER *Silent Gods* 24 The iron-studded massive gate beneath the many storied gopura. **1967** SINGHA & MASSEY *Indian Dances* ii. 41 A permanent visual record of all these karanas adorns the four gopurams or gateways of the great temple at Chidambaram. **1969** *Indian Mus. Jrnl.* V. Suppl., Arunagiri sat under the northern gopura of the temple and did penance for a long time.

gor[1]. *Obs.* exc. *dial.* Also 7 **gorr.** [Of unknown origin; cf. GORB.] An unfledged bird.

1683 F. HODELSTON in *Lond. Gaz.* No. 1860/6 The Old Birds of Prey, with their young Gorrs, which they were training up to swallow Kingdoms at once. **1847–78** HALLIWELL, *Gor*, a young unfledged bird. *Westm.*

gor[2]. *Obs.* exc. *dial.* [Cf. GORMAW.] A sea-gull.

1697 *Phil. Trans.* XIX. 576 Seven sort of Fowls, as Curliew, Sea-Pye, Sea-Swallow, Gorre, and other we want Names for. **1869** in *Lonsdale Gloss.*

gor, dial. f. GORE *sb.*[1]; var. GORE *sb.*[5] *Obs.*; obs. f. GORE *v.*[1]

‖**gorah, gorrah.** Also **goura, gowra.** [Hottentot.] A Hottentot musical instrument (see quot. 1881).

[**1786** SPARRMAN *Cape G.H.* I. 229 This instrument is called a t'Goerra, a name.. tolerably expressive of the sound of the instrument.] **1790** tr. *Le Vaillant's Trav.* II. 104 The *goura* is shaped like the bow of a savage Hottentot, it is of the same size. **1801** J. BARROW *Trav. S. Afr.* I. 149 This instrument was called the *gowra*. **1822–4** BURCHELL *Trav.* I. 458 Their chief was considered a good performer upon the goráh. **1834** PRINGLE *Afr. Sk.* Poem 17 Soothed by the gorrah's humming reed. **1842** R. MOFFAT *Mission Labours S. Afr.* iv. 58 His gorah soothes his solitary hours. **1881** NOBLE in *Encycl. Brit.* XII. 311/1 One [musical instrument] named the 'gorah' was formed by stretching a piece of the twisted entrails of a sheep along a thin hollow stick.. in the manner of a bow and string. At one end there was a piece of quill fixed into the stick, to which the mouth was applied. **1902** *Jrnl. Anthropol. Inst.* XXXII. 156 The *goura*, a stringed-wind musical instrument of the Bushmen and Hottentots. **1905** *Rep. Brit. Assoc.* 529 The *goura* of the Bushmen.. a bow-like instrument having a piece of flattened quill interposed between one end of the string and its attachment to the bow.

‖**goral** (ˈgɔərəl). *Zool.* Also **gooral, goorul, gural.** An Indian antelope (*Cemas goral*).

1834 *Penny Cycl.* II. 89/2 The Goral (*A. goral*).. first described by General Hardwicke in the 'Linnæan Transactions.' **1864** J. A. GRANT *Walk across Africa* iii. 35 Goorul or chamois of the Himalayas. **1876** KINLOCH *Large Game Shooting in Thibet* Ser. II. 21 The Gooral, like the Serow, belongs to the Chamois family.. I have several times seen.. Gooral in the Sewalik hills. **1894** *Westm. Gaz.* 23 Jan. 3/3 There were other kinds of big game, as musk and barking deer, and goral—an animal not unlike the chamois. **1894** *Royal Nat. Hist.* (ed. Lyddeker) II. 257 The goral (*Cemas goral*) of the Himalaya. *Ibid.* 258 Nearly allied to the gorals are the.. serows, or goat-antelopes [*Nemorhædus*]. **1919** *Chambers's Jrnl.* 8 Nov. 777/1, I hoped to get a gural or two on my way. **1922** *Blackw. Mag.* May 558/2 They reminded me of the Himalayan gural. **1925** G. BURRARD *Big Game Hunting* 101, I have always liked gooral meat. **1932** *Discovery* Nov. 344/2 On the wooded crags [in N. Burma] 2,000 feet above the river, there were *gooral*, but it needed dogs to drive them out from cover.

gor-amity (gɒrəˈmaɪtɪ). Also **garamity.** In representations of Negro speech, representing *God almighty*.

1834 T. WENTWORTH *West India Sketch Bk.* II. 16 Da kow no hab no tail, Gor-a-mity brush fry [= if a cow has no tail, God Almighty brushes the flies]. **1835** *Tough Yarns* 158 Gor Amighty send rain,—Gor Amighty send sun: but Gor Amighty send poor nigger too. **1837** *United Service Jrnl.* June 209 Goramity, whar for dem nigger makee me wait? *Ibid.* 211 Tank Garamity,.. me hab de felicity to find my massa. **1891** *Strand Mag.* Oct. 77/1 I'm the gorramighty of the *Biddy McDougal*.

goramy, var. GOURAMI.

goravich, variant of GILRAVAGE.

gorb (gɔːb), *a.* and *sb.* [Of unknown origin; cf. GOR[1]; also GORBLE *v.*[1]] †**A.** *adj.* Greedy; voracious. *Obs.* **B.** *sb. dial.* **a.** A greedy person; **b.** A young bird. *transf.* An infant.

1635 D. DICKSON *Pract. Wks.* (1845) I. 76 The gluttonous or gorb city. **1824** CARLYLE *Let.* 12 Nov. in Froude *Life* (1882) I. xv. 256 Unhappy gorb! I have wished it farther than I need repeat at present. **1825–80** JAMIESON, *Gorb*, a young bird. *Dumfr.* **1880** *Antrim & Down Gloss.*, *Gorb*, a greedy person.

gorbal (ˈgɔːbəl). *Sc.* [? Short for GORBLIN, or derivative of GORB. Cf. GORBLE *v.*[1]] = GOR[1], GORB *sb.*, GORBLIN, GORLIN.

1808 in JAMIESON s.v. *Yeldring*, Children.. often take the bare *gorbals*, or unfledged young, of this bird, and [etc.].

†**ˈgorbellied**, *a.* *Obs.* [f. GORBELLY + -ED[2].] Having a protuberant belly; corpulent.

a **1529** SKELTON *Agst. Garnesche* ii. 36 Gup, gorbellyd Godfrey! **1538** ELYOT *Dict.*, *Doliaris heluo*, a gorbelyed glutton. **1542** UDALL *Erasm. Apophth.* 110a, A great gorrebealyed chuff. *a* **1557** MRS. M. BASSET tr. *More on the Passion* in *More's Wks.* 1402/1 A greate gorbelyed glotton. **1596** SHAKS. *1 Hen. IV*, II. ii. 93 Hang ye gorbellied knaues, are you vndone? **1650** BULWER *Anthropomet.* 259 The Gordians and Muscovites, and other Gorbellied Nations. **1699** R. L'ESTRANGE *Colloq. Erasm.* (1711) 166 A kind of Gorbelly'd Kites, with crooked Beaks and Tallons. **1831** TRELAWNEY *Adv. Younger Son* ix. (1890) 59, I never saw the gorbellied Scotch captain again. **1838** D. JERROLD *Men of Charac.*, *C. Snub* ii. Wks. 1864 III. 421 The gorbellied varlets, with mouths greasy with the goods of cheated worth.

transf. **1596** NASHE *Saffron Walden* F 2 An vnconscionable gorbellied Volume, bigger bulkt than a Dutch Hoy.

†**ˈgorbelly**, *sb.* (and *a.*) *Obs.* exc. *dial.* [? f. *gor*, GORE *sb.*[1] (sense 1) + BELLY. Cf. Sw. dial. *går-bälg*.]

†**1.** A protuberant belly. *Obs.*

1519 HORMAN *Vulg.* 30 He had a fatte necke and a gorbely. **1601** CORNWALLYES *Ess.* II. xxviii. (1631) 22 As if there had beene no grace but in a gorbelly. **1615** T. ADAMS *Sacrifice of Thank.* 18 The Epicure hath a gorbelly. **1674** JOSSELYN *Voy. New Eng.* 21 Finding her [a she-wolf's] Gor-belly stuft with flesh newly taken in. **1725** BAILEY *Erasm. Colloq.* 133 About the size of Vultures.. with crooked Beaks and Gor-bellies. **1790** BURKE *Corr.* (1844) III. 144 Falstaff, reproaching the Londoners.. with their gore-bellies.

b. *nonce-use.* A garment with a loose belly.

1598 E. GILPIN *Skial.* (1878) 48 The French quarter slop, or the gorbelly, The long stockt hose, or close Venetian.

2. A person with a protuberant belly.

1530 PALSGR. 429/1 Se this gorbely, he is so shorte wynded that he can scarsely speke. **1580** NORTH *Plutarch* (1676) 189 They haue called him.. gorebelly, and hook-nosed. **1607** BREWER *Lingua* v. ii, The belching gor-belly hath well nigh killed me. **1694** MOTTEUX *Rabelais* v. (1737) 216 Fat, pursy Gorbellies. **1886** ELWORTHY *W. Somerset Word-bk.*, *Gorbelly*, an over-corpulent person. (Very com.)

†**3.** *attrib.* passing into *adj.* = GORBELLIED *a.* *Obs.*

1532 MORE *Confut. Tindale* Wks. 641/1 Yᵉ church had not prouided for gorbeli glottons. **1581** J. BELL *Haddon's Answ. Osor.* 222b, What if Landes and possessions long times englutted with gorbelly Mouncks became a pray to the spoylers. **1603** DEKKER *Wonderfull Yeare* F ij, My gorbelly Host leapt halfe a yarde from the coarse.

ˈgorbet. *Sc.* and *north.* [? f. GORB + -ET[1].] A young unfledged bird.

? *a* **1557** LYNDESAY *Satyre* [4397] in Pinkerton *Scot. Poems Repr.* (1792) II. 89 Cry lyke the gorbettis of ane kae. **1893** *Northumbld. Gloss.*, *Gorbit*, a newly hatched bird.

ˈgorble, *v.*[1] *Sc.* = GOBBLE *v.*[1]

1728 RAMSAY *Daft Bargain* 10 Raff.. lick'd his thumb, To gorble't up without a gloom. **1832–53** *Whistle-Binkie* (Scot. Songs) (1890) Ser. III. 39 We'll smuir our dule By gorblin' up parritch and cakes.

ˈgorble, *v.*[2] *Sc.* = GOBBLE *v.*[2]

1835 HOGG in *Fraser's Mag.* XI. 357 The earl he gorbled a gruesome laugh.

gorblimey (gɔːˈblaɪmɪ). Also **gaw-, -blime, -blimy.** [Cf. BLIMEY *int.*] Vulgar corruption of the imprecation *God blind me!* See also quots. 1919, 1925.

1896 A. MORRISON *Child of Jago* i. 16 Gawblimy, not what? **1909** J. R. WARE *Passing Eng.*, *Gorblimy* (about 1875). A gutter phrase. **1911** L. STONE *Jonah* I. ix. 105 'Gorblimey! A knock-out!'.. Stinky, with a haphazard blow, had given Chook the dreaded knock-out. **1914** T. A. BAGGS *Back from Front* xix. 92 Gor blimey, 'ow are ye, then, old townie? **1915** A. D. GILLESPIE *Let.* 27 Mar. (1916) 74 Most of the infantry now wear the soft 'Gor'bli'me' hat which looks horrid, but does not give such a mark as the flat-topped 'Brodrick'. **1918** W. J. LOCKE *Rough Road* v. 51 'Gorblime!' said Chipmunk, 'that's the first I 'eard of it.' **1919** *War Terms* in *Athenæum* 8 Aug. 729/1 'Gor-blimey', a soft service cap. **1925** FRASER & GIBBONS *Soldier & Sailor Words*, *Gorblimeys*.. An exclamation or adjective of emphasis. A 'Gorblimey' was the common colloquial term for an unwired, floppy, field-service cap worn by a certain type of subaltern in defiance of the Dress Regulations. Lines from a song, popular before the War, ran:—'He wears Gorblimey trousers An a little Gorblimey 'at.' **1956** J. MASTERS *Bugles & Tiger* 49 A tweed gorblimey cap worn well forward on the head. **1958** *Oxf. Mag.* 27 Feb. 326/1 The British and American tendency is to emphasise the Gorblimey aspect of history, the feelings of the ordinary man on the spot at the time. **1962** *Listener* 31 May 967/1 She offered a gorblimey cheerfulness.

ˈgorblin. *Sc.* [? f. GORB + -LING; cf. GORLIN.] An unfledged bird.

1728 RAMSAY *Answ. to Poverty Poets* ii, [They] gape like gorblins to the sky.

gorbuscha (gɔːˈbʊʃə). Also **garbusche.** [ad. Russ. *gorbúsha*, f. *gorb* hump, humpback.] The humpback salmon, *Oncorhynchus gorbuscha*.

1792 T. PENNANT *Introd. Arctic Zool.* p. ccvii, The Gorbuscha, or Hunch-back, arrives at the same time with the last [*sc.* the keta salmon]. **1884** D. S. JORDAN in G. B. Goode *Nat. Hist. Aquatic Animals* III. 476 This species is known to the Russians still.. by the name of 'Gorbuscha'. **1891** *Fur, Fin & Feather* Mar. 151 The salmon most plentiful in the Alaska waters is known as the humpback or garbusche. **1960** *Guardian* 15 Nov. 6/7 Soviet scientists had been transporting the eggs of gorbuscha from Sakhalin Island.. to the.. rivers of the Kola Peninsula.

†**gorce.** *Obs.* Also 5 **gorte**, 7 **gors**, 8 **goss.** [f. AF. *gortz*, pl. of *gort* (also OF. *gord*, *gourt*, mod.Fr. dial. *gour*, *gourd*):—L. *gurgit-em*, *gurges*, whirlpool. The form *gorce* was taken later for sing. and a pl. formed from it. See also GORE *sb.*[4]] **a.** A whirlpool. **b.** (See quot. 1706.)

[**1350** *Act 25 Edw. III*, Stat. IV. c. 4 Pur ce que Communes passages de neefs & batelx en les grantz rivers dEngleterre si sont sovent foitz destourbez par le lever de gortz. **1472** *Act 12 Edw. IV*, c. 7 Ascuns.. gorces,.. molyns, mille-dammez, etc.] **1480** CAXTON *Ovid's Met.* XIV. i, A lytil gorte.. wherin Sylla bayned her accustomably whan she hade hete. **1628** COKE *On Litt.* 5 b, A deep pit of water, a gors or gulf. **1706** PHILLIPS (ed. Kersey), *Gorce*,.. any stop in a River, such as Wears, Mills, Stakes, etc. which hinder the free Passage of Ships or Boats. **1741** VINER *Abridgm.* XVI. 23 Nusance.. lies for levying of a Goss to intercept the Course of Fish coming from the Sea. [**1891** NORTH in *Times* 13 May 3/5 The construction of such a gort.. was an act of ownership.]

†**gorche.** *Obs. rare*⁻¹. [? distortion of GORGE *sb.*, for the sake of rime.] ? A glutton.

1577 KENDALL *Flowers of Epigr.* 33 One sillie drop of water askt the glotton greedie gorche [*rime* scorche].

gorcock (ˈgɔːkɒk). *Sc.* and *north. dial.* [f. *gor* of obscure origin (hardly, as in the case of next, = GORE *sb.*[1]) + COCK.] The male of the Red Grouse.

1620 *Naworth Househ. Bks.* (Surtees) 128, 2 gorcocks, xᵈ. **1678** RAY *Willughby's Ornith.* 177 The Red Game, called in some places the Gorcock and More-cock, *Lagopus altera Plinii*. **1794** PICKERING in *Burns' Wks.* (1809) IV. 176 Full ninety winters hae I seen, And pip'd where gor-cocks whirring flew. **1813** SCOTT *Trierm.* III. vi, 'Mongst desert hills, where, leagues around Dwelt but the gorcock and the deer. **1856** W. E. AYTOUN *Bothwell* (1857) 48, I thought to hear the gorcock crow, or ouzel whistle shrill. **1882** J. BROWN *John Leech, etc.*, *Dk. Athole* 373 He was.. as prompt and hardy, as heathery as a gorcock.

gorcrow (ˈgɔːkrəʊ). Also 7 **gar-**, 8–9 **gorecrow.** [f. *gor*, GORE *sb.*[1] + CROW.] The Carrion Crow.

1605 B. JONSON *Volpone* I. ii, Raven, and gorcrow, all my birds of prey, That think me turning carcase, now they come. **1632** MARMION *Holland's Leaguer* IV. iii. Dram. Wks. (1875) 71 Out of the wind of me! what, do you think You can put out the eyes of a gorcrow? **1656** *Choyce Drollery* 67 She tript it like a barren Doe, And strutted like a Gar-crowe. **1766** PENNANT *Zool.* I. 167 It [Carrion Crow].. will pick out the eyes of young lambs.. for which reason it was formerly distinguished.. by the name of the gor or gorecrow. **1819** CAMPBELL *Ess. Eng. Poetry* (1861) 71 Human vultures and gorecrows. **1868** BROWNING *Ring & Bk.* x. 579 As the gor-crow treats The bramble-finch, so treats the finch the moth. **1881** *Oxfordsh. Gloss.* Suppl., *Gore-crow.*

gord(e, variant of GIRD *v.*[2], GOURD[2], [3], *Obs.*

gordget, obs. form of GORGET[1].

Gordian (ˈgɔːdɪən), *a.* and *sb.* Also 6 **gordion, -dyon.** [f. L. *Gordi-us* or *Gordi-um* (see sense 1) + -AN. The phrase *nodus Gordius* (used *fig.*) is a conjectural reading in Ammianus Marcellinus XIV. xi. I.] **A.** *adj.*

1. Gordian knot. a. An intricate knot tied by Gordius, king of Gordium in Phrygia. The oracle declared that whoever should loosen it should rule Asia, and Alexander the Great overcame the difficulty by cutting through the knot with his sword.

1611 SHAKS. *Cymb.* II. ii. 34 As slippery as the Gordian-knot was hard. **1891** A. T. PIERSON *Credulity of Incred.* 14 Alexander cut the Gordian Knot, which he had not the skill, patience, or strength to untie.

†**b.** A representation of an intricate knot.

1641 EVELYN *Diary* 1 Sept., The gallery is prettily painted with several huntings, and at one end a gordian knot.

c. *fig.* or allusively: (*a*) A matter of extreme difficulty. ***to cut a Gordian knot***: to get rid of a difficulty by force or by evading the supposed conditions of solution. (*b*) An indissoluble bond. †Also ***Gordian-twined knot***.

(*a*) **1579** FULKE *Heskins' Parl.* 396 Hee had found out a sworde to cutt in sunder this Gordian knot. **1599** SHAKS. *Hen. V*, I. i. 46 Turne him to any Cause of Pollicy, The Gordian Knot of it he will vnloose. **1682** SIR T. BROWNE *Chr. Mor.* II. §13 Death will find some ways to unty or cut the most Gordian Knots of Life. **1735–8** BOLINGBROKE *On Parties* 84 His Sword would have cut the gordian Knot of hereditary Right. **1791** BENTHAM *Panopt.* Pref., The Gordian knot of the Poor Laws not cut but untied. **1887** RIDER HAGGARD *Jess* xxxii, By no other means could the Gordian Knot be cut.

(*b*) **1590** GREENE *Orl. Fur.* (1599) 23 This Gordion knot together counites A Medor partener in her peerelesse loue. *c* **1630** P. FLETCHER *Pisc. Eclogs*, etc. (1633) 61 Strange power of home, with how strong-twisted arms, And Gordian-twined knot, dost thou enchain me! **1788** H. WALPOLE *Remin.* ii. 19 Perhaps too much difficulty of untying the Gordian knot of matrimony.. would be no kindness to the ladies. **1824** BYRON *Juan* XVI. lxxiv, The Gordian or the Geordi-an knot, whose strings Have tied together commons, lords, and kings.

2. Resembling the Gordian knot; consisting of twisted convolutions, intricate, involved.

1606 *Proc. agst. Garnet* S s 3, The binding knot of the late Gordian Conspiracie. **1643** MILTON *Divorce* II. xx, Hereby also dissolving tedious and Gordian difficulties, which have hitherto molested the Church of God. **1667** —— *P.L.* IV. 348 Close the serpent sly, Insinuating, wove with Gordian twine His braided train. **1802–12** BENTHAM *Rationale Judic. Evid.* (1827) III. 193 Some of them [are] such as seem scarce capable of receiving solution but in the Gordian style. **1819** KEATS *Lamia* 47 She was a gordian shape of dazzling hue. **1820** SHELLEY *Ode Liberty* xv, Lift the victory-flashing sword, And cut the snaky knots of this foul gordian word. **1871** R. ELLIS tr. *Catullus* lxiv. 258 Some girt round them in orbs, snakes gordian, intertwining.

†**B.** *sb.*

1. = *Gordian knot.*

1561 T. NORTON *Calvin's Inst.* IV. 152 It is like the Gordian: whiche it is better to breake in sonder, than to labor so much in vndoing it. *a* **1616** BEAUM. & FL. *Bloody Bro.* I. i, My sword, With which the Gordian of your Sophistry Being cut, shall shew th' Imposture. **1643** PRYNNE *Sov. Power Parl.* II. 36 These strongest obligations are all cancelled, these Gordians cut in sunder with the sword of warre. **1709** MRS. MANLEY *Secret Mem.* (ed. 2) II. 195 And who-ever is the Man that unties the Gordian, as some such is always to be found, his Fortune is made.

2. An inhabitant of Gordium; one skilled in tying intricate knots.

1606 EARL NORTHAMPTON in *True & Perf. Relat.* I i 1 a, The hardest knots that the Gordians of our age can deuise to tye.

†**'gordian,** *v. nonce-wd.* [f. prec. adj.] *trans.* To tie in a Gordian knot.

1818 KEATS *Endym.* I. 597 Locks..simply gordian'd up and braided.

gording, variant of GOURDING, *Obs.*

gordlin, variant of GORLIN *Sc.*

Gordon ('gɔːdən). [f. the name of Alexander *Gordon*, 4th Duke of Gordon (1743–1827), who promoted the breed.] In full ***Gordon setter.*** A black and tan setter (cf. SETTER *sb.*[1] 11), used as a gun dog.

1865 *Field* 7 Oct. 255/2 (*heading*) The Black-tan Gordon setter. *Ibid.*, Several of the very best Gordons have even a white foot or feet. **1867** 'OUIDA' *Under Two Flags* I. ii. 27 Three or four Gordon setters, an Alpine mastiff, and two wiry Skyes dashed at their chains. **1907** B. M. CROKER *Company's Servant* xxviii. 278 The dog with the yellow face proved to be the Gordon setter belonging to Major McPherson. **1931** *Times Lit. Suppl.* 26 Nov. 939/2 Three setters (English, Irish and Gordon). **1968** E. H. HART *Encycl. Dog Breeds* 165 The Gordon Setter. The fourth Duke of Gordon..brought into prominence the black and tan setter of Scotland, which eventually, as a breed, adopted his name. *Ibid.*, Gordons have beauty and brains.

‖**Gordonia** (gɔː'dəʊnɪə). *Bot.* [See quot. 1770.] A genus of North-American and Asiatic trees of the camellia or tea family (*Ternstrœmiaceæ*), with large beautiful flowers; a plant of this genus.

1770 ELLIS in *Phil. Trans.* LX. 520, I desire it may have a place among your genera, by the name of Gordonia, as a compliment to our worthy friend, that eminent gardener Mr. James Gordon, near Mile-end. **1865** F. PARKMAN *Huguenots* iv. (1875) 58 Here the rich gordonia..sends down its thirsty roots to drink at the stealing brook.

gore (gɔə(r)), *sb.*[1] Also 4, 7 gorre, 6–7 goar(e, 9 *dial.* gor. [OE. *gor* neut., dung, dirt = MDu., Du. *goor* mud, filth, OHG., MHG. *gor* (mod.Swiss *gur, guhr*, animal dung), ON. *gor* the cud in animals, slimy matter (Sw. *gorr*, dial. *går, gor, gur*, dung, filth, putrid matter).]

1. Dung, fæces; filth of any kind, dirt, slime. *Obs.* exc. *dial.*

c **725** *Corpus Gloss.* 883 *Fimum*, goor. *a* **1000** *Riddles* xli. 72 (Gr.) þæs gores sunu..þone we wifel wordum nemnaþ. *c* **1000** ÆLFRIC *Exod.* xxix. 14 þæs cealfes flæsc and fell and gor. **13..** *E.E. Allit. P.* B. 306 þe gore þer-of me hatz greued & þe glette nwyed. ? *a* **1400** *Morte Arth.* 1130 Bothe þe guttez and the gorre guschez owte at ones. *c* **1400** *St. Alexius* (Laud 622) 1005 His fader sergeauntz alle..gorre on hym gonne þrowe. **1460** *Lybeaus Disc.* 1471 Gore, and fen, and full wast, That was out ykast. **1599** T. M[OUFET] *Silkwormes* 59 Tainting with lothsome gore the common fold. **1641** BEST *Farm. Bks.* (Surtees) 14 Such sheepe likewise as are troubled with the infirmity of chewinge of gorre..A greate parte of their meat, whiles that they are chewinge of it, workes forth of the wykes of their mouthe. **1825** BROCKETT *N.C. Words, Gor, Gore*, dirt, any-thing rotten or decayed.

†**b.** Hardened rheum from the eyes. *Obs.*$^{-1}$

1741 MONRO *Anat. Nerves* (ed. 3) 48 The Gum, or Gore, as we call it, was separated in greater Quantity,..and the Eye-ball itself was diminished. **1808–80** in JAMIESON.

2. Blood in the thickened state that follows effusion. In poetical language often: Blood shed in carnage. †In early use occas. ***blood and gore, bloody gore*** (cf. Du. *bloed en goor*); see also GORE BLOOD.

1563 *Mirr. Mag., Hastings* xxviii, A Souldyours handes must oft be dyed with goare. *c* **1586** C'TESS PEMBROKE *Ps.* LXXVIII. xvii, Zoan plaines..Saw watry clearnes chang'd to bloudy gore. **1602** MARSTON *Antonio's Rev.* I. i. Wks. 1856 I. 76 This warm reeking goare. **1693** DRYDEN *Ovid's Met.* I. 596 Th' expiring serpent wallow'd in his gore. *c* **1760** SMOLLETT *Ode to Indep.* 18 The Saxon prince in horror fled From altars stained with human gore. **1801** SOUTHEY *Thalaba* IX. xx, His talons are sheathed in her shoulders, And his teeth are red in her gore. **1848** LYTTON *Harold* III. ii, Red with gore was the spear of the prelate of London.

¶ Whimsically used for 'blood'.

1799 COLERIDGE *Lett.* (1895) 305, I have three brothers, that is to say, relations by gore.

†**b.** ***(all) (in) a*** (or ***one***) ***gore of blood***: bathed in or besmeared with blood. (Cf. GORE BLOOD 2.) *Obs.*

1661 PEPYS *Diary* 7 Dec., In comes the German back again, all in a goare of blood. **1749** WESLEY *Wks.* (1872) II. 147 She was all in a gore of blood. **1766** H. BROOKE *Fool of Qual.* (1792) I. iv. 147 From their forehead to their shoes they were in one gore of blood. **1784** SIR J. CULLUM *Hist. Hawsted* iii. 171 He's all a Gore of blood. **1824** *Examiner* 15/1 Lying on the ground in a gore of blood.

†**c.** ? A clot, 'gout' (of blood). *Obs. rare*$^{-1}$.

1727 *Philip Quarll* 253 He saw Gores of Blood here and there.

3. *attrib.* and *Comb.* **a.** simple attrib., as (sense 1) †***gore-pit***; **b.** objective, as ***gore-distilling, -dropping***; **c.** instrumental, as ***gore-bedabbled, -drenched, -drowned, -dyed, -fed, -moistened, -spangled, -stained***; **d.** parasynthetic, as ***gore-faced.*** Also **gore-chewer** *dial.* (cf. quot. 1641 in sense 1).

1848 LYTTON *Harold* XI. xi, The tomb Of the bones and the flesh, *Gore-bedabbled and fresh. **1893** *Northumbld. Gloss.*, *Gore-chower, a sheep which, owing to some structural defect in its mouth, is unable to retain or properly masticate its food. **1770** BEATTIE *Ode Peace* I. ii, Murder..shakes her *gore-distilling wings. **1806** J. GRAHAME *Birds Scot.* 169 That *gore-drenched flag. **1848** LYTTON *Harold* V. iii, His sightless and *gore-dropping sockets. **1627** DRAYTON *Agincourt*, etc. 114 Much dismay'd with what had lately hapt, On *Gore-drown'd Gladmore in that bloody shower. **1794** SOUTHEY *Wat Tyler* III. ii, Flattery's incense No more shall shadow round the *gore-dyed throne. **1812** BYRON *Ch. Har.* I. xlviii, *Gore-faced Treason sprung from her adulterate joy. **1801** M. G. LEWIS *Bothwell's Bonny Jane* xxxvi, His hands two *gore-fed scorpions grasp'd. **1811** SCOTT *Don Roderick* xlii, *Gore-moisten'd trees shall perish in the bud. **1508** FISHER *7 Penit. Ps.* vi. Wks. (1876) 18 As a sowe waloweth in the stynkynge *gore pytte, or in the puddell. *a* **1649** DRUMM. OF HAWTH. *Poems* Wks. (1711) 37/1 *Gore-spangled ensigns steaming in the air. **1848** T. A. BUCKLEY *Iliad* 81 Mars, man-slayer, *gore-stained, stormer of walls.

gore (gɔə(r)), *sb.*[2] Forms: 4–6 goore, 4–9 *Sc.* and *north.* gare, 6–8 *Sc.* gair(e, 7–9 goar(e, 4– gore. [OE. *gára* = MDu. *ghere, gheere*, etc. (Du. *geer*), OHG. *gêro, kêro* (MHG. *gêre*, Ger. *gehren, gehre*), ON. *geire* (Sw. dial. *gere*, Da. dial. *gære*), app. related to OE. *gár* spear (see GARE *sb.*[1]), the reference being to the shape of the spear-head. From OHG. the word passed into the Romanic languages; for the forms in these see GYRON.]

1. A triangular piece of land.

†**a.** An angular point, a promontory. (OE. only.)

c **893** K. ÆLFRED *Oros.* I. i. §26 Ispania land is þryscyte..An ðæra garena lið suðwest.

b. A wedge-shaped strip of land on the side of an irregular field (cf. quot. 1881). Now only *dial.*

[**1235–52** *Rentalia Glaston.* (Som. Rec. Soc.) 58 Radulfus tenet unam goram terræ. *c* **1325** in Kennett *Par. Ant.* (1818) I. 571 Duæ rodæ..scilicet le Gores super Shortefurlong.] **1523** FITZHERB. *Surv.* xxi. 39, xxxvi landes, & thre gores fother or pyke, and they be all one thing. **1641** BEST *Farm. Bks.* (Surtees) 43 There is in it 14 through landes and two gares. **1793** *Trans. Soc. Arts* XI. 52 Contained in the head lands and gores, or short lands. **1881** *Leicester Gloss.* s.v., When a field, the sides of which are straight but not parallel, is divided into 'lands' or 'leys', the angular piece at the side is called a gore or pike. **1890** *Gloucester Gloss., Gores*, the short ridges in an unevenly shaped ploughed field.

c. A small strip or tract of land lying between larger divisions. Chiefly *U.S.*

1650 FULLER *Pisgah* I. ii. 34 Which gore or gusset of ground, was called Apherema, that is, a thing taken away, because parted from Samaria, and pieced to Judea. **1703** *Providence (R.I.) Records* (1893) IV. 153 A heape of stones set for a south westerne Corner of a Goare, or Slipe of land. **1733** *Rhode Island Col. Records* (1859) IV. 478 The gore of land (adjoining to Attleborough) in controversy between this colony and the Province of the Massachusetts Bay. **1818** N. MITCHELL in *Mass. Hist. Coll.* VII. 146 A small gore also on the east side of the town..was annexed to Pembroke June 7, 1754. **186.** J. DRAPER *Hist. Spencer* (ed. 2) 12 A gore about one mile wide, lying between Leicester and Spencer. **1887** G. W. SEARS *Forest Runes* p. vii, What New Englanders call a 'gore',—a triangular strip of land that gets left out somehow when the towns are surveyed.

d. ? = GAIR, an isolated fertile strip.

1854 *Jrnl. R. Agric. Soc.* XV. II. 395 Its locality is a narrow gore on the summit of the cinder-bed.

e. (See quots.)

1811 WILLAN *W. Riding Yorksh. Words* in *Archæol.* XVII. (E.D.S.), *Gore*, the lowest part in a tract of country. **1888** *Berksh. Gloss., Gore*, level low-lying land. Most parishes have a field called the 'Gore'.

†**2.** *poet.* The front section of a skirt, wider at the bottom than at the top (cf. sense 3); the lap of a gown, an apron. Hence in extended sense: a skirt, petticoat, gown. Also in phrase ***under gore***, under one's clothes (in ME. poetry often a mere expletive). (Cf. OF. *geron, giron* used in the same senses.) *Obs.*

a **1250** *Owl & Night.* 515 Habbe he isstunge under gore, Ne last his luve no lenger more. *a* **1290** in Horstmann *Altengl. Leg.* (1881) 222 Ich wolde I-witen nouþe Leuedi..Wi þe failleþ gore, Sleue and nammore Of cloþ þat ich I-se. *a* **1300** *Siriz* 5 Wis he wes of lore And gouthlich under gore And clothed in fair sroud. *a* **1310** in Wright *Lyric P.* 26 Glad under gore in gro ant in grys. *c* **1320** *Sir Tristr.* 2868 It was a ferly gin, So heye vnder hir gare It fleiȝe. *c* **1386** CHAUCER *Sir Thopas* 78 An elf-queene shal my lemman be, And slepe vnder my goore. **1406** HOCCLEVE *La Male Regle* 31 Had I thy power knowen or this yore..Nat sholde his lym han cleued to my gore. *c* **1460** *Emare* 198 Þat fayr lady Was godely unther gare. **1570** LEVINS *Manip.* 174/7 A Gore, *gremiale.*

†**b.** The opening in the breast of a gown. (So MDu. *ghere.*) *Obs.*

a **1529** SKELTON *P. Sparowe* 345 My byrde so fayre, That was wont to..go in at my spayre, And crepe in at my gore Of my gowne before.

3. Any wedge-shaped or triangular piece of cloth forming part of a garment and serving to produce the difference in width required at different points, esp. used to narrow a skirt at the waist (cf. sense 2).

c **1325** *Gloss. W. de Biblesw.* in Wright *Voc.* 172 Par devant avet escours E de coste sunt gerouns [*gloss* gores]. *c* **1386** CHAUCER *Miller's T.* 51 A ceynt she werede..A barm-clooth (eek)..ful of many a goore. *Ibid.* 136 (Harl. MS.) A kirtel..Schapen with goores in the newe get. *c* **1440** *Promp. Parv.* 203/2 Goore of a clothe, *lacinia.* *c* **1480** HENRYSON *Test. Cres.* 179 His garmound and his gyte ful gay of grene, With goldin listis gilt on every gair. **1501** DOUGLAS *Pal. Hon.* I. x. 5 In purpour rob hemmit with gold ilk gair. **1530** PALSGR. 226/2 Goore of a smocke, *poynte de chemise.* **1598** FLORIO, *Gheroni*..the gores or gussets of a smocke or shirt, the side peeces of a cloke. **1706** PHILLIPS (ed. Kersey), *Gore*, a piece of Linnen-cloth let into the sides of a Woman's Shift. **1853** KANE *Grinnell Exp.* xx. (1856) 156 The sailors recognized it at once as the gore of a pair of trowsers. **1883** *Knowledge* 13 July 30/1 The skirt..has four gores in front.

†**b.** A triangular piece (cut out of something).

c **1330** *Arth. & Merl.* (Kölbing) 6395 His scheld he clef, god it wot, & of his hauberk a gore & of his aketoun a fot & more.

4. *Her.* A charge formed by two curved lines meeting in the fesse-point, the one being drawn from the sinister or dexter chief and the other from the lowest angle of the base (cf. quot. 1562).

1562 LEIGH *Armorie* (1597) 72 b, He beareth Argent, a Gore Sinister Sable. He that is a coward to his enemie, must beare this, But if it be a dexter Gore, although of Staynand colour, yet it is a good cote for a gentlewoman. **1610** GUILLIM *Heraldry* I. viii. (1660) 45 A Goare Sinister..This [abatement]..is due to him that is a Coward to his enemy. **1706** in PHILLIPS (ed. Kersey): and in mod. Dicts.

5. One of the many triangular or lune-shaped pieces that form the surface of a celestial or terrestrial globe, a balloon, the covering of an umbrella, the dome of a building, etc.

1796 *Specif. Russell's Patent* No. 2144. 3 The globe being covered with printed gores. **1842–59** GWILT *Archit.* §2070 In polygonal domes the curves of the gore will bound the ends of the boards. **1864** *Athenæum* No. 1933. 631/3 Seaming together the gores of his balloon. **1875** KNIGHT *Dict. Mech.* s.v. *Globe*, A very cheap paper globe is now met with, in which the printed gores are brought together edge to edge by a string. **1879** SIR G. SCOTT *Lect. Archit.* II. 171 For each of the triangular gores of the dome we now substitute a vault.

6. *Naut.* **a.** (See quot. 1851.)

1794 *Rigging & Seamanship* I. 91 In sails with a roach-leech, the lower gores are longer. **1851** KIPPING *Sailmaking* (ed. 2) 184, *Gores.*—Angles cut slopewise at one or both ends of such cloths as widen or increase the depth of a sail.

b. 'Angular pieces of plank inserted to fill up a vessel's planking at any part requiring it' (Smyth *Sailor's Word-bk.* 1867).

1875 KNIGHT *Dict. Mech., Gore*, an angular piece of planking used in fitting the skin of a vessel to the frames.

7. *Comb.*, as **gore-coat** (see quot. 1886); **gore-furrow** (see quot.).

1746 *Exmoor Scolding* 154 (E.D.S.) Thy *Gore Coat oll a girred, thy Aead-Clathing oll a' foust. **1886** ELWORTHY *W. Somerset Word-bk.* s.v. *Gore*, A gorecoat is a petticoat made so as to fit closely at the waist without gathering. **1844** H. STEPHENS *Bk. Farm* I. 472 A *gore-furrow is a space made to prevent the meeting of two ridges, and as a substitute for an open furrow between them.

gore, *sb.*[3] = GARE *sb.*[1], a spear or javelin.

c **1250** [see GARE]. **1886** ELWORTHY *W. Somerset Word-bk.*, *Gore*, a long rod tipped with a small spear for driving oxen. Always so called.

†**gore,** *sb.*[4] *Obs.* Also 7 goor. [app. formed as sing. to GORCE, the sibilant ending of which caused it to be taken as pl.] = GORCE.

1523 *Act 14 & 15 Hen. VIII*, c. 13 Diuers newe weres, gores, stackes, and ingins haue bene leuied and enhaunsed. **1657** *Cotton's Abridgem. Records Tower* 57 And now of late daily the said Rivers are stopped and turned aside by Goors, Mills, Piles and Pales.

†**gore,** *sb.*[5] *Obs.* In 6 gor, 7 goare. [a. OF. *gorre.*] = GRANDGORE.

1552 LYNDESAY *Monarche* 5113 Vtheris strange Infirmeteis..As in the Gutt, grauell, and gor. **1614** P. FORBES *Eubulus* viii. (1627) 152 A man hath the Goare in his Legge; which Legge, all-bee-it in an hudge degree festered, yet walketh and mooveth..Nowe, shall the Goare, heere, glorie, that [etc.].

gore (gɔə(r)), *v.*[1] Also 5–6 gor(re, 6–8 goar. [Of obscure etymology; the view that it is f. *gore*, var. of GARE *sb.*[1] spear, is plausible as to sense, but the early Sc. form *gorre* appears to disprove it.]

†**1.** *trans.* To pierce or stab deeply, with a sharp weapon, spike, spur, or the like. *Obs.* exc. as in 2.

a **1400–50** *Alexander* 3645 Þare was..many of Perses Gorred..& grysely woundid. *c* **1400** *Sege Jerus.* (E.E.T.S.) 941 Þe newe emperour..alle þe cite drowe hym; & suþ gored þe gome, þat his guttes alle..in-to his breche felle. *c* **1450** HOLLAND *Howlat* lxv, I am vngraciously gorrit, baith guttis and gall. **1460** CAPGRAVE *Chron.* 189 As he rode ovyr the brigge on was beneth and with a spere gored him. **1513** DOUGLAS *Æneis* II. x. 186 Cruell Pirrus, Quhilk..gorris the fader at the altair but grace. **1535** COVERDALE *Ezek.* xxiii. 46 These shal stone them, and gorre them with their sweardes. *a* **1566** *Merie Tales* in *Skelton's Wks.* (1843) I. Introd. 63 The freere felt hys bellye, &..thought hee had ben gored, and cried out..I am kylled. **1573** *Satir. Poems Reform.* xl. 375 With Gun and Gainȝe thocht thay boist to gor ȝow [*rimes with* befoir ȝow]. **1590** SPENSER *F.Q.* II. vii. 13 The sacred Diademe in peeces rent, And purple robe gored with many a wound. **1600** HOLLAND *Livy* XXXV. XXXV. (1609) 910 He ran with full carriere at him, gored his horse [L. *transfixo equo*]. **1664** H. MORE *Myst. Iniq.* 474 They gore and spurre up the Ass to goe that way. **1690** in Wood *Life* 30 Aug., The two horses..pawed over the iron spikes... Their leggs are goar'd. **1725** POPE *Odyss.* XI. 713 Two ravenous vultures.. Incessant gore the liver in his breast. **1735** SOMERVILLE *Chase* II. 229 Our lab'ring Steeds We press, we gore. **1798** COLERIDGE *Fears in Solit.* 119 As if the fibres of this godlike frame Were gored without a pang. **1820** SCOTT *Monast.* x., No sooner didst thou fall to the ground mortally gored, as he deemed, with his weapon, than [etc.].

transf. and *fig.* *a* **1591** R. GREENHAM *Wks.* (1599) 48 Wee must rather winne men with a louing admonition, then gore them with a sharpe reprehension. **1675** HOBBES *Odyss.* (1677) 23 The ship the sea then gores: The water..wounded and broken roars. **1736** MACHIN in Rigaud *Corr. Sci. Men* (1841) I. 299 It has gored me to think that I was perpetually liable to a just charge of never finishing any thing.

†**b.** With various constructions: To impale *upon*; to dig or scoop *out of*. *Obs.*

1618 BOLTON *Florus* III. x. (1636) 206 Such of the defendents as durst sally out being either cut in peeces in the trenches with the sword, or goared upon the stakes. **1655** FULLER *Ch. Hist.* IX. Ded., Where the violence of the waters aggested the earth, goared out of the hollow valleys.

2. *spec.* Of a horned animal (esp. a bull or ox): To pierce with the horns. Also, rarely, of a boar: To wound with the tusk.

1523 FITZHERB. *Husb.* §70 For els the beastes with theyr hornes, wyll put bothe the horses and the shepe, and gore them in theyr bellyes. **1722** SEWEL *Hist. Quakers* (1795) II. VII. 62 The bull then gored him again with his horns. **1725** POPE *Odyss.* XIX. 527 His tusks oblique he aim'd the knee to goar. **1810** T. COGAN *Ethical Treat. Passions* II. §1 (1813) III. 105 We ascribe vices..to an ox that attempts to gore the attendants. **1834** PRINGLE *Afr. Sk.* iv. 188 My father narrowly escapes being gored by a furious ox. **1865** LIVINGSTONE *Zambesi* xiv. 301 It is the nature of bulls to gore each other.

transf. and *fig.* **1641** J. JACKSON *True Evang. T.* II. 112 Aquinas..was called bos mutus, a dumbe Oxe; and..with two hornes..gored all unbeleevers. **1646** S. MARSHALL *Def. Inf. Baptism* 87 How you avoid being goared by the three hornes of my Syllogisme. **1838** SYD. SMITH *2nd Let. to Archd. Singleton* 11 Billingsgate controversialists, who have tossed and gored an Unitarian. **1841** LONGF. *Wreck Hesp.* xviii, The cruel rocks, they gored her side Like the horns of an angry bull.

b. *absol.*; †also *intr.* to gird *at*.

1626 MIDDLETON *Anything for Quiet Life* V. i. 144 Your wit is still goring at my lady's projects. **1759** ADAM SMITH *Mor. Sent.* II. iii. 213 The dog that bites, the ox that gores, are both of them punished. **1818** SCOTT *Rob Roy* xxi, He's like Giles Heathertap's auld boar; ye need but shake a clout at him to make him turn and gore. **1892** *Blackw. Mag.* Apr. 556 Five or six bulls had stamped and roared and gored and died.

†**gore**, *v.*² *Obs.* Also 6–7 goar. [f. GORE *sb.*¹] Only in **gored, goring**.

1. *trans.* To cover with or as with gore, to besmear *with*, to dabble *in* blood. Only in pa. pple.

1566 DRANT *Wail. Hierem.* K viij b, Preists seruisable to Idols, and gorde in blessed blood. *a* **1592** H. SMITH *Wks.* (1867) II. 338 His sides imbrued and gored with his own blood. **1611** SPEED *Hist. Gt. Brit.* VII. xvii. §6. 289 The Battels ioyned, and the Field goared with bloud, the day was lost vpon the Kings side. **1622** J. REYNOLDS *God's Rev. agst. Murder* II. vii. 87 We haue seene the Theatre of this History, gored with great variety of bloud. **1655** *Theophania* 90 Many of them..lay gored in their own blood.

2. *intr.* To lie soaking *in* blood.

1577 STANYHURST *Descr. Irel.* in *Holinshed* 27/1 They left them goaring in their bloud..and gasping up their flitting ghosts.

Hence **ˈgoring** *ppl. a.*, that forms gore = GORY.

1575 CHURCHYARD *Chippes* (1817) 206 Goring bloode had glutted gasers eye.

gore (gɔə(r)), *v.*³ Also 6 goor. [f. GORE *sb.*²; cf. Du. *geeren*, G. *gehren*.]

1. *trans.* To cut into a gore or gores; to furnish with gores.

1548 HALL *Chron., Hen. VIII* (an. 19) (1550) 166 Cloth of gold..set wyth cut warkes of clothe of syluer plyghted goord fret and folded eche cloth vpon other. **1794** *Rigging & Seamanship* I. 91 Sails, gored with a sweep. **1879** *Scribner's Mag.* XIX. 426/2, I should take out two of the back breadths for an over-skirt—yes—an' gore the others! **1893** GEO. HILL *Hist. Eng. Dress* II. 270 The next fashion was to gore the skirts in every width.

†**2.** *Naut. intr.* To swell or jut *out*. *Obs.*

1627 CAPT. SMITH *Seaman's Gram.* vii. 32 The Clew is.. that which comes goring out from the square of the saile.

3. *trans.* To plough a 'gore'. (See GORING *vbl. sb.*²)

gore variant of GAUR.

ˈgorebill. *local.* [? f. GORE *sb.*³ (= GARE *sb.*¹) + BILL *sb.*¹] A name of the garfish. (Cf. GOREFISH.)

1862 *Chambers's Encycl.* IV. 625/1 It [the Garfish] is sometimes called Greenbone, Gorebill, and Mackerel-guide. **1881** *Cassell's Nat. Hist.* V. 68 The hooks being baited with smelt or a fish called the Gorebill.

†**gore blood, ˈgore-blood.** *Obs.* exc. *dial.* [f. GORE *sb.*¹]

1. Gore-like blood; clotted blood.

1573 TWYNE *Æneid* XII. (1584) S viij, Downe strait he falles, & armour large with goareblood doth embrue. **1594** ? GREENE *Selimus* Wks. 1881–3 XIV. 245 Then teare the old man peecemeal with my teeth, And colour my strong hands with his gore-blood. **1603** KNOLLES *Hist. Turks* (1621) 909 The ground..all stained with gore bloud. **1639** FULLER *Holy War* III. viii. (1640) 122 Leopoldus..fought..till his armour was all over gore bloud. **1685** BAXTER *Paraphr. N.T., Acts* xv. 29 Not eating strangled Creatures in the gore blood.

attrib. **1681** HICKERINGILL *Black Non-Conformist* (1682) A ij, A meer gore-blood Religion.

2. Freq. in phrases. **a.** *all on* (*in, of*) *a gore blood*, all besmeared or covered with blood. (See also A-GORE-BLOOD.) *Obs.* exc. *dial.*

1559 BECON *Displ. Popish Mass* Wks. 1563 III. 48 If ye would..cutte your selues with knyues tyll ye be all on a goreblood [etc.]. **1591** LYLY *Sappho* IV. iii, I was all in a goare bloud. **1631** MABBE *Celestina* XIII. 151 His face..was all blacke and blue, and all of a goare-bloud. **1691** tr. *Emilianne's Obs. Journ. Naples* 233 He..rowled himself stark naked upon Thistles and Thorns..and made all his Body on a Gore-blood. **1774** WESLEY *Wks.* (1872) XI. 74 What, to whip them for every petty offence, till they are all in gore blood? **1840** SPURDENS *Suppl. Forby's Voc. E. Anglia* s.v., 'All of a gore-blood'—a common pleonasm.

b. quasi-*adj.* (*all*) *gore blood*: Gory with blood, besmeared with gore. *Obs.* exc. *dial.*

1631 WEEVER *Anc. Funeral Mon.* 245 Scourged him..so terrible, as..all his body was gore bloud. **1653** H. COGAN tr. *Pinto's Trav.* ix. 29 The Flies and Gnats..bit and stung us in such sort, as not one of us but was gore blood. **1657** TRAPP *Comm. Job* v. 18 He wounds them with the wound of an enemy..and leaves them all gore blood. **1675** HOBBES *Odyss.* (1677) 266 They killing went: all gore-blood was the hall. **1877** *Holderness Gloss.*, *Gor-bleead.*

Hence **gore-bloody** *a.*

1580 HOLLYBAND *Treas. Fr. Tong*, *Ensanglanté*, gore bloudie. **1638** T. HERBERT *Five Mad Shavers*, Shee being thus naked and gore-bloody, they [etc.].

gore copper, variant of GARCOPPER, *Obs.*

1654 WHITELOCKE *Jrnl. Swed. Emb.* (1772) II. 251 To ship ..200 ship-pound, swedish weight, of gore copper.

gorecrow, variant of GORCROW.

gored (gɔəd), *ppl. a.*¹ [f. GORE *v.*¹ + -ED¹.] In senses of the vb.

1577 KENDALL *Flowers of Epigr.* 3 Trust me (saied she) my goared gutts doe put me to no paine. **1590** SPENSER *F.Q.* I. iii. 35 And from his gored wound a well of bloud did gush. **1605** SHAKS. *Lear* V. iii. 320 You twaine, Rule in this Realme, and the gor'd state sustaine. **1747** *Gentl. Mag.* Feb. 93 In dull thought concludes the day, How the gor'd Hack's reward to pay! **1808** J. BARLOW *Columb.* VI. 490 Nor knew the chief..That his gored thigh had first received the ball. **1810** SCOTT *Lady of L.* VI. iv, Mangled limbs, and bodies gored.

†**gored**, *ppl. a.*² *Obs. rare*⁻¹ [f. GORE *v.*² + -ED¹.] (See quot.)

1599 A. M. tr. *Gabelhouer's Bk. Physicke* 336/1 [Prescriptions] For goarred, or congealede bloode.

gored (gɔəd), *ppl. a.*³ [f. GORE *v.*³ and *sb.*² + -ED.]

1. Cut into a gore or gores.

1794 *Rigging & Seamanship* I. 91 The longest gored side of one cloth makes the shortest side of the next. **1891** *Daily News* 19 Sept. 2/1 The gored gowns are now lined throughout.

2. *Her.* (See quot.)

1828–40 BERRY *Encycl. Herald.* I, *Gored*, cut into large arched indents.

†**goree**, *sb.*¹ *slang. Obs.* Also 7 gory. Money. Phrase *old Mr. Goree* (see quot.).

a **1700** B. E. *Dict. Cant. Crew*, *Goree*, Money, but chiefly Gold. *Old-Mr.-Gory*, a piece of Gold. **1725** in *New Cant. Dict.*

goree, *sb.*², **gori** (gɒˈriː). Also gore. [ad. Chinyanja *goli.*] A forked stick used by the Arabs to fasten slaves together by their necks. Also *gori-stick.*

1865 D. & C. LIVINGSTONE *Narr. Exped. Zambesi* v. 137 'Goree', or Slave-stick. **1891** *Life & Work* May [4] This boy ..worked in a gore-stick for two years. **1899** A. WERNER *Captain of Locusts* 243 Uledi and certain men came down.. from the Unango country, bringing with them people tied in gori-sticks. **1921** W. P. LIVINGSTONE *Laws of Livingstonia* III. ix. 213 The slaves..fastened with chains or the gori stick. **1925** *Blackw. Mag.* Aug. 276/2 The young ones already had their necks in the *goree*.

ˈgoree, ˈgory, *a. Her.* [f. GORE *sb.*²; a pseudo-AF. rendering of GORED *ppl. a.*³] (See quots.)

1828–40 BERRY *Encycl. Herald.* I, *Gorée* or *Gory*, in old authors sometimes written *goarée* and *goary*, is the same as *double archée*. **1889** ELVIN *Dict. Heraldry*, *Gored* or *Gorée*, cut into large arched indents.

gore-fish. [? f. *gore*, GARE *sb.*¹] ? = GARFISH. (Cf. GOREBILL.)

1839 COL. HAWKER *Diary* (1893) II. 162 We only got 5 bass..1 flounder, 1 gore fish, and 1..cuttlefish. **1886** R. C. LESLIE *Sea-painter's Log* viii. 164 The long-beaked gore-fish, which when hooked comes along at once, like a sea-serpent, on the top of the water.

†**ˈgorel.** *Obs.* Also 6 gherell. [a. F. *gorel* (*gohorel*), *goreau*, etc. in same sense.] A halter, horse-collar. Also *attrib.*, as *gorel-maker*.

c **1481** CAXTON *Dialogues* (E.E.T.S.) 2/37 Of gorel-makers and joyners. **1526** in Dillon *Calais & Pale* (1893) 81 Item, of a horse coller or gherell.

gorell, variant of GORREL, *Obs.*

gorg, gorgays(e, obs. ff. GORGE, GORGEOUS.

gorge (gɔːdʒ), *sb.*¹ Also 5 goorge, 5–6 gorg. [a. OF. and F. *gorge* = Pr. *gorga*, *gorja*, Sp. *gorga*, Pg. *gorja*, It. *gorga*, *gorgia*:—popular L. **gorga*, **gurga* of unknown origin; the possibility of connexion with L. *gurges*, whirlpool, is very doubtful.]

I. In physical senses.

1. The external throat; the front of the neck; said both of human beings and of animals. *Obs.* exc. *arch.*

? *a* **1400** *Morte Arth.* 3761 He gyrdes hym in at þe gorge with his gryme launce. *a* **1400–50** *Alexander* 4985 All gilden was hire gorg with golden fethirs. **1481** CAXTON *Myrr.* II. viii. 81 The breste and the gorge of hym [the phenix] shyneth. *a* **1529** SKELTON *Ware Hauke* 87 With that he gaue her a bounce Full vpon the gorge. **1586** A. DAY *Eng. Secretary* I. (1625) 73 Taking him [the Rebell] by the gorge. **1819** KEATS *K. Stephen* I. iii, Do not tempt me to throttle you on the gorge. **1866** C. MERIVALE in *Contemp. Rev.* II. 270 The form divine, the graceful gorge, fair breast, and dazzling eyes.

fig. **1579** J. STUBBES *Gaping Gulf* A iij b, We shewe by demonstrative reasons that it goeth to the very gorge of the Church.

†**b.** The dewlap of a bull. ? *nonce-use.*

1591 HORSEY *Trav.* (Hakluyt Soc.) 220 [There was] a goodly fare white bull..his crop or gorg hanging down to his knees before him.

2. The internal throat. Now only *rhetorical*.

1362 LANGL. *P. Pl.* A. XI. 53 God is muche in the gorge of theose grete maystres. *a* **1400–50** *Alexander* 3627 And full of glorand gledis þaim to þe gorge fillis. *a* **1533** LD. BERNERS *Huon* cxxxii. 489 He caste fyre and smoke oute of his gorge lyke a forneyse. *a* **1586** SIDNEY *Arcadia* I. (1590) 62 b, Songs, which the watrie instruments did make their [birds'] gorge deliuer. **1601** HOLLAND *Pliny* I. 339 The vpper part or top of the Wezand, is called the Gorge, or the gullet. **1607** ROWLANDS *Famous Hist.* 41 Forth his smoaking gorge came sulphur smoke. **1821** BYRON *Irish Atavar* xx, Till the gluttonous despot be stuff'd to the gorge! **1832** TENNYSON *Pal. Art* vi, The golden gorge of dragons spouted forth a flood of fountain-foam.

fig. **1876** SWINBURNE *Erechth.* 1358 And the gorge of the gulfs of the battle is wide for the spoil of the world. **1783–94** BLAKE *Songs Exper., Div. Image* 8 The human face [is] a furnace seal'd, The human heart its hungry gorge.

3. *Falconry.* The crop of a hawk. *to bear full gorge*: to be full fed. Hence, in opprobrious rhetorical use, the 'maw', devouring capacity, of a monster, or a person, etc. spoken of as gluttonous, bloodthirsty, or rapacious. *Obs.* exc. *arch.*

c **1450** *Bk. Hawkyng* in *Rel. Ant.* I. 304 The flesch that is in his gorge woll be oversoden if it be ther any while long holdyng. **1486** *Bk. St. Albans* C viij, She goorgith when she fillith hir goorge with meete. **1514** BARCLAY *Cyt. & Uplondyshm.* (Percy Soc.) p. xli, Their greedy gorges are rapt with the smell. **1582** T. WATSON *Centurie of Loue* xlvii. (Arb.) 83 No lure will cause her stoope, she beares full gorge. **1583** [See GARBAGE *sb.*²] **1602** MARSTON *Antonio's Rev.* V. v. Wks. 1856 I. 140 Here lies a dish to feast thy fathers gorge. **1615** LATHAM *Falconry*, *Words of Art* (1633), Gorge, is that part of the Hawke which first receiueth the meat, and is called the craw or crop in other fowles. **1625** GILL *Sacr. Philos.* IV. 23 Nothing could glut the gorges of those bloody Priests. **1641** MILTON *Ch. Govt.* II. Concl. 63 This mighty sailewing'd monster that menaces to swallow up the Land, unlesse her bottomlesse gorge may be satisfi'd with the blood of the Kings daughter the Church. **1852** KINGSLEY *Andromeda* 64 A prey for the gorge of the monster.

fig. **1594** PLAT *Jewell-ho.* I. 29 Doe wee thinke that Nature is bounde to cast vp the treasures of her full gorge amongest vs? **1612–15** BP. HALL *Contempl. O.T.* XVI. iv, So vast are the gorges of some consciences; that they can swallow the greatest crimes. **1814** SCOTT *Ld. of Isles* VI. xxiv, The first are in destruction's gorge.

b. The phrase *a full gorge* properly belongs to sense 3 (cf. *on a full stomach*), but the ambiguity of the adj. led to its being interpreted according to sense 4. (Cf. GORGE *sb.*³)

1553 T. WILSON *Rhet.* 64 The counsailor heareth causes with lesse pain beyng emptie, then he shal be able after a full gorge. **1589** COGAN *Haven Health* cciii. (1636) 195 If..they bee not sicke upon a full gorge, yet they are drousie and heavy. **1642** MILTON *Apol. Smect.* Wks. 1738 I. 132 What though? because the Vultures had then but small pickings, shall we therfore go and fling them a full gorge? *a* **1693** URQUHART *Rabelais* III. xv. 126 Falconers,..when they have fed their Hawks, will not suffer them to fly on a full Gorge. **1727** BRADLEY *Fam. Dict.* s.v. *Capon*, Give the Capon a full Gorge thereof three times a Day.

†**4.** A meal for a hawk. (*to give*) *gorge upon gorge*: a second meal before another is digested; also *transf.* *Obs.*

c **1430** LYDG. *Bochas* II. xxvii. (1494) i jb, They..Forsoke Mars..And to Bachus their hedes gan enclyne Gorge vpon gorge, tyll it drough to nyght. **1575** TURBERV. *Faulconrie* 199 Beware that you gyue hir not gorge upon gorge. *Ibid.* 291 The diseases in Hawkes heads do most commonly breede of giuing them too great gorges. **1615** LATHAM *Falconry* (1633) 107, I haue already forewarned you, to be circumspect in her diet, that it may be of light and coole meate, and small gorges thereof. **1677** N. COX *Gentl. Recreat.* (ed. 2) 247 In the first place, never give them [Hawks] a great Gorge, especially of gross meats.

5. What has been swallowed, the contents of the stomach; in phrases (primarily of *Falconry*) †*to cast* (*up*), *heave, spue up, vomit one's gorge*. Also *to cast the gorge at*: to reject (food) with loathing.

1526 SKELTON *Magnyf.* 1633 To styre vp your stomake you must you forge, Call for a candell, and cast vp your gorge. **1563-87** FOXE *A. & M.* (1684) III. 275 He will vomit his gorge, and cast out floods to overflow him. *c* **1575** *Perfect Bk. Kepinge Sparhawkes* (1886) 20 Castinge the gorge, kepinge her meate longe aboue, or other surfit..be..veary daungerus. **1590** SPENSER *F.Q.* I. iv. 21 And all the way, most like a brutish beast, He spued vp his gorge, that all did him deteast. **1857** GEN. P. THOMPSON *Audi Alt.* I. xvii. 57 Eat horse, or eat dog, or put something into your mouths you have always been taught to cast the gorge at.

fig. **1642** ROGERS *Naaman* 37 Sundry who..haue sent for the minister..and there vomitted up all their gorge, accused and condemned themselves.

b. Freq. used *fig.* in the above phrases to express extreme disgust or (in later use) violent resentment; now commonly *one's gorge rises* (*at* or †*against*). *to rouse* (*stir*) *the gorge*: to make furiously angry.

1532 MORE *Confut. Tindale* Wks. 702/1 [Preachers who] make a man ready to cast his gorge to heare them raue and rage like mad men. **1602** SHAKS. *Ham.* v. i. 207 How abhorred my Imagination is, my gorge rises at it. **1604** —— *Oth.* II. i. 236 Her delicate tendernesse will finde it selfe abus'd, begin to heaue the Gorge, disrelish and abhorre the Moore. **1766** H. BROOKE *Fool of Qual.* Wks. 1792 III. xv. 74 The very gorge of my soul rises against this dæmon. **1809** W. IRVING *Knickerb.* VII. vi. (1820) 485 So insolent..a request would have been enough to have roused the gorge of the tranquil Van Twiller himself. **1863** WHYTE MELVILLE *Gladiators* II. 274 He remembered now that his gorge had risen while he spoke. **1873** H. ROGERS *Orig. Bible* vi. 243 The very thought of whom naturally stirred all the gorge of this Pharisee of the Pharisees. **1877** FARRAR *Days of Youth* iv. 34 In uttering it he would be unable to repress the rising gorge of self-disgust.

II. In transferred (chiefly technical) uses.

6. *Fortif.* The neck of a bastion or other outwork; the entrance from the rear to the platform or body of a work (cf. quot. 1834-47).

1669 *Lond. Gaz.* No. 390/3 But yet the courage of his men prevailing, they won from the Turks the Gorge of that Bastion. **1690** LEYBOURN *Curs. Math.* 586 The greater the Flanks and the Gorge between them are, the better they are. **1762** STERNE *Tr. Shandy* V. xix, We have not a couple of field-pieces to mount in the gorge of that new redoubt. **1812** WELLINGTON in *Gurw. Desp.* IX. 12 The detachment which attacked the work by the gorge had the most serious difficulties to contend with. **1834-47** J. S. MACAULAY *Field Fortif.* (1851) 9 The open or rear part of the redan, and of all other works, is called the gorge. **1876** in VOYLE & STEVENSON *Milit. Dict.*

7. A narrow opening between hills; a ravine with rocky walls, *esp.* one that gives passage to a stream.

1769 GRAY *Let.* Poems (1775) 359 Looking full into the gorge of Borrowdale. **1814** SCOTT *Wav.* xvi, Through the gorge of this glen they found access to a black bog. **1856** STANLEY *Sinai & Pal.* Introd. 39 A mass of high limestone cliffs, with two deep gorges. **1878** HUXLEY *Physiogr.* 157 If the glacier enters a gorge, it becomes contracted.

†**8.** *Farriery.* (See quot.) *Obs.*$^{-1}$ (Cf. GORGED *ppl. a.*[2] 2.)

1610 MARKHAM *Masterp.* II. cx. 391 The gorge or gourded legges, is an ill sorrance, being a grieuous swelling in the neather part of the legges.

9. *Arch.* (See quots.) [All in Fr. use.]

a. 1706 PHILLIPS (ed. Kersey), *Gorge, Gule,* or *Neck,* (in *Architect.*) is the narrowest part of the *Dorick* and *Tuscan* Capitals, lying between the Astragal, above the Shaft of the Pillar, and the Annulets. **1727-41** CHAMBERS *Cycl.*, *Gorge* is also used for the neck of a column; more properly called *collarino*, and *gorgerin*. **1889** in *Century Dict.*

b. 1727-41 CHAMBERS *Cycl.*, *Gorge of a chimney*, is the part between the chambranle and the crowning of the mantle.

c. 1706 PHILLIPS (ed. Kersey), *Gorge*,..a kind of Moulding, hollow on the inside, which is larger, but not so deep as the *Scotia*. **1727-41** in CHAMBERS *Cycl.* **1823** in P. NICHOLSON *Pract. Build.* 585.

d. 1721-41 CHAMBERS *Cycl.*, *Gorge* is sometimes used for a moulding that is concave in the upper part, and convex at bottom; more properly called *gula*, and *cymatium*.

e. 1875 KNIGHT *Dict. Mech.*, *Gorge*, (*Masonry*) a small groove at the under side of a coping, to keep the drip from reaching the wall.

10. *Mech.* The groove of a pulley. [So F. *gorge*.]

1812-16 J. SMITH *Panorama Sci. & Art* I. 308 To prevent the ropes *a* and *b* from rubbing against each other, the upper fixed pulley may have a double gorge. **1875** in KNIGHT *Dict. Mech.*

11. *Angling.* †**a.** A contrivance for disengaging a fishhook, when swallowed (*obs.*$^{-1}$). **b.** A solid object, intended to be swallowed by the fish, to ensure its capture.

1740 R. BROOKES *Art of Angling* I. xiv. 43 As the Pearch generally swallows the Bait..it will be necessary to carry an Instrument..which I call a Gorge. **1883** *Century Mag.* Apr. 900/1 The fish swallowed it, and, the gorge coming crosswise with the gullet, the fish was captured. **1884** *Athenæum* 23 Feb. 254/3 Flints of various sizes.. manufactured for use as fish-hooks, gorges, and sinkers.

12. *U.S.* A mass choking up a narrow passage; esp. in *ice-gorge* (see ICE *sb.* 8).

1884 [see ICE *sb.* 8]. **1886** *Pall Mall G.* 22 Apr. 7/2 The ice gorge near Montreal has been broken.

†**13.** *Pottery. pl.* (See quots.) [Possibly a distinct word: cf. BROWN GEORGE.]

1684 *Dwight's Patent* in Jewitt *Ceramic Art Gt. Brit.* I. 121 Severall new Manufactures of Earthenwares, called by the Names of White Gorges, Marbled Porcellane Vessells, Statues, and Figures, and Fine Stone Gorges and Vessells, never before made in England or elsewhere. **1813** T. FAULKNER *Hist. Acc. Fulham* 27 In the year 1684 Mr. John Dwight..established..a manufactory of earthern wares known under the name of White Gorges. **1879** J. TIMBS in *Cassell's Techn. Educ.* I. 367/2 Specimens of..'Fulham Ware', consisting of white gorges or pitchers.

III. 14. *attrib.* and *Comb.*, as (sense 11) *gorge-bait, -fishing, -hook*; (sense 6) *gorge-curtain, -line*; also **gorge-circle**, in gearing, 'the outline of the smallest cross section of a hyperboloid of revolution' (Webster 1897); †**gorge-millar** *Sc.*, ? a glutton.

1867 F. FRANCIS *Angling* iv. (1880) 132 *Gorge baits of all kinds..were invented by the father of cruelty. **1862** *N.Y. Tribune* 19 Apr. (Cent.), The blindages over the casemates of the *gorge-curtains [were] splintered and shivered. **1898** *Daily News* 14 Dec. 6/4 The abolition of..live or dead *gorge fishing. **1866** *Athenæum* 27 Jan. 131/3 Baited *gorge-hooks. **1875** 'STONEHENGE' *Brit. Sports* I. v. xi. §3. 315 Gorge hooks are either single or double. **1661** S. PARTRIDGE *Double Scale Proportion* 93 The length of the *Gorge-line in the made Fort, is 59,5. **1834-47** J. S. MACAULAY *Field Fortif.* (1851) 109 After having..stretched a cord *mn* four feet above the gorge line [etc.]. **1500-20** DUNBAR *Poems* lx. 26 Gryt glaschew-hedit *gorge-millaris.

†**gorge**, *sb.*[2] *Her. Obs.* [Of unknown origin.] A bearing known only from the drawing given by Leigh; its interpretation was disputed (see quot.).

Not to be confounded with *gorges*, GURGES, which in some mod. books of heraldry appears with the spelling *gorge* or *gurge*.

1562 LEIGH *Armorie* (1597) 103 He beareth Sanguine, a Gorge, Argent. Thoughe this seeme vnlikely to be a water-budget, yet hath it long time bin so taken, and so blazed, and neuer of anie other fashion, then ye see in this escocheon.

gorge (gɔːdʒ), *sb.*[3] [f. next vb.] An act of gorging oneself; a glut (of food, wine, etc.).

1854 SYD. DOBELL *Balder* xxiii. 99 A wreathed wrestler from a gorge of wine, He falls in pride. **1867** F. FRANCIS *Angling* iv. (1880) 105 They have a heavy gorge about once in two or three days. **1890** PETRIE in *Statem. Palestine Explor. Fund* Oct. 228 Thinking of nothing but the perfect gorge all the weary day [of the Ramadan fast].

gorge (gɔːdʒ), *v.* Also 5 **goorge**. [ad. OF. and F. *gorger*, f. *gorge* GORGE *sb.*[1]]

1. *intr.* To fill the gorge; to feed greedily. (In early use, of a bird of prey.) Const. *on, upon.*

13.. *K. Alis.* 5625 Alle hei gorgen as a rauene. **1486** *Bk. St. Albans* C viij, She goorgith when she fillith hir goorge with meete. **1601** SHAKS. *Jul. C.* v. i. 82 On our former Ensigne Two mighty Eagles..pearch'd, Gorging and feeding from our Soldiers hands. **1641** MILTON *Animadv.* Wks. (1851) 233 The very garbage that drawes together all the fowles of prey and ravin in the land to come and gorge upon the Church. **1795** *Gentl. Mag.* July 619/1 He gorged so much at a neighbour's as to stop all the functions of Nature, and he was actually suffocated with a good meal. **1821** SHELLEY *Hellas* 469 They..like hounds of a base breed, Gorge from a stranger's hand, and rend their master. **1891** R. KIPLING *Light that Failed* iii. 44 Dick fell upon eggs and bacon and gorged till he could gorge no more.

fig. **1828** D'ISRAELI *Chas. I*, II. viii. 182 The single passion of D'Ancre was inordinate avarice; he gorged on wealth.

2. *trans.* **a.** To fill the gorge of; to stuff with food; to glut, satiate. Also with *up*. (Cf. ENGORGE 1.)

1486 *Bk. St. Albans* A iv b, How ye shall gyde yow if yowre hawke be full goorged. **1549** LATIMER *1st Serm. bef. Edw. VI* (Arb.) 42 Surueiers there be, yat gredyly gorge vp their couetouse guttes. **1555-8** PHAER *Æneid* III. H iij b, For whan he gorgyd had him self with meates & drinkings drownd. **1591** PERCIVALL *Sp. Dict.*, *Papar*, to gorge vp, to fill the gorge. **1605** SHAKS. *Lear* I. i. 120 He that makes his generation messes To gorge his appetite. **1648** *Hunting of Fox* 21 The Fox..had..so gorg'd his guts that he could not squeeze himself out againe. **1709** STEELE *Tatler* No. 83 ⁋7 Going to a Tavern to Dinner; or after being gorged there, to repeat the same with another Company at Supper. **1725** DE FOE *Voy. round World* (1840) 219 Our men gorged themselves with it [chocolate] and would have no more. **1756** BURKE *Subl. & B.* IV. xxiv, We paint the giant.. plundering the innocent traveller, and afterwards gorged with his half-living flesh. **1826** SYD. SMITH *Wks.* (1867) II. 82 The king of the vultures first gorged himself. **1860** KINGSLEY *Misc.* I. 189 When fish are gorged with their morning meal of green drakes.

b. *transf.* and *fig.*

1596 SHAKS. *1 Hen. IV*, III. ii. 84 Being with his presence glutted, gorg'd, and full. **1639** DU VERGER tr. *Camus' Admir. Events* 84 In this ease and idlenesse of life gorged with wealth. **1719** DE FOE *Crusoe* (1840) II. ix. 199 Heaven can gorge us with our own desires. **1830** SCOTT *Demonol.* vii. 203 Our dungeons are gorged with them. **1844** THIRLWALL *Greece* VIII. lxiii. 216 They were gorging themselves with plunder. **1873** TRISTRAM *Moab* xv. 293 Every press gorged, every sheet of paper occupied.

c. Said of that which is devoured: To glut.

1713 ADDISON *Cato* I. iv, Nor would his slaughter'd army now have lain On Africk's sands..To gorge the Wolves and Vultures of Numidia. **1742** YOUNG *Nt. Th.* v. 468 When his foul basket gorges them no more.

3. To take into the gorge, to swallow; to devour greedily. †Also with *in*.

1614 B. JONSON *Barth. Fair* I. (1631) 15 So it [pig] be eaten with a reformed mouth..not gorg'd in with gluttony, or greedinesse. **1653** WALTON *Angler* I. v. 127 You must fish for him with a strong line..and let him have time to gorge your hook. **1667** MILTON *P.L.* III. 434 As when a Vultur.. Dislodging from a Region scarce of prey, To gorge the flesh of Lambs or yearling Kids. **1817** COLERIDGE *Sibyl. Leaves* (1862) 144 How could I bear To see them gorge their dainty fare? **1848** THACKERAY *Van. Fair* I. xiv. 119 When men of a certain sort..are in love, though they see the hook and the string..they gorge the bait nevertheless.

transf. and *fig.* **1647** N. BACON *Disc. Govt. Eng.* I. lxvi. (1739) 145 The Clergy had not only gotten the game, but gorged it. **1700** BLACKMORE *Job* xx. 87 Tho' he may Riches gorge, the painful Spoil In massy Vomit quickly will recoil. **1742** YOUNG *Nt. Th.* IV. 281 Who is the King of Glory? He who slew The rav'nous foe, that gorg'd all human race! **1816** BYRON *Siege Cor.* xii, On the vulgar yelling press, To gorge the relics of success. **1853** C. BRONTË *Villette* xlii, The storm ..did not lull till the deeps had gorged their full of sustenance.

absol. **1833** MARRYAT *P. Simple* (1863) 76 A glass of grog is a bait that he'll play round till he gorges.

4. a. To fill full, distend (a vein, organ, duct, or other vessel); to choke, choke up. Chiefly in *pa. pple.* (Cf. ENGORGE 1 b.)

1508, 1572 [see GORGED *ppl. a.*[1] b]. **1809** *Med. Jrnl.* XXI. 108 In such cases..the veins have always been found particularly gorged with black blood. **1845** BUDD *Dis. Liver* 381 The lobules of the liver soon become gorged with bile. **1860** TYNDALL *Glac.* II. xx. 336 The water which is supposed to gorge the capillaries of the glacier. **1872** DARWIN *Emotions* viii. 208 During excessive laughter..the head and face become gorged with blood, with the veins distended. **1888** FAGGE *Princ. Med.* (ed. 2) I. 158 [In Relapsing Fever] the kidneys are gorged and swollen.

b. *intr.* Of ice: to become fixed so as to form an obstruction. *U.S.*

1852 *Knickerbocker* XL. 157 After an hour's plunging through the ice, which had accumulated in such masses as almost to 'gorge', we came to where it lay. **1873** J. H. BEADLE *Undevel. West* xxxiv. 738 The ice..gorged against a bluff bank in a short bend of the stream, and dammed the water.

5. To scoop *out* into gorges (see GORGE *sb.* 7).

1849 DANA *Geol.* iii. (1850) 155 The whole surface [is] gorged out with valleys.

Hence **'gorging** *ppl. a.*

1743 *Lond. & Country Brewer* IV. (ed. 2) 284 A strong, gorging, intoxicating Yeast-beaten Ale. **1883** *Athenæum* 29 Dec. 863/3 One passage which ought not to have been inserted..representing us as gorging gluttons.

gorgeable ('gɔːdʒəb(ə)l), *a.* [f. GORGE *v.* + -ABLE.] That can be swallowed.

1883 RUSKIN *Fors Clav.* xciv. VIII. 234 *note*, Chopping up its formerly loved authors..into crammed sausages, or blood-puddings swiftly gorgeable.

gorgeat, obs. form of GORGET[1].

†**gorgeaunt.** *Obs.* [ad. F. *gorgeant*, pr. pple. of *gorger* GORGE *v.*] A boar in its second year.

c **1420** *Venery de Twety* in *Rel. Ant.* I. 151 The boor frist he is a pyg as long as he is with his dame, and whene his dame levyth hym then he is called a gorgeaunt.

gorged (gɔːdʒd), *ppl. a.*[1] [f. GORGE *v.* + -ED[1].] Fed to the full, crammed with food.

1593 SHAKS. *Lucr.* 694 The full-fed Hound, or gorged Hawke. *a* **1626** MIDDLETON *Witch* I. i. 35 Here's marriage sweetly honour'd in gorg'd stomachs And overflowing cups! **1704** SWIFT *Batt. Bks.* (1750) 29 The Refuse of gorged Wolves. **1836** MACGILLIVRAY tr. *Humboldt's Trav.* xvi. 213 The animal lay stretched at full length on the ground, like a gorged cat. **1885** *Truth* 28 May 848/2 A flock of gorged cormorants sitting on rocks by the sea.

transf. **1605** A. WARREN *Poor Mans Pass.* E 3 Some Vsurer ..Whose gorged chests surfet with cramming gold.

†**b.** *Sc.* Stopped up, choked. *Obs.*

1508 DUNBAR *Tua Mariit Wemen* 99 Gory is his tua grym ene gladderrit all about, And gorgeit lyk twa gutaris that wer with glar stoppit. **1572** *Satir. Poems Reform.* xxxvii. 19 Gorgit waters ever gritter growis.

gorged (gɔːdʒd), *ppl. a.*[2] [f. GORGE *sb.*[1] + -ED[2].]

1. *Her.* Having the gorge or neck encircled (with a coronet, etc.).

1610 GUILLIM *Heraldry* III. xxvi. 184 He beareth..a Lion Rampand..Gorged with a Coller. **1708** J. CHAMBERLAYNE *St. Gt. Brit.* I. II. ii. (1743) 53 An unicorn, argent, gorged with a crown. **1763** *Brit. Mag.* IV. 28 On the dexter-side, a lion guardant, or, gorged ducally, argent. **1823** RUTTER *Fonthill* p. xxiii, A Heron's head erased, Or, gorged with a collar. **1868** in CUSSANS *Her.* vi. (1893) 90.

†**2.** *Farriery.* Affected with the 'gorge' (see GORGE *sb.*[1] 8).

1688 *Lond. Gaz.* No. 2395/4 A bright bay Mare,.. something gorged in her near Footlock before. **1701** *Ibid.* No. 3725/4 A slight Nutmeg-grey Mare..gorg'd in both Legs before. **1753** [see DISGORGE *v.* 3].

3. Hollowed out as a gorge or pass. *rare.*

1871 *Vermont Hist. Gazetteer* II. 741/1 Belonging to the mountain scenery..is..a deeply gorged mountain pass.

gorgeer(e, variant of GORGER *sb.*[1], *Obs.*

'gorgeful. *rare*$^{-1}$. [f. GORGE *sb.*[1] + -FUL.] A bellyful.

1611 COTGR., *Saouler*, to glut, cloy, fill, saciate, giue a gorgefull of.

gorgelet ('gɔːdʒlɪt). [f. GORGE *sb.*[1] + -LET; cf. OF. *gorgelete*.] A patch of colour on the throat of a bird.

1872 COUES *Key N. Amer. Birds* 99 The exquisite gorgelets or frontlets of humming birds.

gorgeous ('gɔːdʒəs), *a.* Forms: 5 gorgayse, 6 **gorgays, gorges, gorgyas, gorgyo(u)s(e,**

gorge(o)us(e, 6-7 gorgi(o)us(e, 6- gorgeous. [ad. OF. *gorgias* elegantly or finely dressed, fashionable, gay: of uncertain origin.]

1. Adorned with rich or brilliant colours; sumptuously gay or splendid; showy, magnificent:

a. of persons (with reference to dress).

With quots. 1560 and 1631 cf. GLUTTON 1 b.

c **1495** *Epitaffe* etc. in *Skelton's Wks.* (1843) II. 391 Ladyes, damosels, mynyonat and gorgayse. **1503** HAWES *Examp. Virtue* VI. ix, Impossyble it is for me to dyscouere How gorges she was and gretly magnyfyed. **1507** *Justes of May & June* 117 in Hazl. *E.P.P.* II. 117 Other there were That were Joly and gorgyas in theyr gere. **1560** BECON *New Catech.* Wks. 1564 I. 447 b, That gorgious rych gloton was condemned..because he would shew no mercye to the poore miserable begger Lazarus. **1607** DEKKER *Whore Babylon* Wks. 1873 II. 241, I am not gorgious in attire, But simple, plaine and homely. **1613** WITHER *Sat. Ess.* (1615) 163 And yet the Prince that's gorgioust in array, Must lie as naked as his Groome in clay. **1631** R. H. *Arraignm. Whole Creature* xi. §2. 102 The Georgeous, and glurtenous Gospels Helluoh, that would not feast Lazarvs. **1710** STEELE *Tatler* No. 184 ¶8 My Sister does not affect to be gorgeous in her Dress. **1848** DICKENS *Dombey* iv, Teeming with suggestions of..gorgeous princes of a brown complexion sitting on carpets.

b. of things, esp. dress, decorated rooms, etc.; also of colour.

1533 CRANMER in Ellis *Orig. Lett.* Ser. I. II. 36 Severall bargis deckyd after the most gorgiouse and sumptuous maner. **1545** BRINKLOW *Compl.* xxiv. (1874) 69 What lordes haue more gorgyos houses than thei haue? **1623** SIR F. COTTINGTON in Ellis *Orig. Lett.* Ser. I. III. 142 The late proclamation against gorgeous apparel dispensed with. **1697** DRYDEN *Virg. Georg.* IV. 120 With gorgeous Wings, the Marks of Sov'reign Sway, The two contending Princes make their way. **1794** SULLIVAN *View Nat.* V. 91 The Irish took the field, like their brethren of Britain, in gorgeous array. **1813** BYRON *Br. Abydos* II. iii, All that can eye or sense delight Are gather'd in that gorgeous room. **1851** LAYARD *Pop. Acc. Discov. Nineveh* xiii. 346 Sculptured in alabaster, and painted in gorgeous colours. **1876** BLACK *Madcap V.* xviii. 170 They were in the land of gorgeous sunsets.

c. *transf.* esp. of phraseology and literary colouring; *rarely* of an action: Dazzling.

1561 T. HOBY tr. *Castiglione's Courtyer* I. F iv b, Gorgeous and fine woordes. **1581** J. BELL *Haddon's Answ. Osor.* 263 b, The gorgeous neatnes of Ciceroe's speach. **1635** A. STAFFORD *Fem. Glory* (1869) 47 All morall Vertues whatsoever are no better than gorgious sins. **1857** WILLMOTT *Pleas. Lit.* xxi. 130 The gorgeous tale of genius is always left half told. **1874** DEUTSCH *Rem.* 65 They keep our imagination spell-bound by their gorgeous lore.

2. *colloq.* Used as an epithet of strong approbation. (Cf. *splendid.*)

1883 *Fargo* (Dakota) *Argus* 25 Sept., The northwestern editors, who recently went excursioning over the famous 'Monon Route'..had a gorgeous time. *Mod.* That's gorgeous! How gorgeous!

gorgeously ('gɔːdʒəslɪ), *adv.* [f. GORGEOUS *a.* + -LY².] In a gorgeous manner.

1532 HERVET *Xenophon's Househ.* (1768) 39 Gorgeously peinted with diuers faire pictures. **1535** COVERDALE *Ecclus.* xl. 4 From him that is gorgiously arayed, and weereth a crowne, vntyll him that is but homely and symple clothed. **1598** F. MERES in *Shaks. C. Praise* 21 The English tongue is mightily enriched and gorgeouslie invested in rare ornaments. **1638** SIR T. HERBERT *Trav.* (ed. 2) 168 Banquetting houses, great and gorgeously painted. **1699** BENTLEY *Phal.* 359 The Persons that They introduc'd were not clad so very gorgeously. **1823** RUTTER *Fonthill* 19 The walls..gorgeously glow with a mosaic of the most brilliantly tinted light. **1877** C. GEIKIE *Christ* xxvi. (1879) 293 The people gorgeously appareled, who lived delicately.

gorgeousness ('gɔːdʒəsnɪs). [f. GORGEOUS *a.* + -NESS.] The condition, quality, or state of being gorgeous; splendour; magnificence.

1549 COVERDALE, etc. *Erasm. Par. Jas.* 26 What a gorgiousnes of grene leaues, what a glistering. **1561** T. HOBY tr. *Castiglione's Courtyer* I. F iv, For very suche make the greatnes and gorgeousnes of an Oracion. **1630** BRATHWAIT *Eng. Gentlem.* (1641) 177 Lust, ambition, gorgeousnesse in apparell..and the like. **1698** FRYER *Acc. E. India & P.* 18 We had liberty in this interval to survey the Gorgeousness of his Attire. **1838** LYTTON *Leila* I. iv, The chamber..had a more massive, and if we may use the term, Egyptian gorgeousness. **1868** HAWTHORNE *Amer. Note-bks.* (1879) II. 144 The perfect gorgeousness of autumn.

†**gorger,** *sb.*¹ *Obs.* Also 4-5 gorgere, 5 gorgeer(e, -ier. [a. OF. *gorg(i)ere*, f. *gorge* GORGE *sb.*¹]

1. = GORGET¹ I.

1300 *K. Alis.* 3636 Of Grece he smot a baroun..Thorugh the gargaze and the gorger. **13..** *Coer de L.* 321 Hys pusen therwith gan gon... Hys vyser and his gorgere. *c* **1430** *Pilgr. Lyf Manhode* I. cxx. (1869) 63 With his gorgeer was sum time armed the abbot of Chalyt, thi goode patroun seint William. **1460** *Lybeaus Disc.* 1618 Pysane, aventayle, and gorgere, Fell ynto the felld fer. **14..** *Rom. of Monk* (Sion Coll. MS.) (Halliw.), Nowe I wol sey thee of the gorgier, which shoulde kepe the throte-bolle.

2. A wimple, neckerchief; = GORGET¹ 2.

13.. *Gaw. & Gr. Knt.* 957 þat oþer [lady] wyth a gorger watz gered ouer þe swyre.

Hence †**gorger** *v. trans.*, to fasten a gorger on (a person).

c **1430** *Pilgr. Lyf Manhode* I. cxx. (1869) 63 Whan suich a man armede him with swich a gorgeer, and gorgered him soo, thou shuldest also fastne on gladiche thi gorgeere.

gorger ('gɔːdʒə(r)), *sb.*² [f. GORGE *v.* + -ER¹.]

1. A person or animal that gorges or eats to repletion; a glutton.

1791-1823 D'ISRAELI *Cur. Lit., Anc. Cookery* (Rtldg.) 267/2 Apicius, a name..now synonymous with a gorger, was the inventor of cakes called Apicians. **1883** G. ALLEN *Nat. Studies, Honey Ants* 26 These gorgers might easily become specialized into a honey-bearing set of insects.

2. *Naut.* 'A big haul or heavy deck of fish' (*Cent. Dict.*).

†**gorgeret**¹. *Obs.* [a. OF. *gorgerete* (F. *gorgerette* string of a child's cap), f. *gorge* GORGE *sb.*¹; = Prov. *gorgeyreta*, It. *gorgieretta.*] = GORGET¹ I.

c **1500** *Melusine* xxiv. 175 Vryan drew a short knyff..and threstid it vnder the gorgeret thrugh brandymontis nek.

gorgeret² ('gɔːdʒərɪt). *Surg.* Also 8 gorgoret. [a. F. *gorgeret*, f. *gorge* throat, from the tubular shape of the instrument.] = GORGET².

1758 J. S. *Le Dran's Observ. Surg.* (1771) 257, I introduced a Gorgoret into the Bladder. **18..** *Med. News* XLIX. 315 (Cent.) Over the probe I pass a little gorgeret..this has its blade directed upwards.

gorgerin ('gɔːdʒərɪn). Also 8 gorgerine, 9 gourgerin. [a. F. *gorgerin*, f. *gorge* throat.]

1. *Arch.* = HYPOTRACHELIUM.

1664 EVELYN tr. *Freart's Archit.* 127 Hypotrachelium..is as 'twere the Freeze of the Capitel, and by some so tearm'd, as also the Coller and Gorgerin. **1726** LEONI *Alberti's Archit.* II. 58/1 A Doric Capital, but without any gorgerine. **1842-59** GWILT *Archit.* Gloss., *Collar* or *Colarino*..is sometimes called the neck, gorgerin, or hypotrachelium.

2. = GORGET¹ I. (Cf. It. *gorgierina.*)

1849 JAS. GRANT *Kirkaldy of G.* ix. 86 The culverineers wore a gourgerin and salade, with a sword and dagger. **1869** BOUTELL *Arms & Arm.* viii. 152 The gorgerin, or gorget, completes this head-piece.

gorges, obs. form of GORGEOUS.

gorget¹ ('gɔːdʒɪt). Forms: 5 gorgeat, gorgette, 6 gorgyt, 6-7 gorgett, 7 gordget, gorjet, 6- gorget. [a. OF. *gorgete* (F. dial. *gorgette* a collar), dim. of *gorge* throat.]

1. A piece of armour for the throat. *Obs.* exc. *Hist.*

c **1470** HENRY *Wallace* IV. 661 With ire him straik on his gorgeat off steill. **1484** CAXTON *Chivalry* 62 The gorgette enuyronneth or goth aboute the neck of a knyght by cause it sholde be deffended for strokes and woundes. **1559** *Mirr. Mag., Clifford* viii, As I would my gorget haue vndoen... An headles arrow strake mee through the throte. **1634** FORD *P. Warbeck* III. i. (Stage Direct.), Enter King Henry, with his gorget on. **1715-20** POPE *Iliad* XI. 33 Three glittering dragons to the gorget rise. **1770** LANGHORNE *Plutarch* (1879) II. 732/2 His helmet..was of iron... To this was fitted a gorget of the same metal, set with precious stones. **1808** SCOTT *Marm.* V. ii, Their brigantines, and gorgets light. **1838** PRESCOTT *Ferd. & Is.* (1846) III. xi. 47 The gorget..gave way, and the sword entered his throat. **1859** THACKERAY *Virgin.* lxxii, One of Mr. Walpole's cavaliers with ruff, rapier, buff-coat, and gorget.

b. *transf.* A collar.

1629 J. M. tr. *Fonseca's Dev. Contempl.* 90 A hundred Mules, Sumpter-Clothes on their backes, imbrodered with silke, silver and gold, with their goriets of massie-plate [etc.]. **1663** BUTLER *Hud.* I. ii. 257 He wore, for ornament, a ring; About his neck a threefold gorget. **1820** SCOTT *Ivanhoe* i, It was a brass ring, resembling a dog's collar..On this singular gorget was engraved..an inscription.

2. An article of female dress, covering the neck and breast; a wimple. *Obs.* exc. *Hist.*

1575 LANEHAM *Let.* (1871) 37 A side gooun of kendall green..gathered at the neck with a narro gorget. **1598** YONG *Diana* 71 She had on a light skie coloured petticoate, and vnder that a gorget of so passing fine net-worke. *a* **1635** CORBET *Poems* (1807) 232 To the Ladyes of the New Dresse, That were their gorgets and rayles doune to their wastes. *a* **1659** CLEVELAND *Wks.* (1687) 382 Pray rectifie my Gorget, smooth my Whisk. **1716** LADY M. W. MONTAGU *Let. to C'tess Mar* 14 Sept., I was squeezed up in a gown, and adorned with a gorget and the other implements thereunto belonging. **1826** SCOTT *Woodst.* i, With these grave seniors sate their goodly dames in ruff and gorget. **1843** LYTTON *Last Bar.* IV. vi, Why, Katherine—dame—thy stiff gorget makes me ashamed of thee.

3. An ornament for the neck; a collar of beads, shells, etc.; a necklace.

1570 LEVINS *Manip.* 88/10 A Gorget, *torques.* **1791** W. BARTRAM *Carolina* 370 These champions likewise were well dressed, painted and ornamented with silver bracelets, gorgets and wampum. **1808** PIKE *SourcesIssiss.* II. App. 48, I presented the principal, with a double barrel'd gun, gorget, and other articles. **1870** LUBBOCK *Orig. Civiliz.* ii. (1875) 53 Some also had gorgets of large shells hanging from the neck across the breast.

4. *Mil.* A gilt crescent-shaped badge suspended from the neck, and hanging on the breast, formerly worn by officers on duty.

1786 MACKENZIE *Lounger* No. 87 §7 His sword and gorget were crossed under it [a portrait]. **1816** 'QUIZ' *Grand Master* VIII. 11 Dress'd—gorget, epaulets, and sash, Lion and crown—a perfect dash. **1830** *Ann. Reg.* 124 The gorget to be abolished. **1867** in SMYTH *Sailor's Word-bk.*

†**5.** *Sc.* A kind of pillory. *Obs.*

1635 *Sess. Rec.* in W. McDowell *Hist. Dumfries* xxxii. (1873) 364 Adjudged to pay one dollar and wear the gorgets on Sabbath. **1640-1** *Kircudbr. War-Comm. Min. Bk.* (1855) 40 He shall..stand in the gorgets at the kirk of Balmaghie.

6. *Zool.* †**a.** The pouch or sac under the bill of certain sea-birds. *Obs.*⁻¹

1703 M. MARTIN *Descr. West. Isl. Scotl.* (1816) 283 This Solan Goose..preserves five or six herrings in its gorget entire, and carries them to the nest.

b. A patch of colour on the throat of a bird, insect, etc.

1801 SOUTHEY *Thalaba* III. xxxiii, She view'd his [the locust's] jet-orb'd eyes, His glossy gorget bright. **1820** W. IRVING *Sketch Bk.* II. 382 The golden-winged wood-pecker, with his broad black gorget. **1871** DARWIN *Desc. Man* II. xvi. 188 The male of..one of the humming birds..having a splendid gorget and fine ear-tufts.

7. *Comb.*, as ***gorget-maker***; †**gorget-stead**, the part of the body protected by the gorget.

c **1611** CHAPMAN *Iliad* VII. 12 Beneath his good steele caske it pierc't above his gorget stead. **1656** *Artif. Handsom.* (1662) 85 The Tire-women, the Gorget-makers, the Seamstresses, the Chambermaids.

Hence '**gorgeted** *ppl. a.*, having a gorget.

1861 GOULD *Trochilidæ* IV, *Heliangelus strophianus*, Gorgeted Sun Angel.

gorget² ('gɔːdʒɪt). *Surg.* [Corruption of GORGERET².] A steel instrument having the form of a channel, used in operations for stone, etc.

1740 CHESELDEN *Anat.* (ed. 5) 330 Passing the gorget very carefully in the groove of the staff into the bladder. **1800** *Med. Jrnl.* III. 196 This instrument..cuts easier than the cutting director, or common gorget. **1809** S. COOPER *Dict. Pract. Surg.* 459 Lateral operation as performed at the present day with cutting gorgets. **1839** *Hooper's Med. Dict.* (ed. 7), The gorget is now seldom used; the cutting one being superseded by a simple knife, and the blunt one by the use of the finger.

gorgeus, obs. form of GORGEOUS.

gorgier, variant of GORGER *sb.*¹, *Obs.*

gorging ('gɔːdʒɪŋ), *vbl. sb.* [f. GORGE *v.* + -ING¹.] The action of the vb. GORGE.

1833 I. TAYLOR *Fanat.* vi. 154 The gorging of captives reserved for that very purpose from the slaughter of the field. **1860** HOLLAND *Miss Gilbert* i. 19 Of the gorging of fruits..that followed in the grove back of Dr. Gilbert's house, nothing needs to be said. **1860** TYNDALL *Glac.* II. xx. 337 During this time, the gorging of the capillaries [of a glacier]..must have ceased.

‖**gorgio** ('gɔːdʒɪəʊ). [Romany; in Ger. spelling *gadze, gatscho*; in Sp. spelling *gacho.*] The designation given by gipsies to one who is not a gipsy.

1851 BORROW *Lavengro* I. xvii. 218 Perhaps; but you are of the Gorgios, and I am a Rommany Chal. **1857** —— *Romany Rye* I. x. 135 Marriages..now and then occur between gorgios and Romany chies. **1875** WHYTE MELVILLE *Katerfelto* xi. 118 The Romany in his tent..can be as courteous as the Gorgio in his castle.

gorgious(e, -ius, obs. forms of GORGEOUS.

gorgoil, variant of GARGOYLE.

1841 FERREY *Antiq. Ch. Ch. Priory* 24 There are, also, gorgoils, or water spouts wrought into projecting heads of the most hideous aspect.

Gorgon ('gɔːgən), *sb.* (and *a.*) Also 4-7 gorgone. [ad. L. *Gorgon-em*, *Gorgō*, a. Gr. Γοργώ (pl. Γοργόνες), f. γοργός terrible.]

1. *Gr. Myth.* One of three mythical female personages, with snakes for hair, whose look turned the beholder into stone. The one of most note, and the only one mortal, Medusa, was slain by Perseus, and her head fixed on Athene's shield.

[**1398** TREVISA *Barth. de P.R.* XV. lxx. (1495) 515 Wymmen that were callyd Gorgones Feminine. **1601** HOLLAND *Pliny* I. 148 The Islands called Gorgates, where sometimes the Gorgones kept their habitation.] *c* **1614** SIR W. MURE *Dido & Æneas* II. 528 Whil gastly Gorgones threatne death. **1636** MASSINGER *Bashf. Lover* I. ii, I have seen More than a wolf, a Gorgon! **1667** MILTON *P.L.* II. 628 Gorgons and Hydra's, and Chimera's dire. **1700** CONGREVE *Way of World* v. ii, She is as terrible to me as a gorgon. **1815** SCOTT *Guy M.* iii, Her dark elf-locks shot out like the snakes of a gorgon. **1884** RUSKIN *Pleasures Eng.* (1885) 156 In Greek art, remember to keep yourselves clear about the difference between the Lion and the Gorgon.

†**b.** = DEMOGORGON. *Obs.*

1590 SPENSER *F.Q.* I. i. 37 Great Gorgon, prince of darknes and dead night.

c. Short for *Gorgon's head.*

1796 BURKE *Regic. Peace* I. Wks. VIII. 163 As if the dire goddess..with..her gorgon at her breast, was a coquette to be trifled with.

†**d.** A petrifying influence. *Obs.*

1646 SIR T. BROWNE *Pseud. Ep.* II. i. 54 Chrystall..its immediate determination and efficiency..are wrought by the hand of its concretive spirit, the seeds of petrification and Gorgon within it selfe.

†**2.** An African quadruped; ? the gnu. *Obs.*⁻¹

1607 TOPSELL *Four-f. Beasts* (1658) 206 Among the manifold and divers sorts of Beasts which are bred in Africk, it is thought that the Gorgon is brought forth in that Countrey.

3. A very terrible or very ugly person; esp., a repulsive woman.

a **1529** SKELTON *Sp. Parrot* 503 Was nevyr suche a ffylty gorgon, nor suche an epycure Syn Dewcalyons flodde. **1632** MARMION *Holland's Leaguer* IV. iv, No, my dear Gorgons, I will not have my fame wander without The precincts of your castle. **1670** DRYDEN *Conq. Granada* II. ii, I'll shrowd this Gorgon from all humane view. **1831** DISRAELI *Yng. Duke* I. xi, That gorgon, Lady de Courcy, captured me. **1876** MISS

BRADDON *J. Haggard's Dau.* II. 111 A pretty girl will hardly be a gorgon as a step-mother.

4. *attrib.* and *Comb.* **a.** simple *attrib.* passing into adj. with sense 'petrifying', 'terrible'.

1575 R. B. *Appius & Virg.* C j a, O gorgon Judge, what lawles life hast thou most wicked led! **1633** MASSINGER *Guardian* III. vi, Your Gorgon looks Turn me to stone. **1663** BUTLER *Hud.* I. ii. 783 But Pallas..'twixt the spring and hammer thrust Her gorgon shield. **1690** DRYDEN *Don Sebastian* III. i, Why didst thou not..try the virtue of that Gorgon face, To stare me into statue? **1712** CONGREVE *Ovid's Art Love* III. Wks. 1730 III. 316 It swells the lips and blackens all the Veins, While in the Eye a Gorgon Horror reigns. *a* **1777** POTTER *Æschylus, Prom. Chain'd* 25 From his eyes the gorgon-glare Of balefull lightnings flash'd. **1812** BYRON *Ch. Har.* I. lv, Scarce would you deem that Saragoza's tower Beheld her smile in Danger's Gorgon face. **1827** MISS SEDGWICK *H. Leslie* (1872) II. 251 Feeling as if she had been paralyzed by some gorgon influence.

b. objective and instrumental, as ***gorgon-headed, -like, -mounted*** adjs.

1821 SHELLEY *Prometh. Unb.* IV. i. 291 Quivers, helms, and spears, And *gorgon-headed targes. **1589** NASHE *Anat. Absurd.* 12 See how farre they swerue from theyr purpose, who seeke to garnish such *Gorgonlike shapes. **1848** DICKENS *Dombey* xxiii, As if they had a Gorgon-like mind to stare her youth and beauty into stone. **1836–48** B. D. WALSH *Aristoph. Acharnians* IV. vii, Fetch out my *Gorgon-mounted rounded shield. **1626** SANDYS *Ovid's Met.* IV. Argt., *Gorgon-toucht Sea-weeds To Corall change.

c. Comb. with gen. *gorgon's*: **Gorgon's head**, (*a*) the head of Medusa, or a representation of it; (*b*) 'a kind of basket-fish; a many-rayed ophiurian, as of the genus *Astrophyton*' (*Cent. Dict.*).

1605 *Play Stucley* in Simpson *Sch. Shaks.* (1878) I. 242 His eye is as the Gorgons head to me, And doth transform my senses into stone. **1642** HOWELL *For. Trav.* (Arb.) 73 For they seeme like Bug-beares, or Gorgons heads, to the vulgar. **1690** DRYDEN *Amphit.* V. Wks. 1884 VIII. 99 This is a sight, that, like the gorgon's head, Runs through my limbs, and stiffens me to stone. **1870** BRYANT *Iliad* I. XI. 332 Where glared A Gorgon's-head with angry eyes.

Gorgonean: see GORGONIAN *a.*[2]

gorgoneion (gɔːgəʊˈnaɪən). [a. Gr. (τὸ) γοργόνειον, neut. of γοργόνειος, of or pertaining to a GORGON.] A representation of the Gorgon's head.

1842 BRANDE *Dict. Sci.* etc., *Gorgoneia* [Pl.]. **1850** LEITCH tr. *C. O. Müller's Anc. Art* §177 (ed. 2) 159 A bowl found at Clusium has a gorgoneion with Etruscan inscription. **1880** MURRAY *Grk. Sculpt.* I. viii. 153 On the ægis of Athena in the west pediment had been a gorgoneion of metal. **1895** ELWORTHY *Evil Eye* 158 The Gorgoneion has in all ages been reputed one of the most efficacious of amulets.

gorgo'nesque, *a.* [see -ESQUE.] Having the characteristics of a gorgon; hideous, repulsive.

1888 *Athenæum* 29 Sept. 426/2 A mother-in-law so Gorgonesque even as the ex-*coryphée*.

Gorgonia (gɔːˈgəʊnɪə). *Zool.* Pl. gorgoniæ, -ias. [a. mod.L. *gorgonia*, fem. of *gorgonius*, f. *gorgon-em* GORGON. The name was intended to express its petrified character: cf. GORGON 1 d.] A genus of polyps (family *Gorgoniaceæ*); an individual of this genus; a sea-fan, sea-plume.

1767 ELLIS in *Phil. Trans.* LVII. 433 Most of the Sertularias, Gorgonias. **1775** *Ibid.* LXVI. 1 Zoophytes.. formerly called Ceratophytons, now Gorgoniæ. **1860** MAURY *Phys. Geog. Sea* (Low) xiii. §560 The yellow and lilac fans, perforated like trellis-work, of the Gorgonias. **1883** *Fisheries Exhib. Catal.* (ed. 4) 100 Corals, Sponges and Gorgoniæ. **1885** LADY BRASSEY *The Trades* 297 Some lovely plumes of sea feathers, a species of gorgonia, which had the appearance of ten or a dozen ostrich feathers.

Hence **gor'gonian** *a.*[1], pertaining to the gorgonias or their family. Also *sb.*, a polyp of the family.

1835 KIRBY *Hab. & Inst. Anim.* I. v. 168 In the vicinity of volcanic islands in the Polar seas, corallines and gorgonians [occur]. **1884** *Nature* 17 July 281/1 The numerous species that live clinging to the branches of gorgonians..The gorgonian corals of many species.

Gorgonian (gɔːˈgəʊnɪən), *a.*[2] [f. GORGON + -IAN; cf. L. *gorgoneus*.] Of or pertaining to the Gorgon; resembling the Gorgon, or the effect of the Gorgon's look; Gorgon-like, terrible. Of a shield: Bearing the Gorgon's visage.

1616 B. JONSON *Epigr.* I. cxxxiii. *Famous Voy.*, On one side..Were seene your vgly Centaures..Gorgonian scolds, and Harpyes. **1667** MILTON *P.L.* x. 297 The rest his look Bound with Gorgonian rigor not to move. **1697** DRYDEN *Æn.* VII. 476 Smear'd as she was with black Gorgonean Blood. *a* **1785** GLOVER *Athenaid* XI. 214 Still the sound Of her gorgonian shield my ears retain. **1869** RUSKIN *Q. of Air* §53 The Gorgonian cold, and venomous agony, that turns living men to stone.

†**Gor'gonical**, *a.* *Obs.* [f. as prec. + -IC + -AL[1].] = prec.

1591 HARINGTON *Orl. Fur.* Pref. (1634) ¶iv, The mind of man..killing the earthlinesse of this Gorgonicall nature ascendeth up to the understanding of heavenly things.

Gorgonize (ˈgɔːgənaɪz), *v.* [f. GORGON + -IZE.] *trans.* **a.** To petrify as by the glance of a Gorgon; to render hard or stony. **b.** To gaze at with the look of a Gorgon.

1609 J. DAVIES *Holy Roode* E i b, What Eies so Gorgoniz'd that can endure To see the All-vpholder forc'd to bow? *a* **1631** DONNE *Polydoron* 173 The Stony Jewes had beene Gorgonized before his comming. **1855** TENNYSON *Maud* I. xiii. 21 Curving a contumelious lip, Gorgonised me from head to foot With a stony British stare. **1879** DOWDEN *Southey* i. 5 Ma'am Powell was old and grim, and with her lashless eyes gorgonized the new pupil.

Gorgonzola (gɔːgənˈzəʊlə). A type of blue cheese, usu. made from cow's milk, orig. produced at Gorgonzola, a village near Milan.

1878 [see CAMEMBERT]. **1885** [see EDAM]. **1896** LONG & BENSON *Cheese* 49 The Gorgonzola process. **1910** *Practitioner* Feb. 211 It has become quite an easy matter to make Gorgonzola, Camembert, Pont l'évêque, Gruyère, anything you like, in Nottinghamshire. **1955** *Times* 10 May 12/4 Gorgonzola, the Italian blue veined cheese, on the other hand, is dependent on no unique caves; the process of manufacture is copied elsewhere and Danish cheesemakers send their own brands of Gorgonzola to this country. **1971** *Sunday Times* (Colour Suppl.) 28 Mar. 39/4 *Gorgonzola*, one of Europe's three great blue cheeses, it is naturally veined, creamy, and made of cow's milk.

gorgoret, obs. form of GORGERET[2].

gorgy (ˈgɔːdʒɪ), *a.* [f. GORGE *sb.*[1] + -Y[1].] Full of gorges or ravines.

1891 C. E. DOUGLAS *Diary* 25 Feb. in J. Pascoe *Mr. Explorer Douglas* (1957) iv. 130 I'll have to bridge a few Creeks & Torrents going up to the Glacier, some very ugley gorgy looking gaps are looming up at the head of the flat. **1927** *Blackw. Mag.* Oct. 468/1 As soon as Pyramid Island is reached, the country becomes broken & gorgy [in Tasmania]. **1960** B. CRUMP *Good Keen Man* 135 We struck a few more small waterfalls and a lot of steep, gorgy places where the slippery rocks made travel slow and difficult.

gorgyas, -os, -ous(e, obs. forms of GORGEOUS.

gori: see GOREE *sb.*[2]

gorie, obs. form of GORY *a.*

gorilla (gəˈrɪlə). [An alleged African name for a wild or hairy man (strictly for the female only), preserved (in acc. pl. γορίλλας) in the Greek account of the voyage undertaken by the Carthaginian Hanno in the 5th or 6th c. B.C.; hence adopted in 1847 as the specific name of the ape *Troglodytes gorilla*, first described by Dr. T. S. Savage, an American missionary in Western Africa.] The largest of anthropoid apes, a native of western equatorial Africa; it closely resembles man in its structure, is very powerful and ferocious, and arboreal in its habits.

[**1799** *Naval Chron.* I. 451 Another island full of savage people..whose bodies were hairy, and whom our interpreters called Gorillæ. **1847** P. SAVAGE in *Jrnl. Boston Nat. Hist. Soc.* (*title*) A description of the external characters and habits of *Troglodytes Gorilla*.] **1853** R. OWEN in *Trans. Zool. Soc.* (*title*) Description of Cranium of an adult male gorilla. **1861** DU CHAILLU *Equat. Afr.* i. 1 The fierce untameable gorilla, which approaches nearest, in physical conformation and in certain habits, to man. **1874** LUBBOCK *Orig. & Met. Ins.* i. 6 The chimpanzee and the gorilla must certainly give place to the bee and the ant.

b. *transf.* A person who resembles a gorilla.

1884 SIR S. ST. JOHN *Hayti* iv. 144 Others [of the Haytian negroes] are the meanest-looking gorillas imaginable.

c. *attrib.* and *Comb.*, as ***gorilla-land, -skin***; ***gorilla-built*** adj.

1887 F. FRANCIS Jr. *Saddle & Mocassin* xvii. 293, I saw one deep-chested, gorilla-built fellow. **1897** MARY KINGSLEY *W. Africa* 264 He had a splendid gun, with a gorilla skin sheath for its lock. *Ibid.* 278 To return to that gorilla-land forest.

Gorillagram: see -GRAM.

gorilloid (gəˈrɪlɔɪd), *sb.* and *a.* [f. GORILLA + -OID.] **A.** *sb.* An animal resembling a gorilla. **B.** *adj.* Resembling or characteristic of a gorilla.

1946 F. WEIDENREICH *Apes, Giants & Man* i. 24 (*caption*) Gorilloids. **1949** W. E. LE GROS CLARK *Hist. Primates* 58 Large apes of gorilloid proportions. **1957** L. EISELEY *Immense Journey* 89 Some have..massive gorilloid crests atop their skulls.

gorily (ˈgɔərɪlɪ), *adv.* [f. GORY *a.* + -LY[2].] In a gory manner.

1850 BLACKIE *Æschylus* II. 131 Gorily, gorily thou shalt go! **1864** TENNYSON *Boadicea* 12 Tear the noble heart of Britain, leave it gorily quivering. **1871** R. ELLIS *Catullus* lxiv. 257 Some from a mangled steer toss'd flesh yet gorily streaming.

goring (ˈgɔərɪŋ), *vbl. sb.*[1] [f. GORE *v.*[1] + -ING[1].]

1. The action of the vb. GORE; the action of piercing or stabbing.

1494 FABYAN *Chron.* VII. 580 What with the shotte and gorynge of their horses with the sharpe stakes they stumbelyd one vpon another. *a* **1700** DRYDEN (Ogilv.) His horses' flanks and sides are forc'd to feel The clinking lash, and goring of the steel. *a* **1711** KEN *Anodynes* Poet. Wks. 1721 III. 397 When redhot Needles in my Breast, With confluential Gorings me infest.

†**2.** An alleged name for a company of butchers.

1486 *Bk. St. Albans* F vij, A Goryng of Bochouris.

goring (ˈgɔərɪŋ), *vbl. sb.*[2] [f. GORE *v.*[3] + -ING[1].]

1. a. The action of the vb. GORE; the act of cutting out, or fitting with, gores. **b.** A piece of cloth used as a gore: esp. *Naut.* Also ***goring-cloth***.

1626 CAPT. SMITH *Seaman's Gram.* v. 23 According to the Goaring she is said to spread a great or a little clew. **1769** FALCONER *Dict. Marine* (1780), *Langue de voile*, the goring of a sail, or that part which is next to the leech. **1813** E. S. BARRETT *Heroine* (1815) II. 149 Here was no sloping, or goring, or seaming, or frilling, or flouncing. **1851** KIPPING *Sailmaking* (ed. 2) 184 The goring-cloths are..those which are cut obliquely, and added to the breadth. **1874** MRS. WHITNEY *We Girls* iv. 92 In the midst of measurings and gorings. **1894** *Times* 17 Aug. 9/2 Webbings, gorings, suspenders and braces.

2. The action of ploughing a 'gore'. Also *concr.* = GORE *sb.*[2] 1 b.

1780 A. YOUNG *Tour Irel.* I. 10 Plough with oxen four in a plough; but in goring, or cross-plowing, six. **1886** *S.W. Linc. Gloss.*, *Gorings*, the uneven triangular bits at the side of a field which does not form a parallelogram.

attrib. **1863** *Jrnl. R. Agric. Soc.* XXIV. II. 407 It is not everybody that cares to detain a powerful engine over an awkward headland, or the finishing of a 'goring' corner.

goring (ˈgɔərɪŋ), *ppl. a.*[1] [f. GORE *v.*[1] + -ING[2].] That gores or pierces.

1649 G. DANIEL *Trinarch., Hen. V*, cc, The Stronger Squadron of the french fell in Vpon the goring stakes. **1700** DRYDEN *Fables, Pal. & Arcite* II. 250 He spurred his fiery steed With goring rowels to provoke his speed. *a* **1711** KEN *Preparative* Poet. Wks. 1721 IV. 76 With goring Thorns, and fiery Darts. **1859** F. E. PAGET *Cur. Cumberworth* 72 Wild, mad, goring monsters.

fig. **1578** *Gorgious Gallery Gallant Inuentions, Louers lyfe*, Such goring gripes, such heapes of hideous harmes. **1686** F. SPENCE tr. *Varilla's Ho. Medicis* 85 The burgers of that city having made mighty goaring railleries, and infamous satyrs on the subject of his youth.

goring (ˈgɔərɪŋ), *ppl. a.*[2] [f. GORE *v.*[3] + -ING[2].] Forming a gore. ***cut goring***: cut in the form of a gore.

1627 CAPT. SMITH *Seaman's Gram.* vii. 32 The maine saile must bee cut goring. **1794** *Rigging & Seamanship* I. 91 Topmast..studding sails [are cut] with goring leeches. *Ibid.* I. 136 The cloth at the tack is cut goring to the nock.

gorisoun, ? variant of GARCION, GARSON.

c **1300** *Amis & Amil.* 2449 With hem many a stoute gorisoun, With knyghtes and squiers fale.

gorkem, obs. form of GHERKIN.

1699 EVELYN *Acetaria* (1729) 176 Take the Gorkems, or smaller Cucumbers.

gorlin (ˈgɔːlɪn). *Sc.* Also **gorling, gordlin.** [f. GOR[1]: cf. GORBLIN.] An unfledged bird, a nestling; a very young person.

1721 RAMSAY *Addr. Town-Counc. Edin.* 27 It griev'd me ..By Carlings and Gorlings To be sae sair opprest. **1804** TARRAS *Poems* 3 Or hath the gled or foomart, skaithfu' beast, Stown off the lintie gordlins frae the nest? **1850** *Whistlebinkie* (Scot. Songs) (1890) Ser. II. *Songs Nursery* 33 The wee bird..That feeds its gapin' gorlins a'. **1878** *Cumbld. Gloss.* s.v., 'As neakkt as a gorlin''.

attrib. **1789** DAVIDSON *Seasons* 4 He..sploiting, strikes the stane his grany hit, Wi' pistol screed, shot frae his gorlin doup. **1824** MACTAGGART *Gallovid. Encycl.*, *Gorlin-hair*,.. That hair on young birds before the feathers cometh.

gorm (gɔːm), *v.*[1] Also **gawm.** A vulgar substitute for '(God) damn'.

1849 DICKENS *Dav. Copp.* xxi. 220 Gorm the t'other one. **1850** *Ibid.* lxiii. 618 If a ship's cook..didn't make offers fur to marry Missis Gummidge, I'm gormed. **1883** *Punch* 19 May 230/2 I'm gormed if there was more than six of one and half-a-dozen of the other. **1905** E. PHILLPOTTS *Secret Woman* I. iv, An' coming for to count 'em..be gormed if I didn't find but three! **1907** *Daily Chron.* 9 Mar. 8/5 'Well, I'm gawmed!' exclaimed Mr. Bungard, unable to suppress his surprise. **1910** J. FARNOL *Broad Highway* II. xviii, I'll be gormed if it ain't a'most onnat'ral!

gorm (gɔːm), *v.*[2]: = GAUM *v.*[3]

1928 E. W. HENDY *Lure of Bird Watching* xi. 196 The youngsters sat gorming on its edge, while she stuffed gobbets of bread..into their insatiable maws.

gorm (gɔːm), *v.*[3]: = GAUM *v.*[2] Also with *up*.

1962 *Listener* 1 Nov. 732/3, I have always hoped against hope that one day Mr. Bucknell would..get gormed up in a glue-pot.

gorm (gɔːm), *sb.* Also **gawm.** [cf. GORMLESS *a.* and GAUMLESS *a.*] **a.** An undiscerning person, a fool. **b.** (See quot. 1921.) **c.** (See quot. 1933.)

1912 J. STEPHENS *Crock of Gold* v. xiv. 228 'I must have forgotten about the other one...' 'You gawm!' gritted the sergeant. **1921** F. B. YOUNG *Black Diamond* ix. 106 He asked Abner if he could spare him a gorm. Abner had not the least idea what a gorm was, but the voice explained that it meant a little..bit of tobacco—'for to chew'. **1933** *Amer. Speech* VIII. 49/2 *Gorm*, a mess, a muddle, a poor job. **1936** 'N. BLAKE' *Thou Shell of Death* ii. 33 There's a gorm of a girl comes up from the village every morning. **1959** I. & P. OPIE *Lore & Lang. Schoolch.* x. 181 A brainless gorm. **1969** H. CARVIC *Miss Seeton draws Line* ix. 171 'It's all finished and it's all wunners.' She smiled with pride. 'Isn't it, you great gorm?'

gorma(h, variant of GORMAW.

gormagon, variant of GORMOGON. *Obs.*

gorman, gormand(e: see GOURMAND.

gormandize (ˈgɔːməndaɪz), *sb.* Forms: 5 **gromandise, gormandyse, 6 gourmandice, 6–7 gourmandize, -yse, 6–7 gurman-, -mon-, -mundise, -ize, -yse, 6–9 gormandise, 6– gormandize, gourmandise.** [ad. F. *gourmandise*, f. *gourmand*.] †**a.** Excessive and voracious eating; gluttony (*obs.*). **b.** The habits, tastes, or perceptions characteristic of a GOURMAND; indulgence or connoisseurship in 'good eating'. Now chiefly as an alien word (spelt *gourmandise*).

a **1450** *Knt. de la Tour* (1868) 115 Excesse and gromandise in etyng and drinkinge werithe ayenst the body and the soule. **1533** ELYOT *Cast. Helthe* II. i. (1541) 16 b, Forseene alwaye that they eate without gourmandyse. **1566** DRANT *Horace, Sat.* I. v. C v b, Gurmundyse is fellow-shyp, for so the worlde it calls. **1663** BP. PATRICK *Parab. Pilgr.* xxxii. (1668) 389 If it be but sanctified with a Sermon, Gourmandise is innocent in their account. **1721** in BAILEY. **1814** BYRON *Let. to Moore* 9 Apr., All this gormandise was in honour of Lent. **1833** MACAULAY in Trevelyan *Life & Lett.* I. v. 336, I am to dine on Thursday with the Fishmongers' Company, the first Company for gourmandise in the world. **1849** THACKERAY *Pendennis* I. xx. 185 While the reckless young Amphitryon delighted to show his hospitality and skill in *gourmandise*. **1870** MISS BROUGHTON *Red as Rose* I. 289 Not that this right-hand neighbour labours under any excessive *gourmandise*. **1879** MISS YONGE *Cameos* Ser. IV. xxiii. 250 He followed his life-long passion; not merely for gormandize, but for gluttony.

gormandize (ˈgɔːməndaɪz), *v.* Forms: 6 **gourmandice, -yse, 6–7 gurmandize, 7–9 gourmandise, -ize, (7 go(u)rmondise, -ize, gor-, gurmundize), 7– gormandize.** [f. GORMANDIZE *sb.*]

1. *intr.* To eat like a glutton; to feed voraciously.

1548 ELYOT *Dict.* s.v. *Cibus, Ingurgitare se cibis*,.. to gourmandyse to eate vnmoderately. **1596** SHAKS. *Merch. V.* II. v. 3 Thou shalt not gurmandize As thou hast done with me. **1628** WITHER *Brit. Rememb.* VI. 1565 Like hungry Curres, some alwayes gurmandize. **1693** CONGREVE in *Dryden's Juvenal* (1697) 284 If mod'rate Fare and Abstinence, I prize In publick, yet in private Gormondize. **1768–74** TUCKER *Lt. Nat.* (1852) II. 485 The rich gormandized upon their dainties. **1802** BINGLEY *Anim. Biog.* (1813) I. 97 Their [monkeys'] eyes.. painted their inquietude, their passion to gormandize. **1853** KANE *Grinnell Exp.* xvi. (1856) 124 Gormandizing on the blubber of our game.

2. *trans.* To devour greedily, to gobble up, to take in eagerly. *lit.* and *fig.*

1603 H. CROSSE *Vertues Commw.* (1878) 88 To gurmandize and waste in excesse the good blessings of God. **1603** DRAYTON *Bar. Wars* VI. xxiii. 130 The pamper'd stomack.. Casts vp the surfeit lately gurmundiz'd. **1626** T. H[AWKINS] *Caussin's Holy Crt.* 18 Meere bankrupts, who have allready gourmandized theyr Nobility. **1635** PAGITT *Christianogr.* 205, I lament that.. their livings.. should be sacrilegiously gormandized. **1637** HEYWOOD *Dial. Manhater* Wks. 1874 VI. 191 He hath gormandiz'd a whole hog at a feast. **1775** ADAIR *Amer. Ind.* 100 They gormandize such a prodigious quantity of strong food, as [etc.]. **1886** C. D. WARNER *Their Pilgrimage* xv. (1888) 320 The.. group who have taken all the best seats in the bow, with the intention of gormandizing the views. *a* **1887** H. W. BEECHER in Drysdale *Prov. from Plym. Pulpit* 220 To gormandise books is as wicked as to gormandise food.

†**3.** To feed to excess; to satiate. *Obs.*

1604 T. WRIGHT *Passions* IV. ii. §2. 128 It is impossible that he should be continent in mind, that accustometh to gormandize his belly. **1645** R. BEAKE *Let. fr. Sommer Isl.* in Prynne *Discov. Prodig. Stars & Firebrands* App. (1646) 4 Their bellies and stomacks being well gormondized. **1682** MRS. BEHN *City Heiress* I. i, You cram the Brethren, gormandizing all Comers and Goers. **1773** J. ROSS *Fratricide* v. 604 (MS.) Ripping up The bowels of my Son to gormandize His fell voracity.

¶**4.** As transl. of F. *gourmander*, to keep in check.

1603 FLORIO *Montaigne* II. xi. (1632) 238, I know a man may gourmandize the earnest and thought-confounding violence of that pleasure.

gormandizer (ˈgɔːməndaɪzə(r)). [f. GORMANDIZE *v.* + -ER[1].] One who gormandizes, a glutton.

1589 RIDER *Eng.-Lat. Dict.*, A gormandiser or greate eater. **1615** CROOKE *Body of Man* 64 Those that are great gormandizers are sayd to be.. borne for their bellies. **1665** J. WEBB *Stone-Heng* (1725) 227 From the Licentiousness of this Gurmund.. we brand all luxurious and profuse People with the Nick-name of Gurmundizers. **1715** tr. *Pancirollus' Rerum Mem.* I. I. i. 5 A Gormandizer punish'd for his Gluttony. **1807–8** W. IRVING *Salmag.* (1824) 300 When the guzzlers, the gormandizers, and the wine-bibbers meet together. **1822–34** *Good's Study Med.* (ed. 4) I. 358 In the gormandizers.. who have long habituated themselves to the luxuries of the table.

Hence **ˈgormanˌdizeress** [-ESS], a female glutton.

1842 THACKERAY *Fitz-boodle Papers* Wks. 1879 XVII. 210 There is no reason why she should be.. an ogress, a horrid gormandiseress.

gormandizing (ˈgɔːməndaɪzɪŋ), *vbl. sb.* [f. as prec. + -ING[1].] The action of the vb. GORMANDIZE; excessive eating, gluttony. Also *attrib.*

1597 SHAKS. *2 Hen. IV*, v. v. 57 Leaue gourmandizing: Know the Graue doth gape For thee [etc.]. **1652** C. B. STAPYLTON *Herodian* 48 His night disports and gormandizing diet. *a* **1661** HOLYDAY *Juvenal* 260 Not so much gourmandizing, as daintiness, seems here to be intended. **1835** W. IRVING *Tour Prairies* xxvii, A rude kind of feasting, or rather gormandizing, prevailed throughout the camp. **1837** —— *Capt. Bonneville* III. 15 The gormandizing powers of this worthy, were, at first, matters of surprise and merriment. **1889** JESSOPP *Coming of Friars* iii. 155 The weak point in the monastic life of the thirteenth century was the gormandizing.

gormandizing (ˈgɔːməndaɪzɪŋ), *ppl. a.* [f. as prec. + -ING[2].] That gormandizes; gluttonous.

1596 BP. W. BARLOW *Three Serm.* iii. 119 That Gurmandizing glutton who spent so much vpon his paunch daily. **1657** S. PURCHAS *Pol. Flying-Ins.* 329 Against these gourmandizeing Epicures God grieveth and denounceth a woe. **1712** ARBUTHNOT *John Bull* III. ix, Retrench but a sirloin of beef and a peck-loaf in a week, from thy gormandizing stomach. **1865** TROLLOPE *Belton Est.* xvii. 195 A regiment of lazy, gormandizing servants.

gormaund, obs. form of GOURMAND.

gormaw. *Sc.* and *north. dial.* Also 8–9 **gorma(h, 9 gormer, gormow.** See also GOUL-MAU. [? f. GORE *sb.*[1] + MAW; cf. GORBELLY.] The cormorant.

1500–20 DUNBAR *Poems* xxxiii. 77 The golk, the gormaw, and the gled, Beft him with buffettis quhill he bled. **1722** RAMSAY *Eagle & Robin Redbr.* 15 Greidy Gleds and slie Gormahs. **1847–78** HALLIWELL, *Gorma*, a cormorant. *North.* **1893** *Northumbld. Gloss.*, *Gormer*, the cormorant.

b. (See quot.)

1808–80 JAMIESON, *Gormaw*,.. a glutton, Lanarks. **1878** *Cumbld. Gloss.*, *Gormow*, a clownish fellow; sometimes applied to a great eater.

gormless (ˈgɔːmlɪs), *a.* orig. *dial.* Also 8– (*dial.*) **gaumless, gawm(b)less.** [f. *gaum*, dial. f. GOME notice, understanding + -LESS.] Wanting sense, or discernment. Hence **ˈgormlessness**, the quality of being gormless.

c **1746** J. COLLIER (Tim Bobbin) *Lanc. Dialect* Wks. (1862) 55, I steart like o Wilcat, on wur welly gawmless. **1845** E. BRONTË *Wuthering Heights* xxi, Did I ever look so stupid: so 'gaumless' as Joseph calls it? **1861** WAUGH *Birtle Carter's Tale* 19 Eh, thae greyt, gawmbless foo! Wheer arto for up theer! **1881** 'BASIL' *Love the Debt* iii, You lazy, idle, gaumless good-for-nowt! **1883** in B. WEBB *My Apprenticeship* (1926) iii. 161 Parliament is such a far-off thing, that [they].. say that it is 'gormless meddling with it'. **1925** J. AGATE *Contemporary Theatre 1924* 44 Cordelia is a 'gumph' or, as we say in Lancashire, 'gormless'. **1932** L. GOLDING *Magnolia St.* II. ii. 304 She just went on pulling the [beer] handle and in a moment.. the floor was swilling. 'Mother!' cried little Nellie sharply. 'You *are* gormless!' **1934** A. RANSOME *Coot Club* xix. 233 Ye'd better. He'll ferget the salt else, the gormless old lummocks! **1940** *Illustr. London News* CXCVII. 164/2 He looks at once genial and 'gormless'. **1951** 'E. CRISPIN' *Long Divorce* viii. 84 Pen's been running after a gormless little twerp of a foreign school-master. **1958** *Times* 12 Nov. 3/3 Mr. Danny Ross suffers terrific indignities as the youth and makes his gormlessness not only amusing but genuinely likeable. **1959** *Punch* 17 June 813/2 As a result of this unorthodox treatment Quince's gormless Thespians emerge not as rough comics but as decent, sensible men. **1970** *Daily Tel.* 4 Sept. 11/2 That other skilled writer in the genre.. depended on queers or gormlessness for two West End successes.

†**ˈGormogon.** *Obs.* Also **gormagon.** [Meaningless: pseudo Chinese.] A member of a society imitating the Freemasons, founded early in the 18th c.

1725 *Two Letters* in *Grand Mystery of Freemasons* (ed. 2) 13 The Venerable Order of Gormogons having been brought into England by a Chinese Mandarin. **1729** H. CAREY *Poems* (ed. 3) 206 The Masons and the Gormogons Are laughing at one another. **1731** *Daily Jrnl.* 28 Oct. in *N. & Q.* Ser. IV. IV. 441/2 By command of the Volgi. A general Chapter of the.. Ancient Order of Gor-mogon will be held [etc.]. **1742** POPE *Dunc.* IV. 576 One Rose a Gregorian, one a Gormogon. [*Note.*]A sort of Lay-brothers, Slips from the Root of the Free-Masons. **1747** GRAY *Lett.* Wks. 1884 II. 166, I reckon next week we shall hear you are a free-Mason, or a Gormogon at least. **1791** 'G. GAMBADO' *Ann. Horsem.* v. (1809) 87 The art of riding before a lady on a double horse, vulgarly termed *à la gormagon*.

gormundize, obs. form of GORMANDIZE.

gormy, var. GAUMY *a.*

gornard(e, obs. form of GURNARD.

go-round (ˈgəʊraʊnd). *U.S.* [GO *v.* 90.] The act of going round or something that goes round; *spec.* (*a*) a merry-go-round; (*b*) a fight; a beating; an argument; (*c*) an experience or attempt, esp. an unpleasant one.

1886 *Harper's Mag.* July 172/2 The rink and the go-round opposite the hotel were in full tilt. *Ibid.* 174/1 The rink band opposite.. grinding out its go-round music. **1891** M. E. WILKINS *New Eng. Nun* 382 If I was to say what I thought, it would be something pretty plain. All this go-round——. **1898** E. N. WESTCOTT *David Harum* ii. 13, I had to give him one more go-round.. an' after that I didn't have no more trouble with him. *Ibid.* xvi. 142 Me an' him had a little go-round to-day. **1938** M. K. RAWLINGS *Yearling* xx. 248 Let's knock her [*sc.* a panther] out and leave the dogs have a go-round. *Ibid.* xxiii. 286, I had me a good go-round with them jessies. We cain't see it the same way about killin' 'em. **1968** R. MACDONALD *Instant Enemy* vi. 34 She's a nice girl in serious trouble. This seems to be her second go-round with sex. The first go-round made her suicidal.

gorp, *dial.* var. GAWP *v. intr.*, to gape. Hence **ˈgorping** *ppl. a.*

1915 D. H. LAWRENCE *Rainbow* 19 There he sat stubbornly in his corner at the Red Lion, smoking and musing and occasionally lifting his beer-pot, and saying nothing, for all the world like a gorping farm-labourer. *Ibid.* v. 121 The little crowd at the gate gorps and stretches. **1930** R. CAMPBELL *Adamastor* 43 Funnelled with roaring mouths that gorp like cod. **1961** J. I. M. STEWART *Man who won Pools* 81 The budgerigars in the windows.. must be gorping at them. **1969** —— *Cucumber Sandwiches* 39 He would bring down mediums and other psychically well-accredited persons to gorp and gape at that lake.

gorr, obs. form of GOR[2].

gorrah: see GORAH.

gorre, var. GOR[3]; obs. f. GORE *sb.*[1] and *v.*[1]

†**gorrel.** *Obs.* Also 4, 6–7 **gorrell**, 5 **gorell**, (7 **gorill**). [a. OF. *gorel*, *gorreau*, a pig, hog, related to OF. *gore* fem., sow: of unknown origin.]

1. A fat-paunched person.

1398 TREVISA *Barth. De P.R.* VII. xiii. (1495) 232 Crampe that comyth of replycyon fallyth ofte to fatte men and flesshly and well fedde and gorrelles. **14..** *MS. Laud.* 416 lf. 61 b, Glotony that gorell is þe vjte synne, That men vse oft in delicat fedyng of mete. **1611** COTGR., *Bredailler*, a gorbelly, gorrell, gulch, fatguts.

2. ? A youth, lad, boy.

1530 PALSGR. 226/2 Gorrell a great ladde, *pautonnier*. **1547** SALESBURY *Welsh Dict.*, *Llank ne rhokas*, a gorrell. **1665** COTTON *Scarron.* IV. (1741) 72 She the small Ascanius takes .. And in her lap on tuft of Sorrel Laying the little wanton Gorrel [etc.].

3. *Comb.*, as *gorrel-guts* (also *gorrelled-*); *gorrel-bellied* adj.

1581 J. BELL *Haddon's Answ. Osor.* A vj b, It is an easie matter for every common rascall to vomitt out disdaynefull names of infamous persons as.. Epicures, gorrellguttes, and monsters. **15..** *Old Tom of Bedlam* in *Reliq. Anc. E. Poet.* (1823) III. 190 Gorrel-bellyed Bacchus, gyant-like, Bestryd a strong-beere barrell. *c* **1645** in *Roxb. Ball.* (1886) VI. 321 But if you'r drunk, your wits are sunk, And gorill'd guts will quarrel.

gorrie, obs. form of GORY.

gorrogh, variant of CURRACH.

1670 MILTON *Hist. Eng.* III. Wks. (1851) 104 The Scots and Picts.. from their Gorroghs, or Leathern Frigats, pour out themselves in swarms upon the Land. **1674–81** in BLOUNT *Glossogr.*

gorry (ˈgɒrɪ), *int.* [Substituted for GOD in oaths or exclamations; cf. GOLLY *int.*] In (*by*) *gorry* = (*by*) *God.*

1854 THOREAU *Walden* 162 Then, by gorry, your mind must be there. **1931** G. STERN *Meaning & Change of Meaning* 331 The well-known and well-worn [distortions] *blooming* for *bloody*, *dash*, *darn*,.. *Golly*, *Gorry*,.. and many others, which need not be translated. **1961** R. PARK *Hole in Hill* (1962) xii. 101 'Another dead-end, darn it.' 'By gorry, it isn't,' said Tom jubilantly.

gors, variant of GORCE, *Obs.*

gorse (gɔːs). Forms: 1–6, 9 *dial.* **gorst**, (1, 9 *dial.* **gors, gost**), 6–7 **gorsse**, 7 **gosse**, 7–9 **goss**, (9 **gorz(e**, *dial.* **gurs**), 6– **gorse.** Also *pl.* 1 **gorstas**, 4 **-ez**, 5 **-es**, 6 **gorsses**, 9 **gorses.** [OE. *gorst* (*gors*, *gost*):—Indogermanic type **ghr̥zdo-*, whence L. *hordeum* barley; cf. the ablaut-variant G. *gerst* barley. The root-notion of something bristly or prickly is applicable to both plants.]

1. The prickly shrub *Ulex europæus*; common furze or whin.

c **725** *Corpus Gloss.* 97 *Aegesta*, gors. *Ibid.* 2162 *Voluma*, gorst. *c* **975** *Rushw. Gosp.* Matt. vii. 16 Ah he somnigaþ of þornum winbeȝer oþþe of gorstum ficos. *c* **1050** *Martyrol.* (E.E.T.S.) 146 On wildu hors þæt þa hine drogon on gorstas and on þornas. **13..** *E.E. Allit. P.* B. 99 Waytez gorstez & greuez, if ani gomez lyggez. **1388** WYCLIF *Isa.* lv. 13 A fir tre schal grow for a gorst [ether firse]. **1485** *Nottingham Rec.* II. 400 Wodde, gorstes, brome, or any oder thing growyng. **1523** FITZHERB. *Surv.* 6 b, Yet may he laufully fall and selle all the wode, brome, gorse, fyrs.. and suche other. **1577** B. GOOGE *Heresbach's Husb.* II. (1586) 91 b, The branches are full of prickles as the Gorst is. **1610** SHAKS. *Temp.* IV. i. 180 Tooth'd briars, sharpe firzes, pricking gosse, & thorns. *a* **1635** CORBET *Iter Bor.* (1647) 342 Loe where Richmond in a bed of gorsse Encampt himself orenight, and all his force. **1692** *Act 4 Will. & Mary* c. 23 §9 No person.. shall presume to burne between the second day of February and Twenty fourth of June any Grig Ling Heath Furz Gosse or Ferne. **1784** COWPER *Task* I. 528 The common overgrown with fern, and rough With prickly goss. **1808** SCOTT *Marm.* III. i, Sprung from the gorse the timid roe. **1859** JEPHSON *Brittany* iii. 23, I class gorse among the crops, because it is regularly sown.. as winter food for horses. **1878** *Fraser's Mag.* XVIII. 595 Where gorses gleam with golden smile. **1882** OUIDA *Maremma* I. 62 Grand level stretches of gorse and brushwood.

2. = JUNIPER.

c **1000** *Sax. Leechd.* II. 72 Iuniperi þæt is gorst. *c* **1265** *Voc. Plants* in Wr.-Wülcker 558/14 *Iuniperii*, geneiure, gorst. **1879** BRITTEN & HOLLAND *Plant-n.* 214 Gorst... *Juniperus communis.*

3. *attrib.* and *Comb.* **a.** simple attrib., as *gorse-bud*, *-bush*, *-common*, *-cover*, *-covert*, *-fence*,

-hedge, -tree; *gorse-knife, -slasher*: used for clearing land of gorse. **b.** instrumental, as *gorse-covered, -grown*. Also **gorse-bird, -linnet**, the common linnet; **gorse-chat, -hatch, -hatcher, -thatcher**, local names for the whinchat, stonechat, wheatear, and linnet; **gorse-duck** (see quot.); **gorse-kid**, a bundle of gorse.

1885 SWAINSON *Prov. Names Birds* 65 Linnet... From its frequenting downs and open moors abounding in furze or whin, it is called—*Gorse bird, Gorse hatcher, Gorse thatcher,.. Gorse linnet. **1860** G. H. K. in *Vac. Tour.* 143 We have.. the crackling of the *gorse-buds.. to tell us that nature never sleeps. **1813** *Examiner* 26 Apr. 260/2 They.. threw him into a *gorse-bush. **1848** *Zoologist* VI. 2290 In G[loucestershire] it [the stonechat] is the *gorsechat. **1860** G. H. K. in *Vac. Tour.* 143 A *gorse common, baking in the summer sun. **1780** in Egerton-Warburton *Hunt. Songs* (1883) Introd. 21 At this meeting a fox was found for the first time in the new *gorse cover. **1848** *Zoologist* VI. 2290 The landrail.. in the more western part a 'gurs' or '*gors duck'. **1895** *Daily News* 18 May 8/6 About five-and-twenty horses entered the ring to begin, but after a big ordeal over *gorse fences.. this number was reduced to seven. **1852** R. S. SURTEES *Sponge's Sp. Tour* (1893) 311 They now got.. into a very rushy, squashy, *gorse-grown pasture. **1848** *Zoologist* VI. 2137 *Gorse-hatch, or 'gorse-hatcher' [applied to the female and young of the wheatear]. **1888** F. HUME *Mad. Midas* I. iii, Divided into fields by long rows of *gorse hedges. **1661** PH. HENRY *Diaries* (1882) 79 Two hundred of *Gorse kids [*printed* Goose Kids] cost 6s. 8d. **1885** *Daily News* 1 Dec. 2/1, I hope nobody knows what it is to sit down recklessly on a gorsekid. **1907** 'G. B. LANCASTER' *Tracks we Tread* vi. 80 Randal kicked aside his *gorse-knife—he had been cutting brush in the gully beside. **1848** *Zoologist* VI. 2258 The linnet is a '*gorse linnet', a 'grey linnet'. **1896** R. B. SHARPE *Handbk. Birds Gt. Brit.* 45 The gorse-bushes being such a favourite nesting place that in many places the bird is known as the 'Gorse' Linnet. **1938** 'R. HYDE' *Nor Years Condemn* xiv. 253 We.. were given grubbers and *gorse-slashers. *c* **1440** *Promp. Parv.* 204/1 *Gorstys tre ..*supra in* Fyrrys.

Hence **gorsed** *ppl. a.*, topped with gorse.

1870 *Daily News* 6 June, He [a horse].. snowed the way over the gorsed hurdles, jumping readily from the hand.

Gorsedd ('gɔːsɛð). [W., = throne, tribunal, session.] A meeting of Welsh bards and druids; esp. the assembly which meets each day during a certain period as a preliminary to the eisteddfod. Also *attrib.*

1794 E. JONES *Relicks Welsh Bards* (ed. 2) 60 Likewise, we held a Gorsedd, Tribunal-meeting, or Supreme Congress of the Bards of the Isle of Britain, according to the ancient form of a Druidical Assembly. **1876** *Programme Wrexham Eisteddvod* 6 The Gorsedd will be held every morning.. at 9 o'clock, in a field in Grosvenor Road. **1908** *Daily Chron.* 9 June 5/7 The Eisteddfod.. will be duly proclaimed.. by the Arch-Druid, who will be assisted by the Gorsedd officials and bards. **1909** *Ibid.* 10 June 4/4 The Gorsedd ceremonial takes place within a circle marked out by twelve massive unhewn stones placed a few feet apart. **1928** *Observer* 15 July 11/3 The early morning sessions of the Gorsedd, with the bards in their multi-coloured robes. **1955** *Times* 3 Aug. 3/2 Early this morning the Gorsedd in their cloaking robes, green for the initiates, blue for the bards, and white for the druids, met in the sunlight within the circle of 12 stones to hold the traditional eisteddfod ceremony. **1959** *Manch. Guardian* 5 Aug. 3/1 The Gorsedd ceremony. *Ibid.*, The Gorsedd stones. *Ibid.*, The Gorsedd procession.

gorsoon, variant of GOSSOON.

gorsy ('gɔːsɪ), *a.* Also 6 **gorsty**, 7 **gorssie**, 9 **gorsey**. [f. GORSE + -Y[1].] **a.** Abounding in, covered with gorse. **b.** Of or pertaining to gorse.

1523 FITZHERB. *Surv.* xxv. (1539) 49 Gorsty grounde, the whiche hath ben errable grounde. **1613** *New Direct. Planting Timber* A 4 b, For the planting in Barren, Champion, or Gorssie grounds. **1706** PHILLIPS (ed. Kersey), *Jampnum*, Furze or Gorse; also gorsy Ground. **1766** PENNANT *Zool.* (1768) II. 272 With us it is common on gorsy grounds. **1829** E. JESSE *Jrnl. Nat.* 158 This songster [the linnet].. lives in society, frequenting open commons and gorsy fields. **1870** DISRAELI *Lothair* xiii. 55 Sometimes a gorsy dell and sometimes a great spread of antlered fern. **1885** MRS. PIRKIS *Lady Lovelace* II. xxix. 120 A fresh gorsy smell.

gort, variant of GORCE, *Obs.*

†**gory**, *sb. slang. Obs.*[−1] (See quot.)

1812 J. H. VAUX *Flash Dict.*, *Gory*, a term synonymous with *cove, gill* or *gloak*, and like them, commonly used in the descriptive.

gory ('gɔərɪ), *a.* Also 6 **gorrie**, 6–8 **goary**, 7 **go(a)rie**. [f. GORE *sb.*[1] + -Y[1].]

†**1.** Of blood: Gore-like, clotted. *Obs.*

a **1547** SURREY *Æneid* II. (1557) Bj, Whose sacred fillettes all be sprinkled were With filth of gory blod, and venim rank. **1590** SPENSER *F.Q.* I. xi. 22 Forth flowed fresh A gushing river of blacke gory blood.

2. Covered with gore, stained with blood, bloody.

c **1480** HENRYSON *Mor. Fab.* 38 Thy gorrie gumes and thy bludie snout. **1605** SHAKS. *Macb.* III. iv. 51 Neuer shake Thy goary lockes at me. **1637** MILTON *Lycidas* 62 His goary visage down the stream was sent. **1655** MARVELL *1st Anniv. Govt. Protector* 130 The monster.. shrinking to her Roman denn impure, Gnashes her goary teeth. *a* **1732** GAY *Poems* (1745) I. 17 He.. tears with goary mouth the screaming prey. **1785** BURNS *Winter Nt.* 45 Mad Ambition's gory hand. **1814** SCOTT *Ld. of Isles* VI. xvi, Away the gory axe he threw. *c* **1869** LD. C. E. PAGET *Autobiog.* vii. (1896) 221 The other [hand] held the gory head of a Greek just decapitated.

3. = BLOODY 4.

1586 WARNER *Alb. Eng.* I. vi. (1612) 22 Cerberus with goarie blowes did chace The wounded and the wearie Knight. **1601** ? MARSTON *Pasquil & Kath.* v. 15 The Pistoll is discharg'd; The Act of gorie murder is perform'd. **1606** SHAKS. *Tr. & Cr.* IV. v. 123 The obligation of our bloud forbids A gorie emulation 'twixt vs twaine.

4. Resembling gore; blood-red. *rare.* (Cf. BLOODY 7.) *gory dew*: name of a minute freshwater alga (see quot.).

1822 BYRON *Heaven & E.* I. iii. 211 Until the clouds look gory With the blood reeking from each battle-plain. **1861** H. MACMILLAN *Footn. fr. Nature* 147 [A] curious plant closely allied to the red snow is the *Palmella cruenta* or Gory Dew. **1877** LADY BRASSEY *Voy. Sunbeam* xv. (1878) 268 Waves of blood-red, fiery, liquid lava.. rushed up the face of the cliffs to toss their gory spray high in the air.

goryd ('gɒrɪd). *local.* [ad. Welsh *cored* a weir.] A kind of fishing-weir.

1873 *Act 36 & 37 Vict.* c. 71 Sched. 3 License Duties.. For each.. garth, goryd, box, crib, or cruive, £12. 0. 0.

gorz(e, dial. form of GORSE.

gos, short for GOSHAWK.

1786 BURNS *Brigs of Ayr* 68 Swift as the Gos drives on the wheeling hare. **1891** *Field* 7 Mar. 337/1 The mantle of snow is a fatal barrier to a day's hawking, either with 'gos' or peregrine.

gos, variant of GOSSE[2], *Obs.*

†**gos** = *God's*: see GOD *sb.* 14 a.

1599 [? PEELE] *Sir Clyomon* F j a, Gos bones, turne in that sheep there.

gos, obs. form of GOOSE.

gosain (gəʊ'saɪn). *India.* Also (formerly) **gosaing, gosine, gossein.** [Hindi, etc. *gosāīn* (Skr. *gosvāmin* 'lord of cows', f. *go* cow *sb.*[1]).] A Hindu who professes a life of religious mendicancy.

1774 G. BOGLE in C. R. Markham *Tibet* (1876) 124 The Gosains, the trading pilgrims of India, resort hither in great numbers. **1793** W. HODGES *Trav.* 112 A Gosine, or Hindoo Religious. **1813** J. FORBES *Orient. Mem.* II. 9 This village belongs exclusively to the Gosaings, or Senassees, a caste of religious Hindoo mendicants. **1826** W. B. HOCKLEY *Pandurang Hari* I. 97 About five miles from the city I reached the hut of a Gossein. *Note*, A religious mendicant. **1923** *19th Cent.* Jan. 107 A certain *gosain* or Hindu devotee. **1957** *Encycl. Brit.* XXII. 939/2 Chaitanya himself, as well as his immediate disciples, have come to be regarded as complete or partial incarnations of.. Krishna himself; and their modern successors, the Gosains, share to the fullest extent in the devout attentions of the worshippers.

Goschens ('gəʊʃənz), *sb. pl.* (*Temporary.*) A colloquial name for consols after their conversion from 3 to $2\frac{3}{4}$ per cent by G. J. *Goschen* (Chancellor of the Exchequer) in 1888 (later to $2\frac{1}{2}$).

1889 *Man of World* 29 June (Farmer), The nickname Goschens is going out of fashion. The new $2\frac{3}{4}$ stock is now called by the old name. **1891** *Punch* 4 Apr. 161/1 Securities yielding a larger return than $2\frac{3}{4}$ Goschens. **1903** *Westm. Gaz.* 15 Aug. 7/1 For various reasons, chief of which is the multitude of better-paying investments, the public are not buying Goschens.

gose-: see GOS- or GOOSE-.

gosesomer(e, obs. form of GOSSAMER.

gosh (gɒʃ). [Mincing pronunc. of GOD.] An oath or exclamation, *(by) gosh!, my gosh!* So **'goshawful** *a.* = GOD-AWFUL *a.*; hence **'gosh-,awfulness**; **'gosh-darned** *a.*, God-damned.

1757 FOOTE *Author* II. Wks. 1799 I. 147 Then there's highest—and lowest, by gosh. *c* **1804** C. K. SHARPE *Corr.* (1888) I. 210, I promise, by Gosh (which is the most elegant and classical oath imaginable). **1870** RAMSAY *Remin.* ii. (ed. 18) 26 Such minced oaths as.. losh! gosh! and lovanendie! *a* **1873** LYTTON *Ken. Chillingly* viii, By gosh! I never heard that before. **1906** H. GREEN *At Actors' Boarding House* 169 I'd a been free from that De Shine a long time ago if it wasn't fur the notoriety, an' me so gosh darned sensitive! **1909** H. L. HINDLEY *Gentleman from Hayville* 36 That gosh-awful long-winded, Vermont heestorical society meeting. **1920** F. SCOTT FITZGERALD *This Side Paradise* I. iv. 143 '*The Life of St. Teresa*,' read Alec aloud. 'Oh, my gosh!' **1928** *Daily Express* 9 July 9 Stripped of that language the result is what the flapper critic would call 'goshawful'. **1934** WODEHOUSE *Right Ho, Jeeves* iv. 39 That subtle gosh-awfulness which renders.. my Aunt Agatha the curse of the Home Counties. **1942** M. LOWRY *Let.* (1967) 44 The Goshdarned thing will put you on the spot. **1967** J. FLEMING *No Bones about It* iv. 80 Oh, my gosh! We'll have to have meals in the dining-room. **1967** LORD REITH in *Listener* 30 Nov. 688/3 Blood pouring down my new tunic, my gosh.

goshawk ('gɒshɔːk). Forms: 1 **góshafoc, -uc**, 4–7 **goshauk(e, -hawke**, 6 **gosehauke**, (5–6 **gois(s)halk**, 7 **goshalk**), 6–7 **goosse-hawk(e**, 6 **goushake**, 7 **-hawke, goshhawke**, 7–9 **goss-hawk**, 4, 6– **goshawk**. [OE. *gós-hafoc*, f. *gós* GOOSE + *hafoc* HAWK; cf. ON. *gáshaukr*.] A large short-winged hawk (*Astur palumbarius*, and other species).

c **1000** ÆLFRIC *Gloss.* in Wr.-Wülcker 131/22 *Aucarius*, goshafuc. *c* **1050** *Ags. Voc.* ibid. 285/2 *Accipiter*, goshafoc. **13..** *K. Alis.* 483 Him thoughte a goshauk with gret flyght Setlith on his beryng. **1398** TREVISA *Barth. De P.R.* XII. iii. (1495) 411 The goshawke is in fayrnesse of fethers moost lyke to the Ostrych. **1486** *Bk. St. Albans* D iv, Ther is a Goshawke, and that hauke is for a yeman. *c* **1520** A. WYNDESORE in Ellis *Orig. Lett.* Ser. III. (1846) I. 227 There hathe been.. an Ayerye of goosse hawks contynually there bredyng. **1599** T. M[OUFET] *Silkwormes* 32 Fierce goshawkes with the Phesants had no warre. **1612** *Sc. Bk. Rates* in *Halyburton's Ledger* (1867) 313 Halkis called.. Goshalkis the halk xvli. **1681** FLAVEL *Meth. Grace* vii. 145 A wicked minister is the devil's gosshawk, that goes a birding for hell! **1774** GOLDSM. *Nat. Hist.* (1776) V. 128 The kite or the goss-hawk approach their prey side-ways. **1810** SCOTT *Lady of L.* III. x, Shrill As goss-hawk's whistle on the hill. **1865** *Cornhill Mag.* May 626 Goshawks.. have no chance with anything faster than a rising pheasant; they are excellent for rabbits. **1890** THOMPSON in *Proc. U.S. Nat. Museum* (1891) XIII. 527 *Accipiter atricapillus*, American Goshawk.

attrib. **1818** SCOTT *Hrt. Midl.* xxxix, She hadna the same goss-hawk glance that makes the skin creep.

Goshen ('gəʊʃən). [Heb. *Gōšen* the fertile land allotted to the Israelites in Egypt, in which there was light during the plague of darkness.] Used allusively for: A place of plenty or of light.

1611 R. BOLTON *Comf. Walking* (1625) 13 Thou shalt not find such another illightened Goshen, as this Iland, wherein we dwell. **1683** *Apol. Prot. France* ii. 17, I leave you now to judge whether they are to blame to seek for light in some Goshen. **1759** R. SHIRRA in Johnston *Rem.* (1850) 133 Thereby a land becomes a Goshen—a Valley of Vision. **1820** SCOTT *Monast.* i, The possessions of these Abbeys were each a sort of Goshen, enjoying the calm light of peace and immunity. **1890** *Chamb. Jrnl.* 14 June 369 The tiny dormice gathering their winter hoards from the Goshens of nuts below.

goshenite ('gəʊʃənaɪt). *Min.* [Named by Shepard 1844 after *Goshen* in Massachusetts, where it is found: see -ITE.] A colourless variety of beryl.

1844 C. U. SHEPARD *Min.* I. 143 Goshenite.. [occurs] in rounded crystals with rough surfaces. **1868** DANA *Min.* (ed. 5) 246 Goshenite is a colorless or white variety.

goship, obs. form of GOSSIP.

gosibrede, obs. form of GOSSIPRED.

gosimore, obs. form of GOSSAMER.

goslarite ('gɒzləraɪt). *Min.* [Named by Haidinger 1845; f. *Goslar* a locality in the Hartz, where it is found + -ITE.] A native sulphate of zinc.

1849 NICOL *Min.* 329 Goslarite, Haidinger; Sulphate of zinc. **1884** in DANA *Min.* 647.

'goslet. *U.S.* [f. GOOSE + -LET.] (See quot.)

1884–5 *Riverside Nat. Hist.* (1888) IV. 142 A few diminutive species of geese, the so-called goslets (*Nettepus*).

gos lettuce, variant of *cos lettuce*: see COS *sb.*

1769 MRS. RAFFALD *Eng. Housekpr.* (1778) 11 Split the blanched part of three goss lettuces into four quarters. **1814** LAMB *Lett.* (1837) I. 332 What has gone of.. M—— and his gos-lettuces?

gosling ('gɒzlɪŋ). Forms: α. 5 **geslyng(e**, **gesseling**, 6–9 *Sc.* **gaislin(g**, 7–9 *dial.* **gesling**, (6 *Sc.* **gaysling**, 7 **gazeling**). β. 4–5 **gosselyng**, 5–6 **gos(e)lyng(e**, (6 **gozelyng**), 6–7 **go(o)s(e)ling**, 7–9 **goslin**, (7 **gosselin, gooselin, gozeling**), 6– **gosling.** [Prob. the α form is the earlier: ME. *geslyng*, a. ON. *gæsling-r* (Sw., Da. *gäsling*), f. *gás* GOOSE *sb.*: see -LING. The form surviving in standard Eng. was prob. a new formation on ME. *gōs* GOOSE + -LING; the shortening of the vowel is normal in formations of this kind.]

1. A young goose.

α. *c* **1425** *Voc.* in Wr.-Wülcker 638/17 *Hic anccrulus*, geslyng. **1483** *Cath. Angl.* 154/2 A Geslynge (*A.* Gesseling), *ancerulus*. **1549** *Compl. Scot.* vi. 39 Gayslingis cryit quhilk quhilk. **1653** URQUHART *Rabelais* I. xii, Whether had you rather ride on a gesling or lead a sow in a Leash? **1868** ATKINSON *Cleveland Gloss.*, Gesling.

β. *c* **1430** LYDG. *Hors, Shepe & G.* 191 in *Pol. Rel. & L. Poems* (1866) 21 The goos with her gosselyngis to swyme in the lake. *c* **1440** *Promp. Parv.* 204/2 Goselynge, *anccrulus*. **1465** *Mann. & Househ. Exp.* (Roxb.) 296 Item, my mastyr paid her for a gander, iiij. bredegese, and v. goslynges,.. iiij.s. *a* **1529** SKELTON *E. Rummyng* 460 Two goslynges, That were noughty froslynges. **1603** OWEN *Pembrokesh.* (1891) 118 Yt is saied that this fish [Salmon] and the gooselinge concurre in growth. **1724** SWIFT *Drapier's Lett.* Wks. 1755 V. II. 146 Nature hath instructed even a brood of goslings to stick together, while the kite is hovering over their heads. **1821** CLARE *Vill. Minstr.* I. 18 Other losses too the dames recite, Of chick, and duck, and gosling gone astray.

Proverbs. **1523** SKELTON *Garl. Laurel* 1431 Whan the rayne rayneth and the gose wynkith, Lytill wotith the goslyng what the gose thinkith. **1562** J. HEYWOOD *Prov. & Epigr.* (1867) 159 He that medleth with all thyng, may shooe the goslyng. **1589** PUTTENHAM *Eng. Poesie* III. xxiv. (Arb.) 297 A woman will weepe for pitie to see a gosling goe barefoote. **1590** GREENE *Neuer too late* (1600) 25 As warie as shee was, yet the old Goose could spie the gosling winke. **1862** HISLOP *Prov. Scot.* 9 A gude goose may hae an ill gaislin.

2. *fig.* A foolish, inexperienced person; one who is young and 'green'.

1607 SHAKS. *Cor.* v. iii. 35 Ile neuer Be such a Gosling to obey instinct. **1631** BRATHWAIT *Whimzies, Balladmonger* 19 Guarded with a janizarie of costermongers, and countrey gooselings. **1650** B. *Discollimininium* 21 He let them.. returne home like Goslings as they went. **1766** GRAY *Let. to Nicholls* 26 Aug., You are a green gosling! I was at the same age (very near) as wise as you. **1818** SCOTT *Br. Lamm.* xxv, 'Did ever ony man see sic a set of green-gaislings?' **1824** MRS. CAMERON *Pink Tippet* II. 30 'What a gosling you are, child', said Mrs. Price, 'you know nothing'.

appositive. **1771** *Bachelor* (1773) I. 75 The sentiments of such a gosling critic would not be worth notice. **1780** COWPER *Progr. Err.* 379 Surprised at all they meet, the gosling pair, With awkward gait, stretched neck, and silly stare Discover huge cathedrals built with stone.

3. The figure of a gosling.

a **1535** MORE *Wks.* 1224 Make goselinges in the ashes with a sticke as children do.

4. A catkin or blossom on a tree (see quots.).

1706 PHILLIPS (ed. Kersey), *Gosling*,..a kind of Substance that grows upon a Nut-tree. **1721** in BAILEY. **1736** AINSWORTH *Lat. Dict.* I, Goslin on a nut tree, *nucamentum*. **1766** PENNANT *Brit. Zool.* (1768) II. 304 Its nest..lined..with the goslin or cotton of the sallow. **1847–78** HALLIWELL, *Goslings*, the blossoms of the willow.

5. *attrib.* and *Comb.*, as **gosling-colour**, **gosling-green** (*sb.* and *a.*), a pale yellowish green; **gosling-grass**, **-weed**, local names for *Galium Aparine*, GOOSE-GRASS 2 (Britten & Holland).

1552 HULOET, Goslynge weade herbe, *Rueba minor*. **1600** *Q. Eliz. Wardr.* in Nichols *Progr. Q. Eliz.* (1823) III. 509 Item, one cloak and a saufegarde of gozelinge-colour taphata. **1756** C. LUCAS *Ess. Waters* I. 102 It turns to a pale yellow or gosling green with alcalies. **1766** GOLDSM. *Vic. W.* xii, His waistcoat was of a gosling green. **1807** P. GASS *Jrnl.* 146 We found the southwest branch..of a goslin-green colour. **1835** LONGF. *Outre-Mer* (1851) 285 The nice little man in gosling-green.

go-slow (gəʊ'sləʊ). [f. GO *v.* + SLOW *adv.*] A form of industrial protest in which employees work at a deliberately slow pace. Also *attrib.* Hence **go-'slower**, one who works in this manner. Cf. CA'CANNY.

1930 *Times* 27 Mar. 19/5 The receipts..showed large decreases..due to the recent 'go-slow' movement amongst the men. **1937** *Daily Herald* 11 Feb. 3/1 Drivers on the Morden-Edgware tube and the Bakerloo line had been adopting a 'go-slow' policy, because it is alleged, they resented being reprimanded by inspectors for speeding on bends. **1955** *Times* 12 Aug. 8/4 The men's representatives undertook that there would be no further 'go slows' or stoppages and that every man would work his full shift. **1963** *Listener* 10 Jan. 76/1 A 'go slow' at power stations. **1963** *Times* 12 Jan. 9/5, I would ask potential strikers or 'go-slowers' not to add to the hardship of old people, for whom each winter is a recurring agony.

gosope, obs. form of GOSSIP *sb.*

gospel ('gɒspəl), *sb.* Forms: 1–5 **godspel(l**, 3–4 **goddspel(l**, 4 **godspelle**, **gosspell**, 4–7 **gospell(e**, 5 **gospeel**, **gospille**, 6 **ghospel(l(e**, 3– **gospel**. Also with capital initial in specific uses. [OE. *godspel*, doubtless orig. *gód spel* (see GOOD *a.* and SPELL *sb.*), good tidings (cf. *láð spel* evil tidings), a rendering of the L. *bona adnuntiatio* (*Corpus Gloss.* Int. 117) or *bonus nuntius* ('*Euuangelium*, id est, bonum nuntium, godspel', *Voc. c* 1050 in Wr.-Wülcker 314/8), which was current as an explanation of the etymological sense of L. *evangelium*, Gr. εὐαγγέλιον (see EVANGEL). Cf. Goth. *þiuþspillôn* 'to preach the gospel' (εὐαγγελίζεσθαι), f. *þiuþ-s* good + *spillôn* to announce (cogn. w. SPELL). When the phrase *gód spel* was adopted as the regular translation of *evangelium*, the ambiguity of its written form led to its being interpreted as a compound, *gŏd-spel*, f. GOD + *spel* in the sense 'discourse' or 'story'. The mistake was very natural, as the resulting sense was much more obviously appropriate than that of 'good tidings' for a word which was chiefly known as the name of a sacred book or of a portion of the liturgy. From OE. the word passed, in adapted forms, into the languages of the Teutonic peoples evangelized from England: OS. *godspell*, OHG. *gotspell*, ON. *guð-*, *goðspiall*; in each case the form of the first element shows unequivocally that it was identified with *God*, not with *good*. The ON. form has survived into mod.Icel.; the continental Teut. langs. early discarded the word for adoptions of L. *evangelium*.

Although the *ó* in OE. *gódspel* would necessarily in time have been shortened by the regular operation of phonetic law, it does not appear that this process could have taken place early enough to account for the form of the word in OS. and OHG. The form *gŏdspel* must therefore (as above explained) be due to a misinterpretation of the written form, originating before the word had any oral currency.]

1. a. 'The glad tidings (of the kingdom of God)' announced to the world by Jesus Christ. Hence, the body of religious doctrine taught by Christ and His apostles; the Christian revelation, religion or dispensation. Often contrasted with *the Law*, i.e. the Old Testament dispensation. Phrase, *to preach*, †*minister the gospel*.

c **950** *Lindisf. Gosp.* Matt. ix. 35 Ðe hælend..bodade godspell [so *c* **1000** *Ags. Gosp.*, *c* **1160** *Hatton Gosp.* godspel] rices. *c* **1205** LAY. 29507 Austin þu scalt..beode þer godes goddspel. **1297** R. GLOUC. (Rolls) 1529 Seinte peter..sende seint Marc..vor to preche þen gospel that he adde imaked. *c* **1380** WYCLIF *Sel. Wks.* III. 348 þei letten hem for to preche, and speciali Cristis gospel. **1382** —— *Acts* xx. 24 The gospel of the grace of God. —— *Eph.* i. 13 Whanne ȝe hadden herd the word of treuthe, resceyueden the gospel of ȝoure heelthe. **1548** UDALL, etc. *Erasm. Par. Luke* ix. 88 b, Thei had..debarred a certain man from the fraternitee of mynistryng the ghospell. **1550** LATIMER *Serm. at Stamford* 9 Oct. A vij b, In the whole multytude that professe the gospell, all be not good. **1565** JEWEL *Replie* Wks. III. 170 The Jews saw Christ in the law; the Christians see Christ in the gospel. **1611** BIBLE *1 Thess.* ii. 2. **1649** BP. TAYLOR *Gt. Exemp.* II. xii. 54 The Gospell is therefore a Covenant of grace. **1692** WASHINGTON tr. *Milton's Def. Pop.* M.'s Wks. 1738 I. 473 Let us now consider, whether the Gospel preach up any such Doctrine. **1782** PRIESTLEY *Corrupt. Chr.* I. II. 208 The advantages we at present enjoy by the gospel. **1784** COWPER *Task* II. 342 In strains as sweet As angels use, the Gospel whispers peace. **1827** WHATELY *Logic* App. I. (1850) 202 *Preaching* the Gospel is accordingly often used to include not only the *proclaiming* of the *good tidings*, but the *teaching* of what is to be believed and done, in consequence. **1837** W. IRVING *Capt. Bonneville* III. 156 To spread the light of the gospel in that far wilderness. **1857** MAURICE *Ep. St. John* xiv. 228 That Gospel was the announcement that Jesus Christ had manifested the Life of God. **1876** MOZLEY *Univ. Serm.* i. 3 There is nothing obsolete in the original spirit of the Gospel.

b. Identified by Protestants with their own system of belief, as opposed to the perversions of Christianity imputed by them to their adversaries; also applied by Puritans and modern Evangelicals to the doctrine of salvation solely through trust in the merit of Christ's sacrifice.

1552 [see GOSPELLER 4]. **1565** JEWEL *Def. Apol.* Wks. IV. 213 Ye make yourself game, M. Harding, for that the preaching of the gospel issued first out of Wittenberg, and not from Rome. *Mod.* 'Why don't you go to church?' 'Because the Gospel is not preached there.'

†**c.** *to talk gospel*: to 'talk religion'.

1715 DE FOE *Fam. Instruct.* II. i. (1841) I. 172 Don't thou talk gospel too.

d. *gen.* Any revelation from heaven.

1481 CAXTON *Myrr.* III. xiii. 164 God made neuer so good a gospel but some myghte torne it contrarye to trouthe. **1878** D. CAMPBELL *Rational & True Gospel* xxii. 122 Flowers are gospels of grace and love from the Unseen.

¶ *the Gospel Perdurable*: a book produced in 1255 under the title of *Euangelium Eternum, siue Euangelium Spiritus Sancti*. (See note in Skeat *Chaucer* (1894) I. 447.)

c **1400** *Rom. Rose* 7102.

e. Short for *gospel music*.

1956 M. STEARNS *Story of Jazz* i. 8 It can be heard in the field-holler and the work song, the spiritual and gospel, minstrelsy and ragtime. **1971** *It* 2–16 June 18/3 Oh, yes, it's all well-played stuff, ranging from country thru' rock and blues and gospel. **1979** *Arizona Daily Star* 5 Aug. I. 10/4 Tunes are a mixed bag of rock, calypso, disco, swing and gospel.

2. a. The record of Christ's life and teaching, contained in the books written by the 'four evangelists'.

a **1000** *Andreas* 12 (Gr.) Matheus..se mid Iudeum ongan godspell ærest wordum writan. *c* **1200** ORMIN 1800 Swa summ þe Goddspell kiþeþþ. *c* **1290** *Beket* 2109 in *S. Eng. Leg.* I. 167 For in the godspel it is i-writen þat [etc.]. **1340** HAMPOLE *Pr. Consc.* 4013 In þe godspelle. *c* **1400** *Three Kings Cologne* 59 Wher-of spekeþ þe euangelist in þe godspell. **1794** PALEY *Evid.* I. ix. §3 (1817) 226 Ignatius..speaks of the Gospel..in terms which render it very probable that he meant by the Gospel the book or volume of the Gospels. **1845** S. AUSTIN *Ranke's Hist. Ref.* III. 299 The promises..given to the human race, in the psalms or the gospel.

b. One of the books written by the four Evangelists; †sometimes *pl.* in *sing.* sense. Also applied to certain ancient lives of Christ of a legendary character (*apocryphal gospels*), as *the Gospel of Nicodemus, the Gospel of the Infancy*, etc.

c **1200** *Trin. Coll. Hom.* 71 Vre drihten us seið on þe godspelle þe sein lucas makede. *c* **1290** *S. Eng. Leg.* I. 28/58 þe godspelles of seint Mathev. *a* **1300** *Cursor M.* 21243 Marc..þe gospel [*Fairf.* gosspellis] in itali he wratte. *c* **1315** SHOREHAM 48 Wet he ther redde thou myȝt se Ine seynt Lukes godspelle. **1357** *Lay Folks Catech.* 573 Als saint Iohn saies in his godspel. *c* **1394** *P. Pl. Crede* 257 We ben proued þe prijs of popes at Rome, And of gretest degre as godspelles telleþ. *Ibid.* 709 Wiþ glosinge of godspells þei gods worde turneþ. **1508** FISHER *7 Penit. Ps.* li. Wks. (1876) 119 As is shewed in the gespell [*sic: misprint*] of Luke. **1695** LOCKE *Reas. Chr.* 193 The rest of St. John's Gospel. **1756–7** tr. *Keysler's Trav.* (1760) IV. 397 A beautiful manuscript of the gospels, written in golden letters, in the year 870. **1772** PRIESTLEY *Inst. Relig.* (1782) I. 291 The four gospels are particularly mentioned by Julian. **1845** STODDART in *Encycl. Metrop.* (1847) 145/1 So in the Anglo-Saxon Gospels.

†**c.** In extended sense: The Holy Scriptures.

1393 LANGL. *P. Pl.* C. XI. 234 The godspel ys herageyn, as gomes may reden [Quotes *Ezek.* xviii. 20]. **1483** CAXTON *Cato* H j, The gospel sayth that yf thou wylte lyue longe on the erthe thou must honoure..thy fader and moder.

3. *Eccl.* *the gospel* (*for* or *of the day*): the portion from one of the four gospels read at the Communion Service. (Cf. EPISTLE 3.) *allusively* (cf. 4).

c **1000** *Ags. Gosp.* Matt. xxiv. 42 *marg.*, Ðys godspel sceal to mænies confessores mæsse-dæge. *c* **1175** *Lamb. Hom.* 5 Nu leoue broðre nu ic eou habbe þet godspel iseid. *c* **1200** *Trin. Coll. Hom.* 173 Ðe holi godspel of þis dai specð of ure helende and of two broðren. *a* **1375** *Lay Folks Mass Bk.* App. IV. 642 Forȝete not þe god-spelle For þing þat may bifalle. **1463** *Bury Wills* (Camden) 21 After the gospeel to reherse my name opynly with *De profundis* for my soule. **1548–9** (Mar.) *Bk. Com. Prayer, Communion*, One appointed to reade the Gospel. **1756–7** tr. *Keysler's Trav.* (1760) II. 246 Two desks..on which formerly the epistles and gospels were read. **1877** J. D. CHAMBERS *Div. Worship* 332 The Deacon advances to read the Gospel.

allusively **1545** RAYNOLD *Byrth Mankynde* 110 But these sayinges be nether in the gospell of the day, ne of the nyght. **1601** SHAKS. *Twel. Nt.* v. i. 295 A madmans Epistles are no Gospels, so it skilles not much when they are deliuer'd.

4. Something as 'true as the gospel'; a statement to be implicitly received. Also †with *a*, *no*, and *to take for* (†*a*, *the*) *gospel*.

a **1250** *Owl & Night.* 1268 For-thi seide Alfred swithe wel And his worde was goddspel, That [etc.]. *c* **1374** CHAUCER *Troylus* v. 1265 God wot I wende, O lady bright Criseyde, That every word was gospel that ye seyde! **1496** *Dives & Paup.* (W. de W.) VI. xiii. 254/1 Yet what they saye, the people taketh it for a gospell. **1546** J. HEYWOOD *Prov.* (1867) 46 All is not gospell that thou doest speake. **1559** *Mirr. Mag., Hen. VI*, xxviii, Whose wordes to be no gospel tho, I to my griefe haue found. **1580** LYLY *Euphues* (Arb.) 407 The onely triall that a Ladie requireth of hir louer, it is this..that ..euery gloase [be] a gospell. **1625** *Impeachm. Dk. Buckhm.* (Camden) 212 All the Cardinal sayes is not gospel, for two month's pay is yet behinde. **1678** EVELYN *Mem.* (1857) II. 133 Oates was encouraged, and everything he affirmed taken for gospel. **1712** ARBUTHNOT *John Bull* II. iv, She took them [her dreams] all for the gospel. **1807** CRABBE *Library* 268 And all was gospel that a monk could dream. **1824** BYRON *Juan* XVI. vi, Those holier mysteries which the wise and just Receive as gospel. **1830** GALT *Lawrie T.* II. i. (1849) 43 Offered me two hundred and fifty dollars—gospel, by the living jingo! **1887** G. R. SIMS *Mary Jane's Mem.* 74 It's gospel every word.

5. a. Something that serves as a guide to human action; something that men swear by. **b.** A doctrine 'preached' with fervour as a means of political or social 'salvation'.

a. 1652 MILTON *Sonn. to Cromwell*, Help us to save free conscience from the paw Of hireling wolves, whose Gospel is their maw. **1712** STEELE *Spect.* No. 456 ¶4 The Law of the Land is his Gospel. **1847** L. HUNT *Men, Women & B.* II. xi. 284 Brute force was his law, and contempt of the many his gospel.

b. 1790 BURKE *Fr. Rev.* (ed. 2) 18 The propagators of this political gospel are in hopes their abstract principle would be overlooked. **1829** in Carlyle *Misc.* (1857) II. 87 The Gospel of Economy. **1870** BALDW. BROWN *Eccl. Truth* 274 *La carrière ouverte aux talens* was, according to Mr. Carlyle, the gospel of the Revolution. **1873** HAMERTON *Intell. Life* x. iii. (1875) 351 Is he to go and preach the gospel of the intellect in the kitchen? **1878** HOOKER & BALL *Morocco* 81 We were assured that even here the modern gospel of soap and water has made much progress.

†**6.** = *gospel-oath*. *Obs.*$^{-1}$

1483 CAXTON *Gold. Leg.* 84/2, I toke on a tyme a gospelle in prayeng god that he wold gyue me..contynence..I wente to the bourdel and forgate the gospel upon me.

†**7.** jocularly. *wooden gospels*: the four divisions of a board for the game of tables. *Obs.*

1653 URQUHART *Rabelais* I. xxii, After supper were brought in..the faire wooden Gospels, and the books of the foure Kings, that is to say, many paires of tables and cardes.

8. *attrib.* and *Comb.* **a.** simple attrib., as (sense 1: often = such as accords with, or is enjoined by, the gospel) *gospel-artillery*, *-blessing*, *-champion*, *-church*, *-crew*, *-day*, *-dispensation*, *-duty*, *-freedom*, *-liberty*, *-light*, *-minister*, *ministry*, *-morality*, *music*, *-news*, *-peace*, *-phrase*, *-purity*, *-righteousness*, *-sabbath*, *shout*, *-sufferer*, *-times*, *-trump*, *-union*, *-unity*, *-way*, *-word*; (sense 2) *gospel-record*; (sense 3) *gospel-lectern*. **b.** objective, as *gospel-monger*, *-preacher*, *-preaching*, *singer*, *-teacher*, *-writer*.

c **1660** SOUTH *Serm. Prov.* iii. 17 (1715) I. 34 Pilgrimages, going barefoot, Hair-Shirts, and Whips, with other such *Gospel-Artillery. **1662** STILLINGFL. *Orig. Sacr.* II. vi. §7 The bestowing of such mercies which do suppose the greatest unworthiness of them, as *Gospel blessings do. **1862** E. TROLLOPE in *Rep. Linc. Archit. Soc.* 120 A bold, eager *gospel-champion. **1680** ALLEN *Peace & Unity* 87 And if the Parishioners in a Parish, do usually Assemble together upon the same account [for Communion in Gospel Ordinances], are not those *Gospel Churches as well as the other? **1715** ROWE *Lady Jane Grey* IV. i, There own our Sovereign's Title and defy Jane and her *Gospel-Crew. **1678** BUNYAN *Pilgr.* Apol. (1862) 5, I writing of the Way And Race of Saints, in this our *Gospel-day. **1738** WESLEY *Psalms* CXXX. vi, O that his Mercy's Beams would rise, And bring the Gospel-Day. **1736** BUTLER *Anal.* II. i. 156 This has also a particular Reference to the *Gospel-dispensation. **1658** *Whole Duty Man* xvi. §1 (1687) 126 This is the great *Gospel-duty so often enjoyned us by Christ. *a* **1683** OLDHAM *Ode* Wks. (1685) 99 When Christian Fools were obstinately good, Nor yet their *Gospel-freedom understood. **1877** J. D. CHAMBERS *Div. Worship* 332 The Gospel Pulpitum or Ambo, or the portable *Gospel Lectern. **1687** DRYDEN *Hind & P.* II. 415 The rest some fundamental flaw wou'd see, And call Rebellion *gospel-liberty. **1674** ALLEN *Danger Enthus.* 86 The highest Dispensation of *Gospel-light as ever shined upon the World. *a* **1771** GRAY *Fragm.*, When love could teach a monarch to be wise, And gospel-light first dawn'd from Bullen's eyes. **1768–74** TUCKER *Lt. Nat.* (1852) II. 234 They may..better have recourse to their horse or their apothecary, than to their *gospel-minister. **1721** *Jrnls. Ho. Repr. Mass.* III. 187 The first settled and Ordained Minister ..that Shall Live and Dye in the Work of a *Gospel Ministry. **1831** J. M. PECK *Guide Emigrants* 255 The object is, 'to educate pious, indigent young men for the gospel ministry'. **1764** *Low Life* 90 The *Gospel-Mongers, *alias* Ministers. **1768** BLACKSTONE *Comm.* III. xiii. 218 So closely does the law of England enforce that excellent rule of *gospel-morality of 'doing to others as we would they should do unto ourselves'. **1955** KEEPNEWS & GRAUER *Pict. Hist. Jazz* i. 3 The spirituals and *gospel music that were the Negro's own interpretation of the white man's religion. **1971** *Ink* 12 June 19/1 In an attempt to give *bigness* to their white gospel music, they tried everything from accordion to horns. **1878** BROWNING *La Saisiaz* 75 So preached one his *gospel-news. **1738** WESLEY *Psalms* IV. viii, Of *Gospel-Peace possest, Secure in thy Defence. **1682** DRYDEN *Medal* 191 In *Gospel phrase their Chap-men they betray. **1549** COVERDALE, etc. *Erasm. Par. Philem.* 32 My fellow *ghospell preacher, brother Timothie. —— *Erasm. Par. 2 Tim.* i. 6–12 Thys *ghospell preachynge is committed vnto me. *a* **1861** T. WOOLNER *My Beautiful Lady* (1863) 139 Priests sworn to God, whose daily lives Preached *gospel purity and kindliness. **1833** ROCK *Hierurg.* (1892) I. 247 The *Gospel-record of the institution of the Blessed Eucharist. **1738** WARBURTON *Faith working by Charity* ii. 7 The Law of Nature came to be shunned as a dangerous and fallacious Guide; and Faith, traditional, not scriptural, had usurped its Province of interpreting *Gospel-righteousness. *a* **1711** KEN *Divine Love* Wks. (1838) 278 Thou, O my God, didst ordain the Judaical Sabbath as a shadow of the true *Gospel-sabbath. **1958** 'F. NEWTON' in P. Gammond *Decca Bk. Jazz* v. 73 The great *gospel singers..are the legitimate heirs of Ma Rainey and Bessie Smith, and their rise in the late 1930s and 1940s is one of the most cheering phenomena for the blues-lover. **1959** 'F. NEWTON' *Jazz Scene* iv. 54 A local piano style, based on ragtime and Appalachian *gospel shouts. **1694** KETTLEWELL *Comp. Persecuted* 6, I have directed their eye to the true spirit, duty, and carriage of *Gospel-sufferers. **1550** BALE *Image Both Ch.* II. xi. b vj, They that were monkes, priestes, and friers are nowe become *gospell teachers. **1663** BUTLER *Hud.* I. i. 837, I..do not doubt But bear-baiting may be made out, In *gospel-times, as lawful as is Provincial or parochial classis. **1827** KEBLE *Chr. Y.*, Advent Sund., Again the *Gospel-trump is blown. **1672** *Disc. conc. Evangelical Love* 107 This is that *Gospel-Vnity which we are to labour after. *Ibid.* 108 The means appointed by Christ for attaining *Gospel-Vnion. **1649** in *Milton's Prose Wks.* (1753) I. 387 Such as..invent damnable errors, under the specious pretence of a *gospel-way and new light. **1886** MISS BRADDON *One Thing Needful* ii, He would have England walk in gospel ways. **1538** STARKEY *England* II. iii. 197 Surely thys ys *gospel word. **1768–74** TUCKER *Lt. Nat.* (1852) II. 468 To transmit his Master's doctrines for their benefit in the plainness of a *gospel-writer.

9. Special comb.: **gospel-gossip**, one who is always talking of sermons, texts, etc.; **gospel-hardened** *a.*, rendered incapable of being moved by the gospel, through constant hearing of it; †**gospel-lad**, a COVENANTER; †**gospel-mass-monger** *nonce-wd.*, ? a professed Protestant who favours Romish doctrine; **gospel-oak** (see quot. 1862); **gospel-oath**, an oath sworn upon the gospels, or an oath of an equally binding character; **gospel-place**, a place where the 'gospel' was recited at the perambulation of boundaries; **gospel-right**, a right expressly sanctioned or prescribed in the Gospel; **gospel-sharp**, a Western U.S. term for a Christian minister of religion; **gospel-shop**, a derisive name for a Methodist chapel; **gospel-side**, the side of the altar at which the gospel is read, the north side; **gospel-sin**, sin against the light of the gospel; so ***gospel-sinner***; **gospel song**, a song characterized by its fervour or evangelistic message; **gospel-title**, an indisputable title (cf. 4 and *gospel-right*); **gospel-tree** = *gospel-oak*; **gospel-true** *a.*, as true as the gospel (cf. next); **gospel-truth**, (*a*) the truth or truths contained in the gospel; (*b*) something as true as the gospel (cf. sense 4); **gospelwards** *adv.*, in the direction of the gospel; †**gospelwright**, a composer of a gospel = EVANGELIST I.

1711 ADDISON *Spect.* No. 46 ¶6, I am one of those unhappy Men that are plagued with a *Gospel-Gossip, so common among Dissenters (especially Friends). **1844** J. C. MILLER *Serm.* 2 June 22 Have the Sabbaths and Sermons of a life been in vain? Am I *Gospel-hardened or Gospel-saved? **1871** H. MACMILLAN *True Vine* vii. (1872) 299 Decent church-going professors, who are gospel-hardened. *c* **1679** *Loudon Hill* iii. in Child *Ballads* VII. 107/1 Weel prosper a' the *gospel-lads That are into the west countrie Ay wicked Claverse to demean. **1554** BRADFORD in Coverdale *Lett. Mart.* (1564) 347 Wil the lawes of the realme ..excuse oure *gospell Masse-mongers conscience then? **1830** J. G. STRUTT *Sylva Brit.* 34 The *Gospel Oak near Stoneleigh stands in a little retired coppice. **1862** TOULM. SMITH in *Parl. Remembrancer* Oct. 189 Every one knows how many 'Gospel oaks' there are in different places:—the ancient mark-trees, distinguishing boundaries, and at which the perambulators have, for ages, been accustomed to stand ..while the 'gospel' has been pronounced, cursing him who moves the landmarks. **1891** FLÜGEL *Germ. & Eng. Dict.*, *Auf das Evangelium schwören*, to take a *gospel-oath. **1686** PLOT *Staffordsh.* 318 This it seems they doe too at all *Gospell-places, whether wells, trees, or hills. **1768–74** TUCKER *Lt. Nat.* (1852) II. 102 The landholder having no better *gospel-right to his nine parts than the parson has to his tithe. **1872** 'MARK TWAIN' *Roughing It* xlvii. 333 'What we want is a *gospel-sharp. See?' 'A what?' 'Gospel-sharp. Parson.' **1897** A. H. LEWIS *Wolfville* 50 I've took the trouble to bring a gospel-sharp over from Tucson to do the marryin'. **1902** C. MORRIS *Stage Confidences* 224 There's another gospel-sharp out on the edge of town. **1782** G. PARKER *Hum. Sk.* 88 From Whitfield and Romaine to Pope John range; Each *gospel shop ringing a daily change. *a* **1791** LACKINGTON *Life* xix. (1794) 120 My next enquiry was for Mr. Wesley's Gospel-shops. **1891** *Order Divine Services for Yr.* (Hayes) 52 The people in the centre of the church are incensed first, then those on the Epistle side and lastly those on the *Gospel side. **1647** TRAPP *Comm. 2 Thess.* ii. 10 This is the great *Gospel-sin, punished by God with strong delusions, vile affections, just damnation. **1678** *Yng. Man's Call.* 30 You..are, though but young people, yet old sinners, great sinners, *gospel-sinners. **1905** *Methodist Rev.* LXXXVII. 704 The attitude to take toward the sort of tune ..variously denominated, '*gospel song', 'spiritual song', 'pennyroyal', has cost the Commission a good deal of vexation of spirit. **1959** 'F. NEWTON' *Jazz Scene* ii. 32 Good examples of contemporary negro gospel song groups. **1964** L. NKOSI *Rhythm of Violence* 41 Next time they came we were singing gospel songs. **1763** CHURCHILL *Gotham* I. 9 The Man, who finds an unknown Country out, By giving it a name acquires, no doubt, A *Gospel title. **1648** HERRICK *Hesper.*, *To Anthea* 18 Dearest, bury me Under that Holy oke, or *Gospel-tree. **1801** SHAW *Staffordsh.* II. I. 165 The boundaries..are marked out by what are called Gospel trees, from the custom of having the Gospel read under or near them, by the clergy-man attending the parochial perambulations. *c* **1854** THACKERAY *Wolves & Lamb* (1869) 343 It's all true. *Gospel-true. **1647** TRAPP *Comm. Titus* ii. 12 Every *Gospel-truth strikes at some sin, and thereby may be discerned. **1738** WESLEY *Psalms* CXXXII. v, If..thy Children..The glorious Gospel-Truth obey, The Truth shall make them free indeed. **1833** *Jurist* Feb. 5 It has been believed, nay, clung to as Gospel truth. **1843** HALIBURTON *Attaché* II. vii. 128 Fact I assure you, it's gospel truth. **1865** PUSEY *Truth Eng. Ch.* 272 This is, of course, fundamental Gospel-truth. **1911** BRERETON & ROTHWELL tr. *Bergson's Laughter* i. 41 'A red nose is a painted nose', 'A negro is a white man in disguise', are also absurd to the reason which rationalises; but they are gospel truths to pure imagination. **1880** RUSKIN *Lett. to Clergy* 349 The simplest travelling tinker inclined *Gospel-wards. *c* **1200** ORMIN 5789 Her hafe I nemmnedd nu till 3uw þa fowwre *Goddspellwrihhtess.

Hence **'gospelless** *a.*, devoid of the gospel.

1882–3 J. A. GILFILLAN in Schaff *Encycl. Relig. Knowl.* III. 2602/1 More progress made by them [Indians]..than in all the previous hundred years of gospelless wars. **1896** J. ORR in *Un. Presbyt. Mag.* Oct. 436 His Gospelless Gospel found a hearing.

gospel ('gɒspəl), *v.* [f. prec. sb.; in OE. *godspellian.*] †**a.** *trans.* To preach the gospel to; to imbue with the principles of the gospel, to convert to the gospel; = EVANGELIZE *v.* 3. *Obs.* **b.** *intr.* To preach the gospel. *rare.*

c **1000** *Ags. Ps.* (Th.) lxvii. 12 God ʒifeð gleaw word god-spellendum. *a* **1300** [see GOSPELLING *vbl. sb.*]. *c* **1550** CHEKE *Matt.* xi. 5 Yᵉ blind seeth, and yᵉ laam walketh,..yᵉ deed be raised, and yᵉ beggars be gospeld. **1565** T. STAPLETON *Fortr. Faith* 6 Iff any man doo ghospell vnto yow, besyde that whiche yow haue receyued, be he accursed. **1605** SHAKS. *Macb.* III. i. 88 Are you so Gospell'd, to pray for this good man, And for his Issue, whose heauie hand Hath bow'd you to the Graue? **1659** HOWE in H. Rogers *Life* iv. (1863) 93 They [the army] think it necessary to have the Parliament gospelled or dissolved. **1867** BUSHNELL *Mor. Uses Dark Th.* 196 We have a great many gospeling—that do not come to thought.

Hence **'gospelling** *ppl. a.*

1566 T. STAPLETON *Ret. Untr. Jewel* III. 99 This is the playne dealing of ghospelling Bishoppes. **1579** KNEWSTUB *Confut.* **2 a, The hatred that the Gospelling Churches beare vnto such frensies.

'gospel-book. †**a.** A book containing one or all of the four gospels (see GOSPEL *sb.* 2); hence, loosely, the New Testament or Bible (*obs.*). **b.** A book containing the Gospels (see GOSPEL *sb.* 3), read at the Eucharist.

c **1000** *Canons of Ælfric* §21 in Thorpe *Laws* II. 350 Saltere & pistol-boc & godspell-boc & mæsse-boc. *c* **1200** ORMIN 6458 Nohht ne se33þ þe Goddspellboc þatt Josæp wass þærinne. *a* **1300** *Cursor M.* 21227 O sant mathu þe gospel-bok..wit him he bar. *a* **1400** *Plowman's T.* 595 (Skeat) [They] falsely glose the gospell-book. **1495** *Wills fr. Doctor's Commons* (Camden) 4, I geve to Sir John Blotte a gospell boke, a pistill covered with ledder. **1526** TINDALE *N.T.* To Rdr., All is not gospell that is written in the gospell boke. **1530** —— *Expositions Matt.* v–vii. 48 b, When thou sweryst by the gospell booke, or byble. **1849** ROCK *Ch. of Fathers* III. x. 472 The custom was to set out..every precious vessel and jewelled gospel-book.

gospelize ('gɒspəlaɪz), *v.* Also 7–8 **gospellize.** [f. GOSPEL *sb.* + -IZE.]

†**1.** *trans.* To impart the spirit of the gospel to; to modify according to the spirit of the gospel.

1643 MILTON *Divorce* viii. (1851) 39 And this command thus Gospelliz'd to us hath the same force with that wheron Ezra grounded the pious necessity of divorcing. **1658** GURNALL *Chr. in Arm.* verse 14, xi. §2. II. 269, I had thought, Christ had baptized the Law, and Gospeliz'd it.

2. To preach the gospel to: to convert to Christianity; = EVANGELIZE 3. Now *rare.*

1646 TRAPP *Comm. John* iii. 10 The poor are Gospellized; not only receive it, but are changed by it. **1704** *Elegy Author True born Eng.* xxi. 6 Tho' most suppose his Notions were but wild, To fetch the Jew to Gospellize his Child. **1716** M. DAVIES *Athen. Brit.* I. 100 Where he fulfill'd his foresaid Apostolical Purposes of Gospelizing the Poor, and Disciplining the Proud and Slothful. **1766** DR. CHAUNCY in C. Beatty *Two Months' Tour* (1768) 102 Mr. Thomas Mayhew..began..the work of gospelizing the infidel natives. **1884** *Amer. Missionary* Dec. 392 These two societies are..one in the noble aim of gospelizing the land.

Hence **'gospelized** *ppl. a.*, (*nonce-use*) outwardly modified by the gospel. Also **'gospelizer**, one who 'gospelizes' (*Stand. Dict.*).

1849 STOVEL *Canne's Necess.* Introd. 37 Popery, therefore, ..is evangelical infidelity; a gospelized method of living without God and without hope in the world. *Ibid.* 75 *note*, A gospelized treason against the Lord and his Anointed.

†**gospellary**, *a. Obs. rare*⁻¹. [f. GOSPEL *sb.* + -ARY.] Of or pertaining to the gospel.

1679 *Cloak in its Colours* 8 (T.) Let any man judge how well these gospellary principles of our presbyterians agree with the practice and doctrine of the holy apostles.

gospeller ('gɒspələ(r)). Forms: 1–3 **godspellere,** 3 **godspellare,** 4 **gods speller, god(d)speller, gospello(u)r, gosspel(l)er(e,** 4–5 **gospel(l)ere,** 4–7 **gospeler,** 5 **gospel(l)eer,** 6, (in sense 4) 9 **gospellar,** (6 **ghospeller, gospiller,** 7 **godspeller),** 4– **gospeller.** [f. GOSPEL *sb.* and *v.* + -ER[1].]

1. One of the four evangelists.

971 *Blickl. Hom.* 35 We sceoldan..healdan..þa lara þara feower godspellera. *c* **1175** *Lamb. Hom.* 89 Lucas þe godspellere. *a* **1225** *Ancr. R.* 94 'Hit is a derne halewi' seið sein Johan ewangeliste [C. godspellere] in þe Apocalipse. *a* **1300** *Cursor M.* 13434 þis ilk was ion þe gospeller. *c* **1380** WYCLIF *Serm.* Sel. Wks. I. 397, Oo gospelere expowneþ anoþer. **1387** TREVISA *Higden* (Rolls) IV. 339 þre gospellours that telleþ þe doynge of Crist after þe prisonynge of Iohn Baptiste. **1623** LISLE *Ælfric on O. & N. Test.*, *Mark*, Marke the Gospeller, who followed Peter for instruction. **1674** N. FAIRFAX *Bulk & Selv.* 142 We read from one Gospeller, That after the Lord had spoken he was received up. **1933** V. MCNABB *Nazareth or Social Chaos* iv. 18 This phrase of S. John is all the more striking because he more than the other three gospellers is insistent upon the Will of God.

2. A preacher of the Gospel; a missionary. *rare.*

1673 [R. LEIGH] *Transp. Reh.* 102 The itinerant Gospellers that travel up and down with two penny books. **1847–9** SIR J. STEPHEN *Eccl. Biog.* (1850) I. 114 The migratory gospellers, who in every land toiled, and preached and died.

3. One who reads the Gospel in the Communion Service.

1506 *Mem. Hen. VII* (Rolls 1858) 290 The bishop of Chichester gospeller, the bishop of Norwich epistoler. *a* **1529** SKELTON *Ware Hauke* 120 These be my gospellers, These be my pystillers. **1579** *Wills & Inv. N.C.* (Surtees 1860) 18 To the gospeller and pistoler 6s. 8d. a pece. **1667** *Answ. West to North* 9 Gospelers, Epistelers, Virgers. **1706** PHILLIPS (ed. Kersey), *Gospeller*, he that reads the Gospel in a Cathedral, or Collegiate Church. **1778** *Eng. Gazetteer* (ed. 2) s.v. *Peterborough*, Besides the dean and chapter..here are 8 petty canons,..1 epistler, 1 gospeller. **1849** ROCK *Ch. of Fathers* IV. xii. 186 The deacon and subdeacon [at mass] were sometimes called the 'gospeller' and 'epistoler'. **1874** MICKLETHWAITE *Mod. Par. Churches* 52 The gospeller having received the textus or gospel-book. **1891** S. MOSTYN *Curatica* 12, I was gospeller at my Ordination.

†**4.** A book containing the Gospels (see GOSPEL *sb.* 3); a gospel-book. *Obs.*

1440 in *Eng. Ch. Furniture* (1866) 184 Item a gospeler and a epistolere a year with a plate on them of Copper and gilt. *c* **1530** in Gutch *Coll. Cur.* II. 338 Item oone Booke callid the Gospiller. **1885** *Athenæum* 15 Aug. 215/1 The silver-cased Gospel is placed upon the lectern when the Word is read from the modern Gospellar.

5. a. One who professes the faith of the gospel, or who claims for himself and his party the exclusive possession of gospel truth; in 16–17th c. often applied derisively to Protestants, Puritans, and sectaries. †Also, one learned in the Scriptures.

1533 MORE *Apol.* i. Wks. 846/1 They find a great fault that I handle Tindall and Barns their two newe ghospellers, with no fayrer woordes nor in no more courtes maner. **1547** *Homilies* I. *Agst. Contention* I. (1859) 134 He is a Pharise, he is a Gospeller, he is of the new sort. **1548** UDALL, etc. *Erasm. Par. Matt.* xx. 29–34 With whiche affeccion euery gospeller ought to be sory for other mens harmes. **1552** LATIMER *Serm. at Bexterly* (1607) 273 b, A great number of people pretend the Gospell, and beare the name of Gospelleres, because it is a new thing. **1561** DAUS tr. *Bullinger on Apoc.* (1573) 125 The Gospellers haue once or twise fought vnluckely, and abide euery houre great persecutions: the Papistes ouercome and reioyse. **1615** WADSWORTH in Bedell *Lett.* (1624) 10 Murders which Knoxe and the Geneua Gospellers caused in Scotland. **1674** HICKMAN *Hist. Quinquart.* (ed. 2) 191 His first attempt is to disgrace the Calvinists, by calling them Gospellers. **1638** BUNYAN *Jerus. Sinner Saved* (1886) 72 Nor is [God] so willing to save as some pretended gospellers imagine. **1691** WOOD *Ath. Oxon.* I. 586 Thornden..was a great Gospeller and seemed to all to be an hearty Protestant. **1715** ROWE *Lady Jane Grey* III. i, These Gospellers have had their golden Days..Have trodden down our Holy Roman Faith. **1820** SCOTT *Monast.* xxiii, He began to suspect that he was now in company with one of the gospellers, or heretics. **1837** HAWTHORNE *Twice-t. T.* (1851) II. xvi. 238 Bearing on his breast this label—A Wanton Gospeller. **1858** *Sat. Rev.* V. 273/1 The gentlemanly churchman..did not care to welcome 'the bragging soldier' [Hutten], who might perhaps be followed by a troop of Gospellers. **18..** BLACKIE (Ogilvie), The solemn sepulchral piety of certain North Eastern gospellers.

b. ***hot gospeller***: see as main entry.

'gospel-like, *a.* and *adv.*

A. *adj.*

†**a.** Of persons: Devoted to the principles of the Gospel; cf. EVANGELICAL *a.* 2 a. *Obs.* **b.** Such as is contained in, or comes up to the standard of, the Gospel.

1549 COVERDALE, etc. *Erasm. Par. Thess.* Ded., That Gospellike truth & liberty is almost vtterly chaunged in to hellishe iniquitie. **1553** ? BALE tr. *Bonner's Pref. Gardiner's De vera Obed.* B iv b, No man coulde beleve..yᵗ this good and godly & right gospellike Prince shoulde be falsely betrayed to all the rest of Monarches and Princes. **1597** HOOKER *Eccl. Pol.* v. lxviii. §5 They have by their Religious and Gospel-like behaviour purged themselves of that suspition of Poperie. **1641** J. JACKSON *True Evang. T.* III. 189 See..whether is the more Euangelicall, and Gospell-like. **1671** H. M. tr. *Erasm. Colloq.* 423 Sometimes..a soldiers cloak, slashed hose, do cover a Gospel like mind.

B. *adv.* Agreeably to the doctrines of the Gospel.

1576 WOOLTON *Chr. Man.* M 7, To lyue neglygently, and carnally, or not gospell lyke. **1671** H. M. tr. *Erasm. Colloq.* 426 It was very Gospel-like done.

gospelling ('gɒspəlɪŋ), *vbl. sb.* [f. GOSPEL *v.* + -ING[1].] The action of the vb. GOSPEL.

a **1300** *Cursor M.* 21207 Lukas..wroght..bokes tuin. O gospelling þat tan es kid, þe toþer o þat þe apostels did. **1549** COVERDALE, etc. *Erasm. Par. 2 Tim.* i. 13–18 Their countrefaicte gospellinge beganne to appere. **1652** H. L'ESTRANGE *Americans no Jewes* 63 The discoveries, plantations and gospelling of those people, is a work of longer requisite time..than may be effected before the end of the world. **1845** W. L. ALEXANDER *Mem. J. Watson* 200 Itinerant gospelling was not originally contemplated. **1879** BROWNING *Ned Bratts* 130 The tinker in our cage, Pulled-up for gospelling, twelve years ago. **1884** *Pall Mall G.* 10 Sept. 2/1 We have had blessed experience of the value of the combination of gospelling and healing.

attrib. **1554** T. SAMPSON in Strype *Eccl. Mem.* III. App. xviii. 45 Oh! London, London, is this the gospelling fruit? *Ibid.* 51 If in this gospelling age you have been worthy hearers of the gospel. **1716** M. DAVIES *Athen. Brit.* II. 333 If I mistake not, scarce one ever suffer'd under him for any Opining, Gospelling or Reforming Exertions.

'**gospellist.** *rare.* = GOSPELLER 5.

1845 MOZLEY *Ess., Laud* (1878) I. 165 It was a strange look-out, indeed, if he who had dived into the very arcana of predestinarianism, if the advanced Gospellist was now to expound the Catechism.

† '**gospelly,** *adv. Obs.* [f. GOSPEL *sb.* + -LY[2].] **a.** In accordance with the gospel. **b.** Truthfully.

1545 BRINKLOW *Compl.* 29 Vycarages and personages, thus well and gospelly serued. **1596** NASHE *Saffron Walden* 15 This I can gospelly auouch. **1678** *Yng. Man's Call.* 151 Whatever you do in the matter of religion, do it heartily.. gospelly, and humbly, as in the sight of God.

Gosplan ('gɒsplæn). [Russ. *gosplán*, abbrev. of *Gosudárstvennyĭ plánovyĭ komitét (sovéta minístrov) SSSR*, State Planning Committee (of the Council of Ministers) of the U.S.S.R.] An organization formed in 1921 to draw up plans for the development of the national economy of the U.S.S.R. (The governments of the constituent republics also have Gosplans.)

1926 *Encycl. Brit.* III. 580/1 He [*sc.* Sokolnikov] was.. appointed deputy president of the 'Gosplan', or state-planning commission. **1930** W. H. CHAMBERLIN *Soviet Russia* vi. 136 The main stumblingblock in the path of the Gosplan forecasters. **1938** *Ann. Reg. 1937* 196 The Sovnarkom ordered the Gosplan to finish the schedule for the third five-year period. **1959** *Chambers's Encycl.* IV. 69/1 The state planning commission (Gosplan) set up in February 1921 and given formal status in August 1923. **1962** *Economist* 16 June 1078/2 There is no sign as yet of a budding Gosplan in the Soviet block.

‖**gospodar** ('gɒspədɑː(r)). = HOSPODAR.

1847 MRS. A. KERR *Hist. Servia* 183 From that time he ruled as Gospodar at Zrnareka. **1897** *Longm. Mag.* Dec. 170 All leaped to their feet to salute the Gospodar.

†**goss**[1]. *Sc. Obs.* [? Identical with GOSSE[2], short for GOSSIP. Cf. GOSSY.] (See quot. 1710.)

1710 RUDDIMAN *Douglas's Æneis* Gloss. s.v. *Goddis apis*, God's goss, a silly, but good natured man. **1721** RAMSAY *Elegy P. Birnie* 95 Soon as he wan within the closs, He dously drew in Mair gear fra ilka gentle goss Than bought a new ane.

goss[2] (gɒs). *slang.* [Short for GOSSAMER.] A hat.

1848 *Man in Moon* Feb. 83 When you carry off a 26*s.* beaver be careful to leave a 4*s.* 9*d.* goss in its stead.

goss[3] (gɒs). *slang.* [Origin unknown.] *to give, get goss*: to give, receive punishment.

1840 *Daily Picayune* (New Orleans) 29 July 2/4 Six victims to report this morning—..offences trivial—..Some of them got *gos*, and some got nothing. **1847** J. S. ROBB *Streaks of Squatter Life* 75 —Gin him goss without sweeten' —. **1864** HOTTEN *Slang Dict.* (ed. 3) 146 *To give a man goss*, to require for an injury, to beat, or kill him. **1914** A. A. GRACE *Tale of Timber Town* xxxviii. 173 That's right, ole man. Give 'em goss.

Goss[4] (gɒs). The name of W. H. Goss (1833–1906), of Stoke-on-Trent, used *attrib.* to designate a kind of armorial china orig. manufactured by him.

[**1878** L. JEWITT *Ceramic Art Gt. Brit.* II. v. 224 The works of Mr. William Henry Goss were commenced in 1858 for the production of Parian, ivory-porcelain [etc.]. *Ibid.* 541 Goss's china and parian.] **1906** *Daily Chron.* 31 Aug. 1/7 The Goss china and porcelain. **1926** M. LEINSTER *Dew on Leaf* II. iii. 176 The jingling piano, the goss china, the gummed shells. **1936** G. GREENE *Gun for Sale* iii. 105 Dark curtains and Gosse [*sic*] china. **1969** H. SANDON *Brit. Pott. & Porc.* 112 The title Goss China is nowadays used to describe the huge quantities of holiday mementos, usually on a thin parian body, with the name and crest of the town on it, the shape often in the form of ancient Greek vessels.

goss, variant of GORCE, GORSE.

gossamer ('gɒsəmə(r)), *sb.* and *a.* Forms: 4–5 gosesomer(e, 4–6 gossom(m)er, 5 gossomyre, gossummer, 6–7 gossamour, 7 gosimore, gossamire, -ore, gossem-, -im-, -ymear(e, -e(e)re, gothsemay, -imere, 7–9 gossamere, 8 gossimer, (gosshemere, garsummer), 7– gossamer. [ME. *gos(e)somer(e*, app. f. GOOSE *sb.* + SUMMER *sb.* Cf. the synonymous Eng. dial. *summer-goose* (Craven), *summer-colt*, G. *mädchensommer* (lit. 'girls' summer'), *altweibersommer* ('old women's summer'); also G. *sommerfäden*, Du. *zomerdraden*, Sw. *sommartråd*, all literally 'summer thread'.

The reason for the appellation is somewhat obscure. It is usually assumed that *goose* in this compound refers to the 'downy' appearance of gossamer. But it is to be noted that G. *mädchen-*, *altweibersommer* mean not only 'gossamer', but also a summer-like period in late autumn, a St. Martin's summer; that the obs. Sc. GO-SUMMER had the latter meaning; and that it is in the warm periods of autumn that gossamer is chiefly observed. These considerations suggest the possibility that the word may primarily have denoted a 'St. Martin's summer' (the time when geese were supposed to be in season: cf. G. *Gänsemonat* 'geese-month', November), and have been hence transferred to the characteristic phenomenon of the period. On this view *summer-goose* (which by etymologizing perversion appears also as *summer-gauze*) would be a transposition.]

A. *sb.*

1. A fine filmy substance, consisting of cobwebs, spun by small spiders, which is seen floating in the air in calm weather, esp. in autumn, or spread over a grassy surface: occas. with *a* and *pl.*, a thread or web of gossamer.

c **1325** *Gloss. W. de Biblesw.* in Wright *Voc.* 147 *Filaundre* [*glossed*] gosesomer. *c* **1386** CHAUCER *Sqr.'s T.* 251 On ebbe on flood on gossomer and on myst. **14..** *Bewte will Shewe* 5 in *Pol. Rel. & L. Poems* 45 Twene gold and gossomer is grete difference. *c* **1440** *Promp. Parv.* 205/1 Gossomer, corrupcyon (*H., P.* gossummyr, or corrupcion), *filandrya.* **1592** SHAKS. *Rom. & Jul.* II. vi. 18 A Louer may bestride the Gossamours..And yet not fall. **1627** DRAYTON *Nimphidia* xvii, Foure nimble Gnats the Horses were, Their Harnasses of Gossamere. **1633** MASSINGER *Guardian* II. iv, A bed of gossamire And damask roses. **1659** *Lady Alimony* D 2, Small threeds Thin-spun as is the subtil Gothsemay. **1697** DRYDEN *Virg. Georg.* I. 543 The filmy Gossamer now flitts no more. **1777** W. MASON *Ep. to Dr. Shebbeare* 95 Let my numbers flutter light in air, As careless as the silken Gossimer. **1798** COLERIDGE *Anc. Mar.* III. ix, Are those her sails that glance in the Sun Like restless gossameres? **1813** SHELLEY *Q. Mab* 120 Let even the restless gossamer Sleep on the moveless air! **1847** TENNYSON *Princ.* v. 163 To trip a tigress with a gossamer. **1850** —— *In Mem.* xi. 7 All the silvery gossamers That twinkle into green and gold. *a* **1851** MOIR *October* Poet. Wks. 1852 I. 124 The gossamer..Now floats and now subsides upon the air. **1878** GEO. ELIOT *Coll. Breakf. P.* 34 Weaving gossamer to trap the sun.

b. *transf.* and *fig.* Applied to something light and flimsy as gossamer.

? *a* **1400** *Morte Arth.* 2688 This es bot gosesomere, and gyffene one erles. **1658** EVELYN *Fr. Gard.* (1675) 194 It will ..fly away like the down, or gossemeere of dandelyon. **1827** HOOD *Mids. Fairies* xii, Not measured out against Fate's mortal knives, Like human gossamers. **1855** MOTLEY *Dutch Rep.* VI. i. (1866) 782 A decent gossamer of conventional phraseology was ever allowed to float over the nakedness of unblushing treason. **1871** EARLE *Philol. Eng. Tongue* §233 It would hardly have beseemed such a poet as Chaucer to bring the stroke of his measure down upon such a gossamer.

2. An extremely delicate kind of gauze.

1872 BLACK *Adv. Phaeton* i. 2 A dress of blue, with touches of white gossamer and fur about the tight wrists and neck.

3. a. In England: Originally, an advertising tradesman's name for a make of silk hat recommended as extremely light; hence, used jocularly for a hat generally. **b.** *U.S.* A name for a very light kind of waterproof.

1837 DICKENS *Pickw.* xii, Every hole lets in some air.. wentilation gossamer I calls it. **1851** MAYHEW *Lond. Labour* II. 43, 'I have sold hats from 6*d.* to 3*s.* 6*d.*, but very seldom 3*s.* 6*d.* The 3*s.* 6*d.* ones would wear out two new gossamers.' **1888** *Harper's Mag.* June 139/1 Flinging off his gossamer, and hanging it up to drip into the pan of the hat rack.

4. *attrib.*

1802 BINGLEY *Anim. Biog.* (1813) III. 365 The Gossamer Spider. **1816** KIRBY & SP. *Entomol.* (1843) II. 269 That sight occasionally noticed in fine days in the autumn, of webs—commonly called gossamer webs—covering the earth and floating in the air. **1830** HOOD *Haunted Ho.* III. lxxx, Across the door no gossamer festoon Swung pendulous. **1839** BAILEY *Festus* (1854) 12 The gossamer woof, beaded with dew. **1873** *Sunday Mag.* June 625 The little gossamer thread of hope. **1875** *Encycl. Brit.* II. 296/1 Gossamer lines are merely the threads left by small and immature spiders.

B. *adj.* Of things, both material and immaterial: Light and flimsy as gossamer. Of persons: Frivolous, volatile.

1806–7 J. BERESFORD *Miseries Hum. Life* (1826) I. Introd., Pride and the plague of this gossamer frame of mine. **1843** LYTTON *Last Bar.* I. ii, [Girls] dancing round him with.. gossamer robes that brushed him as they circled. **1847** YOUATT *Horse* xi. 239 The gossamer membrane of..the lobules of the lungs. **1852** DICKENS *Bleak Ho.* xliii, Such an unworldly, uncalculating, gossamer-creature, is a relief to him. **1852** H. ROGERS *Ecl. Faith* (1853) 15 He walks through this bleak world in such a gossamer gauze of transparent 'spiritualism' that [etc.]. **1853** C. BRONTE *Villette* xxvii, There was a kind of gossamer happiness hanging in the air. **1857** W. COLLINS *Dead Secret* III. i. (1861) 75 [He] sighed when the black gossamer ashes floated upward on the draught, and were lost in the chimney. **1879** *Print. Trades Jrnl.* XXIX. 35 A gossamer tissue in imitation of the Japanese. **1888** *Pall Mall G.* 26 Jan. 12/1 Light-weight [India-rubber] goods such as ladies wear, known as gossamer goods. **1893** *Dublin Rev.* Oct. 789 The original authors of this gossamer gossip.

Comb. **1849** JAMES *Woodman* v, That gay gossamer-looking youth, whom the young lord called Hungerford.

Hence '**gossamered** *ppl. a.*, coated with gossamer, gossamer-like.

1860 RUSKIN *Mod. Paint.* V. VI. x. §18 Casting a gossamered grayness and softness of plumy mist along their surfaces far away. **1897** *Q. Rev.* Oct. 344 His [Mr. Austin Dobson's] society is one of picturesque ghosts; of history gossamered.

gossamery ('gɒsəmərɪ), *a.* [f. GOSSAMER *sb.* + -Y[1].] Of the nature of or resembling gossamer; flimsy, unsubstantial; = GOSSAMER *a.*

1790 R. MERRY *Laurel Liberty* (ed. 2) 8 Hang o'er his eye thy gossamery tear. **1794** MATHIAS *Purs. Lit.* (1798) 57 In filmy, gawzy, gossamery lines. **1812** J. WILSON *Isle of Palms* I. 125 A vessel..All rigg'd with gossamery sails. **1845–6** DE QUINCEY *Keats* Wks. 1890 XI. 389 The Italian poet, Marino, had been reputed the greatest master of gossamery affectation in Europe. **1883** *Gd. Words* Dec. 791/2 This orchid is seldom seen without some gossamery spiderwork surrounding it.

gossamire, -ore, -our, obs. ff. GOSSAMER.

†**gossampine.** *Obs.* Also corruptly gossanpine, gassampine, grassapine. [a. F. *gossampin* the shrub *Bombax pentandrum*, which yields a substance similar to cotton = It. *gossampino*, ad. L. *gossympinus* (also *gossypion*). Cf. also It. *gossipina* (Florio) cloth made of this cotton: see GOSSIPINE.] **a.** The shrub *Bombax pentandrum.* **b.** The cotton-like fibre produced from it. **c.** A kind of cloth made of this fibre. Also *attrib.*

1553 EDEN *Treat. Newe Ind.* (Arb.) 14 He weareth a vesture of ye silke called Gossampine. *Ibid.* 21 Their beddes are made of Gossampine cotton. **1594** GREENE & LODGE *Looking Glass* (1598) F iij, On his alters perfume these Turkie clothes, This gassampine and gold ile sacrifice. **1596** LODGE *Marg. Amer.* 125 With gold and silver, silke, and gossanpine threed of many colours, were woven the images of those Gods which the Cuscans most worshipped. **1601** HOLLAND *Pliny* I. 363 Of the Gossampine trees..trees called Gossampines, which yeeld..cotton. **1613** PURCHAS *Pilgrimage* (1614) 907 These Images they made of Gossampine cotten. **1623** COCKERAM *Eng. Dict.* II, Cotton, *grassapine.*

gossan ('gɒzən). *Mining.* Also goz(z)an, gozzen. [Belongs to the dialect of Cornwall, but no Celtic etymon has been found.] Decomposed rock, of a reddish or ferruginous colour (due to oxidized iron pyrites), forming a part of the 'outcrop' of a metallic vein.

1776 PRYCE *Min. Cornub.* 44 Other crude Minerals of no esteem, are those of a ferruginous quality, which the Miners distinguish by the names of Gossan, Cal (more properly Gal), Cockle, &c. Our Gossan Lodes often produce Tin at a shallow level in tolerable plenty..These Gossans or Ochres, are commonly called the Feeders of their respective Metals. **1796** KIRWAN *Elem. Min.* (ed. 2) I. 132 *Brown Tungsten*, Gossan of the Cornish mines. **1808** POLWHELE *Corn.-Eng. Gloss.*, *Gozan*, rust; iron ochre. **1851** RICHARDSON *Geol.* i. 7 Veins of copper are usually found in connexion with an earthy, ochreous stone locally termed gossan. **1854** MURCHISON *Siluria* xvii. 434 There [in North Devon] the matrix or gossan of the lode [of copper ore] is suffused by particles of gold. **1880** *W. Cornw. Gloss.*, *Gossan*, yellow earth just above a vein of metal.

b. *transf.* (See quot.) *dial.*

1880 *W. Cornw. Gloss.*, *Gossan*, an old wig grown yellow from age and wear. **1891** Q. [Couch] *Noughts & Crosses* 36 It was a 'gossan' wig, as we call it in our parts; a wig grown yellow and rusty with age and wear.

Hence **gossa'niferous** *a.*, producing gossan.

1864 in WEBSTER (citing Dana). Hence in later Dicts.

gosse[1], mincing pronunc. of GOD: cf. GOSH.

a **1553** UDALL *Royster D.* III. iv. (Arb.) 52 By gosse and for thy sake I defye hir in deede.

gosse[2], **gos,** short for GOSSIP. (See also GOSS[1], GOSSY.)

1547 BOORDE *Introd. Knowl.* i. (1870) 122 [A Cornishman speaks.] Dup the dore, gos..A, good gosse..Drynke, gosse, to me. **1603** *Philotus* cxlix, This purpois gosse, appeirs to me Sa wonder nyce and strange to be.

gosse, obs. form of GOOSE, GORSE.

gosselin, gosselyng, obs. forms of GOSLING.

gossemeere, obs. form of GOSSAMER.

gossep(pe, obs. form of GOSSIP.

gossip ('gɒsɪp), *sb.* Forms: 1 godsib(b, 4 godsyb(be, -zyb(be, 4–5 gossib(be, 4–7 godsib(be, 5–6 gos(s)y(p)p(e, 5–7 godsip, gossipp(e, gos(s)op(e, 5–8 gossep(pe, 6–7 goship, (5 godsep, -sypp, gossyb(e, 6 ghosseppe, gossup, goshyp(p, godcept, 7 godsepte, ghossip), 6– gossip. [OE. *godsibb* masc. (f. *god* GOD + *sib(b* adj., akin, related: see SIB *a.*) = ON. *guð-sefe* masc., *guð-sifja* fem., OSw. *guzsowir* masc., *gupziff*, *gudzsöff* fem. In ME. a single example is found of a fem. *godzybbe* corresp. to masc. *godzyb* (see quot. 1340 in 1).]

1. One who has contracted spiritual affinity with another by acting as a sponsor at a baptism.

a. In relation to the person baptized: A godfather or godmother; a sponsor. Now only *arch.* and *dial.*

1014 WULFSTAN *Serm. ad Anglos* (Napier) 160 Godsibbas and godbearn to fela man forspilde wide ȝynd þas þeode. **1340** *Ayenb.* 48 Þe zeuende is..of godsone to þe children of his godzyb oþer of his godzybbe. **1590** GREENWOOD *Collect. Sclaund. Art.* G, The rashe, vndiscreete, and vnpossible vowe of the saide gossipps. **1649** EVELYN *Diary* (1827) II. 16 The parents being so poore that they had provided no gossips. *a* **1654** SELDEN *Table T.* (Arb.) 90 Should a great Lady, that was invited to be a Gossip, in her place send her kitchen-maid. **1711** HEARNE *Collect.* (O.H.S.) III. 194 Fully designed to come and stand gossip in person to Dr. Hudson's child. **1770** FOOTE *Lame Lover* I. 12 Do you know that you are new christen'd, and have had me for a gossip? **1819** S. ROGERS *Hum. Life* 34 Now, glad at heart the gossips breathe their prayer. **1856** MISS YONGE *Daisy Chain* I. ix. (1879) 79 I'll find gossips, and let 'em be christened on Sunday. **1876** FREEMAN *Norm. Conq.* V. xxv. 560 The Englishman whose child was held at the font by a Norman gossip..cast aside his own name. **1886** *S.W. Linc. Gloss.* s.v., I suppose the same gossips will do for both.

fig. **1581** J. BELL *Haddon's Answ. Osor.* 407 b, And this place yᵉ Catholicke gosseppes have Christened by the name of Purgatory. **1607** MIDDLETON *Michaelm. Term* III. iv, I would never undertake to be gossip to that bond which I would not see well brought up. **1673** [R. LEIGH] *Transp. Reh.* 8 Who would be Gossip to all the nameless Off-springs of the Press.

†**b.** *transf.* With reference to the christening of a bell. *Obs.*

1563 FOXE *A. & M.* 380 The bel hauing a new garment put vppon it..they goo vnto sumptuous bankets, wherevnto also the Gossips are bidden. **1778** PENNANT *Tour in Wales* (1883) I. 47 A bell..was also christened..The gossips.. were doubtless rich persons.

†**c.** In relation to the parents: (One's) child's godfather or godmother. *Obs.*

c **1325** *Lai le Freine* 42 He schal mi gossibbe be. **1475** SIR J. PASTON in *P. Lett.* No. 766 III. 145 He was fayn to sue to the said Duc..by the meanes of his godsip the Bisshop of Wynchestre. [He was sponsor to the Duke's daughter.] **1494** FABYAN *Chron.* VII. 561 Which Wyllyam..was gossyp vnto the quene. *c* **1610** SIR J. MELVIL *Mem.* (1683) 70, I requested her majesty to be a gossip to the Queen. **1612** DAVIES *Why Ireland*, etc. (1747) 113 The English were forbidden to marry, to foster, to make gossippes with the Irish. **1625** B. JONSON *Staple of N.* Induct., And those Mothers had Gossips (if their Children were christned) as we are. **1698** M. MARTIN *Voy. Kilda* (1749) 76 The Officer ..condescended to be the Impostor's Gossip, i.e. Sponsor at the Baptism of one of his Children. **1893** P. W. JOYCE *Short Hist. Irel.* 88 When a man stood sponsor for a child..he became the child's godfather, and gossip to the parents.

†**d.** In relation to one who acts as godfather or godmother on the same occasion: A fellow-sponsor.

c **1386** CHAUCER *Pars. T.* ¶835 A womman may in no lasse synne assemblen with hire godsib, than with hire owene flesshly brother. *c* **1440** *Promp. Parv.* 204/2 Gossyp, mann, *compater*. Gossyp, woman, *commater*. **1563** BECON *Acts Chr. & Antichr.* Wks. III. 416 Christen Gossippes..those men and women that haue bene Godfathers and Godmothers together of one childe at Baptisme. **1622** FLETCHER *Sp. Curate* II. i, *Lean.* I have heard him say you were gossips too. *Lop.* You did not heare him say to whom. **1666** PEPYS *Diary* 2 Dec., I took my pretty gossip to White Hall with us.

†**e.** *gen. Obs.*

c **1315** SHOREHAM 69 In that cas thou myȝt weddy To thyne wyfes gossibbe. *c* **1386** CHAUCER *Pars. T.* ¶834 Parentele is in two maneres, outher goostly or fleshly; goostly, as for to delen with hise godsibbes.

2. a. A familiar acquaintance, friend, chum. Formerly applied to both sexes, now only (somewhat *arch.*) to women. (A sense apparently derived more immediately from 1 c.)

The expression in quot. 1641 is app. the name of some rustic game or dance.

1362 LANGL. *P. Pl.* A. v. 152 'Ic haue good ale, gossib', quod heo. 'Gloten, woltou asaye'? **1393** *Ibid.* C. VII. 47 What ich gaf for godes loue, to god-sybbes ich tolde. *a* **1450** *Knt. de la Tour* (1868) 79 There was a false bauude that was her godsib. *a* **1529** SKELTON *E. Rummyng* 356 Lo, gossyp, I wys, Thus and thus it is. *c* **1560** INGELEND *Disobedient Child* F ij b, She is to her Gossypes gone to make mery. **1641** BROME *Joviall Crew* II. (1652) D 2 b, He makes us even sick of his sadness, that were wont to see my Ghossips cock to day; mould Cocklebread; daunce clutterdepouch [etc.]. **1766** H. BROOKE *Fool of Quality* (1809) II. 11 Barnaby Boniface, his next neighbour and gossip. **1820** KEATS *Eve St. Agnes* xii, Ah, Gossip dear, We're safe enough; here in this arm-chair sit. **1857** C. BRONTE *Professor* I. xi. 180 The old duenna—my mother's gossip. **1873** OUIDA *Pascarel* I. 65 His mother too, was a gossip of her own.

b. *esp.* Applied to a woman's female friends invited to be present at a birth.

1590 SHAKS. *Mids. N.* II. i. 47 Sometime lurke I in a Gossips bole, In very likenesse of a roasted crab. **1620** *Swetnam Arraign'd* (1880) 44 Bidding of Gossips, calling to Vpsittings. *a* **1661** FULLER *Worthies* (1840) I. xx. 75 They are as good evidence to prove where they were born, as if we had the deposition of the midwife, and all the gossips present at their mothers labours. **1721–1800** BAILEY, *A gossiping*, a merry Meeting of Gossips, at a Woman's Lying in. **1764** *Low Life* 29 Poor labouring Men..are obliged to.. go a Nigiting, i.e. fetching Midwives, Nurses and Gossips. **1805** *Med. Jrnl.* XIV. 258 The officiousness of nurses and gossips. **1858** M. PORTEOUS *Souter Johnny* 31 Whan your nieve the gossip streikit.

transf. **1664** BUTLER *Hud.* II. i. 90 To do the office of a Neighbour, And be a Gossip at his Labour.

3. A person, mostly a woman, of light and trifling character, esp. one who delights in idle talk; a newsmonger, a tattler.

1566 [see 6, *gossip-like*]. **1579** LYLY *Euphues* (Arb.) 52, I will..bring..a visard on my face, for a shamelesse gossippe. **1600** DEKKER *Fortunatus* Wks. 1873 I. 97, I wonder what blind gossip this minx is that is so prodigall. **1614** T. ADAMS *Devil's Banq.* 320 There arise in the end..as many Gospels as Gossips. **1687** DRYDEN *Hind & P.* III. 903 The common chat of gossips when they meet. **1709** HEARNE *Collect.* (O.H.S.) II. 212 John Stevens..a negligent, busy, prating Gossip. **1716** ADDISON *Freeholder* No. 26. 144 A Gossip in Politics is a Slattern in her Family. **1833** HT. MARTINEAU *Loom & Lugger* I. i. 6 If he did not mean the girls to grow up the greatest gossips in the neighbourhood. **1854** EMERSON *Soc. Aims* Wks. (Bohn) III. 176 Why need you, who are not a gossip, talk as a gossip? **1884** MRS. EWING *Mary's Meadow* 13 The Weeding Woman is a great gossip.

4. The conversation of such a person; idle talk; trifling or groundless rumour; tittle-tattle. Also, in a more favourable sense: Easy, unrestrained talk or writing, esp. about persons or social incidents.

1811 *Sporting Mag.* XXXVII. 11, I was up to his gossip, so I took him. **1820** W. IRVING *Sketch Bk.* II. 358 A kind of travelling gazette, carrying the whole budget of local gossip from house to house. **1833** HT. MARTINEAU *Loom & Lugger* I. i. 6 All this gossip about their neighbours. **1849** LD. HOUGHTON in T. W. Reid *Life* (1891) I. x. 439 A sort of focus of political gossip. **1870** E. PEACOCK *Ralf Skirl.* I. 27 We are fond of topographical gossip. **1889** BARRIE *Window in Thrums* 177 My presence killed the gossip on her tongue.

5. With capital initial. Some kind of game. (Cf. *Scandal*.)

1880 *New Virginians* II. 202 We had a few games, 'Gossip', very amusing—I don't know whether English or American.

6. *attrib.* and *Comb.*, as (appositive in senses 2 and 3) ***gossip-nurse***, ***-seer***; (sense 4) ***gossip-exchange***, ***-gleaner***, ***-monger***, ***-mongering***, ***-shop***, ***-writing***; ***gossip-greedy*** adj.; (sense 3) ***gossip-like*** adj. and adv., ***gossip-wise*** adv.; **gossip column**, the column or columns of a newspaper or magazine in which gossip about persons or social events is printed; so ***gossip-columnist***, ***-writer***; †**gossip-cup**, also **gossip's cup** = CAUDLE *sb.*[1]; **gossip-money**, gratuities to the sponsors at a christening; †**gossip-pint-pot**, a hard drinker.

1859 J. BLACKWOOD *Let.* 18 Apr. in *Geo. Eliot's Lett.* (1954) III. 52 We had better set a paragraph afloat... Can you do it in the Athenæum or any of the other weekly literary *gossip columns? **1897** G. MEREDITH *Let.* 20 Dec. (1970) III. 1285, I comply, but love your Gossip Column least. **1930** J. B. PRIESTLEY *Angel Pavement* ii. 57 Mr. Smeeth.. next tried the gossip columns. **1933** H. NICOLSON *Diary* 29 Jan. (1966) 135 A gossip-column writer in a Chicago newspaper. **1938** L. MACNEICE *Earth Compels* 59 It's no go the gossip column. **1962** *Times* 7 June 17/3 Rich gossip-column meat. **1945** KOESTLER *Twilight Bar* 8 Glowworm, poet and *gossip-columnist. **1959** *Times Lit. Suppl.* 4 Sept. 505/2 His friends are song-writers, gossip-columnists, [etc.]. **1633** HART *Diet of Diseased* Introd. 20 A cup of good ale, with some nutmegg, suger, and a tost, a good *gossip cup I confesse. **1594** PLAT *Jewell-ho.* II. 14 If you will make a right *Gossips Cuppe that shall farre exceede all the Ale. **1963** *Times* 25 May 9/7 Everyone will know through the sewing-shop *gossip-exchange. **1853** HICKIE tr. *Aristoph.* (1872) II. 574 Do you say this of me, you *gossip-gleaner? **1904** *Daily Chron.* 12 Dec. 4/4 Another of those scandal books of which the credulous, *gossip-greedy public have.. been treated to a singular crop. **1566** DRANT *Horace's Sat.* II. vi. H viij, Full *gosseplike, the father sage beginnes his fable then. **1599** SHAKS. *Much Ado* V. i. 188, I will leaue you now to your gossep-like humor. **17..** ? E. WARD *Welsh monster* 35 Let him..Tattle but Gossip like, to please 'em. **1845** SYD. SMITH *Irish Rom. Cath. Ch.* Wks. 1859 II. 339/1 The same scenes of altercation take place when *gossip-money is refused at baptisms. **1836** T. HOOK *G. Gurney* xvi. (1850) III. 349 Several of those meddling *gossip-mongers, who invariably infest small country-town society. **1868** E. EDWARDS *Raleigh* I. viii. 119 A few weeks later, Sir Francis Allen informs that great gossip-monger, Anthony Bacon [etc.]. **1893** *Athenæum* 7 Oct. 487/2 What merit it possesses consists in..the mischievous *gossip-mongering of a certain Lady Dahlia Wormwood. **1845** HOOD *Sea Spell* ii, A baby's caul A thing, as *gossip-nurses know, That always brings a squall. **1580** HOLLYBAND *Treas. Fr. Tong* s.v. *Croque*, He is a *gossip pintepot. **1842** F. HOWES *Horace's Sat.* I. ix. 39 Now, now I see the doom approaching near, Which once was told me by a *gossip-seer. **1824** MISS MITFORD *Village* Ser. I. (1863) 208 A *gossip-shop called 'literary'..where he talks and reads newspapers. **1965** M. MORSE *Unattached* v. 153 The Hartford Swimming Club, which he described as 'virtually a gossip shop'. **1863** MRS. C. CLARKE *Shaks. Char.* xviii. 469 Some citizens meet in the street and talk, *gossip-wise, about the ill-ordering of government. **1931** *Punch* 4 Nov. 499/2 Mr. Punch's Crown of Buttered Buns for Deserving *Gossip-Writers goes this week to the creator of the following. **1961** *Ann. Reg. 1960* 6 One pleasing feature of the engagement was that the gossip writers of the press.. had entirely failed to forecast the event. **1936** A. HUXLEY *Olive Tree* 117 Nowhere else in Europe is *gossip-writing a highly paid and creditable profession; nowhere else would such a headline as 'Peer's Cousin in Car Smash' be.. imaginable.

gossip (ˈgɒsɪp), *v.* [f. GOSSIP *sb.*]

†**1.** *trans.* To be a gossip or sponsor to; to give a name to. *Obs.*

1601 SHAKS. *All's Well* I. i. 189 Pretty fond adoptious christendomes That blinking Cupid gossips. **1716** M. DAVIES *Athen. Brit.* II. 241 Arius's..Heathenish Pamphlet, gossop'd by the name of the..Fabulous Thalia (tho' too gentile a Miss for such Mock-Christenings of Sorcery-Ballads).

†**2.** *intr.* To act as a gossip, or familiar acquaintance; to take part (in a feast), be a boon-companion; to make oneself at home. Also *to gossip it*. *Obs.*

1590 SHAKS. *Com. Err.* V. i. 407 With all my heart, Ile Gossip at this feast. **1611** COTGR., *Voisiner*,..to gossip it, or goe to visit neighbours. **1645** MILTON *Tetrach.* Wks. (1851) 220 When sin revels and gossips within the arcenal of law.. this is a faire limitation indeede.

3. a. To talk idly, mostly about other people's affairs; to go about tattling.

1627 DRAYTON *Moon-Calf* 583 Mother Bumby, a mad iocund Mate As euer Gossipt. **1669** H. MORE *Expos. 7 Ep. to 7 Ch.* Pref. b 2, Swarms of men..went gadding and gossipping up and down, telling odd Stories to the people. **1786** MAD. D'ARBLAY *Diary* Oct., I rang vainly for my maid ..she was gossiping out of hearing. **1846** MRS. GORE *Sk. Eng. Char.* (1852) 16 You gossip everywhere, of every thing. **1872** EARL PEMBROKE & G. H. KINGSLEY *S. Sea Bubbles* iii. 70 [We] called and gossipped for an hour with Mr. Saville and his family.

transf. and *fig.* **1784** COWPER *Task* v. 60 Now from the roost, or from the neighb'ring pale, Where..they gossiped side by side. **1856** BRYANT *After Tempest* ii, The cheerful rivulet sung And gossiped, as he hastened ocean-ward. **1863** LONGF. *Wayside Inn, Interl. to Student's T.*, Wild birds gossiping overhead.

b. To write in a gossiping style.

1885 *Manch. Guard.* 20 July 5/5 A writer in *All the Year Round* gossips pleasantly on..the pets of authors.

4. *trans.* To tell like a gossip; to communicate. Also with *around*, *out*, *over*.

1611 HEYWOOD *Gold. Age* I. Wks. 1874 III. 11 It is so Gossipt in the Queenes chamber. **1650** R. STAPYLTON *Strada's Low C. Warres* I. 20 The secret lay not long in the Embers, being gossiped out by a woman. **1786–1805** H. TOOKE *Purley* 122 The substance of the Criticisms..was.. gossiped by the present precious Secretary at War. **1827** CLARE *Sheph. Cal.* 2 And wisdom, gossip'd from the stars. **1880** G. R. SIMS *Ball. Babylon* 30 And they gossiped her story over in language a bit too plain. **1951** AUDEN *Nones* (1952) 5 Pawed-at and gossiped-over By the promiscuous crowd. **1956** W. NEIL tr. *Keller's Bible as Hist.* VII. xxxi. 294 Two unusual dreams..were gossiped around the whole of the ancient orient.

gossipdom (ˈgɒsɪpdəm). [f. GOSSIP *sb.* + -DOM.] The class of gossips as a whole; the realm of gossip.

1892 MANNING *Pastime Papers* 57 Gossipdom has inner *bolge* or circles less innocuous. **1898** F. F. MOORE *Fatal Gift* xxiv. 175 Horace Walpole, the arch-priest of Gossipdom.

gossiper (ˈgɒsɪpə(r)). [f. GOSSIP *v.* + -ER[1].] One who gossips.

1568 TILNEY *Disc. Mariage* E iij a, I cannot but maruayle how a woman of estimation can delite in gadding abrode, to be a gossiper. **1679** SHADWELL *True Widow* I. *ad fin.*, A perpetual Gossiper and Visiter in all Families. **1817** MAR. EDGEWORTH *Tales & Novels, Harrington* xii, Then bitterly I execrated the reporters, and the gossipers, and the letter-writing misses. **1868** E. EDWARDS *Raleigh* I. xiii. 253 Some of the Court gossippers of the day say that the..commission had been offered to Ralegh. **1885** *L'pool Daily Post* 29 Aug. 5/2 Gossipers on the Flags were pleased to notice that cotton remains fair.

gossiphood (ˈgɒsɪphʊd). Now *rare*. Also †**gossiphede**. [f. GOSSIP *sb.* + -HOOD, -HEAD.] †**a.** Spiritual relationship; = GOSSIPRED 1. **b.** A body of gossips (see GOSSIP *sb.* 3).

1502 *Ord. Crysten Men* (W. de W. 1506) II. x. 115 Whan the one or the other ben of lygnage or of ony affynyte, or gossyphede. **1579** TOMSON *Calvin's Serm. Tim.* 56/2 We makes no bones at it to despise & despite God, vnder the name of a gossiphoode. **1856** MISS YONGE *Daisy Chain* II. xi. (1879) 463 It would create a sensation among the gossip-hood of Stoneborough.

†ˈ**gossipine.** *Obs.* [ad. It. *gossipina*: see GOSSAMPINE. Cf. GOSSYPINE *a.*] = GOSSAMPINE.

c **1565** J. SPARKE *Hawkins' Sec. Voy.* in Hakluyt *Voy.* (1600) III. 508 The beds which they [the Indians] haue are made of Gossopine cotton. **1599** HAKLUYT *Voy.* II. II. 91 Who would beleeue, that there were so much gossipine or cotton-wool in China. **1675** tr. *Camden's Hist. Eliz.* IV. (1688) 489 Brasil Wood..and..Gossipine or Cotton.

gossiping (ˈgɒsɪpɪŋ), *vbl. sb.* [f. GOSSIP *v.* + -ING[1].] The action of the vb. GOSSIP.

1. A christening or christening-feast. Now *dial.*

a **1627** MIDDLETON *Chaste Maid* II. i. Wks. (Dyce) IV. 27 You'll to the gossiping Of master Allwit's child? **1728** *Brice's Weekly Jrnl.* (Exeter) 30 Aug., Last Sunday Afternoon was celebrated here a Gossipping, or held a jovial Meeting of Good Wives and Sweethearts, to solemnize the Baptism of a Child. **1756** J. WILLME *Sepherah Shelosh* 201 in *Palatine Note Bk.* (1881) I. 118 At the First Gift of whose Name (commonly called a Gossiping or Up-sit-Feast of Urbanity) there was a very great Rejoising, of many Neighbours and Relations. **1886** ELWORTHY *W. Somerset Word-bk.*, *Gossipping*, a christening feast. Hence the act of frequently attending such gatherings.

†**2.** A meeting of friends and acquaintances, esp. at the birth of a child; also *gen.* a merry-making.

1557 NORTH tr. *Gueuara's Diall Pr.* II. vii. (1568) 96 b, They remember more the gossippinges that they haue to go, then their sinnes, which they ought to lament. **1590** SHAKS. *Com. Err.* V. i. 419 Will you walke in to see their gossipping? **1613** PURCHAS *Pilgrimage* (1614) 506 They chew these leaves; and in their gossippings or visiting of their friends, they are..presented with them. **1721–1800** BAILEY s.v., A gossiping, a merry meeting of gossips at a woman's lying in. **1823** LAMB *Elia* Ser. II. *Child Angel*, Methought..I was present..at an Angel's gossiping.

3. a. The action of talking idly, or tattling; an instance of this. **b.** An assemblage, where this is the chief occupation.

1630 J. TAYLOR (Water P.) *Taylor's Goose* Wks. I. 105/1 The fashion of her prate Our wiues at Gossipings doe imitate. **1712** STEELE *Spect.* No. 310 ¶9 Give us a Speculation on Gossiping. **1765** FOOTE *Commissary* III. Wks. 1799 II. 36 These kind of women are a good deal given to gossiping. **1791** BOSWELL *Johnson* i. (1848) 1/2 A considerable portion is not devoid of entertainment to the lovers of literary gossiping. **1791–1823** D'ISRAELI *Cur. Lit.* (1858) III. 381 The gossiping of a profound politician.. often, by a spontaneous stroke, reveals the individual. **1820** W. IRVING *Sketch Bk.* (1859) 22 They talked those matters over in their evening gossipings. **1870** MISS BRIDGMAN *R. Lynne* I. xvii. 293, I shall be heartily glad to leave this place, with all this impertinent gossiping and scandal.

4. A literary composition of a light and chatty character. *rare.*

1814 L. HUNT *Feast Poets* (1815) 117 Mr. Walter Savage Landor—author of an epic piece of gossiping called Gebir.

5. *attrib.*

1628 EARLE *Microcosm., Meer Gull Citizen* (Arb.) 93 His friendships are a kinde of Gossiping friendships. **1806–7** J. BERESFORD *Miseries Hum. Life* (1826) v. xvi, Those gossiping scenes of a play in which the lacqueys and waiting-maids lay their heads together. **1835** W. IRVING *Tour Prairies* 99 The Captain's lodge.. was a kind of council fire and gossiping place for the veterans of the camp.

gossiping (ˈgɒsɪpɪŋ), *ppl. a.* [f. GOSSIP *v.* + -ING².] That gossips or indulges in light and idle talk: **a.** of persons.

1618 MYNSHUL *Ess. Prison* 21 A prisoner is as much beholding to such leape-frog acquaintance, as a man shaken with the Ague to euery gossipping woman hee meetes. **1692** L'ESTRANGE *Fables* cclxiii. 229 A Bevy of Jolly, Gossipping Wenches. **1846** MRS. GORE *Eng. Char.* (1852) 15 People boast of a new acquaintance, as 'a pleasant gossiping fellow'. **1852** MRS. STOWE *Uncle Tom's C.* vii, The good woman, kindly and gossipping, seemed rather pleased than otherwise with having somebody come in to talk with.

b. of conversation and literary composition.

1709 SHAFTESBURY *Char.* (1711) I. 148 Who..wou'd set her [religion] on the same bottom with Parish-Tales, and Gossiping Storys of Imps, Goblins [etc.]. **1729** LAW *Serious C.* i. 5 If you was to ask him..why he gives himself up to an idle gossiping conversation? **1750** H. WALPOLE *Let. H. Mann* 1 Sept., This I call a very gossiping letter. **1831** MRS. TROLLOPE in L'Estrange *Friendships Miss Mitford* (1882) I. viii. 227 My book is gossiping, and..faithfully true to the evidence of my senses. **1860** DICKENS *Lett.* (1880) II. 111 An idea for my series of gossiping papers. **1882** SERJT. BALLANTINE *Exper.* xix. 194 A gossiping sketch, and claiming no controversial importance.

transf. **1847** LONGF. *Ev.* I. i. 22 Distaffs spinning the golden flax for the gossiping looms.

Hence **ˈgossipingly** *adv.*, in a gossiping manner.

1817 J. GILCHRIST *Intell. Patrimony* 141 The most superficial [philosophers were] public and gossipingly social. **1875** *N. Amer. Rev.* CXX. 209 Such was the formula by which we were first gossipingly made acquainted with the subject.

†**ˈgossiply**, *a. Obs.* [f. GOSSIP *sb.* + -LY¹.] Pertaining to, or characteristic of, a gossip.

1611 COTGR., *Menandé*, surely,..(a Gossiplie oath, or asseueration).

gossipred (ˈgɒsɪprɛd). Also 4 **gossybrede**. [f. GOSSIP *sb.* + OE. *rǣden* condition: see -RED.]

An etymologizing perversion appears in Huloet 1552: 'Goshipbred, or gatheringe of goshyps at the wyne, *syssitia*.'

1. The relationship of gossips (see GOSSIP *sb.* 1 and 2); spiritual affinity. Now only *Hist.* (with reference to Irish customs).

c **1315** SHOREHAM 68 Ase the gossybrede draȝth Ryȝt to ous after crystnynge, So gossibrede draȝeth eke Ryȝt after confermynge. **1387** TREVISA *Higden* (Rolls) I. 357 In gosibrede and holy kynrede. *c* **1430** LYDG. *Min. Poems* (Percy Soc.) 36 Be wel ware of feyned cosynage, And gossiprede. **1494** FABYAN *Chron.* VII. 435 He..assertayned hym of yᵉ gossyprede yᵗ was atwene hym and Blanche his wyfe. **1533** MORE *Debell. Salem* v. Wks. 941/1, I haue none affinitie.. eyther by gossepred or bi mariage. **1612** DAVIES *Why Ireland, &c.* (1747) 181 The like may be said of gossipred or compaternitie which though by the canon lawe it be a spiritual affinity [etc.]. **1646** SIR J. TEMPLE *Irish Rebell.* 8 *marg.*, Alliance by marriage, nurture of Infants, and gossipred with the Irish are high treason. **1807** G. CHALMERS *Caledonia* I. III. x. 458 The custom of fostering, and gossipred, among the Irish. **1861** GOLDW. SMITH *Irish Hist.* 37 The connexion of sponsorship or gossiprede was made a sort of second fosterage.

†**b.** *transf.* Affinity in general. *Obs. rare.*

1674 N. FAIRFAX *Bulk & Selv.* 91 We find some bodies amongst us hold up a Gossipred, that seem to have little or nothing of kinred.

¶**2.** By some mod. writers used for: The habitual action of a gossip or tattler; small-talk; = GOSSIP *sb.* 4.

1828 SCOTT *F.M. Perth* xx, Our poor fellow-citizen.. having been active in spreading these reports, as indeed his element lay in such gossipred. **1859** R. F. BURTON *Centr. Afr.* in *Jrnl. Geog. Soc.* XXIX. 369 The women..collecting in a group upon their little stools indulge in the pleasures of gossipred and the pipe. **1892** MANNING *Pastime Papers* 53 It is a rigorous destiny that Gossipred should have come to signify one of the worst of social vices.

gossipry (ˈgɒsɪprɪ). [f. GOSSIP *sb.* + -RY.]

1. Spiritual relationship: = GOSSIPRED 1.

1550 BALE *Image Both Ch.* III. xviii. Bb. viij b, [Marriage should be forbidden] neither for vowes vnaduised, nor for no popish orders, nor yet for any gossypry. **1861** DASENT *Story Burnt Njal* II. 248, I challenge both these men out of the inquest..for this sake, that one of them is Mord's second cousin by kinship, but the other for gossipry. **1880** *Academy* 21 Aug. 134 There exist many kinds of gossipry besides the usual form connected with christenings.

†**b.** Intimacy. *Obs.*⁻¹

a **1614** J. MELVILL *Diary* (MS.) 36 (Jam.), All gossiprie gade up between him and my uncle Mr. Andrew.

c. *concr.* A relative in general.

1887 BROWNING *Parleyings, Fust & Friends* 12 Greet us thy gossipry, cousin and sib!

2. The practice of gossiping; small talk, gossip; also, a gossiping conversation.

1818 LADY MORGAN *Autobiog.* (1859) 199 'Well, my dear!' as we say in Ireland when we enter on a gossipry. **1819** W. TAYLOR in *Monthly Rev.* LXXXIX. 145 We cannot help being struck with a certain feeling of inanity..of inquiry squandered on the gossipry of the past. **1841** *Blackw. Mag.* XLIX. 362 Any bald disjointed chat—any gossipry—that an accomplished writer may please to descend to. **1876** DOWDEN *Poems* 50 At evening I went back, Walked past the idle groups at gossipry.

b. Gossiping discourse.

1865 *Sat. Rev.* 25 Mar. 348 Girls..are to learn..Greek, to enable them to enjoy..the gossipry of Herodotus.

c. *concr.* A body of gossips.

1853 MRS. BROWNING *Lett.* 16 May, Think kindly of us in the midst of your brilliant London gossipry. **1888** *N. & Q.* 11 Aug. 114 The striking circumstances of it were quite sufficient..to convince all the gossipry of Rome that he was poisoned.

†**ˈgossipship.** *Obs.* [f. GOSSIP *sb.* + -SHIP.] The mutual relation of gossips. Also, the personality of a gossip or sponsor (used as a mock-title). (Cf. GOSSIPRED 1.)

1572 HULOET (ed. Higins), Gosshishippe at a Christening, *lustrica cognatio.* **1591** PERCIVALL *Sp. Dict.*, *Compadrazgo*, gossipship, *Compaternitas.* **1596** NASHE *Saffron Walden* Wks. (Grosart) III. 203 A whole penny-worth of paper, which his Gossipship, that hath the naming of the child, dubs *the Encomium of the Foxe.* **1651** HOWELL *Surv. Venice* 188 (*bis*) To the end that this Goshipship shold no way be a bar or impediment among the Gentlewomen in matter of Mariage. **1677** W. HUGHES *Man of Sin* II. x. 175 Such as were born after such Gossipship was contracted.

gossipy (ˈgɒsɪpɪ), *a.* [f. GOSSIP *sb.* + -Y¹.] Of a literary composition: Characterized by, or full of, gossip. Of a person: Inclined or devoted to gossip.

1818 T. MURDOCH in Smiles *J. Murray* (1891) II. xxii. 67 [It] would soon..sink the journal down to the level of a common gossipy magazine. **1829** DK. BUCKINGHAM *Diary* III. ix. 208 Don't like Florence. The Society is confined, but gossipy to a degree. **1865** *Spectator* 11 Feb. 164 The book, though slight and gossippy, has an interest. **1879** JEFFERIES *Wild Life in S.C.* 83 The old woman's memories were wholly of gossipy family history. **1923** F. M. FORD *Let.* 20 Jan. (1965) 147 Suppose you write me a nice gossipy letter.

Hence **ˈgossipiness**, inclination for gossip.

1890 *Universal Rev.* Apr. 604, I don't ask out of mere gossipiness.

gossom(m)er, gossomyre, obs. ff. GOSSAMER.

gossoon (gɒˈsuːn). Chiefly *Anglo-Irish.* Also 7 **gosoun**, 9 **gosoon**, **gorsoon**. [Alteration of *garsoon* GARCION, GARÇON.] A youth, a boy; a servant-boy, lackey.

1684 J. HAINES *Epil. to Lacy's Sir H. Buffon*, French goûts, that mingle water with their wine, Cry, Ah de French song, gosoun, dat is ver' fine. **1802** MAR. EDGEWORTH *Irish Bulls* (1803) 161 Even the cottiers and gossoons speak in trope and figure. **1841** LEVER *C. O'Malley* vii. 42 The gossoon is gone to look for a pair. **1884** *Times* (weekly ed.) 29 Aug. 14/4 Two or three ragged gossoons were galloping on the flanks of the flock. **1896** *Contemp. Rev.* June 809 Poor unfriended Irish gorsoons.

gossop, obs. form of GOSSIP.

gossopine, variant of GOSSIPINE, *Obs.*

gossummer, gossup, obs. ff. GOSSAMER, GOSSIP.

†**ˈgossy.** *Sc. Obs.* [f. GOSS¹ + -Y.] A crony.

1711 RAMSAY *Elegy Magg Johnston* 87 Let a' thy gossies yelp and yell. **1719** —— *Fam. Epist.* Answer i. 6 In gossy Don's be candle-light. **1721** —— *Poems*, Gloss., *Gossie*, gossip.

gossypine (ˈgɒsɪpaɪn), *a.* [f. mod.L. *Gossypium* (after Pliny's *gossypion*: see GOSSAMPINE), the generic cotton-plant + -INE.] Cottony, flocculent.

1880 GRAY *Struct. Bot.* 413/2 *Gossypine.*

gossypol (ˈgɒsɪpɒl). *Chem.* [a. G. *gossypol* (L. Marchlewski 1899, in *Jrnl. f. prakt. Chem.* LX. 84), f. mod.L. *Gossyp-ium* (see GOSSYPINE *a.*) + -OL.] A toxic phenolic crystalline compound, $C_{30}H_{30}O_8$, that is an important constituent of cotton-seed.

1899 *Brit. Chem. Abstr.* LXXVI. I. 821 (*heading*) Gossypol, a Constituent of Cotton-seeds... When the phenolic constituents of cotton-seed oil are purified..a crystalline product is obtained... This substance, to which the name of *gossypol* is given, has a composition corresponding..with that required for the formula $C_{13}H_{14}O_4$. **1937** *Jrnl. Amer. Chem. Soc.* LIX. 1725/1 A red isomeric form of gossypol has been isolated recently by Podolskaja. This material melts at 184–185° and gives the reactions of ordinary yellow gossypol... Merely grinding the red form in a mortar converts it to the yellow. **1955** *Sci. News Let.* 24 Sept. 196/2 The poison glands, scattered throughout the cotton plant, especially in the seeds, produce a toxic pigment called gossypol. Because of the presence of gossypol, feeding of cottonseed meal was long restricted to cattle and sheep, unaffected by the poison. **1961** L. F. & M. FIESER *Adv. Org. Chem.* xxii. 767 Gossypol..was shown by R. Adams (1938) to be a symmetrically substituted 2,2′-di-(1-naphthol) derivative.

gost, dial. form of GORSE.

gost(e, obs. form of GHOST.

goster, gosther. = GAUSTER *sb.* and *v.*

1734 LADY B. GERMAIN in *9th Rep. Hist. MSS. Comm.* App. iii. (1904) I. 157 Upon which I could not hold, but fell a laughing as loud as Horace could 'goster' himself. **1836** T. POWER *Impress. Amer.* I. 376 Not another word could we coax out of him: he was, however, quite willing and able to make it up in good Irish, and much did I regret not being able to have a 'goster' with him. **1839** W. CARLETON *Fardorougha* (ed. 2) 70 We're idlin' an' gostherin away our time like I dunna what. **1892** *Athenæum* 16 Apr. 496/3 The handsome, selfish Murdough so full of 'gosther' and brag. **1892** EMILY LAWLESS *Grania* II. ii. 91 A gosthering, spending, *having* brood they are and always have been. **1914** JOYCE *Dubliners* 155 He was leaning on the counter..having a deep goster with Alderman Cowley. **1941** L. A. G. STRONG *Bay* 181 Uncle John did not write letters. He would explain that a good gosther and a drink were better than a cold bit of paper.

[**gosting.** Explained in Johnson and some later Dicts. as 'madder': taken from 1736 AINSWORTH *Thesaurus* 1, '*Gosting* (herb), Rubia'. In the Eng.-Lat. part there is: '*Rubia*, Rubia tinctorum, an herb called gosling weed or clivers; madder'. Thus *gosting* in Ainsworth is a mistake for *gosling weed*, which does not mean, however, 'madder', but 'goose-grass' or 'cleavers'.]

†**go-summer.** *Sc. Obs.* Also go o' simmer. [app. identical with GOSSAMER, and exhibiting the orig. sense of that word, not elsewhere recorded: see the etymological note there. The spelling is due to association with GO *v.*; in some Sc. dialects the word has been transformed into *go-harvest*, *goss-hairst* (see Jam.).] The 'St. Martin's summer', a period of summer-like weather in late autumn.

1649 *Cupar Presb. Rec.* in Campbell *Balmerino* (1899) 381 In the last gossummer save one. *a* **1670** SPALDING *Troub. Chas. I* (Bannatyne Club) I. 26 The goe summer, Matchless fair in Murray, but winds, weits, or any storme..the garden herbs revived, July flowers and roses springing at Martinmas. **1790** MORISON *Poems* 112 Our gray hawkit mare Wha last year i' the go o' simmer Broke my fore leg.

got (gɒt), *ppl. a.* [Shortened pa. pple. of GET *v.*: see GOTTEN.] Gained, acquired; gathered as a crop (see the verb). Now only with adv. prefixed, as *ill got, well got.*

1593–1753 [see ILL-GOT]. **1613–16** W. BROWNE *Brit. Past.* II. iv. 80 Fate drew them on to be A greater Fame to our got Victory. **1806** FESSENDEN *Democr.* II. 142 Provided he can save himself Together with his ill got pelf. **1852** *Jrnl. R. Agric. Soc.* XIII. II. 296 The value of well-got hay is duly appreciated.

b. Comb. with advs.: **got-at** (see GET *v.* 38 a, b); **got-up**, artificially produced, elaborated, or adorned, for purposes of effect or deception (see GET *v.* 80 l, m); also, †(well) equipped in a subject.

1818 LADY MORGAN *Autobiog.* (1859) 199 He snubbed me ..for exposing my ignorance to these well got-up Doctrinaires. **1826** R. H. FROUDE *Remains* (1838) I. 86, I believe it to be..a got-up business for effect. **1841** L. S. COSTELLO *Pilgr. Auvergne* I. 336 Plaited collars and delicately got-up linen. **1855** SMEDLEY *Coverdale* xviii, Such follies are very well for got up puppies. **1871** EARLE *Philol. Eng. Tongue* 217 The symbolics in Greek have grown spontaneously, while their Latin analogues have a got-up and cultivated look. **1871** GEO. ELIOT *Middlemarch* I. xii, Stuff and nonsense! I don't believe a word of it. It's all a got-up story. **1880** *Daily Tel.* 3 Dec., The principal publishing houses prepare magnificently got-up books which are works of art in themselves. **1883** *Times* (weekly ed.) 28 Dec. 6/4 Some days after this little got-up play, which seemed to have produced the desired effect. **1891** *Sat. Rev.* 12 Sept. 313/1 The abundance of easily-got-at material.

Hence **got-up** *sb. colloq.*, an upstart.

1881 *Macm. Mag.* XLIV. 383 How dare that 'got-up' give himself airs with his horses and dogs!

gotam, gotamist, obs. ff. GOTHAM, -IST.

gotch (gɒtʃ). *dial.* Also 9 **gotsch**. **a.** A big-bellied earthenware pot or jug.

1674–91 RAY *S. & E.C. Words* 100 A *Gotch*, a large earthen or stone drinking Pot with a great Belly like a Jugg. **1784** SIR J. CULLUM *Hist. Hawsted* iii. 171 A *Gotch*, a jug, or big-bellied mug. **1801** BLOOMFIELD *Rural T.* (1802) 5 A Gotch of Milk I'd been to fill, You shoulder'd me; then laugh'd to see Me and my Gotch spin down the Hill. **1857** BORROW *Romany Rye* (1858) I. 9 Then taking the gotch I fetched water from the spring.

b. *Comb.*: *gotch-eared* adj. **gotch-belly** (see quot.); **gotch-gutted** *a.*, corpulent.

1694 ECHARD *Plautus* 165 Did ye see e'r an old Bald-pated, ..Gotch Gutted, Squint-Ey'd, Sour-Fac'd Rascal? *a* **1825** FORBY *Voc. E. Anglia*, *Gotch-belly*, a fair round belly, much resembling the protuberance of a *gotch.* **1905** C. DRISCOLL *Girl of La Gloria* iii. 21 The *maveriquer*..usually rode a gotch-eared Mexican pony. *a* **1910** 'O. HENRY' *Strictly Business* (1917) ix. 91 You are a concentrated, effete, unconditional, short-sleeved, gotch-eared Miss Sally Walker.

Hence †**ˈgotchy** *a.*, bloated, swollen.

1596 NASHE *Saffron Walden* 48 No French gowtie-leg with a gamash vpon it, is so gotchie and boystrous.

gotcha, gotcher ('gɒtʃə), a representation of the colloq. or vulgar pronunciation of (*I have*) *got you* (see esp. GET *v.* 21 a).

1932 E. WALLACE *When Gangs came to London* xxii. 197 The 'plane was nearing the centre of Cavendish Square, when it suddenly heeled over. Its tail went down and it fell with a crash in the centre of the garden which occupied the middle of the square. 'Gotcher!' It was Jiggs' triumphant voice. **1966** H. WAUGH *Pure Poison* (1967) xviii. 112 'Give her background a once-over on your way to Springfield... You might try for a record of her blood type first. She claims it's O but she doesn't carry any card.' Wilks sighed. 'I gotcha.'

gote (gəʊt). Chiefly *north. dial.* Forms: 4- **gote**, 5-6 **goote**, 6-9 **goat(e**, 7-8 **gott**, 7-9 **gaut**, **goit**, 8-9 **goyt**, 9 **gooat**. See also GOUT. [f. *got-*, wk. root of OE. *ȝéotan* to pour (see YETE *v.*); cf. MLG., MDu. *gote* (mod.Du. *goot*, dial. *geut*) of similar meaning. Cf. also GUT.]

1. A watercourse; any channel for water; a stream.

13.. *E.E. Allit. P.* A. 933 To loke on þe glory of þys gracious gote. *a* **1400-50** *Alexander* 5796 As gotis out of guttars in golanand wedres. **1467** *Nottingham Rec.* II. 380 Two gootes parte of a were, otherwise called a 'fysshe-garth'. **1488** *Will of Welby, Lincoln* (Somerset Ho.), Dreynis Gotes & high weyes. **1694** DE LA PRYME *Diary* (Surtees) 50 There was a plank layd over a little goit or watercourse. **1703** THORESBY *Let. to Ray* in *Philos. Lett.* (1718) 329 Goyts of Mills, where the Stream passes out. **1734** *Rec.* in Cramond *Ann. Banff* (1893) II. 222, 18 feet broad of rock is to be cut from the southmost end of the basson down to the nearest goat or hollow place. **1788** E. PICKEN *Poems* 167 Wi' pettle, owre the rigs I'll stride, At her comman', Or rake the gotts frae paddock-ride To muck the lan'. **1897** *British Weekly* 14 Jan. 232 Reaching the goit, he walked along its muddy banks, its sluggish waters oozing at his feet.

2. A sluice (see quot. 1622).

1531-2 *Act 23 Hen. VIII*, c. 5 §1 Weares fisshgarthes Redels gores gootes.. and other impedimentes in and vppon the same ryuers. **1584** *Lansdowne MS.* 74, lf. 181 b, The saide bancke beinge alreadie charged with three goates. **1622** CALLIS *Stat. Sewers* (1647) 66 Goats be usual Engines .. built with percullesses and doors of timber, stone or brick. **1702** THORESBY in *Phil. Trans.* XXIII. 1159 The.. new Sluice or Goat. **1890** *Blackw. Mag.* Feb. 242, I have often admired the vastness of their gotes and sluices.

3. (See quot.)

1855 ROBINSON *Whitby Gloss.*, *Gaut* or *Gote*, a narrow opening or slip from a street to the shore.

gote, goten, obs. ff. GOAT, GOTTEN.

goter(e, obs. form of GUTTER.

Goth (gɒθ). Forms: 1 **Gota**, 4-5, 7 **Gothe**, 6 *Sc.* **Gotte**, (7 **Got**), 6- **Goth**. [OE. *Gotan* pl. (*Gota* sing.), ad. late L. *Gothī*, *Gotthī*, Gr. *Γόθοι*, *Γότθοι* pl., ad. Goth. **Gutôs* or **Gutans* pl.; cf. Goth. *Gutþiuda* the Gothic people.]

1. One of a Germanic tribe, who, in the third, fourth, and fifth centuries, invaded both the Eastern and Western empires, and founded kingdoms in Italy, France, and Spain.

c **900** tr. *Bæda's Hist.* I. ix. [xi.] (1890) 42 Seo herȝung wæs þurh Alaricum Gotena cyning ȝeworden. *c* **1374** CHAUCER *Boeth.* I. pr. iv. 9 (Camb. MS.) Theodoric þe kyng of gothes .. hadde hise gerneres ful of corn. **1480** CAXTON *Descr. Brit.* 32 These men and these gothes ben all one peple. **1535** STEWART *Cron. Scot.* II. 357 Fair Florence.. Distroyit wes .. Be the gottis perforce that held it than. **1600** SHAKS. *A.Y.L.* III. iii. 9, I am heere with thee, and thy Goats, as the most capricious Poet honest Ouid was among the Gothes. **1613** PURCHAS *Pilgrimage* (1614) 238 Eudo the Goth then King of a great part of France. **1663** GERBIER *Counsel* e iij a, The Gots, who were sent packing by the Mores. **1694** DRYDEN *To Sir G. Kneller* 47 Till Goths and Vandals, a rude northern race, Did all the matchless monuments deface. **1709** SHAFTESB. *Charac.* (1733) I. II. 86 Hardly a Tartar or a Goth would.. reason so absurdly. **1832** W. IRVING *Alhambra* I. 82 The fiery courage of the Arab was at length subdued by the obstinate and persevering valour of the Goth. **1869** LOWELL *Cathedral* Poet. Wks. 1890 IV. 59 Shall not that Western Goth.. Find out, some day, that nothing pays but God.

2. *transf.* **a.** One who behaves like a barbarian, esp. in the destruction or neglect of works of art; a rude, uncivilized, or ignorant person; one devoid of culture and taste. Often associated with *Vandal*.

1663 GERBIER *Counsel* 50 For who would Rob them but Goths and Vandalls. **1735** BERKELEY *Querist* §184 Whether every enemy to learning be not a Goth? **1779** FRANKLIN *Lett.* Wks. 1889 VI. 422, I am sorry for the losses you have suffered by the Goths and Vandals [the British troops]. **1850** W. D. COOPER *Hist. Winchelsea* 135 The successive efforts for ages of the local Goths. **1870** L'ESTRANGE *Miss Mitford* I. v. 114 A horrible Goth of a Scotchman.

b. = GOTHICIST.

[*c* **1812** in W. Thornbury *Haunted London* (1880) App. 465 The Modern Goth.] **1837** *Q. Rev.* LVIII. 66 That preterpluperfect Goth, Mr. S. Pugin.., regrets the mistake of Sir Christopher Wren in the construction of St. Paul's. **1849** T. W. ALLIES *Jrnl. in France* 142 The cathedral [of Milan] itself.. is quite indefinable in the eyes of a thorough-going Goth. **1857** (*title*) A Word to the Goths. **1866** FR. PIUS *Life Fr. Ignatius* xii. 276 The famous Goth [*sc.* Pugin]. **1907** R. A. CRAM *Gothic Quest* 134 Bentley, in some ways perhaps the greatest of all the new Goths of England.

3. *Comb.*

1611 COTGR., *Gothique*, Gothlike; rude, cruell, barbarous. **1887** HISSEY *Holiday on Road* 316 A Goth-like way of settling a difficulty, this, surely.

Gotham ('gɒtəm; often improperly 'gəʊθəm). Also 6 **Gotum**, 6-7 **Got(t)am**.

1. The name of a village, proverbial for the folly of its inhabitants ('wise men of Gotham'). (There is a village so named in Notts., but it is not certain that this was the place alluded to.)

c **1460** *Towneley Myst.* xii. 180 Now god gyf you care, foles all sam, Sagh I neuer none so fare bot the foles of gotham. **1526** *C Mery Talys* (1866) 45 Of the .iii. wyse men of gotam. *c* **1560** *Misogonus* II. iii. 10 (Brandl *Quellen* 441) The wise men of gotum are risen againe. *c* **1568** A. B. (*title*) The Merry Tales of the Mad-men of Gottam (1630). **1603** HARSNET *Pop. Impost.* 61, I doe verily suspect this wonder was acted somewhat neere Gotham and that the Spectators were the Posteritie of them that drowned the Eel. *a* **1700** B. E. *Dict. Cant. Crew*, *Wise Man of Gotham*, a Fool. **1765** FALCONER *Demag.* 48 Let the great monarch ass through Gotham bray!

b. *transf.* Applied to (*a*) Newcastle, (*b*) New York.

1807 W. IRVING *Salmag.* xvii. (1811) II. 155 Chap. cix. of the chronicles of the renowned and antient city of Gotham. **1825** BROCKETT *N.C. Words*, *Gotham*, a cant name for Newcastle. **1852** JUTSON *Myst. N.Y.* xiii. (Farmer), One of the vilest of all hells in Gotham.

†**2.** A 'man of Gotham', a simpleton.

1685 CROWNE *Sir C. Nice* v. Dram. Wks. 1874 III. 351 What a society of Gotam's are here, to laugh at a man for missing a woman?

†**3.** *attrib.* passing into adj.: Of or pertaining to Gotham; foolish, stupid. **Gotham College**: an imaginary institution for the training of simpletons.

1621 BURTON *Anat. Mel.*, Democr. to Rdr. 69 They are all of Gotam parish. **1657** J. SERGEANT *Schism Dispach't* 333 Perhaps it may cause mirth in thee to read such Gottam-absurdities in a Dr. of Divinitie. **1675** COCKER *Morals* 23 But who loves Ignorance before choice Knowledge, A Doctor may commence in Gotham College. **1681** COLVIL *Whigs Supplic.* (1751) p. vi, Some of the society of Gotham college had an intention to burn my lines. **1692-4** R. L'ESTRANGE *Fables* v. (1714) 5 'Tis the Fate of all Gotham Quarrels, when Fools go together by the Ears, to have Knaves run away with the Stakes.

Hence †'**Gothamist**, one who takes after the men of Gotham; a blunderer, a simpleton. '**Gothamite**, (*a*) = GOTHAMIST; (*b*) a New-Yorker.

1589 NASHE *Pref. to Greene's Menaphon* (Arb.) 8 The.. perusing of our Gothamists barbarisme. **1660** T. M. *C. Walker's Hist. Independ.* IV. 78 The Officers of the Army.. a mad crew of Gotamists. **1802** LAMB *Curious Fragments* ii, These were dizzards, fools, gothamites. **1807** W. IRVING *Salmag.* xvii. (1811) II. 160 Whereat the Gothamites.. marvelled exceedingly. **1852** BRISTED *Upper Ten Thous.* ii. 37 The first thing.. that a young Gothamite does is to get a horse.

†'**gothele**, *v. Obs.* In 3-4 **goþele(n**, **-i**, 4 **godele(n**, **-y**. [Echoic.]

1. *intr.* To make a low rumbling noise, as bubbles rising through water, or as is heard in the bowels.

c **1290** *S. Eng. Leg.* I. 314/530 þat ilke druye breth.. þe ȝwile it is in þe watere it goþeleth swyþe loude. **1393** LANGL. *P. Pl.* C. VII. 398 Hus guttes gonne godely [*v.r.* to goþel] as two gredy sowes. *Ibid.* XVI. 99 Thenne shulleþ his gottes godelen [*v.r.* goþelen] and he by-gynne to galpe.

2. *trans.* To slander. Hence '**godeling** *vbl. sb.*

1340 *Ayenb.* 66 Efterward comeþ þe godelinges. þet is huanne þe on godeleþ þanne oþrene. And þet is zuo grat zenne þet þe writynge zayþ, þet huo þet godeleþ his emcristen, he ys acorsed of god.

†'**Gothian.** *Obs.* Also 6 **Gotthian**. [f. GOTH + -IAN.] = GOTH 1.

1548 UDALL, etc., tr. *Erasm. Par. John* i. 9 Neither Scithian, Jewe, Spayneard, Gothian, Englisheman [etc.]. *Ibid. Luke* xix. 26 Gotthians. **1561** DAUS tr. *Bullinger on Apoc.* (1573) 196 He armed agaynst her [Rome] the Gothians, Vandales, and Germanes. *a* **1568** ASCHAM *Scholem.* II. (Arb.) 145 More like vnto the Grecians than vnto the Gothians.

Gothic ('gɒθɪk), *a.* and *sb.* Forms: 7 **Gotic**, **Gotiq(ue**, **Gothicke**, **Gottic**, **Gothiq**, 7-8 **Gothique**, 7- **Gothic**. [ad. L. *gothic-us*, f. *Gothī* (see GOTH). Cf. F. *gothique*.]

A. *adj.*

1. a. Of, pertaining to, or concerned with the Goths or their language.

1611 BIBLE *Transl. Pref.* 5 Vlpilas is reported.. to haue translated the Scriptures into the Gothicke tongue. **1776** GIBBON *Decl. & F.* x. I. 244 Cassiodorus gratified the inclination of the conquerors in a Gothic history. **1845** STODDART *Grammar* 192/1 The Gothic substantive *leik*, body. **1892** WRIGHT (*title*) A Primer of the Gothic Language.

b. = MOZARABIC *a.*

1867 tr. *Guéranger's Life St. Cecilia* xviii. 164 The Gothic Church of Spain, whose Liturgy was compiled by St. Leander, Archbishop of Seville. **1874** *Month* Feb. 223 The old Gothic or Mozarabic rite. **1911** E. B. O'REILLY *Heroic Spain* 235 The Christians who were under Moorish rule.. kept to the old Gothic ritual.

†**2.** Formerly used in extended sense, now expressed by TEUTONIC or GERMANIC.

1647 N. BACON *Disc. Govt. Eng.* I. xl. 96 Nor can any Nation upon earth shew so much of the ancient Gothique Law as this Island hath. *a* **1690** ETHEREDGE *Poems* Wks. (1888) 378 A tawdry ill-bred ramp, Whose brawny arms and martial face Proclaim her of the Gothic race. **1721** SWIFT *Let. to Pope* 10 Jan. Wks. 1841 II. 551/2 As to Parliaments, I adored the wisdom of that Gothic institution which made them annual. **1735-8** BOLINGBROKE *On Parties* 102 Maintaining the Freedom of our Gothick Institution of Government. **1832** PALGRAVE *Eng. Commw.* I. 500 There is no Gothic feudality unless the parties be connected by the mutual bond of Vassalage and Seigniory. **1846** MCCULLOCH *Acc. Brit. Empire* (1854) I. 395 The Gothic blood would seem to have been preserved pretty pure in all the country to the north and east of the Severn and the Exe. **1857** MAURICE *Ep. St. John* xx. 336 He raised up the Gothic or Teutonic race.

absol. **1685** DRYDEN *Albion & Alb.* Pref., This language [Italian] has in a manner been refined and purified from the Gothic ever since the time of Dante.

3. †**a.** Belonging to, or characteristic of, the Middle Ages; mediæval, 'romantic', as opposed to classical. In early use chiefly with reprobation: Belonging to the 'dark ages' (cf. sense 4). *Obs.* [Cf. F. *les siècles gothiques*.]

1695 [see 4]. **1710** SHAFTESBURY *Charact.* (1727) I. III. 217 [The Elizabethan dramatists] have been the first of Europeans, who since the Gothick Model of Poetry, attempted to throw off the horrid Discord of jingling Rhyme. **1762** HURD *Lett. Chiv. & Rom.* 56 He [Spenser] could have planned, no doubt, an heroic design on the exact classic model: Or, he might have trimmed between the Gothic and Classic, as his contemporary Tasso did.. Under this idea then of a Gothic, not classical poem, the *Faery Queen* is to be read and criticized. **1765** H. WALPOLE (*title*) The Castle of Otranto, a Gothic Story. —— *Let. to Cole* 9 Mar., A very natural dream for a head filled like mine with gothic story. **1771** BEATTIE *Minstrel* I. xi, There liv'd in gothic days, as legends tell, A shepherd swain. *Ibid.* I. lx, Here pause, my gothic lyre, a little while. **1773** JOHNSON *Let. to Mrs. Thrale* 21 Sept., A castle in Gothick romance. **1782** COWPER *Table Talk* 564 He sunk in Greece, in Italy he rose, And, tedious years of Gothic darkness past, Emerged all splendour in our isle at last.

b. A term for the style of architecture prevalent in Western Europe from the twelfth to the sixteenth century, of which the chief characteristic is the pointed arch. Applied also to buildings, architectural details, and ornamentation. (Also *transf.* of the wing of an aeroplane).

The most usual names for the successive periods of this style in England are *Early English* (or *First Pointed*), *Decorated*, and *Perpendicular*, q.v.

Our quotations seem to show that the term was taken in the first instance from the French, and employed to denote any style of building that was not classical (Greek or Roman), but used by many writers as if derived immediately from sense 2.

1641 EVELYN *Diary* Aug., This.. towne.. hath one of the fairest Churches, of the Gotiq design, I had seene. **1664** WOOD *Descr. Bampton Castle* in *Wood's Life* (O.H.S.) II. Plate 1, The cheife gate-house where is a ruined entrance, and an old gothick window over it. **1713** WREN in *Parentalia* (1750) 297 This we now call the Gothick Manner of Architecture (so the Italians called what was not after the Roman style). **1739** LABELYE *Short Acc. Piers Westm. Br.* 44 Narrow Gothic Arches, supported by monstrous Piers. **1742** B. LANGLEY *Anc. Archit. Restored* Dissert. i, Every ancient Building which is not in the Grecian Mode is called a Gothic Building. **1750** S. WREN in *Parentalia* 273 They had not yet fallen into the Gothick pointed-arch. **1783** RALPH *Rev. Public Buildings Lond.*, [The tower of St. Michael's, Cornhill, is] in the Gothic style of architecture. **1801** TELFORD & DOUGLAS *Acc. Improvem. Port London* 17 The whole external form of the bridge is to be composed of Gothic tracery. *a* **1839** PRAED *Poems* (1864) I. 69 Some time-honoured Gothic pile. **1880** MISS BRADDON *Just as I am* vii, The cosy chair beside the Gothic fire-place. **1881** RAYMOND *Mining Gloss.*, *Gothic groove*, a groove of Gothic arch section in a roll.

transf. **1959** J. L. NAYLER *Dict. Aeronaut. Engin.* 121 *Gothic wing*, a wing whose plan form is like a Gothic window. **1961** *Flight* LXXX. 966/2 The Super Caravelle wing is of gothic delta plan form with considerable leading edge camber.

c. *nonce-use*. Concerned with Gothic buildings.

1875-7 RUSKIN *Morn. in Florence* (1881) 48 As our Gothic Firms now manufacture a Madonna.

d. Gothic Revival = REVIVAL 1 d. Also *attrib.* So ***Gothic Revivalist***.

1869 C. L. EASTLAKE *Hints Household Taste* (ed. 2) i. 32 The earliest promoters of the Gothic revival appreciated the superficial effect of such features... The glories of the 'fretted vault' were not unfrequently imitated in lath and plaster. **1934** A. HUXLEY *Beyond Mexique Bay* 114 The Gothic revival in England was a product of the Oxford Movement. **1950** *Oxoniensia* XV. 118 Jackson witnessed the evolution of the Gothic Revival. *Ibid.*, They, the Gothic Revivalists, had got the old dead style on its legs and propped it up, but they could not make it walk. **1958** R. LIDDELL *Morea* III. ii. 243 A Gothic revival school building was a relic of the British protectorate. **1963** H. READ *Contrary Experience* III. ix. 276 The Gothic Revival was almost a spent force when Ruskin began to publish *The Stones of Venice* in 1851.

4. Barbarous, rude, uncouth, unpolished, in bad taste. Of temper: Savage.

1695 DRYDEN *Du Fresnoy's Art Paint.* 93 All that has nothing of the Ancient gust is call'd a barbarous or Gothique manner. **1710** SHAFTESB. *Charac.* (1733) I. III. 274 We are not so Barbarous or Gothick as they pretend. *a* **1715** BURNET *Own Time* (1753) V. 222 His [Chas. XII] temper grew daily more fierce and Gothick. **1732** BERKELEY *Alciphr.* v. §13 This Gothic crime of duelling. **1749** FIELDING *Tom Jones* VII. iii, 'Oh more than Gothic ignorance,' answered the lady. **1782** MISS BURNEY *Cecilia* IV. ii, What he holds of all things to be most gothic, is gallantry to the women. **1812** SHELLEY *Lett.* Prose Wks. 1888 II. 384 Enormities which gleam like comets through the darkness of gothic and superstitious ages. **1833** CHALMERS *Const. Man* II. i. (1835) I. 173 Such a gothic spoliation as this. **1841** J. T. HEWLETT *Parish Clerk*

I. 111 Dinner, which was eaten at the gothic hour of one o'clock.

5. *Writing* and *Printing*. †**a.** Used for some kind of written character (? resembling black letter).

1644 EVELYN *Diary* 18–21 Mar., Some English words graven in Gotic characters. **1658** *Ibid.* 27 Jan., He could perfectly reade any of the English, Latine, French, or Gottic letters.

b. In England, the name of the type commonly used for printing German, as distinguished from roman and italic characters. (Formerly, and still in non-technical use, equivalent to *black letter*.)

1781 WARTON *Hist. Eng. Poetry* Diss. iii. III. p. iv, This edition..is in the Gothic letter. **1824** J. JOHNSON *Typogr.* II. i. 10 Black Letter. This letter, which is used in England, descended from the Gothic characters: it is called Gothic, by some; and Old English, by others. **1888** JACOBI *Printers' Voc.*, *Gothic*, an antique character of type similar to black letter. **1895** W. A. COPINGER in *Trans. Bibl. Soc.* II. ii. 111 Gothic type was the first in use..Roman character not being introduced till 1467.

c. Applied in the U.S. to the type called in England GROTESQUE (also *sans-ceriph*, and, by some type-founders, *doric*; formerly *stone letter*).

6. In combination with an adjective formed on a proper name: Gothic and; Gothic in connection with; as ***Gothic-Finnish***, ***-Sarmatian***, ***-Scandinavian***.

1928 C. DAWSON *Age of Gods* iv. 84 The Gothic-Sarmatian kingdom from the Crimea to the lower Danube. **1931** A. SENN in *Jrnl. Eng. & Germ. Philol.* XXX. 143 *(title)* A contribution to Gothic-Finnish relations. **1965** *Language* XLI. 36 The theory of a Gothic-Scandinavian linguistic community distinct from the West Germanic languages.

B. quasi-*sb.* or *sb.*

That which is Gothic. **a.** The Gothic language. **b.** A Gothic building. **c.** Gothic architecture or ornamentation.

1644 EVELYN *Diary* 27 Feb. The style of magnificence then in fashion, which was with too greate a mixture of the Gotic. **1726** LEONI *Alberti's Archit.* Life 4 Ornaments, which..have I know not what in them of Gothick. **1757** SERENIUS *Eng. & Swed. Dict.* (ed. 2) Pref. 2 There are very few that have professedly treated the ancient Gothick. **1762–5** H. WALPOLE *Vertue's Anecd. Paint.* (ed. 2) I. 116 Imitations of the Gothic. *Ibid.* 120 The builders of Gothic. **1825** LOCKHART in *Scott's Fam. Lett.* (1894) II. 308 Then to ..the Castle Chapel—the best by far of all modern Gothics. **1841** LEVER *C. O'Malley* lxxxii. 395 Gazing steadfastly on the fretted gothic of the ceiling. **1858** MAX MÜLLER *Chips* (1880) II. xx. 192 Gothic, as a language, is more ancient than Icelandic. **1915** *Irish Eccl. Record* July 50 Some of these new Gothics were designed by a priest. **1916** *Ibid.* Sept. 209 The fine old walls..gave place to the Gothics.

Hence **Go'thicity**, the quality of being Gothic; **'Gothicky** *a. colloq.*, Gothic-like; †**'Gothicly** *adv.*, in a Gothic manner, barbarously.

1777 W. DALRYMPLE *Trav. Sp. & Port.* xl, The apartments are low..and Gothicly furnished. **1863** *Ecclesiologist* XXIV. 290 The absolute Gothicity of the general idea. **1889** *Athenæum* 16 Feb. 221/1 The crisp, sharp, and firm 'Gothicity' of the direct followers of the Van Eycks. **1893** KATE WIGGIN *Cathedral Courtship* 36 She's going to build a Gothicky memorial chapel somewhere.

†**'Gothical**, *a. Obs.* [f. GOTHIC *a.* + -AL[1].] Gothic.

1612–20 SHELTON *Quix.* I. IV. xv. (1675) 136 Scrolles of Parchment, written with Gothical Characters, but containing Castilian verses.

Gothically ('gɒθɪkəlɪ), *adv.* [f. prec. + -LY[2].] In a manner resembling what is Gothic, in any sense of the adj.

1854 ROSSETTI *Let.* in *Atlantic Monthly* May (1896) 593/2 The words 'Poems by a Painter' printed very gothically indeed. **1876** S. COLVIN *Flaxman's Drawings* 32 He can appreciate and copy Gothic art when he sees it, but he cannot create Gothically. **1885** *Pall Mall G.* 8 Sept. 4/2 A bristling cat with her back gothically arched.

Gothicism ('gɒθɪsɪz(ə)m). [f. GOTHIC *a.* + -ISM.]

1. Rudeness, barbarism; absence of polish or taste; an instance of this.

1710 SHAFTESB. *Charac.* (1727) I. III. 221–2 Barbarity and Gothicism were already enter'd into Arts, ere the Savages had made any Impression on the Empire. **1753** H. WALPOLE *Let. to Gray* 20 Feb., Were I to print any thing with my name, it should be plain Horace Walpole; *Mr.* is one of the Gothicisms I abominate. **1769** J. STRANGE *Acc. Rom. Antiq.* in *Archæologia* (1770) I. 295 Precision in all their works.. distinguishes them [Roman works] from the unmeaning strokes of Gothicism. **1823** J. BADCOCK *Dom. Amusem.* 48 The Oriental gothicism practised by the printers of silk and other handkerchiefs, which now disgrace the national taste. **1823** *New Monthly Mag.* VII. 28 Visiting the galleries and palaces of Rome, I felt an itching to put my Gothicisms on paper. **1828** [J. R. BEST] *Italy as it is* 144 After a long night of tasteless Gothicism.

2. Conformity or devotion to the Gothic style of architecture.

1754 GRAY *Wks.* (1825) 181 Strawberry-Castle..has a purity and propriety of gothicism in it..that I have not seen elsewhere. **1796** MORSE *Amer. Geog.* II. 431 They seem to have lost their ancient taste for gothicism and architecture, and to be returning to Gothicism. **1805** WHITAKER *Hist. Craven* 431 A puerile affectation of what is called Gothicism. **1953** *Archit. Rev.* CXIII. 123/3 The Gothic motifs of Wollaton rightly registered as Gothicism, that is revival and not survival.

3. a. The study of the Gothic language. **b.** Conformity to Teutonic notions. (Cf. GOTHIC *a.* 2.) **c.** A Gothic idiom.

a. 1806 CHALMERS *Exam. Lang. Lyndsay* Wks. I. 160 The singular use of *qu*, and *quh*, which appear, frequently, in Lyndsay..Mr. Sibbald..in his zeal for Gothicism, has endeavoured to derive from an unknown character (⊙) in the Gothic Gospels of Ulphilas.

b. 1847 EMERSON *Repr. Men, Swedenborg* Wks. (Bohn) I. 326 The book had been grand, if the Hebraism had been omitted, and the law stated without Gothicism.

c. 1818 in TODD (with quot. 1806 as example); and in later Dicts.

So **'Gothicist**, one who affects or is conversant with the Gothic style, esp. in architecture.

1861 *Illustr. Lond. News* 13 July 34/1 The Gothicists had no hope of establishing their principle. **1879** SIR G. SCOTT *Recoll.* vii. 321, I so inspired my fellow-pupil, though not much of a gothicist, that he walked there [S. Albans]. **1891** *Athenæum* 15 Aug. 230/3 The craftsmanship of Clovio has never excited the admiration of artists to anything like the same degree as the..illuminations of the Gothic miniaturists, although..the technique of the Gothicists is not for a moment to be compared with Giulio's.

Gothicize ('gɒθɪsaɪz), *v.* [f. GOTHIC *a.* + -IZE.]

†**1.** *intr.* To indulge one's taste for what is 'Gothic' or mediæval. *Obs.*[−1]

1750 H. WALPOLE *Let. H. Mann* 1 Sept. (1833) II. 385 Mr. Whithed has been so unlucky to have a large part of his seat..burnt down; it is a great disappointment to me, too, who was going thither gothicizing.

2. *trans.* **a.** To give a 'Gothic' or mediæval look or character to; to render mediæval.

1808 *Advt. to Strutt's Queen-Hoo Hall* p. iv, The language and manners of the higher ranks are not gothicized. **1843** *Fraser's Mag.* XXVIII. 16 He had early begun to Gothicise it—to stock it with rusty armour and painted glass. **1852** HAWTHORNE *Wonder-Bk., Tanglewood Fire-side* (1879) 148 Your imagination..will inevitably Gothicize everything you touch. **1870** —— *Eng. Note-Bks.* (1879) I. 82 The statue ..was overgrown..with moss and lichens, so that its classic beauty was in some sort gothicized. **1881** SALA in *Illustr. Lond. News* 15 Jan. 51 Garments so Gothicised as to give them a vague resemblance to English matrons and damsels of the 14th and 15th centuries.

b. To give an architecturally Gothic character to; to transform after a Gothic type.

1798 ANNA SEWARD *Let.* 2 Oct. (1811) V. 155 The tenements are to be gothicized. **1821** LAMB *Elia* Ser. I. *Old Benchers I.T.*, They have lately gothicised the entrance to the Inner Temple-hall and the library front. **1824** in Willis & Clark *Cambridge* (1886) I. 565 That..the Provost be hereby authorized..to Gothicise Gibbs's Building. **1851** RUSKIN *Stones Ven.* (1874) I. xiv. 160 Arabic forms of parapet, more or less Gothicised. **1877** J. C. COX *Ch. Derbysh.* II. 349 A pointed east window [was] inserted, and the windows on the South side 'Gothicised.'

Hence **'Gothicized** *ppl. a.* Also **'Gothicizer**, one who Gothicizes.

1804 *Ann. Reg.* 828 Gothicised cottages. **1827** SCOTT *Jrnl.* 3 Oct., The gingerbread taste of modern Gothicisers. **1842** *Blackw. Mag.* LI. 392 Those gothicized severities of the German school.

Gothicness ('gɒθɪknɪs). [f. GOTHIC *a.* + -NESS.] The quality or condition of being Gothic; an instance of this. Also *concr.*, a piece of Gothic ornamentation.

1853 RUSKIN *Stones Ven.* II. vi, Gothicness,—the character which, according as it is found more or less in a building, makes it more or less Gothic. **1872** *Sacristy* II. 5 In these days..'Gothicness' is the sole test of ecclesiastical propriety. **1874** MICKLETHWAITE *Mod. Par. Churches* 175 Projecting canopies and such-like unquiet Gothicnesses.

Gothiglacial (gɒθɪ'gleɪʃɪəl, -ʃəl, -'gleɪsɪəl), *a. Geol.* Also **Gotiglacial** (gɒtɪ-). [f. L. *Gothi-a* country of the Goths + GLACIAL *a.*] Epithet of the second of the three divisions or 'sub-epochs' of the Late Glacial epoch in north-western Europe, when the ice-sheet of the last glaciation retreated from the tip of the Scandinavian peninsula across southern Sweden. Also *absol.* Cf. DANIGLACIAL, FINIGLACIAL *adjs.*

1910 G. DE GEER in *Geologiska Föreningens i Stockholm Förhandlingar* XXXII. 1146 It seems appropriate to designate as *gothiglacial* that part of the late glacial epoch during which the ice-border receded through Götaland—the old Gothia—from Skåne to the great moraines, crossing its northernmost provinces, Dalsland, Västergötland, and Östergötland. **1912** —— in *Compt. Rend. XI Congr. Géol. Internat.* I. 249 Already now I consider it possible to state that we are on the safe side assuming the whole goti-glacial sub-epoch, or the time of the ice-recession from the central parts of Skåne past the old Gotia to the Fennoskandian moraines, almost to amount to, but probably not to exceed 3000 years. **1923**, **1927** [see DANIGLACIAL *a.*]. **1957** J. K. CHARLESWORTH *Quaternary Era* II. 1062 The Gotiglacial tundras of south Sweden. **1960** L. D. STAMP *Britain's Struct.* (ed. 5) xiv. 170 The Gothi-Glacial was the period of the retreat of the ice across southern Sweden and lasted from about 15,000 B.C. to 9,000 B.C.

‖**gothique** (gɔtik). *rare*[−1]. [F. *gothique*, ad. L. *gothicus* GOTHIC.] An antique style of binding.

1818 KEATS *Lett.* Wks. 1889 III. 150, I shall have it bound in Gothique—a nice sombre binding; it will go a little way to unmodernize.

Gothique, obs. form of GOTHIC.

Gothish ('gɒθɪʃ), *a.* Also 7 Gott(h)ish, Gotis(h. [f. GOTH + -ISH.]

1. †**a.** = GOTHIC *a.* 1 (*obs.*). **b.** Resembling what is Gothic; looking like a Goth.

1605 CAMDEN *Rem.* (1637) 51 To give some of them Roman names, to other Gotish names. **1612** BREREWOOD *Lang. & Relig.* vii. 59 The Spanish tongue, as now it is, consisteth of the old Spanish, Latin, Gottish, and Arabick. **1643** PRYNNE *Sov. Power Parl.* App. 58 The Nobility of the Gothish Nation. **1681** COLVIL *Whigs Supplic.* (1751) 49 Great tribulation Follows a Gothish inundation. **1697** tr. *C'tess D'Aunoy's Trav.* (1706) 62 Finding no more among them any Princes of the Race of the Gothish Kings. **1728** MORGAN *Algiers* I. iv. 160 Count Julian, Governor of the Gothish Dominions in Hispania Transfretane. **1830** *Fraser's Mag.* I. 164 What would that..dandy of his age have thought of such worse than Gothish and Hunnish figures?

2. Goth-like, barbarous, tasteless; cf. GOTHIC 4.

1602 *Metam. Tabacco* (Collier) 46 Gotthish Spaniards.. farre more sauage then the Sauages. **1667** WATERHOUSE *Fire Lond.* 66 This late harrass of us by a more than Gottish and Vandalique fire. **1827** *Mirror* II. 36/2 My tyes are regular Gothish. **1863** LD. LENNOX *Biogr. Remin.* II. 145 The flint or M'Adam system..which he pronounces to be quite gothish. **1880** *World* 10 Nov. 10/2 The scenery of the place [Torquay] has been quite spoilt..by Gothish 'improvements'.

†**3.** = GOTHIC 3. *Obs.*

1655 FULLER *Waltham Abbey* 6 A structure of Gothish-building, rather large then neate, firm then fair. **1662** GERBIER *Princ.* 4 Contrary to the very Gothish Custome, who at least did begin their Buttrises from the Ground. **1663** —— *Counsel* d 3 a, The reformation of a Gotis relick building.

Gothism ('gɒθɪz(ə)m). [f. GOTH + -ISM.] Barbarism, bad taste.

1715 M. DAVIES *Athen. Brit.* I. 295 Gothisms and Gallicisms in Religion, as well as in Words. **1827** *Mirror* II. 274/2 Doffing a castor is considered the height of vandalism or Gothism. **1887** *Pall Mall G.* 6 Jan. 6/2 The particular act of Gothism or Vandalism..is the construction of a new road just beyond the 'Spaniards'.

Gothonic (gə'θɒnɪk), *a.* and *sb.* Also †**Gotthonic**. [ad. L. *Gothōn-es* Goths + -IC.] A name introduced by Dr. Gudmund Schütte to include all early Germanic and Scandinavian peoples. **A.** *adj.* Of or belonging to the primitive Germanic stock. **B.** *sb.* The common language of this stock.

1912 G. SCHÜTTE in *Soc. Advancem. Scand. Study, Proc. Ser.* Dec. 93 To avoid ambiguity I have adopted the classical form 'Guttones, Gothones', and from it formed the adjective 'Gotthonic'. **1922** O. JESPERSEN *Lang.* 42 What is now ordinarily called Germanic and which is in this work called Gothonic. *Ibid.* 195 There is a wide gulf between Keltic and Gothonic. *Ibid.*, The oldest Gothonic languages. **1929** J. YOUNG tr. *Schütte's Our Forefathers* p. x, I call our forefathers 'Gothonic nations' so as to avoid the ambiguity attending all the synonyms now in use, both 'Goths', 'Teutons' and 'Germanic nations'. *Ibid.* vi. 152 Long words formed by derivation are at hand even in the oldest recorded Gothonic. **1948** PARTRIDGE *World of Words* (ed. 2) 77 The Teutonic (or Germanic or, better, Gothonic) languages.

gothsemay, gothsimere, obs. ff. GOSSAMER.

Gotic, Gotiq(ue, obs. forms of GOTHIC.

Gotiglacial, var. GOTHIGLACIAL *a.*

gotire, Gotis(h, obs. ff. GUITAR, GOTHISH.

Gotlandian, Gothlandian (gɒt-, gɒθ'lændɪən), *a. Geol.* [ad. F. *gothlandien* (A. de Lapparent *Traité de Géol.* (ed. 3, 1893) II. II. ii. 748), f. *Got-*, *Gothland*, name of an island in the Baltic + -IAN.] Of or pertaining to the geological system between the Ordovician and the Devonian or to the geological period during which it was deposited. Also *absol.* Cf. SILURIAN *a.* and *sb.*[1] 2.

1909 *Cent. Dict.* Suppl. I, *Gothlandian*, noting the uppermost division of the Silurian system of Murchison. **1914** *Proc. Geol. Assoc.* XXV. 213 In northern Gotland reef-formations play a predominant part at certain horizons of both lower and upper Gotlandian age. **1955** G. G. WOODFORD tr. *Gignoux's Stratigr. Geol.* iii. 87 At the beginning of the Gothlandian, the shaly facies seem to have invaded several domains. *Ibid.* 99 At the present time, many British geologists prefer not to use the term Gothlandian, which they deem not precise enough. They replace it by that of Silurian, used in a restricted sense.

go-to, *sb. rare.* [f. phrase (*to*) *go to*: see GO *v.*] ***at one go-to*** = at one GO-OFF.

1853 G. J. CAYLEY *Las Alforjas* I. 132 My letter is getting into the 'own correspondent' style; but I am tired with writing it all at one go-to.

go-to-meeting, *a.* and *sb. colloq.* (orig. *U.S.*). [See GO *v.* VIII.] **A.** *adj.* **a.** Suitable for use on Sundays or at church; *spec.* of clothes: suitable for wearing to church. Cf. *Sunday-go-to-meeting* (SUNDAY *sb.* 1 c). †**b.** Of people: church-going (*obs.*).

1790 R. TYLER *Contrast* III. i, All my tunes [are] go to meeting tunes. **1800** T. G. FESSENDEN *Orig. Poems* (1806) 115 Each scrapes, huzzas, and kicks and bounces, Waves high her go-to-meeting cap. **1835** HALIBURTON *Clockm.* Ser. I. ix, One of those blue-noses, with his go-to-meetin clothes on. **1853** *Harper's Mag.* VII. 562/2 He was looked up to with emulation.. by the 'go-to-meeting' young folk of the town. **1857** HUGHES *Tom Brown* II. v, I want to give you a true picture.. not a kid-glove and go-to-meeting-coat picture. **1868** G. G. CHANNING *Early Recoll. Newport, R.I.* 83, I was quite a go-to-meeting lad. **1870** MISS BROUGHTON *Red as Rose* I. 120 Very few men look their best in their Go-to-Meeting clothes. **1933** O. JESPERSEN *Essentials Eng. Gram.* vii. 74 A *run-away* match, *go-to-meeting* clothes, etc. **1937** C. M. WILSON *Aroostook* 41 A final rinsing for Sunday shirts and go-to-meeting dresses.

†**B.** *sb.* A go-to-meeting garment; usu. *pl. Obs.*

[**1831** *Boston Transcript* 12 Dec. 1/1 They tossed on their 'Sunday-go-to-meetings', and crossed into Jarsey.] **1841** *Chicago Morning Democrat* 26 Feb. 2/1 Their Servant's a regular 'Miss Nancy with her go-to-meetings on'. **1878** R. T. COOKE *Happy Dodd* 70 She didn't never have more'n one caliker gown to her name, an' an old alipacky for a go-to-meeting. **1881** —— *Somebody's Neighbors* 265 He was gone and his shirt an' go-to-meetin's too.

†**gotour.** *Obs.* [? ad. OF. *goutture*, f. *goutte* drop.] ? Running matter from a sore.

14.. *MS. Linc. Med.* lf. 313 (Halliw.) Tak the rutes of morelle.. and lay thame to the fester.. and ever clence it wele of gotours, and wasche it with hate wyne.

gotows, variant of GOUTOUS *Obs.*, gouty.

‖**gotra** ('gəʊtrə). [Skr. *gotrá*.] (See quots.)

1877 M. MONIER-WILLIAMS *Hinduism* xi. 160 All tribes of Brāhmins are divided into *Gotras* or groups of families, according as they are supposed to be derived from one or other of the seven mythical sages. **1902** *Encycl. Brit.* XXIX. 283/2 Members of the three higher castes [of Hindus] are forbidden to marry a woman of the same *gotra* as themselves. Literally a *gotra* means a cattle-yard. **1938** *Nature* 19 Feb. 310/1 The disappearance of totems in favour of gotras of Puranic heroes. **1971** *Illustr. Weekly India* 4 Apr. 9/2 The whole tribe is divided into a certain number of *gotras*, after the name of their patriarchs.

gotsch, variant of GOTCH *dial.*

gott, obs. form of GOTE, GUT.

gotta ('gɒtə), a representation of the colloq. or vulgar pronunciation of (*have*) *got a* or (*have*) *got to* (see GET *v.* 24).

1924 J. BUCHAN *Three Hostages* xviii. 263 He.. went forward as if to take her arm. 'You gotta come along,' I heard. **1929** E. W. SPRINGS *Above Bright Blue Sky* 176 'That oughta be easy,' the sergeant suggested. 'You gotta couple of new pilots that could crash an ice wagon on a prairie.' **1932** T. S. ELIOT *Sweeney Agonistes* 29 But I've gotta use words when I talk to you. **1955** M. HASTINGS *Cork & Serpent* xiv. 210, I gotta little present for you. **1968** A. DIMENT *Gt. Spy Race* iii. 35 Sorry, can't stay, gotta rush.

gotten ('gɒt(ə)n), *ppl. a.* Forms: see GET *v.*; also GOT *ppl. a.* [pa. pple. of GET *v.*]

1. Obtained, acquired, won (chiefly with accompanying adverb). Now *rare*, exc. in ILL-GOTTEN.

c **1340** *Cursor M.* 4913 (Trin.) We haue wiþ vs trussed nouȝt But þing þat we truly bouȝt And so is oure trewe geten þing. *c* **1380** WYCLIF *Sel. Wks.* III. 302 Sathanas.. to whom þei maken sacrifice and omage for þis falsly geten lordischip. **1477** EARL RIVERS (Caxton) *Dictes* 64 Pouertee is better than euyl goten richesse. **1548** HALL *Chron., Edw. IV*, 231 The gain of the nyne gotten battailes. **1580** SIDNEY *Ps.* x. iii, This gotten blisse, shall never part. **1603** KNOLLES *Hist. Turks* (1621) 59 Three or foure yeeres passed in great quietnesse, to the great strengthening of him in those new gotten kingdomes. **1665** MANLEY *Grotius' Low C. Warres* 265 They should not endanger their gotten Honour. **1715–20** POPE *Iliad* x. 596 Haste to the ships, the gotten spoil enjoy. **1820** CHALMERS *Congreg. Serm.* (1838) II. 54 He is apt to be satisfied with the triumphs of his gotten victory. **1894** GLADSTONE *Horace's Odes* 36 On gotten goods to live Contented.

†**2.** = BEGOTTEN 2. *Obs.*

c **1400** *Gamelyn* 365 Of my body heire geten haue I none. *c* **1410** LOVE *Bonavent. Mirr.* vi. (Gibbs MS.), His furst geten sone. *a* **1637** B. JONSON *Elegy on Lady Digby*, Iesus, the only gotten Christ!

3. gotten-up = *got-up* (GOT *ppl. a.* b). *U.S.*

1931 O. NASH *Hard Lines* 47 In a tastily gotten-up flat.

gotter, obs. form of GUTTER.

‖**Götterdämmerung** (gœtər'dɛmərʊŋ). [G., lit. twilight of the gods.] Used *fig.* to denote the complete downfall of a régime, institution, etc.

Popularized by Wagner's use of it as the title of the last opera of the Ring cycle.

1909 C. F. G. MASTERMAN *Condition of Eng.* x. 293 Mr. Wells requires for his *Götterdämmerung* no fresh influx of barbarian hordes. **1930** G. B. SHAW *Perfect Wagnerite* 169 What would he [*sc.* Wagner] have said had he lived to see 1917 in Russia and 1918 in Germany.. such a Götterdämmerung. **1934** *Mind* XLIII. 388 If.. Dr Inge should chance upon a plain unsophisticated Christian, and try to scare him with his Thermodynamic *Götterdämmerung*, would he not be told that the Heavenly Jerusalem was incomparably preferable to the Palestinian, in which there were no abiding habitations? **1949** KOESTLER *Promise & Fulfilment* xv. 170 The Götterdämmerung of British rule in the Holy Land was not in the Wagnerian, but rather in the Dostoievskian style. **1959** *Listener* 1 Oct. 525/1 A totalitarian régime must either prevail absolutely or else it heads straight for some kind of Götterdämmerung.

Gott(h)ish, obs. form of GOTHISH.

gottic, obs. form of GOTHIC.

†**gottling.** *Obs.*[−1] [? f. GOTCH + -LING.] ? A small jug.

1535 *Richmond. Wills* (Surtees) 12, ij panns with a gottling xiij[d].

gotur, obs. form of GUTTER.

gou-: see GOV-.

‖**gouache** (guː'ɑːʃ, gwaʃ). [Fr., ad. It. *guazzo*.] A method of painting with opaque colours ground in water, and mixed with gum and honey so as to form a sort of paste. Also, a painting executed in this way, and the pigment itself.

1882 *Artist* 12 Feb. 53/2 The next step was the exact reproduction of gouache, or water body colour. **1892** *Nation* 13 Oct. 279/2 The title is decorated with allegorical designs painted in gouache.

gouan, obs. form of GOWAN.

goubeyron, obs. form of COB-IRON.

1572 *Richmond. Wills* (Surtees) 152.

gouchf, variant of GOFE *Sc. Obs.*, pillory.

goud, Sc. form of GOLD.

Gouda ('gaʊdə). In full *Gouda cheese*. A flat round cheese orig. made at Gouda in Holland.

1885, 1890, 1902 [see EDAM]. **1902** J. T. LAW *Grocer's Man.* (ed. 2) 326/1 Derbyshire Cheese... One variety is shaped like Gouda cheese, and known as 'Derby Goudas'. *Ibid.* 429/1 Factory Goudas are usually made of skimmed milk in Friesland. **1955** J. G. DAVIS *Dict. Dairying* (ed. 2) 195 *Gouda cheese.* This is a Dutch cheese made from the whole milk of cows. **1971** *Sunday Times* (Colour Suppl.) 28 Mar. 39/1 Gouda, which is made of whole milk, is less soapy [than Edam] and improves remarkably with age when the flesh which is straw yellow in immaturity deepens to a pale mahogany.

goudge, obs. form of GOUGE *sb.*[1]

goudie, gowdie. *Sc.* 'An office-bearer of an incorporation who keeps one of the keys of the Box; also, the name of the office' (Jamieson *Supp.* Add.).

1857 A. WALLACE *Gloaming of Life* iii. (1875) 60 The still more important honours of a 'gowdie' were conferred, in the permission which was then granted to 'snuff the candles and keep the keys'. **18..** *Rules & Regul. Cordiners Glasgow* 3 (Jam. *Supp.* Add.) A Trade's Goudie or keeper of a key of the Box, from among the nine Masters, to hold office for one year.

Goudy ('gaʊdɪ). The name of F. W. *Goudy* (1865–1947), American typographer, used *attrib.* to designate type-faces designed and made by him.

1933 D. L. SAYERS *Murder must Advertise* viii. 132 Re-set in Goudy Bold. **1960** G. A. GLAISTER *Gloss. Bk.* 158/1 Among the more important of the hundred or so types he designed are Village, 1903,.. the old-face Goudy family, 1921. **1962** D. B. UPDIKE *Printing Types* (ed. 3) II. xxiii. 237 For lines set in capital letters on covers and in title-pages, the Goudy Old Style roman capitals are good.

gouf (gɒʊf), *v. Sc.* [? f. ON. *gólf*: see GOAF[1].] *trans.* 'To remove soft earth from under (a structure), substituting sods cut square and built regularly; to underpin' (Ogilvie 1882).

1859 GWILT *Encycl. Archit.* Gloss., *Goufing foundations*, a Scotch term for securing unsound walls by driving wedges or pins under their foundations.

†**goufe.** *Sc. Obs.*[−1] [ad. OF. *goulfe* (F. *golfe*) gulf.] A whirlpool.

1596 DALRYMPLE tr. *Leslie's Hist. Scot.* I. 59 Gret goufes ful of perrellous and deip.

†**gouffre.** *Obs.*[−1] [a. F. *gouffre* gulf.] = GULF.

c **1477** CAXTON *Jason* 117 Argos the goode Maistre saylled so ferre by gouffres and by flotes.

gouge (gaʊdʒ, guːdʒ), *sb.*[1] Also 5 goodg, gow(d)ge, (gourge), 7 goudge. [a. F. *gouge* fem., = Sp. *gúbia*, Pg. *goiva*, It. *gubbia*, *gorbia*:—late L. *gubia*, *gulbia* (Isidore).

Prob. of Celtic origin; cf. OIrish *gulban* ('aculeum'), *gulba* ('rostrum'), OWelsh *gilbin* ('acumine'), mod.Welsh *gylf* beak, Cornish *gilb* boring tool ('foratorium').]

1. A chisel with a concave blade for cutting rounded grooves or holes in wood. In *Surgery*, a similarly-shaped tool used for removing portions of bone, etc.

1495–8 *Naval Acc.* (1896) 240 An yron Goodg with a bolte of yron belongyng to the same. **15..** *Debate Carpenter's Tools* 179 in Hazl. *E.P.P.* I. 85 The gowge seyd: The devyles dyrte Fore anything that thou canne wyrke. **1576** *Richmond. Wills* (Surtees) 261, ij playnes, towe gourges, ij chesells, and ij embowing playnes. **1607** TOPSELL *Four-f. Beasts* (1658) 283 Take a round strong iron toole, half a yard long, and made at the one end in all points like unto the Carpenters gouge. **1676** WORLIDGE *Cyder* (1691) 58 With your quill in form of a goudge. **1678** MOXON *Mech. Exerc.* I. 74 The Gouge.. is a Chissel having a round edge, for the cutting such wood as is to be Rounded or Hollowed. **1807–26** S. COOPER *First Lines Surg.* (ed. 5) 318 If with this instrument he could not remove bone enough, he scrupled not to effect his design by means of a gouge and mallet. **1825** J. NICHOLSON *Operat. Mechanic* 327 To answer the purpose of the common turning gouge. **1885** G. ALLEN *Babylon* ix, Colin.. took up a gouge as if to continue carving the panel.

†**b.** *trenching gouge*: a spade with a concave blade. *Obs.*

1649 BLITHE *Eng. Improv. Impr.* (1653) 69 The Trenching gouge to be vsed as the Spade.

c. A stamping tool for cutting out forms in leather, paper, etc.

1875 in KNIGHT *Dict. Mech.*

d. *Bookbinding.* (See quot. 1895.)

1885 CRANE *Bookbinding for Amateurs* 159 Fig. 135 represents a set of gouges. **1895** ZAEHNSDORF *Hist. Bookbinding* 24 *Gouge*, a curved line or segment of a circle impressed upon the leather. Also the instrument with which it is impressed.

e. *Comb.* **gouge-bit,** a bit shaped at the end like a gouge.

1794 *Rigging & Seamanship* I. 151 *Gouge bit*, a bit smaller than a centre-bit, with a hollow edge at its end like a gouge. **1812–16** J. SMITH *Panorama Sci. & Art* I. 115 The gouge-bit is best adapted for boring small holes in soft wood. **1882** *Rep. to Ho. Repr. Prec. Met. U.S.* 581 A double-gouge bit is used with this machine.

2. *Mining.* (See quot. 1881.)

1877 RAYMOND *Statist. Mines & Mining* 107 It is incased in well-defined walls of metamorphic slate, with a few inches of gouge between the walls and quartz. **1881** —— *Mining Gloss.*, *Gouge*, a layer of soft material along the wall of a vein, favoring the miner, by enabling him after 'gouging' it out with a pick, to attack the solid vein from the side.

3. *U.S. colloq.* **a.** The action of the vb. GOUGE; a scooping out. **b.** A cheat, swindle (cf. GOUGE *v.* 4). 'Also, an impostor' (*Cent. Dict.*).

1845 *N.Y. Tribune* 10 Dec. (Bartlett), This is a clean, plain gouge of this sum out of the people's strong box. **1887** *American* XIV. 344 Another 'gouge' was to charge the women a nominally cost price.. while, as a matter of fact, it was got.. for considerably less.

†**gouge,** *sb.*[2] *Obs.* [a. OF. *gouge*.] A wench.

1828 SCOTT *F.M. Perth* xii, The gouge knows her trade.

gouge (gaʊdʒ, guːdʒ), *v.* Also 6–7 googe, 9 *dial.* gowge. [f. GOUGE *sb.*[1]]

1. a. *trans.* To cut or make holes in, with or as with a gouge.

1570 ABP. PARKER *Let. to Sir W. Cecil* 1 Apr., Corr. (1853) 364 *Quidam filii Beliall* did gouge my poor barge in divers places in the bottom. **1599** M[OUFET] *Silkwormes* 14 As water doth, when pipes of lead or wood are goog'd with punch. **1864** *Daily Tel.* 11 Aug., Great sheets of solid metal .. are gouged and drilled into ragged holes. **1876** CURLING *Dis. Rectum* 107 Unless the surgeon can reach the diseased bone, and, if necessary, gouge it.

b. *intr.* To work with a gouge *at* (something).

1860 *All Year Round* No. 46. 459 An engraver working a little lathe with a sort of fiddlestick, while he gouged delicately at the cornelian signet.

2. *trans.* To cut *out* (a cork), to hollow or scoop *out* (a channel or groove) with or as with a gouge. Also, to hollow *into* (a certain form).

1616 B. JONSON *Devil an Ass* II. i, I will save in cork.. by googing of them out Just to the size of my bottles, and not slicing. **1750** G. HUGHES *Barbadoes* 197 These are succeeded by pods which are lengthways neatly gouged into seven regular channels. **1794** *Rigging & Seamanship* I. 154 The scores.. are gouged out along the outsides. *c* **1850** *Rudim. Navig.* (Weale) 106 It.. is gouged hollow. **1873** J. GEIKIE *Gt. Ice Age* xxiv. 315 Under the influence of rain.. rills and brooklets are gouging out deep trenches in the subsoils and solid rocks.

3. a. To cut or force out with or as with a gouge; to push out (a person's eye) with the thumb. Chiefly with *out* adv. Const. *out of*.

1800 ADDISON *Amer. Law Rep.* 29 M'Birnie.. gouged his eye. **1829** MARRYAT *F. Mildmay* xxi, He had gouged the eye out of a third. **1853** W. IRVING *Life & Lett.* (1864) IV. 129 A pursar of the navy had gouged the bolt out of the wall. **1871** R. ELLIS tr. *Catullus* cviii. 5 Gouged be the carrion eyes some crow's black maw to replenish. **1879** *St. George's Hosp. Rep.* IX. 379 As much as possible of the deep portion was gouged out.

fig. **1815** SOUTHEY *Lett.* (1856) II. 393 If there be a felicitous phrase, he is sure to gouge the sentence. **1845** *N.Y. Tribune* 26 Nov. (Farmer), Very well gentlemen! gouge Mr. C. out of the seat, if you think it wholesome to do it.

b. To force out the eye of (a person). Also *absol.*

1785 GROSE *Dict. Vulg. Tongue*, *Gouge*, to squeeze out a man's eye with the thumb, a cruel practice used by the Bostonians in America. **1796** T. TWINING *Trav. Amer.* (1894) 91 In their common affrays they gouge and commit other barbarities. **1812** COLERIDGE *Lit. Rem.* I. 286 Do they act on the principle that it is prudent to secure the result of the contest by gouging the adversary? **1827** *Blackw. Mag.* Oct. 453/1 When they had gotten him on his back, one gouged him like a Yankee. **1861** DICKENS *Gt. Expect.* xviii, Joe scooped his eyes.. as if he were bent on gouging himself.

4. *U.S.* To cheat, impose upon. Also *absol.*

1875 HOWELLS *Foregone Concl.* iii. (1882) 69 The man's a perfect Jew—or a perfect Christian, one ought to say in Venice; we true believers do gouge so much more infamously here. **1885** B. HARTE *Ship of '49* i, He's regularly gouged me in that ere horsehair spekilation.

5. *Mining.* (See quots. 1964, 1971.) Also more generally, to dig for opal (cf. GOUGING *vbl. sb.*).

1931 M. S. BUCHANAN *Prospecting for Opal in Australia* 8 Gouge your drive, viz., push a cut under the roof searching after the seam of potch. **1936** A. RUSSELL *Gone Nomad* i. 7 In chasing my rainbow I have.. delved for gold; 'gouged' for opal; fossicked for diamonds. **1958** M. D. BERRINGTON *Stones of Fire* 27 We'll gouge.. to start with; and when we strike something we can drive properly. **1964** A. NELSON *Dict. Mining* 202 *Gouging*, working only the rich pockets of ore and leaving the low-grade or marginal ore unmined. **1971** J. S. GUNN *Opal Terminol.* 21 *Gouge*, to cut carefully under the roof searching for a seam of potch [*i.e.* worthless opaliferous material] so that full-scale cutting of the drive can begin.

gou'gee. *nonce-wd.* [f. GOUGE *v.* + -EE[1].] A victim of gouging.
1814 [see GOUGER].

gougeon, obs. form of GUDGEON.

gouger ('gaʊdʒə(r), 'gu:dʒə(r)). [f. GOUGE *v.* + -ER[1].] One who gouges. **a.** One who thrusts out an antagonist's eye. **b.** One who cheats, a swindler.
1814 *Q. Rev.* X. 522 Whenever American sculpture shall exhibit..a combat between two Virginian athletæ, the gouger and the gougee must [etc.]. **1826** T. FLINT *Recoll. Mississippi* 176 It is true there are gamblers and gougers and outlaws. **1840** HALIBURTON *Clockm.* Ser. III. ix, Regular built bruisers too; claw your eyes right out, like a Carolina gouger.
c. *Austral.* An opal-digger. Also, less commonly, a miner seeking other minerals, e.g. copper. Cf. *opal-gouger*.
1898 *Barrier Weekly Post* 17 Sept. 13 The reason assigned for the absence of the 'gouger' from this hill is the extreme hardness of the ground not altogether the absence of opal. **1936** I. L. IDRIESS *Cattle King* xiii. 112 The silver gougers relied for their supplies on bullock-teams from Menindee. **1936** A. RUSSELL *Gone Nomad* vii. 58 Immature opal..was only too often..the usual portion of the gouger. **1937** *Discovery* June 185/2 All their worldly wealth was their copper gouger's outfit. **1948** V. PALMER *Golconda* iii. 19 Leave that piddling hand-to-mouth work to the gougers! Real mining was a long-range business. **1960** *Times Rev. Industry* Mar. 96/3 Because the firm can handle only 650 tons of ore a year from North Queensland copper-gougers —miner-prospectors who rely on established mining companies to treat their ore—the gougers have invited Japanese mining companies to erect a treatment plant. **1968** *Sunday Mail* (Brisbane) 4 Aug. 30/8 Copper gougers were warned last week against southern speculators moving in on Mt. Isa.

gouging ('gaʊdʒɪŋ, 'gu:dʒɪŋ), *vbl. sb.* [f. GOUGE *v.* + -ING[1].] The action of the vb. GOUGE; esp. the action of thrusting out the eye of (a person); an instance of this.
1796 MORSE *Amer. Geog.* I. 654 It was called gouging, and was nothing more nor less than a man, when boxing, putting out the eye of his antagonist with his thumb. **1860** MRS. GASKELL *Life C. Bronte* 20 There were very frequently 'up and down fights'..sometimes with the horrid addition of Pawsing, and Gouging. **1862** DANA *Man. Geol.* 538 The groovings are (1) long straight, parallel lines..or broad scrapings, ploughings, and gougings of the surface. **1877** RAYMOND *Statist. Mines & Mining* 314 Excepting a little 'gouging' done by lessees, the Home Stake [a mine]..has been idle during the year. **1902** *Chambers's Jrnl.* Mar. 175/1 In the 'back blocks' of New South Wales opal is abundant and 'gouging'—the term given to opal-mining—is the chief pursuit of every man on the western side of the Darling River.
attrib. **1881** J. HOOKER in *Nature* No. 619. 444 Ramsay.. explained the formation of so many lake beds in mountain regions by the gouging action of glaciers. **1884** KNIGHT *Dict. Mech.* IV, *Gouging Forceps*,..a bone-gnawing forceps. **1897** *Geog. Jrnl.* IX. 300 This is due to the gouging and tossing action of the eddies [of a sand-shower]. **1971** J. S. GUNN *Opal Terminol.* 21 *Gouging-pick*, short-handled pick, central nosed at both ends of the head, which can be used in a confined space.

gouging, *ppl. a.* [f. GOUGE *v.* + -ING[2].] That practises gouging.
1796 *Gazette of U.S.* (N.Y.) 10 May (Th.), Brave Abraham..Dar'd tell them all..That gouging Gunn had challenged him. **1825** J. K. PAULDING *J. Bull in Amer.* i. 2, I also fully believed that the people were a bundling, gouging, drinking, spitting impious race.

‖**goujat** (guʒa). [a. F. *goujat.*] An army valet; a soldier's boy.
1776 H. WALPOLE in *Gibbon's Misc. Wks.* (1814) II. 158 Employing a goujat to defend the citadel, while the generals repose in their tents.

[**goujeer(s, goujere**, spurious ff. GOOD-YEAR.]

goujon. In sense 1, f. Louisiana Fr., and in sense 2 directly f. Fr.: see GUDGEON *sb.*[1]) **1.** ('gʊdʒən) = BASHAW 3, *Pylodictis olivaris.*
1883 *Nat. Mus. Bull.* No. 27, 491 *Leptops olivaris*..Mud Cat;..Goujon. **1888** [see BASHAW 3]. **1964** H. T. WALDEN *Familiar Freshwater Fishes Amer.* xiv. 201 The flathead catfish has acquired several local names, such as mud catfish, goujon, shovelhead, and yellow cat.
2. (gʊʒɔ̃) *Cookery. pl.* Narrow, deep-fried strips of fish, esp. sole (see quot. 1964).
1940 A. L. SIMON *Conc. Encycl. Gastron.* II. 102/1 *Goujons, En*, fillets of sole cut up in strips, floured and fried. **1964** L. JOYCE-COWEN *Million Menus* 49/a *Goujons de sole*.. cut into strips the size of your little finger..cook in oil and butter so that they look like the tiny Mediterranean fish Goujons. **1975** P. V. PRICE *Taste of Wine* vii. 133/2 *Goujons* (fried strips of sole) with lemon can take a less fine and even a coarse wine.

gouk, variant of GOWK.

gouked, -et, -it, obs. forms of GOWKED.

goul(e, var. GHOUL, GOWL; obs. f. GOOL, GULL.

goulan(d: see GOLLAN(D.

Goulard (gu:'lɑ:d). Also 9 golard. [From the name of Thomas *Goulard*, the French surgeon who first used it.] In full, ***Goulard's extract*** or ***Goulard water***: a solution of sub-acetate of lead, used as a lotion in cases of inflammation.
1806 *Sporting Mag.* XXVII. 65 He first takes the hot water, and having discoloured it with golard or starch, dashed with a little blue [etc.]. **1818** COLERIDGE *Lett.* II. 692, I can so far command myself as to check the intolerable itching by a weak mixture of goulard and rosewater. **1842** BARHAM *Ingol. Leg., Black Mousquetaire* ii. 76 Till her delicate fingers are charr'd With the Steer's opodeldoc, joint-oil, and goulard. *c* **1865** J. WYLDE in *Circ. Sci.* I. 380/1 'Goulard water'..is a weak solution of acetate of lead. **1876** *Trans. Clinical Soc.* IX. 122 Ankle was treated by perfect rest, with Goulard lotion, without effect.

goulash ('gu:lɑ:ʃ, -læʃ). Also goulasch, gulyas, etc. [Hung. *gulyás(hús)*, f. *gulyás* herdsman + *hús* meat.] **1.** A stew or ragout of meat and vegetables highly seasoned. Often called *Hungarian ragout.*
1866 CROWN PRINCESS OF PRUSSIA *Let.* 11 Sept. in R. Fulford *Your Dear Letter* (1971) 97, I have all their favourite dishes cooked..for them—goulash for the Hungarians, and polenta and macaroni for the Italians. **1900** F. B. & W. H. WORKMAN *Ice World Himálaya* 193 Irish stews and *goulasches*, composed of animal odds and ends. **1906** *Westm. Gaz.* 27 Sept. 5/1 The national Hungarian dishes of Gulyas, or ragout, and Paprikahuhn. **1915** WODEHOUSE *Something Fresh* viii, In his hour of affliction it soothed him to read of Hungarian Goulash and Escalloped Brains. **1929** E. LINKLATER *Poet's Pub* i, Sucking-pig, celery, and goulasch. **1958** W. BICKEL tr. *Hering's Dict. Cookery* 426 *Goulash*, a brown beef stew of Hungarian origin, prepared with beef, veal, lamb or pork or a mixture of all with plenty of sliced onions, paprika and other ingredients. **1963** R. CARRIER *Great Dishes of World* 160/1 Hungarian veal gulyas.
2. *Contract Bridge.* A re-deal of unshuffled cards after the hands have been thrown in without bidding.
1927 in E. V. Shepard *Correct Contract Bridge* (1930) 245 When all four players pass, no bid having been made, and the players desire to play a Goulash, the cards shall be redealt by the same dealer... No shuffling of any kind permitted. **1930** *Ibid.* 129 Each player arranges all the cards of a suit in sequence before a goulash deal. **1930** M. KERWIN *How to bid at Contract Bridge* xv. 47 In goulashes lies the greatest gambling element of Contract. **1959** REESE & DORMER *Bridge Players' Dict.* 108 For a goulash hand the cards..are dealt in a manner likely to produce freakish distribution. **1964** *Official Encycl. Bridge* 222/1 *Goulash*, a deal in which the cards are not shuffled, and are dealt five to each player for two circuits, and finally three to each player.

goule, early variant of JOWL.

gouler, variant of GAVELLER *Obs.*, usurer.
c **1380** *R. Brunne's Handl. Synne* 2415 (Dulwich MS.) Now wil I speke of gouleris.

goules, -ez, goulet, obs. ff. GULES, GULLET.

goulf(e, obs. form of GULF.

gouling, variant of GAVELLING *Obs.*, usury.
c **1380** *R. Brunne's Handl. Synne* 2465 (Dulwich MS.) Goulyng haþ a noþer maner.

goulis, obs. form of GULES.

goulp(e, obs. form of GULP.

‖**goum** (gum). Also Goum. [Fr., ad. Arab. *gūm*, dial. var. of *ḳaum* band, troop.] **1. a.** A group of North African tribesmen. **b.** A contingent of North African soldiers (in French service). **2.** Such a tribesman or soldier. So **goumier** (-je), a North African serving in a goum.
1845 *Times* 5 Nov. 5/1 Bou Maza left his dead on the field of battle, and retreated with his goum, composed of about 300 cavalry, without counting a great number of infantry. **1846** *Times* 10 Mar. 6/3 Captain Ducrot, with his Goums and a squadron of Spahis, was the first to overtake the fugitives. **1859** F. C. L. WRAXALL tr. *Mem. Robert-Houdin* II. vii. 185 The strange aspect the capital [of Algeria] assumed on the arrival of the *goums* of the Tell and the South. **1903** *Daily Chron.* 25 Feb. 9/2 Far more interesting, ..was the fantasia of the Goums... The five hundred horsemen assembled at the top of the course. **1907** *Westm. Gaz.* 28 Aug. 5/1 The goumiers are paid for their services, and..pillaging is a crime which is severely punished. **1908** *Ibid.* 17 Mar. 5/1 The first section of the new *goum* from Algeria. **1946** E. LINKLATER *Private Angelo* x. 114 A wild and huge array of tribesmen from the Atlas mountains.. known as Goums. **1955** *Times* 3 May 8/2 A band of 60 Algerian rebels on Sunday night surprised a detachment of 21 goumiers, or native auxiliary troops, in a forest guard post. **1961** B. FERGUSSON *Watery Maze* xii. 315 General Magnan, the French Commander, whose force comprised the 9th Colonial Division, 2,000 Moroccan *goums* and some French commandos. **1961** R. MAUGHAM *Slaves of Timbuktu* 207 In the back were two Goumiers attached to the Commandant's staff and an African servant. **1970** I. ORIGO *Images & Shadows* ix. 242 The Moroccan troops with the Fifth Army, the Goums, who had ransacked everything.

goume, goun, obs. forms of GUM, GOWN.

†**gound.** *Obs.* Forms: 1 gund, 3 gunde, 5 gownde, 7 gound. [OE. *gund* matter, pus, ? = Goth. *gund*, OHG. *gunt*. Cf. ME. *radegound*, REDGUM.] Foul matter, esp. that secreted in the eye.
c **1000** *Sax. Leechd.* II. 46 [Swelling in the neck] Gif se gund biþ þonne onginnende, sio sealf hine todrifþ. *c* **1325** *Gloss. W. de Biblesw.* in Wright *Voc.* 144-5 *Vostre regardz est gracious Mès vos oeyz sunt jaciouz* [*glossed* gundy] *Des oiez outez la jacye* [*glossed* the gunde]. **1426** LYDG. *Pilgr.* 8624 Clenseth a-way [from the eye] al ordure, The gownde, & euery thyng vnpure. *c* **1440** *Promp. Parv.* 206/2 Gownde of þe eye, *ridda, albugo.* **1671** SKINNER *Etym. Ling. Angl.*, Gound,..*sordes oculorum condensatæ per totum agrum Linc. vulgatissime appellantur.*

†'**goundy**, *a. Obs.* Also 3-4 gundy, 6 gowndy, 7 *dial.* gunny. [f. prec. + -Y.] Of the eyes: Full of 'gound' or matter, bleared. Also *fig.*
c **1325** Gundy [see GOUND]. **13..** *MS. Med. Linc.* lf. 283 (Halliw.) For blered eghne and gundy. *c* **1410** LYDG. *Life Our Lady* xxi. (? 1484) divb, The goundy sight Of heretykes. **1412-20** —— *Chron. Troy* II. xii, A goundy eye is deceyued soone. *c* **1450** *ME. Med. Bk.* (Heinrich) 85 Pro oculis qui guttant. i. goundi. *a* **1529** SKELTON *E. Rummyng* 34 Her eyen gowndy Are full vnsowndy. **1684** *Yorksh. Dial.* 263 (E.D.S. No. 76) My Neen are varra sair..They are seay Gunny and Furr'd up [*Gloss.* sore Running Eyes].

goune, obs. form of GOWN.

gounfanoun, obs. form of GONFANON.

goung(e, variant of GONG *sb. Obs.*

gounn, obs. Sc. form of GOWN.

gounne, obs. form of GUN.

goup(p)en, -in, var. GOWPEN *Sc.* and *dial.*

gour, variant of GAUR; obs. form of GIAOUR.

‖**Goura** ('gʊərə). Also gourah. [Native name.] A genus of large crested pigeons inhabiting New Guinea and adjacent islands; a pigeon of this genus.
1855 J. WILSON *Let.* in Hamilton *Mem.* viii. (1859) 313 A gigantic foreign species called the Goura, or Crown pigeon. **1886** *St. Stephen's Rev.* 13 Mar. 14/1 On one side..was set a gourah's picturesque head with its cockatoo-like crest of delicate plumage. **1895** *Daily News* 5 July 5/3 The goura, heron, and bird of paradise are becoming rare.

goura, var. GORAH.

gourami ('gʊərəmɪ, gʊə'rɑ:mɪ). Also goramy, gouramy. [ad. Mal. *gurāmī.*] A large freshwater food fish, *Osphronemus goramy*, of the family Anabantidæ, native to south-east Asia; also, any of various smaller members of the family, freq. kept in aquaria.
1878 F. DAY *Fishes of India* I. 372 At the end of a month numerous fry appear, over which the old gouramies keep watch many days. **1879** *Encycl. Brit.* X. 781/1 Goramy, or Gouramy. **1880** A. GÜNTHER *Introd. Study Fishes* xiv. 185 In the first third of the present century, the Javanese Goramy was acclimatised in Mauritius and Guiana. *Ibid.* II. 517 To this genus belongs the celebrated 'Gourami' (*Osphromenus* [sic] *olfax*), reputed to be one of the best flavoured Freshwater-fishes in the East-Indian Archipelago. **1931** J. R. NORMAN *Hist. Fishes* iv. 81 Some or all of the rays may be drawn out into lengthy filaments, as in the Dwarf Cod-fish (*Bregmaceros*) and Gourami (*Osphronemus*). **1952** H. R. AXELROD *Tropical Fish as Hobby* iii. 55 The *Colisa lalia*, or Dwarf Gourami, is..the smallest of the Gouramis. **1961** E. S. HERALD *Living Fishes of World* 244/1 Although many members of this family have had the term 'gourami' included in their common names, the true gourami, *Osphronemus goramy*, is the only species to which the name should apply.

gourbi ('gʊəbɪ). Also 8 gurbie. [ad. Algerian Arab. *gurbī.*] A tent, or poor dwelling-place, in Northern Africa.
1738 T. SHAW *Trav.* 288 These *Gurbies* are generally raised either with Hurdles, daubed over with Mud, or else they are built out of the Materials of some adjacent Ruins, or with square Cakes of Clay baked in the Sun. **1854** J. R. MORELL *Algeria* 262 The mountains they were now traversing are intersected by very deep and beautiful valleys, up the steep slopes of which were clustered numerous *gourbies*, or huts forming villages. **1895** F. B. & W. H. WORKMAN *Alger. Mem.* 113 In the Province of Constantine the people..live in tents or gourbis made of white or light-coloured canvas. **1908** *Westm. Gaz.* 20 Jan. 2/3, I have watched for thee From my lone gourbi. **1960** *Spectator* 14 Oct. 561 To be a refugee from Algeria means that..you live in a leaky 'gourbi'. **1963** *Economist* 29 June 1352/3 A number [of Alglerians]..must remain..in the 'gourbis', their floorless, mosquito-ridden mud or wattle hovels.

gourd[1] (gɔəd, gʊəd). Forms: 4-6 goord(e, gourde, gowrd(e, (5 gurd, 6 goward(e, gord, 8 goard), 4- gourd. [ad. F. *gourde*, repr. L. *cucurbita.*]
1. a. The large fleshy fruit of the trailing or climbing plants of the N.O. *Cucurbitaceæ*; *spec.* the fruit of *Lagenaria vulgaris*, which when dried and hollowed out is used as a vessel (see 4).
1303 R. BRUNNE *Handl. Synne* 2105 He beheld a fruyt ryȝt feire and swete 'Gourdys' þus men clepe þe name. **1382** WYCLIF *Num.* xi. 5 Into mynde come to vs the goordis [Vulg. *cucumeres*], and the peponys, and the leeke, and the vniowns. *c* **1440** *Promp. Parv.* 203/2 Goord, *cucumer*,

cucurbita. **1533** ELYOT *Cast. Helthe* II. xiv. (1541) 24 Gourdes rawe be vnpleasant in eatinge. **1555** EDEN *Decades* 11 Melones, Gourdes, Cucumers, and suche other, [waxe rype] within the space of .xxxvi. dayes. **1664** EVELYN *Kal. Hort.* (1729) 194 Melons, Cucumbers, Gourds. **1784** COWPER *Task* III. 446 The prickly and green-coated gourd, So grateful to the palate. **1820** KEATS *Eve St. Agnes* xxx, Candied apple, quince, and plum, and gourd. **1862** MERIVALE *Rom. Emp.* (1865) VI. 205 Numbers of unwieldy and bloated gourds.. sun their speckled bellies before the doors.

†**b.** ***wild gourd*** = COLOCYNTH. *Obs.*

1540 RAYNOLD *Byrth Mankynde* 28 Take wyld goward [L. *colocynten*] & seth it in water. **1560** BIBLE (Genev.) *2 Kings* iv. 39 One.. founde, as it were, a wilde vine, and gathered thereof wilde gourdes his garment ful [*Marg.* Which the Apoticaries call colloquintida].

2. a. The plant which bears the fruit; a plant of the N.O. *Cucurbitaceæ*; spec. *Lagenaria vulgaris*, the bottle-gourd. ***bitter gourd*** = COLOCYNTH.

c **1400** *Lanfranc's Cirurg.* 60 þe leeues of a gourde, & þe rote of fenegrek. *c* **1420** *Pallad. on Husb.* IV. 456 The gourde is good this citur nygh to sowe. **1560** BIBLE (Genev.) *Jonah* iv. 6 And the Lord God prepared a gourde, and made it to come vp ouer Ionah. [Earlier versions have *ivy*, *wild vine*, etc.] **1667** MILTON *P.L.* VII. 321 Forth crept The swelling gourd. **1740** DYER *Ruins Rome* 374 The Gourd and Olive brown Weave the light Roof. **1844** HOOD *Haunted H.* xxiii, The gourd embraced the rose bush in its ramble. **1872** OLIVER *Elem. Bot.* II. 175 The fruit of the Gourd sometimes attains an enormous size. **1887** MOLONEY *Forestry W. Afr.* 356 Bottle or Club Gourd (*Lagenaria vulgaris*).

b. Used *allusively*, after *Jonah* iv. 6–10.

1649 JER. TAYLOR *Gt. Exemp.* xv. §19 We should have been but as an Ephemeron, man should have lived the life of a fly or a Gourd. **1658** *Addr.* in Clarendon *Hist. Reb.* xv. §114 All those pleasant gourds, under which we were.. solacing.. ourselves.. how are they withered in a night!

3. Applied to plants of other orders, with fruit resembling that of the *Cucurbitaceæ* (see quots.).

1851 MAYNE REID *Scalp Hunt.* xxii. 160 A small convolvulus, known as the 'prairie gourd', is lying at his feet. **1866** *Treas. Bot.*, *Adansonia digitata*, the Baobab, Ethiopian Sour Gourd, or Monkey-bread. **1887** MOLONEY *Forestry W. Afr.* 337 White Gourd of India (*Benincasa cerifera*, Savi.). Herbaceous plant.

4. a. The 'shell' or whole rind of the fruit dried and excavated, used as a water-bottle, float, rattle, etc. (Cf. CALABASH.)

1596 RALEIGH *Disc. Guiana* 16 He.. called for his Calabaza or gords of the gold beades. **1624** CAPT. SMITH *Virginia* II. 34 Their chiefe instruments are Rattles made of small gourds, or Pumpeons shels. **1774** GOLDSM. *Nat. Hist.* (1776) VI. 139 Whenever the fowler sees a number of ducks settled in any particular plash of water, he sends off two or three gourds to float among them. These gourds resemble our pompions. **1800** WEEMS *Washington* viii. (1810) 57 The servants supplied him with water, which he threw on the fire from an American gourd. **1870** W. M. BAKER *New Timothy* 183 (Cent.) Dozens of gourds hang also suspended from the tops of long and leaning poles, each gourd the home of a family of martins. **1873** OUIDA *Pascarel* I. 6 An empty gourd in which the shrivelled beans of the world's spent pleasures are shaken.

b. = GOURDFUL.

1768 BOSWELL *Corsica* (ed. 2) 288 They put me up a gourd of their best wine. **1893** T. N. PAGE *Marse Chan* etc. 146 She poured a gourd of water over it.

†**5.** *transf.* **a.** A bottle or cup (of any material).

a **1340** HAMPOLE *Psalter* cxviii[i]. 83 For i am made as gourde [Vulg. *sicut uter*] in ryme froste. *c* **1386** CHAUCER *Manciple's Prol.* 82, I haue heer in a gourde A draght of wyn. *a* **1400–50** *Alexander* 3701 Gurds & Goblets of gold althire-finest. *c* **1460** *Towneley Myst.* xii. 483 It is an old by-worde, It is a good bowrde For to drink of a gowrde. **1570** LEVINS *Manip.* 224/15 A Gourd, cup, *calix*. **1583** STANYHURST *Æneis* III. (Arb.) 91 With chuffe chaffe winesops like a gourd bourrachoe replennisht.

†**b.** = CUCURBIT[1] I. *Obs.*

1582 HESTER *Secr. Phiorav.* III. i. 3 Take the water.. and put it into a Goorde of glasse beeyng well luted. **1600** SURFLET *Countrie Farme* III. lxi. 565 The containing vessel [in distilling].. some call it the body or corpulent vessel, or the gourd. **1641** FRENCH *Distill.* i. (1651) 19 Distill this liquor in a glasse gourd. **1683** SALMON *Doron Med.* II. 511 Put this Liquor into a 'Gourd' of Iron.

6. *Her.* A representation of the fruit.

1513 in *Retrospect. Rev.* (1828) II. 520 Sir William Gresley bayryth assur a Lyon sylver passant, and gourds gold. **1828–40** BERRY *Encycl. Her.* II, *Stenkle*, az. three gourds or, stalks upwards.

7. *attrib.* and *Comb.*, as ***gourd-kind***, ***-seed***, ***-shape***; †***gourd-lord*** (cf. sense 2 b); ***gourd-like*** adj. and adv.; ***gourd-shaped*** ppl. a.; †**gourd-fashioned** *a.* (see quot. and *gourd-worm*); **gourd-pear**, a pear shaped like a gourd (L. *pirum cucurbitinum*); **gourd-seed corn, maize** *U.S.*, a variety of Indian corn; **gourd-shell** = sense 4; **gourd tree**, the calabash-tree (see CALABASH 7); **gourd-vine** *U.S.* = sense 2; **gourd-worm**, a name for the fluke (see FLUKE *sb.*[1] 2), and for the segments of the tapeworm, from the resemblance to the seeds of the gourd (cf. CUCURBITIN).

1658 ROWLAND *Moufet's Theat. Ins.* 1110 It breeds round Worms, and *Gourd-fashioned [*sic*: L. *cucurbitinos*], and Ascarides, and all sorts of Worms. **1822–34** *Good's Study Med.* (ed. 4) IV. 353 They [worms] are described as.. sometimes distinctly cucurbitinous, of the fasciola, fluke, or *gourd-kind. **1911** E. M. CLOWES *On Wallaby* ii. 30 The odd impression that all the lodging-houses had sprung up, *gourd-like, to their present proportions the very night after the lease had been signed. **1927** PEAKE & FLEURE *Priests & Kings* 149 The gourd-like form of the earliest Moravian wares seems to indicate an eastern origin. **1952** A. G. L. HELLYER *Sanders' Encycl. Gardening* (ed. 22) 288 *Luffa*,.. stove climbing annual, bearing curious gourd-like fruits. **1659** GAUDEN *Serm. Funeral Bp. Brounrig* 72 We have lived to see many short-lived *Gourd-Lords, created in a chaos of times. **1601** HOLLAND *Pliny* I. 439 As for the *Gourd-pears, they are by nature of a brutish or sauage kind. **1611** COTGR., *Poire de Serteau*, the Allablaster Peare.. or Gourd Peare. **1751** SIR J. HILL *Mat. Med.* II. VI. xvii. 531 The Plant which produces the officinal *Gourd Seed. **1822–34** *Good's Study Med.* (ed. 4) I. 272 The broken-off joints [of the tape-worm] have, when discharged, the appearance of gourd-seeds. **1780** W. DUNBAR *Diary* 27 May in E.O. Rowland *Life W. Dunbar* (1930) 73 Planted white Corn & *goard Seed Corn. **1831** J. M. PECK *Guide Emigrants* II. 38 The species of corn called the gourd seed. **1835** *Knickerbocker* VI. 173 The rich scenery of forty acres of most luxuriant gourd-seed corn. **1872** E. EGGLESTON *End of World* viii. 60 The relative merits of 'gourd-seed' and 'flint corn'. **1827** *Western Monthly Rev.* I. 313 *Gourd-seed maize as high as the waist. **1865** TYLOR *Early Hist. Man.* ix. 270 The frequent adoption of *gourd-shapes in the earthenware of distant parts of the world. **1892** E. REEVES *Homeward Bound* 208 They.. began tuning big, *gourd-shaped guitars and pot-bellied mandolines. *a* **1779** COOK *Voy. Pacific* (1784) II. III. xii. 234 *Gourd-shells, which they convert into vessels that serve as bottles to hold water [etc.]. **1838** T. THOMSON *Chem. Org. Bodies* 520 The balsam.. comes to Europe in small gourd shells. **1854** R. GLISAN *Jrnl. Army Life* (1874) xii. 161 The palm, mango, bread-tree, *gourd-tree, [etc.]. **1876** *Daily News* 22 Sept. 6/1 The roofs of the cottages, in which grow the gourd tree. **1892** *Harper's Mag.* May LXXXIV. 936/2 The rank, malodorous *gourd-vine that straggled over the remains of last year's bean poles. **1756** P. BROWNE *Jamaica* 382 The *Gourd-Worm with a dark-brown head. **1794–6** E. DARWIN *Zoon.* (1801) II. 216 The separate joints are called gourd-worms. **1822–34** *Good's Study Med.* (ed. 4) I. 281 In two patients.. there was room for suspecting, that the gourd-worm had induced epileptic fits. **1846** J. BAXTER *Libr. Pract. Agric.* (ed. 4) II. 274 It bears some resemblance to the seed of the common gourd, and hence is often called the gourd-worm.

†**gourd**[2]. *Obs.* Also 6 gowrde, 6–7 gord(e. [a. OF. *gourt*, *gourd*: see GORCE, GORE *sb.*[4]] (See quots.)

1538 ELYOT *Dict.* Addit., *Aquilegium*, a gourde of water, which cometh of rayne. **1565** COOPER *Thesaurus*, *Colliquiae*, greate gourdes of water runnyng through fieldes. **1589** RIDER *Eng.-Lat. Dict.*, A Gorde of water, which commeth by raine, *aquilegium*. **1670–81** BLOUNT *Glossogr.* (ed. 4), *Gord*,.. a Whirlpool, or deep hole in a River or other waters.

†**gourd**[3]. *Obs.* Also 6–7 gord(e, (7 goade?). [Cf. OF. *gourd* a swindle, 'fourberie', of which Godef. has one example.] A kind of false dice.

1545 ASCHAM *Toxoph.* I. (Arb.) 54 What false dise vse they? as.. dise of a vauntage, flattes, gourdes to chop and chaunge whan they lyste. *c* **1550** *Dice-play* A j b, A bale of Gordes with as many hyghe men as lowe men for passage. **1592** *Nobody and Someb.* I 2 b, Heares fulloms and gourds; heeres tall-men and low-men. **1598** [see FULHAM]. **1606** CHAPMAN *Mons. d'Olive* IV. i. F 3, The Goade, the Fulham, and the stop-kater-tre. **1610** BEAUM. & FL. *Scornf. Lady* IV. (1616) H, Thy dry bones can reach at nothing now, but gords or ninepinnes.

gourde (gʊəd). 'The Franco-American name for a dollar, in use in Louisiana, Cuba, Hayti, etc.' (*Cent. Dict.*)

1858 in SIMMONDS *Dict. Trade.*

†**'gourded**, *ppl. a. Farriery. Obs.* [f. as GOURD-Y + -ED[1].] = GOURDY 2; GORGED *ppl. a.*[2]

1610 [see GORGE *sb.* 8]. **1635** MARKHAM *Faithf. Farrier* (1638) 80 For Gourded or foule swelld Legges. *c* **1720** W. GIBSON *Farrier's Dispens.* (1721) Index Diseases, Legs swelled or Gourded.

†**'gourder**[1]. *Obs.*[−1] [app. f. GOURD[2].] A flooding rain, a 'spate'.

1565 HARDING *Confut. Jewel's Apol.* 195 Let the gourders of raine come downe from you and all other heretikes, let the floudes of worldly rages thrust.

†**'gourder**[2]. ? *Anglo-Irish. Obs.* Identified by Pennant with the Stormy Petrel.

1756 C. SMITH *Hist. Kerry* 186 There is a small bird.. called by the Irish, Gourder. [*Description follows.*] **1802** in MONTAGU *Ornith. Dict.* (1833) 222.

gourdful ('gɔəd-, 'gʊədfʊl). [f. GOURD[1] + -FUL.] As much as a gourd will hold.

1859 R. F. BURTON *Centr. Afr.* in *Jrnl. Geogr. Soc.* XXIX. 335 A guest is received with a gourdful of beer. **1877** SQUIER *Peru* (1878) 538 He responded to all our inquiries by insisting that we should take a gourdful of turbid chicha.

†**'gourding**, *vbl. sb. Farriery. Obs.* Also 7 gording. [f. as next + -ING[1].] Swelling in a horse's legs or joints.

1610 MARKHAM *Masterp.* II. cx. 391 This is the worst gourding, because.. lamenesse will follow it. **1655** THETFORD *Perfect Horse-Man* 163 For Gordings in joynts. Make a very strong Brine of Water and Salt. **1725** BRADLEY *Fam. Dict.* s.v. *Rules for buying horse*, If they be swell'd or big, beware of Sinews, Strains, and Gourdings.

'gourdy, *a.* In 6 goordy. [? a. OF. *gourdi*, pa. pple. of *gourdir* to swell, benumb.]

†**1.** Swollen with stuffing, stuffed out. *Obs.*

1540 PALSGR. *Acolastus* II. iv. M iv, That scrippe or bagge of his.. whiche is now borely or goordy, or stroutted out with moche money.

2. *Farriery.* Of a horse's legs: Swollen (as a morbid condition). Also of a horse so affected. ? *Obs.*

1704 *Dict. Rust.*, *Gourdy-legs* [in Horses] caused by pains or other fleshy Sores. *c* **1720** W. GIBSON *Farrier's Guide* (1722) 241 When Horses are come off a Journey.. to stand in a Stable, their Legs are apt to turn gourdy and swell'd. **1753** J. BARTLET *Gentl. Farriery* xxxvi. 282 If the horse stands too low with his hind legs, most of his weight will rest upon them, and give him the grease, especially if he is at all inclined to be gourdy. **1816** C. JAMES *Milit. Dict.* (ed. 4) 814 Shoulder-pegged horses are so called when they are gourdy, stiff, and almost without motion.

Comb. **1743** tr. *V. Renatus' Distemp. Horses* 278 If an Animal is become gourdy-leg'd.. let him Blood.

Hence **'gourdiness.**

c **1720** W. GIBSON *Farrier's Dispens.* (1721) 252 These are to Discuss hard Swellings, and are particularly of Service in Gourdiness of the Legs. **1803** TAPLIN *Sporting Dict.* I. 335 Gourdiness.. provincial term for swelled legs.

goure, obs. form of GIAOUR.

gourl, gourlie, variants of GURL, GURLY *Sc.*

gourmand ('gʊəmənd, ‖gurmɑ̃). *a.* and *sb.* Forms: 5 (*pl.*) **gourmans**, 6 **gormande**, **gourmound**, 6–7 **gorman**, **gor-**, **gurmond**, **gurmand**, 8 **gormaund**, 7–9 **gourmond**, 6–9 **gormand**, 6– **gourmand**. [a. F. *gourmand*, fem. *gourmande*, adj. and sb., of unknown origin.]

A. *adj.* Gluttonous, greedy; fond of eating.

Now regarded as attributive or appositive use of B.

1530 LYNDESAY *Test. Papyngo* 996 Sillye Saulis, that bene Christis scheip, Ar geuin to hungre gormande wolfis to keip. **1557** NORTH *Gueuara's Diall. Pr.* (1568) 161 The insatiable and gurmand throate. **1693** J. DRYDEN, jun. in *D.'s Juvenal* Sat. xiv. (1697) 345 In Feeding high, his Tutor will surpass, As Heir Apparent of the Gourmand Race. **1725** POPE *Odyss.* XVII. 529 What God has plagu'd us with this gormaund guest? **1824** BYRON *Juan* xv. lxiii, How shall I get this gourmand stanza through? **1849** T. WOOLNER *My Beautiful Lady* (1863) 20, I told of gourmand thrushes, which, To feast on morsels oozy rich, Cracked poor snails' curling niche.

B. *sb.* **1. a.** One who is over-fond of eating, one who eats greedily or to excess, a glutton.

1491 CAXTON *Vitas Patr.* (W. de W. 1495) v. III. 337 b/2 Take none hede to gourmans & glotons whiche ete more than is to theym necessary. **1569** J. SANFORD tr. *Agrippa's Van. Artes* 154 b, Their name passed into the surname of garmands [*sic*: read gurmands *or* gormands] and gluttons. **1580** HOLLYBAND *Treas. Fr. Tong*, *Gormandant, & yvrongnant*, to play the gorman and drunkard. **1599** MARSTON *Sco. Villanie* I. iv, The gurmonds paunch is fed. **1603** B. JONSON *Sejanus* I. i, That great gourmond, fat Apicivs. **1655** MOUFET & BENNET *Health's Improv.* (1746) 154 Greedy Gourmands, that cannot moderately use the good Creatures of God. **1692** LOCKE *Educ.* §14 Many are made Gormands and Gluttons by Custom, that were not so by Nature. **1848** THACKERAY *Van. F.* vi. 49 Jos, that fat *gourmand*, drank up the whole contents of the bowl. **1939** JOYCE *Finnegans Wake* (1964) 235 Our cousin gourmand, Percy, the pup.

†**b.** *fig. Obs.*

1537 LYNDESAY *Deplor. Q. Magd.* 26 O Cruell Deith!.. Gredie gorman! quhy did thow nocht [etc.]. *c* **1580** JEFFERIE *Bugbears* I. ii. 54 in *Archiv Stud. d. neu. Spr.* (1897) XCVIII. 308 O gredy gaping gourmound! o whinyng driveling miser! **1645** MILTON *Colast.* Wks. (1851) 373 The disdain I haue to change a period more with the filth and venom of this gourmand swell'd into a confuter. **1687** DRYDEN *Hind & P.* III. 969 When some lay-preferment fell by chance, The gourmands made it their inheritance.

2. One who is fond of delicate fare; a judge of good eating. In this sense only partially anglicized, and often pronounced (gurmɑ̃). (Cf. GOURMET.)

1758 CHESTERF. *Lett.* 22 Sept. (1774) II. cxx. 427, I dare say, their table is always good, for the Landgrave is a *Gourmand.* **1806** A. HUNTER *Culina* (ed. 3) 263, I appeal to all the thorough-bred Gourmands in every part of the civilized world. **1816** COLERIDGE *Statesman's Man.* (1817) 360 Their best cooks have no more idea of dressing a turtle than the gourmands themselves, at Paris, have of the true taste and colour of the fat! *a* **1839** PRAED *Bachelor* Poems 1864 II. 80 You know that I was held by all The greatest epicure in Hall, And that the voice of Granta's sons Styled me the Gourmand of St. John's. **1845** DARWIN *Voy. Nat.* xx. 464 The slimy disgusting Holuthurizæ.. which the Chinese gourmands are so fond of. **1853** C. BRONTË *Villette* I. x. 182 Fifine was a frank gourmande; any body could win her heart through her palate.

3. *Comb.*, as ***gormand-like*** adv.

1530 LYNDESAY *Test. Papyngo* 1149 The Rauin began.. Full gormondlyke his emptie throte to feid.

†**gourmand**, *v. Obs.* In 5 goormaunde, 6 gourmaund, 7 gurmond. [a. F. *gourmander*, f. *gourmand*: see prec.] **a.** *intr.* To eat greedily or gluttonously. **b.** *trans.* To devour greedily.

a **1450** *Knt. de la Tour* (1868) 9 He chidde his wiff, saieng that she had lost his doughter for leting her haue to moche her wille, and to lete her goormaunde oute of tyme. **1548** UDALL *Erasm. Par. Luke* vi. 25 Whan.. the bealy too whiche gourmaundeth, shal bee consumed, than shal ye bee houngrie and fynde no relief. **1646** G. DANIEL *Poems* Wks. 1878 I. 42 Another.. Gurmonds his Meat.

Hence †**gourmanding** *vbl. sb.* Also †**gourmander** = GOURMAND *sb.* 1.

1542 UDALL *Erasm. Apophth.* 77 b, Thei were vnmeasurable raueners and gourmaunders. *Ibid.* 109 Thyne vnmeasurable gourmaundyng and surfaictyng. **1570** LEVINS *Manip.* 79/36 Gourmander, Gormander, *manduco.* **1582** N. T. (Rhem.) *Luke* vii. 34 Behold a man that is a gurmander. **1603** HOLLAND *Plutarch's Mor.* 467 The Persians are great gourmaunders and greedy gluttons.

gourmanderie. *rare.* [Cf. OF. *gourmanderie*, f. *gourmand.*] Love of good eating.

1823 J. WILSON *Let.* in Hamilton *Mem.* iii. (1859) 107 [He] spent a fortune on French Cooks and gourmanderie. **1825** *Blackw. Mag.* XVII. 70 We strenuously recommend some adequate hand to perform this..service to Grecian literature, and to the great cause of gourmanderie at large.

gourmandice, -ise, -ize, obs. ff. GORMANDIZE.

gourmandism ('gʊəməndɪz(ə)m). Also **gor-**. [f. GOURMAND *sb.* + -ISM.] The principles and practice of a gourmand; love of good fare.

1850 HAWTHORNE *Scarlet L.* Introd. (1883) 35 His gourmandism was a highly agreeable trait. **1869** LADY BARKER *Station Life N. Zealand* ii. (1874) 13 We tried to give a better colouring to our gourmandism by inviting the Captain. **1886** P. FITZGERALD *Fatal Zero* xxii. (1888) 144 D. —— who to his other vices adds that of gormandism.

So †**'gourmandist** [-IST] = GOURMAND *sb.*

1607 CHAPMAN *Bussy D'Ambois* I. i. 3 That (like the grosse Sicilian Gurmundist) Emptie their Noses in the Cates they loue That none may eat but they.

‖**gourmet** (gurmɛ, 'gʊəmeɪ). [F. *gourmet*, repr. of OF. *gourmet, groumet, gromet*, a wine-merchant's assistant, a wine-taster: cf. GRUMMET.] **a.** A connoisseur in the delicacies of the table.

1820 [A. D. MACQUIN] *Tabella Cibaria* 16 *note*, The *gormand* unites theory with practice, and may be denominated *Gastronomer*. The *gourmet* is merely theoretical, cares little about practising, and deserves the higher appellation of *Gastrologer*. **1835** W. IRVING *Tour Prairies* xiv. Crayon Misc. (1863) 80 All relished with an appetite unknown to the gourmets of the cities. **1841** THACKERAY *Mem. Gormandising* Misc. Ess. (1885) 399 The most finished *gourmet* of my acquaintance. **1876** GEO. ELIOT *Dan. Der.* II. xi, Lord Brackenshaw was something of a *gourmet*.

b. *attrib.* and quasi-*adj.*

1904 *Westm. Gaz.* 21 Jan. 8/1 The public in the matter of jokes is gourmand rather than gourmet. **1908** *Athenæum* 11 Apr. 447/3 Few can hope to rival the gourmet-author [of *The Gourmet's Guide to Europe*] in the extent of their experiences. **1967** K. GILES *Death in Diamonds* vi. 111 It was a wonderful, gourmet meal. **1971** M. MCCARTHY *Birds of America* 72 Gift shops selling 'gourmet' food.

Hence (*nonce-wds.*) **'gourmetise** [quasi-Fr. after *gourmandise*], **'gourmetism,** daintiness in eating.

1851 *Fraser's Mag.* XLIV. 605 From the discriminating gourmetise of the young nobleman, to the expansive gourmandise of the voracious grisette, all are more or less gastrological. **1853** JERDAN *Autobiog.* III. viii. 107 To enjoy his refined gourmetism on the cheapest fare.

gournard, gournit, obs. forms of GURNARD.

‖**gourou** ('gu:ru:). Also **goora, guru.** [Presumed to belong to some African lang.] *attrib.* in ***gourou-nut***, the cola or karoo nut.

1870 *Eng. Mech.* 18 Mar. 656/3 Other..names of the kola-nut are; Guru-nut, in Soudan. **1882** J. SMITH *Dict. Pop. Names Plants* 127 Cola or Goora Nuts. **1882** CHRISTY *New Commercial Plants* 62 The Kola nut, also called the Gourou or Ombene seed. **1882** *Lancet* 8 Apr., The Cola, Gourou, or Ombéné nut.

gousberry, gousling, obs. ff. GOOSEBERRY, GUZZLING.

‖**gousblom** ('xəʊsblɒm). *S. Afr.* Pl. **'gousblomme.** [Afrikaans, ad. Du. *goudsbloem*, marigold.] A plant with showy flowers belonging to any of various species of *Arctotis*, *Gazania*, and some other related genera of the family Compositæ.

1822 W. J. BURCHELL *Trav. S. Afr.* I. xi. 229 The term *Goudsbloem*, like too many of the colonial names, is applied gratuitously to various plants, fancied to have a resemblance to the *Marygold*. Different species of *Arctotis* have generally been pointed out to me for it, and sometimes a kind of *Cotula*. **1902** H. J. DUCKITT *Hilda's Diary Cape Housekeeper* 190 In September the ground is literally carpeted with endless varieties of gazenias—local name *Gousbloom*. **1950** *Cape Argus* 5 Aug. 7/5 Namaqualand's most famous flower is the large, brilliant yellow gousblom... Smaller varieties of gousblom are seen in many colours. The arctotis, for example, is a more delicate flower. **1957** *Cape Times* 31 July 1/3 Every piece of uncultivated ground splashed with orange, white and yellow of the gousblomme. **1971** *Ibid.* 28 Aug. 1/7 The display of cinerarias, forget-me-nots, daisies, vygies, gousblomme and kalkoentjies would not be a mass of colour till mid-September.

goussett(e, variant of GUSSET.

gousshe, goust, obs. forms of GUSH, GOÛT.

'goustly, *a. Sc.* and *north. dial.* = GOUSTY.

1513 DOUGLAS *Æneis* VII. Prol. 46. **1825** [see GOUSTY].

goustrous ('gaʊstrəs), *a. Sc.* Also **gowsterous.** [f. Sc. *gouster* to bluster.] Blustering, boisterous

1818 *Edin. Mag.* Oct. 328/2 Black grew the lift wi' gowsterous nicht. **1838** J. STRUTHERS *Poet. Tales* 17 Goustrous winds are owre me blawin'. **1841** CARLYLE in Froude *Life in Lond.* I. 207 It ['Hero Worship'] is a goustrous determined speaking out of the truth about several things.

gousty ('gaʊstɪ), *a. Sc.* and *north. dial.* Also 6 **gowstie,** 7 **goustie,** 9 **gowsty.** Large and empty or hollow; 'dreary in consequence of extent or emptiness, waste, desolate'; also of sound, such as 'is emitted from a place that is empty or hollow' (Jam.).

Sometimes influenced in sense by association with *gust* (of wind), and, in later use, with *ghostly*.

1513 DOUGLAS *Æneis* I. ii. 6 Quhair Eolus the kyng In gowstie cavis [L. *vasto antro*], the wyndis lowde quhisling.. refrenis. *Ibid.* VI. i. 21 That feirfull gousty cave. **1681** GLANVILL *Sadducismus* II. 295 He observed..that the black man's Voice was hough and goustie. **1721** RAMSAY *Ode to Mr. F——*, With ghaists to roam, In gloumie Pluto's gousty dome. **1721** —— *Content* 269 The architecture not so fine as good Nor scrimp nor gousty,—regular and plain. **1808** JAMIESON, *Goustie* 2, what is accounted ghostly, supernatural. **1818** SCOTT *Hrt. Midl.* xiii, I would never have thought for a moment of staying in that auld gousty toom house. **1825** BROCKETT *N.C. Words, Gowsty, gowstly*, ghastly, frightful. Also dismal or uncomfortable, as applied to a house without ceiling, &c. 'What a gowsty hole he lives in.' **1826** G. BEATTIE *John o' Arnha'* Poems 230 A gousty cawdron boil'd an' feamed. **1854** H. MILLER *Sch. & Schm.* x. (1857) 209 The dark, gousty hay-loft into which a light was never admitted. **1875** *Whitby Gloss.* 81 'A gousty spot', said of a ruined building when the wind enters at all points.

Comb. **1662** in Pitcairn *Crim. Trials* III. 607 They [elves] speak gowstie lyk.

gout (gaʊt), *sb.*[1] Forms: 3-7 **goute,** 4 **goutt, gutt(e,** 4-5 **gut(e,** 4-7 **gowt(e,** 6 *Sc.* **gute,** 6-7 *Sc.* **gutt,** 6-8 *Sc.* **gut,** 4- **gout.** [a. OF. *goute, goutte* (F. *goutte*) drop, gout:—L. *gutta* drop, in med.L. applied to gout and other diseases attributed to a 'defluxion' of humours (see Du Cange).]

I. 1. A specific constitutional disease occurring in paroxysms, usually hereditary and in male subjects; characterized by painful inflammation of the smaller joints, esp. that of the great toe, and the deposition of sodium urate in the form of chalk-stones; it often spreads to the larger joints and the internal organs.

The name is derived from the notion of the 'dropping' of a morbid material from the blood in and around the joints.

a. With *a* and *pl.*: orig. perh. referring to an affection of a particular joint; in later use = a fit or attack of the disease, or simply, the disease itself (= b. Cf. FEVER 2). *Obs.*

c **1290** *S. Eng. Leg.* I. 360/39 þare cam a goute In is kneo, of Anguische gret..So longue, þat is kneo to-swal. *a* **1310** in Wright *Lyric P.* xv. 48 A goute me hath ygreythed so, Ant other eveles monye mo. **1377** LANGL. *P. Pl.* B. xx. 191 He ..gyued me in goutes, I may nouȝte go at large. *c* **1400** *Lanfranc's Cirurg.* 235 A man þat haþ arteticam, þat is as myche to seie as a goute. *c* **1450** *ME. Med. Bk.* (Heinrich) 203 Here wyþ anoynte þe goutes. *c* **1566** J. ALDAY tr. *Boaystuau's Theat. World* H ij b, Their legges full of gouts. **1579** LANGHAM *Gard. Health* (1633) 351 For all goutes, seethe the Leekes and Otemeale with sheepes tallow, and apply them hot. **1590** SPENSER *F.Q.* I. iv. 29 And eke in foote and hand A grievous gout tormented him full sore. **1697** DRYDEN *Virg. Georg.* III. 467 From Winter keep Well fodder'd in the Stalls, thy tender Sheep:..That free from Gouts thou mayst preserve thy Care. **1704** F. FULLER *Med. Gymn.* (1711) Pref., There have been some Gouts..which nothing could remove but a very low Diet. **1732** POPE *Ess. Man* II. 149 So, when small humours gather to a gout, The Doctor fancies he has driv'n 'em out. **1822** LD. ELDON in Twiss *Life* (1844) II. 450, I found the King in bed yesterday, He has had a pretty severe gout.

b. *sing.* only (often *the gout*). Phrase, † (*to be*) *in the gout*.

1297 R. GLOUC. (Rolls) 11865 He was al so sik mid goute & oþer wo. *a* **1300** *Cursor M.* 11825 þe gutte þe potagre es il to bete, It fell al dun in-til his fete. *c* **1386** CHAUCER *Nun's Pr. T.* 20 The goute lette hire no-thyng for to daunce. *c* **1450** *M.E. Med. Bk.* (Heinrich) 206 ȝyf hyt be þe hote goute, lef þe lynsed, & ȝyf hyt be þe cold goute, tak hyt. *c* **1450** *Merlin* 91 He fill in a grete sekenesse of the gowte in handes and feet. **1523** FITZHERB. *Husb.* §65 There be beastes, that wyll haue the goute, and moste commonly in the hynder fete, and it wyll cause them to halt. **1535** STEWART *Cron. Scot.* II. 280 Ane greit seiknes him tuke, Quhilk him dalie vexit with gute and gravell. **1587** CHURCHYARD *Worth. Wales* (1876) 59 And legges be lame and gowte creepes in the toes. **1634** LAUD *Let.* 4 Mar. in *Strafforde Lett.* (1739) I. 375 Your Brother tells me you are in the Gout. *a* **1651** CALDERWOOD *Hist. Kirk* (1843) II. 555 He was lying sicke of the gutt. **1726** GAY in *Swift's Lett.* (1766) II. 61 With Mr. Congreve, who has been like to die with a fever, and the gout in his stomach. **1788** GIBBON *Decl. & F.* xlviii. (1869) III. 50 His health was broken by the tortures of the gout. **1806-7** BERESFORD *Miseries Hum. Life* (1826) ii. No. 30 When in the gout, receiving the salutations of a muscular friend, who [etc.]. *a* **1839** PRAED *Poems* (1864) I. 333 I've never had the gout, 'tis true. **1877** ROBERTS *Handbk. Med.* (ed. 3) I. 231 Gout is the chief disease from which rheumatism has to be distinguished.

fig. **1645** MILTON *Colast.* Wks. (1851) 345 The gout and dropsy of a big margent, litter'd and overlaid with crude and huddl'd quotations.

†**c.** ***falling gout***, epilepsy. *Obs.* [med.L. *gutta cadiva* or *caduca*: see Du Cange.]

a **1300** *Cursor M.* 11831 þe falland gute [*Gött.* goutt, *Fairf. & Trin.* euel] he had.

†**d.** *slang.* In names for the venereal disease.

1694 MOTTEUX *Rabelais* V. xxi, The rankest Roan-ague (Anglicé, the Covent-garden Gout). *a* **1700** B. E. *Dict. Cant. Crew, Common-garden-gout*, or rather Covent-Garden. *Ibid., Spanish gout.*

†**2. gout rose, gout roset** [a. OF. *goutte rose*, or with Eng. dim. ending -ET[1]] = COPPER-NOSE 1.

c **1400** *Lanfranc's Cirurg.* 189 Of clooþ þat is clepid fraclis or goute roset. *c* **1450** in *Vicary's Anat.* (1888) App. ix. 229 Vndyr þe nese..lyggys a vayn þat is gud to opyne for þe gut roset. **1541** R. COPLAND *Guydon's Quest. Chirurg.* P ij, For to clense yᵉ mater of gout rose & other infections of the face and mouth. [Cf. *Ibid.* Y j, The *gutta rosa*.]

†**3.** A disease in hawks and other birds; esp. a knob or hard swelling on the feet. *Obs.*

1486 *Bk. St. Albans* C iij, When ye se yowre hawke blaw oftyn tymes: and that it commys of no batyng, ye may be sure she hath the gowte in the throte. *Ibid.*, When ye se yowre hawke may not endew her meete nor remounte her astate, she hath the gowte in the hede and in the Raynes. **1575** TURBERV. *Faulconrie* 258 Many times..the gowte doth befall a Hawke, which is none other thing than a hard tumor and swelling, full of corruption aboute the ioyntes of a Hawkes foote and stretchers. *Ibid.* 345 Of the swelling in a Hawkes foote, which we tearme the pin or pin Goute. **1600** SURFLET *Country Farme* VII. lxvii. 898 Olde Nightingales of the cage..are subiect to gouts and conuulsions in the breast.

4. A disease in wheat, caused by the larva of the gout-fly (see quots. and *gout-fly*).

1828 *Examiner* 344/1 The roots have been destroyed by the *Gout* as it is technically termed. **1860** CURTIS *Farm Insects* 234 *Chlorops tæniopus*..causes the disease termed in Oxfordshire the *gout* in wheat and barley, from the stalk being swollen to thrice its natural size.

II. In the original etymological sense of 'drop'.

5. a. A drop of liquid, esp. of blood. In the later use, after Shakspere, it tends to mean: A large splash or clot.

1503 *Art Good Living & Dying* X iiij, The ewyl rich the qwich may not haue ȝyt oon gowt of Watyr. *Ibid.* Cc v a/1, The .v. tokyng qwych shall go befor the jugement al herbys treys wooddys shal sweyt reed guttys of water, as blood. **1605** SHAKS. *Macb.* II. i. 46, I see thee still; And on thy Blade, and Dudgeon, Gouts of Blood, Which was not so before. **1800** W. R. SPENCER *Beth-gelert* xi, Where'er his eyes he cast, Fresh blood-gouts shock'd his view. **1814** BYRON *Lara* II. vi, Nor gout of blood, nor shred of mantle torn. **1833** M. SCOTT *Tom Cringle* vi. (1859) 121 Gushing streams burst from the mountain sides like gouts of froth. **1839** LOWELL *Summer Storm* Poet. Wks. (1879) 8 Again Plashes the rain in heavy gouts. **1897** MARY KINGSLEY *W. Africa* 304 A high stockade, with its gateway smeared with blood which hung in gouts.

†**b.** *Med.* = DROP *sb.* 3. *Sc. Obs.*

1755 JOHNSON s.v. *Gout* 2, *Gut* for *drop* is still used in Scotland by physicians. **1757** WALKER in *Phil. Trans.* L. 131 To an ounce of common spring-water there was added two gutts of fresh sweet milk. **1765** *Ogilvie & Nairn's Trial* 141 (Jam.) Being interrogated, 'How many guts or drops of laudanum he was in use to take at a dose'; he refuses to answer. **1818** SCOTT *Hrt. Midl.* xii, Not a goutte of his physic should gang through my father's son.

6. A spot of colour resembling a drop. So F. *goutte.* (Cf. GOUTTE *Her.*)

1833 R. MUDIE *Brit. Birds* (1841) II. 17 The parent birds are fed each with 'a drop of the devil's blood!'..and that infernal draught taints the eggs with those streaks and gouts which in fact make them so beautiful.

7. *attrib.* and *Comb.*, as ***gout family, -fit; gout-creating, -ridden, -swollen, -tormented,*** † ***gout-wit-lamed*** ppl. adjs.; **gout-fly,** the fly (*Chlorops tæniopus* or *lineata*) whose larva causes the 'gout' in wheat; † **gout-justice** *nonce-wd.*, ? justice that is halting or tardy, as if with gouty feet; **gout-stone** = CHALK-STONE 3; **gout-stool,** a stool to support the foot when affected by gout; **gout-weed,** a book-name for the plant *Ægopodium Podagraria*; † **gout-wheel-chair,** a wheeled chair used for a gouty patient; **gout-wort** = *gout-weed*.

1802 T. BEDDOES *Hygëia* viii. 166 The *gout-creating action of stimulants. **1829** SYD. SMITH in *Lady Holland's Mem.* (1855) II. 304 My attack..was of the *gout family, but hardly gout itself. *a* **1693** AUBREY *Lives, Milton* (1898) II. 67 He [Milton] would be chearfull even in his *gowte-fitts, and sing. **1881** MISS E. A. ORMEROD *Man. Injur. Insects* 77 From this case the *Chlorops*, or *Gout Fly, comes out towards the end of summer. **1619** MIDDLETON *Love & Antiq.* Wks. (Bullen) VII. 320 Such is *gout-justice, that's delay in right, Demurs in suits that are as clear as light. **1901** A. E. W. MASON *Clementina* xix. 235 [He] told the poor *gout-ridden man that the Princess..had put up at the 'Cervo' Inn. **1961** *Times* 31 July 14/3 The peppery, gout-ridden Don Lope. **1794-6** E. DARWIN *Zoon.* (1801) III. 68 *Gout-stones are formed on inflamed membranes. **1886** MRS. F. H. BURNETT *Little Ld. Fauntleroy* viii. (1887) 157 It was not agreeable to sit alone..with one foot on a *gout-stool. **1597-8** BP. HALL *Sat.* IV. i. 21 His *gout-swolne fist Gropes for his double Ducates in his chist. *a* **1711** KEN *Hymns Evang.* Poet. Wks. 1721 I. 61 Internal Fire, and *Gout-tormented Feet. **1776** WITHERING *Brit. Plants* I. 181 *Goutweed, *Ægopodium*. **1854** S. THOMSON *Wild Fl.* III. (ed. 4) 296 The root of the gout-weed (*Ægopodium*). **1667** EVELYN *Diary* 9 Dec., I found him in his garden..sitting in his *gout wheel-chair. **1595** CHAPMAN *Ovid's Banq. Sences* (1639) 15 They are cripple minded, *Gowt-wit lamed. **1597** GERARDE *Herbal* II. ccclxxii. 849 Herba Gerardi, is called in English Herbe Gerard, Aish-weed, and *Goutwoort. **1670** JOHN SMITH *England's Improv. Reviv'd* 225 Goutwort.. The very bearing of this Herb about one easeth the pains of the Gout.

gout (gaʊt), *sb.*[2] Also 6, 7, 9 **gowt.** [? var. of GOTE; but cf. F. *égout* (OF. *esgout*) sewer.]

†**1.** ? A stream or flow of water. (Cf. GOTE 1, quot. *a* 1400-50.)

c **1400** *Sege Jerus.* 561 Baches woxen ablode aboute in þe vale, & goutes fram gold wede as goteres þey runne.

2. A channel for water; a sluice; a covered drain or culvert.

1598 BARCKLEY *Felic. Man* IV. 315 The ages past haue discharged all their mallice into the age we liue in, as into a gowt or sinke. **1610** HOLLAND *Camden's Brit.* I. 237 With

Common Sewes, or Sinks (they call them Goutes) made to run under the ground. **1800** W. CHAPMAN *Witham & Welland* 29 Vast quantities of water..which used to enter through the Gowt at Langarl. *c* **1818** BRITTON *Lincolnsh.* 557 At the lower end of these are sluices, guarded by gates, termed gowts or gouts. **1851** *Jrnl. R. Agric. Soc.* XII. II. 308 During that time the doors of the gouts used to be over-rode. *Ibid.* 312 The narrow band of salt marsh..is drained by sea-gouts through the frontier banks. **1886** *S.W. Linc. Gloss.*, *Gowt*, or *Gote*, a drain, or channel for water. **1890** *Gloucester Gloss.*, *Gout*, a covered drain or culvert.
attrib. **1682** in Nicholls *Forest Dean* xv. 233 Through wch the gout water must necessarily run for draining of the worke.

‖**goût** (gu:), *sb.*[3] Also 7–9 goust, 9 *Sc.* gou, goo. [F. *goût*, earlier *goust*:—L. *gustus* taste. Cf. GUST, GUSTO.] = TASTE in various senses.

1. Flavour or savour (of food, etc.). †***high goût***: cf. HAUT-GOÛT 1.

1751 *Affect. Narr. Wager* 97, I question if any Food we ever tasted at home had so high a *Gout*, as these four legged Animals, in that Day of Scarcity. **1753** L. M. tr. *Du Boscq's Accomplish'd Woman* III. 147 Hunger gives a goût to our daily food. **1817** *Blackw. Mag.* II. 305/1 There is a nameless *gout* in certain of the dishes done up here, that reminds me [etc.]. **1830** M. DONOVAN *Dom. Econ.* I. 257 The beer spirit will have the abominable *goût* of the yest. **1870** RAMSAY *Remin.* vi. (ed. 18) 247 *Gou*, taste, smell.

2. Liking, relish, zest, fondness. Const. *for*.

1586 MARY Q. SCOTS *Let. to C. Paget* 20 May in Tytler *Hist. Scotl.* (1864) IV. 118 If you see and perceive the same ambassador to haue goust in these overtures, and put you in hope of a good answer thereunto. **1729** *Woodward's Fossils*, Publ. to Rdr. p. vi, A Direction to any one that has a Goût for the like Studies. **1789** A. BURN *Who fares best?* (1810) 10 Relished a dish of fine-flavoured tea with as high a goût as you or any man ever did. *a* **1810** J. HENRY *Camp. agst. Quebec* (1812) 73 Simpson warmed some of this in water, and ate with gout. To me it was nauseous. **1814** MAD. D'ARBLAY *Wanderer* V. 375 A lad for whom he had a great goust. **1822** *Sporting Mag.* IX. 220 The public *goût* for the most licentious..songs. **1896** CROCKETT *Grey Man* xii. 86 Having..no goo for a minister meddling in the bickerings of men.

3. The faculty of perceiving and discriminating savours; the faculty of aesthetic appreciation; one's individual judgement or predilection in such matters; also, nice perception, good taste.

1706 *Art of Painting* (1744) 348 There are three sorts of taste in painting. The natural *gout*, the artificial, and the *gout* of each nation. **1706** HEARNE *Collect.* (O.H.S.) I. 307 Paragraphs unagreeable and distasteful to the goust and palate of the..Presbyterians. **1739** CIBBER *Apol.* (1756) II. 154 It seems the goust of that age was not so nice and delicate in these matters. **1741** TAILFER, etc. *Narr. Georgia* Pref. 9 We catch Fish with a Hook baited to their particular Goût. **1743** FIELDING *Wedding-Day* III. viii. Wks. 1771 III. 356 This last opera..is too light for my goût. **1747** *Gentl. Mag.* 202 The opinion of the cardinal was however so much to the goût of his majesty, that [etc.].

¶**b.** One who affects taste.

1684 J. HAINES *Epil. to Lacy's Sir H. Buffon*, French goûts, that mingle water with their wine, Cry, Ah de French song, gosoun, dat is ver' fine.

4. Style or manner in which a work of art is executed, as judged by connoisseurs; also, a prevailing or fashionable style in matters of taste.

1717 BERKELEY *Tour in Italy* Wks. 1871 IV. 523 His [Perugino's] drapering every one knows to [be] of a little gout. **1751** SMOLLETT *Per. Pic.* (1779) II. xlii. 55 We have more taste..than to relish the productions of such a miserable gout. **1751** *Student* I. 35 Learn'd in each goût, and vers'd in ev'ry fashion.

†**gout**, *v. Obs. rare.* In 5 gowt(e. [a. OF. and F. *goutter*, f. *goutte* drop.] *intr.* To drop. Of a candle: To gutter.

a **1400** *Med. MS.* in *Archæol.* XXX. 408 Gowtyth. *c* **1440** *Promp. Parv.* 206/2 Gowton, as candelys, *gutto.*

gout: see *go out* s.v. GO *v.* 87 s.

‖**goûter** (gute). [Fr., f. *goûter* to taste.] A light afternoon repast; five-o'clock tea.

1792 *Wynne Diaries* 16 July (1935) I. 158 When you go anywhere you are shure to find a tea and a good gouté prepared. **1794** *Ibid.* 28 Apr. 149 We went to a Gouter at Thiergarten. *c* **1854** C. BRONTË *Professor* (1857) I. viii. 136 My 'goûter' (a meal which answers to our English 'tea'). **1905** *Westm. Gaz.* 28 Sept. 2/1 At five o'clock we return home to a sort of afternoon tea; or goûter,..wines, cakes, and fruit being served, as well as tea. **1958** R. GODDEN *Greengage Summer* iv. 37 'There wasn't any tea,' said Vicky; we had not learned about the French children's goûter yet.

goutify (ˈgaʊtɪfaɪ), *v.* [f. GOUT *sb.*[1] + -(I)FY.] *trans.* To make gouty, afflict with gout. Chiefly in **ˈgoutified** *pa. pple.* and *ppl. a.* So **goutifiˈcation** *nonce-wd.*

1749 SMOLLETT tr. *Gil Blas* II. i. (1782) I. 114 We perceived the old goutefied canon buried as it were in an elbow chair. **1756** W. TOLDERVY *Hist. Two Orphans* IV. 100 Goutify your dewbeaters!..What right have you to ask questions of me? **1757** COLE in Clark *Cambridge* 83 Old men, sometimes goutified, and not well able to get upstairs. **1824** *Blackw. Mag.* XVI. 2 The physician will hear the masterly defence of Claret against the charge of goutification. **1832** M. SCOTT *Ibid.* XXXII. 22 An old rich goutified coffee-planter.

goutish (ˈgaʊtɪʃ), *a.* [f. GOUT *sb.*[1] + -ISH.] **a.** Of persons: Somewhat gouty; predisposed to gout. **b.** Pertaining to, or of the nature of, gout.

a. **1398** TREVISA *Barth. De P.R.* XVII. vi, Powder þerof [of Aloes]..helpeþ goutische men. *a* **1649** DRUMM. OF HAWTH. *Fam. Ep.* Wks. (1711) 146 The tables [are] for goutish and apoplectick persons to make them move their joints. **1810** SOUTHEY in *Q. Rev.* IV. 337 The excessive heat of their apartments, and the bad custom of sitting close to the fire, dispose them to be goutish when exposed to the least cold.
b. **1700** SIR E. HARLEY in *14th Rep. Hist. MSS. Comm.* App. II. (1894) 617 It pleased God yesterday to visit me with pain and faintness, goutish and scorbutick. **1737** HERVEY *Mem.* II. 492 Imagining the Queen's pain to proceed from a goutish humour.

†**ˈgoutous**, *a. Obs.* Also 5 **gowtus, gowttous, gotows.** [ad. OF. *gutus* (F. *goutteux*), f. OF. *gout(t)e* GOUT *sb.*[1]] **a.** Of persons: Gouty. Also *absol.* **b.** Of meats: Apt to cause gout (cf. GOUTY 2 c).

a. **14..** in *Rel. Ant.* I. 196 In hys contree was a quene, Gowtus and croket. *c* **1430** *Pilgr. Lyf Manhode* II. xc. (1869) 108, I hatte Peresce, the goutous, the encrampised. *c* **1440** *Promp. Parv.* 206/2 Gotows mann, or womann (*P.* gotorous), *guttosus.*
b. *c* **1440** in *Househ. Ord.* (1790) 473 Forbere goutous metes, an unholsome. **14..** *MS. Med. Linc.* lf. 310 (Halliw.) Luk ay that he ette no gowttous mette.

‖**goutte** (gu:t). *Her.* Also 4 **gowte**, 9 **goute.** [Fr.: see GOUT *sb.*[1]] A small drop-shaped figure (of specified tincture), used as a charge.

a **1400** *Morte Arth.* 3759 That bare of gowles fulle gaye, with gowces [? *read* gowtes] of syluere. **1838** *Penny Cycl.* XII. 143/2 When the field, charge or supporter is covered with *goutes*, or *drops*, it is called *gutty.* **1868** CUSSANS *Her.* iv. 71 The terms *d'eau, de sang*, &c., are not always employed when blazoning Gouttes; it is equally correct..to blazon Gouttes by their Tinctures.

goutté, goutty, *Her.* See GUTTÉ.

gouty (ˈgaʊtɪ), *a.* [f. GOUT *sb.*[1] + -Y[1].]

1. Affected with gout; subject to gout.

c **1422** HOCCLEVE *Jereslaus's Wife* 713 Potagre and gowty & halt he was eek. *a* **1533** LD. BERNERS *Gold. Bk. M. Aurel.* Let. v. Cc iij, O ye olde gowtie people, ye forget youre selfe, and runne in poste, after the lyfe. **1581** SAVILE *Tacitus' Hist.* I. ix. (1591) 6 Hordeonius Flaccus..a man aged and gowtie. **1602** *Return fr. Parnass.* II. ii. (Arb.) 23 Ought his gowty fists then first with gold be greased? **1611** TOURNEUR *Ath. Trag.* II. v. Wks. 1878 I. 64 My legge is not goutie. *a* **1668** DAVENANT *Gondibert* I. vi. 37 Not giving like to those, whose gifts though scant Pain them as if they gave with gowty hand. **1693** DRYDEN *Persius* v. 78 Knots upon his Gouty Joints appear. **1712** STEELE *Spect.* No. 472 ¶1 Would such gouty Persons administer to the Necessities of Men disabled like themselves. **1772** FRANKLIN *Lett.* Wks. 1887 IV. 538 But I being gouty of late, seldom go into the city. **1875** B. MEADOWS *Clin. Observ.* 46 A gentleman..of gouty habit, and habitually dyspeptic.
absol. **1799** *Med. Jrnl.* I. 151 Dyspepsia, the inseparable companion of the gouty.
fig. **1656** COWLEY *Ode to Wit* iv, 'Tis not to force some lifeless Verses meet With their five gowty feet. **1735** BERKELEY *Querist* §424 Whether the want thereof [money] doth not render the state gouty and inactive?

†**b.** Of birds: cf. GOUT *sb.*[1] 2. *Obs.*

1600 SURFLET *Country Farme* VII. lvi. 887 The nightingale hauing beene two or three yeeres in the cage, becommeth goutie: nowe when you shall perceiue it, annoint her feet with butter.

†**c.** Of a horse's legs: Swollen, affected with swellings. Also of the animal so affected. *Obs.*

1523 FITZHERB. *Husb.* §56 Yf thou shalte by oxen for the ploughe, se that they be yonge, and not gowty. **1577** B. GOOGE *Heresbach's Husb.* III. 115 The legges and the thyes [of a horse]..ought to be euen, straight, and sound, not gouty..with much fleshe and vaynes [*citra venarum ac carnium obesitatem aut tumorem aliquem*].

2. Of or pertaining to gout; of the nature of gout.

1615 CROOKE *Body of Man* 285 To make a calculous impression in the Kidneys, or a gowty impression in the ioyntes is onely proper to the seede. **1724** BLACKMORE *Treat. Consumpt.* 23 There are likewise other Causes of Blood-spitting; one is the Settlement of a gouty Matter in the Substance of the Lungs. **1748** RICHARDSON *Clarissa* I. v. 31 Under the torture of a gouty paroxysm. **1846** G. E. DAY tr. *Simon's Anim. Chem.* II. 477 Gouty concretions, which frequently form on the joints of the hands and feet. **1865** CARLYLE *Fredk. Gt.* XV. v. VI. 16 The neuralgic maladies press sore, and the gouty twinges. **1879** M. PATTISON *Milton* 151 He was very abstemious in his diet, having to contend with a gouty diathesis.

b. Used during an attack of gout.

1733–4 BERKELEY in Fraser *Life* vi. (1871) 215, I hope..to be able to put on my gouty shoes. **1777** SHERIDAN *Sch. Scand.* IV. i, Here's an old gouty chair of my grandfather's. **1794** MRS. A. M. BENNETT *Ellen* IV. 59, I..will take my old seat on the gouty stool, and tell my dear grandfather [etc.]. **1825** *Morisoniana* (1831) 218 The gouty patient may now..burn his gouty shoes.

c. Having a tendency to produce gout.

1802 T. BEDDOES *Hygëia* viii. 164 The weaker wines of France are reputed more gouty than those in common use among the English. **1897** *Allbutt's Syst. Med.* III. 182 Champagnes, especially the sweeter sorts, are undoubtedly gouty wines.

3. *transf.* and *fig.* Swollen or bulging, so as to be out of shape or disproportioned; distorted with swellings or protuberances; tumid.

1595 COPLEY *Wits, Fittes & Fancies* 41 He that euermore alleadgeth in his conuersation other mens sayings, is like a gowty naile, that cannot enter the wood, except an augar make the way before. **1663** J. SPENCER *Prodigies* (1665) 105 This humour in Historians hath made the body of ancient History in some parts so gouty and monstrous. *a* **1704** T. BROWN *Collect. Dial.* I. 18 You cannot imagine what a Mortification it is for a Noble Author..to have his Song tagg'd with half a dozen gouty Stanzas by a Grub street Hand. **1790** HERSCHEL in *Phil. Trans.* LXXX. 477 The p. arm [of Saturn's ring] is a little gouty. **1848** JOHNSTON in *Proc. Berw. Nat. Club* II. No. 6. 310 There is no mistaking this mite from its size..and its gouty unfashioned legs. **1875** *Encycl. Brit.* II. 441/2 Rustic masonry, ill-formed festoons, and gouty balustrades.

b. Of the stems of vegetables, and their joints; also of thread: Full of knots or knobs, knotty. *Obs.* exc. *dial.*

1597 GERARDE *Herbal* I. xii. §2. 14 Long and slender stemmes, jointed with many knobbie and gowtie knees. **1677** HOLYOKE *Dict.*, *Crassa Minerva*, spun with a gouty thread, bungling work. **1713** DERHAM *Phys.-Theol.* VIII. vi. Note *hh* (1727) 391 Which..makes the young Shoots tumify, and grow knotty and gouty. **1896** *Warwicksh Gloss.*, *Gouty*, knobby, knotty: usually applied to rough thread, worsted, silk, etc.

†**4.** Of land: Boggy (see quot. 1790). *Obs.*

1686 PLOT *Staffordsh.* 109 The black moorish and gouty grounds of the Moorelands. **1790** W. MARSHALL *Midl. Co.* II. 437 *Gouty*, diseased and swelled by subterraneous water; as boggy tumours, at the bottom, or on the side of a hill.

5. *Comb.*, as ***gouty-bagged, -handed, -legged*** adjs.; **gouty-stem (tree)**, the Australian baobab (*Adansonia Gregorii*).

1599 NASHE *Lenten Stuffe* 33 Holy S. Taurbard, in what droues the *gouty bagd Londoners hurry down [etc.]. *a* **1613** OVERBURY *A Wife* (1638) 153 His liberality can never be said to be *gowty-handed. **1611** COTGR., *Podagre*, *gowtie-legd. **1846** STOKES *Discov. Australia* II. iii. 115 The *gouty-stem tree..bears a very fragrant white flower, not unlike the jasmine. **1889** MAIDEN *Usef. Nat. Plants Austral.* 60 *Sterculia rupestris*..The 'Bottle-tree' of N.E. Australia, and also called 'Gouty-stem', on account of the extraordinary shape of the trunk.

Hence **ˈgoutily** *adv.*; **ˈgoutiness**, tendency to gout *lit.* and *fig.*; **ˈgoutyish** *a.*, somewhat gouty.

1632 SHERWOOD *s.v.*, Goutinesse, *la douleur de la goutte.* **1700** WALLACE in *Phil. Trans.* XXI. 541 All have been frequently here except Captain Diego who is Goutyish. **1820** *Q. Rev.* XXIII. 180 An Englishman is encumbered with a certain goutiness of mind. **1864** HAWTHORNE *Dolliver Rom.* (1879) 53 He had met the grim old wreck of Colonel Dabney, moving goutily. **1890** *Brit. Med. Jrnl.* 25 Jan. 184/1 There is probably more gout and goutiness in London than in any other spot on the globe.

gouv-: see GOV-.

†**ˈgouvernant.** *Obs. rare*[−1]. In 5 -aunt. [a. F. *gouvernant*, pr. pple. of *gouverner* to GOVERN.] A governor (of a country).

1475 *Bk. Noblesse* 41 Prince Richarde duke of Yorke..being at two voiages lieutenaunt and gouvernaunt in Fraunce.

‖**gouvernante** (guvɛrnɑ̃t). Cf. GOVERNANTE. [F. *gouvernante*, fem. pr. pple. of *gouverner* to GOVERN.]

†**1.** A female ruler of a country. *Obs.*

1751 CHESTERF. *Let.* 28 Oct., Misc. Wks. 1777 II. 372 If..your Catharines and Marys of Medicis, your Anns of Austria, &c., should prove the model of your *gouvernante.* **1772** *Hartford Merc.* Suppl. 18 Sept. 3/1 The King of Sweden had nominated her Gouvernante of Swedish Pomerania.

2. a. A housekeeper (to a bachelor or widower). *rare.* **b.** A chaperon or duenna. **c.** A governess; a female teacher. (Cf. GOVERNANTE 2, 3, 4.)

a. **1772** GRAVES *Spirit. Quix.* III. vii. (1783) I. 145 My sister..became reserved to me, in order to recommend herself more effectually to our gouvernante. [Explained by context.] **1788** H. WALPOLE *Narr. Rousseau* 141 Rousseau..crossed the country with his gouvernante.
b. **1716** ADDISON *Free-holder* No. 4 ¶3 The old and wither'd Matrons, known by the frightful Name of *Gouvernantes* and *Duegnas.* **1800** MAR. EDGEWORTH *Belinda* (1833) I. xi. 200 A beautiful young girl, and an elderly lady whom they took for her gouvernante. **1838** LYTTON *Calderon* iii, She was living with an old relation, or *gouvernante.*
c. **1781** HAYLEY *Tri. Temper* I. 150 What ills the little female haunt, The testy nurse, th' imperious gouvernante. **1828** MISS MITFORD *Village* III. 113 During the church-wardenship of Farmer Brookes, no less than three village gouvernantes arrived at Aberleigh. **1865** *Look before you leap* I. 179 Disregarding her gouvernante, she went straight to Neville.

gove (gəʊv), *v. Sc.* Also 4–6 **gowe**, 6 **gofe, goif, goyf**, 8 **gauve**, 8–9 **goave.** [Of obscure origin: connexion with *gow*, GAW *v.*, of similar meaning, cannot be traced.]

1. *intr.* To gaze, stare; to stare stupidly.

c **1375** *Sc. Leg. Saints, Thomas* 82 And mete & drink vald nocht assay, bot to þe hewine ves govand ay. *Ibid.* 7 *Sleperis* 329 A-bout hyme fast þan gowit he, gyf he mycht ony þane se. **1501** DOUGLAS *Pal. Hon.* III. xx, Thus in a stair, quhy standis thow stupifak, Gouand all day. **1508** DUNBAR *Tua Mariit Wemen* 287 Apon the galland for to goif it gladit me agane. **1513** DOUGLAS *Æneis* v. vi. 136 Than leuch that riall prence on hym to goif. *c* **1560** A. SCOTT *Poems* (S.T.S.) 56 The blenkyne of ane e Ay gart the goif and glaik. **1728** RAMSAY *2nd Answ. Somervile* 35 Nae mair they'd gaunt and gove away, Or sleep or loiter out the day. **1786** BURNS *Interview Ld. Daer* iv, How he star'd and stammer'd, When goavan, as if led wi' branks..He in the parlour hammer'd. **1813** HOGG *Queen's Wake, Kilmeny* (1814) 187 The wild beasts of the forest came And goved around, charmed and amazed. **1819** W. TENNANT *Papistry Storm'd* (1827) 150 A tumbler at a fair, Whair thousands round him goave and stare. **1894** Crockett *Lilac Sunbonnet* 44 The dull cattle that 'goved' upon her.

2. *trans.* 'To examine; to investigate' (Jam.). **1513** Douglas *Æneis* viii. iv. 68 Sic way he wrocht that, quha thair tred lyst gove, Na takynnys suld convoy thaim to his cove.

gove, obs. form of goave *v.*

gove, obs. and dial. pa. t. of give *v.*

govel(e, -er(e, obs. ff. gavel *sb.*[1], gaveller.

goverment, obs. form of government.

†**'govern**, *sb. Obs. rare.* [f. the vb.; cf. F. *gouverne* (from 14th c.), Pr. *govern-s*, Pg., It. *governo*, Sp. *gobierno*.] Government. *c* **1300** *Beket* (Percy Soc.) 1792 That his bischopriche hadde ibeo: withoute govern and rede.

govern ('gʌvən), *v.* Forms: 3–7 **governe**, (4 **governi**, 5 **goveryne, gouverne**), 4–6 **gowern(e**, 3– **govern**. [a. OF. *governer* (F. *gouverner*) = Pr., Pg. *governar*, Sp. *gobernar*, It. *governare*:—L. *gubernāre* to steer (a vessel), hence to direct, rule, govern, ad. Gr. κυβερνᾶν to steer.]

1. *trans.* To rule with authority, esp. with the authority of a sovereign; to direct and control the actions and affairs of (a people, a state or its members), whether despotically or constitutionally; to rule or regulate the affairs of (a body of men, corporation); to command the garrison of (a fort). **1297** R. Glouc. (Rolls) 1036 Cassibel þat noble prince was inou & þat lond gouerned wel. *c* **1330** R. Brunne *Chron.* (1810) 37 Sone after þi daies þe reame salle men se Gouerned þorgh aliens kynde. **1389** *Eng. Gilds* (1870) 46 An Aldirman ..able and konyng to reulen and gouern þe company. *c* **1400** Maundev. (Roxb.) xii. 53 Þe sepulcre of Ioseph Iacob son, þat gouerned Egipte. *a* **1400–50** *Alexander* 3387 Þe same cure is a kyng..To gy & gouerne his gomes. *a* **1533** Ld. Berners *Huon* xxi. 62, I delyueryd to hym all my londes to gouerne. **1617** Moryson *Itin.* ii. 116 Captaine Thomas Williams with his Company, being left to governe the new Fort. **1651** Hobbes *Leviath.* ii. xxvi. 139 Govern them by the same Lawes, by which they were governed before. **1709** Steele *Tatler* No. 29 ¶7 There is no governing any but Savages by other Methods than their own Consent. **1764** Goldsm. *Trav.* 372 In every soil..those that think must govern those that toil. **1856** Froude *Hist. Eng.* (1858) I. ii. 163 From the accession of Henry VII, the country had been governed by a succession of ecclesiastical ministers. *fig.* **1635** Quarles *Embl.* i. xv. 31 Lord..Can thy flockes be thriving, when the fold Is govern'd by a Fox?

b. said of the Deity. *c* **1374** Chaucer *Boeth.* i. pr. vi. 17 (Camb. MS.) Syn þat thow ne dowtest nat that þis world be gouerned by god. *c* **1450** *St. Cuthbert* (Surtees) 571 Grete god þat gouernes all. **1535** Coverdale *Job* xxxvi. 31 By these thinges gouerneth he his people. *a* **1677** Barrow *Serm.* xxiii. Wks. 1686 III. 260 Can we..peruse the Records of everlasting destiny by which the World is governed? **1859** Kingsley *Lett.* (1878) II. 73 It is a fearful look-out when God has to govern a nation because it cannot govern itself.

†**c.** To be in command of (a force, an army); to lead (a choir). *Obs.* **1297** R. Glouc. (Rolls) 8205 Þe baldewines tueye.. gouernede þe ost mid hor poer beye. **1375** Barbour *Bruce* xii. 499 The battall that schir Eduard Gouernyt and led. **1387** Trevisa *Higden* (Rolls) VII. 81 Or elles berynge a cope to governe þe queere [L. *chorum rexit*].

d. To direct and control (a person, the members of a household) with the authority of a superior. ? *Obs.* *a* **1340** Hampole *Psalter* xxii[i]. 1 Lord gouerns [Vulg. *regit*] me & nathynge sall me want. *c* **1340** *Cursor M.* 10804 (Trin.) If..she no husbonde had I-had hir to haue gouerned & lad. **1413** *Pylgr. Sowle* (Caxton) iv. xxxviii. (1859) 64 They ordeyne and gouerne hym, ryght as he were to yonge within age, and couthe nought gouerne hym seluen. **1450–1530** *Myrr. our Ladye* 16 He taught her grammer and songe, & gouerned her & her housholde. **1577** B. Googe *Heresbach's Husb.* i. (1586) 16 She must..looke to the Kitchin..gouerne the maides, and keepe them at their woorke. **1679** Hobbes *Behemoth* iii. (1682) 242 Some others were sent thither [to the universitie] by their Parents, to save themselves the trouble of governing them at home, during that time wherein Children are least governable.

e. *absol.* To exercise the function of government. The phrase 'the king reigns but does not govern', app. first used by French writers, is intended to characterize those monarchies (e.g. that of England) in which the action of the sovereign is mainly confined to the selection of responsible ministers. *c* **1400** Maundev. (1839) v. 38 And this regnede longe & governed wisely. **1601** Shaks. *Twel. N.* i. ii. 24 Who gouernes heere? **1699** Temple *Ess. Pop. Discontents* Wks. 1731 I. 260 Every Prince should govern as He would desire to be governed if he were a Subject. **1710** Swift *Examiner* No. 18 ¶5 When this Man governed in that Island. **1845** M. Pattison *Ess.* (1889) I. 16 The throne was occupied by a minor, whose mother..governed as regent for him. **1861** May *Const. Hist.* I. i. 6 The king reigned, but his ministers governed. **1874** Stubbs *Const. Hist.* I. ii. 36 He reigns but does not govern. **1897** *Daily News* 3 May 5/5 In a Crown Colony..the Governor governs; in a free one he reigns.

2. To sway, rule, influence (a person, his actions, etc.); to direct, guide, or regulate in conduct or actions. (Said of persons: also of motives, etc.) *c* **1440** *Promp. Parv.* 206/2 Gouernyn, and mesuryn in manerys, and thewys, *moderor*. **1597** Bacon *Ess., Followers & Friends* (Arb.) 36 To be gouerned [**1625** *adds* (as we call it)] by one is not good. **1601** Shaks. *Jul. C.* i. iii. 83 Our Fathers mindes are dead, And we are gouern'd with our Mothers spirits. *a* **1631** Donne *Paradoxes* (1633) D 3 How then shall this nature gouerne vs, that is gouerned by the worst part of vs? **1662** *Bk. Com. Prayer, Pr. for all Conditions of Men*, We pray for the good estate of the Catholick Church; that it may be so guided and governed by thy good Spirit that [etc.]. **1704** Swift *T. Tub* Apol., Not that he would have governed his judgment by the ill-placed cavils of the sour. **1709** Steele *Tatler* No. 66 ¶5 Ordinary Minds are wholly governed by their Eyes and Ears. *a* **1754** J. McLaurin *Serm. & Ess.* (1755) 17 Eternal motives are the only motives that should govern immortal Souls. **1882** Miss Braddon *Mt. Royal* II. iii. 39, I did not allow myself to be governed by Lady Cumberbridge's gossip. **1883** Froude *Short Stud.* IV. i. iii. 41 The archbishop..was aware of the motives by which the papal decisions were governed.

†**b.** To master, prevail over. *Obs.* **1592** Shaks. *Ven. & Ad.* 42 Backward she push'd him, as she would be thrust, And govern'd him in strength, though not in lust.

†**c.** To guide, direct, lead (*in* some course); to guide *to* or *towards* an object. *Obs.* **1382** Wyclif *Isa.* xlix. 10 The rewere of them shal gouerne [L. *reget*] them and at the welles of watris ȝyuen hem to drinke. *c* **1400** Maundev. (Roxb.) xvii. 80 Þe nedill ..by þe whilk schippe men er gouerned in þe see. **1549** *Bk. Com. Prayer, Litany*, That it may please thee to rule and gouerne thy holy Churche vniuersall in the right waye. *c* **1600** Shaks. *Sonn.* cxiii. 2 And that which gouernes me to goe about, Doth part his function, and is partly blind. *a* **1635** Corbet *Poems* (1807) 116 As a straying starr intic't And governd those wise-men to Christ. **1704** Swift *Mech. Operat. Spirit* (1711) 294 By what kind of Practices the Voice is best govern'd towards the Composition and Improvement of the Spirit. **1737** Whiston *Josephus, Hist.* i. i. §5 He that governed the elephant was but a private man.

d. To regulate, determine the course or issue of (an event, etc.). *a* **1625** Fletcher *Witt without Money* iii. i, 'Tis not folly, But good discretion, governs our main fortunes. **1798** Wellesley in Owen *Desp.* 46 The attempts which they have already made to interfere in governing the succession. **1863** Kinglake *Crimea* (1877) II. xii. 156 At the storming of Constantine..he really helped to govern the events.

e. Of things, *esp.*, in astrological use, of the stars: To hold sway over, influence, determine the motions or nature of. **1390** Gower *Conf.* II. 109 O Phebus, which the daies light Governest til that it be night. *Ibid.* III. 106 Of alle thinges the matere,..Of thing above it [this erthe] stont governed, That is to sain of the planetes The cheles both and eke the hetes. *Ibid.* 127 Wherof the firste regiment..Governed is of signes thre. *c* **1566** J. Alday tr. *Boaystuau's Theat. World* B vij b, Beastes..nature hath given them a complection so well ruled and governed, that they never take more than is requisite for their nourishment. **1591** Shaks. *Two Gent.* ii. vii. 74 But truer starres did gouerne Protheus birth. **1631** Widdowes *Nat. Philos.* (ed. 2) 10 Saturne is a star of a leaden colour,..governing malancholike persons. **1664** Power *Exp. Philos.* Pref. 15 What-soever is invisible..is little enquired; and yet these be the things that govern Nature principally. **1671** R. Bohun *Wind* 86 Here in England, the Eastern [Winds] usually govern the spring..but generally the Western ingrosse the greatest part of the yeare.

†**f.** To determine the key of (a musical composition). *Obs. rare*⁻¹. **1597** Morley *Introd. Mus.* 156 Your song being gouerned with flats it is vnformall to touch a sharpe eight.

3. *intr.* To hold sway, prevail, have predominating or decisive influence. **1596** Shaks. *Merch. V.* iii. v. 63 Let it be as humors and conceits shall gouerne. **1606** —— *Ant. & Cl.* ii. ii. 150 From this houre, The heart of Brothers gouerne in our Loues. **1626** Bacon *Sylva* §453 It hath been received, that a smaller Pear, grafted upon a Stock that beareth a greater Pear, will become great. But I think..the Cions will govern. **1669** Marvell *Corr.* cxiv. Wks. 1872–5 II. 274 After the ablest men have employed all their art..yet chance will governe at last. **1884** *Chr. Commonwealth* 21 Feb. 448/1 Since then we have been asking whether policy or principle is to govern in matters of this kind.

4. *refl.* To direct or regulate one's actions; †to conduct oneself, behave, act (in a specified way). **1375** Barbour *Bruce* ii. 588 On this maner thaim gouernyt thai, Till thai come to the hed off tay. *c* **1386** Chaucer *Melib.* ¶28 If ye gouerne yow by sapience, put awey sorwe out of youre herte. *a* **1450** *Knt. de la Tour* (1868) 3 To teche my doughtres..how thei shulde gouerne hem. *c* **1460** *Urbanitatis* 22 in *Babees Bk.*, Loke..þat þow gouerne þe welle. **1608** Armin *Nest Ninn.* 29 Fooles that want wit to gouerne themselves well. **1651** Marius *Bills of Exchange* 8 Advice..ought to be given by the first Post that..the deliverer may know..how to govern himself. **1715** Nelson *Addr. Pers. Qual.* 257 If in this Extremity the poor Widow had governed herself by the Measures of this Age, in a few Days she had perished with hunger. **1745** *De Foe's Eng. Tradesman* ii. (1841) I. 17 Intimating that you can or cannot answer this order, that I may govern myself accordingly. **1778** Burke *Corr.* (1844) II. 248 You have..a great country to govern; and I have no doubt of the principles on which you govern yourself in the management of it.

†**5.** *trans.* To administer, manage, order (affairs, an undertaking, an establishment, household, etc.). *Obs.* **1382** Wyclif *1 Tim.* v. 4 If ony widew hath sone, or children of sones, lerne sche first for to gouerne hir hous. *c* **1440** *Promp. Parv.* 206/2 Governe a towne, *villico*. **1480** Caxton *Chron. Eng.* ccxxxiv. 255 That thurgh his counceil and gouernaunce al thynge shold be gouerned and dressyd. **1535** Coverdale *1 Sam.* xviii. 17 Be stronge now, & gouern the warres of the Lorde. **1588** Shaks. *Tit. A.* v. ii. 139 Whiles I goe tell my Lord..How I haue gouern'd our determined iest. **1610** *Histrio-m.* vi. 92 Il hast thou govern'd thy prosperity. That canst not smile in meere adversity. **1617** Moryson *Itin.* i. 238 So as all the rest chose him for their guide, and to governe their expences. **1672** Evelyn *Diary* 31 May, My Lord Sandwich was prudent as well as valiant, and always govern'd his affaires with successe and little losse. **1741** Richardson *Pamela* II. 108 The Ladies and Gentlemen would make me govern the Tea-table, whatever I could do.

†**6.** To attend to, care for, look after (a person); esp. to tend or treat in respect to health. *Obs.* *c* **1386** Chaucer *Shipman's T.* 261 Governeth yow also of your diete Atemprely, and namely in this hete. **1523** Ld. Berners *Froiss.* I. cxcix. 236 And there he gouerned hymselfe so well, that he was healed. *a* **1533** —— *Huon* cxliv. 540 That ye kepe this lady in your house clothyd and apareyled and as well gouernyd. **1541** R. Copland *Guydon's Quest. Chirurg.* N j, Howe ought he to be gouerned that wyll be letten blode before he do blede. **1658** A. Fox *Wurtz' Surg.* ii. x. 85 Govern the party in his diet, as you were told at the Head-wounds. **1675** Temple *Let. to Sir J. Williamson* Wks. 1731 II. 332, I never knew any Sickness of a Great Man so well govern'd as his. **1680** Walton in *Four C. Eng. Lett.* 69 His pensions..were given to a woman that governed him.

†**b.** To tend, treat (plants). *Obs.* **1572** Mascall *Art Planting & Graffing* 49 How to guide and gouerne the sayde trees. **1658** Evelyn *Fr. Gard.* ii. vii. (1675) 258 They are all of them to be Planted, and governed like Raspes. **1669** J. Rose *Eng. Vineyard* v. (1675) 27 Thus you shall also govern your Vineyard the third year.

†**7.** To work or manage (a ship, the sails, the helm). *Obs.* *c* **1375** *Sc. Leg. Saints, Ninian* 525 & sa, þat patent gouernande, haile and sounde he com to lande. **1387** Trevisa *Higden* (Rolls) IV. 63 Hem lakked schipmen to governe here schippes [L. *remiges..ad naves regendas*]. *c* **1440** *Partonope* 3157* The bote was governde in the see. **1565** Cooper *Thesaurus, Auxilia nautica*, the sterne and other instrumentes, wherby the shippe is gouerned. **1617** Moryson *Itin.* iii. 135 A Venetian ship governed by Greekes. **1653** H. Cogan tr. *Pinto's Trav.* xx. 71 An hundred and sixty Mariners, both for rowing, and for governing the sails. **1671** R. Bohun *Wind* 253 [The hurricane] came to such an height, that..7 men could scarce govern the Helme. **1697** Potter *Antiq. Greece* iii. xiv. (1715) 124 Ships of Burden were commonly govern'd by Sails.

†**b.** [after L.] To steer. In quot. *absol. Obs.* **1675** Hobbes *Odyss.* (1677) 61 Then he astern sate down and governed.

†**8.** To manage, manipulate, work, control the working of (an implement, machine, etc.); to regulate (a fire). *Obs.* *c* **1385** Chaucer *L.G.W.* 1209 *Dido*, The fomy brydle with the bit of gold Governyth he. *c* **1386** —— *Monk's T.* 407 Thus can ffortune hir wheel gouerne and gye. **1602** Shaks. *Ham.* iii. ii. 372 Gouerne these Ventiges with your finger and thumbe. *a* **1631** Donne *80 Serm.* (1640) vii. 64 What can a graine of dust work in governing the balance? **1694** Salmon *Bate's Dispens.* i. (1713) 150/1 The Fire is to be so governed, as to hinder the Oil from boiling. **1797** *Monthly Mag.* III. 222 Twelve pins, placed in two rows diagonally on the barrel, which the stud on the rack governs, by the turn of the pinion on the rack. **1807** Robinson *Archæol. Græca* iv. ix. 376 They rendered them [battering-rams] useless by cutting with long scythes the ropes by which they were governed.

9. To hold in check, curb, bridle (esp. one's passions). †Also, to keep or restrain *from*. **1513** Bradshaw *St. Werburge, Ball. to St. W.* 31 Governe my lyfe from all actes daungerous. **1597** Shaks. *2 Hen. IV*, ii. ii. 180 *Bar.* I haue no tongue, sir. *Page.* And for mine Sir, I will gouerne it. **1605** —— *Lear* v. iii. 161 Go after her, she's desperate, gouerne her. **1719** De Foe *Crusoe* ii. x, Neither could he govern his passion. **1729** Butler *Serm.* Wks. 1874 II. 39 If he puts on any..face of religion, and yet does not govern his tongue, he must surely deceive himself. **1870** Dickens *E. Drood* viii, I appeal to you to govern your temper. **1873** Hamerton *Intell. Life* ii. iv. 72 An ambitious man will govern himself for the sake of his ambition, and withstand the seductions of the senses.

10. To constitute a law or rule for; to be applicable to as a determining principle or limiting condition; to serve as a precedent, rule, or type for; esp. in *Law*, to serve in determining or deciding (a case). **1818** Cruise *Digest* (ed. 2) IV. 398 The case of Peacock v. Spooner having been decided by the House of Lords, must govern this case. **1834** McMurtrie *Cuvier's Anim. Kingd.* 1 The laws which govern those beings. **1861** J. R. Greene *Man. Anim. Kingd., Cœlent.* 70 This rule does not appear to govern the nectocalyces in the last-mentioned group. **1884** Ld. Coleridge in *Law Times Rep.* L. 46/1 The principles laid down in that case are applicable to and govern this. **1885** C. H. Anderson in *Law Rep. 14* Q. Bench Div. 727 There is no break in the section, and the words 'in any highway', govern all that follows. **1890** Sir H. C. Lopes in *Law Times Rep.* LXIII. 692/2 The law there stated clearly governs this case. **1891** J. P. Lilley *Lord's Day & Servants* ii. i. 88 Should not this thought largely govern the service of Congregational praise. *absol.* **1818** Cruise *Digest* (ed. 2) VI. 398 Sir Joseph Jekyll, in Papillon v. Voyce said, the intention if lawful shall govern.

11. *Grammar.* Of a word, chiefly a verb or prep.: To require (a noun or pronoun) to be *in* a certain case, or a verb to be *in* a certain mood; to be necessarily followed by (a certain case or mood). †Formerly also of the subject: To determine the number and person of (the verb). *Obs.* **1530** Palsgr. 74 Pronownes be suche as..may governe verbes to be of lyke nombre and parson with them. **1612** Brinsley *Grammar-Schoole* 98 The word gouerning or directing, to be placed before those which it gouerneth or directeth. *c* **1620** A. Hume *Brit. Tongue* ii. v, With *s*, it [the genitive] precedes the word quherof it is governed. **1620** T. Granger *Div. Logike* 58 A verbe substantive..governing two datives, one of the person, and another of the thing. **1877** Whitney *Essent. Eng. Gram.* iii. 32 We speak of both verbs and prepositions as governing in the objective the word that is their object. **1881-7** CUMMINS *Friesic Gram.* § 195 Prepositions governing the dative and accusative. **1892** J. WRIGHT *Primer Gothic* § 291 The genitive is also governed by certain adjectives.

absol. **16..** MAUGER *Fr. Gram.* (T.), In our language evermore Words that govern go before.

governable ('gʌvənəb(ə)l), *a.* [f. GOVERN *v.* + -ABLE.] Capable of being governed (in senses of the verb).

1647 CLARENDON *Hist. Reb.* II. § 81 The earls of Essex and Holland.. were thought less governable by those councils. **1659** *Gentl. Calling* IV. iii. 400 They become more tame and governable ever after. **1664** EVELYN *Sylva* xxiii. 59 There is not a more tonsile and governable Plant in Nature. **1679** [see GOVERN *v.* 1 d]. **1684** OTWAY *Atheist* I. (1735) 24 Will you promise me..to be very governable, and very civil. **1703** DAMPIER *Voy.* III. 111 The Ship was very governable, and Steer'd incomparably well. **1737** BRACKEN *Farriery Impr.* (1757) II. 81 He may prove mild and governable. **1768-74** TUCKER *Lt. Nat.* (1852) II. 412 To keep him in ignorance, that he may be ductile and governable. **1819** R. CHAPMAN *Jas. VI,* 127 Where the same religion is unanimously professed, the subjects are more governable and peaceable. **1880** G. MEREDITH *Tragic Com.* (1881) 185 Alvan in love was not likely to be governable by prudent counsel.

Hence ˌ**governa'bility**, '**governableness**, the state or quality of being governable; '**governably** *adv.*, in a governable manner.

1775 ASH, *Governableness.* **1853** RUSKIN *Stones Ven.* II. App. xii. 393 By its perfect governableness it [oil-colour] permits the utmost possible fulness and subtlety in the harmonies of colour. **1863** P. S. WORSLEY *Poems* 12 The god Infused a soul more governably mild. **1872** BAGEHOT *Physics & Pol.* (1876) 25 We reckon, as the basis of our culture, upon an amount of order, of tacit obedience, of prescriptive governability. **1876** MISS O'MEARA *F. Ordnam* 267 He was a confirmed optimist in his estimate of the goodness and governableness of mankind in general.

†**governail.** *Obs.* Forms: 4-5 **governayl(l(e,** 4-6 **governaile, -aill(e, -al(e,** 5-6 **governall(e,** (5 **governaly, -ele, -ell, -naille, -yl),** 4- **governail.** [a. OF. *governail* (F. *gouvernail*), *governaille*:—L. *gubernāculum*, pl. *gubernācula* rudder, f. *gubernāre* to steer: see GOVERN *v.*]

1. The rudder of a ship; also, the use of the rudder, steering.

c **1375** *Sc. Leg. Saints, Magdalena* 210 Put in a bat apone þe se bot gouernale. **1382** WYCLIF *Jas.* iii. 4 Schippis..ben born aboute of a litel gouernayle. *c* **1430** *Pilgr. Lyf Manhode* II. xliv. 93 The gouernayle which is within ledeth it. *c* **1477** CAXTON *Jason* 112 b, His gouernaile brack in more thenne a thousand pieces. **1483** —— *Gold. Leg.* 222 b/2 Thenne they recited to her the myracle..how they were comen wythout ony gouernayle of the Shippe. **1561** EDEN *Arte Nauig.* A iij b, Tipho fyrst founde the gouernall or rudder.

2. The action, method, or function of governing; government; authority.

In early use often *pl.*, after L. *gubernacula.*

c **1374** CHAUCER *Boeth.* I. pr. vi. 17 (Camb. MS.) With which gouernayles takestow heede þat [the world] is gouerned. **1375** BARBOUR *Bruce* XVI. 358 Of the marchis than had he The gouernale and the pouste. *c* **1380** WYCLIF *Serm.* Sel. Wks. II. 254 Wiþouten his governaile mut þe Chirche nedis perishe. **1388** —— *Prov.* i. 5 A man vndur-stondinge shal holde gouernails. *c* **1400** *Apol. Loll.* 12 A clene man was in þe court, & spak to hem þat had gret gouernaile in þe court. *c* **1407** HOCCLEVE *Min. Poems* (1892) 59 Glad cheerid Somer to your gouernaille And grace we submitte al our willynge. *c* **1470** HENRY *Wallace* VIII. 16 Thai..Besocht him..To cum and tak sum gouernaill on hand. *c* **1500** *Blowbol's Test.* 112 in Hazl. *E.P.P.* I. 96 Lucina hath the governale of the salt floodes. *a* **1555** LYNDESAY *Tragedie* 71 Off all Scotland I had the Gouernall. **1597** *Guistard & Sismond* I. Bj, His fame had never spot in all his governall.

b. Period of government, reign. Also, form of government, dispensation.

c **1420** *Chron. Vilod.* st. 424 In to þe governell of Quene Elvyne. **1432-50** tr. *Higden* (Rolls) I. 31 The firste gouernayle was from Abraham to Moysen. *Ibid.* VII. 119 The firste yere of his governayle [*Trevisa* duchery].

c. *concr.* One who governs, a ruler. Also, the community governed; a state.

c **1395** *Plowman's T.* 1078 Shuld holy churche have no heed? Who shuld be her governayl? *a* **1400** *Relig. Pieces fr. Thornton MS.* (1867) 33 All of a gouernaylle hafe we a ffadyr. **1597-8** BP. HALL *Sat.* IV. v. 19 Thousands beene in euery gouernall, That liue by losse, and rise by others fall.

d. Management, contrivance. Also, tending, treatment (of plants, wounds).

c **1475** *Partenay* 5561 Other gift bere hens shall by no gouernaill; Then grett mischaunce to purchace and haue. **1502** ARNOLDE *Chron.* 168 The gouernaile of thes plantis is dowblyng of beryng of frute. **1541** R. COPLAND *Guydon's Formul.* R iv, The gouernall accomplysshynge the entencyon after the vlceracyon is to drye the rottennesse. **1590** SPENSER *F.Q.* II. xii. 48 He of this gardin had the governall.

e. Behaviour, self-control; rule of conduct.

1375 BARBOUR *Bruce* XI. 161 He set ledaris till Ilk battale, Knawyn war of gud gouernale. *c* **1420** *Chron. Vilod.* st. 259 þis was þe governyl þey token hem to þe moder and þe douȝter y ffer. *c* **1470** HARDING *Chron.* XXXVI. i, His ire excede[d] his wytte and gouernall. *c* **1475** *Partenay* 844 Ye take A wif vnknow what is sche, Neither haue knewlich of hir gouernail, Ne of hir kinrede. **1597-8** BP. HALL *Sat.* IV. vi. 48 The fashions of their liues and Gouernals.

governance ('gʌvənəns). Forms: 4-6 governaunce, (5 governaunc, -awnce), 4-6 go(u)verna(u)nce, -a(u)ns(e, (6 govirnance, guevernans), 4- governance. [a. OF. *gouvernance*, f. *gouverner*: see GOVERN and -ANCE. Cf. med.L. *gubernantia* (14th c.).]

1. The action or manner of governing (see senses of the vb.); the fact that (a person, etc.) governs.

c **1380** WYCLIF *Sel. Wks.* III. 346 þis stiward..failiþ in governaunce of þe Chirche. *c* **1391** CHAUCER *Astrol.* Contents, As wel for the governance of a clokke as for to fynde the altitude Meridian. **1477** EARL RIVERS (Caxton) *Dictes* 69 To remembre and se to the good gouernaunce of his people. **1548** UDALL *Erasm. Par.* Pref. 2 By Goddes gouvernaunce. **1628** COKE *On Litt.* Pref., Good governance and full right is done to every man. **1643** MILTON *Divorce* II. iii. (1851) 69 Without any wry thoughts cast upon divine governance. *a* **1677** BARROW *Pope's Suprem.* (1680) 57 The Bishop's governance should be so gentle and easie, that men hardly can be unwilling to comply with it. **1850** J. H. NEWMAN *Diffic. Anglic.* 7 It is but one aspect of the state, or mode of civil governance. **1866** FERRIER *Grk. Philos.* I. xiv. 427 The strict governance of his own passions. **1873** BROWNING *Red Cott. Nt.-cap* IV. 50 All my belongings..I have submitted wholly..to your rule and governance. **1879** FARRAR *St. Paul* I. 319 A fresh proof of the immediate governance of God. **1884** *Longm. Mag.* Mar. 493 Rules..for the governance of racing.

b. Controlling, directing, or regulating influence; control, sway, mastery.

1398 TREVISA *Barth. De P.R.* v. i. (1495) 100 The ouer membres gyuyth influence and gouernance to the nether. **1789** BURNEY *Hist. Mus.* (ed. 2) IV. v. 186 An irascible spirit under no great governance. **1863** KINGLAKE *Crimea* (1876) I. vii. 113 A power..which could exert more governance over Turkish statesmen. **1883** RUSKIN *Art Eng.* (1884) 225 Over these hours and colours of the scene, his governance was all but complete.

†**c.** *in* or *under* (a person's) ***governance***: subject to his control. So *to have, hold, take in governance. Obs.*

c **1375** *Sc. Leg. Saints, Mathias* 126 þe towne..quhare pylat presydent was, & had in gouernance þe place. *c* **1385** CHAUCER *L.G.W.* 1044 *Thisbe*, Fortune that hath the world in governaunce. *c* **1430** *Hymns Virg.* (1867) 58 Two in gouernaunce it takid, An aungel freende, an aungil foo. **1450-1530** *Myrr. our Ladye* 31 Saint Benet had many abbeys under hys gouernaunce. **1500-20** DUNBAR *Poems* xlv. 10 Discretioun and considerance Ar both out of hir [love's] gouirnance. **1531** ELYOT *Gov.* I. xiii. (1534) 48 b, Vertue hath all thinge vnder gouernaunce. **1533-4** *Act 25 Hen. VIII*, c. 22 § 11 Your said issue..shalbe & remaine.. at and in the gouernance of their naturall mother. **1548-9** (Mar.) *Bk. Com. Prayer, Communion*, The heartes of kynges are in thy rule and gouernaunce. *c* **1560** A. SCOTT *Poems* (S.T.S.) iii. 24 Body and gudis to hair in govirnance. **1593** SHAKS. *2 Hen. VI*, I. iii. 50 What, shall King Henry be a Pupill still, Vnder the surly Glosters Gouernance? **1824** BENTHAM *Anarchical Fallacies* Wks. 1843 II. 520 The governed are to have the governors under their governance.

†**d.** The state of being governed; good order; esp. in *to set in governance. Obs.*

1390 GOWER *Conf.* III. 339 And thus the faders ordenaunce This londe hath set in governaunce. *c* **1400** *Rom. Rose* 4958 Elde [can]..set men..In good reule and in governaunce. **1590** SPENSER *F.Q.* II. x. 38 Whose countries he redus'd to quiet state, And shortly brought to civile governaunce.

2. The office, function, or power of governing; authority or permission to govern; †the command (of a body of men, a ship).

c **1386** CHAUCER *Wife's Prol.* 814 He yaf me al the bridel in myn hond To han the gouernance of hous and lond. *c* **1400** MAUNDEV. (Roxb.) xvii. 77 [þai] will noȝt suffer men to hafe gouernaunce of þe rewme. *c* **1449** PECOCK *Repr.* Prol. 1 Seint Poul ȝeueth not to Thimothe the instruccioun of eny hiȝer gouernaunce than [etc.]. **1477** EARL RIVERS (Caxton) *Dictes* 14 He that hath grete myght & gouernaunce in this worlde ought to haue no grete reioyssyng. **1491** *Act 7 Hen. VII*, c. 20 § 1 The King..Willeth..that Thomas Lovell Knyght have the guydyng and governaunce of the seid Edmond. *c* **1500** *Melusine* xxxvi. 254 And gaaf hym the gouernaunce of a houndred men of armes. *a* **1546** G. WISHART tr. *Confes. Fayth Sweserlandes* in *Wodr. Soc. Misc.* (1844) 11 Holy wrytte..shulde be the owne interpretour, the rule of charite and faythe hauynge gouernaunce. **1563** B. GOOGE *Eglogs* (Arb.) 102 And thou that hast the gouernance of all, O myghty God. **1759** ROBERTSON *Hist. Scot.* (1813) II. App. i. 133 They may commit the governance thereof to the next heir of the crown. **1884** J. PAYNE *Tales fr. Arabic* I. 112 And Kisra the king invested him with the governance of one of the provinces of his empire.

†**b.** quasi-*concr.* That which governs; governing person or body. *Obs.*

a **1533** LD. BERNERS *Gold. Bk. M. Aurel.* viii. (? 1573) Ej, For certayne they that haue the charge of a prynce, be the.. gouernance of people. **1601** HOLLAND *Pliny* I. 3 Beleeue we ought, this Sun to be..the principall gouernance of nature. **1643** PRYNNE *Sov. Power Parl.* II. 60 Persons of estate.. elected to counsell and assist the governance.

†**3.** The manner in which something is governed or regulated; method of management, system of regulations. In Pecock often: A rule of practice, a discipline. *Obs.*

c **1400** MAUNDEV. (1839) xxii. 232 Now schalle I tell ȝou the Governance of the Court. **1421** *Petition* in Sharp *Cov. Myst.* (1825) 181 Hit wer good Governauns, that every ward kept hem within her own ward. *c* **1449** PECOCK *Repr.* I. i. 5 That no gouernaunce is to be holde of Cristen men the seruice or the lawe of God, saue [etc.]. **1456** *Sc. Acts Jas. II* (1814) II. 46/1 Item as to the feird artikill belangand þe pestilence and gouernance þerof The clergy thinkis þ^t [etc.]. **1559** N. BACON in Strype *Ann. Ref.* (1824) I. ii. 78 A thing to be eschewed in all good governances. **1660** R. COKE *Power & Subj.* 207 To enquire of the Foundation, Erection, and Governance of Hospitals.

†**4.** Conduct of life or business; mode of living, behaviour, demeanour. Also *pl.* proceedings, doings.

c **1374** CHAUCER *Troylus* II. 170 (219) Her tale was broght to the ende, Of her astate, and of her governaunce. *c* **1400** *Destr. Troy* 656 All your gate and your gouernaunse graidly to telle. **1423** JAS. I *Kingis Q.* lxxxviii, Folk of religioun, That from the warld thaire gouernance did hide. **1426** LYDG. *De Guileville's Pilgr.* (E.E.T.S.) 3567, I ha..suffryd ..That ye, by your gouernauncys My custommys & myn ordynauncys..Ye han ytournyd at your wyl. **1428** *Surtees Misc.* (1888) 9 Yat ye sayd John Lyllyng fra yan furth suld be of gude governance and trew in all his bying and hys sellyng. *c* **1460** FORTESCUE *Abs. & Lim. Mon.* xx, Many men wil than be of better gouernaunce. **1481** CAXTON *Myrr.* I. v. 18 That procedeth of theyr folissh and outrageous gouernaunce. **1508** DUNBAR *Tua Mariit Wemen* 259 Be constant in ȝour gouernance, and counterfeit gud maneris. **1581** LAMBARDE *Eiren.* I. v. (1588) 31 Sufficient men.. learned in the Lawe and of good gouernance. **1591** SPENSER *Muiopot.* 384 He likest is to fall into mischaunce, That is regardles of his governaunce. **1656** STANLEY *Hist. Philos.* VI. (1701) 243/1 Wise Princes ought not to be admired for their Government, but Governance.

†**b.** Discreet or virtuous behaviour; wise self-command. *Obs.*

c **1392** CHAUCER *Compl. Venus* 9 In him is bountee, wisdom, governaunce, Wel more then any mannes wit can gesse. **1600** HOLLAND *Livy* XLII. lxii. (1609) 1152 The manner..was, in time of adversitie to bear all out and set a good countenance, but in prosperitie to hold an even hand and to use governance [L. *moderari animos*].

†'**governancy.** *Obs.* [f. as prec.: see -ANCY.] = GOVERNANCE 2.

1693 *Col. Rec. Pennsylv.* I. 414 And as to other reasons rendred for the Superseding our proprietor's governancie. [**1794** *Laura & Augustus* II. 50, I preferred the lieutenant governancy of Dominica.]

†'**governante.** *Obs.* Also 7-8 **governant.** [Anglicized form of GOUVERNANTE.]

1. A female governor or ruler.

1698 FRYER *Acc. E. India & P.* 132 An Old Gentlewoman ..the Governant of the Womens Quarters. **1763-5** SMOLLETT *Hist. Eng.* xxii. (1827) III. 282 The administration of the government devolved upon the princess, as governante during her son's minority.

2. A mistress of a household; a housekeeper.

1668 L'ESTRANGE *Vis. Quevedo* (ed. 3) 46, I saw Envy there drest up in a Widow's Vail, and the very Picture of the Governant of one of your Noblemen's Houses. **1700** CONGREVE *Way of World* v. i, This was your Merchandize you dealt in, when I..made you Governante of my whole Family! **1793** MRS. INCHBALD *Midn. Hour* I. i, I am..the general governante of the whole house. **1816** SCOTT *Old Mort.* vi, 'Mercifu' powers!' exclaimed the governante.

3. A woman who has charge of a young person; a governess, a female teacher; a chaperon, duenna.

1639 T. BRUGIS tr. *Camus' Mor. Relat.* 232 What diligence soever widowed fathers use to finde out good governants, they never find any whose eyes be so vigilant over their daughters as their mothers. **1674-81** in BLOUNT *Glossogr.* **1685** CROWNE *Sir C. Nice* IV. Dram. Wks. 1874 III. 310 Other nations, by their spies and governantes, are at great toil and charges to be cuckolds. **1688** in Ellis *Orig. Lett.* Ser. II. IV. 114 The Lady Marquis of Powis, governante to the Prince. **1709** STEELE *Tatler* No. 9 ⁋3 The young Lady saw her good Governante on her Knees. **1711** E. WARD *Quix.* I. 373 To Steal a Squint at One another when Jealous Governant sits by. **1756** COWPER in *Connoisseur* No. 119 ⁋4 The governantes at the boarding-school teach Miss to be a good girl. **1796** J. MORSE *Amer. Geog.* II. 265 A lady of a Polish grandee,..attended by..an old gentlewoman for her governante. **1823** SCOTT *Peveril* v, Mistress Ellesmere..laid her orders upon Deborah, the governante, immediately to carry the children to their airing in the park.

†**gover'nation.** [f. GOVERN *v.* + -ATION.] = GOVERNANCE, in various senses.

Erroneously substituted for GOVERNANCE in some late MSS. (hence in certain editions) of Chaucer *Astrol.* Prol. 59 ('the gouernance of a clokke') and *Somnours Tale* 186 ('Aron, that hadde the temple in gouernaunce').

†**governator.** *Obs. rare*⁻¹. [ad. It. *governatore*: see GOVERNOR.] A governor.

1522 J. CLERK in Ellis *Orig. Lett.* Ser. III. I. 312 There be deputed for gouernators here, for this first moneth of the Popis absence, the Cardinall *Sanctæ Crucis primus Episcopus Cardinalis*, The Cardinall Sedunen [etc.].

†**governatrice.** *Obs. rare*⁻¹. [a. It. *governatrice*:—L. *gubernātrīc-em*, fem. agent-n. f. *gubernare* to GOVERN.] A female governor.

1532 CRANMER *Let.* in Strype *Cranmer* (1694) App. 6 The Diate..was lately held in Flandres, where the Quene of Hungary is governatrice.

governayl, -ayll(e, vars. GOVERNAIL, *Obs.*

governed ('gʌvənd), *ppl. a.* [f. GOVERN *v.* + -ED¹.] In senses of the vb.

1686 J. SCOTT *Chr. Life* (1747) III. 435 The Church, by Christ's own Institution, is a governed Society of Men. **1824** L. MURRAY *Eng. Gram.* (ed. 5) I. 261 The sign of the possessive should be annexed to each of the governed nouns. **1861** T. WOOLNER *My Beautiful Lady* (1863) 158 A well-planned city in a governed land That [etc.].

absol. **1596** SPENSER *State Irel.* Wks. (Globe) 649 This inconvenience..is..more hardly to be redressed in governour than in the governed. **1681** NEVILE *Plato Rediv.* 30 It was instituted for the good and preservation of the Governed. *a* **1832** MACKINTOSH *Lit. Soc. Bombay* Wks. 1846 II. 577 The security of the governed cannot exist without the security of the governors. **1855** MACAULAY *Hist. Eng.* xiv. III. 393 This great contract between the governors and the governed.

governele, -ell, variants of GOVERNAIL, *Obs.*

†**governeress.** *Obs.* Also 4 governowresse, 4–7 governeresse, 5–6 governouresse, 6 gouvernres. [ad. OF. *gouverneresse*, fem. of *gouverneur* GOVERNOR.] A female governor; = the later GOVERNESS, in various senses.

*c*1366 CHAUCER *A.B.C.* 141 He hath thee maked.. governeresse of hevene. *c*1368 —— *Compl. Pite* 80 Shal Crueltee be your governeresse? *c*1422 HOCCLEVE *Jereslaus' Wife* 298 A yong doghtir haue I.. Of which I wolde.. Thow tooke on thee to be gouerneresse, And teche hire. 1430–40 LYDG. *Bochas* I. viii. (1544) 15 b, She was their iudge and their gouerneresse. *c*1430 *Pilgr. Lyf Manhode* I. viii. (1869) 6, I am gouernouresse of alle thinge, and of alle harmes j am leche. 1490 CAXTON *Eneydos* xxvii. 96 She was maister ouer him & gouerneresse. 1553 EDW. VI *Lit. Rem.* (Roxb.) II. 571 If i died wᵗout issu, and there were none heire masle, then the L. Fraunces to be gouvernres. 1555 W. WATREMAN *Fardle Facions* I. i. 27 To Ceres (thei Sacrificed and did honour) as gouerneresse of the earth. 1577 [see GOVERNESS *sb.* 2 quot. 1587]. 1652 *Orders Barthol. Hosp.* (1885) 21 You [the Matron] shall also as the chiefe Governeresse.. have speciall regard to the good ordering.

governess (ˈgʌvənɪs), *sb.* [shortened form of GOVERNERESS: see -ESS.]

1. a. A woman who governs (e.g. a kingdom, province, a community, religious institution); a female governor or ruler. *Obs.* exc. as *nonce-use.* †Formerly often applied to the presiding or ruling goddess (of a department of nature, art, etc.).

1483 CAXTON *Gold. Leg.* 296/2 Thappostle halowed to god Ephygene the kynges doughter and made her maystresse and gouuernesse of moo than two hondred Vyrgyns. 1539 *Act 31 Hen. VIII*, c. 13 §2 Abbottes, priours, abbesses, prioresses, and other ecclesiasticall gouernors & gouernesses of such late monasteries. 1548 HALL *Chron., Hen. VIII* (1550) 145 The Lady Margaret gouernesse of Flaunders. 1577 HARRISON *England* II. xxiii. (1877) I. 352 Minerva was the cheefe goddesse and governesse of those waters. 1590 GREENWOOD *Collect. Sclaund. Art.* B iij b, All true Christians.. acknowledg her Maiestie to be the supreame maiestrate and gouernesse of all persons. 1610 HOLLAND *Camden's Brit.* I. 718 The Abbay.. whereof her selfe was first Governesse. 1663 DAVENANT *2nd Pt. Siege Rhodes* II. Dram. Wks. 1873 III. 325 As if our sex's governess, the moon, Had plac'd us but for sport on fortune's lap. 1703 J. SAVAGE *Lett. Antients* lx. 174 As it is a great Cruelty in Barbarians to make Slaves of their Wives, so is it no less a Folly in us Romans, to let them be our Governesses. 1730 A. GORDON *Maffei's Amphith.* 168 Diana, the Governess of all kinds of Hunting. 1737 WHISTON *Josephus, Hist.* I. iii. §1 John had left her to be the governess of the public affairs. 1749 FIELDING *Tom Jones* VIII. vii, The landlady was.. absolute governess in these regions. 1754 RICHARDSON *Grandison* (1781) IV. xviii. 143 The governesses or matrons of the society I would have to be women of family. 1797 MRS. RADCLIFFE *Italian* xxv. (1824) 665 This lady was a shining example to governesses of religious houses. 1826 C. BUTLER *Life Grotius* xiv. §3. 219 His mother was named by the states Governess of the United Provinces. 1875 MISS BIRD *Sandwich Isl.* (1880) 65 The governess of Hawaii, the Princess Keelikolani, has a house on the beach.

†**b.** *fig.* of things personified. *Obs.*

1561 T. NORTON *Calvin's Inst.* I. xvii. (1634) 90 That providence, which is the governesse of all things. 1587 GOLDING *De Mornay* xx. (1617) 345 Religion is the gouernesse of all vertues. 1604 T. WRIGHT *Passions* II. ii. 58 The Will, being the governesse of the Soule. 1611 SPEED *Hist. Gt. Brit.* VI. xvii. §5. 97 The Prouince reduced to the obedience of the fatall Gouernesse Rome. 1643 MILTON *Divorce* II. xx. (1851) 116 To teach us that charity is the high governesse of our beleefe. 1706 Z. CRADOCK *Serm. Charity* (1740) 25 Eternal damnation may be.. the instrument of wise men, but the mistress and governess of fools only.

†**2. a.** A woman who has charge or control of a person, esp. of a young one. *Obs.*

1587 HOLINSHED *Chron.* III. 335/2 The Ladie Marie of Biskie, gouernesse [1577 gouerneresse] of the King of Castile and Leon. 1615 G. SANDYS *Trav.* III. 180 Virgins who neuer past the bounds of their Couents but on Sundayes onely (and then attending on their seuerall Gouernesses). 1653 H. COGAN tr. *Pinto's Trav.* liii. 209, I Nhay Nivolau, a poor woman, Governess, and Tutress of my Son, an Orphan, do prostrate my self before thee. 1688 *Lond. Gaz.* No. 2360/4 He [the infant son of James II] being then in the Arms of the Lady Governess, the Right Honourable the Lady Marchioness of Powis. 1771 SMOLLETT *Humph. Cl.* 6 Apr., To Mrs. Jermyn, My worthy governess may believe me.

b. A female teacher; an instructress; now chiefly, one so employed in a private household. (The current use.)

1712 STEELE *Spect.* No. 314 ¶8 Pray proceed to detect the male administration of governesses as successfully as you have expos'd that of pedagogues. 1759 *Ann. Reg.* 425 The mistress of the school is called *governess*, for the word *mistress* has a vulgar sound with it. 1762 GOLDSM. *Cit. W.* lxxxviii, Their language-masters, music-masters, hair-frizzers, and governesses, are all from abroad. 1804 G. ROSE *Diaries* (1860) II. 187 The head governess for the.. princess. 1850 C. M. YONGE *Langley School* xix. 172 There is governess gone to Mr. Howard's. 1884 PAE *Eustace* 22 But in two years thereafter he had married the governess. 1890 'L. FALCONER' *Mlle. Ixe* (1891) 16 'For my part', said Mrs. Merrington,.. 'I think good looks are rather out of place in a governess'. 1939 F. THOMPSON *Lark Rise* xi. 204 There was no assistant mistress; Governess taught all the classes simultaneously.

3. The wife of a Governor. *Obs.* exc. as jocular nonce-use.

1697 tr. *C'tess D'Aunoy's Trav.* (1706) 22 The Lady Governess of the Town drew near to me. 1814 HEYNE *Tracts India* 345 The common wood strawberry.. was introduced by the Right Hon. Lady Powis when Governess at Madras. 1855 THACKERAY *Newcomes* I. 234 Lady Trotter, the Governess of St. Kitts, you know.

4. *attrib.* and *Comb.*, as ***governess-instructor***, ***-tongue***, ***-trade***; ***governess-like***, ***-made***, ***-moulded***, ***-taught***, ***-trained*** adjs.; **governess-cart, -car**, a light two-wheeled vehicle with seats at the sides only, face to face; **Governess-General** (cf. 3), the wife of a Governor-General; **governess-pupil, -student**, a girl or young woman who is being trained to be a governess.

1893 *Chicago Exhib., Catal. Brit. Section* 171 The 'Governess Car'—a small wagonette body, without boot, hung—on elliptic springs, and with a deep cranked axle—very near the ground, and used either with a donkey or very small pony. 1878 *Porcupine* 16 Nov. 516/1 The brothers of the Governess-General arrived at the station. 1909 *Westm. Gaz.* 5 July 5/2 The governess-instructor stood at the right and the nursery-governess at the left. 1928 *Manch. Guardian Weekly* 10 Aug. 114/1 Some of them—and this applies chiefly to.. the calfas and elderly governess-like slaves—are gradually selling off the treasures that their sojourn in the Palace brought to them. 1934 H. G. WELLS *Exper. Autobiogr.* II. ix. 769, I have already said that Tyrell's mind was governess-made. *Ibid.* 771 Another of these governess-moulded minds. *a*1900 *Mod. Advt.* Governess-student required. 1934 H. G. WELLS *Exper. Autobiogr.* II. ix. 772, I declare that the greatest present dangers to the human race are those governess-trained brains which apparently monopolize the Foreign Offices of the world. 1906 *Westm. Gaz.* 28 Aug. 2/1 That governess-taught conception of the classics. 1892 HARDY *Well-Beloved* (1897) I. ii. 20 To drown the local ballads by songs purchased at the Budmouth fashionable music-sellers', and the local vocabulary by a governess-tongue of no country at all. 1816 JANE AUSTEN *Emma* II. xvii. 324, I was not thinking of the slave-trade..; governess-trade, I assure you, was all that I had in view.

Hence (*nonce-wds.*) **ˈgoverness-dom, ˈgovernesshood**, the state of being a governess; **ˈgovernessless** *a.*, without a governess; **ˈgovernessship**, the office of a governess.

1866 *Q. Rev.* No. 238. 515 If but a few such women would combine here and there to elevate the tone of *governess-dom. 1867 E. YATES *Forlorn Hope* xv. 183 She was always on the look-out for that knight who was to come and deliver her from the bonds of *governesshood. 1859 FREEMAN in Stephens *Life* (1895) I. 245, I am still houseless, as well as boroughless, and am soon going to be *governessless. 1826 MISS MITFORD *Village* Ser. II. (1863) 403 She.. proceeded to give me the history of her successive *governess-ships. 1862 *Spectator* 13 Dec. 1390/1 She seems to have finally abandoned governessship.

governess (ˈgʌvənɪs), *v.* [f. the sb.]

1. *intr.* (Only in gerund.) To work or earn one's living as a governess.

1826 MISS MITFORD *Village* Ser. II. (1863) 405 Sixteen years of governessing.. might well have.. tamed that romantic imagination. 1848 C. BRONTË *J. Eyre* (1857) 276 You will give up your governessing slavery at once. 1860 SALA *Lady Chesterf.* 43 The girls had to go out governessing. 1882 *Spectator* 11 Feb. 182 Governessing was the only occupation open to 'ladies' without means.

2. *trans.* To act as governess to; to teach.

1847 C. M. YONGE *Scenes & Characters* xiii. 162 She has been governessed and crammed till she is half sick of all reading! 1852 *Tait's Mag.* XIX. 346 Esther yet remains single, and governesses her brother's rising family. 1884 *Harper's Mag.* Oct. 692/2 I'm going to 'governess' the children of a Mrs... Caryl.

governessy, *a.* [f. GOVERNESS + -Y.] Having the characteristics of a governess.

1872 *Spectator* 30 Mar. 406/1 Mary Garth has none of her mother's didactic precision, none of her *governessy* qualities—if one may be permitted to coin a word. 1879 C. M. YONGE *Magnum Bonum* II. xxv. 498 [She] has broken out of all her primmy governessy crust. 1893 *Westm. Gaz.* 6 Apr. 3/1 Miss C. is sometimes a little prim and *governessy. 1963 *Times* 24 May 15/4 It is an ungrateful task, but her governessy approach does not make the best of it.

governing (ˈgʌvənɪŋ), *vbl. sb.* [f. GOVERN *v.* + -ING¹.]

1. The action of the vb. GOVERN. (rarely *pl.*)

*a*1300 *Cursor M.* 7414 Saul was yeitt in sted o king, Bot he moght do na gouerning. *c*1400 *Rom. Rose* 7266 To such folk .. Shuld princes & these lordes wyse Take alle her londes & her thinges, Bothe werre & pees, in gouernynges. 1450–70 *Golagros & Gaw.* 1320 Sen vourschipfull Wawane has wonnyn to your handis The senyory in gouernyng. 1661 MILTON *Gram.* II. Wks. (1847) 469/1 Governing, wherby one part of speech is govern'd by another. 1843 CARLYLE *Past & Pr.* IV. i, It was a valorous Governing.

†**2.** = GOVERNMENT, esp. in phrases ***to have the governing of***; (***to have***) ***in***, ***under one's governing***.

*c*1340 *Cursor M.* 7402 (Trin.) Þe kyngdome to haue in gouernyng. *c*1385 CHAUCER *L.G.W.* 581 *Cleopatra*, Tholome the kyng, That al Egypte hadde in his governyng. 1389 *Eng. Gilds* (1870) 116 Other fundacion or gouernynge is noughte in oure gilde. 1450–70 *Golagros & Gaw.* 1169 Ye ar gaderit in grosse.. vndir my gouernyng. 1523 LD. BERNERS *Froiss.* I. clxxxvii. 221 The towne, wherof I haue the gouernynge. 1590 SPENSER *F.Q.* III. ix. 44 And Troy againe out of her dust was reard To sitt in second seat of soveraine king Of all the world, under her governing.

†**3.** Conduct, mode of action. Also, means of living; livelihood. *Obs.*

1375 BARBOUR *Bruce* VI. 383 He valde se his gouernyng, That hade the castell in keping. *c*1475 *Rauf Coilȝear* 447 Gangand with laidis, my gouerning to get. 1500–20 DUNBAR *Poems* xli. 2 Be ȝe ane luvar, think ȝe nocht ȝe suld Be weill adwysit in ȝour gouerning? ?*a*1550 *Freiris Berwick* 360 in *Dunbar's Poems* (S.T.S.) 297 For in her hairt scho had ane persaving That he had knawin all hir governing.

governing (ˈgʌvənɪŋ), *ppl. a.* [f. GOVERN *v.* + -ING².] That governs, in sense of the vb.

governing body: a designation (in some cases the only term officially recognized) for the body of managers of a hospital, public school, etc.

1635 *Gram. Warre* D 6 b, Betweene the word gouerning and gouerned. 1647 CLARENDON *Hist. Reb.* IV. §125 And so they were both invested in those offices, to the no small displeasure of the governing party. 1653 R. SANDERS *Physiogn.* 157 He will be somewhat covetous because of the governing Sign. 1701 ATTERBURY *Serm.* vii. (1726) I. 274 God's Governing Providence, by which he holds the Balance of Nations. 1736 BUTLER *Anal.* I. iii. Wks. 1874 I. 62 Man is the acknowledged governing animal upon the earth. 1824 L. MURRAY *Eng. Gram.* (ed. 5) I. 399 When a verb in the infinitive mood, follows its governing verb [etc.]. 1875 JOWETT *Plato* (ed. 2) I. 113 Knowledge is certainly a governing power. 1887 *Daily News* 30 May 5/1 M. Grévy.. had most of the governing men.. on his side. 1901 *Westm. Gaz.* 20 Apr. 2/3 He [*sc.* Whitty] originated the term 'governing classes'. 1903 G. B. SHAW *Man & Superman* p. xxiv, We know now that there is no hereditary 'governing class' any more than a hereditary hooliganism. 1938 *New English Weekly* 21 July 276/1 It may be that behind the apparent split in governing-class opinion there is a conflict of financial interests.

Hence **ˈgoverningly** *adv.*

1884 C. H. PARKHURST *Serm.* in *Bibl. Soc. Rec.* Dec. 178 We infer that somewhere some one mind has worked governingly on these forty musicians.

†**ˈgovernless**, *a. Obs.* [f. GOVERN *v.* + -LESS.] Without government, ungoverned.

1621 BP. R. MOUNTAGU *Diatribæ* II. ii. 368 These things were thus done as in a gouernlesse City, with all licentiousnesse. 1624 CAPT. SMITH *Virginia* V. 190 This done, because they would not be gouernlesse when his Deputiship was expired, there was a generall assembly, and by that Election Kendall was confirmed to succeed still Gouernor. 1679 SIR T. BROWNE *Wks.* (1848) 453 These are the sad ends of many dissolute and governless persons.

government (ˈgʌvənmənt). Also 6 gouver(n)ment, 6–7 goverment. [a. OF. *governement* (F. *gouvernement*), f. *governer*: see GOVERN *v.* and -MENT. In the main, this word may be considered to have superseded GOVERNANCE.]

1. The action of governing (see senses of the vb.).

a. The action of ruling; continuous exercise of authority over the action of subjects or inferiors; authoritative direction or regulation; control, rule.

*c*1566 J. ALDAY tr. *Boaystuau's Theat. World* H iv b, A king or a prince.. that hath under his governement so manye thousands of men. 1666 PH. HENRY *Diaries* (1882) 184 That the Governmᵗ of the Church of Christ ought to bee manag'd by the Ministers of Christ. 1729 BUTLER *Serm.* Wks. 1874 II. 45 The government of the tongue.. relates chiefly to conversation. 1758 S. HAYWARD *Serm.* i. 4 We are all under its [sin's] power and government. 1827 POLLOK *Course T.* x, God's eternal government approved. 1849 MACAULAY *Hist. Eng.* vi. II. 88 The Dean was charged with the government of a.. number of youths of high connections. 1859 TENNYSON *Enid* 1043 They.. [horses], like creatures gently born,.. felt Her low firm voice and tender government.

b. *spec.* The action of ruling and directing the affairs of a state; political rule and administration.

1789 BENTHAM *Princ. Legisl.* vii. §1 The business of government is to promote the happiness of the society by punishing and rewarding. 1841 E. MIALL in *Nonconf.* I. 1 At present we have government in excess. 1860 MILL *Repr. Govt.* i. (1865) 1 Government is a problem to be worked like any other question of business. 1895 MORLEY in *Daily News* 30 May 2/1 All government is difficult.

†**c.** Management. *Obs.*

1587 MASCALL (*title*) Government of Cattel. 1660 SHARROCK *Vegetables* 22 The whole government and husbandry of hemp from the seed to the distaffe is like this of flax.

†**d.** Working or propelling (a ship). *Obs.*⁻¹

1697 POTTER *Antiq. Greece* III. xiv. (1715) 124 All the three ways of Government [of Ships] viz. by Sail, Oar, and Cords, were upon Occasion made use of.

e. Guidance (in action). *Obs.* exc. in commercial and official epistolary use (cf. F. *gouverne*, Sp. *gobierno*).

1712 ARBUTHNOT *John Bull* I. ix, If she submits to my government, she will be abroad in a little time. 1824 L. MURRAY *Eng. Gram.* (ed. 5) I. 227 Examples.. which may serve as some government to the scholar. *Mod.* (*Comm.*) Please send me, for my government, a copy of your correspondence with Mr. A.

†**2.** The manner in which one's action is governed. **a.** In physical sense: Management of the limbs or body; movements, demeanour; also, habits of life, regimen. **b.** In moral sense: Conduct, behaviour; becoming conduct, discretion. *Obs.*

a. *c*1566 J. ALDAY tr. *Boaystuau's Theat. World* E ij, Here you may see his life and governement, whilst he is inclosed in his mothers wombe. 1590 SPENSER *F.Q.* I. ix. 10 Their God himselfe.. Shott many a dart at me with fiers intent; But I them warded all with wary government. 1601 CHESTER *Love's Mart.* lxvii, Running, vaulting, and Actiuitie And other exercise of gouernement. 1612 in *Crt. & Times Jas. I* (1849) I. 203 The disease.. must have its ordinary course, and the less physic the better, but only sweating, and an orderly course of keeping and government.

b. 1483 CAXTON *G. de la Tour* B viij, The goode knyght.. was wyse and of grete gouernment in repreuying of the lady. 1596 SPENSER *F.Q.* IV. v. 20 Whose beauties wonderment

She lesse esteem'd then th' others vertuous government. **1604** SHAKS. *Oth.* III. iii. 256 Feare not my gouernment. **1633** FORD *'Tis Pity* I. i, How did the university applaud Thy government, behaviour, learning, speech. **1639** T. BRUGIS tr. *Camus' Mor. Relat.* 319 He tooke into his house one of his sisters, a maid of government and judgement.

3. a. The office or function of governing or ruling; authority to govern; †the command of an army or fortress (*obs.*).

1584 POWEL *Lloyd's Cambria* 69 The rule and Gouernment of North Wales. **1590** SPENSER *F.Q.* I. x. 37 The first.. Of all the house had charge and governement, As Guardian and Steward of the rest. **1593** SHAKS. *3 Hen. VI*, IV. vi. 24, I here resigne my Gouernment to thee. **1610** —— *Temp.* I. ii. 75 The Government I cast vpon my brother. **1651** HOBBES *Gov. & Soc.* x. §16. 163 The government it self, or the administration of its affairs, are better committed to one, then many. **1685** BAXTER *Paraphr. N.T.* Matt. x. 2 Peter had a priority, though no Government over the rest. **1700** TYRRELL *Hist. Eng.* II. 915 He was.. perswaded.. to accept the Government of Dover Castle. **1727** DE FOE *Syst. Magic* I. i. (1840) 18 Prometheus obtained the government of a part of Armenia. **1872** J. L. SANFORD *Eng. Kings, Chas. I*, 333 He would learn.. to look upon government as an absolute function of the Sovereign.

†b. An appointment as governor. *Obs.*

1617 MORYSON *Itin.* II. 68 Hee.. had made offer to resigne the gouernement he had in the Prouince of Connaght. **1647-8** COTTERELL *Davila's Hist. Fr.* (1678) 9 Those few small governments which yet remained in their family. **1769** *Junius Lett.* iv. (1804) I. 37 My silence may have been purchased by my government.

†c. The post of gouvernante or governess. *Obs.*[-1]

1804 G. ROSE *Diaries* (1860) II. 196 Lady Pembroke had been offered the government of the Princess Charlotte.

4. a. The fact that a particular person governs.

1559 AYLMER (*title*) An Harborowe for Faithfull and Trewe Subiectes, agaynst the late blowne Blaste, concerninge the Government of Women. **1759** ROBERTSON *Hist. Scot.* (1813) I. II. 72 The government of a Queen was unknown in Scotland. **1841** ELPHINSTONE *Hist. Ind.* II. 195 The government of Warangól was never restored. **1879** RYDBERG *Magic Mid. Ages* iv. 175 Never has there been a time when a divine and universal government was so much despaired of as in the Middle Ages.

†b. Period of rule, tenure of office. *Obs.*

1603 SHAKS. *Meas. for M.* IV. ii. 141 His fact till now in the gouernment of Lord Angelo, came not to an vndoubtfull proofe. **1617** MORYSON *Itin.* II. 2 The time of my owne being in Ireland, in the Lord Mountjoy his Governement. **1664** MARVELL *Corr.* Wks. 1872-5 II. 153 [I] shall pray to God to bless your Majesty with a long and happy Government.

5. The portion of country ruled over by a governor, a province; also as a specific name for a subdivision of a kingdom or empire, as formerly in France and in Russia (= Russian *guberniya*). Also, occas., the territory united under a common rule, as a kingdom, republic, principality, etc.

1603 SIR D. CARLETON in Ellis *Orig. Lett.* Ser. I. III. 82 Which was payde owt of his goverment of Jersy. **1617** MORYSON *Itin.* I. 245 To make a present to a Cady, returning from his governement to Constantinople. **1624** N. DE LAUNE tr. *Du Moulin's Logick* 54 As when we divide.. France into seventeene governments. **1700** DRYDEN *Fables, Baucis & Philemon* 20 To Phrygian realms, my Grandsire's Government. **1705** ADDISON *Italy* Ded., When I pass'd through most of the Protestant Governments in Europe. **1710** WHITWORTH *Acc. Russia* (1758) 53 In 1710, the Czar.. divided the Empire into eight governments. **1759** WHEELOCK in F. Chase *Hist. Dartmouth Coll.* (1891) I. 6, I was upon the same road to New Haven when that Doctor passed through this government. **1840** THIRLWALL *Greece* VII. 127 The governments west of the Euphrates. **1894** *Daily News* 24 Mar. 5/3 The manufacture of Russian lace.. is spread over many governments.

6. a. The system according to which a nation or community is governed; form or kind of polity. Often with defining word indicating either the nature of the community governed, as in ***civil*** or ***political, church*** or ***ecclesiastical government***, or the kind of organization adopted, as in ***monarchical, oligarchical, republican government; episcopal, presbyterian government.***

1553 BRENDE *Q. Curtius* 48 He passed.. vnto the inwarde partes of Egypt, and set a staie and order of the gouerment of the countrey. **1588** *Marprel. Epist.* (Arb.) 4 The Church gouerment prescribed in the worde. **1604** EDMONDS *Observ. Cæsar's Comm.* 28 Gouernment is defined, to be an establishing of order best fitting the maintenance of a people, in a peaceable and happie life. **1605** CAMDEN *Rem.* 2 Gouernement Ecclesiasticall, and Civill. **1660** MILTON *Free Commw.* 3 Depriving our selves the instant fruition of that free government which we have so dearly purchasd. *a* **1698** TEMPLE *Hist. Eng.* (1699) 9 Their Government was like that of the ancient Gauls, of several small Nations under several petty Princes. **1733** POPE *Ess. Man* III. 303 For Forms of Government let fools contest. **1735-8** BOLINGBROKE *On Parties* 142 A Government by Will, never prevail'd in Britain. **1748-9** GRAY *Let.* Poems (1775) 201 The three sorts of government, Despotism, the limited Monarchy, and the Republican. **1769** ROBERTSON *Chas. V* (1813) VI. VI. 107 But Loyola.. appointed that the Government of his order should be purely monarchical. **1771** *Junius Lett.* xlvii. 249 The government of England is a government of law. **1809-10** COLERIDGE *Friend* (1865) 103 Government must have originated in choice and an agreement. **1874** BANCROFT *Footpr. Time* i. 43 Government, in early times, was very imperfectly organized.

b. Short for *instrument of government*.

1654 CROMWELL *Sp.* 12 Sept. in *Carlyle*, The Gouernment was to be read. **1654** *Perfect Account* (Thomason Tracts DXCI. No. 21. 1245) This day was extant the Government of this Commonwealth by his Highness special commandement.

7. The governing power in a state; the body of persons charged with the duty of governing. This may be viewed in two aspects, giving rise to two distinct senses of the word, which however often coincide in use. **a.** As a permanent entity (cf. 'the Crown', 'Parliament', etc.), irrespective of the changes in the persons who hold office. Hence often practically equivalent to STATE, esp. when used *attrib.* **b.** As constituted afresh by the appointment of a number of persons to certain official positions; in England, synonymous with *ministry* or *administration*. Often used without article. ***to form a government***: said of the action of the prime minister in filling up those offices, the holders of which are jointly with himself responsible for the administration of the country.

1702 LUTTRELL *Brief Rel.* (1857) V. 212 The government yet has not any account of it. **1779** R. BAKER *Remarks* 35 [Condemns as 'barbarous' the custom of saying 'government' instead of 'the government']. **1801** BP. TOMLINE in Stanhope *Life Pitt* II. 395 A Roman Catholic Bill, which Government stands pledged to Ireland to introduce into the Imperial Parliament. **1817** SOUTHEY in *Life & Corr.* (1850) IV. 239 Government are acting like themselves. **1817** *Parl. Deb.* 347 A direct charge against the Government of Ireland. **1828** PALMERSTON in Bulwer *Life* I. v. 217 The Duke of Wellington has been employed since.. the 9th in taking steps to reorganize the Government. **1844** H. H. WILSON *Brit. India* I. 105 The suspension of military operations.. for several years afforded the British Government opportunity to [etc.]. **1860** MILL *Repr. Govt.* (1865) 137/2 In all questions between a government and an individual, the presumption in every Englishman's mind is, that the government is in the wrong. **1868** G. DUFF *Pol. Surv.* 17 The Liberal Government.. is neither so strong nor so wisely composed as we might wish. **1875** JEVONS *Money* (1878) 246 The United States government tried a similar experiment. **1879** MCCARTHY *Own Times* II. xxiii. 197 If the resolution had been passed, the Government must have resigned. **1880** *Our Nat. Responsibility for Opium Trade* 4 The Indian Government is the greatest manufacturer in the world. **1888** BRYCE *Amer. Commw.* I. 119 *note*, In America people usually speak of the President and his ministers as the 'administration', not as the 'government'. **1893** *Daily News* 2 May 5/5 Her Majesty's Government had not only to consider Egypt, but [etc.].

c. *pl.* Short for *government securities*. *U.S.*

1885 *Boston* (Mass.) *Jrnl.* 30 Apr. 1/3 Money Steady—Governments Firmer—Stocks Higher.

8. *Grammar.* The influence of one word over another, according to established usage, in determining the case of a noun or pronoun or the mood of a verb; the effect of this influence.

1755 in JOHNSON. **1762** BP. LOWTH *Introd. Eng. Gram.* (1838) 157 Adverbs have no government. **1824** L. MURRAY *Eng. Gram.* (ed. 5) I. 267 This position of the pronoun sometimes occasions its proper case and government to be neglected. *Ibid.* 285 Participles have the same government as the verbs from which they are derived. **1859** H. ALFORD *Grk. Test., Heb.* ix. 15 IV. I. 173 The severing of a genitive in government from its governing noun is not uncommon in our Ep[istle].

9. *attrib.* and *Comb.*, as (sense 7) ***government-account, -act, -borough, -candidate, -money, -office, -price, -property, -rent, -secretary, -timber***; objective, as ***government-making***; instrumental, as ***government-appointed, -backed, -certificated, -controlled, -directed, -financed, -held, -issued, -imposed, -made, -mounted, -organized, -run, -sponsored, -supported, -worked*** adjs. Also †**government-general**, the territory under the control of a governor-general; **government house**, the official residence of a governor; also jocularly in the colonies the residence of the owner or manager of an estate; **government-man**, (*a*) a man connected with the government, an official; †(*b*) *Austral.*, a convict; **government-paper**, bonds, exchequer-bills, or the like, issued by a government; **government-securities**, (*a*) = prec.; (*b*) *slang*, handcuffs or fetters generally; **government-signpost** *slang*, the gallows; **government-stroke** (*Austral.*), a convict's stroke or rate of work; **government surplus**, unused equipment sold by the government through retailers; **government-valve** = SAFETY-VALVE.

1809 A. HENRY *Trav.* 58 A clerk, who managed the Indian trade here, on *government account. **1828** P. CUNNINGHAM *N.S. Wales* (ed. 3) II. 304 It.. renders.. *government-acts less liable to be made objects of personal cavil or animosity. **1909** *Westm. Gaz.* 10 June 4/1 The *Government-appointed Air Committee stepped in. **1963** *Rep. Comm. Inquiry Decimal Curr.* i. 1 in *Parl. Papers 1962-3* (Cmnd. 2145) XI. 195 Following reports in 1959 by Government-appointed committees, Australia will adopt a decimal currency in 1966. **1951** A. L. ROWSE *England of Elizbeth* iv. 116 The Merchant Adventurers, the great *government-backed body of exporters. **1861** MAY *Const. Hist.* I. i. 15 The king.. wrested *government boroughs from the ministers. **1812** *Sporting Mag.* XXXIX. 177 The agent of the *Government-Candidates. **1909** *Westm. Gaz.* 11 Oct. 4/1 Four.. *Government-certificated schoolmistresses answered an advertisement. **1964** M. GOWING *Brit. & Atomic Energy* xii. 329 Everyone agreed that a *Government-controlled Experimental Establishment should be created. **1959** G. D. MITCHELL *Sociol.* ix. 148 In industry or in *government-directed organisations. **1964** *Ann. Reg. 1963* 189 To this end the U.S.A. on 6 February imposed a prohibition on U.S. *government-financed cargoes to foreign merchant ships engaged in trade with Cuba. **1803** WELLESLEY in Owen *Desp.* 623 The *Government-General repeatedly derived important advantages from the full command of those ports during the last war. **1965** H. KAHN *On Escalation* iii. 60 A *government-held village. **1802** A. ELLICOTT *Jrnl.* 43 The Governor.. consented that we should meet at the *government house. **1803** in *Ann. 8th Congress* 2 Sess. 1507 A Government house, stables, and garden. *a* **1828** D. WORDSWORTH *Jrnl. Tour Continent* 11 Sept. in *Jrnls.* (1941) II. 269 The bathing-house, a square building, is as conspicuous as a Government House. *a* **1830** W. HICKEY *Mem.* (1960) viii. 124, I.. posted away to the Government House and made my request in person. **1845** STOCQUELER *Handbk. Brit. India* (1854) 139 The Government House was built about the year 1804. **1960** *Farmer & Stockbreeder* 15 Mar. 66/1 The reward for this patriotic effort has been a *Government-imposed cut of £9 million in the guarantees. **1964** A. WYKES *Gambling* 335 The latter are *government-issued bonds. **1907** *Westm. Gaz.* 7 Nov. 1/3, I could not smoke the filthy *Government-made stuff that French people call tobacco. **1905** *Ibid.* 30 Dec. 2/2 *Government-making is a great sport for the public. **1828** P. CUNNINGHAM *N.S. Wales* (ed. 3) II. 109 When fairly domiciliated, they are more respectfully spoken of under the loyal designation of **government-men*, the term *convict* being erased by a sort of general tacit compact from our Botany dictionary. **1843** HALIBURTON *Attaché* II. viii. 142 That government man, that spoke in their favour, warn't his speech rich? **1883** *Graphic* 17 Mar. 262/3 They never settle down as thousands of our 'Government men' cheerfully did in Australia after they had their freedom. **1776** FOOTE *Bankrupt* II. Wks. 1799 II. 120 He is in the receipt of some *government money. **1907** *Daily Chron.* 1 Apr. 4/6 A special *Government-mounted messenger was carrying the document along a country road. **1891** *Pall Mall G.* 27 Aug. 6/2 *Government offices were principally held by young men who were distinguished for their extraordinary insolence and incompetence. **1946** *Nature* 19 Oct. 529/2 What stands out from these discussions.. is.. a distrust.. of *Government-organised or -sponsored research. **1802** *Edin. Rev.* I. 105 The privilege of using twenty millions of *government-paper for a certain limited time. **1837** HT. MARTINEAU *Soc. Amer.* II. 87 The soldiers have disposed of their lands much under the *government price. **1832** G. DOWNES *Lett. Cont. Countries* I. 489 A quantity of *government property has been destroyed by the inundation. **1828** P. CUNNINGHAM *N. S. Wales* (ed. 3) II. 323 The internal taxes and *government rents are collected by a colonial treasurer. **1964** A. WYKES *Gambling* x. 241 Britain's *government-run lottery.. is commonly called 'Premium Bonds'. **1828** P. CUNNINGHAM *N.S. Wales* (ed. 3) II. 323, To a *government secretary residing in the colony is consigned all epistolary correspondence. **1860** *Slang Dict.*, **Government signpost.* **1946** *Nature* 13 July 39/2 In its opinion, a *government-sponsored public corporation financed by the Exchequer is, in general, the most suitable agency. **1856** W. W. DOBIE *Recoll. Visit Pt. Phillip* iii. 47 Government labourers.. were breaking stones with what is called 'the *government stroke', which is a slow-going, anti-sweating kind of motion. **1890** BOLDREWOOD *Col. Reformer* (1891) 236 Regular Government stroke, as we say in this country. **1956** *Nature* 18 Feb. 312/2 Graduates who take up government or *government-supported jobs related to national defence. **1952** 'E. C. R. LORAC' *Murder in Mill-Race* xv. 151 Grey blankets, (good '*government surplus'). **1962** 'O. MILLS' *Headlines make Murder* xiii. 146 He kept a short-wave Government-surplus radio. **1803** *Edin. Rev.* II. 39 Reserving the best timber on the estates as *government-timber. **1860** *Merc. Marine Mag.* VII. 216 The vessel was loaded at 25 lb. upon the *government valve. **1900** *Daily News* 20 Apr. 3/2 *Government-worked mines.

Hence **'governmentist**, a partisan of the (Papal) government; †**'governmentship** = GOVERNORSHIP.

1615 *Nottingham Rec.* (1889) IV. 339 Hee.. shall.. at all tymes duringe his gouernmentshipp geue accompte vnto them of all the saied beddinge. **1862** SEVERN *Roman Jrnls.* in *Atlantic Monthly* May (1892) 637 The governmentists swear that Victor Emmanuel is all the time in league with this 'sacrilegious brigand' [Garibaldi].

governmental (gʌvən'mɛntəl), *a.* [f. GOVERNMENT + -AL[1].] Of or pertaining to government, or to *the* government of a country, etc.

1744 F. MOORE *Voy. Georgia* in *Coll. Georgia Hist. Soc.* (1840) I. 96 The governmental view.. was, with numbers of free white people, well settled to strengthen the southern part of the English settlements. **1781** S. PETERS *Hist. Connect.* 171 One part out of seventy-three of all governmental taxes. *Ibid.* 286 A religious test.. will ever keep all churchmen.. from governmental employments in Connecticut. **1791** PAINE *Rights of Man* II. Introd. (1792) 2 Emigrants.. of diversified professions of religion, retiring from the governmental persecutions of the old world. **1804** W. TAYLOR in *Ann. Rev.* II. 318 The contribution *fonçière*, and the *recette exterieure* are in fact the chief sources of governmental income. **1861** GEN. P. THOMPSON *Audi Alt.* III. clvii. 163 They want to lay down a precedent, that there shall be no examination into governmental misdoings. **1879** H. SPENCER *Data of Ethics* xvi. §109. 285 What is the ethical warrant for governmental authority?

Hence **govern'mentally** *adv.*; also **,govern'mentalism**, a disposition to enlarge or render general the legitimate sphere of government activity; **,govern'mentalist**, one who entertains this disposition.

1848 *Tait's Mag.* XV. 319 They have the fixed idea of Governmentalism... They wish that the Government, so that it be democratic, should dare all, do all, hold all. **1884** *19th Cent.* July 120 No book governmentally unorthodox was sanctioned. **1894** *Contemp. Rev.* May 671 The chief purpose of human existence became.. in the eyes of these governmentalists, to supply a State revenue out of blood and sweat. **1897** *Westm. Gaz.* 9 Oct. 5/1 Any Governmentally-managed colony.

governor ('gʌvənə(r)). Forms: 4–9 governour, 4–6 governo(u)re, 5–6 -owre, (4 -ur, 6 -er), 4– governor. [ad. OF. *governeür* (F. *gouverneur*) = Sp. *gobernador*, It. *governatore*:—L. *gubernātōrem*, f. *gubernāre* to GOVERN.]

†**1.** A steersman, pilot, captain of a vessel. *Obs.*

c **1330** R. BRUNNE *Chron.* (1810) 153 Of Helianore schip he was hir gouernour. **1382** WYCLIF *Acts* xxvii. 11 Sothli centurioun bileuede more to the gouernour, and to the lord of the schipp, than to..Paul. *c* **1430** *Pilgr. Lyf Manhode* II. xc. (1869) 108, I am þilke þat maketh þe gouernour slepe amiddes þe ship..whan he hath lost oþer broken the steerne. **1475** *Bk. Noblesse* 58 Some goithe to set up the saile and take it downe as the governoure the maister avisithe hem. *c* **1530** L. Cox *Rhet.* E vij b, Of the whiche vessell the one man was both owner and gouernour. **1611** BIBLE *Jas.* iii. 4 Yet are they [ships] turned about with a very small helme, whithersoeuer the gouernour listeth.

2. a. One who governs, or exercises authoritative control over, subjects or inferiors; a ruler.

governor of the feast: used in the Bible of 1611 as transl. of Gr. ἀρχιτρίκλινος (*John* ii. 8, 9).

13.. *K. Alis.* 1714 Darie, the kyng of alle kynges.. Governor of lewed and lerid. *c* **1386** CHAUCER *Knt.'s T.* 3 Of Atthenes he was lord and gouernour. *a* **1400–50** *Alexander* 1936 (Dubl.) Sir Dary..Gouernour of ilke grome. & god all þi-seluen. *c* **1400** *Ywaine & Gaw.* 1222 Wemen..most nedes have a governowre. *c* **1430** *Syr Tryam.* 849 Than hath that lady gente Chosyn hym with comyns assente, To be hur governowre. **1460** *Lybeaus Disc.* 1525 Ho ys yowre governowre? They seyde, Kyng Artour. **1531** ELYOT *Gov.* I. iii, There can be no perfect publike weale without one capital and soueraigne gouernour. **1548–9** (Mar.) *Bk. Com. Prayer, Litany*, Edward the Sixt, thy seruaunt our kyng and gouernour. **1596** SHAKS. *Merch. V.* III. ii. 167 Her gentle spirit Commits it selfe to yours to be directed, As from her Lord, her Gouernour, her King. **1651** HOBBES *Leviath.* II. xviii. 94 The greatest pressure of Soveraign Governours, proceeded not from [etc.]. **1695** LD. PRESTON *Boeth.* IV. 186 When the Happiness of the Governours is in some measure diffused. **1775** JOHNSON *Tax. no Tyr.* 17 Without the consent of their countrymen or governours. **1802** WORDSW. *Sonn.*, '*I grieved for Buonaparte*', 'Tis not in battles that from youth we train The Governor who must be wise and good. **1847** EMERSON *Repr. Men, Napoleon* Wks. (Bohn) I. 370 History is full, down to this day, of the imbecility of kings and governors. **1867** *Gd. Words* 1 Feb. 132/2 The parent is made known to the child, not merely as a benefactor, but as a moral governor.

b. Said of the Deity, or of the persons in the Trinity; also of a heathen divinity.

a **1300** *Cursor M.* 18366 Lauerd and godd he sal be ur, And euer mar vr gouernur. **13..** *E.E. Allit. P.* C. 199 Hatz þou, gome, no gouernour ne god on to calle. *c* **1440** *York Myst.* xlvii. 33 Jesu Criste, our gouernoure. **1552** ABP. HAMILTON *Catech.* (1884) 3 The haly spreit quhilk is ane daily techeour and governour of the hail universal kirk. **1678** CUDWORTH *Intell. Syst.* I. iii. 110 The Deity, or that perfect Mind, which is the supreme Governour of all things. **1710** PRIDEAUX *Orig. Tithes* i. 18 Being given to them by God not as General Governor of the World..but [etc.]. **1817** A. BONAR *Serm.* II. x. 218 The infinitely wise moral Governor of the world.

c. Said of things more or less personified.

c **1385** CHAUCER *L.G.W.* Prol. 170 Welcome Sommer, oure governour and lorde. **1398** TREVISA *Barth. De P.R.* v. ii. (1495) 102 The heede is gouernoure and ruler of all the body. **1513** BRADSHAW *St. Werburge* I. 3084 The day was gouernour over the nyght. **1526** *Pilgr. Perf.* (W. de W. 1531) 18 b, Whiche grace, vnder god, is the chefe gouernour of mannes soule. **1726** BUTLER *Serm. Rolls* ii. 42 This Faculty was placed within to be our proper Governour.

3. a. An official appointed to govern a province, country, town, etc. Now used as the official title of the representative of the Crown in a British colony or dependency; also of the executive head of each of the United States.

1390 GOWER *Conf.* III. 178 When he made a governour.. Of province or of region. **1535** COVERDALE *2 Kings* xxv. 23 The kynge of Babilon had made Godolias gouernoure. **1579** LYLY *Euphues* (Arb.) 51 Don Ferardo one of the chiefe gouernours of the citie. **1673** RAY *Journ. Low C.* 9 Brussels ..where the Spanish Governour of these Provinces.. usually resides. **1683** *Col. Rec. Pennsylv.* I. 57 Wm. Penn, proprietery and Governer of Pensilvania. **1742** HUME *Ess., Taxes* (1777) I. 368 The emperor..must allow all the bashaws and governors to oppress and abuse the subjects. *a* **1832** MACKINTOSH *Review Milton's Nephews* Wks. 1846 II. 505 While the grandson of Milton resided at Madras..it is somewhat remarkable that the elder brother of Addison should have been the Governor of that settlement. **1840** THIRLWALL *Greece* VII. 5 Here [at Alexandria] he found reason to remove the governor whom he had left there.

b. The officer in command of a fortress or garrison.

1647 CLARENDON *Hist. Reb.* IV. §207 Sending an order to the governor of Portsmouth that nobody should be admitted into that town and fort. **1663** *Flagellum, or O. Cromwell* (1672) 85 Stafford the Governour of the Castle basely betrayed it to Cromwell. **1837** *King's Regul. & Ord. Army* 23 To Governors, who have not Commissions as General Officers, all Guards within their Garrisons are to turn out with presented Arms, and beat one Ruffle. **1898** FORSYTH in *Expositor* Oct. 268 The governor of a besieged town.

4. One who bears rule in an establishment, institution, society, etc. Now chiefly as an official title, sometimes applied only to the head of an institution (e.g. in the Bank of England, where the 'Governor' is chosen from a body of 'Directors'), sometimes to each member of a governing body, as often in the case of charitable institutions. *spec.* One who is in charge of a prison.

c **1386** CHAUCER *Monk's Prol.* 52 Thou art..a gouernour, wyly and wys. **1427** in Heath *Grocer's Comp.* (1829) 4 John de Wellys, Alderman and gouernour. **1535** COVERDALE *Isa.* xxii. 15 Go in to the treasury vnto Sobna the gouernoure, and saye [etc.]. *c* **1566** J. ALDAY tr. *Boaystuau's Theat. World* H viij b, The rector or governor of one onlye Churche or congregation. **1577** HANMER *Anc. Eccl. Hist.* (1619) 493 Governer of the Monastery in Constantinople. **1607** in *Hist. Wakefield Gram. Sch.* (1892) 68 The usher being convented by the Governours and admonished. **1697** DAMPIER *Voy.* (1702) I. 525 Withal I think it worth the care of the Owners or Governours of the Factory..to lay Pipes to convey the Fountain Water to the Shore. **1721** STRYPE *Eccl. Mem.* II. II. xiv. 362 The Governour of the Hospital of Christ's-Church in London. **1807** SOUTHEY *Lett. fr. Eng.* II. xxxix. 162 Of late years the office of jailor has become of considerable importance, and ennobled by the title of Governor. **1864** C. M. YONGE *Trial* II. vii. 137 Mr. Ernescliffe sent in his card at the governor's house... They were told that the prisoner they wished to see was at work. **1884** J. PAYN *Some Lit. Recoll.* 42 It came under the notice of the Governor of Woolwich Academy. **1897** O. WILDE *Let.* 1 Apr. (1962) 514 Of the many, many things for which I have to thank the Governor there is none for which I am more grateful than for his permission to write fully to A[lfred] D[ouglas]. **1911** *Encycl. Brit.* XXII. 366/1 The convict.. exercises and goes to chapel..in the society of others, but holds no communication with them; his only intercourse with his fellow-creatures is when he is visited by the governor, chaplain, schoolmaster or trade instructor. **1965** T. PARKER *Plough Boy* III. i. 196 Then the governor come in ..rabbiting..about 'respite' or 'reprieve' or something like that.

†**5.** The commander of a company, esp. an armed force, naval or military. *Obs.*

13.. *Gaw. & Gr. Knt.* 225 'Wher is,' he sayd, 'þe gouernour of þis gyng?' *c* **1385** CHAUCER *L.G.W.* 1060 *Dido*, His Meinie That hadde founde here lord here gouernour. *c* **1400** *Destr. Troy* 4819 Agamynon, the gouernour. *c* **1450** HOLLAND *Howlat* xxvi, Goiss Halkis war governouris of the gret oist. **1553** EDEN *Treat. Newe Ind.* (Arb.) 34 They elected a new gouernoure of theyr nauie. **1604** SHAKS. *Oth.* II. i. 55 My hopes do shape him for the Gouernor. *a* **1625** FLETCHER *Love's Pilgr.* IV. i. (1647) 18/2 *Rod. within.* Ho, Governor [*ed.* 2 gunner] make a shot into the Town, *a shot.*

†**6.** One who has charge of a young man's education and occupations; a tutor, esp. of a prince or young noble. *Obs.*

1577 RHODES *Bk. Nurture* in *Babees Bk.* 63 And thus by the Chylde yee shall perceiue the disposytion of the Gouernour. **1591** SHAKS. *1 Hen. VI*, I. i. 171 To Eltam will I, where the young King is, Being ordayn'd his speciall Gouernor. **1638** SIR H. WOTTON in *Four C. Eng. Lett.* 53 Attending the young Lord S. as his governor. **1654** *Nicholas Papers* (Camden) II. 146, I will..recommend unto his Majesty care the placing some such Governor over the Duke of Gloucester as may understand the moralls of a Prince; and I pray beleeve it is 3 weekes very strict observance that makes me see the difference betwixt a schoole-master and a Governor. **1692** LOCKE *Educ.* §94 The great Work of a Governour is to fashion the Carriage and form the Mind. **1752** CHESTERF. *Lett.* (1792) III. cclxxix. 279 Others..are sent abroad in servitude to some aukward pedantic Scotch governor. **1788** *New Lond. Mag.* 153 Mr. Hobbs..travelled with him as his governor into France.

7. *colloq.* or *slang.* **a.** An employer (cf. sense 4). **b.** Applied by young men to their fathers. **c.** Used as a vulgar form of address to a man.

a. 1802 K. WHITE *Rem.* I. 83, I have made such a proficiency in the law, as has ensured me the regard of my governors. **1838** DICKENS *O. Twist* xxxi, Tell your governor that Blathers..is here.

b. 1827 *Sporting Mag.* XX. 70, I was accompanied on this occasion by my Governor. **1847** HARE *Vict. Faith* 107, I allude to the habit which sons have in speaking of their father,..to call him governor, as the vulgar phrase is. **1853** 'C. BEDE' *Verdant Green* I. x, I suppose the bills will come in some day or other, but the governor will see to them. **1888** E. J. GOODMAN *Too Curious* vi, I will not fail to let you know ..how the governor is going on.

c. 1844 DICKENS *M. Chuzz.* xxiii. 284 'My youngest died last week.' 'I'm sorry for it, governor, with all my heart,' said Mark. **1852** *Punch* 2 Oct. 152/1 (*caption*) I say, Guvner, give us a hist with this 'ere bilin' o' greens! **1866** *Night in Workh.* 37 'Is this anything like wot you've lost, guv'ner?'

8. *Machinery.* A self-acting contrivance for regulating the passage of gas, steam, water, etc., esp. the supply of any one of these to a machine, in order to ensure an even and regular motion.

1819 REES *Cycl.* XXIII. s.v. *Mill-work*, These regulators [in a mill] are usually termed governors. **1825** J. NICHOLSON *Operat. Mechanic* 38 Governors or flying-balls are very frequently used in the wind-mills employed for grinding flour. **1832** BABBAGE *Econ. Manuf.* iii. (ed. 3) 27 That beautiful contrivance, the governor of the steam-engine. **1849–50** WEALE *Dict. Arch.*, etc. s.v., The governor is a machine for regulating and equalizing the flow of gas from the gasometers to the street-mains. **1864** *G. Buchanan & Co.'s Descr. List Machinery* i. 53 The addition of a governor or regulator for adjusting the supply of water to the wheel. **1879** *Dickens' Dict. London*, s.v. *Gas*, The pressure of gas to a house is..regulated by a wet governor. **1918** E. M. ROBERTS *Flying Fighter* 63 By means of a governor, the speed of the lorries was being limited to fifteen miles an hour. But we discovered that if the ball in the governor was held up we could get as much as twenty-five miles out of the motor. **1940** 'GUN BUSTER' *Return via Dunkirk* I. iv. 40 They do forty miles per hour, and can do eighty if you take the governor off. **1961** *Lancet* 2 Sept. 549/2 We might consider obliging the police to seal a governor set at 50 m.p.h. into the carburation of everything on wheels.

9. A particular fly used in angling.

1856 KINGSLEY *Let.* May in *A. Locke* (1876) p. lvii, Fished all the morning... Killed eight on 'March brown' and 'governor', by drowning the flies. **1867** F. FRANCIS *Angling* vi. (1880) 243 The Governor..is a very useful fly on many waters. **1884** *St. James's Gaz.* 21 June 6/2 The artificial fly known as the 'governour', which is intended for an imitation of the ground bee.

10. *attrib.* and *Comb.* (chiefly sense 8), as ***governor-apparatus***, ***-burner***, ***-house***, ***-reed***, ***-valve***; also **governor-block**, one of a pair of cast-iron blocks pivoted to the axle-clamp in the railway automatic compression-brake (*Cent. Dict.*).

1865 *Morning Star* 3 Nov., The servants..were employed putting up '*governor' apparatus on the pipes attached to the gasometer. **1891** *Anthony's Photogr. Bull.* IV. 346 A Peebles' *governor burner..forms an excellent arrangement. **1895** *Daily News* 14 Oct. 7/7 The saving effected by needle governor burners..will soon pay for their cost. **1895** *Daily News* 17 Dec. 3/5 A fire..occurred in the *governor house of Worthing Gasworks. **1892** *Pall Mall G.* 27 Apr. 7/2 Regulated by a simple screw contrivance to vibrate at the exact rate of the distant transmitter or *governor reed. **1875** KNIGHT *Dict. Mech.*, **Governor-valve*, a valve in a steam-pipe operated by the governor to vary the area of steam.

governorate ('gʌvənərət). [f. GOVERNOR + -ATE[1], after *consulate*, etc.] **a.** A province or portion of country ruled by a governor, esp. in the Ottoman empire and subsequently in Egypt. **b.** The residence of a governor. **c.** The office of governor.

1899 *Standard* 8 Apr. 4/2 Suakim will form a separate Governorate. **1900** *Pilot* 1 Sept. 263/1 Samos, the freest of Turkish governorates. **1926** *Blackw. Mag.* Mar. 412/1 Kena ..is the Mudirieh, or Governorate town, of the province which embraces Luxor. **1930** CHESTERTON *Four Felons* 25 The gardens round the Governorate. **1961** B. FERGUSSON *Watery Maze* xvi. 402 The block of flats behind the Governorate [at Port Said]. **1962** *Economist* 17 Nov. 673/1 Another..is in the running for one or two important governorates.

'governor-'general. A governor who has under him deputy- or lieutenant-governors.

[**1556** J. HEYWOOD *Spider & F.* xcv. 98 You [spiders] (welnie) brought flies: to graunt to agree, You: as head gouernou[r]s generall bee.] **1586** LD. BURGHLEY in *Leycester Corr.* (Camden 1844) 267 My lord of Leicester hath accepted the title of governor-generall of those provinces. **1684** *Lond. Gaz.* No. 1979/3 The humble Address of Your Majesty's Lieutenant and Governor-General of Your Colony and Dominion of Virginia. **1796** MORSE *Amer. Geog.* II. 455 Corfu..the residence of the governor-general over all the other islands. **1828** P. CUNNINGHAM *N.S. Wales* (ed. 3) II. 303 New South Wales and Van Dieman's Land are under the jurisdiction of a governor-general..with a lieutenant-governor under him for each colony. **1854** SIR G. C. LEWIS *Lett.* (1870) 281 It is, certainly, a very singular accident, that a small society such as that of Merton should have sent out two successive Governors-General of Canada. **1858** J. B. NORTON *Topics* 76 As to how far the Governor-General [of India] has deserved well of his country..it is difficult for me to form an opinion.

Hence **'governor-'generalship**, the office of governor-general; also his term of office.

1833 T. HOOK *Widow & Marquess* i, A blue riband, and the governor-generalship of India, were the marks at which he aimed. **1881** *Athenæum* 12 Feb. 255/1 The two years of his Governor-Generalship.

governorship ('gʌvənəʃɪp). [f. GOVERNOR + -SHIP.]

1. The office of a governor.

1658 BRAMHALL *Schisme garded* xii. §1. 216 His [the Pope's] First Movership and his First Governourship, are but generall unsignificant Termes. **1663** PEPYS *Diary* 29 Apr., He ought to have expected and had the governorship upon the death or removal of the former governor. **1828** P. CUNNINGHAM *N.S. Wales* (ed. 3) II. 236 His merits could not have raised him to a governorship quite so quickly, unless he had founded a governorship himself. **1859** LANG *Wand. India* 364, I want the governorship..at the Cape. **1884** *Law Times* 20 Sept. LXXVII. 346/2 Mr. Lloyd, the late warder in charge, having been promoted to the governorship of Huntingdon prison.

2. The exercise or tenure of the office of governor.

1644 PRYNNE & WALKER *Fiennes's Trial* 31 His Governourship of Bristoll, was the foundation of the impeachment. **1812** L. HUNT in *Examiner* 21 Sept. 602/1 This Foundation has..attracted some..attention, with respect to its governorship and economy. **1888** B. W. RICHARDSON *Son of Star* III. ix. 139 He hates governorship, and yet he continues to govern. **1891** S. C. SCRIVENER *Our Fields & Cities* 75 How do they reconcile governorship of ten cities with Christian virtues if the governor Herod was properly called a fox?

governyl, variant of GOVERNAIL *Obs.*

govey, govy ('gʌvɪ), hypocoristic [-Y[6]] forms of *governess.*

1903 *Westm. Gaz.* 28 Mar. 2/2 I'm trying to avoid the govy difficulty by sending my girls to classes. **1904** H. O. STURGIS *Belchamber* xx. 272, I am..just your old govey that you loved when you were a little boy.

gow (gaʊ). [Shortening and adaptation of Chinese *yao-kao* (Mathews), opium. f. *yao* drug + *kao* an oily, fatty substance, esp. an unguent.] A drug; *spec.* opium. Hence **'gowster**, a drug addict.

1922 *Dialect Notes* V. v. 182 Terms for opium. *Gow*, a Chinese word which..is meaningless unless allied with another Chinese word. **1926** J. BLACK *You can't Win* xii. 159 You're in with what gow I've got. **1933** *Amer. Speech* VIII.

II. 27/1 When one has contracted the [drug] habit..he is.. hitting the gow. **1942** BERREY & VAN DEN BARK *Amer. Thes. Slang* §509.19 *Gowster*,.. esp. an opium addict.

gow, ? error for *goll*, variant of GALE *sb.*[1]

1598 FLORIO, *Acaro*, wilde Mirtle or gow.

gow, var. GAW *v. Obs.*, Sc. variant of GULL.

gowai, gowhai, varr. KOWHAI.

gowan ('gaʊən). *Sc.* and *north. dial.* Also 7 gouan. [app. a dial. variant of GOLLAN(D.]

1. A general name for various yellow or white field flowers. When used without defining word, now always denoting the Common Daisy (*Bellis perennis*).

1570 *Satir. Poems Reform.* xv. 5 ȝe greinis, grow gray; ȝe gowanis, dune. *a* **1605** MONTGOMERIE *Misc. Poems* xli. 10 The feildis ouerflouis With gouans that grouis. **1701** J. BRAND *Orkney* (1703) 31 We saw the pleasantest mixture of Gowans..or Daisies white and yellow..that ever we had occasion to see. **1785** BURNS *Death & Dr. Hornbook* xxiii, His braw calf-ward where gowans grew, Sae white and bonie. **1802** WORDSW. *Farewell* 22 Thou, like the morning in thy saffron coat, Bright gowan, and marsh-marigold, farewell. **1812** J. WILSON *Agric. Renfrewsh.* 136 (Jam.) Some of the prevailing weeds of the meadows and grass lands are ..ox-eye, or large white gowan, Chrysanthemum leucanthemum [etc.]. **1856** MRS. CARLYLE *Lett.* II. 284 The hearts of these two old women are as fresh as gowans. **1895** CROCKETT *Men of Moss Hags* i. 1 The dales and holms were pranked out with white hawthorn and broad gowans.

2. With qualifications, as **ewe gowan, May gowan**, the Common Daisy; **gule gowan**, the Corn Marigold; **horse gowan** (see HORSE 28 c); **lucken gowan**, the Marsh Marigold; **open gowan**, the Globe-flower; **witch gowan**, the Globe flower, also the Dandelion; **yellow gowan**, any species of Ranunculus, also applied generically to all the yellow flowers mentioned above. (See Britten and Holland *Plant-n.* 1878–86.)

1721 RAMSAY *Richy & Sandy* 35 While on burn banks the Yellow Gowan grows. **1724** —— *Yng. Laird & Katy*, We'll pou the daisies on the green The lucken gowans frae the bog. **1810** CROMEK *Rem. Nithsdale Song* 110 *note*, Witch-gowan flowers, are large yellow gowans, with a stalk filled with pernicious sap. **1842** HARDY in *Proc. Berw. Nat. Club* II. No. x. 14 In Lanarkshire..the phrase, yellow gowans, yet flourishes as the common name of the creeping meadow crowfoot (*Ranunculus repens*). *Ibid.* 19 *note*, Ye'll get round again, if ye had your fit (foot) on the May gowan.

Hence **'gowaned** *ppl. a.*, full of gowans; covered with gowans; **'gowany** *a.* = GOWANED.

1725 RAMSAY *Gentle Sheph.* II. ii, O Peggy!.. Sweeter than gowany glens or new mawn hay. *a* **1774** FERGUSSON *King's Birthday* Poems (1845) 4 Doggies play and lambies sport, On gowany braes. **1804** TARRAS *Poems* 80 On yon gowan'd lawn she was seen. **1818** SCOTT *Hrt. Midl.* xlv, The green was even, gowany, and fair. **1841** *Fraser's Mag.* XXIV. 351 They sat on the gowany bank. **1847** J. HALLIDAY *Rustic Bard* 265 Clear is Allan's siller stream, An' sweet her gowan'd lea.

go-way (bird): see GO-AWAY.

gowbin, variant of GOBBON *sb. Obs.*, gobbet.

gowcht, variant of GOFE *Sc. Obs.*

gowdge, obs. form of GOUGE *sb.*[1]

'gowdie. *Sc. dial.* [Local pronunciation of GOLDY.] The fish *Callionymus Lyra*.

1810 NEILL *List Fishes* 4 (Jam.) *Callionymus Lyra*, Dragonet; Chanticleer, or Gowdie. **1836** YARRELL *Brit. Fishes* I. 261 The Gemmeous Dragonet. Yellow Skulpin. *Cornwall.* Gowdie. *Scotland.*

'gowdy. *Sc.* [? = GOLDI(LOCKS).] Used only in phr. ***heels ower gowdy***: see HEEL *sb.*[1] 15 b.

gowe, var. GAW *v. Obs.*; obs. f. GOVE *v. Sc.*

gower, gowern(e, obs. ff. GIAOUR, GOVERN.

gowff (gouf), *v. Sc.* [Connected with *gowff* GOLF *sb.*] *trans.* To strike.

a **1796** BURNS *Song, When Guilford good* ix, But word an' blow, North, Fox, and Co. Gowffed Willie like a ba', man.

gowff, variant of GOFE, GOLF.

gowge, variant of GOUGE.

gowife, variant of GOFE *Sc. Obs.*

gowk (gaʊk), *sb.* Orig. *Sc.* and *north. dial.* 4–6 gok(e, 5–6 gowke, golk, (6 *Sc.* goilk), 6–8 gouk, 6–9 gouk, 7– gowk. [a. ON. *gaukr* = OE. *ȝéac* (see YEKE), OHG. *gouh* (MHG. *gouch*, G. *gauch*):—OTeut. **gauko-z*.]

1. The cuckoo.

c **1325** *Song* 5 in *Rel. Ant.* I. 291, I ga gowlende a-bowte, al so so dos a goke [*rime-word* bok]. ? *a* **1400** *Morte Arth.* 927 Thare galede þe gowke one greuez fulle lowde. *c* **1450** HOLLAND *Howlat* lxiv, The Tuchet and the gukkit Golk. **1483** *Cath. Angl.* 161/2 A Goke (*A.* A Goke, A Gotoo), *cuculus.* **1500–20** DUNBAR *Poems* xxxiii. 77 The golk, the gormaw, and the gled, Beft him with buffettis quhill he bled. **1544** TURNER *Avium Præcip. Hist.* D 3 b, De cvcvlo.. Anglicé a cukkouu, & a gouke. **1688** R. HOLME *Armoury* II. 274/2 The Cuckow is in some parts of England called a Gouke. **1786** BURNS *Let. to R. Muir* 20 Mar., I hope, some time before we hear the gowk, to have the pleasure of seeing you at Kilmarnock. **1841** SELBY in *Proc. Berw. Nat. Club* I. No. 9. 253 The numbers of the cuckoo or gowk (*Cuculus canorus*) which visit us. **1882** *Lanc. Gloss.*, *Gowk*, the cuckoo.

2. A fool: a half-witted person. [So G. *gauch.*]

a **1605** POLWART *Flyting w. Montgomerie* 23 Gowke, wyt mee not to gar thee greit; Thy tratling, truiker, I sall tame. *a* **1605** MONTGOMERIE *Sonn.* lxx. 9 Art thou a god? No—bot a gok disguysit. **1725** RAMSAY *Gentle Sheph.* v. i, What ails thee, gowk! to mak sae loud ado? **1777** BRAND *Pop. Antiq.* (1849) I. 139 April Gouks. **1795** BURNS *Heron Ballads* iv, A lord may be a gouk, Wi' ribbon, star, and a' that. *a* **1810** TANNAHILL *Poems* (1846) 21 The gowk's possest I ween. **1858** R. S. SURTEES *Ask Mamma* xliv. 196 A gowk of an Englishman, who gained an audience under a mistaken notion. **1893** 'Q.' [Couch] *Delect. Duchy* 154 You gowk!

3. Phrases. ***to give the gowk to***: to befool. ***to hunt the gowk***: to go on a fool's errand.

1728 RAMSAY *Mercury in Quest of Peace* 81 Has Jove then sent me amang thir fowk, Cry'd Hermes, here to hunt the gowk? ? *a* **1800** *Sweet Willie* xxi. in Finlay *Sc. Ball.* (1808) II. 66 Ye hae gien me the gowk, Annet, But I'll gie you the scorn.

4. *attrib.* and *Comb.* esp. with gen. *gowk's*, as **gowk's-errand** = *fool's-errand* (see ERRAND 2 c); **gowk('s)-meat, gowk-oats** (see quots.); **gowk's-spittle** = CUCKOO-SPIT[2]; **gowk's-storm**, †(*a*) a storm of short duration; (*b*) a spring gale which occurs at the time of the cuckoo's arrival. Also **gowk-like** *a.*, foolish.

1823 CORBETT *Petticoat Tales* I. 227 'Somebody', continued Robin, 'sent them on a *gowk's errand, to look for smuggled whiskey in my house'. **1823** LOCKHART *Reg. Dalton* I. 234 Though Archy Keith might have done a very *gowk-like thing when he joined their cloth [etc.]. **1778** LIGHTFOOT *Flora Scot.* (1792) 238 Wood Sorrel, *Anglis.* *Gouke-meat, *Scotis.* **1879** BRITTEN & HOLLAND *Plant-n.* 217 Gowk (or Gowks) Meat. 1. *Orchis mascula* and *O. Morio.* 2. *Oxalis Acetosella.* **1893** *Northumbld. Gloss.*, **Gowk-oats*, late sown oats. The season for sowing oats is usually during the month of March. When by chance the sowing is delayed till April they are gowk-oats. **1824** MACTAGGART *Gallovid. Encycl.*, **Gowk-spittles*, a white frothy matter common on the leaves of plants, about the latter end of the summer and beginning of autumn. **1847** J. WILSON *Chr. North* (1857) I. 138 The slaver of gowk's-spittle. **1594** HUNTLY *Let. to Earl Angus* in Tytler *Hist. Scot.* (1864) IV. 225 [Huntly spoke of the king's rumoured campaign as likely to turn out a] '*gowk's storm'. *a* **1691** SIR S. MACKENZIE *Mem.* (1721) 70 That being done he hop'd that this was but a gowk storm. **1849** W. THOMPSON *Nat. Hist. Birds Irel.* I. 357 The peasantry look forward with the greatest interest every spring for what they call the 'Gowk (cuckoo) Storm', that takes place about the end of April or the beginning of May, when the note of this bird is heard. **1899** H. C. HART in *Trans. Phil. Soc.* 11 The portion shed from the plant and driven ashore by May storms, usually by that storm known as the 'cuckoo storm' or 'gowk storm'.

gowk (gaʊk), *v. rare.* Also 6 gouk. [? f. prec.; but *goukis* in the first quot. may be a spelling of *guckis*: see GUCK *v.*] *intr.* To stare foolishly.

1513 DOUGLAS *Aeneis* VIII. Prol. 94 Sum goukis quhill the glas pyg grow full of gold ȝit. **1873** MISS BROUGHTON *Nancy* II. 154 Bobby, Tou-Tou and I, having no one to..gowk amorously up at us, are sitting in a row in our pew.

gowked (gaʊkɪd), *ppl. a. Sc.* Forms: 6 gouket, 7 gowkit, 8 gouked, goukit, 9 gowket, 7– gowked. [app. an alteration of GUCKED, assimilated to GOWK.] Foolish.

a **1605** MONTGOMERIE *Flyting w. Polwart* 88 Ȝour gryses grunȝie is graceless and gowked. **1622** [SCOT] *Course Conformitie* ii. 27 Their apparell, their trayns, fleshly pleasure, and gowkit gloriositie. **1637** RUTHERFORD *Lett.* (1862) I. 351 Yet there is no gowked (if I may so speak) nor fond loue in Christ. **1790** MORISON *Poems* 187 Fool goukit chield, sic stuff as that to true.

Hence **'gowkedly** *adv.*, **'gowkedness.**

c **1570** ARBUTHNOT in Pinkerton *Maitland Poems* (1786) 141 Alace, men hes the wyit! That geves sa gouketlie Sic rewleris onperfyte. **1883** G. MACDONALD *D. Grant* I. xxiv. 257 Mrs. Brookes paused, lost in contemplation of the gowkedness of Eppy.

†**gowl**, *sb.*[1] *Obs.* Also 6 goule, goawle. See also GOLE, GOOL. [a. OF. *goule*, *gole* (mod. *gueule*):—L. *gula* throat.]

1. The throat. Also, the front of the neck.

1513 DOUGLAS *Æneis* IX. ix. 86 Or as a ravanus bludy wolf throu slycht Hyntis in his gowl. *Ibid.* x. xii. 94 Joifful he bradis tharon dispituusly, Wyth gapand goule. **1565** GOLDING *Ovid's Met.* VI. 139 Their voices still are hoarse and harsh, their throats have puffed goawles.

2. (See quot. 1893; cf. L. *fauces.*)

1638 H. ADAMSON *Muses Threnodie* vi. 177 From thence we, passing by the Windie gowle, Did make the hollow rocks with echoes yowle. **1893** *Northumbld. Gloss.*, *Gowl, Gool*, a hollow passage or pass between hills.

gowl (gaʊl), *sb.*[2] *Sc.* and *north. dial.* [f. GOWL *v.*[1]] A howl, a yell, a loud cry.

1805 *Water Kelpie* in Whitelaw *Bk. Sc. Ballads* (1875) 504 The troublit pool conveyit the gowl Down to yon echoin' rock. **1862** J. BROWN in *Illustr. Melbourne Post* 26 July, Anybody, even a beggar, by a *gowl*, and a threat of eye, could send him off howling. **1878** *Cumbld. Gloss.*, *Gowl*, the howl of a dog. **1894** CROCKETT *Raiders* 377, I..burst out in a kind o' gowl o' anger.

gowl (gaʊl), *sb.*[3] *Obs.* exc. *dial.* Also 7, 9 goul. [Possibly connected with ON. *gul-r* yellow.]

A gummy secretion in the eye. (Cf. GOUND.)

1665 COTTON *Scarron.* IV. (1741) 125 The Page was got as far as Atlas Back on his way, ere he could free 'um From Gowl and Matter, fit to see him. **1882** *Lanc. Gloss.*, *Goul*, a yellow secretion in the eyes of children.

Hence †**'gowly** *a.*, full of 'gowl'. *Obs.*

1601 WEEVER *Mirr. Mart.* B iij, With that I stretcht my lims along the bed, Hauing no power to ope my gowlie eyes.

gowl (gaʊl), *v.*[1] Chiefly *Sc.* and *north. dial.* Forms: 4 goule(n, 5 gole, 9 *dial.* goal, goul, 7 gule, 5– gowl. [a. ON. *gaula*, perh. an extended form, with *-l-* suffix, of the root **gau-*, ON. *gøyja* (:—**gaujan*) to bark. But cf. YOWL.] *intr.* To howl, yell, cry bitterly or threateningly; also, to whine. Said of men and animals.

c **1300** *Havelok* 164 He greten, and gouleden. **1340** HAMPOLE *Pr. Consc.* 477 Unnethes es a child born fully þat it ne bygynnes to goule and cry. *c* **1375** *Sc. Leg. Saints, Clement* 93 Scho goulyt, & grat, & rawe hir hare. **14..** *Tundale's Vis.* (1893) 1179 He gret, he gowled, he was fulle wo. *c* **1425** WYNTOUN *Cron.* IV. xxiv. 2096 Hundys.. gowland in gret multytude. **1552** LYNDESAY *Monarche* 5487 Wylde beistis..Gowland with mony gryslye grone. **1802** R. ANDERSON *Cumberld. Ball.* 53 Our Jenny she gowled, ay, like ought. **1813** HOGG *Queen's Wake, Kilmeny* (1814) 183 The lion..gowled at the carle, and chased him away. **1895** *Lakeland & Iceland Gloss.*, *Gowl*, to cry with a whine, as a dog does.

b. *transf.* of the wind.

1724 RAMSAY *Tea-t. Misc.*, '*O Steer her up*', Let's have pleasure while we're able..And let wind and weather gowl. **1855** ROBINSON *Whitby Gloss.*, *Goul* or *Goal*, to blow in strong draughts, as wind through a narrow passage. **1886** STEVENSON *Kidnapped* xxvi. 271 When the wind gowls in the chimney and the rain tirls on the roof.

Hence **'gowling** *vbl. sb.* and *ppl. a.*

1340 HAMPOLE *Pr. Consc.* 6109 þe day of gretyng and goulyng. **13..** *Minor Poems fr. Vernon MS.* xxxiii. 248 Goulyng and grisbatyng of tethe. **14..** *Tundale's Vis.* (1893) 398 Cryyng and golyng and dolfulle dynne. *c* **1450** HOLLAND *Howlat* iv, At the quhilk he [an Howlat] couth growe, And made gowlyne. **1513** DOUGLAS *Æneis* VI. ix. 50 Murnyng, granyng, gowlyng, and duleful beir. **1552** LYNDESAY *Monarche* 6008 Thare salbe gowlyng and gretyng. **1650** *Minutes Aberdour Sess.* in Ross *Aberdour* (1885) 326 He heard one great guleing voice and dinne in the hollow. **1786** BURNS *Ded. to G. Hamilton* 96 May ne'er misfortune's gowling bark Howl thro' the dwelling o' the Clerk!

gowl (gaʊl), *v.*[2] *Obs.* exc. *dial.* [f. GOWL *sb.*[3]] *trans.* To stop *up* with 'gowl'.

1637 BP. HALL *Rem. Prophaneness* 32 There is a kind of earthliness in the best eye, whereby it is gouled up. **1886** *S.W. Linc. Gloss.* s.v., Her eyes have been clean gowled up.

gowl, obs. form of GAVEL *sb.*[1]

c **1380** *R. Brunne's Handl. Synne* 2394 (Dulwich MS.) It is boþe gowl & þefte.

gowl, variant of GHOUL; obs. form of GULL.

gowlan, variant of GOLLAND.

gowlare, gowler, variants of GAVELLER.

c **1380** *R. Brunne's Handl. Synne* 2419 (Dulwich MS.) Ȝif þou of ony gowlere with wrong a-wey his good bere.

gowle, variant of GAVEL *sb.*[1]

gowlfe, obs. form of GULF.

gowl(l)es, -is, -ys, obs. forms of GULES.

gowlon, variant of GOLLAND.

gowme, obs. form of GUM.

gown (gaʊn), *sb.* Forms: 4–6 goun(e, 4–7 gowne, (6 *Sc.* gounn, 8–9 *vulgar* gownd), 4– gown. [a. OF. *goune, gone, gonne* fem., a Com. Rom. word = Pr. *gona*, OSp. *gona*, It. *gonna*:—med.L. *gunna*, used in the 8th c. by St. Boniface for a garment of fur permitted to elderly or infirm monks. A late L. *gunna* 'skin, fur', is quoted from a scholiast on Verg. *Georg.* III. 383, and in Byzantine Gr. γοῦνα is common as the name of a coarse garment, sometimes described as made of skins.

The origin of the Rom. word is obscure. Some scholars regard it as of Celtic origin, comparing the Welsh *gŵn*, Irish *fúan* 'lacerna', which are referred by Stokes (Fick's *Idg. Wb.*[4] II. 281) to an OCeltic **vo-ouno-*, f. *vo-* (= Gr. ὑπό under) + root *ou-* to clothe (cf. L. *ex-u-ĕre, ind-u-ĕre, sub-ū-cula*). But Loth (*Rev. Celt.* XX. 353) raises phonological objections, and believes the Welsh word to be adopted from Eng. (as are the Irish *gúnn*, Gael. *gùn*, Manx *goon*). In any case the Celtic origin of the Rom. word does not seem to accord with the geographical probabilities. Albanian has *gunë* cloak, but it is uncertain whether this is native or adopted from Gr.]

1. A loose flowing upper garment worn as an article of ordinary attire.

a. By men. (See also senses 3 and 4.)

13.. *E.E. Allit. P.* B. 145 þow art a gome vngoderly in þat goun febele. **1375** BARBOUR *Bruce* XIX. 352 A gown on his armyng he had. *c* **1460** J. RUSSELL *Bk. Nurture* 904 Syr, what Robe or govn pleseth it yow to were to day? **1483** *Act 1 Rich. III*, c. 12 §1 No Merchant Stranger..shall bring into this Realm..Clasps for Gowns. **1532–3** *Act 24 Hen. VIII*, c. 13 No man vnder the degree of a barons sonne..shall weare any maner of veluet in their gownes. *a* **1586** C'TESS PEMBROKE *Ps.* CXLVIII. v, You, that proud of native gown Stand fresh and tall to see. **1607** SHAKS. *Timon* III. vi. 120, I haue lost my Gowne. **1815** ELPHINSTONE *Acc. Caubul* (1842) II. 199 He wears an Uzbek shirt and a gown, over which is a girdle.

b. By women. In mod. use, a garment fitting close to the upper part of the body with flowing skirts; = FROCK 4.

In the 18th c. it was the ordinary word; subsequently it was to a great extent superseded in colloquial use by *dress*, but has latterly been somewhat more common, esp. in fashionable use, as applied to a dress with some pretension to elegance, and in Comb. as *dinner-*, *tea-gown*. In the U.S. it has always been the current word.

1397 in Dugdale *Monasticon Angl.* (1846) IV. 194 Quod non utantur..jupis Anglicè gounes. *a*1450 *Knt. de la Tour* (1868) 65 This woman had tenne diuerse gownes and as mani cotes. 15.. *Adam Bel & Clym of Clough* 73 in Ritson *Anc. P.P.* 8 They gave to her a ryght good goune. 1557 *Tottel's Misc.* (Arb.) 198 Girt in my giltlesse gowne, as I sit here and sow. 1598 Shaks. *Merry W.* iv. ii. 81 Quicke, quicke, wee'le come dresse you straight: put on the gowne the while. 1663 Pepys *Diary* 10 Nov., The Queene..hath bespoke herself a new gowne. 1716 Lady M. W. Montagu *Let. to C'tess Mar* 8 Sept., I have not yet been at Court, being forced to stay for my gown. 1750 H. Walpole *Lett. H. Mann* (1834) II. ccxiii. 330 Several women have made Earthquake gowns—that is warm gowns to sit out of doors all tonight. 1801 Mar. Edgeworth *Angelina* iii. (1832) 48 Betty Williams' heavy foot was set upon the train of Clara's gown. 1856 Mrs. Browning *Aur. Leigh* i. 5 Women..With rosy children hanging on their gowns. 1882 Miss Braddon *Mt. Royal* III. viii. 162 There is no end to the variety of her gowns.

c. *fig.*

*c*1586 C'tess Pembroke *Ps.* lxxiv. xvi, The winters frosty gowne. *a*1649 Drumm. of Hawth. *Poems* Wks. (1711) 15/1 In gloomy gowns the stars this loss deplore.

2. = DRESSING GOWN, NIGHTGOWN.

1597 Shaks. *2 Hen. IV*, iii. ii. 197 Come, thou shalt go to the Warres in a Gowne: we will haue away thy cold. 1722 De Foe *Col. Jack* (1840) 216, I came down..in my gown and slippers. 1762 Goldsm. *Cit. W.* lxxvii. ¶4 The nobility receiving company in their morning gowns. 1778 James *Diss. Fevers* (ed. 8) 40 On Saturday morning, about three o'clock, it was observed his breast had sweated through his shirt and gown. 1907 *Yesterday's Shopping* (1969) 758 Dressing Jackets, Tea Jackets, and Gowns... Graceful Gown. In Nuns' Veiling, accordion pleated, trimmed white embroidery. 1969 E. McGirr *Entry of Death* iii. 51 She wears thick Viyella pyjamas... And her gown... Brushed nylon, a kind of housecoat really.

3. Used as the name of the flowing outer garment worn by the ancients, esp. the Roman toga. Hence after Roman usage: 'The dress of peace' (J.).

1387 Trevisa *Higden* (Rolls) I. 243 Virgil clepeþ the Romayns togati; þat beeþ men i-cloþed in gownes. *Ibid.* V. 293 He was i-cloþed in a consuls gowne [L. *trabea*]. 1612 Davies *Why Ireland*, etc. (1747) 129 After that the Roman attire grew to be in account, and the gowne to be in use among them. 1627 May *Lucan* ii. 409 His best attire rough gownes, such as of old Was Roman weare. 1658 Dryden *Cromw.* xx, He Mars deposed, and arms to gowns made yield. 1701 tr. *Le Clerc's Prim. Fathers* (1702) 287 The Rhetorical Exercises which Young Men applied themselves to, when they had put on the thorough White Gown—that is, at Seventeen or Eighteen Years of Age. 1887 Bowen *Virg. Æneid* i. 282 Lords of the world, thy Romans, the race of the glorious gown.

4. A more or less flowing outer robe indicating the wearer's office, profession, or status:

a. as worn by the holder of a civil or legal or parliamentary office, e.g. an alderman, a judge, magistrate; also *collect.* the magistracy. ***furred gown***: that worn by an alderman.

1377 Langl. *P. Pl.* B. xiii. 227 And fewe robes I fonge or furred gounes. 1486 *Surtees Misc.* (1888) 53 The Maire and Aldermen, cled in long gownys of skarlet. 1596 Spenser *State Irel.* 49 The person that is gowned, is by his gown put in minde of gravitie. 1622 Fletcher *Beggars Bush* ii. i, To the field we are not prest; Nor are called into the Towne, to be troubled with the Gowne! 1681 Dryden *Abs. & Achit.* 193 Oh, had he been content to serve the Crown, With Virtues only proper to the Gown. 1785 Wolcot (P. Pindar) *Wks.* 1816 I. 80 Skinner in his aldermanic gown. 1820 Byron *Mar. Faliero* v. iii, Robed in their gowns of state. 1842 Browning *Pied Piper* iii, And as for our Corporation —shocking To think we buy gowns lined with ermine For dolts that can't or won't determine [etc.]. 1886 *Manch. Exam.* 14 Jan. 5/6 Mr. Peel..wore a wig, but had not yet donned the flowing gown which is the distinguishing mark of his office [the Speakership]. 1888 Bryce *Amer. Commw.* (1889) I. xxii. 227 The justices [of the Supreme Court] wear black gowns.

b. as distinctive of the legal or clerical profession. Hence, The profession itself, and *collect.* the members of it. †***lawyer of both gowns***: one versed in both common and ecclesiastical law.

1564 *Brief Exam.* ***** iij b, The Gowne that you..would so gladly minister in, seemeth to come eyther from Turkes or Papistes. 1601 Shaks. *Twel. N.* iv. ii. 1, I prethee put on this gown, and this beard, make him beleeue thou art Sir Topas the Curate. 1641 Bp. Lincoln *Sp.* 24 May in Cobbett *Parl. Hist.* (1807) II. 798 Calvin and Beza, whilst they lived, carried all the counsel of the state of Geneva under their own gowns. 1641 Sir E. Dering *Sp. on Relig.* 20 Nov. xiv. (1642) 63 Lawyers of both Gownes. 1649 Milton *Eikon.* xvi, How constantly the Preist puts on his Gown and Surplice, so constantly doth his praier put on a servile yoak of Liturgie. 1682 Dryden *Medal* 306 The Cut-throat Sword and clamorous Gown shall jar. 1697 tr. *C'tess D'Aunoy's Trav.* (1706) 101 It is a surprizing thing, the number of Employs for men of the Sword and the Gown, which his Majesty every day bestows. 1708 *Brit. Apollo* No. 84. 1/2 The Gown was the Intention of your Studies. 1770 Goldsm. *Des. Vill.* 184 Children..pluck'd his gown, to share the good man's smile. 1784 J. Potter *Virt. Villagers* II. 135, I have now taken the gown [i.e. holy orders], agreeable to my good father's wishes. 1855 Macaulay *Hist. Eng.* xiii. III. 250 His gown was torn to shreds over his head: if he had a prayer book in his pocket it was burned. *Mod.* (*N. Linc.*) He goes as gain'and popery as he can wi'out hevin' his gown pulled off.

fig. 1601 Shaks. *All's Well* i. iii. 99 It [honestie] will weare the Surplis of humilitie ouer the blacke-Gowne of a bigge heart.

c. as the distinctive costume of a member of a University, varying in form, colour, etc., with the academical standing or degree of the wearer (as in phr. †***man of his gown***). ***cap and gown*** (see CAP 4 b).

1665 Needham *Medela Medic.* 253 It is not a Gown, or Degrees taken in Universities, which constitute the Physician. 1668 Maynwaring *Compl. Physitian* 169 By their pragmatick Insolencies and upbraiding men of the Gown. 1707 Guinnet in Hearne *Collect.* 23 Dec. (O.H.S.) II. 84 The Exercises, that are appointed Gentlemen of his Gown. 1748 Johnson *Vanity Hum. Wishes* 138 The strong contagion of the gown. 1764 *Oxford Sausage* 30 My Wife's Ambition and my own Was that this Child should wear a Gown. *a*1839 Praed *Poems* (1864) II. 131 A scholar, in my cap and gown. 1868 M. Pattison *Academ. Org.* iv. 72 The scholar's gown, now a robe of honour, was a badge of social inferiority.

5. *collect. sing.* The resident members of a University. Now only without article and in opposition to *town*.

1659 Wood *Life* (O.H.S.) I. 292 Challenging also the gowne it self to oppose what they did and said. 1764 *Oxford Sausage* 17 Ben Tyrrell, Cook of high Renown, To please the Palates of the Gown, At Three-pence each, makes Mutton-Pies. 1828 *Sporting Mag.* XXI. 428 Parties of five or six, both 'gown' and 'town', were parading abreast. 1854 'C. Bede' *Verdant Green* ii. iii, When Gown was absent, Town was miserable. 1891 *Pall Mall G.* 30 May 4/3 'Town' and 'Gown' joined in harmony.

6. *attrib.* and *Comb.*, as ***gown-piece***, ***-skirt***, ***-sleeve***, ***-tail***; **gown-boy**, a boy belonging to a scholastic foundation, esp. to that of the Charterhouse; †**gown-cloth**, a piece of material to make a gown; †**gown-crook**, a hook on which gowns are hung; **gown-fashion** *adv.*, after the fashion of a gown; †**gown-rule**, civilian government (in Rome); †**gown-sept**, the clan or nation of the gown or toga (= L. *gens togata*).

1558 Thackeray *Newcomes* I. ii. 18, I have seen his name carved upon the *Gown Boys' arch. 1886 Sir. F. H. Doyle *Remin.* 29 A gown-boy at the Charterhouse. *c*1386 Chaucer *Sompn. T.* 544 Thou shalt haue anon A *goune clooth. 1452 in Willis & Clark *Cambridge* (1886) I. 337 The said prouost shal yif to the said Robert..yerly duryng his lyf a gownecloth in sute with his gentilmen. 1549 in H. Hall *Eliz. Age* (1886) 191 A gowne clothe for George Darrell..xl^s. 1573 *Richmond. Wills* (Surtees 1853) 235 To ye wyfe of Wiliam my son..a pare of *gowne krokes. 1891 Miss Dowie *Girl in Karp.* 13 Their coarse white linen dresses, made *gown-fashion in one piece. 1821 *Blackw. Mag.* VIII. 616 The spangled *gown-piece, fancy-figured o'er. 1851 Mayhew *Lond. Labour* I. 374 The gown-pieces were rolled loosely together. 1627 May *Lucan* vii. 71 [Cicero] In whose *gown-rule fierce Catiline did feare The peacefull axes. 1583 Stanyhurst *Æneis* i. (Arb.) 27 Iuno..with mee newlye shal enter In leage with Romans, and *gownesept charelye tender. 1870 Morris *Earthly Par.* II. iii. 85 Holding her *gownskirt in her hand. 1894 —— *Wood beyond World* x. 59 She..hastily covered up her legs with her gown-skirt. *c*1489 Caxton *Blanchardyn* xix. 61 Vnto hym she gaffe one of her *gowne sleues. 1889 T. Hardy *Mayor Casterbridge* iv, A woman with her gown-sleeves rolled up. 1772 *Ann. Reg.* 213 Her legs and hands tied, and her *gown tail muffled over her head. 1818 Scott *Hrt. Midl.* xvii, I.. canna climb up to that high window to see sae muckle as her gown-tail.

Hence †'**gownist**, one who is entitled to wear a gown; '**gownlet** *nonce-wd.*, a small gown.

1586 Warner *Alb. Eng.* v. xxvii. (1589) 120 Those inricht our Gownests. 1890 Sarah Duncan *Social Departure* 107 Cuddling her small person up..in her swathing gownlet.

gown (gaʊn), *v.* [f. GOWN *sb.*]

1. *trans.* To dress in a gown.

*c*1485 *Digby Myst.* (1882) v. 726 Here entrithe vj. Iorours in a sute gownyde with hoodes a-bowte her neckes. 1592 Warner *Alb. Eng.* vii. xxxvii. (1612) 186 Empson and Dudley, fur'd Esquires, more harmefull being gown'd. 1609 Rowlands *Whole Crew Gossips* 22 Nay Ile be sworne it makes my purse-strings cracke, To ruffle her in her pride, and gowne her backe. 1700 Dryden *Fables, Flower & Leaf* 161 In velvet white as snow the troop was gown'd. 1842 Tennyson *Gardener's Dau.* 125 Gown'd in pure white..she stood. 1890 Mrs. Hungerford *Born Coquette* I. viii. 73 Should she elect to gown herself in the latest Paris fashions.

transf. and *fig.* 1590 Spenser *F.Q.* ii. xii. 67 Th' yuorie in golden mantle gownd. 1633 P. Fletcher *Pisc. Ecl.* v. ii, The warmer sunne his bride hath newly gown'd. *a*1850 Rossetti *Dante & Circ.* i. (1874) 206 The man who in Love's robe is gowned May say that Fortune smiles upon his lot.

2. *intr.* for *refl.* To put on a gown.

1896 *Durham Univ. Jrnl.* XII. 81 One or two men in different parts of the Hall who had not gowned were politely requested to do so.

gownd, vulgar form of GOWN.

gownde, variant of GOUND *Obs.*

gowned (gaʊnd), *ppl. a.* [f. GOWN *v.* + -ED[1].]

1. Dressed in a gown, in various senses of the word.

1590 Spenser *F.Q.* i. xii. 5 A noble crew about them waited round Of sage and sober peres, all gravely gownd. 1617 Moryson *Itin.* iii. 171 The Venetians are gowned, yet by night going to visit their Mistresses, weare short Spanish cloakes. 1651 Jer. Taylor *Serm. for Year* i. xvii. 215 Well might all the gowned Romans fear when Pompey fled. *a*1764 R. Lloyd *Poetry Professors* 113 These sons of gowned ease Proud of the plumage of Degrees. 1805 Wordsw. *Prelude* iii. (1850) 75 Happy is the gowned youth, Who only misses what I missed. 1888 Amy Levy *Reuben Sachs* xi. 162 Their gorgeously gowned and bejewelled women.

absol. 1885 *Century Mag.* XXIX. 508 Shall we begrudge the wigged and gowned their rations of wit?

†**2. a.** Used as the equivalent of L. *togāta* (*fābula*), the epithet of the class of plays that dealt with Roman characters and incidents. **b.** ***gowned war***, ***warfare***: 'warfare' waged in the law-courts. (Cf. GOWN *sb.* 3, 4 b.) *Obs.*

1640 Somner *Antiq. Canterb.* 207 One equally experienced in both warfares, the armed and gowned. *a*1661 Holyday *Juvenal* 1 Shall one sweat, Whiles his gown'd comique scene he does repeat? 1665 Cowley *Agric.* Wks. (1684) 105 The Camps of Gowned War.

gownless ('gaʊnlɪs), *a.* [See -LESS.] Not provided with or not wearing a gown.

1895 Hardy *Jude* ii. vii. 144 Two devil-may-care young men who proved to be gownless undergraduates. 1901 'L. Malet' *Sir R. Calmady* iv. i, The picture of those reportedly gownless backs had depressed him abominably.

gownsman ('gaʊnzmən). Also 6–8 **gownman**. [f. GOWN *sb.* + MAN; cf. *craft(s)man*, *draught(s)man*, *sword(s)man*, etc.]

†**1.** (Used to translate L. *togātus*.) An adult Roman; a Roman as distinguished from one of another nation. *Obs.*

1579–80 North *Plutarch* (1676) 443 He called Lucullus, Xerxes the Gownman, as if he would have said, Xerxes the Roman. *Ibid.* 959 Four years after that, he became a Gownman, though he were but young.

2. One wearing the gown, or 'dress of peace' (cf. GOWN *sb.* 3 and L. *togātus*); a civilian, in contradistinction to a soldier.

1607–12 Bacon *Ess., Seditions & Troubles* (Arb.) 414 But lett such one, be an assured one..holding good Correspondence with the gowne Men. 1643 Wither *Campo Musæ* 15 The Gownman, must a Swordman, learne to be. 1699 T. C[ockman] *Tully's Offices* (1706) 77 The Publick receives as much Benefit from Gownsmen..as it doth from Soldiers. 1719 D'Urfey *Pills* II. 253 Let the politick Gown-man Tread the Mazes of the State. 1757 Burke *Abridgm. Eng. Hist.* Wks. X. 455 It was rather a military spirit, than that of the gownman. 1759 Hume *Hist. Eng.* (1806) IV. lx. 516 The soldiery..were more desirous of serving under a young prince of spirit and vivacity than under a committee of talking gown-men. 1849 Macaulay *Hist. Eng.* ix. II. 485 Military men are seldom disposed to take counsel with gownsmen on military matters.

3. One who wears a gown as an indication of his office, profession, or standing. **a.** A member of the legal profession; a lawyer, barrister, or judge.

1627 May *Lucan* iii. 155 To play the Gowneman now He had forgot. 1673 Kirkman *Unlucky Cit.* 174 Instead of Gown-men pleading at the Bar, they found Sword-men fighting at the Barriers. *a*1735 Ld. Lansdowne *Poems, Beauty & Law* 35 Was't a vain promise and a gownman's lie? 1858 Polson *Law & L.* 60 He was a legal monk, a cloistered gownsman.

b. A member of the clerical profession; a clergyman. Now *rare*.

1641 Shirley *Cardinal* ii. iii. (1652) 20 But let the purple Gownman place his engins I' th' dark that wounds me. 1671 M. Bruce *Good News in Evil T.* (1708) 24 You will not haunt the companie of Betrayers of Him, call them Gown-men, or call them Kirk-men as they will. 1697 Vanbrugh *Relapse* v. iii, Lory, take care of this reverend gown-man in the next room a little. 1794 Mathias *Purs. Lit.* (1798) 53 Levite gownsmen hugg'd their ignorance. 1821 Joanna Baillie *Metr. Leg., Columbus* xl, A mission'd gownsman o'er the sea Was sent. 1855 Macaulay *Hist. Eng.* xvi. III. 627 A gownsman who pushed himself into a battle..strongly excited William's spleen.

c. A member of a university; often in contrast with *townsman*. ***gownsman of the foundation*** = FOUNDATIONER.

1665 Needham *Medela Medic.* 249 The idle sort of Gownmen, lazing in their Studies over the Pagan Books of Institutions. *c*1670 Hobbes *Dial. Com. Laws* (1840) 144 Books which are commonly read by gownmen. 1688 Smith in *Magd. Coll. & Jas. II* (O.H.S.) 243 Gownsmen of the Foundation. 1721 Amherst *Terræ Fil.* ii. (ed. 3) 10 The traiterous gown-men proceeded gradually from one corruption to another. 1750 W. Dodd *Poems* (1767) 38 The bevy bright of gownsmen blythe. 1791 'G. Gambado' *Ann. Horsem.* vii. (1809) 96 My dear Miss S—— will perhaps ride away with some other Gownsman. 1823 Lamb *Elia* Ser. ii. *Poor Relations*, The distance between the gownsmen and the townsmen..is carried to an excess. 1889 Jessopp *Coming of Friars* vi. 277 The townsmen soon discovered that the gownsmen were gainers by the new plan.

†**d.** A member of a municipal corporation. *Obs.*

1675 Otway *Alcibiades* i. i. (1687) 6 Heavy Gown-men clad in formal Furrs. 1681 *Lond. Gaz.* No. 1656/2 The Mayor and Aldermen..together with the Common Council, and all the Gown men of that Corporation, to the number of about fourscore.

4. *Sc.* = BEADSMAN 2 b. *rare*$^{-1}$.

1886 Stevenson *Kidnapped* xv. 138 Our lowland beggars —even the gownsmen themselves, who beg by patent—had a louting, flattering way with them.

gowp, Sc. form of GULP *sb.* and *v.*

gowpen ('gaʊpən). *Sc.* and *dial.* Forms: 3 goupynes (*pl.*), 6–7 gopin(g, 6–9 gowpin(g, (8 gapen, gouppen, 9 gowpan, 7, 9 goppen), 8–9 goupen, -in, gowpen. [a. ON. *gaupn* (Norw. dial. *gaupn*, Sw. *göpen*, Da. *gievn*, *giøvn*, in the Dict. of 1802) = OHG. *coufana* (MHG. *goufen*). Cf. YEPSEN.

The original sense of the Teut. word was prob. the single hand hollowed, the sense of 'double handful' being expressed by the plural. The ON. word seems to occur only as pl.; in mod.Scand. dialects the sing. is used, with varying sense.]

1. The two hands placed together so as to form a bowl (†formerly *pl.* in the same sense). Hence, usually, as much as can be contained in the hands so placed; a 'double handful'.

c **1325** *Gloss. W. de Biblesw.* in Wright *Voc.* 147 *note*, (Sloane MS.) Amedous les mayns, voides ou pleyns, En Fraunz apellom les galeyns [*glossed by* goupynes]. **1536** BELLENDEN *Boece's Hist. Scot.* (1821) I. p. lviii, Bot gevis ane gowpin, orellis sum thingis mair abone the just mesure that they sell. **1724** RAMSAY *Tea-T. Misc., South Sea Sang*, When we came to London Town We dream'd of gowd in gowpings here. **1805** MACNEILL *Poet. Wks.* (1812) II. 105 Our laird has fine houses and guineas in gowpins. **1827** SCOTT *Antiq.* Advt., A handful of meal (called a gowpen) was scarce denied by the poorest cottager. **1871** GIBBON *Lack of Gold* vi, He took out a gowpen of the grain. **1872** J. G. MURPHY *Comm. Lev.* xvi. 12 *Handsful*, the full of the gowpens in Old English phrase. **1893** *Northumbld. Gloss.*, *Gowpen*, the hollow of both hands placed together.

fig. **1819** W. TENNANT *Papistry Storm'd* (1827) 118 Flang frae her lap rejoicingly Goupins o' glory down.

b. *Sc. Law.* A perquisite allowed to a miller's servant.

a **1765** ERSKINE *Inst. Law Scot.* II. ix. §19. 314 The sequels are the small parcels of corn or meal given as a fee to the servants,..they pass by the name of..*bannock*, and *lock*, or *gowpen*. **1818** SCOTT *Hrt. Midl.* xiii. *note*, The expression *lock*, for a small quantity of..corn, meal, flax, or the like, is still preserved, not only popularly, but in a legal description, as the *lock* and *gowpen*, or small quantity and handful, payable in thirlage cases, as in-town multure.

2. The grasp of a hand, the fist.

1788 PICKEN *Poems* 111 An honest chiel..Juste ram'd it [a letter] in my gowpen. **18..** *Tom Linn* xxiii. in Maidment *New Bk. Old Ball.* (1844) 54 Hold me fast, let me not go, Or from your goupen break.

gowpenful ('gaupənfʊl). *Sc.* and *dial.* [f. GOWPEN + -FUL.] A 'double handful' (see GOWPEN 1).

1674-91 RAY *N.C. Words* 32 *Gopingfull*, as much as you can hold in your Fist. **1789** DAVIDSON *Seasons* 13 Who for a knife Or penny whissle, will part wi' their gold In gopinfu's. **1852** CARLYLE *Let.* in Froude *Life in Lond.* (1884) II. xx. 107 An old Russian countess yesternight sat playing Gowpanfuls of gold pieces every stake. **1871** W. ALEXANDER *Johnny Gibb* xxxiv. (1873) 193, I wudna gi'en a goupenfu' o' sheelocks for yer chance. **1887** J. SERVICE *Life Duguid* ix. 53, I myself have gathered a gowpenful of flinty arrowheids on the sands of Ardeer.

gowra, var. GORAH.

gowrde, obs. f. GOURD *sb.*[1]; var. GOURD *sb.*[2] *Obs.*

gowrie, obs. variant of COWRIE.

1723 *Pres. State Russia* I. 336 White Shells, commonly called Gowries or Blackamores Teeth. **1777** PENNANT *Zool.* IV. 99 *Cypræa*, Gowrie..This genus is called Cypræa and Veneria, from its being peculiarly dedicated to Venus.

gowsbery, obs. form of GOOSEBERRY.

gowshe, obs. form of GUSH.

gowt, variant of GALT *Obs.* exc. *dial.*

1641 BEST *Farm. Bks.* (Surtees) 141 Halfpence a peece for the gowtes or bore pigges.

gowt(e, obs. f. GOUT *sb.*[1]; var. GOUT *sb.*[2] and *v. Obs.*

gowylsought, var. GULESOUGHT *Obs.*, jaundice.

goy (gɔɪ). Pl. goyim ('gɔɪjɪm), goys. Fem. 'goyah. [Heb. *gōy* people, nation, pl. *gōyim*.] A Jewish designation of a non-Jew, a Gentile. Hence '**goyish** (also **goyisch**, etc.) *a.*, resembling, in the manner of, having the characteristics of, a goy.

Quot. 1835 may not belong here.

1835 [see GUY *sb.*[2] 3 c]. **1841** BORROW *Zincali* I. x. 159 The children of Roma and those of Israel..are..dispersed among the Gentiles, whom they hate and despise, under the names of Busnees and Goyim. **1892** I. ZANGWILL *Childr. Ghetto* I. vi. 158 The *Goyah*, which is literally heathen female, did everything required on the Sabbath. **1919** F. HURST *Humoresque* 205 A goy play-actor. *Ibid.*, She reproaches me with having brought about this *goy* mix-up! **1931** 'D. STIFF' *Milk & Honey Route* vi. 64 Jewish hobos are so scarce that when business gets low the agencies will sometimes help the 'goys' or gentile hobos. **1940** E. POUND *Cantos* lii. 11 Paying for a big jews' vendetta on goyim. **1950** *Penguin New Writing* XL. 35 He would join the others in speaking derisively of the Dropper and his girl as a couple of Goys. **1959** M. LEVIN *Eva* 32 My father..had spoken of the Austrians as..among the best of the *goyim*. **1959** H. SLESAR *Grey Flannel Shroud* (1960) viii. 125 My mother..never really approved of Sword's Point [a district]; it was a little too *goyisher*..for her. **1960** *Commentary* Aug. 131 We got pros for the Yiddish parts and for the English roles I'm lining up all my *goyishe* friends. **1963** *Guardian* 23 Dec. 4/5 It would certainly have gone against their Jewish grain..to follow so *goyish* a custom. **1964** S. BELLOW *Herzog* (1965) 28 A Christian lady came... Beside his bed, the goyische lady sat in her long skirts.

Goyaesque (gɔɪjə'ɛsk), *a.* Also Go'yesque. [f. the name of Francisco de *Goya* y Lucientes (1746-1828), Spanish painter + -ESQUE.]

Having the character of the pictures by Goya.

1934 R. CAMPBELL *Broken Record* 108 Squalid Goyesque groups of hags in conversation. **1939** *Burlington Mag.* Apr. 154/2 Not..Goyaesque in spirit. **1959** *Listener* 30 Apr. 774/2 A Goyesque ruthlessness. **1961** *Times* 24 May 16/6 A Goyaesque print of a massacred family.

goyal, variant of GOYLE.

goyazite ('gɔɪəzaɪt). *Min.* [Named by Damour 1864 after *Goyaz*, a town in Brazil: see -ITE.]

Phosphate of aluminium and calcium found in small yellow grains in the diamond sands.

1884 *Amer. Jrnl. Sci.* Ser. III. XXVIII. 237 Damour has given the name goyazite to a phosphate of alumina and lime.

goye, obs. form of JOY.

goyf(f, variant of GOFE *Sc. Obs.*, pillory.

goyle (gɔɪl). *dial.* Also 7 goile, 9 **goyal**. A deep trench, a ravine.

1617 LANE *Cont. Sqr.'s T.* 414 Canac, his daughter.. whome theare hee made right perfect in the skilles of ridinge goiles, plaines, ruffetes, dales, and hills. **1869** BLACKMORE *Lorna D.* iii, We were come to a long deep 'goyal', as they call it on Exmoor. **1873** *Q. Rev.* CXXXV. 146 Dartmoor abounds in..traces of a very numerous population, which.. found its chief occupation in streaming for tin—the 'goyles' or deep trenches of their old works being everywhere visible. **1886** in Elworthy *W. Somerset Word-bk.* s.v., A scramble down into the goyal; a clatter up the other side. **1894** BEATRICE WHITBY *Mary Fenwick's Dau.* III. 123 There are landmarks down, and 'goyles' blocked up. **1902** A. CONAN DOYLE *Hound of Baskervilles* ii. 24 Three of them..rode forward down the goyal. **1963** *Times* 26 Apr. 16/6 On my left tumbles the brook at the bottom of a deep gully—what we call in Devon a goyal—deep enough to take a horse and cart.

goym, Sc. variant of GOME[1]. *Obs.*

†**goynire**. *Obs.*[−1] [ad. OF. *guinier* (F. *guignier*), f. *guine* (F. *guigne*: see GEAN) a small kind of cherry.] A kind of cherry-tree.

1572 MASCALL *Art of Planting & Graffing* 16 The healme Cherrie, which is graft on the wilde goynire (which is an other kinde of grate Cherrie).

goys, obs. form of GOOSE.

†'**goyster**. *Obs.*[−1] Corrupt form of AGISTOR.

1523 FITZHERB. *Surv.* 28 b, And than may the kepars, regarders, goysters, and other offycers of suche forest and chases, haue parfyte knowledge what townshyppe the catell is of.

goyster, goyt, variants of GAUSTER, GOTE.

gozan, variant of GOSSAN.

gozel(l, variant of GUZZLE *Obs.* or *dial.*, ditch.

gozeling, gozelyng, obs. forms of GOSLING.

gozell ('gəʊzəl). *dial.* Also 9 gozill. [ad. F. *groseille* gooseberry or currant.] (See quots.)

1657 W. COLES *Adam in Eden* clxxvi. 274 The black sort is generally called..in English Black Currans, as other are Red and White; but the White are called Gozell in some parts of Kent. **1866** *Treas. Bot.* 546/1 *Gozell*, the gooseberry *Ribes uva-crispa*. **1879** BRITTEN & HOLLAND *Plant-n.*, Gozill. 1. *Ribes rubrum*. 2. *Ribes Grossularia*.

Gozitan ('gəʊzɪtən), *sb.* and *a.* [f. *Goz(o*, name of an island near Malta + *-itan* as in NEAPOLITAN.] **A.** *sb.* An inhabitant of Gozo. **B.** *adj.* Of or pertaining to Gozo.

1870 *Malta & Gozo Vade Mecum 1871* 83 Gozo is under the rule of the Governor of Malta... The Gozitans return 1 member to Council. **1958** SITWELL & JONES *Malta* vi. 69 Plenty of the Gozitan boats of peculiar design. **1962** *Times* 10 Feb. 11/6 A diminutive motor-vessel squeezes in..and this is the event of the Gozitan day. **1963** *Guardian* 17 May 11/4 The intricate carving at which the Gozitans excel.

†'**gozle**, *v. Obs. rare*[−1]. Cf. GUZZLE *v.* [ad. OF. *gosillier* (F. *gosiller*) to pass as if through the throat, f. OF. *gosillier* throat (F. *gosier*).]

intr. ? To trickle.

1650 BULWER *Anthropomet.* 114 He that drinketh, lifteth up the vessel, and not touching it with his lips, receives the water by those little holes, the which doth gozle and make a pleasing noise.

gozzan, variant of GOSSAN.

gozzard ('gɒzəd). [repr. OE. **góshierde*, with normal shortening of the vowel of the initial syllable; the literary form *gooseherd* is due to recomposition.] = GOOSEHERD.

14.. *Voc.* in Wr.-Wülcker 566/34 *Aucarius*, a gosherde. *c* **1440** *Promp. Parv.* 204/1 Gosherde, *aucarius, aucaria*. **1771** PENNANT *Tour Scotl. in 1769* (1790) 10 A person called a Gozzard attends the flock and twice a day drives the whole flock to water. **1773** BARRINGTON in *Phil. Trans.* LXIII. 287 The shepherd..knows each of them, and can swear to them, if they are lost; as can the Lincolnshire gosherd to each goose. **1804** BEWICK *Brit. Birds* (1847) II. 240 This business requires the attendance of the Gozzard (Gooseherd) a month at least. **1893** BARING-GOULD *Cheap-Jack Z.* II. 48 Why should gaulters and bankers only have double pay? Why not molers and gozzards also?

gozzen, variant of GOSSAN.

†**gra.** *int. Obs. rare.* [app. repr. Irish *a ghráidh* 'my dear', in English books commonly rendered *agra(h* or ARRAH.] An exclamation ascribed to Irishmen.

1707 FARQUHAR *Beaux Stratagem* IV. i, I am your Priest, Gra; and your Conscience is under my Hands. **1771** SMOLLETT *H. Clinker* 24 Apr., to Sir W. Phillips, Now I believe you are my friend, sure enough, gra.

Graafian ('grɑːfɪən), *a. Anat.* [f. the name of R. de Graaf, a Dutch anatomist (1641-73) + -IAN.]

In ***Graafian follicle, vesicle***, one of the small sacs in the ovary of mammals in which the ova are matured.

1841 tr. *Cruveilhier's Descr. Anat.* I. 616 In the midst of this tissue..the Graafian vesicles are deposited. **1849-52** TODD *Cycl. Anat.* IV. 838/1. **1873** T. H. GREEN *Introd. Pathol.* (ed. 2) 183 Dilatation of the Graafian follicles.

grab (græb), *sb.*[1] *Anglo-Indian.* Also 7 grob, 8 grabb, gurab, 9 ghurab. [a. Arab. *ɣurāb*, lit. 'raven', applied to a kind of galley.] A large coasting-vessel, drawing very little water, built with a prow and usually two-masted, used in the East (see quots. 1763, 1839).

1680 MORDEN *Geog. Rect.* (1685) 405 The desperate attacks made..by 1500 of his men in three Ships and four Grabs. **1698** FRYER *Acc. E. India & P.* 174 Admiral of his Fleet of Grobs and Boats. **1763** R. ORME *Hist. Milit. Trans. Ind.* I. 401 The grabs have rarely more than two masts, although some have three;..they are built to draw very little water, being very broad in proportion to their length, narrowing however from the middle to the end, where instead of bows they have a prow. **1773** E. IVES *Voy.* 43 One Grab of 18 guns, and several other vessels. **1824** HEBER *Jrnl.* (1828) I. i. 11 Their grabs, which still have an elongated bow ..are often very fine vessels. **1839** H. MALCOM *Trav. S.E. Asia* II. 357 *Gloss.*, *Grab*, a square-rigged Arab coasting vessel, having a very projecting stem, and no bowsprit. It has two masts. **1878** TRELAWNY *Shelley*, etc. (1887) 84 A Persian dhow, an Arab grab, or a Chinese junk.

b. *Comb.*, as ***grab-brig, -ketch, -snow, -vessel***; ***grab-service*** (see quot. 1867).

1831 TRELAWNY *Adv. Younger Son* I. 177 De Ruyter now took me on board of an Arab *grab brig. **1790** BEATSON *Nav. & Mil. Mem.* II. 40 His fleet..consisted of eight *grab-ketches [etc.]. **1867** SMYTH *Sailor's Word-bk.*, **Grab service*, country vessels first employed by the Bombay government against the pirates; afterwards erected into the Bombay Marine. **1806** *Naval Chron.* XV. 470 The *Grab Snow *Generous Friends*,..burthen about two hundred tons. **1800** *Asiatic Ann. Reg., Chron.* 22/2 They perceived a *grab vessel at anchor.

grab (græb), *sb.*[2] [f. GRAB *v.*]

1. a. A quick sudden clutch, grasp, seizure, or attempt to seize.

1824 DE QUINCEY *Incognito* Wks. XI. 3 The chairman, unable to control his impatience, made a grab at it. **1835** HALIBURTON *Clockm.* Ser. I. viii, He makes a grab at me, and I shuts the door right to on his wrist. **1839** MARRYAT *Diary Amer.* Ser. I. II. 111, I rose gently with both hands ready for a grab.

b. The action or practice of grabbing. ***game of grab*** (? cf. sense 5 and *grab game* in 6), ***policy of grab***: in recent journalistic use often applied opprobriously to rapacious proceedings in political or commercial affairs. ***up for grabs***: open to offer; easily obtainable (*slang* (chiefly *U.S.*)).

1883 LD. WEMYSS in *St. James's Gaz.* 16 July, They..are playing a game of 'grab' for the farmer's vote. **1884** *Pall Mall G.* 13 Sept. 3/1 The fatal inauguration of the policy of grab by Lord Beaconsfield in 1878. **1888** *Daily News* 12 Dec. 4/8 Part of a policy called by fine people annexation and by common people grab. **1893** BESANT *Ivory Gate* 236 The selfishness of mankind as illustrated by the universal game of Grab. **1897** *Westm. Gaz.* 24 Nov. 1/3 The newly invented game of 'grab' in Africa. **1945** L. SHELLY *Jive Talk Dict.* 35 *Up for grabs*, easy to make gal. **1954** BERREY & VAN DEN BARK *Amer. Thes. Slang* (ed. 2) §356/7 *Up for grabs*, easy to pick up. **1967** *Boston Globe* 5 Apr. 51/5 Right now every position is up for grabs. Every player is going to get a shot. **1968** *Globe & Mail* (Toronto) 3 Feb. B3/3 At the time that General Bakeries made its bid, Mr. Conrad said the Ogilvie companies appeared to be 'up for grabs'. **1971** *Financial Mail* (Johannesburg) 26 Feb. 675/2 So the hotel reservations set-up looks up for grabs.

2. The thing grabbed. *Sc.*

1777 SIR M. HUNTER *Jrnl.* (1894) 27 Grab was a favourite expression among the Light Infantry, and meant any plunder taken by force. **1824** MACTAGGART *Gallovid. Encycl.*, *Grabs*, little prizes. **1825-80** JAMIESON, *Grab*,..the number of objects thus seized.

3. One who grabs: **a.** A body-snatcher, resurrectionist; **b.** A catchpoll, bumbailiff, policeman. ? *Obs.*

1823 *Spirit Publ. Jrnls.* (1824) 178 When bailiffs and grabs hunt us up in the East. **1830** S. WARREN *Diary Physic.* I. xvi. 370 Sir ——'s dressers and myself, with an experienced 'grab', that is to say, a professional resurrectionist—were to set off from the Borough. **1849** ALB. SMITH *Pottleton Leg.* xv. 123 Do you want to..have the grabs point at us as swindlers? **1919** B. BOOTH in H. Begbie *Life Wm. Booth* (1920) ii. 24 My father was a Grab, a Get. **1958** *Amer. Speech* XXXIII. 225 Less frequently used among nonmusicians..are..*shamus, fuzz, grab* (all meaning policeman).

4. A mechanical device or implement for clutching or gripping objects (see quots.).

1865 A. M. EATON *Diary* 14 Oct. in *West. Pennsylvania Hist. Mag.* (1935) XVIII. 205 We saw a 'grab' an instrument designed to get out tools stuck in any well. **1875** KNIGHT *Dict. Mech.*, *Grab*,..the term is especially applied to devices for withdrawing pipes, drills, reamers, etc., from artesian, oil, and other wells. **1881** *Proc. Instit. Civil Engin.* LXV. 312 A modification of the bucket [dredger]..with strong curved steel arms..to which the makers have given the name of 'grab'. **1881** *Standard* 16 Nov. 2/5 The accident was caused by the plate having slipped from the 'grab' by which it was being lifted. **1893** *Times* 10 July 13/6 Grain cargoes.. discharged..by the use of hydraulic cranes and tubs or Priestman's grabs. **1897** *Daily News* 10 Sept. 8/5 Hydraulic cranes drop down their 'grabs' into the loose grain in the hold of the vessel like a huge pair of jaws. They come up the next instant with a mouthful of about three-quarters of a ton, and spit it out into a hopper. **1955** *Times* 19 May 7/6 Cranes and mechanical grabs heave up loads of what the council call 'reluctant London clay'.

5. a. A children's game at cards, in which when two or more cards of equal value are on the table together the player who is quickest to recognize and 'grab' them adds them to his own hand. Cf. also ANIMAL C. 1.

1900 in *N.E.D.* **1941** H. G. WELLS *You can't be too Careful* II. i. 46 They had a pack of real cards..and gambled with them at *Beat your Neighbour out of doors* and *Grab*.

b. *Chess.* Applied to a particular class of problems: in full ***grab theme***. (See quot. 1913.)

1909 A. C. WHITE *Knights & Bishops* p. iii. **1913** —— *Sam Loyd* 357 The Grab Theme... The theme includes, in its broadest sense, all problems where a Black piece is captured on two or more squares... In its narrower sense it is limited to the problems where a particular Black piece is captured on two or more squares by a single White piece or by two White pieces of the same kind. *Ibid.* 359 The Grab by the concerted action of the two White Knights is extremely pretty. **1943** B. HARLEY *Mate in Three Moves* 52 The grab theme..is essentially a brutal and monotonous business. **1963** M. LIPTON et al. *Chess Probl.* 259 A doubling of the grab theme, in which a black unit is captured on a number of different squares, leading to zugzwang.

6. *attrib.* and *Comb.*, chiefly in the names of various appliances for seizing or clutching, as ***grab-crane***, ***-digger***, ***dredger***, ***-iron***, ***-line***, ***-machine***; also **grab-bag** (*U.S.* at fancy fairs), a bag containing various articles, into which one may dip on payment of a certain sum; also *fig.*; **grab bar**, a bar fitted as a handhold, esp. one grasped for stabilization or support; **grab bucket** = BUCKET *sb.*[1] 3 b; **grab-coup** = *grab-game (a)*; **grab-game**, (*a*) (see quot. 1859); (*b*) the policy of 'grabbing' territories, etc.; **grab handle**, a handle fitted in a motor car to assist passengers entering or alighting, or to steady them when the car is moving; **grab-hook**, any hook for grabbing, *spec.* (see quot. 1887); *pl.* (*Naut. slang*) fingers; **grab-racket** *U.S.*, a disorderly scramble, in which each person 'grabs' what he can; **grab rail, strap**, a rail or strap inside a motor vehicle for standing passengers to hold.

1855 M. M. THOMSON *Doesticks* xvi. 135 [A] young woman wanted me to invest in the '*grab bag'; [I] gave half a dollar, and fished in. **1879** *N.Y. Tribune* 23 Sept. (Cent.), It is a grab-bag from which every disappointed politician hopes to draw a prize. **1886** *Harper's Mag.* Jan. 237 The woodman's axe now resounded with the busy notes of preparation for a dive into nature's great grab-bag. **1960** *20th Cent.* May 460 Sociology is the great intellectual grab-bag of our times. **1967** *Canadian Ann. Rev.* 1966 6 It met strong resistance from those who supported the traditional formula of a grab-bag of promises. **1967** C. O. SKINNER *Madame Sarah* xii. 269 Sarah would hold out a grab bag from which each child drew a number. **1959** *Home Safety Rev.* Winter 21/2 Install *grab bars next to bathtub and in showers. **1967** *Gloss. Caravan Terms (B.S.I.)* 2 *Grab bars, grab handles*, bars or handles fitted to the outside of the bodywork to assist in manhandling the caravan. **1970** *Globe & Mail* (Toronto) 28 Sept. 10/2 (Advt.), Bathroom safety aids..grab bars and safety rails. **1985** *New Age* Winter 22/2 Corridors, passages and bathrooms should have hand-rails; and one or two 'grab bars' might be worth considering for the bedroom. **1885** *Marine Engin.* 1 Aug. 139/2 (*heading*) Recent applications for patents..7333 C. W. Hunt. Dredging or *grab buckets. **1823** 'JON BEE' *Dict. Turf*, *Grab-coup, modern practice of gambling, adopted by the losers, thus the person cheated or *done*, takes his opportunity, makes a dash at the depository of money, or such as may be down for the *play* and *grabs* as much as possible, pockets the proceeds, and fights his way out of the house. **1895** *Daily News* 15 Apr. 8/2, [For sale by auction,] 30 steam, hand, and *grab cranes. **1936** *Oxoniensia* I. 81 Without their ready co-operation and their keenness to save everything possible from the very teeth of their '*grab'-digger, we should not have been able to record and preserve such a wealth of detail in advance of the gravel-digging. **1909** *Man. Seamanship* (*H.M.S.O.*) II. xiii. 224 In hard ground it would be necessary to loosen the earth..or dig a hole with a *grab dredger. **1846** R. B. SAGE *Scenes Rocky Mts.* xxxii. 282 Provided you won't attempt the *grab game on us. **1859** BARTLETT *Dict. Amer.*, *Grab Game*, a mode of swindling or rather stealing, practised by sharpers ..Bets are made..when a dispute is purposely planned, in the midst of which one of the confederates seizes or 'grabs' the money at stake and runs off. The term is also used in a more general sense to signify stealing and making off with the booty. **1864** R. B. KIMBALL *Was he successful* ix. 116 A bold, daring, unscrupulous man, who, in the language of his acquaintances, practised the grab-game. **1895** *Forum* (N.Y.) May 265 This eventuated in preventing the grab-game of France. **1959** *Observer* 1 Mar. 21/6 The..walnut screen rail with *grab handle. **1961** *Times* 28 Mar. 4/6 Large 'grab' handles of a flexible material fitted to the roof above each of the four doors are useful when passengers are entering or leaving. **1970** *Motoring Which?* Apr. 50/1 Armrests were only fair, but the passenger had a good grab handle. **1608** TOPSELL *Serpents* (1658) 713 Taking up their Nets, at one place they did hang so fast, as without breaking they could not pull them out of the water, wherefore they set their *Grab-hooks unto them to loose them. **1887** JEFFERIES *Field & Hedgerow* (1889) 179 The grapnel kept at every village draw-well is called the grab-hook. **1889** *Cent. Dict.*, *Grab-hook*, in angling, a hook made by fixing four large fish-hooks in a piece of lead. **1905** *Terms Forestry & Logging* 38 *Grab hook*, a hook having a narrow throat, adapted to grasp any link of a chain. **1946** J. IRVING *Royal Navalese* 86 *Grabhooks*, fingers. **1887** *Pall Mall G.* 22 Sept. 11/1 Priestman's *grab machine is now set to work to excavate the earth from the centre of the caisson. **1892** STEVENSON & OSBOURNE *Wrecker* (ed. 2) 219 Now boss!..is this to be run shipshape? or is it a Dutch *grab-racket? **1955** E. K. WENLOCK *Kitchin's Road Transport Law* (ed. 10) 94 A clear height of 5 ft 10 in excluding any *grab rail or strap shall extend over all space intended for use by standing passengers. **1963** *Times* 21 May 5/6 Sensible points include a padded grab-rail.

grab (græb), *v.* [Corresponds to MDu., MLG. *grabben*, mod.Sw. *grabba*; perh. an onomatopœic modification of the root of GRIP.]

1. *trans.* To grasp or seize suddenly and eagerly; hence, to appropriate to oneself in a rapacious or unscrupulous manner. Phr. ***to grab hold of*** (cf. HOLD *sb.*[1] 2).

1589 RIDER *Eng.-Lat. Dict.*, To Grabbe, or grabble, *vide* to graple. **1801** A. WILSON *Poems & Lit. Prose* (1876) I. 86 Old..witches..butter from churns are eternally grabbing. **1820** J. W. CROKER in Smiles *J. Murray* (1891) II. xxiii. 86, I will go to the Museum and grab them, as my betters have done before me. **1873** G. C. DAVIES *Mount. & Mere* xviii. 164 He grabbed it hard and fast. **1878** BROWNING *Poets Croisic* cvii, How did it happen that gross Humbug grabbed Thy weapons? **1881** *Macm. Mag.* XLV. 39 Little dark-brown creatures..armed each with four needle-like talons, ready to grab cruelly the hand put within reach. **1888** *Times* (weekly ed.) 21 Dec. 16/3 You had done what is called 'grab' that land. **1894** *Forum* (N.Y.) Dec. 401 John Bull is not habitually slow to run up his flag on any available spot he may safely grab. **1894** A. CONAN DOYLE *Mem. Sherlock Holmes* 123 The fellows evidently grabbed hold of anything they could get. **1900** BAYLY & BRISCOE *Chrons. Country Cricket Club* (1908) x. 111, I was walking outside the cricket grounds and you grabbed hold of me.

absol. **1841** EMERSON *Lect.*, *Man the Reformer* Wks. (Bohn) II. 243 To have somewhat left to give, instead of being always prompt to grab.

2. a. To 'collar', capture, or arrest (a person).

1800 *Sporting Mag.* XVI. 26 Agreed to grab about a dozen old acquaintances. **1811** *Lex. Balatronicum* s.v., The pigs grabbed the kiddey for a crack. **1829** *Ann. Reg.* 117 He is sure Benning did not grab, or endeavour to collar Wickliffe. **1845** BARHAM *Ingol. Leg.*, *Bros. Birchington*, My bailiff grabb'd Dick when he should have nabb'd Bob. **1894** H. NISBET *Bush Girl's Rom.* 115 A very dangerous young criminal..whom I reckon we won't be able to grab in a hurry.

b. To arrest the attention of (a person); to make an impression on. *slang.*

1966 *Gramophone Popular Record Catal.* (Artist Section) Dec. 190/2 *Sinatra, Nancy... How Does That Grab You?* Not the lovin' kind; Shadow of your smile;..How does that grab you darlin'?; Bang, bang. **1968** *Canadian Mag.* 15 June 27/2 D'you think *that* will grab them? **1970** *Daily Tel.* (Colour Suppl.) 18 Sept. 46/4, I suppose, as my daughter puts it, 'life is whatever grabs you'. **1971** *Post* (Cape ed.) 9 May 9/5 Elton John is big but if his music doesn't grab you then it just doesn't grab you.

3. a. *intr.* To make a grab or snatch *at* (U.S. *for*).

1852 MRS. STOWE *Uncle Tom's C.* xii. 107 A stick of candy, which he eagerly grabbed at. **1867** TROLLOPE *Chron. Barset* I. xxxvii. 325 She stretched out her hand to grab at the ledger. **1885** *N.Y. Weekly Sun* 13 May 5/1 He made a jump for the knife and Short grabs for it at the same time.

b. Of the brakes of a motor vehicle: to act harshly or jerkily.

1919 FRASER & JONES *Motor Vehicles* xxxi. 328 If the brakes grab or screech a few drops of castor oil..may stop the trouble. **1962** *Which?* (Suppl.) July 90/1 The brakes 'grabbed' very badly, because the friction pad assemblies on the front wheels had moved in the caliper units.

4. *slang.* ***to grab on***: to get along, live.

1861 MAYHEW *Lond. Labour* III. 139 Between the two I do manage to grab on somehow.

5. *Comb.*: **grab-all**, (*a*) one who grabs everything, a rapacious person; (*b*) a bag to carry odds and ends (Farmer *Slang* 1893).

1872 *Sunday Times* 18 Aug. 2/3 The mean and contemptible grab-alls of that government which professes to study the people's interest. **1895** CROCKETT *Men of Moss Hags* xxiii. 163 Robert Grier of Lag, who was a very grab-all among them.

Hence **grabbed** *ppl. a.*, **'grabbing** *vbl. sb.*

1788 W. EDEN in *G. Rose's Diaries* (1860) I. 74 There remained merely the finding and grabbing some respectable office for life. **1891** *Star* 5 Nov. 4/1 The grabbed rights of way mentioned recently. **1895** *Daily News* 25 Oct. 6/3 The Chitral principality is now within the English sphere, to borrow a term which international diplomacy owes to the grabbing-up of Africa. **1919** FRASER & JONES *Motor Vehicles* xxii. 235 Cone clutches are usually faced with leather..the leather becomes hard and dry resulting in 'grabbing'. **1959** *Motor Man.* (ed. 36) iv. 71 Quite elaborate springing arrangements may be built into the clutch disc to avoid 'grabbing' when the friction surfaces are just on the point of gripping.

grabbable ('græbəb(ə)l), *a. nonce-wd.* [f. GRAB *v.* + -ABLE.] That may be grabbed.

1823 *Spirit Publ. Jrnls.* (1824) 110 The 'Old Minstrel Act' would.. make them grabbable as rogues and vagabonds. **1892** *Sat. Rev.* 12 Nov. 571/1 The southern half of Northern Africa is in a condition much more 'grabbable', and attention to it is specially desirable that it be not grabbed by other nations than England.

grabbe, obs. variant of CRAB *sb.*[2]

1578 LYTE *Dodoens* VI. xxx. 696 Roundish leaues, somwhat like the leaues of a gribble, grabbe tree, or wilding.

†**'grabbedness.** *Obs. rare*[−1]. [A variant of, or an error for CRABBEDNESS.] Unevenness.

1563 GOLDING *Cæsar* (1565) 234 b, The grabbednes of the top of a place to a falling grounde hath in it great aduantage.

grabber ('græbə(r)). [f. GRAB *v.* + -ER[1].] One who or that which grabs; *esp.* in (or short for) the combination **land-grabber**, used chiefly in Ireland as a term of reproach for one who takes a holding from which another has been evicted.

1849 T. MILLER in G. W. M. Reynolds *Myst. of Lond.* V. lxxvi. 243/1 Instead of making you either a..buzzman, grabber, or sneak, we..makes a cracksman of you at once. **1859** *Slang Dict.*, *Grabbers*, the hands. **1880** *Daily Tel.* 27 Oct. 5/8 A tenant farmer, whom Mr. Healy denounced as a land grabber. **1889** *Daily News* 24 May 5/8 He was questioned about boycotting and intimidation..He had.. said he would not hurt a hair of the grabber's head. **1920** R. MACAULAY *Potterism* I. iii. 37 He thinks Johnny's a profiteer, too, because of the ribbons and things... It's in the blood. We're grabbers. **1961** NEW ENGLISH BIBLE *I Cor.* v. 10, I was not, of course, referring to pagans who lead loose lives or are grabbers and swindlers or idolaters. *Ibid.* vi. 10 No thieves or grabbers or drunkards..will possess the kingdom of God.

grabbit (boat) hook. = *grab-hook.*

1936 J. GRIERSON *High Failure* v. 92, I made fast, to the first small buoy which I could see, by means of the Grabbit boathook and my special gear for mooring-up single-handed. **1948** *Shell Aviation News* cxxv. 20/3 The pilot using a short boathook fitted with a grabbit hook engages the strop on the buoy.

grabble ('græb(ə)l), *sb.* [f. GRABBLE *v.*]

†**1.** A grapple or struggle. ***to come to a grabble***: to come to handgrips. *Obs.*

1650 CROMWELL *Let.* 30 July (Carlyle), Our bodies of horse..came to a grabble with them.

2. *Angling.* ***to fish*** (†***lie***) ***on*** or ***upon the grabble*** (see quots. 1726, 1787).

1726 *Gentl. Angler* 149 To lie upon the Grabble, is when a running Bullet or flat Piece of Lead keeps the Line firm on the Bottom of the River; so that the Link, to which the Hook is fastened, may play about with the Current of the Water. **1787** BEST *Angling* (ed. 2) 168 Fishing on the grabble is when the line is sunk with a running plummet fast to the bottom, so that the hook-link plays in the water. **1861** *Illustr. Lond. News* 4 May 425/1 The best way is to angle upon the grabble for them [eels] with a lobworm.

grabble ('græb(ə)l), *v.* Also 6–8 **grable**. [Corresponds to Du. *grabbelen* (which has been used in all the senses below exc. 5), a frequentative of *grabben* GRAB *v.*]

1. *intr.* To feel or search with the hands, to grope about. Sometimes ***to grope and grabble*** (cf. Du. *grapen en grabbelen*).

1579–80 NORTH *Plutarch* (1676) 294 Grabling all night in the dark..through wild Olive Trees, and high Rocks. **1581** B. R. *Herodotus* 103 b, Where after they have placed hym, they leave hym grabling in that place, and departe their way. **1630** *God's Power & Prov.* in *Churchill's Collect. Voy.* (1704) IV. 811 We were fain to grabble in the dark (as it were) like a blind Man for his way. **1630** J. TAYLOR (Water P.) *Wks.* III. 13 Ile grable for Gudgeons or fish for Flounders. **1640** SHIRLEY *Arcadia* III. ii, Thou must stoop..And grabble for't [gold] in ground. **1658** A. FOX *Wurtz' Surg.* I. vi. 22 To what end is it, to groap and to grable so much in Wounds? **1712** ARBUTHNOT *John Bull* II. xiii, My Blood chills about my Heart, at the thought of these Rogues, with their bloody Hands grabbling in my Guts, and pulling out my very Entrails. **1727** *Philip Quarll* 178 Grabling round a nautious Weed for fulsome Worms. **1823** *Ann. Reg.*, *Chron.* 141 They continued grabbling for about five minutes, as if looking for something they had lost. **1824** *Hist. Murder Weare* 127 He was grabbling about in the water with a sponge. **1841** *Blackw. Mag.* L. 155 To wade through Hegel..is merely to grope and grabble and to gnaw at the root of one's own growth. **1869** *Lonsdale Gloss.* s.v., 'To grabble for trout;' *i.e.* to grope in holes for them.

b. *trans.* with cognate obj. To feel (one's way).

1627 W. D. tr. *A. d' Audigier's Tragi-com. Hist.* 37 Hee, being in the darke, grabling his way, with one hand upon the raile of the staires [etc.]. **1842** BLACKIE in *Tait's Mag.* IX. 752 Sending the unaided pupil to grope and grabble his way by the help of them [grammars, etc.] only.

2. *intr.* To sprawl or tumble about on all-fours; to scramble (for money, etc.).

1736 AINSWORTH *Lat. Dict.* 1, To lie grabbling on the ground, *humi prostratus jacere*. **1741** RICHARDSON *Pamela* I. 202 A few Scratches on his Face, which..I suppose he got by grabbling among the Gravel, at the Bottom of the Dam. **1851** S. JUDD *Margaret* I. xvii, Some of the boys were..sent grabbling on their faces down the hill. **1888** *Berksh. Gloss.* s.v., I drowed the apples among the bwoys an' let um' grabble vor um.

3. = GRAPPLE *v.* 8. *rare.*

1835 ANSTER tr. *Faustus* II. I. (1887) 47 With dragons let the old drake grabble. **1895** *E. Anglian Gloss.*, *Grabble*, to resist, to contend, to grapple with.

†**4.** *trans.* To handle rudely or roughly. *Obs.*

1684 DRYDEN *Disappointm.* Prol. 60 The doughty bullies ..Invade and grabble one another's punk. **1687** MIEGE *Gt. Fr. Dict.* II, To Grabble or handle untowardly...as, to grabble (or grope) a Wench. **1746** *Exmoor Courtship* (E.D.S.) 376 Es wont ha' ma Tetties a grabbled zo. **1790** J. B. MORETON *W. Ind. Isl.* 146 [They] grabble, grasp and jostle each other to get the best.

5. To seize, to appropriate to oneself.

1796 *Grose's Dict. Vulg. Tongue* (ed. 3) s.v., To grabble the bit; to seize any one's money. **1857** SIR F. PALGRAVE *Norm.*

& Eng. II. 581 The rich armour..and all the precious articles which decked Otho's pavilion they grabbled and got.

b. *intr.* To grap or snap *at* (something).

1837 *New Monthly Mag.* L. 108 Every hungry dog.. began to grabble at the tempting morsel.

Hence ˈ**grabbling** *vbl. sb.*

a **1654** SELDEN *Table-T.* (Arb.) 99 He puts his hands in his Pockets, and keeps a grabling and a fumbling. **1687** MIEGE *Gt. Fr. Dict.* II, Grabbling, *l'action de manier quêque Chose de mauvaise grace.* **1691** TRYON *Wisd. Dictates* Pref. 2 The Grabling of the poor dark Spirit of Man after Truth. **1736** AINSWORTH *Lat. Dict.* I, A grabbling, *contrectatio.*

grabby (ˈgræbɪ), *sb. slang.* A Service (esp. Naval) term for a foot-soldier.

1868 WHYTE MELVILLE *White Rose* I. x. 121, I shouldn't like to be a 'Grabby'.. I'd rather be a private in the cavalry than an officer in the regiment of *feet!* **1916** *Chambers's Jrnl.* Jan. 11/1 Being about five miles out from the shore, we knew that the local 'grabbies' would not see us. **1919** 'ETIENNE' *Strange Tales from Fleet* 123 'Do you mean the grabby's dinner-party we gave?' inquired the.. first lieutenant.

grabby (ˈgræbɪ), *a. colloq.* [f. GRAB *v.* + -Y[1].] Having a tendency to grab; greedy, grasping.

1910 A. ROSS in *Penguin Dict. Mod. Quots.* (1971) 196/1, I don't believe in publishers who wish to butter their bannocks on both sides while they'll hardly allow an author to smell treacle. I consider they are too grabby together and like Methodists they love to keep the Sabbath and everything else they can lay their hands on. **1924** E. FERBER *So Big* xiv. 245 'What's the matter with her hands?'.. 'They're brown, and awfully thin and sort of—grabby.' **1942** BERREY & VAN DEN BARK *Amer. Thes. Slang* 279 *Avaricious; Greedy,* Grabby, a hog for,.. on the make, piggy. **1953** E. HAHN *J. Brooke* vi. 99 James was not particularly patriotic, nor grabby on behalf of Britain. **1970** J. H. VANCE *Deadly Isles* xi. 76 Nice when they don't steal my copra. Some people are pretty grabby.

graben (ˈgrɑːbən). *Geol.* Pl. **grabens, graben** (after G. pl. *gräben*). [a. G. *graben* ditch, introduced in its Geol. sense by E. Suess (*Antlitz d. Erde* (1883) I. I. iii. 166).] A depression in the earth's surface bounded by faults; a rift valley.

1896 J. W. GREGORY *Great Rift Valley* xii. 220 This left a great open Rift Valley (or, to use Prof. Suess's term, a 'Graben'). **1910** *Encycl. Brit.* X. 598/1 Crust-blocks resembling 'graben' and 'horsts'. **1913** *Bull. Geol. Soc. Amer.* XXIV. 201 The broad valley, or graben, of the middle Rhine is inclosed by maturely dissected scarps. **1968** R. W. FAIRBRIDGE *Encycl. Geomorphol.* 485/1 The association of volcanism with grabens is well known. **1970** *Nature* 18 Apr. 247/1 The whole region is a large graben which has been filled with up to 3 km of evaporites.

grace (greɪs), *sb.* Also 4–5 gras(e, (4 grass, greace). [a. F. *grâce* = Pr., Sp. *gracia*, Pg. *graça*, It. *grazia*, semi-popular a. L. *grātia* (1) pleasing quality, attractiveness, (2) favour, goodwill, (3) gratitude, thanks; f. *grātus* pleasing, GRATEFUL.]

I. Pleasing quality, gracefulness.

1. The quality of producing favourable impressions; attractiveness, charm. Now usually with more restricted application: The attractiveness or charm belonging to elegance of proportions, or (especially) ease and refinement of movement, action, or expression. †In 16–17th c. *occas.* Pleasantness of flavour.

1382 WYCLIF *Prov.* i. 9 That ther be added grace to thin hed. *Ibid.* xxii. 11 Who looueth clennesse of herte, for the grace of his lippis shal han the king frend. **1390** GOWER *Conf.* III. 27 Her eyen.. her nase.. her redde lippes eke,.. All that he seeth is full of grace. **1530** PALSGR. 35 As it was first written in the Romant tonge, it hath a marveylous grace. **1551** TURNER *Herbal* I. (1568) D iv b, They haue in sauces a proper plesantnes by them selues or a peculiar grace as some speake nowe adayes. **1587** GOLDING *De Mornay* xi. 155 Without the blacke, the white could haue no grace. *a* **1625** BEAUM. & FL. *Custom Country* II. i, My Nephew.. Had been a happy man had he ne'er knowne What's there in grace and fashion. **1661** LOVELL *Hist. Anim. & Min.* 227 They are best.. eaten hot, for if cold they loose much of their grace. **1674** PLAYFORD *Skill Mus.* I. ii. 47 We use to say of a man that he sings with much Grace, or little Grace. **1693** DRYDEN *Ep. to Congreve* 19 All below is strength, and all above is grace. **1698** —— *Monum. Maiden Lady* 8 Her limbs were formed with such harmonious grace. **1709** STEELE *Tatler* No. 94 ¶1 It gives new Grace to the most eminent Accomplishments. **1753** HOGARTH *Anal. Beauty* x. 52 There is only one precise serpentine line that I call the line of grace. **1785** REID *Intell. Powers* VIII. iv. (1803) 561 The last and noblest part of beauty is grace. **1844** DISRAELI *Coningsby* VI. ii, Grace, indeed, is beauty in action. **1870** H. MACMILLAN *Bible Teach.* ix. 186 It is not possessed of showy-coloured flowers; but is distinguished for the grace of its foliage. **1871** R. ELLIS tr. *Catullus* iii. 2 Weep all men that have any grace about ye. **1875** JOWETT *Plato* (ed. 2) V. 15 The long speeches.. have never the grace and harmony which are exhibited in the earlier dialogues. **1888** BRYCE *Amer. Commw.* III. cvi. 539 The Americans have gained more than they have lost by equality. I do not think the upper class loses in grace. **1890** BOLDREWOOD *Col. Reformer* (1891) 150 Miss Frankston rode.. extremely well, and with an unconscious grace.

b. In a weaker sense: Seemliness, becomingness, favourable or creditable aspect. Chiefly in ***a good grace***; hence ***a bad, an ill grace***, an unbecoming appearance. Now somewhat *rare* (cf. c).

a **1586** SIDNEY *Arcadia* II. (1590) 175 The same words in my Ladie Philocleas mouth, as from one woman to another (so as there were no other bodie by) might haue had a better grace; and perchance haue found a gentler receipt. **1667** TEMPLE *Let. to Ld. Arlington* Wks. 1731 II. 35 The first Pace of the War being made in Flanders, loses all the good Grace which the French endeavour'd to give their Invasion. **1711** STEELE *Spect.* No. 6 ¶4 All which is supported by no other Pretension, than that it is done with what we call a good Grace. *a* **1715** BURNET *Own Time* (1823) I. 334 That it would have a good grace in them to seem zealous for it. *a* **1751** BOLINGBROKE (J.), They would have ill grace in denying it. **1833** HT. MARTINEAU *Vanderput & S.* v. 83 As soon as she could with any grace leave the company. **1856** FROUDE *Hist. Eng.* (1858) I. i. 35 Henry.. retired with a good grace from an impossible position. **1856** LEVER *Martins of Cro' M.* 598 Incidents.. which came off with an ill-grace on the table of a Court of Justice.

c. Hence (with mixture of branch II), ***with a good grace***, with a show of willingness, as though pleased to do so; ***with a bad*** or ***ill grace***, with ill-concealed reluctance, ungraciously.

1754 HUME *Hist. Eng.* (1761) I. viii. 170 Becket, though with the worst grace imaginable, was induced to comply with the royal mandate. **1778** MISS BURNEY *Evelina* (1794) II. 138 May I.. hope that you will pardon the ill-grace with which I have submitted to my disappointment? **1836** *Backwoods Canada* 17 When the tide fails cast anchor, and wait with the best grace we can. *Ibid.* 74 With a marvellous ill grace the men took up their oars when their load was completed. **1858** DICKENS *Lett.* (1880) II. 81, I submit with the worst grace possible.

†**d.** ***to do*** (a person, a thing) ***grace***: to become, reflect credit on, set in a good light, embellish; also, to do honour *to*. So ***in grace of***: in honour of. *Obs.*

1590 SHAKS. *Mids. N.* IV. i. 139 They.. Came heere in grace of our solemnity. **1596** —— *1 Hen. IV*, II. i. 79 Troiens that.. are content to doe the Profession some grace. *c* **1600** —— *Sonn.* xxviii, I tell the Day.. thou do'st him [the day] grace when clouds doe blot the heauen. *Ibid.* cxxxii, O, let it then as well beseeme thy heart To mourne for me since mourning doth thee grace. **1602** —— *Ham.* II. ii. 53 Thy selfe do grace to them, and bring them in. **1806** CUMBERLAND *Mem.* (1807) I. 155 Further to do me grace, he was pleased to put into my hands a very.. elaborate report of his own drawing up.

2. a. An attractive or pleasing quality or feature. †Formerly often in phrase ***goods and graces.***

1340 *Ayenb.* 79 Zuyche guodes and zuiche graces wyþoute doþ ofte kuead. *a* **1450** *Knt. de la Tour* (1868) 91 No woman shulde be proude of the goodes and graces that God hathe sent her. **1692** DRYDEN *Eleonora* Ded., The nice touches, which give the best resemblance, and make the graces of the picture. **1741** RICHARDSON *Pamela* (ed. 3) II. 257, I never before saw so young a Lady shine forth with such Graces of Mind and Person. **1749** SMOLLETT *Regicide* I. vi, Possess'd of ev'ry manly grace. **1798** FERRIAR *Eng. Historians* 236 The affectation of unattainable graces only adds distortion to clownishness. **1836** SIR H. TAYLOR *Statesman* xxxi. 237 It is a grace in flattery so to let fall your compliments as that [etc.]. **1888** BRYCE *Amer. Commw.* I. vii. 97 Washington.. cultivates the graces and pleasures of life with eminent success.

†**b.** quasi-*concr.* Something that imparts beauty; an ornament; the part in which the beauty of a thing consists. *Obs.*

1599 SHAKS. *Hen. V*, II. Prol. 28 By their hands, this grace of Kings must dye. **1645** EVELYN *Mem.* (1857) I. 176 A noble piece of architecture.. which is the grace of the whole Corso. **1658** tr. *Porta's Nat. Magick* IX. vii. 238 Curl'd Hair seems to be no small Grace and Ornament to the Head. **1700** DRYDEN *Flower & Leaf* 313 A spreading laurel stood, The grace and ornament of all the wood. **1837** DICKENS *Let.* 8 May (1965) I. 258 A young and lovely girl, who has been the grace and ornament of our home for the whole time of our marriage, died here yesterday.

c. A procedure, attitude, etc. adopted with a view to grace. *Obs.* exc. in ***airs and graces***, affectations of elegance of manners.

1607 HIERON *Wks.* I. 76 It is a common grace of some, to vse some words or sentences of scripture instead of iests and prouerbs in their common talke. **1608** ROWLANDS *Humors Looking-Gl.* 21 Then forth they goe after the drunken pace, Which God he knowes was with a reeling grace. **1848** THACKERAY *Van. Fair* xxxix, Old Sir Pitt.. chuckled at her airs and graces, and would laugh by the hour together at her assumptions of dignity and imitations of genteel life.

3. *Mus.* An embellishment consisting of additional notes introduced into vocal or instrumental music, not essential to the harmony or melody. (Cf. *grace-note* in sense 21 b.)

1657 R. LIGON *Barbadoes* (1673) 12 No Graces, Double Relishes, Trillos, Gropos, or Piano forte's, but plain as a packstaff. **1659** C. SIMPSON *Division Viol.* 9 Graces done with the Fingers, are of two sorts: viz. smooth and shaked. *Ibid.*, In ascending, it makes that Grace which we call a Plain-beat. **1674** PLAYFORD *Skill Mus.* I. 38 Those excellent Graces and Ornaments to the good manner of singing, which we call Trills, Grupps [etc.]. **1806** CALLCOTT *Mus. Gram.* vi. 61 The principal Graces of Melody are the Appoggiatura, the Shake, the Turn and the Beat. **1866** ENGEL *Nat. Mus.* iii. 118 The bagpipe tunes of the Scotch are full of graces. **1878** F. TAYLOR in Grove *Dict. Mus.* I. 43 The agrémens or graces peculiar to Old English music.

4. *Mythology.* One of the sister-goddesses (= L. *Grātiæ*, Gr. *Χάριτες*) regarded as the bestowers of beauty and charm, and portrayed as women of exquisite beauty. Usually spoken of (after Hesiod) as three in number, Aglaia, Thalia, and Euphrosyne.

1579 SPENSER *Sheph. Cal.* Apr. 115 She shalbe a grace To fyll the fourth place. **1590** —— *F.Q.* I. i. 48 And eke the Graces seemed all to sing, Hymen Iō Hymen! dauncing all around. **1606** SHAKS. *Tr. & Cr.* I. ii. 257 Had I a sister were a Grace, or a daughter a Goddesse, hee should take his choice. **1624** MASSINGER *Parl. Love* II. iii, To swear that Venus leads The Loves and Graces from the Idalian green. **1632** MILTON *L'Allegro* 15 Euphrosyne.. Whom lovely Venus, at a birth, With two sister Graces more, To ivy-crownèd Bacchus bore. **1675** COTTON *Burlesque upon Burl.* 108 Thy Mistress Venus, and the Graces. *a* **1721** PRIOR *Celia to Damon* 46 On this forehead.. The Loves delighted, and the Graces play'd. **1780** COWPER *Progr. Err.* 337 The Graces too.. Felt each a mortal stab in her own breast. **1847** TENNYSON *Princ.* II. 13 The Muses and the Graces, group'd in threes, Enring'd a billowing fountain in the midst.

transf. **1802** MRS. JANE WEST *Infidel Father* I. 88 Lady Languish, the beauty of the year.. softness, susceptibility, and an affectation of weakness almost to fragility, were the distinguishing traits of this reigning grace. **1830** J. G. STRUTT *Sylva Brit.* 53 These three graces of the forest form a group within sight of the house. **1846** MRS. GORE *Eng. Char.* (1852) 40 The three black graces—law, physic, and divinity.. claim her successively as their own. **1886** RUSKIN *Præterita* I. 322 [Taglioni] the Grace of her century.

5. ***the graces*** (= F. *le jeu des grâces*): a game played with hoops and pairs of slender rods, so called (according to Littré) because it develops graceful movement of the arms.

One of the players takes a hoop upon two rods, held one in each hand; he then draws the rods rapidly across each other, with the effect of sending the hoop into the air to be caught by another player on his pair of rods.

1842 A. COMBE *Princ. Physiol.* (ed. 11) 185 The play called the graces is also well adapted for expanding the chest, and giving strength to the muscles of the back. **1855** in OGILVIE, Suppl. [**1871** M. COLLINS *Mrq. & Merch.* III. vii. 189 The younger members.. were laughing over a game of *les Graces.*]

II. Favour.

6. a. Favour, favourable or benignant regard or its manifestation (now only on the part of a superior); favour or goodwill, in contradistinction to right or obligation, as the ground of a concession. Somewhat *arch.* †***of grace***: as a matter of favour and not of right. †***in grace of***: in favour of, for the benefit of. (Cf. sense 14.)

c **1275** LAY. 6616 Ware he mihte of his men eni grace finde. *a* **1300** *Cursor M.* 5425 If i [Jacob, addressing Joseph] euer fand grace wit þe. *c* **1330** R. BRUNNE *Chron.* (1810) 62 Harold.. had þe kynge's grace. **1362** LANGL. *P. Pl.* B. XII. 114 If men it wol aske.. and bidden it of grace. *c* **1400** MAUNDEV. (1839) v. 34 He moste get grace of him and leve to go. **1480** CAXTON *Chron. Eng.* ccxliii. 293 The kyng for hir manfulnesse and of his grace toke hir quarel in to his honde. *a* **1533** LD. BERNERS *Gold. Bk. M. Aurel.* (1546) Bb, They haue rather merited pardon by theyr ignoraunces, then praysyng or grace by theyr wysedome. **1577** FENTON *Gold. Epist.* 195 Alexander Seuerus published a lawe in grace of the Christians. **1590** SPENSER *F.Q.* I. ix. 39 Is not great grace to helpe him over past, Or free his feet that in the myre sticke fast? **1597** HOOKER *Eccl. Pol.* v. ix. §3 Through meere voluntarie grace or beneuolence. **1623** MASSINGER *Dk. Milan* IV. ii, All the grace I hitherto have done you was bestowed With a shut hand. **1652** H. COGAN tr. *Scudery's Ibrahim* III. v. 108 Having received it of grace from the hand of your enemy. **1677** DRYDEN *Prol. Circe* 28 Perhaps, if now your grace you will not grudge He may grow up to write, and you to judge. **1700** —— *Flower & Leaf* 598 Of her grace she gave her maid to know The secret meaning of this moral show. **1709** PRIOR *Imit. Anacreon*, The Herd of Criticks I defie.. Regardless of their Grace, or Spight. **1821** SCOTT *Kenilw.* xvii, The marks of grace which Elizabeth from time to time shewed to young Raleigh. **1878** M. A. BROWN *Nadeschda* 56 Prince Wladmir looked with grace Upon the old and tried retainer. **1883** *Law Times* 20 Oct. 409/2 The Treasury, though professing to make some acknowledgment by way of grace for inventions adopted by the Crown, has [etc.]. **1891** *Law Rep., Weekly Notes* 78/1 The applicants came to the Court for an act of grace, and they must take it on proper terms.

b. Said with reference to God. (See also 11 a.)

c **1175** *Lamb. Hom.* 49 Godalmihtin haueð isceaweð us wel muchele grace. *a* **1300** *Cursor M.* 17095 God.. send us space al of his grace, ur wranges here to right. *c* **1330** *King of Tars* 910 Forth wente Sir Cleophas, To the court thorw godes gras. *c* **1460** FORTESCUE *Abs. & Lim. Mon.* xii. (1885) 139 God.. gyff hym grase to augmente is reaume. **1583** STUBBES *Anat. Abus.* II. (1882) 1 How farre purpose you to trauell this way by the grace of God? **1585** T. WASHINGTON tr. *Nicholay's Voy.* XVII. vii. 40 b, Untoo the seconde time, in which (yf God give me grace) shalbe described [etc.]. **1655–61** WALTON *Angler* iv. (ed. 3) 76 A grace of God Ile give you a Sillibub of new Verjuice. **1864** TENNYSON *En. Ard.* 190 Annie, this voyage by the grace of God Will bring fair weather yet to all of us. **1872** A. LANG *Ball. & Lyr. Old France* 11 Mock not at us that so feeble be, But pray God pardon us out of His grace.

c. Hence in phrase ***by the grace of God*** (tr. L. *Dei gratia*), appended to the formal statement of the titles of sovereigns, and formerly also of ecclesiastical dignitaries; perh. with mixture of sense 11 a.

1495 in *Extracts Aberd. Reg.* (1844) I. 55 James, be the grace of God kinge of Scottis. *c* **1532** DU WES *Introd. Fr.* in *Palsgr.* 1019 Henry by the grace of God lyveng kyng victorious [etc.]. **1611** BIBLE Ded., Iames by the grace of God King of Great Britaine. **1837** CARLYLE *Fr. Rev.* I. I. ii, Louis, King by the Grace of God.

†**d.** ***save your grace***: an apologetic phrase = 'may it not displease you', 'by your leave'. *Obs.*

c **1386** CHAUCER *Melib.* ¶104 Whereas ye seyn that alle wommen been wikke, Saue youre grace certes ye despisen alle wommen in this wyse. *c* **1400** MAUNDEV. (Roxb.) xx. 92 After my feble witte me thinke, saue þaire grace, þat it es mykill mare.

e. ***by grace of***: by virtue of, 'thanks to'.

1852 BRIMLEY *Ess., Esmond* 259 The Chevalier St. George ..misses being James the Third.. by grace of his own exceeding baseness.

†**f.** ***hard grace***: displeasure, ill-will, severity. (See also sense 10.) *Obs.*

c **1384** CHAUCER *H. Fame* III. 496 This Eolus, with harde grace, Held the wyndes in distresse. *c* **1386** —— *Sompn. T.* 520 Lo sires quod the lord with harde grace Who herd euere of swich a thyng er now? —— *Can. Yeom. Prol. & T.* 636 This chanoun took his cole with harde grace.

g. ***grace and favour house, residence***, etc.: accommodation held 'by grace and favour' of the Crown, the Government, or other owner.

1909 *Daily Chron.* 7 May 1/2 Someone to whom the King may grant a 'Grace and Favour' residence will find himself bound to pay for.. work which he had not ordered. **1953** 'M. INNES' *Christmas at Candleshoe* i. 14 Benison is a Grace and Favour house, the patronage of which is vested in two or three powerful persons in the City. **1956** MONCREIFFE & POTTINGER *Blood Royal* 54 Others contain 'grace and favour' apartments, for rewarding distinguished servants of the country in their retirement. **1967** *Whitaker's Almanack* 652/1 The Minister of Public Buildings and Works reported in Parliament.. that, of 140 grace and favour residences, [etc.].

7. The condition or fact of being favoured. †***in grace***, in favour (*obs.*). †(***a person's***) ***grace***, ***good grace*** (obs.), now only, after Fr. idiom, (***a person's***) ***good graces***: (his) favour and good opinion.

1463 *Bury Wills* (Camden) 24 That he stonde welle and cler in the kynggez grace. *c* **1477** CAXTON *Jason* 64 b, Ye shewe well howe that aboue all other ye haue me in your grace. *c* **1489** —— *Blanchardyn* xli. 153 And how he was in her goode grace, and she lyke wyse in his. **1586** PUTTENHAM *Eng. Poesie* I. vi. (Arb.) 27 This [the custom of Princes] brought the ryming Poesie in grace. **1596** DRAYTON *Leg.* Pref., In Pierce of Gaveston there is given to the Minions, and Creatures of Princes, a very faire warning, to use their Grace with their Royall Patrons, modestly. **1599** SHAKS. *Much Ado* II. i. 32 Till all graces be in one woman, one woman shall not come in my grace. *c* **1620** FLETCHER *False One* II. i, The red Pharsalian feilds.. Where killing was in grace, and wounds were glorious. **1670** COTTON *Espernon* III. x. 498 He would not however in return offer him his good Graces. [*Sidenote*] Not otherwise to be rendred without spoiling the sense. **1672** DRYDEN *Marr. à la Mode* II. i, A gentleman.. who understands the *grand monde* so well.. may pretend to the good graces of a lady. **1675** EVELYN *Mem.* (1857) II. 110 A sprightly young lady, much in the good graces of the family. **1711** STEELE *Spect.* No. 76 ¶4 The Men themselves shall think thus meanly or greatly of themselves, as they are out or in the good Graces of a Court. **1727** COLDEN *Hist. Ind. Nations* 112 Adario.. resolved.. to recover the good Graces of the French. **1757** FOOTE *Author* I. Wks. 1799 I. 133 The booksellers have.. refused to employ me; you, Sir, I hear, are in their graces. **1855** MACAULAY *Hist. Eng.* xii. III. 221 The one who had the largest share of James's good graces seems to have been Cartwright. **1858** CARLYLE *Fredk. Gt.* II. xiii. (1865) I. 124 Their progress.. in the grace of Karl, was something extraordinary. **1875** JOWETT *Plato* (ed. 2) III. 304 These gentlemen.. do not seem to be in your good graces. **1882** *Macm. Mag.* XLVI. 65/2 The band.. and the guard of honour.. ran each other hard for the first place in the islanders' good graces.

8. a. An instance or manifestation of favour; a favour conferred on or offered to another.

1297 R. GLOUC. (Rolls) 6505 He [Canute].. þoȝte on þe vaire grace þat vr louerd him sende. **13..** *Guy Warw.* (A.) 1058 He.. þonked god of þat gras. **1390** GOWER *Conf.* III. 37 Sithe it so is, That Lazar may nought do me this.. I wolde pray an other grace. **1470-85** MALORY *Arthur* x. ii, Thou hast a fayre grace of me this daye, that I shold rescowe the. **1603** KNOLLES *Hist. Turks* (1621) 45 Andronicus.. proudly rejected the graces offred. **1659** B. HARRIS *Parival's Iron Age* 101 This Peace was received by all the Subjects of the King, as a speciall grace sent them from God. **1859** TENNYSON *Elaine* 381 Do me this grace, my child, to have my shield In keeping till I come. **1871** R. ELLIS tr. *Catullus* lxvi. 71 A grace I here implore thee, if any Word should offend.

b. An exceptional favour granted by some one in authority, a privilege, a dispensation. *Obs.* exc. *Hist.* ***expectative grace*** (see EXPECTATIVE *a.* 1 a).

c **1400** *Rom. Rose* 5128 If thou scape yit, atte laste, Fro Love.. Certeyn, I holde it but a grace. **1554** *Act 1 & 2 Phil. & M.* c. 8 §33 Dispensations and Graces given by such Order as the publick Laws of the Realm then approved. **1587** FLEMING *Contn. Holinshed* III. 362/2 The highest pontife or bishop granted these foresaid graces to father Robert Persons & Edmund Campion. **1651** HOBBES *Leviath.* (1839) 30 The benefit which a sovereign bestoweth on a subject, for fear of some power and ability he hath to do hurt to the commonwealth, are not properly rewards; for they are not salaries.. nor are they graces. **1697** DRYDEN *Æneid* VI. 196 But, to return and view the chearful Skies,.. To few great Jupiter imparts this Grace. **1777** BURKE *Let. Affairs Amer.* Wks. III. 165 To protect the king's loyal subjects, and to grant to them.. the common rights of men, by the name of graces? **1824** SYD. SMITH *Wks.* (1859) II. 55/2 Charles I. took a bribe of 120,000*l.* from his Irish subjects, to grant them what in those days were called Graces, but in these days would be denominated the Elements of Justice. **1827** HALLAM *Const. Hist.* (1876) I. vi. 339 It was resolved to announce certain intended graces in the speech from the throne. **1848** WHARTON *Law Lex.*, *Grace*, a faculty, license or dispensation. **1878** LECKY *Eng. in 18th C.* II. vi. 115 These Graces, the Irish analogue of the Petition of Rights.

†**c.** Permission to do something; leave. *Obs.*

a **1300** *Cursor M.* 26285 þan mai his biscop do him grace, wijf to tak wijt hir to liue. *c* **1400** *Rom. Rose* 4080 No man mo into this place Of me to entre shal have grace. *c* **1400** *Destr. Troy* 826 Wold ye graunt me your grase goodly to wende, I wold boune me to batell. **14..** *Sir Beues* (Pynson) 1379 + 9 There shal no man haue grace.. Agaynst my wyl to lye me by Nor do me shame nor velany!

†**d.** A mark of divine favour, a mercy. *Obs.*$^{-1}$

1523 LD. BERNERS *Froiss.* I. xxii. 31 It was a fayre grace that the Kynge had nat ben taken.

†**e.** A gratuity or 'douceur'. *Obs.*

1769 S. PATERSON *Another Trav.* II. 144 An English coachman, postboy, or waterman, generally expects some grace from the passengers, over and above his fare.

9. In University language. **a.** †Originally, a dispensation, granted by the Congregation of a University or by some Faculty in it, from some of the statutable conditions required for a degree. As in the English universities the full performance of such conditions ceased to be enforced, the 'grace' came to be an essential preliminary to any degree. Hence the word has now the sense: **b.** The leave of Congregation to take a degree. **c.** Other decrees of the Governing Body, being very often dispensations from the permanent statutes, were sometimes styled *graces*, and at Cambridge every such decree is called a Grace of the Senate. **d.** In mod. use, the term is also applied to the permission which a candidate for a degree is required to obtain from his College or Hall.

14.. *Nom.* in Wr.-Wülcker 719/41 *Nomina domorum et rerum ecclesiasticarum, Hec gracia*, a grace. **1529** *Act 21 Hen. VIII*, c. 13 §12 Doctours, and Bachelers of Dyvynyte [etc.] which shalbe admytted to any of the said Degrees by any of the Unyversitees of this Realme and nat by Grace onely. **1573** HARVEY *Letter-bk.* (Camden) 2 Mr. Nuce was requestid to put up our graces the next morning. **1623** in *Crt. & Times Jas. I* (1849) II. 408 They say, it was a stolen congregation, and yet he got his grace but by three votes. **1665** J. BUCK in G. Peacock *Stat. Cambridge* (1841) App. B. 66 Then a Bedel carrieth all the Graces that passed unto the Proctors. **1709** HEARNE *Collect.* (O.H.S.) II. 294 His grace was denied. **1741** in Fowler *Hist. C.C.C.* (O.H.S.) 280 Every Undergraduate of the Foundation before his Grace is proposed, shall be examined publicly. **1841** G. PEACOCK *Stat. Cambridge* 21 When graces were submitted by the chancellor to the approbation of the senate, the proctors collected the votes and announced the decision. **1882** L. CAMPBELL *Life Maxwell* xii. 348 The Chair of Experimental Physics in the University of Cambridge was founded by a Grace of the Senate on 9th. Feb. 1871. **1887** *Cambridge Univ. Calendar* 2 Except supplicats for degrees, no Grace can be offered to the Senate without three days previous notice. **1898** *Oxford Univ. Calendar* 73 [Conditions required for degrees] The Grace or consent of the Candidate's College or Hall.. and of Congregation, which depend upon his conduct and character.

transf. **1600** HOLLAND *Livy* XXII. x. (1609) 437 In this forme of wordes was the bill propounded unto the people. Pleaseth it you, that this grace may passe and the thing done with your assent in this wise?

†**10.** The share of favour allotted to one by Providence or fortune; one's appointed fate, destiny, or lot; hap, luck, or fortune (good or bad). ***hard grace***, ***evil grace***, ***a sorry grace***: (a stroke of) ill luck (cf. sense 6 f). *Obs.*

1297 R. GLOUC. (Rolls) 7492 Ȝut was willames grace þulke day so god þat he nadde no wounde. **13..** *Coer de L.* 2 Lord Jesus.. Suche grace and vyctorye Thou sente to Kyng Rychard. *c* **1320** *Seuyn Sages* (W.) 658 For that schild, that naked was, Mani bade th'emperice evel gras! *c* **1330** R. BRUNNE *Chron.* (1810) 181 Richard oste forth ran, & grace bifor him ford, Auht jornes he wan with in þe Sarazins lond. Philip þat þer lay to spede had he no grace. **13..** *Gaw. & Gr. Knt.* 2480 Wylde wayez in þe worlde Wowen now ridez, On Gryngolet, þat þe grace hade geten of his lyue. *c* **1374** CHAUCER *Troylus* I. 713 Nomore harde grace May sitte on me, for-whi þer is no space. *c* **1380** *Sir Ferumb.* 3591 þar hadde þe Saraȝyns yule grace, For of dede men lay fuld þe place, & oþre bygunne to fle. *c* **1384** CHAUCER *H. Fame* III. 700 Eolus.. Go, blow this folk a sory grace. *c* **1386** —— *Can. Yeom. Prol.* 112 Peter! quod he, god yeve it harde grace. *c* **1400** *Ywaine & Gaw.* 687 A faire grace yit fel him swa, Al if it smate his hors in twa, And his spors of aither hele, That himself passed so wele. *c* **1450** LONELICH *Grail* lv. 486 Pellean.. that thorwgh bothe hypes I-Maymed was atte batayllE Of Rome, swich was his gras. ? *c* **1475** *Sqr. lowe Degre* 176 Ye must.. ryde through many a peryllous place, As a venterous man to seke your grace. **1513** MORE *Rich. III* Wks. 35/1 Elizabeth, whose fortune and grace was after to bee Quene. **1535** STEWART *Cron. Scot.* (1858) I. 9 In thair passage [they] mony perrell fand.. Sic wes thair grace ȝit haif tha chapit all. **1561** *Child-Marriages* 80 Further beynge demaundid why she did.. play the hoore: she answeris, 'her grace was no better'. **1591** SHAKS. *Two Gent.* III. i. 146, I.. Doe curse the grace, that with such grace hath blest them.

11. In scriptural and theological language.

a. (Also ***the grace of God*** or ***free grace***). The free and unmerited favour of God as manifested in the salvation of sinners and the bestowing of blessings. ***doctrines of grace***: by Calvinists applied esp. to the doctrines of election, predestination, etc. For *covenant, dispensation, throne of grace*, see the respective words.

a **1225** *Leg. Kath.* 298 He.. of his grace makeð ham pæt ha beon eche. *a* **1300** *Cursor M.* 21627 þe grace o godd es gret and gode. *c* **1300** *Harrow. Hell* 241 Loverd, for thi muchele grace, Graunte us in heovene one place! **1382** WYCLIF *Titus* ii. 11 The grace of God.. hath apperid to alle men, techinge [etc.]. *c* **1450** *St. Cuthbert* (Surtees) 1009 þe grace of god him calde þarto. **1613** PURCHAS *Pilgrimage* (1614) 306 Holding that they are saved by Merit, without Law or Grace. **1675** BAXTER *Cath. Theol.* II. I. 263 Is there anything that more.. destroyeth the honour of free grace. **1781** COWPER *Expostul.* 213 But grace abused brings forth the foulest deeds. **1863** A. RALEIGH *Quiet Resting Pl.* viii. (1865) 145 Grace.. the free and unmerited favor of God. **1875** MANNING *Mission H. Ghost* ii. 35 The word grace signifies the free and gratuitous operation of God.

¶ Used for: The source of grace, God.

1601 SHAKS. *All's Well* I. iii. 226, I will tell truth by grace it self I sweare. *Ibid.* II. i. 163. **1605** —— *Macb.* v. viii. 72 This.. by the Grace of Grace, We will performe.

b. The divine influence which operates in men to regenerate and sanctify, to inspire virtuous impulses, and to impart strength to endure trial and resist temptation. Often spoken of as ***the grace of God, of our Lord, of the Holy Spirit***, or as imparted through the sacraments; also, in Roman Catholic use, as proceeding from the Virgin Mary.

Used with many defining words, usually translations from scholastic Latin. ***prevenient grace***: the grace which produces the repentance and faith without which the ***grace of justification*** cannot be received. ***sufficient grace***: the grace which (merely) renders the soul capable of performing a supernatural act, in contradistinction to ***efficacious grace***, the grace which really effects the end for which it is given. For *means of grace, saving grace*, see MEANS, SAVING *ppl. a.* ***the grace of Orders*** (see quot. 1869).

c **1200** *Vices & Virtues* 23 Ðurh godes grace þu hes hafst forsaken. *c* **1220** *Bestiary* 119 Ðurg grace off ure drigtin. *a* **1225** *St. Marher.* 2 þe grace of þen holi gost. *a* **1240** *Lofsong* in *Cott. Hom.* 207 Ich halsi þe þet ðu bi-seche him .. þurh þe grace of fuluht. *a* **1300** *Leg. Rood* (1871) 32 To salomon heo com.. þoru grace þat our lord hire ȝef. *a* **1340** HAMPOLE *Psalter* xix. 6 Ilkan.. þat is enoynt with þe grace of þe halygast. **1382** WYCLIF *2 Cor.* xiii. 14 The grace of oure Lord Ihesu Crist.. be with ȝou alle. **1500-20** DUNBAR *Poems* xlvii. 85 Is non but grace of God I wiss, That can in ȝewth considdir thiss. **1535** COVERDALE *Acts* xviii. 27 He helped them moch which beleued thorow grace. **1538** BALE *Thre Lawes* 824 When we went to Berye And to our lady of grace. **1591** SHAKS. *1 Hen. VI*, v. iv. 40 Chosen from aboue By inspiration of Celestiall Grace. **1678** BARCLAY *Apol. Quakers* (1841) 284 The way whereby Christ helpeth, assisteth, and worketh with us is by his grace. *a* **1700** DRYDEN *Creator Spirit* 13 Plenteous of grace, descend from high. **1738** WESLEY *Psalms* v. ii, On Thee, O God of Purity, I wait for hallowing Grace. **1841** B'NESS BUNSEN in Hare *Life* II. i. 18 That you may have grace to make the use intended of the present bitter dispensation. **1869** HADDAN *Apost. Succ.* i. (1879) 13 A belief in the *grace of Orders*; i.e. in the necessity, and in the spiritual effectiveness, of a proper formal ordination. **1873** BROWNING *Red Cott. Nt.-Cap* 226 They wanted faith.. The many get their grace and go their way Rejoicing.

c. The same regarded as a permanent force, having its seat in the soul.

c **1325** *Song Passion* 52 in *O.E. Misc.* (1872) 198 Marie ful of grace. **1340** HAMPOLE *Pr. Consc.* 1011 For ilk man sal hafe þar a place To wone ay in ioy, þat here has grace. **1382** WYCLIF *Luke* i. 28 The aungel gon yn to hir seide, Heil, ful of grace. **1634** CANNE *Necess. Separ.* (1849) 135 In cases of this nature, grace is best tried. **1684** BUNYAN *Pilgr.* II. 123 There is no Grace, where there is no fear of God. **1707** NORRIS *Treat. Humility* iii. 158 By grace.. I understand.. the inward operation of God's spirit super-naturally assisting our natural faculties. **1821** WORDSW. *Sonn., Eng. Reformers in Exile*, Blest Is he who can, by help of grace, enthrone The peace of God within his single breast! **1871** MORLEY *Voltaire* (1886) 2 They realised life as a long wrestling with unseen and invincible forces of grace, election and fore-destiny.

personified. **1500-20** DUNBAR *Poems* lxxii. 113 With greiting glaid be than come Grace, With wourdis sweit saying to me. **1784** COWPER *Tiroc.* 30 Umpire in the strife That Grace and Nature have to wage through life.

d. The condition of one who is under such divine influence. More fully ***a state of grace***. Also in ***to fall from grace*** (see FALL *v.* 1 c).

1382 WYCLIF *Gal.* v. 4 Ȝe that ben iustified in the lawe han fallen awey fro grace. **1500-20** DUNBAR *Poems* lxxiii. 13 Bend up thy saill, and win thy port of grace. **1502** *Ord. Crysten Men* (W. de W. 1506) I. vi. 51 These holy persons the whiche.. were deed in the estate of good grace. **1632** LITHGOW *Trav.* I. 7 The flying from evil, is a flying to grace. **1643** [ANGIER] *Lanc. Vall. Achor* 12 Many of them have proved practicall Arminians, practising falling from Grace. **1754** SHERLOCK *Disc.* viii. I. 247 For all the Children of God are in a state of Grace. **1852** ROBERTSON *Lect. Ep. Cor.* xlvi. (1863) 345 A state of grace is the state in which all men are, who have received the message of salvation which declares God's goodwill towards them.

e. An individual virtue or excellence, divine in its origin. Also in phr. ***to have the grace*** (to do something): cf. sense 13 b.

1303 R. BRUNNE *Handl. Synne* 26 Syþyn of þe twelue poyntes of shryfte And of þe twelue gracys of here ȝyfte. *c* **1340** *Cursor M.* 10062 þerfore is she called in places Modir of pite and of graces. **1537** *Inst. Chr. Man* in *Formul. Faith* (1856) 49 Gifts and graces I knowledge and professe that they proceed from this Holy Spirit. *a* **1628** PRESTON *Effectual Faith* (1631) 112 There is no grace that God gives but he hath tryals for it afterward. **1641** HINDE *J. Bruen* xxxiv. 108 They that have the grace to live unto the Lord, shall never [etc.]. **1642** ROGERS *Naaman* Ep. Ded. 1 The Graces of Selfe-deniall and Faith are like those two pillars of Iachin and Boaz. **1844** LINGARD *Anglo-Sax. Ch.* (1858) II. i. 14 The dignity and graces of the priesthood were conferred by prayer. **1852** ROBERTSON *Lect. Ep. Cor.* xxv. (1863) 183 A grace is that which has in it some moral quality. **1875** E. WHITE *Life in Christ* III. xx. (1876) 294 It leads to a general acknowledgement of worldly virtues as Christian graces.

12. ***year of grace***: a year as reckoned from the birth of Christ. *arch.*

[After med.L. *anno gratiæ*, used by chroniclers (e.g. Gervase of Canterbury *a* 1200); cf. *anno salutis*, ANNO DOMINI.]

1297 R. GLOUC. (Rolls) 7838 þo deide he in þe ȝer of grace a þousend.. & four score & seuene. **1303** R. BRUNNE *Handl. Synne* 3 þe yeres of grace fyl þan to be A þousynd and þre hundrede and þre. **1387** TREVISA *Higden* (Rolls) V. 363 The ȝere of grace seven hondred ȝere and fiftene. **1477** EARL RIVERS (Caxton) *Dictes* 1 The yere of grace a thousand, CCCC. lxxiij. **1603** KNOLLES *Hist. Turks* 36 He departed the thirteenth of February in the yeare of Grace 1163. **1897**

Literature 11 Dec. 233/2 At the present year of grace we have had published but ten of these parts.

13. In senses *transf.* or weakened from 11.

†**a.** In things: Beneficent virtue or efficacy. ***grains of grace***: seeds endowed with some wholesome quality. *Obs.*

a **1300** *K. Horn* 571 þe stones beoþ of suche grace.. þat þu ne schalt in none place Of none duntes beon ofdrad. ? *a* **1366** CHAUCER *Rom. Rose* 1099 Yit the stoon hadde suche a grace, That he was siker in every place. *c* **1450** HOLLAND *Howlat* iii, Granes of grace, Mendis and medicyne for mennis all neidis. **1592** SHAKS. *Rom. & Jul.* II. iii. 15 O mickle is the powerfull grace that lies In Plants. **1604** E. G[RIMSTONE] tr. *D'Acosta's Hist. Indies* I. iii. 13 The workes of God haue (I know not what) secret and hidden grace and vertve.

b. In persons: Virtue; an individual virtue; sense of duty or propriety; esp. in phrase ***to have the grace*** (to do something): cf. sense 11 e.

1530 *Compend. Treat.* (1863) 56 They have no grace one to beware of another. **1591** SHAKS. *Two Gent.* v. iv. 165, I think the Boy hath grace in him, he blushes. **1600** —— *A. Y. L.* III. iv. 2 Haue the grace to consider, that teares do not become a man. **1605** —— *Macb.* IV. iii. 91 The King-becoming Graces, As Iustice, Verity [etc.]. **1652–62** HEYLIN *Cosmogr.* III. (1673) 60/2 For matters of Religion the People of this Land were priviledged above all others, had they had the grace to make good use of it. **1667** PEPYS *Diary* 30 Dec., Captain Cocke.. would have borrowed money of me; but I had the grace to deny him. **1706** STANHOPE *Paraphr.* III. 444 Only One poor Samaritane of the whole Number had the Grace to come back. *c* **1780** PARR in E. H. Barker *Parriana* (1829) II. 101 Markham shewed some grace in his neutrality. **1781** COWPER *Expostul.* 79 They had the grace in scenes of peace to show The virtue they had learned in scenes of woe. **1816** SCOTT *Antiq.* vi, He blushes again, which is a sign of grace. **1851** LONGF. *Gold. Leg.* III. *Square in front Cathedral* 78 In the church.. will be represented a Miracle-Play; and I hope you will all have the grace to attend. **1892** STEVENSON *Across the Plains* 14, I put my patronage away for another occasion, and had the grace to be pleased with that result.

14. a. Favour shown by granting a delay in the performance of an action, or the discharge of an obligation, or immunity from penalty during a specified period; as in ***a day's***, ***fortnight's***, ***moment's***, etc. ***grace***. ***year of grace*** (at the Universities: see quot. 1726). ***time of grace***, a close time (for beasts of the chase). ***day of grace*** (Theol.), the period allowed for repentance.

1711 HEARNE *Collect.* (O.H.S.) III. 126 Mr. Greenwood had a year's Grace. **1726** AMHERST *Terræ Fil.* xl. 212 When a college-living falls, the person chosen to succeed.. is allow'd a year of grace (as it is call'd), at the end of which he must resign either his living or his fellowship, as he thinks best. **1801** STRUTT *Sports & Past.* I. i. 17 The time of grace begins at Midsummer, and lasteth to Holyrood-day. **1855** MACAULAY *Hist. Eng.* xxii. IV. 775 A fortnight's grace was allowed. **1859** TENNYSON *Elaine* 681 But he pursued her, calling, 'Stay a little! One golden moment's grace!' **1878** J. P. HOPPS *Jesus* x. 38 Your long day of grace is gone. **1895** MARIE CORELLI *Sorrows Satan* v. (1897) 53, I give you a day's grace to decide.

b. Comm. ***days of grace***, the period (in England 3 days) allowed by law for the payment of a bill of exchange, after the expiration of the term for which it is drawn. Similarly, the period allowed for the payment of a premium of insurance or the like, after the date at which it is said to be due.

In present practice, the date at which a bill is said to be due is the last of the 'days of grace'. Thus a bill payable '60 days after sight' is due (in England) on the 63rd day after acceptance, and if it is discounted the discount is calculated to that day.

a **1731** DE FOE *Eng. Tradesman* (1732) I. xxv. 360. **1767** BLACKSTONE *Comm.* II. 469. **1780** T. JEFFERSON *Corr.* Wks. 1859 I. 261, I suppose, that your drafts in favor of the quarter-master, if attended with sixty days' grace, may be complied with to a certain amount. **1809** R. LANGFORD *Introd. Trade* 12 They have the.. allowance of three days grace for payment. **1848** WHARTON *Law Lex.*, *Grace* , days of... It was originally a gratuitous favour.. but custom has rendered it a legal right. **1849** FREESE *Comm. Class-bk.* 27 'Days of grace:'.. in Brazil when the word *preciso* is not added.. 15 days are allowed on inland bills, and 6 days on foreign bills. **1866** CRUMP *Banking* v. 103 The 'grace' allowed upon bills varies considerably in different countries.

15. a. Mercy, clemency; hence, pardon or forgiveness. Now *rare* or *arch.*

1297 R. GLOUC. (Rolls) 11818 Wiþoute eni grace he suspendede echone [of the bishops]. *c* **1375** *Lay Folks Mass Bk.* (MS. B) 81 Gyue me grace & forguenes of my mys-dede. *c* **1386** CHAUCER *Doctor's T.* 236 Goode fader shal I dye? Is ther no grace? is ther no remedye? **1411** *Rolls of Parlt.* III. 650/2 Wherof I beseke yow of grace and mercy. **1462** J. RUSSE in *Paston Lett.* No. 460 II. 113 The Lord Summyrset had wretyn to hym to come to grace. **1559** *Mirr. Mag., Dk. Suffolk* xxv, There was no grace, but I must loose my head. **1570** *Satir. Poems Reform.* xiii. 216 Syne hangit him but grace vpon the Gallous. **1613** HEYWOOD *Silver Age* I. i. Wks. 1874 III. 86 [Thou] Stand'st at our grace, a captiue. **1652** H. COGAN tr. *Scudery's Ibrahim* III. i. 34 Soliman.. swore he would punish him.. though my Master employed all his power to obtain his grace.. Seresbeg's Wife and Children.. humbly besought him to grant them the grace of her Husband and their Father. **1667** MILTON *P.L.* I. 111 To bow and sue for grace With suppliant knee. **1718** HICKES & NELSON *J. Kettlewell* II. xxxviii. 145 That they might not Reject the King's Grace.. freely offered. **1842** MACAULAY *Lays Anc. Rome, Horatius* lvii, 'Now yield thee', cried Lars Porsena, 'Now yield thee to our grace'. **1867** FREEMAN *Norm. Conq.* (1876) I. App. 749 Ulf, finding himself forsaken of all men, asks for grace.

Proverb. **1546** J. HEYWOOD *Prov.* (1867) 8 In space comth grace. *a* **1553** UDALL *Royster D.* III. iii. (Arb.) 47.

b. ***act of grace***: a formal pardon, *spec.* a free and general pardon, granted by Act of Parliament.

(The phrase also occurs under sense 6.)

1648 *Eikon Bas.* ix. 53 Is this the reward and thanks I am to receive for those manie Acts of Grace I have lately passed? **1655** FULLER *Ch. Hist.* IX. vi. §12 Seventy priests.. were, by one act of Grace, pardoned, and sent over beyond sea. **1729** G. JACOB *Law Dict.* s.v., Acts of Grace. **1827** HALLAM *Const. Hist.* (1876) III. xv. 114 In the next [parliament] William took the matter into his own hands by sending down an act of grace. **1839** THIRLWALL *Greece* VI. xlix. 185 He also celebrated his victory by an act of grace.

16. a. In ***his***, ***her***, ***your***, ***my lord's***, ***the king's***, etc. ***(good) grace***, serving as a complimentary periphrasis for *he*, *she*, *you*, etc. *Obs.* exc. *arch.*

c **1430** *Syr Gener.* (Roxb.) 1870 To his lord he went a pase, And broght him tithinges from hir goode grace. **1481** CAXTON *Reynard* (Arb.) 117 And yf your good grace will ony thyng late me haue knowleche of it. **1529** ALWARD *Let. to Cromwell* in Cavendish *Life Wolsey* (1827) 487 My lords grace went again into the kyngs highnes beyng then in his pryvie chamber. **1541** BARNES *Wks.* (1573) 316/1 No man maibee admitted into his seruice excepte that hee first sweare to bee an enemy vnto the kyngs grace of England. **1559** ABP. HETHE in Strype *Ann. Ref.* I. App. vi. (1824) 405 The lord Cardinall Poles good grace. **1591** SHAKS. *1 Hen. VI*, v. iii. 33 A goodly prize, fit for the diuels grace. **1605** in *Crt. & Times Jas. I* (1848) I. 39 The rebels came but two hours too late to have seized upon the person of my Lady Elizabeth's grace. **1830** GEN. P. THOMPSON *Exerc.* (1842) I. 317 If the King wants a yacht, or Her Majesty's Grace would like a few acres of real lace.

b. A courtesy-title now only given to a duke, a duchess, or an archbishop. Formerly used in addressing a king or queen. (Cf. G. *Euer Gnaden.*)

Now usually written with capital.

1500–20 DUNBAR *Poems* lix. 14 Ȝour Grace beseik I of remeid. **1549** LATIMER *6th Serm. bef. Edw. VI* (Arb.) 158 (*heading*), Sermon.. whych he preached before the kynges Maiesty wyth in hys Graces Palaice at Westminster. **1596** SHAKS. *1 Hen. IV*, I. ii. 19 God saue thy Grace, Maiesty I should say. **1602** —— *Ham.* III. iv. 3 Tell him.. your Grace hath scree'nd, and stoode betweene Much heate, and him. **1605** CAMDEN *Rem.* Surnames 138 As for Grace, it beganne about the time of Henry the fourth. Excellent Grace vnder Henry the sixt. **1630** WADSWORTH *Pilgr.* vii. 75 Intelligence was giuen to the Archbishops Grace of Canterbury. **1639** EARL TRAQUAIR in *Hamilton Papers* (Camden) 97 To the Marquis of Hamilton. Pleas your Grace. **1687** DRYDEN *Ep. to Sir G. Etherege* 75 His Grace of Bucks has made a farce. **1711** SWIFT *Jrnl. Stella* 28 Dec., We have given his grace some hopes to be one of our Society. **1780** COWPER *Progr. Err.* 105 Will Avarice.. give place, Charmed by the sounds —'Your reverence' or 'Your grace'? **1824** BYRON *Juan* XVI. xxxiv, *Her* Grace replied, *his* Grace was rather pain'd [etc.]. **1844** DISRAELI *Coningsby* I. i, Let me present to your Grace —Mr. Coningsby. **1872** EARL PEMBROKE & G. H. KINGSLEY *S. Sea Bubbles* viii. 221 The daintiest Alderney in her grace's fancy dairy.

17. Hence †**a.** The high position or dignity of an archbishop, etc. (*obs.*). **b.** in the nonce-verb, ***to 'Your grace'*** (a person).

1631 WEEVER *Anc. Funeral Mon.* 224 A Doctor of the Canon Law, who by degrees came to this Metropolitan Grace of Canterbury. *Ibid.* 309 To forsake his pontificall Grace and Dignitie. **1862** TENNYSON *Let. to Dk. of Argyll* Feb., If you call me Mr Tennyson any longer, I think that I must Your-grace you till the end of the chapter.

†**18. a.** In the names of some plants: (*a*) ***grace of God*** (= L. *Gratia Dei*), species of *Hypericum*, esp. *H. perforatum*; (*b*) *Geranium pratense*; (*c*) *Gratiola officinalis*; (*d*) (see quot. 1607); (*e*) ***herb (of) grace*** (see HERB-GRACE). *Obs.*

1597 GERARDE *Herbal* II. clxviii. 467 Hedge Hyssope is called in Latin.. *Gratia Dei*, or the Grace of God. *Ibid.* Table Eng. Names, Grace of God, or S. Johns Grasse. **1607** TOPSELL *Four-f. Beasts* 126 *Elapho[bo]scum*: (that is, as some call it Harts eye, others Hart-thorne, or grace of God, others wilde Ditany).

†**b.** ***grace of God*** (tr. med.L. *gratia Dei*): a composition used as a plaster. *Obs.*

c **1450** *ME. Med. Bk.* (Heinrich) 189–190.

III. †**19.** *pl.* Thanks, thanksgiving. Also ***to do, give, make, render, yield graces***. Cf. F. *rendre grâces*, L. *gratias agere*. *Obs.*

1382 WYCLIF *1 Cor.* x. 30 Therfore if I take part with grace, what am I blasfemyd, for that I do graces or thankyngis? *c* **1386** CHAUCER *Melib.* ¶838 Yeldynge graces and thankynges to hir lord Melibee. *a* **1400–50** *Alexander* 5394 Makis he gracis to his goddis. **1480** CAXTON *Ovid's Met.* x. vi, Venus, ryght puissante lady, I adoure, thanke, and rendre graces. **1483** —— *Gold. Leg.* 438 b/2 He toke breed & yeldyng graces to god the fader brosyd and gaue it to his dyscyples. *a* **1533** LD. BERNERS *Gold. Bk. M. Aurel.* (1546) sig. I, I.. gyue great graces to my goddes of my good happe.

20. (Till the 16th c. almost exclusively *pl.* in sing. sense; now only *sing.*) A short prayer either asking a blessing before, or rendering thanks after, a meal. Frequent in phrase ***to say grace(s.***

a **1225** *Ancr. R.* 44 Ower graces.. biuore mete & efter.. & mid te miserere goð biuoren ower weouede & endeð ðer þe graces. *c* **1330** R. BRUNNE *Chron. Wace* (Rolls) 16086 Þe borde was leyd, þe cloþ[es] spred, þe graces seyd. [*c* **1340** *Cursor M.* 13496 (Trin.) Ihesus blessed þis breed wiþ grace.] **1377** LANGL. *P. Pl.* B. XIV. 62 As holywrit witnesseth whan men segge her graces, *Aperis tu manum tuam* [etc.]. *c* **1440** *Ipomydon* 313 Whan they had ete and grace sayd. *c* **1500** *Melusine* xxxvi. 241 After they had dyned, graces were said. **1526** TINDALE *Matt.* xxvi. 30 When they had sayd grace they went out. **1588** J. UDALL *Diotrephes* (Arb.) 6 He would needs saye grace (forsooth) before and after supper. *a* **1639** SUCKLING *Poems* (1646) 19 Long graces do But keep good stomachs off that would fall too. **1680** DRYDEN *Prol. to Cæsar Borgia* 42 But mark their feasts.. The Pope says grace, but 'tis the Devil gives thanks. **1705** HICKERINGILL *Priest-cr.* II. vi. 62 Until Mr. Say-Grace has blest the Cup, and said a short Grace. **1760–72** H. BROOKE *Fool of Quality* (1808) I. 68 The latter grace was said, and the cloth taken away. **1791** *Heroic Ep. to Priestley* in *Poet. Reg.* (1808) 395 With simile and face, Each longer than a Presbyterian grace. **1856** EMERSON *Eng. Traits, Univ.* Wks. (Bohn) II. 89 A youth came forward.. and pronounced the ancient form of grace before meals. **1881** BESANT & RICE *Chapl. of Fleet* I. viii, The dinner was at times scanty,.. a grace before the meat, and a grace after.

IV. 21. *attrib.* and *Comb.*, as ***grace-covenant***, ***-giver***, †***-market***, ***-token***; ***grace-doing*** vbl. sb.; †***grace-empaled***, ***-followed***, ***-giving***, ***-like***, ***originating***, ***-restoring***, ***-thirsty***, ***-working*** adjs.

1892 WESTCOTT *Gospel of Life* 260 The *grace-covenant with Abraham. **1382** WYCLIF *Isa.* li. 3 Ioȝe and gladnesse shal be founde in it, *gracedoing and vois of preising. **1615** T. ADAMS *Bl. Devil* 75 To restraine his savage fury from forraging his *Grace-empaled Church. **1598** SYLVESTER *Du Bartas* II. ii. II. *Babylon* 589 Amos' son.. *Grace-followed, grave, holy, and eloquent. **1588** A. KING tr. *Canisius' Catech.* 153 Christ is our propiciatour and *grace-geuar. **1887** H. O. WAKEMAN *Ch. & Puritans* 121 All the *grace-giving powers of the Church. **1636** B. JONSON *Discov.*, *Consuetudo*, etc. Wks. (1641) 119/1 They have the Authority of yeares, and out of their intermission doe win to themselves a kind of *grace-like newnesse. **1820** W. TOOKE tr. *Lucian* I. 71 Homer bestows on your locks the epithet of grace-like. **1645** RUTHERFORD *Tryal & Tri. Faith* (1845) 93 No purse is Christ's *grace-market. **1851** W. ANDERSON *Exposure Popery* (1878) 126 The words Ego te absolvo penetrate to the Soul with *grace-restoring power, just as the water of baptism 'reached' it with *grace-originating power. *a* **1633** T. PIERSON *Expos.* 84 *Ps.* (1647) 49 *Grace-thirsty soules. **1842** MANNING *Waiting Invis. Ch.* Serm. 1848 I. 340 The *grace-tokens of the Cross. **1849** ROCK *Ch. of Fathers* II. 283 The brightsomeness of the Gospel was dimmed in becoming shorn of many of its *grace-working ordinances.

b. Special comb., as **grace-drink** *Sc.*, 'the drink taken by a company after the giving of thanks at the end of a meal' (Jam.); **grace-hoop**, 'a hoop used in playing the game called *graces*' (Worcester 1860); **grace-note** = sense 3; also *transf.*; †**grace-stroke** (after F. *coup de grâce*: see COUP *sb.*[3] 5 e), in quots. used for (*a*) a finishing touch, (*b*) an elegant touch or feature; †**grace-term** (*Oxford University*), a term of the period required for a degree, in which residence was customarily dispensed with; †**grace-wife**, a midwife.

1725 RAMSAY *Gentle Sheph.* I. i, When we hae tane the *grace-drink at the well. **1788** BURNS *Let. to Clarinda* 18 Feb., I am just going to propose your health by way of grace-drink. **1823** CRABB *Technol. Dict.*, **Grace Note* (*Mus.*), any note added to a composition as a decoration or improvement. **1864** ENGEL *Mus. Anc. Nat.* 361 These passages.. are considered only as grace-notes introduced according to the fancy of the singer. **1896** STEVENSON *Kidnapped* xxv, Variations which, as he went on, he decorated with a perfect flight of grace-notes, such as pipers love, and call the 'warblers'. **1927** *Blackw. Mag.* Dec. 827/1 A lady was holding forth, a born narrator, recklessly lavish of grace-notes and embroidery. **1957** J. BRAINE *Room at Top* xx. 177 The extra refinement, the grace-note, was Jack's waving away of my offer to buy the drinks. **1960** *Guardian* 30 Sept. 12/5 Its architecture, for all its English grace-notes, is fundamentally international. **1701** *Scot. Characterized* in *Harl. Misc.* (1811) VII. 377 Your intentions led you to our neighbouring kingdom of Scotland, to perfect and give the *grace-stroke to that very liberal education you have so signally improved in England. **1686** F. SPENCE tr. *Varillas' Ho. Medicis* 262 A piece wherein the character and grace-stroaks the Greek poetry possess'd.. were restored in the highest point of their perfection. **1853** 'C. BEDE' *Verdant Green* II. x, He and Mr. Bouncer had together gone up to Oxford, leaving Charles Larkyns behind to keep a *grace-term. **1465** *Reg. St. Nicholas' Ch.* in Brand *Hist. Newcastle* (1789) II. 362 *note*, [A midwife is styled] '*grace-wyfe.' **1672** in *12th Rep. Hist. MSS. Comm.* App. VII. (1890) 382 Given to the grace-wife and nurse 15s. **1829** BROCKETT *N.C. Words* (ed. 2), *Grace-wife*, an old provincial name for a midwife; still retained by the vulgar.

grace (greɪs), *v.* [In sense 1, a. OF. *gracier* to thank, also, as in mod.F., to pardon (a criminal), f. *grace* GRACE *sb.*; in the other senses f. prec.]

†**1.** *trans.* To thank. Only in *pass. subj.*

a **1225** *Ancr. R.* 366 Igraced beo his milce! **13..** *Coer de L.* 3772 Graced be Jesu Cryst our Lord. **1377** LANGL. *P. Pl.* B. VI. 126 Lord, y-graced be ȝe!

†**2. a.** To show favour or be gracious to; also, to countenance. *Obs.*

c **1440** *Sir Gowther* 65 She praid to Crist and Marie mylde, Shulde hire grace to have a Childe. **1590** SPENSER *F.Q.* I. x. 64 Then shall I soone.. so God me grace, Abett that virgins cause disconsolate. **1596** *Ibid.* VI. xii. 16 To tell her how the heavens had her graste To save her chylde. **1604** MARSTON *Malcontent* II. v. D 3 And therevpon you graced him?.. Tooke him to fauour? **1626** L. OWEN *Spec. Jesuit.* (1629) 33 The Pope would not grace the Iesuites Author, or founder, vntill they had first greased him in the fist.

†**b.** To favour with permission *to* do something.

1639 FULLER *Holy War* III. i. (1647) 109 He was graced to wear his shoes of the Imperiall fashion.

3. To endow with (heavenly) grace.

1634 BP. HALL *Wks.* II. 50 Hee that can (when hee will) convince the obstinate, will not Grace the disobedient. **1637** RUTHERFORD *Lett.* (1862) I. 289 The honourable cause which ye are graced to profess is Christ's own truth. **1701** BEVERLEY *Glory of Grace* 4 He hath Graced, or invested with

Grace. 1961 F. J. Ripley *Last Gospel* xii. 114 God may have graced them more than he has graced us.

4. a. To lend or add grace to, to adorn, embellish, set off; to adorn *with* some becoming quality.

a 1586 Sidney *Arcadia* i. (1633) 39 He left nothing unassayed, which might disgrace himselfe, to grace his friend. 1588 Shaks. *L.L.L.* v. ii. 74. 1606 J. Carpenter *Solomon's Solace* i. 3 They were graced with an excellent memory. 1609 Douland *Ornith. Microl.* 184 Most commonly it [the high Tenor] graceth the Base, making a double Concord with it. 1658 Cokaine *Trappolin* ii. ii. Dram. Wks. (1874) 141 One grac'd with all the virtues. 1693 Dryden *Ovid's Met.* i. 759 Thou shalt returning Cæsar's triumph grace. 1712 Arbuthnot *John Bull* iii. iii, He.. mounted upon the bottom of a Tub, the inside of which he had often graced in his prosperous days. 1767 Sir W. Jones *Seven Fountains* Poems (1777) 46 A table with a thousand vases grac'd. 1828 D'Israeli *Chas. I*, I. vi. 204 This chivalric Earl..was just the hero to grace a desperate cause. 1857 Livingstone *Trav.* ii. 43 The eland..would grace the parks of our nobility more than deer. 1877 Dowden *Shaks. Prim.* vi. 73 A Midsummer Night's Dream was written to grace the wedding of some noble person.

b. *Mus.* To add grace-notes, cadenzas, etc., to.

1659, 1780, 1836 [cf. gracing *vbl. sb.*^{1}] 1824 Scott *Redgauntlet* let. x, Then taking the old tune of Galashiels for his theme, he graced it with a number of wild, complicated, and beautiful variations. 1876 Stainer & Barrett *Dict. Mus. Terms* s.v., Music for viols was also *graced* in various ways. 1882 in Ogilvie; and in later Dicts.

†**c.** *to grace out*: to make to appear favourably. *Obs.*

1606 Day *Ile of Guls* Prol. A 2 Hath he not a prepard company of gallants, to aplaud his iests, and grace out his play? 1622 Rowlands *Good Newes & Bad* 33 A Sutor, that a wealthy widow pli'd, To grace out his bad fortunes did prouide Vpon his credit, for an outward show, That gallantly he might a wooing goe.

5. a. To confer honour or dignity upon; to honour *with* a title or dignity. Also, to do honour or credit to.

1585 T. Rogers *39 Art.* Pref. (1607) 22 The doctrine in this land allowed, and publicly graced and embraced of all sorts. 1588 Shaks. *L.L.L.* i. i. 3 Let Fame..then grace vs in the disgrace of death. 1591 —— *Two Gent.* i. iii. 58 How happily he liues, how well-belou'd, And daily grac'd by the Emperor. *c* 1592 Marlowe *Jew of Malta* Prol., Grace him as he deserves, And let him not be entertain'd the worse Because he favours me. 1594 Plat *Jewell-ho.* iii. 17 Such as shall commend and grace the wormwood beyond the hoppe. 1601 R. Johnson *Kingd. & Commw.* (1603) 171 Leaving his son..whome the king graced with his fathers regency. 1605 Shaks. *Macb.* iii. iv. 45 Pleas't your Highnesse To grace vs with your Royall Company? *a* 1626 Bacon *Max. & Uses Com. Law* Pref. (1636) 1 Thereby not onely gracing it in reputation and dignity, but also [etc.]. 1631 Massinger *Believe as you List* v. ii, Hee was My creature! and in my prosperitie, prowde To holde dependance of mee, though I grac'd hym With the title of a freinde. 1701 W. Wotton *Hist. Rome* 341 He was immediately graced with the Title of Princeps. 1810 Scott *Lady of L.* i. xxiii, He bade that all should ready be, To grace a guest of fair degree. 1859 Tennyson *Elaine* 223 So ye will grace me..with your fellowship O'er these waste downs.

†**b.** With complement: To name or designate honourably. *Obs.*

1667 Milton *P.L.* xi. 169, I [Eve] who first brought death on all, am graced The source of life.

†**6.** To give pleasure to, to gratify, delight. *Obs.*

a 1586 Sidney *Arcadia* i. (1633) 1 This place, where we last..did grace our eyes upon her ever-flourishing beauty. 1594 Shaks. *Rich. III*, iv. iv. 74 What comfortable houre canst thou name, That euer grac'd me with thy company. 1670 Dryden *Conq. Granada* i. i. (1701) 385 When fierce Bulls run loose upon the place And our bold Moors their Loves with danger grace. 1703 Rowe *Fair Penit.* i. i. 304 At sight of this black Scrowl, the gentle Altamont..Shall droop ..And never grace the Publick with his Virtues.

†**7.** To say 'grace' over (a meal). *Obs.*

1644 Bulwer *Chirol.* 140 The same gesture we use in gracing our meals.

†**8.** To confer a degree upon (a person) by a 'grace'. *Obs.*

1573 G. Harvey *Letter-bk.* (Camden) 9 Almost al the toun ar gracid yea and admittid too alreddi.

9. To address by the title 'your grace'.

c 1610 Sir J. Melvil *Mem.* (1683) 124 Cringe low, Grace him at every word.

Hence **'gracing** *ppl. a.*

1601 Chester *Love's Mart.* (1878) 142 In that great gracing word shalt thou be counted Louing to him, that is thy sworne louer. *a* 1684 Leighton *Exp. Lect. Rom.* Wks. (1868) 332 The apostle recommends that gracing grace of humility.

grace, obs. form of grass.

'grace-cup.

The cup of liquor passed round after grace is said; the last cup of liquor drunk before retiring, a parting draught. (Cf. *grace-drink*, grace *sb.* 21 b.)

1593 *Rites of Durham* (Surtees) 68 A great mazer, called the Grace-cup. 1647 Trapp *Comm. Mark* xiv. 25 That grace-cup (as they call it) after which they might not eat any thing more till the day following. 1687 Dryden *Hind & P.* ii. 680 A grace-cup to their common Patron's health. *c* 1718 Prior *Ladle* 115 The grace-cup serv'd, the cloth away. 1816 Scott *Old Mort.* iii, Such as..were..obliged to partake of a grace-cup with their captain before their departure. 1828 —— *F.M. Perth* xxviii, A bowl, called the grace-cup, made of oak, hooped with silver. 1886 Willis & Clark *Cambridge* III. 381 As soon as Grace had been said, and the grace-cup had been passed round, the seniors were to retire to their studies.

fig. 1679 Dryden *Troilus & Cr.* Pref., Thus in *Mustapha*, the Play should naturally have ended with the Death of Zanger, and not have given us the grace Cup after Dinner, of Solyman's Divorce from Roxolana. 1786 *Francis the Philanthropist* III. 173 The epilogue, or grace-cup, to wash down the meal..had not yet exceeded the *vos valete & plaudite*.

graced (greɪst), *ppl. a.* [f. grace *sb.* or *v.* + -ed.]

Endowed with grace; favoured; having a grace or graces; embellished, etc. Also *well graced*.

1593 Shaks. *Rich. II* v. ii. 24 After a well grac'd Actor leaues the Stage. 1605 —— *Macbeth* iii. iv. 41 Here had we now our Countries Honor roof'd, Were the grac'd person of our Banquo present. —— *Lear* i. iv. 267 More like a Tauerne, or a Brothell, Then a grac'd Pallace. 1605 Bacon *Adv. Learn.* ii. xviii. §5. 68 Their well graced fourmes of speech. *c* 1630 Naunton *Fragm. Reg.* (Arb.) 52 A maxime of more discretion for the conduct and management of their now graced Lord and Master. 1645 Rutherford *Tryal & Tri. Faith* (1845) 40 All graced persons are privileged persons. 1701 Cibber *Love Makes Man* iv. ii, I'm little practis'd in the Rules of grac'd Behaviour. 1797 Mary Robinson *Walsingham* III. 260 The graced affections growing from the pure and feeling heart. *Ibid.* IV. 38 That graced complacency which seems to experience pleasure in harmonizing the feelings of others. 1832 Standish *Maid of Jaen* 44 All wears devotion's solemn face austere, From the grac'd altar to the black'ned bier. 1880 *Academy* 23 Oct. 300 The best graced of our English actresses.

graceful ('greɪsfʊl), *a.* [f. grace *sb.* + -ful.]

†**1.** Full of divine grace; spiritually profitable; (of persons) holy. *Obs.*

c 1420 *Anturs of Arth.* xx, þes arne þe graceful giftes of þe holy goste. *c* 1430 Lydg. *Ball. Commend. Our Lady* 52 Som drope of graceful dewe to us propyne. *c* 1449 Pecock *Repr.* i. xiii. 66 The seid reeding was to hem so graceful, and so delectable. 1611 Shaks. *Wint. T.* v. i. 171 You haue a holy Father, A gracefull Gentleman.

†**2.** Of persons: Possessed of graces of character, virtuous. *Obs.*

1605 Camden *Rem.* (1637) 171 Their gracefull issue Prince Charles, the Lady Elizabeth. *a* 1715 Burnet *Own Time* (1724) I. 171 A Royal family of three Princes and two Princesses, all young and graceful persons.

†**3.** Favourable, friendly. *Obs.*

1606 Shaks. *Ant. & Cl.* ii. ii. 60, I Your Partner in the cause 'gainst which he fought, Could not with gracefull eyes attend those Warres Which fronted mine owne peace.

†**4.** Conferring grace or honour. *Obs.*

1595 Spenser *Epithal.* 3 Others to adorne, Whom ye thought worthy of your gracefull rymes.

5. Possessed of pleasing or attractive qualities. Now in more restricted sense (cf. grace *sb.* 1): Elegant in form, proportions, movement, expression, or action. Of actions: esp. acts of courtesy, concessions, and the like: Felicitously well-timed or becoming.

a 1586 Sidney *Arcadia* iii. (1590) 248 b, Their countenaunces full of a gracefull grauitie. 1599 Shaks. *Much Ado* iii. iv. 42 But for a fine queint gracefull and excellent fashion, yours [i.e. your gowne] is worth ten on't. 1624 Wotton *Arch.* ii. 108 Of this Plastique Art, the chiefe vse with vs is in the gracefull fretting of roofes. 1647 Clarendon *Hist. Reb.* i. §120 He was..a graceful speaker upon any subject. 1662 J. Davies tr. *Mandelslo's Trav.* 4 The King..was a very handsome graceful person. 1698 Fryer *Acc. E. India & P.* 285 To these he has given.. graceful Houses. 1725 Pope *Odyss.* xviii. 182 He shook the graceful honours of his head. 1742 Richardson *Pamela* IV. 121 She was one of the gracefullest Figures in the Place. 1766 Fordyce *Serm. Yng. Wom.* (1767) II. xiii. 224 In your sex manly exercises are never graceful. 1809 Roland *Fencing* 7 This position is not so graceful as the old one. 1826 Disraeli *Viv. Grey* vi. i, A magnificently cut chandelier, which threw a graceful light upon a sumptuous banquet table. 1849 Macaulay *Hist. Eng.* v. I. 665 She left a paper written, indeed, in no graceful style, yet such as was [etc.]. 1856 Stanley *Sinai & Pal.* iii. (1858) 168 A dome graceful as that of St. Peter's. 1860 Tyndall *Glac.* i. iii. 27 It [a chamois] was a most graceful animal.

quasi-*adv.* 1712–14 Pope *Rape Lock* v. 7 Clarissa graceful waved her fan.

gracefully ('greɪsfʊlɪ), *adv.* [f. graceful *a.* + -ly^2.] In a graceful manner, with grace, becomingly, elegantly.

a 1586 Sidney *Arcadia* ii. (1633) 122 Not Musidorus, no nor any man liuing..could..deliuer that strength more nimbly, or become the deliuery more gracefully. 1605 in *Crt. & Times Jas. I* (1848) I. 42 The bridegroom carried himself as gravely and gracefully as if he were of his father's age. 1607–8 *Ibid.* 73 Being very gracefully attired. 1647 Clarendon *Hist. Reb.* i. §65 He..had the habit of speaking very gracefully and pertinently. 1698 Fryer *Acc. E. India & P.* 66 Panes of Oister-shells for their Windows (which as they are cut in Squares, and polished, look gracefully enough). 1711 Addison *Spect.* No. 102 ¶7 This teaches a Lady to quit her Fan gracefully when she throws it aside. 1746–7 Hervey *Medit.* (1818) 160 See how gracefully it erects its majestic head! 1838 Dickens *Nich. Nick.* xxx, Sticking his other arm gracefully a-kimbo. 1858 Froude *Hist. Eng.* III. xiii. 129 He was taking precautions..to enable him to yield gracefully to necessity should necessity arise. 1860 Tyndall *Glac.* i. ix. 63 The..moraine.. forming at first a gracefully winding curve. 1876 Ouida *Winter City* xi. 334 The most gracefully-worded appeal possible.

gracefulness ('greɪsfʊlnɪs). [f. as prec. + -ness.] The quality or state of being graceful.

†**1.** Possession of graces; excellence of character. *Obs.*

1611 Beaum. & Fl. *King & No K.* ii. i, If you Can find no disposition in yourself To sorrow, yet, by gracefulness in her, Find out the way, and by your reason weep.

†**2.** Graciousness, kindness, disposition to favour.

1640 W. Mountague & Digby in Rushw. *Hist. Coll.* iii. (1692) I. 161 We shall certainly preserve his Gracefulness to us.

3. The quality of being graceful or elegant in form, proportions, movement, action, or expression. Originally in wider sense: Beauty, charm.

a 1586 Sidney *Arcadia* ii. (1633) 106 All her parts were decked with some particular ornament..her eyes with majestie, her countenance with gracefulnesse, her lips with lovelinesse. 1627 Hakewill *Apol.* iii. viii. (1635) 293 Petrarchs Thuscan gracefulnesse. 1647 Clarendon *Hist. Reb.* i. §14 The beauty and gracefulness..of his person. 1657 R. Ligon *Barbadoes* (1673) 13 With far greater Majesty, and gracefulness, than I have seen Queen Anne, descend from the Chair of State, to dance. 1724 Swift *Use Irish Manuf.* Wks. 1755 V. ii. 7 He..could..talk more than six, without either gracefulness, propriety or meaning. 1756 Burke *Subl. & B.* iii. xxxii, Gracefulness is an idea not very different from beauty. 1815 Chalmers *Let.* in *Life* (1851) II. 29 An unsoiled gracefulness and brilliancy of character. 1821 Lamb *Elia* Ser. i. *Grace bef. meat*, These exercises.. have little in them of grace or gracefulness. 1832 Tennyson *Eleanore* 50 The luxuriant symmetry Of thy floating gracefulness.

graceless ('greɪslɪs), *a.* [f. grace *sb.* + -less.]

1. a. Not in a state of grace, unregenerate; hence depraved, wicked, ungodly, impious. ***graceless florin*** (see quot. 1870).

1399 Langl. *Rich. Redeles* i. 25 Graceles gostis gylours of hem-self, That..sawe no manere siȝth saff solas and ese [etc.]. *c* 1440 *Jacob's Well* (E.E.T.S.) 161 þe peple schal be graceles, vnmyȝty in batayle, & vnstedfast in þe feyth of holy cherch. 1534 Sir T. More *Dialogue of Comfort* ii. v. Wks. (1557) 1174/2 Lette no manne sinne in hope of grace..he shall either gracelesse goe linger on carelesse, or with a care fruitlesse, fall into despayre. 1603 Knolles *Hist. Turks* (1621) 256 He was glad..to receive at his hypocriticall hands a graceless blessing for his better speed. *a* 1625 Beaum. & Fl. *Knt. Malta* i. i, White innocent sign, thou dost abhor to..grace these graceless projects of my heart! 1659 D. Pell *Impr. Sea* 96 Hereby you do a great deal more bolster graceless fellows in their wickedness, than you are aware of. 1715 De Foe *Fam. Instruct.* i. iv. (1841) 85 Even our father and mother themselves have been negligent, godless and graceless. 1733 Pope *Ess. Man* iii. 307 For modes of Faith let graceless zealots fight. 1738 Warburton *Serm. 2 Pet.* i. 5–7 (1745) 11 The graceless Furniture of the old Man with his Affections and Lusts. 1818 Scott *Hrt. Midl.* xvi, There's a minister in the Tolbooth—wha will ca' it a graceless place now? 1853 Marsden *Early Purit.* 305 They [pilgrim fathers] saw the graceless intruders wasting their substance in riot. 1870 H. W. Henfrey *Guide to Study Eng. Coins* ii. 137 The usual letters D.G., for Dei Gratia, were omitted... This raised a storm of remonstrance against this coinage [of 1849], which at once received the name of the 'godless' or 'graceless florin'. 1897 [see godless *a.*].

b. Wanting sense of decency or propriety.

1508 Dunbar *Flyting w. Kennedie* 127 The gallowis gaipis eftir thy graceles gruntill. *a* 1586 Sidney *Arcadia* ii. (1633) 108 In sooth (answered Dametas with a gracelesse scorn) the Lad may prove well enough, if [etc.]. 1642 Fuller *Holy & Prof. St.* v. xiv. 412 To mouth an oath with a gracelesse grace. 1714 Addison *Spect.* No. 559 ¶3 The graceless Youth, in less than a quarter of an Hour, pulled the old Gentleman by the Beard. 1753 Eliz. Carter *Lett.* (1808) 325, I am afraid you have thought me rather graceless about the visit to North End. 1795 Macneill *Will & Jean* iii. vi, Villain! wha wi' graceless folly Ruin'd her he ought to save. 1822 W. Irving *Braceb. Hall* xv. 126 Their feathered school has turned out the most untractable and graceless scholars. 1830 D'Israeli *Chas. I*, III. Pref. 6 It would be graceless in me, not to add, that I was honoured by a promise of aid. 1849 Cobden *Speeches* 80, I have heard that some graceless wight once said that [etc.]. 1885 *Manch. Exam.* 10 Apr. 5/2 If graceless insults are levelled at them they are not worthy a reply.

c. *absol.* Of a person or persons. Also in *sing.* only as sb., a graceless person.

c 1386 Chaucer *Can. Yeom. Prol. & T.* 525 O graceles, ful blynd is thy conceite. 1508 Dunbar *Flyting w. Kennedie* 222 Our gallowis gaipis; lo! quhair ane greceles gais. 1591 Shaks. *1 Hen. VI*, v. iv. 14 Gracelesse, wilt thou deny thy Parentage. 1675 Baxter *Cath. Theol.* ii. vi. 124 Do the Armenians hold that the Wills of the graceless and unsanctified are freed from sinful habits? 1858 Carlyle *Fredk. Gt.* vi. vi. (1872) II. 206 Rejoicing to find something of a soldier in the young graceless, after all. 1874 Spurgeon *Treas. Dav.* Ps. xcii. 12 Contrasts the condition of the righteous with that of the graceless.

†**2.** Lacking favour. *Obs.*

c 1374 Chaucer *Troylus* i. 781 How wost þow so þat þow art graceles? *c* 1475 *Rauf Coilȝear* 786 It war ane graceles gude that I war cummin to. 1579 Spenser *Sheph. Cal.* Aug. 113 If for gracelesse griefe I die.

†**3.** Merciless, unfeeling, cruel, pitiless. *Obs.*

1588 *Marprel. Epist.* (Arb.) 29 His honor could not obtaine this small suit at your graceles hands. 1596 Spenser *F.Q.* v. xii. 18 He shund his strokes, where ever they did fall, And way did give unto their gracelesse speed. *a* 1658 *Johnie Armstrong* in *Wit Restord* 32 Asking grace of a graceles face.

4. Wanting grace, charm, or elegance, unlovely.

1638 Junius *Paint. Ancients* 37 The most ill-favoured and gracelesse Pictures most commonly wrought by them that [etc.]. 1823 P. Nicholson *Pract. Build.* 490 Crowns, coronets, mitres, and similar graceless objects. *a* 1850 Rossetti *Dante & Circ.* i. (1874) 134 Lady she seems of such high benison As makes all others graceless in men's sight. 1884 *St. James's Gaz.* 26 Jan. 6/1 The composition is graceless, the colour sombre, and the handling broad.

†**5.** (See quot.) *Obs.*$^{-0}$

1727 BOYER *Fr. Dict.* II, Graceless (that has not said Grace) *qui n'a point rendu graces.*

Hence **ˈgracelessly** *adv.*

c **1440** *Jacob's Well* (E.E.T.S.) 126 þanne þei deyin gracelesly. **1581** SIDNEY *Apol. Poetrie* (Arb.) 71 The French ..hath not one word, that hath his accent in the ..*Antepenultima*, and little more hath the Spanish: and therefore, very gracelesly may they vse *Dactiles.* **1608** T. MORTON *Preamb. Encounter* 115 Which must haue beene either giddily rash, or gracelesly false. **1659** D. PELL *Impr. Sea* 227 *note*, Thy life lyes at the stake to answer his whom thou gracelesly goes about to take away. **1846** H. TORRENS *Remarks Mil. Lit. & Hist.* I. 96 The horses, bridleless, moving gracelessly with the neck stiff and the head stretched out. **1894** H. NISBET *Bush Girl's Rom.* 238 He had taken favours all his life, gracelessly and as his due.

gracelessness (ˈgreɪslɪsnɪs). [See -NESS.] The quality or condition of being graceless.

1588 *Marprel. Epist.* (Arb.) 5 What hath beene written against the gracelesnes of your Archbishoprick. **1598** FLORIO, *Sgratia*, a disgrace, a gracelesnes or vnhandsomnes. **1614** T. ADAMS *Devil's Banq.* 22 Wee finde Grace compared to Fire, and gracelessnesse to water. **1653** BAXTER *Meth. Peace Consc.* 366 To be Tempted is no sign of Gracelessness. **1816** *Edin. Rev.* XXVI. 313 The gay swordsmen..carry off their gracelessness as a matter of course. **1881** SWINBURNE *Mary Stuart* II. iii, To crave grace of her for his gracelessness.

†**ˈgracely**, *a. Obs. rare*⁻¹. [f. GRACE *sb.* + -LY¹.] = GRACEFUL.

1648 MARKHAM *Cheap Husb.* (ed. 7) 21 That maketh him [the horse]..to straiten his rings with gracely [**1623** (ed. 3) a gracefull] comelinesse.

gracer (ˈgreɪsə(r)). [f. GRACE *v.* + -ER¹.] One who graces or gives grace to.

1592 GREENE *Groat's w. Wit* (1617) F 2 Thou famous gracer of Tragedians. *c* **1611** CHAPMAN *Iliad* Ep. Ded., Through all the pomp of kingdoms still he shines, And graceth all his gracers. **1635** D. DICKSON *Pract. Writ.* (1845) I. 165 The Saviour of the world..the gracer of the unworthy.

ˈgraceship. ? *nonce-wd.* [f. GRACE *sb.* (sense 16 b) + -SHIP.] Used as a title for a duke.

1822 *Blackw. Mag.* XII. 696 His graceship of Brandon has but little to stand on.

†**ˈgracify**, *v. Obs. rare.* [f. GRACE *v.* + -(I)FY.] *trans.* To impart grace to, to beautify.

1575 LANEHAM *Let.* (1871) 8 Grapes in Clusters, whyte and red, gracified with their Vine leauez. *Ibid.* 50 Much gracified by du proporcion of four eeuen quarterz.

gracile (ˈgræsɪl), *a.* Also 7 gracill. [ad. L. *gracil-is* slender.] Slender, thin, lean.

1623 COCKERAM II, Leane, *gracill.* **1657** TOMLINSON *Renou's Disp.* 465 It's tail like that of other Serpents, grows more gracile by degrees. **1721–92** in BAILEY. **1818** J. BROWN *Psyche* 30 Words daily grow more short and gracile. **1824** LANDOR *Wks.* (1846) I. 246/1 Unswathe his Egyptian mummy; and..you disclose the grave features and gracile bones of a..cat. **1832–4** DE QUINCEY *Cæsars* Wks. 1862 IX. 47 In person he was tall, fair, gracile.

¶ By some recent writers misused (through association with *grace*) for: Gracefully slender.

1871 ROSSETTI *Poems, Love's Nocturn* xi, Where in groves the gracile Spring Trembles. **1888** *Harper's Mag.* Apr. 733/2 Girls..beautiful with the beauty of ruddy bronze,—gracile as the palmettoes that sway above them.

Hence **ˈgracileness.**

1727 in BAILEY vol. II.

†**ˈgracilent**, *a. Obs.*⁻⁰ [ad. L. *gracilent-us*, irregularly f. *gracilis* GRACILE.] Slender, thin.

1727 in BAILEY vol. II.

gracilescent (græsɪˈlɛsənt), *a.* [ad. L. *gracilescent-em*, pr. pple. of *gracilescĕre* to become slender, f. *gracilis* GRACILE.] Becoming slender, narrowing.

1856–8 W. CLARK *Van der Hoeven's Zool.* II. 301 Tail short, broad at the base, suddenly gracilescent.

†**gracilious**, *a. Obs. rare.* [f. L. *gracil-is* GRACILE + -IOUS.] = GRACILE *a.*

1688 R. HOLME *Armoury* II. 374/1 Gracilious Fish..are.. slender, small, thin, soft and weak.

gracilis (ˈgræsɪlɪs). *Anat.* [L., = slender.] Also ***musculus (adductor) gracilis***: a superficial muscle on the medial side of the thigh, passing from the hip-bone to the tibia, and acting as an adductor of the hips and a flexor and medial rotator of the leg.

1615 H. CROOKE *Descr. Body Man* xxxvii. 804 The second muscle of the Legge which is also called *Gracilis* or the slender muscle. **1685** S. COLLINS *Syst. Anat.* I. xviii. 111 The *Gracilis*..is inserted with a round Tendon into the inside of the *Os Tibiæ.* **1727** CHAMBERS *Cycl.* I. 176/1 *Gracilis*, in anatomy, a muscle of the leg, thus called from its slender shape. **1858** H. GRAY *Anat.* 281 The *Gracilis* is the most superficial muscle on the inner side of the thigh. **1964** *Cunningham's Textbk. Anat.* (ed. 10) 353/1 The gracilis arises by a tendon, short, thin, and wide, from the lower half of the edge of the pubic symphysis.

gracility (grəˈsɪlɪtɪ). [ad. L. *gracilitāt-em*, f. *gracilis* slender: see GRACILE and -ITY.] **1.** The state or character of being gracile; slenderness, leanness.

1623 COCKERAM, *Gracilitie*, leannesse. **1661** LOVELL *Hist. Anim. & Min.* 431 Gracility of the part. **1707** FLOYER *Physic. Pulse-Watch* 53 By the dryness we describe the gracility or hardness; and by the humidity the plumpness or obesity of the habit of the Body. **1833** SIR W. HAMILTON *Discuss.* (1853) 126 It [a book] was accordingly subjected to a process of extenuation, out of which it emerged, reduced to a little more than a third of its original gracility. **1855** MILMAN *Lat. Chr.* XIV. ix. (1864) IX. 313 As the niches became..narrower the saints..shrunk to meagre gracility.

2. *fig.* Of literary style: unornamented simplicity.

1900 T. W. WRATISLAW *A. C. Swinburne* 146 The dexterous verses *To a Cat* are in a lighter tune than usual, recalling the gracility of Hugo. **1906** *Academy* 1 Sept. 201/2 Their spontaneity, their *gracility*, to borrow a word from the Latin, is perfect.

gracing (ˈgreɪsɪŋ), *vbl. sb.*¹ [f. GRACE *v.* + -ING¹.] The action of the verb GRACE in the various senses; an instance of this; also quasi-*concr.*

1591 LYLY *Endym.* II. ii. 24 Let us stand aside, and let him use his garbe, for all consisteth in his gracing. **1607** HIERON *Wks.* I. 177 Haman..was..forced by the kings commandement to bee the chiefe in the gracing and honouring of Mordecai. **1611** COTGR., *Decoration*, a decoration..trimming, gracing. **1615** JACKSON *Creed* IV. II. vii. §3 Unless his faith have quelled all trust all pride or glory in these gracings. **1659** C. SIMPSON *Division Viol.* 9 Graceing of Notes is performed two Wayes; viz. by the Bow, and by the Fingers. **1780** T. TWINING *Recr. & Studies* (1882) 76 In gracing, he [a singer] does the most beautiful.. things I ever heard. **1808** E. S. BARRETT *Miss-led General* 152 Laces, tags, points, edgings, facings, gracings, and such stuff. **1836** *New Monthly Mag.* XLVIII. 304 Her father reduced the art of gracing more nearly to a science than any other musician of his time.

gracing (ˈgreɪsɪŋ), *vbl. sb.*² *slang.* Also greycing. Contracted form of ***greyhound racing*** (see GREYHOUND 4).

1928 *Star* 8 June, Gracing at Wimbledon. **1928** *Daily Express* 20 July 17/5 Greycing... Programmes..for tonight's greyhound racing meetings. **1935** E. C. ASH *Bk. Greyhound* viii. 141 Greyhound Racing, or 'Gracing', as it is sometimes termed, started in 1926.

graciosity (greɪʃɪˈɒsɪtɪ). Also 5 graciousete, 7 gratiositie. [Late ME. *graciousete*, ad. F. *gracieuseté*, f. *gracieux* GRACIOUS; afterwards refash. after L. *grātiōsitās*: see GRACIOUS and -ITY.] The quality or state of being gracious, graciousness.

c **1477** CAXTON *Jason* 32 Alle they had wondre and meruaylle of the beaute graciousete wytte and perfection of Iason. **1603** HOLLAND *Plutarch's Mor.* 15 Like as of Valiant he derived Valour..so also of Gracious, he comes in with Gratiositie. **1837** CARLYLE *Fr. Rev.* I. III. vi, With a delicate graciosity of manner covering unutterable things. **1878** H. M. STANLEY *Dark Cont.* I. iii. 57 With diplomatic blandness and graciosity.

‖**gracioso** (greɪʃɪˈəʊsəʊ; in Sp. graθiˈoso). Also 7 gratioso. [Sp.; etymologically = GRACIOUS *a.* In sense 1, perh. from the It. *grazioso.*]

†**1. a.** ? An attractive person. **b.** A court favourite. *Obs.*

1650 BULWER *Anthropomet.* (1653) 133 We in this Island ..doe no way like of a shooing-horn-like Nose; neither do wee esteem such to be *gratiosos.* *a* **1670** HACKET *Abp. Williams* I. (1692) 114 The Lord Marquess of Buckingham, then a great Gratioso, was put on by the Prince to ask the King's liking to this Amourous Adventure. *Ibid.* II. 195 He knew not whether it were a Synastria, a Star which reigned at both their Births, that made him a Gratioso to so brave a Lady. **1670** TEMPLE *Let.* Wks. 1720 II. 224 Passing his Time with his Virginals, his Dwarfs, and his Graciosoes.

2. The buffoon of Spanish comedy.

1749 SMOLLETT *Gil Blas* VII. vi. (1782) III. 38 At length the Gracioso presented himself to open the scene. **1808** SCOTT *Dryden's Wks.* I. 77 The character of the gracioso, or clown. **1837** *Q. Rev.* LIX. 78 The principal character in these lighter afterpieces is the 'Gracioso', who has superseded the 'Introitu', the clown or rustic, who in the older, less artificial Spanish plays spoke to the audience and explained what was going on. **1881** MAX MÜLLER *Sel. Ess.* I. v. 422 A Brahman, who acts the part of gracioso in the Indian drama.

Hence **graciˈosoly** *adv.* (*nonce-wd.*) [-LY²], in the manner of a 'gracioso'.

1879 E. FITZGERALD *Lett.* I. 443 The Italian Carnival ended with somewhat of the same Burlesque Ceremonial, but was thought to mimic too Graciosoly that of the Church.

gracious (ˈgreɪʃəs), *a.* Forms: 4–5 gracios(e, 4–6 graciouse, (4 -iouce), -ius(s, -yous(e, (5 -yows), 5–6 grac(i)eux, 6–7 gratious, (6 -ius), 4– gracious. Also GRATIOSE. [a. OF. *gracious* (mod.F. *gracieux*) = Pr. *gracios* Sp. *gracioso* (also as sb.: see GRACIOSO), Pg. *gracioso*, It. *grazioso*, ad. L. *grātiōsus*, f. *grātia*: see GRACE and -OUS.

The L. word usu. means 'enjoying favour', 'attracting favour, pleasing'. In mod.Fr. the prevailing meaning is 'graceful'; but all the senses below have existed in Fr. use.]

†**1.** Enjoying grace or favour; in good odour, acceptable, popular. Also of actions: Winning favour or goodwill. Const. *to*, *with*. *Obs.*

13.. *Coer de L.* 6456 It was to Richard a gracious dede. **1573** G. HARVEY *Letter-bk.* (Camden) 20, I am sorie I am so litle gratius in Pembrook that I cannot yit..obtain mi grace. **1602** WARNER *Albion's Eng.* XI. lxi. 268 Alreadie was he gratious both with her and all the Court. **1613** in *Crt. & Times Jas. I* (1848) I. 279, I marvel he would offer himself, knowing how little gracious he is. **1613** BEAUM. & FL. *Captain* v. iv, I am a handsome gratious fellow amongst women. **1647** CLARENDON *Hist. Reb.* IV. §339 Spies were set upon..all..discourses, which fell from those, who were not gracious to them. **1658** CLEVELAND *Rustick Rampant* Wks. (1687) 400 Ever babling those things which he fancied would be Gracious to the Multitude. **1691** RAY *Creation* (1714) 379 Which renders persons gracious and acceptable in the eyes of others. **1727** SWIFT *Let. to Writer of Occas. Paper* Wks. 1778 XI. 129 You are not supposed to be very gracious among those who are most able to hurt you. **1760–72** H. BROOKE *Fool of Quality* (1809) IV. 92 This man wanted to be gracious with my pretty young wife. **1821** HAGGART *Life* 55, I..got very gracious with the dub coves, on account of my being a quiet orderly prisoner.

2. a. Of a character likely to find favour; having pleasing qualities. Now somewhat *arch.* or *poet.*

1303 R. BRUNNE *Handl. Synne* 5805 He ys a man ful gracyous Gode to wynne on to þine hous. **1340–70** *Alex. & Dind.* 954 Al þat growus in þe ground of graciouce þingus. *c* **1380** WYCLIF *Sel. Wks.* I. 91 Grace is a manere in man bi which he is graciouse to God. **1398** TREVISA *Barth De P.R.* XVII. xxiii. (Tollem. MS.), Cipresse..haþ bitter leues, and violent smel, and graciouse schadowe. **1490** CAXTON *Eneydos* xv. 54 The byrdes renewen theyre swete songe gracyouse. *c* **1491** *Chast. Goddes Chyld.* 10 Among al bestes there is a gracious best whiche men call *apes.* **1509** FISHER *Funeral Serm. Hen. VII*, Wks. (1876) 269 His speche gracyous in dyuerse languages. **1530** PALSGR. 314/1 Gracyouse in spekyng, *facont, facunde.* **1585** T. WASHINGTON tr. *Nicholay's Voy.* I. xix. 23 b, They woulde endevour..too make the Bascha condescend to a better and more gracious composition. **1601** WEEVER *Mirr. Mart.* A viij b, Ioyned to a Citie, to the sight most gratious. **1768** H. WALPOLE *Hist. Doubts* 108 The body..was found almost entire, and emitted a gracious perfume. **1842** S. LOVER *Handy Andy* Pref. 5 If to paint one's country in its gracious aspect has been a weakness. **1852** M. ARNOLD *Empedocles on Etna* I. i. 6 How gracious is the mountain at this hour! **1863** HAWTHORNE *Our Old Home* 107 A thousand shrubs and gracious herbs. **1864** TENNYSON *Aylmer's F.* 240 A gracious gift to give a lady, this!

†**b.** Endowed with grace or charm of appearance, attractive; also in more limited sense, graceful, elegant. *Obs.*

1340–70 *Alisaunder* 182 Grete yien & graie, gracious lippes. **13..** *E.E. Allit. P.* A. 933 To loke on þe glory of þys gracious gote. *c* **1386** CHAUCER *Clerk's T.* 556 A man child she bar by this Walter ffull gracious and fair for to biholde. *c* **1400** MAUNDEV. (1839) vi. 69 Toward the Est ende of the Cytee, is a fulle fair Chirche and a gracyouse. *a* **1400–50** *Alexander* 4909 Ane of þe graciousest gomes þat euire god fourmed. *c* **1500** *Melusine* lxi. 366, I desyre none other thing erthly nor none other I shal not aske nor take of you, but only your gracyous body. *c* **1590** GREENE *Fr. Bacon* ix. 174 Gracious as the morning star of heaven. **1604** MARSTON *Malcontent* II. iv. D 3, Hee is the most exquisite in forging of veines..dying of haire [etc.] that euer made an old Lady gratious by torchlight. **1607–12** BACON *Ess., Beauty* (Arb.) 210 In beautie that of favour is more then that of collour, and that of decent and gracious mocion, more then that of favour. **1613–39** I. JONES in Leoni *Palladio's Archit.* (1742) I. 38 The Wave..instead of the Ovolo, in my Judgment is very gracious. **1649** EVELYN *Mem.* (1857) III. 45 His person is not very gracious, the small-pox having put out one of his eyes: but he is of good shape.

c. ***gracious living***: an elegant way of life, esp. with reference to the proprieties and niceties in standards of housekeeping. Occas. ironical. Hence ***gracious liver.***

[**1932** Q. D. LEAVIS *Fiction & Reading Public* 319 Cf. the following advertisement taken at random from one of the luxurious women's magazines: Those who golf at St. Andrews..shop in the Rue de la Paix..those who live graciously, are fastidious in their choice of ships.] **1937** *New Yorker* 16 Jan. 24/3 Many a shoe wholesaler has learned more about what constitutes a Pattern of Gracious Living. **1945** *Palestine Post* 26 Oct. 7/6 American magazines..are all geared to some super-glamourized Gracious Living in relation to the opinion of the neighbours. **1951** J. CANNAN *And All I Learned* ix. 154, I don't demand luxury..but I do like gracious living. **1953** K. AMIS *Lucky Jim* xiv. 145 It should be possible for the right man to stop, or at least hinder, her from being a refined gracious-liver and arty-rubbish-talker. **1958** *Observer* 13 Apr. 9/3 One of the main problems the Russians are wrestling with to-day is how to achieve 'gracious living'. **1959** 'M. DERBY' *Tigress* iii. 129 The suburban vulgarity of gracious living. **1969** M. PUGH *Last Place Left* xxiii. 178 In a booming bistro..we sat hard against a gracious liver who called the bread the club of death.

3. Characterized by or exhibiting kindness or courtesy; kindly, benevolent, courteous. Now *rare* (chiefly *poet.*) exc. with some notion of sense 4.

a **1310** in Wright *Lyric P.* xvi. 52 Heo is dereworthe in day, Graciouse, stout, ant gay. *c* **1400** *Destr. Troy* 13553 Iff ye haue ferkit any fode to þis frith now, Bes gracius, for goddes loue, ges me som part! **1450–70** *Golagros & Gaw.* 389 Schir Gawyne the gay, gude and gracius. *c* **1477** CAXTON *Jason* 29 They had neuer seen none so courtays ne so gracious. **1598** MARSTON *Pygmal.* xv. 127 Be gracious vnto him that formed thee. **1859** TENNYSON *Guinevere* 326 Sir Lancelot..Was gracious to all ladies. **1871** BLACKIE *Four Phases* i. 41 An essentially selfish motive can often be traced beneath the gracious surface.

4. a. Condescendingly kind, indulgent and beneficent to inferiors. Now only of very exalted personages (cf. b), or in playful or sarcastic applications.

1390 GOWER *Conf.* II. 141 Be gracious and do largesse. *Ibid.* III. 190 It sit a king to be pitous Toward his people and gracious. **1543** *Extracts Aberd. Reg.* (1844) I. 190 Quher-for we beleif your lordschip wilbe so graciuss to pardon ws to remane at hame at this tym. **1713** SWIFT *Let. to Miss Vanhomrigh* Lett. 1766 II. 285 When I am fixed anywhere, perhaps, I may be so gracious to let you know, but I will not promise. **1787** MAD. D'ARBLAY *Diary* Oct., She [the Queen] almost regularly came to my room, and spent the time in gracious converse. **1791** BURKE *App. Whigs* Wks. VI. 102 The gracious intentions of his sovereign. **1838** DICKENS *Nich. Nick.* iii, I am sure I am very much obliged to you at least, sir, said Miss La Creevy in a gracious manner. **1849**

MACAULAY *Hist. Eng.* vi. II. 125 He now proclaimed that he had been only too gracious when he had condescended to ask the assent of the Scottish Estates to his wishes. **1855** *Ibid.* xiii. III. 320 He was a gracious master, a trusty ally, a terrible enemy. **1876** TROLLOPE *Autobiogr.* vii. (1883) I. 168 [He] turned out to be a duke,—and a duke, too, who could speak English! How gracious he was to us, and yet how thoroughly he covered us with ridicule.

b. Used as a courteous epithet in referring to kings, queens, or dukes, their actions, etc.

c **1330** R. BRUNNE *Chron.* (1810) 133 Þan was Inglond in pes & charite, & alle in Henry gracious kyng & fre. *a* **1413** PR. OF WALES *Let. to Hen. IV* in *Facsim. Nat. MSS.* I. 36, I recomande me to yowr good & gracieux lordship. **1530** *Privy Purse Exp. Hen. VIII* (1827) 22 Paied to ij Nonnes of Caunterbury by way of the kinges gracieux rewarde xl*s*. **1555** EDEN *Decades W. Ind.* (Arb.) 52 Owr noble and gratious prince kynge Phylyppe. **1559** *Bk. Com. Prayer, Litany*, Our most gracious Quene, and gouernour. **1571** *Act 13 Eliz.* c. 29 §2 In the third yeare of her Highnes most gratious Raigne. **1638** M'QUIS HAMILTON *Let. to Chas. I* in *H. Papers* (Camden) 21 Your Ma[tts] most gratious letter of the 29. **1771** *Junius Lett.* xlix. 253 The gracious prince who governs this country. **1845** S. AUSTIN *Ranke's Hist. Ref.* II. 112 The voice of the majority decides that my gracious master shall not be written to.

†**c.** ***gracious Lord*** [= F. †*gracieux seigneur*], a name given to some fish. *Obs.*

1694 MOTTEUX *Rabelais* IV. lx. 236 Rock fish, Gracious Lords, Sword fish [etc.].

5. a. Of the Deity, Christ, the Virgin Mary: Disposed to show or dispense grace, merciful, compassionate, benignant.

1340 HAMPOLE *Pr. Consc.* 133 How mercyful and gracyouse God es. **1393** LANGL. *P. Pl.* C. xv. 134 And god is ay gracious . . to alle þat gredeþ to hym. *c* **1410** HOCCLEVE *Mother of God* 81 Thy gracious bountee spredith al aboute. *c* **1430** *Hymns Virg.* 99 Graciose crist! my soule þou haue. **1535** COVERDALE *2 Kings* xiii. 23 The Lorde was gracious vnto them, and had mercy vpon them. **1576** FLEMING *Panopl. Epist.* 444 The moste mightie and gratious God . . prolong your life in health and prosperitie. **1635** A. STAFFORD *Fem. Glory* (1869) 148 Under the shadow of Thy gratious Wing. **1650** HUBBERT *Pill Formality* 122 So great, so good, and so gratious a God. **1687** DRYDEN *Hind & P.* I. 64 But, gratious God, how well dost thou provide For erring judgments an unerring Guide? **1738** WESLEY *Psalms* II. viii, I heard my Gracious Father say [etc.]. *Ibid.* v. i, O Lord, incline thy gracious Ear. **1847** TENNYSON *Princ.* II. 174 A pack of wolves! the Lord be gracious to me! **1871** MORLEY *Voltaire* (1886) 2 A gracious, benevolent and all-powerful being. **1876** MOZLEY *Univ. Serm.* xi. (1877) 218 God is so gracious that He gives man faith and a religious spirit upon his asking for it. **1877** MACLEAR *Mark* i. 36 His gracious presence was not to be confined to Capernaum.

quasi-*adv.* *a* **1617** P. BAYNE *Lect.* 269 Therefore the Lord hath dealt marvellously gracious with us.

b. *ellipt.* as a substitute for the name of God. In various exclamations, as ***gracious! Ah*** (***Oh***) ***gracious! good gracious!*** †***goodly and gracious! O my gracious! gracious me! gracious sake!***, etc. See also GOODNESS 5.

1713, 1744 [see GOODLY *a.*]. **1768** GOLDSM. *Good-n. Man* I. Wks. (Globe) 616/1 Good gracious! can I believe my eyes or my ears! **179.** PEGGE *Derbicisms* I. (E.D.S.) s.v., Ah gracious! an exclamation for ah gracious God! or, ah be gracious unto me! **1794** MRS. A. M. BENNETT *Ellen* I. 18 'Gracious!' she exclaimed. *a* **1839** PRAED *Poems* (1864) II. 65 Shot in a duel too! good gracious! **1850** MRS. CARLYLE *Lett.* II. 137 My startled look and exclamation, 'Oh, gracious!' **1856** WHYTE MELVILLE *Kate Cov.* i, But we women—gracious! if we only take the trouble, we can turn the whole male sex round our little fingers. **1856** MRS. STOWE *Dred* I. xi. 144 'Married! O, my gracious! **1884** PAE *Eustace* 14 Gracious me, how does she come to be the sister of that huge salmon-fisher? **1885** HOWELLS *Silas Lapham* (1891) I. 77 'By gracious! . . there ain't anything like that in this world for business.' **1893** 'Q.' [Couch] *Delect. Duchy* 155, 'I hope to gracious you'm goin' to keep it up.'

†**6.** Characterized by or endowed with divine grace, godly, righteous, pious, regenerate. *Obs.*

a **1300** *Cursor M.* 2081 Noe, þat gracius and god. *c* **1380** WYCLIF *Sel. Wks.* III. 457 Þat all men . . schul . . calle hem moste holy faderis, and most blessid and moste mercyful and gracius. **1533** MORE *Answ. Poysoned Bk.* Wks. 1137/1 All the olde holy expositours of the scripture, whiche were good menne and gracious. *a* **1635** SIBBES *Confer. Christ & Mary* (1656) 100 A gracious Christian never wanteth arguments of assurance of salvation. **1641** J. JACKSON *True Evang. T.* II. 102 Grace of Regeneration . . introduceth gracious habits of sweetnesse, peace and love. **1669** BUNYAN *Holy Citie* 130 All the holy and truly gracious Souls that are with him on the Mount Zion. **1738** WESLEY *Psalms* LXXX. xv, Error in ten thousand shapes Would every gracious Soul beguile. **1757** —— *Wks.* (1872) XIII. 202, I could not deny his being a gracious person.

†**7.** Happy, fortunate, prosperous. *Obs.*

1340–70 *Alex. & Dind.* 193 Alixandre . . þat grete god amon in graciouce timus Bi-gat on olimpias þe onurable quene. **1387** TREVISA *Higden* (Rolls) I 321 Insule Fortunate þat beeþ þe gracious ilondes. *c* **1460** *Towneley Myst.* xiii. 244 Bot were I not more gracyus and rychere befar, I were eten outt of howse and of harbar. **1603** SHAKS. *Meas. for M.* v. i. 76, I . . desir'd her, To try her gracious fortune with Lord Angelo, For her poore Brothers pardon. **1611** —— *Wint. T.* III. i. 22 Goe: fresh Horses, And gracious be the issue.

†**8.** Given by way of indulgence or mercy: **a.** ***gracious day*** (see quot.); **b.** said of a mortal thrust given to one in great pain (cf. *coup de grace*). *Obs.*

1703 MAUNDRELL *Journ. Jerus.* (1732) 141 Some one of the Standers by is permitted to give him a gracious stab to the Heart. **1726** AMHERST *Terræ Fil.* xlii. 233 Some of these days are called gracious days, because upon them the respondent is not obliged to stay in the schools above half the time, which respondents upon other days are.

9. *Comb.*

1868 LD. HOUGHTON *Select. fr. Wks.* 29 A strife of gracious-worded difference.

†'**graciousize**, *v. Obs. rare.* [f. GRACIOUS + -IZE.] *trans.* To render 'gracious', to endow with heavenly grace.

1701 BEVERLEY *Glory of Grace* 9 Our Investiture with Grace, or our being Gratiousciz'd in all these great Points of Salvation. *Ibid.* 21 We are thus Invested with Grace, or Graciousciz'd from Eternity to Eternity.

Hence '**graciousized** *ppl. a.* (in quot. *absol.*)

1701 BEVERLEY *Glory of Grace* 39 So that Grace Appears in such an Excellency and Glory of the Graciouscizd.

graciously ('greɪʃəslɪ), *adv.* [f. GRACIOUS + -LY[2].] In a gracious manner.

1. 'In a pleasing manner' (J.); with grace, attractively, gracefully. Now *rare.*

13.. *E.E. Allit. P.* B. 488 Gracyously vmbe-grouen al with grene leuez. **1641** HINDE *J. Bruen* xxxi. 99 He . . shewed his religion very graciously in his government. **1890** *Spectator* 25 Oct. 496/1 One of the most gracious of poetic solecisms when graciously employed.

2. With kindness, friendliness, or gracious condescension.

c **1380** WYCLIF *Serm.* Sel. Wks. I. 91 Feiþ is a ȝifte of God, and so God may not ȝyve it to man but ȝif he ȝyve it graciousely. *c* **1430** *Syr Gener.* (Roxb.) 1898 Thoo ansuered she ful graciouslie with myld chere. *a* **1440** *Sir Eglam.* 679 So gracyously he come hur tylle. **1548–9** (Mar.) *Bk. Com. Prayer, Litany*, Graciously loke vpon our afflyctions. **1567** *Gude & Godlie Ball.* (S.T.S.) 116 Thow oppinnis furth thy hand full graciuslie. **1654** *Nicholas Papers* (Camden) II. 70 If his majestie will be graciously pleased to come amongst us. **1697** DRYDEN *Virg. Past.* I. 62 He . . graciously decreed My Grounds to be restor'd. **1725** BERKELEY *Proposal*, etc. Wks. III. 218 If his Majesty would graciously please to grant a Charter for a College. **1744** H. WALPOLE *Lett. H. Mann* (1834) I. xcviii. 334 He went yesterday and was most graciously received. **1847** JAMES *J. Marston Hall* vii, My New Lord received me very graciously. **1878** J. P. HOPPS *Jesus* v. 20 He spoke to her so graciously and forgivingly, that [etc.]. **1880** MRS. FORRESTER *Roy & V.* I. 23 She smiled very kindly and graciously at him in return.

†**3.** Through, or by means of, divine grace.

1303 R. BRUNNE *Handl. Synne* 12073 How þou . . ouercomest hym gracyously. *c* **1449** PECOCK *Repr.* III. v. 305 Not alle men ben in lijk maner . . disposid naturali and gracioseli. **1526** *Pilgr. Perf.* (W. de W. 1531) 81 b, What so euer he aske of god he shall optayne it gracyously. **1534** MORE *On the Passion* Wks. 1324/2 If you receive and eate vertuouslye the tone into your body, you receiue the tother graciouslye into youre soules. **1596** DALRYMPLE tr. *Leslie's Hist. Scot.* IV. 254 In Hevinn his reward gratiouslie has he obteynet. **1603** SHAKS. *Meas. for M.* II. iv. 77 Let [me] be ignorant, and in nothing good, But graciously to know I am no better.

†**4.** With good luck or fortune, fortunately.

1330 R. BRUNNE *Chron.* (1810) 72 Þe reame of Inglond so graciously he gatte. **1382** WYCLIF *Gen.* xxx. 11 The which aftir conseyuynge bryngynge forth a child, seide, Gracyously. **1387** TREVISA *Higden* (Rolls) V. 301 He . . ruled þe Longo-bardes swiþe graciousliche long tyme. *Ibid.* VII. 35 So al þat þere were, [were] dede oþer i-hurt ful sore, outtake Dunston alone þat scapede graciousliche and wyseliche. *c* **1400** MAUNDEV. (Roxb.) xv. 70 He gouerned it wisely and graciousely.

graciousness ('greɪʃəsnɪs). [f. GRACIOUS *a.* + -NESS.] The quality or state of being gracious.

1. Pleasing or attractive quality or condition, charm, winning grace, esp. of manner.

c **1385** CHAUCER *L.G.W.* 1675 *Medea*, Of thyn tunge the infynyt graciousnesse. **1530** PALSGR. 227/1 Graciousnesse, *gracievseté*. **1751** JOHNSON *Rambler* No. 147 ¶5 He possessed some Science of Graciousness and Attraction which Books had not taught. **1850** LYNCH *Theo. Trin.* vii. 134 Beautiful things . . have a graciousness that wins us. **1885** *Manch. Exam.* 4 Feb. 3/3 He discourses, with a pensive graciousness which is irresistibly charming, of three departed friends.

†**b.** = GRACEFULNESS.

1652–62 HEYLIN *Cosmogr.* I. (1682) 261 The . . gratiousness of the Bell tower.

2. Courtesy, politeness; now esp. condescending courtesy.

1638 BAKER tr. *Balzac's Lett.* (1654) (vol. III.) 13 Such is your graciousnesse, that it is impossible to fall foule with you. *Ibid.* (1638) 216, I did not looke to finde so great a graciousnesse. **1647** CLARENDON *Hist. Reb.* IV. §85 The graciousness and temper of this answer, made no impression in them. **1741** RICHARDSON *Pamela* II. 126 His Graciousness to this fine Gentleman and myself. **1751** JOHNSON *Rambler* No. 165 ¶12 The Barber . . seized me by the Hand with honest Joy in his Countenance, which I repressed with a frigid Graciousness. **1824** MISS MITFORD *Village* Ser. I. (1863) 171 The letter was . . received with the most cordial graciousness. **1855** MACAULAY *Hist. Eng.* xvii. IV. 230 The only words in his Declaration which had any show of graciousness. **1872** J. L. SANFORD *Eng. Kings, Chas. I*, 342 He . . effaced the memory of his previous insinuating graciousness.

3. Mercifulness or compassionateness (of the Deity). Also *occas.* kindness (of fortune).

1585 ABP. SANDYS *Serm.* XV. 264 No tongue can expresse, neither any minde conceiue this gratiousnesse. **1599** SANDYS *Europæ Spec.* Q 4 b, Vnless the gratiousness of God stirre vppe some worthy Princes of renowne, and reputation, with both sides to enterpose their wisedome. *a* **1665** J. GOODWIN *Filled w. the Spirit* (1867) 305 The exceeding graciousness and condescension of his nature. **1811** *Henry & Isabella* II. 2 In the midst of her calamities, she thought it a graciousness still left in her fate, to have escaped the connection. **1872** SPURGEON *Treas. Dav.* Ps. cxii. 4 His justice is . . seasoned with graciousness.

†**4.** Possession of grace, moral excellence. *Obs.*

a **1691** BP. T. BARLOW *Rem.* (1693) 437 The Acts derive their Graciousness from the Habits, and not *è contra.* *a* **1711** KEN *Serm.* Wks. (1838) 116 Graciousness is honoured as a participation of the Divine nature, appropriated to no other than saints.

grackle ('græk(ə)l). Also 8 **gracule**, 9 **grakle.** [Anglicized form of the generic name *Gracula*, a mod.L. fem. corresponding to L. *grāculus* jackdaw.]

1. A name applied to various birds originally included in the genus *Gracula* (see quot. 1893).

1772 FORSTER in *Phil. Trans.* LXII. 400 The *Gracula Quiscula*, Linn. or shining Gracule. **1782** LATHAM *Gen. Synopsis Birds* I. II. 455 *Gracula religiosa*, Minor Grakle. *Ibid.* 457 *Gracula calva*, Bald Grakle. **1816** KIRBY & SP. *Entomol.* (1843) I. 244 The purple grackle. **1842** BRANDE *Dict. Sci.*, etc. s.v. *Gracula*, The bird commonly called the mino grackle (*Gracula religiosa* of Linnæus). **1850** LYELL *2nd Visit U.S.* II. 150 The boat-tailed grackle (*Quisqualus*). **1865** TRISTRAM *Land Israel* ix. 209 My first specimen of the beautiful grakle (*Amydrus tristrami*). **1893** NEWTON *Dict. Birds*, *Grackle* . . a word . . restricted to members of the Families *Sturnidæ* (starling) belonging to the Old World, and *Icteridæ* belonging to the New. Of the former those to which it has been most commonly applied are the species variously known as Mynas, Mainas and Minors of India . . and especially the *Gracula religiosa* of Linnæus. . . In the New World the name Grackle has been applied to several species of the genera *Scolecophagus* and *Quiscalus*. . . The best known are the Rusty Grackle, *S. ferrugineus* . . and *Q. purpureus*, the Purple Grackle or Crow-Blackbird. **1896** *Westm. Gaz.* 28 Oct. 6/3 The black-throated grackle-cock.

2. *Angling.* The name of an artificial fly.

1894 *Outing* (U.S.) XXIV. 227/1 Bass flies of proved merit include grackle, all the palmers, [etc.].

†'**gracy**, *a. Obs. rare*$^{-1}$. [f. GRACE *sb.* + -Y[1].] Full of teaching about grace, evangelical.

1661 PEPYS *Diary* 14, Apr., Heard Mr. Jacomb, at Ludgate, upon these words, 'Christ loved you and therefore let us love one another,' and made a gracy sermon, like a Presbyterian.

grad[1], abbrev. of GRADUATE *sb.* 1; also of UNDERGRADUATE *sb.* 1.

1871 L. H. BAGG *4 Years at Yale* 45 *Grad*, abbreviation for graduate. **1893** W. K. POST *Harvard Stories* p. ix, Reverend grads., from the tales I have heard ye tell, I opine that the undergraduate is still the same. **1920** F. SCOTT FITZGERALD *This Side of Paradise* (1921) iv. 143 Amory 'ran it out' at a great rate, bringing the most eccentric character to dinner, wild-eyed grad students, preceptors with strange theories. **1950** M. MARPLES *University Slang* 184 The provincial universities . . have even produced analogous abbreviations [to undergrad], such as grad = graduate (Durham, 1934 +) and post-grad = post-graduate (Leeds, 1940). **1957** W. H. WHYTE *Organization Man* xxi. 269 Only 27·3 per cent of high school grads aged twenty-five to thirty-four . . were inter-state migrants. **1958** *Times* 3 Nov. 6/1 Town and gown in Cambridge have . . been inclined to settle their differences through fists . . and once again conflict is causing some concern, this time under the heading of 'grads' versus 'teds'. **1969** *Daily Tel.* 10 Mar. 1/4 Cambridge police were last night looking for three youths who beat up Rajeer Dhavan, 22, undergraduate son of the Indian High Commissioner, in the latest episode of 'grad-bashing'.

grad[2] (græd). [prob. f. GRAD(E *sb.*] = GRADE *sb.* 1 b.

1909 in WEBSTER. **1953** *Amer. Jrnl. Physics* XXI. 294 Proposed symbols for physical units. . . Grad ($\equiv 10^{-2}$ rt. angle). **1959** G. & R. C. JAMES *Math. Dict.* (ed. 2) 176/2 *Grad*, one-hundredth part of a right-angle in the centesimal system of measuring angles, also called a grade or degree.

grad[3], abbrev. of GRADIENT *sb.* 5, used chiefly in symbolic contexts.

1909 J. G. COFFIN *Vector Analysis* v. 102 The vector . . is called the gradient or the slope of V . . and is written grad V or slope V. *Ibid.* 103 It remains to show that the operator ∇ applied to V gives the grad. **1957** R. S. LONGHURST *Geom. & Physical Optics* xix. 393 If ϕ is a scalar point function, grad ϕ is a vector. **1962** T. M. APOSTOL *Calculus* II. iv. 170 The notation grad f is also used instead of ∇f.

gradal ('greɪdəl), *a. rare.* [irregularly f. L. *grad-us* degree + -AL[1]; used instead of the regularly formed adj. *gradual*, to avoid ambiguity.] Of or pertaining to degree.

1872 E. TUCKERMAN *Genera Lichenum* p. vi, He conceives then that while less weight . . should be given to spore-differences of a mere gradal character . . more [etc.].

‖**gradale.** *Obs.*$^{-1}$ [med.L. *gradāle* sb., neut. of late L. *gradālis* adj., f. *grad-us* step.] = GRADUAL *sb.*

a **1746** LEWIS in Gutch *Coll. Cur.* II. 168 A Gradale or Grail, so called from the Gradales contained in it . . The Gradales, or what is gradually sung after the Epistle.

gradan, variant of GRADDAN *Sc.*

gradate (grə'deɪt), *v.* [Back formation from GRADATION.]

1. With reference to colour: **a.** *intr.* To pass by imperceptible grades from one tone or shade to another; to shade off. Const. *into.*

1753 HOGARTH *Anal. Beauty* xii. 96 Retiring shades, which gradate or go off by degrees. **1775** C. DAVY *Bourrit's Glac. Savoy* (1776) 113 The deeper colour of a single neighbouring mountain, which gradated from top to bottom. **1823** *Examiner* 186/1 The light . . admirably gradates into and contrasts the solemn dark on the shore.

b. *trans.* To cause so to pass by imperceptible grades.

1853 RUSKIN *Stones Ven.* III. ii. §21. 47 Let the reader take the two extreme tints and carefully gradate the one into the other. **1857** —— *Elem. Drawing* iii. 219 It is not enough ..that colour should be gradated by being made merely paler or darker at one place than another.
absol. **1857** RUSKIN *Elem. Drawing* i. 20 If you cannot gradate well with pure black lines, you will never gradate well with pale ones. **1874** R. TYRWHITT *Sketch. Club* 70 Now gradate over the gray to nothing with a little vermillion and yellow ochre.

2. *trans.* To arrange in steps or grades (material or immaterial). ? Only in *passive*. Const. *into*. Also with *off*.
1869 A. W. WARD tr. *Curtius' Hist. Greece* II. III. i. 254 The surrounding heights are gradated off in artificial terraces up to their summit. **1885** BLACK *Wh. Heather* in *Longm. Mag.* VI. 126 In the old country, where society is gradated into ranks.

3. *Chem.* (? *U.S.* only.) 'To bring to a certain strength or grade of concentration; as, to gradate a saline solution' (Webster 1897); 'to concentrate as by evaporation' (Funk's *Stand. Dict.*). Cf. GRADUATE, GRADUATION, GRADUATOR.
Hence **gra'dated** *ppl. a.*
1846 RUSKIN *Mod. Paint.* (1851) II. III. I. v. §16 Compare the gradated colours of the rainbow with the stripes of a target. **1863** E. V. NEALE *Anal. Th. & Nat.* 179 These currents would produce, in all substances possessing a 'gradated' structure, secondary currents circulating round them. **1886** *Spectator* 18 Dec. 1711 Glowing with rich and carefully gradated colour.

†**gradately**, *adv. Obs.* Also 5 **graditly**, 6 **gradatlye**. [f. **gradate* adj. (ad. L. *gradātus* furnished with steps) + -LY².] By degrees; *spec.* in *Her.* (cf. ENGRADED, ENGRAILED).
1486 *Bk. St. Albans, Her.* D ij b, They ar calde armys engradit for they ar made of ij colouris the wich graditly ar broght to gedir oon coloure in to an other coloure. **1572** BOSSEWELL *Armorie* II. 27 Two colors, or any mettal or colour, be gradately inferred one into the other, that no partition, but onely the Purflue maie be seene betwene them. **1599** A. M. tr. *Gabelhouer's Bk. Physicke* 113/1 The same being liquefactede, then take Minii lb. j. verye finelye pulverisatede, and gradatlye mixe the same therwith.

‖**gradatim** (grəˈdeɪtɪm), *adv.* [L. *gradātim* by degrees, f. *gradus* step.] Step by step, gradually.
1583 STUBBES *Anat. Abuses* F iiij b, Three or foure degrees of minor ruffes, placed *gradatim*, step by step one beneath another. **1669** WORLIDGE *Syst. Agric.* (1681) 301 The vast quantities of water that flow over our heads in stormy or rainy weather, which..do *gradatim* diffuse themselves upon the Earth. **1694** SALMON *Bate's Dispens.* I. (1713) 132/1 Make a gentle Fire first, which increase *gradatim* to the fourth Degree. **1785** D. LOW *Chiropodologia* xii. 104 Let them be bathed in water, tepid at first, and rendered afterwards, *gradatim*, more warm.

gradation (grəˈdeɪʃən). Also 6–7 gradacion. [ad. L. *gradātiōn-em*, n. of action f. *grad-us* step: see GRADE *sb.* and -ATION. Cf. F. *gradation* (1520 in sense 8 a, which is the earliest recorded sense also in English.]

†**1.** The process of advancing step by step; a course of gradual progress. *Obs.*
1589 GREENE *Menaphon* (Arb.) 39 Loue..should enter into the eye, and by long gradations passe into the heart. *c* **1630** RISDON *Surv. Devon* (1810) 14, I purpose my beginning in the east part..my gradation into the south with the sun. **1727** DE FOE *Syst. Magic* I. ii. (1840) 43 Knowledge had its gradations too, and though it must be confessed it was a very slow rate, yet some advances they did make. **1750** CHESTERF. *Lett.* (1792) II. ccxviii. 340, I am very well satisfied with the progress you have made in that language.. according to that gradation you will [etc.].

†**b.** Period of advance; length of career. *Obs.*⁻¹
1613–16 W. BROWNE *Brit. Past.* I. iv, They civilly had spent their lives gradation As meeke and milde as in their first creation.

2. A series of successive conditions, qualities, events, etc., forming stages in a process or course. (In early instances prob. suggested by 8 a.) ? *Obs.*
1549 LATIMER *5th Serm. bef. Edw. VI* (Arb.) 139 What was the waye they walked?.. They stouped after gayne.. What folowed?.. They toke..brybes..What then?.. They turned Iustice vpsedowne [see 1 *Sam.* viii. 3]..Here is the Deuyles genealogye. A gradation of the Diuyles making. **1614** B. JONSON *Barth. Fair* III, The care I had of that civil young man..drew me to that exhortation, which drew the company..which drew the cut-purse; which drew the money; which drew my brother Cokes his loss; which drew on Waspe's anger; which drew on my beating: a pretty gradation! **1675** SOUTH *Serm. Ingratitude* (1715) 429 So certain it is, by a direct Gradation of Consequences from this principle of merit, that [etc.]. **1717** L. HOWEL *Desiderius* 12 Love of God is to be attain'd by a gradation of religious Virtues. **1739** CIBBER *Apol.* (1756) I. 49 That such a pile of English fame and glory..should..so..moulder away in one continual gradation of political errors. **1781** GIBBON *Decl. & F.* xxvii. III. 29 The son..attained, in the regular gradation of civil honours, the station of consular of Liguria.

3. *pl.* Steps, progressive movements. Now only in immaterial sense, stages of transition or advance.
1599 *Warn. Faire Wom.* II. 3 You have..by gradations seen how we have grown Into the main stream of our tragedy. **1662** J. BARGRAVE *Pope Alex. VII*, etc. (1867) 129 The Cameleon..winding its tail about the sticks of the cage, to help and secure its gradations. **1671** TILLOTSON *Serm.* ii. 103 The several gradations by which men at last come to this horrid degree of impiety. **1712** STEELE *Spect.* No. 430 ¶2, I hope you will..give us the History of Plenty and Want, and the natural Gradations towards them. **1861** M. PATTISON *Ess.* (1889) I. 48 The Steelyard passed with the rest of the parish by the same easy gradations from the old to the new faith.

†**b.** *sing.* A means of gradual transition. *Obs.*
1710 CROMWELL *Let. to Pope* 3 Aug., 'Tis an interpolation indeed, and serves for a gradation to the Cœlestial Orb.

†**4.** *pl.* Configurations or arrangements resembling a flight of steps. *Obs. rare.*
1698 FRYER *Acc. E. India & P.* 260 The Foundations Black Marble with gradations to the bottom. **1727** SWIFT *Gulliver* III. i. 181, I could see the sides of it encompassed with several gradations of galleries. **1802** tr. *A. La Fontaine's Reprobate* II. 279 They then descended the gradations of the rock together.

5. A scale or series of degrees in rank, merit, intensity, or difference from some particular type; the fact or condition of including or being arranged in a series of degrees.
1677 HALE *Prim. Orig. Man.* 158 Although perchance existing Individuals may not be actually Infinite, yet certain it is that the potential gradation of things may be potentially Infinite. **1783** *Phil. Trans.* LXXIII. 206, I plainly observed a gradation in the damage done to the buildings..in proportion as the countries were more or less distant from this supposed center of the evil. **1808** J. WEBSTER *Nat. Phil.* 170 This changes by gradation into an orange, thence into a yellow, and as the rays rise higher, into a green, blue, indigo, and violet. **1831** BREWSTER *Nat. Magic* vi. (1833) 153 Hence there will necessarily arise a gradation of density. **1832** HT. MARTINEAU *Life in Wilds* vii. 96 No man can be more sensible than I am of the advantages of a gradation of ranks in society. **1856** EMERSON *Eng. Traits, Relig.* Wks. (Bohn) II. 96 The gradation of the clergy..makes them the link which unites the sequestered peasantry with the intellectual advancement of the age. **1863** H. COX *Instit.* III. vi. 670 The present system of a gradation of officers, each imposing a check upon the other. **1864** H. SPENCER *Biol.* I. 6 The several compounds of oxygen with nitrogen, present us with an instructive gradation. **1879** MACLEAR *Mark* ix. 105 There is order and gradation in the hierarchy of blessed spirits.

†**b.** Position in a scale, relative rank. *Obs.*
1604 SHAKS. *Oth.* I. i. 37 Preferment goes by Letter, and affection, And not by old gradation, where each second Stood Heire to th' first. **1802** tr. *A. La Fontaine's Reprobate* I. 39 She had received a better education than was generally bestowed on others of the same gradation in life.

6. *pl.* Degrees of rank, merit, intensity, etc.; successively differing varieties of form or properties, constituting a series intermediate in character between two conditions or types.
1605 BACON *Adv. Learn.* II. vi. §2. 23 The sober and grounded inquiry [as to angels, etc.] which may arise..out of the Gradacions of Nature is not restrained. **1660** *Trial Regic.* 41 The Indictment contains many Circumstances, and Gradations, in the Treason. **1758** JOHNSON *Idler* No. 7 ¶9, I cannot pretend to inform our generals through what gradations of danger they shall train their men to fortitude. **1783** BURKE *Rep. Affairs Ind.* Wks. 1842 II. 9 They thought it not unnecessary here to state the gradations in the service. **1793** HOLCROFT *Lavater's Physiog.* ii. 20 Who shall enumerate the gradations between insect and man? **1813** BAKEWELL *Introd. Geol.* (1815) 447 Granite, porphyry, sienite, green-stone and basalt pass by..insensible gradations into each other. **1836** MACGILLIVRAY tr. *Humboldt's Trav.* xxiv. 370 In this district are displayed in a remarkable manner the gradations of vegetation. **1856** MASSON *Ess.* x. 473 Thus..prose passes into verse by visible gradations. **1875** DARWIN *Insectiv. Pl.* iii. 58 There were gradations in the completeness of the process.

7. The action of arranging in a series of grades.
1858 WHEWELL *Novum Org. Renovatum* 220 The method of gradation consists in taking a number of stages of a property in question, intermediate between two extreme cases which appear to be different.

8. a. *Rhet.* = CLIMAX I. ? *Obs.*
1538 ELYOT *Dict.*, *Climax*, a ladder, and the fygure callydde gradation. **1553** T. WILSON *Rhet.* 109 Gradacion is when we reherse the worde that goeth nexte before, and bryng another woorde thereupon that encreaseth the matter, as though one should go vp a paire of staiers, and not leaue til he come at the toppe. **1573** G. HARVEY *Letter-bk.* (Camden) 51 In time, bi his troth, for ani thing he knew.. this verri gradation he usid himself with me at that time. **1627** H. BURTON *Baiting Pope's Bull* 29 Concluding this clause with a rhetoricall gradation, that neither the prison, the racke, nor death it selfe should daunt them. **1681** FLAVEL *Meth. Grace* xiv. 277 We may observe a notable climax or gradation in those Scriptures that speak of His glory. **1727–41** CHAMBERS *Cycl.*, *Gradation*, in rhetoric, is when a series of considerations or proofs is brought, rising by degrees, and improving each on the other.

†**b.** *Logic.* = SORITES. *Obs. rare.*
1727–41 CHAMBERS *Cycl.*, *Gradation*, in logic, is an argumentation, consisting of four or more propositions, so disposed, as that the attribute of the first is the subject of the second; and the attribute of the second, the subject of the third; and so on, till the last attribute come to be predicated of the subject of the first proposition.

†**9.** *Alch.* 'Exaltation' or raising to a higher degree (see quot. 1612). *Obs.*
1612 WOODALL *Surg. Mate* Wks. (1653) 271 Gradation is an exaltation of Metals in the degree of affections, where by weight, colour, and constancy they are brought to an excellent measure, but the substance unaltered: so Gold is rubified, fixed, and purified. **1641** FRENCH *Distill.* vi. (1651) 188 Pour upon it..*Aqua regia*, and the water of gradation. **1727–41** CHAMBERS *Cycl.*

10. *Fine Arts.* **a.** *Painting.* An insensible passing from one colour or shade to another.
1727–41 CHAMBERS *Cycl.* s.v., The painters also use the word gradation for an insensible change of colour, by the diminution of the teints and shades. **1762–71** H. WALPOLE *Vertue's Anecd. Paint.* (1786) I. 84 Blues, reds, greens and yellows not being blended in the gradations. **1821** CRAIG *Lect. Drawing* iv. 228 To gratify the sight, by delicate contrasts, and impossible gradations. **1846** RUSKIN *Mod. Paint.* (1851) II. III. I. v. §16 What curvature is to lines, gradation is to shades and colours... Absolutely without gradation no natural surface can possibly be. **1873** HAMERTON *Intell. Life* II. i. (1875) 50 The amateur..finds that the gradation of his sky will not come right. **1887** *Q. Rev.* CLXIV. 109 In the production of gradations of effect in gold the Japanese stand alone.

b. *Archit.* (See quot.)
1727–41 CHAMBERS *Cycl.*, *Gradation*, in architecture, signifies an artful disposition of parts, rising, as it were, by steps, or degrees, after the manner of an amphitheatre; so that those placed before do no disservice..to those behind.

c. *Mus.* 'A diatonic ascending or descending succession of chords' (Brande *Dict. Sci.* etc. 1842).
1876 STAINER & BARRETT *Dict. Mus. Terms*, *Gradation* (F.), *Gradazione* (I.), gradation; by degrees of the scale.

11. *Philol.* = ABLAUT. Also, a modification (of a vowel) resulting from ablaut.
1870 SWEET in *Trans. Philol. Soc.* I. 3 *Au* being the second 'gradation' of *u*... The first gradation of *u* is *eû*. **1887** SKEAT *Princ. Eng. Etymol.* x. §134. 156 Some of the older vowel-sounds..are to a certain extent connected by what is known as 'gradation,' or in German, *ablaut.*

¶**12.** = GRADUATION. *rare*⁻¹ (possibly misprint).
1759 GOLDSM. *Enquiry into Pres. State* etc. (1774) 43, I have sometimes attended their disputes at gradation.

Hence **gra'dationed** *ppl. a.*, formed by or with gradations.
1805 W. TAYLOR in *Ann. Rev.* III. 288 Under a gradationed representation, the electoral body..become the real constituents. **1808** —— *Ibid.* VI. 269 To depute by universal suffrage, but gradationed delegation, the wisest depositaries of their wishes respecting [etc.].

gradational (grəˈdeɪʃənəl), *a.* [f. GRADATION + -AL¹.] Pertaining to, or characterized by, gradation.
1842 DE QUINCEY *Wks.* (1863) XIII. 327 A slow and gradational transition of the population into its present physical condition. **1866** ODLING *Anim. Chem.* 47, I.. pointed out that even the most remote members were distinguished from one another by gradational differences only. **1868** *Lyell's Princ. Geol.* (ed. 10) II. III. xliii. 482 We are only beginning, by aid of paleontology, to trace back the passage through a series of gradational forms. **1880** G. MEREDITH *Tragic Com.* xviii. (1892) 252 It was easier to remain incredulous notwithstanding the gradational distinctness of the whispers.

Hence **gra'dationally** *adv.*
1864 OWEN *Power of God* 6 The delicately and gradationally adjusted densities of the humours for correcting spherical and chromatic aberration. **1884** *19th Cent.* Feb. 336 To regard them [a class of diseases], not as uniformly marked out, one from another, by well-defined boundaries, but as shading off gradationally one into another.

gra'dationary, *a. rare*⁻¹. [f. GRADATION + -ARY.] Marked by gradations.
1824 *Examiner* 594/2 The foundations of her present prosperity, if less splendid, are more gradationary and permanent.

gradative (grəˈdeɪtɪv), *a. rare*⁻¹. [f. (on the analogy of GRADATION) L. *grad-us* step: see -ATIVE.] Advancing by grades or steps. Hence **gra'datively** *adv.*, step by step.
1818 J. BROWN *Psyche* 58 A system-builder you commence, But drawn gradatively from thence, Would quit your doctrine. **1840** J. H. GREEN *Vital Dynamics* 39 The law ..that the progressive phases of the embryo correspond to the abiding forms, which are preserved in the total organism of animated nature, as typical of its gradative evolution.

gradatlye, variant of GRADATELY *adv. Obs.*

gradatory (ˈgreɪdətərɪ), *sb.* [as if ad. L. **gradātōrium*, f. *gradus* step.] A flight of steps, esp. those leading from the cloisters to the choir of a church.
1670 in BLOUNT *Glossogr.* (ed. 3). **1703** T. N. *City & C. Purchaser* 159. **1721–1800** in BAILEY. **1859** HOLLAND *Gold F.* xiii. 142 That which is above us, in allotment, gift, and acquisition, forms so many steps of the gradatory that leads from the cells where we do penance, to the temple.

gradatory (ˈgreɪdətərɪ), *a.* [as if ad. L. **gradātōrius*, f. *grad-us* step.]
1. Proceeding by steps or grades. *rare.*
1793 ANNA SEWARD *Lett.* (1811) III. 202 The chain of subordination, which binds the various orders of national society in one common form of polity; that gradatory junction, which can alone give vigour and effect to the laws. *Ibid.* 243 Could this gradatory apostasy [of Macbeth] have been shown us. *Ibid.* 253. **1843** *Fraser's Mag.* XXVIII. 566 We find assembled, in its continuous extent of gradatory links, the whole chain of serving maidenhood.

2. Adapted for stepping (see quot.).
1842 BRANDE *Dict. Sci.* etc., *Gradatory*, a term applied in Mammalogy to the extremities of a quadruped which are equal or nearly so, and adapted for ordinary progression on dry land.

graddan (ˈgrædən), *sb. Sc.* Also 7 **gradȝan**, 8 **graddon, graydon**, 9 **gradan, gradden**. [Gaelic and Irish *gradan*, f. *gread-aim* I scorch.]
Parched grain (see quot. 1854, and quots. s.v. GRADDAN *v.*). Also *attrib.*, as ***graddan-bread, -cake, -meal.***
a **1605** MONTGOMERIE *Misc. Poems* liv. 5 Insteid of grene gynger ȝe eit gray gradȝan. **1703** M. MARTIN *Descrip. West.*

Isl. 204 The ancient way of dressing Corn, which is yet us'd in several Isles, is call'd Graddan. *c* **1730** BURT *Lett. N. Scotl.* (1818) II. 170 This Oatmeal is called graydon meal. *c* **1750** MAXWELL *Let.* in Smiles *Engineers* (1861) II. 97 The tenants in general lived..on..groats, milk, graddon ground in querns turned by the hand [etc.]. **1790** PENNANT *Tour Scotl.* (ed. 5) 323 The lasses are merry at their work of grinding the Graddan. **1806** R. JAMIESON *Quern Lilt* in Sir G. Douglas *Scott. Minor Poets* (1891) 117 Grind the gradden—grind it. **1808** J. WALKER *Econom. Hist. Hebrides* II. 368 To make gradan bread. **1828** SCOTT *F.M. Perth* xxv, The graddan cake will keep her white teeth in order. **1854** H. MILLER *Sch. & Schm.* v. (1857) 104 Gradden-meal, i.e. grain dried in a pot over the fire, and then coarsely ground in a hand-mill.

graddan ('grædən), *v. Sc.* [f. GRADDAN *sb.*] *trans.* To parch (grain) in the husk (see quots.). Hence **'graddaned** *ppl. a.*, **'graddaning** *vbl. sb.*

1773 BOSWELL *Jrnl. Tour Hebrides* 9 Sept., There were oat-cakes, made of what is called graddaned meal, that is, meal made of grain separated from the husks, and toasted by fire. **1774** PENNANT *Tour Scotl. in 1772*, 280 The corn is graddan'd, or burnt out of the ear, instead of being thrashed. *Ibid.* 281 Graddened corn was the parched corn of Holy Writ. **1864** GREENSHIELDS *Ann. Lesmahagow* 34 The process of graddening was conducted thus.

gradde, pa. t. GREDE *v. Obs.*

grade (greɪd), *sb.* [a. F. *grade*, ad. L. *grad-us* step; cf. Sp. and It. *grado*. (The regular representative of L. *gradus* in OF. was *gré*: see GREE.)

Not in Johnson 1755; noted by Todd 1819 as not yet in established use.]

1. *Math.* †**a.** A degree of angular measurement, or of latitude or longitude; the 90th part of a right angle or quadrant; = DEGREE 9, 9 b. *Obs.*

c **1511** *1st Eng. Bk. Amer.* (Arb.) Introd. 29/2 They of Lussbone in vnder yat forsayde linie .xxxix. grade and one halfe. **1571** DIGGES *Pantom.* I. *Elem.* c, A Quadrant is.. diuided in 90 portions, which partes are named grades or degrees. **1593** EALE *Dialling* 60 The Grades or Degrees are found in the upper head of this Table, and the Minutes pertaining to the degres on yᵉ left side.

b. In the centesimal mode of dividing angular quantity: The hundredth part of a right angle.

1801 DUPRÉ *Neolog. Fr. Dict.* 127 *Grade*..the grade, or decimal degree of the meridian. **1833** SNOWBALL *Plane Trigonom.* (1837) 5 To find the relation between E and F, the number of degrees and grades contained in the same angle BAC. **1968** *Times* 24 June 25/5 May I make a plea that the makers of theodolites cease producing circles marked in the sexagesimal system and use the metric system—that is, divide a right angle into 100 grades?

†**2.** One of a flight of steps; = DEGREE 1. *Obs.*$^{-1}$

1698 FRYER *Acc. E. India & P.* 286 Causeways..at every Tank ascended or descended by Marble Grades, while the Horse-way was sloped.

3. A step or stage in a process; rarely *spec.* a step in preferment. (Cf. DEGREE 2.)

1796 W. TAYLOR in *Monthly Rev.* XIX. 517 If a quantity of paper-money pass through all the successive grades of depreciation. **1798** —— in *Monthly Mag.* VI. 553 He was a skilful pupil, and had attained the highest grade of initiation. **1851** CARPENTER *Man. Phys.* (ed. 2) 238 That highest grade of development which it [the brain] possesses in Man. **1875** JOWETT *Plato* (ed. 2) IV. 403 The steps or grades by which he rises from sense and the shadows of sense to the idea of beauty and good. **1879** G. MEREDITH *Egoist* xxxix. (1889) 385 As a barrister, diplomatist, or a general, he would have won his grades. **1884** tr. *Lotze's Metaph.* 434 Countless different grades which it [the soul] traverses by degrees when first it is being formed.

4. a. A degree or position in the scale of rank, dignity, social station, eminence, proficiency, etc. (Cf. DEGREE 4.)

1808 E. S. BARRETT *Miss-led General* 32 At seventeen, having hopped, skipped, and jumped through all the inferior grades..he became colonel. **1830** HERSCHEL *Stud. Nat. Phil.* 67 If on comparing the *very* lowest states in civilized and savage life, we admit a difficulty in deciding to which the preference is due, at least in every superior grade we cannot hesitate a moment. *a* **1862** BUCKLE *Civiliz.* (1869) III. v. 288 Teachers of every grade, from village school-masters to tutors in private families. **1866** CRUMP *Banking* ii. 47 Unfortunate officers of all grades. **1868** J. H. BLUNT *Ref. Ch. Eng.* I. 396 The minor orders were holy orders as well as the three higher grades of the ministry. **1873** BURTON *Hist. Scot.* VI. lxxiii. 321 He was a man of an inferior grade and nature. **1890** BOLDREWOOD *Col. Reformer* (1891) 215 The companionship of some one nearly approaching his own grade.

b. A number of persons holding the same relative social rank or official dignity; a class.

1827 *Linc. & Lincolnsh. Cabinet* 7 Any artist skilled in delineating the lower grades of human life. **1837** DICKENS *Pickw.* ii, The solicitors' wives and the wine merchant's wife headed another grade. **1858** J. B. NORTON *Topics* 112 Regulating the numbers and grades to be withdrawn for staff employ. **1873** BURTON *Hist. Scot.* VI. lxvii. 101 Promotion in the higher grades of the Church. **1888** BRYCE *Amer. Commw.* II. xlix. 253 The public Schools..are everywhere and in all grades gratuitous. **1897** *Daily News* 24 Feb. 7/5 All grades of railway employés were now organized.

c. A class at school in relation to advancement. (Cf. GRADED *ppl. a.* 2.) *N. Amer.*

1835 *Southern Lit. Messenger* I. 275 In the first and second grades boys and girls are schooled together. **1852** *Indiana Hist. Soc. Publ.* III. 619 Qualified to teach in any of the grades, from the primary to the grammar school. **1903** A. B. HART *Actual Govt. Amer. Conditions* 543 Many cities have public kindergartens, which take children of 4 to 5 years of age in hand and teach them simple beginnings. The next division is usually the primary, extending over 3 to 6 years, followed by about 4 years of the grammar school; these two systems taken together are often called simply 'the grades'. **1904** O. H. LANG in *Forum* (U.S.) Oct. 268 Polite conduct and usages might advantageously be taught in the grades and in the high school. **1906** C. A. MCMURRY (*title*) Course of study in the eight grades. **1909** *Springfield* (Mass.) *Weekly Republican* 18 Feb. 2 In the British isles the classes are designated standards and these are supposed to correspond to our grades. **1934** W. SAROYAN *Daring Young Man* (1935) 75 A little girl named Maxine, in the third grade. **1967** *Atlantic Monthly* Apr. 102/2 My plan after being passed out of Grade VIII, King Edward School, was to go with my best girlfriend. **1968** *Globe & Mail* (Toronto) 3 Feb. 8/4 Ontario ..will have public French education from Grade 1 through university. **1970** *Publ. Amer. Dial. Soc. 1968* L. 50 Attended Memphis public schools. Completed fifth grade.

d. A mark (usu. alphabetical) indicating an assessment of the year's work, examination papers, etc., of a student.

1886 *Ann. Rep. Pres. Harvard 1885–6* 72 The marks received by a student in the several studies of his college course have until now been combined to determine the grade of his degree. **1889** *Harvard Faculty Rec.* 15 Oct., Any member of the graduating class who has attained Grade C or a higher grade in eighteen courses [etc.]. **1963** BARNARD & LAUWERYS *Handbk. Brit. Educ. Terms* 101 *Grading*, a method of placing pupils in groups according to their academic attainment in examinations or tests. Frequently five grades, named A, B, C, D, E, are used. **1964** MRS. L. B. JOHNSON *White House Diary* 10 June (1970) 163 Her grades were excellent and she planned to go to the University of Southwestern Louisiana. **1966** *Rep. Comm. Inquiry Univ. Oxf.* II. 68 Where more than three A levels in different subjects had been taken, the rating is based on the three best grades. *Ibid.* 463 Questionnaire for Schools Survey... What had been their performance in 'A' Level examinations (subjects attempted and grades achieved).

5. a. In things: A degree of comparative quality or value. **b.** A class of things, constituted by having the same quality or value.

1807 J. MARSHALL *Life of Washington* V. 213 To talents of the highest grade, he united a patient industry. **1816** U. BROWN *Jrnl.* in *Maryland Hist. Mag.* (1915) X. 274 Jack Oaks of the meanest grade. **1818** H. B. FEARON *Sk. Amer.* 30 Neither trades are (to use an Americanism) of the first grade. *Ibid.* 191 Because their neighbour's face was (to use their own phrase) a grade darker than their own. **1833** HT. MARTINEAU *Berkeley the Banker* I. v. 99 On either side of Miss Egg, various grades of tippets and bonnets. **1853** KINGSLEY *Hypatia* v. 60 The furniture of the chamber was but a grade above that of the artisan's. **1880** *Manch. Guard.* 27 Nov., Low grades [of cotton] are again decidedly dearer. **1884** *York Herald* 26 Aug. 7/2 Tea: The tone of the market is firm, and most grades are rather dearer. **1893** SELOUS *Trav. S.E. Africa* 354 The ore was of such low grade that it would not pay to work it.

c. ***grade A, Grade A***: of the highest grade in value, of the best or highest quality; hence *colloq.* (occas. ironically), extremely good, first-rate.

1911 *Proc. 5th Ann. Conf. Amer. Assoc. Medical Milk Commissions* 100 On or soon after the first of January 1912, there will be three grades of milk, A, B, and C. Grade A —for infants, children, and adults certified (or equivalent such as guaranteed)... Grade B—for adults only, Pasteurized... Grade C—for cooking purposes only. **1920** *Collier's* 20 Mar. 35/3 All you could see was her little peaches and grade A cream face stickin' out over the top. **1935** N. MITCHISON *We have been Warned* IV. 385 She'd always insisted on Grade A milk. **1936** A. THIRKELL *August Folly* i. 10 A very fine herd of cows which supply Grade A milk, at prices fixed by the Milk Marketing Board. **1942** O. NASH *Good Intentions* 45 Give me a grade-A May day. **1948** H. R. DAVIDSON *Prod. Market. Pigs* iv. 51 The 'basic price' was the price for a Grade C pig in each class. Bonuses above and reductions below the basic prices applied to Grades A and B and to D and E. **1968** R. STOUT *Father Hunt* (1969) xiv. 161 If the fingerprints didn't match we were left with a Grade A mess.

6. *Path.* Of a disease: Degree or condition of intensity.

1803 *Med. Jrnl.* X. 369 The subordinate forms and grades of fever, not arrested within forty-eight or seventy-two hours, invariably passed on to the malignant grade of disease. **1822–34** *Good's Study Med.* (ed. 4) I. 645 The captain..died with every symptom of the highest grade of yellow remittent fever. **1858** COPLAND *Dict. Pract. Med.* II. 444/2 Partial Insanity—the simpler forms and slighter grades of mental disorder. **1897** *Allbutt's Syst. Med.* II. 404 Those cases in which the fever attains a high grade.

7. With reference to animals: A result of cross-breeding, a hybrid. Now *techn.* in cattle-breeders' language, a variety of animal produced by crossing a native stock with a superior breed; also *attrib.*

1796 MORSE *Amer. Geog.* I. 196 The other sort is..the Ranging Bear, and seems to be a grade between the preceding and the wolf. **1851** J. F. W. JOHNSTON *Notes N. Amer.* I. vi. 164 Most of the stock are *grades*, as they are called, or crosses of the pure Devon bull with the older stock of the country. **1852** *Trans. Mich. Agric. Soc.* III. 142 A few full blood Saxons; the rest are a grade sheep. *Ibid.* 182 My cattle are yet grades, and am getting rid of them as fast as possible. *Ibid.* 184 One good grade sow. **1857** *Ibid.* VIII. 707 The greatest show, however, for number and size, was among the grades and natives. **1882** *Rep. Maine Board Agric.* XXVI. 168 In every dairy of six cows I would keep not less than two Jerseys, or their grades. **1883** C. WILSON in *Harper's Mag.* Jan. 272/2 Grade animals in a well-managed dairy can be made..quite as productive as thorough-breds. **1883** *Pall Mall G.* 21 Sept. 12/1 Hereford grade steer calves. **1891** *Daily News* 24 Nov. 5/4 There is room for a..trade in fat grade lambs between Canada and Britain. **1939** [see AFRIKANER 2]. **1945** *New England Homestead* 13 Oct. 9/2 If you mess around with breedin' purebreds a while longer you'll be so much in love that you'll never go back t' keepin' grades. **1949** *Caribbean Q.* I. II. 36 A small herd of grade red poll cattle was maintained. **1970** *Daily Nation* (Nairobi) 16 Jan. 17/4 Cattle rearing is not encouraging but grade cattle has [*sic*] been introduced in some areas.

8. *Zool.* **a.** In the genetic classification of animals, a group constituted by the fact that its members are presumed to have branched from the common stem at about the same point of its development.

1877 E. R. LANKESTER *Notes on Embryology*, etc. in *Qly. Jrnl. Microsc. Sci.* New Ser. XVII. 440 [The writer refers to *grade* as a new term introduced by himself.] Whilst all other terms indicate branches of the pedigree diverging from a very nearly common point..the various 'grades' are introduced to separate the starting-points of the branches; a certain advance in differentiation of structure separates the branches of a higher grade from those of a lower.

b. A group of animals at a similar level of development, but not necessarily having a common genetic origin. Cf. CLADE *sb.*²

1957 J. S. HUXLEY in *Nature* 7 Sept. 455/2 Stasi-genesis results in the formation of delimitable and persistent anagenetic units, or grades. **1958** —— in *Uppsala Univ. Årsskrift* VI. 27 The best general term for such anagenetic units would seem to be *grade*. **1961** G. G. SIMPSON *Princ. Animal Taxon.* iv. 126 That grade is..now known to have been reached independently by a considerable number of different clades. **1967** R. E. BLACKWELDER *Taxon.* xiii. 220 It is not uncommon to interpolate such levels as Branch, Grade, and Series between Subkingdom and Phyla.

9. *Philol.* **a.** The position occupied in an ablaut-series by a particular vowel or form of a root. **b.** Applied (after Grimm's use of G. *grad*) to denote the class of a consonant as 'tenuis' or 'media' (see quot. 1872). *rare*$^{-1}$.

1872 BEAMES *Comp. Gram. Aryan Lang. India* I. iii. 190 Initial consonants retain the grade of each organ in the purest and truest way..By the expression 'grade' must be understood the two classes of tenues and mediæ. **1891** MAYHEW *O.E. Phonology* p. xvi, The double colon (::) occurring between forms of words, is used to indicate 'ablaut' or change of grade in a vowel series.

10. *U.S.* **a.** In a road, railway, etc: Amount of inclination to the horizontal; rate of ascent or descent; = GRADIENT *sb.*

1835 *Jrnl. Franklin Inst.* XV. 230 From whence it [the route of a proposed railroad] continues in nearly a direct course, rising at a grade of about twenty feet to the mile. **1840** TANNER *Canals & Rail Roads U.S.* 78 The grades vary from a level to an inclination of 1 in 330. **1888** BRYCE *Amer. Commw.* III. VI. cxiv. 641 A railroad line of gentle grade. **1898** in *Westm. Gaz.* 19 Jan. 2/1 The relations that should exist between the grade of a sewer, its size, and the volume of flush water required to produce a given effect. **1898** in *Daily News* 81 May 10/3 The river you enter after leaving Lake Lebarge..has a big grade.

b. An inclined portion of a railway or road; a slope, an ascent or descent. Also DOWN GRADE, UP GRADE.

1811 *Deb. Congress U.S.* (1853) 8 May 2171/1 Each grade of the [Cumberland] road to be perfectly levelled. **1850** R. GLISAN *Jrnl. Army Life* (1874) ii. 12 The cars are moved on these heavy grades by stationary engines. **1861** *Harper's Mag.* Jan. 147/1 The descent of the 'grade' was the next rough feature in our day's journey... The trail on the grade was slippery with sleet, and walking upon it was out of the question. **1883** *Times* 27 Mar. 3/6 Owing to the incomplete condition of the grades previously made..rapid progress could not be made. **1888** *Scribner's Mag.* Aug. 191 Jack never tires of telling what his engine did when 'she was going up Rattlesnake Grade'. **1890** BOLDREWOOD *Col. Reformer* (1891) 150 The..rush of the express train..adown the flying grades. **1895** *Daily News* 10 Sept. 3/5 A passenger train went off the rails at the bottom of a downward grade. **1896** R. KIPLING *Seven Seas* 57 His whistle waked the snow-bound grade.

fig. **1893** *Daily News* 26 June 2/5 Trade is on the upward grade.

c. *U.S. local.* In mining districts: A portion of road.

1877 RAYMOND *Statist. Mines & Mining* 278 The surface works of the mine are situated about 300 feet above the 'grade', or stage-road. **1883** STEVENSON *Silverado Sq.* 70 Entered the Toll road, or, to be more local, entered on 'the grade'.

d. *Physical Geogr.* The condition of a river in which, after initial down-cutting of its bed, further down-cutting is balanced by aggradation; a state of equilibrium between the erosion of material from a river-bed and the deposition of fresh sediment; also, the profile of a river or part of one throughout which this condition exists; ***at grade***, in this condition.

In quots. 1876, 1894 the sense is closer to 'slope' (GRADE *sb.* 10).

[**1876** G. K. GILBERT in *Amer. Jrnl. Sci.* CXII. 100 In this way a stream, which has a supply of debris equal to its capacity, tends to build up the gentler slopes of its bed and cut away the steeper. It tends to establish a single, uniform grade. **1894** W. M. DAVIS in *Jrnl. Geol.* II. 78 In certain cases, it seems to be possible for a stream to cut down its profile to a gentler grade in its early adolescence than is suitable to later adolescence and maturity.] **1902** —— in *Ibid.* X. 89 The use of 'grade', in the sense here advocated, was almost reached by Gilbert. *Ibid.* 92 The development of grade depends on the spontaneous adjustment of the capacity of a river to do work, and the quantity of work to be done by the river. **1934** C. R. LONGWELL et al. *Outl. Physical Geol.* iii. 42 In places where there is an approximate balance between erosion and deposition, the stream is said to be graded or at grade. **1936** *Geogr. Jrnl.* LXXXVII. 25 At least twice the river cut down to grade and had begun to widen its channel when rejuvenation forced it to trench further. **1942**

O. D. VON ENGELN *Geomorphol.* viii. 134 Maintenance of grade consists of a continuous, infinite series of adjustments between volume, slope, and sediment supply. **1963** D. W. & E. E. HUMPHRIES tr. *Termier's Erosion & Sedimentation* v. 106 The profile is actually a composite curve, showing breaks at each important confluence and irregularities caused by the nature of the rocks which it crosses. It is a uniform slope varying regularly, a 'grade'. **1970** O. T. JONES in G. H. DURY *Rivers & River Terraces* iii. 75 Between Carmarthen and Fanog the Towy is graded to present sea-level, and the tributaries which enter it are at grade with the existing river.

e. ***to make the grade***: to reach the proper standard, to be successful. orig. *U.S.*

1912 J. SANDILANDS *West. Canadian Dict.* 20 Make the grade, make the running. **1921** S. FORD *Inez & Trilby May* ix. 168 It's Gwendolyn that's got to do the hustling. Three days! I doubt if she can make the grade. **1922** *Collier's* 7 Oct. 5/1, I don't think he can make the grade. **1930** *Publishers' Weekly* 5 July 29/1 Can the seasonal bookshop make the grade, and under what conditions? **1932** A. D. POWELL *Venusberg* xxxiii. 235 How will it feel when the Recording Angel calls your bluff for the last time? How many of us will make the grade? **1958** *Listener* 9 Oct. 568/3 A would-be thief who cannot make the grade. **1958** *Times* 24 Oct. 14/7 Word spread quickly round the village: my cottage had made the grade.

11. Of a surface: Degree of altitude; level. *rare.* ***at grade*** (U.S.): on the same level.

1849 *Acts & Resolves Prov. Mass. Bay* 126 Number of public ways crossed at grade, Number of railroads crossed at grade. **1851** C. L. SMITH tr. *Tasso* I. lxxv, Swollen beyond his wonted grade, That river.. O'ertops his banks. **1869** *Congress. Globe* 24 Mar. 252/3 Does not the junction road.. cross the streets.. at grade?.. No, sir; it crosses them above grade in nearly every instance. **1880** FITZGIBBON *Trip to Manitoba* xiv. 164 The immense cost of filling up and levelling to bring the line to the proper grade. **1890** *Boston* (Mass.) *Jrnl.* 26 Aug. 4/2 Petition.. for leave to cross the Grand Trunk tracks at North Stratford at grade.

12. *Comb.*, **grade-crossing** *N. Amer.*, a place where a road and a railway, or two railways cross each other at the same level, a level crossing; **grade line** (see quot.); **grade school** = *graded school* (see GRADED *ppl. a.*[1]); **grade teacher** *N. Amer.*, a teacher in a grade school.

1890 *Boston Jrnl.* 26 Aug. 4/2 (*caption*) Want a *Grade Crossing. **1894** STEAD *If Christ came to Chicago* 2 The spot of green light which arrests traffic across the grade crossing of the railway. **1906** *Daily Colonist* (Victoria, B.C.) 27 Jan. 2/4 (*heading*) Fatal Grade Crossing Accident. **1840** TANNER *Canals & Rail Roads U.S.* 249 **Grade line*, or profile, is a prescribed line which governs the construction of a rail-road. **1869** *Daily News* 20 Dec., At a meeting of the Social Science Association.. a paper will be read by Mr. Edwin Pears, 'On *Grade Schools, and on Scholarships between Primary and Grade Schools, and to the Universities'. **1967** *Boston Globe* 5 Apr. 51/6 The Celtics have been the greatest since Muhammad Ali was in grade school. **1970** *New Yorker* 14 Nov. 209/1 College, high-school, and grade-school teaching is unsatisfactory almost everywhere. **1906** *Springfield* (Mass.) *Weekly Republican* 12 Apr. 6 The *grade teachers attempting little.. except setting the class to sing music already familiar. **1909** G. STRATTON-PORTER *Girl of Limberlost* ix. 165 She gathered.. all sorts of natural history specimens and sold them to the grade teachers.

†**grade**, *v.*[1] *Obs. rare*$^{-1}$. [aphetic form of DEGRADE.] *trans.* To degrade.

a **1400–50** *Alexander* 2430 (Dublin MS.) Thar as he giltyd me ayayns, I hym gradit haue.

grade (greɪd), *v.*[2] [f. GRADE *sb.*]

†**1.** *trans.* To admit to a (specified) degree at a University. *Obs.*$^{-1}$

1563 FOXE *A. & M.* 403/1 Returning the same yere, he was graded doctor, at the expences of elector Frederick, according to the solempne manner of scholes.

†**2.** To lay out (the plan of a country) by degrees of latitude and longitude. *Obs. rare*$^{-1}$.

1600 HAIES in Hakluyt *Voy.* III. 152 Also some obserued the eleuation of the pole, and drewe plats of the countrey exactly graded.

3. a. To arrange or place in grades or classes; to class (persons, schools, etc.) according to dignity, merit, or advancement; to sort (produce) according to quality; to determine the grades or degrees of.

1659 EEDES *Wisdom's Justif.* 34 They that turn many to righteousness shall be graded in glory accordingly. **1880** FITCH *Lect. Teaching* (1881) 48 When Schools are rightly graded each will have its own complete and characteristic course. **1882** *Harper's Mag.* Dec. 123/2 Seats were graded according to rank in the churches. **1884–5** *Riverside Nat. Hist.* (1888) IV. 179 Grading our groups on a somewhat different principle.. we include the two species of boat-bill .. in the sub-family Cochleariinæ. **1885** *Pall Mall G.* 13 June 6/1 It is a comparatively simple matter to grade American wheat. **1889** MARG. LEE *Faithf. & Unf.* xi. 125 He despises Maud, and grades me with her. **1890** *Westm. Rev.* Apr. 351 Society grades the wrong of killing, and gives names to the degrees.

b. To blend with other things, so as to affect the grade or quality of.

1889 *Times* 23 Oct. 5/4 Cider.. is again graded with other apple juices, so as to produce either sweet or dry cider.

c. To colour with shades or tints which pass insensibly one into another.

1871 [see GRADING *vbl. sb.* a]. **1882** *Athenæum* 7 Jan. 23/1 The sky is tenderly graded from the vapours of the horizon to the clear blue of the zenith. **1893** BAILDON *Rescue*, etc. 81 Pencilled, painted, grained and graded.

d. *intr.* Of produce: To take a specified grade.

1891 *N.Y. Tribune* 30 Oct. 7/3 (Funk) They have had no frost and the wheat is grading nearly all No. 1 hard.

4. *trans.* To reduce (the line of a road, railway, or canal) to levels or practicable gradients.

1835 [see GRADING *vbl. sb.* c]. **1840** TANNER *Canals & Rail Roads U.S.* 155 The line is graded for two tracks, only one of which.. has been laid down. **1870** EMERSON *Soc. & Solit., Civiliz.* Wks. (Bohn) III. 8 When the Indian trail gets widened, graded, and bridged to a good road, there is a benefactor. **1881** HUGHES *Rugby, Tennessee* 49 His duties.. in grading and superintending the walks, interfered with the garden. **1888** BRYCE *Amer. Commw.* II. II. li. 287 Cities were .. compelled to grade, pave, and sewer streets without inhabitants.

absol. **1858** *Times* 25 Aug. 6/3 We are sending out men.. to survey, to level, to grade.

fig. **1870** LOWELL *Among my Bks.* Ser. I. (1873) 263 Hugh Peter grades the sharp descent from the apostolic to the practical with an et cetera.

5. *Stock-breeding.* To cross with some better breed. ***to grade up***: to improve the breed of (stock) by grading.

1873 *Rep. Vermont Board Agric.* II. 92 He.. thought he should improve the color of his butter by grading his herd with Jersey blood. **1887** F. FRANCIS Jr. *Saddle & Mocassin* ix. 161 It encourages you to go to the expense of turning in good bulls and grading up your stock.

6. *Philol.* In *passive*: To be altered by gradation or ablaut.

1887 SKEAT *Princ. Eng. Etymol.* x. §155. 170 The Teut. E may be 'graded' to A on the one hand, and O on the other.

7. In occasional uses: **a.** To wear *away* the surface of so as to produce a regular slope. **b.** To cut (steps) at regular intervals.

1841 CATLIN *N. Amer. Ind.* (1844) I. x. 69 By the action of water, the country seems to have been graded away. **1896** HOWELLS *Impressions & Exp.* 230, I.. mount some steps graded in the rock at one place.

8. *intr.* To pass imperceptibly from one grade *into* another. Also with *down, off, over, toward, up.* Also, ***to grade up***: to take rank with a higher grade or class (cf. 5); ***to grade up with***: to compare with, to be like.

1892 R. D. SALISBURY in *Ann. Rep. Geol. Surv. New Jersey 1891* 74 While the drumlin type is fairly distinct, drumlins grade into hills which are not drumlins. **1903** *Harper's Mag.* July 186 The type graded downward into the lower invertebrates. **1907** 'O. HENRY' *Heart of West* i. 5 When a man marries a queen he ought to grade up with her. **1921** *Brit. Mus. Return* 157 Rock-crystal grading into quartzite, from.. Minas Geraes, Brazil. **1922** C. E. MULFORD *Black Buttes* xiv. 227 Strikes me funny, though, the way they [*sc.* the new cattle] grade up. **1925** ODELL in E. F. Norton *Fight for Everest, 1924* 292 This granite.. frequently graded off into pegmatite. **1927** HALDANE & HUXLEY *Anim. Biol.* ix. 198 The activity grades down from one pole of the egg to the other. **1943** J. S. HUXLEY *Evol. Ethics* iv. 26 Ethics grades over into the prescriptions of totem and tabu. **1952** P. ABRAHAMS *Path of Thunder* II. ii. 91 If the whites and the black people were equal, if there were no colour bar, if a black man could go to Parliament and had all the same rights as a white man, and the Coloured people wanted to grade toward the whites, then it would be all right. **1971** *Nature* 1 Jan. 16/1 Basalt, up to 2 km thick, grades downwards into gabbro and metamorphic rocks.

9. To read and mark (a student's paper) with a grade.

1931 H. F. PRINGLE *Theodore Roosevelt* I. iii. 37 Lodge.. graded their papers with undue severity. **1948** *Christian Sci. Monitor* 22 Apr. 4/3 The robot prof. is a machine that automatically grades homework and examination papers, at the rate of 10 a minute.

-grade, an adj. suffix repr. L. *-gradus* stepping, walking (f. stem of *gradus* step, *gradī* to step, walk), occurring in a few L. compounds, e.g. *retrōgradus* RETROGRADE, *tardigradus* TARDIGRADE. Hence in mod.L. scientific formations, as *digitigradus* DIGITIGRADE, *plantigradus* PLANTIGRADE.

gradeability (greɪdəˈbɪlɪtɪ). [GRADE *sb.* + ABILITY.] The ability of a vehicle to climb a gradient at an efficient speed.

1952 *Automobilist* Jan. 10 Hill climbing. Per cent of gradeability. Synthetic rubber tires 4·3%... Winterized mud-snow tires 7·6%... Tire chains 23·5%. **1959** *Chambers's Encycl.* IX. 572/1 Even though a vehicle may have a relatively poor top gear 'gradeability' it must still be able to climb all ordinary road gradients with its full load on low gear. **1967** *Jane's Surface Skimmer Systems 1967–68* 99/1 Characteristics.. Gradeability, forward slope 60%. Gradeability, side slope 30%.

graded (ˈgreɪdɪd), *ppl. a.* [f. GRADE *sb.* and *v.*[2] + -ED.]

1. a. Formed like a flight of steps.

1850 *Ecclesiologist* XI. 113 Three graded sedilia.. with trefoiled heads. **1865** *Athenæum* No. 1984. 612/3 A graded, low, broad wall. **1874** J. THOMSON *City Dreadful Nt.* xxi. (1880) 52 The bronze colossus of a wingèd Woman Upon a graded granite base foursquare.

b. *Her.* Of a cross: = DEGRADED *ppl. a.*[2]

1874 *Papworth's Coats of Arms* 607/1 Arg., a cross graded of three sa.—Wyntworth. **1894** *Parker's Gloss. Her.* 161 s.v. *Cross.*

2. Divided or arranged according to grades of rank, quality, etc. ***graded school*** (chiefly U.S.): 'a school divided into departments taught by different teachers, in which the children pass from the lower departments to the higher as they advance in education' (*Cent. Dict.*).

1859 *Amer. Cycl.* V. 553/2 A system of graded schools for each town. **1867** *Nation* (N.Y.) 12 Sept. 207 He especially recommends that our system of graded schools be imitated in the large towns of England. **1873–6** JENKIN *Electr. & Magnet.* (ed. 3) 197 Sir William Thomson has given the name of graded galvanometer to an instrument constructed as above, and [etc.]. **1877** BLACKIE *Wise Men* 32 Thus earth and fire, the heavy and the light, Are bound together by the graded kinds of air and water.

3. Of a road, etc.: Reduced to levels or practicable gradients.

1840 TANNER *Canals and Rail Roads U.S.* 151 The graded surface of the road. **1847** EMERSON *Repr. Men, Napoleon* Wks. (Bohn) I. 371 'There shall be no Alps', he said; and he built his perfect roads, climbing by graded galleries their steepest precipices. **1857** R. TOMES *Amer. in Japan* iii. 82 Here are to be found wide and well-graded streets. **1882** W. H. BISHOP in *Harper's Mag.* Dec. 60/2 A half mile of graded road-bed alone remains.

4. Of cattle: Improved by crossing with a superior breed.

1876 H. T. WILLIAMS *Pacific Tourist* 185/2 The immense range fenced in at this point is occupied by a select herd of graded stock. **1879** *U.S. Dept. Agric. Spec. Rep., No. 12. Invest. Dis. Swine* 187 The graded calves of this county have this year suffered severely by a disease called black-leg. **1887** F. FRANCIS Jr. *Saddle & Mocassin* ix. 161 Graded cattle are more valuable, ain't they?

5. *Physical Geogr.* Of a river or its profile: at grade (see GRADE *sb.* 10 d); having attained grade.

1894 W. M. DAVIS in *Jrnl. Geol.* II. 77 Mr. Gilbert has recently suggested to me that a stream in this condition of balance between degrading and aggrading might be called a graded stream; and its slope, a graded slope. **1934** C. R. LONGWELL et al. *Outl. Physical Geol.* iii. 42 When a part of a main stream reaches grade, the local tributaries soon become graded with respect to it. **1944** A. HOLMES *Princ. Physical Geol.* x. 154 When the profile is developed so that it everywhere provides the necessary minimum gradient, it is called a graded profile or a profile of equilibrium. **1946** L. D. STAMP *Britain's Struct.* v. 47 A river tends to reach a state of equilibrium and its longitudinal profile will form a smooth curve from source to mouth. When it reaches this stage a river is said to be graded. **1970** [see GRADE *sb.* 10 d].

gradely (ˈgreɪdlɪ), *a.* Now only *dial.* Also †**graithly.** Forms: α. 3 **græi[þ]lich, greiðlic,** 4 **grathly, graythely, greiþli,** 9 *dial.* **grathely.** β. *dial.* 8 **greidly,** 8–9 **greadl(e)y,** 9 **graadly, graid(e)l(e)y, gradely.** [ME. *greiðlic*, a. ON. *greiðlig-r*, f. *greið-r* GRAITH *a.* + *-lig-r* -LY[1].]

1. Of persons, their actions and attributes.

†**a.** in early use, with somewhat uncertain meaning: ? Ready, prompt. *Obs.*

c **1205** LAY. 445 þene king he grette mid greiðlicre speche. *Ibid.* 10039 Bruttes heo gretten mid græi[þ]lichen worden. *a* **1375** *Joseph Arim.* 88 Heo grauntede þenne to ben at his grace; And sone aftur þat gretnede þat greiþli mayde.

b. in mod. dialectal use, a general term of commendation; chiefly with reference to character: Decent, respectable, worthy; *occas.* of a girl, comely, good-looking. Also, 'regular', thorough.

c **1746** J. COLLIER (Tim Bobbin) *View Lanc. Dial.* Wks. (1862) 67 Yed's os greadly o Lad as needs t' knep oth' Hem of a keke. **1781** J. HUTTON *Tour to Caves* Gloss., Greidly, well-meaning, or any thing good in its kind. **1790** MRS. WHEELER *Westmld. Dial.* (1821) 48 Hees rackend a varra graadly man. **1840** S. BAMFORD *Life of Radical* xiii. 84 Yore a graidley felley for owt 'at I kno' to th' contrary. **1866** WAUGH *Home Life Factory Folk* xi. 105 Thoose hens.. rooten abeawt th' heawse just th' same as greadley Christians. **1877** MRS. F. H. BURNETT *That Lass o' Lowrie's* (1887) 31 He's a graidely foo', he is.

c. *predicatively* (cf. the *adv.*). Well in health.

1851 C. BRONTE *Let.* in *C. B. & her Circle* (1896) 312 Her beloved papa and mama.. are living and 'gradely'. **1865** LAYCOCK *Mi Gronfeyther* in Harland *Lanc. Lyrics* 192 He never wur gradely no moor. **1877** MRS. F. H. BURNETT *That Lass o' Lowrie's* (1887) 170 I'm feelin' a trifle graidelier than I ha' done.. Things is lookin up.

2. Of things: **a.** Excellent, suitable, handsome.

a **1300** *Cursor M.* 18409 Hu come þe sa grathli gode þat þou on schuldre bers a rode? ? *a* **1400** *Morte Arth.* 187 Gumbaldes graythely, fulle gracious to taste. **1863** KINGSLEY *Water-Bab.* 12 This is a hard road for a gradely foot like that. **1865** *Hard Times* in Harland *Lanc. Lyrics* 305 Th'art nooan so feaw, yet, wench, if thae'd gradely clooas to wear. **1877** MRS. F. H. BURNETT *That Lass o' Lowrie's* (1887) 189 It's the graideliest book tha ivver seed.

b. in mod. dial. use: Real, proper.

18.. *Three Dial. by Toddle* 19 My gradely name is Harry Shareall. **1865** WAUGH *Lanc. Songs* 9 But aw've no gradely comfort, my lass, Except wi' yon childer and thee. **1865** RAMSBOTTOM *Gooin' to Schoo'* in Harland *Lanc. Lyrics* 302 A gradely plague it's bin to me—It's been a gradely blessin' too.

Hence †**ˈgradeliness.**

c **1425** *St. Elizabeth of Spalbeck* in *Anglia* VIII. 115/30 Wiþ fulle deuoute sighynges and goostly greydlynes.. abidynge mekely þe comynge of hir sauyoure.

gradely (ˈgreɪdlɪ), *adv.* Now only *dial.* Also †**graithly.** Forms: α. 4 **graitli, grayþ(e)ly,** 4–5 **grayth(e)ly,** 4–6 **grath(e)ly,** 7 *dial.* **greathly,** (4 **gra(i)þeli, graith(e)li, grathli, grayþliche, graytli, -ly, gre(i)þli, greythly,** 6 *Sc.* **graithlie**). β. 4 **graideli,** 5 **graidly, greidly,** 8–9 **greadly,** 9 **gradeley, graidely,** 6– **gradely.** [ME. *grayþly, graydely*, a. ON. *greiðliga*, f. *greið-r* GRAITH *a.*]

†**1.** Promptly, readily. *Obs.*

a **1300** *Cursor M.* 741 Graitli taght he him þe gin How he suld at þe wif be-gin. **13..** *E.E. Allit. P.* B. 341 Ful grayþely gotz þis god man & dos godez hestes. *c* **1350** *Will. Palerne* 948 But ȝe graunt him ȝour grace, him greiþli to help.. his liif nel nouȝt for langour, last til to-morwe. *c* **1400** *Ywaine & Gaw.* 3208 Graithly hit he tham ogayn. **1450–70** *Golagros & Gaw.* 54 Grant me, lord, on yone gait graithly to gay.

2. Carefully, exactly; properly; quite, really; well.

1340 Hampole *Pr. Consc.* 645 Behalde..graythely and loke. **1393** Langl. *P. Pl.* C. xxi. 324 Hit is nat greythly getyn, ther gyle is þe rote. *c* **1400** Maundev. (Roxb.) xv. 70 Þe whilk..descryued me þe maners of oþer cuntrees.. graythely and..verraily. *c* **1460** *Towneley Myst.* xv. 152 Tent thou to that page grathly. **1515** Barclay *Egloges* iv. (1570) c. iv/3 If thou haue all these thou mayst grathly carpe. **1585** Jas. I *Ess. Poesie* (Arb.) 14 Let Readers think they fele the burning heat, And graithly see the earth [etc.]. **1597** Montgomerie *Cherrie & Slae* 327 Quhais schaddow is in the river schew, Als graithlie glancing, as they grew. **1674** Ray *N.C. Words, Greathly,* handsomely, towardly. *c* **1746** J. Collier (Tim Bobbin) *View Lanc. Dial.* Wks. (1862) 51, I cannaw tell thee greadly. **1850** *N. & Q.* Ser. i. II. 334/2 Most frequently it is precisely equivalent to 'very', as in the expression a gradely fine day. **1865** R. R. Bealey *My Johnny* in Harland *Lanc. Lyrics* 89 Aw dunnot like to think o' that, An' yet it's gradely true. **1865** Waugh *Lanc. Songs* 70 For when hoo's gradely donned, hoo'll look As grand as th' queen o' Shayba.

grader (ˈgreɪdə(r)). [f. grade *v.*[2] + -er[1].]

1. A person employed: **a.** in grading produce (see grade *v.*[2]); **b.** in grading roads (see grade *v.*[2] 4).

a. **1889** *Columbus* (Ohio) *Dispatch* 22 Nov., Graders whose business is to classify cotton for English markets. **1893** *Westm. Gaz.* 7 Mar. 9/3 The wool was duly delivered..and a large number of graders put to work preparing it for cleaning.

b. **1870** *Times* 5 Sept. 5 Track-laying will be commenced next week, and will be pushed forward after the graders as fast as the iron is received. **1883** W. H. Bishop in *Harper's Mag.* 825/2 The grader of streets will probably follow the.. mining capitalist.

2. A machine for 'grading' (in various senses).

1868 *Rep. U.S. Commissioner Agric.* (1869) 361 The side tracks [should be] kept in order by the use of the grader. [*Plate,* Improved Rut Scraper and Grading Machine.] **1884** Knight *Dict. Mech.* Suppl., *Grader* (Railway). A temporary track is laid, and from a platform and caboose car on this track a double plow is rigged out to throw up a track. *Ibid., Grader,* an earth scraper. **1888** *Wine, Spirit & Beer* 8 Mar. 142/2 The machine consists of two separate frames, one containing the half-corn separator, feed-hopper and elevator, and the other the grader. **1953** R. J. C. Atkinson *Field Archaeol.* (ed. 2) ii. 58 For stripping large areas a bulldozer or grader is to be preferred. **1963** A. Lubbock *Austral. Roundabout* 11 The roads are kept up by a 'grader', a kind of steamroller with a wide scraper attached in front. **1963** *Field Archaeol.* (Ordnance Survey) (ed. 4) 14 When a grader is removing topsoil as a preliminary to the extension of a chalk pit it may reveal ditches, post-holes, beam slots, rubbish pits [etc.]. **1971** *Timber Trades Jrnl.* 21 Aug. 26/2 No grading machine is in operation at present in Sweden, but the major sawmillers are actively studying the potential offered by machine graders.

Gradgrind (ˈgrædgraɪnd). Name of the mill-owner in Dickens's *Hard Times* (1854), 'a man of facts and calculations', used allusively for: one who is hard and cold, and solely interested in facts. Hence **ˈGradgrinding, ˈGradgrindery.**

1855 *Putnam's Mag.* Jan. 76/2 There have not been wanting travelled Gradgrinds to assure us that the song from his lips was a humbug and a sham. **1871** E. Eggleston *Hoosier Schoolmaster* (1872) v. 37 You, my Gradgrind friend, you think me sentimental. **1920** *Glasgow Herald* 14 Aug. 5 A..metropolis of ant-like industry and social Gradgrindery. **1924** *Ibid.* 18 Apr. 8 A nation of Gradgrinds, immersed in work and money-getting, and denying themselves and their employees any opportunity of recreation. **1925** *Public Opinion* 7 Aug. 122/1 The gradgrinding system. **1927** *United Free Ch. Mission Rec.* Sept. 379/2 These self-appointed Gradgrinds seem to imagine that their actions are pleasing to the Almighty. **1958** R. Williams *Culture & Society* i. v. 94 Public commissions, Blue Books, Parliamentary legislation—all these, in the world of *Hard Times*—are Gradgrindery. **1968** *Listener* 25 July 124/1 Sidney and Beatrice [Webb] instructed Asquith, Balfour, Churchill... Gradgrinds they may have been—it is Beatrice's own self-description—but one cannot deny them greatness. **1971** *Where?* Oct. 308/1 The interest motif can be just as bewildering as Gradgrindery, and it should be put into reverse; namely, it is the teacher's task to make interesting *that which is relevant.*

gradi, gradiate, obs. ff. greedy, graduate.

gradient (ˈgreɪdɪənt), *a.* and *sb.* [ad. L. *gradient-em* pr. pple. of *gradī* to walk, f. *grad-us* step.]

A. *adj.*

1. a. Of animals: Characterized by taking steps with the feet, as their distinctive mode of progression; walking, ambulant.

1641 Wilkins *Math. Magick* ii. iv. (1648) 174 Amongst these gradient Automata, that iron spider mentioned in Walchius is more especially remarkable. **1663** R. Boyle *Usef. Exp. Nat. Philos.* i. ii. 40 But it is not so conspicuous in gradient animals (if I may so speak) as in swimming ones. **1668** Wilkins *Real Char.* 161 Oviparous Beasts..Gradient; having four feet. **1822** T. Taylor *Apuleius* 300 There are animals adapted to the several parts, the volant living in the air, and the gradient on the earth.

b. *Her.* Said of a tortoise depicted as walking.

1780 Edmondson *Her.* II. Gloss. **1828–40** Berry *Encycl. Her.* I.

2. Of a railway line: Rising or descending by regular degrees of inclination. *rare*$^{-0}$. (? A figment.)

1855 in Ogilvie, Suppl. Hence in mod. Dicts.

B. *sb.*

1. a. Of a road or railway: Amount of inclination to the horizontal; degree of slope; = grade *sb.* 10.

This sense can hardly have been evolved from that of the Lat. pple. or the Eng. adj.; possibly it was a new formation on *grade,* after the supposed analogy of *quotient.*

1835 *Railway Mag.* Dec. 264 The line of Railroad here proposed..passing over the most easy and beautiful tract of country..with the most favourable gradients. **1836** *Dubl. Rev.* May 225 In describing the gradients of a railway, it is usual to state the rise per mile in feet. **1836** *Mech. Mag.* 6 Aug. XXV. 317 In a contemporary journal there appears a violent tirade against the word gradient as at present used by civil engineers. **1861** Smiles *Engineers* II. 429 One in thirty being about the severest gradient at any part of the road. **1868** Peard *Water-Farm.* xi. 111 Wherever they have been constructed on a gradient of 1 in 9..they have answered admirably. **1880** Haughton *Phys. Geog.* v. 241 The uniformly increasing gradient with which the pampas everywhere rise. **1884** *American* VIII. 86 The road was built with needlessly steep gradients.

fig. **1868** W. H. Dixon *Spirit Wives* I. xv. 159 That duality in the soul of nature..led by an easy gradient into a state of manners, as between brother and sister, which [etc.].

b. A part of a road which slopes upward or downward; a portion of a way not level.

1845 *Rep. Brit. Assoc. 1844* ii. 96 It was necessary that that railway should present long and very steep gradients. **1915** R. B. Holt *Tramway Track Constr. & Maintenance* ix. 114 The wear on the rails on all parts of the gradient, both on the up track and on the down track, is exceedingly irregular. **1971** *Homes & Gardens* Aug. 90/1 The train..could be heard puffing like an old man, 'Chuff, chuff, chuff', as it travelled up the gradient approaching the cutting. **1971** *Daily Tel.* (Colour Suppl.) 27 Aug. 12/3 Snow drove into our faces and on the steep gradients where skis had to be removed we stumbled in deep powder.

2. *transf.* Orig., the proportional amount of rise or fall of the barometer or thermometer in passing from one region to another. Now in wider use: a continuous increase or decrease in the magnitude of any quantity or property along a line from one point to another; also, the rate of this change, expressed as the change in magnitude per unit change in distance.

The 'barometric gradient' is expressed in hundredths of an inch to a degree of a great circle; thus 'a gradient of 4 means that over a distance of 60 nautical miles, the barometer rises $\frac{4}{100}$ or $\frac{1}{25}$ of an inch' (Huxley *Physiogr.* 95).

1870 Everett *Deschanel's Nat. Philos.* xiii. 168 Generally speaking, the wind blows from regions of high to regions of low barometer, and with greater force as the barometric gradient is steeper. **1876** Tait *Rec. Adv. Phys. Sci.* xi. 263 The temperature will fall off by a uniform gradient. **1878** Huxley *Physiogr.* 95 If the isobars run close together it shows that the gradient is high, and therefore the winds will be strong. **1880** *Times* 11 Aug. 11/6 Gradients for westerly winds lay over Scotland, and for easterly winds over the Bay of Biscay. **1882** *Nature* XXVI. 11 The primary cause of cyclones, according to Ferrel, is a horizontal temperature gradient. **1886** J. A. Fleming *Short Lect. Electr. Artisans* vii. 122 Along the lead there is a regular fall or gradient of [electrical] pressure. **1892** W. Peddie *Man. Physics* ix. 132 The rate of variation of density per unit of length is *r*... The quantity *r* is generally called the 'concentration-gradient'. **1898** *Proc. R. Soc.* LXIII. 364 The kathode fall is constant for all pressures and currents whilst the potential gradient along the rest of the tube is variable. **1902** Poynting & Thomson *Prop. Matter* xviii. 205 The ratio of the stress to the velocity gradient is called the viscosity of the fluid. **1910** *Encycl. Brit.* V. 891/2 This outflow of heat necessitates a rise of temperature with increase of depth. The corresponding gradient is of the order of 1°C. in 100 ft. **1948** Glasstone *Textbk. Physical Chem.* (ed. 2) iv. 260 The gradient is actually negative, that is the concentration decreases from left to right. **1957** *Encycl. Brit.* X. 681/2 He proposed to measure the rate of change or gradients in the gravitational field. **1962** A. R. W. Hayes *Revision Physics* 98 We must measure..the uniform temperature gradient along the bar—found from readings of thermometers placed in mercury ..in holes bored in the specimen. **1970** *Nature* 19 Dec. 1225/1 There is a gradient of dormancy within the spikelet, the larger proximal seed being less dormant than the smaller distal seed, while a much smaller third seed..is extremely dormant.

b. *spec.* in *Embryol.,* such an increase or decrease, along an axis of an organism or a part, in the potential for developing into an organ or in a related bodily process.

1911 [see *axial gradient*]. **1915** C. M. Child *Individuality in Organisms* iii. 65 Gradients in rate of cell division, size of cells, condition or amount of protoplasm in the cells, rate of growth, and rate and sequence of differentiation are very characteristic features of both animal and plant development. Such gradients are definitely related to the axes of the individual or its parts, and are..expressions of axial metabolic gradients. **1924** Bellamy & Child in *Proc. R. Soc.* B. XCVI. 141 In a protoplasm of specific hereditary constitution, such a gradient is adequate as the initiating factor in the axial differentiation characteristic of that species. **1927** [see field *sb.* 17 c]. **1953** J. S. Huxley *Evol. in Action* i. 29 Gradients exist in the developing organism—gradients in metabolism, growth-potential, and other factors. Genes altering the shape and intensity of such gradients will affect a number of parts simultaneously. **1957** [see field *sb.* 17 c]. **1970** F. Crick in *Nature* 31 Jan. 420/1 It is an old idea that 'gradients' are involved in embryological development... Many of the gradients to which Child referred seem more likely, in retrospect, to be the results of development rather than its cause. An outsider to embryology has the impression that in recent years gradients have become a dirty word. *Ibid.* 422/1 If this approach serves to make the idea of diffusion gradients respectable to embryologists it will have served its purpose.

3. *Math.* A rational integral function of a number of quantics of assigned weights, which is of one degree and one weight throughout (Prof. Elliott).

1887 Sylvester in *Amer. Jrnl. Math.* IX. 2 A rational intergral homogeneous and isobaric function (or, to avoid a tedious periphrasis, say a gradient). **1895** Elliott *Algebra Quantics* 145, 146, 233.

4. The degree of steepness of a graph at any point, measured by the tangent of the angle between the horizontal axis and either the line (if straight) or the tangent to the curve; (see also quot. 1937).

1897 H. Lamb *Elem. Course Infinitesimal Calculus* ii. 67 It is convenient to have a name for the property of a curve which is measured by the derived function. We shall use the term 'gradient' in this sense. **1937** E. J. McShane tr. *Courant's Diff. & Integral Calculus* (ed. 2) I. xi. 90 The slope or gradient of the curve is given by tan *a,* and hence the term *gradient* is occasionally used for the derivative of the function represented by the curve. **1942** C. E. K. Mees *Theory Photogr. Process* xix. 702 The *D,* log *E* curve continues..into the region of decreasing exposure with constantly decreasing gradient. **1958** A. Barton *Introd. Coordinate Geom.* v. 64 A line whose gradient is zero is parallel to the *x*-axis; as the gradient increases the line gets steeper. *Ibid.* 66 Two lines are..perpendicular if the product of their gradients is -1.

5. *Math.* A vector function whose components along the co-ordinate axes are the partial derivatives with respect to the corresponding variables of a given scalar function; it is denoted by ∇f (see del) or by grad *f,* where *f* is the scalar function.

1901 E. B. Wilson *Vector Analysis* iii. 138 The vector sum which is the resultant rate of increase of V is denoted by ∇V... The terms gradient and slope of *V* are..used for ∇V. **1936** E. J. McShane tr. *Courant's Diff. & Integral Calculus* II. iii. 89 The direction of the gradient is the direction in which the function increases most rapidly. **1966** *McGraw-Hill Encycl. Sci. & Technol.* II. 413/1 There are three differentiation processes that are of conceptual value in the study of vectors: the gradient of a scalar, the divergence of a vector, and the curl of a vector.

6. *attrib.* and *Comb.,* as **gradient wind** *Meteorol.,* the (hypothetical) wind whose direction is that of the geostrophic wind but whose speed is calculated by allowing for the effect on the geostrophic wind of the centrifugal force that results from its curved path.

1908 E. Gold *Barometric Gradient & Wind Force* 24 We can construct a scale..which shall give..the Beaufort number corresponding to the theoretical gradient wind for straight isobars for any pressure distribution. **1928** [see geostrophic *a.*]. **1966** *McGraw-Hill Encycl. Sci. & Technol.* VI. 244/2 The gradient wind is a good approximation to the actual wind and is often superior to the geostrophic wind, particularly when the flow is strongly curved in the cyclonic sense.

gradienter (ˈgreɪdɪəntə(r)). *U.S.* Also -or. [f. prec. + -er[1].] A small instrument used by surveyors for determining gradients, etc.

1884 in Knight *Dict. Mech.* Suppl., *Gradientor.* **1889** in *Century Dict.*

gradin, gradine[1] (ˈgreɪdɪn, grəˈdiːn). [a. or ad. F. *gradin,* ad. It. *gradino,* f. *grado* grade *sb.*]

1. One of a series of low steps or seats raised one above the other.

1834 Beckford *Italy* I. 140 A semi-circular niche, with seats like the gradines of a diminutive amphitheatre. **1851** Sir F. Palgrave *Norm. & Eng.* I. 709 The Pontiff Formosus received him on the gradins of St. Peter's Basilica. **1862** Rawlinson *Anc. Mon.* I. v. 334 This monument..tapering gently towards the summit, which is crowned with three low steps, or gradines.

b. *Mining.* (See quot.)

1839 Ure *Dict. Arts,* etc. 839 The working is disposed in the form of steps (*gradins*), placed like those of a stair.

2. A shelf or ledge at the back of an altar.

1877 Lee *Gloss. Litorg. & Eccl. Terms, Gradin* 1. A French term for a step behind and above the level of the altar-slab for placing the cross and candlesticks upon..2. The term 'gradine' has been recently introduced into the Church of England. It corresponds with that already defined. **1887** *Ch. Times* 23 Sept. 746/3 The altar is well raised, and a gradine above it bears the legal ornaments. **1890** Gasquet & Bishop *Edw. VI & Bk. Com. Prayer* 59 *note,* The modern introduction of *gradins* is a witness to the scruple felt at placing anything on the altar beyond what was necessary for the sacrifice. **1891** *Ch. Times* 4 Dec. 1180/4 Flowers may stand on the gradines on every Sunday in the year.

gradine[2] (grəˈdiːn). [a. F. *gradine.*] A toothed chisel used by sculptors.

1860 in Worcester. **1883** Helen Zimmern in *Mag. of Art* Oct. 517/2 All the instruments in the sculptor's profession are indicated—the modelling tool..the point, the gradine, even down to the very screw-jack.

grading (ˈgreɪdɪŋ), *vbl. sb.* [f. grade *v.*[2] + -ing[1].] The action of the vb. grade[2].

1. *gen.* (See the senses of the vb.)

1871 *Athenæum* 29 Apr. 531/1 The art of the painter has supplied that subtle grading of light and tone which all enjoy. **1882** C. L. Brace *Gesta Chr.* 400 The grading and separation of prisoners. **1886** *Athenæum* 11 Dec. 789/2 [The picture] gives with delightful truth..and aërial grading a view near the mouth of the Thames.

2. *spec.* **a.** The action or process of sorting (produce) into grades according to quality. Also *attrib.*

1883 E. INGERSOLL in *Harper's Mag.* June 75/2 It descends another story upon patented grading screens, which sort out the larger-sized grains from the smaller. *Ibid.* 76/2 The first operation..is the grading of the middlings. **1887** *Contemp. Rev.* May 699 The odious elevator, against which they preferred the charges of false grading.

b. The action or process of reducing (a road, etc.) to practicable gradients; *concr.* a graded portion of a road. Also *attrib.*

1835 *Jrnl. Franklin Instit.* XV. 233 The amount of labour in grading, fixing rails, and forming all other parts of the road. **1840** R. H. DANA *Bef. Mast* xix. 55 The grading of the road..they could easily understand. **1875** KNIGHT *Dict. Mech.*, *Grading-scraper*, a large two handled shovel drawn by a pair of horses..It is used in road-making [etc.]. **1877** RAYMOND *Statist. Mines & Mining* 130 Fifteen miles..were cleared of brush and some grading was done last year. **1881** 'MARK TWAIN' *Tramp Abr.* xvii. 134 The heavy work in..the new railway gradings is done mainly by Italians.

c. The placing of school teachers or pupils in groups according to ability and other qualifications.

1903 A. B. HART *Actual Govt. Amer. Conditions* 543 The number of children is great enough to allow complete grading. **1923** *N.Z. Educ. Gaz.* 3 Apr. 39/1 Revised grading-marks will reach all primary-school teachers this month. **1923** *Ibid.* 1 Oct. 157/1 The grading of primary-school teachers. **1958** S. ASHTON-WARNER *Spinster* 90, I have tried.., giving far more to my work than many a crack Infant Mistress in town, dancing upward on the grading list. **1963** [see GRADE *sb.* 4 d].

‖**gradino** (gra'dino). [It.: see GRADIN.] **a.** = GRADIN 2. **b.** A work of painting or sculpture intended to ornament the 'gradin' of an altar.

1883 C. C. PERKINS *It. Sculpt.* 18 An altar whose 'gradino' is covered with extremely flat reliefs sculptured by Alphonso Lombardi. **1886** *Athenæum* 4 Sept. 312/2 His [Civitali's] niche is secured in the Temple of Fame, not in the central line..but in some modest *gradino*, like those on his own altarpieces and monuments.

gradiometer (greɪdɪ'ɒmɪtə(r)). [f. GRADI(ENT *sb.*: see -METER.] **a.** Any of various surveying instruments used for setting out gradients or for measuring the gradient of a slope (see quots.).

1899 W. G. BLIGH *Notes on Instruments Engin. Field-Work* v. 89 The ordinary type of level is always at a disadvantage when the ground is sloping. To overcome this difficulty..a variation has been made..which permits the telescope to be inclined. One of these is Stanley's Patent Gradiometer, an excellent combination of the level and clinometer. **1940** *Chambers's Techn. Dict.* 384/2 *Gradiometer*, an instrument for setting out long uniform gradients; it consists of a level that may be elevated or depressed, by known amounts, by means of a vertical tangent screw. **1960** H. L. MICHAEL in K. B. Woods et al. *Highway Engin. Handbk.* ii. 11 Devices called 'gradiometers' or 'inclinometers', essentially bubble tubes graduated to read either percentage of grade or degree of incline, have been constructed to obtain grade information.

b. An instrument for measuring the gradient of a field, esp. the horizontal gradient of the earth's gravitational or magnetic field.

1929 *Mining Mag.* XL. 272 (*heading*) The gravity gradiometer. *Ibid.* 277 On account of its small size and its rapid speed of operation the gradiometer is admirably adapted for use in confined spaces such as underground mine galleries. **1934** *Trans. Amer. Inst. Mining & Metall. Engineers* CX. 383 At right angles to the magnetic meridian ..a positive gradient implies that the vertical component of the magnetic field is increasing to the east. In the magnetic meridian, the effective component is that in the magnetic vertical plane through the center of the gradiometer. **1957** *Encycl. Brit.* X. 681/2 In a design by Shaw and E. Lancaster-Jones [of an instrument for the measurement of gravity gradients] the beam system is made irresponsive to 'curvature' effects and is called a gravity gradiometer. **1971** *Sci. Amer.* Aug. 70/2 During the time when the moon was inside this region of very steady magnetic fields we sent commands to the instrument that enabled it to function as a gradiometer.

†**gradionately**, *adv.* *Obs.*$^{-1}$ [A humorously bombastic formation: perh. Nash meant to write *gradationately*.] In regular gradation or sequence.

1599 NASHE *Lenten Stuffe* 41 To recount..how he came to be king of fishes, and gradionately how from white to red he changed, would require as massive a toombe [i.e. tome] as Hollinshead.

graditly, variant of GRADATELY *adv.* *Obs.*

gradocol ('grædəʊkɒl). Also Gradocol. [See quot. 1931.] Used *attrib.* in ***gradocol membrane***: a membrane made by the controlled evaporation of a collodion solution, having a high uniformity of pore size and used as a filter, esp. for viruses.

1931 W. J. ELFORD in *Jrnl. Path. & Bacteriol.* XXVIII. 507, I propose to refer to these new membranes as gradocol membranes, since they are products of a graded coagulation of collodion. **1953** RHODES & VAN ROOYEN *Textbk. Virol.* (ed. 2) I. ii. 12 Suspensions of virus particles are filtered through a series of 'gradocol' membranes of varying degrees of porosity, and the filtrates tested for the presence of virus. **1964** WILSON & MILES *Princ. Bacteriol. & Immunity* (ed. 5) I. xl. 1166 In estimating the size of virus particles ultrafiltration through Gradocol membranes is widely used.

gradometer (grə'dɒmɪtə(r)). [f. GRAD(E *sb.*: see -METER.] Any instrument for measuring the gradient of a slope or the deviation from the horizontal.

1901 J. H. BULLARD *U.S. Pat.* 685,569, This invention relates to gradometers, and has for its object the construction of an instrument of this class adapted especially to use on self-propelled vehicles... The usual curved glass tube..is provided with graduation-marks, indicating the per cent. of inclination of the device relative to the horizen [*sic*]. **1904** GOODCHILD & TWENEY *Technol. & Sci. Dict.* 266/1 *Gradometer*, an instrument for measuring the angle of dip of a rock formation or mineral deposit. **1924** F. CALDWELL *U.S. Pat.* 1,492,156, Improvement in Gradometers..relates to the visible indication of the grade up or down on which a vehicle..is travelling or standing, on which an aircraft is travelling, or the extent to which a ship is rolling or pitching.

†**graduable**, *a.* *Obs.* *rare*$^{-1}$. [f. med.L. *graduāre* (see GRADUATE *v.*) + -ABLE.] Entitled to an academic degree.

1513 *Bk. Keruynge* in *Babees Bk.* (1868) 284 Clerkes that ben gradewable..may syt at the squyers table.

gradual ('grædjuːəl), *sb.* [ad. med.L. *graduāle* sb., orig. neut. of *graduālis* adj.: see next.]

1. An antiphon sung between the Epistle and the Gospel at the Eucharist, so called because it was sung at the steps of the altar or while the deacon was ascending the steps of the ambo. (Cf. GRAIL[1] 1.)

1563–83 FOXE *A. & M.* 1402/1 The Responsorie, which is called the Graduall (beyng wont to be song at the steps going vp). **1656** BLOUNT *Glossogr.*, *Gradual*, that part of the Mass which is said or sung between the Epistle and the Gospel, as a grade or step from the first to the later. **1849** ROCK *Ch. of Fathers* I. III. 217 A part of a psalm was chanted between the Epistle and the Gospel, which..came to be called the gradual. **1896** *Ch. Times* 14 Aug., A special Collect, Epistle, and Gospel have been licensed for this festival by the Bishop of the diocese, and the proper Introit and Gradual were also used.

2. A book of such antiphons. = GRAIL[1] 2.

1619 BRENT tr. *Sarpi's Counc. Trent* (1629) 752 Authority may bee giuen to reforme Missals, Breuiaries, Agends, and Graduals. **1674** in BLOUNT *Glossogr.* (ed. 4). **1782** BURNEY *Hist. Mus.* (1789) II. ii. 137 The following is another alleluja from an ancient Gradual. **1846** MASKELL *Mon. Rit.* I. p. xxxiii, It certainly is not easy, if it be possible, to lay down express signs by which the Antiphoner and the Gradual are always to be distinguished. **1866** J. H. BLUNT *Annot. Bk. Com. Prayer* 68 A third [volume] for the Anthems, called the Antiphonarius or Gradual.

†**3.** The steps of an altar. *Obs.* (? *nonce-use.*)

1693 DRYDEN *Ovid's Met.* I. 506 Before the gradual, prostrate they ador'd: The pavement kiss'd; and thus the saint implor'd.

gradual ('grædjuːəl), *a.* Also 6 -ale, 7 -all. [ad. med.L. *graduāl-is*, f. *gradu-s* step. Cf. F. *graduel.*]

†**1.** Of or pertaining to degree; only in ***gradual difference*** = difference in degree. *Obs.*

a **1652** J. SMITH *Sel. Disc.* VI. ii. (1821) 190 Besides this gradual difference between Moses and the prophets, there is [etc.]. **1651** BAXTER *Saints' Rest* III. xi. §12 A Moral specifical difference is usually founded in a Natural Gradual difference. **1658** —— *Saving Faith* §2. 15 The difference is only gradual, and not specifical.

†**b.** *Mus.* ***gradual tone*** = DEGREE 11 a. *Obs.*

1665 C. SIMPSON *Princ. Pract. Musick* 3 All Musick..is formed of Seven Gradual Tones, or Degrees of Sound.

†**2.** *Mus.* Corresponding to the degrees of the natural scale; giving the 'natural' notes. *Obs.*

1694 W. HOLDER *Harmony* (1731) 118 The Breves representing the Tones of the broad Gradual Keys of an Organ; the Semibreves representing the narrow Upper Keys.

†**3.** Arranged in, or admitting of, degrees or gradation. *Obs.*

1541 R. COPLAND *Guydon's Quest. Chirurg.* G ij b, And in both the endes of yᵉ same ben pyttes receyuynge the roundnesses, Towarde the elbowe ben receyued yᵉ roundnesses graduales of the adiutory [L. *rotunditates gradatas adiutorii*]. **1641** J. JACKSON *True Evang. T.* III. 168 A graduall expression, growing up to the height of its emphasis by foure steps. **1667** MILTON *P.L.* v. 483 Flowers and their fruit, Man's nourishment, by gradual scale sublimed, To vital spirits aspire. **1677** HALE *Prim. Orig. Man.* 129 Moral Evidence is gradual, according to the variety of circumstances. **1712** STEELE *Spect.* No. 270 ¶1 So great an Assembly of Ladies placed in gradual Rows.

4. Of a process: Taking place by degrees; advancing step by step; slowly progressive. Of a slope: Gentle, not steep or abrupt.

1692 LOCKE *Educ.* §184 By a gradual Progress from the plainest and easiest Historians, he may at last come to read the most difficult and sublime of the Latin Authours. **1701** GREW *Cosm. Sacra* II. viii. 80 The Transition from Humane into Perfect Mind, is made by a Gradual Ascent. **1736** BUTLER *Anal.* I. iii. Wks. 1874 I. 65 The complete success of virtue, as of reason, cannot..be otherwise than gradual. **1781** GIBBON *Decl. & F.* xxix. III. 105 The gradual discovery of the weakness of Arcadius and Honorius. **1821** KEATS *Isabella* xxxii, Isabel By gradual decay from beauty fell. **1840** TANNER *Canals & Rail Roads U.S.* 73 The ascents and descents of the summits are very gradual, not exceeding 30 feet per mile. **1844** EMERSON *Lect., New Eng. Ref.* Wks. (Bohn) I. 260 A gradual withdrawal of tender consciences from the social organizations. **1854** H. MILLER *Sch. & Schm.* xxiv. (1860) 269/1 The increasing roll of the sea, showed the gradual shallowing of the water. **1875** JOWETT *Plato* (ed. 2) V. 66 We should consider how gradual the process is by which..a legal system..becomes perfected.

b. *poet.* in *nonce-uses.* Of objects with regard to form, movement, etc.: Tapering; sloping gradually; moving or changing gradually.

1739 G. OGLE *Gualtherus & Griselda* 5 The rounded Turret, and the gradual Spire. **1742** COLLINS *Odes* ix. 40 Thy dewy fingers draw The gradual dusky veil. **1762** FALCONER *Shipwr.* I. 744 Along the arch the gradual index slides. **1850** MRS. BROWNING *Poems* I. 75 Back to the gradual banks and vernal bowers. **1890** W. WATSON *Wordsworth's Grave*, etc. 71 How welcome—after drum and trumpet's din—The continuity, the long slow slope And vast curves of the gradual violin!

c. quasi-*adv.* (*poet.*)

1736 THOMSON *Liberty* IV. 227 Arts gradual gather Streams. **1793** GILB. WHITE *Invit. Selborne* 80 There spreads the distant view, That gradual fades till sunk in misty blue. **1801** SOUTHEY *Thalaba* v. xlii, Gradual as by prayer The sin was purged away. **1808** J. BARLOW *Columb.* III. 2 Now twenty years these children of the skies Beheld their gradual growing empire rise. **1813** SCOTT *Rokeby* II. ii, What prospects, from his watch-tower high, Gleam gradual on the warder's eye! **1850** LYNCH *Theo. Trin.* v. 82 Now, gradual, earth withdraws from view.

5. ***gradual psalms***: fifteen psalms (cxx–cxxxiv) each of which is entitled in the A.V. 'Song of Degrees', in R.V. 'Song of Ascents'; in the Vulgate *Canticum graduum*, in the LXX ᾠδὴ ἀναβαθμῶν = Heb. *shir hammaʿalōth*, the sense of which is disputed. (Cf. F. *psaumes graduels.*)

1656–81 in BLOUNT *Glossogr.* **1864** PUSEY *Lect. Daniel* v. 319 Some of the gradual psalms suit well to the habitual low estate of the returned exiles. **1893** C. L. MARSON *Psalms at Work* (1894) 178/1 The gradual psalms..were for the ascent to the Temple.

Hence '**gradualness.**

1842 PUSEY *Crisis Eng. Ch.* 16 We..have been exempt from the degree of trial to which a younger generation is exposed, through the very gradualness with which our conceptions of the Unity of the Church came upon us. **1883** H. DRUMMOND *Nat. Law in Spir. W.* ii. (1884) 92 The gradualness of growth is a characteristic which strikes the simplest observer.

gradualism ('grædjuːəlɪz(ə)m). [f. GRADUAL *a.* + -ISM.] The principle or method of gradual as opposed to immediate change. Orig. used with reference to the abolition of slavery. (Cf. IMMEDIATISM.)

1835 H. G. OTIS in *Liberator* V. 144 *Immediatism*..is the opposite of *gradualism*, another new coinage. **1846** HT. MARTINEAU *Hist. Peace* III. IV. viii. 13 The unsound method of 'gradualism' in the abolition of slavery. **1855** —— *Autobiog.* (1877) III. 233 He got his gradualism assented to in Parliament. **1865** LOWELL *Reconstruction* Prose Wks. 1890 V. 237 We have purposely avoided any discussion on gradualism as an element in emancipation. **1931** *Time & Tide* 5 Sept. Suppl. 19/2 The reading of the facts now most popular in the Labour Movement will inevitably strengthen enormously the 'dictatorship of the Proletariat' solution... 'This,' remarked one of the younger Labour M.P.'s the other day, 'is the end of gradualism.' **1959** *Times* 16 Mar. 9 Gradualism is to continue to be Mr. Gomulka's agricultural watchword [in Poland]. **1963** *Economist* 15 June 1134/1 Gradualism is in disfavour with increasing numbers of Negroes. **1965** *Listener* 3 June 812/2 We were thinking in terms of the politics of democracy and gradualism, of separate African states, each different. **1969** *Times* 6 Jan. 9/2 The best hope for Ulster..is..to allow the gradualism of Captain O'Neill's ministry to go forward, without direct intervention from Westminster.

'**gradualist** *sb.* and *a.* [f. GRADUAL *a.* + -IST.] **A.** *sb.* An advocate of gradual action.

1835 H. G. OTIS in *Liberator* V. 744 The Colonization Society..are gradualists. **1880** *Libr. Univ. Knowl.* (N.Y.) IX. 235 Mr. Lundy, like most of the anti-slavery men of that day was a gradualist, fearing..that a sudden emancipation would be dangerous to the public welfare.

B. *adj.* Also **gradua'listic.** Of or pertaining to gradualism.

1926 *Glasgow Herald* 25 Jan. 10 The duty of the Left Wing would be to fight with all its power against evolutionary and gradualistic theories. **1931** *Economist* 17 Oct. 698/2 It [*sc.* Labour] now sees no chance of securing these ends by merely gradualist methods within the general structure of the capitalist system. **1931** *Time & Tide* 7 Nov. 1273/1 And this most effective body of Labour is gradualist, not revolutionary. **1945** *Chicago Daily News* 4 Oct. 12/7 On a higher level of thought, we've labeled ourselves 'gradualists'; and stilled any uneasy twinge of conscience by assuming that everything will wash out in the fullness of time. **1947** KOESTLER in *Partisan Rev.* XIV. II. 142 You know that we are a reformist, gradualist movement. **1953** K. BRITTON *J. S. Mill* v. 170 Such a solution..allows us to regard inductive inference as inconclusive and gradualistic. **1960** *20th Cent.* Nov. 391 The fighters of the country are not generally the gradualists. **1961** *Listener* 21 Dec. 1059/2 We cannot sit back and *hope* that..Africa will retain our gradualist and liberal traditions.

graduality (grædjuː'ælɪtɪ). [f. GRADUAL *a.* + -ITY.] The quality or condition of being gradual, in various senses of the adj.

1646 SIR T. BROWNE *Pseud. Ep.* VI. x. 322 Which..others [ascribe] to the graduality of opacity and light. **1662** J. CHANDLER *Van Helmont's Oriat.* 134 An accident being on both sides graduated, cannot lay aside its graduality. **1806** W. TAYLOR in *Monthly Mag.* XXI. 417 The accessory ideas of graduality and of change from internal causes are associated with the term. **1869** *Fortn. Rev.* 1 Oct. 423 *note*, A striking instance of the graduality of the evolution of fetichism will be found in 'Fiji and the Fijians'. **1871** R. H. HUTTON *Ess.* (1877) I. 42 The graduality of the stages by which life ascends.

gradually ('grædju:əlɪ, 'grædʒ(j)u:əlɪ), *adv.* [f. GRADUAL *a.* + -LY².]

†**1.** In respect of degree. (Cf. GRADUAL *a.* 1.)

1649 *Bounds Publ. Obed.* (1650) 61 They..differ but gradually, just as the morning and the noon light do. 1660 F. BROOKE tr. *Le Blanc's Trav.* a iv, Saving Faith..is not only Gradually, but Specifically distinct from all common Faith. 1665 BOYLE *Occas. Refl.* (1848) 73 This use of Occasional Meditations, though it do but gradually differ from some of those that have been already mentioned. 1701 GREW *Cosmol. Sacra* II. viii. 83 Wherein Human Reason doth not only Gradually, but Specifically differ, from the Phantastick Reason of Brutes.

†**2.** In a graduated scale; by gradations; by degrees of relationship or rank. *Obs.* (Cf. GRADUAL *a.* 3.)

1673 *Rep. Committee, Ho. of Lords* in *Peerage* (1710) I. 263 The Petitioner, being the Heir gradually and lineally descended from the said Lord Clifton. 1678 CUDWORTH *Intell. Syst.* I. iv. 206 Several Distinct Substances, gradually subordinate to one another. 1704 *Phil. Trans.* XXV. 1626 Some of 'em gradually bigger than others. 1715 *Lond. Gaz.* No. 5371/3 If a Lieutenant inform against a Captain..he shall have his Company, so proceeding gradually to a Colonel. 1755 YOUNG *Centaur* ii. Wks. 1757 IV. 156 There are three kinds of happiness on earth, gradually less, and less.

3. By a gradual process; little by little; by degrees.

1646 SIR T. BROWNE *Pseud. Ep.* VI. x. 323 The effects of whose activity are not precipitously abrupted, but gradually proceed to their cessations. 1715 DE FOE *Fam. Instruct.* I. i (1841) 21 You must understand it gradually, my dear, a little at a time. 1776 ADAM SMITH *W.N.* I. xi. (1869) I. 220 These metals are not likely to become gradually cheaper. 1807 T. THOMSON *Chem.* (ed. 3) II. 262 Acetous acid gradually becomes acetic acid when distilled repeatedly off dry muriate of lime. 1860 TYNDALL *Glac.* I. vii. 47 The ice.. being gradually melted. 1880 L. STEPHEN *Pope* vi. 157 We are softened into pity as the strong mind is seen gradually sinking into decay.

graduand (,grædju:'ænd). *Sc.* [ad. med.L. *graduand-us*, gerundive of *gradu-āre* to GRADUATE.] One about to be graduated or to receive a university degree.

1882 in OGILVIE. 1890 *Star* 14 June 1/6 As they were introduced each made a spasmodic effort to get into conversation with the graduand.

graduate ('grædju:ət), *a.* and *sb.* Also 5–7 **graduat**, 6 **graduatt**, 7 **gradiate**. [ad. med.L. *graduāt-us*, pa. pple. of *graduāre* to GRADUATE, f. *gradu-s* step, degree.]

A. *pa. pple.* and *ppl. a.* Equivalent to the later GRADUATED.

1. Admitted to or holding a university degree. *Obs.* exc. as an attrib. use of the sb., e.g. 'the graduate members of the university'.

1494 FABYAN *Chron.* VII. 455 The Frenshe kyng this yere put to deth one maister Henry de Malestrete, a graduat man. 1563–7 BUCHANAN *Reform. St. Andros* Wks. (1892) 13 The examinatouris salbe graduat, ane in theologie, ane that has red in philosophie. 1591 R. TURNBULL *Expos. Jas.* 95 For the word is the word, whether a Doctor of diuinitie preach it, or a man learned, yet not graduat. 1637 GILLESPIE *Eng. Pop. Cerem.* III. iv. 73 Graduate men should under-stand better what they speake off. 1637–50 ROW *Hist. Kirk* (Wodrow Soc.) 447 Shortlie thereafter, he wes graduat in Padua, *Doctor utriusque Juris*. 1687 W. SHERWIN in *Magdalen Coll.* (O.H.S.) 216 There was a Cloth laid in the Hall for the Undergraduate Fellow above the Graduate Demies. 1753 HANWAY *Trav.* (1762) I. IV. liv. 248 *note*, Dr. Cooke, now a graduate physician in Scotland.

2. Arranged by steps or degrees. Now *rare*.

1628 FELTHAM *Resolves* II. xcii. 268 From whom all things, by a graduate Derivation, haue their light, life, and being. 1658 FRANCK *Northern Memoirs* (1694) 170 Nor got our Ship the Mediums of Motion, but by Argument of Force..which forced her by graduate Means, till arriving in this Ness. 1789 E. TATHAM *Chart & Scale Truth* (1790) I. 42 Beginning with the Genus, passing through all the graduate and subordinate stages. 1855 LYNCH *Rivulet* xxx. i, The starry ranks..In graduate scale of might, They all are sons of light.

B. *sb.*

1. One who has obtained a degree from a university, college or other authority conferring degrees.

In the U.S. sometimes used for: A pupil who has completed a school course and passed the final examination.

1479 *Paston Lett.* No. 830 III. 246 Master Edmund, that was my rewler at Oxforth..kan tell yow, or ellys any oder gradwat. 1509–10 *Act 1 Hen. VIII*, c. 14 No manne undre the degree of a Gentilman excepte Graduates of the Universities. 1563–7 BUCHANAN *Reform. St. Andros* Wks. (1892) 15 Chosin be the hayl graduattis of the vniuersite. 1586 (*title*) A Discourse of English Poetrie..By William Webbe Graduate. *a* 1613 OVERBURY *A Wife* (1638) 123 His Ambition is, that he either is or shall be a Graduate. *a* 1657 LOVELACE *Poems* (1864) 251 Fair Cam saw thee matriculate At once a tyro and a graduate. 1733 BRAMSTON *Man of Taste* 17 Of Graduates I dislike the learned rout, And chuse a female Doctor for the gout. 1773 J. ADAMS *Diary* in *Works* II. 321 Their academy [in Phila.] emits from nine to fourteen graduates annually. 1776 ADAM SMITH *W.N.* V. i. (1869) II. 347 The privileges of graduates in arts, in law, in physic, and divinity. 1858 DORAN *Crt. Fools* 124 He held the University graduates in very absolute contempt. 1861 *Amer. Cycl.* XII. 396 The whole number of pupils who have been connected with the school is 3,408, of graduates 1,158. 1888 ANNA K. GREEN *Behind Closed Doors* iii, He is a graduate of the Medical School. 1952 *Manch. Guardian Weekly* 18 Sept. 13/2 To an astonishing degree Groton graduates have made names for themselves in public life.

2. *transf.* One who is advanced in any art, career, occupation, or profession; a proficient. Now *rare*.

1582 N. LICHEFIELD tr. *Castanheda's E. Ind.* xiv. 36 b, The Maisters which teach them be graduats in the weapons which they teach. *c* 1600 *Songs Costume* (Percy Soc.) 120 None but graduates can proceede In sinne so far till this they neede. 1625 FLETCHER *Fair Maid of Inn* IV. ii, I would be a graduate, sir, no freshman. 1642 SIR E. DERING *Sp. on Relig.* xvi. 86 Your gradiate in the schoole of warre will tell you, that [etc.]. 1658 T. WALL *Charac. Enemies Ch.* (1659) 34 To be a graduate in ungraciousness. 1883 E. INGERSOLL in *Harper's Mag.* Jan. 206/2 The Americans employed are very often graduates of the Maine woods.

3. A graduated cup, tube, or flask; a measuring glass used by apothecaries and chemists; the quantity contained in such a glass.

1883 HALDANE *Workshop Rec.* Ser. II. 114 A graduate that has contained tincture of iron. 1895 *Westm. Gaz.* 6 July 1/3 Though his black eyes were starting out with pain he said nothing till a graduate of oil had been poured on.

4. *attrib.*, as ***graduate course***, ***school***, ***student***, etc.

1871 L. H. BAGG *4 Years at Yale* 112 Delta Phi has also four alumni associations, or 'graduate chapters'. 1880 *Harvard Catal.* 190 (*heading*) Graduate department. *Ibid.*, Any Graduate course which is taken by less than three students may be withdrawn at the option of the Instructor. 1880 *Harper's Mag.* July 251/2 The solution of the difficulty lies in..putting the extra studies in the graduate courses. 1893 *Bryn Mawr Program* 34 The most distinguished place among graduate students will be held by the Fellows. 1895–6 *Cal. University Nebraska* 37 The Graduate School provides for advanced University work on the basis of completed undergraduate studies. 1926 *Encycl. Brit.* II. 318/2 The period under review [1909–26] was marked by constant developments in the graduate schools of the university [*sc.* Harvard]. 1951 M. MCLUHAN *Mech. Bride* 43/2 The Harvard methods and pursuits differ little from those of any other graduate school. 1958 *Times Lit. Suppl.* 10 Oct. 578/2 Just another piece of graduate-student exhibitionism.

graduate ('grædju:eɪt), *v.* [f. med.L. *graduāt-*, ppl. stem of *graduāre* (in sense 1), f. *gradu-s* step, Cf. F. *graduer*.]

I. In University phraseology.

1. *trans.* To admit to a university degree. Also with complement, indicating the degree obtained. (Cf. sense 3.) Now *rare* exc. *U.S.*

1588 PARKE tr. *Mendoza's Hist. China* xiv. 95 To commence or graduate such students as haue finished their course. 1602 CAREW *Surv. Cornwall* I. (1723) 61 John Tregonwel, graduated a Doctor and dubbed a Knight, did his Prince good seruice. *c* 1645 HOWELL *Lett.* (1650) I. 3 Transplanting me thence to Oxford, to be graduated. 1693 *Apol. Clergy Scot.* 106 An insinuation that he was not graduated Doctor in the University. 1723 in B. Peirce *Hist. Harvard Univ.* (1833) 128 The Theses of the Batchelours to be graduated at Commencement. 1766 T. CLAP *Hist. Yale Coll.* 23 [He] upon his Return was graduated at this College 1724. 1844 EMERSON *Lect., New Eng. Ref.* Wks. (Bohn) I. 262 Some thousands of young men are graduated at our colleges in this country every year. 1884 *Harper's Mag.* Nov. 813/1 The class of '76 was graduated with six men.

fig. 1622 MABBE tr. *Aleman's Guzman d'Alf.* I. 75 With him I ranne over the whole course of my misfortunes, since the first time that I was graduated and tooke degree in them. *a* 1661 FULLER *Worthies, Durham* (1662) I. 316 This Fresh-man Colledge lived not to be matriculated, much less (not lasting seven years) graduated, God in his wisdom seeing the contrary fitter.

†**2.** Of an acquirement, etc.: To qualify (a person) for a degree or as a proficient in an art, etc.

1624 WOTTON *Archit.* 43 As if the very tearms of Architraues, and Frizes, and Cornices..were enough to graduate a Master of this Art. 1654 WHITLOCK *Zootomia* 434 Among haire-braind Judgments, a hairelesse Chin graduateth him a hopefull, and gifted young man in their esteem. 1664 POWER *Exp. Philos.* III. 184 It has been held accomplishment enough to graduate a Student, if he could but stiffly wrangle out a vexatious dispute of some odd Peripatetick qualities. 1829 SOUTHEY *Sir T. More* II. 53 The course of life there was better adapted to graduate young men in the brutalizing habits of the society wherewith they were soon to mingle.

3. a. *intr.* To take a university degree. Also (*U.S.*), to complete a high school course and receive a diploma.

1807 SOUTHEY *Espriella's Lett.* II. 76 Four years are then to be passed at college before the student can graduate. 1808 *Monthly Mag.* Oct. 224/1 He [Mandeville] graduated at Leyden in 1691. 1839 MARRYAT *Diary Amer.* Ser. I. III. 304, I married her a month after she had graduated. 1866 ODLING *Anim. Chem.* Pref. 6 Among students, especially those about to graduate. 1882 I. M. RITTENHOUSE *Jrnl.* in *Maud* (1939) 77 The very minute that she found out she was too far behind the class to graduate she stopped school. 1892 *Times* 8 Mar. 10/1 In 1837 he graduated from Yale College. 1935 H. NICOLSON *Dwight Morrow* i. 14 Dwight was..able to graduate from High School at the premature age of fourteen.

b. *transf.* To qualify (*as*); also, to pass through a course of education or training in order to qualify.

1829 SOUTHEY *Sir T. More* II. 11 One who was preparing to graduate as a Saint. 1850 SIR A. DE VERE *Pict. Sketches* I. 201 It is only when it has graduated as a nation, that a race completes its being. 1867 J. HATTON *Tallants of B.* viii, Richard Tallant was graduating very successfully in the Blackguard school. 1871 M. COLLINS *Mrq. & Merch.* I. x. 308 Their sisters..have graduated in the saloons of western London.

II. *gen.*

4. a. *trans.* To divide into degrees; to mark out into portions according to a certain scale.

1594 BLUNDEVIL *Exerc.* VII. xii. (1636) 667 To graduate the first side of your staffe..you must lay the Ruler to the Centre A. 1665 *Phil. Trans.* I. 31 An Instrument for Graduating Thermometers to make them Standards of Heat and Cold. *a* 1691 BOYLE *Hist. Air* (1692) 79, I have not seen any cylinder that hath been well graduated, 12 or 16 degrees being the most that are set upon the common weather-glass. 1748 *Anson's Voy.* II. v. 182 The thermometer..graduated according to the method of Farenheit. 1816 J. SMITH *Panorama Sci. & Art* II. 266 Sometimes the wire *o q* is graduated. 1834–47 J. S. MACAULAY *Field Fortif.* (1851) 301 Graduate that tangent, and place the crest of the traverse on a parallel plane ten feet above it. 1881 ANDERSON in *Nature* No. 626. 618 One of the frames is graduated.

b. To arrange in gradations; to adapt *to* (something) by graduating; to apportion the incidence of (a tax) according to a certain scale.

1610 HEALEY *St. Aug. Citie of God* 460 They..begin to graduate the ages past. 1644 DIGBY *Man's Soul* xi. 436 The pure soule would apply it selfe therevnto, according to the proportion of her iudgements, and as they are graduated and qualifyed. 1761 *Descr. S. Carolina* 28 Those superior and general Laws of Nature whereby Heat and Cold in every Climate are commonly understood to be chiefly governed and graduated. 1816 J. SCOTT *Vis. Paris* (ed. 5) 123 There are editions of the works of all the established authors, graduated for every description of taste. 1832 W. IRVING *Alhambra* (1875) 121 The Alhambra possesses retreats graduated to the heat of the weather. 1841 MYERS *Cath. Th.* IV. §50. 434 A scale of ranks in society graduated according to the natural ascent of gifts and powers and moral attainments. 1860 READE *Cloister & H.* II. 334, I called little Kate's hand a Kardiometer, or heart-measurer, because it graduated emotion, and pinched by scale. 1863 FAWCETT *Pol. Econ.* IV. ii. (1876) 543 The proposal to graduate the Income-tax seems to sanction the principle that it is desirable to impose a penalty upon the accumulation of wealth.

c. *intr.* for *refl.* To adapt oneself to a certain scale; to fall into grades or degrees.

1796 [see GRADUATING below]. 1832 HT. MARTINEAU *Each & All* iv. 61 Our affections graduate according to a truer scale then that of hereditary rank. 1898 [see GRADUATING below].

†**d.** *trans.* To carry *up* through a series of ascending degrees. *Obs.*

1694 'S. S.' *Loyal & Impart. Satirist* Ded. 2 We shall be graduated up, through all the decent forms of Ingenious Cruelty..to a more Solemn and Ceremonious Death.

†**5. a.** To improve the grade or quality of; *spec.* in *Alch.* to transmute (a metal, an essence) into one of a higher grade. *Obs.*

1646 SIR T. BROWNE *Pseud. Ep.* VI. xii 338 Dyars.. advance and graduate their colours with Salts. 1655 G. S. *Let.* in Hartlib *Ref. Commw. Bees* 25 The tincture of the Concrete whence it was produced, which then being graduated beyond its own nature, leaveth its dye in grain. 1662 J. SPARROW tr. *Behme's Rem. Wks., Consid. upon Stiefel* 7 Which..reneweth the Essences, viz. the Forms of the Dark-world to the Fire-Life, and highly graduates or Exalts them and transmutes them into another thing. 1669 BOYLE *Cert. Physiol. Ess.* etc. (ed. 2) 76 The Tincture was capable to transmute or graduate as much Silver as equall'd in weight that Gold from whence the Tincture was drawn.

b. To concentrate (a solution) by evaporation. So F. *graduer* (Littré). (Cf. GRADATE *v.* 3, GRADUATOR c.)

1828–32 WEBSTER, *Graduate*,..8 In chimistry, to bring fluids to a certain degree of consistency.

6. *intr.* To pass by degrees or gradations; to change gradually; *spec.* in *Geol.*, *Bot.*, and *Zool.*, said of a species or variety, or a kind of tissue passing gradually into another. Const. *into*, also with *away*.

1786 GILPIN *Observ. Pict. Beauty* I. p. xxxi, To make lights graduate as they ought. 1792 *Minstrel* (1793) II. 232 This tender sympathy of sorrow, imperceptibly to themselves, graduated to a still more tender sympathy of affection. 1799 KIRWAN *Geol. Ess.* i. 209 The sandstone in the vicinity of Prague graduates into hornstone, and even into granite. 1832 DE LA BECHE *Geol. Man.* (ed. 2) 407 This sandstone graduates into the inferior conglomerates. 1833 LYELL *Princ. Geol.* III. 362 In Shetland a granite composed of hornblende, mica, felspar, and quartz, graduates in an equally perfect manner into basalt. 1859 DARWIN *Orig. Spec.* vi. (1873) 135 Climate and height or depth graduate away insensibly. 1868 —— *Anim. & Plants* I. v. 139 Carriers ..graduate through foreign breeds into the rock-pigeon. 1884 tr. *De Bary's Phaner. & Ferns* 127 The elements bordering on the thin-walled tissue may graduate into the latter.

Hence '**graduating** *vbl. sb.* (also *attrib.*) and *ppl. a.*

1786 GILPIN *Observ. Pict. Beauty* II. Expl. p. ix, A graduating light, a graduating shade, or a graduating distance, are all beautiful. 1796 KIRWAN *Elem. Min.* (ed. 2) I. 455 The whole graduating series must be of the same origin. 1840 R. H. DANA *Bef. Mast* xxviii. 96 The full account of the exercises at the graduating of my own class. 1887 *Spectator* 15 Oct. 1389 The highest distinction that could be conferred on a graduating student. 1893 GUNTER *Miss Dividends* 19 She is in the habit of going to West Point, to graduating exercises. 1898 *Westm. Gaz.* 20 Jan. 5/1 Lines of ribbon velvet in graduating widths trimmed it up to the waist.

graduated ('grædju:eɪtɪd), *ppl. a.* [f. GRADUATE *v.* + -ED.] In senses of the vb.

†**1.** ? Formed by or consisting of steps. *Obs.*

1655 H. L'ESTRANGE *Chas. I*, 137 The Communion Table he injoyned to be placed at the East end, upon a graduated advance of ground.

2. That has received or holds a university degree; in later use chiefly, that has a medical degree, fully qualified. Now *rare*.

1665 NEEDHAM *Medela Medicinæ* 212 Call men what you will, because they are neither graduated nor incorporated. **1678** *Quacks Academy* 5 Graduated Doctors, and Book-learned Physicians. **1774** WARTON *Hist. Eng. Poetry* (1775) II. 131 The king's Laureate was nothing more than 'a graduated rhetorician'. **1784** COWPER *Task* II. 739 Ignorance.. With parrot tongue performed the scholar's part, Proceeding soon a graduated dunce. **1818** *Art Preserv. Feet* Pref. 6 Such complaints appear more worthy the notice of the graduated and licensed operator. **1824** SCOTT *St. Ronan's* xiii, 'By my faith, Captain MacTurk' said the Doctor 'you speak as if you were graduated!' **1833** SYD. SMITH in *Mem.* (1855) II. 346 Scarlet-fever awes me and is above my aim. I leave it to the professional and graduated homicides.

b. *transf.* That has passed through a course of training; qualified.

1828 P. CUNNINGHAM *N.S. Wales* (ed. 3) II. 252 The whole aim of regularly graduated thieves is, to be able to lead a riotous life of eating, drinking, and profligate sociality with each other.

3. Marked with lines to indicate degrees, grades, or quantities.

1762 FALCONER *Shipwr.* II. 434 In vain he spreads the graduated chart. **1774** M. MACKENZIE *Maritime Surv.* v. 61 Make the Needle level with the graduated Circle in the Box. **1806** *Med. Jrnl.* XV. 12 The equal length of the screws.. being ascertained by means of a graduated measure. **1858** GREENER *Gunnery* 41 When the powder explodes the spring is forced forward, and moves an index round a graduated circle. **1882** MINCHIN *Unipl. Kinemat.* 94 The graduated roller may be fixed anywhere on an arm attached rigidly to *AB*.

4. Arranged in grades or gradations; arranged according to the degree of difficulty or importance; advancing or proceeding by degrees.

1678 NEWTON *Let. R. Boyle* in *Boyle's Wks.* (1772) I. p. cxii, Now the space between the limits EFGH and IKLM, I shall call the space of the æther's graduated rarity. **1800** tr. *Lagrange's Chem.* II. 343 Put equal parts of these two salts into two retorts, and expose them to a strong, equal, graduated fire. **1837** H. H. WILSON *Sánkhya Káriká* 107 The formation of ideas is, in all cases, a graduated process. **1856** FROUDE *Hist. Eng.* (1858) I. v. 426 The military organization of society required a graduated uniform. **1861** MILL *Utilit.* v. 87 Graduated taxation, taking a higher percentage from those who have more to spare. **1868** PEARD *Water-Farm.* vi. 71 A natural fall of the ground would enable the manager to arrange them in a graduated series. **1896** HOW & LEIGH *Hist. Rome* 309 The old policy of graduated privilege and regular promotion fell into oblivion. *Mod.* Graduated readings in Chinese.

b. *Ornith.* (See quot.)

1842 BRANDE *Dict. Sci.*, etc., *Graduated*, in Ornithology, when the quill-feathers of the tail increase in length by regular gradations. Hence **1860** in WORCESTER; and in later Dicts.

†'**graduately**, *adv. Obs. rare.* [f. GRADUATE *a.* + -LY[2].] By grades or degrees; gradually.

1628 FELTHAM *Resolves* II. lxv. 187 The stones are graduately concimented, and there is none that subsisteth alone. *Ibid.* II. xc. 260 So Warre is begotten out of Peace, graduately, and ends in Peace immediately.

graduateship ('grædju:ət-ʃɪp). [f. GRADUATE *sb.* + -SHIP.] **a.** The period during which one is a graduate. **b.** The condition of being a graduate.

1644 MILTON *Areop.* (Arb.) 64 It is no new thing.. for a parochiall Minister.. to finish his circuit in an English concordance and a topic folio, the gatherings and savings of a sober graduatship. **1854** LOWELL *Cambridge* (*U.S.*) *Thirty Yrs. Ago* Prose Wks. 1890 I. 82 So, by degrees, there springs up a competition in longevity, the prize contended for being the oldest surviving graduateship.

gradu'atical, *a. rare.* [f. GRADUATE *sb.* + -IC + -AL[1].] Of or pertaining to graduates. ˌ**gradu'atically** *adv.*, *nonce-wd.*, as a graduate should.

1612 WEBSTER *White Devil* III. i, I most graduatically thanke your Lordship. **1837** *Fraser's Mag.* XVI. 661 On this and other matters graduatical (if that be the proper adjective) we shall discuss.. hereafter.

graduation (grædju:'eɪʃən). [f. GRADUATE *v.*: see -ATION.] The action of graduating.

1. a. The action or process of dividing into degrees or other proportionate divisions on a graduated scale. **b.** *pl.* Lines employed to indicate degrees of latitude and longitude, quantity, etc.; *sing.* †a single line on which these are marked; also *collectively*, the aggregate of lines employed. **c.** The manner in which something is graduated. †**d.** Position on a map as indicated by degrees. *Obs.*

a. 1833 HERSCHEL *Astron.* ii. 105 The result will be liable to two sources of error—that of graduation and that of observation. **1837** WHEWELL *Hist. Induct. Sci.* II. 269 The slightest casualty happening to such an instrument, or any doubt whether the method of graduation has been rightly applied, make it unfit for the jealous scrupulosity of modern astronomy. **1869** ROSCOE *Elem. Chem.* (1871) 27 The graduation and use of thermometers. **1880** BLYTH in *Encycl. Brit.* XI. 27/2

b. 1594 BLUNDEVIL *Exerc.* VII. xxxi. (1636) 702 The line of degrees of Latitude, otherwise called the Graduation of the Card. **1611** SPEED *Hist. Gt. Brit.* v. v. 2 The length thereof, measured by the graduations to both extremes. **1773** *Gentl. Mag.* XLIII. 115 The experiments which he has made.. have enabled him to form a graduation for the thermometer of quick-silver that really expresses equal differences of heat. **1812** WOODHOUSE *Astron.* xl. 390 By reading off its graduations. **1849** HERSCHEL in *Man. Sci. Enq.* 287 The graduation is in the stem of the screw, which is prolonged to receive and defend it. **1875** KNIGHT *Dict. Mech.* 1001/1 Sometimes the stopper is hollow, forms a cup, and has graduations for doses of certain amounts.

transf. **1874** *Edin. Rev.* No. 285. 92 Moving.. among the stars, and.. marking its course over those illuminated graduations of the nocturnal sky.

c. 1653 H. COGAN tr. *Pinto's Trav.* x. 32 As may easily be seen by the cards and globes of the world, if so be their graduation be true. **1860** TYNDALL *Glac.* I. xxiv. 169 A thermometer, the graduation of which.. he feared was not low enough.

d. 1611 SPEED *Theat. Gt. Brit.* v. (1614) 9/2[Chichester] whose graduation for Latitude is remooved from the Equator unto the degree fiftie, fiftie five minutes.

2. a. Arrangement in degrees or gradations; 'regular progression by succession of degrees' (J.).

1658 ROWLAND *Moufet's Theat. Ins.* 1051 Whence they [Scorpions] are so forcible with poyson, and have a kinde of graduation (that I may use Paracelsus) in the use of it. **1692** TRYON *Good House-w.* ii. (ed. 2) 27 Diseases that have.. crept on by degrees.. will require the like Graduation in the Cure. **1701** GREW *Cosmol. Sacra* II. vii. 72 The graduation of the Parts of the Universe, is likewise necessary to the Perfection of the whole. **1865** GROTE *Plato* I. xviii. 524 Graduation, or ordination of objects as former and latter, first, second, third, etc. **1868** M. PATTISON *Academ. Org.* iv. 73, I do not regret the abolition of the graduation of rank.

b. An elevation by degrees into a higher condition; also quasi-*concr.* a step in the process, a degree.

1643 SIR T. BROWNE *Relig. Med.* I. §38 We enjoy a being and life in three worlds, wherein we receive most manifest graduations. **1657** G. STARKEY *Helmont's Vind.* Ep. to Rdr., A strong Diaphoretick, curing the Cough and all Feavers and Agues, except of the highest graduation. **1818** BYRON *Ch. Har.* IV. clvii, Until thy mind.. unroll In mighty graduations part by part, The glory which at once upon thee did not dart. **1863** MRS. C. CLARKE *Shaks. Char.* xvii. 445 [Justice] Silence [in *2 Hen. IV*] is an embryo of a man,—a molecule,—a graduation from nonentity towards intellectual being.

†**3.** *Alch.*, *Chem.*, etc. **a.** The process of tempering the composition of a substance to a required degree; the process of refining an element, a metal. *Obs.*

1477 NORTON *Ord. Alch.* v. in Ashm. (1652) 57 So manie graduations your wisdome must attaine. **1570** DEE *Math. Pref.* 7 In their [Phisicians] Art of Graduation, and compounde medicines. **1646** SIR T. BROWNE *Pseud. Ep.* II. iii. 68 Of greater repugnancy unto reason is that which he delivers concerning its graduation, that heated in fire & often extinguished in oyle of Mars or Iron, it acquires an ability to extract or draw forth a naile fastened in a wall. **1669** W. SIMPSON *Hydrol. Chym.* 57 Degrees of the graduation of the sulphurs. **1683** PETTUS *Fleta Min.* I. (1686) 211 If you will do something more for the Graduation sake it may be done.

b. The process of concentrating (brine, etc.) by evaporation. Also *attrib.*

1839 URE *Dict. Arts* 1087 Sea-water.. may be concentrated.. by graduation. At Salza, near Schönebeck, the graduation-house is 5817 feet long.

4. *Gunnery.* (See quot.)

1828 J. M. SPEARMAN *Brit. Gunner* (ed. 2) 380 The horizontal column at the bottom of the table.. is the graduation, or common difference, of the several piles.

†**5.** *U.S. Railways.* Formerly used for GRADING, GRADIENT.

1840 TANNER *Canals & Rail Roads U.S.* 163 The maximum graduation.. being about thirty feet per mile. *Ibid.* 249 *Graduation*, the act of modifying or adjusting a roadway into a particular line. In rail-road making, it signifies the process by which a required grade is obtained.

6. The action of receiving or conferring a university degree, or a certificate of qualification from some recognized authority. Also, the ceremony of conferring degrees. Chiefly *Sc.* and *U.S.* Also *attrib.*

a **1639** SPOTTISWOOD *Hist. Ch. Scot.* III. (1655) 163 Every Earl's son at his entry should give 40s. with so much at his graduation. **1723** *Wodrow Corr.* (1843) III. 29 In a very little time after his graduation, he was advanced to be a Regent or Professor of Philosophy in that University. **1776** ADAM SMITH *W.N.* v. i. III. ii. II. 361 There was nothing equivalent to the privileges of graduation, and to have attended any of those schools was not necessary, in order to be permitted to practise any particular trade or profession. **1858** MASSON *Milton* (1859) I. 183 The most important formality connected with the graduation. **1876** GRANT *Burgh Sch. Scot.* II. v. 172 The rector [of the grammar School of Aberdeen] indulged the boys with.. plays.. sometimes at the graduation. **1901** *Daily News* 2 Mar. 4/7 There are only seven signatures of Milton known, the first occurring in the Graduation Book of Cambridge, 1628–9. **1903** *N.Y. Times* 7 Oct. 6 The annual graduation exercises of the schoolship St. Mary's were held last night on board the ship. **1906** M. E. W. FREEMAN *By Light of Soul* 217 Maria dressed herself in her graduation gown.

graduator ('grædju:eɪtə(r)). [f. GRADUATE *v.* + -OR.] One who or that which graduates. **a.** One who graduates (see GRADUATE *v.* 4) glasses, instruments, etc. **b.** An instrument for dividing any line, whether straight or curved, into small regular portions; a dividing-engine. **c.** A contrivance for concentrating a solution by means of rapid evaporation.

1828–32 WEBSTER, *Graduator*, an instrument for dividing any line, right or curve, into equal parts. **1839** URE *Dict. Arts* 618 These tubes serve to allow the air.. to circulate freely through the graduator [in vinegar making]. **1898** *Daily News* 24 Sept. 10/6 Glass Graduator (Medical) wanted.

†**graduatory**, *a. Obs. rare*[−1]. [ad. L. type *graduātōrius, f. med.L. *graduāre* to GRADUATE: see -ORY.] Having the property of graduating metals (see GRADUATE *v.* 5).

1691 BOYLE *Exper. & Observ. Phys.* iv. 104 Sulphur of Mars, which.. the others.. speak of as a graduatory Substance (as to some Metals).

[**graduction**: Error for GRADUATION (sense 1 and 3 b).

1849 CRAIG. **1860** WORCESTER [citing *Brande*; but edd. 1843, 1853, and 1866 of *Dict. Sci.*, etc., read *Graduation*] Hence in some later Dicts.]

‖**gradus** ('greɪdəs). Short for *Gradus ad Parnassum* 'a step to Parnassus', the Latin title of a dictionary of prosody until recently used in English public schools, intended as an aid in Latin versification, both by giving the 'quantities' of words and by suggesting poetical epithets and phraseology. Hence applied to later works of similar plan and object; also extended as in ***Greek gradus***, and *transf.*

The earliest edition of the 'Gradus' in the British Museum is that of Cologne 1687; there was a London edition in 1691.

a **1764** R. LLOYD *Poetry Professors* 6 What reams of paper will be spoil'd! What graduses be daily soil'd By inky fingers, greasy thumbs, Hunting the word that never comes! **1810** BENTHAM *Packing* (1821) 69 The arguments you have to encounter—together with whatsoever other appropriate epithets and phrases.. are furnished by the *Courtier's and Lawyer's Gradus.* **1827** J. B. MOZLEY *Lett.* (1885) 8, I should like to have a Greek Gradus, if there is such a book [Written æt. 14]. **1857** HUGHES *Tom Brown* II. iii, The three fell to work with Gradus and dictionary upon the morning's vulgus.

attrib. **1887** *Athenæum* 25 June 831/1 A fair descriptive passage is spoilt by a commonplace or gradus epithet.

grady ('greɪdɪ), *a. Her.* [app. f. GRADE after heraldic adjs. in *-y*, ad. F. *-é*, *-ée*.] Of a line or ordinary: Cut into steps. Of a cross: Springing from steps; degraded.

1828–40 BERRY *Encycl. Her.* I, *Grady*, represents steps or degrees, and one battlement upon another, sometimes termed battled, embattled, and grady embattled. *Ibid.* s.v. *Cross*, *Cross grady*, fixed to, or on steps or degrees. **1894** *Parker's Gloss. Her.* 223 *Battle embattled*, or *battled grady*, is a name given to a figure having, as it were, an extra battlement, but, as usual for these fanciful names, no examples are given.

grady. obs. form of GREEDY.

†**Græcaster.** *Obs. rare*[−1]. In 8 Gre-. [f. L. *Græc-us* + -ASTER.] ? = GREEKLING.

1716 M. DAVIES *Athen. Brit.* III. *Orig. Physick* 46 Some Grecaster about Constantin's Time translated most of the Latin old Country-Tracts into Greek.

Græcian, obs. form of GRECIAN.

Græcism, Grecism ('gri:sɪz(ə)m). Also 5 **Gryscysme**, 6–7 **Græcisme**, 7 **Grecisme**. [ad. F. *grécisme*, ad. med.L. *Græcismus*, f. *Græcus* GREEK.]

†**1.** The *Græcismus*, a grammatical treatise in Latin verse of the 12th century. *Obs. rare*[−1].

c **1450** *Cov. Myst.* (Shaks. Soc.) 189 In alle this scyens is non us lyke In Caton, Gryscysme, nor Doctrinal.

2. An idiom, or a grammatical or orthographical feature, belonging to the Greek language; esp. as used by a speaker or writer in another language.

1570 LEVINS *Manip.* 146 Græcisme, *Græcismus.* *a* **1610** HEALEY *Theophrastus* To Rdr. (1636), The French is elegant enough.. and has many Graecismes. **1693** DRYDEN *Juvenal* Ded. (1697) 13 No Man has so happily copy'd the Manner of Homer; or so copiously translated his Grecisms. **1712** ADDISON *Spect.* No. 285 ¶9 Milton.. has infused a great many Latinisms as well as Græcisms.. into the Language of his Poem. *a* **1800** COWPER *Comm. Milton's P.L.* I. 335 A Græcism, and taken from the ουδ' απιθησε.. of Homer. **1880** EARLE *Philol. Eng. Tongue* §150 In one instance it is written *sch* where nothing but the simple *sc* is heard, as *school*. This is probably a Grecism. **1881** G. W. MOON *Revisers' Eng.* vii. (1882) 20 The maintenance of pure idiomatic English, in opposition to the Grecisms into which the Revisers have occasionally been betrayed.

3. The spirit or style characteristic of the Greeks in art, mode of thought or expression, and the like; adoption or imitation of these; an instance of this.

1609 BIBLE (Douay) II. Index, Sectes of Panimes, Barbarisme, Scythisme, and Grecisme. **1642** FULLER *Holy & Prof. St.* III. xxiv. 221 The influence of the Grecian Empire on the Persians had then spiced them with a smack of Grecisme. **1669** GALE *Crt. Gentiles* I. I. xii. 76 Words, which savor not more of Grecisme, than of the Illyric. **1806** *Edin. Rev.* VII. 489 The which apotheosis of Alexander was one grand Grecism. *a* **1849** H. COLERIDGE *Ess.* (1851) I. 31 The ridiculous affectation of Grecism that was prevalent in the decline of Rome. **1851** RUSKIN *Stones Ven.* I. App. xvii. 392 Every stunted Grecism and stucco Romanism, into which they are now forced to shape their palsied thoughts. **1851** CARLYLE *Sterling* I. iv. (1872) 29 There is.. especially in his early writings, a certain tinge of Grecism. **1871**

RUSKIN *Fors Clav.* (1896) I. xxiii. 463 The singular Grecism in Shakespeare's mind.

Græcize, Grecize (ˈgriːsaɪz), *v.* [ad.L. *Græcizāre*, f. *Græc-us* GREEK: see -IZE.]

1. *trans.* To assimilate to what is Greek; to give a Greek cast, character, or form to.

1692 R. L'ESTRANGE *Josephus, Antiq.* i. (1733) 3 Josephus endeavours to Grecize, and shape the history of the Jews as like as he could to those of the Greeks and Romans. **1827** G. HIGGINS *Celtic Druids* 200 *note*, This word, as usual, they Græcised. **1853** RUSKIN *Stones Ven.* III. iv. §35. 194 Whatever is..in any way Grecized or Romanized. **1861** J. G. SHEPPARD *Fall Rome* vii. 390 Hilderic..succeeded to the throne without dispute, though entirely Grecized by education and long residence in Constantinople. **1880** T. HODGKIN *Italy & Inv.* II. ii. II. 81 *note*, His habit of Grecising the names of undoubted Huns.

2. *intr.* **a.** To favour the cause of the Greeks. *rare*$^{-1}$. **b.** To become Greek-like; to adopt Greek expressions, idioms, modes of life, etc.

1840 *Blackw. Mag.* XLVII. 646 To Graecize or not to Graecize had become a test of patriotic feeling. **1879** FARRAR *St. Paul* I. 126 One who 'Græcises' in language or mode of life. **1892** *Guardian* 18 May 743/3 The MS. quite certainly does not Latinise but Graecises.

Hence **ˈGræcized** *ppl. a.*, **ˈGræcizing** *vbl. sb.* and *ppl. a.*

18.. KITTO *Hist. Bible* Introd. (1873) 34 (Funk) This is what enraged them so much against the Hellenistic, or Grecizing Jews, who read the Septuagint Greek version in their synagogues. **1860** ELLICOTT *Life Our Lord* vii. 316 *note*, It is..probable that they were complete strangers, but attracted to Philip by his Grecized name. **1861** TRENCH *Comm. Ep. to 7 Ch. Asia* 82 *Νικόλαος* is no more than a grecizing of this name [Balaam]. **1861** STANLEY *East. Ch.* i. (1869) 14 The early Roman Church was but a colony of Greek Christians or Grecised Jews. **1884** EARLE *Ags. Lit.* 2 He lamented even in his time the Grecising of his mother-tongue.

Græco-, Greco- (ˈgriːkəʊ), mod. combining form of L. *Græcus* GREEK. Like other comb. forms of ethnic adjs. (as ANGLO-, CELTO-, FRANCO-, GALLO-[1], TURCO-), it is modelled on the form occuring in Greek compounds like *Συροφοίνιξ*, and in late L. imitations of these, like *Gallogræcus*. Apart from the words *Græcomania*, *Græcophil*, which are formed strictly on Gr. analogies, it occurs only in compound adjs. (now always written with hyphen), the sense of which is either 'relating to the Greek settlements or states established in certain regions abroad', as in ***Græco-Asiatic***, ***-Bactrian***, ***-Phrygian***, or 'partly Greek and partly something else', as in ***Græco-Latin***, ***-Mohammedan***, ***-Oriental***, ***-Trojan***, ***-Turkish***.

1667 WATERHOUSE *Fire Lond.* 82 The Græcatrojan [*sic*] Horse out of which marched many of the Hectors of Englands courage. **1680** H. DODWELL *Two Lett.* (1691) 227 You shall find them together collected in three Greco-Latine folio's, by Valesius. **1849** GROTE *Greece* II. lxxiii. (1862) VI. 433 He sought also to compose the dissensions and misrule which had arisen..in the Greco-Asiatic cities. **1855** MILMAN *Lat. Chr.* XIV. iii. (1864) IX. 108 This Mohammedan, or Graeco-Mohammedan philosophy was as far removed from the old, stern, inflexible Unitarianism of the Korân, as [etc.]. **1861** J. G. SHEPPARD *Fall Rome* xii. 659 The new Greco-oriental philosophy of Alexandria. **1888** *Academy* 21 Jan. 38/2 After the destruction of the Græco-Bactrian power in those regions. **1898** *Expositor* Dec. 438 Many little touches throughout..place the reader in the Graeco-Phrygian cities of Asia Minor.

b. Græco-Roman *a.*, *spec.* of a style of wrestling, resembling that used by the ancient Greeks and Romans, in which attacks are directed only at the upper part of the body.

1888 *Antiqua Mater* Pref. 9 The Græco-Roman literature of the second century. **1901** J. W. MCWHINNIE *Mod. Wrestling* 7 Graeco-Roman wrestling, as now practised all over the civilised world, is understood to be a last-century continental revival of the athletic contests which figured prominently in the festivities of ancient Greece and Rome. **1934** [see ALL-IN 2]. **1968** G. KENT *Pict. Hist. Wrestling* viii. 175 Alberg laid claim to the Greco-Roman championship of the world.

Græcomania (ˌgriːkəʊˈmeɪnɪə). [f. GRÆCO- + Gr. *μανία* madness (see MANIA).] A mania for things Greek. Hence **Græcoˈmaniac**, one possessed by Græcomania.

1800 B. CROWTHER (*title*) The Rabies Piratica, its history, symptoms, and cure; also the Furor Hippocraticus or Græcomania, with its treatment. **1854** KEIGHTLEY *Myth. Anc. Greece & It.* (ed. 3) 447 Each succeeding age saw the Græcomania increase. **1897** *Nation* (N.Y.) 28 Jan. 75/1 Aesthetic emotion was never anything more than a pose with the Grecomaniacs of the Empire.

Græcophil (ˈgriːkəfɪl). Also 9 **Grecophil**. [f. GRÆCO- + Gr. *φίλος* friend. A newspaper word.]

A lover of Greece or of what is Greek.

1889 *Pall Mall G.* 24 Oct. 7/2 Greece has always been grateful to the German Grecophils for sacrificing their money and their lives in the fight for Greek independence.

grædde, pa. t. of GREDE *v. Obs.*

graet(e, obs. form of GRATE, GREAT.

Grætian, obs. form of GRECIAN.

‖**graf** (grɑːf). Also 7 **graff**. [G. *graf*: see also GRAVE *sb.*[3]] The German equivalent of COUNT and EARL.

1630 J. TAYLOR (Water P.) *Wks.* III. 86 This towne..is wholely and solely belonging to the Graff or Graue of Shomburgh. *a* **1690** ETHEREDGE *Poems* Wks. (1888) 378 These form'd the jewel erst did grace The cap of the first Graf o' th' race. *a* **1849** MANGAN *Poems* (1859) 113 The Graf came never—the Graf was dead. **1852** SIR J. STEPHEN *Lect. Hist. Fr.* (ed. 2) I. 63 Each Herizog and Graf was regarded as supreme.

grafe, obs. form of GRAVE *v.*[1]

graff (grɑːf, -æ-), *sb.*[1] *arch.*; superseded in ordinary use by GRAFT. Forms: *α.* 4–6 **graf(e**, 4–7 **graffe**, 4– **graff**. *β.* 6 **greffe**, **grefe**. *γ.* 5–6 **gryf(fe**, 6–7 **griff(e**. [a. OF. *grafe*, *greffe* (mod.F. *greffe*), semi-popular ad. late L. *graphium*, ad. Gr. *γραφίον*, *γραφεῖον* stylus, f. *γράφειν* to write. The sense 'stylus, pencil' is common in OFr.; the transferred sense of 'scion, graft' was suggested by the similarity of shape.

The OFr. word was adopted in Du. both in the original and the transferred sense: MDu. *greffie*, *griffie*, mod.Du. *griffie*, *grif*, whence perh. the *γ* forms above. Du. has also a form *grift*, with which cf. Eng. *grift*, GRAFT *sb.*]

1. A shoot or scion inserted in another stock: = GRAFT *sb.*[1] 1.

1398 TREVISA *Barth. De P.R.* XVII. ii. (1495) 595 The beste is whan the graffe and the stocke ben lyke. *c* **1440** CAPGRAVE *Life St. Kath.* II. 1247 Liche a gryf am I I-planted be God vp-on a old stok. **1523** FITZHERB. *Husb.* §138 Thou must get thy graffes of the fayrest lanses that thou canste fynde on the tree. **1530** PALSGR. 227/2 Grefe, *ente*. **1664** EVELYN *Kal. Hort.* (1729) 190 Gather Cyons for Graffs before the Buds sprout. **1703** POPE *Vertumnus* 13 Now the cleft rind inserted graffs receives. **1823** COBBETT *Weekly Reg.* 29 Mar. 827 Trees with very fine bloom coming from graffs imported the year before last. **1859** TENNYSON *Vivien* 477 A Gardener putting in a graff.

fig. **1570** DEE *Math. Pref.* 2 What commodity..is to be looked for, as well of graff as stocke. **1593** SHAKS. *Lucr.* 1062 This bastard graff shall never come to growth. *a* **1603** T. CARTWRIGHT *Confut. Rhem. N.T.* (1618) 85 Out of the griffe of transfiguration, it were strange to gather the fruite of Transubstantiation. **1661** BOYLE *Style Holy Script.* 141 The Word, which Saint James pronounces able to save our Souls, he describes as a Graff. **1826** E. IRVING *Babylon* II. 329 With occasional allusions to the Gentile graff, which was graffed into that ancient and everlasting stock.

2. A twig, shoot, scion; *gen.* a branch, plant: = GRAFT *sb.*[1] 2.

1555 EDEN *Decades* 162 They wyll suffer owre corne, graffes and frutes to bee consumed of woormes. **15..** *Robin Hood* (Ritson) 128, I have a staff of another oke graff. **1567** TURBERV. *Epit.* etc. 5 b, How coulde so barraine soyle bring forth so good a Graffe? **1583** STUBBES *Anat. Abus.* II. (1882) 82 If he can get a graffe of this tree loden with..apples. **1613–16** W. BROWNE *Brit. Past* II. iv, On a Cypresse Graffe ..they hung this Epitaph. **1831** T. L. PEACOCK *Crotchet Cas.* xii. (1887) 135 We can no more [etc.], than we can flourish the oaken graff of the Pindar of Wakefield.

fig. a **1393** LANGL. *P. Pl.* C. II. 201 Loue is..þe graffe of grace and grayþest wey to heuene. **1509** BARCLAY *Shyp of Folys* (1570) 44 b, Roote out the graffes of your olde offence. **1522** MORE *De quat. Noviss.* Wks. 85/1 Litle meruail it is though enuy be an vngracious grafe. For it cometh of an vngracious stocke.

†**3.** An act of grafting. In quot. *transf. Obs.*

1610 DOULAND *Var. Lute-lessons* B 2 b, But if the letter that we doubt of, be placed not alone, but with one or more other letters, which coniunction we for this time will call a griffe, then the difficultie is greater.

4. *attrib.* and *Comb.*, **graffshoot** = sense 1; **graff-stock**, a stock on which to graft.

1502 ARNOLDE *Chron.* (1811) 169 To haue frute without cores, loke thou haue a sufficient graffstok and doo therwith as I said before. **1860** T. MARTIN *Horace* 226 The russet fig adorns the tree, that graffshoot never knew.

graff (grɑːf, -æ-), *sb.*[2] *Obs.* exc. *Hist.* Also 7–9 **graffe**, 8 **grauff**. [prob. ad. MDu. *grave* wk. masc. = GRAVE *sb.*[1]] A trench serving as a fortification; a dry or wet ditch; a foss or moat; *rarely*, a canal (in Holland). Cf. GRAFT *sb.*[2]

1637 R. MONRO *Exped.* I. 69 The enemy forsaking our workes unconquered, the graffe filled with their dead bodies. **1641** EVELYN *Diary* 19 Aug., It is by extraordinary industry that as well this Citty, as generaly the townes of Holland, are so acommodated wth graffs, cutts, sluces, moles, and rivers. *a* **1674** CLARENDON *Hist. Reb.* VIII. §6 The walls [of Arundel Castle] were very strong, and the graff broad and deep. **1706** MAULE *Hist. Picts* in *Misc. Scot.* I. 61 It had a deep grauff and a drawbridge. **1759** B. MARTIN *Nat. Hist. Eng.* II. Cambridge 95 Two Graffs between the three Ramparts. **1791** LUCKOMBE *Beauties Eng.* I. 286 Another very large camp and prodigious works, the graff being inwards and outwards. **1850** WARBURTON *Reginald Hastings* I. 13 The Saxon palace had been..surrounded by a graff, or moat, in the reign of Rufus. **1898** *Blackw. Mag.* Oct. 518/2 A bristling monstrosity of sconces, graffes, fussies, stackets and crenelles.

transf. **1637** R. MONRO *Exped.* I. 29 Retiring to one corner of his Kingdom, to prevent the losse of the whole, being naturally fortified with a broad graffe, as the isle of Britaine.

graff (grɑːf, -æ-), *sb.*[3] Also 6 **graffe**, 7 **grafe**, **griffe**. [perh. a variant of GRAFT *sb.*[3]]

1. = GRAFT *sb.*[3] 1: usually ***spade('s) graff***. ? *Obs.*

1523 FITZHERB. *Husb.* §124 Dygge vp the muldes a spade-graffe depe. **1601** HOLLAND *Pliny* II. 466 There was found in Dalmatia a vaine of gold ore within one spades griffe in the first turfe of the ground. **1649** BLITHE *Eng. Improv. Impr.* iv. (1653) 23 Thou must go half one Spades grafe deep at lest.

2. *dial.* = GRAFT *sb.*[3] 2.

1875 PARISH *Sussex Gloss.*, *Graff* or *Graffing Tool*, a curved spade, generally made of wood shod with iron, used by drainers.

graff (grɑːf, -æ-), *v.*[1] *arch.*; in ordinary use superseded by GRAFT *v.* Forms: *α.* 4–7 **graffe**, 5 **graffyn**. *β.* 6 **greffe**. *γ.* 5 **gryffe(n**, **-yn**, 7 **griffe**. [f. GRAFF *sb.*[1]; recorded earlier than the equivalent OF. *grafier*, mod.F. *greffer*.]

1. *trans.* To insert (a scion of one tree) into a different stock: = GRAFT *v.*[1] 1.

1377 LANGL. *P. Pl.* B. v. 137, I was sum tyme..the couentes gardyner..for to graffe ympes. **1388** WYCLIF *Rom.* xi. 19 The braunchis ben brokun, that Y be graffid in. **14..** *Songs & Carols* (Warton Club) 35 The fayrest mayde of this toun preyid me For to gryffyn here a gryf of myn pery tre. **1523** FITZHERB. *Husb.* §137 A peare or a warden wolde be graffed in a pyrre-stocke. **1574** HYLL *Planting* 86 Ye may graffe your graffes full as long as two or three trunchions. **1621** AINSWORTH *Annot. Pentat.* Lev. xix. 19 (1639) 115 He ..graffeth one tree in another. **1706** J. GARDINER *Rapin's Gard.* (1728) 167 To graff a fruitful Branch on barren Trees.

fig. c **1430** *Pilgr. Lyf Manhode* I. cvi. (1869) 56 She hath be graffed bi subtile art and ioyned to this burdoun. **1548–9** (Mar.) *Bk. Com. Prayer* (Collect 7th Sund. Trinity), Graffe in our hartes the loue of thy name. *a* **1553** UDALL *Royster D.* I. i. (Arb.) 12 In these twentie townes..Is not the like stocke, whereon to graffe a loute. **1605** CAMDEN *Rem.* (1637) 41 We graffe upon French words those buds, to which that soile affoordeth no growth. *a* **1645** D. FEATLEY in *Fuller's Abel Rediv.* (1651) 542 Of all the fruitfull trees in our Paradise he chose to griffe his meditations upon the Apocalipse upon Abbot his stocke. **1692** LOCKE *Educ.* §200 The proper Stock whereon afterwards to graff the true Principles of Morality and Religion. **1695** E. WELCHMAN *Husbandm. Man.* (1707) 43 A Man is by the Baptism of Repentance graffed into the body of Christs Church. **1828** E. IRVING *Baptism* II. Wks. 1864 II. 286 When God is visiting a people in his wrath..no new branches are graffed into Christ. **1878** BROWNING *Poets Croisic* 139 Never hope to graff A second sprig of triumph there! **1882** FREEMAN *Reign Will. Rufus* II. vii. 455 The old stock was neither cut down nor withered away; but a new stock was graffed upon it.

1536 LADY BRIAN in Ellis *Orig. Lett.* Ser. II. II. 82, I trust to God & her teeth were well graft. **1579** SPENSER *Sheph. Cal.* Feb. 242 So longe haue I listened to thy speche, That graffed to the ground is my breche. **1598** SYLVESTER *Du Bartas* I. iv. 220 Twelve [Houses] in that rich Girdle greft Which God gave Nature for her New-Years-gift. **1608** A. WILLET *Hexapla in Exod.* 685 They [the horns of the altar] were made out of the same matter and wood, not griffed in. **1624** GEE *Foot out of Snare* v. 38 [His] legs cut off at the knees..were, without the help of any Artist, graffed on again. **1648** GAGE *West Ind.* xii. 54 In the walls whereof was graffed betwixt stone and stone a skull with the teeth outwards.

2. *absol.* and *intr.* To insert a graft or grafts.

1483 CAXTON *Gold. Leg.* 251 b/2 Ypolyte took his legge.. and tooke and set it in his place like as on graffyth in a tree. **1523** FITZHERB. *Husb.* §136 It is conuenyent to lerne howe thou shalt graffe. **1572** MASCALL *Plant. & Graff.* Exhortation, Before ye doe intend to plant or Graffe, it shall be meete to haue good experience in thinges meete for this Arte. **1658** tr. *Porta's Nat. Magic* III. v. 68 Nature, saith he [Pliny], hath taught how to graffe with a seed. **1693** EVELYN *De la Quint. Compl. Gard.* II. 106 We might Graff in the Cleft, during the Months of November [etc.].

fig. **1676** DRYDEN *Epil. Man of Mode*, So brisk, so gay, so travailed, so refined, As he took pains to graff upon his kind.

3. *trans.* To insert a graft in (a stock). Also *vaguely* (= GRAFT *v.*[1] 3).

1564 GOLDING *Justine* XLIII. (1570) 175 They lerned to plant and graffe their olyues. **1575** GASCOIGNE *Posies* 190 To griffe a pippine stocke, when sappe begins to swell. **1613** PURCHAS *Pilgrimage* III. vii. 227 Date trees, amongst which there are two growing out of one stock exceeding high, which their Prophet forsooth graffed with his owne hande. **1693** EVELYN *De la Quint. Compl. Gard.* II. 107 April is likewise Convenient to Graff Vines. **1820** SCOTT *Abbot* xxxviii, I scarce remember the pear-mains which I graffed here with my own hands some fifty years since.

†**4.** To implant. *lit.* and *fig.* = GRAFT *v.*[1] 4.

c **1420** *Pallad. on Husb.* I. 115 Seedis newe eschewe To sowe or graffe. *c* **1450** LONELICH *Grail* xlii. 108 Ouer the Se Cowndyed scholen ȝe be Into the lond that is to ȝow behote, there-Inne to Gryffen Many A Rote. **1553** T. WILSON *Rhet.* 18 God hath graffed & geuen man power therunto, wherof these are deriued. **1573** BARET *Alv.* G 419 There is a sober thriftinesse graffed in thy race and kinred naturally.

5. *Comb.*, †**graff-horn** (see quot.).

1611 COTGR., *Cuco cocuant*, a cuckold-maker, a Graffe-horne.

graff, *v.*[2] *Obs.* exc. *dial.* [variant of GRAVE *v.*] *intr.* To dig.

1387–8 T. USK *Test. Love* Prol. 5 Dul wit and a thoughtful soule so sore have myned and graffed in my spirites. **1875** Graffing [see GRAFF *sb.*[3] 2].

graff, var. GRAVE *sb.*[1]; obs. f. GRAF, count.

graffage (ˈgrɑːfɪdʒ, -æ-). *dial.* [? f. GRAFF *sb.*[2] + HEDGE.] (See quots.)

1798 J. JEFFERSON *Let. to J. Boucher* 19 Mar. (MS.), [Hampshire words] Graffage..a wooden frame somewhat like a Stile, placed in a bank, where there is a water-course. **1835** MISS MITFORD *Country Stories* (1850) 29 They clean the graffages, clear out the moat-like ditches. **1883** *Hampshire Gloss.*, *Graffage*, a railed fence at the junction of two ditches, or where a ditch abuts on a road at right angles.

graffane, obs. form of GRIFFAUN.

†**graffed**, *ppl. a. Obs.* [f. GRAFF *v.*[1] + -ED[1].] = GRAFTED *ppl. a.* 1.

14.. *Voc.* in Wr.-Wülcker 590/3 *Insitus*, planted or graffed. *c* **1449** PECOCK *Repr.* I. xiii. 69 Receue ȝe it as a graffid word. **1557** *Tottel's Misc.* (Arb.) 190 Ah thinke her graffed loue can not so sone decay. **1598** GRENEWEY *Tacitus' Ann.* (1604) 182 A true and woorthy plant to receiue his fathers Empire, which a graffed son by adoption now possessed.

†**graffer**[1]. *Obs.* Also 5 **graffare, -ere, gryffar(e**. [f. GRAFF *v.*[1] + -ER[1].] = GRAFTER 1.

c **1440** *Promp. Parv.* 212/1 Gryffare, or graffare, *insertor.* **1565** JEWEL *Repl. Harding* 544 Husbandmenne, and Ditchers, and Heardmenne, and Graffers. **1572** MASCALL *Plant. & Graff.* Exhortation, Thus much haue I thought meete to declare vnto the Planters and Graffers. **1693** EVELYN *De la Quint. Compl. Gard., Refl. Agric.* 47 We shou'd not be much better Graffers than we now are without that Knowledge.

†**graffer**[2]. *Obs.* Also 7 **graphiere.** [ad. F. *greffier*: see GREFFIER.] A notary.

1513-4 *Act 5 Hen. VIII*, c. 1 Preamb., Officers..called Notaries otherwise called Graffers to accepte take and recorde the knowlege of all contractes. **1607** COWELL *Interpr.*, *Graffer*, signifieth as much as a notary or scrivener. **1615** HOBY *Curry-combe* v. 238 Wee will say the Graphiere was a knaue.

graffing ('grɑːfɪŋ, -æ-), *vbl. sb.* [f. GRAFF *v.*[1] + -ING[1].] = GRAFTING *vbl. sb.*[1] in various senses.

1398 TREVISA *Barth. De P.R.* IX. xxx. (1495) 366 Lente is tyme of graffynge for in Lente graftes ben grafted on the trees. *c* **1420** *Pallad. on Husb.* IV. 36 Another seith ther graffying nigh the grounde Is best, ther esili they comprehende And preue. **1571** HANMER *Chron. Irel.* (1633) 187 Manuall labour, as..planting and greffing for daily wages. **1575** *Art of Planting* 19 There be many wayes of graffinges. **1611** SPEED *Hist. Gt. Brit.* VI. xlvii. §11. 165 This Emperor was..from the graffing of his neck, to the groin very long, but from thence somewhat short and bow-legged withal. **1667** DRYDEN *Wild Gallant* II. i. Wks. 1882 II. 53 But I fear we shall not have the graffing of the horns. **1672** —— *Conq. Granada, Defence Epil.* 169 By this graffing, as I may call it, on old words, has our Tongue been Beautified by the three fore-mention'd Poets. **1840** R. H. DANA *Bef. Mast* xxxv. 134 The neat work upon the rigging, —the knots.. pointings, and graffings. **1876** SWINBURNE *Erechth.* 199 For the first fair graft of his graffing. **1884** BLACK *Jud. Shaks.* ii, Left to his weeding and graffing.

attrib. **1523** FITZHERB. *Husb.* §136 Thou must haue a graffynge-sawe. *Ibid.*, Thou must haue also a graffynge knyfe. **1591** PERCIVALL *Sp. Dict.*, *Encensar tierra para plantar*, to set graffing stockes. **1661** OGILBY *King's Coronation* 30 All Sorts of Graffing, and Gardening Tools.

‖**graffito** (graf'fito, grə'fiːtəʊ). *Antiq.* and *Art.* Pl. graffiti (graf'fiti, grə'fiːtiː). [It. *graffito*, f. *graffio* a scratch.] A drawing or writing scratched on a wall or other surface; a scribbling on an ancient wall, as those at Pompeii and Rome. Also, a method of decoration in which designs are produced by scratches through a superficial layer of plaster, glazing, etc., revealing a ground of different colour; chiefly *attrib.*, as in ***graffito-decoration, -pottery, -ware.***

1851 D. WILSON *Preh. Ann.* (1863) II. IV. iv. 286 The slight scratching of many of the Maeshowe Runes, and the consequent irregularity and want of precision in the forms.. of what, it must be remembered, are mere graffiti. **1873** SYMONDS *Grk. Poets* xi. 242 Even the Graffiti of Pompeii have scarcely more power to reconstruct the past and summon as in dreams the voices and the forms of long since buried men. **1873** MRS. PALLISER tr. *Jacquemart's Hist. Ceramic Art* 619 Index, Graffito decoration.

transf. **1877** A. B. EDWARDS *Up Nile* xxi. 653 Visited by crowds of early travellers, who have as usual left their neatly-scribbled graffiti on the walls. **1886** DOWDEN *Shelley* I. v. 179 She sang pleasantly; and could scribble such graffiti as may be found in school-girls' copy-books.

graft (grɑːft, -æ-), *sb.*[1] Forms: α. 5 grafte, 6- graft. β. 6 gryft, 6-7 grift(e. [A modification of the earlier GRAFF *sb.*[1]

The precise formation is uncertain. Possibly due to the use of *graft* as pa. t. and pa. pple. of GRAFF *v.*[1] But there has been much phonetic confusion between (f) and (ft) at the end of words; cf. *draft* as a variant of *draff*. The forms *grif* under GRAFF *sb.*[1] and *grifte* above may perh. be influenced by the Du. *grif, grift* (recorded from 16th c.); in Du. it is uncertain whether the *-t* is a suffix or phonetically excrescent.]

1. A shoot or scion inserted in a groove or slit made in another stock, so as to allow the sap of the latter to circulate through the former.

1483 *Cath. Angl.* 162/1 A Grafte, *surculus.* **1554** *Acc. Edw. VI* in *Trevelyan Papers* (Camden) II. 15 Sir John Wulfe.. maker and deviser of the Kinges herbors and plantes of grafts. **1560** BECON *Catech.* Wks. 1564 I. 435 b, Is there any man..will cal a young gryft of the first yeres gryfting fruteles and barren. **1649** J. ELLISTONE tr. *Behmen's Epist.* v. §49 A plant or grift that is set, doth worke so long till it putteth forth its branches. **1774** GOLDSM. *Nat. Hist.* (1776) III. 96 This tumour every day buds forward from the point like the graft of a tree. **1813** SIR. H. DAVY *Agric. Chem.* (1814) 253 The graft is only nourished by the sap of the tree to which it is transferred. **1878** J. BULLER *40 Y. in N. Zealand* I. viii. 63 Fruitful orchards are the outcome of grafts I introduced.

fig. **1547** BECON *Agst. Adultery* Wks. 1560 II. 161 b, If God spared not the natural braunches, neyther wyll he spare vs that be but graftes, if we commit lyke offences. **1650** DAVENANT *Gondibert* Pref. (1673) 3 New grafts of old wither'd words. **1844** H. H. WILSON *Brit. India* I. I. viii. 579 The legislative encouragement yielded to missionary labours was also a graft upon the original design. **1871** BROWNING *Pr. Hohenst.* 1524 A devil's-graft on God's foundation-stone. **1885** *Act 48 & 49 Vict.* c. 73 §8 The interest vested in him by such order shall..be deemed to be a graft upon the previous interest of the tenant in the holding.

†**2.** A twig or off-shoot fit for use in grafting; a scion, sucker; hence *gen.* a branch, plant. *Obs.*

1587 FENNER *Song of Songs* iv. 13 Thy gryfts they are, as of A pomgranat orchard. **1606** BRYSKETT *Civ. Life* 2 To transport from..forraine countries..strange grafts, plants and flowers. **1624** QUARLES *Sion's Sonets* xii. 13 My love is like a Paradise, beset With rarest grifts, whose fruits..The world nere tasted.

fig. **1576** FLEMING *Panopl. Epist.* Epit. A b, This younge impe and flexible grifte..bent not his listening eare unto others lore. **1587** TURBERV. *Trag. T.* etc. (1837) 345 No tree can take so deep a roote as grifts of faithful love. **1598** DRAYTON *Heroic. Ep.* x. 81 Edward the top-Branch of that golden Tree..I his Graft, of eu'ry Weed o'r-growne. **1600** FAIRFAX *Tasso* XVII. lxxix. 311 And in Bauaria's field transplanted new This Romane grift florisht, encreast and grew. **1614** RALEGH *Hist. World* I. I. ii. §6. 32 God gaue vnto man all kinde of seeds and grafts of life.

3. *Surg.* 'A portion of living tissue transplanted from one place to another on the same or another organism, with a view to its adhesion and growth' (Billings *Med. Dict.* 1890); also, the operation or its result, the adhesion and growth of such new tissue.

1871 J. WOODMAN *Notes Transpl. or Engraft. Skin* 19, I took three small pieces of skin from her own arm and engrafted them... On the fourth day I removed the plaster, and with it one of the grafts. **1886** *Dict. Pract. Surg.* (ed. Heath) I. 616 These grafts may be placed at any part of a healing granulation-surface, and may grow there, forming islets of skin. *Ibid.* 618 The preservation of the periosteum is not essential to the success of the graft..When an osseous graft is about to be effected, the part into which the graft is to be placed ought to be first prepared. **1913** *Interstate Med. Jrnl.* XX. 573 Only the peripheral part of thyroid grafts persisted, the central part becoming necrotic... Regeneration was complete at the end of three months, and the graft differed from a normal gland by an infiltration of connective tissue. **1970** *Oxford Times* 16 Jan. 1/1 This is the first transplant operation to be carried out at the hospital. The other kidney graft in Oxford was at the Radcliffe Infirmary two years ago. **1970** *Nature* 28 Feb. 851 Liver grafts may be less exacting in their genetical requirements than those of kidney.

4. [From the vb.] **a.** The process or product of grafting (see combinations in 5); also, a variety produced by grafting, a kind (of fruit).

1847 BARHAM *Ingol. Leg.* Ser. III. *Jarvis's Wig*, On the precise graft of the espalier of Eden, Sanchoniathon Manetho, and Berosus are undecided.

b. The place where the scion is inserted in the stock.

1802 FORSYTH *Fruit-trees* i. 8 Taking off the worst branches first,..always cutting as near to the graft as possible. **1898** L. H. BAILEY *Pruning-bk.* 263 The grafting of the main trunk has some disadvantages, because a bad fork is apt to occur at the graft.

5. *attrib.* and *Comb.* (in sense 3), as ***graft-growth, surface, theory***; **graft-hybrid** (see quot.); **graft-hybridism, -hybridization**, the process of hybridizing by means of a graft.

1868 DARWIN *Var. Anim. & Plants* I. xi. 390 If..we must admit the extraordinary fact that two distinct species can unite by their cellular tissue, and subsequently produce a plant bearing leaves and sterile flowers intermediate in character between the scion and stock..Such plants, if really thus formed, might be called graft-hybrids. *Ibid.* II. xxvii. 365 The case would become one of graft-hybridism. **1875** *Ibid.* (ed. 2) I. xi. 423 The number of new forms produced by graft-hybridisation. **1886** *Syd. Soc. Lex.*, *Graft theory*, a theory which attributes the causation of disease to organic particles detached from the body of a diseased person, which becoming engrafted into a healthy person set up a diseased process in his body similar to that which existed in the body of the person from which they were detached. **1897** *Allbutt's Syst. Med.* III. 726 The interesting process of implantation or graft growths from a growth in one part of the intestines to another has been already referred to. **1897** W. ANDERSON *Surg. Treat. Lupus* 14 The graft surface has a better appearance than that of an ordinary cicatrix.

†**graft**, *sb.*[2] *Obs.* [a. MDu. *graft* fem. and neut. (MDu. and Du. *gracht* fem.), f. *graven* to dig. Cf. next and GRAFF *sb.*[2]] A ditch; a moat; Also (in Holland) a street on either side of a canal.

1641 EVELYN *Diary* (1889) I. 26 The Keiser's or Emperor's Graft, which is an ample and long street. **1644** PRYNNE & WALKER *Fiennes's Trial* App. 11 The Castle was a very large stong Hold, fortified with a very broad deepe ditch, or graft. **1653-4** WHITELOCKE *Jrnl. Swed. Emb.* (1772) II. 292 The grafts of the workes are large and deep, full of water on all sides. **1683** *Apol. Prot. France* iv. 46 They caught a Soldier measuring the Graft and the Wall in order to scale the place. **1737** G. SMITH *Curious Relat.* I. iii. 387 All the rest which the Canals, Grafts, and Rivers are fill'd with, being salt, or at least brackish.

graft (grɑːft, -æ-), *sb.*[3] [a. (? or cognate with) ON. *grǫft-r* action of digging:—OTeut. **graftu-z* masc., f. **grab-* GRAVE *v.* to dig.]

1. The depth of earth that may be thrown up at once with a spade; a 'spit'. Often ***spade('s) graft.***

1620 MARKHAM *Farew. Husb.* (1625) 41 Within a spades graft of the vpper swarth of the earth. **1681** CHETHAM *Angler's Vade-m.* iv. §9 (1689) 38 You yourself may dig one spade Graft, deep in Sandy heathy ground. **1792** *Trans. Soc. Arts* X. 139 We dug..one spade's graft (about nine inches deep, and seven inches wide) into the quick sand. **1802** *Ibid.* XX. 191 The drains were generally made two grafts deep. **1848** *Jrnl. R. Agric. Soc.* IX. I. 55, I then dug a trench.. throwing the first graft of good soil on one side.

2. A kind of spade, used in digging drains.

1894 *S.E. Worc. Gloss.*, *Graft* or *Grafting-tool*, a narrow crescent-shaped spade used by drainers.

graft (grɑːft, -æ-), *sb.*[4] *slang.* [Perh. a transferred use of prec. in the original sense 'digging'.] **a.** Work, *esp.* hard work. **b.** A trade, craft.

1853 J. ROCHFORT *Adv. Surveyor N.Z.* v. 47, I could make more money by 'hard graft', as they call labour in the colonies. **1890** *Glouc. Gloss.*, *Graft*, work. **1890** *Melbourne Argus* 16 Aug. 13/1 It is when hard graft has to be done.. that they're troubled a bit. **1891** *Sheffield Gloss.*, Suppl., *Graft*, work. 'Well, I've got some graft to do now'. **1896** *Pop. Sci. Jrnl.* IV. 255 The roadster proper is distinguished from the tramp by having a 'graft' or in other terms a visible means of support. **1933** *Bulletin* (Sydney) 15 Nov. 20/3 Another three miles' tramping, and four hours' hard graft. **1968** *Times* 27 June 25/1 This view is that salvation..is to be won by long, hard graft by industrial management. **1971** *Observer* 14 Mar. 7/7 They're too busy turning down 14 per cent pay offers to fuss about the three-quarters of a million out of graft.

graft (grɑːft, -æ-), *sb.*[5] *colloq.* (orig. *U.S.*). [Origin uncertain. Perhaps a use of GRAFT *sb.*[4] 'work' (cf. *job*); but some authorities connect it with GRAFT *sb.*[1] with the notion of 'excrescence'.]

The obtaining of profit or advantage by dishonest or shady means; the means by which such gains are made, esp. bribery, blackmail, or the abuse of a position of power or influence; the profits so obtained.

1865 *Nat. Police Gaz.* (N.Y.) 8 July 1/3 'Twas handy that we were so related, as, when about a 'graft', or 'doing stur', both sisters could keep each other company. **1886** W. NEWTON *Secrets Tramp Life Revealed* 14 This 'Guide' cannot work this 'graft' alone, for he has to have a good supply for stock, a bag of 'snide' or base coins. **1889** in J. B. Thoburn *Hist. Oklahoma* (1916) I. xxix. 407 The enterprising individual sold water at so much a drink until he was ousted from his profitable graft. **1896** ADE *Artie* i. 3 To the church show—the charity graft. **1901** 'J. FLYNT' *World of Graft* ii. 12 Chi ain't no free soup kitchen. The City Hall people want their graft just as much as I [*sc.* a criminal] do. **1903** H. HAPGOOD *Autobiogr. Thief* (1904) ii. 34 In those days..Moll-buzzing, as well as picking pockets in general, was an easy and lucrative graft. *Ibid.* x. 205 The boy had a much better chance to learn the graft than I had when a kid, for my father was an honest man. *Ibid.* 222, I was too sleepy those days to go out of town much on the graft. **1903** *Daily Chron.* 21 Oct., A Chicago paper has the headline, 'Labour revolts at paying graft'. *Ibid.* 3 Nov. 5/3 Are you ready to support a government of law against a government of 'graft', an administration of the city's resources in the interest of the public and of the public treasury, against their dissipation for the benefit of a favoured few? **1904** *Ibid.* 17 Feb. 3/5 Glimpses are also given of the shady side of American politics, where 'graft' is only another word for plunder. **1904** *Athenæum* 30 Apr. 560 In New York 'graft' is thieves' patter for stealing. **1905** *Daily Chron.* 13 Sept. 5/2 It is now the turn of the War Department to start a campaign against 'graft' among the officials of the army. **1909** *Westm. Gaz.* 13 Oct. 5/4 Showing how Tammany robs the city, bribes the judges, protects criminals, and generally carries on the game of graft, an Americanism for bribery, corruption, and illicit commission. **1915** *Lit. Digest* (N.Y.) 21 Aug. 340/1 There is no evidence that Minister Sullivan received any money or participated in any way in what has come to be known as 'graft'. **1928** *Sat. Even. Post* 4 Feb. 35/1 'We had a slick graft' he told me, 'We was taking about two hundred smackers a week.' **1945** C. S. LEWIS *Hideous Strength* xi. 301 Here was a world of plot within plot, crossing and double crossing, of lies and graft and stabbing in the back. **1970** *Daily Tel.* 13 Jan. 2/4 Victims in a wave of graft, corruption and fear were making regular payments for protection.

b. *attrib.* and *Comb.*

1905 *Daily Chron.* 26 May 5/2 He..says he is tired of 'graft' politics and the sale of city franchises to monopolies [in Philadelphia]. **1908** *Ibid.* 24 Dec. 1/6 During the hearing of the latest 'graft' scandal here [*sc.* in Pittsburgh] evidence was given that sixty members of the City Council received 45,000 dollars as bribe money. **1908** 'O. HENRY' *Gentle Grafter* 48 I'd like, myself, to hedge a bet or two in the graft game. **1910** *Westm. Gaz.* 4 Apr. 7/2 He expressed himself as overwhelmed with..shame at the stain which had been revealed by the graft exposures upon the fame of the city [*sc.* Pittsburgh]. **1955** D. W. MAURER in *Publ. Amer. Dial. Soc.* XXIV. 150 Is there already a well-established, well-oiled graft-machine set up to process all *fixed* cases?

graft (grɑːft, -æ-), *v.*[1] Forms: α. 5 grafte, 6- graft. β. 6-7 grift(e, 9 *dial.* grift. γ. 9 *dial.* greft. [variant of GRAFF *v.* See GRAFT *sb.*[1]]

1. *trans.* To insert (a shoot from one tree) as a graft (see GRAFT *sb.*[1]) into another tree. Const. *in, into, on, upon.* Also with advs. *in, together.*

1483 *Cath. Angl.* 162/1 To Grafte, *inserere, surculare.* **1535** COVERDALE *Isa.* xvii. 10 Thou hast also set a fayre plante, & grafted a straunge braunch. **1616** SURFL. & MARKH. *Country Farme* 36 He shall get Grifts to graft. **1741** *Compl. Fam.-Piece* II. iii. 362 Upon the white English sort of Jessamine, now graft the Spanish. **1859** DARWIN *Orig. Spec.*

ix. (1873) 245 No one has been able to graft together trees belonging to quite distinct families.

b. *transf.* and *fig.* To insert or fix *in* or *upon* something, with the result of producing a vital or indissoluble union. (Cf. sense 6.)

1531 TINDALE *Exp. 1 John* ii. (1538) 23 All they that are grafted into Christe to followe hys doctrine. **1548–9** (Mar.) *Bk. Com. Prayer, Communion* (Collect ad fin.), Graunt.. that the wordes..may through thy grace, bee so grafted inwardly in our heartes. **1605** BACON *Adv. Learn.* II. xxv. §5. 110 God..doth grift his revelations and holy doctrine upon the notions of our reason. **1650** FULLER *Pisgah* 389 Each of them [pillars] having half a cubit of their shaft lost in their height, as running in, and hid in his Chapiter grafted upon it. **1774** GOLDSM. *Nat. Hist.* (1776) III. 99 The horns may in every respect, be resembled to a vegetable substance, grafted upon the head of an animal. **1786** SIR J. REYNOLDS *Disc.* xiii. (1876) 73 No Art can be grafted with success on another art. **1822–34** *Good's Study Med.* (ed. 4) I. 149, I have observed that dyspepsy is often grafted upon an hysterical or hypochondriacal diathesis. **1856** FROUDE *Hist. Eng.* (1858) I. i. 2 The Northern nations grafted the religion and the laws of the Western empire on their own hardy natures. **1876** E. MELLOR *Priesth.* 208 The Lord's Supper, while a new institution, was in its forms grafted upon the Paschal meal.

c. *intr.* for *refl. rare* (? *U.S.*).

1884 HORNER *Florence* I. i. 24 The Florentine artist..only adopted those principles which grafted most readily on his preconceived ideas. **1894** *Forum* (U.S.) July 564 If possible, the theme should graft on to a vigorous and well grown stock of native interest.

2. *absol.* and *intr.* To insert a graft or grafts. Const. as in sense 1.

1626 BACON *Sylva* §415 If you graft vpon the Bough of a Tree, and cut off some of the old Boughs, the new Cions will perish. **1816** J. SMITH *Panorama Sci. & Art* II. 640 The method of propagating the cider-fruit trees in Herefordshire, is by grafting. **1860** EMERSON *Cond. Life, Power* Wks. (Bohn) II. 332 Here is question, every spring, whether to graft with wax, or whether with clay.

transf. and *fig.* **1685** *Loyal Poems* 132 But of all Pates, Cit has the softest one; 'The better', cries the Wife, 'to graft upon'. **1713** WARDER *True Amazons* 154 If any of more Intellect..will graft upon this stock.

3. *trans.* To fix a graft or grafts upon (a stock). Also *vaguely*, to perform the operation of grafting on (a tree), to produce (fruits) by grafting.

1624 QUARLES *Sion's Sonets* xx. 8 To see my Stockes, so latelie grifted, sprout. **1707** *Curios. in Husb. & Gard.* 256 You graft it with Grafts of an Apple-tree. **1795** KNIGHT in *Phil. Trans.* LXXXV. 292, I have since grafted some very old trees with cuttings from seedling apple-trees of five years old. **1823** COBBETT *Weekly Reg.* 12 July 98 Stocks have.. been grafted with English cuttings. **1845** *Florist's Jrnl.* 77 On grafting the Chinese Azalea. **1887** BOWEN *Virg. Eclog.* IX. 51 Graft thy pears, O Daphnis, the fruit thy sons shall enjoy.

4. In loose or *transf.* uses: To plant, implant.

1562 TURNER *Baths* Pref., Their nature whiche Almighty God grafted in them [the birds]. **1580** LYLY *Euphues* (Arb.) 473 They that feare theyr vines will make too sharpe wine, must..graft next to them Mandrage. **1771** *Muse in Min.* 110 From page to page thro' Nature's folio flies, Where hoary wisdom grafts her aching eyes.

5. *Naut.* To cover (a ring-bolt, block-strop, etc.) with a weaving of small cord or rope-yarns.

c **1860** H. STUART *Seaman's Catech.* 31 How do you point and graft a rope? *Ibid.* 81 Two hammock lashings..pointed and grafted at the ends.

6. *Surg.* To transplant (a piece of skin, tissue, etc.) into a different part of the body, or from one animal to another.

1868 DARWIN *Var. Anim. & Plants* II. xxvii. 369 The tail of a pig has been grafted into the middle of its back. **1897** *Allbutt's Syst. Med.* III. 203 The experiment of grafting a portion of the extirpated pancreas outside the abdominal cavity in the muscles of the external walls.

7. *U.S.* To repair (boots) by adding new soles and 'foxing' the uppers.

1859 in BARTLETT *Dict. Amer.*

graft, *v.*[2] *dial.* [Variant of GRAFF *v.*[2]] *intr.* To dig. Hence **'grafting** *vbl. sb.*, in **grafting-spade, -tool** (see quots.).

1823 CRABB *Technol. Dict., Grafting Tool*, a kind of curved spade made very strong for the purpose of digging canals. **1883** GRESLEY *Gloss. Cool Mining, Grafting spade*, a long narrow-plated spade for digging clay. *Mod. dial.* (*Kent*), A grafting-tool would suit best for digging that clite.

graft, *v.*[3] *slang.* [? transferred use of prec.; cf. GRAFT *sb.*[4]] *intr.* To work. Hence **'grafting** *vbl. sb.*

1859 HOTTEN *Slang Dict.* 47 *Graft*, to go to work. **1878** *Graphic* 6 July 2/2 Perhaps in a generation or two Paddy will fail us. He will have become too refined for hard 'grafting'. **1890** *Melbourne Argus* 9 Aug. 4/2 'You graftin' with him?' 'No, I'm with Johnson'. **1936** J. CURTIS *Gilt Kid* ii. 19 'Where did you graft in Wandsworth?' 'Cleaner.' **1958** *Times* 18 Oct. 3/3 But his 90 minutes in the middle were worth many nets, and he was quite imperturbable in the way he grafted along [at cricket]. **1966** A. PRIOR *Operators* xvi. 246 The great mass of mugs were law-abiding..doing as they were told, working, grafting.

graft (grɑːft, -æ-), *v.*[4] *colloq.* (orig. *U.S.*). [f. GRAFT *sb.*[5]] *intr.* To practise 'graft'; to make money by shady or dishonest means.

1859 *Nat. Police Gaz.* (N.Y.) 14 May 3/4 Liz Thompson and her husband..do not intend going out to 'graft' until the summer season sets in, when they are going to Newport, Saratoga, and other fashionable watering resorts, at which game she made out so good last season. **1863** *Illustr. London News* 13 June 658/3, I am progressing wonderfully, and I expect Poll and Bob will be able to go out with me and graft (pick pockets) in a few days. **1895** *McClure's Mag.* Feb. 247/2 He had been 'grafting' with a 'mob' of pickpockets at county fairs. **1903** H. HAPGOOD *Autobiogr. Thief* (1904) ii. 48, I know some thieves who, although they have grafted for twenty-five years, have not yet 'done time'. **1905** D. G. PHILLIPS *Plum Tree* 61, I don't see how those in politics that don't graft, as they call it, are any better than those that do. Would they get office if they didn't help on the jobs of the grafters? **1960** *Observer* 25 Dec. 7/6 Anybody who had neglected to have a nice tickle during the late autumn would be out grafting for all he was worth. **1967** J. MORGAN *Involved* 27 They used to graft together..they pulled one or two big capers.

Hence **'grafting** *vbl. sb.*[3] and *ppl. a.*

1859 MATSELL *Vocabulum* 39 *Grafting*, working; helping another to steal. **1901** 'J. FLYNT' *World of Graft* 78 They make their living, such as it is, by grafting. **1904** *Treasury* Oct. 8/2 We excel other countries in the phenomenal corruption of our city Governments and Legislatures. The evil system of 'grafting', so called, extends everywhere. **1912** F. J. HASKIN *Amer. Govt.* 71 Large business houses felt the loss from the petty grafting of stamps by office boys. **1921** *Glasgow Herald* 13 June 9 The efforts of professional and grafting Irish agitators. **1960** *Observer* 25 Dec. 7/7 Christmas Day was not likely to be a big grafting day for various reasons.

graftage ('grɑːftɪdʒ, -æ-). [f. GRAFT *v.*[1] + -AGE.] The action of grafting or fact of being grafted.

1895 BAILEY *Horticulturists' Rule-bk.* (ed. 3) 283.

grafted ('grɑːftɪd, -æ-), *ppl. a.* [f. GRAFT *v.*[1] + -ED[1].] In senses of the vb. *lit.* and *fig.*

1570 DEE *Math. Pref.* 2 That mighty..*Mathematicall Tree*, with his Chief armes and second (grifted) branches. **1606** G. W[OODCOCKE] tr. *Justin's Hist.*, etc. Kk5b, Being hated of al men for his grafted cruelty. **1697** DRYDEN *Virg. Georg.* IV. 214 He knew..For Fruit the grafted Pear-tree to dispose. *a* **1700** B. E. *Dict. Cant. Crew, Grafted*, made a Cuckold of. **1707** *Curios. in Husb. & Gard.* 73 The Pores of the grafted Branch. **1719** LONDON & WISE *Compl. Gard.* xxxvi. 155 For an old grafted Peach-Tree, the grand Remedy of short'ning may not avail. **1828** P. CUNNINGHAM *N.S. Wales* 161 A few dozen grafted trees..will in a few years insure you a very fair crop of fruit. **1892** *Daily News* 11 July 4/3 'Companions' anxious for situations for which no special skill or training is required, only patience and a sort of grafted cheerfulness.

b. *Her.* (See quots.)

1765–77 PORNY *Heraldry* Gloss., *Grafted*. This is said of that part of the Escutcheon which is jointed or inserted into the other..The fourth Quarter is Mars, Brunswick, and Lunenburgh impaled, with ancient Saxony grafted in point. **1868** CUSSANS *Her.* ii. 46 To these may also be added what is sometimes called *Grafted*, but would be better expressed by *Party per Pale and Chevron*.

grafter[1] ('grɑːftə(r), -æ-). [f. GRAFT *v.*[1] + -ER[1].]

1. One who grafts trees.

1616 SURFL. & MARKH. *Country Farme* 347 The furniture and tooles wherewith a grafter should be furnished..are [etc.]. **1668** BOYLE *Cert. Physiol. Ess.* (1669) 91, I am inform'd by the trails of more than one of the most skilful and experienc'd Grafters of these parts, that [etc.].

†**2.** The original tree from which a scion has been taken for grafting upon another tree. *Obs.*

1599 SHAKS. *Hen. V*, III. v. 9 Shall..Our Syens, put in wilde and sauage stock, Spirt vp so suddenly into the Clouds, And ouer looke their Grafters? *a* **1770** CHATTERTON *Consuliad* 48 Monarchs! Of mole-hills, oyster-beds, a rock; These are the grafters of your royal stock.

3. A tool used in grafting (see quot.).

1884 KNIGHT *Dict. Mech.* Suppl., *Grafter*, a fine-toothed, pointed, narrow-bladed, hand-saw, used in sawing off limbs and stocks for the insertion of grafts.

grafter[2] ('grɑːftə(r), -æ-). [f. GRAFT *v.*[2] + -ER[1].] = GRAFT *sb.*[3] 2.

1877 *N.W. Linc. Gloss.*, *Grafter*, a long iron spade used for digging hard ground, especially by workmen engaged in making drains and banks.

grafter[3] ('grɑːftə(r), -æ-). *colloq.* (orig. *U.S.*). [f. GRAFT *sb.*[5] or *v.*[4] + -ER[1].] **1.** One who makes money by shady or dishonest means; a thief; a swindler.

1899 'J. FLYNT' *Tramping with Tramps* 394 *Grafter*, a pickpocket. **1900** *Daily Express* 22 June 5/3 American thieves, hotel robbers, 'bunco steerers', 'grafters', 'con' men, and 'crooks' of every degree. **1901** 'H. MCHUGH' *John Henry* 49 No more swell Sandwich Salons for me, where the grafters want to butt in all the while. **1903** *Westm. Gaz.* 16 July 10/1 Camp followers, adventurers, and a weird aggregation of grafters. **1916** S. LEACOCK *Ess. & Lit. Stud.* 205 All the world loves a grafter—at least a genial and ingenious grafter—a Robin Hood who plunders an abbot to feed a beggar, an Alfred Jingle, a Scapin, a Raffles. **1926** E. WALLACE *Yellow Snake* ix. 76 You're not exactly wrapping up your words now... You've called me a grafter and a crook. **1967** J. MORGAN *Involved* 82 She's a straight bird.. not a grafter.

2. One who practises 'graft', esp. in public life; a politician, official, etc., who misuses his position in order to reap dishonest gain or advantage.

1896 *Columbus* (Ohio) *Dispatch* 20 Apr. 3/8 Most of the 'grafters' have left the town, and not many of them will remain here. **1904** F. LYNDE *Grafters* xxiv. 298 You were to crush the grafters in this railroad struggle—show them up. **1904** *Daily Chron.* 28 Mar. 3/5 Kuropatkin shares with Prince Khilkoff, the Minister of Railways, the distinction of being one of the few high officials who are not called grafters. **1908** *Ibid.* 16 Nov. 1/7 Many of his 'grafter' friends will be tried for attempted murder. **1914** G. ATHERTON *Perch of Devil* I. 58 And although she has her pestilential politicians, her grafters.., yet ability and talent make good as always. **1935** A. J. CRONIN *Stars look Down* III. vi. 526 They've always been a set of grafters down there; local government has been one long sweet laugh. **1958** S. ELLIN *Eighth Circle* (1959) II. viii. 95 And what happens to somebody who.. isn't a born grafter? They make him one, that's what!

grafter[4] ('grɑːftə(r), -æ-). *colloq.* [f. GRAFT *v.*[3] + -ER[1].] One who works; a (hard) worker.

1900 H. LAWSON *On Track* 41 'What are we to do now?' enquired Andy, who was the hardest grafter, but altogether helpless, hopeless, and useless in a crisis like this. **1906** E. DYSON *Fact'ry 'Ands* vi. 62 Several of the piece-workers, confirmed grafters, toiled with swift fingers. **1913** W. K. HARRIS *Outback in Austral.* 24 Shared and shared alike, the loafer with the grafter. **1927** *Glasgow Herald* 19 Mar. 9 The visiting eight are heavy and expert in the tight, and to meet them we have a pack which contains at least three players who are by no means 'grafters'. **1959** *Times* 24 Jan. 3/7 He is a grafter rather than a fluent striker, with little back-lift, plenty of concentration, and a willingness to use his feet.

grafting ('grɑːftɪŋ, -æ-), *vbl. sb.*[1] [f. GRAFT *v.*[1] + -ING[1].] The action of GRAFT *v.*[1]

1. The action of inserting a graft (see GRAFT *sb.*[1] 1). For *cleft-, crown-, saddle-, tongue-, whip-*, etc. *grafting*, see the sb. which forms the first member.

1483 *Cath. Angl.* 162/1 A Graftynge, *insicium*. **1560** [see GRAFT *sb.*[1] 1]. **1666** BOYLE *Orig. Formes & Qual.* 129 'Tis worth observing..what happens both in ordinary graftings, and especially in that kind of Insition..which is commonly call'd Inoculation. **1807** *Med. Jrnl.* XVII. 196 New and superior species of apples may be produced from seed: and ..impregnating the pollen was found to be an advantageous substitute for grafting. **1860** DELAMER *Kitch. Gard.* (1861) 143 The reader is strongly advised to take lessons in grafting and budding.

fig. **1833** LAMB *Elia* Ser. II. *Wedding*, The hurry a beloved child is sometimes in to tear herself from the paternal stock, and commit herself to strange graftings. **1865** TYLOR *Early Hist. Man.* ii. 22 The grafting of the English, French or German grammar and dictionary on the gesture-language.

†**2.** The place where a graft is inserted; its junction with the stem. Also *transf. Obs.*

1601 HOLLAND *Pliny* II. 271 It riseth vp with a four cornered stem..hauing many concauities or holes like armpits in the grafting of the branches to the said stem.

3. In various technical senses: **a.** *Naut.* 'An ornamental weaving of fine yarns, etc., over the strop of a block; or applied to the tapered ends of the ropes, and termed pointing' (Smyth *Sailor's Word-bk.* 1867; see also quot. 1815). **b.** *Surg.* The transference of a portion of skin, etc. to another part of the body, or to another body. **c.** *Carpentry.* 'A scarfing or endwise attachment of one timber to another, as in attaching an extra length or false pile to one already driven' (Knight *Dict. Mech.* 1875). **d.** *Knitting.* (See quot. 1880.)

1815 *Falconer's Dict. Marine* (ed. Burney), *Grafting a rope*, the act of unlaying the two ends of it, placing the strands one within the other, as for splicing, and stopping them at the joining. The yarns are then opened out, split, and made into knittles for pointing. **1841** LADY WILTON *Art Needlework* (ed. 3) xx. 317 There is..darning—grafting—and patching. **1858** SIMMONDS *Dict. Trade, Grafting*,.. knitting new feet to stockings. **1880** *Plain Knitting* 33 This ..grafting..is joining two pieces together, and is useful in joining a new foot to an old leg. **1888** H. MORTEN *Sk. Hosp. Life* 66 We must try grafting on that boy..who was burnt. You don't mind parting with a few portions of your epidermis, I suppose? **1896** *Allbutt's Syst. Med.* I. 207 No authentic instance..is at present forthcoming of the grafting of human carcinoma upon any of the lower animals. **1897** W. ANDERSON *Surg. Treat. Lupus* 14 The advantages of epidermic grafting..are obvious.

4. *attrib.* and *Comb.*, as ***grafting chisel, knife, saw, time***; **grafting clay, wax**, a mixture of clay or wax and other ingredients, forming a composition with which to cover the united parts of a scion and stock in grafting.

1483 *Cath. Angl.* 162/1 A Graftyngtyme, *insicio*. **1727** BRADLEY *Fam. Dict.* s.v. *Grafting*, Then must the Gardener ..cut it with his Grafting Knife in the Shape of a Wedge. **1727–41** CHAMBERS *Cycl.* s.v. *Engrafting*, Clay, mixed with horse-dung, [etc.]..; also..grafting wax. *Ibid.*, In this cleft, the grafting chissel, or wedge, is put to keep it open. **1802** FORSYTH *Fruit-trees* vi. 79 The Composition..should be rather softer than grafting-clay generally is. **1875** KNIGHT *Dict. Mech.* 1001/2 *Grafting-saw*, a tenon-saw for cutting off stocks for grafting.

grafting, *vbl. sb.*[2]: see GRAFT *v.*[2]

grafting, *vbl. sb.*[3]: see GRAFT *v.*[4]

graftling ('grɑːftlɪŋ, -æ-). [f. GRAFT *sb.* + -LING.] A small tree on which a graft has been set.

a **1618** SYLVESTER *St. Lewis* 88 The Gardner's Care over some Graftlings choice.

graftonite ('grɑːftənaɪt, -æ-). *Min.* [f. *Grafton*, name of a village in New Hampshire, U.S.A.: see -ITE[1].] A pink to brown crystalline phosphate of calcium and bivalent iron and manganese, $(Fe,Mn,Ca)_3(PO_4)_2$, usually found associated with triphylite.

1900 S. L. PENFIELD in *Amer. Jrnl. Sci.* CLIX. 20 (*title*) On graftonite, a new mineral from Grafton, New

Hampshire, and its intergrowth with triphylite. **1968** *Amer. Mineralogist* LIII. 742 Graftonite is a phosphate mineral of wide occurrence.

Graham[1] ('greɪəm). Also **graham**. The name of Sylvester Graham (1794–1851), used *attrib.* to designate unbolted wheaten flour, and bread or biscuit prepared from this. Also *absol.* = Graham bread.

1834 *Knickerbocker* IV. 305 'Hail!' said I, 'thou pure, unadulterated substitute—Graham bread!' **1834** W. L. GARRISON in *Life* (1885) I. 428 If they are Grahamites we have a fine spring of water in our cellar, and plenty of Graham flour upstairs. **1859** *Amer. Agriculturist* May 150/2 (*caption*) Graham biscuits or bread. **1874** *Rep. Vermont Board Agric.* II. 509 Large enough to hold the flour, the meal, the rye, the graham, butter. **1882** 'M. HARLAND' *Eve's Daughters* 443 Eat lightly—dry bread or biscuit, Graham crackers—anything that is easy of digestion. **1896** *Godey's Mag.* Feb. 207/1 When Mr. Dives turns from his recondite menu to nibble at wheaten grits and graham bread. **1947** J. STEINBECK *Wayward Bus* 220 It's got graham crackers instead of crust. **1957** G. CARSON *Cornflake Crusade* (1959) iv. 53 They shared their beans, boiled rice, graham bread and puddings. **1958** L. C. PRITCHETT *Cabin at Medicine Springs* (1959) xiv. 118 Ma often..made gruel out of coarse graham flour.

Graham[2] ('greɪəm). [The name of Thomas *Graham* (1805–69), Scottish chemist.]

Graham's law: that the rates of diffusion and of effusion of a gas are inversely proportional to the square root of its density.

1845 TODD & BOWMAN *Physiol. Anat. & Physiol. Man* II. xxix. 409 Oxygen being the lighter gas, a larger quantity is required to replace the carbonic acid; 81 parts of the latter will require 95 of the former to replace it according to Graham's law, that the diffusion volume of different gases varies inversely as the square root of the density. **1946** GLASSTONE *Elem. Physical Chem.* iv. 86 The results of Graham's law of diffusion have been used to determine gas densities by measuring the time required for a definite volume of the gas to effuse through a small hole in a thin metal plate.

Grahamism ('greɪəmɪz(ə)m). *U.S.* [f. GRAHAM[1] + -ISM.] The vegetarian principles advocated by Sylvester Graham (1794–1851). So **'Grahamite**[1], a follower of Graham.

1834 [see GRAHAM[1]]. **1839** C. F. BRIGGS *Adv. H. Franco* II. iii. 27 'Have you got the dyspepsia?' asked Mrs. D. 'Ain't you a Grahamite?' asked Mr. D. **1845** LOWELL *Lett.* (1894) I. 87, I am becoming more and more inclined to Grahamism every day. **1864** B. TAYLOR *H. Thurston* iii. 45 They were Grahamites for a year or two—lived on bran bread and turnips, boiled wheat and dried apples. **18..** *N.Y. Med. Jrnl.* XI. 567 (Cent.) Grahamism was advocated and practised by many. **1879** WEBSTER, Suppl., *Grahamite*. **1957** G. CARSON *Cornflake Crusade* iv. 49 The Grahamite was required not to drink water with his meals.

grahamite[2] ('greɪəmaɪt). *Min.* [Named by Waitz in 1865, after the Messrs. *Graham*, in whose mine it was found: see -ITE.] A bituminous compound of several hydrocarbons, similar to asphaltum.

1866 *Amer. Jrnl. Sci.* XCII. 420 Wurtz has proposed the name Grahamite..for the pitch-black Albertite-like mineral of Virginia. **1880** *Libr. Univ. Knowl.* VIII. 139 Grahamite is black, and has a variable luster.

Grahamize ('greɪəmaɪz), *v.* [f. *Graham* + -IZE. (Sir James Graham, as Home Secretary, had Mazzini's letters so opened in 1844.)] *trans.* To cause (letters) to be opened when passing through the post. Hence **'Grahamizing** *vbl. sb.* So (*rarely*) **'Grahaming** *vbl. sb.*

1883 *Manch. Guard.* 8 Feb. 4 Postmasters in country towns..are much under temptation to follow their masters in the General Post-Office in 'Grahamising' letters and telegrams. **1888** *Times* 18 Dec. 8/4 Mr. Sexton asked to what extent the practice of 'Grahamizing' letters was now carried. **1892** W. B. SCOTT *Autobiog. Notes* I. 121 He was the friend of Mazzini in the discovery of the Grahaming of letters by the Post Office.

graial, obs. form of GRAIL[1].

graid, obs. pa. pple. of GRAITH *v.*

graid(e)ly, -ley, dial. variant of GRADELY.

grail[1] (greɪl). Forms: 4 **graiel, graell**, 4–5 **grayel**, 4–9 **grayle**, 5–6 **grale, grayll(e**, 5–9 **graile**, 6 **graial, greyle**, 6– **grail**. [ad. OF. *grael*:—Eccl. L. *gradāle*, var. *graduāle*. GRADUAL.]

1. = GRADUAL *sb.* 1.

13.. *Metr. Hom.* (Harl. MS.) 514 in *Minor Poems fr. Vernon MS.* 188 By ierom and ambrose ordained es To sing þe graell [*v.r.* grayel] at þe mes. *c* **1380** WYCLIF *Sel. Wks.* III. 202 þei neden to have..expositouris on þe gospellis and pistelis, more þan Graielis and oþere bokis of song. **1398** TREVISA *Barth. De P.R.* IX. xxviii. (1495) 364 In Ester weke the Grayle is songe wyth Alleluya. *c* **1460** *Towneley Myst.* xvi. 205 Lefe pystyls and grales; Mes, matyns, noght avalys, All these I defende. **1493** *Festivall* (W. de W. 1515) 33 The greyle is not sayd for those yt ben newe crystened. *a* **1529** SKELTON *P. Sparow* 441 The pecocke so prowd, Bycause his voyce is lowde..He shall syng the grayle. **1553** BECON *Reliques of Rome* (1563) 124 Pope Gelasius the fyrst brought in ye Grayll, commaunding that the people shoulde sing it. **1893** J. CHRISTIE *Acc. Parish Clerks* 15 Ability to read the Epistles and Lessons, to sing Responsals, Grails, and other parts of the Service.

2. = GRADUAL *sb.* 2.

c **1440** *Promp. Parv.* 207/1 Grayle, boke..*gradale*. **1459** *Test. Ebor.* II. (Surtees) 227 The best Mes boke..the lesse Antiphoner of iiij, a Graile, a Manuell. **1504** *Churchw. Acc. St. Mary Hill, London* (1797) 105 A manuell, a legend, 2 solomes and grayles. **1549–50** *Act 3 & 4 Edw. VI*, c. 10 (1553) 13 b, All bookes called Antiphoners, Missales, Grailes, Processionalles [etc.]. **1577–87** HOLINSHED *Chron.* III. 1146/1 One of the gard lift vp to him into the pulpit a masse booke and a graile. **1774** WARTON *Hist. Eng. Poetry* (1840) I. Diss. ii. 88 Among the books they found there, were one hundred psalters, as many grayles, and forty missals. **1818** SCOTT *Rob Roy* ix. **1849** ROCK *Ch. of Fathers* II. vi. 202 Upon the outstretched wings of the large brazen eagle lay open the Grail.

grail[2] (greɪl). Also 4, 9 **greal**, 5, 7, 9 **graal**, 6 **graile**. [ad. OF. *graal, grael, greel, greil* = Pr. *grasal, grazal* whence OCat. *gresal-s*):—med.L. *gradālis* a cup or platter, of uncertain origin; commonly referred to a popular L. type **crātālis*, f. **crātus* altered form of L. *crāter* cup.] ***the (Holy) Grail, the Saint Grail*** or SANGRAIL: in mediæval legend, the platter used by our Saviour at the Last Supper, in which Joseph of Arimathea received the Saviour's blood at the cross.

The fortunes of 'the Holy Grail' (OF. *le saint graal*, whence Malory has the corrupt form *sancgreal*: see SANGRAIL), and the adventures undergone in the search for it by various knights of Arthur's Round Table, form an important part of the matter of mediæval romance. According to one story, it was brought by Joseph of Arimathea to Glastonbury (see the 14th cent. *Joseph Arim.*, where it is called 'þe dische wiþ þe blode'). Sometimes the Grail or Sangreal has been erroneously supposed to be the cup or chalice used at the Last Supper.

c **1330** *Arth. & Merl.* (Kölbing) 2222 Til he wer born þat schuld do al Fulfille þe meruails of þe greal. *c* **1450** *Merlin* 59 The peple that were ther-at cleped this vessell that thei hadden in so grete grace, the Graal. **1590** SPENSER *F.Q.* II. x. 34 Ioseph of Arimathy..brought with him the holy graile (they say). **1685** STILLINGFL. *Orig. Brit.* i. 13 And for all that I can see, the holy Graal deserves as much credit as the Book taken out of Pilat's Palace. **1833** LONGF. *Drift-Wood* Prose Wks. (1886) I. 301 The former, indeed, founded upon the marvels of the Saint Graal, contain nothing but strange and miraculous adventures. **1842** TENNYSON *Sir Galahad* 42 Three angels bear the holy Grail.

fig. **1876** LANIER *Psalms of West* 505 Godly Hearts that, Grails of gold, Still the blood of Faith do hold. **1894** STEAD *If Christ came to Chicago* 110 The quest of the almighty dollar is their Holy Grail.

¶ ? Misused (for rime) in the sense of 'cup'.

In recent Dicts. this passage is given as authenticating a sense 'foam' for GRAIL[3].

1653 *Exaletation of Ale* vii. in *F. Beaumont's Poems* M 3 b, To see how it flowers and mantles in grayle.

grail[3] (greɪl). *Poet.* Also 6 **graile, grayle**. [Of unknown origin, perh. a contraction of GRAVEL.] Gravel.

1590 SPENSER *F.Q.* I. vii. 6 This gentle knight..lying downe upon the sandie graile, Dronke of the streame. **1591** —— *Vis. Bellay* 157 The golden grayle that bright Pactolus washeth. **1647** H. MORE *Song of Soul* III. I. xxii, Like torch that droppeth down..Lies now in darknesse on the grail, or stone. **1840** BROWNING *Sordello* VI. 447 The silver globules and gold-sparkling grail At bottom.

grail[4] (greɪl). Also 9 **graille**. [a. F. *grêle* of the same meaning, f. *grêler* to make slender, *spec.* taper and smooth (the teeth of a comb), f. *grêle* slender.] A comb-maker's file. Hence **'grailing** *vbl. sb.*, the process of finishing the teeth of a comb with the grail.

1688 R. HOLME *Armoury* III. 383/2 A Comb-makers Grail ..is a long, flat, and broad Tool on the Back, and the other side wrought into Teeth like a Saw. **1875** KNIGHT *Dict. Mech.*, *Graille*, a single-cut file, or float, having one curved face and a straight one, used by comb-makers. **1878** *Encycl. Brit.* VI. 178/2 They [combs] then pass to the 'grailing' department, where, by means of special forms of files or rasps, known as grails and topers, the individual teeth are rounded or bevelled, tapered, and smoothed.

†**grail**[5]. *Obs.*[−1] [Cf. OF. *gravele* a fish, also GRAYLING and GRAVELING.] Some kind of fish.

1587 HARRISON *England* III. iii. in Holinshed *Chron.* I. 224 Besides the salmons..we haue the trout, barbell, graile, powt, cheuin, pike [etc.].

[**grail**[6]. Error for BRAIL *sb.*[1] (sense 3).

[**1486** *Bk. St. Albans* a viij b, The same federis ye shall call the brayles or the brayle federis.] **1671** SKINNER *Etymol. Ling. Angl.* IV, *Grayle feders*, or *Graylles*, vox quæ apud solam Jul. Barns occurrit lib. de re Falconaria [*i.e.* quot. 1486], à Fr. G. *Gresle*, Gracilis. **1847** in HALLIWELL [citing *Blome*; but not found there]. Hence in some later Dicts.]

†**grailing**, *vbl. sb. Obs.* [aphetic form of ENGRAILING.] = ENGRAILING *vbl. sb.*

1502 *Privy Purse Exp. Eliz. of York* (1830) 14 Making of six tapettes for the sompter horses, with the lynyng, grayling, jagging..viijs. **1511** *St. Papers Hen. VIII*, II. II. 1497, 2 doz. green foil for 'grayling' the battlements, 8*d.*

grailing, obs. form of GRAYLING.

graille, variant of GRAIL *sb.*[4]

graim, obs. form of GRAME *sb.*

grain (greɪn), *sb.*[1] Forms: 3–6 **greyn(e**, 4 **grein(e**, 4–7 **grayn(e**, 5, 7 **grane**, (6 **grene**, 5 *pl.* **grennys**), 6–7 **graine**, 5– **grain**. [Two formations: (1) a. OF. *grain, grein* (mod.F. *grain*) = Pr. *gran, gra*, Sp. *grano*, Pg. *grão*, It. *grano*:—L. *grānum* a grain, seed; (2) a. OF. *grain(n)e* (mod.F. *graine*) seeds collectively, seed = Pr., Sp., It. *grana*:—pop. L. *grāna* fem., orig. pl. of *grānum*.]

I. Seed; seed of cereal plants, corn.

†**1. a.** A single seed of a plant, esp. one which is small, hard, and roundish in form. (After 15th c. almost exclusively: The stone or pip of a fruit.)

13.. *E.E. Allit. P.* A 31 Vch gresse mot grow of graynez dede. **1398** TREVISA *Barth. De P.R.* XVII. lxxxi. (1495) 652 A greyne is the leest party both of the sede and of the tree, in euery greyne is both pyth and rynde. *a* **1400–50** *Alexander* 1984 Loo, here a gloue full of graynes I graythe þe to take. *c* **1420** *Pallad. on Husb.* III. 805 Ek peris men deuyde, And pike awey the greyne of euery side. **1486** *Bk. St. Albans* C vij b, Take ye greynes of shaffelegre. **1502** ARNOLDE *Chron.* 167 Wan ye mone is in tauro it is good tyme to plante trees of graynes and pepins. **1528** PAYNELL *Salerne's Regim.* G iv b, The lyuer is fatted with them [grapes]..if they be clensed from y graynes or kyrnels. **1607** TOPSELL *Four-f. Beasts* (1658) 335 The stones or grains of *Vitis Alba*, otherwise called Brionie. **1684** *Contempl. State Man* I. iv. (1699) 45 Life..is so frail and slippery, that..even the Grain of a Grape hath been able to..over-throw it. **1796** H. HUNTER *St. Pierre's Stud. Nat.* (1799) II. *Explan. Plates* 11 Aquatic grains have characters entirely opposite to those which are produced on the mountains. **1823** J. BADCOCK *Dom. Amusem.* 187 A grain of a raisin.

fig. **1377** LANGL. *P. Pl.* B. XIX. 269 Grace gaue greynes, the cardynales vertues, And sewe hem in mannes soule. **1390** GOWER *Conf.* I. 14 They no greine of pite sowe. *a* **1400–50** *Alexander* 5622 Sum grayne of godhede..was growen ȝow within. **14..** *Purif. Marie* in *Tundale's Vis.* (1843) 135 That he..lyke a dowve bysyly aspye Wher he of vertu gedur may the greyne. *c* **1440** *Psalmi Penitent.* (1894) 16 Yn my flesch ther nys non helthe, Therfor, of grace sende me greynus.

†**b.** ***in the grain***: in the stage of forming or producing seed. *Obs.*

1613 PURCHAS *Pilgrimage* VIII. ii. (1614) 734 Where Wheate and Mays will not grow, but so vnequally, that at one instant, some is in the grasse, other in the graine.

2. *spec.* A seed or corn of a cereal plant.

In botanical language a grain of a cereal plant is not a 'seed' but a 'fruit' of the kind called CARYOPSIS.

c **1380** WYCLIF *Serm.* Sel. Wks. II. 35 þe secounde fruyt, of the sixtiþe greyn. **1426** LYDG. *De Guil. Pilgr.* (E.E.T.S.) 3315 She hadde..Off a lytel barly greyn Makyd an Er large & pleyn. **1450–1530** *Myrr. our Ladye* 201 Blyssed be thow.. that haste sowen a grayne of the beste whete in the best lande. **1613** PURCHAS *Pilgrimage* (1614) 764 At the end of every song,..laying downe two or three Graines of Wheate. **1806** HUTTON *Course Math.* I. 25 The original of all weights used in England, was a grain or corn of wheat, gathered out of the middle of the ear. **1842** GRAY *Struct. Bot.* vii. §2 (1880) 295 A Caryopsis or Grain. **1885** GOODALE *Physiol. Bot.* (1892) 181 The so-called 'grains' of the cereals are fruits instead of seeds.

3. *collect. sing.* **a.** The fruit or seed of wheat and the allied food-plants or grasses (†*rarely* of beans, etc.); the plants themselves whether reaped or standing; = CORN *sb.*[1] 3, 4. †Also ***grain of wheat.***

In England the colloquial word for this sense is *corn*, which in the U.S. has a different application.

c **1315** SHOREHAM 30 Jesus seyth the vygne be hys, And eke the greyn of wete. **1362** LANGL. *P. Pl.* A. VII. 112 Schal no greyn that heer groweth gladen ow at neode. *c* **1386** CHAUCER *Prol.* 595 Wel wiste he, by the droghte, and by the reyn, The yielding of his seed and of his greyn. *c* **1420** *Pallad. on Husb.* I. 217 Eek hillis yeld is Wel gretter grayn and fewer, then in feeld is. **1467** in *Eng. Gilds* (1870) 382 Barly ne malte ne none other greyne. *c* **1550** *Decay Eng. by Shepe* (E.E.T.S.) 98 Euery ploughe to sell .xxx. quarters of grayne by the yeare. **1598** W. PHILLIP *Linschoten* xxxvii. 71 They have a custome..to cast corn and other graine vpon the ground to feed birds and beastes withal. **1632** LITHGOW *Trav.* II. 66 A Girnell for grayne. **1697** DRYDEN *Virg. Georg.* III. 797 The lab'ring Swain Scratch'd with a Rake, a Furrow for his Grain. **1727–46** THOMSON *Seasons, Summer* 361 Wide flies the tedded grain. **1740** SOMERVILLE *Hobbinol* II. 133 The ripen'd Grain, whose bending Ears Invite the Reaper's Hand. **1753** J. BARTLET *Gentl. Farriery* i. 2 Beans afford the strongest nourishment of all grain. **1774** GOLDSM. *Nat. Hist.* (1776) V. 344 All this tribe..feeding upon grain. **1817–8** COBBETT *Resid. U.S.* (1822) 4 The general harvest for grain (what we call corn) is a full month earlier than in the South of England! **1847** TENNYSON *Princ.* Concl. 89 A lord of fat prize-oxen and of sheep..A pamphleteer on guano and on grain. **1879** J. D. BURNS *Mem. & Rem.* 422 The husbandman employs different processes in preparing his grain for use.

b. A particular species of corn. †Also *pl.* Crops of grain.

c **1400** MAUNDEV. (1839) xxxi. 310 Corn of dyverse greynes and of Ryzs. *c* **1460** FORTESCUE *Abs. & Lim. Mon.* (1714) 95 This Realme gave to their Kyng..the ixth Scheff of their Graynys. **1494** FABYAN V. cxxxvi. 122 Whete & other graynes were at an excedyng pryce. **1544** tr. *Littleton's Tenures* 15 b, If the lesse sowe the lande & the lessour.. before that his graynes be rype puttith him out, yet [etc.]. **1704** *Old Tour in Scotl.* in *Blackw. Mag.* Feb. (1818) 520/2 Barley is a sumer grain, and beer a winter grain. **1732** ARBUTHNOT *Rules of Diet* I. 250 Mays not so easily brought to Fermentation as other Grains. **1767** A. YOUNG *Farmer's Lett. to People* 310 The grain, or grass, which seems best to suit it [the soil]. **1825** *Philos. Jrnl.* 25 Apr., The grains which extend farthest to the north in Europe are barley and oats. **1870** J. YEATS *Nat. Hist. Comm.* 128 Wheat is the chief grain of temperate and sub-temperate climates.

c. *fig.* (Cf. a like use of L. *farina*.)

1622 MABBE tr. *Aleman's Guzman d'Alf.* II. iii. 27 [Those men] are both of one graine, sowne and reaped vnder one and the same Moone, bread of the same meale.

4. Specialized applications of the plural. **a.** (in full ***grains of Paradise***: in early use also *sing.*):

The capsules of *Amomum Meleguetta* of Western Africa (cf. CARDAMOM b), used as a spice and in medicine; called also ***Guinea grains*** (see GUINEA).

?a1366 CHAUCER *Rom. Rose* 1369 Clowe-gelofre, and licoryce, Gingere, and greyn de Parys [orig. *Graine de paradis*]. c1386 —— *Miller's T.* 504 But first he cheweth greyn and lycorys, To smellen swete. c1420 *Liber Cocorum* (1862) 38 Take..Of maces, cloves and graynys also. c1460 J. RUSSELL *Bk. Nurture* 126 Graynes of paradise, hoote & moyst þey be. 1542 BORDE *Dyetary* (1870) 286 Graynes be good for the stomake and the head. 1614 B. JONSON *Barth. Fair* IV. iv, I'ld cure him now..with..garlike, long pepper, and graines. 1669 WORLIDGE *Syst. Agric.* (1681) 225 Steep the Regulus of Antimony in Ale, with a little of the Spice called Grains. 1705 BOSMAN *Guinea* 305 Malagueta, otherwise called Paradise-Grains, or Guinea Pepper. 1743 *Lond. & Country Brew.* IV. 288 When I found it [Two-Penny Drink] left a hot Tang behind it, it gave me just Reason to believe they had used Grains of Paradise, or long Pepper, both which will save Malt. 1812 J. SMYTH *Pract. of Customs* (1821) 96 Guinea Grains and Grains of Paradise are considered by the Trade, as one and the same article. 1850 KINGSLEY *Alt. Locke* viii, 'Beer poisoned wi' grains o' Paradise and *cocculus indicus*.'

b. Refuse malt left after brewing or distilling.

In the first quot. the sense seems to be 'malt'.

1583 T. STOCKER tr. *Trag. Hist. Civ. Wars Low C.* I. III. 118b, And the fift day, they made ordenaunces concerning their flesh victual, and Graynes, which they began to bake [orig. *gasteaus de brassin qu'on commençoit a cuyre*]. *Ibid.*, The greater sort of the common people dronk water, by reason that the grains was baked into bread. 1595 *Manch. Ct. Leet Rec.* (1885) II. 94 No persone..shall sell any Draffe graynes or branne by any other measure then onlye by the measure that they by..theire corne bye. 1616 SURFL. & MARKH. *Country Farme* 105 There is also two other Foods ..excellent for Hogges: the first whereof is Ale or Beere Graines. a1659 CLEVELAND *Coachman* 16 There's Difference in the Reins Of Horses fed with Oats, and fed with *Grains*. 1718 BATES in *Phil. Trans.* XXX. 880 The feeding Cows with Distillers Grains was a new Custom. 1751 JOHNSON *Rambler* No. 138 ¶13, I met Miss Busy carrying grains to a sick cow. 1846 J. BAXTER *Libr. Pract. Agric.* II. 34 Brewers' grains. In Norfolk, grains have been employed as a manure. 1880 *Daily Tel.* 9 Jan., Advt., Owing to the deficient root crop..stockowners should use oil or stout grains.

†**c.** = DUCKWEED. (Also *greens*: see GREEN *sb.*)

1578 LYTE *Dodoens* I. lxxi. 107 In English water Lentils, Duckes meate, and Graynes. 1597 GERARDE *Herbal* II. cclxxxvii. 690 Ducks meate: some terme it after the Greek water Lentils, and of others it is named Graines.

5. †**a.** A berry, grape. (So F. *grain*.) *Obs.* **b.** One of the parts of a collective fruit. **c.** (See quot. 1829.)

a. c1315 SHOREHAM 23 Ase the wyne to gadere flouthe Of manye greyne ytake. 1388 WYCLIF *Lev.* xix. 10 Nethir in thi vyner thou schalt gadere reysyns and greynes falling down [Vulg. *racemos et grana cadentia*]. c1400 *Lanfranc's Cirurg.* 273 þe cure herof is with electuari maad of greynes of lauri. c1430 *Pilgr. Lyf Manhode* II. cxlvii. (1869) 134, I serue of vinegre and of vergeous, and of greynes þat ben soure and greene. 1660 F. BROOKE tr. *Le Blanc's Trav.* 155 Excellent Grapes..which they..load and unload..without hurting the least grain. 1693 EVELYN *De la Quint. Compl. Gard.* I. 157 The Chassela's..is a very sweet Grape..its grain or Berry is large and crackling.

b. 1674 tr. *Scheffer's Hist. Lapland* 141 Each Berry being divided as it were into graines of a pale yellow color. 1859 W. S. COLEMAN *Woodlands* (1862) 106 The grains of which it [the dewberry] is composed are..covered with fine bloom.

c. 1829 LOUDON *Encycl. Plants* 1100 The segments of the flowers of Rumex have tubercles which are called grains.

II. Senses originally transferred from 1 and 2.

†**6.** A bead, esp. one of the beads of a rosary (so F. *grain*); also, a pearl. *Obs.*

a1310 in Wright *Lyric P.* xi. 38 A grein in gold that godly shon. 1579 FULKE *Heskins' Parl.* 456 Their graines of the Trinitie, and such other gaudes. 1630 WADSWORTH *Pilgr.* iii. 18 They haue..Meddals and hallowed graines from his holinesse. 1662 J. DAVIES tr. *Mandelslo's Trav.* 254 They sold us a fat Sheep..for 7. or 8. grains of Coral or Agat, and a Capon for 3. or 4. grains of counterfeit Coral.

7. a. A small, hard, usually roundish particle (e.g. of sand, gold, salt, pepper). ***with a grain of salt*** (fig.): see SALT.

c1290 *S. Eng. Leg.* I. 417/486 þare nas inne [the grave of S. John] nouȝt bote smale greynes..i-cleoped Manna in holi write. 1384 CHAUCER *H. Fame* II. 183 And moo berdys in two oures..then greynes be of sondes. c1440 *Jacob's Well* (E.E.T.S.) 303 Grauel & sande han stonys and greynys wyth-oute noumbre. c1500 *Melusine* xxi. 128 One grayne of peper alone smertith more on mans tonge than doth a sacke full of whete. 1601 R. JOHNSON *Kingd. & Commw.* (1603) 167 In manie rivers are found graines of gold. *Ibid.*, Hee maketh graines of salt and pepper to passe for current coine. 1651 HOBBES *Leviath.* III. xlii. 270 The Multiplication of a grain of Mustard-seed. 1667 MILTON *P.L.* VIII. 17 This Earth, a spot, a grain, An atom, with the Firmament compar'd. 1687 A. LOVELL *Thevenot's Trav.* I. 124 The surface of them [obelisks in Egypt] seems to be covered with little grains. 1719 DE FOE *Crusoe* (1840) I. iii. 44 Gold-dust, Guinea grains. 1799 *Scot. Described* (ed. 2) 16 Gold has been gathered in Grains among the sands of the Elvan. 1813 J. THOMSON *Lect. Inflam.* 289 The smooth surface..is..raised into a number of small eminences, like grains or papillæ. These little eminences are termed granulations. 1838 E. BROWN *Serm.* iii. 45 What so insignificant in the inanimate creation as a grain of dust? 1871 R. ELLIS tr. *Catullus* lxxxvi. 4 In all that bodily largeness, Lives not a grain of salt, breathes not a charm anywhere. 1888 F. HUME *Mad. Midas* I. ii, A paper full of grains of gold.

b. *spec.* Of gunpowder: A particle of definite size, varying according to requirements. (Also *poet.* in collective sense.) Also *attrib.* in *large*, *small*, etc. ***grain powder***.

1667 MILTON *P.L.* IV. 817 The Smuttie graine, With sudden blaze diffus'd, inflames the Aire. *Ibid.* VI. 515. 1714 GAY *Trivia* III. 384 The smutty Train With running blaze awakes the barrell'd Grain. 1769 FALCONER *Dict. Marine* (1780) I 4 b, The powder..expands so as to occupy a much greater space than when in grains. 1846 GREENER *Sci. Gunnery* 248 All barrels have a size of grain that will suit them best. 1859 F. A. GRIFFITHS *Artil. Man.* (1862) 92 Large grain, or common powder.

c. Of incense (see quot.).

1853 ROCK *Ch. of Fathers* III. II. 98 A deacon sang..the blessing of this candle, as well as of the incense, large knobs of which, or as they are now called 'grains', were stuck up on it at one part of this ceremony.

†**d.** A lump or nugget (of gold). *Obs. rare.*

1613 PURCHAS *Pilgrimage* (1614) 913 That admirable graine of gold..weighed in the first finding..many thousand crowns.

e. Any of the irregularly shaped discrete particles or crystals in a rock or a metal, usu. but not necessarily small.

(i) *Petrol.* 1813 R. BAKEWELL *Introd. Geol.* ii. 25 *Granitic*, composed of grains or crystals closely united without a cement. 1836 *Edin. New Philos. Jrnl.* IX. 268 It [*sc.* the granite] is not throughout pure, but is occasionally mixed with the gneiss,..or its ingredients, especially felspar, are disseminated in grains or crystals. 1882 A. GEIKIE *Text-bk. Geol.* II. ii. 140 Pitchstone... Examined microscopically, it is found to consist of glass in which are diffused..angular or irregular grains, or more definitely formed crystals. 1939 A. JOHANNSEN *Descr. Petrogr.* (ed. 2) I. iii. 31 When the constituents [of the rock] are..from walnut to cocoanut size, it is very coarse-grained. Occasionally rocks are of still larger grain; certain pegmatites, for example, have grains of several cubic meters or more in size. 1970 *Encycl. Brit.* X. 163/1 The high-silica rocks are generally light coloured and their excess of silica is expressed in abundant grains of quartz.

(ii) *Metallurgy.* 1899 EWING & ROSENHAIN in *Phil. Trans. R. Soc.* A. CXCIII. 355 When the polished surface of a metal, such as gold or iron, is lightly etched, and is then examined by means of normally reflected..light, the surface appears divided up into a number of areas separated by more or less polygonal boundaries. These areas are the sections of the crystalline grains which constitute the mass of the metal. 1923 GLAZEBROOK *Dict. Appl. Physics* V. 392/2 A section cut parallel to the direction of extension shows that the metal still consists of an aggregate of grains, but instead of a system of equi-axed crystals we now find grains elongated in the direction of extension. 1953 *Science News* XXIX. 36 The atoms [in a metal] are..aligned in small regions called grains; one grain containing rows of atoms lying at an angle to the rows in the neighbouring grains. 1965 W. A. TILLER in R. W. Cahn *Physical Metall.* ix. 431 The main volume of the ingot generally consists of a zone of long columnar grains and a zone of equiaxed grains.

f. *Aeronaut.* A piece of solid propellant of the shape and size used in a rocket engine.

1952 K. W. GATLAND *Devel. Guided Missile* 125 Tiny Tim... Solid-propellent (4 × 40 lb solventless extruded ballistite grains, discharge through 24 nozzles). 1954 *Ibid.* (ed. 2) i. 34 The smokeless propellants used in modern rocket projectiles..may be produced in the form of tubes, or grains, of any desired length and thickness. 1962 F. I. ORDWAY et al. *Basic Astronautics* x. 417 Early solid rocket grains were ignited at one end and burned 'cigarette fashion' along the chamber. 1966 *McGraw-Hill Encycl. Sci. & Technol.* XI. 606/2 In some rockets there is more than one grain inside the same combustion chamber.

8. The smallest English and U.S. unit of weight (for the origin see quot. 1542); now = $\frac{1}{5760}$ of a lb. Troy, $\frac{1}{7000}$ of a lb. avoirdupois. ***diamond grain*** (see quot. 1883). ***fine grain*** (see FINE *a.* 2 b).

1542 RECORDE *Gr. Artes* (1575) 202 After the statutes of Englande, the least portion of waight is commonly a Grayne, meaning a grayne of corne or wheate, drie, and gathered out of the middle of the eare. 1660 BOYLE *New Exp. Phys. Mech.* vi. 59 We found the weight increas'd onely by one Grain. 1670 DRYDEN *2nd Pt. Conq. Granada* Epil., None of 'em, no not Johnson in his Height, Could pass, without allowing Grains for Weight. 1684 R. WALLER *Nat. Exper.* 77 A pair of Scales that turned with the $\frac{1}{64}$ part of a Grane. 1747 WESLEY *Prim. Physick* (1762) 84 Take from eight to twelve Grains of Calomel. 1825 J. NICHOLSON *Operat. Mechanic* 763 The assayers' grains are called fine grains. 1870 JEVONS *Elem. Logic* xxvi. 222 When a chemist analyses a few grains of water. 1883 A. H. CHURCH *Precious Stones* vii. 50 It [the carat] is, however, spoken of as being equal to 4 grains, the grains meant being 'diamond' grains, and not ordinary troy or avoirdupois grains. Thus a diamond grain is but .7925 of a true grain.

9. In figurative applications of senses 7 and 8: The smallest possible quantity; esp. in negative contexts. For the phr. ***grains of allowance*** cf. quot. 1670 in sense 8.

1377 LANGL. *P. Pl.* B. x. 139, I myȝte gete no greyne of his grete wittis. 1559 *Mirr. Mag., Clifford* ii. 3 My faultes be out so playne..That though I would I can not hide a grayne. 1593 DRAYTON *Eclog.* 5 If there so much be left but as a Graine, Of the great stock of antike Poesie. 1629 CHAPMAN *Juvenal* 16 His forme and prime..May well allow him some few Graines of pride. 1643 MILTON *Divorce* I. iv. (1851) 31 The lonelinesse which leads him still powerfully to seeke a fit helpe, hath not the least grain of a sin in it. 1647 TRAPP *Comm. 1 Pet.* i. 6 When our hearts grow a grain too light, God seeth it but needfull to make us heavy through manifold temptations. 1648 ROUSE *Balm Love* 10 Thou must give every Saint those graines of allowance which the Apostle gives him. 1654 WARREN *Unbelievers* 98 The *Minor* are the words of Christ..and need not a graine of allowance. 1676 [see ALLOWANCE 9]. 1706 HEARNE *Collect.* 9 Apr. (O.H.S.) I. 221 A..stupid Blockhead, without one Grain of Learning. 1713 STEELE *Englishman* No. 1. 5 Your Man.. might have given some Grains of Allowance to a good Droll for being a bad Politician. 1735-8 BOLINGBROKE *On Parties* 69 He had not a Grain of Pride, or Vanity, in his whole Composition. 1775 SHERIDAN *Rivals* II. i, A little less simplicity with a grain or two more sincerity. 1868 J. H. BLUNT *Ref. Ch. Eng.* I. 360 Nor is it probable that it ever had a grain of truth in it. 1879 TOURGEE *Fool's Err.* xxxiii. 217 An inferior race, whose evidence, at best, would have to be taken with many grains of allowance. 1894 DRUMMOND *Ascent Man* 391 Wedded life without a grain of love.

III. With reference to dyeing. [OF. *graine*; the kermes was believed to consist of seeds or berries.]

10. *Hist.* The Kermes or Scarlet Grain (see ALKERMES 1); in later use also applied to Cochineal. Also, the dye made from either of these.

1335-6 *Durham Acct. Rolls* 527 Ij li. de grayn. 1340 *Ayenb.* 107 Zuo moche ydept yne grayne. 1465 *Mann. & Househ. Exp.* (Roxb.) 164 My Mastyre delyverd..of crymeson owt of greyn, ij. yerdes. 1488-9 *Act 4 Hen. VII*, c. 8 And a brode yerde of Wollen cloth of ony other Colour out of grayne. 1502 ARNOLDE *Chron.* (1811) 87 To sarse syfte and trye out the beste greyne and ther wyth dye and greyne their owne clothes. 1601 HOLLAND *Pliny* I. 461 The Scarlet grain..which commeth of the Ilex. 1617 MORYSON *Itin.* III. I. iv. 96 The Spaniards and Portugals brought graine for Scarlet Dye. 1649 BP. REYNOLDS *Hosea* vi. 68 The grace of God unto the purposes of men is like graine to colours died. 1861 HULME tr. *Moquin-Tandon Med. Zool.* II. III. i. 71 The Common Cochineal..was supposed to be a small berry or grain, known as 'Shining Grain'. 1883 *Contemp. Rev.* Sept. 427 The chief reds were scarlet..and grain, imported from Portugal.

fig. 1578 W. CLOWES in Lyte *Dodoens* Commend., Lyte, whose toyle hath not bene light, to dye it in this grayne. 1626 T. AILESBURY *Passion Serm.* 23 Tyranny cloatheth him with one purple, died in the purest graine of his bloud.

b. ***to dye*** (rarely, ***to put***) ***in grain***: orig. to dye in scarlet grain or kermes; afterwards, to dye in any fast colour, to dye in the fibre, or thoroughly (see note on ENGRAIN *v.*).

c1386 CHAUCER *Sqr.'s T.* 503 So depe in greyn he dyed his colours. 1580 NORTH *Plutarch* (1676) 7 This sail..was not white, but red, died in grain, and of the colour of Scarlet. 1650 FULLER *Pisgah* IV. vi. 99 These colours not being dyed in grain, lose much of their lustre, and gloss in washing. 1715 *Lond. Gaz.* No. 5387/4 His new invented Art of Printing, Dying or Staining of Calicoes in Grain. 1742 SHENSTONE *Schoolmistress* vi. 48 Her apron, dy'd in grain, as blue, I trowe, As is the hare-bell.

fig. 1567 R. EDWARDS *Damon & Pithias* (1571) Bij a, A Villaine for his life, a Varlet died in Graine. 1598 DRAYTON *Heroic. Ep.* ix. 124 Greene, Scroope, and Bushy dye his fault in graine. 1651-3 JER. TAYLOR *Serm. for Year* 92 Our Reason is first stained..with the Dye of our Kindred, and Countrey, and our Education puts it in grain. 1670 LASSELS *Voy. Italy* I. 221 Its a Gentry dyed in grain, that is, its both witty and rich. 1731 SWIFT *Strephon & Chloe* 85 She, a goddess dy'd in grain, Was unsusceptible of stain. 1775 BURKE *Corr.* (1844) II. 4 My American measures..have a certain unity of colour which has stood wearing for upwards of nine years... It is indeed dyed in grain.

c. ***in grain*** [short for ***dyed in grain***, or a rendering of F. *en graine*], adjectival phrase = dyed scarlet or crimson, fast dyed; hence in figurative use, esp. with contemptuous epithets, as *ass*, *fool*, *knave*, *rogue*, etc.: Downright, by nature, pure and simple, genuine, thorough. Also as ***predicate***, indelible, ineradicable, INGRAINED. See also INGRAIN *a.*

c1386 CHAUCER *Sir Thopas* 16 His rode is lyk scarlet in grayn. 1441 *Pol. Poems* (Rolls) II. 208 Farewelle, velvet, and clothes in grayn. 1531 in Weaver *Wells Wills* (1890) 22 Maud K. my gowne off vyolett yn grayne. a1577 *Misogonus* I. iv. 17 (Brandl *Quellen* 434), Now by me, trwlye, thou art a knaue, an grane. 1590 SHAKS. *Com. Err.* III. ii. 108 *Anti.* That's a fault that water will mend. *Dro.* No sir, 'tis in graine, Noahs flood could not do it. 1599 MINSHEU *Dial. Sp. & Eng.* (1623) 34 Go to, make an end babler in graine. 1601 SHAKS. *Twel. N.* I. v. 255 *Vio.* Excellently done, if God did all. *Ol.* Tis in graine sir, 'twill endure winde and weather. 1606 *Choice, Chance*, etc. (1881) 3 Here are conceits of diuerse colours, some in graine and none but will bide the weather. 1611 COTGR. s.v. *Game*, *Fol à la haulte game*, an arrant foole..; an Asse in graine. 1613 WITHER *Motto, Nec Habeo* (1633) 518 To maintain a habit for my Minde Of Truth in graine. c1650 *Roxb. Ballads* (1886) I. 317 Then Drawer, go fill a Quart, and let it be Claret in graine. a1661 FULLER *Worthies* (1840) II. 551 Some who properly may be termed knaves in grain. 1698 CROWNE *Caligula* II. Dram. Wks. (1874) IV. 377 Princes are slaves in purple, slaves in grain. 1719 D'URFEY *Pills* (1872) IV. 60 No Woman should deceive my Thought, With Colours not in Grain. 1759 STERNE *Tr. Shandy* I. xxi, My father, as I told you, was a philosopher in grain. 1793 T. JEFFERSON *Writings* (1859) IV. 5 Dumourier was known to be a scoundrel in grain. 1840 CARLYLE *Misc.* II. 84 Being palpably a Turk in grain, his intents are wicked. 1862 *Sat. Rev.* XIV. 370/2 To paint himself as a saint in grain, but a sinner by accident. 1863 KEBLE *Life Bp. Wilson* xvii. 540 He was an antiquarian in grain, and delighted in exact observation. 1886 R. BOYLE in *Trans. New Shaks. Soc.* 585 Massinger's corrupt female natures are in grain.

11. Dye in general, esp. a fast dye; colour, hue. Now only *poet.*

1377 LANGL. *P. Pl.* B. XVI. 59 Of o gretnesse, and grene of greyne thei [this thre piles] semen. c1394 *P. Pl. Crede* 230 His kyrtel of clene whijt..Hyt was good y-now of ground, greyn for to beren. 1587 M. GROVE *Pelops & Hipp.* (1878) 100 Ne to change that colour sad, for any other graine. 1593 DRAYTON *Eclog.* III. 132 Beta shall have the firstling of the Fold, Yea, though the Hornes were of the purest gold, And the fine Fleece, the richest purple Graine. 1632 MILTON *Penseroso* 31 All in a robe of darkest grain. 1649 G. DANIEL *Trinarch., Rich. II*, 96 To make his Course-spun beare a Graine Fitt for a finer Thred. 1712 ADDISON *Spect.* No. 412 ¶4 In Birds..we often see the Mate determined in his Courtship by the single Grain or Tincture of a Feather.

1801 SOUTHEY *Thalaba* I. 22 The ebony..With darkness feeds its boughs of raven grain. **1849** LYTTON *K. Arthur* II. lxxxv, Cloth of comely grain.

fig. **1641** MILTON *Ch. Govt.* (1851) 132 By this is seene.. whose vertue is of an unchangeable graine, and whose of a slight wash. **1647** N. BACON *Disc. Govt. Eng.* I. xxxix. (1739) 59 Then might that Penance be reduced to a Ransom (according to the grain of the offence). **1660** H. THURMAN in Wood *Life* 21 Oct. (O.H.S.) I. 370 Sins of so deep a graine as of killing a king. **1782** J. TRUMBULL *M'Fingal* II. (1795) 37 T' evade these crimes of blackest grain, You prate of Liberty in vain.

IV. Granular texture.

12. a. A roughness of surface, giving the appearance of 'grains' (sense 7) or small roundish bodies side by side. Hence in an engraving or drawing, a granular appearance produced by dots or lines.

1390 GOWER *Conf.* III. 27 He seeth her front is large and pleine Withoute frounce of any greine. **1607** TOPSELL *Serpents* (1658) 791 The little Lizard, or Stellion starred in body grain [L. *atris stellatus corpore guttis*]. **1625** BACON *Transl. cert. Ps.* 8 The Compasse heauen, smooth without graine or fold, All set with Spangs of glitt'ring Stars vntold. **1646** SIR T. BROWNE *Pseud. Ep.* III. xxiii. 168 The tooth of a Morse or Sea-horse in the midst of the solider part containing a curdled graine. **1715** GAY *Trivia* I. 46 And Show'rs soon drench the Camlet's cockled Grain. **1812** R. H. in *Examiner* 25 May 329/1 We regret that the..Artist does not clear out his copper a little better, so as to obviate a want of clearness of grain. **1821** CRAIG *Lect. Drawing* vii. 401 These cracks..when bit in, form what is called the grain of the work. **1968** *Gloss. Terms Offset Lithogr. Printing* (*B.S.I.*) 21 *Grain*, a roughened state of a lithographic surface which assists the retention of moisture and control of the image.

b. *Photogr.* An appearance of mottling or granulation in a negative.

1890 *Anthony's Photogr. Bull.* III. 173 The former, owing to a certain amount of grain, are not adapted to make good sharp lantern plates.

13. *spec.* Of leather: **a.** The rough or wrinkled surface resulting from the growth of papillæ.

1607 TOPSELL *Four-f. Beasts* (1658) 527 They leave it [pigskin] to the sadlers and to them that cover books—for which cause it is much better then either sheep or goats skins, for it hath a deeper grain. **1612** DRAYTON *Poly-olb.* xiv. 233 The staple deepe and thicke, through, to the very graine. **1876** SCHULTZ *Leather Manuf.* 19 The grain must be fully preserved.

b. = *grain-side* (see 19 below).

1851 MAYHEW *Lond. Labour* I. 443 The skin is 'split'.. That known as the 'grain' (the part to which the fleece of the animal is attached) is very thin. **1885** *Harper's Mag.* 276/2 Grains and splits together are again 'pin-wheeled'.

c. A similar surface produced artificially.

1530 [see GRAIN *v.*[1] 6]. **1687** A. LOVELL tr. *Thevenot's Trav.* II. 34 These [little dents]..make that grane which we see in Chagrin. **1839** URE *Dict. Arts* 769 A grain is formed upon the flesh side with the roughened lead plate or grainer of the curriers. **1879** *Cassell's Techn. Educ.* IV. 88 The grain is made by passing a ball of boxwood, with grooves in it, over the skin many times. *Ibid.*, Skins..marked with a handsome full grain of considerable size.

d. Short for *grain-leather* (see sense 19).

1895 *Montgomery Ward Catal.* 516/1 A shoe..made from the finest grade of English imported grain... This grain consists of a very fine selection of calfskin, finished on the grain side. **1897** *Sears, Roebuck Catal.* 193/3 Ladies' Bright Grain Button Shoe. **1930** *Daily Tel.* 1 Dec. 15/1 Washable Grain Cape Gloves. **1949** D. WOODROFFE *Stand. Handbk. Industr. Leathers* i. 16 The grain is dressed for handbags, luggage, men's dress belts.

14. The texture of any substance; the arrangement and size of its constituent particles, appearing in an exposed surface or in a cross-cut or fracture: **a.** in flesh or skin.

c **1600** *Grobiana's Nuptialls* Prol. (*Bodl. MS.* 30, fol. 13 a), Such as ne're swathed their feete in socks, for feare of the graine of their owne bodies. **1634** MILTON *Comus* 750 Coarse complexions, And cheeks of sorry grain. **1697** DAMPIER *Voy.* (1698) I. iv. 91 The lean Flesh is black, and of a course grain. **1747** MRS. GLASSE *Cookery* xxi. 162 The hen [of the pheasant], if young, has smooth Legs, and her Flesh of a curious Grain. **1762–71** H. WALPOLE *Vertue's Anecd. Paint.* (1786) IV. 51 The head of an old woman..in which the grain of the skin, the hairs [etc.] were represented with the most exact minuteness. **1823** J. BADCOCK *Dom. Amusem.* 68 Dark persons observed to have skin of a finer grain than fair persons. **1840** DICKENS *Old C. Shop* iii, His hands, which were of a rough coarse grain, were very dirty.

b. in wood (cf. sense 15).

c **1640** J. SMYTH *Lives Berkeleys* (1883) I. 161 My selfe havinge..told theire [Oakes'] ages..by the graine..made in a circle in every kind of tree by the yearly assent and consolidation of the sapp. **1664** EVELYN *Sylva* (1679) 17 The Timber is far better, and of a finer grain, which grows upon the Mountains. **1672–3** GREW *Anat. Plants* IV. iv. §3 (1682) 153 Giving the Leaf, as it were, a different Grain. **1725** POPE *Odyss.* v. 302 The clouded olive's easy grain. **1815** J. SMITH *Panorama Sci. & Art* I. 91 Mahogany..grown on rocks is the..closest in the grain.

c. in stone, metal, etc.

1703 MOXON *Mech. Exerc.* 57 The English-steel..breaks Fiery, with somewhat a course Grain. **1793** SMEATON *Edystone L.* §218 *note*, A large flat stone, of a close grain. **1832** G. R. PORTER *Porcelain & Gl.* i. 11 The grain in both the Chinese and Saxon pieces appeared compact, smooth, and shining; while that of the French ware was less close.. and its grain resembled sugar. **1878** HUXLEY *Physiogr.* 22 Close in grain as the rock may appear to the eye.

d. *Soap-making.* (See quot. 1885.)

1884 A. WATT *Soap-making* vi. 59 When a sample of the paste, after being allowed to cool, is firm and solid, and exhibits a good grain or 'feather' when cut, the soap is finished. **1885** W. L. CARPENTER *Manuf. Soap & Candles* i. 12 The appearances known as 'grain' or 'strike' in a hard soap, and 'fig' in a soft soap, are due to the crystalline character of soap.

e. *concr.* Internal substance.

1579 SPENSER *Sheph. Cal.* Feb. 203 The Axes edge did oft turne againe, As halfe vnwilling to cut the graine. **1600** HAKLUYT *Voy.* (1810) III. 237 The graine of the bone is somewhat more yellow than the Ivorie. **1622** DRAYTON *Poly-olb.* xxvi. 255 The lustie Salmon..Whose graine doth rise in flakes, with fatnesse interlarded. **1873** SPON *Workshop Receipts* Ser. I 362/1 The middle of the blade [of whalebone] is of a looser texture than the rest, and is called the grain, being composed of coarse, bristly hairs.

fig. *a* **1627** HAYWARD *Edw. VI* (1630) 82 They liued..as brothers glued together but not vnited in graine.

15. The longitudinal arrangement of fibres or particles, in lines or veins more or less parallel along which the material is more easily cloven or cut than in any other direction: **a.** in wood, producing often the effect of a pattern. ***grain upset***: *Naut.* (see quot. 1867).

1565 COOPER *Thesaurus*, *Vndatim crispæ mensæ*. Plin. Tables hauynge grayne lyke waues of water. **1606** SHAKS. *Tr. & Cr.* I. iii. 8. **1674** tr. *Scheffer's Lapland* 47 When the grain of the wood, running from the bottom to the top of the tree, winds it self from the right hand to the left. **1703** MOXON *Mech. Exerc.* 68 The Grain of the Wood lying along the length of the Bench. **1801** KNIGHT in *Phil. Trans.* XCI. 344 There is..in every kind of wood, what workmen call its grain, consisting of two kinds, the false or bastard, and the true or silver grain. **1825** J. NICHOLSON *Operat. Mechanic* 599 Having the grain of the wood to run in the same direction with the rail. **1834** MRS. SOMERVILLE *Connect. Phys. Sci.* xvi. (1849) 150 The facility with which the vibrations of sound are transmitted along the grain of a log of wood is well known. **1865** DICKENS *Mut. Fr.* I. vi, The light shone full upon the grain of certain panels. **1867** SMYTH *Sailors' Word-bk.*, *Grain upset*, when a mast suffers by buccles, it is said to have the grain upset.

b. in flesh.

1591 A. W. *Bk. Cookrye* 20 b, Take Venison and cut it as the graine goeth.

c. in coal, stone, etc.: Lamination; stratification; plane of cleavage.

1664 POWER *Exp. Philos.* III. 169 Those Magnetical Atoms that strike..through the Body of every petty Loadstone, accordingly as they are best received by the Grain or Bait of the said Stone. **1703** T. N. *City & C. Purchaser* 254 Common Stones have a cleaving Grain, (as they lie in the Quarry,) and a breaking one; the first..runs parallel with the Horizon; the other is perpendicular to it. **1793** SMEATON *Edystone L.* 194 The grain of the laminated moorstone.. being nearly parallel thereto. **1830** HERSCHEL *Study Nat. Phil.* 31 Rock-crystal and Iceland spar..have a grain which glass has not. **1842–76** GWILT *Archit.* Gloss., *Grain*, in wood or stone, is the line of direction in which either may be split transversely. **1860** J. PRESTWICH in *Phil. Trans.* CL. 295 As the gun-flint makers observe, 'flint has no grain'. It has not in fact the slightest cleavage. **1867** W. W. SMYTH *Coal & Coalmining* 145 Banks are..worked across the grain of the coal. **1881** RAYMOND *Mining Gloss.*, *Grain*, of coal, the lines of structure or parting parallel with the main gangways.

d. In paper.

1922 *Paper Trade Jrnl.* 15 June 50/2 *Grain*... In paper the direction of manufacture on the machine, as 'across the grain'. **1924** *Ibid.* 7 Feb. 56/2 *Grain direction*, the direction in which the fibers flow on a papermaking machine. **1949** *Manual of Style* (*Chicago Univ. Press*) (ed. 11) 251 Paper resists bending and folding against the grain. For this reason printers take care to make sure that the grain will run vertically in the completed book, in order that..the book pages will lie flat when the book is opened. **1961** J. P. CASEY *Pulp & Paper* (ed. 2) III. xvii. 1258 The grain of paper must be taken into account in measuring all physical properties.

16. *fig.* (from senses 14 and 15). Quality, nature, temper; inclination, tendency.

(In first quot. other senses are possible: cf. 3 c and 11 *fig.*)

1641 MILTON *Prel. Episc.* (1851) 80 All men would have readily seen what grain the testimony had bin of. **1664** DRYDEN *Rival Ladies* Ded., To work and bend their stubborn Minds, which go not all after the same Grain. *a* **1677** BARROW *Serm.* Wks. 1716 III. 159 Crossing the Grain of our Nature and Desires. *a* **1715** BURNET *Own Time* (1766) I. 148 The king ought to govern them according to the grain of their own inclinations. **1786** *Har'st Rig* 61 The master hardly can restrain Their thrawart humour and cross grain. **1866** ALGER *Solit. Nat. & Man* IV. 329 He was separated from ordinary persons in grain and habits. **1876** GEO. ELIOT *Dan. Der.* II. xvi. 129 Hatred of innocent human obstacles was a form of moral stupidity not in Deronda's grain. **1884** *Pall Mall G.* 11 Sept. 3/1 Mr. Broadhurst is a representative English workman of the best grain.

b. Phr. ***against*** (also, ***contrary to***) ***the grain***: contrary to one's disposition or inclination; esp. in ***to go against the grain***.

1650 HUBBERT *Pill Formality* 65 O this goes against the grain, this cannot be indured. *a* **1659** OSBORN *Characters*, etc. (1673) 630 To whom in all things you are bound to obey, though contrary to the grain of Prudence it self. **1691–1701** NORRIS *Ideal World* II. xii. (1704) 514 That which seems.. more against the grain of common prejudice. **1694** DRYDEN *Love Triumph.* v. Wks. (1884) VIII. 462 It goes against the grain to give it them. **1778** H. LAURENS in Sparks *Corr. Amer. Rev.* (1853) II. 119 Such provision will be against the grain of the people. **1826** SCOTT *Jrnl.* 12 July, I have dawdled and written letters sorely against the grain all day. **1832** TENNYSON '*Love thou thy land*' 22 Cut Prejudice against the grain. **1861** HUGHES *Tom Brown at Oxf.* xliv. (1889) 421, I followed your advice at last, though it went against the grain uncommonly. **1875** JOWETT *Plato* (ed. 2) III. 91 The mind..unlike the body, must not be made to work against the grain. **1886** STUBBS *Lect. Study Hist.* Pref. 5 The lectures were written under the pressure of statutory compulsion, and against the grain.

17. *pl.* A preparation used in 'graining' leather: = GRAINER[2] 1 a. (In recent Dicts.)

V. *attrib.* and *Comb.*

18. General relations: **a.** simple attrib., as (sense 3) ***grain-barge***, ***-barn***, ***-bin***, ***-boat***, ***-box***, ***-cart***, ***-chamber***, ***-country***, ***-crop***, ***-department***, ***-farm***, ***-field***, ***-food***, ***-land***, ***-market***, ***-merchant***, ***-mill***, ***-port***, ***-room***, ***-sack***, ***-ship***, ***-trade***; (sense 4 b) ***grain-tub*** (in quot. *fig.*); (sense 7 e) ***grain-boundary***, ***-size***; (sense 8) ***grain-weight***; (sense 10 c) ***grain-dyer***, ***dyeing***; (sense 15) ***grain-ways*** adv. **b.** objective, as (sense 3) ***grain-carrier***, ***-crusher***, ***-dealer***, ***-divider***, ***-dryer***, ***-farmer***, ***-grower***, ***-huller***, ***-rubber***, ***-scourer***, ***-separator***; ***grain-carrying***, ***-grinding***, ***-growing***, vbl. sbs.; ***grain-carrying***, ***-cutting***, ***-eating***, ***-growing***, ***-raising*** ppl. adjs. **c.** instrumental, as (sense 3) ***grain-fed***, ***-laden*** adjs.

1902 S. E. WHITE *Blazed Trail* xxix. 204 They were locked through after some delay on account of the *grain barges from Duluth. **1844** *Knickerbocker* XXIII. 439 Let us drop into the '*grain-barn'. **1879** B. F. TAYLOR *Summer-Savory* xiii. 112 The pulpit, with the architecture of a *grain-bin and two stories high. **1891** KIPLING *Light that Failed* 122 An Odessa *grain-boat. **1920** *Jrnl. Inst. Metals* XXIII. 462 This is rather deep etching, but the *grain boundaries were revealed better than by light etching. **1957** D. MCLEAN *Grain Boundaries in Metals* i. 1 A grain boundary in a piece of metal is the boundary separating two crystals (or 'grains') that differ either in crystallographic orientation, composition, or dimensions of the crystal lattice, or in two or all of these properties. **1872** *Rep. Vermont Board Agric.* I. 312 A convenient *grain-box and root-cellar are great aids. **1908** E. NOBLE (*title*) The *grain carriers. **1892** *Pall Mall G.* 9 May 7/1 The Russian *grain-carrying trade. **1901** *Daily Chron.* 19 Aug. 5/7 Twenty-nine grain-carrying ships, chartered for European ports. **1709** *Brit. Apollo* II. No. 70. 3/1 A plain Cart, By Wights ycleped call'd a *Grain-Cart. **1887** H. H. JACKSON *Between Whiles* i. 26 A winding staircase outside led to what had been the *grain-chamber. **1799** J. ROBERTSON *Agric. Perth* 347 Oats and barley were consequently poured down from the Highlands of Perthshire in great quantities towards those provinces of the county that are called *grain-countries. **1822** J. LAING *Voy. Spitzbergen* 34 The *grain crop consists of a small kind of black or grey oats, and a species of barley. **1850** *Rep. U.S. Comm. Patents, Agric. 1849* 113 Their newly invented horse-powers..their seed sowers and *grain-crushers..do much to expedite the labors of the farm. **1850** *Mary Wedlake's Priced List Farming Implements* 16 (*heading*) A General Grain Crusher, Crushing the smallest Pulse and the largest: viz., Lentils and Beans. **1838** H. W. ELLSWORTH *Valley Upper Wabash* v. 47, I have a plan..to introduce the mowing and *grain-cutting machine into this state. **1840** C. MATHEWS *Politicians* 5 To the invading *grain-dealer, the voracious statesman sends a furious inspector. **1868** *Rep. Iowa Agric. Soc. 1867* 158 Near the river a portion [of the corn crop is] sold to grain-dealers where it finds a market at St. Louis. **1800** *Asiat. Ann. Reg.* IV. 56/2 The *grain department was placed under his charge. **1893** *Jrnl. R. Agric. Soc.* Dec. 716 The *grain dividers are secured to the steel framing in a very substantial manner. **1884** *Cassell's Fam. Mag.* Feb. 189/1 Large *grain-dryers..weighing from three to four tons each. **1791** HAMILTON *Berthollet's Dyeing* I. II. iv. I. 192, I wish..that the distinction between *grain and other dyers was abolished. **1714** MANDEVILLE *Fab. Bees* (1733) II. 153 In some of these arts, especially *grain or scarlet-dying, there are processes really astonishing. **1842** A. COMBE *Physiol. Digestion* (ed. 4) 68 The granivorous or *grain-eating birds. **1799** J. ROBERTSON *Agric. Perth* 400 In *grain-farms..the body of the soil must be meliorated before it can be rendered productive. **1804** J. BARROW *Trav. S. Afr.* II. vi. 386 The population of this colony may be reduced into four classes. .. 3. *Grain-farmers. **1959** *Cape Times* 2 July 2/8 Grain farmers are now anxiously looking out for rain for their young crops. *c* **1804** MRS. SHERWOOD *Life* xvii. (1847) 289 A *grain-fed sheep had been killed in the morning. **1817–18** COBBETT *Resid. Amer.* (1822) 96 My hay-fields and *grain-fields. **1845** F. DOUGLASS *Life* (1846) 12 The black-smithing, cartwrighting, coopering..and *grain-grinding, were all performed by the slaves. **1863** D. G. MITCHELL *My Farm* 131 A professed *grain-grower. **1927** PEAKE & FLEURE *Peasants & Potters* 22 Grain is a more sustaining diet than whelks and limpets, and the grain-growers had more time and more energy to improve the amenities of their surroundings. **1963** *Times* 13 Mar. 10/7 Stalin accused some of the 'respected grain-growers' of staging a sit-down strike and leaving workers and the Red Army without bread. **1813** *Niles' Weekly Register* IV. 385/2 The public vigilance and scorn must aid the legal authorities; and so it will, in the *grain-growing states. **1858** J. A. WARDER *Hedges & Evergreens* I. x. 144 Just as..grain-growing prevails, we find the fences are legally considered inclosures for the cattle, or barriers against them. **1868** *Rep. Iowa Agric. Soc. 1867* 148 The enemies to grain-growing are numerous. **1872** W. R. GREG *Enigmas* ii. 83 The average yield of the splendid grain-growing provinces in America. **1850** *Rep. U.S. Comm. Patents 1849* 302 What I claim..is covering..*grain hullers with vulcanized India rubber. **1852** C. W. H[OSKINS] *Talpa* 112 A *grain-laden Dutchman clearing out of harbour. **1817** S. R. BROWN *Western Gaz.* 84 It proves to be excellent *grain land. **1938** *Times Lit. Suppl.* 19 Mar. 181/1 A distinction between grainland, paying tax or rent in kind, and vine-, orchard- and garden-land, paying money-dues. **1871** SCHELE DE VERE *Americanisms* (1872) 481 *Grain* is used in America as *corn* is in England,..the papers quote therefore daily an account of the *Grain Market. **1838** *Lett. fr. Madras* (1843) 225 The *grain-merchants want to hoard it. **1870** J. K. MEDBERY *Men & Myst. Wall St.* 335 All our great grain-merchants..do the same. **1867** H. LATHAM *Black & White* 27 Ellicott..dammed up the Patapsco..and built *grain-mills there. **1891** *Times* 26 Oct. 4/4 From..the Pacific *grain ports..chartering has been almost at a standstill. **1893** GUNTER *Miss Dividends* 187 Great *grain-raising plains. **1873** J. G. BEADLE *Undevel. West* xxv. 524 The other officials and employes were..in charge of [the] *grain room. **1889** *Jrnl. Derbysh. Archæol. Soc.* XI. 40 Found associated with..*grain-rubbers. **1868** *Rep. Iowa Agric. Soc. 1867* 420 We are not behind the rest of the world in inventive skill, for we have invented..Kent's *grain scourer. **1883** E. INGERSOLL in *Harper's Mag.* June 75/2 It is fed down into the *grain separators..which sift out the chaff. **1928** L. P. SMITH *Words & Idioms* 12 The basket.. hoisted by the Egyptian *grainships as an ensign. **1935** *Discovery* Feb. 61/2 These photographs give a good idea of life on a grain ship. **1912** SEXTON & PRIMROSE *Outl. Metallurgy Iron & Steel* (ed. 2) xliv. 545 The *grain-size is reduced to very small dimensions by each pass through the rolls, or by each blow of the hammer. **1956** W. EDWARDS in D. L. Linton *Sheffield* 13 Inferior thickness and grain-size of sandstones. **1958** F. E. ZEUNER *Dating Past* (ed. 4) 21 Varves ..composed of sand below (grain-size chiefly 1·0–0·1 mm.) and silty clay in their upper portion (grain-size under 0·1 mm., chiefly 0·1–0·01 mm.). **1966** D. G. BRANDON *Mod. Techniques Metallogr.* 246 Etched grain boundaries are commonly 1μm or so in width at the low magnifications usually used in grain-size analysis. **1889** *Kansas Times & Star* 22 June, The new Missouri inspection law..will seriously hurt the *grain trade here. **1661** K. W. *Conf. Charac.* (1860) 63 They are resolved to..chock and stifle it in the *graintub of resistance. **1811** *Self Instructor* 519 Holding it *grainways to the light. **1706** PHILLIPS (ed. Kersey) *s.v.*, A *Grain-weight of Gold-Bullion is worth two Pence. **1862** H. SPENCER *First Princ.* II. vi. §61 (1875) 192 The portion of metal called a grain-weight.

19. Special comb.: **grain-bag**, lit., a bag for holding corn; *humorously*, a corn-dealer; **grain-block**, an over-accumulation of grain from the lack of transport; **grain-colour**, (*a*) scarlet dye; (*b*) a fast colour; also a cloth dyed with this; **grain-cradle** = CRADLE *sb.* 7 (Knight *Dict. Mech.* 1875); **grain-cut** *a.* (*Shipbuilding*), of timber, cut athwart the grain (see quot.); **grain-elevator** (see ELEVATOR 3 a, b); **grain-founder** = *grain-sick*; **grain-gold**, †(*a*) gold dust; (*b*) gold formed into grains by heat after 'parting'; **grain growth**, an increase in the average grain size of a metal; **grain-intoxication**, that arising from the use of musty grain; **grain-leather**, leather dressed with the 'grain-side' outwards; **grain-moth**, a moth (esp. *Tinea granella*) whose larvæ devour grain in storehouses; **grain-oriented** *a.*, (of steel) having had the grains oriented predominantly in one direction in order to modify the magnetic properties; **grain-poisoning**, see *grain-intoxication*; **grain-process**, a process in photographic engraving in which a granular texture is given to the plate; **grain roll**, an iron roller made by casting the metal in sand; **grain-sick**, a disease in cattle, consisting of an excessive distension of the rumen with food; **grain-side**, the side of a skin on which the hair grew, opposed to *flesh-side*; **grain-soap, -stone** (see quots.); **grain tin** (see TIN); **grain-tree** *Her.*, an imaginary plant bearing kermes grains (see quot.); **grain-weevil**, a small weevil which injures stored grain; **grain-whisky** (see quot.).

1890 R. KIPLING in *Fortn. Rev.* XLVII. 171 A son of some *grain-bag sat with me at meat. **1899** *Academy* 11 Feb. 184/1 Blankets, grain-bags, and all-wool coats were woven everywhere. **1891** *Pall Mall G.* 11 Nov. 6/3 It will be impossible to avoid a *grain block this year. **1632** SHERWOOD s.v., *Graine-colour, or in graine, *teinct en grain.* **1647** S. CLARKE *Looking Glasse* (1657) 25 True grace is not like a slight staine, but a durable die, and grain-colour which can never be washed out. **1709** *Lond. Gaz.* No. 4540/6 The best broad Italian colour'd Mantua's at 6*s.* 9*d.* per Yard, and grain Colours in proportion. **1778** *Eng. Gazetteer* (ed. 2) s.v. *Stroud*, Famous for dying scarlet broad cloth, and for all other grain colours. **1824** *18th Congress 1 Sess.* H.R. Doc. No. 25, 7 Improvement in *grain cradle [patented March 24, 1823, by] Isaac Babcock. **1845** *Cultivator* New Ser. III. 17 My method is to..cut with a grain cradle previous to the first frost. **1897** *Sears, Roebuck Catal.* 50/3 Morgan Grain Cradle, 4 fingers, grape vine pattern, wood brace, ring fastening, silver steel scythe. **1923** J. H. COOK *50 Yrs. Old Frontier* 3 Sturdy sons of the forest, they could swing the scythe or the grain-cradle from sunup to sundown. **1830** HEDDERWICK *Nav. Arch.* 113 *Grain-cut, is when a timber is formed from a straight piece of wood, so that the direction of the fibre does not follow the curve of the timber. **1852** L. B. MACKINNON *Atlantic & Transatlantic Sketches* I. 57 To accelerate the introduction of the cargo, a *grain-elevator was employed. This novel machine pumped the grain from barges,..in a continuous stream into the ship's hold... It was..accurately measured in the operation. **1873** 'MARK TWAIN' & WARNER *Gilded Age* xxii. 203 Pictures of wharves, crowded with steam boats, and of huge grain elevators on the bank. **1905** *Macm. Mag.* Nov. 47 The wheat..is warehoused ready for shipment in grain-elevators, which are large rectangular buildings of great height, consisting of vertical bins, some of which are a hundred feet in depth. **1926** *Daily Colonist* (Victoria, B.C.) 3 Jan. 1/2 Chief of the commercial buildings contemplated is the proposed new grain elevator of the Panama-Pacific Grain Terminals Company. **1967** *Canadian Ann. Rev. 1966* 283 Among the buildings deferred were a large grain elevator in Prince Rupert and several proposed government buildings in Ottawa. **1890** BILLINGS *Nat. Med. Dict.*, *Grain-founder or *Grain-sick.* **1695** WOODWARD *Nat. Hist. Earth* IV. 222 'Tis by this means [Rain] chiefly that the *Grain-Gold, upon all the Golden Coast..in Guinea, is displayed. **1825** J. NICHOLSON *Operat. Mechanic* 766 It [the parted gold after being made red-hot] is then called Grain Gold. **1850** W. COLTON *Deck & Port* xiv. 397 Each has a bag of grain-gold in his hand, which he must double or lose. **1928** *Jrnl. Iron & Steel Inst.* CXVII. 920 *Grain growth started at the surfaces of the samples by small grains of iron absorbing the diffusing metal, and extended by migration of grain boundaries in the direction of the diffusing force. **1897** *Allbutt's Syst. Med.* II. 792 Rare..are the *grain intoxications in our own country. **1858** SIMMONDS *Dict. Trade*, *Grain-leather, a name for dressed horse-hides. **1885** WATT *Leather Manuf.* xxvii. 341 Leather which has to be blackened on the flesh side is differently treated to grain leather. **1842** T. W. HARRIS *Insects Injur. Veget.* 363 The European *grain-moth (*Tinea granella*), in its perfected state, is a winged insect. **1855** *Cycl. Agric.* (ed. Morton) II. 989 *Tinea granella* (the little Grain or Corn Moth). **1932** METCALF & FLINT *Fund. Insect Life* viii. 273 Among the most destructive and best-known species [of Gelechiidæ] are the pink bollworm.., the Angoumois grain moth. **1967** S. O. NELSON in Kilgore & Doutt *Pest Control* iii. 107 The Angoumois grain moth and the lesser grain borer were more resistant to control by infrared treatment. **1951** *Trans. Amer. Inst. Electr. Engineers* LXX. 840/1 The successful application of *grain oriented strip steel to turbine generators, marks an important new step in the field of power generation. **1960** *Times* 11 Feb. 17/3 A modern plant for the integrated and continuous processing of ultra-low-loss grain-oriented electrical quality sheet and strip. **1897** *Allbutt's Syst. Med.* II. 792 There are three well-known modes of *grain poisoning. **1890** W. J. GORDON *Foundry* xi. 216 There are other *grain processes besides this one. **1904** HARBORD & HALL *Metallurgy of Steel* xvi. 291 Such rolls cost from 50 to 100 per cent. more than those cast in sand, and known as '*grain rolls'. **1932** E. GREGORY *Metallurgy* i. 18 Small amounts of chromium also bring about considerable grain refinement, which is desirable in ordinary 'grain' rolls used for roughing purposes. **1834** W. YOUATT *Cattle* 436 The disease is recognised in town-dairies by the name of *grain-sick*; in some parts of the country it is termed *maw-bound*. **1848** *Rural Cycl.* II. 486 In mild cases of grainsick. **1858** SIMMONDS *Dict. Trade* s.v. *Grain-leather*, Goat, seal, and other skins, blacked on the *grain side for women's shoes, &c. **1884** WATT *Soap-making* 11 If the plastic soap be now removed and cooled while the solution is pressed out, it will have become so solid as scarcely to receive an impression from the finger. In this condition it is called *grain soap. **1756** P. BROWNE *Jamaica* 50 *Grain-stone*, the stones of this kind are easily known by their hardness and granulated appearance. **1780** EDMONDSON *Heraldry* II. Gloss., *Grain-tree..Three sprigs of this tree vert, fructed gu. is the crest of the Dyers' Company. **1848** *Rural Cycl.* II. 487 *Grain-weevil.* See *Calandra.* **1887** *Daily News* 27 Sept. 5/3 *Grain whisky, i.e. made of barley in the grain stage, and not of malt.

grain (greɪn), *sb.*[2] Forms: 4–5 greyn(e, 4–6 **grane**, 4–7 **grayn**(e, 6–7 **graine**, 7 **grein**, 7– **grain**. Also 9 (*pl.*, sense 5 b) **grainse**. [ad. ON. *grein* division, distinction, branch (Da. *green*, Sw. *gren* branch).]

†**1.** *pl.* The fork of the body, the lower limbs.

a **1300** *Cursor M.* 7449 O bodi gret, o granis lang. **1506** *Kal. Sheph.* 100 Libra [gouerneth] the nauyll, the graynes, the partyes vnder the haunches. **1612** DRAYTON *Poly-olb.* i. 12 Then Corin up doth take The Giant twixt the grayns.

2. A bough or branch. Also, the fork between two boughs. *Obs.* exc. *dial.*

1501 DOUGLAS *Pal. Hon.* I. 26 Not throw the soyl bot muskane treis sproutit..Moch, all waist, widderit, with granis moutit. **1513** —— *Æneis* IV. viii. 73 The souchand bir quhissillis amang the granis. **1597–8** BP. HALL *Sat., Defiance to Envie* 5 Ye prouder pines Whose swelling graines are [etc.]. **1633** —— *Hard Texts* 113 His head was caught fast within the graines of a spreading oke. **1652** GAULE *Magastrom.* 315 The Faulconer climing up to fetch down his Hawke, a grayne of a branch got hold of his neck, and there he hung. *a* **1700** *Ballad* in W. McDowall *Hist. Dumfries* v. (1873) 63 Five [men] he hang'd upon a grain. **1821** CLARE *Vill. Minstr.* I. 75 While, underneath their mingling grains, The river silver'd down the plains. **1863** ATKINSON *Danby, Grain*,..the branch of a tree.

fig. **1513** DOUGLAS *Æneis* x. Prol. 65 Thocht thir persons [of the Trinity] be seuerall in thre granis. **1596** DALRYMPLE tr. *Leslie's Hist. Scot.* II. 418 Afor he cuttit of had and snedit al the branches and graines of his superstitione.

3. †**a.** An arm (of the sea); a branch or 'fork' (of a stream). *Obs.* **b.** A valley branching out of another. *dial.* (Cf. HOPE *sb.*[2])

a. *a* **1400–50** *Alexander* 2451 A grayne of þe grete see þaim aboute glidis. **1533** BELLENDEN *Livy* (1822) v. 420 Divide it first with small granis and burnis.

b. 1542 *Newminster Cartul.* (Surtees) Introd. 18 Such as inhabyte in one of those hoopes, valyes, or graynes. **1813** HOGG *Queen's Wake* (1871) 56 Astonished mid his open grain [the hind] sees round him pour the sudden rain. **1897** MARY BRYCE *Mem. J. Veitch* II. 51 Resisting the appeal of 'grain' and 'hope' to sit in the narrow room.

†**4.** ? The blade of a weapon. *Obs.*

13.. *K. Alis.* 6537 Theo horn [of a rhinoceros] is scharp as a sweord, Bothe by the greyn and at ord. **13..** *Gaw. & Gr. Knt.* 211 A spetos sparþe..þe hede of an elnȝerde þe large lenkþe hade, þe grayn al of grene stele & of golde hewen, þe bit burnyst bryȝt.

5. One of the prongs of a fork. *Obs.* exc. *dial.*

1486 *Nottingham Rec.* III. 242 A hoke with iij. greynes to drawe vp stones out of the water. **1606** HOLLAND *Sueton.* 147 With three graines like an ele speare. **1641** HINDE *J. Bruen* xlvi. 147 The two greins of the pikell ran on both sides of his leg, and hurt him not. **1681** CHETHAM *Angler's Vade-m.* i. §3 (1689) 3 A Stick of Hasle, which hath two grains, or is forked. **1861** *Jrnl. R. Agric. Soc.* XXII. II. 305 A fork with three grains or prongs. **1864** ATKINSON *Stanton Grange* 220, I cut a stick wiv tweea grains. Two grains? What are they? What you quality wad call a fork.

Comb. **1674–91** RAY *S. & E.C. Words, Grain-staff*, a quarter-staff with a pair of short tines at the end, which they call *grains*.

b. Also **grane**. Freq. as *pl.* (commonly construed as *sing.*; formerly also spelt *grainse*): A fish-spear or harpoon with two or more 'grains' or prongs.

1815 M. G. LEWIS *Jrnl. W. Ind.* (1834) 43 The five-pronged *grainse*, which arms his hands, Your scales is doomed to gore. **1851** *Chambers' Papers for People* No. 52. 7 The sailmaker..personated Neptune..and..flourished a three-pronged grainse. **1865** WILCOCKS *Sea-Fisherman* 137 The instrument known as the grains consists of five harpoons in one..attached to a stiff light ashen staff with a ball of lead at the top. **1882** *Worcester Exhib. Catal.* iii. 55 Harpoons and shifting grains for whale fishing. **1883** *Fisheries Exhib. Catal.* 195 Eel spears, porpoise and dolphin grains. **1899** F. T. BULLEN *Idylls of Sea* xvii. 136 A few good lines and hooks, and a set of granes. **1951** R. CAMPBELL *Light on Dark Horse* xx. 285, I went on fishing, with my spare grane (fish-spear).

grain (greɪn), *v.*[1] Also 4, 6 **greine**, **greyne**, 6 **graine**, **grayne**. [f. GRAIN *sb.*[1]]

1. *intr.* To produce grain; to yield fruit. Of corn: To form its grains.

1390 GOWER *Conf.* II. 155 The lond began to greine, Which whilom hadde be bareine. **1598** FLORIO, *Ingranellare*, to growe to cornes or little graines, to graine. **1604** E. G[RIMSTONE] *D'Acosta's Hist. Indies* VII. ix. 519 Much Mays (which is their corne) already grained, and in the eare. **1924** *Glasgow Herald* 12 Nov. 16 Arable ground would grain even faster than it does if the dole-fed masses of the great cities, such as Buenos Aires and Sydney, were to be induced to lend a hand at the plough.

fig. **1390** GOWER *Conf.* II. 389 It floureth but it shall not greine Unto the fruit of rightwisnesse.

†**b.** *passive.* To spring (from a seed). *Obs.*

1387–8 T. USK *Test. Love* II. iii. 124 Al mortal folk of one sede arn greyned.

2. a. *trans.* To cause (sea-water) to deposit grains (of salt). **b.** To form (sugar, tin, etc.) into grains. **c.** *intr.* for *refl.* Of salt, syrup, etc.: To form into grains.

1706 *Phil. Trans.* XXV. 2265 The Sea-Water being in hot Countries grained in Pans called Salt-Marshes. **1748** *Ibid.* XLV. 363 To make the Salt grain better, or more quickly form into Chrystals. **1791** *Ann. Reg.* 94 The sugar of this tree was capable of being grained. **1791** HAMILTON *Berthollet's Dyeing* I. III. i. I. 236 The tin should be grained by melting it, and pouring it into agitated water. **1865** *Trans. Ill. Agric. Soc.* V. 566 The yield of stalk was enormous but the sirup made from it was quite dark, and refused to grain. **1893** R. WELLS *Toffy & Sweets* 7 When lump or crystallised sugars are boiled to the heat..of 250 degrees, the sugar is liable to grain, and to turn out a solid mass on the slab. **1906** *Daily Chron.* 31 Oct. 8/5 When the syrup has boiled for fifteen minutes add the chestnuts and stir the mixture until it 'grains' and turns white.

3. *Brewing. trans.* To free from grain; separate the grain from.

1882 [see GRAINING *vbl. sb.*[1]].

4. To dye in grain (see GRAIN *sb.*[1] 10 c).

1530 PALSGR. 574/1 A man may grayne a clothe what colour so ever it be dyed in. **1538** ELYOT *Dict.*, *Coccum*, grayne wherwith cloth and silke is grayned. **1862** O'NEILL *Dict. Calico Printing & Dyeing* s.v. *Kermes*, Colours dyed with them [Kermes] were said to be *grained*, or *engrained*.

fig. **1682** SIR T. BROWNE *Chr. Mor.* 9 Persons lightly dipt, not grain'd in generous honesty, are but pale in goodness, and faint hued in integrity. **1897** *Sunday Sch. World* June 199/1 These vices were not merely grained into the life of the common people.

5. To give a granular surface to. (Cf. GRAIN *sb.*[1] 12, and GRAINER[1] 3.)

1888 *Daily News* 1 June 6/5 For drawing in what is termed the chalk manner the stone is first 'grained' by being rubbed against a similar stone, with a little fine white sand between the two. **1891** [see GRAINER[1] 3].

6. *Leather-dressing.* **a.** To remove the hair from (skins). **b.** To soften or raise the grain of (leather, etc.). (Cf. GRAIN *sb.*[1] 13.)

1530 PALSGR. 574/1, I grayne ledder, I make it by tannyng crafte to have a grayne, *je besanne.* **1841** CATLIN *N. Amer. Ind.* (1844) II. xlii. 64 The women are drying meat, and 'graining' buffalo robes. **1849** RUXTON *Life Far West* 15 Than whom no more..expert trapper ever..grained a beaver-skin. **1896** *Daily News* 6 Nov. 2/3 A Leather Finisher graining and setting a skin.

7. To paint in imitation of the 'grain' of valuable woods or of marble. Also *absol.*

1798 [see GRAINED *ppl. a.*[1]]. **1827** WHITTOCK *Paint. & Glaz. Guide* ii. 25 Spread the megilp over one panel at a time, and grain that completely before proceeding to another. **1876** T. HARDY *Ethelberta* (1890) 100, I can..grain in every kind of wood. **1877** *Paperhanger, Painter, Grainer*, etc. 112 Care should be taken in graining maple, not to put too much colour on.

8. *trans.* To feed with grain. *U.S.*

1852 H. MELVILLE *Pierre* 40 No one grained his steeds, but himself. **1874** *Rep. Vermont Board Agric.* II. 406 Older sheep should be grained the first of the season, after which they may do without till the first of March. **1949** *Sat. Even. Post* 9 Apr. 132/4 We throwed our drive into a pole-fence pasture, grained Blaze and Blackie's *grullo*, then went up to the main house.

grain, *v.*[2] [f. GRAIN *sb.*[2]] †**1.** *refl.* To branch; to divide. *Obs. rare.*

1664 POWER *Exp. Philos.* I. 56 The hairs do grain and fork themselves (when grown too long).

2. *trans.* To spear (fish) with a grains.

1892 STEVENSON & OSBOURNE *Wrecker* xii. 196 Something struck me right through the forearm and stuck there. I put my other hand up, and, by George, it was the grain; the beasts had speared me like a porpoise. 'Cap'n!' I cried... 'They've grained me.'

grain, variant of GRANE *v. dial.*, to throttle.

grainage (ˈgreɪnɪdʒ). [f. GRAIN *sb.*[1] + -AGE.]

†**1.** Crop of grain. *Obs.*[−1]

1610 W. FOLKINGHAM *Art of Survey* I. x. 26 We could plausibly approoue the light and easie Tillage and rich Graynage, by Winterton in Norfolke.

2. *Farriery.* Mangy tumors which sometimes form on the legs of horses.

1847 in CRAIG.

grainage, mod. spelling of GRANAGE *Hist.*

grainary, obs. form of GRANARY.

graine (greɪn). Also **grain**. [Fr.] The eggs (†or an egg) of the silkworm; cf. SEED *sb.* 6 a.
1835 URE *Philos. Manuf.* II. vi. 230 The eggs or grains of the silk-worm are covered with a liquid, which glues them to the piece of cloth or paper on which the female is made to lay them. **1887** *Encycl. Brit.* XXII. 58/2 The eggs of the silkworm, called *graine*, are hatched out by artificial heat. *Ibid.* 59/2 The sources of healthy graine became fewer and fewer. **1887** *Colonial & Indian Exhib., Rep. Col. Sect.* 337. **1930** R. CUTHILL tr. *Schober's Silk & Silk Industry* i. 14 Silkworm eggs (graine) are bluish violet granules. *Ibid.* 31 Persia itself does not produce good graine. **1941** C. J. HUBER in *Matthews' Textile Fibers* (ed. 5) xvii. 680 The production of industrial eggs by cocoon raisers consisted of..43 per cent grain method where the eggs are distributed in 10-, 20-, and 30-grain unit receptacles.

grained (greɪnd), *ppl. a.*[1] [f. GRAIN *v.*[1] + -ED[1].] In senses of the vb.
1. Dyed in grain.
c **1400** *Beryn* 3065 Beryn & these romeyns were com in good array as myȝt be made of woll & of colour greynyd. **1455** *Sc. Acts Jas. II* (1814) II. 43/2 All Erlis sall vse mantilles of brown granyt opyn befor. **1488–9** *Act 4 Hen. VII*, c. 8 Wollen Cloth of the fynest making scarlet grayned. **1534** in Weaver *Wells Wills* (1890) 203 To my brother Wm. Trotte my grayned gowne. **1577–87** HOLINSHED *Scot. Chron.* (1806) I. 2 The most costlie skarlets, pliant gloves and manie other grained and delicate clothes.
fig. **1602** SHAKS. *Ham.* III. iv. 90 Thou turn'st mine eyes into my very soule, And there I see such blacke and grained spots, As will not leaue their Tinct.
2. Formed into grains.
1800 tr. *Lagrange's Chem.* II. 43 For this purpose, put grained zinc into a matrass. **1856** OLMSTED *Slave States* 673 Sugar in a pure crystallized or grained state. **1867** SMYTH *Sailor's Word-bk.*, *Grained-powder*, that corned or reduced into grains from the cakes, and distinguished from mealed powder, as employed in certain preparations.
3. Of leather (see GRAIN *v.*[1] 6).
1714 *Fr. Bk. of Rates* 81 Skins..Grain'd per Piece 00 08. **1807** P. GASS *Jrnl.* 32 Captain Lewis gave them a grained deer skin to stretch over a half keg for a drum. **1880** *Print. Trades Jrnl.* XXXI. 11 Imitation Russia grained leather.
4. Painted to imitate the 'grain' of wood or the markings of marble.
1798 TAYLOR *Builder's Price Bk.* in *Archit. Publ. Soc. Dict.*, Mahogany grained. **1871** *Amer. Encycl. Printing* (ed. Ringwalt), *Grained*, colored in imitation of the grain of woods, marbles, etc., as in the ornamentation of marbled papers.

grained (greɪnd), *ppl. a.*[2] [f. GRAIN *sb.*[1] + ED[2].] Having a grain or grains.
1. Having grains, seeds, or particles. *Obs.* exc. in parasynthetic derivatives, as ***large-, small-grained***.
1611 COTGR., *Grenu*, grained, full of graine, of seed, of graines. **1721–1800** in BAILEY. **1733** J. TULL *Horse-hoing Husbandry* 164 Small-grain'd Wheat.
2. Of wood, stone, leather, flesh, etc.: Having a grain, or granular structure or surface (see GRAIN *sb.*[1], senses 12–15). Often in parasynthetic derivatives, as ***coarse-, smooth-grained***. (Cf. also CROSS-GRAINED, FINE-GRAINED.)
a **1529** SKELTON *E. Rummyng* 32 Her skynne lose and slacke, Grained [*v.r.* Greuyned] lyke a sacke. **1597** A. M. *Guillemeau's Fr. Chirurg.* 54/1 The fleshe verye rubicund and grayned as we woulde desire. **1632** SHERWOOD, Grained wood, *madre, madriér*. **1822–34** *Good's Study Med.* (ed. 4) IV. 464 The corium..presented the same grained appearance that is observable in a section of the hides of the larger quadrupeds. **1847** SMEATON *Builder's Man.* 137 Passages are usually painted, if some handsome grained wood be not introduced. **1885** W. L. CARPENTER *Soap & Candles* vi. 161 To produce a grained soft-soap..it is essential to use pure potash lye. **1890** W. J. GORDON *Foundry* xi. 216 There is one [grain process] in which a grained glass is used.
3. *Bot.* Having tubercles, as the segments of the flowers of the *Rumex*.
1818 WITHERING *Brit. Plants* (ed. 6) IV. 7 *Lichen graniformis.* Tubercles black..granulated..Grained Lichen. **1829** LOUDON *Encycl. Plants* 293 *Rumex Patientia*.. Valves cordate entire: one grained.

grained (greɪnd), *ppl. a.*[3] Now *dial.* [f. GRAIN *sb.*[2] + ED[2].] Having tines or prongs; forked. Also ***two-, three-grained***.
1513 DOUGLAS *Æneis* III. iv. 42 With treis clois bilappit round about, And thik harsk granit pikis standand out. **1523** FITZHERB. *Husb.* §41 An hole bored in the borde with an augur, and therin a grayned staffe of two fote longe. **1597** SHAKS. *Lover's Compl.* x, So slides he downe vppon his greyned bat. **1613–14** *N. Riding Rec.* II. 37 A man presented for an assault with a two graned staff. **1844** J. TOMLIN *Mission, Jrnls.* 240 A hoe, a three grained fork intended as a sort of hand harrow. **1878** *Cumbld. Gloss.*, *Grain't*, forked; divided.

†**grainel**. *Sc. Obs. rare*$^{-1}$. [variant of GARNEL, GIRNEL.] A granary.
1584 HUDSON *Du Bartas' Judith* I. (1611) 13 Their sick and old at home do keep the skore And ouer grainels great they take the charge.

grainer[1] ('greɪnə(r)). [f. GRAIN *v.*[1] + -ER[1].] One who or that which grains.
1. *Leather-dressing.* **a.** (See quots. and cf. BATE *sb.*[3]). **b.** A tool either for taking off the hair of skins, or for producing the appearance of 'grain'.
a. 1813 SIR H. DAVY *Agric. Chem.* (1844) 237 The contents of the grainer, as the pit is called in which soft skins are prepared by dung, must form a very useful manure. **1852** MORFIT *Tanning & Currying* 350 This alkaline lye consists of water impregnated with pigeon's or hen's dung, and is technically termed a grainer, or bate. **1895** *E. Anglian Gloss.*, *Grainer*, a vat used in tanning—in the second operation.
b. 1839 [see GRAIN *sb.*[1] 13 c]. **1852** MORFIT *Tanning & Currying* 384 When nearly dry, the lustre is given with a finely grooved pummel, or grainer, passed over in both directions.
2. *Salt-making.* (See quot.; cf. GRAIN *v.*[1] 2 c.)
1880 *Libr. Univ. Knowl.* XIII. 77 The liquid is drawn into other vats called 'grainers'..[in which] the salt forms very rapidly. **1884** KNIGHT *Dict. Mech.* Suppl. 778/2.
3. (See quot. and cf. GRAIN *v.*[1] 5.)
1891 *Labour Commission* Gloss., *Grainers*, men in the printing industry who grain stone with sand for artists doing what is called 'chalk work'.
4. A house-painter's graining-tool.
1858 in SIMMONDS *Dict. Trade*; and in later Dicts.
5. One who paints in imitation of the grain of wood or the markings of marble.
1837 WHITTOCK *Bk. Trades* (1842) 356 The Grainer, who admirably imitates the grains of woods, marbles, etc. **1887** *Paperhanger, Painter, Grainer*, etc. 105 Graining is the imitation, strictly speaking, of woods, although the term 'grainer' is often used..to signify a painter of marbles as well as of woods. **1891** *Daily News* 21 Jan. 3/8 A sign writer and grainer.

grainer[2] ('greɪnə(r)). [f. GRAIN *v.*[2] + -ER[1].] One who uses a pronged fish-spear.
1894 *Outing* (U.S.) XXIV. 56/1 Many grainers wore long rubber waders.

grainer, variant of GRANER *Obs.*

grainering ('greɪnərɪŋ), *vbl. sb.* [f. GRAINER[1] + -ING[1].] The preparation of hides with a grainer or bate.
1857 *Encycl. Brit.* XIII. 307/1 Tanning is preceded by what is called *abating* or *grainering*. **1882** *Ibid.* XIV. 386/1 The skins are washed in the dash wheel, and under-go a process of *bating* or *grainering*. **1897** C. T. DAVIS *Manuf. Leather* (ed. 2) 153 The operation of immersing hides and skins intended for the manufacture of pliable leathers, in an alkaline solution consisting of the dung of chickens, pigeons, dogs, or in bran water..is termed either 'bating', 'abating', 'grainering', 'reducing', 'drenching', or 'puring'.

grainery, variant of GRANARY.

‖**graineur** (grɛnœr). [F. *graineur*, also *greneur*. Cf. GRAINE.] A producer of silkworm eggs.
1913 J. H. LONGFORD *Evol. New Japan* vii. 87 French and Italian graineurs, while eager to buy her raw silk, were still more eager to buy the eggs of her healthy silk-worms in order to replenish their own exhausted stock. **1919** R. C. RAWLLEY *Econ. Silk Ind.* v. 80 In the province of Var there are 'graineurs' or seed-producers.

grainger, obs. form of GRANGER.

graininess ('greɪnɪnɪs). [f. GRAINY *a.* + -NESS.] The quality of being grainy or granular; granularity. Also *fig.*
1921 *Chem. Abstr.* XV. 476 Graininess in photographic deposits. *Ibid.*, The word 'graininess' is used to denote the inhomogeneity of the deposit due to aggregations of particles. **1923** A. E. CONRADY et al. *Photogr. as a Sci. Implement* iv. 199 *Graininess or granulation.* The 'grain' of the developed image so far considered is the size of the silver particle. *Ibid.*, Corresponding to every stage of magnification..a certain degree of granulation or 'graininess' will exist. **1956** E. M. HUTTEN *Lang. Mod. Physics* iii. 96 The concept of probability, and statistics, is used to 'smooth out' the graininess in the particle picture. **1966** *New Statesman* 25 Feb. 269/1 Like so many television originals, his play's a Victorian genre-painting disguised under contemporary black-and-white graininess.

graining ('greɪnɪŋ), *vbl. sb.*[1] [f. GRAIN *v.*[1] + -ING[1].]
1. a. The action of GRAIN *v.*[1] in various senses.
1823 P. NICHOLSON *Pract. Builder* 417 Graining is the imitating, by means of painting, various kinds of rare woods ..and likewise various species of marble. **1837** WHITTOCK *Bk. Trades* (1842) 409 [Soap-boiling] This agitation indeed, is found so mainly conducive to the required *graining*, as the workmen call the required coagulation. **1882** tr. *Thausing's Beer* iv. 198 The graining of wort from wheat is difficult on account of the tenacious layer of grains. **1894** HARRIS *Techn. Fire Insur. Comm.*, *Graining*, a tanning process, in which the skins are placed in an alkaline solution. **1951** R. MAYER *Artist's Hand-bk.* xii. 379 *Graining.* The grain is imparted to the stone by grinding its surface with flint, sand, or other abrasive. **1961** T. LANDAU *Encycl. Librarianship* (ed. 2) 154/1 *Graining*, preparation of the surface of metal lithographic plates by grinding them with a muller and sand or mechanically, by pebbles and abrasive.
b. quasi-*concr.* The result of this action, *esp.* in house-painting. In quot. 1856 = GRAIN *sb.*[1] 14 b.
1834 *West Ind. Sk. Bk.* II. 3 No graining, and painting, and lettering, to engage the attention of the passer by. **1856** R. A. VAUGHAN *Mystics* (1860) I. VI. viii. 269, I remember the very graining of the wood of his lance. **1892** *Pall Mall G.* 5 Oct. 2/2 To whom the lie of the strata in a quarry-cliff says no more than the combed graining on a deal door. **1896** R. KIPLING *Seven Seas* 73 Bone-bleached my decks, wind-scoured to the graining.
2. *Coinage.* †**a.** A ring of grain-like protuberances on the face of a coin close to its edge (= F. *grènetis*). *Obs.* **b.** A ring of fine concave grooves round the edge of a coin; = MILLING.
1664 EVELYN tr. *Freart's Archit.* Ep. Ded. 15 Its just and equal roundness, the Grenetis or graining which is about it [etc.]. **1691** LOCKE *Money* Wks. 1727 II. 96 The Engines which..mark the Edges..with a Graining, are wrought secretly. **1726** LEAKE *Hist. Acc. Eng. Money* 109 Those [coins] with the Graining or Letters upon the Edge. **1752** LOUTHIAN *Form of Process* (ed. 2) 171 Marking of Money round the Edges, with Letters or Grainings. **1887** *Roy. Proclam.* in *Standard* 18 May 3/2 Every Sixpence should have the same..impression..with a graining upon the edge.
3. *Comb.*, as ***graining block, board, gouge, machine, roller, tool***; **graining comb**, a tool resembling a comb, used by house-painters for graining.
1688 R. HOLME *Armoury* III. 352/1 A Graining Board..is a Board with Nicks in after the manner of a Saw, if you look sideways at it, but turn it up and you will perceive the Nicks, Teeth or Riggets (call them which you will) run quite a-thwart the Board. **1706** PHILLIPS (ed. Kersey), *Graining-board*, a Board made with Nicks, or Teeth like a Saw, and us'd by Curriers in graining their Leather. **1846** R. B. SAGE *Scenes Rocky Mts.* xxxiii. 288 Near this is his 'graining block', planted aslope, for the ease of his operative in preparing his skins for the finishing process in the art of dressing. **1875** KNIGHT *Dict. Mech.*, *Graining machine* (Leather manufacture), a machine having rollers with raised, parallel, straight, or diagonal threads, which indent the goat or sheep skins and confer the wrinkled appearance to morocco leather. *Ibid.*, *Graining-tool* [= graining comb]. **1875** T. SEATON *Fret Cutting* 141 The details of the hair and curls must now be worked out with fine hollow gouges and graining gouges. **1881** YOUNG *Every Man his own Mechanic* §1603 The leather and metal graining combs with which graining in imitation of any kind of wood is done. Graining rollers are made for imitating various kinds of wood. **1959** R. HOSTETTLER et al. *Techn. Terms Printing Industry* (ed. 3) 114/1 Graining machine for offset plates. **1960** G. A. GLAISTER *Gloss. Bk.* 158/2 *Graining boards*, boards or metal plates used by the binder to produce a diced effect on covers. The boards have a pattern in relief of parallel lines running diagonally.

graining ('greɪnɪŋ), *vbl. sb.*[2] [f. GRAIN *v.*[2] or *sb.*[2] + -ING[1].]
1. a. The point of forking or bifurcation. **b.** One of the prongs or tines of a fork.
1641 BEST *Farm. Bks.* (Surtees) 51 Betwixt the two grainings of the rake shafte they tye a stringe. **1877** *N. W. Linc. Gloss.* s.v., If you cut the cherry-tree top off above the grainings, it will be sure to grow. **1886** *S.W. Linc. Gloss.*, *Grainings*, the forks, or joinings of the large boughs of a tree.
2. The method or practice of taking fish with a pronged spear (see GRAIN *sb.*[2] 5 b).
1889 in *Century Dict.*

graining ('greɪnɪŋ), *sb.* [Of unknown origin.] A small fresh-water fish, *Leuciscus Lancastrensis*.
1772 PENNANT *Tour Scotl.* (1774) 11 In this river [Mersey] ..is found a fish called the Graining..in some respects resembling the dace, yet is a distinct and perhaps new species. **1863** H. C. PENNELL *Angler Nat.* 158 The Graining is a very rare and local fish, in habits and food some-what resembling the trout. **1875** 'STONEHENGE' *Brit. Sports* I. v. i. 306 The Graining is scarcely found anywhere but in the Mersey and its tributaries.

†**grainish**, *a. Obs.* [f. GRAIN *sb.*[1] + -ISH.] Having somewhat of a grain. (See GRAIN *sb.*[1] 13.)
1653 R. SANDERS *Physiogn.* 183 The skin grainish, like an Ox or Goat.

grainless ('greɪnlɪs), *a.* [f. GRAIN *sb.*[1] + -LESS.] Devoid of grain or grains, in the various senses of the sb.
1882 *Cornhill Mag.* Feb. 204 The barley had to be cut down green and grainless. **1890** ABNEY *Treat. Photogr.* (ed. 6) 138 The paper employed should be as tough and grainless as possible. **1894** *Outing* XXIV. 124/2 We could hear them [mice] working to and fro through the grainless fodder.

grainy ('greɪnɪ), *a.* [f. GRAIN *sb.*[1] + -Y[1].]
1. a. Consisting of grain-like particles; granular. Also of a particle: Grain-like.
1611 COTGR., *Granuleux*, Grainie, seedie. **1709** *Phil. Trans.* XXVI. 497 You will always be able to discover the grainy Particles thereof. **1780** J. T. DILLON *Trav. Spain* (1781) 218 Soft grainy pyrites. **1891** *Times* 17 Oct. 4/5, 750 bags grainy Peruvian at 15*s.* 6*d.* **1940** A. L. M. SOWERBY *Wall's Dict. Photogr.* (ed. 15) 350 A negative is said to be 'grainy' when an enlargement from it shows the structure of the image. **1947** J. STEINBECK *Wayward Bus* 33 He was tired and his skin felt grainy. **1961** G. MILLERSON *Technique Telev. Production* iii. 42 Pictures will be indistinct, smeary, lifeless, and scintillating with the grainy effect of picture-noise. **1967** *Times* 27 Dec. 11/1 The coarsely grainy photography which not very long ago was a sign of spontaneity and originality. **1970** *Nature* 5 Sept. 1064/1 The very dark and grainy appearance of many of the photographs.
b. Of a voice or sound: rough, gritty.
1963 W. K. ROSE in *Lett. Wyndham Lewis* p. xxi, The everyday tone of Lewis's voice—grainy, insistent. **1969** *Listener* 20 Mar. 398/2 Jack Bruce's bass-guitar work..on the live tracks has a wonderfully grainy, growling sound.
2. Full of grain or corn.
1755 in JOHNSON. **1792** ROGERS *Pleasures Mem.* I. (1810) 12 We watched the emmet to her grainy nest. **1819** WIFFEN *Aonian Hours* (1820) 47 They [the ants] throne prosperity in grainy hives.

3. Resembling the surface grain of wood.
1858 *Edin. Rev.* July 9 It presented on its surface the grainy ripple of primeval seas.

graip (ˈgreːp). *Sc.* and *north. dial.* Also 4–9 grape, 6 graype. [a. ON. *greip* fem. (recorded only in the sense 'space between thumb and fingers, grip, grasp'; but cf. OSw. *greep*, mod.Sw. *grep*, Da. *greb* fork) corresponding to OE. *grāp* fem., grasp, f. OTeut. root **grīp*: see GRIP, GROPE.]

1. A three- or four-pronged fork used as a dung-fork or for digging.
1459 *Durham Acct. Rolls* (Surtees) 89, j scala, j Grape, j Shepecroke. **1483** *Cath. Angl.* 163/1 A Grape; *vbi* forke, *tridens* (A.). **1559** *Wills & Inv. N. C.* (Surtees 1853) 171 A kowter, a soke, a muk fowe, a graype, 2 yerne forks, [etc.]. **1785** BURNS *Halloween* xviii, The graip he for a harrow taks. **1799** ROBERTSON *Agric. Perth* 176 Potatoes..are raised in October..with the three pronged forks used for dung (provincially grapes). **1817** *Blackw. Mag.* I. 161/1 A graip, a sort of large three-pronged fork used about farm offices. **1822** SCOTT *Pirate* xvii, He shook his graip aloft. **1894** *Superfluous Woman* (ed. 4) I. 74, I must just give her the graip..and bid her lift a potato.

†**2.** ? A handful, piece. *Obs.*[−1]
c **1475** *Rauf Coilȝear* 471 Greit Graipis of Gold his Greis [*i.e.* greaves]..And his Cussanis cumlie schynand.

graip, variant of GRAPE *sb.*[3]

graip, Sc. and north. dial. variant of GROPE *v.*

graise, obs. form of GRAZE *v.*[2]

graisle, variant of GRASSIL *v. Sc. Obs.*

grait, obs. form of GRAITH *v.*, GREAT *a.*

graith (greɪθ), *sb.* In later use only *Sc.* Forms: 4 graiþ, 4–6 grayth(e, 5 greiþe, -yþe, 5–6 grath, (7 greath), 4– graith. [a. ON. *greiðe* wk. masc.:—OTeut. type **garaiðon-* or **garaiðjon-*, cognate with OE. *ȝerǽde* str. neut., trappings, equipage:—OTeut. type **garaiðjo*[m], f. OTeut. **ga-* prefix (see Y-) + **raið* -: see READY *a.* For the development of sense cf. GEAR.]

†**1.** A state of preparation; readiness; good order. ***to do in graith***: to put in readiness. ***in graith***: in proper order; also, without delay. ***out of graith***: out of order. *Obs.*
c **1330** R. BRUNNE *Chron.* (1810) 193 Þei stand alle to gode graith, whan þou ert þam among. *Ibid.* 307 Whan it were don in grayth þe weddyng of Margarete. *a* **1375** *Joseph Arim.* 66 In gret Anguisse ȝe ben þat nis not God greiþe. ? **14..** *Mandeville & the Souden* 63 in Hazlitt *E.P.P.* I. 157 Now.. lowsit is Sathanesse, That sett this ward thus owt of graythe. *c* **1450** MYRC 587 Lete name hyt [a child] þare, ȝef hyt schule in greyþe fare. **1460** *Towneley Myst.* iii. 482 He may happyn to day come agane or none With grath.

2. Equipment in general; apparel, attire, dress, articles of dress.
a **1300** *Cursor M.* 4796 Giue me mi graith and lat me ga. **15..** *Chalmerlan Ayr* c. 22 (in *Sc. Acts* I.), þai [sowtaris] mak schone butis and vther graitht of the lethir or jt be barkit. **1637–50** J. ROW *Hist. Kirk* (Wodrow Soc.) 462 What meanes..this short skarlet cloake, and all this gay graith of yours? *a* **1774** FERGUSSON *Braid Claith* Poems (1845) 9 He..Bids bauld to bear the gree awa With a' this graith. **1785** BURNS *Holy Fair* vii, Here, farmers gash, in ridin graith Gaed hoddin by their cotters.

b. Armour.
c **1420** *Anturs of Arth.* 436 We arene one owre gamene, we ne hafe no gude graythe. **1550** LYNDESAY *Sq. Meldrum* 414 Go dres yow in your graith. **1828** SCOTT *F.M. Perth* v, I will sleep like a sentinel, with my graith about me. *a* **1851** MOIR *Ruins Seton Chapel* iii. Poet. Wks. 1852 I. 189 Clad in their robes of state or graith of war.

c. Harness.
1663 SPALDING *Troub. Chas. I* (Bannatyne Club) I. 12 The earle..directed..his led horse with his graith to the Bog. **1799** J. ROBERTSON *Agric. Perth* 96 The driver..can.. save the harness (graith) better than in any other position. **1850** W. INNES in Hamilton *Chr. Sabbath* (1852) 225 *note*, Removing the harness from off one of his team, or as a Scotchman would say, taking off the graith.

3. Apparatus, implements, gear, tackle; a structure, contrivance. See also *plough-graith*, *spinning-graith*. (Cf. GEAR *sb.* 5.) *Obs.* exc. *dial.*
c **1375** *Sc. Troy-bk.* II. 2360 Bot now we dress our graith þarfore. *a* **1400–50** *Alexander* 5518 Foure Griffons full grym, he in þat graythe festes. **1497** in *Ld. Treas. Acc. Scotl.* (1877) I. 349 Item, giffin for xiij stane of irne to mak grath to Mons new cradill. **1513** DOUGLAS *Æneis* VI. v. 120 For myself tuik I nane sa gret feir, As of thi schip..Spulȝeit of hir graith. **1786** BURNS *Scotch Drink* x, When Vulcan gies his bellows breath, An' ploughmen gather wi' their graith. **1792** A. WILSON *2 Men sawing Timber*, Ye're tempin Providence, I swear, To raise your graith sae madly here. *a* **1810** TANNAHILL *Poems* (1846) 53 Wha may cast by their brewin graith Baith pat and pail.

†**4.** Possessions in general; wealth, money. *Obs.*
1500–20 DUNBAR *Poems* lxvi. 85 Greit abbais grayth I nill to gather. **1552** LYNDESAY *Monarche* 4753 Thay haif spred thare Net..on gold, and vther graith. **1603** *Philotus* xiv, Tak another be the neck, Quhen ȝe the graith haue gottin. **1786** BURNS *Inventory* 3, I send you here a faithfu' list O' gudes and gear, and a' my graith.

5. Material, stuff (for a particular purpose); now *esp.* in *Sc.* soapy water, soap-suds. (Cf. GEAR *sb.* 10.)
1513 DOUGLAS *Æneis* IV. xi. 105 Bid hir..the bestis, and the blude, And clengeing graith, scho knawis, with hir bring. **15..** *Chalmerlan Ayr* c. 24 (in *Sc. Acts* I), þai [tailȝeouris] sow with fals graith. **1572** *Sc. Acts Jas. VI* (1814) III. 77/1 Certane particular persounis hes applyit the stanes, tymber and uther graith pertening thairto, to thair awin particular use. **1583** *Satir. Poems Reform.* xlv. 339 Suppoise the devill maid that graith, The seiknes sua ouersett my fayth, At that tyme, to asswage my sair, I wald have tane it. **1725** RAMSAY *Gentle Sheph.* I. ii, We're not yet begun To freath the graith.

b. 'Things'. (Cf. GEAR *sb.* 9 c.) *Obs.*
1790 A. WILSON *Poems* 209 Tho' Beagles Hornings an' sic graith Glowre roun' they ne'er sal dread me.

†**graith**, *a.* and *adv. Obs.* Forms: 3 greið, 4 grath(e, grayþ, 4–5 graiþ, graith(e, grayth(e, (4 greythe, 5 greithe, grayd). [a. ON. *greið-r* = OE. *ȝerǽde* ready:—OTeut. **garaiðjo-*, f. **ga-* prefix (see Y-) + *raið-*: see READY. Cf. G. *bereit*.]

A. *adj.*

1. Of persons: Prepared, ready. Of things: Ready, prompt, handy.
a **1225** *Ancr. R.* 16 Þis word siggeð euer vort ȝe beon al greiðe. *a* **1300** *Cursor M.* 5105 (Gött.) Als suith as we mai be graith, we sal do as ȝe haue said. **13..** *Gaw. & Gr. Knt.* 597 Bi þat watz Gryngolet grayth, & gurde with a sadel. **1375** BARBOUR *Bruce* IV. 759 The euill spirit, That gaf rycht graith ansueir hir to. *c* **1400** *Cato's Morals* 191 in *Cursor M.* App. iv. 1671 Wiþ lernyng & teyching growes graiþ kunnyng. *c* **1400** *Destr. Troy* 5719 The secund sort [of ships]..Were graither of gouernaunce. *c* **1420** *Anturs of Arth.* vi, Syr Gauan, graythest of alle Was laft with Dame Gaynour. *c* **1460** J. RUSSELL *Bk. Nurture* 880 Agayne he riseth vp, make redy youre fote shete in þis maner made greithe. *c* **1475** *Rauf Coilȝear* 389 Graith thocht of the grant had the gude King.

b. With *of*: Furnished or provided with; possessed of, acquainted with.
c **1400** *Destr. Troy* 2536 Þat any gome shuld be graithe of our goddes wille. *a* **1400–50** *Alexander* 1865 And he þat graithist is of gudis gird all to poudire. *c* **1450** *St. Cuthbert* (Surtees) 6660 And of cristes leuing make þaim graythe.

2. Of a road: Direct. Of a measure: Exact.
c **1340** *Cursor M.* 24143 (Fairf.) Na graiþer gate of gammen is here. **1352** MINOT *Poems* vi. 28 The bare rade, withouten rese, Unto Cane the graythest gate. **1377** LANGL. *P. Pl.* B. I. 203 Loue is..the graith gate that goth into heuene. **1393** *Ibid.* C. VII. 230 A galon for a grote and ȝut no grayþ mesure.

b. Of a sign, truth, etc.: Clear, plain. Also *absol.* as sb., ***the graith***, the truth.
c **1325** *Metr. Hom.* 99 The erthe bar als ful graith witnes Igain the Jowes wrangwisnes, For it schewed with graithe takening, That Crist was Godd of all thing. *c* **1375** *Sc. Leg. Saints, Placidas* 891 He..be þar taknis grath wit had þat þai war his twa sonnis dere. **1393** LANGL. *P. Pl.* C. XI. 242 Ac þe godspel ys a glose þere hudynge þe greythe treuthe. *c* **1394** *P. Pl. Crede* 34 Sire..þe graiþ þou me telle.

c. Of a stroke: Clean, unimpeded.
c **1470** HENRY *Wallace* V. 76 Wallace mycht nocht a graith straik on him gett.

B. *adv.* Readily; clearly, plainly.
c **1340** *Cursor M.* 26592 (Fairf.) þe quilk graiþ þe salle be kende & þou wille here þis boke til ende. *c* **1394** *P. Pl. Crede* 232 Canstou me graiþ tellen To any worþely wiȝt þat wissen me couþe Whou y schulde conne my Crede? *c* **1450** MYRC 346 Teche hem also welle and greythe.

graith (greɪθ), *v. Obs.* exc. *dial.* Forms: 3 *Orm.* greȝȝþen, 3–4 greiþ, greyþ(e, (3 græiðen, greiþi), 3–6 greith(e, 4 graiþ(e, grayþ, 4–5 graithe, graþ, greyth(e, 4–6 grayth(e, 4–7 grath, (4 grait, greþ, greiȝ, 5 greth, 6 greath, 9 grathe), 4– graith; also 4–5 *pa. pple.* 4 greyt, graid. [a. ON. *greiða*, f. *greið-r* ready: see GRAITH *a.*]

1. *trans.* To make ready, prepare, put in order, repair; also, to procure.
c **1200** ORMIN 11087 He wollde shæwenn Whatt gate he wollde greȝȝþenn uss To winnenn eche blisse. *c* **1205** LAY. 8058 þe king lette..græiðen heore iweden. **1297** R. GLOUC. (Rolls) 4920 + 75 (Harl. MS.) Þus wax stryf bytuene hem, hii greyþed her host vaste. *a* **1300** *Cursor M.* 3532 His broþer he faand gueand his tent To grayth a riche pulment. **13..** *E.E. Allit. P.* C. 53 What grayþed me þe grychchyng bot grame more seche? **13..** *Guy Warw.* (A.) 2501 Þi palays þou schalt grayþi. *c* **1374** CHAUCER *Boeth.* I. pr. IV. 19 Þat .I. had[de] grayþed deep to alle goode men. *c* **1400** *Prymer* in Maskell *Mon. Rit.* II. 62 Greithe a sikir weie: so that we seynge god be glad euermore. *c* **1460** *Towneley Myst.* xxvii. 286 Lo, here a borde and clothe laide, And breed theron, all redy graide. *c* **1475** *Rauf Coilȝear* 143 Of sic taillis they began, Quhill the supper was graid. **1513** DOUGLAS *Æneis* IV. v. 92 Pas, son, in haist, graith thi wingis in effect. **1601** *Vestry Bks.* (Surtees) 135 For mending the wheeles, and graithing the bells against the cronation day. **1609** SKENE *Reg. Maj.* 156 Of coukes graithand or makand reddie flesh or fishe. **1851** GREENWELL *Coal-trade Terms Northumb. & Durh.* 29 *Grathe*, to put in order, to dress; to replace a worn bucket-leather.

†**2.** *refl.* To prepare oneself, get ready. Often with *inf.* Rarely *intr.* for *refl. Obs.*
c **1230** *Hali Meid.* 17 Leccherie ananriht greiðeð hire wið þat to weorren oþi meidenhad. *a* **1300** *Cursor M.* 20180 Has he sete me ani dai þat i wit in me grait mai? *c* **1400** *Destr. Troy* 5970 Þai graithet to fle. *a* **1400–50** *Alexander* 2873 Þat he suld graythe him to ga as him his god chargis. *c* **1460** *Towneley Myst.* x. 76 Grayth the, gabriell, and wende. **1535** STEWART *Cron. Scot.* I. 642 That euerilk Scot..Within ane da sould graith thame for to gone. *a* **1650** *Scotish ffeilde* 55 in Furniv. *Percy Folio MS.* I. 215 Thus he greathes him godly ..with a grat host.

†**b.** with *to*, *toward*, or an adv. implying motion: To prepare to go, shape one's course, betake oneself. *Obs.*
c **1250** *Gen. & Ex.* 1738 He..greiðet him ðeðenward wið sped. *a* **1300** *Cursor M.* 17810 Ful smertli þai þam þider graid. *c* **1330** R. BRUNNE *Chron.* (1810) 300 Þei..smertly did þam grayth Toward Dun Bretayn. ? *a* **1400** *Morte Arth.* 1266 Graythe ȝowe to ȝone grene wode. *c* **1400** *Melayne* 1595 Oure Oste..graythes þam to Melayne walle. *c* **1450** *St. Cuthbert* (Surtees) 1600 To maumetry þai þaim graythe.

3. To equip, furnish; to array (in clothes, armour); to dress (a person); to fit out (a vessel); to bedeck, ornament. Also with *up*.
1297 R. GLOUC. (Rolls) 8955 Pouueremen wel ofte in to hire chambre heo drou..& greiþede hom vaire inou. *a* **1300** *Cursor M.* 5190 'Gif me mi clathes', þan said he, 'And hastily þat we graithed be'. *c* **1320** *Sir Tristr.* 670 Graiþed y wil he be, And seþþen schewe him as kniȝt. *c* **1350** *Will. Palerne* 2731 On [schip] þat was gayly greyt to go to þe seile. *c* **1394** *P. Pl. Crede* 195 Þat cloister..wiþ lauoures of latun louelyche y-greithed. ? *a* **1400** *Morte Arth.* 589 Iche prynce with his powere appertlyche graythede. *c* **1420** *Anturs of Arth.* xl, Syr Gauan the gode was graythet in grene. **1500–20** DUNBAR *Poems* xliii. 28 Send in ȝour steid ȝour ladeis grathit vp gay. **1535** STEWART *Cron. Scot.* (1858) I. 223 The Romanis war sa weill graithit into geir. **1560** ROLLAND *Crt. Venus* II. 1033 Thair proud palphrais was graithit Incontinent, In glansand geir and best abillement. *a* **1775** *Hobie Noble* v. in Child *Ballads* VII. clxxxix. 2/1 Then Hobie has graithd his body weel. **1803** R. ANDERSON *Cumberld. Ball.* 72 Oft graith'd in aw their kurk-gawn gear. **1855** ROBINSON *Whitby Gloss.* s.v., 'Bonnily graithed,' handsomely dressed. 'Badly graithed', ill dressed. 'Get the table graithed', set out.
refl. **1297** R. GLOUC. (Rolls) 7642 Þat folc of denemarch.. Greiþede hom mid gret poer. **13..** *Guy Warw.* (A.) 1917 Gii him graiþed. *c* **1386** CHAUCER *Reeve's T.* 389 Thise clerkes.. greythen hem, and tooke hir hors anon. *c* **1470** HENRY *Wallace* I. 277 His modyr graithit hir in pilgrame weid. **1513** DOUGLAS *Æneis* VIII. vii. 69 Thou the grathis for to fecht. **1593** R. BARNES *Parthenophil, Sonn.* xlix. in Arb. *Garner* V, A Fiend which doth in Graces' garments grath her.

†**b.** ***to graith in the grave***: to give burial to.
1535 STEWART *Cron. Scot.* II. 112 He..Richt gloriouslie gart graith him in his graif. *Ibid.* 295. *a* **1600** *Battle of Harlaw* in *Evergreen* (1761) I. 80 He vowed..All the hale Lands of Ross to haif, Or ells be graithed in his Graif.

†**c.** *fig.* To treat, 'serve' in some (unwelcome) manner. *Obs.*
c **1320** *Sir Tristr.* 1095 Mo þat hider wil ride, Þus grayþed schul ȝe be. *c* **1375** *Sc. Leg. Saints, Eugenia* 374 Se hou-gat ȝone monk has grapit me. **1569** N. HUBERT *Confess.* in H. Campbell *Love-lett. Mary Q. Scots* 207 He should graith me in such a sort as I never was in my life.

†**4. a.** = MAKE in various senses: To make up, compose; to build, set *up*; to constitute; to represent. *Obs.*
a **1300** *Cursor M.* 550 Of þir things i haf her said was adam cors to-gedir graid. *c* **1400** *Destr. Troy* 1664 In the cheffe of þe choise halle, chosen for þe kyng, Was a grounde vp graid with gresis of Marbill. *a* **1400–50** *Alexander* 1874 Syn gostid godesses & gods ere graythid neuir to dye. *Ibid.* 4499 For marcure was manslaȝt, a mammlere of wordis, ȝe graith him to be gouenoure & god of þe tonge.

†**b.** To put *on*. *Obs.*
c **1350** *Will. Palerne* 2933 Gode crounes of gold on here hedes graiþed. *a* **1400–50** *Alexander* 790* [Alexander] Grathez on þis gay gere & þen a gilt sadyll.

†**'graithful**, *a. Obs. rare.* [f. GRAITH *sb.* + -FUL.] Prompt, speedy.
a **1300** *Cursor M.* 13184 Þe mining lastes yeitt bi yeir, Wit a greithful soth vengeance.

graithing (ˈgreɪθɪŋ), *vbl. sb. Obs.* exc. *dial.* [f. GRAITH *v.* + -ING[1].] The action of the vb. GRAITH; preparation; furnishing; also *concr.* furniture, attire.
a **1340** HAMPOLE *Psalter* lxiv. [lxv.] 10 Þou grayth þe mete of þaim, for swa is þe graythynge of it. *a* **1350** *Kindh. Jesu* 1250 Cloth..of swiþe guod greiþingue. **1495** in *Ld. Treas. Acc. Scot.* (1877) I. 267 To Dauid Caldwell, to the grathing of his chalmeris..xviijs. **1786** BURNS *On Naething* v, Some quarrel the Presbyter gown, Some quarrel Episcopal graithing. **1881** MRS. ANNIE ELLIS *Sylvestra* I. 92 The lass was..willing, but sadly in want of 'graithing'. **1884** *Gd. Words* 202 It's a bit of bonnie graithin.

graithly, older form of GRADELY *a.* and *adv.*

†**'graithness.** *Obs. rare.* [f. GRAITH *a.* + -NESS.] Readiness, promptitude.
c **1400** *Destr. Troy* 4509 And your graithnes may gretly the grekes auaile.

graive, graivie, obs. ff. GRAVE, GRAVY.

grakle, variant of GRACKLE.

grale, obs. form of GRAIL[1].

grallatorial (grælәˈtɔәrɪәl), *a. Ornith.* [f. mod.L. *grallātōri-us*, (f. L. *grallātor* one who walks on stilts, f. *grallæ* stilts) + -AL[1].] Pertaining to the order *Grallatores*, which consists of long-legged wading birds, such as the crane, heron, etc.
1835 SWAINSON *Nat. Hist. Quadrupeds* §310 Comparing them..with other grallatorial types. **1860** GOSSE *Rom. Nat. Hist.* 198 Spoonbills, ibises and other..grallatorial birds.
So **'grallatory** = prec.
1855 in H. CLARKE; and in later Dicts.

grallic ('grælɪk), *a.* *Ornith. rare.* [f. L. *grall-æ* stilts + -IC.] Of or pertaining to the *Grallæ* or wading birds.

1828-32 in WEBSTER; and in later Dicts.

gralline ('grælaɪn), *a.* *Ornith.* [f. L. *grall-æ* stilts + -INE.] = GRALLIC.

1888 *Nature* 20 Dec. 180/1 The large order of the Charadri-ornithes has split into aquatic and gralline types.

gralloch ('grælɒx), *sb.* Also -ock. [a. Gael. *grealach* intestines.] The viscera of a dead deer.

1882 OGILVIE, *Grallock.* **1886** WALSINGHAM & PAYNE-GALLWEY *Shooting* (Badm. Libr.) II. iii. 93 The gralloch showed nothing but clover and grass.

gralloch ('grælɒx), *v.* Also 9 **garlock, grallock, grulloch.** [f. prec.] *trans.* To disembowel (properly, a deer).

1848 *Fraser's Mag.* XXXVIII. 313 Having flayed and garlocked the elk, he cut off one of its haunches. **1863** OUIDA *Held in Bondage* (1870) 55 We think no toil or trouble too great to hear the ping of the bullet, and see the deer grallocked at last. **1894** SIR J. D. ASTLEY *50 Y. my Life* I. 297 We had to gralloch our pig ourselves, for the natives would not touch them.

Hence **'gralloched** *ppl. a.*

1897 *Outing* (U.S.) XXIX. 440/1 We bore our gralloched game..on double shoulder poles.

gram[1] (græm). Also 8 **gramm.** [ad. Pg. *grão* (formerly sometimes written *gram*):—L. *grānum* GRAIN.] The chick-pea, a kind of vetch, *Cicer arietinum.* Sometimes called ***Bengal gram.*** The name is extended to any kind of pulse used as food for horses.

1702 in J. T. Wheeler *Madras Old. Time* (1861) II. 10 Their allowance three times a week is but a quart of rice and gram together for five men a day. **1732** PIKE in *Phil. Trans.* XXXVII. 231 Boil a Peck of Gramm..to a Jelly. **1879** MRS. A. E. JAMES *Ind. Househ. Managem.* 71 Your stock of gram should be kept in a large tin-lined chest or box.

b. *attrib.*, as ***gram-bread, -contract, -field; gram-fed*** ppl. a.

1799 WELLINGTON in Gurw. *Desp.* (1844) I. 47 You mentioned some time ago that Purneah would bid for the gram contract when it was offered. **1849** SIR C. NAPIER in *Life* (1857) IV. 201 A man..with a self-sufficient idea, that no one 'can know India' except through long experience of brandy, champagne, gram-fed [*printed* grain-fed] mutton, cheroots and hookahs. **1869** E. A. PARKES *Pract. Hygiene* (ed. 3) 228 Gram bread or cakes have been occasionally used in India for Europeans. **1880** G. ABERIGH-MACKAY *Tour Sir Ali Baba* 127 All the gram-fed secretaries and most of the alcoholic chiefs were there.

gram[2], **gramme** (græm). [a. F. *gramme*, ad. late L. *gramma*, Gr. γράμμα, a small weight. The spelling *gram* is now preferred to *gramme* in scientific use.]

In the Metric System, the unit of weight; the weight of a cubic centimetre of distilled water at the maximum density, weighed *in vacuo.* It equals 15.432 grains. Later redefined as a unit of mass equal to 1/1000 of a KILOGRAM, although it is still used as a unit of force equal to the *gram force.*

1797 *Nicholson's Jrnl.* Aug. 197 From the gramme are deduced by multiplication or division all the weights superior and inferior. **1810** *Naval Chron.* XXIV. 300 The monetary unit is a piece of silver weighing five grams. **1846** G. E. DAY tr. *Simon's Anim. Chem.* II. 160 The mean amount of free lactic acid excreted daily..was 2·167 grammes. **1877** *Rep. Brit. Assoc. 1876* II. 32 In the system already adopted by the British Association Committee on Dynamical and Electrical Units..the Centimetre, the Gram, and the Second were taken as the units of length, of mass, and of time. [*Note*] The spelling Gram, instead of Gramme, for the English word is adopted..in accordance with the spelling put forward in the Metric Weights and Measures Act, 1864, which legalizes the use of the Metric System. **1889** *Anthony's Photogr. Bull.* II. 360 A solution of 50 grams of ferrocyanide of potassium in 100 water. **1892** *Proc. Amer. Assoc. Adv. Sci. 1891* 176 Rules for the orthography and pronunciation of chemical terms... Gramme. **1894** J. PARKER *Thermodynamics* 3 The weight of a gramme has no definite value unless we specify the place where the weight is to be found, because the weight of a given mass is not quite the same in all parts of the world... The weight of a gramme at Paris is 980·868 dynes. **1898** *Rev. Brit. Pharm.* 54 A true cubic centimetre is the volume of 1 gramme of water at 4° C. **1911** KAYE & LABY *Tables Physical & Chem. Constants* 3 Mass. Unit—the gramme, 1/1000 of the International Prototype Kilogramme. **1954** *Amer. Jrnl. Physics* XXII. 298/1 Weighing in grams..is extremely familiar even though few calculations are carried out in this system [*sc.* the metric gravitational system], conversion usually being made to the cgs system. **1958** *Van Nostrand's Sci. Encycl.* (ed. 3) 1744/2 The abbreviation gf is used to indicate gram (force), the unit of force, which is defined as the weight of a one-gram mass under the action of a gravitational acceleration of 980·665 cm/sec². **1966** J. R. PARTINGTON *Gen. & Inorg. Chem.* (ed. 4) i. 7, 1 mol. wt. of a gas at S.T.P...in grams occupies 22·4 lit. **1967** *Units & Standards of Measurement: Mechanics* (*H.M.S.O.*) (ed. 4) 10 These densities..are expressed in terms of grammes per millilitre. **1970** *Spec. Univ. Syst. desig. Linear Density Textiles* (*B.S.I.*) 5 The linear density in 'tex' expresses the mass in grammes of one kilometre of yarn.

b. *attrib.* **gram-atom**, the quantity of an element having a mass in grams numerically equal to its atomic weight; **gram calorie** = CALORIE b; **gram-centimetre**, a unit equivalent to the 'work' done in raising a mass of one gram vertically one centimetre; **gram-degree, -equivalent** (see quots.); **gram force**, a unit of force equal to the weight of a mass of 1 gram, esp. under standard gravity; also called ***gram*** and ***gram weight***; **gram-ion**, the quantity of an ionic substance having a mass in grams numerically equal to the atomic weight of the ion or the sum of the atomic weights of the constituent atoms; **gram-molecule**, the quantity of a substance having a mass in grams numerically equal to its molecular weight; so ***gram-molecular*** adj.; **gram-rad**, a unit of the energy absorbed by any quantity of a substance when irradiated with ionizing radiation, equal to 100 ergs; **gram weight** = *gram force.*

1899 *Jrnl. Chem. Soc.* LXXVI. II. 587 The magnetic susceptibility of a number of the elements,..has been determined. The coefficient of susceptibility for each element, when divided by the number of *gram-atoms per litre, gives the atomic magnetism. **1938** R. W. LAWSON tr. *Hevesy & Paneth's Man. Radioactivity* (ed. 2) i. 7 A divalent ion requires 96,500 coulombs to deposit half a gram-atom. **1902** *Encycl. Brit.* XXXIII. 280/1 Small calorie or *gramme calorie. **1951** *Engineering* 29 June 792/2 Expressed in the absolute units of the C.G.S. system,..he had found that a gram-calorie was equal to 4·181 Joules, and the mean gram-calorie corresponded to 4·187 Joules. **1875** EVERETT *Illustr. Centimetre Gramme* p. x, 1 *gramme-centimetre = 9·18 × 10² ergs nearly. **1870** —— tr. *Deschanel's Nat. Philos.* xxxi. 427 The *gramme-degree (Centigrade) is the quantity of heat required to raise a gramme of water 1° (Centigrade). **1897** WEBSTER, **Gram equivalent* (Electrolysis), that quantity of the metal which will replace one gram of hydrogen. **1909** *Gram force [see *pound force* s.v. POUND *sb.*[1] 4]. **1966** KAYE & LABY *Tables of Physical & Chem. Constants* (ed. 13) 12 It is often convenient to use submultiples and multiples of these units, e.g., gramme-force (gf), ounce-force (ozf). **1898** *Jrnl. Chem. Soc.* LXXIV. II. 210 The contraction which occurs when a substance is dissolved in water is proportional to the concentration of the solution.. the contraction is about 13·5 c.c...for every dissolved *gram ion of an electrolyte. **1902** J. MCCRAE tr. *Arrhenius' Text-Bk. Electrochem.* i. 9 One gram-ion of chlorine signifies 35·45 grams of chlorine in the ionic condition (Cl). **1906** A. SMITH *Introd. Gen. Inorg. Chem.* xii. 199 It is called, therefore, the *gram-molecular volume (G.M.V.) or the molar volume... It may be defined as that volume which contains one mole (gram-molecular weight) of any gas at 0° and 760 mm. **1931** E. C. MILLER *Plant Physiol.* ii. 51 A solution made up after this manner is termed a 'molar', ..'gram-molecular', or 'molecular' normal solution. **1878** *Gram molecule [see MOLECULE 1 c]. **1894** G. S. NEWTH *Text-bk. Inorg. Chem.* I. vii. 56 The number of grammes of a substance, equal to the number which represents its molecular weight, is spoken of as the gramme-molecule. **1958** W. K. MANSFIELD *Elem. Nucl. Physics* i. 2 It follows that a gramme-molecule of any substance contains the same number of molecules. **1954** *Brit. Jrnl. Radiol.* XXVII. 243/2 Integral absorbed dose is the integration of the energy absorbed throughout a given region of interest. The unit is the *gramme-rad. 1 gramme-rad = 100 ergs. **1963** QUIMBY & FEITELBERG *Radioactive Isotopes in Med. & Biol.* viii. 120 The maximum permissible dose to a normal individual in 3 months is 3 rads of radiation to the whole body... For a 70 kg man this would be an integral dose of 210,000 gram-rads. **1871** *Phil. Mag.* 4th Ser. XLII. 375 The value of *T* is about ·074 of a *gramme weight per centimetre. **1894** J. PARKER *Thermo-dynamics* 3 The value of this arbitrary unit of pressure is found to be 1033·279 gramme-weights, or 1,013,510 dynes, per square centimetre. **1960** *Amer. Jrnl. Physics* XXVIII. 480/1 The weight of a body is a force measured in dynes or gram weight.

Gram[3] (græm). Also **gram.** The name of H. C. J. *Gram* (1853-1938), Danish physician, used *attrib.* and in the possessive to designate his method of staining bacteria and the iodine solution he employed in this method, as ***Gram('s) method, solution, stain*** (so ***Gram-stained, -staining*** ppl. adjs.). Hence ***Gram-positive, -negative*** adjs., respectively staining, or not staining, by Gram's method.

1884 *Brit. Med. Jrnl.* 6 Sept. 487/2 Gram's method gives good results with many bacteria. **1886** E. M. CROOKSHANK *Introd. Pract. Bacteriol.* 246 (*index*) Gram's solution. **1902** R. T. HEWLETT *Man. Bacteriol.* (ed. 2) iii. 91 By this method the ordinary Gram-staining organisms are stained. **1903** W. D. FROST *Lab. Guide Elem. Bacteriol.* (ed. 3) i. 60 (*heading*) Gram's stain. **1907** *Practitioner* Aug. 277 The Boas-Oppler bacillus is Gram-positive, whereas the normal bacillary flora of the large intestine is mainly Gram-negative. **1908** PARK & WILLIAMS *Pathogenic Micro-organisms* (ed. 3) xii. 133 A Gram-stained smear may show all Gram-negative or all Gram-positive bacteria. **1949** H. W. FLOREY et al. *Antibiotics* II. xv. 632 The active agent inhibited the growth of certain gram positive pathogenic organisms and gram negative cocci. **1961** *Lancet* 29 July 228/1 To avoid errors due to contamination, Gram-stained films of the growth were examined. **1963** H. BURN *Drugs, Med. & Man* (ed. 2) xx. 202 Most of the bacteria which stain by the gram stain.. are sensitive to the action of penicillin. **1964** M. HYNES *Med. Bacteriol.* (ed. 8) v. 44 All [bacteria] may be placed into one of two broad groups according to whether they stain by Gram's technique. *Ibid.* v. 45 The organisms are first stained with methyl-violet or gentian-violet and then treated with iodine as a mordant; Gram-positive bacteria then resist decolourization by alcohol.

gram[4] (græm), colloq. abbrev. of (*a*) TELEGRAM or CABLEGRAM; also **'gram**; (*b*) GRAMOPHONE.

1891 'F. LESLIE' *Let.* 24 Aug. in W. T. Vincent *Recoll. F. Leslie* (1893) II. xxv. 140, I wired you *date of production and result*, and sincerely hope the 'grams reached you safely. **1928** *Sunday Express* 19 Aug. 1 Grams: 'Mould-board, London.' Phones: 1615 1616 East. **1960** WODEHOUSE *Jeeves in Offing* iii. 37 What's a guffin?.. That's what she calls you in her latest 'gram. **1964** —— *Frozen Assets* iii. 51, I cabled the New York lawyers asking if..there was some small legacy coming my way, and back comes this gram informing me that I cop the lot.

1959 *New Statesman* 26 Dec. 904/3 The thing he wanted to buy most in the world was a gram and lots of jazz records. **1970** *Guardian* 24 Dec. 9/3 There was Edmundo Ros and his Cuban band on the gram.

gram, obs. form of GRAME *sb.*; var. GRAME *a.*

-gram (græm), repr. (chiefly) Gr. γράμμα something written, letter (of the alphabet). The older Eng. sbs. with this ending fall into three classes: (1) adaptations of actual or assumable Gr. sbs. in -γραμμα, derived from vbs. f. prep. + γράφειν to write, and expressing the result of the action of the verb, as *anagram, diagram, epigram, paragram, program* (usu. in Fr. spelling *programme*); (2) compounds of a Gr. sb. with γράμμα, f. legitimately assumable Gr. types, as *chronogram*, and (later) *ideogram, logogram*; (3) compounds of a numeral with γράμμα, or more frequently with γραμμή line, of which the Gr. type, where one exists, is a neut. adj. in -γραμμον, as *monogram, hexagram, pentagram.* (Yet a fourth kind of formation has one example in LIPOGRAM.) In the year 1857 the need for a shorter term for 'telegraphic message' was supplied by the introduction of *telegram* (previously proposed in 1852), which violates Gr. analogy, as an adv. like τῆλε could not correctly form a compound with a vb. or sb., but which was found so convenient that it quickly became established, and has been adopted into several foreign langs. Later formations suggested by this word are the hybrids *cablegram* for 'cable telegram', *pistolgram* for an instantaneous photograph. Another recent formation, also suggested by *telegram*, but not open to the same objection, is *phonogram* for the record of sound made by the phonograph. In the denominations of weight in the metric system, *decagram(me, kilogram(me*, etc., *-gram(me* is the word GRAM², GRAMME.

2. In various (often humorous) combinations based on *telegram*, denoting a message delivered by a representative of a commercial greetings company, *esp.* one outrageously dressed to amuse or embarrass the recipient, in the manner indicated by the first element, as ***Gorillagram*** (proprietary in the U.S.), ***Rambogram, strippergram***, etc. See also KISSOGRAM.

1979 *Maclean's Mag.* 19 Nov. 17/1 For singing-telegram junkies bored by the same old song and dance, Cookie climbs into a furry suit to deliver Gorillagrams. **1980** *Official Gaz.* (U.S. Patent Office) 17 June TM104 *Gorillagram.* Eliot Corey Stein... Filed 12-11-78. **1981** *N.Y. Times* 20 Apr. 5/5 Mary Flatt..said its services include..the 'Bellygram', which is sung by a singer in a belly-dancing attire. **1982** *Private Eye* 16 July 22/4 (Advt.), Singing telegrams, Gorillagrams,..Strip-a-Grams..for..anniversaries etc. **1983** K. BRYSON et al. *Compl. Naff Guide* 46 Send a girlfriend a male singing strippergram on her birthday. **1985** *Time* 24 June 72/3 Youngsters will soon be able to pop Rambo vitamins, and New Yorkers can send a Rambogram, in which a Stallone look-alike will deliver a birthday message or carry out a tough assignment.

grama[1], **gramma** ('grɑːmə, 'græmə). See GAMA GRASS. [a. Sp. *grama* a sort of grass.] A name for several low pasture grasses abundant in the western and south-western United States, esp. *Bouteloua oligostachya.*

1844 J. GREGG *Commerce of Prairies* I. 160 A highly nutritious grass called *grama.* **1851** MAYNE REID *Scalp Hunt.* xix, Our horses refreshed themselves on the 'grama' that grew luxuriantly around.

attrib. and *Comb.* **1828** A. WETMORE *Diary* 28 July in *U.S. Senate 22nd Congress 1st Sess.* Doc. 90 (1832) 39 Our mules have been recently much benefitted by the *gramme grass*, the best pasturage between the Atlantic and Pacific Ocean. **1851** MAYNE REID *Scalp Hunt.* xxvi. 194 There the grama grass is longer and more luxuriant. **1887** F. FRANCIS Jr. *Saddle & Mocassin* xii. 230 The dry crowsfoot gramma grass that clothed the country. *Ibid.* xiii. 249 The gramma-carpeted foot-hills and plateaux of the Sierra Madre.

grama[2] ('grɑːmə). [Skr. *grāma.*] A scale used in Indian music.

1807 J. D. PATERSON in *Asiatick Researches* IX. 446 (*title*) On the Grāmas or Musical Scales of the Hindus. *Ibid.* 457 The scale is denominated *Grāma* (literally village) because there is in it the assemblage of all the notes. **1891** C. R. DAY *Mus. & Musical Instr. S. India* ii. 15 The srutis are differently arranged in grāmas, or scales, three in number. **1913** E. CLEMENTS *Introd. Study Indian Mus.* i. 2 First came the *Grāmas*, which may be regarded as collections of notes definitely related to one another by musical intervals. **1954** *Grove's Dict. Mus.* (ed. 5) IV. 456/2 *Grāma* means 'village' and thus 'scale' or 'collection of notes'. **1968** *Indian Mus. Jrnl.* V. 49 The whole framework of *grāma* and its adjuncts was evolved on the basis of the actual musical practice that had crystallised as *Jāti-s.*

gramaire, obs. form of GRAMMAR.

gramarcy, obs. form of GRAMERCY.

gramari-: see GRAMM-.

gramarye ('græmərɪ). *Obs.* exc. *arch.* Also 4 **grammarie**, 5 **gramery**, **-ory**, 9 **gramarie**, **-ary**, **grammary(e**, **gramowrie**. [a. OF. **gramarye*: see GRAMMAR.]

†**1.** Grammar; learning in general. *Obs.*

c **1320** *Seuyn Sag.* (W.) 183 Therinne was paint..eke alle the seven ars The first so was grammarie. *c* **1460** *Towneley Myst.* xii. 242 Yee speke all by clerge..Cowth ye by youre gramery reche vs a drynk, I shuld be more mery. *Ibid.* xxx. 253, I se thou can of gramory and som what of arte. **1483** *Cath. Angl.* 162/2 Gramery, *gramatice.*

2. Occult learning, magic, necromancy. Revived in literary use by Scott.

For the connexion between senses 1 and 2 see quot. 1870 (cf. GLAMOUR, and F. *grimoire*).

c **1470** *K. Estmere* 144 in Percy *Reliq.*, My mother was a westerne woman, And learned in gramarye. **1805** SCOTT *Last Minstr.* III. xi, Whate'er he did of gramarye Was always done maliciously. **1832** J. P. KENNEDY *Swallow B.* xxx. (1860) 298 It was like casting a spell of 'gramarie' over his opponents. **1870** LOWELL *Among my Bks.* Ser. I. (1873) 96 All learning fell under suspicion, till at length the very grammar itself..gave to English the word gramary. **1883** *Century Mag.* XXVII. 203 All white from head to foot, as if bleached by some strange gramarye.

gramaryen, -one, -oun, obs. ff. GRAMMARIAN.

gramash (grə'mæʃ). Also 8 **gramashen**, 9 **gramoche**. [Sc. var. GAMASH.] = GAMASH.

1681 COLVIL *Whigs Supplic.* (1751) 24 He had on each leg a gramash. **1813** E. PICKEN *Poems* I. 124 I've guid gramashens worn mysel'. **1816** SCOTT *Old Mort.* i, Gramoches or leggins, made of thick black cloth, completed his equipment. **1862** HISLOP *Prov. Scot.* 163 Put your shanks in your thanks and mak gude gramashes o' them.

†**gramaun'gere.** *Obs.*⁻¹ [a. OF. *grant mangier* great meal.] A great meal.

Not from the orig. Fr., which has 'do you think you can eat up all the pagans by yourselves?'

c **1400** *Rowland & O.* 1052 Charles with his stronge powere Schall thynk this a grete gramaungere.

‖**Gramdan** (grɑːm'dɑːn). Also **gram-dan**, **gramdan**. [Hindi, f. *grām-a* village + *dān* gift.] In India, (a movement for) the free gift of a village for the benefit of the community. Cf. BHOODAN.

1957 *Economist* 28 Sept. 1037/1 The most specifically Indian political innovation since Mahatma Gandhi's satyagraha was bhoodan, the gift of land. Acharya Vinoba Bhave, its founder, has now extended it to gramdan, the gift of villages. **1958** [see BHOODAN]. **1959** HOUGH & MADHAVA DAS *Co-op. Movement in India* (ed. 4) 425 The problem of meeting the credit needs of the *gramdan* villages in Koraput. **1969** *Times* 13 Oct. (Indian Suppl.) p. vi/7 The movement is at present in its second stage: that of *Gramdan*... So far all that is being done is to collect 'declarations of intent' on prescribed forms, a village being declared *Gramdan* when at least 75 per cent of its population has signed the form... Only after 80 per cent of the villages in a state have been brought under *Gramdan* in this manner, would the implementing of the declared intentions be taken up. **1971** *Catholic Worker* Feb. 7/2 We see in a gramdan village how a meeting house, a nursery, a village store, a school, a milk cooperative can be started through voluntary cooperation.

grame (greɪm), *sb. Obs.* exc. *arch.* Forms: α. 1–2 **grama**, 4–6 **gram**, (4 **graim**, 6 **gramm**), 3– **grame**. β. 2–4 **grome**. [OE. *grama*, related to *gram* GRAME *a.* Cf. GREME *sb.*]

†**1.** Anger, wrath, ire. *Obs.*

α. *c* **1000** ÆLFRIC *Gen.* xix. 25 God towearp þa swa mid graman þa burȝa. —— *Hom.* II. 120 Wel hi sind Dere ȝehatene forðan ðe hi sind fram graman ȝenerode. *a* **1175** *Cott. Hom.* 223 þa nam he mulcene gramen and andan to ðan mannum. *a* **1300** *Cursor M.* 2423 þe king was radd for godds gram. *c* **1380** *Sir Ferumb.* 596 Olyuere stert vp hol & sound; & spekeþ til him wyþ grame. *c* **1430** *Syr Tryam.* 1223 Hyt ys grete schame On a hors to wreke thy grame! **1501** DOUGLAS *Pal. Hon.* II. 220 Out on sic gram I will haue na repreif. **1621** AINSWORTH *Annot. Ps.* ii. 5 Grame, grimnesse or fierceness of countenance.

β. *a* **1225** *Juliana* 26 þe reue rudnede ant o grome grede. *c* **1300** *Passion our Lord* 72 in *O.E. Misc.* 39 þe Gywes ..þerof hi hedde grome. *c* **1325** *Body & Soul* 70 Mid Godes grom.

2. Grief, sorrow; harm. In *pl.* Troubles.

α. *c* **1000** *Sax. Leechd.* III. 212 Æppla gaderian graman ȝe[tacnað]. *c* **1200** *Trin. Coll. Hom.* 67 Mid te bitere grame þat alle synfulle men schule þolen on domes dai. *a* **1300** *Cursor M.* 8405 He is wis and o redi tung þat neuer serued grefe ne grame. *a* **1340** HAMPOLE *Psalter* xiv. 4 þat..he dide to his neghburgh iuel ne gram. **1480** *Robt. Devyll* 44 That valyuant knyght am I That saved youe thre tymes fro grame. **1513** DOUGLAS *Æneis* IV. Prol. 161 All ȝour solace sall returne in gram. ? *a* **1548** *Smyth & Dame* 218 in Hazl. *E.E.P.* III. 209 Age doth me mvche grame. **1597** *N. Mother's Blessing* E6, Gif thou haue an euill name It will turne the to grame. **1865** SWINBURNE *Masque Q. Bersabe* 114 By Termagaunt that maketh grame. **1872** ROSSETTI *Staff & Scrip* Poems (ed. 6) 49 God's strength shall be my trust, Fall it to good or grame 'Tis in his name.

β. *c* **1205** LAY. 1435 ȝe doð þan kinge muchel scome: þer fore ȝe sculen han grome. *c* **1275** *Sinners Beware* 335 in *O.E. Misc.* 83 þu vs hauest iwroht þes schome And alle þene eche grome. *c* **1306** *Pol. Songs* (Camden) 219 Oure wajour turneth us to grome.

†**grame**, *a. Obs.* Forms: α. 1 **gram**, 3 *Orm.* **gramm**, 3–5 **gram**, 4– **grame**. β. 1, 3 **grom**. [OE. *gram*, *grǫm* = OHG., OS. *gram*, ON. *gram-r*, f. Teut. root **gram-*, *grem-*: see GRIM.] **a.** Angry; vexed; furious. *transf.* of heat: Fierce. **b.** Grieved, sorrowful.

α. *Beowulf* (Z.) 778 þær þa graman wunnon. *c* **1000** *Ags. Gosp.* Matt. xxvi. 10 Hwi synt ȝe grame [Vulg. *molesti*] þysum wife? *c* **1200** ORMIN 7145 Maþþew..seȝȝþ..þatt tatt unnfæle Herode king Wass gramm & grill. *c* **1250** *Gen. & Ex.* 1228 Bi ðe desert a-wei che nam, In ard weie and hete gram. *c* **1275** LAY. 24774 þe he greteþ mid his grame wordes. *c* **1300** *Havelok* 2469 God was him gram. *c* **1330** R. BRUNNE *Chron.* (1810) 106 Hir dede dos him fulle gram. *c* **1440** *Gaw. & Gol.* 471 To greif thair gomys gramest that wer. **1560** *Proude Wyues Pater noster* 190 in Hazl. *E.P.P.* IV. 160 Forbere your husbonde whan he is grame.

β. *c* **893** K. ÆLFRED *Oros.* II. iv. §6 He swa grom wearð on his mode. *a* **1250** *Owl & Night.* 992 Hweþer is betere of twere twom, That mon beo bliþe oþer grom.

2. *absol.* as *sb. pl.* Devils. [So OS. *gramon*, ON. *gramer.*]

c **1175** *Lamb. Hom.* 103 He..maceð of cristes leoman heoranna [*read* horena] leoman and of godes husa gromena wuniunge.

†**grame**, *v. Obs.* Forms: α. 3 **gramie(n**, 3– **grame**. β. 3 **gromien**. [f. GRAME *a.* Cf. GREME *v.*]

1. *impers.* as in (*it*) *grames me*: I am grieved, vexed, displeased, in distress.

α. *c* **1200** *Trin. Coll. Hom.* 69 þanne ne þarf us noðer gramien, ne shamien. *c* **1275** LAY. 25216 Fol sore ous may samie and wel sore gramie. *c* **1380** *Sir Ferumb.* 691 Oþer weys þee schal grame. **14..** *Pilgrim's Sea Voy.* (E.E.T.S.) i. 3 Many a man hit gramys, When they begyn to sayle.

β. *c* **1205** LAY. 25216 Ful swiðe us mæi scomien: and ful swiðe us mæi gromien. *a* **1225** *Leg. Kath.* 2075 þe king walde weden, swa him gromede wið ham.

2. *intr.* To be vexed or displeased; to fret.

α. *a* **1300** *Cursor M.* 17836 (Gött.) Wid þair hertis gun þai grame. **1399** LANGL. *Rich. Redeles* Prol. 41, I wolde be gladde þat his gost myȝte..grame if it greued him. *a* **1420** HOCCLEVE *Min. Poems* (1892) 43 Stif stande in þat & yee shuln greeue & grame. **1526** SKELTON *Magnyf.* 1864 The crane and the curlewe thereat gan to grame.

β. *a* **1225** *Juliana* 66 þe reue gromede þat he grispatede aȝein þet wod he walde iwurðen.

3. *trans.* To anger, grieve, vex.

c **1320** R. BRUNNE *Medit.* 548 And for a lytyl wurde þou wylt men grame. *c* **1350** *Barlam & Jos.* (Bodl. MS.) 908 þæt þu me hast gramyd þin hert auȝt be sor. *c* **1450** *Cov. Myst.* (Shaks. Soc.) 27 Gret schame it is us nakyd to se, Our lord God thus to grame. *c* **1460** J. RUSSELL *Bk. Nurture* 348 þan may þe sewere his lord serue & neythur of yow be gramed.

Hence †'**graming** *vbl. sb.* and *ppl. a.*

c **1175** *Lamb. Hom.* 33 A þer [in helle] is waning and graming and toþen grisbating. *c* **1205** LAY. 6127 þa seide Gudlakes sune mid gromiende speche, ȝif [etc.].

grameer, obs form of GRAMMAR.

†'**gramely**, *a. Obs.* Forms: 1 **gram(u)lic**, 3 **gromelich**. [OE. *gram(u)lic*, f. *gram*, *grama* (see GRAME *a.* and *sb.*) + *-lic* -LY¹.] Wrathful.

c **1000** ÆLFRIC *Judges* iv. 2 He hiȝ þa betæhte sumum gramulican cininge. *a* **1225** *St. Marher.* 9 Vnseheliche godd ..hwas wreððe is swa gromelich þæt helle ware ant heouenes ant alle cwike þinges cwakieð þer aȝeines.

†'**gramely**, *adv. Obs.* Also 1 **gramlíce**, 5 **gramly**. [OE. *gramlíce*, f. *gram* GRAME *a.* + *-líce* -LY².] Angrily, furiously, grievously.

c **1000** *Ags. Ps.* lxxvii. 20 Hi..gramlice be Gode spræcan. *c* **1450** *St. Cuthbert* (Surtees) 1037 þe childe was greued and gramly gret.

gramenite ('greɪmənaɪt). *Min.* [ad. G. *gramenit* (f. L. *grāmen* grass). Named by Krantz in 1857.] A grass-green variety of chloropal.

1858 *Amer. Jrnl. Sci.* Ser. II. XXVI. 351 Gramenite comes..from Menzenberg in the Siebengebirge. **1868** DANA *Min.* 461 Gramenite has a grass-green color.

gramenivorous: see GRAMIN-.

gramer, obs. form of GRAMMAR.

gramercy (grə'mɜːsɪ), *int. phr. Obs.* exc. *arch.* Forms: 4, 6 **grand**, **graunt(e mercy**, (4 **grant merci**, **-y**, **gromercy**, 4–5 **gramarcy**), **-erci**, 5 **gray mercy**, **gremercy**, **gromersy**, (**-essye**, **-esty**), 5–6 **gramercye**, (6 **garmercye**, **grammercie**), 6–7 **gramercie**, (7 **g'rammercy**, 7–8 **gra'mercy**, **gran mercé**), 4– **gramercy**. *Pl.* 6 **gram(m)ercies**, **-sies**, 7 **gramercyes**, 8 **gray mercies**. [a. OF. *grant merci*; *grant* great (see GRAND *a.*) + *merci*: see MERCY.

The primary sense of *merci* was 'reward, favour gained by merit'; hence *grant merci* originally meant 'may God reward you greatly': cf. GOD-A-MERCY. Both *grant merci* and *merci* without the adj. came to be used interjectionally = 'thanks', in which use the shorter form survives in mod.Fr.]

1. = Thanks; thank you. Formerly also in *pl.* Const. *for*, †*of*.

13.. *Coer de L.* 1371 Quod the kyng: 'Frendes, gromercy!' *c* **1330** R. BRUNNE *Chron.* (1810) 145 Philip..Said often grant mercy. **1390** GOWER *Conf.* III. 317 She saith: Graunt mercy, leve sir. *a* **1400** *Octouian* 1291 Graunt marcy, my lord the kyng. *c* **1420** *Sir Amadace* (Camd.) lii, The king.. bede, 'Gromersy, gentulle knyȝte!' *a* **1440** *Sir Degrev.* 785 'Maydame', sche seid, 'gramercy Of thi gret cortesy'. ? **1507** *Communyc.* (W. de W.) Ciij, Graunte mercy Iesu croppe and rote Of al frensshypp. **1563** FOXE *A. & M.* 734/1 Winchester, Winchester, grand mercy for your wine. *c* **1590** GREENE *Fr. Bacon* iii. 88 Gramercies Peggy look for me ere long. **1594** *True Trag. Rich. III*, 67 Richmond, gramercies for thy kinde good newes. **1598–9** FORDE *Parismus* I. (1661) 187 Gramercies, quoth he, for thy good will. **1607** SHAKS. *Timon* II. ii. 69 Gramercies good Foole: How does your Mistris? **1691** RAY *Creation* II. (1704) 438 Grammercy, Socrates, that is good Counsel indeed. **1820** SCOTT *Ivanhoe* vi, Gramercy for thy caution. **1842** BARHAM *Ingol. Leg.* Ser. II. *Nell Cook*, Gramercy for thy benison!

†**b.** *Indirectly*, with *dat.* of agent or instrument (later with *to*): = Thanks *to*; by the instrumentality of. So, proverbially, ***gramercy horse!*** (app. an allusion to the story quoted s.v. GOD-A-MERCY). *Obs.*

1426 *Paston Lett.* No. 7 I. 26 Evere gremercy God, and ye. *c* **1450** LONELICH *Grail* lii. 757 Gromesty God and that good Man. **1489** CAXTON *Faytes of A.* IV. vii 248 To the whiche thing god gramercy the kynge of fraunce..hathe wel aduysed. **1591** HARINGTON *Orl. Fur.* XXXVI. liv, Though the shield brake not, gramercy charme. *c* **1640** WILSON *Inconstant Ladie* II. iv. (1814) 45 Hee's gon. Gramercy, horse! **1713** ROWE *Lady Jane Grey* III. i. (1720) 43 They have confin'd me long, Gra'mercy to their Goodness, Pris'ner here. *a* **1734** NORTH *Exam.* I. ii. §140 Gran Mercé to his Authors the Libellers of that Time.

2. ? Used as an exclamation of surprise or sudden feeling; = 'mercy on us!'

Johnson, 1755, who regards the word as shortened from *grant me mercy*, gives this as the only application of the word; but both his examples belong to sense 1. The quots. from Heywood and Ross seem to show that the word was sometimes actually used as Johnson says; but the instances in 19th c. may be merely based on his explanation.

1607 HEYWOOD *Wom. killed w. Kindnesse* (1617) A3b, Gramercies brother, wrought her too't already. **1624** —— *Captives* IV. i. in Bullen *O. Pl.* IV, Gramercyes, I in truth much suffered for thee, Knowing how rashly thou exposd thyself To such a turbulent sea. **1768** ROSS *Helenore* 24 Gray-mercies she replies, but I maun gang. **1798** COLERIDGE *Anc. Mariner* 111, Gramercy! they for joy did grin. **1843** LYTTON *Last Barons* I. v, Gramercy, it seems that there is nothing which better stirs a man's appetite than a sick bed.

†**3.** quasi-*sb.* The salutation 'thanks' or 'thank you'. Hence in phrases, as ***worth gramercy***, worth giving thanks for, of some value or importance. ***no gramercy***, no occasion for deserving thanks; no special merit; similarly, ***what gramercy? for gramercy***: for a 'thank-you'; for nothing or next to nothing; gratis. (Cf. GOD-A-MERCY 2.) *Obs.*

c **1485** *Digby Myst.* (1882) iv. 410 Is this theire gramercy? is this theire reward? **1548** HALL *Chron., Hen. IV* (1809) 530 The Kyng..sendeth to you great gramercies. **1548** UDALL, etc. *Erasm. Par. Mark* viii. 57 Suche a one as loketh for summe thankes or gramercies. **1549** COVERDALE *Erasm. Par. Peter* 7 But what garmercye were it, yf you suffre when you are buffetted for naughtye doinges? **1551** ROBINSON tr. *More's Utop.* (Arb.) 121 Payinge very lytle for them, yea mooste commonlye gettynge them for gramercye. **1572** GASCOIGNE 100 *Flowers* 274 The Ladies all saluted him & he gaue them the gramercy. **1576** HOLINSHED *Chron.* III. 56 Rendering to him and his armie a thousand gramersies. **1578** TIMME *Caluine on Gen.* 279 It was no gramercie to him, that his wife's honesty was not put in hazard. **1579–80** NORTH *Plutarch* (1676) 966 He made Corn to be distributed to the People at a very mean price to some, and for gramercy to the poor. **1581** MULCASTER *Positions* xxxix. (1887) 219 Where desire to do good, and good for gramercie be the true ends of most honour. *a* **1610** HEALEY *Epictetus' Man.* xvii. (1636) 21 Nothing is gotten for gramercy. **1624** BP. R. MOUNTAGU *Gagg* 153 Workes of compulsion are not worth Gramercy. **1641** MILTON *Animadv.* ii. Wks. 1738 I. 84 So have we our several Psalms for several occasions, without gramercy to your Liturgy. **1641** BROME *Joviall Crew* IV. ii, No Ladies live such lives. *Mer.* Some few, upon necessity, perhaps, But that's not worth g'rammercy. **1643** SIR T. BROWNE *Relig. Med.* 37, I cannot relate the history of my life ..with a..bare gramercy to my starres. **1644** MILTON *Areop.* (Arb) 51 What grammercy to be sober, just, or continent? *a* **1670** HACKET *Abp. Williams* I. (1692) 174 The Duke returned him no Gra-mercy, being resolute to out-face Envy.

gramere, -ery, obs. ff. GRAMMAR, GRAMARYE.

gramicidin (græmɪ'saɪdɪn). *Chem.* [f. GRAM³ + *-i* + -CID(E + -IN¹.] Any of several polypeptides produced by *Bacillus brevis* which have antibiotic properties, esp. against Gram-positive bacteria, and are used externally to treat local infections; orig. considered a single compound.

1940 HOTCHKISS & DUBOS in *Jrnl. Biol. Chem.* CXXXII. 791 Three crystalline preparations highly bactericidal for Gram-positive microorganisms have been obtained... The third substance, which we have named gramicidin, is concentrated by repeatedly recovering the fraction which remains soluble in alcohol. **1967** HUNTER & SCHWARTZ in Gottlieb & Shaw *Antibiotics* I. 642 Counter-current distribution techniques resolved gramicidin into four groups of polypeptides now specifically designated as gramicidins A, B, C, D. **1969** *New Scientist* 10 July 65/2 The antibiotics which are produced include..gramicidin and tyrocidin.

graminaceous (græmɪ'neɪʃəs), *a.* [f. L. *grāmin-*, *grāmen* grass + -ACEOUS.] = GRAMINEOUS.

1847 in CRAIG. **1871–2** *Cassell's Techn. Educ.* II. 231/1 Nitrogenous manures are more peculiarly adapted for graminaceous plants, such as the meadow-grasses and the cereals. **1898** 'ROLF BOLDREWOOD' *Romance Canvas Town* viii. 104 So they [sheep] roamed unattended..enjoying abundant food and water with perfect immunity from the graminaceous scourge [a spiked grass].

†**gramine.** *Her. Obs.* [ad. L. *grāmineus*: see GRAMINEOUS.] Of grass. Only in ***garland gramine*** (tr. L. *corona graminea*).
1572 BOSSEWELL *Armorie* II. 96 b, The field is of the Diamond, an Helmet Pearle, ensigned with a Garlande gramine. **1610** GUILLIM *Heraldry* IV. xvi. (1660) 347 Yet is the same Garland Gramine..most honourable and noble.

gramineal (grəˈmɪnɪəl), *a.* [f. as next + -AL[1].] = next.
1658 PHILLIPS, *Gramineous*, or *Gramineal*, grassie or made of grasse. Whence in later Dicts.

gramineous (greɪˈmɪnɪəs), *a.* [ad. L. *grāmine-us* (f. *grāmin-*, *grāmen* grass) + -OUS.] Of or pertaining to grass; resembling grass; grassy; *spec.* belonging to the N.O. *Gramineæ*.
1658 [see GRAMINEAL]. **1668** WILKINS *Real Char.* 73 Gramineous Plants not used by men for Food, may be distributed into such as are more properly called Grasses [etc.]. **1750** G. HUGHES *Barbadoes* 169 From the top rises a long gramineous spike. **1881** ELWES tr. *A. de S. Pinto's How I crossed Afr.* I. v. 101 It flows through vast plains, slightly undulated and clothed with gramineous plants.
Hence **graˈmineousness**.
1727 in BAILEY vol. II.

graminiferous (græmɪˈnɪfərəs), *a.* [f. mod. assumed L. **grāminifer* (f. L. *grāmin-*, *grāmen* grass + *-fer* bearing) + -OUS.] Bearing or producing grass.
1834 MRS. SOMERVILLE *Connect. Phys. Sci.* xxvi. (1849) 294 The graminiferous plains of South America.

graminifolious (græmɪnɪˈfəʊlɪəs), *a.* [f. L. *grāmin(i)-* (see prec.) + *foli-um* a leaf + -OUS.] Having leaves resembling those of grass.
1731 in BAILEY vol. II; and in mod. Dicts.

graminiform (grəˈmɪnɪfɔːm), *a.* [f. as prec. + -(I)FORM.] Having the form of grass; resembling grass.
In mod. Dicts.

graminivorous (græmɪˈnɪvərəs), *a.* Also 8 **gramen-**. [f. mod.L. *grāminivor-us* (f. L. *grāmin-*, *grāmen* grass + *-(i)vorus* devouring) + -OUS.] Eating or feeding on grass.
1739 S. SHARP *Surgery* xxix. 168 The gramenivorous kind [of Brutes]. **1746** R. JAMES *Introd. Mouffet's Health's Improv.* 43 Graminivorous Animals. **1785** J. DOUGLAS *Antiq. Earth* 7 An animal that is both grameniverous and carniverous. **1840** ARNOLD in Stanley *Life* (1844) II. App. C. 422 The graminivorous [animals] become so numerous as to eat up all the young trees. **1873** E. SMITH *Foods* 102 Rookpie..has a fulness and lusciousness of flavour which excels any dish of graminivorous birds.

graminology (græmɪˈnɒlədʒɪ). [f. L. *grāmin-* (see prec.) + -(O)LOGY.] The science of grasses; a treatise on grasses.
In some mod. Dicts.

gramiˈnose, *a.* *Obs.*[−0] [ad. L. *grāminōs-us* grassy, f. *grāmin-* *grāmen* grass: see -OSE.] = GRAMINOUS.
1727 in BAILEY vol. II.

†**gramiˈnosous**, *a.* *Obs.*[−1] [f. L. *grāminōs-us* f. *grāmin-*, *grāmen* grass + -OUS.] = next.
1623 in COCKERAM.

graminous (ˈgræmɪnəs), *a.* ? *Obs.* [ad. L. *grāminōsus*: see prec. and -OUS.] **a.** Covered with grass; grassy. **b.** = GRAMINEOUS.
1659 D. PELL *Impr. Sea* 422 All manner of vermine lye very much couchant in every field, and graminous place. **1769** E. BANCROFT *Nat. Hist. Guiana* 54 Ginger..From its stalk [rise] several long narrow graminous leaves. **1798** in *Spirit Publ. Jrnls.* (1799) II. 152 The cow had discharged her graminous digestion in a very ludicrous abundance. **1811** J. PINKERTON *Petral.* II. Introd. 12 Silex..found in the straw of graminous plants.

gramly, varient of GRAMELY *adv. Obs.*

†**gramm.** *Obs. rare*[−1]. [ad. Gr. γράμμα in same sense.] What is written; a phrase.
1647 WARD *Simp. Cobler* (*title-p.*) This is no time to feare Apelles gramm: *Ne sutor quidem ultra crepidam.*

gramm, gramma, var. GRAME, GRAMA[1].

grammalogue (ˈgræməlɒg). *Shorthand.* [f. Gr. γράμμα + λόγος word: cf. *analogue*, *catalogue*.] A word represented by a single sign; also, a letter or character representing a word (more correctly called LOGOGRAM).
1845 I. PITMAN *Manual Phonogr.* §30 (ed. 7) 19 Grammalogue, a letter-word; a word represented by a logogram. **1857** *Ibid.* §137 (ed. 10) 50 The positions of the grammalogues, above, on, and through the line, are determined by their vowels. **1864** *Social Sci. Rev.* Mar. 224 Grammalogues and phraseology are rather freely employed. **1892** *Pall Mall G.* 3 Oct. 7/2 Contractions and 'grammalogues' had to be devised by each man for himself.

grammar (ˈgræmə(r)), *sb.* Forms: 4-5 gram(m)ere, 4-6 gramer, 4-7 grammer, (4 gramaire, 5 gramayre, -eer), 6- grammar. [ad. OF. *gramaire* (F. *grammaire*), an irregular semipopular adoption (for the form of which cf. OF. *mire* repr. L. *medicum*, *artimaire* repr. L. *artem magicam* or *mathematicam*) of L. *grammatica*, ad. Gr. γραμματική (scil. τέχνη art), fem. of γραμματικός adj., of or pertaining to letters or literature, f. γράμματα letters, literature, pl. of γράμμα letter, written mark, f. root of γράφειν to write. Cf. Pr. *gramaira* (prob. from Fr.). Old Fr. had also a learned adoption of the L. word, *gramatique*, parallel with Sp. *gramática*, Pg., It. *grammatica*, G. *grammatik*, Welsh *gramadeg*.

In classical Gr. and L. the word denoted the methodical study of literature (= 'philology' in the widest modern sense, including textual and æsthetic criticism, investigation of literary history and antiquities, explanation of allusions, etc., besides the study of the Greek and Latin languages. Post-classically, *grammatica* came to be restricted to the linguistic portion of this discipline, and eventually to 'grammar' in the mod. sense. In the Middle Ages, *grammatica* and its Rom. forms chiefly meant the knowledge or study of Latin, and were hence often used as synonymous with learning in general, the knowledge peculiar to the learned class. As this was popularly supposed to include magic and astrology, the OF. *gramaire* was sometimes used as a name for these occult sciences. In these applications it still survives in certain corrupt forms, F. *grimoire*, Eng. GLAMOUR, GRAMARYE.]

1. a. That department of the study of a language which deals with its inflexional forms or other means of indicating the relations of words in the sentence, and with the rules for employing these in accordance with established usage; usually including also the department which deals with the phonetic system of the language and the principles of its representation in writing. Often preceded by an adj. designating the language referred to, as in *Latin*, *English*, *French* grammar.

In early Eng. use *grammar* meant only Latin grammar, as Latin was the only language that was taught grammatically. In the 16th c. there are some traces of a perception that the word might have an extended application to other languages (cf. quot. 1530 under GRAMMATICAL 1); but it was not before the 17th c. that it became so completely a generic term that there was any need to speak explicitly of '*Latin* grammar'. Ben Jonson's book, written *c* 1600, was app. the first to treat of 'English grammar' under that name.

As above defined, grammar is a body of statements of fact—a 'science'; but a large portion of it may be viewed as consisting of rules for practice, and so as forming an 'art'. The old-fashioned definition of grammar as 'the art of speaking and writing a language correctly' is from the modern point of view in one respect too narrow, because it applies only to a portion of this branch of study; in another respect, it is too wide, and was so even from the older point of view, because many questions of 'correctness' in language were recognized as outside the province of grammar: e.g. the use of a word in a wrong sense, or a bad pronunciation or spelling, would not have been called a *grammatical* mistake. At the same time, it was and is customary, on grounds of convenience, for books professedly treating of grammar to include more or less information on points not strictly belonging to the subject.

Until a not very distant date, Grammar was divided by Eng. writers (following the precedent of Latin grammarians) into Orthography, Etymology, Syntax, and Prosody, to which Orthoëpy was added by some authors. All these terms (except Syntax) were used more or less inaccurately (see the several words). The division now usual is that into Phonology, treating of the sounds used in the language, Accidence, of the inflexional forms or equivalent combinations, and Syntax, of the structure of sentences; the branch of grammar dealing with the functions of the alphabetic letters is usually treated along with the phonology.

1362 LANGL. *P. Pl.* A. XI. 131 Gramer for gurles, I gon furste to write. **1398** TREVISA *Barth. De P.R.* XVII. iii. (1495) 604 Holy wrytte wol not al way be subget to the rules of gramer. *c* **1400** *Lanfranc's Cirurg.* 8 He muste studie..in gramer, þat he speke congruliche. **1485** CAXTON *Chas. Gt.* 29 After that Charles was Instructe in gramayre & other scyences. **1577** tr. *Bullinger's Decades* (1592) 161 Dionysius ..set vp a schoole and taught children their Grammer. **1605** BACON *Adv. Learn.* II. xvi. §4 (1873) 168 Concerning speech and words, the consideration of them hath produced the science of Grammar. **1619** FOTHERBY *Atheom.* II. xiii. §1 (1622) 346 The naturall, and..homogeneall parts of Grammer, be two, Orthology, and Orthography. **1620** GRANGER *Div. Logike* 8 That part of every proposition that goeth afore in reason..is the Theme. In grammar it is called the nominative case. *a* **1637** B. JONSON *Eng. Gram.* I. i. (1640) 35 Grammar is the art of true and well speaking a Language: and writing is but an Accident. **1669** MILTON *Acced. Gram.* (1847) 457 Latin Grammar is the Art of right understanding, speaking or writing Latin. **1741** WATTS *Improv. Mind* xx. Wks. (1813) 164 Grammar is nothing else but rules and observations drawn from the common speech of mankind in their several languages. **1752** HUME *Ess. & Treat.* (1777) I. 95 Men..had no relish for the seemingly minute observations of grammar and criticism. *a* **1774** PEARCE *Serm.* I. xii. 250 If a man, who professes himself a master of grammar, is always found to be speaking improperly. **1824** L. MURRAY *Eng. Gram.* (ed. 5) 25 English grammar is the art of speaking and writing the English language with propriety. **1869** FARRAR *Fam. Speech* iv. 120 Grammar consists in accidence, syntax and analysis.

transf. **1644** BULWER *Chiron.* 99 Amongst which Grammars by gestures, the postures of the Fingers..have been contrived into an Alphabet. **1678** CUDWORTH *Intell. Syst.* 5 They who are skilled in the Grammar of the Heavens may be able from the several Configurations of the Stars, as it were Letters to spell out future Events.

b. ***general, philosophical*** or ***universal grammar***: the science which analyses those distinctions in thought which it is the purpose of grammatical forms more or less completely to render in expression, and which aims to furnish a scheme of classification capable of including all the grammatical categories recognized in actual languages. ***historical grammar***: the study of the historical development of the inflexional forms and syntactical usages of a language. ***comparative grammar***: the comparative treatment of the phenomena of two or more related languages, with the object of determining the nature and degree of their relationship.
1751 HARRIS *Hermes* Wks. (1841) 117 These different analysings or resolutions constitute what we call 'philosophical or universal grammar'. **1872** MORRIS *Hist. Outlines Eng. Accid.* i. §4 b, Comparative Grammar informs us that the radical part of the verb is *lov* (or *luf*). **1892** SWEET *Eng. Gram.* i. §6 General grammar (*philosophical grammar*) ..is..concerned with the general principles which underlie the grammatical phenomena of all languages.

2. A treatise or book on grammar.
1530 PALSGR. Ep. Ded. v, Folowyng the order of Theodorus Gaza, in his grammer of the Greke tonge. **1588** SHAKS. *Tit. A.* IV. ii. 23, I read it in the Grammer long agoe. *c* **1620** HUME *Brit. Tongue* (1865) 2 You wald cause the universities mak an Inglish grammar to repres the insolencies of sik green heades. *c* **1645** HOWELL *Lett.* v. 31 You desired me lately to procure you Dr. Davies Welsh Grammer. **1693** DRYDEN *Juvenal* p. lxxxvj, We have yet no English *Prosodia*, not so much as a tolerable Dictionary, or a Grammar. **1751** HARRIS *Hermes* Wks. (1841) 169 We are taught in common grammars that verbs active require an accusative. **1894** V. HENRY (*title*) A short comparative Grammar of English and German.
transf. and *fig.* *a* **1617** P. BAYNE *Comm. Coloss.* i. 16 (1634) 82 The booke of the Creatures: though it be not so good as the Grammar of the Scripture which doth describe Him plainely, yet it is a good primmer for us to spell in. **1836** EMERSON *Nature, Language* Wks. (Bohn) II. 152 Did it need ..this host of orbs in heaven, to furnish man with the dictionary and grammar of his municipal speech? **1865** TYLOR *Early Hist. Man.* ii. 16 Ideas which do not come within the scope of the very limited natural grammar and dictionary of the deaf and dumb.

3. An individual's manner of using grammatical forms; speech or writing judged as good or bad according as it conforms to or violates grammatical rules; also speech or writing that is correct according to those rules.
a **1586** SIDNEY *Arcadia* III. (1598) 366 An answer farre out of all Grammer. **1657** TRAPP *Comm. Ps.* xvi. 4 It was the Serpents grammar that first taught men to decline God in the plurall number. **1672** DRYDEN *Almanzor* II. *Def. Epilogue* Wks. 1883 IV. 231 The sense is here extremely perplexed; and I doubt the word *they* is false grammar. *a* **1700** —— (J.), *Varium et mutabile semper femina*, is the sharpest satire that ever was made on woman; for the adjectives are neuter, and animal must be understood to make them grammar. **1842** MACAULAY *Fredk. Gt.* Ess. (1865) III. 209 He had German enough to scold his servants ..but his grammar and pronunciation were extremely bad. **1855** —— *Hist. Eng.* IV. xviii. 245 The letter may still be read with all the original bad grammar and bad spelling.

4. The phenomena which form the subject-matter of grammar; the system of inflexions and syntactical usages characteristic of a language.
Languages not possessing an elaborate system of inflexions and concords are often said to have 'little' or 'no grammar.' This seems to have been partly the meaning of the reproach against the English language quoted by Sidney *Apol. Poetrie* (Arb.) 70, 'that it wanteth Grammer'; though it may also have meant that English had not been refined and improved, as the classic tongues were supposed to have been, by the labours of grammarians.
1846 WRIGHT *Ess. Mid. Ages* I. i. 8 To know the grammar of a language it is necessary to know the reasons of the grammar. **1860** MARSH *Lect. Eng. Lang.* i. 13 In English, having no grammar, we have till lately possessed no grammars, and we still want a dictionary. **1886** DOUSE *Introd. Gothic* Prelim, ch. §6 The distinctive features of Teutonic Grammar.

5. †**a.** Used for LATIN, or the Latin language. ***by grammar***: in Latin. (Cf. GRAMMAR-SCHOOL.)
c **1320** *Seuyn Sag.* (W.) 106 He made the boke of Catoun clere, That es biginyng of gramere. *c* **1460** *Towneley Myst.* xii. 387 Virgill in his poetre sayde in his verse, Even thus by gramere as I shall reherse [a Lat. quot. follows]. **1532** MORE *Confut. Tindale* Wks. 723/1 In our owne time, of al that taught grammer in England, not one vnderstode ye latine tongue. **1546** *Eng. Gilds* (1870) 198 A scolemaster of Gramer. **1576** GASCOIGNE *Steele Gl.* (Arb.) 77 That grammar grudge not at our english tong Bycause it stands by Monosyllaba And cannot be declind as others are.

†**b.** Scholarship generally, literature.
c **1500** *Melusine* lxii. 370 For as I fele & vnderstand by the Auctours of gramaire & phylosophye they repute..this present hystorye for a true Cronykle & thinges of the fayry.

c. The name of a class in certain Jesuit schools or colleges.
1629 J. WADSWORTH *Pilgr.* iii. 13 Father Lacy, the Reader of Poetry, and Master of the Syntax. Father Henry Bentley and Father Iohn Compton of Grammer. **1667** in *Cath. Rec. Soc. Publ.* III. 63 He was newly entered into grammer. *Ibid.* 69 Answering to hard and intrecat questions publickly in our Refectory even the first week he was in grammer. **1773** in *Mem. Stonyhurst Coll.* (1881) 22 The former Master of Poetry, the latter of Grammar, at Bruges. **1837** J. C. FISHER in *Ushaw Mag.* (1904) Dec. 262-3. **1904** *Ibid.* June 201 On Tuesday, May 19th, Syntax played Grammar.

d. Short for GRAMMAR SCHOOL. Also *attrib.*

1950 J. CANNAN *Murder Included* iv. 62 He won a scholarship to Harborough Grammar, but his father wouldn't let him take it up. **1959** I. & P. OPIE *Lore & Lang. Schoolch.* xvi. 356 The home-work toilers are called 'Grammar grubs'. *Ibid.*, At Caistor, in Lincolnshire, the Moderns chant: Grammar fleas, [etc.]. **1964** A. PRIOR *Z Cars Again* xv. 147 A 'girl in the Grammar' meant much to a family in that neighbourhood. **1965** *Listener* 22 July 125/1 'Grammar grubs,' the secondary school-boys shouted at us, and we passed by, noses lifted, precociously dignified.

6. *transf.* **a.** The fundamental principles or rules of an art or science. **b.** A book presenting these in methodical form. (Now *rare*; formerly common in the titles of books.)

1642 FULLER *Holy & Prof. St.* III. xiii. 185 Manly sports are the Grammer of Military performance. **1792** A. DUNCAN *Mariner's Chron.* (1804) II. 33 A small geographical grammar. **1796** W. TAYLOR in *Monthly Rev.* XIX. 551 It forms a most valuable grammar of antient geography. **1809** J. GOLDSMITH (*title*) A brief Grammar of the Laws and Constitution of England. **1835** E. NEWMAN (*title*) The Grammar of Entomology. **1856** O. JONES (*title*) Grammar of Ornament. **1870** J. H. NEWMAN (*title*) An Essay in aid of a Grammar of Assent. **1882** W. SHARP *Rosetti* v. 315 The young poet may be said to have reached the platform of literary maturity while he was yet learning the grammar of painting. **1894** *Daily News* 23 Nov. 7/1 He might..have studied the pure grammar of his art for a longer time. **1958** *Listener* 18 Sept. 441/2 Reizenstein's dissonances do not make one 'sit up' in the way Haydn's do if we attend to his musical grammar. **1963** *Times* 5 Mar. 15/1 The grammar of the film was established.

7. *attrib.* and *Comb.*, as ***grammar-book, -construction, -learning, -monger, -pamphlet, -pedant, -rule, -shop*** (humorous), ***-tree, -word***; ***grammar-ridden*** adj. Also †**grammar-boy**, a pupil at a grammar-school, a boy still learning his (Latin) grammar; †**grammar-castle**, ? humorously for a grammar-school; **grammar-child**, ? = *grammar-boy*; †**grammar-college**, a school for teaching Latin attached to a college (cf. GLOMEREL, GLOMERY); **grammar-figure** (see FIGURE *sb.* 22); **grammar-grinding**, instruction in grammar, pedantic instruction generally (cf. *gerund-grinding*); **grammar-lad** = *grammar-boy*; **grammar-learning**, †(*a*) the subjects taught in a grammar-school, Latin and Greek; (*b*) the learning of grammar; **grammar-scholar** = *grammar-boy*.

1503 *Bury Wills* (Camden) 229 Myn portoose and all my *gramer bokys. **1578** ASCHAM *Scholem.* (Arb.) 27 Let the Master..teach his Scholer, to ioyne the Rewles of his Grammer booke, with the examples of his present lesson. **1820** W. COBBETT *Grammar* (1847) §233 The loose and imperfect definitions of my grammar-book yielded me no clue to a disentanglement. **1590** NASHE *Pasquil's Apol.* I. C iij, A rodde for the *Grammer boy, he dooth nothing but wrangle about words. *a* **1641** BP. R. MONTAGU *Acts & Mon.* (1642) 188 For Grammar boyes know, that she [Cassandra] in love to virginitie, deceived Apollo her Suiter. **1895** RASHDALL *Univ. Europe* I. v. §5. 482 It was only when the students were mere Grammar-boys that they were governed like schoolboys. **1670** EACHARD *Cont. Clergy* 14 Whose parts and improvements duely considered will scarce render them fit governours of a small *grammar-castle. **1557** *Order Hospitalls* G viij, Such a one of the *Grammer children as can redilest write. **1886** WILLIS & CLARK *Cambridge* I. Introd. 58 Bingham was establishing his modest *grammar-college in connection with Clare Hall. **1605** JAS. I *Sp. in last Session* B iv, I did..interpret..some darke phrases therein, contrary to the ordinary *Grammar construction of them. **1657** J. SMITH *Myst. Rhet.* 176 Transposition is a *Grammar figure whereby one letter is put for another. **1898** *Daily News* 3 Feb. 6/2 The preliminary *grammar-grinding of the old method is enough to destroy love for the classics. **1644** MILTON *Areop.* (Arb.) 56 As if they were no more then the theam of a *Grammar lad under his Pedagogue. **1628** T. SPENCER *Logick* 59 Aptnes vnto laughing, and *Grammar-learning, is predicated of man. **1709** *Lond. Gaz.* No. 4533/3 Persons of eminent Ability in teaching Grammar Learning. **1845** R. W. HAMILTON *Pop. Educ.* iv. (ed. 2) 69 Our ambition is to base all upon Grammar learning. **1833** J. C. HARE in *Philol. Mus.* II. 215 A *grammar monger's language would be like a sluggish monotonous canal. **1864** W. CORY *Lett. & Jrnls.* (1897) 114 After all I was to be nothing but a third-rate grammar-monger. **1716** M. DAVIES *Athen. Brit.* I. 23 The forementioned John Stanbridge wrote also several *Grammar-Pamphlets. **1726** AMHERST *Terræ Fil.* xxxi. 165 The tyranny of a school is nothing to the tyranny of a college, nor the *grammar-pedant to the academical one. **1906** *Westm. Gaz.* 28 Aug. 1/3 Opportunities for experiment are not often forthcoming in our much-examined and *grammar-ridden schools. **1935** R. PAGET *This English* 7 English..is much less grammar-ridden than most other languages. **1565** JEWEL *Def. Apol.* (1611) 625 Some Popes be so voide of Learning, that they vnderstand not the *Grammar Rules. **1693** C. DRYDEN in *D.'s Juvenal* (1697) 183 Be sure he knows exactly Grammar-Rules. **1580** SIR R. MANWOOD in Boys *Sandwich* (1792) 224 *note*, There be not so many *grammer-schollers as do furnish the school-house. **1654** SIMEON ASHE *Funeral Serm.* 6 June (1656) 53 While he was a Grammar-Scholar, this calling he chose. **1774–81** WARTON *Hist. Eng. Poetry* (1840) II. xxxv. 552 Grammar scholars. *c* **1836** SYD. SMITH in *Cornh. Mag.* Feb. (1865) 224 You may call it an university, it will only be a *grammar-shop. **1693** DRYDEN *Juvenal* (1697) 146 Who climbs the *Grammar-Tree, distinctly knows Where Noun, and Verb, and Participle grows. **1685** COTTON tr. *Montaigne* I. 597 Metaphors and allegories and other *grammer words.

grammar (ˈɡræmə(r)), *v. rare.* [f. the sb.] †**a.** *intr.* To discuss grammar. *Obs.*[−1] †**b.** *trans.* To ground *in* something as in the rudiments of grammar. *Obs.* **c.** To classify, as the parts of speech in grammar.

1593 G. HARVEY *Pierces Supererog.* Wks. (Grosart) II. 246 When I am better grammered in the Accidents of his proper Idiotisme. *a* **1616** BEAUM. & FL. *Laws of Candy* II. i, *Erot.* I can, I doe, I will. *Gonz.* She is in her Moods and her Tences: Ile Gramer with you. And make a triall how I can decline you. **1682** BUNYAN *Holy War* 32 These two..did much more Grammer and settle the common people in hurtful ways. **1883** R. H. BUSK in *N. & Q.* Ser. VI. VIII. 51 Groups of phenomena which have been gathered, and grammared, and ranged into sciences.

grammarian (ɡrəˈmɛərɪən). Forms: 4–5 **gramarien**, 4–7 **-ian**, 5–6 **-yen**, (5 **gramarion**, **-yone**, **-youn**, **grammaryon**, 6 **-yan**, **-yen**, **-ien**), 6– **grammarian**. [a. OF. *gramarien* (F. *grammairien*), f. *gramaire* GRAMMAR: see -IAN.]

1. One versed in the knowledge of grammar, or of language generally; a philologist; often signifying also a writer upon, or teacher of grammar.

c **1380** WYCLIF *Serm.* Sel. Wks. I. 376 Gramariens and devynes. **1387** TREVISA *Higden* (Rolls) V. 161 Donatus þe gramarian. **1412–20** LYDG. *Chron. Troy* II. x, To sewe his style in my translation Worde by worde like the construction After the maner of gramariens. **1509** BARCLAY *Shyp of Folys* (1570) 105 The great Gramarians and pleasaunt Oratours. **1583** T. WATSON *Poems* lxviii. (Arb.) 104 Suidas mentioned an other Telephus, an excellent Grammarian of Pergamus. **1600** O. E. *Rep. Libel* I. i. 9 Not vnlike hungrie Grammarians, that are descanting still of the calamities of Troie, and yet see not their owne domesticall miseries. **1643** SIR T. BROWNE *Relig. Med.* II. §8, I have seene a Grammarian toure, and plume himselfe over a single line in Horace. **1681** NEVILE *Plato Rediv.* 123, I know some Criticks, who are rather Grammarians than Lawyers, have made a distinction between *elegerim* and *elegero*. *a* **1704** T. BROWN *Sat. Antients* (1730) I. 22 They have commented upon him like grammarians not philosophers. **1727–41** CHAMBERS *Cycl.* s.v., The denomination grammarian is, like that of critic, now frequently used as a term of reproach; a mere grammarian; a dry, plodding grammarian, etc. **1771** SMOLLET *Humph. Cl.* 19 May, They serve only as exceptions; which, in the grammarian's phrase, confirm and prove a general canon. **1798** H. K. WHITE *On being confined at school* iii, All that arithmeticians know, Or stiff grammarians quaintly teach. **1861** HOOK *Lives Abps.* (1869) I. vii. 436 The homilies of Elfric the Grammarian. **1876** JAS. GRANT *Burgh Sch. Scotl.* II. xiii. 359 *note*, He educated a grammarian not inferior to himself.

2. †**a.** A pupil engaged in the study of grammar; a grammar-school boy. *Obs.*

1571 *Vestry Minutes St. Olave's, Southwark* in *Lett. Lit. Men* (Camden) 65 He should have twentye marks by the yere..to teache so many gramaryens as we think shall be found meet for the same. **1607** in *Hist. Wakefield Gram. Sch.* (1892) 71 Because this schole is not ordained for petties but for grammarians.

b. A member of the class named 'Grammar' in certain Jesuit schools or colleges.

1705 in *Ushaw Mag.* (1903) Dec. 298. **1837** J. C. FISHER *Ibid.* (1904) Dec. 250 In the cyphering school with the Grammarians and High Fig[ures]. **1904** *Ibid.* Mar. 98.

3. *attrib.* and *Comb.*

1586 WARNER *Alb. Eng.* v. xxvii. (1589) 119 Grammarian-like, in order words significant to speake. **1853** WHEWELL in Todhunter *Acct. W.'s Writ.* (1876) II. 376 The absurd iniustice of our grammarian critics.

Hence **graˈmmarianism** [see -ISM], the principles or practice of a grammarian.

1846 in WORCESTER, quoting *Ch*[*ristian*] *Ob*[*server*]. Hence in later Dicts.

grammarie, obs. form of GRAMARYE.

†**grammariour.** *Obs.* [f. as prec. + *-our*, -OR.] = GRAMMARIAN 1.

1536 BELLENDEN *Cron. Scot.* (1821) I. 231 About this time war mony clerkis profound in every science: as..Donatus, gramariour;..with mony otheris. **1597** LOWE *Chirurg.* (1634) 34 Speaking of Antioch mediciner, and Telephus grammariour. **1617** *Sc. Acts Jas. VI* (1816) IV. 576/1 With þe mansis, ȝairdis, and croftis of the Canonist, ciuilist, mediciner, and grammarior.

†ˈ**grammarize**, *v. Obs. rare*[−1]. [f. GRAMMAR *sb.* + -IZE.] *trans.* To give a certain grammatical structure to.

1746 W HORSLEY *Fool* (1748) I. 174 You find some modern Performances so exquisitely grammarised and pointed, and the Meaning so blinded and obscured, that one is at a Loss to determine whether it is Wrote in our own Language, or in Cypher.

grammarless (ˈɡræməlɪs), *a.* [f. GRAMMAR *sb.* + -LESS.] Having no grammar.

1. a. Of a language: Destitute of a system of grammatical forms, or of features susceptible of grammatical treatment. **b.** Of persons, speech, compositions: Showing ignorance of grammar.

1823 *Blackw. Mag.* XIV. 294 Miserable, bald, and even grammarless English is employed. **1868** FARRAR in *Jrnl. Philology* No. 2. 20 Chinese has been for thousands of years monosyllabic and grammarless. **1891** *Harper's Mag.* July 220/1 Ours is really a grammarless language. **1891** *Daily News* 14 Feb. 5/1 Futile romances, tasteless, senseless, grammarless.

2. Having no book of grammar. *nonce-use.*

1854 *Fraser's Mag.* L. 317 Battling, grammarless and dictionaryless, with a work in a strange idiom.

grammar school. A school for teaching grammar.

1. The name given in England to a class of schools, of which many of the English towns have one, founded in the 16th c. or earlier for the teaching of Latin. They subsequently became secondary schools of various degrees of importance, a few of them ranking little below the level of the 'public schools'. Since the Education Act of 1944, any secondary school with a 'liberal' curriculum including languages, history, literature, and the sciences, as distinct from technical or modern schools.

1387 TREVISA *Higden* (Rolls) V. 51 At Alexandria he heeld a gramer scole. **1454** *E.E. Wills* (1882) 133 For to fynde to gramer scole my cosyn, his sone William. **1523** FITZHERB. *Husb.* §147, I lerned two verses at grammer-schole. **1593** SHAKS. *2 Hen. VI*, IV. vii. 37 Thou hast most traiterously corrupted the youth of the Realme, in erecting a Grammar Schoole. **1616** R. C. *Times' Whistle* ii. 845 The foole Was never farther than the grammer schoole. **1647** *Laws Massachusetts* (1672) 136 Where any Town shall increase to the number of one hundred Families..they shall set up a Grammar School. **1711** STEELE *Spect.* No. 157 ⁋1 The many Heart-aches and Terrors, to which our Childhood is exposed in going through a Grammar-School. **1809** KENDALL *Trav.* III. lxxvii. 197 It differs therefore in nothing from the other grammar schools, called academies. **1858** DE QUINCEY *Autobiog. Sk.* Wks. II. 268 At the little town of Hawkshead..a grammar-school (which, in English usage, means a school for classical literature) was founded. **1874** GREEN *Short Hist.* vi. §4. 305 The grammar schools of Edward the Sixth and of Elizabeth..had changed the very face of England. **1876** BANCROFT *Hist. U.S.* V. xxii. 577 They provided for a school in each town, a grammar-school in each county, and a university in the state. **1963** BARNARD & LAUWERYS *Handbk. Brit. Educ. Terms* 101 *Grammar school*,..The term nowadays is used for a secondary school with an academic curriculum, particularly suited for preparing pupils for entry to the universities or professions.

attrib. **1826** SYD. SMITH *Wks.* (1869) 529 An Hamiltonian makes, in six or seven lessons, three or four hundred times as many exchanges of English for French or Latin, as a grammar schoolboy can do. **1898** J. K. JEROME *Second Thoughts of Idle Fellow* 266, I like to think of him [Shakespeare] as poacher, as village ne'er-do-well, denounced by the local grammar-school master.

2. *U.S.* 'In the system of graded common schools in the United States, the grade or department in which English grammar is one of the subjects taught' (*Cent. Dict.*).

1860 WORCESTER, *Grammar-School*..2. A school next in rank above a primary school and below a high school. (U.S.) **18..** *Amer. Cycl.* VI. 424 (Cent.) After passing through the primary grade..the pupil enters the grammar school.

grammarye, variant of GRAMARYE.

†**grammates**, *sb. pl. Obs.*[−1] [? ad. Gr. γράμματα, pl. of γράμμα letter.] Rudiments; first principles.

1633 FORD *Broken Hrt.* I. iii, C 2 b, These Apish boyes, when they but tast the Grammates, And principals of Theory, imagine They can oppose their teachers.

grammatic (ɡrəˈmætɪk), *a.* [ad. L. *grammaticus*, ad. Gr. γραμματικ-ός, f. γράμματ-, γράμμα letter. See -IC.] = GRAMMATICAL *a.* 1 and 2.

1599 H. BUTTES *Dyets drie Dinner* E viij, Other expound it mystically, and not according to the grammaticke sense. **1644** MILTON *Educ.* Wks. (1738) I. 136 They [Novices] having but newly left those Grammatic Flats and Shallows ..do for the most part grow into hatred and contempt of learning. *c* **1645** HOWELL *Lett.* I. II. §5 xxvii. (1650) 164 To frame Grammatic toiles to curb her. **1762** WARBURTON *Doctr. Grace* I. viii. Wks. 1788 IV. 575 What was thus inspired was the terms together with that grammatic congruity in the use of them, which is dependent thereon. **1814** W. TAYLOR in *Monthly Rev.* LXXIII. 455 Grammatic studies were understood at Alexandria to comprehend all that we call philology. **1829** *Blackw. Mag.* XXVI. 504 True wisdom all grammatic stuff disowns. **1884** *Science* III. 794/2 To judge from their lexical and grammatic character, the dialects have evolved in the following historic order from the parent language.

grammatical (ɡrəˈmætɪkəl), *a.* [f. as prec. + -AL[1]. Cf. F. *grammatical* (1536 in Hatz.-Darm.).]

1. a. Of or pertaining to grammar.

grammatical gender: the kind of gender (found in the great majority of Indo-European and Semitic langs.) which is not determined by the real or attributed sex; opposed to *natural gender*.

1530 PALSGR., Ep. Ded. v, The accidentes..and other preceptes grammaticall. *a* **1586** SIDNEY *Arcadia* II. (1633) 122 The beautie of vertue..taught them with far more diligent care, than grammatical rules. **1591** PERCIVALL *Sp. Dict.* Gram. B, I haue taken in hand to deale with this Grammaticall treatise. **1603** FLORIO *Montaigne* II. xii. 305 Most of the occasions of this worlds troubles are Grammatical. Our sutes and processes proceed but from the canvasing and debating the interpretation of the Lawes. **1620** GRANGER *Div. Logike* 127 Grammaticall comparison: which hath two degrees, comparative, and superlative. **1644** BULWER *Chiron.* 98 Glancing at the same Grammaticall expressions. **1781** WARTON *Hist. Eng. Poetry* Diss. iii. (1840) I. p. cciv, Berchorius probably compiled this work for the use of his grammatical pupils. **1804** BP. HORSLEY *Serm. on Christ's Descent* 13 It is of great importance to remark, though it may seem a grammatical nicety, that the prepositions..have been supplied by the translators. **1841** BORROW *Zincali* II. II. iii. 140 The pure Gypsy language, with all its grammatical peculiarities. **1875** WHITNEY *Life Lang.* iii. 39 The Anglo-Saxon had grammatical gender.

b. *Logic.* Of or relating to the mere arrangement of words in the sentence or proposition, in contrast to its logical structure. So esp. ***grammatical form, subject.*** (Opp. *logical form*, etc.)

1874 W. S. JEVONS *Princ. Sci.* vi. 137 Another..difficulty is to decide when a change is merely grammatical and when it involves a real logical transformation. Between a *table of wood* and a *wooden table* there is no logical difference. **1883** F. H. BRADLEY *Princ. Logic* I. i. §17 It is false that the grammatical subject is the reality of which the predicate is held true, yet in every judgment there must be a subject. *Ibid.* III. I. ii. 394 But this differs from the result given by Professor Jevons in nothing except grammatical form. **1903** B. RUSSELL *Princ. Math.* iv. 48 The question is: what logical difference is expressed by the difference of grammatical form? **1910** —— in Whitehead & Russell *Principia Mathematica* I. Introd. iii. 66 The proposition must be capable of being so analysed that what was the grammatical subject shall have disappeared. **1933** L. S. STEBBING *Mod. Introd. Logic* (ed. 2) ix. 153 The point that is of importance is to distinguish the *grammatical* subject of a sentence from the *logical* subject of the proposition expressed by the sentence. **1951** A. FLEW *Ess. on Logic & Lang.* 7 It would be absurd, but it would also be easy, to be misled by the grammatical similarity of 'It goes on to London' to 'It goes on to Infinity'. **1959** P. F. STRAWSON *Individuals* II. v. 148 Grammatical classifications do not unequivocally or clearly declare their own logical rationale.

c. *Philol.* ***grammatical change*** [tr. G. *grammatischer wechsel*]: the system of contrasting consonants found in the strong verb in Germanic languages, exemplifying Verner's Law.

1926 *Language* II. 177 Another article by Braune..on what he calls 'The Grammatical Change in the Inflection of the German Verb'. **1934** PRIEBSCH & COLLINSON *German Lang.* II. i. 95 Grammatical change (*grammatischer Wechsel*), which is limited in Gothic to a few cases..is well preserved in O.H.G. **1963** J. T. WATERMAN *Perspectives in Linguistics* 49 Grimm..had been especially impressed by the curious interplay of stop and spirant in the morphology of the strong verb, applying the term 'grammatical change' to this phenomenon.

d. Of languages: having relatively greater structural resources, and relying less on lexical richness.

1937 J. ORR tr. *Iordan's Introd. Romance Ling.* 287 Where there is greater solidarity between the semantic and the formal associations, the signs appear less arbitrary, and these he [*sc.* Saussure] calls grammatical languages. **1959** W. BASKIN tr. *Saussure's Course in Gen. Linguistics* II. vi. 133 We might say that languages in which there is least motivation are more lexicological, and those in which it is greatest are more grammatical. **1962** S. ULLMANN *Semantics* iv. 105 It was one of Saussure's most important discoveries that the proportion of transparent and opaque words varies characteristically... 'Grammatical' languages..favour the transparent type.

2. ***grammatical sense***: that sense of a text which is obtained by the simple application of the rules of grammar to the words, without reference to any extraneous considerations; the literal sense. So ***grammatical category, feature, form, meaning, interpretation,*** †***translation, word*** (see quots.).

1526 *Pilgr. Perf.* (W. de W. 1531) 211 b, As the lettre of these wordes (as to the grammaticall sense) pretendeth or sheweth. **1597** HOOKER *Eccl. Pol.* v. xiii. (1611) 205 In as much as by plaine grammaticall construction Church doth signifie no other thing than the Lords house. **1651** HOBBES *Leviath.* IV. liv. 350 They had not transgressed the Grammaticall sense thereof. **1654** R. WHITLOCK *Zootomia* Pref. a vj, As for my declining in many places Grammaticall Translations, it is to bring the Sense neerer my Purpose. **1769** *Junius Lett.* xix. 88, I trouble not myself with the grammatical meaning of the word expulsion; I regard only its legal meaning. **1891** H. A. STRONG et al. *Hist. Lang.* xx. 343 The grammatical categories of substantive, adjective, and verb correspond to the logical categories of substance, quality, and..occurrence. **1924** O. JESPERSEN *Philos. Gram.* ii. 44 The paradigmatic arrangement is not one of grammatical form. *Ibid.* iii. 54 The grammatical category of number evidently corresponds to the distinction found in the outside world between 'one' and 'more than one'. **1925** P. RADIN tr. *Vendryes' Lang.* ii. 90 To the concepts expressed by means of morphemes, we give the name grammatical categories. Thus, gender, number, person, tense and mood, interrogation and negation,..etc., are grammatical categories in languages where these concepts are expressed by special morphemes. **1933** BLOOMFIELD *Lang.* x. 166 A simple feature of grammatical arrangement is a grammatical feature or taxeme... The utterance *Run!*, for example, contains two grammatical features (taxemes), namely, the modulation..and the selective feature. *Ibid.*, The smallest meaningful units of grammatical form may be spoken of as tagmemes. *Ibid.* 169 Some pitch-scheme.., in English at any rate, lends it a grammatical meaning such as 'statement', 'yes-or-no question', 'supplement-question', or 'exclamation'. *Ibid.*, The grammatical forms of a language can be grouped into three great classes. **1958** C. F. HOCKETT *Course in Mod. Ling.* xxvii. 231 A *specific* grammatical category is an element in a system or a class in a classification: English plural, Spanish masculine, Latin accusative. **1963** *Listener* 3 Jan. 21/2 The feeling of climax comes..from increasing syntactical concentration. More merely grammatical words—'see', 'are', 'was', 'is'—are omitted. **1964** M. JOOS *Eng. Verb* iv. 81 The necessity of distinguishing between lexical meaning and grammatical meaning. **1966** G. N. LEECH *Eng. in Advertising* ix. 88 'Grammatical words' such as prepositions, pronouns, and auxiliary verbs. **1968** M. BLACK *Labyrinth of Lang.* iv. 85 The totality of rules that determine the correct use of a given word or expression may be said to specify the grammatical form of that word or expression.

3. Of speech, composition, etc.: Conforming to the rules of grammar.

1752 JOHNSON *Rambler* No. 206 ¶11, I have laboured to refine our language to grammatical purity. **1861** CRAIK *Eng. Lit. & Lang.* II. 538 [Carlyle's style is] with all its startling qualities, one of the most exactly grammatical in our literature. *Mod.* The sentence is grammatical, but not quite idiomatic.

4. *transf.* Of or pertaining to, also strictly conforming to the 'grammar' or formal principles of an art.

1846 RUSKIN *Mod. Paint.* II. II. i. §20 The..grammatical accuracy of the tones of Turner. **1890** *Anthony's Photogr. Bull.* III. 426 To secure 'grammatical' or perspective truth the horizon line of such background must be brought opposite the lens.

b. *Mus.* ***grammatical accent***: the accent regularly occurring at the beats of a bar; opposed to *oratorical accent*.

1833 *Penny Cycl.* I. 72/2. **1889** H. C. BANISTER *Music* (ed. 14) §362.

†**5.** *absol.* and *sb. pl.* The subjects taught in a grammar-school. *Obs.*

1691 WOOD *Athen. Oxon.* I. 12 John Constable.. Educated in Grammaticals under William Lilye, in Academicals in an antient Hostle sometimes called Byhem ..Hall. **1716** M. DAVIES *Athen. Brit.* II. 328 Robert Talbot ..He was educated in Grammaticals in Wikeham-School.

Hence **gra'mmaticalness**, the quality of being grammatical.

1650 *Vindic. Hammond's Addr.* 43 §88 To justifie the Grammaticalnesse of these words. **1897** F. HALL in *Nation* (N.Y.) LXIV. 357/2 Not without entertaining a very original notion of grammaticalness can Mr. Philpson say what he says about *expect*.

grammaticality (grəˌmætɪ'kælɪtɪ). *Linguistics.* [f. prec. + -ITY.] The quality of being grammatical (sense 3).

1961 A. A. HILL in *Word* XVII. 1 (*title*) Grammaticality. **1965** *Language* XLI. 403 Within such a framework, deviance as well as grammaticality can tentatively be made explicit. **1968** J. LYONS *Introd. Theoret. Ling.* ix. 422 Grammaticality is that part of the acceptability of utterances which can be accounted for in terms of the rules.

grammaticalize (grə'mætɪkəlaɪz), *v.* *Linguistics.* [f. GRAMMATICAL *a.* + -IZE.] To express by means of the grammatical structure; to adopt as a grammatical requirement. Usu. in *pass.*

1937 J. ORR tr. *Iordan's Introd. Romance Ling.* 337 A similar order [*sc.* inversion in interrog. sentences] is observable in other languages, but has not become 'grammaticalized' as in French. **1961** *Brno Studies* III. 10 The position of the word within the sentence context is grammaticalized to a much higher degree in analytical than in synthetic languages. **1968** J. LYONS *Introd. Theoret. Ling.* ix. 438 We cannot assume..that such notions..will necessarily be 'grammaticalized', rather than 'lexicalized', in the structure of any particular language.

Hence **graˌmmaticali'zation**, the action or process of grammaticalizing.

1955 *Archivum Linguisticum* VII. I. 28 The affectivity of reprise has been weakened by grammaticalization. **1965** *Language* XLI. 107 The creation of oppositions through grammaticalization.

grammatically (grə'mætɪkəlɪ), *adv.* [f. GRAMMATICAL *a.* + -LY[2].] In a grammatical manner.

1. In accordance with the rules of grammar.

1589 FLEMING (*title*) The Georgiks of Publius Virgilius Maro.. Grammaticallie translated into English meter by A. F. **1651** HOBBES *Leviath.* IV. xliv. 341 Which words, if taken grammatically [etc.]. *a* **1661** FULLER *Worthies, Yorksh.* (1662) III. 189 This is called the Petrifying well (how grammatically I will not engage). **1720** WATERLAND *Serm. Christ's Divinity* vi. Wks. 1823 II. 128 The words will grammatically bear this construction. **1776** *Trial of Nundocomar* 52/2 He..speaks it [Moors] more grammatically than common Bengalers do. **1802** SYD. SMITH *Wks.* (1867) I. 13 Those who write grammatically, and those who do not. **1865** E. C. CLAYTON *Cruel Fortune* II. 220 To ascertain whether it was grammatically correct and properly spelt.

2. In accordance with the 'grammar' or rules of an art. (For quot. 1477 cf. GRAMARYE 2.)

1477 NORTON *Ord. Alch.* v. in Ashm. (1652) 59 Conjoyne your Elements Grammatically. **1883** *Harper's Mag.* Sept. 571/2 These works of Mr. Haight's are grammatically 'correct' Gothic.

grammaticaster (grə'mætɪkæstə(r)). Also 7 grammaticastre. [ad. med.L. *grammaticaster* 'scriba, notarius', f. *grammatic-us*; see GRAMMATIC and -ASTER.] A petty or inferior grammarian. (Used in contempt.)

1601 B. JONSON *Poetaster* I, He tells thee true, my noble neophyte; my little grammaticaster, he does. **1659** PECKE *Parnassi Puerperium* 21 Upon Hallus the Grammaticastre. **1716** M. DAVIES *Athen. Brit.* I. 23 He was censur'd as a vain and noisy Grammaticaster..by the most intelligent part of his Profession. **1880** M. COLLINS *Th. in Garden* I. 20 The construction..would have been clear enough to the keenest grammaticaster.

†**grammatication.** *Obs.* [f. GRAMMATIC + -ATION.] A grammatical discussion; a discussion of points in grammar.

1582 G. MARTIN *Discov. Corrupt. Script.* vii. §43. 131 Gentle Reader, beare with these tedious grammatications, fitter to be handled in Latin, but necessarie in this case also. **1680** DALGARNO *Didascalophos* vi. 52 Being free from all anomoly, æquivocalness, redundancy, and unnecessary Grammatications.

gra'mmaticism. Now *rare.* [f. GRAMMATIC + -ISM.] A point or principle of grammar; a grammatical definition.

1610 HEALEY *St. Aug. Citie of God* 421 Wee may not drawe (nay wrest) the gospell to those grammaticismes. *a* **1634** LEIGHTON *Comm.* 1 *Pet.* ii. 25 If we would contest Grammaticisms, the word here is passive. **1678** OWEN *Mind of God* viii. 227 Other Glossaries from whose Grammaticismes and Vocabularys some do countenance themselves in curious and bold conjectures. **1836** G. S. FABER *Answ. Husenbeth* 19 *note*, A brother Romanist..could readily point out an undoubted inaccurate translation of an exactly parallel grammaticism as made by a protestant divine.

grammaticize (grə'mætɪsaɪz), *v.* [f. GRAMMATIC + -IZE.]

1. *trans.* To render grammatical; to reduce to grammatical rules.

1780 JOHNSON in *Boswell* lxx. (1848) 660/1, I always said, Shakspeare had Latin enough to grammaticize his English. **1811** NICHOLS *Fuller's Worthies, Wales* II. 561 *note*, This was the very first attempt to embody, to arrange, or to grammaticize this language. **1837** J. E. MURRAY *Summer in Pyrenées* I. 42 Prior to the period when Democritus grammaticised the Latin language.

2. *intr.* To discuss grammatical points.

1673 BP. WARD *Apol. Myst. Gosp.* 44 Gramaticizing pedantically, and criticising spuriously, upon a few Greek Particles.

grammatist ('græmətɪst). [ad. F. *grammatiste*, ad. med.L. *grammatista*, ad. Gr. γραμματιστής, f. γράμματ-, γράμμα letter. Cf. F. *grammatiste* (1575 in Hatz.-Darm.).] **a.** A grammarian, a student of grammar; chiefly used disparagingly. **b.** After Greek usage: A teacher of letters.

1589 FLEMING *Virg. Georg.* To Rdr., A direct order of construction for the releefe of weake Grammatists. **1609** HOLLAND *Amm. Marcell.* XIV. v. Annot. a ij, *Eculei*..Not instruments of burning plates, like unto an horse..like as some Grammatists have imagined. **1635** BRATHWAIT *Arcad. Pr.* 170 Rhemnius Palæmon, that arrogant Grammarian, or rather Grammatist. **1798–1805** TOOKE *Div. Purley* (1860) 101 *note*, The constant excuse of them all, whether Grammatists, Grammarians, or Philosophers. **1849** GROTE *Greece* II. lxv. VIII. 351 A general suppression of the higher class of teachers or professors, above the rank of the elementary (teacher of letters or) grammatist.

Hence **gramma'tistical** *a.*, befitting a grammatist.

1837 LANDOR *Pentameron* Wks. 1846 II. 323/1 The affectation of Ovid was light and playful; Virgil's was wilful, perverse, and grammatistical.

grammatite ('græmətaɪt). *Min.* [Named in 1801 by Haüy, f. Gr. γράμματ-, γράμμα, letter, line, in allusion to a line seen on some of the crystals: see -ITE.] A synonym of tremolite.

1802 *Paris as it was* II. lxix. 387 Tremolite or grammatite of Haüy, in the same place. **1813** *Amer. Min. Jrnl.* IV. 229 Grammatite or Tremolite is found among the limestone. **1868** DANA *Min.* 233.

†'**grammatol.** *Obs. rare*[−1]. In 6 **gramatol.** [Arbitrary formation, app. suggested by L. *grammaticus* and *-olus* dim. ending.] A smatterer.

a **1529** SKELTON *Sp. Parrot* 319 Nodypollys and gramatolys of smalle intellygens.

grammatolatry (græmə'tɒlətrɪ). [f. Gr. γραμματο-, combining form of γράμμα letter + λατρεία worship: see -LATRY.] The worship of letters; adherence to the letter (of Scripture). So **gramma'tolator** [cf. *idolator*], a stickler for the forms of words.

1847 BUCH tr. *Hagenbach's Hist. Doctr.* II. 230 This rigid adherence to the very letter of Scripture (Grammatolatry). **1869** *Southern Rev.* July 42 Webster and Trench are both guilty of grammatolatry, in regarding certain changes in words as 'details of spelling'. *Ibid.*, As a grammatolator he follows certain dictionaries..in suppressing a useful word pronounced *pleat*, by making it sound like *plate*, because book-makers present it under the form of 'plait'. **1871** R. D. OWEN *Debatable Land* 99 The worship of words is more pernicious than the worship of images; grammatolatry is the worst species of idolatry.

grammatophore ('græmətəfɔə(r)). [f. Gr. γραμματο- (see prec.) + -φορος bearing.] A book-name for the Australian genus *Grammatophora* of lizards, esp. *G. muricata*.

1845 J. E. GRAY *Catal. Lizards B.M.* 251 The Grammatophore. *Grammatophora muricata.*

gramme[1]: see GRAM[2].

Gramme[2] (græm). The name of the Belgian electrician Zénobe Théophile *Gramme* (1826–1901), used attrib. to designate a form of dynamo armature introduced by him in 1870 (***Gramme ring, armature, winding,*** etc.).

1884 F. KROHN tr. *Glaser de Cew's Magn. & Dyn.-Electr. Mach.* 255 The inductive actions in the coils of a Gramme ring. *Ibid.*, The ring of the Gramme machine. **1893** HAWKINS & WALLIS *Dynamo* 115 The first or 'Ring' method ..is also frequently called the 'Gramme' winding. *Ibid.* 193

In the Gramme-wound ring armature the number of loops and the number of inductors are identical.

grammer, obs. form of GRAMMAR.

grammercies, -mersies, pl. ff. GRAMERCY.

grammetre (ˌgræmˈmiːtə(r)). [f. GRAM², GRAMME + METRE.] A unit of 'work', being that done in raising a mass of one gramme vertically to the height of one metre.

1873 in *Rep. Brit. Assoc.* 225 The unit of work being but little more than the hundred thousandth part of a grammetre.

†**ˈgrammic**, *a. Obs.*—⁰ [ad. Gr. γραμμικ-ός linear, f. γραμμή line.] (See quot.)

1727 BAILEY vol. II, *Grammick*, made by Lines; demonstrated by Lines. Also **1730–6** (folio).

grammite (ˈgræmaɪt). *Min.* [Named in 1802 by Karsten (*Grammit*), f. Gr. γραμμή line, from its fibrous appearance: see -ITE.] Obsolete synonym of wollastonite.

1826 EMMONS *Min.* 216. **1854** DANA *Min.* 156.

grammopetalous (ˌgræməʊˈpɛtələs), *a. Bot.* [f. *grammo-*, irreg. comb. form of Gr. γραμμή line + πέταλον leaf + -OUS.] Having linear petals.

1847 in CRAIG; and in later Dicts.

Grammy (ˈgræmɪ). orig. *U.S.* [f. GRAM⁴ (*b*) or GRAM(OPHONE, after EMMY.] Any of several golden statuettes awarded annually for outstanding achievement in the recording industry by the American National Academy of Recording Arts and Sciences; also used as a proprietary service mark (*U.S.*) with reference to these awards.

1959 *Variety* 30 Sept. 45/5 The National Assn. of Recording Arts & Sciences' all-out membership drive prior to its first Grammy Award Show..has already been bolstered by 200 new members. *Ibid.* 7 Oct. 63/4 (*heading*) Nominations for Grammys. **1968** *N.Y. Times* 16 June 68/5 Another album, 'Goin' Out of My Head', won a Grammy award as the best instrumental jazz performance of 1966. **1970** *Official Gaz.* (U.S. Patent Office) 10 Mar. TM86 Service Marks. Class 100... *Grammy.* National Academy of Recording Arts and Sciences. **1977** *Rolling Stone* 5 May 31/2 Getting something like a Grammy nomination means a lot. **1984** *Sounds* 1 Dec. 22/6 So they stuck out two independent albums,..put out an EP on Slash, got a grammy and have now released an album.

gramoche, variant of GRAMASH.

gramophile (ˈgræməfaɪl). [f. GRAMO(PHONE + -PHILE.] An enthusiast of the gramophone and gramophone records.

1922 C. MACKENZIE in *Daily Tel.* 2 Sept. 5/3, I wish Stevenson could have had a gramophone in Samoa... I feel sure that he would have become a 'gramophile'. **1926** *Gramophone* IV. 294/2 The price of the instrument..(£120) is such that the number of gramophiles who could afford to possess one must be strictly limited. **1927** *Observer* 11 Dec. 22/3 Records of Ravel's Quartet in F..that have received the composer's imprimatur. They will..please the increasing number of gramophiles who look to the [National Gramophonic] society for work of particular excellence. **1932** *Gramophone* July 60 (*heading*) Borodin for the gramophile. **1958** *Times* 19 Apr. 7/3 The ordinary gramophile is beginning to demand his high fidelity as a packaged whole.

gramophone (ˈgræməfəʊn), *sb.* Also **grammophone.** [app. formed by inversion of PHONOGRAM. The spelling *grammo-* (not the inventor's) is an attempt to make the word look more like a correct formation.] **1.** An instrument for the reproduction of recorded sound, similar in principle to the phonograph but using, instead of a drum, a flat disc containing a spiral groove; a stylus is allowed to rest in the groove as the disc is rotated on a turntable, and the vibrations communicated to the stylus by the iregularities in the groove are transformed into sound vibrations. (In the U.S., *phonograph* is the generic name for such an instrument.) In its modern form, with an electric motor, electronic amplification, and one or more loud-speakers, it is now more commonly termed a 'record-player'.

The earliest gramophones were also used to cut records, using blank discs.

1887 *Pat. Off. Gaz.* 8 Nov. 620/2 Gramophone [patented by] Emile Berliner, Washington, D.C. **1888** *Times* 13 Jan. 12/3 His [Edison's] original phonograph has received important modifications.. in..Mr. Berliner's grammophone. **1896** *Critic* 21 Nov. 322/2 A man who uses a gramophone..talks into his machine, and hands the records over to his typewriter, who reads them off on her gramophone, and writes them out on the typewriter. **1899** E. WHARTON *Greater Inclination* 59 Her voice..was like a voice reproduced by a gramophone: the real woman seemed far away. **1906** *Daily Chron.* 26 Nov. 4/7 What's wearing me to skin and bone? My neighbour's grinding gramophone. **1913** B. CLEMENTS-HENRY *Gramophones & Phonographs* 5 The disc machine is known as the 'gramophone', and the cylinder machine as the 'phonograph'. **1917** A. WAUGH *Loom of Youth* II. i. 89 Every night closed with a feed in Mansell's big study, while the gramophone strummed out rag-time choruses. **1921** P. A. SCHOLES *Learning to Listen* p. xv, The accumulated results of their already large experience of the educational use of the Gramophone. **1922** O. MITCHELL *Talking Machine Industry* iv. 31 The gramophone, or disc machine, has..practically ousted the older invention from the English market. **1923** T. S. ELIOT *Waste Land* III. 256 She smoothes her hair with automatic hand, And puts a record on the gramophone. **1928** GALSWORTHY *Swan Song* II. iv. 140 'What is the most pitiable sight in the world?'.. 'Oh! I think—a rich man listening to a bad gramophone.' **1952** GODFREY & AMOS *Sound Recording & Reproduction* i. 33 The chief advantage of the gramophone over the phonograph as claimed by Berliner was this comparatively simple method of producing copies. **1955** *Times* 3 May 6/2, 10s. notes were found stuffed in the horn of a gramophone in his bedroom. **1967** *Times Rev. Industry* Mar. 41/3 The Gramophone Co. was refused the right to the trade mark 'Gramophone' in 1910. **1971** *Daily Tel.* 4 Nov. 12/4 Antoine speaks posthumously to the back-biting assembly through the horn of a 1913 gramophone.

2. *attrib.* and *Comb.*, as ***gramophone bank, needle, pick-up, recital, rights***; **gramophone-cut**, the form of record-cutting in which the recording stylus vibrates parallel to the surface of the disc; **gramophone record**, a flat disc on which sound has been recorded for reproduction by a gramophone, the recording taking the form of a spiral groove usu. starting at the periphery.

1941 *B.B.C. Gloss. Broadc. Terms* 14 *Gramophone bank*, group of turn-tables and other equipment for playing gramophone records or disc recordings. **1913** B. CLEMENTS-HENRY *Gramophones & Phonographs* 4 The so-called 'gramophone-cut'. **1907** *Yesterday's Shopping* (1969) 1038/1 Only genuine Gramophone Needles should be used to play Gramophone Records. **1960** J. RAE *Custard Boys* I. v. 51 When he spoke it sounded as though a gramophone-needle was scratching across worn grooves in his throat. **1929** WILSON & WEBB *Mod. Gramophones* x. 230 The change-over from radio to gramophone pick-up is effected by means of a switch. **1962** A. NISBETT *Technique Sound Studio* 247 *Crystal microphone or gramophone pick-up.* This generates a signal by means of a crystal bimorph. **1913** G. F. ROWELL *Hints about Gramophone* 11 A gramophone recital. **1888** *English Mechanic* 24 Aug. 558/2 (*heading*) The preparation of grammophone and telephone records. **1918–19** *T. Eaton & Co. Catal.* Fall & Winter 369/2 The Gramophone Record Needles here listed..are made of good hard steel. **1924** P. A. SCHOLES *1st Bk. Gramophone Rec.* p. vii, Many of the best 'tunes'..await their enjoyment in the form of Gramophone Records. **1941** *Libr. Assoc. Rec.* Aug. 149/1 The report..records that Herefordshire County Library is one of the few possessors of a Gramophone Record Library in the country. **1947** *Ibid.* Sept. 224 (*title*) A gramophone record library service. *Ibid.* 224/1 The gramophone record library..comes at a time when there is a growing demand for music by the best artists. **1964** P. J. GUY *Disc Recording & Reproduction* v. 68 Up till a few years after the last world war, nearly all gramophone records were recorded at 78 r.p.m. with coarse grooves..and would accommodate only 4–4½ minutes of programme on a 12-in. record. **1971** *Radio Times* 16/23 Dec. 26/4 8.0 am. News... 8.5 Aubade. Gramophone records of music by Parry, Delius, Elgar, and Grainger. **1921** A. E. HOUSMAN *Let.* 20 Mar. (1971) 184, I do not want revenue from gramophone and mechanical rights.

ˈgramophone, *v.* [f. the sb.] *trans.* To reproduce by means of the gramophone; to record for the gramophone. Also *fig.* and *absol.* Hence **ˈgramophoned** *ppl. a.*

1908 *Daily Chron.* 8 Apr. 3/7 The Tories are canvassing, 'gramophoning', &c. **1926** G. B. SHAW *Let.* 14 Sept. (1960) 104 Albert Coates has gone to London for 10 days to gramophone the Ninth Symphony. **1927** *Sunday Express* 28 Aug. 5/2 America's noise was gramophoned everywhere. **1928** *Manch. Guardian Weekly* 10 Aug. 113/4 The perils of a syndicated or grammophoned press. **1931** *Times Lit. Suppl.* 17 Dec. 1024/3 If it be true that the novel..is to be dramatized, filmed, gramophoned and everything else, one can only remark that this is another example of the incalculability of public taste. **1935** N. MITCHISON *We have been Warned* IV. 463 Bubbling voices and laughter, penetrated by gramophoned jazz.

gramophonic (græməˈfɒnɪk), *a.* [-IC.] Of, pertaining to, or of the nature of the gramophone or gramophone records.

1905 *Westm. Gaz.* 2 Sept. 9/1 She has what I call a 'gramophonic mind'—that is, she assimilates other people's ideas and then rolls them off as if they were her own. **1915** *Morning Post* 4 Mar. 4/4 A gramophonic reproduction of a tune which was being played in Berlin. **1921** P. A. SCHOLES *Learning to Listen* p. xiv, The illustrated volume to which this one is, frankly, a gramophonic companion. **1927** *Observer* 24 Apr. 4/3 The National Gramophonic Society.. issues the first of its orchestral records. **1946** *Penguin Music Mag.* I. 122 That a margin of extra time should be allowed —to be filled up if necessary by the time-honoured gramophonic stop-gap. **1965** *Listener* 3 June 837/2 Recording Wagner's *Götterdämmerung*... The biggest achievement in gramophonic history.

Hence **gramoˈphonically** *adv.*, in a gramophonic manner; by or on a gramophone.

1911 W. J. LOCKE *Clementina Wing* xx, A stupendous woolly lamb..which, on something being done to its anatomy, opened its mouth and gramophonically chanted the 'Jewel Song' from Faust. **1913** *Christian* 3 Jan. 10/1 To find..the daily Press..giving voice to facts instead of gramophonically repeating the sentiments uttered by huge vested interests. **1924** P. A. SCHOLES *1st Bk. Gramophone Rec.* 30 The only piece of our great Purcell gramophonically available was the song *Nymphs and Shepherds.* **1948** *Scrutiny* XV. 337 The now gramophonically celebrated Concertgebouw Orchestra.

gramophonist (græˈmɒfənɪst, ˈgræməfəʊnɪst). [-IST.] One who uses or operates a gramophone; a 'gramophile'. (Not in current use.)

1907 *Daily Chron.* 12 Dec. 7/4 The gramophonist will redistribute the pearls of wisdom which have fallen from the lips of great Unionist statesmen to crowds of admiring villagers. **1923** *Weekly Dispatch* 4 Feb. 2, I must modestly disclaim being a passionate gramophonist (if that is the word). **1924** P. A. SCHOLES *1st Bk. Gramophone Rec.* 123 The description..will..be thought sufficient by many gramophonists. **1934** C. STONE in H. C. Bryson *Gramophone Record* p. xii, The true gramophonist will prefer to melt an old worn-out favourite and shape it into a flower-bowl.. rather than to drop it into the dustbin.

gramophony (græˈmɒfənɪ, ˈgræməfəʊnɪ). [f. GRAMOPHONE, after *telephony*.] The art of the gramophone; gramophonic reproduction. (Not in current use.)

1925 P. A. SCHOLES *2nd Bk. Gramophone Rec.* p. xix, It is one of the regrettable features of gramophony to-day that the songs of Schubert..are not to be obtained. **1927** *Daily Mirror* 10 Dec. 12/3 An impression is rapidly gaining ground that the whole future of gramophony rests with the electrical 'pick-up'.

gramory, gramowrie, vars. GRAMARYE.

gramp (græmp). [Abbrev. of GRANDPAPA.] A colloq. or dial. substitute for *grandfather*.

1898 in *Eng. Dial. Dict.* **1912** A. N. LYONS *Clara* xxvii. 297 'You see,' explained the maiden, 'we be going to Gramp's.' **1959** E. POUND *Thrones* xcvi. 4 And a wolf acting as guide Till it thought gramp looked too hungry. **1966** 'L. LANE' *ABZ of Scouse* II. 25 That ther kid's ther dead spit of 'is gramp.

grampas(se, obs. form of GRAMPUS.

†**ˈgrampell.** *Obs.* Also 7 **crampell, grample.** [Cf. obs. F. *grampelle* (Cotgr.).] A kind of crab.

1598 FLORIO, *Paguro*, a kind of creuis or crafish called a grit, a grampell, or a punger. **1608** TOPSELL *Serpents* 312 The Sea-fish called Gryff or Grample. **1611** FLORIO, *Màia*, a kind of Crab called a Crampell.

grampisce, -pois, -pos, obs. ff. GRAMPUS.

grampus (ˈgræmpəs). Forms: 6 **graundepose, grampoys,** 7 **grampas(se, -pisce, -po(i)s, grandpisce,** (*pl.* **granspices**), 8 **grampuss,** 7– **grampus.** [Early 16th c. *graundepose*, app. an etymologizing alteration (after GRAND *a.*) of the earlier GRAPEYS of the same meaning. Most of the forms of the last syll. are paralleled in the case of PORPOISE *sb.*; but some show assimilation to L. *piscis* fish.]

1. The popular name of various delphinoid cetaceans, having a high falcate dorsal fin and a blunt rounded head, and remarkable for the spouting and blowing which accompanies their movements.

In popular use, the name seems to be more frequently applied to the formidable 'killer' (*Orca gladiator*). But it is also applied to an inoffensive cetacean resembling this in size and general appearance, but differing in the smaller size and number of the teeth. For the latter, which Cuvier had placed in the genus *Delphinus*, the Eng. word *grampus* was adopted by J. E. Gray, 1846, as a mod.L. generic name; the only species certainly determined is *G. griseus*, sometimes called *cow-fish*. According to some authorities, the name is also applied to the pilot- or ca'ing whale (*Globice-phalus*).

a **1529** SKELTON *Sp. Parrot* 309 With porpose and graundepose he may fede hym fatte. **1593** NASHE *Christ's T.* 15, Sea-monsters, such as the Whale, the Grampoys, the Wasser-man. **1624** CAPT. SMITH *Virginia* VI. 231 We espied eight or ten Saluages about a dead Grampus. **1634** WOOD *New Eng. Prospect* (1865) 36 The snuffing Grampus. **1655** E. TERRY *Voy. E. India* 7 God hath made to take his pastime in the Sea; Granspices, or lesser whales, Sharkes [etc.]. **1674** JOSSELYN *Voy. New Eng.* 10 Here likewise we saw many Grandpisces or Herring-hogs, hunting the scholes of Herrings. **1675** CROWNE *Country Wit* II. Dram. Wks. 1874 III. 39 My master is a leviathan in love, and I am a very grampois. **1686** GOAD *Celest. Bodies* II. viii. 264, I do not add the Legend of Two Grampisces stranded, or taken at Greenwich. **1755** T. H. CROKER *Orl. Fur.* VI. xxxvi, The grampus and the monsters of the sea Move on disturbed from their accustom'd sloth. **1776** GOLDSMITH *Anim. Nat.* VI. 188 The whale or the grampus are terrible at any time; but are fierce and desperate in the defence of their young. **1812** S. ROGERS *Written in Highlands* 35 The grampus, half-descried, Black and huge above the tide. **1848** DICKENS *Dombey* v, Coughing like a grampus. **1888** *Strange MS. in Copper Cylinder* 12 All around us..grampuses were gambolling.

b. *Naut.* phr. ***to blow the grampus*** (see quots.).

1829 MARRYAT *F. Mildmay* iv, The buckets of water which were..poured over me by the midshipmen, under the facetious appellation of 'blowing the grampus'..could [not] rouse my dormant energies. **1867** SMYTH *Sailor's Word-bk.* 346 *Blowing the grampus*, sluicing a person with water, especially practised on him who skulks or sleeps on his watch.

c. *transf.* A person given to puffing and blowing.

1836 DICKENS *Pickwick* xxv, 'The boy breathes so very hard while he's eating, that we found it impossible to sit at table with him'. 'Young grampus!' said Mr. Weller. **1851** MAYNE REID *Scalp Hunt.* vi. 47 The blustering old grampus of a governor is to honour the ball with his presence.

2. *Metallurgy.* (See quot.)

1881 RAYMOND *Mining Gloss.*, *Grampus* (U.S.), the tongs with which bloomary loups and billets are handled.

3. *attrib.* and *Comb.*, as ***grampus-oil***; also **grampus-whale** = sense 1.

1883 *Fisheries Exhib. Catal.* 202 *Grampus oil, used for lubricating fine machinery. **1744** tr. *Boerhaave's Instit. Med.* 191 The *Grampus Whale. **1879** *Daily News* 23 Aug. 6/2 A large cetacean called a grampus whale.

†**gran**[1]. *Obs. rare*$^{-1}$. [? Short for GRANDFATHER; cf. *gaffer*.] A jocular term for a rustic.

1592 GREENE *Conny Catching* II. 4 Meanely attired like some plaine gran of the Countrey.

gran[2] (græn). A childish or familiar shortening of *granny* or *grandmother*.

1863 DICKENS in *All Year Round* 3 Dec. 11/2 And now dear Gran let me kneel down here where I have been used to say my prayers. **1890** E. LYTTON *Let.* 16 Apr. in E. Lutyens *Blessed Girl* (1953) iii. 29 Mother had a telegram last night to say that Gran is dead. **1908** *Westm. Gaz.* 8 Feb. 12/3 People say it was just because Gran lived so vividly that she flickered out like a candle come midsummer. *Ibid.*, The lady who received the Grans. **1960** R. DANIEL *Death by Drowning* iii. 40 By the time she gets back to 'Mum' and 'Gran' she'll be wet through. **1960** *Sunday Express* 10 July 15/5 There is Gran Tatlock, tired and crusty after bringing up a family of 11.

gran, obs. form of GROAN *v.*

grana, pl. GRANUM.

†**granada**. *Cookery. Obs.* = GRENADE[2].

1806 A. HUNTER *Culina* (ed. 3) 24 A Granada. Take the caul laid over a leg of veal..put upon it a layer of the flitch part of bacon; then a layer of high-seasoned forcemeat; then [etc.].

granada, -ade, obs. ff. GRENADO, -ADE[1].

granadeer, granadier, obs. ff. GRENADIER.

granadilla, grenadilla (grænə-, grɛnə'dɪlə). Also 7 **granadille**, 7-8 **-dil**, 9 **granadillo**, **grenadillo**. [a. Sp. *granadilla*, dim. of *granada* pomegranate.] A name applied to various tropical species of the Passion-flower; esp. to *Passiflora quadrangularis* or its fruit, which is much esteemed as a dessert fruit.

1613 PURCHAS *Pilgrimage* (1614) 734 The flower of the Granadille they say..hath the markes of the Passion. **1707** *Curios. in Husb. & Gard.* 205 Granadils, or Passion-Flowers. **1741** *Compl. Fam.-Piece* II. iii. 408 We have also.. Granadilla, Guernsey Lilly [etc.]. **1760-72** tr. *Juan & Ulloa's Voy.* (ed. 3) I. 287 The granadilla resembles a hen's egg in shape, but larger. The outside of the shell is smooth and glossy, and of a faint carnation colour, and the inside white and soft. **1786** P. FRENEAU *Santa Cruz* 159 in *Poems* 139 Plump grenadilloes and güavas grey. **1803** T. WINTERBOTTOM *Sierra Leone* I. iii. 57 The [Sierra Leone] company have also introduced..the granadillo. **1825** CALDCLEUGH *Trav. S. Amer.* I. ii. 26 The fruit of the passion flower, or grenadilla of the Spaniards. **1859** R. THOMPSON *Gardener's Assist.* 33 Musas, Granadillas, Guavas, or other tropical plants bearing fruit. **1875** MISS BIRD *Hawaii* 134 Orange blossoms, and the great granadilla or passion flower. **1894** *Times* 31 Jan. 13/5 The tropical verandah, with the grenadillas trained along the latticework.

b. *attrib.*, as ***granadilla vine***; also **granadilla tree**, the *Brya Ebenus* of Jamaica.

1756 P. BROWNE *Jamaica* 327 The Granadilla Vine. This plant..produces an agreeable cooling fruit. **1864** GRISEBACH *Flora W. Ind.* 784 Granadilla tree: *Brya Ebenus.*

Granadine ('grænədiːn), *a.* [ad. Sp. *granadino* pertaining to Granada.] Of or pertaining to Granada, a province of southern Spain (formerly a Moorish kingdom).

1865 H. O'SHEA *Guide to Spain* 183/1 Alpine peaks.. shine forth in the African sun like a mass of sparkling mother-of-pearl, to use the metaphoric definition of the Granadine Arab poets. **1959** *Times* 5 Aug. 9/6 But his rule marked the beginning of two centuries of Granadine grandeur. **1961** *John o' London's* 9 Feb. 137/3 The differences between Castilian, Sevillean, and Granadine solutions of similar architectural problems. **1962** Y. MALKIEL in Householder & Saporta *Probl. Lexicogr.* 12 Granadine Arabic. **1963** *Times* 16 Feb. 4/3 He describes his play as a 'Granadine' poem of the twentieth century divided into different gardens, with scenes for singing and for dancing.

†**Gra'nado.** [app. a corrupt form of the name of the Spanish city Granada: cf. -ADO.] Only in *Granado silk, silk of Granado.*

1582 *Rates Custom ho.* E iiij a, Silk of Granado black the pound xxs. **1592** GREENE *Upst. Courtier* Wks. (Grosart) XI. 221 The Netherstocke was of the purest Granado silke. *a* **1618** *Rates Merchandize* K 3 b, Granado silke black.

granado, obs. form of GRENADO.

†'**granage.** *Obs.* In mod. Dicts. grainage. [AF., f. *grain*: see GRAIN *sb.*[1] and -AGE. Du Cange has med.L. *grannagium*, perh. a duty on corn.] (See quot. 1685.)

a **1582** DYER *Cases* (1592) 352 b, Vn custome en la Citie de Londres appeale granage. **1685** *Termes de la Ley* 427 Granage, is a Duty in London, viz. the twentieth part of Salt Imported by an Alien, and due to the Mayor. **1820** TOMLINS *Law Dict.* (ed. 3), *Grainage.*

granand, obs. pr. pple. of GROAN *v.*

granar(d, var. ff. GRANER *Obs.*, granary.

granary ('grænərɪ). Forms: 6-8 **grainary**, (7 **-ie**), 8-9 **grainery**, 6-7 **granarie**, 6- **granary**. [ad. L. *grānārium*, f. *grān-um* corn, GRAIN *sb.*[1] Some of the obs. forms were influenced by GRAIN *sb.*] A storehouse for grain after it is threshed.

1570 LEVINS *Manip.* 104/24 A Granarie, *granarium.* **1623** MIDDLETON *Tri. Integrity* Wks. (Bullen) VII. 389 Sir Simon Eyre..built Leadenhall, a granary for the poor. **1669** WORLIDGE *Syst. Agric.* (1681) 56 The principal use of a Granary is against a very dear year. **1714** *Fr. Bk. of Rates* 195 There should be an immediate Search made into all Grainaries, Farm-Houses, &c. **1788** GIBBON *Decl. & F.* (1869) III. lii. 247 The public granaries and arsenals were abundantly replenished. **1800** L. W. WYATT *Archit. Designs* 19 Waggon and Implement Houses, with Grainaries over them. **1824** MISS MITFORD in L'Estrange *Life* (1870) II. ix. 184 An old granary to which we mount by outside wooden steps. **1879** J. WRIGHTSON in *Cassell's Techn. Educ.* IV. 415/2 The granaries should extend as two wings eastward and westward from it [the corn-barn].

b. *transf.* and *fig.* Said chiefly of a country or region which produces an abundance of grain and from which supplies of corn are obtained.

1570 T. NORTON tr. *Nowel's Catech.* (1853) 220 Fruits of godliness to be bestowed and laid up in the barn and granary of the kingdom of heaven. **1605** CAMDEN *Rem.* 3 The Store-house and Granary of the whole westerne world. **1632** MASSINGER *Maid of Hon.* I. i, Sicily..when 'twas styled the Granary of Great Rome. **1665** BOYLE *Occas. Refl.* (1848) 17 An Ant..onely carries away that [corn] which she finds ready form'd into its little Granary or Repository. **1680** MORDEN *Geog. Rect.* (1685) 189 Alenteio passes for the Granary of Portugal, by reason of the Corn which it produces. **1728-46** THOMSON *Spring* 76 May your rich soil ..be th' exhaustless granary of a world! **1796** MORSE *Amer. Geog.* I. 162 This Island..was called the granary of Canada, which it furnished with great plenty of corn. **1822-34** *Good's Study Med.* (ed. 4) III. 97 The man voluntarily starves himself in the granary of plenty. **1878** BOSW. SMITH *Carthage* 6 Palestine was the granary of Tyre, supplying it with corn and oil.

c. *attrib.*, as ***granary-crevice, floor, -keeper, -man, -register, -rent.***

1839 CARLYLE *Chartism* iii. 120 Stop up the *granary-crevice. **1833** TENNYSON *May Queen, N.Y. Eve* 45 She'll find my garden-tools upon the *granary-floor. **1886** HARRIS *Techn. Dict. Fire Insur.* 131 *Granary-keepers' utensils cannot be insured in the same item as grain. **1677** YARRANTON *Eng. Improv.* 116 In these publick Granaries, the Corn is kept..a whole year, for a Half-peny a Bushel; and the *Granary-Man gets by it. *Ibid.* 132 Receiving a Ticket from the *Granary-Register, of a certain quantity of Corn there lodged. *Ibid.* 137 Fourteen thousand Quarters will come to 350*l.* for *Granary-Rent yearly.

Hence **granary** *v. trans.*, to store in a granary.

1862 RUSKIN *Unto This Last* iv. 154 A remarkably light crop, half thorns and half aspen leaves, sown, reaped, and granaried by the 'science' of the modern political economist.

†'**granat.** *Obs.*$^{-1}$ [a. Du. *granaat*, ad. It. *granato*: see GRENADE.] = GRENADE.

a **1637** B. JONSON *Underwoods, Execr. Vulcan* 206 Vse your Petarres, and Granats, all your fine Engines of Murther.

†'**granate**, *sb.*[1] *Obs.* Also 7 **granat, grenat.** [ad. med.L. *grānāt-um* (OF. *grenat*): see GARNET[1].] = GARNET[1].

a **1400-50** *Alexander* 3344 þe ferd degre a Granate, a gracious gemme. **1555** EDEN *Decades* (Arb.) 234 A granate which we commonly caule a garnet. **1600** HAKLUYT *Voy.* (1810) III. 451 Certaine small stones broken which are in Colour somewhat like Granates. **1601** HOLLAND *Pliny* XXXVII. vii. II. 618 The common Grenat also of Carchedon or Carthage, is said to doe as much... These Grenats are found upon the hills among the Nasamons. **1655** FULLER *Ch. Hist.* III. iv. §4 The red Granat [signified] Charity. **1750** tr. *Leonardus' Mirr. Stones* 104 Granate,..a Stone of the Carbuncle Kind. **1796** MORSE *Amer. Geog.* II. 16 Norway produces crystals, granates, amethysts [etc.].

†'**granate**, *sb.*[2] *Obs.* Also 7 **gran(n)et.** See GARNET[2]. [a. L. (*pōmum*) *grānātum*, OF. (*pome*) *grenate*: see POMEGRANATE. Cf. GRENADE[1].]

1. The pomegranate.

1568 SKEYNE *The Pest* (1860) 34 Vyne of granatis. **1605** TIMME *Quersit.* III. 149 Thou maiest extract out of the barke of..granates, a substance comming most neere to the vertue of vitriol. **1641** G. SANDYS *Paraphr. Song Sol.* VI. v, To see ..Granets blooming on their Stems. **1694** SALMON *Bate's Disp.* II. (1713) 634/2 Syrup of Clove-gilly-flowers, Limons, or Granates. **1698** FRYER *Acc. E. India & P.* 247 Figs, Prunes, Grannet, Chestnut..and all those we call Wall-Fruit.

b. *attrib.*, as ***granate-apple.***

a **1622** AINSWORTH *Annot. Song Sol.* iv. 13 Granate-apples, so named because they are full of granes or kernels.

2. Short for 'granate-colour'. (In quot. 1805 used to render F. *grenat*: see GRENAT.)

1750 tr. *Leonardus' Mirr. Stones* 111 Some of them are of a Citron Colour, others of a Granate..the Granate of the Colour of the Flower of a Pomegranate Apple. **1805** tr. *A. La Fontaine's Hermann and Emilia* I. 245 The old lady wore a mantle of black velvet, ornamented with granate.

†'**granate**, *a. rare*$^{-0}$. [ad. L. *grānāt-us*, f. *grān-um* GRAIN *sb.*[1]] Having many grains. (Cf. GRANATED.)

1706 PHILLIPS (ed. Kersey), *Granate*, that has many Grains, as *granate Marble.*

†'**granate**, *v. Obs. rare*$^{-1}$. [f. L. *grānāt-us* formed into grains.] *trans.* To form into grains; to granulate. Hence **granated** *ppl. a.*

1688 BURNET *Lett. State Italy* (1708) 242 Pillars..of granated Marble. **1750** G. HUGHES *Barbadoes* 143 A subtile resinous juice perspires through the leaves,..which by the heat of the sun is granated and entirely incrusts them.

granate, obs. variant of GRANITE.

†**granatine.** *Min. Obs.* [ad. F. *granatin* (Daubenton, with somewhat different application); formed arbitrarily on L. *grān-um*, with reference to its derivative GRANITE.] Kirwan's name for the class of granitoid rocks consisting of three ingredients. (Cf. GRANITIN.)

1796 KIRWAN *Elem. Min.* (ed. 2) I. 342.

granatite, *Min.*, variant of GRENATITE.

†**granator.** *Obs.* Chiefly *Sc.* Also 5 **granitar**, 6 **graniter.** See also GARNETER, GRINTER. [ad. F. *grenetier*, f. (by substitution of suffix) *grenier* GARNER.] One who has charge of a granary or grange.

? **14..** *Charter Aberbroth.* fo. 126 in Macfarlane 433 (Jam.) Memorandum, that the Granitar sete na teynds to na baronis, nether landit men, without sikkir soverte of husband-men, except them that has the commone sele, and our seil, the gryntar beyng for the tyme. **1535** LYNDESAY *Satyre* 2495 Thir is my Graniter [ed. E.E.T.S. Grainter], and my Chalmerlaine, And hes my gould and geir vnder thair cuiris. **1647** HAWARD *Crown Revenue* 33 Three Yeomen granators: Fee a peice per diem 9*d.*

†'**granch**, *v. Obs. rare.* [Onomatopœic; cf. *grind, cranch.*] **a.** *intr.* Of the teeth: To gnash. **b.** *trans.* (see quot. 1886).

1736 AINSWORTH *Lat. Dict.*, *Mandūcus*,..a bugbear, or hobgoblin..with wide jaws and great teeth granching, shown at plays. **1886** CUNLIFFE *Rochdale-with-Rossendale Gloss.*, *Granch*, to crunch between the teeth with noise.

grand (grænd), *a.* and *sb.* Also 4-6 **graunt(e**, 5-6 **grawnt(e**, 6-7 **graund**, 7 **gran** (Howell). [a. OF. *grand, grant* (AF. also *graund, graunt*, mod.F *grand*), the Com. Rom. word for 'great' = Pr. *gran(t)-z*, Sp., Pg., It. *grande* (shortened *gran* before a sb.):—L. *grand-em*, in class. L. full-grown, big; in late popular L. superseding *magnus* in all its uses. Some scholars regard the word as cogn. w. Gr. βρενθύεσθαι to swagger.

The nature of the contexts in which the Fr. word was introduced into English accounts for the development which its meaning has undergone. In some of the mod. uses, the nearest Fr. equivalent is *grandiose.*]

A. *adj.*

†**1.** *the Grand*: = 'the Great' [F. *le grand, la grande*] as an epithet of a famous person, city, or country. *Obs.*

a **1400-50** *Alexander* 5668 Baxe, Bayon, & Burdeux, & Bretayn þe graunt. *c* **1440** *Bone Flor.* 26 Syr Otes the grawnt hyght that gome. **1484** CAXTON *Fables of Æsop* 2 He was.. borne in grece not ferre fro Troye the graunt. **1529** RASTELL *Pastyme* (1811) 26 Theodose the Graunte.

2. a. Used in official titles (chiefly after Fr. or other Romanic originals), with the sense: Chief over others, highest in rank or office. Now chiefly *Hist.* or with reference to foreign countries; in England there are still officials called *Grand Almoner, Grand Falconer* (see the sbs.); and the adj. forms part of titles of office amongst Freemasons, Odd Fellows, Good Templars, etc.

Grand Pensionary, Pensioner, the title of the prime minister or president of the Council of Holland, when a republic. ***Grand Vicar***, in France, the representative of a bishop in the administration of ecclesiastical affairs. ***Grand Vizier***, the chief minister of the Turkish empire. Also GRAND-CAPTAIN, GRAND-DUKE, GRAND-MASTER.

1609 BIBLE (Douay) *1 Macc.* xii. 20 To Onias the grand-priest [Vulg. *sacerdoti magno*]. **1613** PURCHAS *Pilgrimage* (1614) 738 Cabot..was constituted Grand Pilot of England by King Edward the sixt. **1688** *Answ. Talon's Plea* 5 The Chapters..name for Grand Vicar those whom the King intends to bestow the Bishopricks upon. **1708** *Lond. Gaz.* No. 4429/6 Letters from Warsaw..say, That at the desire of the Grand General, and other Confederate Senators [etc.]. **1709** STEELE *Tatler* No. 13 ¶2 We hear from the Hague.. That Monsieur de Torcy hath had frequent Conferences with the Grand Pensioner. **1714** MANDEVILLE *Fab. Bees* (1733) I. 245 A grand pensionary of Holland. **1727-41** CHAMBERS *Cycl.* s.v., In the French polity and customs, there are divers officers thus denominated, which we frequently retain in English; as *grand* almoner, *grand* ecuyer, *grand* chambellan, *grand* voyer, &c. **1767** BLACKSTONE *Comm.* II. 54 In the king's presence and under the direction of his grand justiciary. **1781** COWPER *Truth* 104 No grand inquisitor could worse invent. **1795** ANDERSON *Narr. Brit. Embass. China* vii. 87 The grand mandarin of the place sent to inform the Ambassador that [etc.]. **1847** MRS. A. KERR *Hist. Servia* 268 The Deputies were referred to the new Grand Vizier. **1855** EMERSON *Misc.* 136 A grand marshal.

b. Similarly in the titles of sovereigns; as GRAND SIGNIOR, ***Grand Turk***, the Sultan of Turkey (*arch.*). †***Grand Tartar***, the Great Mogul.

1588 PARKE tr. *Mendoza's Hist. China* 407 The prouince of Cambaya, subiect vnto the grand Tartar, or Mogor. **1860** WHYTE MELVILLE *Holmby House* I. 87 Who..had smoked his chibouque with the Grand Turk at Stamboul. **1860** SALA *Baddington Peerage* xliii, Whether..he felt as happy as the Grand Turk.

3. a. [Orig. a transferred use of 2; cf. ARCH-*prefix* 2.] Qualifying a personal designation, with the sense: Pre-eminent, chief; supremely deserving of the appellation. ? *Obs.*

1584 R. Scot *Discov. Witchcr.* xvi. ii. 471 The grandfoole their ghostlie father. **1593** Shaks. *Rich. II*, v. vi. 19 The grand Conspirator, Abbot of Westminster. **1594** —— *Rich. III*, iv. iv. 52 That excellent grand Tyrant of the earth. **1599** B. Jonson *Ev. Man out of Hum.* ii. i, Thou Grand Scourge, or Second Untruss of the time. **1609** Hieron *Chr. Jrnl.* Wks. 1614 I. 21 Sathan is our grand-enemy. **1662** Stillingfl. *Orig. Sacr.* i. iii. §2 Near that very place where the grand Ancestors of the world had their chief abode and residence. **1671** Milton *P.R.* i. 159 To conquer Sin and Death, the two grand foes. **1686** Wood *Life* 10 Aug., On the same morning on which he died..his only sister..was married..shewing herself thereby either a grand fool or a grand beast. **1778** R. James *Dissert. Fevers* (ed. 8) 32 Doth it not expel the Grand Enemy from every stronghold with irresistible force?

†**b.** Eminent; great in reputation, position, scale of operations, etc. *Obs.*

c **1540** tr. *Pol. Verg. Eng. Hist.* (Camden) I. 67 The garrison of the olde grande warriers [L. *ueteranorum præsidium*]. **1667** Milton *P.L.* ii. 507 And forth In order came the grand Infernal Peers. **1742** *Lond. & Country Brew.* i. (ed. 4) 10, I have heard a great Maltster that lived towards Ware say, he knew a grand Brewer, that melted near 200 Quarters a week.

absol. **1667** Milton *P.L.* x. 427 There kept thir watch the legions, while the Grand In council sat.

4. *Law.* **a.** Used with the sense of 'great' or that of 'principal, chief' in various designations (chiefly Anglo-Fr. in origin) of actions or agents, tribunals, etc.; opposed to *petty* or *common*. For *grand assize*, *cape*, *compounder*, *distress*, *inquest*, *jury*, *larceny*, *serjeanty*, etc. see the sbs.

1562 *Act 5 Eliz.* c. 1 §5 Such as be of the Grand Company of every Inn of Chancery. **1600** Holland *Livy* i. 31 In the grand-leetes and solemne elections of Magistrates, everie man had not prerogative alike. **1688** R. Holme *Armoury* iii. 310/1 Grand Rogues have sometimes their Ears Nailed to the Pillory.

b. ***grand day.*** (See quots.)

1656 Blount *Glossogr.*, *Gawdy* or *Grand days*. In the Inns of Court there are four of these in the yeer, that is, one in every Term. **1708** *Termes de la Ley* 372 Grand Days are those which are solemnly kept in every Term in the Inns of Court and Chancery, viz. In Easter Term, Ascention Day; in Trin. Term, St. John Baptist; in Michaelmas Term, All Saints; in Hillary Term, the Feast of the Purification of the B. Virgin. And these are no days in Court.

5. a. Of things, events, etc.: Great or important above all others of the kind; chief, main.

1597 Ingmethorp *Serm. 2 John* Ep. Ded., You have enameld as it were..that graundbenefite with infinite other kindnesses. *c* **1645** Howell *Lett.* i. xxix. (1650) 48 That Gran Universall-fire which shall happen at the day of judgment. *Ibid.* vi. 201 Solomon..wrote divers books which were lost in the gran Captivity. **1662** Stillingfl. *Orig. Sacr.* ii. vii. §11 The time was not yet come wherein the grand mystery of mans salvation by the death of the Son of God was to be revealed. *c* **1680** Beveridge *Serm.* (1729) I. 374 This first and grand promise was absolutely made to all mankind. **1713** Gay *Guardian* No. 11 ¶3 The Use of the Grand Elixir to support the Spirits of Human Nature. **1720** Swift *Mod. Educ.* Wks. 1755 II. ii. 32 The noblest blood of England having been shed in the grand rebellion. **1727–41** Chambers *Cycl.*, *Elixir*,..Sometimes [used] for an universal medicine..called, by way of excellence, the grand elixir. **1739** Wesley *Wks.* (1872) I. 179 The grand article of my expense is food. **1784** Cowper *Task* vi. 184 Evincing, as she [Nature] makes The grand transition, that there lives and works A soul in all things, and that soul is God. **1849** E. B. Eastwick *Dry Leaves* 10 The grand want is that of dams across the principal streams. **1889** J. Bennett *Billiards* v. (ed. 5) 41 But if so played, and this is the grand point, position is lost.

b. Preceded by *a*, or with sb. in plural: Of first-rate magnitude, value, or importance.

1611 Hieron *Spirit. Sonship* 12 These and the like be the grand imployments of the times. **1654** Whitlock *Zootomia* 70 No grand Alteration here below, but..she [the moon] must be made Author of it. *c* **1687** Dryden *Ep. to Sir G. Etherege* 38 In grand affairs thy days are spent, In waging weighty compliment With such as monarchs represent. **1705** Berkeley *Commonpl. Bk.* Wks. 1871 IV. 460 The not distinguishing 'twixt Will and ideas is a grand mistake with Hobbs. **1769** *Junius Lett.* xi. 46 You have united this country against you on one grand constitutional point. **1842** Miall in *Nonconf.* II. 2 We declared the establishment to be a grand imposture. **1850** Robertson *Serm.* Ser. iii. ii. (1872) 25 So then..vice is nothing more than a grand imprudence. **1870** Baldw. Brown *Eccl. Truth* 264 It would be a grand mistake to say that Christianity created feudalism. **1878** Huxley *Physiogr.* 179 A grand movement of water from the polar towards the equatorial regions. **1891** *Law Times* XC. 419/2 The old reticence of the Bench was a grand safeguard of its dignity.

6. Used to designate a comprehensive unity in relation to its constituent portions. Now only in ***grand total*** (formerly †***grand sum***), the sum of the sums of several groups of numbers.

1576 Fleming tr. *Caius' Dogs* in Arb. *Garner* III. 232, I will express and declare in due order, the grand and general kind of English Dogs, the difference of them [etc.]. **1597** Hooker *Eccl. Pol.* v. iii. §3 The Christian world it selfe being deuided into two graund parts. **1610** Healey *St. Aug. Citie of God* 549 The summe of 10 is added to the grandsumme. **1611** Hieron *Spirit. Sonship* 11 As I haue giuen you a bill, as it were of particulars, so I will now in a word tender vnto you the graund sum of all. **1613** Shaks. *Hen. VIII*, iii. ii. 298 Produce the grand summe of his sinnes, the Articles Collected from his life. **1816** A. C. Hutchison *Pract. Obs. Surg.* (1826) 311 The subjoined document, shewing the total number of seamen and marines received into the three hospitals..making the grand total of 96,000.

7. a. With reference to physical magnitude: Main, principal. *Obs.* exc. as in b.

1601 Holland *Pliny* II. 471 The grand cirque or shew-place at Rome. **1606** Shaks. *Ant. & Cl.* iii. xii. 10, I was of late as petty to his ends As is the Morne-dew on the Mertle leafe To his grand Sea. **1708** *Lond. Gaz.* No. 4478/2 In order to drain the Ditch before the Grand Breach..Getting all things in a Readiness for the Passage of the Grand Ditch. **1753** Franklin *Lett.* Wks. 1840 V. 314 May not the small electrized clouds rise up to the main body, and by that means occasion so large a vacancy, as that the grand cloud cannot strike in that place?

b. Of a specified part of a building (as a gateway, an entrance-hall, a saloon, etc.): Main, principal. Applied only to objects that are magnificent in size and adornment, and therefore apprehended as implying these qualities.

1806 R. Cumberland *Mem.* ii. 154 The bas-relieves at the back of the grand altar. **1855** Macaulay *Hist. Eng.* xxii. IV. 789 The Swedish Minister alighted at the grand entrance. **1860** Sala *Baddington Peerage* xlv, On the grand staircase there were rows of exotic plants in boxes.

8. a. Used (instead of 'great' in various senses) in anglicized Fr. phrases, where the sb. is rendered by its etymological equivalent; ***Grand Army*** = Grande Armée; ***grand manner*** [after F. *grande manière*], the style of plastic art suited for noble subjects and vast design; also *attrib.* and *transf.*; ***grand passion*** = grande passion.

Somewhat similar are the quasi-proper names *The Grand Canal* (Venice, tr. It. *Il Gran Canale*), *The Grand Canal* of Ireland (1765), *The Grand Junction*, *Grand Surrey*, *Grand Union Canal*; *The Grand Hotel*; and similar designations, where the choice of *grand* instead of *great* was suggested by the associations of senses 9 and 10.

1660 F. Brooke tr. *Le Blanc's Trav.* 166 When the King goes..to the grand chase, he takes along abundance of Pioneers, to stop up the Avenues. *a* **1704** T. Brown *Praise Poverty* Wks. 1730 I. 101 It [Homer's poem] was..to stir his countrymen up against the exorbitant power of the Asiatick Grand Monarch. **1775** T. Campbell *Diary* 27 Apr. (1947) 87 Revisited the exhibition of the Royal Academy & am confirmed in my opinion of the grand manner of Barrys Venus lamenting over Adonis. **1827** Scott *Napoleon* V. viii. 190 This formidable assemblage of troops, laying aside the appellation of the Army of England, was hereafter [*sc.* from 1805] distinguished by that of the Grand Army. **1850** Thackeray *Pendennis* II. v. 47 My father was a General of the Grand Army. *Ibid.* xxii. 210, I..am the person who eight years ago had a grand passion. **1850** C. M. Yonge (*title*) Kenneth, or the Rearguard of the Grand Army. **1860** Sala *Baddington Peerage* xlix, Henceforth he carries his arm in a sling, and wears an extra ribbon, even as a veteran of Napoleon's grand army. **1905** A. Bennett *Tales of Five Towns* i. 170 He seemed to sink luxuriously into this grand passion of hers. **1905** *Daily Chron.* 28 Dec. 3/1 The Royal Academy tradition of the Grand Manner in painting. *Ibid.*, Sculpture groups, illustrating a classical theme, built up on Grand Manner traditions. **1925** F. F. Potter in *Teacher's World* July Extra No., The boys of Manchester Grammar School were engaged in a project in the grand manner, when they drained, levelled, and turfed their playing fields. **1929** A. Huxley *Do what you Will* 138 Where there are no psychological or external restraints, the Grand Passion does not come into existence. **1957** E. H. Gombrich *Story of Art* xxv. 381 David and his school cultivated the Grand Manner. **1962** 'H. Lourie' *Question of Abortion* ix. 76 We amuse each other... But it doesn't necessarily mean a grand passion or marriage. **1971** *Guardian* 14 Jan. 2/4 La Madeleine..began as a neo-Greek temple dedicated to the glory of Napoleon's Grand Army.

b. *Mus.* (See quot. 1879.)

1724 *Explic. For. Words Musick*, *Grande*, is Great, or Grand, and is used to distinguish the Great or Grand Chorus from the rest of the Musick. **1825** Danneley *Encycl. Mus.*, *Grand*, this word is sometimes appended to others; as, a grand sonata, a grand overture, a grand chorus, and is synonymous with the term full, as full chorus, full organ, etc. **1879** *Grove's Dict. Music*, *Grand*, a word much in use in England till within a few years to denote a classical composition of full dimensions or for full orchestra... A grand sonata or a grand concerto meant one in complete classical form.

9. a. Of a ceremony, public performance, or the like: Characterized by great solemnity, splendour, or display; conducted with great form and on a great scale.

1735 *Lond. Daily Post* 21 Apr. No. 145/3 On Thursday last..was held the Annual Grand Feast of Free and Accepted Masons. **1802** Mar. Edgeworth *Moral T.* (1816) I. xviii. 147 His apparel was..finished, and ready for the grand day. **1837** Dickens *Pickw.* vii, 'The grand Match is played to-day, I believe', said Pickwick. **1860** Sala *Baddington Peerage* xlvii, The last grand entertainment of the fashionable season being over. **1871** Miss Yonge *Cameos* II. xxxiv. 353 The last Parliament had been a very grand one. **1893** Furnivall in *Three Kings' Sons* Forewords 6 There are grand wedding festivities.

b. Of persons, their belongings or surroundings: Fine, splendid, gorgeously arrayed. Also more widely: Giving evidence of wealth or high social position; recognized as belonging to, or characteristic of, the 'great world.'

1766 Goldsm. *Vic. W.* xxiii, They usually rode out together in the grandest equipage that had been seen in the country for many years. **1848** Thackeray *Van. Fair* li, The mothers grand, sumptuous, solemn, and in diamonds. *Ibid.*, She was placed at the grand exclusive table with his Royal Highness. **1860** Sala *Baddington Peerage* xlii, A forced adieu to fine houses, grand company, and the Grimaldi Club? **1861** Thackeray *Four Georges* (1869) 92 She [Q. Charlotte] was..a very grand lady on state occasions, simple enough in ordinary life.

sarcastically. **1884** W. C. Smith *Kildrostan* 47, I found her not At all. She is too grand to see me now.

c. Used as adv. *colloq.*

1775 Johnson *Let. Mrs. Thrale* 22 May, Beattie has called once to see me. He lives grand at the Archbishop's.

d. ***grand-scale*** adj. (cf. scale *sb.*[3] 13 b).

1959 *Listener* 29 Jan. 217/3 Today these works [of Wagner] are truly 'popular', the latest addition to the unquestioned grand-scale masterpieces. *a* **1963** L. MacNeice *Astrol.* (1964) i. 20 These [eclipses] (and comets) are still assumed to portend grand-scale happenings. **1964** I. L. Horowitz *New Sociol.* 22 A theoretical option to narrow empiricism and grand-scale rationalism.

10. With reference to emotional effect. **a.** Of natural objects, architecture, etc.: Impressing the mind with a sense of vastness and magnificence; imposing by reason of beauty coupled with magnitude.

1712 Addison *Spect.* No. 414 ¶4 There is generally in Nature something more Grand and August, than what we meet with in the Curiosities of Art. **1756** Burke *Subl. & B.* ii. x, I have ever observed, that colonnades and avenues of trees of a moderate length, were without comparison far grander, than when they were suffered to run to immense distances. **1784** Cowper *Task* vi. 249 What he views of beautiful or grand In nature, from the broad majestic oak To the green blade. **1859** Hamilton *Mem. J. Wilson* ii. 31 The interior of the Church is very grand. **1860** Tyndall *Glac.* i. ii. 12 The scene from the summit..was exceedingly grand. *Ibid.* xi. 82 The clouds were very grand—grander indeed than anything I had ever before seen. **1885** *Athenæum* 23 May 669/3 Grand surges move in ranks..till they beat furiously on the shore.

b. Hence of ideas, style, composition, design, etc.: Lofty and dignified in conception, treatment, or expression; conceived or planned in a large and majestic manner. ***grand style***: a style fitted to the expression of lofty ideas and great subjects in literature and art.

a **1755** Young (J.), A voice has flown To re-enflame a grand design. **1758** S. Hayward *Serm.* xvi. 469 A variety of the most grand similitudes. **1772** *Ann. Reg.* 161 It gave what is called the grand stile to invention, to composition, to expression. **1784** Cowper *Task* v. 678 Be most sublimely good, verbosely grand, And with poetic trappings grace thy prose. **1790** Burke *Fr. Rev.* Wks. V. 156 It is not clear, whether in England we learned those grand and decorous principles, and manners..from you, or whether you took them from us. **1859** Gwilt *Archit.* (ed. 4) Gloss., *Grand*, a term used in the fine arts, generally to express that quality by which the highest degree of majesty and dignity is imparted to a work of art. **1868** Lowell *Dryden* Prose Wks. 1890 III. 173 This is certainly..in what used to be called the grand style, at once noble and natural. **1875** Bryce *Holy Rom. Emp.* vi. (ed. 5) 79 The grand vision of a universal Christian empire was utterly lost in the isolation.

c. Of persons: Imposing by nobility of moral or intellectual character. Also with reference to appearance or manner: Stately, noble, dignified.

1832 Tennyson *Sisters* vi, He look'd so grand when he was dead. **1847** —— *Princ.* i. 185 She look'd as grand as doomsday and as grave. **1848** Lowell *Lamartine* iii, Now thou'rt thy plain, grand self again. **1877** E. R. Conder *Bas. Faith* i. 7 Religion has proved herself equally able to dominate the grandest intellects, and to elevate the humblest. **1878** R. H. Hutton *Scott* iii. 30 With that grand unconcern characteristic of elderly persons in high position. **1883** Mrs. Rollins *New Eng. Bygones* 56 They were all three grand men, sensible, honest, and carrying weight in town affairs. **1897** P. Warung *Tales Old Regime* 25 Bowing the while in the grand manner.

d. In recent use, the adj. in sense 10 has acquired an idiomatic frequency of application to sbs. qualified by *old*.

'The Grand Old Man' (jocularly 'G.O.M.') was from 1882 a current journalistic appellation for W. E. Gladstone. It appears (in quotation marks) in *Punch* 17 June 280/1.

[**1802** Coleridge *Dejection* 2 The grand old ballad of Sir Patrick Spence.] **1833** Tennyson *Lady Clara Vere de V.* 51 The grand old gardener [*late edd.* The gardener Adam] and his wife smile at the claims of long descent. **1850** —— *In Mem.* cxi, He bore without abuse The grand old name of gentleman. **1850** C. Brontë *Let.* 12 June in Mrs. Gaskell *Life* (1857) II. 162 A sight of the Duke of Wellington at the Chapel Royal (he is a real grand old man). **1860** Hook *Lives Abps.* I. 150 The grand old man [Theodore of Tarsus]. **1868** J. H. Blunt *Ref. Ch. Eng.* I. 349 So the grand old abbot..was taken to Wells. **1877** Jennings *Field Paths & Green Lanes* 37 A delightful old church..rendered a true pilgrim's shrine..by its grand old tower. **1887** M. Arnold *Kaiser dead* vii, Since, 'gainst the classes, He heard, of late, the Grand Old Man Incite the masses.

e. With *not*, etc. Of persons: indisposed, unwell.

1934 N. Marsh *A Man lay Dead* viii. 145 'May I see your patient, Doctor Young?'.. 'She's not so grand,' he said doubtfully. **1951** E. Coxhead *One Green Bottle* x. 257 You don't look too grand... Are you sure you're all right? **1960** H. Pinter *Room* 98, I told him you hadn't been too grand.

11. Used as a general term to express strong admiration: 'Magnificent', 'splendid'. *colloq.*

1816 Pickering *Voc. U.S.*, *Grand.* Much used in conversation for very good, excellent, fine, &c. *Ex.* This is grand news; he is a grand fellow; this is a grand day. *New England.* **1866** *Derbysh. Gloss.* in *Reliquary* Jan. 160 *Grand*, good, superior. 'Hay! it wor grand, lads, that ale wor.' **1876** *Whitby Gloss.* s.v., 'Here's a grand day', very fine weather. **1894** Crockett *Raiders* 156 They'll bide..at at the Herd's Hoose, or Cassencary belike, that's a graund hauf o' smugglers and gypsies. **1898** Ranjitsinhji *With Stoddart's Team* iii, The Melbourne ground was..in grand condition as regards the turf.

ironically. **1889** J. K. Jerome *3 Men in a Boat* 257 Up he would march to the head of the punt, plant his pole, and then run along right to the other end, just like an old punter. Oh! how grand!

12. a. Combinations and special collocations, as *grand-looking*, *-made* adjs.; **grand action**, the action of a grand pianoforte; **grand-bob**, ? = grand-sire bob (see GRANDSIRE 6); **Grand Canyon** *Geol.* [name of the gorge of the Colorado River in Arizona, U.S.A.], a rock formation laid down during the pre-Cambrian era in the south-western U.S.A.; hence, in local use to designate the geological period during which these rocks were formed; **grand chain**: see CHAIN *sb.* 5 f; **grand committee** (*Parliament*), (*a*) *Hist.*, each of the four committees (for religion, for grievances, for courts of justice, and for trade) annually appointed by the House of Commons until 1832 (though they had long before that date ceased actually to sit); †also, in 17th c., often used for 'committee of the whole house'; (*b*) now, the ordinary unofficial designation of the two 'standing committees' (each of 60 to 80 members) since 1882 appointed every session for the consideration of bills relating severally to matters of Law and Trade; **Grand Cordon, Cross** (see CORDON *sb.* 6, CROSS *sb.* 19); **grand cru**, wine of a superior quality (cf. CRU); **grand fir**, *Abies grandis*, a large fir native to the west coast of North America; **Grand Fleet**, (*a*) the 18th-cent. fleet based at Spithead; (*b*) the name during the war-period 1914–16 for the British Battle Fleet operating in the North Sea; †**grand hound**, ? a mastiff; **grand-junctioner** (*U.S.*), ? a director of the 'Grand Junction' railway; **grand lodge** (see LODGE); †**grand-maund**, a gabion; **Grand National**, the great steeplechase established in 1839 and run annually at Aintree, Liverpool, in the first week of the flat-racing season; **grand-paunch**, (*a*) a glutton; (*b*) a 'corporation', large abdomen; **grand pianoforte, piano**, a large pianoforte, usually harp-shaped and horizontal, whose size admits of the most effective arrangement of the mechanism (for *grand-upright*, *upright-grand*, see UPRIGHT *a.*); **grand prize**, anglicization of GRAND PRIX 2; **grand quarter** *Her.*, see quots. and cf. *grand-quartering*; **grand quartering** *Her.* (see quot.); †**grand relief**, ? = ALTO-RELIEVO; **Grand Remonstrance** (see REMONSTRANCE *sb.* 3 b); **grand slam** (see SLAM *sb.*[2] 2 b); **grand unified theory** *Physics*, a theory in which the strong, the weak, and the electromagnetic interactions are treated mathematically as different manifestations of a single force; abbrev. *GUT* s.v. G III. f.

1810 in Southey *Comm.-pl. Bk.* IV. 391 The ringers to ring one peal of *grand bobs. **1876** J. W. POWELL *Rep. Geol. Eastern Portion Uinta Mount.* 70 The *Grand Cañon Group rests unconformably upon the crystalline schists... Fossils have been found at the base of the Grand Cañon series... Red Creek Quartzite and Grand Cañon schists..are believed to be Eozoic. **1925** J. JOLY *Surface-Hist. Earth* viii. 131 The third (the Killarney or Grand Canyon) closing pre-Cambrian time. **1958** R. C. MOORE *Introd. Hist. Geol.* (ed. 2) iv. 61/2 Collectively, they are called the Grand Canyon Sequence of rocks. **1626** *Jrnl. Commons* 4 Apl. I. 843 The *grand committee to sit at two of the clock. **1640** [see COMMITTEE]. **1644** VICARS *God in Mount* (1644) 69 A grand-Committee of both Houses. **1891** *Guardian* 4 Mar. 341/2 The Tithe Bill..is to be further put into shape by a grand committee. **1905** A. L. SIMON *Hist. Champagne Trade England* ix. 119 There are three groups of famous growths in Champagne... These..may be called the *Grands Crûs of Champagne. **1932** E. HEMINGWAY *Death in Afternoon* i. 11 The Grand crus of Medoc. **1951** N. MITFORD *Blessing* II. ix. 230 'Quite an honourable wine,' said Sigi, 'but not grand cru.' **1965** A. SICHEL *Penguin Bk. Wines* 132 *Grand cru* or *grand vin*. Any wine bearing this description on the label must contain at least 11° of alcohol from the natural sugar of the grapes before the addition of extra sugar at the time of fermentation. **1897** G. B. SUDWORTH *Nomencl. Arborescent Flora U.S.* 54 *Abies grandis*... *Grand or Oregon White Fir. **1913** S. B. ELLIOTT *Important Timber Trees U.S.* II. 192 The important Western Firs are Grand Fir (*Abies grandis*), White Fir (*Abies concolor*), [etc.]... It is proposed by Mr. Sudworth to discard the appellation 'white' and adopt that of 'grand' in its place, making it Grand Fir. **1969** *Northwest* (Sunday Oregonian Mag.) 14 Dec. 21/3 While our familiar Douglas fir is still the most popular species..the..Grand firs are very close seconds especially in container plants. **1745** R. GOADBY *Life & Adv. B. M. Carew* 119 Impressed Men, who were all put on board the Winchester,..and carried to the *grand Fleet then lying at Spithead. **1914** J. R. JELLICOE in *Times* 16 Sept. 8/6 The officers and men of the Grand Fleet beg that you will convey to their comrades of the British Army their intense admiration for the magnificent fight they have made. **1919** —— *Grand Fleet 1914–16* iii. 34 The Grand Fleet may be said to have come into being only at the outbreak of the War, when it was so christened. **1922** *Encycl. Brit.* XXXII. 294/1 Up to the outbreak of war, Rosyth was regarded as the principal base and headquarters for the Grand Fleet. **1966** A. J. MARDER *From Dreadnought to Scapa Flow* III. vi. 207 The moral ascendancy of the Grand Fleet over the High Seas Fleet remained and, if anything, was stronger. **1548** HALL *Chron., Rich. III*, 35 Semblable my cousyne therle of Rychemonde ..wyll surelye attempte lyke a fierce *grandhounde, other to byte or to perce me on the other syde. **1860** EMERSON *Cond. Life* iii. (1861) 58 Railroad presidents, copper-miners, *grand-junctioners [etc.]. **1878** GEO. ELIOT in J. W. Cross *Life* (1885) III. 327 The Crown-Prince is really a *grand-looking man. **1850** MRS. BROWNING *Poems* I. 213 His lips and jaw, *Grand-made and strong, as Sinai's Law. **1579** DIGGES *Stratiot.* 113 *Graund Maunds, or Gabbions. **1839** *Sporting Rev.* Mar. 164 The *Grand National Steeple Chase. **1866** *Field* 10 Mar. 199/3 Why should he be a favourite for the Grand National? **1886** EARL OF SUFFOLK & BERKS. *Racing & Steeple-chasing* 352 Tom Olliver won three Grand Nationals. **1894** J. D. ASTLEY *Fifty Yrs. Life* II. 281, I hoped to be able to pick out the winner of the Grand National when the weights appeared. **1967** *Observer* Suppl. 1 Oct. 36/1 The Prime Minister is on the verge of his first political success: he is about to save the Grand National. **1601** HOLLAND *Pliny* II. 11 Our *grand-panches..haue deuised for themselues a delicat kind of meat out of corn and grain. **1606** —— *Sueton.* 270 He became disfigured and blemished..with a fat grand-panch. **1797** *Monthly Mag.* III. 145 Their newly invented *grand and square Piano Fortes. **1834** MEDWIN *Angler in Wales* I. 273 It was a grand piano of Broadwood's. **1876** STAINER & BARRETT *Dict. Mus. Terms* 353/2 Pianofortes have been named from..the size, as *piccolo*, *semi-grand*, and *full grand*. **1879** STAINER *Music of Bible* 25 A grand pianoforte, which contains more strings than any other instrument in use. **1866** *Lond. Gaz.* 26 June 3645/2 Paris Universal Exhibition of 1867... 17 *grand prizes, each of the value of 2000 f. **1880** *Rep. Paris Univ. Exhib. 1878* II. 365, 100 Grand Prizes and exceptional awards in money. **1869** J. E. CUSSANS *Handbk. Heraldry* ii. 45 If one or more of these quarters should be subdivided into other like divisions, it is said to be Quarterly-quartered; and the quarter thus quartered is called a *Grand quarter. **1896** J. WOODWARD *Her.* II. 102 It may happen that one of the heiresses whose arms are to be quartered, herself bore a quartered coat, in this case the quarter appropriated to her contains her whole bearings..and..is called a Grand-quarter. **1969** FRANKLYN & TANNER *Encycl. Dict. Heraldry* 271/1 In Scotland, quarters are limited to four, but each may be a grand quarter, i.e. a quarter which is itself quarterly of four sub-quarters. **1889** ELVIN *Dict. Heraldry*, s.v. *Marshalling*, a *Grand Quartering..usually accompanies the assumption of a second name, and unites the two associated coats so inseparably, that if they come to be Marshalled with other quarterings they are no longer (as in other cases) spread out among them, but they still remain together as a Grand Quartering. **1768** E. HOLDSWORTH *Dissert. Virgil* 95 The famous base at Pozzuoli..on which are fourteen figures in *grand relief. **1978** *Nuclear Physics* B. CXXXV. 85 We have mainly studied three aspects of *grand unified theories of the strong, weak, and electromagnetic interactions. **1979** Grand unified theory [see UNIFIED *ppl. a.* 2]. **1982** *McGraw-Hill Yearbk. Sci. & Technol. 1982–3* 440/1 The last, and the most ambitious, stage of unification deals with the possibility of combining grand unified and gravitation theories into a superunified theory.

b. used (after Fr. example) to denote the second degree removed in ascent or descent of relationship, as GRANDFATHER, GRANDSON, etc. So †*grand-forefather*; also *transf.* in nonce-uses, as *grand-patron*, *-pupil*. †Also (?*nonce-use*) repeated *grand-grand-father* = great-grandfather.

Of combinations of this kind, the oldest are GRANDAME and GRANDSIRE, which appear in the 13th c.; GRANDFATHER and GRANDMOTHER *sb.* are not found until late in the 15th c. In Fr. *grand* is restricted to a degree of *ascent*, the corresponding degree downwards being expressed by *petit* (little).

1578 TYMME tr. *Calvin on Genesis* 235 His great graunde graunde father. **1599** H. BUTTES *Dyets Drie Dinner* D vj, When our grand-forefathers had a long time lived with Acorns. **1825** BENTHAM *Indications* 14 Say patron and grandpatron, as you say son and grandson. Grand patronage is not so valuable as patronage. *Ibid.* 16 Wherever you can see a grand patron other than the king, seeing the king, you see a great grand patron. **1883** P. SCHAFF *Apostolic Chr.* 678 Irenaeus..a spiritual grand-pupil of John.

B. quasi-*sb.* and *sb.*

1. quasi-*sb.* **a.** ***the grand***: that which is grand; the lofty, magnificent, sublime.

1742 YOUNG *Nt. Th.* IX. 843 The grand of nature is th' Almighty's oath, In Reason's court, to silence Unbelief. **1794** MRS. RADCLIFFE *Myst. Udolpho* i, The taste they create for the beautiful and the grand. **1821** CRAIG *Lect. Drawing* iv. 228 The grand calls for the accompanying aid of wild forests.

b. ***to do the grand***: to make a great display; to put on airs. *slang.* (See DO *v.* 11 j.)

1893 in FARMER *Slang*.

†**2.** *sb.* [a. Sp., It. *grande.*] = GRANDEE. *Obs.*

1606 EARL NORTHAMPTON *True Perfect Rel.* Oo 3 a, Then fell the Grands of Italy to renounce all duetie. **1614** SELDEN *Titles Hon.* 206 The Grands (all Dukes among them are Grands, and some Marquesses and Counts)..shall bee honord with *Vuestra Sennoria* i. your Lordship. **1669** *Lond. Gaz.* No. 352/3 To whom His Majesty has been pleased in favour to the Count, as a Grand of Portugal, to give her the Priviledge of a Stool before the Queen.

†**3.** *ellipt.* (See quot.) *Obs. rare*$^{-1}$.

1670 COTTON *Espernon* I. IV. 151 Betwixt these Forts..he caus'd a Grand to be erected, that is to say, a greater Fort.

4. a. Among Freemasons, any of the officers whose titles contain the adj. **b.** In some convivial clubs, the title of the chairman. Also ***Noble Grand, Vice Grand***, the chairman and vice-chairman of a lodge of Odd Fellows.

1747 W. HORSLEY *Fool* (1748) II. 165 The Fools being assembled, the Grand..attended by the Vice, and the other Officers of Folly, assum'd the Chair. **1765–6** GOLDSM. *Ess., Clubs* (Globe) 284/2 The Grand, with a mallet in his hand, presided at the head of the table... My speculations were soon interrupted by the Grand, who had knocked down Mr. Spriggins for a song. **1821** LAMB *Elia* Ser. I. *All Fools' Day*, Gebir, my old free-mason, and prince of plasterers at Babel, bring in your trowel, most Ancient Grand! **1840** DICKENS *Old C. Shop* xiii, The Glorious Appollers, of which I have the honour to be Perpetual Grand.

5. A grand pianoforte.

1840 *Penny Cycl.* XVIII. 142 In flat instruments, especially grands, there is a difficulty in giving strength to the bracing. **1876** STAINER & BARRETT *Dict. Mus. Terms* 352/2 By means of this invention [the upright action] a pianoforte can be made which will occupy a space about a fourth of the depth of the 'grand'. **1891** *St. James's Gaz.* 26 Mar. 5/2 She..begins the preliminary scramble on the hired grand.

6. *Sugar manuf.* (West Indian). The largest evaporating pan of a battery. [ad. F. *grande.*]

1839 URE *Dict. Arts* 1202 The skimmings of the *grand* are thrown into a separate pan. [**1875** KNIGHT *Dict. Mech.* has the Fr. form *grande.*]

7. [G. (a. Fr.) *grand*, formerly *grando* (see quot. 1893).] In the game of skat, a bid to play with only the four matadores (knaves) as trumps. Varieties of this are called ***solo grand, gucki grand, tournee grand, open grand*** (or ***grand ouvert***).

[**1893** 'L. HOFFMAN' tr. *Hertefeld's Skat* 7 In *Grando*, the only trumps are the four knaves. *Ibid.* 46 The basis value is in *Grando Tourné*, 12; in *Grando Solo*, 16; and in *Grando Ouvert*, 24.] **1906** R. F. FOSTER *Skat Manual* 121 This he can do by declaring a Grand. **1957** *Encycl. Brit.* XX. 727/2 The games in which only knaves are trumps are called grand (or grando). *Ibid.*, Solo grand is played without use of the skat. In open grand the player's entire hand is exposed before the opening lead, and the player contracts to win every trick.

8. *slang* (orig. *U.S.*). A thousand dollars. Also occas., a thousand pounds. (The *sing.* form is often used for the *pl.*)

1921 *Collier's* 26 Mar. 24/2 'A hundred and fifty grands!' I breathed. 'You're cuckoo.' *Ibid.* 27 Aug. 4/3 '*I lose twenty-five thousand dollars!*'.. Twenty-five grand! **1924** G. C. HENDERSON *Keys to Crookdom* 406 Grand. $1,000. Called 'a grand'. **1931** E. LINKLATER *Juan in America* IV. x. 359 D'you think I'd pay a hundred grand for protection if it wasn't worth it? **1932** *Amer. Mercury* Jan. 16, I don't know how much it is, but I suppose around ten, twelve, fifteen grand. **1946** *People* 7 Apr. 2/3, I stepped out with the spree-bent suckers..into this..world..where the black market boys..gamble in 'grands' (£1,000). **1958** *Times* 25 Feb. 5/3 He wanted his 'whack of the grand'. **1967** *Sunday Tel.* 23 Apr. 6/1 One 26-year-old [criminal]..insisted that he picked up a regular £1,000 a week working with a professional gang. 'Honest, a grand or a couple of grand isn't really big stakes in my game.'

†**grand**, *v. Obs. rare.* In 7 graund. [f. GRAND *a.*] *trans.* To make greater, 'magnify'.

1602 J. DAVIES *Mirum in Modum* G 3 b, Which Grands his Goodnesse, and augments his fame. **1607** —— *Summa Totalis* xvi. B, His Iustice to extenuate To graund his Grace is sacrilegious.

grandævity, -ous, var. ff. GRANDEVITY, -OUS.

grand air. [properly Fr., but pronounced like the Eng. words of identical form and etymology.] An air of distinction; a noble appearance; also (in bad sense) an affected dignity or loftiness of manner.

1775 H. WALPOLE *Lett.* (1857) VI. 212, I like the hotel d'Harcourt; it has *grand air* and a kind of Louis XIV old fashionhood. **1863** OUIDA *Held in Bondage* 3 He had more of the 'grand air' about him than anyone else I had ever seen. **1881** H. JAMES *Portr. Lady* xxxv, The proportions of the windows, and even the details of the cornice, had quite the grand air.

Hence **grand-aired** *a.*, having a grand air.

1881 *Academy* 5 Mar. 167 Worried by a severe aunt and a grand-aired cousin.

grandam, grandame ('grændəm, -deɪm). *arch.* Forms: 4–5 graun-, grawndam, 5–6 grauntdam(e, 6 graundame, grandhame, grandamme, 6–9 grand-dame, 3, 6– grandame, 6– grandam. See also GRANNAM. [a. AF. *graund dame*: see GRAND *a.* 12 b and DAME, DAM[2]; the use of *dame*, 'lady' in the sense of 'mother' seems to be AF. only. This word is in Eng. the oldest of the terms of relationship formed with *grand.*]

1. = GRANDMOTHER *sb.* 1.

a **1225** *St. Marher.* 22 In hire grandame hus þat wes icleopet Clete. **1390** GOWER *Conf.* I. 90 A lady..So olde she might unnethes go, And was grauntdame to the dede. *c* **1400** *Destr. Troy* 13593 His graundam full graidly grippit hym onone. **1509** FISHER *Funeral Serm. Hen. VII* (Colophon), My lady ye Kynges graundame. **1556** *Chron. Gr. Friars* (Camden) 96 The xxvij. of June [1555] was kept the obijt of the kynges grandhame. **1595** SHAKS. *John* I. i. 168, I am thy grandame Richard. **1818** SCOTT *Hrt. Midl.* ix, These blunders occasioned grief to his grand-dame. **1841–4** EMERSON *Ess., Self-Reliance* Wks. (Bohn) I. 28 We are like children who repeat by rote the sentences of grandames and tutors. **1871** R. ELLIS tr. *Catullus* lxxxiv. 6 So grandsire, grandam alike did agree.

Proverb. **1611** COTGR. s.v. *Apprendre*, (An idle, vaine, or needlesse labour) we say, to teach his grandame to grope ducks.

b. (In form **grandam** only.) Of animals: The dam's dam. (See DAM *sb.*[2])

1839 URE *Dict. Arts* 1308 By coupling the female [ewe] thus generated, with such a male..another improvement of one-half will be obtained, affording a staple three-fourths finer than that of the grandam.

2. An ancestress (said of Eve); = GRANDMOTHER *sb.* 2.

1620 T. PEYTON *Glasse of Time* I. 30 Our grandame Eue. **1628** GAULE *Pract. Theories* (1629) 9 One should ryse from her Loynes, to recouer his Grand-dames fall; and pash that wily Serpents head. **1724** *Weekly Jrnl.* 25 Jan. 2769/1 When Grandame Eve first invented the Needle to sew Fig Leaves together. **1820** SCOTT *Abbot* iv, Who, wise and good as she was, was yet a daughter of grandame Eve.

3. An old woman; a 'gossip'.

c **1550** BALE *Apol.* 54 Some superstycyouse grandame, or some olde dottynge Sir Dauy. **1553** T. WILSON *Rhet.* 77 b, This olde grandamme was devoutelye kneling upon her knees. **1837** HAWTHORNE *Twice-Told T.* (1851) I. xix. 285 The skinny ugliness of a shrivelled grandam.

4. *fig.* (Chiefly *appositive.*)

1602 *Narcissus* (1893) 734 And so I died and sunke into my grandam..earth. **1606** DEKKER *Sev. Sinnes* vii. (Arb.) 43 This ancient and reuerend Grandam of Citties. **1630** J. TAYLOR (Water P.) *Wks.* I. 98 That Ale is Grandam Natures brewing. *a* **1649** DRUMM. OF HAWTH. *Poems* Wks. (1711) 34 From out their grand-dame earth they fain would fly. **1812** COMBE *Picturesque* XIX. (Chandos) 72 In Grandame Nature's vast collection.

5. *attrib.* (quasi-*adj.*) as in †**grandam gold**, hoarded wealth; †**grandame words**, old or obsolete words.

1598 E. GILPIN *Skial.* (1878) 63 Some blame deep Spencer for his grandam words. **1663** DRYDEN *Wild Gallant* IV. i, Frances has one hundred and twenty pieces of old grandam-and-aunt gold left her. **1700** —— *Fables* Pref. (Globe) 504 They..would..hard him up, as misers do their grandam gold, only to look on it themselves.

Hence †'**grandameship** *humorous.*

1649 DAVENANT *Love & Honour* II. 8 Ile teach Her Grandameship to mump, and marry too.

'grand-aunt. [See GRAND *a.* 12 b.] One's father's or mother's aunt; a great-aunt.

18.. *Burd Isbel & Sir Patrick* xxxii. in Child *Ballads* (1892) IV. 421/2 He calld upon his gude grand-aunt. **1826** MISS MITFORD *Village* Ser. II. (1863) 346 Tom..had had the good luck..to take the fancy of a rich relation, a grand-aunt. **1860** SALA *Baddington Peerage* xxxvii, Various comments..were made on his beautiful grand-aunt.

‖**grand battement** (grɑ̃ batəmɑ̃). [Fr.] A ballet exercise in which both legs are kept straight and one leg is raised into the air and brought down again, with the function of loosening the hip joints.

1830 [see BATTEMENT]. **1888** S. D. HEADLAM *Theory Theatr. Dancing* x. 59 *Grands battements* enable a dancer to turn her legs completely outwards, and give much facility to the motions of her thighs. **1933** C. W. BEAUMONT *Primer Class. Ballet* 34 *Grands battements*, which means *large beatings*, are used to loose the hip-joints and to turn out the legs from the hips. **1952** KERSLEY & SINCLAIR *Dict. Ballet Terms* 27 *Grands battements* are taken next. The student throws one leg high to front, side or back, the knee straight and the foot pointed, keeping the rest of the body as still and as upright as possible.

†**grand captain.** *Obs.* [See GRAND *a.* 2; cf. F. *grand capitaine*, Sp. *gran capitan.*] A chief captain or commander.

1534 WHITINTON *Tullyes Offices* I. (1540) 17 Pomphilius graunde capitayne, gouerned a certayne prouynce. **1559** *Mirr. Mag., Dk. Suffolk* xxi, Their graund Captaine Blewberd. **1561** DAUS tr. *Bullinger on Apoc.* (1573) 162 b, On the other side fighteth the Dragon, as Graundcaptayne of this warre. **1606** SHAKS. *Ant. & Cl.* III. i. 9 Thy grand Captaine Anthony Shall set thee on triumphant Chariots.

grandchild ('grændtʃaɪld, 'græntʃaɪld). [See GRAND *a.* 12 b.] The child of one's son or daughter.

1587 GOLDING *De Mornay* xvii. 271 Zoroastres (as is written of him) was Noes graundchilde. **1607** SHAKS. *Cor.* v. iii. 24 And in her hand The Grandchilde to her blood. **1640** YORKE *Union Hon.* 80 Edward, Lord Russell, grand-childe to Francis, Earle of Bedford. **1753** *Scots Mag.* Mar. 158/1 He has left 113 children, grandchildren, and great-grand-children. **1838** LYTTON *Alice* 19 She was sure she should like the grandchild of her dear Mrs. Leslie.

fig. **1661** COWLEY *Disc. Govt. O. Cromwell* Wks. 1710 II. 667 'Twas a Beginning..Fit for a Grand-Child of the Deity. **1810** SCOTT *Fam. Lett.* 10 Dec. (1894) I. 197 Though I have these theatrical grandchildren, as I may call them, I have seen none of them.

‖**grand coup** (grɑ̃ ku). [Fr.: see COUP *sb.*[3]]

1. A great and important stroke or hit; a bold and successful effort.

1813 BYRON *Let. to Moore* 22 Aug. in Moore *Life* (1832) II. 234, I hope you are going on with your *grand coup*—pray do—or that damned Lucien Buonaparte will beat us all. **1856** C. F. ADAMS in *Life & Wks. J. Adams* I. 352 Justly was it denominated by one who had spent his life in the diplomatic service, a '*grand coup*'. **1883** *Standard* 17 Sept. 5/2 (Stanford), [The police] then make a *grand coup* all at once.

2. *Whist* and *Bridge*. The getting rid of a superfluous trump by ruffing a winning card from the opposite hand.

1874 'CAVENDISH' *Whist* (ed. 10) 130 Sometimes..a player has a trump too many. To get rid of this trump..is to play the grand coup. **1939** N. DE V. HART *Bridge Players' Bedside Bk.* xxxvii. 116 This ruffing of a winner to use up an embarrassing trump constituted the Grand Coup. **1952** I. MACLEOD *Bridge* xiv. 169 *Grand Coup*... It is a simple exercise in trump reduction and the fact that you trump winners alone distinguishes it from its humbler cousin the trump coup. **1964** *Official Encycl. Bridge* 222/2 *Grand coup*, a play by which declarer deliberately shortens his trump holding by ruffing a winner in order to achieve a finessing position over an adverse trump holding in an end position.

grand-dad, grandad ('grænddæd, 'grændæd). [See GRAND *a.* 12 b.] A childish or affectionate word for GRANDFATHER.

1819 BYRON *Juan* II. cxxxvii, His hardships were comparative To those related in my grand-dad's 'Narrative'. **1865** *Look before you leap* I. 18 A ward of my granddad's. **1889** P. H. EMERSON *Eng. Idyls* 17 Grandad, what did granny say?

So **gran(d-)dada** = GRAND-DAD.

1698 FARQUHAR *Love & Bottle* I. (1699) 6 And so you left them to Grand Dada! **1871** G. MEREDITH *H. Richmond* III. xii. 205 Her mind was simply obedient to her grandada's wish.

'gran(d-)daddy. [See prec.] **1. a.** = GRAND-DAD.

1769 MAD. D'ARBLAY *Early Diary* (1889) I. 41 My Grand-Daddy is here to-night, to the very great satisfaction of us all.

b. *fig.* Also used *colloq.* with *of* to designate something large, notable, etc., of its kind. Cf. FATHER *sb.* 1 h.

1956 *Amer. Speech* XXXI. 255 This [*sc.* a spoonerism by a radio announcer] is known as the 'grandaddy' of all bloopers. **1960** *Woman's Own* 23 July 54/4 That young fellow is going to have the granddaddy of all headaches for about a week. **1961** M. BEADLE *These Ruins are Inhabited* (1963) xi. 156 The granddaddy of all electrical storms dumped a cloudburst. **1965** R. & D. MORRIS *Men & Snakes* vi. 132 The mythical Serpent of Midgard has been described as the grand-daddy of all sea-serpents. **1968** *New Yorker* 18 May 60 I've had some granddaddies of hangups.

2. *transf.* Also **gran(d-)daddy-longlegs** = DADDY-LONG-LEGS b.

1808 A. WILSON *Let.* in *Poems & Lit. Prose* (1876) I. Pref. 6 A species of Acaris, vulgarly called Longlegs, Grandady, [etc.]. **1875** 'MARK TWAIN' *Sk. New & Old* 130 The learned and aged Lord Grand-Daddy-Longlegs..had been sitting in deep study, with his slender limbs crossed. **1890** W. D. HOWELLS *Boy's Town* 201 You must not kill a granddaddy-long-legs, or a lady-bug, it was bad luck. **1907** *Dialect Notes* III. 188 Don't kill that grandaddy-long-legs; he won't hurt you.

'grand-daughter. [See GRAND *a.* 12 b.] **a.** The daughter of one's son or daughter.

1611 BIBLE *2 Kings* viii. 26 Athaliah the daughter of Omri [*marg.* or granddaughter]. **1625-8** tr. *Camden's Eliz.* Introd. (1630) 7 Lady Iane Grey, grand-daughter to the second sister of King Henry the eighth. **1749** FIELDING *Tom Jones* XVIII. xiii, The tattling of his little grand-daughter, who [etc.]. **1818** CRUISE *Digest* (ed. 2) II. 18 The grand-daughter married without consent.

b. *transf.* Of a mare.

1891 *Daily News* 26 Oct. 3/5 Kairouan, a grand-daughter of Hermit..won in a canter.

c. *Path.* in *attrib.* use (see quots.).

1885 W. ROBERTS *Urin. & Renal Dis.* III. xiii. (ed. 4) 635 In rare cases the secondary cysts contain a tertiary series (grand-daughter cysts). **1897** *Allbutt's Syst. Med.* II. 1118 Such cysts..may give rise to a numerous progeny of daughter or even granddaughter bladders.

d. *attrib.* **grand-daughter clock**, a clock similar to, but smaller than, a grandfather clock; also *ellipt.*

1940 *Chambers's Techn. Dict.* 385/2 *Granddaughter-clock*, a long-case clock about 3½ ft. high, with movement usually provided with lever escapement; a grandfather-clock in miniature. **1962** E. BRUTON *Dict. Clocks* 83 *Grand-daughter clock*, modern clock of grandfather style standing under about 4 ft. 6 in. high. **1968** R. THOMSON *Antique Amer. Clocks & Watches* iii. 80 The New England tall clock reached the pinnacle of development about 1810... On the right is a miniature (or 'granddaughter') in the same style.

Grand Duchess.

a. The wife or widow of a Grand Duke. **b.** A lady holding in her own right the sovereignty of a duchy. **c.** In pre-revolutionary Russia: A daughter of the Tsar.

a **1757** P. H. BRUCE *Mem.* (1782) 125 The Imperial princess, consort to the czarowitz, was brought to bed of a daughter..who..had the title of grand duchess given her. **1862** *Illustr. Lond. News* 5 July 19/2 Her Royal Highness the Grand Duchess of Mecklenburg Strelitz. **1874** *Graphic* 3 Jan. 18/2 The Grand Duchess Marie of Russia.

Grand Duchy. The territory ruled by a Grand Duke or Duchess.

1835 *Penny Cycl.* III. 260/2 The grand-duchy of Baden. **1839** *Ibid.* XIII. 62/1 The Grand Duchy of Tuscany.

Grand Duke. [a. F. *grand duc*, a literal rendering of It. *granduca*, G. *groszherzog*, Russian *velikiĭ kniaz*. See DUKE.]

1. a. The title of the sovereigns of certain European countries (called Grand Duchies); the rank so designated is understood to be one degree below that of king. **b.** In pre-revolutionary Russia, the title of any of the sons of an emperor. (Cf. DUKE 2, 2 c.)

The title seems to have been first assumed by the ruler of Tuscany in the 16th c. Before Peter the Great, the sovereign of Russia was styled 'Grand Duke of Muscovy' in European diplomacy.

a **1693** LUDLOW *Mem.* (1698) II. 507 A Fleet..was sent..to require satisfaction from the Grand Duke of Tuscany. **1833** *Penny Cycl.* I. 309/2 On his death, his next brother, the Grand Duke Constantine, was proclaimed king at Warsaw. **1835** *Ibid.* III. 260/1 The executive and judicial powers in Baden are vested in the grand duke. **1875** T. MARTIN *Prince Consort* I. 214 The Emperor [of Russia] had been in England before..when Grand-Duke.

2. A name of the Great Eagle Owl (*Bubo ignavus*). [F. *grand duc*: cf. DUKE 5.]

1855 OGILVIE, Suppl., *Grand-duke*, the great horned owl (*Bubo maximus*), a species but rarely met with in the British Islands. **1882** OUIDA *Maremma* I. 125 A great grand-duke owl..flew heavily by her. **1895** *Daily News* 3 July 5/4 All sorts of owls save the one known in France as the Grand Duke.

Hence **grand-'ducal** *a.*, of or belonging to a Grand Duke; **grand-'ducalist** *a.*, that supports grand-ducal power or rule; **grand-'dukedom**, the possessions or title of a Grand Duke.

1833 ALISON *Hist. Europe* (1850) II. lxxv. §57. 371 Tearing from his brow the grand-ducal crown of Poland. **1860** SALA *Baddington Peerage* xliv, Before the magnificence of his titles and possessions German grand-dukedoms..paled their ineffectual fires. **1864** *Daily Tel.* 3 Oct., Where the population is republican in the lower classes, and Granducalist in the higher. **1885** AGNES M. CLERKE *Pop. Hist. Astron.* ii. 35 Grand-ducal patronage.

‖**grande amoureuse** (grɑ̃damurøz). [Fr.] A woman of passion; a woman skilled in the arts of love.

1925 A. HUXLEY *Those Barren Leaves* v. i. 341 She found herself..playing the part of the *grande amoureuse*. **1937** *Times Lit. Suppl.* 30 Oct. 796/3 She [*sc.* Pepita] became a very popular dancer at other European capitals and, obviously, a *grande amoureuse*. **1966** G. GREENE *Comedians* I. iii. 82 She could have played the *grande amoureuse* with the English tourist. **1967** *Times* 23 Oct. 6/4 Kedrova [a Russian actress] is yet another version of the grande amoureuse—..who weeps for her Cherry Orchard—..and for her worthless lover.

‖**Grande Armée** (grɑ̃darme). [Fr.] Napoleon's main army, from the campaign of 1805 to that of 1814.

1844 W. SIBORNE *Hist. War France & Belgium* I. ii. 20 The renowned '*grande armée*' of Imperial France. **1896** G. A. HENTY *Through Russian Snows* vii. 142 All believed that the Grande Armée would be invincible. **1942** C. OMAN *Britain against Napoleon* x. 302 Her army could not compare in numbers with the *Grande Armée*. **1958** *Listener* 18 Sept. 441/2 A son of an officer of the Grande Armée. **1969** *Times* 31 May 17/6 When the Emperor got back to Paris in December, 1812, he organized a new *Grande Armée*.

‖**grande dame** (grɑ̃d dam). [Fr.] A great lady; a lady of rank and dignified bearing. Also as *attrib. phr.*

1744 H. WALPOLE *Let.* 8 May (1857) I. 301, I have seen her but once, and found her..*très grande dame*. **1775** A. STORER *Let.* 29 July in *Hist. MSS. Comm. 15th Rep. App. VI.* (1897) 281 And little Ursula a finer lady, from being at Bath, than ever, there being no such *grande dame* there as herself. *c* **1845** C. BRONTË *Professor* (1857) viii. 140 A licence of manners..such as our venerable grand-dames would recoil from. **1855** J. S. MILL *Let.* 15 Jan. in F. A. Hayek *J. S. Mill & Harriet Taylor* (1951) 215 O those grandes dames how all vestige of the very conception of strength or spirit has gone out of them. **1862** THACKERAY *Philip* i, She had been a great beauty, and was a perfect *grande dame* always. **1865** 'OUIDA' *Strathmore* I. ii. 35 Or you've made love to some grande dame because it answered a political purpose. **1908** *Daily Chron.* 21 Feb. 3/2 Mrs. Saker, who is an accomplished player of 'grand-dame' parts. **1936** *Burlington Mag.* Apr. p. xv/2 A Florentine *grande dame* seated in a canopied carriage. **1969** *New Yorker* 11 Oct. 43/1 A *grande dame* caught in the middle of dressing.

grandee (græn'di:). Forms: 6-7 **grande**, 7 **grandie**, **-dy**, 7- **grandee**. [a. Sp., Pg. *grande* great (person): see GRAND *a.*] A Spanish or Portuguese nobleman of the highest rank.

1598 PARSONS *Ward-Word to Hasting's Watch-Word* viii. 116 One of his Grandes in Spayne. **1610** B. JONSON *Alch.* III. iii, *Dol.* What is he, Generall? *Fac.* An *Adalantado*, A *Grande*, girle. **1631** DEKKER *Match me in Lond.* I. Wks. 1873 IV. 143 The Dons and Grandi'es. **1638** FORD *Lady's Trial* I. ii. (1639) C 2 b, Under a pretence of being Grandee of Spain, and cousin to twelve Princes. **1705** *Lond. Gaz.* No. 4161/3 To exasperate the Spanish Grandees. **1814** WELLINGTON in Gurw. *Desp.* (1838) XII. 34 They raised me to the dignity of a Grandee of Spain of the first class. **1833** LONGF. *Outre-Mer* Prose Wks. 1886 I. 141 A muleteer bestrides his beast of burden with the air of a grandee.

b. *transf.* and *gen.* A person of high rank or position, or of eminence in any line.

1605 BACON *Adv. Learn.* II. xvi. §3. 59 The cutting off and keeping low of the Nobilitie and Grandes. **1621** BURTON *Anat. Mel.* Democr. to Rdr. (1651) 35 In a great person..a right honorable Grandy, tis not a venial sin. **1648-9** C. WALKER *Relat. & Observ.* I The said Leading men or Grandees (for that is now Parliament language) First divided themselves into two factions. *a* **1661** HOLYDAY *Persius* (1673) 339 Tertullian..a *Grande* in learning. **1664** H. MORE *Myst. Iniq.* 435 The Pope and Cardinals and other Grandees of that Church. **1691** WOOD *Ath. Oxon.* II. 582 He was offer'd by one of the Grandees of the H. of Commons to keep all that he had. **1726** AMHERST *Terræ Fil.* xiii. 62 Their footmen, who are the next grandees of the university. **1776** ADAM SMITH *W.N.* I. xi. (1869) I. 216 The retinue of a grandee in China or Hindostan. **1847** EMERSON *Repr. Men, Goethe* Wks. (Bohn) I. 393 These grandees of European scientific history. **1855** MACAULAY *Hist. Eng.* xviii. IV. 134 This commercial grandee, who in wealth, and in the influence which attends wealth vied with the greatest nobles of his time. **1863** GEO. ELIOT *Romola* II. vi, Quite a typical Florentine grandee.

appositive. **1652** BENLOWES *Theoph.* x. iii. 179 No grandee patron court I.

†**c.** *fig.* applied to things.

1621 LAUD *Serm.* 24 Mar. (1622) 37 Three Grandies are met together; Blessing, Ioy, and Hope. **1686** GOAD *Celest. Bodies* II. iv. 194 The Planet Mars..hath been reckoned one of the Grandees in Aetherial Regions. **1827** H. HEUGH *Jrnl.*

in Macgill *Life* (1852) x. 292 Ben Nevis..the monarch among the mountain grandees of Scotland.

Hence **gran'deeism** *nonce-wd.*

1850 S. G. Osborne *Gleanings* 238 Landed grandeeism is all very well in its way. **1885** *Spectator* 13 June 775 Mr. Bartley's justification of himself is from end to end an attack on 'grandeeism'.

‖**grande épreuve** (grɑ̃deprœv). [Fr., lit. 'great test'.] An international motor-race.

1955 *Autocar* 10 June 802/1 Francorchamps, the setting for the second of the European *grandes épreuves*, contrasts with Monaco. **1958** *Times* 4 Aug. 8/5 In 1956, his first season as a member of the Ferrari team, he won two of the *grandes épreuves*—the French and Belgian Grands Prix. **1959** *Times* 1 June 16/1 For him there is the added satisfaction of winning his first *grande épreuve*.

grandeeship (græn'diːʃɪp). [f. GRANDEE + -SHIP.] The position or dignity of a grandee.

1776 H. Swinburne *Trav. Spain* xlii. (1779) 386 The Conde de Altamira has no less than nineteen grandeeships centered in his person. **1879** Lowell *Lett.* (1894) II. 268 The duke represents ten grandeeships of the first class.

fig. **1890** *Blackw. Mag.* CXLVII. 177/1 He inherited..his father's grandeeship of manner.

‖**grande passion** (grɑ̃d pasjɔ̃). [Fr.] An overmastering love for another person; an engrossing love affair.

1823 Byron *Juan* XII. lxxvii, And if in fact she takes to a *grande passion*, It is a very serious thing indeed. **1847** C. Brontë *Jane Eyre* xv. 278 A French opera-dancer..towards whom he had once cherished what he called a 'grande passion'. **1854** 'C. Bede' *Verdant Green* II. xi. 95 Despite the hindrance which the *grande passion* is supposed to bring to the student. **1865** 'Ouida' *Strathmore* I. ii. 30 The perpetual gallantries, the never-ending, ever-changing *grandes passions*..that were characteristic of the Sabreur. **1938** *Times Lit. Suppl.* 24 Sept. 612/2 So many Lives have been written without any mention of the *grande passion*. **1960** J. Bayley *Characters of Love* ii. 84 Troilo—after several affairs—is now embarked on a *grande passion*.

‖**grande sonnerie** (grɑ̃d sɔn(ə)ri). [Fr., = great striking, chiming.] (See quot. 1960.)

1938 H. Cescinsky *Old English Master Clockmakers* iii. 13 There are..quarter-strike, chiming, 'Grand Sonnerie', and musical clocks. **1960** H. Hayward *Antique Coll.* 133/2 *Grand sonnerie*, a system of clock striking whereby the hour and the quarter are struck at each quarter. The earliest known example is the movement..made by Tompion about 1676–80. **1963** *Times* 12 Jan. 10/6 A late eighteenth-century *grande sonnerie* mantel clock.

‖**grande tenue** (grɑ̃d təny). [Fr.] Full dress; *esp.* full military costume. Also *fig.* (See also s.v. EN *prep.*)

1849 C. Brontë *Shirley* II. v. 132 Peter Augustus came up, all in 'grande tenue', gloved and scented. **1865** 'Ouida' *Strathmore* I. x. 171 The ease of the dressing-gown after the restraint of the *grande tenue*. **1880** in *Manchester Stage 1880–1900* (1900) 145 Mme. Bernhardt shows the possession of the *grande tenue* necessary for classic tragedy. **1886** *Athenæum* 24 Apr. 560/2 The little soldier..is almost a caricature; the *grande tenue* is so ridiculous as to lose the charm which belongs to grotesqueness. **1952** C. Day Lewis *Grand Manner* 23 Lost, too, are the rhetoric of pulpit and parliament, the ceremonious style of letter-writing, the high-flown leading article—all that *grande tenue* in everyday communication which, though not directly the source of a poetic grand manner, seems so often to be its concomitant.

grandetza, variant of GRANDEZZA *Obs.*

grandeur ('grændjʊə(r)). Also 7 granduer, 7–8 grandure, grandour, 8–9 grandor. [a. F. *grandeur*, f. *grand* great; see GRAND *a.*

Being a word of late adoption, it retains the Fr. form *-eur* of the suffix; attempts to anglicize the form were made in the 17–18th c., and again by Landor.]

†**1. a.** Loftiness, height; tall stature. **b.** Greatness (in amount or degree). *Obs. rare.*

c **1500** *Melusine* xxi. 120 Whan he considered the grandeur & the facion of Vryan. **1632** Lithgow *Trav.* v. 191 Their circle spred tops, do kisse..the lower cloudes; making their grandure over-looke the highest bodies of all other aspiring trees. **1658** Jas. Webb tr. *Calprenede's Cleop.* VIII. i. 4 Consolations, which..sweetened the Grandure of their displeasure.

2. Greatness of power or rank, eminence, puissance. Now somewhat *rare.*

1616 Bullokar, *Grandour*, greatnesse. **1632** Lithgow *Trav.* x. 497 Gentry..All which in each degree, as they illuminat the soyle with grandure, so [etc.]. **1654** tr. *Scudery's Curia Pol.* D 2 a, Freely to renounce Glory and Granduer, to pass from a Throne to an Hermitage. **1657** *North's Plutarch* (1676) Add. Lives 40 [Charlemain] attained to that grandure that no French King could ever before compass. **1704** Hearne *Duct. Hist.* (1714) I. 437 The great number of Coyns and Inscriptions continually dug up in this Place, are so many Instances of its Lustre and Grandeur. **1741** Middleton *Cicero* II. xii. 563 This was the old constitution of Rome, by which it had raised itself to all its grandor. [So spelt elsewhere in this book.] **1815** Elphinstone *Acc. Caubul* (1842) II. 147 They still fondly recal the ancient grandeur of their tribe. **1871** Blackie *Four Phases* i. 26 Estimating our national grandeur by the visible pomp of gigantic machinery.

b. *pl.* Titles or positions implying 'grandeur'; also quasi-*concr.*

1708 *Deplor. St. New Eng.* 21 in *Sewall's Diary* (1879) II. 118* To Strut among his Neighbours, with the Illustrious Titles of, Our Major, and, The Captain, or, His Worship. Such magnificant Grandeurs, make many to Stagger Egregiously! **1897** W. C. Hazlitt *Ourselves* 78 Freemasonry enables them to associate on equal terms with Brother Magnificences and Grandeurs.

3. Transcendent greatness or nobility of intrinsic character.

1669 Gale *Crt. Gentiles* I. I. i. 2 This Grandeur, and sovereign Perfection of God. **1692** Dryden tr. *St. Euremont's Ess.* 204 The Grandeur of the Soul cannot consist with the filthiness of Avarice. **1692** tr. *Sallust* 4 Deeds require Words to equal their Grandeur. **1712** Addison *Spect.* No. 487 ¶8 There seems something in this Consideration that intimates to us a natural Grandour and Perfection in the Soul. **1742** Young *Nt. Th.* IV. 486 To none man seems ignoble, but to man; Angels that grandeur, men o'erlook, admire. **1797** Mrs. Radcliffe *Italian* ii. (1826) 16, I am ready to sacrifice inferior duties to the grandeur of a principle which ought to expand all hearts and impel all actions. **1832** tr. *Sismondi's Ital. Rep.* xii. 263 Men of the fifteenth century perceived honour in a murder..and historic grandeur in conspiracy. **1841–4** Emerson *Ess.*, *Circles* Wks. (Bohn) I. 131 The great man will not be prudent in the popular sense; all his prudence will be so much deduction from his grandeur. **1856** Alger *Solit. Nat. & Man* III. 92 The solitary often occupy themselves with trivialities instead of grandeurs.

4. The quality of being 'grand' (see GRAND *a.* 4) or imposing as an object of contemplation; sublimity, majesty. Also, an instance of this.

1748 Hartley *Observ. Man* I. iv. 419 The Grandeur of some Scenes and the Novelty of others. **1784** Cowper *Tiroc.* 10 That form [*sc.* man's], the labour of Almighty skill..bespeaks control, But borrows all its grandeur from the soul. **1817** Moore *Lalla R.* (1824) 151 Lebanon, Whose head in wintry grandeur towers. **1846** Wright *Ess. Mid. Ages* I. ii. 49 The solemn and majestic grandeur of their Gothic churches. **1868** Longf. in *Life* (1891) III. 121 Switzerland ..outbids the imagination by its grandeurs and perpetual surprises. **1874** Green *Short Hist.* vii. §7. 413 The genius of Shakspere rising year by year into supremer grandeur.

b. of style, composition, etc.

1662 Stillingfl. *Orig. Sacr.* III. i. §15 The grandeur..of the whole books of the Æneids. **1699** Bentley *Phal.* 297 Euripides was accused by Aristophanes..for debasing the Majesty and Grandure of Tragedy. **1870** J. H. Newman *Gram. Assent* II. x. 441 Who can deny the superhuman grandeur and impressiveness of that sacred book, the Apocalypse? **1897** *Westm. Gaz.* 3 Nov. 4/3 The grandeur which is the chief characteristic of the Latin hexameter.

5. Conscious greatness, lofty dignity. †Also, in bad sense, haughtiness, arrogance. *Obs.*

1644 [H. Parker] *Jus Pop.* 20 That arrogant tumor or grandour of mind which is incompatible with brotherly demeanour. **1647** Clarendon *Hist. Reb.* II. §48 The earl of Essex, still preserving his grandeur and punctuality, positively refused to meddle in the treaty. **1797** Godwin *Enquirer* I. vi. 41 The tranquil grandeur of an elevated mind. **1851** Landor *Popery Brit. & For.* 60 Disdain for popularity, unobtrusive wisdom, sedate grandor. **1856** Emerson *Eng. Traits, Race* Wks. (Bohn) II. 23 As you go North..as you enter Scotland, the World's Englishman is no longer found..there is a rapid loss of all grandeur of mien and manners.

6. Magnificence or splendour of appearance, style of living, trappings, etc., such as attends wealth or high station. Also *pl.*

1652 H. Cogan tr. *Scudery's Ibrahim* I. v. 111, I have a desire..to acquaint her with all the magnificences, and all the grandeurs which you have quitted for her sake. **1672** Marvell *Reh. Transp.* I. 26 He undertook to abate of our Episcopall Grandeur, and condescended indeed to reduce the Ceremonious Discipline in these Nations to the Primitive Simplicity. **1711** Shaftesb. *Charac.* (1737) III. 173 The love of grandure and magnificence, wrong turn'd, may have possess'd his imagination over-strongly with such things as frontispieces, parterres, equipages [etc.]. **1784** Cowper *Task* v. 158 Nor wanted aught within, That royal residence might well befit, For grandeur or for use. **1847–8** H. Miller *First Impr.* xviii. (1857) 314, I was placed rather high for witnessing with the right feeling the gauds and the grandeurs [of the Lord Mayor's procession]. **1856** Emerson *Eng. Traits, Aristocracy* Wks. (Bohn) II. 80 The English go to their estates for grandeur. The French live at court, and exile themselves to their estates for economy. **1868** Earl Wilton *Sports of Eng.* 91 Louis then returned to his palace ..ready to proceed with the other methodical..grandeurs of the day. **1878** Mrs. Stowe *Poganuc P.* xi. 93 Leghorn bonnets were a newly-imported test of station, grandeur and gentility in Poganuc.

Hence †**'grandeurship** = GRANDEESHIP.

1692 tr. *C'tess D'Aunoy's Trav.* (ed. 2) 112 The Heiress of the House and Grandeurship of Castle Rodrigue.

grandeval (græn'diːvəl), *a. rare.* [f. L. *grandæv-us* + -AL[1].] Of a great age, old, ancient.

1650 H. More *Obs.* in *Enthus. Triumph.* (1656) 103 Reverend Master Aristotle, that grandeval Patriarch in points of Philosophy. **1846** Mozley *Ess., Carlyle's Cromwell* (1878) I. 231 There..the one grandeval element of Power exists alone.

†**gran'devity.** *Obs.* Also 7 grandævity. [ad. L. *grandævitās*, f. *grandævus*: see next and -ITY.] Great or old age.

1623 Cockeram, *Grandeuitie*, old or great age. **1661** Glanvill *Van. Dogm.* xv. 141 Upon a true account the present age is the worlds Grandævity. **1664** H. More *Myst. Iniq.* 347 A confirmation of the grandevity of the Apostle at that time. **1682** —— *Annot. Glanvill's Lux O.* 185 Whom Dr. More for his Function and Grandevity sake handles so respectfully. **1688** R. Holme *Armoury* II. 403/2 Grandaevity.

†**gran'devous,** *a. Obs. rare*$^{-1}$. In 7 grandævous. [f. L. *grandævus* aged, f. *grand-is* great, GRAND + *ævum* age: see -OUS.] Aged, old.

1682 H. More *Annot. Glanvill's Lux O.* 211 So grave and grandævous a person as he. **1721–1800** in Bailey.

Hence †**gran'devousness.**

1727 Bailey (vol. II), *Grandævousness*, greatness of Age.

‖**gran'dezza, gran'deza.** *Obs.* Also 7 grandetsa. [It. *grandezza*, Sp. *grandeza* :—popular L. type **granditia*, f. *grand-is*: see GRAND *a.*] Grandeur, greatness, magnificence; also, an instance of this, a distinguished honour or privilege.

1642 Howell *For. Trav.* (Arb.) 40 If he be there at the arrivall of the Plate-Fleet..he shall see such a Grandeza, that the Roman Monarchy in her highest florish never had the like. *c* **1645** —— *Lett.* I. II. III. xvii. (1650) 62 Amongst other Grandezas which the King of Spain conferr'd upon our Prince, one was the releasment of Prisoners. **1652** J. Hall *Height Eloquence* p. xxxiv, They are overshadowed with Grandezza's and beauties. **1663** *Flagellum, or O. Cromwell* (1672) 37 The credit of this Atchievement was industriously cryed up at Westminster, and all the Grandezza's of Scriptural Ovation fitted and accommodated thereto. **1675** H. Teonge *Diary* (1825) 87 This island [Cyprus]..had in it 30 cittys, of which there still remaine many worthy memorables of their pristin grandetsa's.

grandfather ('grændfɑːðə(r), 'grænfɑːðə(r)). Forms: 5 grawntefader, grauntfadyr, -ir, graunfadre, 6– grandfather. [f. GRAND *a.* 12 b + FATHER; after F. *grandpère.*]

1. a. The father of one's father or mother.

1424 [Implied in GRANDFATHERLESS]. **1432–50** tr. *Higden* (Rolls) II. 259 Sarug, grawntefader to Thare the fader of Abraham. *c* **1449** Pecock *Repr.* II. iii. 150 Lo here lieth my fadir and there lieth my graunt fadir. **1481** Caxton *Reynard* (Arb.) 74 His fadre and his graunfadre. **1546** *Eng. Gilds* (1870) 197 Kinge Edward graundfather to Richard the second. **1591** Shaks. *Two Gent.* III. i. 295 La. Who begot thee? *Sp.* Marry, the son of my Grand-father. **1615** Crooke *Body of Man* 305 The markes which were in the body of the Grandfather do often appeare in the Grand-childe. **1751** Earl Orrery *Remarks Swift* (1752) 204 Your grandfather sustained the character, which he had so early acquired, to the last moment of his life. **1827** J. F. Cooper *Prairie* I. iii. 42, I wish it was hot noon now, grand'ther.

appositive. **1871** Fraser *Life Berkeley* i. 6 The supposed grandfather-collector was a natural son of the first Lord Berkeley of Stratton.

b. *fig.* and *humorous.* (*occas.* quasi-*adj.*)

1624 Donne *Serm.* cxxx. Wks. 1839 V. 336 Here are risen grandfather and great-grandfather sins quickly, a froward generation. **1655** Baxter *Quaker Catech.* 10, I have no such Infallibility, nor your Grandfather the Pope neither. **1709** Sacheverell *Serm.* 5 Nov. 22 The Grand-Father of Falshood, the Devil. **1961** P. Barry *Unwillingly to School* xvi. 221 There's been the grandfather of a mix-up somewhere. **1971** *Daily Tel.* 18 Dec. 10 Sir Julian Huxley, whom Peter Scott yesterday described as the 'grandfather' of the World Wildlife Fund.

†**2.** *Sc.* Used for 'great grandfather' = GRANDSIRE 2. *Obs.*

a **1651** Calderwood *Hist. Kirk* (1843) II. 174 His grandfather, goodsir, and father, had served his predecessors, and some of them lost their lives under their service.

3. A male ancestor; a forefather.

1613 Hieron *Christian's Jrnl.* Wks. I. 2 Our grand-father Adam. **1638** Sir T. Herbert *Trav.* (ed. 2) 329 The habit they weare, differs not from their grandfather Adams. **1650** Trapp *Comm. Gen.* v. 32 Shem..was in dignity preferred, before his brother, to be grandfather to the Messiah.

4. a. A kind of dance. (Cf. GRANDPAPA b and GRANDPÈRE.)

1897 *Pall Mall Mag.* Aug. 445 One of the last dances was an old-fashioned country dance, called 'the grand-father', when each couple in turn passed along holding a handkerchief, over which all the others had to jump.

b. Short for *grandfather clock* (see sense 5).

1894 F. J. Britten *Former Clock & Watchmakers* 175 Some of these primitive 'grandfathers' were exceedingly narrow in the waist. **1906** *Bazaar, Exch. & Mart Suppl.* 3 Oct. 1302/3 Wanted, old grandfathers, brass arched dials. **1909** E. Rickert *Beggar in Heart* 1 The house is so still I can hear grandfather ticking on the stairs with the door shut. **1967** B. Palmer *Treasury Amer. Clocks* 1 Grandfathers were the first type of clocks to be made in the Colonies.

5. *Comb.*, as **grandfather's beard, chair** (see quots.); **grandfather clause** *U.S. colloq.*, a clause in the constitutions of some Southern states, exempting from suffrage restrictions the descendants of men who voted before the Civil War; also *transf.*; **grandfather's clock** [suggested by a song which was popular about 1880], a furniture-dealer's name for the kind of weight-and-pendulum eight-day clock in a tall case, formerly in common use; also **grandfather clock** (now the usual name); **grandfather-long-legs** = DADDY-LONG-LEGS (cf. GRAN(D-)DADDY 2).

1883 *Hampsh. Gloss.*, *Grandfather's beard*, a species of *Equisetum* (mare's tail). **1892** *Pall Mall G.* 2 June 1/3 The new easy-chair..is called the grandfather's chair. It is roomy and soft, and on each side at the top has two projections, something like the peaks of a Gladstone collar. **1900** *Congress. Rec.* 22 Jan. 1033/1 The grandfather clause will not avail those citizens who..are unable to pay their poll tax. **1903** *N.Y. Evening Post* 22 Dec. 6 It is proposed [in Maryland] to remodel the Constitution so as to exclude colored men from voting. The usual Southern method is followed, 'grandfather clause' and all. **1906** W. H. Fleming *Slavery* 44 This proviso was popularly known as the 'Grandfather clause'. **1948** *Georgia Hist. Q.* Mar. 1 In 1898, Louisiana wrote the notorious 'Grandfather Clause' into its constitution. [**1876** H. C. Work *Grandfather's Clock*, My grandfather's clock was too large for the shelf, So it stood ninety years on the floor.] **1892** J. F. Kendal *Hist. Watches* 153 Longcase or 'Grandfathers'' clocks. **1910** *Encycl. Brit.* VI. 552/2 The long or 'grandfather' clock dates from about the fourth quarter of the 17th century. **1922** O. Mitchell *Talking Machine Industry* vi. 68 Others use weight-driven mechanism[s] like those of the old-fashioned grandfather's clocks. **1928** J. E. HASWELL *Horology* 74 A typical grandfather clock. **1952** H. GORDON *Antiques* ii. 36 A particular development associated with the [Restoration] period was the first appearance of the 'Grandfather' clock. **1970** G. SAVAGE *Dict. Antiques* 191 *Grandfather clock*, a comparatively recent term for the long-case clock.

Hence **'grandfatherhood**, the condition of being a grandfather; **'grandfatherland** (*nonce-wd.*), the 'fatherland' of one's parents; **'grandfatherless** *a.*, without a grandfather; hence *'grandfatherlessness*; **'grandfatherly** *a.*, of, befitting, or resembling a grandfather; also *transf.*; **'grandfathership**, the fact of being a grandfather.

1856 J. GROTE in *Cambridge Ess.* 85 The similarity (arising from its relation of parentage, or more properly of *grandfatherhood) between our language and the Latin in many words. **1892** *Blackw. Mag.* CLI. 224/1 Some.. vague idea of relationship and grandfatherhood. **1864** E. BURRITT *Walk Lond. to John O'Groat's* 317 The *grandfatherland of fifty millions who now speak its language beyond the sea. **1424** *E.E. Wills* (1882) 57 þan shall he be left.. *grauntfaderles. **1885** D. C. MURRAY *Rainbow Gold* III. v. ii. 25 Grandfatherless persons whose manners smacked of mine and foundry. **1896** *Blackw. Mag.* Apr. 595 That salve for *grandfatherlessness, indifference to rank and the opinions of others. **1824** COLERIDGE *Lett., Convers.*, etc. (1836) II. 167 My *Grandfatherly love and kisses to the Fairy Prattler. **1850** HAWTHORNE *Scarlet L.* viii. (1883) 138 He was a grandfatherly sort of person. **1856** EMERSON *Eng. Traits, Race* Wks. (Bohn) II. 29 What substantial, respectable, grandfatherly figures. **1880** *New Virginians* I. 95 A grand-fatherly rat. **1883** *B'ham Weekly Post* 1 Sept. 4/5 The *grandfathership of the Norwich Lincolne is impossible.

'grandfather, *v. rare.* [f. GRANDFATHER *sb.*] *trans.* **a.** ***to grandfather up***: ? to flatter with excess of deference. **b.** ***to grandfather*** (a thing) ***on***: *fig.* [after FATHER *v.*] to impute to (a person) as its mediate originator.

1748 RICHARDSON *Clarissa* (1811) I. 331 Nor would I advise that you should go to grandfather up your cousin Morden. **1893** A. BIRRELL *Res Judicatæ* 99 Alexander Knox ..on whom the Tractarian movement has been plausibly grandfathered.

grandfer, granfer ('grænfə(r)), dial. shortening of GRANDFATHER.

1874 HARDY *Far fr. Mad. Crowd* viii, Ah, he's his grandfer's own grandson. **1889** A. GISSING *Both of this Parish* I. i. 21 'E be a good girl to look after your old granfer. **1930** *Daily Express* 23 May 10/3 What is good enough for granfer is good enough for us, look'ee.

‖**grand feu** (grɑ̃ fø). [Fr., lit. great fire.] (See quot. 1960.)

1863 W. CHAFFERS *Marks Pott. & Porc.* 164 When the mark is not indented on the paste, or baked with the porcelain when at its greatest heat (*au grand feu*), it gives no guarantee for its genuineness. **1906** S. W. BUSHELL *Chinese Art* II. 37 Under-glaze copper red (*rouge de cuivre*) of the *grand feu*. **1959** G. SAVAGE *Antique Coll. Handbk.* 227 Tin-enamelled wares are usually decorated in colours applied directly at the same time as the glaze (high-temperature colours, or colours of the *grand feu*). **1960** R. G. HAGGAR *Conc. Encycl. Cont. Pott. & Porc.* 210/1 *Grand feu*, a term introduced by Brongniart for the hottest kiln, used for firing the glaze of hard-paste porcelain. *Grand feu* colours are those which require a high temperature to fire them.

†**grandgore.** *Obs.* Chiefly *Sc.* Forms: α. 5-6 **grantgor, grand gor(e**; β. 6 **glengoir**, 7 **glangore**, 7-8 **glengore**. [a. OF. *grand gorre*: *grand* great + *gorre* syphilis.] Syphilis.

α. **1497** *Min. Town Counc. Edin.* in *Phil. Trans.* XLII. 421 This contagious sickness callit the Grandgor. **1497** in *Ld. Treas. Acc. Scotl.* I. 356 Item, to ane woman with the grantgore.. iijs. vjd. **1509** *Register Privy Seal Scot.* in Pitcairn *Crim. Trials* I. 110* To hele þe said vmqle Schir Lancelote of þe infirmite of þe grantgor. **1529** LYNDESAY *Compl. King* 286 Ihone Makerery, the kyngis fule,.. For his rewarde, gat the grand gore. **1535** STEWART *Cron. Scot.* II. 313 No canker, fester, gut, or ȝit grandgor.

β. **15..** *Rowllis Cursing* 63 in Laing *Anc. Pop. Poetry* 213 The strangelour and grit glengoir. *a* **1605** MONTGOMERIE *Flyting w. Polwart* 297 The glengore, gravell, and the gut. **1621** J. TAYLOR (Water P.) *Taylors Goose* Wks. (1630) I. 105/2 Luxurious, letcherous Goates, that hunt in Flockes, To catch the Glangore, Grinkums, or the Pockes. **1716** *He winna be guidit by me* in *Jacob. Songs* (1887) 115 God send him a heavy glengore, too, For that is the death he will die.

attrib. **1500-20** DUNBAR *Poems* xiv. 19 So mony glengoir markis Within this land was nevir hard nor sene. **1508** —— *Flyting w. Kennedie* 83 Fy! glengoir loun, fy! fy!

grandgosier, obs. form of GRANGOUSIER.

grand guard. Also 6 **graungarde**, 7 **grangard**. [f. GRAND *a.* + GUARD *sb.*; in sense 1 app. a. OF. **grant garde*.]

1. 'A piece of plate armour used in the fifteenth and sixteenth centuries in the tournament. It covered the breast and left shoulder, forming an additional protection for that side of the body; and it was affixed to the breastplate by screws, and hooked on the helmet' (*Fairholt's Costume*, 1885).

1546 HALL *Chron., Hen. VIII* an. 5 (1550) 29 The one bare ye helme, the seconde his graungarde. **1602** WARNER *Alb. Eng.* XII. lxix. (1612) 291 The Poldrons, Grangard, Vambraces, Gauntlets for either hand. **1612** *Two Noble K.* III. vi, You care not for a grand-guard? **1898** VISC'T DILLON in *Archæol. Jrnl.* Ser. II. V. 313 The grandguard and pasguard are ornamented with the same designs.

2. (See quot. 1802.)

1703 *Lond. Gaz.* No. 3923/2 A Party of 1200 of the Enemy's Horse and Dragoons.. attempted to surprise our Grand Guard. **1763** MUNRO in J. Grant *Hist. India* (1876) I. xix. 104/2, I.. ordered in our advance posts and grand-guards. **1802** C. JAMES *Milit. Dict.*, *Grand Guard*, a guard composed of three or four squadrons of horse, commanded by a field officer, posted about a mile and a half from the camp, on the right and left wings, towards the enemy, for the better security of the camp. **1844** *Regul. & Ord. Army* 267 The Grand Guards of Cavalry are to be formed, and the Horses picketed.

Grand Guignol (grɑ̃ giɲɔl). [Fr. (= Great Punch), the name of a theatre in Paris.] A dramatic entertainment in which short pieces of a sensational or horrific kind are played successively. Also *transf.* Hence **Grand Guigno'lesque, Grand 'Guignolish** *adjs.*; **Grand 'Guignolism.**

1908 *Sat. Rev.* 397/2 To act well in the Grand-Guignol postulates.. as much art as in any other theatre. *Ibid.* 398/1 The most typically Grand-Guignolesque thing in the programme. **1920** H. B. IRVING in M. Level *Crises* p. iii, M. Level has given literary expression of a high order to the compact horrors of the Grand Guignol. **1922** *Westm. Gaz.* 1 Dec., Violent eccentricity is on the decrease; I have seen Salons of a much more Grand Guignol character than this one. **1923** *Daily Mail* 12 June 8 'The Drums of Oude'.. is perhaps unequalled as a one-act thriller outside frank Grand Guignolism. **1928** *Daily Tel.* 27 Mar. 6 'The Unknown', a morbid Grand Guignolesque conception rendered tolerable .. by the actor's arresting personality. **1958** *Listener* 7 Aug. 211/2 Nor did any Grand Guignolish nonsense spoil his story which was full of genuine horror. **1961** A. WILSON *Old Men at Zoo* iv. 214 Did you see this grand guignol of Leacock's yesterday morning?.. The destruction of the lynx had a morbid effect on the spectators. **1967** *Times* 3 Oct. 11/5 Many more [secrets] perished with the death of the sinister man who managed Stalin's *Grand Guignol* in the last years. **1969** *Observer* 12 Jan. 26/5 The film winds, with brilliant clarity, through a maze of shadowy emotions to a splendidly Grand-Guignolesque ending.

†**gran'dific**, *a. Obs. rare.* [ad. L. *grandific-us*, f. *grandi-s* great + *-ficus* making: see -FIC.]

1727 BAILEY vol. II, *Grandifick*, doing great Things. **1782** W. STEVENSON *Hymn Deity* 23 In those grandific works.. Where perfect fitness, beauty, use, unite.

grandiflora (,grændɪ'flɔərə), *a.* [a. mod.L. *grandiflora* a specific epithet often used in the names of large-flowered plants, f. L. *grandi-s* great + FLORA.] Bearing large flowers.

1901 *Vegetables & Flowers from Seeds* (Sutton & Sons) 274 The single [Petunia] flowers are of the fine Grandiflora type. **1933** *Jrnl. R. Hort. Soc.* LVIII. 393 *Phlox Drummondii nana compacta*.. are similar to the well-known grandiflora type. **1938** *Harper's Mag.* Nov. 668/2 We, the unholy innocents, study the bulb catalogue and order one dozen paper-white Grandiflora Narcissus. **1952** V. GOLLANCZ *My Dear Timothy* 279 Grandiflora geraniums. **1960** *Times* 9 Jan. 9/1 For those who like larger flowered petunias.. the 'grandiflora' types are excellent. **1970** C. LLOYD *Well-Tempered Garden* iii. 273 Would a devotee of wild gladioli and of the dwarf or small-flowered hybrids ever desert them in preference for the heavy, showy spikes of the Grandiflora types?

†**grandify**, *v. Obs.* [f. L. *grandi-s* (see GRAND *a.*) + -FY.] *trans.* To make great.

1683 E. HOOKER *Pref. Ep. Pordage's Mystic Div.* 92 Whom that.. God mai saluifi, fortifi and grandifi.

grandilo'quacity. *nonce-wd.* [See next and LOQUACITY.] A piece of grandiloquence.

1814 *Q. Rev.* XII. 48 His visit to France is only a pleonasm or grandiloquacity for a trip from Dover to Calais.

grandiloquence (græn'dɪləkwəns). [f. next: see -ENCE.] The quality of being grandiloquent; a lofty or imposing style of speech or writing.

1589 PUTTENHAM *Eng. Poesie* III. v. (Arb.) 162 And therefore of learned duke asketh martiall grandiloquence, if [etc.]. **1603** HOLLAND *Plutarch's Mor.* 1158 Her grandiloquence and stout resolutions in her speech. **1669** GALE *Crt. Gentiles* I. III. x. 96 The Grandiloquence of Plato. **1791** BOSWELL *Johnson* 3 Apr. an. 1773, One cannot help smiling sometimes at his affected grandiloquence. **1840** CARLYLE *Heroes* (1858) 321, I find in Johnson's Books.. a measured grandiloquence, stepping or rather stalking along in a very solemn way. **1856** MASSON *Ess.* iv. 137 In lyrical grandiloquence, Dryden was in his natural element. **1880** MCCARTHY *Own Times* III. xlvi. 411 Both the vagueness and the grandiloquence were doubtless deliberate.

grandiloquent (græn'dɪləkwənt), *a.* [f. L. *grandiloqu-us*, of the same meaning, f. *grandi-s* big, great (see GRAND *a.*) + *-loquus* speaking, f. root of *loquī* to speak. For the ending (after *eloquent*) cf. *magniloquent* and Sp. *grandilocuente*, It. *grandiloquente*.] Of a person, his language, style of writing, etc.: Characterized by swelling or pompous expression.

1593 NASHE *Strange Newes* Wks. (Grosart) II. 253, I.. admire your aged Muse, that may well be grand-mother to our grandeloquentest Poets at this present. **1656** BLOUNT *Glossogr.*, *Grandiloquent*, that useth great words, that hath a high stile. **1827-48** HARE *Guesses* Ser. II. (1873) 361 Men are ambitious of saying grand things, that is, of being grandiloquent. **1837-9** HALLAM *Hist. Lit.* IV. IV. v. §17 230 To imitate the grandiloquent strains of Pindar. **1840** POE *Gold Bug* Wks. 1864 I. 60 'I sent for you', said he, in a grandiloquent tone. **1868** HELPS *Realmah* viii. (1876) 178 You should have heard him dilate upon it in his grandiloquent way. **1888** BURGON *Lives 12 Gd. Men* I. i. 35 An enthusiastic (and of course a grandiloquent) admirer of the future President.

absol. **1829** LYTTON *Disowned* 18 A prodigious love of the grandiloquent.

Hence **gran'diloquently** *adv.*, in grandiloquent language.

1865 E. C. CLAYTON *Cruel Fort.* II. 119 You talk very grandiloquently about taking an interest in me. **1870** *Spectator* 27 Aug. 1039/2 That insignificant chain of hills which geographers grandiloquently term the Ural Mountains.

gran'diloquism. *nonce-wd.* [f. L. *grandiloqu-us* (see prec.) + -ISM.] The practice of using grandiloquent language.

1836 *Monthly Rev.* Aug. 526 But everything that is Russian appears, according to the author's colouring, so superior to what exists any where else, that we must take his testimony with some caution.. His grandiloquism proves too much.

grandiloquous (græn'dɪləkwəs), *a.* Also 7 **grandiloquious.** [f. L. *grandiloqu-us* (see prec.) + -OUS.] Grandiloquent.

1592 G. HARVEY *Pierce's Super.* 177 What grandiloquous epithets.. have they bestowed. **1689** G. HARVEY *Curing Dis. by Expect.* xxi. 175 The blazoning of their vertues are so grandiloquious. **1806** SOUTHEY in *Ann. Rev.* IV. 60 His grandiloquous style often obscures.. his meaning. **1832** AUSTIN *Jurispr.* (1879) II. xxx. 560 Grandiloquous talk. **1863** *N. & Q.* Ser. III. III. 334 Notwithstanding the grandiloquous flourish about the 'French, Spanish, and Portuguese Authorities of the order'.

†**gran'diloquy.** *Obs.*$^{-0}$ [ad. L. **grandiloquium*: cf. *soliloquium* soliloquy.] Lofty speech.

1663 BULLOKAR, *Grandiloquy*, high, lofty, big-speaking. **1676** in COLES.

†**grandinous**, *a. Obs.*$^{-0}$ [ad. L. *grandinōsus*, f. *grandin-*, *grandō* hail.] (See quot.)

1656 BLOUNT *Glossogr.*, *Grandinous*, full of hail, subject to hail. **1755** in JOHNSON.

†**grandio.** *Obs.* [Cf. GRANDO[1].] A grandee.

1650 TRAPP *Comm. Gen.* x. 8 A Magnifico, a Grandio, such a one as sought to make himself great even to a proverb.

grandiose ('grændɪəʊs), *a.* [a. F. *grandiose*, ad. It. *grandioso* (whence also Sp., Pg. *grandioso*), f. L. *grandi-s* (It., Sp., Pg. *grande*) great (see GRAND *a.*); for the suffix see -OSE, -OUS.]

1. Producing an effect or impression of grandeur or greatness; characterized by largeness of plan or nobility of design.

1843 EMERSON *Misc. Papers, Carlyle* Wks. (Bohn) III. 317 This grandiose character pervades his wit and his imagination. **1850** LEITCH tr. *C. O. Müller's Anc. Art* §290 (ed. 2) 322 Amphitheatres.. in the simple and grandiose taste of the Hellenic architects. **1855** BROWNING *In a Balcony* 132 Things painted by a Rubens.. All better, all more grandiose than the life. **1874** H. R. REYNOLDS *John Bapt.* viii. 506 Those who saw the grandiose form of the Baptist. **1897** DOWDEN *Fr. Lit.* IV. iii. 303 In *Les Ruines*.. he recalls the past like 'an Arab Ossian', monotonous and grandiose.

2. Of speech, style, deportment, etc. Characterized by formal stateliness; often in disparaging sense: Aiming at an effect of grandeur, pompous.

1840 THACKERAY *Paris Sk.-bk., Napoleon* (1869) 118 Our author speaks of the Emperor's advent in the following grandiose way. **1847** DE QUINCEY *Sp. Mil. Nun* xii. Wks. 1862 III. 34 Mr. Urquiza entered first, with a strut more than usually grandiose. **1850** W. IRVING *Goldsmith* xii. 150 He carried into the bookselling craft somewhat of the grandiose manner of the stage. **1865** DICKENS *Mut. Fr.* I. xvi, What is it that we call it in our grandiose speeches? **1876** GEO. ELIOT *Dan. Der.* v. xxxix. 363 His grandiose air was making Mab feel herself a ridiculous toy to match the cottage piano. **1892** A. BIRRELL *Res Judicatæ* ii. 58 Gibbon .. Milton.. as the one is our grandest author, so the other is our most grandiose.

grandiosely ('grændɪəʊslɪ), *adv.* [f. prec. + -LY[2].] In a grandiose manner.

1858 DORAN *Crt. Fools* 331 A Pole grandiosely named Corneille de Lithuanie. **1879** MCCARTHY *Own Times* I. 425 Lord George Bentinck talked grandiosely. **1888** *Harper's Mag.* July 220 All this is now repeated for us more imposingly, more grandiosely.

grandiosity (grændɪ'ɒsɪtɪ). [f. GRANDIOSE + -ITY.] The quality of being grandiose.

1839 HALLAM *Hist. Lit.* III. III. vi. §47. 573 There is.. something of a *grandiosity* in the sentiments and language, which shows us that Shakspeare had not read that history without entering into its spirit. **1862** *Sat. Rev.* XIV. 573/2 Mr. Balme's book.. is disfigured, in regard to style, by.. a pervading grandiosity of manner. **1881** M. ARNOLD *Byron* in *Macm. Mag.* XLIII. 372/2 That 'daring, dash, and grandiosity', of Byron, which are indeed so splendid. **1887** LOWELL *Old Eng. Dramatists* (1892) 36 Marlowe.. constantly pushes grandiosity to the verge of bombast.

grandisonant (græn'dɪsənənt), *a. rare.* [f. L. *grandi-s* great + *sonant-em*, pr. pple. of *sonā-re* to sound. Cf. GRANDISONOUS.] Stately-sounding.

1684 H. MORE *Answer* 276 The expressions are so high, sublime, and grandisonant. **1685** —— *Paralip. Prophet* 381 That grandisonant Speech was uttered by Nestorius. **1827** WILSON in *Blackw. Mag.* XXI. 503 The grandisonant name of The Glory of Mount Pleasant.

Grandisonian (grændɪˈsəʊnɪən), *a.* [f. *Grandison* (see below) + -IAN.] Of deportment, manner, etc.: Of or resembling that of Sir Charles Grandison, the hero of S. Richardson's novel of that name.

The character was intended by the author to represent his ideal of a perfect gentleman. The stately and formal courtesy, and the chivalric magnanimity, ascribed by Richardson to his hero, are the features of the character most prominent in allusive references.

1829 *Westm. Rev.* X. 179 To say the truth, our exquisite sports nothing at all Grandisonian either in morals or manners. **1859** CARLYLE *Let.* 13 Apr. in Sir C. G. Duffy *Convers. w. Carlyle* (1892) 203 A man of scrupulous veracity, correctness and integrity, a kind of Grandisonian style of magnanimity, both in substance and manner, visible in all his conduct. **1881** STEVENSON *Virg. Puerisque* 58 They treat them to Grandisonian airs. **1882** TUCKERMAN *Hist. Eng. Fiction* (1884) 197 The Grandisonian manners are not to be taken as a picture of contemporary fashion.

So also the *nonce-wds.* **Grandiˈsonianism**, Grandisonian manner or style; **ˈGrandisonize** *v. trans.*, to escort in a Grandisonian fashion.

1824 *Blackw. Mag.* XV. 224 Will your ladyship permit me to have the honour of Grandisonizing you into the next apartment? **1882** A. W. WARD *Dickens* 116 He becomes a really fine picture, unmarred by any Grandisonianisms in either thought or phrase, of a true gentleman.

grandisonous (grænˈdɪsənəs), *a.* [f. late L. *grandison-us* (f. *grandi-s* GRAND *a.* + *son-*, root of *sonus* sound): see -OUS.] = GRANDISONANT.

1674 PETTY *Disc. Dupl. Proportion* A v, Grandisonous or Euphonical Nonsence. **1727–1800** BAILEY, *Grandisonous*, that maketh a great Sound. **1870** MUSGRAVE *Ramble Brittany* I. 107 The opera-house rejoicing in the grandisonous designation of L'Académie Impériale de la Musique.

†**ˈgrandity.** *Obs.* [ad.L. *grandităs*, f. *grandis*: see GRAND and -ITY. OF. had *grandité*.] Grandeur, stateliness. Also, an attribute or mark of greatness.

1589 PUTTENHAM *Eng. Poesie* III. xxiv. (Arb.) 302 And in a Prince it is decent to goe slowly, and to march with leysure, and with a certaine granditie rather than grauitie. **1605** CAMDEN *Rem.*, *Poems* 1 Our Poets..excell in granditie and grauity. **1689** T. PLUNKET *Char. Gd. Commander* 34 Inheritor..of his ample territories and other grandities. **1839** J. ROGERS *Antipopopr.* x. ii. 252 Beings so unequal in dignity and grandity.

†**ˈgrandize,** *v. Obs. rare*$^{-1}$. [f. GRAND *a.* + -IZE.] *trans.* To make grand or great.

1660 FULLER *Mixt Contempl.* Ser. I. xlvi. 310 The many mountains of our age grandised by the unlawful ruin of others.

‖**grand jeté** (grɑ̃ ʒəte). [Fr.: see JETÉ.] A ballet-step (cf. JETÉ and see quot. 1957).

1930 CRASKE & BEAUMONT *Theory & Pract. Allegro Class. Ballet* 37 (*heading*) Grand jeté en attitude. **1941** C. W. BEAUMONT *3rd Primer Class. Ballet* ii. 16 *Grand jeté*, as its name implies, is a step of big elevation, executed *en tournant en diagonale*. **1948** A. CHUJOY tr. *Vaganova's Basic Princ. Class. Ballet* vii. 76 For execution on the stage, grand jeté demands an entirely different approach than the small jeté. **1957** G. B. L. WILSON *Dict. Ballet* 154 *Grand jeté*,..a leap from one foot to the other, finishing in any required position. **1960** *Spectator* 4 Nov. 691 Held in the air, momentarily frozen in a *grand jeté*. **1962** *Ibid.* 2 Mar. 272 His sensational *grand jeté* from the Kirov ballet naturally helped to establish him. **1962** *Times* 27 Nov. 14/7 The generous *grands jetés*.

grand-juror, jury, etc.: see JUROR, etc.

†**ˈgrandling.** *Obs. rare*$^{-1}$. [f. GRAND *a.* + -LING.] A 'grand' person, an aristocrat.

a **1637** B. JONSON *Underwoods, Sp. according to Horace* Wks. (1640) 215 But he that should perswade to have this done For education of our Lordings; Soone Should he [not] heare of billow, wind, and storme From the Tempestuous Grandlings.

grandly (ˈgrændlɪ), *adv.* [f. GRAND *a.* + -LY².] In a grand manner; magnificently, splendidly, grandiosely, etc.

1654 Z. COKE *Art Logick* Ep. Ded. (1657) A iij b, To Tranquility of Government, Corruption of Manners, and Mazing Errors are grandly opposite. **1658–9** *Burton's Diary* (1828) IV. 243 The Chair..takes a little too much on him, but grandly. **1785** BOSWELL *Tour Hebrides* 348 There was something grandly horrible in the sight. **1841–4** EMERSON *Ess.*, *Over-Soul* Wks. (Bohn) I. 122 A mind that is grandly simple. **1863–5** J. THOMSON *Sund. at Hampstead* IV. iv, Mary and Dick so grandly Parade suburban streets. **1882** MRS. OLIPHANT *Lit. Hist. Eng.* I. 3 Means which are dimly or grandly traceable across the ages. **1888** STEEL & LYTTLETON *Cricket* (Badm. Libr.) xi. 347 Lyttleton..was grandly caught by Webbe close to the ropes. **1890** B. WYNNE *Our Hardy Fruits* 20 It [a pear] does grandly against a house wall.

‖**grand mal** (grɑ̃ mal). [Fr., = the great sickness.] General convulsive epilepsy with loss of consciousness; epilepsis gravior. Sometimes artificially induced as part of electro-shock treatment. (Cf. PETIT MAL.)

[**1842** J. JACKSON *Inquiry into Nature & Causes of Epilepsy* 10 The peculiar giddiness or momentary state of half consciousness, to which epileptics are so liable, is indeed an imperfect seizure, and differs only in degree and duration from the state called catalepsy; it is termed by the French 'vertige epileptique' or 'petit mal', in contradistinction to the perfect seizure, or 'grand mal'.] **1879** *Encycl. Brit.* VIII. 479/2 There are two well-marked varieties of the epileptic seizure... To these the terms *epilepsia gravior* and *epilepsia mitior*, *le grand mal* and *le petit mal*, are usually applied. **1948** *Jrnl. Nerv. & Mental Dis.* CVIII. 296 No patient was treated with petit mal seizures, and a grand mal response was achieved with each single treatment in each patient. **1960** M. SPARK *Bachelors* i. 10 The patient might learn to exercise some control during the *petit-mal* stage to stand him in good stead during the *grand-mal* convulsions. **1965** J. POLLITT *Depression & its Treatment* iv. 50 Electro-convulsive treatment..is still the most rapid and effective treatment. It consists of the passage of a brief alternating electric current across the anterior temporal regions of the head to induce a grand mal convulsion.

grandmamma (ˈgrændməmɑː, ˈgrænməmɑː). Also **grandmama.** [See GRAND *a.* 12 b.] A colloquial synonym of GRANDMOTHER *sb.* Also **ˈgrandma, ˈgrandmammy.** (For the status of these forms see MAMMA, MA, MAMMY¹.)

1749 J. CLELAND *Mem. Woman of Pleasure* I. 140 The maid..added, that she was sure this usage of her sweet young master, would be the death of his grand-mamma. **1763** *Brit. Mag.* IV. 495 O discretion! thou'rt a jewel, Or our grand-mammas mistake. **1781** COWPER *Retirement* 515 Your prudent grandmammas, ye modern belles, Content with Bristol, Bath, and Tunbridge Wells. **1813** *Examiner* 29 Mar. 204/1 To frighten children and grandmammas. **1825** C. M. WESTMACOTT *Eng. Spy* I. 158 At our old grand-mamma's in St. Clement's. **1836** DICKENS *Let.* 30 July (1965) I. 159 Perhaps you will fill up the blank, and place 'Grandmama' and 'Grandpapa' at the top. **1866** GEO. ELIOT *F. Holt* i. 34 You shall have nothing to do now but to be grandmamma on satin cushions. **1867** W. JAMES *Let.* 26 Sept. (1920) I. 105, I remember days passed in Grandma's old house in Albany. **1871** L. M. ALCOTT *Little Men* iii. 30 Mrs. Bhaer with Daisy and her own two boys drove into town, to pay the weekly visit to Grandma. **1894** CROCKETT *Lilac Sunbonnet* 38 But, grandmammy dear, I thought that [etc.]. **1939** JOYCE *Finnegans Wake* 580 To make grim grandma grunt and grin again.

Grand Marnier (grɑ̃ marnje). [Fr.; *grand* great, fine, and *Marnier*-Lapostolle, name of manufacturer.] A French cognac-based liqueur.

1905 *Daily Chron.* 28 Apr. 6/7 A publican who supplied Benedictine to several customers who asked for Grand Marnier was fined £5. **1910** *Encycl. Brit.* VII. 636/1 A lighter variety of Curaçoa, made with fine brandy, is known as 'Grand Marnier'. **1924** GALSWORTHY *White Monkey* II. ii, He went to a cupboard and returned with two small glasses of a brown fluid. 'Have a Grand Marnier?' **1958** A. L. SIMON *Dict. Wines* 85/1 *Grand Marnier*, popular French liqueur with an orange flavour and a Cognac brandy basis. **1962** *Cocktails* (Cunard Line) Grand Marnier 2/6.

grand master.

†**1.** The chief officer of a royal household. *Obs.*

1549 LATIMER *1st Serm. bef. Edw. VI* (Arb.) 32 God is great grand mayster of the Kynges house, and wil take accompt of euery one that beareth rule therin, for the executing of their offices. **1556** *Chron. Gr. Friars* (Camden) 55 The lord Richard Ryche was made chaunseler of Ynglond, and the lord Sent Jone that was lorde grandemaster gave it up. **1748** LADY M. W. MONTAGU *Let. to W. Montagu* 25 Dec., She came attended with the greatest part of her court; her grand-master.., the first lady of her bedchamber [etc.].

2. a. The head of one of the military orders of knighthood, *e.g.* the Hospitallers, Templars, etc.

1553 BECON *Reliques of Rome* (1563) 59 Of the Templares orders. For when their g[r]aundmaster, Iames Burgonion was burnt at Paris [etc.]. **1603** KNOLLES *Hist. Turks* (1638) 59 Otto, grand master of the Templars. **1777** WATSON *Philip II* (1839) 67 The sieur de la Valette, grand-master of the knights of Malta. **1802** G. ROSE *Diaries* (1860) I. 515 The present inclination..was to leave the nomination of a Grand Master to the Knights. **1820** SCOTT *Ivanhoe* xxxviii, On an elevated seat..sat the Grand Master of the Temple.

b. The head of the order of Freemasons (or of a 'province' of this), or of later societies which imitate its constitution, as the Odd Fellows, etc.

1724 *Weekly Jrnl.* 25 Jan. 2769/1 Sampson..was accounted Grand Master of that Fraternity [Free Masons]. **1753** *Scots Mag.* Sept. 426/2 George Drummond, of the society of Free Masons in Scotland Grand Master. **1840** DICKENS *Old C. Shop* xiii, The Perpetual Grand Master of the Glorious Appollers.

†**3.** A leading member of a trade guild. *Obs.*

1615 J. STEPHENS *Satyr. Ess.* 293 [He] is never free of the Company,..till he hath drunk out his Apprentise-hood among the graund Masters.

4. *Chess.* (Freq. written as one word.) Orig. the title accorded to a player who won first prize in a great international tournament (opp. *Master* in national tournaments). Now often used more generally of an unusually skilled player. Also *attrib.* and *transf.* Hence **grandˈmasterly** *a.*

1927 *Brit. Chess Mag.* XLVII. 61 Yates made a characteristic recovery and added to his growing bag the scalps of two 'grand masters'. **1936** *Chess Rev.* (N.Y.) Jan. 17 (*title*) A Gallery of Grandmasters. **1936** B. HARLEY *Chess & its Stars* 121 The ultra-caution which is merely a symptom of her progress to the grand-master class of chess. **1937** *Chess* III. 116 The victory was achieved by the only one of the Grand Masters who had not received a retainer: Keres! **1946** *Brit. Chess Mag.* LXVI. II. 50 Grandmaster Lilienthal..insistently advises us to study the Slav defence. **1952** *Sci. Amer.* May 30 To take an apt title from the terminology of chess players, Sherrington was a grand-master of science. **1955** *N.Y. Times* 20 Feb. 2/5 United States chess players..will oppose the famous Soviet grandmasters who have maintained world supremacy ever since their series of victories during 1954. **1965** *New Statesman* 9 Apr. 590/1 Here..is a case of..truly grandmasterly chess. **1967** *Times* 11 Feb. 12/5 What constitutes a grandmaster at chess?.. The term itself is supposed to have been invented by the Tsar to describe the competitors in the great international tournament at St. Petersburg in 1914. *Ibid.* 14 Nov. 6/3 He [*sc.* a Russian grandmaster since 1939] attributed much of the deterioration in chess to changes in the rules of the World Chess Federation, made in the 1950s. Abandoning the procedure under which the title of grandmaster could be won only by taking first prize in a tournament, the federation liberalized the rules to permit the title to be conferred upon any player winning 55 per cent of the points in a tournament.

Hence **grandˈmastership,** the office or position of grandmaster.

1769 ROBERTSON *Chas. V*, I. Wks. 1826 III. 241 She bequeathed to Ferdinand..the grand-masterships of the three military orders. **18..** LOWELL *Leg. Brittany* Poet. Wks. 1890 I. 95 He had spared no thought's or deed's expense, That by and by might help his wish to clip Its darling bride,—the high grandmastership. **1882–3** SCHAFF *Encycl. Relig. Knowl.* I. 49 King Ferdinand now united the grand-masterships of St. James, Calatrava, and Alcantara to the crown.

grandmaternal (ˌgrændməˈtɜːnəl), *a.* Somewhat *jocular.* [f. GRAND *a.* + MATERNAL *a.*] Of, pertaining to, or befitting a grandmother; grandmotherly.

1790–1811 COMBE *Devil upon Two Sticks* (1817) I. 260 Maternal or grand-maternal pleasures will not, I fear, compose any part of the happiness of her life. **1862** *Sat. Rev.* 8 Feb. 155 In spite of paternal protests and grand-maternal tears, the fatal miscalculation was expiated on the block. **1880** G. MEREDITH *Tragic Com.* vii. (1892) 91 He named a grandmaternal date for the year of the baroness's birth.

‖**Grand Monarque** (grɑ̃ mɔnark). [Fr.] The title given to Louis XIV. Also *transf.*, a supreme and absolute ruler.

1699 M. LISTER *Journey to Paris* 25 There are an infinite number of Busto's of the Grand Monarque every where put up by the Common People. **1716** ADDISON *Freeholder* No. 10 ¶6 His Governours of Towns and Provinces, who form'd themselves upon the Example of their *Grand Monarque*, practised Rapine, Violence, Extortion. **1842** BARHAM *Ingol. Leg.* 2nd Ser. 22 'Twas the *Grand Monarque's* birthday. **1856** BAGEHOT *Coll. Works* (1965) I. 379 How gravely admirable to see the *grand monarque* shaved, and dressed, and powdered. **1911** *Encycl. Brit.* XVII. 42/2 Louis was singularly well fitted by his physical and intellectual gifts for the rôle of *Grand Monarque* and he played it to perfection. **1933** D. OGG *Louis XIV* 250 This fact may temper enthusiasm for the cult of the *Grand Monarque*. **1967** D. W. BROGAN in L. Norton tr. *Mem. St.-Simon* I. p. xix, Saint-Simon shows us the King with..his 'courage never to submit or yield' which enabled him..to be in 1715 still *le grand monarque*.

‖**grand monde** (grɑ̃ mɔ̃d, ˈmɒnd). [Fr., = great world.] The beau-monde, the 'upper ten'.

1704 SWIFT *Tale Tub* ii. 57 A Sect arose, whose Tenents [*sic*] obtained and spread very far, especially in the *Grand Monde*, and among every Body of good Fashion. **1725** —— *Let.* 29 Sept. in *Corr. Pope* (1956) II. 324, I am now returning to the noble Scene of Dublin in the Grande [*sic*] Monde. **1823** BYRON *Juan* XIV. xlii, She was a fine and somewhat full-blown blonde,..For several winters in the grand, *grande* [sic] *monde*. **1892** W. JAMES *Let.* 29 Apr. (1920) I. 319 Strange to say, altho' practically bed-ridden for years, her mental atmosphere..was altogether that of the *grand monde*. **1925** D. H. LAWRENCE *St. Mawr* 13 Mrs. Witt ..always expected to find the real *beau monde* and the real *grand monde* somewhere or other.

grandmother (ˈgrændmʌðə(r), ˈgrænmʌðə(r)), *sb.* Also 5 **graunt(e)moder,** 6 **graundemoder, -mother,** 7 **gran-mother.** [See GRAND *a.* 12 b.]

1. a. The mother of one's father or mother.

1424 [Implied in GRANDMOTHERLESS]. **1483** CAXTON *Gold. Leg.* 429/1 The graunte moder of Saynt aldebaulte. **1496** *Plumpton Corr.* (Camden) p. c, Sir Robert Babthorp, kt. or Dame Elizabeth his wife, grauntfeder & grauntmoder to the said Elizabeth. **1535** COVERDALE *2 Tim.* i. 5 The vnfayned faith..which dwelt first in thy graundemother Lois, and in thy mother Eunica. *c* **1645** HOWELL *Lett.* I. II. vi. ii. 182, I made another Latin Speech to the Duke, touching his Gran-Mothers death. **1671** LADY MARY BERTIE in *12th Rep. Hist. MSS. Comm.* App. v. 23 Her grandmother sent a chaire for her. **1788** H. WALPOLE *Remin.* ii. 18 It was the portrait of her grandmother. **1860–1** FLO. NIGHTINGALE *Nursing* 26 A great-grandmother, who was a tower of physical strength, descending into a grandmother, perhaps a little less strong.

b. Phrases. ***this beats my grandmother***: said of something that excites astonishment. ***teach your grandmother to suck eggs*** (see EGG *sb.* 4 b). ***your grandmother!***: said of something with which one disagrees. (Cf. GRANNY 1 c.)

1870 'MARK TWAIN' *Screamers* (1871) 50 'Shake the tree —' ' Shake your grandmother! Turnips don't grow on trees!' **1874** TROLLOPE *Phineas Redux* II. xiii. 111 'Did you see her?' said Ned... 'See your grandmother.' **1883** *Harper's Mag.* 889/2 Well, this does beat my grandmother, I must say! **1909** GALSWORTHY *Joy* I, *Mrs. Hope.* You'll just attend to what I say and look into that mine! *Colonel.* Look into your grandmother! **1911** G. B. SHAW *Getting Married* 268 *Lesbia.* I hate..sentimental people. *Mrs. George.* Oh, sentimental your grandmother! **1934** E. WAUGH *Handful of Dust* ii. 22 'I think she [*sc.* a horse] put in a short step.' 'Short step my grandmother.'

c. *fig.*

1626 *Will of Carew* (Somerset Ho.), My body to my grand-mother the Earth. **1650** B. *Discolliminium* 15 Ignorance is the Grand-mother of mistaken Necessity. **1774** J. ADAMS in *Fam. Lett.* (1876) 46, I strolled away to mother church, or rather to grandmother church. I mean the

Romish chapel. **1870** E. A. FREEMAN in W. R. W. Stephens *Life & Lett.* (1895) II. 9 Atholl..built himself the grandmother of pews. **1879** B. TAYLOR *Stud. Germ. Lit.* 5 If the Gothic language be the legitimate mother of the Old German, it must also be, through the Saxon, the grandmother of English. **1959** *Woman* 24 Oct. 12/1 My mother and Laura Simmonds, who had lived in each other's pockets since the age of five, had the very grandmother of a row.

d. ***Grandmother's (Foot)steps***, name of a children's game in which one player stands with his back turned to the rest and the others try to approach him in a stealthy manner and touch his back without his seeing them move. The person in front is allowed to turn round often and without warning and any player caught moving is sent back to the starting-line.

1937 'N. BLAKE' *There's Trouble Brewing* i. 30 The children's game called 'Grandmother's Steps'. **1945** E. WAUGH *Brideshead Revisited* 122 She took hold of her subject in a feminine, flirtatious way... She played 'grandmother's steps' with it, getting nearer the real point imperceptibly while one's back was turned, standing rooted when she was observed. **1956** L. MCINTOSH *Oxford Folly* 204 We were playing grandmother's footsteps. **1966** J. BETJEMAN *High & Low* 37 A game of Grandmother's Steps on the vicarage grass.

2. A female ancestor.

1526 *Pilgr. Perf.* (W. de W. 1531) 76 The fourth thynge that is dispraysed in our graundmother Eue, was that she was curyous. **1588** SHAKS. *L.L.L.* I. i. 266 With a childe of our Grandmother Eue, a female. **1606** HIERON *Truth's Purchase* Wks. (1613) I. 61 Our grand-mother Heuah. **1642** FULLER *Holy & Prof. St.* v. iii. 366 Satan tempted our grandmother Eve.

3. *attrib.* (quasi-*adj.*)

a **1649** DRUMM. OF HAWTH. *Cypress Grove* Wks. (1711) 119 What excellency is there in it, for which he should.. repine to be at rest, and return to his old grandmother dust? **1649** E. SPARKE in J. Shute *Sarah & Hagar* Pref. A 3 a, Our grave Author..was..master of those three Grandmother-Languages inscribed on the Cross of Christ, besides some others of their progeny. **1814** *Prophetess* III. iii, I held him here with these grandmother hands.

4. grandmother clock, a clock resembling a grandfather clock, but with a smaller case. Also *ellipt.*

1922 H. S. BARRETT *A.B.C. Hist. Antique Eng. Furnit.* 86 By Grandmother clocks I refer to clocks not exceeding about 5 ft. to 6 ft. in height. **1927** *Daily Tel.* 6 Dec. 3/7 A grandmother clock with brass dial. **1930** *Aberdeen Press & Jrnl.* 31 May 8/3 The gift to ex-Constable Jamie was a beautiful grandmother clock. **1931** H. SUTCLIFFE *Persons Unknown* i. 11 The quieter pendulum-swing of the slim clocks known as 'grandmothers'. **1965** E. TUNIS *Colonial Craftsmen* vi. 145 In addition to the taller clocks, there were also 'grandmother' clocks about five feet high, controlled by shorter, half-second pendulums. **1967** B. PALMER *Treasury Amer. Clocks* 23 Grandmother clocks are diminutive editions of grandfather clocks, standing four feet or less in height.

Hence **'grandmotherhood**, the condition or fact of being a grandmother; **'grandmotherism**, the relation of being a grandmother; **'grandmotherless** *a.*, without a grandmother.

1424 *E.E. Wills* (1882) 57 þan shall he be left..graunt-moderles. **1806** ANNA SEWARD *Lett.* (1811) VI. 324 The apparent grandmotherism seems now reversed between us. **1846** DE QUINCEY *Sophocles' Antigone* Wks. 1860 XIV. 201 Surely..she will command that reverence from you, by means of her grandmotherhood, which by means of her ethics she might not.

'grandmother, *v.* [f. the sb.] *trans.* and *intr.* To take care of as a grandmother; to behave in a grandmotherly way (towards); to be the grandmother of. Hence **'grandmothering** *vbl. sb.* (Cf. GRANDMOTHERLY *a.*)

1901 KIPLING *Kim* xv. 396 When one cannot dance in the festival one must e'en look out of the window, and grandmothering takes all a woman's time. **1903** H. JAMES *Better Sort* 42 Do you mean by his idea his proposal that I should grandmother his wife? **1923** *Chambers's Jrnl.* Feb. 102/1 A frail little lady who had grandmothered a hefty brood of men. **1929** *Daily Express* 8 Jan. 8/7 Political power has naturally passed into the hands of people with a passion for grandmothering. *Ibid.* 12 Jan. 8/7, I refuse to believe that Britons are so excessively unmanly as to be driven to this state of grandmothering. **1966** E. H. JONES *Margery Fry* xv. 203 Agnes was grandmothering two schoolboy evacuees.

grandmotherly ('grænd-, 'grænmʌðəlɪ), *a.* [f. GRANDMOTHER *sb.* + -LY[1].] Pertaining to or befitting a grandmother. Now often *fig.* of government, legislation, etc.: Characterized by a trivial minuteness of detail in its regulations, as if the governed were children incapable of protecting their own interests.

1842 C. WHITEHEAD *Richard Savage* (1845) III. vii. 390 But this device is grandmotherly. **1871** *Daily News* 7 Apr., They have abjured all attempt to rule Paris except by a grandmotherly kind of coaxing. **1874** MRS. J. W. HORNE *Sex & Educ.* 17 A good old grandmotherly doctrine, handed down from parent to child. **1880** *Harper's Mag.* LX. 914 'Now Jerome', said Irene, in the advising grandmotherly manner she often assumed. **1883** *Athenæum* 8 Sept. 309/3 The enterprising traveller had set their rather grandmotherly regulations at defiance. **1888** LOWELL *Prose Wks.* (1890) VI. 218 Those theories of grandmotherly government which led to our revolt from the mother country. **1889** JESSOPP *Coming of Friars* vi. 277 There was no grandmotherly legislation in those days.

grand-nephew. [See GRAND *a.* 12 b.] The son of a nephew or niece.

a **1639** WOTTON *Will* in Walton *Life* (1651) c 9 My two Grand-nephews Albert Morton..and Thomas Bargrave. **1826** MISS MITFORD *Village* Ser. II. (1863) 346. **1860** SALA *Baddington Peerage* xxix, I'll have you out, were you twenty times my grand-nephew.

grandness ('grændnɪs). [f. GRAND *a.* + -NESS.] The state or quality of being grand; magnificence, splendour, grandeur. Also, a grand action.

1722 WOLLASTON *Relig. Nat.* v. (1724) 80 The grandness of this fabric of the world. **1871** BROWNING *Balaust.* 1252 He did too many grandnesses, to note Much in the meaner things about his path. **1873** MRS. WHITNEY *Other Girls* x. (1876) 160 It's good to have grandness somewhere, or else nobody would have any place to stretch in. **1893** W. A. P. MARTIN in Barrows *Parl. Relig.* II. 1142 Had Columbus realized the grandness of his discovery.

grand-niece. [See GRAND *a.* 12 b.] The daughter of a nephew or niece.

1830 in BOOTH *Analyt. Dict.* **1832** MARRYAT *N. Forster* xxxix, The colonel..requested his grand-niece to accept of his hospitality. **1860** SALA *Baddington Peerage* xliv, Lord Baddington the fourth had not deemed his grand-nieces worthy of a thought..The grand-niece-in-law had hitherto pertinaciously refused to hold any intercourse with Lord Baddington's widow.

†**'grando**[1]. *Obs.* [pseudo-Sp., from the notion that Sp. masc. sbs. end in *-o*. Cf. GRANDIO.] = GRANDEE.

1623-4 MIDDLETON & ROWLEY *Sp. Gipsy* II. i. 28 In th' opinion of the best, grandoes, dukes, marquesses, condes, and other titulados. **1634** S. R. *Noble Soldier* II. i. in Bullen *O. Pl.* I. 283 Grandoes and Lords of Spaine be witnesse all What here I cancell.

‖**'grando**[2]. *Obs.* [L. *grandō* hail; in early modern physiology used for a minute granular body.] (See quot.)

1650 SIR T. BROWNE *Pseud. Ep.* III. xxvii. (ed. 2) 151 Whether it [the chicken] be not made out of the grando, gallature, germe or tredde of the egge..doth seem of lesser doubt.

Grand Old Party. *U.S. politics.* [See GRAND *a.* 10 d.]

†**1.** The Democratic party. *Obs.*

Used without capitals and perhaps not specific.

1879 *Congress. Record* 11 June 1913/1 We are for national politics now. We come back to the grand old party of the North. **1888** *Ibid.* 10 May 3981/1, I am glad that I am a member of that grand old party that assures a better trade to our people, larger wages &c.

2. The Republican party. Now usu. in abbreviated form *G.O.P.*

1876 *Cincinnati Comm.* in *Harper's Weekly* (1884) 576/3 Grand Old Party. **1884** *N.Y. Tribune* 15 Oct. 4/5 'The G.O.P. doomed,' shouted the *Boston Post*... The Grand Old Party is in condition to inquire [etc.]. **1888** *Congress. Record* 1 May 3598/1 Old Farmer: Is this Democratic doings or Republican doings? Collector: O, it is the doings of the G.O.P.,—the grand old party,—the Republican party. **1898** *Ibid.* 7 Jan. 444/1 Has the Grand Old Party (G.O.P.) so called never been corrupt? Has it never had dishonest men in it? **1904** *N.Y. Even. Post* 25 Aug. 6 A close examination of Republican speeches fails to reveal an instance in which the Democracy is portrayed as on a parity with the Grand Old Party. **1960** *Detroit News* 16 Aug. 18B/1 The Nixon influence..has sought to capitalize on the new appeal of the GOP. **1964** KNEBEL & BAILEY *Convention* vi. 88 Right now, this has the makings of the closest G.O.P. nomination contest since the Eisenhower-Taft fight in 1952.

grand opera. [See GRAND *a.* 8 b.] Serious opera without spoken dialogue.

1803 *Lett. Miss Riversdale* II. 317 A few nights of the *Grand Opera*..will bring you over to my opinion. **1879** *Grove's Dict. Music, Grand Opera*..The term—fast becoming obsolete—is French..and denotes a lyric drama in which spoken dialogue is excluded, and the business is carried on in melody or recitative throughout. **1879** [see OPERA 3]. **1954** *Grove's Dict. Mus.* (ed. 5) III. 757/1 Grand Opera, a term with a definite meaning in French, unlike the English 'grand opera', which..is useless for classification, since it is loosely used to mean serious as distinct from comic opera. **1967** *Listener* 5 Oct. 443/1 She [*sc.* Melba].. bulldozed her initially reluctant countrymen into a fervid admiration for Grand Opera. **1967** *Times* 7 Oct. 12/8 After 12 years in opera—both light and grand—soprano Joyce Blackham is to appear in her first West End musical.

grandpapa ('grændpəpɑː, 'grænpəpɑː). [See GRAND *a.* 12 b and PAPA.] **a.** A colloquial substitute for GRANDFATHER. Also **grandpa.**

1753 *Scots Mag.* Apr. 188/1 There is my grandpappa. **1836-48** B. D. WALSH *Aristoph., Knights* IV. i, Don't you see 'tis empty, Dear grand-papa? **1875** JOWETT *Plato* (ed. 2) I. 194 They..call him grandpapa's master.

b. ***grandpapa dance.*** (Cf. GRANDFATHER 4.)

1898 O. BROWNING *Peter Gt.* vi. 52 The 'Grandpapa' dance of which Peter was particularly fond.

Also **'grandpappy, 'grandpop** (PAPPY *sb.*[1], POP *sb.*[6]).

1890 *Texas Siftings* 22 Nov. 10/1 'Grandpop,' said he, 'did you know that there was flying fish?' **1919** *Dialect Notes* V. 39 Gran'-pappy. **1931** H. CRANE *Let.* 10 Jan. (1965) 363 Spinoza (Einstein's grandpop) furnishes plenty of discipline. **1936** F. CLUNE *Roaming round Darling* xiii. 107 Grandpop betrayed them, and at daybreak the police attacked. **1938** M. K. RAWLINGS *Yearling* x. 92 Now Grandpappy, I kin see you settin' there on your stoop. **1946** M. LOWRY *Let.* 26 Dec. (1967) 134 Just like the old days of my grandpappy. **1948** D. BALLANTYNE *Cunninghams* (1963) I. xviii. 96 'You don't say, grandpop,' Joy said. **1953** 'N. BLAKE' *Dreadful Hollow* iv. 51 Have a glass of port, won't you? It's rather delish. Grand-pop laid it down. **1959** [see BREAK *sb.*[1] 8 k].

grandparent ('grændpɛərənt). [See GRAND *a.* 12 b.] A parent of a parent.

1830 in BOOTH *Analyt. Dict.* **1868** WALT WHITMAN *Poems* 137 The white-haired Irish grand-parents. **1875** T. W. HIGGINSON *U.S. Hist.* v. 31 Their grandparents had told them of a country far to the west.

So **grandparentage**, the state or condition of being a grandparent or of having grandparents.

1889 *Nature* 24 Jan. 299/2 Families differently grouped according to their parentage and grandparentage. **1896** *Daily News* 10 Jan. 3/6 Such a life as might be expected from his grand-parentage.

grandparental (grændpə'rɛntəl), *a.* [See -AL.] Of, belonging to, or derived from a grandparent or grandparents.

1903 *Lancet* 18 Apr. 108/1 Cases in which the taint was grandparental. **1929** *19th Cent.* Dec. 810 A collateral relative at the level of the grandparental or great-grandparental generation. **1930** R. A. FISHER *Genet. Theory Nat. Selection* 198 The grandparental effect..is subject to somewhat large sampling errors. **1958** *New Biology* XXVI. Pl. 3(b), At the base of the parent corm is the remains of the connexion to the 'grandparental' corm.

‖**grand pas.** *Obs.* Also anglicized 7 **grand paw.** [Fr.; lit. 'great step'.] In quots. used for: A stylish manner of walking.

1667 LACY *Sauny the Scot* II. Dram. Wks. (1875) 336 Where didst thou learn the grand pas, Peg? It becomes thee rarely. **1698** FRYER *Acc. E. India & P.* 139 They are taught little more than the Grand Paw, and to make a Salam. **1822** SCOTT *Pirate* xiv, The story, like a horse on the *grand pas*, seemed to be advancing with rapidity, while, in reality, it scarce was progressive at the rate of a yard in a quarter of an hour.

grandpaternal (ˌgrændpə'tɜːnəl), *a.* Somewhat *jocular.* [f. GRAND *a.* + PATERNAL *a.*] Of or befitting a grandfather; grandfatherly.

1844 MRS. BROWNING *Let.* 20 Feb. in *Lett. to R. H. Horne* (1877) I. xxxviii. 245 You give me grand-paternal advice sometimes. **1884** E. YATES *Recoll.* I. ii. 40 The finances of the grand-paternal establishment.

‖**grandpère** (grɑ̃pɛr). [Fr.; lit. 'grandfather'.] A variety of the cotillon (*Cent. Dict.*).

1835 *Woman* I. 171 Are not the forms of dance more recently introduced, the Galoppe, Mazurka, Cotillon, Grandpere, 'romping'?

grandpisce, obs. form of GRAMPUS.

grandpop: see GRANDPAPA.

Grand Prix (grɑ̃ priː). [Fr., = great or chief prize.] **1. a.** (In full ***Grand Prix de Paris.***) An international horse race for three-year-olds established in 1863 and run annually in June at Longchamps, Paris. **b.** Any of certain motor-races held annually in different countries and governed by international rules.

1863 *Times* 3 June 9/4 The great event which had been looked forward to with such deep interest..both in England and France,..resulted in the victory of an English horse... The Grand Prix de Paris was looked forward to by the partisans of Lord Clifden, Saccharometer, and the Ranger. **1866** *Field* 10 Mar. 199/3 Some of our English friends, too, are travelled gentlemen, who go to the Grand Prix. **1899** [see ASCOT]. **1902** *Encycl. Brit.* XXIX. 336/2 The Grand Prix de Paris, an international race for three-year-olds, run at Longchamps... The first Grand Prix fell to an English horse. **1908** *Westm. Gaz.* 2 Apr. 4/3 The drivers have now definitely been selected for the team of three Austin cars entered for competition in the Grand Prix race. **1922** *Encycl. Brit.* XXXI. 1003/2 In 1911 began a new series of races for the *Grand Prix* of the Automobile Club of France. **1923** W. J. LOCKE *Moordius & Co.* viii. 99 Already, after the Grand Prix, the ultra fashionables were leaving Paris. **1931** *Times* 5 June 4/6 To-day's practice for the Irish Grand Prix Race for motor-cars. **1958** [see GRANDE ÉPREUVE]. **1959** *Chambers's Encycl.* IX. 559/1 In 1906 the French organized the first Grand Prix on a circuit near Le Mans, and by making it open to all, instead of to three cars only from each country, set the pattern for all future races. **1960** *Times* 28 Sept. 16/5 The cars to be run..will comprise three Grand Prix cars. **1966** *Times* 14 Feb. 6/3 Grand prix racing under the new 3-litre Formula 1 gets into its stride this year.

2. *gen.* The highest prize awarded for products in some particular line at an exhibition.

Also in anglicized form, *grand prize*: see GRAND *a.* 12.

1880 *Rep. Paris Univ. Exhib. 1878* II. 425. **1916** *Oxf. Univ. Press Gen. Cat.*, The Twenty-three Grands Prix Awarded to the Oxford University Press At International Exhibitions 1889-1911.

grandrills. [Cf. DRILL *sb.*[5]] (See quot.)

1882 CAULFEILD & SAWARD *Dict. Needlework, Grandrills*, a dark grey material, made of cotton..and employed for the making of stays; a description of coarse Jean.

'grandship. *nonce-wd.* The personality of a 'Grand' (see GRAND B. 4).

1747 W. HORSLEY *Fool* (1748) II. 165 The Grand, he pray'd for Silence to the Herd; at length..Clamour ceas'd, and thus his Grandship open'd.

‖**grand siècle** (grɑ̃ sjɛkl). [Fr., = great century or age.] The reign of Louis XIV, the classical or 'Augustan' age in France. Also *transf.*

1838 *Westm. Rev.* XXXI. 7 Many a Liberal or Republican critic will stand up stiffly..for the *grand siècle.* **1912** L. STRACHEY *Landmarks Fr. Lit.* v. 133 While the masterpieces of the *Grand Siècle* served no ulterior purpose..those of the eighteenth century were works of propaganda. **1937** *Burlington Mag.* Dec. 294/2 An essay in praise of the *grand siècle.* **1963** *House & Garden* Mar. 97/1 The hundred years from 1811 to 1911 deserve to be called the *Grand Siècle* of wine.

grand signior. Forms: see SIGNIOR. [ad. It. *gran signore* 'great lord': see GRAND and SIGNIOR. Some of the forms are assimilated to the Fr. equivalent *grand seigneur.*]

1. ***the Grand Signior***: the Sultan of Turkey.

1592 WOTTON *Let. to Ld. Zouch* 6 Aug. in *Reliq.* (1685) 683 The Gran Seignior yet liveth in Croatia. **1598** B. JONSON *Ev. Man in Hum.* I. i. Wks. (1616) 9 Our Turkie companie neuer sent the like to the Grand-Signior. **1610** GUILLIM *Heraldry* III. xiv. (1660) 177 Embassador for many years to the Grand Signeur from the King..of England. **1713** WARDER *True Amazons* (ed. 2) 59 The Grand Seignior with all his Janizaries about him. **1774** GOLDSM. *Nat. Hist.* (1776) II. 399 [The Zebra] It is frequent with the African ambassadors to the court of Constantinople, to bring some of these animals with them, as presents for the Grand Seignior. **1847** MRS. A. KERR *Hist. Servia* 445 Intending..to lay some complaints before the Effendi of the Grand Signior.

†**2.** A great noble. *Obs.*

The F. *grand seigneur* is occasionally used in recent English books in this sense.

1601 HOLLAND *Pliny* II. 81 The Grand-siegniors and great men of the citie. *Ibid.* 526 M. Valerius Maximus.. beeing one of the grand-seigneiurs of Rome. [**1860** WHYTE MELVILLE *Holmby Ho.* I. 142 A Paladin in the field, a *grand seigneur* in the drawing-room.]

grandsire ('grændsaɪə(r), 'grænsaɪər). Forms: see GRAND *a.* and SIRE; also 4 **graunsire, -ser,** 5 **granser, grawn(e)sire, -syre,** 6 **graynser;** *Sc.* 6 **grant-, grandschir,** 7 **grandsher, -ir,** 9 **gran(d)sher,** *dial.* **gransir.** [a. AF. *graunt sire*: see GRAND *a.* 12 b and SIRE.]

1. = GRANDFATHER 1. *arch.* and *dial.*

c **1290** *Beket* 473 in *S. Eng. Leg.* I. 120 Bi þe kingus daye henries þat ovre graunt-sire was. **1297** R. GLOUC. (Rolls) 6353 Vor he wilnede vorto ligge is grantsire ney. **1387** TREVISA *Higden* (Rolls) II. 259 Sarug was Abraham his fader graunsire. *c* **1400** *Destr. Troy* 2169 Synkes not in your sowle þe sorow of your graunser. **1474** CAXTON *Chesse* 53 Counceyllour of his fader his grauntsire and of his grauntsirs fader. **1477** EARL RIVERS (Caxton) *Dictes* 124 Hys grauntsirs [*misprinted* gramitsirs] fader was an harper and meter of landes. **1501** *Plumpton Corr.* (Camden) 151 All the estayts made by your graynser and father. **1587** *Mirr. Mag., Q. Cordila* vi. 1 My grandsire Bladud hight. **1605** CAMDEN *Rem.* 212 My father was King of England..and his father my grandsire was also King of England. **1697** POTTER *Antiq. Greece* (1715) I. I. xxvi. 169 If an Heiress is contracted lawfully in full Marriage by a Father or Grand-sire. **1725** POPE *Odyss.* XIX. 566 His grandsire sent him to the sylvan chace. **1814** SCOTT *Ld. of Isles* II. xxvii, By Woden wild, (my grandsire's oath). **1863** LONGF. *Wayside Inn* Prel. 112 The sword his grandsire bore. **1876** *Whitby Gloss., Gransir,* grandfather.

b. The sire of a sire (of an animal, esp. a horse).

1881 *Encycl. Brit.* XII. 184 Another chestnut [horse], but with the characteristic black spots of his grandsire.

c. †***first grandsire, great grandsire*** = great-grandfather. (See also GREAT *a.* 21 b.)

c **1400** *Destr. Troy* 13602 Aschatus..þat is my fader so fre, and þi first graunser.

2. *Sc.* A great-grandfather. (Cf. GRANDFATHER 2.)

1543 *Sc. Acts Mary* (1814) II. 432/1 Or souerane ledyis feder..hir guidschir, & grantschir. **1592** *Sc. Acts Jas. VI* (1814) III. 619/1 His maiesties vmquhile darrest grandschir. **1609** SKENE *Reg. Maj.* 91 The father, gudsher, and grandsher. **1641** *Sc. Acts Chas. I* (1870) V. 696/2 The estate..Hes beine possest be me my father gudshir and grandshir thir thriescoir and ten yeires bygane. **1806** *R. Jamieson's Pop. Ball.* I. 292 His gransher, his gutsher, his daddie.

3. A forefather, progenitor. *arch.*

c **1290** *S. Eng. Leg.* I. 52/182 þe kyng Alfred, is graunt-sire, þat hous a-rerd hadde. **1573** TWYNE *Æneid* x. (1584) Q v, Thy soule vnto thy grandsiers gosts..I send. **1599** H. BUTTES *Dyets drie Dinner* A aiij, Our Grand-sire Adam. **1693** C. DRYDEN in *J. D.'s Juvenal* vii. (1697) 182 In Peace, ye Shades of our Great Grandsires rest. **1847** TENNYSON *Princ.* I. 6 Some sorcerer, whom a far-off grand-sire burnt Because he cast no shadow. **1896** F. HALL in *Nation* (N.Y.) LXII. 157/2 Our colonial grandsires of course stressed the first syllable in *hired man.*

appositive. **1649** MILTON *Eikon.* xx. Wks. (1847) 321/1 So did..our grandsire papists in this realm.

4. A man of an age befitting a grandfather; an old man. *arch.*

1596 SHAKS. *Tam. Shr.* IV. v. 50 Do good old grandsire, & withall make known Which way thou trauellest. **1819** W. TENNANT *Papistry Storm'd* (1827) 10 Auld grandshers at their doors sat beikin'.

5. *attrib.* (quasi-*adj.*)

1592 SHAKS. *Rom. & Jul.* I. iv. 37 For I am prouerb'd with a Grandsier Phrase. **1637** N. WHITING *Albino & Bellama* (1638) 85 Yet had their pleasure not a grand-sire life. **1856** R. A. VAUGHAN *Mystics* VIII. iv. (1860) II. 56 Yon grey promontory, about whose grandsire knees the waves are gambolling.

6. *Bell-ringing.* A particular method of ringing the changes on a ring of bells; its varieties are designated ***grandsire cinque, grandsire bob, grandsire triples,*** etc.

1671 *Tintinnalogia* 95 Grandsire is the best and most ingenious Peal that ever was composed, to be rang on five bells. *Ibid.* 102 This Peal of Grandsire..is the absolute foundation from whence the excellent Peal of Grandsire bob (on six bells) had its beginning and method. **1671, 1677** [see BOB *sb.*[5]]. **1798** in *Gentl. Mag.* (1825) XCV. I. 298 A full and compleat peal of grandsire tripples, consisting of 5040 changes. **1809** in Southey *Comm.-pl. Bk.* IV. 390 A peal of grandsire-bob-cators containing 126 changes. **1872** ELLACOMBE *Ch. Bells Devon* iii. 40 The College Youths rang at..S. Bride's, London, the first peal of 5000 grandsire cinques on twelve bells. **1883** *B'ham Daily Post* 19 Oct. 7 A peal of 10,176 changes of grandsire majors..This is the longest peal ever rung..upon hand-bells.

grandson ('grændsʌn, 'grænsʌn). [See GRAND *a.* 12 b.] A son's or daughter's son.

1586 WARNER *Alb. Eng.* II. xi. (1589) 48 Alcæus grand-sonne searching long the Thefts he could not finde. **1655** SIR E. NICHOLAS in *N. Papers* (Camden) II. 280 Which only hath bin obstructed by my grandsonnes treachery. **1734-5** LORD C. in *Swift's Lett.* (1766) II. 211 These works shall be the first foundation of the libraries of my three grand-sons. **1765-9** BLACKSTONE *Comm.* (1793) 248 Stephen..was indeed the grandson of the conqueror, by Adelicia his daughter. **1866** GEO. ELIOT *F. Holt* i. 24 She expected a little grandson also.

b. *transf.* of a horse.

1881 *Encycl. Brit.* XII. 184/1 The Darley Arabian's line is represented..through his son Flying Childers, his grandsons Blaze and Snip, and his great-grandson Snap. *Ibid.* 185/2 The Baron..and his grandson Blair Athol.

c. Comb. ***grandson-in-law.***

1898 *Daily News* 19 Dec. 5/1 If a grandson-in-law is a grandson.

Hence **'grandsonship.**

1856 DONALDSON in *Cambridge Ess.* 30 Among the Romans, a man, of whom grand-sonship could not be predicated, was dubbed a *terræ filius.*

grandstand, grand-stand. [GRAND *a.* 12.]

1. The principal stand for spectators at a race-course, football ground, etc.

1834 *N.Y. Sporting Mag.* Nov. 169/1 At the Grand Stand Chapple let him go, and he won by a length in a canter. **1841** TATTERSALL *Sport. Arch.* 91 The first brick of the Grand Stand at Ascot was laid on the 5th of December, 1838. **1872** EARL PEMBROKE & G. H. KINGSLEY *South Sea Bubbles* i. 20 On arriving at the course we were placed in the grand stand. **1961** F. C. AVIS *Sportsman's Gloss.* 28/1 *Grand Stand,* that part of the football ground generally containing the business offices, dressing rooms, press box, reserved and special seats, etc.

2. *attrib.* Intended to impress the spectators in the grandstand; as good as if viewed from a grandstand. So ***grandstand finish,*** a close and exciting finish to a sporting contest; ***grandstand play*** (U.S.), a way of playing a game with an eye to the applause of the spectators in the grandstand.

1888 M. J. KELLY *Play Ball* viii. 39 It's little things of this sort which makes [*sic*] the 'grand stand player'. They make impossible catches, and when they get the ball they roll all over the field. **1893** W. K. POST *Harvard Stories* 308 They all hold on to something or clasp their knees tightly—to faint or fall over would be a grand-stand play. **1904** *Utica* (N.Y.) *Observer* 23 June 6 The ultimatum to the Sultan of Morocco, 'Perdicaris alive or Raisuli dead' was a good one. But telegraphing it to the National Convention at Chicago made it look very much like a grand stand play. **1906** S. FORD *Shorty McCabe* (1908) xiii. 276, I makes a grandstand finish, and then has the nerve to face the audience and do a matinée bend. **1942** E. PAUL *Narrow St.* xx. 163 Then [André] Breton made another grandstand play. **1958** *Spectator* 1 Aug. 172/2 Dumaine's shrewdness and his grandstand view of French post-war history. **1958** F. C. AVIS *Boxing Ref. Dict.* 49 *Grand stand finish,* very vigorous exchanges of blows in the final round of a boxing contest. **1967** *Bucks Examiner* 6 Oct. 2/1 He..had a grandstand view of Sir Francis [Chichester] and his yacht.

Hence **'grandstand** *v. intr.,* to perform with an eye to the applause of the spectators in the grandstand. Also **'grandstander,** (*a*) one who occupies a seat in a grandstand; (*b*) one who 'grandstands'.

1891 *Sporting Times* (N.Y.) 23 May 3/3 During the four New York games there were never less than 2,200 people at a game, and 50 per cent of the patrons here were 'grand-standers'. **1900** *Cincinnati Enquirer* 23 June 1/9 [Kentucky will go for McKinley] if Teddy can only be secured to do some 'Grand Standing'. **1914** S. BLYTHE *Fakers* 163 That old grandstander, Rollins, is making a good deal of a row over the franchise matter. **1920** C. H. STAGG *High Speed* vii. 121 A car like that, and in the hands of a grand-stander! **1927** K. NICHOLSON *Barker* 132, I ain't grand-standin' an' I'm tellin' you what I'm goin' to do. **1935** M. M. ATWATER *Murder in Midsummer* xiii. 120 'Sure, he's grandstanding,' said Matter. **1935** E. S. GARDNER *Case of Howling Dog* xv. 151 The public will think you're simply grandstanding for the purpose of getting a big fee out of the trial. **1948** *Sat. Even. Post* 24 July 21/1 Editorial blasts..have described the general in many unflattering terms—namely: a blunderer; a grandstander; a bull in a china shop; a trouble causer. **1970** B. KNOX *Children of Mist* v. 114 Adam Jennings loves a chance to grandstand. This was made to order.

grand tour. [Originally Fr. = 'great circuit'; but now apprehended as an English phrase.]

a. A tour of the principal cities and places of interest in Europe, formerly supposed to be an essential part of the education of young men of good birth or fortune. Chiefly in phr. ***to make the grand tour.***

[**1670** LASSELS *Voy. Italy* Pref. a vj, And no man understands Livy and Cæsar..like him who hath made exactly the *Grand Tour* of France and the *Giro* of Italy.] **1748** RICHARDSON *Clarissa* (1768) IV. 261 Should we not make the Grand Tour upon this occasion? **1748** SMOLLETT *Rod. Rand.* i. (1760) I. 3 You have made the grand tour. **1837** *Penny Cycl.* VII. 56/2 In 1714 he [Chesterfield] left the University to make the usual grand tour of Europe. **1869** ROGERS *Pref. to Adam Smith's W.N.* I. 12 Young men of fortune and fashion made what was called the 'grand tour' under the guidance of a tutor.

b. *transf.* ***to take the grand tour of***: to make the circuit of, go round.

1843 HALIBURTON *Attaché* I. xv. 270 The decanters now take the 'grand tour' of the table. **1970** *Sci. Jrnl.* May 9/3 The 'grand tour of the planets' (the opportunity at the end of this decade to send a single rocket around Jupiter, Saturn and the outer planets, using the gravitational pull of each planet it passes to send it on to the next one). **1971** *Daily Tel.* 2 Dec. 6 (Advt.), The complete story of man's conquest of the moon—glimpses of the future and the fantastic 'grand tour' of the planets.

Hence **grand-tour** *v., nonce-wd.,* to 'make the grand tour'.

1886 RUSKIN *Præterita* I. 392 [They] were grand-touring in Italy and Sicily.

'grand-uncle. [See GRAND *a.* 12 b.] One's father's or mother's uncle; a great-uncle.

1475 *Bk. Noblesse* 19 He also..was crouned king of Fraunce..be the gret mighte..of his graunt oncle Henry cardinalle of Englande. **1777** ROBERTSON *Hist. Amer.* I. I. 52 He promoted it with all the ardour of his grand-uncle. **1834** MRS. CARLYLE *Lett.* I. 12 My present maid has a grand-uncle in town. **1881** J. GRANT *Cameronians* I. ii. 24, I won't consult grand-uncle on *that* matter, Cousin Hew.

†**grane,** *sb. Obs.* Also 3-4 **grone.** [Not in OE., but app. in ablaut relation to the synonymous GRIN *sb.*[1]] A snare, trap; a noose. (Cf. GIRN *sb.*[1])

a **1225** *Ancr. R.* 134 Leste heo beo ikeiht þuruh summe of þe deofles gronen. *Ibid.* 278 So lutel þing is edmodnesse & so smel þet no grone ne mei hire etholden. **13..** *Metr. Hom.* (Vernon MS.) in *Archiv Stud. d. neu. Spr.* LVII. 247/1 He sauh al þe eorþe was sprad wiþ panters and wiþ grones blake. *c* **1380** WYCLIF *Wks.* (1880) 437 þes two lawis ben granes [*misprinted* graues] to þe fend to gnare men in his net. —— *Sel. Wks.* III. 198 þe day of dome schal come as a snare, or grane. **1382** —— *Amos* iii. 5 A brid shal falle in to grane of erthe. —— *Judith* ix. 13 Be he taken with the grane of his eȝen in me. —— *Matt.* xxvii. 5 He hangide hym with a grane. *c* **1430** LYDG. *Min. Poems* (Percy Soc.) 203 That fro hir gravys [? *read* granys] and hir snare Goth not awey that comyth between.

grane (greɪn), *v. Obs.* exc. *dial.* Also 7, 9 **grain,** 9 *dial.* **green.** [f. prec.; the form *green* may belong to GRIN *v.*] *trans.* To choke, strangle.

1613 PURCHAS *Pilgrimage* (1614) 112 One executioner on one side, and another on the other, graned him [the condemned person] with a linnen cloth about his neck, pulling the same till they forced him to gape. **1674-91** RAY *S. & E.C. Words* 101 To *Grain* or *Grane*; to choak or throttle. **1806** BLOOMFIELD *Wild Flowers* 43 Till I was nearly gran'd outright He hugg'd so woundly hard. **1823** MOOR *Suffolk Words, Green,* throttle—choak. A tight collar is said to green a horse. **1895** *E. Anglian Gloss., Grain,* to gripe the throat; to strangle.

grane, obs. f. GRAIN; northern f. GROAN.

grane, var. of GRAIN *sb.*[2] 5 b.

†**granell,** *v. Obs. rare*[−1]. [Variant of GIRNEL *v.*] *trans.* To store *up* in a granary.

1621 BOLTON *Stat. Irel.* 43 (Act 8 Edw. IV) Diverse persons..have used to buy..great store of corns to granell up the same to sell upon a dearth.

†**graner.** *Obs.* Forms: 5-7 **graner,** 6 **grayn-, grainard, granier, grayner,** 6-7 **granar, (granard).** [ad. F. *grenier*; the forms have been variously influenced by GRAIN and GRANARY. Cf. GARNER.]

1. Some utensil belonging to a brewery; perh. a vessel for holding grain.

1413 *E.E. Wills* (1882) 22 Y be-quethe to..Ion, 1 graners, an a flot, an a planer.

2. A granary, garner.

1531 ELYOT *Gov.* II. ix. (1537) 128 b, They lacked corne in their graynardes. **1538** BALE *Enterlude John Bapt.* in *Harl. Misc.* (1808) I. 110 He wyll brynge the wheate into hys barne or grayner. **1548** UDALL, etc. *Erasm. Par. Matt.* iii. 12 He shal vtterly cleanse his floore, & ley vp the wheat in his granard. **1565** COOPER *Thesaurus, Comes horreorum,* the ouerseer of the graner and bakehouse..in a princes house. **1579** TOMSON *Calvin's Serm. Tim.* 639/1 They haue..their graniers and their caues full. **1583** STANYHURST *Æneis* IV. (Arb.) 109 Much lyk when pismers theire corner in granar ar hurding, Careful of a winter nipping, in barns they be piling. **1610** HEALEY tr. *Vives on St. Aug. Citie of God* XV. xxvi. 567 The graner or place where meate was kept for all the creatures [in the Ark]. **1613** R. C. *Table Alph.* (ed. 3), *Garnar, Granar,* corne chamber. **1628** WITHER *Brit. Rememb.* IV. 1362 Our Granards filled, and our Gates made strong.

granfer: see GRANDFER.

grange (greɪndʒ), *sb.* Forms: 4-7 **graunge,** (4-5 **gronge,** 5 **grawnge,** 6 **grandge, graynge, granege),** 4- **grange.** [a. AF. *graunge* (F. *grange*):—med.L. *grānea, grānica* f. *grān-um* GRAIN *sb.*[1]]

1. A repository for grain; a granary, barn. *arch.*

a **1300** *Cursor M.* 4689 Garners and Granges fild [he] wit sede. *c* **1384** CHAUCER *H. Fame* II. 190 And eke of loves mo eschaunges Than ever cornes were in graunges. **1489** CAXTON *Faytes of A.* IV. ix. 253 A man..brought to losse and domage by fortune of fyre in his hous or in his grange. **1523** LD. BERNERS *Froiss.* I. xviii. 25 All these cariagis were sette in voyde granges and barnes. **1634** MILTON *Comus* 175 When, for their teeming flocks and granges full, In wanton dance they [unlettered hinds] praise the bounteous Pan. **1853** TURNER *Dom. Archit.* II. 119 The grange was equivalent to our modern barn, where the corn is placed before it is thrashed. **1853** M. ARNOLD *Scholar-Gipsy* xiii, And thou hast climb'd the hill..Then sought thy straw in some sequester'd grange. **1873** HALE *In His Name* i. 3 Beyond, she could see large farms with their granges.

2. An establishment where farming is carried on; †also, *rarely*, a group of such places, a village (*obs.*). Now applied to: A country house with farm buildings attached, usually the residence of a gentleman-farmer.

c **1300** *Havelok* 764 Forbar he neythe[r] tun, ne gronge, þat he ne to-yede with his ware. **1377** LANGL. *P. Pl.* B. XVII. 71 The Samaritan..ladde hym so forth on lyard to *lex-christi*, a graunge. *a* **1529** SKELTON *Col. Cloute* 421 Of an abbaye ye make a graunge. **1530** PALSGR. 227/1 Graunge or a lytell thorpe, *hameau.* Graunge, *petit uillage.* *c* **1550** BALE *K. Johan* (Camd. Soc.) 23 Our changes are soch that an Abbeye turneth to a graunge. **1563-87** FOXE *A. & M.* (1596) 38/1 Polycarpus..hid himselfe in a grange or village not farr off from the citie. **1606** HOLLAND *Sueton.* 193 It received moreover graunges [L. *rura*] with cornefields, vine yards, pastures and woodes. **1622** FLETCHER *Prophetess* v. iii, Make this little grange seem a large empire. **1623** COCKERAM, *Graunge*, a lone house in the Countrey, a Village. **1703** T. N. *City & C. Purchaser* 159 *Grange*,..a Building which hath Barns, Stables, Stalls, and other necessary Places for Husbandry. **1721** STRYPE *Eccl. Mem.* II. xxx. 503 A Messe and a Grange called Badley Grange, of the Value of 42 Shillings in Cheshire. **1849** W. IRVING *Crayon Misc.* 300 One of these renovated establishments, that had but lately been a mere ruin, and was now a substantial grange. **1850** TENNYSON *In Mem.* xci, The thousand waves of wheat, That ripple round the lonely grange. **1876** BANCROFT *Hist. U.S.* I. xvii. 508 They were scattered in lonely granges.

b. esp. *Hist.* An outlying farm-house with barns, etc. belonging to a religious establishment or a feudal lord, where crops and tithes in kind were stored.

c **1386** CHAUCER *Miller's T.* 482 He is wont for tymber for to go, And dwellen at the grange a day or two. *c* **1440** *Gesta Rom.* xlviii. 368 (Add. MS.) All here studie is granges, shepe, nete, and rentes. **1598** HAKLUYT *Voy.* I. 97 Great lordes have cottages or graunges towards the South, from whence their tenants bring them millet. **1726** AYLIFFE *Parergon* 88 Of this sort were their Granges and Priories. **1816** SCOTT *Antiq.* iii, A grange, or solitary farm-house, inhabited by the bailiff, or steward, of the monastery. **1868** YONGE *Cameos* (1877) I. viii. 52 He..harassed a few brethren of the Abbey of Croyland, who inhabited a grange not far from Spalding. **1874** GREEN *Short Hist.* iii. §6. 145 [They] turned aside to a grange of the monks of Abingdon.

†**3.** A country house. *Obs.*

1552 HULOET, *Graunge*, or manour place without the walls of a citie, *suburbanum.* **1587** TURBERV. *Trag. T.* (1837) 98 His wife abode A three myles off the towne, where he had buylte a graunge. **1592** DANIEL *Compl. Rosamond* Poems (1717) 47 Soon was I train'd from Court, T' a solitary Grange. **1611** COTGR., *Beauregard*, a Summer house, or Graunge; a house for pleasure, and recreation. **1614** RALEIGH *Hist. World* II. v. iii. §16. 454 Eight yeeres..had hee been absent out of the Citie, and liued in his Countrie Grange. **1630** DONNE *Serm.* xxxix. 391 The Grange or country house of the same Landlord. **1633** HEYWOOD *Eng. Trav.* III. Wks. 1874 IV. 43 Who can blame him to absent himselfe from home, And make his Fathers house but as a grange, For a Beautie so Attractiue.

†**4.** *fig.* in various senses. *Obs.*

1557 *Tottel's Misc.* (Arb.) 179 [Thou] The heape of mishap of all my griefe the graunge. **1580** LYLY *Euphues* (Arb.) 265 Though England be no graunge, but yeeldeth euery thing. **1581** T. HOWELL *Deuises* (1879) 201 Where al delights condemde are shut, in sharp repentance grange. **1596** SPENSER *F.Q.* VII. vii. 21 Ne have the watry foules a certaine grange Wherein to rest. **1632** LITHGOW *Trav.* IX. 385 It [Sicily] was also aunciently called the Grange of the Romanes.

5. *U.S.* A lodge or local branch of the order of 'Patrons of Husbandry', an association for the promotion of the interests of agriculture.

1875 C. F. ADAMS in *N. Amer. Rev.* CXX. 405 The great convention of the Granges held at Springfield, Ill. **1880** *Libr. Univ. Knowl.* (U.S.) VII. 9 *Grange*,..used in the U.S. since 1867, as the familiar name of the state and subordinate organizations of the 'patrons of husbandry', a national association of agriculturists.

6. *attrib.* and *Comb.*, as ***grange account, farm,*** †***horse,*** †***house, keeper,*** †***place;*** **grange apple**, a particular variety of apple; †**grange-gotten** *a.*, ? born in a grange, descended from farmers.

1892 KIRK *Abingdon Acc.* p. xxxi, This account is followed by a *grange account of Mercham. **1823** J. BADCOCK *Dom. Amusem.* 48 A new variety has been produced between this and the *Grange apple. **1878** MACLEAR *Celts* vii. (1879) 118 All flocked forth from their little *grange farms near the monastery. **1586** WARNER *Alb. Eng.* v. xxv. (1589) 112 *Grange-gotten Pierce of Gauelstone, and Spensers two like sort, Meane Gentlemen. **1667** DUCHESS OF NEWCASTLE *Life Duke of N.* (1886) 152 *Grange horses, hackney horses, manage-horses..and others. **1589** GREENE *Menaphon* (Arb.) 85 It is long since wee met, and our house is a *Grange house with you. **1590** *Tarlton's News Purgat.* 48, I would haue thee staye at our little graunge house in the Countrey. **1701** *Grange-keeper [see GRANGER 1]. *c* **1340** *Cursor M.* 5044 (Fairf.) þai..þe stiwarde fande atte a *grange place [*Cott.* garner] soiournande. **1590** GREENE *Roy. Exch.* Wks. (Grosart) VII. 242 Sequestrating himself in a graunge place.

†**grange**, *v.* *Obs. rare*⁻¹. [? f. prec.] *trans.* Perh. a fig. use of a vb. meaning 'to engross (corn)'.

c **1595** in Birch *Mem. Q. Eliz.* (1754) I. 355 This ruffianry of causes I am daily more and more acquainted with, and see the manner of dealing, which groweth by the queen's straitness to give these women, whereby they presume thus to grange and huck causes.

granger ('greɪndʒə(r)). Also 7 **grangier, grainger.** [a. AF. *graunger* (F. *grangier*), f. *grange* GRANGE *sb.*]

1. One who is in charge of a grange; a farm-bailiff; also, ? a tenant-farmer.

c **1112** in *Mem. St. Giles's, Durh.* (Surtees) 196 *note*, Undecimus erit Graunger et Custos Carucarum. **1583** STANYHURST *Æneis* IV. (Arb.) 109 Soom grangers with goade iads restye be pricking. **1601** HOLLAND *Pliny* I. 225 As if he had slain his Grangier, or Bailif of his husbandry. **1641** BEST *Farm. Bks.* (Surtees) 97 His tenants the graingers are tyed to come themselves, and winde the woll. **1689** *Def. Liberty agst. Tyrants* 4 To the end that God might be acknowledged Lord, and they his grangers and vine dressers. **1701** *Cowell's Law Dict.*, *Grangerus*, the Granger, or Grange-keeper, an Officer belonging to Religious Houses, who was to look after their Grange. **1877** F. G. LEE *Gloss. Eccl. Terms* 140 The granger who takes charge of the garners and barns of a religious house.

2. *U.S.* **a.** A member of a 'grange' (see GRANGE 5).

1875 C. F. ADAMS in *N. Amer. Rev.* CXX. 395 The time has now come when the Granger can be looked upon as a phenomenon of the past. **1896** *Daily News* 3 Nov. 2/4 The leading Grangers were afraid to go into politics.

b. A farmer (see quot. 1887).

1887 I. R. *Lady's Ranche Life Montana* 121 They call the farmers here 'grangers', as distinct from ranch-men or stock-men... The granger is held in low estimation by the stock-man. **1889** *Century Dict.*, *Granger*, a farmer, a countryman (Humorous. *U.S.*).

c. *pl.* Short for *granger shares.*

1885 *Atlantic Monthly* Apr. 449/1 One has but to mention the word 'railway', and there arises to the mind a congeries of difficult questions dealing with Western 'grangers'. **1897** *Daily News* 17 June 3/1 Other stocks reacted, Grangers leading the railways.

3. *attrib.* (sense 2), as ***granger law, movement, party;*** **granger road** (*U.S.*), one of the railways which convey grain from the Western States; **granger shares** (*U.S.*), shares in the granger roads.

1887 *Contemp. Rev.* May 700 The rash '*granger' laws of more than a decade ago firmly established the principle. **1875** C. F. ADAMS in *N. Amer. Rev.* CXX. 395 That *Granger movement, which..has played a most prominent part in the politics of certain of the North-western States. **1888** BRYCE *Amer. Commw.* II. II. xlvi. 202 The farmers associated themselves in societies called 'Granges'..for the promotion of agriculture, and created a *Granger party, which secured drastic legislation against the railroad companies. **1892** *Pall Mall G.* 31 Aug. 7/1 The *granger roads gained 16 per cent. in net. **1881** *Chicago Times* 12 Mar., High-priced *granger shares.

Grangerize ('greɪndʒəraɪz), *v.* [f. *Granger* (see below) + -IZE.

In 1769 James Granger published a 'Biographical History of England', with blank leaves for the reception of engraved portraits or other pictorial illustrations of the text. The filling up of a 'Granger' became a favourite hobby, and afterwards other books were treated in the same manner.]

trans. To illustrate (a book) by the addition of prints, engravings, etc., especially such as have been cut out of other books.

1882 SALA in *Illustr. Lond. News* 4 Nov. 463/3 Mr. Ashton's 'Social Life in the Reign of Queen Anne'..would be a capital book to grangerise. **1885** *Pall Mall G.* 12 Feb. 4/2 He..proceeded to 'Grangerize' or illustrate it, by the insertion of his mass of materials.

Hence **'Grangerized** *ppl. a.*, **'Grangerizing** *vbl. sb.* Also **,Grangeri'zation**, the action of Grangerizing; **'Grangerizer** = GRANGERITE; **'Grangerism**, the practice of Grangerizing; **'Grangerite**, one who Grangerizes.

1886 *Athenæum* 9 Oct. 468/3 A very handsome '*grangerized' copy of Byron's 'English Bards and Scotch Reviewers'. **1886** *Pall Mall G.* 23 July 5/2 A great piece of *Grangerizing is now on view..— a copy of James Granger's 'Biographical History of England'. **1885** *Standard* 24 Jan. 5/3 By inlaying each page with the accumulated material for its *Grangerisation, he turns a quarto into a folio. **1889** *N.Y. Tribune* 13 Jan. (Cent.), The portraits of actors will be paged separately, with blank backs, for the benefit of *Grangerizers. **1896** *Bookseller's Catal.*, The value to a Grangerizer of this huge collection of portraits cannot be over-estimated. **1882** SALA in *Illustr. Lond. News* 4 Nov. 463/3 The only drawback to *Grangerism is that [etc.]. **1881** A. LANG *Library* 20 *Grangerite. **1885** *Pall Mall G.* 11 June 6/1 A fine specimen of the Grangerite art. **1889** *Bookworm* 362 Granger's History was the first book extended by the introduction of extra prints illustrative of its text, and Mr. Granger was the original Extra-illustrator, the father of the noble band of Grangerites.

‖**Grangousier.** Also 6 **grandgosier.** [Use of *Grangousier* (= F. *grand gosier* 'great throat'), proper name of a character in Rabelais.] One who will 'swallow' anything. Also *attrib.*

c **1580** JEFFERIE *Bugbears* III. i. in *Archiv Stud. d. neu. Spr.* (1897) 25 He gave me thys swete ware to be grime our grandgosier withall. **1871** G. MEREDITH *Richmond* liii, Our grangousier public.

†**'grangy**, *a.* *Obs. rare*⁻¹. [f. GRANGE *sb.* + -Y.] Rustic.

c **1541** *Answ. Papystic. Exhort.* 6 Ther meters all mangye Rashe, rurall, and grangye.

graniferous (grə'nɪfərəs), *a.* [f. L. *grānifer* (f. *grāni-*, *grānum* GRAIN + *-fer* bearing) + -OUS.] Producing or bearing grain or seed like grain.

1656 BLOUNT *Glossogr.*, *Graniferous*, that beareth grains, or kernels. **1668** WILKINS *Real Char.* II. 112 Graniferous Evergreen Shrubs. **1688** R. HOLME *Armoury* II. 115/2 Graniferous seed pods bearing small seed like grains. **1794** MARTYN *Rousseau's Bot.* xviii. 252 Fiddle-dock has the valves notched about the edges, one of them usually graniferous. **1843** HUMBLE *Dict. Geol. & Min.*, *Graniferous*, pods which bear seeds like grains.

graniform ('grænɪfɔːm), *a.* [f. L. *grān-um* GRAIN + -(I)FORM.] Formed like a grain or as if composed of grains; *spec.* in *Anat.* and *Bot.*

1778 CAMPER in *Phil. Trans.* LXIX. 157 Little graniform bones. **1797** *Ibid.* LXXXVII. 207 The inner surface of the horns was graniform. **1829** LOUDON *Encycl. Plants* 441 *Mesembryanthemum parvifolium*..Leaves graniform expanded bluntly. **1830** R. KNOX *Béclard's Anat.* 354 A.. very painful graniform or pisiform subcutaneous tumour. **1840** PAXTON *Bot. Dict.*, *Graniform*, formed like grains of corn.

granilite ('grænɪlaɪt). *Min.* Now *rare.* [Introduced by Kirwan; f. L. *grāni-*, comb. form of *grān-um* GRAIN + -LITE.] A granular aggregate of more than three ingredients (see quot. 1796).

1794 KIRWAN *Elem. Min.* (ed. 2) I. 346 Granilite. Under this denomination, we may comprehend all granites that contain more than three constituent parts. **1799** —— *Geol. Ess.* 166 By granitic compounds, I mean granitines, granitells, and granilites. **1865** in PAGE *Handbk. Geol. Terms* (ed. 2) s.v. *Granitelle.*

Hence **grani'litic** *a.*

1799 KIRWAN *Geol. Ess.* 123 This granilitic rock.

‖**granilla** (grə'nɪlə). [Sp., dim. of *grana*: see GRAIN *sb.*[1]] An inferior quality of cochineal, consisting of the dried bodies of small or half-grown cochineal-insects.

1812 J. SMYTH *Pract. of Customs* (1821) 96 Granilla is the refuse of Cochineal, in small grains. *a* **1873** CALVERT *Dyeing & Calico-printing* (1876) 208 There is often a second production of cochineal before the wet season sets in; if so, it is scraped off with a knife and dried, but it is of inferior quality, and is sold under the name of *granilla.*

granita (gra'nita). Pl. **granite** (gra'nite). [It. (cf. GRANITE).] **a.** = GRANITE 2. **b.** An iced drink.

1869 'MARK TWAIN' *Innoc. Abr.* xxiii. 174 People at small tables [in Venice]..smoking and taking *granita* (a first cousin to ice-cream). **1963** *Times* 14 Jan. 11/5 No account of Italian sweets would be complete without mention of the ices, and of these the simplest and perhaps the best are the *granite*, sorbets or water ices. **1968** R. COLLIN *Locust on Wind* iii. 25 A tall glass of *granite*, crushed ice in fresh lemon juice. **1970** SIMON & HOWE *Dict. Gastron.* 205/1 In Italy *granita* heralds the first sign of summer.

granite ('grænɪt). Also 8 **granate, granet.** [ad. It. *granito* (orig. a ppl. adj. = 'grained'), f. *grano* GRAIN *sb.* The It. word has been adopted in most of the European langs.: F. *granit* (cited in Hatz.-Darm. from 1690), Sp., Pg. *granito*, Ger., Sw., Da. *granit*, Du. *graniet.*

The 18th c. form *granate* is due to etymologizing identification of the word with GRANATE *a.* Cf. *granated marble*, s.v. GRANATE *v.*]

1. a. A granular crystalline rock consisting essentially of quartz, orthoclase-feldspar, and mica, much used in building.

It varies in colour, light grey being the predominating tint. Other varieties are white and light red or pink.

[**1613-39** I. JONES in Leoni *Palladio's Archit.* (1742) II. 49 A. Pannels of Porphyry. B. Ditto of Granito.] **1646** EVELYN *Mem.* (1857) I. 232 Columns of great height, of Egyptian granite. **1670** LASSELS *Voy. Italy* II. 236 Pillars..all of a granite, or speckled marble. **1718** LADY M. W. MONTAGU *Let. to Abbe Conti* 31 July, Vast pieces of granite..are daily lessened by the prodigious balls that the Turks make from them for their Cannon. **1759** JOHNSON *Rasselas* xxxvii, Palaces and temples will be demolished to make stables of granate. **1762** *Phil. Trans.* LII. 510 The school-house all of square granet. **1814** SCOTT *Ld. of Isles* III. xv, Huge terraces of granite black. **1851** LAYARD *Pop. Acc. Discov. Nineveh* xiii. 341 A country..rich in stone and costly granites. **1860** TYNDALL *Glac.* I. vii. 50 The Aiguille..piercing with its spikes of granite the clear air. **1868** LOSSING *Hudson* 364 The mansion is built of blue granite. **1887** RUSKIN *Præterita* II. 233 The tremendous granites of the Grimsel.

b. *fig.* Applied to 'stony', hard-headed, or hard-hearted persons. Often *attrib.* and *Comb.* (cf. *granite-like* in 3 b).

1839 J. R. LOWELL *Ye Yankees* 3 in *Uncoll. Poems* (1950), Stern granite hearted ones! **1902** *Daily Chron.* 12 Nov. 5/6 That granite-headed ship-owner, Sir Alfred L. Jones. **1908** *Ibid.* 7 Nov. 4/4 His countenance expressed neither the sweetness and tenderness of the saint nor the granite severity of the prophet. **1916** *Punch* 14 June 398/2, I stole a look at Hercules over my shoulder, but he was granite. **1920** C. JERDAN *Scott. Clerical Stories* viii. 164 Strong-boned, granite-headed, and endowed with all kinds of vitality.

2. *U.S.* 'A kind of rough-grained water-ice or sherbet. Also called *rock-punch* and *rock ice-cream*' (*Cent. Dict.*).

1887 *N.Y. Tribune* 7 Apr. (Cent.), Granites..must be frozen without beating, or even much stirring, as the design is to have a rough, icy-substance. **1892** *Star* 14 May 4/3 Delicious 'granites' in custard glasses.

3. *attrib.* and *Comb.*

a. *simple attrib.* or quasi-*adj.* Consisting of or made of granite. ***the granite capital*** or ***city***, Aberdeen. ***the granite State***, New Hampshire, U.S.

1703 MAUNDRELL *Journ. Jerus.* (1732) 126 Granite Pillars. **1813** SCOTT *Trierm.* III. x, A pile of granite fragments. **1842** J. F. COOPER *Jack o' Lantern* I. iv. 112, I come from New Hampshire, or what we call the Granite state. **1846** J. BAXTER *Libr. Pract. Agric.* (ed. 4) I. 343 Granite mountains are known at a distance by their rounded tops. **1862** BURTON *Bk. Hunter* (1863) 307 Aberdeen, the granite capital of the far north. **1892** *Pall Mall G.* 21 Sept. 6/1 A well-known surgeon..in the granite city. **1898** *Daily News* 10 May 8/2 A..thoroughfare..paved with granite setts.

b. objective and instrumental, as ***granite-dispersion***; ***granite-dispersing***, ***-like***, ***-sprinkled*** adjs.

1879 *Q. Jrnl. Geol. Soc.* XXXV. 431 The *granite dispersing capacity of Kirkcudbrightshire must have been very great. *Ibid.*, The great Kirkcudbrightshire *Granite-dispersion. **1839** BAILEY *Festus* viii. (ed. 1848) 90 The first and *granite-like effect Of things. **1849** COBDEN *Speeches* 20 The granite-like hardihood and consistency of the man. **1867** R. S. HAWKER *Prose Wks.* (1893) 147 A boundless reach of *granite-sprinkled moor.

c. Special comb.: **granite-porphyry** = GRANOPHYRE; **granite-quartzy** *a.*, intermediate between granite and quartz; **granite ware**, (*a*) pottery with a speckled colouring imitating that of granite; (*b*) the name given to a kind of enamelled ironware.

1885 GEIKIE *Text-bk. Geol.* II. II. vii. (ed. 2) 140 *Granophyre* (*Granite-porphyry)—a rock composed of a compact, but thoroughly crystalline (microgranitic) base, through which are porphyritically dispersed crystals of felspar, mica, and quartz (often doubly terminated). **1882** CAPELLO & IVENS *Benguella to Yacca* II. 232 We find..the ground to be composed of *granite-quartzy rock. **1895** *Tradesman's List*, Pie Dishes—Best White *Granite Ware.

granitell ('grænɪtɛl). *Geol.* Also granitel, -elle, -ello. [F. *granitelle*, a. It. *granitello*, dim. of *granito* GRANITE.] A binary granite, or granular aggregate of two ingredients (see quot. 1794).

1794 KIRWAN *Elem. Min.* (ed. 2) I. 343 Mr. D'Aubenton calls the aggregate of quartz and shorl, or of quartz and hornblende, *Granitell*..To avoid all ambiguity, I would propose to denote all these duplicates in general, by the name granitell. **1802** PLAYFAIR *Illustr. Hutton. Theory* 312 It is no matter whether the rock be a syenite, a granitelle, or a real granite. **1802–3** tr. *Pallas's Trav.* (1812) I. 523 This monument appears to be formed of hard granitel, a fossil composed of quartz sand and granite interspersed with particles of black mica. **1848** SIR J. G. WILKINSON *Dalmatia & Montenegro* I. 221 A small-grained granite or granitello. **1879** RUTLEY *Study Rocks* xii. 211 Semi-granite or granitell is a rock..consisting of a crystalline-granular admixture of felspar and quartz.

granitic (græ'nɪtɪk), *a.* [f. GRANITE + -IC. Cf. F. *granitique.*]

1. Of, pertaining to, or of the nature of granite; composed of, or containing, granite. Of water: Obtained from granite soils.

1794 KIRWAN *Elem. Min.* (ed. 2) I. 357 Granitic Porphyry. **1798** *Phil. Trans.* LXXXVIII. 127 The quartz and mica..indicate a granitic origin. **1807** HEADRICK *View Min. Arran* 57 A granitic vein intersects the strata. **1833** LYELL *Princ. Geol.* III. 364 Conditions necessary to produce the granitic texture. **1862** TYNDALL *Mountaineer.* 56 A large prism of granite, or granitic gneiss. **1864** NEALE *Seaton. Poems* 130 How those granitic temples rise. **1868** LOCKYER *Elem. Astron.* cxc. 80 The older rocks of the granitic series. **1869** E. A. PARKES *Pract. Hygiene* (ed. 3) 21 Generally the granitic water is very pure. **1879** D. M. WALLACE *Australas.* xi. 223 One-sixth of the area of the colony is granitic.

2. *fig.* Hard, rigid, unimpressionable.

1862 WRAXALL *Hugo's Misérables* III. xii. 64 The granitic solidity of certain celebrated prose. **1876** DOUSE *Grimm's L.* xxxvi. 76 Much less shall we dream of the Holethnic speech as of one rigid and granitic whole. **1884** C. L. PIRKIS *Judith Wynne* II. iii. 33 His face..was granitic in its effacement of all human feeling. **1886** *Edin. Rev.* Jan. 137 The granitic, patriarchal figure of Job..is strikingly conceived.

granitical (græ'nɪtɪkəl), *a. rare.* [f. prec. + -AL[1].] = prec.

1796 MORSE *Amer. Geog.* I. 179 *note*, Granitical [rocks]. **1797** POLWHELE *Hist. Devonsh.* I. 146 If..we bow down to this granitical god. **1802** *Edin. Rev.* I. 57 Everywhere schistose or granitical, it [the island] exhibits no trace of volcano. **1802** *Paris as it was* II. lxix. 385 Granitical rocks, fossil shells. **1843** in HUMBLE *Dict. Geol. & Min.*

graniticoline (grænɪ'tɪkəlɪn, -aɪn), *a.* [f. GRANITE + L. *colĕre* to inhabit + -INE.] Of a lichen: Growing upon or attached to granite.

1889 in *Century Dict.*

granitiferous (grænɪ'tɪfərəs), *a.* [f. GRANITE + -(I)FEROUS.] Granite-bearing.

1852 TH. ROSS *Humboldt's Trav.* III. xxxii. 383 Layers of chloritic, granitiferous slate.

granitification (grænɪtɪfɪ'keɪʃən). [f. GRANITE + -(I)FICATION.] The action of forming, or the process of being formed, into granite.

1843 in HUMBLE *Dict. Geol. & Min.*

granitiform (græ'nɪtɪfɔːm), *a.* [f. GRANITE + -(I)FORM.] Resembling granite (see quot. 1876).

1833 LYELL *Princ. Geol.* III. 353 We find also..granitiform porphyries intruding themselves into granite. —— *Elem. Geol.* (1865) 705 The talcose gneiss assumes a granitiform structure. **1876** PAGE *Adv. Text-Bk. Geol.* vii. 125 The epithets granitoid and granitiform..are applied to rocks having some resemblance to granite, though not decidedly of granitic nature.

granitin ('grænɪtɪn). *Min.* Now *rare.* Also **granitine.** [f. GRANITE + -IN (used arbitrarily); app. altered from GRANATINE.] A granular aggregate of three mineral ingredients, one or more differing from those which compose granite.

1799 KIRWAN *Geol. Ess.* 325 Hornblende, a stone which enters into the composition of..many granitines, and of most traps. **1811** PINKERTON *Petral.* I. 196 Grey granite, with nodules of granitin. **1865** in PAGE *Handbk. Geol. Terms* (ed. 2) s.v. *Granitelle*, Granitine.

granitite ('grænɪtaɪt). *Min.* Also **-yte.** [f. GRANITE + -ITE.] A variety of granite (see quot. 1879).

1875 *Ure's Dict. Arts* (ed. 7) II. 734. **1879** RUTLEY *Stud. Rocks* xii. 210 Granitite is a term given to those varieties of granite which contain a certain amount of plagioclase (oligoclase). **1887** DANA *Man. Min. & Petrogr.* (ed. 4) 470 Biotite granite (*granityte*).

granitization (grænɪtaɪ'zeɪʃən). *Geol.* [f. GRANIT(E + -IZATION.] The process by which granitic rocks are formed from other rocks; formerly also, the injection of granite into a rock. Also **'granitized, 'granitizing** *ppl. adjs.*

1893 A. GEIKIE *Text-bk. Geol.* (ed. 3) 579 Round some bosses of granite the adjacent rocks are injected or impregnated with such an abundance of minute threads or veins of granite substance..that they are said to be 'granitized'. *Ibid.* 604 This impregnation or granitization has been strongly insisted upon by M. Michel Lévy. **1944** *Proc. Geol. Assoc.* LV. 78 The view..that the granitising material must have varied with the rocks undergoing granitisation. **1963** D. W. & E. E. HUMPHRIES tr. *Termier's Erosion & Sedimentation* p. vii, Many mechanical, physical and chemical phenomena resulting from internal geodynamic processes, such as folds, metamorphism and granitization, are only known by their effects. **1965** G. J. WILLIAMS *Econ. Geol. N.Z.* i. 1/1 This gneiss probably represents an intensely metamorphosed and granitized complex of ancient sediments.

‖**granito.** In 7 *erron.* garnito. [It. *granito* 'a kind of speckled stone' (Florio, 1611).] ? Granite. In quot. *attrib.*

1644 EVELYN *Diary* 4 Nov., At the entrance of this stately Palace stand 2 rare and vast fountaines of garnito stone. [**1656** BLOUNT *Glossogr.*, *Granito* (Ital.), a kind of speckled stone or marble very common at Milan, and other parts of Italy.]

granitoid ('grænɪtɔɪd), *a.* and *sb.* [f. GRANITE + -OID.] **A.** *adj.* Resembling granite; having the granular-crystalline structure of granite.

1839 MURCHISON *Silur. Syst.* I. xxxi. 418 Small yellowish green veins ramifying through the granitoid and syenitic rocks. **1843** PORTLOCK *Geol.* 508 Granitoid mica schists. **1856** KANE *Arct. Expl.* II. App. ii. 308 Numerous granitoid islands. **1881** GEIKIE in *Macm. Mag.* XLIV. 426 A huge erratic of the usual granitoid gneiss. **1885** H. O. FORBES *Nat. Wand. E. Archip.* 333 No rock of a sedimentary or granitoid character could I detect.

B. *sb.* A granitoid rock.

1794 KIRWAN *Elem. Min.* (ed. 2) I. 369 Still many aggregates are daily met, which cannot be arranged under any general denomination now in use. Hence I would propose to call them, if any of their constituent parts can be considered as a basis, *Porphyroids*; if none can be considered as a basis, *Granitoids*. **1811** PINKERTON *Petral.* I. 209 Such [rocks]..as perfectly resemble granite, but are of a very different modification, are here styled granitoids.

Hence **grani'toidal** *a.* = GRANITOID *a.*

18.. NEWBOLD in Stocqueler *Handbk. Brit. Ind.* (1854) 305 Granitoidal gneiss.

granitone ('grænɪtəʊn). *Min.* ? *Obs.* Also **graniton.** [ad. It. *granitone*, augmentative of *granito* GRANITE.] (See quot. 1794.)

[**1794** KIRWAN *Elem. Min.* (ed. 2) I. 345 The aggregate of felspar and mica is called *Rapakivi*..; when the felspar exceeds, it forms a durable stone, called in Italy *Granitone.*] **1811** PINKERTON *Petral.* I. 203 Graniton may also be denominated, from the mica assuming the size of plates of talc. **1816** *Edin. Rev.* XXVI. 163 Granitone is found in almost every situation where serpentine exists.

granitor, variant of GRANATOR.

†**granitose**, *a. Obs.* [f. GRANITE *a.* + -OSE.] Having some of the characteristics of granite.

1811 PINKERTON *Petral.* I. 128 Weight, sometimes granitose, sometimes carbonose. *Ibid.* II. 181 A rock whose base is a mixture of felspar and black hornblende, both in small grains..in this kind of granitose paste are contained tolerably regular crystals of..felspar.

granitous ('grænɪtəs), *a. rare*[−1]. [f. GRANITE + -OUS.] Of the nature of granite.

1868 G. STEPHENS *Runic Mon.* I. 345 Granitous graystone.

granivorous (grə'nɪvərəs), *a.* [f. mod.L. *grānivor-us* (f. L. *grāni-*, *grānum* grain + *vor-āre* to devour).] That feeds on grain.

1646 SIR T. BROWNE *Pseud. Ep.* VII. xiv. 368 Some kinde of granivorous bird. **1713** DERHAM *Phys.-Theol.* VI. iii. 362 Granivorous Quadrupeds. **1774** HUNTER in *Phil. Trans.* LXIV. 311 In granivorous birds..one single organ answers both to the teeth and stomach of granivorous quadrupeds. **1848** CARPENTER *Anim. Phys.* 163 This crop is of enormous size in some of the granivorous birds.

†**grank**, *v. Obs.* [App. a frequentative formation on northern *grane* GROAN *v.*, with suffix *-k*, as in *tal-k*, *wal-k*.] *intr.* To groan.

c **1460** *Towneley Myst.* xvii. 45 Bot settys me downe, and grankys, and gronys, And lygys and restys my wery bonys, And all nyght after grankys and goonys, On slepe tyll I be broght.

Hence †**grank** *sb.*, a groan; †**'granking** *vbl. sb.*

1513 DOUGLAS *Æneis* VII. ix. 56 The deyr, so deidly woundit..enteris in his stall..wyth mony grank and grone. **1807** STAGG *Poems* 48 Hout man! what signifies repeynin? Owr grankin, snifteran, twistin, tweynin.

grannam ('grænəm). *Obs.* exc. *dial.* Forms: 6– **granam**, 8 **granum**, 7– **grannam**, **-um**, (9 **grannan**). [colloq. pronunc. of GRANDAM.] A grandmother; an old woman.

1597 SHAKS. *Rich. III*, II. iv. 30 (Qo.) Granam this would haue beene a biting iest. *a* **1625** BEAUM. & FL. *Lover's Progr.* IV. i, Ghosts never walk till after midnight, if I may believe my grannam. **1679** *Confinement* 30 Old Granams shake their empty heads, and cry, I long before read this his destiny. **1714** GAY *What d'ye call it* II. i. 19 Oft my kind Grannam told me—Tim, take warning. *a* **1763** SHENSTONE *Odes* (1765) 205 Such breeding as one's granam preaches. **1817** COLERIDGE *Zapolya* IV. ii, Find grannam out a sunny seat. **1818** *Blackw. Mag.* III. 406 The first was Moll, the namesake of her grannum. **1825** *Sporting Mag.* XVI. 404 My grannan, God rest her old soul! **1876** *Whitby Gloss.*, *Grannam*,..grandmother.

b. *Phrases.*

1631 MASSINGER *Emperor East* IV. ii, By my granam's ghost, 'Tis a wholesome Zaying! **1632** BROME *Court Beggar* II. Wks. 1873 I. 212 As I hope for my Grannums blessing. **1651** H. MORE *2nd Lash* in *Enthus. Triumph.* (1656) 243 In the rest of your answer you do but teach your Grannam to crack nuts. *a* **1700** B. E. *Dict. Cant. Crew* s.v. *Bit*, He has bit his Grannam; he is very Drunk. **1797** WOLCOT (P. Pindar) *Livery Lond.* II. Wks. 1812 III. 449 They teach forsooth their grannum to suck eggs!

c. *attrib.* and *Comb.*, as †***grannam-like*** adv.; †**grannam-gold** (see GRANDAM 5).

a **1700** B. E. *Dict. Cant. Crew*, *Grannam-gold*, old Hoarded Coin. **1711** E. WARD *Quix.* I. 27 Poor Dobbin..Grannum like, had much ado To mumble what he could not chew.

Hence †**'grannamish** *a.*, old-womanish.

1672–3 MARVELL *Reh. Transp.* Wks. (Grosart) III. 516 A grannamish and doating superstition.

grannom, granam ('grænəm, -æm). A kind of fly (see quots.); also an imitation of it used in fly-fishing.

1787 BEST *Angling* (ed. 2) 112 The Granam-fly is a four-winged fly; as it swims down the water its wings lie flat on its back, it has a small bunch of eggs of a green colour which gives it the name of the Green-tail-fly. **1834** MEDWIN *Angler in Wales* I. 29 The first dropper was a granam, or green-tail. **1889** CHOLMONDELEY-PENNELL *Fishing* (Badm. Libr.) 283 The grannom..is a reddish brown insect, not uncommon in the bushy reaches of many southern streams.

granny, grannie ('grænɪ). Also 7 **grannee**, 8 **grany**, *Sc.* **graunie.** [See -IE, -Y[4]; the dim. is prob. formed on *grannam*, GRANDAM, rather than on GRANDMOTHER *sb.*] **1. a.** A familiar, endearing, or contemptuous synonym of GRANDMOTHER *sb.* Also used loosely for 'an old woman', 'a gossip'.

1663 DRYDEN *Wild Gallant* II. i, I never knew your Grand-mother was a Scotch woman..: pray whistle for her, and lets see her dance : come—whist Grannee! **1785** BURNS *Addr. Deil* v, My reverend Graunie. **1810** *Cromek's Rem. Nithsdale Song* 51 The gladness which dwells in their auld grannie's ee. **1816** *Gentl. Mag.* LXXXVI. I. 522 This old grannie..sends a message to the Earl. **1821** CLARE *Vill. Minstr.* I. 22 What things were seen in granny's younger days. **1856** MISS MULOCK *J. Halifax* xxxix. (ed. 22) 414 'Me want to see Grannie and Uncle Guy.' **1861** MAX MÜLLER *Chips* (1880) II. xxiv. 247 Stories..for which we are indebted to the old grannies in every village. **1889** *Harper's Mag.* Feb. 376/1 'Fairly good holy images thou hast here, granny'..said I to the old woman.

fig. **1726** AMHERST *Terræ Fil.* viii. 36 From the earliest accounts that we have of these two contending grannies [Oxford and Cambridge] they were untoward cross grain'd baggages from children.

b. *Phrase.* (Cf. GRANDAM 1 b.)

1793 FITZGERALD in *European Mag.* xxvi. 387 Go teach your granny. **1845** *Lond. Jrnl.* I. 191 Now they are taught to teach their grannies how to suck eggs.

c. ***your granny!***: used as an exclamation suggesting derision or disbelief. (Cf. GRANDMOTHER *sb.* 1 b.)

1838 J. C. NEAL *Charcoal Sks.* 35 'War!' ejaculated the party; 'oh, your granny!' **1858** GEO. ELIOT *Scenes Cler. Life* I. 65 'Well,' suggested John,..'you should wet the bottom of the *duree* a bit, to hold it from slippin'.' 'Wet your granny!' returned the cook. **1863** *Ladies' Repository* XXIII. 482/2 'Repose, your granny,' answered Addie, who, when vexed never stopped for elegant phrases. **1876** 'MARK TWAIN' *Tom Sawyer* xxv. 193 'Do they hop?' 'Hop—your granny! No.' **1939** 'F. O'BRIEN' *At Swim-two-Birds* i. 13, I open several books every day, I answered. You open your granny, said my uncle.

2. *U.S. local.* A nurse or midwife. (Cf. GRANNY *v.*)

1794 WASHINGTON *Let.* Writings 1892 XIII. 18 An application was made to me by Kate at Muddy hole.. to serve the negro women (as a Grany) on my estate.

3. *dial.* A stupid person, 'old woman'.

1887 *S. Chesh. Gloss.*, *Granny*, a simpleton: used of both sexes. **1897** *Daily News* 20 Dec. 8/5 Characterising the.. officials as a set of what they called in Scotland grannies, a parcel of old women [etc.].

4. Short for *granny knot*.

1865 in *Slang. Dict.* *a* **1894** STEVENSON *St. Ives* cxxxiv. (1898) 283 He tied his knots into 'grannies'.

5. *U.S.* 'A duck, the south-southerly or old-wife. More fully, *old granny*' (*Cent. Dict.*).

6. Short for *granny bond. colloq.*

1981 *Sunday Times* 23 Aug. 45/6 (*heading*) 'Grannies' in lead. **1982** *Ibid.* 10 Oct. 57/1 It's time to throw out your 'grannies'—they are no longer earning their keep. The reason people are ditching their 'grannies' is plain to see.

7. *Comb.*, as ***granny-armchair, collarette, dress, glasses, gown, hat, print, skirt***; **granny bashing, battering** *colloq.*, the assault or mugging of elderly persons; *spec.* violence towards an elderly member of one's family, esp. one's grandmother; **granny bond**, a familiar name for an index-linked National Savings certificate available originally only to a person of pensionable age; **granny bonnet, muff**, a bonnet or muff of a shape resembling those of Victorian grandmothers; **granny flat**, a self-contained living unit for an elderly relative forming part of or detached from the family home; **granny knot** = *granny's knot*; **granny's bend, knot** (see quots.); **granny's nightcap**, *dial.* name for various plants.

1946 KOESTLER *Thieves in Night* 146 There were mattresses, saucepans, a cuckoo-clock, a *granny-armchair, a bicycle and even a bird-cage. **1975** *Observer* 7 Sept. 2 (*heading*) Doctor warns on *granny-bashing. **1979** E. DEEPING *Caring for Elderly Parents* vi. 116 'Granny-bashing' is now well established on the list, along with 'mugging' and 'football hooliganism'. **1981** *Pulse* 24 Oct. 45 (*heading*) Granny bashing signs are passing GPs by. **1975** G. BURSTON in *Brit. Med. Jrnl.* 6 Sept. 592/3 Perhaps general practitioners.. and casualty officers.. should become as conscious of *granny-battering as they are now aware of baby-battering. **1984** M. EASTMAN *Old Age Abuse* 9 The term 'granny battering' has in recent years caught the imagination of the so-called helping professions as well as the media. **1977** *Sunday Times* 4 Sept. 71/5 The 1,200,000 pension-age people (men over 65, women over 60) who have money tucked away in National Savings Retirement certificates—now endearingly known as *granny bonds. **1981** *Times* 31 July 1/7 Granny bonds are to be made available to everyone from September 7. **1984** *Daily Tel.* 17 Dec. 12/2 Bonuses on granny bonds not encashed.. increased the value of investments by.. £269 million. **1894** *Daily News* 30 Oct. 6/6 *Granny bonnets are revived. **1880** *Queen* 10 July (Advt.), The 'Granny' shade hat,.. The '*Granny' collarette. **1909** *Westm. Gaz.* 3 Apr. 15/2 The best dress-makers are preparing what they call '*Grannie' dresses. **1966** *Punch* 29 June 946/1 The social columns continue to keep us informed in their eager girlish way about where the 'in' crowd are currently surging in their Granny dresses, Stalin caps, sawn-off skirtlets and mini-beards. **1965** *New Society* 16 Sept. 22/1 The idea of '*grannyflats' was put forward.. attached to family houses. These might well satisfy a widow or widower's desire for independence while enabling them to live in close contact with their family. **1981** 'M. INNES' *Lord Mullion's Secret* ix. 70 It seemed wholly amiable in the Mullions to incorporate this not particularly close kinswoman in their household, even if it was on what was coming to be known as the granny-flat principle. **1968** J. HUDSON *Case of Need* III. i. 171 She had a flower painted on her cheek, and large, blue-tinted *granny glasses. **1970** *Guardian* 22 June 1/1 A mop-headed youth with granny glasses. **1965** J. HART *File for Death* iv. 31 The girl, dressed in a long *granny gown and wearing a bright pink hairnet. **1880** *Granny hat [see *granny collarette* above]. **1967** *Boston Sunday Globe* 23 Apr. A 28/3 These favorites will be offered along with the teens' 'granny hats'. **1905** *Eng. Dial. Dict.* Suppl., Granny-knot. **1932** KIPLING *Limits & Renewals* 196 They'd been busy since light unpickin' the wire granny-knots this so-called Noo Navy had tied 'em in with. **1959** *Listener* 7 May 808/2 The bag.. that took half an hour to rope up with eighteen feet of clothes-line and about forty granny-knots. **1897** *Daily News* 23 Jan. 6/3 The *Granny-muffs have been found to be really less warm. **1961** *Sunday Express* 28 May 15/2 Small black-on-grey '*Granny' prints. **1867** SMYTH *Sailor's Word-bk.*, **Granny's bend*, the slippery hitch made by a lubber. **1853** THOREAU *Jrnl.* 25 July in *Writings* (1906) XI. 335, I had been all the while tying what is called a *granny's knot. *c* **1860** H. STUART *Seaman's Catech.* 1 This knot.. will not jam as a 'granny's' knot would do. **1867** SMYTH *Sailor's Word-bk.*, *Granny's knot*, a term of derision when a reef-knot is crossed the wrong way, so as to be insecure. It is the natural knot tied by women or landsmen, and derided by seamen because it cannot be untied when it is jammed. **1966** H. YOXALL *Fashion of Life* viii. 76 In the autumn of 1965.. girls in Los Angeles started a fad for wearing '*granny' skirts, down to their heels. **1863** *Phytologist* New Ser. VI. 416 The *Caltha palustris* is called 'May-blobs' by the children who gather the flower in the meadows near Warwick; they also call the Wood Anemone (*A. nemorosa*) '*Granny's Nightcap'. **1892** C. M. YONGE *Old Woman's Outlook* 119 The odd red-calyxed *Geum rivale*, called by the village children Granny's nightcaps. **1893** DARTNELL & GODDARD *Gloss. Wilts.* 69 *Granny* (or *Granny's*) *Nightcap*, (1) *Anemone nemorosa*,.. Wood Anemone.. (2) *Aquilegia vulgaris*,.. Common Columbine.. (3) *Convolvulus sepium*,.. Great Bindweed.. (4) *Convolvulus arvensis*,.. Field Bindweed.

Hence '**granny** *v.*, *U.S. local, trans.*, to act as a 'granny' (sense 2) to.

1897 RUTH M. STUART *In Simpkinsville* 85 She grannied yore mother when you was born.

Granny Smith. [f. the name of Maria Ann *Smith* ('Granny Smith'), d. 1870.] An Australasian variety of apple, which is bright green and suitable for eating raw or cooked.

1895 *Agric. Gaz. N.S. Wales* VI. 900, I think that.. Granny Smith's Seedling.. would be worth a trial. *Ibid.*, If it is desirable to go in more for the late home market, then I would include.. Granny Smith's Seedling. **1932** *Discovery* July 220/2 Australasia has Granny Smith, Cleopatra, Jonathan, Sturmer, Pippin etc., which excel. **1933** *Bulletin* (Sydney) 11 Jan. 12 Seventy years ago there dwelt in the isolated hamlet of Eastwood.. an old lady named Smith.. the original source of the 'Granny Smith' apple. **1943** *Gen* 10 Apr. 60/2 The stubby 'Granny Smith' apple tree on the lawn. **1960** W. A. BEATTY *Treas. Austral. Folk Tales* 186 The Granny Smith is unique among apples inasmuch that there is none its equal for cooking purposes, it is a splendid eating apple, and when stored keeps better than any other variety.

‖**grano**[1] ('grano). Pl. **grani** ('grani). [It.; = GRAIN *sb.*[1]] A money of account in Southern Italy and the Mediterranean, = about $\frac{1}{12}$*d.* sterling (1900).

1858 in SIMMONDS *Dict. Trade.* **1860** *Merc. Marine Mag.* VII. 57 A Neapolitan.. Decree imposes a Light Due of four grani per ton.

grano[2] ('grænəʊ), abbrev. GRANOLITHIC *sb.*

1940 *Archit. Rev.* LXXXVIII. 40 The floor of the stoep is finished in shiny black grano. **1951** *Ibid.* CIX. 290 A wood roof with corrugated asbestos covering, wood and grano floors. **1958** J. S. SCOTT *Dict. Civ. Engin.* 165 *Granolithic* or *grano*, a screed of cement, sand, and granite chippings floated over concrete floors to give a smooth, hard-wearing surface about 1½ in. thick.

granodiorite (ˌgrænəʊ'daɪəraɪt). *Petrogr.* [f. *grano-*, taken as combining form of *granite* (cf. GRANOPHYRE) + DIORITE.] Any of the plutonic igneous rocks intermediate in composition between true granite and quartz-diorite, which are similar in appearance to granite but are usu. darker in colour; *esp.* one in which there is at least twice as much plagioclase as alkali feldspar.

1893 W. LINDGREN in *Amer. Jrnl. Sci.* 3rd Ser. XLVI. 203 On the Survey maps of the Gold Belt of the Sierra Nevada, of which district Mr G. F. Becker is geologist in charge, it has therefore been determined to indicate this rock as granodiorite, which term it is hoped will find general acceptance. **1932** A. JOHANNSEN *Descr. Petrogr.* II. 323 Granodiorites occur as intrusive bodies, in the same manner as granites, and often form huge masses. **1961** *Bull. Board Celtic Stud.* XIX. 167 A magnificent implement [*sc.* a Neolithic axe-head] made of an augite granodiorite, almost certainly of Pembrokeshire origin. **1965** G. J. WILLIAMS *Econ. Geol. N.Z.* xiv. 216/1 The central granite consists of types ranging from pink, generally porphyritic, alkali granites to the more common white to grey biotite calc-alkali granite, adamellite or granodiorite.

granola (græ'nəʊlə). Chiefly *N. Amer.* [Cancelled trade-mark: see GRAIN *sb.*[1], GRANULAR *a.*, and -OLA; the earlier *Granūla* (registered 1876 as 'cooked granulated wheat' by Austin Jackson & Co., Dansville, N.Y.), is a different product.] †**a.** With capital initial. Formerly, a proprietary name for a breakfast cereal devised by W. K. Kellogg, consisting of wheat, oats, and cornmeal baked and ground into granules. *Obs.*

1886 *Trade Marks Jrnl.* 24 Mar. 275 *Granola*,.. A product for food. **1928** *Official Gaz.* (U.S. Patent Office) 8 Nov. 288 The Battle Creek Food Company, Battle Creek, Mich... Granola.

b. A mixture of rolled oats, wholewheat flour or wheatgerm, nuts, dried fruits, oils, and other 'natural' ingredients toasted and sold as a breakfast cereal, biscuit-like snack, etc. (Not proprietary in this sense.)

1970 *Time* 16 Nov. 63/1 Rows of unfamiliar foodstuffs are appearing in middle-class cupboards: brown rice by the bucketful, as well as packages of ad[z]uki, granola, gomasio, ginseng and miso. **1974** *Daily Colonist* (Victoria, B.C.) 16 July 17/1 Increasingly, consumers are becoming aware of the low nutritional value of traditional breakfast cereals, and more and more they are turning to the granola products which offer more in the way of grain cereals combined with nutritious products such as raisins, nuts and seeds. **1976** C. BONINGTON *Everest Hard Way* 213 Doug Scott revealed his cravings for granola and French nougat. **1977** *Time* 9 May 62/3 Williams' happier ending is blended for the granola '70s. **1984** S. BELLOW *Him with his Foot in his Mouth* 89 Katrina woke the girls and told them to dress and come downstairs for their granola. **1985** *New Yorker* 3 June 73/1 She drank the juice and ate a granola bar.

granolithic (grænəʊ'lɪθɪk), *a.* (and *sb.*) [f. *grāno-* (taken as combining form of L. *grānum* GRAIN *sb.*[1]) + Gr. λίθος stone + -IC.] The designation of a particular kind of concrete. Hence, of buildings, etc.: Made of 'granolithic' concrete. Also as *sb.*, = granolithic concrete.

1881 P. STUART *Brit. Pat.* 610 4 The granit and cement is mixed... This composition, which I call 'granolithic', is spread on the concrete so as to embed the iron rods. **1883** *Fisheries Exhib. Catal.* 35 Patent Granolithic Steps for Harbours. **1893** *Daily News* 3 Oct. 2/6 The corridors are floored with the well-known granolithic concrete. **1909** *Pall Mall Gaz.* 12 Apr. 2/2 An inscription in brass letters set in granolithic. **1956** DAVIES & PETTY *Building Elem.* ix. 282 Special abrasive aggregates can be added to the granolithic to provide a non-slip surface.

†**granons**, *pl. Obs. rare*[−1]. [a. OF. *grenon* (*guernon, gernon*, etc.), of Teut. origin; cf. ON. *grǫn* moustache.] The whiskers (of a cat).

1607 TOPSELL *Four-f. Beasts* 104 If the long haires growing about her [the cat's] mouth (which some call *Granons*) be cut away, she looseth hir corage.

granophyre ('grænəʊfaɪə(r)). *Geol.* [First introduced in Ger. form *granophyr* by Vogelsang 1872; f. G. *gran*(it) granite + (por)*phyr* porphyry.] (See quot. 1882.)

1882 GEIKIE *Text-bk. Geol.* II. II. iii. 90 Vogelsang has proposed to classify this type [Porphyritic] in three divisions: 1st, Granophyre, where the ground-mass is a microscopic crystalline mixture of the component minerals, with a sparing development of an imperfectly individualized magma; 2nd, Felsophyre,..; 3rd, Vitrophyre. **1885** [see *Granite-porphyry*]. **1894** *Naturalist Mag.* 298/16 Buttermere granophyres, Yewdale breccias [etc.]. **1897** GEIKIE *Anc. Volcanoes Gt. Brit.* I. 17 The protrusion of the gabbros and granophyres which mark later stages of the same continuous volcanic history.

Hence **grano'phyric** *a.*, composed of granophyre.

1897 GEIKIE *Anc. Volcanoes Gt. Brit.* I. 20 The felsitic and granophyric dykes of Skye.

granose (greɪ'nəʊs), *a. rare*[−0]. [ad. L. *grānōsus*, f. *grānum* GRAIN *sb.*[1]: see -OSE.] Full of, or resembling, grains.

1727 BAILEY vol. II, *Granose*, full of Grains. **1889** *Century Dict.*, *Granose*, in *entom.*, having the form of a string of grains or beads; moniliform, as the antennæ of many insects.

grant (grɑːnt, -æ-), *sb.*[1] Forms: see the vb. [f. the vb.] The action of granting; the thing granted.

†**1. a.** Consent, permission. **b.** Promise. **c.** Admission, acknowledgement. Also, what is agreed to, promised, admitted, etc. *Obs.*

a. *a* **1225** *Ancr. R.* 238 þeo uihteð treouliche þet.. hwuch so euer þe lust beo.. wiðsiggeð þe graunt þerof. *a* **1300** *Cursor M.* 8380 Giue it to quam-sum þou will, For mi grant sal þou haf þer-till. **13..** *E.E. Allit. P.* A. 317 Ȝet of graunt þou myȝtez fayle. **1387** TREVISA *Higden* (Rolls) II. 119 By graunt of Kingislus, kyng of West Saxon, þe firste Birinus ordeyned a cee at Dorchestre. **1389** *Eng. Gilds* (1870) 39 He hath oblisshed him-self, bi his avow and his owen graunt, to [etc.]. *c* **1450** MYRC 399 But heo haue grawnte of hyre husbonde. *c* **1572** GASCOIGNE *Fruites of Warre* (1831) 214 The noble Prince gaue graunt to my request. **1602** MARSTON *Antonio's Rev.* I. i. Wks. 1856 I. 75 Could I avoyde to give a seeming graunt Unto fruition of Antonios love. **1613** HEYWOOD *Silver Age* I. Wks. 1874 III. 88 Gaine by thy grant, life; thy deniall, death. **1648** BOYLE *Seraph. Love* (1660) 46 [You] might have found yourself as sensibly disappointed by her Grant, as you were by her Change.

b. *c* **1300** *Cursor M.* 17956 (Arundel MS.) Whenne fyue þousonde ȝeer are past.. þenne shal god his grante fulfille. *c* **1380** WYCLIF *Serm.* Sel. Wks. II. 86 þei hadden graunt of Crist þat he Wolde algatis have mercy. **1412–20** LYDG. *Chron. Troy* I. vi, To perfourme your hestes & your graunt. *c* **1475** *Rauf Coilȝear* 76 The King was blyth.. Of the grant that he had maid. **1575** CHURCHYARD *Chippes* (1817) 98 A wyfe, a queane, did make the French a graunt Upon this rocke in sight of Leeth to stand.

c. **1503** in *Extracts Aberd. Reg.* (1844) I. 431 It was sufficiently pruit befor the said assis, and als be his avne gravnt, that the said William [etc.]. **1552** T. WILSON *Logike* 57 This is the vse of Reduction by a contradictorie, violently to force the graunt of our saiyng. **1565** JEWEL *Repl. Harding* (1611) 116 By M. Hardings owne grant, we may iustly claime prescription. *a* **1612** DONNE *Βιαθανατος* (1644) 121 To grant that we may wish death to be in heaven.. is.. somewhat more dangerous.. a graunt. **1631** CHAPMAN *Cæsar & Pompey* Plays 1873 III. 177 Your happy exposition of that place.. Euicts glad grant from me you hold a truth. **1659** HAMMOND *On Ps.* Pref. 17 The very objection is a grant that the Psalms contein devotions [etc.]. *a* **1700** DRYDEN (J.), This grant destroys all you have urg'd before.

2. The action of according (a request, a favour asked for).

? *a* **1366** CHAUCER *Rom. Rose* 851 She of hir love graunt him made. **1530** PALSGR. 363 There is no graunt made lyberally, if it be demaunded neglygently. **1599** SHAKS. *Much Ado* I. i. 319 The fairest graunt is the necessitie. **1624** DE LAUNE tr. *Du Moulin's Logick* 86 If a Prince hath granted something to one Citizen, another Citizen may pretend, that the like grant ought to be made unto him also. **1686** J. SCOTT *Chr. Life* (1747) III. 474 The Grant of Remission was wholly in his Will and Pleasure. *a* **1847** MRS. SHERWOOD *Lady of Manor* (1860) V. xxix. 71 Punished with the grant of my wishes. **1892** LD. ESHER in *Law Times Rep.* LXVII. 211/2 The grant or refusal of an injunction upon a matter of law is appealable.

3. a. An authoritative bestowal or conferment of a privilege, right, or possession; a gift or assignment of money, etc. by the act of an administrative body or of a person in control of a fund or the like.

c **1380** WYCLIF *Sel. Wks.* III. 348 But ȝif þei han oþir title þan ben bullis of þe pope, or graunt of him, þei [etc.]. **1550** CROWLEY *Epigr.* 763 Heare is to se Your seale at a graunte of a pluralitie. **1673** *Essex Papers* (Camden) I. 67, I know not whether Mr Brunker may have deceiv'd you in his assurances concerning ye Grant of ye Phœnix Parke. **1719** W. WOOD *Surv. Trade* 174 To oblige the Persons, who.. are in Possession.. by virtue of old Grants, either to settle, or sell them [lands]. **1759** ROBERTSON *Hist. Scot.* (1813) I. 111. 231 The grant of the earldom of Murray to the prior of St.

Andrews was confirmed. **1771** *Junius Lett.* lxvii. 332 You hastened the grant with an expedition unknown to the treasury. **1824** R. STUART *Hist. Steam Engine* 34 Fifty years after the grant of the patent. **1841** W. SPALDING *Italy & It. Isl.* II. 69 His [Pepin's] invasion had been preceded by his famous Grant to the Popes. **1855** MACAULAY *Hist. Eng.* xv. III. 539 He obtained a grant of all the lands..belonging to Jesuits in five or six counties. **1870** ROGERS *Hist. Gleanings* Ser. II. 234 The primary business of both houses was the grant of money. **1874** GREEN *Short Hist.* viii. §3. 481 The Commons restricted their grant of certain Customs duties.. to a single year.

b. The thing granted; a tract of land, a sum of money, etc. which is the subject of a formal grant. Also ***capitation-grant*** (see CAPITATION 3); ***grant in aid of***: see also GRANT-IN-AID.

1815 ELPHINSTONE *Acc. Caubul* (1842) II. 197 The revenues..are consumed in grants to learned and religious men. **1851** HT. MARTINEAU *Hist. Peace* v. iv. (1877) III. 246 In 1834 the government obtained from Parliament the first grant in aid of education. **1860** TYNDALL *Glac.* I. xxiv. 169 A small grant of money to purchase thermometers, &c. **1869** CLARIDGE *Cold Water-cure* 136 Jenner..was voted two grants in parliament. **1897** MARY KINGSLEY *W. Africa* 355 The Chambers voted a grant towards the expenses. **1897** *Mag. Art* Sept. 254 The trustees of polytechnics are apt to judge of the success of the classes by the amount of grant earned.

4. *Law.* **a.** A conveyance by deed or other written instrument. †**b.** Formerly in more restricted application: A conveyance of such property (viz. incorporeal hereditaments) as can pass only by deed. ***to be*** or ***lie in grant***: (of property) to be of a nature transferable only by deed.

1596 SPENSER *State Irel.* Wks. (Globe) 611/2 The act of the parent, in any lawfull graunt or conveyaunce. **1607** COWELL *Interpr.* s.v., A thing is said to lie in graunte which cannot be assigned with out deed. *a* **1626** BACON *Max. & Uses Com. Law* xiv. (1636) 56 Grants are never countermandable..in respect of the nature of the conveyance. **1628** COKE *On Littleton* §259. 172 Grant. *Concessio* is in the Common law a conueyance of a thing that lies in grant, and not in Liuerie, which cannot passe without Deed. **1642** ROGERS *Naaman* 362 Heaven is theirs in the grant and reversion. **1766** BLACKSTONE *Comm.* II. 317 Grants, *concessiones*; the regular method by the common law of transferring the property of incorporeal hereditaments, or, such things whereof no livery can be had. **1817** W. SELWYN *Law Nisi Prius* (ed. 4) II. 1053 Where the plaintiff complains of an injury to an easement, it will be incumbent on him (unless he can shew an express grant) to carry his evidence ..as far back as possible. **1844** WILLIAMS *Real Prop.* i. (1877) 19 A grant to A. B. simply now confers but an estate for his life. **1848** WHARTON *Law Dict.* s.v., A grant of personalty is more properly termed an assignment or a bill of sale.

5. Chiefly *U.S.* The name given to a portion of land in the occupation of specified persons. ***New Hampshire Grants***: now the State of Vermont.

1719 W. WOOD *Surv. Trade* 321 Silver Mines lately discovered to be within the Grant of Monsieur Croizat. **1777** A. HAMILTON *Wks.* (1886) VII. 514 They may be obliged to increase their attention to this matter by keeping a body of men somewhere about the Grants. **1842** L. MUNSELL in *M. Cutler's Life*, etc. (1888) I. 133 There [were] only a few hunters just below the falls, or what is called Clark's grant. **1863** *Amer. Cycl.* XVI. 73/2 The country west of the Connecticut was only known at that time [1760] by the name of 'New Hampshire grants'. **1876** BANCROFT *Hist. U.S.* IV. xxv. 502 Men poured in from towns in the Grants.

6. *attrib.* and *Comb.*, as (sense 3b) ***grant-money***; ***grant-earning*** (so ***grant-earner***), ***-giving*** adjs.; †**grant-parole**, ? respite.

1909 *Daily Chron.* 8 Sept. 6/3 Boys who will reach this age [14] between now and next Easter are inferior *grant-earners as compared with boys who can put in a full year's attendance. **1892** *Daily News* 19 Oct. 5/4 The attendance of considerable numbers of *grant-earning children. **1900** H. G. WELLS *Love & Mr. Lewisham* xxv. 231 Some grant-earning grammar-school. **1960** *Farmer & Stockbreeder* 16 Feb. 146/1 (Advt.), In Britain, Canadian Douglas fir plywood has been designated a grant-earning material. **1963** *Higher Educ.* (Cmnd. 2154) xiv. 213 The increased burden on the local *grant-giving authorities. **1964** J. S. HUXLEY *Ess. Humanist* 267 The great grant-giving..agencies such as the U.N. [etc.]. **1893** *Westm. Gaz.* 27 May 5/1 A number of men have been 'hustled' out of the place in order to get their *grant money. **1616** B. JONSON *Devil an Ass* v. vi, H'hath sent thee *grant-paroll by me to stay longer A moneth here on earth.

grant (grɑːnt, -æ-), *sb.*[2] *U.S.* [? var. GRAND *sb.* 6.] 'In brewing, a copper or iron vessel into which the wort flows from the clarifying battery, and from which it is lifted into the wort-pan' (*Cent. Dict.*).

grant (grɑːnt, -æ-), *v.* Pa. t. and pa. pple. **granted**. Forms: 3 **granti**, 3–7 **graunt(e**, 4 **grant(t)e**, **granty**, 5–6 **grawnt(e**, (5 **grawunt**, **grownte**), 3– **grant**. Also *Pa. t.* 4 **gra(u)nt**; *Pa. pple.* 4–6 **gra(u)nt**. [a. AF. *graunter*, *granter*, OF. *graanter*, *greanter*, altered form of *craanter*, *creanter*:—pop. L. type **crēdentāre*, f. *crēdent-em* pr. pple. of *crēdĕre* to entrust, believe.]

†**1.** *intr.* To agree, consent; to assent to the request of (a person: const. *dat.*); to agree or consent *to* or *to do* (rarely *at do*) something. *Obs.*

a **1300** *Cursor M.* 16851 Ioseph..Ne granted neuer wit wil ne werc, to þair gret felunni. **1340** *Ayenb.* 225 Þe ilke bernþ þet to zenne graunteþ. **1375** BARBOUR *Bruce* IV. 352 I grant thar-till; To ly heir mair war litill skill. *c* **1385** CHAUCER *L.G.W.* 2665 *Hypermnestra*, [Egiste commanded his daughter, with threats, to kill her husband;] And, for to passyn harmles of that place, She grauntyth hym. **1390** GOWER *Conf.* III. 338 He..graunteth with hem for to wende. *c* **1400** MAUNDEV. (Roxb.) xxx. 138 Þai graunted at do all þat he wald bidd þam do. *c* **1400** *Sowdone Bab.* 250, I graunte to be his derlynge. *c* **1440** *Jacob's Well* (E.E.T.S.) 198 þe freendys prayed þe preest to ley þe dede body on his asse. þerto grauntyd he hem. **1485** CAXTON *Paris & V.* 15 At these words graunted Parys to goo to the sayd Ioustes. **1523** LD. BERNERS *Froiss.* I. ccxliii. 363 He graunted to the warr with an yuell wyll. *a* **1547** SURREY *Æneid* II. 164 Assigning me To the altar; whereto they graunted all. **1593** SHAKS. *3 Hen. VI*, I. i. 245 The Souldiers should haue toss'd me on their Pikes, Before I would haue granted to that Act.

2. *trans.* To agree to, promise, undertake.

†**a.** Const. *dat.* of person, and *acc.* of thing. *Obs.*

c **1250** *Gen. & Ex.* 1423 Ðo gan ðat moder and laban Rebecca freinen ðor for-ðan, And ȝhe it grantede mildelike. *c* **1305** *St. Cristopher* 77 in *E.E.P.* (1862) 61 He grantede þis anon. **1390** GOWER *Conf.* II. 243 She graunteth and behight him this. *c* **1400** *Destr. Troy* 978 And he hir graunted þat gate with a good wille. *a* **1400–50** *Alexander* 516 'Þat graunt I gudly,' quod þe gome. **1559** *Mirr. Mag., Hen. VI*, xxvii, Aduise wel ere they graunt, but what they graunt, perfourme.

b. with *inf.* (preceded by *to*) or *clause* as obj. *Obs.* exc. in legal documents.

c **1420** *Chron. Vilod.* st. 141 Þe Kyng of Denmark ȝold hym anon þo And granted crystenmon ever to be. *c* **1450** *Merlin* 23 They that shull come to seche me, have graunted their lorde that they shull me sle. **1484** CAXTON *Fables of Æsop* II. xi, To promytte & graunte to gyue to the that whiche thou neuer leuest to me. **1512** J. WASTELL in Willis & Clark *Cambridge* (1886) I. 609 The said John Wastell graunteth to gyff...xx. markes. **1558** in *Vicary's Anat.* (1888) App. v. 186 The said T. D...couenaunteth and graunteth, to and with the said T. V...that if he [etc.]. **1647** N. BACON *Disc. Govt. Eng.* I. (1739) 200 Do you grant to hold and keep the Laws and rightful Customs, which the Commonalty of your Realm shall have chosen? **1818** CRUISE *Digest* (ed. 2) IV. 68 A. covenanted, granted, and agreed that B. should have the land.

3. To accede to, consent to fulfil (a request, prayer, wish, etc.).

a **1225** *Ancr. R.* 34 Holdeð hine ueste, uort he habbe igranted ou al þet ȝe euer wulleð. *c* **1275** LAY. 14152 Þe bet we wolleþ cweme þe ȝef þou þis wolt granti me [**1205** ȝif þu þis ȝettest me]. *c* **1290** *S. Eng. Leg.* I. 20/33 And grauntede al his bone. *a* **1300** *Cursor M.* 13988 Iesus grant him his praier. **1390** GOWER *Conf.* I. 182 The souldan graunteth her axinge. *c* **1450** *Mirour Saluacioun* 3878 So crist..what eure sho wille aske grauntis he hire fauourably. **1526** *Pilgr. Perf.* (W. de W. 1531) G b, Yf I sholde graunt you at all tymes your affeccyons and desyres. **1600** J. LANE *Tom Tel-troth* 110 O graunt my suit. **1697** DRYDEN *Virg. Georg.* I. 63 Use thyself betimes to hear and grant our Pray'rs. **1797** MRS. RADCLIFFE *Italian* iii. (1826) 20 Grant me then the only request I have to make. **1867** SMILES *Huguenots Eng.* vii. (1880) 126 The authorities at once cheerfully granted all that they asked.

4. a. To allow or concede as an indulgence; to permit or suffer (a person) to have (something); to bestow or confer as a favour, or in answer to a request. Const. *dat.* of person, and *acc.* of thing.

1297 R. GLOUC. (Rolls) 11552 Leue him was igraunted god wot to wuch ende. *a* **1300** *Cursor M.* 2506 (Cott.) Was nan þai raght þai grantid grith. *Ibid.* 25340 Grant vs þi maght til oþer sua forgiue þair sin, þat [etc.]. *c* **1340** *Ibid.* 20011 + 894 (B.M. Add. MS.) Þe archibisshop..haþ graunted xl daies to pardoun to alle þat þis vie wol here. *c* **1374** CHAUCER *Anel. & Arc.* 188 Sheo ne graunted him in hir lyvynge No grace. *c* **1380** WYCLIF *Serm.* Sel. Wks. I. 132 First Crist apperide to þes holy wommen, fer to graunt a privylegie to womman's kynde. **1390** GOWER *Conf.* III. 219 God to hem that ben well thewed Hath yove and graunted the victoire. *c* **1400** *Rom. Rose* 2986 He me graunted ful gladly The passage of the outer hay. *a* **1450** *Knt. de la Tour* H iv b, He graunted his [Absalon's] grace and pardon. **1484** *Surtees Misc.* (1888) 41 God graunte & gyff thaym joy and comforth. *c* **1500** *Lancelot* 456 Grant ws dais three. *a* **1586** SIDNEY *Arcadia* III. (1590) 274 To onely thee thou seest we graunt this speciall grace Vs to attend. **1651** HOBBES *Leviath.* II. xviii. 93 When he has granted all he can, if we grant back the Soveraignty, all is restored. *c* **1709** PRIOR *Callimachus' Hymn to Jupiter* 116 Great father! grant us virtue, grant us wealth. **1711** *Fingall MSS.* in *10th Rep. Hist. MSS. Comm.* App. v. 172 By his granting better conditions to the garrison. **1841** LANE *Arab. Nts.* I. 102 Granting him a delay of three days. **1855** MACAULAY *Hist. Eng.* xii. III. 208 It was an Act purporting to grant entire liberty of conscience to all Christian sects. **1860** TYNDALL *Glac.* I. viii. 60 He had..the good sense..to grant me the liberty I requested. **1871** R. ELLIS *Catullus* xvii. 7 This rare favour, a laugh for all time, Colonia, grant me. **1885** MABEL COLLINS *Prettiest Woman* x, Why might he not grant himself one more sight of her at the door of the Church.

†**b.** With a *thing* as subj. or as indirect obj.: To allow to have. *Obs.*

c **1420** *Pallad. on Husb.* I. 105 Thikke and drie, espie & graunte hit rest. **1668** CULPEPPER & COLE *Barthol. Anat.* II. vi. 98 A smal valve..grants entrance to the blood into the right Ventricle.

†**c.** To sanction, permit (an action). *Obs.*

c **1386** CHAUCER *Melibeus* 22 Attempree weping is nothing defended to him that sorweful is..but it is rather graunted him to wepe..But thogh attempree weping bee y-graunted, outrageous weping certes is defended.

d. with *inf.* or *clause* as obj.; *rarely* with obj. and compl.

c **1250** *Old Kent. Serm.* in *O.E. Misc.* 36 Þider lord granti us to cumene. *c* **1380** WYCLIF *Last Age Chirche* p. xxxvi, þe whiche semlant he graunte us to see. *a* **1400–50** *Alexander* 1826 Bot wald ȝe grant vs to gaa & gefe vs ȝour lefe. **1513** DOUGLAS *Æneis* I. viii. 51 O hie princes, quham to Jupiter hes grant To beild ane new cietie. **1535** COVERDALE *Isa.* xxvi. 13 Graunte, that we may only hope in the. **1570–6** LAMBARDE *Peramb. Kent* (1826) 207 They graunt him to take it with him. **1607** SHAKS. *Cor.* II. i. 156 The Gods graunt them true. **1720** STRYPE *Stow's Surv.* I. I. viii. 35/2 Our Lord Richard the King..hath granted..That all the Kidels that are in the Thames be taken away. **1834** SOUTHEY *Lett.* (1856) IV. 384 God grant that I may find you well enough..for a morning walk.

e. In *pa. pple.* as a polite rejoinder to an apology.

1902 KIPLING *Traffics & Discoveries* (1904) 238 'Granted —granted as soon as asked,' he said, unbending. 'I *did* think it a shade odd at the time.' **1924** —— *Debits & Credits* (1926) 311 '..I beg your pardon..' 'Granted.' **1926** R. MACAULAY *Crewe Train* II. v. 103 When others craved their pardon for stepping on their toes, their reply was, 'Granted.' **1951** E. COXHEAD *One Green Bottle* v. 115 'Pardon?' said Cathy, momentarily bewildered; whereat Mr. Derwent..replied: 'Oh-er, granted.' **1967** 'H. CALVIN' *Nice Friendly Town* vi. 87 She yawned a great yawn and said, 'Sorry.' 'Granted,' I said.

5. a. To bestow or confer (a possession, right, etc.) by a formal act. Said of a sovereign or supreme authority, a court of justice, a representative assembly, etc. Also, in *Law*, to transfer (property) from oneself to another person, especially by deed.

c **1305** *Pilate* 82 in *E.E.P.* (1862) 113 Þemperour.. grantede pilatus al þat lond to holde bi maistrie. **1390** GOWER *Conf.* III. 103 Asia..Was granted by commune assent To Sem. **1463** *Bury Wills* (Camden) 17, I graunte hem fulle pover. **1485** WRIOTHESLEY *Chron.* (1875) I. 1 A great taske and disme grawnted to the Kinge. **1605** CAMDEN *Rem.* 138 Granted by Patents. **1625** BACON *Ess., Friendship* (Arb.) 181 Where Friendship is, all Offices of Life, are as it were granted to Him, and his Deputy. **1632** SANDERSON *Serm.* 436 God the Father hath graunted vs..a new Patent. **1651** HOBBES *Leviath.* III. xlii. 302 The Power here granted belongs to all Supreme Pastors. **1766** BLACKSTONE *Comm.* App. II. §2 They the said Abraham Barker and Cecilia his Wife..do, and each of them doth, grant, bargain, sell, release, and confirm unto the said [D. E. and F. G.;], their heirs and assigns, All that the capital messuage called Dale Hall. **1817** W. SELWYN *Law Nisi Prius* (ed. 4) II. 725 Granting letters of administration, belongs to the prerogative court of the archbishop of that province. **1849** MACAULAY *Hist. Eng.* ii. I. 193 The Commons alone could legally grant him money. **1858** BUCKLE *Civiliz.* (1873) II. viii. 575 They granted charters to the towns and privileges to the inhabitants. **1883** *Law Reports* 11 Q. Bench Div. 545 (*headnote*) An attachment granted to enforce compliance with the order of court.

b. with advs., in technical phrases: ***to grant*** (land, a title) ***away***, ***out***. †***to grant forth*** (a warrant): to issue.

1583 STUBBES *Anat. Abus.* II. (1882) 16 The other officers who grant foorth the warrants, the Subpœnas. **1661** A. BROME *Royalist's Answ.* ii. Songs 75 All titles of honours.. being granted away With the grantees stay. **1844** WILLIAMS *Real Prop.* i. (1877) 2 The lands thus confiscated were granted out by the Conqueror to his followers. **1849** MACAULAY *Hist. Eng.* x. II. 657 The estates of accused persons had been granted away before conviction. **1876** DIGBY *Real Prop.* I. i. §2. 14 The grantee of the land is to be entitled to grant the land away to whomsoever he pleases in his lifetime.

†**6.** To yield, give up. Also with *over*. *Obs.*

1390 GOWER *Conf.* III. 122 For Libra graunteth him [i.e. Scorpion] his ende Of eighte sterres. *a* **1400–50** *Alexander* 3103 Þi meche we beseke..to grant vs oure modire..out of bande. *a* **1586** SIDNEY *Arcadia* I. (1590) 42 b, Palladius not accustomed to grant ouer the possession of him self vpon so vniust titles, with sword drawne gaue them so rude an answer, that [etc.]. **1613** PURCHAS *Pilgrimage* (1614) 331 Certain Thracian women.. granted their haire to this purpose.

7. To admit, confess, acknowledge. Now only in a more restricted use: To concede to an actual or hypothetical opponent (a proposition) to be used as a basis of argument.

a. with obj. either *acc.* with *inf.* or a clause introduced by *that* (often suppressed), rarely *how*. In this sense the imperative mood, the pres. pple. (used *absol.*) and the pa. pple. often introduce an adverbial (concessive) clause.

c **1340** *Cursor M.* 27428 (Fairf.) A man..grauntis [*Cott.* yetes]..þat he is falling in misliking. *c* **1375** *Sc. Leg. Saints, Laurentius* 366 Þat ypolyt..before al had granttyt þare, þat he had bene a cristine mane. **1411** *Rolls of Parlt.* III. 650/1 The sayd Robert wold nouht graunte that he had submytted hym in that mater. *a* **1450** *Le Morte Arth.* 1652 There he grauntyd a monge hem alle..How in an appelle he dede the galle. **1558** BP. WATSON *Seven Sacram.* xxi. 123 A synner maye graunt and confesse, that he hathe not considered thys great kyndenes of God. **1581** MULCASTER *Positions* xxi. (1887) 237 But graunting thinges there to be well done already. **1604** E. G[RIMSTONE] *D'Acosta's Hist. Indies* I. v. 16 They graunt there is a Heaven on this other part of the world. **1659** D. PELL *Impr. Sea* 73 Grant they never used drinking and bezling before they came to Sea..they will soon finde out the art. **1659–60** PEPYS *Diary* 11 Jan., I went to see Mrs. Jem, who was in bed, and now granted to have the small-pox. **1674** tr. *Scheffer's Lapland* 4 Granting there were antiently such names..it remaines doubtfull [etc.]. **1711** STEELE *Spect.* No. 4 ¶5, I grant her Dress is very becoming, but [etc.]. **1849** MACAULAY *Hist. Eng.* ii. I. 156 Grant that such a man had, by his recent services, fairly earned his pardon. Yet [etc.]. **1849** RUSKIN *Sev. Lamps* iv. § I. 94 Only asserting that to be beautiful which I believe will be granted me to be so without dispute. **1853** J. H. NEWMAN *Hist. Sk.* (1876) 161 Granting that that downfall is to come, it is reasonable [etc.]. *a* **1861** T. WOOLNER *My Beautiful Lady* (1863) 128, I grant a few, the greatest, live content. **1884** tr. *Lotze's Metaph.* 101 Granted that two Beings, *A* and *B*, are so independent of each other..then [etc.].

b. with *sb.* or *pron.* as obj. Also *absol.*

a **1340** HAMPOLE *Psalter* xxi. 15 In dust of ded thou has me broght. This says he, noght grauntand it, for his body rot noght. **1375** BARBOUR *Bruce* XIX. 48 The lord sowlis hass grantit thar The deid in-to plane parliament. **1428** *Surtees Misc.* (1888) 3 He gart yarof, als he graunted, ix^{xx} peces & xij. **1526** TINDALE *Acts* xxiii. 8 The phariseies graunt bothe. **1596** SHAKS. *1 Hen. IV*, II. iv. 390, I grant ye, vpon instinct. **1611** BIBLE *Transl. Pref.* 1 This will easily be granted, by as many as know story. **1612** in *Extracts Aberd. Reg.* (1848) II. 312 Patrick Gordoune.. being accusit for trubling of this burght.. in drawing of ane sword, and persewing thairwith Gilbert Leslie.. graunted the drawing of his sword to the said Gilbert, and persewing him thairwith. **1671** GREW *Anat. Plants* I. Ep. Ded., Like the first Principles of Mathematical Science, they are.. granted by all. **1709** BERKELEY *Th. Vision* §15 Though we should grant the real existence of those optic angles. **1774** GOLDSM. *Nat. Hist.* (1776) I. 107 This granted, we shall take something more. **1848** KEBLE *Serm.* Pref. 41 If thus much be granted,.. how is not our principle conceded? **1879** GEO. ELIOT *Coll. Breakf. P.* 287 We settle first the measure of man's need Before we grant capacity to fill.

c. with obj. and complement: To admit or concede (a person or thing) to be so and so. *rare.*

1387 TREVISA *Higden* (Rolls) IV. 367 Vienna was þo i-graunted the place of corsynge. *a* **1400–50** *Alexander* 3125 And if [he] grant him noȝt de-grayd. **1602** SHAKS. *Ham.* II. ii. 100 Mad let vs grant him then. **1653** WALTON *Angler* 139 [I] haue not tryed it; yet I grant it probable. **1730** SWIFT *Traulus* I. 83 Grant him but a drone at best. **1810** SCOTT *Lady of L.* II. xiv, I grant him brave, But wild.

d. To admit the existence of. *Obs. rare*$^{-1}$.

a **1619** FOTHERBY *Atheom.* I. vi. §3 (1622) 46 For, of necessitie hee granteth him [God], though of impotencie hee blaspheme him.

grantable ('grɑːntəb(ə)l, -æ-), *a.* [f. GRANT *v.* + -ABLE.] Capable of being granted.

1548 GEST *Pr. Masse* in H. G. Dugdale *Life* App. i. (1840) 81 Thee sayd bread and wine reteygne styl theyr own natures, whyche is grantable. **1565** *Act 8 Eliz.* c. 4 §3 The former Offence wherein Clergy is not Grantable being not then known. **1648** D. JENKINS *Wks.* 15 No priviledge of Parliament is grantable for treason. **1690** LEYBOURN *Curs. Math.* 225 The Principles of Geometry, consisting of Definitions, Postulates, (or grantable Truths) [etc.]. **1765** BLACKSTONE *Comm.* I. 258 These letters are grantable by the law of nations. **1798** MALTHUS *Popul.* II. xi. (1806) II. 52 Lands which were not cultivated by the proprietor within a limited time were declared grantable to any other person. **1869** *Act 32 & 33 Vict.* c. 115 §11 Any Licence grantable by a Secretary of State.. may.. be granted by the Commissioner. **1879** *Edin. Rev.* CL. 551 In America new trials became grantable, but in England not.

'grant-aided, *a.* [Cf. GRANT-IN-AID.] Of a school or other institution: assisted by an allowance from government or official funds. Hence, by back-formation, **grant-aid** *v. trans.*, to afford financial support of this kind to (a school, etc.). Also **grant-aid** *sb.*, short for GRANT-IN-AID; **grant-aiding** *a.*

1927 CARR-SAUNDERS & JONES *Soc. Struct. Eng. & Wales* 120 Grant-aided secondary schools. **1930** *Times Educ. Suppl.* 18 Oct. 436/4 One-quarter of the grant-aided schools were now co-educational. **1933** *Planning* I. XII. 8 In road transport the adoption after the war of a national system of classified numbering and a policy of rapid grant-aided development opened the way to a national policy for road transport. **1943** *Our Towns. A Close-up* iii. 96 The Board [of Education] should.. ensure, by special grant-aid if necessary, the observance of a minimum standard of hygiene. **1944** H. C. DENT *Educ. Act 1944* 71 A point of interest is that for the first time the Minister is empowered to grant-aid educational research. *Ibid.* 72 Special agreement schools will, under Clause 102, be grant-aided in accordance with the special agreement in respect of each school. **1959** *20th Cent.* Nov. 345 Independent Television.. is no less concerned with programmes on current affairs than the grant-aided corporation. **1962** *Economist* 13 Oct. 148/2 The function.. will be largely that of a grant-aiding body.

granted ('grɑːntɪd, -æ-), *ppl. a.* [f. GRANT *v.* + -ED^{1}.] In senses of the vb.

1. Bestowed, allotted.

1700 DRYDEN *Ovid's Met.* VIII. *Baucis & Philem.* 196 Tablets hung for gifts of granted vows. *a* **1770** JORTIN *Serm.* (1771) IV. i. 2 He daily returned thanks for the granted favor. **1829** H. MURRAY *N. Amer.* II. III. v. 490 In the granted and located districts called the Concessions, two sevenths are retained. **1860** ELLICOTT *Life Our Lord* ii. 67 The granted issue of all his longings and all his prayers. **1876** RUSKIN *Fors Clav.* VI. lxi. 22 It shall be in a constantly progressive relation to the granted years of my life.

2. Admitted, acknowledged.

1640 BP. HALL *Chr. Moder.* (Ward) 36/2 We have reason to take it for a granted truth. **1677** DRYDEN *State Innoc.* Apol. Wks. 1883 V. 124 If they will take it as a granted principle, it will be easy to put an end to this dispute. **1897** W. C. HAZLITT *Ourselves* 50 A gratuitous superstructure on granted or presumed premises.

b. *to take for granted*: to regard as not requiring proof, or as likely to be admitted by every one. † *to give for granted*: see GIVE *v.* 31 b.

1615 J. STEPHENS *Satyr. Ess.* 265 He takes it for granted, that hee can grace or disgrace any man at his pleasure. **1718** *Freethinker* No. 57 ¶2, I have hitherto taken my Beauty for Granted. **1771** *Junius Lett.* liv. 287, I take the facts he refers to for granted. **1826** DISRAELI *Viv. Grey* I. vi, I want you to take no theological dogmas for granted. **1883** F. M. PEARD *Contrad.* xx, She had taken Dorothy's happiness too much for granted. **1894** H. NISBET *Bush Girl's Rom.* 182 He was perfectly frank with Worrogonga who, he took for granted, knew about his assumed character.

¶ Confused use.

1678 CUDWORTH *Intell. Syst.* I. v. 774 He.. takes it as a thing for granted, that this [the soul] is.. in every part of the body.

Hence **'grantedly** *adv.*, admittedly.

a **1638** MEDE *Chr. Sacrif.* Wks. (1672) 355 And this so generally and grantedly as could never have been.. unless [etc.].

grantee (grɑːn'tiː, -æ-). *Law.* Also 5–6 **graunte,** 6–7 **grauntee.** [f. GRANT *v.* + -EE.] The person to whom a grant or conveyance is made.

1491 *Act 7 Hen. VII*, c. 5 §1 The grauntes.. aske deduccions and allowaunces at every quinzime. **1523** FITZHERB. *Surv.* 21 b, The grauntee maye distreyne for the same rent bycause of the clause of dystresse. **1647** N. BACON *Disc. Govt. Eng.* I. xxxi. (1739) 47 The Estate that was granted, depended partly on the condition of the Grantee. **1745** *Season. Adv. Protest.* 7 Many of Cromwell's Grantees, ..joyfully put themselves under the Protection of great Men. **1862** MERIVALE *Rom. Emp.* (1865) VII. lvi. 63 The grantees.. had squandered their grants as fast as they had obtained them. **1875** POSTE *Gaius* III. §32 The praetor's grant of possession only makes the grantee a quasi successor.

granter ('grɑːntə(r), -æ-). Also 4 **grant-, grauntar,** 5–6 **grawnt-, graunter.** See also GRANTOR. [f. GRANT *v.* + -ER^{1}.] One who grants.

c **1400** *Apol. Loll.* 8 In þis caas are comynli grauntars of pardoun. **1483** *Cath. Angl.* 164/1 A Grawnter, *largitor* vel *-trix.* ? *a* **1500** *Chester Pl.* (E.E.T.S.) vii. 591 Hayle, graunter of happe! **1523** FITZHERB. *Surv.* 22 He wyll distreyne for the rent or serve a writ of annuyte agaynst the graunter. *a* **1586** SIDNEY *Arcadia* III. (1590) 263 So that both sides being desirous, and neither granters, they brake of conference. **1616** B. PARSONS *Magistr. Charter* 4 To begin first with the granter, with whom every well-drawne charter first beginneth. **1774** T. WEST *Antiq. Furness* (1805) 188 When that life is determined by the dissolution of the body politic, the granter takes it back by reversion. **1827** HONE *Every-day Bk.* II. 121 The granters of the venison. **1883** LD. CRAIGHILL in *Law Rep.* 9 App. Cases 312/2 The power of the granter to deal with her estate under the radical right is plain.

Granth (grʌnt). Also **Grantha,** †**Grooht, Grunth.** [Hindi *granth* book, code, a. Skr. *grantha* tying, knot, literary composition, book, text, f. *granth, grath* to tie.] The sacred scriptures of the Sikhs.

1798 G. FORSTER *Journey f. Bengal to England* I. xi. 255 A book, entitled the *Grunth*,.. is the only typical object which the Sicques have admitted into their places of worship. **1837** G. R. SIDDONS in *Jrnl. Asiatic Soc. Bengal* VI. I. 480 The Granthas, or sacred books, of the Dadupanthi Sect. **1838** E. EDEN *Let.* 10 Dec. in *Up Country* (1866) II. i. 7 There was a large collection of priests, sitting in a circle, with the 'Grooht', their holy book, in the centre. **1839** H. BEVAN *30 Yrs. India* II. i. 7 This compilation is called *Granth*, and is held at least in as high veneration by the Sikhs as the Bible by Christians. **1852** J. M. HONIGBERGER *35 Yrs. in East* I. 99 The Gooroos, or priests of the Sikhs, did the same, from their holy scripture called Grunthsaheb. **1877** *Good Words* 699 Nanuk was rather the bard, who handed down in his Grunth the verses of Kubeer and other fakeers. **1877** E. TRUMPP tr. (*title*) The Ādi Granth or Holy Scriptures of the Sikhs. **1901** *N. Amer. Rev.* Feb. 303 The Sikh still.. visits the temple to listen to the reading of the Granth. **1927** *Daily Tel.* 22 Feb. 11/5 Three hundred Sikhs, carrying the Granth Sahib, or Holy Book,.. were attacked by infuriated Moslems. **1934** H. H. GOWEN *Hist. Religion* xxiii. 347 The fifth Guru, in 1601, compiled the sacred book known as the *Adi Granth* which is now reverenced almost as a god. *Ibid.*, When the tenth Guru died the succession was regarded as closed and the *Adi Granth* remained the sole authority. **1961** P. SPEAR *India* xxii. 249 The fifth Guru, Arjun, compiled the Adigranth, or first scripture of the community, containing many devotional poems which are now continuously recited by devotees in the Golden Temple. *Ibid.* Guru Gobind lost his sons in battle; after his death in 1708 the guruship lapsed and its place was taken by the Sikh scriptures or Granth Sahib as the sole object of worship.

Grantha ('grʌntə). Also **Grantham.** [Skr. *grantha* (see prec.).] A South Indian alphabet used by the Tamil Brahmans for the Sanskrit transcripts of their sacred books.

1874 A. C. BURNELL *Elem. S. Indian Palæogr.* ii. 34 The name 'Grantha' by which the E. coast variety has been known for some centuries indicates that it was merely used for 'books' or literary purposes. **1883** I. TAYLOR *Alphabet* II. x. 334 Across the whole breadth of India two alphabetic types are superimposed—one was a cursive script..; the other being a literary alphabet, represented in the north by the Devanagari, in the south by the Grantha. **1959** V. CRONIN *Pearl to India* vi. 86 One discovery Nobili soon made: Grantham was not, as Europeans thought, a name for Sanskrit, but merely the angular script evolved by the Tamils to write Sanskrit. **1962** D. DIRINGER *Writing* vi. 147 South-Indian.. Grantha.

grant-in-aid. [GRANT *sb.*^{1} 3 b.] A sum granted, esp. by a government or institution, to a school, institution, scholar, etc. Also *attrib.*

1881 GLADSTONE *Sp. at Leeds* 7 Oct., I am an enemy of the present system of what are called grants in aid. **1890** G. B. SHAW *Let.* 26 Sept. (1965) 266 That the London Society shall make a grant-in-aid of £15. **1899** YOUNGSON *Punjab Mission* xxiii. 196 From fees and Government grants, according to the grant-in-aid system, the schools are in some cases self-supporting. **1906** *Daily Chron.* 21 May 7/4 Mr. Hart Davies suggests that in future there should be two kinds of schools—'State' schools and 'grant-in-aid' schools. **1941** *Ann. Reg. 1940* 260 The grant-in-aid from the British Government.. was almost doubled. **1946** *Nature* 10 Aug. 208/2 It has been decided to adopt a scheme of senior research fellowships and grants-in-aid to operate over the next two years. **1955** *Times* 30 June 17/3 The grant-in-aid of $8,000,000 in goods and services under the U.S.A./Jordan pact of June, 1954, has done much to encourage the realization of these various plans. **1959** *N. & Q.* Dec. 448, I am indebted to the University of Alabama Research Committee for a grant-in-aid which has enabled me to carry on research at Harvard University. **1971** *Nature* 12 Feb. 444/3 For the financial year 1970–71 the budget of the centre is £975,000, of which £589,000 is grant-in-aid.

granting ('grɑːntɪŋ, -æ-), *vbl. sb.* [f. GRANT *v.* + -ING^{1}.] The action of the vb. GRANT.

1340 *Ayenb.* 47 Zuyche grantinges byeþ alneway deadlich zenne. *c* **1386** CHAUCER *Knt.'s T.* 1581 Swich strif ther is bigonne For thilke grauntyng.. That [etc.]. **1587** R. HOVENDEN in *Collect.* (O.H.S.) I. 206, I was deceaved in the graunting. *c* **1600** SHAKS. *Sonn.* lxxxvii, How do I hold thee but by thy granting? **1673** *True Worship God* 19 To return something to the gods for the granting of their desires. **1798** in Picton *L'pool Munic. Rec.* (1886) II. 223 The granting of bounties to seamen. **1824** *Ibid.* 341 Relative to the granting of leases. **1895** L. J. TROTTER *Life Dalhousie* vi. 114 The mere granting of land to a Railway Company.

granting ('grɑːntɪŋ, -æ-), *ppl. a.* [f. GRANT *v.* + -ING^{2}.] That grants, in senses of the vb.

1593 Q. ELIZ. tr. *Boeth.* I. 11 Thassurance of a graunting conscience diminishith it self in a sorte, as oft as bosting receauith rewarde of fame. **1890** *Daily News* 14 Mar. 7/1 'The case' cannot be sent to the High Court because it is not signed by the granting magistrate.

† **grantise.** *Obs.* [a. OF. *grantise*, f. *granter* to GRANT.] The action of the vb. GRANT; concession; permission.

a **1300** *Siriz* in *Anecd. Lit.* (1844) 12 I-wis nou maiȝt thou ben above, For thou havest grauntise of hire love. *c* **1330** R. BRUNNE *Chron.* (1810) 134 Com þe Scottis Kyng, & asked Henry a bone Of grantise of grace, to haf his Seignorie. *Ibid.* 208 Of som he had grantise his wille forto do.

grantor (grɑːn'tɔː(r), -æ-). *Law.* [a. AF. *grantor*, agent-n. of *granter* to GRANT: see -OR. Cf. GRANTER.] One who makes a grant or conveyance in legal form.

a **1626** BACON *Max. & Uses Com. Law* xiv. (1636) 56 A foundation of an interest in the grantor. **1642** tr. *Perkins' Prof. Bk.* i. §1. 1 Unto a Grant, a Grantor, Grantee, and a thing granted are requisite. **1765** BLACKSTONE *Comm.* I. 478 Their privilege even of purchasing from any living grantor is greatly abridged. **1792** J. BELKNAP *Hist. New Hampsh.* III. 276 A conveyance is not valid against any other person but the grantor, unless it be thus acknowledged and recorded. **1818** HALLAM *Mid. Ages* (1872) I. 196 Saying masses for the benefit of the grantor's family. **1883** *American* VI. 270 In England, if the grantor cannot sign, he may make his mark.

b. In quasi-legal language.

a **1740** WATERLAND *Regeneration* Wks. (1823) VI. 348 Regeneration on the part of the Grantor, God Almighty, means admission or adoption into sonship..: and on the part of the grantee, viz. man, it means his birth, or entrance into that state of sonship. **178.** KNOX *Liberal Educ.* xlviii. Wks. 1824 IV. 186 For the sake of the grantors, the practice [of 'granting testimonia of morals and proficiency'] ought to be put an end to, unless [etc.].

‖ **gran turismo** (gran tu'rizmo). [It., lit. great touring.] A touring-car (see quot. 1967). Abbrev. *G.T.* (see G III. f).

1960 *Times* 28 Sept. 16/5 Sports and *gran turismo* cars. **1961** I. FLEMING *Thunderball* ix. 90 He had.. a white convertible Lancia Gran Turismo. **1963** *Observer* 24 Nov. 37/3 What the Italians call the Gran Turismo.. is a high-performance car with good luggage space, very comfortable seats for two and.. occasional seats. **1967** E. RUDINGER *Consumer's Car Glossary* (ed. 2) 52 *GT*, short for *gran turismo*, or grand touring. Originally a car designed particularly for covering long distances at high speeds, now sometimes used to describe a sporty version of an ordinary car.

‖ **granula** ('grænjʊlə). Pl. **granulæ**; also 7 **granulaes.** [mod.L. *grānula*, irreg. dim. of *grānum* grain = late L. *grānulum.*] = GRANULE.

1658 R. FRANCK *North. Mem.* (1821) 130 Shining stones that look not unlike to golden granulaes. **1781** THOMPSON in *Phil. Trans.* LXXI. 252 From 50 to 70 granulæ or particles of unfired powder were driven through the screen. **1832** LINDLEY *Introd. Bot.* I. iii. 207 *Granula*; large sporules, contained in the centre of many Algæ; as in Gloionema of Greville. **1866** *Treas. Bot.* 548/2 *Granula*.. Among fungals it sometimes expresses a spore-case.

granular ('grænjʊlə(r)), *a.* [f. late L. *grānulum*, dim. of *grānum* GRAIN *sb.*^{1} + -AR.]

1. a. Consisting of grains or granules; existing in the condition of grains or granules.

1794 SULLIVAN *View Nat.* I. 493 Mountains, which consist of lime stone or marble of a granular or scaly texture. **1826** HENRY *Elem. Chem.* I. 480 Steel is granular. **1831** BREWSTER *Nat. Magic* xiii. (1833) 339 The fluid.. leaves behind it a sort of granular residue. **1841** BRANDE *Chem.* 682 Massive and granular gypsum is found in this country in the red marl or new red sandstone accompanying the salt-deposits in Cheshire. **1868** *Daily Tel.* 15 July, Dynamite.. is a solid granular explosive. **1897** *Allbutt's Syst. Med.* II. 935 To these granular zinc or finely divided copper is added.

b. *granular pearlite Metallurgy*, a constituent of carbon steels produced by the disintegration of plates of pearlite into ferrite and spheres of cementite; divorced pearlite.

1910 C. H. DESCH *Metallogr.* xvii. 372 The cementite forms granular masses or oval globules, surrounded by areas of ferrite. This granular pearlite may be of all degrees of coarseness. **1958** A. D. MERRIMAN *Dict. Metallurgy* 115/1 *Granular pearlite*, a structure produced when pearlite steels are annealed for long periods at temperatures below, but approximating to, the lower critical point.

2. Having a granulated surface or structure. *Path.* Of diseased structures, diseases: = GRANULATED 3.

1833 SIR C. BELL *Hand* (1834) 210 On the [foot] pads or cushions of the cat, the cuticle is rough and granular. **1874** G. LAWSON *Dis. Eye* 13 There is..one form of granular lids produced by vesicular granulations. **1875** H. C. WOOD *Therap.* (1879) 374 A widespread granular or fatty degeneration of the tissues. **1878** T. BRYANT *Pract. Surg.* I. 292 Granular ophthalmia. **1879** HARLAN *Eyesight* v. 54 It [catarrhal ophthalmia]..may..end in the condition known as granular lids. **1897** *Allbutt's Syst. Med.* IV. 373 Most frequently the granular kidney comes on insidiously with no early symptoms.

3. Of the nature of a granule or granules.

1834 McMURTRIE *Cuvier's Anim. Kingd.* 177 Their [geckos'] skin is studded above with very small granular scales. **1867** J. HOGG *Microsc.* I. ii. 67 The granular particles seen among the pollen grains of plants. **1870** ROLLESTON *Anim. Life* 128 A series of raised granular but minute tubercles.

Hence **granu'larity**, granular condition or quality. **'granularly** *adv.*

1882 VINES *Sachs' Bot.* 520 The apical cells of these internal rows are distinguished by their size and by the granularity of their protoplasm. **1894** *Brit. Jrnl. Photogr.* XLI. 24 Its surface being free from granularity or roughness.

granulary ('grænjʊlərɪ), *a.* [f. late L. *grānulum* (see prec.) + -ARY[2].] = GRANULAR.

1646 SIR T. BROWNE *Pseud. Ep.* II. v. 87 Salt-peter, Smal-coale, and Brimstone..proportionably mixed, tempered, and formed into granulary bodies. **1850** ARVINE *Cycl. Relig. Anecd.* 832 Bone-grinders..by steam-engines and powerful machinery, reduced them to a granulary state. **1852** TH. ROSS *Humboldt's Trav.* II. xxiv. 512 Vallies, which contain magnetic sands (granulary oxidulated iron).

granulate ('grænjʊleɪt), *a.* [f. as prec. + -ATE[2] 2.] = GRANULATED *ppl. a.* 2.

1793 MARTYN *Lang. Bot.*, *Granulata radix*, a granulate root. **1826** KIRBY & SP. *Entomol.* IV. 273 Granulate (*Granulata*), beset with many granules like shagreen. **1852** DANA *Crust.* I. 464 Hands elongate..granulate above and somewhat pilose. **1870** HOOKER *Stud. Flora* 231 Arbutus..berry globose, granulate.

¶ In pseudo-L. combining form *granulato-*, as ***granulato-capitate, -costate, -serrulate, -striate*** adjs.

1852 DANA *Crust.* I. 169, 217, 418. **1887** PHILLIPS *Brit. Discomyc.* 246.

granulate ('grænjʊleɪt), *v.* [f. as prec. + -ATE[3].]

1. *trans.* To form into granules or grains.

1666 BOYLE *Orig. Formes & Qual.* 370 We take then the finest Gold we can procure, and having either Granulated it or Laminated it [etc.]. **1670** W. CLARKE *Nat. Hist. Nitre* 30 Gun-powder, which is of greater power granulated. **1787** M. CUTLER in *Life*, etc. (1888) II. 398 The sap is.. granulated, by the simple operation of boiling. **1794** G. SMITH *Laboratory* I. 102 Take one part of yellow arsenic, and one part of copper, and melt and granulate. **1825** J. NICHOLSON *Operat. Mechanic* 719 The gold to be mixed should be previously granulated. **1861** W. H. RUSSELL in *Times* 12 July, The juice of the cane is expressed, boiled, granulated, and prepared for the refiner. **1879** *Cassell's Techn. Educ.* IV. 191/2 The metal is first granulated, by throwing it while melted into cold water.

b. *intr.* for *refl.* To take the form of granules or grains; to become granular.

1667 SPRAT *Hist. Roy. Soc.* 193 The Juyce of Wine, when it is dry'd, does alwayes granulate into Sugar. **1681** GREW *Mus. Reg. Soc.* 224 The principal knack..is in making the Juyce, when sufficiently boil'd to kerne or granulate. **1830** LINDLEY *Nat. Syst. Bot.* 287 Its stalk is employed to bring sugar to a good grain when it..cannot be made to granulate properly by the application of lime alone. **1839** CLARKE *Trav. Russ.* 53 They place it in a caldron over a charcoal fire, until the powder begins to granulate.

2. *trans.* To raise in granules or small asperities; to roughen the surface of.

1691 RAY *Creation* I. (1692) 120 The gullet..thick set, or as it were granulated, with a multitude of Glandules. **1767** GOOCH *Treat. Wounds* I. 319 When the *Dura Mater* is granulated with flesh, the sindon or lint, moistened with ..*Tinct. Myrrhæ* and *Aq. Calcis*, is a good application.

b. To unite (two surfaces) as if by granulation.

1846 LANDOR *Minor Prose Pieces* Wks. II. 458/2 They are all grafts, imperfectly granulated on an uncongenial stock.

3. *intr.* in *Path.* Of a wound, ulcer, etc.: To develop a number of small prominences, producing a roughened appearance, as if sprinkled with granules.

1737 BRACKEN *Farriery Impr.* (1757) II. 180 The Flesh must granulate, otherwise such Wounds could never heal. **1804** ABERNETHY *Surg. Obs.* 87 Mr. Hunter tried various stimulating means to induce the cyst to granulate. **1835-6** TODD *Cycl. Anat.* I. 604/2 Few or no abscesses granulate till they are exposed. **1879** T. BRYANT *Pract. Surg.* II. 5 The wound that is left being allowed to granulate.

granulated ('grænjʊleɪtɪd), *ppl. a.* [f. GRANULATE *v.* + -ED[1].] In senses of the vb.

1. a. Of metals, sugar, gunpowder, etc.: Formed into granules. **b.** Consisting of granules, or grainlike bodies.

1694 SALMON *Bate's Dispens.* (1715) 427/1 Refined granulated Silver. **1727** BRADLEY *Fam. Dict.* s.v. *Corn setting Engine*, A rich compost..such as dry or granulated pigeon's dung. **1806** GALPINE *Brit. Bot.* 55 Fruit granulated. **1814** *Sporting Mag.* XLIV. 151 A quantity of granulated powder. **1834** MRS. SOMERVILLE *Connex. Phys. Sci.* xxxvii. (1849) 434 Many [nebulæ] have a granulated appearance. **1837-8** MACGILLIVRAY *Withering's Brit. Plants* (ed. 4) 7 A Granulated Root consists of numerous small bulbs or scales strung together. **1842** PARNELL *Chem. Anal.* (1845) 3 Prepared by boiling granulated tin..with concentrated hydrochloric acid. **1853** SOYER *Pantroph.* 217 There are two sorts of caviar: granulated caviar, and sack caviar. **1859** R. F. BURTON *Centr. Afr.* in *Jrnl. Geogr. Soc.* XXIX. 189 The latter [sugar] is generally made of granulated honey. **1875** KNIGHT *Dict. Mech.*, *Granulated-steel.* Melted pig-iron is scattered by a wheel into a cistern of water, and thus reduced to fragments. These are imbedded in powdered hematite or sparry iron ore, and subjected to furnace heat. **1896** *Allbutt's Syst. Med.* I. 391 Granulated malt extract dissolved in milk constitutes a grateful variety of readily digestible food.

2. Having the surface raised in granules or small prominences. ***granulated glass***, a kind of roughened glass used in stained windows.

1677 PLOT *Oxfordsh.* 140 The one plain and smooth, the other granulated on the out-side. **1758** *Descript. Thames* 216 The Turbot has a rough granulated Skin full of exceeding small Prickles. **1802** PALEY *Nat. Theol.* v. (ed. 2) 72 It would be too much to assert that the skin of the dog fish was made rough and granulated on purpose for the polishing of wood. **1821** CRAIG *Lect. Drawing* iv. 200 Chisseled..to represent.. the granulated surface of the human skin. **1863** BERKELEY *Brit. Mosses* iii. 15 In some genera the walls of the cells..are strongly granulated. **1877** W. THOMSON *Voy. Challenger* I. iv. 256 The surface of the carapace is granulated, not spiny. **1877** W. JONES *Finger-ring* 61 The whole is overlaid with funiform wire ornaments and granulated work. **1894** *Brit. Jrnl. Photogr.* XLI. 28 A granular-surfaced or granulated paper.

b. Having the appearance of being raised in granules; mottled.

1885 AGNES CLERKE *Pop. Hist. Astron.* 210 The term 'granulated', suggested by Dawes in 1864, best describes the mottled aspect of the solar disc.

3. *Path.* Characterized by the presence of granulations or small grain-like bodies; = GRANULAR *a.*

1835-6 TODD *Cycl. Anat.* I. 426/2 A man who was found on post-mortem examination to have granulated kidneys. **1896** *Daily News* 3 Apr. 5/6 The astounding statement that 'granulated ophthalmia is chiefly a pauper disease'.

granulating ('grænjʊleɪtɪŋ), *vbl. sb.* [-ING[1].] The action of the vb. GRANULATE; granulation.

1793 J. HUNTER *Treat. Blood*, etc. II. vii. Wks. 1837 III. 488 This process is called granulating, or incarnation. **1872-6** VOYLE & STEVENSON *Milit. Dict.* (ed. 3), *Granulating*, an operation in the manufacture of gunpowder which follows the process of 'pressing' the cake, whereby it becomes reduced to grains of different sizes.

attrib. **1807-26** S. COOPER *First Lines Surg.* (ed. 5) 143 When a wound begins to heal by the granulating process. **1856** KANE *Arct. Expl.* I. xxv. 336 Hard to realize that they could be formed by the ordinary granulating processes of the winter snows. **1873** SPON *Workshop Rec.* Ser. I. 145/2 It is then fed into the granulating machine.

granulating ('grænjʊleɪtɪŋ), *ppl. a.* [-ING[2].] That granulates, in senses of the vb.

1710 T. FULLER *Pharm. Extemp.* 102 It [*i.e.* the draught] ..potently expels..granulating Tartar. **1873** T. H. GREEN *Introd. Pathol.* (ed. 2) 244 It may be continuously discharged from the surface, as in a granulating wound. **1896** *Allbutt's Syst. Med.* I. 407 The high arterial pressure so commonly associated with granulating kidneys.

granulation (grænjʊ'leɪʃən). [n. of action f. GRANULATE *v.*: see -ATION. Cf. F. *granulation.*]

1. *gen.* The action or process of forming into granules or grains; the process or condition of being so formed.

1612 WOODALL *Surg. Mate* Wks. (1653) 271 Granulation proper to Metals, by infusion on fire,..is their comminution into granula, or very small drops like *Grana Paradisi.* **1670** W. CLARKE *Nat. Hist. Nitre* 88 The Reason of the Granulation of this Powder [gunpowder]. **1799** G. SMITH *Laboratory* I. 78 Granulation is easily performed, by pouring, leisurely, the melted metal between the twigs of a new birch broom..in a pail of water. **1822** IMISON *Sci. & Art* II. 117 It is mixed with lead to assist its granulation in making small shot. **1839** URE *Dict. Arts* 1142 The neutro-saline matter present in the spent lye is essential to the proper granulation and separation of the saponaceous compound. **1862** *New Syd. Soc. Year-bk.* 168 On the Granulation of Medicines.

fig. **1886** *Pall Mall G.* 2 Aug. 1/2 Italy and Germany have been redeemed from the granulation which for so many ages has made them mere ropes of sand.

b. *concr.* A granular formation.

1759 MOUNTAINE in *Phil. Trans.* LI. 288 On the projections of the wainscot, I found several granulations, and longer pieces of the wire. **1875** H. C. WOOD *Therap.* (1879) 184 In frogs poisoned with prussic acid a rounded form of the corpuscles was commonly exhibited, and sometimes granulations were present. **1879** tr. *De Quatrefages' Hum. Species* 72 The anthers scarcely ever enclose veritable pollen, but merely irregular granulations.

2. *Path.* The formation of grain-like prominences on sores when healing; the development of granules in diseased structures.

1786-7 J. HUNTER *Lect. Princ. Surg.* xii. Wks. 1835 I. 368 But on all internal canals suppuration does not necessarily lead to granulation. **1813** J. THOMSON *Lect. Inflam.* 215 That which Mr. Hunter calls union by granulation would, in the language of Galen, have been union by the third intention. **1848** CARPENTER *Anim. Phys.* 302 But if inflammation be permitted to arise, the repair takes place by a process termed granulation. **1886** *Syd. Soc. Lex.* s.v., Healing by granulation.

fig. **1895** J. J. RAVEN *Hist. Suffolk* 57 Then set in slowly and irregularly a kind of granulation, if we may use a comparison from the healing of a wound.

b. *concr.* in *pl.* The grain-like bodies so formed.

1739 S. SHARP *Surg.* Introd. 24 Tents in Wounds, by resisting the growth of the little Granulations of the Flesh, in process of time harden them. **1789** T. WHATELY in *Med. Commun.* II. 387, I..felt a loose piece of bone lying in a bed of granulations within the cavity of the tibia. **1804** ABERNETHY *Surg. Obs.* 54 Granulations formed, and a cicatrix took place. **1807-26** S. COOPER *First Lines Surg.* (ed. 5) 141 Granulations are formed by an exudation of coagulating lymph from the vessels of the wounded or exposed surface. **1813** J. THOMSON *Lect. Inflam.* 149 Granulations sometimes form on the surfaces of inflamed serous membranes. **1855** HOLDEN *Hum. Osteol.* (1878) 13 Every surgeon must have witnessed how sensitive are granulations from bone. **1878** T. BRYANT *Pract. Surg.* I. 5 The grey granulations or tubercles are apparently derived from some pre-existing inflammation.

3. *Bot.* and *Zool.* **a.** The formation of granular bodies on the surface of a plant, a crustacean, etc. **b.** *concr.* The granular structure, or in *pl.* the granules, so formed.

1796 WITHERING *Brit. Plants* IV. 45 Branches generally incrusted with small granulations. **1843** FORBES in *Proc. Berw. Nat. Club* II. No. 11. 79 Among the granulations numerous large stomata. **1852** DANA *Crust.* I. 447 A smooth even surface, excepting a neat miliary granulation. **1859** R. F. BURTON *Centr. Afr.* in *Jrnl. Geogr. Soc.* XXIX. 142 The folds and wrinkles which form by granulation upon the oblongs where the bark has been removed for its fibre. **1872** NICHOLSON *Palæont.* 75 A short robust stem, which is marked with flutings and superficial granulations. **1884** BOWER & SCOTT *De Bary's Phaner.* 104 In the pointed warts there is often stratification and granulation.

4. *attrib.*, chiefly *Path.* (see sense 2), as ***granulation-growth, -mass, -sarcoma, -tissue, -tumour.***

1899 J. HUTCHINSON *Archives Surg.* X. 157 Over these [pustules] the nail softened and a little *granulation growth protruded. **1898** *Ibid.* IX. 347 Being attended by the production of a *granulation-mass. **1886** *Syd. Soc. Lex.*, **Granulation sarcoma*, the ordinary form of simple or round-celled *Sarcoma.* **1873** T. H. GREEN *Introd. Pathol.* (ed. 2) 270 The serous membrane becomes infiltrated with young cells, which form a *granulation-tissue beneath the layer of proliferating endothelium. **1888** C. H. FAGGE *Princ. & Pract. Med.* (ed. 2) I. 114 Under the term '*granulation-tumours' he [Virchow] describes the various lesions which are produced by syphilis, leprosy and glanders.

granulative ('grænjʊlətɪv), *a.* *Path.* [f. GRANULATE *v.* + -IVE.] Characterized by granulation.

1883 MACALISTER tr. *Ziegler's Pathol. Anat.* I. § 117.163 It was Virchow who invented the term 'granulative growth' or 'granuloma' for these formations.

granulato-: see under GRANULATE *a.*

granulator ('grænjʊleɪtə(r)). [f. GRANULATE *v.* + -OR.] One who or that which granulates; *spec.* a granulating-machine.

1839 URE *Dict. Arts* 1202 The syrup is transferred into wooden chests or boxes..called coolers, but which are more properly crystallizers or granulators. **1873** SPON *Workshop Rec.* Ser. I. 145/2 A small stream of water enters the granulator; the movement of the machine rolling the damp grains constantly among the dry meal powder, causes the latter to [etc.]. **1888** *Engineer* LXVI. 273/1 This gentleman saw white sugar come out of spouts, and heard a granulator revolving at the rate of 300 rotations per minute.

granule ('grænju:l). [ad. late L. *grānul-um* (dim. of *grānum* GRAIN *sb.*[1]), either directly, or through F. *granule.*] A small grain; a small compact particle; a pellet. Employed *spec.* in *Zool.* and *Bot.*, also in *Astron.* and *Pharm.* (see quots.).

1652 CHARLETON *Darkn. Atheism* 45 Those Granules of sand, which suffice to make up the vast bulk of the World. **1664** BOYLE *Exper. & Consid. Colours* iii. 41 With an excellent Microscope..the assisted Eye could discern particular Granules, some..Blew, and some..Yellow. **1796** WITHERING *Brit. Plants* IV. 112 Fructifications terminating, swelling with seed-bearing granules. **1797** M. BAILLIE *Morb. Anat.* (1807) 281 Small granules of stone are sometimes found in the tubular portion of the kidneys. **1804** ABERNETHY *Surg. Obs.* 98 They resemble pearl barley, but the granules are generally smaller. **1826** KIRBY & SP. *Entomol.* IV. 273 *Granule*, a very minute elevation. **1834** McMURTRIE *Cuvier's Anim. Kingd.* 491 The animal bark which envelopes it is mixed with calcareous granules. **1835** LINDLEY *Introd. Bot.* (1848) I. 350 The pollen grains are often called granules. **1840-51** E. WILSON *Anat. Vade M.* 572 The smallest lobule is apparently composed of granules, which are minute cæcal pouches. **1849** MURCHISON *Siluria* x. 241 The granules of the skin. **1867-77** G. F. CHAMBERS *Astron.* I. i. 36 Granule is the best word to describe the luminous particles on the Sun's surface. **1871** NAPHEYS *Prev. & Cure Dis.* III. iv. 691 Very small pills are called granules. **1876** tr. *Wagner's Gen. Pathol.* 88 Colorless protoplasm, which..contains shining fat-like granules. **1879** RUTLEY *Study Rocks* x. 107 Granules of augite are common.

b. *attrib.*

1855 tr. *Wedl's Pathol. Histol.* II. v. 287 The fine-molecular cell becomes a granule cell. *Ibid.* 291 Colossal granule-masses. **1881** *Syd. Soc. Lex.*, *Cell, granule*, a term applied by His to a cell, like an ordinary white blood cell, found in the stroma of the ovary. Also, generally applied to cells in main part consisting of granules. **1882** THOMSON, etc. *Quain's Elem. Anat.* (ed. 9) II. 312 The inner or granule layer. **1886** *Syd. Soc. Lex.*, *Granule-layer of cerebellum*, the inner nuclear layer of the grey matter of the cortex of the cerebellum. *Ibid.*, *Granule masses*, the same as *giant Cells.*

granuliferous (grænjʊ'lɪfərəs), *a.* [as if f. L. *grānulifer* (f. *grānul-um* granule + -(*i*)*fer* bearing) + -OUS.] Bearing or producing granules or granulations.

1840 in PAXTON *Bot. Dict.* **1847** CRAIG, *Granuliferous*, full of granulations, as in the shell Mitra granulifera. **1886** in *Syd. Soc. Lex.*

granuliform (græ'njuːlɪfɔːm), *a.* [f. L. *grānul-um* granule + -(I)FORM.] Having a granular structure.

1847 in CRAIG. **1852** DANA *Crust.* I. 236 Teeth.. granuliform. **1887** PHILLIPS *Brit. Discomyc.* 257 Margin entire, denticulated; when dry closed, granuliform.

granulite ('grænjʊlaɪt). *Geol.* [f. GRANULE + -ITE.] A rock consisting of feldspar and quartz intimately mixed. Hence **granu'litic** *a.*, composed of or containing granulite.

1849 DANA *Geol.* xiii. (1850) 564 A variety of granulite. **1879** RUTLEY *Study Rocks* x. 142 They are especially common in granulites. **1888** *Engineer* LXV. 379/2 The light-banded granulitic gneisses or Wiltshire type. **1894** BARING-GOULD *Deserts S. France* I. 11 There are the eruptive rocks, granite and granulite.

granulo- ('grænjʊləʊ), used as a combining form of L. *grānulum* GRANULE, to describe a substance which is 'granular and ——', as in *granulo-adipose*, *-crystalline*, *-fatty*, *-pulpy* adjs. Also in wider use, as in GRANULOCYTE, GRANULOMETRIC *a.*

1845 DARWIN *Voy. Nat.* v. (1873) 100 This granulo-pulpy matter was in process of being converted into ova. **1886** *Syd. Soc. Lex.*, *Granulo-adipose*, containing, or consisting of, granules and fatty matter. *Ibid.*, *Granulo-fatty*, relating to granules and to fat.

granulocyte ('grænjʊləʊsaɪt). *Med.* [f. GRANULO- + -CYTE.] Any cell that contains or is destined to contain (conspicuous) granules in its cytoplasm; *spec.* any of the mature granular leucocytes (comprising neutrophils, eosinophils, and basophils) or the immature precursors of these cells.

1906 G. A. BUCKMASTER *Morphol. Normal & Path. Blood* iv. 87 According to Pappenheim, all the members of the three groups of erythroblasts, lymphocytes, and granulocytes originate from an ancestral lymphocyte. **1951** WHITBY & HYNES *Med. Bacteriol.* (ed. 5) v. 61 The body falls a ready prey to infections of all sorts when the bone-marrow for any reason fails to produce granulocytes. **1960** *McGraw-Hill Encycl. Sci. & Technol.* VII. 485/2 Of the three kinds of white cells found in normal blood, the granulocytes, the lymphocytes, and the monocytes, it is the granulocytes that are largely affected in most forms of leukopenia. **1968** PASSMORE & ROBSON *Compan. Med. Stud.* I. xxvi. 12/1 The time taken for maturation of a granulocyte in the bone marrow prior to its release into the circulation is believed to be of the order of 3–4 days. **1971** T. L. LENTZ *Cell Fine Structure* 282 (*heading*) Endometrial granulocyte. *Ibid.*, The granulocyte has been implicated in the secretion of the peptide hormone relaxin.

Hence **granulo'cytic** *a.*

1908 *Practitioner* Feb. 244 A form of lymphatic (*i.e.*, non-granulocytic) leucocythaemia occurs, in which the parent cells have given rise to an excessive formation of Türk's 'stimulation' cells. **1962** *Lancet* 27 Jan. 209/1 We thus came to the tentative conclusion that in the marrow of our standard guineapig.. the small lymphocyte functioned as a stem cell for both the red cell and the granulocytic series.

granulocytopenia (ˌgrænjʊləʊsaɪtəʊ'piːnɪə). *Med.* [f. prec. + Gr. πενία poverty.] A condition characterized by an abnormally small number of granulocytes in the blood.

1931 H. N. HARKINS in *Arch. Internal Med.* XLVII. 408 In this article the terms agranulocytosis and agranulocytic angina are used interchangeably for the Schultz syndrome specifically, and the general term granulocytopenia is used to include atypical and related cases. **1951** A. GROLLMAN *Pharmacol. & Therapeutics* i. 27 One of the most feared reactions observed in drug idiosyncrasies is granulocytopenia which may progress to agranulocytosis. **1961** *Lancet* 22 July 208 Patients with hepatitis were separated into two groups... In the treated group there was ..1 episode of mild granulocytopenia lasting two weeks.

granulocytosis (ˌgrænjʊləʊsaɪ'təʊsɪs). *Med.* [f. as prec. + -OSIS.] The presence of an abnormally large number of granulocytes in the blood.

1937 KRACKE & GARVER *Dis. Blood* I. ii. 23 *Granulocytosis*, the accumulation of an unusual number of granulocytes in the blood stream. **1940** R. L. HADEN *Princ. Hematol.* (ed. 2) ix. 161 Granulocytosis (increase in polymorphonuclear cells) may be classified as follows. **1947** *Radiology* XLIX. 301/2 This leukocytosis has been found.. to be predominantly a granulocytosis in the rabbit and the chicken. **1961** *Lancet* 12 Aug. 377/2 In all patients there was a granulocytosis.

granuloma (grænjʊ'ləʊmə). *Path.* [f. L. *grānul-um* GRANULE, after the analogy of GLAUCOMA and other words of Gr. origin.] 'A term invented by Virchow to include certain neoplasms which generally do not advance in structure beyond the stage of granulation tissue, and which usually proceed to ulceration' (*Syd. Soc. Lex.* 1886). Also with qualifying L. adj., as *granuloma inguinale*, a chronic, probably venereal infection produced by the bacterium *Calymmatobacterium* (*Donovania*) *granulomatis* and characterized by creeping granulomatous lesions in the inguinal and genital regions.

1861 BUMSTEAD *Ven. Dis.* (1879) 442 These cells belong to the group called by Virchow granuloma. **1897** *Allbutt's Syst. Med.* II. 804 In nodular leprosy, however, the granuloma of the skin..[is] characteristic. **1918** *Jrnl. Med. Res.* Jan. 427 Granuloma inguinale is endemic in certain tropical and subtropical countries. **1957** *Encycl. Brit.* XXIII. 48/1 In all cases of suspected *granuloma inguinale*, syphilis should be thoroughly ruled out.

Hence **granu'lomatous** *a.*, of or pertaining to granuloma.

1883 MACALISTER tr. *Ziegler's Pathol. Anat.* I. §117. 162 In most of the granulomatous disorders we may have not merely a diffusion of the disease throughout the individual organism, but [etc.]. **1898** P. MANSON *Trop. Diseases* xxvii. 423 A.. granulomatous, encrusted eruption.

granulomatosis (ˌgrænjʊˌləʊmə'təʊsɪs). *Med.* [f. *granulomat-a*, pl. of GRANULOMA + -OSIS.] Any condition characterized by multiple granulomas.

1911 DORLAND *Med. Dict.* (ed. 6) 360/1 Granulomatosis. **1966** WRIGHT & SYMMERS *Systemic Path.* I. xxiv. 726/1 Some of these are cases of Wegener's granulomatosis and show the necrotizing granulomatous foci in the nose.. and lung.. that are characteristic of this condition.

granulometric (ˌgrænjʊləʊ'mɛtrɪk), *a.* [ad. F. *granulométrique* (R. Feret 1892, in *Ann. d. Ponts et Chaussées* IV. 15): see GRANULO- and METRIC *a.*[1] and *sb.*] Pertaining to the distribution of grain sizes in a sample of sand, etc.

1905 L. C. SABIN *Cement & Concrete* xi. 163 Thus, all of the sands tested had the same 'granulometric' composition. **1964** *Economist* 28 Mar. 1254/1 Granulometric measurements of the alluvial deposits. **1970** R. C. SELLEY *Anc. Sedim. Environm.* i. 5 The granulometric analysis of ancient sediments is a declining art, to the delight of laboratory technicians.

granulose (grænjʊ'ləʊs), *sb.* and *a.* [f. as GRANULOMA + -OSE.] **A.** *sb.* One of the essential constituents (the other being cellulose) of the starch granule, which gives a blue colour with iodine, and is converted into sugar by the saliva.

1875 BENNETT & DYER *Sachs' Bot.* 589 A grain of starch leaves behind a skeleton containing very little solid material when the granulose has been extracted. **1878** KINGZETT *Anim. Chem.* 48 Starch consists of an outer coating of cellulose enclosing alternating layers of granulose.

B. *adj.* = GRANULAR.

1852 DANA *Crust.* I. 245 Areolets plane, granulose.

granulous ('grænjʊləs), *a.* Also 6 **granuluse.** [f. GRANULE + -OUS.] = GRANULAR, in various senses.

1547 BOORDE *Brev. Health* ii. 2 A fatte matter in the browes the whiche be granuluse aggregacions. **1699** *Bucaneers Amer.*, *Exploits Sir H. Morgan* 30 A sort of granulous flower or meal. **1741** MONRO *Anat. Bones* (ed. 3) 19 The.. Marrow.. is granulous, or composed of very small Grains. **1791** HAMILTON *Berthollet's Dyeing* I. I. III. ii. 249 There is obtained a granulous precipitate. **1841** JOHNSTON in *Proc. Berw. Nat. Club* I. No. 9. 275 The back convex, roughish or granulous. **1872** NICHOLSON *Palæont.* 193 The surface of the cell may be either smooth and entire, spinous or granulous. **1887** *Pall Mall G.* 22 July 4/2 That terrible eye disease known as granulous ophthalmia.

granum ('grɑː-, 'greɪnəm). *Bot.* Usually as pl. **'grana.** [a. G. *granum* (A. Meyer *Das Chlorophyllkorn in chem. morphol. und biol. Beziehung* (1883) ii. 24), a. L. *grānum* grain.] Any of the discs which are arranged in stacks in the chloroplast, which are formed of membranes and in which the chlorophyll is incorporated.

1894 S. H. VINES *Student's Text-bk. Bot.* I. I. 100 The chlorophyll appears to exist in an oily solution, and to be confined to the fibrillar portions of the plastid, in the form of droplets (*grana*). **1898** H. C. PORTER tr. *Strasburger's Text-bk. Bot.* I. i. 57 The fundamental substance of the chlorophyll bodies is itself colourless, but contains numerous coloured drops, which are termed Grana. These consist of an oleaginous substance, which holds various pigments in solution. **1966** R. B. PARK in Vernon & Seely *Chlorophylls* ix. 286 The chlorophyll fluorescence is seen to reside primarily in the grana stacks. **1967** KIRK & TILNEY-BASSETT *Plastids* i. 30 Most of the thylakoids in a granum extend beyond the edge of the granum.

graocracy (greɪ'ɒkrəsɪ). *nonce-wd.* [f. Gr. γραο-, γραῦς an old woman + -κρατία government.] Government by an old woman or old women.

1830 *Blackw. Mag.* XXVII. 484 Madame de Genlis's admired and lamented graocracy.

grap, obs. f. GRAPE *sb.*[1]; var. GRAPE *sb.*[3], GRAPPE *sb.*

grapas, -pays, variant forms of GRAPEYS *Obs.*

grape (greɪp), *sb.*[1] Also 3–7 grap, 4 graap. [a. OF. *grape*, *grappe* fem., bunch of grapes (also *crape*; mod.F. *grappe*, north-eastern dialects *crappe*), prob. a vbl. sb. from *graper* to gather grapes with a vine-hook, f. *grape* hook, ultimately f. Teut. *krappon- (OHG. *krapfo*) hook. Cf. It. *grappare* to seize, *grappa* hook, *grappo* act of seizing, *grappo*, *grappolo*, bunch of grapes, Sp. *grapa* hook, Pr. *grapa* hook, claw, *grap-s* hollow of the hand.

The change of meaning which the word underwent in passing from Fr. to Eng. seems to be due to the fact that it was first adopted in plural and collective uses, from which a new sense of the sing. was afterwards evolved. The comb. *win-grape* appears for 'cluster of grapes' in *Gen. & Ex.* 3710.]

1. a. One of the berries, growing in clusters on a vine, and from the juice of which wine is made. Also *grape of wine*. Chiefly *pl.*; in poetry often *sing.*, as quasi-*collect.*

the grapes are sour (now usu. *sour grapes* (see SOUR *a.* 9 c)): said proverbially with allusion to Æsop's fable of 'The Fox and the Grapes', when a person is heard to disparage something which it is suspected he would be glad to possess if he could.

c **1290** *S. Eng. Leg.* I. 231/424 A luytel foul.. brouȝte a gret bouȝ Fol of grapus swyþe rede. *a* **1300** *Cursor M.* 4468 (Götting.) Vpon pis tre, on ilk a bohw Methoght þar hing grapis [*Cott.* winberis] enohw. *c* **1315** SHOREHAM 30 That schel be to thys sacrement Ryȝt of the grape of wyne. **1382** WYCLIF *Deut.* xxxii. 32 The graap of hem graap of gal, and the cluster moost bittre. —— *Matt.* vi. 16 Whether men gaderen grapis of thornys, or fijgis of breris? *a* **1400** *Pistill of Susan* 84 On grapes þe goldfinche þei gladen and glees. *c* **1420** *Liber Cocorum* (1862) 22 Take persole.. grene Grapus, and stope thy chekyns with wynne. **1471** RIPLEY *Comp. Alch.* v. xiii. in Ashm. (1652) 151 Thou shalt have Graps ryght as the Ruby red. **1587** *Mirr. Mag.*, *Pinnar* i. 7 On vine growes the grape, and not the biter hop. **1667** MILTON *P.L.* IV. 259 The mantling Vine Layes forth her purple Grape. **1697** DRYDEN *Virg. Georg.* IV. 805 Like a large Cluster of black Grapes they show. **1732** ARBUTHNOT *Rules of Diet* I. 247 Grapes, taken in Moderate Quantities, help the Appetite. **1760** A. MURPHY *Way to keep Him* I. 5 You'd be glad to have me! —But sour Grapes, my Dear. **1855** LONGF. *Hiaw.* II. 235 Grapes in purple clusters. **1876** 'MARK TWAIN' *Tom Sawyer* vi. 62 Another boy said 'Sour grapes!' **1923** A. HUXLEY *Antic Hay* xiii. 190 The concert had begun. 'Never mind,' said Gumbril. 'We shall get in in time for the minuetto. It's then that the fun really begins.' 'Sour grapes,' said Emily, putting her ear to the door. 'It sounds to me simply too lovely.' **1958** C. P. SNOW *Conscience of Rich* xxxv. 261, I have never been able to understand the fascination which makes my brother Philip and others wish to spend their entire lives in this neighbourhood. I once said as much to Hannah, and she replied that it was sour grapes on my part.

fig. **1526** *Pilgr. Perf.* (W. de W. 1531) 290 A taste of the fyrst rype grapes of the gyfte of heuenly wysdome. **1857** TROLLOPE *Barchester T.* xlvi, Mr. S... said, as plainly as a look could speak, that the grapes were sour.

b. With some word prefixed that indicates the species or variety, as ***Black Hamburgh***, ***Fox***, ***Frontignac***, ***Muscadine***, ***Muscat***, ***Muscatel***, ***Sweetwater***, etc. ***grape***.

1736 AINSWORTH *Eng.-Lat. Dict.* sv., Muscadine grapes. **1741** *Compl. Fam.-Piece* II. iii. 389 These Grapes: White Muscadine,.. black Cluster,.. white sweet Water. *Ibid.* 394 White Morillon, red Morillon, Currant Grape. **1802** *Brookes' Gazetteer* (ed. 12), *Lipari*.. abounds with the currant grape.

c. Put for the juice of the grape, or wine.

1636 [see FRONTIGNAC]. **1708** J. PHILIPS *Cyder* II. 397 Nor can the Poet Bacchus' Praise indite, Debarr'd his Grape. **1859** FITZGERALD tr. *Omar* xlii, He bid me taste of it; and 'twas—the Grape! **1898** T. HARDY *Wessex Poems* 56 We rolled rich puncheons of Spanish grape.

†**2.** *transf.* The berry or fruit of other plants.

c **1400** *Lanfranc's Cirurg.* 137, I seie þat oile of rosis.. þat schal be maad of grapis of olyue trees þat ben not ripe is not oyntuose. **1551** TURNER *Herbal* I. C iv b, Anagyris.. hath a fruyte in long horned coddes.. whiche when the grape is ripe wexeth harde. **1578** LYTE *Dodoens* III. vii. 323 Whan [the spadix and spathe of the arum are] gone, the bunche.. of beries also or grapes, doth at length appeere. **1601** HOLLAND *Pliny* II. 161 Of the grapes which this Palma Christi or Ricinus carieth, there be made excellent weiks or matches for lamps and candles.

3. a. The plant that produces grapes; the vine; chiefly with some word prefixed, as in 1 b.

14.. *Voc.* in Wr.-Wülcker 578/7 *Depastino*, to do away grapys. **1657** AUSTEN *Fruit Trees* I. 59 The Fox Grape is a faire large Fruit, and a very great bearer. **1870** YEATS *Nat. Hist. Comm.* 174 The grape varies in the colour, form, size, and flavour of its fruit.

b. *transf.* ***seaside grape*** = *grape-tree* (q.v. in 9).

1756 P. BROWNE *Jamaica* 209 The Mangrove or Sea-side Grape.. The berries are generally about the size of common grapes. **1792** M. RIDDELL *Voy. Madeira* 87 The *coccoloba uvifera*, or sea-side grape. (In some mod. Dicts. s.v. *Seaside.*)

4. *Mil.* = GRAPE-SHOT. Now only *collect. sing.* and apprehended as a shortened form; formerly also *pl.*

1687 A. LOVELL tr. *Thevenot's Trav.* I. 282 The six Scopa Coperta Pieces were charged with bunches of Grapes. [**1747** Cf. GRAPE-SHOT.] **1798** LD. MORPETH in *Anti-Jacobin* 14 May (1852) 129 Sacrilegious grape and ball Deform the works of Stone and Steel. **1804** NELSON in Nicolas *Disp.* (1845) V. 399 Have your guns loaded with grape. **1823** BYRON *Juan* VII. xxix, A fire of musketry and grape. **1828** J. H. MOORE *Pract. Navig.* (ed. 20) p. iv, The Number of Shot contained in Grapes of different sizes. **1833** ALISON *Hist. Europe* (1849–50) II. vi. §55. 49 They turned a gun, loaded with grape, on the entering column. **1868** KINGLAKE *Crimea* (1877) III. i. 57 Some buildings.. afforded good cover against grape.

5. *Farriery. pl.* **a.** A diseased growth resembling a bunch of grapes on the pastern of a horse, mule, etc. (Cf. F. *grappes.*) **b.** A similar growth on the pleura.

1600 SURFLET *Country Farme* I. xxvii. 189 Graps.. are moules and scabbes on the heeles. *Ibid.* 193 The grapes. **1753** J. BARTLET *Gentl. Farriery* xliv. 323 Excrescences, such as . . grapes, &c. are best removed by the knife. **1810** *Sporting Mag.* XXXVI. 271 Grapes upon the heels, of long standing and dry, are incurable. **1897** *Allbutt's Syst. Med.* II. 21 Tuberculosis of the pleura [in cattle] in the form of 'grapes' may occur without the lungs being affected.

6. In various applications: †**a.** (See quot. 1644.) *Obs.* **b.** The knob or pommel at the rear end of a cannon; formerly called the CASCABEL. †**c.** A particular size of paper; also *grape-paper. Obs.*

1611 COTGR., *Papier raisin*, Grape paper. **1644** BULWER *Chiron.* 75 The top or grape of the left Index. **1864** WEBSTER, *Grape of a cannon*, the cascabel or knob at the butt. **1891** A. MORRIS *Watermarks* in *Paper Record* 8 Sept. 65/1 The names of the principal sizes of *papier vergé* have been handed down to us, and . . have suggested watermarks. Rising from the smallest sheet to the largest, they are as follows:—Bell, pot, écu, crown, shell, grape, large grape, jesus, great eagle, and great world.

7. Short for *grape-hop* (see 9).

1861 *Illustr. Times* 5 Oct. 222 The ordinary 'grape', and the rank 'colegates' of Sussex and the Wealds of Kent.

8. *attrib.* and *Comb.*: **a.** simple attributive, as ***grape-arbour***, ***-bunch***, ***-cluster***, ***-cutting***, ***-harvest***, ***industry***, †***-kernel***, ***-mildew***, ***-pip***, ***-rot***, ***-seed***, ***-skin***, ***-stalk***, ***-time***; **b.** objective, as ***grape-culture***, ***-cutter***, ***-gatherer***, ***-gathering***, ***-gleaning***, ***-grower***, ***-growing***, ***-picker***, ***-picking***, ***-treader***; ***grape-bearing*** adj.; **c.** instrumental, as ***grape-crowned***, ***-loaded***, ***-thickened*** adjs.; **d.** parasynthetic, as ***grape-hued***, ***-seeded***, ***-shaped***, ***-sized*** adjs.; **e.** similative, as ***grape-bloom***, ***-green***, ***-like*** adjs.; ***grape-ways***, ***-wise*** advs.

1810 F. CUMING *Sk. Tour W. Country* 167 He has opened a little publick garden behind his house, which he calls Vaux-hall. It has a most luxuriant *grape arbour, and two or three summer houses! **1898** M. DELAND *Old Chester Tales* 107 They were sitting in the grape-arbor with a little table between them. **1907** *Chicago Evening Post* 4 May 15 (Advt.), Fine summer home on good lake; grape arbors; garden. **1898** *Archæol. Æliana* XIX. III. 193 Prof. Stephens calls it a *grape-bearing vine. **1926** M. LEINSTER *Dew on Leaf* 214 *Grape-bloom darkness. **1950** D. GASCOYNE *Vagrant* 27 Rockets released to-night rush up to rape the grape-bloom sky. *a* **1661** HOLYDAY *Juvenal* 238 Bees, like a long *grape-bunch settle on Some temple's top. **1552** HULOET, *Grape cluster or cluster of grapes . . *racemus*. **1627** DRAYTON *Elegies, On Lady Aston's Depart.* 52 *Grape-crowned Bacchus. **1859** H. DE CARADEUC *(title)* Treatise on *Grape-Culture. **1382** WYCLIF *Jer.* vi. 9 Conuerte thin hond, as a *grape kuttere to a basket. **1768** WASHINGTON *Diaries* (1925) I. 267 Planted out *Grape Cuttings. **1848** *Rep. U.S. Comm. Patents 1847* 469 The landlord to furnish the dwelling house . . fruit trees and grape cuttings at his own expense. **1535** COVERDALE *Jer.* vi. 9 *Grape gatherer. **1599** H. BUTTES *Dyets drie Dinner* B iij, That Grapes are verie nourishing, is well seene by the Grape-gatherers in the time of Vintage. **1580** HOLLYBAND *Treas. Fr. Tong, Grappage*, *grape-gathering. **1791** *Visible World* 57 When the time of grape-gatherings is come. **1611** BIBLE *Micah* vii. 1, I am . . as the *grape gleanings of the vintage. **1893** R. NOEL *Swimmer* 47 *Grape-green all the waves are. **1896** *Daily News* 7 Nov. 6/2 Another good combination would be navy blue and grape green. **1862** *Rep. U.S. Comm. Patents 1861: Agric.* 525 At present there are very few practical *grape growers who ever saw such a document. **1889** *Harper's Mag.* Jan. 261/2 The better class of laboring agriculturists, grape-growers, and stock-raisers. **1970** Grape-grower [see *grape-picker* below]. **1573** BARET *Alv.* G 440 *Grape harueſt . . *Vindemia*. **1898** ZANGWILL *Dreamers Ghetto* xv. 462 He thought of last year's grape-harvest ruined by a thunderstorm. **1883** E. INGERSOLL in *Harper's Mag.* Feb. 433/2 He let it slip from his *grape-hued lips. **1887** MOLONEY *Forestry W. Afr.* xi. 157 West Africa is not without its promise of a development of the *grape industry. **1483** *Cath. Angl.* 163/1 A *Grape kyrnelle, *acinus*. **1619** T. MILLES tr. *Mexia's Treas. Anc. & Mod. Times* II. 380/1 A very delicate and *Grape-like gumme. **1832** TENNYSON *Dream Fair Wom.* 219 The valleys of *grape-loaded vines that glow Beneath the battled tower. **1871** H. MACMILLAN *True Vine* v. (1872) 229 Every one has heard of the terrible *grape-mildew. **1923** R. HERRICK *Homely Lilla* 68 She found herself laughing freely with the *grape-pickers. **1970** *Times* 14 July 8/1 The poverty-ridden grape pickers, most of them semi-literate Mexican-Americans, have brought the wealthy grape growers to the negotiating table. **1897** MISS HARRADEN *Hilda Strafford* 199 It was the *grape-picking season. **1863** *Horticulturist* Sept. 287/2 *Grape Rot and Mildew. **1886** *Harper's Mag.* June 44/1 When mildew and grape-rot first appear. **1786** WASHINGTON *Diaries* (1925) III. 36 Tho' the ground was nearly prepared for my *grape Seeds, I could not sow them on acct. of the Weather. **1897** *Allbutt's Syst. Med.* III. 885 Grape-seeds or grains of wheat. **1887** MOLONEY *Forestry W. Afr.* 423 Large or *Grape-seeded Amomum. **1849** MURCHISON *Siluria* iv. 74 *Grape-shaped heads. **1822–34** *Good's Study Med.* (ed. 4) IV. 228 Cells oval, currant-sized or *grape-sized. **1897** *Allbutt's Syst. Med.* III. 885 A portion of a *grape-skin is very remarkably imitated by [etc.]. **1820** KEATS *Hyperion* I. 33 Empty shells were scatter'd on the grass, And *grapestalks but half bare. **1832** TENNYSON *Eleänore* 36 Youngest Autumn, in a bower *Grape-thicken'd from the light. **1548** UDALL, etc. *Erasm. Par. Mark* xii. 2 And when *grape time was cum, he sent his seruaunt to the same husbandmen. **1889** WILDE *Birthday of Little Princess* in *Paris Illustré* 30 Mar. 207/2 At vintage time came the *grape-treaders. **1931** *Times Lit. Suppl.* 29 Jan. 68/4 The proud young grape-treader defying her rustic lover. **1727** BRADLEY *Fam. Dict.* s.v. *Currants*, Branches . . to which a round Point hangs *Grape-ways. *Ibid.* s.v. *Hop*, The Flowers . . rang'd *Grapewise.

9. Special combs.: **grape-belt**, a belt of country in which grapes grow; **grape-berry moth** (*U.S.*) = *grape-moth* (*Cent. Dict.*); **grape-brandy**, brandy distilled from grapes or wine without admixture of any other ingredient; **grape-cake**, the mass of grape-skins, etc. which remains after the juice has been pressed out of the grapes; **grape-cure**, the treatment of disease by a diet consisting mainly of grapes; **grape-eater**, the Australian bird *Zosterops chloronotus*; **grape-essence**, an artificial flavouring liquid composed of chloroform, various ethers, tartaric acid, and other ingredients (*Syd. Soc. Lex.* 1886); **grape-fern**, a plant of the genus *Botrychium*, so called from the appearance of the fructification; †**grape-flower** = *grape-hyacinth*; **grape-fungus**, a mould (*Oidium Tuckeri*) which attacks the vine, vine-mildew (Cassell, 1882); †**grape-gall** (see quot.); **grape hop**, a variety of hop (see quot.); **grape-hopper** (*U.S.*), an insect destructive to vine-leaves (Funk's *Stand. Dict.*); **grape-house**, a glass-house in which grapes are grown, a vinery; **grape hyacinth** (see HYACINTH 2 b); **grape-louse** (*U.S.*), 'the vine-pest or phylloxera' (*Cent. Dict.*); †**grape-monger**, a wine-bibber; **grape-moth** (*U.S.*), a small moth, *Eudemis botrana*, the larva of which devours grapes (Webster, 1897); **grape-nuts**, the trade name for a breakfast cereal, a patent preparation of maize or wheat in a crisp granular form; **grape-paper** (see 6 c); **grape-pear**, *Amelanchier Botryapium*; †**grape-press**, a wine-press; **grape-scissors**, scissors used either for thinning the bunches on the vine, or for dividing them at table; **grape-sugar** = DEXTROSE or GLUCOSE; **grape-tree**, (*a*) in W. Indies, a tree of the genus *Coccoloba*; (*b*) a grape-vine; **grape-weevil** (*U.S.*), a weevil (*Cæliodes* or *Craponius inæqualis*), which destroys green grapes; **grape-wine**, a 'home-made' wine, made of grapes; **grape-worm** (*U.S.*), the larva of a grape-moth (Webster, 1897); **grape-wort**, the baneberry, *Actæa spicata*; also, *Bryonia dioica* (Britten & Holland, *Plant-n.* 1879).

1897 BAILEY *Princ. Fruit-growing* 41 The famous Chautauqua *grape-belt is confined to a strip about two to three miles wide lying upon Lake Erie. **1871** *Trans. Ill. Agric. Soc.* VIII. 158 The *Penthina Vitivorana*, or *Grape-berry moth. **1892** *Pall Mall G.* 7 Nov. 7/2 They testify to its purity as a genuine *grape brandy. **1897** *Allbutt's Syst. Med.* II. 228 The best alcoholic stimulants for the acute stage [of small-pox] are good grape brandy [etc.]. **1830** M. DONOVAN *Dom. Econ.* I. 249 The *grape-cake which remains after the wine has been pressed out is called by the French *les marcs de raisin*. **1862** J. A. SYMONDS *Biog.* (1895) I. 202 The *grape cure cured her. **1848** J. GOULD *Birds of Austral.* IV. 82 *Grape- and Fig-eater. **1597** GERARDE *Herbal* I. lxxi. 105 The *Grape flower is called Hyacinthus Botryoides. *Ibid.* lxxii. 105 Of Muscari or Musked grape flower. **1753** CHAMBERS *Cycl. Supp.*, **Grape galls*, . . a name given by authors to a species of protuberances resembling clusters of grapes . . which are found hanging from the oak at some seasons of the year. **1838** *Penny Cycl.* XII. 288/2 The varieties most esteemed are the *Grape Hop [etc.]. **1881** WHITEHEAD *Hops* ii. 11 Grape Hops, so called because the cones hang in clusters like bunches of grapes. **1789** E. DARWIN *Bot. Gard.* II. (1791) 28 *note*, Vines in *grape-houses. **1825** COBBETT *Rur. Rides* 457, I noticed . . a very curiously constructed grape house; that is to say a hot-house for the raising of grapes. **1733** MILLER *Gardener's Dict.*, *Muscari*, Musk or *Grape Hyacinth. **1882** Grape hyacinth [see HYACINTH 2 b]. **1897** [see *baby's breath* (BABY *sb.* B. 2)]. **1950** G. BRENAN *Face of Spain* vi. 146, I picked a blue grape hyacinth, the only flower growing there among the rushes. **1606** DEKKER *Sev. Sinnes* iii. (Arb.) 27 When the *Grape-mongers and hee are parted. **1898** *Off. Gaz. U.S. Pat. Off.: Trade Marks* 14 June 1657/1 Cereal food for human consumption. Postum Cereal Company, Limited, Battle Creek, Mich. . . *Grape-Nuts. . . Used since December 1, 1897. **1902** *Granta* 3 May 286/1 It will be a pleasant puzzle for your readers to discover where the Grape-Nuts come in. **1903** *Army & Navy Co-op. Soc. Price List* Sept. 11/2 Grape Nuts . . per packet, about 2 lb. 0/7. **1905** CHESTERTON *Heretics* 136 There is more simplicity in the man who eats caviar on impulse than in the man who eats grape-nuts on principle. **1927** T. E. LAWRENCE *Let.* 8 Sept. (1938) 536 You [*sc.* E. M. Forster] called your novel-book 'a sauceful of last week's grapenuts'. **1956** *Trade Marks Jrnl.* 18 Apr. 243/1 Grape-Nuts. . . General Foods Corporation . . City of White Plains, State of New York, . . Manufacturers. **1840** PAXTON *Bot. Dict.*, *Grape-pear. **1882** *Garden* 15 Apr. 263/3 The Grape Pear . . differs . . from other trees in flower at this season by its peculiarly graceful twiggy growth. **1615** CROOKE *Body of Man* 446 From whence, as wine from a *grape-presse, the bloud poured out of the veines and arteries is squeesed into the whole braine. **1861** MRS. BEETON *Bk. Househ. Managem.* 802 *Grape-scissors, a melon-knife and fork, and nutcrackers, should always be put on the table, if there are dishes of fruit requiring them. **1881** BLACKMORE *Christowell* iii, 'Father', cried Rose . . running up to him, with her long grape-scissors in her hand. **1887** *Lady* 20 Jan. 38/3 Baskets of fruit ornamented either end of the table, and the grape-scissors were in the form of a solemn-looking stork. **1831** J. DAVIES *Manual Mat. Med.* 411 *Grape sugar. **1879** FOSTER *Phys.* App. 673 Grape-sugar, or dextrose (glucose). **1697** DAMPIER *Voy.* I. 392 The *Grape-tree grows with a strait Body . . and hath but few Limbs or Boughs. The Fruit grows in Clusters, all about the Body of the Tree . . They are much like such Grapes as grow on our Vines, both in shape and colour, and they are of a very pleasant Winy taste. **1725** SLOANE *Jamaica* II. 129 Mangrove Grape-tree. **1753** CHAMBERS *Cycl. Supp.* s.v. *Grapes*, A muscadine grape-tree was raised from a cutting of a parent vine. **1756** P. BROWNE *Jamaica* 210 The Mountain Grape-Tree . . is looked upon as a fine timber-wood. *c* **1830** *Houlston Tracts* III. No. 90. 2 The house . . with a grape-tree running up the wall. **1884–5** *Riverside Nat. Hist.* (1888) II. Index, *Weevil, grape 341. **1718** A. HILL *(title)* Essays . . ; on English *Grape-Wines. **1839** URE *Dict. Arts* 1304 Drained grape wine. **1858** HOMANS *Cycl. Comm.* 1974/1 Grape wine. **1548** TURNER *Names of Herbes* 84 It [Christopheriana] may be called in englische *Grapwurt, because it hath many blacke beries in the toppes lyke grapes.

Hence †'**grapeful** *a.*, abounding in grapes or vines; '**grapeless** *a.*, having no grapes; wanting the flavour of grapes; '**grapelet**, a small grape; also *transf.*; †'**grapeling** = GRAPELET.

1616 CHAPMAN *Homer's Hymn to Apollo* 42 And made the sea-trod ship arive them nere The grapefull Crissa. *c* **1620** T. ROBINSON *M. Magd.* 17/219 To pick yᵉ ruddy grapelets, was their aime. **1694** MOTTEUX *Rabelais* v. xvi. (1737) 68 Those little Grapelings. **1755** E. MOORE in *World* No. 153 (1772) III. 290 Rusty hams . . stale game, green fruit, and grapeless wines. **1844** MRS. BROWNING *Rhapsody Life's Progr.* iv, Thy small head . . with its grapelets of gold.

grape, *sb.*[2] [a. OF. *grape*, *grappe* (= F. *grappin*): see GRAPE *sb.*[1]] †**a.** ? A hook. *Obs.* **b.** (in Cornwall) = GRAPNEL 2.

1493 *Acta Dom. Conc.* (1839) 315/1 A bankure, four cuschingis, twa grapis of siluer, a spone owrgilt. **1823** T. BOND *E. & W. Looe* 76 *note*, A grape or grapnell is a small anchor, generally used for mooring boats.

†**grape**, *sb.*[3] *Sc. Obs.* Also 5 graip, 7 grap(pe. [? altered form of GRIPE *sb.*[3], influenced by *grape*, *graip* GROPE *v.*] A vulture.

c **1480** HENRYSON *Mor. Fab.* vi. v, The foxe was clerk . . The gled, the grape [*v. rr.* graip, grip] at the bar couth stand, As aduocatis. **1533** BELLENDEN *Livy* I. (1822) 12 Apperit to Remus sex grapis, afore ony foul aperit to Romulus. **1611** COTGR., *Vaultour*, a Vulture, Geire, Gripe, or Grap. **1615** T. THOMAS *Lat. Dict.*, *Vultur*, a ravenous birde called a vulter, a geyre or grappe.

†**grape**, *v. Obs.* [f. OF. *grape* GRAPE *sb.*[2]] *trans.* = GRAPPLE *v.* 1.

1523 LD. BERNERS *Froiss.* (1812) I. ccxcii. 435 They hadde graped their shyppes toguyder with hokes of yron.

grape, obs. f. GRAIP *sb.*; Sc. and north f. GROPE.

graped (greɪpt), *ppl. a.* [f. GRAPE *sb.*[1] + -ED[2].] Having the grapes (see GRAPE *sb.*[1] 5 a and b).

1810 *Sporting Mag.* XXXVI. 271 The farrier . . succeeded in cutting away the fungous and graped flesh. **1886** *Chesh. Gloss.* s.v., Cattle are said to be graped when the lungs become tuberculated, and adhere to the side.

grapefruit ('greɪpfruːt). Also **grape-fruit**. [f. GRAPE *sb.*[1] + FRUIT *sb.*; so called because it grows in clusters.] The globular fruit of *Citrus paradisi*, having a yellow skin and pale yellow (occas. pink), juicy, acid pulp. Also *attrib.* and *Comb.*, as ***grapefruit cocktail***, ***juice***, ***knife***, ***marmalade***.

1814 J. LUNAN *Hortus Jamaicensis* II. 171 The shaddock was originally regarded by Linneus as only a variety of the orange. . . There is a variety known by the name of *grape-fruit*, on account of its resemblance in flavour to the grape; this fruit is not near so large as the shaddock. **1859** BARTLETT *Dict. Amer.*, *Grape Fruit*, a variety of *Citrus racemosus*. Barbadoes. **1885** LADY BRASSEY *The Trades* 305 'Grape-fruit' . . It looks and tastes much like a shaddock . . it does not bear the slightest resemblance to a grape. **1904** *Daily Chron.* 4 May 10/5 The grapefruit, which is gradually growing in popularity in England. **1911** 'M. RONALD' *Century Cook Bk.* Suppl. 600 Grape-fruit marmalade. **1926–7** *Army & Navy Stores Catal.* 581/3 Grape Fruit Knife . . Grape Fruit Spoon . . Grape Fruit Fork. **1930** J. CANNAN *No Walls of Jasper* vii. 125 She bought some grape fruit for dinner. **1934** R. STOUT *Fer-de-Lance* v. 67 I'll have grapefruit juice. **1935** M. MORPHY *Recipes of all Nations* 598 (*heading*) Crab and grapefruit cocktail. *c* **1938** *Fortnum & Mason Catal.* 65/2 Knives . . Grape Fruit, English—each 3/-. **1959** J. BRAINE *Vodi* vii. 108 'Have a drink with me. Gin-and-orange?' . . 'Thanks very much, I'll have a grapefruit juice if you don't mind.' **1967** K. GILES *Death & Mr Prettyman* viii. 145 Breakfast in bed . . kidneys and her grapefruit marmalade. **1967** *Listener* 12 Jan. 53/1 Modern hotels (complete with . . grapefruit cocktails, and roast lamb).

†**grapelage**. *Obs.*[−1] [ad. F. *grappillage*, in same sense.] Grape-gleaning.

a **1603** T. CARTWRIGHT *Confut. Rhem. N. T.* (1618) 507 The grapelage of the vine, or the gleaning of the harvest, are not to be counted good corne and grapes, because they are rare and scattered heere and there.

grapell, obs. form of GRAPPLE *sb.*

grapenel(le, obs. forms of GRAPNEL.

†'**graper**. *Obs.* [? f. *grape* GROPE *v.* + -ER[1].] The part of a lance by which it was grasped.

14.. in *Archæol.* XVII. 291 Officers of armys shewyng their mesure of theire speris garneste, that is cornall, vamplate & grapers all of acise that they shall just with.

graper, variant of GRAPPER *Obs.*

grapery ('greɪpərɪ). [f. GRAPE *sb.*[1] + -ERY.] A building, made mainly of glass, in which grapes are grown; a plantation of vines; a vinery.

1812 MISS EDGEWORTH *Absentee* vi, She led the way to a little conservatory, and a little pinery, and a little grapery. **1815** *Hist. Decastro* I. 175 Mr. Decastro . . planted graperies. **1848** THACKERAY *Van. Fair* xlii, A fine villa . . where there were beautiful graperies and peach-trees. **1885** *Ch. Times* 2 Apr. 269/2 Pineries, graperies, hot-houses, and the like.

'grape-shot. [f. GRAPE *sb.*[1]] Small cast iron balls, strongly connected together, so as to form a charge for cannon (see quots. 1769 and 1867).

1747 *Gentl. Mag.* 308 The violence of the grape and round shot. **1769** FALCONER *Dict. Marine* (1780) M m b, Grape-shot is a combination of balls, put into a thick canvas-bag, and corded strongly together, so as to form a sort of cylinder, whose diameter.. is adapted to the cannon. **1794** SOUTHEY *Botany Bay Eclog.* iii, The chain and the grape-shot roll splintering around. **1809** *Med. Jrnl.* XXI. 446 A middle aged man, of the name of Robinson.. was wounded by a grape shot. **1867** SMYTH *Sailor's Word-bk.* 346 A round of grapeshot consists of three tiers of cast-iron balls arranged, generally three in a tier, between four parallel iron discs connected together by a central wrought-iron pin. **1876** BANCROFT *Hist. U.S.* VI. xxxix. 211 The two columns, heedless of musketry and grapeshot, gained the center of the works nearly at the same moment.

Hence **grapeshot** *v. trans.*, to fire upon with grape-shot.

1876 RUSKIN *Fors Clav.* VI. lxv. 145 Not until England has had to stone.. some of the children she has got: or at least to grapeshot them.

'grape-stone. [f. GRAPE *sb.*[1] + STONE.]

1. The seed of a grape.

1589 RIDER *Eng.-Lat. Dict.* 678/16 A Grape stone, or kernell in grapes, *vinacea*. *a* **1627** MIDDLETON & ROWLEY *Changeling* III. iii. 45 There's a spider in the cup! no, 'tis but a grape-stone. **1656** COWLEY *Misc.*, *Elegy Anacreon* (1669) 41 In Deaths Hand the Grape-stone proves As strong as Thunder is in Joves. **1703** PRIOR *Ode to Col. Villiers* 54 A Fly, a Grape-stone, or a Hair can kill.

2. *Min.* Occas. used for BOTRYOLITE.

1860 *Nicholson's Jrnl.* XXVI. 273 On the Botryolite, or Grapestone.

'grape-vine. Now chiefly *U.S.* and *Austral.*

1. The vine which bears grapes; any species of the genus *Vitis*, esp. *V. vinifera.*

1736 PEGGE *Kenticisms* (E.D.S.), *Grape-vine*, a vine. **1844** MARG. FULLER *Wom. 19th C.* (1862) 59 An isle.. perfumed by the blossoming grape-vine which draped its bowers. **1851** LONGF. *Gold. Leg.* II. v. *Foot of Alps*, Blossoms of grape-vines scent the sunny air. **1884** ROE *Nat. Ser. Story* x. in *Harper's Mag.* Sept. 537/1 The grape-vine.. can endure an unusual degree of drought.

2. In various applied senses: **a.** Orig., a canard: current during the American civil war, and shortened from 'a despatch by grape-vine telegraph' (Funk's *Stand. Dict.*). Now in general use to indicate the route by which a rumour or a piece of information (often of a secret or private nature) is passed.

a **1867** B. F. WILLSON *Old Sergeant* vii. (Funk) Just another foolish grape-vine. **1891** *Century Mag.* Mar. 713/2 The 'grape-vine' spoke to us of little else. **1934** J. T. FARRELL *Studs Lonigan* (1936) II. xv. 337 Down there at that express company they find out about everything a guy does. They got the best grapevine in the world. **1948** *Daily Tel.* 3 Sept. 4/5 The guerrillas know the jungle, and they have an almost incredible 'grapevine' which gets information from one State to another with uncanny speed. **1955** *Times* 11 June 9/6 Of the younger men, the Moscow grape-vine reported that Mr. Shepilov, editor of *Pravda*, was coming forward to strengthen the party theoreticians. **1962** K. ORVIS *Damned & Destroyed* vii. 54 Hurrying a message through the grapevine to the trafficker. **1970** *New Yorker* 3 Oct. 100/2 The art-world grapevine buzzed with rumors.

b. A hold in wrestling (Farmer).

1968 T. CLAYTON *Handbk. Wrestling Terms & Holds* 103 (*caption*) Double grapevine with arm tieup.

c. A figure in skating.

1868 G. ANDERSON *Skating* iii. (ed. 2) 36 The Canadian Grape-Vine.. I saw it beautifully performed last winter, and it looks like a curious interlacing and juggling of the feet. **1903** *Westm. Gaz.* 30 Dec. 3/2 The expert dons his skates and glides.. off with the air of one to whom threes, grape-vines,.. and other mysterious figures are.. familiar. **1952** VISC. TEMPLEWOOD in *Skating with T. D. Richardson* xiii. 104 In days long ago it was the fashion to perform a series of two-footed movements called grapevines.

3. *attrib.*, as ***grape-vine journalist, method, moth, rumour, telegraph*** (see 2 a), ***telegraphic*** adj., ***weevil, wire.***

1959 *Economist* 4 Apr. 20/2 The grapevine journalists have been listening; up to Thursday morning the grapevine still had not yielded any word. **1942** *Daily Tel.* 31 Aug. 3/4 Each province is presumed to have a leader.. whose instructions are transmitted by 'grapevine' methods from one person to another. **1950** *N.Z. Jrnl. Agric.* Oct. 326/1 The caterpillars of the grapevine moth, which found its way to New Zealand from Australia in recent years, depredate vines by devouring the foliage and damaging the developing grapes. **1941** AUDEN *New Year Let.* III. 61 The careless victor never knew Their grape-vine rumour would grow true. **1889** FARMER *Americanisms* s.v., During the Civil War exciting news of battles not fought and victories not won were said to be received by grape-vine telegraph. **1936** J. G. BRANDON *Pawnshop Murder* iii. 26 I'll see what I can get over the 'grapevine' telegraph. **1951** *John o' London's* 17 Aug. 494/2 First with the news was.. the little old man who cleans our windows... He is our grapevine telegraph. **1953** A. W. FIELDING *Stronghold* I. i. 5, I had long ago ceased to wonder at the workings of their grape-vine telegraph. **1864** in *Southern Hist. Soc. Papers* (1876) I. 437 Many 'grape-vine' telegraphic reports are afloat in camp. **1950** *N.Z. Jrnl. Agric.* Oct. 326/1 The grapevine weevil can cause considerable damage by eating the leaves, shoots, and bunches. **1907** J. L. GIVEN *Making Newspaper* xiii. 230 Not often does a telegraph editor.. manufacture news, or, in the vernacular, employ the 'grapevine wire'.

grapey, var. GRAPY *a.*

†grapeys. *Obs.* Also 4 **graspeys, crospays, gra(y)pays,** 5 **grappays.** [a. OF. *grapois, graspeis* (also *craspois*):—med.L. *crassum piscem* (*crassus* fat, *piscis* fish). In the 16th c. the word became by etymologizing alteration GRAMPUS.] The flesh of the grampus (prob. not distinguished from that of other cetaceans).

[*c* **1112** '*Laws of Æthelred*' in Thorpe *Laws* I. 300 Homines de Rotomago qui veniebant cum vino vel craspice dabant rectitudinem sex sol. de magna navi, et vicesimum frustum de ipso craspice.] **1324-5** *Durham Acc. Rolls* (Surtees) I. 15 In 2 petr. de Graypays rem. post comp. *Ibid.* I. 42 In grapays emp. 10d. **1390** *Earl Derby's Exped.* (Camden) 19 Pro j barella parua de crospays ibidem empta. *Ibid.* 221 In vno cado de graspeys. *c* **1420** *Liber Cocorum* (1862) 45 To serve on fysshe day with grappays. *c* **1430** *Two Cookery-bks* I. 59 Crabbe au Creueys, Graspeys [etc.]. **1489** *Paston Lett.* No. 906 III. 347 Bales, sturgion, porpeys, or grapeys.

graph (grɑːf, -æ-), *sb.*[1] [Orig. an abbreviation of *graphic formula*: see GRAPHIC.]

1. A kind of symbolic diagram (used in *Chemistry, Mathematics*, etc.) in which a system of connexions is expressed by spots or circles, some pairs of which are colligated by one or more lines. Also, *occas.* the system expressed by one of these diagrams. In abstract terms: A finite, non-empty set of elements together with a set (empty or non-empty) of unordered pairs of these elements.

'Graphs' were first employed (under the name of 'graphic formulæ': see GRAPHIC *a.* 5) in Chemistry for expressing the relations of the elements forming a compound. The application to Mathematics (app. also the shortened name) is due to Sylvester.

1878 SYLVESTER in *Amer. Jrnl. Math.* I. 65 The graph to nitric anhydride. *Ibid.* 79 Chemical graphs.. are to be regarded as mere translations into geometrical forms of trains of priorities and sequences having their proper habitat in the sphere of order. *Ibid.* 126 *note*, Whilst I was only able, in certain cases, to represent in terms of the roots of the parent quantic, the quantitative constitution of a form pictured by a graph.. he [Clifford].. has found the universal pass key to the quantification of graphs. **1879** *Proc. Lond. Math. Soc.* XI. 2 On Clifford's Graphs.. Dr. Spottiswoode. **1884** *Amer. Jrnl. Math.* VI. 382 The Method of Graphs applied to Compound Partitions. **1931** *Proc. Nat. Acad. Sci.* XVII. 122 Suppose we assign to each vertex of a graph a color in such a way that each pair of vertices joined by an arc are of different colors. **1966** *McGraw-Hill Encycl. Sci. & Technol.* VI. 255/2 If points represent people and lines their interrelationships, then a graph may be used to depict the structure of a social group. **1967** H. C. SNEYD tr. *Kaufmann's Graphs* i. 10 The map of all the roads in a country.. forms a graph. **1969** F. HARARY *Proof Techniques in Graph Theory* i. 1 By far the most celebrated problem concerning graphs is the Four Color Conjecture. **1971** W. L. PRICE *Graphs & Networks* i. 1 Many problems of sequencing and scheduling can be looked upon as problems in graph and network theory. *Ibid.* ii. 7 If the set *A* is empty and the graph consists only of nodes, the result is called a null graph.

2. *Alg.* A graphical representation of the locus of a function; the traced curve of an equation. In wider use: A line or curve representing the variation of one quantity with another, each quantity being measured along one of a pair of axes at right angles.

1886 CHRYSTAL *Algebra* I. 307 The representative point will therefore trace out a continuous curve.. This curve we may call the graph of the function. *Ibid.* 380 Draw the graphs of the two functions $3x - 5$ and $5x + 7$. **1926** *Encycl. Brit.* III. 643 (*caption*) Graph showing consumption per head of tea and sugar in the United Kingdom in each year 1864–1913. **1951** ROBERTS & MILLER *Heat & Thermodynamics* (ed. 4) v. 155 The graph of entropy as a function of magnetic temperature is obtained by plotting this temperature against the calculated change of entropy. **1962** A. R. W. HAYES *Revision Physics* I. 27 For a wire subjected to a stretching force four points on the load-extension graph can be distinguished. **1963** L. NOBLES in H. M. Burlage et al. *Physical & Techn. Pharm.* ii. 63 The plotting of a graph will establish quickly the meaning of a set of experimental data. **1971** *Nature* 24 Sept. 271/1 These data are easier to comprehend in the form of a graph (Fig. 1).

3. Special Comb.: **graph theory**, the mathematical theory of the properties and applications of graphs (sense 1); hence **graph-theoretic** *a.*

1959 *Jrnl. Math & Physics* XXXVIII. 104 (*heading*) A *graph theoretic method for the complete reduction of a matrix with a view toward finding its eigen values. **1973** *Nature* 6 July 60/1 In some papers.. numerical analysis and operations research are investigated from a graph theoretic point view, whilst in others computing techniques are applied to graph-theoretic problems. **1953** HARARY & NORMAN *Graph Theory as Math. Model in Social Sci.* p. iv, It soon became apparent that a whole cluster of substantive problems in psychology and sociology may be treated fruitfully by a branch of mathematics known as '*graph theory'. **1964** *Sci. Amer.* Apr. 126/2 Today graph theory is a flourishing field. It is usually considered a branch of topology (because in most cases only the topological properties of graphs are considered). **1977** B. ANDRÁSFAI *Introductory Graph Theory* v. 113 The degree of each vertex of *G* is $k_1 + k_2 + .. k_m$ and, similarly, the degree of the product of some polynomials is also equal to the sum of the degrees of the factors. This similarity illustrates a strong connection between algebra and graph theory.

graph (grɑːf, -æ-), *sb.*[2] *colloq.* [Abstracted from CHROMOGRAPH, HECTOGRAPH, etc.] An apparatus of the nature of the chromograph, hectograph, etc., for taking copies of writing by pressing it on a gelatinous surface.

1884 *Advt.*, The Cyclostyle. No press, no washing, no graph.

graph (grɑːf, -æ-), *sb.*[3] *Philol.* [ad. Gr. γραφή writing; cf. DIGRAPH[1].] A visual symbol representing a phoneme or a segment or feature of speech; esp., a letter, or one of its occurrent forms, or a combination of letters.

1933 BLOOMFIELD *Lang.* xvii. 294 For the writers, the *gh* was now a mere silent graph, indicative only of vowel-quantity. **1953** *Medium Ævum* XXII. 14 The Exeter Book has one example of a clear t-graph where a 3 would normally be expected. **1958** C. F. HOCKETT *Course in Mod. Ling.* lxii. 544 In Egypt certain graphs very early came to represent syllables rather than morphemes. **1968** *English Studies* XLIX. 513 The graphs *t* and *d* in post-stress, intervocalic position can be ambiguous. **1970** A. CAMERON et al. *Computers & O.E. Concordances* 49 In the final printout, a simple graphic accommodation was employed to designate .. the Old English graphs, ash, eth, and thorn.

graph (grɑːf, -æ-), *v.*[1] *Math.* [ad. Gr. γράφ-ειν to write.] *trans.* To trace (a curve) from its equation; to trace the curve corresponding to (a given equation). Also *fig.* Hence **'graphing** *vbl. sb.*

1898 PERRY *Applied Mechanics* 21 Students will do well to graph on squared paper some curves like the following. *Ibid.* 2. Graph $y = a + bx$. *Ibid.* 1 The graphing of functions on squared paper. **1951** M. MCLUHAN *Mech. Bride* 79/1 When producers want to know what the public wants, they graph it as curves. **1964** *Listener* 20 Aug. 280/1 The book graphs and annotates the hostility between generations.. and this is shaming to read. **1966** I. JEFFERIES *House Surgeon* iii. 31 Anybody graph the survival rates against the day of admission?

graph (grɑːf, -æ-), *v.*[2] *colloq.* [f. GRAPH *sb.*[2]] *trans.* To reproduce in a number of copies by means of a 'graph'. Also *absol.*

1880 *Stationer* XXXV. 3 We graphed by the dozen. **1894** *Westm. Gaz.* 4 July 8/1 The Matabeleland News.. is 'graphed' in manuscript.

-graph (grɑːf, -æ-), repr. F. *-graphe*, L. *-graphus*, Gr. *-γραφος*. The Greek termination was used to form adjectives, sometimes in the passive sense of 'written', e.g. αὐτόγραφος written with one's own hand, χειρόγραφος written with the hand; sometimes in the active sense, 'that writes, delineates, or describes', chiefly used *absol.* as sbs., 'one who writes, delineates, or describes': e.g. ζωγράφος a painter from life, βιβλιογράφος a writer of books, γεωγράφος a delineator of the earth, a geographer. Many of the passive formations in *-γραφος* have been anglicized, being for the most part used both as adjs. and sbs., as in ***autograph, chirograph, holograph.*** These words have been imitated in a few modern sbs. formed on Gr. types, as *lithograph, photograph*; and these in turn have been imitated in hybrid formations, such as *pictograph*; jocular nonce-words, like ***hurrygraph*** for 'a hurried sketch', are occasionally met with. The Gr. active formations in *-γράφος*, where they have been anglicized, take in mod.Eng. the ending -GRAPHER, which is used also for new formations denoting persons (exceptions, such as *calligraph*, are rare). The great bulk of the words in *-graph* is composed of technical terms of very recent invention, mostly formed on Gr. elements, and expressing the general sense of 'that which writes, portrays, or records', as *actinograph, heliograph, hygrograph, ideograph, phonograph, seismograph, telegraph*, etc.

graphematic (græfɪ'mætɪk), *a. Linguistics.* [f. GRAPHEM(E + -ATIC.] = GRAPHEMIC *a.*

1956 A. MCINTOSH in *Trans. Philol. Soc.* 42 The complexity.. of a full graphematic analysis of a text. **1959** *Brno Studies* I. 15 The graphematic difference. **1969** *Computers & Humanities* IV. 131 The graphematic oppositions are being grouped as to their positions and analyzed statistically.

grapheme ('græfiːm). *Linguistics.* [f. GRAPH *sb.*[3] + -EME; cf. MORPHEME.] The class of letters and other visual symbols that represent a phoneme or cluster of phonemes, as e.g. the grapheme ⟨f⟩ consists of the ALLOGRAPHS *f, ff, F, Ff, gh, ph*, and *Ph* which represent the phoneme /f/ in *fun, huffy, Fingal, Ffoulkes, cough, graph*, and *Philip* respectively; so, in a given writing system of a given language, a feature of written expression that cannot be analysed into smaller meaningful units.

1935 W. F. TWADDELL *Defining Phoneme* 54 It would clarify the issue if these units might be called 'graphemes'. **1937** R. H. STETSON in *Mélanges Ling. et Philol. offerts à J. van Ginnekin* 353 The unit of writing may be called the grapheme. **1951**, etc. [see ALLOGRAPH[2]]. **1955** H. A. GLEASON *Introd. Descr. Ling.* xxi. 302 A writing system consists of a set of graphemes plus certain characteristic features of their use. **1958** A. A. HILL *Introd. Ling. Struct.* 443 The grapheme for /+/ was normally the blank space left between words. **1964** R. A. HALL *Introductory Linguistics* xliv. 265 In the Greek alphabet, the grapheme ⟨σ⟩ 'sigma', corresponding to our ⟨s⟩, has the two allographs ς (occurring only at the end of a word, before space) and σ (used elsewhere).

graphemic (grəˈfiːmɪk), *a.* and *sb. Linguistics.* [f. GRAPHEM(E + -IC.] **A.** *adj.* Of or relating to graphemes. **B.** *sb. pl.* **graphemics**. The study of systems of written symbols (letters, etc.) in their relation to spoken languages.

1951 STOCKWELL & BARRITT (*title*) Some Old English graphemic-phonemic correspondences. **1951** E. PULGRAM in *Word* VII. 19 It is precisely that parallelism of phonemics and graphemics which renders feasible a phonemic transcription. **1953** J. B. CARROLL *Stud. of Lang.* ii. 13 This branch of linguistics has been termed graphemics by some linguists, and graphonomy by others. **1958** A. A. HILL *Introd. Ling. Struct.* 442 Graphemic symbols are enclosed in angle marks (⟨⟩). **1964** R. A. HALL *Introductory Linguistics* xliv. (*heading*) Graphemics.

Hence **graˈphemically** *adv.*

1956 *Trans. Philol. Soc.* 50 Graphemically irrelevant variations in the shape of *p.* **1964** *Language* XL. 167 One-syllable words, graphemically defined, have the same part-of-speech assignments.

-grapher (grəfə(r)), an ending of many Eng. words of Greek derivation. First found in the earlier half of the 16th c. The analogy of *astronom-er* (really f. *astronomy*, but having the appearance of being f. L. *astronom-us* + -ER[1]) naturally suggested the use of the suffix *-er* as a means of anglicizing L. words in *-ˈographus* without altering their rhythm, as in *cosmographer* (recorded 1527). In the 16th c. there also occur a few derivatives in *-er* from nouns in *-graphy*, as *geographier* (1542), *chronographier* (1548), but these were soon superseded by the forms in *-grapher*. (In CHIROGRAPHER, q.v., the ending has a different source.) From the latter part of the 16th c. the formation with *-grapher* has been the normal mode both of anglicizing a real or assumed Gr. word in *-γράφος* (see -GRAPH) denoting a personal agent, and of providing a personal designation correlative to sb. in -GRAPHY denoting an art or science. It would often be impossible to determine in which of these two ways an individual word actually originated; but the question is unimportant, because Gr. words in *-γράφος* were themselves influenced in sense by their derivatives in *-γραφία*, so that, e.g. *γεωγράφος* meant not so much 'one who describes the earth' as 'one versed in *γεωγραφία*'.

The suffix *-ist* has sometimes been used instead of *-er* in anglicizing Gr. words in *-γράφος* or forming derivatives from sbs. in *-graphy*; cf. *biographist* for the more usual *biographer*; *telegraphist* is more common than *telegrapher*.

graphic (ˈgræfɪk), *a.* and *sb.* [ad. L. *graphic-us*, Gr. *γραφικ-ός*, f. *γραφή* drawing or writing. Cf. F. *graphique*.]

A. *adj.* †**1.** Drawn with a pencil or pen. *Obs.*

a **1637** B. JONSON *Underwoods, Eupheme* ix, [God] can Find..our closest creeks and corners, and can trace Each line, as it were graphick in the face.

2. Of or pertaining to drawing or painting. ***graphic arts***: the fine arts of drawing, painting, engraving, etching, etc.; also, the techniques of production and design involved in printing and publishing; ***graphic design***: graphics (sense B. 2 below); so ***graphic designer***.

1756 *Epitaph* in *H. Walpole's Vertue's Anecd. Paint.* (1786) V. 269 With..all the genius of the Graphic Art, His fame shall each succeeding artist own. **1811** LAMB *Guy Faux* Misc. Wks. (1871) 374, I only notice the print as being one of the earliest graphic representations which woke my childhood into wonder. **1872** RUSKIN *Eagle's N.* §123 This faculty of sight..is the only proper faculty which the graphic artist is to use in his inquiries into nature. **1882** P. G. HAMERTON (*title*) The Graphic Arts: a Treatise on the Varieties of Drawing, Painting and Engraving. **1949** *Sci. Amer.* Nov. 29 The new Graphic Arts Research Foundation, whose work is supported by 139 newspapers, printing firms and other interested groups. **1956** H. WILLIAMSON *Methods Bk. Design* Pref., Principles of graphic design which apply to all kinds of book production. **1967** Graphic design [see sense B.3 below]. **1967** KARCH & BUBER *Offset Processes* ii. 9 Of the many methods and procedures used in the graphic arts, letterpress and offset-lithography account for 66·1% in monetary value. **1971** PERRY & ALDRIDGE *Penguin Bk. Comics* (ed. 2) Bastard title p., Alan Aldridge is one of the most original and creative graphic designers... His unique style of illustration has appeared in countless magazines, newspapers, record sleeves, posters.

3. Producing by words the effect of a picture; vividly descriptive, life-like.

1669 GALE *Crt. Gentiles* I. III. i. 15 He shews..that Poesie was..a graphic Art, or Art of Imitation. *a* **1745** SWIFT *On D. Jackson's Picture* 1 Whilst you three merry poets traffic To give us a description graphic Of Dan's large nose in modern Sapphic. **1830** CUNNINGHAM *Brit. Paint.* II. 228 They are all..graphic copies of common life. **1852** MRS. STOWE *Uncle Tom's C.* i, Expressions, which not even the desire to be graphic in our account shall induce us to transcribe. **1856** FROUDE *Hist. Eng.* (1858) I. iii. 265 A Venetian..wrote..to Henry, informing him in a very graphic manner of the treatment to which..he had been exposed. **1872** DARWIN *Emotions* xi. 260 A graphic description of the face of a young Hindoo at the sight of castor-oil.

4. a. Of or pertaining to writing; fit to be written on.

1774 WARTON *Hist. Eng. Poetry* (1778) II. 157 [Chatterton] became a skilful practitioner in various kinds of handwriting. Availing himself therefore of..his facility in the graphick art..he [etc.]. **1851** D. WILSON *Preh. Ann.* (1863) II. IV. ii. 289 The scribe executing his graphic art. **1854** SYD. DOBELL *Balder* xxiii. 87, I would..make eloquent The graphic bark of beech! **1877** E. R. CONDER *Bas. Faith* v. 197 Letters, hieroglyphics, or any kind of graphic symbol. **1882** SKEAT in *Trans. Philol. Soc.* 1880-1 III. *176 If we now collate the two copies, we find..certain variations which are merely graphic, and of no linguistic significance.

b. Of a mineral: Presenting on the surface, or in the fracture, an appearance of written or printed characters. ***graphic gold, ore*** or ***tellurium***: = SYLVANITE. ***graphic granite*** (see quot. 1859).

1814 AIKIN *Man. Min.* 70 Graphic tellurium. Graphic Gold. **1823** URE *Dict. Chem.*, *Graphic-ore*, an ore of tellurium, occurring in veins in porphyry in Transylvania. **1828** *Amer. Jrnl. Sci. & Arts* XIV. 362 Granite, is..graphic, when [etc.]. **1838** *Penny Cycl.* XI. 355/2 The felspar in graphic granite is almost one huge crystallized mass. **1859** PAGE *Hand-bk. Geol. Terms, Graphic Granite*..a binary compound of felspar and quartz—the quartz being disposed through the felspar matrix like lines of Arabic writing. **1868** DANA *Min.* (ed. 5) 81 Graphic Tellurium. **1879** RUTLEY *Study Rocks* xii. 211 The so-called graphic-granite..in which the quartz..roughly resembles Hebrew characters.

5. a. Pertaining to the use of diagrams, linear figures, or symbolic curves.

graphic formula: in chemistry, a formula (see FORMULA 3 b) in which lines are employed to indicate the connexions of the elements represented by the symbols. (Cf. GRAPH *sb.* 1.) ***graphic method, solution***: a method of solving problems (e.g. in *Statics*; occas. in *Algebra*) by the construction of a diagram from which the result is obtained by direct measurement instead of calculation. ***graphic method***: the method of recording movements of a part of the body by some automatic instrument, e.g. the movement of the pulse by the sphygmograph.

1866 FRANKLAND *Lect. Notes Chem. Students* iii. 24 Graphic notation..is founded almost entirely upon the doctrine of atomicity, and consists in representing graphically the mode in which every bond in a chemical compound is disposed of. *Ibid.*, The following comparative examples of symbolic and graphic formulæ. **1870** ATKINSON *Ganot's Physics* §216 M. Duhamel's graphic method..consists in fixing a fine point to the body emitting the sound, and causing it to trace the vibrations on a properly prepared surface. **1883** *Amer. Jrnl. Math.* VI. 174 A Graphic Method of Solving Spherical Triangles. **1884** *Science* III. 164/1 Graphic representations are always specially valuable to the reader. **1897** *Allbutt's Syst. Med.* III. 326 A continuous graphic record of the blood pressure was obtained by means of a manometer.

b. Of a geometrical proposition, or a branch of geometry: Concerned with position and form, not with measurement. Opposed to *metric*.

1865 CLIFFORD *Math. Papers* (1882) 80 It may be possible to state the same theorem in two ways, so as to make it either metric or graphic.

6. ***graphic equalizer***: a device enabling the quality of an audio signal to be varied by adjusting its strength in each of a series of frequency bands independently, each band having its own control (usu. a slider).

1969 *Jrnl. Audio Engin. Soc.* XVII. 20/1 This circuit could easily be adapted to be a section of a graphic equalizer. **1976** *Gramophone* May 1826/2 The graphic equalizer is not for every hi-fi customer, because it does require some skill, time and patience in usage... JVC was the first to offer in their stereo and four-channel receivers a relatively simple 5-ganged sound equalisation system which went beyond the conventional tone controls. **1984** *Listener* 3 May 21/1 (Advt.), It also boasts a twin deck cassette player with Dolby B and C and a stereo amplifier with graphic equalizer.

B. *sb.* **1. a.** *pl.* The technical use of diagrams and figures as an aid to mathematical calculation or to engineering or architectural design.

1889 R. H. SMITH (*title*), Graphics: or the Art of Calculation by Drawing Lines. **1898** PERRY *Applied Mechanics* 1 One teacher seems to think that applied mechanics is simply the study of kinematics and mechanisms..another, that it is mere graphics. **1912** D. A. LOW (*title*) Practical geometry and graphics. **1929** W. ABBOTT *Pract. Geom. & Engin. Graphics* 3 In Part I considerable space has been devoted to Engineering Graphics, particularly to the applications of graphical integration. **1960** *McGraw-Hill Encycl. Sci. & Technol.* IV. 615/1 Engineering graphics includes preparation of drawings that show the shape of objects.

b. *pl.* The production of diagrams, patterns, etc., by means of a computer.

1966 *Sci. Amer.* Sept. 184 (*caption*) Perspective drawing of a vehicle designed for reentry from space was produced by a computer-graphics program. **1969** *Computers & Humanities* IV. 66 Production of Visual Material by Computer. The formal name of this category is computer graphics, but you might prefer calling it computer art. **1970** *Ibid.* 172 By concentrating on a single graphics language, each student will have the opportunity to prepare a computer-generated film sequence.

2. *pl.* Design and decoration that involves typographic elements; the production of pictures, diagrams, etc., in association with text.

1960 *Design* Sept. 79/1 The type of credits designed by Saul Bass are an isolated example of good graphics for movies. **1965** *Amer. N. & Q.* Apr. 122/1 A graphics exhibition centering on the production of a recent book published by the famous Gehenna Press. **1967** M. MCLUHAN *Medium is Massage* (back-flap of dust-cover), Quentin Fiore is a distinguished graphics designer and artist. **1971** *Guardian* 12 Oct. 8/2 Graphics, textile design, ceramics..and many other design courses.

3. An example of the graphic arts or of graphic design; also, a diagram, pattern, picture, etc., produced by means of a computer.

1961 in WEBSTER. **1967** *Listener* 2 Mar. 296/3 There is an exhibition of Polish graphics. These are not prints but examples of graphic design... Typography is used as an essential element in the design rather than as adjunct to photography and illustration. **1969** *Computers & Humanities* IV. 66 Since the first computers used typewriters and punched cards, the first graphics were illustrations using clever combinations of typing characters, or simple arrays of holes. **1970** *Guardian* 17 June 12/6 At present neither multiples nor graphics (that is prints of all kinds) sell in really mass editions.

Hence **ˈgraphicly** *adv. rare*[−0]. (In mod. Dicts.) **ˈgraphicness**, vividness of description.

1861 GEIKIE & WILSON *Mem. E. Forbes* xi. 330 This is brought out with a melancholy graphicness in his letters to Mr. Thompson. **1890** *Illustr. Sporting & Dram. News* 13 Sept. 23/3, I went on to describe with equal graphicness encounters with beasts.

-graphic (ˈgræfɪk), the ending of the adjs. correlative in sense with the sbs. in -GRAPH, -GRAPHER, -GRAPHY, represents Gr. *-γραφικός*, which occurs in a few words derived from adjs. or sbs. in *-γράφος* (see -GRAPH), some of which have been anglicized, as *ἱστοριογραφικός historiographic*. Any of the Eng. adjs. in *-graphic* might conceivably have been formed on an assumed Gr. type, but it is probable that they have been mostly formed with suffix -IC directly on Eng. sbs. in *-graphy* (or less frequently *-graph*). The prevailing sense is 'of or pertaining to —— graphy'.

graphical (ˈgræfɪkəl), *a.* [f. GRAPHIC *a.* + -AL[1].] †**1.** Clearly traced. (Cf. GRAPHIC *a.* 1.) *Obs.*

1626 BACON *Sylva* §503 For as they grow, so the Letters [scratched on trees or fruit] will grow more large, and Graphicall.

2. = GRAPHIC 2. †Also, skilled in drawing.

1610 W. FOLKINGHAM *Art of Survey* 1 The Survey of Possessions is the Arte by which their Graphicall Description is particularized. **1669** FLAMSTEED in Rigaud *Corr. Sci. Men* (1841) II. 84 Some person indued with a celestial wit and a graphical hand not unemulous of it. **1788** V. KNOX *Winter Even.* II. v. ii. 195 All graphical representations of God the Father are to be disapproved. **1810** SYD. SMITH *Female Educ.* Wks. (1850) 177 The highest exertions of musical or graphical skill. **1828** W. IRVING in *Life & Lett.* (1864) II. 347 He..is eager for all kinds of graphical illustrations, fac-similes, &c.

3. = GRAPHIC 3. Now *rare.*

1644 BULWER *Chiron.* Prælud., The whole Nation of the Greekes were Comœdians; for..in graphicall assimilating and imitating the affections, there were few of any Nation could match them. **1650** TRAPP *Comm. Exod.* x. 14 See a graphical description of a like plague threatened. *Joel* ii. 4-11. **1658** J. ROBINSON *Eudoxa* 84 Every Line being a Graphical Pourtraict of Christ. **1777** G. FORSTER *Voy. round World* II. 9 Every part answered the graphical description which the Spaniards have given. **1825** CARLYLE *Schiller* III. (ed. 2) 162 'Wallenstein's Camp'..paints with much humour and graphical felicity the manners of that rude tumultuous host. **1830** MISS MITFORD *Village* Ser. IV. (1863) 193 One of the finest sketches which Mr. Crabbe's graphical pen ever produced.

absol. **1845** *Blackw. Mag.* LVIII. 387 Such a sentiment..asks not the happinesses of humour, wit, fancy, of the graphical and the characteristic.

4. Of or pertaining to writing; consisting of letters. (Cf. GRAPHIC 4.) †***graphical stone***, graphic granite (see GRAPHIC 4 b).

1643 SIR T. BROWNE *Relig. Med.* II. §2 The Finger of God hath left an Inscription upon all his works, not graphical, or composed of Letters, but [etc.]. **1802** PLAYFAIR *Illustr. Hutton. Theory* 322 The graphical stone of Portsoy must..be admitted to differ materially from that of Daouria. **1881** W. R. SMITH *O. T. in Jew. Ch.* vi. 168 The Septuagint translation was made from a copy, which shared many graphical errors of our present Hebrew.

5. = GRAPHIC 5. ***graphical method*** = 'graphic method'. ***graphical statics***: statics as studied by the 'graphic method'.

1784 in *Phil. Trans.* LXXV. 144 If there is a possibility of drawing a graphical figure that represents nearly the orbit under consideration. **1801** J. JONES tr. *Bygge's Trav. Fr. Rep.* xiv. 306 Lieutenant Maindon's graphical method of ascertaining the distance between the sun and moon. **1837** WHEWELL *Hist. Induct. Sci.* (1857) I. 153 The graphical methods of geometry. **1863** ATKINSON *Ganot's Physics* 187 Graphical methods of studying vibratory movements. **1878** SYLVESTER in *Amer. Jrnl. Math.* I. 73 Such a proposition ought to admit of graphical proof. **1886** CHRYSTAL *Algebra* I. 306 To obtain a graphical representation of the variation of the function *f*(*x*). **1890** BEARE tr. *Cremona's Graphical Statics* (title), Two Treatises on the Graphical Calculus and Reciprocal Figures in Graphical Statics. **1898** PERRY *Applied Mechanics* 1 Teachers who spend most of the time on graphical statics, or the graphing of functions on squared paper.

Hence **ˈgraphicalness**.

1882 in OGILVIE; and in recent Dicts.

graphically ('græfɪkəlɪ), *adv.* [f. GRAPHICAL *a.* + -LY².] In a graphic or graphical manner.

†**1.** By means of drawing or painting. *Obs.*

1658 SIR T. BROWNE *Hydriot.* ii. 11 Urnes.. handsomely described, and graphically represented by the Learned Physician Wormius.

2. As in a picture; clearly, picturesquely, vividly.

1576 NEWTON *Lemnie's Complex.* Ep. Rdr., Which .. abuse manye learned Clerkes bewaylinge haue.. by wryting and otherwise graphicallye depainted. [**1623** COCKERAM, *Graffically*, cunningly done.] **1655** BP. J. RICHARDSON *Observ. O.T.* 419 Very Rhetorical delineations do follow of their miseries by this invasion of Nebuchadnezzar, graphicaly as in a Map described. **1698** FRYER *Acc. E. India & P.* 290 None more Graphically expresses them than these Facetious Verses. **1711** J. DENNIS *Publick Spirit* 11 To paint the Manners of our own Times graphically. **1833** J. RENNIE *Alph. Angling* Pref. 13, I sallied out one day to the river Ayr, with a bent pin for a hook, as Christopher North has described so graphically and well. **1883** *Eng. Illustr. Mag.* Nov. 68/2 The sea-banks and droves of the north.. tell us more graphically than any records, how the 'Marshland' was won from the raging sea.

3. †**a.** In the manner of writing (*obs.*); **b.** by means of or in respect of written signs.

1609 B. JONSON *Masque Queens* Wks. (1616) 964 After it, succeeded their third dance; then which, a more numerous composition could not be seene, Graphically disposed into Letters and honoring the name of.. Prince Charles. **1861** F. HALL in *Jrnl. Asiat. Soc. Bengal* 197 *note*, The original [Sanskrit] does not graphically characterize *v* from *b*. *Mod.* The verbs *rede* and *read* differ only graphically; in etymology and pronunciation they are the same word.

4. By the use of graphic methods; by the construction of diagrams or graphs.

1771 PEMBERTON in *Phil. Trans.* LXI. 450 All the particulars usually inquired into in solar eclipses may.. be assigned graphically with scale and compass. **1834** MRS. SOMERVILLE *Connect. Phys. Sci.* xxxvii. (1849) 417 A curve is thus constructed graphically by means of the angles of position and the corresponding times of observation. **1866** ODLING *Anim. Chem.* 27 We should.. represent populin graphically.. by the residues of three circles conjoined with one another. **1879** SPOTTISWOODE in *Proc. Lond. Math. Soc.* X. 209 Graphically, the form itself will be represented by —o—; —o—) or . . . . **1882** MINCHIN *Unipl. Kinemat.* 215 The velocity at *P* may be graphically represented.. as the resultant of two forces from *P* towards *A* and *B*. **1886** CHRYSTAL *Algebra* I. 333 Solve graphically the equation $x^3 - 16x^2 + 71x - 129 = 0$. **1895-6** *Cal. Univ. Nebraska* 253 The measurements are plotted graphically upon a chart.

graphiologist (græfɪ'ɒlədʒɪst). [f. next + -IST.] = GRAPHOLOGIST.

1851 W. J. COPLESTON *Mem. Bp. Copleston* 3 We prognosticate, without the aid of the graphiologist, clear thought and methodical accuracy.

graphiology (græfɪ'ɒlədʒɪ). [irreg. f. Gr. γράφ-ειν to write + -(O)LOGY. The word seems to have been invented (in sense 1) by some of the advertising practitioners of the art about 1850.]

1. = GRAPHOLOGY 2.

1854 LADY LYTTON *Behind Scenes* I. I. ii. 67 If there is anything in graphiology.

2. a. The science or 'art of writing or delineation, or a treatise on that art' (Ogilvie, Suppl., 1855). *rare*⁻⁰. **b.** Methods of graphic representation.

1880 *Daily Tel.* 20 Oct., Everything connected with the graphiology of heraldry is of the weakest.. character.

-graphist: see note under -GRAPHER.

graphite ('græfaɪt). [First in Ger. form *graphit* (Werner, 1789); f. Gr. γράφ-ειν to write (because used for pencils) + -ITE. Cf. F. *graphite* (Haüy, 1801, in Hatz.-Darm.).] **a.** One of the crystalline allotropic forms of carbon (see CARBON *sb.* 1), called also BLACK LEAD *sb.* and PLUMBAGO.

1796 KIRWAN *Elem. Min.* (ed. 2) II. 58 Plumbago, Graphite of Werner. **1849** D. CAMPBELL *Inorg. Chem.* 13 Carbon occurs.. in six-sided plates in graphite. **1871** B. STEWART *Heat* (ed. 2) §27 The bore contains a small index made of iron or graphite. **1896** *Trans. Amer. Soc. Mech. Engineers* XVII. 106, I have.. advised the introduction of graphite of fine grades, and specially purified, wherever.. great loads are to be carried on heavy and slow-moving machinery. **1963** GREGORY & PITT in F. J. PEARSON *Nuclear Power Technol.* ix. 228 The extract properties of the graphite cannot be predicted and all batches have to be tested for their neutron absorption properties.

b. *attrib.* and *Comb.*, as ***graphite moderator, pile, reactor***; ***graphite-moderated*** adj.

1945 H. D. SMYTH *Gen. Acct. Devel. Atomic Energy Mil. Purposes* 63 The prospects for a graphite pile with helium cooling looked promising. *Ibid.* 68 The lattices.. consisted of lumps of uranium imbedded in the graphite moderator. *Ibid.* 79 In a typical graphite-moderated pile a neutron that has escaped from the uranium into the graphite travels on the average about 2·5 cm between collisions. **1950** *Amer. Speech* XXV. 24 Reactors may be named according to fuel (uranium reactor), moderator (graphite reactor), [etc.]. **1958** *Times Rev. Industry* Aug. 7/1 Britain will depend mainly on the gas-cooled, graphite-moderated type reactor, using natural uranium. **1962** *Newnes Conc. Encycl. Nuclear Energy* 511/1 With gas-cooled reactors the graphite moderator normally acts as a guide for the fuel elements.

Hence **graphited** ('græfaɪtɪd) *a.*, supplied with graphite as a lubricant; also (of a lubricant), having had graphite added to it.

1922 *Autocar* 10 Nov. 997 Graphited oilless bushes are freely used. **1939** J. I. CLOWER *Lubricants* v. 65 Perhaps the chief advantage of graphited oils and greases is their ability to form films of graphite on the bearing surfaces of mechanical devices. **1955** A. F. BREWER *Basic Lubrication Pract.* iv. 61 Bronze and cadmium-base graphited alloys involve somewhat lower maximum operating temperature ranges.

graphitic (grə'fɪtɪk), *a.* [f. GRAPHITE + -IC.] Of or pertaining to graphite; having the nature of graphite. ***graphitic acid*** (see quot. 1864).

1864 WATTS *Dict. Chem.* II, *Graphitic acid*.. an acid discovered by Brodie.. and produced from graphite by the repeated action of chlorate of potassium and nitric acid. **1877** LE CONTE *Elem. Geol.* II. (1879) 346 The graphitic and anthracitic varieties of coal. **1878** LAWRENCE tr. *Cotta's Rocks Class.* 199 Graphitic Granite, with graphite in the place of mica. **1881** RAYMOND *Mining Gloss.*, *Graphitic carbon*, that portion of the carbon in iron or steel which is present as graphite.

graphitization (,græfɪtaɪ'zeɪʃən). [f. GRAPHIT(E + -IZATION.] **1.** A process in which an allotrope of carbon becomes wholly or partly converted into graphite or becomes more graphitic in nature; also, the graphitic character of the resulting carbon.

1899 E. G. ACHESON in *Jrnl. Franklin Inst.* 3rd Ser. CXLVII. 484 One [form of the product] consists of.. articles made out of amorphous carbon,.. which will afterwards be heated in an electric furnace and converted.. into graphite. I have been.. using the furnaces of the Carborundum Company to produce the graphitization. **1951** *Proc. R. Soc.* A. CCIX. 215 Graphitization [of the coal] does not occur because the crystallites are in random orientation and the pore structure remains intact. **1956** *Nature* 4 Feb. 239/1 Short periods of oxidation of the coal.. decreased the graphitization of the carbon. **1958** *Sci. News* L. 118 The graphite obtained from the Dayton, Ohio, meteorite.. is like the graphite obtained by graphitization of diamond. **1970** *New Scientist* 5 Feb. 253/2 They may not reach the same degree of graphitization as in the absence of oxidation.. but they can still be reasonably graphitic.

2. A kind of corrosion in which grey cast iron becomes soft and porous, the metallic iron constituents being converted to corrosion products whilst the graphite is left intact; graphitic softening.

1916 *Yorks. Post* 4 Apr. 8/1 An instance [of internal disintegration] may be taken from the 'graphitisation' of iron pipes, a form of decay to which cast iron is liable when buried in the ground. **1941** *Nature* 22 Mar. 343/2 Cast iron behaved well in air, but when submerged was very liable to 'graphitization', the outer form being retained but the interior being converted into a spongy mass without strength. **1967** FONTANA & GREENE *Corrosion Engin.* iii. 71 White cast iron has essentially no free carbon and is not subject to graphitization.

3. The formation of graphite from combined carbon in a ferrous alloy.

1919 *Jrnl. Iron & Steel Inst.* XCIX. 569 Graphite is always to be seen in an ingot which was slowly cooled, even when there is practically no silicon, which was formerly supposed to be necessary in graphitisation. **1951** W. B. SHANNON in W. E. Benbow *Steels in Mod. Industry* xiii. 275 Of the carbide forming elements, chromium is particularly effective in inhibiting graphitization. **1961** *Metals Handbk.* (ed. 8) I. 587/3 Graphitization lowers the room-temperature strength somewhat by removing the strengthening effects of finely dispersed carbides.

graphitize ('græfɪtaɪz), *v.* [f. as prec. + -IZE.] **1.** *trans.* **a.** To convert (an allotrope of carbon) into graphite, to make more graphitic.

1899 E. G. ACHESON in *Jrnl. Franklin Inst.* 3rd Ser. CXLVII. 485, I have also graphitized some tons of carbon plates, to be used in making dynamo and motor brushes. **1912** W. L. LANDIS in Rogers & Aubert *Industr. Chem.* xii. 276 After such a run the granulated coke forming the heating core has been graphitized. **1952** *Mineral. Mag.* XXIX. 805 Attempts were also made to graphitize diamonds in a carbon arc.

absol. **1910** *Encycl. Brit.* XII. 365/1 In graphitizing *en masse* large lumps of anthracite are treated in the electric furnace.

b. To cause the combined carbon in (a ferrous alloy) to form graphite; to convert (a carbon-containing constituent of a ferrous alloy) into graphite and something else.

1919 *Jrnl. Iron & Steel Inst.* XCIX. 582 Carbon-iron alloys within the range 2·0 to 4·3 per cent. carbon, when.. slowly cooled past the eutectic freezing temperature 1130° C., were partially graphitised. **1934** *Chem. & Ind.* 14 Dec. 1052/2 With the aid of silicon, which breaks down or graphitizes the iron carbide.., the bulk of the carbide can be converted to iron and graphite. **1937** EPSTEIN & SISCO *Alloys Iron & Carbon* II. x. 369 All the remaining austenite changes to ferrite and cementite; the remaining cementite has, therefore, still to be graphitized. **1960** LAING & ROLFE *Man. Foundry Pract.* (ed. 3) x. 366 In the manufacture of whiteheart.. the white iron is not only graphitised, but the carbon is also very largely removed.

2. *intr.* **a.** Of a ferrous alloy: to undergo a change characterized by the conversion of the combined carbon into graphite. **b.** To change into graphite.

1919 *Bull. Amer. Inst. Mining & Metall. Engineers* July 1068 The gray iron.. begins to graphitize further at temperatures lower than those at which there is initial graphitization of the white iron. **1920** *Jrnl. Iron & Steel Inst.* CII. 293 White pig iron always graphitises when annealed at a temperature above 1000°. **1961** *Metals Handbk.* (ed. 8) I. 587/3 Many of these steels do not graphitize completely. **1968** C. G. KUPER *Introd. Theory Superconductivity* i. 11 Diamond at room temperature shows no tendency to graphitize. **1970** *New Scientist* 5 Feb. 252/2 The non-graphitizing type [of carbon] can be induced to graphitize by the use of a catalyst.

Hence **'graphitizable** *a.*, convertible into graphite; so **,graphitiza'bility**; **'graphitizing** *ppl. a.*, that graphitizes or brings about graphitization; also as *vbl. sb.*

1904 *Electrochem. Ind.* II. 492/2 When carbon is raised to the graphitizing temperature its properties will depend largely on the kind of amorphous carbon used. **1920** *Jrnl. Iron & Steel Inst.* CII. 288 This process continues.. until the temperature falls below the graphitising range. **1930** *Engineering* 11 July 58/1 Work carried out on the influence of nickel on cast iron has.. demonstrated that nickel is, like silicon, a graphitising agent. **1951** *Proc. R. Soc.* A. CCIX. 198 Those non-graphitic carbons which, on heating to temperatures between 1700 and 3000° C, form graphitic carbons will be called graphitizing carbons. *Ibid.* 203 At a certain temperature.. there is formed, in a non-graphitizing carbon, a certain proportion of graphitic or graphitizable carbon. *Ibid.* 207 The graphitizability of a carbon is apparently related to its colloidal or fine-pore structure. **1970** *New Scientist* 5 Feb. 252/2 With increasing temperatures the structure and properties of graphitizing carbons approach those of graphite. *Ibid.* 253/1 A synthetic fibre of the graphitizable type.

graphitized ('græfɪtaɪzd), *ppl. a.* [f. prec. + -ED¹.] That has undergone graphitization; that has been graphitized.

1899 *Jrnl. Franklin Inst.* CXLVII. 484 The life or efficiency of these graphitized electrodes is many times that of the same electrodes ungraphitized. **1930** *Jrnl. Iron & Steel Inst.* CXXI. 355 Values for pure graphite and the graphitised silicon alloy. **1951** *Proc. R. Soc.* A. CCIX. 203 The small amount of graphitic carbon which is formed in certain non-graphitizing carbons is more highly graphitized than is a true graphitizing carbon heated under the same conditions. **1963** H. R. COPSON in LaQue & Copson *Corrosion Resistance of Metals & Alloys* (ed. 2) i. 15 Superficially the casting appears unattacked, but the graphitized layer is soft and weak.

graphitizer ('græfɪtaɪzə(r)). [f. as prec. + -ER¹.] A substance that is added to molten metal to promote the formation of graphite rather than a carbide.

1940 *S.A.E. Jrnl.* Aug. 28/3 In a summary of the effect of the various elements of cast iron on its micro-structure when other variables are considered constant, it is brought out.. that nickel acts as a graphitizer, promoting machinability. **1959** H. F. TAYLOR et al. *Foundry Engin.* xii. 319 Grain refiners and graphitizers probably promote nucleation in the melt by introducing 'foreign' nuclei into the liquid metal.

graphitoid ('græfɪtɔɪd), *a.* [f. GRAPHITE + -OID.] Having the appearance of graphite. Also **graphi'toidal** *a.*

1858 T. GRAHAM *Elem. Chem.* (ed. 2) II. 668 Graphitoïdal Boron. *Ibid.* 672 Silicon, like boron, may be obtained in three states analogous to the amorphous, graphitoïdal, and diamond forms of carbon. **1875** *Ure's Dict. Arts* (ed. 7) II. 735 Graphitoid carbon destined to form the pencils used for the electric light. **1880** *Nature* XXI. 409 A substance.. from which it [carbon] crystallises out partly in graphitoidal, partly in adamantine forms.

graphiure ('græfɪjʊə(r)). Also *erron.* **graphyure.** [ad. mod.L. *graphiūrus*, f. Gr. γραφεῖον a pencil + οὐρά tail.] A South African rodent, with a tail ending in a pencil of hairs.

1849 *Sk. Nat. Hist., Mammalia* IV. 31 Cape Graphiure. **1849** tr. *Cuvier's Anim. Kingd.* 111 The Graphyures.. scarcely differ from the Dormice externally, but have weaker jaws and a longer.. intestinal canal.

grapholite ('græfəlaɪt). [f. Gr. γραφο-, combining form of γραφή writing + -LITE.] Any species of slate suitable for writing on.

1796 KIRWAN *Elem. Min.* (ed. 2) I. 238 Grapholite (Argillaceous genus), gives a white streak, and is generally used to write upon.

graphologist (grə'fɒlədʒɪst). [f. next + -IST.] A person versed in graphology.

1885 *Pall Mall G.* 29 Sept. 3/2 Engaging a graphologist to judge the candidates by their handwriting. **1890** *Ibid.* 8 Sept. 7/1 The confessions of a lady graphologist. **1932** C. MORGAN *Fountain* II. v. 62 Lewis did not examine the handwriting as a graphologist would have examined it. **1961** *Evening Standard* 2 Aug. 12/5 Please write in longhand (we are.. graphologists).

graphology (grə'fɒlədʒɪ). [f. Gr. γραφο-, combining form of γραφή writing + -λογία discourse: see -LOGY. (Substituted, as more correct, for the earlier GRAPHIOLOGY. Cf. F. *graphologie*.)]

1. The study of handwriting.

1882 *Athenæum* 23 Sept. 402/3, I work with a method and principles of criticism different from his in comparative graphology and palæography. **1886** *Syd. Soc. Lex.*, *Graphology*, a study or description of handwriting in relation to the changes from the ordinary which occur in some diseases, such as general paralysis. **1960** M. SPARK *Bachelors* i. 11 Ronald got a job in a small museum of graphology in the City... To Ronald's museum came criminologists from abroad, people wishing to identify the dates of manuscripts, or the handwriting attached to documents of doubt.

2. *esp.* The art or science of inferring a person's character, disposition, and aptitudes from the peculiarities of his handwriting.

1886 *Pall Mall G.* 15 Feb. 10/2 He sought in graphology indications of capacity and disposition. **1887** *Blackw. Mag.*

May 642/1 Phrenology and graphology are admitted to take rank as acknowledged sciences. **1891** J. F. NISBET *Insanity Genius* 149 Graphology contains no doubt a substratum of truth.

3. The system of graphic formulæ; the notation used for graphs.

1878 SYLVESTER in *Amer. Jrnl. Math.* I. 79 Any tendency to disturb or complicate the existing graphology.

4. *Linguistics.* The study of written and printed symbols and of writing systems (see quot. 1964).

1961 A. MCINTOSH in *Archivum Linguisticum* XIII. 107, I have used the word 'graphology' in a sense which is intended to answer, in the realm of written language, to that of 'phonology' in the realm of spoken language. **1962** D. DIRINGER *Writing* 21 Graphology, 'the science of writing', is more concerned with the subject from the biological and psychological points of view than in terms of its history. **1964** M. A. K. HALLIDAY et al. *Linguistic Sci.* ii. 50 Graphology..includes orthography, punctuation, and anything else that is concerned with showing how a language uses its graphic resources to carry its grammatical and lexical patterns.

Hence **grapho'logic, grapho'logical** *adjs.*, of or pertaining to graphology; **grapho'logical** *a.*, **grapho'logically** *adv.*

1891 *N. Y. Tribune* 23 Dec. 3/5 (Funk) The afternoon session of the trial was taken up with the testimony of the graphological experts. **1895** *Daily News* 4 Dec. 6/6 Important graphologic researches. **1964** M. A. K. HALLIDAY et al. *Linguistic Sci.* ii. 50 The 'graphological' level of language, whatever the nature of the script, is characterized by its own distinctive pattern, just as is the level of phonology. **1964** A. MCINTOSH in *Archivum Linguisticum* XVI. 79 These two graphs should at least be recognised as graphologically (even if not graphemically) contrastive.

graphomania (græfəʊ'meɪnɪə). [f. Gr. γραφο- (see GRAPHOLOGY) + MANIA.] A mania for writing. So **grapho'maniac**, one who has graphomania.

1827 (*title*), The Cheilead..being Violent Ebullitions of Graphomaniacs. **1840** *Fraser's Mag.* XXII. 765 An unnecessary act of impolitic graphomania. **1895** *19th Cent.* Apr. 611 The restless repetition of one and the same strain of thought is characteristic of graphomania. **1895** *Athenæum* 15 June 765/1 The graphomaniac is defined [by Max Nordau] as a being 'with an insatiable desire to write, though he has nothing to write about except his own mental and moral ailments'.

graphometer (grə'fɒmɪtə(r)). Also 8 **-metre**. [ad. F. *graphomètre* (1597 in Hatz.-Darm.), f. as prec. + μέτρον measure.] A mathematical instrument, used for measuring angles in surveying; otherwise called a semi-circle. †Also, a goniometer used in crystallography.

1696 PHILLIPS, *Graphometer.* **1712** J. JAMES tr. *Le Blond's Gardening* 81 Instruments made use of for tracing upon the Ground..are the Graphometre, or Semicircle, and the Square. **1773** *Gentl. Mag.* XLIII. 457 Making use of the graphometer to take the angles of depression. **1802** *Nicholson's Jrnl. Nat. Phil.* I. 132 Description of the graphometer, or instrument of Cit. Carangeau for measuring the angles of Crystals. **1842** in BRANDE *Dict. Sci.*, etc. Hence in some mod. Dicts.

grapho'metric, *a.*[1] [f. prec. + -IC.] Pertaining to or ascertained by a graphometer.

In mod. Dicts.

So **grapho'metrical** *a.*[1] = prec.

1828-32 in WEBSTER; and in later Dicts.

grapho'metric, *a.*[2] (*sb.*) *Math.* [f. *grapho-* (taken as comb. form of GRAPHIC, in sense 5 b) + METRIC.] Applied by Clifford to a class of functions which pertain equally to graphic and metric geometry. Hence as *sb.*, a graphometric function.

1865 CLIFFORD *Math. Papers* (1882) 85 Now this function belongs to Metric Geometry..But it also belongs to Graphic Geometry because it is unaltered by projection or linear transformation. On these accounts I propose to call it a Graphometric function... I shall, in what follows, pay particular attention to Graphometrics.

graphophone ('græfəfəʊn). [f. Gr. γράφ-ειν to write + φωνή voice, sound.] The name of one of the instruments for recording and reproducing sound. (Cf. PHONOGRAPH.)

1886 *Boston Herald* (Mass.) 16 July, The 'graphophone', or improved phonograph. **1892** *Mod. Mechanism* (ed. Benjamin) 606 The Bell-Tainter graphophone.

Hence **grapho'phonic** *a.*, of or pertaining to a graphophone.

(In some recent Dicts.)

graphoscope ('græfəskəʊp). [f. Gr. γραφο-, γραφή writing, drawing + -σκόπος observing: see -SCOPE.] An apparatus containing a magnifying lens arranged for viewing engravings, photographs, etc.

aerial graphoscope: a contrivance for presenting the image of an object, projected upon the atmosphere as upon a screen.

1879 H. GRUBB in *Trans. R. Dublin Soc.* 186 Viewed with both eyes through a single magnifying lens, such as is supplied with the graphoscope. **1897** *Dublin Rev.* Apr. 403 The photographing of the vision shown by an aerial graphoscope.

graphospasm ('græfəspæz(ə)m). [f. as prec. + SPASM *sb.*] Writer's cramp.

In some recent Dicts.

graphotype ('græfətaɪp), *sb.* [f. as prec. + TYPE.] **a.** A process for producing a design in relief for surface-printing; also, the block or plate so produced. **b.** (See quot. 1877.)

1866 *Chamb. Jrnl.* XXVIII. 271 Mr. Hitchcock, an American, has invented a process for preparing wood-blocks for the printing of pictures, diagrams, and so forth, to which he gives the name of *graphotype*. **1866** *Brande's Dict. Sci.* etc. II. 61 Some graphotypes are said to rival in beauty and delicacy the best engravings. **1877** *Echo* 22 Oct. 4/1 Under the term graphotype may be included the several systems of reproducing copies of letters which are rapidly finding their way into commercial circles.

Hence **'graphotype** *v. trans.*, to print by means of the graphotype; **'graphotyping** *vbl. sb.* (in quot. *attrib.*); **grapho'typic** *a.*, of or pertaining to the use of the graphotype.

1866 *Sat. Rev.* 31 Mar. 384 Unlearned readers..will not easily make out why the graphotypic and the typographic arts should be so closely allied in nomenclature and so different in fact. **1866** *Spectator* 29 Dec. 1469 Twenty-one illustrations..graphotyped by the Graphotyping Company.

graphy ('græfɪ). *Philol.* [ad. Fr. *graphie* system of writing.] A graphic symbol representing a phoneme; = GRAPH *sb.*[3]

1955 *Trans. Philol. Soc.* 138 The characteristic insular graphies of the later twelfth century *boef, beof, bøf* do not deserve to be dismissed as Anglo-Normanisms. **1962** DAVIS & WRENN *English & Medieval Stud.* 56 Whereas original long *e* and *o* are not infrequently represented by the graphies *ee* and *oo*, original short *e* and *o* are never so represented. **1968** *Medium Ævum* XXXVII. 87 The same graphy appears in the same manuscript in the form *beniscun*. **1970** *Jrnl. Eng. Place-Name Soc.* II. 16 The graphy *gu* for [g] before *e, i* arose in French after initial *gw* had been reduced to *g* at some time before the late twelfth century.

-graphy (grəfɪ), = F., G. *-graphie*, Sp. *-grafía*, It. *-grafia*, L. *-graphia*, repr. Gr. -γραφία in sbs. adapted from Gr. or formed on Gr. types. The Gr. sbs. in -γραφία are abstract nouns of action or function derived from the sbs. (or adjs.) in -γράφος (see -GRAPH, -GRAPHER). Many of these have been adapted in Eng. (usually through the medium of other langs.), and many other compounds of Gr. elements on the analogy of them have been formed in Eng., or adapted from Fr. or mod.Lat. Some of the words with this ending denote processes or styles of writing, drawing, or graphic representation, as *brachygraphy, calligraphy, stenography, cryptography, lithography, photography*. More commonly they are names of descriptive sciences, as *geography, bibliography* (cf. the Gr. βιβλιογραφία, which means the writing of books), *astrography, cometography, petrography, selenography*, etc. Hybrid formations with this ending are rare, *stratigraphy* being almost the only example that has obtained general currency. All sbs. in *-graphy* have actual or potential correlative agent-nouns in *-grapher* and adjs. in *-graphic, -graphical*.

graphyure, erroneous variant of GRAPHIURE.

'graping, *vbl. sb.* [Cf. BLACKBERRYING.] The gathering of grapes.

1854 THOREAU *Walden, House-Warming* (1884) 256 In October I went a-graping to the river meadows.

†**'graping,** *ppl. a. nonce-wd.* Bearing grapes.

1610 G. FLETCHER *Christ's Vict.* II. xlv, Over the hedge depends the graping Elme.

graple, obs. form of GRAPPLE *sb.* and *v.*

graplin, grap-line, corrupt ff. GRAPPLING 3.

grapnel ('græpnəl), *sb.* Forms: 4-7 **grapenel(le**, 6-9 **grapnell**, 7 **grabnel(l, (grapnail)**, 9 **grapnall**, 6- **grapnel**. [a. AF. **grapenel*, dim. of *grapon*, of the same meaning; cf. mod.F. *grapin, grappin* grapnel.]

1. An instrument with iron claws intended to be thrown by a rope for the purpose of seizing and holding an object, esp. an enemy's ship.

Quots. 1373, 1485-6, may belong to 2.

1373 in H. T. RILEY *Lond. Mem.* (1868) 369, 1 grapenel, 1 cheyne. *c***1385** CHAUCER *L.G.W.* 640 *Cleopatra*, In goth the grapenel so ful of crokes Among the ropes, and the shering-hokes. **1485-6** *Naval Acc., Hen. VII* (1896) 45 Grapenelles of Iren with chenes. **1679** *Lond. Gaz.* No. 1393/1 His men..cry'd out, Cut away; which they did.. leaving on Board us their Grapnails. **1878** A. S. MACKENZIE *Paul Jones* I. iii. 59 (Funk) The grapnels were triced up to the yard-arms, ready for falling on the enemy's decks. **1884** *Mil. Engineering* I. II. 100 Grapnels may be used for escalading.

†**b.** A harpoon. *Obs.*

1663 PEPYS *Diary* 6 May, They have catched often, in Greenland, whales with the iron grapnells that had formerly been struck into their bodies covered over with fat.

2. A small anchor with three or more flukes, used esp. for boats, and for securing a balloon on its descent. †*to come to grapnel*: to come to anchor.

[**1373, 1485-6**: see 1.] **1556** W. TOWRSON in Hakluyt *Voy.* (1589) 101 We wayed our Grapnel and went away. **1624** CAPT. SMITH *Virginia* II. 24 Having lost our Grapnell among the rocks. **1631** PELLHAM *Mirac. Preserv. Englishm. Greenland* 16 Casting our Grabnell or Anchor over-board. **1748** *Anson's Voy.* III. vii. 360 Eighteen half gallies..came to grapnel a-head of the *Centurion*. **1836** MARRYAT *Midsh. Easy* xxiii. 87 The boats were to..drop their grapnels till daylight. **1864** *Daily Tel.* 10 June, The grapnel was lowered; it took the ground at once; and the balloon slowly descended.

transf. and *fig.* **1851** H. MELVILLE *Whale* ii. 8 With anxious grapnels I had sounded my pocket. **1857** HUGHES *Tom Brown* II. ii, To lay hold of the working boys and young men of England by any educational grapnel whatever. **1877** THOMSON *Voy. Challenger* I. iii. 176 The form of the spicules which make up the structure of the substance of the sponge, and the form of the double grapnel of the sarcode.

3. A name for various implements for grasping or clutching (see quots.).

1875 KNIGHT *Dict. Mech.*, *Grapnalls*, a heavy tongs used for dragging logs, chunks, stones, etc. **1881** RAYMOND *Mining Gloss.*, *Grapnel*, an implement for removing the core left by an annular drill in a bore-hole, or for recovering tools, fragments, etc., fallen into the hole.

4. *attrib.* and *Comb.*, as ***grapnel-anchor, -rope***; **grapnel-plant** = *grapple-plant* (see GRAPPLE *sb.* 6).

1706 in PHILLIPS (ed. Kersey), **Grapnel-Anchors*, a sort of Anchors..without Stocks, and having four Flooks. **1631** PELLHAM *Mirac. Preserv. Englishm. Greenland* 21 Taking up an old Harping Iron..& fastning a *Grapnell Roape unto it, out lanch't wee our Boate. **1711** W. SUTHERLAND *Shipbuild. Assist.* 133 Grapnel-rope Cabl'd. **1867** SMYTH *Sailor's Word-bk.*, *Grapnel-rope*, that which is bent to the grapnel by which a boat rides, now substituted by chain.

Hence **'grapnel** *v. trans.*, to catch or seize with a grapnel.

1890 *Pall Mall G.* 2 June 5/1 His balloon, in descending, grapnelled a tree, and he was dashed to the ground.

†**grapoud.** *Obs.*[−1] [a. OF. *grapaud*, var. of *crapaud*.] = CRAPAUD 2.

*c***1475** *Pict. Voc.* in Wr.-Wülcker 768/36 *Hec pama*, a grapoud [*printed* grapond].

grappa ('græpə). [It.] A brandy distilled from the skins, pips, and stalks of the grapes after they have been pressed for wine-making. (Cf. MARC.)

1893 in *Funk's Stand. Dict.* **1921** *Chambers's Jrnl.* 6 Aug. 575/1 We drew our bombs and our *grappa*, and soon we were whirling..to the attack. **1929** E. HEMINGWAY *Farewell to Arms* iv. 25 He poured two glasses and we touched them... The grappa was very strong. **1947** DYLAN THOMAS *Let.* 20 May (1966) 307 He was..drinking, by the gallon, grappa. **1960** C. DAY LEWIS *Buried Day* i. 25 Auden and I were sitting by the Grand Canal soaking up grappa. **1971** M. MCCARTHY *Birds of America* 247 He accepted a *grappa* on the house.

†**grappe,** *sb. Obs.* Also **grap**. [a. F. *grappe* bunch (of grapes).] A cob (of maize).

1693 SIR R. BULKLEY in *Phil. Trans.* XVII. 938 Now out of each Grain came up 3, 4, 5, or 6 Stems..every of which Stems had four, three, or two of these Grappes. *c***1700** BP. KENNETT *MS. Lansd.* 1033 (Halliwell), *Grap*, an ear of Virginia corn.

†**grappe,** *v. Obs.* [Cf. ONorthumb. pa. t. *ʒegræppde* (app. related to *grápiʒa* GROPE *v.*) 'apprehendit'; also GRIP *v.*, GRASP *v.* In the earliest instances it may be miswritten for *grap(e*, northern form of GROPE *v.*] **a.** *intr.* To feel with one's hands, to grope. **b.** *trans.* To grip, grasp.

*a***1300** *Cursor M.* 17141 Put in and grappe, mi suet freind, Tak ute mi hert bituix þine hend. **1382** WYCLIF *Deut.* xxviii. 29 Thow shalt graasp [*v.r.* grappe, **1388** grope] in myddday, as is woned a blynd man to graasp in derknissis. **1483** CAXTON *Knt. de la Tour* civ. 139 They founde a foule orible tode within her body, that grapped her herte with her pawes .. [The toad said] Whan thou herdest her confession, y was vpon her herte, and grapped it so sore with my iiij pawes.. that [etc.].

grappe, variant of GRAPE *sb.*[3]

†**'grapper.** *Obs.* Also 5-6 **graper**. [? f. OF. *grape, grappe*, hook, clamp.] A grappling-hook.

1485 *Naval Acc. Hen. VII* (1896) 50 Grapers of Iren. **1495** *Ibid.* 193 Grappers of yron with cheynes to the same. **1523** LD. BERNERS *Froiss.* I. I. 72 They had great hokes, and grapers of yron, to cast out of one shyppe into another. **1548-50** THOMAS *Ital. Dict.*, *Rampicone*, a graper or claspe of yron. **1625** J. GLANVILL *Voy. to Cadiz* 61 We fastned grappers in her, and soe towed her a head. **1676** H. MORE *Remarks* 145 Without the help of vellicles, hooks, or grappers.

grappier ('græpɪə(r), ‖grapje). [Fr., f. *grappe* (as in *grappes de la chaux*).] One of the hard lumps of unslaked material sometimes left in hydraulic lime after it has been slaked. In Comb., as **grappier cement**, cement made by grinding grappiers to a powder.

1897 *Jrnl. Soc. Chem. Ind.* XVI. 889/1 The hardest burned portions, called 'Grappiers', of the celebrated Teil hydraulic lime. **1905** E. C. ECKEL *Cements* 185 Grappier cements are made by grinding finely the lumps of unburned and overburned material which remain when a hydraulic lime is slaked. **1922** A. P. MILLS *Materials of Construction* (ed. 2) I. iv. 30 As a rule all of the grappiers are finely ground under millstones and a certain proportion is added to the lime... The ground grappiers are also separately marketed as a special cement known as grappier cement. **1970** F. M. LEA *Chem. Cement & Concrete* (ed. 3) ii. 12 Such sintered lumps are sometimes separated and form, after grinding, the French 'grappier' cement, a product closely akin to the natural cements.

grapple ('græp(ə)l), *sb.* Forms: 6-7 grap(p)ell, graple, (6 grapull), 6- grapple. [In branch I, prob. a. OF. *grapelle, dim. of *grape* hook; cf. '*grappil*, the graple of a ship' (Cotgr.; not elsewhere found). In branch II, f. the vb.]

I. An implement for grappling or laying hold.

1. = GRAPNEL 1.

1530 PALSGR. 574/1, I fasten two shyppes of warre togyther with a grappell, *jagrappe*. **1546** LANGLEY *Abridgm. Pol. Virg.* III. xi. 80 b, Anacharsis..inuented the Grapull or Tacle of a ship. **1602** J. CLAPHAM *Hist. Gt. Brit.* I. III. xix. (1606) 151 They gave an assault to the wall..and with grapples, and such like engines, pulled downe..a great part thereof. **1650** R. STAPYLTON *Strada's Low C. Warres* VIII. 8 The enemie chasing him with Grapples in their hands, that is, long poles headed with iron hooks, or hooks at the end of long ropes. **1700** DRYDEN *Fables, Cymon & Iph.* 281 But Cymon soon his crooked grapples cast, Which with tenacious hold his foes embraced. **1774** GOLDSM. *Grecian Hist.* II. 202 They likewise cast iron grapples, to throw on the enemy's works, and tear them away. **1842** ARNOLD *Hist. Rome* III. xlv. 287 The end of the lever, with an iron grapple affixed to it, was lowered upon the Roman ships. **1869** *Echo* 3 Feb., He procured grapples, and brought it [a dead body] to the bank.

transf. and *fig.* **1587** *Mirr. Mag., Rudacke* vii, Ambition out sercheth to glory the greece, The staire to estate, the graple of grace. **1658** ROWLAND *Moufet's Theat. Ins.* Ep. Ded., The petulant Crab-lice, with their grapples, wherewith they perpetually lance mans skin between the hair with their mouth, and stick on faster than Cockles do to the rocks. **1667** JER. TAYLOR *Dissuas. fr. Popery* II. I. vii. 207 The fear of the two deaths, which are the two arms and grapples of iron by which the Church of Rome takes and keeps her timorous, or conscientious, Proselytes. **1712** BLACKMORE *Creation* (1786) 68 The creeping ivy, to prevent its fall, Clings with its fib'rous grapples to the wall. **1877** *Five Yrs.' Penal Servit.* iii. 246 Anything she once put her grapples on she slipped inside.

†**2.** = GRAPNEL 2. *to be at a grapple*: to be at anchor. *Obs.*

1623 WHITBOURNE *Newfoundland* 59 Two small Boates, Anchors and a small Grapple..were found in the Sea. **1657** R. LIGON *Barbadoes* (1673) 81 A Grapple that holds the long-Boat of a Ship. **1749** F. SMITH *Voy. Disc.* II. 147 Off Sea Horse Point, where the Boat found a pretty Stream being at a Grapple. **1804** *Naval Chron.* XI. 360 Cables, or chains, to which it is fixed by means of grapples, to prevent its drifting outwards. **1807** G. CHALMERS *Caledonia* I. I. ii. 100 An iron grapple, or anchor, was discovered with one of these canoes.

†**3.** = CLAMP *sb.*[1] 1. *Obs.*

1767 MONTAGU in *Phil. Trans.* LVII. 441, I endeavoured with a..hanger to cut off a small piece of the grapple [used 'to fasten or tie the shaft' of a pillar 'to the base'].

4. a. A name given to various contrivances and implements for clutching and grasping.

1593 HOLLYBAND *Dict.*, *Agraphe*, a buckle of a girdle, a claspe, or brace, a graple. **1875** KNIGHT *Dict. Mech.*, *Grapple*, a grasping tongs, used in various shapes and for many purposes. **1884** *Ibid.* Suppl., *Grapple*, a pair of claws grasping a beam or rafter as a means of suspension of a tackle for hoisting hay in a barn, or merchandise in a warehouse.

b. 'A tool with spring jaws which are closed by striking the fish' (Knight *Dict. Mech.* Suppl. 1884).

1872 *Game Laws Maine* in *Fur, Fin & Feather* (1872) 162 No person shall be allowed to take or catch any pickerel with spears, hooks or grapples.

II. [f. the vb.] **5. a.** The action of grappling, or grappling *with*; the state of being grappled; the grip or close hold of a wrestler; a contest in which the combatants grip one another. Said also of immaterial contests.

1601 SHAKS. *Twel. N.* V. i. 59 A bawbling Vessell was he Captaine of..With which such scathfull grapple did he make, With the most noble bottome of our Fleete, That [etc.]. **1602** —— *Ham.* IV. vi. 18 In the Grapple, I boorded them. **1654** WHITLOCK *Zootomia* 306 The variety of Graples a Christian hath for time. **1671** MILTON *P.R.* IV. 567 Antæus ..oft foiled, still rose..Fresh from his fall, and fiercer grapple joined. **1701** C. WOLLEY *Jrnl. N.Y.* (1860) 55, I.. ordered him to fetch a kit full of water and discharge it at them, which immediately cool'd their courage, and loosed their grapple. **1710** STEELE *Tatler* No. 173 ¶1 The Knowledge of the Cornish Hug, as well as the Grapple. **1741-3** WESLEY *Extract of Jrnl.* (1749) 14 An hour after I had one more grapple with the enemy, who then seem'd to collect all his strength. **1814** SCOTT *Ld. of Isles* III. xxix, One beneath his grasp lies prone, In mortal grapple overthrown. **1836** J. GILBERT *Chr. Atonem.* ii. (1852) 38 The grapple of a tiger, or the more sparing resolution of the elephant. **1841** MIALL in *Nonconf.* I. 2 A final grapple with ecclesiastical tyranny. **1873** HOLLAND *A. Bonnic.* xviii. 278 Henry..in a fierce grapple with his antagonist, threw him. **1891** G. MEREDITH *One of our Conq.* III. x. 203 Presently he was at quiet grapple with her mind. **1894** CROCKETT *Raiders* 222, I ..longed to..come to grapples with a dozen Faas.

b. Applied to a friendly meeting, ? a handshake. ? *nonce-use.*

1809 MALKIN *Gil Blas* VII. vii, The burning desire of having a grapple with Phenicia.

III. 6. *attrib.* and *Comb.*, as ***grapple-closing***; **grapple-iron** = *grappling-iron* (*lit.* and *fig.*); **grapple-plant**, a South African herb, *Uncaria* (or *Harpagophytum*) *procumbens*, the fruit of which has many projecting claw-like hooks; **grapple-shot**, a projectile attached to a cable, with hinged flukes which catch in the rigging of a ship in distress; **grapple-wood**, some West Indian tree.

1851 MRS. BROWNING *Casa Guidi W.* 115 Those whom she-wolves suckle Will bite as wolves do, in the *grapple-closing Of adverse interests. **1661** BOYLE *Spring Air* II. ii. (1682) 31 For I further demand how the Funiculus comes by such hooks or *graple-irons to take fast hold. **1786** BURNS *Dream* xiii, Then heave aboard your grapple airn. **1822-4** BURCHELL *Trav.* I. 536 The beautiful *Uncaria procumbens*, or *Grapple-plant was not less abundant. **1893** J. T. BENT *Ruined Cities Mashonaland* 17 Lurking in the grass is the Grapple plant, the *Harpagophytum procumbens*. **1884** KNIGHT *Dict. Mech.* Suppl., **Grapple shot*. **1750** G. HUGHES *Barbadoes* 217 *Grapple-wood. This shrubby tree hath a reddish-grey bark.

grapple ('græp(ə)l), *v.* Also 6 grap(p)el(l, 6-9 graple. [f. the sb.; in some uses app. influenced by association with GROPE, GRIP, GRASP.]

1. *trans.* To seize or hold (a ship, etc.) with a grapnel; to fasten *to* something with grappling-irons.

1530 PALSGR. 574/1 Their shyppes were grappelled so faste togyther that one chaunce of fyre burned them bothe. **1599** HAKLUYT *Voy.* II. II. 168 The gallies were grapled to the Centurion in this maner. **1600** HOLLAND *Livy* XXVI. xxxix. (1609) 614 They closed and grappled their ships together. **1638** SIR T. HERBERT *Trav.* (ed. 2) 11 To grapple her, our fleet divided all night, but saw her not. **1647** W. BROWNE tr. *Gomberville's Polexander* I. i. 24 Iphidamantus ship..was grapled with a Turke. **1754** T. GARDNER *Hist. Dunwich* 225 A fourth Fire Ship grappled him. **1774** HUTCHINS in *Phil. Trans.* LXV. 132 A large piece of ice, to which the three ships were grappled. **1838** W. WARE *Lett. fr. Palmyra* II. xiv. 152 The bridge was in the very act of being thrown and grappled to the ramparts. **1847** GROTE *Greece* II. xlvii. (1862) IV. 198 The ships on both sides..were grappled together. **1871** MISS YONGE *Cameos* II. iv. 54 The King wished to grapple this vessel and take it.

refl. **1647** W. BROWNE tr. *Gomberville's Polexander* I. 31 He gave then his Gunners charge to shoot into the sailes, and to his Mariners to grapple themselves with the body of the ship.

†**b.** To take hold of (the bottom) with a grapple or anchor. Also, *to grapple hold*.

1583 STANYHURST *Æneis* I. (Arb.) 23 Wheere sea tost nauye remayning Needs not too grapple thee sands with flooke of an anchor. **1825** T. JEFFERSON *Autobiog.* Wks. 1859 I. 82 To throw an anchor ahead, and grapple further hold for future advances of power.

c. *fig.* or with reference to what is immaterial: To fasten as with a grapple; to attach closely and firmly.

1599 SHAKS. *Hen. V*, Prol. 18 Follow, follow: Grapple your minds to sternage of this Nauie. **1602** —— *Ham.* I. iii. 62 The friends thou hast, and their adoption tride, Grapple them to thy Soule, with hoopes of Steele. **1785** BURKE *Sp. Nabob Arcot* Wks. IV. 228 Never to be torn from thence, but with those holds that grapple it to life. **1853** MAURICE *Proph. & Kings* iv. 70 Let us grapple this faith to our inmost souls. **1887** J. HUTCHISON *Lect. Philippians* Pref. 7 Some abrupt but significant phrase at once grapples his argument upon the personal feelings of those to whom he writes.

d. To take *up* with a grapnel. *rare.*

1865 DICKENS *Mut. Fr.* III. ii, They've grappled up the body.

2. *intr.* for *refl.* To fasten oneself firmly (*to* an object) by means of a grapple. Also *fig.* (Cf. 8.)

1563 B. GOOGE *Eglogs* viii. (Arb.) 67 Death..Coms saylyng fast, in Galley blacke, and whan he spyes hym neare, Doth boorde hym strayght, and grapels fast And than begyns the fyght. **1748** F. SMITH *Voy. Disc.* I. 42 The Piece of Ice we grappled to had a Pond upon it. **1861** P. LEYS *Mem. J. Maclaren* viii. 51 Those elementary principles.. had grappled to the heart of him, and conquered it.

3. *intr.* To 'fish' *for* with a grapnel.

1799 A. BURN *Mem.* (1816) IV. 189 When we had light and time to grapple for the cable.

4. *trans.* To take hold of (a person or thing) with the hands; to seize; to grip firmly; *hence*, to come to close quarters with.

1583 STANYHURST *Æneis* III. (Arb.) 90 Of my feloes I saw that a couple he grapled. *a* **1704** T. BROWN *Sat. Antients* Wks. 1730 I. 23 As Horace is a true Proteus..they have.. grappled him as well as they could. **1719** DE FOE *Crusoe* II. xii. (1840) 247 He grappled the pagan, and dragged him by main force out of their own boat into ours. **1762** FALCONER *Shipwr.* II. 166 In vain to grapple pendent ropes they try. **1791** COWPER *Iliad* IV. 560 Man grapples man. **1830** CAPT. H. CROW *Mem.* 233 Uttering a loud yell of triumph, [they] grappled the poor fellow as their prisoner of war. **1834** PRINGLE *Afr. Sk.* viii. 275 Grappling its antagonist by the throat with its fore-paws. **1865** KINGSLEY *Herew.* v. 114 Whoever she grappled she would never let go. **1898** A. H. S. LANDOR *Forbidden Land* II. lxxxii. 131 The soldiers.. grappling me, and lifting me bodily off my feet.

fig. **1854** J. S. C. ABBOTT *Napoleon* (1855) II. xxxiii. 613 The profundity of his doctrine, which grapples the mightiest difficulties. **1894** C. N. ROBINSON *Brit. Fleet* 71 With the same purpose did the Dutchmen (1594-7) grapple the icy perils of the North-East Passage.

b. To snatch *up*. *rare.*

1775 ADAIR *Amer. Ind.* 111 They fly about to grapple up a kind of chalky clay, to paint themselves white.

c. *poet.* To fasten in the grip of irons. *rare.*

1833 MRS. BROWNING *Prometh. Bound* Poems I. 142 Here's an arm at least Grappled past freeing.

5. *intr.* To take a firm hold, as with a grapple, esp. in wrestling; to get a tight grip of another; to contend with another in close fight. Also with *together*. (Cf. 8 b.)

1583 STANYHURST *Æneis* II. (Arb.) 58 With righthands grapling thee tops of turret ar holden. **1596** SPENSER *F.Q.* IV. iv. 29 As two wild boares together grapling go. *a* **1611** BEAUM. & FL. *Maid's Trag.* v. ii, Your Grace and I Must grapple vpon euen tearmes no more. **1644** MILTON *Educ.* Wks. 1738 I. 139 To tug or grapple, and to close. **1700** DRYDEN *Pal. & Arc.* III. 57 Greyhounds,..A match for pards in flight, in grappling for the bear. **1709** STEELE & SWIFT *Tatler* No. 70 ¶10 A large French Mongrel..when he grapples, bites even to the Marrow. **1825** J. NEAL *Bro. Jonathan* I. 271 They drew up—made play..grappled anew. **1858** DORAN *Crt. Fools* 338 They grappled and commenced wrestling.

fig. **1644** MILTON *Areop.* (Arb.) 74 Let her [Truth] and Falshood grapple.

6. To make movements with the hands, as if to grasp some object: to grope. Const. *after, at, for, to.* Also with *about* adv. *rare.* (? *Obs.*)

1596 LODGE *Marg. Amer.* 137 He grapled about the floore among the dead bodies. **1742** YOUNG *Nt. Th.* IV. 349 Is praise the perquisite of ev'ry paw, Tho' black as hell, that grapples well for gold? **1766** H. BROOKE *Fool of Quality* (1809) III. 126, I kept aloof, however, for fear he should grapple at me, and sink us both together. **1810** SCOTT *Lady of L.* VI. iv, Fierce was their speech, and, 'mid their words, Their hands oft grappled to their swords. **1815** *He must be married* II. ii, Modesty! is it that you would be grappling after?

†**b.** To mount *up* by clutching or grasping.

1598 GRENEWEY *Tacitus' Ann.* I. xiv. (1622) 27 They.. grappled vp to the toppe of the trench [L. *summa valli prensant*].

7. *Manège* (see quot.).

1727 BAILEY vol. II, To *Grapple* [with Horsemen] is when a Horse lifts up one or both his Legs at once, and raises them with Precipitation, as if he were a curveting. **1727-41** in CHAMBERS *Cycl.*

8. grapple with ——.

a. *Naut.* To make one's ship fast to (an enemy) with grappling-irons; to come to close quarters with.

1632 J. HAYWARD tr. *Biondi's Eromena* 61 Metaneone.. hastened to grapple with the Galley. **1687** A. LOVELL *Thevenot's Trav.* I. 283 Laid us on board, and grappled with us on the Starboard side. **1759** HUME *Hist. Eng.* (1806) IV. lxv. 808 He sunk three fire-ships, which endeavoured to grapple with him. **1783** WATSON *Phillip III* (1839) 71 As the Dutch..could navigate their ships with greater dexterity, they were enabled to avoid grappling with the Spaniards. **1868** E. EDWARDS *Raleigh* I. vii. 111 To advise the..Admiral ..to grapple with the enemy's ships and board them.

b. To grip as in wrestling; to seize with hands and arms; to close with bodily.

1624 CAPT. SMITH *Virginia* III. x. 84 The President prevented his shoot by grapling with him. **1711** ADDISON *Spect.* No. 13 ¶3 He would fall at the first Touch of Hydaspes, without grappling with him. **1801** SOUTHEY *Thalaba* v. xl, The undefended youth Sprung forward.. And grappled with him breast to breast. **1870** E. PEACOCK *Ralf Skirl.* III. 253 Some one was grappling with Milo [a bloodhound]. **1880** HARTING *Extinct Brit. Anim.* I. 19 As the animal rose to grapple with the dogs. **1883** FROUDE *Short Stud.* IV. I. x. 124 He grappled with Tracy and flung him to the ground.

c. To encounter hand to hand; to battle or struggle with.

1593 SHAKS. *2 Hen. VI*, I. i. 257 Then will I..in my Standard beare the Armes of Yorke, To grapple with the house of Lancaster. **1648** GAGE *West Ind.* xviii. 129 Some of them fear not to encounter..and to graple in the rivers.. with Crocodiles. **1850** SCORESBY *Cheever's Whalem. Adv.* xi. (1859) 147, I..saw with horror one of our men..grappling with the waves. **1867** FREEMAN *Norm. Conq.* (1876) I. v. 288 The valiant burghers had already learned to grapple with the Dane on his own element.

d. *fig.* or with reference to immaterial things.

1631 R. H. *Arraignm. Whole Creature* xiii. §1. 168 We will come (as in a Land, or Sea-fight) to grapple and gripe, with Vanities. *a* **1688** BUNYAN *Dying Sayings* (1767) I. 48 Who can grapple with the wrath of God? **1748** *Anson's Voy.* III. viii. 374 This is usually a power too mighty for reason to grapple with. **1807** WORDSW. *Wh. Doe Rylstone* II. 150, I.. Presumed to grapple with their scorn.

e. *esp.* To try to overcome (a difficulty, etc.); to try to accomplish, take in hand (a task, etc.); to try to deal with (a question, etc.); to try to solve (a problem, etc.).

1830 J. W. CROKER in *C. Papers* 10 May, He did not at all grapple with the real question. **1851** D. WILSON *Preh. Ann.* (1863) I. ii. 51 Science grapples with such startling phenomena. **1865** W. PENGELLY in H. Pengelly *Life* xi. (1897) 170, I am glad to find you are grappling with the question. **1888** BRYCE *Amer. Commw.* II. xxxvi. 3 The new historical school..will doubtless grapple with this task.

Hence '**grappling** *ppl. a.*

1666 DRYDEN *Ann. Mirab.* lxxxiv, Two grappling Ætna's on the ocean meet And English fires with Belgian flames contend. **1705** ADDISON *Italy* 307 Antæus here and stern Alcides strive, And both the grappling Statues seem to live. **1814** CARY *Dante, Par.* XXVI. 54 All grappling bonds, that knit the heart to God, Confederate to make fast our charity.

†'**grapplement.** *Obs. rare*$^{-1}$. [f. GRAPPLE *v.* + -MENT.] A grappling, a close grasp in fighting.

1590 SPENSER *F.Q.* II. xi. 29 Downe him stayd With their rude handes and gryesly graplement.

grappler ('græplə(r)). [f. GRAPPLE *v.* + -ER[1].] One who or that which grapples: **a.** a grappling-iron, a grapnel; **b.** one who grapples or grapples *with* (an object); **c.** (see quot.); **d.** *slang*, a hand.

a. **1628** LE GRYS tr. *Barclay's Argenis* 251 By casting..[a] grappler upon the wall, which presently laid hold on the stones. **1830** S. WARREN *Diary Physic.* (1832) I. xvi. 380 The grapplers, with ropes attached to them, were then fixed in the sides. **1897** *Daily News* 17 May 6/7 He gently lowered the grappler and swung it to and fro to try and catch the clothing of the body.

b. **1832** L. HUNT *Translations* Poems 249 Atlas, grappler of the stars. **1865** MRS. WHITNEY *Gayworthys* xxvii. (1879) 276 Grappler as he was with realities.
c. **1838** *Penny Cycl.* XI. 87/1 A [gas] retort..was emptied by a sort of grated iron or basket, called a grappler.
d. **1852** HAZEL *Yankee Jack* ii. 9 'Give us your grappler on that, old fellow!' said Paul,..seizing the merchant's hand.

grappling ('græplɪŋ), *vbl. sb.* In sense 3 corruptly **graplin, grap-line.** [f. GRAPPLE *v.* + -ING[1].]

1. The action of the vb. GRAPPLE.

1601 CORNWALLYES *Ess.* x, To lay hold at the grappeling of ships until the losse of both hands, and then to hold by the teeth. **1607** HIERON *Wks.* I. 225 To beare the shock and brunt of the first grapling. **1748** F. SMITH *Voy. Disc.* I. 42 It becoming, soon after the Ship's grappling, a close Body of Ice. **1894** H. NISBET *Bush Girl's Rom.* 238 The different stages [in an illness] of mad fury, savage grappling, abject terror [etc.].

†**2.** A place where one may grapple a vessel. Also *to come, bring to a grappling*: to come to anchor (cf. GRAPNEL 2). *Obs.*

1712 W. ROGERS *Voy.* 166 We rowed till 12 at Night, judg'd it High Water, and came to a Graplin. **1740** WHITEFIELD in *Life & Lett.* (1756) 330 The wind being high and contrary we were obliged to come to a Grapling, near an open Reach. **1772–84** COOK *Voy.* (1790) I. 21 The long-boat having filled with water, they had brought her to a grapling, and quitted her. *Ibid.* V. 1680 Two others were ordered out, to fish at a grappling near the shore.

3. *concr.* **a.** A grappling-iron; = GRAPPLE *sb.* 1. In first quot. *collect.* = implements for grappling.

1598 BARRET *Theor. Warres* 134 The iron workes, cables anchors and grappling. **1626** CAPT. SMITH *Accid. Yng. Sea-men* 19 Boord him on his weather quarter, lash fast your graplins. **1718** ROWE tr. *Lucan* 82 The crooked Grappling's steely Hold they cast. **1719** DE FOE *Crusoe* I. x. 163, I had made me a kind of an Anchor; with a piece of a broken graplin. **1875** BEDFORD *Sailor's Pocket Bk.* vi. (ed. 2) 228 A grappling..should be kept handy in the bows of the boat. *fig.* **1887** HALL CAINE *Deemster* xxvii. 170 'We're rael sorry, and we know your heart was gript to him with grapplins'.

b. = GRAPNEL 2, GRAPPLE 2.

1626 CAPT. SMITH *Accid. Yng. Sea-men* 16 The streame Anchor, graplings or kedgers. **1676** T. GLOVER in *Phil. Trans.* XI. 625 The sloop-man dropped his grap-line. **1725** DE FOE *Voy. Round World* (1840) 116 They hove over their grappling in five fathom water. **1793** SMEATON *Edystone L.* §149 The yawl's grappling got so fast among the rocks, that it could not be weighed. **1808** A. PARSONS *Trav.* viii. 168 Boats..with two anchors or graplins to each boat. **1833** M. SCOTT *Tom Cringle* xv. (1859) 381 Stand by with the grapplings.

4. *attrib.* and *Comb.*, as ***grappling-engine, -instrument***, etc.; **grappling-hook, -iron** = GRAPNEL.

1618 BOLTON *Florus* (1636) 77 The hands of yron, and other the *grappling engine of the Romans, the enemy made much sport at. **1622** DRAYTON *Poly-olb.* xix. (1748) 334 In hulks with *grapling hooks to hunt the dreadful whale. **1625** HEYLIN *Cosmogr. America* (ed. 2) 783 We are indebted..for grapling-hookes to Anacharsis. **1660** BOYLE *New Exp. Phys. Mech.* xxxiii. 245 Hooks, or other *grappling Instruments. **1538** ELYOT *Dict.*, *Harpa*, a *grapelyng yron, for to close shyppes togyther. **1766** H. BROOKE *Fool of Quality* (1809) IV. 139 The grappling-iron of a corsair. **1828** SCOTT *F.M. Perth* vii, The Red Rover, casting out grappling irons.. jumped on the deck. **1845** JAMES *A. Neil* II. i, Hand me that grappling iron, my man.

grapse, obs. form of GRASP *v.*

grapsoid ('græpsɔɪd), *a.* [f. mod.L. *graps-us* + -OID.] Of or pertaining to the genus of crabs denominated *Grapsus*, or the family *Grapsidæ*.

1852 DANA *Crust.* I. 48 There are Cancroidea that approach the Grapsoid species in the distant eyes. **1934** *Nature* 29 Sept. 500/1 Species of cancroid, grapsoid and spider crabs in the Gulf of California. **1941** [see AUTOTOMY].

So **grap'soidian** *a.* and *sb.*

1838 *Penny Cycl.* XI. 359/2 *Grapsoidians*, a natural group of brachyurous crustaceans.

graptolite ('græptəlaɪt). *Palæont.* [f. Gr. γραπτό-ς painted or marked with letters + -LITE; in sense 1 ad. mod.L. *graptolithus* (Linnæus).]

†**1.** Any stone exhibiting a resemblance to a drawing. *Obs.*

1838 *Penny Cycl.* XI. 363/1 The Florentine, or ruin marble, the dendritical ramifications on many limestones, and the moss-like forms in agates, &c., were ranked [by Linnæus] as Graptolites. **1847** in CRAIG.

2. A fossil zoophyte of the genus *Graptolites* (or *Graptolithus*) or of the family of which this genus is the type.

(The graptolites are known from their impressions on the surface of hard shales, resembling markings with a slate pencil. Some suggest the form of a quill pen.)

1841 *Trans. Geol. Soc.* Ser. II. (1842) VI. 558 Graptolites were found at Robleston..in calcareous shales. **1872** NICHOLSON *Palæont.* 11 If the Graptolites belong to certain genera, we may be sure that we are dealing with lower Silurian Rocks.

Comb. **1863** A. C. RAMSAY *Phys. Geog.* vi. (1878) 83 The graptolite-bearing mud.

Hence **grapto'litic** *a.*, of or pertaining to graptolites; containing graptolites.

1843 PORTLOCK *Geol.* 231 Another graptolitic bed in Fermanagh. **1849** MURCHISON *Siluria* v. 96 The supposed fucoids..belong to graptolitic or other zoophytes. **1880** RAMSAY in *Times* 26 Aug. 5/3 The Lower Silurian graptolitic rocks at Corswall Point in Wigtonshire.

graptoloid ('græptəlɔɪd), *a.* [f. GRAPTOL-ITE + -OID.] Resembling a graptolite; belonging to the division *Graptoloidea* of hydroids.

1872 W. S. SYMONDS *Rec. Rocks* v. 143 He thought these branched, plant-like bodies would prove eventually to be graptoloid animals.

graptomancy ('græptəmænsɪ). *rare*[−1]. [f. Gr. γραπτό-ς written + μαντεία divination. Cf. BIBLIOMANCY.] Divination by handwriting.

1818–60 WHATELY *Commpl. Bk.* (1864) 187 To convince those who deride graptomancy..that there must be something in it.

grapull, obs. form of GRAPPLE *sb.*

grapy ('greɪpɪ), *a.* Also **grapey.** [f. GRAPE *sb.*[1] + -Y[1].]

1. Of or pertaining to grapes or to the vine; composed or savouring of grapes.

1594 PLAT *Jewell-ho.* II. 15 That little acquaintance which I haue had with the grapie God. **1633** P. FLETCHER *Purple Isl.* VII. lxxiii, His soul quite sousèd lay in grapy blood. **1717** ADDISON *Ovid, Metam.* III. 800 The grapy clusters spread On his fair brows. **1717** GAY *Ovid, Metam.* IX. 198 And on the marble altar's polish'd frame Pours forth the grapy stream. **1837** *Fraser's Mag.* XVI. 162 'Surely', said the corks, 'we have been acquainted before?' 'Unquestionably', answered the wine, with a grapy kiss, 'we have'. **1863** B. TAYLOR *H. Thurston* I. 70 Neither of these gentlemen possessed a particle of the grapy bloom in either cell of the double heart. **1962** *Harper's Bazaar* Aug. 33 The plummy, grapey tones of the harvest. **1968** *Daily Tel.* 17 Dec. 13 There is nothing astringent about it [*sc.* a variety of Madeira]—it is always 'grapey'.

†**2.** As the epithet of the CHOROID coat of the eye. (Cf. UVEA.) *Obs.*

1398 TREVISA *Barth. De P.R.* v. v. (Tollem. MS.), Aftyr þis foloweþ þe curtel þat is called 'uvea', grapi, and haþ þat name for he is liche in coloure to a blak grape. **1615** H. CROOKE *Body of Man* 671 The grapy membrane which is diuersly coloured would be seene. **1696** J. EDWARDS *Demonstr. Exist. God* II. 30 The anterior part only is that which should be call'd grapy. It is generally black in man, and therefore hath the name because it resembles the skin of a black grape when 'tis press'd.

3. Affected with 'grapes' (see GRAPE *sb.* 5).

1838 *Penny Cycl.* XII. 313/1 The grapy heels are a disgrace to the stable in which they are found.

4. *Comb.*, as ***grapy-blue*** adj.

1825 J. NEAL *Bro. Jonathan* III. 313 The stupid little half open eyes were of that strange, dull, grapy blue colour, common to beast or baby.

gras(e, obs. form of GRACE, GRASS, GRAZE.

grasett, variant of GRAZET(T.

†**grash,** *sb. Obs. rare*[−1]. [f. the vb. Cf. CRASH *sb.*[3]] A bout or attack.

a **1610** BABINGTON *Comf. Notes Num.* xxxi. Wks. (1615) II. 181 Miserable man whom a little Flea can vex, whom one grash of an Ague can pluck downe.

†**grash,** *v. Obs.* [Onomatopœic. Cf. GNASH *v.*, CRASH *v.* 3.] *trans.* and *intr.* = GNASH *v.*

1563 *Mirr. Mag., Collingbourne* xviii, Here Tyraunt Rychard played the eager Hog, His grashyng tuskes my tender grystels shore: His bloudhound Lovell playd the ravenyng Dog. **1570** T. PRESTON *Lament. fr. Rome* etc. in Collier *Old Ball.* (Percy Soc.) 71 Poll nose, rube eye Grash the teth, drawe mouth awrye. **1577** KENDALL *Trifles* 7 No chillyng cold, no scaldyng heate, No grashyng chaps of monsters greate. **1607** TOPSELL *Four-f. Beasts* 126 The Serpent seeing her aduersary lifteth her necke aboue the ground, and grasheth at the Hart with her teeth.

grashop, variant of GRASSHOP, *Obs.*

grasier, -or, obs. forms of GRAZIER.

grasle, variant of GRASSIL, *Sc. Obs.*

grasoune, variant of GERSUM, *Obs.*

1640 *Bk. War Committee Covenanters* 16 My Lady Kenmure's dewties, grasounes and uthers.

grasp (grɑːsp, -æ-), *sb.* Also 6–7 **graspe.** [f. the vb.]

1. That which is fitted to grasp or clutch, or to be grasped or clutched; the fluke of an anchor, a handle. Now only *Naut.* the handle of an oar.

1561 EDEN *Arte Nauig.* A iij b, The *Thirreni* founde the vse of the anker of one graspe or flooke. **1600** SURFLET *Countrie Farme* II. lxxi. 421 Two boords..in the midst.. made fast to a little sticke or woodden pin in manner of a graspe, by which one may handle them. **1883** in CLARK RUSSELL *Sailors' Lang.*

2. The action of grasping; a gripping or fast hold; the grip of the hand; †an embrace.

1606 SHAKS. *Tr. & Cr.* IV. ii. 13 Beshrew the witch! with venomous wights she stayes..but flies the graspes of loue. **1690** DRYDEN *Don Sebastian* III. (1692) 46 This hand and this [sword] have been acquainted well; It shou'd have come before into my grasp, To kill the Ravisher. **1752** YOUNG *Brothers* IV. i. Wks. 1757 II. 272 Stubborn is the grasp of dying men. **1800** SOUTHEY *Thalaba* III. xxxii, From his [a bird's] relaxing grasp a Locust fell. **1855** TENNYSON *Maud* I. xiii. ii, I long'd..To give him the grasp of fellowship. **1855** BAIN *Senses & Int.* II. i. §7 (1864) 85 The grasp of the hand is the result of an extensive muscular endowment. **1884** M. MACKENZIE *Dis. Throat & Nose* II. 206 His power of grasp with the left hand was..less than normal.

transf. **1869** BOUTELL *Arms & Arm.* i. 5 The shaft with the arrow-head within its grasp was bound round with bands.

†**b.** *fig.* with allusion to wrestling. *to come to (the) grasp*: to come to close quarters. *Obs.*

c **1583** BURLEIGH *Adv. to Eliz.* in *Harl. Misc.* (1811) VII. 62 As King of Spain, without the Low Countries he may trouble our skirts of Ireland, but never come to grasp with you. **1589** *Pappe w. Hatchet* (1844) 17, I would it were come to the grasp, we would show them an Irish tricke. **1590** NASHE *Pasquil's Apol.* I. B iv b, I looke for scholasticall graspes, and aunswers to so graue and weightie arguments.

c. ***within*** *(one's)* ***grasp***: close enough to admit of being grasped. Similarly ***ready to one's grasp. beyond one's grasp***: out of one's reach. Chiefly *fig.*

a **1674** CLARENDON *Hist. Reb.* VIII. §84 They looked upon it [York] as their own, and had it even within their grasp. **1803** J. BRISTED *Tour Highlands* I. 296 No inducement could prevail upon me to trust myself within the grasp of this amorous Bacchante. **1831** DE QUINCEY *Parr* Wks. (1890) V. 15 Had volume the second of that same folio with which he [Dr. Johnson] floored Osborne happened to lie ready to the prostrate man's grasp, nobody can suppose [etc.]. **1871** FREEMAN *Norm. Conq.* (1876) IV. xvii. 27 He was restoring lands most of which were quite beyond his grasp.

3. *fig.* **a.** Firm hold or control; possession, mastery.

1605 SHAKS. *Macb.* IV. iii. 36, I would not be the Vilaine that thou think'st, For the whole Space that's in the Tyrants Graspe. **1634** MILTON *Comus* 357 Within the direful grasp Of savage hunger, or of savage heat. **1699** POMFRET *Love Triumph. over Reason* 55 I'll not see my charge..Into the grasp of any ruin run. **1811** W. R. SPENCER *Poems* 33 In the grasp of death. **1849** MACAULAY *Hist. Eng.* v. I. 619 He was in the grasp of one who never forgave. *a* **1852** WEBSTER *Wks.* (1877) IV. 133 To rescue liberty from the grasp of executive power. **1875** BRYCE *Holy Rom. Emp.* xiv. (ed. 5) 225 Albert I tried in vain to wrest the tolls of the Rhine from the grasp of the Rhenish electors.

b. Intellectual hold; *esp.* comprehensive mastery of the whole of a subject; hence, mental comprehensiveness.

1683 TEMPLE *Mem.* Wks. 1731 I. 474 The Prince and Pensioner, who alone had so full a Grasp of the Business in Holland, as to [etc.]. **1713** BERKELEY *Guardian* No. 70 ¶7 It is too big for the grasp of a human intellect. **1817** CHALMERS *Astron. Disc.* i. (1852) 39 Though His mind takes into its comprehensive grasp, immensity and all its wonders. **1830** COLERIDGE *Table-t.* 11 May, Those enormously prolix harangues are a proof of weakness in the higher intellectual grasp. **1867** A. BARRY *Sir C. Barry* i. 13 Gaining a thorough grasp of his art. **1875** E. WHITE *Life in Christ* I. i. (1878) 7 In health the mind is strong, in sickness it loses its energy and grasp. **1878** R. W. DALE *Lect. Preach.* i. (ed. 2) 15 We think we have a grasp of new truth. **1884** M. CREIGHTON in *Contemp. Rev.* XLVI. 144 No historian has ever had so large a grasp as Ranke of the fundamental principles of history. **1889** RUSKIN *Præterita* III. 19 A succession of men of immense mental grasp.

†**4.** Twilight. [? Another word; cf. GRISPING, GROPSING.]

1650 USSHER *Annals* Age vi. (1658) 296 And then, removing his Camp without any noise, in the grasp of the evening, encamped upon the bank of the River Nile.

5. *Comb.*: **grasp-hold,** hold for the grasp.

1851 SIR F. PALGRAVE *Norm. & Eng.* I. 619 Some branch which might furnish grasphold for his hands.

grasp (grɑːsp, -æ-), *v.* Forms: 4 **graasp,** (5 **craspe, grapse),** 4–7 **graspe,** 4– **grasp.** [ME. *graspen*, metathesis of *grapsen*, perh. repr. OE. **græpsan*:—OTeut. type **graipisôn*, f. **graip-* GROPE *v.* Cf. LG., EFris. *grapsen* to grasp, snatch, *graps* a grasp.

With the rare form *craspe* (sense 1), perhaps a distinct word, cf. ON. *krafsa*, 'to paw or scratch with the feet' (Vigf.).]

†**1.** *intr.* To make clutches with the hand. Often used as synonymous with GROPE. Often with *after, to, towards, upon, with. Obs.* exc. as in b.

1382 WYCLIF *Deut.* xxviii. 29 Thou shalt graasp [**1388** grope] in myddai, as is woned a blynd man to graasp in derknissis. **1398** TREVISA *Barth. De P.R.* VII. xx. (1495) 237 The blynde puttyth forth the honde all abowte gropyng and graspynge. **1415** HOCCLEVE *To Sir J. Oldcastle* 347 O! wher-to graspen yee so fer, and grope After swich thyng. *a* **1420** —— *De Reg. Princ.* 212 Þou graspist [*v.r.* grapsest] heer & þere, as doþ þe blynde. *c* **1440** *Bone Flor.* 678 Owt of ther sadyls they felle besyde, And graspyd to odur gere. *c* **1450** *Merlin* 649 Than he began to craspe after his arme, for to take from hym his swerde out of his honde. **1593** SHAKS. *2 Hen. VI*, III. ii. 172 His hands abroad display'd as one that graspt And tugg'd for Life, and was by strength subdude. **1814** *Sorceress* I. iii, Why do you shake and grasp upon me so? **1828** SCOTT *F.M. Perth* ii, His irritated opponent.. grasped towards his own side, as if seeking a sword or dagger.

fig. **1742** YOUNG *Nt. Th.* VII. 2042 This, this is thinking free, a thought that grasps Beyond a grain, and looks beyond an hour.

b. *to grasp at*: to make a clutch at, to try to seize. Chiefly with immaterial obj. or *fig.* Also, To accept with avidity (an offer, etc.).

1677 [see GRASPING *vbl. sb.*]. *a* **1698** TEMPLE *Ess. Constit. & Int. Empire* Wks. 1731 I. 87 No Monarchy having ever grasped at so great an Empire there. **1718** PRIOR *Solomon* I. 741 Alas! we grasp at Clouds, and beat the Air, Vexing that spirit we intend to clear. **1755** J. MCLAURIN *Serm. & Ess.* 25 Covetousness often loses what it has by grasping at more. **1781** COWPER *Progr. Error* 22 Like quicksilver, the rhetoric they display, Shines as it runs, but, grasped at, slips away. **1840** THIRLWALL *Greece* VII. lviii. 267 Teutames grasped at their offers. **1849** MACAULAY *Hist. Eng.* vii. II. 252 There was little doubt that..by grasping at too much, the government would lose all. **1850** W. IRVING *Goldsm.* iii. 54, I readily grasped at his proposal. **1859** TENNYSON *Enid* 1573

Geraint..grasping at his sword. **1868** HELPS *Realmah* xvi. (1869) 441 Recovering himself he grasped at the balcony. **1898** J. CAIRD *Univ. Addr.* 7 Grasping at a premature and false simplicity.

transf. **1850** TENNYSON *In Mem.* ii, Old Yew, which graspest at the stones That name the under-lying dead.

†**c.** To make the motion of embracing or encircling something with the arms; to grapple *with.*

a **1586** SIDNEY *Arcadia* III. (1590) 269 Nisus grasping with Amphialus, was with a short dagger slaine. *Ibid.* 293 b, Argalus..ranne in to graspe with him, and so [they] closed together. **1613–16** W. BROWNE *Brit. Past.* II. i, Some villaine's outrage..Might graspe with her. **1647** W. BROWNE tr. *Gomberville's Polexander* III. 136, I cannot conceive through what urgency so many unfortunate people should be compell'd hither to graspe with death. **1766** H. BROOKE *Fool of Quality* (1809) IV. 157 She now grasped about his neck, half-smothering him with the repetition of her kisses and caresses.

2. *trans.* To clutch at; to seize greedily.

1642 DENHAM *Cooper's H.* 18 Kings, by grasping more than they can hold, First made their Subjects, by oppression, bold. **1656–9** B. HARRIS *Parival's Iron Age* (ed. 2) 92 He who grasps much, holds little.

Proverb. **1855** H. G. BOHN *Coll. Eng. Prov.* 99 Grasp no more than thy hand will hold. *Ibid.* 365 Grasp all, lose all.

absol. *a* **1700** DRYDEN (J.), Like a miser 'midst his store, Who grasps and grasps 'till he can hold no more. **1844** THIRLWALL *Greece* VIII. lxii. 147 He was..willing to let his friends grasp and enjoy as they were able.

3. To seize and hold firmly with the hand. *to grasp the nettle*: *fig.* to attack a difficulty boldly.

a **1586** SIDNEY *Arcadia* II. (1590) 199 b, O foole that I am, that thought I coulde graspe water and binde the winde. **1593** SHAKS. *2 Hen. VI*, V. i. 97 Thy Hand is made to graspe a Palmers staffe. **1602** MARSTON *Antonio's Rev.* IV. iii. Wks. 1856 I. 126 She graspt my hand, And kissing it, spake thus. **1638** SIR T. HERBERT *Trav.* (ed. 2) 83 Curroon (longing to graspe the Diadem) commands [him] to begin the fight. **1687** A. LOVELL *Thevenot's Trav.* I. 124 A fruit like Oranges, but so big, that one cannot grasp them with both hands. **1708** E. SMITH *Phædra & Hipp.* II. (1709) 20 Now he devours her with his eager Eyes, Now grasps her Hands. **1782** COWPER *Gilpin* 91 He grasp'd the mane with both his hands, And eke with all his might. **1816** J. SMITH *Panorama Sci. & Art* II. 286 If two..silver spoons, be grasped one in each hand [etc.]. **1860** TYNDALL *Glac.* I. iii. 29 He stretched forth his right hand, which I grasped firmly in mine. **1884** SIR S. ST. JOHN *Hayti* Introd. 10 It was hoped..that, grasping the nettle with resolution, he might suffer no evil results.

b. *fig.* or in immaterial sense. (See also 6.)

1602 MARSTON *Antonio's Rev.* III. i. Wks. 1856 I. 106 Graspe the sterne bended front Of frowning vengeance with unpaized clutch. **1612–16** W. BROWNE *Brit. Past.* II. i, She [Hagar] chose (apart) to graspe one death, alone, Rather than by her babe a million. **1782** COWPER *Retirement* 756 We ..grasp seeming happiness, and find it pain. **1833** I. TAYLOR *Fanat.* vi. 204 The anguish that grasps the heart of his judge! **1875** JOWETT *Plato* (ed. 2) IV. 86 Like wrestlers, let us approach and grasp this new argument. **1878** R. W. DALE *Lect. Preach.* vi. (ed. 2) 167 Grasp your thoughts firmly and let your sentences take their chance.

†**4.** To clasp in the arms, embrace; also with *in. to grasp up* (transf.): to hem in. *Obs.*

1606 SHAKS. *Tr. & Cr.* III. iii. 168 A fashionable Hoste, That slightly shakes his parting Guest by th' hand; And with his armes out-stretcht, as he would flye, Graspes in the commer. **1657** W. DILLINGHAM *Comm. Sir F. Vere* Ep. Rdr., With three times that number he had grasped up the Prince and his men against the sea-shore. **1684**? DRYDEN in *Miscell.* I. 204 The City Dame..to her Country-house retires, Where she may bribe, then grasp some brawny clown, Or her appointed Gallant come To feed her loose desires. **1766** H. BROOKE *Fool of Quality* (1809) IV. 142 Seating her fondly on his knee, and grasping her to his bosom.

5. To hold firmly as with the fingers; to grip.

1774 GOLDSM. *Nat. Hist.* (1776) IV. 261 It sometimes happens that the object is too large for the [elephant's] trunk to grasp. **1799** *Med. Jrnl.* II. 246 The fimbriæ..are gradually expanding themselves, so as to grasp and completely enclose the ovaria. **1851** CARPENTER *Man. Phys.* (ed. 2) 513 The operation of grasping and swallowing the food..is accomplished through the agency of the Nervous system. **1871** B. STEWART *Heat* §83 The tire is put on hot.. on its contraction in cooling, it grasps the wheel with great force.

6. To lay hold of with the mind; to become completely cognizant of or acquainted with; to comprehend.

1680 H. MORE *Apocal. Apoc.* 3 The Eternal Iehovah, who graspeth all past, present, and to come in the eternity of His Wisdom and Power. **1720** WATERLAND *Eight Serm.* 85 In one comprehensive View grasping the whole System. **1781** V. KNOX *Liberal Educ.* xi. 108 The memory will grasp and retain all that is sufficient for the purposes of valuable improvement. **1835** I. TAYLOR *Spir. Despot.* iii. 94 The one party did not grasp the immortal destinies of the other. **1837–8** SIR W. HAMILTON *Logic* vii. (1860) I. 120 Conception..expresses the act of comprehending or grasping up into unity the various qualities by which an object is characterised. **1875** JOWETT *Plato* (ed. 2) III. 367 Philosophers only are able to grasp the eternal and unchangeable. **1881** BESANT & RICE *Chapl. of Fleet* I. viii. (1883) 62 Kitty only imperfectly grasped the rudiments of the science.

Hence **grasped** *ppl. a.* Also ***grasped-at.***

1814 *Apostate* III. iii, With grasped dagger and blanch'd quiv'ring lip. **1889** *Spectator* 14 Dec. 829 A much-desired and eagerly grasped-at excuse.

graspable (ˈgrɑːspəb(ə)l, -æ-), *a.* [f. GRASP *v.* + -ABLE.] That may be grasped.

1818 KEATS *Endym.* II. 673 His every sense had grown Ethereal for pleasure; 'bove his head Flew a delight, half graspable. **1868** BROWNING *Ring & Bk.* I. 1275 While life was graspable and gainable. **1887** E. GURNEY *Tertium Quid* II. 60 Short and graspable pieces of musical combination.

grasp-all. *nonce-wd.* [obj. comb. f. GRASP *v.*] One who clutches at everything, a greedy person.

1802 MRS. JANE WEST *Infidel Father* I. 256 The latter have long possessed a prescriptive right to the titles of epicures and graspalls.

grasper (ˈgrɑːspə(r), -æ-). [f. GRASP *v.* + -ER[1].]

†**1.** A grappling-iron. *Obs.* (Cf. GRASPLE.)

1553 BRENDE *Q. Curtius* IV. 40 The bandes and graspers wherwith yᵉ galaies were fastened together.

2. One who grasps (*at*); a grasping person.

1601 Q. ELIZ. *Sp. to last Parl.* 2, I neuer was any greedy scraping grasper. **1632** SHERWOOD, A grasper, *grippeur.* **1736** AINSWORTH *Eng.-Lat. Dict.* s.v., A grasper at, *qui aliquid captat.* **1755** JOHNSON, *Grasper*, one that grasps, seizes, or catches at. **1851** MAYHEW *Lond. Labour* (1861) II. 233 When it is not followed by a like diminution in the selling price of the article, and the wages of which the men are mulct go to increase the profits of the capitalist, the employer alone is benefited, and is then known as a 'grasper'. **1895** R. BLATCHFORD *Merrie Eng.* xv. 116 The great bulk of our graspers and grubbers value money for what it will bring.

graspeys, variant of GRAPEYS, *Obs.*

grasping (ˈgrɑːspɪŋ, -æ-), *vbl. sb.* [f. GRASP *v.* + -ING[1].] The action of the vb. GRASP.

1546 J. HEYWOOD *Prov.* (1867) 80 Gredy graspyng gat it. **1647** SANDERSON *Serm.* II. 215 Ambitious spirits, who, for the grasping of a vast and unjust power..have [etc.]. **1647** CLARENDON *Hist. Reb.* IV. §239 The grasping of the militia of the kingdom into their own hands..was..desired the Summer before. **1677** GILPIN *Demonol.* (1867) 408 They lick themselves whole by an overforward grasping at such passages of Scripture. **1841** EMERSON *Lect.*, *Man Reformer* Wks. (Bohn) II. 247 Let the amelioration in our laws of property proceed from the concession of the rich, not from the grasping of the poor. **1864** BURTON *Scot. Abr.* I. ii. 99 The history of almost every man's rise in the world consists of a succession of graspings and holdings.

attrib. **1876** *Clinical Soc.* IX. 146 The hand had regained ordinary grasping power.

grasping (ˈgrɑːspɪŋ, -æ-), *ppl. a.* [-ING[2].]

1. That grasps, in senses of the vb.; tenacious.

1577 KENDALL *Flowers Epigr.* 93 b, And lastly deme thy fethered bedde, alwaies thy graspyng graue. **1590** SPENSER *F.Q.* I. i. 20 It forst him slacke His grasping hold. **1816** SHELLEY *Alastor* 531 Nought but knarled roots of ancient pines Branchless and blasted, clenched with grasping roots The unwilling soil. **1883** G. ALLEN in *Knowledge* 20 July 34 The big grasping claws..in a crab.

2. *fig.* Eager for gain, greedy, avaricious.

1748 RICHARDSON *Clarissa* I. 126 The less, surely, ought I to give into these grasping views of my brother. **1771** BURKE *Sp. Middlesex Election* Wks. X. 65 This is..a difficult thing to the corrupt, grasping and ambitious part of human nature. **1813** SCOTT *Rokeby* IV. xxviii, My wealth, on which a kinsman nigh Already casts a grasping eye. **1855** MACAULAY *Hist. Eng.* xxi. IV. 555 He was generally thought interested and grasping.

Hence ˈ**graspingly** *adv.*, ˈ**graspingness**.

1748 RICHARDSON *Clarissa* I. 124 To take all that good-nature, or indulgence..confers shews..a graspingness that is unworthy of that indulgence. **1832** LYTTON *Eug. Aram* I. vii, To be more graspingly selfish. **1873** M. ARNOLD *Lit. & Dogma* (1876) 201 Faults of self-assertion, graspingness, and violence. **1885** C. LOWE *Bismarck* II. 357 The Pope had proved himself to be graspingly unwise. **1890** *Eng. Illustr. Mag.* Dec. 209 Hard were their backs as anvils of steel, and graspingly arched nipper-armed claws before them.

†ˈ**grasple,** *sb.* [variant of GRAPPLE *sb.*: cf. next.] = GRAPPLE *sb.* I.

1553 BRENDE *Q. Curtius* IV. 40 b, They deuised longe rafters to the which they fastened grasples of Iron and great hokes. *Ibid.* 41 The grasples [*ed.* **1570**, fol. 60 b, grasplers] letten downe (which be called corui) toke violently away many of the souldiers that were within the shyppes.

†ˈ**grasple,** *v. Obs.* [variant of GRAPPLE *v.*, influenced by association with GRASP *v.*] *trans.* and *intr.* = GRAPPLE *v.* 4 and 8 a.

1553 BRENDE *Q. Curtius* IV. 41 b, The cynquereme graspeled with her. **1555** EDEN *Decades* 188 Suche as can not grasple or take holde of any thynge.

Hence †**graspler** = GRAPPLER a.

1553 [see GRASPLE *sb.*].

graspless (ˈgrɑːsplɪs, -æ-), *a.* [f. GRASP *sb.* + -LESS.] **a.** Without grasp or grip; loose, relaxed. **b.** Not admitting of a grasp, i.e. of being grasped.

1794 COLERIDGE *On Friend Who Died of Fever* 43 From my graspless hand Drop Friendship's precious pearls, like hour-glass sand. **1849** *Tait's Mag.* XVI. 348/2 Where Past and Future wholly are submerged In one vast, graspless, Present infinite. **1886** *Blackw. Mag.* CXL. 259 In its graspless hold her hand Felt that the sceptre shivered. **1894** HALL CAINE *Manxman* VI. x. 390 It fell from his graspless fingers to the floor.

grass (grɑːs, -æ-), *sb.*[1] Forms: *α.* 1 græs, (*pl.* grasu), 3–5 gres, 3–6 gras, (3 grace, graes, 4 grece, grees), 4 gris(e, 4, 6 griss(e, 4–6 gress(e, 4–7 grasse, (5 graas, grase, graz), 6– grass. *β.* 1 gærs, gers, subsequently *Sc.* and *north. dial.* 4, 6–9 gers(e, 4–6 gyrs(s, 5–6 gyrse, 5, 9 girss, 6, 9 gerss, 6–9 girs(e. [Com. Teut.: OE. *græs, gærs* str. neut. = OFris. *gres, gers*, OS. *gras* (MDu. *gras, gars, gers*, mod.Du. *gras*), OHG. (MHG., mod.Ger.), ON. (Sw. *gräs*, Da. *græs*), Goth. *gras*:—OTeut. **grasoᵐ*, f. OTeut. root **gra-*: *grô-* (whence MHG. *gruose* young plants; also GREEN *a.*, GROW *v.*):—OAryan **ghrā-* to grow, whence L. *grāmen* grass.]

1. a. Herbage in general, the blades or leaves and stalks of which are eaten by horses, cattle, sheep, etc. Also, in a narrower sense, restricted to the smaller non-cereal *Gramineæ* (see 3), and plants resembling these in general appearance. In early use often *pl.*, but now only *collect. sing.*

c **725** *Corpus Gloss.* 864 *Fenum*, graes. *c* **897** K. ÆLFRED *Gregory's Past.* xxiii. 173 Sua sua maneȝra cynna wyrta & grasu beoð ȝerad. *c* **1000** *Andreas* 38 (Gr.) Hie hiȝ & gærs for meteleaste meðe ȝedrehte. *c* **1200** ORMIN 15467 Swa fele kinne wasstmess Off gresess, & off tres. *c* **1205** LAY. 3905 þat heo frete þet corn & þat graes. *c* **1250** *Gen. & Ex.* 3049 Trees it for-brac, and gres, and corn. *a* **1300** *Cursor M.* 11109 (Gött.) He..liued wid rotis and wid grise [*Cott.* gress]. *c* **1340** *Ibid.* 4563 (Trin.) Floures & greses [*other texts* gress(e)] þerynne I fond. *c* **1380** WYCLIF *Wks.* (1880) 388 Lilyes & grasse þat growen in þe felde. **1393** LANGL. *P. Pl.* C. XVI. 244 Bestes by gras & by greyn and by grene rotes. *c* **1425** WYNTOUN *Cron.* I. xiii. 11 Sum steddys growys sa habowndanly Of Gyrs, þat [etc.]. **1447** BOKENHAM *Seyntys* (Roxb.) 296 Whan a flode rysyth up heye Gres goth undyr. **1484** CAXTON *Fables of Æsop* V. i, Of a mule whiche ete grasse in a medowe nyghe to a grete forest. **1504** *Plumpton Corr.* (Camden) 187 She hath no gresse to hir cattell. **1513** DOUGLAS *Æneis* III. iv. 25 Trippis eik of gait, but ony keipar, In the rank gersis pasturing on raw. **1549** *Compl. Scot.* vi. 37, I past to the greene hoilsum feildis..to resaue the sueit fragrant smel of tendir gyrssis. **1597** MIDDLETON *Wisdom Solomon* xvi. 25 Is grass man's meat? no, it is cattle's food. **1637** B. JONSON *Sad Sheph.* I. i, Her treading would not bend a blade of grasse! **1755** J. MCLAURIN *Serm. & Ess.* 110 The least pile of grass is an effect of infinite power. **1774** GOLDSM. *Nat. Hist.* (1776) II. 315 Quadrupedes, that feed upon grass. **1817** COLERIDGE *Sibyll. Leaves* (1862) 117 The grass was fine, the sun was bright. **1837** EMERSON *Addr., Amer. Schol.* Wks. (Bohn) II. 179 The human body can be nourished on any food, though it were boiled grass and the broth of shoes. **1883** *Gd. Words* 3 His foot caught in a tuft of grass. **1894** CROCKETT *Raiders* xviii. 165 There's a handfu' o' girse to brew mair milk.

fig. **1535** COVERDALE *Is.* xl. 6 All flesh is grasse [*so later versions*; *Wyclif* hei]. **1858** HAWTHORNE *Fr. & It. Jrnls.* II. 12 Without running into the high grass of latent meanings and obscure allusions.

b. *Proverbs.*

c **1440** CAPGRAVE *Life St. Kath.* II. 253 The gray hors, whyl his gras growyth, May sterue for hunger, þus seyth þe prouerbe. *c* **1530** R. HILLES *Common-Pl. Bk.* (1858) 140 Whyle the grasse growyth the hors stervyth. **1869** HAZLITT *Eng. Prov. & Phrases* 467 Where the Turk's horse once treads, the grass never grows.

c. In figurative phrases. ***between grass and hay*** (see quots.). ***to cut one's own grass***: to earn one's own living (*slang*). ***to cut the grass from under a person's feet***: to foil, thwart, trip him up. †***to give grass*** (a rendering of L. *dare herbam*): to yield, to surrender. ***to let no grass grow*** (or ***the grass does not grow***) ***under one's feet*** (or †***on one's heel, beneath one's heels***): giving the idea of moving or acting briskly, making the most of one's time. †***to pluck the grass to know where the wind sits***: to interpret the signs of the times.

a **1553** UDALL *Royster D.* III. iii. (Arb.) 48 There hath grown no grasse on my heele since I went hence. **1588** GREENE *Pandosto* (1843) 13 Willing that the grasse should not be cut from under his feete. **1597–8** HALL *Sat., Defiance to Enuie* 105 Needs me give grasse unto the conquerers. **1607** TOPSELL *Four-f. Beasts* (1658) 210 The hare..leaps away again, and letteth no grass grow under his feet. *a* **1670** HACKET *Abp. Williams* II. (1692) 16 No Man could pluck the Grass better, to know where the Wind sat; no Man could spie sooner from whence a Mischief did rise. **1672** MARVELL *Reh. Transp.* I. 278 You are all this while cutting the grass under his feet. **1743** ELLIS *Mod. Husb.* III. I. 78 April and September are reckoned the worst Months to make Butter in, because then the Season is between Grass and Hay. **1828** SCOTT *Jrnl.* 29 Mar., I have let no grass grow beneath my heels this bout. **1848** in *Amer. Speech* (1935) X. 40 *Betwixt hay & grass*, between Boyhood & Manhood. **1855** MACAULAY *Hist. Eng.* xvi. III. 619 The King answered that he had not come to Ireland to let the grass grow under his feet. **1868** *Morning Star* 8 June, It is the habit of costermongers and that class of people to make their children useful—to make them 'cut their own grass'. **1877** *5 Yrs.' Penal Serv.* iii. 242 'Cut her own grass!..what is that?' ..'Why, purvide her own chump—earn her own living.' **1884** EDNA LYALL *We Two* v, [He] was not a man who ever let the grass grow under his feet. **1891** H. C. BUNNER *Zadoc Pine* 17 He..got a couple of eggs cooked for his private supper... The eggs were, as he told Mr. Bryan, 'kinder 'twixt grass and hay'.

d. *slang.* Green vegetables.

1867 in SMYTH *Sailor's Word-bk.* 347.

e. Marijuana, used as a drug. *slang* (orig. *U.S.*).

1943 *Time* 19 July 54 Marijuana may be called..grass. **1945** L. SHELLY *Jive Talk Dict.* 25 *Grass reefers*, marijuana cigarettes. **1967** *Boston Sunday Herald* 26 Mar. IV. 1/1 According to one Federal Narcotics Bureau agent, California 'is flooded with marijuana', which is better known by the increasing numbers who smoke it as 'pot', 'grass' and 'Mary J.'. **1968** A. DIMENT *Gt. Spy Race* vi. 88 Pure Grass cigarettes, at two dollars a pack and none of your watering down with tobacco. **1969** *Win* 15 May 31/2, I consider grass and mescaline to be extremely important and inherent parts of this social revolution.

2. A kind of grass; one of the various species of plants spoken of collectively as grass.

†**a.** A small herbaceous plant, a (medicinal) herb. *Obs.*

1297 R. GLOUC. (Rolls) 1011 Vor men þat beþ enuenimed, þoru graces of þe londe Idronke hii beþ iclansed sone þoru godes sonde. **1320–30** *Horn Ch.* in Ritson *Metr. Rom.* III. 316 Go.. And geder parvink and ive, Gresses that ben of main. *c* **1340** *Cursor M.* 8453 (Fairf.) þe kinde of þingis lered he baþ of tree and grissis fele [*Cott.* þe kind o thinges lerd he, Bath o tres, and gress fele]. **13..** *Minor Poems fr. Vernon MS.* (E.E.T.S.) 575/275 Macer þe strengþe of grases telles, Boþe of crop and Rote. *c* **1375** *Sc. Leg. Saints, Symon & Judas* 24 And of þe cure, thru þe wrocht is But ony medycyne ore gris [L. *medicamentis aut herbis*]. *c* **1386** CHAUCER *Sqr.'s T.* 145 Euery gras that groweth vp on roote she shal eek knowe. *c* **1400** *Rowland & Otuel* 993 To hym commes þat lady clere & greses broghte þat fre, þat godd sett in his awenn herbere. *c* **1440** *Boctus* (*Laud MS.* 559 lf. 4 b), Many a grasse and many a tree. **1587** MASCALL *Gov. Cattle, Horses* (1627) Index, The fiue grasses that draw a wound. Oculus Christi, Madder, Buglosse [etc.].

fig. **1393** LANGL. *P. Pl.* C. xv. 23 Grace is a gras ther-fore to don hem eft growe.

b. One of the non-cereal *Gramineæ*, or any species of other orders resembling these in general appearance. Often preceded by a defining word, with which it forms the designation of some particular species; as *blue-*, *bunch-*, *dog-*, *St. John's*, *saw-*, *silk-*, *spear-* (etc.) *grass*, for which see those words. ***grass of the Andes***: an oat-grass, *Arrhenatherum avenaceum*. ***grass of Parnassus*** (also ***Parnassus grass***): a name for *Parnassia palustris*.

Turner speaks of the 'right' or 'true' grass, intending to indicate one particular species of plant as properly entitled to the name; but his notions seem to have been vague. He regarded the 'true' grass as identical with 'great grass'.

1548 TURNER *Names of Herbes* 41 Gramen is called.. in english great grass. **1562** —— *Herbal.* II. 13 The roote of the right Grasse brused and layde to byndeth woundes together an closeth them vppe. **1578** LYTE *Dodoens* IV. li. 509 Of the grasse of Parnasus.. This herbe groweth in moyst places. **1597** GERARDE *Herbal* II. ccxciv. 692 Parnassus Grasse, or white Liuerwoort. **1854** S. THOMSON *Wild Fl.* III. (ed. 4) 230 One of the handsomest of our moss plants, the *Parnassia palustris*, or grass of Parnassus.

c. In agricultural use: Any of the species of plants grown for pasture, or for conversion into hay.

1677 PLOT *Oxfordsh.* 153 Grasses, the usual name for any Herbage sown for Cattle, especially if perennial. **1886** C. SCOTT *Sheep-Farming* 25 This should be more particularly attended to on rotation grasses, where rye-grass forms very often a large proportion of the herbage.

d. *Bot.* Any plant belonging to the order *Gramineæ* (*Graminaceæ*), which includes most of the plants called 'grass' in the narrower popular sense (see 1) together with the cereals (barley, oats, rye, wheat, etc.), the reeds, bamboos, etc.

1611 COTGR. s.v. *Aiguillette, Aiguillettes d'armes*, the hearbe, or grasse, called Ladies laces, white Cameleon grasse, painted, or furrowed grasse. **1672** GREW *Anat. Plants, Idea Philos. Hist.* §11 Amongst the several Sorts of Grass, there are some which match all those of Corn; which is but a greater kind of Grass. **1759** B. STILLINGFL. *Observ. Grasses* Misc. Tracts (1762) 365 By grasses are meant all those plants, which have a round, jointed and hollow stem. **1776** WITHERING *Brit. Plants* (1796) I. 130 The great solicitude of nature for the preservation of grasses is evident from this; that the more the leaves are consumed, the more the roots increase. **1828** STARK *Elem. Nat. Hist.* II. 379 *Tabanus pratensis*.. Inhabits Europe, in meadows, the larvæ destroying the roots of grasses. **1869** RUSKIN *Q. of Air* §79 The grasses are essentially a clothing for healthy and pure ground. **1887** *Chamb. Jrnl.* IV. 583 Oil or otto of geranium ..is produced in India..by distillation of andropogon grasses with water.

3. An individual plant of grass †or corn; a blade or spire of grass. Now only in *pl.*, and somewhat *rare*.

13.. *E.E. Allit. P.* A. 31 Vch gresse mot grow of graynez dede. *c* **1350** *Will. Palerne* 27 þat litel child listely lorked out of his caue.. to gadere of þe grases þat grene were & fayre. *c* **1384** CHAUCER *H. Fame* III. 263 (Pepys MS.) They wer sett as thikk as owches Full of the fynest stones faire.. As grasses growen in a mede. *c* **1440** *Jacob's Well* (E.E.T.S.) 214 Alle levis of treen, euery gresse on erthe, euery droppe of watyr in þe se & land. *c* **1460** *Towneley Myst.* i. 238 Gresys and othere small floures. **1523** FITZHERB. *Husb.* §20 Dernolde groweth vp streyght lyke an hye grasse. *a* **1533** FRITH *Wks.* (1573) 75 If euery grasse of the ground were a man as holy as euer was Paule or Peter. **1577** KENDALL *Flowers of Epigr.* 12 b, In midst of all, thy sconse is balde: there allies are to see: Wherein not half a grasse doth growe so bald, and bare they be. **1662** J. DAVIES tr. *Mandelslo's Trav.* 11 In the Country all about this City, there is not so much as a grasse to be seen. **1848** DICKENS *Dombey* i, Strange grasses were sometimes perceived in her hair. **1850** TENNYSON *In Mem.* xxi, I take the grasses of the grave, And make them pipes whereon to blow.

4. †**a.** The blade stage of growth, in phr. ***in the grass*** (lit. and fig.); corn in the blade. *Obs.*

c **950** *Lindisf. Gosp.* Mark iv. 28 Forðon eorðo wæstmiað ærist gers [*c* **1000** *Ags. Gosp.* gærs], æfterðon ðone ðorn, soððа full hwæte in eher. **1340** *Ayenb.* 28 þet corn.. is uerst ass ine gerse, efterward ine yere. **1579** TOMSON *Calvin's Serm. Tim.* 432/1 Our faith is yet in the grasse. **1589** GREENE *Orpharion* Wks. (Grosart) XII. 34 Fancy long helde in the grasse, seldom prooues a timely Haruest. **1613** [see GRAIN *sb.*[1] 1 b]. **1733** J. TULL *Horse-Hoing Husbandry* 71 *note* 2 Wheat falls sometimes whilst 'tis in Grass, and before it comes into Ear.

b. *Gardening.* Applied to the young shoots of the onion. Also, the young shoots of the carnation.

1820 T. HOGG *Pract. Treat. Culture of Carnation* 48 The propagation by piping..ought to commence as soon as the shoots or grass is [*sic*] ready. **1836** N. PATERSON *Manse Garden* (1860) 189 The young shoots [of carnations] near the ground which do not run to flower are denominated grass. *Ibid.* 190 Pipings (as the grass shoots taken off and stuck in the ground are called)..will take root. **1885** SUTTON *Cult. Veget. & Fl.* 81 The Onion makes a weak grass that cannot well push through earth that is caked over it. **1925** W. WATSON *Gardener's Assistant* (ed. 4) V. 22/1 The 'grass', or young growths produced at the base of the plant, form the layers.

5. a. Pasture; the condition of an animal at pasture. In phrases (***to be, run***) ***at grass, to go, put, send, turn*** (***out***) ***to grass***.

1471 SIR J. PASTON in *P. Lett.* No. 670 III. 7 That Phelypp Loveday put the othyr horse to gresse ther. **1523** FITZHERB. *Husb.* §85 It wyl leaste appere, whan he [the horse] is at grasse. **1593** SHAKS. *2 Hen. VI*, IV. ii. 75 In Cheapside shall my Palfrey go to grasse. **1607** TOPSELL, *Four-f. Beasts* (1658) 313 Let him rest, or run at grasse for a week or more. **1611** BEAUM. & FL. *Knt. Burn. Pestle* IV. v, The sturdy steed now goes to grass, and up they hang his saddle. **1650** R. GELL *Serm.* 8 Aug. 21 Nebuchadnezzar was put to grasse. **1662** J. DAVIES tr. *Olearius' Voy. Ambass.* 257 His Elephant.. being then at Grasse, it was so long ere they could bring him. **1674** tr. *Martiniere's Voy. N. Countries* 77 Our Guids unharnessed our Elks and turn'd them to Grass. **1675** *Lond. Gaz.* No. 988/4 Lost at Grass April 9..a bay Gelding. **1708** J. C. *Compl. Collier* (1845) 34 Turn them out in Summer time to Grass. **1753** J. BARTLET *Gentl. Farriery* i. 4 Horses, whose feet have been impair'd by quitters..or any other accidents, are also best repaired at grass. **1855** TENNYSON *Brook* 139 The Squire had seen the colt at grass.

b. *fig.* The phrases under 5 a are applied to persons, with the notion of being dismissed from one's position or 'rusticated', or of going away for a holiday, being free from fixed engagements, etc.

1589 *Hay any Work* 6 If his worship and the rest of the noble clergie Lords weare turned out to grasses. **1630** J. TAYLOR *Wks.* (Water P.) II. 110/1 Wiues might vnable husbands turne to grasse. **1646** *Unhappy Game Sc. & Eng.* 12 When the king hath got all, hell turne your brethren to grasse. **1673** DRYDEN *Marr. à la Mode* III. i, When I have been at grass in the summer, and am new come up [to town] again. **1700** CONGREVE *Way of World* III. xviii, I'll turn my wife to grass. **1786** MACKENZIE *Lounger* No. 78 ¶6 [Our three boys] were sent to an academy in Yorkshire, to grass, as my husband phrased it. **1794** *Gentl. Mag.* Dec. 1085 Soho, Jack!..very nigh being sent to grass, hey? **1801** in *Spirit Publ. Jrnls.* (1802) V. 361 Then no longer let mortals repine, If to grass sent from Oxon or Granta. **1838** D. JERROLD *Men of Charac.* II. xvii. 264, I think I can send you to grass somewhere in Essex. **1887** A. BIRRELL *Obiter Dicta* Ser. II. 64 He had long been an author at grass, and had no mind..again to wear the collar.

¶ Misused for GREASE *sb.* 1 b.

c **1650** *Carle off Carlile* in *Percy Folio* III. 64 The gray hounds..drew downe the deere of grasse.

6. Pasture sufficient for the animal or number of animals specified; grazing.

858 *Charter of Æthelberht* in *O.E. Texts* 438, IIII oxnum gers. **1493** *Mem. Ripon* (Surtees) III. 164 Pro j hors gresse in parva prata apud Topclyf, 2*s.* **1790** MRS. WHEELER *Westmld. Dial.* (1821) 14 Yee mun kna we tewk sum gerse for her. **1799** J. ROBERTSON *Agric. Perth* 59 They have not only a house, but generally a cow's grass to afford milk to their families. **1880** in *Daily News* 13 Dec. 3/1 There is not as much as the grass of a goat.

7. a. Land on which grass is the permanent crop; pasture-land. Also, the condition of such land. Also † ***to lay to grass***.

1609 SKENE *Reg. Maj.* 86 Moueable escheit is, as be pasturing of cattell or beastes in the lands, or girse of Lords sundrie tymes. **1767** A. YOUNG *Farmer's Lett. to People* 99 Half the lands of a farm, but more particularly of a small or middling one, ought to be grass. **1793** WASHINGTON *Lett.* Writ. 1891 XII. 400 Preparing the second lot of the mile swamp for the purpose of laying it to grass. **1893** *Westm. Gaz.* 13 Nov. 6/2 At that time the whole of the land was under cultivation. Now the land had all gone down to what people called grass, but he called it weeds.

b. with reference to the hunting-field.

1861 WHYTE MELVILLE *Mkt. Harb.* 28 'I'm going down to the grass.' 'Grass!' grunted the listener. ' Where be that?' 'Well, I'm going to see what sport they have in the Shires.' **1867** TROLLOPE *Chron. Barset* I. xxiv. 204 A man very well known both in the City and over the grass in Northamptonshire.

8. The yearly growth of grass; hence, the season when the grass grows, spring and early summer. ***eating its fifth grass***: in its fifth year.

1485 *Sc. Acts Jas. III* (1814) II. 170/2 It is thocht expedient..that our souueran lord causs his Justice airis to be haldin vniuersaly in al partis of his Realme, twys in þe ȝere anys on the girss, and anys on the Corne. **1598** SYLVESTER *Du Bartas* II. i. IV. *Handie-crafts* 415 Whom seven-years-old at the next grass he ghest. **1649** DAVENANT *Love & Honour* v. Dram. Wks. 1873 III. 184 She writes a hundred and ten, sir, next grass. **1685** *Lond. Gaz.* No. 2061. 2/2 A Black brown Gelding..six years old last Grass. **1705** *Ibid.* No. 4120/3 Every Owner..must send a Certificate from the Breeder that his Horse is really no more then 6 the Grass before he Runs. **1799** J. ROBERTSON *Agric. Perth* 312 Good wedders, eating their fifth grass, sold in the year 1793 at eighteen shillings. **1826** MISS MITFORD *Village* Ser. II. 49 She is five years old this grass. **1859** G. MEREDITH *R. Feverel* xxiv. (1885) 181 When did ye meet?—last grass, wasn't it?

9. a. The grassy earth, grass-covered ground; *esp.* ground covered with grass closely mown and rolled, forming a lawn in a public or private garden. Phr. ***keep off the grass***: a notice frequently posted in a park or garden to which the public are admitted; also used *fig.* as a warning not to take liberties, encroach, or interfere. †In early use ***into, under grass*** = into or in the grave.

a **1300** *Cursor M.* 5811 'Lauerd', he said, 'I ber a wand'. 'þou kest it on þe gress, i bidd'; 'Gladli, lauerd', and sua he didd. **13..** *E.E. Allit. P.* A. 245 In to gresse þou me aglyȝte. **1375** BARBOUR *Bruce* II. 361 The gress woux off the blud all rede. **1390** GOWER *Conf.* II. 45 Forth she wente prively.. All softe walkend on the gras. *c* **1400** *Gamelyn* 69 A-none as he was dede & under gras graue. **1773–83** HOOLE *Orl. Fur.* XXIII. 39 On the verdant grass, Beneath the covering trees, her limbs she throws. **1840** DICKENS *Old C. Shop* xvi, They were two men who were seated in easy attitudes upon the grass. [**1846** *Punch* 12 Sept. 113/2 If from the gravel pathway hard He turn to tread the verdant sward,..What bids his happy dream to pass?—'Get off the Grass! Get off the Grass!'] **1850** *Punch* 5 Oct. 144/1 The public, who are here and there 'requested to keep off the grass'. **1877** 'RITA' *Vivienne* I. i, The grasses are crimsoned with tulips; every nook is sweet with odours of sheltered violets. **1897** W. S. MAUGHAM *Liza of Lambeth* v. 59 'Na then,' she said, 'keep off the grass!' [i.e. don't take liberties with me]. **1904** *Daily Chron.* 27 Oct. 4/7 'Now, then, some girl can tell me about grass. What is grass?' The protagonist of the class..gave the definition. 'Please, it's what you got to keep off of.' **1925** P. GIBBS *Unchanging Quest* xxi. 156 Of course you wouldn't be left alone to do what you like under some forms of government. Not entirely under ours, as you'll find if you don't keep off the grass, old lad. **1953** K. AMIS *Lucky Jim* xx. 211 What I want to say to you is, keep off the grass, that's all. You're causing nothing but trouble by behaving as you are.

b. The earth's surface above a mine. Also ***to be at grass, to bring, come to grass***.

1776 PRYCE *Min. Cornub.* 322 Grass or at Grass, signifies on the surface of the earth. 'Is Tom Treviscas underground?' 'No; he's at Grass.' **1801** HITCHINS in *Phil. Trans.* XCI. 160 One hundred and fifty-five fathoms below the surface, or, as the miners call it, from grass. **1843** *Penny Cycl.* XXV. 32 The quantity [of mineral] brought to the surface, or, as it is technically called, to grass. **1855** *Cornwall* 288 Let us now watch the men ascending from the mine after work. This is what they call 'coming to grass'. **1890** *Goldfields Victoria* 14 About 70 tons [of quartz] are now at grass awaiting crushing.

c. *slang.* The ground. ***to go to grass***: to come to the ground, be knocked down; also (*U.S.*) to die; to be ruined; in the imperative = 'go and be hanged'. ***to send to grass***: to fell to the ground, to knock down; *lit.* and *fig.* ***to hunt grass***: be knocked down.

a **1625** BEAUM. & FL. *Little Fr. Lawyer* IV. v. (1647) 69 Away, good Sampson; You go to grass else instantly. **1816** *Sporting Mag.* XLVIII. 181 Lancaster..was..much exhausted, and soon found his way on the grass. **1848** DURIVAGE *Stray Subjects* 95 A gentleman..declared that he might go to grass with his old canoe, for he didn't think it would be much of a shower, anyhow. **1872** MARK TWAIN *Innoc. at Home* ii. (1882) 271 When you get in with your left I hunt grass every time. **1876** HINDLEY *Cheap Jack* 237 Elias was sent to grass to rise no more off it. **1894** *Nation* (N.Y.) 18 Jan. 39/3 Several of the McKinleyites were sent to grass in the course of the debate. **1894** ASTLEY *50 Years Life* I. 82, I naturally went to grass through having too much steam on to be able to pull up in time.

d. *Electr.* A fuzzy appearance along the time base-line of a cathode-ray tube display due to random, fluctuating deflections caused by electrical noise.

1947 *Amer. Speech* XXII. 154 The radar-man..speaks of 'losing the pip in the grass'. *Ibid.*, *Grass*,..electronic haze at the bottom of the screen. **1957** RAWNSLEY & WRIGHT *Night Fighter* iv. 58 'What's all that stuff?'.., 'Grass,..it's like the background noise of a wireless set.' **1961** PARTRIDGE *Dict. Slang* Suppl. 1116/2 *Grass* was the normal 'picture' seen on certain types of radar cathode-ray tube, as distinct from the signals produced by aircraft, etc. It looked like waving grass. **1969** *Sunday Mail Mag.* (Brisbane) 16 Feb. 1/3 'Grass'—useless noise from outer space.

10. Short for *sparrow-grass*, corrupt form of ASPARAGUS. Now *vulgar*.

1747 MRS. GLASSE *Cookery* xiv. 234 Boil some Grass tender, cut it small and lay it over the Eggs. **1764** FOOTE *Mayor of G.* II. Wks. 1799 I. 181 A hundred of grass from the Corporation of Garrat. *a* **1845** HOOD *Public Dinner* 61 You then make a cut on Some Lamb big as mutton; And ask for some grass too. **1852** DICKENS *Bleak Ho.* xx, Will you take any other vegetables? Grass? Peas? Summer Cabbage? **1898** *Garden* 1 May 318/1 In warm localities established beds will be affording a welcome supply of serviceable 'grass'.

11. *Printing.* Casual employment; jobbing work.

1888 *Daily News* 16 July 7/1 Good jobbing hands wanted on grass. **1893** *Ibid* 5 June 8/5 Reader (practical)..wants Two or Three Days' or Nights' Grass, or steady situation.

12. *slang.* A police informer. (See also GRASSER[2], GRASSHOPPER 1 c.)

1932 A. GARDNER *Tinker's Kitchen* 283 *Grass*, an informer. **1936** J. CURTIS *Gilt Kid* ii. 22 Tell you the details and then you'll do the gaff on your jack..or else turn grass. **1954** 'N. BLAKE' *Whisper in Gloom* ii. 31 He was a nark, nose, snout, grass, squeaker, or whatever coarse word is current for it. **1955** P. WILDEBLOOD *Against Law* 105 'What are grasses?' I asked. 'Informers. Short for "grasshoppers", which is rhyming slang for "shoppers", meaning people who go to the cop-shop and squeal on their friends.' **1961** *Guardian* 6 Dec. 4/5 Throughout the gaols..the word 'grass' is an abbreviation for grass-snake, which..means informer.

13. *attrib.* and *Comb.* **a.** simple attributive, as ***grass-blade, -bud, -country, -fen, -field, -ground, -haulm, -heath, -holding, -holm,***

-park, -patch, -path, -pollen, -prairie, -ranch, -road, -seed, -shears, -slope, -spire, -stalk, -stem, -track, -tuft, -veld (S. Afr.), *-walk*; *grass-like* adj. **b.** objective or objective genitive, as *grass-catcher, -champer, -eater, -farmer, -mower*; *grass-clipping, -mowing* (in quot. *attrib.*), *-picking* vbl. sbs. **c.** instrumental, as *grass-bowered, -carpeted, -clad, -covered, -cushioned, -embroidered, -fed, -grown, -muffled, -roofed, -woven* adjs. **d.** parasynthetic, as *grass-leaved* adj.

1831 CARLYLE *Sart. Res.* III. viii, Through every *grass-blade. **1934** T. S. ELIOT *Rock* ii. 84 Glow-worm glowlight on a grassblade. **1949** E. POUND *Pisan Cantos* lxxxiii. 124 When the mind swings by a grass-blade an ant's forefoot shall save you. **1804** J. GRAHAME *Sabbath* (1808) 45 Larks, descending to their *grass-bowered homes. **1847** EMERSON *Poems* (1857) 126 Pondering shadows, colors, clouds, *Grass-buds and caterpillar-shrouds. **1889** WESTGARTH *Austral. Progr.* 253 Pretty vistas of *grass-carpeted open forests. **1895** *Montgomery Ward Catal.* 392/3 *Grass Catcher..has new device for attaching to mower. **1971** *CGA Ann. Price List* 39/2 Motor Mowers..(4-stroke) complete with grass catcher. **1599** NASHE *Lenten Stuffe* 25 All the foure footed rablement of herbagers and *grasse champers. **1870** MORRIS *Earthly Par.* I. II. 456 Midst sunny *grass-clad meads. **1954** J. R. R. TOLKIEN *Fellowship of Ring* ii. 73 He lifted the astonished Sam, shears, *grass-clippings and all, right through the window. **1966** G. W. TURNER *Eng. Lang. Austral. & N.Z.* iv. 68 *Lawn mowings* in Beatrix Potter's *The Tale of the Flopsy Bunnies* was rendered *grass clippings*. **1875** W. S. HAYWARD *Love Agst. World* 10 A beautiful *grass-country. **1880** C. R. MARKHAM *Peruv. Bark* 154 A *grass-covered..region. **1861** W. F. COLLIER *Hist. Eng. Lit.* 400 The *grass-cushioned crags of Sandy-Knowe. **1649** G. DANIEL *Trinarch., Hen. IV*, lv, Hee [Soliman] only swept the Grasse, They the *Grasse-Eaters. **1894** T. TILTON *Chameleon's Dish* 5 Odin's coast With all its twenty-thousand bays And *grass-embroidered water-ways. **1894** *Times* 10 Dec. 10/4 The grass land being occupied by *grass farmers. **1638** PENKETHMAN *Artach.* I iij b, A *grasse fed Ox 16s. **1880** *Vermont Agric. Rep.* VI. 26 Time was when the butchers of Brighton claimed that they could distinguish between the grass-fed beef fattened in this valley, and that from other sections, by its superior quality. **1892** A. C. GUNTER *Miss Dividends* (1893) 213 What's champagne muscle to grass-fed muscle, you dainty cut of New York. **1960** *Times* 1 Oct. 7/6 Grass-fed cattle. **1865** KINGSLEY *Herew.* I. Prel. 16 The rich *grass-fen. **1806** J. GRAHAME *Birds Scot.* 9 Joined by her mate [she] to the *grass-field flies. **1765** A. DICKSON *Treat. Agric.* ix. (ed. 2) 225 This plough is used for breaking up *grass-ground. **1788** COWPER *Lett.* 21 Feb., Abounding with beautiful grass-grounds, which encompass our village. **1735** THOMSON *Liberty* IV. 718 Desolating Famine, who delights In *grass-grown Cities, and in desart Fields. **1865** KINGSLEY *Herew.* I. i. 27 The great labyrinth of grass-grown banks. **1882** VINES *Sachs' Bot.* 845 The nodes of *grass-haulms. **1936** *Discovery* Jan. 24/2 The unique '*grass-heath' of fescue and bent grasses. **1964** V. J. CHAPMAN *Coastal Veget.* vi. 148 Many of them can be regarded as 'grass-heath' species. **1894** *Times* 10 Jan. 6/4 A *grass-holding which he could use for the benefit of himself and his family. **1818** SCOTT *Hrt. Midl.* l, It wad be better laid out on yon bonny *grass-holms, than lying useless here in this auld pigg. **1830–7** MCGILLIVRAY *Withering's Brit. Plants* (ed. 4) xxiii. 377 *Atriplex littoralis*. *Grass-leaved Sea Orache. **1883** F. M. BAILEY *Synop. Queensld. Flora* 693 Grass-leaved fern. **1776** WITHERING *Brit. Plants* (1796) II. 7 Leaves thread-shaped, *grass-like. **1894** *Country Gentlemen's Catal.* 240 A 'Stamford' *Grass Mower. **1913** W. J. LOCKE *Stella Maris* xii. 165 The grass-mower driven over the grass. **1825** COBBETT *Rur. Rides* (1885) II. 14 In harvest and *grass-mowing time. **1850** MRS. BROWNING *Poems* II. 2 Our steeds, with slow *grass-muffled hoofs Tread deep the shadows through. **1806** *Gazetteer Scotl.* (ed. 2) 557 The surface is agreeably diversified with hill and dale, heath, moss, meadow, corn, and *grass parks. **1841** CATLIN *N. Amer. Ind.* (1844) II. xxxiii. 19 In a *grass-patch. **1828** MISS MITFORD *Village* Ser. III. 156 Mrs. Lucas ..was walking pensively up and down the *grass-path of the pretty flower-court. **1802** *Edin. Rev.* I. 221 *Grass-picking is only known in the windward islands. **1921** *Amer. Jrnl. Bot.* VIII. 473 Liefmann..found 2,500,000 grains of *grass pollen in one square meter. **1957** *Granta* 9 Mar. 19/2 The girl sneezed with the grass-pollen. **1851** MAYNE REID *Scalp Hunt.* i. 11 This is the '*grass-prairie', the boundless pasture of the bison. **1905** *Westm. Gaz.* 20 May 4/1 One of the main objects of the Bill was to get rid of the agricultural slums by splitting up the *grass-ranches. **1846** W. E. FORSTER 28 Sept. in Reid *Life* (1888) I. vi. 183 The *grass roads here [in Ireland] are far better than our Yorkshire roads. **1828** P. CUNNINGHAM *N.S. Wales* (ed. 3) II. 104 The wretched stone and turf-walled and *grass-roofed hovels they inhabit. **1765** *Mus. Rust.* IV. 383 *Grass-seeds gathered clean from the fields. **1880** *Vermont Agric. Rep.* VI. 32, I cannot recommend the use of oats in connection with grass seed. **1965** *R. Tucker & Sons Catal.* (Autumn) 48 We have considerable experience of Lawn Grass Seed... Many types of grass seed sold are quite unsuitable for making good lawns. **1770** WARING in *Phil. Trans.* LXI. 372 On the *grass-slopes here. **13..** *Adultery* 113 in *Archiv Stud. d. neu. Spr.* LXXIX. 420 þow euery *gress-spyre were a preste þat growyth upon goddys grounde Owte of þese-peyns þei cowd not me relese. **1867** 'T. LACKLAND' *Homespun* I. 99 The busy spiders..had spun slenderest ropes of very gossamer, and swung them across from one grass spire to another. **1861** WHYTE MELVILLE *Mkt. Harb.* 49 Ere he reached the *grass-track he meant to follow, the fog was denser than ever. **1891** KIPLING *Light that Failed* i. 10 Maisie was picking *grass-tufts. **1909** *Westm. Gaz.* 11 Dec. 16/1 Only recovering his feet after much floundering in one of the sandy hollows which occur between the grass-tufts. **1933** R. TUVE *Seasons & Months* iv. 165 Shepherds tending sheep on green grass-tufts. [**1844** J. BACKHOUSE *Narr. S. Afr.* 115 The Hottentots..could obtain from one to two rixdollars a day in the *Gras *Veld*, grass field.] **1958** *Cape Argus* 1 Nov. (Mag. Section) 11/1 We have exchanged.. grassveld for karoo. **1971** *Nature* 6 Aug. 374/3 This animal originally occurred extensively in..the central and southern Cape grassveld. **1712** J. JAMES tr. *Le Blond's Gardening* 44 We usually make a *Grass-walk in the Middle. **1885** *Century Mag.* XXIX. 657/2 His [the Bedouin's] drinking-vessels are gourds and *grass-woven bowls.

14. Special comb., as †**grass-acre** = GRASS-EARTH; **grass-bar**, a bar in a river, inlet, or harbour overgrown with grass (*Cent. Dict.*); **grass-bass**, a freshwater edible fish (*Pomoxys sparoides*) of the U.S.; †**grass-bed**, *poet.* one's grave, also, the 'field' on which a warrior dies; **grass-beef**, the flesh of grass-fed oxen; **grass-bird**, (*a*) a name for various American sandpipers, esp. *Tringa maculata*; (*b*) in Australasia, one or more species of *Sphenœacus*; **grass-bleached** *pa. pple.*, bleached by exposure on grass; so *grass-bleaching* vbl. sb.; **grass-box**, the receptacle on a lawn-mower into which the cut grass is projected; **grass-butter**, butter made from the milk of cows at grass; **grass-captain** *Cornwall* (see quot. and CAPTAIN *sb.* 8); **grass carp**, a vegetarian fish, *Ctenopharyngodon idella*, native to Asia, sometimes introduced elsewhere to control aquatic vegetation; **grass-cat** (see quot.); **grass-chat** = WHINCHAT; **grass-cock**, one of the small cocks into which grass is formed from the windrow; **grass-cold**, a slight cold or catarrh affecting horses; **grass-comber**, a sailor's term for one who has been a farm-labourer; †**grass-corn**, *Phalaris canariensis*; **grass court**, a grass Lawn Tennis court; **grass-cut** = *grass-cutter* (*a*); **grass-cutter**, (*a*) [corruption of a synonymous Hindustani *ghāskaṭ, ghāskaṭā*], in India, a native employed to cut and bring in grass for horses; (*b*) = *grass-hand* (*a*); (*c*) *slang* (see quots.); (*d*) = *cane-rat* (CANE *sb.*[1] 10); **grass-drake** = CORN-CRAKE; **grass-eating** *a.* = *grass-feeding* adj.; **grass-feeding** *a.*, graminivorous; **grass-finch**, (*a*) a common American sparrow (*Poœcetes gramineus*); (*b*) any Australian finch of the genus *Poëphila*; **grass fire**, a fire that destroys an area of grass; **grass-fish** (see quot.); **grass-flesh**, the flesh gained by an animal 'at grass' (in quot. *fig.*); **grass-frog**, the common frog, *Rana temporaria*; †**grass-girl**, ? a woman of loose character; **grass grub**, a New Zealand grass-eating grub, the larva of a cockchafer beetle, *Odontria zealandica*; **grass-guard**, a man or body of men in charge of animals grazing; **grass-hand**, (*a*) a compositor temporarily engaged; (*b*) an irregular cursive hand used by the Chinese and Japanese in business and private writing; **grass hawser** *Naut.* (see *grass rope* below); **grass hockey** *Canad.*, hockey played on grass, as opp. ice hockey; **grass-hole** *U.S.* (see quot.); †**grass-honey**, ? honey collected from the flowers of grass; **grass-hook**, a sickle for cutting grass; **grass-horse**, ? a horse 'at grass', or one living exclusively on grass; **grass-house**, †(*a*) the cottage of a GRASSMAN; (*b*) = next; **grass-hut**, in India and Polynesia, a hut with walls and roof of grass-stalks; **grass-ill**, a disease of lambs (see quot.); **grass-lamb**, (*a*) a lamb suckled by a dam which is running on pasture land and giving rich milk; (*b*) the flesh of the same; **grass-lawn**, a fine gauze-like material, the colour of unbleached linen, suitable for summer dresses; **grass-line** (*a*) *N.Z.*, the line or level on a mountain above which no grass grows; (*b*) = *grass rope*; **grass-linen**, a kind of fine grass-cloth; †**grass-mail**, rent for grass or the privilege of grazing; **grass-mare**, a mare 'at grass' (cf. *grass-horse*); **grass-meal** *Sc.*, so much grass as will keep an animal for the season; †**grass-money**, ? money received for the grazing of animals on the common land of a parish; **grass-moth**, one of many small moths of the genus *Crambus* or family *Crambidæ*, found in dry meadows; **grass-nail** (see quot. 1851); †**grass-nurse**, a wet-nurse; **grass-oil**, one of several fragrant essential oils, obtained in India by distillation from grasses (*Andropogon* and other genera), and used in perfumery; **grass-orphan** *nonce-wd.* [after GRASS-WIDOW], a child whose parents have gone away for a time; †**grass-ox**, a grass-fed ox, an ox 'at grass'; **grass-parakeet**, an Australian parakeet of the genus *Euphema* or *Melopsittacus*; **grass-parrot** , a small brightly-coloured Australian parrot of the genus *Neophema* or *Psephotus*; †**grass-pen**, an enclosed piece of land planted with grass; **grass-pile** *Sc.*, a blade of grass; **grass-pink** *U.S.* (see quot.); †**grass-poly**, a book-name for *Lythrum Hyssopifolia*; **grass-potato** (see quot.); **grass-quit**, one of several finches of tropical America, esp. species of *Phonipara*; **grass-right** *Austral.*, a right of pasturage; **grass rope** *Naut.*, a rope made of coir; **grass scythe**, a scythe for mowing grass; †**grass-sea**, the Sargasso sea; **grass-seeder** *N.Z.*, a person who gathers grass-seed for sale; also *attrib.*; hence **grass-seeding** *vbl. sb.*, the act of gathering grass-seed; †**grass-sick** *a.* (see quot. and cf. *grass-ill*); **grass sickness**, an equine disease, usually fatal, which can occur when a horse is put on to certain pastures; **grass-siding**, a border of grass at the side of a road; †**grass-silver**, money paid for grass or grazing; **grass skirt**, a skirt made from long grass and leaves secured to a waistband, orig. worn by the hula dancers of some Pacific islands; **grass-snake**, (*a*) the common ringed snake (*Tropidonotus natrix*); (*b*) the common green snake of the United States; **grass-snipe** *U.S.* = *grass-bird* (*a*); **grass-sparrow** = *grass-finch* (*a*); **grass-spirit**, spirit distilled from grasses; **grass-sponge**, an inferior kind of sponge from Florida and the Bahamas; **grass-spring** *poet.*, the springing up of grass, renewal of vegetation; **grass staggers** = GRASS TETANY; **grass-table** *Arch.* = EARTH-TABLE; †**grass-taffety** (cf. GRASS-CLOTH); **grass verge**, a strip of grass at the side of a garden path or road; **grass-warbler** *Austral.*, a bird of the genus *Cisticola*; **grass-way** = *grass-siding*; **grass-weed** = *grass-wrack*; †**grass-week** (see quot.); **grass-work**, †(*a*) a piece of lawn for ornamental purposes; (*b*) the work of a mine that is carried on above ground (cf. 9 b); hence *grass-worker*; †**grass-worm**, an earth-worm; **grass-wrack**, a seaweed (*Zostera marina*), with grass-like leaves; **grass wren**, any of several small Australian birds of the genus *Amytornis*; **grass-yard** = GREEN-YARD 3. Also GRASS-CLOTH, GRASS-EARTH, GRASS-PLAT, -PLOT, GRASS-WIDOW, etc.

c **1300** *Battle Abbey Custumals* (1887) 60 Et vocatur ista arrura *grasacra. *Ibid.* 66 Præter Garsacram operandam. **1897** *Outing* (U.S.) XXX. 437/2 The calico, or *grass bass, a showy, mottled fellow, sometimes a foot long. *c* **1000** *Ags. Ps.* cii[i]. 15 þonne he gast ofȝifeð, syþþan hine *gærs-bedd sceal wunian. *c* **1205** LAY. 23985 Uppen þan gras-bedde his gost he bi-læfde. **1521** LD. DACRES in *Archæol.* XVII. 203 Ther is, whiche shal alwey be redie, unto *grisse Beif com, vj fed oxen. **1573** TUSSER *Husb.* xii. (1878) 28 When Mackrell ceaseth from the seas, John Baptist brings grassebeefe and pease. **1799** J. ROBERTSON *Agric. Perth* 371 These are disposed of to English and south country drovers, for grass-beef. **1784–5** *Grass-bird [see *grass-finch* below]. **1847** in Gosse *Birds Jamaica* 252 The Grass-birds remind me much of the European Sparrow. **1865** GOULD *Handbk. Birds Austral.* I. 399 *Sphenœacus galactotes*, Tawny Grass-bird. *Ibid.* 400 *Sphenœacus gramineus*, Little Grass-bird. **1893** NEWTON *Dict. Birds*, *Grass-bird*, a general name in America..for the smaller Sandpipers..but applied by Gould..to two species of Australian birds which he referred to the genus *Sphenœacus* of Strickland. *a* **1845** HOOD *Sonn., On Mrs. Nicely*, Spotless in linen, *grass-bleached in her fame. **1842** BARHAM *Ingol. Leg.* Ser. II. *Aunt Fanny*, '*Grass-bleaching' will bring it To rights 'in a jiffy'. **1894** *Country Gentlemen's Catal.* 289 The *Grass Box can be placed either behind or in front of the cutters. **1660** HEXHAM *Dutch Dict.*, *Begrasde boter*, *grasse butter. **1776** PRYCE *Min. Cornub.* 174 The *Grass-Captain, who directs the separation of the Ore again above ground. **1855** *Cornwall* 137 'Grass captains'..being engaged chiefly on the surface works, or 'at grass'. **1885** D. J. MACGOWAN in *Bull. U.S. Fish Comm.* V. 240 Some [Chinese minnows] fatten on grass, and are called '*grass carp'. **1964** *Listener* 17 Sep. 429/1 Grass carp have been keeping Chinese rivers clear of weed for millions of years, and they have been cultivated for food in Chinese fishponds for the past 2,000 years. **1971** *Nature* 15 Jan. 154/1 The Asiatic grass carp, *Ctenopharyngodon idella*, a gross browser on aquatic vegetation. **1892** W. H. HUDSON *Nat. La Plata* 14 The *grass-cat not unlike Felis catus..but a larger, more powerful animal. **1845** *Zoologist* III. 1058 Whinchat or *Grasschat, *Saxicola rubetra*. **1641** BEST *Farm. Bks.* (Surtees) 33 They..putte two or three *grasse-cockes inone. **1846** J. BAXTER *Libr. Pract. Agric.* (ed. 4) I. 385 These lesser staddles, though last spread, are first turned, then those which were in grass-cocks. **1812** SINGER *Agric. Surv. Dumfries* 380 There is a *grass-cold, as the farmers call it, that seldom does much harm, or lasts long. **1832** SIR J. CAMPBELL *Mem.* I. xi. 293 Passengers of the class which is known by the name of *grass-combers. **1887** BESANT *The World Went* II. xxix. 309 Luke was a grass comber and a land swab. **1548** TURNER *Names of Herbes* 62 Phalaris.. because it is partly lyke grasse and partly lyke corne, it may be called *grasse corne. **1659** TORRIANO, *Falúride* [sic], the weed Grasse-corn. **1883** *Lawn Tennis for 1883* 98 One of the most important accessories to a *grass court..is a good lawn mower. **1930** W. S. MAUGHAM *Cakes & Ale* iv. 48 She's got quite a good grass court and she does one very well. **1879** MRS. A. E. JAMES *Ind. Househ. Managem.* 46 If you keep horses, you will require a syce for each horse, and a *grasscut. **1789** I. MUNRO *Narr. Milit. Oper. Coromandel Coast* iii. 28 An Horsekeeper and *Grasscutter at two pagodas. **1824** BP. HEBER *Jrnl.* (1828) II. 45, I should..give a gratuity of two rupees among the wood and grass-cutters. **1853** C. M. SMITH *Working-Man's Way in World* ii. 20 My father was a grass-cutter for twenty years on the *Morning* ——. **1918** *Independent* 6 July 11 This plane with clipped wings which keep it no more than six feet above the ground is variously nicknamed by the aviators 'grass-cutter', 'creeper', 'two-spot'. **1930** BROPHY & PARTRIDGE *Songs & Slang 1914–18* 128 *Grass-cutters*, small bombs dropped by aeroplanes on camps and bivouacs behind the lines, bursting on hitting the ground and scattering shrapnel pellets at a low level. **1944** *Word Study* Apr. 4/2 Grass Cutter. This is what pilots call the A-20A Attack Plane because it flies so low. **1946** G. S. Cansdale *Animals W. Afr.* 62 Next in size is the Cutting Grass, Grass Cutter or Cane Rat. **1961** *Times* 12 May 18/7 We had also acquired a dried grass-cutter, a sort of bush-rat. **1885** Swainson *Prov. Names Birds* 177 *Grass drake. **1888** *Amer. Naturalist* XXII. 260 The *Grass-Eating Thrips. **1904** W. H. Hudson *Green Mansions* ix. 117, I have found you.. and your grass-eating dogs as well! **1946** *Nature* 28 Dec. 928/2 The grass-eating, short-tailed, or meadow vole. **1859** Darwin *Orig. Spec.* iii. (1872) 58 *Grass-feeding quadrupeds. **1784–5** Pennant *Arct. Zool.* (1792) II. 65 *Grass Finch.. Inhabits New York.. Called the Grey Grass-bird. **1865** Gould *Handbk. Birds Austral.* I. 421 *Poëphila mirabilis*, Beautiful Grass-Finch. *Ibid.* 422 *Poëphila acuticauda*, Long-tailed Grass-Finch. **1869** J. Burroughs in *Galaxy Mag.* Aug. 172 The field or vesper-sparrow, called also grass-finch. **1882** W. R. Ludlow *Zululand* xxi. 182 As we approached the Umslatoos, we came in sight of an immense *grass fire. **1891** R. Wallace *Rural Econ. Austral. & N.Z.* xxii. 296 It must not be forgotten that a bush-fire or a grass-fire at a wrong season is one of the greatest causes of loss.. to the stock-owner in Australia. **1927** W. Plomer *I speak of Africa* i. 13 Thirty miles away a grass-fire gave the air a bluish tinge. **1967** *Evening News* 2 Nov. 7/1 (*heading*) Clamp-down on grass-fires [on railway embankments]. **1885** C. F. Holder *Marvels Anim. Life* 139 In Eastern seas we find the *grass-fish (Nemichthys) which is invariably seen upright among the grass it resembles. **1803** Windham 9 Dec. in Amyot *Sp. Parl.* (1812) II. 131 They were men.. who.. had not yet got their *grass-flesh off. **1901** H. Gadow *Amphibia & Reptiles* 253 The habits of the *Grass-frog are essentially terrestrial. **1931** H. W. Parker in W. P. Pycraft *Standard Nat. Hist.* xii. 498 The Common English Grass-frog may be taken as an example of the normal structure and commoner habits of the whole group. **1691** J. Wilson *Belphegor* Prol., Dram. Wks. (1874) 291 What makes you leave a fair wife at home For a *grass-girl, or some odd homely Joan? **1910** *N.Z. Jrnl. Agric.* 15 Aug. 223 No means are yet known for the thorough control of the New Zealand *grass-grub. **1946** *Nature* 21 Dec. 920/1 The Entomology Division has focussed its attention on the grass-grub, the major insect pest affecting pastures [in N.Z.]. **1969** *N.Z. News* 9 Apr. 7/1 Grass grub and porina caterpillar, numbered among the most devastating of New Zealand pasture pests, face a three-pronged attack. **1751** Lady Luxborough *Let. to Shenstone* 27 May, My eyes have.. forty-three troop-horses to observe scampering.. which, with the tent of the *grass-guards, really makes the scenery pretty. **1758** Washington *Let. Writ.* 1889 II. 57 We have been obliged, for the sake of our Cattle, to move the grass guard to Cresaps, 15 miles hence. **1875** Southward *Dict. Typogr.* 44 It is a frequent occurrence for a casual *grass-hand to take more wages than a regular book-hand. **1881** McClatchie in *Encycl. Brit.* XIII. 586/1 This style consists of the ordinary cursive hand .. and also of what is termed the 'grass' hand, which is very much abbreviated and exceedingly difficult to acquire. **1897** *Grass hawser [see *grass rope* below]. **1921** *Daily Colonist* (Victoria, B.C.) 2 Apr. 1/1 The Victoria *Grass Hockey Club is holding a practice this afternoon. **1964** *Maclean's Mag.* 16 Nov. 81/2, I.. do solemnly swear never to waste company time arguing.. or raving about.. lawn bowling and grass hockey. **1809** Kendall *Trav.* II. xxxviii. 39 [Ponds] that being filled only in the wet seasons, and affording grass in the dry, are denominated *grass-holes. **1658** Rowland *Moufet's Theat. Ins.* 908 From thence it takes the name of *grasse-honey.. respect being had to those things from which it is collected or gathered. **1812** *Niles' Weekly Reg.* II. 131/1 The purveyor of public supplies advertises for.. 1000 *grass hooks. **1858** J. A. Warder *Hedges & Evergreens* 97 Using for the purpose [of pruning] a strong knife about two feet long, or a common grass-hook. **1969** *Sears, Roebuck Catal.* 1079 Craftsman Grass Hook. Traditional scythe type, heat-treated, 12½-in. blade adjusts to two cutting angles. *c* **1647** Boyle *Mem.* in Wks. 1744 I. *Life* 12 As when in summer we take up our *grass-horses into the stable, and give them store of oats, it is a sign, that we mean to travel them. **1691** *Lond. Gaz.* No. 2716/4 Stolen.. a Grass Horse. **1557** *Richmond. Wills* (Surtees 1853) 102 To every *grisse house within the parishe which hath no corne growing, one busshell of rye. **1892** Jas. Kennedy *Mem. M. S. Kennedy* v. 57 There was a grass-house belonging to a banya half a mile in another direction. **1884** *Leisure Hour* Feb. 84/1 The central building [of a house in Fiji].. formed the family sitting-room.. Mr. L.'s room lay beyond—a *grass hut all by itself. **1807** Duncan in *Prize Ess. Highl. Soc. Scot.* III. 351 When about three weeks old, and beginning to make grass a part of their food.. a straggling lamb or two will sometimes die of what is called the *Grass ill. **1747** Mrs. Glasse *Cookery* xxi. 160 *Grass Lamb comes in in April or May. **1793** *Misc. Ess.* in *Ann. Reg.* 379/1 The vicinity to Smithfield market makes early grass-Lambs an object of considerable importance. **1895** *Daily News* 2 Aug. 6/6 *Grass-lawn.. formed the material of many of the prettiest dresses. **1892** C. E. Douglas in J. Pascoe *Mr. Explorer Douglas* (1957) 176 It is very common all along the ranges close to the *grass line. **1909** *Man. Seamanship* II. x. 180 A grass line attached to a breaker should be towed astern in case.. the boat missed the towing ship. **1941** J. Masefield *Nine Days Wonder* 25 Various devices were tried for heaving off strings of boats together on messengers of grass-line. **1959** *Tararua* XIII. 45 *Scrubline* for the upper limit of the scrub seems to be confined to New Zealand as does the corresponding *grassline*. **1866** Mrs. Whitney *L. Goldthwaite* viii. (1867) 175 A strip of sheer, delicate *grass-linen, which needle and thread.. were turning into a cobweb border. **1479** *Acta Dom. Conc.* (1839) 41/1 He Resavit þe said scheipe in gresing fra þe said lady & tuke & is pait of his *gerss male þarfor. **1752** J. Stewart in *Scots Mag.* June (1753) 286/1, 10 l. Scots was in payment of the grass-mail of cattle. *a* **1640** Massinger *Very Woman* III. v, How she holds her nose up, like a jennet In the wind of a *grass-mare! **1799** J. Robertson *Agric. Perth* 232 The *grass-meal of a sheep.. is valued at two or three shillings. **1597** *MS. Grassmen's Bk. St. Giles's, Durham*, Delyvered of the *grasse money. **1837** *Penny Cycl.* VIII. 136/1 *Crambus*, a genus of moths.. called in England the Veneers, and sometimes *grass-moths. **1824** Mactaggart *Gallovid. Encycl.*, *Grass-nail. **1851** H. Stephens *Bk. of Farm* (ed. 2) II. 339/1 The blade [of the scythe] is further supported by the addition of the light stay C, termed the grass-nail. **1797** *Monthly Mag.* III. 34 Girls of this description, are.. eagerly sought for, under the appellation of *grass-nurses. **1844** Hoblyn *Dict. Med.*, *Grass-oil of Namur*, a volatile oil procured, according to Royle, from the Andropogon Calamus aromaticus. **1887** Moloney *Forestry W. Afr.* 454 The oil produced in the Namar district of the Nerbudda Valley is sometimes called grass-oil of Namar. **1893** Sarah Grand *Heavenly Twins* (1894) III. ii. 252 Poor *grass-orphans. *a* **1483** *Liber Niger* in *Househ. Ord.* 17 [Solomon had] dayly x stalled oxen very great and xx great *grasse oxen. **1840** J. Gould in *Proc. Zool. Soc.* VIII. 147 Those [birds] now exhibited were three new species of small *Grass Parrakeets. **1848** —— *Birds Austral.* V. pl. 37 *Euphema chrysostoma*, Blue-banded Grass-Parrakeet. [Six other species named.] **1884–5** *Riverside Nat. Hist.* (1888) IV. 355 The zebra grass-parakeet, *Melopsittacus undulatus*. **1913** G. M. Mathews *List Birds Austral.* 138 Neophema pulchella. Red-shouldered *Grass-Parrot. **1936** A. Russell *Gone Nomad* vi. 44 'It's out there!' he continued pointing to a flock of budgerigars flashing across the plain. 'Them grass parrots are makin' in fer it.' **1966** Eastman & Hunt *Parrots of Australia* 153 Characteristics of Neophema Group... Known as Grass Parrots because they are strictly ground-feeders on grass and herbaceous seeds. **1790** J. B. Moreton *Mann. W. Ind.* 57 One hundred oxen.. will require a good convenient *grass-penn to feed them. **1513** Douglas *Æneis* xii. Prol. 92 The *gers pilis. **1746** E. Erskine *Serm.* Wks. 1871 III. 320 The rocks and trees and grass piles. **1894** *Harper's Mag.* Mar. 566 The sweet pogonia or *grass-pink of our sedgy swamps (*Pogonia ophioglossoides*). **1633** Johnson *Gerarde's Herbal* ii. clxxviii. 581 Cordus first mentioned it, and that by the Dutch name of *Grasse Poley, which name we may also very fitly retaine in English. **1764** *Mus. Rust.* I. 356 There are several ways of breeding potatoes in Ireland.. First, On rich clay land without any manure, vulgarly called *grass potatoes. **1847** Gosse *Birds Jamaica* 249 Yellow Face *Grass-Quit, *Spermophila olivacea*. [And other species.] **1893** Newton *Dict. Birds*, *Grass-quit*, applied in Jamaica to some species of the genus *Phonipara*, or.. *Euethia*. **1890** 'Rolf Boldrewood' *Col. Reformer* (1891) 318 Their *grass-rights, their.. herds and their flocks. **1882** Nares *Seamanship* (ed. 6) 147 Veer a buoy or small boat astern by the *grass rope [**1897** (ed. 7) 141 by a grass hawser]. **1573** Tusser *Husb.* (1878) 37 A brush sithe and *grasse sithe. **1787** Washington *Diaries* (1925) III. 243 Called on my return at French's where I had begun with grass Scythes (a cradle having been found not to answer). **1908** *Sears, Roebuck Catal.* 522 (*caption*) Double rib extra grade all steel grass scythe. **1700** S. L. tr. *Fryke's Voy. E. Ind.* 219 From thence we pass'd to the Gras-Zee, or *Grass-Sea, so called from the Grass which grows there, so that the Sea appears just like a Meadow. **1922** C. G. Turner *Happy Wanderer* 211 The official issue of clothing is a wide-brimmed '*grass-seeder' straw hat. **1936** C. R. Allen *Poor Scholar* xix. 202 The grass-seeder would entrust his cheque to the squatter. *Ibid.*, *Grass-seeding is conducive to a princely thirst. *Ibid.* 204 Grass-seeding is rather characteristic of these parts [Banks Peninsula]. **1607** Topsell *Four-f. Beasts* (1658) 62 When Oxen come first of all after Winter to grasse, they fall *grasse-sick. **1920** *Glasgow Herald* 9 Sept. 9 The discovery of a bipolar organism in *grass-sickness. **1923** *Daily Mail* 18 June 7 The disease in horses known as grass sickness which first appeared in Forfarshire in the summer of 1909... The principal symptoms are paralysis of the palate and gullet, causing inability to swallow. **1955** Gaiger & Davies *Vet. Path. & Bacteriol.* (ed. 4) xxix. 555 It would appear, therefore, as if little or no immunity is left by an attack of grass sickness. **1852** R. S. Surtees *Sponge's Sp. Tour* (1893) 224 The *grass-siding of Orlantire Park wall favouring their design, they increased the trot to a canter. **1346–7** *Durham Acct. Rolls* (Surtees) 743 *Gressiluer.. Et in herbag. empt. pro Joh'e de Haliden Hospit. superueinent. et equis Hostillarii xi *s*. [**1898** J. R. Musick *Hawaii* vi. 79 Kalakaua's hula girls sometimes danced nude but the usual costume is a skirt made of grass, coming to the knees.] **1937** C. Gessler *Hawaii* xxix. 334 The *grass skirt introduced in Kalakaua's time survives in Hawaii mainly for sale to tourists. **1938** R. Finlayson *Brown Man's Burden* 68 She loved to dance the hulas in that bright-coloured grass skirt. **1949** M. Mead *Male & Female* ii. 27 They [*sc.* anthropologists] are accused of having.. put on a grass skirt or a loin-cloth. **1970** *Observer* (Colour Suppl.) 15 Feb. 20/2 Cruise passengers [are] very much in so far as the multitude of small shops selling dress materials and grass (plastic grass) skirts go. **1863** Atkinson *Stanton Grange* 219, I seed a *grass-snake come out of the corn near me. **1884–5** *Riverside Nat. Hist.* (1888) III. 370 With the common people it [*Tropidonotus natrix*] is known as the ringed or grass-snake, and is often tamed. **1883** *Encycl. Amer.* I. 530/1 The *grass sparrows (*Poœcetes gramineus*). **1830** M. Donovan *Dom. Econ.* I. 251 *Grass Spirit.. procurable in great quantities from the various kinds of grass. **1883** W. S. Kent in *Fisheries Bahamas* 47 Another variety of the coarse-fibred series is the *Grass-sponge (*Spongia equina*, var. *cerebriformis*). **1840** Browning *Sordello* iii. 327 Leaf-fall and *grass-spring for the year:—for us! **1878** *Grass staggers [see stagger *sb.*[1] 2]. **1889** [see loco *sb.*[1]]. **1960** *Farmer & Stockbreeder* 29 Mar. 99/1 A disorder of cattle and sheep which is now more wide-spread than is generally realized has been christened with a host of names. The commonest is 'grass staggers', because it generally occurs in grazing animals and those which are affected tend to stagger. **1969** *Times* 13 Oct. 14/6 No accurate estimate has been made of the toll that grass staggers, or hypomagnesaemia, takes of beef cattle. *a* **1490** Botoner *Itin.* in R. Willis *Archit. Nomencl. Mid. Ages* (1844) 26 Altitudo turris Sancti Stephani Bristoll continet in altitudine from the *grasse [*glossed* erth] table to the gargyle est 21 brachia, id est 42 virgas. *c* **1693** in *Dict. Arch.* (Arch. Publ. Soc.) s.v., A Bill of work done for ye Lord Scudamore .. at the two ends of the house, below ye grass table. **1867** Gwilt *Archit.* Gloss. Add., Earth Table, or Ground Table, and Grass Table. **1696** J. F. *Merchant's Ware-ho.* 27 This sort is made of the same stuff your *Grass Taffeties are. **1824** Loudon *Encycl. Gard.* (ed. 2) §1338 Verge-shears.. are chiefly used for trimming the sides of box-edgings and *grass-verges. **1930** *Morning Post* 12 June 12/5 He was within four feet of the grass verge and was unable to avoid the approaching motor cycle. **1937** *Sunday Times* 10 Jan., Nearly all the new roads have broad central 'reserves' and broad grass verges on each side. **1963** *Radio Times* 14 Mar. 5/1 Even if there was a grass verge or something handy to wipe a toe-cap you would have to lie face down and drag yourself along. **1865** Gould *Handbk. Birds Austral.* I. 349 Great *Grass-warbler. Exile Grass-Warbler. Lineated Grass-Warbler. **1927** *Sunday Express* 17 July 17/5 Sometimes the road was so bad that, dodging between the trees, they left it for the flat *grass-way beside it. **1836** W. A. Bromfield *Flora Vectensis* 537 *Zostera marina* ..*Grassweed. **1706** Phillips (ed. Kersey), **Grass-week*, rogation-week, so call'd in the Inns of Court and Chancery, because the commons of that week consist chiefly of sallets, with hard eggs, green sauce, etc. **1712** J. James tr. *Le Blond's Gardening* 23 A *Grass-work, encompassed with Cases and Yews, with Water-works in the Middle. **1727–41** Chambers *Cycl.* s.v., Small pieces of grass-work, as knots, shell-work.. cut-work.. etc. must always be laid with turf. **1855** *Cornwall* 164 Here is the 'grass-work' of a great Copper Mine. *Ibid.* 289 The *grass-workers.. have stopped work. **1658** Rowland *Moufet's Theat. Ins.* 929, I have seen him [the hornet] to eat of *grasse worms. **1776** Withering *Brit. Plants* 554 *Grasswrack. **1838** Audubon *Ornith. Biogr.* IV. 10 Its subsistence.. is chiefly derived from the grass-wrack or Eel-grass, *Zostera marina*. **1961** R. W. Butcher *New Illustr. Brit. Flora* II. 595 The Common Grass-wrack or Eelgrass is a stout to slender, green, marine plant with compressed, keeled, much-branched stems. **1898** Morris *Austral. Eng.* 519/1 *Grass W[ren]*... Called by Gould the *Textile Wren*. **1934** A. Russell *Tramp-Royal in Wild Australia* xvii. 103 The grass wren he called the 'jump-along'. **1965** *Austral. Encycl.* IV. 363 All grass-wrens, though able to fly fairly well, move mainly on foot, and with remarkable speed. **1841** Tattersall *Sport. Archit.* 75 A *grass-yard adjoining the kennel.

† **grass**, *sb.*[2] *Obs. rare*[−1]. [a. F. *gras* (*des cadavres*).] = adipocere.

1793 Beddoes *Sea Scurvy* 96 The soap or grass is said.. not to constitute above $\frac{1}{10}$ or $\frac{1}{12}$ of the body.

grass (grɑːs, -æ-), *v.* [f. grass *sb.*[1] Cf. graze *v.*[1]]

† **1.** *trans.* To plunge or sink in grass. *Obs.*

c **1460** *Towneley Myst.* xii. 189 *Primus Pastor*. How pastures oure fee? *Garcio*. Thay ar gryssed to the kne. *a* **1670** Hacket *Abp. Williams* II. (1692) 20 One Arrow must be shot after another, though both be grast, and never found again.

2. *trans.* † **a.** To feed (cattle) on grass, to graze. Also, of land: To yield grass enough for. *Obs.* **b.** To supply (cattle) with grass.

c **1500** *Three Kings Sons* (E.E.T.S.) 112 They wolle likken me to a Bocher that gressith beestes. **1523** Fitzherb. *Surv.* xix. (1539) 39 Howe many cattel it wyll grasse. **1584** *Vestry Bks.* (Surtees) 15 Yt is.. agreed.. that everie iiij pounde rent within this parrishe.. shal gras winter and somer one shepe. **1594** *Privy Council* 10 Mar. in Arb. *Garner* I. 301 For the.. grassing of beefs and muttons. **1617** Sir R. Boyle in *Lismore Papers* (1886) I. 162 He to grass 14 hed of cattles till Michas. *c* **1710** Celia Fiennes *Diary* (1888) 130 Breeding and grasseing Cattle. **1766** W. Gordon *Gen. Counting-ho.* 467 Grassing the highland cows. **1871** Blackie *Four Phases* i. 43 You expect.. your cow when well grassed, to give good milk.

3. a. *intr.* To produce grass, become covered with grass.

1573 Tusser *Husb.* xxxv. (1878) 84 With otes ye may sowe it, the sooner to grasse, more soone to be pasture to bring it to passe. **1861** Sir T. F. Buxton in *Peaks, Passes, & Glaciers* Ser. II. I. 284 Three mighty ramparts.. of which.. the youngest has hardly commenced grassing on its outer side.

b. *trans.* To cover with grass or turf. Chiefly with advs. To lay *down* turf upon; to enclose *in* a grass-covered grave; to cover *over* with a growth of grass, or with turf.

1832 L. Hunt *Translations* 242 I'd just as lief be buried, tomb'd and grass'd in. **1849** *Jrnl. R. Agric. Soc.* X. I. 18 If they plough it up and take a crop of oats.. they leave it to time and nature to grass it over again. **1888** T. Hardy *Wessex Tales* I. 203 The new house had so far progressed that the gardeners were beginning to grass down the front. **1895** J. Brown *Pilgrim Fathers* viii. 211 The graves being levelled and grassed over. *a* **1900** *Mod.* I intend to have that piece of ground grassed.

4. To lay or stretch on the grass or on the surface of the ground: **a.** To lay out (flax, etc.) on grass for the purpose of bleaching.

1765 *Mus. Rust.* IV. 460 Short heath is the best field for grassing flax. *Ibid.* 461 Experience only can fully teach a person the signs of flax being sufficiently grassed. **1847** *Jrnl. R. Agric. Soc.* VIII. II. 455 It is not intended to grass the flax immediately that it is taken out of steep.

b. *slang*, passing into general use: To knock or throw (an adversary) down; to fell; *spec.* in Rugby and Australian National Football.

1814 *Sporting Mag.* XLIV. 70 A terrific blow on the mouth, which floored or grassed him. **1848** Dickens *Dombey* xliv, He was severely fibbed by the Larkey one, and heavily grassed. **1864** C. Clarke *Box for Season* II. 76 He.. fell head foremost into the pit of Professor Sharp's stomach ..grassing him at once. **1883** Besant *All in Garden Fair* I. Introd. 12 His foot caught in a tuft of grass, and he was grassed. **1937** in Partridge *Dict. Slang*. **1963** *Times* 13 June 13/3 In Rugby football no try could be simply converted; the oval had to be propelled through the uprights and players were not tackled but grassed. **1968** Eagleson & McKie *Terminology Austral. Nat. Football* II. 13 *Grass*, knock a player to the ground by a hip or a shoulder bump.

fig. **1826** J. Wilson *Noct. Ambr.* Wks. 1855 I. 162 At the first facer Hume or Voltaire is grassed and gives in.

c. To bring (a fish) to bank.

1856 Kingsley in *Life* (1877) I. 490 We'll.. Whoop like boys at pounders Fairly played and grassed. **1861** Hughes *Tom Brown at Oxf.* III. iii. 52 The intense delight of grassing your first big fish after a nine months' fast. **1894** *Field* 9 June 832/1 One of the anglers.. grassed six brace.

d. To bring down (birds, game) by a shot.

1871 *Daily News* 8 Apr. 5 The excitement of grassing blue rocks. **1889** H. O'Reilly *50 Years on Trail* 21, I lost no time in grassing another [antelope].

e. *Cricket.* To drop (a catch).

1960 E. W. SWANTON *W. Indies Revisited* v. 124 Illingworth had a very sharp, low c and b chance from Sobers. He grassed it.

5. *intr.* Of animals: To crop the grass; to graze.

1859 CORNWALLIS *New World* I. 198 The horses had been left grassing at a short remove.

6. *Trade slang.* **a.** *trans.* To discharge from work for a time (usually for misbehaviour).

1881 *Lanc. Gloss.* s.v., What's up wi' yor Jim? Why, he wur drinkin'; and th' mestur grassed him for a fortnit.

b. *intr. Printing.* To do casual or jobbing work. (Cf. GRASS *sb.* 11.)

1894 *Westm. Gaz.* 19 Feb. 7/3 The society is dead against pluralists, and does not allow men with a full 'claim'—*i.e.* 54 hours' work a week—to 'grass' anywhere else.

7. *Mining.* To bring to the surface.

1890 *Goldfields Victoria* 28 This company have about 30 tons of good stone grassed from their 50 foot shaft.

8. *trans.* and *intr.* To betray (someone); to inform the police about (someone). (Cf. GRASS *sb.*[1] 12.) *slang.*

1936 J. CURTIS *Gilt Kid* xxvii. 269 Anyhow it was a dirty trick grassing his pals. **1938** G. GREENE *Brighton Rock* III. ii. 118, I wouldn't grass, Spicer said, unless I had to. **1958** F. NORMAN *Bang to Rights* 86 What is more he didn't grass any one else. **1963** *Daily Tel.* 28 Feb. 15/7 *(heading)* 'Grassing' discussed at Co-op murder trial. *Ibid.*, The underworld code dealing with criminals in prison who 'grass' or inform on colleagues was discussed. **1965** J. PORTER *Dover Two* vii. 77 It won't come out! Not unless you start grassing.

†**grassant**, *a. Obs.* [ad. L. *grassant-em*, pres. pple. of *grassārī* to roam about, lie in wait.] Roaming about, or lying in wait, with evil intent. Of diseases, etc.: Raging.

1659 GAUDEN *Tears Church* II. xi. 183 Those innovations and mischiefs which are now grassant in England. **1674** R. GODFREY *Inj. & Ab. Physic* 169 Those violent and stubborn Diseases which are grassant and assail us in our dayes. *a* **1734** NORTH *Exam.* II. v. §42 (1740) 339 Thieves, Malefactors and Cheats, every where grassant.

grassapine, corrupt var. GOSSAMPINE, *Obs.*

†**grassate**, *v. Obs.*[−1] [f. ppl. stem of L. *grassārī* (see prec.).] *intr.* Of a disease: To rage.

1652 GAULE *Magastrom.* 259 The Delphian oracle being consulted about a great plague grassating among the Ionians, it was answered [etc.].

†**grassation**. *Obs.* [ad. L. *grassātiōn-em* rioting, n. of action f. *grassārī* (see prec.).] The action of making violent attacks; also, lying in wait to attack; assailing, assault.

1610 DONNE *Pseudo-Martyr* 52 This claime to that Kingdome was..reuiued againe by Tyrannicall force, by violent grassation, and by the robbery of Princes. **1627–77** FELTHAM *Resolves* II. viii. 176 If in Vice there be a perpetual Grassation, there must be in virtue a perpetual Vigilence. **1652** MARBURY *Comm. Habbak.* I. 1 Do not the Jesuits.. incense the King thereof to grassation and destruction of all that have not the mark of the beast? **1656–81** BLOUNT *Glossogr.*, *Grassation*, a robbing, killing, assailing. **1680** H. MORE *Apocal. Apoc.* 80 Notwithstanding the grassations of these Imposters, the truly Apostolick Church would be kept safe.

†**grassator**. *Obs.* [a. L. *grassātor* in same sense, agent-n. f. *grassārī*: see prec.] A footpad, waylayer, violent assailant.

1602 F. HERING *Anatomyes* A iij b, You haue cut off great numbers of Grassators and Robbers. **1686** RENWICK *Serm.* xxi. (1776) 273 They shall involve themselves in compliance with wicked tyrants and grassators.

ˈ**grass-cloth**. **a.** A fine light cloth, resembling linen, woven from the fibres of the inner bark of the **grass-cloth plant** (*Boehmeria nivea*). **b.** A thick fabric made in the Canary islands from some vegetable fibre.

1857 R. TOMES *Amer. in Japan* iv. 92 Long flowing robes of yellow and blue grass-cloth. *a* **1858** N. WILSON in Homans *Cycl. Comm.* 845 My entire success in the cultivation of the China grass-cloth plant (*Bœhmeria nivea*) introduced [into Jamaica] in 1854. **1868** *Rep. U.S. Commissioner Agric.* (1869) 306 A water net..is made of grass-cloth or some coarse material. **1883** BURTON & CAMERON *To Gold Coast* I. v. 125 The articles of dress [in the Canaries] were grass-cloth, thick as matting [etc.]. **1884** *Weekly Scotsman* 9 Feb. 1/7 The grass cloth of the Chinese ..is said to rival the best French cambric in softness and fineness of texture.

†**grass-earth**. *Obs.* Also 3 -hurde, 4 -herth(e, 8 -hearth, -hurt. [OE. *gærs-ierþ*, f. *gærs* GRASS *sb.*[1] + *ierþ* ploughing, EARTH *sb.*[2]] The November ploughing of grass-land.

c **1050** *Rect. Sing. Pers.* in Thorpe *Ags. Laws* I. 434 Toeacan ðam iii æceras to bene & ii to gærs-yrðe. **1235–52** *Rentalia Glaston.* (Somerset Rec. Soc.) 109 Quos aquietabit per garshurde. *c* **1300** *Battle-Abbey Custumals* (1887) 89 Et post festum Sancti Martini, arrabunt domino j acram, que vocatur Grasherþe [*printed* Grasherxe] qui habent carrucas. **1363** in Kennett *Par. Antiq.* (1818) II. 137 Ad arandam terram domini..quod vocatur Gras-herth. **1706** PHILLIPS (ed. Kersey), *Grass-hearth*, or grass-hurt, was anciently a custom in some places, for the tenants to bring their ploughs, and do one day's work for their lord.

grassed (grɑːst, -æ-), *ppl. a.* [f. GRASS *sb.*[1] and *v.* + -ED.]

1. Grown or covered with grass. Also *grassed-down*.

1731 MEDLEY *Kolben's Cape G. Hope* I. 79 The Chamtouers..are possess'd of a fine flat country, well grass'd and watered. **1835** J. BATMAN in Cornwallis *New World* (1859) I. App. 404 We passed through an open forest ..with excellently grassed surface. **1875** KATH. S. MACQUOID *My Story* II. xix. 288 When I reached the grassed slope, I found the frozen grass very slippery. **1884** J. G. BOURKE *Snake Dance Moquis* xxxi. 343 A country well grassed with 'grama'. **1960** *Times* 23 Jan. 11/4 The rest of the grassed-down area. **1967** *Heretaunga Plains* (Ministry of Works, N.Z.) 49/1 A crop rotation programme is normally observed and this provides for grassed-down periods (for grass seed and stock fattening) which improve soil fertility.

2. *Golf.* Of a golf-club (see quot. 1890).

1878 'CAPT. CRAWLEY' *Football* etc. 83 (Golf) *Grassed*, a term used instead of spooned, to signify the backward slope of a club-face. **1883** *Cassell's Bk. Sports & Past.* 51 The golfer's tools..consisting of the play-club, the grassed-driver [etc.]. **1890** HUTCHINSON *Golf* (Badm. Libr.) 59 The 'grassed club' which was in reality nothing but a driver with a slightly filed-back face.

grasser[1] (ˈgrɑːsə(r), -æ-). *U.S.* [f. GRASS *sb.*[1] + -ER.[1]] A calf brought up on grass as distinguished from one fed on prepared food.

1881 *Chicago Times* 1 June, Several droves of Texas 'grassers' were among the fresh arrivals.

grasser[2] (ˈgrɑːsə(r), -æ-). [f. GRASS *v.* 8 + -ER[1].] = GRASS *sb.*[1] 12.

1950 P. TEMPEST *Lag's Lexicon* 97 *Grasser.* One who gives information. A 'squealer' or 'squeaker'. The origin derives from rhyming slang: grasshopper—copper; a 'grass' or 'grasser' tells the 'copper' or policeman. **1966** 'L. LANE' *ABZ of Scouse* 46 *Grasser*, a police informant; a stool-pigeon. **1968** 'P. ALDING' *Circle of Danger* vii. 57 Five minutes alone with you and he'll be babbling like a grasser. **1968** R. JEFFRIES *Traitor's Crime* iii. 31 'How reliable was the original information?' 'As reliable as any information is from a grasser.'

‖**grasserie** (grasəri). [Fr., f. *gras* fat.] A virus disease of silkworms, characterized by yellowing of the skin and liquefaction of the internal tissues.

1836 F. G. COMSTOCK *Pract. Treat. Culture Silk* II. 40 *(heading)* The grasserie.—The period at which the Worms are most subject to this disease, is before the second moulting, and in the third and fourth ages. **1879** C. U. RILEY *Silkworm* 14 Silkworms..may become yellow, limp, and die of a malady called *grasserie* or jaundice. **1923** *Nature* 24 Mar. 411/2 Flacherie is of less importance in mulberry worms, while grasserie is stated to cause loss to all species. **1943** W. BORAH *Silk Raising in Colonial Mexico* vi. 64 Normally,..grasserie is a moderate scourge which does not result in epidemics. *Ibid.* 65 Even when confined to single silk houses, however, grasserie..can reduce or ruin many a crop.

grass-green, *a.* (and *sb.*) (Stress variable.) [Cf. MDu. *grasgroene* (Du. *grasgroen*), MHG. *grasgrüene* (G. *grasgrün*), ON. *grasgrønn* (Da. *græsgrøn*, Sw. *gräsgrön*).]

1. Green as grass; having the colour of grass.

a **700** *Epinal Gloss.* 298 *Carpassini*, gresgro[e]ni. **13..** *K. Alis.* 299 Mercury he made gras-grene. *a* **1593** MARLOWE *Jew of Malta* I. (1633) B 2, Iacints, hard Topas, grasse-greene Emeraulds. **1641** FRENCH *Distill.* vi. (1651) 193 There will remaine..a grasse-green Liquor. **1812** SIR H. DAVY *Chem. Philos.* 424 Oxide of nickel is employed to give colours to enamels and porcelain; in different mixtures it produces brown red, and grass green tints. **1842** TENNYSON *Lancelot & Guinevere* 24 A gown of grass-green silk she wore. **1884–5** *Riverside Nat. Hist.* (1888) III. 369 *Tragops prasinus*..is a beautiful grass-green animal, living in the jungles of India.

b. quasi-*sb.* and *sb.* (the *adj.* used *absol.*).

1657 R. LIGON *Barbadoes* (1673) 83 All sorts of yellows, with their shadows intermixt with grass greens. **1696** BP. PATRICK *Comm. Exod.* xxviii. (1697) 542 The colour of it is a Grass-green; wonderfully refreshing. **1792** CHARLOTTE SMITH *Desmond* III. 120 Lined with sky blue, or grass green. **1843** PORTLOCK *Geol.* 513 A..light oil-green colour, occasionally grass-green, and passing into bottle-green.

2. Green with grass.

1602 SHAKS. *Ham.* IV. v. 31 At his head a grasse-greene Turfe. **1742** SHENSTONE *Schoolmistress* 273 When my bones in grass-green sods are laid. **1767** F. FAWKES *Idyll. Theocritus* xiii. 32 And grass-green meads pronounc'd the summer near. **1830** TENNYSON *Circumstance* 6 Two graves grass-green beside a gray church-tower.

†**grasshop**. *Obs.* Forms: 1 gershoppe, gærs-, græshoppa, 3 gresseoppe, 3–4 gresshop(p)e, 5 gyrssoppe, 4–6 gres-, grishop, grysope, 4, 6 gressop, 6 grass-, gressoppe, 6–7 grashop. [OE. *gærs-hoppe*, *-hoppa*, f. *gærs* GRASS *sb.*[1] + *hoppa*, related to *hoppian* HOP *v.*[1] Cf. Sw. *gräshoppa*, Da. *græshoppe*.] A grasshopper, locust.

c **825** *Vesp. Psalter* cviii. 23 Ascecen eam swe swe gershoppe [*c* **1000** *Ags. Ps.* gærshoppa]. *c* **975** *Rushw. Gosp.* Matt. iii. 4 His mete þanne wæs græshoppa. *c* **1250** *Gen. & Ex.* 3065 Moyses siðen and aaron Seiden..To-morȝen sulen gresseoppes cumen. *a* **1387** *Sinon. Barthol.* (Anecd. Oxon.) 16 *Cicada*, gressehope. **14..** *Voc.* in *Wr.-Wülcker* 707/7 *Hec cicada*, a grysope. **1496** *Bk. St. Albans*, *Fishing* i j b, A grete greshop. *a* **1529** SKELTON *P. Sparowe* 134 Lorde, how he wolde hop After the gressop! **1565** COOPER *Thesaurus*, *Achetæ*,..greshops that chirpe lowde and pleasantly. **1607** WALKINGTON *Opt. Glass* 32 Phydias merited great praise for his Scarabee, his Grashop, his Bee.

grasshopper (ˈgrɑːshɒpə(r), ˈgræs-), *sb.* [f. GRASS *sb.*[1] + HOPPER[1]. Cf. LG. and Flemish (Kilian) *grashopper*, MSw. *gräshoppare*, G. *gräshupfer*.]

1. a. A name for orthopterous insects of the families *Acridiidæ* and *Locustidæ*, remarkable for their powers of leaping, and the chirping sound produced by the males (see quot. 1880). Occas. with allusion to Eccl. xii. 5.

(Coverdale sometimes uses the word where both the later versions and Wyclif have *locust*.)

14.. *Voc.* in Wr.-Wülcker 572/32 *Cicada*, a grashoppere. **14..** *MS. Sloane* 4 lf. 80 in *N. & Q.* Ser. III. (1864) VI. 4/1 Also a greshopper ys good, for dyuers fysshes must haue diuers baytys. **1526** *Pilgr. Perf.* (W. de W. 1531) 165 They be blessed & happy that wyll apply & dispose themselfe with the greshopper to lepe vp as hye as they may. **1579** SPENSER *Sheph. Cal.* Oct. 11 Such pleasaunce makes the Grashopper so poore. **1611** BIBLE *Eccl.* xii. 5 The grashopper shall be a burden. *c* **1611** CHAPMAN *Iliad* III. 161 As in well-growne woods, on trees, cold spinie grashoppers Sit chirping. **1692** L'ESTRANGE *Fables* ccxvii. 189 An Ant and a Grasshopper. **1727–46** THOMSON *Summer* 446 Scarce a chirping grasshopper is heard Thro' the dumb mead. **1771** SMOLLETT *Humph. Cl.* 24 May, My uncle..bolted through the window as nimble as a grasshopper. **1880** *Encycl. Brit.* XI. 60/1 In Britain the term is chiefly applicable to the large green grasshopper (*Locusta viridissima*)..and to smaller and more obscure species of the genera *Stenobothrus*, *Gomphocerus*, and *Tettix*. **1882** *Contemp. Rev.* Aug. 230 The principal breeding grounds of that formidable pest, the locust or grass-hopper, known to entomologists as *Caloptenus spretus*. **1886** BESANT *Childr. Gibeon* II. vi. II. 54 These old people hear the voice of the grasshopper continually..They hate the voice of the grasshopper.

b. *fig.* As a term of derision or reproach.

1561 DAUS *Bullinger on Apoc.* (1573) 114 The Pope.. defending them [errors] by his vngratious Grashoppers that eate vp all thynges. **1581** J. BELL *Haddon's Answ. Osor.* 28 b, For I accompt it sufficient to pinche that seely abject grashopper Dalmada now & then in the chase. **1788** MAD. D'ARBLAY *Diary* 13 Feb., In two minutes more he will be somewhere else, skipping backwards and forwards; what a grasshopper it is! **1935** *N. & Q.* CLXIX, 365 Use of animal names as epithets to man... *Grasshopper*, undependable; mental effort inconstant and purpose shifting. **1968** *Listener* 27 June 827/3 My natural inclination was to watch the screen for a moment, then look away, then look back again. This, after I began to study my own behaviour, turned out to be the way I watched not just the news but all television. I was the grasshopper viewer; and, I suspect, but one of millions of grasshopper viewers.

c. *Rhyming slang* = COPPER *sb.*[4] Also ellipt. *grass.* (Cf. also quot. 1955 s.v. GRASS *sb.*[1] 12.)

1893 in FARMER & HENLEY *Dict. Slang.* **1907** *Daily Chron.* 1 Apr. 4/4 The criminal classes always speak of policemen as 'grasshoppers'. **1938** F. D. SHARPE *Sharpe of Flying Squad* 330 *Grasshopper*, a policeman. **1939** H. HODGE *Cab, Sir?* xv. 222 A policeman is the usual cockney 'Grass' (copper, grass-hopper). **1950** [see GRASSER[2]].

d. (See quot. 1956.) *U.S. slang.*

1942 *Pop. Sci.* Jan. 63 Grasshoppers...that's what the army calls its new odd-job planes. **1956** W. A. HEFLIN *U.S.A.F. Dict.* 234 *Grasshopper*, any small, light, cabin monoplane used for observation, liaison, or training.

†**2.** An alleged name for the hare. *Obs.*

a **1325** *Names Hare* in *Rel. Ant.* I. 133 The grashoppere.

3. In a pianoforte: = HOPPER[1] 9.

1807 *Specif. W. Southwell's Patent* No. 3029. 2 The end of the grasshopper hath pressed up the connecting rod *l*, *h*, which by its pressure on the tail of the hammer, hath caused it to give the stroke. **1845** G. DODD *Brit. Manuf.* IV. 160 To give the technical terms applied to all these little pieces would be of no use; for after saying that the key acts on the grass-hopper..we have done but little towards explaining the particular construction and action of each.

4. An artificial bait for fish.

1867 F. FRANCIS *Angling* viii. (1880) 298 The grasshopper, so-called,..though actually an artificial bait, in nowise resembles a grasshopper. **1889** 'JOHN BICKERDYKE' *Bk. All-round Angler* III. 99 The 'grasshopper' is cast in likely spots and worked with a sink-and-draw motion near the bottom.

5. *attrib.* and *Comb.*, as ***grasshopper-like*** adj.; **grasshopper-beam**, a form of working-beam in steam-engines, pivoted at one end instead of in the centre (hence ***grasshopper-engine***, ***-principle***); **grasshopper-lark** = *grasshopper-warbler*; **grasshopper-march** (see quot.); **grasshopper mouse**, either of two species of North American mice belonging to the genus *Onychomys*; **grasshopper-sparrow**, a small sparrow of the U.S. of the genus *Coturniculus*, so called from its note; †**grasshopper-spring** (see quot. 1794); **grasshopper-warbler**, a small warbler, *Locustella nævia*, so called from its note; **grasshopper year**, a year when the crops are destroyed by grasshoppers.

1875 KNIGHT *Dict. Mech.*, *Grasshopper-beam. **1888** *Lockwood's Dict. Mech. Engin.*, *Grasshopper engine. **1768** G. WHITE *Selborne* xvi. (1789) 45 The *grasshopper-lark began his sibilous note in my fields last Saturday. **1827** HONE *Every-day Bk.* II. 514 The..little grasshopper lark.. runs whispering within the hedgerows. **1768** G. WHITE *Selborne* xix. (1789) 55 This last [sort of willow-wren].. makes a sibilous *grasshopper-like noise. **1884** *Brit. Stand. Handbks. Sports & Past.* II. IV. 23 The *Grasshopper March. Jump along the bars backwards and forwards with both arms. The arms of course must be bent a little to give the necessary spring. **1904** W. T. HORNADAY *Amer. Nat. Hist.* vii. 91/1 The *Grasshopper Mouse..strongly resembles the white-footed mouse. **1964** E. P. WALKER et al. *Mammals of World* II. 779/2 Grasshopper mice live in practically any shelter they can find at ground level. **1890** W. J. GORDON *Foundry* 100 By the side of the winding engine is the long row of blowing engines, on *grasshopper and other principles. **1883** *Encycl. Amer.* I. 530/1 The *grasshopper sparrows (*Coturniculus passerinus, C. henslowi, C. lecontii*). **1794** W. FELTON *Carriages* (1801) II. 188 The *grass hopper spring is a peculiarly formed spring which fixes under the shaft of a one-horse chaise to the axletree. **1822** *Monthly Mag.* Oct., Modern coaches, constructed of one piece, and resting on what are called grasshopper springs. **1839–43** YARRELL *Hist. Birds* I. 263 The *Grasshopper Warbler is found within a few miles north of London, and also in Surrey. **1880** *Scribner's Monthly* July 458/1 Then came 1875 and 1876, which were '*grass-hopper years' when no crops of consequence were raised in the whole state. **1949** *Chicago Tribune* 5 June 1/3 He predicted it will be the worst grasshopper year since 1936.

Hence **'grasshoppering** *vbl. sb.*, (*a*) living improvidently like a grasshopper (in quot. *attrib.*); (*b*) fishing with a 'grasshopper' bait; **'grasshopperish** *a.*, somewhat resembling a grasshopper; **'grasshoppery** *a.* = *grasshopperish* adj.

1803 M. G. LEWIS *Let.* 9 Nov. in *Mem. T. Moore* (1856) VIII. 46, I thought it high time that your grashoppering system should be at an end, and that you should begin to collect a provision of corn against the winter. **1872** W. S. SYMONDS *Rec. Rocks* vi. 199 In former days, when 'grasshoppering' was allowed there, I have taken many a basketful [of grayling] from the gravelly Teme. **1883** 'EHA' *Tribes on my Frontier* 80 Long-legged, green, grasshopperish animals. **1921** 'K. MANSFIELD' *Let.* 21 July (1928) II. 121 If only one could make some small grasshoppery sound of praise. **1926** *Brit. Weekly* 2 Sept. 456/4 She announces the result in her little grasshoppery voice.

'grasshopper, *v.* [f. the sb.] *intr.* To live, or jump, like a grasshopper. Also with *over*.

1873 J. H. BEADLE *Undevel. West* xxxii. 704 When they spar [= push (a steam-boat) with poles] thus on both sides, they are said to 'grasshopper over'. **1956** 'A. GILBERT' *Riddle of Lady* i. 12 [We] enjoy ourselves .. by working. We shouldn't get any fun out of grasshoppering. **1966** D. VARADAY *Gara-Yaka's Domain* iii. 32 All others were ignored, even one that grass-hoppered directly into her path. **1966** J. FOWLES *Magus* xxxvii. 230 My mind travelled up to the Bonnards, and grasshoppered from them to Alison.

†**grassil**, *v. Sc. Obs.* Also 6 graisle, grasle. [Perh. echoic.] *intr.* To make a harsh noise; to creak, rattle; also quasi-*trans.*, to make a harsh noise with (the teeth or tusks), to gnash.

1513 DOUGLAS *Æneis* I. ii. 60 Sone eftir this, of men the clamour rais, The takles graislis, cabillis can freit and frais. *Ibid.* III. x. 17 Grassilland his teth, and rummesand full hie. *Ibid.* VIII. iv. 103 Grasling his teith, and byrnand full of ire.

'grassiness. ('grɑːsɪnɪs, 'græs-). [f. GRASSY + -NESS.] The quality or state of being grassy.

1727 BAILEY vol. II, *Grassiness*, the having or fulness of grass. **1787** WASHINGTON *Diaries* (1925) III. 199 The harrow was ordered to preceed it once, or as many times as the ground from the clodiness or grassiness of it, should appear to need it. **1924** C. MACKENZIE *Heavenly Ladder* x. 138 The infinitely various earthy odours and the cool grassiness of the place allayed his feverish regrets.

grassing ('grɑːsɪŋ, -æ-), *vbl. sb.* [f. GRASS *sb.*[1] or *v.* + -ING.[1]]

1. The action of the vb. in various senses. **a.** Spreading out (flax, etc.) on the grass for bleaching (see GRASS *v.* 4 a). **b.** *Printing.* The taking of casual work (see GRASS *v.* 6 b.).

1780 A. YOUNG *Tour Irel.* I. 224 Taking out and grassing [Flax] .. 0. 5. 0. **1797** —— *Agric. Suffolk* 121 The grassing [of hemp] requires about five weeks. **1844** SPROULE *Flax* (1846) 23 Too little watering is given in this country, trusting to the grassing afterwards to make up the deficiency. **1875** SOUTHWARD *Dict. Typogr.* 44 Many compositors earn a good income by grassing. **1888** JACOBI *Printers' Voc.*, *Grassing*, a compositor taking occasional jobs, or assisting on a newspaper.

2. *Sc.* **a.** The place for cutting turfs and for grazing cattle. **b.** The privilege of grazing in a specified place.

1557 in *10th Rep. Hist. MSS. Comm.* App. v. 388 The pasture and grassing of Capney-vaugh. **1630–56** SIR R. GORDON *Earld. Sutherland* (1813) 344 The ffealing and girsing of Aldinalbanagh. *Ibid.* 351 Sir Robert gave vnto John Robsone some lands about Dounrobin, with the girsin of Badinlogh. **1632** *Rec. Inverness Presbyt.* (Scot. Hist. Soc., 1896) 25 They went and measured and marched the Gleib and grassing thereof as followeth. **1825** BROCKETT *N.C. Words* s.v. *Whittle*, An harden sark, a guse grassing, and a whittle gait, were all the salary of a clergyman, not many years ago, in Cumberland.

†**3.** The laying on of a first or ground colour; the colour itself. *Obs.*

1538 ELYOT *Dict.*, *Sublitio*, the grounde colour, wheron the colour is layde, in cloth dyed it is callyd grasynge perfyte. **1570** LEVINS *Manip.* 136/17 Y[e] Grasing of cloths, *sublitio.*

grass land, grassland. orig. *U.S.* [GRASS *sb.*[1]] Land producing grass; pasture or grazing land. Also *attrib.*

1682 in C. W. Manwaring *Digest Early Connecticut Probate Rec.* III. 114 In any corn feild or grass land. **1697** *Connecticut Col. Rec.* IV. 212 About one acre of grasse land in the said meddowe. **1765** *Mus. Rust.* III. 325 Twenty Acres of Grass-Land. **1807** J. BARLOW *Columb.* v. 300 The conscious flocks .. spread thro the grassland. **1846** J. BAXTER *Libr. Pract. Agric.* (ed 4) I. 5 Grass-land, when of good quality, is of the greatest value. **1903** W. R. FISHER tr. *Schimper's Plant-Geogr.* II. i. 174 A good grassland climate is .. composed of the following elements. **1920** *Nature* 27 May 408/2 It is too often the case that grassland is left to take care of itself, and that no steps are taken for its improvement. **1954** M. BERESFORD *Lost Villages* v. 148 From 1445 to 1491 he had been near Warwick at the heart of the grasslands. **1959** A. MCLINTOCK *Descr. Atlas N.Z.* 41 During the 1920s farmers adopted the idea of intensive grassland farming. **1971** *Sci. Amer.* July 86/1 The Serengeti National Park is an area of 5,600 square miles of grassland and open woodland.

grassless ('grɑːslɪs, -æ-), *a.* [f. GRASS *sb.*[1] + -LESS.] Without grass; devoid of grass.

1591 SYLVESTER *Du Bartas* I. ii. 574 Then, Fields seem grassless, Forests leaf-less all. **1610** *Mirr. Mag.* IV. Induct. 44 Nought else vpon the grasselesse ground, but winter's waste was seene. **1809–10** COLERIDGE *Friend* (1863) II. 41 Upon the yet grassless grave she threw herself down. **1865** MERIVALE *Rom. Emp.* VIII. lxvi. 218 Bare limestone rock, treeless, grassless, and waterless.

†**'grassman.** *Sc.* and *north. dial. Obs.* Forms: see GRASS *sb.*[1]

1. = COTTIER 1. [So MSw. *grässäte.*]

[*c* **1150** in Chalmers *Caledonia* (1807) I. 720 De Hurdmannis, et Bondis, et Gresmannis.] **1461** *Will* in *Ripon Ch. Acts* 100 Item lego cuilibet husbandman de Nid, xijd. Item cuilibet gresman de eadem, vjd. **1521** *Test. Ebor.* (Surtees) V. 134 Item I will that every house of gresse men w[t]in the towne of Besynby have ijd. a pece. **1607** *N. Riding Rec.* (1883) I. 94 Rich. Taylor, grasseman presented for using the trade of a badger. **1663** SPALDING *Troub. Chas. I* (1792) II. 187 There was not a lock, key, band, nor window left unbroken down daily to the tenants, cottars and grassmen. **1825–80** JAMIESON, *Grass-man* .. This word has now fallen into disuse, but is still perfectly intelligible to elderly people, Aberd., who recollect the time when *Girseman* and *Cottar* were used as quite synon[ymous].

2. A man who took charge of the common lands of a parish.

1597 *Mem. St. Giles's, Durham* (Surtees) 9 Expenses for this present yere 1579 beeing gyrsmen John Taylor & Robert Hudspethe. **1646** *Vestry Bks.* (Surtees) 192–3 Itt is ordered by the 24[tie] thatt the Grasemen for the yeares 1644 and 1645 shall make accompt of all receipts and disbursements to the new elected Grasemen. **1737** *Durham MS. Bk.*, Grassmen for ye Year. **1846** BROCKETT *N.C. Words* (ed. 3), *Grassmen*, officers of great antiquity in the borough of Gateshead, whose duty was to look after the herbage or grass. **1893** in *Northumbld. Gloss.*

Grassmann ('grɑːsmən, 'græs-). The name of Hermann *Grassmann* (1809–77), German mathematician and polymath, used in the possessive to designate his discoveries, esp. ***Grassmann's Law*** (Philol.): see quot. 1960 and LAW *sb.*[1] 17 c.

1891 MAX MÜLLER *Science of Lang.* II. v. 270 The following are the principal words in which, according to Grassmann's Law, double media in Gothic can be accounted for: Sk. *Gardh* .. Sk. *Dabh* [etc.]. **1935** G. K. ZIPF *Psycho-Biol. Lang.* iii. 81 We view in turn the conditions under which Grassmann's Law operated in Sanskrit and Greek. **1939** L. H. GRAY *Foundations of Lang.* 70 A noteworthy form of incontiguous dissimilation is seen in the operation of Grassmann's Law. **1960** S. POTTER *Lang. in Mod. World* x. 152 According to Grassmann's Law of the dissimilation of aspirates, the speakers of these ancient languages could not tolerate the aspirated plosives *ph th kh* at the beginning of two successive syllables. Wherever such a sequence of sounds developed, they just de-aspirated one of them, generally the first. *Ibid.*, Grassmann's law cannot fail to warm the heart of every true-born philologist.

'grass-plat, -plot. [f. GRASS *sb.*[1] + PLAT, PLOT. In the compound word *plot* app. is the older form, though the simple *plat* is found in 1611.] A piece of ground covered with turf, sometimes having ornamental flower-beds upon it.

α. **1697** C. LESLIE *Snake in Grass* (ed. 2) 333 Upon a Grass-Plat before his Window .. I saw some Women, very busie with their Bibles. **1727** HALL in *Phil. Trans.* XXXV. 309 The Snake being ty'd and pinn'd down to a Grass-plat. **1766** GOLDSM. *Vic. W.* viii, Mr. Thornhill .. intended that night giving the young ladies a ball by moonlight, on the grass plat before our door. **1818** HAZLITT *Eng. Poets* iv. (1870) 95 Artificial grass-plats [and] gravel-walks. **1897** *Pall Mall Mag.* Dec. 553 A statue in the centre of the grassplat.

β. **1610** SHAKS. *Temp.* IV. i. 73 Here on this grasse-plot, in this very place To come, and sport. **1685** TEMPLE *Wks.* (1720) I. 183 Grass-Plots bordered with Flowers. **1770** WARING in *Phil. Trans.* LXI. 370 We have it plentifully .. on the grass-plots about this house. **1876** MISS BRADDON *J. Haggard's Dau.* II. 17 The picture of grassplot and flower-bed.

grass root. [GRASS *sb.*[1]] Usu. in *pl.*

1. *lit.* The root of a plant of grass.

1766 T. AMORY *J. Buncle* (1825) III. 108 Petrified twigs of trees, shrubs, and grass-roots.

2. *fig.* **a.** The fundamental level; the source or origin.

Some of the later examples are influenced by sense b.

1901 KIPLING *Kim* xiv. 371 Not till I came to Shamlegh could I meditate upon the Course of Things, or trace the running grass-roots of Evil. **1907** *Putnam's Monthly* July 483/1 Carter had taken out wonderful grass-root values from the first. **1947** H. READ (*title*) The grass roots of art. **1952** *Times* 22 Mar. 7/4 Pushkin and Bakunin were only two of many famous men who were .. given an opportunity to study at leisure what would now be called the 'grass-roots' of Russian civilization. **1960** *Times* 13 Jan. 21/7 Thus the jobs themselves generate a range of industrial development at the grass-roots of the economy. **1963** *Listener* 21 Feb. 323/2 The modernization of agriculture requires the most skilled combination of central direction and grass-roots co-operation for success. **1966** *Oxf. Univ. Gaz.* 23 Dec. 438/2 If one goes back, to use a dull cliché, to the grass roots of academic life, .. then it seems to me the Franks proposals follow logically. **1969** *Oz* May 32/3 Some of the attitudes and values to be found inherent in the music at its grass roots level.

b. *Politics.* Used *spec.* to describe the rank-and-file of the electorate or of a political party. Also *attrib.* orig. *U.S.*

1912 *McClure's Mag.* July 324/1 From the Roosevelt standpoint, especially, it was a campaign from the 'grass roots up'. The voter was the thing. **1935** *Nation* 19 June 697/2 'No crisis so grave has confronted our people' since the Civil War, Mr. Lowden told the grassroots convention at Springfield. **1948** *Times Lit. Suppl.* 13 Mar. 143/4 The self-governing congregation is a unique element in English 'grass-root' democracy. **1955** *Times* 12 Aug. 9/6 These are the complaints at grass-root level; in more sophisticated circles the N.L.M. politicians talk of disregard of minority rights and incipient dictatorship. **1959** *Listener* 30 April 746/2 The rather narrow oligarchic regime of President Ngo Dinh Diem [in South Viet-Nam] .. seems to be losing contact with the 'grass roots'. **1966** *New Statesman* 25 Mar. 410/1 The grassroot Tory still prefers to touch his forelock and reverence his 'betters'.

Hence **'grass-rooted** *ppl. a.*, **'grass rooter.**

1935 *Harper's Mag.* Sept. 484/1 'We believe,' the embattled Republican Grass Rooters resolved, [etc.]. *Ibid.* 489/2 Do we hear the Grass Rooters, the financial interests, and the industrialists raising their voices in protest against this usurpation? **1947** *Chicago Times* 28 June 13/4 Other straw polls in other states indicate that Republican 'Grass rooters' quite generally feel the same way. **1957** D. DAVIE *Winter Talent* 21 Grass-rooted goodness and a joy unmixed Parch unbaptized inside a droughty head.

grass tetany. [ad. G. *grastetanie* (Sjollema & Seekles 1930, in *Biochem. Zeitschr.* CCXXIX. 358).] A disease in cattle caused by magnesium deficiency, occurring esp. when there is a change of diet such as from indoor feeding to outdoor grazing.

1933 *Jrnl. Biol. Chem.* May 636 It is interesting that Sjollema and coworkers have studied in a comprehensive manner a bovine disease which they term grass tetany. **1955** J. G. DAVIS *Dict. Dairying* (ed. 2) 1132 The term 'Grass Tetany' is frequently used to designate a disorder of dairy cows which may occur a week or so after the cows are first admitted to grass in springtime. **1960** *Farmer & Stockbreeder* 29 Mar. 78/1 It is important to ensure that animals have the necessary amount of magnesium in their diet to avoid the danger of grass tetany. **1967** *Times* 28 Dec. 7/3, I remember about 15 years or so ago when I first started spraying my pastures with magnesium sulphate as a preventive against grass tetany.

grass time. [Cf. GRASS *sb.*[1] 8.] The time of year when animals are at grass.

c **1386** CHAUCER *Reeve's Prol.* 14 Gras tyme is doon, my fodder is now forage. **1637** EARL STRAFFORDE *Lett.* II. 60 A Place which .. affords Sport to pass over a Grass-time. **1838** JAS. GRANT *Sk. Lond.* 302 'Here's a capital good 'un, Sir; three years old next grass-time, Sir', was the recommendation of his donkey, which was given by a fourth.

¶ Misused for *grease-time.* (Cf. GRASS *sb.*[1] 5 ¶.)

1590 COKAINE *Treat. Hunting* C iv, You must beware that you offer not to hunt the Bucke before the first day of Grasse time.

'grass-tree. A name given to several Australasian trees. The liliaceous genus *Xanthorrhœa*; *Richea dracophylla* and *R. pandanifolia* of Tasmania; the *Pseudopanax crassifolium* of N. Zealand; the cabbage-tree of New Zealand, *Cordyline australis*; the juncaceous plant *Kingia australis*.

1802 D. COLLINS *Acc. N.S. Wales* II. 153 A grass tree grows here, similar .. to that about Port Jackson. **1852** *Zoologist* X. 3383 The curious *Xanthorrhœa hastilis*, or grass-tree, with tall spear-like flower-stalks, eight feet high. **1866** *Treas. Bot.* 550/2 Grass-tree, Xanthorrhæa; also *Richea dracophylla*, and *Kingia australis*. **1867** HOCHSTETTER *New Zealand* 132 Here and there, in moist places, arises isolated the 'grass-tree' or 'cabbage-tree' (Ti of the natives; *Cordyline australis*). **1878** W. W. SPICER *Handbk. Plants Tasmania* 125 (Morris) *Richea pandanifolia*, H., Giant Grass Tree. **1889** T. KIRK *Flora New Zealand* 59 It [*Pseudopanax crassifolium*] is commonly called lancewood by the settlers in the North Island, and grass-tree by those in the South. **1893** MRS. C. PRAED *Outlaw & Lawmaker* II. 5 A stony ridge, with weird-looking grass trees, lifting their blackened spears.

grassum(me, obs. form of GERSUM.

grass widow. [Certainly f. GRASS *sb.*[1] + WIDOW; cf. the equivalent MLG. *graswedewe* (= sense 1), Du. *grasweduwe*, Sw. *gräsenka*, Da. *græsenke*; also G. *strohwittwe* (lit. 'straw-widow'). The modern continental Teut. words seem to have chiefly sense 2 below, but dialect glossaries often give sense 1 as locally current. The etymological notion is obscure, but the parallel forms disprove the notion that the word is a 'corruption' of *grace-widow*.

It has been suggested that in sense 1 *grass* (and G. *stroh*) may have been used with opposition to *bed*; cf. the etymology of BASTARD. Sense 2 may have arisen as an etymologizing interpretation of the compound (cf. GRASS *sb.* 5 b) after it had ceased to be generally understood; in Eng. it seems to have appeared first as Anglo-Indian.]

1. An unmarried woman who has cohabited with one or more men; a discarded mistress. ?*Obs.*

1528 MORE *Dyaloge* III. xiii. 86 b, Tyndall wolde by thys waye make saynt Poule to say thus. Take & chese in but such a wydow as hath had but one husbande at onys .. I thynke saynt Powle ment not so. For then had wyuys ben in his time lytel better than grasse wydowes be now. For they be yet as seuerall as a barbours chayre & neuer take but one at onys. **1582** *Reg. Bk. Stoke-by-Nayland, Suffolk* Jan., The 31 day was buri'd Marie the daught[r] of Elizabeth London graswidow. *a* **1700** B.E. *Dict. Cant. Crew* s.v., *Widows Weeds*. A *Grass-Widow*, one that pretends to have been Married, but never was, yet has Children. **1760** GOLDSM. *Goddess of Silence* Misc. Wks. 1837 I. xxvi. 329, I have made more matches in my time than a grass widow. **1785** GROSE *Dict. Vulg. Tongue* s.v., *Widow's Weeds*, A grass widow, a discarded mistress.

2. A married woman whose husband is absent from her.

1846 J. J. HOOPER *Taking Census* ii. 183 John Green's sister, (the grass widder, as lives with 'em,) she goes to her battling bench. **1853** E. CLACEY *Lady's Visit Gold Diggings Austral.* 255 The absence of so many of 'the lords of creation' in pursuit of what they value..more than all the women in the world—nuggets. The wives thus left in town to deplore their husbands' infatuation, are termed 'grass-widows'—a mining expression. **1859** LANG *Wand. India* 4 Grass widows in the hills are always writing to their husbands, when you drop in upon them. **1865** *Englishm. Mag.* Aug. 138 The pretty grass-widow..is going because every one else is gone. **1884** LADY DUFFERIN *Viceregal Life India* (1889) I. i. 4 Expectant husbands come out to meet the 'grass widows' who have travelled with us.

Hence **grass-'widow** *v. intr.*, to live as a grass-widow; **'grass-widowed** *ppl. a.*, temporarily living apart from one's husband; **grass-'widowhood**, the condition of a grass-widow; also *transf.* So also **grass-widower**, [cf. G. *strohwittwer*, lit. 'straw-widower'], a man living apart from his wife; hence **grass-'widowerhood**, the condition of a grass-widower.

1862 *Rocky Mt. News* (Denver) 14 June (Th.), David is a bachelor again, or rather a 'grass-widower'. **1872** W. B. DONNE *Euripides* ix. 186 The real Helen..passed the score of years between the visit of Paris to Sparta and the fall of that city in a respectable grass-widowhood. **1878** *Life in the Mofussil* II. 100 The Clergyman..was a grass widower, his wife being at home. **1881** W. E. NORRIS *Matrimony* III. 92 Asking Nina how long her period of grass-widowhood was going to last. **1886** *N.Y. Evening Post* 22 May (Farmer), All the grass-widowers and unmarried men. **1887** *Sat. Rev.* 30 Apr. 624 The female plant..was brought to Europe before the male, and so, berryless, may be said to have suffered a grass-widowhood of some eighty years. **1892** *Critic* (U.S.) 12 Mar. 154/1 She and her husband lived charmingly—apart, 'grass-widowing' here and there. **1894** J. KNIGHT *Garrick* xvi. 301 Johnson..insisted upon a grass widowhood before they proceeded to another election. **1926** W. J. LOCKE *Stories Near & Far* 112 She could never resolve the problem whether she would have been happier or unhappier in a grass-widowed state. **1930** HARWOOD & BROWNE *Cynara* 34 We're celebrating his grass-widowerhood.

grassy ('grɑːsɪ, -æ-), *a.* [f. GRASS *sb.*[1] + -Y[1]. Cf. MDu. *grasich*, Du. *grazig*, G. *grasig*.]

1. Covered with grass, abounding in grass.

1513 DOUGLAS *Æneis* XI. xi. 76 The speir onon..Furth of the gresy swaird he hes vptane. **1579** SPENSER *Sheph. Cal.* June 6 The grassye ground with daintye Daysies dight. **1593** SHAKS. *Rich. II*, III. iii. 50 Goe signifie as much, while here we march Vpon the Grassie Carpet of this Plaine. **1667** MILTON *P.L.* V. 391 Rais'd of grassie terf Thir Table was. **1725** POPE *Odyss.* III. 535 To lead A well-fed bullock from the grassy mead. **1820** SCOTT *Ivanhoe* i, The sun was setting upon one of the rich grassy glades of the forest. **1870** MORRIS *Earthly Par.* II. III. 11 A narrow vale, that lay, Grassy and soft betwixt the pine-woods bound.

2. Of or pertaining to grass; consisting of or containing grass.

1697 DRYDEN *Virg. Past.* V. 39 The thirsty Cattel, of themselves, abstain'd From Water, and their grassy Fare disdain'd. **1727-41** CHAMBERS *Cycl.* s.v. *Graminea*, The grassy crown, *corona graminea*, was but rarely conferred; and for some signal exploit. **1752** F. FAWKES *Descrip. May* 96 As fast as cattle the long summer's day Had cropt the grassy sustenance away. **1818** KEATS *Endym.* III. 1027 How happy once again in grassy nest! **1821** CLARE *Vill. Minstr.* II. 84 Big drops bow the grassy stems. **1846** J. BAXTER *Libr. Pract. Agric.* (ed. 4) II. 185 This is a good course if the wheat stubble can be depended on to produce grass enough to furnish a sufficient dressing of ashes..but if there is reason to expect the wheat stubble will not be sufficiently grassy [etc.].

3. Resembling grass in colour, form, habit, or smell.

1567 MAPLET *Gr. Forest* 22b, The Topaze, as Plinie sayth, is a Gem of grassie colour. **1596** GOSSON *Quippes Upst. Gentlewomen* 99 in Hazl. *E.P.P.* IV. 254 The swarthie-blacke, the grassie-greene. **1668** WILKINS *Real Char.* 98 Hatchet vetch..being long and slender, of grassy leaves. **1725** POPE *Odyss.* XV. 510 Aboard they heave us, mount their decks and sweep With level oar along the grassy deep. **1807** J. E. SMITH *Phys. Bot.* 474 The great genus of *Carex*..and some other grassy plants, are found here. **1812** BYRON *Ch. Har.* II. liv, The wearied eye Reposes gladly on as smooth a vale As ever Spring yclad in grassy dye. **1849** RUSKIN *Sev. Lamps* iii. §17. 83 The sharp, grassy, intricate leafage [of the black spruce fir]. **1931** H. CRANE *Let.* 11 Sept. (1965) 379 A marvelous stillness and grassy perfume pervade the district. **1957** G. E. HUTCHINSON *Treat. Limnol.* I. xvii. 901 Blue-green algae are described as having a grassy odor.

4. *Comb.*

1770 GOLDSM. *Des. Vill.* 360 The cooling brook, the grassy-vested green. **1804** BEWICK *Brit. Birds* (1847) II. 240 On whose grassy-margined pools they feed.

grasyar, -er, obs. forms of GRAZIER.

grat, obs. form of GREAT *a.*; obs. pa. t. of GREET *v.*[2]

grate (greɪt), *sb.*[1] Also 6 **gratte**. [app. a. med.L. *grata* (? used in monastic Latin for a lattice), ad. It. *grata* grate, gridiron, hurdle, alteration of *grate*:—L. *crātem*, *crātis* hurdle. (Godef. has one example of OF. *grate* with the sense 'hurdle', which may be from monastic Latin.)]

1. A framework of bars or laths, parallel to or crossing each other, fixed in a door, window, or other opening, to permit communication while preventing ingress. Now somewhat *rare*; cf. GRATING *vbl. sb.*[2]

c **1440** *Promp. Parv.* 207/2 Grate, or trelys wy(n)dowe ..*cancellus*. **1523** [see sense 9]. **1530** PALSGR. 227/1 Grate of a windowe, *trelis de fer*. **1535** COVERDALE *2 Kings* i. 2 Ochosias fell thorow y[e] grate in his chamber at Samaria. **1590** SPENSER *F.Q.* I. viii. 36 But in the same [doore] a little grate was pight, Through which he sent his voyce. **1602** MARSTON *Antonio's Rev.* II. iii. Wks. 1856 I. 99 Antonio kisseth Mellida's hand: then Mellida goes from the grate. **1687** A. LOVELL tr. *Thevenot's Trav.* I. 190 At present there is no more but a Window with a Grate. **1697** CONGREVE *Mourning Bride* I. i, While his jailor slept, I through the grate Have softly whispered and inquired his health. **1716** LADY M. W. MONTAGU *Let. to Lady X.*, 1 Oct., The young Count of Salmes came to the grate.. and the Abbess gave him her hand to kiss. **1778** FOOTE *Trip Calais* II. Wks. 1799 II. 354 The father and mother of that amiable child are now at the grate. **1805** SCOTT *Last Minstr.* I. Introd. ii, The embattled portal-arch he pass'd, Whose ponderous grate and massy bar Had oft roll'd back the tide of war. **1837** CARLYLE *Fr. Rev.* III. I. v, The grate which led to our quarter opened anew.

2. A similar framework (or, sometimes, a perforated plate) for other purposes, esp. for closing an orifice without intercepting the passage of fluids; *rarely*, †a gridiron.

1412-20 LYDG. *Chron. Troy* II. xi, Voydyng fylthes lowe into the grounde Thorough grates made of yron perced round. **1718** STEELE *Fish Pool* 168 Great advantage is effected by large grates at the head and stern..of the vessel. **1750** [see *grate-iron* in 10 below]. **1755** JOHNSON, *Grill*, to broil on a grate or gridiron. **1825** T. COSNETT *Footman's Directory* 62 If the spout of the tea-pot gets furred up, have a small piece of wire or wood to push up and down it, but be careful not to break the grate of it in so doing.

†**3.** The railing round a monument, building, etc.

a **1400** *Stacyons of Rome* 603 in *Pol. Rel. & L. Poems* 136 A-bowte that stoone a grate there is of Irne. **1519** in Glasscock *Rec. St. Michael's* (1882) 36 Item pd to Rase Thomas for dygyng of the holis for the grate iiijd. *Ibid.*, Item to Jardefeld for tymber for the chirche grate..Item to Hothe the Carponter for makyng of the tymber werke at the south gate and grate of the chirche yerd. *a* **1645** HABINGTON in *Proc. Worc. Hist. Soc.* II. 223 The grate of iron inclosinge the tombe. **1872** O. SHIPLEY *Gloss. Eccl. Terms*, *Grate*, an ornamental iron screen around a monument.

4. A frame of metal bars for holding the fuel in a fireplace or furnace. Hence, the fireplace itself.

1605 TIMME *Quersit.* III. 191 A grate shall be layed, wherein the coales of fire must lie. **1608** A. WILLET *Hexapla in Exod.* 614 The wood was laid in order vpon that grate, and so burned, which grate was all of brasse. **1611** BIBLE *Exod.* xxvii. 4. **1712** STEELE *Spect.* No. 308 ¶2 An old-fashioned Grate consumes Coals, but gives no Heat. **1779** BOSWELL in *Life Johnson* 10 Oct., Why, Sir, do people play this trick which I observe now, when I look at your grate, putting the shovel against it to make the fire burn? **1800** tr. *Lagrange's Chem.* I. 97 You must make it pass through the grate of the furnace. **1848** DICKENS *Dombey* vi, Throw those shoes under the grate. **1875** J. SMITH *Temperance Reform.* iii. 96 The cold and cheerless grate.

†**5.** *transf.* **a.** (See quot.) Cf. GRATING *vbl. sb.* 3. **b.** Applied to the chequers on the door-post of a tavern. *Obs.*

1598 HAYDOCKE tr. *Lomazzo's Tracte Artes*, etc. II. v. xxiv. 217 The third part is wrought with a Grate [*marg.* Which is an instrument made with crossing of lines], or insteede thereof with a glasse set betweene the eie of the Painter, and the thing seene. **1622** MASSINGER & DEKKER *Virgin Martyr* III. iii, I see then a tavern and a bawdy-house have faces much alike; the one hath red grates next the door, the other hath peeping-holes within doors.

6. *Mining.* A screen used when stamping ores.

1776 W. PRYCE *Min. Cornub.* Expl. Terms, *Grate*, an iron plate punched full of small holes; which belongs to the stamping mill, and sizes the stampt Ore. **1839** URE *Dict. Arts* 749 The grate..is a grid composed of square bars of iron..placed horizontally, and parallelly to each other, an inch apart. **1875** *Ure's Dict. Arts* (ed. 7) II. 736 *Grate*,..a metal plate pierced with small holes; it is fixed in front of the stamps in which ore is pounded, and through the holes the finely divided matter makes its escape. **1881** RAYMOND *Mining Gloss.*, *Grate*..See *Screen* (as applied to stamps).

†**7.** A barred place of confinement for animals, also, a prison or cage for human beings. *Obs.*

1552 in Glasscock *Rec. St. Michael's* (1882) 93 Of the Mayor and burges for the gaol called the grate p[r] a[m] xijd. **1598** SHAKS. *Merry W.* II. ii. 8 Else you had look'd through the grate, like a Geminy of Baboones. **1603** KNOLLES *Hist. Turks* (1638) 220 Shut vp in an yron cage made like a grate, in such sort as that he might on euery side be seen. **1610** HEALEY *St. Aug. Citie of God* XII. xxvi. (1620) 443 These gods..are but the forgers of our prisons..our iaylors, locking vs in those dolorous grates and wretched fetters. **1613** PURCHAS *Pilgrimage* IV. v. 365 Lions and Leopards in grates were carried before him. **1652** BENLOWES *Theoph.* XIII. lxxxiii. 247 The folded flocks are pent In hurdled Grates. **1759** JOHNSON *Rasselas* v, He was now impatient as an eagle in a grate. **1777** HOWARD *Prisons Eng.* (1780) 287 Every debtor that lies in the common grate.

†**8.** One of the spaces between the bars of a grating. *Obs. rare.*

1523 LD. BERNERS *Froiss.* I. xxxix. 53 He Caused to be made without the towne, a barrers ouerthwart the strete lyke a grate, nat past half a fote wyde euery grate. **1649** G. DANIEL *Trinarch.*, *Rich. II*, ccl, As were his Cage too straite; Like wilder Birds, soe pent, prolls, till he find A hole, by Chance, or any wider Grate.

9. *attrib.* and *Comb.*, as ***grate-bar***, ***-work***; ***grate-fashion***, ***-wise*** advs.; **grate-area** = *grate-surface*; **grate-fire**, a fire in an open grate; †**grate-iron**, (*a*) = GRIDIRON; (*b*) see quot. 1750; **grate-room**, in some furnaces, a chamber with a grate beneath it; **grate-shavings**, shavings of wood or curled strips of paper for filling fireplaces in summer; **grate-surface**, the area in square feet covered by the fire-bars of a furnace or boiler.

1888 *Lockwood's Dict. Mech. Engin.*, s.v. *Grate Area. **1896** *Daily News* 20 Apr. 5/2 In a Yarrow boiler..the total grate area is forty and a quarter square feet. **1832** *Edin. Rev.* LVI. 124 The *grate-bars which support the fuel. **1659** TORRIANO, *Bastoncello*..a certain paste bak't in moulds, and *grate-fashion contrived. **1907** *Daily Chron.* 30 Nov. 4/4 When other reformers insist on our abolishing *grate fires altogether. **1909** E. BANKS *Myst. Frances Farrington* 87 Your utterly useless, but expensive, grate-fire. **1574** HELLOWES *Gueuara's Fam. Ep.* (1577) 178 The *grateyron of S. Laurence. **1577** tr. *Bullinger's Decades* (1592) 315 In his time was Saint Laurence..broiled vpon a grate yron. **1750** BLANCKLEY *Nav. Expos.*, Grate-irons are to loosen the Mud and Sullage of the Docks, which lodge in the Grates of the Drains. **1883** CHANCE in Powell *Princ. Glass-making* 111 These *grate-rooms are sunk several feet below the level of the bed of the furnace. **1899** *Longman's Mag.* Aug. 331 Statia gazed at the fireplace, decorated with what are known as *grate-shavings and silver paper. **1854** RONALDS & RICHARDSON *Chem. Technol.* (ed. 2) I. 255 The usual dimensions..are 1 square foot of *grate surface for a consumption of 20 lbs. of coal per hour. **1613** PURCHAS *Pilgrimage* IX. v. 844 A grediron..with billets laid thereon, and other sticks on them *grate-wise. **1736** AINSWORTH *Lat. Dict.*, *Transenna*,..any *grate-work, a lattice before a window.

†**grate**, *sb.*[2] *Obs.* [f. GRATE *v.*[1]] = GRATER[1].

14.. *Voc.* in Wr.-Wülcker 596/8 *Micatorium*, a grate. *Ibid.* 609/44 *Scalprum*, a grate, or a shaue. **1472** *Durham Acct. Rolls* (Surtees) I. 246 Item j grate pro zinzebr'. **1530** PALSGR. 227/1 Grate for bredde, *gragevr a payn*. **1609** W. M. *Man in Moone* (Percy Soc.) 18 When you lie like a nutmegge in a grate. **1674** RAY *Collect. Words, Prepar. Tin* 121 An iron-plate perforated with small holes like a grate.

†**grate**, *sb.*[3] *Obs. rare.* [a. Flem. *graet* = Du. *graat*, G. *grat*.] The backbone of a fish.

1481 CAXTON *Reynard* (Arb.) 7 Ye ete the good plays allone and gaf hym nomore than the grate or bones.

†**grate**, *sb.*[4] *Obs. rare*[−1]. [f. GRATE *v.*[1]] Collision (of weapons). Cf. GRATE *v.*[1] 6.

1460 *Lybeaus Disc.* (Kaluza) 1675 He smitte his schaft in grate. **1509** HAWES *Past. Pleas.* XXXIV. xx, Ye shall not nede to feare The stroke of swerde or yet the grate of spere.

†**grate**, *a. Obs.* Also 6 **gret**. [ad. L. *grāt-us* with the same meanings; according to Brugmann = Skr. *gūrtá* welcome:—OAryan *gr̥̄to-*, from the same root as Gr. γέρας reward. Cf. F. *grate* (Cotgr.).]

1. Pleasing, agreeable, acceptable.

1523 Q. MARGARET in *St. Papers Hen. VIII*, IV. 56 For it vold be ryght gret to me, gyf I myght do it. **1543** BECON *Nosegay* C j b, Nothynge can be gyuen to vs more grate, acceptable & pleasaunt than this your gyfte nowe promised. **1596** DALRYMPLE tr. *Leslie's Hist. Scot.* I. 130 Quhen the name of king was maist grate and thankful to thame al. **1665** SIR T. HERBERT *Trav.* (1677) 311 Coho or Coffee..however ingrate or insapory it seems at first, it becomes grate and delicious enough by custom.

2. Thankful, grateful.

1565 COOPER *Thesaurus*, *Gratus*..That remembreth or recompenseth a good turne: grate: thankeful. **1567** R. MULCASTER *Fortescue's De Laud. Leg.* (1572) 107b, He that is once made free, be he grate or ingrate, is adjudged to enjoy his Freedome still. **1573** DAVIDSON in *Satir. Poems Reform.* xl. Ded. I. 277 As..I wald let my gude will and grate mynd ..appeir towardis ȝow. **1596** DALRYMPLE tr. *Leslie's Hist. Scot.* III. 190 He labouris how to find the way to mak sum significatione of his grate mynd, for the benefites..quilkes afortymes frome the King of Scottis he had receuit.

Hence †**'grately** *adv.*

1533 BONER in *St. Papers Hen. VIII*, XI. 410 His Majestie toke all the same very grately and acceptablie.

grate (greɪt), *v.*[1] [a. OF. *grate-r* (mod.F. *gratter*) = Pr., Sp. *gratar*, It. *grattare*; Com. Rom. ad. Teut. **krattôjan* (OHG. *chrazzôn*, mod.Ger. *kratzen* to scratch, Sw. *kratta*, Da. *kratte* to rake).]

†**1.** *trans.* To scrape, file, abrade; to rub harshly, scarify, excoriate. *Obs.*

14.. *Voc.* in Wr.-Wülcker 610/2 *Scarifacio*, to grate. **1514** BARCLAY *Cyt. & Uplondyshm.* (Percy Soc.) p. li, Alle the night longe shall he his sides grate. **1593** NASHE *Christ's T.* 76a, Some of them haue grated and sawed theyr smooth tender skinnes, with hayre shirts. **1597** A. M. tr. *Guillemeau's Fr. Chirurg.* 33b/2 We muste then grate the bone with a peculiare Raspatorye. **1598** FLORIO, *Grattuggiare*, to shaue as curriers leather, to grate. **1649** BP. HALL *Cases Consc.* (1650) 105 Why may he not unrivet, or grate an iron wherewith he is fettered? **1650** FULLER *Pisgah* III. xii. 343 The edges of the Cross grating his late whip-furrowed back. **1660** F. Brooke tr. *Le Blanc's Trav.* 333 'Tis sharp and grates the throat of those that are not used to it.

b. with complement: To wear *away, down, to nothing*, etc. by abrasion. Chiefly *fig. arch.*

1555 W. Watreman *Fardle Facions* I. vi. Gjb, They gather a kynde of great shelle fysshe, whose shelles they grate open with stones. **1602** Marston *Ant. & Mel.* III. Wks. 1856 I. 36 Thou wouldst even grate away thy soule to dust. **1606** Shaks. *Tr. & Cr.* III. ii. 195 When..mightie States characterlesse are grated To dustie nothing. **1859** Tennyson *Vivien* 621 Who..Read but one book, and ever reading grew So grated down and filed away with thought.

2. In culinary and pharmaceutical use: To reduce to small particles by rasping or rubbing against a rough or indented surface; to pulverize by means of a grater. Often with *prep.*: To grate and allow the powder to fall *in, into, over* something. ***to grate off***: to grind down.

c **1420** *Liber Cocorum* (1862) 40 Take rawe chese anone And grate hit in disshes mony on. *c* **1430** *Two Cookery-bks.* I. 6 þanne grate fayre brede and cast þer-to. *c* **1440** *Promp. Parv.* 207/2 Grate gynger..*frictico*. **1530** Palsgr. 574/1, I grate breed or spyce. **1578** Lyte *Dodoens* III. xlvii. 384 Like vertue hath the roote if it be scrapte or grated very small. **1612** Woodall *Surg. Mate* Wks. (1653) 355 Take Bayberries..dry them..then powder them, or for a need grate them. **1626** Bacon *Sylva* §458 Artichoakes will bee lesse prickly, and more tender, if the Seeds haue their Tops dulled or grated off vpon a Stone. **1732** *Phil. Trans.* XXXVII. 432 His Tongue [was] dry enough to grate a Nutmeg. **1769** Mrs. Raffald *Eng. Housekpr.* (1778) 173 Take the inside of a penny loaf, grate it fine. **1853** Soyer *Pantroph.* 92 The Indians grate this root [ginger] in their broth or ragoût. **1871** Napheys *Prev. & Cure Dis.* II. i. 405 A little nutmeg grated over the surface.

†**b.** *fig.* To examine rigorously. *Obs.*

?**1538** Latimer *Let. to Cromwell* in *Remains* (1845) 405 After such sort, much grating of him, and yet finding no other thing in him, we [etc.].

3. *fig.* To affect painfully, as if by abrasion; to fret, harass, irritate. Now *rare.*

1555 Eden *Decades* 96 It grated the bowels of suche as harde hym. **1591** Spenser *M. Hubberd* 1334 Grinding his teeth, and grating his great heart. **1602** Shaks. *Ham.* III. i. 3 Grating so harshly all his days of quiet With turbulent and dangerous Lunacy. **1613** F. Robarts *Revenue Gospel* 136 What they doe now is to grate and oppresse the poore minister. **1655** Fuller *Ch. Hist.* III. ii. §3 Others ..could not endure to be so ..frequently grated with the shame of the sin they had committed. **1665** J. Webb *Stone-Heng* (1725) 110 Untruths..wherewith at present he grateth your Ears. **1741** Blackstone *Lawyer's Farew. to Muse* 52 With sounds uncouth, and accents dry, That grate the soul of harmony. **1748** Richardson *Clarissa* (1811) VII. 380 The matter begins to grate me most confoundedly. **1826** J. Wilson *Noct. Ambr.* Wks. 1855 I. 63 This outrageous merriment grates my spirits. **1892** H. H. Furness *Shaks. Tempest* 21 Such a mere bare iteration grates me as somewhat un-Shakespearian.

†**b.** *intr.* for *refl.* To be affected unpleasantly, fret. *Obs.*

1555 Eden *Decades* 7 He shall feele his bowelles grate with a certen horroure. **1590** Spenser *F.Q.* I. i. 19 That when he heard, in great perplexitie His gall did grate for griefe and high disdaine.

4. *intr.* ***to grate on*** or ***upon***: †**a.** To oppress or harass with exactions or importunities; to make burdensome demands upon. *Obs.*

1532 *St. Papers Hen. VIII*, II. 159 His Graces Counsaile here..verelie hath so sore gratid uppon my litle substaunce that I had, that [etc.]. **1544** *Privy Counc.* ibid. IX. 578 His Highnes thought Him a Prince of so grete and noble a courage, that He wold not grate any further upon Him, until [etc.]. **1598** Shaks. *Merry W.* II. ii. 6, I haue grated vpon my good friends for three Repreeues for you. **1611** Speed *Hist. Gt. Brit.* IX. viii. (1632) 580 His Prelates greedily grating on him to empouerish his meanes. **1619** Fletcher *M. Thomas* I. ii, I know your Nature's sweet enough, and tender, Not grated on, nor curb'd. **1633** Bp. Hall *Hard Texts, N.T.* 75 Do not grate on the subject in exacting more tribute..than the law hath appointed for you. *a* **1656** Hales *Gold. Rem.* (1673) 205 God..permitted not the Jews to grate too much upon the bordering Nations. **1705** Hickeringill *Priest-cr.* II. iii. 33 The Law..prohibiting Marriages..Contributes accidently..to fill the Register's Purses,..and grates hard upon the People, especially the Poor.

b. To have an irritating effect *on* or *upon.*

1635 R. Bolton *Comf. Affl. Consc.* iv. 21 Of all other passions of the Soule, sadnesse and griefe grates most upon the vital spirits. **1677** *Gov. Venice* 48 These sort of reflections..grate upon their Equality. **1744** Swift *Serm. Mut. Subj.* 10 Although this Doctrine of subjecting ourselves to one another may seem to grate upon the Pride and Vanity of Mankind,..yet[etc.]. **1827** Hallam *Const. Hist.* (1876) II. viii. 87 All mention, therefore, of calling parliament grated on his ear. **1847** Disraeli *Tancred* II. xvi, She never grated for an instant on his high ideal. **1878** Geo. Eliot *Coll. Breakf. P.* 339 Your itch to choose What grates upon the sense.

†**c.** To offend against, be derogatory to. *Obs.*

1676 Glanvill *Ess. Philos. & Relig.* Ep. Ded. a, Being cautious to abstain from all expressions, that grate on the Honour of God, as you are free from any that can give just offence unto man.

†**5.** *trans.* (Cf. 4 a.) To obtain by oppression or importunity. *Obs.*

1540 Hen. VIII in *St. Papers Hen. VIII*, VIII. 410 Ye shal not..entre any further with him in the twoo poyntes, wherby he grate more of youe, wherby to chalenge the same. **1541** Hen. VIII *ibid.* 644 They seame..to grate a further pryvileage by a graunte of our progenitour King Edwarde the Thirde, thenne before was alledged. **1542** Paget *ibid.* IX. 51 For great store of money they have not,..and [he] hath alredy grated as much as He can get.

†**6. a.** *trans.* To make (a weapon) strike or 'bite'. **b.** *intr.* Of a weapon: To strike or bite. Const. *on. Obs.*

1412-20 Lydg. *Chron. Troy* III. xxii, On Meneste he gan his spere grate. **1525** Ld. Berners *Froiss.* II. clxviii. 190 b, Their speres grated nat, if they had, by moost lykelhod they had taken hurte. **1530** Palsgr. 574/1, I grate, as a weapen dothe upon harnesse or any sharpe thynge and harde upon a nother, *je amors*. *a* **1633** Austin *Medit.* (1635) 255 Whence comes it, that Bullets or Arrowes often grate on us, and yet hurt us not? *a* **1700** *Ballad Geo. Barnwell* 152 Ere I would want, were I a man..On father, friends and all my kin I would my talons grate.

7. *trans.* **a.** To rub harshly together, 'grind' (the teeth). **b.** Of a thing: To rub against (another thing) harshly, producing a jarring sound.

1555 Eden *Decades* 20 Fretinge and gratinge his teethe as it had bin a lyon of Libia. **1590** Spenser *F.Q.* II. vii. 34 Thereat the feend his gnashing teeth did grate. **1593** Shaks. *Lucr.* 306 The threshold grates the doore to haue him heard. **1604** T. M. *Black Bk.* in *Middleton's Wks.* (Bullen) VIII. 8 They grate with their hard naily soles The stones in Fleet-street. **1607** Topsell *Four-f. Beasts* (1658) 540 Then champeth he with his mouth, grateth and gnasheth his teeth one against another. **1633** T. James *Voy.* 15 The..corners of the Ice did grate vs with that violence, as I..thought it would haue grated the plankes from the Ships sides. **1821** Keats *Lamia* I. 224 His galley now Grated the quay-stones. **1834** Medwin *Angler in Wales* I. 57 When it [the dingy] grates the sand.

8. *intr.* To rub *against* with a harsh, grinding noise; to move creakingly; to sound harshly.

1596 Shaks. *1 Hen. IV*, III. i. 132, I had rather heare a..dry Wheele grate on the Axle-tree. **1597** Hooker *Eccl. Pol.* V. xxxvi. §4 We are not so nice as to cast away a sharp knife because the edge of it may sometimes grate. **1637** Milton *Lycidas* 124 Their lean and flashy songs Grate on their scrannel pipes of wretched straw. **1759** Adam Smith *Mor. Sent.* VI. III. i. 493 The vile rust, which makes them [wheels] jarr and grate upon one another. **1794** Mrs. Radcliffe *Myst. Udolpho* xxvi, The great doors of the hall, which grate so heavily. **1797** —— *Italian* xii, A key grated in the lock. **1814** Byron *Corsair* I. xiv, Till grates her keel upon the shallow sand. **1853** Kingsley *Hypatia* xxii. 275 At last his cell-door grated on its hinges. **1864** Tennyson *En. Ard.* 773 Turning softly like a thief, Lest the harsh shingle should grate underfoot.

b. *trans.* In poetical nonce-uses: To produce (discordant sound) by jarring movement; to proclaim by a grating cry.

1667 Milton *P.L.* II. 881 Th' infernal dores..on their hinges grate Harsh Thunder. **1847** Tennyson *Princ.* IV. 107 Marsh-divers..Shall croak thee sister, or the meadow-crake Grate her harsh kindred in the grass.

c. *trans.* To utter (words) in a harsh tone.

1921 Galsworthy *To Let* II. v. 165 Gradman grated: 'Rather extreme at your age, sir; you lose control.' **1969** J. Ross *Dead at First Hand* i. 8 'I'm a gambler, Rogers,' he grated.

†**9.** *intr.* To 'harp' or dwell querulously *upon* a subject. *Obs.*

1542 Paget in *St. Papers Hen. VIII*, VIII. 686 It pleased Him to devise with me of the mariage now in treaty for Your Majesties doughter, albeit He did grate sumwhat at the furst upon this terme, bastarde. **1562** J. Heywood *Prov. & Epigr.* (1867) 109 Cha so grated on the new, cha forgot tholde. **1567** *Triall Treas.* (1850) 18 Gredy-gutte maketh them continually to grate On the mock of this world, which he thinketh permanent. **1573** G. Harvey *Letter-bk.* (Camden) 48 Here wuld be matter gud plenti, both for them to grate uppon and to brute abroad in the town. **1625** W. Pemble *Justif. Faith* (1629) 197 Who are very ready, when it fits their humour, to grate sore vpon the bare words and letter of a text. **1698** F. B. *Modest Censure* 17 Mr. Boyle..grates on the Doctor's breeding.

grate (greɪt), *v.*² [f. Grate *sb.*¹]

†**1.** *trans.* To confine within 'grates' or bars.

1528 More *Dyaloge* I. xiv. 18 b/2 Aftere she was gratid within iren grates aboue in the rood loft where it was byleued that she liued without any mete or drynke only by angels fode.

2. To fit or furnish with a grate or grating.

1547 Boorde *Introd. Knowl.* xxxix. (1870) 220 The sepulcre is grated rounde aboute wyth yrone. **1577** B. Googe *Heresbach's Husb.* IV. (1586) 172 b, Be sure that you have them well grated, that the Fish can by no meanes passe through. **1629** Massinger *Picture* IV. ii, The windows grated with iron! **1644** Evelyn *Diary* 12 Nov., A well.. grated over with iron. **1766** Goldsm. *Vic. W.* xxv, One large apartment, strongly grated. **1776** G. Semple *Building in Water* 106 You are to grate the Bottom with two Courses of six Inch Plank, crossing one another. **1821** Byron *Sardan.* II. i. 419 The gates That grate the palace, which is now our prison.

†**3.** To put on a grate or grid. *Obs. rare*$^{-1}$.

1598 Florio, *Gratellare*, to grate, to broyle vpon a grid-iron.

grate, variant of Grote *v. Obs.*, to weep.

grated ('greɪtɪd), *ppl. a.*¹ [f. Grate *v.*¹ + -ed¹.] In senses of the vb.

a. Pulverized with a grater.

c **1430** *Two Cookery-bks.* 14 Caste þer-to gratyd brede. **1598** *Epulario* D ij, Straw them ouer with grated Cheese. **1747** Mrs. Glasse *Cookery* ix. 99 Add some grated bread. **1872** C. W. Heaton *Exper. Chem.* IV. iii. 312 The liquid pressed out from the grated potatoes.

b. Of the teeth: Rubbed harshly together.

1590 Spenser *F.Q.* II. v. 14 [He]..gan to grind His grated teeth for great disdeigne.

†**c.** Scarified. *Obs.*

a **1699** J. Beaumont *Psyche* XXIII. cxli, And yet thy grated Throat is not so dry, As are thy now exhausted Eyes.

grated ('greɪtɪd), *ppl. a.*² [f. Grate *sb.*¹ and *v.*² + -ed².] Having a grate or grating, latticed.

1786 S. Henley tr. *Beckford's Vathek* (1868) 113 A vast cataract, visible in part through the grated portals. **1792** Burke *Negro Code* Wks. IX. 285 Grated port-holes between the decks. **1840** Dickens *Barn. Rudge* lxxiii, The grated window. **1876** Farrar *Marlb. Serm.* vi. 57 Through the grated lattice he saw the wild-eyed charioteers.

grateful ('greɪtfʊl), *a.* Also 6 greate full, 6–8 gratefull, 7 *Sc.* grytfull. [f. Grate *a.* + -ful (q.v. with regard to the unusual formation).]

1. Pleasing to the mind or the senses, agreeable, acceptable, welcome. Now only of things.

1553 Brende *Q. Curtius* v. 72 Hys comming was very greate full vnto the kynge. **1609** Heywood *Brit. Troy* IX. ii, Chast,—nothing better; wanton,—nothing worse, The gratefulst Blessing, or the greatest Curse. **1656-9** B. Harris *Parival's Iron Age* (ed. 2) 99 Nor ever had the Catholicks a more gratefull Victorie. **1670** G. H. tr. *Hist. Cardinals* II. II. 146 He is so far from being hateful, he is exceedingly grateful to the people of Rome. **1694** Salmon *Bate's Dispens.* I. (1713) 468/1 It is given..dissolved in some grateful Vehicle. **1725** Pope *Odyss.* IV. 542 In grateful sleep. **1761** Churchill *Night* Poems I. 81 Then in Oblivion's grateful cup I drown The galling sneer. **1774** Goldsm. *Nat. Hist.* (1776) VII. 367 Fishermen are careful to provide themselves with these insects, as the most grateful bait. **1814** Scott *Wav.* viii, Enjoying the grateful and cooling shade. **1866** Dk. Argyll *Reign Law* ii. (ed. 4) 55 This is a doctrine ..grateful to scientific men who are afraid of being thought hostile to Religion.

2. Of persons, their actions and attributes: Feeling gratitude; actuated by or manifesting gratitude; thankful.

1552 Dk. Northumbld. *Let.* 7 Dec. in Tytler *Edw. VI*, II. 148, I love not to have to do with men which be neither grateful nor pleasable. **1552** *Bk. Com. Prayer, Communion*, The humble and gratefull acknowledgeynge of the benefites of Christe. **1601** Shaks. *All's Well* II. i. 132, I cannot giue thee lesse to be cal'd gratefull. **1601** *Extracts Aberd. Reg.* (1848) II. 219 Ane grytfull rememberance. **1667** Milton *P.L.* XI. 864 With uplifted hands, and eyes devout, Grateful to Heav'n. **1696** Tate & Brady *Ps.* c. 3 Your grateful Hearts and Voices raise. **1738** Wesley *'How happy they, O King of Kings'* v, Our Hearts we'll on his Altars lay, A grateful Sacrifice. **1754** Richardson *Grandison* IV. xxii. 166 You oppress me, Sir, by your goodness! I cannot speak my grateful sensibilities. **1826** Disraeli *Viv. Grey* VI. i, Hailed by the grateful plaudits of all present. **1831** Lytton *Godolphin* 7 Heaven knows what either you or I have to be grateful for. **1841** W. Spalding *Italy & It. Isl.* II. 326 Gazing up at the Saviour in the first return of consciousness, amazed, grateful, and adoring. **1873** Miss Broughton *Nancy* I. 277 We always have a longer, gratefuller grace than usual, on Sundays.

absol. **1876** Mozley *Univ. Serm.* ix. 192 Everything from the grateful soothes—their looks, their words.

b. Of land: Responsive to the labour bestowed on it, fertile.

1832 Lander *Adv. Niger* III. xvii. 47 Afterwards..the soil was more rich and grateful, and the country more varied.

gratefully ('greɪtfʊlɪ), *adv.* [f. Grateful *a.* + -ly².] In a grateful manner; so as to give pleasure; with gratitude; thankfully.

1548 Elyot *Dict.*, *Grate*, kyndely, thankefully, gratefully. **1585** T. Washington tr. *Nicholay's Voy.* I. vi. 5 The king lent him one of his gallies & did further gratefully furnish him of tallowe and other thinges. **1597** A. M. tr. *Guillemeau's Fr. Chirurg.* *v, I intreate all men to receave gratefully this my laboure. **1635-56** Cowley *Davideis* I. 782 'Twas God himself that here tun'd every Toung; And gratefully of him alone they sung. *a* **1688** Cudworth *Immut. Mor.* (1731) 183 Finding something akin to its self in those Harmonious Airs, some Foot-steps and Resemblances of it self gratefully closing with them. **1741** Watts *Improv. Mind* I. xv. (1868) 135 This sort of study detains the mind by the perpetual occurrence and expectation of something new, and that which may gratefully strike the imagination. **1782** V. Knox *Ess.* xxxviii. I. 174 Science gratefully attributes to the same source a library and observatory. **1833** Sir R. Grant in Bickersteth *Chr. Psalmody* 16 O gratefully sing His pow'r and his love. **1860** Dickens *Uncomm. Trav.* xvi, I am gratefully particular in this reference to him.

gratefulness ('greɪtfʊlnɪs). [f. as prec. + -ness.] The quality of being grateful (see the adj.).

1581 Sidney *Apol. Poetrie* (Arb.) 47 The humane consideration of vertuous gratefulness. **1600** Abp. Abbot *Exp. Jonah* 427 Where he powreth foorth most benefits, he expecteth most gratefulnesse. **1627-77** Feltham *Resolves* II. lxix. 305 The gratefulness of his wit and parts. **1688** Norris *Theory Love* II. ii. 86 The particular gratefulness of one or two particular strings. **1764** Harmer *Observ.* XXVIII. iv. 196 Sweet wine, such as was used in royal palaces for its gratefulness. **1823** Lamb *Elia* Ser. II. *Amicus Redit.*, Dolefully trailing a length of reluctant gratefulness. **1858** J. Martineau *Stud. Chr.* 18 The gratefulness with which he accepted from the government the promise of a grant. **1884** *Manch. Exam.* 13 Nov. 8/5 The gratefulness of this provision [of ice cream] may be estimated when it is remembered that..the thermometer ranged from 95° to 100° in the shade.

†**'grateless**, *a.*¹ *Obs. rare.* [f. Grate *a.* + -less (on the analogy of *grateful*).] Ungrateful, thankless.

1577 Kendall *Flowers of Epigr.* 24 Lest she thee call churle gratelesse and vnkinde. **1594** Carew *Tasso* (1881) 19 Nor Eurard, nor Gernier, must slip my mind, To passe in gratelesse silence more then loth.

grateless (ˈgreɪtlɪs), *a.*[2] [f. GRATE *sb.*[1] + -LESS.] Without a grate, having no grate.

1808 J. BARLOW *Columb.* VI. 34 What grateless dungeons groan beneath the ground! **1876** M. M. GRANT *Sun-Maid* iv, The chimney was open and grateless.

†**grateolent**, *a. Obs. rare*⁻⁰. [f. L. *grātē*, adv. of *grātus* pleasant + *olent-em*, pres. pple. of *olēre* to smell (after *graveolent*).] 'Well savouring, smelling pleasantly' (Blount *Glossogr.* 1656).

grater[1] (ˈgreɪtə(r)). Also 4 -our, 5 -ere. [a. OF. *grateor*, *gratour* (13th c. in Godef., of a person), f. *grater* to GRATE *v.*[1]

In sense 1 possibly (in spite of the form) a. OF. **gratoir* (mod.F. *grattoir*, first in Cotgr. 1611) or **gratoire* (found only in 16th c.).]

1. An instrument with a rough indented surface used for grating or rasping; *esp.* a kitchen utensil, having a rasping surface formed by punching holes which raise protuberances, and used for grating ginger, nutmegs, etc.

1390–1 *Earl Derby's Exped.* (Camden) 24 Pro j gratour. **1555** W. WATREMAN *Fardle Facions* II. viii. 185 People.. muche like vnto dogges, with mouthes roughe like a grater. **1577** FRAMPTON *Joyful News* III. (1596) 103 They.. grate it in certeyne Graters, which are made of Needles. **1664** POWER *Exp. Philos.* I. 5 The Common Fly: her eyes are most neatly dimpled with innumerable little cavities like a small grater or thimble. **1741** *Compl. Fam.-Piece* I. ii. 154 Take raw Carrots and scrape them clean, grate them with a Grater. **1824** SOUTHEY *Bk. of Ch.* (1841) 183 They bound chains round the body, which eat into the flesh; or fastened graters upon the breast and back. **1872** C. W. HEATON *Exper. Chem.* IV. iii. 311 Rasp some potatoes on a grater. **1875** KNIGHT *Dict. Mech.*, *Grater* (Book-binding), an iron instrument used by the forwarder in rubbing the backs of sewed books after pasting.

†**2.** A scraper. *Obs.*

1580 HOLLYBAND *Treas. Fr. Tong.*, *Vn racloir*, a grater, a scraper. **1688** R. HOLME *Armoury* III. 315/2 A Dough scrape, or a Grater.. with this they scrape and cleanse the sides and bottom of the Kneading Trough from the Dough that sticks to it.

b. *Her.* A glazier's tool figured in the arms of the Glaziers' Company.

1780 EDMONDSON *Her.* II. Gloss. **1847** *Gloss. Herald.*, *Grater* or *Glaziers' Nippers*, called also *Grazier*, or *Grosing-iron*.

†**3.** One who or that which grates; chiefly *fig.* said of a person (or thing) that performs some harassing, exhausting, or 'wearing' process. *Obs.*

14.. *Voc.* in Wr.-Wulcker 610/3 *Scarifactor et Scarifactrix*, a gratere. **1549** CHALONER *Erasm. Folly* T ij a, I requyre you not to be overscrupulous graters of the bare woords. **1566** in Harington *Nugæ Ant.* 145 Those that be the great graters for gayne and profitt. **1581** MULCASTER *Positions* xxxvii. (1887) 145 Repulse in great hope is a perillous grater. **1611** COTGR., *Racleur*, a scraper, a rasper, a grater. **1628** EARLE *Microcosm.*, *Graue Diuine* (Arb.) 24 He is no base Grater of his Tythes, and will not wrangle for the odde Egge.

†**grater**[2]. *Obs.* [Perh. an extension of GRATE *sb.*[1], or possibly merely an error.] App. a kind of wooden grating or hurdle.

1598 FLORIO, *Aggratticare*,.. to make grater-wise, to make like a hurdle, to hurdle. ?**1623** J. TAYLOR (Water P.) *Wks.* (1630) III. 103/2 Washing boules, and beetles went to wracke, old graters and stooles were turn'd to ashes, mouse-traps and tinder boxes came to light.

†**grates**, *sb. pl. Obs.* [a. L. *grātes*.] Thanks.

c **1485** *Digby Myst.* (1882) v. 190 What grates I ough to god a-geyn.

grath, obs. f. GRAITH; var. GROWTH[2] *Obs.*

grathely, var. GRADELY *a.* and *adv.*

‖**Gratia Dei** (ˈgreɪʃ(ɪ)ə ˈdiːaɪ). [L. = 'grace of God'. Cf. GRACE *sb.* 18.]

1. A name for the Hedge Hyssop (*Gratiola officinalis*); formerly also applied to the Lesser Centaury (*Erythræa Centaureum*) and *Geranium pratense*.

13.. *Old Med. MS.* in *Archæol.* (1844) XXX. 382 Gracia Dei yt growyth in mede. *c* **1400** in *Med. Wks. 14th C.* (Henslow, 1899) 53 An herbe þat [is] y-clipyd gratia dei. **1578** LYTE *Dodoens* I. xxxiii. 48 The seuenth [Geranium] is called Gratia Dei: in English also Gratia Dei. *Ibid.* VI. xii. 673 Hedge Hysope.. Some do call it in Latine, *Gratia Dei*, Howbeit it is nothing lyke *Gratia Dei*, or *Gratiola*, which is a kinde of the lesse Centaury. **1706** PHILLIPS (ed. Kersey), *Gratia Dei*,.. a kind of lesser Centaury. **1866** *Treas. Bot.* 550/2 Gratia Dei, *Gratiola officinalis*.

†**2.** A kind of plaster. *Obs.*

c **1450** *ME. Med. Bk.* (Heinrich) 187 Thys gratia dei vsede þe lady bechampe. **1669** PHILLIPS, *Gratia Dei*, a Plaister, made of Wax, Rosen, Suet, Turpentine, Mastick, and Olibanum.

graticulation (grətɪkjʊˈleɪʃən). [ad. F. *graticulation*, f. *graticuler*, f. *graticule* (see next).] The division of a design or plan into squares with the object of reproducing accurately in the process of enlargement or reduction the proportions in detail of the original; *concr.* a surface so divided.

1727–41 in CHAMBERS *Cycl.* **1735** in DYCHE & PARDON *Dict.* **1859** in GWILT *Encycl. Archit.* (ed. 4) Gloss. **1887** GEN. WALKER in *Encycl. Brit.* XXII. 714/1 Graticulation. The sheets of paper on which the details of the survey of any large area of country are to be laid down must be furnished with a system of conventional lines, drawn with a view to assimilate the margins of contiguous sheets, and to form a graticulation within which the details may be accurately inserted.

graticule (ˈgrætɪkjuːl). [a. F. *graticule*, ad. med.L. *grāticula*, for *crāticula* gridiron, dim. of *crātis* hurdle.] **1.** A design or plan divided into squares to facilitate its proportionate enlargement or reduction; the style or pattern of such a division.

1887 GEN. WALKER in *Encycl. Brit.* XXII. 714/1 The graticule is sometimes rectangular, sometimes spherical, sometimes a combination of both.. Spherical graticules are constructed in various ways.

2. A transparent plate or cell bearing a grid, cross-wire, or scale, designed to be used with an optical instrument or cathode-ray oscilloscope for the purpose of positioning, measuring, or counting objects in the field of view; the scale, grid, etc., on such a plate. Hence **ˈgraticuled** *ppl. a.*, fitted with a graticule.

1914 *Handbk. Artill. Instrum.* 42 In front of the eye-piece is fixed.. a diaphragm, with spider's web graticules attached to it. **1919** *Trans. Opt. Soc.* XX. 277 Generally the graticules are on glass and it is usual to refer to the complete discs or plates with the measuring scales or marks on them, as 'graticules'. *Ibid.* 286 Graticuled binoculars are not used much for peace purposes. **1920** *Nature* CV. 563/1 Such motion being observed by a plate micrometer or 'graticule' in the observing telescope. **1922** *Encycl. Brit.* XXXII. 243/1 Graticuled binoculars. **1924** L. C. MARTIN *Opt. Meas. Instr.* 27 The use of lines engraved on a glass (a graticule) is finding an increasing favour. **1952** M. TRIPP *Faith is Windsock* ii. 34 By means of a line-of-flight marker, a controllable circular graticule and a movable compass ring, the relative position of the aircraft and a ground feature could be ascertained. **1966** *McGraw-Hill Encycl. Sci. & Technol.* IX. 430/1 Practically all laboratory oscilloscopes have calibrated horizontal sweeps so that time interval measurements may be read directly from a graticule over the cathode-ray tube screen. **1970** E. M. SLAYTER *Optical Methods in Biol.* xii. 282 When exact measurements are required, however, an ocular can be used in which a ruled scale (graticule) is incorporated. The graticule is placed at the first focal plane of the 'eye lens' of the ocular. **1971** *Physics Bull.* July 398/2 A graduation line is centred in the microscope eyepiece graticule.

†**gratiˈfactory**, *a. Obs. rare*⁻¹. [f. GRATIFY, after *satisfactory*.] Gratifying.

a **1665** J. GOODWIN *Filled w. the Spirit* (1867) 270 All such things which are gratifactory and pleasing unto the flesh.

†**graˈtific**, *a. Obs. rare*⁻⁰. [ad. L. *grātific-us*, f. *grātus* pleasing, thankful: see -FIC.]

1727 BAILEY vol. II, *Gratifick*, grateful, thankful.

gratification (grætɪfɪˈkeɪʃən). [ad. (directly or through F. *gratification*) L. *grātificātiōn-em*, n. of action f. *grātificārī* to GRATIFY.]

1. The action of gratifying, or the fact of being gratified: **a.** Requital, satisfaction; the giving of pleasure, the doing of a favour.

1598 FLORIO, *Gratificatione*, a gratification. **1603** HOLLAND *Plutarch's Mor.* 434 They.. called for him agaîne, not so much by way of gratification and to do him a pleasure, but [etc.]. **1611** SPEED *Hist. Gt. Brit.* IX. xvi. §37 (1614) 601 To make himselfe one of the greatest of England, by this gratification of the French, with his Masters charge and dishonour. **1633** T. MORTON *Disch. Imput.* 233 They, who masque the visages of Sins with the vizard of Virtues; calling Drunkennesse Good-fellowship.. Bribery gratification. *a* **1862** BUCKLE *Civiliz.* (1873) III. v. 308 Men, in the pursuit of wealth, consider their own gratification oftener than the gratification of others.

†**b.** Expression of pleasure or satisfaction; congratulation. **c.** Thanksgiving. *Obs.*

1599 HAKLUYT *Voy.* II. 306 Whereupon she sent an upper gown of cloth of gold very rich.. with a letter of gratification. **1620** SHELTON *Quix.* IV. x, Many other Words of Compliment and Gratification pass'd between Don Quixote and Don Ferdinando. **1660** F. BROOKE tr. *Le Blanc's Trav.* 363 The.. whole multitude.. with hymns and gratifications [Fr. *actions de grâces*].

d. The satisfaction or indulgence of, or compliance with (a feeling, desire, etc.).

1669 STILLINGFL. *Serm.* v. (1673) 85 The pleasure of humane life lies in the gratifications of the senses. **1736** BUTLER *Anal.* I. iii. Wks. 1874 I. 54 The gratification itself of every natural passion must be attended with delight. **1807** G. CHALMERS *Caledonia* I. II. vi. 292 Little advantage seems to have been obtained, beyond the gratification of hatred. **1809** W. IRVING *Knickerb.* IV. v. (1849) 221 Nothing so soon awakens the malevolent passions as the facility of gratification. **1860** MILL *Repr. Govt.* (1865) 50/1 The gratification of his love of domineering.

2. The state of being gratified or pleased; enjoyment, satisfaction, pleasurable feeling.

1712 STEELE *Spect.* No. 454 ¶7 If they could learn with me to keep their minds open to Gratification, and ready to receive it from any thing it meets with. **1713** BERKELEY *Guardian* No. 55 ¶10 A natural gratification attends good actions. **1875** JOWETT *Plato* (ed. 2) I. 152 Gratification is of the mind when receiving wisdom and knowledge, but pleasure is of the body. **1876** MOZLEY *Univ. Serm.* vii. (1877) 148 A compassionate person derives a true gratification from the exercise of his affection.

b. with *a* and *pl.* An instance of this; a thing that gratifies or pleases; a source of pleasure or satisfaction.

1711 STEELE *Spect.* No. 151 ¶4 He little knows the perfect Joy he loses, for the disappointing Gratifications which he pursues. **1750** JOHNSON *Rambler* No. 80 ¶3 That insatiable demand of new gratifications, which seems.. to characterize the nature of man. **1798** W. BLAIR *Soldier's Friend* 92 The use of butcher's meat.. or fermented liquors, and all those gratifications that are so agreeable to idle people. **1859** W. ANDERSON *Discourses* (1860) 97 By the 'things on earth' are denoted the gratifications of sense.

3. Something given to gain favour, or as a recompense for anything done or to be done; a reward, recompense, gratuity; in bad sense, a bribe.

1576 *Extracts Aberd. Reg.* (1848) II. 27 The said Mr. Alex[r]. procuris for thame in all thair actionis and caussis.. without gratificatioun and recompensatioun, frelie on his awin expenssis. **1607** TOPSELL *Four-f. Beasts* (1658) 367 The Lioness requited the same with such gratification as lay in her power, for she brought him very many sheep-skins to clothe and cover him. **1624** *Impeachm. Dk. Buckhm.* (Camden) 87 Giveing the gratification of twoe thowsand poundes. **1642** ROGERS *Naaman* 382 All who went unto them for advice, offered them a gratification. **1751** SMOLLETT *Per. Pic.* (1779) I. xxvii. 244 She would not bestow upon him any pecuniary gratification. **1828** I. R. BEST *Italy* 372 A presentation to the Pope costs about forty shillings in gratifications to the servants of the household. **1849** MACAULAY *Hist. Eng.* vi. II. 65 Six thousand guineas was the smallest gratification that could be offered to so important a minister.

b. *Mil.* (See quot.) Cf. GRATUITY 3.

1802 C. JAMES *Milit. Dict.* s.v., In the Royal Artillery, gratifications, or voluntary subscriptions for the relief and support of the wives of deceased officers, are conducted on the most liberal plan.. Gratification likewise means a certain allowance in money which is made to prisoners of war.

†**4.** A concession. *Obs. rare.*

1677 HALE *Prim. Orig. Man.* II. vii. 187, I am no way satisfied with this Gratification of that Author to the *Præ-Adamitæ*.

†**5.** A term of uncertain meaning, formerly in use in the colony of Massachusetts; also *attrib.*, *gratification lot*. *Obs.*

1637 *Rec. Dedham, Mass.* (1892) III. 33 That Lott wch John Dwite hath layd out for a freind in grateficacion. **1638** *Ibid.* 45 Assigned vnto Jno. Dwite.. 6 acres at the lower end of the greate medowe next ye River in pte of his graceficacion Lott. **1640** *Ibid.* 74 Graunted to John Dwite Twelue acres of planting grownd to make up his grateficacion Lott.

†**ˈgratificator.** *Obs. rare*⁻⁰. [agent-n. in L. form, f. *grātificārī* to GRATIFY.] One who gratifies.

1755 BAILEY (ed. Scott), *Gratificator*, one that performs the act of gratifying.

gratified (ˈgrætɪfaɪd), *ppl. a.* [f. GRATIFY *v.* + -ED[1].] Pleased, satisfied, etc. Hence **ˈgratifiedly** *adv.*, with pleasure or satisfaction.

1818 T. MOORE *Mem.* (1853) II. 213 With many gratified acknowledgments of their high opinion. **1854** MARION HARLAND *Alone* xxi, Mrs. Grant.. raised her spectacles to look at her, and smiled gratifiedly. **1861** WHYTE MELVILLE *Mkt. Harb.* 76 'Never was better, sir', answers gratified John, with a touch of his hat. **1897** MARY KINGSLEY *W. Africa* 243 'All Fan now', says Singlet in anything but a gratified tone of voice.

gratifier (ˈgrætɪfaɪə(r)). [f. GRATIFY *v.* + -ER[1].] One who gratifies, rewards, or requites.

1549 LATIMER *3rd Serm. bef. Edw. VI* (Arb.) 97 A bryber, a gyft taker, a gratifier of rytche men. **1660** H. MORE *Myst. Godl.* v. xiv. 169 Other Eminent persons.. who were great gratifiers of the natural life of man. **1825** *New Monthly Mag.* XV. 2 Secret gratifiers of their passions.

gratify (ˈgrætɪfaɪ), *v.* [ad. F. *gratifier* (16th c. in Hatz.-Darm.), or L. *grātificārī*, f. *grātus* pleasing, thankful: see -FY.]

†**1.** *trans.* To show gratitude to (a person) in return for benefits received, esp. in a practical manner; to reward, requite. *Obs.*

c **1540** tr. *Pol. Verg. Eng. Hist.* VIII. (Camden) I. 291 Edwarde was verie desierus to seeme to gratifie the duke for his owlde hospitalitie and interteinement. **1570** *Satir. Poems Reform.* x. 410 To quhome.. he schew his greit clemence, Thocht thou with tressoun hes him gratifeit. **1578** T. N. tr. *Conq. W. India* 30 Al we of this navie wil gratifie your gentlenesse and good service that ye shal do unto us. **1607** SHAKS. *Cor.* II. ii. 44 It remaines.. To gratifie his Noble seruice. **1655** STANLEY *Hist. Philos.* III. (1701) 123/1 To Dionysius he imparted some Dialogues and was gratified by him, with whom he lived untill he was deposed.

†**b.** To give thanks to. *Obs.*

1599 B. JONSON *Cynthia's Rev.* IV. iii, In behalf of the males, I gratifie you. *a* **1646** J. GREGORY *Assyrian Mon.* in *Posth.* (1650) 193 So far Diodorus: whom after ages may for ever gratifie for this pretious monument of Antiquitie.

2. To make a present (usually of money) or give a gratuity to, esp. as a reward or recompense, or as a bribe; to remunerate; to fee. †Also, to reward (an action, services, etc.). Now *arch.* and with a mixture of sense 4.

1590 GREENE *Neuer too late* (1600) 22 Francesco.. gaue her all the money in his purse, so that she returned so highly gratified [etc.]. **1596** SHAKS. *Merch. V.* IV. i. 406 Anthonio, gratifie this gentleman. **1613** WITHER *Abuses Stript.* I. vi. in *Juvenilia* (1633) 47 The Messenger he richly gratifies. **1639** FULLER *Holy War* v. xxvii. (1647) 276 They must pay the Guardian both for their victuals and for their welcome, and gratifie his good words and looks. **1672** *Merch. Adv. Newc.* (Surtees) 216 To gratifie his servant with 40s. for secureing the same. **1679** *Boston Rec.* (1881) VII. 127 Voted that the Select men gratifie the scauengers for cleereinge the streetes. **1763** SMOLLETT *Hist. Eng.* (1800) III. 278 The services done by the colonies in North America during the war were gratified with the sum of £122,246. **1855** MACAULAY *Hist.*

Eng. xxi. IV. 552 The only answer which they had been able to extract from Cook was that there were some great persons whom it was necessary to gratify. **1856** OLMSTED *Slave States* 252 Those engaged in almost all employments superior to that of field-hands in the Southern States, are, nearly always, 'gratified' with some sort of wages. **1883** C. J. WILLS *Mod. Persia* 76 We left the tomb, after having gratified the two Jews.

†**3.** To express pleasure at (an event); to give a welcome to (a person). *Obs.*

1548 HALL *Chron., Henry VII* an. 15 (1550) 51 b, While the kyng laye thus at Caleys the archeduke Philip sent to him diuerse notable personages..to gratefye and welcome hym into those partes. **1553** BRENDE *Q. Curtius* IV. 32 Caryeng unto him a crowne of golde, in gratifieng yᵉ victory he had won. **1588** GREENE *Pandosto* (1607) 51 The Courtiers and Knights appointed Iustes and Turneyes, to signifie their willing mindes in gratifying the Kings hap. **1612** SKELTON *Quix.* III. x. I. 208, I do with all my Heart gratifie the Signs of Affection and Courtesy which you have used towards me.

4. To give pleasure or satisfaction to; to please, satisfy, oblige; to do a favour to.

1568 GRAFTON *Chron.* II. 47 The Bishops and Priestes.. were contented yet to ayde him with money. For the which thing, he being desyrous to gratefie them againe, caused it to be ordeyned and enacted [that]. **1574** J. STUDLEY tr. *Bale's Pageant Popes* 99 b, The Soldan..deuised howe to gratifye the Pope and to slay his ennemye. **1595** *Locrine* II. iii. 151 If you mean to gratify such poor men as we be, you must build our houses by the tavern. **1651** HOBBES *Leviath.* III. xli. 264 Pilate himself (to gratifie the Jews) delivered him to be crucified. **1662** *Bk. Com. Prayer* Pref., Not to gratifie this or that party. **1775** BURKE *Corr.* (1844) II. 32 Since you are gratified by hearing of us. **1830** D'ISRAELI *Chas. I*, III. vi. 85 The King was always highly gratified by a present of a painting from his ambassadors. **1831** BREWSTER *Newton* (1855) II. xv. 73 Varignon was much gratified at having brought about this reconciliation.

†**b.** *intr.* for *refl.* To rejoice. *Obs.*

1811 *Ora & Juliet* II. 157 It is to be hoped..you will not retreat again from the world, to gratify on the mischief you have increased in my poor heart.

5. To please by compliance; to give free course to; to humour, indulge, satisfy (a desire, feeling, etc.); †to comply with (a request, a command), to concede (an objection).

1662 STILLINGFL. *Orig. Sacr.* II. i. §6 Suppose we at present, to gratifie so far the objection, that these Laws were brought..under Moses his name. **1665** BOYLE *Occas. Refl.* IV. xix. (1848) 281 'Tis not the Body, but the unruly Fancy, that is Gratify'd. **1703** ROWE *Fair Penit.* III. i. 769 Has not your Daughter giv'n her self to Altamont To gratifie a Father's stern Command? **1711** STEELE *Spect.* No. 260 ¶1 My Appetites are increased upon me with the Loss of Power to gratify them. **1729** BUTLER *Serm.* Wks. 1874 II. 13 Mankind have ungoverned passions which they will gratify at any rate. **1798** FERRIAR *Illustr. Sterne* ii. 47 The book is not sufficiently entertaining to gratify much expectation. **1855** PRESCOTT *Philip II*, I. II. viii. 238 His vanity was gratified by the homage..paid him.

†**6.** To render pleasing or acceptable; to grace.

1577 KENDALL *Flowers of Epigr.* 65 b, With sweet perfumes and flowers, my graue doe you not gratifie. **1588** SHAKS. *L.L.L.* IV. ii. 161 If..it shall please you to gratifie the table with a Grace. *a* **1672** WREN in Gutch *Coll. Cur.* (1781) I. 243 The King (though highly gratified both with courage and understanding). **1698** FRYER *Acc. E. India & P.* 19 All things..strive to gratify the Life of Man.

Hence **'gratifying** *vbl. sb.*

1555 EDEN *Decades* To Rdr. (Arb.) 49 The gratifyinge of vniuersal mankind. **1591** PERCIVALL *Sp. Dict., Gratificacion*, gratifying. **1611** COTGR., *Gratification*, a gratification or gratifying.

'gratifying, *ppl. a.* [-ING².] That gratifies; affording pleasure, pleasing, satisfying.

1611 FLORIO, *Gratifico*, gratifying. *a* **1617** BAYNE *On Eph.* (1658) 68 Wee come from that gratifying Mother, child-bearing grace, to that grace which is freely given to us. **1794** MATHIAS *Purs. Lit.* (1798) 393 Dr. W's criticisms..are often very just, curious, and gratifying. **1847** JAMES *Convict* i, I have something to propose which I think will be gratifying to you. **1849** MACAULAY *Hist. Eng.* ii. I. 269 Beyond his reign there was the gratifying prospect of a long series of Protestant sovereigns.

Hence **'gratifyingly** *adv.*

1822 *Examiner* 428/1 Sportsmen..will..be most gratifyingly attracted by this beauty. **1831** CARLYLE *Sart. Res.* II. x, Fruits of my unseen sowing gratifyingly meet me here and there.

gratility (grəˈtɪlɪtɪ). In the Shakspere passage the clown's humorous perversion for *gratuity*; so jocularly used by Scott.

1601 SHAKS. *Twel. N.* II. iii. 27 ..I sent thee sixe pence for thy Lemon, hadst it? *Clo.* I did impeticos thy gratillity. **1829** SCOTT *Jrnl.* 5 June, Cadell lent me £10 —— funny enough, after all our grand expectations, for Croesus to want such a gratility.

‖**gratin** (gratẽ). *Cookery.* [Fr., f. *gratter*, earlier *grater* GRATE *v.*¹] **a.** A manner of preparing viands by treating them with raspings of bread and cooking them between two fires so as to produce a light crust; hence, the dish so cooked; *spec.* the light crust on the surface of such dishes, now usu. formed by a sprinkling of breadcrumbs or grated cheese browned in the oven or under the grill. (See also quots. 1846 and 1877, where the meaning given may be the result of some error.) Hence phr. ***au gratin*** (o gratẽ): cooked in this way; also, as *sb.*

1806 J. SIMPSON *Compl. Syst. Cookery* 139 Crayfish au gratin. **1844** THACKERAY in *New Monthly Mag.* July 418 Eels, salmon, lobsters, either *au gratin* or in cutlets. **1846** FRANCATELLI *Mod. Cook* p. xii, *Gratins*, a term applied to consolidated soups and sauces; also to certain dishes of high character, consisting of game, poultry, fish, vegetables, or maccaroni, &c., improved by great care and finish, through the use of concentrated sauces or gravies. *Ibid.* 56 Farce of fat livers for gratins. **1846** A. SOYER *Gastronomic Regenerator* 112 Sole au gratin. *Note*, In France we have silver dishes on purpose for *au gratins*, in which they are dressed and served to table, the gratin adhering to the bottom of the dish. **1877** *Cassell's Dict. Cookery*, *Gratin* is a French forcemeat. It may be made either of the lean part of veal or the breast and wings of a fowl. **1889** A. B. MARSHALL *Cookery Bk.* 219 Maccaroni au Gratin. **1897** NANSEN in *Daily News* 9 Feb. 8/4 A fish gratin made of powdered fish and Indian meal and train oil. *a* **1936** KIPLING *Something of Myself* (1937) v. 144 The diamond's tip bubbled like cauliflower *au gratin*. **1964** *Good Housek. New Cooking* v. 57 *Egg and Spinach Au Gratin*... Sprinkle on the remaining cheese and grill until golden.

b. *attrib.*

1889 A. B. MARSHALL *Cookery Bk.* 17 Gratin Sauce (for Fish). **1901** C. H. SENN *New Cent. Cook. Bk.* 599 Butter a silver-plated gratin-dish. **1902** *Daily Chron.* 15 Feb. 8/4 Drain and turn into a gratin dish,..cover with fine breadcrumbs. **1965** *House & Garden* Dec. 84/3 A *gratin* dish often does contain cheese, but it is not a vital ingredient.

c. *transf.* The 'upper crust' of society.

1934 E. F. THOMAS *Portrait of Widow* iii. 28 Did you chance to know the Duchesse de Mallincourt in Paris? She always received the *gratin* of the American colony. **1959** *Sunday Times* 17 May 15/4 She belonged to the Edwardo-Georgian *gratin*. **1967** S. PAKENHAM *Sixty Miles from England* xiv. 185 Madeleine Lemaire had one of the most famous Paris salons, where all but the very highest *gratin* of the French nobility congregated.

Hence **'gratinate** *v.* [after F. *gratiner*: see -ATE³], to cook (food) *au gratin*.

1902 in WEBSTER Suppl.

grating (ˈgreɪtɪŋ), *vbl. sb.*¹ [f. GRATE *v.*¹ + -ING¹.] The action of the verb GRATE.

1. The action of breaking into small particles by rasping or rubbing; also, the product of this.

c **1440** *Promp. Parv.* 207/2 Gratynge of brede, *micacio. Ibid.*, Gratynge of gyngure, and oþer lyke, *frictura.* **1725** BRADLEY *Fam. Dict.* s.v. *Lemon tree*, Mix some Gratings of Lemon therewith. **1856** KANE *Arct. Expl.* I. xxxi. 434, I have to give him a grating of potatoes.

2. The action of rubbing harshly against something; hence, the discordant sound made by this.

1611 FLORIO, *Grattalice*, a grating, a scraping. **1626** BACON *Sylva* §275 The grateing of a Saw when it is sharpned ..setteth the Teeth on edge. **1657** W. MORICE *Coena quasi Κοινὴ* Pref. 22 If my stile seeme to be keene and peircing.. they have sharpned it by hard grating. **1760** YOUNG in *Phil. Trans.* LI. 847 The grating, that is always to be felt, when the two broken ends of a bone are moved against one another. **1812** BYRON *Ch. Har.* II. xiii, The grating of his chain. **1842** MRS. F. TROLLOPE *Visit Italy* II. xiii. 231 The ear almost fancies it can catch the grating of a Roman chariot wheel. **1894** CROCKETT *Raiders* 122 The grating of the oars of the boat against the sides of the cave.

3. *fig.* Irritation, fretting, harassing. (See GRATE *v.*¹ 3 and 4.)

a **1716** SOUTH *Serm.* XI. i. 26 The difficulties, the hard grating, and afflicting contrariety that bears to the flesh.

grating (ˈgreɪtɪŋ), *vbl. sb.*² [f. GRATE *sb.*¹ and *v.*² + -ING¹.]

1. The action of GRATE *v.*² *rare.*

1611 COTGR., *Grillement*..also a grating, or shutting vp with grates.

2. a. A framework of wooden or metal bars; a piece of cross-barred work; = GRATE *sb.*¹ 1, 2.

1739 LABELYE *Short Acc. Piers Westm. Bridge* 14 The Foundation of every Pier should be laid on a strong Grating of Timber. **1769–80** FALCONER *Dict. Marine, Grating*, a drain whereon to lay new tarred cordage. **1810** *Hull Improv. Act* 34 Drains gutters sinks or watercourses, grates or gratings. **1873** *Act 36 & 37 Vict.* c. 71 §39 Gratings shall be placed..across the head and tail race of mills. **1874** HELPS *Soc. Press.* iii. (1875) 39 A stench..came up through all the neighbouring gratings.

b. *esp. Naut.* The open wood-work cover for the hatchway.

1626 CAPT. SMITH *Accid. Yng. Sea-men* 14 A grating, netting or false decke for your close fights. **1711** W. SUTHERLAND *Shipbuild. Assist.* 43 As many Gratings as can possibly..be placed for causing Lights on the Plan below, as also to give vent to the Smoke of Powder in Time of Service. **1828** P. CUNNINGHAM *N.S. Wales* (ed. 3) II. 204 Looking down through the main-hatchway gratings. **1873** *Act 36 & 37 Vict.* c. 88 Sched. i, Hatches with open gratings, instead of the close hatches which are usual in merchant vessels.

c. The perforated plate used for separating large from small ore; also, the process of sorting ore with grates.

1869 R. B. SMYTH *Goldf. Victoria* 612 *Grating*, a piece of thin sheet-iron, in which about 100 holes..to the square inch are punched. It is fixed in front of the stamper-box.

†**3.** A scoring or ruling of a surface. *Obs.*

1678 MOXON *Mech. Exerc.* I. 71 You will quickly wear the courser grating of the Grind stone off the edge on that side.

4. *Optics.* An arrangement of parallel wires in a plane, or a surface of glass or polished metal ruled with a series of very close fine parallel lines, designed to produce spectra by diffraction.

1877 G. F. CHAMBERS *Astron.* x. iii. (ed. 3) 847 A diffraction grating, that is, a piece of glass ruled with very fine close lines. **1882** TAIT in *Encycl. Brit.* XIV. 607/2 Let us next consider the effect of a grating, a series of parallel wires placed at small equal intervals, or a piece of glass or of speculum metal on which a series of equidistant parallel lines have been ruled by a diamond point. **1893** SIR R. BALL *Story of Sun* 109 He was able to rule a grating..with as many as 43,000 lines to the inch.

5. *attrib.* and *Comb.*, as ***grating-bar, -constant, -iron, photograph, space, spectrometer***; **grating-deck** (see quot. 1867); **grating spectrum**, a diffraction spectrum produced by a grating.

1597 A. M. tr. *Guillemeau's Fr. Chirurg.* 33/2 Without greate paynes we can not fasten theron with the grating iron. **1867** SMYTH *Sailor's Word-bk.*, *Grating-deck*, a light movable deck, similar to the hatch-deck, but with open gratings. **1897** P. WARUNG *Tales Old Regime* 97 The man who filed away the grating-bars would be first out of the shaft. **1926** R. W. LAWSON tr. *Hevesy & Paneth's Man. Radioactivity* iv. 44 The grating space of a Rowland grating is about 10^{-4} cm. **1938** *Ibid.* (ed. 2) iv. 49 The 'grating constant' is here the distance between two adjacent lattice planes in the crystal. **1941** *Nature* 24 May 643/2 The spectrum was obtained from a discharge tube of the type described by Pearse and Gaydon, and grating photographs were taken (dispersions 2·6 and 1·9 A./mm.) in the region λλ 6400–4900. **1963** G. TROUP *Masers & Lasers* (ed. 2) viii. 149 The fluorescent light emitted from the ends and from the sides was examined, using a grating spectrometer capable of resolving the R_1 and R_2 lines.

grating (ˈgreɪtɪŋ), *ppl. a.* [f. GRATE *v.*¹ + -ING².] That grates, in senses of the vb.

1. Abrading, rasping; affecting painfully, as if by abrasion; irritating, fretting, 'wearing'.

1563 B. GOOGE *Eglogs*, etc. (Arb.) 85 In Countreye growes, no gratynge grudge. **1611** FLORIO, *Grattugina*, a grating trull. **1643** SIR T. BROWNE *Relig. Med.* I. §44 The grating torture of a disease. **1643** BURROUGHES *Exp. Hosea* v. (1652) 251. I have a grating conscience within me. **1710** STEELE *Tatler* No. 225 ¶2 A Man is allowed to say the most grating Thing imaginable to another. **1720** WATERLAND *Vind. Christ's Divinity* xv. 222 Those Positions..were too grating upon, and too shocking to every pious Christian at that Time. **1734** tr. *Rollin's Anc. Hist.* (1827) VIII. XIX. vii. 186 The yoke of obedience and submission always grating to kings. **1766** *Gent. Mag.* Feb. 72/2 Its skin was rough, scaly, and grating, like that of a sea-dog or seal. **1798** MALTHUS *Popul.* (1806) I. I. ii. 17 Reduced to the grating necessity of forfeiting his independence. **1858** LYTTON *What will he do* I. iv, Pride is a garment all stiff brocade outside, all grating sackcloth on the side next to the skin. **1876** GEO. ELIOT *Dan. Der.* VI. xlv, This speech was grating to Deronda.

†**2.** Of persons, their qualities, etc.: Grinding, oppressive. *Obs.*

1653 HOLCROFT *Procopius* Pref. A ij b, He severely indites ..Tribonianus the Questor of grating avarice. **1673** *Essex Papers* (Camden) 83 In all his Majesties 3 Kingdomes, there lives not a more grating man than Sʳ Willᵐ Petty.

3. That makes a grinding or creaking sound, as of two rough bodies grating together; hence, sounding harsh or discordant.

1718 LADY M. W. MONTAGU *Let. to Lady Rich* 10 Oct., Their music at the opera..was abominably grating. **1756** BURKE *Subl. & B.* I. ii, Suppose..a man..to have his ears wounded with some harsh and grating sound. **1803** J. LEYDEN *Scenes of Infancy* I. 67 The Scythed Car on grating axle rings. **1886** HALL CAINE *Son of Hagar* I. Prol., The ghastly face answered ill to the grating laugh that followed.

Hence **'gratingly** *adv.*

1683 KENNETT tr. *Erasm. on Folly* 56 The mind is freed from those cares, which would otherwise gratingly afflict it. **1857** *Chamb. Jrnl.* VII. 199 Fiendish laughter, gratingly, piercingly loud. **1873** MASSON *Drumm. of Hawth.* vi. 107 It does come a little gratingly in the context of the inter-changed letters.

†**gratinȝied,** *ppl. a. Sc. Obs. rare.* [f. OF. *gratigner, gratiner*, recorded only in the sense to scratch; but cf. F. *égratigner* to pink.] Pinked.

1578 *Inv. R. Wardr.* (1815) 230 Ane uther [cloak] of quheit satine granteinyeit. **1657** *Sp. Fife Laird* in Watson *Collect.* (1706) I. 29 Ev'n his whole shirt his skin doth hide. Gowpherd, Gratinȝied [*printed* Gratnizied].

‖**Gratiola** (græˈtaɪələ). *Bot.* [mod.L. f. *grātia* grace: so called from the supposed medicinal virtues of the plants. Cf. F. *gratiole.*] A genus of scrophulariaceous plants, the best known species of which is *G. officinalis*, the Hedge Hyssop.

1579 LANGHAM *Gard. Health* (1633) 295 Gratiola, or gratia Dei, boyle it and drinke it, or eate it in any kinde of meat to open the belly freely. **1712** tr. *Pomet's Hist. Drugs* I. 86 A Plant found in France, which the Botanists call Gratiola. **1811** A. T. THOMSON *Lond. Disp.* (1818) 187 The sensible qualities of gratiola are strongest when it is in flower. **1847** E. J. SEYMOUR *Severe Dis.* I. 92 A vinous infusion of gratiola.

gratiolin (græˈtaɪəlɪn). *Chem.* [f. prec. + -IN. Cf. F. *gratioline* (Littré).] A bitter resinous principle obtained from *Gratiola officinalis.*

1886 in *Syd. Soc. Lex.*

†**gratiose,** *a. Obs. rare.* [ad. L. *grātiōs-us*, f. *grātia* grace.] Of or pertaining to (Divine) grace (cf. GRACIOUS).

1678 GALE *Crt. Gentiles* IV. III. i. 15 The Soul..is remotely, passively and naturally capacitated for the reception of gratiose infusions.

gratiositie, obs. form of GRACIOSITY.

gratis (ˈgreɪtɪs, ˈgrætɪs, ˈgrɑːtɪs), *adv.* and *a.* [L. *grātīs*, contr. from *grātiīs* lit. out of favour or kindness, abl. pl. of *grātia* grace, favour.]

A. *adv.*

1. For nothing; freely, without any return made or expected; without charge, cost, or pay; gratuitously. ***free gratis*** (see FREE C b).

1477 NORTON *Ord. Alch.* Introd. in Ashm. (1652) 3 Heaven doth all things gratis give. *a* **1541** WYATT *Certayne Ps.* li. The Author 16 The justyce.. That *gratis* hys grace to men doth departe. **1583** STUBBES *Anat. Abus.* II. (1882) 84 Hee may sometimes..preach the word of God abroad in other places, but then he ought to doe it *gratis*. *a* **1592** H. SMITH *God's Arrow agst. Atheists* v. (1593) Q, If they be Iustified *gratis*, freely (as hee affirmeth), then are they Iustified withoot any desert of theirs. **165.** MILTON *Consid. touching Hirelings* (1851) 343 Unless every Minister were, as St. Paul, contented to teach *gratis*. **1678** DRYDEN *Limberham* I. i. (1680) 6, I do all *gratis*, and am most commonly a loser. **1726** SWIFT *Gulliver* IV. xi, They were sure the Captain would carry me *gratis* to Lisbon. **1840** ALISON *Hist. Europe* I. §34 (1849-50) VIII. 153 In the evening the theatres were all opened gratis. **1848** MILL *Pol. Econ.* I. I. §4 (1876) 18 No one will give anything for that which can be obtained gratis.

†**b.** Scot-free, without penalty. *Obs. rare.*

1601 W. PARRY *Trav. Sir A. Sherley* 30 So the wench went away *gratis* with the money.

†**2.** Without a reason or due cause; unjustifiably, gratuitously. *Obs.*

1582 *N.T.* (Rhem.) *John* xv. 25 They hated me gratis. **1621** BP. R. MOUNTAGU *Diatribæ* II. 332 But grant we that which you assume *gratis*..yet [etc.]. **1661** BOYLE *Style of Script.* (1675) 103 That this may not appear to be said *gratis* let us consider, that [etc.]. **1676** HALE *Contempl.* I. 466 Exposing my body *gratis* to unnecessary dangers. **1686** W. HARRIS tr. *Lemery's Course Chem.* I. xviii. (ed. 3) 422 Perhaps it will be said, I do here suppose *gratis* that the Oil of Vitriol does contain fiery particles. **1818** CRUISE *Digest* (ed. 2) V. 397 The vouchee came in *gratis* before the writ of summons.

B. *adj.*

1. Given or done for nothing; free, gratuitous.

1659 T. PECKE *Parnassi Puerp.* 64 No Chinke no Drink; Nothing is Gratis now. **1663** GERBIER *Counsel* B v b, One of the publick lectures (which as all the other were *gratis*). **1717** RAMSAY *Elegy Lucky Wood* 38 She had the gate sae well to please, With gratis beef, dry fish, or cheese. **1765** FOOTE *Commissary* II. i. (1773) 39 You will permit me to expunge the obligation by an instantaneous and gratis lecture on that species of eloquence peculiar to ladies. **1767** S. PATERSON *Another Traveller* I. 143 The third [table being] for gratis-passengers and servants. *Ibid.* I. 262 The British-museum is the only gratis-shew in England. **1833** L. RITCHIE *Wand. by Loire* 204 He..treated the people to gratis representations of mysteries. **1869** CARLYLE in *Mrs. Carlyle's Lett.* III. 250 His gratis practice of medicine. **1879** H. SPENCER *Data of Ethics* 255 Sympathetic gratification which costs the receiver nothing, but is a gratis addition to his egoistic gratifications.

2. Exempting from payment. *rare.*

1752 J. LOUTHIAN *Form of Process* (ed. 2) 45 As also *gratis* Warrands are granted to Prisoners, That Clerks, Macers and others, may serve without Fee or Reward.

gratitude ('grætɪtjuːd). Also 6-7 *Sc.* gratitud, (6 gratituid). [a. F. *gratitude* (15th c. in Godef. *Compl.*), or ad. late L. *grātitūdo, -inem*, f. *grātus* pleasing, thankful.]

1. The quality or condition of being grateful; a warm sense of appreciation of kindness received, involving a feeling of goodwill towards the benefactor and a desire to do something in return; gratefulness.

1565 COOPER *Thesaurus, Gratitudo*, Kindnes: gratitude: thankefulnes. **1601** SHAKS. *All's Well* IV. iv. 6 Which gratitude Through flintie Tartars bosome would peepe forth, And answer thankes. **1605** —— *Lear* II. ii. 182 Thou better know'st The Offices of Nature, bond of Childhood, Effects of Curtesie, dues of Gratitude. **1710** LADY M. W. MONTAGU *Let. to Bp. Burnet* 20 July, I am sensible of the gratitude I owe to so much goodness. **1855** MACAULAY *Hist. Eng.* xii. III. 206 He..expressed his gratitude to the natives of Ireland for having adhered to his cause. **1878** J. P. HOPPS *Princ. Relig.* vi. 22 Gratitude urges us to repay kindness.

b. (with *a* and *pl.*) An instance of this; an expression of thankfulness. Now *rare.*

1660 F. BROOKE tr. *Le Blanc's Trav.* 255 The people.. presented us with birds of divers kinds, for which we shewed a gratitude, but accepted nothing. **1682** SIR T. BROWNE *Chr. Mor.* 105 Common gratitude must be kept alive by the additionary fewel of new courtesies: but generous gratitudes ..have thankful minds for ever. **1894** BLACKMORE *Perlycross* 11 A thrush..broke forth into a gratitude of song.

†**2.** Grace, favour; a favour. Chiefly *Sc. Obs.*

1500-20 DUNBAR *Poems* ix. 97 Nocht thanking The of gratitud nor grace That thow me wrocht. **1524** WOLSEY in *St. Papers Hen. VIII*, IV. 204 Without considring the manyfolde gratitudes that the Kinge hathe and intendeth to shewe unto theym. **1527** ANGUS *ibid.* 484 The greit kyndnes and humanite, speciall favouris, and diverse gratitudes done to me be the Kingis Hienes. **1535** STEWART *Cron. Scot.* II. 112 Beseikand him of his greit gratitude. He wald prouyde for thame ane king or prince. *Ibid.* III. 364 The gratituidis war done to me befoir. *c* **1557** in G. Cavendish *Wolsey* (1893) 202 In consideracion of all those gratitudes receyved at my lords hands.

†**3.** A free gift; a gratuity, reward; *esp. Sc.* a grant or contribution of money made to the sovereign. *Obs.* (Cf. *benevolence.*)

1535 *Sc. Acts Jas. V* (1814) II. 344/2 Ane gratitude Is grantit to þe kingis grace be þe thre Estatis of his realme, for Supportatioune of sik necessar Errandis as his grace hes ado. **1555** *Extracts Aberd. Reg.* (1844) I. 293 To grant to gif ane compositioune, propyne, and gratitud to our said souerane lady. **1597** *Ibid.* (1848) II. 158 To pay Robert Lyndesey, pylot, the sowme of fourtie merkis, for ane gratitude for the sey kart presentit this day be him to the prouest. **1610** J. FORBES *Certaine Rec.* (1846) II. III. 422 His Majestie had caused mak proclamation offering great gratituds and immunities to any who sould apprehend him. **1699** *Advt.* in Doran *Saints & Sinners* (1868) II. 155 He shall have the moveables restored, giving a reasonable gratitude.

,gratitudi'narian, *a. nonce-wd.* [f. late L. *grātitūdo, -inem* (see prec.), after *latitudinarian.*] Making a show of gratitude.

1794 COLERIDGE *Let.* 6 July, Lett. (1895) I. 72 You are averse to gratitudinarian flourishes.

grattage (grataʒ). *Med.* [Fr., = scraping, f. *gratter* to scrape, scratch (see GRATE *v.*[1]).] The scraping or scrubbing of a surface (as the conjunctiva in cases of trachoma) to remove granulations.

1890 in BILLINGS *Med. Dict.* **1895** S. STEPHENSON *Epidemic Ophthalmia* 143 Scarification of the conjunctiva, combined in various ways with 'brassage' and 'grattage', has been recommended. **1911** A. DARIER in W. L. Pyle *Internat. Syst. Ophthalmic Pract.* xvii. 217 Hypertrophic blepharitis ..is best treated surgically by..longitudinal incision and grattage of the entire palpebral border. **1949** M. WIENER *Surg. Eye* (ed. 2) xiii. 200 The upper lid is grasped with the Darier grattage forceps, the male blade engaging the conjunctival surface about 4 mm. away from the lid margin.

gratte, obs. form of GRATE *sb.*[1]

gratten ('grætən). *south. dial.* Also 6-8 **grotten**, 8 **grotton**, 9 **grattan**, 7- **gratton**. [? Repr. OE. **grǽd-tún*, f. *grǽd* 'ulva', coarse grass (cf. GREEDS) + *tún* enclosure (see TOWN).] A stubble-field, stubble. Also, the after-grass growing in the stubble.

1572 GOOGE *Heresbach's Husb.* III. (1577) 149 b [Young pigs] may well feed vpon strawe, and grottens. **1625** MARKHAM *Inrichment Weald of Kent* 10 Vpon that fallow or Gratten, (as we call it,) you shall doe well to sow it with Pease. **1674** RAY *S. & E.C. Words* 67 A Gratton..Stubble. Kent. **1675** in *Phil. Trans.* X. 295 The grass will be so good immediately after Tillage, that we commonly mow it the first year: This is call'd mowing of gratten. **1736** PEGGE *Kenticisms* (E.D.S.), *Grotten*. **1750** ELLIS *Mod. Husbandm.* V. I. xxii. 101 Now turn your Cows and Hogs into your enclosed Stubble-fields as the first Cattle proper for this Purpose, or, as some call them, into Grattons and Eddishes. **1789** *Trans. Soc. Arts* I. 121 Two acres Wheat Gratten. **1860** *Jrnl. R. Agric. Soc.* XXI. II. 385 A barley-stubble, or gratten, of the required dimensions. **1884** R. BRIDGES *Return of Ulysses* II. 451 Yet mayst thou see on me The sign of what I have been, and I think Still from the gratten one may guess the grain.

gratters, colloq. (school and university) for *congratulations*: see -ER[6]. (Cf. CONGRATTERS.)

1903 D. COKE *Sandford of Merton* xiii. 98 'Gratter [*sic*], Sandford,' he said, 'on your rowing to-day.' **1906** —— *Bending of Twig* xii, Gratters, Marsh, on being monitor. **1919** W. DEEPING *Second Youth* xiii, Right-ho! Good luck and gratters!

†**'grattishing.** *Obs.*[−1] The dung (of a deer).

1611 COTGR., *Fumées en plateaux*, flat grattishing, fewmishing (or dung) of a Deere.

‖**grattoir** (gratwar). *Archæol.* [Fr., f. *gratter* to scrape, scratch.] A flint scraping tool in which the working edge is at the end of the blade or flake and lies across its long axis; an 'end-scraper'. (Cf. SCRAPER 4 e.)

1872 [see SCRAPER 4 e]. **1887** *Amer. Antiquarian* IX. 341, 4000 grattoirs, blades, knives and saws. **1915** W. J. SOLLAS *Anc. Hunters* (ed. 2) 298 The grattoirs or end scrapers are generally short and rough. *Ibid.* 485 The characteristic keeled grattoir. **1926** *Guide Antiquities Stone Age* (Brit. Mus.) (ed. 3) 130 A good specimen of the double end-scraper, consisting of a flintflake rounded at both ends on one face only by use as a plane (*grattoir*) is here illustrated.

†**'gratuit**, *a. Obs. rare.* Also 6 gratuite. [ad. F. *gratuite* (16th c.) or L. *grātuīt-us* GRATUITOUS.] Free, gratuitous.

1550 VERON *Godly Sayings* (1846) 17 The heavnlye & gratuite benefytes of God. *c* **1561** —— *Free-will* 29 a, The trust, that they oughte to haue..in his gratuite and free grace. **1644** ABP. MAXWELL *Sacrosancta Regum Majestas* 71 The gratuit concession of princes.

Hence **gra'tuitly** *adv.*, freely, gratuitously.

a **1586** *Satir. Poems Reform.* xxxvi. 137 Had ȝe him gevin but pryce, gratuitlie, Be benefeit ȝow thinkand þairto bound.

†**gra'tuital**, *a. Obs.* [f. L. *grātuīt-us* (see next) + -AL[1].] Free, gratuitous.

1594 BP. J. KING *Jonas* xxviii. (1599) 382 To iustifie you with the power of his free gratuitall grace. **1615** T. ADAMS *White Devill* 13 What!..thy Master, Judas, thy Friend.. and canst not endure anothers gratuitall kindnesse towards him? **1637** R. HUMPHREY tr. *St. Ambrose* Pref., A gratuitall and free gift in Iesus Christ our Lord. *a* **1641** BP. MONTAGU *Acts & Mon.* (1642) 189 So to dispense of his graces partially, stands not with the justice of God, howsoever convenient enough for gratuitall dispensation.

gratuitous (grə'tjuːɪtəs), *a.* [f. L. *grātuīt-us* free, spontaneous, voluntary (cogn. w. *grātia* favour, *grātus* pleasing) + -OUS. Cf. obs. F. *gratuiteux.*]

1. Freely bestowed or obtained; granted without claim or merit; provided without payment or return; costing nothing to the recipient; free.

1656 JEANES *Fuln. Christ* 38 How that the Father hath given unto the Sonne..to have life in himselfe..; not by any gratuitous gift, but by natural generation. *a* **1690** E. HOPKINS *Expos. Lord's Prayer* (1692) 97 Our Pardon is free and gratuitous; for whatsoever God doth he doth it freely.. without respect to any former deserts, or expectations of any future recompence. **1692** L'ESTRANGE *Fables* cccvii. 270 We are..given to Mistake the Gratuitous Blessings of Heaven, for the Fruits of our Own Industry. **1841** W. SPALDING *Italy & It. Isl.* III. 371 Besides this number, the gratuitous schools received 5584 children. **1867** SMYTH *Sailor's Word-bk.*, *Gratuitous money*, a term officially used for bounty granted to volunteers in Lord Exmouth's expedition against Algiers. **1868** M. PATTISON *Academ. Org.* v. 200 A student ..attends with more assiduity a course for which he has paid money, than one which is gratuitous. **1870** EMERSON *Soc. & Solit.*, *Farming* Wks. (Bohn) III. 59 The earth is a machine which yields almost gratuitous service to every application of the intellect.

b. *spec. Sc. Law.* Of a charter or deed: Made or granted without any value given in return.

1773 ERSKINE *Inst. Sc. Law* II. iii. §22. 189 A charter which proceeds merely from the love and favour which the granter hath for the grantee, is said to be granted for a lucrative or gratuitous cause. *Ibid.* III. viii. §45. 566 The institute can defeat the substitution, even by a gratuitous deed. **1872** *Bell's Princ. Law Scotl.* §64 (ed. 6) 33 Obligations which are, as free gifts, voluntarily undertaken, or at least without an adequate consideration, are called gratuitous.

2. Done, made, adopted, or assumed without any good ground or reason; not required or warranted by the circumstances of the case; uncalled-for; unjustifiable.

1691 RAY *Creation* I. (1692) 17 The second Motive they had to introduce this gratuitous Declination of Atoms, the same Poet gives us. **1790** BURKE *Fr. Rev.* 95 But as these occasions may never arrive, the mind receives a gratuitous taint. **1844** H. H. WILSON *Brit. India* III. 507 A gratuitous interference with private rights. **1844** LINGARD *Anglo-Sax. Ch.* (1858) I. App. A. 318 A gratuitous and unfounded supposition. **1860** J. PAYN *Bateman Househ.* xxi. 260 The innuendo conveyed in the notice is not only malicious and cruel, but a gratuitous lie. **1876** GEO. ELIOT *Dan. Der.* lviii. IV. 179 There never was more gratuitous sinning.

b. Of the agent: Performing the action implied without reason or justification.

1864 SALA in *Daily Tel.* 29 Sept., I should be held up to execration as a malignant slanderer and a gratuitous liar.

†**3.** Requiring no proof; axiomatic. *Obs. rare.*

1775 JOHNSON *Tax. no Tyr.* 1 Of these gratuitous and acknowledged truths it is often the fate to become less evident by endeavours to explain them.

gratuitously (grə'tjuːɪtəslɪ), *adv.* [f. prec. + -LY[2].] In a gratuitous manner.

1. Without cost to the recipient; without any claim or merit on his part; free of charge.

1716-17 BENTLEY *Serm.* xi. 374 Gratuitously given us by the good-will of our Maker. **1773** ERSKINE *Inst. Sc. Law* II. iii. §25. 190 He who makes over a subject gratuitously is understood to transfer it barely as it was vested in himself when he made the grant. **1776** ADAM SMITH *W.N.* I. xi. I. (1869) I. 159 The distributions of corn frequently made to the people, either gratuitously, or at a very low price. **1804** W. TENNANT *Ind. Recreat.* (ed. 2) I. 70 The children of such as have died..are admitted gratuitously into this school. **1867** SMILES *Huguenots Eng.* i. (1880) 18 The bishop also distributed the four Gospels gratuitously among the poor.

2. Without sufficient cause, reason, or ground; unjustifiably, unwarrantably, unnecessarily.

1697 BENTLEY *Diss. Ep. Phalaris* 43 But there is a learned Greek Professor..who, after he has asserted the credit of Euripides's Letters, gratuitously undertakes to apologize for These too, about this matter of the Dialect. **1774** BP. S. HALLIFAX *Roman Civil Law* Pref. xvi, Those, who apply to the study of the Common Law, often boast, and sometimes gratuitously enough, of this distinction. **1799** KIRWAN *Geol. Ess.* 385 The vast size of the most ancient species of fish he ascribes to the great heat which he gratuitously supposes the sea to have originally possessed. **1845** LD. HOUGHTON in T. W. Reid *Life* (1891) I. viii. 359 It is assumed (I think gratuitously) that Peel is going to repeal the Corn Laws. **1875** E. WHITE *Life in Christ* I. ii. (1878) 14 The most gratuitously perverse misinterpretations. **1880** MᶜCARTHY *Own Times* IV. xlviii. 22 Gratuitously offensive.

gratuitousness (grə'tjuːɪtəsnɪs). [f. as prec. + -NESS.] The quality or state of being gratuitous.

1727 BAILEY vol. II, *Gratuitousness*, free Bestowment, without Expectation of Reward or Recompence. **1845** H. ROGERS *Ess.* I. iii. 139 The perfect gratuitousness of salvation. **1852** *Ibid.* I. vii. 363 We can hardly excuse the perfect gratuitousness of his hypotheses. **1879** M. PATTISON *Milton* xiii. 190 Here it is not..so much the unnatural character of the incident itself, as its gratuitousness which offends.

‖**gra'tuitum.** *Obs.* Also (? *erron.*) gratuito. [L. *grātuītum*, neut. of *grātuītus* adj.: see GRATUITOUS. The use of the L. adv. *grātuītō* as sb. may be a blunder imputed to the ignorant speaker.] A free gift.

1602 *2nd Pt. Return fr. Parnassus* II. iv. 673 Fy father, thou must not call it selling, thou must say is this the gentleman that must haue the gratuito? *Ibid.* 692 When thou haue gotten me the gratuito of the liuing. *a* **1670** BP. HACKET *Christian Consolations* iv. in *Bp. Jer. Taylor's Wks.* (1828) I. 131 And the gratuitum which God gives, is a thousand-fold greater than the present which we bring.

gratuity (grə'tjuːɪtɪ). Also 6 gratuite, gratuyte, 7 gratuetie, -ty, (greatuetie). [ad. F. *gratuité* (14th c. in Hatz.-Darm.), or med.L. *gratuitās* 'beneficium', gift, also used as a title of honour, f. *grātia, grātus* (cf. GRATUITOUS).]

†**1.** Graciousness, favour, freq. used of Divine grace or favour; a favour, a kindness. *Obs.*

1523 HEN. VIII in Strype *Eccl. Mem.* (1721) I. iii. 43 Some manifest Demonstration of Gratuity and Kindness.

1532 Bennet in Froude *Hist. Eng.* (1881) I. 403, I have not at any time found his Holiness more tractable or propense to show gratuity unto your Highness than now of late. 1543–4 *Act 35 Hen. VIII*, c. 12 His maiestie..shewed vnto him dyuers and sundrye inestimable gratuities and amities. 1546 Gardiner *Decl. Joye* xlviij b, Whereby we shuld knowlege his gratuite & goodnes to be so moch the more towardes vs. 1568 Grafton *Chron.* II. 501 All these kindnesses suffised not, nor all these gratuities auayled not to make this king James friendly to the realme of Englande. 1646 Evance *Noble Ord.* 14 It is not Gods contract with his people, to honour them, that honour him, but Gods gratuitye. [1818 Jas. Mill *Brit. India* II. v. iv. 440 By concluding a peace, before the reduction of the fort, any allowance to the army was a matter of gratuity, not of right.]

†**b.** A gratuitous concession. *Obs.*

*c*1555 Harpsfield *Divorce Hen. VIII* (1878) 155 Let us now by way of gratuity grant..that she was a virgin. 1641 Milton *Ch. Govt.* v. 15 In the former place he tels us he forbeares to take any argument of Prelaty from Aaron..In the latter he can forbeare no longer, but repents him of his rash gratuity..and stiffly argues that [etc.].

2. A gift or present (usually of money), often in return for favours or services, the amount depending on the inclination of the giver; in bad sense, a bribe. Now applied exclusively to such a gift made to a servant or inferior official; a 'tip'.

1540 Hen. VIII in *St. Papers Hen. VIII*, VIII. 410 We entende not to charge Ourself with geving any thing, eyther for a recompense or a gratuite. 1594 R. Ashley tr. *Loys le Roy's Variety of Things* 44 b, The Countries..gave certaine gratuites and giftes to the king. 1603 Holland *Plutarch's Mor.* 43 That faire mare Aetha, which he gave him as a gift and gratuitie. 1626 Sir R. Boyle in *Lismore Papers* (1886) II. 190 [He] sent the town of yoghall..a hundreth pownds ster: for a further gratuety: to the poor of that corporacon. 1637 Earl Cork *Diary* ibid. Ser. I. V. 19, iiij[li] ster: in money ..as a greatuetie from me. 1662 J. Bargrave *Pope Alex. VII* (1867) 137 The Cravat &c...were sent me by one Mr. Tymothy Couley..by way of gratuity, he being one of the 162 slaves that I redeemed from Argeers. 1712 Addison *Spect.* No. 471 ¶7 When he [Caesar] had given away all his Estate in Gratuities among his Friends. 1758 Johnson *Idler* No. 29 ¶4, I.. had a small gratuity above my wages. 1768–74 Tucker *Lt. Nat.* (1852) II. 387 Any gratuity given to Pharaoh or other princes, to resign up their right of dominion over their slaves. 1803 Jane Porter *Thaddeus* viii. (1831) 70 The treasury was soon filled with gratuities from the nobles. 1818 Cruise *Digest* (ed. 2) IV. 501 No gift or gratuity to an attorney, beyond his fair professional demands..shall be permitted to stand. *c*1830 in N. Wood *Treat. Rail Roads* (1838) 740 No gratuity to be allowed to be taken by any guard, porter, or other servant of the company. 1855 Thackeray *Newcomes* I. 231 The post-boys quite stared at the gratuity he gave them. *Mod.* The attendants at this restaurant are forbidden to receive gratuities.

†**b.** Payment; wages. *Obs.*

*a*1637 B. Jonson *Underwoods, Petition Poor Ben to Chas. I*, A large hundred marks annuitie, To be given me in gratuitie For done service and to come. 1647 in Rushw. *Hist. Coll.* IV. II. 825 The treasurers of the Army do forthwith advance a months Gratuity for the Army. 1673 in *Scotsman* 21 Aug. (1885) 7/4 To Mr. Geo. Sinclare..by gratuitie for his attendance and advyce..£66 13*s.* 4*d.* 1832 tr. *Sismondi's Ital. Rep.* xvi. 347 They were to pay a gratuity of 80,000 crowns to the army which besieged them.

3. *spec.* **a.** A bounty given to soldiers on re-enlistment, retirement, or discharge. **b.** (See quot. 1815.)

[1698 Ludlow *Mem.* (1698–9) II. 819 Promising them their whole Arrears, constant Pay, and a present Gratuity.] 1804 Wellington in Gurw. *Desp.* (1837) IV. 442 Sir John Kenaway received Lieut. Colonel's gratuity upon the same occasion. 1815 *Falconer's Dict. Marine* (ed. Burney), *Gratuity*, in the royal navy, is a recompense or royal bounty made by his Majesty to the widows, orphans, and mothers of sea and marine officers slain in fight with the enemy. *Ibid.*, Gratuities to Officers wounded in Fight with the Enemy, and to Seamen hurt in the service. 1898 *Daily News* 11 July 7/1 When the Commander-in-Chief calls upon 'an officer who has not been guilty of misconduct' to retire, the Secretary for War decides his rate of gratuity.

†**4.** = gratitude 1; also, reciprocity, recompense. *Obs.*

1614 Lodge *Seneca* 96 The fault is not through our default, but for that disabilitie preventeth our gratuity. 1640 Yorke *Union Hon. Battles* 24 The King to testifie his gratuity Knighted Walworth. 1660 F. Brooke tr. *Le Blanc's Trav.* 346 The Captaine, in gratuity [orig. *par reciproque*], gave to the cheife of them a handsome sword.

5. = gratuitousness. *rare.*

1858 Hawthorne *Fr. & It. Jrnls.* I. 267, I like this overflow and gratuity of device with which Gothic sculpture works out its designs. 1861 *Times* 22 Aug., It is merely gratuitous to talk of a paradox. And the gratuity is all the more marked when [etc.]. 1882 Stevenson *Fam. Stud.* 365 Such disinterestedness and beautiful gratuity of affection as there is between friends of the same sex.

†'**gratulance.** *Obs. rare*[−1]. [f. L. *grātulārī* (see gratulate) + -ance.] A fee, gratuity.

1608 Machin *Dumbe Knt.* v, Come, there is Some odde disburse, some bribe, some gratulance, Which makes you locke up leasure.

gratulant ('grætjʊlənt), *a.* [ad. L. *grātulant-em*, pr. pple. of *grātulārī* (see gratulate).] Expressing pleasure, joy, or satisfaction; congratulatory.

1471 Ripley *Comp. Alch.* Pref. in Ashm. (1652) 121 Of Hierarchycall Jubylestes the gratulant gloryfycation. 1790 H. Boyd *Sheph. Lebanon* in *Poet. Reg.* (1808) 135 The mind expands. Its opening faculties in general blow All gratulant, receive the genial ray. 1794 Coleridge *Destiny Nations*, The white-robed multitude of slaughtered saints At Heaven's wide-opened portal gratulant Receive some martyr'd patriot. 1868 Milman *St. Paul's* x. 240 St. Paul's rang with a gratulant thanksgiving. 1897 D. P. Todd in *Nation* (N.Y.) LXV. 392/3 Hundreds of people..all gratulant to the man whose well-directed munificence had provided [etc.].

†'**gratulate,** *a. Obs. rare.* [ad. L. *grātulāt-us*, pple. of *grātulārī* (see next).] To be rejoiced at; pleasing, gratifying.

1603 Shaks. *Meas. for M.* v. i. 535 Thanks good friend, Escalus, for thy much goodnesse, There's more behinde that is more gratulate.

gratulate ('grætjʊleɪt), *v.* Now *arch.* and *poet.* Also 7 **gratulat.** [f. L. *grātulāt-*, ppl. stem of *grātulārī* to manifest one's joy, congratulate, rejoice, give thanks, f. *grātus* pleasing, thankful.]

1. *trans.* To express joy at the coming or appearance of; to welcome, hail; to greet, salute.

1556 Abp. Parker *Ps.* xcvii. Argt., This Psalme in sprite: doth gratulate Christes kingdome cleare: immaculate. 1596 *Edw. III*, I. ii. 9 Dear aunt, descend and gratulate his highness. 1616 Chapman *Homer's Hymn to Hymen* Plays 1873 III. 122 Euery flowre and weed Looks vp to gratulate thy long'd for fruites. 1671 Milton *P.R.* iv. 434 The birds ..Cleared up their choicest notes..To gratulate the sweet return of morn. 1681 T. Jordan *London's Joy* 7 The Seven Champions..are come To gratulate my Lord, and guard you from Mutinous Mischiefs. 1746 Akenside *Hymn to Naiads* 101 Thames..with words Auspicious gratulates the bark. 1784 Cowper *Task* v. 820 When every star, in haste To gratulate the new-created earth, Sent forth a voice. 1799–1805 Wordsw. *Prelude* xi. 469 Some other spring, which by the name Thou gratulatest. 1822 —— *Sonn. Waldenses*, As the lark Springs from the ground the morn to gratulate.

2. To express or manifest joy at or on account of (an event, a happy condition, etc.); = congratulate 2.

1584 Peele *Arraignm. Paris* i. iii, The muses give you melody to gratulate this chance. 1596 Harington *Metam. Ajax* 93, I hope all the Innes of court will gratulate the present flourishing estate of our Lincolnes Inne. 1603 B. Jonson *Sejanus* iv. ix, I gratulate the newes. 1637 Heywood *Royall King* i. i. Wks. 1874 VI. 7 The Embassadors that come..To gratulate our famous victories. 1699 Cibber *Xerxes* i, And come with pious Joy, to gratulate your Triumphs. 1828 Scott *F.M. Perth* xxviii, The minstrels sent forth their gayest notes to gratulate Eachin's succession.

†**b.** const. *to, unto* (the person), or with simple *indirect obj. Obs.*

1591 Lambarde *Archeion* Ep., To gratulate unto You, that Honourable place wherunto you are right worthily advanced. 1624 Bacon *Let.* 9 Oct., Wks. 1874 XIV. 521, I cannot but..gratulate his Majesty the extreme prosperous success of his business. 1658 W. Burton *Itin. Anton.* 159 My Author gratulates to his own good luck this discovery. 1693 Dryden *Ovid's Met.* xii. 27 Calchas..with a smiling glance Thus gratulates to Greece her happy chance.

3. To express joy or satisfaction to (a person) on a happy event; to compliment, felicitate; = congratulate 4. Const. *on, upon, †in.*

1598 Florio, *Gratulare*, to gratulate, to reioice with. 1621 Cade *Serm.* Ep. Ded., Well, then, may I gratulate our Commonwealth, that is so much blessed with wise and worthy men. 1644 Milton *Jdgm. Bucer* (1851) 299 So as I may justly gratulat mine own mind with due acknowledgment of assistance from above. 1726 De Foe *Hist. Devil* ii. iv. (1840) 218 Where do his devotees gratulate one another and congratulate him more than at church? 1742 *Mem. Lady Harriot Butler* II. 50, I gratulate you upon it with all my heart. 1831 Scott *Ct. Robert* xxxii, Some.. gratulated him upon his most unexpected return to the service of his country. 1871 B. Taylor *Faust* (1875) I. iv. 83, I gratulate thee on thy new career!

refl. 1672 Sir T. Browne *Let. to Friend* §22 The heirs and concerned relations gratulating themselves in the sober departure of their friends. 1678 Marvell *Def. John Howe* Wks. 1875 IV. 232 Hereupon The Discourse..highly gratulates It self in three instances. 1823 Scott *Quentin D.* Introd., Your authors.., if they have children, [may] gratulate themselves that the peck-loaf may be had for sixpence.

†**b.** *absol.* or *intr.* To offer congratulations.

1601 B. Jonson *Poetaster* ii. ii, We all come to gratulate, for the good report of you.

†**4.** To be grateful or show gratitude for; also, to express gratitude to (a benefactor) *for*; to thank. *Obs.*

1590 Greene *Orl. Fur.* (1599) 31 But friendly gratulate these fauours found. 1645 Pagitt *Heresiogr.* (1662) 279 To acknowledge and gratulate that harmony, which God hath been pleased..to blesse. 1652 F. Kirkman *Clerio & Lozia* 120 After he had submissively gratulated him for the honour. 1667 Waterhouse *Fire Lond.* 149 To Gratulate the Kindness..I have had from any person or thing with frequency of acknowledgment. 1673 Marvell *Reh. Transp.* II. 399, I cannot but gratulate my good fortune rather than my wisdom, that I have travelled such an Author through with no more extravagancy.

†**5.** To reward or recompense (a service, etc.).

*a*1611 Beaum. & Fl. *Maid's Trag.* i. ii, To gratulate So great a seruice done at my desire. 1612 Heywood *Apol. Actors* G 4, I could not choose but gratulate your honest indeauours with this short remembrance. 1633 Marmion *Antiquary* v. Dram. Wks. (1875) 290 I'll find some office To gratulate thy pains.

†**6.** To gratify, please. *Obs.*

*a*1592 Greene *Jas. IV* Prelude, To gratulate thee I brought these antics to show thee some sport in dancing. 1627–77 Feltham *Resolves* i. xix. 33 Nay many times to gratulate the company, we are fain to force our selves to unworthiness. 1809 Campbell *Gertr. Wyom.* i. xxvi, I will teach thee..To pay with Huron blood thy father's scars, And gratulate his soul rejoicing in the stars.

Hence '**gratulating** *vbl. sb.* and *ppl. a.*

1639 Sanderson *Serm., Ad Aulam* ix. (1689) 490, I note it, not without much rejoycing and gratulating to us of this Church. *a*1711 Ken *Christophil* Poet. Wks. 1721 I. 468 Seeing God pleas'd, the heavenly Quire In gratulating Hymns conspire. 1803 Wordsw. *Blind Highland Boy* xliv, A gratulating voice, With which the very hills rejoice. 1850 De Quincey in H. A. Page *Life* (1877) II. xvii. 67 To pass through innumerable stations of gratulating comrades.

gratulation (grætjuː'leɪʃən). Now somewhat *rare.* Also 5 **gratulacyon,** 6 **-acion,** *Sc.* **-atioun.** [ad. L. *grātulātiōn-em*, n. of action f. *grātulārī* to gratulate.]

1. A feeling of gratification, joy, or exultation; rejoicing in heart. (Now only with mixture of sense 3, implying self-congratulation upon some good fortune.)

1482 *Monk of Evesham* (Arb.) 106 Y wote not whedir sorow or deuocyon or compassion or gratulacyon drawyn nowe myne onhappy soule dyuers weyes. 1577 tr. *Bullinger's Decades* (1592) 537 With great ioie of hart and godlie gratulation. 1644 Milton *Areop.* (Arb.) 31 The joy and gratulation which it brings to all who wish and promote their Countries liberty. 1732 Berkeley *Alciphr.* iii. §3 That gratulation and delight in beholding the virtuous deeds of other men. 1751 Johnson *Rambler* No. 141 ¶9 You would look with some gratulation on our success. 1809 W. Irving *Knickerb.* iii. ii. (1820) 169 Listening with silent gratulation to the clucking of his hens. 1842 Miall in *Nonconf.* II. 1 Our great and growing success cannot but be to ourselves a matter of gratulation. 1885 C. Mercier in *Mind* X. 16 Gratulation is the feeling of which congratulation is the expression.

2. Manifestation or expression of joy; *esp.* with *a* and *pl.*, an instance of this; a rejoicing.

1549 Coverdale, etc. *Erasm. Par. Thess.* 6 It is more worthy gratulacions and reioycinges. 1649 Roberts *Clavis Bibl.* 387 The mutual gratulations and contentment of Christ and the Church in one another. 1741 Middleton *Cicero* I. iv. 262 The people came out to receive him with all imaginable gratulations and expressions of joy for his happy return. 1863 Mary Howitt *F. Bremer's Greece* I. viii. 259 After an hour's entertainment and gratulation, every one went home. 1874 Motley *Barneveld* (1879) II. xiii. 82 The coronation..had gone on with pomp and popular gratulations. 1895 *Atlantic Monthly* LXXVI. 91 The.. gratulations with which the four hundredth anniversary of the discovery of America was lately heralded.

3. The expression of pleasure or gratification at a person's success, good fortune, or the like; compliment, felicitation, congratulation.

1542 Udall *Erasm. Apoph.* ii. 316 To whom where many of y[e] nobles resorted in the waye of gratulacion, & of kepyng hym coumpaignie. 1622 Bacon *Hen. VII* 42 After this Complement, and some gratulation for the Kings victorie, they fell to their errand. 1646 Sir T. Browne *Pseud. Ep.* iv. ix. 200 As a gratulation for the one, and a deprecation from the other. 1807 Crabbe *Parish Reg.* ii. Wks. 1834 II. 184 The crowd Stood humbly round, and gratulation bow'd. 1827 Scott in *Croker Papers* 25 Apr. (1884), I cannot but add my sincere gratulation upon your keeping a good house over your head. 1828 —— *F.M. Perth* xxxiv, The victors had the general meed of gratulation.

b. An instance of this; a complimentary or congratulatory speech.

1614 Raleigh *Hist. World* ii. (1634) 492 When Diagoras had seen his 3 Sons crowned for their severall victories in those games, one came running with this gratulation..'Die Diagoras for thou shalt not clime up to heaven'. 1631 Massinger *Believe as You List* ii. i, Their gratulations for his safetie. 1751 Johnson *Rambler* No. 97 ¶21 Gratulations pour in from every quarter. 1848 Clough *Bothie* ix. 143 Be it recounted in song..Who gave what at the wedding, the gifts and fair gratulations. 1891 J. Winsor *Columbus* viii. 177 True science places no gratulations higher than those of its own conscience.

†**4.** A joyful greeting; a welcome. *Obs.*

1589 (*title*) A Skeltonicall Salutation, Or Condigne gratulation. 1630 *Tinker of Turvey, Gent. T.* 58 Hearing such a scholler-like gratulation, seeing by this salute, that [etc.]. *a*1638 Mede *Disc. Luke* Wks. (1672) i. xxiv. 91 Secondly, a Gratulation rendring the reason thereof, Because of Peace on Earth. [1815 Lamb *Lett.* (1888) I. 299 He was one of those who would have hailed your return.. with the complacent gratulations of a philosopher anxious to promote knowledge as leading to happiness.]

†**5.** Expression of thanks, thanksgiving; also, an instance of this. *Obs.*

1579 Fenton *Guicciard.* 352 The King vsing towards them at their departure a very small gratulation [It. *piccoli segni di gratitudine*] of their seruices past. 1592 Greene *Groat's-w. Wit* (1617) 26 Roberto..returned him thankefull gratulations. *a*1677 Manton *Serm. Ps. cxix.* 65 Wks. 1872 VII. 200 Warm in petitions, but cold, raw, and infrequent in gratulations.

†**6.** Reward, recompense; = gratification 3.

1611 Speed *Hist. Gt. Brit.* viii. vii. §50. 408 The Duke.. forthwith granted their desires: whereupon they drew out store of gold to present him in way of gratulation. 1628 Wither *Brit. Rememb.* vi. 505 He askt, and had a willing gratulation, From one both rich and of another Nation.

'**gratulatorily,** *adv.* [f. next + -ly[2].] By way of congratulation, thanks, or greeting.

1620 Donne *Serm.* xlii. 416 To Exclaime gratulatorily in his behalfe *Quanta fidei vis. a*1638 Mede *Disc. Luke* Wks. (1672) i. xxiv. 91 Or both causally and gratulatorily thus, Glory be to God in the highest [etc.]. 1880 Miss H. A. Duff *Honor MacMichael* I. ii. 46 His brother heard..of his engagement, and wrote gratulatorily.

gratulatory ('grætjʊlətərɪ), *a.* (*sb.*) Also 6–7 **gratulatorie.** [ad. med.L. **grātulātōri-us*, f.

grātulārī to GRATULATE; see -ORY and cf. obs. F. *gratulatoire*.]

1. Expressing joy or gratification for the good fortune, etc. of another; conveying gratulation; congratulatory, complimentary.

1577 HANMER *Anc. Eccl. Hist.* (1619) 183 That Sermon gratulatorie of the repairing of the Churches. **1622** PEACHAM *Compl. Gent.* x. (1634) 92 His gratulatory verse to King Henry upon his Coronation day. *a* **1656** USSHER *Ann.* (1658) 795 He was entertained with gratulatory acclamations. **1763** CHESTERF. *Let. to Faulkner* 4 Jan., Lett. 1892 III. 1287, I take it for granted, that some of your many tributary wits have already presented you with gratulatory poems. **1867** PARKHAM *Jesuits N. Amer.* vi. (1875) 68 He gave an outcry of delight, echoed by gratulatory cries from all present. **1871** *Daily Tel.* 14 Sept., Lord Derby could hardly use other than gratulatory language to an audience of great manufacturers. He therefore felicitated them on the material prosperity of the present year.

†**b.** Bearing or charged with congratulations. *Obs. rare.*

1655 *Nicholas Papers* (Camden) 195 The Gratulatory Ambassador to the new Pope.

†**2.** Expressing gratitude or thanks; made as a thankoffering. In theological language, spec. applied to sacrifices 'of thanksgiving' as opposed to propitiatory sacrifices. *Obs.*

a **1555** BRADFORD in Foxe *A. & M.* (1563) 1204/1 The sacrifice of the churche is no propiciatorie sacrifice but a gratulatorie sacrifice. **1576** FLEMING *Panopl. Epist.* 100 A gratulatorie letter, that is, an Epistle of thankes. *a* **1631** DONNE *Serm.* lv. (1640) 549 The Psalme hath..a Gratulatory part, a sacrifice of thankesgiving. **1670** *Devout Commun.* (1688) 163 Let me do something gratulatory..Let me give myself a thank-offering to him. **1675** L. ADDISON *State Jews* (1676) 121 They make a gratulatory Oration unto God, for that he has been pleased to assist and accept their Services. **1739** WATERLAND *Eucharist* Wks. 1823 VIII. 263 Whereas formerly he had disowned any propitiatory sacrifice, content with gratulatory, after the Protestant way.

†**3.** *sb.* An expression of gratulation, a congratulatory speech. *Obs. rare.*

a **1734** NORTH *Lives* (1826) III. 385 The chief failing that appeared in him was an over repetition of gratulatories and compliments.

†**'gratuling**, *ppl. a. Obs. rare*$^{-1}$. [f. OF. *gratuler* (ad. L. *grātulārī*: see GRATULATE) + -ING[2].] Congratulating, gratulant.

1622 FLETCHER *Beggar's Bush* II. i, Where's Oratour Higgen with his gratuling Speech now, In all our names?

†**'graty**, *a. Obs. rare*$^{-0}$. [f. GRATE *sb.*[1] + -Y[1].] Consisting or full of grates; like a grate.

1611 COTGR., *Grilleux*, gratie; full of grates; made like a grate.

grauff, obs. form of GRAFF *sb.*[2]

graulse, (graul), Anglo-Irish f. GRILSE.

'grauly, *a. rare*$^{-1}$. [Meant for an equivalent of G. *gräulich*.] Grisly, causing a shudder.

1848 LYTTON *K. Arthur* x. v, In many a grauly flock..the she-bears sprawling play'd. *Ibid., foot-note. Grauly* and *grausame* are both adjectives which belong to the Saxon element of the language and are fairly reclaimed from the German. The Scotch indeed have preserved the first.

graunch (grɔːntʃ), *v. dial.* and *N.Z.* [Onomatopœic: cf. GRANCH *v.*] *intr.* To make a crunching or grinding sound; *trans.*, to cause to make such a sound; hence, to damage (a mechanism of some kind). Also **'graunching** *vbl. sb.*; **'graunchy** *a.*, difficult, testing.

1881 A. B. EVANS *Leics. Words* 163 *Graunch*, var. of 'crunch' and 'scrunch', to crush or grind with a noise; crash. 'I'm sure it freezes, for I heard the ice *graunching* under the wheels of the carriage.' **1954** *Dominion* (Wellington, N.Z.) 1 July, As far as I know 'to graunch' means to damage an engine, instrument, machine, etc., by using wrong tools and/or repair methods, and a 'graunch-artist' is 'a person who does that'. *Ibid.* 9 July, The first time I heard the word [graunch] was some time in '39 or '40, and it was used by an English airman. To the best of my knowledge it originated in the R.A.F. and was pronounced 'garraunch' to reproduce the sound of a plane as it crashed and slid... Later it became a one-syllable word and refers to any metal torn or damaged by force. **1957** *Evening Post* (Wellington) 17 Apr. 8 (*headline*) Graunch!—Bang goes more than the door. **1959** D. BEATY *Cone of Silence* xxviii. 288 'Have you tried this new take-off technique?' 'Yes sir..we're in for a hell of a graunching.' **1964** *Observer* (Colour Suppl.) 11 Oct. 42/1 Many people 'graunch' their gears. **1965** *N.Z. Listener* 27 Aug. 9/1 John Pascoe himself knew that editing an encyclopaedia would be a lengthy project. 'When I started I knew it was a graunchy job. But then I've always liked long graunchy jobs. It's tied in with my youthful experiences of long distance running... I rather like long, slow patient plodding.' **1968** *Dominion Sunday Times* (Wellington) 10 Apr. 2/3 They said they could hear the ship 'graunching' on the rock.

graund, obs. form of GRAND.

†**graundcie.** App. var. of *craunce*, CRANTS.

1592 GREENE *Upst. Courtier* H, Such brooches, such bracelets, such graundcies, such periwigs.

graundepose, obs. form of GRAMPUS.

graunser, obs. form of GRANDSIRE.

graunt, -ar, -er, -e(e, obs. ff. GRANT, -ER, -EE.

graunt(e mercy, variant of GRAMERCY.

‖**graupel** ('graʊp(ə)l). *Meteorology.* [G. *graupel(-wetter)*.] Soft hail.

1889 *Weather Rep.* 4 Mar., Occasional showers of graupel, sleet, and snow have been recorded. **1894** BLACKMORE *Perlycross* 238 The snow, or soft hail (now known as graupel).

‖**grauwacke** ('graʊvakə). *Geol.* Also 8 grauwacken, 9 grawacké, grauwack. [Ger., f. *grau* GREY + *wacke* WACKE.] = GREYWACKE.

1794 KIRWAN *Elem. Min.* (ed. 2) I. 235 Its [Argillite's] transitions are into..grau-wacken [etc.]. **1806** DAVY in *Phil. Trans.* XCVII. 10 Grauwackè from North Wales. **1828** G. YOUNG *Geol. Surv. Yorksh. Coast* 55 The hard porphyritic-looking rocks..usually designated by the harsh-sounding name grawacké. **1840** *Trans. Geol. Soc.* Ser. II. (1842) VI. 558 The fossiliferous grauwacke which constitutes the chief mountain masses of the right bank of the Rhine. **1876** SMILES *Sc. Natur.* viii. (ed. 4) 131 The hills, which descend to the coast, are composed of hard grauwacke.

attrib. **1832** DE LA BECHE *Geol. Man.* (ed. 2) 41 Detritus from the grauwacke slates. **1842** H. MILLER *O.R. Sandst.* ii. (ed. 2) 56 The harder grauwacke schists. **1851** RICHARDSON *Geol.* viii. (1855) 246 The ancient grauwacke limestones.

gravaile, obs. form of GRAVEL.

gravamen (grə'veɪmɛn). Pl. **gravamina** (grə'veɪmɪnə). [a. late L. *gravāmen* a physical inconvenience, in med.L. a grievance, f. *gravāre* to load, f. *gravis* heavy, GRAVE *a.*]

1. A grievance.

1647 WARD *Simp. Cobler* 58 Is your *Advisera* such a *Suavamen* to you, that hath been such a *Gravamen* to Religion and Peace? **1708** S. SEWALL *Diary* 9 Feb. (1879) II. 216 [We] found this to our Comfort..which was a gravamen for many years. **1857** SIR F. PALGRAVE *Norm. & Eng.* II. 24 Charles gave Hagano the higher room..The real gravamen, however, appears to have been Hagano's affectionate though rough fidelity.

2. †**a.** A formal complaint or accusation. *Obs.*

1647 JER. TAYLOR *Lib. Proph.* Ep. Ded. 38 It is not safe..to extend the gravamen and punishment beyond the instances the Apostles make. **1774** BP. S. HALLIFAX *Roman Civ. Law* (1775) 126 In an Appeal, whether from a Gravamen or the Sentence, an Inhibition is issued from the Superior Court to the Inferior, to stop Proceedings. **1880** *Lit. World* 30 July 65/2 A gravamen brought forward by the Diet in opposition to the royal demands.

b. *Eccl.* A memorial presented by the Lower House of Convocation to the Upper representing the existence of disorders or grievances in the church.

1602 *Archpriest Controv.* (Camden) II. 13 They willed vs to bring our probations for the Grauamina we had put up against the Archpriest. **1869** *Daily News* 18 June, Archdeacon Hale presented a gravamen characterising the measure now before Parliament in very strong terms. **1889** *John Bull* 2 Mar. 145/3 Archdeacon Denison's *gravamen* just presented to Convocation is a most doleful document. **1899** *Westm. Gaz.* 9 Feb. 9/1 The Prolocutor thought the Archdeacon was travelling beyond the words of the *gravamen*.

3. The particular part of an accusation that bears most heavily on the person accused.

1832 MCCHEYNE in *Mem.* i. (1844) 12 It constitutes the very gravamen of the charge against the unrenewed man that he has affection for his earthly parent..but none for God! **1839** BROUGHAM *Sk. Statesmen, Ld. Mansfield* Ser. I. 115 The great gravamen, too, of these charges against him is his leaning towards the Americans. **1840** MILL *Diss. & Disc.* (1859) I. 151 The gravamen of the charge against the principle of utility seems to lie in a word. **1887** LOWELL *Democr.* 19 The real gravamen of the charge lies in the habit it has of making itself generally disagreeable.

†**gravament.** *Obs.* [ad. L. *gravāmentum* f. *gravāre*: see prec.] A grievance.

1537 LATIMER *To Cromwell* Rem. (1845) 378 Mr. Nevell shall deliver to you a bill of the gravaments of two or three of the fellows, most given to good letters.

†**gra'vaminous**, *a. Obs.* Also 8 *erron.* graviminous. [f. L. *gravāmin-*, *gravāmen* + -OUS.] Grievous, annoying, distressing.

1659 D. PELL *Impr. Sea* 19 A dishonour unto God, and a gravaminous burthen to the ships and men they go amongst. **1713** S. SEWALL *Diary* 19 Nov. (1879) II. 412 Gen[l]. Nicholson mention'd it as graviminous that the Shops were shut up. **1721** WODROW *Hist. Suffer. Ch. Scot.* (1829) II. 146 The parliament made new and gravaminous laws.

gravat, variant of CRAVAT.

†**gravative**, *a. Obs.* [ad. L. type **gravātīv-us* f. *gravāre*; see GRAVAMEN.] 'Applied to the feeling of pain accompanied by a sense of weight' (*Syd. Soc. Lex.* 1886).

1572 J. JONES *Bathes of Bath* I. 7 b, Heauy or grauatiue paine is caused in an Aposteme in a membre not sensible. **1668** CULPEPPER & COLE *Barthol. Anat.* I. xvii. 47 Persons having the Stone in their Kidneys have..gravative..pains. **1710** T. FULLER *Pharm. Extemp.* 151 Such [illnesses] as gravative Head Ach.

grave (greɪv), *sb.*[1] Forms: 1 græf, 4–6 graf(e, 5, 8–9 *Sc.* graff, (4 greve, 5 grawe, 6 *Sc.* graif, graiwe), 3– grave. [OE. *græf* str. neut. = OFris. *gref*, OS. *graf*, OHG. *grap*:—OTeut. type **grabo*^{m}; a parallel type is **grabâ* fem., represented by ON. *grǫf* (Da. *grav*, Sw. *graf*), Goth. *graba*; f. root of OE. *grafan* to dig, GRAVE *v.*[1]

The normal mod. representative of OE. *græf* would be *graff*; the ME. disyllabic *grave*, from which the standard mod. form descends, was prob. due to the especially frequent occurrence of the word in the dat. (locative) case.]

1. a. A place of burial; an excavation in the earth for the reception of a corpse; †formerly often applied loosely to a receptacle for the dead not formed by digging, as a mausoleum.

a **1000** *Seafarer* 97 (Gr.) þeah þe græf wille golde streȝan broþor his ȝeborenum. *c* **1250** *Gen. & Ex.* 3184 Oc ðe ail haueð so wide spiled, ðat his [Joseph's] graue is ðor vnder hiled. *a* **1300** *Cursor M.* 21063 First he did his graf to deluen. *c* **1330** R. BRUNNE *Chron.* (1810) 290 To þat stede he ferd, þer he was laid in graue. *c* **1385** CHAUCER *L.G.W.* 903 *Thisbe*, We preyen yow..That in o graue y-fere we moten lye. *a* **1400–50** *Alexander* 4451 Graffis garnyscht of gold & gilten tombis. *c* **1440** *Promp. Parv.* 207/2 Grave, solempnely made, or gravyn..*mausoleum*. *c* **1460** *Towneley Myst.* xxvi. 54 Dede men also rose vp sone, Outt of thare grafe. **1535** STEWART *Cron. Scot.* I. 594 He..With all honour wnto his graif is gone. **1548–9** (Mar.) *Bk. Com. Prayer, Burial Dead*, When they come at the graue. **1590** SHAKS. *Mids. N.* v. i. 387 The graues, all gaping wide, Euery one lets forth his spright. **1607** DEKKER *Roaring Girle* Wks. 1873 III. 107, I must not to my graue, As a drunkard to his bed. **1687** A. LOVELL tr. *Thevenot's Trav.* I. 58 When the Grave is filled up, they erect a stone. **1756–7** tr. *Keysler's Trav.* (1760) III. 97 Here in one grave are deposited the remains of Constantia..and..her daughter. **1794** BURNS '*O Death, hadst thou but spar'd his life*', E'en as he is, cauld in his graff. **1821** BYRON *Cain* III. i, Compose thy limbs into their grave. **1861** WRIGHT *Ess. Archæol.* I. vii. 142 The Anglo-Saxons..dug a rather deep rectangular grave..often of considerable dimensions. *a* **1876** G. DAWSON *Lect. Shaks.* etc. (1888) 62 When your grave comes to be dug, will the diggers weep?

transf. **1590** SPENSER *F.Q.* III. x. 42 We will blyndfolded ly, Ne privy bee unto your treasures grave.

†**b.** *holy grave* = HOLY SEPULCHRE.

a **1455** HOLLAND *Houlate* xxxv, The haily graif. *Ibid.* xxxvii, The haly graf. **1481** CAXTON *Reynard* (Arb.) 108, I wyl goo for you to the holy graue. *c* **1511** *1st Eng. Bk. Amer.* (Arb.) Introd. 31/2 They seke the holy graue to Iherusalem.

c. A grave-mound. Also transf., ***dead men's graves*** (see quot.).

1868 DICKENS *Uncomm. Trav.* xxi, Gravely making hay among the graves. **1869** R. B. SMYTH *Goldf. Victoria* 609 *Dead-men's Graves*, applied to country generally basaltic, where, owing to the unequal decomposition of the underlying rock, humps like graves occur.

d. In various fig. and proverbial expressions. †***into the grave of hell***: into the lowest depth. ***secret as the grave***: kept as a close secret. ***to make a person turn in his grave***: said fancifully or hyperbolically of the effect of something which was abhorrent to the person in his lifetime. ***some one is walking over my grave*** (see quot. 1868). ***one foot in the grave*** (see FOOT *sb.* 26 a.) ***to dig the grave of***: to cause the ruin, downfall, end of (a person or thing).

c **1585** CARTWRIGHT in R. Browne *Answ. Cartwright* 88 It shoulde followe that that assembly..shoulde from the hyest heauen fall into the graue of hell. **1738** SWIFT *Pol. Conversat.* i. 84 *Miss* [shuddering]. Lord! there's somebody walking over my Grave. **1832** L. HUNT *Sir R. Esher* (1850) 89 The correspondence I kept as secret as the grave. **1859** H. KINGSLEY *G. Hamlyn* xxxi. (1860) 268 Sometimes somebody would walk over my grave, and give me a creeping in the back. **1868** HOLME LEE *B. Godfrey* xiv. 77 Joan shuddered —that..convulsive shudder which old wives say is caused by a footstep walking over the place of our grave that shall be. **1883** *Harper's Mag.* Apr. 768/1 Somebody's walking over your grave, they say, when you feel so. **1888** BRYCE *Amer. Commw.* I. xii. 159 Jefferson might turn in his grave if he knew of such an attempt to introduce European distinctions of rank into his democracy. **1934** F. SCOTT FITZGERALD *Let.* 8 Dec. (1963) 397 Of course any *apologia* is necessarily a whine to some extent; a man digs his own grave and should, presumably, lie in it. **1963** *Listener* 31 Jan. 207/2 The delegation called for the convening of a conference next month to 'dig the grave' of the Federation.

e. with omission of the article (after a prep.).

1548 UDALL, etc. *Erasm. Par. Luke* xx. 38 Now wer Abraham, Isaac, and Jacob, at that tyme alreadie buiried in graue. **1662** HICKERINGILL *Serm.* Wks. 1716 I. 286 Few or none went down to Grave in peace.

2. a. Regarded as the natural destination or final resting-place of every one. Hence sometimes put for: The condition or state of being dead, death. †***to the grave***: till death. (***to bear a mark***) ***to one's grave***: all one's life. ***to find one's grave***: to meet one's death.

c **1380** WYCLIF *Wks.* (1880) 17 Crist sparid not to visyte pore men..in þe colde greue. **14..** *Songs & Carols 15th C.* (Percy Soc.) 66 Thei wyl gyffe a man a mark that he xal ber it to hys grafe. **1535** COVERDALE *Gen.* xlii. 38 Yf eny mysfortune shulde happen vnto him..ye shulde bringe my graye hayre with sorowe downe vnto the graue. **1624** QUARLES *Job* vi. 39 Both Rich and Poore are equal'd in the Grave. **1634** SIR T. HERBERT *Trav.* 168 My course came next, though not to die, yet to goe neere the Grave. **1656–9** B. HARRIS *Parival's Iron Age* (ed. 2) 244 France, where he soon found his grave. **1674** tr. *Martiniere's Voy. N. Countries* 113 And thinking by bleeding and purgation to recover their Patients, sent many of them to the Grave. **1707** WATTS *Hymn*, '*Life is the time to serve the Lord*', There are no Acts of Pardon pass'd In the cold Grave to which we haste. **1723** *Pres. State Russia* II. 129, I am, to the Grave, full of good Wishes towards you. **1726** SWIFT *Gulliver* IV. xi,

The Savages..discharged an Arrow, which wounded me deeply on the inside of my left Knee (I shall carry the Mark to my Grave). **1726** DYER *Grongar Hill* 92 Between the cradle and the grave. **1738** WESLEY *Psalms* VI. iii, I cannot thank Thee in the Grave. **1750** GRAY *Elegy* ix, The path of glory leads but to the grave. **1815** SHELLEY *Alastor* 720 Birth and the grave, that are not as they were.

b. with personification: = Death or Hades.

1611 BIBLE *Hosea* xiii. 14 O death, I will be thy plagues, O graue [WYCLIF, COVERDALE hell(e)], I will be thy destruction. *Ibid. 1 Cor.* xv. 55. **1615** CLEAVER *Proverbs* 175 No might..can rescue him out of the hand of the graue.

3. In enlarged rhetorical use: Anything that is, or may become, the receptacle of what is dead. So ***liquid, watery grave***.

1559 *Mirr. Mag.*, *Jack Cade* xxi, Than were on poales my parboylde quarters pight, And set aloft for vermine to deuower, Meete graue for rebels that resist the power. **1632** LITHGOW *Trav.* VII. 326 Their dead Corpes were cast over Board, in a boundlesse graue to feed the fishes. **1655** FULLER *Ch. Hist.* III. iii. §15 Ptolemais (the Grave General of the Christian Army). **1821** BYRON *Heaven & E.* I. iii, Not even a rock from out the liquid grave. **1865** KINGSLEY *Herew.* vi. 127 They had only just escaped a watery grave. **1874** LISLE CARR *Jud. Gwynne* I. vi. 170 He had carried her..out of a grave of fire. **1895** MAGUIRE in *United Service Mag.* July 373 The country between the Balkans and Constantinople would have been the grave of the entire Russian Army. **1898** J. R. ILLINGWORTH *Divine Immanence* vi. 137 The body ceases to be the spirit's organ, and becomes first its prison, and then its grave.

4. An excavation of any kind; a pit or trench. *Obs.* exc. in sense of a trench for earthing up potatoes and other roots.

1526 *Pilgr. Perf.* (W. de W. 1531) 276 b, It is wryten in the lawe of Moyses That no man sholde dyg ony pyt, or open ony graue or cesterne, but he sholde couer it agayne..lest [etc.]. **1847** HALLIWELL, *Grave*,..a potato-hole. *Linc.* **1857** *Jrnl. R. Agric. Soc.* XVIII. I. 108 Potatoes are brought out of the 'hogs', or 'graves', or 'pits'. **1890** *Morning Post* 26 Dec. 6/2 The mangold and potato graves have also suffered considerably.

5. *attrib.* and *Comb.* **a.** simple attributive, as *grave-brass, -clod, -field, -garth, -ground, -group, -hill, -lid, -linen, -mound,* † *-neighbour, -place, -rail, -side* (also *attrib.*), *-slab, -stead, -worm*; *grave-like* adj. **b.** objective, as *grave-maker, -raker, -robber*; *grave-digging* (cf. GRAVE-DIGGER), *-making, -robbing* vbl. sbs. **c.** adverbial (of destination) and instrumental, as *grave-bound, -riven* adjs. **d.** locative or originative, as *grave-interment*; *grave-born* adj.

1596 DRAYTON *Mortimeriados* 34 Lyke *graue-borne gosts, amaz'd and mad with feare. **1825** D. L. RICHARDSON *Sonnets* 10 The *grave-bound Pilgrim never can return. **1849** ROCK *Ch. of Fathers* I. II. 187 Our old English *grave-brasses. **1847** CRAIG, **Graveclod*, a lump of earth belonging to a grave. **1749** FIELDING *Tom Jones* XVI. v, The *grave-digging scene next engaged the attention of Partridge. **1868** G. STEPHENS *Runic Monuments* 1026/1 *Grave-fields. **1937** *Jrnl. R. Anthrop. Inst.* 233 To point out to me the sight of the grave-field. **1963** *Times Lit. Suppl.* 18 Jan. 44/2 The Viking character of the Gnezdovo grave-field. **1880** ROSSETTI *Ballads & Sonn.* 273 As in a *gravegarth, count to see The monuments of memory. **1874** GREEN *Short Hist.* i. §2. 9 The *grave-ground of Addington. **1937** *Jrnl. R. Anthrop. Inst.* 232 Nothing is said as to the original composition of the *grave-groups. *a* **1835** MRS. HEMANS *Song of Tomb* Poems (1875) 340 He must ride o'er the *grave-hills..with stormy speed. **1894** ATKINSON *Old Whitby* 62, I have taken 3 axe-hammers from grave-hills on the Danby and Skelton moors. **1658** SIR T. BROWNE *Hydriot.* Introd. i. 3 Poppæa, the wife of Nero, found a peculiar *grave enterment. *c* **1340** *Cursor M.* 14332 (Trin.) þe *graue lid awey þei kist. **1764** *Oxford Sausage* 63 O haste thee from thy *grave-like Grot! **1847** DE QUINCEY *Secret Societies* Wks. 1863 VI. 269 You may sit in that deep grave-like recess. **1836** LANE *Mod. Egypt* II. xv. 285 It is common, also, for a Mooslim, on a military expedition..to carry his *grave-linen with him. **14..** *Nom.* in Wr.-Wülcker 722/30 *Hic bostarius*, a *grafmakere. **1602** SHAKS. *Ham.* v. i. 34 Gardiners, Ditchers, and Graue-makers. **1654** WHITLOCK *Zootomia* 63 Hee being to work too fast for the Grave-maker. **1602** SHAKS. *Ham.* v. i. 74 Has this fellow no feeling of his businesse, that he sings at *Graue-making? **1894** E. H. BARKER *Two Summers Guyenne* 239 There is..very little grave-making, except by mounds and wooden crosses. **1603** DEKKER *Wonderfull Yeare* D iv, The colde companie of his *graue neighbours. **1665** WALTON *Life Hooker* in *Hooker's Wks.* (1888) I. 78 The poor clerk had many rewards for shewing Mr. Hooker's *grave-place. **1874** STUBBS *Const. Hist.* I. iv. 64 The researches into the grave-places of the nations. **1732** E. FORREST *Hogarth's Tour* 4 Hogarth.. untrussed upon a *grave-rail. **1631** WEEVER *Anc. Funeral Mon.* 51 The *graue-rakers, these gold-finders are called theeues. **1850** MRS. BROWNING *Poems* I. 318 The poet sings upon the earth *grave-riven. **1845** *Ecclesiologist* IV. 291 The sin of *grave-robbing. **1838** J. L. STEPHENS *Trav. Greece*, etc. 27/1 The Greeks returned, and, taking up the body, carried it to the *grave-side. **1865** MRS. WHITNEY *Gayworthys* xix. (1879) 172 How many a heart has felt that graveside solemnity. **1894** H. SPEIGHT *Nidderdale* 190 Two well preserved *grave-slabs. **1884** A. LANG *Custom & Myth* 286 The ghosts that haunt ancient *grave-steads. **1815** MILMAN *Fazio* (1821) 53, I had rather *grave-worms were on thy lips than that bad woman's kisses.

6. Special comb.: **grave-board**, a board, inscribed with symbolic figures, set upright over the graves of N. American Indians; **grave-clad** *a. nonce-wd.*, clad in grave-clothes; **grave-cloth**, ? a pall; **grave-cover**, a stone slab covering a grave; **grave-deep** *a. nonce-wd.*, deep as the grave; **grave-digging** *ppl. a.*, epithet of certain insects (see GRAVE-DIGGER 2); † **grave-fellow**, a companion in the grave; **grave-find**, an object or a number of objects found in a grave; **grave-furniture** = *grave-goods*; **grave-goods** *pl.*, valuables deposited with a corpse in the grave; **grave-hoard**, a quantity of objects buried with a corpse; † **grave-jelly**, corruption, rottenness; **grave-man, -master**, a sexton; **grave-mound**, a hillock, or a barrow or tumulus, indicating the site of an interment, a burial-mound; **grave-plant**, *Datura sanguinea* (*Syd. Soc. Lex.* 1886); † **grave-porer**, one who is poring over or looking towards his grave; an aged man; **grave-post** = *grave-board*; **grave-trap** *Theatr.* (see quot. 1886); also *fig.*; † **grave-wax** = ADIPOCERE. Also GRAVE-CLOTHES, GRAVE-DIGGER, GRAVESTONE, GRAVEYARD.

1851 SCHOOLCRAFT *Indian Tribes* I. 356 At the head of the grave a tabular piece of cedar, or other wood, called the adjedatig, is set. This *grave-board contains the symbolic or representative figures which record, if it be a warrior, his totem. **1862** MAX MÜLLER *Chips* (1880) I. xiv. 318 The inscriptions which are found on the Indian graveboards. *a* **1802** HOME *Alonzo* IV, Why should I fear to see a *grave-clad ghost? **1646** in C. W. Manwaring *Digest Early Conn. Probate Rec.* (1904) I. 16, 1 *graue cloath 3 s. **1764** *Rec. Amherst* (1884) 28/1 Voted To provide..a grave Cloth for the use of the District. **1925** V. WOOLF *Common Reader* 35 The Prior of Bromholm sent word that the grave-cloth was in tatters. **1875** J. T. FOWLER in *Archæologia* XLV. 385 The *grave-covers indicated in Browne-Willis's plan. **1850** MRS. BROWNING *Poems* II. 227 Give him room! Room for the dead in Paris! welcome solemn And *grave-deep. **1847** CRAIG s.v. *Grave*, *Grave-digging or burying beetle. **1851** GOSSE *Naturalist's Soj. Jamaica* 147 The labour of the bee is play compared with the efforts of the grave-digging Sphex. **1642** FULLER *Holy & Prof. St.* III. v. 164 For he that was buried with the bones of Elisha..recovered his life by lodging with such a *grave-fellow. **1681** FLAVEL *Meth. Grace* xviii. 327 When guilt shall neither be our bed fellow, nor grave-fellow. **1868** G. STEPHENS *Runic Mon.* I. p. x, At what era they came, is not known. *Grave-finds show that it was as early as some time..before Christ. **1937** *Discovery* 152/1 The excavation of the churchyard produced virtually nothing in the way of *grave furniture. **1939** G. CLARK *Archæol. & Society* iii. 55 Any archaeologist digging in England would give his head to find grave-furniture in anything approaching such a state of preservation as that in the young Pharaoh's tomb. **1883** *Daily News* 7 Nov. 5/3 Burying their dead with weapons and *grave-goods. **1894** —— 11 Jan. 5/2 For want of *grave hoards, very little will be known about us in some three thousand years or less. **1657** REEVE *God's Plea* 32 [He] will ere long be taken off from his leggs, lye upon a death-couch, be carried out by Bearers, and consume to *grave-gelly. **1821** COMBE *Wife* II. (1869) 273 The bold *grave-man at the meeting Gave the rude clown so sound a beating, That [etc.]. **1622** MABBE tr. *Aleman's Guzman d'Alf.* II. 220 Committed over to the Curate, Sexton, or *Grave-master. **1859** REEVE *Brittany* 137 Running to and fro over the *grave-mounds. **1583** STANYHURST *Æneis* IV. (Arb.) 117 To clap on shoulders his bedred *grave-porer old sire! **1840** *Southern Lit. Messenger* VI. 191/1 When an Indian dies, it is his family or surname, that is put on his *grave-post, or *adjedatigwon*. **1851** SCHOOLCRAFT *Indian Tribes* I. 356 After which the bones are buried, and the grave-posts fixed. **1855** LONGF. *Hiaw.* xiv. 18 On the grave-posts of our fathers Are no signs, no figures painted. **1844** J. R. PLANCHÉ *Drama at Home* I. 8 I'll propose her [*sc.* Ophelia] to be resident directress, with a bed in the *grave trap. **1859** E. FITZBALL *35 Yrs. Dram. Author's Life* II. 211 On one side, was the grave trap made use of in 'Hamlet'. **1886** *Stage Gossip* 69 The grave-trap is the one in centre of the stage, or nearly so, and is so called on account of its use in the grave scene in 'Hamlet'. **1919** M. BEER *Hist. Brit. Socialism* I. II. viii. 251 He was then firmly convinced that England..was tottering to the brink of the grave-trap in which exhausted nations disappear from the scene of history. **1854** MAYNE *Expos. Lex.*, **Grave-wax*. **1865** PAGE *Handbk. Geol. Terms* (ed. 2), *Grave-wax*, a familiar term of adipocere, because occasionally found in grave-yards.

† **grave**, *sb.*[2] *Obs.* [OE. *græf*, f. root of *grafan* GRAVE *v.*[1]] A graven image.

11.. *Voc.* in Wr.-Wülcker 541/15 *Sculptura*, græf. *a* **1300** *E.E. Psalter* xcvi. 7 Alle schente be þat bidden graues als. *Ibid.* cv. 19 And a kalfe in Oreb maked þai, And baden þe graue.

grave (greɪv), *sb.*[3] *local.* Forms: 3 **greȝȝfe, greyve**, 5 **grafe**, 5–6 **grayve**, 6 **greyff**, 5– **grave**. [a. ON. *greife*, of obscure origin; prob. a. OS. **grêbio* (MLG. *grêve*) = G. *graf* GRAVE *sb.*[4] (In South Yorkshire documents of the 16th c. GRIEVE *sb.* and *grave* are used indifferently.)]

† **a.** A steward, a person placed in charge of property (*obs.*). **b.** In certain parts of Yorkshire and Lincolnshire, each of a number of administrative officials formerly elected by the inhabitants of a township.

c **1200** ORMIN 18365 Icc amm sennd biforenn himm Hiss bidell & hiss greȝȝfe. *a* **1300** *Havelok* 266 Schireues he sette, bedels, and greyues. ? **14..** *Benedictine Rule* 374 in *Engl. Studien* II. 65 A priores may knaw wele þan, Sche beres þe charch of a hirdman; And als a graue bihoues hir be, þat cure hase tayn to kepe hir fe. **14..** *Nom.* in Wr.-Wülcker 683/33 *Hic villicus, Hic prepositus*, a grafe. *c* **1450** *Bk. Curtasye* 576 in *Babees Bk.*, Of þe resayuer he [tresurere] shalle resayue Alle þat is gedurt of baylé and grayue. *Ibid.* 589 Grayuis, and baylys, and parker. *c* **1478** *Plumpton Corr.* (Camden) 39 To the welfare of our soveraigne lord the King and you, nothing they will pay, with-out your said tenants will fray with them, whearfore they are in regage to divers of your graves. **1524** *Par. Accts. Ecclesfield, Yorks.*, Our lady greyffs haith maid their acownc. **1527** *Ibid.*, Owr lady grayves..haith maid theyr Recknyng and they ayr in debet iij[li]. xj[s]. ij[d]. *c* **1599** *Acct. Bk. W. Wray* in *Antiquary* XXXII. 278 The vsuall order of election of all & singuler Reves & graves, belonging to the prebendes w[th]in the colligiat churche or minster..in Ripon. **1605** SALTERN *Ant. Laws Gt. Brit.* E 2 b, The Saxons ..called their Nobles by a name of the same signification, viz. Earles or eldermen, a name of nobilitie vnknowne in their owne Countrie; where (as I take it) they are called *Graues* or *Greues*, signifying a gouernor, which name also they brought hither, and it remaineth in some vse to this day. **1610** *Louth Accts.* (1891) 95 Item payde for a Supper for the graves & theire wyues..iiij *li.* iiij *s.* **1710** in Morehouse *Kirkburton & Graveship of Holme* (1861) 140 We, y[e] Jury sworn for the lord of the Manor of Wakefield above-said, upon our Inquiry into the old Rentalls and Evidences concerning our said Graveship of Holme, find and present y[t] there are 61 Graves within our said Graveship.

attrib. **1861** MOREHOUSE *Kirkburton & Graveship of Holme* 140 After revising the grave roll, they subscribed the following declaration.

† **grave**, *sb.*[4] *Obs.* [ad. MDu. *grave* (Du. *graaf*) = GRAF. Now only as the second member of compound titles, as *landgrave, margrave, palsgrave*.] A foreign title = COUNT 1; chiefly used of the counts of Nassau.

1605 SYLVESTER *Du Bartas* II. iii. iv. *Captaines* 63 When, with the rest of all his Hoast, the Grave Marcheth amain to give the Town a brave..[*sidenote*, Signifieth but an Earl, but here it is usurped for the chiefe Captaine Josuah]. **1609** DEKKER *Guls Horne-bk.* v. 23 Then you may discourse how honorably your Graue vsed you; obserue that you call Graue Maurice your Graue. **1638** FORD *Lady's Trial* IV. ii, Her father was greve Hans van Herne. *a* **1718** PENN *Treat. Oaths* Wks. 1782 II. 485 Here follow two letters, of the Graue of Nassau, and Prince of Orange.

grave (greɪv), *a.*[1] (*sb.*[5]). [a. F. *grave*, ad. L. *grave-m, gravis* heavy, important. Cf. Sp., Pg., It. *grave*.

The popular Fr. representative of L. *grav-em* is *grief*; see GRIEF *a.*]

A. *adj.*

† **1.** Of persons: Having weight or importance; influential, respected. (Sometimes used as an epithet of respectful address.) Of authors, books, maxims, advice: Weighty, authoritative. *Obs.*

1541 PAGET in *St. Papers Hen. VIII*, VIII. 644 Remitting the consyderation of the same to your most excellent wisedom and grave judgement. **1557** NORTH tr. *Gueuara's Diall Pr.* 1272/6 Nowe I knowe, that thou art no lesse graue in making [= writing, composing], then gracious in teaching. **1583** FULKE *Defence* Answ. to Pref. 16 Let him preferre those Scriptures which the greater number and grauer churches do receiue. *a* **1592** GREENE *Alphonsus* IV. Wks. (Rtldg.) 240/2 Welcome, grave sir, to me. **1599** THYNNE *Animadv.* (1875) 22 Chaucer was a grave manne, holden in greate credyt. **1602** ROWLANDS *Tis Merrie when Gossips meete* 23 There's an old graue Prouerbe tell's vs that Such as die Maydes, doe all lead Apes in hell. **1604** E. G[RIMSTONE] *D'Acosta's Hist. Indies* I. i. 2 Theodoret a very grave Authour, follows Crysostome in this opinion. **1607** SHAKS. *Cor.* II. ii. 46 Most reuerend and graue Elders. **1622** SPARROW *Bk. Com. Prayer* (1661) 15 Our Churches direction in this particular, is grave and conform to ancient rules. **1657** J. SMITH *Myst. Rhet.* 203 Your determination is ..repugnant to the grave advice of your knowing friends. **1701** GREW *Cosm. Sacra* III. iii. 108 Once, the Roman State [was] of all others the most celebrated for their Virtue; as the Gravest of their own Writers, and of Strangers..do bear them witness. **1741** MIDDLETON *Cicero* I. v. 347 By imposing so shameful a task upon the gravest man in Rome [Cato]. **1749** H. WALPOLE *Lett.* (1848) II. 260 He is a grave man, and a good speaker.

2. Of works, employments, objects of consideration: Weighty, important; in later use chiefly, requiring serious thought, serious.

1592 SHAKS. *Ven. & Ad.* Ded. 4, I..vowe to take aduantage of all idle houres, till I haue honoured you with some grauer labour. **1602** *2nd Pt. Return fr. Parnass.* I. ii. 307 Could but a grauer subiect him [*sc.* Shakspere] content, Without loues foolish lazy languishment. **1828** SCOTT *F.M. Perth* x, When our council is assembled, we will treat of graver matters. **1868** HELPS *Realmah* xv. (1876) 415, I shall merely reply by asking you in turn some grave questions.

b. Now *esp.* in unfavourable sense, of faults, evils, difficulties, responsibilities, etc.: Highly serious, formidable. Of diseases or symptoms: Serious, threatening a fatal result.

1824 LANDOR *Imag. Conv.* Ser. I. II. 110 The fault is graver than the reproof. **1858** BRIGHT *Sp. India* 24 June, Grave errors had been committed in that country. **1866** G. MACDONALD *Ann. Q. Neighb.* i. (1878) 4 Grave doubts as to whether I was in my place. **1885** *Manch. Even. News* 16 July 2/3 If to-night's news be true, the position is very grave indeed. **1885** *Law Reports* 29 Chanc. Div. 797 There has been a grave breach of duty resulting in heavy loss. **1888** FAGGE *Princ. & Pract. Med.* (ed. 2) I. 174 This [meteorism] is a grave symptom. **1896** *Allbutt's Syst. Med.* I. 190 In poisoning from phosphorus, &c., and in the grave anæmias. *a* **1900** *Mod.* Grave news from the front.

3. Of persons, their character, aspect, speech, or behaviour: Marked by weighty dignity; of reverend seriousness. In later use with wider sense, of temperament, feeling, or their manifestations: Serious, not mirthful or jocular; opposed to *gay*.

1549 LATIMER *5th Serm. bef. Edw. VI* (Arb.) 143 The Judge at the enpanelynge of the queste hadde hys graue-lookes. **1598** MARSTON *Pygmal.* v. 161 That which I deemed Bacchus surquedry, Is graue, and staied, civill, Sobrietie. **1667** MILTON *P.L.* II. 300 With grave Aspect he rose, and in his rising seem'd A Pillar of State. **1709** LADY M. W. MONTAGU *Let. to Miss Anne Wortley* 21 Aug., This letter is a good deal grave, and, like other grave things, dull. *a* **1721** PRIOR *Cantata* 10 Youth on silent wings is flown: Graver years come rolling on. **1721** BERKELEY *Prev. Ruin Gt. Brit.* Wks. III. 204 At a time when the nation ought to be too grave for such trifles. **1802** WOLCOT (P. Pindar) *Pitt & his Statue* Wks. 1812 IV. 510 His grave Lordship and grave wig Both with the first importance big. **1828** SCOTT *F.M. Perth* xxi, He should be subjected to the charge of some grave counsellor. **1848** DICKENS *Dombey* iv, Solomon looked a little graver as he finished his dinner. **1868** J. H. BLUNT *Ref. Ch. Eng.* I. 329 The Prior of Durham writes a grave letter to him. **1889** 'ROLF BOLDREWOOD' *Robbery under Arms* xxviii, There was old George sitting on the bench as grave as a judge. **1897** *Literature* 190/2 The grave-and-gay verse so characteristic of this poet.

absol. **1676** GLANVILL *Ess. Philos. & Relig.* VI. 17 The Grave and the Sober, whose Judgements we have no reason to suspect to be tainted by their Imaginations. **1725** POPE *Odyss.* XIV. 522 The grave in merry measures frisk about.

b. Of movements, also of music, tones of voice, etc.: Expressive of or befitting serious feelings, serious, solemn.

1585 T. WASHINGTON tr. *Nicholay's Voy.* III. xiv. 98 They go with a grave, fayre, and soft pace. **1597** MORLEY *Introd. Mus.* 177 You must..if you have a graue matter, applie a graue kinde of musick to it. *Ibid.* 181 A kinde of staide musicke ordained for graue dauncing. **1611** SHAKS. *Wint. T.* I. ii. 173 We two will walke (my Lord) And leaue you to your grauer steps. **1660** F. BROOKE tr. *Le Blanc's Trav.* 312 When he saw the Monks with grave steps draw nearer the bed [etc.]. **1687** A. LOVELL tr. *Thevenot's Trav.* I. 30 That way of saluting is very grave. **1859** DICKENS *T. Two Cities* I. v, The children had ancient faces and grave voices. **1897** W. WATSON *Hope World*, etc. (1898) 24 The Song of Mingling flows Grave, ceremonial, pure.

4. Of colour, dress, etc.: Dull, plain, sombre, not gay or showy.

1611 COTGR., s.v. *Fol*, Graue clothes make dunces often seeme great Clarkes. **1725** DE FOE *Voy. round World* (1840) 267 A mantle..dyed in two or three grave brown colours. **1756** NUGENT *Gr. Tour, Italy* III. 86 Their dress is grave and becoming. **1811** *Self Instructor* 520 Every part has equally received the pumice..exhibiting a dead grave appearance. **1849** RUSKIN *Sev. Lamps* vi. §12. 174 Vigorous oppositions of light and shadow, and grave, deep, or boldly contrasted colour. **1863** GEO. ELIOT *Romola* (1880) I. Introd. 3 The folds of his well-lined black silk garment.. hang in grave unbroken lines from neck to ankle.

quasi-*adv.* **1805** EMILY CLARK *Banks of Douro* I. 18 Though so young, she dressed plain and grave, to give her an older appearance.

5. [After L. *gravis*.] Physically ponderous, heavy. *Obs.* or *arch.*

1570 LEVINS *Manip.* 42/44 Graue, *grauis, grandis*. *c* **1611** CHAPMAN *Iliad* v. 752 In her violent hand she takes his graue, huge, solid lance. **1682** *Weekly Mem. Ingen.* 356 Some few others are equally grave with the water within which they are. **1805** WORDSW. *Waggoner* I. 13 The mountains against heaven's grave weight Rise up.

6. Of sounds: Low in pitch, deep in tone; opposed to *acute*. ***grave accent*** (see ACCENT 1, 2). ***grave harmonic*** (see HARMONIC B. 2).

1609 DOULAND *Ornith. Microl.* 71 A graue accent is made in the end of a complete sentence. **1669** HOLDER *Elem. Speech* 99 The Acute accent raising the Voice in some certain Syllables, to a higher, i.e. more acute Pitch or Tone, and the Grave depressing it lower. **1706** A. BEDFORD *Temple Mus.* ii. 19 The Verse was also mixt with acute and grave Sounds. **1727-41** CHAMBERS *Cycl.* s.v., The thicker the chord, or string, the more grave the tone, or note. **1779** [see ACUTE *a.* 5]. **1831** BREWSTER *Nat. Magic* ix. (1833) 229 Dr. Wollaston has also shown that this is true also of very grave sounds. **1876** STAINER & BARRETT *Dict. Mus. Terms, Grave* (1) Deep in pitch; as grave hexachord, the lowest hexachord in the Guidonian system. **1881** *Nature* No. 616. 358 A low booming tone to which musicians give the name of the grave harmonic.

7. *attrib.* and *Comb.* Chiefly parasynthetic, as ***grave-browed, -coloured, -eyed, -faced, -hearted, -looking, -toned, -visaged*** adjs.

1861 W. F. COLLIER *Hist. Eng. Lit.* 41 *Grave-browed men. **1768-74** TUCKER *Lt. Nat.* (1852) II. 25 A morning gown of a *grave coloured flowered damask. **1861** W. F. COLLIER *Hist. Eng. Lit.* 155 *Grave-eyed philosophers. *a* **1699** J. BEAUMONT *Psyche* xiii. 21 Those *grave-fac'd Bloodhownds..those Elders. **1863** ATKINSON *Stanton Grange* 96 The grave-faced assurance the young man gave him. **1642** VICARS *God in Mount* (1644) 75 The grey-headed but not *grave-hearted Citizens of London. **1825** J. NEAL *Bro. Jonathan* III. 237 A thoughtful, *grave-looking personage. **1828** MISS MITFORD *Village* Ser. III. 273 It was a grave-looking mansion. **1751** WESLEY *Wks.* (1872) XIV. 80 A word that has no accent on the last syllable is termed a *grave-toned. **1843** LYTTON *Last Bar.* I. i, Here is my *grave-visaged headman.

B. *sb.* A grave accent; †a grave note.

1609 [see ACUTE *a.* B]. **1727** BOYER *Dict. Fr.-Eng.* s.v. *Accent grave*..the Accent Grave, the Grave. **1728** R. NORTH *Mem. Musick* (1846) 28 A right downe singing, with acutes and graves. **1824** J. JOHNSON *Typogr.* II. iii. 36 Vowels marked with a grave..; è has a grave when it stands for a word by itself.

‖**grave** (grav, 'grave), *a.*[2] *Mus.* [F. *grave* or It. *grave* = GRAVE *a.*[1]] A term indicating a slow and solemn movement.

1683 PURCELL *3-Pt. Sonnatas* To Rdr., The English Practitioner..will find a few terms of Art perhaps unusual to him, the chief of which are these following: *Adagio* and *Grave*, which import nothing but a very slow movement: [then *Largo*, etc.]. **1724** *Explic. For. Words Mus.* 36 *Grave*, signifies a very Grave and Slow Movement, somewhat faster than Adagio, and slower than Largo. **1762** STERNE *Tr. Shandy* VI. xi, What Yorick could mean by the words *lentamente*,—*tenutè* [sic],—*grave*,—and sometimes *adagio*, —as applied to theological compositions..I dare not venture to guess. **1848** RIMBAULT *First Bk. Piano* 65 *Grave*, a very slow and solemn degree of movement.

grave (greɪv), *v.*[1] Forms: *Inf.* 1 grafan, 3 graven, (5 gravyn), 4–7 grave, (5 grafe, grawe, 6 greve, *Sc.* graife, 7 greave), 4– grave. *Pa. t.* 1 gróf, 4 grof(e, (grufe), 4–5 grove, (5 grave); *weak forms*: 4–6 gravede, 4– graved. *Pa. pple.* 1 (á-, be-)grafen, 4–6 grave, (5 *Sc.* grawin, 6 graffin), 3– graven; also 3, 5 igrave(n, 4–5 ygrave; *weak forms*: 4– graved, (5 -id, *Sc.* -it, 6 -yd); also 4 igraved. [A Com. Teut. str. vb.; OE. *grafan* (pa. t. *gróf, gróf*on, pa. pple. *-grafen*) to dig, to engrave (cf. *begrafan* to bury: see BEGRAVE), OS. *bigraban* to bury, OLow Frankish *gravan* to dig, (MDu., Du. *graven* to dig), OHG. *graban* to dig, carve, (MHG., G. *graben* to dig; *begraben* to bury, *eingraben* to engrave), ON. *grafa* to dig, to bury (Sw. *grafva, gräfva*, Da. *grave*), Goth. *graban* to dig, f. OTeut. root **grab*-, *grôb*- (whence GRAVE *sb.*[1], GROOVE *sb.*):—pre-Teut. **ghrăbh*-. Cognates are found in OSl. *grebą* I dig (also, I row), *grobŭ* ditch, Lettish *grebju* I scrape. Connexion with Gr. γράφειν, to write, is no longer accepted by philologists. The str. pa. t. died out in the 15th c.; in the pa. pple. the str. form is still the prevailing one.

The F. *graver*, to engrave, is an adoption of the Teut. vb.; its compound *engraver* became Eng. as ENGRAVE *v.*, which has nearly superseded the native word in this sense.]

I. 1. *intr.* To dig. *Obs.* exc. *dial.* †Also *fig.*

a **1000** *Riddles* xxii. 2 (Gr.) Ic..be grunde græfe. *a* **1000** *Boeth. Metr.* viii. 57 Se forma feohȝitsere..grof æfter golde. *c* **1400** MAUNDEV. (Roxb.) xxix. 132 At þe last þai schall dryfe him to þe hole whare he come oute. And þan schall þai grafe after him. **1412** HOCCLEVE *De Reg. Princ.* 83 He [*sc.* þoght] graueþ deppest of seekenesses alle. *c* **1450** *St. Cuthbert* (Surtees) 2377 And he stode grauand with a spade. **1674-91** in RAY *N.C. Words*. **1867** J. P. MORRIS *Siege o' Brou'ton* 5 (Lanc. Gloss.) Jinny Dodgon ran into t' garden, whār her āld man was greavin'.

2. *trans.* To dig, form by digging; to dig out, excavate. Also with *out, up*. † ***to grave away***: to get rid of by digging. Now *rare* exc. *dial.* in ***to grave peat(s, turf***.

a **1000** *Riming Poem* 71 (Gr.) þæt ic grofe græf. *a* **1300** *Cursor M.* 17288 + 134 It was in maner of a hows þat crist laide in was, Grauen depe in a roche. *a* **1300** *E.E. Psalter* vii. 16 þe slough he opened and it groue he. **1340-70** *Alex. & Dind.* 7 þei..hadde graue on þe ground many grete cauys. *c* **1385** CHAUCER *L.G.W.* 678 *Cleopatra*, And next the shryne a pit thann doth she grave. *c* **1400** MAUNDEV. (Roxb.) ix. 35 þe pitte þer þai graue it vpp. *c* **1425** *St. Eliz. of Spalbeck* in *Anglia* VIII. 109/15 Sche..strekith oute hir fynger & puttith to hir eyen..as sche wolde graue hem oute or bore hem in. **1483** *Cath. Angl.* 163/2 To Grave, *cespitare, fodere*. **1535** COVERDALE *Jer.* xviii. 14 Maye the springes off waters be grauen awaye. —— *Ezek.* iv. 2 Stronge diches are grauen on euery syde off it. **1552** LYNDESAY *Monarche* Prol. 278 That sors..Off Hylicone..That Longeous..did graue in tyll his syde. **1557** *Rec. Scotter Manor* in *N.W. Linc. Gloss.* s.v., No man shall graue any turves in thest car nor in Rany[how] vpon payne for euery dayes work, iij[s] iiij[d]. **1560** BIBLE (Genev.) *Isa.* xxii. 16 He that..graueth an habitacion for him self in a rocke. **1641** BEST *Farm. Bks.* (Surtees) 70 We grave up a rownde sodde with a spade. **1747** STOVIN in *Phil. Trans.* XLIV. 571 The Pit he was graveing Peat in. **1794** *Trans. Soc. Arts* XII. 126 And the earth [was] graved up, where each plant was to stand, one spit deep. **1884** *Gd. Words* 76 Out on the top was an old man graving turf. **1896** M. BEAUMONT *Joan Seaton* 61 'So he graved that [a dike] to carry my water off from t' beck.'

II. To bury. [Not recorded in OE., which has *begrafan* in this sense; cf. ON. *grafa*.]

3. To deposit (a corpse) in the ground, in a tomb; to bury, inter. *Obs.* or *arch.*

In the later examples prob. apprehended as a derivative of GRAVE *sb.*[1]

c **1250** *Gen. & Ex.* 3778 Ðarð noman swinken hem [*sc.* Korah, Dathan, and Abiram] to grauen. *a* **1300** *Cursor M.* 3213 In ebron groue hir abraham. *Ibid.* 17660 All we cund þe mikel graim For iesu þou grufe [*Gött.* grof] his licam. *c* **1300** *Havelok* 2528 In the tun ther Grim was grauen. *c* **1340** *Cursor M.* 6962 (Trin.) Joseph bones þei wiþ hem lede And þere grauen [*Cott., Gött.* grof] hem in þat stede. **1375** BARBOUR *Bruce* IV. 309 At Ierusalem thus trowit he Gravyn in the burch to be. **1430-40** LYDG. *Bochas* I. iv. (1544) 8 a, After tyme her father was ygraue. *c* **1440** *York Myst.* xxiv. 140 What tyme þat he was graued in graue. *c* **1450** *Cov. Myst.* (Shaks. Soc.) 227 That he must now in cley be graue. **1513** DOUGLAS *Æneis* Epitaph, Now stant I graue in Naplys the cite. **1535** STEWART *Cron. Scot.* II. 298 Ewgenius..grauit wes..in Ecolumkill. **1602** *2nd Pt. Return fr. Parnass.* III. v. 1442 Dead things are graued. **1632** MASSINGER & FIELD *Fatal Dowry* III, Would I had seen thee graved with thy great sire. **1876** JAS. GRANT *One of the '600'* ix. 80 They told you that I was dead too and graved in yonder kirk.

fig. **1597-8** BP. HALL *Sat.* III. ii. 23 Thine ill deserts cannot be graued with thee.

†**b.** To deposit or hide under ground. *Obs.*

a **1300** *Cursor M.* 16923 Nu is þe croice grauen vnder greit and iesus vnder stan. *c* **1386** CHAUCER *Wife's T.* 209 For al the metal ne for oore That vnder erthe is graue. *c* **1420** *Pallad. on Husb.* VI. 45 Sarment, or stre, or loppe in hit be graued.

†**c.** To swallow up in or as in a grave. *Obs.*

a **1340** HAMPOLE *Psalter* vi. 5 Hell graues synful men. **1607** SHAKS. *Timon* IV. iii. 166 Ditches graue you all. *c* **1611** CHAPMAN *Iliad* XV. 317 The throtes of dogs shall graue His manlesse lims.

III. To engrave.

4. To form by carving, to carve, sculpture. *lit.* and *fig.*; also *absol.* *Obs.* exc. *poet.*

c **1000** *Ags. Ps.* (Th.) lxxvii[i]. 58 Hi..him woh-godu worhtan and grofun. **1382** WYCLIF *Hab.* ii. 18 What profitith the sculptile for his maker grauede it. **1398** TREVISA *Barth. De P.R.* XVI. lxviii. (1495) 575 Men that graue loue it [Marbyl callyd Caristium] wel. *c* **1400** *Destr. Troy* 8744 Like ymages were all, abill of shap, & craftely grauen. *c* **1430** *Hymns Virg.* 104 Make not þi god þat man haþ graue. **1535** COVERDALE *2 Esdras* xiii. 6 Beholde, he graued himself a greate mountayne. **1671** MILTON *P.R.* I. 253 Affirming it thy Star new graven in Heaven. **1706** STANHOPE *Paraphr.* III. 373 Images that our distempered Fancies first form and grave to themselves, and then fall down and worship them. **1878** H. PHILLIPS *Poems fr. Span. & Ger.* 14, I graved for thee a silver god.

†**b.** in pa. pple. = CHISELLED 2. *Obs. rare*[−1].

1650 BULWER *Anthropomet.* 88 Eares graven, somewhat short, soft, and delicate.

†**5. a.** To cut into (a hard material); in quots. *fig.* **b.** To mark by incisions; to ornament with incised marks; = ENGRAVE *v.* 2. *Obs.*

13.. *Test. Christi* (Vernon MS.) in *Archiv Stud. neu Spr.* LXXIX. 428 þe seles þat hit was seled wiþ þei were grauen vp-on a stiþ. *c* **1374** CHAUCER *Troylus* II. 1192 (1241) Hard was it youre herte for to graue. *Ibid.* III. 1413 (1462) What proferestow thi light here for to selle Go selle it hem þat smale selys grauen. **1399** LANGL. *Rich. Redeles* I. 40 It [the croune] was ffull goodeliche y-graue with gold al aboute. ?*a* **1400** *Morte Arth.* 3463 His gloves gayliche gilte, and gravene by þe hemmys, With graynes of rubyes fulle gracious to schewe. *a* **1400-50** *Alexander* 3343 þe thrid of a Topas a-tyred & trelest & grauen. *c* **1470** HENRY *Wallace* VIII. 107 Hys glytterand glowis grawin on athir sid. **1592** SHAKS. *Ven. & Adon.* 376 Being steeld, soft sighes can neuer graue it [thy heart]. **1677** HALE *Prim. Orig. Man.* IV. iv. 324 A..Watch, curiously wrought, graved, and enameled.

c. *nonce-use.* To mark as with engraved lines.

1865 GEIKIE *Scen. & Geol. Scot.* i. 1 Man..graves the country with lines of roadway.

6. To engrave (an inscription, figures, etc.) upon a surface. Also, to engrave (a surface) *with* (letters, etc.). Hence, to record by engraved or incised letters. *arch.*

c **1205** LAY. 7636 þer on weoren igrauen Feole cunne bocstauen. *c* **1305** *Edmund Conf.* 91 in *E.E.P.* (1862) 73 Aue maria gracia plena: þuse four wordes were ido & igraued in his ring of golde. **1377** LANGL. *P. Pl.* B. XV. 507 That rode thei honoure, That in grotes is ygraue, and in golde nobles. **1390** GOWER *Conf.* III. 73 A ring, wherin a stone Was set and grave therupon A sonne. *a* **1400-50** *Alexander* 201 All þe sawis of þaire Syre..þare gan þai graithly þam graue in golden lettirs. **1463** *Bury Wills* (Camden) 15 My smale tablys of ivory gravyn with ymages. **1551** ROBINSON tr. *More's Utop.* II. (Arb.) 148 A piller of stone with the dead mans titles therin graved. *c* **1600** NORDEN *Spec. Brit., Cornw.* (1728) 64 A fayre earthen pott gylded and grauen with letters. **1624** CAPT. SMITH *Virginia* III. vi. 62 There setting vp crosses, and graving our names in the trees. **1727** DE FOE *Syst. Magic* I. vi. (1840) 140 Ham..caused the rules and precepts to be graved in metal. **1750** GRAY *Elegy* xxix, Approach and read..the lay Graved on the stone beneath yon aged thorn. **1840** DICKENS *Old C. Shop* xvi, Wreaths less liable to wither..than some which were graven deep in stone and marble. **1869** BLACKMORE *Lorna D.* i, Go and see my name John Ridd graven on that very form. **1887** BOWEN *Virg. Æneid* VI. 20 Graved on the doors is the death of Androgeos.

absol. **1430-40** LYDG. *Bochas* II. xv. (1554) 54 Sethes children..Made two pillers where men myght graue. *c* **1614** SIR W. MURE *Dido & Æneas* I. 492 Some grave in brasse; some kyth their craft in stone. **1877** C. GEIKIE *Christ* xiii. (1879) 127 Seeking wisdom when you are old is like writing on water; seeking it when you are young is like graving on stone.

b. *fig.* To impress deeply, to fix indelibly; = ENGRAVE *v.* 3 c.

1390 GOWER *Conf.* I. 60 Min hert is growen into stone, So that my lady there upon Hath suche a printe of loue grave, That [etc.]. *c* **1460** ROS *La Belle Dame* 281 in *Pol. Rel. & L. Poems* (1866) 61 Yf suche bileve be in your mynde y-grave. **1526** *Pilgr. Perf.* (W. de W. 1531) 239 And he wolde that we sholde greue them in y[e] tables of our hertes. **1559** *Primer* in *Priv. Prayers* (1851) 38 O Christ..Faith in our hearts set and grave. **1580** SIDNEY *Ps.* XXV. iv, Let those things thy remembrance grave, Since they eternall essence have. **1690** LOCKE *Hum. Und.* I. iv. §20. 34 To what purpose should Characters be graven on the Mind, by the finger of God. **1725** POPE *Odyss.* XVIII. 156 Hear my words and grave them in thy mind! *a* **1839** PRAED *Poems* (1864) II. 107 Until my heart shall cease to beat,..That kind blue eye and golden hair, Eternally are graven there. **1851** HAWTHORNE *Snow Image, Gt. Stone Face* (1879) 52 His wrinkles and furrows were inscriptions that Time had graved. **1890** *Spectator* 8 Nov. 639/2 With this conviction well graved into his mind. **1898** J. CAIRD *Univ. Serm.* 71 Features on which time had graven its seemingly indelible impress.

†**7.** To portray or copy in an engraving; = ENGRAVE *v.* 4. *Obs.*

a **1631** DONNE *Serm.* i. (1634) 2 That earth, which if we will cast it all but into a map, costs many moneths labour to grave it. **1690** EVELYN in *Pepys' Diary* VI. 171, I am deceived if he has not graved most of the Chancellors. **1707** SLOANE *Jamaica* I. p. xlix, The figures of some of these instruments are hereafter graved. **1818** W. ALLSTON in *W. Irving's Life & Lett.* (1864) I. 398 The time the engraver demands for graving my drawing.

grave (greɪv), *v.*[2] Also 7 greave. [Of obscure origin; possibly f. F. *grave* = *grève* shore.

The guess that the word is a derivative of *graves*, GREAVES, rests on the baseless and unlikely assertion that that substance was formerly used in the operation. The vb. occurs much earlier than the sb.]

trans. To clean (a ship's bottom) by burning off the accretions, and paying it over with tar or some composition, while aground on a beach, or placed in a specially-constructed dock. (Cf. BREAM *v.*[1])

1461 in *10th Rep. Hist. MSS. Comm.* App. v. 301 No maner shipp of aliennts..to be sette agrounde to be graved in no manere place within the francheise of the saide citie. **1600** W. MAGOTHS in Hakluyt *Voy.* III. 839 Wee stayed in this harborough 17 dayes, to graue our ship & refresh our wearied people. **1668** *Lond. Gaz.* No. 279/4 Yesterday were launched, the Monmouth and Mary, which are new Graved and re-fitted. **1692** in *J. Smith's Seaman's Gram.* xvi. 78 *To greave a Ship*, is to bring her to lye dry a ground, to burn off her old filth. **1719** DE FOE *Crusoe* II. xiii. (1840) 248 Our carpenter being prepared to grave the outside of the ship. **1769** FALCONER *Dict. Marine* (1780), *Fourches de carene*, breaming-hooks..used to hold the flaming furze..to a ship's bottom when graving. **1891** C. CREIGHTON *Hist. Epidemics* 585 They graved the ship there and remained twenty-six days.

grave (greɪv), *v.*[3] *rare*[−0]. *Mus.* [f. GRAVE *a.*[2]] *trans.* To render (a note or tone) grave.

1864 in WEBSTER; and in later Dicts.

grave, obs. Sc. form of GROVE.

grave-clothes, *sb. pl.* [f. GRAVE *sb.*[1] + CLOTHES.] The clothes or wrappings in which a corpse is laid out for burial.

1535 COVERDALE *John* xi. 44 And ye deed came forth bounde hande and fote with graue clothes. **1590** SPENSER *F.Q.* II. xi. 20 Like a ghost he seem'd whose grave-clothes were unbound. **1633** G. HERBERT *Temple, Dawning* 15 Christ left his grave-clothes. **1679** J. GOODMAN *Penit. Pardoned* III. ii. (1713) 287 Without so much as his grave-clothes about him. **1820** SHELLEY *Vision Sea* 57 The sharks and the dog-fish their grave-clothes unbound. **1857** KEBLE *Eucharist. Adorat.* 17 Angels..employed chiefly, as far as we are told, in guarding His tomb and grave-clothes.

graved (greɪvd), *ppl. a.* [f. GRAVE *v.*[1] + -ED[1].] In senses of the vb. †**a.** Buried (*obs.*). **b.** = GRAVEN. *rare.*

a **1547** SURREY *Æneid* IV. 42 Cinders, thinkest thou, mind this? or graved ghosts? **1552** ABP. HAMILTON *Catech.* (1884) 37 Thou sal nocht mak to the..ony gravit ymage. **1566** Q. ELIZ. in Strype *Ann. Ref.* (1709) I. xlix. 532 Without she saw some glimpse of their following surety after her graved bones. **1873** MRS. PALLISER tr. *Jaquemart's Ceram. Art* 288 The first [of the writers cited] only mentions the paintings on engobe, while the second attaches himself to the graved decoration.

grave-digger (ˈgreɪvdɪgə(r)). [f. GRAVE *sb.*[1]]

1. a. One whose employment it is to dig graves.

1593 NASHE *Christ's T.* to Rdr., Wks. (Grosart) IV. 4 He hath proued him selfe to be the only Gabriel Graue-digger vnder heauen. **1702** STEELE *Funeral* I. i. 5 The Grave digger of St. Timothie's in the Fields. **1749** FIELDING *Tom Jones* XVI. v, I never saw in my life a worse grave-digger. **1838** DICKENS *O. Twist* v, The grave-digger shovelled in the earth.

†**b.** One who digs up or violates graves. *Obs.*

1631 WEEVER *Anc. Funeral Mon.* 51 These Tombe-breakers, these graue-diggers.

2. A name given to various insects that bury the bodies of small animals and insects, for the use of their larvæ on quitting the egg: *esp.* a beetle of the genus *Necrophorus*, called also *burying-beetle* and *sexton*; also, a digger-wasp, e.g. one of the genus *Sphex*.

[**1847** Grave-digging: see GRAVE *sb.* 6.] **1851** GOSSE *Nat. in Jamaica* 146 We perceive the Sphex at work..we discover by narrow watching that she is digging the hole; and hence the negro children have given her the appropriate title of grave-digger. **1884–5** *Riverside Nat. Hist.* (1888) II. 385 On account of their habit of burying small dead vertebrate animals, in which they lay their eggs, these beetles [of the genus *Necrophorus*] are often called sextons or grave-diggers.

3. *fig.* (See quots.)

1887 F. GALE *Game of Cricket* 193 Let me say a word to captains..about the gravediggers... They grow despondent for lack of encouragement, and there is a sameness in constantly bringing up the rear. **1896** *Daily Tel.* 21 Aug. 3/2 Too much 'route-marching, pipe-claying, and starching' tends to dulness and apathy, whilst it leads the British soldier, when off duty,..to make too free an acquaintance with the 'grave-digger' [*sc.* strong drink], as it is termed in India. **1934** LEWIS *Lang. Cricket* 111 *Grave diggers*, the last batsmen of a side in the order of going in to bat. **1949** I. DEUTSCHER *Stalin* 94 Labelled by Lenin 'the liquidators', the grave-diggers of the party. **1957** C. HUNT *Guide to Communist Jargon* l. 163 According to Marx, the proletariat is brought into existence by the capitalist system, of which it is destined to be the 'grave-digger'.

Hence **gravediggership**, a gravedigger's office.

1894 CROCKETT *Lilac Sunbonnet* 139 Anxious for his grave-diggership.

†**gravedinous**, *a. Obs. rare*[−0]. [ad. L. *gravēdinōsus*, f. *gravēdō*: see next and -OUS.] Drowsy, heavy-headed.

1721 in BAILEY.

†**gravediny.** *Obs. rare*[−1]. [f. L. *gravēdin-*, *gravēdō*.] = GRAVEDO.

1620 VENNER *Via Recta* (1650) 241 Dolorous Gouts, gravedinie of the head..are not apt to be bred by parsimony.

graveditie, obs. form of GRAVIDITY.

†**gravedity.** *Obs. rare*[−1]. [irreg. f. GRAVEDO.] = GRAVEDO.

1547 BOORDE *Brev. Health* lxiv. 18b, The cause of so muche slepynge doth come..of great graveditie in the head thorowe reume.

‖**gravedo** (grəˈviːdəʊ). [L. *gravēdō* heaviness (in the limbs or head), f. *gravis* heavy.] A cold in the head; coryza.

1706 PHILLIPS (ed. Kersey), *Gravedo*, Heaviness: Also the Pose or stuffing of the Head, a Disease. **1744** ARMSTRONG *Preserv. Health* I. 319 Fierce coughs will teize you..Or moist Gravedo load your aching brows. **1781** JOHNSON *Let. to Mrs. Thrale* 23 Oct., The Gravedo is not removed. **1803** *Med. Jrnl.* X. 140 The..affections of the chest and head, the cough, gravedo, sneezing, vertigo, and catarrh. **1886** in *Syd. Soc. Lex.*

†ˈ**graveful**, *a. Obs. rare*[−1]. [irreg. f. GRAVE *a.*[1] (*sb.*[1]) + -FUL.] Full of gravity.

1621 LADY M. WROTH *Urania* 442 Then appeared an ancient grauefull old man speaking these words.

gravel (ˈgrævəl), *sb.* Forms 4–7 gravell, (4 gravaile, -ayl, -eil, 5 gravylle, 6 gravele, grawell), 5 gravelle, 3– gravel. [a. or ad. OF. *gravele*, *gravelle* in senses 1, 2, 2b, mod.F. *gravelle* in sense 4, dim. of OF. *grave* gravel, coarse sand, also sea-shore (mod.F. *grève*) = Pr., Cat. *grava*; of Celtic origin, cf. Welsh *gro*, Cornish *grou*, Bret. *grouan* gravel; possibly cogn. w. OE. *gréot* GRIT *sb.*[1]]

†**1.** Sand. ***quick gravel***: quicksand. ***gravel of gold, golden gravel***: see GOLDEN 3. *Obs.*

a **1300** *Cursor M.* 2347 Naman suld cun sume ne neuen.. Namar þen grauel in þe see. *a* **1325** *Prose Psalter* lxxvii[i]. 31 He rained..volatils feþered as grauel of þe se. *a* **1340** HAMPOLE *Psalter* i. 1 The rightwisman passis that way swiftly, as he that gas on qwik grauel, that gers him synk that standis thar on. *c* **1374** CHAUCER *Boeth.* III. metr. x. 74 (Camb. MS.) Alle the thinges that the Ryver tagus geueth yow with hys goldene grauayles. *c* **1400** MAUNDEV. (Roxb.) xxxiii. 150 In þat riuer er many precious stanes..and mykill grauell of gold. *c* **1450** *Mirour Saluacioun* 1624 My synne passes in noumbre the gravell..in the see. **1477** EARL RIVERS (Caxton) *Dictes* 9 All is lost that is geuen vnto them right as the reyne falleth vpon the grauel. **1590** SPENSER *F.Q.* III. iv. 18 All the gravell mixt with golden owre. **1712** SWIFT *Midas* Wks. 1755 IV. I. 4 People travel From far to gather golden gravel.

2. a. A material consisting of coarse sand and water-worn stones of various sizes, often with a slight intermixture of clay, much used for laying roads and paths. (In early use not clearly distinguished from sense 1.)

a **1300** *Cursor M.* 9938 Four strandes rinnes suete Thoru þat grauel and þat grett. ? *a* **1366** CHAUCER *Rom. Rose* 127 Tho saugh I wel The botme paved everydel With gravel, ful of stones shene. **1398** TREVISA *Barth De P.R.* XVI. i. (1495) 552 Grauell and sonde is more harde in substaunce than comyn erthe. **1503** HAWES *Examp. Virt.* x. 9 The hall paued was..With none other grauell but precyous stones. **1542–3** *Act 34 & 35 Hen. VIII*, c. 9 §6 Anie maner of balast rubbish grauell or any other wracke, or filth. **1585** T. WASHINGTON tr. *Nicholay's Voy.* I. xvi. 17 With great valleyes full of gravel and large stones very painful too goe upon. **1613** SHAKS. *Hen. VIII*, I. i. 155 Proofes as cleere as Founts in July, when Wee see each graine of grauell. **1653** WALTON *Angler* i. 22 The Cuttle-fish, being then hid in the gravel, lets the smaller fish nibble and bite the end of it. **1679–88** *Secr. Serv. Money Chas. & Jas.* (Camden) 105 [Amount paid] for the carting of gravel..and laying the gravell upon the walks in St. James's Park. **1710** STEELE *Tatler* No. 179 ⁋8 A spacious Walk of the finest Gravel. **1756–7** tr. *Keysler's Trav.* (1760) II. 431 There is one great defect in the Italian gardens, viz. the want of gravel for the walks. **1799** *Med. Jrnl.* I. 258 The soil consists chiefly of rich clay, loam, and sharp gravel. **1813** BAKEWELL *Introd. Geol.* (1815) 253 Gravel is evidently an alluvial production. **1833** LYELL *Princ. Geol.* III. 146 During the gradual rise of a large area..several kinds of superficial gravel must be formed. **1872** R. B. SMYTH *Mining Statist.* 34 Strata of gravel and coarse sands. **1886** W. HOOPER *Sk. Acad. Life* (Durham) 38 The fragment may be utterly pounded down, till it becomes gravel or even sand.

b. *fig.* and in allusions to Prov. xx. 17.

c **1440** *Jacob's Well* (E.E.T.S.) 282 Takyth a spade, & deluyth out þis grauel of obstinacye fro þe herte, tunge, & dede. **1535** COVERDALE *Prov.* xx. 17 Euery man liketh the bred that is gotten with disceate, but at the last is mouth shalbe fylled with grauell. **1597** HOOKER *Eccl. Pol.* v. lxii. §16 Shall this be thought to turne cælestiall bread into grauell? **1605** BP. HALL *Medit. & Vowes* II. §77, I will not envie the gravell in the unjust mans throte. *a* **1639** W. WHATELEY *Prototypes* III. xxxix. (1640) 19 Wealth gotten by grinding the poore, shall never prove good meale. God will mixe it with gravell to them that eate it. **1649** BP. HALL *Cases Consc.* (1650) 19 What you thus get is but stolne goods..and will prove at the last no other than gravell in your throat.

c. *Geol.* and *Mining.* A stratum of this material, *esp.* one that contains gold. ***pay gravel***: gravel containing gold enough to yield a profit.

1849 MURCHISON *Siluria* xix. 473 The various ages of golden gravels or Drifts. **1872** RAYMOND *Statist. Mines & Mining* 81 Several companies..are taking out pay gravel. Webster & Co...have struck gravel from 2 feet to 6 feet in thickness which prospects very rich. **1876** WHITNEY in *Encycl. Brit.* IV. 701/2 It was not long before it was discovered that the so-called 'high-gravels'—that is, the detrital deposits of Tertiary age—contained gold. **1882** *Rep. to Ho. Repr. Prec. Met. U.S.* 622 *Gravel.*—The term refers to the water-worn pebbles or bowlders which occur generally as a more or less compact conglomerate, immediately overlying the bed-rock. *Ibid.* 623 The term red gravel is given to the brownish or reddish colored conglomerate which forms the top and overlies the blue gravel.

3. *U.S.* = BALLAST 5. (See quot.)

1868 LOSSING *Hudson* 280 Many vessels are employed in carrying away lime, limestone, and 'gravel' (pulverized limestone, not fit for the kiln). [Cf. *gravel-car, -train* in 8.]

4. *Path.* A term applied to aggregations of urinary crystals which can be recognized as masses by the naked eye (as distinguished from *sand*); also, the disease of which these are characteristic. 'Also popularly used to indicate pain or difficulty in passing urine with or without any deposit' (*Syd. Soc. Lex.* 1886).

c **1400** *Lanfranc's Cirurg.* 274 If þe grauel of his vrine be whit: þan þe stoon is in þe bladdre. **15..** *Almanak for 1386*, 24 Rede gravel bytokens ache, and þe stoon in þe raynes. **15..** in *More's Wks.* 1434, I had a while talked with him..of his diseases bothe in his brest of olde, & his reynes nowe, by reason of grauel and stone. ? *a* **1550** *Freiris Berwik* 40 in *Dunbar's Poems* (1893) 286 For he wes awld, and micht nocht wele travell, And als he had ane littill spyce of gravell. **1655** CULPEPPER *Riverius* XIV. ii. 379 The Spaniards void much Gravel, and yet are not subject to the stone. **1709** STEELE *Tatler* No. 89 ⁋8, I am very much afflicted with the Gravel. **1796** MORSE *Amer. Geog.* II. 351 Those [waters] of St. Amand cure the gravel and obstructions. **1846** J. BAXTER *Libr. Pract. Agric.* (ed. 4) I. 74 Afflicted with symptoms of gravel, and other calculous affections. **1874** VON BUREN *Dis. Genit. Org.* 357 Gravel is more frequently seen in summer than at other seasons, on account of the greater activity of the skin.

†**5.** *Farriery.* = GRAVELLING *vbl. sb.* 2. *Obs.*

1675 *Lond. Gaz.* No. 988/4 Stolen..A Coal black Nag.. the further Foot before his Hoof is cut for a Gravel.

6. *Brewing.* Applied to yeast-cells swimming in beer with the appearance of fine gravel.

1882 tr. *Thausing's Beer* II. §2. ii. 596 It is a bad sign if the beer..is not transparent, when it has an appearance as if a veil was drawn over it, when no 'gravel' can be perceived.

7. *Financial slang.* (See quot.)

1884 *Pall Mall G.* 2 Feb. 5/1 A result of the appearance of *gravel*, as the phrase is when the supply of money in the market is growing bare.

8. *attrib.* and *Comb.* **a.** simple attributive, as (senses 2a, c) ***gravel-bank, bar, -bed, -claim, -deposit, -diggings, -drive, -ground*** (also attrib.), ***-heap***, †***-heart*** (fig.), ***-mill, -mine, -mining, -path, -place, -soil, -spit, -sweep, -terrace, -working***; (sense 3) ***gravel-car, -train***; **b.** parasynthetic, as ***gravel-pathed, -bottomed*** adjs.; **c.** instrumental, as ***gravel-spread, -strewn*** adjs.

1877 RAYMOND *Statist. Mines & Mining* 122 There being ..no cemented strata to obstruct the washing down of the *gravel-banks. **1821** T. NUTTALL *Jrnl. Trav. Arkansa* vii. 136 Four miles above Dardennes commences the first *gravel-bar, accompanied by very rapid water. **1968** R. M. PATTERSON *Finlay's River* 20 We followed the trail through the water-lilies and slipped over the last gravel bar into the little stream that calls itself the Crooked River. **1852** C. W. HOSKINS *Talpa* 202 It broke away into a perfect *gravel-bed. **1864** J. A. GRANT *Walk across Africa* 38 Clear, *gravel-bottomed river M'gazee. **1960** *Times* 13 Feb. 9/4 Clean gravel-bottomed reaches..will also yield good quality roach. **1875** KNIGHT *Dict. Mech.*, *Gravel-car, a railway ballast-wagon. **1882** *Rep. to Ho. Repr. Prec. Met. U.S.* 12 Permitting the development of the *gravel claims. **1873** J. GEIKIE *Gt. Ice Age* (1894) 559 In the deep and broad valleys so formed we encounter a second series of *gravel deposits. **1877** RAYMOND *Statist. Mines & Mining* 35 There are about forty acres on this claim, all rich *gravel-diggings. *a* **1450** *Fysshynge w. Angle* (1883) 22 He [the trout] wyl not be but yn cleyn *grauel grounde watur and yn a streme. **1632** SHERWOOD, A *gravell-heape, *gravoir*. **1603** SHAKS. *Meas. for M.* IV. iii. 68 Unfit to liue, or die: oh *grauell heart. **1882** *Rep. to Ho. Repr. Prec. Met. U.S.* 624 The gravel must then be crushed in a *gravel mill. **1881** RAYMOND *Mining Gloss.*, *Gravel-mine*, U.S. An accumulation of auriferous gravel. **1882** *Rep. to Ho. Repr. Prec. Met. U.S.* 13 Two of the principal gravel mines in the State. **1877** RAYMOND *Statist. Mines & Mining* 93 The extensive *gravel-mining operations of Nevada County. **1840** DICKENS *Old C. Shop* xvi, The old man and the child quitted the *gravel path. **1898** *Month* Nov. 482 A trim *gravel-pathed garden. **1580** HOLLYBAND *Treas. Fr. Tong*, *Vne sablonnière*, a *grauell place. **1897** OMOND *Fletcher of Saltoun* vi. 86 The *gravel soil, and the salubrious climate [of London]. **1874** GREEN *Short Hist.* i. §2. 8 The little *gravel-spit of Ebbsfleet. **1855** TENNYSON *Daisy* 34 Where oleanders flush'd the bed Of silent torrents, *gravel-spread. **1927** W. G. KENDREW *Clim. Cont.* (ed. 2) 241 The rivers, whose beds, dry, wide, and *gravel-strewn in summer, often become filled in a few hours in winter by swollen torrents. **1810** *Splendid Follies* II. 104 The Ellercott family drove round the *gravel sweep of Mistley Manor. **1888** J. PAYN *Myst. Mirbridge* III. xl. 120 The noise of wheels and hoofs upon the gravel-sweep. **1873** J. GEIKIE *Gt. Ice Age* (1894) 514 The low-level *gravel-terraces and moraines of the inner zone. **1881** *Chicago Times* 18 June, The *gravel train was backing up the track. **1881** 'MARK TWAIN' *Tramp Abr.* xxxvi. 375, I have not jumped to this conclusion; I have travelled to it per gravel train, so to speak. **1882** *Rep. to Ho. Repr. Prec. Met. U.S.* 641 The cars and track used in the *gravel workings.

9. Special comb.: **gravel-brook**, a brook that flows over a gravel-bed; **gravel court**, a lawn-tennis court with a gravel surface; **gravel-crusher, -crushing** *ppl. a.*, *slang* (see quots.); **gravel culture**, a hydroponic method of plant cultivation, using beds of gravel supplied with nutrient solutions; **gravel eye, -eyed** adj. (see quot. 1951); **gravel-grass**, *Galium verum* (*Syd. Soc. Lex.* 1886); **gravel-plant**, *Epigæa repens* (*Syd. Soc. Lex.* 1886); **gravel-powder**, 'coarse gunpowder, otherwise known as pebble-powder' (Knight *Dict. Mech.* Suppl. 1884); **gravel-rash** *colloq.*, abrasions caused by a fall on a gravelly or rugged surface; **gravel-root**, *Eupatorium purpureum* (*Treas. Bot.* 1866);

gravel-throated *a.* = *gravel-voiced*; **gravel voice**, a thick, husky voice; so **gravel-voiced** *a.*

1591 *Troub. Raigne K. John* II. (1611) 85 Here are my proofes, as cleere as *grauel brooke. **1890** C. G. Heathcote *Lawn Tennis* xv. 294 *Gravel courts, though at first sight attractive, have many serious defects. **1934** T. S. Eliot *Rock* i. 30 In the land of lobelias and tennis flannels.. The nettle shall flourish on the gravel court. **1889** Barrère & Leland *Dict. Slang* *Gravel-crusher* (military), a soldier compelled to tramp about a square at defaulter's drill. **1901** *Daily News* 9 Jan. 5/2 The 'gravel-crushers' (as the dismounted service is generically known). **1918** E. S. Farrow *Dict. Mil. Terms, Gravel crushers*, a slang expression equivalent to doughboy or infantry soldier, and the French *fiflot*. **1948** Partridge *Dict. Forces' Slang* 86 *Gravel-crusher*, a Drill Instructor; a P.T. Instructor. (Mostly Air Force.) **1900** *Kynoch Jrnl.* Feb.–Mar. 63/2 Cyclists.. act more in conjunction with and as the eyes of their *gravel-crushing comrades. [**1936** Withrow & Biebel in *Jrnl. Agric. Res.* LIII. 697 Fine gravel.. appears to be the most suitable for this type of culture.] **1940** A. Laurie *Soilless Culture Simplified* viii. 136 The advantage often claimed for sand or *gravel culture—that of increased production—can easily be overstressed. **1942** Laurie & Ries *Floriculture* v. 104 If flat-bottomed concrete benches have already been built, they can be converted to gravel culture. **1966** *New Scientist* 23 June 784/3 Gravel culture may also open possibilities for basic food production in malnourished countries. **1855** *Poultry Chron.* III. 9/1 The Suabian Pigeons.. have generally a turned crown, *gravel eye, and clean feet. **1879** L. Wright *Pract. Pigeon Keeper* 101 An altogether red, gravel, or orange eye is a decided fault. **1951** E. Haedy *A–Z Pigeon Guide* 71 *Gravel-eyed*, white or pearl eye with red mixed in it. **1860** *Slang Dict.*, *Gravel-rash, a scratched face,—telling its tale of a drunken fall. **1891** *Standard* 21 Oct. 3/1, I admitted him and then saw he had the gravel-rash. [**1942** Berrey & Van den Bark *Amer. Thes. Slang* §188.7 *Gravel-throat*, a granular enunciation. *Ibid.* §422.9 *Gravel-throat*, one with a husky granular voice.] **1955** *Jazzbook 1955* 45 Joseph 'De De' Pierce, *gravel-throated vocalist. **1962** K. Orvis *Damned & Destroyed* viii. 157 A gravel-throated switchboard cop. **1947** *Time* 24 Nov. 29 The very sound of Earl Long's *gravel voice. **1958** *Times* 5 July 4/1 The umpire's voice echoed the gravel voice on the radio which tells us what 'the next object will be' in a parlour game. **1947** *Time* 29 Dec. 15 *Gravel-voiced Joe Curran, president of the National Maritime Union. **1952** *Ibid.* 2 June 46/2 When *Collier's* hired gravel-voiced Louis Ruppel as editor three years ago, it knew it was buying a whirl-wind. **1963** *Daily Tel.* 25 Nov. 1/2 Dallas's detective chief, Capt. Will Fritz, a gravel-voiced Texan who sports a white cowboy hat.

gravel ('grævəl), *v.* [f. prec. sb.]

1. a. *trans.* To cover, lay, or strew (a street, etc.) with gravel or sand. †Also, to sprinkle (a newly-written document) with sand (*obs.*).

1543 *Churchw. Acc. St. Giles, Reading* 67 For Amerciamentes for Cristyne Mores hous because it was not gravelled iiij*d*. **1549** Wriothesley *Chron.* (1877) II. 29 All the streates of the City of London beinge gravelled. **1607** Tourneur *Rev. Trag.* I. iii. Wks. 1878 II. 27 And in a world of Acres Not so much dust due to the heire t'was left to, As would well grauell a petition. **1661** Pepys *Diary* 22 Apr., The streets all gravelled, and the houses hung with carpets before them, made brave show. **1712** J. James tr. *Le Blond's Gardening* 45 This Way of Gravelling and Beating Walks. **1753** in Picton *L'pool Munic. Rec.* (1886) II. 137 That the Public Walk.. be repaired and gravell'd. **1833** Ht. Martineau *Briery Creek* ii. 44 Half of it [the bridge] is prettily gravelled. **1841** Marryat *Poacher* xxvii, The road was newly-gravelled.

†b. To smother or choke with gravel or sand; also with *up*: *lit.* and *fig.* *Obs.*

1602 Fulbecke *2nd Pt. Parall.* 74, I see your inuention and memorie are not grauelled nor dryed vp, parched as it were with summers drought. **1635** Quarles *Embl.* I. vii. 5 O thou the fountain of whose better part Is earth'd, and gravell'd up with vain desire. **1669** Worlidge *Syst. Agric.* (1681) 274 Now leave off watring your Meadows, lest you gravel or rot your Grass. **1686** R. P. in *Phil. Trans.* XX. 383 The Towns have either of them a great Beck (as we call it) or Current of Water running through them, which by the first Flood were gravel'd up.

†c. To injure with grit or sand. *Obs.*

1608 Armin *Nest Ninn.* (1880) 45, I fearefull presume not to looke into the milstone, least I grauell my eye sight.

†2. To bury in gravel or sand; to overwhelm with gravel; hence *fig.* to suppress, stifle. *Obs.*

1577–87 Holinshed *Chron.* II. 29/2 The dead bodies need not in that Iland to be gravelled. **1583** Stanyhurst *Æneis* IV. (Arb.) 106 Graueling in his hert [L. *sub corde premebat*] his sorroful anguish. **1686** R. P. in *Phil. Trans.* XX. 382 Several Houses were quite demolished, and not a Stone left; others gravel'd to the Chamber-Windows.

†3. To run (a ship) aground on the gravel or beach, mud, etc. Also, in *passive*, of a person: To be set fast in sand or mud. *Obs.*

1582 N. T. (Rhem.) *Acts* xxvii. 41 When we were fallen into a place betwene two seas, they graveled the ship. **1597–8** Bp. Hall *Sat.* III. vi. 14 Till the blacke Carauell Stands still fast grauel'd on the mud of hell. **1605** Camden *Rem., Wise Sp.* 189 William Conquerour when he invaded this Iland, chanced at his arrivall to be graveled, and one of his feet stacke so fast in the sand, that he fell to the ground. **1660** F. Brooke tr. *Le Blanc's Trav.* 271 Our Almadie was so fast gravell'd, we were forced to unload.

fig. **1594** Nashe *Unfort. Trav.* 21 So grounded and grauelled were they in this opinion. **1596** —— *Saffron Walden* 96 At a Commensment dinner.. he graueld and set a ground both him and his brother. **1606** Ford *Honor Tri.* (1843) 25 Ere I wade further, and be grauel'd in the owze, and quicksand of my own intention. *a* **1610** Healey *Cebes* (1636) 167 They are so graueled in the quick-sands of erroneous ignorance. **1613** Wither *Abuses Stript & Whipt* Occas. this Wk. 90, I was gravell'd, like a ship that's grounded. **1648** Earl Westmoreland *Otia Sacra* (1879) 78 A great Professor, Master of Israel, once was gravelled Upon that Shelf. **1682** Norris tr. *Hierocles* Pref. *a* 3 Whosoever denies the possibility.. must necessarily gravel himself upon one of these Absurdities.

4. *fig.* but without explicit reference to 3. **a.** To set fast, confound, embarrass, non-plus, perplex, puzzle.

1548 *Detect. Unskil. Physic.* Pref. 2 in Recorde *Urin. Physick* (1651), He is much troubled.. for his being graveld at what is wrote against Aristotle. **1566** Drant *Horace's Sat.* I. x. E v, As yf some passyng man shoulde.. sweate agayne to grauayle thee. *c* **1590** Marlowe *Faust.* i. 111, I.. have with concise syllogisms Gravell'd the pastors of the German church. **1600** Shaks. *A.Y.L.* IV. i. 74 Nay, you were better speake first, and when you were grauel'd for lacke of matter, you might take occasion to kisse. *a* **1617** Hieron *Penance for Sinne* Wks. 1619 II. 168 Nicodemus, a Pharise by profession and breed, is grauelled in the Doctrine of Regeneration. **1638** Laud *Wks.* (1853) V. 213 Not propounding studied subtilties to gravel and discourage young students. **1662** J. Davies tr. *Olearius' Voy. Ambass.* 106 He.. would not speak the Muscovian, but the Polish language, purposely to gravel the other. **1672** Marvell *Reh. Transp.* I. 30 The Surveyor was gravell'd, being asked whence that City should be supplied with water. **1706** Stanhope *Paraphr.* III. 162 Such is that Passage by which our Saviour gravell'd the Scribes and Pharisees. **1741** Watts *Improv. Mind* I. xiii. §18 To manage his argument so well as to puzzle and gravel the respondent. **1768–74** Tucker *Lt. Nat.* (1852) II. 118 The free-thinker.. is not so prone to anger as the bigot, except now and then when gravelled in argument. **1796** Coleridge *Poems, Fire, Famine & Slaughter* Pref., The subtle and witty atheist that so grievously perplexed and gravelled him [Bishop Hall]. **1841–4** Emerson *Ess., Intellect* Wks. (Bohn.) I. 135 The wisest doctor is gravelled by the inquisitiveness of a child. **1850** Whipple *Ess. & Rev.* (ed. 3) I. 105 We might hear.. Socrates gravel a sophist with his interrogative logic. **1862** *Sat. Rev.* 5 July 23 It imparts a certain air of connexion and design, where the writer is gravelled for want of either.

b. Of a question, difficulty, practice, subject of discussion, etc.: To prove embarrassing to; to confound, perplex, puzzle. Also *U.S.* To irritate, to 'go against the grain with'.

1601 Dent *Pathw. Heaven* 254 This question would grauell a great number. **1633** Hart *Diet of Diseased* I. ix. 33 Foure, or five daies abstinence, either from meate or drinke, will gravell most men and women. **1681** R. Wittie *Surv. Heavens* 18 A ready Answer.. to the difficulties that gravel others about this stupendous Motion of the Sun. **1710** Berkeley *Princ. Hum. Knowl.* I. §97 It will perhaps gravel even a philosopher to comprehend it. **1794** Burns *Let. to G. Thomson* 19 Oct., These English songs gravel me to death. **1871** Hay *Banty Tim* 15 It gravels me like the devil to train Along o' sich fools as you. **1883** 'Mark Twain' *Life Mississippi* xiv. 138 It 'gravels' me, to this day, to put my will in the weak form of a request, instead of launching it in the crisp language of an order. **1886** Lowell *Lett.* (1894) II. 321, I wasn't thinking so much of the studies as of the method of teaching.. when I wrote what gravels you.

5. *Farriery.* in *passive* and *intr.* Of a horse, or its feet: To be injured by particles of gravel or sand being forced between the shoe and the hoof.

1593 *Steward's Acc. Shuttleworths* Sept. (Chetham Soc.) I. 100 Dressing of a mare foot, gravelled at Lostoke, iij*d*. **1593** G. Giffard *Dial. Witches* (1843) 118, I would carie him to the smith to search if he were not pricked or graveld. **1657** H. Crowch *Welsh Trav.* 15 His blistered feet were gravelled. **1688** *Lond. Gaz.* No. 2411/4 One black Mare,.. above 14 hands, and has been gravel'd of her neare Foot. **1710** *Ibid.* No. 4674/8 The near Foot before pared very near towards the Heel, having been gravelled. **1737** Bracken *Farriery-Impr.* (1756) I. 352 By such injudicious Practice the Horse often gravels.

6. *intr.* = dust *v.*[1] 3 b.

1870 D. P. Blaine *Encycl. Rur. Sports* §2618 Where they [*sc.* partridges] bask at noontide, and where they preen, scratch, and gravel.

7. (See quot.)

1902 C. J. Cornish *Naturalist on Thames* 216 In winter the eelman goes 'gravelling', that is, scooping up gravel from the bottom to deepen any part of the channel.

gravel-blind, *a.* Orig. *high-gravel-blind*, in Shaks. a jocular intensive synonym for sand-blind. Hence used by later writers for 'nearly stone-blind'. Also *fig.*

1596 Shaks. *Merch. V.* II. ii. 38 This is my true begotten Father, who being more than sand-blinde, high grauel-blinde, knows me not. **1818** Scott *Hrt. Midl.* xxxi, One old woman, who, being nearly 'high-gravel blind', was only conscious that something very fine and glittering was passing by. **1841** Prescott in Ticknor *Life* (1864) 95 *note*, Pity that his love for the ancients made him high gravel-blind to the merits of the moderns. **1845** Hood *Tim Turpin* 1 Tim Turpin he was gravel blind. **1887** E. Gilliat *Forest Outlaws* 240 There be a power of signs to tell us what's coming, if we were not gravel-blind.

graveless ('greɪvlɪs), *a.* [f. grave *sb.*[1] + -less.] Having no grave; devoid of graves.

1606 Shaks. *Ant. & Cl.* III. xiii. 166 Till.. my braue Egyptians all.. Lye grauelesse. **1855** T. Guthrie *Ezekiel* (1856) 335 There is a griefless, graveless land. **1864** Neale *Seaton. Poems* 18 Their graveless bones are left to bleach.

†gravelin. *Obs. rare*$^{-1}$. ? Some kind of waterfowl; ? = gravell.

1621 *Naworth Househ. Bks.* (Surtees) 169, 5 mallerds and gravelins, xx[d].

graveling ('grævəlɪŋ). Also 9 gravelin, gravelling. [Of obscure origin; OF. had *gravele* as the name of some fish, perh. the minnow.] The parr or young salmon.

1587 Harrison *Descr. Eng.* III. iii. in Holinshed *Chron.* 224 A salmon is the first yeare a grauellin. **1744** *Anc. & Pres. State County Down* 235 A delicate small Fish.. called .. in some Parts a Graveling. **1776** Twiss *Tour Irel.* 97 Roach, lamprey, and jenkins or graveling, which is a species of small trout. **1836** Yarrell *Brit. Fishes* II. 50 The Parr, or Samlet. The terms Brandling, Fingerling, Skirling, Gravelling.. &c. .. referring either to some quality or habit observed in other species. **1861** *Act 24 & 25 Vict.* c. 109 §4 All migratory fish of the genus salmon, whether known by the names.. gravelling, shed, scad.. or by any other local name.

gravelish ('grævəlɪʃ), *a.* [f. gravel *sb.* + -ish.]

1. Of the nature of gravel; containing an admixture of gravel.

1530 Palsgr. 314/2 Gravelysshe belongyng to the nature of gravell, *areneux*. **1649** Blithe *Eng. Improv. Impr.* xxxv. (1653) 228 Very warm earth, either a little gravellish or sandish. **1806** *Gazetteer Scotl.* (ed. 2) 328 The soil is light, shallow, and gravellish, but tolerably fertile.

2. Resembling, or indicative of, the disease called gravel.

1757 Whytt in *Phil. Trans.* L. 214 In February 1737 he began to take soap; and after 1743 never had any gravelish symptoms. **1789** Saunders *Ibid.* LXXIX. 105 Gravelish complaints.. are.. unknown here. **1806** Forsyth *Beauties Scotl.* IV. 412 The waters.. are of great service in gravelish, scorbutic, and scrophulous affections. **1831** Sir J. Sinclair *Corr.* II. 437, I am sorry to find.. that you continue troubled with gravelish complaints.

†gravell. *Obs. rare*$^{-1}$. Also **grevell**. ? Some kind of waterfowl; ? = gravelin.

1618 *Naworth Househ. Bks.* (Surtees) 79, 2 gray hens, a grevell and a teele, xiiij[d]. **1622** *Ibid.* 191 A gravell and a woodcock, vij[d].

gravelled ('grævəld), *ppl. a.* [f. gravel *v.* (? and *sb.*) + -ed.]

1. Covered or laid with gravel; †consisting of gravel.

1400–1507 *Churchw. Acc., St. Mary Hill, Lond.* (Nichols 1797) 90 The Procession church yard with its gravelled causey. **1563** Hyll *Art Garden.* II. lvi. (1608) 141 The Radish in no wise agreeth to be sowen either in a sandy or grauelled ground. **1597** Tofte *Laura* in *Alba* (1880) Introd. 41 And venter for to sayle in th' Ocean strong, Though now on graueld shore it fearfull staies. **1712** *Order* 1 July in *Lond. Gaz.* No. 5028/1 The South side of the Gravelled Coach Road. **1813** Scott *Trierm.* II. Interlude ii, And grant the lounger seldom strays Beyond the smooth and gravell'd maze. **1840** Dickens *Barn. Rudge* lviii, He was taken handcuffed across the gravelled area. **1888** E. J. Goodman *Too Curious* iv, A gravelled path led from the outer gate.

2. In various transf. and fig. senses. **a.** Perplexed, puzzled. **†b.** Of a ship: Beached, stranded. **†c.** Of a horse: (see gravel *v.* 5). **†d.** *gravelled ashes* (see quot. 1706: = F. *cendre gravelée*).

1579 J. Field *Calvin's Serm.* Ded., Receiuing nothing but that which standeth to the lyking of their humors & graueled consciences. **1611** Cotgr., *Aggravé*,.. also, grauelled, or, as a ship, fast on the ground. **1630** J. Taylor (Water P.) *Wks.* I. 90/1 The Pricke in the sole, the Loose in Hoofe, the Graueld, the Foundring, and the Shedding of the haire. **1660** Hexham *Netherdutch Dict.*, A Gravelled horse, *een verstijft paerde*. **1706** Phillips (ed. Kersey), *Gravelled Ashes*, (among Chymists) the Lees of Wine dry'd and burnt to Ashes. **1736** Bailey *Househ. Dict.* 44 Fill a kettle or stew-pan half full of water, into which put.. a penny-worth or two of Gravelled-Ashes. **1865** Dickens *Mut. Fr.* II. IV. xii. 262 He never did know such a move,.. he never had been so gravelled. **1967** *Listener* 7 Dec. 763/2 Sir Francis Chichester, temporarily gravelled for an admired man of the past, appealed to the studio audience for names.

e. Of a voice: cf. *gravel voice*.

1958 *Listener* 26 June 1071/2 A gravelled voice with superb powers of timing.

'graveller. *rare*$^{-1}$. [f. gravel *v.* + -er[1].] A proposition that 'gravels' one, a 'poser'.

1674 Fairfax *Bulk & Selv.* 106 For so he takes off the graveller, *Indivisibile junctum indivisibili non facit majus*.

gravelling ('grævəlɪŋ), *vbl. sb.* [f. gravel *v.* + -ing[1].]

1. The action of laying down gravel. Also, a gravelled surface.

1577 *Nottingham Rec.* IV. 169 We present ye caussey.. to be in dekye for lack of gravelyng. **1659** Torriano, *Arenaménto*, any gravelling or sanding. **1726** W. King in *Nat. Hist. Irel.* 111 Gravelling is a great improvement in this country. **1751** Labelye *Westm. Br.* 26 This Bridge (its Paving and Gravelling excepted) will want no considerable Repairs. **1883** W. H. Bishop in *Harper's Mag.* 825/2 What cutting and filling! what gravelling and paving!

†2. *Farriery.* A disease in a horse's foot (see gravel *v.* 5). *Obs.*

1523 Fitzherb. *Husb.* §114 Grauelynge is a hurte, that wyll make a horse to halte, and commethe of grauell and lyttell stones, that goth in betwene the shough and the herte of the fote. **1580** Blundevil *Order Curing Horses Dis.* cxliv. 62 b, The Graueling.. is a fretting vnder the foote most commonlie in the inside, and sometime in the outside. **1639** T. de Gray *Compl. Horsem.* 107 Prick, stab, graveling, quitterbone, or other hurt within the foote. **1706** in Phillips (ed. Kersey). **1727–41** in Chambers *Cycl.*

gravelling ('grævəlɪŋ), *ppl. a.* [f. gravel *v.* + -ing[2].] Puzzling; perplexing.

1686 Goad *Celest. Bodies* II. vii. 248 Men shall never give an account of these Great Questions if they deny our Influences,.. the Question is so gravelling. **1691** Norris *Pract. Disc.* 206 The most gravelling Problem of all the Heathen Philosophy. **1720** Wodrow *Life Bruce* (1843) 64 This was one of the most gravelling things Mr. Bruce had met with.

gravelly ('grævəlɪ), *a.* [GRAVEL *sb.* + -Y[1].]

1. † **a.** Abounding in sand; sandy (*obs.*). **b.** Full of or abounding in gravel; consisting of or containing gravel; strewn with gravel. Also, resembling gravel.

1382 WYCLIF *Ecclus.* xxv. 27 As a graueli steeȝing vp [Vulg. *sicut ascensus arenosus*]. **1398** TREVISA *Barth. De P.R.* XVII. clxxx. (1495) 721 In grauely londes and to lene the vyne ouerdryeth and faylleth. *c* **1400** MAUNDEV. (1839) xiii. 150 The See that men clepen the gravely See. **1578** LYTE *Dodoens* I. iii. 8 The wilde groweth..in barren soyle and grauelly grounde. **1590** BARROUGH *Meth. Physick* 239 He must vse fishes of grauelly waters. **1606** BIRNIE *Kirk-Buriall* (1833) 3 Sown in corruption, dishonour, and weaknes, in the grauely fielde of the graue. **1609** BIBLE (Douay) *Ecclus.* xxv. 27 As the goeing up a gravelie [**1611** sandy] way. **1677** PLOT *Oxfordsh.* 94 Filled with a kind of gravelly earth. **1713** DERHAM *Phys. Theol.* III. ii. Note vi, The Sand was at last so gravelly, that it hinder'd our boring any deeper. **1774** GOLDSM. *Nat. Hist.* (1862) I. vi. 31 Gravelly marble. **1807** G. CHALMERS *Caledonia* I. I. iii. 105 A Roman cinereal urn of a gravelly brown earth. **1830-3** LYELL *Princ. Geol.* (1875) II. III. xl. 375 Certain species prefer a sandy, others a gravelly, and some a muddy sea-bottom. **1847** J. WILSON *Chr. North* (1857) II. 21 The large trouts came to the gravelly shallows. **1873** J. GEIKIE *Gt. Ice Age* xi. 146 Yellowish gravelly sand.

2. *Path.* Of the nature of gravel (see GRAVEL *sb.* 4); characterized by, or arising from, the presence of gravel. (Cf. GRAVELISH.)

1607 TOPSELL *Four-f. Beasts* (1658) 536 They make an emplaister of Bacon to scatter gravelly matter in the bladder. **1743** DR. BANYER in *Phil. Trans.* XLII. 633 The Treatment of a gravelly Case. **1793** BEDDOES *Calculus* 20 He had been perfectly free from any gravelly symptoms till within a few weeks. **1807** VANCOUVER *Agric. Devon* (1813) 420 Consumptive and gravelly cases were more frequently heard of in different parts of this district. **1897** *Allbutt's Syst. Med.* III. 162 Seldom or almost never do gravelly paroxysms coincide with the arthritic paroxysms.

† **3.** Containing gritty particles. *Obs.*

a **1640** DAY *Parl. Bees* II. (1881) 20 An almes that by a Niggards hand is serv'd Is mold and gravelly bread. **1727** BRADLEY *Fam. Dict.*, *Gravelly*, a Term used concerning certain Pears, which..have a kind of small Stones or Gravel in them, especially towards the Core; thus they say the great Musk is too gravelly.

4. *Financial slang.* (Cf. GRAVEL *sb.* 7.)

1887 ATKINS *House Scraps* 15 Stock Exchange Idioms:—Getting gravelly here.

5. *transf.* Of a voice (cf. *gravel voice*).

1944 *Harper's Mag.* June 38/1 The tired, imperturbable man aboard the carrier flagship called his orders over the gravelly-voiced TBS (talk between ships). **1958** *Listener* 7 Aug. 203/1 Sunderland's gravelly voice insinuating that they were all a dead loss. **1959** 'F. NEWTON' *Jazz Scene* vii. 135 The gravelly and expressive voice of the great Louis Armstrong. **1971** *Daily Tel.* 13 Oct. 15/3 William Costello ..provided the gravelly voice of Popeye the sailor in film cartoons.

Hence '**gravelliness**, gravelly quality.

1649 BLITHE *Eng. Improv. Impr.* (1653) 9 Another cause [of the earth's barrenness] is Rockiness, Stoniness, and Gravelliness.

† '**gravelous**, *a. Obs.* [a. F. *graveleux* (14th c. in Hatz.-Darm.), f. *gravele* GRAVEL *sb.*: see -OUS.] **a.** Abounding in gravel; gravelly. **b.** Resembling grains of gravel or sand; granular.

c **1420** *Pallad. on Husb.* III. 612 Welwrought faat lond they loue, And sondy, cleyi, grauelous they lothe. **1541** R. COPLAND *Guydon's Quest. Chirurg.* Rj, Loke on the flesshe that abydeth in the cloute and yf it be graueylous and troublous it is a great token. **1758** J. S. *Le Dran's Observ. Surg.* (1771) 259 This gravellous Abscess.

'**gravel-pit.** An excavation from which gravel (or †sand) is or has been obtained.

c **1440** *Promp. Parv.* 207/2 Gravel pytte, *arenarium.* **1611** TOURNEUR *Ath. Trag.* II. iv. Wks. 1878 I. 54 Hee's fall'n into the grauell-pit. **1683** *Lond. Gaz.* No. 1786/4 Stolen or Strayed out of the Grounds near Kensington Gravel-pits, a fine shaped brown Mare. **1878** HUXLEY *Physiogr.* Pref. 7 The gravel pit whence the roads are mended.

'**gravel-stone.** [f. GRAVEL *sb.* + STONE *sb.*]

1. One of the stones of which gravel is mainly composed; a pebble. Also *fig.*

c **1440** *Jacob's Well* (E.E.T.S.) 304 þise grauelstonys, þat is, coueytous thoutys..arn so scharpe & hevy as grauel. **1535** COVERDALE *Isa.* xlviii. 19 Thy sede shal be like as the sonde in the see, & the frute of thy body like the grauel stones thereof. **1650** JER. TAYLOR *Funeral Serm. C'tess Carbery* 4 The unevenness of a gravel-stone. **1697** DRYDEN *Virg. Georg.* IV. 286 Bees bear Gravel Stones, whose poising Weight Steers thro' the whistling Wind their steddy Flight. **1795** ANDERSON *Narr. Brit. Emb. China* viii. 99 The lateral parts are laid with gravel stones. **1849** JAMES *Woodman* vii, Mingled with small gravel stones and thick loam.

† **2.** A kind of stone, having the appearance of consolidated gravel; ? conglomerate. *Obs.*

1715 LEONI *Palladio's Archit.* (1742) I. 91 Stone, or Gravel-stone, or any soft Stone.

† **3.** = CALCULUS I. *Obs.*

1606 HOLLAND *Sueton.* 74 Voiding at length little gravell-stones by urine, he was eased of that paine.

gravel-walk. An alley or path in a garden or pleasure-ground, laid with gravel.

1663 GERBIER *Counsel* gj a, Gravell walkes. **1782** V. KNOX *Ess.* lxxv. I. 323 My garden was laid out in gravel walks, intersecting each other at right angles. **1849** LYTTON *Caxtons* 39 Divided by three winding gravel walks. **1859** JEPHSON *Brittany* iii. 28 The quadrangle is laid out in grass-plats and gravel-walks.

gravely ('greɪvlɪ), *adv.* [f. GRAVE *a.*[1] (*sb.*[1]) + -LY[2].] In a grave manner.

1. Seriously, soberly, solemnly.

1553 *Bp. Gardiner's True Obed.* Translator to Rdr. A vi, How these incarnate deuils could so aduisedlye, so grauelie, and so confidently say yea than, & so impudently..saie nay now. **1591** LAMBARDE *Archeion* (1635) 125 The Kings alwayes most gravely and considerately repelled that sort of attempt. **1680** OTWAY *Orphan* III. iv. 948 My Lord's not haughty nor imperious Nor I gravely whimsical. *a* **1688** VILLIERS (Dk. Buckhm.) *Chances* IV. ii. (1714) 155 Don Frederick has sent away this Wench, for all he carries it so gravely. **1766** GOLDSM. *Vic. W.* xx, When asked his opinion he would gravely take me aside and ask mine. **1785** REID *Intell. Powers* 36 Would any man think it worth while to reason gravely with such a person? **1828** SCOTT *F.M. Perth* xxxiii, He raised his eyes, and said very gravely, 'My lord in these most melancholy documents' [etc.]. **1856** KANE *Arct. Expl.* II. ix. 97 It makes me write gravely, for I am far from well. **1882** F. W. H. MYERS *Renewal of Youth* 54 With souls rejoicing gravely to rejoice.

† **2.** With dignity. *Obs.*

1596 SHAKS. *1 Hen. IV*, II. iv. 478 If thou do'st it halfe so grauely, so maiestically, both in word and matter, hang me vp by the heeles. **1653** R. SANDERS *Physiogn.* 151 A mocker and insolent, going proudly and gravely. **1697-9** DAMPIER *Voy.* (1702) I. 397 Having paced it gravely about the Streets till 2 or 3 a clock in the Morning, their Idols were carry'd with much Ceremony into the Temple.

3. In an important degree; seriously.

1885 F. TEMPLE *Relat. Relig. & Sci.* vi. 171 The consideration of this incompleteness gravely modifies the conclusion. **1895** F. HALL *Two Trifles* Introd. p. vi, That journal..would be gravely compromised in character.

graven ('greɪv(ə)n), *ppl. a.* [pa. pple. of GRAVE *v.*[1]]

1. Sculptured, hewn.

1382 WYCLIF *Exod.* xx. 4 Thow shalt not mak to thee grauen thing [**1388** a grauen ymage]. **1552** ABP. HAMILTON *Catech.* (1884) 31 Thai quhilkis makis a graven ymage. **1585** T. WASHINGTON tr. *Nicholay's Voy.* II. iii. 33 The foundations..are made of graven stone without morter or playster. **1897** W. WATSON *Hope World*, etc. (1898) 18 A God for ever jealous grown Of carven wood and graven stone.

b. quasi-*sb.* A graven image.

1609 BIBLE (Douay) *Ps.* lxxvii. 58 In their gravens [Vulg. *in sculptilibus suis*] they provoked him to emulation.

2. Carved on a surface, engraved.

1821 JOANNA BAILLIE *Metr. Leg.*, *Columbus* lviii, Some ardent youth..will..Read fondly o'er and o'er his graven name. **1863** P. S. WORSLEY *Poems & Transl.* 8 Huge valves, embossed with graven gold. **1871** R. ELLIS tr. *Catullus* xxv. 7 The rings from Thynia quaintly graven.

graveness ('greɪvnɪs). [f. GRAVE *a.*[1] (*sb.*[1]) + -NESS.] The quality or state of being grave; seriousness, solemnity and sobriety of behaviour; gravity.

1577-87 HOLINSHED *Chron.* I. 18/1 Grauenesse in countenance, and shew of apparell. **1606** MARSTON *Fawne* III. Wks. 1856 II. 62 Your once steady gravenes. **1655** CULPEPPER *Riverius* I. vii. 29 Graveness of actions. **1719** D'URFEY *Pills* II. 318 A graveness palls the Cupid. **1865** WRIGHT *Hist. Caricature* viii. 138 The graveness and air of importance with which he regards it, would lead us to suppose that the barrel contains wine. **1875** TENNYSON *Q. Mary* v. ii, Had put off levity and put graveness on.

Gravenstein ('grɑːvənʃtaɪn). [The German name for Graasten, a village in Denmark formerly in Schleswig-Holstein, Germany.] A variety of dessert apple, which has large fruit with yellow, red-streaked skin.

1821 *Trans. Hort. Soc. Lond.* IV. 216 Mr. John Wilmot sent specimens of the Gravenstein Apple, the produce of a tree imported from Holland. **1841** J. LINDLEY *Pomologia Britannica* III. 98 What the English call the Gravenstein is an Apple of great merit. **1860** R. HOGG *Fruit Man.* 10 Gravenstein... Large, round, flattened at the ends, and angular... A very valuable apple. **1908** L. M. MONTGOMERY *Anne of Green Gables* xxix. 325 Mr. Harmon Andrews took second prize for Gravenstein apples. **1969** *Oxf. Bk. Food Plants* 52 *'Gravenstein'* is often considered the best flavoured apple in Northern Germany and Denmark. It is a fairly large fruit, its strong sweetness balanced by a marked acidity and a penetrating scent.

† **graveolence, -ency.** *Obs. rare*[−0]. [ad. L. *graveolentia*, f. *graveolent-em* GRAVEOLENT.] A rank, offensive smell.

1623 COCKERAM, *Graueolentie*, a stincking sauour. **1658-78** PHILLIPS, *Graveolence.* **1676** COLES, *Graveolence.* **1696** PHILLIPS, *Graveolencie.* **1727** BAILEY vol. II, *Graveolency.*

graveolent (grə'viːələnt), *a.* [ad. L. *graveolent-em*, *graveolens*, f. *grave*, advb. neut. of *gravis* heavy + *olent-em*, *olens*, pres. pple. of *olēre* to smell.] Having a strong or offensive smell; rank, fetid.

1657 TOMLINSON *Renou's Disp.* 212 Odoraments objected to the nose in great quantity are graveolent. **1669** BOYLE *Contn. New Exp.* II. (1682) 186 The Butter..was yellow and something graveolent, yet it was edible. **1721** in BAILEY. **1755** in JOHNSON. **1833** LYTTON *Eng. & English* II. 236 He strives to buoy himself from 'the graveolent abyss' of his infamy. **1862** G. A. LAWRENCE *Barren Honour* I. 5 Such playful missiles as graveolent eggs. **1875** *Anderida* II. vii. 137 The soul..smelled the graveolent vapours of Avernus.

graver ('greɪvə(r)). Also 5 gravowre. [f. GRAVE *v.*[1] + -ER[1]. Cf. F. *graveur* (14th c. in Hatz.-Darm.).]

† **1.** One who digs or digs up (turf). *Obs.*

1483 *Cath. Angl.* 163/2 A Graver, *cespitator, cultor, fossor.* **1610** *Assessment Wages Norf.* in *Eng. Hist. Rev.* (1898) XIII. 524 A graver of Flaggs & Turfes vd.

2. One who carves or engraves. † **a.** A sculptor.

c **1430** *Freemasonry* 504 Gravers and ymage-makers. **1430-40** LYDG. *Bochas* II. xv. (1494) hj b, Callicrates a grauer moost notable Of white yuor..His hande his iye so iuste were and so stable Of an ampte to graue out the lykenesse. *c* **1440** *Promp. Parv.* 208/2 Gravowre, *sculptor.* *a* **1533** LD. BERNERS *Gold. Bk. M. Aurel.* iv. (1536) 7b, Romulus..honoured greatly grauers in stone. **1585** T. WASHINGTON tr. *Nicholay's Voy.* II. viii. 42 Sonnes of Antherme the most renowned carver and graver of Images. **1601** HOLLAND *Pliny* II. 564 A cutter and grauer in marble. **1628** COWLEY *Piramus & Th.* xxiv, Just like a Marble Statue did he stand Cut by some skilful Graver's artful hand.

b. = ENGRAVER I. Now *rare.*

1398 TREVISA *Barth. De P.R.* XVI. ix. (Tollem. Ms.), Grauers use þe peces þerof to signe and to þurle preciouse stones. **1483** *Cath. Angl.* 163/2 A Gravere (*A.* Graver of wode or metelle), *celator, sculptor.* **1564-78** BULLEYN *Dial. agst. Pest.* (1886) 25 A liuely grauer of Seales. **1623** B. JONSON in *Shaks. Wks.* To Rdr., Wherein the Grauer had a strife with Nature, to out-doo the life. *a* **1674** CLARENDON *Hist. Reb.* XIV. §70 He had lately imploy'd a Graver to prepare a Great Seal. **1762-71** H. WALPOLE *Vertue's Anecd. Paint.* (1786) I. 164 Cellini being rather a sculptor than a graver. **1859** C. BARKER *Assoc. Princ.* ii. 49 The piety..of our early gravers, enchasers, and designers.

3. A tool. **a.** A cutting or shaving tool of any kind. † **b.** A sculptor's chisel. **c.** An engraver's tool; a burin. (Now the principal use.) **d.** 'An instrument used for turning iron after it has been roughed out by the heel-tool' (Ogilvie). † **e.** 'A Barber Chirurgeons Instrument for the taking Scales off from the Teeth' (Phillips 1678).

a. 1548 ELYOT *Dict.*, *Scobina*, an instrument that bowiers vse to shaue their bowes with called a grauer. **1703** MOXON *Mech. Exerc.* 217 The Tool, which is commonly a Graver. **1714** GAY *Fan* I. 134 Some work the File, and Some the Graver guide. **1836** SIR G. HEAD *Home Tour* 182 As the cylinder revolved, the graver, or cutting tool was fixed.

b. 1636 B. JONSON *Discov.*, *Virorum schola respub.* (1640) 128 What figure of a Body was Lysippus ever able to forme with his Graver..?

c. 1662 EVELYN *Chalcogr.* i. 9 The Burin (for so they [the French] tearm the Instrument which we [call] the Graver). **1763** H. WALPOLE *Catal. Engrav.* (1765) 83 George White afterwards made use of the graver for forming the black spot in eyes, and sharpening the light. **1812-16** J. SMITH *Panorama Sci. & Art* I. 38 With a graver, or some finely pointed steel instrument, draw a line upon the plate. **1889** J. HIRST in *Archaeol. Inst. Jrnl.* No. 181. 29 Thick feathers delicately finished with a graver.

† **graveress.** *Obs. rare*[−1]. [ad. F. *graveresse*, f. *graver* to engrave.] A female engraver.

c **1430** *Pilgr. Lyf Manhode* III. xvii. (1869) 144 A graueresse of false seles.

† '**gravery.** *Obs.* [f. GRAVE *v.*[1] + -ERY 1 b.] The employment of an engraver; engraving.

1601 HOLLAND *Pliny* II. 537 Neither shall you euer heare of any piece either of picture or grauerie and embossing, that came out of a seruile hand. **1695** PEPYS *Let.* in *Academy* 9 Aug. (1890) 111/1, I will with all y[e] speed I can, enable my selfe to say something to you ab[t] our Gravery.

Graves (grɑːv). [Fr. (pl.), a name for gravelly sandy parts of the Bordeaux country.] A wine produced in the Graves district of France.

1605 P. ERONDELL *French Garden* xi. sig. L7[v] What wine will it please you to drink? Claret wine, Graue wine,.. Greeke wine? **1630** J. TAYLOR (Water P.) *Wks.* Fff 4/1 The French Frontiniacke, Claret, Red nor White, Graues nor High-Country could our hearts delight. **1833** C. REDDING *Hist. Mod. Wines* 148 Macau produces seven or eight hundred tuns of red Graves. **1908** E. & A. VIZETELLY *Wines of France* 81 Cérons..produces a fine white Graves. **1935** *Punch* 30 Jan. 131/1 Add one bottle champagne cider and one bottle Sauterne or Graves, and stir again. **1971** *Times* 10 Nov. (Wines Suppl.) p. vi (Advt.), White Bordeaux... Chateau Olivier 1967 Graves 86p.

graves, obs. form of GREAVES.

graveship ('greɪvʃɪp). [f. GRAVE *sb.*[3] + -SHIP.] **a.** The office of a grave; = GRIEVESHIP. **b.** In the West Riding of Yorkshire, a district, in some instances a subdivision of a large parish, in others comprising a number of parishes; so called as having formerly been administered by a grave or a body of graves.

1460 in *Ripon Ch. Acts* (Surtees) 365 Thomæ Walworth pro le graveship, 12*s.* 8*d.* **1653** in Morehouse *Kirkburton & Graveship of Holme* (1861) 145 King James being heretofore seized in fee of two water corne mills in Holmefirth, being a graveship within the Manor of Wakefield, in the countie of York. **1793** *Local Act 33 Geo. III*, An Act for Dividing and Inclosing the Open Common Fields..and Waste Grounds, within the Townships or Graveships of Wakefield, Stanley, Wrenthorpe [etc.]..in the Parish of Wakefield. **1861** MOREHOUSE *Kirkburton & Graveship of Holme* 141 In 1828 an act was obtained for enclosing all the common and waste lands within the graveship of Holme.

Gravesian ('greɪvzɪən), *a.* [f. the name of R. R. *Graves* (1895–1985) + -IAN.] Resembling in matter, style, or quality the work or manner of

Robert Ranke Graves, poet, novelist, and man of letters.

1961 *Times* 7 Jan. 9/5 Sir Cedric Hardwicke reads..and adopts exactly the approved Gravesian tone. **1968** *Listener* 6 June 736/3 There is an almost Gravesian myth now discovered by Burgess in the Kell deposit.

Graves's disease. *Med.* [f. the name of Dr. R. J. *Graves* of Dublin, who in 1835 recognized the individuality of the disease.] 'The diseased condition also called Basedow's disease and exophthalmic goitre. It is characterised by enlargement of the thyroid, protrusion of the eyeballs, and persistent palpitation' (*Syd. Soc. Lex.* 1886).

1868 tr. *A. Trousseau's Clin. Med.* xix. 548 Graves's disease is not necessarily attended with disease of the heart. **1874** LAWSON *Dis. Eye* 348 Exophthalmic Goitre.—Graves's Disease. **1887** *Lancet* 11 June 1196/2 An apparently well-authenticated case of Graves' disease.

gravestone, grave-stone ('greɪvstəʊn). [f. GRAVE *sb.*¹ + STONE *sb.*]

†**1.** A stone coffin. *Obs. rare*⁻¹.

a **1225** *St. Marher.* 22 Ich..dude hit i graue stan in hire grandame hus.

2. A stone placed over a grave, or at the entrance of a tomb; in later use also applied to an upright stone at the head or foot of a grave, bearing an inscription.

1340 *Cursor M.* 17370 (Trin.) Of aungels one Had lifte awey þe graue stone. **1387** TREVISA *Higden* (Rolls) VII. 79 Of þe swetynge of þe gravestone þere is taken a forwetynge or tokenynge of þe pope sone for to deie. *c* **1450** *St. Cuthbert* (Surtees) 6373 He kyst þe graue stane. **1502** *Bury Wills* (Camden) 93, I will ouer my grave be leid a graveston of marbull. **1566** in Peacock *Eng. Ch. Furniture* (1866) 112 The alter stones one is broken and pauith the church, thother is laid for a graue stonne. **1607** SHAKS. *Timon* IV. iii. 380. **1722** DE FOE *Plague* (1840) 26 He saw a ghost walking upon such a gravestone there. **1821** CLARE *Vill. Minstr.* I. 211 Where the grave-stone meets the eye. **1845** D. JERROLD *St. Giles* xxi. (1851) 213 [He] rose from the grave-stone, whereupon..he was wont to sit. **1884** PAE *Eustace* 79 Cast the shadows of the gravestones on the silent graves.

†**'gravet.** *Obs. rare*⁻¹. [f. GRAVE *a.*¹ (*sb.*¹) + -ET¹.] A grave person.

1583 STANYHURST *Æneis* I. (Arb.) 22 In this blooddye riot they soom grauet [L. *pietate gravem*] haplye beholding Of geason pietee, doo throng and greedelye listen.

gravet, obs. form of GRAVY.

Gravette (grə'vɛt). *Archæol.* [f. *La Gravette*, name of a site in the Dordogne.] Name of a long, narrow knife-like flint of Upper Palæolithic date, having a sharp cutting-edge and blunted back. Usually ***Gravette point.***

1911 W. J. SOLLAS *Ancient Hunters* viii. 218 A new form of implement came into use. This is a pointed flake, carefully retouched all along the cutting edge; it..is known as the type of La Gravette. *Ibid.*, (*caption*) The La Gravette Point. **1920** QUIGGIN & HADDON *Keane's Man Past & Pr.* 12 Finely worked knife-like blades (Châtelperron point, Gravette point). **1921** R. A. S. MACALISTER *Text-bk. Europ. Archaeol.* I. 368 The Gravette point..is a flake having one edge treated with secondary chipping and the other left sharp and untouched. *Ibid.* 369 In some Gravette knives the chipped edge is not straight, but has a kind of hump. **1932** *Antiquity* VI. 364 A number of points of gravette character ..combine with the burins to suggest an upper Palaeolithic facies. **1959** *Chambers's Encycl.* V. 448 Straight knife-blades with blunted back (La Gravette blade), steep scrapers, end-of-blade scrapers, burins or chisels, usually with straight working-end, have been found. **1963** R. CARRINGTON *Million Years of Man* xii. 147 One of the uses of their *gravettes* was to decorate the ivory of the slaughtered mammoths.

Gravettian (grə'vɛtɪən), *a.* and *sb. Archæol.* [See GRAVETTE + -IAN.] **A.** *adj.* Of, characteristic of, or designating the Upper Palæolithic culture represented by remains found at La Gravette, France. **B.** *sb.* **a.** The Gravettian culture. **b.** A man or woman of this culture.

1938 D. A. E. GARROD in *Proc. Prehist. Soc.* IV. 23, I would suggest for these two very closely related levels the names of Lower Gravettian and Upper Gravettian respectively. *Ibid.*, The theory of an eastern centre of dispersion for the Gravettian. **1940** V. G. CHILDE *Prehist. Communities* i. 13 Gravettians whose kinsmen and ancestors had specialized in hunting big game. *Ibid.*, Gravettian tools. **1946** F. E. ZEUNER *Dating Past* ix. 289 From the beginning of LGl_2 onwards..the archaeological succession is clear. It is a surprisingly rapid one. While the middle Aurignacian may have lasted into this time, upper Aurignacian or Gravettian dominates, both in the west ('western' Gravettian) and in the east (Predmost or 'eastern' Gravettian). **1947** J. & C. HAWKES *Prehist. Brit.* (ed. 2) i. 17 The next stray bands to arrive were Gravettians, a people with a rather more northerly range than their predecessors, who in south Russia and else-where had used their human wits to prey successfully upon the formidable mammoth herds. **1952** V. G. CHILDE *New Light Most Anc. East* (ed. 4) ii. 19 Even in Africa Minor great heaps of small shells in the deserts and rock shelters yield blade industries..Caspian and Oranian—comparable to the Châtelperronian and Gravettian of Europe. **1952** *Proc. Prehist. Soc.* XVIII. 105 Examples of the Upper Aurignacian, with backed 'Gravettian' points, often microlithic in their size and delicacy, are found in the Ardèche and Gardon caves. **1953** A. L. KROEBER *Anthrop. Today* 173/2 It is possible that further excavations in the plains region of southern Russia will reveal that the Gravettian was derived from this source. **1967** *Listener* 30 Mar. 426/1 Among the Upper Paleolithic tools which appear first in these two Greek caves are narrow flint blades which have been intentionally blunted down one side, and they are said to belong to a culture called the Gravettian.

graveward ('greɪvwəd), *adv.* and *a.* [f. GRAVE *sb.*¹ + -WARD.]

A. *adv.* Towards the grave; in quot. *fig.*

1871 G. MACDONALD *Wks. Fancy & Imag.*, *Gospel Women* VI. i, She..Her eyes hath graveward sent.

B. *adj.* Tending towards the grave or death.

1855 M. BRIDGES *Pop. Mod. Hist.* 436 All trod the same graveward path. **1863** W. LANCASTER *Praeterita* 54 Until the tale of years disorb my hand, And set a graveward darkness on my brain.

gravewards ('greɪvwədz), *adv.* [f. GRAVE *sb.*¹ + -WARDS.] = GRAVEWARD *adv.*

1880 J. PAYN *Confid. Agent* III. 255 Whenever I thought of Sabey and the little one I sank gravewards.

gravewis, obs. form of GRIEVOUS.

graveyard ('greɪvjɑːd). [f. GRAVE *sb.*¹ + YARD.]

1. A burial-ground.

1773 P. V. FITHIAN *Jrnl.* (1900) 74 He meant it for a Satire upon the neglect of the people in suffering their Grave-Yard to lie common. **1806** M. L. WEEMS *Lett.* (1929) II. 344 Constantly walking over the grave yard of Foreigners. **1822** J. F. COOPER *Spy* (1831) xiv. 168 The grave-yard was an enclosure on the grounds of Mr. Wharton. **1825** J. NEAL *Bro. Jonathan* I. 20 Moving slowly..on their way to the grave-yard. **1855** MACAULAY *Hist. Eng.* xvi. III. 621 The..desolate graveyard of Donore. **1882** 'MARK TWAIN' *Innoc. at Home* iii. 278 A desperado..who 'kept his private graveyard', as the phrase went.

transf. **1843** *Quincy* (Ill.) *Whig* 7 Jan. 2/6 The iron steamer Valley Forge has been sunk at the 'Grave Yard' below St. Louis. **1853** KANE *Grinnell Exp.* xlii. (1856) 389, I remember..coming to a little graveyard of ice-tablets. **1879** *Chambers's Jrnl.* 18 Oct. 663/2 Those whose biographies lie in the sub-editorial desk—'grave-yard' this compartment is grimly called. **1933** P. A. EADDY *Hull Down* vii. 157 She had gone ashore on what was known as the 'Graveyard', on the northern side of the entrance to the Kaipara River. **1953** R. GRAVES *Poems* 30 Must the book end, as you would end it, With testamentary appendices And graveyard indices? **1965** *New Statesman* 7 May 715/2, I survived part of adolescence in the despair of Dundee, that industrial graveyard of the Thirties. **1969** *Daily Tel.* 8 Feb. 1 The M1 motorway was a graveyard of cars abandoned across all six lanes.

2. *attrib.* and *Comb.*, as ***graveyard cough, test; graveyard-minded*** adj.; **graveyard shift, watch** (see quots.).

1873 J. H. BEADLE *Undevel. West* 33, I was shaken by an ominous graveyard cough. **1890** E. DOWSON *Let.* 11 Feb. (1967) 137, I have a graveyard cough of the most alarming dimensions. **1948** I. BROWN *No Idle Words* 71 No doubt Housman did overplay the lads, lightfoot or grave-yard-minded. **1907** *Collier's* 26 Jan. 14/1 From the saloons came the clink of the chips. For it was the 'grave-yard gamblers' shift... The small hours of the morning..are theirs. **1908** *Sat. Even. Post* 7 Nov. 27/2 A month later he and his fellows went on 'graveyard' shift. 'Graveyard' is the interval between twelve, midnight, and eight in the morning. **1965** 'E. MCBAIN' *Doll* (1966) ii. 22 The afternoon shift is from four p.m. to midnight. And the graveyard shift is midnight to eight a.m. **1957** *Brit. Commonw. Forest Terminol.* II. 85 *Graveyard test*, a test conducted out of doors on pieces of timber in contact with the ground to determine their durability. **1927** G. BRADFORD *Gloss. Sea Terms* 76/1 *Graveyard watch*, the middle watch or 12 to 4 a.m., because of the number of disasters that occur at this time. **1928** *Papers Mich. Acad. Sci. & Arts* X. 297 Graveyard watch, the watch from midnight till 4 A.M., so called on account of the silence throughout the ship. **1933** J. H. MCCULLOCH *Million Miles in Sail* vii. 125 Without this arrangement..the 'graveyard watch'—or..the middle watch..would fall to the lot of the same men each night.

†**'graviate.** *Obs.* [f. GRAVE *sb.*⁴ + -ATE; cf. *landgraviate.*] The territory ruled by a 'grave'.

1728 BAILEY, s.v. *Graves-End* [explains this name to mean] the end of the graviate or County.

gravic ('grævɪk), *a.* [irreg. f. L. *gravis* GRAVE *a.*¹ (*sb.*¹) + -IC.] Pertaining to or causing gravitation.

1864 in WEBSTER. Hence in recent Dicts.

gravicembalo (grævɪ'tʃɛmbələʊ), It. corruption of CLAVICEMBALO.

1858 SIMMONDS *Dict. Trade*, Gravecembalo. **1899** KELLETT & NAYLOR tr. *Bie's Hist. Pianoforte* 133 When Italy decided..to replace the Gravicembalo by the pianoforte. **1958** A. JACOBS *New Dict. Mus.* 151 *Gravicembalo*, harpsichord.

gravid ('grævɪd), *a.* Also 6 **gravide.** [f. L. *gravid-us*, f. *gravis* burdened, heavy (see GRAVE *a.*¹ (*sb.*¹). Cf. F. *gravide.*] Pregnant, heavy with young.

1597 A. M. *Guillemeau's Fr. Chirurg.* 2 b/2 Woemen when they are gravide with Childe. **1638** SIR. T. HERBERT *Trav.* (ed. 2) 24 A carefull husband [*sc.* a dolphin] over his gravid associate. **1799** W. G. BROWNE *Trav. Africa*, etc. xxi. 344 If the mother..become gravid. **1799** J. BURNS (*title*), The Anatomy of the Gravid Uterus. **1846** J. BAXTER *Libr. Pract. Agric.* (ed. 4) I. 344 They are gravid four months and a half. **1866** J. B. ROSE tr. *Ovid's Fasti* II. 658 Gravid she grew with twins. **1867** F. FRANCIS *Angling* i. (1880) 51 Numbers of barbel..in a gravid state.

fig. **1648–1702** JOS. BEAUMONT *Psyche* VII. ci, Let The gravid Universe deliver'd be From pangs. *Ibid.* XVII. cxv, Resolving..to ease the fount Of her impatient gravid Eyes. **1873** *St. Paul's Mag.* II. 225 That grave and gravid journal the *Lectern.* **1882** *St. James's Gaz.* 28 Mar., They are not merely gravid with ideas but have a plan to produce.

Hence **'gravidness**, gravidity.

1727 in BAILEY vol. II.

‖**gravidad.** *Obs. rare*⁻¹. In quot. *erron.* gravidud. [Sp. *gravedad* GRAVITY.] Gravity.

1641 *Witt's Recreations* No. 579. N 5, He has Of Gravidud a dose full in his face.

†**'gravidate**, *v. Obs. rare.* [f. L. *gravidāt-*, ppl. stem of *gravidāre* to burden, f. *gravidus* GRAVID; see -ATE³.] **a.** *intr.* To be gravid or pregnant. **b.** *trans.* To make heavy, make gravid. Hence **'gravidated** *ppl. a.*, pregnant.

1623 COCKERAM II, To be with Childe, *Grauidate.* **1657** TOMLINSON *Renou's Disp.* 220 Of which wines we should drink moderately..for they gravidate the head. *a* **1677** BARROW *Serm. Matt.* i. 20 Wks. 1686 II. 349 Whence her womb is said..to have been *gravidated* or great with child.

†**gravi'dation.** *Obs.* Also 8 *erron.* **gravitation.** [ad. L. **gravidātiōn-em*, f. *gravidāre* (see prec.).] The condition or fact of being pregnant.

1450 *Mirour Saluacioun* 924 Whare of shuld sho conceyue this grauidacioune. **1623** COCKERAM II, A being great with Childe, *Pregnation, Grauidation.* **1654** VILVAIN *Theorem. Theol.* i. 8, The usual time or term of womens gravidation. **1665–6** *Phil. Trans.* I. 388 Pregnant Bitches..at certain times of their gravidation. **1720** WELTON *Suffer. Son of God* I. ii. 20 Her Gravitation..was free from many of the Infirmities common to others of her Sex. *Ibid.* iii. 59 Who can conceive..the Graces Thou hast received during the Nine months of thy Gravitation!

gravidity (grə'vɪdɪtɪ). Also 6 **graveditie.** [f. L. *graviditās*, *-tātem*, f. *gravidus* GRAVID. Cf. F. *gravidité.*] The state of being gravid; pregnancy.

1651 WITTIE *Primrose's Pop. Err.* II. 76 The urine is not changed by the graviditie it selfe, but onely by the suppression of the flowers. **1732** ARBUTHNOT *Rules of Diet* 402 The Signs of Gravidity and Obstructions are hard to be distinguish'd in the beginning. **1822–34** *Good's Study Med.* (ed. 4) IV. 118 During the period of a determined gravidity. **1880** tr. *H. von Ziemssen's Cycl. Med.* IX. 244 Gravidity manifestly induces..a predisposition to the disease.

†**graviers**, *sb. pl. Obs.* [Origin and form doubtful; Dekker *Belman Lond.* (1608) E 3 prints *graniers.*] False dice of some kind.

c **1550** *Dice-play* A j b, The names of Dyce..A bale of light grauiers. *Ibid.* C iv, Light grauiers there be..forged cleane against the apparaunt vantage. **1608** DEKKER *Belman Lond.* (ed. 2) E 3 A Bale of light Graniers.

gravific (grə'vɪfɪk), *a.* [f. L. *gravi-s* heavy + -FIC.] That makes heavy or produces weight.

1807 *Edin Rev.* X. 147 The particles by which this effect is brought about, are called by Le Sage the gravific. **1862** SIR H. HOLLAND *Ess.* i. 15 Hypotheses..such as that of gravific atoms permeating all space. **1881** *Nature* XXIII. 462 Regarding the gravific aether as simply a stationary gas.

gravigrade ('grævɪgreɪd), *a.* and *sb. Zool.* [f. mod.L. *Gravigrada* (see below), f. *gravi-s* heavy + *grad-ī* to step, walk.]

A. *adj.* 'Walking heavily'; of or belonging to the extinct edentate group *Gravigrada*, which, includes the Megatherium and the Mylodon.

1884 in CASSELL.

B. *sb.* A name formerly given to heavy-paced animals, such as the elephant; now, an animal of the group *Gravigrada* (see A).

1847 CRAIG, *Gravigrades*, a name given by Blainville to Mammalia, comprising such heavy-paced animals as the elephant. **1849** *Sk. Nat. Hist., Mammalia* III. 109 MM. Blainville and Duméril consider the dinotherium to have been allied to the lamantins, or 'aquatic gravigrades'. **1899** *Westm. Gaz.* 31 July 3/2 He regards it as a living representative of the *Gravigrades* of Argentina, and has given it the name of *Neo-Mylodon Listai.*

†**gra'viloquence.** *Obs.*⁻⁰ [f. L. *gravis* GRAVE *a.* + *loquī*, *loquent-* to speak.] (See quot.)

1656 BLOUNT *Glossogr.*, *Graviloquence*, a grave speech, or a speaking gravely.

gravimeter (grə'vɪmɪtə(r)). *Physics.* [ad. F. *gravimètre* (Guyton de Morveau, 1797), f. L. *gravi-s* heavy: see -METER.] **1.** A kind of hydrometer (resembling Nicholson's), for determining the specific gravity of bodies, whether liquid or solid.

1797 *Nicholson's Jrnl.* June 110 Description of a Gravimeter, or Instrument for measuring the Specific Gravity of Solids and Fluids. By Citizen Guyton. **1801** J. JONES tr. *Bygge's Trav. Fr. Repub.* v. 120 Determining the Specific gravity of a calcedon by means of Guiton's gravimeter. **1868** *Nat. Encycl.* I. 991 For fluids of greater specific gravity than water..an instrument..which was invented by Guyton de Morveau, and is designated 'Gravimeter', may be used.

2. Any instrument designed to measure the variation in the force of gravity from one place to another; usu. applied to those which involve determining the force exerted on a suspended mass.

1932 *Physics* II. 124 (*caption*) Diagram of gravimeter. *Ibid.* 128 (*caption*) The gravimeter in the field. **1940** *Geogr. Jrnl.* XCV. 135 An exhaustive test of all modern gravimeters should be made..to compare the Lejay astatic pendulum, the new Nörgaard instrument, the gravimeters depending on the properties of helical springs..and finally the

Nörgaard and Halck patterns of hydro-static gravimeter. **1955** *Sci. Amer.* Sept. 165/1 The pendulum is still the standard for absolute values of gravity, but nowadays the instrument most commonly used is the gravimeter, a supersensitive version of the ordinary spring scale. The earth's pull is measured by the amount of stretching of a thin wire of silica or invar (a nickel-steel alloy) on which a small weight hangs. **1957** [see *gravity meter* s.v. GRAVITY 8 b].

Also **gravi'metric, gravi'metrical** *adjs.*, pertaining to the gravimeter or to gravimetry; **gravi'metrically** *adv.*, by means of the gravimeter; in respect of measurement by weight; **gra'vimetry**, measurement of weight.

1858 THUDICHUM *Urine* 39 In the generality of diseases the gravimetry of urine gives very meagre results as yet. **1866** ODLING *Anim. Chem.* 100 By comparing the items gravimetrically instead of volumetrically. **1873** RALFE *Phys. Chem.* 216 Gravimetric [method], in which the substance after isolation from the mixture is weighed in the balance. **1883** ATKINSON *Ganot's Physics* (ed. 11) §185 This apparatus [volumometer or sterometer], is of great value in determining the gravimetrical density of gunpowder. **1884** *Pharmaceut. Soc. Prosp.* 13 Volumetric and Gravimetric Quantitative Analyses. **1935** *Geogr. Jrnl.* LXXXV. 199 Conditions of gravimetric survey. **1955** *Sci. Amer.* Sept. 170/3 The fundamental idea of the gravimetric method of mapping, and of the present world-wide gravity measuring program, is that the undulations of the geoid and its tilt at every place can be computed from the observed gravity anomalies.

graving ('greɪvɪŋ), *vbl. sb.*[1] [f. GRAVE *v.*[1] + -ING[1].] The action of GRAVE *v.*[1]

†**1.** Digging. *Obs.*

a **1340** HAMPOLE *Psalter* xxi. 17 *Foderunt manus meas & pedes meos*.. He says thai grof, forto shew the mykilnes of his pyne, vgly grauynge in hend and fete. *Ibid.* lxxix. 17 *Incensa igni & suffossa*.. Bot swilke kyndilynge and swilke grafeynge sall perishe and be dampnyd. **1411** *Rolls Parlt.* III. 650/1 Certein Commune of Pasture, and Turfgravyng. *c* **1440** *Promp. Parv.* 208/1 Gravynge, or delvynge, *fossio*. **1486** *Nottingham Rec.* III. 242, iij. warkmen.. grauyng of soddes to fill among þe wattilles. [**1620** *Naworth Househ. Bks.* (Surtees) 134 To John Marsam for graving x dayes woork of peates.]

†**2.** (With possessive pron.) Burial. *Obs.*

c **1340** HAMPOLE *Prose Tr.* (1866) 7 Till his grauynge it semyde als þe ayere gafe seruese. *c* **1440** *York Myst.* xvii. 286 This mirre will I giffe to þi grauyng. *c* **1460** *Towneley Myst.* xiv. 557 To thy grauyng this myr of me Resaue the tyll.

†**3. a.** Carving, sculpturing. **b.** Incision of lines, etc. in stone, metal, and the like. *Obs.*

1362 LANGL. *P. Pl.* A. III. 55 Bote god to alle good folk such grauynge defendet [*B-text adds* To writen in wyndowes of here wel dedes]. **1382** WYCLIF *Isa.* xlv. 20 The Jentiles.. that rereden vp a tocne of ther grauyng. **1398** TREVISA *Barth. De P.R.* XVI. xxvii. (1495) 562 All kyndes of the stone Calcedonius wythstondeth grauynge. **1603** KNOLLES *Hist. Turks* (1621) 1326 Foure other vessels made of fishes bones whereas the art seemed miraculous in the graving. *a* **1619** FOTHERBY *Atheom.* II. xiv. §6 (1622) 361 The Arte of Graving, in all kinde of mettals. **1727** DE FOE *Syst. Magic* I. vi. (1840) 141 The writing and graving upon hard stones.

c. *concr.* Something cut or carved; a carving, sculpture; an inscription. *Obs.* or *arch.*

1382 WYCLIF *Ezek.* xl. 22 The wyndowis therof, and porche, and grauyngis. *c* **1440** LYDG. *Balade* in *Harvard Studies* (1897) V. 193 Neuer in gravyng nor in portrature Sawe I depict so fayre a creature. *c* **1510** BARCLAY *Mirr. Gd. Manners* (1570) G iv, The housholder.. Ought not to be noted for sumptuous building, Nor by outwarde grauing, or workes curious. **1609** BIBLE (Douay) *Ezek.* xl. 37 The graving of palme-trees in the front therof. **1647** W. BROWNE tr. *Gomberville's Polexander* IV. iii. 258 The walls were adorned with the same metall and gravings. **1703** T. N. *City & C. Purchaser* 268 Triglyph.. signifies a hollow Graving like 3 Furrows. **1801** SOUTHEY *Thalaba* IV. xv, Belike you can interpret then the graving Around this Ring!

fig. **1648** *Eikon Bas.* 63 Gravings and characters which by just and lawful oaths were made upon their souls.

d. A grooving.

1877 RAYMOND *Statist. Mines & Mining* 419 If Mr. Krom's graving and facing of his rolls obviate the difficulties heretofore experienced with that form of crusher.

4. The engraving (of a design, picture, etc.) on a metal plate or wood block. *Obs.* or *arch.*

1646 *Crashaw's Steps to Temple* Pref. 21 His skill in Poetry, Musicke, Drawing, Limming, graving. **1661** EVELYN *Mem.* (1857) I. 365 Prince Rupert showed me.. the new way of graving called mezzo-tinto. **1712** J. JAMES tr. *Le Blond's Gardening* Ded., The graving of the Plates. **1753** T. GRAY *Let.* Wks. 1884 II. 234, I am surprised at the print, which far surpasses my idea of London graving. **1762** H. WALPOLE *Vertue's Anecd. Paint.* I. iv. (1765) 66 He [Holbein] learned besides, graving, casting, modelling, and architecture.

b. An engraved plate or an impression from it. *Obs.* or *arch.*

1760 RAPER in *Phil. Trans.* LI. 806 *note* 2 His plans seem to be inverted, as gravings commonly are. **1823** J. BADCOCK *Dom. Amusem.* 138 This steel graving should have a hole drilled in one of its corners.

5. *attrib.*, as ***graving iron, knife, skill, steel, stick***; **graving tool**, (*a*) the tool used by an engraver, a graver; (*b*) *dial.* (see quot. 1877).

14.. *Nom.* in Wr.-Wülcker 727/15 *Hec revictica*, a *grawyngern. **1580** BARET *Alv.* G 481 A grauing iron, a shauing knife, *scalprum*. **1577** KENDALL *Flowers Epigr.* 64 b, When as he graues in wood, a *grauyng knife. **1784** COWPER *Tiroc.* 300 The wall on which we tried our *graving skill. **1676** COLES, *Graver*, a *graving-steel. **1580** HOLLYBAND *Treas. Fr. Tong*, *Vn Burin*, a *grauing sticke. **1591** PERCIVALL *Sp. Dict.*, *Buril*, a *grauing toole. **1877** *N.W. Linc. Gloss.*, *Graving-tool*, a spade used in making drains.

graving ('greɪvɪŋ), *vbl. sb.*[2] [f. GRAVE *v.*[2] + -ING[1].] The action of GRAVE *v.*[2]; the cleaning of a ship's bottom by scraping or burning, and coating with tar; *concr.* = *graving-stuff*.

1627 CAPT. SMITH *Seaman's Gram.* ii. 13 Grauing is onely vnder water. **1673** *Phil. Trans.* VIII. 6192 More cheap and durable than any Sheathing or Graving hitherto used. **1780** in FALCONER *Dict. Marine*. **1867** in SMYTH *Sailor's Word-bk.*

b. *Comb.*, as **graving beach** (see quot.); **graving bowl** *dial.* (see quot.); **graving dock**, a dock into which vessels are floated to be graved; = DRY DOCK (see also DOCK *sb.*[3] 4); **graving piece**, a small piece of wood inserted to repair a defect in a plank; †**graving place** = *graving dock*; **graving slip** = *graving beach*; **graving stuff**, the materials used in graving.

1867 SMYTH *Sailor's Word-bk.*, **Graving Beach* or *Slip*, a portion of the dockyard where ships were landed for a tide. **1880** *Antrim & Down Gloss.*, **Graving bowl*, a gratuity paid to ship carpenters when they have completed the repair of a vessel, on bringing her out of the graving dock. **1840** *Evid. Hull Docks Comm.* 53 *Graving docks. **1894** *Times* 1 Oct. 6/3 Her Majesty's ship Ringarooma was yesterday placed in the graving dock at Cockatoo Island for repairs. **1803** in *Naval Chron.* XV. 219 The ship-wrights attending the caulkers to let in *graving pieces. **1628** LE GRYS tr. *Barclay's Argenis* 353 Part of his Fleet being shaken with the storme was brought vpon *greuing places. **1693** *Lond. Gaz.* No. 2849/2 The *Mermaid* Fire-ship, as she lay at the Graving Place in Cattwater, was.. unhappily set on Fire. **1702** *Ibid.* No. 3849/4 *Graving-stuff.

gravish ('greɪvɪʃ) *a.* [f. GRAVE *a.*[1] (*sb.*[1]) + -ISH.] Somewhat grave.

1751 R. PALTOCK *P. Wilkins* I. v. 32 A gravish Sailor came and sat down by me. **1866** CARLYLE *Irving*, Remin. (1881) I. 151 Hat of gravish breadth of brim.

†**gravisonous,** *a. Obs. rare*[−0]. [f. L. *gravisonus* (f. *gravis* heavy + *sonus* sound) + -OUS.] Having a deep or heavy sound.

1727–90 in BAILEY.

‖**gravitas** ('grævɪtɑːs, -æ-). [See GRAVITY.] = GRAVITY 3.

1924 *Manch. Guardian Weekly* 10 Oct. 313 He never sheds a certain Roman *gravitas*. **1958** *Spectator* 30 May 698/2 A certain *gravitas* in the atmosphere of the Scottish universities. **1961** *Times* 2 Aug. 11/6 Its leading articles, and even its news coverage, will have a superb Victorian *gravitas*. **1961** *Listener* 30 Nov. 901/2 As for the Prime Minister [of Nigeria], to see him at close quarters is to recognize the true *gravitas* of the statesman. **1969** *Ibid.* 20 Mar. 376/2 *Gravitas*, the heavy tread of moral earnestness, becomes a bore if it is not accompanied by the light step of intelligence.

'gravitate, *a. nonce-wd.* [f. L. *gravit-ās* + -ATE.] Endowed with gravity.

1827 COLERIDGE *Notes & Lect. on Shakespeare* (1849) II. 157 The particles themselves must have an interior and gravitate being.

gravitate ('grævɪteɪt), *v.* [f. mod.L. *gravitāt-*, ppl. stem of *gravitāre*, f. *gravis* heavy, *gravitās* weight, GRAVITY. Cf. 17th c. F. *graviter*.]

†**1.** *intr.* To exert weight or pressure; to press *upon* (*on*); also of heavy bodies, to move or tend to move downward by their own weight. *Obs.*

In early natural philosophy, bodies classed as heavy were said to gravitate, and bodies classed as light to levitate, in consequence of their tendency to 'seek their own place'.

1644 DIGBY *Nat. Bodies* (1645) 112 The weights.. do not gravitate or weigh so much.. when the aire is thick and foggy. **1660** BOYLE *New Exp. Phys. Mech.* xvii. 110 The one gravitating, the other pressing with equal force upon the subjacent Mercury. **1661** —— *Spring of Air* I. iv. (1682) 9 When the lower finger is removed then the Cylinder of Mercury, which before gravitated upon the Finger comes to gravitate upon the restagnant Mercury. **1664** POWER *Exp. Philos.* II. 107 By which [experiment] it.. appears, that water does gravitate in its own Sphære (as they phrase it). **1678** HOBBES *Decam.* Wks. 1845 VII. 140 Water does not gravitate on any part of itself beneath it. **1782** A. MONRO *Compar. Anat.* (ed. 3) 29 The lymph.. gravitating upon the inferior part of the ventricles may.. elongate and produce them. **1788** REID *Aristotle's Log.* VI. ii. 144 In the ancient philosophy.. Many things were assumed under that character without a just title [e.g.].. that bodies do not gravitate in their proper place. **1808** BENTHAM *Sc. Reform* 38 The.. burthen of patronage, which, by Right Honourable persons in your Lordship's.. station, has always been felt to gravitate with so severe a pressure. [**1822** IMISON *Sci. & Art* I. 135 As all parts of the atmosphere gravitate, or press upon each other.]

†**b.** *trans.* To weigh down, oppress. *Obs.*

1754 H. P. *Hiberniad* i. 6 People.. condemned to Tracts of Land, and gravitated by an Atmosphere baneful to them.

2. *intr.* To be affected by gravitation; to move or tend to move by the force of gravity *towards* a body, as the planets of the solar system towards the sun, and bodies near and on the earth towards its centre, etc.

1692 BENTLEY *Boyle Lect.* 225 The sun, moon, and all the planets do reciprocally gravitate one toward another. **1712** BLACKMORE *Creation* II. (1736) 57 That matter is with active force endu'd, That all its parts magnetic pow'r exert, And to each other gravitate. **1726** tr. *Gregory's Astron.* I. 99 The Secondary Planets of Jupiter gravitate towards Jupiter.. and both the Primary and Secondary Planets gravitate towards the Sun. **1739** tr. *Algarotti's Newton's Philos.* (1742) II. 41 All Bodies here below gravitate, and if left to themselves descend. **1822** IMISON *Sci. & Art* I. 16 As all bodies gravitate towards the earth, so does the earth gravitate towards all bodies. **1834** MRS. SOMERVILLE *Connect. Phys. Sci.* i. (1849) 7 The satellites also gravitate to their primaries. **1868** LOCKYER *Guillemin's Heavens* (ed. 3) 436 Systems of bodies which gravitate round a central body.

b. To sink or fall by, or as by, gravitation: to tend to reach a low level; to settle down (*into* a place). *lit.* and *fig.*

1823 CHALMERS *Posth. Wks.* (1849) VI. 410 The soul sinks and gravitates again to the dust of its own kindred earthliness. **1847–9** HELPS *Friends in C.* (1851) I. 31 They gravitate into their old way very soon. **1851** ROBERTSON *Serm.* Ser. II. xi. (1864) 143 The soul gravitates downward beneath its burden. **1856** FROUDE *Hist. Eng.* I. 142 Thus were the various parties in the vast struggle which was about to commence gravitating into their places. **1879** *Rep. St. George's Hosp.* IX. 400 The intestinal contents.. had gravitated behind the ascending colon to the region of the cæcum.

c. *trans.* To cause to descend or sink by gravitation; *spec.* in *Diamond-digging*, to manipulate (the gravel) after washing, so that the heavy stones sink to the bottom (in quot. 1894 *absol.*).

1894 *Pop. Sci. Monthly* XLV. 473 These are sufficiently near the shore to be used to dig materials from to be gravitated down to the dam. **1894** *Graphic* 4 Aug. 129/2 [In diamond-digging] there is the gravitating machine, which has the same effect on the gravel as gravitating by hand.

3. *transf.* and *fig.* (*intr.*) To move or tend to move towards a certain point or object as a natural goal or destination; to be strongly attracted (to some centre of influence).

1673 MARVELL *Reh. Transp.* II. 187 A Lecture.. upon the Centers of Knowledge and Ignorance, and how and when they Gravitate and Levitate. **1776** ADAM SMITH *W.N.* I. vii. (1869) I. 62 The market price.. is continually gravitating towards the natural price. **1777** BURKE *Let. to Fox* Wks. IX. 154 We must gravitate towards them, if we would keep in the same system, or expect that they should approach towards us. **1837** SIR R. PEEL in *Croker Papers* (1884) 5 July, A King.. is the centre towards which all business gravitates. **1865** MERIVALE *Rom. Emp.* VIII. lxvi. 245 Rome.. was the place to which the imperial pilgrimages gravitated. **1873** BURTON *Hist. Scot.* VI. lxv. 26 The Irish no longer, as of old, gravitated to Scotland. **1875** MERIVALE *Gen. Hist. Rome* lxxiv. (1877) 616 The common feeling of mankind was slowly gravitating towards the new religion.

Hence **'gravitated** *ppl. a.* Also **'gravitater**, a workman who 'gravitates'.

1727 BAILEY vol. II, *Gravitated*, weighed, poised. **1822–34** *Good's Study Med.* (ed. 4) II. 469 The lungs were of a pale grey, without any marks of gravitated blood. **1894** *Graphic* 4 Aug. 129/2 [Diamond-digging] Then the washing begins. A bucketful of gravel is put into a fine-mesh sieve, .. and a 'nigger' takes it,.. shaking it so as to wash the gravel. He then passes it to the 'gravitater'.. the gravitater, by dexterous manipulation, causing all the heavy stones to sink to the bottom and come together in the centre.

gravitating ('grævɪteɪtɪŋ), *vbl. sb.* [f. GRAVITATE *v.* + -ING[1].] The action of the vb. GRAVITATE; gravitation. In quots. *attrib.* passing into *adj.* = gravitative. Also *Comb.*, as **gravitating-machine** (see GRAVITATE *v.* 2 c).

1665 *Phil. Trans.* I. 31 About the variations in the Moon, and its gravitating principle. **1692** BENTLEY *Boyle Lect.* vii. 244 The Gravitating Power of each of them is exactly proportional to their Matter. *a* **1711** KEN *Hymnarium* Poet. Wks. 1721 II. 145 To see all Nature's Course, Harmonious kept by gravitating Force. **1817** J. SCOTT *Paris Revisit.* (ed. 4) 387 A general gravitating tendency towards the centre of the state. **1860** TYNDALL *Glac.* II. xix. 329 We have a certain amount of gravitating force stored up.

gravitating ('grævɪteɪtɪŋ), *ppl. a.* [f. GRAVITATE *v.* + -ING[2].] That gravitates; †exerting weight or pressure (*obs.*); moving or tending to move by gravitation.

1718 J. CHAMBERLAYNE *Relig. Philos.* (1730) II. xvii. §40 Set a Cup full of Water under the Receiver of an Air-pump, then draw off the gravitating Air. **1794** J. HUTTON *Philos. Light*, etc. 244 The gravitating matter which is proper to this globe. **1853** KANE *Grinnell Exp.* xlv. (1856) 411 The opposing face of the berg varies with every change of its gravitating centre. **1881** GREENER *Gun* 83 Manton's latest improvement in flint-locks was the gravitating stop. **1893** TYNDALL in *Daily News* 5 Jan. (1894) 5/4 Lifted on the wings of hope and then let fall like a simple gravitating mass without a pinion.

gravitation (grævɪ'teɪʃən). [ad. mod.L. *gravitātiōn-em*, n. of action f. *gravitāre* to GRAVITATE. Cf. F. *gravitation*.]

1. *Physics.* **a.** The action or process of gravitating; in early use, the falling of bodies to the earth or their sinking to their lowest level; in later use applied in wider sense to the process of which this is an instance, the moving or tending to a centre of attraction.

c **1645** *Enquiry* in *Harl. Misc.* (Malh.) V. 501 If the opinion be true, that gravitation is from the magnetism of the earth, then, the more remote from the earth, the less is the gravity. **1664** POWER *Exp. Philos.* II. 104 This Experiment seems onely to evince the gravitation of Ayr condensed. **1713** BERKELEY *Guardian* No. 126 ¶6 The mutual gravitation of bodies. **1797** M. BAILLIE *Morb. Anat.* (1807) 65 Where blood too is accumulated in any part of a lung after death, from gravitation, it is always of a dark colour. **1812–16** PLAYFAIR *Nat. Phil.* II. 308 How the gravitation toward distant bodies, such as the Sun and Moon, may affect the Earth's rotation on its axis. **1831** BREWSTER *Newton* (1855) I. ii. 26 If the moon was thus kept in her orbit by gravitation to the earth, or, in other words, its attraction. **1888** *Pall Mall G.* 23 Mar. 5/1 The substitution of irrigation by gravitation instead of by pumps.

b. The amount or degree of such attraction.

1812–16 PLAYFAIR *Nat. Phil.* II. 266 The gravitation of one planet to another, is expressed by the quantity of matter in each, divided by the square of the distance.

2. The attraction of one body for another, or the effective force of one body moving towards another; the tendency of every particle of matter towards every other particle, of which the fall of bodies to the earth is an instance.

The ***law of gravitation***, according to which the attractive force of bodies varies directly as their masses and inversely as the square of the distance between them, was discovered by Sir Isaac Newton.

1646 SIR T. BROWNE *Pseud. Ep.* IV. vii. 196 In carcasses warme..there doe exhale and breathe out vaporous and fluid parts, which carry away some power of gravitation. **1692** BENTLEY *Boyle Lect.* 225 The gravitating power of each of them [planets]..arises from the several gravitations or attractions of all the individual particles that compose the whole mass. **1728** PEMBERTON *View Newton's Philos.* 17 This power of gravitation extends up to the moon, and causes that planet to gravitate..towards the earth. **1728** POPE *Dunc.* II. 318 Whirlpools and storms his circling arm invest, With all the might of gravitation blast. **1813** SIR H. DAVY *Agric. Chem.* ii. (1814) 31 One of the most important properties belonging to matter is Gravitation. **1829** SCOTT *Anne of G.* ii, The power of gravitation determined a direct and forward descent. **1837** WHEWELL *Hist. Induct. Sci.* (1857) II. 181 They..obeyed the law of universal gravitation. **1860** MAURY *Phys. Geog. Sea* (Low) ii. §95 But for the forces of gravitation the waters of the Mississippi would remain at its fountain. **1877** HUXLEY *Physiogr.* xxi. (1878) 371 The force by which the iron rushes to the earth is called gravitation.

3. *transf.* and *fig.* The fact or condition of being attracted towards an object or point of influence; natural tendency (*to* or *towards*); in bad sense, tendency to sink to a low level.

1644 DIGBY *Man's Soul* Concl. 454 The vehemence and intensenesse of any pleasure, is proportionable..to the grauitation, bent, and greatnesse that such a subiect hath to the obiect that delighteth it. **1688** NORRIS *Theory Love* I. iii. 26 That moral Gravity and Gravitation of the Soul impress'd on her by the universal Good acting attractively upon her. **1784** COWPER *Task* v. 588 That low And sordid gravitation of his pow'rs To a vile clod. **1805** WORDSW. *Prelude* II. 243 The gravitation and the filial bond Of Nature that connect him with the world. **1862** MERIVALE *Rom. Emp.* (1865) IV. xxxii. 2 We shall..observe the general gravitation of the whole machine towards a more absolute despotism. **1876** E. MELLOR *Priesth.* viii. 372 That strong gravitation towards evil. **1883** GILMOUR *Mongols* xxxii. 373 Russia has toleration for all religions, but the gravitation is towards..the Greek Church.

4. *attrib.* and *Comb.*, as ***gravitation law***, ***supply*** (cf. sense 1. quot. 1888); **gravitation battery** = *gravity battery* (see GRAVITY 8b); **gravitation constant** = *gravitational constant*; **gravitation measure** (see quot. 1875); **gravitation stamp** = *gravity stamp* (see GRAVITY 8b); †**gravitation unit** = *gravitational unit* (obs.).

1883 JENKIN *Electr. & Magnet.* (ed. 7) 227 Gravitation batteries are like the Menotti's with the sawdust removed. **1889** *Cent. Dict.* s.v. *constant*, The gravitation constant is about 0·0000000658 of a c.g.s. unit. **1894** *Nature* 2 Aug. 330/2 This G, the gravitation constant, or as I prefer to call it..the Newtonian Constant of Gravitation, has nothing to do with that other quantity generally written *g*, which represents the attraction of the earth's surface. **1910** *Encycl. Brit.* XII. 385/1 The law of gravitation states that two masses M_1 and M_2, distant *d* from each other, are pulled together each with a force $G.M_1M_2/d^2$, where G is a constant for all kinds of matter—the gravitation constant. **1850** H. MILLER *Footpr. Creat.* xiii. (1874) 242 Such..would be the direct effects of this gravitation law. **1875** EVERETT *Illustr. C. G. S. Syst. Units* 13 Force is said to be expressed in gravitation-measure when it is expressed as equal to the weight of a given mass. **1894** T. K. ROSE *Metallurgy Gold* 99 Californian 'gravitation' stamps are in general use..for crushing gold ores. **1914** W. GOWLAND *Metallurgy Non-Ferrous Metals* 200 A modern heavy gravitation stamp. **1896** *Westm. Gaz.* 30 July 7/2 It [the water] will be served by a gravitation supply under a net head of about 65ft. **1872** *Rep. Brit. Assoc.* 1871 II. 29 The object of the paper was to urge the necessity of giving names to *absolute* units of force and energy, that is, units not varying with locality, like the gravitation units vulgarly employed (pound, foot-pound, &c.), but defined by reference to specified units of length, mass, and time. **1885** A. MACFARLANE *Physical Arithmetic* xxxiii. 192 Work is also measured in terms of gravitation units, by taking the corresponding gravitation unit of force instead of the absolute unit of force.

gravitation, erron. form of GRAVIDATION.

gravitational (grævɪˈteɪʃənəl), *a.* [f. GRAVITATION + -AL¹.] **a.** Of, pertaining to, or caused by gravitation; employing the principle or law of gravitation (sense 2).

gravitational astronomy: a system of astronomy based, as by Sir Isaac Newton, on the theory of gravitation; also called *theoretical astronomy*; so *g. astronomer*.

1855 B. POWELL *Ess.* 78 All kinds of physical agents..thermotic, electric, chemical, molecular, gravitational, luminiferous. **1869** DUNKIN *Midn. Sky* 148. 27 Several double stars suspected to belong to a common gravitational system. **1876** NEWCOMB in *N. Amer. Rev.* CXXIII. 101 Theoretical astronomy is a term somewhat too vague and inclusive; and 'gravitational astronomy' somewhat too narrow. **1881** SIR R. BALL in *Eng. Mech.* 17 June 349/1 Modern gravitational astronomers. **1889** *Chamb. Jrnl.* 16 Mar. 163/1 Venus has nearly the same gravitational power as the earth. **1893** SIR R. BALL *Story of Sun* 75 The gravitational method of finding the Sun's distance.

b. Special collocations: ***gravitational constant***: in classical physics, the constant of proportionality in the equation relating the strength of the gravitational attraction between two bodies to their mass and their separation, equal to approx. $6{\cdot}67 \times 10^{-11}$ N. m.² kg.⁻² ($6{\cdot}67 \times 10^{-8}$ dyne cm.² gm.⁻²); symbol *G*; ***gravitational mass***: the mass of a body as measured by the force exerted on it by a gravitational field; cf. *inertial mass*; ***gravitational potential***: the potential of a gravitational field, the gradient of which at any point is equal in magnitude and direction to the field at that point; ***gravitational system*** (***of units***): a system of units based on a fundamental unit of weight rather than a unit of mass; ***gravitational unit***: a unit the value of which depends upon the value of *g*, the acceleration due to gravity; formerly called *gravitation unit*; ***gravitational water***: the water in saturated soil which can drain away under the influence of gravity; ***gravitational wave***: (*a*) = *gravity wave*; (*b*) a periodic variation in gravitational field-strength which is propagated through space (the existence of such waves is not yet established with certainty).

1904 *Science* XIX. 928/2 The adoption of this unit of mass involves a change in the numerical value of the gravitational constant. **1966** *McGraw-Hill Encycl. Sci. & Technol.* VI. 264 Determining the gravitational constant by a suitable experiment is therefore equivalent to 'weighing the Earth'. **1918** A. S. EDDINGTON *Rep. Relativity Theory Gravitation* i. 11 In astronomy..the masses of heavenly bodies are measured by their gravitational effects; naturally we cannot legitimately apply (7.8) to gravitational mass without a full discussion of the law of gravitation. **1955** *Sci. Amer.* June 32/2 The theory of general relativity was constructed on the basis of a physical observation of the equivalence of inertial and gravitational mass under certain simple circumstances. **1928** NEWMAN & SEARLE *Gen. Prop. Matter* iii. 59 To move this unit mass from one point to another in the gravitational field would require an expenditure of work against the attraction. The amount of this work..is called the difference in gravitational potential at the points. **1938** W. M. SMART *Stellar Dynamics* ii. 32 The motion of an individual star at any instant will be determined by the gravitational potential of the system. **1971** *Sci. Amer.* May 69/1 Light emitted from such an object would have to overcome an immense gravitational potential and would be red-shifted just as it is in quasars. **1888** *Proc. Physical Soc.* X. 41 To find J in the metre-kilogram-second gravitational system, when it is given in the British gravitational system. **1899** W. WATSON *Text-bk. Physics* I. x. 85 Such a system of units is called a gravitational system, and it is this system which is almost exclusively used by engineers. **1966** KAYE & LABY *Tables of Physical & Chem. Constants* (ed. 13) 6 It is convenient to distinguish the basic units of force in gravitational systems from the basic units of mass in other systems by using the symbols kgf for the kilogramme-force and lbf for the pound-force. **1896** NICHOLS & FRANKLIN *Elem. Physics* I. iii. 31 (*heading*) Gravitational units of force. **1923** H. MOORE *Textbk. Interm. Physics* viii. 67 The English gravitational unit of power is one foot-pound per second. **1954** *Amer. Jrnl. Physics* XXII. 293/2 The gravitational unit of force..is related to the weight of the standard object. [**1897** L. J. BRIGGS in *U.S. Bur. of Soils Bull.* No. 10, 6 The water contained in a soil may be considered to be of three kinds—gravitation water, capillary water, and hydroscopic water.] **1907** C. W. BURKETT *Soils* iv. 40 Three kinds of water are present in soils: gravitational water, capillary water, and hydroscopic water. Immediately after a rain, gravitational water, or that which will move under the influence of gravity, is present in the soil. **1917** MOSIER & GUSTAFSON *Soil Physics & Management* xvii. 217 The movement of gravitational water down-ward through the soil by the force of gravity is called percolation. **1960** TEUSCHER & ADLER *Soil & its Fertility* vii. 85 Gravitational water is of next to no importance for plant growth. **1899** W. WATSON *Text-bk. Physics* III. i. 345 The large waves seen on the surface of the sea are well-known examples of gravitational waves. **1941** B. HAURWITZ *Dynamic Meteorol.* xiv. 276 (*heading*) Wave motion at the free surface of a single layer. Gravitational waves. **1963** *Meteorol. Gloss.* (*Met. Office*) 120 *Gravity wave*, a type of wave, also referred to as a gravitational wave, in which the controlling forces are gravity and buoyancy. **1906** E. E. FOURNIER D'ALBE *Electron Theory* x. 191 If we had any means of creating or destroying matter, we could produce gravitational waves of infinite wave-length. **1922** A. S. EDDINGTON in *Proc. R. Soc.* A. CII. 278 The chief point of practical interest in the problem of the spinning rod is the question whether its energy is gradually carried away by the gravitational waves which are created, so that the rotation would slow down. **1937** EINSTEIN & ROSEN in *Jrnl. Franklin Inst.* CCXXIII. 43 The approximate method of integration of the gravitational equations of the general relativity theory leads to the existence of gravitational waves. **1970** *Sci. Amer.* 58/3 Einstein's general theory of relativity predicts that gravitational waves should be produced by matter that is accelerating with respect to the observer. **1971** *Nature* 15 Jan. 185/2 Weber has..presented a plausible case for believing that his detectors may indeed have monitored frequent and sharply pulsed gravitational waves, which seem to be emanating from the centre of our galaxy.

Hence **graviˈtationally** *adv.*, by gravitation.

1887 SIR W. THOMSON *Sun's Heat* in *Gd. Words* 150 Pieces of matter gravitationally attracted together. **1935** *Discovery* Dec. 352/2 Meteorites are gravitationally drawn towards the Earth. **1965** J. D. NORTH *Meas. of Universe* 417 Using Whittaker's and McCrea's idea of gravitational mass ..and restricting his attention to what he termed a 'gravitationally steady-state' in which σ is held to a constant value, McVittie found [etc.]. **1968** R. A. LYTTLETON *Myst. Solar Syst.* ii. 77 The requisite pressure arises gravitationally.

gravitative (ˈgrævɪteɪtɪv), *a.* [f. GRAVITATE *v.* + -IVE.] Of, pertaining to, or produced by gravitation.

1799 SIR H. DAVY in Beddoes *Contrib. Phys. & Med. Knowl.* 40 When the repulsive motion eminently predominates over the cohesive and gravitative attraction. **1818** COLERIDGE in *Rem.* (1836) I. 216 The particles themselves [of the human body] must have an interior and gravitative being. **1855** H. SPENCER *Princ. Psychol.* (1872) II. VI. xii. 156 The attributes of Heavy and Light; which indicate amounts of gravitative force in relation to bulk. **1891** *Nature* 26 July 291 That the heat developed by the falling together of the earth's materials arose simply from their gravitative potential energy.

graviton (ˈgrævɪtɒn). *Physics.* [f. GRAVIT(ATION + -ON.] A hypothetical sub-atomic particle thought of as propagating the action of gravitational force.

1942 *Chem. Abstr.* XXXVI. 6074 Plane waves of a particle with spin 2 (graviton). **1960** *New Scientist* 2 June 1433/2 To produce gravitons, one would need rapidly varying gravitational fields. Such fields are familiar in astronomy and accompany double stars. However..it will be a very long time before (astronomical) gravitons can be detected even if these exist. **1971** *Sci. Amer.* May 22/2 This fact, together with the small value of the gravitational constant, means that only one graviton (the quantum of gravitational radiation) would be emitted by an atom or a molecule for every 10^{43} photons (light quanta) emitted.

† **ˈgravitoned**, *a. Obs. rare*⁻¹. [f. L. *gravis* deep, heavy + *tonus*, Gr. τόνος TONE + -ED².] Deep-toned.

1657 REEVE *God's Plea* Ep. Ded. Relig. Cit. 9 They are not yet come to her [Nineveh's]..paroxisms of conflicts, gravitoned accents of prayer.

gravity (ˈgrævɪtɪ). Also 6 gravite(e, -yte, -etie, -ytye. [ad. F. *gravité* (12–13th c. in Hatz.-Darm.) or L. *gravitāt-em*, *gravitās*, n. of quality f. *gravis* heavy, weighty: see GRAVE *a.*¹ (*sb.*¹) The word was first introduced in figurative senses, corresponding generally to the Eng. senses of the adj. The primary physical sense of the Lat. word came into Eng. first in the 17th c.]

I. The quality of being GRAVE.

1. †**a.** Weight, influence, authority. *Obs.*

1534 WHITINTON *Tullyes Offices* I. (1540) 2 Plato if he wolde have practysed this maner of persuadynge, he might have persuaded with singular gravytie. **1535** *St. Papers Hen. VIII* (1849) VII. 614 So in all their procedinges..they shew themselffes to be men of gravyte and wisedom. **1620** BRENT tr. *Sarpi's Counc. Trent* I. (1676) 95 To send Ambassadours, men of gravity and authority. **1728** MORGAN *Algiers* II. iv. 290 Why should these Circumstances be mentioned by a Historiographer of such gravity. **1741** MIDDLETON *Cicero* II. x. 406, I would not have you think, that any Letters were ever read in the Senate of greater weight than yours, both for the eminent merit of your services, and the gravity of your words and sentiments.

†**b.** As a title of honour or respect. *Obs.*

1618 *Barnevelt's Apol.* Ded. A ij, I offer it to you with all singular affection, and bending submission to your grauitie. **1629** PRYNNE *New Antith.* Pref. 2 It cannot be unknown to your gravities, that [etc.]. **1781** GIBBON *Decl. & F.* xvii. II. 24 Your Gravity, your Excellency, your Eminence [etc.].

c. Of a ceremony, proceedings, etc.: Solemnity.

1647 CLARENDON *Hist. Reb.* III. §10 The earl was, with more clamour than was suitable to the gravity of that supreme court, called upon to withdraw. **1689** EVELYN *Corr.* 12 Aug. (1879) III. 445 There was at least something of more grauity and forme kept up. **1716** LADY M. W. MONTAGU *Let. to C'tess Mar* 14 Sept., The whole [drawing-room] passes with a gravity and air of ceremony that has something very formal in it. **1849** MACAULAY *Hist. Eng.* vi. II. 40 The gravity and pomp of the whole proceeding made a deep impression even on the Nuncio. **1855** PRESCOTT *Philip II*, v. 83 The process went on with suitable gravity.

d. Something grave; a grave or serious subject, speech, or remark. *Obs.* or *arch.*

1609 *Shakspere's Tr. & Cr.* (Qo. 1) Epist. ¶ ij, You should see all those grand censors, that now stile them [Playes] such vanities, flock to them for the maine grace of their grauities. **1850** L. HUNT *Autobiog.* II. x. 18 He seldom ventured on a gravity, but in echo of another's remark. **1871** GEO. ELIOT in J. W. Cross *Life* (1885) III. 131, I read aloud..books of German science, and other gravities. *Ibid.* III. 325 We are deep among the gravities.

2. Grave, weighty, or serious character or nature; importance, seriousness: †**a.** of literary productions, style, etc. (*obs.*); **b.** of events, facts, conditions.

1519 *Interl. Four Elem.* (Percy Soc.) 3 They myght, yf they wolde, in our Englyshe tonge Wryte workys of gravyte. **1533** SIR T. MORE *Debell. Salem* Wks. 964/2 The iudges parte is to see that the punishemente passe not the grauitie of the offence. **1594** HOOKER *Eccl. Pol.* I. x. §9 To punish the injury committed according to the gravity of the fact. **1649** MILTON *Eikon.* viii. Wks. (1847) 295/2 Empty sentences that have the sound of gravity, but the significance of nothing pertinent. **1659** PEARSON *Creed* (1839) 203 The gravity of every offence must needs increase proportionably to the dignity of the party offended. **1790** BURKE *Fr. Rev.* Wks. V. 74 The wise will determine from the gravity of the case. **1878** BOSW. SMITH *Carthage* 213 He was himself alive to the gravity of the occasion. **1883** J. PARKER *Tyne Ch.* 274 Great questions should be considered in a spirit worthy of their gravity.

3. Weighty dignity; reverend seriousness; serious or solemn conduct or demeanour befitting a ceremony, an office, etc.; staidness. In later use with wider application: Seriousness or sobriety (of conduct, bearing, speech, temperament, etc.); opp. to *levity* and *gaiety*.

1509 BARCLAY *Shyp of Folys* (1570) 233 Let these fooles auoyde this mad misuse, And folowe the right way of vertuous grauitie. **1549** *Compl. Scot.* vii. 70 Sittand in ane chair..kepand grite grauite, heffand ane beuk in his hand. **1585** T. WASHINGTON tr. *Nicholay's Voy.* II. xxv. 66 Marching with great gravitie. **1597** MORLEY *Introd. Mus.* 166 Those songs which are made for the high key be made for more life, the other in the low key with more grauetie and staidnesse. **1598** SHAKS. *Merry W.* III. i. 57, I neuer heard a man of his place, grauity, and learning, so wide of his owne respect. **1642** FULLER *Holy & Prof. St.* III. xxi. 209 Gravity in the ballast of the soul. **1647** CLARENDON *Hist. Reb.* I. §185 He was a man of very morose manners and a very sour aspect, which in that time was called gravity. **1689–90** TEMPLE *Ess. Pop. Discontent* Wks. 1731 I. 259 Gravity often passes for Wisdom, Wit for Ability. **1698** FRYER *Acc. E. India & P.* 70 Our Entertainment was truly Noble, and becoming the Gravity of the Society [Jesuits]. **1703** MAUNDRELL *Journ. Jerus.* (1732) 145 Let. 2 Their Religion is fram'd to keep up great outward Gravity. **1771** MACKENZIE *Man Feel.* xl. (1803) 77 The natural gravity of her temper..was such as not easily to be discomposed. **1823** LAMB *Elia* Ser. II. *Poor Relations*, His deportment was of the essence of gravity. **1837** W. IRVING *Capt. Bonneville* III. 39 Captain Bonneville sat..listening to them with Indian silence and gravity. **1868** STANLEY *Westm. Abb.* i. (ed. 2) 13 His manners presented a singular mixture of gravity and levity. **1894** HALL CAINE *Manxman* III. vii. 142 She grew uneasy at the settled gravity of his face.

II. In physical senses.

4. †**a.** The quality of having weight, ponderability; the tendency to downward motion, regarded in ancient physics as a property inherent in certain bodies (opposed to *levity*, or the upward tendency ascribed, e.g., to the element of fire). *Obs.*

1622 MALYNES *Anc. Law-Merch.* 62 But Aristotle his reasons are generally approued, to proue the earths stabilitie in the middle or lower part of the world, because of grauitie and leuitie. **1625** N. CARPENTER *Geog. Del.* I. iv. (1635) 85 Grauity or heauinesse is nothing els but an inclination of the parts of the Earth, returning to their naturall place. **1626** BACON *Sylva* §704 Similitude of Substance will cause Attraction, where the Body is wholly freed from the Motion of Grauity. **1646** SIR T. BROWNE *Pseud. Ep.* II. iii. 72 To overcome the resistance of its gravity and to lift it up from the earth. **1656** STANLEY *Hist. Philos.* VI. (1701) 250/2 Heaven hath neither gravity nor levity: this is manifest from its motion which is circular, not from the center which is proper to light things, nor to the center, as is proper to heavie, but about the center. **1665** GLANVILL *Scepsis Sci.* xi. 63 Gravity, which makes great bodies hard of Remove. **1678** HOBBES *Decam.* viii. 84 Gravity is an Intrinsecal Quality by which a Body so qualified descendeth perpendicularly towards the Superficies of the Earth.

b. Weight, heaviness; chiefly = *specific gravity* (see c), but occasionally the weight of an individual portion of matter, a definite amount of weight. Not now in scientific use, exc. in ***centre of gravity*** (see CENTRE *sb.* 16).

1641 WILKINS *Math. Magick* I. iii. (1648) 15 With this kinde of Ballance, it is usuall by the help onely of one weight, to measure sundry different gravities. **1650** BULWER *Anthropomet.* 122 Their gravity and weight may also offend the upper Lip. **1664** POWER *Exp. Philos.* II. 105 The reason why the Quicksilver descends at all in the first Experiment, is from its exceeding gravity. **1722** WOLLASTON *Relig. Nat.* ix. 213 Inanimate bodies, which have different gravities. **1750** JOHNSON *Rambler* No. 69 ¶8 Liquors of different gravity and texture which never can unite. **1805–17** R. JAMESON *Char. Min.* (ed. 3) 265 The degrees of gravity of minerals. **1807** HUTTON *Course Math.* II. 149 The weights, or gravities, of bodies near the surface of the earth, are proportional to the quantities of matter contained in them. *c* **1860** FARADAY *Forces Nat.* i. 21 Let us examine it with regard to the amount of its heaviness, or its gravity.

c. specific gravity. The degree of relative heaviness characteristic of any kind or portion of matter; commonly expressed by the ratio of the weight of a given volume to that of an equal volume of some substance taken as a standard (viz. usually water for liquids and solids, and air for gases). Abbreviated ***sp. gr.***

Since the weights of bodies are proportional to their masses, their specific gravities are in the same ratio as their densities; and in some scientific books the term *density* has displaced *specific gravity*.

1666 BOYLE in *Phil. Trans.* I. No. 14. 234 In case its (specifick) gravity were considerably alter'd. **1685** *Phil. Trans.* XV. 1004 As if they were different fluids, of different specifick gravities (as the word is now a-days) or (as it was wont to be called, and I think, better) Intensive gravity, one from the other. **1696** WHISTON *Theory Earth* I. (1722) 61 Fluids are..as capable of all degrees of Density and specifick Gravity, as Solids. **1758** REID tr. *Macquer's Chym.* I. 234 As the fire carries off the most aqueous part, the other which remains in the retort increases in specific gravity. **1822** IMISON *Sci. & Art* I. 120 The Hydrometer is the most eligible instrument for finding the specific gravity of fluids. **1831** LARDNER *Hydrost.* viii. 135 By the weights of equal bulks bodies may be separated and arranged in species. Hence the term *specific weight* or *specific gravity*. **1868** LOCKYER *Elem. Astron.* ix. §50 (1879) 311 The mean density, or specific gravity, of its materials. **1870** ATKINSON *Ganot's Physics* (ed. 4) §24 The relative density of a substance is generally called its *specific gravity*.

fig. **1841–4** EMERSON *Ess., Spir. Laws* Wks. (Bohn) I. 66 The permanence of all books is fixed by..their own specific gravity, or the intrinsic importance of their contents.

d. ***specific gravity beads*** or ***bulbs***: small hollow glass spheres used in determining the specific gravity of a liquid (see quot. 1884). ***specific gravity bottle*** or ***flask***: an instrument for determining the specific gravity of a liquid by a comparison of the weight of a given volume of it with that of an equal volume of a standard liquid under the same conditions of temperature and pressure; a pycnometer.

1863 ATKINSON *Ganot's Physics* §99 Specific gravity flask. **1881** *Ibid.* (ed. 10) §122 The pyknometer or specific gravity bottle. **1884** A. DANIELL *Princ. Physics* 198 Specific-gravity bulbs. Bulbs are sold which are known to float without rising or sinking in liquids of the sp. gr. marked in numbers upon them. A number of them are thrown into the liquid; those which bear too high a number sink, those which are too light rise; the one exactly corresponding, if there be one, is at rest anywhere in the fluid.

5. The attractive force by which all bodies tend to move towards the centre of the earth; the degree of intensity with which a body in any given position is affected by this force, measured by the amount of acceleration produced. Also often in wider sense, the degree of intensity with which one body is affected by the attraction of gravitation exercised by another body. *absol.* A force equal to the accelerating force of gravity; abbrev. *g*.

Some writers who restrict the word to terrestrial attraction apply it to the resultant of the earth's attraction of gravitation and the centrifugal force due to the earth's rotation, while others apply it to the gravitational component only.

1692 BENTLEY *Boyle Lect.* iv. (1724) 126 Without Gravity, the whole Universe..would have been a confused Chaos. *a* **1721** KEILL *Maupertuis' Diss.* (1734) 53 The Gravity in A towards γ being = π. **1756** BURKE *Subl. & B.* IV. i, If I were to explain the motion of a body falling to the ground, I would say it was caused by gravity. **1812** WOODHOUSE *Astron.* xxxiv. 329 A mean force tending to diminish the Moon's gravity to the Earth. **1816** KIRBY & SP. *Entomol.* (1843) II. 219 These ubiquitaries—some flying about—others pacing against gravity up the walls or upon the ceiling. **1837** BREWSTER *Magnet.* 246 A pendulum, oscillating by the action of gravity. **1854** —— *More Worlds* iv. 70 An accurate calculation of the force of gravity upon Jupiter. **1867** HERSCHEL *Fam. Lect. Sci.* 90 *note*, A force directed to the sun differing by a mere infinitesimal from its direct gravity. **1879** THOMSON & TAIT *Nat. Phil.* I. 230 Thus, approximately, the poundal is equal to the gravity of about half an ounce. **1945** *Jrnl. Exper. Zool.* C. 398 A sample of lobster-serum was..subjected to ultracentrifugation in a small air-turbine..machine at approximately 120,000 gravities. **1949** W. LEY *Conquest of Space* (1950) 44 If we assume the average acceleration of a moonship amounts to 4 *g* (gravities), which is something we are sure the pilot can stand.

†**6.** Heaviness, sluggishness (of bodily condition). *Obs.*$^{-1}$ (a Latinism).

1610 HEALEY *St. Aug. Citie of God* XXII. xv. (1620) 838 About thirty yeares man is in his full state and from that time he declineth to an age of more grauity and decay.

7. Of sounds: Lowness of pitch.

1669 HOLDER *Elem. Sp.* 18 There may be other ways of discriminating the voice, e.g. by Acuteness and Gravity. **1721** A. MALCOLM *Treat. Mus.* 539 All this seems plainly to put the Difference of the Tones only in the Acuteness or Gravity of the Whole. **1828** BUSBY *Mus. Man., Gravity*, a word used in contradistinction to *acute*: depth of sound. **1889** H. C. BANISTER *Music* (ed. 14) §2 The pitch—acuteness or gravity—of a musical sound depends upon the rapidity of the vibrations which produce it.

III. 8. *attrib.* and *Comb.*

a. simple attrib.

1882 *Rep. to Ho. Repr. Prec. Met. U.S.* 650 The mill itself is put up on the terrace or 'gravity' plan, the movement of ore in process of treatment being always down. **1894** *Outing* (U.S.) XXIV. 173/2 The house was..held together nominally by a little mud and mortar, in reality by virtue of being laid in the gravity line.

b. Special comb.: **gravity anomaly**, the difference between the observed acceleration due to gravity at a point on the surface of the earth (or another planet) and a value derived either from calculations of the geoid or from observations at some reference point; **gravity balance**, a type of torsion balance formerly used to measure the variation in the force of gravity from one place to another; **gravity battery, cell**, a galvanic battery or cell in which the liquids are kept apart by the force of gravity alone; **gravity-collapse structure** (see quot. 1961); **gravity conveyor**, a conveyor in which material slides, rolls, or falls under its own weight, the rate of descent being determined by friction; also, a conveyor in which the material is contained in freely suspended buckets kept upright by gravity; **gravity dam**, a dam that resists the pressure of the water by its weight; **gravity die-casting**, die-casting in which the metal is poured into the mould rather than forced in under pressure; a casting so made; **gravity escapement** (see quot. 1884); **gravity meter** = GRAVIMETER 2; **gravity-railroad**, 'a railroad in which the cars move down an inclined plane, or a series of inclined planes, under the action of gravity alone' (*Cent. Dict.*); **gravity stamp**, a machine for crushing ore in which a heavy weight is repeatedly raised by a revolving cam and allowed to drop on the ore; **gravity survey** (see quot. 1923); **gravity tank**, a fuel container from which the petrol is fed by gravity to the engine; **gravity water system** (see quot. 1940); **gravity wave**, a wave on the surface of a liquid in which the dominant force is gravity rather than surface tension; also, a wave in the atmosphere propagated because of gravity; **gravity-wedge**, a wedge that falls into position, when released, by the force of gravity alone; **gravity wind** (see quot. 1959).

1912 HAYFORD & BOWIE *Effect of Topography & Isostatic Compensation upon Intensity of Gravity* 112 A study was made to see if a possible relation could be discovered between the *gravity anomalies..and the geoid contours. **1924** H. JEFFREYS *Earth* ix. 121 It is seen from an examination of the formula for the gravity anomaly that only the second term arises from the attraction of the mountain itself. **1959** B. F. HOWELL *Introd. Geophysics* xxi. 326 Positive rather than negative gravity anomalies would be expected in the regions into which more mass is sliding. **1969** Z. KOPAL *Moon* xiii. 202 Local concentration of denser material would accelerate overflying spacecraft; and, conversely, negative gravity anomalies would slow the motion down. **1899** THRELFALL & POLLOCK in *Phil. Trans. R. Soc.* A. CXCIII. 215 (*title*) On a quartz thread *gravity balance. *Ibid.* 216 Our..attempts to construct a gravity balance began in September, 1889. **1923** GLAZEBROOK *Dict. Appl. Physics* III. 403/1 In Threlfall and Pollock's gravity balance a quartz thread is mounted horizontally and is attached, at one end to a spring which takes up variations of tension, and at the other end to an axle which can be rotated, in line with the thread. **1870** ATKINSON *Ganot's Physics* (ed. 4) §704 A kind of battery has been devised in which the porous vessel is entirely dispensed with, and the separation of the liquids is effected by the difference of density. Such batteries are called **gravity batteries*. **1876** PREECE & SIVEWRIGHT *Telegraphy* 31 The so called 'Gravity' batteries. **1936** HARRISON & FALCON in *Q. Jrnl. Geol. Soc.* XCII. 91 (*title*) *Gravity collapse structures and mountain ranges, as exemplified in south-western Iran. **1961** J. CHALLINOR *Dict. Geol.* 95/2 *Gravity-collapse structures*, structures, in stratified rocks, produced on the limbs of (simple) folds as a result of collapse under the force of gravity. **1910** *Encycl. Brit.* VII. 56/1 The *gravity or tilting bucket conveyor can be used as a combined elevator and conveyor. **1966** *McGraw-Hill Encycl. Sci. & Technol.* III. 447/2 The most economical means for lowering articles and materials is by gravity conveyors. **1940** *Chambers's Techn. Dict.* 388/1 *Gravity dam. **1957** *Encycl. Brit.* VII. (*caption*, facing p. 8), Solid masonry gravity dams. **1971** N. SMITH *Hist. Dams* ii. 33 A gravity dam is in general a straight wall of masonry or earth which resists the applied water-pressure because of its sheer weight. **1940** *Chambers's Techn. Dict.* 388/1 **Gravity diecasting*, a process by means of which castings of various alloys are made in steel or cast-iron moulds, the molten metal being poured by hand. **1960** *Metallurgia* LXI. 65/2 Although there are many methods of producing castings in aluminium alloys, only three are of major importance, namely sand casting, gravity die casting, and pressure die casting. **1964** S. CRAWFORD *Basic Engin. Processes* (1969) xi. 246 Gravity die castings are generally superior in structure and strength to both sand castings and pressure die castings. **1850** DENISON *Clock & Watch Making* 71 The most simple ..form of the *gravity escapement is this. **1884** F. J. BRITTEN *Watch & Clockm.* 115 *Gravity Escapement*, an escapement in which impulse is given to the pendulum by a weight falling through a constant distance. **1941** J. M. BRUCKSHAW in *Proc. Physical Soc.* LIII. 449 The present interest in *gravity meters arises from two..considerations. *Ibid.* 452 It is by no means an easy matter to produce a gravity meter..which..is robust and sufficiently transportable to be employed in the field. **1955** *Sci. Amer.* Sept. 164/1 The only way we can trace its girth and plot its distances accurately is to travel over its surface with a gravity meter, measuring the tiny differences in gravity from point to point as a guide to the ups and downs of the globe's undulating shape. **1957** *Encycl. Brit.* X. 677/1 The gravity meter or gravimeter is simply a spring balance comprising a constant mass supported by a spring system, the changes in elongation of which may be read with precision. **1903** R. H. RICHARDS *Ore Dressing* I. v. 144 *Gravity stamps are lifted by cams and drop by their own weight. **1965** E. J. PRYOR *Mineral Processing* (ed. 3) iv. 60 The gravity stamp..is a fixed-path machine. It is obsolescent, its place being taken by the rod mill. **1913** *Q. Jrnl. Geol. Soc.* LXIX. p. lxxxii, A *Gravity Survey seems clearly to be called for. **1923** GLAZEBROOK *Dict. Appl. Physics* III. 398/1 The primary object of a gravity survey is to obtain values of the force and direction of gravity at various points of the sea-level surface. **1959** *New Scientist* 5 Feb. 274/2 The Americans are now planning an airborne seismic and gravity survey of the central section of the supposed *graben*, in Marie Byrd Land. **1917** 'CONTACT' *Airman's Outings* 225 A small *gravity tank for his machine, to be used when the pressure tank is ventilated by a bullet. **1934** V. M. YEATES *Winged Victory* 48 A small reserve supply [of fuel] in the gravity tank. **1940** *Chambers's Techn. Dict.* 388/1 **Gravity water system*, a system in which flow occurs under the natural pressure due to gravity. **1960** R. DAVIES *Voice from Attic* 99 The same unpleasing charts of the sexual organs (the male, like plans for a gravity water system; the female like the skull of an elk, with vastly branching antlers). **1877** *Proc. Lond. Math. Soc.* IX. 22 The following particular cases..are here tabulated for convenience:—$V \propto \lambda$, $U = 0$, Reynold's disconnected pendulums. $V \propto \lambda^{\frac{1}{2}}$, $U = \frac{1}{2}V$, Deep-water *gravity waves. $V \propto \lambda^0$, $U = V$, Aërial waves, &c. $V = \lambda^{-\frac{1}{2}}$, $U = \frac{3}{2}V$, Capillary water waves. $V \propto \lambda^{-1}$, $U = 2V$, Flexural waves. **1930** N. SHAW *Man. Meteorol.* III. i. 30 The genesis of gravity-waves in air is not generally understood. **1957** *Jrnl. Marine Res.* XVI. 107 At wind velocities between 16 and 20 knots it is common for capillary waves having the same velocity as the gravity waves to ride just at the beginning of the crest of the gravity waves. **1971** *Nature: Physical Sci.* 29 Mar. 99/2 The excitation of atmospheric gravity waves by a nuclear test in the atmosphere. **1888** *Pall Mall G.* 23 Oct. 2/2 A very simple but effective *gravity-wedge safety apparatus. **1928** N. SHAW *Man. Meteorol.* II. 255 Katabatic winds.. Such winds are *gravity-winds which pay no attention to isobars until they get into the open where they have time to adjust themselves to the requirements of the earth's rotation. **1959** R. E. HUSCHKE *Gloss. Meteorol.* 259 *Gravity wind*, a wind.. directed down the slope of an incline and caused by greater air density near the slope than at the same levels some distance horizontally from the slope.

Hence **'gravityship**, used as a mock title.

1772 NUGENT tr. *Hist. Friar Gerund* I. 370 God forgive his Gravityship the very Reverend Father Provincial.

'gravity-fed, *a.* [See FEED *v.* 7, 8 c.] Supplied with material by the action of gravity; utilizing a gravity feed. Hence (as a back-formation) **'gravity-feed** *v. trans.*, to supply (material) in this way.

1908 *Westm. Gaz.* 20 Feb. 4/2 The gravity-fed oil-pump. **1936** *Archit. Rev.* Dec. p. lxii/3 The hopper is so designed that the fuel is gravity-fed into the back of the fire space. **1962** *Times* 26 Mar. 5/3 Automatic gravity-fed boilers. **1971** *New Scientist* 18 Mar. 626/2 The normal pre-1950s reservoir makes use of upland topography to capture a volume of water and gravity-feed it to the towns.

'gravity(-)feed, *sb.* [FEED *sb.* 5. Cf. prec.] A supply system that makes use of gravity to maintain the flow of material; the supplying of material in this way. Also *attrib.*

1914 *Programme Isle of Man Tourist Trophy Races* 9/1 Either gravity or pressure feed may be used. **1925** A. W. JUDGE *Carburettors* 142 The three systems of fuel supply used on motor vehicles are as follows: (1) The Gravity Feed. (2) Pressure Feed. (3) Vacuum Feed. **1934** *Aircraft Engin.* Nov. 286/1 The simplest form of petrol system is one employing direct gravity feed to the engine. **1961** *Listener* 12 Oct. 583/2 A more automatic type is the gravity-feed boiler, generally using a special grade of small anthracite. **1964** S. CRAWFORD *Basic Engin. Processes* (1969) xi. 246 Molten metal at the correct temperature is poured from a ladle under gravity feed into a split metal die.

gravo-, bad combining form of GRAVE *a.*

1807 J. THELWALL in *Monthly Mag.* XXIII. 30 Their distinctions of gravo-acute and acuto-grave or circumflexes.

† **'gravous**, *a. Obs. rare.* [f. L. *grav-is* or Eng. GRAVE *a.* + -OUS, possibly influenced by *grievous.*] Grave. So † **'gravously** *adv.*, gravely.

1535 *St. Papers Hen. VIII* (1849) VII. 614 Pausing in every degree, and proceding in a gravous sorte, with mature advise and deliberation. **1548** HALL *Chron., Edw. IV* (an. 22) (1550) 56 Grauous matters, concernyng the welthes of bothe the Realmes. *Ibid.* (an. 23) 59 b, If wee..would..in our myndes grauously ponder the fraile..imbecilitie of our humayn nature. *Ibid., Hen. VII* (an. 1) 3 He would that there should be elected the most prudent & grauous persons of euery countie.

gravure[1] ('greɪvjʊə(r)). *rare*⁻¹. [f. GRAVE *v.*[1] + -URE. Cf. F. *gravure* engraving.] The fact of being graven or engraved.

1876 LANIER *Poems, Dedication*, Symbol of gravure on his heart to be.

gravure[2] (gravy:r, 'grævjʊə(r), -'jʊə(r)). [Shortened from PHOTOGRAVURE.] The process of engraving by means of photography; a print produced by this process. Also *attrib.*

1893 *Daily News* 29 June 5/4 Accompanied by numerous Woodbury gravure illustrations. **1896** *Ibid.* 11 June 3/1 A number of Herkomer gravures, including portraits..and copies of well-known pictures.

gravy ('greɪvɪ). Forms: 4-5 **gravé**, 5 **gravey, greve, grovy**, (7 **gravet**), **greavie, -y**, 8 **graivie**, 7-8 **gravie**, 5- **gravy**. [Of obscure origin.

The receipts quoted under sense 1 below are substantially identical with receipts in OF. cookery books, in which the word is *grané*. For the OF. word the reading *grané* seems certain (though in printed texts *gravé* usually appears); it is prob. cogn. with OF. *grain* 'anything used in cooking' (Godef.), and with GRENADE[2], GRENADINE; cf. also *faus grenon* = 'gravy bastard'. But in the Eng. MSS. the word has nearly always either a *v* or a letter which looks more like *u* than *n* (the only exception being in the 'table' to *Liber Cocorum*, which has thrice *grane*, while the text has *graue*). As the ME. word was therefore identical in form with the mod. word, it seems difficult, in spite of the difference in sense, to regard them as unconnected. In the present state of the evidence, the most probable conclusion is that the OF. *grané* was early misread as *gravé*, and in that form became current as a term of English cookery.]

† **1.** Some kind of dressing used for white meats, fish, and vegetables, which seems to have consisted of broth, milk of almonds, spices, and (usually) wine or ale. ***gravy bastard***: app. an inferior imitation of this. *Obs.*

?*c* **1390** *Form of Cury* (1780) 22 Connynges in Grauey. Take Connynges..and drawe hem with a gode broth with almandes blanched and brayed, do þerinne suger and powdor gynger. *Ibid.* 59 Oysters in Gravey. Schyl Oysters and seeþ hem in wyne and in hare own broth, cole the broth thrugh a cloth, take almandes blaunched, grynde hem and drawe hem up with the self broth & alye it wiþ floer of Rys and do the oysters þerinne, cast in powder of gynger, suger, macys. *c* **1420** *Liber Cocorum* (1862) 25 For tenchis in gravé. Sethe þy tenchis..Grynd peper and safron with ale..With tenchis brothe, þou temper hit. **14..** *Voc.* in Wr.-Wülcker 586/4 *Garus*, greue. [Cf. *Ibid.* 740/38 *Hic garus*, a fyscbrowe.] **14..** *MS. Arundel* in *Househ. Ord.* (1790) 446 Eles in Grave. Take almondes and grinde hem [etc.]. *c* **1430** *Two Cookery-bks.* 13 Oystres en grauey. *Ibid.*, Oystrys in grauy bastard...take þe water of þe Oystrys, & ale, an brede y-straynid..an put it on a potte, an Gyngre, Sugre, Saffron, powder pepir, and Salt. *Ibid.* 33 Whyte Pesyn in grauey. *c* **1450** *Ibid.* 101 A litul gravey of þe pike. *c* **1470** *Noble Bk. Cookry* (Napier 1882) 117 To mak tenche in grave, tak.. your tenche and sethe hym and alay it with myed bred pepper and saffron and temper it with the tenches brothe, then lay the tenche in a platter and poure on the grave. *c* **1475** *Pict. Voc.* in Wr.-Wülcker 789/35 *Hec promulada* [? = **promulsida, promulsis*] grovy. **1508-13** *Bk. Keruynge* (W. de W.) B 4 Sprottes is good in sewe..oystres in ceuy, oysters in grauy, menewes in porpas.

2. a. The fat and juices which exude from flesh during and after the process of cooking; a dressing for meat or vegetables made from these with the addition of condiments.

1591 A. W. *Bk. Cookrye* 4 Boile it [a Swan] vntill it be somwhat thick, and put in two spoon full of the grauye of the Swan. **1600** SHAKS. *2 Hen. IV*, I. ii. 184 *Iust.* There is not a white haire in your face but should haue his effect of grauity. *Falst.* His effect of grauy, grauie, grauie. **1601** HOLLAND *Pliny* II. 312 The grauie or dripping..of the Hyænes liuer, newly taken out of the body. **1615** CHAPMAN *Odyss.* XVIII. 62 There are now at fire Two brests of Goat: both which, let Law set downe Before the man..With all their fat and greauie. **1638** RAWLEY tr. *Bacon's Life & Death* (1650) 47 Gravies of Meat..Are good for old Persons. **1661** LOVELL *Hist. Anim. & Min.* Introd., The gravet of rosted meat. **1709** ADDISON *Tatler* No. 148 ¶1 A whole roasted Ox, (which was certainly the best Way to preserve the Gravy). **1769** MRS. RAFFALD *Eng. Housekpr.* (1778) 69 When you dish it [a tongue] up, pour a little brown gravy. **1846** MRS. GORE *Eng. Charac.* (1852) 109 The pure and transparent gravies of France. **1868** JEWRY *Model Cookery* 270 Serve it up hot with a rich gravy poured round it.

b. *transf.* Also in phr. ***goose without gravy*** (see GOOSE *sb.* 1 d); ***to stew in one's own gravy***, to be bathed in sweat.

1699 E. WARD *London Spy* IX. 14 He reliev'd us out of our Purgatory [a bath], and carried us to our Dressing Room, which gave us such Refreshment after we had been thus long stewing in our own Gravy, that [etc.]. *a* **1845** HOOD *Widow* iii, As if..to soothe his grave with sorrow's gravy [*i.e.* tears].

c. *Theatrical slang.* (See quot. 1952.)

1864 P. PATERSON *Glimpses Real Life* x. 107 The farce.. was gone through with equal rapidity—of course, all the 'points' were carefully given, 'cartfuls of beefsteaks and bucketsful of gravy' especially. **1952** W. GRANVILLE *Dict. Theatr. Terms* 92 *Gravy*, easy laughs from a friendly audience. (2) Good lines, or business, in a farce or comedy.

d. Money easily acquired; an unearned or unexpected bonus; a tip. Hence ***to ride (board) the gravy train*** (or ***boat***), to obtain easy financial success. *slang* (orig. *U.S.*).

1910 *Sat. Even. Post* 30 July 13/1 Stick him for all you can. You're a hard worker, and you mustn't let some-body else git the gravy. **1927** *Amer. Speech* II. 276 *Gravy train*, sinecure. **1932** WODEHOUSE *Hot Water* i. 30 'Sixty thousand dollars' worth, at least.' Mr. Slattery was impressed. Sixty grand, he agreed, was pretty good gravy. **1933** *Amer. Speech* Feb. 32/1 *Ride a gravy train*, to continue to receive more than one's deserts. **1934** J. O'HARA *Appointment in Samarra* (1935) 11 If you sell two Cadillacs a month, you make expenses, and anything over that is so much gravy. **1939** E. S. GARDNER *D.A. draws Circle* (1940) xv. 269 We started riding the gravy train like I said. **1942** D. POWELL *Time to be Born* (1943) viii. 180 An apartment which he was able to furnish almost completely with 'gravy'—sofas, mattresses, gadgets pressed on him by earnest manufacturers in hopes of public mention of their products. **1948** MENJOU & MUSSELMAN *It Took Nine Tailors* 141 Once you get on the Hollywood gravy boat, it is no trick to make money; the trick is to keep it. **1952** M. MCCARTHY *Groves of Academe* (1953) x. 197 There was a moment in the spring when the whole Jocelyn sideshow seemed to be boarding the gravy train, on to fatter triumphs of platitude and mediocrity. **1960** *Guardian* 17 Oct. 16/3 In 1960, says the cool Bob Kennedy, if his brother gets 55 [electoral votes]..'anything else will be gravy'. **1967** *Sun* 20 Apr. 5/8 The tip is called the gravy, and when there is a mix-up at the table and two diners leave separate tips, it becomes double gravy. **1968** *Globe & Mail* (Toronto) 17 Feb. 8/1 In the past 10 years, the Manitoba Government has reaped about $8-million from the Downs (more than $1-million last year). This revenue is almost pure gravy.

3. *attrib.* and *Comb.*, as ***gravy-boat, -salt, sauce, soup, spoon***; instrumental, as ***gravy-dripping*** adj.; **gravy beef**, a part of the leg of beef which is cooked for the sake of its gravy; **gravy-eyed** *a.* (see quot.).

1747 MRS. GLASSE *Cookery* ii. 39 Lay a Pound of *Gravy Beef..over your Chickens. **1895** *Montgomery Ward Catal.* Index, *Gravy Ladles and Boats. **1916** *Daily Colonist* (Victoria, B.C.) 7 July 7/1 (Advt.), Covered Gravy Boats with Plate. **1970** SIMON & HOWE *Dict. Gastron.* 206 *Gravy boat*, the name commonly given to a low, boatshaped container used to dispense gravies, sauces etc. **1886** W. J. TUCKER *E. Europe* 175 Digging his dirty, *gravy-dripping knife into the salt-cellar. **1785** GROSE *Dict. Vulg. Tongue*, **Gravey eyed*, blear eyed, one whose eyes have a running humour. **1907** *Yesterday's Shopping* (1969) 33/1 *Gravy Salt ..pkt., 0/1. **1958** J. CANNAN *And be a Villain* iii. 68, I went down to the shop for your gravy salt. **1769** MRS. RAFFALD *Engl. Housekpr.* (1778) 24 To make the *gravy sauce, put a little brown gravy into a sauce-pan, with one anchovy. **1694** MOTTEUX *Rabelais* v. xvii. (1737) 74 *Gravy Soupe. **1765** GOLDSM. *Ess.* xxv. 227 He drank gravy-soup when he could get it. **1813** *Sporting Mag.* XLII. 135 A basin of gravy-soup ..was placed before him. **1844** DICKENS *Mart. Chuz.* i, A *gravy spoon.

gravylle, gravyn, obs. ff. GRAVEL, GRAVE *v.*[1]

grawacke, variant of GRAUWACKE.

grawe, obs. form of GRAVE, GROW.

grawell, obs. form of GRAVEL.

grawin, obs. pa. pple. of GRAVE *v.*[1]

grawls, Anglo-Irish form of GRILSE.

grawous, obs. form of GRIEVOUS.

gray, etc.: see GREY.

grayboyle, obs. form of GARBOIL.

1620 *Concession to J. Merrick* in Rymer *Fœdera* (1710) XVII. 256 The late Troubles and Grayboyles happened in that State.

graydon, grayel, obs. ff. GRADDAN, GRAIL[1].

graylag: see GREYLAG.

grayle, var. GRAIL[1]; obs. f. GRAIL[3], gravel.

grayling ('greɪlɪŋ). Also 5 **gra-, gray-, grelyng(e, grayllyng(h)e**, 6-7 **grailing**, 7-8 **greyling**, 8 **gragling**. [f. *gray*, GREY *a.*: see -LING.]

1. A freshwater fish of the genus *Thymallus* (family *Salmonidæ*), of a silvery-grey colour and characterized by a long and high dorsal fin.

The common European grayling is *Thymallus vulgaris*; other species are *T. signifer*, the American or Alaskan grayling, and *T. ontariensis*, the Michigan grayling.

a **1450** *Fysshynge w. angle* (1883) 15 Ye schall angle..For þe trowyt the grelyng and þe barbel..with a lyne of ix herys. *Ibid.* 17 A dubbed hooke for the troute & gralyng. *a* **1490** BOTONER *Itin.* (1778) 358 Yn Wye water sunt pisces, trouthes, cullys, loches, anguillæ, grayllynghes. **1496** *Bk. St. Albans, Fishing* h 6 b, The grayllynge by a nother name callyd vmbre is a delycyous fysshe to mannys mouthe. **1577-87** HARRISON *England* I. xiv. in *Holinshed* (1807) I. 123 In this riuer [Wie] be vmbers, otherwise called grailings. *a* **1672** WILLUGHBY *Icthyogr.* (1686) Tab. N 8, A Greyling or Omer. **1787** BEST *Angling* 39 The Gragling, Grayling or Umber. This fish has three different names given it, according to the different parts of England where it is found. **1855** TENNYSON *Brook* 58 And here and there a lusty trout, And here and there a grayling. **1867** F. FRANCIS *Angling* viii. (1880) 294 If the trout be the gentleman of the streams, the grayling is certainly the lady. **1873** G. C. DAVIES *Mount. & Mere* xi. 89 The tender-mouthed grayling. **1882** *Michigan & its Resources* 29 Brook trout and grayling are plenty in some of the small rivers of the northern counties.

b. An Australian fish, *Prototroctes marœna*, closely resembling the English grayling.

1880 W. SENIOR *Travel & Trout* 94 The cucumber mullet ..I have long expected to be a grayling. **1882** TENISON-WOODS *Fish of N. S. Wales* 109 (Morris) The Australian grayling, which in character..is almost identical with the English fish of that name. **1889** *Cassell's Picturesque Austral.* (1890) IV. 206 The river abounds in the delicious grayling or cucumber fish.

c. (See quot.)

1889 'JOHN BICKERDYKE' *Bk. All-round Angler* III. 95 *note*, In parts of Ireland grilse are termed grayling, and in the markets of the Midlands pollan..is sold as Irish grayling.

2. A common butterfly (*Hipparchia Semele*), so called from the grey under-side of the wings.

1819 G. SAMOUELLE *Entomol. Compend.* 241 *Hipparchia Semele* (grayling, or rock underwing). **1841** WESTWOOD *Brit. Butterflies* 68. **1893** MORRIS *Brit. Butterflies* 51. **1893** *Daily News* 1 Feb. 8/2 The grayling. This quiet coloured butterfly is a native of stony hill sides.

3. *attrib.* and *Comb.*, as ***grayling-angler, -fishing, -fly***; **grayling sky**, a sky of a silvery-grey colour.

1894 H. NISBET *Bush Girl's Rom.* 6 The motionless figure as it lies under that grayling sky. **1889** 'JOHN BICKERDYKE' *Bk. All-round Angler* III. 97 The best Test grayling-flies. **1898** *Speaker* 29 Oct. 515/2 Your grayling angler casts it [his fly] in very different fashion.

graymalkin, variant of GRIMALKIN.

gray mercy, obs. variant of GRAMERCY.

graymill ('greɪmɪl). Also 6 **gray mil(e, myle**, 7 **greimile**. [Etymological perversion (after *gray*, GREY *a.*) of F. *grémil* GROMWELL. (A further corruption is *grey millet*: see GREY *a.* 10.)] = GROMWELL.

1548 TURNER *Names of Herbes* 49 Lithospermon is called of the Herbaries Milium solis, in englishe Grummel, but it shoulde be called Gray myle. **1551** —— *Herbal* II. 40 Lithospermon..is called gray mil of the blewish gray color that it hath. **1565** COOPER *Thesaurus, Lithospermum*..Some take it to be grummell, or gray mile. **1601** HOLLAND *Pliny* (1634) II. 284 Of all herbes that be, there is none more wonderful than Greimile. **1611** COTGR., *Gremil*, the hearb Gromill, Grummell, or Graymill. **1756** WATSON *Leicestersh. Plants* in *Phil. Trans.* XLIX. 814 Gromwell, Gromil, or Graymill.

grayn(e, grayth(e, obs. ff. GRAIN, GRAITH.

grayvez, graz, obs. ff. GREAVES, GRASS.

graze (greɪz), *sb.* [f. GRAZE *v.*[2]]

1. An act or instance of grazing, touching lightly, or rubbing against, a surface in passing: said esp. of shot; also, 'the point at which a shot strikes and rebounds from earth or water' (Smyth *Sailor's Word-bk.* 1867).

1692 in *Capt. Smith's Seaman's Gram.* II. xxvi. 136 The Graze of the Bullet at the first Shot. **1864** *Daily Tel.* 7 June, Dividing the sum of all the distances, taken from the muzzle to the first graze. **1876** *Daily News* 30 Sept. 2/2 Common shell..which gave a range of about 3,000 yards at the first graze. **1879** PROCTOR *Pleas. Ways Sci.* v. 112 All successive grazes [of a ray of light] would be indicated to us by accessions of lustre. **1899** *Speaker* 11 Nov. 133/1 The difficulty is..to secure a fuze sufficiently delicate to act on graze.

2. A superficial wound or abrasion, caused by an object rubbing against the skin of the body.

1847 *Illustr. Lond. News* 10 July 30/1 A few grazes and bruises were all the evils. **1891** E. PEACOCK *N. Brendon* I. 151 Quite a slight wound, just a graze of the arm.

graze (greɪz), *v.*[1] Forms: 4–8 grase, (5 gresyn, 6 grease), 6– graze. [OE. *grasian*, f. *gras-*, *græs* GRASS *sb.*[1]; cf. MDu., MHG. *grasen* (Du. *grazen*, G. *grasen*), Sw. *gräsa*, Da. *græsse*, trans. and intr.]

1. *intr.* Chiefly of cattle: To feed on growing grass and other herbage.

c **1000** *Sax. Leechd.* III. 200 [Se þe] oxan grasiende ȝesihþ siȝe ceapas [*read* ceapes] ȝetacnað. **1390** GOWER *Conf.* I. 142 Lich an oxe under the fote He graseth. *c* **1430** LYDG. *Min. Poems* (1840) 121 Nature hathe..Ordeyned..Sheepe in theyr pasture to grase day and nyght. **1585** T. WASHINGTON tr. *Nicholay's Voy.* II. viii. 40 b, Driving them [partridges] in the daye time too goe grase in the mountaynes. **1624** CAPT. SMITH *Virginia* IV. 111 Our Hogs and Cattell haue twentie miles circuit to graze in securely. **1784** COWPER *Task* VI. 774 The lion, and the libbard, and the bear Graze with the fearless flocks. **1837** W. IRVING *Capt. Bonneville* I. 102 The poor jaded horses were turned out to graze. **1879** STAINER *Music of Bible* 2 The god..found a mountain tortoise grazing near his grotto. **1894** J. T. FOWLER *Adamnan* Introd. 51 The cows that grazed in the monastic pastures.

b. *Proverb.*

1509 BARCLAY *Shyp of Folys* (1570) 189 Suche as they most gladly dead would haue Eateth of that goose that graseth on their graue. **1599** PORTER *Angry Wom. Abingt.* (1841) 25 'The goose that graseth on the greene', quoth he, 'May I eat on when you shall buryed be!' **1632** in *Crt. & Times Chas. I* (1848) II. 177 He looks fresh, and enjoys his health..so that if any other prelate do gape after his benefice, his grace, perhaps, according to that old and homely proverb, [may] eat of the goose which shall graze upon his grave.

2. *transf.* and *fig.* **a.** 'To move on devouring' (J.). ? *Obs.* **b.** *humorously* of persons: To feed. Also *to send to graze*: to send packing, turn out.

1579 SPENSER *Sheph. Cal.* Sept. 113 Sike mischiefe graseth hem emong. **1592** SHAKS. *Rom. & Jul.* III. v. 190 Graze where you will, you shall not house with me. *a* **1626** BACON *War w. Spain* (1629) 10 As euery State lay next to the other that was oppressed, so the fire perpetually grazed. **1675** T. TURNOR *Case Bankers & Creditors* (ed. 3) 35 This Wildfire..had now grazed almost throughout the whole Realm. **1733** SWIFT *Legion Club* 215 Will you, in your faction's phrase, Send the clergy all to graze? **1824** LADY GRANVILLE *Lett.* (1894) I. 304 Mr. Drummond..does no harm grazing at the bottom of a long table. **1872** EARL PEMBROKE & G. H. KINGSLEY *S. Sea Bubbles* ix. 230 Mosquitoes that are grazing coolly on one's hands.

3. *trans.* To feed on, eat (growing grass or other herbage). Chiefly *poet.*

1667 MILTON *P.L.* IV. 253 Flocks Grasing the tender herb. **1697** DRYDEN *Æneid* VI. 889 Their Steeds around, Free from their Harness, graze the flow'ry Ground. **1712** POPE *Messiah* 77 The lambs with wolves shall graze the verdant mead. **1784** COWPER *Task* V. 785 Brutes graze the mountain-top with faces prone.

fig. **1791** BOSWELL *Johnson* 1 July, an. 1763 *note*, He is the richest authour that ever grazed the common of literature.

†**b.** *transf.* Said of fish. *Obs. rare.*

1697 DRYDEN *Virg. Georg.* IV. 568 This Neptune gave him, when he gave to keep His scaly Flocks, that graze the wat'ry deep.

4. *causal.* To put (cattle) to feed on pasture; also, to tend while so feeding.

1564 GOLDING *Justin's Hist.* II. (1570) 10 b, They feede & graze theyr cattell wandering through the desertes. **1596** SHAKS. *Merch. V.* I. iii. 92 When Iacob graz'd his Vncle Labans sheepe. **1613** WITHER *Epithal.* in *Juvenilia* (1633) 372 We drive our flocks a field to graze them. **1707** J. ARCHDALE *Descr. Carolina* 31 A Cow is grased near as cheap as a Sheep here in England. **1846** MCCULLOCH *Acc. Brit. Empire* (1854) I. 181 Great numbers of cattle, and of long-wooled sheep, are grazed in the fens. **1863** FAWCETT *Pol. Econ.* II. viii. (1876) 239 Labourers who have been accustomed to graze a cow..upon a common.

5. *intr.* (or *absol.*) To pasture cattle.

c **1645** T. TULLY *Siege of Carlisle* (1840) 34 Capt Philipson jun. grased in the same place. **1660** SHARROCK *Vegetables* 21 A delicate grasse..upon which..you may graze with cattle or horse. **1668** *Ormonde MSS.* in *10th Rep. Hist. MSS. Comm.* App. v. 79 Your petitioners, and those that grase with them, have..noe way to bring their cattell to the markett. **1892** *Within Hour Lond.* xiii. 266 My own friends, who grazed on the marshes.

6. *trans.* To put cattle to feed on (grass, land, etc.); † *to graze up*, to exhaust by grazing.

1601 R. JOHNSON *Kingd. & Commw.* (1603) 161 Driving on til they have grazed al up. **1707** MORTIMER *Husb.* 16 Some graze their Land till Christmas, and some longer. **1783** JOHNSON in *Boswell* 18 Apr., You may graze the ground when the trees are grown up. **1861** *Jrnl. R. Agric. Soc.* XXII. II. 420 The young grass should not be grazed. **1880** JEFFERIES *Gt. Estate* viii. 150 A pasture field..which it was believed had been grazed for fully two hundred years.

7. *intr.* Of land: To produce grass; to serve for grazing. *Obs.* exc. *dial.*

1625 BACON *Ess., Building* (Arb.) 551 The Quarters to Graze, being kept Shorne, but not too neare Shorne. **1626** —— *Sylva* §600 The Ground will be like a Wood, which keepeth out the Sunne; And so continueth the Wet; Whereby it will neuer graze (to purpose) that yeare. **1649** BLITHE *Eng. Improv. Impr.* (1653) 10 The unsuitable unnaturall laying down of Land to Graze. **1707** MORTIMER *Husb.* 28 Those Lands that Graze speedily. *a* **1825** FORBY *Voc. E. Anglia*, *Graze*, to become covered with the growth of grass.

Hence **grazed** (greɪzd), *ppl. a.* Also **'grazer**, an animal that grazes.

1649 BLITHE *Eng. Improv. Impr.* (1653) 113 Grazed Lands. **1667** MILTON *P.L.* I. 486 Lik'ning his Maker to the Grazèd Ox. **1708** J. PHILIPS *Cyder* I. 104 After them the Cackling Goose, Close-grazer, finds wherewith to ease her Want. **1856** WHITTIER *Panorama* 254 Like the crowned grazer on Euphrates' shore.

graze (greɪz), *v.*[2] Also 7 graise, 8 grease. [Of obscure etymology. The sense closely approaches that of *glaze*, GLACE *v.* (see esp. 2 b below), of which this may possibly be an altered form due to the influence of GRATE *v.* Prof. Skeat suggests that the word may be a transferred use of prec., the sense 'to take off the grass close down to the ground' having passed into the sense 'to touch lightly in passing'; cf. 'a close *shave*'; also G. *grasen* 'to roll and bound, said of cannon-balls' (Flügel), and quots. 1632 and 1642 under sense 2.]

1. *trans.* To touch (a surface) lightly in passing; esp. to roughen or abrade (the skin or a part of the body) in rubbing or brushing past. Also, to suffer slight abrasion of (a part of one's body).

1604 SHAKS. *Oth.* IV. i. 279 Whose solid vertue The shot of Accident, nor dart of Chance Could neither graze, nor pierce? **1701** *Cowell's Interpr.* s.v. *Grass-Hearth*, As we still say, the Skin is gras'd, or slightly hurt. **1814** SCOTT *Wav.* li, The bullet grazed the young lady's temple. **1863** FR. A. KEMBLE *Resid. in Georgia* 51 At six o'clock our little canoe grazed the steps. **1868** LOCKYER *Elem. Astron.* iii. §23 (1879) 125 Some comets..approach so close to the Sun as almost to graze its surface. **1869** MRS. STOWE *Oldtown Folks* xiv. (1870) 132 She fell and grazed her arm sadly.

fig. **1809** MALKIN *Gil Blas* XI. vii. ¶1 His self-love was grazed now and then. **1849** MACAULAY *Hist. Eng.* v. I. 644 The civil war had barely grazed the frontier of Devonshire. **1887** J. C. MORISON *Service of Man* (1889) xv, How nearly we grazed a fratricidal war with our American kinsfolk..dwells in all memories.

b. Said of a ray of light; *spec.* To meet (a curve) tangentially.

1839 G. BIRD *Nat. Philos.* 308 The luminous ray could only graze the surface of the medium ABD. **1860** TYNDALL *Glac.* I. xxv. 178 The sun's..rays..grazing the summit of the mountain. **1863** CHALLIS in *Notices R. Astron. Soc.* XXIII. 235 Hitherto it has been supposed that a ray from a star..may pass through the atmosphere in a course which grazes, or is a tangent to, the interior globe.

c. To rub (oneself) against a surface in passing.

1870 DICKENS *E. Drood* iii, You..keep close to the house yourself and squeeze and graze yourself against it.

2. *intr.* To move so as to touch something lightly in passing, or so as to produce slight abrasion. †In early use, of a bullet: To ricochet.

1632 *Shaks.'s Hen. V*, IV. iii. 105 (2nd Folio) Marke then abounding valour in our English: That being dead, like to the bullets grasing [*Quartos & 1st Folio* crasing], Breake out into a second course of mischiefe. **1642** FULLER *Holy & Prof. St.* v. i. 358 Those bullets which graze on the ground do most mischief to an army. **1662** J. DAVIES tr. *Olearius' Voy. Ambass.* 267 An Arrow came grazing through my hair. **1732** LEDIARD *Sethos* II. x. 420 The edge of the buckler..graz'd pretty hard along his arm. **1796** H. HUNTER tr. *St. Pierre's Stud. Nat.* (1799) I. 212 So that the fresh breezes..may graze along the shores of Chili and Peru. **1853** KANE *Grinnell Exp.* xlv. (1856) 410 Sometimes running into a berg, or grazing against its edge. **1859** TENNYSON *Vivien* 171 Faintly-venomed points Of slander, glancing here and grazing there.

b. said of a ray of light.

a **1641** BP. R. MOUNTAGU *Acts & Mon.* (1642) 78 Then be the tops of the mountaines graised on by the beames appearing.

Hence **grazed** (greɪzd), *ppl. a.*

1890 *Daily News* 13 Oct. 7/1 A slight grazed wound over the right eye.

graze (greɪz), *v.*[3] *dial.* [? Back-formation from GRAZIER; connexion with F. *engraisser* of like meaning seems improbable.] *trans.* and *intr.* To fatten. Also, to weigh (a specified weight) after fattening.

1787 W. MARSHALL *Norfolk* (1795) II. 380 *To Graze*, to fat. **1854** *Jrnl. R. Agric. Soc.* XV. II. 419 A 20 weeks' old pig will graze 7 score, and on the average they reach 20 score at 12 months' age: they have been grazed to 29 score within the 12 months. **1886** ELWORTHY *W. Somerset Word-bk.*, *Graze*, 1. To fatten; to become fat—applied to cattle, but quite as much to stall-fed as to grass-fed. 2. To weigh after fattening —applied to a pig..'I have a great sow I reckon will graze up pretty nigh thirty score.'

grazeable ('greɪzəb(ə)l), *a.* Also **grazable**. [f. GRAZE *v.*[1] + -ABLE.] That may be grazed.

1649 BLITHE *Eng. Improv. Impr.* (1653) 50 Many times in February..they are grazeable with great cattell. **1787** W. MARSHALL *Norfolk* II. 277 The water is thrown from the grazable parts into these reed-ronds.

grazery: see GRAZIERY.

grazet(t. Now *rare.* Also 7 gras-, gresett, 8 grazzet. [? corruption of F. *grisette*, a cheap woollen stuff of grey colour.] A kind of woollen stuff.

1696 *Lond. Gaz.* No. 3181/4 An Orange and Black Gresett Gown lined with Black. *Ibid.* No. 3199/4 A Grasett Mantua Gown black and white, lined with black Silk. **1701** *Ibid.* No. 3701/4 Mercery Goods, viz... Estemines, Russels,.. Elatches, Grazets. **1719** D'URFEY *Pills* (1872) I. 222 Tho' Grazzet she wears. **1719** J. ROBERTS *Spinster* 346 Some of them [*sc.* stuffs] are quite lost, and thrown out of sale, such as..flowered grazetts. **1745** in J. F. Watson *Ann. Philad.* (1830) 179 (Advt.), Turkettees, grassetts, [etc.]. **1894** A. M. EARLE *Costume Colonial Times* 120 Grazzets, a dress-stuff appearing in lists in the [Boston] *News Letter* from 1712 to 1768, often specified as 'changeable grazzets'. **1933** E. SITWELL *Five Variations* 2 To make more glittering the gowns of these Smooth nymphs that wear a grazet petticoat.

grazier ('greɪʒ(ɪ)ə(r)). Forms: 6–8 grasier, (6 -ior, -yar, grazyer, 6–7 grasyer), 7– grazier. [f. *gras* GRASS *sb.*: see -IER. Quots. 1580 and 1611 seem to indicate that the word became more or less identified with the 16–17th c. F. *graissier* (f. *graisse* fat, GREASE *sb.*). Cf. GRAZE *v.*[3]]

†**1.** Used to render med.L. *viridarius* VERDERER.

1502 *Charter of Forests* in Arnolde *Chron.* (1811) 210 To theis twoo swanmotis shall com togedur our foresturs grasyers & woodwalkers.

2. One who grazes or feeds cattle for the market.

1523 FITZHERB. *Husb.* §40 Thou grasier, that hast many shepe in thy pastures. **1562** TURNER *Herbal* II. 52 They that are grasiers, vse the hole herbe in the stede of grasse and hay. **1580** HOLLYBAND *Treas. Fr. Tong*, *Vn Graissier*, a grasier. **1606** DEKKER *Sev. Sinnes* II. (Arb.) 20 Marching not like a plodding Grasyer with his Droues before him, but like a Citty-Captayne. **1611** COTGR., *Graissier*,..a Grasier, or fattener of cattell. *a* **1639** W. WHATELEY *Prototypes* II. xxvi. (1640) 71 He brought them up..to be Grasiers, as we call them, to breed Cattell, Sheep, Oxen, Camels, Goats, and the like. **1678** R. L'ESTRANGE *Seneca's Mor.* (1702) 47 A Grasier fats his Cattel to bring them to a better Market. **1710** SWIFT *Baucis & Phil.* 118 Presently he feels His Grazier's Coat fall down his Heels. **1787** W. MARSHALL *Norfolk* (1795) II. 380 *Graziers*, fatters of cattle; whether their food be grass, turneps, or oilcake. **1838** DICKENS *Nich. Nick.* xxxv, Broad-brimmed white hat, such as a wealthy grazier might wear. **1853** J. H. NEWMAN *Hist. Sk.* (1873) II. I. i. 3 The savage.. chooses to be a grazier rather than to till the ground.

b. Proverbial and allusive uses.

a **1520** *Vox Populi* 65 in *Skelton's Wks.* (1843) II. 401 Grasyers and regraters, Withe to many shepemasters, That of erable grounde make pasture, Are thei that be these wasters. **1583** STUBBES *Anat. Abus.* II. Eij, Insaciable cormorants, greedie grasiers..who hauing raked togither infinite pasture, feed all themselves, and will not sell for anie reasonable gaine. **1872** E. W. ROBERTSON *Hist. Ess.* 134 'To life like a grazier' or to turn arable land into pasture continued to be a reproach cast upon some of the great English land owners at so late a period as the 16th century.

Hence (*nonce-wds.*) **'grazierly** *a.*, pertaining to or like that of a grazier; **'grazierdom**, the realm or world of graziers.

1599 NASHE *Lenten Stuffe* Ep. Ded. A iij, Thou..spendest more..then in a whole yeare thou gettest by some grasierly gentilitie thou followest. **1822** BP. HEBER in *Jer. Taylor's Wks.* (1839) I. p. cxi, In a respectable grazierly style, on horseback, and in a white coat. **1828** CARLYLE *Misc.* (1857) I. 230 Do battle against the intrusions of Grocerdom and Grazierdom.

graziery ('greɪʒ(ɪ)ərɪ). Also 8 grasery, grazery. [f. GRAZIER: see -ERY.] **a.** The business of a grazier; the grazing of cattle. **b.** Grazing-ground, pasture. *rare.*

1731 MEDLEY *Kolben's Cape G. Hope* II. 288 Where the Governour Adrian van der Stel had for some time a grasiery. **1760–72** tr. *Juan & Ulloa's Voy.* (ed. 3) I. 341 In the territory of Pasto, grasiery is a very profitable article. **1762** tr. *Busching's Syst. Geog.* III. 777 Grasery is the principal occupation. *Ibid.* 580 The inhabitants derive their principal subsistence from grazery. **1799** W. TOOKE *View Russian Emp.* II. 98 Sedulously attending to agriculture, graziery, and even to mining. *c* **1843** CARLYLE *Hist. Sk. Jas. I & Chas. I* (1898) 58 Fishing, fowling, graziery and peaceable cutting of peat.

grazing ('greɪzɪŋ), *vbl. sb.*[1] [f. GRAZE *v.*[1] + -ING[1].]

1. The action of GRAZE *v.*[1]; pasturing.

c **1440** *Promp. Parv.* 210/2 Gresynge, of beestys fedynge, *pastura*. *a* **1520** *Vox Populi* 41 in *Skelton's Wks.* (1843) II. 401/1 Suche and suche, That of late are made riche, Have to, to, to myche By grasyng and regratinge. **1594** R. ASHLEY tr. *Le Roy's Interch. Course of Things* 28 a, There is no doubt but that pasturage, grasing, and shepheardrie, were before husbandrie and tillage. **1674** tr. *Scheffer's Lapland* 19 The Laplanders live by hunting and grasing. **1846** J. BAXTER *Libr. Pract. Agric.* (ed. 4) II. p. xix, The mode of grazing in Romney Marsh and East Kent. **1867** D. G. MITCHELL *Rural Stud.* 275 Where he may watch his Alderneys at their quiet grazing.

†**b.** *fig.* in phr. *to send a grazing*, etc. = to send to grass, etc. (see GRASS *sb.*[1], 5 b). *Obs.*

1533 MORE *Apol.* xxxvi. Wks. 901/2 Hys remembraunce was good inoughe, saue that it went about in grasing til it was beaten home. *a* **1632** T. TAYLOR *God's Judgem.* II. iv. (1642) 53 Being tyred with his new Peere, he turned her off to grazing. **1688** KENNET in *Magd. Coll.* (O.H.S.) 258 The several counties whither we were sent a grazing. **1693** *Humours of Town* 23 The young Cully sends him out a-grazing like Nebuchadnezzar, with scarce a Shirt to his back.

2. Grazing ground, pasture-land, pasture.

1517 *Domesday Inclos.* (1897) I. 220 Wher ther was ij plowys wele ocupyd, now yt ys retorned to pasteure and grasyng. **1588** R. PARKE tr. *Mendoza's Hist. China* 181 They doo feede them commonly in the fieldes of rice, for that they haue no other grasinges. **1752** J. STEWART in *Scots Mag.* (1753) 295/1 Having..taken grasings south for the cattle. **1816** SCOTT *Old Mort.* i, The grazings on which their grandsires fed their flocks and herds. **1893** LYDEKKER *Horns & Hoofs* 147 In open plains, where there is good grazing.

3. *attrib.* and *Comb.*, as ***grazing country, ground, land, rights***; ***grazing-like*** adj.; **grazing guard**, a guard placed over the cattle of an army whilst grazing.

1626 BACON *Sylva* §595 If the Ground be Grazing Ground. **1707** MORTIMER *Husb.* 13 A second sort of grazing Ground. **1835** J. BATMAN in Cornwallis *New World* (1859) I. 404 The same open, grazing-like land is every where seen. **1867** SMILES *Huguenots Eng.* Pref. (1880) 6 Down to a comparatively recent period, it [England] was a great grazing country. **1890** 'ROLF BOLDREWOOD' *Col. Reformer* (1891) 254 Their owners commenced to grumble if the Rainbow cattle fed over their grazing rights. **1893** *Westm. Gaz.* 19 Dec. 4/2 Captain Borrow and Sir John Willoughby ..galloped out of laager..and headed them off back to the grazing guard.

'grazing, *vbl. sb.*[2] [f. GRAZE *v.*[2] + -ING[1].] The action of GRAZE *v.*[2]; the touching or rubbing of a surface in passing so as to turn it up or roughen it; abrasion.

a **1693** LUDLOW *Mem.* (1698) I. 59 With the grazing of a Bullet upon the Face of one of the Servants. **1709** STEELE *Tatler* No. 77 ¶ 1 By the lucky grazing of a bullet on the Roll of his Stocking.

grazing ('greɪzɪŋ), *ppl. a.*[1] [f. GRAZE *v.*[1] + -ING[2].] That grazes. **a.** Of an animal: That feeds on growing grass.

1590 SPENSER *F.Q.* I. vii. 19 Whiles he had keeping of his grasing steed. **1725** POPE *Odyss.* XVII. 620 The grazing ox and browzing goat. **1871** R. ELLIS tr. *Catullus* lxii. 49 A flower privily growing, Hid from grazing kine. **1880** MUIRHEAD *Gaius* Digest 632 He who..killed another man's slave or grazing quadruped.

b. That keeps cattle at grass.

1769 *De Foe's Tour Gt. Brit.* I. 5 Great part of the lands ..are held by the Farmers, Cowkeepers, and Grasing-Butchers.

'grazing, *ppl. a.*[2] [f. GRAZE *v.*[2] + -ING[2].] That grazes; that touches or rubs lightly in passing or moving; abrading.

c **1693** *Ad Populum Phaleræ* I. 65 More dangerous than grazing Ball that flew. **1834–47** J. S. MACAULAY *Field Fortif.* (1851) 148 An oblique direction should be given to the loop-holes..to obtain a grazing fire. **1842** TENNYSON *St. Sim. Styl.* 115 A grazing iron collar grinds my neck. **1872–6** VOYLE & STEVENSON *Milit. Dict.* (ed. 3) s.v., When the trajectory is low and nearly parallel to the ground, and when the projectile strikes the object..at a less angle than 10°, this is termed grazing fire. **1881** LD. RAYLEIGH in *Nature* XXV. 64 By giving the light a more nearly grazing emergence.

Hence **'grazingly** *adv.*, so as to graze.

1881 *Cornh. Mag.* Dec. 710 The course of any comet may well chance to be so directed as to carry it straight towards the very centre of the sun, instead of passing grazingly by his orb as did the comet of 1843.

‖**grazioso** (gratsi'oso), *adv.* and *a. Mus.* [It. = gracious, graceful.] A direction denoting that a composition is to be played in a graceful manner.

1806 T. BUSBY *Dict. Mus.* (ed. 2), *Grazioso*,..a term implying that the movement to which it is prefixed is to be performed in a smooth, flowing, and graceful style. **1935** D. F. TOVEY *Ess. Mus. Analysis* II. lxi. 138 The seventh variation (grazioso 6/8) is the crowning point of new melody and new lusciousness. **1965** *Listener* 24 June 953/1 During an early scene with Moses, Aaron's *grazioso* line..is first accompanied by counter-lines on the divided cellos.

gre, variant of GREE.

†**'greable**, *a. Obs.* [a. OF. *greable* (1207 in Godef.), f. *greer* to approve of, grant, consent to, please: see GREE *v.* and -ABLE.] = AGREEABLE, in various senses; fitting, accordant, compliant, pleasing, etc.

1401 *Pol. Poems* (Rolls) II. 112 The greable gardoun for al opin sclaundris. **1412–20** LYDG. *Chron. Troy* I. vi, A certayne hour..To our intent that shalbe most greable. **1463** ASHBY *Prisoner's Refl.* 104 Poems (E.E.T.S.) 4 To chaung my lyf to god greable. *c* **1500** *Melusine* xxxix. 305 They were greable that he shuld be professed monke. **1503** HAWES *Examp. Virt.* vii. 15, I therto had not ben greable. **1526** SKELTON *Magnyf.* 201 To se howe greable we are of one mynde. **1528** LYNDESAY *Dreme* Epistle 28 Tyll sic ane Prince to be so greabyll! **1548** UDALL, etc. tr. *Erasm. Par. Matt.* xii, 26 And howe is it likely and greable all diuelles beyng ennemyes of men. **1647** W. BROWNE tr. *Gomberville's Polexander* I. i. 14, I know not what greable and pleasant fantasie.

Hence †**'greably** *adv.*, agreeably.

a **1455** HOLLAND *Howlat* lxvi, The Pape begynnis the grace, as greably ganit. *c* **1500** *Partenay* 1543 Honestly was don The mariage And weddyng greabilly.

gread, obs. form of GREED.

†**greade.** *Obs.* Also 4 grede. [OE. *gréada*, wk. masc.] Bosom, lap.

c **897** K. ÆLFRED *Gregory's Past.* xiii. 77 Ða ðe berað on hira greadum ða a libbendan fatu. *c* **1000** *Ags. Gosp.* Luke xvi. 23 He..geseah feorran abraham & lazarum on his greadan. **13..** *K. Alis.* 4187 He dronk of that wyn rede, The coppe he putte undur his grede. *Ibid.* 4196. **13..** *Seuyn Sag.* (W.) 1802 And whan..the bichche lith in thi grede. **1340** *Ayenb.* 196 Ac þe wyse zayþ þet me do þe elmesse in-to þe greade of þe poure.

greade, variant of GREDE *sb.* and *v. Obs.*

greadly, variant of GRADELY *a.* and *adv.*

greadye, greaf, obs. forms of GREEDY, GRIEF.

Greakishe, obs. form of GREEKISH.

greal, variant of GRAIL *sb.*[2]

greane, obs. form of GREEN.

grease (gri:s), *sb.* Forms: 3–5 grece, 4 grees(s)e, 4–5 grese, grees, greece, (4 greis, -ys, 5 gris, gresse, gres, 6 gress, 7 greese), 6–7 greace, 6– grease. See also CREESH. [a. OF. *graisse, greisse, gresse, craisse, creisse, cresse* (mod.F. *graisse*) = Pg. *graixa*, It. *grascia*:— popular L. **crassia*, f. *crassus* (F. *gras*) adj., fat; cf. the synonymous Sp. *grasa*, It. *grassa*, which represent the fem. of the adj.]

†**1. a.** The fat part of the body of an animal; also, corpulence, fatness. *Obs.*

a **1340** HAMPOLE *Psalter* xvi. 11 Bestis þat waxis iolife when þai ere ful of grese. **1398** TREVISA *Barth. De P.R.* v. lvii. (1495) 173 The marowe of the bones is lyke to fatnesse or to greys. *c* **1400** *Destr. Troy* 3838 Polidarius was..Full grete in the grippe, all of grese hoge. *c* **1430** *Pilgr. Lyf Manhode* I. cxiii. (1869) 59 Thou art to fat and haste to miche grees vnder the wynge. **1541** R. COPLAND *Guydon's Quest. Chirurg.* C iij, Howe many maners of greas be there? Answere. Two. The one is withoutforth nere to the skynne, & that proprely is called adeps or fatnes. And y[e] other is inwarde & nyghe to the bely, & proprely is called auxunge or fat grease. **1638** F. JUNIUS *Paint. of Ancients* 246 Every Artificer must know..that he likewise must lose some grease and part with his grosse humors if ever he meaneth to be.. strong. **1672** MARVELL *Reh. Transp.* I. 123 So he might take down our Grease and Luxury, and keep the English courage in breath and exercise.

b. Chiefly in *Hunting*. The fat of a boar, hare, hart, etc. ***in the time*** or ***season of grease***: when the game is fat and fit to kill. ***in grease, in prime*** or ***pride of grease***: fat and fit for killing; also *transf.* of a hawk or horse. ***deer of grease, goose of grease, hart of grease*** (see HART 1 b), ***hen of grease***, etc.: a fat deer, goose, etc.

c **1330** R. BRUNNE *Chron.* (1810) 64 Whan Harald or þe kyng wild com þider eftsons In þe tyme of g[r]ese, to tak þam venysons. ? *a* **1400** *Morte Arth.* 658 That nane werreye my wylde, botte Waynour hir seluene, And þat in þe sesone whene grees es assignyde. *c* **1440** *Ipomydon* (ed. Kölbing) 3571 A noble dere off gresse. *c* **1460** J. RUSSELL *Bk. Nurture* 409 Capon & hen of hawt grees þus wold þey be dight. **1513** *Bk. Keruynge* in *Babees Bk.* 272 Capon or henne of grece. **1576** TURBERV. *Venerie* 217, I have termed their fatte greace and so is it to be called of all beastes which praye. **1607** TOPSELL *Four-f. Beasts* (1658) 311 Foundering cometh when a Horse is heated, being in his grease and very fat. **1610** GUILLIM *Heraldry* III. xiv. (1660) 166 The fat of a Boare and Hare is termed Greace. **1615** LATHAM *Falconry* (1633) 42 When she [your Hawke] is in the prime of her grease, the least heat she can take is all too much. **1667** DRYDEN & NEWCASTLE *Sir M. Mar-all* IV. i. D.'s Wks. 1883 III. 56 Crammed capons, pea-hens, chickens in the grease. **1678** RAY *Willughby's Ornith.* App. 409 There is a scurvy quality in some Hawks proceeding from pride of grease, or being high kept. **1727** BRADLEY *Fam. Dict.* s.v. *Hounds*, For entring the Hound at a Hart or Buck, let him [*sc.* the Hart or Buck] be in prime of Grease. **1814** SCOTT *Wav.* xii, The roe ..never being in what is called *pride of grease*, he is also never out of season. **1881** GREENER *Gun* 509 The harts are 'in grease' from August to the middle of October.

†**c.** Short for *hart* or *deer of grease* (see 1 b). *Obs.*

c **1440** *Ipomydon* (Kölbing) 370 Tomorrow..Loke ye be all redy dight..In the forest to take my grese.

d. Phrases (chiefly *fig.*), as ***to chafe, fret, fry, melt, stew, sweat in one's own grease*** (cf. FRY *v.*[1] 3). ***to melt one's grease***: to exhaust one's strength by violent efforts.

13..–1684 [see FRY *v.*[1] 3]. *a* **1569** KINGESMYLL *Man's Est.* viii. (1580) 41 Must we needes be still sweating in the greace of our own fleshly wickednesse? **1598** SHAKS. *Merry W.* II. i. 69 Till the wicked fire of lust haue melted him in his owne greace. **1608** ARMIN *Nest Ninn.* (1880) 59 There hee sat fretting in his owne grease. *c* **1645** HOWELL *Lett.* I. IV. xv. (1655) I. 181 The adventurous Earl Henry of Oxford..was set upon a desperat Work, wher he melted his grease, and so ..died. **1663** TUKE *Adv. Five Hours* I. in *Anc. Brit. Drama* III. 415/1 There they stew In their own grease till morning. ? **17..** *R. Hood & Gold. Arrow* in Child *Ballads* (1888) III. 224/2 So we'll leave him chafing in his grease. **1838** SOUTHEY *Doctor* cxliv. V. 96 The day was exceedingly hot, and..Rubios's horse was overheated, and, as the phrase was, melted his grease.

2. a. The melted or rendered fat of animals, esp. when it is in a soft state: often with a qualifying sb., specifying the kind of fat, as ***bear's grease***, GOOSE-GREASE, ***swine's grease***, etc.; †***white grease***, lard. Hence, by extension, oily or fatty matter in general, esp. such as is used as a lubricant.

c **1290** *S. Eng. Leg.* I. 12/375 Þat fuyr was i-maud of col and grece. **1297** R. GLOUC. (Rolls) 8485 Hii..wilde fur wiþ pich & grece wiþ ginnes In caste. **13..** *Coer de L.* 1552 Talwgh and grese menge alsoo. **1377** LANGL. *P. Pl.* B. XIII. 63 Egges yfryed with grece. *c* **1420** *Liber Cocorum* (1862) 14 Gode brothe with wyte grece thou no3t forsake. *c* **1430** *Two Cookery-bks.* 8 Take oynonys, and schrede hem..an frye in a panne of fayre grece. **1523** FITZHERB. *Husb.* §43 Let thy terre be medled with oyle, gose grease, or capons grease. **1545** RAYNOLD *Byrth Mankynde* (1564) 62 b, Annoynt.. with..some of the greases spoken of before. **1634** SIR T. HERBERT *Trav.* 16 They delight to..make their skin glister with grease and char-cole beat together. **1678** *Massacre Irel.* 6 One fat man they murthered and made Candles of his grease. **1783** JOHNSON in *Boswell* 18 Apr., They..extract a grease from them [bones] for greasing wheels. **1816** J. SMITH *Panorama Sci. & Art* II. 821 *heading*, Taking grease out of paper. **1825** J. NICHOLSON *Operat. Mechanic* 172 Causing the piston-rod to work through a close collar stuffed with hemp and grease. **1889** *Scribner's Mag.* Aug. 215/2 The expenditure for lubricating oils, waste, and greases alone amounts to more than $150,000 per annum.

b. in various expressions, with reference to the qualities of grease, as oiliness, combustibility, etc.

1650 *Sc. Metr. Ps.* cxix. 70 As fat as grease they be. **1843** HALIBURTON *Attaché* II. xii. 211 As slick as grease. **1860** SALA *Looking at Life* 147 His goods absuming away from him like grease in fire.

†**c.** A salve (for the scab in sheep). *Obs.*

1523 FITZHERB. *Husb.* §44 Those that be wasshen, wyll not take scabbe after (if they haue sufficient meate) for that is the beste grease that is to a shepe, to grease hym in the mouthe with good meate.

d. *dial.* Butter; *spec.* rancid or inferior butter.

1788 W. MARSHALL *Yorksh.* II. 196 The firsts and seconds [of butter] go to the London market, the 'grease' to the woollen-manufactory in the west of Yorkshire. *Ibid.* 333 *Grease*, rancid butter, of the lowest degree. **1919** *Athenæum* 8 Aug. 727/2 When 'gyppo' or 'grease' was asked for at mealtimes, gravy or butter (?) was meant. **1928** *Papers Mich. Acad. Sci. & Arts* X. 297 *Grease*, butter. **1953** J. MASEFIELD *Conway* (ed. 2) III. 165 As to the food..we had many names for it;..grease for butter.

3. A disease which attacks the heels of a horse (see quot. 1865).

1674 *Lond. Gaz.* No. 898/4 A Chesnut coloured Horse,.. his grease faln into his Legs. *Ibid.* 962/4 One black Gelding, ..the Greece in his Heels behind of both Feet. **1737** BRACKEN *Farriery Impr.* (1757) II. 172 There are some gummy-leg'd Horse very apt to the Grease and Scratches. **1799** *Med. Jrnl.* I. 2 What farriers term the grease in the heels of horses. **1865** YOUATT *Horse* xv. (1872) 354 Grease is a specific inflammation of the sebaceous follicles of the skin of the heels..followed by an increased morbid secretion.

4. The oily matter in wool; also, wool before it is cleansed of this. ***in the grease***: that has not been cleansed after shearing.

1835 URE *Philos. Manuf.* 98 Shreds of flannel which having been freed from grease by washing, are readily moistened. **1863** S. BUTLER *1st Yr. in Canterbury Settlement* x. 160 If you wash [the sheep]..you should do it thoroughly ..otherwise you had better shear in the grease i.e. not wash. Wool in the grease weighs about one third heavier. **1886** HARRIS *Techn. Fire Insur.*, Wool 'in the grease', that is, in the fleece, as it is taken from the sheep. **1895** *Daily News* 3 Oct. 7/4 Merino wools in the grease. **1898** *Johannesburg Star* 19 Mar. 1/2 The Colonial wool auction was opened on Tuesday ..Grease showed a farthing advance on last sales rates.

5. *slang* and *dial.* (See GREASE *v.* 4.) **a.** Money given as a bribe. **b.** Flattery, wheedling, 'soft sawder'.

1823 'JON BEE' *Dict. of Turf*, *Grease*, a bonus given to promote the cause of anyone. **1877** *N.W. Linc. Gloss.*, *Grease*, flattery. 'I should like him a vast sight better if he hed n't so much of his grease'. **1959** N. MAILER *Advts. for Myself* (1961) 123 You should have seen the grease job I gave to Carter. I'm dumb, but man, he's dumber.

6. *attrib.* and *Comb.*, as ***grease-maker, -mark***; ***grease-free, -laden, -sodden, -spotted*** adjs.; **grease-ball**, (*a*) a medicinal ball of grease for giving to a horse; (*b*) *U.S. slang*, a derogatory term for a foreigner, esp. applied to one of Mediterranean or Latin American origin; **grease-band** (see quot. 1953); hence **grease-band** *v. trans.*; **grease bird**, a name for the Canada Jay (*Perisoreus canadensis*); **grease boil** *N.Z.*, a boil caused by contact with the grease in sheep's wool; **grease-box** = *grease-pot*; also *grease axle box* (see quot.); **grease-bush** = *grease-wood*; **grease-cap** = GREASER 1 d; **grease-cock, cup**, a cock or cup by means of which machinery is supplied with grease; †**grease-fallen** *a.*, affected with 'grease' (sense 3); **grease-fish** = *candle-fish* (see CANDLE *sb.* 7); †**grease grown** *a.*, grown greasy or fat; **grease-gun** (see quot. 1963); †**grease-heels** = sense 3; **grease-horn**, a horn in which grease is carried for lubricating purposes; hence *fig.* (*dial.*), a flatterer; **grease-jack**, 'an apparatus for improving the finish of leather' (*Cent. Dict.*); **grease-man**, one employed to grease machinery; †**grease-molten** *a.* (see quot.); **grease monkey** *slang*, a mechanic; **grease mould** (see quot.); **grease-paint**, a composition used by actors in painting their faces; **grease-pan** (see quot. 1960); **grease-patch**, a piece of greased cloth in which the bullets of some kinds of rifles were wrapped (see PATCH *sb.*); **grease-pot**, a vessel containing grease for lubricating, etc.; *spec.* in *Archery* and in *Tin-plating* (see quots.); **grease-pox**, the disease produced by inoculation from the 'grease' (see 3) of a horse's heels; **grease-proof** *a.*, impermeable to grease; **grease-season, -time**, the period when the deer are 'in grease'; **grease-spot**, (*a*) a spot of grease (on clothes, etc.); (*b*) *slang* (see quot. 1860); (*c*) a spot of grease used in photometry; so ***grease-spot photometer***; **grease-tight** *a.* = *grease-proof* adj.; **grease-trap**, an appliance for catching grease in a drain (cf. *fat-trap*, FAT *sb.*[2] 6 c); **grease-wood**, a name for various stunted and prickly chenopodiaceous shrubs, of the genera *Sarcobatus*, *Atriplex*, etc., which contain oil and are found in dry alkaline valleys of the western U.S.

1926-7 *Army & Navy Stores Catal.* p. xlv/5 *Grease Balls. **1934** *Amer. Ballads & Folk Songs* (1957) 559 Our grease-ball is a goddam dirty bum. **1958** S. ELLIN *Eighth Circle* (1959) II. xvii. 176 A certain Mr. García—some greaseball who runs a lunch stand. **1969** I. KEMP *Brit. G.I. in Vietnam* xii. 193 The gunner was..Rick Francese; tormented with such unflattering names as 'Wop' and 'Greaseball' and mercilessly teased..about his Sicilian extraction, he was at the same time universally liked and enormously respected. **1900** W. D. DRURY *Bk. Gardening* 1093 *Grease-bands put round the trees..will prevent the females from ascending. *Ibid.* 1100 As a preventive measure all orchard trees should be grease-banded in autumn, using Willesden or similar grease-proof paper. **1930** J. COUTTS et al. *Compl. Bk. Gardening* 704 The stake supporting the tree must also be grease-banded. **1953** *Brit. Commonw. Forest Terminol.* I. 71 *Grease band*, a band of sticky or greasy material applied to a stem, as a barrier to insects. **1965** *Listener* 7 Oct. 555/3 In really big fruit trees, you can get control of, say, caterpillar, by grease-banding now. **1892** W. PIKE *North. Canada* 123 The Whisky Jack..In the mountains of British Columbia he is the Hudson's Bay bird or *grease bird. **1926** J. DEVANNY *Butcher Shop* vii. 73 Hone Reki is pretty bad with *grease boils. **1956** G. BOWEN *Wool Away!* (ed. 2) iv. 52 When a shearer does get grease boils he should rest with the legs up. **1856** FORD *Archery* vii. 46 The *grease box is generally made of wood, horn, or ivory. **1888** *Lockwood's Dict. Mech. Engin.* s.v. *Axle-Box*, Axle boxes are called oil axle boxes, or grease axle boxes, as they are constructed for using one or the other lubricant. **1875** *N. Amer. Rev.* CXX. 5 The valleys [are covered] with *greasebush and sage. **1924** A. W. JUDGE *Mod. Motor Cars* I. 245 Screw-down *grease caps are generally provided, and a turn should be given every time the car is used for more than a few miles. **1839** R. S. ROBINSON *Naut. Steam Eng.* 155 The instrument is then fixed in the *grease cock of the cylinder. *Ibid.* 37 Its upper surface forms a *grease cup, where melted tallow, or oil, is kept constantly lubricating the piston. **1688** *Lond. Gaz.* No. 2386/4 A dark brown Gelding ..a little *grease-fallen. **1711** *Ibid.* No. 4847/4 The further Foot behind Grease fallen. **1908** *Practitioner* Sept. 488 Cyllin obstetrical lubricant..has the advantage that it is *grease-free. ?*a* **1400** *Morte Arth.* 1101 *Greesse growene as a galte. **1917** *Catal. T. Eaton* Spring & Summer 282/1 in *Shopper's View of Canada's Past* (1969) 194 Ford *Grease and Oil Gun, made specially to fill rear axle housing with grease. **1923** *Daily Mail* 11 May 12, I liked very much the accessibility of all the greasers on the car. Every one can easily be reached with a grease gun without any acrobatic feats. **1963** R. F. WEBB *Motorists' Dict.* 117 *Grease gun*, a tool or device designed to pump grease into the required place under high pressures. **1753** BARTLET *Gentl. Farriery* xxi. 190 An alterative for surfeits, molten grease, hide-bound, *grease-heels, &c. **1641** BEST *Farm. Bks.* (Surtees) 32 The tooles that mowers are to have with them, are sythe, shafte,..and *grease-horne. **1837** LOCKHART *Scott* vii, A grease-horn for his scythe. **1855** ROBINSON *Whitby Gloss.*, *A Greasehorn*, a flatterer. **1857** C. BRONTE *Professor* I. v. 76 Smoothfaced snivelling greasehorn! **1890** A. CONAN DOYLE *Firm of Girdlestone* (1926) 238 *Grease-laden hold. **1862** MAYHEW *Lond. Labour* IV. 13 Soap Boilers and *Grease Makers. **1898** *Century Mag.* Jan. 403/2 Lever men, engineers and '*greasemen' had rushed up from the engine-room. **1885** MABEL COLLINS *Prettiest Woman* vii, These walls..bore the *grease-marks of ages. **1706** PHILLIPS (ed. Kersey), **Grease-molten*, a Distemper in a Horse, when his Fat is melted by over-hard Riding, or Labour. **1928** L. GRAVATT *Pioneers of Air* 251 All the way down the line we find them from skilled draftsmen in a polished office to the '*grease monkeys' with blackened faces and smeary over-alls. **1946** V. TEMPEST *Near Sun* viii. 63 Flight mechanics and fitters, known in the Battle of Britain as 'grease monkeys' but generally called in the Royal Air Force 'Erks'. **1959** *Times Lit. Suppl.* 27 Nov. 700/3 In Australia he was impressed by the 'grease-monkey' at Broken Hill who could afford to run a racing stable. **1882** J. SMITH *Dict. Pop. Names Plants* 185 Tallow stores are often infested with a microscopic fungus, known as *Grease Mould (*Mucorini phycomyce*). **1888** *Pall Mall G.* 1 Sept. 3/1 He only used such materials as [are] in every actor's make-up box—*grease-paint, rouge, lining-pencil, and powder. **1928** H. CRANE *Let.* 27 Apr. (1965) 324 Hawaii..the Pollyanna greasepaint pinkpoodle paradise. **1944** L. MACNEICE *Christopher Columbus* 16 The grease-paint voice will stick out all the more when there is no real grease-paint to look at. **1958** *Listener* 9 Oct. 578/1 'The Vortex', faithfully performed in 1920 greasepaint voices, is a very poor play. **1936** *Burlington Mag.* July 26/2 Candlesticks with candle-holders and *grease-pans. **1960** H. HAYWARD *Antique Coll.* 134/1 *Grease-pan*, the circular dish beneath the nozzle of a candlestick into which grease from the burning candle might drip. **1887** *Whitaker's Almanack* 542/1 The *grease patch was discontinued with the adoption of the Minié rifle. **1801** T. ROBERTS *Eng. Bowman* 289 **Grease-pot*, a small box ..containing the composition used in lubricating the fingers of the shooting-glove. **1839** URE *Dict. Arts* 1253 (*Tin-plate*) A range of rectangular cast-iron pots is set over a fire-flue.. The first..is the tin-pot;..the third is the grease-pot. **1834** *Good's Study Med.* (ed. 4) II. 356 *Grease-pox seems to have succeeded as well as small-pox. **1895** *Montgomery Ward Catal.* 573/1 Waxed Butter Paper, *grease proof. **1900** Grease-proof [see *grease-band* above]. **1910** *Daily Chron.* 8 Mar. 3/3 Each loaf..is packed and sealed in a paper wrapper, which is grease-proof and germ-proof. **1940** L. A. G. STRONG *Sun on Water* 201 Secreted about her were various parcels of food, and it was the stiff greaseproof paper in which they were wrapped that gave off the cracklings. *a* **1562** G. CAVENDISH *Wolsey* (1893) 137 His hyghnes rode in his progresse, with Mistresse Anne Boleyn in his company, all the *grece season. **1883** ANNIE THOMAS *Mod. Housewife* 126 A mere *grease-sodden mass. **1829** in *Amer. Speech* (1965) XL. 129, I hit a man..dere was nothing left, Sept a little *grease spot. **1839** *Mag. Dom. Econ.* IV. 214 *Grease-spots may be removed from woollen cloths by [etc.]. **1843** HALIBURTON *Attaché* II. viii. 143 If you was to look at me with a ship's glass you wouldn't see a grease spot of it in me. **1860** *Slang Dict.*, *Grease-spot*, a minute remnant, the only distinguishable remains of an antagonist after a terrific contest. **1882** *Encycl. Brit.* XIV. 584/1 Bunsen has recently suggested the very simple expedient of making a grease-spot on white paper for photometric purposes. When the paper is equally illuminated from both sides, the grease-spot cannot be seen except by very close inspection... The amounts of light are as the squares of the distances of the sources from this point [*sc.* the grease-spot]. **1911** R. S. CLAY *Treat. Pract. Light* xviii. 388 The grease-spot photometer is perhaps the most sensitive to scattered light. **1923** GLAZEBROOK *Dict. Appl. Physics* IV. 416/2 As a convenient example, the simple form of the Bunsen grease-spot photometer may be described. **1824** in *Spirit Publ. Jrnls.* (1825) 346 His inexpressibles..were napless, *grease-spotted, and ventilated at the knees. **1925** A. W. JUDGE *Mech. Car* 163 The nipples are..*grease-tight and dust-excluding. *a* **1562** G. CAVENDISH *Wolsey* (1893) 211 My lord contynued at Southwell untill the latter end of *grease tyme. **1884** G. E. WARING in *Century Mag.* Dec. 264/2 There have been invented various forms of *grease-trap. **1851** MAYNE REID *Scalp Hunt.* xi. 81 A plain covered with artemisia and clumps of hideous *greasewood. **1883** W. H. BISHOP in *Harper's Mag.* Mar. 502/2 The 'grease-wood' is a large bush which is said to burn just as well green as dry.

grease (griːz, griːs), *v.* Forms: 4 **greese**, 5 **grece**, **gresse**, 6 **grese**, **greace**, 7 **greaze**, 6– **grease**. [f. prec. Cf. F. *graisser* (1539 in Hatz.-Darm.).]

1. a. *trans.* To smear or anoint with grease.

c **1440** *Jacob's Well* (E.E.T.S.) 237 þe feendys grecyd here lyppes wyth here oynementys..& þanne þe folk iangelyd. **1481** CAXTON *Reynard* (Arb.) 46 Reynard thenne dyde grece his shoes..and dyd hem on. *c* **1500** *Melusine* xxi. 142 Flaxe grecyd with oyle and mixtyouned with brymstone. **1618** *Barnevelt's Apol.* D 3 b, By Gods grace. [*note*] Which lies in your bootes, after the kitchin-wench hath greased them. **1662** J. DAVIES tr. *Mandelslo's Trav.* 255 Their hair..grows not much, though they grease it perpetually. **1675** WYCHERLEY *Country Wife* III. i, A confessor! just such a confessor as he that, by forbidding a silly hostler to grease the horse's teeth, taught him to do 't. **1853** SOYER *Pantroph.* 178 Grease well the inside of a dish.

b. To make greasy, to soil with grease or fat.

a **1613** OVERBURY *Charac. Puny-Clarke* Wks. (1856) 113 He..greases his breeches extremely with feeding without a napkin. **1648** GAGE *West Ind.* iv. 14 In daily greazing his white habit with handling his fat Gammons of Bacon. **1704** SWIFT *T. Tub* §7. 144 A Treatise..never to be thumb'd or greas'd by Students. **1873** J. RICHARDS *Wood-working Factories* 68 If the bearings have to be oiled in the usual manner, the belt is sure to become greased by the waste oil.

fig. **1893** 'Q.' [Couch] *Delect. Duchy* 66 A still black pool, greased with eddies.

2. To apply a salve of tallow and tar to (sheep). Also *absol.*

c **1380** WYCLIF *Wks.* (1880) 439 þe þridde offiss þat falliþ to persouns is to greese þer scabbid sheep. **1401** *Friar Daw's Reply* in *Pol. Poems* (Rolls) II. 63 Go, grees a shoep undir the taile. **1523** FITZHERB. *Husb.* §40 And than let the shepeherde go belte, grese, and handel all those that he hath drawen. **1641** BEST *Farm. Bks.* (Surtees) 29 Before which time, wee cannot conveniently grease our lambes. *Ibid.*, Yow are to see the weather sette att a certane before yow beginne to grease.

3. a. To lubricate with grease.

1462 in *Brit. Mag.* (1834) VI. 263 Hys Fellowe schall greese ye bellys and Fynde gresse therto. **1530** PALSGR. 574/2 He greaseth his carte to make it go the better. **1598** BARRET *Theor. Warres* V. iii. 134 To annoynt and grease the axle-trees of the carriages. **1780** COWPER *Progr. Err.* 439 The carriage bowls along and all are pleased, If Tom be sober, and the wheels well greased. **1851** D. JERROLD *St. Giles* xxii. 219 Silently went the window up..as though greased by some witch. **1885** SIR A. L. SMITH in *Law Times* LXXIX. 331/2 To keep the machinery greased.

b. *transf.* To make to run easily.

1883 R. HALDANE *Workshop Rec.* Ser. II. 165 Confectionary..Spinning..Boil clarified syrup to 'caramel' ..The moment it is at crack, add a little acid to 'grease' it.

4. *fig.* **a.** With direct reference to the literal senses. Phr. ***to grease the wheels*** (fig.): to make things run smoothly; to provide the entertainment, pay the expenses.

c **1440** *Jacob's Well* (E.E.T.S.) 260 As a carte-qweel, drye & vngrecyd, cryeth lowdest of oþere qwelys; So, þou drye & noȝt grecyd wyth grace grucchyst lowdest. **1575** GASCOIGNE *David's Salut. to Betzabe* 33 Posies 289 She greazde this guest with sause of Sorcerie. **1607** SHAKS. *Timon* IV. iii. 195 Ingratefull man with Licourish draughts And Morsels Vnctious, greases his pure minde, That from it all Consideration slippes. **1809** MALKIN *Gil Blas* II. ix. ¶4 To-day, the wheels are greased by your humble servant. **1857** SIR A. H. ELTON *Below the Surface* (1860) 327 The party I mean is a glutton for money, but I will do my best with him. I think a hundred pounds..would grease his wheels.

b. To ply with money, to bribe; also, †to enrich; orig. in phrases ***to grease*** (a person's) ***hand*** or ***palm***, †***to grease*** (a person) ***in the hands, palm, fist***. (Cf. F. *graisser la patte à quelqu'un.*) ***to grease the fat pig*** (or *sow*) (fig.): to give to those who do not lack.

1526 SKELTON *Magnyf.* 438 Wyth golde and grotes they grease my hande. **1528** ROY & BARLOWE *Rede me* (Arb.) 54 With rewardes they must hym greace. **1562** J. HEYWOOD *Dialogue containing Proverbs* I. xi. sig. D4[v] What should we (quoth I) grease the fat sow in thars. **1573** TUSSER *Husb.* lxviii. (1878) 159 How husbandrie easeth, to huswiferie pleaseth, And manie purse greaseth with siluer and gold. **1581** J. BELL *Haddon's Answ. Osor.* 400 b, Y[e] shavelynges.. dare not abide to be greaced in the handes. **1591** *Troub. Raigne K. John* (1611) 20 The Pope and Popelings shall not grease themselues With gold and groates. **1648** MILTON *Tenure Kings* 6 While pluralities greas'd them thick and deepe. **1651** WOOD *Life* Aug. (O.H.S.) I. 178 His engineer was greased in the fist. **1670** J. RAY *Coll. Eng. Prov.* 178 To grease a fat sow on the A... **1707** J. STEVENS tr. *Quevedo's Com. Wks.* (1709) 249, I greas'd the Goaler..with three Pieces of Eight. **1791** 'P. PINDAR' *Works* (1794) I. 287 'And then why vore?' the peepel rail:— 'To greaze a vat ould pig in the tail—*Old Weymouth* o' Long Leat.' **1807** 'CERVANTES HOGG' *Rising Sun* III. 42 You would imply that, if we were greased in the palm, we should, like them, be ready to turn a courtier. **1883** C. J. WILLS *Mod. Persia* 294 In Persia, justice, though at times very blind, is never slow unless her palm is greased. **1923** *Daily Mail* 7 Aug. 8/6 These instances of extravagance, which seem to recall the old saying of greasing the fat pig.

c. †To gull, cheat (*obs.*). Also *dial.*, to flatter, wheedle.

1621 FLETCHER *Wildgoose Chase* IV. ii, Am I greas'd once again? *a* **1625** —— *Mad Lover* V. iv, So; you are greas'd, I hope. (*Aside.*) **1634** MASSINGER *Very Woman* IV. iii, She's finely greased! **1877** *Holderness Gloss.*, *Grease*, to flatter; to fawn upon.

5. To cause (a horse) to become affected with 'grease'. Also *intr.* of a horse: To become so affected.

1737 BRACKEN *Farriery Impr.* (1756) I. 341 More Horses are greased by bad looking to, than by hard Riding. *Ibid.*, I have had but one [boy] that could truly be said to be so careful, that you could not grease one [horse] whilst under his Care. *Ibid.* 345 They would grease and scratch sooner before than behind. *a* **1845** HOOD *T. of Trumpet* lv, The wishes that Witches utter Can..Grease horses' heels.

grease, obs. form of GRAZE *v.*[1]

greased (griːzd, griːst), *ppl. a.* [f. GREASE *v.* + -ED[1].]

1. Smeared, anointed, or lubricated with grease.

greased pole = greasy pole (see GREASY *a.* 9). Phr. ***as quick as***, or ***like***, ***greased lightning*** (colloq.): used to denote extreme quickness of movement.

a **1529** SKELTON *Agst. Garnesche* ii. 5 (Your) lothesum lere to loke on, lyke a gresyd bote dothe schyne. **1552** HULOET, Greased or dressed wyth grease or fat, *ædipatus*. Greased or anoynted wyth grease, *vnctus*. **1697** DAMPIER *Voy.* (1702) I. 537 They rub Soot over the greased parts. **1789** NICHOLSON in *Phil. Trans.* LXXIX. 273 Grease the cylinder by turning it against a greased leather. **1833** *Boston, Lincoln*, etc. *Herald* 15 Jan. 3/6 He spoke as quick as 'greased lightning'. **1849** D. CAMPBELL *Inorg. Chem.* 73 The mouth of the bottle is secured by a greased stopper. **1871** L. STEPHEN *Playgr. Europe* xiii. (1894) 306 Others..put it [mountaineering] on a level with the passion for climbing greased poles. **1880** MALLESON *Ind. Mutiny* III. 470 Sir John Lawrence arrived at the conclusion that the mutiny was due to the greased cartridges, and to the greased cartridges only.

b. *fig.* Bribed.

1693 DRYDEN *Persius* iii. (1697) 444 Envy not the Store Of the greaz'd Advocate, that grinds the Poor.

c. (See quot. Cf. GREASE *sb.* 4.)

1848 ARNOULD *Mar. Insur.* III. vii. II. 1025 The hides were found to be in a state of incipient putrefaction..; they were all, as it is termed 'greased', the hair coming off in the fingers of those who handled them.

2. Of a horse: Affected with 'grease'.

1710 *Lond. Gaz.* No. 4695/4 A..Gelding..lately greas'd in the..Feet. **1720** *Ibid.* No. 5831/4 The..Preparation of Antimony..cures Greased Heels. **1759** STERNE *Tr. Shandy* I. x. (1760) 43 His horse was either clapp'd, or spavin'd or greaz'd. *c* **1785** BEWICK *Waiting for Death* in A. Dobson *Bewick & Pupils* ix. 155 Becoming greased, spavined, [etc.], he was judged to be only fit for the dogs.

greaser (ˈgriːzə(r), ˈgriːsə(r)). [f. GREASE *v.* + -ER[1].]

1. †**a.** One who greases (sheep). **b.** One who cleans and lubricates machinery, etc. with grease. *spec.* an engineer on a ship.

1641 BEST *Farm. Bks.* (Surtees) 30 Wee provide usually sixe or seaven greasers; and they will grease..sixe lambes a day. **1832** *Examiner* 168/2 The sinecure place of greaser to the King's state-carriage wheels. **1888** L. A. SMITH *Music of Waters* 38 And who do you think was second greaser? **1889** G. FINDLAY *Eng. Railway* 169 The train is accompanied by a staff of..greasers who keep a vigilant watch on each side of it. **1890** *Columbus* (Ohio) *Disp.* 17 July, The head firemen [in steamers] are called 'greasers', and they oil and clean the machinery. **1899** *Daily News* 3 Oct. 3/4 The nine men..are all said to be firemen or greasers. **1906** *Daily Chron.* 20 Mar. 3/6 Every A.B. signing on for a British ship must prove that he has served already at least three years as an ordinary seaman on a British vessel, and that every fireman, greaser, &c., has served two years as trimmer, &c. **1909** J. R. WARE *Passing Eng.* 147/1 *Greaser* (Navy, 1860–82), a scornful way of describing naval engineers. **1942** *Penguin New Writing* XV. 9 Seamen don't salute bloody greasers.

c. (See quot. 1906.)

1906 L. CLAREMONT *Gem-Cutter's Craft* 100 The heavy material among which are the diamonds..is..passed through a machine called the 'greaser', which consists of a shaking table made of five shallow steps..coated with a thick layer of grease, and the diamonds adhere to the grease while the remainder of the gravel is washed away. **1962** F. C. PHILLIPS *Smith's Gemstones* (ed. 13) xx. 276 In this ingenious machine, the 'jigger' or 'greaser' as it is commonly termed, the concentrates are washed over a series of galvanized-iron trays, which are covered with a thick coat of grease.

d. A device for lubricating the parts of a motor vehicle with grease.

1908 *Westm. Gaz.* 17 Nov. 5/2 Greasers are fitted every-where necessary. **1923** [see *grease-gun* s.v. GREASE *sb.* 6]. **1924** A. W. JUDGE *Mod. Motor Cars* I. 245 The shackle pins.. should be provided either with screw-down greasers or dust-proof oil cups.

2. a. *U.S. slang.* 'A native Mexican or native Spanish American: originally applied contemptuously by Americans in the south-western United States to the Mexicans' (*Cent. Dict.*).

1849 RUXTON *Life Far West* 4 The Greasers payed for Bent's scalp, they tell me. *Note*, The Mexicans are called 'Spaniards' or 'Greasers' (from their greasy appearance) by the Western people. **1872** C. KING *Mountain. Sierra Nev.* vi. 113, I thought them not worse than the average Californian greaser. **1883** B. HARTE *Carquinez Woods* vii. 154 *note*, *Greasers*—Californian slang for a mixed race of Mexicans and Indians.

attrib. **1855** FRANK MARRYAT *Mount. & Mole Hills* xiv. 263 The term 'greaser camp' as applied to a Mexican encampment is truthfully suggestive of the filth and squalor the passing traveller will observe there. **1888** *Century Mag.* Oct. 836 The cowboys..fairly stormed the 'Greaser'—that is, Mexican—village.

b. An objectionable person; a sycophant. (Cf. GREASE *sb.* 5 b.)

1900 J. S. FARMER *Public School Word-Book* 100 *Greaser*, ..a cad. **1911** D. COKE *Wilson's* vii. 74 Dick could not help wondering..what possible breach of House discipline could brand a fellow as a beastly greazer. **1958** *Spectator* 7 Feb. 163/1 The dismissive contempt the little greaser had so richly earned. **1959** I. & P. OPIE *Lore & Lang. Schoolch.* x. 191 *Grease* is a very popular word in school just now, and seems to be short for 'greaser'—i.e. sycophant, soft-soaper, teacher's pet.

c. A term applied, orig. in California, later elsewhere, to long-haired youths who, as members of a group or gang, ride about habitually on motor-cycles (in California, in 'hot rods').

1964 *San Francisco Examiner* 26 Jan. I. 14 The boy distinguished..'the Surfers'..from less-favored individuals called 'Greasers', who indulge in such gauche activities as drag-racing, putting grease on their hair, smoking marijuana and dancing the Twist. **1965** *Sun* 8 June 7/7 You can call rockers Greasers if you like... Greasers just means they have to put a lot of work into bikes. **1969** *Guardian* 23 Sept. 5/1 The London Street Commune.. intends forming a 'working coalition between greasers, skinheads, and beats'. **1970** *Daily Mirror* 31 Mar. 24/4, 200 teenagers—both skin-heads and 'greasers', who are long-haired youths—fought for two hours with bricks and chains. **1971** *Daily Tel.* (Colour Suppl.) 3 Sept. 41 The surfers used to refer to the hotrodders neither as hotrodders nor as Hair Boys, but as 'greasers'. **1971** *It* 7–21 Oct. 21/3 From the very start he seemed bound for Angeldom, leading a young pack of greasers down Leyton Baths on a regular basis and battling with the Mods.

greasily ('griːzɪlɪ, 'griːsɪlɪ), *adv.* Also 6 greasely. [f. GREASY + -LY².] In a greasy manner; with or as with grease; so as to grease; *fig.* unctuously; †indecently (quot. 1588; cf. F. *parler gras*).

1588 SHAKS. *L.L.L.* IV. i. 139 You talke greasely, your lips grow foule. **1607** BEAUM. & FL. *Woman-hater* I. i, He hath followed your court..from place to place.. as faithfully as your spits and your dripping-pans have done, and almost as greasily. **1642** MORE *Song of Soul* I. II. lxxvii, His sweaty neck did shine right greasily. **1868** *Less. Mid. Age* 74 A hoary reprobate..having professed some penitence in the last hours of life..was greasily held forth from a certain pulpit as a noble Christian character.

greasiness ('griːzɪ-, 'griːsɪnɪs). [f. GREASY + -NESS.] The quality or condition of being greasy; fattiness; oiliness; unctuousness. With *pl.* A greasy or fatty article.

1552 HULOET, Greasines, or spottes of grease, or filthynes, *squallor*. **1658** A. FOX *Wurtz' Surg.* II. xx. 131 These [knees] ought not at all to be annointed, much less must any greasiness or moisture come to it. **1669** BOYLE *Absol. Rest in Bodies* 20 Upon the most of these stones after they are cut, there appears always as it were a kind of greasiness or unctuosity. **1801** ANNA SEWARD *Lett.* lxxiii. (1811) V. 408 The slippery greasiness of a damp day keeps me within doors. **1832** G. R. PORTER *Porcelain & Gl.* 297 This substance..will, through its greasiness, indispose the glass from taking the colour properly. **1845** BUDD *Dis. Liver* 230 Greasiness of the skin. **1890** S. J. DUNCAN *Social Departure* 184 Split fish and unimaginable greasinesses to eat.

greasing ('griːzɪŋ, 'griːsɪŋ), *vbl. sb.* [f. GREASE *v.* + -ING¹.] The action of the vb. GREASE.

1. a. Smearing, anointing, lubricating, etc. with grease. In Protestant literature of the 16th c. often used contemptuously for 'anointing', as practised by Roman Catholics.

c **1440** *Promp. Parv.* 210/2 Gresynge, or a-noyntynge (*P.* with grece), *saginacio*. **1560** *1st Bk. Discipl. Ch. Scot.* xvi. (1836) 82 The clipping of their crownes, the greasing of their fingers [etc.]. **1574** J. STUDLEY tr. *Bale's Pageant Popes* Ep. Rdr. *b iv, How can that foundation stand which is made of earth and claye,..Popes miters,..annoyntings and greazings, blessings [etc.]. **1591** PERCIVALL *Sp. Dict.*, *Untura*, greasing, anointing, *vnctio*. **1641** BEST *Farm. Bks.* (Surtees) 29 For Greasinge of Lambes. Soe soone as harvest is done and past, wee beginne to looke after greasinge of our hogges. **1748** F. SMITH *Voy. Disc.* I. 183 The Greasing themselves..with..Bears Grease. **1886** W. J. TUCKER *Life E. Europe* 175 The greasing and twiddling and twirling of their moustaches.

b. *fig.* The action of bribing, in phr. *a greasing of palms*. Also an instance of this, a bribe.

c **1661** MARQ. ARGYLE *Will* in *Harl. Misc.* (1746) VIII. 30/1, I take all their Lands, Estates, and whatever Scotland is worth, not to be worth a Suit, much less the Overplus of a Greasing. **1887** T. A. TROLLOPE *What I remember* III. ii. 32 Certain columns..might, by good management, and certain greasing of certain palms, be acquired at no very great cost.

c. See quot. and cf. GREASED *ppl. a.* 1 c.

1848 ARNOULD *Mar. Insur.* III. vii. II. 1025 This greasing [of hides] is a partial fermentation.

2. *concr.* Grease (for lubrication).

1598 BARRET *Theor. Warres* V. iii. 135 Barrels to cary.. greasing for the axeltrees.

3. = GREASE *sb.* 3. ? *Obs.*

1756 C. LUCAS *Ess. Waters* III. 205 Those dropsical tumors of horses legs, which our ferriers call greasing.

†'**greasling.** *Obs. rare*⁻¹. [f. GREASE *v.* + -LING. Cf. *shaveling*.] A contemptuous term for a Roman Catholic priest. (See prec. 1 a.)

1583 GOLDING *Calvin on Deut.* lxx. 426 Yᵉ Pope.. attibuting it to his owne clergie, as he termeth them, yᵗ is to wit to yᵉ stinking rabble of his powlshorn greaslings.

greasy ('griːzɪ, 'griːsɪ), *a.* Forms: 6 gresy, 6–8 greasie, 7 greazie, -y, (greezy), (9 greecy), 7– greasy. [f. GREASE *sb.* + -Y¹.]

1. a. Smeared, covered, or soiled with grease; foul with grease. Often said of persons or their clothes.

1514 BARCLAY *Cyt. & Uplondyshm.* (Percy Soc.) p. xxxviii, Gresy lippes & slimy bearde. *c* **1515** *Cocke Lorell's B.* 2 His hosen gresy upon his thyes. **1598** SHAKS. *Merry W.* III. v. 92 Ram'd me in with foule Stockings, greasie Napkins [etc.]. **1660** BLOUNT *Boscobel* I. (1680) 61 An old gray, greazy hat. **1700** T. BROWN tr. *Fresny's Amusem. Ser. & Com.* 21 A Fat Greasie Porter. **1726** LEONI *Alberti's Archit.* II. 108/2 If the glass be perfectly clean and not greasie. **1867** MISS BRADDON *Run to Earth* I. i. 2 The paper on the walls was dark and greasy with age. **1890** HARRIS *Techn. Dict. Insur. Chem.*, *Greasy waste*, Greasy matter (such as cotton and other oily material, and oily rags). **1892** *Speaker* 30 July 141/2 Little children who make themselves greasy with roast turkey at Christmas.

b. as a contemptuous or abusive epithet.

a **1529** SKELTON *Agst. Garnesche* iii. 35 Wherto xulde I wryght Of soche a gresy knyght? **1600** SHAKS. *A.Y.L.* II. i. 55, I quoth Iaques, Sweepe on you fat and greazie Citizens. **1641** MILTON *Ch. Govt.* II. Concl. (1851) 179 Not Epicurus, nor Aristippus..but would shut his school dores against such greasy sophisters. **1792** A. WILSON in *Poems & Lit. Prose* (1876) II. 38 Ye ugly, greasy, girnin' tyke. **1825** J. NEAL *Bro. Jonathan* II. 91, 'I do wonder what sich great, nasty, good-for-nothin'—greecy—snappish—'. Come, come, our major—none o' that.

†2. Anointed or 'smeared' with 'grease' or chrism. (A contemptuous term applied to R.C. priests in reference to unction.) *Obs.*

1545 BRINKLOW *Compl.* xxiv. H iv b, Thus for lukers sake the gresy canonistes nosell the peple in Idolatry. **1579** FULKE *Heskins' Parl.* 118 That greasie order of shauelings. **1583** STUBBES *Anat. Abus.* II. (1882) 70 He [the Pope], being a greasie priest, and smered prelate, hath no more authority than other oiled shauelings haue.

3. Composed of or containing grease; of the nature of grease. Of food: Containing a disproportionate quantity of grease. †*greasy stomach* (? nonce-use): an appetite for oily food.

1592 tr. *Junius on Rev.* xiii. (1599) 16 Her greasie Chrisme which hee doubteth not to preferre before Baptisme. **1622** MALYNES *Anc. Law-Merch.* 40 Oyle and all greasie things are light, and therefore swimme aboue, and burne. **1634** SIR T. HERBERT *Trav.* 211 [Dodos] are reputed of more for wonder then food, greasie stomackes may reeke after them. **1674** OWEN *Holy Spirit* (1693) 77 The Papacy may content themselves with their Chrysme, or greasie Unction. **1794** SULLIVAN *View Nat.* II. 44 The greasy bituminous particles raised from the sea. **1828** SCOTT *F.M. Perth* xxii, Thy greasy ointment will hiss as it drops upon the wound. **1838** T. THOMSON *Chem. Org. Bodies* 922 The fixed oil..gave a greasy stain to paper. **1840** HOOD *Up Rhine* 216 When a German dish is not sour it is sure to be greasy. **1883** C. J. WILLS *Mod. Persia* 296 The native mode of cookery is extravagant, and possibly a little greasy.

fig. **1606** SHAKS. *Tr. & Cr.* V. ii. 159 The..greazie reliques Of her ore-eaten faith.

4. a. Of wool: Containing a natural grease (see GREASE *sb.* 4); used *spec.* of wool before it has been cleansed of this. Also of flannel.

1600 SHAKS. *A.Y.L.* III. ii. 55 We are still handling our Ewes, and their Fels you know are greasie. **1707** MORTIMER *Husb.* 177 See that they [sheep]..have a soft, greasie, well curled close Wooll. **1712** ARBUTHNOT *John Bull* III. i, She would not keep herself in a constant sweat with greasy flannel. **1883** *Leisure Hour* 242/1 The specifications of the state of the wool, *i.e.* whether 'greasy' or 'scoured'.

b. *absol.* as *sb.* 'Greasy' wool.

1883 *Times* 25 May 11 Western Cape lambs' wool and some descriptions of Natal greasies. **1890** *Daily News* 24 Feb. 7/3 Good deep combing greasys..have shown less decline.

5. Of a horse: Affected with the 'grease'.

1701 *Lond. Gaz.* No. 3741/4 A Sorrel Mare..subject to greasy Heels. **1813** *Sporting Mag.* XLII. 55 Stiff and greasy horses. **1844** STEPHENS *Bk. Farm* II. 226 It is a disgrace for any steward..to allow his horses to become greasy.

6. a. Having the appearance or 'feel' of containing or being covered with grease.

1703 MOXON *Mech. Exerc.* 241 Greasy clammy Stone. **1794** KIRWAN *Elem. Min.* I. 41 As to the Feel, we may distinguish those that are rough, smooth, or greasy. **1843** PORTLOCK *Geol.* 92 The chalk is..very splintery and greasy. **1856** HENSLOW *Bot. Dict.*, *Greasy*, where the surface feels as though it were rubbed with grease. **18..** *Gilder's Manual* 88 (Cent.) Should the presence of mercury or a bad deposit prevent the [burnishing] tool from producing a bright surface [in electroplating], the object is said to be greasy.

b. Of a road, etc.: Slippery or slimy with mud or moisture.

1801 [implied in GREASINESS]. **1806–7** J. BERESFORD *Miseries Hum. Life* (1826) II. viii, When the ground is what the vulgar call greasy. **1836** DICKENS *Sk. Boz, Streets* ii, Just enough damp gently stealing down to make the pavement greasy. **1869** G. MORGANS in *Eng. Mech.* 10 Dec. 293/1 The rails about stations generally being what is termed 'greasy'. **1894** ASTLEY *50 Years Life* II. 83 The ground was very greasy and slippery.

c. *dial.* (See quot. 1787.)

1735 SOMERVILLE *Chase* I. 161 Whose nice Scent O'er greasy Fallows, and frequented Road, Can pick the dubious Way. **1787** W. MARSHALL *Norfolk* (1795) II. 380 *Greasy*, foul, grassy: spoken of fallows or other plowed grounds.

d. Of the weather or the sky: 'Thick', 'dirty'.

a **1825** FORBY *Voc. E. Anglia* s.v., The sky is greasy. **1875** BEDFORD *Sailor's Pocket Bk.* iv. (ed. 2) 86 The harder, more 'greasy', rolled, tufted, or ragged [clouds look]—the stronger the coming wind will prove.

7. Filthy, obscene, low; esp. of language.

1588 [implied in GREASILY]. **1598** MARSTON *Sco. Villainie* I. iii. 79 Chaste cells, when greasie Aretine For his rank Fico, is surnam'd diuine. **1614** B. JONSON *Bart. Fair* II. i, Let's away, her language grows greasier than her pigs. **1687** SETTLE *Refl. Dryden* 5 His greasy Jest. **1814** *Way to win Her* III. i, Kettle of fish! O fie; how could you possibly pick up so coarse and greasy an idea?

8. Of manners, expression of countenance, voice, etc.: Disagreeably 'unctuous', 'oily'.

1848 THACKERAY *Bk. Snobs* xlvi, With a..greasy simper —he fawns on everybody. **1871** LEGRAND *Cambr. Freshman* 367 A greasy voice struck his ear.

9. Combinations and special collocations, as ***greasy-headed***, ***-heeled***, ***-smelling*** adjs.; † **greasy chin** *slang* (see quot.); **greasy fritillary**, a species of butterfly (see quot.); **greasy pole**, a pole rubbed with grease to make it harder to climb or walk upon (commonly used as an object of diversion at fairs or village sports); **greasy spoon (restaurant)** *slang* (orig. *U.S.*), a cheap and inferior eating-house; **greasy steam** (see quot.).

1785 GROSE *Dict. Vulg. Tongue*, **Greasy chin*, a treat given to parish officers in part of commutation for a bastard; called also eating a child. **1844** WESTWOOD *Brit. Butterflies* 37 *Melitæa Artemis*, the *greasy fritillary. **1798** CHARLOTTE SMITH *Yng. Philos.* I. 103 Cropped *greasy-headed joskins's. **1711** *Lond. Gaz.* No. 4902/4 Given to be *greasie-heal'd. **1813** *Sporting Mag.* XLII. 54 Greasy-heeled, and broken-winded horses. **1851–61** MAYHEW *Lond. Labour* III. 199 We had a day's sport, consisting of *greasy-pole climbing, jumping in sacks [etc.]. **1886** T. HARDY *Mayor Casterbr.* xvi, They erected greasy-poles for climbing. **1899** *Strand Mag.* May XVII. 529 The walking the greasy pole for a pig is a very old form of pastime. It is nearly always the last item in a regatta programme. **1607** TOPSELL *Four-f. Beasts* (1658) 185 A filthy and *greasie-smelling old man. **1925** *Writer's Monthly* June 486/2 **Greasy spoon*, a low-class restaurant. **1951** *Time* 31 Dec. 29/2 They [*sc.* the Marx brothers]..ate in coffee pots and greasy spoons. **1966** C. HIMES *Heat's On* iii. 25 A room behind a greasy-spoon restaurant. *Ibid.*, The cook came from the greasy spoon. **1968** L. DEIGHTON *Only when I Larf* viii. 110 Bob said he was hungry and wanted to pull up at every greasy spoon we passed. **1888** *Lockwood's Dict. Mech. Engin.*, **Greasy Steam*, steam which becomes its own lubricant by a mechanical admixture of grease therewith.

great (greɪt), *a.*, *adv.*, and *sb.* Forms: 1 gréat, (gréæt, gréot), 2 grat-e, 3 græt, *Kent.* griat, 3–6 gret(e, 4 *Kent.* grat, 4–6 grett(e, greet(e, grait, 5–6 greate, greatt(e, (5 greth, 6 graete, 7 grat), 6 *Sc.* greit, gryt(t, 6–9 *Sc.* grit, 9 *Sc.* grite, gryte, 3– great. β. 4 gert(t, 6 gertte, 9 *dial.* girt, gurt. (See also GREATER, GREATEST.) [Com. WGer.: OE. *gréat* = OFris. *grât*, OS. *grôt* (MDu., Du. *groot*), OHG., MHG. *grôz* (G. *grosz*):—OTeut. **grauto-*:—pre-Teut. **ghroudo-*. (Wanting in Gothic and Scandinavian.)

On the assumption that the primary sense is 'coarse' (sense 1 below), some scholars regard the word as cognate with ON. *graut-r* porridge, OE. *grút* fine meal, *grot* particle, *grytta* coarse meal, *gréot* sand, gravel, ON. *griót* stones. But the connexion is not free from difficulty, as the cognates of these words outside Teut. point to a root meaning 'to pound', a sense from which that of the adj. is not easily derived. It has been suggested (Stokes in Fick *Idg. Wb.*⁴ II. 119) that a cognate of the Teut. adj. may exist in the OIrish *gruad* (?:—pre-Celtic **ghroudes-*) cheek (? lit. 'thick or fleshy part' of the face; cf. sense 2 below, and the contrasted notion in OE. *þunwang* lit. 'thin cheek', the temples). The prevailing senses in OE. are 'coarse, thick, stout, big'; but the word also appears as an intensive synonym of *micel* MICKLE, which in the later language it superseded. In OHG. *grôz* had the senses of 'big, awkwardly large', and of 'pregnant', but was also used as a synonym of *mihhil* (though not with reference to length); in OS. *grôt* is recorded only in the sense of 'great', in which it is less frequent (and possibly more emphatic) than *mikil*. The development by which *great* has superseded *mickle* (not only in Eng. but also in Du., Ger., and Fris.) may be illustrated by reference to the mod. colloquial substitution of *big* for *great*, and to the supersession of L. *magnus* in Rom. by *grandis* big, full-grown (see GRAND *a.*).

In this word, as in *break*, the influence of the preceding *r* has caused ME. (ɛː) to be represented by (eɪ) instead of the usual (iː); cf. *broad* with (ɔː) instead of (əʊ). The pronunciation (griːt) was, however, very common, and approved by the majority of orthoepists, throughout the 18th c.; it seems to have been merely an artificial fashion. Many modern dialects have (grɛt), and others have metathetic forms such as (g(ʌ)rt); a common Sc. form, esp. in senses 1 and 2, is *gryte* (greiᵗ).]

A. *adj.*

I. Thick, coarse, massive, big.

1. a. Composed of large particles; coarse of grain or texture. Of diet: Coarse, not delicate. In *Old Cookery*, applied sometimes to boiled meat in contradistinction to roast. *Obs.* exc. *Sc.* (in form *grit* or *gryte*).

909 *Grant* in Birch *Cartul. Sax.* (1887) II. 290 Tu hund greates hlafes & þridde smales. *c* **1000** *Sax. Leechd.* I. 138 Cnuca mid greatum sealte [L. *cum sale marino*]. *c* **1200** *Trin. Coll. Hom.* 163 His alter cloð is great and sole, ac hire chemise smal and hwit. *a* **1225** *Ancr. R.* 10 Mid hore greate maten & hore herde heren. *Ibid.* 418 Nexst fleshe schal mon werien no linene cloð bute ȝif hit beo of herde and of greate heorden. **1398** TREVISA *Barth. De P.R.* VI. xi. (1495) 195 A seruaunt woman . . is fedde with grete mete and symple [L. *grossioribus cibis reficitur*]. *Ibid.* VII. lv. 268 Stone and grauell . . comyth namely of drynke of slymy water and of grete dyete. *c* **1425** *Voc.* in Wr.-Wülcker 661 *Caro salsa*, salt flesche. *Ibid.* 662 *Caro grossa*, grete flesche. *Caro assata* [printed *assota*], rost flesche. *c* **1440** *Anc. Cookery* in *Househ. Ord.* (1790) 435 Take onyons and mynce hom grete. *c* **1460** FORTESCUE *Abs. & Lim. Mon.* ii. (1885) 114 A pouere cote . . made of grete caunuas, and callid a frokke. *a* **1483** *Liber Niger* in *Househ. Ord.* (1790) 24, vi messes of greete mete and rost. **1614** *Compt bk. D. Wedderburne* (S.H.S.) 250 Aucht hundreth bolls great salt. *Mod. Sc.* That meal (*or* salt) is ower gryte; I like it sma'.

†b. Said of the air: Thick, dense. *Obs.*

1398 TREVISA *Barth. De P.R.* XIV. xlvi. (1495) Fj/2 Therfore valeyes ben demyd by assaye hote & trowbly with grete ayre & thycke & many vapours.

2. Thick; stout, massive, bulky, big. (Opposed to *small* in its original sense of 'slender'.) *Obs.* exc. *Sc.* (in form *grit* or *gryte*).

a. Of things.

c **888** K. ÆLFRED *Boeth.* xxxviii. §2 Great beam on wuda. *c* **1000** ÆLFRIC *Hom.* I. 52 Greatum haȝolstanum. *c* **1050** *Voc.* in Wr.-Wülcker 415/7 *Grossas et graciles*, great and smæl. **11..** *O.E. Chron.* (1892) 5 (Laud MS.) Ða ȝenamon þa Walas & adrifon sumre ea ford ealne mid scearpum pilum greatum innan þam wetere. *c* **1320** *Sir Beues* (A.) 1884 Þe staf, þat he to fiȝte ber, Was twenti fote in lengþe be tale, Þar to gret & noþing smale. *c* **1386** CHAUCER *Doctor's T.* 37 And Phebus dyed hath hir tresses grete Lyk to the stremes of his burned hete. *c* **1450** *Bk. Curtasye* 359 in *Babees Bk.*, A stafe, A fyngur gret two wharters long. [**1547** BOORDE *Introd. Knowl.* xxxvi. (1870) 212 They haue gret lyppes, and nottyd heare.] ? *a* **1800** *Earl of Aboyne* in Child *Ballads* (1892) IV. 312 Wi her fingers sae white, and the gold rings sae grite. *a* **1900** *Mod. Sc.* He had a stick as gryte as your airm.

†b. Of persons and animals: Stout, corpulent.

c **1050** *Suppl. Ælfric's Voc.* in Wr.-Wülcker 172/14 *Corpulentus*, ðiccul. *Grossus*, græat. **10..** *O.E. Chron.* an. 1017 (MS. D) Æþelward Æȝelmeres sunu [þæs] greatan. *c* **1250** *Gen. & Ex.* 2098 Ðeden ut-comen vii. neet, Euerilc wel swiðe fet and gret. *c* **1300** *Leg. St. Gregory* 1024 Fisches þre þat were boþe gret and long. *c* **1369** CHAUCER *Dethe Blaunche* 954 Euery lyth Fattysh, flesshy, not grete therwith.

3. a. Pregnant; far advanced in pregnancy: app. orig. referred to the stoutness of the body. Chiefly with *with* (*child*, etc.); †*occas.* with *of*. †Also said of the body. (Cf. BIG *a.* 4.) *arch.* and *dial.*

c **1200** ORMIN 2479 Ȝho wass waxenn summ del græt & . . wass wiþþ childe. **13..** *Minor Poems fr. Vernon MS.* (E.E.T.S.) 639/52 Virgyn Marie . . gret with childe. *c* **1460** *Towneley Myst.* x. 158 Hyr body is grete, and she with childe! **1483** CAXTON *Gold. Leg.* 217/2 To whom her husbond answerd . . dame . . thou art grete and the perylles of the see ben wythout nombre thou myghtest lyghtely perysshe. **1549** *Compl. Scotl.* vi. 60 Ane nobil princesse callit martia grit vitht child. **1638** SIR T. HERBERT *Trav.* (ed. 2) 24 Dolphins . . go great 10 months. **1647** A. ROSS *Myst. Poet.* viii. (1675) 157 Being great of Paris, she dreamed that she had a burning fire-brand in her belly. **1657** R. LIGON *Barbadoes* (1673) 55 She chanc'd to be with Child, . . and being very great, and that her time was come to be delivered. **17..** in *Herd's Coll. Sc. Songs* (1776) II. 58 O silly lassie, what wilt thou do? If thou grow great, they'll heez thee high. **1779–81** JOHNSON *L.P.*, *Savage* Wks. II. 245 The child, with which she was then great. **1842** TENNYSON *Walking to Mail* 80 She [a sow] . . Lay great with pig, wallowing in sun and mud.

†b. *fig. Obs.*

1602 MARSTON *Antonio's Rev.* II. iii, My heart is great of thoughts. *Ibid.* IV. iii, Art not great of thanks To gratious heauen? **1606** CHAPMAN *Gentl. Usher* Plays 1873 I. 308 The Asse is great with child of some ill newes. **1608** SHAKS. *Per.* v. i. 107, I am great with woe, and shall deliver weeping. **1654** Z. COKE *Logick* (1657) Ep. Ded. A iij b, The smattering Soul of Lapsed man . . often taking shewes and shadowes for substances, gets the minde great of Distemperature.

†4. Full or 'big' with courage, emotion, anger, sorrow, or pride; angry, grieved; proud, arrogant. Often qualifying *heart* (cf. GREAT-HEARTED). *Obs.*

c **1205** LAY. 569 Heo comen to gadere mid greatere heorte. *Ibid.* 25292 We habbeoð writen ibroht þe word swiðe grate [*c* **1275** grete]. *a* **1225** *Ancr. R.* 342 Of alle kudde & kuðe sunnen, ase of prude, of great heorte, oðer of heih heorte. **1297** R. GLOUC. (Rolls) 2855 Is herte was so gret uor is fader deþe þere. *Ibid.* 6314 Edmond . . is grete herte wiþ drou & ensentede to is rede. *a* **1300** *Cursor M.* 5949 His hert wex gret and gan to greue. *c* **1400** *Destr. Troy* 12234 Than Telamon . . spake Grete wordes . . all in grym yre. *a* **1450** *Knt. de la Tour* (1868) 126 The wise Sarra, that made no gret ansueres vnto her chambrere. *c* **1460** *Towneley Myst.* xxvii. 55 He [Jesus] spake neuer, by nyght ne day, No wordes greatte. **1470–85** MALORY *Arthur* XVI. ix, They wente betynge hym . . but he said neuer a word as he whiche was grete of herte. **1484** CAXTON *Fables of Æsop* II. v, Men ought not to doubte al folk which ben of grete wordes and menaces. **1593** SHAKS. *Rich. II*, II. i. 228 My harte is great: but it must break with silence. **1597** —— *2 Hen. IV*, IV. iii. 121 The Heart; who great, and pufft up with his Retinue, doth any Deed of Courage. **1608** DOD & CLEAVER *Expos. Prov. xi. & xii.* 6 So standeth the case with all proud persons, theire great heart doth threaten some greate mischiefe to bee nigh vnto them. *a* **1784** in Scott *Minstr. Scot. Bord.* (1802) I. 143 Dickie's heart it grew sae grit, That the ne'er a bit o't he dought to eat. **1832** MOTHERWELL *Jeanie Morison* 79 Oh! say gin e'er your heart grows grit Wi' dreamings o' langsyne?

5. Of the sea, a river: Having the water swollen or high; in high flood. *dial.*

a **1670** SPALDING *Troub.* (Bannatyne Club) I. 174 Seeing they wanted the boats, and that they could not ryde the watter, it being great. **1687** A. LOVELL *Thevenot's Trav.* II. 3 We had a very great Sea from the West. **1692** SYMSON *Descr. Galloway* (1823) 30 A rivulet called Pinkill Bourn, which is sometimes so great, that [etc.]. **1760–72** tr. *Juan & Ulloa's Voy.* (ed. 3) II. 252 There is no possibility of landing on account of the great sea.

II. Having a high position in a scale of measurement or quantitative estimation. (Opposed to *small*, *little*.)

With words like *as*, *so*, *how*, the adj., like some other adjs. and advs. of cognate meaning (cf. FAR *adv.* 6), admits of being used in a weakened sense, expressing size or quantity in the abstract. Thus 'as great as' may mean merely 'equal in size or amount to', without any implication that the things compared are 'great'. See also GREATER.

6. a. Of material objects, with reference to size.

In unemotional use the word in this application is now superseded by *large* or (colloquially) *big*. To use *great* with reference to size now implies either some kind of feeling on the speaker's part, or a mixture of some other sense of the adj. Thus 'I found a *large* table in my room' would simply state a fact, but if *great* were used the sentence would indicate annoyance, amusement, or surprise. Often preceding a partly synonymous adj., as in ***great big***, ***great thick***, etc. The adj. has never had, like the F. *grand* and the G. *grosz*, the sense of 'tall'; if used with reference to stature it expresses some feeling such as surprise, contempt, or admiration, as in 'that great boy', 'a great tall man'.

a **1300** *Cursor M.* 393 Þe sterns, gret and smale. **13..** *K. Alis.* 5245 He maden fyres vertuous Fyve hundreth, vche gret als an hous. **1340** *Ayenb.* 238 Þe vissere heþ more blisse uor to nime þe gratne viss þane ane littlene. *c* **1380** WYCLIF *Sel. Wks.* III. 415 Þis burgeys of þo cyte schewed hom a grett hous strewid. *c* **1440** *Jacob's Well* (E.E.T.S.) 80 Grete fyssches are takyn in þe nett, & slayn; smale fyssches scapyn throuȝ þe nett. **1542** *Inv. R. Wardrobe* (1815) 71 Item, twa gryt barrallis ourgilt. **1542** UDALL *Erasm. Apoph.* 130 When he sawe greate wyde gates . . where as the toune was but a litle preaty pyle. **1562** TURNER *Herbal* II. 120 It [raspberry] hath . . no great howky prickes at all. **1585** T. WASHINGTON tr. *Nicholay's Voy.* II. iii. 33 Within a great rock eighteen or twentie baths small and great. **1596** DALRYMPLE tr. *Leslie's Hist. Scot.* VI. 309 Frome a grett heid he is namet Canmoir. **1610** SHAKS. *Temp.* IV. i. 153 The Clowd-capt Towres, the Gorgeous Pallaces, The solemne Temples, the great Globe it selfe . . sall dissolue. **1715** M. DAVIES *Athen. Brit.* I. 249, I saw once in a Barn a Weasel and a great hugy Rat engage. **1748** RICHARDSON *Clarissa* (1811) II. i. 8 A great over grown, lank-haired, chubby boy. **1766** ELIZ. GRIFFITH *Lett. Henry & Frances* IV. 272 Little Master Jacky Thompson is returned from the West-Indies, a great big Man. **1809** MALKIN *Gil Blas* I. v. ¶9 A great bloated horse-godmother. **1818** SHELLEY *Rev. Islam* X. xxiii. 2 The great fountain in the public square. **1819** —— *Cyclops* 222 A great faggot of wood. *Ibid.* 620 A great oak stump. **1841** LYTTON *Night & Morning* II. xi. 58, I send you a great big sum of 20*l.* **1849** MACAULAY *Hist. Eng.* vi. II. 98 The charge of his great diocese was committed to his judges, Sprat and Crewe. **1884** JEFFERIES *Red Deer* 33 Heath-poults, the female of black-game, fly like a great partridge. **1961** L. P. HARTLEY *Two for River* 94 It was a great big thing, the size of a small haystack.

b. Of letters = CAPITAL. Also in the names of some large sizes of type-bodies, as ***Great Canon***, ***Great Primer***. See also PRIMER *sb.*[1] 3 a. ***great A***: capital A.

1565 COOPER *Thesaurus*, *Grandis litera*, a great capitall letter. **1594** *Selimus* H i b, I began to sweare all the crisse crosse row ouer, beginning at great A, litle a, til I cam to w, x, y. **1594** BLUNDEVIL *Exerc.* III. I. xx. (1636) 324 Six Columnes, every front or head whereof is noted with three great letters, D.M.S., signifying degrees, minutes, and seconds. **1601** SHAKS. *Twel. N.* II. v. 97 Thus makes she her great P's. **1602** J. COOKE *Gd. Wife fr. Bad* III. i. (1614) E ij b, I was fiue yeare learning cris-crosse from Great A, and fiue yeere longer comming to F. **1634** PEACHAM *Gentl. Exerc.* 16 Pensills of Broome, with which they shadow great letters with common Inke in Coppy bookes. **1683** MOXON *Mech. Exerc.* II. 13 Great Primmer . . Great Cannon. *Ibid.* 20, English and upwards are accounted great Bodies. **18..** in Halliwell *Nursery Rhymes* (1842) 131 Great A, little a, Bouncing B, The cat's in the cupboard, And she can't see. **1860** READE *Cloister & H.* lxi, Few minds are big enough to be just to great A without being unjust to capital B.

c. In the names of certain animal and vegetable species or varieties, distinguished by their larger size from others belonging to the same genus or popularly called by the same name. (Cf. GREATER.)

a **1387** *Sinon. Barthol.* (Anecd. Oxon.) 12 *Bardana*, an clote, gert burr. *Ibid.* 16 *Consolida media*, grete dayeseghe. *a* **1450** *Fysshynge w. angle* 15 The Dare & þe greyt Roche . . þe greyt cheven . . þe greyt Trowt. **1530** PALSGR. 227/2 Great hasyll nutte, *aueleine*. Great hounde, *alant*. **1548** TURNER *Names of Herbes* 42 Hieracium is of two kyndes. The one is called in latin Hieracium magnum. It may be called in englishe greate Haukweede. *Ibid.* 70 Particalis salix is the greate Wylowe tree. **1678** RAY *Willughby's Ornith.* 99 The great Horn-Owl or Eagle-Owl. **1756** SIR J. HILL *Brit. Herbal* II. 420 Great Hercules Allheal. **1802** BINGLEY *Anim. Biog.* (1813) II. 273 The black or great ostrich. **1832** *Veg. Subst. Food* 188 The Great Cat's-Tail is a perennial reed . . a native of Britain. **1861** MISS PRATT *Flower, Pl.* VI. 396 Great Horse-tail, Great Water Horsetail, or Great Mud Horsetail. **1882** *Garden* 4 Feb. 71/1 The Great St. John's Wort. **1896** NEWTON *Dict. Birds* 967 The Great Titmouse, *Parus major*.

d. Forming part of the specific designations of other objects, e.g. in the names of constellations, as ***Great*** (formerly †***Greater***) ***Bear***, ***Great Dog***; of anatomical structures, as ***great artery***, †***great bone*** (the sacrum), ***great pelvis***, etc. (See the sbs.)

†***great arm***, ***great hand***: used by the early anatomists for the arm and hand together. Similarly ***great foot***: see FOOT *sb.* I c.

1594 BLUNDEVIL *Exerc.* VI. vi. (1636) 616 The Meridian Altitude of the great dog called *Canis maior*. **1615** CROOKE *Body of Man* 215 The marrow of the great or holy bone. **1676** MOXON *Tutor Astron.* (ed. 3) 220 *Canis Major*, the Great Dog, it consisteth of 18 Stars. *a* **1715** BURNET *Own Time* (1724) I. III. 394 He received a deep wound by a knife struck into his thigh, that pierced the great artery. **1718** J. CHAMBERLAYNE *Relig. Philos.* (1730) I. viii. §1 The Vessel which is called the Aorta, Arteria magna, or Great Artery. **1842** E. WILSON *Anat. Vade M.* (ed. 2) 352 The Great Cardiac Vein commences at the apex of the heart. **1857** BULLOCK *Cazeaux' Midwif.* 27 The great pelvis has a very irregular figure, and forms a species of pavilion to the entrance of the pelvis. **1868** [see BEAR *sb.*[1] 3]. **1886** *Syd. Soc. Lex.* s.v., Great dorsal muscle, the *Latissimus dorsi* . . Great serrate muscle, the *Serratus magnus*.

e. Prefixed to the names of many English villages or towns, to distinguish them from places having identical names with the prefix *Little*, as in Great Malvern, Great Snoring (Norfolk); similarly to names of rivers, as the Great Ouse; to names of streets, as Great Portland Street.

f. In quasi-superlative sense, of a specified part of a building; of a particular building, monument, square, etc. in a town: Main, principal. (Cf. GRAND 7 b.)

1598 STOW *Surv. Lond.* 385 William Rufus builded the great Hall there [Westminster] about the yeare of Christ, 1097. **1624** WOTTON *Archit.* II. 103 If the great Doore be Arched with some braue Head, cut in fine Stone or Marble for the Key of the Arch. **1822** SHELLEY *Chas. I*, 114 You torch-bearers advance to the great gate. **1900** *Ch. Times* 2 Feb. 119/3 Canon Gore will lecture on the Apostles' Creed . . in the Great Hall of the Church House.

†7. Grown up; full-grown. Chiefly in *Hunting* language, of animals above a particular age (see quots.). *Obs.*

1485 CAXTON *Chas. Gt.* 27 A quarter of moton, or ij hennes, or a grete ghoos. **1486** *Bk. St. Albans* E ij, A grete hynde a grete bucke and a fayre doo My sonnys where ye walke call ye hem so. *a* **1533** LD. BERNERS *Huon* v. 9 We be grete ynow to be made knyghtes. *a* **1547** in *Gentl. Mag.* (1813) May 427 Grene Gesse from Ester till mydsomer yᵉ pece, vjjd. Gesse grett from mydsomer tell shroftyde yᵉ pece, viijd. *a* **1700** B. E. *Dict. Cant. Crew*, *Great Buck*, the Sixth Year. *Great Hare*, the Third Year and afterwards. **1774** [see BUCK *sb.*[1] 1 b].

8. a. Of collective unities, numbers, quantities, dimensions, etc. For ***great deal***, ***many***, see those words.

c **950** *Epist. Alex.* in *Anglia* IV. 143 Ða [the columns] wæron unmetlice greate he[ah]nisse upp. [But the orig. has *ingenti grossitudine atque altitudine*; cf. sense 2.] *c* **1205** LAY. 306 Ane heorde of heorten swiðe greate. **1297** R. GLOUC. (Rolls) 616 Þe quene . . gret ost made & strong. *c* **1400** *Destr. Troy* 1178 Comyn to þe kyng in companies grete, Mony stithe man. **1411** *Rolls of Parlt.* III. 650/1 Greet noumbre of men armed. *c* **1420** *Sir Amadas* (Weber) 123 A marchande [was he] . . and had greyt rentes be yere. *c* **1460** FORTESCUE *Abs. & Lim. Mon.* ix. (1885) 130 How necessarie it is þat the kynge haue grete possescions. **1658** JER. TAYLOR *Let.* in *12th Rep. Hist. MSS. Comm.* App. v. 5 Her duty to you . . does . . make a very great part of her religion to God. **1662** JOHN SMITH *England's Improv. Reviv'd* (1670) 269 Great part of their Fish is sold in other Countries for ready Money. **1725** DE FOE *New Voy.* (1840) 349 These lower lands lay great part of the year under water. **1827** HALLAM *Const. Hist.* (1842) I. 429 Military tenures . . bound great part of the kingdom to a stipulated service. **1849** MACAULAY *Hist. Eng.* i. I. 106 To raise a great army had always been the King's first object.

†b. A great number or quantity of; many, much. Also *absol. Obs.*

1430–40 LYDG. *Bochas* VIII. i. (1554) 177 b, Full great bloud shad in that mortall fyght. **1447** BOKENHAM *Seyntys* Introd. (Roxb.) 4, I was taryed wyth greth reyn. *c* **1470** HARDING *Chron.* XXX. iii, Greate people dyed. **1561** HOLLYBUSH *Hom. Apoth.* 5 a, Let him take thereof in hys mouth so great as a small beane. **1676** HOBBES *Iliad* II. 134 Great Dust they raised.

c. ***the great body***, ***majority***, ***part***, etc.: the larger portion or section (of).

1849 MACAULAY *Hist. Eng.* ii. I. 159 To no such plan could the great body of Cavaliers listen with patience. **1895** F. HALL *Two Trifles* 2 Nor is this the sole uncouth trait that sullies the written style of the great body of our fellow-countrymen.

d. ***great gross***, twelve gross, 1728. ***great hundred***, a 'long hundred', 120. †***great million***, a billion. (See the *sbs.*)

1533–4 [see HUNDRED 3]. **1625** GILL *Sacr. Philos.* I. 101, 1,124,002,590,827,719,680,000, that is, one thousand one hundred twentie foure millions of great millions, two thousand five hundred and ninetie great millions, eight hundred twenty seven thousand seven hundred and nineteene millions, sixe hundred and fourescore thousand. **1640** in Entick *London* (1776) II. 166 Catling, the great gross, qt. 12 small gross of knots. **1812** J. SMYTH *Pract. of Customs* (1821) 125, 120 Ells, or one great hundred. **1866** ROGERS *Agric. & Prices* I. x. 171 The hundred yards of canvas are the great hundred of 120.

†e. ***a shilling great***: a money of account equal to twelve Flemish groats. ***a pound great*** (= 'pound of groats'): 20 'shillings great'. *Obs.*

c **1483** CAXTON *Dial. Fr. & Eng.* (1900) 51/25 A pounde grete, Moneye of flaundres. **1518** *Extracts Aberd. Reg.* (1844) I. 94 Tua s. grett Flandris money. **1527** *Ibid.* 119 Gilbert Menzeis, provest, tua lib. grit. **1546** *Ibid.* 234 Ane Flemis ell of welwet cost xi s. grit.

9. ***a great while***, † ***season***, † ***time***: a long while. ***great age***, † ***years***: advanced age.

c **1330** R. BRUNNE *Chron.* (1725) 22 So fer bare a woulfe þe hede, & kept it a grete while. *c* **1400** *Ywaine & Gaw.* 1667 Thare he lifed a grete sesowne With rotes and raw venysowne. **1603** KNOLLES *Hist. Turks* (1621) 489 That he should in so great yeares be set upon by two of his own sonnes. **1610** SHAKS. *Temp.* III. iii. 105 Like poyson giuen to worke a great time after. **1634** SIR T. HERBERT *Trav.* 108 His great yeares were more propense to ease then tumult. **1662** STILLINGFL. *Orig. Sacr.* I. v. §2 The great age of some men in ancient times, who are supposed to have lived 1000 years. **1674** tr. *Scheffer's Lapland* 3 Saxo making mention of such a Country a great while before. **1709** STEELE *Tatler* No. 128 ¶7, I..have for a great while entertained the Addresses of a Man who I thought lov'd me more than Life.

10. a. Of qualities, emotions, conditions, actions, or occurrences; with reference to degree or extent.

a **1175** *Cott. Hom.* 231 þat [he] heom wolde ȝearceon anæ grate laðienge and þider ȝeclepien all his underþeod. *c* **1205** LAY. 2284 Moni greatne dunt..þolede ich on folde. *Ibid.* 26396 þæ andswarede þe kaisere mid grættere wræððe. **1297** R. GLOUC. (Rolls) 7730 He was..of grete strengþe. *a* **1300** *Cursor M.* 14219 His kin..for þair frend gret murning made. **1340** *Ayenb.* 222 He mai habbe grat merite ase to þe zaule. ? *a* **1366** CHAUCER *Rom. Rose* 251 Som greet mischaunce, or greet disese. *c* **1380** WYCLIF *Sel. Wks.* III. 301 Gret ypocrisie. *c* **1430** *Syr Tryam.* 135 Grete worde of hym aroos. *a* **1450** *Le Morte Arth.* 1102 She deide for gre[t] louyng. **1450** W. LOMNER in *Paston Lett.* No. 93 I. 126 Wretyn in gret hast at London. **1506-7** *Old City Acc. Bk.* in *Archæol. Jrnl.* XLIII, To the gertte coost & damage of all the suters befor named & to ther grett hyndranse. **1521** FISHER *Serm. agst. Luther* Wks. (1876) 313 To the graete trouble and vexacyon of his chyrch. **1548** UDALL, etc. *Erasm. Par. John* xviii. 40 The Iewes..with a great lowde voyce cryed [etc.]. **1561** WINȜET *Cert. Tractates* i. Wks. 1888 I. 6 Sa gret vproir, tumult, and terrible clamour. **1573-80** BARET *Alv.* H 333 The great heates are abated. **1624** N. DE LAUNE tr. *Du Moulin's Logick* 176 A man of great capacitie. **1670** WOOD *Life* 12 Nov., He had, in his great reading, collected some old words for his use. **1714** HEARNE in *Lett. Lit. Men* (Camden) 355, I will take great care of them. **1736** FIELDING *Pasquin* v. Wks. 1784 III. 301 Places, requiring learning, and great parts. **1845** M. PATTISON *Ess.* (1889) I. 22 The Bishop..whose great popularity at Tours..made him a person of much consideration. **1849** MACAULAY *Hist. Eng.* vi. II. 101 The agitation was great in the capital. **1857** BUCKLE *Civiliz.* I. ii. 42 Great ignorance is the fruit of great poverty.

† **b.** Of the pulse: High. *Obs.*

1707 FLOYER *Physic. Pulse-Watch* 27 The Pulse is called great, high, or a full Pulse.

III. In figurative extensions of branch II; important, elevated, distinguished.

11. a. Of things, actions, events: Of more than ordinary importance, weight, or distinction; important, weighty; distinguished, prominent; famous, renowned.

1297 R. GLOUC. (Rolls) 9287 þe gret oþ þæt he suor. **1448** *Extracts Aberd. Reg.* (1844) I. 16 The quilk to do lelely and treuly the forsaid personis hes sworn the gret ath. **1565** COOPER *Thesaurus* s.v. *Magnus, Magnum facere*, to doe some great mattier. **1655** DIGGES *Compl. Ambass.* 90 Great matters..could not but be full of great difficulties. **1675** tr. *Machiavelli's Prince* xvii. (Rtldg. 1883) 107 Instances of Hannibal's great conduct. **1760** C. JOHNSTON *Chrysal* II. I. ii. 10, I dream'd..that I saw you at court, on some *great* occasion. **1764** GOLDSM. *Trav.* 42 These little things are great to little man. **1821** BYRON *Stanzas* (first line), O talk not to me of a name great in story. **1825** LAMB *Vision of Horns* in *Eliana* (1871) 31 This shows that use is a great thing. **1840** J. H. NEWMAN *Lett.* (1891) II. 315, I do not think anything great of the Continental churches, as you seem to think, or of the Roman Catholics at home. **1849** MACAULAY *Hist. Eng.* iv. I. 469 The executive government could undertake nothing great without the support of the Commons. *Ibid.* vi. II. 100 The great foundations of Eton, Westminster, and Winchester. *Ibid.* vii. II. 227 He had studied no great model of composition, with the exception.. of our noble translation of the Bible. **1865** TENNYSON *Captain* 19 He..Hoped to make the name Of his vessel great in story. **1872** *Punch* 21 Sept. 118/2 If you can't command an entire language, it's a great thing to have a small effective force at your disposal for manœuvres. **1887** LOWELL *Old Eng. Dram.* (1892) 76 There is the same confusion at times of what is big with what is great.

b. Of times, days, etc.: Having important results; critical. (See also *Great day* in 20.)

a **1400** *Prymer* 69 A greet dai, & a ful bitter. **1703** ROWE *Fair Penit.* I. i. 148 That minute sure was lucky. Oh 'twas great. **1849** MACAULAY *Hist. Eng.* vi. II. 35 The great day of the Exclusion Bill. **1879** FARRAR *St. Paul* (1883) 202 It is one of the great moments in the ascensive work begun by Stephen.

c. (With *the.*) Important among all others of the kind; pre-eminent in importance; chief, main.

c **1374** CHAUCER *Troylus* III. 456 (505)þere was some Epistel hem by-twene, That wolde..wel contene Neigh half þis bok..How sholde I þanne a lyne of it endyte? But to þe grete effect. **1662** STILLINGFL. *Orig. Sacr.* II. v. §7 This.. was the great rule the Jews went by. **1676** tr. *Guillatiere's Voy. Athens* 175 Their Doctrine..is at this day the great Theme of our Schools. **1834** MEDWIN *Angler in Wales* II. 3 We have been able to scan a few of the secondary causes.. of nature, and think we are thus prepared to form some feeble notion of the First Great Cause. **1840** DICKENS *Barn. Rudge* xxxix, The great attraction was a pamphlet called The Thunderer.

d. As applied to nations, cities, etc., this sense blends with the literal senses relating to spatial or numerical magnitude (see 6, 8); esp. in ***great power***. In poetical use the adj. sometimes precedes the name of a city, etc.

13.. *K. Alis.* 1476 His lettres come In to the cite of gret Rome. [Cf. **1483** CAXTON *Dial.* 22/22 The pope of rome, which duelleth at auynyon, that by right shold be at gret rome (Fr. *c* 1340 *a grand romme*).] **1398** [see CITY 2]. **1606** SHAKS. *Tr. & Cr.* v. ix. 10 Great Troy is ours. **1612** BACON *Ess., Greatn. of Kingdoms* (Arb.) 468 He could not fiddle; but he could make a small Towne to become a great Citie. **1722** SEWEL *Hist. Quakers* (1795) I. 7 The Quakers..are become a great people. **1735-8** BOLINGBROKE *On Parties* 11 They, who are eager..to sacrifice her Commerce, by intangling Her..with the other great Powers of Europe. **1791** MRS. RADCLIFFE *Rom. Forest* i, La Motte avoided the great towns. **1863** [see POWER *sb.*[1] 6 b]. **1876** CARLYLE *Let.* Nov. in H. J. Nicoll *Carlyle* (1885) ix. 231 The thing to be desired is concord between the three Great Powers. **1955** *Times* 11 May 10/3 Diplomatists remark, however, that Moscow invariably speaks of a meeting of the Great Powers rather than the four Powers. **1965** *New Statesman* 30 Apr. 686/3 An agreement with Russia which would restore Germany's great-power status.

12. a. Of persons: Eminent by reason of birth, rank, wealth, power, or position; of high social or official position; of eminent rank or place. (In poetry often prefixed to a proper name.) ***the great world*** [= F. *le grand monde*]: aristocratic society.

1297 R. GLOUC. (Rolls) 10111 An grete erles doȝter. *a* **1300** *Cursor M.* 12063 þe gret lauerdinges. **1340** *Ayenb.* 256 Senekes zayþ þet þer ne lackeþ to greate lhordes bote zoþ ziggeres. *c* **1460** FORTESCUE *Abs. & Lim. Mon.* vi. (1885) 122 The payment off the wages and ffees off the kynges grete officers. **1585** T. WASHINGTON tr. *Nicholay's Voy.* II. xxii. 59 b, Which is not to be reputed as spoken of the women of bare estate or condition, but likewise of the great and notable dames. **1615** J. STEPHENS *Satyr. Ess.* 266 Let him liue about great persons and his best discourses will be lye-blowne with tales of honour. **1660** F. BROOKE tr. *Le Blanc's Trav.* 81 Dishes..much esteemed, and sought for by the Great Ones. **1709** STEELE *Tatler* No. 2 ¶3, I avoid speaking of Things which may offend Great Persons. **1778** MISS BURNEY *Evelina* xxiv. (1784) 201 During her residence in the great world. **1816** SCOTT *Antiq.* xxix, The secrets of grit folk..are just like the wild beasts that are shut up in cages. **1849** MACAULAY *Hist. Eng.* x. II. 562 The great man, at whose frown, a few days before, the whole kingdom had trembled. **1851** E. FITZGERALD *Lett.* (1894) I. 272 Thackeray says he is getting tired of being witty, and of the great world. **1891** E. PEACOCK *N. Brendon* I. 181 Mr. Dickson was a great man in Sparston.

b. Applied (more or less conventionally) to the Deity, or deities; also, to saints.

Great Mother, tr. L. *mater magna*, i.e. Cybele.

1340-70 *Alex. & Dind.* 193 þat grete god amon. ? *a* **1400** *Ipomadon* (Kölbing) 395 Grette god kepe the in hele. **1591** SHAKS. *1 Hen. VI*, I. i. 154 To keepe our great Saint Georges Feast withall. **1594** —— *Rich. III*, v. v. 8 Great God of Heauen, say Amen to all. **1606** —— *Tr. & Cr.* iv. v. 198 By great Mars, the Captaine of vs all. **1629** MILTON *Hymn Nativ.* 120 While the Creator great His constellations set. **1728** POPE *Dunc.* I. 269 The Great Mother. [*Note*] *Magna mater*, here applied to Dulness. **1802** *Hymn*, Great God, what do I see and hear? **1871** R. ELLIS tr. *Catullus* xxxiv. 1 Great Diana protecteth us. *Ibid.* xxxv. 18 The Great Mother he surely sings divinely. **1898** DOYLE *Trag. Korosko* vi. 156 That we should go cheerfully whither the Great Hand guides us.

c. In exclamations, as ***Great Cæsar***, ***Scott***, ***Sun!***, meaningless euphemisms for *Great God!* Also ***Great-Scott*** v. intr.

1876 BESANT & RICE *Gold. Butterfly* I. viii. 164 Great sun! I think I see it now. *Ibid.* II. xiii. 195 Great Jehoshaphat!.. can't you see when a gentleman is on the stump? **1885** 'F. ANSTEY' *Tinted Venus* 60 Great Scott! I must be bad! **1889** J. K. JEROME *Three Men in Boat* vi. 81 Great Cæsar! man,.. you don't mean to say you have covered over carved oak with blue wall-paper? **1892** *Tit Bits* 19 Mar. 416/1 (Farmer) Great Cæsar! There you go again! **1902** 'MARK TWAIN' in *Harper's Weekly* 6 Dec. 9/1 'Ger-reat *Scott!*' ejaculated the Major... The secretary said, wonderingly: 'Why, what are you Great-Scotting about, Major?' **1947** *Mind* LVI. 356 Lord Russell mentions an exciting moment in 1894... He suddenly had a flash of apparent insight..exclaiming: 'Great Scott, the ontological argument is sound!' **1963** WODEHOUSE *Stiff Upper Lip, Jeeves* i. 10 'You don't mean that old crumb was there?' I said, Great-Scott-ing.

d. ***the Great*** (following a proper name): (*a*) merely as an honorific epithet (*obs.* or *arch.*); (*b*) appended as a title to the names of certain historical persons, chiefly monarchs, implying both that the person so designated is the most famous person of the name, and that he ranks among the great men of history. (Cf. GRAND *a.*[1])

The latter use, which is paralleled in all the modern European langs., is inherited from the similar application of L. *magnus*, Gr. ὁ μέγας. But in modern times the adj. in this formula has come to be apprehended in sense 15.

1382 WYCLIF *Rev.* xvii. 5 Babilon the greet, modir of fornycac, ouns, and of abhomynacions of erthe. *c* **1400** *Destr. Troy* 10474 Agamynon the gret. **1485** CAXTON *Chas. Gt.* 24 This noble Charlemayn, otherwyse called Charles the grete. **1553** EDEN *Treat. Newe Ind.* (Arb.) 5 That myghtie kyng..Alexander the great. **1588** SHAKS. *L.L.L.* v. i. 136 It pleased them to thinke me worthie of Pompey the great. **1658** BROWNE *Gard. Cyrus* ii. 41 Charles the great. **1833** *Penny Cycl.* I. 294/2 Alexander III., commonly called the Great, son of Philip II. king of Macedon. **1862** BURTON *Bk. Hunter* (1885) 159 Napoleon was little, so was Frederic the Great [etc.].

e. In the titles of certain sovereigns. ***the Great King***: in *Greek History*, the King of Persia. For ***the Great Cham, Mogul, Turk***, see CHAM, etc.

1849 GROTE *Greece* II. lxii. (1862) V. 397 The Great King.

f. Used in official titles with the sense: Chief over others; = GRAND *a.* 2; e.g. ***great duke, master*** (hence ***great mastership***), ***preceptor, prior*** (hence † ***great prior's herb***, tobacco), etc. (Cf. HIGH.) *Obs.* exc. in ***Lord Great Chamberlain***.

1532 DU WES *Introd. Fr.* in *Palsgr.* 916 The great chamberlayn, *le chambrier.* **1547** *Extracts Aberd. Reg.* (1844) I. 248 Grit admirale of Scotland. **1547** GARDINER *Let. to Dk. Somerset* in Foxe *A. & M.* (1563) 741 When I was in commission with my Lord great master and the Erle of Sowthampton. **1577** FRAMPTON *Joyful News* II. 42 b, Others haue named it [tobacco] the greate Priours hearbe, for that hee caused it to multiplie in Fraunce, more then any other. **1591** SHAKS. *1 Hen. VI*, IV. vii. 70 Great Marshall to Henry the sixt. **1632** MASSINGER *Maid of Hon.* II. v, When this, the glorious badge Of our Redeemer, was conferred upon thee By the Great Master [of the Order of St. John of Malta]. **1667** *Observ. Burning Lond.* in *Select. Harl. Misc.* (1793) 448 That the great duke..had so depopulated the country. **1707** *Lond. Gaz.* No. 4322/2 His Grace made a Visit to the Great Pensionary. **1721** *Ibid.* No. 5918/1 The Pope's Bulls for the Great Mastership of St. Lazarus. **1727-41** CHAMBERS *Cycl.* s.v., We say, the lord great chamberlain, the great marshal of Poland, &c. **1756-7** tr. *Keysler's Trav.* (1760) I. 274 The count of Provana, great hospitaler. **1848** *Secret Societies, Templars* 244 The Great-priors, Great-preceptors, or Provincial Masters..of the three Provinces of Jerusalem, Tripoli, and Antioch. **1881** J. RUSSELL *Haigs* v. 101 Alexander Home of that Ilk..who then [1490] held the high office of Great Chamberlain of Scotland.

g. In the derisive titles ***the Great Unpaid, Unwashed***: see the ppl. adjs.

h. ***great*** (***white***) ***father, chief***, etc. (also with capital initials). A term of address orig. used by American Indians to refer to the President of the United States; now usu. *transf.* and ironical. Cf. CHIEF *sb.* 6 b.

1808 Z. M. PIKE *Sources Mississ.* 5, I spoke to them [*sc.* Indians] to the following purport: 'That their great father, the president of the United States, [etc.]'. **1832** F. TROLLOPE *Dom. Manners* I. xx. 314 All the chiefs who.. have come to negociate with their great father, as they call the President. **1881** *Harper's Mag.* Apr. 671/1 Spotted Tail has been to the Great Father's house so often that he has learned to tell lies and deceive people. **1936** *Time* 25 May 11/1 The Indians came bearing gifts, a blanket for the Great White Father [*sc.* President Roosevelt], a ring for the Great White Mother. **1937** *Discovery* Sept. 276/1 The 'Proclamation of the Great White King' which granted this clan 'complete protection from the interference of strangers in this reserved area which the White King had given'. **1960** *Ontario Legislature Debates* 6 Dec. 247/2 And when they had it arranged, the great white father blows into town and gives the people a party. **1963** *Amer. Speech* XXXVIII. 272 The disparaging use of the term *Great White Father* for the superintendent, an unpopular authoritarian figure, appears to be limited to the staff, only half of whom are Indian. **1966** *Listener* 15 Dec. 895/1 To call a discussion influenced by such low-grade remarks as these..'a brisk intellectual exercise' can only suggest how little the great white scientist expects of the natives. **1966** 'A. YORK' *Eliminator* iv. 73 She acknowledges you as the great white chief.

13. Of things: Pertaining to or occupied by persons of high place or rank.

c **1340** *Cursor M.* 596 (Trin.) þou maist aske wiþouten blame, Whi god him ȝaf so greet a name. **1612** BACON *Ess.* (*title*), Of Great Place. **1613** PURCHAS *Pilgrimage* (1614) 427 When any of great place dyeth. *a* **1678** C'TESS WARWICK *Autobiog.* (Percy Soc.) 13 He was descended from a very great and honourable family. **1709** HEARNE *Collect.* (O.H.S.) II. 197 He being not of great Birth, as appears from his arms. **1855** MACAULAY *Hist. Eng.* xi. III. 24 The great office of Groom of the Stole. **1863** KINGSLEY *Water-Bab.* 7 They were going to a very great house. **1875** JOWETT *Plato* (ed. 2) I. 298 He was of a great family, and a man of influence at Athens.

† **14.** Distinguished in appearance; of lofty or imposing aspect; 'of elevated mien' (J.). *Obs.*

1585 T. WASHINGTON tr. *Nicholay's Voy.* II. xi. 46 Certayne monumentes of olde walles beyng of great apparence. **1687** A. LOVELL *Thevenot's Trav.* I. 56 They wear this Cap..with a Handkerchief of fine stuff, wrought with flowers of Gold and Silk, which makes them look Great. **1697** DRYDEN *Æneid* I. 708 Such Dido was; with such becoming State, Amidst the Crowd, she walks serenely great.

15. Of persons: Extraordinary in ability, genius, or achievement.

a. With explicit reference to some special department or kind of activity. (Qualifying an agent-noun or some equivalent personal designation; also predicatively with *in* or *as.*)

1340 HAMPOLE *Pr. Consc.* 665 þe grete clerk Innocent. **1601** SHAKS. *Twel. N.* IV. ii. 11 A great scholler. **1605** —— *Oth.* I. i. 19 A great Arithmatician. **1718** *Freethinker* No. 63 ¶5 The Great Poet, and the Great Painter, think alike. **1852** TENNYSON *Death Wellington* 30 Great in council and great in war. **1893** *Bookman* June 82/2 The great magician. **1894** *Law Times* XCVII. 387/2 If he was great as an advocate, he was still greater as a judge.

b. In wider sense (usually qualifying *man*): Eminent in point of mental or moral attainments or magnitude of achievement; of transcendent qualities in thought or action; exhibiting signal excellence in some important work. In recent use, the designation is often felt to imply in addition more or less attribution of loftiness and integrity of character.

1709 HEARNE *Collect.* (O.H.S.) II. 247 That Great and Good Man, Dr. Henry Aldrich. **1792** BURKE *Corr.* (1844) III. 419 He is a great man, eloquent in conception and in language. **1861** J. PYCROFT *Ways & Words* 19 We may call all men Great who have succeeded in stamping their character on the generations among which they lived. **1870** MORRIS *Earthly Par.* III. IV. 320 A great man art thou grown; Thou know'st not fear or lies. **1875** JOWETT *Plato* (ed. 2) I. 201 Themistocles, Pericles, and other great men. *Ibid.* V. 75 The truly great man is not a lover of himself but of justice. **1898** J. CAIRD *Univ. Serm.* 261 The great man is he who approaches more nearly than others to the ideal of man's nature.

c. Of the soul, ideas, etc.: Lofty, magnanimous, noble.

1726 GAY *Fables* I. xvii. 19 Great souls with generous pity melt. **1751** JOHNSON *Rambler* No. 185 ⁋12 Nothing can be great which is not right. **1847** TENNYSON *Princ.* IV. 119 Great is song Used to great ends. **1884** (*title*) Great Thoughts from Master Minds. **1897** H. DRUMMOND *Ideal Life* 107 Great living is being appreciated for its own sake.

16. In certain colloquial or trivial uses developed from the preceding senses.

a. *predicatively.* Having considerable knowledge (of a subject) or extraordinary skill (in doing something); const. *at*, †*in*. ***great on***: of considerable knowledge or experience in, conversant with; hence, much interested in or occupied with. ***a great one for*** (cf. ONE 15c).

1784 R. BAGE *Barham Downs* I. 344 The very air of the south of France is almost a specific for it [consumption], to say nothing of the faculty there, who are peculiarly great in this malady. **1844** DICKENS *Christm. Carol* iii, At the game of How, When and Where, she was very great. **1859** THACKERAY *Virgin.* xvi, He was great at cooking many of his Virginian dishes. **1862** TYNDALL *Mountaineer.* x. 82, I am not great at finding tracks. **1877** SPURGEON *Serm.* XXIII. 95 A great hand with his cricket-bat. **1878** JEFFERIES *Gamekeeper at H.* i. 12 He is very 'great' on dogs. **1884** GILMOUR *Mongols* xxvii. 323 They are also great on fur caps, and one may sometimes meet a man wearing a cap worth as much as all the rest of his clothes put together. **1927** C. ASQUITH *Black Cap* 100 Now Mrs. Mingle, unlike Hetty, had been a great one for reading. **1934** T. S. ELIOT *Rock* i. 13 There's David. One o' them fancy lads—a good soldier and fond o' the ladies—but a great one for 'is church. **1957** J. KIRKUP *Only Child* ix. 127 Isa was a great one for the proprieties.

b. Of surpassing excellence; hence, used as a (more or less) rapturous term of admiration: 'Magnificent', 'splendid', 'grand', 'immense'. Also as *int.* *U.S.* and *colloq.* In *Racing* and *Coursing*, in phr. ***to run a great filly, dog***, etc.: said of a horse or dog that runs a fine race.

1809 W. IRVING *Knickerb.* (1849) 88 She..could get along very nearly as fast with the wind ahead, as when it was a-poop, and was particularly great in a calm. **1839** MARRYAT *Diary Amer.* Ser. I. II. 225 The word great is oddly used for fine, splendid. 'She's the greatest gal in the whole Union'. **1868** G. WILKES *Introd. to H. Woodruff's Trotting Horse Amer.*, At the end of a few years [he] gave a *great* animal to the country in place of what had been only a *good* animal before. **1895** *Daily News* 18 Oct. 3/2 Amphora and.. Attainment, the two top weights in the Orleans Nursery, ran a great race. **1897** R. KIPLING *Capt. Courageous* i. 5 Say, wouldn't it be great if we ran one [a boat] down? **1897** *Daily News* 20 Feb. 9/2 [In hare-coursing] Gallant ran a great dog. **1898** *Ibid.* 20 June 7/2 Winsome Charteris ran a great filly. **1967** *Listener* 12 Oct. 465 Great! I see a great headline. **1968** *Ibid.* 26 Sept. 423/2 Gary's mum's bread pudding is *great*. **1969** D. FRANCIS *Enquiry* v. 66 'We're going down to the yard.' 'Great,' said Roberta... 'I'll come too.'

17. Qualifying a descriptive sb.

a. Qualifying the designation of (*a*) a person or (*b*) a thing, with the sense: Eminently entitled to the designation, especially remarkable for the quality indicated.

(*a*) *c* **1380** WYCLIF *Wks.* (1880) 81 Men ben grete foolis þat bien þes bulles of pardon so dere. **1460** *Paston Lett.* No. 349 I. 512 Radclyf and ȝe bene grete frendes. **1525** LD. BERNERS *Froiss.* II. cxl. [cxxxvi.] 391 A Scotte (who be great theves) had stollen hym awaye. **1622** in *Crt. & Times Jas. I* (1848) II. 306 Sir Anthony Magnie, a great papist. **1726** SHELVOCKE *Voy. round World* (1757) 83 When we came into the channel, our pilot seemed to be as great a stranger to it as myself. *a* **1715** BURNET *Own Time* (1724) I. 202 One Mrs. Steward, reckoned a very great Beauty. **1802** H. MARTIN *Helen of Glenross* I. 106 He and his great friend here had a row about her. **1828** P. CUNNINGHAM *N.S. Wales* II. 249 A great scoundrel. **1871** W. ALEXANDER *Johnny Gibb* ix, The dominie's nae gryte deykin at the common coontin' 'imsel'. **1891** E. PEACOCK *N. Brendon* I. 177 Plumer and Thornton were great friends.

(*b*) *a* **1599** SPENSER *State Irel.* Wks. (Globe) 672/2 A Burse-holder over them should not onlye be a greate indignitye, but also a daunger. **1674** tr. *Scheffer's Lapland* 93 They are persuaded 'tis a great preservative of health. **1676** tr. *Guillatiere's Voy. Athens* 15 We observed the Standard of Savoy, as great a rarity as the other. **1698** FRYER *Acc. E. India & P.* 340 Unless there happen to be Trees, which is a great chance in such Sandy, Wild, and Desert Places. **1719** DE FOE *Crusoe* I. xx. (1840) 361 It was a great chance we were not all devoured. **1837** *Penny Cycl.* VII. 15/2 In this state it is a great dainty for those who disregard a pungent and fetid smell. *a* **1900** *Mod.* The exhibition was a great fiasco.

b. With an agent-noun or its equivalent: That is much in the habit of performing the action. Also, with sb. indicating employment, function, ownership, etc.: That is such on a large scale.

c **1290** *S. Eng. Leg.* (1887) I. 319 He schal beo..Of nesche her and no-þing crips, gret slepare and slovȝ þar-to. *a* **1300** *Cursor M.* 2205 Reuer and man-queller gret. *c* **1386** CHAUCER *Prol.* 339 An householdere, and that a greet was he. **1573** LOD. LLOYD *Pilgr. Princes* (1586) 140 A fishe called Varus..is a great murtherer and a spoyler of Frogges. **1599** H. BUTTES *Dyets drie Dinner* K viij, The Jewes are great Goose-eaters. **1601** SHAKS. *Twel. N.* I. iii. 90, I am a great eater of beefe. **1631** WEEVER *Anc. Funeral Mon.* 323 To marry so great an inheritrix. **1670** LADY MARY BERTIE in *12th Rep. Hist. MSS. Comm.* App. v. 21 So grat a hors woman. **1706** POPE *Let. to Wycherley* 10 Apr., The great Dealers in Wit. **1870** W. ARNOT in A. Fleming *Life* x. (1877) 442 They are great introducers, hand shakers, questioners. **1894** *Season* X. No. 9. 36/2 For great dancers plain satin shoes are the most economical.

18. Much in use or request; high in favour *with*; favourite. In some cases hardly distinguishable from sense 19.

c **1430** *Life St. Kath.* (1884) 92 He was so gret wyth þe Emperour. **1481** CAXTON *Reynard* (Arb.) 73 She was grete wyth the quene and wel belouyd. **1530** PALSGR. 426, I am in favour, or I am great, or in conceyte with a person. **1598** HAKLUYT *Voy.* I. 64 It is his desire also that they should become great or in fauour with God in heauen. **1685** STILLINGFL. *Orig. Brit.* iv. 190 This St. German was so great with Hilary, Bishop of Arles, that [etc.]. **1704** *Key to Dk. Buckhm.'s Rehearsal* III. i. (Arb.) 70 [Ay, 'tis pretty well; but he does not Top his Part.] A great Word with Mr. Edward Howard.

19. Intimate, familiar, friendly; 'thick' *with*. Now only *dial.* [App. not directly connected with *great friends* (sense 17a).]

1483 *Vulgaria abs Terentio* 3 b, They are grete or homely to gydre. **1516** in E. Lodge *Illustr. Brit. Hist.* I. ix. (1791) 19 My Lord Cardynall & Sr Willm Compton be marvelous gret. **1662** J. BARGRAVE *Pope Alex. VII* (1867) 111 The General of the Jesuits order and he, you may be sure, were great. **1668–9** PEPYS *Diary* 16 Jan., The Duchess of York and the Duke of York are mighty great with her. **1690–1** LADY RUSSELL *Let.* 5 Feb., The dean and he are not great; that is, I mean the dean is not his creature. **1707** HEARNE *Collect.* (O.H.S.) II. 61 Mr. Laughton..was very great with most of the Non-Jurors. **1714** SWIFT *Imit. Horace* II. vi. 85 My lord and he are grown so great, Always together, *tête à tête.* **1725** RAMSAY *Gentle Sheph.* III. ii, Awa, awa! the deil's owre grit wi' you. **1726** DE FOE *Hist. Devil* II. vii. (1840) 261 As great as the devil and Dr. Faustus. **1728** VANBR. & CIB. *Prov. Husb.* III. Wks. (1730) 249, I love her dearly already, we are growing very great together. **1788** COWPER *Let.* 6 May, Wks. 1836 VI. 153 When people are intimate, we say they are as *great* as two inkle-weavers. **1799** T. MOORE *Let.* 14 Nov. in *Mem.* (1853) I. 96 Johnson and I got very great: he is to introduce me to Colman, the manager and author. **1877** *N.W. Linc. Gloss.* s.v., Sam's very great wi' Mr... If he'd nobbut keep fra drink he mud stop there for ivver. **1877** *Holderness Gloss.* s.v., Oor lad an your's is varry greeat just noo.

IV. Combinations.

20. In syntactical combination with sbs., forming designations for the most part normally preceded by the definite article.

Great Bible, the name commonly given to the English version of the Bible by Coverdale in 1539; sometimes applied also to the revised editions of this, esp. to Cranmer's Bible of 1540; **Great book** [F. *grand livre* 'ledger'], the general list of the creditors of the (French) state; **Great British Public**, a jocular, usu. ironic, way of referring to the British people; cf. *G.B.P.* (s.v. G III. f); **Great Canon**, (*a*) *Greek Ch.* the longest canon of odes (see CANON *sb.*[1] 7b); (*b*) *Printing* (see 6b and CANON *sb.*[1] 11); **Great Cham**, a nickname applied to Samuel Johnson; **Great Dane** (see DANE 2); **Great day**, (*a*) the Day of Judgement (see DAY *sb.* 8b); (*b*) Easter Day; (*c*) a feast- or fast-day of high importance; **(Great) Deliverer**, a title given to King William III; **Great fast**, the season of Lent; **Great forty days**, the forty days which intervened between Christ's resurrection and ascension; the corresponding season in the ecclesiastical year from Easter to Ascension Day; **great game**, (*a*) golf; (*b*) spying; **Great house**, (*a*) a designation often given to the principal house of a district, usually that of a large proprietor; (*b*) *slang* or *dial.*, the workhouse: usually called *big house*; **great insertion**, the section of St. Luke's Gospel, ix. 51–xviii. 14, which is independent of St. Mark; **Great lake**, a humorous term for the Atlantic Ocean; **Great Lakes** (see LAKE *sb.*[4]); **Great Leap Forward**, an attempt begun in 1958 by which the leadership of the People's Republic of China sought to stimulate industrial and other forms of production by the use of advanced techniques, and thereby transform China rapidly into a modern socialist state; also *ellipt.* as *Great Leap*, and *transf.*; † **Great mean (string)** *Mus.* (see quot.); **great omission**, St. Mark vi. 45–viii. 26, which is omitted in St. Luke; **great red spot** *Astr.*, an oval feature in the outer gas of the planet Jupiter, occas. red but now usu. pink in colour; † **great relief**, ? = ALTO-RELIEVO; † **great road** [F. *grande route*], the high road; **great thought**, a maxim, an apophthegm; now freq. used ironically; **great tradition**, a phrase employed by F. R. Leavis (1895–1978) to denote the corpus of great English fiction; **Great War**, (*a*) the French Revolutionary and Napoleonic Wars, 1793–1815; (*b*) the war which began on 28 July 1914 with hostilities between Austria-Hungary and Serbia, and ultimately involved the majority of the nations of the world; it was suspended by armistice 11 Nov. 1918; **Great week** = HOLY WEEK; **Great White Way**, Broadway in New York City, in reference to the brilliant street illumination. See also *Great* ASSIZE *sb.*, BRITAIN, CHARTER (*sb.*[1] 1a), CIRCLE (*sb.* 2a, b), CLIMACTERIC, COMMONER (3), DEATH *sb.* (7b), ENTRANCE (2), GENERALS (B. 2e), HABIT (*sb.* 2b), HORSE (*sb.* 21), INQUEST (*sb.*), OATH, ORGAN, PLAGUE, POX, SCALE, SCHISM, SEA, SEAL, TITHE, TOE, YEAR[1], etc.; also main words below.

1553 (*title*) The Bible in Englishe according to the translation of the *great Byble. **1835** *Penny Cycl.* IV. 374/2 The Great Bible, or Cranmer's. **1882** H. MORLEY *Eng. Lit.* 254 In April of the same year, 1539, appeared Coverdale's revision of Tyndal's work and his own, in the folio known as Cromwell's (or the Great) Bible. **1809** R. LANGFORD *Introd. Trade* 54 Inscriptions on the *Great Book of the French National Debt cannot be attached. **1866** J. BLACKWOOD *Let.* 26 June in *Geo. Eliot's Lett.* (1955) IV. 279 The '*Great British Public' is not yet sufficiently aware of the book [sc. *Felix Holt*] to affect the sale. **1924** J. DOE in M. Joseph *Journalism for Profit* xii. 210 The next business in hand is getting on the right side of the Great British Public. **1927** T. E. LAWRENCE *Let.* 30 Dec. (1938) IV. 562 The soul of the great British public will be turned with rage at its surfeit of my rareness and virtuosity. **1932** Q. D. LEAVIS *Fiction & Reading Public* I. iii. 38 The major achievements of contemporary novelists appear to be unknown even by name to that part of the community journalists call the Great British Public. **1968** 'L. MARSHALL' *Blood on Blotter* xvi. 108 The Great British Public would sooner eat dry bread and processed cheese..in a house they thought was tops, than enjoy a good meal in a place that didn't have any reputation. **1850** NEALE *Holy Eastern Ch.* 876 The *Great Canon, sung on Thursday of Passion Week [*read* the 4th Week of Lent]..at Lauds, after the fifty-first Psalm. **1759** *Great Cham [see CHAM]. **1958** P. KEMP *No Colours or Crest* vii. 146, I would jerk awake to find myself declaiming one of the magisterial pronouncements of the Great Cham. **1542–5** BRINKLOW *Lament.* 2 b, What shalbe layed agaynst you at the *greate daye of the Lorde. **1583, 1690** [see DAY *sb.* 8b]. **1710** WHITWORTH *Acc. Russia* (1758) 39 On great days a little fish, or milk, if it is not a fast. **1751** JORTIN *Serm.* (1771) V. iii. 54 Such sinners are reserved for the judgement of the great day. **1812** BRADY *Clavis Calend.* I. 285 Easter Sunday was..antiently called the Great Day, and the Feast of Feasts. **1886** C. M. YONGE *Chantry House* I. x. 92 There was a dissenting chapel, old enough to be overgrown with ivy.., erected by the Nonconformists in the reign of the *Great Deliverer. **1898** S. WEYMAN *Shrewsbury* xi. 101 'The Deliverer', as the Whig party still love to call him, landed at Torbay. **1969** *Listener* 9 Oct. 475/2 A gilded equestrian statue of William III. Erected in 1734..and inscribed 'To the Great Deliverer'. **1868** ROMANOFF *Sk. Greco-Russ. Ch.* 120 The *Great Fast approaches, preceded by three preparatory weeks. **1844** G. MOBERLY (*title*) The Sayings of the *Great Forty Days, between the Resurrection and Ascension. **1866** J. BLACKWOOD *Let.* 26 Apr. in *Geo. Eliot's Lett.* (1955) IV. 245 The old golf ball maker's shop is associated in my mind..with elevating talks about 'the *great game'. **1901** KIPLING *Kim* vii. 183 When he comes to the Great Game he must go alone—alone, and at peril of his head. **1961** *Guardian* 17 Mar. 10/7 Some John Buchan hero, busily playing the Great Game for Queen and Country. **1964** 'J. WELCOME' *Hard to Handle* ii. 28 Originally the Secret Service..was entrusted to amateurs..who played 'the great game', as they romantically called it, amongst themselves. **1809–10** COLERIDGE *Friend* (1818) I. 251 The mansion of a neighbouring Baronet, awfully known to me by the name of THE *GREAT HOUSE. **1834** *West Ind. Sketch Bk.* I. 161 To leeward of 'the great house'. *note* The 'great house' is a term commonly applied by the Negroes to the proprietor's dwelling, in contradistinction to their own. **1851** BORROW *Lavengro* III. xix. 232 'What do you mean by the great house?' 'The workhouse'. **1877** L. JENNINGS *Field Paths & Green Lanes* xiii. 178 'Why, Sir', said he, 'we be a goin' to kill him [a sheep] directly after dinner for the great house'. **1911** J. V. BARTLET in *Stud. Synoptic Problem* 336 The part of Luke's Gospel prior to the *Great Insertion. **1927** A. H. MCNEILE *Introd. N.T.* 26 The next non-Marcan block, [Luke] ix. 51–xviii. 14, containing more than 30 per cent. of the Third Gospel, is often called the 'Great Insertion'. **1772** in Sparks *Life & Writ. Gouv. Morris* (1832) I. 19, I know others that never saw the east side of the *great lake. [**1958** *China Reconstructs* May 14 (*heading*) 1958—Year of the Forward Leap.] **1958** *N.Y. Times* 18 Nov. 6/3 Jawaharlal Nehru talked of what Peiping likes to call the *great 'leap forward' campaign—of millions of people being herded into communes, of steel furnaces sprouting in everyone's backyard, of peasants being marched to the fields like soldiers to the parade ground. **1959** *Economist* 25 Apr. 322/1 The People's Congress opened in Peking last Saturday; Mr Chou En-lai, the prime minister..reviewed the government's past achievements and future plans. His oration was later described as a 'book of history and poetry summing up the success of China's great leap forward'. **1963** D. J. DWYER in *China Now* (1974) xi. 234 The tremendous spurt in coal production recorded in 1958 was ..directly related to the official 'Great Leap Forward' of that year. **1971** *Guardian* 25 Nov. 12/2 Peking through two great leaps forward—the New Literature Movement in 1919 and the Han Character Simplification Movement in 1955 —evolved new ideographs. **1972** *Korea Times* 18 Nov. 2/1 We now anticipate a great leap toward the 1980s in national advancement, with the per capita national income to reach the $1,000 level by 1981. **1975** A. WATSON *Living in China* v. 130 The collapse of many of the Great Leap policies also led to a cut back in these irregular schools and universities. **1983** G. PRIESTLAND *At Large* 66 Members [of the General Synod of the Church of England] have been bombarded with letters and petitions either imploring them to take the great leap forward [to unity with Nonconformist churches], or warning them to stay where they are. **1674** PLAYFORD *Skill Mus.* II. 92 The Bass-Viol..is usually strung with six strings..which..are known by six several Names; the first ..is called the Treble; the second the small Mean; the third, the *Great Mean. *Ibid.* 112 For the Tuning of your Violin ..the Bass or fourth string is called G sol re ut..the third or great Mean, D la sol re. **1911** J. C. HAWKINS in *Stud. Synoptic Problem* 61 This well deserves its usual name of St. Luke's '*great omission'. **1927** A. H. MCNEILE *Introd. N.T.* 26 Whether intentionally or not he [*sc.* St. Luke] omits [Mark] vi. 45–viii. 26, which is sometimes called the 'Great Omission'. **1881** *Monthly Not. R. Astr. Soc.* XLI. 44 The *great red spot..has maintained a constancy of appearance and regularity of motion. **1936** F. REH *Astron. for Layman* xviii. 243 Occasionally a more or less fixed spot appears. Such a spot is the so-called 'great red spot'..still faintly visible in good photographs. **1967** P. MOORE *Amat. Astron. Gloss.* 61 Of particular interest is the *Great Red Spot*, which can be traced on drawings made as long ago as 1631. It became prominent in 1878, and is still conspicuous, though it has been known to vanish temporarily. It is decidedly pinkish in colour; its exact nature is uncertain, though presumably it is a solid or semi-solid body floating in Jupiter's outer gas. **1654–66** LD. ORRERY *Parthenissa* (1676) 518 The Plinth of each of them was beautified with Sculptures of *great Relieve. **1772** SIMES *Mil. Guide* (1781) 12 The heavy artillery in general keeps the *great road. **1821** HAZLITT *Table-T* xi. 253 *Great thoughts reduced to practice become great acts. **1913** C. MACKENZIE *Sinister St.* I. I. iv. 48 A calendar of Great Thoughts was roughly divested of ninety-eight great thoughts at once, in order that ..a correct announcement should celebrate the ninth of April. *a* **1916** 'SAKI' *Coll. Short Stories* (1930) 407 A William the Conqueror calendar..with a quotation of one of his greatest thoughts for every day in the year. **1925** A. HUXLEY *Along Road* I. 67 There is nothing more dismal than a 'Great Thought' enunciated by an author who has not himself the elements of greatness. **1969** K. GILES *Death cracks Bottle* iii. 23 'How nice!' said Noni, with what passed with her for wit. 'Any more great thoughts on offer?' **1948** F. R. LEAVIS *Great Tradition* i. 7 By '*great tradition' I mean the tradition to which what is great in English fiction belongs. **1969** *Guardian* 21 Aug. 8/3 The inheritors of Leavis's Great Tradition..mutter about pretentious, jumped-up, pulp writers. **1970** *Ibid.* 16 Sept. 10/3 You can't go on writing Leavisite criticism when you've reviewed everything that relates to the great tradition. **1971** *Human World* Nov. 88 The Great Tradition from Jane Austen to Conrad is that of the fine individual consciousness, typically considered under the aspect of conscience, implying self-knowledge and self-transcendence. **1887** R. D. BLACKMORE (*title*) Springhaven. A tale of the *Great War. **1911** J. W. FORTESCUE (*title*) British Statesmen of the Great War 1793–1814. **1914** *Maclean's Mag.* Oct. 53/1 Some wars name themselves... This is the Great War. **1915** GRAHAME-WHITE & HARPER (*title*) Aircraft in the Great War. **1921** A. HUXLEY *Crome Yellow* xxii. 238 Luther was reality—like the Great War. **1922** S. WEYMAN *Ovington's Bank* i. 7 By that coach had come eleven years before, the news of the abdication of the Corsican and the close of the Great War. Laurelled and flagged, it had thrilled the town a year afterwards with the tidings of Waterloo. **1923** [see *gallery-play* s.v. GALLERY *sb.* 12 b]. **1925** D. H. LAWRENCE *Refl. Death Porcupine* 61 Even the great war does not alter our civilization one iota, in its total nature. **1937** [see ATROCITY 5]. **1969** A. TOYNBEE *Experiences* II. iii. 221 'The Great War'—as, until the fall of France, the British continued to call the First World War in order to avoid admitting to themselves that they were now again engaged in a war of the same magnitude. **1659** H. L'ESTRANGE *Alliance of Divine Offices* v. 151 It [Holy Week] became to be stiled also The *great Week. **1812** BRADY *Clavis Calend.* I. 266 The week was called the 'Great Week', in token of the inestimable blessings bestowed upon mankind, through the merits and sufferings of our Saviour. **1901** A. B. PAINE (*title*) The *great white way. **1908** G. V. HOBART *Go to It* 22 Eight weeks since we left Chicago, three shows to the bad, and still a thousand miles from the Great White Way. **1936** H. MILLER *Black Spring* 248 The Great White Way is blazing with spark-plugs. **1967** *Act One Scene Two* II. Nov./Dec. 12/3 All we can do is to keep our bit of the Oxford Playhouse staked out worthily along the Great White Way.

21. Prefixed to certain terms denoting kinship (viz. *uncle, aunt, nephew, niece*, and the compounds of *grand-*), to form designations for persons one degree further removed in ascending or descending relationship. The prefix may be repeated any required number of times to express progressively more and more remote degrees of relationship. Nonce-uses of the prefix are ***great-cousin, -father, -sire*** (see below), and perh. ***great kinsman*** (Shaks. *Rom. & Jul.* IV. iii. 53, where however the adj. may have sense 12). [After F. *grand* (see GRAND A. 12 b), which follows the example of Latin *avunculus magnus* great-uncle, *amita magna* great-aunt.]

a. great-uncle, -aunt, a father's or mother's uncle, aunt; **great-nephew, -niece**, a son's or daughter's nephew, niece; †**great-cousin** (*nonce-wd.*), a first cousin once removed; †**great father, sire,** (*nonce-wds.*), a grandfather.

1656 W. D. tr. *Comenius' Gate Lat. Unl.* §752. 235 Above these are, great-unkle and *great-aunt by the father's side, unkle and aunt by the father's side in the third degree. **1870** LUBBOCK *Orig. Civiliz.* iv. (1875) 188 When great uncles and aunts are termed grandfathers and grandmothers. **1742** *Collectanea* (O.H.S.) II 387 He..had a *great-cousin master of an estate. *Ibid.* 388. **1484** CAXTON *Æsop* v. i. (1889) 128 And the mule ansuerd, my *grete fader was a hors. **1581** MARBECK *Bk. of Notes* 176 Chore (which was the *great Nephew of the Patriarke Leui). **1689** WOOD *Life* 20 Dec., The said Mathew Slade also was great nephew, as 'tis said, of Mathew Slade who wrote against Vorstius. **1884** *Harper's Mag.* Feb. 481/2 The *great-niece of Mrs. Barbauld. **1704** N. N. tr. *Boccalini's Pol. Touchstone* 95 in *Adv. fr. Parnassus* III, He prov'd himself a Grand Child worthy his *great Syre by his Mother's side. **1438** *Rolls of Parlt.* V. 438 His Uncle Humfrey Duc of Gloucestre, his *grete Uncle H. Cardinal of England. *a* **1547** *Will Hen. VIII* in Pote *Hist. Windsor Cas.* (1749) 51 The tombes and aultars of King Henry VI. and also of King Edward IV. our great Uncle and graunt-father. *a* **1850** ROSSETTI *Dante & Circ.* I. (1874) 241 Geri, son of Bello Alighieri, and Dante's great-uncle. **1896** *Daily News* 23 Apr. 5/4 The Prince de Joinville, at once great-uncle and grandfather of the bride.

b. With compounds of *grand*: **great-grandfather, -grandmother**, a grandfather's or grandmother's father, mother (also *transf.* a remote male or female ancestor); so ***great-grandmamma, -grandparent, -granduncle; great-grandfatherly, -grandparental*** adjs.; **great-grandchild**, a grandchild's child; **great-grandson, -granddaughter**, a grandson's or granddaughter's son, daughter; so ***great-grandniece***. Also †**great-grandame**, a great grandmother, †**great-grandsire**, a great-grandfather.

1538 ELYOT *Dict.*, *Proauia*, my *great grandame. **1665** NEEDHAM *Medela Medic.* 33 Diseases of the Female Sex grown more severe than they were in the days of their great Grandames. **1753** *Scots Mag.* Mar. 158/1 He has left 113 children, grandchildren, and *great-grandchildren. **1827** JARMAN *Powell's Devises* (ed. 3) II. 301 In Hussey *v.* Berkeley, Lord Northington expressed an opinion that the word grandchildren would, without further explanation, comprehend great grandchildren. **1753** *Scots Mag.* Oct. 525/2 Miss Cromwel, *great-granddaughter of Oliver Cromwel. **1882** J. H. BLUNT *Ref. Ch. Eng.* II. 29 A great-granddaughter of Henry VII, Lady Jane Grey. **1513** BRADSHAW *St. Werburghe* I. 367 Ermenrycus, kynge of Kent ..Vnto whom Engystus was *great-graundfather. **1555** HARPSFIELD in *Bonner's Homilies* 7 Oure great graundefather Adam. **1599** SHAKS. *Hen. V*, I. ii. 146 You shall reade that my great Grandfather Neuer went with his forces into France. **1624** DONNE *Serm.* cxxx. Wks. 1839 V. 336 Here are risen grandfather and great-grandfather sins quickly, a froward generation. **1834** GEN. P. THOMPSON *Exerc.* (1842) III. 40 The Flemings are the great-grandfathers of us English. **1869** MRS. STOWE *Oldtown Folks* xix. (1870) 198 Supposing I were a minister, as my father, and grandfather and great-grandfather were before me. **1903** *Daily Chron.* 2 Jan. 5/2 Is 1903 to revert to the *great-grandfatherly ways of 1803? **1826** MISS MITFORD *Village* Ser. II. 133 A doting, scolding *great-grandmama. **1530** PALSGR. 227/2 *Great graunde mother, *aielle*. **1597** J. PAYNE *Royal Exch.* 41 Our great grand mother Eve. **1712** ADDISON *Spect.* 295 ⁋2 The Doctrine of Pin-money is of a very late Date, unknown to our Great Grandmothers. **1804** EUGENIA DE ACTON *Tale without a Title* I. 45 Trustee to her *great-grand-niece. **1883** *Cornh. Mag.* June 718 Our *great grandparents appear to have been excessively enamoured of masquerades. **1929** *19th Cent.* Dec. 810 A collateral relative at the level of the grandparental or great-grandparental generation. **1577** tr. *Bullinger's Decades* (1592) 145 Y^e *great grandsire. **1599** SHAKS. *Hen. V*, I. ii. 103 Goe..to your great Grandsires Tombe, From whom you clayme. **1636** G. SANDYS *Paraphr. Ps.* xliv. 1 Wee have heard our Fathers tell The Wonders..To them by their great Grandsires told. **1814** CARY *Dante, Par.* xv. 90 My Son And thy great-grandsire. **1716** ADDISON *Freeholder* No. 9 (1751) 49 No Body ever doubted that King George is *Great Grandson to King James the first. **1808** SCOTT *Mem. Early Life* in Lockhart *Life* (1839) I. 5 William Scott of Raeburn, my *great-grand-uncle. **1922** JOYCE *Ulysses* 123 His granduncle or his *greatgranduncle.

c. With repetition of *great*. **great(-great)**, *colloq.* an ancestor or descendant of 'great (-great)' degree.

1651 tr. *Wotton's Panegyr. K. Chas.* in *Reliq.* 138 Your Great Great-Grand-father Henry the Seventh. **1747** *Gentl. Mag.* 199 At his death he was grandfather to 56, great grandfather to 19, great great grandfather to 11, and great great great grandfather to 4. **1819** BYRON *Juan* I. lvi, Her great great grandmamma. **1823** LOCKHART *Reg. Dalton* II. ii. (1842) 105 That old body that says she is Shakespeare's great-great-great-great-great-great-grand-niece-in-law. **1825–7** HONE *Every-day Bk.* II. 899 The infant's godfathers ..were..his great-great-great-great uncle; and..his great-great-great uncles. His godmothers..were..his great-great-great-great aunt;..his great-great-grandmother; and ..his great-grandmother. **1867** FREEMAN *Norm. Conq.* (1876) I. App. 723 Can we conceive a man marrying the great-great niece of his own brother-in-law? **1870** RAMSAY *Remin.* i. (ed. 18) 4 My distinguished great-great-great-uncle, Bishop Burnett. **1884** *Illustr. Lond. News* 20 Dec. 602/1 The great-great-great-granduncle of the present Lord Walsingham. **1896** *Westm. Gaz.* 3 Oct. 7/2 A great-great-granddaughter of the author of the 'School for Scandal'. **1905** MRS. H. WARD *Marriage W. Ashe* I. ii. 33 'We—you and I—are a little bit cousins too, aren't we?'.. 'Was our "great-great" the same person?' he said, laughing. **1907** A. QUILLER-COUCH *Major Vigoureux* xxii, Your grandfathers and grandmothers, and right back into the greats and great-greats. **1926** W. R. INGE *Lay Thoughts* 181 Its great-great-grand-offspring.

22. a. In parasynthetic adjectives, as ***great-armed, -boned, -eared, -grained, -headed, -leaved, -lipped, -minded*** (so ***great-mindedness***), ***-named, -nosed,*** †***reasoned, -sized, -souled, -spirited, -witted***, etc.; **great-bellied**, having a big belly; pregnant; *fig.* 'big' with events, etc.; **great-eyed**, *lit.* having large or prominent eyes, as some animals; *fig.* far-seeing, taking a large view; †**great-kind**, of great or noble birth; **great-mouthed**, *fig.* loud-voiced; boastful, bragging; †**great-stomached**, high-spirited (see STOMACH); †**great-wombed**, having a large abdomen. †**b.** as complement to a pass. pple., as ***great-grown, -made***.

1798 SOUTHEY *Cross Roads* viii, I wish It were a *great-arm'd chair! **1572** B. GOOGE *Heresbach's Husb.* III. (1577) 114 b, The Mares..to haue large bodyes..*greate bellyed, with large and square brest and buttockes. **1586** T. B. *La Primaud. Fr. Acad.* I. 520 Plato..requireth that great bellied women should give themselves to walking. **1647** J. TRAPP *Comm. Matt.* vi. 34 Thou knowest not what this great-bellied day may bring forth. **1665** NEEDHAM *Medela Medic.* 343 Great-bellied Women. **1591** PERCIVALL *Sp. Dict.*, *Ossudo*, *great boned. **1634** BRERETON *Trav.* (1844) 51 A man..not great-boned nor large-sized. **1797–1804** BEWICK *Birds* I. 64 The eagle-owl or *Great eared owl. **1617** MINSHEU *Voc. Hisp. Lat.*, *Ojudo, Magnoculus*, *great-eyed. **1847** EMERSON *Repr. Men, Plato* Wks. (Bohn) I. 306 The great-eyed Plato proportioned the lights and shades after the genius of our life. **1621** BURTON *Anat. Mel.* I. ii. II. i. (1651) 66 Hart, and Red Deer..a strong and *great grained meat. *c* **1450** *Merlin* 117 He helde a shorte *grete growen spere, sharp grounden. **1593** SHAKS. *3 Hen. VI*, IV. viii. 63 Away.. And take the great-growne Traytor vnawares. *c* **1394** *P. Pl. Crede* 84 Grey *grete-hedede quenes. **1885** SWAINSON *Prov. Names Birds* 160 Pochard..Also called..Great-headed wigeon. *c* **1450** *St. Cuthbert* (Surtees) 7502 A *grete kynd [L. *natu nobilis*] man and a wyse. **1868** *Rep. U.S. Commissioner Agric.* (1869) 200 The *great-leaved magnolia (*Magnolia macrophylla*) is a superb tree of tropical appearance. **1591** PERCIVALL *Sp. Dict.*, *Becudo*, *great-lipped. **1645** QUARLES *Sol. Recant.* v. 13 Oft have I seen encreasing riches grow To be their *great-made Owners overthrow. **1876** GEO. ELIOT *Dan. Der.* lxii. IV. 233 Always poor..but..*great-minded. *a* **1586** SIDNEY *Arcadia* I. (1590) 70 b, For in her euery thing was goodly and stately; yet so, that it might seeme that *great-mindednes was but the auncient-bearer to humblenes. *a* **1832** BENTHAM *Deontol.* (1834) II. 62 Magnanimity is a word which, for popular use, might be conveniently translated into great-mindedness. **1600** ABP. ABBOT *Exp. Jonah* 215 *Great-mouthed Gloriosoes. **1607** TOPSELL *Four-f. Beasts* (1658) 126 This village dog ought to be..great mouthed, or barking bigly. **1387–8** T. USK *Test. Love* I. viii. (Skeat) l. 112 How many *greate named, and many greate in worthinesse losed. **1653** R. SANDERS *Physiogn.* 158 He is *great-nosed. **1529** MORE *Dyal.* 14 b/2 *Grete reasoned men and phylosophers haue dowted therof. **1606** SHAKS. *Tr. & Cr.* III. iii. 147 A *great siz'd monster of ingratitudes. *Ibid.* v. x. 26 Thou great siz'd coward. **1848** BUCKLEY *Iliad* 248 The *great-souled son of Oïleus. **1628** FORD *Lover's Mel.* I. i, My *great-spirited Sister. **1607** TOPSELL *Four-f. Beasts* (1658) 240 More liberty: where-withal a generous and *great stomached Beast is much delighted. **1519** *Interl. Four Elem.* (Percy Soc.) 5 A *great wytted man may sone be enrychyd, That laboryth and studyeth for ryches only. **1297** R. GLOUC. (Rolls) 7731 Suiþe þikke mon he was & of grete strengþe *Gret wombede & ballede. **14..** *Voc.* in Wr.-Wülcker 567/18 *Bafer*, gret-wombed.

B. *adv.*

1. In a great degree; to a great extent; greatly, exceedingly, highly; much; very. *Obs.* exc. *dial.*

In †*great cheap* (CHEAP *sb.* 8, 9) the word is not an adv. *a* **1300** *Cursor M.* 7233 Þare es nan sa gret mai greif Als traitur dern and priue theif. *c* **1394** *P. Pl. Crede* 501 In beldinge of tombes þei trauaileþ grete To chargen her chirche-flore. **1535** COVERDALE *Susanna* 4 Now Ioachim.. was a greate rich man. **1556** *Chron. Gr. Friars* (Camden) 6 Thys yere was a grete dere yere. **1593** SHAKS. *2 Hen. VI*, IV. i. 379 Say that he thriue, as 'tis great like he will [etc.]. **1609** ROWLANDS *Dr. Merrie-man* 6 Horses that labour great, Are cast in ditches for the Dogges to eate. **1736** PEGGE *Kenticisms* (E.D.S.), *Great*, very; as 'great much', very much. **1855** ROBINSON *Whitby Gloss.*, *Great likly*, very likely. 'Ay, ay, great likly, great likly'.

†**2.** Grossly, coarsely. (Cf. A. 1.) *Obs.*

c **1440** *Ipomydon* 1789 Fole, he sayd, þou bourdist grete.

†**3.** In a great, eminent, or distinguished fashion; imposingly. *Obs.*

1698 FRYER *Acc. E. India & P.* 279 To pay their Respects to their Governor in Chief, who receives them very great. **1698** M. LISTER *Journ. Paris* (1699) 105 He lives great, and has a House which joins upon the King's Library.

†**4.** Arrogantly, presumptuously, proudly. *Obs.*

1699 T C[OCKMAN] *Tully's Offices* (1706) 130 'Tis a very unbecoming thing for a Man to talk great of himself in Discourse.

†**5.** With force; loudly. *Obs.*

1533 ELYOT *Cast. Helthe* (1541) 51 a, Nothinge doth profite unto helthe of the body, but to inforce him selfe to synge great, for therby moch aire drawen in by fetching of breth, thrusteth forth the breast and stomake.

6. *Comb.* **a.** In syntactic combination with a pres. or pa. pple. of a verb which may be qualified by *great* or *greatly*, as †***great-begotten***, †***-born, -counselling, -doing*** (implied in adv. †***gret doendely***), ***-triumphing***. **b.** With an adj. (hyphened), as ***great-important***, i.e. highly important.

1382 WYCLIF *Isa.* xii. 5 Syngeth to the Lord, for gret doendely he dide. *c* **1430** *Syr Gener.* (Roxb.) 1155 He was grete borne. **1615** J. STEPHENS *Satyr. Ess.* 66 There is nothing more allied to faction then for a great-begotten to prevaile in governement before his time. **1627** DRAYTON *Agincourt*, etc. 39 Some great-borne Frenchman. **1711** *Fingall MSS.* in *10th Rep. Hist. MSS. Comm.* App. v. 137 His great-triumphing army. *Ibid.* 138 Athlone..being the great-important pass into the province of Connaught. **1848** BUCKLEY *Iliad* 28 Great-counselling Jove.

C. as quasi-*sb.* and *sb.*

I. The adj. used *absol.*

1. a. As *plural*: Great persons; freq. in the collocation *great and small*. Now usually ***the great***: those who are great, eminent, or distinguished by rank, wealth, position, or the like.

1399 LANGL. *Rich. Redeles* III. 250 By gouernaunce of grete and of good age. *a* **1420** HOCCLEVE *De Reg. Princ.* 2830 By þe grete, poer folk ben greuyd. *Ibid.* 5049 Men say two grete may nat in o sak. *c* **1440** *Ipomydon* 96 All spake of hym, bothe grete & smalle. **1651** HOBBES *Leviath.* II. xxx. 180 So as the great, may have no greater hope of impunity. **1654**

WHITLOCK *Zootomia* 97 Quacking Mountebanks are admitted in the Bed-chambers of great and small. **1757** GRAY *Progr. Poesy* (end), Beneath the Good how far—but far above the Great. **1781** GIBBON *Decl. & F.* xxxi. III. 208 The houses and society of the great. **1785** BURNS *Holy Willie's Prayer* xii, [He] has sae monie takin arts, Wi' grit an' sma'. **1834** J. H. NEWMAN *Par. Serm.* (1837) I. ii. 19 Supported by the great and the many. **1849** MACAULAY *Hist. Eng.* ii. I. 161 The masques which were exhibited at the mansions of the great.

b. (With *the.*) That which is great; great things, aspects, qualities, etc. collectively; †also, great quantity, large amount (*obs.*).

1557 NORTH tr. *Gueuara's Diall Pr.* 107 a/2 Haue no respecte to ye litel which we do offer; but to ye great, which (if we were able) we would giue. **1787** CANNING in *Microcosm* No. 30 ¶7 Uniting the great and sublime of epic grandeur with the little and the low of common life. **1791** COWPER *Yardley Oak* 87 Comparing still The great and little of thy lot. **1809–10** COLERIDGE *Friend* vi. (1887) 25 To exclude the great is to magnify the little. **1847** EMERSON *Repr. Men, Uses Gt. Men* Wks. (Bohn) I. 274 The search after the great is the dream of youth. **1864** LUCY AIKIN *Mem.* 157 The same misapprehension everywhere of the grand for the great.

†**c.** ***a great***: something great. *Obs.*

1303 R. BRUNNE *Handl. Synne* 2366 Many smale makeþ a grete. **1592** WYRLEY *Armorie, Ld. Chandos* 82 No earthly great, but wasted is with time.

d. ***a great***, a large part or amount. ***no great***, not a great deal, nothing great; *adv.* not much. *U.S. colloq.*

1724 *Essex Inst. Hist. Coll.* XXXVI. 337 Mackey's sloop sunk at Boston, & spoild a great of our English goods. **1854** 'O. OPTIC' *In Doors & Out* (1876) 186 I've got consider'ble, but I don't care no great about sellin' it. **1885** A. GRAY *Lett.* (1893) 772 No great to see, except a spick and span new Hotel. **1890** *Harper's Mag.* Apr. 715/1, I wa'n't no great of a boy, an' let little things wear on me. *Ibid.* Dec. 146/2, I hadn't been round no great in New York, an' there ain't no general store there.

†**2. a great** (see AGREAT *adv.*), **at the great**. By the piece; wholesale. *Obs.*

1523 FITZHERB. *Husb.* §134 To sell the toppes as they lye a greatte. **1646** J. GREGORY *Notes & Obs.* Pref. (1650) 16 The way to doe this..will not be to doe the work a great, and undertake the whole or any considerable part of the Booke by one man. **1727** BOYER *Fr. Dict.* II. s.v., To take Work at the great, or a-great, *Entreprendre un Ouvrage.*

3. by the great, †**by great**. **a.** Of work done: At a fixed price for the whole amount; by task; by the piece. Now *dial.*

1523 *MS. Acc. St. John's Hosp., Canterb.*, Paied to a carpenter by grete for mendyng of Myster Collettis house. **1573** TUSSER *Husb.* lvii. (1878) 129 To let out thy haruest, by great or by day, let this by experience leade thee a way. By great will deceiue thee, with lingring it out, by day will dispatch, and put all out of dout. **1581** LAMBARDE *Eiren.* IV. iv. (1588) 471 If any Artificer or Labourer..taking any worke by the great. **1635** SIR E. VERNEY in Lady Verney *Mem. V. Fam.* (1892) I. 128 If you fiend him fidle about his woarke, agree with him by the great. **1667** PRIMATT *City & C. Builder* 55 Many workmen had rather agree by the Great, and find all materials, than for workman-ship only. **1712** ADDISON *Spect.* No. 505 ¶7, I..interpret by the great for any Gentlewoman who is turned of Sixty, after the rate of half a Crown *per* week. *a* **1734** NORTH *Lives* (1826) III. 294 To..keep hirelings in garrets, at hard meat, to write and correct by the great. **1764** FOOTE *Mayor of G.* I. Wks. 1799 I. 162, I have contracted to physic the parish-poor by the great. **1851** *Jrnl. R. Agric. Soc.* XII. II. 404 [In Lincolnshire] In harvest..the cutting is done 'by the grate'..Hay-mowing, corn-cutting, &c., are commonly executed by the 'grate'. **1862** MRS. GROTE *Collect. Papers* 158 [Buckinghamshire] Piece-work or 'by the grate'.

†**b.** Of buying and selling: In large quantities, in gross, wholesale. *Obs.*

1592 NASHE *P. Penilesse* (Shaks. Soc) 48 A merchant..that sells commodities of good cheere by the great. **1623** COCKERAM, *Staple*, any Towne..appointed for Merchants..to carrie their..commodities vnto, for the better sale of them to other Merchants by the great. **1634** PEACHAM *Gent. Exerc.* I. x. 38 A friend of mine was notably cozened in a bargaine of timber hee bought by the great, in a mistie morning. *a* **1640** DAY *Parl. Bees* (1881) 73 You..Bought wax and honey up by th' great.

†**c.** *transf.* and *fig.* In large quantities or numbers; in the mass; 'by wholesale'. *Obs.*

1579–80 NORTH *Plutarch* (1676) 925 Not..to carry away their dead bodies by great altogether, but every city one after another. **1607** MIDDLETON *Michaelm. Term* IV. ii, Do they not thrive when they utter most, and make it away by the great. *a* **1625** FLETCHER *Nice Valour* I. i, Bastinadoes by the great. **1670** DRYDEN *1st Part Conq. Granada* II. i. Wks. 1883 IV. 50 Death did at length so many slain forget, And lost the tale, and took them by the great. **1755** CARTE *Hist. Eng.* IV. 237 They are apt to swallow every thing by the great which they see in print.

†**4. in great**. [Cf. F. *en grand, en gros*, G. *im groszen*, Du. *in 't groot.*] *Obs.*

a. In the mass, in the bulk; in or for the whole amount, piece, etc.; in the gross, wholesale; by the piece; = *by the great* (see 3). (Also occas. ***in the great, in greats.***)

c **1430** *Pilgr. Lyf Manhode* I. liv. (1869) 32 Thinketh not..þat it sufficeth to biholde and thinke þe sinnes in gret. **1472** OSBERN in *Paston Lett.* No. 710 III. 71 Selle non in gret, but make fagottes and astell. **1480** *Wardr. Acc. Edw. IV* (1830) 126 For binding and dressing of thre smalle bookes..price in grete vjs. viijd. **1486** *Naval Acc. Hen. VII* (1896) 17 By couenaunte with him made in great. **1486** *Nottingham Rec.* III. 246 For dykyng..to a man hired in grete xxd. *c* **1530** TINDALE *Matt.* v–vii. 52 b, The publycans bought in greate ye emperours tribute. **1577–87** HOLINSHED *Chron.* III. 833/2 The labourers would in no wise labour by the daie, but all by taske & in great. **1598** *Extracts Aberd. Reg.* (1848) II. 168 That na inhabitant..gadder the same [victuall] in gryt, and keip the same to ane darth. **1631** in *Burgh Laws Dundee* (1872) 5 July, For selling of salt in greats. **1659** WILLSFORD *Scales Comm., Archit.* 3 When bricks are deare, and lime is cheap, the workman by the Great will use more morter. **1670–98** LASSELS *Voy. Italy* I. 103 Before I come to the particulars of what I saw in Florence, I will consider it in great, and then come to the retail of it. **1790** BENTHAM *Wks.* (1838–43) X. 233 Accustomed to view things in the great, this virtue, if it be one, costs me no less, perhaps, than most people. **1792** BURKE *Corr.* (1844) IV. 16 For want of ever dealing in the great, they do not know, that, though multitudes may be deluded, they never can be bribed.

b. ***all in great***: 'all told', in all.

1533 MORE *Answ. Poysoned Bk.* Wks. 1038/2 In that part also the man bringeth in two places all in great, whych he hathe pyked out..among al my bookes.

c. In large letters.

a **1641** SUCKLING *Sessions of Poets* xxviii. in *Fragm. Aurea* (1646) 11 Not a man in the place But had discontent writ in great [*ed.* **1648** at large] in his face.

d. On a large scale: usually said by comparison with something smaller but of the same proportions. (Also occas. ***in the great.***)

1652 H. COGAN tr. *Scudery's Ibrahim* II. iii. 49 Having demanded of this pretended Painter, whether he could work in great, as well as in little. **1672** DRYDEN *Marr. à la Mode* Ded. 1 Being that in little, which your lordship is in great. *c* **1705** *Soul of World* in Somers *Tracts* II. 234 The World itself is, after a Sort, an Animal in great. **1769** J. WATT in *Q. Rev.* (1858) CIV. 433 The necessary experience in great was wanting. **1795** BENTHAM *Wks.* (1838–43) X. 307 The Duke..gave him orders for making some [baggage-wagons] in the great [from a small model].

†**5. of great**. In the bulk; in its entirety. *Obs.*

1502 [see AGREAT *adv.*].

6. *attrib.*: **great work** *dial.*, work done by the piece, 'piece-work'. (See 3 a, 4 a.)

1855 *Cycl. Agric.* (ed. Morton) II. 723 *Gret* (Beds., Worc.), gret-work, or great-work, is piece-work. **1889** A. T. PASK *Eyes Thames* 148 They can earn 18*s.* a week, doing piece-work, or, in market-garden parlance, 'great-work'.

II. As *sb.*

7. A great, eminent, or distinguished person.

c **1400** *Destr. Troy* 7018 Serdill..Slogh a grete of þe grekes. *Ibid.* 11735 While this gode was in gederyng the grettes among. **1635** HAKEWILL *Apol.* 538 So have wee had three Greats, not in name only but in deed, such as were Constantine the great..and Charles the great. *a* **1649** DRUMM. OF HAWTH. *Poems* Wks. (1711) 40/2 Till thou the greatest be among the greats. **1912** E. POUND in *Poetry* I. I. 7 You also, our first great, Had tried all ways. **1947** R. DE TOLEDANO *Frontiers of Jazz* xvi. 176 The passing of another one-time great. **1959** *Encounter* Aug. 32/1 Their admiration for coloured greats like Tusdie and Maria really *meant* something to them. **1963** J. WALSH *Shroud* (1964) viii. 73 Statues and paintings of the greats of French science and literature. **1965** *Listener* 17 June 894/1 Tilden was an all-time great with no technical weakness anywhere. **1970** *Times* 13 July 3/1 El Vino has been the haunt of Fleet Street's greats and not-so-greats for nearly a century.

†**8.** The chief part; the main point; the sum and substance; the general drift or gist (of a story). *Obs.*

c **1369** CHAUCER *Dethe Blaunche* 1242 (Fairf. MS.), I kan not now wel counterfete Hyr wordys, but this was the grete Of hir answere. *c* **1374** —— *Troylus* v. 1036 He refte here of þe grete of al here peyne. *c* **1381** —— *Parl. Foules* 35 Of his centence I wole ȝow seyn the greete. *c* **1385** —— *L.G.W.* Prol. 574 That thou reherce of al hir lyfe the grete. **1430–40** LYDG. *Bochas* IX. xxxiv. (1554) 214 Of your complaynt say to me the grete. *c* **1450** *Merlin* 315 The grete of this mater longeth vn-to hym.

†**9. a.** Thickness. **b.** Greatness, magnitude. *Obs. rare.*

[*c* **950** *Epist. Alex.* in *Anglia* IV. 147 Unȝemetlicre gryto and micelnysse, L. *vincens grossitudine.*] *a* **1300** *Cursor M.* 8244 (Gött.) Þat was þe stauin for to strenthe, And knaw þe wax of gret and lenthe. **1629** CHAPMAN *Juvenal* v. 213 Before him see a huge Goose-liuer set; A Capon cramb'd, euen with that Goose for great [L. *anseribus par altilis*].

10. greats (*Oxford Univ. colloq.*). The final examination for the degree of B.A.; now applied *esp.* to the examination for Honours in Literæ Humaniores. The earlier name was GREAT GO. (Cf. *smalls.*)

1853 'C. BEDE' *Verdant Green* II. xi, The little gentleman was going in for his Degree, *alias* Great-go, *alias* Greats. **1861** HUGHES *Tom Brown at Oxf.* I. x. 163 In our second term we..begin to feel ourselves at home, while both 'smalls' and 'greats' are sufficiently distant to be altogether ignored if we are that way inclined. **1884** G. ALLEN *Strange Stories* 175 Since I have begun reading philosophy for my Greats. **1897** *Westm. Gaz.* 12 June 1/3 There are..more entries for Modern History than for Classical Greats.

†**great**, *v. Obs.* Forms: 1 **gréatian**, 3 **greaten**, (*pa. pple.* **igret**), 3–5 **grete**, 6 **great**. [OE. *gréatian* (= OHG. *grôzên*, mod.Ger. dial. *groszen*), f. *gréat* GREAT *a.*]

1. *intr.* To become great, thick, or large; to increase; *occas.* with reference to pregnancy.

c **897** K. ÆLFRED *Gregory's Past.* xi. 68 Hwæt on ðæs siweniȝȝean eaȝum beoð ða æplas hale, ac ða bræwas greatiað [*Hatton MS.* greatiȝað; L. *grossescunt*]. *a* **1225** *Ancr. R.* 128 Swin ipund ine sti uorte uetten, & forte greaten aȝein þe cul of þer eax. **1297** R. GLOUC. (Rolls) 1556 His [Nero's] wombe bigan to greti. *a* **1300** *Cursor M.* 4700 Sua bigan þe derth to grete. **13..** *K. Alis.* 452 The lady greted with yonge bon. *a* **1330** *Syr Degarre* 155 Here wombe greted more and more. *c* **1420** *Pallad. on Husb.* VII. 20 That the corn may grete [L. *grandescere*]..They sayn, is good to lete (hit) ly vnbounde. *Ibid.* 25 Yf hit [wheat] be ripe, is forto se If al the lond attonys rody grete [L. *si æqualiter spicarum populus maturato rubore flavescat*].

2. *trans.* To make great; to increase; to magnify, aggrandize.

a **1225** *Juliana* 11 An godd þat is igret wið euches cunnes gode. *c* **1420** *Pallad. on Husb.* II. 241 The plauntis bigge a depper delf desireth And larger space, as wynd may hem to shake: That gretith hem [L. *ut..a ventis frequentibus agitata grandescat*]. **1605** SYLVESTER *Du Bartas* II. iii. III. *Law* 649 This false Politick, Plotting to Great himself, our deaths doth seek.

great-aunt: see GREAT *a.* 21 a.

great-coat, greatcoat (ˌgreɪtˈkəʊt, ˈgreɪtˌkəʊt).

'The Dicts. mark the stress as '*greatcoat* or '*great,coat*; in England the stress seems to be usually on the last syllable, less frequently equal.' (N.E.D.)

A large heavy overcoat; a top-coat.

1661–85 *Househ. Ord.* 362 None shall presume to come into Our Privy Chamber..in cloakes, or great coates, or in bootes. **1714** *Post Boy* No. 2970 Horsemens Great-Coats made of a good West-Country Drab Cloth. **1768–74** TUCKER *Lt. Nat.* (1834) 441 The hood of a great-coat. **1826** SCOTT *Jrnl.* 16 Dec., Came home through a cold easterly rain without a greatcoat. **1881** BESANT & RICE *Chapl. of Fleet* I. 203 Heavy greatcoats with triple capes.

Hence **great'coat** *v. trans.*, to dress in a greatcoat; **great'coatless** *a.*, without a great-coat.

1882 *Daily News* 10 Apr. 5/2 The prudent man still great-coats himself. **1887** *Ibid.* 27 Dec. 5/1 He fled, great-coatless, into the snow. **1891** *Pall Mall G.* 1 Apr. 6/1 'We are sitting out of doors, greatcoatless and hatless', writes a correspondent from Lago Maggiore on Easter Sunday.

great-coated, *a.* [f. prec. sb. + -ED[2].] Dressed in or wearing a great-coat.

1750 JENYNS *Mod. fine Lady* 74 Great-coated tenants her arrival greet. **1798** JANE AUSTEN *Northang. Abb.* (1833) II. xi. 175 Henry came, booted and great-coated, into the room. **1824** MISS MITFORD *Village* Ser. I. 277 How often have I seen him on a cold winter morning, with a face all frost and business, great-coated up to the eyes. **1884** *Punch* 22 Nov. 249/2 Listening to a great-coated military band in late October at 9 p.m.

great-cousin: see GREAT *a.* 21 a.

greate full, obs. form of GRATEFUL.

greaten (ˈgreɪt(ə)n), *v.* Now *arch.* [f. GREAT *a.*: see -EN[5].]

†**1.** *intr.* To become pregnant; = GREAT *v.* 1. *Obs.*

a **1375** *Joseph Arim.* 88 Sone aftur þat gretnede þat greiþli Mayde.

2. *trans.* To render great or greater in size or amount; to increase, augment, enlarge, magnify.

1626 R. HARRIS *Hezekiah's Recov.* 5 This must greaten our thankes. **1633** BP. HALL *Occas. Medit.* (1851) 64 It is the nature of that element, to greaten appearing quantities. **1641** J. JACKSON *True Evang. T.* III. 201 It will easily so appeare, without any flow of words to greaten it. *a* **1658** CROMWELL in *2nd Narr. late Parl.* in *Harl. Misc.* (1745) III. 467 That some should so enrich and greaten them-selves in the Ruin of others. **1667** PEPYS *Diary* 14 June, Every thing concurred to greaten the fire. **1682** BUNYAN *Holy War* 18 To promote thee to honour, and to greaten thy liberty. **1724** R. WELTON *Subst. Chr. Faith* 89 As men proceed in wickedness, as they greaten and aggravate their sins. **1850** MRS. BROWNING *Poems* I. 237 The whole strain being multiplied And greatened. **1877** FURNIVALL *Introd. to Leopold Shaks.* 83 This fault he shared, but he wilfully greatend it. **1889** LOWELL in *Atlantic Monthly* LXIV. 148 Greatened by the watery lens.

3. To render eminent, prominent, distinguished, or important; to increase the rank or power of; to exalt, aggrandize. Also *refl.* and *absol.*

1614 RALEIGH *Hist. World* v. i. §4. 552 The Athenians, who hoped to have greatned themselves in Sicily, by the division and civil war, were disappointed of their expectations. **1650** FULLER *Pisgah* II. vi. 151 Cana..greatened with Christs first miracle. **1662** PETTY *Taxes* 28 So much doth the means of facilitating carriage greaten a city. **1707** NORRIS *Treat. Humility* iv. 146 Weary in seeking ways to greaten and advance themselves.

b. To exalt mentally or spiritually; chiefly in good sense, to elevate or ennoble (the mind).

1647 SPRIGGE *Anglia Rediv.* Address (1854) 9 Whose minds are so greatened as that you will look upon no small things. **1659** J. ARROWSMITH *Chain Princ.* 275 An humble spirit greatned by continual converse with the great God. **1698** M. HENRY *Life Philip H.* ix. (1699) 131 The Grace of Christ in the Spirit..greatens and guides the Spirit. **1742** YOUNG *Nt. Th.* I. 84 Virtue, or purpos'd virtue, still be Thine..This greatens, fills, immortalizes All. **1747** HERVEY *Medit.* II. 21 An uniform Air of ineffable majesty greatens, exalts, ennobles the whole.

absol. *a* **1849** J. C. MANGAN *Poems* (1859) 388 For valour, truth, and comely bloom, For all that greatens and adorns.

4. *intr.* Of material and immaterial things: To become great or greater; to increase in size, dimension, or extent; to assume large proportions.

a **1716** SOUTH *Serm.* (1744) X. 336 Being committed against an infinite majesty, it [sin] greatens, and rises to the height of an infinite demerit. **1746** HERVEY *Medit.* (1818) 78 Influenced by these considerations, thy views will greaten. **1839** BAILEY *Festus* iii. (1848) 25 That curse is ever greatening. **1856** MRS. BROWNING *Aur. Leigh* I. 1065 My blue eyes greatening in the looking-glass. **1861** A. K. H. BOYD *Recreat. Country Parson* Ser. I. (1862) 70 The subject greatens on me, but the paper dwindles. **1874** G. DAWSON

Our Shaks. Club 115 As we grow he [Shakespeare] grows, and as we greaten he greatens.

Hence **'greatened** *ppl. a.*, **'greatening** *vbl. sb.* and *ppl. a.*

1614 RALEIGH *Hist. World* IV. ii. §9. 473 Rather to the greatning of others than himself. **1646–7** J. HALL *Poems* 91 And there my greatned selfe disperse As wide as thought. **1677** GALE *Crt. Gentiles* III. 24 The greatening and advancing of themselves. **1678** N. TATE *Brutus of Alba*, My greatening soul aspires to range like thee, In unknown worlds. **1856** MRS. BROWNING *Aur. Leigh* v. 420, I called the artist but a greatened man. **1861** *All Year Round* V. 14 To glut the greatening bonfire. **1884** J. PULSFORD in *Chr. World* 11 Sept. 688/2 As you go on your ever greatening way.

greater ('greɪtə(r)), *a.*, *adv.*, and *sb.* Forms: 1 grýttra, 3–4 grettur, -yr, 4–5 gratter, -ur, gretter, -or, 5–6 greter, 4–6 *Sc.* gretar, (5 greiter, 6 grytur, greter, greitar, greittar, 6–9 gritter), 6– greater. [OE. *grýttra* (**gríetra*, Anglian **grétra*):—OTeut. **grautizon-*, comparative of **grauto-* GREAT *a.*; but it is doubtful whether any of the later forms descend directly from this, most if not all being, like the now current form, refashioned on the positive. See -ER[3].]

A. *adj.*

1. a. The comparative of GREAT in various senses.

c **950** *Epist. Alex.* in *Anglia* IV. 151 Wæron hie [serpents] swa greate swa columnan ʒe eac sume.. gryttran. *a* **1225** *Ancr. R.* 420 Euer me is leouere so ʒe don gretture werkes. Ne makie none purses.. ne blodbendes of seolke, auh schepieð.. chirche cloðes, and poure monne cloðes. *a* **1300** *Cursor M.* 11078 O wijf.. was neuer born nan A greter barn þan sant iohan. *c* **1386** CHAUCER *Prol.* 197 He hadde of gold ywroght a curious pyn: A loue knotte in the gretter ende ther was. *c* **1400** *Destr. Troy* 3874 Was neuer kyng.. his knightes more louet, Ne gretter of giftes to his goode men. *c* **1460** FORTESCUE *Abs. & Lim. Mon.* vi. (1885) 122 We beyre moch gretter charges yerely than done the Scottis. **1549** *Bk. Com. Prayer, Athan. Creed*, And in this trinitie none is afore nor after other: none is greater nor lesse then other. **1588** A. KING tr. *Canisius' Catech.* 75 We culd neuer wishe ane gryter benefit nor yat Christ Iesus our lord.. suld sa giv him self haill for vs. *a* **1605** MONTGOMERIE *Sonn.* xii, Can candle lou give fyr a griter heet? **1605** SHAKS. *Macb.* I. iii. 65 Lesser then Macbeth, and greater. **1611** JONSON *Catiline* II. (Chorus), Great father Mars, and greater Ioue. **1654** JER. TAYLOR *Real Pres.* 193 The greater your reason is against it, the greater excellency in your obedience. **1664** PEPYS *Diary* 15 July, He says that he is as great with the Chancellor, or greater, than ever in his life. **1748** *Earthquake Peru* i. 39 A French Toise, or Fathom, is about five Inches greater than the English. **1860** TYNDALL *Glac.* I. ii. 16 The sound.. appears to come from greater and greater distances.

b. *the greater part*, †*sort*, etc.: the larger of two parts into which any whole or quantity is divided; the more considerable number or quantity (of); the majority.

1578 TIMME *Caluine on Gen.* 42 The greater sort do agree that this word [image] is distinguished from Likeness. **1585** T. WASHINGTON tr. *Nicholay's Voy.* I. iv. 3 b, The greater part of us went a shoare to see the Ilande. **1601** SHAKS. *Jul. C.* IV. ii. 29 The greater part, the Horse in generall Are come with Cassius. **1603** —— *Meas. for M.* III. ii. 145 The greater file of the subiect held the Duke to be wise. **1781** C. JOHNSTON *John Juniper* II. 249 The characters in tragedy are, for much the greater part, out of common life. **1829** LANDOR *Wks.* (1846) II. 210/1 The greater number of men .. are disposed, on most occasions, rather to virtue than to vice. **1861** M. PATTISON *Ess.* (1889) I. 45 The greater part of the area was covered with the lofty warehouses.

c. Applied to and descriptive of towns (to indicate the inclusion of adjoining boroughs, suburbs, etc.) and countries (with dependencies, etc.).

1616 T. CORYAT *Traveller for English Wits* 12 *Traiecto Tigride*, I entred Armenia the greater: After that, Media the lower. *Ibid.* 19 My whole perambulation of this Asia the greater. **1868** Greater Britain [see BRITAIN *sb.* 1]. **1882** *Encycl. Brit.* IV. 834/1 The London police district, or 'Greater London', is divided into two police jurisdictions, that of the metropolitan police,.. and that of the City police. **1898** *Appletons' Dict. of N.Y.* (title-page), First 'Greater New York' Edition. *Ibid.* p. iii, The present edition of this book is the first to deal with the territory of the 'Greater New York' as constituting one municipality. **1939** *Ann. Reg. 1938* 190 After the Anschluss with Austria, Czechoslovakia was surrounded on three sides by Greater Germany. **1955** *Times* 2 Aug. 6/5 Motorists living in the Greater London area were on the roads early in the morning bound for the seaside or the country. **1958** *Listener* 21 Aug. 274/2 Apart from Greater London and Greater Birmingham all the conurbations were either increasing their population at a rate far lower than the nation as a whole or (in the case of Greater Manchester) were even losing population.

†**2.** Older, elder. [A Latinism.] *Obs.*

c **1380** WYCLIF *Wks.* (1880) 383 He þat is gratter of ʒow, loke þat he be made as ʒongar in sympilnes. **1535** COVERDALE *1 Sam.* xvii. 28 And Eliab his greater brother herde him talke with the men.

†**3.** Pregnant. *Obs. rare.*

c **1375** *Sc. Leg. Saints, Theodera* 550 Syne eftyre of tyme in processe Hapnyt þat scho gretare wes, & hyr frendis sperit ʒarne Quha with hyr gat þat barne.

4. In special or technical use, opposed to *lesser*. **a.** *Astron.* in names of certain constellations, as ***the Greater Dog***, † ***the Greater*** (now ***Great***) ***Bear***. Also † ***greater circle*** = 'great circle': see CIRCLE. **b.** *Mus.* Applied to intervals now usually called MAJOR. **c.** in names of plants. **d.** in names of animals, esp. birds. **e.** *Anat.* **f.** (see quot.).

a. 1551 RECORDE *Cast. Knowl.* (1556) 263 The lesser Beare .. the greater Beare. **1638** J. CHILMEAD tr. Hues' *Tractatus de Globis* III. ii. (1889) 80 Of the Circumference of the Earth, or of a Greater Circle. **1674** MOXON *Tutor Astron.* (ed. 3) 209 *Ursa Major*, the Greater Bear. **1727–51** CHAMBERS *Cycl.* s.v., The Equator, meridian, ecliptic, verticals, &c. are great or greater circles of the sphere: and the parallels, tropics, &c. lesser circles.

b. 1597 MORLEY *Introd. Mus.* Annot., The greater halfe note is that distance which is betwixt *fa* and *mi*. **1674** PLAYFORD *Skill Mus.* III. 11 A sixth beneath the Bass is a third above, and if it be the lesser sixth, then is the third above the greater third. **1727–51** CHAMBERS *Cycl.* s.v. *Diesis*, Enharmonical Diesis is the difference between a greater and lesser semi-tone. **1818** BUSBY *Gram. Music* 317 Greater Sixth. **1887** BROWNING *Parleyings, Chas. Avison* iv, The key Was.. C.. with the Greater Third.

c. 1776–96 WITHERING *Brit. Plants* (ed. 3) III. 745 Greater Knapweed. **1861** MISS PRATT *Flower Pl.* IV. 75 Greater Broom-rape. *Ibid.* 215 Greater Bladderwort. *Ibid.* 255 Greater Plantain. *Ibid.* V. 305 Greater Water Plantain.

d. 1876 SMILES *Sc. Natur.* xi. (ed. 4) 213 A Greater Shrike or Butcher Bird. **1885** SWAINSON *Prov. Names Birds* 208 Greater Black-backed Gull (*Larus marinus*). *Ibid.* 215 Greater loon.

e. 1872 MIVART *Elem. Anat.* 180 The deep concavity.. called the greater ischiatic notch.

f. 1614 SELDEN *Titles Hon.* 344 Barons with the rest vpward wee call the Greater Nobilitie, the others beneath them the Lesse Nobilitie.

¶**5.** ***Greater Britain***: see BRITAIN.

†**6.** *Comb.*, forming comparatives to the combinations of GREAT *a. Obs.*

1562 TURNER *Herbal* II. 101 Wilde lekes.. greater heded then they were that I saw about Bon. **1597** BACON *Coulers Good & Euill* v. (Arb.) 144 Men whose living lieth together in one Shire, are commonly counted greater landed then those whose livings are dispersed.

†**B.** *adv.* In a greater degree. *Obs.*

1496 *Dives & Paup.* (W. de W.) I. xlii. 82/1 Greter sodayne deth wyste I neuer than thet men had than.

C. quasi-*sb.* and *sb.* **a.** The adj. used *absol.* and *ellipt.* ***the greater***: that or those of greater size, importance, eminence, etc. ***a greater***: a person or thing which is greater (than another).

1388 WYCLIF *Isa.* xxxii. 5 He that is vnwijs schal no more be clepid prince, and a gileful man schal not be clepid the grettere [Vulg. *major*]. **1607** SHAKS. *Timon* IV. iii. 6 The greater scornes the lesser. **1620** T. GRANGER *Div. Logike* 121 Negations of unequals are of the greater, or lesse, or of both together. **1845** McCULLOCH *Taxation* I. i. (1852) 51 Unless a method should be found of taking a greater from a less. **1898** MORLEY in *Westm. Gaz.* 27 June 10/1 We mourn for one of the greater among the servants of mankind.

†**b.** (One's) superior. *Obs.*

1480 CAXTON *Chron. Eng.* ccxxxii. 251 Kyng Edward his gretter and his fadre. **1627** J. CARTER *Plaine Expos.* 85 They come farre short, not onely of some of their compeeres and greaters especially, but of many very base creatures. **1667** MILTON *P.L.* v. 172 Thou Sun, of this great World both Eye and Soule, Acknowledge him thy Greater. **1671** —— *P.R.* I. 279 He.. first Refused on me his baptism to confer, As much his greater, and was hardly won.

Hence † **'greaterness**, the condition or quality of being greater.

1625 GILL *Sacr. Philos.* I. xi. (1635) 59 The working of God is infinite.. for otherwise there should bee a greaternesse in being, and a lessenesse in working. *c* **1705** BERKELEY *Commonpl. Bk.* Wks. 1871 IV. 485 Why should we judge her [i.e. the horizontal moon] to be greater? What connexion betwixt the same angle, further distant, and greaterness?

greatest ('greɪtɪst), *a.* (*sb.*) and *adv.* Forms: 3–5 grettest, (5 -yst, -ist, -ust), 4 gretest, 4–5 grattest, -ist, gretest, *Sc.* -ast, (5 grattes, -us), 6– greatest. *β.* 3–5 greste. [f. GREAT *a.* + -EST; app. not recorded in OE.]

A. *adj.* **1. a.** The superlative of GREAT in various senses.

c **1290** *S. Eng. Leg.* I. 220/17 Nou is þe se [of] Occean grettest and mest al-so. **1340** *Ayenb.* 44 Huanne me.. beggeþ be þe gratteste wyʒtes, oþer be þe grattestе mesures, and zelleþ by þe leste. *c* **1380** WYCLIF *Sel. Wks.* III. 398 One of þo grattest synnes of alle. *c* **1386** CHAUCER *Reeve's T.* 134 The gretteste clerkes been noght the wysest men. **1398** TREVISA *Barth. De P.R.* XVII. ii. (1495) 598 The grettest tree synkyth not in water though it be heuy. *c* **1420** *Sir Amadas* (Weber) 306 The grattes maysters yede hym beforne. *c* **1460** FORTESCUE *Abs. & Lim. Mon.* xii. (1885) 138 Whan any rysinge hath be made.. the pouerest men þeroff haue be þe grettest causers and doers therin. **1604** E. G[RIMSTONE] *D'Acosta's Hist. Indies* I. xx. 67 Birds faile in their flight, yea, those of the greatest wing, vpon the passage of so great a Gulph. **1683** A. D. *Art Converse* 40 The greatest swearers are commonly the greatest liars. **1834** SIR H. TAYLOR *Artevelde* I. I. v, The world knows nothing of its greatest men. **1871** R. ELLIS tr. *Catullus* xlix. 1 Greatest speaker of any born a Roman, Marcus Tullius. **1895** LD. ESHER in *Law Times Rep.* LXXIII. 701/2, I have the greatest respect and admiration for American decisions.

β. *a* **1225** *Ancr. R.* 66 Ower greste, & ower lodlukeste sunnen. *c* **1315** SHOREHAM 8 Of alle other sacramens Thes sevene beth the greste. *c* **1420** *Chron. Vilod.* st. 490 In my greste nede.

b. ***greatest part***: the largest amount or proportion (of); the majority (cf. GREATER A. 1 b).

1604 E. G[RIMSTONE] *D'Acosta's Hist. Indies* IV. xxxiii. 300 In many partes of the Indies, and I thinke in the greatest part, small cattell do not increase and profite well. **1644** BP. HALL *Rem. Wks.* (1660) 133 The greatest part of the Romish Doctors. **1648** LD. BYRON in *Hamilton Papers* (Camden) 166 The greatest part of Lancashire, Cheshire, and North Wales. **1660** F. BROOKE tr. *Le Blanc's Trav.* 3 The greatest part of our company were reprobate persons. **1741** JOHNSON *Debates in Parlt.* (1787) I. 358 Both inn-holders and soldiers are, for the greatest part, of this rank and temper. **1771** T. HULL *Sir W. Harrington* (1797) I. 180 It attracted his eyes greatest part of the evening. *a* **1774** GOLDSM. *Grecian Hist.* I. 194 He died.. aged threescore and five years, the greatest part of which he had spent in the intrigues and bustles of active employment.

c. ***greatest happiness of the greatest number*** (see HAPPINESS 2 b). **d.** ***greatest common measure*** (see MEASURE).

†**2.** Eldest. (Cf. GREATER A. 2.) *Obs.*

1535 COVERDALE *1 Sam.* xviii. 17 Saul sayde vnto Dauid: Beholde my greatest [*Wyclif*, more, *A.V.* elder] doughter Merob wyl I geue the to wyfe.

3. *absol.* and *ellipt.* (quasi-*sb.*)

c **1350** *Will. Palerne* 1196 He slou six of þe grettes. *c* **1400** *Destr. Troy* 1006 The grettyst of Grise gremyt þerat. *c* **1420** *Anturs of Arth.* xxxiii, My nome is Syr Galrun.. The grattus [*Douce MS.* grettest, *Thornt. MS.* gretteste] of Galway, of greuys and of gillus. **1450–70** *Golagros & Gaw.* 1168 Al the gretest Of gomys that grip has. *c* **1470** HENRY *Wallace* I. 133, Vij score thai led off the gretast that thai fand Off ayris with thaim. **1602** DEKKER *Satire mastix* A 4 b, *Ad Lectorem*.. It shall not be amisse.. first to beholde this short Comedy of Errors and where the greatest enter to giue them in stead of a hisse, a gentle correction. **1634** SIR T. HERBERT *Trav.* 163 Mecha (neere which.. is buried their greatest Mahomet). **1784** COWPER *Task* II. 168 Since from the least The greatest oft originate. **1852** TENNYSON *Death Wellington* 29 Our greatest yet with least pretence. **1946** *Jazzways* I. 104/1 'Duke's the greatest' is certainly the easiest cliché tossed around swing circles. **1954** *Time* 8 Nov. 70 A term of high approbation in the swing era.. is 'the greatest'. **1964** *Globe & Mail* (Toronto) 30 Nov., Joe Kapp and Willie Fleming swung in a jubilant jig, and Kapp hollered, 'Baby, you're the greatest.' **1970** *New Yorker* 17 Oct. 39/1 Everything about this broad spelled class,.. she was the greatest.

†**B.** *adv.* Most greatly or highly; most. *Obs.*

1553 in Strype *Eccl. Mem.* II. 369 Articles.. gathered.. by the greatest learned men of the bishops.

great go. [See GREAT *a.* and GO *sb.*[1]] *Univ. slang.* The final examination for the degree of B.A. (At Oxford now called *greats*.) (Cf. *little go*.)

1820 *Gentl. Mag.* XC. I. 32 At present the examination [at the University of Oxford] is divided into a Little-go and a Great-go. **1825** C. M. WESTMACOTT *Eng. Spy* I. 137 An examination that would far exceed the perils of the great go. *Ibid.* 141 When he enters upon life, action, or profession, both the *little go*, and the *great go*, he will find to be a *by go*; for he will find that he has gone by the best part of useful and substantial learning; or that it has gone by him. **1841** THACKERAY *K. of Brentford* vii, His little go and great go He creditably pass'd. **1876** 'P. PYPER' *Mr. Gray & Neighb.* I. 74 Young Mr. Applebee had managed to pass his 'great go' at Oxford, just about the time the living fell vacant.

great-grandfather, etc.: see GREAT *a.* 21 b.

great-great-: see GREAT *a.* 21 c.

greath, obs. form of GRAITH.

great-head ('greɪthɛd). *U.S.* [f. GREAT *a.* + HEAD *sb.*: see quot. 1844.] An American name for the golden-eye, *Clangula glaucion*.

1844 J. P. GIRAUD *Birds Long Island* 334 *Fuligula clangula* —Linn. Golden-eye... By some it is called 'Great Head', from its beautiful, rich, and thickly-crested head. **1888** G. TRUMBULL *Game Birds* xxiii. 79 *Glaucionetta clangula americana*. American Golden-eye.. At Seaford (Hempstead), L.I., Great-head.

great-hearted, *a.* (Stress variable.) [f. GREAT *a.*: see HEARTED.]

†**a.** High-spirited; proud. *Obs.* **b.** Having a noble or generous heart or spirit; magnanimous; great-souled.

1398 [see GREAT-WILLY]. **1398** TREVISA *Barth. De P.R.* XII. xxi. (1495) 427 The faucon is soo grete hartyd that yf he fayllyth of his pray in the fyrste flyghte and rees, in the seconde he takyth wreche on hymself. *c* **1440** *Promp. Parv.* 210/2 Grete hertyd, and bolde, *magnanimus*. Grete hertyd, not redy to buxumnesse *pertinax, inflexibilis*. *a* **1450** *Knt. de la Tour* (1868) 26 Alle women that ben gret herted and misansueringe her husbondes. **1647** CLARENDON *Hist. Reb.* I. §66 The earl.. was as great-hearted as he, and thought the very suspecting him to be an injury unpardonable. **1842** BROWNING *Cavalier Tunes, Marching Along*, Great-hearted gentlemen, singing this song. **1848** BUCKLEY *Iliad* 102 Great-hearted, brazen-voiced Stentor. **1880** G. MEREDITH *Tragic Com.* (1881) 172 Alvan was great-hearted: he could love in his giant's fashion.

Hence **great'heartedness**, †(*a*) High-spiritedness (*obs.*). (*b*) Nobility or generosity of heart, magnanimity.

1813 *Examiner* 31 May 349/2 The courage and great-heartedness of the people of England. **1844** LOWELL *Lett.* (1894) I. 79 If they give us nothing else, they give us at least a feeling of great-heartedness and exaltation. **1880** G. MEREDITH *Tragic Com.* (1881) 283 Wives he should have by fifties and hundreds if he wanted them, she thought in her great-heartedness. **1895** J. SMITH *Message of the Exodus* xviii. 264 In His great-heartedness our Father is tolerant of mere human frailty.

†**greathede.** *Obs.* [f. GREAT *a.* + -*hede*, -HEAD. Cf. MHG. *grôzheit*, G. *grôszheit*, MLG. *grôtheit*, Du. *grootheid*.] Greatness.

a **1340** HAMPOLE *Psalter* lxx. 9 Synge .i. all day þi gretehede. *Ibid.* cxliv. 3 Of his gretehede is nane ende. *c* **1380** WYCLIF *Sel. Wks.* III. 22 Falle on hem dreede and qwaking in þe greetheed of þin arm.

greatish ('greɪtɪʃ), *a.* [f. GREAT *a.* + -ISH.] Somewhat great.

1866 CARLYLE *Remin.* (1881) II. 185, I now.. see it had been, as she called it, 'a great success', and greatish of its kind. **1870** [Lady Verney] *Lettice Lisle* 41 'You do a greatish deal, Gabriel, up and down' said the child.

great-line, 'greatline. Also grettlin, gritline. A long line used in deep-sea fishing for cod, ling, etc. Also *attrib.*, as *great-line fish, fishing.*

a **1600** *Aberdeen Reg.* (Jam.), Gryt lyne fische, sic as leing, turbat, keling, & skaitt. **1866** *Banffsh. Gloss.*, *Grettlin*, a great-line; the line used for catching the larger kinds of fish; as cod, ling, etc. **1867** Smyth *Sailor's Word-bk.*, *Great-line fishing*, that carried on over the deeper banks of the ocean.. It is more applicable to hand-fishing, as on the banks of Newfoundland, in depths over 60 fathoms. **1879** Holdsworth in *Encycl. Brit.* IX. 262/1 The cod or 'great lines' are of the same description as those used for haddock fishing, but have longer snoods and the hooks farther apart. It is unnecessary to speak of the manner in which these long-lines are worked. **1883** *Fisheries Exhib. Catal.* 13 One Greatline placed in a basket.

†**greatly,** *a. Obs.* [f. great *a.* + -ly[1]. Cf. MHG. *grôzlîch*, MDu. *grotelijc.*] Great.

c **1450** *Merlin* 65 Gretly was the kynge at that feeste, and ioyfull and mery. **1450-70** *Golagros & Gaw.* 377 Thai war courtes and couth thair knyghthed to kyth, Athir vthir wele gret in gretly degre.

greatly ('greɪtlɪ), *adv.* Forms: see great *a.* [f. great *a.* + -ly[2]. Cf. MHG. *grôz(e)lîche*, MDu. *grotelike*, Du. *grootelijks.*]

1. To a great extent, in a great degree; extensively, exceedingly; highly; much, very.

a. qualifying verbs and pples.

c **1200** *Trin. Coll. Hom.* 13 He sineгeð gretliche, for þe holie boc hit forbet. *a* **1225** *Ancr. R.* 426 And þe ancre legge on eiðer sum penitence more upon þe ilke þet gret-luker haueð agult. *c* **1330** *Arth. & Merl.* 1137 So gretliche sche awondred was, þat hir chaunged blod & fas. **1340** *Ayenb.* 47 Ne weneþ naȝt gratliche zeneȝy. *c* **1386** Chaucer *Melib.* ¶2736, I can nat seen that it mighte greetly harme me, though I toke vengeaunce. *a* **1400-50** *Alexander* 472 þou has giltid, but noȝt gretly. **1484** Caxton *Æsop* III. ii, I thanke the gretely. **1525** Ld. Berners *Froiss.* II. ccxvii. [ccxiii.] 671 That he had many of his men slayne, and that the batayle had cost hym greatly. **1590** Spenser *F.Q.* I. iv. 20 He.. greatly shunned manly exercise. **1596** Drayton *Leg.* iv. 660 He that first stirr'd in the Churches cause, Against Him greatliest that oppugned it. **1604** Shaks. *Oth.* III. i. 18 To heare Musicke, the Generall do's not greatly care. **1665** Evelyn *Mem.* (1827) IV. 146 Such as have lived long in Universities do greately affect words and Expressions no where in use beside. **1742** Young *Nt. Th.* VIII. 785 They, first, Themselves offend, who greatly please. **1756** P. Browne *Jamaica* 221 The bark is greatly esteemed among the tanners. **1849** E. E. Napier *Excurs. S. Africa* II. 287 Gigantic shrubs, greatly resembling our English yew. **1875** Jowett *Plato* (ed. 2) I. 55, I should greatly prefer a real friend to all the gold of Darius. **1880** Geikie *Phys. Geog.* ii. §10. 66 Evaporation is greatly helped by wind.

b. qualifying adjs. and advs. Somewhat *arch.* exc. with comparatives or words implying comparison.

a **1300** *Cursor M.* 11634 Sco was gretli in dute. *c* **1350** *Will. Palerne* 1292 þan was þemperour greteli glad. **1579** Tomson *Calvin's Serm. Tim.* 548/1 To the ende that euery man may..be greatlyer afraide. **1636** Chardin *Coron. Solyman* (1686) 16 His long Experience in Affairs rendered him greatly considerable. **1691** T. H[ale] *Acc. New Invent.* 12 Lead-sheathing greatly cheaper than that of Wood. **1749** Lady Luxborough *Let. to Shenstone* 28 Dec., I..think it an ornament greatly in taste. **1768** H. Walpole *Hist. Doubts* 70, I shall show that it is greatly probable. **1817** A. Bonar *Serm.* II. xv. 318 All the names of excellence..are greatly too mean to declare the Saviour's worth. **1824** Landor *Wks.* (1846) I. 183/2 Here the bow is greatly a better weapon than the musket. *a* **1856** H. Miller *Test. Rocks* i. (1857) 66 The skate and dog fish are greatly less rare. **1873** Ruskin *Fors Clav.* xxx. (1896) II. 131 Her mother and brother were greatly proud of her. **1886** R. Kipling *Departm. Ditties* 12 Careless and lazy is he, Greatly inferior to Me.

2. On a large scale; in large numbers; largely. ? *Obs.*

1670 R. Coke *Disc. Trade* 51 Any business which is more freely managed may be greatlier managed than if it were more restrained. **1792** Burke *Corr.* (1844) III. 420 The funeral of dear Sir Joshua. It will be greatly attended.

b. For a great or the most part; mainly, chiefly. *rare.*

1742 Young *Nt. Th.* I. 112 They greatly live a life on earth Unkindled, unconceiv'd. **1865** Grote *Plato* I. v. 178 We now enter upon the second or dialectic period; passed by Plato greatly at Megara.

†**3.** With a 'great' voice; loudly. *Obs.*

1340 *Ayenb.* 156 He [þe asse] beginþ zinge grat-liche.

4. In a great manner. **a.** Magnanimously, nobly; grandly. †**b.** Eminently, illustriously. **c.** With brilliant success. *Obs.*

a **1400** *Prymer* (1891) 44 Oure lord gretly dyde with us. We been maad ioyful. ? **14..** *Death & Life* 3 in Furniv. *Percy Folio* III. 56 Give vs grace on the ground the greatlye to serve, For that royall red blood that rann from thy side. **1435** Misyn *Fire of Love* I. xiv. 30 Hermetis lyffe þerfore is grett, if it gretely be done. **1599** Shaks. *Hen. V*, Epil. 5 Small time: but in that small, most greatly liued This Starre of England. **1670** Dryden *1st Pt. Conq. Granada* v. ii, It is for you, brave man..Greatly to speak, and yet more greatly do. **1678** —— *Limberham* v. i, My Comfort is, I fell greatly. **1713** Addison *Cato* IV. iv, The brave youth..Who greatly in his country's cause expired. **1713** Pope *Prol. Addison's Cato* 22 A brave man struggling in the storms of fate, And greatly falling with a falling state. **1725** —— *Odyss.* II. 312 What he greatly thought, he nobly dar'd. **1764** Foote *Patron* III. Wks. 1799 I. 357 If your piece had been greatly receiv'd, I would have declared Sir Thomas Lofty the author; if coldly, I would have owned it myself. **1784** Cowper *Task* VI. 820 All were once Perfect, and all must be at length restored. So God has greatly purpos'd. **1876** Ouida *Winter City* viii. 238 It was a great theme greatly treated.

5. In or to a high rank or position. *rare.*

a **1800** T. Bellamy *Beggar Boy* (1801) II. 142, I am not greatly born, like you. **1815** Jane Austen *Emma* I. viii. 53 You encourage her to expect to marry greatly. **1830** Gen. P. Thompson *Exerc.* (1842) I. 293 It matters not..how many ensigns shall have greatly risen through all the gradations of command.

great-nephew: see great *a.* 21 a.

greatness ('greɪtnɪs). [f. great *a.* + -ness: in OE. (**grēatnes*) *grētnys.*]

†**1.** Thickness, coarseness; stoutness. *Obs.*

c **1020** *Rule St. Benet* (Logeman) lv. 92 þara þinga eallra be bleo ne ðððe gretnysse [L. *grossitudine*] na cidan. *c* **1400** *Lanfranc's Cirurg.* 200 If it so be þat þis greetnes [= swelling] come of malancolious blood or of greet fleume. **14..** *Voc.* in Wr.-Wülcker 587/22 *Grossitas*, gretenesse. *c* **1440** *Eng. Conq. Irel.* 89 Forto aquenche that gretnes he put hym-Selfe to ful mych trauayl that vnneth he lette his body haue enny reste. *a* **1450** *Fysshynge w. angle* (1883) 16 And your floyt for on heyr be no bygger a pese for ij herys as a beyn for xij heres as a walnot and so forthe euery lyne aftur hys gretnes. **1536** in *Gentl. Mag.* (1813) May 427 Euery Essex byllet conteyn in lenght iij footte, w[t] the carfe; in gretnes in mydes xv ynches.

†**b.** Pregnancy. *Obs.*

c **1450** *Merlin* 86 Thus was the kynge wedded to Ygerne, and kepe her till her gretnesse apered. **1565** Cooper *Thesaurus*, *Grauiditas*, greatnesse with childe, or with yonge. **1634** T. Johnson *Parey's Chirurg.* (1649) 594 Certain infallible signs of greatness with child. *Ibid.*, In this greatness of childe-bearing.

2. The attribute of being great in size, extent or degree; †loudness (of voice); †force (of the pulse).

a **1300** *Cursor M.* 27033 Wan-hope es..quen man for grettnes of his gilt has tint þe hope o merci. *c* **1380** Wyclif *Serm.* Sel. Wks. I. 117 The puple woundrid herof for gretnesse of þe myracle. *c* **1400** Maundev. (Roxb.) xii. 50 It es also called a see, for þe greteness þeroff. *c* **1500** *Melusine* xxxviii. 304 They were al abasshed of hys gretnes, For he was xv foot of lengthe. **1585** T. Washington tr. *Nicholay's Voy.* II. xxi. 59 b, The greatnes & magnificence of the costly & sumptuous Thermes. **1614** Bp. Hall *Recoll. Treat.* 902 For greatnesse of number, hugenesse of quantity, strangenesse of shapes. **1682** Bunyan *Holy W.* 143 They shouted with that greatness of voice. **1707** Floyer *Physic. Pulse-Watch* II. 168 We must endeavour to preserve the natural Strength, Greatness, Celerity and Crebrity [of the pulse]. **1767** A. Young *Farmer's Lett. People* 79 The greatness of rent which a little farm bears. **1774** Goldsm. *Nat. Hist.* (1776) I. 215 The Zara, and the Coanza, from the greatness of whose openings into the sea..we form an estimate of the great distance from whence they come. **1898** T. Adamson *Stud. Mind in Christ* x. 248 He saw the difficulty and greatness of his task.

†**b.** semi-*concr.* Great bulk. *Obs. rare.*

1595 Daniel *Civ. Wars* II. vii, Goodly riuers (that haue made their graues, And buried both their names and all their good Within his greatnes, to augment his waues).

†**3.** Magnitude or size in the abstract. *Obs.*

1377 Langl. *P. Pl.* B. XVI. 59 On o more thei growed, And of o gretnesse and grene of greyne thei semen. *c* **1440** *Anc. Cookery* in *Househ. Ord.* (1790) 472 Make rounde pelettes of the gretnesse of an ey. **1488-9** *Act 4 Hen. VII*, c. 22 The said gold..not wrought in gretnesse of threde and in colour according to the outeward shewe. **1512** *Act 4 Hen. VIII*, c. 19 §14 Nott regardyng the quantitie greatnesse or smalnes of the same penyes. **1551** Recorde *Cast. Knowl.* (1556) 271 These starres..are distincte into diuers measures of lyght, and namely 8, which are called the first greatnes, the second [etc.]. **1553** Eden *Treat. Newe Ind.* (Arb.) 15 An Elephant excedeth in greatnes thre wilde oxen. **1613** Purchas *Pilgrimage* (1614) 506 The flowres in forme and greatnesse are like to those of the Orange-tree. **1654** Z. Coke *Art Logicke* (1657) 29 Greatnesse is extension, or stretching out ..Of greatnesse, the subject is said to be equal or unequal. **1765** A. Dickson *Treat. Agric.* (ed. 2) 339 That the weight of the roller bear a proportion to the greatness of the diameter.

4. Eminence of rank or station; great or exalted rank, place, or power; eminence, distinction, importance. *Occas.* in *pl.*

c **1400** *Destr. Troy* 3312 Ye..souerain of all, Shalbe worshipped..And honouret..To be gouernet in your grettenes, most godely of other. **1595** Shaks. *John* IV. ii. 94 It is apparant foule-play, and 'tis shame That Greatnesse should so grossely offer it. **1601** —— *Twel. N.* II. v. 158 Some are become great, some atcheeues greatnesse, and some haue greatnesse thrust vppon em. **1634** Sir T. Herbert *Trav.* 3 These Iles were unknowne in Romes greatnesse. **1638** *Ibid.* (ed. 2) 103 He had small joy of his greatnes. **1650** Earl Monmouth *Senault's Man become Guilty* 101 Those who think to better their condition by revolting are oft undone by their rebellion, and fal from their legitimate greatnesses for having sought after unjust ones. **1652** H. Cogan tr. *Scudery's Ibrahim* II. iv. 64, I was..to abandon her to grief and despair, and so return again to enjoy all those greatnesses. **1729** Butler *Serm.* Wks. 1874 II. 85 The grave, the end of all temporal greatness. **1751** Johnson *Rambler* No. 153 ¶21 Wealth..commands the ear of greatness. **1809** W. Irving *Knickerb.* VII. i. (1849) 385 It is the mystery which envelopes great men, that gives them half their greatness. **1849** Macaulay *Hist. Eng.* i. I. 4 Nothing in the early existence of Britain indicated the greatness which she was destined to attain. **1877** Mrs. Oliphant *Yng. Musgrave* I. 4 The old greatness of the house.

b. of God.

a **1325** *Prose Psalter* cl. 2 Herieþ hym efter þe michelnes of his gretnes. **1388** Wyclif *Deut.* v. 24 Lo! oure Lord God schewide to vs his maieste and greetnesse [**1382** mychylnesse]. **1597** Hooker *Eccl. Pol.* v. vi. §2 Betokening the greatnesse of God. **1611** Bible *1 Chron.* xxix. 11 Thine, O Lord, is the greatness, and the power, and the glory. **1895** W. Watson *Hymn to Sea* 8 Man and his greatness survive, lost in the greatness of God.

†**c.** Used as a title. (Cf. highness 2 b.) *Obs.*

1588 Shaks. *L.L.L.* v. i. 113 Some certaine speciall honours it pleaseth his greatnesse to impart to Armado a Souldier. *Ibid.* v. ii. 894 Most esteemed greatnesse, wil you heare the Dialogue that the two Learned men haue compiled? **1638** Sir T. Herbert *Trav.* (ed. 2) 137 After six dayes attendance his Greatnesse was pleased to visit Sheraz. **1697** Dryden *Virg. Georg.* I. 62 Int'rest thy Greatness in our mean Affairs. **1766** H. Brooke *Fool of Quality* (1808) I. Ded. ix, Your greatness was pleased to demand, whether this romance was wholly on my own invention.

5. Inherent nobility or dignity (of mind, character, action, or expression); grandeur.

1597 Hooker *Eccl. Pol.* v. vi. §1 The greatness and dignity of all manner actions is measured by the worthiness of the subject from which they proceed. *c* **1665** Mrs. Hutchinson *Mem. Col. Hutchinson* (1846) 27 He had..a sweet greatness that commanded love. **1697** Dryden *Ess. Virg. Georg.* (1721) I. 199 This Language..has a Natural Greatness in it. **1718** *Freethinker* No. 6 ¶5 True Greatness of Mind consists in manfully supporting Misfortunes. **1793** V. Knox *Pers. Nobility* xlii. Wks. 1824 V. 93 Greatness of soul is more necessary to make a great man, than the favour of a monarch and the blazonry of the herald. **1855** Macaulay *Hist. Eng.* xx. IV. 530 She received the intimation of her danger with true greatness of soul. **1856** Ruskin *Mod. Paint.* III. IV. iii. §5 Greatness of style consists, then: first, in the habitual choice of subjects of thought which involve wide interests and profound passions, as opposed to those which involve narrow interests and slight passions. **1892** Jas. Brown *Serm.* 183 It is the surest test of greatness that a man can act alone.

6. Intimacy or familiarity *with*. *Obs.* or *arch.*

1625 Fletcher *Noble Gent.* III. iii, Your greatnesse with the people. **1668** Etheredge *She Wou'd if she cou'd* IV. ii. Wks. (1723) 151 The access which his greatness with Sir Oliver has giv'n him daily to me. **1731** E. Calamy *Life* (1830) I. i. 60 His greatness with him did not in the sequel turn to his honour or advantage. **1897** D. H. Fleming *Mary Q. Scots* 460 *note*, Bothwell's greatness with the Queen.

great-niece: see great *a.* 21 a.

greats: see great C. 10.

greats, obs. and dial. pl. of grit *sb.*[2]

Great Spirit. [tr. Ojibway *kitchi manitou*: see Manitou.] The supreme spirit or deity recognized by the North American Indians.

1703 tr. *Lahontan's New Voy. N. Amer.* II. 19 All the Savages are convinced..that Man was not made by chance, and that he's the Work of a Being superior in Wisdom and Knowledge, which they call the Great Spirit, or the Master of Life, and which they Adore in the most abstracted and spiritual manner. **1805** J. Sibley in *Deb. Congr. U.S.* (1852) 9th Congr. 2nd Sess. 1076 The Great Spirit placed on an eminence, near this lake, one family of Caddoques. **1812** *Niles' Weekly Reg.* II. 81/1 We return thanks to the Great Spirit for the many favors he has bestowed upon us. **1836** [see spirit *sb.* 4]. **1855** Longf. *Hiaw.* i. 96 Listen to the words of warning, From the lips of the Great Spirit. **1869** C. L. Brace *New West* xi. 140 Their idea of a Great Spirit is undoubtedly a reflex of Christian teachings. **1873** J. Miller *Life amongst Modocs* (1876) xix. 264 The Indians said the Great Spirit made this mountain [*sc.* Shasta] first of all. **1958** *Native Voice* (Sp. ed.) 48/1 'Woe! Woe! My children,' cried the wise Chief. 'Do you not know that those who harm one of the Great Spirit's creatures will suffer in a like way.'

greatt(e, greatter, obs. ff. great, greater.

†**'greatumly,** *adv. Sc. Obs.* Forms: 4-6 **gretumly,** 4 **grettum-,** 6 **greattum-, greitum-, gritum-, grittum-, grytum-,** 7 **greatumlie, -ly.** [app. f. ME. **grētum* (advb. formation on great, after OE. *miclum* greatly, orig. dat. pl. of *micel* mickle) + -ly[2]. Cf. Sc. *hailumlie* wholly.]

= greatly 1 a. Chiefly used with vbs. expressing emotion.

1375 Barbour *Bruce* III. 668 Full gretumly thankyt him the king. *Ibid.* IX. 619 Thai that saw thame so stoutly Cum on thame, dred thame gretumly. *Ibid.* xii. 364 Quha sa varrayis vrangwisly, Thai faynd god all too gretumly. *c* **1375** *Sc. Leg. Saints, Thomas* 196 þat blith ves grettumly of his cumynge. **1513** Douglas *Æneis* IX. i. 56 Full gretumly the goddis..Besekand till attend to hys prayer. **1535** Stewart *Cron. Scot.* II. 498 How King Constantyne was grittumelie commouit of the Tynsall of his Lordis. **1567** *Gude & Godlie Ball.* (S.T.S.) 143 My spreit rejoysis gretumlie. **1568** Skeyne *The Pest* (1860) 31 The oile of Scorpionis.. supportis greitumlie. **1588** A. King tr. *Canisius' Catech.* 109 S. Cyprian in this respect commends grytumlie S. Cornelius Pap and Martyr. **1637-50** Row *Hist. Kirk* (Wodrow Soc.) 9 Whilk speeches made the people glade, and confirmed the Master of the schoole..and all these that had any knowledge of the trueth greatumlie.

great-uncle: see great *a.* 21 a.

†**great-willy,** *a. Obs.*[−1] [f. *great will* (see great *a.* 4) + -y[1].] High-spirited, strong-willed, proud.

1382 Wyclif *Judg.* v. 15 Ruben aȝens hym diuydide, of greet willi [**1388** greet hertyd] men is foundun stryuynge.

†**greatwort.** *Obs.* [OE. *grēate wyrt* 'thick plant': see great *a.* 2 and wort.]

a. In OE., some bulbous plant = L. *hieribulbus*. **b.** In ME., Elecampane, *Inula Helenium*.

c **1000** *Sax. Leechd.* I. 118 Ðeos wyrt þe man hieribulbum and oðrum naman greate wyrt nemneþ. *c* **1265** *Voc. Plants* in Wr.-Wülcker 554/12 *Elna enula*, ialne, gretwurt.

†**greave**[1]. *Obs.* Forms: 4-7 greve, 6-7 **greave**, (4 *Sc.* grewe, 6 *pl.* grevous, *Sc.* greis, graiwis, 7 greeve, grieve). [OE. *grǽfa* wk. masc. or *grǽfe* fem.:—prehistoric *graibjon-, f. *graibo- GROVE.]

1. a. (OE. only.) Brushwood. **b.** *pl.* Branches, twigs. (Used once by Drayton as *sing.*)

a **1000** *O.E. Chron.* an. 852 (Laud MS.) He scolde ȝife ilca ȝear in to þe minstre sixtiȝa foðra wuda and twælf foður græfan and sex foður ȝearda. *c* **1385** CHAUCER *L.G.W.* Prol. 159 Of silk I-broudede ful of grene grevys. *c* **1386** —— *Knt.'s T.* 649 To maken hym a gerland of the greues, Were it of wodebynde or hawethorn leues. **1501** DOUGLAS *Pal. Hon.* Prol. 22 The birdis sat on twystis and on greis. **1563** WINȜET *Wks.* (1890) II. 59 God forbid, I say, that in this spiritual paradise, of the graiwis [orig. L. *surculis*] of cannal and balme, fra hand spring wp guild and humlokis. **1567** TURBERV. *Ovid's Ep.* 27 How oft have we of grasse and greaves preparde a homely bedde? **1593** DRAYTON *Moses* II. 248 A swarming cast of Bees..Pressing each plant, and loading eu'ry greaue. **1612** —— *Poly-olb.* xiii. 215 Hid among the leaves, Some in the taller trees, some in the lower greaves.

2. A thicket.

c **1050** *Voc.* in Wr.-Wülcker 406/33 *Frondosis dumis*, þæm ȝehilmdum græfum. *c* **1100** *Ibid.* 517/36 *Per dumos*, þurh græfan. *c* **1200** ORMIN 9209 Whærse iss all unnsmeþe get þurrh bannkess & þurrh græfess. **13..** *Sir Tristr.* 14 Þis greues wexen al gray, þat in her time were grene. *c* **1374** CHAUCER *Troylus* v. 1144 By hedge, by tre, by greue. **1375** BARBOUR *Bruce* v. 13 All grewis begouth to spryng. *c* **1420** *Pallad. on Husb.* II. 149 Ther as wrecched greues [L. *misera virgulta*] Sour lond, to weet, or salt is, neuer delue. **1460** *Lybeaus Disc.* 551 A logge they dyghte of leves, In the grene greves. **1470-85** MALORY *Arthur* VI. xvi, There with al came oute syre phelot oute of the greuys sodenly. ?*c* **1475** *Hunt. Hare* 107 Yonder syttes [the hare] in a greyve. **1590** SPENSER *F.Q.* III. x. 42 It is best..that ye doe leave Your treasure.. Either fast closed in some hollow greave, Or buried in the ground from jeopardy. **1600** FAIRFAX *Tasso* III. vi. 40 The winde in houltes and shadie greaues A murmur makes, among the boughes and leaues. **1609** HOLLAND *Amm. Marcell.* XIX. viii. 134 We made speed through greves and groves [L. *per dumeta et silvas*] toward the high mountains.

greave[2] (griːv). Chiefly *pl.* Forms: *pl.* 4 grayvez, grevez, 5 greves, grevys, *Sc.* greis, 6-7 graves, 7 greeves, greves, 6- **greaves**. *sing.* 6- **greave**, (6 greve, 7 grieve). [a. OF. *greve* shin, armour for the legs (12th c. in Littré), of unknown origin; cf. Sp. *grebas*, *grevas* (Minsheu).]

1. Armour for the leg below the knee.

13.. *Gaw. & Gr. Knt.* 575 His legez lapped in stel with luflych greuez. *c* **1425** WYNTOUN *Cron.* IX. viii. 847 Cusseis or greis or braseris. **1463** *Mann. & Househ. Exp.* (Roxb.) 215 To Cakebrede ffor a harneyse complet, ssave salatt and grevys, v. marc. **1557** GRIMALD in *Tottell's Misc.* (Arb.) 122 Zoroas..The carelesse king there smote, aboue the greaue, At thopening of his quishes. **1603** DRAYTON *Bar. Wars* II. xi, Marching in Greaves, a Helmet on her Head. **1622** F. MARKHAM *Bk. Warre* V. ii. 166 From the close Caske downe to the Greaue. **1671** MILTON *Samson* 1119 Put on..thy broad habergeon, Vaunt-brass and greves, and gauntlet, and thy spear. **1715-20** POPE *Iliad* XVIII. 707 The greaves of ductile Tin. **1813** BYRON *Br. Abydos* II. ix, The greaves below his knee that wound With silvery scales were sheathed and bound. **1832** TENNYSON *Lady of Shalott* III. 4 The sun came dazzling thro' the leaves, And flamed upon the brazen greaves Of bold Sir Lancelot. **1873** SYMONDS *Grk. Poets* v. 133 The burnished brazen greaves that hang upon the wall.

†**2.** The part of the leg on which the greave is worn; the shin, leg. *Obs.*

1600 *New Yr.'s Gift* in Nichols *Progr. Q. Eliz.* (1823) III. 474 A slender greve swifter than roe.

3. *Comb.*, as ***greave-stud***.

1601 HOLLAND *Pliny* XXII. xxii, A grieve-stud or leg harneis-naile.

†**greave**[3]. *Obs.*[−1] [ad. F. *grève*: see GRAVEL.] The sandy shore of a river.

1579 FENTON *Guicciard.* II. (1599) 80 The french men forbare not to march, partly upon the breach or greaue of the riuer, partly by the skirts or stretching out of the bancke.

greave, obs. form of GRAVE, GRIEF, GRIEVE *v.*

greaved (griːvd), *a.* [f. GREAVE *sb.*[2] + -ED[2].] Furnished with greaves.

[**1848** BUCKLEY *Iliad* 75 Exhorting the well-greaved Greeks to fight.] **1894** *Q. Rev.* CLXXVIII. 341 Those who have come forward thus light-heartedly bucklered and greaved.

transf. **1865** E. BURRITT *Walk to Land's End* 342 Bold headlands that stood greaved with granite.

greaves, graves (griːvz, greɪvz), *sb. pl.* Also 7 graives, 9 *dial.* groves. [app. originally a term of the whale fisheries; ad. LG. *greven* pl. (whence Sw. dial. *grevar*, Da. *grever*), corresp. to OHG. *griubo*, *griobo* (MHG., G. *griebe*), which agrees in form with OE. *gréoua* (= *gréofa) 'olla'.] The fibrous matter or skin found in animal fat, which forms a sediment on melting and is pressed into cakes to serve as meat for dogs or hogs, fish-bait, etc.; the refuse of tallow; cracklings.

1614 G. MARKHAM *Cheape & Good Husb.* 97 Chandlers Graiues [*printed* Graines], which is the dregges and offall of rendred Tallow, as hard skinnes, kels, and fleshly lumpes. **1631** PELLHAM *Mirac. Perserv. Englishm. Greenland* 14 Lading this other Shallop..with the Graves of the Whales that had beene there boyled this present yeare. **1673** MARVELL *Reh. Transp.* II. Wks. II. 283 It was observed that he was wont still to put more graves than all the rest in his porridge. **1735** LEDIARD *Naval Hist.* 521 They [had] to feed on mouldy Frittars and Greaves of Whales. **1740** R. BROOKES *Art of Angling* I. xxii. 59 Graves, to be had at the Tallow-Chandlers for a Ground-Bait. **1770-4** A. HUNTER *Georg. Ess.* (1804) VI. 229 A farmer in Surrey used graves from the Tallow-Chandlers, with very great success on sandy soil. **1844** J. T. HEWLETT *Parsons & W.* xxi, A cake of greaves. **1867** F. FRANCIS *Angling* xiv. (1880) 500 Greaves or Scratchings is the refuse skin, etc., from the tallow-melters. **1893** *Northumbld. Gloss.*, *Greaves, Groves*, tallow-chandler's refuse. **1894** *Times* 30 July 6/2 Roach are taking gentles, barbel lobworms, greaves, and gentles.

greavie, greavy, obs. forms of GRAVY.

greaze, obs. form of GREASE *v.*

grebe (griːb). Also 8 griebe, greb. [a. F. *grèbe*, of unknown origin]

1. The name for the diving birds of the genus *Podiceps* or family *Podicipedidæ*, characterized by a short body, flattened and lobed feet set far behind, and the almost entire absence of tail.

(**great**) **crested grebe**, the largest European species, *Podiceps cristatus*. **eared g.**, *P. nigricollis*. **Slavonian** or **horned g.**, *P. auritus* (or *cornutus*). **little g.**, the Dabchick or Didapper, *P. pluviatilis* (or *minor*). **spear-billed** or **western g.**, the *Æchmophorus occidentalis* of North America.

1766 PENNANT *Zool.* (1768) II. 393 *note*, The Grebes and Divers are placed in the same genus. **1773** *Gentl. Mag.* XLIII. 219 The crested Griebe. **1814** COL. HAWKER *Diary* (1893) I. 92, I got..18 ox-birds and 1 dusky grebe. **1863** *Spring Lapland* 36, I fancy they confounded it [the smew] with the red-necked grebe. **1863** BARING-GOULD *Iceland* 327 Neither M. Preyer nor Mr. Fowler found the little grebe in the island. **1873** G. C. DAVIES *Mount. & Mere* iii. 18 That upright, stick-like object moving along the surface is the neck and head of a great crested grebe, swimming low in the water to escape observation.

2. The plumage of the grebe.

1859 W. H. GREGORY *Egypt* I. 260, I secured the pad of the breast, which was as soft as grebe. **1899** *Westm. Gaz.* 26 Oct. 3/2, I want everybody who owns a brown cloth costume to trim it with grebe.

3. *attrib.*, as ***grebe-feathers***, ***-hat***, ***-muff***, ***-plumage***, ***-skin***; **grebe-cloth**, a cotton cloth with a downy surface on one side.

1882 CAULFEILD & SAWARD *Dict. Needlework*, **Grebe Cloth*, a cotton cloth, made very much in the style of Swanskin. **1781** S. E. BURNEY in *Mad. D'Arblay's Early Diary* (1889) II. 267 Part of the trimming is composed of *greb feathers. **1885** *Daily Tel.* 22 Dec. 6/2 Protective Acts have almost banished from the markets the sea-gull and *grebe hats which were once so common. **1887** *Pall Mall G.* 9 Aug. 5/1 Some years ago, when *grebe muffs were 'the rage', that rage nearly extinguished a beautiful race of birds. **1781** MAD. D'ARBLAY *Let. to Mrs. Thrale* 11 Jan., The [dress].. is to be trimmed with *grebeskins and gold. **1882** O'DONOVAN *Merv Oasis* I. 312 Here, at all times of the day, hemp, silk, cotton, tobacco, and grebe skins are to be seen.

greble, obs. form of GRIBBLE, crab tree.

grebyche, -bytch, vars. GREYBITCH *Obs.*

grecale, variant of GREGALE.

†'**Grecan**, *a.* and *sb.* *Obs.* Also grekin. [? ad. med.L. *Græcān-us, f. *Græcus* GREEK.]

A. *adj.* Grecian, Greek. **B.** *sb.* A Greek.

a **1400-50** *Alexander* 5504 A grete glauir & a glaam of grekin tongis. **1422** tr. *Secreta Secret, Priv. Priv.* (E.E.T.S.) 122 Olde bokis of the grecanys. *Ibid.* 129 The grecanys (or grekis, whych you semyth beste Englyshe).

†**Gre'canic**, *a.* *Obs.* [ad. L. *Græcānic-us*, f. *Græc-us* GREEK.] Of or pertaining to Greece, the Greeks, or their language. So †**Gre'canical** *a.*

1601 HOLLAND *Pliny* II. 596, I must not forget one kind of pauing more, which is called Grecanicke. **1669** GALE *Crt. Gentiles* I. II. ii. 15 O in women is the Grecanic termination; as Dido. **1678** *Ibid.* IV. III. i. 21 The Grecanic terme whereby the efficacitie of Divine concurse is expressed in the Scriptures is ἐνέργεια. **1678** CUDWORTH *Intell. Syst.* I. iv. Contents §17 Orpheus, commonly called by the Greeks, The Theologer, and the Father of the Grecanick Polytheism. *Ibid.* 326 Casaubon..affirms all the Philosophy ..to be merely Platonical and Grecanical but not at all Egyptian.

†'**Grecanize**, *v.* *Obs.* [f. as GRECAN + -IZE. Cf. GERMANIZE.] = GRECIANIZE.

1611 COTGR., *Grecanizant*, Grecanizing, or Grecianizing it; speaking Greeke; imitating a Grecian. **1740** WARBURTON *Div. Legat.* IV. §5 II. 222 This quaint Improvement on an Egyptian Blunder, by some driveling grecanized [*ed.* 1788 Greek] Mythologist.

Grecaster: see GRÆCASTER.

grece (griːs). *Obs.* exc. *dial.* Forms: α. 4-6 grese, 4-8 greece, 4-9 **greese**, (6 greesse, greysse, greis(s, 6-8 gresse, 7 grees, greice), 4-9 **greece**. β. 5-6 **gryse**, 6-7 grice, grise, 6-9 griece, (7 griese, grize). [a. OF. *grez*, *greyz*, *greis*, pl. of *gré* GREE *sb.*[1], taken as a collective sing. in sense of 'flight of steps, staircase'; contemporaneously a double plural *greces*, *greeses* was formed and used with the meaning 'flight of steps' and 'steps in a flight'; whence in the 15th c. a sing. form *grece* was deduced (sense 2 c).]

1. A flight of stairs or steps; a stairway.

α. *a* **1300** *Cursor M.* 10584 (Gött.) A grece þer was of steppis fiftene. **13..** *E.E. Allit. P.* B. 1590 Glydes doun by þe grece & gos to þe kyng. **1382** WYCLIF *Ezek.* xl. 6 He stiede vp by the greese therof. **1449** in Willis & Clark *Cambridge* (1886) II. 10 Thei shull make the Rofes..with all the Midilwalles and the greses to the seid houses perteyning. **1509** HAWES *Past. Pleas.* (Percy Soc.) 16 A grece there was, y-chesyled all of stone Out of the rocke. *a* **1533** LD. BERNERS *Huon* xxxviii. 119 He mountyd upe the grese of the palayes. **1622** BACON *Hen. VII*, Mor. & Hist. Wks. (Bohn) 431 The lord archbishop, upon the greece of the quire, made a long oration. **1777** HOOLE *Comenius' Vis. World* (ed. 12) 86 They go up into the upper stories by greeses, and winding-stairs. **1869** J. P. MORRIS *Gloss. Furness*, *Grece*, the inclined way to a barn or granary, when built over a shippon or stable. **1882** *Lanc. Gloss.*, *Greese*, stairs, steps.

β. *c* **1475** *Partenay* 1427 On grice went vp, the kyng on bed thay founde. **1481-90** *Howard Househ. Bks.* (Roxb.) 122 He schal..make the gryse as my Lord wyll desyre yt. **1674** RAY *N.C. Words* 22 Grees or Griece, Stairs.

fig. **1549** COVERDALE, etc. *Erasm. Par. Heb.* 11 That lawe ..was geuen for a season, to thentente it shoulde be a certaine griece or stayre to bring vs at the length to a better hope. **1587** *Mirr. Mag.*, *K. Rudacke* vii, Ambition out sercheth to glory the greece.

2. a. *pl.* Steps or stairs (collectively); a set or flight of stairs; = sense 1.

c **1340** *Cursor M.* 10588 (Laud) This may but of iij^e yere old Went on the grecys [*other MSS.* grece, grees] I ere of told. *a* **1400-50** *Alexander* 332 Gase him doune be þe grecis a-gayn fra þe sale. *c* **1440** *Generydes* 1531 Downne of the greses he felle the hede before, And brake his nek. **1463** *Bury Wills* (Camden) 20 The litil botrie vndir the gresys. **1527** ANDREW *Brunswyke's Distyll. Waters* Bij, And the panne shal be set upon a hye steyre or gryses. **1557** N. T. (Genev.) *Acts* xxi. 35 When he came vnto the greces, he was borne of the souldiers, for the violence of the people.

b. *pl.* Steps or stairs (in a flight); *spec.* in *Her.* with the spelling **grieces** (whence GRIECED *a.*).

α. *c* **1400** MAUNDEV. (1839) vi. 70 At the right syde, as men comen dounward 16 Greces. *c* **1450** *Mirour Saluacioun* 1161 Salomones Throne was with sex greces exaltate. **1533** WRIOTHESLEY *Chron.* (1875) I. 21 A table sett at the upper ende of the hall, going upp twelve greeses. **1681** KEEPE *Monum. Westm.* (1682) 31 Ascending from this Picture by two or three Greeses or steps, until you come to the Rails that compass in the High Altar.

β. **1549** THOMAS *Hist. Italie* 30 Certayn skaffoldes of borde, with grices or steppes one aboue an other. **1566** in Peacock *Eng. Ch. Furniture* (1866) 81 The steers or gryses coming vpp to the altare. **1603** B. JONSON *K. Jas.' Entertainm. Fenchurch* 108 The daughters of the Genius..in a spreading ascent, upon severall grices, help to beautifie both the sides. **1610** GUILLIM *Heraldry* IV. ix. (1611) 212 A crosse crossed, mounted upon three grieces. **1681** COTTON *Wond. Peak* (ed. 4) 79 Fair round Stairs, some fifteen grieses high Land you upon a Terrass. **1688** R. HOLME *Armoury* III. 459/2 A pillar mounted on Grices or Stepps. **1869** CUSSANS *Her.* (1893) 116 *Grieces*, steps or Degrees.

transf. and *fig.* **1380** WYCLIF *Wks.* (1880) 420 þey gon not to heuene bi greesis þat god haþ ordeyned to lede þidur. **1540** MORYSINE *Vives' Introd. Wysd.* Pref. A v b, The steppes and grices, wherby..my lord your father..hathe clymed to nobilitie. **1606** J. RAYNOLDS *Dolarney's Prim.* (1880) 64 Phœbus..Climbing the lofty gresses of the skies. **1611** SPEED *Hist. Gt. Brit.* IX. viii. §46 Neither is the Popes reuenge thus appeased, some higher greeces yet remaine, on which his Greatnesse..must display it selfe. **1625** W. MORRELL *New Eng.* in *Ferdinando Gorges* (Prince Soc., Boston) 129 Whose hayre is cut with greeces, yet a locke Is left [cf. **1565** COOPER *Thesaurus*, *Comam in gradus frangere*, to turne or set the heare in facion of greeses].

c. *sing.* A single step or stair in a flight.

α. **1448** *Will of Hen. VI* in Willis & Clark *Cambridge* (1886) I. 355, vj. grecis to be before the high auter, with the grece called *gradus chori*. **1491** CAXTON *Vitas Patr.* (W. de W. 1495) I. xlvii. 87 b/2 The deuyll threwe her downe from the hyghest grece to the loweste. **1549** LATIMER *2nd Serm. bef. Edw. VI* (Arb.) 67 The top of the ladder, or first greese. **1607** COWELL *Interpr.* s.v. *Constable*, Staffel in their language signifieth a grees or steppe of a paire of staires. **1641** PRYNNE *Antip.* I. i. 26 Upon the third or fourth Greice of those steps he was slaine.

β. **1559** *Will of Sir R. Tyson* (Somerset Ho.), The lowest Grice of the Alter. **1604** SHAKS. *Oth.* I. iii. 200 Let me..lay a Sentence, Which as a grise, or step may helpe these Louers. **1640** SOMNER *Antiq. Canterb.* 166 The third or fourth griece or step of the Pulpitum.

fig. **1601** SHAKS. *Twel. N.* III. i. 135 *Vio.* I pittie you. *Ol.* That's a degree to loue. *Vio.* No not a grize: for tis a vulgar proofe That verie oft we pitty enemies. **1607** —— *Timon* IV. iii. 16 Euerie grize of Fortune Is smooth'd by that below. **1636** FEATLY *Clavis Myst.* li. 720 How low must the descent be where humility is the uppermost greece.

3. *attrib.* ***grece-head***, the top of a flight of stairs.

1556 *Richmond. Wills* (Surtees) 91 The lytyll chamber at the greisshedde. **1559** *Ibid.* 123 One standing bed stede being in the grecehed chamer. **1583** in *Ripon Ch. Acts* 380 In the chamber over grese head. **1876** *Whitby Gloss.*, *Grees-heead*, the stair-head.

grece, obs. f. GRASS, GREASE, GREEK; pl. of GREE *sb.*[1] and [3]; variant of GRIS *sb.* and *a.* *Obs.*

grecelled, obs. form of GRIZZLED *a.*

Grecian ('griːʃ(ɪ)ən), *a.* and *sb.* Also 6 Grecien, Grecyon, Grætian, Gretian, 6-8 Græcian. [f. L. *Græci-a* Greece + -AN. Cf. OF. *grecien.*]

A. *adj.* **1. a.** Of or pertaining to Greece or its inhabitants; characteristic of the Greeks; resembling what is Greek; Greek. Now *rare* exc. with reference to style of architecture and facial outline.

1577 KENDALL *Flowers of Epigr.* 98 Doest muse with skill of Grecian tongue, how Ladie Iane was fraight. As sone as euer she was borne she was a Grecian straite. **1585** T. WASHINGTON tr. *Nicholay's Voy.* II. xxiv. 65 b, If..a Græcian woman [do marry] with a Perot Franco. **1596** SHAKS. *Merch. V.* v. i. 5 In such a night Troilus..sigh'd his soule toward the Grecian tents Where Cressed lay that night. **1667** MILTON *P.L.* IV. 212 Great Seleucia, built by Grecian kings. **1674** JOSSELYN *Voy. New Eng.* 181 No trading for a stranger with them, but with a Grecian faith, which is not to part with your ware without ready money. **1712** ADDISON *Spect.* No. 287 ¶10 So different are the Genius's which are formed under Turkish Slavery and Grecian Liberty. **1756–7** tr. *Keysler's Trav.* (1760) II. 452 It consists of three arches, and is of Grecian marble. **1797** MRS. RADCLIFFE *Italian* i. (1826) 5 Her features were of the Grecian outline. **1838** THIRLWALL *Greece* II. 157 The period when Grecian history begins to be genuine and connected. **1847** TENNYSON *Princ.* Prol. 225 A Gothic ruin and a Grecian house. **1866** E. MASSON tr. *Winer's Gram. N.T. Diction* p. vi, Hellenic..is the Attic Dialect, as modified in Athens itself, from the reign of Alexander the Great,—the period of its becoming the language of the educated throughout the Grecian world.

b. In specialized collocations: **Grecian bend**, an affected carriage of the body, in which it is bent forward from the hips; †**Grecian calends** (see CALENDS 3 b); **Grecian coil** (see quot. 1966); **Grecian curve** = *Grecian bend*; †**Grecian dog** [misinterpretation of GREW-HOUND], a greyhound; **Grecian fire**, (*a*) = Greek fire (see FIRE *sb.* 8 b); (*b*) a kind of firework; **Grecian horse**, the wooden horse by means of which Troy was captured; **Grecian knot**, a method of dressing women's hair in imitation of the ancient Greek fashion; **Grecian leather, netting** (see quots.); **Grecian nose**, one that is straight and continues the line of the forehead; **Grecian plait**, an elaborate plait of hair made from about thirteen strands; **Grecian slipper**, a shop name for a soft slipper cut low at the side; **Grecian splice** *Naut.* (see quot. 1883).

1821 *Etonian* No. 8 (1822) II. 219 In person he was of the common size, with something of the *Grecian bend, contracted doubtless from sedentary habits. **1869** *Daily Tel.* 1 Sept. 3/3 Some [girls] affect what is called the 'Grecian bend'. **1886** *Cornhill Mag.* Dec. 618 He likes a smart young woman with a Grecian bend. **1806** MOORE *Devil among Schol.* 66 He..never paid a bill or balance Except upon the *Grecian Kalends. **1874** C. M. YONGE *Lady Hester* v. 115 Her black hair in the *Grecian coil we used to wear. **1966** J. S. COX *Illustr. Dict. Hairdressing* 66 *Grecian coil*, a kind of spiral roll by which the front hair on either side of a middle parting is brought forward onto the forehead and from the forehead rolled spirally towards the ears. **1846** J. G. SAXE *Progress* (1847) 18 'She stoops to conquer' in a '*Grecian curve'. **1607** TOPSELL *Four-f. Beasts* (1658) 114 Among the divers kinds of hunting Dogs, the Gray-hound or *Grecian Dog..deserveth the first place. **1774** WARTON *Hist. Eng. Poetry* (1840) I. 161 This *fyr Gregeys*, or *Grecian fire, seems to be a composition belonging to the Arabian chemistry. **1833** MARRYAT *P. Simple* (1863) 51 Blue lights and Catherine-wheels, mines and bombs, Grecian-fires and Roman-candles. **1847** CRAIG, *Grecian-fire*. **1802** A. HAMILTON *Wks.* (1886) VII. 244 To admit foreigners indiscriminately to the rights of citizens..would be nothing less than to admit the *Grecian horse into the citadel of our liberty and sovereignty. **1931** *Queen* 25 Feb. 38/1 Little twists of hair, *Grecian knots and thick, soft plaits that clip on the back of the head..can be obtained very cheaply. **1852** MORFIT *Tanning & Currying* (1853) 369 Buffalo, or '*Grecian leather'. This leather is made of buffalo-skins, and differs from other kinds in being tanned with myrtle-leaves instead of oak-bark. **1882** CAULFIELD & SAWARD *Dict. Needlework* 360 *Grecian Netting, used for purses when worked with fine silks, and for curtains and toilet cloths when worked with knitting cotton. **1830** T. E. HOOK *Maxwell* viii, A beautiful girl,..—Italian eyes—*Grecian nose. **1873** L. TROUBRIDGE *Life amongst Troubridges* (1966) ii. 8 She has..a very good long, straight Grecian nose. *c* **1845** C. BRONTË *Professor* (1857) II. xix. 58 Her plenteous brown hair arranged in smooth bands on her temples, and in a large *Grecian plait behind. **1851** *Ladies' Compan. & Monthly Mag.* July 266/2 The 'Grecian' plait, and the 'basket' or 'chain plait', and the 'cable plait', are repeated again and again in various forms. **1968** J. IRONSIDE *Fashion Alphabet* 188 *Plait..Grecian*, a more complicated version of the braid. **1926–7** *Army & Navy Stores Catal.* 654/1 Red, blue or brown leather *Grecian Slippers, with heels. **1953** J. W. JOHNSON in J. H. Thornton *Textbk. Footwear Manuf.* IX. 520 The Grecian slipper usually has a folded or bagged edge and orthodox methods of closing are employed. **1970** *Harrods Christmas Catal.* 15/3 Grecian slipper with shiny patent stripes. 87/-..Man's Shop, ground floor. **1883** *Man. Seamanship for Boys* 124 A *Grecian Splice [description follows]. *Ibid.* 125 There is also another way to make a Grecian splice, by making all the yarns into foxes, leaving no heart... This splice is also used for tailing a smaller to a larger size rope, when it has to travel through a block. **1944** C. W. ASHLEY *Bk. Knots* 434/2 (*heading*) The Grecian Shroud Splice.

†**2.** Belonging to the Greek Church. *Obs. rare.*

a **1600** HOOKER *Eccl. Pol.* VI. iv. §10 Grecian catholic bishops.

B. *sb.*

1. a. A native or inhabitant of Greece; a Greek. *Obs.* or *arch.*

1547 BORDE *Introd. Knowl.* xxi. 176 Except he be a lord or a Grecyon. **1571** DIGGES *Pantom.* IV. Pref. Tj, The Romanes and other Latin writers..haue not shamed to borrow of the Gretians these and many other termes of arte. **1601** SHAKS. *All's Well* I. iii. 75 Was this faire face the cause, quoth she, Why the Grecians sacked Troy? **1697** POTTER *Antiq. Greece* III. i. (1715) 1 The Wars of the ancient Grecians. **1727** DE FOE *Syst. Magic* I. ii. (1840) 41 The great Egyptian Thebes, a city much more ancient than the nation of the Grecians. **1817** BYRON *Beppo* xi, Black eyes, arch'd brows, and sweet expressions still; Such as of old were copied from the Grecians.

allusively. **1773** GRAVES *Spirit. Quixote* XI. xiv. (1783) III. 230 A well-booted Grecian [cf. ἐϋκνήμιδες Ἀχαιοί Hom. *Il.* I. 17] in a fustian frock and jockey cap.

b. [tr. Gr. Ἑλληνιστής.] A Jew of the Dispersion who spoke Greek; a Grecian Jew; = HELLENIST 1.

1611 BIBLE *Acts* vi. 1 There arose a murmuring of the Grecians [*R.V.* Grecian Jews] against the Hebrewes. **1831** E. BURTON *Eccl. Hist.* ii. (1845) 48 The Grecians were those foreign Jews, who since the captivity had lived in great numbers in different countries, and generally spoke Greek as the prevailing language. **1860** TRENCH *Serm. Westm. Abb.* viii. 82 A 'Greek' is a Gentile.. ; but a 'Grecian' is a Jew, quite as much a Jew, as truly as the stock of Abraham, as the Hebrew; and with only the difference that..he, or his fathers before him, had unlearned the Hebrew tongue and spake the Greek language.

2. a. One learned in the Greek language; a Greek scholar.

1557 NORTH tr. *Gueuara's Diall Pr.* 190 a/2 He became a great Gretian and latinest. **1577** HELLOWES *Gueuara's Chron.* 75 Adrian being so great a Grecian..compounded certaine workes in Heroicall Metre. **1577** [See A. 1]. **1612** BRINSLEY *Lud. Lit.* 239 All painfull students would be found to profit exceedingly, and to become rare Grecians in a little time. **1677** HALE *Prim. Orig. Man.* To Rdr. 4, I was a better Grecian in the 16th than in the 66th year of my life. **1705** HEARNE *Collect.* 10 July (O.H.S.) I. 3 One of the Græcians of Glocester Hall. **1790** COWPER *Lett.* 30 Apr., I know him [Dr. Madan] to be a rare old Grecian. **1817** W. IRVING in *Life & Lett.* (1864) I. 360 He is a great favorite of Doctor Parr, and is very anxious to make me acquainted with that formidable old Grecian. **1890** MARGOLIOUTH *Ecclus. in Semitic Lit.* 14 The great Grecian, whose recent death closes the most brilliant period of Greek scholarship in this century, Prof. Cobet, of Leyden.

b. A boy in the highest class at Christ's Hospital (the Blue-coat School).

1820 LAMB *Ess.* Ser. I. *Christ's Hosp.*, The young men.. who, under the denomination of Grecians, were waiting the expiration of the period when they should be sent, at the charges of the Hospital, to one or other of our Universities. **1851** MAYHEW *Lond. Labour* (1861) I. 217 The two brothers ..were both scholars of Christ's Hospital. They were second Grecians, and might have gone to college.

†**3.** A member of the Greek Church. *Obs.*

1547 BORDE *Introd. Knowl.* xx. 173 The Greciens do erre & swere in mani articles concerning our fayth. *a* **1600** HOOKER *Eccl. Pol.* VI. iv. §9 The Grecians' canon for some one presbyter in every church to undertake the charge of penitency..continued in force for the space of about two hundred years. **1635** PAGITT *Christianogr.* I. i. (1636) 30 The Papists, under the Pope of Rome, The Grecians, under the Patriarch of Constantinople. **1766** ENTICK *London* IV. 404 A chapel..where the Grecians perform divine service.

4. *slang.* An Irishman: = GREEK *sb.* 6.

1853 J. GARWOOD *Million-peopled City* 303 The descendants [of the Irish immigrants] are called 'Irish Cockneys', and the new-comers are called 'Grecians'. **1879** J. BRITTEN in *N. & Q.* 5th Ser. XII. 147 In many places —e.g. London, Liverpool, and Manchester—young Irishmen, on their first arrival in England, are known as Grecians.

Grecianize ('griːʃ(ɪ)ənaɪz), *v.* [f. prec. + -IZE.] †**a.** *intr. to Grecianize it*: (see quot. 1611). *Obs.* **b.** *trans.* To render Grecian. Hence '**Grecianized**, '**Grecianizing** *ppl. adjs.*

1611 COTGR., *Grecizer*, to Grecianize it; to play the Grecian; or to speak Greek. **1884** *Edin. Rev.* Apr. 459 All the attempts of the dominant party to Grecianise the people failed. **1893** F. ADAMS *New Egypt* 67 When..the Grecianised Macedonian barbarians fell upon the East. **1897** *Daily News* 1 Sept. 6/2 Apollo is a Grecianized form of the Sanscrit Apa-var-yan. **1898** E. S. WALLACE *Jerus. the Holy* xv. 297 The Grecianizing influences that were alienating the people from their pure Jehovah worship.

grecing ('griːsɪŋ). *Obs.* exc. *dial.* Also 5–6 **gresyng**, 6 **grees-**, **gres(s-**, **griessing**, 7 **gresin**, **grison**, 7, 9 *dial.* **grissens**. [f. GRECE *sb.* + -ING[1].] Chiefly *pl.* Steps in a flight; flights of steps; stairs. Rarely *sing.* A step; also, ? a flight of steps (quot. *c* 1500).

A flight of stone steps at Lincoln is called 'The *Grecian* stairs'; the appellation (which is mentioned in 1724 by Stukeley *Itin. Curios.* I. 84) is prob. a corruption of *grecing*. At York also a flight of steps called 'The Grecian steps' is said formerly to have existed.

c **1400** MAUNDEV. (1839) xx. 220 Thei maken ther of Grecynges & Pileres. **1448–9** in Willis & Clark *Cambridge* (1886) II. 10 Tymber for gresynges and Midelwalles to the seides howses perteynyng. *c* **1500** in G. Peacock *Stat. Cambridge* (1841) App. A. 24 The Father of Dyvinite shall sytt in the myddys of the Gresynge before the Hyghe Auter. **1549** LATIMER *6th Serm. bef. Edw. VI* (Arb.) 170 Ther is an other way to go doune, by gressinges. **1563–83** FOXE *A. & M.* II. 1960/1 Makyng their prayers at the gresings they so proceeded into the stalles. **1673** *Yorks. Dial.* 42 (E.D.S. No. 76) 112 Hee stack his Schackfork up i' th' Esins, An' tuke his Jerkin of o' th' Gresins. **1674–91** RAY *N.C. Words* s.v. *Grees*, In Norfolk they call them *Grissens*. **1787** W. MARSHALL *Norfolk* (1795) II. 380 *Grissons*. **1847–89** HALLIWELL, *Greesings*..Still in use, pronounced *grissens*.

fig. **1654** H. L'ESTRANGE *Chas. I* Pref. (1655) A ij, Some.. who..should not have been permitted, so much as to step over the threshold of Gods house, were notwithstanding advanced to the highest grison of Church Dignities? *Ibid.* 118 An abomination whose every grison and step should we climbe, we shall not be able in the hole Repertory of Fame to finde its parallel.

Grecism, Grecize, Greco-: see GRÆC-.

Greckes, obs. pl. form of GREEK.

‖'**Greco.** *Obs.* [It. = GREEK.]

1. The north-east wind. (Cf. GREGALE.)

1555 EDEN *Decades* 185 Passynge by the lyne of the Diameter where the compasse makethe the difference of saylynge by the wynde cauled *Greco*, (that is North East) and *Magistral*, (that is south west).

2. A kind of wine.

1644 EVELYN *Diary* 29 Nov., From hence, we went to taste some rare Greco. **1645** *Ibid.* 7 Feb., Vineyards, where formerly grew the most incomparable Greco.

‖**Grecque** (grɛk). [In sense 1 F. *grecque*, fem. of *grec* GREEK.]

1. *Arch.* A Greek fret.

1836 MACGILLIVRAY tr. *Humboldt's Trav.* xix. 280 The edge is encircled by meanders, labyrinths, and grecques, with narrow lines variously combined. **1855** KINGSLEY *Westw. Ho!* xxv, A handsome earthen tube..painted with quaint grecques and figures of animals. **1887** *Athenæum* 23 Apr. 548/3 The basket-work of the Chilkaht Indians is superb..presenting all sorts of lovely designs in bands, crosses..and grecques.

2. A kind of coffee-strainer or 'percolator'; a coffee-pot fitted with such a strainer. ? *U.S.*

1864 in WEBSTER.

gredaline, variant of GRIDELIN.

gredde, pa. t. GREDE *v. Obs.*

†**grede**, *sb. Obs.* Forms: 3 **grade**, **gred.** [f. GREDE *v.* Cf. I-GREDE.] A cry; outcry; noise.

c **1250** *Gen. & Ex.* 3230 On moysen he setten a gred. 'Beð nu stille', quað moyses. *Ibid.* 3717 Ðis folc ðo sette up grot and gred. **13..** *K. Alis.* 5204 Michel was the pleynt and the grade That the folk hadden y-made. *Ibid.* 5470 Hy [olyfauntz] ne haue so mychel drade, Of nothing as of hogges grade.

†**grede**, *v. Obs.* Forms: 1 **grǽdan**, (*3rd pers. pres. ind.* **grǽt**), 2–3 **greden**, 3–4 (*3rd pers. pres. ind.* **gret**) **gred**, 3–5 **grede**, (3 **greade**, 4 **graden**, **gredyn**, **graide**, 5 **greyde**). *Pa. t.* 3–4 **gradde**, **gredde**, (3 **grædde**, 5 **grad**). *Pa. pple.* 3–4 **igrad**, 4 **ygrad**, **ygred**. [OE. *grǽdan*, of unknown origin; the resemblance in sound and sense with *grǽtan* GREET *v.*[2] is remarkable; in the 3rd pers. sing. pres. *grǽt* the two vbs. coincide.]

1. *intr.* To cry, cry out, shout; to wail.

c **1000** *Sax. Leechd.* II. 182 Hine mon sceal swiðe hlude hatan grædan oððe singan. *c* **1205** LAY 8634 Al þæt folc þe he lædde, lude hit grædde [*c* **1275** gradde]. *a* **1240** *Ureisun* in *Cott. Hom.* 199 Biuoren þine uote ich wulle liggen and greden. **1297** R. GLOUC. (Rolls) 9781 Loude gradde þe luþer kniȝt smiteþ alle to grounde. **13..** *K. Alis.* 2751 They of Thebes can graden, And for him gret deol maden. *c* **1330** *Florice & Bl.* (1857) 449 The maid al for drede Bigan to schricken an to grede. **1340** *Ayenb.* 56 Þe maȝe gret and zayþ [etc.]. *c* **1425** *Eng. Conq. Irel.* i. 4 Sho grad and cried as thogh he nam hir agaynes hir will. *c* **1450** *Cov. Myst.* (Shaks. Soc.) 361, I must nedys sore wepe and grede.

b. Said of birds; of the cock: To crow; etc.

c **897** K. ÆLFRED *Gregory's Past.* lxiii. 459 Ðonne græt se lareow swa swa kok on niht. *a* **1000** *Riddles* xxv. 3 (Gr.) Ic.. græde swa gos. *a* **1250** *Owl & Night.* 1149 Hwane þu havest a niht igrad, Men beoþ of þe wel sore ofdrad. *c* **1380** *Sir Ferumb.* 2804 Þow schalt him haue to-morwe or niȝt, þat þe cok hym graide. **1398** TREVISA *Barth. De P.R.* XII. Introd. (Tollem.MS.), Yf a crane leseþ his felawschipe he fleþ vp ful hyȝe and gredeþ and cryeþ.

c. with *cognate obj.* To utter (a cry), sing (a song).

13.. *K. Alis.* 2771 Mony foul crye was y-grad. **1387** TREVISA *Higden* (Rolls) I. 237 At nyȝt for drede Truly no song doþ he grede.

d. with quoted words, in direct or indirect speech.

c **1250** *Gen. & Ex.* 3585 Ðo gredde he lude, 'goð me to, Alle ðe god luuen so'. *c* **1250** *Kent. Serm.* in *O.E. Misc.* 33 Grede we to him Merci and sigge we him lord sauue us. **1297** R. GLOUC. (Rolls) 2665 He bigan to grede anon Nimeþ ȝoure sexes. **13..** *Life Jesu* (Horstm.) 628 Men gradden aboute þat þe spouse cam anon. *c* **1330** *King of Tars* 610 On Tirmagaunt he gon to grede..'Fy on ow everichon!' **1400–10** CLANVOWE *Cuckow & Night.* xxvii, For that skil 'ocy! ocy!' I grede. **1480** CAXTON *Chron. Eng.* cxcvii, The vileyns..grad on high, yelde yow, traytours, yelde yow.

2. With prepositions: To cry or call *after*, *on*, *upon*, *to*, *till* (a person), *after*, *upon* (a thing).

a **1225** *Ancr. R.* 244 Þe oðer deouel..gredde lude to Seinte Bartholomeu. *Ibid.* 284ȝif eni is þet naueð nout þe heorte þus afeited..grede on ure Louerd. *Ibid.* 330 Mid þus onwille halsunge, [she] weopeð & gret efter sume helpe. **1297** R. GLOUC. (Rolls) 1885 Deserites bigonne alle on him grede. *c* **1300** *Havelok* 2703 He cam driuende up-on a stede, And bigan til him to grede. **13..** *Guy Warw.* (A.) 3337 After Gij loude he gradde þo. **1340** *Ayenb.* 212 Þeruore ssolle we ofte grede to god þet he ous loki uram þo þieues. **1390** GOWER *Conf.* I. 336 She with him no reste hadde For ever upon her love he gradde. **1393** LANGL. *P. Pl.* C. x. 76 Gurles, that greden after fode. **14..** *Ps.* li. in *Pol. Rel. & L. Poems* 251 Aftur gostliche grace I grede. **1480** CAXTON *Chron. Eng.* cxcvii. 175 Sir Andrew ageyne grad vpon Syr thomas companye yolling as a wode wolf.

3. To announce with a loud voice; to proclaim, publish; to proclaim (a person) to be (something).

c **1305** *St. Dunstan* 101 in *E.E.P.* (1862) 37 He drof him out of Engelond: and let him grede fleme. **13..** *Guy Warw.* (A.) 805 A turnament he haþ don grede. *c* **1315** SHOREHAM 71 For erthe the banes y-gred He that the treuthe maketh. *Ibid.* 122 Wanne..pays [hys] i-grad for hyre love Of angeles in-place. **1460** *Lybeaus Disc.* (Kaluza) 771 For love of his lemman..He haþ do crie and grede; Who so bryngeþ a fairir oon, A gerfaucoun..He schall have to mede.

4. *trans.* To beg loudly for; to implore.

1340–70 *Alex. & Dind.* 606 Þei scholde hasteli ȝou here.. Whan ȝe greden ȝour grace to graunte ȝour wille. **1390** GOWER *Conf.* III. 16 Grace he gradde and grace he had.

5. To accuse *of* (a crime).

a **1450** *Le Morte Arth.* 1572 Thou, that hyr of treson gredys.

grede, obs. form of GREED; var. GREADE *Obs.*

gredel(le, obs. form of GIRDLE, GRIDDLE.

gredeline, variant of GRIDELIN.

gredely, obs. form of GREEDILY.

grederne, obs. form of GRIDIRON.

gredi(e, gredil(e, obs. ff. GREEDY, GRIDDLE.

gredi3, obs. form of GREEDY.

grediliche, -li(e, -like, -ly, obs. ff. GREEDILY.

† **greding**, *vbl. sb. Obs.* [f. GREDE *v.* + -ING[1].] Crying; outcry; wailing; supplication.

c **1275** LAY. 23564 þar was weping strong þar was gredinge a-mong. **1340** *Ayenb.* 212 Zuych gredinge cacheþ þe þyeues þet byeþ þe dyeulen þet ous wayteþ ous to robbi. **1398** TREVISA *Barth. De P.R.* XII. x. (1495) 420 Crowes token reyne with gredynge and cryenge. *a* **1400** *Jeremie's Tokens* (E.E.T.S.) 156 So longe þat þai..he[r] gredyng forberen.

grediren, -irne, -iron, obs. ff. GRIDIRON.

gredyl(e, -yly, obs. ff. GRIDDLE, GREEDILY.

gredyre, -yrne, -yron, obs. ff. GRIDIRON.

gree (griː), *sb.*[1] *Obs.* exc. *Sc.* Forms: *sing.* 4–6 gre, 4–9 gree, (6 graie), 6–7, 9 grie. *pl.* 4–6 greis, 5 grece, 4–7 grees, (5 greez, 6 gries); cf. GRECE. [a. OF. *gré* (pl. *greis, greyz*: see GRECE) = It., Sp. *grado*, Pg. *grao*:—L. *gradum* step. Cf. DEGREE, GRADE.]

† **1.** A step in an ascent or descent; one of a flight of steps; = DEGREE 1. In quots. 1303 and 1382, a flight of steps. *Obs.*

1303 R. BRUNNE *Handl. Synne* 1562 She was beryyde, as fyl to be, Be syde an auter before þe gre. **1382** WYCLIF *Neh.* viii. 4 Esdras scribe stod vpon a treene gree [**1388** the grees of tree], the whiche he hadde maad to speken in [**1388** theron]. *c* **1400** MAUNDEV. (Roxb.) viii. 31 By syde þe hie awter er iiii greez to gang vp at to þe toumbe of alabastre. *c* **1420** *Pallad. on Husb.* I. 463 Thre grees or iiij is up thereto to go. **1447** BOKENHAM *Seyntys* (Roxb.) 59 She stey up from gre to gree. **1483** CAXTON *Gold. Leg.* 73/2 A trone of yuorye ..whiche had vi grees or stappes. **1555–8** PHAER *Æneid* I. B ij b, The brasen grees afore the dores dyd mount. **1610** HOLLAND *Camden's Brit.* II. 25 One onely ascent by which hardly one by one can passe up, and that with a labour by grees or steps. **1693** J. WALLACE *Orkney* 44 Bishop Stewart enlarged it [the Cathedral Church] to the East, all above the Grees.

† **b.** *canticle* or *song of grees*: 'Song of Degrees', 'Gradual Psalm' (see GRADUAL *a.* 5). *Obs.*

1382 WYCLIF *Ps.* cxix. [cxx.] *heading*, The song of grees [**1388** greces]. *a* **1420** *Wyclif's Bible, Ps.* 2nd Prol., The canticlis of grees ben in noumbre of fiftene. **1483** CAXTON *Gold. Leg.* 273 b/2 Thou gauest to me syngyng the cantycle of grees sharpe arowes and cooles wastyng.

† **2.** *fig.* A step or stage in a process, etc., esp. one in an ascending or descending scale; = DEGREE 2. *Obs.*

a **1340** HAMPOLE *Psalter* cxix. 1 He herd me, settand me in greis of steghynge. *c* **1380** WYCLIF *Serm.* Sel. Wks. II. 269 þe grees of cunnynge and joie here must nedis passe. *c* **1420** *Pallad. on Husb.* IV. 471 Ther humour is ek erth and ayer wel warme, That fruyt to fruyt fro gre to gre succedith. *c* **1470** HENRYSON *Mor. Fab.* v. (Parl. Beasts) ii, It followis weill be ressoun naturall, And gre be gre, of richt comparisoun: Of euill cumis war, of war cumis werst of all. **1513** DOUGLAS *Æneis* VI. Prol. 97 As he tuichis greis seir in pane, In blis, elykwys sindry stagis puttis he. **1589** R. BRUCE *Serm.* (1843) 32 The first gree of preparation stands in contrition.

† **3.** A 'step' in direct line of descent; a degree of relationship; = DEGREE 3. *greis defendant* (Sc.): forbidden degrees. *Obs.*

c **1315** SHOREHAM 69 The sibbe mowe to-gadere nau3t The foerthe grees wythinne. *c* **1340** *Cursor M.* 1464 (Fairf.) Iareth þat was þe .v. gree [*Cott.* kne] fra Seth. **1387** TREVISA *Higden* (Rolls) I. 409 Nigh kyn þey wil bee þey he passe an hondred gree. *c* **1425** WYNTOUN *Cron.* IX. xxvii. 56 He and he Wes evynlike in topir Gre. **1535** STEWART *Cron. Scot.* II. 112 He him self wes narrest to thair croun, Fra Dioneth the fourt grie cuming doun. **1571** *Satir. Poems Reform.* xxvii. 100 Kin of Kingis discendit grie be gre. **1617** in Pitcairn *Crim. Trials Scot.* III. 424 He was within greis-defendant with the Hous of Bass.

† **4.** A stage or position in the scale of dignity or rank; relative social or official rank, grade, order, estate, or station; = DEGREE 4. In quot. 1450, a rank or class of persons. *Obs.*

13.. *S.E. Legendary* (MS. Bodl. 779) in *Archiv. Stud. neu. Spr.* LXXXII. 402/46 He ordeyned þat ech man þat prest wolde be scholde vndirfong þe ordres fro gre to gre—wit-oute lope & defaute þat þey I-taken were. **1382** WYCLIF *Gen.* xl. 13 Pharao..schal restore thee to the bifore had gree. *c* **1385** CHAUCER *L.G.W.* 1313 *Dido*, She..profreth him to be His thral, his servant in the leste gree. *c* **1440** *Promp. Parv.* 208/2 Gre, or worthynesse, *gradus*. *c* **1450** *St. Cuthbert* (Surtees) 4901 þai spared na elde na gre. *c* **1450** HOLLAND *Howlat* 407 All gretest of gre. **1493** *Festivall* (W. de W. 1515) 7 To understande all the grees Of ye worlde. **1520** *Caxton's Chron. Eng.* IV. 38/2 He ordeyned that he that was worthy sholde ascende gree by gree to his ordre, fyrst benet, than colet, subdecon, deacon, and than preest. *a* **1555** LYNDESAY *Tragedie* 47 Gre by gre, vpwarte I did ascende; Swa that in to this realme did neuer ryng So gret one man as I, vnder ane kyng. **1579** SPENSER *Sheph. Cal.* July 215 He is a shepheard great in gree. **1590** GREENE *Orl. Fur.* (1599) 50 Proude that thou art, I recke not of thy gree.

5. Pre-eminence; superiority; mastery; victory in battle; hence, the prize for a victory. *to bear, get, have, take, win the gree.* Now *Sc.*

1320–30 *Horn Ch.* 319 That day Horn the turnament wan ..He toke the gre, that was a swan. **13..** *Sir Beues* (E.) 3769 + 4 A turnement sche haþ don crye..for to see, What kny3t ys to han þe gree. *c* **1386** CHAUCER *Knt.'s T.* 1875 Duk Theseus leet crye, To stynten alle rancour and enuye, The gree as wel of o syde as of oother. **1393** LANGL. *P. Pl.* C. XXI. 103 The gree 3ut hath he geten for alle hus grete wondes. *c* **1450** HOLLAND *Howlat* 448 To James lord Douglas thow the gre gaif, To ga with the kingis hart. **1470–80** MALORY *Arthur* VI. vii, The gree was gyuen to kynge Bagdemagus. **1480** CAXTON *Chron. Eng.* cviii. 90 In this batayll..the gree of the felde [was] left with the danoys. **1513** DOUGLAS *Æneis* V. ii. 52 Quha best on fute can ryn lat se, To preif his pith, to wersill, and beir the gre. *a* **1578** LINDESAY (Pitscottie) *Chron. Scot.* XIX. ix. (1899) I. 198 Prayand to god that he micht haue that graie and victorie of him quha was his enemye. *a* **1605** in *Montgomerie's Poems* (1887) 274 The Muses wald have gevin the grie To her, as to the Aperse. **1686** G. STUART *Joco-ser. Disc.* 22 Of aw the pipers I did see, This piper Tony wan the 'gree. **1795** BURNS *For a' that and a' that* v, That sense and worth, o'er a' the earth, May bear the gree, and a' that. **1818** SCOTT *Hrt. Midl.* xxix, The Cu'ross hammermen have the gree for that. **1837** R. NICOLL *Poems* (1843) 91 Whether be it wark or play, The gree was wi' our auld gudeman. **1858** M. PORTEOUS *Souter Johnny* 29 Ower them a' for classic style It bears the gree.

† **6.** A degree, step, or grade in intensity or amount; = DEGREE 6. *Obs.*

c **1386** CHAUCER *Merch. T.* 131 Ther nys no thyng in gree superlatyf, As seith Senek, aboue an humble wyf. *c* **1400** *Rom. Rose* 5743 They nil, in no maner gree, Do right nought for charitee. **1460–70** *Bk. Quintessence* II. (1866) 22 þerfore þe feuere agu is þe posityue degree, and in þe superlatyue degree, comparatif gree and superlatif gree. **1552** LYNDESAY *Monarche* 6053 That Lantern of the Heuin Sall gyf more lycht, be greis sewin, Nor it gaue sen the warld began. **1563** WINSET *Four Score Thre Quest.* Wks. 1888 I. 68 We ar in mony greis of luue naturalie coniunit. —— *Wks.* (1890) II. 57 In al greis of aigis and tymes.

† **7.** In mediæval physics: = DEGREE 6 c. *Obs.*

1398 TREVISA *Barth. De P.R.* XVI. vii. (1495) 556 Quycke syluer as Plato sayth is hote and moyst in the fourth degree though some men deame that it is cold in the same gree. *c* **1400** *Lanfranc's Cirurg.* 86 In consideringe þe complexioun of al þe body..& þe gre of þe medicyn. **1547** BOORDE *Brev. Health* clv. 56 This fleume which is swete, gree for gree is hote and moyst lyke the ayer.

† **8.** An academical degree; = DEGREE 7 a. *Obs.*

c **1449** PECOCK *Repr.* I. xvi. 90 Y wolde grees of scolis to be take. **1494** FABYAN *Chron.* 3 By hym that neuer yet any ordre toke, Or gre of Scole, or sought for great cunnynge, This werk is gaderyd. **1508** DUNBAR *Flyting w. Polwart* 397, I sall degraid the, graceles, of thy greis.

† **9.** *Geom.* (*Astron.*, *Geog.*, etc.) The unit of the sexagesimal measurement of angles or circular arcs; = DEGREE 9.

1412–20 LYDG. *Chron. Troy* Prol. (1513) A 1 b, The tyme of yere, shortly to conclude When .xx. grees was phebus altitude. **1423** JAS. I. *Kingis Q.* xxi, Passit bot myd-day foure greis evin. **1426** *Pol. Poems* (Rolls) II. 140 The bulle.. twenty grees Entred was the hed of the dragoun. **1536** BELLENDEN *Cron. Scot., Descr. Alb.* xiii, The last and out-maist Ile is namit Hirtha; quhare the eleuatioun of the pole is lxiii greis.

gree (griː), *sb.*[2] Now *arch.* Also 4–6 gre. [a. OF. *gré, gred, gret* (11th c. in Littré), mod.F. *gré* pleasure, goodwill, will (cf. MAUGRE = *mal gré*) = Pr. *grat-z*, It., Sp., Pg. *grado*:—L. *grātum*, neut. subst. of *grātus* pleasing, grateful. The word was taken over into English chiefly in phrases (see the various senses).]

† **1.** Favour, goodwill. *Obs.*

a **1300** *Cursor M.* 1656 (Gött.) 3e eyth [= eight], for 3ou treu leute, Alone i haue granted mi gre [*Trin.* graunted gre, *Cott.* mi sagh(t)]. *c* **1400** *Sowdone Bab.* 2850 And [*read* God] graunte him gree and grith. **1590** SPENSER *F.Q.* II. iii. 5 But for in court gay portaunce he perceiv'd And gallant shew to be in greatest gree.

b. **in gree** (also *at, to gree*: cf. AGREE *adv.*, ENGREE): with goodwill or favour, with kindly feeling or pleasure, kindly, in good part. Chiefly in phr. *to take, accept, receive in gree.* [F. *prendre, recevoir, avoir en gré, servir à gré.*]

? *a* **1366** CHAUCER *Rom. Rose* 42 God graunte in gree that she it take For whom that it begonnen is! *c* **1374** —— *Troylus* II. 480 (529) My lowe confessioun Accepte in gre. *c* **1386** —— *Clerk's T.* 1095 Vs oghte Receyuen al in gree that god vs sent. *c* **1415** LYDG. *Temp. Glas* 1085 Boþe 3e and I mekeli most abide To take agre [*v.rr.* at gre, in gre]. *c* **1430** —— *Min. Poems* (Percy Soc.) 22 My simple makyng for to take at gree. **1481** CAXTON *Myrr.* I. xiv. 47 That after his deth..god receyueth hym in gree. *a* **1577** GASCOIGNE *De Profundis* Wks. (1831) 203 And thou (good God) vouchsafe in gree to take This woefull plaint. **1597–8** BP. HALL *Sat.* IV. ii. 85 Soone as he can kisse his hand in gree, And with good grace bow it below the knee. **1600** FAIRFAX *Tasso* x. x. 181 Accept in gree..the words I spoke. **1894** F. S. ELLIS *Reynard Fox* 230 A man should hold his friends in gre, And his foes hate but tardily.

c. *with* or *in good* (*goodly*) *gree*: with goodwill [F. *de bon gré*].

1542 UDALL *Erasm. Apopth.* 259 So ye graciousnesse of this prince tooke in good gree the eiuill wille of bothe the saied parties against hym. **1590** SPENSER *F.Q.* I. v. 16 Which she accepts with thankes and goodly gree. **1609** HOLLAND *Ammianus* XXVII. 313 Having..wrought the souldiers to accept thereof in good gree and willingly. **1885** BURTON *Arab. Nts.* (1887) III. 349 Replied the smith, 'With gladness and goodly gree'.

2. *to do* or *make gree*: to give satisfaction (for an injury). Also, *to make one's gree to* or *with* (a person): to do what will satisfy him; to give satisfaction *to*, come to terms or make one's peace *with*. Also, *to make* (a person's) *gree*.

c **1290** *Childh. Jesus* (Horstm.) 455 To his freont make þi gre Oþur þou worst i flem of þis contre. *Ibid.* 1430 To Josepe he maude is gre With guode wille. [**1377** *Act 1 Rich. II* c. 6 §1 Qe..le clerc..eit la prisone tange il avera fait gree a la partie.] **1412** HOCCLEVE *De Reg. Princ.* 621 þat I, with lownesse & humylitee, To my curat go scholde, & make his gree. **1413** *Pilgr. Sowle* (Caxton) I. xxxviii. (1859) 42 Thus shalt thou make thy gree with Iustyce, that Mercy and she be finally acorded. *c* **1440** *Partonope* 2149 He thenketh fast how that he To his Lord myght make his gre. *c* **1492** *Gest of Robyn Hode* cviii. in Child *Ballads* (1888) III. 61/2 Holde my londes in thy honde Tyll I haue made the gree! **1613** SIR H. FINCH *Law* (1636) 297 No Wardein of the Fleet shall suffer any prisoner in execution to goe out of prison.. without making gree to the partie. **1697** *View Penal Laws* 121 Then the Sheriff have the Hawk, making gree to him that did take him. **1764** BURN *Poor Laws* 11 He shall be imprisoned till he justify himself, and make gree to the party.

† **b.** *unto gree*: with a view to satisfaction, as an indemnity. *Obs. rare.*

c **1400** *Destr. Troy* 11595 The grekes for hor greme vnto gre asken Gret sommes, forsothe, to hor sad harmes.

† **3.** (One's) good pleasure; will, desire; consent. *by his gree* (quot. 1483): of its own accord. *of the gre*: of (one's) own accord, voluntarily. *out of gree*: contrary to one's pleasure or desire; hence amiss. [F. *à son gré, de* (*son*) *gré, contre son gré.*] *Obs.*

13.. *E.E. Allit. P.* C. 348 Lene me þy grace For to go at þi gre. *c* **1330** R. BRUNNE *Chron.* (1810) 272 þe erle..did no maner wik, þe Kyng gaf him his gre. *Ibid.* 308 He wild not do þer gre, þat terme þat he sette. ? *a* **1400** *Morte Arth.* 2645 It es the gifte of Gode, the gree es hys awene. *Ibid.* 2748 Here are galyarde gomes that of the gre seruis. **1417** *E.E. Wills* (1882) 27, I will þat myn executours do her gre. **1481** CAXTON *Godfrey* cxciii. 283 It was not knowen..whether it was taken from hym by constraynt or yf he delyuerd it with his gree and wyll. **1483** —— *Gold. Leg.* 196 b/1 The dore that was soo locked opened by his gree by hym self. **1513** DOUGLAS *Æneis* IX. Prol. 80 Quhar ocht is bad, gais mys, or owt of gre. **1632** *Womens Rights* 18 Whosoever..shall in his life time without gree of his lord, marry. [**1666** PEPYS *Diary* 25 Nov., Against the *gré*..of my Lord Treasurer. **1692** O. WALKER *History Illustr.* I. vii. 119 Against the gré of the Senate.] *a* **1734** NORTH *Lives* (1742) 9 History..(after the partial Gree of the late Authors) has been, to all good Purposes, silent of him.

† **gree**, *sb.*[3] *Obs. rare.* ? Weeping, mourning.

1555 ABP. PARKER *Ps.* xxx. 70 Thou tournst from mee my wo and gree, to myrth in cherefull voyce. **1590** GREENE *Mourn. Garm.* (1616) 53 With hearts griefe and eyes greee [*sic*]. Eyes and heart both full of woes.

gree, *v. Obs.* exc. *dial.* Also 5–6 gre, 6 *Sc.* grie. [aphetized from AGREE *v.*, or f. GREE *sb.*[2] Cf., however, OF. *gréer*, which may be the direct source.] = AGREE *v.*, in various senses.

† **1.** *trans.* Of a person: To please, to satisfy. = AGREE 1 b. *Obs.*

1468 *Plumpton Corr.* (Camden) 19, I stand in doubt whether Mr. Midleton & Mr. Ros greed you & Sir John Malivera thereof or no.

† **2.** To make (persons) pleased; to reconcile, conciliate (several persons, or one *with* another); also, to arrange or settle (a matter). *Obs.*

1570 *Satir. Poems Reform.* xxi. 75 Now thay tak on hand to gre 3ow With all the tother syde. **1596** DALRYMPLE tr. *Leslie's Hist. Scot.* VI. 342 Edward king of Jngland..was chosen arbiter to grie this mater. *Ibid.* IX. 154 In hauie and sair seiknes he takis Jornay, of that mynd to grie thame. **17..** *Jacobite Relics* (ed. Hogg 1819) I. 146 They're fallen out among themselves, Shame fa' the first that grees them!

† **3.** *refl.* and *intr.* (for *refl.*) To become well-disposed or favourable; to consent, accede. *Obs.*

c **1440** *Generydes* 1141, I gre me wele In your presence to travell day by day. **1490** CAXTON *Eneydos* vi. 29 They.. accorded and greed to do all hir wyll. **1523** LD. BERNERS *Froiss.* I. civ. 125 They within desyred respyte to gyue an answere, the which was agreed; and whan they had counsayled the parties greed. **1578** HUNNIS *Hyvef. Hunnye* Gen. xxxvi. 28 If. 86 Shall not all their substance greatte And cattell that they have Be ours if we gree thereunto? **1591** HARINGTON *Orl. Fur.* v. xxxii, To trie the matter thus they greed both.

4. To come into accord or harmony; to come to terms *with* (a person), *on, upon* (a matter); to make an agreement.

c **1380** WYCLIF *Serm.* Sel. Wks. II. 144 3if þis be herd of Pilat we shulen gree wiþ him, and make 3ou sikir. *c* **1566** *Merie Tales* in *Skelton's Wks.* (1843) I. Introd. 69 The miller ..greed with the sexten of the churche to haue the key of the churche dore. **1574** *Mirr. Mag., Nennius* x, Till with their creditours they gree. **1591** SHAKS. *Two Gent.* II. iv. 183 All the means Plotted, and 'greed on for my happinesse. **1597** BRETON *Scholler & Souldiour* (1599) 30, I will either have it give it or gree upon it. **1606** SHAKS. *Ant. & Cl.* II. vi. 37 Then, to send Measures of Wheate to Rome; this greed vpon, To part with vnhackt edges. **1786** BURNS *To G. Hamilton* iii, My word of honour I hae gi'en,..To try to get the twa to gree. **1822** SCOTT *Nigel* xxxi, All..*consentiunt in eundem*—gree on the same point. **1824** MISS FERRIER *Inher.* xvii, It's you that has made us cast out, and it's you that maun make us 'gree. **1878** *Cumbld. Gloss.*, *'Gree*, agree. They're about 'greean for a horse.

5. To be in harmony in opinion, way of life, etc.; to be of the same mind; to be friends; also of things, to be in accord or harmonious.

1500–20 DUNBAR *Poems* liii. 5 The ane futt ȝeid ay onrycht, And to the tother wald not gree. **1523** SKELTON *Garl. Laurel* 275 Whos heuenly armony was so passynge sure, So truely proporsionyd, and so well did gree. **1532** HERVET *Xenophon's Househ.* (1768) 23 Vtterynge our myndes one to an other, if we myght gree in one tale. *c* **1540** J. REDFORD *Mor. Play Wit & Sci.* (Shaks. Soc.) 39 We wyll gre better, or ye pas hence. **1594** MARLOWE & NASHE *Dido* III. i, Weapons gree not witt my tender years. *c* **1600** SHAKS. *Sonn.* cxiv, Mine eie well knowes what with his gust is greeing. **1620** T. PEYTON *Glass Time* 49 Neptune himselfe with foure great riuers greeing, To deck the bosome which gaue Adam being. **1768** ROSS *Helenore* 108 Like twa sisters, ye will live an' gree. *a* **1774** FERGUSSON *Poems* (1845) 5 As lang's there's pith into the barrel, We'll drink and gree. **1814** SCOTT *Wav.* xxxvi, They're just neighbour-like..and nae wonder they gree sae weel.

Hence ˈ**greeing** *ppl. a.*, concordant.

a **1547** SURREY *Æneid* (Roxb. Club) 125 The people cried with sundry greeing shouts To bring the horse to Pallas temple blive.

greece, -cy, obs. forms of GREASE, GREASY.

greed (griːd), *sb.* Orig. *Sc.* Also 7 **gread, griede**. [Back formation from GREEDY. (OE. had dat. pl. *grǽdum* used advb. = 'with greediness'.)]

Inordinate or insatiate longing, esp. for wealth; avaricious or covetous desire. Const. *of*.

1609 S. GRAHAME *Anat. Humours* 38 b, Whose avarice and gread of geare is such, that they care not whom with they joyne, so being they be ritch. **1618** LITHGOW *Pilgr. Farew.* (sig.) E, Is hee poore, then faine hee would bee rich; And rich, what tormentes his great griede doth feele. **1786** BURNS *Twa Dogs* 144 Some rascal's pridefu' greed to quench. **1828** SCOTT *F.M. Perth* xvii, The Duke of Albany is generally hated for his greed and covetousness. **1863** FAWCETT *Pol. Econ.* II. ii. 130 Many..attach to competition the stigma of selfish greed. **1870** MORRIS *Earthly Par.* I. II. 515 If greed of power and gold have led thee on. **1874** GREEN *Short Hist.* i. §2. 10 The greed of plunder drew fresh war-bands from the German coast.

greed (griːd), *v. rare.* [f. GREED *sb.*]

a. *intr.* To indulge one's greed; to be avaricious; to have an eager longing *for*. **b.** *trans.* To long for.

c **1685–8** *Huntingd. Ploughman's Compl.* in *Roxb. Ballads* (1890) VII. 32 On wealth her mother's mind was bent, she greeded out of measure. **1843** *Blackw. Mag.* LIII. 176 You might the horrent jaws survey, Griesly, and greeding for their prey. **1848** LYTTON *Harold* XI. xi, The ravens sit greeding, And watching, and heeding..And ravens sit greeding Their share of the bones.

greede, variant of GREDE *v. Obs.*

†ˈ**greedilaik.** *Obs.* In 3 **grediȝleȝȝc**. [f. GREEDY *a.* + ON. *-leik-r*, -LAIK.] Greediness.

c **1200** ORMIN 3994 All modiȝleȝȝc, & grediȝleȝȝc, & irre, & gluterrnesse. *Ibid.* 4560 Wæpenn god & strang..ȝæn ȝittsunng & grediȝleȝȝc.

greedily (ˈgriːdɪlɪ), *adv.* Forms: *α.* 1 **grǽdelice**, 2 **gredliche**, 4–6 **gredely**, (6 **greedely(e)**; *β.* 1 **grǽdilice**, 2–3 **grediliche, -like**, 4–6 **gredyly**, (4 **gredili, -ly**, 6 **gredilie**), 6– **greedily**. [Two synonymous words seem to have coalesced: (1) OE. *grǽdelíce* (= ON. *gráðuliga*), f. **grǽd* (*u*-stem, = ON. *gráð-r*, Goth. *grêdus*: see GREED *sb.*) + *líce* -LY²; (2) OE. *grǽdi(ȝ)líce*, f. *grǽdiȝ* GREEDY + *-líce* -LY². The former, if it had survived into mod.Eng., would have become **greedly*; it is uncertain how far the *α* forms represent this type, as in the 16th c. they might be misspellings for *greedily* (cf., however, GREEDLY *a.*).

A similar coalescence occurs in the case of OE. *hefelíce*, *hefiȝlíce* HEAVILY. Perh. in both cases the derivative of the adj. should be regarded as a refashioned form, arising when the primitive sb. had ceased to be in common use. For the *-e-* representing the thematic vowel of a long *u*-stem in composition, cf. **feldefare* (written *feldeware*): see FIELDFARE.]

1. As one that is hungry or thirsty; with keen appetite; hungrily, ravenously, voraciously.

c **1000** *Hexameron of St. Basil* (Norman) xx. 28 Ðonne him hingraþ he yt grǽdilice. *c* **1175** *Lamb. Hom.* 123 And þa ifelde þe deofel þene hoc þe he er gredliche forswealh. *c* **1220** *Bestiary* 321 He drinkeð water gredilike. *a* **1300** *Cursor M.* 27905 To ette ouer gredyly. *a* **1340** HAMPOLE *Psalter* Cant. 497 Bird of swalugh þat gredily askis mete. *c* **1440** *Jacob's Well* v. 35 Þe smyth bad an-oþer man castyn of his breed to þe hog, & þe swyn eet it gredyly. **1574** HYLL *Conject. Weather* vii, If the Oxen feede greedelyer. **1667** MILTON *P.L.* x. 562 Greedily they pluck'd The Fruitage fair to sight. **1725** DE FOE *Voy. round World* (1840) 189 Flour and oil which the men had fallen greedily upon. **1856** KANE *Arct. Expl.* I. xxiv. 318 Some..were greedily waiting for the shell-fish and sea-urchins which the old bird busied herself in procuring for them.

in fig. context. **1535** COVERDALE *Jer.* xv. 16 When I had founde thy wordes, I at them vp gredely. **1583** STUBBES *Anat. Abus.* II. (1882) 92 If they heare him not..greedily and thirstily thereby to profit. **1590** SPENSER *F.Q.* I. v. 9 Cruell steele so greedily doth bight. *Ibid.* I. vi. 38 To see their blades so greedily imbrew, That dronke with blood yet thirsted after life. **1665** BOYLE *Occas. Refl.* v. iii. (1848) 306 Death..devour'd them as greedily, as they did those Birds.

b. Applied to the behaviour of material substances, to indicate rapidity of absorption or combination. (Cf. GREEDY 1 b.)

1584 COGAN *Haven Health* ccxvii. 218 Sweete wines through their sweetenesse are greedily drawen of the members. **1671** J. WEBSTER *Metallogr.* xiii. 203 Wherein Minerals that strike upon the Lunar passages are greedily refreshed. **1799** *Med. Jrnl.* I. 408 Nitrous gas..tends..to lessen the respirable portion, from its strong attraction for oxygen, which it greedily combines with to the point of saturation. **1878** HUXLEY *Physiogr.* 42 The drier and hotter the air happens to be, the more greedily does it drink up this moisture.

2. As one that is greedy of gain; avariciously, covetously, rapaciously.

c **1000** ÆLFRIC *Hom.* I. 66 He ȝymð grǽdelice his teolunge. *c* **1380** WYCLIF *Serm.* Sel. Wks. I. 166 Siche þat gaderen gredili Cristis patrimonye. *c* **1400** *Apol. Loll.* 113 Þei..gredyly gon abowt to geyt al þat þey may. **1635** R. BOLTON *Comf. Affl. Consc.* vi. (ed. 2) 38 And there gather Grace greedily as the most griping Usurer graspeth gold. **1874** GREEN *Short Hist.* v. §2. 227 The eyes of the feudal baronage turned greedily on the riches of the Church.

3. With manifestation of strong desire; with avidity or eagerness; eagerly; †jealously, zealously, fervently (*obs.*).

c **1200** *Trin. Coll. Hom.* 173 Hie iseð bineðen hem deflen þe hem grediliche kepeð. **1398** TREVISA *Barth. De P.R.* XVIII. xci. (1495) 839 The frogge..cryeth gredyly and makyth moche noyse. *a* **1400–50** *Alexander* 1435 His men & all þe messedones maynly ascendis And þai of Grece gredely girdis vp eftire. **1548** UDALL, etc. *Erasm. Par. Matt.* xi. 7–15 There is now no more to doe, but feruently and gredely to take that which..is now presently offered. **1575–85** ABP. SANDYS *Serm.* xviii. 211 Greedilie expecting their looked for time. **1581** J. BELL *Haddon's Answ. Osor.* 291 Some places that are ouer greedely geuen to sectes and deuisions. **1631** WEEVER *Anc. Funeral Mon.* 40 Greedily affected to view the sacred Sepulchres. *a* **1680** BUTLER *Rem.* (1759) I. 25 Those who greedily pursue Things wonderful, instead of true. **1710** BERKELEY *Princ. Hum. Knowl.* §141 This notion has been greedily embraced and cherished by the worst part of mankind. **1845** FORD *Handbk. Spain* 113 The candles lighted in these processions..are greedily purchased by women at treble their original cost. **1852** H. ROGERS *Ecl. Faith* (1853) 279 Miraculous legends have been most greedily taken up by the vast majority of mankind.

greediness (ˈgriːdɪnɪs). Forms: see GREEDY. [f. GREEDY + -NESS.] The attribute of being greedy. Const. as in the adj.

1. Excessive longing for food or drink, or avidity in the consumption of it; gluttony, voracity, ravenousness.

1426 LYDG. *De Guil. Pilgr.* 13044 Gredynesse Off sundry metys and deyntes. *c* **1440** *Jacob's Well* 144 For mete is good to man..so mesure be kepte, & þe sause þerto be dreed of god, þat gredynes be left. **1526** *Pilgr. Perf.* (W. de W. 1531) 99 b, Voracite or gredynesse in eatyng. **1575** *Brieff Disc. Troubles Franckford* (1846) 11 As the harte chased pantethe for gredines off waters. **1641** J. JACKSON *True Evang. T.* I. 73 There is too much of the greedinesse of the Wolfe still remaining. **1744** BIRCH *Life Boyle* B.'s Wks. I. 10 Philaretus was little given to greediness, either in fruits or sweetmeats. **1840** DICKENS *Old C. Shop* v, He chewed tobacco and water-cresses at the same time and with extraordinary greediness. **1856** MACAULAY *Biog., Johnson* (1867) 88 He contracted a habit of eating with ravenous greediness.

2. Excessive eagerness or longing for wealth or gain; covetousness, avarice, rapacity, greed.

1154 *O.E. Chron.* (Laud. MS.) an. 1086 He wæs on ȝitsunge be feallan & grǽdinæsse he lufode mid ealle. *c* **1175** *Lamb. Hom.* 103 Heo [auaritia] is helle iliche, forðon þet hi ba habbeð unafillendliche gredinesse. *a* **1225** *Ancr. R.* 416 Ne beo non þe grediure uorto habben more. Þeo gredinesse [is] rote of hire bitternesse. *c* **1380** WYCLIF *Serm.* Sel. Wks. I. 178 Gredynesse and avarice letten þes two partis. **1426** LYDG. *De Guil. Pilgr.* 9034 The costys & the gret expense That thow dost hym for to plese, And hys gredynesse tapese. **1535** COVERDALE *Eph.* iv. 19 To worke all maner of vnclennes euen with gredynesse [so **1611** and **1881**; WYCLIF in coueityse; Gr. ἐν πλεονεξίᾳ]. **1661** BRAMHALL *Just Vind.* vi. 134 The greediness and extortion of the Court of Rome. **1855** MACAULAY *Hist. Eng.* xiii. III. 296 In excuse for his greediness, it ought to be said that he was the poorest noble of a poor nobility. **1884** A. R. PENNINGTON *Wiclif* vi. 193 Greediness for wealth. **1885** *L'pool Daily Post* 11 Apr. 5/1 To explain off-hand the greediness of Russia in the Afghanistan direction.

3. Excessive longing or desire in general; eager longing; eagerness, keenness.

1553 BRENDE *Q. Curtius* IX. 183 The gredines of glory & the vnsaciable desire of fame, made no place to seme to far. **1590** SPENSER *F.Q.* I. viii. 6 Eger greedinesse through every member thrild. **1594** SHAKS. *Rich. III*, III. vii. 7 Th' vnsatiate greedinesse of his desire. **1665** BOYLE *Occas. Refl.* v. x. (1848) 336 A Greediness of Knowledge, that is impatient of being confin'd. **1668** *Lond. Gaz.* No. 232/3 The people are with greedinesse expecting the issue of the ensuing Diet. **1752** HUME *Ess. & Treat.* (1777) II. 175 With what greediness are the miraculous accounts of travellers received. **1794** PALEY *Evid.* II. ii. (1817) 58 A topic which is always listened to with greediness. **1849** MACAULAY *Hist. Eng.* ii. I. 179 Men flew to frivolous amusements..with the greediness which long and enforced abstinence naturally produces.

greediron, obs. form of GRIDIRON.

†**greedly**, *a. Obs. rare*⁻¹. In 6 **greadlye**. [f. *greedly* adv.; see GREEDILY.] Greedy.

a **1546** BECON *Gov. Vertue* Wks. 1564 I. 260 b, Adam and Eue by satisfying theyr greadlye appetite in eatynge the forbidden fruit.

greeds (griːdz), *pl. dial.* [Repr. OE. *grǽd* 'ulva' (coarse grass, water-weeds), pl. *grǽdas* 'gramina'. Cf. GRATTEN, GROWTH².]

1. Straw manure.

1736 J. LEWIS *Hist. Isle Tenet* (ed. 2) 37 *Greeds*, the Straw, in a Place or Barton to make Dung of. **1855** *Cycl. Agric.* (ed. Morton) II. 723/2 *Greeds*, (Kent) long manure in the straw-yard.

2. Applied to Duckweed and Pondweed.

1863 PRIOR *Plant-n.* 99 *Greeds*, now applied to the Pondweed tribe. *Potamogeton.* **1879** BRITTEN & HOLLAND *Plant-n.* 233 Greeds, *Lemna minor*, L.

greedy (ˈgriːdɪ), *a.* Forms: 1 **grǽdiȝ**, 2–3 **gradi, -y**, 2–6 **gredi**, 3 **grediȝ**, 3–4 **gredie**, 4–7 **gredy**, 6 **greadye**, 6 *Sc.* **grydy**, 6–7 **greedie**, 6– **greedy**. [OE. *grǽdiȝ* = OS. *grâdag*, OHG. *grâtag*, ON. *gráðug-r* (OSw. *grådig*, Da. *graadig*), Goth. *grêdags*:—OTeut. **grǽdago-*, *-ugo-*, f. **grǽdu-z* (Goth. *grêdu-s* hunger, ON. *gráð-r* hunger, greed, OE. *grǽd* in dat. pl. *grǽdum* eagerly), cognate with Skr. *grdh* to be greedy.]

1. Having an intense desire or inordinate appetite for food or drink; ravenous, voracious, gluttonous. †In some of the earlier quots. the meaning is simply: Hungry. Const. *of* (OE. *genitive*); †also *after, on, upon, (for) to* have something (*obs.*).

Beowulf (Z.) 121 Wiht unhælo grim and grǽdiȝ ȝearo sona wæs, reoc and reþe. **971** *Blickl. Hom.* 211 Þa fynd..heora gripende wæron swa swa grǽdiȝ wulf. *a* **1000** ÆLFRIC *Hom.* I. 216 Þam grǽdiȝan fisce, þe ȝesihð þæt æs, and ne ȝesihð ðone angel ðe on ðam æse sticað. *c* **1175** *Lamb. Hom.* 123 Þenne bið he gredi þes eses and forswoleȝeð þene hoc forð mid þan ese. *c* **1200** *Vices & Virtues* (1888) 139 Sobrietas..makeð þanne mann maðfull ðe was to grady. *a* **1225** *Ancr. R.* 324 Hwou gredie hundes stondeð biuoren þe borde. *c* **1250** *Gen. & Ex.* 1494 Iacob wurð war he was gredi. *c* **1325** *Body & Soul* 43 in *Map's Poems* (Camden) 340 Thyne mete..That thou were gredi for to frete. **1393** LANGL. *P. Pl.* C. VII. 398 Two gredy sowes. **1575–85** ABP. SANDYS *Serm.* iii. 53 The foxe is rauenous, greedie on his pray. **1697** DRYDEN *Virg. Georg.* II. 756 The falling Mast, For greedy Swine provides a full repast. **1725** POPE *Odyss.* IX. 427 He said, and greedy grasped the heady bowl. **1733–39** J. TULL *Horse-Hoing Husbandry* 86 Most sorts of Cattle are greedy of it. **1767** T. HUTCHINSON *Hist. Mass.* II. i. 100 As greedy after their prey as a wolf. **1772** *Ann. Reg.* 96/2 This snake is very greedy of milk. *a* **1839** PRAED *Poems* (1864) I. 180 Greedy hawk must gorge his prey.

fig. *a* **1000** *Phœnix* 507 (Gr.) Liȝ..grǽdiȝ swelȝeð londes frætwe. **1572** GASCOIGNE *Dan Barthol. of Bathe* Hund. Flowers 429, I seeke a greedy graue, To make an ende of all these stormes and strife. **1610** G. FLETCHER *Christ's Vict.* I. xxix, Cooz'ning the greedie sea, pris'ning their nimble prey. **1654–66** LD. ORRERY *Parthenissa* (1676) 651, I..knew the Vessel was founder'd, had struck, or sprung some greedy Leak. **1715–20** POPE *Iliad* IX. 288 The first fat offerings, to the immortals due, Amidst the greedy flames Patroclus threw. **1843** CARLYLE *Past & Pr.* II. xv. (1845) 158 The..noise of greedy Acheron. **1860** B. TAYLOR *Pine Forest of Monterey* Poems (1866) 321 Look from the greedy wave.

b. said of the stomach, etc.; also of the appetite. See also GREEDY-GUT(S.

1514 BARCLAY *Cyt. & Uplondyshm.* (Percy Soc.) p. xli, Their greedy gorges are rapt with the smell. **1526** *Pilgr. Perf.* (W. de W. 1531) 99 b, To stuffe & fyll the gredy gutte of thy bely with delycate meetes. **1599** H. BUTTES *Dyets drie Dinner* A a iv b, Yet soft and fayre: oregreedy jawes Eate not their meale with decent pause. **1634** SIR T. HERBERT *Trav.* 211 Her appetite strong and greedy. **1644** DIGBY *Nat. Bodies* (1645) 353 The stomack, when it is greedy of meate, draweth it selfe up towards the throate.

c. said of chemical substances which absorb with avidity. ? *Obs.*

1758 REID tr. *Macquer's Chym.* I. 278 The Acid of the Phosphorus..is very greedy of moisture. **1791** W. NICHOLSON tr. *Chaptal's Elem. Chem.* (1800) III. 63 The oil is more drying or greedy of oxigene. **1800** tr. *Lagrange's Chem.* I. 194 When the air is very greedy of moisture.

d. greedy glede *dial.*, a kite; also the name of a children's game (Jam.). †**greedy worm**: see quot. 1585; = *hungry worm* (see HUNGRY *a.* 4).

1508 DUNBAR *Flyting* 146 As gredy gleddis, ȝe gang With polkis to mylne, and beggis baith meill and schilling. **1530** PALSGR. 227/1 Gredy wormе that is in a dogges tong. *a* **1568** *Wyf of Auchtermuchty* 51 By thair cumis the gredy gled, And likkit vp five [gaislingis]. **1585** LUPTON *Thous. Notable Th.* (1675) 33 If the little nerve under a Whelp's tongue (commonly called the greedy worm) be taken away, it keeps the same safe after from being mad. **1627** BP. HALL *Pharis. & Chr.* Wks. 417 O thou worldling, which hast the Greedy-worme vnder thy tongue, with Esaies dogges, and neuer hast enough. **1768** ROSS *Helenore* 10 At greedy-glad, or warpling o' the green, She 'clipst them a'. **1802** G. MONTAGU *Ornith. Dict.* 282 Greedy glead. **1885** SWAINSON *Prov. Names Birds* 137 Greedy gled.

2. Eager for gain, wealth, and the like; avaricious, covetous, rapacious. Const. as in sense 1.

a **1000** *Sal. & Sat.* 344 (Gr.) Sum to lyt hafað godes grǽdiȝ. *c* **1175** *Lamb. Hom.* 105 God nele þet we beon gredie ȝitseras. *a* **1200** *Moral Ode* 264 And weren to gredi of solure and of golde. *c* **1200** *Trin. Coll. Hom.* 195 Þe deuel is gredi uppen woreld richeise and gredi him to winende. *a* **1225** *Ancr. R.* 416 Ne beo non þe grediure uorto habben more. *c* **1380** WYCLIF *Sel. Wks.* III. 347 Men seien þat preestis ben moost gredy purchasours in erþe. *c* **1400** *Rom. Rose* 5696 An usurer..Shal never for richesse riche bee But..Scarce, and gredy in his entent. *c* **1500** *Plumpton Corr.* (Camden) 148 Praying that ye wille content unto this bringer, my Cousin Robert Hastings, iiij mark & xxd. now dew unto him at this Martymasse last, which is right gredy therupon. **1648** GAGE *West Ind.* xxi. 202 A wolvish, greedy, and covetous heart.

1697 DRYDEN *Virg. Georg.* I. 72 That Crop rewards the greedy Peasant's pains. **1752** HUME *Pol. Disc.* ii. 33 Nor is a porter less greedy of money, which he spends on bacon and brandy, than a courtier, who purchases champagne and ortolans. **1841** W. SPALDING *Italy & It. Isl.* III. 209 Unscrupulous and greedy power. **1844** THIRLWALL *Greece* VIII. 461 The..exactions of corrupt magistrates, and their greedy officers.

absol. *c* **1400** *Rom. Rose* 5791 If these gredy..Loveden, and were loved ageyn..Such wikkidnesse ne shulde falle.

3. In wider sense: Eager, keen; †eagerly active, zealous (*obs.*); eagerly or keenly desirous *of* or †*to do* (something).

a **1300** *Cursor M.* 27597 O pride becums als wainglory, þat es to be o roos gredi. *c* **1400** *Destr. Troy* 1370 The Grekes were full gredy, grippit hom belyue, Prayen and pyken mony priuey chambur. **1540** COVERDALE *Fruitf. Less.* To Rdr. A4b, O, how euill doth it become a beleeuer to be irefull and greedie of vengeance. **1553** LATIMER *Serm. Lincolnsh.* vii. (1562) 118b, So all oure prelates byshops and curates..should be so paynful, so gredy in castyng their netts, that is to say, in preachyng Gods worde. **1600** FORMAN *Autobiog.* (1849) 11 He was soe gredy on his bocke. **1646** SIR T. BROWNE *Pseud. Ep.* I. viii. 34 A greater enquirer of truth, but too greedy a receiver of it. **1734** tr. *Rollin's Anc. Hist.* XIX. v. (1827) VIII. 160 The populace, who are ever greedy of novelty. **1784** COWPER *Task* III. 671 The rank society of Weeds, Noisome, and ever greedy to exhaust The impoverished earth. **1884** *Sat. Rev.* 12 July 38/1 The people of the United States are seldom greedy of legislation.

fig. *c* **1374** CHAUCER *Troylus* III. 1709 (1758) The see, that gredy is to flowen. **1899** FINDLAY in *Expositor* Feb. 94 Dogmatic theology, greedy of proof-texts.

4. Of actions, qualities, emotions, and the like: Characterized by or manifesting intense or eager desire; keen, eager.

c **1385** CHAUCER *L.G.W.* Prol. 105 My besy goost..To sene this flour so yonge..Constrayned me with so gredy desyre. **1568** T. HOWELL *Arb. Amitie* (1879) 37 Most greedy gripes with plunging paines, do pierce my ruthfull hart. **1590** SPENSER *F.Q.* I. viii. 29 He himselfe with greedie great desyre Into the castle entred forcibly. *Ibid.* 48 With griping talaunts armd to greedy fight. **1647** CLARENDON *Hist. Reb.* v. §394 [Which] begot a greedy hope, and expectation in him that this petition would have been..an introduction to peace. **1667** MILTON *P.L.* IX. 257 With greedy hope to find His wish and best advantage. **1698** FRYER *Acc. E. India & P.* 18 Had not my greedy Eye espied a House more eminently seated. **1749** FIELDING *Tom Jones* VIII. xiv, He and Partridge sat with greedy and impatient ears. **1838** DICKENS *Nich. Nick.* xxii, Smike listened with greedy interest.

†**5.** *transf.* Of spoil, prey: Greedily pursued. *Obs.*

1586 MARLOWE *1st Pt. Tamburl.* II. ii, Being void of martial discipline, All running headlong after greedy spoils. **1648** GAGE *West Ind.* xxi. 187 The monster..thinking to have made some of us his greedy prey.

6. *adv.* or quasi-*adv.*

1599 MINSHEU *Sp. Gram.* 83 To a greedi eating horse, a short halter. **1612** ROWLANDS *More Knaues Yet* 16 A desp'rate fellow fell to eate salt Beefe: Feeding so greedy that the rest admir'd.

7. *Comb.*, as ***greedy-minded*** adj.

1577 NORTHBROOKE *Dicing* (1843) 48 A greedy minded man..may be, and is a couetous man. **1613** HIERON *Wks.* I. 259 Greedy minded men, which seeke by all meanes to secret and keep close the treasure they haue found.

'greedy-gut(s. Now *dial.* and *vulgar.* [See GREEDY and GUT.] A voracious eater; a glutton, gormandizer.

1550 LEVER *Serm.* (Arb.) 63 Disceitful Merchauntes, couetous greedyguttes, and ambicious prollers, whiche canne neuer haue ynough. **1579** TOMSON *Calvin's Serm. Tim.* 638/1 Euerie one of vs woulde swimme in pleasures of this worlde, and play the greedie guts without all measure. **1613** T. GODWIN *Rom. Antiq.* (1674) 68 A glutton or greedy gut which cannot abstain from his food till grace be said. **1736** AINSWORTH *Lat.-Eng. Dict.*, *Lurco*, a glutton, a belly-god, a greedygut, a great eater. **1950** A. WILSON *Such Darling Dodos* 210 'Greedy guts,' he said smiling, as she took a second helping of water-cress. **1959** *Elizabethan* Apr. 10/1 'Here, steady on with the sugar, greedy guts, you've taken it all,' Friday shouted.

attrib. **1647** TRAPP *Marrow Gd. Auth.* in *Comm. Ep.* 606 Such are our greedy-gut Cormorants.

greef(e, obs. form of GRIEF.

greegree ('gri:gri:). Also 8 **griggory,** 8–9 **grigri,** 9 **gregre(e.** [Presumed to be of African origin; in F. *grisgris* (Littré).]

1. An African charm, amulet, or fetish.

1698 FROGER *Voy.* 14 They wear about their Neck, Arms, and Legs, and even bind about their Horses, little leathern Bags, which they call Grisgris, in which are enclosed certain Passages of the Alcoran..to secure them from venemous Beasts, etc. **1788** J. MATTHEWS *Voy. Sierra Leone* vi. 133 Every griggory is assigned its particular office: one is to preserve him from shot, one from poison [etc.]..and when a man happens to be killed..they only say his griggory was not so good as the person's who occasioned his death. **1803** T. WINTERBOTTOM *Sierra Leone* I. xv. 258 In all the Bullom and Timmanee towns greegrees are placed to prevent the incursion of evil spirits or witches. **1861** DU CHAILLU *Equat. Afr.* xix. 337 Next in order, after the idols, come the charms or greegrees, called by them *monda*. Greegree..is a term of European origin. **1865** LIVINGSTONE *Zambesi* xxv. 523 The images, horns or other articles called greegrees. **1931** R. ALDINGTON *Colonel's Daughter* v. 287 He shared with her the common but essentially mystic passion for gadgets—the white man's mechanical grigris. **1935** G. GORER *Africa Dances* I. iii. 47 The great majority of both Catholics and Protestants believe in the efficacy of amulets or grisgris. **1956** M. STEARNS *Story of Jazz* (1957) v. 48 Even today, voodoo drugstores in New Orleans are doing a profitable business in *gris-gris* or magic charms.

¶**2.** Misused for *greegree man* (see 4).

1848 WHITTIER *Slaves of Martinique* 8 As the gregree holds his Fetich from the white man's gaze apart.

3. The ordeal tree of Guinea, *Erythrophleum guineense.*

1847 in CRAIG. **1866** *Treas. Bot.* 551/1 Gregre tree, *Erythrophleum guinense.*

4. *attrib.* and *Comb.*, as ***gree-gree bag, maker; gree-gree man,*** a fetisheer, 'medicine-man'.

1788 J. MATTHEWS *Voy. Sierra Leone* 107 The only trades in use amongst them are those of the carpenter, blacksmith, and griggory maker. *Ibid.* 133 They tell many wonderful stories of their griggory men. **1861** DU CHAILLU *Equat. Afr.* viii. (ed. 2) 96 Even the little children are covered with these talismans, duly consecrated by the doctor or greegree man of the tribe. **1897** MARY KINGSLEY *W. Africa* i. 19 The leather-work that meets with the severest criticism from the Christian party is the talisman or gri-gri bags.

Greek (gri:k), *sb.* Forms: *pl.* 1 **Cré(a)cas, Gré(a)cas,** 3 **Greckes,** *Orm.* **Grickess,** 4 **Greks, Grekis,** 4–5 **-ys,** 4–6 **-es,** 5 **Grecys.** *sing.* 5 ? **Grece,** 6 **Greke,** 6–7 **Greeke,** 7– **Greek.** See also GREW. [In branch I: The OE. *Crécas* pl., corresponds to OHG. *Chrêch, Chriech* (MHG. *Kriech*), Goth. *Krêks*:—**Krêko-z*, an early Teut. adoption of L. *Græcus*, pl. *Græcī* (see below), the name applied by the Romans to the people called by themselves Ἕλληνες. The substitution of *k* for *g* is commonly accounted for by the supposition that the Teut. initial *g*, when the word was adopted, still retained its original pronunciation (ɣ), so that *k* would be the Teut. sound nearest to the Latin *g*. In all the Teut. langs. the word was ultimately refashioned after Latin, with change of *k* into *g*; hence OE. *Grécas* pl. beside *Crécas*, MDu. *Grieke* (Du. *Griek*), mod.Ger. *Grieche*, ON. *Grikkir* pl. In branch II the sb. is an absolute use of GREEK *a.*

The L. *Græcī* is ad. Gr. Γραικοί, said by Aristotle (*Meteor.* I. xiv) to have been the prehistoric name of the Hellenes in their original seats in Epirus. The word is app. an adjectival derivative of *Graius*, which is used in Latin as a poetical synonym of *Græcus*. Recent scholars think the name may have been brought to Italy by colonists from Eubœa, where there is some evidence of its having existed: see Busolt *Gr. Gesch.* I.[2] 198.]

I. 1. a. A native of Greece; a member of the Greek race.

c **893** K. ÆLFRED *Oros.* v. xii. §4 þa foran hi on Crecas. *c* **900** tr. *Bæda's Hist.* IV. xxxii. [xxxi.] (1890) 378 Mid þa aðle ȝeslæȝene..þe Grecas nemnað paralysis. *c* **1200** ORMIN 17560 Forr werelld iss nemmnedd Cossmos, Swa summ þe Grickess kiþenn. *c* **1275** LAY. 801 Leteþ þe Greckes [*earlier text* þa Grickisca] glide to grunde. **1398** TREVISA *Barth. De P.R.* XIX. cxxviii. (1495) 935 All rounde thynges ben callyd Mala amonge the Grekys. *c* **1400** *Destr. Troy* 40 Homer ..þat with the Grekys was gret. *c* **1400** tr. *Secreta Secret., Gov. Lordsh.* (E.E.T.S.) 66 þe bigynnyge of Philosophye hadden Indes, Grecys, Percys and Latyns. **1535** COVERDALE *John* xii. 20 There were certayne Grekes (among them that were come vp to Ierusalem to worshipe at the feast). **1605** DANIEL *Ulisses & Siren* 1 Come worthy Greeke, Ulisses, come. **1662** STILLINGFL. *Orig. Sacr.* III. ii. §2 Those who were renowned among the Greeks for wisdome and learning. **1839** THIRLWALL *Greece* II. XIV. 216 The artful Greek..persuaded Darius of his innocence. **1842** PRICHARD *Nat. Hist. Man* 200 The Greeks are generally tall, and finely formed. **1871** J. CAIRD *Univ. Serm.* (1898) i. 19 The Greek with his hereditary love of freedom and art. **1875** JOWETT *Plato* (ed. 2) III. 31 A Greek in the age of Plato.

b. Proverb. ***when Greek meets Greek, then comes the tug of war***: the now usual perversion of Nathaniel Lee's line (see quot. 1677).

1677 LEE *Rival Queens* IV. ii. 48 When Greeks joyn'd Greeks, then was the tug of War. **1839** LEVER *H. Lorrequer* (1857) 104 When short whist for five-penny points sets in —then Greek meets Greek and we'll have it. **1863** READE *Hard Cash* xxxv, Meantime unknown to these bewildered ones, Greek was meeting Greek only a few yards off.

2. A member or adherent of the Greek Church.

c **1380** WYCLIF *Wks.* (1880) 332 þe þridde maner & leste yuel, þat men seyn þat greks han, is þat þe prest preyeþ þat god assoyle hym. **1547** GARDINER *Let.* 21 May in Foxe *A. & M.* (1583) 1343/2 There is nothyng more commended vnto vs christen men in both the Churches of the Greekes and Latins then lent is. **1696** tr. *Du Mont's Voy. Levant* 190 Both the Greeks and Romanists were extremely griev'd for the Loss of their Saint. **1727–41** CHAMBERS *Cycl.* s.v., Of the seven Latin sacraments..the Greeks only admit of five. **1885** *Catholic Dict.* 389/2 The Greeks generally were averse to the addition of the 'Filioque', and to the use of unleavened bread in the Eucharist. *Ibid.* 392/1 In addition to Lent, the Greeks keep the fast of 'the Mother of God'.

†**3.** A Hellenized Jew; = GRECIAN B. 1 b. *Obs.*

1382 WYCLIF *Acts* vi. 1 In tho dayes..grucchinge of Greekis is maad aȝens Ebrews. **1685** BAXTER *Paraphr. N.T., Acts* vi. 1 Those Jews that understood the Greek Tongue, and used the Greek Translation of the Scripture, were called Greeks.

4. A cunning or wily person; a cheat, sharper, esp. one who cheats at cards. (Cf. F. *grec.*)

1528 ROY & BARLOW *Rede me*, etc. II. (Arb.) 117 In carde playinge he is a goode greke. **1568** *Sat. Poems Reform.* ix. 217 A cowle, a cowle for such a Greek Were fitter for to wear. **1664** *Floddan F.* vii. 69 Giles Musgrave was a Guileful Greek. **1794** *Sporting Mag.* III. 227 The waiter pillages the greek, The greek the spendthrift fleeces. **1812** COMBE *Picturesque* XIX. (Chandos) 75 If I may with freedom speak, I take you for a very Greek. **1823** MONCRIEFF *Tom & Jerry* II. v, Come lads, bustle about; play will begin—some of the Pigeons are here already, the Greeks will not be long following. **1854** THACKERAY *Newcomes* I. xxxvi. 361 He was an adventurer, a pauper, a blackleg, a regular Greek. **1884** *Sat. Rev.* 16 Feb. 202/1 Without a confederate the..game of baccarat does not seem to offer many chances for the Greek.

5. Qualified by *merry, mad, gay*: A merry fellow; a roysterer; a boon companion; a person of loose habits.

See GRIG *sb.*[1] 5; the relation between the two words is uncertain.

1536 *Rem. Sedition* 7b, Whom can they refuse, when smythes, coblers, tylers, carters, and such other gay grekes, seme worthy to be theyr gouernours? *a* **1553** UDALL *Royster D.* I. i. (Arb.) 11 Mathewe Merygreeke. He entreth singing. **1583** BABINGTON *Commandm.* viii. (1637) 75 O he is a merry greeke, a pleasant companion, and in faith a good fellow. **1597** *Return fr. Parnass.* I. i. 265 Thou seems a mad Greeke, and I have lovd such ladds of mettall as thou seems to be from mine infancie. [**1606** SHAKS. *Tr. & Cr.* IV. iv. 58 A wofull Cressid 'mong'st the merry Greekes.] **1611** *Coryat's Crudities, Panegyr. Verses*, Ulysses was a merry Greek they say So Tom is, and the Greeker of the tway. **1635** HEYWOOD *Philocothonista* 44 To title a drunkard by, wee..strive to character him in a more mincing and modest phrase; as thus:—Hee is a good fellow, or A boone Companion, A mad Greeke, A true Trojan. **1650** HOWELL *Ep. Ded. to Cotgr.*, They tearm in French, a boon companion or merry greek, *Roger bon temps.* **1694** MOTTEUX *Rabelais* v. (1737) 216 Merry-Greeks with crimson Snouts.

6. *slang.* An Irishman. (Cf. GRECIAN.)

1823 'JON BEE' *Dict. Turf*, *Greek*—Irishmen call themselves Greeks—none else follow the same track to the east; throughout this land, many unruly districts are termed Grecian. **1851** MAYHEW *Lond. Labour* I. 226 We had the Greeks (the lately arrived Irish) down upon us more than once. **1872** *Standard* 3 Sept. 5/2 'Greek', as some of your readers are aware, is colonial slang for 'Irish'.

II. [absol. use of the adj.: see etymology.]

7. The language of a native of Greece or one of Greek race; the Greek language. Also, a particular form or period of the language, as ***late Greek, Ionic Greek, modern Greek.***

[*c* **975** *Rushw. Gosp.* Matt. xxvii. 46 Hælend miclæ stefnæ cwæþende in grec [*MS.* gc] god min god min for-whon forletes þu mec.] *c* **1391** CHAUCER *Astrol.* Prol., Suffise to the thise trewe conclusiouns in englissh, as wel as suffisith to thise noble clerkes grekes thise same conclusiouns in grek. *c* **1400** MAUNDEV. (1839) ii. 10 The Table aboven his Heved ..on the whiche the Title was writen, in Ebreu, Grece and Latyn. *a* **1400–50** *Alexander* 5009 Sothly..þe son-tree.. Entris in with yndoyes & endis in greke. **1534** STARKEY *Let. to Cromwell* in *England* (1878) p. x, The knolege of both tongys bothe latyn and greke. **1573** LOD. LLOYD *Marrow Hist.* (1653) 127 Cato being aged in his last years went to school to Ennius, to learn the Greek. **1623** B. JONSON in *Shaks. Wks.* (1st Fo.) Pref. verses, And though thou hadst small Latine, and lesse Greeke. **1668** WILKINS *Real Char.* I. i. §3. 3 The Greek was anciently of very great extent, not onely in Europe, but in Asia too, and Afric. **1700** MAIDWELL in *Collect.* (O.H.S.) I. 310 Masters for Græc and Latin. **1718** LADY M. W. MONTAGU *Let. to Lady Rich* 16 Mar., In Pera they speak Turkish, Greek, Hebrew [etc.]. **1727–41** CHAMBERS *Cycl.* s.v., Modern or vulgar Greek, is the language now spoken in Greece. *Ibid.*, The modern Greek has divers new words not in the antient. **1866** E. MASSON *Winer's Gram. N.T. Diction* Introd. (ed. 6) 15 The Grammar of Later Greek..has not..been completely and systematically investigated. **1899** *Oxford Univ. Cal.* 15 The Regius Professor of Greek.

8. Unintelligible speech or language, gibberish. Also ***heathen Greek*** (rarely ***Hebrew-Greek***). (Cf. *Hebrew.*) ***St. Giles's Greek***: slang.

1600 DEKKER *Grissil* II. i. (Shaks. Soc.) 17 *Far.* Asking for some Greek poet, to him he falls..but I'll be sworn he knows not so much as one character of the tongue. *Rice.* Why, then it's Greek to him. **1601** SHAKS. *Jul. C.* I. ii. 282–7 He spoke greeke..those that vnderstood him, smil'd at one another, and shooke their heads: but..it was Greeke to me. **1610** B. JONSON *Alch.* II. v, *Svb.* Is *Ars sacra*..A heathen language? *Ana.* Heathen Greeke, I take it. *Svb.* How? heathen Greeke? *Ana.* All's heathen, but the Hebrew. **1647** COWLEY *Mistress, Discretion* ii, Joynture, Portion, Gold, Estate..Are Greek no Lovers understand. **1769** WESLEY *Jrnl.* 1 July (1827) III. 360, I knew this was heathen Greek to them. **1785** GROSE *Dict. Vulg. Tongue, Greek.* St. Giles's Greek, the slang lingo, cant, or gibberish. **1828** P. CUNNINGHAM *N.S. Wales* (ed. 3) II. 52 A number of the slang phrases current in St. Giles's Greek. **1840** DICKENS *Barn. Rudge* i, I am a stranger, and this is Greek to me. **1886** SIR F. H. DOYLE *Remin.* 239 As unintelligible to the person addressed as if it had been Hebrew-Greek. **1892** *Nation* (N.Y.) 7 July 13/1 Schubert clothed his melodies in wondrous harmonies, which were 'Greek' to his contemporaries.

9. *pl. Typogr.* Greek characters or types.

1894 W. G. RUTHERFORD in *Class. Rev.* 82 Believing that the new Greeks are likely to be..widely adopted.

III. 10. *attrib.* and *Comb.*, as (sense 1) ***Greek-peopled, speaking*** adjs., (sense 7) ***Greek factory.*** (See also GREEK *a.* 2.)

1856 EMERSON *Eng. Traits, Universities* Wks. (Bohn) II. 91 Oxford is a *Greek factory, as Wilton mills weave carpet. **1896** *Westm. Gaz.* 11 Nov. 2/2 The *Greek-peopled islands. **1898** *Daily News* 6 Oct. 3/1 There are *Greek-speaking villages in Syria.

Hence **'Greekess,** a female Greek, a Greek woman; **'Greekless** *a.*, having no Greek; without knowledge of Greek.

1846 WORCESTER (citing Taylor), *Greekess.* **1902** J. LONDON *Let.* 3 Mar. (1966) 277 Charmian sends her love to Greek and Greekess and all the Crowd. **1891** *Q. Rev.* Jan. 217 An appreciable number of Greekless boys wish to go to the Universities. **1891** *Pall Mall G.* 1 Dec. 3/2 It is intended apparently to institute a Cambridge B.Sc. degree for which there shall be a Greekless Little-Go.

Greek (gri:k), *a.* Also 5–6 **Greke,** 6 *Sc.* **Greik,** 6–7 **Greeke,** (8 **Græc**). [f. GREEK *sb.*, under the influence of L. *Græcus* and F. *grec* adjs., of which it might indeed be regarded as a direct adoption. It is not recorded before the 14th c., and did not supplant GREEKISH in general use until the 17th c.]

1. a. Of or pertaining to Greece or its people; Hellenic.

c **1391** CHAUCER *Astrol.* Prol., Thise noble clerkes grekes. **1552** LYNDESAY *Monarche* 1993 The auld Greik Historitiane Diodorus. **1674** PRIDEAUX *Lett.* (Camden) 23, I will determin all cronologicall controversys which have been ever moved in the Greeke history. **1833** TENNYSON *Œnone* 257, I will not die alone..leaving my ancient love With the Greek woman. **1872** RUSKIN *Eagle's N.* §168 Every Greek hero called himself chiefly by his paternal name.

b. Of buildings, works of art, physiognomy, etc.: Resembling what prevailed in Greece, Grecian.

1847 TENNYSON *Princ.* Prol. 11 And me that morning Walter show'd the house, Greek, set with busts. **1888** F. HUME *Mad. Midas* I. iii, The straight Greek nose.

2. a. As the designation of a language (see GREEK *sb.* 7). Hence, of words, idioms, grammar, etc.: Belonging to or characteristic of the Greek language. Of literary compositions: Written in the Greek language. ***Greek fathers***: those early Christian fathers (see FATHER *sb.* 3 b) who wrote in Greek. (In uses like *Greek professor*, *Greek scholar*, the word is perh. in most cases to be regarded as the sb. used attrib.)

1548 UDALL, etc. *Erasm. Par.* I. Pref. 14 b, The Greke diuines. **1573** LOD. LLOYD *Marrow Hist.* (1653) 127 Terentius Varro was almost forty years old, before he took a Greek book in hand, and yet proved excellent in the Greek tongue. **1596** SHAKS. *Tam. Shrew* II. i. 101 This small packet of Greeke and Latine bookes. **1644** MILTON *Educ.* Wks. (1847) 99/1 The ill habit..of wretched barbarizing against the Latin and Greek idiom, with their untutored Anglicisms. **1654** WHITLOCK *Zootomia* 162 Stout Defenders of the Faith..that..are ready to make their own Testament, if they see a Greek one. **1711** SHAFTESB. *Charac.* (1737) III. 241 A foreign protestant divine, and most learned defender of religion, making the best excuse he can for the Greek-fathers. **1727–41** CHAMBERS *Cycl.* s.v., In the living tongues, are still preserved a vast number of Greek terms of art. *Ibid.* s.v. *Accent*, Wetstein, Greek professor at Basil. **1838** *Penny Cycl.* XI. 435/1 Such doctrines as..were confirmed by the Greek fathers of the church. **1845** STODDART *Gram.* in *Encycl. Metrop.* I. 164/1 The Greek or Latin construction. **1866** E. MASSON *Winer's Gram. N.T. Diction* Introd. (ed. 6) 15 The Greek diction of the sacred writers. *Ibid.* 21 It was in classical Greek philology that this pernicious empiricism was first exploded. **1895** W. A. COPINGER in *Trans. Bibliogr. Soc.* II. II. 111 Lascaris's *Greek Grammar* was probably the first book printed in Greek characters.

b. ***Greek letter fraternity, order, society*** (U.S.): a club of students, denoted by two or three Greek letters; as the Phi Beta Kappa (φ β κ) society.

1888 BRYCE *Amer. Commw.* III. VI. cii. 454 The absence of colleges constituting social centres within a university has helped to develop..the Greek letter societies. **1894** H. GARDENER *Unoff. Patriot* x. 146 He encouraged them to join the..Greek letter orders which admitted discussion of such topics. **1898** *B'ham Weekly Post* 22 Jan. 3/4 This [Kansas] farmer was a Greek-letter fraternity man.

3. The distinctive epithet of that section of the Christian Church (commonly known also as the *Eastern* or (*Holy*) *Orthodox Church*, and now representing the major Christian denominations of Greece, Russia, and other Eastern European countries), which acknowledge the primacy of the Patriarch of Constantinople and which formally renounced communion with the Roman see in the 9th century A.D. Also applied to its clergy, rites, buildings, etc.

1560 BECON *New Catech.* v. Wks. 1564 I. 433, I passe ouer the other auncient fathers and doctours bothe of the Greke and Latin churches. *a* **1600** HOOKER *Eccl. Pol.* VI. iv. §8 The Greek church first, and in process of time the Latin altered this order [of public penitence]. **1727–41** CHAMBERS *Cycl.* s.v., The Romanists call the Greek church, the Greek schism. **1838** *Penny Cycl.* XI. 435/2 The Greek convents follow the strict rule of St. Basilius. *Ibid.* 436/1 The Greek church under the Turkish dominion has preserved almost entirely its antient organization. **1877** A. W. THOROLD in *Gd. Words* 17 The iconostas, or screen, which in Greek churches separates the body of the church from the sanctuary.

4. a. In specific names of things of actual or attributed Greek origin or referred to Greek style or usage:

Greek braid (***ornament***), braid arranged in the pattern of a fret (see FRET *sb.*[1] 3 b); **Greek bread**, a kind of cake or biscuit; **Greek Calends** (see CALENDS 3 b); **Greek chorus**, used *transf.*, in comparisons, etc., to indicate the wise, sympathetic comments or open wailing of the chorus in Attic tragedies (see CHORUS 1); **Greek cross** (see CROSS *sb.* 18); **Greek embroidery** (see quot.); **Greek fire** (see FIRE *sb.* 8 b); **Greek fret** = FRET *sb.*[1] 3 b; **Greek gift**, a gift covering some act of treachery, with allusion to Virgil *Æn.* II. 49, *timeo Danaos et dona ferentes*; **Greek god**, (*a*) used *transf.* and in comparisons to denote a paragon of male physical beauty; (*b*) a short hairstyle with curls close to and all over the head; **Greek key** (also ***Greek design, pattern***) = *Greek fret*; **Greek lace** = *Greek point*; **Greek masonry** (see quots.); †**Greek pitch** (L. *pix Græca*) = COLOPHONY; **Greek point**, a kind of needle-made lace.

1894 H. NISBET *Bush Girl's Rom.* 251 She..began touching the *Greek-braid ornament on the edge of her skirt with trembling fingers. **1893** D. RADFORD *Autobiog.* 24 *Greek bread forced into fingers through a mould by pressure. **1863** F. NIGHTINGALE in C. Woodham-Smith *F. Nightingale* (1951) xvii. 291 She [*sc.* Queen Victoria] always reminds me of the woman in the *Greek chorus..wailing out her inexpressible despair. **1893** E. F. BENSON *Dodo* I. iii. 56 He had no desire to interrupt this rapid monologue of Dodo's. He was quite content to play the part of the Greek chorus. **1913** J. VAIZEY *College Girl* xxiii. 319 Hannah, as Greek Chorus, interposed moral remarks. **1947** A. HUXLEY *Let.* 9 Mar. (1969) 568, I visualize him as a kind of philosophical recluse, who comments upon all that is happening from the vantage ground of eternity, and acts as a kind of Greek chorus. **1962** J. BRAINE *Life at Top* v. 78 'You show him, Killer. You show him.' It was like a Greek chorus. **1725** HENLEY tr. *Montfaucon's Antiq. Italy* (ed. 2) 20 The Church is built in the shape of a *Greek Cross. **1839** YEOWELL *Anc. Brit. Ch.* xii. (1847) 135 Greek crosses; that is, having four short equal limbs. **1882** CAULFEILD & SAWARD *Dict. Needlework*, **Greek Embroidery*, this is a modern work..and consists in arranging upon a flat foundation pieces of coloured cloth or silk, in arabesque designs, and attaching these to the material with Chain, Herring-bone, and other Embroidery stitches. **1828** TYTLER *Hist. Scot.* (1864) I. 80 [Edward I] gave orders for the employment of a new and dreadful instrument of destruction, the *Greek fire, with which he had probably become acquainted in the East. **1850** ROBERTSON *Serm.* Ser. III. i. (1872) 9 It is like the Greek fire used in ancient warfare, which burnt unquenched beneath the water. **1872** RUSKIN *Fors Clav.* II. xxiii. 8 The pattern known as the '*Greek fret'. **1885** *Times* (weekly ed.) 27 Nov. 11/3 [It] would be worse than a *Greek gift. *a* **1910** W. F. BUTLER *Autobiogr.* (1911) iii. 42, I often look now as soldiers pass and marvel what has become of those old *Greek gods. **1955** E. COXHEAD *Figure in Mist* iv. 106 It was irritating that Greek gods should drop off the bus and suddenly reduce Matthew to insignificance. **1968** J. IRONSIDE *Fashion Alphabet* 193 *Greek god*, introduced in 1967, a close haircut with flat curls all over the head as seen in statues of Apollo. **1968** *Guardian* 7 Oct. 7/1 They will give you Greek god treatment, a tight mass of tiny curls. **1969** G. SIMS *Sand Dollar* v. 72 He emerged from the sea looking like a Greek god, his hair bleached nearly white. **1970** O. JOHN *Diamond Dress* viii. 90 Don't stand there like some Greek god! You've got about three minutes in which to get dressed. **1897** *Daily News* 16 Jan. 6/5 Tailor-made gowns are finished on the skirt with three or five rows of braiding, usually in trefoil or *Greek key pattern. **1899** *Ibid.* 19 Apr. 2/1 A Greek key design in sugarwork. **1865** F. B. PALLISER *Hist. Lace* v. 74 The greater part of the conventionally termed *Greek lace is really the Venetian reticella; the designs are of geometric fashion, and often of Oriental character. **1880** L. HIGGIN *Handbk. Embroidery* 63 Design for quilt... To introduce squares of Greek or guipure lace. **1960** H. HAYWARD *Antique Coll.* 134/1 'Greek lace', a name given to drawn and cut work embroidery, often combined with geometrical needlepoint or pillow lace. **1727–41** CHAMBERS *Cycl.* s.v. *Masonry*, **Greek Masonry*. **1847** SMEATON *Builder's Man.* 107 Greek masonry is that..where every alternate stone..is made of the whole thickness of the wall. **1657** W. COLES *Adam in Eden* cclix. [414] The Pomanders, Chaines and Bracelets that are made of..*Greek-pitch are effectuall to warm the brain. **1727–41** CHAMBERS *Cycl.* s.v. *Pitch*, Greek Pitch, or Spanish Pitch, is that boiled in water till it have lost its natural smell. **1882** CAULFEILD & SAWARD *Dict. Needlework*, **Greek Point*. Also known as Roman Lace.. This needle made lace is one of the earliest made, being worked in the Ionian Isles..during the fifteenth century.

b. In specific names of plants and animals, as ***Greek nettle, Greek tortoise, Greek valerian***: see the sbs. **Greek rose** [transl. of L. *rosa græca*], a book-name for the Campion.

1601 P. HOLLAND *Pliny* II. 83 The Rose Campion, which our men call the Greeke Rose, and the Greekes name Lychnis.

Hence **Gree'kesque** *a.* [cf. It. *grechesco*], resembling what is Greek; **'Greekified** *ppl. a.* [see -FY], rendered Greek in style or character, fashioned on a Greek model; †**Greekly** *adv. Obs.*, in a Greek fashion; in the Greek language; **'Greekness**, Greek character or quality.

1620 GRANGER *Div. Logike* 292, I say of the same kinde Greekely termed homogeneous. **1654** VILVAIN *Epit. Ess.* I. lxxxiv, T' hav the books of the old Testament Greekly transfer'd. *a* **1861** MRS. BROWNING *Lett. R. H. Horne* (1877) II. liv. 96 The necessary name 'Psyche' drew me towards the propriety of holding a certain Greekness in the other names. **1874** RUSKIN *Fors Clav.* (1896) II. xliii. 388 The Greeks sometimes got their own way, as a mob; but nobody, meaning to talk of liberty, calls it 'Greekness'. **1879** SIR G. SCOTT *Lect. Archit.* I. 100 In the nave of Nôtre Dame every vestige of this Greekesque foliage is got rid of.

†**Greek**, *v. Obs.* [f. GREEK *sb.* Cf. L. *Græcārī*.]

1. *to Greek it*: to follow the practice of the Greeks; to play the Greek scholar.

1615 G. SANDYS *Trav.* 79 [Drinking]..sometimes as many together as there were letters contained in the names of their mistresses.. Insomuch that those were prouerbially said to greeke it that quaft in that fashion. **1660** DURHAM *Life R. Harris* 14 The Bishop..tries his Examinate a little in Divinity, but most in other Learning and Greek, where the Bishops strength lay, but so long they both Greeked it, till at last they were both scoted, and to seek for words. **1799** E. DU BOIS *Piece Fam. Biog.* II. 20 As to the t'other dead fellow, I never could greek it at all, that's flat.

2. Only in *gerund* and *vbl. sb.*: To cheat at cards. (Cf. GREEK *sb.* 4.) *slang.*

1817 *Sporting Mag.* L. 284 A discovery of Greeking at Brighton, has made considerable noise this month in the sporting world. **1819** *Hermit in Lond.* III. 263 Then greeking transactions came on the tapis. **1825** C. M. WESTMACOTT *Eng. Spy* II. 247 *note*, Elements of Greeking.

Greekdom ('gri:kdəm). [f. GREEK *sb.* + -DOM.]

1. The realm of Greeks, the Greek world; also, a Greek state or community.

1843 CARLYLE *Past & Pres.* III. v. 216 The old Romans also could not *speak*, for many centuries:—not till the world was theirs; and so many speaking Greekdoms, their logic-arrows all spent, had been absorbed and abolished. **1868** B. CRACROFT *Ess.* II. 72 The original of the 'Arabian Nights' is probably separated by quite as wide an interval from modern Asiatic life as 'Homer' from modern Greekdom.

2. The fraternity of 'Greeks' or sharpers (see GREEK *sb.* 4).

1861 *All Year Round* 334 The ranks of modern Greekdom, are..recruited by individuals who have been brought to ruin by wastefulness and debauchery.

Greekery ('gri:kərɪ). *rare.* [f. GREEK + -ERY.] The practices of Greeks.

†**1.** *contemptuous.* Customs or practices (in general) of the Greek Church. *Obs.*

1680 *Dial. betw. Pope & Phanatick* 11 They [the Greek Church] are no more true Protestants than the Church of England; for they have Bishops and Liturgies, Rites and Ceremonies, and such kind of Greekery.

2. Cheating, card-sharping. (See GREEK *sb.* 4.)

1823 *Spirit Publ. Jrnls.* (1824) 414 No art..requires so much practice as Greekery. **1861** *All Year Round* 29 June 334 Nothing is less likely to reform a man, and bring him back to an orderly and economical life, than the practice of Greekery.

Greekesque, Greekified: see under GREEK *a.*

Greekish ('gri:kɪʃ), *a.* and *sb.* Forms: 1 grécisc, 2–3 grekisc, (2 gerkisc), 3 grikisc, grickischs, 3–4 grickisshe, (4 *north.* greckes, grekkis), 4–5 crekische, crekkyshe, grekkisch, grekyssch, -eshe, 5–6 grekish(e, -ysh, -ysshe, (6 greakishe), 6– Greekish. [In branch I, repr. OE. *crécisc*, *grécisc* (= OHG. *crêhhisc*, *crêchisc*), f. *Créc-as*, *Grêc-as* (see GREEK *sb.*) + *-isc*, -ISH. In branch II, a new formation on GREEK *sb.* or *a.* + -ISH.]

A. *adj.*

I. 1. Of or pertaining to Greece or the Greeks; Greek, Grecian. *arch.*

a **1300** *Cursor M.* 2121 (Gött.) All on þis side þe grekkisch [*Trin.* grickisshe, *Cott.* greckes, *Fairf.* grekkis] see. *a* **1400** *Octouian* 1837, I suede hem to the Grekyssch see. **1412–20** LYDG. *Chron. Troy* II. xiii, They met a grekishe shyp. **1491** CAXTON *Vitas Patr.* (W. de W. 1495) I. clix. 168 b/2 He beynge there amonge the grekysshe Phylosophers. **1591** SPENSER *Virg. Gnat* 547 The..famous light of all the Greekish hosts. **1599** HAKLUYT *Voy.* II. 187 A Greekish Carmosell which came into Africa to steal Negroes. **1600** SURFLET *Countrie Farme* VI. xvi. 760 To make wine like vnto greekish wine. **1606** SHAKS. *Tr. & Cr.* I. iii. 221 All the Greekish heads, which with one voyce Call Agamemnon Head and Generall. **1610** HOLLAND *Camden's Brit.* (1637) 207 Diodorus Siculus..went on with the Greekish historie. **1678** CUDWORTH *Intell. Syst.* I. iv. §18. 309 The very Names of many of the Greekish Gods were originally Egyptian. **1703** T. N. *City & C. Purchaser* 45 An ancient sort of Greekish Bricks. **1812** W. TENNANT *Anster F.* I. 3 Muse, that from top of thine old Greekish hill, Didst the harp-fing'ring younker view. **1870** MORRIS *Earthly Par.* II. III. 163 A certain island-man of old..Voyaged awhile in Greekish seas.

†**2.** With reference to the language, its words, phrases, etc.; = GREEK *a.* 2. Also *occas.* of a person: Speaking Greek. *Obs.*

c **900** tr. *Bæda's Hist.* IV. ii. (1890) 258 Heora discipulas wæron wel ȝelærde ȝe in Grecisc ȝereorde ȝe in Lædenisc. *c* **1175** *Lamb. Hom.* 117 Episcopus is gerkisc noma. *c* **1200** ORMIN 4304 Writenn o Grickisshe boc. *Ibid.* 4307 Affterr Grickisshe spæche. *c* **1374** CHAUCER *Boeth.* I. pr. I. 21 (Sk.) In the nethereste hem or bordure of thise clothes men redden..a Grekissh P, that signifyeth the lyf Actif. **1481** CAXTON *Godefroy* 215 The latyns vnderstode no grekysshe language. **1578** BANISTER *Hist. Man* I. 10 The outward part ..spreadyng like vnto the winges of Battes, called therfore by the Grekish name, πτερυγοειδεις. **1594** CAREW *Tasso* (1881) 17 Two hundred followed of the Greekish tong. **1647** R. STAPYLTON *Juvenal* 87 They speake all Greeke.. Wilt thou, fourescore and six, be Greekish now?

†**3.** Of or pertaining to the Eastern Church: = GREEK *a.* 3. *Obs.*

1606 G. W[OODCOCKE] tr. *Justin's Hist.* LI 2 a, Andronicus Paleologus the elder..returned againe to the Greekish Rites. **1614** BP. HALL *Recoll. Treat.* 459 The Greekish Church (so the Russes tearm themselves). **1639** GENTILIS *Servita's Inquis.* (1676) 865 The power of punishing Offences in the Greekish Church, hath always been in the Prince.

4. In special collocations: †**Greekish fire** = Greek fire (see FIRE *sb.* 8 b); †**Greekish hay**, a leguminous plant, FENUGREEK; †**Greekish nettle**, Greek Nettle, *Urtica pilulifera.*

c **1205** LAY. 628 Stal fiht heo makeden, mid Grickisce fure. *a* **1225** *Ancr. R.* 402 Grickischs fur is imaked of reades monnes blode. *c* **1420** *Pallad. on Husb.* I. 702 For wont of gresse, on trefoil lette hem byte On gooldis wilde, on letuce, greekish hey. *c* **1450** *Alphita* (Anecd. Oxon.) 193 Crekische nettle [*MS.* netche]. **1489** CAXTON *Faytes of A.* II. xxxix. 162 Grekys fyre may be so called wel by cause that it was first founde by the grekys beyng at the sege byfore troye.

II. 5. Somewhat Greek in style or character; resembling Greek persons or things; characteristic of a Greek or Greeks.

a 1568 ASCHAM *Scholem.* II. (Arb.) 157 *Id quod vulgò amat fieri*, for *solet fieri*, is but a strange and grekysh kind of writing. **1581** MULCASTER *Positions* xxvii. (1887) 104 Such people, as though barbarous in nature, yet by traine and learning, were become greekish. **1583** FULKE *Defence* xxi. 507 So many Greekish and Latine-like terms. **1610** HEALEY *Vives on St. Aug. Citie of God* I. iv. 9 The truely Greekish leuity. **1786** BURNS *Ordination* xi, There, Learning, with his Greekish face, Grunts out some Latin ditty. **1862** MERIVALE *Rom. Emp.* (1871) V. xli. 83 They condemned as undignified and Greekish any superfluous abundance of words. **1872** F. HALL *Recent Exempl. False Philol.* 61 *note*, We have but few Greekish words in *-ist* so purely formed as *agonist*, *antagonist* [etc.].

b. Used for: Pagan, heathen.

1851 CARLYLE *Sterling* I. vii. 67, I find at this time his religion is as good as altogether Ethnic, Greekish, what Goethe calls the Heathen form of religion.

†**B.** *absol.* and *sb. Obs.*

a. The Greek language. **b.** *pl.* Greeks.

c **1050** *Byrhtferth's Handboc* in *Anglia* (1885) VIII. 302 Concurrentes on grecisc synt ȝecwedene epacte. *c* **1175** *Lamb. Hom.* 63 Bred on grikisce is Larspel to us. *Ibid.* 93 Weren heo grekisce oðer romenisce oðer egiptisse oðer of hwulche londe swa heo weren þet þe lare iherden. *c* **1205** LAY. 798 Leteð þa Grickisca [*c* **1275** Greckes] gliden to grunde.

Hence **'Greekishly** *adv.*, after the Greek fashion, in accordance with Greek idiom.

1831 *Blackw. Mag.* XXX. 118 Cowper calls him, more simply and Greekishly, 'compasser of earth'.

Greekize (ˈgriːkaɪz), *v. rare.* [f. GREEK + -IZE.] *trans.* = GRÆCIZE I. So **'Greekism** = GRÆCISM 2; **'Greekist**, a student of Greek.

1796 COLERIDGE *Lett.* (1895) 182 But I forgot that you are not a Greekist. **1800** W. TAYLOR in *Monthly Mag.* IX. 564 Miss was a pedant in as short a time as ever pedant yet took to become Greekised. **1803** SOUTHEY in Robberds *Mem. W. Taylor* I. 452–3 You have ruined your style by Germanisms, Latinisms and Greekisms. **1841** D'ISRAELI *Amen. Lit.* (1867) 130 Du Bartas, and others, imbued with Attic literature, Greekised the French idiom.

†**'Greekland.** *Obs.* [f. GREEK *sb.* + LAND.] The land of the Greeks; Greece.

c **1000** ÆLFRIC *Hom.* I. 558 Dionisius ȝewende on ðam timan from Greclande. *c* **1200** ORMIN 16423 An staff þatt iss ȝehatenn *MY* Affterr Gricclandess spæche. *c* **1205** LAY. 327 He iwende sorhful ouer sea streames into Griclonde [*c* **1275** Greclonde]. **1535** COVERDALE *Acts* xx. 2 He came in to Grekelonde & there abode thre monethes. *a* **1568** —— *Bk. Death* III. x. (1579) 292 The kynge of Barbarie..whom he [Themistocles] before had driuen out of Greekeland.

Greek-like (ˈgriːklaɪk), *a.* [f. GREEK *a.* + -LIKE.] Resembling what is Greek in style or character.

1847 LD. LINDSAY *Chr. Art* I. 65 Grouping most picturesquely with the varied architectural lines of the Greek-like city [Ancona] it looks down upon.

Greekling (ˈgriːklɪŋ). [f. GREEK *sb.*[1] + -LING, after L. *Græculus* dim. of *Græcus*.] A little or insignificant Greek; a degenerate, contemptible Greek; in quot. 1880, one who contemptibly affects Græcisms.

1636 B. JONSON *Discov.* (1640) 128 Which of the Greekelings durst ever give precepts to Demosthenes? **1667** DRYDEN *Ess. Dram. Poesie* Dram. Wks. 1725 I. 30 The talkative Greeklings (as Ben Johnson calls them). **1850** BLACKIE *Æschylus* I. 331 'Tis one of the many tricks of that wisdom of words which the curious Greeklings sought..in the rough Gospel of St. Paul. **1861** *Q. Rev.* CX. 472 The hack jeer of the upstarts of the time at all Greeks as 'Greeklings', and all philosophers as babblers. **1870** BRYANT *Iliad* I. II. 46 Ye abject Greeklings, Greeks no longer. **1880** F. A. MARCH *Spelling Reform* 25 *Ake* also is restored and *ache* turned over to the Greeklings. **1881** *Times* 6 Apr. 12/1 The commercially-minded little Greekling.

Greekly, Greekness: see under GREEK *a.*

†**'greement.** *Obs.* Forms: 5–6 grement, 6 griment, 9 greement. [perh. aphetic form of AGREEMENT. Cf., however, OF. *greement*, which may be the direct source, and GREE *v.*] Agreement, consent, accord.

c **1400** *Destr. Troy* 9384 Agamynon..by grement of all.. Meuyt vnto Missam. **1483** CAXTON *Gold. Leg.* 409 b/2 Alle byleueden by theyr gremente or for fere or for doute of Swerde. **1523** LD. BERNERS *Froiss.* I. cliv. 183 The kyng.. dyd set them in acorde and grement. **1559** *Mirr. Mag.*, *Jack Cade* i, Or was it courage that made mee so ioly, Which of the starres and bodyes grement grow? **1596** DALRYMPLE tr. *Leslie's Hist. Scot.* x. 455 Tha gyue ouer thair disputeng, but ony concord or kynd of griment. **1813** W. BEATTIE *Tales* 19 Ye'll make amends when ye come back. Gueed greement's best.

green (griːn), *a.* and *sb.* Forms: 1 grœni, gréne, 2–7 grene, 4–6 grenn(e, greyn(e, 4–7 greene, gren, 6 greane, grein(e, gryne, 7 grien, 5– green. [OE. *gréne* = OFris. *grêne*, OS. *grôni* (MDu. *grone*, Du. *groen*), OHG. *gruoni*, *kruoni* (MHG. *grüene*, G. *grün*), ON. *grœnn* (Da. *grøn* Sw. *grön*):— OTeut. **grônjo-*, f. OTeut. root **grô-*, whence GROW *v.* Cf. GRASS.]

A. *adj.*

I. With reference to colour.

1. The adjective denoting the colour which in the spectrum is intermediate between blue and yellow; in nature chiefly conspicuous as the colour of growing herbage and leaves.

a. Said of foliage, grass, and the like.

a **700** *Epinal Gloss.* 298 *Carpassini*, gresgro[e]ni. *c* **1000** *Sax. Leechd.* I. 72 Wið earena sar ȝenim þære ylcan wyrte leaf þonne heo grenost beo. *c* **1250** *Gen. & Ex.* 2775 Ðo saȝ moyses, at munt synay..fier brennen on ðe grene leaf. *a* **1300** *Cursor M.* 1256 Þat gresse..euer has siþen ben gren. **1390** GOWER *Conf.* II. 188 Like to the tree with leves grene, Upon the which no fruit is sene. **1590** SPENSER *F.Q.* III. v. 40 A dainty place..Planted with mirtle trees and laurells greene. **1610** SHAKS. *Temp.* II. i. 52 How lush and lusty the grasse looks? How greene? **1727** *Philip Quarll* (1816) 11 Grass, which, though as dry as..hay, was as green as a leek. **1838** T. THOMSON *Chem. Org. Bodies* 919 Many kilns have two floors, on the uppermost of which the greener hops are laid. *Ibid.* 976 The green colouring matter of plants. **1843** JAMES *Forest Days* ii, It will make your wheat look ten times greener. **1870** MORRIS *Earthly Par.* II. III. 2 Green grows the grass upon the dewy slope.

b. Said of the sea (properly, of the sea near the shore), and hence of Neptune.

a **1500** *Chaucer's Dreme* 1267 Sailing..Over the waves high and greene. **1606** SHAKS. *Ant. & Cl.* IV. xiv. 58, I, that with my Sword, Quarter'd the World, and o're greene Neptunes backe With Ships, made Cities. **1611** —— *Wint. T.* IV. iv. 28 The greene Neptune. **1667** MILTON *P.L.* VII. 402 Fish that..Glide under the green Wave. **1850** JAS. WILSON *Let.* in *Mem.* vii. (1859) 258 The deep green sea is at your feet. **1867** SMYTH *Sailor's Word-bk.*, *Green Sea*, a large body of water shipped on a vessel's deck; it derives its name from the green colour of a sheet of water between the eye and the light when its mass is too large to be broken up into spray.

c. Of other things.

c **725** *Corpus Gloss.* (Hessels) A 957 *Aurocalcum*, groeni aar. *c* **1200** *Trin. Coll. Hom.* 163 Hire winpel is wit..and hire mentel grene oðer burnet. *a* **1300** *Cursor M.* 9983 Þe roche..þat painted es wit grene heu. *c* **1330** R. BRUNNE *Chron.* (1810) 174 Þe sailes..some were blak & blo, Som were rede & grene. **1398** TREVISA *Barth. De P.R.* XIX. xix. (1495) 875 Hunters clothe themself in grene for the beest louyth kyndely grene colours. *c* **1420** *Liber Cocorum* (1862) 37 Bothe grene and rede thow may hit make, With iuse of herbz. **1463** *Bury Wills* (Camden) 16 A bagge of grene silk. **1500–20** DUNBAR *Poems* lxxxvii. 37 The emerant greyne. **1677** HORNECK *Gt. Law Consid.* vii. (1704) 340 He that looks on a green glass, fancies all things he looks upon to be green. **1687** A. LOVELL *Thevenot's Trav.* I. 6 The whiteness of the Earth..makes many Commanders and Knights to wear green Spectacles. **1727** *Philip Quarll* (1816) 26 Trees where the greener sort of monkies harbour. **1768–74** TUCKER *Lt. Nat.* (1852) II. 451 The gifted priestess among the Quakers is known by her green apron. **1805** *Med. Jrnl.* XIV. 237 Pain in his head, attended with vomiting, and purging, of a green and bilious matter. **1828** STARK *Elem. Nat. Hist.* I. 250 Wing-coverts green, with red margins. **1839** URE *Dict. Arts*, *Green Dye* is produced by the mixture of a blue and yellow dye, the blue being first applied. **1879** HARLAN *Eyesight* v. 63 A green light at night marks the 'starboard' or right-hand side of a vessel.

d. The particular shade is expressed by words prefixed, as *light*, *dark green*; *almond-*, *apple-*, *bottle-*, *bronze-*, *emerald-*, *lettuce-*, *olive-green*, etc.; also GRASS-GREEN, SEA-GREEN. See also B.

1648–60 HEXHAM *Dutch Dict.*, *Appel-groen*, Apple-greene. **1727–46** THOMSON *Summer* 11 The dark-green grass. **1868** *Rep. U.S. Commissioner Agric.* (1869) 79 A most beautiful metallic golden-green colour. **1887** *Lady* 20 Jan. 38/3 Pink satin bags, tied with bow and ends of bronze-green satin ribbon. **1899** *Daily News* 2 Sept. 7/2 A lining of lettuce-green batiste. *Ibid.* 16 Sept. 7/2 A beautiful dress is in almond-green cloth.

e. Forming compound adjs. with the names of other colours, as *green-and-gold*.

1831 J. H. NEWMAN *Lett.* (1891) I. 242 A beetle I picked up at Torquay was as green and gold as the stone it lay upon. **1882** DE WINDT *Equator* 100 The *Brookeana*, a beautifully-marked green-and-black butterfly.

f. Applied to meat that is putrid from long keeping, with reference to the green surface tint which it acquires.

1863 *Morning Star* 1 Jan. 5, I know men..who would not touch a hare unless it was regularly 'green' before cooking.

†**g.** ***green gown.*** In phr. ***to give a woman a green gown***: to roll her, in sport, on the grass so that her dress is stained with green; hence *euphemistically* (cf. quot. 1825–80). *Obs.*

a **1586** SIDNEY *Arcadia* I. (1598) 84 Then some greene gownes are by the lasses worne In chastest plaies, till home they walke arowe. **1599** GREENE *Geo. a Greene* Wks. (Grosart) XIV. 140 Madge pointed to meete me in your wheate-close..And first I saluted her with a greene gowne, and after fell as hard a-wooing as if the Priest had bin at our backs, to haue married vs. **1602** MUNDAY *Pal. Eng.* II. v. (1639) D, At length he was so bold as to giue her a greene gowne when I feare me she lost the flower of her chastity. **1648** HERRICK *Hesper.*, '*Corinna's going a Maying*' (1869) I. 71 Many a green-gown has been given. *a* **1700** B. E. *Dict. Cant. Crew*, *Green gown*, a throwing of young Lasses on the Grass and Kissing them. **1714** A. SMITH *Lives Highwaym.* I. 281 Our Gallant being dispos'd to give his Lady a Green Gown, she deny'd his Civility. **1764** *Low Life* (ed. 3) 73 Servants..meeting their acquaintance according to Appointment in the Fields, and giving and taking Green Gowns from each other. **1825–80** JAMIESON, *Green Gown*, the supposed badge of the loss of virginity, Roxb.

h. Phr. ***to see anything green in*** (*one's*) ***eye***: to detect any signs of gullibility. Cf. sense 8 d. (Now more usually as in B. 2 c.) *vulgar.*

1851 MAYHEW *Lond. Labour* II. 41 I'm not a tailor, but I understands about clothes, and I believe that no person ever saw anything green in my eye. **1863** READE *Hard Cash* xxiv, Do—you—see—anything—green—in this here eye?

i. Used of lights and signals on the road, railway, etc., to indicate that the traffic is free to proceed (see also quot. 1970). Hence fig. phr. (*to give*) ***the green light***, (to give) permission to proceed on a course of action; also ***green-light*** as *v. trans.* Cf. GREEN *sb.* 7 e.

1883 *Encycl. Brit.* XX. 238 *Railway Signals*... At night the place of semaphores or disks is supplied by large and powerful lamps with reflectors... In general practice, two lights..are shown,—red and green. **1937** T. RATTIGAN *French without Tears* III. i. 126 We had a bottle of wine and got pretty gay, and all the time she was giving me the old green light. **1954** WODEHOUSE *Jeeves & Feudal Spirit* xxii. 216 Carry on, old sport. You have the green light. **1968** *Highway Code* 44 *Traffic light signals*... *Green* means you may *go on* if the way is clear... *Green arrow* means that you may go in the direction shown by the arrow. **1968** F. MULLALLY *Munich Involvement* ii. 15 'Anything else I can do for you?' Her smile green-lighted the innuendo. **1968** *Times* 19 Feb. 3/7 The Greek revolutionary rulers have warned King Constantine not to attempt to return to his throne until the Papadopoulos Government gives him the green light. **1968** *Guardian* 11 Apr. 1/2 A more selective system of Customs questioning of passengers..is provided for in the finance bill published yesterday... Those who have anything to declare will go through a 'red' channel... Those who have nothing to declare will pass through a 'green' channel. **1968** *Listener* 27 June 837/2 But Professor Barnard decided to take a chance and have a go—and as so often happens, his example triggered off attempts by a whole host of imitators who had been impatiently waiting for the green light. It now seems sadly obvious that the light was not green. **1970** *Daily Tel.* 16 Dec. 3/2 He calmly drove through the 'green' channel, indicating he had nothing to declare.

j. Used to denote the colour of absinthe, esp. in ***green peril***; also *ellipt.*

1889 E. DOWSON *Let.* 18 Feb. (1967) 36, I have not felt myself since my generous allowance of the potent green on Thursday & was right 'orf' the fascinating fluid yesterday. **1905** *Westm. Gaz.* 4 May 12/1 Some statistics.. of the growth of the absinthe habit in France seem to justify the alarmists who speak of the beverage as 'the green peril'. **1908** *Daily Chron.* 21 May 1/5 This taxing of the 'green peril' will no doubt be popular.

k. Phr. ***to have green fingers*** (or ***a green thumb***), to be unusually successful in making plants grow; also *transf.*; hence ***green-fingered*** adj.

1934 R. ARKELL (*title*) Green fingers. **1943** R. CARSON *Bride saw Red* xvii. 203 Plants don't grow for me, but my wife's got a green thumb. **1943** S. CLOETE *Congo Song* xvi. 150 Some men have green fingers. Plants like them. They can make things grow because they love them. **1946** *Nature* 28 Dec. 941/2 The arts of budding and grafting can only be fully acquired by observing the green-fingered dexterity of the experienced propagator. **1949** *Eng. Studies* I. 2 Yet we are such born meddlers, and so convinced..that we have 'green fingers' of the spirit to give help and guidance in these difficult years. **1962** R. PAGE *Educ. Gardener* 16 To have 'green fingers' or a 'green thumb' is an old expression which describes the art of communicating the subtle energies of love to prosper a living plant. **1962** *Listener* 19 July 89/1 Every kind of briar, of bush rose, of rare bulb, and flowering tree flourished under her green thumb. **1963** [see AGIN *prep.*]. **1966** *Lancet* 31 Dec. 1461/2 Trees like this..would soon be produced by hybridisation and plant-hormones under the green-fingered genius of him and his helpers. **1969** *Daily Tel.* 26 Apr. 6/6 'Success with money is often accidental,' she sighed. 'One needs "green fingers" to make it grow.'

2. a. Covered with a growth of herbage or foliage; verdant; (of trees) in leaf. ***green acres*** (see quot. 1831). ***the Green Island, Green Erin***: Ireland. ***green field(s)***: used *attrib.* to denote building away from existing developments.

847 *Charter* in *O.E. Texts* 434 On grenan pytt. **1045** *Charter of Eadweard* in Kemble *Cod. Dipl.* IV. 98 Andlang ðæs wuduweȝes on ðone grene pað. *c* **1325** *Gloss. W. de Bibbesw.* in Wright *Voc.* 159 *Vert choral*, a grene balke. *c* **1386** CHAUCER *Friar's T.* 86 Wher rydestow under this grene shawe? *c* **1400** MAUNDEV. (Roxb.) viii. 28 Þat gardyne es all way grene. *c* **1450** *St. Cuthbert* (Surtees) 6624 He kepid bestys on pasture grene. *a* **1533** LD. BERNERS *Huon* xlvii. 157 The erthe was so fayre and grene. **1613** PURCHAS *Pilgrimage* (1614) 648 These Trees are alway greene: some have leaves twice a yeare. **1648** GAGE *West Ind.* xiv. 90 Harboured in a green plot of ground resembling a meadow. **1665** G. HAVERS *P. della Valle's Trav. E. Ind.* 89 The very walls of the Gardens are all green with moss. **1667** MILTON *P.L.* IV. 626 Yon flourie Arbors, yonder Allies green. **1700** DRYDEN *Flower & L.* 132 On the green bank I sat, and listened long. **1725** POPE *Odyss.* XX. 356 Who..urged for title to a consort queen, Unnumbered acres, arable and green. **1784** COWPER *Task* I. 222 Perch'd upon the green-hill top. **1831** LOUDON *Encycl. Agric.* (ed. 2) 1206 The Marquis of Hertford..has 64,000 green acres; that is, land capable of tillage, and independently of bog and mountain. **1841** LANE *Arab. Nts.* I. 102 Having in his hand a branch of a green tree. **1860** TYNDALL *Glac.* I. xvi. 118 We were soon upon the green alp. **1962** *Economist* 24 Mar. 1150/1 Continental shipyards..had the advantage of being rebuilt *de novo*, often on 'green field' sites, after wartime destruction. **1968** *Times* 9 Nov. 2/3 It would not be a 'green fields' new town but an addition to an existing development, or in an open space.

transf. *c* **1645** HOWELL *Lett.* (1650) II. *The Vote*, Sound sleeps, green dreams. **1847** EMERSON *Poems* (1857) 60 Thou ..The green silence dost displace With thy mellow, breezy bass.

b. ***green road***: a permanent farm-road giving access to fields, etc.; an untarred road (see also quot. 1938). ***green way***, †***gate***: a way well covered with verdure; hence *fig.* the pleasant path, the 'broad way'. (Cf. *primrose path*.)

In the earlier versions of the *Moral Ode* there appears to have been confusion between the riming words.

a 1200 *Moral Ode* 339 in *Lamb. Hom.* 179 Læte we þe brode stret and þe wei bene.. Go we þene narewe wei and þene wei grene. *c* 1275 *Ibid.* 335 in *O.E. Misc.* 70 Lete we þeo brode stret and þene wey grene.. Go we þene narewe wey þene wey so schene. *c* 1290 *S. Eng. Leg.* I. 6/179 Ȝwane þou comest to þe heued of þis valeie a grene wei þov schalt wiende, þat gez euene riȝt puyr est and to parays gez þat on ende. *c* 1325 in Kennett *Par. Antiq.* (1818) I. 578 Seynt Edburges grene wey. *c* 1540 *Pilgr. T.* 13 in *Thynne's Animadv.* (1865) App. i. 77 The gren gat I had more delit to folow then of deuotion to seke the halowe. *a* 1674 MILTON *Sonn.* ix. 2 Lady, that in the prime of earliest youth Wisely hast shunned the broad way and the green. 1895 *E. Angl. Gloss., Green Way*, a road over turf between hedges, usually without gates. 1900 *Eng. Dial. Dict.*, Green-road. 1938 *Oxoniensia* III. 9 These limits embrace all the country between.. the Northamptonshire forest-land on the one hand, and, on the other, all the land immediately visible or accessible from the 'green road' leading from the eastern counties to the Wiltshire Downs. 1943 *N. & Q.* CLXXV. 203 Green-road. Farm-road to fields. Kent. 1968 *Guardian* 11 July 3/6 The estate will.. be broken into four units, each separated from the others by wide spaces, which the planners call 'greenway lungs'. 1970 *Times* 26 Aug. 10/3 A plan for turning two railway lines.. into greenways for walkers, horseriders, and cyclists.. has been sent to Somerset and Devon county councils.

c. Of a season of the year: Characterized by abundance of verdure; hence, of a winter or Christmas: Mild, temperate.

1412–20 LYDG. *Chron. Troy* I. v. (1513) B v, Whan that grene vere Ypassed were aye fro yere to yere And May was come the monthe of gladnesse. ?*c* 1430 *Purif. Marie* in *Tundale's Vis.* (1843) 135 The comyng of greene veer, with fresch buddes new. 1642 FULLER *Holy & Prof. St.* III. xix. 202 A green Christmas is neither handsome nor healthfull. 1721 KELLY *Sc. Prov.* 30 A green yule makes a fat Churchyard. 1832 TENNYSON *Early Sonn.* ix, The pits Which some green Christmas crams with weary bones. 1898 *Daily News* 5 Mar. 5/2 Good English poultry.. with prices for the most part high. Owing to the green winter, however, they are not nearly so high as usual.

3. a. Of the complexion (often ***green and wan***, ***green and pale***): Having a pale, sickly, or bilious hue, indicative of fear, jealousy, ill-humour, or sickness. (Cf. Gr. χλωρός green, pale.) So ***the green eye***, the eye of jealousy (cf. GREEN-EYED *a.*). See also GREEN SICKNESS.

a 1300 *Signs bef. Judgem.* 63 in *E.E.P.* (1862) 9 Wel grene and wan sal be is [the sun's] liȝt and þat for dred so hit sal be. *c* 1300 *Havelok* 470 Al-so he wolde with hem leyke, þat weren for hunger grene and bleike. *a* 1310 in Wright *Lyric P.* 92 So muchel y thenke upon the that al y waxe grene. 1525 LD. BERNERS *Froiss.* II. lxxxiii. [lxxx.] 251 The duke.. waxed pale and grene as a lefe. 1605 SHAKS. *Macb.* I. vii. 37 Was the hope drunke, Wherein you drest your selfe? Hath it slept since? And wakes it now to looke so greene, and pale, At what it did so freely? *a* 1650 *Eger & Grime* in Furniv. *Percy Folio* I. 356 Now thou art both pale and greene. 1701 CIBBER *Love Makes Man* II. ii, The wholsomest Food for green consumptive Minds. 1783–94 BLAKE *Songs Innoc., Nurse's Song* 4 My face turns green and pale. *a* 1845 HOOD *Lamia* v. 278 Sir Lycius now Must have the green eye set in his head. 1863 READE *Hard Cash* xliii, The doctor was turning almost green with jealousy. 1887 RIDER HAGGARD *Jess* xxxi, The Boers halted and consulted, except Jacobus, who went on, still looking very green.

b. ***green jaundice***, a species of JAUNDICE which imparts a green hue to the complexion.

1822–34 *Good's Study Med.* (ed. 4) I. 340 In green jaundice the patient rarely recovers. *a* 1823 M. BAILLIE *Wks.* (1825) I. 89 The green jaundice occurs more frequently at the middle and more advanced periods of life.

4. Consisting of green herbs, plants, or vegetables,

c 1460 J. RUSSELL *Bk. Nurture* 97 Beware of saladis, grene metis, and of frutes rawe. 1607 TOPSELL *Four-f. Beasts* (1658) 59 From April unto June give them Grasse, and such green meat as may be found abroad. 1804 W. TENNANT *Ind. Recreat.* (ed. 2) II. 12 The grand desideratum of Indian husbandry, the want of green food for cattle. 1879 F. POLLOK *Sport Brit. Burmah* I. 234 To keep an elephant in health, his green food should be constantly changed.

5. a. When applied to fruits or plants, the designation of colour often implies some additional sense: (*a*) Unripe, immature; (*b*) young and tender; (*c*) full of vigorous life, flourishing; (*d*) retaining the natural moisture, not dried.

c 1000 *Sax. Leechd.* II. 216 Pintreowes þa grenan twigu. *a* 1300 *Cursor M.* 6044 Þat beist þan gneu vp al bidene þat þe thoner left, bath ripe and grene. 1377 LANGL. *P. Pl.* B. VI. 300 Thanne pore folke for fere fedde Hunger ȝerne With grene poret and pesen. *c* 1384 CHAUCER *H. Fame* III. 134 Pipes made of grene corne. *c* 1450 *St. Cuthbert* (Surtees) 463 Grene resches a few he schare. *c* 1450 *M.E. Med. Bk.* (Heinrich) 141 Take grene walnotes wyþ alle þe hulkes. 1526 *Pilgr. Perf.* (W. de W. 1531) 108 b, Hurte the grene blade, & you shall haue no whete there. 1578 LYTE *Dodoens* I. xviii. 28 Chamœpitys greene pound.. and layde upon great woundes.. cureth the same. 1620 VENNER *Via Recta* vii. 116 The greene and ripe Figs are hot and moyst in the first degree. 1657 R. LIGON *Barbadoes* (1673) 80 There is alwaies some green, some ripe, some rotten grapes in the bunch. 1665 BOYLE *Occas. Refl.* (1848) 68 Green Fruit, though of a good Kind, will not easily be shaken down. [1667 MILTON *P.L.* XI. 435 The green Eare, and the yellow Sheaf.] 1700 S. L. tr. *Fryke's Voy. E. Ind.* 174 They Boil [it] with a deal of green Pepper. 1853 SOYER *Pantroph.* 119 Green walnuts were much esteemed; they were served at dessert. 1872 BLACK *Adv. Phaeton* xx. 284 My dear, this is worse than eating green apples. 1884 *Public Opinion* 3 Oct. 436/1 Beware of green fruit.

b. ***green corn*** (U.S.), the unripe and tender ears of maize, commonly cooked as a table vegetable.

1716 B. CHURCH *Hist. Philip's War* (1865) I. 170 This season'd his Cow-beaf so that with it and the dry'd green-corn.. he made a very hearty Supper. 1817 J. BRADBURY *Trav. Amer.* 114 Sweet corn, is corn gathered before it is ripe, and dried in the sun: it is called by the Americans green corn, or corn in the milk. 1882 *Garden* 25 Mar. 191/3 To go to America for a good.. head of green Corn.

II. *transf.* and *fig.* Connoting qualities which in plants or fruits are indicated by green colour.

6. Full of vitality; not withered or worn out.

a. *rarely* of material things. †Of the bones (*Sc.*): Full of marrow; esp. in phr. ***to keep the bones green***: to maintain good health. ***in the green tree*** (after Luke xxiii. 31, Gr. ἐν τῷ ὑγρῷ ξύλῳ, Vulg. *in viridi ligno*): under conditions not involving pressure or hardship.

c 950 *Lindisf. Gosp.* Luke xxiii. 31 Forðon ȝif in groene tree [*Ags. Gosp.* on grenum treowe: similarly in all later versions] ðas doað in dryȝi huæd bið? *a* 1300 *Cursor M.* 16663 Quen suilk in grene tre es wroght, in dri sal mikel mare. 1513 DOUGLAS *Æneis* I. x. 6 Within hir banis grene The hote fyir of luif to kendle. 1577 HANMER *Anc. Eccl. Hist.* (1619) 148 Their fresh and greene bodies. 1788 E. PICKEN *Poems* (1813) II. 41 Tak a skair O' what may keep the banes just green. 1824 SCOTT *St. Ronan's* x, Ye might.. have gotten.. a Commissaryship.. to keep the banes green. 1890 W. E. NORRIS *Adrian Vidal* xiv, If this was done in the green tree, what would be done in the dry?

b. of immaterial things, *esp.* the memory of a person or event; also in ***green old age***.

c 1380 WYCLIF *Wks.* (1880) 408 A curat shulde preche to þe puple treuþis of goddis lawe þat euere ben grene. 1390 GOWER *Conf.* I. 85 For ever it is a liche grene The great love which I have. 1513 DOUGLAS *Æneis* I. ix. 54 Thi honour and thi fame sall euir be grene. 1535 STEWART *Cron. Scot.* I. 549 The rancour wes so ruttit in thair hairt, And in thair mynd so recent and so grene, That [etc.]. 1579 FENTON *Guicciard.* I. (1599) 6 The example is fresh and greene, that [etc.]. 1583 STUBBES *Anat. Abus.* I. (1879) 100 The remembrance wherof is yet green in their heds. 1634 T. JOHNSON tr. *Parey's Chirurg.* I. v. (1678) 5 Those we say, are beginning to grow Old, or in their green Old-age. 1666 BUNYAN *Grace abounding* §233 (1692) 108 Those Graces of God that now were green on me. 1766 GOLDSM. *Vic. W.* xiv, His green old age seemed to be the result of health and benevolence. 1821 LAMB *Elia* Ser. I. *Old Benchers*, He is yet in green and vigorous senility. 1840 DICKENS *Barn. Rudge* lxiii, My heart is green enough to scorn and despise every man among you. 1855 MACAULAY *Hist. Eng.* xiv. III. 413 In youth his habits had been temperate; and his temperance had its proper reward, a singularly green and vigorous old age. 1888 BURGON *Lives 12 Gd. Men* II. vii. 121 Memorials, which will keep his memory fresh and green for many a long year. 1896 A. DOBSON *18th Cent. Vign.* Ser. III. i. 8 His still green recollections of that memorable night.

†**7.** Of tender age, youthful. *Obs.*

1412–20 LYDG. *Chron. Troy* I. v. (1555) C vi b, This is affyrmed of them that were ful sage And specially whyle they be grene [*ed.* 1513 *reads* tendre] of age. *c* 1450 *Merlin* 287 The children were tendre and grene. 1475 *Bk. Noblesse* 44 Johan duc of Bedforde.. in his grene age was lieutenaunt of the marchis. 1508 DUNBAR *Gold. Targe* 155 Syne tender Youth come wyth hir virgyns ying, Grene Innocence, and schamefull Abaising. 1563 B. GOOGE *Eglogs* vi. (Arb.) 53 Eche thyng is easely made to obaye, whyle it is yong and grene. 1601 CORNWALLYES *Ess.* II. xlviii. (1631) 304 The world in his greenest time lay in the arms of ignorance. 1611 BIBLE *Transl. Pref.* 4 In that new world and greene age of the Church. 1664 MARVELL *Corr.* Wks. 1872–5 II. 181, I never yet saw a Prince.. whose young mind did in his greenest years promise and threaten so much and so handsomely. 1697 DRYDEN *Virg. Georg.* III. 263 While yet his Youth is flexible and green. 1742 YOUNG *Nt. Th.* v. 633 Tho' grey our Heads, our Thoughts and Aims are green. 1748 RICHARDSON *Clarissa* (1811) VIII. 128 A little time hence, the now-green head will be grey. 1808 J. BARLOW *Columb.* VII. 577 Green in years But ripe in glory. 1814 *Intrigues of a Day* III. iii, As the proverb says, a grey head is often placed on green shoulders. 1818 SCOTT *Rob Roy* i, Your greener age and robust constitution promise longer life.

8. Unripe, immature, undeveloped. Often with mixture of sense 9; also with conscious allusion to the literal use in sense 5.

a. Of things, chiefly immaterial; Not fully developed, matured, or elaborated.

c 1300 *Prov. Hendyng* in *Rel. Ant.* I. 111 He wol speke wordes grene, Er þen hue buen rype. 1426 LYDG. *De Guil. Pilgr.* 2707 Correcte a cause grene & newe. 1594 PLAT *Jewell-ho.* II. 35 Vntill som better clarke confirme this greene conceipt. 1687 DRYDEN *Hind & P.* III. 855 To ripen green revenge your hopes attend. 1727 DE FOE *Syst. Magic* I. i. (1840) 2 At that time the knowledge of Nature was very green and young in the world. 1792 BURKE *Corr.* (1844) III. 394 The Regency,.. when Price's sermon appeared, was still green and raw. 1860 READE *Cloister & H.* xxxviii. (1896) 110 Thy beard is ripe, thy fellow's is green; he shall be the younger. 1876 GEO. ELIOT *Dan. Der.* IV. lxix. 346 But these are green resolves.

b. Applied to young birds.

1660 FISHER *Rustick's Alarm* Wks. (1679) 226 They run like a company of Green-guls with Shells on their Heads. 1884 *St. James's Gaz.* 22 Aug. 4/2 Good sportsmen look upon the blackcock as not being sufficiently ripe for the gun at the date.. the bird being green and tender.

c. Of persons, their powers or capacities: Immature, raw, untrained, inexperienced. So ***green hand*** (cf. HAND 8). Also in sporting use, of animals: Untrained.

1548 UDALL, etc. *Erasm. Par. Luke* vi. 75 Unlearned and rawe or grene in cunning. *c* 1573 CARTWRIGHT *Reply to Whitgift's Answ.* 27 Hauing a contrary precept giuen, that no newe plant, or greene christian, should be taken to the ministerie. 1585 T. WASHINGTON tr. *Nicholay's Voy.* III. xiv. 97 b, As they were young of yeeres and age, they should also bee greene of sense and judgment. 1588 SHAKS. *L.L.L.* I. ii. 94. 1603 KNOLLES *Hist. Turks* (1621) 744 He being an old commander, and halfe blind, saw more in the matter than all those greene captaines with their sharpe sight. 1639 FULLER *Holy War* I. xii. (1640) 18 Green striplings unripe for warre. 1735 DYCHE & PARDON *Dict.* s.v., A young or inexperienced Person in Arts, Sciences, &c. is sometimes said to be green. 1822 LAMB *Elia* Ser. I. *Some old Actors*, Green probationers in mischief. 1845 STOCQUELER *Handbk. Brit. India* (1854) 102 Boys and girls, green in mind though blooming in person. 1864 C. F. HALE *Life with Esquimaux* I. 91 Being a stranger in the place and a green hand, I found it very difficult to get a berth. 1871 S. SMILES Jr. *Boy's Voy. Round World* xiii. (1875) 136, I had gone out parrot-potting, with another young fellow almost as green as myself. 1876 *Coursing Calendar* 5 Mr Vyner's puppy appearing to run very green to commence with. 1880 A. H. HUTH *Buckle* I. iv. 246 [He] chooses his course while his mind is yet green and unformed. 1889 C. BOOTH *Labour & Life People* I. 232 At first the new master will live on 'green' labour. 1894 ASTLEY *50 Years Life* II. 75 Actea ran very green, and had a small boy on her back. 1894 *Times* 10 Jan. 11/5 Very early in her voyage she encountered a very severe storm, and that with a green crew. 1897 *Outing* (U.S.) May 110/2 Trained coach-horses.. as well as green stock. 1965 *Observer* (Colour Suppl.) 30 May 34 *Running green*, a horse that gets upset by the crowd and the noise and other unfamiliar surroundings.

d. Hence, of persons, their ideas or actions: Simple, gullible; characterized by, or displaying, simplicity. So phr. ***to be not as green as one is cabbage-looking***: to be less of a fool than might be assumed.

1605 CHAPMAN *All Fooles* IV. i, You're green, your credulous; easy to be blinded. 1695 CONGREVE *Love for L.* IV. xiii, He hadn't a Word to say, and so I left 'n, and the green Girl together. 1753 *Scots Mag.* Oct. 490/2 Green.. I continued even in externals near two years. 1825 C. M. WESTMACOTT *Eng. Spy* I. 236 *note*, 'Chaunting' a horse to a green one. 1838 *Lett. fr. Madras* (1843) 219 Ladies who are very blue are apt to be rather green. 1844 DICKENS *Mart. Chuz.* xxvii, I've been and got married. That's rather green, you'll say. 1861 HUGHES *Tom Brown at Oxf.* iv. (1889) 36 Most readers.. will think our hero very green for being puzzled at so simple a matter. 1884 PAE *Eustace* 35 The chap is precious green for one of his inches. 1898, 1922 [see CABBAGE *sb.*[1] 1 d]. 1931 E. RAYMOND *Mary Leith* IV. ii. 318, I ain't the sort to be taken in by his gaff. I may look a fool.. but I'm not as green as I'm cabbage-looking. 1969 J. N. SMITH *Is he Dead, Miss ffinch?* xviii. 117 Women don't have a sense of direction... But I'm not as green as I'm cabbage-looking. 1970 J. FLEMING *Young Man, I think you're Dying* i. 16 Mind you, she's not as green as she's cabbage-looking, she never leaves you alone in the room.

9. That has not been prepared by drying; hence, in wider sense, not ready for use or consumption.

a. Of wood, vegetable products, or things made of these: Not thoroughly dried, unseasoned.

1477 EARL RIVERS (Caxton) *Dictes* 65 Grene wode is hotter than the other whan it is wel kyndeled. 1523 FITZHERB. *Bk. Husb.* §24 If the rake be made of grene woode, the heed wyll not abyde vppon the stele. 1600 SHAKS. *A.Y.L.* III. iii. 90 One of you wil proue a shrunke pannell, and like greene timber, warpe, warpe. 1604 E. GRIMSTONE *Hist. Siege Ostend* 29 Certaine Gabions.. being too greene or wet. 1611 BIBLE *Judg.* xvi. 7 If they binde mee with seuen greene withs [*marg.* Or, newe coards, Heb. moist], that were neuer dried. 1749 ERSKINE *Serm.* Wks. 1871 III. 367 A green yoke is galling and uneasy to the cattle. 1777 G. FORSTER *Voy. round World* I. 498 It had unfortunately been packed into new, or what are called green casks. 1881 *Chicago Times* 1 June, Lumber Rep., Quotations for cargoes of green lumber.

b. Of flesh, fish: Freshly killed or taken; unsalted; uncured; undried. Of meat: Uncooked, underdone, raw. Of ham, bacon: Undried, unsmoked.

c 1460 [see GREEN-FISH 1]. 1577 HARRISON *England* III. i. in Holinshed I. 221/2 Of these [swine] some we eat greene for porke, and other dried vp into bakon. 1607 TOPSELL *Four-f. Beasts* (1658) 463 Their Oxen, Camels, and Sheep, eat fishes after they be dryed, for they care not for them when they be green. 1651 *Manch. Crt. Leet Rec.* (1887) IV. 68 For sellinge a stirke beefe w[ch] wee were informed had the turne and for sellinge a quarter of greene beefe the same day. 1697 DAMPIER *Voy.* (1729) I. 538 Their Legs are wrapt round with Sheeps-guts.. These are put on when they are green. 1714 *Fr. Bk. of Rates* 42 Fish-Cod dry.. *Ditto* Green. 1725 WATTS *Logic* I. iv. §8 We say, the Meat is green when it is half-roasted. 1796 MRS. GLASSE *Cookery* iii. 26 A green ham wants no soaking. 1814 PEGGE *Suppl. to Grose, Green*, raw, not done enough. 1845 DISRAELI *Sybil* VI. vii, "Tis the tenpence a pound flitch', said the comely dame.. 'I have paid as much for very green stuff', said Mrs. Mullins. 1879 *Cassell's Techn. Educ.* IV. 352/2 The sides are re-stacked and salted.. They are now 'green bacon', and only require drying and smoking.

c. Of a skin or hide: Raw, untanned, unseasoned. (***green hide*** is freq. written with a hyphen or as a single word, esp. when used attrib.)

1577 HANMER *Anc. Eccl. Hist.* VIII. xxiii. (1585) 163 A yong man.. was wrapped together with a dogge and a serpent in a greene oxe hyde, and caste into the depth of the sea. 1727–41 CHAMBERS *Cycl.*, *Green hide*, is that not yet tanned, or dressed, but such as taken off from the carcase. 1840 R. H. DANA *Bef. Mast* xxx. 111 Wheel-ropes made of green hide, laid up in the form of ropes. 1852 MORFIT *Tanning & Currying* (1853) 148 It would be greatly to the interest of the tanner.. if all hides were imported in a green state, that is, merely salted. 1881 A. C. GRANT *Bush Life Queensland* iii. (1882) 21 A long-handled whip with thong of raw salted hide, called in the colony 'greenhide'. *Ibid.* viii. 72 A strongly plaited greenhide-halter was now slipped over the head. 1889 'ROLF BOLDREWOOD' *Robbery under Arms* xxiv, Most of 'em were.. winding up greenhide buckets filled with gravel from shafts. 1893 SELOUS *Trav. S.E. Africa* 92 This skin.. was the green hide of an eland bull.

d. Of clay, bricks, pottery, etc.: Undried, unburnt, unfired. ***green sand***: 'sand used for moulds without previous drying or mixture' (Raymond *Mining Gloss.* 1881); see also quot. 1839.

1825 J. NICHOLSON *Operat. Mechanic* 463 When the clay is in one peculiar state, called the green state. **1831** J. HOLLAND *Manuf. Metal* I. 71 *Green sand*, as that used in moist casting, in contradistinction to dry, is termed by the workmen. **1839** URE *Dict. Arts* 516 Moulding in green sand.—The name green is given to a mixture of the sand as it comes from its native bed, with about one twelfth its bulk of coal reduced to powder, and damped in such a manner as to form a porous compound. **1875** [see GREEN-HOUSE 2]. **1882** *Chamb. Jrnl.* 80 (*Pottery*) The salt-glaze process must essentially modify the ornamentation of the ware, since it receives it in the stage of raw or green clay. **1884** KNIGHT *Dict. Mech.* Suppl., *Green Ware* (*Ceramics*), articles just molded or otherwise shaped, before drying and baking.

10. Unaltered by time or natural processes; fresh, new.

a. Of a wound: Recent, fresh, unhealed, raw.

1297 R. GLOUC. (Rolls) 8670 To winchestre he was ilad al mid is grene wounde. *c* **1400** *St. Alexius* (Laud 622) 316 Wiþ his blood & peynes grene. **1541** R. COPLAND *Galyen's Terap.* 2 Dj, Is nat that to cure an vlcere as a grene wounde? **1612** WOODALL *Surg. Mate* Wks. (1653) 73 Resina..is excellent for the cure of green and fresh wounds. **1625** BACON *Ess.*, *Revenge* (Arb.) 503 A Man that studieth Revenge, keepes his owne Wounds greene, which otherwise would heale. *a* **1682** SIR T. BROWNE *Tracts* 15 Pouring oil into a green wound. **1760** HOME *Siege Aquileia* 111, Like a green wound, At first I felt it not. **1780** BURKE *Sp. Bristol previous to Elect.* Wks. III. 366 Whilst the wounds of those I loved were yet green. **1866** CONINGTON *Æneid* VI. (1867) 193 Her death-wound bleeding yet and green.

fig. **1642** FULLER *Holy & Prof. St.* V. x. 393 Making the green wound of an errour fester into the old soare of an Heresie.

b. Retaining the traces of newness; perceptibly fresh or recent. *Obs.* exc. in technical uses.

15.. *Aberd. Reg.* (Jam.), New and grein graves. **1611** COTGR., *Peindre à fraiz*, to paint with water-colours on a greene, or new-mortered, wall. **1679** *Trials of Wakeman* &c. 30 He believes that the hand that writ the Letter..and the Bill that he saw green..were the same. **1721** PERRY *Daggenh. Breach* 87 The Mischief that must ensue if the Tide went over such a green Bank or Wall of Earth. **1739** 'R. BULL' tr. *Dedekindus' Grobianus* 174 Bid 'em be jogging, while their Boots are green. **1776** G. SEMPLE *Building in Water* 49 To preserve the green Mortar..from being washed away before it would get proper Time to cement. **1878** F. S. WILLIAMS *Midl. Railw.* 653 If the fire is 'green' (that is, if coals have only lately been put on).

c. †Of oil, wine, etc.: Unmatured, not mellowed by keeping; also, in favourable sense, fresh, not rank or stale (*obs.*). Also (*Sc.*) of milk: That has recently begun to flow (after childbearing, calving, etc.).

1483 *Vulgaria abs Terentio* 15 b, This wyne is ouyr grene, that is ryper. **1519** HORMAN *Vulg.* 41 A cuppe of grene [L. *austerum*] wyne. **1606** HOLLAND *Sueton.* 22 His Host set before him..olde ranke oile in steed of greene, sweet, & fresh. **1607** TOPSELL *Four-f. Beasts* (1658) 197 Two ounces of this Goats-grease, and a pinte of green Oyl mixed together. **1616** SURFL. & MARKH. *Country Farme* 632 Such greene wines..are..more hurtfull than any other. **1712** STEELE *Spect.* No. 264 ¶5 It [Port] strengthens Digestion.. which green Wines of any kind can't do. **1768** ROSS *Helenore* 6 Reed that her milk gat wrang fan it was green. **1825–80** JAMIESON, *Green-milk*, milk of a cow just calved, Banffs.

†**d.** Of persons: recently recovered from an illness (const. *of*). Of a mother: recently delivered. ***green in earth***: just buried. *Obs.*

1592 SHAKS. *Rom. & Jul.* IV. iii. 42 Where bloody Tybalt, yet but greene in earth, Lies festring in his shrow'd. **1598** R. BERNARD tr. *Terence, Adelphi* V. vii, Its the better a great deale then the greene woman be brought hither thro the streets. **1660** FULLER *Mixt. Contempl.* (1841) 250 England is this green woman, lately brought to bed of a long-expected child, Liberty. **1706** *Lond. Gaz.* No. 4254/4 William Coster ..green of the Small-pox. **1825–80** JAMIESON, *Green cow*, a cow recently calved; denominated from the freshness of her milk.

11. Of, pertaining to, or supporting environmentalism (esp. as a political issue); that belongs to or supports an ecological party; *loosely*, environmentalist, ecological. Cf. sense 17 of the sb. below.

The association of the colour *green* with the environmentalist lobby, esp. in Europe, dates from the early 1970s in West Germany, notably with the *Grüne Aktion Zukunft* Green Campaign for the Future, and the *grüne Listen* green lists (of ecological election candidates), both of which emerged mainly from campaigns against nuclear power stations.

1971 [see GREENPEACE]. **1973** *Courier-Mail* (Brisbane) 4 June 8/10 'Green' bans have been introduced by the New South Wales Building and Construction Workers' Union. **1977** *Undercurrents* June–July 38/1 What of local elections in France, and, most importantly, the 'Green' party in Paris? **1978** *Economist* 14 Jan. 39/1 European politics are turning green; or so the ecologists would have us believe. *Ibid.*, The Lower Saxons, whose party is known as the Green Environment List or, more euphoniously, as the Green party, consider themselves in the front line of the ecological movement. Their state has seen some violent demonstrations against nuclear power stations. **1979** *Now!* 21–27 Sept. 71/1 The rebuff to 'green', environmentalist ideals is displayed by the drop in the Centre Party's vote from 24 to 18 per cent. **1985** *Times* 25 Apr. 13/6 Dr David Clark, Labour MP for South Shields and Opposition spokesman on 'green' issues. **1985** *Sunday Times* 22 Sept. 2/8 The 5,000-strong Ecology Party swapped its 'too middle class' name for the Green Party at its annual conference in Dover yesterday.

III. Combinations.

12. General combinations: **a.** parasynthetic and instrumental, as ***green-backed***, ***-bodied***, ***-bordered***, ***-boughed***, ***-breasted***, ***-capped***, ***-curtained***, ***-decked***, ***-edged***, ***-embroidered***, ***-faced***, ***-feathered***, ***-fringed***, ***-garbed***, ***-glazed***, ***-grown***, ***-haired***, ***-headed***, ***-hearted***, ***-hewed***, ***-leaved***, ***-legged***, ***-mantled***, ***-recessed***, ***-ribbed***, ***-seeded***, ***-shaded***, ***-shadowed***, ***-sheathed***, ***-striped***, ***-suited***, ***-throated***, ***-twined***, ***-turfed***, ***-veined***, ***-waved*** adjs.; also ***green-flesh***, †***green-leave*** (= having green leaves), ***green-leafy*** adjs.

1792 MAR. RIDDELL *Voy. Madeira* 77 The *green-backed cavally (*gasterosteus Carolinus* Lin.). **1839** R. REEVE *Mem.* (1898) I. 104 A neat *green-bodied glass chariot. **1891** C. JAMES *Rom. Rigmarole* 22 The *green-bordered road was white with dust. **1776** MICKLE tr. *Camoens' Lusiad* 257 The *green-boughed forests by the lawns of Thames. **1645** QUARLES *Sol. Recant.* ii. 46 Teach her to slide..through the fluid veynes Of the *green breasted stream-embroydred Plaines. **1922** JOYCE *Ulysses* 499 A *greencapped dark lantern. **1963** G. MCINNES *Road to Gundagai* x. 154, I saw ..some green-capped boys marching. **1859** MRS. CARLYLE *Lett.* III. 5 The elegant *green-curtained bed. **1583** STANYHURST *Æneis* III. (Arb.) 74 From thence wee trauayled to the *greenedeckt gaylye Donysa. **1727–46** THOMSON *Summer* 698 For oft these valleys shift Their *green-embroidered robe to fiery brown. **1916** H. G. WELLS *Mr. Britling* I. v. 138 *Green-faced and pitiful under an anaesthetic. **1655** MOUFET & BENNET *Health's Improv.* (1746) 169 Yet [geese] being taken whilst they are young, *green feather'd, and well fatted. **1855** BROWNING *De Gustibus, Men & Women* 149 A girl bare-footed brings and tumbles Down on the pavement, *green-flesh melons. **1686** *Lond. Gaz.* No. 2126/4 A..Saddle *green-fring'd round the Seat. **1808** SCOTT *Marm.* VI. Introd., The *green-garb'd ranger. **1891** HODGKIN *Ex. Early Eng. Pottery* Introd. 9 The *Green-glazed Ware, with a buff body..is called Tudor ware. **1807** DOR. WORDSWORTH in *Mem. of Coleorton* (1887) I. 220 The floor of the alley..is simply meant to be *green-grown, which it will in a short time be with short moss. **1776** MICKLE tr. *Camoens' Lusiad* 475 The *green-hair'd Nereids tend the bowery dells. **1847** EMERSON *Poems* (1857) 24 The green-haired forest. **1807–8** W. IRVING *Salmag.* (1824) 335 The *green-headed monkey of Timandi. **1852** DICKENS *Bleak-Ho.* xxxvii, He is such a cheery fellow..Fresh and *green-hearted! **1508** DUNBAR *Tua Mariit Wemen* 11 Ane holyn hewinlie *grein hewit. *a* **1849** J. C. MANGAN *Poems* (1859) 357 Each *green-leafy bosk and hollow. **1607** ROWLANDS *Famous Hist.* 39 Where shady trees Embrac'd each other in their *green-leave arms. *c* **1620** Z. BOYD *Zion's Flowers* (1855) 39 It will be still *Greene leaved. **1861** MISS PRATT *Flower. Pl.* IV. 61 Green-leaved Hound's-tongue. **1678** RAY *Willughby's Ornith.* 299 The *green-leg'd Horseman. **1831** CARLYLE *Sart. Res.* III. viii, A hugh Troglodyte Chasm, with frightful *green-mantled pools. **1820** KEATS *Lamia* I. 144 Into the *green-recessed woods they flew. **1796** WITHERING *Brit. Plants* (ed. 3) III. 308 *Green-ribbed Spleenwort. **1880** *Plain Hints Needlework* 73 The other varieties are Nankin cotton, *green-seeded, etc. **1909** *Westm. Gaz.* 15 May 6/2 A *green-shaded city nestling oasis-like in its arena. **1854** 'G. GREENWOOD' *Haps & Mishaps* 19 Every hill & *green-shadowed vale..spoke to my heart. **1955** P. LARKIN *Less Deceived* 36 Green-shadowed people sit, or walk in rings. **1833** TENNYSON *Poems, Lady of Shalott* 8 The *greensheathed daffodilly. **1870** MORRIS *Earthly Par.* I. I. 191 *Greenstriped onions. **1859** TENNYSON *Guinevere* 22 All the court *Green-suited, but with plumes that mock'd the may, Had been, their wont, a-maying. **1861** J. GOULD *Trochilidæ* II, *Delattria viridipallens*, *Green-throated Cazique. **1851** H. MELVILLE *Whale* II. xii. 92 His *green-turfed, flowery Nile. **1933** W. DE LA MARE *Fleeting* 101 Meek harebell hung her head Over the green-turfed chalk. **1848** ELIZA COOK *Xmas Song of Poor Man* i. 6 A merry Christmas to ye all, Who sit beneath the *green-twined roof. **1895** *Oracle Encycl.* I. 565/2 The *green-veined white butterfly. **17..** *Sir Patrick Spens* xv. in Child *Ballads* (1885) II. 22/2, I see the *green-waved sea.

b. complemental, as ***green-dropping***, ***-glimmering***, ***-growing***, ***-shining*** adjs.; ***green-stain*** vb.

1592 SHAKS. *Ven. & Ad.* 1176 She crop's the stalke, and in the breach appeares, *Green-dropping sap, which she compares to teares. **1859** TENNYSON *Lancelot & Elaine* 482 A wild wave..*Green-glimmering toward the summit. **1841** LONGF. *Childr. Lord's Supper* 81 E'en as the *green-growing bud is unfolded when spring-tide approaches. **1858** TENNYSON in *Mem.* (1897) I. 428 One great wave, *green-shining, past..high up beside the vessel. **1856** AIRD *Poet. Wks.* 22 Clover leaves *green-stain his corduroys.

c. qualifying the names of other colours (= greenish, greeny), as ***green-black***, ***-blue***, ***-gold***, ***-golden***, ***-grey***, ***-yellow*** adjs. (occas. sbs.).

1849 D. CAMPBELL *Inorg. Chem.* 281 Leaving this oxide in *green-black, anhydrous, lustrous crystals. **1844** LOUISA S. COSTELLO *Béarn & Pyrenees* II. 41 A broad space of clear *green-blue sky was seen. *a* **1843** SOUTHEY *Comm.-pl. Bk.* Ser. II. (1849) 602 That *green-gold beetle, the most splendid of British insects. **1868** W. CORY *Lett. & Jrnls.* (1897) 240 Light on steep *green-grey slopes. **1876** 'SARAH TYTLER' *What She came through* xli, The green-grey or 'water of the Nile', dear to the hearts of artists. **1849** D. CAMPBELL *Inorg. Chem.* 297 From black, becoming blue-green, *green-yellow, deep-red.

13. a. Special collocations: **Green Beret**, the nickname for a member of the British, and later the American, Army Commandos; **green-book**, a book with a green cover, *spec.* an official publication of the Indian Government (cf. BLUE-BOOK); †**green box**, an upper box at a theatre; **green butter**, a savoury butter (see also quot. 1938); **green card**, an international insurance document required by motorists taking their cars abroad; **green-charge**, gunpowder of which the ingredients have been mixed but have not yet undergone the incorporating process; †**green coffer**, ? a strong box covered with green cloth (cf. GREEN CLOTH); **green crop**, a crop used for food while in a green or unripe state, as opposed to a grain crop, hay crop, etc.; **green cross**, designating a poison gas shell marked with a green cross, or its contents; **green curtain** *Theatr.* (see quot. 1961); **green ebony**, the wood of the West Indian tree *Jacaranda ovalifolia*; also of *Excœcaria glandulosa*; **green fat**, the green gelatinous portion of the turtle, highly esteemed by epicures; **green fingers** *pl.*, **-fingered** *a.* (see GREEN *a.* 1 k); †**green-finned** *a.*, of oysters (see *green oyster* below); **green fire**, a pyrotechnical composition, consisting of sulphur, potassium chlorate, and a salt of barium, which burns with a green flame; **green flash** (see quot. 1925); **green gill** (*U.S.*), the condition of oysters when tinged green by feeding on confervæ (cf. GREEN *v.*[1] 2 b); so **green-gill**, **-gilled** *adjs.*, affected with 'green gill'; **green gland**, 'one of a pair of large glands in Crustacea, supposed to serve as kidneys' (Webster 1890); **green glass**, a coarse kind of glass of a green colour, bottle-glass; **green goods** *pl.*, (*a*) counterfeit greenbacks (see GREENBACK *sb.* 1); also *attrib.*; (*b*) vegetables and fruit, greengroceries; **Green Jackets** *pl.*, a name applied to the King's Royal Rifle Corps and the Rifle Brigade, from the dark green colour of their uniforms; **green-jerkin**, one who wears a green jerkin, a forester; **Green Line**, a service of green express coaches in London and the Home Counties; also *attrib.*, as ***Green Line coach***; **Green Linnets** *pl.* (see quots.); **green manure**, a mass of growing plants ploughed while green into the soil, for the purpose of enriching it; hence ***green-manuring*** vbl. sb.; **Green Mountain State**, the state of Vermont, U.S.A.; **green oak**, the wood of oak branches stained green by a parasitic fungus (used in the manufacture of 'Tunbridge ware'); **green oyster**, an oyster coloured green (see GREEN *v.*[1] 2 b), formerly regarded as a delicacy; **green paper** (see quot. 1969); **green-plot** = GRASS-PLOT; **green pound**, the unit of account in which prices of agricultural commodities fixed by the Common Agricultural Policy of the European Common Market are converted into sterling (the exchange value of the green pound is established annually); the similar unit in which such prices are converted into the Irish punt; **green ray** = *green flash*; **green revolution**: see REVOLUTION *sb.* 6 d; **green ribbon**, a ribbon of green colour worn (*a*) as the badge of the King's Head Club, consisting of supporters of the Duke of Monmouth (1679–1685); used *attrib.* in †***green ribbon club***, ***man***; (*b*) as part of the insignia of the Order of the Thistle; **green rod**, the rod borne as the symbol of office by the Gentleman-ushers of the Order of the Thistle; †**green rushes**, fresh rushes spread on the floor of a house in honour of a guest who is a great stranger; hence used as an exclamation of surprise or welcome on seeing a person who has been absent a long while; **green salad**, a salad made from one or more ingredients, esp. lettuce, chicory, cucumber, watercress, etc., freq. served with French dressing; **green-salted** *a.*, salted down without tanning; **green-seal**, *attrib.* of certain brands of wine, distinguished by a green seal on the cork; **green-shaving** *Leather-dressing* (see quot.); **green-side** *dial.*, grassy land, pasture land, grass, turf; **green-soil**, soil in which 'green crops' are raised; hence **green-soil** *v.*, to provide with such a soil; †**green-staff**, one who carries a green staff; **green-stick** *Path.*, a term applied to a kind of fracture (see quot. 1885); **Green Striper** (see quot. 1948); **green-stuff**, vegetation, herbage; *pl.* a commercial term for green vegetables; **green syrup** *Sugar-manuf.*, the syrup which flows off from the 'loaves'; **green table**, a table covered with green cloth; hence (*a*) *Hist.* the board of Covenanting notables which ruled Scotland in 1638–1641; (*b*) a gaming table; **green tail**, a kind of diarrhœa incident to deer; **green tar** (see quot. 1864); **green tea** (see TEA *sb.* 1 b); **green thumb** (see GREEN *a.* 1 k); **green-ware**, †(*a*) = *greenstuffs*; (*b*) see 9 d; **green water**, †(*a*) some remedy for venereal disease; (*b*) *Med.*, a name for the lochia in the later stage; (*c*) the condition of the river Nile when the water is low and consequently unwholesome.

For *green apron, ginger, hasting, pea, pip, tea*, etc., see the sbs.

1949 H. St. G. Saunders (*title*) The *Green Beret. The story of the Commandos. 1955 *Mountaineer* (Fort Carson, Colo.) 2 Dec., Twelve of the green beret Special Forces troops will jump in the next test scheduled today. 1962 *Army* June 34/2 Before each exercise starts, the Green Berets—Special Forces guerrilla leaders—have the advantage of being established in the area first. 1964 C. B. Colby *Special Forces* 18 In the top photo a 'Green Beret' takes to the air over the cornice of a hotel. 1968 *Listener* 22 Aug. 229/2 The Green Berets, as the Special Forces are nicknamed, are guerrilla teams who live in the bush and work with bigger detachments of South Vietnamese. 1970 A. Sinclair *Guevara* iii. 40 Che['s]..manual..even serves as a text-book for the Green Berets and other North American counterinsurgency special forces. 1970 *Sunday Times* 22 Nov. 23/6 Southampton [football team], as notorious as the Green Berets for their policy of search and destroy. 1892 *Times* 14 Apr. 7/3 The results of these studies stand embodied in a '*Green-book', of extraordinary interest. 1751 *Guide to Stage* 10 Unless they [ladies] take a fancy to pass away the time *en deshabille* in a *green-box. 1808 Earl Carlisle *Thoughts on Stage* 10 [Formerly] women of the town quietly took their stations in the upper boxes, called the green boxes. 1889 A. B. Marshall *Cookery Bk.* ii. 38 Montpellier or *green butter. 1938 *Thorpe's Dict. Appl. Chem.* (ed. 4) II. 187/2 'Green butters' (*i.e.* vegetable tallows which may be coloured artificially to resemble Borneo tallow). 1951 *Good Housek. Home Encycl.* 495/1 *Green butter*, a savoury spread used for biscuits, sandwiches, etc. 1965 *Sunday Times* (Colour Suppl.) 5 Sept. 96/2 To make Green Butter; cream butter with garlic.. chopped parsley..lemon juice, salt and pepper. 1959 *Motor Man.* (ed. 36) xi. 263 The motorist must get from his insurers a '*Green Card', which confirms that he has Third Party insurance cover. 1963 *Daily Tel.* 29 Nov. 1/4 Green cards were introduced 10 years ago. 1969 J. Leasor *Week of Love* v. 90 I've owned the car outside for years. I've all the papers.. Green card. Log book. 1876 Voyle *Milit. Dict.*, *Green Charge. 1896 *Globe* 10 Nov. 3/3 A 'greencharge explosion' took place at Messrs.—— Gunpowder Mills. *a*1483 *Liber Niger* in *Househ. Ord.* (1790) 65 Thys Countyng-house hathe assigned hym one charyotte complete & a sompter horse for the *grene coffyrs. 1842 Johnson *Farmer's Encycl.*, *Green crops, crops which are consumed on the farm in their unripe state. 1918 E. S. Farrow *Dict. Mil. Terms*, *Green cross shell, very dangerous asphyxiating shell, first used by the Germans, filled with diphosgene or phosgene. 1928 *Daily Express* 22 May 1/2 An immense steel flask of phosgene, the notorious Green Cross poison gas employed by Germany with such deadly effect during the war. 1931 Brophy & Partridge *Songs & Slang 1914–18* (ed. 3) 314 *Green cross shell*, an enemy gas-shell of an emetic and lachrymatory nature. 1805 *Wynne Diaries* 15 June (1940) III. 172 The Ballets have in general been curtailed..but this evening the *Green Curtain..dropped at twenty minutes after Eleven. 1826 *Life & Times Frederick Reynolds* I. i. 16, I was much surprised by seeing a person put his head through the hole in the green curtain. 1859 J. R. Planché *Love & Fortune* 31 Then amidst your applause may the green curtain fall. 1961 Bowman & Ball *Theatre Lang.* 162 *Green curtain*, a heavy outer curtain, traditional from the time of the Restoration, but now outmoded, serving variously as an act drop, fire curtain, etc. 1849 *Weale's Dict. Terms*, *Green ebony wood..is used for round rulers, turnery, marquetry-work, &c.; it is also much used for dyeing. 1858 Simmonds *Dict. Trade*, *Green-ebony*, a wood obtained from the *Jacaranda ovalifolia*, a native of the West Indies. 1830 Booth *Analyt. Dict.* I. 101 The more highly prized *Green Fat..is found.. round the abdomen. 1846 Soyer *Gastron. Regenerator* 85 Make choice of a good turtle..take out the interior, which throw away, first collecting the green fat which is upon it. 1870 Dubois *Cosmopolitan Cookery* 56 To prepare the turtle-soup..add to it some pieces of the green fat. *c*1645 Howell *Lett.* (1650) II. ii. 12, I have sent you..two barrells of Colchester oysters..I presume they are good, and all *green finnd. 1912 *Nature* 6 June 351/2 The well-known phenomenon of the *green flash at sunset. 1925 R. Clements *Gipsy of Horn* 125 For the first time I saw the 'Green Flash', as it is called. Just as the sun is about to sink below the horizon a flash of vivid green seems to leap from it. It only lasts a second and is gone. 1931 *Discovery* Apr. 112/2 The Green Flash is an interesting meteorological phenomenon. 1950 *Caribbean Q.* II. ii. 40 In the West Indies..we have the finest opportunities for observing the phenomenon of the Green Flash..the bright green-blue light flashed from the sun at the moment of sunrise and at sunset. 1963 Green flash [see *green ray* below]. 1881 Ingersoll *Oyster Industry* (10th Census U.S.) 185 In 1880 what the oystermen call the 'green-gill' began to affect the planted oysters in Back river. *Ibid.* 245 In Virginia, are to be found in the markets what are called 'green-gill' oysters. Some say they are diseased... The negroes claim that they are the best in Richmond. 1660 Boyle *New Exp. Phys. Mech.* xxxvi. 277 The courser sort of Glass (which the Trades-men are wont to call *Green-glass). 1838 Dickens *O. Twist* xxvii, A pint green-glass bottle. 1888 *Boston Transcript* (Farmer), Get a good melon, and if you can't tell for yourself by that intuition which is the best guide in such matters, then trust to your *green goods grocer's judgement. 1888 *Troy Daily Times* 3 Feb. (Farmer), The green goodsman escaped, for the only proof against him was [etc.]. 1891 Gunter *Miss Nobody* iii. xix. 223 The janitor..states that in his opinion, Stillman, Myth and Co. were in the 'green-goods' business. 1920 E. Bok *Autobiogr.* (1921) 99 A market dealer in green goods. 1824 in Sir. H. Smith *Autobiogr.* (1901) I. 3 'Well, I will make you a Rifleman, a *green jacket,' says the General. 1927 *Observer* 1 May 19 The Duke [of Connaught] loves the Green Jackets best of all in spite of his other military associations. 1970 *Times* 24 Nov. 3/6 Men of the Green Jackets created a very favourable impression of their verbal dexterity. 1826 Scott *Woodst.* xvii, By the force of his buffcoats and his *greenjerkins. 1932 *Times* 6 Feb. 14/3 *Green Line Coaches, Limited, announce that arrangements have been made for the acquisition of the Skylark Motor Coach Company..and the London to Ongar service of Associated Coaches... Licences held by the above companies to be regranted to Green Line Coaches. 1935 A. E. W. Mason *They wouldn't be Chessmen* v. 67 He..was almost run over by a Green Line charabanc. 1940 Auden *Another Time* 77 Went by Green Line bus. 1961 J. Stroud *Touch & Go* ii. 21 'How do we get there?' 'Train, I suppose. Or Green Line.' 1968 *Times* 22 Aug. 3 (*heading*) New towns are proposed within the Green Line range. 1870 Brewer *Dict. Phrase & Fable* 365/2 *Green Linnets, the 39th Foot, so called from the colour of their facings. 1901 'Linesman' *Words by Eyewitness* (1902) 191 Dorsets and Middlesex (famous old corps, with famous old *sobriquets*, 'Green Linnets' and 'Die-Hards'). 1925 Fraser & Gibbons *Soldier & Sailor Words* s.v. *Nicknames, Green Linnets, The*: The Dorsetshire Regiment. Through the 1st Battalion, as the 39th Foot. From the green facings. 1842 J. F. W. Johnston *Agric. Chem.* 141 Among *green manures the use of fresh sea-ware deserves especial mention. *Ibid.* 139 The practice of *green manuring has been in use from very early periods. 1838 *N.Y. Advert. & Express* 7 Feb. 3/4 A Mr. Fletcher of Vermont, the only Administration member from the *Green Mountain States [*sic*]. 1948 *Vermont Q.* July 74 It is of much historic interest to the Green Mountain State. 1887 Phillips *Brit. Discomyc.* 147 *Green oak. 16.. in Sprat *Hist. Roy. Soc.* (1667) 308 *Green Oysters, Commonly called Colchester-Oysters. 1858 Eyton *Oyster* 27 The 'green Oyster' formerly in such high repute, is now gone out of fashion. 1967 K. Robinson in *Hansard Commons* 6 Nov. 644, I wish to make a statement concerning the administrative structure of the medical and related services for which I am responsible. I shall..set out my views, probably in the form of a *Green Paper, as a basis for public discussion and wide consultation. 1969 *Times* 1 Mar. 8/8 Green Papers..originated with the D[epartment] [of] E[conomic] A[ffairs] in 1967. *Ibid.*, Mr. Michael Stewart.. defined a Green Paper as 'a statement by the Government not of policy already determined but of propositions put before the whole nation for discussion'. 1970 *Daily Tel.* 10 Apr. 2/1 Doctors are divided over the second Green Paper on the future structure of the National Health Service. *Ibid.*, The Green Paper, put forward for discussion, proposes the scrapping of the present hospital boards and committees. 1712 J. James tr. *Le Blond's Gardening* 28 A large double Walk, and a *Green-Plot in the Middle. 1828 J. R. Best *Italy* 410 It is approached by a neglected, unplanted, unfenced green-plot. 1974 *Financial Times* 14 Sept. 12/3 Britain and Ireland have what is labelled a *Green Pound because sterling is floating in relation to the currencies of other EEC members. 1979 *London Rev. Bks.* 25 Oct. 19/2 Because of green-pound devaluations British farm prices.. rose about 12 per cent in this period. 1987 *Times* 27 May 9/4 Mr Jopling has dismissed as 'not enough' a devaluation of nearly 4 per cent in Britain's 'green pound', the special money used in agricultural trade. 1906 W. Marriott *Hints to Meteorol. Observers* (ed. 6) 66/2 *Green ray, a flash of greenish-blue light seen, when the sun's disc appears or disappears, in a sunrise or sunset on a clear horizon. 1963 *Meteorol. Gloss.* (*Met. Office*) (ed. 4) 120 On still rarer occasions a 'green flash' or 'green ray', also lasting a few seconds, shoots above the horizon from the upper limb. 1971 *Islander* (Victoria, B.C.) 7 Mar. 2/2 It was in March I saw the rarely seen green ray. Twice..when the sun had almost disappeared the very top of its disc seemed to shoot upward, sudden and brilliant, in an emerald flame. 1680 A. Allam *Let. Wood* 12 Nov. (Bodl. MS. *Wood F.* 39 fol. 35) Prat's sonn..hath listed himself in to the *Green Ribbon Club. 1681 Wood *Life* 12 Jan. (O.H.S.) II. 512 Sr. Southby was put aside, for being a green ribband man and saying that 'the old king' [Charles I] 'died justly', and speaking against the bishops and other things. 1725 *Lond. Gaz.* No. 6344/1 The Earls..had the Honour to be invested with the Green Ribbon. 1810 G. Rose *Diaries* (1860) II. 482 His Royal Highness mentioned the vacancies of a Blue, a Green, and a Red Riband. 1815 *Sporting Mag.* XLV. 295 May I congratulate you, my Lord, on having the Green ribband? 1868 Cussans *Handbk. Her.* xviii. (1893) 246 The Officers attached to this Noble Order [of the Thistle] are: the Dean; Lord Lyon, King-of-Arms; and the Usher of the *Green Rod. 14.. *London Lyckpeny* xi. in Skeat *Spec. Eng. Lit.* 26 '*Ryshes grene', an other gan grete. 1589 Greene *Menaphon* (Arb.) 85 Indeede Doron..it is long since wee met..when you come you shall haue greene rushes, you are such a straunger. 1602 Breton *Wonders worth hearing* (Grosart) 5 Greene rushes. M. Francisco it is a wonder to see you heere in this Country. 1891 A. B. Marshall *Larger Cookery Bk.* x. 416 *Green Salad à la Bretonne... Take two hearts of well-washed and dried crisp lettuce. 1939 *Vogue's Cookery Bk.* 69 Fennel is another herb that adds distinction to an ordinary green salad. 1969 P. Highsmith *Tremor of Forgery* xi. 108 They had scrambled eggs with fried salami and a green salad. 1885 C. T. Davis *Leather* i. 55 *Green salted [hides] are those that have been salted and are thoroughly cured. 1871 Legrand *Cambr. Freshm.* 8 After having discussed a bottle of his particular *green-seal claret. 1885 *Harper's Mag.* Jan. 275/1 The hides are next trimmed with a knife..and '*green-shaving' in turn removes the roughness from the flesh side of the skin. 1613–16 W. Browne *Brit. Past.* ii. iii, A christall rill Which from the *greenside of the flowry bancke Eat doune a channell. 1796 W. Marshall *W. Eng.* I. 326 *Greenside*, grass, turf, greensward. 1880 *W. Cornw. Gloss.*, *Green side*, land kept in pasture. 'The green side is the most profitable after all'. 1805 Forsyth *Beauties Scotl.* II. 66 The soils..are.. arranged into two kinds; namely, light and clayey. The former is called turnip or *green soil. 1899 Rider Haggard in *Longm. Mag.* May 45 Our original idea was to *greensoil the whole of this little field. *a*1618 Sylvester *Hymn of Alms* 240 But reverend *Green-Staves, what's all this to you? 1885 Sir W. Roberts *Treat. Urin. & Ren. Dis.* i. (ed. 4) 8 When sharply bent they [flax-fibres] break with a '*green-stick' fracture. 1885 *Syd. Soc. Lex.*, *Greenstick fracture*, a form of fracture of a long bone in which whilst one side of the bone is broken the other is only bent. It occurs chiefly in the soft bones of children. 1948 Partridge *Dict. Forces' Slang 1939–45* 87 *Green Striper, an officer in the Special Branch of the R.N.V.R. who wears an emerald-green stripe between the gold lace on his sleeves. 1951 A. H. Cherry *Yankee R.N.* 417 The third was Lieut. Archie Pitt, *Starling's* green-striper Asdic specialist. 1851 Mayhew *Lond. Labour* II. 97/1 Street sellers of '*green stuff', including watercresses, chickweed and gru'n'sel, turf, &c. 1891 *Daily News* 30 Dec. 2/7 The potato trade is very flat. Greenstuffs in more than adequate supply for the slack demand. 1895 *Atlantic Monthly* Mar. 340 Fields of greenstuff and forage. 1839 Ure *Dict. Arts* 1209 The syrup which flows off spontaneously is called *green syrup. *a*1670 Spalding *Troub. Chas. I* (1828) I. 119 He took also with him to the *Grein Table, the marquess' boy..with ane other called Gordon..for alleadged saying they would shoot Felt Lesslie. 1825 Brockett *N.C. Words.*, *Green-table*, the large table in the Guildhall, of Newcastle. 1861 Thackeray *B. Lyndon* ix, His [the merchant's] bales of dirty indigo are his dice..and the sea is his green table. 1892 *Daily News* 24 Mar. 5/7 'Do that', say the Ryhope miners, 'and then we will meet you round a green table and discuss this question of markets and prices'. 1847 Halliwell *Green-tail*, a diarrhœa in deer, to which they are often subject. *North.* 1750 G. Hughes *Barbadoes* 50 *Green Tar. *a*1864 Gesner *Coal, Petrol.*, etc. (1865) 43 There is a petroleum spring in St. Andrew's parish, Barbadoes. The product of this spring has been sold under the name of 'green tar', and 'Barbadoes tar'. 1744–50 W. Ellis *Mod. Husbandm.* IV. iii. 104 Turneps, Clover and other *Green-ware. 1629 Massinger *Picture* iv. ii, He's acquainted With the *green water, and the spitting-pill's Familiar to him. 1841 F. H. Ramsbotham *Obstet. Med. & Surg.* 192 Before its final departure it becomes of a serous character possessing a greenish tint; it is then known, in the language of the lying-in room, by the name of the *green waters*. 1896 *Daily News* 22 July 5/3 We are now in the middle of the unhealthiest period of the year in this country—the season of 'the green water'.

b. In names of animals: **green bass**, the black bass (see bass *sb.*[1] 1 b); **green bird** = greenfinch 1; **green blights**, plant-lice, aphides; **green bone**, (*a*) the garfish; (*b*) the viviparous blenny; **green-bottle**, a fly (*Musca Cæsar*) having a green body; **green bug**, ? a kind of plant-louse [cf. F. *punaise des bois*]; **green-cod**, †(*a*) = green-fish 1; (*b*) the Coal-fish, *Gadus virens*; (*c*) the Cultus Cod, *Ophiodon elongatus*; **green cormorant**, a name in Ireland for the shag, *Phalacrocorax graculus*; **green crab**, the common shore crab, *Carcinus mænas*; **green dolphin**, an aphid, *Acyrthosiphon pisum*, that attacks peas and other Leguminosæ; **green drake**, an angler's name for the common May-fly, *Ephemera vulgata*; **green eel** (Australian), *Muræna afra*; **green grosbeak** = greenfinch 1; **green heron**, an American heron (*Ardea virescens*) with dark green back and wings; **green-leek**, an Australian parrakeet (see quot.); **green linnet** = greenfinch 1; **green-louse**, a plant-louse or aphis; **green mamba**, a venomous African snake, *Dendraspis angusticeps* or *D. viridis*; **green monkey**, the West African race of the grass monkey, *Cercopithecus æthiops*; formerly used for several other monkeys with greenish fur; **green pigeon**, a pigeon of the genus *Treron*, which is widely distributed in Africa south of the Sahara and southern Asia; **green plover**, the lapwing; **green-pollack**, the coal-fish; **green racer** *U.S.*, a popular name for several snakes belonging to the genera *Coluber* and *Masticophis*; **green swallow**, the short-bill, *Phibalura flavirostris*, of Brazil (Craig 1847); **green-tail** (*fly*), a name for the grannom fly; **green-tree ant**, the common Queensland ant; **green-wing**, the green-winged teal, *Querquedula crecca* of Europe, *Q. carolinensis* of America. For *green grasshopper, leech, lizard, monkey, turtle, woodpecker*, etc., see the sbs. Also greenback, greenfinch, etc.

1883 *Fisheries Exhib. Catal.* (ed. 4) 160 Black, White, and *Green Bass. 1897 *Outing* (U.S.) XXX. 438/1 The boys called the rock bass the 'black bass', while large and small-mouth black bass were known as 'green' bass. 1678 *Lond. Gaz.* No. 1321/4 A green Parroket..about the bigness of a *Green Bird. 1838 *Penny Cycl.* XI. 437/1 The mules bred between a hen-canary and a greenbird. 1851 Mayhew *Lond. Labour* II. 60/1 Greenfinches (called green birds, or sometimes green linnets, in the streets). 1879 Rossiter *Dict. Sci. Terms*, *Green blights = Aphidæ: insects belonging to Homoptera. 1710 Sibbald *Fife* 53 *Acus altera major Bellonii*; our Fishers call it the Gar fish..Some call it the *Green-bone. 1805 G. Barry *Orkney Isl.* 291 The Viviparous Blenny (*blennius viviparus*), from the colour of the back-bone, has here got the name of greenbone. 1883 E. P. Ramsay *Food-Fishes N.S. Wales* 29 *Belone ferox*, the 'Long Tom' of the fishermen, 'green-bone', and 'gar-fish' of Europeans. 1862 *All Year Round* 13 Sept. 7 The *green-bottle, *Musca Cæsar*, thrives best on carrion and corpses. 1712 J. James tr. *Le Blond's Gardening* 173 Insects that attack Fruit-Trees..as *Green-Bugs [orig. F. *punais*], Ear-Wigs. 1750 [see green-fly 2]. 1838 *Lett. fr. Madras* (1843) 205 There is nothing I dislike so much in India as those green bugs. 1667 *Lond. Gaz.* No. 195/1 A French Vessel of 70 Tuns laden with *Green Cod. 1880–4 F. Day *Fishes Gt. Brit. & Irel.* I. 295 *Gadus virens*..Coal-fish..also locally as ..green-cod, green-pollack, gray-lord. 1884–5 *Riverside Nat. Hist.* (1888) III. 253 The cod-fish (*Ophiodon elongatus*) ..is also called bastard cod, cultus cod, green cod, buffalo cod, etc. 1883 *Fisheries Exhib. Catal.* (ed. 4) 115 *Green Cormorant. 1863 J. G. Wood *Nat. Hist.* III. 580 Any living thing that can be caught becomes prey to the *Green-Crab. 1850 *Rep. U.S. Comm. Patents, Agric. 1849* 339 These plants are often smothered with lice, or *green-dolphin, as they are termed. 1876 G. B. Buckton *Monogr. Brit. Aphides* I. 134 *Siphonophora pisi*... Vulgariter. Green Dolphin. 1926 F. V. Theobald *Plant Lice Gt. Brit.* I. 132 This common aphid is usually spoken of as the Green Pea Louse or Green Dolphin. 1676 Cotton *Walton's Angler* ii. 323 The *Green-drake and Stone-fly. 1787 [see grey A. 8, *grey-drake*]. 1884 [see drake *sb.*[1] 4]. 1883 E. P. Ramsay *Food-Fishes N.S. Wales* 30 *Conger labiata* and *Muræna afra*, the 'rock' and '*green' eels. 1838 *Penny Cycl.* X. 483/1 The *Green Grosbeak or Greenfinch. 1785 T. Pennant *Arctic Zool.* II. 447 *Green Heron... *Ardea virescens*. Lin. Syst. 238... Inhabits from New York to South Carolina. 1855

Knickerbocker XLVI. 222 Night-herons, snowy-herons, green-herons, and little-herons construct their nests so closely together that four or five hundred of them may be counted upon twenty or thirty cedars. **1883** *Century Mag.* 653 Among the most common birds are the green heron. **1848** J. Gould *Birds Austral.* V. pl. 15 *Polytelis Barrabandi*, ..*Green-leek of the Colonists of New South Wales. **1678** *Green Linnet [see greenfinch 1]. **1893** Newton *Dict. Birds* 383 Greenfinch or Green Linnet, as it is very often called. **1822–34** *Good's Study Med.* (ed. 4) I. 264, I have seen ..a hop-ground completely overrun and desolated by the *aphis humuli* or hop *green-louse. **1882** C. C. Hopley *Snakes* ix. 154 Another African snake, the '*Green Mamba', has such very bad manners that it not only hisses, but spits and darts at you. **1912** F. W. Fitzsimons *Snakes S. Afr.* (ed. 2) vi. 196 Green Mambas are always found in the forests, clumps of tangled creeper-covered bush, and wooded valleys. **1969** J. L. Cloudsley-Thompson *Zool. Tropical Afr.* iv. 74 Although longer, heavier and more terrestrial than the forest-dwelling green mamba..it [*sc.* the black mamba] is not confined to the ground. [**1727** Green monkey (see monkey *sb.* 1).] **1840** *Cuvier's Anim. Kingd.* 57 Several of these smaller kinds are very common in Guinea. Allied to them are the larger *green Monkeys. **1866** *Proc. Zool. Soc.* 80 The animals were undoubtedly referable to the common Green Monkey (*Cercopithecus callitrichus*, Geoffr.) of Western Africa. **1965** D. Morris *Mammals* 150 The most important [grass monkeys] are: the West African form, known as the Green Monkey, with a very dark face and a stronger greenish tinge in its fur; the East African form [etc.]. **1967** *New Scientist* 9 Nov. 330/2 Green monkey fever has baffled microbiologists throughout the world. **1832** J. Gould *Century of Birds* Tab. lviii, The present as well as the preceding species, together with several others, are known to the natives of India by the general name of the *Green Pigeon. **1884** Layard & Sharpe *Birds S. Afr.* 557 This species [sc. *Treron calva*] is easily distinguished from the other Green Pigeons of South Africa by its grey tail. **1928** H. Whistler *Popular Handbk. Indian Birds* 297 The Green Pigeon is found almost throughout India, Burma and Ceylon, and farther east. **1952** Mackworth-Praed & Grant *Birds E. & N.E. Afr.* I. 486 The normal voice of all Green Pigeons is most curious, it is a sort of clucking whistling yap. **1967** D. Goodwin *Pigeons & Doves of World* 300 In both the wedge-tailed and pin-tailed green pigeons there are some morphological differences. **1610** W. Folkingham *Art of Survey* iv. iii. 83 Gray, *Greene and Bastard Plover. **1883** V. Stuart *Egypt* 383 Underneath the left-hand tower of the pavilion may be observed a bird squatting on a bowl..it represents a green plover. **1880–4** *Green pollack [see *green cod* above]. **1870** *Amer. Naturalist* III. 124 *Green Racer (*Boscanion vetustus*). I saw one dead specimen of this snake along Hell Gate River. **1957** A. H. & A. A. Wright *Handbk. Snakes U.S. & Canada* I. 464 Green racer... *Masticophis taeniatus schotti.* **1787, 1834** *Green-tail [see grannom]. **1847** Leichhardt *Jrnl.* ix. 294 It was at the lower part of the Lynd that we first saw the *green-tree ant. **1895** *Outing* (U.S.) Dec. 212/1 They were soon joined by more *green-wings.

c. In names of plants and fruits: **green arrow**, dial. corruption of Green Yarrow, *Achillea Millefolium*; **green ash**, a variety of the ash tree (see quot. 1882); **green-bind**, a variety of hop; **green brier**, an American name for *Smilax* (*Treas. Bot.* 1866); **green broom**, the common broom, *Sarothamnus* or *Cytisus scoparius*; **green dragon**, (*a*) the plant *Dracunculus vulgaris* (formerly *Arum D.*) = dragon[1] 14; (*b*) the U.S. plant *Arisæma Dracontium*, dragon-root (Webster 1864); †**green endive**, *Lactuca virosa* or *L. Scariola*; †**green fillet**, a kind of apple (see quot.); **green laver**, an edible seaweed, *Ulva Lactuca* and *U. latissima*, also called locally ***green oyster*** (Morris *Austral Eng.*) and ***green sloke*** (Jam.); †**green mustard**, a name for pepperwort, *Lepidium latifolium*; **green rose**, *Rosa chinensis viridiflora*; **green withe**, a climbing orchid of Jamaica, *Vanilla claviculata*; **green-wort**, sneeze-wort, *Achillea Ptarmica*. For *green hellebore, osier, rose, spleen-wort, thistle*, etc., see the sbs. Also greengage, greenheart, green sauce, greenweed.

1886 *Suffolk Rime* in Britten & Holland *Plant-n.* s.v. *Arrow*, *Green 'Arrow, Green 'Arrow, you bears a white blow. **1898** Rider Haggard in *Longm. Mag.* Oct. 500, I found the wildflower called Green-arrow in bloom. **1843** Marryat *M. Violet* xliv. 367 A luxuriant growth of noble timber, such as..blue and *green ash. **1882** *Garden* 23 Sept. 273/1 The green Ash..so called from the colour of the young shoots. **1805** R. W. Dickson *Pract. Agric.* (1807) II. 233 This plant [the hop]..has several varieties, as the red-bind, the *green-bind, the white-bind. **1733** Miller *Gard. Dict.* (ed. 2), *Cytiso-genista*, Common (or *Green) Broom. **1840** Paxton *Bot. Dict.*, **Green Dragon.* **1548** Turner *Names of Herbes* 45 *Lactuca*..The thyrde sorte is called in latin Lactuca syluestris, in englishe *greene Endyue, the Poticaries haue longe abused thys herbe for right Endyue. **1676** Beal in *Phil. Trans.* XI. 587 Green Cider..made of a *green fillet, as they called it, where they had other kinds of fillets. This which I commend..was a small, round, and green Apple full of black spots. **1829** Loudon *Encycl. Plants* 941 The *green laver which, stewed with lemon juice, is so much esteemed in England, is the Ulva lactuca. **1597** Gerarde *Herbal* Suppl., *Green Mustard is Dittander. **1911** E. Willmott *Genus Rosa* I. 80 The curious *Green Rose belongs to this section [sc. *chinensis*]. It is in no way beautiful, but is remarkable from having all its floral organs transformed into leaves. **1932** 'J. Hill' *Curious Gardener* viii. 126 The 'Green Rose', which appeared about seventy years ago in America..is some-times listed in catalogues. **1962** G. S. Thomas *Shrub Roses of Today* x. 122 [*Rosa*] *chinensis viridiflora* (*R. monstrosa*). The 'Green Rose'. **1725** Sloane *Jamaica* II. 160 *Green-with. This plant hangs down from the branches of trees. **1854** S. Thomson *Wild Fl.* iii. (ed. 4) 241 The *greenwort, or *Achillea ptarmica.*

d. In names of mineral and chemical substances: †**green brass** = verdigris; **green diallage**, (*a*) diallage, a variety of pyroxene; (*b*) = smaragdite, a variety of amphibole; **green drops**, 'a coloured solution of corrosive sublimate' (*Syd. Soc. Lex.* 1886); **green earth** = glauconite; **green gold**, an alloy of gold and silver; **green iron ore** = dufrenite; **green lead ore** = pyromorphite; **green marble** = serpentine; **green mineral** = malachite. For *green bice, copperas, iodide of mercury, salt of Magnus, vitriol*, etc., see the sbs. Also greenstone.

1398 Trevisa *Barth. De P.R.* xvii. clxxxviii. (1495) 729 Vyneygre fretyth metalles and gendreth therof dyuers colours: as Serusa of leed, *grene brasse of copur and Lazurium of syluer. **1837** Dana *Syst. Min.* 305 *Green Diallage, Kokkolit, Baikalit. **1794** Kirwan *Elem. Min.* (ed. 2) I. 196 *Green Earth. **1843** Portlock *Geol.* 212 Green Earth is common, lining the cavities in amygdaloid throughout the basaltic range. **1799** G. Smith *Laboratory* I. 72 An alloy of silver with gold produces *green gold. **1825** J. Nicholson *Operat. Mechanic* 724 To heighten the colour of Green Gold. **1935** W. G. Hardy *Father Abraham* iii. iii. 265 They opened the chests and yellow gold blinded his eyes and massy bars of silver and green gold. **1951** J. R. Partington *Gen. & Inorg. Chem.* (ed. 2) xiii. 353 *Electrum* is a native alloy of gold and 15–45 p.c. of silver; green gold contains 10 p.c. of silver: these alloys were called *asem* in ancient Egypt. **1864** Watts *Dict. Chem.* II. 944 **Green Iron Ore*, native ferric phosphate. *Ibid.*, **Green lead ore*, arsenio-phosphate of lead with chloride of lead. **1879** Rossiter *Dict. Sci. Terms*, **Green marble* = Serpentine. **1844** Hoblyn *Dict. Med.*, **Green mineral*, a carbonate of copper, used as a pigment.

B. *sb.*

1. The adj. used *absol.* That which is green; the green part of anything.

c **1000** *Sax. Leechd.* I. 398 Bere siþþan ða turf to circean ..& wende man þæt grene to ðan weofode. **1764** Foote *Patron* I. Wks. 1799 I. 331 Sever the green [i.e. the 'green fat' of turtle] from the shell with the skill of the ablest anatomist.

2. a. Green colour. In *pl.* = different tints of green. †*in green*: on a (heraldic) field of green. *Obs.*

c **1205** Lay. 24652 þat heo wolden of ane heowen heore claðes habben. Sum hafde whit sum hafden ræd, sum hafde god grene æc. *a* **1225** *Ancr. R.* 150 Grene ouer alle heowes froureð mest eien. *c* **1386** Chaucer *Sec. Nun's Prol.* 90 Or, for she whitnesse hadde of honestee, And grene of conscience, and of good fame The sote savour, 'lilie' was hir name. *c* **1475** *Rauf Coilȝear* 455 He bair grauit in Gold and Gowlis in grene..Ane Tyger. **1644** Digby *Mans Soul* (1645) 39 By severall compoundings of these extreames, reds, blewes, yellowes, greenes, and all other intermediate colours may be generated. **1667** Milton *P.L.* vii. 479 In all the liveries deck'd of Summer's pride, With spots of gold and purple, azure and green. **1687** B. Randolph *Pres. St. Archipelago* 107 The sea had a continual passage over us, so as our Deck was covered with a green. **1704** Pope *Windsor For.* 216 In the clear azure gleam the flocks are seen, And floating forests paint the waves with green. **1821** Craig *Lect. Drawing* iii. 176 Light-yellow has much clearness and beauty on purple and green. **1873** Symonds *Grk. Poets* xii. 404 Its [the olive's] pearly greys and softened greens.

b. with defining word prefixed, indicating a particular kind of shade of green, as ***cedar, celandine, emerald, grape, leek, parrot, pea, Russian, sea, Spanish, vine-leaf green***, etc.

a **1500** *Flower & Leaf* 35 Leves new..Some very rede, and some a glad light grene. **15..** [see *goose-turd*: goose *sb.* 7]. **1611** Cotgr., *Verd gay*, a Popiniay greene..*Verdet*, Spanish greene. **1658** W. Sanderson *Graphice* 84 The best is Cedar-green. **1727–41** Chambers *Cycl.* s.v., The dyers make divers shades, or casts of green, as light green, yellow green, grass green, laurel green, sea green, dark green, parrot green, and celadon green. *c* **1750** Shenstone *Elegies* iv. 2 Near some lone fane or yew's funereal green. **1805–17** R. Jameson *Char. Min.* (ed. 3) 67 *Verdigris-green* is emerald-green mixed with much Berlin-blue, and a little white... *Mountain-green* is emerald-green, mixed with much blue, and a little yellowish-grey... *Leek-green* is emerald-green, with bluish-grey and a little brown. It is the Sap-green of painters. **1818** *La Belle Assemblée* XVII. No. 106. 38/6 The most fashionable colours in this material are, vine-leaf green [etc.]. **1881** J. Grant *Cameronians* I. i. 7 One [of his eyes] was a species of bilious green. **1899** *Daily News* 16 Sept. 7/4 Lovely shades of green, such as grape, pistachio, and reed-green.

c. ***(to see any) green in one's eye***: signs of inexperience or gullibility. (Cf. A. 1 h.)

1859 *Slang Dict.* s.v., 'Do you see any green in my eye?' ironical question in a dispute. **1883** Atkin *House Scraps* (1887) 161 Major P——'s unco' sly, There is no green about his eye. **1894** Blackmore *Perlycross* 189 Sergeant, do you see any green in my eye? **1936** F. Clune *Roaming round Darling* xxii. 219 The governor, however, hadn't any green in his eye, so in despair Andy smuggled a letter to Dr John Dunmore Lang. **1966** O. Norton *School of Liars* vi. 106 'You don't have to believe all you hear.'.. He leant forward and pulled down his lower eyelid. 'See any green, Mrs Sumner?'

3. A green dye or pigment; usually with some defining word prefixed, as ***bladder, Brunswick, chrome, emerald, Hungary, mineral, mountain, Paris, Prussian, Saxon, Scheele's, Veronese***, etc.

1611 Cotgr. s.v. *Chevre, Verd de chevre*, a kind of sand whereof Painters make their greenes. **1727–41** Chambers *Cycl.* s.v., *Mountain Green* or *Hungary Green*, is a sort of greenish powder found..among the mountains of Kernausent in Hungary. The painters make use of this Colour for a grass green. **1816** J. Smith *Panorama Sci. & Art* II. 556 Sulphate of indigo is used for Saxon greens. **1839** Ure *Dict. Arts* 793 *Malachite*, or mountain green. *Ibid.* 1094 Scheele's Green, is a pulverulent arsenite of copper. **1849** D. Campbell *Inorg. Chem.* 218 When to a solution of sulphate of copper a solution of carbonate of potash is added, it gives a blue precipitate, which on boiling assumes a green tint; it..is known in commerce as mineral green. **1887** *Amer. Naturalist* XXI. 481 The insecticide employed was Paris green. **1892** *Pall Mall G.* 4 Apr. 3/1 Paris green, an insoluble arsenite of copper.

4. Green clothing or dress, *lit.* and *fig.*; †green cloth. †Also *pl.* green dresses.

c **1320** *Sir Tristr.* 1380 A schip wiþ grene and gray, Wiþ vair and eke wiþ griis. *c* **1350** *Parl. Three Ages* 122 He was gerede all in grene. *c* **1385** Chaucer *L.G.W.* Prol. 117 Now hadde the tempre sonne..clothede hym [the earth] in grene al newe a-geyn. **14..** *Ipomadon* 657 (Kölbing) A hunter all in grene. **1412** Hoccleve *De Reg. Princ.* 696 And where ben my gounes of scarlet,..blewes sadde & lighte, Grenes also. **1673** [R. Leigh] *Transp. Reh.* 112 Would not exchange his royal purple for a forresters green. **1810** [see greenman 1].

5. *Antiq.* As the distinctive colour of one of the factions in the circus. Also *pl.* the adherents of this faction. (Cf. faction *sb.* 2 b.)

1693 Congreve in *Dryden's Juvenal* Sat. xi. 35 The Green have won the Honour of the Day. **1884** *19th Cent.* Dec. 999 What light is thrown on the history of Byzantium by talking of the 'Blues' and the 'Greens'?

6. The emblematic colour of Ireland (suggested by 'Green Erin': see A 2); hence adopted as the distinctive colour of the 'nationalist' party.

1797 *Song, 'The Shan van vocht'*, What colour should be seen Where our fathers' homes have been, But our own immortal Green? *c* **1798** *Song, 'The Wearing of the Green'*, They are hanging men and women for the wearing of the green. *c* **1798** Hope in Madden *Lit. Rem. United Irishm.* (1887) 99 We fell to work, hammer and tongs, The Orange and Green both together.

7. a. Elliptically for a green species or variety of an animal or a substance, the nature of which is explained by the context, *e.g.* a green bird, etc.

1895 *Outing* (U.S.) XXVI. 69/2, I made out the blue yellow-back,..the blackpoll and the black-throated green. **1897** *Ibid.* XXX. 380/2 It seems that they were out of tobacco, and had been able to get only the 'long green' that the mountaineers used.

b. = *green tea.*

1728 [see tea *sb.* 1 a]. **1835** Dickens in *Bell's Life* 4 Oct. 1/1 Two ounces of seven and sixpenny green. **1838** —— *O. Twist* iii. ii. in *Bentley's Misc.* IV. 115 Half a pound of seven and sixpenny green, so precious strong..it'll go nigh to blow the lid of the teapot off. **1903** *Westm. Gaz.* 4 Feb. 4/2, 4,000,000 lb. of black tea had been taken off the market last year by being converted into greens.

c. *fig.* A greenhorn, simpleton. (Cf. A. 8 d.)

Cf. *Verdant Green*, the name of the hero in the title of the story (1853–6) of Oxford university life by 'Cuthbert Bede'. **1825** *Spirit of Pub. Jrnls. 1823* (ed. 2) 63 It appears that George Charteris..had been 'doing' the *green*, and taking in the 'deep ones', quite in the gull-catching style, for a considerable period. **1837** Dickens *O. Twist* xviii, 'Well, well,' said the Dodger... 'That hasn't got anything to do with young Green here.' **1840** G. Thompson *Newgate Calendar* 280, I then with my comrade stole from a green twelve shirts..and some stockings. **1841** *Southern Lit. Messenger* VII. 54/2, I knifed a flat-boat Hoozier—took his lucre—Went up the country—rifled twenty *greens.*

d. Also *pl.* Money. *slang* (orig. *U.S.*). Cf. greenback *sb.* 1 and *long green* (long *a.*[1] 18).

1925 *Flynn's Mag.* in Partridge *Dict. Underworld* (1968) 307 *Greens*, paper currency; bank notes. **1942** Berrey & Van den Bark *Amer. Thes. Slang* §559/5 *Paper money*..the green, green boys,..greens, the long green. **1951** E. Paul *Springtime in Paris* vi. 125 'A banker!.. Nobody comes on this scene wearin' any green,' said another taller Negro. **1961** *New Statesman* 21 July 81/2 The hours proved to be from four to half eleven in the morning and the greens would amount to eight ten a week. **1962** L. Deighton *Ipcress File* vi. 44 At five shillings a dose that's a lot of green. **1968** *Scottish Daily Mail* 3 Jan. 6 What had been 'dough' in the 20's and became 'readies' and 'greens' in the 50's turned up again as 'bread'. **1971** 'R. Crawford' *Badger's Daughter* i. ii. 24 When finally we did lay our mitts on a nice pile of green, Arthur simply knuckled under to luxury.

e. A green light, lamp, flare, etc., meant as a signal. Cf. green *a.* 1 i.

1953 R. Chisholm *Cover of Darkness* ii. 30 At last I was given a 'green', but the dim pattern of aerodrome lights made little sense by this time. **1962** J. Braine *Life at Top* ii. 31 The car in front of me stalled and I missed the green. **1962** J. Glenn in *Into Orbit* 213 You have a green. You look good on attitude. **1963** *Amer. Speech* XXXVIII. 119 *In the green*, slang expression meaning that all instruments show safe readings. Many of the instruments have colored markings on them: red for danger, yellow for caution, and green for safe ranges. **1963** 'W. Haggard' *High Wire* xi. 116 Overhead there was the unmistakable clatter of a helicopter, then another. Somebody fired a green.

f. Marijuana of poor quality. *slang* (orig. *U.S.*).

1957 J. Kerouac *On Road* (1958) 184 He got hold of some bad green, as it's called in the trade—green, uncured marijuana. **1969** R. R. Lingeman *Drugs from A to Z* 86 *Green*, a 'grade' of marijuana sometimes of relatively low potency because it is low in resin content. **1969** *Observer* 12 Jan. 30/3 Everybody was talking pot last week (or Mary Jane, tea, grass, weed, hay, boo, gage, green or technically *cannabis sativa*).

8. Greenness, as indicative of vigorous growth or youth; vigour, youthfulness, virility; phr. ***in the green***, in the period of youthful growth or vigour.

c **1586** C'tess Pembroke *Ps.* xcii. iv, Like cedar high, And like date-bearing tree, For greene and growth the just shall be. **1597** Middleton *Wisdom Solomon* xi. 21 Man had..

perish'd in the spring-time of his green. **1850** TENNYSON *In Mem.* lxxv, Thy leaf has perish'd in the green. **1866** NEALE *Sequences & Hymns* 26 How this saplessness shall flush to green. **1886** C. H. PARKHURST *Serm.* 15 May, in Crafts *Sabb. for Man* 267 All disobedience is anarchy, young anarchy, anarchy in the green.

9. Verdure, vegetation, greenery.

c **1386** CHAUCER *Frankl. T.* 523 The bittre frostes with the sleet and reyn Destroyed hath the grene in euery yerd. **1426** LYDG. *De Guil. Pilgr.* 3814 With newe grene agayn Clothen the busshes in ther maner. **1563** B. GOOGE *Eglogs* i. (Arb.) 31 The Ram..forceth ground (yat spoyld of grene Did lye), newe grene to yelde. **1657** R. LIGON *Barbadoes* (1673) 50 Poor Sambo..and as good a natur'd poor soul, as ever wore black, or eat green. **1710** ADDISON *Tatler* No. 218 ¶1 This Summer..while the Green was new. **1725** POPE *Odyss.* v. 90 Vines..With purple clusters blushing through the green. **1882** F. W. H. MYERS *Renewal of Youth* 183 All the scarlet flowers and tossing green.

†**10.** A tree, herb, or plant. Also *spec.*, an evergreen. (Mostly in plural.) *Obs.*

a **1300** *E.E. Psalter* xxxvi. 2 Als wortes of grenes [Vulg. *olera herbarum*] tite fal sal þai. **1593** T. WATSON *Tears Fancie* xlvii. Poems (Arb.) 202 How each pleasant greene, Will now renew his sommers liuerie. **1664** EVELYN *Kal. Hort.* (1729) 196 Myrtles, Laurels, and other curious Greens. **1679–88** *Secr. Serv. Money Chas. & Jas.* (Camden) 121 Several orange trees and other greens. **1688** R. HOLME *Armoury* II. 86/2 Greens are such Trees or Herbs as are green all the year. **1698** M. LISTER *Journ. Paris* (1699) 204 Their Oleanders, Laurels, Lentiscus's and most other Greens had suffered miserably. *c* **1710** C. FIENNES *Diary* (1888) 142 A large fountaine..with flower potts and Greens set round ye Brimm. **1711** POPE *Temp. Fame* 2 In that soft season when descending show'rs Call forth the greens, and wake the rising flow'rs. **1719** YOUNG *Revenge* V. ii, How every green is as the ivy pale!

11. *plural.* †**a.** The green parts of a plant or flower. *Obs.*

c **1600** *Acc. Bk. W. Wray* in *Antiquary* XXXII. 80 Take the leaues of Blew violetes seperated from theire stalkes and grenes. **1620** MARKHAM *Farew. Husb.* II. xvii. (1668) 84 That the wind and Sun may get into it, and dry the greens more sufficiently.

b. Freshly-cut branches or leaves, or other greenery used for decoration. Now *U.S.*

1697 DRYDEN *Virg. Georg.* I. 192 The peaceful Ground, Which only Turfs and Greens for Altars found. **1702** *Lond. Gaz.* No. 3842/2 A Triumphal Arch..adorned with Greens and Flowers. **1767** DODD *Pious Memory* 44 Poems 194 Strew thy greens and flowers so sweet. **1878** MRS. STOWE *Poganuc P.* IV. (ed. 3) 30 The Christmas greens in the church. **1897** *Globe* 18 Feb. 6/4 The staircase was 'trimmed with green', to use the expression current in the States.

c. Green vegetables such as are boiled for the table. *colloq.*

In London applied *spec.* to certain smaller varieties of the cabbage kind, and to the young sprouts of cabbage. In dialectal use the specific application varies. The American Dicts. refer to spinach and the leaves of dandelion and beet as the examples of what would be called 'greens'.

1725 DE FOE *Voy. round World* (1840) 91 Fresh provisions ..such as roots, greens, hogs, and fowls. **1748** *Anson's Voy.* II. iii. 141 Greens, as wild celery, nettle-tops, etc. **1749** WESLEY *Acc. Sch. Kingswood* 5 Bacon and Greens. **1783** MAD. D'ARBLAY *Diary* 15 July, At Mr. Garrick's table [he] called out to a very timid young woman to help him to some greens. **1816** SCOTT *Antiq.* xxxv, A few half-cold greens and potatoes. **1825** JAMIESON, *Green Kail*, I. That plain species of green colewort which does not assume a round form like savoys, or become curled; called German Greens. **1843** PEREIRA *Food & Diet* 382 The Cabbage Tribe includes the Cabbage (both white and red), the Savoy, Greens, the Cauliflower, and Broccoli. **1846** J. BAXTER *Libr. Pract. Agric.* (ed. 4) I. 149 The Dwarf winter greens not being required to attain much size before the winter. **1860** DELAMER *Kitch. Gard.* (1861) 169 Clear away the..rotting leaves from the lower part of the stems of broccoli, savoys, and other winter greens. **1861** DU CHAILLU *Equat. Afr.* viii. (ed. 2) 93 The leaves [of the manioc]..make excellent 'greens'. **1883** *Encycl. Amer.* I. 199/2 Vegetables, which he [the Western man] prefers to call *greens*, he does not know, unless it be in the shape of *roasting ears*.

sing. **1779** FORREST *Voy. N. Guinea* 86 We found near the Moodo's house, the green, called by the Malays Assimum.

†**d.** Green food. *Obs.*

1727 *Philip Quarll* (1816) 54 Finding by the greens in its mouth it was not a beast of prey.

†**e.** The plant Duckweed. (Cf. *grains*, GRAIN *sb.* 4 c.) *Obs.*

1516 *Gt. Herbal* cclix. (1529) Pj, De lenticula aque. Grenes or duckes meate.

f. Sexual activity, esp. intercourse. *slang.*

1889 BARRÈRE & LELAND *Dict. Slang* I. 429 'To have one's *greens*', to have sexual intercourse. **1893** FARMER & HENLEY *Slang* III. 206/1 *To have, get,* or *give one's greens*, to enjoy, procure, or confer the sexual favour. Said indifferently of both sexes. **1963** C. CONNOLLY *Bond strikes Camp* 3 Section A make a study of the kind of greens the big shots go in for. Sometimes we know more about what these people are like between the sheets than they do themselves. **1963** L. MEYNELL *Virgin Luck* vii. 164 Mr. Cahill..is an adult male with healthy instincts. He wants his greens regularly. **1967** G. GREENE *May we borrow your Husband?* 27 Why not go after the girl?..She's not getting what I believe is vulgarly called her greens.

12. a. Grassy ground; a grassy spot. Now *rare.*

c **1300** *Havelok* 2840 Sket was þe swike on þe asse leyd, And led vntil þat ilke grene. *c* **1330** R. BRUNNE *Chron.* (1810) 2 Ine..wente to þe bataile in a fulle faire grene. *c* **1400** *Destr. Troy* 7732 The grete horses on the grene girdon abacke. *c* **1460** *Towneley Myst.* iii. 534 Behald on this greyn nowder cart ne plogh is left. **1603** KNOLLES *Hist. Turks* (1621) 966 All enriched with goodly gardens and pleasant greenes. **1625** BACON *Ess., Gardens* (Arb.) 558 The Greene hath two pleasures; The one, because nothing is more Pleasant to the Eye, then Greene Grasse kept finely shorne; The other, because it will giue you a faire Alley in the midst [etc.]. **1667** MILTON *P.L.* IV. 325 Under a tuft of shade that on a green Stood whispering soft. **1715** POPE *Iliad* III. 223 Though some of larger stature tread the greene. **1832** TENNYSON *Pal. Art* xxvii, In some fair space of sloping greens. **1877** BLACK *Green Past.* xix, You..nearly put your foot in it by chaffing old Chorley about selling the piece of green.

b. A piece of public or common grassy land situated in or near a town or village, from which it often takes its name; a 'village green'.

1477 *Extracts Aberd. Reg.* (1844) I. 35 Adam Strath till haue the Schripraw, with the Grene. **1509** *Mem. Ripon* (Surtees) III. 172, j grangia juxta Bondegate Greyn in tenura relictæ Joh. Tomlynson. *c* **1533** SIR T. MORE *Confut. Barnes* Wks. 792/2 If Barns had not tolde vs so, we woulde haue went that Christe had bode hym..tarye till he coulde geate all the knowen catholike church together vpon a Greene. **1606** *Nottingham Rec.* IV. 280 Common balkes and greens within and about the feilds of this towne. **1718** *Freethinker* No. 80. 173 Every Holiday, she danced upon the Green. **1770** GOLDSM. *Des. Vill.* 7 Sweet Auburn! loveliest village of the plain, How often have I loiter'd o'er thy green. **1805** FORSYTH *Beauties Scotl.* II. 131 The principal market for sheep and lambs..is held on a large green. **1835** THIRLWALL *Greece* I. x. 389 Sports, not essentially different from those of our village greens. **1870** E. PEACOCK *Ralf Skirl.* III. 234 On the southern side of Wivilby was a little green. **1888** P. DARYL *Ireland's Disease* 8 Dublin is provided with fine public gardens and splendid parks, which are here called greens.

c. A piece of grassy land used for some particular purpose, as ***bleaching-green***, BOWLING-GREEN. In *Golf*, the putting-ground (more fully, ***putting-green***); sometimes = the whole links or field.

1646–1825 [see BOWLING-GREEN]. **1847–8** H. MILLER *First Impr.* xv. (1857) 249 A long green ribbon of flat meadow, laid down in the middle of the landscape like a web on a bleaching green. **1849** *Chambers' Inform.* II. 654/1 The holes are situated at the different ends and sides of the green, at irregular distances. **1878** 'CAPT. CRAWLEY' *Football, Golf,* etc. 83 *Green*, a name for the Putting-ground, or for the Links or field. **1886** *Act 49 & 50 Vict.* c. 59 §14 Any lands being an orchard, bleach-green, walled garden, haggard, or yard. **1890** *John Bull* 5 Apr. 225/3 There will soon be more greens in England than in Scotland.

†**13.** *pl.* = GREEN SICKNESS. *Obs. slang.*

1719 D'URFEY *Pills* I. 313 The Maiden..that's vex'd with her Greens.

14. a. Short for GREEN MAN or *Jack-in-the-green.*

1835 DICKENS *Sk. Boz, Scenes* xx. (1892) 159 For some few years the dancing on May-day began to decline; small sweeps were observed to congregate in twos or threes, unsupported by a 'green'.

b. Phr. ***on the green***: on the stage (see GREENGAGE 2).

1940 *N. & Q.* 29 June 462/2 'On the Green' is perfectly good rhyming slang for 'On the Greengage' = on the stage. As such, it is familiar to every touring actor, stage-door keeper and stage-hand of over forty, and is in constant use to-day. **1957** *Times Lit. Suppl.* 6 Dec. 742/1 If a modern producer asks his stage-manager to summon down a man from the flies, we might well hear the cry: 'Bill, come down on the green a minute.'

15. *pl.* = *green syrup* (see A. 12).

1889 *Century Dict.* s.v., The last greens, after three successive crystallizations of sugar, are purified and form the golden syrup of commerce.

†**16.** A seton. (Cf. A 10 a.)

1781 P. BECKFORD *Hunting* (1802) 124 A green, or seton, in the neck, is of great relief in most disorders of the eyes.

17. *pl.* The members or supporters of an ecological party, esp. that in W. Germany (*die Grünen*); those committed to environmentalism or ecology, esp. as a political issue. Cf. sense 11 of the adj. above.

1978 *Economist* 14 Jan. 39/2 The Greens are more likely to take votes from the Social Democrats and the Liberals than from the Christian Democrats. **1979** *Listener* 6 Dec. 775/3 Chancellor Schmidt..is now facing the possibility that the votes of the so-called 'greens' (ecology-conscious citizens) may decide whether his government survives. **1982** *New Society* 22 July 129/1 *Die Grünen* in Germany: a federation of broad interests forged..from three major citizen action groups...British greens believe such a federation is possible ..here. **1983** *Times* 24 Feb. 17/8 It has to be recognized that the world's economic story is now developing in a manner that goes the Greens' way. **1986** *New Socialist* Sept. 4/2 If the government's greens..get their way, then the pollution from Drax B may yet be cleaned up.

18. *attrib.* †Of or pertaining to 'greens' or vegetables, as ***green market, shop, stall, woman*** [cf. G. *grünmarkt*, Du. *groenmarkt, groenwijf*]. Also, Of or pertaining to a bowling-green or golf-links, as ***green(s) committee, -fee, -keeper, -keeping, -man, -putter, -record.***

1896 *Rules of St. Andrews* in J. Kerr *Golf-bk. E. Lothian* App. p. xxii, When the *Green Committee consider it necessary, a telegraph board shall be used to give the numbers for starting. **1909** *Westm. Gaz.* 5 May 12/4 The green committee did not consider that golf was a game likely to be benefited by inclusion in any programme of the Olympic Sports. **1926** WODEHOUSE *Heart of Goof* vii. 230 The Greens Committee..have altered the Mossy Heath course. **1909** *Westm. Gaz.* 20 Oct. 12/2 The committee suggested the charge of a *green fee of one shilling a round on each player. **1962** *Punch* 21 Nov. 746/2 The economy-size golfer only needs a narrow course and a green-fee. **1971** 'D. HALLIDAY' *Dolly & Doctor Bird* ii. 22 Greens fees eight dollars, power cart ten dollars, balls eighteen dollars fifty the dozen. And a complete set of clubs and bag... Four hundred dollars? **1705–30** S. GALE in Nichols *Bibl. Topog. Brit.* III. 47 Neat apartments..for servants and the *green-keeper. **1890** HUTCHINSON *Golf* (Badm. Libr.) xii. 293 The green-keeper, engaged by the club at a certain annual salary to look after the ground. **1907** *Westm. Gaz.* 18 Oct. 3/1 All that has gone past him, like the scientific *green-keeping. **1961** *Technology* Oct. 257 Courses are also held in horticulture and greenkeeping. **1905** *Westm. Gaz.* 10 Feb. 3/1 The *green-men use various liquids to bring the worms to the top, where they may be swept away and destroyed. **1928** *Daily Express* 3 Jan. 9/2 After the snow had fallen greenmen tried to clear it away by flooding the course with hosepipes. **1604** E. GRIMSTONE *Hist. Siege Ostend.* 115 They slue 2 Souldiers in the *greene market. **1881** *Green putter [see PUTTER *sb.*[2] 2 a]. **1902** *Westm. Gaz.* 28 July 4/1 Had Herd not been badly bunkered at the fourteenth hole he would probably have beaten the *green record. **1908** *Ibid.* 22 June 9/4 At the age of sixteen he..had won a scratch medal and broken a green-record. **1753** PRINGLE in *Phil. Trans.* XLVIII. 47 At a *green-shop in the little Old Bailey. **1848** THACKERAY *Van. Fair* xxxvii, Who had subsisted..by the exercise of a mangle, and the keeping of a small green shop. **1755** FIELDING *Voy. Lisbon* Pref., Every sort of trash that can be picked up at the *green-stall, or the wheel-barrow. **1799** *Founders Fr. Repub.* I. 440 An aunt, who kept a green-stall [etc.]. **1760** C. JOHNSTON *Chrysal* (1822) I. 9 Peg Sprout, the *green-woman's daughter.

green (griːn), *v.*[1] Forms: see the adj. [OE. *grénian* (= OHG. *gruonên*), f. *gréne* (see prec.).]

1. *intr.* To become green, as growing herbage; *occas.* to appear or look green; to become covered with verdure, to be 'clothed' with green. (Also with *over.*)

a **1000** *Boeth. Metr.* xi. 57 (Sedgefield) Hæfð se ælmihtiʒa ..ðæt ʒewrixle ʒeset..wyrta growan, leaf grenian. *a* **1225** *Ancr. R.* 150 Hwonne þe rinde is aweie, ne nouðer hit ne bereð frut, ne hit ne greneð þerefter ine lufsume leaues. *c* **1230** *Hali Meid.* 35 þi rudi neb schal leanen & as gres grenen. **1340** *Ayenb.* 95 þyse þri þinges..deþ al greny and flouri and bere frut. *c* **1440** *Promp. Parv.* 210/1 Grenyn or growe grene, *vireo*. *c* **1500** *Death & Life* 73 in Furniv. *Percy Folio* III. 59 The grasse that was gray greened beliue. **1612** STURTEVANT *Metallica* (1854) 98 Freestone greeneth presently with the first wet and raine. **1800** *Monthly Mag.* IX. 464 On the fields where green'd the wheat. **1833** L. A. STANLEY in *Mem. Quiet Life* (1874) I. xii. 482 Larches all greening and every hedge ready to burst into full leaf. **1858** MAYHEW *Upp. Rhine* iv. §2 (1860) 204 The Rhine..has been gradually greening in tint as we ascended the upper portion of the stream. **1883** STEVENSON *Silverado Sq.* (1886) 17 The new lands, already weary of producing gold, begin to green with vineyards. **1899** *Daily News* 15 Apr. 8/1 The wild-rose briars will be shooting strongly, the elder greening over.

2. *trans.* To colour or dye green; to soil or stain with green; to impart a green colour to; to cover with verdure or vegetation (also with *over*); to 'clothe' with green.

1570 B. GOOGE *Pop. Kingd.* 10 The Rest with silver garnisht is, and plaited fine and neat Least it shoulde greene his holy hands. **1606** SYLVESTER *Du Bartas* II. iv. II. 1175 God Almighty..Plaid the Painter, when he did so gild The turning globes, blew'd seas & green'd the field. **1727–41** CHAMBERS *Cycl.* s.v., All the greens are first dyed in blue, then taken down with woad, verdegris, etc. and then greened with the weed. **1730–46** THOMSON *Autumn* 1258 Whatever greens the Spring, When Heaven descends in showers. **1769** MRS. RAFFALD *Eng. Housekpr.* (1778) 342 Nothing is more common than to green pickles in a brass pan. **1818** KEATS *Endym.* I. 217 Have not rains Green'd over April's lap? *a* **1851** MOIR *Poems, Glen Roslin* x, Moss now greens the chapel walls. **1854** R. S. SURTEES *Handley Cross* (1898) II. 280 He has begun greening his breeches' knees among the hazel bushes. **1882** BURTON & CAMERON *To Gold Coast for G.* (1883) I. iii. 75 The heap of ruins has long been greened over. **1891** T. HARDY *Tess* I. iii, The..white frock ..which she had so carelessly greened..on the damping grass.

b. *Oyster-culture.* To turn (oysters) green in the gills by putting them in pits. Also *absol.*

16.. *Green Oysters* in Sprat *Hist. Roy. Soc.* (1667) 308–9 To prove that the Sun operates in the greening, Tolesbury Pits will green only in Summer; but that the Earth hath the greater power, Brickel-Sea Pits green both Winter and Summer: and for a further proof, a Pit within a foot of a greening Pit will not green. **1748** MORANT *Colchester* I. (1768) 92 All oysters are naturally white in the body, and brown in the fins. In order to *green* them, they are put into Pits [etc.]. **1825** CROMWELL *Hist. Colchester* II. 295 But this distinction of Colchester from other oysters is rapidly wearing away: indeed, it may be said, That few or none of them are now ever *greened*.

†**c.** *Plumbing.* To rub (new sheet-lead) with some green vegetable (see quot. and GREENING *vbl. sb.*[1] 2). *Obs.*

1703 T. N. *City & C. Purchaser* 195 He scraped the Metal bright, having first..green'd it (as they phrase it), all round about, to prevent the Sodder's taking any where but where they scrape it.

3. *slang.* To make to appear 'green', simple, or gullible; to hoax, take in, humbug.

1884 *Pall Mall G.* 17 Sept. 7/1 Some of the little victims of over-pressure had, at any rate, enough spirit in them to 'green' their visitor pretty freely. **1888** T. C. BUCKLAND *Eton in 1836–41* in *Longm. Mag.* XII. 153 Some mild attempts were made to 'green me', as boys call it. **1898** *Daily News* 15 July 2/2, I have greened all the Spaniards.

green (griːn), *v.*[2] *Sc.* Forms: 6 gren(e, 6–8 grein(e, 8 greene, grien, 6, 8– green. [perh. a metathetic form of ON. *girna* (= OE. *ʒiernan*, Northumb. *ʒiorna*: see YEARN *v.*).] *intr.* To desire earnestly, to yearn, to long *after, for.*

a **1300** *Cursor M.* 15511 (Gött.) Lang es siþen gane þat grened [*Cott., Fairf.* ʒerned] i haue þis ilk mete, mast at ete of ane. *Ibid.* 16167 (Gött.) Herodes grenid him to se and of his come was faine. **1513** DOUGLAS *Æneis* VIII. Prol. 45 Sum grenis quhill the gers grow for his gray meyr. *Ibid.* 51 Sum grenis eftir a gus, To fars his wame full. **1570** *Satir. Poems Reform.* xii. 114 Sum feiris yair flesche, sum grenis to gadder crounis. **1585** JAS. I *Ess. Poesie* (Arb.) 67 He..greind Ʒit fast for day, and thocht the nicht to lang. *a* **1605** MONTGOMERIE *Misc. Poems* xxxii. 5 Not that I grene ȝour honour to degraid. **1795** BURNS *Election* 76 Walie, That griens for the fishes an' loaves. **1831** *Blackw. Mag.* XXIX. 6 The feck o' them gae'n sickly, and greenin' for hame. **1838** A. RODGER *Poems* 108 Nae woman o' judgment need green To be rubbit, like me, for a kiss. **1862** HISLOP *Prov. Scot.* 40 Breeding wives are aye greening.

Hence **'greening** *vbl. sb.*[2] and *ppl. a.*[2]

1585 JAS. I *Ess. Poesie* (Arb.) 23 When greening great for fame aboue my pears Did make me lose my wonted chere and rest. **1597** MONTGOMERIE *Cherrie & Slae* 508 Frae anes that thou thy grening get, Thy paine and trauel is forȝet. **1637** RUTHERFORD *Lett.* lxxxv. (1862) I. 217 Longing and dwining and greening of sick desires. *Ibid.* clx. (1894) 296 Oh, if He would..let my greening soul see it! **1710** RUDDIMAN *Gloss. to Douglas' Æneis* s.v. *Grene*, A greening wife i.e. a woman with child that hath an extreme longing for some kind of meat, which, if it be denied her, will (as they say) do harm to her or the child. **1737** RAMSAY *Sc. Prov.* (1797) 33 Greening wives are ay greedy. **1755** FORBES *Ajax's Sp.*, *Shop Bill* 39 Perhaps I may their greening stench 'ere I hae done.

green, dial. var. GRANE *v.*, GRIN *v.*[1]

green, obs. form of GRIN *sb.*[1]

greenable ('gri:nəb(ə)l), *a.* [f. GREEN *v.*[1] + -ABLE.] Capable of being made green.

1882 *Athenæum* 25 Nov. 704/1 Aniline blacks formed in the cold are greenable, but if developed at a temperature higher than 70° Centigrade they are ungreenable.

greenage ('gri:nɪdʒ). *rare*[−1]. [f. GREEN *a.* + -AGE.] Assemblage of green hues.

1874 WOOD *Out of Doors* 82 The dried stalks of last year's vegetation, which..are wonderfully effective in toning down the dappled greenage of the living leaves.

greenback ('gri:nbæk), *sb.* [f. GREEN *a.* + BACK *sb.*[1]] A thing that has a green back.

1. a. The popular name for one of the legal-tender notes of the U.S., first issued in 1862 and so called from the devices printed in green ink on the back. Also, 'by extension, any note issued by a national bank in the U.S.' (Funk's *Stand. Dict.*).

1862 *Times* 23 Dec. (Amer. Corr.), Bonds, greenbacks, and postage currency paper..are..to do all the duty of money in this unhappy land. **1870** LONGF. in *Life* (1891) III. 143 Never having known the difference between a bank-note and a greenback. **1966** *New Yorker* 22 Oct. 164 We observe him on his way to Mexico with a suitcase full of green-backs.

b. *attrib.* **greenback party**, a party in U.S. politics, which advocated that 'greenbacks' should be made the sole currency of the country.

1878 *N. Amer. Rev.* CXXVII. 103 The greenback issue has rapidly gained strength. **1884** *Boston* (Mass.) *Jrnl.* 26 July, Hon. Charles Jenkins, twice candidate of the Greenback party in Ohio for Governor. **1888** BRYCE *Amer. Commw.* II. III. lvi. 369 The Greenback party..held a national Nominating Convention in 1876. **1893** *Nation* (N.Y.) 27 Apr. 306/1 The greenback controversies that supervened after the close of the war.

2. As the name of animals. (Cf. *blue-back*, *red-back*.) **a.** The garfish, *Belone vulgaris*. **b.** The American golden plover, *Charadrius dominicus*, also called *golden-back*. **c.** *U.S.* A humming-bird of the genus *Panoplites*. **d.** *slang.* A frog.

1778 *Eng. Gazetteer* (ed. 2) s.v. *Warrington*, In the river are caught sturgeons, greenbacks [etc.]. **1869** J. BURROUGHS in *Galaxy Mag.* Aug., VIII. 170 The finest songster among the Sylvia..is the blackthroated greenback. **1880–4** DAY *Fishes Gt. Brit. & Irel.* II. 148 *Belone vulgaris*..green-bone or green-back. **1893** FARMER *Slang*, *Greenback* (common), a frog.

3. A book with a green back. (Cf. *yellow-back*.)

1893 FARMER *Slang*, *Greenback*..(University), one of Todhunter's series of mathematical text-books. (Because bound in green cloth.) **1953** R. FULLER *2nd Curtain* iv. 61 The quart bottle of beer, the Penguin greenback, incongruous modernities. **1960** E. MORGAN in M. Barry *Television Playwright* 357 Harry re-enters with the book, a green-back Penguin.

4. A deficiency disease of tomatoes, shown by the calyx end of the fruits failing to ripen.

1926 *Ann. Appl. Biol.* XIII. 338 Exposure of the fruits to excessive sunlight causes a type of blotchiness known as 'green back' if the nitrogen and potash supply is inadequate. **1943** T. WALLACE *Diagnosis Mineral Deficiencies in Plants* iv. 32 Tomato plants have a high requirement for potassium. When the element is deficient..fruits often fail to ripen evenly, and may show sharply defined, green patches near the stalks (green-back). **1961** *Amat. Gardening* 21 Oct. Suppl. 25/1 *Green-back*, a common tomato disorder in which the fruits do not ripen completely but remain green near the stalk.

5. *Surfing slang.* = GREENIE.

1965 H. A. KLEIN *Surfing* iii. 58 Australian surfers use the picturesque word 'greenbacks' for a swell as it peaks higher and higher but has not yet begun to spill 'white water' down its front face. **1965** J. POLLARD *Surfrider* ii. 20 Just out a little further are the 'green-backs', the unbroken waves. **1970** [see GREENIE].

Hence (*U.S.*) **'greenbacker**, a member of the greenback party. **'greenbackism**, the principles of the greenback party, advocacy of those principles.

1878 *N. Amer. Rev.* CXXVII. 103 The millions who call themselves Greenbackers. **1882** PLAYFAIR in *Macm. Mag.* XLV. 336 The greenbackers advocate an internal, inconvertible, non-exportable currency. **1883** *American* VI. 5 Without criticising his Greenbackism at all. **1888** BRYCE *Amer. Commw.* II. III. lvi. 368 The Greenbackers, who arose soon after the end of the war..demand a large issue of greenbacks. **1892** *N. Amer. Rev.* CLIV. 745 Greenbackism was strongly tinctured with the sentiment of Nationalism.

greenback ('gri:nbæk), *v. rare.* [f. GREEN *a.* + BACK *sb.*[1]] *trans.* To bind in a green cover.

1828 SOUTHEY *Lett.* (1856) IV. 99 Bailey's next job will be to green-back the 'Parnaso Italiano', fifty-six vols.

green bag, green-bag. A bag made of green material such as was used formerly (the colour being now blue) by barristers and lawyers for documents and papers. Also *attrib.* †**b.** Hence *slang* (hyphened and stressed *'green-bag*), a lawyer.

1677 WYCHERLEY *Plain Dealer* III. i, You Green Bag Carrier, you Murderer of unfortunate Causes, the Clerks Ink is scarce off of your fingers. *a* **1700** B. E. *Dict. Cant. Crew*, *Green-bag*, a Lawyer. **1712** ARBUTHNOT *John Bull* II. iii, I am told, Cousin Diego, you are one of those that have under-taken to manage me, and that you have said you will carry a Green Bag your self, rather than we shall make an end of our Law-Suit. **1817** COBBETT *Pol. Reg.* 8 Feb. 181 There is a green bag full of papers..laid before Parliament. **1817** *Parl. Deb.* 1866 When green bags were introduced by the noble lord opposite, they were..referred to committees. **1885** BREWER *Reader's Handbk.*, *Green-Bag Inquiry.* A green bag full of documents, said to be seditious, was laid before parliament by lord Sidmouth, in 1817. An 'inquiry' was made into these documents, and it was deemed advisable to suspend the Habeas Corpus Act. **1897** BARRÈRE & LELAND *Dict. Slang* s.v., 'What's in the green bag?' *i.e.*, what is the charge to be preferred against me?

green baize. [See BAIZE *sb.*] Baize of a green colour, such as is used to cover office tables or gaming tables; hence used *transf.* for such a table. Also *attrib.*

1801 C. WILMOT *Diary* 29 Nov. (1920) 4 Even after trunks, Pocket Books, Writing Cases, Green baize bags, &c., were quietly deliver'd in. **1812** *Dramatic Censor 1811* col. 362 'Tis bekase I'm a poet you see, That I kiver my head with green baize. **1843** *Ecclesiologist* II. 31 The carving however being concealed by a green-baize lining. **1852** [see BAIZE *sb.* 3]. *c* **1870** B. HARTE *Brown of Calaveras*, He pushed open a green-baize door. **1880** [see BAIZE *sb.* 2].

Hence **green-baized** *a.*, covered with green baize.

1836–9 DICKENS *Sk. Boz* (1850) 52/1 A small, green-baized, brass-headed-nailed door. **1818** KEATS *Let.* 7 July (1958) I. 319 A nice carpeted Room with Sofa hair bottomed chairs and green-baized mehogany.

green belt. [BELT *sb.*[1] 5 a.] An officially designated belt of open countryside in which all development is severely restricted, usu. enclosing a built-up area and designed to check its further growth.

1932 S. FREESE *Ten-Year Plan* 8 This had once been a 'green belt of country' as spoken of so glibly by the town-planning 'experts' of to-day. **1935** *Planning* 26 Feb. 3 Mr. Herbert Morrison's offer of a sum of £2 millions to neighbouring local authorities in order to create a green belt round London represents a belated assumption by the L.C.C. of the wider responsibilities already recognised last century by the City Corporation. **1937** *Daily Herald* 15 Jan., (*headline*) Green belt maps televised. **1937** *Discovery* Nov. 328/2 To draw the attention of the cities and towns of England to the need for safeguarding the country in their immediate vicinity by means of the establishment of green belts. **1945** P. ABERCROMBIE *Greater London Plan 1944* ii. 29 One of the first attempts to prevent the expansion of London was made by Queen Elizabeth..on 7th July, 1580, in a proclamation from Nonsuch Palace near Ewell in Surrey (now interestingly enough one of the properties secured as part of the Green Belt). **1958** *Listener* 19 June 1022/3 Parking facilities in the 'green belt' areas. **1961** E. A. POWDRILL *Vocab. Land Planning* iii. 34 Green belts have at least three specific functions: to prevent the unrestricted sprawl of large built-up areas; to provide areas of unspoilt country-side wherein people from the towns can find recreation and enjoyment; and to provide for the continued use of farmland, woodland, heath and common land. **1972** *Daily Tel.* 1 Jan. 2/1 Mr Page, Minister for Local Government and Development, is working on a scheme for extending green-belt policy so that it becomes..a more general protection of the countryside.

'green-blind, *a.* Suffering from the variety of colour-blindness in which the retina is insensitive to green light-rays. Hence **green-blindness**, the condition of being green-blind.

1881 LD. RAYLEIGH in *Nature* XXV. 66 The test of green-blindness would be the possibility of matches between colours which to normal eyes appear green and purple, or green and grey. **1888** *Amer. Jrnl. Psychol.* Feb. 311 The fact lately placed beyond all doubt by König and Dieterici, that those that are born color-blind fall naturally into two great groups, the red and green blind. **1890** H. ELLIS *Criminal* iii. 117 He met with one case (green-blindness) among 460 criminals tested with Holmgren's wools. **1892** *Pall Mall G.* 28 June 3/3 A colour-blind person will match drabs, pinks, and yellows with grass-green, blues and violets with light purple or rose, and dark green or light green with light red, according as he is 'red-blind' or 'green-blind'.

green cheese.

a. New or fresh cheese (see GREEN *a.* and CHEESE *sb.*[1] 2 a). **b.** An inferior kind of cheese prepared from skim milk or whey. **c.** Cheese coloured green (usually only in parts, with a pattern) with sage; also called *sage cheese.*

The saying ***to believe that the moon is made of green cheese*** (for which see CHEESE *sb.*[1] 2 a) might belong to any of these senses; perh. sense c is the most likely, the reference being to the variegated surface of the moon.

1362 LANGL. *P. Pl.* A. VII. 268, 'I haue no peny', quod Pers, 'poletes to bugge, Nouther gees ne grys, bote twey grene cheeses'. *c* **1430** *Two Cookery-bks.*, 48 Take 3olkys of Eyroun..& grene chese putte ther-to. **1542** BOORDE *Dyetary* xiii. (1870) 266 There is .iiii. sortes of chese, whiche is to say, grene chese, softe chese, harde chese, and spermyse. Grene chese is not called grene by the reason of colour, but for the newnes of it. **1546** GARDINER *Decl. Art. Joye* (Quarto ed.) 73 All is noth worth a greane chease. **1599** H. BUTTES *Dyets drie Dinner* N vij, Greene or new cheese, newly made, nourisheth..more then salt and olde. **1605** *Tryall Chev.* III. i. in Bullen *O. Pl.* III. 305 How did he looke? Faith, scurvily, my lord, like a greene cheese. *a* **1658** CLEVELAND *May Day* v, Fields with Curds and Cream like green-cheese lie. **1727** BOYER *Dict. Royal* II, Green Cheese (with Herbs in it), *fromage persillé.* **1839** *Mag. Dom. Econ.* IV. 241 In Gloucestershire there is another species of cheese, generally known by the name of 'green cheese', or 'sage cheese'. *c* **1865** *Circ. Sci.* I. 355/2 In its abundance of fat, cream-cheese is the richest: while green cheese, prepared from whey..is the poorest of all.

green cloth, greencloth.

1. In full, *Board of Green Cloth*: A department of the Royal Household, consisting of the Lord Steward and his subordinates, which has control of various matters of expenditure, and legal and judicial authority within the sovereign's court-royal, 'with power to correct all offenders, and to maintain the peace of the verge or jurisdiction of the court-royal, which extends every way two hundred yards from the gate of the palace' (Wharton *Law Lex.*). (So called from the green-covered table at which its business was originally transacted.)

1536 in *Gentl. Mag.* (1813) May 427 Thomas Hatterlyf and Edwarde Weldon, clerks of the greenclothe. **1539** *Househ. Ord.* (1790) 228 Calling unto them the Cofferer, Clerke of the Greencloth, and one of the Clerkes-Comptrollers. **1604** BACON *Sp. conc. Purveyors* in *Resuscit.* (1657) 7 As to the Court, of the Green-Cloth, ordained, for the Provision, of your Majesties most Honourable Houshold, we hold it Ancient, we hold it Reverent. **1658** OSBORN *Q. Eliz.* (1673) 428 The Green cloth (a Court only intending Provision and Carriages). **1692** LUTTRELL *Brief Rel.* (1857) II. 571 Mr. Isack, secretary of the green cloth, is dead. *Ibid.* III. 489 Mr. comptroller has complained to the green cloth against Mr. Story for keeping musick and revelling in his house on the fast day. **1711** SWIFT *Jrnl. to Stella* 11 Aug., Wks. 1824 II. 329, I dined to-day at the green cloth. **1719** D'URFEY *Pills* II. 103 The Queen..with good store of Dishes for the Greencloth does provide, To treat all Strangers heartily. **1806** CUMBERLAND *Mem.* (1807) I. 209, I put his [Lord Halifax's] Green Cloth upon a liberal, but regulated establishment. **1895** *Whitaker's Alm.* 92 Lord Steward's Department. Board of Green Cloth, Buckingham Palace. **1897** *Daily News* 2 Feb. 7/4 The Board of Green Cloth..pointed out that complimentary orders did not entitle the trade to the use of the Royal arms.

b. *attrib.*

? **1616** BACON *Advice to Sir G. Villiers* Wks. 1826 VI. 448 For the green-cloth law, take it in the largest sense, I have no opinion of it, farther than it is regulated by the just rules of the common laws of England.

†**2.** A kind of linen. *Obs.*

1769 *De Foe's Tour Gt. Brit.* IV. 181 Here is a Manufacture of Linen, as there is upon all the Coast of Fife, and especially for Green-cloth, as it is called.

3. *colloq.* The green baize covering of a billiard or gaming table; hence, the table itself.

1871 LEGRAND *Camb. Freshm.* 127 [They] strolled into Green's to pass a social hour over the board of green cloth at the game of pool. **1881** J. GRANT *Cameronians* I. ii. 28 Trying..his fortune at 'the board of green cloth'. **1891** *Review of Rev.* July 24 Gambling on the green cloth.

green coat, 'green-coat. **a.** *gen.* One who wears a green coat. **b.** *spec.* One of the scholars in certain charity schools (cf. BLUE COAT 3); *attrib.* in ***Green-coat Hospital, institution.***

1647 STAPYLTON *Juvenal* xi. 244 By that lowd shout the green-coats [i.e. the 'green' faction in the circus] have the best. **1766** ENTICK *London* IV. 411 In Tothill-side there is..the Green Coat-hospital, for the poor fatherless children of this parish. **1859** SALA *Tw. round Clock* (1861) 81 A foot-man..a dull knave, who no more resembles the resplendent flunkey of Eaton Square..than does the cotton-stockinged 'green-coat' of the minor theatres. **1899** *Daily News* 15 Sept. 5/1 In addition to the Blue Coat School, there were also Black Coat and Green Coat institutions in Westminster.

So **green-coated** *a.*, having or wearing a green coat or covering.

1784 COWPER *Task* III. 446 The prickly and green-coated gourd. **1898** *Daily News* 25 Mar. 3/2 The leading companies of green-coated cadets.

greened (gri:nd), *a.* [f. GREEN *a.* or *v.*[1] + -ED[1].] Rendered green; covered with verdure.

1852 G. W. CURTIS *Wanderer in Syria* 319 It sweeps for ever around an old greened wall below. **1892** *Pall Mall G.* 10 Feb 3/1 Whenever we got to the top of a ridge we beheld another ridge beyond it, with the thin greened hay-track going up it straight as a dart.

Greeneian ('gri:nɪən), *a.* Also Greene-ian, Greenian. [f. the name of the English writer Graham *Greene* (b. 1904) + -IAN.] Typical of, or resembling the style, matter, or quality of the works of Graham Greene.

1961 *Encounter* Apr. 70 The idiom is often satisfyingly Greeneian—there is an ample provision of those new proverbs of hell. **1963** *Punch* 26 June 938/1 'Under the Garden'..begins in the cold Greene-ian manner. **1968** *Listener* 10 Oct. 475/1 A palpable difference between Greene and Amis is that everything Greenian is available in the first of his 'Catholic' novels..while there is something approaching an emergent moral philosophy in Amis.

Greeneland ('griːnlænd). [f. the name *Greene* (see prec.) + LAND *sb.*; with a pun on GREENLAND.] A term used to describe the world of depressed seediness reputedly typical of the setting and characters of the novels of Graham Greene.

1940 A. C. MARSHALL in *Horizon* May 369 'The seedy level!' That is the location of Greeneland. **1966** D. LODGE *Graham Greene* 3 Over Clapham Common solitary walkers move with bowed heads through the slanting rain..in West Africa the laterite roads turn a fragile pink at sundown, then are swallowed by darkness. These are some characteristic scenes from a country of the mind known internationally as Greeneland. **1970** G. GREENE *Brighton Rock* p. x, Some critics have referred to a strange violent 'seedy' region of the mind..which they call Greeneland, and I have sometimes wondered whether they go round the world blinkered. 'This is Indo-China,' I want to explain, 'this is Mexico, this is Sierra Leone carefully and accurately described. I have been a newspaper correspondent as well as a novelist.'

greener[1] ('griːnə(r)). *slang.* [f. GREEN *a.* + -ER[1]; but cf. G. *ein grüner*, a 'green' one.] A 'green' or inexperienced workman; a raw hand: esp. a foreigner who has recently arrived in the country in search of work.

1888 *Times* 20 Sept. 7/4 The master sweater gets hold of a new hand, a greener, as he is termed, and pays him a shilling a day. **1890** *Pall Mall G.* 3 July 2/1 So long as the influx of 'greeners' gives the sweaters an inexhaustible supply of labour. **1892** ZANGWILL *Childr. Ghetto* I. 48 He was a 'greener' of the greenest order, having landed at the docks only a few hours ago. **1893** FARMER *Slang*, *Greener*,.. specifically employed of inexperienced workmen introduced to fill the place of strikers.

Greener[2] ('griːnə(r)). Applied to rifles, cartridges, etc., made by, or according to the designs of, W. *Greener* (1806–1869), gunsmith and author, or his son, W. W. Greener, gunsmith and author.

1895 *Montgomery Ward Catal.* 450/1 Facile Princeps Greener..fine Damascus barrels... No better shooting gun at any price. **1901** *Kynoch Jrnl.* Apr.–May 93/2 Diagrams obtained with a Greener ·310 rifle and orthoptic sights. **1902** *Ibid.* Apr.–May 84/1 Of these cartridges the Greener sharpshooter is probably the most popular. **1918** E. S. FARROW *Dict. Mil. Terms* 271 *Greener bullet*, one of the first bullets made to take the grooves by the expanding action of the powder. It had a conical pewter wedge which was driven into a cavity in the base of the bullet by the powder and forced the outer walls of the bullet into the grooves. **1921** *Outward Bound* June 45/1 Tucking away his valuable Greener under his arm. **1949** H. WADMAN *Life Sentence* 21 One of the beaters gave me a gun—it was a Greener.

greenery ('griːnərɪ). [f. GREEN *a.* or *sb.* + -ERY.]

1. Green foliage or vegetation; verdure.

1797 COLERIDGE *Kubla Khan* 11 Here were forests ancient as the hills, Enfolding sunny spots of greenery. **1856** MRS. BROWNING *Aur. Leigh* I. 574 The out-door world with all its greenery. **1876** GREEN *Stray Stud.* 388 Steeps clothed from top to bottom in the thick greenery of the lemon or orange. **1893** R. KIPLING *Many Invent.* 203 After an hour's riding through the greenery, he heard a rustle.

2. Green branches or leaves used for decoration. (Rarely *pl.*)

1867 TROLLOPE *Chron. Barset* I. xvi. 132 The greeneries of the winter had not been stuck up in the old-fashioned, idle way. **1885** LADY BRASSEY *The Trades* 495 The pictures.. wreathed with myrtles, and other greenery. **1887** BOWEN *Virg. Æneid* IV. 459 In snow-white fillets and festal greenery crowned.

3. A place where plants are reared, kept, or exhibited.

1847 CRAIG, *Greenery*, a place for green plants. **1893** *Westm. Gaz.* 10 Apr. 5/3 The greeneries of the Thiergarten.

greenery-yallery ('griːnərɪ 'jælərɪ), *a. colloq.* [f. GREEN *a.* + *yaller*, vulgar pronunc. of YELLOW *a.*, with ending *-ery* repeated to produce a jingling compound.] Of, pertaining to, or affecting the colours green and yellow, in accordance with the style or fashion of the aesthetic movement of the late nineteenth century; hence, typical of this movement; affected.

1880 W. S. GILBERT *Patience* II. 37 A greenery-yallery, Grosvenor Gallery, Foot-in-the-grave young man. **1886** 'S. COOLIDGE' *What Katy did Next* (1887) iii. 59 She had chosen a 'greenery, yallery' paper for her walls. **1896** *Amer. Bookman* III. 131/1 The greenery-yallery school would have found no disciple in him [*sc.* Dickens]. **1896** MRS. H. WARD *Sir G. Tressady* 194 You needn't wear greenery-yallery gowns, you know. **1945** E. WAUGH *Brideshead Revisited* ii. 49 Nothing greenery-yallery about her. So gay, so correct, so unaffected. **1956** C. WILLOCK *Death at Flight* ii. 18 Two articles, including the one about the boy artist, dealt with the more greenery-yallery end of the Arts.

greenes, -ess(e, obs. forms of GREENNESS.

green-eyed (griːnaɪd), *a.* (Stress variable.) [f. GREEN *a.* + EYE *sb.* + -ED[2]; cf. EYED 1 b.] Having green eyes. ***the green-eyed monster*** (in and after Shakspere): jealousy. (Cf. GREEN *a.* 3.) Hence *fig.* Viewing everything with jealousy.

1596 SHAKS. *Merch. V.* III. ii. 110 Shuddring feare, and greene-eyed ielousie. **1604** —— *Oth.* III. iii. 166 Oh, beware my Lord, of ielousie, It is the greene-ey'd Monster. **1627** MILTON *Vacation Exer.* 43 How green-eyed Neptune raves. **1653** R. SANDERS *Physiogn.* 152 Well-featured, round-faced, flaxen-haired, green-eyed. *c* **1800** H. K. WHITE *Genius* I. i, Green-eyed Grief, and dull Despair. **1804** *Sporting Mag.* XXIII. 284 What he had uttered was under the influence of the 'green-eyed monster'. **1854** S. DOBELL *Balder* xi. Poet. Wks. 1875 II. 57 Hellebore, like a girl-murderess, Green-eyed and sick with jealousy. **1883** MISS BRADDON *Phantom Fort.* xxxviii, (1884) 335 Devoured by the gnawing of the green-eyed monster.

greenfeed ('griːnfiːd). Chiefly *Austral.* and *N.Z.* [f. GREEN *a.* + FEED *sb.*] Forage grown to be fed fresh to livestock. Also *attrib.*

1898 *Bulletin* (Sydney) 30 Apr. 31/4 A large hairy dairyman began to tell how many pounds of butter his little 'yaller' heifer..yielded in a week... For ten minutes nothing could be heard but 'pounds', 'quarts',..'separators', 'green feed', and 'Ayrshire'. **1916** *N.Z. Jrnl. Agric.* 20 Sept. 190 The wise dairyman will provide sufficient soilage (green-feed-producing crops) and silage to make good all possible shortage of pastures in summer or winter. **1928** *Bulletin* (Sydney) 12 Jan. 31/2 Although green feed is essential for poultry, it should be given in moderation and regularly. **1947** E. A. MCCOURT *Music at Close* 51 By the end of May the spring rush was over and all the crops in except late oats and greenfeed. **1950** *N.Z. Jrnl. Agric.* July 37/2 Maize for greenfeed is sown at the rate of 2 bushels per acre. **1960** *Farmer & Stockbreeder* 23 Feb. 61/3 They claim that it gives a greater tonnage of green-feed per acre than any other variety. **1967** *Heretaunga Plains* (Ministry of Works, N.Z.) 45/2 Many farmers grow lucerne, chou moellier, and greenfeed ryecorn.

greenfinch ('griːnfɪnʃ). [See GREEN *a.*[1] and FINCH. Cf. G. *grünfink*, Du. *groenvink.*]

1. A common European bird of the family *Fringillidæ*, *Coccothraustes* or *Ligurinus chloris*, so called from its green-and-gold plumage. Called also *green linnet*. **Chinese greenfinch**, *Ligurinus sinicus.*

c **1532** DU WES *Introd. Fr.* in *Palsgr.* 912 The grene fynche, *la verdiere.* **1544** TURNER *Avium Præcip. Hist.* F 3 De Ligvrino sive Spino..Anglicè a grene finche. **1678** RAY *Willughby's Ornith.* 246 The Green-finch: Chloris..It is bigger than a House-Sparrow..It is called by some the Green Linnet. **1766** PENNANT *Brit. Zool.* (1768) II. 330 The greenfinch does not begin his [flight] till the frost sets in. **1894** R. B. SHARPE *Handbk. Birds Gt. Brit.* I. 32 In summer the Greenfinch is somewhat shy, but in winter it is found in flocks in the fields and farmyards along with Sparrows and Chaffinches.

2. The Texas sparrow (*Embernagra rufivirgata*).

1883 *Encycl. Amer.* I. 530/1 The green finch (*Embernagra rufivirgata*) of Texas.

3. *slang.* One of the Pope's Irish guard.

1865 *Daily Tel.* 1 Nov. 5/3 *Point d'argent, point de Suisse* —a saying applicable alike to every contingent, from the Franco-Belgian down to the 'greenfinches' of Old Ireland.

green-fish ('griːnfɪʃ). [See GREEN *a.* 9 b.]

†**1.** Fresh, unsalted fish; *spec.* applied to cod before it has been salted or cured. (Cf. HABERDINE.) *Obs.*

c **1460** J. RUSSELL *Bk. Nurture* 851 Grene sawce is good with grene fisch. **1540** *Old City Acc. Bk.* in *Archæol. Jrnl.* XLIII, It. for a grene ffysshe a goyle of sawmond and for a haberdyne. **1580** HOLLYBAND *Treas. Fr. Tong.*, *Moruë*, or *Mouluë*, *poisson*, a fishe called Codde, or greene fishe. *a* **1625** BEAUM. & FL. *Bonduca* IV. i, [It] shews thee like a long Lent, thy brave body turn'd to a tail of green-fish without butter. **1623** WHITBOURNE *Newfoundland* 79 Two hundred thousand dry fish, ten thousand of large greene fish. **1630** J. TAYLOR (Water P.) *Wks.* I. 119/2 If..euery house in this Kingdome did spend but the quantity of two Haberdine or Greenfish in a week. **1655** MOUFET & BENNET *Health's Improv.* 155 Whilst it [Codling] is new, it is called green-fish; when it is salted it is called Ling. **1682** J. COLLINS *Salt & Fishery* 90 Green-Fish (*alias* Staple Fish as they call it) cured with a good Salt, proves excellent. **1694** MOTTEUX *Rabelais* IV. lx. (1737) 247 Green-fish, Sea-Batts, Cod-Sounds. **1736** AINSWORTH *Eng.-Lat. Dict.*, A green fish, *asellus.* **1867** SMYTH *Sailor's Word-bk.*, *Green-fish*, cod, hake, haddock, herrings, &c. unsalted.

2. a. *local.* The coal-fish. **b.** *U.S.* (See quot. 1884–5).

1880–4 F. DAY *Fishes Gt. Brit. & Irel.* I. 297 *Gadus pollachius*..Names.— Pollack: whiting-pollack.. Sometimes termed greenling or green-fish. **1884–5** *Riverside Nat. Hist.* (1888) III. 183 The blue-fish (*Pomatomus saltatrix*)..in parts of Virginia and North Carolina it is known as green-fish.

'green-fly.

1. *Angling.* A particular kind of artificial fly.

1686 BLOME *Gentl. Recreat.* II. 182/1 The Shell-flye, Termed also the Green-fly, hath his body made of Greenish-wooll. **1832** MAR. EDGEWORTH *Absentee* viii, The green-fly, and the moorish-fly.

2. An aphis or plant-louse, so called from its colour. Usually *collect. sing.*

1744–50 ELLIS *Mod. Husbandm.* III. I. xv. 184 An Insect seldom, or never, misses attacking our green Cherries with so much Diligence and Fury, as to spoil great Numbers of them, by eating into their very Stone; and because of this hollow Operation, we call them Ladlemen, or the Green Fly, or Bug. **1849** *Florist* 35 Flowers in windows..are peculiarly liable..to be infested with green-fly (*Aphis*). **1882** *Garden* 18 Mar. 174/1 If green-fly makes its appearance, fumigation with Tobacco smoke is the only remedy.

greengage ('griːngeɪdʒ). Also 9 **green-gedge.** [f. GREEN *a.* and the surname *Gage* (see quot. 1759–65).] **1.** A variety of plum of roundish shape, green colour, and fine flavour. Also *attrib.* in ***greengage plum, tart.***

1724 R. BRADLEY *New Improvements of Planting & Gardening* (ed. 4) 222 Queen Mother; Green Gage, Violet. **1759–65** COLLINSON in *Hortus Collinsonianus* 60, I was on a visit to Sir William Gage..he told me that..in compliment to him the Plum was called the Green Gage; this was about the year 1725. **1769** MRS. RAFFALD *Eng. Housekpr.* (1778) 220 To preserve Green Gage Plumbs. **1802** FORSYTH *Fruit-trees* ii. 13 The Green Gage Plum is of an exquisite taste, and eats like a sweatmeat. **1813** W. TAYLOR in *Monthly Mag.* XXXV. 232 The Cadiz plum, or green-gedge. **1891** C. JAMES *Rom. Rigmarole* 105 The question of a greengage-tart for dinner.

2. *Rhyming slang.* (*a*) the stage (cf. GREEN *sb.* 14 b); (*b*) *pl.* wages.

1931 *Even. Standard* 19 Aug. 10/1 We speak of..the stage as the 'green-gage'. **1931** 'G. ORWELL' *Coll. Essays* (1968) I. 71 Greengages, meaning wages. **1932** P. P. *Rhyming Slang* II. 20 *Greengages*,..Wages. **1964** *Guardian* 2 Mar. 7/6 The money? Greengages we call it, greengages—wages. You'll be surprised. In a lot of places it's a fiver a night.

green goose. [See GREEN *a.*; the use of the word in opposition to *stubble-goose* suggests GREEN *sb.*]

1. A young goose, a gosling. ? Now *dial.*

The precise application of the term with respect to age and condition varies with the locality (see quots.).

1564 in Gross *Gild Merch.* (1890) II. 279 The furste course: frometye, rost byffe, grene gese, weale. **1588** SHAKS. *L.L.L.* I. i. 97 The Spring is neare when greene geesse are a breeding. **1589** COGAN *Haven Health* (1636) 156 The greene goose is better than the stubble goose. **1620** VENNER *Via Recta* iii. 66 Young Geese, which are commonly called greene-Geese. **1741** *Compl. Fam.-Piece* III. 509 Stubble Geese or Green Geese should be kept in the Dark, and fatted with ground Malt mixed with Milk. **1821** J. HODGSON in J. Raine *Mem.* (1857) I. 342 We dined with my aunt, and had a green goose, four months old, to dinner. **1877** *N.W. Linc. Gloss.*, *Green goose*, a goose killed at midsummer time. A goose under four months old. **1881** *Oxfordsh. Gloss.* Suppl., *Green geese*, unfatted geese. They should be eaten on Old Michaelmas Day.

2. A simpleton; = GOOSE *sb.* 1 f. *rare.*

1768 GRAY *Let.* 25 Feb., Wks. 1836 IV. 113 The true title of this part of his work [Boswell's *Corsica*] is, a Dialogue between a Green-goose and a Hero. **1877** DOWDEN *Shaks. Prim.* vi. 130 Here Troilus, the noble green-goose, goes through his youthful agony of ascertaining the unworthiness of her to whom he had given his faith and hope.

green gown: see GREEN A. 1 g.

greengrocer ('griːn,grəʊsə(r)). [See GREEN and GROCER.] A retail dealer in vegetables and fruit.

1723 *Lond. Gaz.* No. 6188/9 Samuel Stubley..Green-Grocer. **1791** BOSWELL *Johnson* an. 1753 (1847) 81/1 Covent-garden, where the green-grocers and fruiterers were beginning to arrange their hampers. **1793** WOLCOT (P. Pindar) *Ep. to Pope* Wks. 1812 III. 198 As from their shops Green-grocers for the palate Deal Garden-stuff of all complexion. **1816** *Sporting Mag.* XLVII. 255 A green grocer of Brighton was convicted..for..exposing in his shop..twenty partridges and two hares. **1860** W. G. CLARK in *Vac. Tour* 17 A species of tax..is levied [in Naples] upon cabmen, small greengrocers, fishmongers, and other tradesmen.

Hence **'green,groceress** [see -ESS] *rare*, a female greengrocer. **'green,grocery** [see -ERY], the business of a greengrocer; the articles retailed by a greengrocer. Also *attrib.*

1806 H. SIDDONS *Maid, Wife & Widow* II. 28 Retailers of chandlery and green-grocery. **1848** THACKERAY *Van. Fair* xxxvii, Mr. Raggles himself had to supply the green-groceries. **1868** MRS. H. WOOD in *Argosy* June 46 A miserable greengrocery shed. **1884** *Academy* 16 Feb. 107/3 The motherly Genoese greengroceress..is a charming sketch. **1885** *Law Times* 16 May 47/1 In the present case the business of greengrocery was not ancillary to that of grocery. **1899** *Westm. Gaz.* 25 Jan. 9/1 Exposing green-grocery for sale on the carriage way.

Greenham ('griːnəm). [f. the name of *Greenham* Common in Berkshire, southern England.] ***Greenham woman***: any of the women who established a women's peace camp (see PEACE *sb.* 17 a) at Greenham Common in 1981 to protest about the deployment of nuclear weapons at the U.S. airbase there and elsewhere. Also ***Greenham Common woman.***

1982 *Sunday Times* 19 Dec. 32/3 In September 1981..the Greenham women were still a long way off their present notoriety. **1982** *Guardian* 13 Dec. 12/2 The work of the women's lib movement is growing ugly and facetious, trampling over ideals of unity and the love of all people to use the Greenham Common women's dedication and commitment to make an abrasive and belittling point. **1983** *Guardian Weekly* 4 Dec. 5 Not least of it is the success of the Greenham women in preventing the effective deployment of the first batch of cruise missiles. **1985** *New Statesman* 27 Sept. 6/2 Katrina conducted her own defence and read to the court the notorious 'SAS' letter sent to CND which said that a Greenham woman would be framed.

†**'greenhead**[1]. *Obs.* [f. GREEN *a.* + -HEAD.] Greenness. Also *fig.* (see GREEN A. 8).

c **1325** *Gloss. W. de Bibbesw.* in Wright *Voc.* 171 *Verdoure*, grenhed. **1340** *Ayenb.* 94 Þe holy writ comparisoneþ þe zaule and of þe guode manne an of þe guode wyfmanne to ane uayre gardyne uol of grenhede. *c* **1386** CHAUCER *Man of Law's T.* 65 In hire is heigh beautee, with oute pride, Yowthe, with oute grenehede or folye. *c* **1440** *Promp. Parv.* 210/1 Grenehed, or grenenesse, *viriditas, viror.*

green head, 'greenhead[2]. [f. GREEN *a.* + HEAD *sb.*]

†**1.** (See HEAD *sb.* 2 a.) A young, immature, or untrained intellect. *Obs.*

1588 J. UDALL *Diotrephes* (Arb.) 11 Euerye yoong boy will take vpon him to teache the ancient, and to reproue them, for that their greene heades thinke not to bee true. **1591** R. TURNBULL *Expos. Jas.* 175 To whom..in the conceits of their grene heads, they wil not obey. **1694** F. BRAGGE *Disc. Parables* xi. (1706) I. 373 The Difference between living under the mild and prudent Government of his Father, and being left to the Conduct of his own ill instructed and green Head.

2. (See HEAD *sb.* 7.) A raw, inexperienced person; a simpleton; an ignoramus. ? *Obs.*

1589 *Marprel. Epit.* B ij, The author of the Learned Discourse, and 500 green heads more that are on their side. **1600** HOLLAND *Livy* XXXVIII. lii. (1609) 1017 With the checks and taunts of certaine greene heads and busie youths. **1652** BP. PATRICK *Funeral Serm.* in *J. Smith's Sel. Disc.* 526 Holy and pious counsels for the teaching of rawer and greener heads. *a* **1700** B. E. *Dict. Cant. Crew, Green-head*, a very raw Novice or inexperienc'd Fellow. **1742** RICHARDSON *Pamela* III. 311 Hadst thou been a born Fool, or a raw Greenhead, or a doting Greyhead. **1781** COWPER *Conversat.* 626 Some green heads, as void of wit as thought. **1820** SCOTT *Monast.* xvii, Methinks there is use for the grey hairs on the old scalp, were it but to instruct the green head by precept and by example.

†**3.** One entitled to wear the green turban, a descendant of Mahomet. *Obs.*

1609 BIDDULPH in T. Lavender *Trav.* (1612) 71 There was a Sheriffe or a Green-head in Aleppo, whom they account Mahomets kindred. **1625** PURCHAS *Pilgrims* II. 1623 The cadie of Tripoly being a Green-head that is one of the Parentage of Mahomet.

4. One of several biting flies of the family Tabanidæ, esp. *Tabanus nigrovittatus.*

1837 A. WETMORE *Gaz. Missouri* 65 In the early settlement of the country, the value of the prairies was under-rated by a knowledge of the mischievous power vested in the greenheads, or prairie fly. **1838** E. FLAGG *Far West* II. 107 (Th.), [My horse was] severely troubled by that terrible insect, so notorious all over the West, the large green-bottle prairie fly, called the 'greenhead'. **1888** J. KIRKLAND *McVeys* 18 What can be the matter with that horse?.. Is he crazy? Pretty near, I guess, with a greenhead on him somewhere where he can't get at it. **1951** E. PAUL *Springtime in Paris* v. 113 He twitched like a steer which green-heads were biting.

5. An Australian ant, *Ectatomma metallicum.*

1907 W. W. FROGGATT *Austral. Insects* 93 The 'Green-head', *Ectatomma metallicum*, is a common ant of medium size that lives in small communities under stones or logs. **1926** *Glasgow Herald* 19 Dec. 6 The greenhead is the most vicious attacker of man. **1970** E. F. RIEK in *Insects of Australia* (C.S.I.R.O.) xxxvii. 910/2 One specimen is recorded from the nest of *Ectatomma metallicum*, the green-head ant.

Hence †**green-headed** *a.*, raw, inexperienced.

1569 NEWTON *Cicero's Old Age* 43 a, Such youthly prankes and exercises, as lustye and greene-headed galantes do enure themselues withal. **1593** *Tell-Troth's N.Y. Gift* 31 Those are greene headed that long for reformations. **1649** ROBERTS *Clavis Bibl.* 214 Rehoboam's tyrannical Answer.. according to the advice of his green-headed Counsellours. **1684** BUNYAN *Pilgr.* II. 179 That with green-headed Ignorance I would presume to go on to the Gate.

greenheart ('griːnhɑːt). [See GREEN *a.* and HEART *sb.* 18, 30.]

1. The name of several West Indian trees remarkable for the quality of their wood. **a.** A large lauraceous tree of Guiana, *Nectandra Rodiæi*, which furnishes very hard timber. **b.** The cogwood tree, *Ceanothus Chloroxylon.* **c.** A small rhamnaceous tree, the *Colubrina ferruginosa* of Jamaica. **d.** *bastard* or *false greenheart*, a small myrtaceous tree, *Calyptranthes Chytraculia.*

1756 P. BROWNE *Jamaica* 187 The Greenheart or Cogwood tree.. It is generally esteemed one of the best timber-woods in the island. *Ibid.* 239 Bastard Green-heart ..is generally reckoned an excellent timber-wood. **1769** E. BANCROFT *Nat. Hist. Guiana* 333 They contentedly recur to the use of Sipera, or Green-Hart-tree Apples. **1839** M. J. HIGGINS *Ess.* (1875) xvii, Moras, greenhearts, and silk-cotton trees, rearing their heads far above the other giants of the forest. **1858** *Penny Cycl.* Supp. II. 682/2 The Bibira, or Greenheart Tree. **1875** BEDFORD *Sailor's Pocket Bk.* ix. (ed. 2) 336 The Morra and Greenheart of British Guiana.

2. The timber of *Nectandra Rodiæi*, used in shipbuilding, for fishing-rods, etc. Also *attrib.*

1794 *Rigging & Seamanship* I. 151 *Green-heart*, a wood imported from the West Indies, used for the pins of blocks. **1863** *Times* 19 Mar. 14/2 In the main and lower decks, teak, mahogany, and greenheart are used almost exclusively. **1875** J. D. HEATH *Croquet Player* 26 Handles are generally made of ash, but greenheart and Canadian rock elm are more springy and elastic. **1884** *Times* 26 Mar. 10 New greenheart planks have been put in where the worst chafing had occurred. **1887** J. CUMMINS *Catal., Hints to Anglers*, The best Rods are composed of Hickory butts, Greenheart centres, with Greenheart or Washaba tops.

b. A fishing-rod made of this wood.

1884 *Blackw. Mag.* Mar. 344/1 It was an Irish greenheart. **1894** *Ibid.* July 67 The rod..was a 13-foot single-handed greenheart with one splice.

'greenhew. *Obs.* exc. *Hist.* Also 7 **greenhuge, -hue.** [? f. GREEN *a.* + HEW *v.*; cf. Da. *hug* sb.]

1. The green parts of trees in a wood or forest; VERT. Also *attrib.*

1598 MANWOOD *Lawes Forrest* viii. §4. 46 If the people of a whole towneship doe make wast in the greene hew of the Forrest. **1621** *Naworth Househ. Bks.* (Surtees) 150 Received of Chr. Harding.. for green-huge, ij[s]. viij[d]. **1648** COKE *4th Inst.* lxxiii. 299 The Kings Officers within his Forest have charge of Venison, and of Vert or Green hue for the maintenance or preservation of the Kings game. **1774** T. WEST *Antiq. Furness* (1805) 85 They may take unto themselves green hew, or wood, out of my woods. *Ibid.* 97 Customary rents, encroachment rents, hen rents, greenhew rents.

2. The right to cut greenery for fodder; payment for such a right.

1869 *Lonsdale Gloss., Green-hew*, the right of cutting hollies and evergreens in winter for sheep, etc. **1895** *Lakeland Gloss., Greenhew*, a word found in old manorial writings, used for the payment of cutting trees upon an estate by the tenant.

green hide, greenhide: see GREEN *a.* 9 c.

greenhorn ('griːnhɔːn). [See GREEN *a.*]

†**1.** An appellation given to an animal, ? orig. to an ox with 'green' or young horns. *Obs.*

c **1460** *Towneley Myst.* ii. 25 Io furth, greyn-horne! and war oute gryme! Drawes on.. What! will ye no forther, mare?

†**2.** A recently-enlisted soldier; a raw recruit.

1650 *Relat. Fight near Leith* (1806) 214 The Scotch king being upon the castle-hill to see his men, which he called his Green Hornes, beaten. **1682** C. IRVINE *Hist. Scot. Nomencl.* 241 *Tyrones*, fresh-water Souldiers, or new levyed; Greenhorns: also it signifieth novices in any profession.

3. A raw, inexperienced person, *esp.* a novice in a trade (cf. GREENER); an ignoramus; hence, one easily imposed upon, a simpleton.

1682 [see sense 2]. **1753** *Scots Mag.* Oct. 490 The scale.. consists of eight degrees; Greenhorn, Jemmy, Jessamy, Smart, Honest Fellow, Joyous Spirit, Buck, and Blood. *Ibid.* Peculiarities which..would have denominated me a *Greenhorn.* **1790** J. B. MORETON *Mann. W. Ind.* 92 Overseers are glad to get green-horns, because they can impose hardships on them. **1806** SURR *Winter in Lond.* (ed. 3) I. 176 If we stand that..we should be greenhorns. **1835** W. IRVING *Tour Prairies* xx. 175 He..looked down upon them with contempt as greenhorns, little versed in the noble science of woodcraft. **1859** GREELEY *Overland Journ.* 359 The chances for 'big strikes' in the mines are few, and greenhorns cannot share them. **1885** RIDER HAGGARD *K. Solomon's Mines* ii. (1886) 29, I suppose you are not hoaxing us? It is, I know, sometimes thought allowable to take a greenhorn in.

attrib. **1845** COL. HAWKER *Diary* (1893) II. 255 Some greenhorn dandies.

Hence **'greenhornism**, the character or condition of a greenhorn, inexperience.

1831 DISRAELI *Yng. Duke* IV. vi, As for Lady Afy, he execrated the greenhornism which made him feign a passion and then get caught where he meant to capture. **1844** COL. HAWKER *Instruct. Yng. Sportsm.* 491 Nothing, therefore, betrays greenhornism more than expecting to make a shot under the latter circumstance.

green-house, greenhouse ('griːnhaʊs).

1. [f. GREEN *sb.* 10.] A glass-house in which delicate and tender plants are reared and preserved.

1664 EVELYN *Kal. Hort.* (1729) 198 Set your..Windows and Doors of the Green-houses and Conservatories open. **1683** —— *Diary* 30 Oct., Greene houses for oranges and mirtles. **1712** J. JAMES tr. *Le Blond's Gardening* 75 Green-houses are large Piles of Building like Galleries..for preserving Orange-Trees, and other Plants..during the Winter. **1742** *Phil. Trans.* XLII. 56 Thermometers, Hygrometers and Barometers.. adapted to the Use of Green-houses. **1858** GLENNY *Gard. Every-day Bk.* 94/1 The house ought now to be enriched by plants from the greenhouse and hothouse.

b. *attrib.*, as ***greenhouse cactus, plant, shrub***; **greenhouse bug** (see quot.); **greenhouse effect** *Meteorol.*, the phenomenon whereby the surface and the lower atmosphere of a planet are maintained at a relatively high temperature owing to the greater transparency of the atmosphere to visible radiation from the sun than to infra-red radiation from the planet.

1797 HOLCROFT tr. *Stolberg's Trav.* (ed. 2) III. lxxx. 232 The cistus with us is a green-house plant. **1845** *Florist's Jrnl.* 15 A hardy and very pretty greenhouse shrub. **1848** *Rural Cycl.* II. 525 *Greenhouse-bug*, scientifically *Coccus Hesperidum*, a heteropterous insect of the gallinsecta or coccidæ family. **1858** GLENNY *Gard. Every-day Bk.* 140/1 Greenhouse Cacti and Epiphyllums. **1937** G. T. TREWARTHA *Introd. Weather & Climate* i. 25 The so-called greenhouse effect of the atmosphere. **1962** F. I. ORDWAY et al. *Basic Astronautics* iii. 78 On Mars the greenhouse effect is not expected to be very significant. **1968** *Observer* 17 Nov. 9/5 Carbon dioxide..is responsible for a 'greenhouse' effect which allows in heat from the sun but prevents it escaping back into space.

2. *Pottery.* A house in which 'green ware' (see GREEN *a.* 9 d) is left to dry, before being placed in the kiln.

1875 *Ure's Dict. Arts* (ed. 7) III. 614 The [bisque] ware being finished from the hands of the potter is brought by him upon boards to the 'green-house', so called from its being the receptacle for ware in the 'green' or unfired state.

3. *Aeronaut. slang.* (See quots.)

1941 *Life* 24 Mar. 85/1 In the slang of the Royal Air Force man, the cockpit of his plane is the 'pulpit' or 'office', the glass covering over it the 'greenhouse'. **1942** *Gen* 1 Sept. 14/1 A fighter pilot..pulls the 'greenhouse'—cockpit cover—over him. **1944** *Word Study* Apr. 4/2 *Greenhouse.* This is what pilots call the glass cockpit covering over observation and similar planes. **1947** AUDEN *Age of Anxiety* (1948) i. 18 'Why have They killed me?' wondered Bert, our Greenhouse gunner.

Greenian ('griːnɪən), *a.* (*sb.*) [f. the name of the English mathematician George *Green* (1793–1841) + -IAN.] *Greenian functions*: a class of functions introduced by George Green, serving to represent the distribution of electricity on an ellipsoid.

1875 CAYLEY *Math. Papers* (1896) IX. 393 In the present Annex, I in part reproduce Green's process for the integration of this equation by means of a series of functions, which are analogous to Laplace's Functions, and may be termed 'Greenians'. *Ibid.* 394 These functions ϕ of the variables $\alpha, \beta, .., \gamma$ are in fact the Greenian Functions in question.

greenie ('griːnɪ). *Surfing slang.* [f. GREEN *a.* + -IE.] A large wave before it breaks.

1962 *Austral. Women's Weekly* (Suppl.) 24 Oct. 3/2 *Greenie*, a big wave before it breaks into white foam. **1970** *Studies in English* (Univ. of Cape Town) I. 27 A wave can be a mere *green back*, or *greenie*, but more often it is a *roller, grinder, pounder* or *dumper.*

greening ('griːnɪŋ), *sb.* [f. GREEN *a.* + -ING[3]. In sense 1 cf. *hasting.* Cf. MDu. *groeninc*, Du. *groening* kind of apple.]

1. The name of a fruit. †**a.** A variety of pear. Also ***greening-pear.*** *Obs.*

1600 SURFLET *Country Farme* III. xlix. 537 Garden, tender or delicate peares such as are the..hasting, mollart, greening, butter peare [etc.]. **1611** COTGR., *Poire de verdelet*, the Greening; a tender and delicate Peare. **1632** SHERWOOD, s.v., A greening peare, *verdelet.*

b. An apple, which is green when ripe.

1664 EVELYN *Pomona* iv. 13 Russetings and Greenings. **1676** WORLIDGE *Cyder* (1691) 210 The Greening is also another old English fruit of a green colour. **1846** J. BAXTER *Libr. Pract. Agric.* (ed. 4) I. 59 Winter Sauce Apples.. Yorkshire greening. **1868** *Rep. U.S. Commissioner Agric.* (1869) 474 Winthrop Greening..Rhode Island Greening.

2. = GREENERY 2.

1895 *Daily News* 24 June 7/1 Horses' heads are crowned with greening.

greening ('griːnɪŋ), *vbl. sb.* [f. GREEN *v.*[1] + -ING[1].] The action of GREEN *v.*[1] in various senses.

1. The action or process of becoming green or covered with verdure.

a **1300** *Cursor M.* 16867 On þe morn o þat grening, þe tre als ar was dri. **1817** KEATS *Sleep & Poetry* 171 The tender greening Of April meadows. **1883** STALLYBRASS tr. *Grimm's Teut. Myth.* III. 959 *note*, The withering or greening of a tree is bound up with the fate of a country.

2. a. The process of rendering green or imparting a green colour, as in *Plumbing* (see GREEN *v.*[1] 2 c), *Pickling, Oyster-culture*, etc.

16.. [see GREEN *v.*[1] 2 b]. **1703** T. N. *City & C. Purchaser* 195 This Greening is only rubbing it with some green Vegetable; it matters not what..and..the Sodder..by reason of the Greening easily peel'd off. **1806** A. HUNTER *Culina* (ed. 3) 83 Whenever the juice of spinage is used for greening. **1879** *Cassell's Techn. Educ.* IV. 184/2 The fattening and greening of the oysters.

b. *concr.*

1892 *Encycl. Cookery* (ed. Garrett) I. 719 *Greening*, a vegetable colouring matter made by expressing the juice of spinach. Occasionally used in confectionery and for other culinary purposes.

c. In sense of GREEN *v.*[1] 3.

1879 *Boy's Own Paper* 18 Jan. 3/2 Leave to others the shamming, The 'greening' and 'cramming', In fun and in earnest, be true, boys! **1907** *Daily Chron.* 29 Jan. 3/3 The method of 'greening' is the schoolboy trick of making a statement which is a fabrication and getting another boy to believe it.

3. *attrib.* †**greening pit**, a pit in which oysters are 'greened' (see GREEN *v.*[1] 2 b); †**greening weed**, a plant used for dyeing green; = GREENWEED.

16.. *Greening pit [see GREEN *v.*[1] 2 b]. **1588** L. M. tr. *Bk. Dyeing* 18 Put therein two pound of *grening weede. **1751** CHAMBERS *Cycl.* s.v., If urine, citron-juice, or spirit of vitriol, be cast on a green ribband, it becomes blue; by reason the yellow of the greening-weed is thereby exhaled and consumed; so that nothing but blue remains behind. **1761** J. WHITE *Art's Treasury* 6.

'greening, *ppl. a.*[1] [f. as prec. + -ING[2].]

1. Growing or becoming green.

1800 *Monthly Mag.* IX. 465 The war-steed's hoof-mark hide with greening ears, Twine round the elm once more the trampled vine! **1827** CLARE *Sheph. Cal.* 24 The greening plain. **1835** TENNYSON *Early Spring* ii, From skies of glass A Jacob's ladder falls On greening grass. **1850** —— *In Mem.* cxli, Where now the seamew pipes, or dives In yonder greening gleam. **1858** BAILEY *Age* 52 Slowly greening woods Make dim the distant view.

2. That causes to become green.

1846 *Jrnl. R. Agric. Soc.* VII. II. 494 The sun's scorching and greening influence.

greening, *vbl. sb.*[2] and *ppl. a.*[2]: see GREEN *v.*[2]

greenish ('griːnɪʃ), *a.* [f. GREEN *a.* + -ISH.] Somewhat green.

c **1384** CHAUCER *H. Fame* III. 557 Suche a smoke gan out wende..Blak bloo grenyssh, swart rede. **1398** TREVISA *Barth. De P.R.* XIX. xix. (1495) 875 Melancoly: that is blacke by meane of vnkynde Colera: that is rusty and grenysshe: and is founde grene. **1530** PALSGR. 314/2 Grenysshe, *verdastre.* *c* **1580** JEFFERIE *Bugbears* IV. iii. in *Archiv Stud.*

neu. Spr. (1897), The flame that it gave was greenish, pale, and dimme. **1626** BACON *Sylva* §512 There is a Greenish Prime-Rose, but it is Pale, and scarce a Greene. **1707** *Curios. in Husb. & Gard.* 91 A wild Oat, while 'tis yet greenish. **1771** SMOLLETT *Humph. Cl.* 6 May, Her eyes are not grey, but greenish, like those of a cat. **1872** HUXLEY *Physiol.* ix. 221 When the eye is turned aside to the white paper a greenish spot will appear.

b. *Comb.*, qualifying adjs. or sbs. of colour.

1644 EVELYN *Diary* 21 Nov., It was transparent, of a greenish yellow. *a***1691** BOYLE *Hist. Air* (1692) 223 The filings exposed to the air, changed colour, and became a greenish blew. **1776** WITHERING *Brit. Plants* (1796) II. 385 Bloss[oms] greenish white. **1803** CHENEVIX in *Phil. Trans.* XCIII. 296 The supernatant liquor of the precipitate..is sometimes of a fine greenish-blue. **1879** ROOD *Chromatics* x. 141 The greenish-grey tints of the mosses.

Hence '**greenishness**, greenish quality.

1727 in BAILEY vol. II. **1865** *Intell. Observ.* No. 40. 277 A certain greenishness.

†'**greenkin.** *Obs.*⁻¹ [f. GREEN *a.* + -KIN.] A person clad in green or wearing green colours.

1601 HOLLAND *Pliny* II. 471 *marg.*, Some were called *Prassini* that ran for the prise, *i.* Greenkins.

Greenland ('gri:nlənd). [f. GREEN *a.* + LAND *sb.*[1], ultimately after the equivalent ON. *Grœnland*, whence Sw., Da. *Grönland*, adopted in Du. *Groenland*, G. *Grönland*.

According to *Islendingabók* vi, the land was so named by its discoverer in 986 'because it would induce settlers to go there, if the land had a good name'.]

1. A large island or small continent to the north-east of North America. Used *attrib.* in **Greenland dove** (see DOVE 1 c); **Greenland falcon** or **gerfalcon**, the whitest of the gerfalcons (*Falco candicans*); **Greenland poppy** ? = *Iceland poppy*; **Greenland turtle** = *Greenland dove*; **Greenland whale**, the Arctic Right Whale (*Balæna mysticetus*); **Greenland yard**, a yard where whales are cut up and the blubber boiled, etc.

1678 RAY *Willughby's Ornith.* 326 That bird which in Holland they call the Greenland-Dove. **1797–1804** BEWICK *Birds* (1847) I. 8 The Greenland Falcon, *Falco Grænlandicus.* **1840** *Evid. Hull Docks Comm.* 14 Greenland-yards on both sides. **1842** BRANDE *Dict. Sci.* etc., *Balæna*, the Greenland whale. **1867** SMYTH *Sailor's Word-bk.*, *Greenland Dove*, the puffinet, called scraber in the Hebrides. **1882** *Garden* 10 June 400/2 The Greenland Poppy..has a delicate odour. **1884–5** *Riverside Nat. Hist.* (1888) V. 201 In form the Greenland whale is the most ungraceful of mammals. **1885** SWAINSON *Prov. Names Birds* 218 Sea turtle, or Greenland turtle. **1896** R. B. SHARPE *Handbk. Birds Gt. Brit.* II. 191 The Greenland Gyr-falcon, *Hierofalco candicans.*

2. *slang.* The country of greenhorns.

1838 DICKENS *O. Twist* viii, 'A new pal', replied Jack Dawkins, pulling Oliver forward. 'Where did he come from?' 'Greenland'.

Greenlander ('gri:nləndə(r)). [f. prec. + -ER[1].]

1. A native or inhabitant of Greenland.

1774 GOLDSM. *Nat. Hist.* (1776) II. 217 It is common with them [Greenlanders], when they see a quiet..stranger, to say that he is almost as well bred as a Greenlander. **1842** PRICHARD *Nat. Hist. Man* 504 The Greenlanders believed in the existence of spirits, good and evil.

†**2.** A vessel of some kind (? resembling a Greenland whaler in build). *Obs.*

1692 *Lond. Gaz.* No. 2815/4 In her way home [she] took a French Greenlander, of 22 Guns, and 42 Men.

Greenlandic (gri:n'lændɪk), *a.* and *sb. rare.* [f. GREENLAND + -IC.] **A.** *adj.* Of or pertaining to Greenland, its language and its inhabitants. **B.** *sb.* The language of Greenland.

1813 E. HENDERSON in *Life* iii. (1859) 116 Another merchant has promised to get the Greenlandic Testaments forwarded. **1883** A. C. THOMPSON *Morav. Missions* vi. 250 The translation of the Scriptures into Greenlandic. **1887** *Science* X. 287 Written in the modern Greenlandic alphabet.

Greenlandish ('gri:nləndɪʃ), *a.* [f. as prec. + -ISH.] Characteristic of Greenland.

In mod. Dicts.

Greenlandite ('gri:nləndaɪt). *Min.* [f. GREENLAND + -ITE.] A variety of garnet.

1837 DANA *Syst. Min.* 351.

Greenlandman ('gri:nləndmən). [f. GREENLAND + MAN *sb.* Cf. *Indiaman.*] A vessel engaged in the Greenland whale-fishery.

1794 *Naval Chron.* XXIV. 102 One man was killed belonging to the Greenlandman. **1827** J. WILSON *Noctes Ambr.* Wks. 1855 II. 4, I sud hae nae great objections to be a whale in the Polar Seas. Gran' fun..wi' ae thud o' your tail, to drive in the stern-posts o' a Greenlandman.

greenless ('gri:nlɪs), *a.* [f. GREEN *sb.* + -LESS.] Without greenness or verdure.

*a***1618** SYLVESTER *Mem. Mortal.* xxv. Wks. (Grosart) II. 217 But, Beauty, Grace-lesse, is a Saile-lesse Bark, A greenlesse Spring. **1854** *Tait's Mag.* XXI. 218 Birds..held their chattering synods..among the greenless boughs. **1896** HENSLOW *Wild Flowers* 169 This is a greenless fleshy root-parasite.

greenlet ('gri:nlɪt). [f. GREEN *a.* + -LET; app. formed to render the etymological sense of L. *vireō*.] A name for the numerous species of small greenish American singing-birds of the genus *Vireo* or family *Vireonidæ*.

1831 SWAINSON *Fauna Bor. Amer.* II. 233, 1. *Vireo olivaceus* (Bonaparte), Red-eyed Greenlet. *Ibid.* 235, 2. *Vireo Bartramii* (Swainson), Bartram's Greenlet. *Ibid.* 237 *Vireo longirostris* (Swainson), Long-billed Greenlet. **1869** J. BURROUGHS in *Galaxy Mag.* Aug., The Vireos, or Greenlets, are a sort of connecting-link between the Warblers and the true Fly-catchers. **1884–5** *Riverside Nat. Hist.* (1888) IV. 513 The greenlets reach their highest development in the genus *Cyclorhis.* **1895** C. DIXON in *Fortn. Rev.* Apr. 645 The Vireonidæ or greenlets.

greenling ('gri:nlɪŋ). *rare.* [f. GREEN *a.* + -LING.] = GREEN-FISH 1 and 2 a.

In quot. 1440 *grene lynge* may be two words, *green ling*, but the fact that *leenge* is the spelling of *ling* sb. in the *Promp. Parv.* militates against this supposition.

*c***1440** *Promp. Parv.* 210/1 Grene lynge, fyshe (*S.* grenlynge, *P.* grenelynge). **1847** HALLIWELL, *Greenling*, same as Greenfish. **1880–4** [see GREEN-FISH 2].

greenly ('gri:nlɪ), *adv.* [f. GREEN *a.* + -LY[2].]

1. With a green colour; with green vegetation; so as to look green.

1583 STANYHURST *Æneis* IV. (Arb.) 113 With twisted garland and leau's, spred greenlye, she garnisht Thee place of her burial. **1816** BYRON *Ch. Har.* III. xlvi, Grey but leafy walls, where Ruin greenly dwells. **1856** MRS. BROWNING *Aur. Leigh* I. 572 The straight small bed was curtained greenly. **1864** LOWELL *Fireside Trav.* 198 The valley widens greenly toward other mountains. **1881** MISS YONGE *Lads & Lasses Langley* iv. 149 Rows of hops, with the sun glancing greenly through on the waving clusters.

2. *fig.* Chiefly with reference to growing vegetation: Freshly, vigorously, youthfully.

1633 P. FLETCHER *Purple Isl.* I. iii, Two gentle swains Whose sprouting youth did now but greenly bud. **1815** BYRON *Parisina* xx, The rest shall bloom and live All greenly fresh. **1871** R. ELLIS tr. *Catullus* lxiv. 232 Look that warily then deep-laid in steady remembrance These our words grow greenly. **1879** MRS. HOUSTON *Wild West* 249, I could not flatter myself that in the hearts of even one of those whom I had striven to aid my memory would greenly live. **1886** W. ALEXANDER *St. Augustine's Holiday* 142 If he have wrinkles they are greenly hid.

3. In an inexperienced or unskilful manner; unskilfully; with simplicity. *arch.*

1599 B. JONSON *Cynthia's Rev.* v. ii, He, greenly credulous, shall withdraw thus. **1599** SHAKS. *Hen. V*, v. ii. 149, I can-not looke greenely: nor gaspe out my eloquence. **1602** —— *Ham.* IV. v. 83 We haue done but greenly In hugger-mugger to interre him. **1820** SCOTT *Monast.* xxx, I must assist you, I reckon, for you are setting very greenly about this gear.

'**greenmail.** *Stock Market* (orig. *U.S.*). [f. GREEN *a.* + BLACK)MAIL; cf. GREEN *sb.* 7 d.] The practice of purchasing enough shares in a firm or trading company to threaten a take-over, thereby forcing the owners to buy them back at a premium in order to retain control of the business. Freq. *attrib.*

1983 *National Law Jrnl.* (U.S.) 21 Mar. 23/4 Corporations are scurrying to combat a perceived threat from those professional investors who practice 'greenmail'—putting pressure on a company to get a buy-out for cash. **1984** *Daily Tel.* 16 June 17 The Disney settlement is the latest and biggest in a recent spate of 'greenmail' deals. **1984** *Times* 15 Oct. 17/6 Two leading companies in the United States are introducing schemes to help ward off the threat of unwelcome takeover bids or attempts of 'greenmail'. **1986** *N.Y. Times* 13 Nov. D1/1 CPC may have revived 'greenmail' by moving to get Ronald O. Perelman off its back, some Wall Street players contend.

Hence as *v. trans.*, to subject (a company) to greenmail; also *absol.*; '**greenmailer**, one who engages in greenmail.

1984 *Washington Post* 14 May (Business Suppl.) 25/4 The only beneficiaries are..the greenmailers, who are encouraged to use the tactic again and again. **1984** *Financial Times* 27 Sept. 32/7 It is not every year that CJR will have the chance to greenmail St Regis. **1985** *Harper's Mag.* Jan. 62/2 Gulf..suggested that Pickens..was therefore nothing but a mischievous greenmailer. **1985** *Observer* 24 Nov. 40/2, I don't buy stock to greenmail. **1986** *Sunday Times* 6 Apr. 59/4 Fears of a consortium bid to break up the company or greenmail it—buy off the shares held by those threatening to make a bid.

green man, greenman.

†**1.** A man dressed up with greenery to represent a wild man of the woods, who took part in outdoor shows, masques, triumphs, and the like; a Jack-in-the-green. *Obs.*

The common tavern sign of 'The Green Man and Still' seems to have been suggested by the arms of the Distillers' Company, the supporters of which are two Indians. The sign-painters represented the Indian by a 'Green man' (in the above sense), and this figure was afterwards replaced by that of a man clothed in green, a forester, often Robin Hood. (See 'Larwood' & Hotten *Signboards* 148.)

1638 KIRKE *7 Champions* III. H 2, Have you any squibs in your Country? any Green-men in your shows? **1654** GAYTON *Pleas. Notes* I. vi. 19 The strange Feasts of the Greenmen, Whiflers, Marshals, and his Ministers. **1687** TAUBMAN *London's Tri.* 7 Besides Green-men, Swabs, Satyrs, and Attendants innumerable. *a***1716** BAGFORD in 'Larwood' & Hotten *Signboards* (1866) 367 They are called woudmen or wildmen, thou' at thes day we in ye signe call them Green Men, couered with grene boues. **1801** STRUTT *Sports & Past.* IV. iii. 282 The actors formerly concerned in the pyrotechnical shows..were called monstrous wilde men; others were frequently distinguished by the appellation of green men; and both of them were men whimsically attired and disguised with droll masks [etc.]. **1810** CRABBE *Borough* XI. 229 But the Green-Man shall I pass by unsung, Which mine own James upon his sign-post hung? His sign, his image,—for he once was seen A squire's attendant, clad in keeper's green.

2. A fresh, raw, or inexperienced man; a 'green hand'; *spec.* in whale-fishing, one who had not been to sea before. *Obs.* exc. *Hist.*

1682 J. COLLINS *Salt & Fishery* 99 The third of the Men that go a Fishing being Green-Men, that never were at Sea before. **1690** CHILD *Disc. Trade* (1694) 228 Boat-keepers enter very few new or green men. **1699** *Act 10 Will. III*, c. 25 §10 Every Master of any Fishing Ship going to Newfoundland..shall have in his Ship's Company every fifth Man a Green-man (that is to say) not a Seaman, or having been ever at Sea before. **1786** *Act 26 Geo. III*, c. 26 It shall and may be lawful for the Hirer or Employer of any such Green Men engaged in the said Fishery, to advance to any such Green Man, during the Time he shall be in his Service, a Sum not exceeding Five Pounds. **1867** SMYTH *Sailor's Word-bk.*, *Green-men*, the five supernumerary seamen who had not been before in the Arctic Seas, whom vessels in the whale-fishery were obliged to bear, to get the tonnage bounty. [**1886** H. CLARKE in *Science* VIII. 604, I am afraid we would have killed a green man, travelling and working as we did.]

3. A name for *Aceras anthropophora*; in full ***green man orchis***.

1829 LOUDON *Encycl. Pl.* 752.

†**greenmans.** *Old Cant.* [f. GREEN *a.*: the second element occurs also in *darkmans*, *lightmans*, etc.] The field, the country.

1610 ROWLANDS *Martin Mark-all* E iv, Greenemans, the fields.

greenness ('gri:nnɪs). Forms: see GREEN *a.*; also 1 grénes, 4–6 grenes, greness(e, grennes, (4 grenis, 6 greenes, grienesse), 7 greeness(e. [OE. *grénnes*, f. *gréne* GREEN: see -NESS.] The quality or condition of being green.

1. a. The green colour of growing vegetation. Hence *concr.* or semi-*concr.* Verdure.

*c***900** tr. *Bæda's Hist.* III. viii. [x.] (1890) 180 þære stowe grennis [*v.l.* grenes] & fæȝernis. *a***1300** *Cursor M.* 8034 Passed war a thusand yere, Sin þai war planted in þat place, In grenes ai wit godds grace. **1398** TREVISA *Barth. De P.R.* IX. xxxii. (1495) 369 Pentecoste is tyme of myrth and of grenesse for namly thenne herbes ben grene. *c***1450** *Mirour Saluacioun* 1071 In aarons ȝerde we fynde of braunches the grennesse. **1561** T. NORTON *Calvin's Inst.* I. xvi. (1634) 82 Out of seeds warmed in the bosome of the grounde, he draweth a budding greennesse. **1634** SIR T. HERBERT *Trav.* 209 Here is store of box trees, whose growth and greennesse, afford profit and delight. **1712** J. JAMES tr. *Le Blond's Gardening* 143 The little Greenness it affords..makes it seldom used in Gardens. **1821** LAMB *Elia* Ser. I. *New Year's Eve* (1860) 46 Sun and sky..and the greenness of fields. **1825** COBBETT *Rur. Rides* 469 There never yet was a summer ..when the downs did not retain their greenness to a certain degree.

b. Green colour of the sea and other things.

*a***1300** *Cursor M.* 9987 þe grennes lastand euer in ay Bitakens end o þat maiden. **1398** TREVISA *Barth. De P.R.* XVI. lxviii. (1495) 574 Marbyll hyghte Marmor & hath yᵉ name of Grekys: for grenesse [L. *a viriditate vocatur*] as Ysido[r] sayth. **1561** DAUS *Bullinger on Apoc.* (1573) 65 Grennes signifieth the everlastyngnesse of God, and that he quickeneth and kepeth all thynges alyue. **1597** A. M. *Guillemeau's Fr. Chirurg.* 29/2 Ther remayneth somtimes a viriditye or greenes about the apertione. **1661** LOVELL *Hist. Anim. & Min.* 259 When they bite, there followeth great.. greennesse or blacknesse of the wound. **1756–7** tr. *Keysler's Trav.* (1760) I. 231 The contrast of the white foam, with the natural greenness of the water, has a charming effect. **1824** MISS MITFORD *Village* Ser. I. 226 She used to accuse my French greys of blueness..and my greens of their greenness. **1871** TYNDALL *Fragm. Sci.* (1879) I. vi. 226 The greenness of the sea is physically connected with the matter which it holds in suspension.

2. a. Unripeness (in fruits, etc.) as indicated by green colour.

*c***1450** LYDG. & BURGH *Secrees* 1942 Looke they be rype and of good swetnesse, Strong in substance, no grenness let be sene. **1634** SIR T. HERBERT *Trav.* 183 Bananas or Plantanes..They will ripen though you first plucke them in their greenesse. **1719** LONDON & WISE *Compl. Gard.* 161 Care must be had not to uncover them till they have attain'd their proper size, and begin to lose the great Greenness they had.

b. Immaturity or tenderness (of age).

*a***1420** HOCCLEVE *De Reg. Princ.* 964 In grenesse Of youthe. **1557** *Tottel's Misc.* (Arb.) 167 The grenes of my youth cannot therof expresse The proces. **1579** FENTON *Guicciard.* I. 18 What with the greennes of his yeares aspiring nowe to xxij. **1631** WEEVER *Anc. Funeral Mon.* 225 Considering the greenesse of his age. **1753** SMOLLETT *Ct. Fathom* (1784) 17/2 The greenness of his years secured him from any suspicion of fallacious aim. **1762** A. MURPHY *Life Fielding* 14 (F.'s Wks. 1771 I.), Considering the greenness of his years, the sensibility of his temper, and the warmth of his imagination.

c. *gen.* Immaturity, crudity.

1574 J. STUDLEY tr. *Bale's Pageant Popes* 37 Antichrist as it were appearing aboue the grounde: who grewe still forwarde from grenenesse to ripenesse. **1617** HALES *Serm.* in *Gold. Rem.* (1673) 10 If..St. Paul required diligent reading, and expressly forbad greenness of Scholarship. **1641** MILTON *Reform.* I. (1851) 12 The greennesse of the Times, the weake Estate which Qu. Mary left the Realme in. **1856–81** MRS. H. O. CONANT *Eng. Bible* xxvi. 216 The prelates were seeking to conceal the greenness of their new church from the popular eye under this garb of antiquity. **1875** JOWETT *Plato* (ed. 2) V. 148 The greenness of our argument will ludicrously contrast with the ripeness of our ages.

d. Rawness, inexperience. **e.** Simplicity, gullibility.

1548 UDALL, etc. *Erasm. Par. Mark* iv. 26–9 The grenenes of innocencie. **1740** DYCHE & PARDON *Dict.*, *Greenness*.. also the rawness, unskilfulness, or imperfection of any person in a trade, art, science, &c. **1838** JAS. GRANT *Sk. Lond.* vi. 205 Instances of perfect simplicity or 'greenness'. **1848** THOREAU *Maine W.* (1894) 17 A Province man was betraying his greenness to the Yankees by his questions. **1853** DE QUINCEY *Autobiog. Sk.* Wks. I. 61, I had an opportunity of displaying my exemplary greenness. **1875** tr. *Comte de Paris' Hist. Civ. War Amer.* I. 228 When McDowell alleged the greenness of his troops, as they say in English.

f. Of horses: want of training. (See GREEN *a.* 8 c.)

1900 *Daily Mail* 30 Apr. 4/3 They were due to the greenness of many of the horses, to the fact that they were not acclimatised. **1927** *Ibid.* 30 June 13 The failure of Mrs. Whitburn's colt at Ascot may have been due to greenness.

3. The vigour or freshness of growth; vitality.

a **1649** DRUMM. OF HAWTH. *Poems* Wks. (1711) 53/1 With fragrant greenness of Thy grace Our blasted souls of wounds release. **1675** TRAHERNE *Chr. Ethics* App. 561 Enmities and disgraces.. fall like storms and showers upon budding vertues in their spring and greeness. *a* **1716** SOUTH *Serm.* (1744) X. ii. 44 The hypocrite's hope.. for a while gives growth and greenness to his comforts. **1843** *P. Parley's Ann.* IV. 249 The affection of a child gives a greenness to old age.

4. a. Freshness, newness. ? *Obs.*

1553 BRENDE tr. *Q. Curtius* K iv, Through yᵉ grene-nesse of their woundes they felt litle paine. **1616** SURFL. & MARKH. *Country Farme* 635 There is great difference betwixt that tartnesse or sowrenesse, which is an accidentall vice or fault in wines, and that greenenesse or sharpenesse, which is a naturall tast and relish in them. **1651** tr. *Bacon's Life & Death* 5 This .. preserves them [Grains] also in that Greennesse, that they are fit and serviceable to make Bread.

†**b.** The condition of being fresh from child-bearing. *Obs.*

1624 HEYWOOD *Gunaik.* IV. 169 Canace by reason of her greenenes and weake estate, not able to make her escape.

greenockite ('griːnəkaɪt). *Min.* [Named by Jameson in 1840 after Lord *Greenock*: see -ITE.] Native sulphide of cadmium, found usually in yellow coatings, rarely in crystals.

1844 ALGER *Min.* 573 Sulphuret of Cadmium. Greenockite of Prof. Jameson. **1855** BREWSTER *Newton* I. x. 213 The refractive index.. of greenockite. **1892** DANA *Min.* 69.

greenovite ('griːnəvaɪt). *Min.* [Named by Dufrenoy in 1840 after G. B. *Greenough*: see -ITE.] A variety of titanite having a reddish colour due to manganese.

1844 ALGER *Min.* 613. **1892** DANA *Min.* 714.

Greenpeace ('griːnpiːs). [f. GREEN *a.* (see sense 11) + PEACE *sb.*] The name of an international organization which campaigns actively in support of general conservation and the protection of the environment.

[**1971** *Sun* (Vancouver, B.C.) 4 Sept. III. 29/1 Those of us on board the Greenpeace will be deliberately ignoring the warning.] **1972** R. KEZIERE *Greenpeace* 3 A bringing-together of the peace and environmental movements... Greenpeace seemed like a concept that might create such an alliance. **1976** *Facts on File* 10 Apr. 250/3 The International Fund for Animal Welfare March 17 and the Greenpeace Foundation of Vancouver March 24 ended their respective campaigns to protest and disrupt the annual hunting of baby seals off Newfoundland's Northern coast. **1977** *Maclean's Mag.* 21 Feb. 64/1 The shambling New Brunswick Liberal .. is about to be subjected to the piranha-like peckings of Greenpeace, the scruffy band of ecofreaks who take on nations—and usually win. **1985** *Times* 26 Sept. 12/1 Greenpeace was christened.. as Mr McTaggart set sail one day from Vancouver. 'It was just some guy on the dock... He.. shouted, "Green! Peace!" and that was that.'

green-peak ('griːnpiːk). Also **-peek.** [A rendering of It. *picchio verde* or F. **pic-vert* (now *pivert*).] The Green Woodpecker, *Gecinus viridis*.

1598 FLORIO, *Picchio verde*, a birde called a greene peake. **1611** COTGR., *Pic verd*, the Greene-peake, or ordinarie Woodpecker. **1772–84** COOK *Voy.* (1790) III. 937 The greenpeak is all over green, except two red spots, one on its breast, and another on its head, and is a very beautiful bird. **1847–78** HALLIWELL, *Green-peak*, a woodpecker. *Linc.*

'green-room.

1. A room in a theatre provided for the accommodation of actors and actresses when not required on the stage, probably so called because it was originally painted green. *transf.* The players who frequent the green-room. Phr. ***to talk green-room***: to talk theatrical gossip.

1701 CIBBER *Love Makes Man* IV. iv, I do know London pretty well, and the Side-box, Sir, and behind the Scenes; ay, and the Green-Room, and all the Girls and Women-Actresses there. **1736** FIELDING *Pasquin* I. Wks. 1882 X. 140 Sir, the Prompter and most of the players are drinking tea in the Green-room. **1809** MALKIN *Gil Blas* II. viii. ¶3 Characters.. as eccentric as any *bona roba* of the green-room. **1820** BYRON *Blues* II. 78 Sir, the green-room's in rapture. **1839** LEVER *H. Lorrequer* xvi, We talked 'green-room'. **1885** J. K. JEROME *On the Stage* 71 Where a green room was originally provided, it has been taken by the star or the manager, as his or her private room.

attrib. **1809** MALKIN *Gil Blas* III. x. ¶4 Our green-room goddess. **1812** *Examiner* 21 Sept. 602/2 Few Authors.. would enter a green-room cabal. **1823** W. IRVING in *Life & Lett.* (1864) II. 141 The colonel.. is a green-room veteran, and has written for the London theatre. **1887** BESANT *Kath. Regina* xv, Actors' gossip and green-room whispers.

2. A room in a warehouse or factory for the reception of goods in a 'green' state, such as cloth fresh from the weaving factory, undried pottery, etc. (Cf. GREEN-HOUSE 2.)

In recent Dicts.

'green-sand, 'greensand.

1. *Min.* and *Geol.* **a.** = GLAUCONITE, green earth. **b.** A variety of sandstone, usually imperfectly consolidated, consisting largely of glauconite. **c.** A formation consisting largely of this sandstone; denominated ***Upper*** or ***Lower Greensand*** from the position of the stratum relatively to the gault.

1796 KIRWAN *Elem. Min.* (ed. 2) II. 149 Green sand of Peru. Its colour is grass green; of the consistence of sand. **1830** LYELL *Princ. Geol.* I. 477 Marine strata about the age of our chalk and green-sand. **1847** ANSTED *Anc. World* x. 228 The Upper Greensand is generally barren of fossils. **1873** DAWSON *Earth & Man* ix. 229 The mineral Glauconite or 'green-sand'. **1875** —— *Dawn of Life* v. 99 Glauconite.. gives by the abundance of its little bottle-green concretions the name of green-sand to formations of this age. **1876** PAGE *Adv. Text-Bk. Geol.* xviii. 339.

attrib. **1865** *Reader* No. 118. 377/2 Greensand fossils. **1868** *Rep. U.S. Commissioner Agric.* (1869) 69 Greensand marls.

2. (See GREEN *a.* 9 d.)

green sauce, 'greensauce. *Obs.* exc. *dial.*

1. A sauce of a green colour made from herbs and eaten with meat. (Cf. 2, quot. 1883.)

c **1460** [see GREEN-FISH 1]. **1591** PERCIVALL *Sp. Dict.*, *Morteruela*, greene sauce, *Moretum*. **1599** H. BUTTES *Dyets drie Dinner* P ij b, Greene Sauce. Made of sweete hearbes, as .. a clowe or two, and a little Garlicke. *a* **1612** HARINGTON *Salernes Regim.* (1634) 68 Sauce for Mutton, Veale, and Kid, is greene sauce, made in Summer with Vinegar or Verjuyce, with a few spices, and without Garlicke. **1661** LOVELL *Hist. Anim. & Min.* 117 Pork..; when powdered it's best to be eaten with green sauce. **1747** MRS. GLASSE *Cookery* ii. 42 You must either put good Gravy, or Green-sauce in the Dish. **1847–89** HALLIWELL, *Green-sauce*, sour dock or sorrel mixed with vinegar and sugar. *North.*

2. A name for field sorrel, *Rumex acetosa* and wood sorrel, *Oxalis acetosella*.

1620 VENNER *Via Recta* vii. 149 This proueth that Greenesauce is.. wholsome against contagion. **1645** N. DRAKE *Siege Pontefract Cas.* (Surtees Soc. 1861) 37 We had allso a boy about 9 yeares of age (as he was getting of greene sawse..) was dangerously shott in the belly. **1790** in W. MARSHALL *Midl. Co.* II. 438. **1862** C. P. JOHNSON *Useful Pl. Gt. Brit.* 64 The Wood-Sorrel [*Oxalis acetosella*], ..or Green-sauce. **1883** *Almondb. & Huddersf. Gloss.*, *Green sauce*, *Rumex acetosa*,.. much used formerly as a sauce with meat, especially veal.

greenshank ('griːnʃæŋk). A large sandpiper, *Totanus glottis*; probably so called from its olive-coloured legs. Cf. REDSHANK (*T. calidris*).

1766 PENNANT *Zool.* (1776) II. 375 *Limosa, et glottis*.. Green Shank. **1863** *Spring Lapl.* 351 Perhaps one of the commonest of our waders here was the greenshank. **1890** LUMHOLTZ *Cannibals* 56 At Thompson I found an old acquaintance from Europe, the greenshank.

†**'greenship.** *Obs. rare*⁻¹. In 4 greneschipe. [f. GREEN *a.* + -SHIP.] Greenness.

13.. *Cast. Love* 709 So is þe foundement al grene, þat to þe roche faste liþ.. For þe greneschipe lasteþ euere, And his heuh ne leseþ neuere.

greensick ('griːnsɪk), *a.* ? *Obs.* [Back-formation from GREEN SICKNESS.] Affected with green sickness; also *fig.* 'morbid', 'sickly'.

1681 *Broadside, Canto on Miracle wrought by the D. of M[onmouth]*, But O the Greensick Girls may boast This Duke hath cur'd Them to His Cost. **1684** tr. *Bonet's Merc. Compit.* III. 93 Green-sick persons are unfit for exercise. **1807** OPIE in *Lect. Paint.* (1848) 316 Those greensick lovers of chalk, brickdust, charcoal, and old tapestry. **1822–34** *Good's Study Med.* (ed. 4) IV. 83 There is even ground for carrying the term, with other authors, still further, and applying it to green-sick boys, as well as green-sick girls.

green sickness, green-sickness (ˌgriːn'sɪknɪs). [See GREEN *a.* 3.] An anæmic disease which mostly affects young women about the age of puberty and gives a pale or greenish tinge to the complexion; chlorosis.

1583 GREENE *Mamillia* Wks. (Grosart) II. 36 His daughter beeing at the age of twentie yeeres, would.. fall into the green sicknes for want of a husband. **1584** J. RAYNOLDS *Proph. Haggai* iv. (1649) 53 Like them that are troubled with the greene sicknesse. **1678** DRYDEN *Limberham* IV. i. Wks. 1883 VI. 82 Languishing maids in the green-sickness. **1707** FLOYER *Physic. Pulse-Watch* 225 The Pulse in the Green-Sickness beats 90. **1746** R. JAMES *Introd. Moufet's Health's Improv.* 21 The Mischief that young Girls do themselves, who are inclined to.. the green Sickness, by taking great Quantities of Chalk, Lime, and other Absorbents. **1846** MRS. CARLYLE *Lett.* I. 385 She.. had quite lately had the green sickness.

b. *transf.* and *fig.* (often with reference to the morbid appetite which characterizes chlorosis).

1596 NASHE *Saffron-Walden* Wks. (Grosart) III. 166 It will then appeare.. whose wit hath the greene sicknes. **1597** SHAKS. *2 Hen. IV*, IV. iii. 100 A kinde of Male Green-Sicknesse. *a* **1658** CLEVELAND *Antiplatonic* iv, Virtue's no more in Womankind But the Green sickness of the Mind. **1675** BROOKS *Gold. Key* Wks. 1867 V. 142 Curiosity is that green-sickness of the soul, whereby it longs for novelties, and loathes sound and wholesome truths. **1682** *Loyal Satirist* in Somers *Tracts* (1812) VII. 68 What a desperate green-sickness is the land fallen into, thus to doat on coals and dirt, and such rubbish divinity! **1881** STEVENSON *Virg. Puerisque* 104 There is some meaning in the old theory of wild oats; and a man who has not had his greensickness and got done with it for good, is as little to be depended upon as an unvaccinated infant.

c. *attrib.* and *Comb.* (= GREENSICK *a.*), esp. in ***green-sickness girl, maid***, etc.

1592 SHAKS. *Rom. & Jul.* III. v. 157 Out you greene sicknesse carrion, out you baggage, You tallow face. **1598** E. GILPIN *Skial.* (1878) 46 Bad green-sicknes wines. **1628** FORD *Lover's Mel.* III. ii, What a green-sickness-liver'd boy is this! **1651** CLEVELAND *Poems* 42 Why, my Muse, like a Green-sicknesse-Girle, Feed'st thou on coals and dirt? **1733** CHEYNE *Eng. Malady* Introd. (1734) 2 Sunk even below the Weakness of a Green-sickness Maid. **1767** A. CAMPBELL *Lexiph.* (1774) 169 Just as a green-sickness girl, when gorged with chalk and trash, nauseates the nicest dainties.

Hence **green-sicknessed** *a.*, green-sick.

1673 F. KIRKMAN *Unlucky Cit.* 176 Never did Green-sickness'd Girl long with half so much earnestness for Chalk or Oatmeal. *c* **1720** BP. RUNDLE in Butler *Life Hildesley* (1799) 185 Thy [*sc.* Sir R. Steele] works will.. cure all the green-sicknessed appetites that will seize on the gay and young, without so friendly a cordial.

green-sleeves. A woman wearing green sleeves; the name given to an inconstant lady-love, who is the subject of a ballad published in 1580 (see quot.), which, together with the tune to which it was sung, became very popular; hence, a name for the ballad and the tune themselves.

1580 in Arber *Stationer's Reg.* (1875) II. 376 A newe northe[r]n Dittye of ye Ladye Greene Sleves. **1584** C. ROBINSON *New Sonet of Ladie Green Sleeues* in Roxb. Ball. (1887) VI. 398 Green-sleeues was all my ioy, Green-sleeues was my delight: Green-sleeues was my heart of gold, and who but my Ladie Green-sleeues? **1598** SHAKS. *Merry W.* II. i. 64. *Ibid.* v. v. 22 Let it thunder to the tune of Greene-sleeues. **1717** PRIOR *Alma* II. 320 Old Madge, bewitch'd at Sixty one, Calls for Green Sleeves, and Jumping Joan.

green snake. *U.S.*

1. One of two green harmless snakes of the U.S.

1791 W. BARTRAM *Carolina* 275 The green snake is a beautiful innocent creature. **1880** *Libr. Univ. Knowl.* VII. 84 Green Snake.. common through most of the U.S...; long, slender, and entirely harmless.

2. An air-plant resembling the snake.

1883 A. J. ADDERLEY *Fisheries Bahamas* 17 One of the most remarkable of them [air-plants] is the green-snake, which looks exactly like a long serpent made of coloured india-rubber.

greensome ('griːnsəm), *a.* [See -SOME¹.] = GREENY *a.* 2.

1901 *Westm. Gaz.* 19 Oct. 2/1 The goat.. browsed.. quite close to a suit, a shirt, and other man's belongings that were strewn on the bank of a greensome bywater. **1908** *Ibid.* 15 June 2/3 Good-day, good-day! bright hazel there, What makes you so greensome?

green-stone, 'greenstone. [f. GREEN *a.* + STONE *sb.*; in sense 1 ad. G. *grünstein*.]

1. *Geol.* A term of wide and varying application, but usually comprising the greenish-coloured eruptive rocks containing feldspar and hornblende (or augite), such as diorite, melaphyre, etc.

1805 *Edin. Rev.* VI. 235 The name *grünstein* or green-stone has been given by Werner to a rock composed of horneblende and feldspar. **1813** BAKEWELL *Introd. Geol.* (1815) 117 Transitions from granite to sienite and green-stone may sometimes be observed in the same block. **1826** W. PHILLIPS *Outl. Min. & Geol.* (ed. 4) 151 The Diabase, Diorite and Amphibolite of French authors, and the Grünstein of the German School, seems to include both Green-stone and Hornblende rock. **1856** PAGE *Adv. Text-Bk. Geol.* §119 The greenstones (whinstones of Scotland) are less compact, more granular [etc.]. **1857** R. TOMES *Amer. in Japan* xii. 283 Several quarries of trachyte, or green-stone, are worked in the neighbourhood. **1862** SMILES *Engineers* III. 297 A remarkable bed of whinstone or green-stone.

attrib. **1830** LYELL *Princ. Geol.* I. 175 A large block of greenstone-porphyry. **1842** MILLER *O. R. Sandst.* viii. (ed. 2) 183 The greenstone bed of Salisbury Crags. **1875** CROLL *Climate & T.* xxvii. 442 A Greenstone boulder.

2. *Min.* = NEPHRITE, a variety of jade.

1772–84 COOK *Voy.* (1790) I. 125 Many of these Indians wore pieces of green-stone round their necks which were transparent, and resembled an emerald. These being examined, appeared to be a species of the nephritic stone. **1849** DANA *Geol.* xvii. (1850) 636 The greenstone, usually called jade, used for ornaments, and also in making hatchets. **1859** A. S. THOMSON *Story N. Zealand* I. I. vii. 140 The greenstone composing these implements of war is called nephrite by mineralogists.. The most valuable kind is as clear as glass with a slight green tinge. **1892** F. R. CHAPMAN (*title*) The Working of Greenstone by the Maoris.

attrib. **1859** A. S. THOMSON *Story N. Zealand* I. I. vii. 140 Of these [weapons] the greenstone meri was the most esteemed. **1885** *Times* (weekly ed.) 30 Jan. 13/2 Their [the natives of New Guinea] principal instrument is a green-stone adze.

3. 'A very hard and close-textured stone used for putting the last edge on lancets and other delicate surgical instruments.' (*Cent. Dict.*)

4. (See quot.)

1874 G. LAWSON *Dis. Eye* 16 Sulphate of Copper, or a combination of this salt with alum, 'lapis divinus', or 'green stone'.

greensward (ˈgriːnswɔːd). For forms see SWARD. Turf on which grass is growing.

1600 HOLLAND *Livy* XXIII. xix. (1609) 487 When the enemies had turned up with a plough all the green sord. **1616** SURFL. & MARKHAM *Country Farme* 662 Except you leaue such large space of greeneswarth betwixt it and the corne-lands, that [etc.]. **1637** B. JONSON *Sad Sheph.* I. ii, I am To cut the Table out o the greene sword. *Ibid.* I. v, On every greene sworth, and in every path. **1661** WALTON *Angler* xvi. (ed. 3) 221 When you see men ploughing up.. greenswards, then follow the plough. **1709** POPE *Jan. & May* 621 The Knights so nimbly o'er the greensward bound. **1792** S. ROGERS *Pleas. Mem.* I. 147 Oft as he turned the greensward with his spade. **1842** BARHAM *Ingol. Leg., Netley Abbey*, There they lie on the greensward strown. **1854** HAWTHORNE *Eng. Note-Bks.* (1879) I. 325 The garden is..set out with greensward and gravel-walks.

b. *attrib.*, as ***greensward ground***; **greensward way** = *green way*, lit. and fig. (see GREEN *a.* 2 b).

1691 DRYDEN *K. Arthur* II. ii, Trembling bogs, that bear a greensward show. **1697** —— *Æneid* III. 291 We spread the Tables, on the greensword Ground. **1703** SAVAGE *Lett. Antients* viii. 46 He..had an easy greensword Way to whatever else he had a mind to persue. **1808** SCOTT *Marm.* IV. iv, The green-sward way was smooth and good.

Hence **ˈgreenswarded** *a.*, covered with greensward.

a **1847** ELIZA COOK *Old Mill-Stream* i. 2 The greenswarded paradise watered by thee. **1870** HUXLEY *Lay Serm.* iii. (1874) 48 Greenswarded courts.

greenth (griːnθ). [f. GREEN *a.* + -TH[1]; one of Walpole's coinages: cf. *gloomth*.] Verdure.

1753 H. WALPOLE *Lett. to Montagu* lvi, I found my garden brown and bare, but these rains have recovered the greenth. **1856** MASSON *Ess.* vii. 372 In the poetry of Keats..there is an excess of greenth and vegetable imagery. *c* **1860** G. H. LEWES in Mathilde Blind *Geo. Eliot* xii. 164 Under a broad sweep of sky and the greenth of the uplands round her. **1876** GEO. ELIOT *Dan. Der.* IV. xxx. 251 Amidst the gleams and greenth of summer.

green wax, ˈgreenwax. *Obs.* exc. *Hist.* Sealing-wax of a green colour; hence **b.** A seal of green wax, such as was affixed to documents delivered by the Exchequer to sheriffs. **c.** An estreat or other document bearing this seal; also ***process of green wax***. **d.** The fines or amercements exacted in accordance with such a document.

[**1299** *Act 27 Edw. I, Stat. de Finibus* c. 9 Nomina omnium qui..debita per viridem ceram ab eis exacta solverunt.] **1377–8** *Durham Acc. Rolls* (Surtees) 586 In soluc. facta vicecomiti Northumbr. pro le Grenewax, 13*s.* 4*d.* *c* **1460** *Towneley Myst.* xxx. 284 Rasers of the fals tax, And gederars of greyn wax. **1461** *Plumpton Corr.* (Camden) 2, I trust to God for to gett you downe your greene wax if that I may, thof it cost you mony. *c* **1500** *God Speed the Plough* 69 in *P. Pl. Crede* (1867) 71 Then commeth the grenewex which greveth vs sore, With ronnyng in reragis it doth vs sorowe Inough. **1523** FITZHERB. *Surv.* 28 The whiche afterwarde is estreyted agayne and sende downe to the shiryffes of euery countie..and it is called grene waxe. **1577–87** HOLINSHED *Chron.* III. 124/1 Hugh Pateshull, treasuror of the exceker, which was treasuror of the greenewax, or of the seale. **1613** SIR H. FINCH *Law* (1636) 487 Of Sherifes and greene waxe. **1618** in *Crt. & Times Jas. I* (1849) II. 61 Sir Thomas Edmondes is in concert with the duke, to farm the green wax, as they call it, or the seal of the exchequer. **1668** in *10th Rep. Hist. MSS. Comm.* App. v. 76 A processe of green wax issued to the Sheriff of Sligo for £300 arreares of rent to his Majestie. **1747** *Lond. Gaz.* No. 8626. 1/1 All Manner of Fines, Forfeitures and Sums of Money, commonly called Green Wax Monies.

greenweed (ˈgriːnwiːd). [f. GREEN *a.* + WEED.]

1. The plant *Genista tinctoria*, so named from its dyeing properties; also extended to other species.

1599 HAKLUYT *Voy.* II. 163 Yellowes and greenes are colours of small prices in this realme, by reason that Alde and Greenweed wherewith they be died be naturall here. **1807** CRABBE *Parish Reg.* III. 169 When strayed her lambs where gorse and greenweed grow. **1830–7** MACGILLIVRAY *Withering's Brit. Plants* xvii. 282 *Genista pilosa.* Hairy Green-weed..*G. anglica.* Needle Green-weed. Petty Whin. **1894** WRIGHT & DEWAR *Johnson's Gardener's Dict.*, Greenweed. *Genista pilosa* and *tinctoria.*

2. A green sea-weed.

1856 WOODWARD *Mollusca* III. 444 For marine aquaria, the green-weeds (Ulva, Enteromorpha, and Bryopsis) are better oxygen-producers than the red sea-weeds.

Greenwell (ˈgriːnwəl). [f. the name of William *Greenwell* (1820–1918), archæologist and angler.] In full ***Greenwell's glory***: A trout fly designed by the Revd. W. Greenwell. Also, a salmon fly of his invention.

1879 W. HENDERSON *Life Angler* xxi. 237, 104 fish [trout], chiefly captured with the 'Greenwell's Glory' fly. *Ibid.* xxii. 251 'The Greenwell' fly did most execution [of salmon]. **1899** E. GREY *Fly Fishing* viii. 216 In wet fly fishing for trout I am content with March-browns, Greenwell's glories, [etc.]. **1920** H. MAXWELL in F. Francis *Bk. Angling* 177 The Greenwell salmon fly, a favourite on the Tweed. **1928** W. F. R. REYNOLDS *With Fly Only* 65 Perhaps an iron blue or two, and a few Greenwells. **1961** A. C. WILLIAMS *Dict. Trout Flies* (ed. 3) II. 197 There can be no fly the name of which is better known to the general public than the great Greenwell's Glory which is as it should be, for a more generally useful wet fly has never been made.

Greenwich (ˈgrɪnɪdʒ, ˈgrɛn-, -ɪtʃ). A town on the south bank of the Thames adjoining London on the east, famous for its astronomical observatory and its hospital formerly occupied by naval pensioners; used *attrib.* in † **Greenwich barber** *slang*, a retailer of sand from the Greenwich pits (Grose *Dict. Vulg. Tongue* 1785); † **Greenwich-goose** *slang*, a pensioner of Greenwich Hospital (*ibid.*); **Greenwich stars**, 'those used for lunar computations in the nautical ephemeris' (Smyth *Sailor's Word-bk.* 1867); **Greenwich time**, mean time for the meridian of Greenwich, adopted as the standard time by English astronomers.

1861 DICKENS *Gt. Expect.* xxv, At nine o'clock every night, Greenwich time..the gun fires. **1893** G. E. MATHESON *About Holland* 31 The Dutch railway companies have, however, recently adopted Greenwich time.

Greenwich Village (ˈgrɛnɪdʒ ˈvɪlɪdʒ). The name of a quarter of New York, used *attrib.* to denote the Bohemian outlook and way of life typical of many of its inhabitants. So **Greenwich Villager.**

1924 H. CRANE *Let.* 12 Jan. (1965) II. 170, I wish you could meet some of my friends, who are not the kind of 'Greenwich Villagers' that you may have been thinking they were. **1931** *Ibid.* 22 June IV. 376 Peggy (Baird) will be here [*sc.* in Mexico] in a few days—I'd rather..she didn't step into a truly Greenich Village scene. **1962** *Listener* 4 Oct. 529/2 It was opposed to..socialists, capitalists, Greenwich Villagers, pedants, and Prohibition. **1968** *Ibid.* 3 Oct. 434/3 Muggeridge impressed me as very much a Bloomsbury type, or what in New York we would perhaps call a Greenwich Village type.

ˈgreen-winged, *a.* [GREEN *a.* 11 a.] Having green wings: in spec. names or descriptions of animals.

1637 T. MORTON *New Eng. Canaan* 68 Teales, there are of two sorts, greene winged, and blew winged. **1849** C. LANMAN *Lett. Alleghany Mts.* ix. 73 The Cherokees relate that there once existed among these mountains a very large bird, which resembled in appearance the green winged hornet. **1861** MISS PRATT *Flower. Pl.* V. 204 Green-winged Meadow Orchis. **1895** *Outing* (U.S.) XXVII. 211/2 A pair of green-winged teal.

greenwood (ˈgriːnwʊd). [See GREEN *a.* 2.]

1. A wood or forest when in leaf. It is taken as the typical scene of outlaw life, hence ***to go to the greenwood***: to become an outlaw.

13.. *K. Alis.* 677 Now con Alisandre..In grene wode of huntyng. *a* **1400** CLANVOWE *Cuckoo & Night.* 100, I herde.. A Nightingale so lustily singe That with her clere vois she made ringe Through-out al the grene wode wyde. *c* **1500** *Notbrowne Maid* 89 in Hazl. *E.P.P.* II. 276, I muste too The grene wode goo Alone a bannysshed man. *a* **1641** BP. R. MONTAGU *Acts & Mon. Ch.* (1642) 385 Some who lived in the greene Woods, and haunted the wilde Forests. **1755** JOHNSON, *Greenwood*, a wood considered as it appears in the Spring or Summer. It is sometimes used as one word. **1810** SCOTT *Lady of L.* IV. xii, Merry it is in the good green-wood. **1828** —— *F.M. Perth* xxviii, Rock and greenwood rang to harp and pipes. **1855** KINGSLEY *Heroes, Theseus* II. 213 They hammered together till the greenwoods rang. **1884** RUSKIN *Lect. at Oxf.* in *Pall Mall G.* 10 Dec. 11/2 A bit of Alpine snow, of Greek sea, or of English greenwood.

b. *attrib.*, as ***greenwood adventurer, bower, glen, life,*** † ***linde, path, shade, side, tree.***

15.. *Adam Bel* 404 in Ritson *Anc. Pop. Poetry* 20 Cloudesle walked a lytle besyde, And loked vnder the grenewood linde. *c* **1510** *Lytell Geste R. Hode* III. (1847) I. 173 They..dyde them strayt to Robyn Hode Under the grene wode tre. **1600** SHAKS. *A.Y.L.* II. v. 1. **1729** T. COOKE *Tales* 128 Him to the greenwood Shade they gently bore. **1808** SCOTT *Marm.* II. Introd., Foresters in green-wood trim. **1810** —— *Lady of L.* IV. xxiv, His coat was all of the greenwood hue. **1856** FROUDE *Hist. Eng.* (1862) I. 69 The Robin Hood ballads..breathe the warm genial spirit of the old greenwood adventurers.

† **2.** = GREENWEED 1. *Obs.* (Perh. a misprint.)

1776 WITHERING *Brit. Plants* 441 Greenwood, *Genista.*

greeny (ˈgriːnɪ), *sb.* [f. GREEN *a.* + -Y.]

1. *Theatr. slang.* The curtain of a theatre.

1821 EGAN *Tom & Jerry* xiii. (1870) 357 It is far more difficult to please the company behind Greeny; I beg pardon, sir, I should have said than the audience before the curtain.

2. A greenish-coloured bird. **a.** *dial.* The greenfinch or green grosbeak. **b.** *Austral.* A schoolboy's name for the white-plumed honey-eater, *Ptilotis penicillata.*

1825 BROCKETT *N.C. Words*, *Greeney*, the green grosbeak. **1896** *Australasian* 11 Jan. 73/1 (Morris) The members of the feathered tribe known to young city 'knights of the catapult' as greenies.

3. A greenhorn; a freshman at a university.

1834 SOUTHEY *Doctor* I. II. 157 He was entered among the Greenies of this famous University [Leyden]. **1852** JUDSON *Myst. N.Y.* III. ix. 58 Anybody could know that these was took by a greeny. **1887** *Congregationalist* 7 Apr. (Farmer), Jim said I was a greeny.

greeny (ˈgriːnɪ), *a.* Also 6 griny. [f. GREEN *a.* + -Y[1].]

† **1.** Green, verdant. Also *fig.* Vigorous. *Obs.*

1593 Q. ELIZ. *Boethius, De Consol.* I. metr. i. 7 Happy griny Youthe. *Ibid.* III. metr. viii. 3 Seake not the Golde in griny tre. **1602** DAVISON *Rhapsody* B 11 The scorching heate of Summer Sun..Thy [*sc.* Earth]..pride of all thy greeny haire defaceth. **1620** SHELTON *Quix.* III. xiii. 81 A Nymph of the greeny Grove. **1630** J. TAYLOR (Water P.) *Sculler* Wks. III. 27/2, I that on greenie grasse could lay me downe. **1669** FLAVEL *Husb. Spirit.* (1770) 203 In a greeny seat Of shady oak. **1674** PLAYFORD *Skill Mus.* I 64 When merry Lads are playing Each with his bonny Lass Upon the greeny grass.

2. Somewhat green, greenish.

1826 MISS MITFORD *Village* Ser. II. 192 A sky-blue sash.. not the poor, thin greeny colour which usually passes under that dishonoured name. **1897** VIZETELLY *Zola's Rome* 444 The second floor dining-room was so gloomy, saddened by the greeny half-light of the courtyard.

b. quasi-*adv.* qualifying adjs. of colour.

1884 FENN *Sweet Mace* III. ii. 18 A greeny olive snake raised its head. **1891** H. HERMAN *His Angel* 209 His countenance was of a greeny ashen. **1898** *Blackw. Mag.* Sept. 375/2 The greeny white of breaking water.

green-yard, greenyard (ˈgriːnjɑːd). An enclosure covered with grass or turf (not paved). In various specific applications.

† **1.** At Norwich (see quot. 1870). *Obs.*

1578 *Joyf. Receiving Q. Eliz. Norwich* C iij b, M. Churchyard brought Mercurie..into the greene yard vnder the..bedchamber window, out of the which, the Queenes Maiestie looked. **1644** BP. HALL *Rem. Wks.* (1660) 101 Preacht..in the Green-Yard of Norwich. *a* **1656** *Ibid.* 63 The Leaden Crosse, which had been newly sawne downe from over the Green-Yard Pulpit. **1870** *Murray's Handbk. Essex*, etc. 206 The Green Yard of the monastery [Norwich], in which was a cross, where sermons were occasionally preached.

2. An enclosure for the reception of stray animals and vehicles; a pound.

1720 *Lond. Gaz.* No. 5866/2 Two Stables in the Green-Yard without Aldermanbury-Postern. **1824** *Bell's Life* in *Spirit Publ. Jrnls.* (1825) 135 If you don't take charge of the coach, I'll take it to the green-yard, and yourself to the watch-house. **1852** *Househ. Words* 23 Oct. 136 Phaetons that should properly have been sequestrated in the Greenyard of oblivion..long since. **1862** *Times* 16 Aug. 11/3 The greenyard belonged to the defendant's ancestors and was not a parochial greenyard or pound. **1889** VINCENT *Police Code* (ed. 6) 90 In nearly every parish there is a greenyard or pound, where animals found straying or in the possession of prisoners, may be kept at certain charges. **1893** *Daily News* 12 Dec. 5/3 'Green yard'..is the metropolitan equivalent for the village 'pound'.

3. A grass yard for hounds to take exercise in.

1828 *Sporting Mag.* XXIII. 23 Great care should be taken in keeping the green-yard in order. **1841** TATTERSALL *Sport. Archit.* 84 The large green yard..should adjoin the apartments for the young hounds.

† **Grees,** *sb. pl. Obs.* Also **gres, grece.** [App. ad. L. *Græcī* pl.] Greeks.

a **1300** *Cursor M.* 7060 In his time was troi nomyn, And thoru þe grece [*Gött.* grekis, *Fairf.* greges, *Trin.* grekes] ouercomyn. **1387** TREVISA *Higden* (Rolls) I. 175 Whan þe grete Constantyn made Constantinopolim þe cheef sete of þe emperour of Rome, þan were þe Grees [L. *gens Græcorum*] i-cleped Romanij..And anon to þis day þe Grees [L. *Græci*] clepeþ nouȝt hem self Grees, but Romayses. *Ibid.* IV. 271 þe Grees [*v.r.* Gres].

grees, obs. form of GRASS.

grees, grees(s)e, obs. forms of GREASE.

grees(e, greesse: see GRECE.

greesing, obs. form of GRECING.

greesly, greest, obs. forms of GRISLY, GRIST.

† **greet,** *sb.*[1] *Obs.* [f. GREET *v.*[1]] The action of GREET *v.*[1]; a greeting.

c **1590** GREENE *Fr. Bacon* ix. 205 Let me that joy in these consorting greets..Yield thanks for all these favours to my son. *a* **1616** BEAUMONT *Sonnet* Poems (1640) 4 The broken marrow bone is sweet, The token doth adorn the greet. *a* **1634** RANDOLPH *De Magnete* 64 Poems (1638) 31 She dares goe forth alone..and with a winning greet The tumour of his high swolne breast asswage.

greet (griːt), *sb.*[2] *Obs.* exc. *Sc.* Also 3–4 gret, 3–6 grete, 5 greit, 6 greete. [f. GREET *v.*[2]]

1. Weeping, lamentation; also, a cry of sorrow.

c **1250** *Gen. & Ex.* 3888, xxx. daiȝes ðat folc in wep Wið bedes, and gret, and teres wep. *a* **1300** *Cursor M.* 14008 þar-wit sco fell on suilk a grete. **13..** *Sir Beues* (A.) 3129 Iosian ..spak to hire wiþ loude gret. *c* **1420** *Anturs of Arth.* 324 (Douce MS.) With a grisly grete þe goste a-wey glides. *c* **1480** HENRYSON *Orpheus* 139 in *Bannatyne MS.* (Hunter. Club) 927 Now weip with me..And all thy game thow change in gole and greit. **1513** DOUGLAS *Æneis* XII. ii. 49 Persew me nocht thus with ȝour grete and teris. **1579** SPENSER *Sheph. Cal.* Aug. 66 *Per.* Well decked in a frocke of gray. *Wil.* Hey, ho, gray is greete [*Gloss.* weeping and complaint]. **1591** GREENE *Maiden's Dream* iv, A golden hind ..Whose valed eares bewraid her inward greet. *a* **1650** *Sir Lambewell* 61 in Furniv. *Percy Folio* I. 146 Sobbing & greet. *a* **1801** R. GALL *Poems* (1819) 76 The widow's greet, the baby's cry He winna lout to hear. **1898** BULLOCK *Mem. Congreg. Ch. Aberdeen* viii. 101 His admonitions were not the less powerful though given with 'the greet in his throat'.

† **2.** A prayer or entreaty. *Obs. rare*$^{-1}$.

c **1400** *Destr. Troy* 2757 þai grauntid the grete with a glad chere.

greet (griːt), *v.*[1] Forms: 1 grétan, grētan, (3 græten, 3 *Orm.* gretenn, 4 greten), 3–5 grete, (5 greth, gretyn), 6–7 greete, 6– greet. *Imper.* 4 greet. *Pa. t.* (2 greite), 3–5, 7 gret, 3–6 grett(e, 5 grete, (6 gryte), 6– greeted. *Pa. pple.* 3 gret, (igrette), 4 grett, (5 greet), 8– greeted. [Com. WGer.: OE. *grétan* wk. vb., corresponds to OFris. *grêta*, OS. *grôtian* (Du. *groeten*), OHG. *gruozzan* (MHG. *grüezen*, mod.G. *grüszen*):—WGer. **grôtjan*, related to **grôto-z*, **grôtâ* sb. (MHG. *gruoz*, mod.G. *grusz* masc.; MDu. *groet* masc. and fem., Du. *groet* masc.).

The primary sense is uncertain; the senses of early occurrence in continental Teut. are 'to approach', 'to call upon', 'to provoke or compel to action', 'to attack', 'to irritate, annoy', 'to address, salute', In mod.Ger. and Du. as in Eng. the sense 'salute' has become the prominent one, such other senses as survive being now apprehended as transferred from this. (The sb., which may be only a back-formation, expresses the action of the vb. in all senses.) The ultimate etymology is equally uncertain with the radical meaning; many scholars refer the word to OAryan **ghrōd-*: *ghrēd-* to resound (see GREET *v.*[2]), on which supposition the primary sense should be 'to call on'; another view is that the Teut. root **grôt-* is an extension of the root which appears in Gr. as χρα̃ with the sense 'to approach closely, touch', etc.]

†**1.** *trans.* In various senses which did not survive beyond OE.: To approach, come up to; to begin upon, begin to treat or handle, take in hand. *Obs.*

a 700 *Epinal Gloss.* 210 *Convenio*, groetu *vel adjuro*. [*c* 950 *Lindisf. Gosp.* Luke viii. 28 þætte ðu mec ne ȝegoroeta (*ne me torqueas*).] *c* 1000 *Endowments of Men* 49 in *Exeter Bk.*, Sum mid hondum mæȝ hearpan gretan. *c* 1000 *Soul & Body* 139 Ðeah ðe wyrmas ȝyt ȝifre gretaþ. *c* 1000 ÆLFRIC *Gram.* ix. (Z.) 49 On scortne as ȝeendiað grecisce naman, ac we ne gretað nu ða.

†**2.** To assail, attack. *Obs.* (After 15th c. prob. only as a transferred or ironical use of sense 3.)

Beowulf (Z.) 3080 þæt he ne grette gold-weard þone. *c* 893 K. ÆLFRED *Oros.* v. ii. §2 Siþan wæs eallum þæm oþrum swa micel eȝe from him þæt hi hiene leng gretan ne dorstan. *a* 1000 *Cædmon's Gen.* 1755 (Gr.) Gif ðe æniȝ eorðbuendra mid wean greteð. *c* 1300 *Havelok* 1811 Wit þe barre so he him grette. 13.. *K. Alis.* 3789 A duyk of Perce sone he mette With his launce he him grette. *c* 1330 R. BRUNNE *Chron.* (1810) 18 Harald of Donesmore vppon Done him mette Vibrand.. with suerd so him grette, þat þorghout his armes Wibrand alle to hewe. *c* 1440 *Ipomydon* 1140 Ipomydon so Campanus grette, That knyght and stede.. Felle on hepe, in mydde the place. [1594 MARLOWE *Edw. II*, I. iv. 266 How easily might some base slave be suborn'd To greet his lordship with a poniard. 1880 J. O'HAGAN *Song of Roland* ccxxviii, I will him body to body greet, Give him the lie with my brand of steel.]

3. To accost or address with the expressions of goodwill or courtesy usual on meeting; to offer in speech or writing to (a person) the expression of one's own or another's friendly or polite regard. Now only *literary*. †Formerly often ***to greet*** (a person) ***fair, friendly, well.***

Beowulf 614 Cwen.. grette.. guman on healle. *c* 1000 *Ags. Gosp.* Mark xv. 18 Ongunnon hine þus gretan hal wes þu iudea cyning. *c* 1175 *Lamb. Hom.* 121 þet folc.. hine greite and cleopede king on bismer. *c* 1205 [see FAIR *adv.* 2]. *a* 1300 *Cursor M.* 4339 Quen he had hir hend-li gret. *c* 1325 *Lay le Freine* 257 The abbesse and the nonnes alle, Fair him gret in the gest-halle. *c* 1380 *Sir Ferumb.* 2170 Go forth.. & gret wel my doȝtre dere. *c* 1410 LOVE *Bonavent. Mirr.* iv. (Gibbs MS.), What tyme þat oure blessed lady grette Elizabeth. *c* 1470 HENRY *Wallace* v. 974 Rycht gudlye he with humylness him gret. 1553 Q. MARY in Strype *Eccl. Mem.* III. App. i. 3 We grete you well. 1603 SHAKS. *Meas. for M.* IV. v. 13 There's other of our friends Will greet vs heere anon. 1706 PHILLIPS (ed. Kersey), *To Greet* (old Word), to salute. 1742 BLAIR *To W. Law* 115 If.. thou greets Heaven's King, and shoutest through the.. streets. 1794 SIR W. JONES *Instit. Hindu Law* ii. §132 The wife of his brother.. must be saluted every day; but his paternal and maternal kinswomen need only be greeted on his return from a journey. 1805 SCOTT *Last Minstr.* I. xxii, Greet the Father well from me. 1866 G. MACDONALD *Ann. Q. Neighb.* xxix. (1878) 501, I had passed Jane Rodgers.. and having just greeted her, had gone on.

fig. 1590 SPENSER *F.Q.* I. ii. 19 He, tumbling doune alive With bloudy mouth his mother earth did kis, Greeting his grave. 1601 WEEVER *Mirr. Mart.* Ev, With neare embracements Weeuer, Mersey met, And both together th' Irish Seas they gret. 1601 SHAKS. *Twel. N.* II. iv. 62 Not a friend greet My poore corpes.

b. *absol.*

c 1250 *Gen. & Ex.* 2864 God.. of israel ðe bode sente, and greteð wel, ðat, bi ði leue, hise folc vt-fare. 1588 SHAKS. *Tit. A.* I. i. 90 There greete in silence as the dead are wont. 1591 —— *1 Hen. VI*, IV. iii. 42 Away, vexation almost stoppes my breath, That sundred friends greete in the hour of death. 1700 DRYDEN *Pal. & Arc.* II. 191 None greets, for none the greeting will return.

c. To salute *with* words or gestures; *transf.* to receive at meeting or arrival *with* some speech or action (whether friendly or otherwise) in lieu of salutation.

a 1000 *Juliana* 164 in *Exeter Bk.*, Hy þa se æðeling grette.. bliþum wordum. *a* 1225 *Ancr. R.* 430 Greteð þe lefdi mid one Aue Marie. *a* 1300 *Cursor M.* 15014 Ald and yong, bath less and mare, Wit a word alle him grett. *c* 1440 CAPGRAVE *Life St. Kath.* III. 1444 My sone gretheth yow now wyth his good blyssyng. 1450–1530 *Myrr. our Ladye* 78 When he gryte her with thys Aue. 1589 PUTTENHAM *Eng. Poesie* I. xxvi. (Arb.) 67 The same Musicians.. greeted them with a Psalme of new applausions. 1703 ROWE *Fair Penit.* I. i. 252 The Gifts With which I greet the Man whom my Soul hates. 1835 W. IRVING *Tour Prairies* 58 Our arrival at the camp was greeted with acclamation. 1840 DICKENS *Old C. Shop* xvi, The merry man was the first to greet the strangers with a nod. 1852 TENNYSON *Death Wellington* 21 No more in soldier fashion will he greet With lifted hand the gazer in the street. 1868 —— *Lucretius* 7 The woman.. ran To greet him with a kiss.

†**d.** To honour (a person) *with* a gift. *Obs.*

a 1225 *Leg. Kath.* 798 To beon mid gold & gersum igrette. 1362 LANGL. *P. Pl.* A. v. 187 He that repenteth rathest schulde arysen aftur And greten sir Gloten with a galun of ale.

†**e.** In Spenser: to offer congratulations on (an achievement, etc.); const. *unto* or *dative*.

1596 SPENSER *F.Q.* v. iii. 14 Thether also came.. Florimell.. To greet his guerdon unto every knight. *Ibid.* 15 Florimell.. godly gan to greet his brave emprise. *Ibid.* xi. 15 She towards him in hast her selfe did draw To greet him the good fortune of his hand.

f. Of cries, demonstrations: To be addressed to or evoked by (a person or incident), to 'hail'.

1874 GREEN *Short Hist.* viii. §3. 487 Shouts of assent greeted the resolution.

†**g.** To gratify, please. *Obs.*

a 1592 GREENE *Jas. IV*, I. i, You greet me well if so you will her good. 1608 SHAKS. *Per.* IV. 38, I finde It greets mee as an enterprize of kindnesse performd to your sole daughter.

4. To receive or meet with demonstrations of welcome.

1605 SHAKS. *Lear* V. i. 54 We will greet the time. *c* 1611 CHAPMAN *Iliad* XXIV. 152 Let him greet alone The Grecian nauie. 1682 TATE *Abs. & Achit.* II. 628 Who.. greet thy landing with a trembling joy. 1786 BURNS *To Mountain Daisy* 11 The bonnie Lark.. Wi' spreckl'd breast, When upward-springing, blythe, to greet The purpling east. 1849 MACAULAY *Hist. Eng.* iii. II. 295 The cavalcade.. was greeted two miles from the city by the bishop and clergy. 1855 *Ibid.* xii. III. 242 The whole population.. came to the shore to greet them.

†**b.** *intr.* To meet *with*. *Obs.*

1599 MASSINGER, etc. *Old Law* I. i, You have a Lodge, sir, So far remote from way of passengers That seldome any mortall eye does greet with it.

5. Of a thing: To present itself to. Now only of sights or sounds: To meet (the eye, ear).

1698 FRYER *Acc. E. India & P.* 43 The Sea on one side greets its Marble Walls. 1871 FREEMAN *Norm. Conq.* (1876) IV. xviii. 160 The pageant which had greeted his eyes as he entered Le Mans. 1872 JENKINSON *Guide Eng. Lakes* (1879) 307 A wide extent of sea greets the eye.

greet (griːt), *v.*[2] Now only *Sc.* and *north. dial.* Forms: 1 **grétan, gréotan,** 3–5 **grete,** 4–5 **gret,** 4–6 **greete,** 6 **grate, griet,** 6–7 **greit,** 7– **greet.** *Pa. t.* 3–5 **gret(t,** 4 **grete,** 5 **grette;** 3, 5–9 **grat.** *β.* 5 **gretid.** *Pa. pple.* 3 **graten, i-groten,** 4 **greten,** 5 **gret,** 9 **grutten.** [Two distinct but synonymous words have here coalesced: (1) OE. *grǣtan* (only in Anglian form *grétan*), presumably a redupl. str. vb. with pa. t. **grét*, pa. pple. **grǣten* (a wk. pa. pple. occurs once in the pl. *begrétte*), corresp. to OS. *grátan* (only once in pa. t. *griat*, v.r. *griot*) to weep, MHG. *grazen* (wk.) to cry out, rage, storm, ON. *gráta*, pa. t. *grét* (Sw. *gråta*, Da. *græde*), Goth. *grêtan*, pa. t. *gaigrôt*:—OTeut. **grǣtan*, f. OAryan root **ghrēd-*: *ghrōd-* found also in Skr. *hrād* to resound (cf. GREET *v.*[1]); (2) OE. *gréotan* (pa. t. **gréat*, **gruton*, pa. pple. **groten*) = OS. *griotan*, *greotan*; possibly evolved from a pa. t. of the redupl. vb. *grǣtan*; possibly a compound with prefix **ga-* of the synonymous str. vb. found in OE. as *réotan*. Prof. Sievers suggests that both vbs. may descend from a common pre-Teut. root **ghrēud-*, the long diphthong being differentiated into Teut. *ǣ* and *eu*.

The gloss '*mereo* [= *mæreo*], groeto' in the Corpus Glossary is difficult to explain; most prob. *groeto* is simply miswritten for *gréto* (or *gréoto*)' owing to confusion with GREET *v.*[1]]

1. *intr.* To weep, cry, lament, grieve; †*rarely* said of the eyes.

Beowulf 1342 þeȝne moneȝum se þe æfter sinc-gyfan on sefan greoteþ. *c* 725 *Corpus Gloss.* 1305 *Mereo*, groeto. *a* 900 CYNEWULF *Crist* 991 Beornas gretað. *a* 1000 *Sal. & Sat.* 376 (Gr.) Heo.. sceall oft.. greotan. *c* 1250 *Gen. & Ex.* 2341 So e gret, ðat alle hise wlite wurð teres wet. *a* 1300 *Cursor M.* 15006 Almast for ioi þai grette. *a* 1340 HAMPOLE *Psalter* lv. 13 The eghen may grete. 1375 BARBOUR *Bruce* III. 347 At leve-takyng the ladyis gret, And mak thar face with teris wet. *c* 1400 MAUNDEV. (Roxb.) xi. 46 Petre grette full tenderly, when he had forsaken Criste. *c* 1450 *St. Cuthbert* (Surtees) 570 þe childe was sary and þerfore grett. 1549 *Compl. Scot.* vi. 39 The turtil began for to greit, quhen the cuschet ȝoulit. 1557 *Tottell's Misc.* (Arb.) 252 Graunt grace to him that grates therfore with sea of saltish brine. 1579 SPENSER *Sheph. Cal.* Apr. 1 Tell me, good Hobbinoll. what garres thee greete? 1632 BROME *North. Lasse* v. vi. Wks. 1873 III. 93 I'le near greet for that sir, while I have your love. 1714 RAMSAY *Elegy J. Cowper* 1, I wairn ye a' to greet and drone. 1791 BURNS '*There'll Never be Peace*' iii, My seven braw sons for Iamie drew sword, And now I greet round their green beds in the yerd. 1824 SCOTT *Redgauntlet* let. xi, Dougal.. neither grat nor graned. 1889 BARRIE *Window in Thrums* 174 'Leely', said Jamie, 'dinna greet, an' I'll never do't again'. 1893 STEVENSON *Catriona* 109, I sat down and grat like a bairn.

b. with *cognate obj.* To shed (tears).

c 1300 *Havelok* 285 For hire was mani a ter i-groten. 1450–70 *Golagros & Gaw.* 1141 The king.. Grat mony salt tere. *c* 1460 *Towneley Myst.* xxviii. 331 The teres thou grett when thou rasid lazare. 1719 RAMSAY *Richy & Sandy* 43 Hing down ye'r heads, ye hills, greet out ye'r springs.

†**2.** *trans.* To weep for, lament, bewail. *Obs.*

a 900 CYNEWULF *Crist* 1571 Hu þa wom-sceaþan hyra ealdȝestreon.. sare greten. *c* 1330 R. BRUNNE *Chron. Wace* (Rolls) 15613 For þyng þat þou hast greten sore. *a* 1340 HAMPOLE *Psalter* lx. 2 Whils i grete my syn.

†**3.** *intr.* To cry or call out in supplication or in anger. Const. *after, on, upon, till, to*. *Obs.*

c 1250 *Gen. & Ex.* 3659 He greten up-on moysen, And he to god made his bi-men. *a* 1300 *Cursor M.* 15624 To-quils he lai in orisun, he wit [*Fairf.* til, *Trin.* on] his fader grett. *c* 1330 R. BRUNNE *Chron.* (1810) 148, I am Thomas ȝour hope, to whom ȝe crie & grete. *c* 1410 LYDG. *Life Our Lady* xvi. (? 1484) c iv, Where as she sat in hir oratorye With herte ententyf.. Grete to god and all hir ful mynde. 1513 DOUGLAS *Æneis* VIII. Prol. 34 The gud wyffe gruling befor God gretis eftir grace.

†**4.** To beseech (a person) with tears. *Obs. rare.*

1562 A. SCOTT *Poems* (S.T.S.) i, 224 Greting grit God to grant thy Grace gude ȝeir.

greet, obs. and dial. form of GRIT.

greet(e, obs. form of GREAT *a.*

greeter[1] ('griːtə(r)). [f. GREET *v.*[1] + -ER[1].] One who greets, or salutes.

1552 HULOET, Greter or brynger of a gretynge, *salutiger*. 1611 COTGR., *Saluëur*, a saluter, a greeter. 1780 MAD. D'ARBLAY *Diary* May, She used to be my constant elbow companion, and most smiling greeter. 1853 MISS SHEPPARD *Ch. Auchester* II. 116 Only half the students had returned, and they.. were standing in self-interested fraternities, broken by groups and greeters. 1868 *Daily News* 6 July, The outbursts of cheering that would have greeted him if the greeters had not been [etc.].

greeter[2] ('griːtə(r)). *Sc.* [f. GREET *v.*[2] + -ER[1].] One who 'greets' or cries.

17.. *Yng. Ronald* xvii. in Child *Ballads* (1898) V. 183 I've heard greeters at your school-house.. But for to hear an auld man greet, It passes bairns' play.

greeting ('griːtɪŋ), *vbl. sb.*[1] [f. GREET *v.*[1] + -ING[1].] **a.** The action of GREET *v.*[1], in various senses; an instance of this, *esp.* a salutation. ***sendeth greeting***: a translation (now *arch.*) of the Lat. and Gr. epistolary formulæ of salutation, *salutem* (*dicit*), χαίρειν; also with ellipsis of the vb.

c 900 tr. *Bæda's Hist.* II. x. (1891) 124 Bonefatius papa sende Eadwine gretinge. *c* 950 *Lindisf. Gosp.* Luke i. 29 And ȝeðohte huliȝ wæs ðios groeteng. *a* 1225 *Leg. Kath.* 207 Gretunge, keiser, walde wel bicumen þe.. ȝef [etc.]. *c* 1275 in *O.E. Misc.* 100 From heouene in-to eorþe god gretynge he sende. *a* 1300 *Cursor M.* 17647 Ioseph sli greting þam gaf, 'Godds peis mot yee alle haf'. *c* 1350 *Will. Palerne* 4883 A gay greting was þer gret wan þei togedir met. *c* 1380 WYCLIF *Serm.* Sel. Wks. II. 9 Whanne Elizabeth herde þe greting of Marie. 1444 *Extracts Aberdeen Reg.* (1844) I. 399 James, be the grace of God kyng of Scottis, to the alderman and balleis of our burgh of Aberden gretyng. *c* 1450 *Merlin* 47 My lady sente me to yow, and sendeth yow gretinge, and sente yow this letter. 1535 COVERDALE *2 Macc.* xi. 27 Kynge Antiochus sendeth gretinge vnto the councell and the other people of the Iewes. 1593 SHAKS. *Rich. II*, I. iii. 254 Oh to what purpose dost thou hord thy words, That thou returnst no greeting to thy friends? 1597 —— *2 Hen. IV*, IV. i. 27 Health, and faire greeting from our Generall. 1611 BIBLE *Jas.* i. 1 Iames.. to the twelue tribes which are scattered abroad, greeting. 1685 BAXTER *Paraphr. N.T.*, *3 John* 1. 13–14 Kind Remembrances and Greetings are suitable to Christian Fellowship. 1805 WORDSW. *Waggoner* I. 54 Where once the Dove and Olive-Bough Offered a greeting of good ale To all who entered Grasmere Vale. 1863 GEO. ELIOT *Romola* lxiv, Tito did not kneel, but simply made a greeting of profound deference. 1876 GREEN *Stray Stud.* 51 Everybody meets everybody with greetings on the warmth and the sunshine.

b. *Comb.*, as ***greeting-place, -word***; **greeting(s)-card**, a card sent to relatives and friends at Christmas (or another festival); **greeting stamp** (see quot.); **greeting(s) telegram**, a coloured and illustrated telegram form conveying congratulations for weddings, birthdays, etc.

1898 *Weekly Budget* (Christmas Suppl.) 24 Dec. 14/5 (*heading*) Yule-tide parcel.. containing:.. *greeting cards, [etc.]. 1907 *Westm. Gaz.* 10 Dec. 12/1 The sending of the Royal greeting-cards is also a very big business. 1936 *Discovery* Dec. 366/2 Attractive greeting cards for Christmas use. 1951 *Catal. Exhibits, S. Bank Exhib. Festival of Britain* 49/2 Greetings Cards. 1967 F. MULLALLY *Prizewinner* iv. 57 She had been behind the counter, serving a woman with greetings cards. 1867 R. S. HAWKER *Prose Wks.* (1893) 114 The tree which marked the *greeting-place of master Bunsby. 1936 *Discovery* Dec. 378/2 Christmas seals, which are little *greeting stamps used for sticking on the flaps of Christmas letters and on parcels. 1937 *Rep. Proc. 14th Conf. ASLIB* 76 The design of a new '*greetings' telegram. 1952 M. STEEN *Phoenix Rising* ii. 51 The floor was littered with the gilt envelopes of 'greeting' telegrams. 1967 V. CANNING *Python Project* vi. 110 The British Post Office.. would deliver it as a greetings telegram with a border of fluffy rabbits, song birds and nosegays. *c* 1200 ORMIN 2799 Rihht affterr þatt tin *greting word Wass cumenn i min ære.

greeting ('griːtɪŋ), *vbl. sb.*[2] Now only *Sc.* and *north. dial.* [f. GREET *v.*[2] + -ING[1].] The action of GREET *v.*[2]; lamentation, weeping.

a 1300 *Cursor M.* 24624 For mi greting ful sare þai grett. 1340 HAMPOLE *Pr. Consc.* 1451 Now es laghter and now es gretyng. 1375 BARBOUR *Bruce* III. 514 Thocht I say that thai gret, sothly It wes na greting propyrly. *c* 1400 MAUNDEV. (Roxb.) ix. 34 þe vale of Mambre, þat es at say þe Vale of Gretyng. *c* 1400 *Destr. Troy* 3491 What gretyng & gremþ growes vnto þe? 1533 BELLENDEN *Livy* v. (1822) 428 Ane huge clamoure, mingit sum parte with skirll and greting of wiffis and barnis. 1588 A. KING *tr. Canisius' Catech.* 210 Griting and gnashing of teeth.

attrib. *a* 1300 *Cursor M.* 17947 (Gött.) þat þu þe suink naght.. wid greting praier for to gett þe oyle þat god in hight has sett.

greeting ('griːtɪŋ), *ppl. a.*[1] [f. GREET *v.*[1] + -ING[2].] That greets, salutes, etc.

1890 *Daily News* 3 Oct. 3/4 The greeting cheers from all parts of the hall.

Hence '**greetingly** *adv.*

1834 *Tait's Mag.* I. 339 It hails the lov'd child greetingly.

greeting (ˈgriːtɪŋ), *ppl. a.*² *Sc.* [f. GREET *v.*² + -ING².] That 'greets' or weeps.

1588 A. KING tr. *Canisius' Catech.* 39 With greitting eyes vaiting for ws in the coaste of the heavenlie countrie. **1676** W. ROW *Contn. Blair's Autobiog.* x. (1848) 210 Away with him, he is a greeting devil.

† **ˈgreetingful,** *a. Obs. rare*⁻¹. [f. GREETING *vbl. sb.*² + -FUL.] Sorrowful, tearful.

a **1340** HAMPOLE *Psalter* xvii. 10 A gretyngful prayer of men þat does penaunce.

greetingless (ˈgriːtɪŋlɪs), *a.* [f. GREETING *vbl. sb.*¹ + -LESS.] Without greeting or welcome.

1890 JEAN MIDDLEMASS *Two False Moves* I. v. 64 A greetingless coming home.

† **ˈgreety,** *a. Obs. rare*⁻¹. In 4 **grety.** [f. GREET *v.*² + -Y¹.] Inclined to shed tears.

c **1350** *Med. MS.* in *Archæologia* XXX. 351 Take rwe heysele & mengys wᵗ hony For wattryd eyne & to grety.

greevance, obs. form of GRIEVANCE.

greeve, var. GREAVE *sb.*¹ *Obs.*; obs. f. GRIEVE.

greeves, obs. pl. of GREAVE *sb.*³, GRIEF.

greeze, greaze (griːz). *Westminster School slang.* [Orig. unknown.] (See quots.)

1881 W. A. PECK in C. E. Pascoe *Everyday Life in our Public Schools* 115 Few..will forget how they pressed through the surrounding 'greeze' (*Anglice* crowd), fought their way up to the notice-board. **1884** F. H. FORSHALL *Westm. School* i. 14 In my first week I learnt the meaning of 'the greaze'. **1927** *Weekly Times* 10 Mar. 267/2 The historical scramble for the pancake, or the 'Pancake Greeze', as it is called by the boys, took place. **1934** *Times Educ. Suppl.* 17 Feb. 1/3 Two pancakes had to be tossed at Westminster School on Tuesday for the annual 'greeze'.

greezy, obs. form of GREASY.

gref(e, obs. form of GRAFF *sb.*¹, GRIEF, GRIEVE.

grefeous, obs. form of GRIEVOUS.

† **greff(e.** *Obs.* [a. F. *greffe*:—L. *graphium*: see GRAFF *sb.*¹] A graving instrument, a style.

[*c* **725** *Corpus Gloss.* 997 *Graffium*, gref.] *a* **1300** *Cursor M.* 21315 Þe first his greff of irin was. **1483** CAXTON *Gold. Leg.* 113 b/2 A greffe is proprely callid a poyntel to wryte in tablis of waxe.

greff(e, obs. form of GRAFF, GRIEF, GRIEVE.

greffier (ˈgrɛfɪə(r), Fr. grefje). Also 7 **grephier,** 8 **griffier.** [a. F. *greffier*, f. *greffe*: see GRAFF *sb.*¹]

1. A registrar, clerk, or notary. Chiefly with reference to foreign countries or to the Channel Islands.

1590 in A. Collins *Lett. & Mem. State* (1746) I. 304 Artsens, the Greffier to the States. **1608** BP. HALL *Epist.* I. v. 56 The Grephier of that Towne. **1676** TEMPLE *Let. to Sir J. Williamson* Wks. 1731 II. 414, I will endeavour to engage them either to write themselves to their Resident at Vienna, or, at least, to order the Greffier to do it. **1728** CHESTERF. *Let. to Ld. Townshend* 14 Dec., Some things might be communicated to the Pensionary in confidence, which he would not tell the Greffier. **1759** B. MARTIN *Nat. Hist. Eng.* I. Guernsey 128 There is an Officer called a Griffier, who.. tenders the Oaths. **1841** C. MACKAY *Mem. Pop. Delusions* III. 205 A rich *greffier* paid him a large sum of money that he might be instructed in the art. **1882** STEVENSON *Fam. Stud.* 250 The very greffier, entering it in his register.

2. A white hunting dog. *Obs.*

1576 TURBERV. *Venerie* 4 Of the nature and complexions of whyte dogges called Baux, and surnamed Greffiers.

greffon, obs. form of GRIFFIN.

gref(f)ul, greful(l, obs. forms of GRIEFFUL.

greg(e, obs. form of GRIG *sb.*¹

gregal (ˈgriːgəl), *a.* Also 6 **gregall.** [ad. L. *gregāl-is*, f. *greg-*, *grex* flock, crowd, multitude.]

1. Pertaining to a flock, or to the multitude. *rare.*

c **1540** tr. *Pol. Verg. Eng. Hist.* (Camden) I. 68 Caractacus ..was brought to Rome emonge other gregall captives. **1656** BLOUNT *Glossogr.*, *Gregal*, of the same flock or company, common. **1873** W. S. MAYO *Never again* vii, For this gregal conformity there is a cause and an excuse.

† **2.** = GREGARIOUS. *Obs.*

1607 TOPSELL *Four-f. Beasts* (1658) 557 When once his flesh is tickled with lust, he groweth tame, gregal and loving. **1658** ROWLAND *Moufet's Theat. Ins.* 921 A winged Insect, gregal or hearding. *Ibid.*, He is a..flocking or gregal creature.

‖ **gregale** (greˈgale). Also **grigale, grecale.** [It.; app. repr. a late L. **græcāle-m*, f. L. *Græcus* GREEK *a.*] The north-east wind in the Mediterranean. Cf. GRECO¹.

1804 C. B. BROWN tr. *Volney's View Soil U.S.* 135–6 In Egypt, where it is named *grigale*, I found it gloomy, chilly, and oppressive. **1867** SMYTH *Sailor's Word-bk.*, *Grecale*, a north-eastern breeze off the coast of Sicily, Greece lying N.E. **1883** *Encycl. Brit.* XV. 340 The 'gregale'..is a strong north-east wind which occasionally blows in the winter months with great fury and force for two or three days together.

gregarian (grɪˈgɛərɪən), *a. rare.* [f. L. *gregāri-us* (see GREGARIOUS) + -AN.] Belonging to the herd or common sort. Of a soldier: Common, private (= L. *gregārius miles*).

1632 SIR T. HAWKINS tr. *Mathieu's Vnhappy Prosperitie* I. 112 Even as the meanest gregarian souldier. **1640** BP. H. KING *Serm.* 16 Those Gregarian sparks, those Plebeian lesser Starres, which people the skie. *c* **1645** HOWELL *Lett.* (1650) III. 2 The Gregarian Soldiers and gross of the Army is well-affected to him.

Hence **greˈgarianism,** the practice of collecting in flocks or companies.

1881 *Truth* 13 Oct. 460/1 The tendency to gregarianism is nowhere more manifest than along the Riviera.

gregarine (ˈgrɛgərɪn), *a.* and *sb.* *Zool.* [f. mod.L. *Gregarina* (f. L. *gregāri-us*: see GREGARIOUS), the typical genus of the *Gregarinidæ.*]

A. *adj.* Of or pertaining to the genus *Gregarina* or class *Gregarinida* of protozoans, parasitic chiefly in insects, molluscs, and crustacea.

a **1900** In recent Dicts. **1903** E. A. MINCHIN in E. R. Lankester *Treat. Zool.* I. II. 152 The first notice of a gregarine parasite. *Ibid.* 161 Gregarine spores. **1968** R. D. MANWELL *Introd. Protozool.* (ed. 2) xxiii. 463 Some features of gregarine life cycles have already been briefly considered.

B. *sb.* One of the *Gregarinida.*

1867 J. HOGG *Microsc.* II. ii. 368 The Gregarines observed in the flesh of oxen. **1884** A. SEDGWICK tr. *Claus' Zool.* I. 208 The Gregarines are found mainly in Invertebrata.

So **gregaˈriniform** *a.*, shaped like a gregarine; **greˈgarinous** *a.*, afflicted with or possessing gregarines (*Syd. Soc. Lex.* 1886).

1897 *Allbutt's Syst. Med.* II. 728 *note*, The malarial organism being a gregariniform parasite capable of living in the body of man or in the body of mosquito.

gregarious (grɪˈgɛərɪəs), *a.* [f. L. *gregāri-us* (f. *greg-*, *grex* flock, herd) + -OUS.]

1. *Nat. Hist.* Of classes or species of animals: Living in flocks or communities, given to association with others of the same species.

1668 WILKINS *Real Char.* 135 Being gregarious, swimming together in great multitudes. **1678** RAY *Willughby's Ornith.* II. 196 Stares are gregarious birds, living and flying together in great flocks. **1701** GREW *Cosm. Sacra* III. ii. §38. 99 Those which are the most useful, fly not singly, as other Birds, but are commonly Gregarious; as the Partridge, Lark, Teal. **1774** GOLDSM. *Nat. Hist.* II. 41 This is practised among all gregarious animals. **1851–6** WOODWARD *Mollusca* 68 *Philonexis.*—Gregarious in the open sea. **1875** LYELL *Princ. Geol.* II. 340 A gregarious species of butterfly.

b. *transf.* Of persons: Inclined to associate with others, fond of company.

1789 MRS. PIOZZI *Journ. France* I. 369 Society! gregarious dame! **1822** SYD. SMITH *Wks.* (1859) II. 2/1 A very gregarious profession, that habitually combines and butts against an opponent with a very extended front. **1853** C. L. BRACE *Home Life Germ.* 188 We like being together well enough, but our gregarious tendencies are nearly always for some earnest object. **1896** MRS. CAFFYN *Quaker Grandmother* 70 She's not a gregarious person. Society and she have choked each other off some time ago.

2. *Bot.* Growing in open clusters.

1829 LOUDON *Encycl. Plants* 995 *Agaricus fusipes* ..gregarious. **1870** HOOKER *Stud. Flora* 131 *Saxifraga granulata*..Gregarious, glandular-hairy.

3. *Path.* Closely collected, clustered.

1822–34 *Good's Study Med.* (ed. 4) I. 256 Occasionally, however, this species [intestinal calculus] is found gregarious, instead of solitary. *Ibid.* IV. 440 They [pimples] are sometimes solitary, but more frequently gregarious.

4. Of or pertaining to a flock or community; characteristic of or affecting persons gathered together in crowds.

1833 I. TAYLOR *Fanat.* iii. 60 The enthusiasm of gregarious rage..puts contempt upon death. **1855** DICKENS *Lett.* (1880) I. 401 An instance of the gregarious effect of an excitement. **1876** LOWELL *Among my Books* II. 210 His faith in the gregarious advancement of men was afterwards shaken. **1876** MOZLEY *Univ. Serm.* xiii. 236 Mere religious zeal is a gregarious thing..like other gregarious affections, which are caught by men in company.

Hence **greˈgariously** *adv.*, **greˈgariousness.**

1688 R. HOLME *Armoury* II. 374/1 *Gregariously*, such as swim by Flocks, Troops, or Companies together. **1818** TODD, *Gregariously, Gregariousness.* **1834** MEDWIN *Angler in Wales* I. 177 It is evident that they prey gregariously. **1840** DE QUINCEY *Style* Wks. 1859 XI. 233 That marked gregariousness in human genius had taken place amongst the poets and orators of Rome, which [etc.]. **1870** LOWELL *Study Wind.* 151 Men acting gregariously. **1874** HELPS *Soc. Press.* xii. 154 A vile gregariousness of thought and feeling.

gregarization (grɛgəraɪˈzeɪʃən). [f. mod.L. *gregaria*, used to describe a locust during the gregarious phase of its life + -IZATION.] The swarming of locusts.

1939 J. S. KENNEDY in *Trans. R. Ent. Soc.* LXXXIX. 531 The 3rd stage in the outbreak process is termed 'Gregarisation', that is, the development of typically gregarious behaviour as a result of intensive aggregation. **1947** *New Biol.* III. 22 The whole process of gregarisation is a matter of interplay between the insect and the environment. **1970** *Sci. Jrnl.* Jan. 65/1 Phase change plays a central part in the population changes of locusts, but exactly what conditions produce gregarization and swarms is not known.

† **ˈgregary,** *a. Obs. rare*⁻¹. In 7 **gregarie.** [ad. L. *gregāri-us*: see GREGARIOUS.] Pertaining to the common herd, ordinary, undistinguished.

1640 BP. HALL *Episc.* III. ix. 53 Men that gave their blood for the Gospell and imbraced their fagots, flaming, which many gregarie professours held enough to carry cold.

† **greˈgation.** *nonce-wd.* [f. L. *greg-*, *grex* flock + -ATION.] A crowd, multitude (see quot.).

1621 BP. ANDREWES *Serm.* (1641) II. 156 It is the vertue (this of Concord) that is most proper..to a Congregation; without it a gregation it may be, but no Congregation.

grege, obs. form of GRIG *sb.*¹

grège (greɪʒ, grɛʒ), *a.* and *sb.* Also **greige.** [F. *grège* raw (silk).] (Of) a colour between beige and grey.

1926 *Dry Goods Economist* 18 Sept. 13 Vera Dexter designed this sports dress of Belding's Crêpe in grège and beige. **1927** *Weekly Dispatch* 6 Nov. 10 The newest colours [for stockings]..are a deep peach-beige, light tan, and a soft grège shade something between a fawn and a grey. **1928** *Daily Express* 3 Apr. 5/4 Different shades of beige and greige are most in demand. **1931** *Times* 21 May 19/4 A gown of greige satin. **1949** *Brit. Colour Council Dict. Colours* III. 9/2 The colour names of Ecru, Beige and Grège..mean exactly the same thing—the colour of the condition of cloth in its raw, unbleached state. **1960** *Harper's Bazaar* Oct. 22 Wool-belted in Bronze, Ebony, Cypress, Graphite, Greige, Roan and African Violet.

gregeis, variant of GREGOIS *Obs.*

† **gregge,** *v. Obs.* Also **grege.** [Aphet. form of *agregge*, AGGREGE q.v.]

1. *trans.* To aggravate, make more grave.

1340 HAMPOLE *Pr. Consc.* 2991 Some sal haf..þe dropsy to grege þair angwyse. *c* **1380** WYCLIF *Serm.* Sel. Wks I. 134 We greggen oure synne. **1382** —— *Ecclus.* viii. 18 Lest parauenture he gregge his eueles in thee.

2. To make heavy; also, to make dull (the ear).

1382 WYCLIF *1 Sam.* v. 6 Forsothe the hoond of the Lord is greggid vpon the Azothis. —— *Isa.* lix. 1 Lo! ther is not abreggid the hond of the Lord, that sauen he mai not, ne agreggid [*v.r.* greggid] is his ere, that he ful out here not.

greggle, var. GREYGLE *dial.*, wild hyacinth.

ˈgregicide, *a. nonce-wd.* [f. L. *greg(i)-*, *grex*, flock, crowd + -CIDE 1; after *regicide.*] Involving the slaughter of the common people.

1796 (*title*) Thoughts on the prospect of a Gregicide War, in a Letter to the right hon. Edmund Burke.

† **Gregion, -oun,** *a.* and *sb. Sc. Obs.* [Alteration of *gregyus* GREGOIS, suggested by *Graiugenum* Æn. III. 550.] **A.** *adj.* Grecian. **B.** *sb. pl.* Greeks.

1513 DOUGLAS *Æneis* II. vii. 56 Ane Gregioun swerd. *Ibid.* xii. 51 Nor go to serve na matroun Gregioun. *Ibid.* III. viii. 85 The Gregionis herbry, and fronteris suspek We left behind.

‖ **grego** (ˈgreɪgəʊ). Also 8 **grieko.** [a. some Rom. form of L. *Græcus* GREEK *a.*; cf. Sp. *griego*, Pg. *grego*, It. *greco.*] A coarse jacket with a hood, worn in the Levant. Also *slang*, a rough great-coat.

1747 *Adv. Kidnapped Orphan* 54 Manly..lent him a warm Grego, or long jacket lined with fur. **1768** J. BYRON *Narr. Patagonia* (ed. 2) 151 All my cloaths consisted of an old short grieko, which is something like a bearskin. **1809** *Naval Chron.* XXI. 215 They wear..a *grego*, or thick shaggy great coat, with a hood. **1825** C. M. WESTMACOTT *Eng. Spy* II. 175 A good grego in a winter's watch. **1836** MARRYAT *Midsh. Easy* xix, Their gregos, or night great-coats with hoods. **1840** —— *Poor Jack* xxxviii, The..men..had lain down in their gregos and pilot-jackets.

attrib. **1851** H. MELVILLE *Whale* iii. 25 He takes about a double handful of shavings out of his grego pocket.

† **ˈGregois,** *a.* and *sb. Obs.* Forms: 4–5 **gregeis, -eys, -ies, gregois, -oyse,** (4 **gergeis**), 5 **gregyows,** 6 *Sc.* **gregyus.** [a. OF. *gregois*, dial. var. of *greseis*:—late L. *græciscus*, f. *Græcu-s* GREEK *a.*]

A. *adj.* only in *fyr gregeys* = Greek fire. **B.** *sb.* A Greek.

13.. *K. Alis.* 2433 Eche of his men a Gregeis. **13..** *Coer de L.* 2575 Many barel ful off fyr Gregeys. *c* **1350** *Will. Palerne* 2200 Alle gergeis for grame gonne take here leue. *Ibid.* 5104 But go we now from þe gregoyse & ginne of anoþer. *c* **1375** *Sc. Leg. Saints, Martha* 46 Þe quhilk, quhatthinge It ourtuke As fyr gregois brynt at a luke. **1390** GOWER *Conf.* II. 230 The Gregois hadden mochel peine. *c* **1400** tr. *Secreta. Secret., Gov. Lordsh.* (E.E.T.S.) 77 And oon old Gregeys of hem shewyd and sayde. *c* **1450** *Guy Warw.* 7927 (C.) There were Gregyows many a wonne, Or he hyt gate, that were slone. **1513** DOUGLAS *Æneis* II. vii. 22 Bot first encounteris ws Androgeus, With a greit cumpany of the Gregyus.

Gregorian (grɪˈgɔərɪən), *a.* and *sb.* [ad. mod.L. *gregoriānus* (whence F. *grégorien*), f. late L. *Gregorius* (a. Gr. *Γρηγόριος*), a man's name (commonly rendered in Eng. by the adapted form *Gregory*); in senses A 3, 4, B 1 used with reference to the Eng. surname *Gregory*: see -AN, -IAN.]

A. *adj.*

1. Of or pertaining to Pope Gregory I (who reigned 590–600); chiefly applied to the ancient system of ritual music, otherwise known as *plain-chant* or *plain-song* (characterized by free rhythm, a limited scale, etc.), which is founded on the *Antiphonarium* of which Gregory is presumed to have been the compiler. So ***Gregorian chant, music, tones***, etc.

1653 URQUHART *Rabelais* I. xliii, Throughly besprinkled with holy water..that by the virtue as well of that Gregorian water as of the starres..they might [etc.]. **1751** CHAMBERS *Cycl.* s.v. *Chant*, The plain, or Gregorian chant, is where the choir and people sing in unison, or all together in the same manner. **1776** HAWKINS *Hist. Mus.* I. 346 He [Gregory] formed that ecclesiastical music so grave and edifying, which at present is called the Gregorian music. **1782** BURNEY *Hist. Mus.* II. 12 The ancient Gregorian chants that are come down to us. *Ibid.* 14, I shall..give a short example of each mode in Gregorian notes. **1855** STANLEY *Mem. Canterb.* i. (1857) 10 Every one who has ever heard of Gregory, has heard of his Gregorian chants. **1867** MACFARREN *Harmony* i, 18 The so-called Gregorian scales. **1872** O. SHIPLEY *Gloss. Eccl. Terms, Gregorian Tones*, a collection of chants compiled by S. Gregory the Great, consisting of eight tones, four of which, called authentic, he is said to have found, to which he added another four, plagal. **1876** STAINER & BARRETT *Dict. Mus. Terms* 362/2 The usual notes of the Gregorian Plain Song.

2. Of, pertaining to, or established by Pope Gregory XIII. ***Gregorian calendar***: see CALENDAR 1; so ***Gregorian style*** = 'new style'. ***Gregorian epoch***, the time from which the Gregorian calendar dates (1582).

1642 FULLER *Holy & Prof. St.* IV. xix. 336 The Gregorian account goes ten dayes before the computation of the English calendar. **1649** MILTON *Eikon.* Pref. Wks. (1851) 333, I shall suspect their Calendar more then the Gregorian. **1700** MOXON *Math. Dict., Gregorian Year*, the New Account, or New Style, instituted upon the Reformation of the Calendar, by Pope Gregory the 13th..Anno Domini, 1582. **1709** STEELE *Tatler* No. 39 ¶2 The Gregorian Computation was the most regular. **1751** CHAMBERS *Cycl.* s.v., The year 1726 is the 144th year of the Gregorian epocha. *Ibid.*, The old, or Julian, and new, or Gregorian style. **1872** O. SHIPLEY *Gloss. Eccl. Terms, Gregorian Style*, the new style invented by Gregory XIII. to correct the Julian.

3. The distinctive epithet of the kind of reflecting telescope invented by J. Gregory (died 1675).

1761 DUNN in *Phil. Trans.* LII. 191 My Newtonian reflector shewed objects clearer than the generality of Gregorian reflectors. **1831** BREWSTER *Optics* xlii. 350 The Gregorian telescope is shown in fig. 167. **1878** NEWCOMB *Pop. Astron.* II. i. 124 This form has an advantage over the Gregorian in that the telescope may be made shorter.

†**4.** ***Gregorian tree***, the gallows. (Cf. GREGORY 2.)

1641 *Mercur. Pragmat.* (Farmer), He Doth fear his fate from the Gregorian tree. **1785** GROSE *Dict. Vulg. Tongue, Gregorian tree*, so named from Gregory Brandon, a famous finisher of the law.

B. *sb.*

1. A variety of wig worn in the sixteenth and seventeenth centuries, said by Blount 1670 to be named after the inventor, Gregory, a Strand barber.

1598 FLORIO, *Perucca*, a periwig or gregorian of counterfait haire. *a* **1612** HARINGTON *Epigr.* III. (1633) 32 A quaint Gregorian to thy head to binde. **1639** DRUMM. OF HAWTH. *Consid. to Parlt.* Wks. (1711) 186 That no man wear a Gregorian or periwig, unless he have a testimonial from a town-clerk, that he is either bald, sickly, or asham'd of white hairs. **1658** BRAITHWAIT *Honest Ghost* 46 Pulling a little downe his gregorian, which was displac't a little by hastie taking off his Bever.

Comb. **1598** FLORIO, *Perucchiera*, a periwig or gregorian maker.

2. A member of a society (often classed with the Freemasons), which existed in England in the eighteenth century.

c **1742** in Hone *Every-day Bk.* II. 525 All other institutions, whether..Gregorians..or Free-Masons. **1742** POPE *Dunc.* IV. 576 One Rose a Gregorian, one a Gormogon. **1765** SMOLLETT *Trav.* xxvii. (1766) II. 54 These associations ..may be compared to the Free Masons, Gregoreans, and Antigallicans of England. **1810** CRABBE *Borough* x. 349 Griggs and Gregorians here their meetings hold.

3. †**a.** One who is versed in Gregorian music (*obs.*). **b.** A Gregorian chant.

1609 DOULAND *Ornith. Microl.* 9 The Gregorians (whom the Church of Rome doth imitate) marking all the lines with one colour. *Ibid.* 27 The authorities of the Gregorians admit no such Song. *a* **1873** S. WILBERFORCE in Burgon *Lives* 12 *Gd. Men* (1888) II. 59, I assure you I never hear a Gregorian without feeling a wish to lie down on my stomach and howl.

Hence **Gre'gorianist**, one who advocates the use of Gregorian chants; **Gre'gorianize** *v. trans.*, to render Gregorian in style; *intr.* to use or advocate the use of Gregorian music; whence **Gre'gorianizing** *vbl. sb.*, **Gre'gorianizer**.

1866 *Pall Mall G.* 3 Apr. 9/1 Imagine the Gregorianizing of the musical taste of a generation which [etc.]. **1884** *Ch. Times* 28 Nov. 905/4 Very largely the fault of the Gregorianizers. *Ibid.* 906/1 A reductio ad absurdum of extreme Gregorianizing. *Ibid.* 906/4 Our rough and ready Gregorianists.

Gregory ('grɛgərɪ). [Uses of the proper name.]

†**1.** App. a 'gallant'. *Obs.*

1599 MASSINGER, etc. *Old Law* III. ii, Faith, and I've other weapons for the rest too, I have prepard for em, if ere I take My Gregories heere agen.

†**2.** A hangman. *Obs.* (Cf. GREGORIAN A. 4.)

Gregory Brandon, common hangman of London in the reign of James I. was succeeded in office by his son Richard (*d.* 1649) who was commonly called 'Young Gregory'.

[**1642** *Merc. Aulicus* 553 This mighty gentlemans stollen Venison will not be sweet, when Gregory shall demand his fees.] *a* **1658** CLEVELAND *To T. C.* 10 Wks. (1687) 262 Are Rocks and Halters grown so dear That there's no perishing but here? Do no Committee yet survive Those cheaper Gregories of Men alive?

†**3.** The name of an old game. *Obs.*

1801 STRUTT *Sports & Past.* IV. iv. (1876) 513 Pick-point ..and Gregory, occur in a description of the children's games in the sixteenth century.

4. *Anglo-Irish.* A feast held on St. Gregory's day (12 Mar.). In quot. 1804 used for: An evening party.

1804 LADY HUNTER in *Sir M. Hunter's Jrnl.* (1894) 216, I have been at one or two gregorys—stupid card-parties, where you are crammed with tea, coffee and cakes, and then in an hour or two cold turkey, ham, and profusion of tarts, etc. **1830** W. CARLETON *Traits & Stor. Irish Peasantry* (1843) I. 321 To-morrow we will have our Gregory; a fine faste, plinty of poteen, and a fiddle. **1892** L. L. K. in *N. & Q.* 20 Aug. 145/2 'Gregories' were at one time common all over Europe.

Gregory-powder. Also shortened **Gregory.** [f. the name of James *Gregory*, a Scottish physician (1758–1822).] The 'compound powder of rhubarb' (*Pulvis rhei composita*) of the British Pharmacopœia. Usually called ***Gregory's powder***.

[**1850** BEASLEY *Druggist's Rec. Bk.* 163 Gregory's Powder.] **1886** *Pall Mall G.* 28 Aug. 4/2 However beautifully the Gregory powder of morality is apparelled in the currant jelly of story and incident. **1897** RAMSAY *Every Day Life Turkey* viii. 265 He made a face like a child at a dose of 'Gregory'. **1898** *Blackw. Mag.* Nov. 606 She once forced me to swallow a gregory-powder.

gregoyse, variant of GREGOIS *Obs.*

gregre(e, variant of GREEGREE.

†**gregs**, *sb. pl. Obs.* Also 7 **gregg(e)s**. [ad. F. *grègues*, app. a. Pr. *gregas*, fem. pl. of *grec* adj.] Galligaskins or breeches.

1611 COTGR., *Gregues*, wide Slops, Gregs, Gallogascoines. **1653** URQUHART *Rabelais* II. vi, His breeches..were not deep and large enough, but round streat caniond gregs.

gregyows, variant of GREGOIS *Obs.*

greho(u)nde, obs. form of GREYHOUND.

greice, obs. form of GRECE.

greidly, obs. form of GRADELY *dial.*

greif(e, obs. form of GRIEF, GRIEVE.

grein(e, obs. form of GRAIN, GREEN.

greis, obs. form of GREASE, GRECE.

greis, obs. Sc. pl. of GREAVE *sb.*[1], *sb.*[3]

greisbok, variant of GRYSBOK.

greisen ('graɪz(ə)n). *Min.* [Ger.; a dial. var. of *greisz*, f. *greiszen* to split.] A granitic rock with crystalline-granular texture, consisting chiefly of quartz and mica. Hence '**greisening** *vbl. sb.*, **greiseni'zation**, the pneumatolytic conversion of granite of similar rocks into greisen.

1878 LAWRENCE tr. *Cotta's Rocks Class.* 312 Greisen, a compound of quartz and mica. **1879** RUTLEY *Study Rocks* xii. 211 Greisen is a granular-crystalline rock, consisting of quartz and mica, the latter usually lithia-mica. **1907** REID & FLETT *Geol. Land's End District* iv. 58 There is not much evidence to show whether the tourmalinisation preceded, accompanied or followed the greisening. **1920** A. HOLMES *Nomencl. Petrol.* 114 The process whereby igneous emanations transform granite into greisen is called greisening or greisenisation. **1934** *Q. Jrnl. Geol. Soc.* XC. 348 Greisenization is always regarded as a typical example of pneumatolysis. **1962** W. T. HUANG *Petrol.* iv. 97 Three main types of alteration primarily due to the action of volatiles or pneumatolysis are connected with the intrusion of granitic plutons. They are tourmalinization, greisening, and kaolinization. **1970** *Mineral. Abstr.* XXI. 39/2 The author discusses the chemical changes involved in greisenization.

†'**greisiler.** *Obs. rare*⁻¹. [ad. OF. *groisillier* (F. *groseillier*).] A gooseberry bush.

c **1430** *Pilgr. Lyf Manhode* II. cxlvii. (1869) 133 More sharp than brambere, or thorn, or greisiler.

greisly, obs. form of GRISLY, GRIZZLY.

greiss, greist, obs. forms of GRECE, GRIST.

greistled, obs. form of GRIZZLED *a.*

greit, obs. Sc. form of GREAT *a.*

greit, obs. form of GREET *sb.*[2], *v.*[2], GRIT *sb.*[1]

greith(e, obs. form of GRAITH.

greive, greivo(u)s, obs. ff. GRIEVE, GRIEVOUS.

greizlie, obs. form of GRISLY.

Greke, Grekin, obs. ff. GREEK, GRECIAN.

'**greking.** *Obs.* exc. *Sc.* Forms: α. 3 **griking(e**, 4 ? **graykyng**, 5 **gryking**, 6 **greiking, greking**, 9 **greyking.** β. 3 **griging** 4 **grygynge.** [Corresponds to MDu. *grakinge, griekinge* of the same meaning; app. a derivative, with *-k*-suffix, from the root of ON. *grýja* to dawn (viewed by Noreen as cogn. w. *grá-r* GREY *a.*, though belonging to a different ablaut series). Cf., however, the synonymous Du. *krieken* (older *kriecke*) and Eng. CREEK *sb.*[2], SCREAK, SCREIGH.] Break (of day), dawn.

a **1300** *E.E. Psalter* cvii. 2 In þe grikinge rise sal I. **13..** *K. Alis.* 5413 Thise duden the oost mychel noye, In the gravkyng [*so clearly in MS.*] of the daye. ? *a* **1400** *Morte Arth.* 2510 The grygynge of the daye. *c* **1425** *Thomas of Erceld.* I. 2 In þe grykyng of þe day, Me a lone as I went. **1513** DOUGLAS *Æneis* IV. xi. 4 Quhen the quene The first greking of the day has sene. *Ibid.* VII. Prol. 115 Approching neir the greiking of the day. **1802** J. SIBBALD *Chron. Sc. Poet.* IV. Gloss., *Greke, greking*, peep, peeping, break of day. **1875** J. VEITCH *Tweed* 139 Ere greyking of the misty morn.

Grekish(e, grekkisch, obs. ff. GREEKISH.

Grelling ('grɛlɪŋ). The name of Kurt *Grelling*, an early 20th-cent. German logician, used *attrib.*, *absol.*, in the possessive, and coupled with that of L. *Nelson*, to designate the paradox of heterologicality, which they discovered and published in 1907; as ***Grelling antinomy*** (also ***Grelling-Nelson antinomy***), ***Grelling's paradox***, etc. (The paradox is sometimes referred to as *Weyl's contradiction*, by a mistaken attribution.)

1937 A. SMEATON tr. *Carnap's Logical Syntax of Lang.* §60a. 211 (*heading*) Grelling's antinomy. **1955** A. N. PRIOR *Formal Logic* III. iii. 287 A particularly clear example is.. Grelling's paradox about 'heterological'. **1960** P. SUPPES *Axiomatic Set Theory* i. 10 The third..semantical paradox ..is the Grelling-Nelson paradox..of heterologicality. **1962** W. & M. KNEALE *Devel. Logic* xi. 656 Grelling's paradox has to do with a newly invented word. **1963** G. T. KNEEBONE *Math. Logic* iv. 128 The Grelling-Nelson antinomy (1908). **1966** L. J. COHEN *Diversity of Meaning* (ed. 2) §26. 214 Similar antinomies, like the Grelling, may arise. **1966** W. V. QUINE *Ways of Paradox* i. 6 Thus viewed, Grelling's paradox seems unequivocally falsidical.

‖**grelot** (grəlo). [Fr.] A small globular metal bell, worn on harness, etc.

1854 BADHAM *Halieut.* ii. 31 The boatmen..keep tense upon strong stretchers hung with grelots, a floating net, and so ring in a great number of fish to the tinkling of these bells. **1888** *Pall Mall G.* 29 Feb. 10/1 This..bridal robe was covered with flounces, edged with pretty silver grelots.

†**greme**, *sb. Obs.* Also 4 **grem.** [ad. ON. *gremi*:—OTeut. type **gramjo-*, f. **gramo-* GRAME *a.*]

1. Anger; wrath.

13.. *E.E. Allit. P* B. 16 þay..hym to greme cachen. **13..** *Propr. Sanct.* (Vernon MS.) in *Archiv Stud. neu. Spr.* LXXXI. 94/30 Jerusalem, Jerusalem, þou slest and stonest prophetes wiþ grem. *c* **1460** *Towneley Myst.* vi. 73 He slo not, for old greme, these moders with thare barne teme.

2. Grief, harm.

13.. *Gaw. & Gr. Knt.* 2251, I schal gruch þe no grwe, for grem þat fallez. *c* **1400** *Destr. Troy* 603 With no gaudys me begyle, ne to grem brynge. *c* **1435** *Torr. Portugal* 1929 Hym to kepe frome greme.

Hence †'**gremeful** *a.*, sad; sorrowful.

a **1300** *Signs bef. Judgem.* 156 in *E.E.P.* (1862) 11 So sore i-worþ adrad iwis of ihsu crist-is gremful wreche.

†**greme,** *v. Obs.* Forms: 1–2 **gremian**, 3 **gremen, -ien**, (4 **grem**), 4– **greme.** Also pa. pple. 3 **i-gremet.** [OE. *grẹmian* = OHG. *gremjan, gremen*, ON. *gremja*, Goth. *gramjan*, f. OTeut. **gramo-* GRAME *a.* Cf. GRAME *v.*]

1. *trans.* To anger, grieve; to vex.

c **893** K. ÆLFRED *Oros.* IV. i, He..þa ðe elpendas.. gremede. *c* **1000** *Ags. Gosp.* Mark xv. 29 þa ðe forð-stopon hine gremedon & hyra heafod cwehton. *c* **1175** *Lamb. Hom.* 25 He gremeð ure drihten. *a* **1225** *St. Marher.* 12 Stute nu uuele gast to gremien me mare. *a* **1250** *Owl & Night.* 931 The niȝtingale was i-gremet. *c* **1300** *Havelok* 441 þat he shulde[n] him nouth greme. *c* **1400** *Destr. Troy* 12153 Scho ..myche gremyt þe grekes in hir grete angur.

b. *impers.* (*it*) *gremes me*, etc.: I, etc. am grieved.

a **1310** in Wright *Lyric P.* x. 36 Heo me bed go my gates, lest hire gremede. **13..** *E.E. Allit. P.* C. 42 Bot lenge whereso-euer hir lyst, lyke oþer greme.

2. *intr.* To become angry, be vexed.

c **1400** *Destr. Troy* 1006 The grettyst of Grise gremyt þerat. *c* **1460** *Anturs of Arth.* 524 (Douce MS.) And Gawayne greches þerwith, and gremed ful sare.

Hence '**greming** *vbl. sb.* and *ppl. a.*

c **1205** LAY. 23489 Græmende segges gras-bæd isohten. ? *a* **1500** *Chester Pl.* (Shaks. Soc.) II. 197 Ther is reminge, greminge, veramente.

grement: see GREEMENT.

gremercy, obs. form of GRAMERCY.

gremial ('gri:mɪəl), *a.* and *sb.* [ad. late L. *gremiālis*, f. *gremi-um* the lap, bosom.]

A. *adj.*

1. Of or pertaining to the bosom or lap. Of a friend: Intimate (cf. *bosom-friend*). *Obs.* exc. in ***gremial veil*** (Eccl.) = B. 2.

a **1631** DONNE *Serm.* xvii. 167 Centricall Gold, viscerall Gold, gremiall Gold, Gold in the Matrice and womb of God. **1659** T. PECKE *Parnassi Puerp.* 153 Cæsar entreated, by a gremial Friend; To certifie him, when Stern Mars did end. **1669** *Address Yng. Gentry Eng.* 72 A repentance that will snatch you out of their [prostitutes'] gremial graves. **1721–1800** in BAILEY. **1853** DALE tr. *Baldeschi's Ceremonial* 81 The gremial veil, which serves as an apron for the bishop.

2. Dwelling within the 'bosom' of a university or society, resident. Also as the epithet of the ordinary or full members of a society as distinguished from honorary members. *Obs.* exc. *Hist.*

1730 J. TAYLOR *Music Sp. Camb.* 10 By the Model of this single Day, The gremial Doctor shapes his awkward Way. **1739** J. HILDROP *Ess. Freethinking* 14 All such as should at any time offer themselves as Candidates to be Gremial or Honourary Members of our Society. **1841** G. PEACOCK *Stat. Cambridge* App. A. 17 *note*, Gremial masters of arts were allowed to wear silk in their gowns and hoods.

3. Of or pertaining to the internal affairs of a corporation or society, confined to its members.

1880 W. SMITH & CHEETHAM *Dict. Chr. Antiq.* II. 1713 It was the rule for the prior to be elected from among the inmates of the monastery; in other words, the election was to be 'gremial'.

B. *sb.*

1. A resident member (of a university or other society). *Obs.* exc. *Hist.*

1563 FOXE *A. & M.* 937/1 That done they came all into the Quere, and there helde the conuocation of the Uniuersitie, being gremials. **1574** M. STOKYS in G. Peacock *Stat. Cambridge* (1841) App. A. 17 At Generall Processyons all Inceptours that war no Gremyallys shall goo before the Regentys. **1655** FULLER *Ch. Hist.* VIII. iii. §45 They were made as capable of Degrees, as if admitted Gremials in the University. —— *Waltham Abb.* 20 And now was not Waltham highly honoured.. when amongst those fourteen [Commissioners], two were her Gremials, the forenamed Nicholas living in Waltham, and this John, having his name thence, because birth therein. **1665** J. BUCK in G. Peacock *Stat. Cambridge* (1841) App. B. 84 The Bedels deliver verses and Groats to all Drs. present, as well Strangers as Gremials. **1694** STRYPE *Cranmer* II. vi. 162 These things made him always cast a favourable aspect upon the Universities, and especially that of Cambridg.. which the Governors and the rest of the Gremials very well knew. **1702–8** CHAMBERLAYNE *St. Gt. Brit.* I. III. xi. (1707) 470 In several Colleges the Gremials are dispenc'd with from taking their Batchelor of Divinity's Degree. **1841** G. PEACOCK *Stat. Cambridge* App. A. 17 *note, Gremials*, who were regents or non regents, were punished by suspension, *ab omni datione* [etc.].. whilst *non gremials*.. were suspended *ab omni gradu* [etc.]. **1855** HEYWOOD tr. *Early Camb. Stat.* 17 No gremial in the congregations of masters shall utter any words publicly except in Latin.

2. *Eccl.* A silken apron placed on the bishop's lap when celebrating Mass or conferring orders.

1811 *Chron.* in *Ann. Reg.* 65 The scarf, the cross, the gremial, and the mitre of the bishop. **1853** DALE tr. *Baldeschi's Ceremonial* 114 The Bishop having been divested of the mitre and gremial, rises.

† **'gremious,** *a. Obs. rare*⁻⁰. [f. L. *gremium* lap, bosom + -OUS.] = GREMIAL *a.*

1656 BLOUNT *Glossogr.*, *Gremious*, pertaining to the lap or bosom.

gremlin ('grɛmlɪn). orig. *R.A.F. slang.* [Orig. unknown, but probably formed by analogy with GOBLIN.] **1.** A mischievous sprite imagined as the cause of mishaps to aircraft; later, an embodiment of mischance in other activities.

1941 C. GRAVES *Thin Blue Line* ix. 123 As he flew round, he wished that his instructor had never told him about the Little People—a mythological bunch of good and bad fairies originally invented by the Royal Naval Air Service in the Great War... Those awful little people, the Gremlins, who run up and down the wing with scissors going 'snip, snap, snip' made him sweat. **1942** *Observer* 8 Nov. 6/5 Behaviour of.. machines couldn't always be explained by.. laws of aerodynamics. And so, lacking a Devil, the young fliers.. invented a whole hierarchy of devils. They called them Gremlins, 'on account of they were the goblins which came out of Fremlin beer bottles'. They were the genii loci of the R.A.F. messes in India and the Middle East, where Fremlin's beer bottles were plentiful. **1943** C. GRAVES *Seven Pilots* 89 'Any Gremlin trouble last night?' Wing Commander Prall asked Paddy... 'None, thank goodness,' Paddy replied. **1944** *Times* 12 Aug. 2/1 The King said that on his way back from Italy they thought they heard a gremlin in the royal aeroplane. **1944** *Amer. Speech* XIX. 280 Gremlins are mythical creatures who are supposed to cause trouble such as engine failure in aeroplanes, a curious piece of whimsy-whamsy in an activity so severely practical as flying. Now the gremlin seems to be extending its sphere of operations, so that the term can be applied to almost anything that inexplicably goes wrong in human affairs. **1955** M. GILBERT *Sky High* xi. 163 'I hope you had a comfortable night,' she said. 'Not a single gremlin,' said Tom. **1958** *Times* 20 Feb. 5/2 A gremlin in the organ that had decided to add a noisy C sharp to the beautiful soft D major chords. **1959** *New Statesman* 2 May 611/3 Unfortunately the misprint gremlin has raised its ugly head in my letter to you on 18 April. **1969** *Daily Tel.* 15 Aug. 4/3 Gremlins were at work on this column yesterday and a 7 p.c. stake of the Furness Withy equity appeared in print as 27 p.c.

2. *Surfing.* **a.** A young surfer. **b.** A trouble-maker who frequents the beaches but does not surf. *slang.*

1961 *Life* 1 Sept. 51 If [a beginner's] surfing career goes well, he will be a 'gremlin' in a few years. **1965** J. M. KELLY *Surf & Sea* 286 Gremmie or gremlin, a young inexperienced surf enthusiast to whom nothing counts in life but surf-board and water. Also, an uncomplimentary term applied to those who hang around the beaches for reasons other than surfing. **1967** *Internat. Surfing* III. III. 23 There is really a lot of talent running around these days in the form of young gremlins. **1967** J. SEVERSON *Great Surfing* (Gloss.), *Gremlin*, a trouble-maker; one whose misdeeds cause surfing beaches to be lost and gives surfing a bad name.

gremmie ('grɛmɪ). *Surfing slang.* Also **gremmy**. [Shortened form of GREMLIN.] = GREMLIN 2. Also *attrib.*

1962 T. MASTERS *Surfing made Easy* 64 *Gremmies*, young poor mannered surfers. **1965** *N.Z. Listener* 17 Dec. 4/5 Surfers.. are.. antagonistic towards learners ('gremmies'). **1967** *Internat. Surfing* III. III. 13 About girl surfers, they are great to surf with until you are driving left and some gremmy girl takes off in front of you and goes straight off, forcing you to straighten out. **1968** *Surfer Mag.* Jan. 35/1 He worked all morning with several beach gremmies piling 12-foot sections of plywood and rocks into a small reef on the wet sand.

† **gremth.** *Obs.* [app. repr. OE. **gremðu* = Middle Ger. *gremde*:—WGer. **gramiþa*, f. **gram-* GRAME *a.*] Anger; rage.

1340–70 *Alisaunder* 279 þe gremþe of þo grim folke glod to his hert. *c* **1350** *Will. Palerne* 2080 þe grewes for gremþe ginneþ on me werre. *c* **1400** *Destr. Troy* 1720 þe harmys þat we haue, & þe hoge lose; That the Grekes in hor gremþ vs to grefe broght. *Ibid.* 2545 Let other men Aunter, abill þerfore, ffor to shunt vs of shame, shend of our foos, And venge vs of velany & of vile gremþ [*printed* gremy: *see Errata*].

gren, obs. form of GREEN.

gren, var. or obs. f. GRIN *sb.*[1], *v.*[1] and *v.*[2]

‖**grenache** (grənaʃ). [Fr., the name of a sweet wine grape.] A sweet wine, usually drunk with dessert, produced in the Languedoc-Roussillon region of France.

1851 C. REDDING *Hist. Mod. Wines* vi. 151 Good Grenache wine is made in the communes of Banyuls sur Mer, Collioure, Port Vendres, and some in the canton of Rivesaltes. **1946** G. MILLAR *Horned Pigeon* xxii. 372 There was good *grenache* for an *apéritif*. **1958** A. L. SIMON *Dict. Wines* 86 *Grenache*, a sweetish red or tawny dessert wine from the Pyrénées (Roussillon) made chiefly in the *Banyuls* district from Grenache grapes. **1963** L. DURRELL in *Holiday* Jan. 74/3 A *Blanc de Blanc* to accompany the *pâté* and the fish, and then a *grenache*.

grenade (grɪ'neɪd), *sb.*[1] Forms: α. 6–7 **granade**; β. 7– **grenade**. [a. F. *grenade* fem., a. Sp. *granada* (also Pg.) pomegranate (see GARNET); hence transf. = sense 2 below. See also GRENADO.]

†**1.** A pomegranate. *Obs.* (Cf. GRANATE *sb.*[2])

α. *c* **1532** DU WES *Introd. Fr.* in *Palsgr.* 912 Granades, *grenades*. **1664** EVELYN *Kal. Hort.* (1729) 211 Water young planted Shrubs.. as Orange-Trees, Myrtles, Granades.

β. **1654** WHITELOCKE *Jrnl. Swed. Emb.* (1772) I. 375 He.. sent.. a present of citrones, grenades, and curious spanish comfitures.

2. a. A small explosive shell, usually of metal, thrown into the trenches or among clusters of the enemy. It is now thrown only by hand: see HAND-GRENADE. ***rampart grenade***, one to be rolled down the rampart to harass the besieging enemy.

α. **1591** *Garrard's Art Warre* 317 For preparations against the assault you must not be destitute of all sorts of arteficial fire, as Trompes, Granades, Bullets. *c* **1645** T. TULLY *Siege Carlisle* (1840) 38 Diverse were pitifully burned by the granade. **1658** R. FRANCK *North. Mem.* (1694) 16 Sin, like a Granade, tears up all before it.

β. **1709** STEELE *Tatler* No. 80 ¶9 The Charge began with the Fire of Bombs and Grenades. **1767** SIMES *Mil. Medley* (1768), *Grenade* is an iron orbicular case.. filled with powder, to be thrown by the grenadiers amongst the enemy in an attack. **1855** MACAULAY *Hist. Eng.* xvii. IV. 81 A brave French refugee with a grenade in his hand was the first to climb the breach. **1863** KINGLAKE *Crimea* (1876) I. xiv. 242 That.. grenades should be secretly placed in the houses of the men.

fig. *a* **1657** LOVELACE *Poems* (1864) 193 An icy breast in it betray'd Breaks a destructive wild granade. **1886** *Pall Mall G.* 30 Sept. 1/1 The bludgeon of downright calumny, and the mud grenade of libellous abuse are more in vogue nowadays than the rapier of wit or the barbed dart of polished sarcasm.

b. A glass receptacle to be thrown in order to burst and disperse its contents; e.g. ***drain grenade***, one filled with a strong-smelling fluid, to be used in detecting a leakage in a drain; ***fire-grenade***, a fire-extinguisher, = HAND-GRENADE 2.

1891 *E.A. Parkes' Pract. Hygiene* 110 Glass grenades charged with pungent chemicals. **1893** TAYLOR *Sanit. Inspector's Handbk.* 103 A similar test is the 'Banner drain grenade', an appliance made of thin glass charged with pungent and volatile chemicals. **1895** *Army & Navy Coöp. Soc. Price List* Sept. 286 New Hand Fire Grenade.

3. *attrib.*, as ***grenade-launcher, pouch, -thrower***.

1959 C. OGBURN *Marauders* (1960) iv. 125 The Japanese .. redoubled the fire of their *grenade launchers. **1969** I. KEMP *Brit. G.I. in Vietnam* iv. 83 There was a good deal of shouting from the garrison, several of whom started to fire grenade launchers into the night. **1836** *Hist. Rec. Life Guards* 47 A *grenade pouch. **1920** *Glasgow Herald* 14 Apr. 9 For one moment Commander-in-Chief and *grenade-thrower stood hand in hand looking long and confidently into each other's eyes.

grenade (grɪ'neɪd), *sb.*[2] *Cookery.* [Alleged to be Fr.; perh. f. *grain* GRAIN *sb.*[1], with the etymological sense of 'something spiced' (cf. OF. *grané* mentioned s.v. GRAVY); perh. a transferred use of *grenade* pomegranate. (Cf. GRENADINE[1] and GRANADA.)] (See quot. 1706.)

1706 PHILLIPS (ed. Kersey), *Grenade*,.. in Cookery, a Dish, of larded Veal-collops bak'd in a Stew-pan between two Fires, with six Pigeons and a Ragoo in the middle, and cover'd on the top and underneath with thin slices of Bacon. **1730–6** in BAILEY (folio). **1892** *Encycl. Cookery* (ed. Garrett) I. 719 Grenades with Cherry Sauce.

gre'nade, *v.* [f. GRENADE *sb.*[1]] *trans.* To attack with grenades.

1849 A. H. CLOUGH *Lett. & Rem.* (1865) 144 The simple truth would appear to be, that we have been grenaded, not bombarded. **1947** DYLAN THOMAS *Let.* 29 May (1966) 309 Our little spankers make so much noise I cannot work anywhere near them. God grenade them. **1959** C. OGBURN *Marauders* (1960) iv. 120 The sound of anything stirring was to be instantly grenaded.

Grenadian (grɪ'neɪdɪən), *a.* and *sb.* Also **Grenadan.** [f. *Grenada*, an island in the W. Indies + -IAN.] **A.** *adj.* Of or pertaining to Grenada. **B.** *sb.* An inhabitant of Grenada.

1923 A. ASPINALL *Pocket Guide to West Indies* (ed. 4) vi. 142 Grenadians.. have been acquiring land. **1950** *Caribbean Q.* II. II. 21 He is the product of urbanization, and, be he Grenadian, or Hindu or Trinidad creole, he has rapidly taken on characteristics of his own. **1962** *Listener* 5 July 9/2 The Grenadans have also a French tradition of desperate political remedies. **1967** V. S. NAIPAUL *Mimic Men* I. v. 82 We had a Grenadian woman cleaner. **1969** G. SIMS *Sand Dollar* iv. 55 Pleasure before business. That's a good old Grenadian motto. **1969** 'I. DRUMMOND' *Man with Tiny Head* x. 124 Some Grenadans tried talking to her in French, but she could not understand their debased slaves' argot, nor they her Parisian.

† **grenadier**[1]. *Obs.* [a. F. *grenadier*, f *grenade* GRENADE *sb.*[1] 1.] A pomegranate tree.

1632 LITHGOW *Trav.* v. 207 The best Carobiers, Adams Apples, and Grenadiers that grow on the earth is here [Damascus].

grenadier[2] (grɛnə'dɪə(r)). Forms: 7 **grenadeer**, (**granatier**), 7–8 **granadeer, -dier**, 8 **granider**, 7– **grenadier.** [a. F. *grenadier*, f. *grenade* GRENADE *sb.*[1] sense 2.]

1. a. Originally, a soldier who threw grenades. At first four or five were attached to each company, but, later, each battalion or regiment had a company of them. Though grenades went out of general use in the eighteenth century, the name of 'grenadiers' was retained for a company of the tallest and finest men in the regiment. Now, however, in the British army, the word is retained only in the name of the ***Grenadier Guards*** (*colloq.* ***Grenadiers***), the first regiment of household infantry.

1676 tr. *Guillatiere's Voy. Athens* 405 If I went on with these Grenadeers, I would if possible, escape. **1678** EVELYN *Diary* 29 June, Now were brought into service a new sort of soldiers call'd *Granadiers*, who were dextrous in flinging hand granados. **1686** *Lond. Gaz.* No. 2106/4 Capt. Cornwallis's Company of Grenadiers in the Holland Regiment. **1714** GAY *Sheph. Week* Prol. 48 For Peace allays the Shepherd's Fear Of wearing Cap of Granadier. **1776** C. LEE in Sparks *Corr. Amer. Rev.* (1853) I. 202, I have formed two companies of grenadiers to each regiment. **1800** WELLINGTON in Gurw. *Desp.* (1837) I. 164, I was in hopes that the grenadiers and the cavalry would have joined Lieut. Colonel Maclean. *a* **1839** PRAED *Poems* (1864) I. 91 Guarded by griefs and grenadiers. **1853** SIR H. DOUGLAS *Milit. Bridges* (ed. 3) 137 These were speedily followed by six companies of grenadiers in boats.

b. *attrib.* as ***grenadier-bonnet, -cap, -company, -guard; grenadier-like*** adj.

1837 CARLYLE *Fr. Rev.* II. vi. vi. 396 Demoiselle Théroigne has on her *grenadier-bonnet. **1749** FIELDING *Tom Jones* VII. xiv, When the centinel first saw our hero approach, his hair began gently to lift up his *grenadier-cap. **1772** *Ann. Reg.* 73/2 Serjeant of the *grenadier company of the Royal Scots. **1844** H. H. WILSON *Brit. India* I. 363 The grenadier company of the 3rd volunteer native battalion. **1752** FIELDING *Amelia* I. iv, Her father-in-law.. was in the *grenadier guards. **1878** BROWNING *Poets Croisic* 132 *Grenadier-like, marching to assault.

c. *transf.* A person with the build of a grenadier.

1805 E. CAVANAGH *Let.* 20 Aug. in Londonderry & Hyde *Russ. Jrnls. M. & C. Wilmot* (1934) II. 182 In walk'd a Grenadier of a Man with a silver Tray. **1879** R. L. STEVENSON *Trav. Donkey* 105, I found two other guests. One was a country parish priest... He was a grenadier in person with the hale colour and circular wrinkles of a peasant. **1929** W. FAULKNER *Sartoris* (1954) 30 That straight, grenadier's back of hers. **1949** M. LASKI *Little Boy Lost* iii. 57 No child of mine could ever have reminded this grenadier of her Isidor.

2. a. A South African weaver-bird, *Pyromelana* (or *Ploceus*) *oryx*, with vivid red and black plumage. Also ***grenadier grosbeak, waxbill.***

1751 G. EDWARDS *Nat. Hist. Birds* IV. 178 The Grenadier .. This Bird was brought from Angola..; his Note is not very agreeable, it resembling the Winding-up of a Clock. **1802** BINGLEY *Anim. Biog.* (1813) II. 161 The Grenadier

Grosbeak is of about the size of a sparrow. The body is..of a beautiful red colour. **1875–84** R. B. SHARPE *Layard's Birds S. Afr.* 474 *Uræginthus granatinus*, Grenadier Waxbill.

b. The fish *Macrurus fabricii* or *M. rupestris* (*Cent. Dict.* 1889).

Hence **grena'dierly** *adv.*, after the manner of a grenadier; †**grena'diership**, the position or function of grenadier.

1676 tr. *Guillatiere's Voy. Athens* 405 In order to my Grenadiership, they had..put a linnen bagg full of Grenadoes about my shoulders. **1829** LANDOR *Wks.* (1846) 557/2 In the midst of her finery, she tosses down her gin grenadierly.

grenadilla: see GRANADILLA.

grenadin (ˈgrɛnədɪn). [Fr.: see GRENADINE[1].] A French variety of carnation (see quot. 1910).

1904 R. P. BROTHERSTON *Bk. Carnation* 18 The French Grenadin, truly a biennial, both single and double, with small flowers of a sweet scent, and extraordinarily floriferous. **1910** T. W. SANDERS *Carnations* 45 Grenadin Carnations. A Continental strain of dwarf habit, growing about 1 ft. high, and bearing scarlet or white flowers. **1928** L. J. COOK *Carnation Culture* (ed. 5) viii. 69 What is known as the Grenadin Carnation is a race possessing a dwarf, stiff habit of growth.

grenadine[1] (ˈgrɛnədiːn). *Cookery.* [a. F. *grenadin*: cf. GRENADE *sb.*[2]] (See quots.)

1706 PHILLIPS (ed. Kersey), *Grenadin*, a sort of Farce, or stuff'd Meat laid upon thin slices of Bacon in a Baking-pan, with a hollow place to receive a Fowl cut into Halves and dress'd in a Ragoo. **1736** BAILEY *Househ. Dict.* 247 Ducks in Grenadines..Glaze them..pour a cullis of ham into the dish, put in the grenadine, and serve them up hot. **1846** FRANCATELLI *Mod. Cook* p. xii, *Fricandeau* and *Grenadins* consist of the primest parts of veal, or fillets of poultry, &c. smoothly trimmed, larded, and brightly glazed with a concentration of their own liquor.

grenadine[2] (ˈgrɛnədiːn). Also 8 **grenadin**. [a. F. *grenadine*; ? f. the name of the Spanish city *Granada*.] An open silk or silk and wool textile used for dresses.

1852 E. TWISLETON *Let.* 15 July (1928) ii. 30, I..went in my purple Grenadine..and my lace bonnet. **1865** *Pall Mall G.* 13 May 4 Their handsome moiré or grenadine. **1869** MRS. PALLISER *Lace* xv. (ed. 2) 183 From its being a grenadine, not a shining silk, a common error prevails that it is of thread. **1879** GEO. ELIOT *Theo. Such* (ed. 2) 178 Ophelia in fleshings and a voluminous brevity of grenadine. **1890** *Daily News* 24 Mar. 6/1 Very light and transparent woollen materials of the kind that used to be called barège, mousseline-de-laine, and grenadine.

attrib. **1861** MRS. GASKELL *Let.* 23 May (1966) 652 Silk barège *scarf* shawls, 35s—grenadine *shawls* ditto. **1864** *Daily Tel.* 8 June, A charge of £59 for one grenadine dress and trimmings.

grenadine[3] (grɛnəˈdiːn). [ad. F. (*sirop de*) *grenadine*, f. *grenade* GRENADE *sb.*[1]] A syrup made from pomegranates (or other fruit).

1896 F. B. & W. H. WORKMAN *Algerian Mem.* 43 We found syrup of grenadine, or pomegranate with water, a delicious drink. **1905** W. J. LOCKE *Morals Marcus Ordeyne* xii. 148, I..restore her to beatitude with grenadine syrup and soda-water. **1906** *Daily Chron.* 21 July 8/5 One of them, prepared from ripe gooseberries, is particularly delicious. It is called grenadine. **1913** C. MACKENZIE *Sinister St.* I. I. ix. 130 Michael thought grenadine sucrée was just as nice as it looked. **1958** R. GODDEN *Greengage Summer* ix. 106 Mademoiselle Zizi had joined us for drinks; we had the pink grenadine sirop.

grenado (grɪˈneɪdəʊ). *arch.* Forms: α. 7–8 **granado(e**, 7–9 **granada**, (7 **granida**). β. 7– **grenado**. [ad. Sp. *granada*: see GRENADE *sb.*[1] and -ADO.]

1. = GRENADE[1] 2.

α. **1611** N. T. in Coryat *Crambe* b j a, Of some Oxe-hide in Styx long drenched, Or that had some Granada quenched. [*Marg.* A warlike engine otherwise called a Mortar, vsually quenched with wet Hides.] **1626** CAPT. SMITH *Accid. Yng. Sea-men* 32 Iron bals, granadoes, trunkes of wilde fire. **1652–62** HEYLYN *Cosmogr.* II. (1682) 126 Mortar-pieces and Granado's in proportion to them. *a* **1670** HACKET *Abp. Williams* I. (1693) 75 One..trouled out a Motion crammed like a Granada with obsolete Words. **1675** *Lond. Gaz.* No. 1052/2 The Besiegers began to shoot from six Mortar-pieces into the Town, Granadoes of 2 and 300 pound each. **1686** GOAD *Celest. Bodies* II. iv. 200 So have I seen a Granado in the Air, fuming as it went along in a sullen silence. **1690** NORRIS *Beatitudes* (1692) 67 More like Granidas shot into a Town, than Inhabitants of it. **1727** A. HAMILTON *New Acc. E. Ind.* II. xli. 105 We saluted them with a Shower of twenty or thirty Granadoes. **1761** STERNE *Tr. Shandy* III. xvi, It would have broke the cerebellum (unless indeed the skull had been as hard as a granado).

β. **1676** tr. *Guillatiere's Voy. Athens* 404 Those who were to throw the Grenadoes. **1729** SHELVOCKE *Artillery* IV. 173 Very old Grenado's..shaped perfectly like a Cube or Parallelopiped. **1807–8** W. IRVING *Salmag.* (1824) 364 More fell to our port is the cargo she bears Than grenadoes, torpedoes, or warlike affairs. **1865** CARLYLE *Fredk. Gt.* XVIII. xiii. (1872) VIII. 41 Stoffeln..began firing shells and incendiary grenadoes at a great rate.

fig. *c* **1645** HOWELL *Lett.* I. VI. xlii, Fires..kindled at first by a Granado hurl'd from his brain. **1651** BIGGS *New Disp.* ⁋ 170. 131 Those mortar-pieces and granadoes of Physick. **1677** YARRANTON *Eng. Improv.* 14, I will now shoot a Granado into London..I hope 'twill make them look about them.

2. = GRENADE[1] 1.

1656 BLOUNT *Glossogr.*, *Granado*, a Pomegranat, an apple filled with delicious grains.

3. *attrib.* and *Comb.*, as ***grenado gun***, ***-maker***, ***-man***, ***mortar***, ***shell***, ***shot***; †***grenado-netherstock***, some fashion of hose.

1690 LUTTRELL *Brief Rel.* (1857) II. 42 There have been lately ship't away..several *granado guns. **1670** CLARENDON *Ess.* Tracts (1727) 183 Gun-smiths, or *granado-makers. **1676** tr. *Guillatiere's Voy. Athens* 404 Above thirty were cut off by those *Grenado men. **1631** PREMPART *Siege Busse* 25 Twoo *Granado Morters. **1599** MARSTON *Sco. Villanie* 167 Ribanded eares, *Granado-netherstocks, Fidlers, scriueners [etc.]. **1684** J. PETER *Siege Vienna* 80 Certain *Granado Shells he had Invented, not of Glass or any Metal, but of Potters Clay wrought..to the hardness of Iron. **1790** BEATSON *Nav. & Mil. Mem.* I. 100 A party..was ordered to march next to them, with the grenado shells in bags. **1705** SIR E. WALKER *Hist. Disc.* I. 38 Firing the Magazine within with a *Granado shot.

‖**grenat** (grəna). [Fr.: see GARNET[1].] Used *attrib.*: Of a deep red colour, like that of garnet.

1851 *Harper's Mag.* II. 432/2 While others [head-dresses] of a grenat color, are sable and gold. **1852** LD. MALMESBURY *Mem. Ex-minister* (1884) I. 365 Lady ——, in a *grenat* velvet and blue bonnet.

grenat: see GRANATE.

gre'natiform, *a. rare*⁻⁰. [f. GRENAT-ITE + -I)FORM.] Having the form of grenatite.

1828–32 in WEBSTER; and in later Dicts.

grenatite (ˈgrɛnətaɪt). *Min.* Also **granatite**. [f. F. *grenat* garnet + -ITE.] = STAUROLITE.

1804 R. JAMESON *Syst. Min.* I. 76 Grenatite..is dark reddish brown. **1805–17** —— *Char. Min.* 178 There are two planes of junction which unite, crossing each other, as in the mineral named grenatite. **1837** DANA *Min.* 355 Prismatoidal Garnet M. Grenatite, Staurotide H. [**1868** p. 388 Granatite. **1892** p. 558 Grenatite, Granatite]. **1859** PAGE *Handbk. Geol. Terms*, *Grenatite*, prismatoidal garnet; known also as Staurotide, Staurolite, or Cross-stone.

grench, variant of GRINCH *Obs.*

grene, obs. f. GRAIN, GREEN; var. GRIN *sb.*[1], *v.*[1]

grenes, -ess(e, -is, obs. forms of GREENNESS.

grenetine (ˈgrɛnɛtiːn). [f. *Grenet*, the name of its French inventor + -INE.] A pure transparent gelatin, obtained from the skin and cartilage of young animals (*Syd. Soc. Lex.* 1886).

1843 PEREIRA *Food & Diet* 221 Grenetine is extracted from bones.

Grenfell (ˈgrɛnfəl). [Name of Sir Wilfred Thomason *Grenfell* (1865–1940), English medical missionary who in 1893 founded the Labrador Medical Mission.] Used *attrib.* in ***Grenfell cloth***, the proprietary name for a tough, closely woven, windproof cotton fabric. Also ***Grenfell clothing***.

1926 *Trade Marks Jrnl.* 3 Nov. 2471/2 *Grenfell Cloth*.. Cotton Piece Goods made in England. **1933** W. GRENFELL *40 Yrs. Labrador* x. 126 The first thing in clothing is the material—impervious to wind and water, light in weight, inexpensive, tough, smooth on the outside so as to shed snow... Just such a material can be ordered through our offices..and the English firm·which invented it calls it 'Grenfell cloth'. **1933** G. D. ABRAHAM *Mod. Mountaineering* x. 186 Closely woven, wind-proof cloth is best, such as 'Grenfell' cloth, which is made in Manchester. **1947** G. G. DENNY *Fabrics* (ed. 6) 34 *Grenfell cloth*, closely woven, water-repellent, windproof fabric made of Egyptian cotton. .. Uses: sports clothes, shower curtains, upholstery, drapery. **1955** 'G. CARR' *Corpse at Camp Two* i. 20 His Grenfell clothing and so forth would be turned over to you.

grengasite (ˈgrɛŋgəsaɪt). *Min.* [Named by Hisinger 1831 after *Grängesberg* in Sweden, where it is found: see -ITE.] A variety of chlorite occurring in radiated groups of hexagonal crystals.

1844 DANA *Min.* 525 Grengasite..has a specific gravity of 3·1.

grenier, variant of GRANER *Obs.*, a granary.

1604 E. G[RIMSTONE] *D'Acosta's Hist. Indies* V. xxviii. 413 They take a certaine portion of the most fruitefull of the Mays that growes..the which they put in a certaine grenier which they doe call *Pirua*.

grenn(e, grennes, obs. ff. GREEN, GREENNESS.

grenne, obs. form of GRIN *sb.*[1] and *v.*[2]

†**grent**, *v. Obs.* [? onomatopoeic; cf. GRIN, GRINT, GRUNT *vbs.*] *intr.* **a.** To gnash the teeth. **b.** ? To grunt or groan. Hence **'grenting** *vbl. sb.*

13.. *K. Alis.* 5846 He grented als a bore. **1387** TREVISA *Higden* (Rolls) IV. 11 Þan at soper..Alisaundre was i-poysoned, and grent [L. *ingemuit*] as he were i-stiked wiþ a knyf þoruȝ þe body. **1388** WYCLIF *Matt.* xxii. 13 There schal be wepyng and grentyng of teeth. **14..** *Lat.-Eng. Voc.* in Wr.-Wülcker 613/44 *Strido*, to grenne or grente with the theth.

Grenzbegriff (ˈgrɛntsbəgrɪf). *Philos.* [G., f. *grenze* limit, boundary + *begriff* concept.] In Kantian philosophy, a concept which shows the limitation of sense-experience; a limiting concept (also *limit-concept*, *limitative conception*); also, loosely, a conception of an unattained ideal.

[**1787** KANT *Kritik der reinen Vernunft* (ed. 2) 310 Der Begriff eines Noumenon ist also bloss ein Grenzbegriff.] **1893** P. CARUS *Primer of Philos.* 98 The straight line..must be taken as a *Grenzbegriff*, i.e., a conception which denotes the utmost limit to be reached by a certain operation. **1896** W. JAMES *Will to Believe* (1897) 16 Objective evidence is never triumphantly there; it is a mere aspiration or *Grenzbegriff*, marking the infinitely remote ideal of our thinking life. **1908** —— *Meaning of Truth* (1909) xii. 239 The notion of an *absolute* reality inevitably arises as a *grenzbegriff*. **1941** *Mind* L. 309 Kant's 'thing in itself', understood either as a transcendent real or as a Grenzbegriff, could be only a prolific source of error.

greot(e, obs. form of GRIT *sb.*[1]

grep(e, obs. f. GRIP; obs. pa. t. of GRIPE *v.*[1]

Grepo (ˈgrɛpəʊ). [G. *gre(nz)po(lizei* frontier police.] An East Berlin border guard.

1964 L. DEIGHTON *Funeral in Berlin* v. 31 The Grepo nodded. **1966** R. THOMAS *Spy in Vodka* (1967) xiii. 136 'We run to an apartment building directly in front of the wall.' 'What are the Vopos and Grepos doing all this time?' **1967** J. GARDNER *Madrigal* iv. 74 The Vopos and Grepos..were all young men,..each one washed from childhood into the Communist pattern.

gres, obs. f. GRASS, GREASE; var. GRIS *a.*

‖**grès** (grɛ). [Fr.] Stoneware. ***grès de Flandres***, Cologne ware.

1872 LADY C. SCHREIBER *Jrnl.* (1911) I. 153 Perez.. showed us a grès de Flandres jug. **1874** *Ibid.* 244 The collection..chiefly consists of Grès and Delft. **1882** *Hamilton Sale Catal.* No. 950 A Pilgrim's Bottle, of old grès-de-Flandres stone ware. **1902** *Encycl. Brit.* XXXI. 875/1 The influence of the Japanese potters on the production of *grès* in France. **1962** D. M. BILLINGTON *Technique Pottery* 206 *Grès de Flandres*, the salt-glazed stoneware of the Low Countries.

†**'gresco.** *Obs.* An old game at cards.

1605 CHAPMAN, etc. *Eastward-Ho* IV. i, My Prentise.. would play his hundred pound at Gresco, or Primero, as familiarly..as any bright peece of Crimson on 'hem all. **1611** FLORIO, *Nassáre*, to play or cast at the by, at hazard or gresco.

grese, obs. form of GREASE, GRECE, GRICE.

†**gresell**, *v. Obs. rare*⁻¹. [a. OF. *gresiller*, *greziller* 'to wrigle..; to curle, twirle, frizle haire' (Cotgr.)] *intr.* Of hair: To stand on end.

1490 CAXTON *Eneydos* xvi. 64 His heeres byganne to gresell [Fr. orig. *hericer*], & dresse vpward.

gresell, obs. form of GRIZZLE *v.*

gresett, variant of GRASETT *Obs.*

†**'Greshamist.** *Obs.* [f. the proper name *Gresham* + -IST.] A fellow of the Royal Society, which in its early days met at Gresham College. So **'Greshamite**.

1665 OLDENBURG *Let. to Boyle* 29 Aug. in *B.'s Wks.* (1744) V. 334 There were some of our Greshamists that thought one or other of the two former comets might be seen again, after some time. *a* **1700** B. E. *Dict. Cant. Crew*, *Greshamite*.

Gresham's law: see LAW *sb.*[1] 17 c (*d*).

gresing, variant of GRECING *Obs.*, steps.

gresle, gresli, obs. ff. GRIZZLE *a.*, GRIZZLY.

gresone: see GRISON *a. Obs.*

gress(e, obs. form of GRECE, GRASS *sb.*[1]

gressam, variant of GERSUM.

gressell, obs. form of GARSIL, GRISTLE.

†**'gressible**, *a. Obs.* [f. L. *gress-*, ppl. stem of *gradī* to walk: see -BLE.] Able to walk.

c **1600** *Timon* v. iv. (Shaks. Soc.) 86 A two legd liuing creature, gressible, vnfeathered. **1610** GUILLIM *Heraldry* III. xiii. (1611) 124 Some are gressible, hauing feete, and some creeping or gliding as serpents.

†**'gressile**, *a. Obs. rare*⁻¹. [f. as prec.: see -ILE.] = prec.

1659 D. PELL *Impr. Sea* 193 Terrestrial. And under this term I would comprehend, 1. Gressile, 2. Volatile, 3. Reptile. *Ibid.* 244 Those creatures that are Gressile. **1730–6** BAILEY (folio), *Gressile*, of or pertaining to steps.

†**'gressive**, *a. Obs. rare*⁻¹. [f. as prec.: see -IVE.] Taking steps, walking.

1668 WILKINS *Real Char.* 239 Gressive.

gressome, variant of GERSUM *sb.* and *v.*

1558 *Lanc. Wills* (Chetham Soc.) III. 79 Richard Hall for the gressome of his horse iiij[li]. **1564–78** BULLEYN *Dial. agst. Pest.* (1886) 10 Muche reisyng of rentes and gressomyng of men, causyng greate dearth, much pouertie.

gressorial (grɛˈsɔərɪəl), *a. Zool.* [f. mod.L. *gressōri-us* (f. *gressor*, agent-n. f. L. *gradī* to walk) + -IAL.] Adapted for stepping or walking, formed for or having the habit of walking, ambulatory.

1842 BRANDE *Dict. Sci.*, etc., *Gressorial*, in Ornithology, is applied to the feet of birds which have three toes forward, two of which are connected, and one behind. **1852** DANA

Crust. II. 825 The family of gressorial Gammarids. **1856–8** W. CLARK *Van der Hoeven's Zool.* I. 649 Feet of trunk all gressorial. **1877** COUES & ALLEN *N. Amer. Rod.* 532 The forelimbs small and neat, indicating predominance of prehensile over merely gressorial faculties.

So **gre'ssorious** *a.*

In recent Dicts.

†**grest.** *Obs. rare.* Also **gresses.** [app. ad. L. *gressus* step.] A footboard.

1563 *Ludlow Churchw. Acc.* (Camden) 115 For makynge of a grest for my lorde to knele upon. **1569** *Ibid.* 137 Payd ffor ijᵒ. sawed bordes to make a gresses to sett under the singing mens ffeete.

grest, gresy, obs. ff. GRIST, GREASY.

gresyn, obs. form of GRAZE *v.*¹

gret, obs. f. GREAT, GREET *sb.*², GRIT *sb.*¹

gret: see GREDE *v. Obs.*, GREET *v.*¹ and ².

gretch, obs. form of GRUTCH *v.*

Gretchen ('greɪtʃən). [The name of the ignorant girl seduced by Faust in Goethe's play.] A girl resembling Gretchen; a German girl or woman. Also used *attrib.* to denote typically German hairstyles, etc., as ***Gretchen braid, plait,*** etc.

1890 *Amer. Mail Order Fashions* (1961) 11 Linen Lawn Gretchen Apron. **1905** *Daily Chron.* 16 Jan. 8/5 The English hairdressers are rejoicing..in the new Gretchen plait. **1913** D. H. LAWRENCE *Sons & Lovers* xi. 284 'Then why shouldn't we belong to each other altogether?'..'I know it's a lot to ask,' he said; 'but there's not much risk for you really—not in the Gretchen way.' **1917** —— in *Seven Arts* July 283 No, but really, Marta, you're not going to wait any more—really! It's stupid for you to play Gretchen—your eyes are much too green. **1940** 'GUN BUSTER' *Return via Dunkirk* II. x. 162 With that flaxen hair and those blue eyes they reminded one of a couple of typical Saxon Gretchens. **1952** KOESTLER *Arrow in Blue* x. 85 Seducing rustic Gretchens who were either the innkeeper's or the miller's daughter. **1966** J. S. COX *Illustr. Dict. Hairdressing* 67/2 *Gretchen style*, a hair style usually worn by young girls, in which the hair, 6" to 10" long, is worn in tightly plaited stiff plaits hanging over or just behind the ears. **1970** *Sunday Times* 8 Feb. 61/4 Gretchen braids wound round small chignoned heads.

grete, obs. form of GREAT, GREET, GRIT *sb.*¹

†**'gretful,** *a. Obs.* [? altered form of BRETFULL; but cf. GREAT B. 6.] Quite filled, full.

c **1400** *Destr. Troy* 331 Grete greues full grene, gretfull [*printed* grecfull] of dere. *Ibid.* 13826 A Grydell full gay, gret-full of fiche.

greth, obs. f. GREAT *a.*, GRAITH *v.*; var. GRITH.

gretian, obs. form of GRECIAN.

Gretna Green ('grɛtnə 'griːn). The name of a village in Dumfriesshire just across the Border, used *attrib.* in reference to the custom by which runaway couples from England have been married there according to Scots law, without the parental consent required in England for those who have not attained their majority. Also *ellipt.* as ***Gretna.***

Such marriages first became common after Lord Hardwicke's Act of 1753, prior to which it was possible to contract a valid marriage in England clandestinely. Since then lack of parental consent, while not invalidating an English marriage, has meant that it is virtually impossible to get the ceremony performed. The convenience for elopers of a Scottish marriage has been reduced by successive Acts of Parliament, notably by the Marriage (Scotland) Act of 1939, prior to which a valid marriage could be contracted in Scotland merely by a declaration of consent by the two parties before a witness (traditionally the village blacksmith).

[**1791** C. STUART *Gretna Green* II. 19 Never think of dying a maid, for that would be setting a bad example, and Gretna Green might then go a begging.] **1813** [see BLACKSMITH]. **1823** GALT *Entail* III. x. 95 Whomsoever ye hear giving me the wyte o' ony sic Gretna Green job, I redde ye put your foot on the spark, and not let it singe my character. **1852** *Househ. Words* V. 199/2 It was my impression Gretna marriages were quite matters of the past. *Ibid.* 201/1 Old Colthard..was the first regular Gretna Green parson. **1863** *Chambers's Encycl.* V. 106/2 The Gretna Green marriages may yet be resorted to by English parties, provided the intended husband comply with this requisite [*sc.* 21 days' residence in Scotland]. **1904** *Daily Chron.* 17 Feb. 7/1 Caroline, Marchioness of Queensberry..was the heroine of a genuine Gretna Green marriage. *Ibid.*, The period of the Gretna Green weddings..extended over almost exactly a century. **1959** *Chambers's Encycl.* VI. 590/2 Gretna marriages still attracted the sentimental until the Scottish irregular marriage..was abolished in 1939. **1968** D. J. STEEL et al. *Nat. Index Parish Registers* I. 317 Information on the history of Gretna marriages.

grett(e, obs. form of GREAT *a.*, GRIT.

gretumly, variant of GREATUMLY *Sc. Obs.*

greu, variant of GREW *sb.*¹ *Obs.*

†**greund.** *Obs.* Also 6 grewand, -end, 6–9 grewnd, 9 grune. [app. a contracted form of ME. *grehund* GREYHOUND.]

c **1420** *Anturs of Arth.* 126 (Douce MS.) The grete greundes were agast of þe gryme bere. **1513** in Glover *Hist. Derby* (1829) I. App. 61 A Greundes hed sylver and sabull quartered. **1519** *Presentm. Juries* in *Surtees Misc.* (1888) 32 That no man kepe no hown, grewand, nor spanzell. **15..** SIR P. DRAYCOTT in Lodge *Illustr.* (1791) I. 6 They [staggys] was not only cowrssyd wᵗ sum grewnds, but also wᵗ horsmen. **1567** GOLDING *Ovid's Met.* VII. 93 She gaue me eke a goodly Grewnd. **1591** HARINGTON *Orl. Fur.* XLVI. cxxi, Still the Grewnd prevailes. **1816** *Sporting Mag.* XLVIII. 204/1 Those spaded bitches appeared to have been grunes or greyhounds. **1865** *Derbysh. Gloss.* in *Reliquary* V. 159/2 *Grewnd*, a greyhound.

greut, variant of GROOT *sb.*¹

Greuze (grœz). The name of J. B. *Greuze* (1725–1805), French painter, used in ***Greuze-like*** adj., resembling a figure in his pictures. Also ***Greuze-ish.***

1860 O. W. HOLMES *Elsie Venner* xxi. 232 A lax, ..*Greuze*-ish looking blonde. **1905** *Westm. Gaz.* 13 May 5/2 'This is my first dance!' said a young and very pretty girl with a Greuze-like face. *Ibid.*, We did not know whether that remark applied to the Greuze-like young girl. **1948** L. SPITZER *Linguistics & Lit. Hist.* 178 Her Greuze-like décolleté.

grevance, obs. form of GRIEVANCE.

greve, obs. f. GRAVE *a.*, GREAVE, GRIEF, GRIEVE.

greveous, obs. form of GRIEVOUS.

Grevillea (grɪ'vɪlɪə). *Bot.* [mod.L., named by R. Brown in 1809 after Charles Francis *Greville*, Vice-President of the Royal Society (Morris).] A large genus of trees (N.O. *Proteaceæ*) of Australia and Tasmania; (also with lower-case initial) a tree or shrub of this genus.

1853 *Hooker's Jrnl. Bot.* V. 313 Two Grevilleas with scarlet flowers. **1882** *Garden* 25 Nov. 462/2 The Grevilleas are among the easiest of plants to grow. **1888** *Cassell's Picturesque Australasia* (1890) III. 138 Graceful grevilleas, which in the spring are gorgeous with orange-coloured blossoms.

grevious, grevos(e, etc., obs. ff. GRIEVOUS.

Grévy's zebra ('greɪvɪz 'ziːbrə, 'zɛbrə). [tr. of *Equus grevyi* (A. Milne-Edwards 1882, in *La Nature* 3 June 13/1), f. the name of F. P. J. Grévy (1807–91), president of the French Republic.] A member of a species of zebra, *Equus grevyi*, found in southern Ethiopia and Somalia.

[**1882** *Proc. Zool. Soc.* 721 Mr. Sclater exhibited some photographs of the new Zebra, lately named *Equus grevyi* by M. A. Milne-Edwards.] **1891** W. H. FLOWER *Horse* 196/2 (*index*) Zebra, Grevy's. **1894** *Proc. Zool. Soc.* 320 Grévy's Zebra was, I think, first shot in Somaliland by Colonel Paget. **1910** R. E. DRAKE-BROCKMAN *Mammals of Somaliland* 105 Grevy's zebra seems to prefer undulating rocky bush country to any other. **1931** *Times Educ. Suppl.* 7 Nov. 11 This species is known as Grevy's zebra, and is taller and slimmer than the true zebra. **1957** R. CAMPBELL *Portugal* 46 The shimmering skin of a Grevy's zebra. **1965** D. MORRIS *Mammals* 353 Grévy's Zebra is the largest and most narrowly striped of the zebras.

†**Grew,** *sb.*¹ and *a. Obs.* (After 15th c. chiefly *Sc.*) Forms: 3–4 **greu, gru,** (3 **gryu,** 4 **griu**), 4, 5 **grw,** 4–6 **grew(e,** 5, 6 **grue,** (5 **griewe**). [a. OF *griu*:—L. *Græcum* GREEK.]

A. *sb.*

1. The Greek language, Greek.

c **1275** *Passion our Lord* 470 in *O.E. Misc.* 50 Hit wes iwryten on ebreu, on gryv, and latyn. *a* **1300** *Cursor M.* 16689 Of hebru, gru, and latine. **1387** TREVISA *Higden* (Rolls) II. 245 þey torned Holy Writte out of Ebrew in to Grewe. **1450–1530** *Myrr. our Ladye* 90 Thys worde Hympne is a worde of grew. *c* **1480** HENRYSON *Orpheus* vi, The first in grew was callit Euterpe. **1560** ROLLAND *Crt. Venus* I. 181 Thus was he clad, and with letteris of grew In fine Scriptour, I saw it writtin new.

2. A Greek.

a **1300** *Cursor M.* 19740 Paulus..fast disputed wit þe gruus. *c* **1350** *Will. Palerne* 2080 And þe grewes for gremþe ginneþ on me werre. *c* **1400** *Lanfranc's Cirurg.* 180 If a man desiriþ for to haue blac heeris as doiþ greuis & spay-nardis, þanne make þis tincture.

3. The land of the Greeks, Greece.

1387 TREVISA *Higden* (Rolls) I. 193 For Minerua in þe speche of Grewe hatte Athena. **1432–50** tr. *Higden* (Rolls) I. 37 In the reigne of men of Grewe. *c* **1480** HENRYSON *Orpheus* iv, The grete lordis of grewe.

B. *adj.* Greek.

c **1400** MAUNDEV. (Roxb.) x. 39 Writen in Grew lettres. **1401** *Pol. Poems* (Rolls) II. 91 Heresie, that is Grw, is divisioun on Latyn. **1513** DOUGLAS *Æneis* I. Prol. 114 Lyk as in Latyne bene Grew termes sum. *Ibid.* III. iv. 1 Strophades in Grew leid ar nemmit so, In the grete see standand ilis two.

grew (gr(j)uː), *sb.*² *Sc.* and *north. dial.* [Shortened form of GREW-HOUND.] A greyhound.

1815 SCOTT *Guy M.* xxii, Five grews, and a wheen other dogs. **1826** J. WILSON *Noct. Ambr.* Wks. 1855 I. 124, I.. worry him as if I were a grew, and him a bit leveret. **1868** G. MACDONALD *R. Falconer* I. 37 'What wad the grew be efter, but maukin?' returned Miss Letty. **1893** *Northumbld. Gloss.*, *Grew*, a greyhound.

b. *Comb.*, as ***grew-bitch, -whelp.***

1536 BELLENDEN *Cron. Scot.* (1821) I. 38 Grew-quhelpis. **1814** PEGGE *Suppl. to Grose*, *Grew-bitch*, a greyhound bitch. York.

grew (gr(j)uː), *v. Sc.* [f. GREW *sb.*²] *intr.* To go coursing with greyhounds.

1825 J. WILSON *Noct. Ambr.* Wks. 1855 I. 62 Thine too skatin, and curlin, and grewin.

grew, pa. t. of GROW *v.*; var. GRUE *sb.* and *v.*

grewe, obs. f. GRIEVE; Sc. var. GREAVE *sb.*¹ *Obs.*

grewel, grewell(e, obs. forms of GRUEL.

grew-hound ('gr(j)uːhaʊnd). *Obs.* exc. *Sc.* Forms: 4 **grewhounde,** 5 **grewhonde, grohund, grou, grw hund,** 5–6 **grew hund, grew-hund, grewe hound,** 7–9 **grewhound,** 9 **grue hound.** [app. an etymologizing alteration (as if meaning 'Greek hound': see GREW *a.*) of GREUND.] A greyhound.

? *a* **1400** *Morte Arth.* 1075 He grevede as a grewhounde. *c* **1440** *Gesta Rom.* lxxviii. 398 (Add. MS.) The grewhonde of aubry had kepte iiij. dayes the dede body of his mayster from briddes and bestes. **1473** in *Ld. Treas. Acc. Scotl.* (1877) I. 44 To fech a grew hund to the king. **1580** *Wills & Inv. N.C.* (Surtees 1860) 20 One brace of blacke grewe houndes. **1668** *N. Riding Rec.* VI. 124 Two Croft yeomen presented for keeping grewhounds. *a* **1802** *Ld. Thomas & Fair Annie* xxiv. in Child *Ballads* (1885) II. 70/2 Gin..I were a grew hound..Soon worried they a' should be. **1887** *Scotsman* 4 Mar. 2/2 Grue hound (steel grey) found; if not claimed in three days will be sold.

grewnd, variant of GREUND *Obs.*

grewsome, obs. form of GRUESOME.

grewt, variant of GROOT *sb.*¹

grex (grɛks). *Biol.* [a. L. *grex* flock.] A clump of myxamœbæ formed during a phase of the life cycle of cellular slime moulds, the Acrasina or Acrasiomycetes. Also *attrib.*

1962 B. M. SHAFFER in M. Abercrombie *Adv. Morphogenesis* II. 112 In the second phase, the aggregate has a fairly definite shape, whatever its origin, and reactions that are foreign to those of the component cells: *it* has become the individual. As no existing words connoting 'many-in-oneness' seem to be available, the name *grex*—the classical product of ad-gregation—is put forward for it. *Ibid.* 162 If the grex cells move like stream cells, we must again consider to what extent they are guided by acrasin. **1971** *Nature* 4 June 329/2 Although the aggregate can differentiate directly into a fruiting body it usually migrates as a coordinated irritable whole in the form of a tapered cylinder called the grex.

grey, gray (greɪ), *a.* and *sb.* Forms: α. 1 **grǽᵹ,** 3–4 **grai,** 4–6 **graye,** (6 **graie,** *Sc.* **gra**), 4– **gray.** β. 1 **gréᵹ, gréiᵹ, gréi,** 3 **grei,** 3–4 **greye,** 4 **grey3e,** 4– **grey.** [OE. *grǽᵹ* = OFris. *grê*, MDu. *grau, gra* (Du. *grauw*), OHG. *grâo*, pl. *grâwe* (MHG. *grâo*, mod.G. *grau*), ON. *grá-r* (Sw. *grå*, Da. *graa*), repr. two OTeut. types **grǽgo-* and *grǽwo-*:—pre-Teut. **ghrēgʷho-* (or **ghrēgh-wo-*, the suffix *-wo-* being frequent in colour-adjs.), with variable accent. Outside Teut. no affinities have been found; the word has no connexion with OHG. *grîs* (Ger. *greis*), whence F. *gris*.

Each of the current spellings has some analogical support. The only mod.Eng. words repr. OE. words ending in *-ǽᵹ* are *key* (which is irrelevant on account of its pronunciation), *whey*, and *clay*. If we further take into consideration the words repr. OE. words in *-ǽᵹe*, viz. *blay* or *bley*, *fey*, *wey*, we have three (or four) instances of *ey* and only two (or one) of *ay*. On the other hand, this advantage in favour of *grey* is counterbalanced by the facts that *clay* is the only word of the five which is in very general use, and that *grey* is phonetically ambiguous, while *gray* is not. With regard to the question of usage, an inquiry by Dr. Murray in Nov. 1893 elicited a large number of replies, from which it appeared that in Great Britain the form *grey* is the more frequent in use, notwithstanding the authority of Johnson and later Eng. lexicographers, who have all given the preference to *gray*. In answer to questions as to their practice, the printers of *The Times* stated that they always used the form *gray*; Messrs. Spottiswoode and Messrs. Clowes always used *grey*; other eminent printing firms had no fixed rule. Many correspondents said that they used the two forms with a difference of meaning or application: the distinction most generally recognized being that *grey* denotes a more delicate or a lighter tint than *gray*. Others considered the difference to be that *gray* is a 'warmer' colour, or that it has a mixture of red or brown (cf. also the quot. under 1 c below). In the twentieth century, *grey* has become the established spelling in the U.K., whilst *gray* is standard in the United States. There seems to be nearly absolute unanimity as to the spelling of 'The Scots *Greys*', 'a pair of *greys*'. As the word is both etymologically and phonetically one, it is undesirable to treat its graphic forms as differing in signification.]

A. *adj.*

1. a. The adjective denoting the colour intermediate between black and white, or composed of a mixture of black and white with little or no positive hue; ash-coloured, lead-coloured.

Said of sea, sky, and cloud when not illuminated by the sun.

a **1000** *Cædmon's Gen.* 2865 (Gr.) Ac hine se halᵹa wer gyrde grǽᵹan sweorde. *a* **1000** *Boeth. Metr.* v. 8 Oft smylte sæ suðerne wind, grǽᵹe glashlutre, grimme ᵹedrefeð. *c* **1000** ÆLFRIC *Saints' Lives* II. 324 þa læᵹ se grǽᵹa wulf þe bewiste þæt heafod. *a* **1300** *Cursor M.* 9886 þis castel..It es hei sett a-pon þe crag, Grai [*Gött.* Gray] and hard. *a* **1400–50** *Alexander* 1330 He mas to graue sum in grete & sum in gray marble. **1527** ANDREW *Brunswyke's Distyll. Waters* F ij b, It is rede that the graye water snakes engendreth them with the eale. **1590** SPENSER *F.Q.* I. ii. 28 Two goodly trees..did spred Their armes abroad, with gray mosse overcast. **1597** SHAKS. *2 Hen. IV*, II. iii. 19 It stucke vpon him, as the Sunne In the gray vault of Heauen. **1817** COLERIDGE *Sibyll. Leaves* (1862) 274 The night is chill, the cloud is gray. **1857** WILLMOTT *Pleas. Lit.* xi. 49 A coarse coat of gray cloth. **1874** BLACKIE *Self-Cult.* 14 Ask yourself..not what you saw printed on a gray page, but what you see pictured in the glowing gallery of your imagination.

β. *a* **700** *Epinal Gloss.* 473 *Glaucum*, heuui *vel* grei. *c* **725** *Ags. Voc.* in Wr.-Wülcker 21 *Feruginius*, greiȝ. *a* **1225** *Ancr. R.* 12 Her inne is religiun & nout iþe wide hod..ne iðe greȝe kuuele. *c* **1250** *Gen. & Ex.* 1723 Sep or got, haswed, arled, or grei, Ben don fro iacob fer a-wei. *c* **1315** SHOREHAM 145 Sonne and mone and sterren greyȝe. **1466** *Paston Lett.* No. 549 II. 270 For grey lynen cloth and sylk frenge for the hers. **1576** TURBERV. *Venerie* 184 As touching their heare they have a grey coate..waxyng greyer and greyer the elder that they bee. **1662** J. DAVIES tr. *Olearius' Voy. Ambass.* 207 Clad in a grey Garment. **1724** DE FOE *Mem. Cavalier* (1840) 237, I had pistols under my grey frock. **1820** BYRON *Mar. Fal.* IV. ii, The air puts on A morning freshness..The sea looks greyer. **1821** CRAIG *Lect. Drawing* iii. 184 Your next proceeding will be to insert the grey tints. **1841** BROWNING *Pippa* Introd. 209 Down the grass path grey with dew. **1882** OUIDA *Maremma* I. 178 The plain grew yellower and the sky greyer. **1884** *West. Daily Press* 17 Dec. 3/5 Capes of curled Crimean lamb—so often called grey astrakan.

Proverb. **1546** J. HEYWOOD *Prov.* v. (1874) 22 When all candles bee out all cats be gray. [**1605** SHAKS. *Lear* III. vi. 47 (Qos. 1-2) Pur the cat is gray.] *a* **1700** in B. E. *Dict. Cant. Crew*, s.v. *Joan*. **1809** E. S. BARRETT *Setting Sun* I. 80 All Cats are grey in the dusk.

b. with prefixed word indicating some particular shade of grey, as *dark*, *light*, *sad*, *silver*, *slatey*, *whitish*, etc.; cf. B. 4 b; also DAPPLE-GREY, IRON-GREY.

a **1000** ÆLFRIC *Voc.* in Wr.-Wülcker 163/25 *Elbus*, deorce-græȝ. **1799** G. SMITH *Laboratory* II. 311 Dubbing of the down of a sad grey cat. **1843** MACAULAY *Lays Anc. Rome, Battle Regillus* xi, High on a gallant charger Of dark-grey hue he rode. **1859** SEMPLE *Diphtheria* 272 Thin elastic layers, of a whitish-grey colour. **1883** *Truth* 31 May 747/1 A very becoming gown of silver-grey surah.

¶ **c.** (See quot.)

1885 *Field's Chromatography* iii. 38 *note*, The distinction between grey and gray should be carefully observed. Grey is composed only of black and white; the term gray is applied to any broken colour of a cool hue, and therefore belongs to the class of chromatic colours.

2. Epithet: (*a*) of the Cistercian monks; (*b*) of the Franciscan friars; (*c*) of the sisters of the third order of St. Francis, on account of the colour of their habits. See also GREY FRIAR.

c **1290** *S. Eng. Leg.* I. 149. 1497 Greye Monekes of Cisteos. **1297** R. GLOUC. (Rolls) 9072 Vor þe ordre of greye monekes þoru him me broȝte Verst here in to engelond. *c* **1300** *Beket* 1228 Tuelf myle he ȝeode grete ynouȝ to a grei abbeye, That me clipeþ Clermareys, of greye monekes. **1567** *Gude & Godlie Ballatis* (S.T.S.) 205 The Sisteris gray, befoir this day, Did crune within thair cloister. *a* **1596** in Shaks. *Tam. Shr.* IV. i. 148 It was the Friar of Orders gray. **1796** MARY ROBINSON *Angelina* III. 24 The grey sisters were endowed with five hundred marks a year, to say masses for the souls of the unhappy lovers. *a* **1832** SCOTT *Grey Brother* xxvi, He..there was aware of a Grey Friar..'Now, Christ thee save!' said the Grey Brother.

3. Of the eyes: Having a grey iris.

α. *a* **1310** in Wright *Lyric P.* 39 Gret hire wel, that swete thyng, with eȝenen gray. *c* **1420** *Anturs of Arth.* 599 (Ireland MS.) Dame Gaynour, with hur gray een. **1548** HALL *Chron., 3 Rich. III* (1809) 416 His eyes gray shynynge and quicke. **1611** COTGR. s.v. *Verd*, *Oeil verd*, a gray eye.

β. *c* **1386** CHAUCER *Reeve's T.* 54 This wenche thikke and wel ygrowen was, With kamuse nose and eyen greye as glas. *a* **1440** *Sir Eglam.* 861 Hys eyen grey was crystalle stone. **1591** SHAKS. *Two Gent.* IV. iv. 197 Her eyes are grey as glasse. [MALONE in Shaks. *Wks.* 1821 IV. 118 By a *grey* eye was meant what we now call a *blue* eye.] **1891** E. PEACOCK *N. Brendon* II. 42 Keen, searching, grey eyes.

4. a. Of a horse: Having a grey coat.

α. **1380** in *Test. Karl.* (1893) 143, J equum graye. **1398** TREVISA *Barth. De P.R.* XVIII. xxxix. (1495) 800 The colour in horses is now redde now blacke now whyte now graye now dyuers. **1590** SPENSER *F.Q.* II. i. 18 But under him a gray steede he did wield. **1601** SHAKS. *Twel. N.* III. iv. 315 Ile giue him my horse, gray Capilet. **1897** *Times* 17 Feb. 8/2 The intended reorganization..will not prevent the Scots Greys retaining their gray horses.

β. **1390-1** *Earl Derby's Exped.* (Camden) 5 Edmundo Bugge pro j equo grey. **1595** *Nottingham Rec.* IV. 62 Unus equus juvencus, coloris grey et baye. **1843** MACAULAY *Lays Anc. Rome, Battle Regillus* xxviii, Horses black and grey. **1865** TROLLOPE *Belton Est.* vii. 73 An old grey horse.

b. Proverb. ***the grey mare is the better horse***: the wife rules the husband. Hence, in allusion to this proverb, simply ***the grey mare***: the wife who rules her husband.

1546 J. HEYWOOD *Prov.* (1867) 52 The grey mare is the better hors. *c* **1645** HOWELL *Lett.* I. IV. ix, To suffer the Gray-mare sometimes to be the better Horse. **1700** R. CROMWELL *Let.* in *Eng. Hist. Rev.* (1898) XIII. 117 Shee tells him (as being the gray mare) he could not goe. **1726** *Adv. Capt. R. Boyle* 2 She began to tyrannize over my Master,..and soon prov'd, as the Saying is, The grey Mare to be the better Horse. **1847** TENNYSON *Princ.* v. 441 The gray mare Is ill to live with, when her whinny shrills From tile to scullery. **1876** MISS YONGE *Womankind* xxii. 183 The grey-mare may keep down the husband who chose her,..but she cannot restrain her growing-up sons.

5. a. Used to describe the dull or cold light of twilight, or of a day when the sky is overclouded.

α. *a* **1400-50** *Alexander* 2044 Begynnys sone in þe gray day as any gleme springis. *c* **1401** LYDG. *Flour Curtesye* 9 The same tyme, I herde a larke singe Ful lustely, agayn the morowe gray. **1526** *Pilgr. Perf.* (W. de W. 1531) 85 Lyke as the gray mornynge breketh & spryngeth before ye presence of the sonne. **1860** TYNDALL *Glac.* I. ii. 19 In the gray light of the evening.

β. *c* **1380** WYCLIF *Serm.* Sel. Wks. II. 145 Eerli and in þe grey day Camen wymmen to se þe sepulcre. **1730** T. BOSTON *Mem.* 286 It was a grey day with some pleasant blinks. **1780** COWPER *Progr. Err.* 82 Grey dawn appears. **1816** BYRON *Prisoner Chillon* ix, For all was blank, and bleak, and grey, It was not night—it was not day. **1870** E. PEACOCK *Ralf Skirl.* III. 86 In the grey twilight. **1898** *Mag. Art* Feb. 212 Those [painters]..for whom Nature is only at her best on a nice grey day.

b. *fig.* Not bright or hopeful; dismal, gloomy; sad, depressing; esp. in phr. *to go a grey gate* (dial.). *spec.* Of a person: dull, anonymous, 'faceless'. Cf. *sb.* 5 c.

1721 KELLY *Scot. Prov.* 380 You'll gang a gray Gate yet..you will come to an ill End. **1783-94** BLAKE *Songs Innoc., Earth's Answer* 6 Her locks cover'd with grey despair. **1820** *Blackw. Mag.* June 281 Its a sad and sair pity to behold youthfu' blood gaun a gate sae gray. **1846** BROCKETT *N.C. Words* (ed. 3), He has gane a grey gate. **1871** J. CAIRD *Univ. Serm.* (1898) i. 12 The solace of a life perhaps hard and grim and grey. **1874** BLACKIE *Self-Cult.* 44 The student who stays at home, and learns in a gray way only from books. **1884** E. LYALL *We Two* xxxii, Those were grey years, Erica. **1967** [see *sb.* 5 c]. **1969** *Times* 8 Aug. 3/3 The identity of these grey men of politics should be revealed. **1969** *Sunday Times* (Colour Suppl.) 9 Nov. 80/3 Oh no, it's no myth. When he leaves university he is often very, very grey. **1969** *Gandalf's Garden* IV. 22/2 What about the Universities? (Surely ranking among Britain's most proficient and prolific in the churning out of grey people.)

c. Used in various collocations in the place of *black* to indicate a less extreme form of the activity, object, etc. See also *grey market*, *grey-out* (8 a below).

1966 *Punch* 14 Dec. 900/2 *A Hero of Modern Industry*..could, I suppose, be described as a grey rather than a black comedy, on the grounds that no one actually gets killed. **1967** *Economist* 29 Apr. 487/3 The grey list..cannot strictly be defined as a banned list, but the Ministry of Health has drawn up for doctors' guidance, ten pages of drugs..that it would prefer them not to prescribe. **1970** *Guardian* 26 Mar. 26/4 As for the over-prescribing doctors, it was not just the black sheep we had to worry about. It was the grey sheep too.

6. a. Of the hair or beard: That is turning white (as with age or grief).

This use is of somewhat late appearance in Eng., but now one of the most prominent applications of the word.

α. **13..-1440** [see GREY-HAIRED *a.*]. **1535** COVERDALE *Prov.* xx. 29 A gray heade, is an honoure vnto the aged. **1581** MARBECK *Bk. of Notes* 60 Like an olde man in a graie beard. *a* **1631** DONNE *Poems* (1650) 8 When with my browne, my gray haires equall be. **1769** *Junius Lett.* xxiii. 112 Can gray hairs make folly venerable?

β. **1577** STANYHURST *Descr. Irel.* iv. 39 in *Holinshed*, In which well such as loath greie heares are accustomed to diue. **1599** SHAKS. *Much Ado* V. i. 65, I..with grey haires and bruise of many daies, Do challenge thee. **1653** R. SANDERS *Physiogn.* 169 Hairs, black, red, flaxen, and white or grey. **1725** WATTS *Logic* II. iii. §2 Remember that a grey Beard does not make a Philosopher. **1797** SOUTHEY *K. Charlemain* xviii, [He] kiss'd his long grey grizzle beard. **1816** BYRON *Prisoner of Chillon* 1 My hair is grey, but not with years. **1883** *Gd. Words* 640 His grizzled hair was greyer.

b. Of a person: Having grey hair; grey-haired.

α. *c* **1483** CAXTON *Dialogues* (E.E.T.S.) 44/24 He may no more for age; he is alle graye. **1626** BACON *Sylva* §739 Divers with us that are grown Gray. **1784** COWPER *Task* II. 633 We grow early gray, but never wise.

β. **1596** SHAKS. *1 Hen. IV*, II. iv. 499 That grey Iniquitie, that Father Ruffian. **1742** YOUNG *Nt. Th.* II. 386 Who knows not this, tho' Grey, is still a Child. **1855** PRESCOTT *Philip II*, I. I. v. 64 He had grown grey in the service of the court. **1865** KINGSLEY *Herew.* xv. 196 He had got somewhat greyer in the last ten years. **1898** J. HUTCHINSON *Archives Surg.* IX. No. 36. 343 He was a thin grey man.

c. *fig.* Also, ancient, old.

1662 GLANVILL *Lux Orient.* i. (1682) 2 If..this Grey Dogma clear all doubts. **1742** SHENSTONE *Schoolmistress* 95 Herbs for use, and physic, not a few Of grey renown. **1814** SCOTT *Ld. of Isles* IV. vii, Mac-Kinnon's chief, in warfare grey. **1826** LAMB *Elia* Ser. II. *Pop. Fallacies*, Our spirits showed grey before our hairs. **1842** MIALL in *Nonconf.* II. 249 [The state-church's] errors and superstitions are venerably grey.

d. Belonging to old age; hence (of advice, experience, etc.), mature.

α. **1602** MARSTON *Antonio's Rev.* IV. v, I tell thee, youth, age knows, yong loues seeme grac't, Which with gray cares, rude iarres, are oft defac't. **1627-47** FELTHAM *Resolves* I. 200 The Macedonian proved himself a better Physician for calumny by his bounties; than his Philosophers by their gray advisements. **1693** T. CREECH in *Dryden's Juvenal* xiii. (1697) 322 When sixty Years have spread Their gray Experience o'er thy hoary Head! **1874** L. MORRIS *Song Two W.* Ser. II. ii, Gray wisdom comes with time and age.

β. **1775** SHERIDAN *Rivals* 2nd Prol., Is grey experience suited to her youth? **1866** RUSKIN *Crown Wild Olive* Pref. 33 This..you may win, while yet you live; type of grey honour, and sweet rest.

e. Of a person: white-skinned. *U.S. Black slang.* Cf. *sb.* 5 b.

1962 *Times Lit. Suppl.* 21 Sept. 706/3 The 'grey boys', as Mr. Simmons calls white men. **1965** E. LACY *Moment of Untruth* iv. 69 Funny thing with grey chicks... They're always so sure their white skin is the sexiest ever. *Ibid.* vii. 112, I appreciate your socking that lousy grey dick.

7. General combinations: **a.** qualifying the names of other colours, as ***grey-black***, ***-brindled***, ***-brown***, ***-green***, ***-white***, etc. Also GREY-BLUE.

1796 WITHERING *Brit. Plants* (ed. 3) IV. 63 Foliage grey brown. *Ibid.* 269 Gills watery white changing to grey green. **1804** COLERIDGE *Lett.* (1895) 482 Nothing green meets your eye—one dreary grey-white. **1839** BAILEY *Festus* vii. (1848) 74 Gray-green oaks. **1849** D. CAMPBELL *Inorg. Chem.* 329 Glucina, or its compounds..become grey-black. **1891** *Daily News* 3 Dec. 5/1 Our wild cat..was a fine, powerful animal, grey brindled.

b. parasynthetic and instrumental, as ***grey-boughed***, ***-breasted***, ***-cheeked***, ***-clad***, ***-coloured***, ***-crowned***, ***-faced***, ***-girdled***, ***-gowned***, ***-hooded***, ***-moustached***, ***-nebbed***, ***-seeded***, ***-slated***, ***-sloped***, ***-speckled***, ***-streaken***, ***-tinted***, ***-winged***.

1844 W. BARNES *Poems Dorset Dial.* 122 The *grey-boughed withy's a-leanen lowly. **1752** SIR J. HILL *Hist. Anim.* 480 The *grey-breasted and reddish-breasted Charadrius. **1893** B. TORREY *Footpath-Way* 94 The evergreens immediately about the house were full of *gray-cheeked thrushes. **1895** *Century Mag.* Aug. 499/1 *Gray-clad, white-bonneted sisters of charity. **1530** PALSGR. 314/1 *Gray coloured as ones eyes be, *vair*. **1883** STEVENSON *Treas. Isl.* III. xiii, Grey-coloured woods. **1852** S. F. BAIRD in H. Stansbury *Exped. Valley Gt. Salt Lake* 317 (*heading*) Leucosticte Tephrocotis,..*Gray-crowned Finch. **1945** BAKER *Austral. Lang.* xii. 211 The Grey-crowned Babbler is known also as apostle-bird, [etc.]. **1830** MARY HOWITT in *W. Howitt's Seasons* (1837) 137 The *grey-faced mountain-sheep. **1821** CLARE *Vill. Minstr.* I. 9 *Grey-girdled eve, and morn of rosy hue. **1591** *Troub. Raigne K. John* (1611) 50 *Gray-gown'd good face, coniure ye, Nere trust me for a groat. **1634** MILTON *Comus* 188 The *gray-hooded Ev'n Like a sad Votarist in Palmers weeds Rose from the hindmost wheels of Phœbus waine. **1866** HOWELLS *Venet. Life* xviii. 273 The *gray-moustached papa. **1870** MORRIS *Earthly Par.* III. IV. 85 And o'er the wrack of Senlac field Full fed the *grey-nebbed raven wheeled. *Ibid.* II. III. 46 The long *grey-seeded grass. **1897** J. C. HODGSON *Hist. Northumbld.* IV. 55 The old *grey-slated house. **1870** MORRIS *Earthly Par.* II. III. 506 That sad fight within the *grey-sloped vale. **1895** A. NUTT in Meyer *Voy. Bran* I. 155 Steeds with *grey-speckled manes. **1854** R. S. SURTEES *Handley Cross* (1898) I. 148 *Grey-streaken locks. **1870** MISS BRIDGMAN *Ro. Lynne* I. vii. 106 That's what makes life appear so dull and *gray-tinted to me. **1899** *Edin. Rev.* Jan. 43 Her twin footprints are *grey-winged pigeons.

c. complemental, as ***grey-grown***, ***-lit***, ***-mouldering*** adjs.

1727-46 THOMSON *Summer* 225 The daw, The rook, and magpie, to the *grey-grown oaks..direct their lazy flight. *a* **1881** ROSSETTI *House of Life* viii, Thine eyes *grey-lit in shadowing hair above. **1740** DYER *Ruins Rome* 33 Globose and huge, *Grey-mouldring Temples swell.

8. a. Special collocations, as **grey area** (see quot. 1968); **grey band** (see quot.); **grey bark**, a variety of Peruvian bark (see BARK *sb.*[1] 7); also *attrib.*; **grey box**, an Australian tree, esp. *Eucalyptus moluccana*; **grey bread** *Sc.*, 'bread made of rye; perhaps also, of oats' (Jam.); **grey cells** *colloq.* = *grey matter*; **grey cloth**, unbleached cloth; **grey eminence** = ÉMINENCE GRISE; **grey-frieze**, frieze of a grey colour; hence ***grey-friezed*** adj., made of grey frieze; **grey goods** (see quots.); **grey groat**, an emphatic equivalent of *groat*; also used as the type of something of little value (cf. *brass farthing*, BRASS *sb.* 7); **grey leaf** = *grey speck*; **greymail** *colloq.* (*U.S. Law*) [after BLACKMAIL], (a ploy involving) a threat by the defence, esp. in a spy trial, to expose government secrets unless charges are dropped; **grey market**, a less extreme form of black market; **grey matter**, the grey-coloured matter of which the active part of the brain is composed; also *fig.*; **grey meal**, the refuse and sweepings of a meal-mill; dirty meal (Jam.); **grey millet** = GRAYMILL, GROMWELL (in Cassell 1882); **grey oak**, any of several American oaks, esp. *Quercus coccinea* or *Q. borealis*; **grey oil**, olive oil and lanolin containing mercury; **grey-out** *Aeronaut.*, a less severe form of black-out; so **grey-out** *v. intr.*, to suffer a 'grey-out'; also **greying-out** *vbl. sb.*; **grey paper**, ? an unbleached paper, used chiefly for wrapping (in some dialects now = *brown paper*); also, a grey-tinted drawing paper; **grey parson** (see quot.: cf. *grey-coat(ed parson)*); **grey pea** (see PEA); **grey pine**, either of two North American pines, *Pinus banksiana* or *P. sabiniana*; †**grey plack** *Sc.*, a plack containing an alloy of silver; **grey powder** (see quot. 1866); also *attrib.*; **grey russet** (see quot. *a* 1825); **grey scale** (see quot. 1959); also *attrib.*; **grey school** (see quot.); **grey slag** (see quot.); **grey sour, souring**, in *Bleaching*, the process of immersing cloth in dilute acid; **grey speck**, a disease in oats caused by a manganese deficiency and characterized by specks on the leaf-blades; **grey steep**, a steep or bath used in the process of *grey souring*; **grey stock** (see quot. 1852, and cf. GRIZZLE *sb.*[3]); **grey wethers** (see quots.); **grey willow**, one of several willow trees or bushes with grey foliage or down, esp. *Salix sericea* or *S. cinerea*; **grey wood** (see quot. 1934).

1963 *Times* 22 May 9/3 Within urban areas Mr. Wates said there were vast '*grey' areas—he mentioned Fulham, Battersea and Islington—which could not be classified as slums but were in need of rebuilding. **1968** *Guardian* 18 Mar. 8/1 The 'grey areas'—the term now often used for parts of the country which are in poor or declining economic health, but not so dramatically stricken..[as] the development areas. **1970** *Daily Tel.* 9 Apr. 21/4 Local authorities in administrative counties which include development areas and intermediate ('grey') areas will be able to borrow up to 50 p.c. of their capital finance needs from the Public Works Loans Board in 1970–1971. 1828 *Amer. Jrnl. Sci. & Arts* XIV. 366 Saliferous Rock.. Subdivisions.—..*Grey-band, the uppermost layers of bluish grey sandrock. 1863 DANA *Man. Geol.* 232 Flagstone, —a gray, laminated quartzose sandstone, called 'gray band'. 1837 *Penny Cycl.* VII. 172/1 Of the pale [Cinchona] barks, three varieties are known in English commerce..2 *Gray, silver, or Huanuco bark. 1880 C. R. MARKHAM *Peruv. Bark* 228 At Huanuco, a town on the verge of the grey bark region. 1879 F. VON MUELLER *Eucalyptographia* I, The tree [sc. *E. goniocalyx*] passes among the woodmen as Blue and White Gum-tree, in the other case as *Grey or Bastard Box. 1884 A. NILSON *Timber Trees N.S.W.* 136 *Grey box*, Eucalyptus saligna. Myrtaceæ. 1944 F. CLUNE *Red Heart* 51 Colson noted the grey box and whitewood trees became sparser. 1969 *Age* (Melbourne) 24 May 24/5 The estate is natural bushland crowded with grey box, [etc.]. 1535 STEWART *Cron. Scot.* III. 476 Wes nane that tyme that durst so hardy be..to mak him remeid, Or him support with ane byte of *gra breid. 1606 ROLLOCK *2 Thess.* xvi. 201 He is the honester man that will..sit down with gray bread conquest by his labour, nor he who eates all dilicates with idlenesse. 1920 A. CHRISTIE *Mysterious Affair at Styles* x. 226 'This affair must all be unravelled from within.' He tapped his forehead. 'These little *grey cells. It is "up to them"—as you say over here!' 1960 WODEHOUSE *Jeeves in Offing* iii. 38 You can't hold down an editorial post on an important London weekly paper without being fairly well fixed with the little grey cells. 1930 *Aberdeen Press & Jrnl.* 1 Apr. 8/4 Plain *greycloth—that is, unbleached cloth, or cloth dyed in the piece. 1959 *Listener* 9 July 46/2 The weavers manufacture, from the yarn, cloth in an unfinished state, known as grey cloth. 1968 Grey cloth [see *grey goods* below]. 1941 A. HUXLEY (*title*) *Grey Eminence. 1945 R. HARGREAVES *Enemy at Gate* 151 Bismarck's 'grey eminence', the enigmatic Holstein. 1956 F. SWINNERTON *Background with Chorus* 78 The parts played by men not visibly figuring in 'movements'—the grey eminences whose unpublished efforts give new ideas currency and new authors, or old authors, great places in literature. 1965 *Listener* 21 Oct. 614/1 That grey eminence of British communism Mr Palme Dutt. *a* 1653 GOUGE *Comm. Heb.* xi. 37 In wearing shirts of hair, *Gray-freeze, or other like course raiments. 1650–66 WHARTON *Wks.* (1683) 350 The glittering Tissue, and the *gray-friz'd Gown. 1954 *Textile Terms & Defs.* 21 **Grey goods*, woven or knitted fabrics as they leave the loom or knitting machine, i.e. before any bleaching, dyeing, or finishing treatment has been given to them. 1968 J. IRONSIDE *Fashion Alphabet* 231 *Grey cloth* or *goods*, woven fabric before it is dyed or printed. 1587 HARRISON *England* II. ii. (1877) I. 63 Of thise portion poore saint Peter did neuer heare, of so much as one *graie grote. *c* 1592 MARLOWE *Jew of Malta* IV. iv, I'll not leave him worth a grey groat. 1820 SCOTT *Abbot* iv, I would have been his caution for a grey groat against salt water or fresh. 1928 F. T. BROOKS *Plant Dis.* ii. 15 On some alkaline soils oats cannot be grown profitably on account of a disease known as *Grey-leaf. 1973 M. PEI *Double Speak in Amer.* 66 '*Graymail'..is summarized by psychiatry professor Ray Birdwhistell based on the principle 'I will do something bad to you if you do something bad to me.' 1978 *Washington Post* 1 Nov. A14/2 A recent study by the Senate Intelligence Committee recommended substantial changes in court procedure to cope with this problem (as well as others that arise in 'graymail' cases) by permitting wider use of secret hearings. 1985 *N.Y. Times* 1 Apr. A21/1 The indictment was originally blocked because the department wanted to be sure that no 'greymail'—threats to expose national secrets—would be used in the defense. 1946 *Life* 1 Apr. 32/1 In the Rocky Mountain region there is a *gray market in toilet paper. 1952 *Economist* 15 Nov. 451/1 My own experience is that the effect of the grey or black market is grossly exaggerated by the Ministry's estimate of 50 per cent of home production. 1963 *Listener* 14 Feb. 275/2 In the countryside there is a gigantic grey market where the collective farms get together to defeat the demands of the state [*sc.* Czechoslovakia]. 1969 *Times* 16 July 9/6 It was suggested that instead of the grey market where a few doctors deliberately overprescribed [heroin] and addicts sold off their surplus supplies there would be a..black market. 1840 G. ELLIS *Anat.* 45 The *grey matter of the third ventricle entirely conceals the crus of the fornix. 1894 A. ROBERTSON *Nuggets*, etc. 33 These..thoughts rushed over the grey matter of Bill's brain, as the wind rushes through the tree-tops. 1897 MARY KINGSLEY *W. Africa* 673 Whether he does this by adding convolutions or piling up his gray matter we will leave for the present. 1647 in *Laird of Logan* (1878) 578 [A man was called before the Presbytery for calling his minister's doctrines] Dust and *Gray Meal. 1697 *Rec. Early Hist. Boston* (1880) VI. 8 From thence to another wallnut tree and so straight to a *gray oak. 1813 H. MUHLENBERG *Catal. Plant.* 87 Upland willow-oak, or gray oak. 1832 D. J. BROWNE *Sylva Amer.* 261 The Gray Oak is found farther north than any other species in America. 1908 N. L. BRITTON *N. Amer. Trees* 290 Gray Oak—*Quercus borealis*. 1908 *Practitioner* Sept. 467 The use of *grey-oil in subcutaneous injections. 1945 *Reader's Digest* May 43/2 Formerly a pilot had only two chances:..or go in all the way and turn sharply, incurring enough G to *grayout or blackout. 1946 A. M. LOW *How Secrets Work* 153 The first noticeable effect is a 'grey-out' due to a reduced pressure on the capillaries at the back of the eye. 1956 J. E. JOHNSON *Wing Leader* iii. 44 The Spit protests and shudders, and when the blood drains from your eyes you 'grey-out'. 1962 W. SCHIRRA in *Into Orbit* 46 When a man is pulling heavy Gs in the normal sitting position, the blood drains down from his head, and he can have a grey-out or a black-out. 1961 *New Scientist* 25 May 457/3 At slightly lower *g*, the individual experiences *greying-out: there is an overall dimming of vision and loss of peripheral vision. 1549 BALE *Journ. & Serche of Leylande* Pref. B i b, Thys stuffe [the contentes of two noble lybraryes] hath he occupyed in the stede of *graye paper. 1600 NASHE *Summer's Last Will* B 4 An other that ranne in det..aboue foureteene thousand pound in lute strings and gray paper. 1878 RUSKIN *Notes* 50 The material used by Turner in his drawings on grey paper. 1784 SIR J. CULLUM *Hist. Hawsted* iii. 171 A *Grey parson, a layman, who hires the tithes of the parson. 1810 F. A. MICHAUX *Arbres* I. 16 *Pinus rupestris*... *Grey pine.., dénomination donnée..en Canada. 1832 D. J. BROWNE *Sylva Amer.* 240 In Nova Scotia and the state of Maine, where it is rare, it is called Scrub Pine, and in Canada, Gray Pine. 1908 N. L. BRITTON *N. Amer. Trees* 37 This tree [sc. *Pinus sabiniana*], also called Gray pine..occurs locally in the foothill region of western California. 1923 L. H. BAILEY *Cultivated Evergreens* iii. 103 The gray pine, *Pinus Banksiana*, is found farther northward than any other American pine. 1956 B. R. MORTON *Native Trees of Canada* (ed. 5) 16 Banksian pine [is also called] grey pine. 1591 *Sc. Acts Jas. VI* (1814) III. 526/2 For all vther allayed money, quhilk is subiect to refyning, as babeis, thre penny grottis, twelf penny grottis, and *gray plakkis. 1842 C. RIDLEY *Let.* 4 Dec. (1958) ix. 111 Baby is not quite well. I consulted Sir John Fife, who gave him *grey powder. 1866 SQUIRE *Comp. Med. Chest* 18 Grey Powder. *Hydrargyrum cum Creta*... A mild mercurial. 1883 D. J. LEECH in *Encycl. Brit.* XVI. 34/2 Grey powder..consists..of mercury and chalk. 1897 J. HUTCHINSON *Archives Surg.* VIII. No. 31. 220 The grey-powder pill..he regards as a tonic. 1377 LANGL. *P. Pl.* B. xv. 162 A goune of a *graye russet. *a* 1529 SKELTON *E. Rummyng* 54 In her furred flocket, And gray russet rocket. *a* 1825 FORBY *Voc. E. Anglia*, *Grey-russet*, coarse cloth of a dull grey colour, commonly preceded by the epithet *dandy*. 1940 *Chambers's Techn. Dict.* 389/2 *Grey scale. 1957 V. J. KEHOE *Technique Film & T.V. Make-Up* i. 23 (*caption*) The Gray Scale. Diagrammatic representation of gradation from white to black, the in-between shades being tones of gray. 1959 W. S. SHARPS *Dict. Cinematogr.* 101/1 *Grey scale*, a graduated range of tones extending from white to black, with intermediate greys consisting of intermixed white and black. 1961 G. MILLERSON *Technique Telev. Production* iii. 45 (*caption*) Sample paint-cards and materials are compared on camera with a standard grey-scale chart. 1968 *Brit. Med. Bull.* XXIV. 262/2 The grey scale is a graded series of densities from transparent (white) to black. 1804 R. GRAHAM *Fisherm. Let. to Propriet. Fisheries Solway* 8 (Jam.) Those too, it is probable, spawn sooner than the last and largest species, called the *Grey Scool, which appear in the Solway and rivers about the middle of July. 1853 URE *Dict. Arts* (ed. 4) II. 653 Those [lumps of partly-fused ore] which are so far agglutinated by the heat, as to be quite hard, and further known by their brightness, being picked out.. They are called '*grey slags'. 1875 J. PATON in *Encycl. Brit.* III. 816/2 *Gray Sour. 1844 G. DODD *Textile Manuf.* ii. 51 The process of '*grey souring', in which the cloth passes through a machine..containing very dilute sulphuric acid. 1928 *Jrnl. Dept. Agric. S. Austral.* XXXI. VII. 696 (*title*) *Grey speck (manganese deficiency) disease of oats... For many years the Grey Speck disease of oats has been known to occur on certain alkaline soils in Holland, Norway, Sweden, Denmark, and Germany. *Ibid.* 704 In the pots treated with nitrate of soda and cyanamide the Grey Speck symptoms were worst. 1929 *Ann. Appl. Biol.* XVI. 497 It does not seem to have been recognised that the symptoms of the Grey Speck disease are essentially the symptoms of manganese deficiency. 1947 *Sci. News* V. 88 Manganese is essential for healthy plant life. Its deficiency in soil..leads to plant diseases such as grey speck of oats. 1812–16 J. SMITH *Panorama Sci. & Art* II. 546 Bainbie, or *Gray Steep. 1793 *Misc.* in *Ann. Reg.* 378 The bricks called *greystocks, for the outside of houses. 1852–61 *Archit. Publ. Soc. Dict.*, *Grey stock*, a brick made of common earth and thoroughly burnt in a close clamp; it is so called to distinguish it from the place brick on the one hand, and the red stock or kiln burnt brick on the other. 1794 J. B. S. MORRITT *Let.* 13 Nov. (1914) vi. 143, I saw a hill covered with stones and *grey-wethers, but could not make out many of the foundations he mentions. 1835 *Penny Cycl.* III. 163/2 Detached oolitic sandstones of various sizes, known by the name of the Grey Wethers. 1863 LYELL *Antiq. Man* 137 Great blocks of hard sandstone of the kind called in the south of England 'grey-weathers'. 1895 *Murray's Devon* 138/1 The Grey Wethers—2 circles [of stones] which nearly touch each other, like the Cornish 'Hurlers'... These blocks are very like sheep, when seen from a little distance. 1813 H. MUHLENBERG *Catal. Plant.* 91 *Gray willow. 1861 *Trans. Ill. Agric. Soc.* IV. 448 Mr. Overman has the Pennsylvania Gray Willow—the most rapid growing variety he has ever known. 1930 J. E. KIRKWOOD *N. Rocky Mt. Trees & Shrubs* 88 The Gray Willow, so called in allusion to its covering of long gray hairs, is variously understood by various authors. 1951 *Dict. Gardening* (R. Hort. Soc.) IV. 1852/1 *S[alix] cinerea*. Grey Willow...almost wholly covered with grey down. 1933 *Times Educ. Suppl.* 15 Apr. 115/3 The former is faced with Indian silver *greywood. 1934 *Archit. Rev.* LXXVI. 70/1 Sycamore has also been used in decorative work and furniture, dyed and known as 'greywood' or steamed and known as 'weathered' sycamore. 1952 H. H. SAYLOR *Dict. Archit.* (1963) 79 *Greywood*,..used extensively in England for decorative woodwork and veneer.

b. In the names of animals, as **grey bass**, a sea-fish said to belong to the perch family, but to resemble the mullet in taste; **grey-bird**, a dial. name for (*a*) the thrush (*Turdus musicus*), (*b*) the linnet (*Linota cannabina*); **grey crow**, the Hooded Crow, *Corvus cornix* (cf. GREY-BACK 4); **grey dog**, the Scottish hunting dog (Jam.); **grey-drake**, a species of *Ephemera* (cf. *green-drake*); **grey duck**, the gadwall; **grey eagle** *U.S.*, 'a young golden eagle' (Funk's *Stand. Dict.*); **grey falcon**, (*a*) the hen-harrier (*Circus cyaneus*); (*b*) (see quot. 1847); **grey-fin**, a variety of trout found in the Tweed; **grey-fish**, (*a*) a local Sc. name for the COAL-FISH at a certain stage of its growth; (*b*) *U.S.* the common dogfish; **grey fly**, perhaps a dor-beetle; **grey fowl**, grouse when in its winter plumage; **grey-fox** (see quot. 1884–5); **grey-jumper** *Austral.* (see quot.); **grey linnet**, **lizard** (see LINNET, LIZARD); **grey lord** = *grey-fish*; **grey-midge** *Angling*, the name of an artificial fly; **grey mullet** (see MULLET); **grey-necked** *a.*, epithet of a group of crows, *esp.* the Hooded Crow, *Corvus cornix*; **grey nurse** *Austral.* (see quot.); **grey owl**, **parrot** (see the sbs.); **grey pate** (see quot.); **grey perch** *U.S.*, the fresh-water drum (see DRUM *sb.*[1] 11); †**grey pie** (see quot.); **grey pike** = HORN-FISH 2; **grey plover**, **sandpiper**, **seal**, **shark**, **shrike**, **skate**, **snail**, **snapper** (see the sbs.); **grey snake** (see quots.); **grey snipe**, 'the dowitcher in winter plumage' (Webster 1897); **grey squirrel** (see SQUIRREL); **grey trout** (see TROUT); **grey whale**, *Rhachianectes glaucus*; **grey wolf**, the common wolf, *Canis lupus*; also *fig.* (see quot. 1904).

1747 MRS. GLASSE *Cookery* xxi. 163 *Gray Bass comes with the Mullet. 1787 GROSE *Prov. Gloss.*, **Grey-bird*, a thrush. 1885 SWAINSON *Prov. Names Birds* 64 Linnet (*Linota cannabina*)... Grey: or Grey bird (Westmoreland; North of Ireland). From its dull colouring in winter. 1837 MACGILLIVRAY *Hist. Brit. Birds* I. 529 *Grey Crow. 1808 J. WALKER *Ess. Nat. Hist.* xiii. 475 Canis Scoticus venaticus. Gesn.—Scot. The *Grey Dog. 1787 BEST *Angling* (ed. 2) 26 *Grey-drake, Found in general where the Green-drake is, and in shape and dimensions perfectly the same, but almost quite another colour, being of a paler and more livid yellow. 1884 [see DRAKE[1] 4]. 1885 SWAINSON *Prov. Names Birds* 157 Gadwall..*Grey duck. 1688 *Grey Eagle [see EAGLE 1 b]. 1688 R. HOLME *Armoury* II. xi. 233/1 The *Grey Falcon.. The whole Body..is..Cinereous, tending to blew. 1802 G. MONTAGU *Ornith. Dict.* 230 Grey Falcon. A name for the Hen Harrier. 1847 CRAIG, *Grey-falcon*, the common or Peregrine Falcon. 1847 T. STODDART *Angler's Comp.* 210 The *grey-fin or bull-trout smolt. 1923 W. A. HERDMAN *Founders Oceanogr.* 310 People..are prejudiced against 'dog-fish', so the [United States] Bureau [of Fisheries] altered the name of the latter to 'gray-fish'. 1793 *Statist. Acc. Scot., Argylesh.* VIII. 92 A species of fish taken on this coast, which goes by the general name of *Grey fish. 1848 *Life Normandy* (1863) I. 283 It was some time before I knew that stainloch, grey-fish, seath, cudding, and poddly, were all one fish at different ages. 1637 MILTON *Lycidas* 27 What time the *gray fly winds her sultry horn. 1752 HILL *Hist. Anim.* 31 The grey Fly or trumpet Fly. 1864 THOREAU *Cape Cod* vii. (1894) 167 Probably he would not hear much of the 'gray-fly' on his way to Virginia. 1815 SCOTT *Guy M.* xxii, And for the moor-fowl, or the *grey-fowl, they lie as thick as doos in a dooket. 1887 *Pall Mall G.* 26 Nov. 5/1 In the full pride of the steely winter plumage the November grouse or grey-fowl seems to revel in conscious ability to outwit all enemies. 1781 PENNANT *Hist. Quadrup.* I. 241 *Grey fox. 1884–5 *Riverside Nat. Hist.* (1888) V. 411 The well-known species, the Gray Fox *V[ulpes] cinereo-argentatus*, shares the characters of the coast fox, but is larger. 1898 MORRIS *Austral English*, **Grey-jumper*, name given to an Australian genus of sparrow-like birds, of which the only species is *Struthidea cinerea*, Gould. 1698 MARTIN *Voy. St. Kilda* 30 The coast of St. Kilda, and the lesser Isles, are plentifully furnished with variety of..Cod, Ling..Turbat, *Graylords, Sythes. 1836 YARRELL *Brit. Fishes* II. 170 Among the Scotch islands the Coal-fish is called..Grey-Lord. 1799 G. SMITH *Laboratory* II. 311 *Grey-midge or gnat. 1866 R. C. BEAVAN in *Intell. Observ.* No. 50. 104 Corvus splendens (Viellot), the '*Grey-necked Crow' of some. 1894 R. B. SHARPE *Handbk. Birds Gt. Brit.* I. 12 Of the grey-necked section our Hooded Crow is the most familiar species. 1898 MORRIS *Austral English*, **Grey Nurse*, a New South Wales name for a species of Shark, *Odontaspis americanus*, Mitchell, family *Lamnidæ*, which is not confined to Australasia. 1917 *Chambers's Jrnl.* Sept. 589/2 The gray nurse, like the white shark, is noted for its daring ferocity. 1969 *Man* (Austral.) Mar. 12/2 There's even been grey nurse hooked here, and a blue marlin that had been hunted over from the deep-sea beds. 1766 PENNANT *Zool.* (1768) II. 304 The young bird [goldfinch] before it moults, is grey on the head; and hence it is termed by the bird-catchers a *grey pate. 1688 R. HOLME *Armoury* II. xi. 235/1 The Bucher Bird, or Shrike..This Bird is of some called..a *Grey Pie. 1863 J. G. WOOD *Nat. Hist.* III. 134 The *Grey Snake of Jamaica (*Dromicus ater*). 1884–5 *Riverside Nat. Hist.* (1888) III. 379 The genus *Diemenia* includes several Australian forms..The gray-snake *D. reticulata*..is uniformly gray above and greenish below. 1870 *Game Laws Penn.* in *Fur, Fin & Feather* (1872) 120 No person shall kill, capture, take ..any *gray snipe. 1860 *Merc. Marine Mag.* VII. 213 The California *Grey Whale. 1883 G. B. GOODE *Rev. Fish. Indust. U.S.* 62 The Pacific gray-whale, or devil-fish, *Rhachianectes glaucus*. 1814 LEWIS & CLARK *Hist. Exped. Missouri* (1815) I. 206 We caught..a large *gray wolf. 1831 J. M. PECK *Guide Emigrants* 162 The large grey wolf, or *canis lupus* of Linneus, is not very plenty. 1880 *Harper's Mag.* July 171/1 You will find bear and the great gray wolf..in the wilderness. 1904 *Grand Rapids Even. Press* 8 June 4 In plain words, a gray wolf, in Chicago phraseology, is a professional grafter. 1936 D. MCCOWAN *Anim. Canad. Rockies* iii. 30 The grey wolf, also known as timber wolf and formerly as buffalo wolf, is grey in colour with a liberal sprinkling of black and brown in the coat. 1964 E. P. WALKER et al. *Mammals of World* II. 1152/1 Two species of wolves are recognized: *C. lupus*, the gray or timber wolf, and *C. niger*, the red wolf.

c. In the names of minerals, etc., as **grey antimony** (see ANTIMONY 2); **grey (cast) iron**, cast iron that has a grey fracture and contains most of its carbon in the form of flakes of graphite; **grey cobalt** (see COBALT 1 b); **grey copper (ore)**, tetrahedrite; **grey ore**, chalcocite; **grey oxide**, 'black-turpeth' (*Cent. Dict.*); **grey tin**, a grey powdery allotrope of tin, to which ordinary (white) tin is converted at low temperatures; so **grey modification**.

1802 *Phil. Mag.* XII. 28 By increasing the dose of carbon you increase the fusibility, and it passes at length into the state of *gray cast iron. 1824 T. TREDGOLD *Pract. Ess. Strength of Cast Iron* (ed. 2) i. 7 Gray cast-iron is used for artillery, and is sometimes called gun-metal. 1880 *Encycl. Brit.* XIII. 281/2 A coarse-grained crystalline structure results, the product being then termed grey cast iron. 1967 *Times Rev. Industry* Mar. 76/1 High production costs amounting to over £98 per ton of grey cast iron. 1839 URE *Dict. Arts* 301 *Gray cobalt..is a compound of cobalt with iron, arsenic, sulphur, and nickel. 1836 MACGILLIVRAY tr. *Humboldt's Trav.* xxvi. 396 Most of it is obtained from sulphuretted silver, arsenical *gray-copper [etc.]. **1770** *Cronstedt's Min.* 192 Mineralized..with sulphur alone.. Grey copper-ore. **1665** D. DUDLEY *Metallum Martis* 47 The *Gray Iron..is most fined, and more sufficient to make Bar-Iron with, and tough Iron to make Ordnance, or any Cast Vessels, being it is..more malliable and tough, then the other two sorts. **1911** *Daily Colonist* (Victoria, B.C.) 28 Apr. 1/6 Fire..destroyed the blacksmith and forging shop, the machine shops and the Grey iron and brass founders. **1955** *Times* 15 July 2/6 Qualified Metallurgist preferably with experience with malleable and grey iron. **1965** *Economist* 23 Oct. p. xxii/2 Even a quick look at the processes of grey-iron castings—the type of iron used for the bulk of auto castings—shows up the fundamental differences. [**1879** *Jrnl. Chem. Soc.* XXXVI. 888 The grey modification of tin was found to be electronegative towards ordinary tin.] **1911** *Encycl. Brit.* XXIX. 996/2 When exposed for sufficient time to very low temperatures (to − 39°C for 14 hours), tin becomes so brittle that it falls into a grey powder, termed the **grey modification*. **1729** WOODWARD *Nat. Hist. Fossils* 181 A grey Marcasite..Another, very like the fore-going. It consists mainly of Sulphur and Arsenick, and seems to hold a little Bismuth. The Miners call this *Grey-Ore. From the Duke of Somerset's Works..Cumberland. **1809** A. HENRY *Trav.* 212, I found several veins of copper-ore, of that kind which the miners call gray ore. **1881** RAYMOND *Mining Gloss., Gray ore* (Corn.), copper-glance. **1886** *Jrnl. Chem. Soc.* L. 124 The author concludes that only the following allotropic modifications may be regarded as different:—*Grey tin..; rhombic tin..; and tetragonal tin. **1933** *Jrnl. R. Aeronaut. Soc.* XXXVII. 540 Tin shows a maximum ductility at about 100°C., and becomes increasingly brittle at lower temperatures, until, at 18°C., the change to its allotropic form, 'grey tin', commences. **1950** N. V. SIDGWICK *Chem. Elements* I. 552 The change from white to grey tin at low temperatures is very slow. **1965** PHILLIPS & WILLIAMS *Inorg. Chem.* I. iii. 67 The transition of diamond to graphite, which involves a profound change of structure, requires a total energy change per atom of as little as 0·02 eV as does the change of white to grey tin.

B. *sb.* **1. a.** Grey material or clothing.

c **1230** *Hali Meid.* 43 Ah under hwit oðer blac & ase wel vnder grei as under grene & gra ha [Pride] lukeð iþe heorte. *c* **1530** *Crt. of Love* 1096 O why be som so sorry and so sad, Complaining thus in blak and whyte and gray? Freres they ben, and monkes, in good fay. *c* **1590** GREENE *Fr. Bacon* iii. 69 Proportiond as was Paris, when, in grey, He courted Œnon in the vale by Troy. **1618** *Naworth Househ. Bks.* (Surtees) 100, v. yards of gray for Creak, at 16ᵈ a yard. **1640** tr. *Verdere's Rom. Rom.* III. 54 He espied a young Hermit in a long Gown of gray. **1832** G. DOWNES *Lett. Cont. Countries* I. 293 A blind old man, dressed in gray.

b. *techn.* Unbleached material; *spec.* see quot. 1884. (Cf. GREY-BACK 6.) Also phr. *in the grey*. (Cf. *grey cloth, grey goods* in sense A. 8.)

1860 S. JUBB *Hist. Shoddy-Trade* 40 Short Ends were sold to the merchants..in the grey. **1884** W. A. HARRIS *Dict. Insur. Chem.* (1890) 49 The greys' used under the pieces which were being printed were used until they had become ..loaded with colour. **1891** *Labour Commission* Gloss., *The grey* is a term used in the cotton and worsted trade to describe pieces of yarn or 'slubbing' as they come from the looms before going through any process of dyeing or finishing. **1929** *Times* 7 Feb. 9/3 There were thousands of piece goods coming into this country 'in the grey' to be dyed here.

attrib. **1844** G. DODD *Textile Manuf.* ii. 48 The cotton-cloth—is brought to the bleach-works, in the 'grey' state.

c. The uniform of the Southern troops in the American Civil War. *U.S.*

1863 *Rebellion Rec.* V. II. 72 An Irishman of the Seventeenth New-York came up to the General,..driving three prisoners in gray before him. **1866** J. C. GREGG *Life in Army* xviii. 172 They were refused admission..on the ground of their uniform; when if they had been dressed in rebel gray..no doubt they would have met with a warm welcome. **1886** F. C. BAYLOR *On Both Sides* II. viii. 429 A military society composed of men who had worn the gray. **1948** *Realty & Building* 15 May 11/2 Colonel John was a Johnny Reb who delighted in telling of the exploits of the boys in gray.

d. *pl.* Grey flannel trousers. Also (colloq.) *greyers* [see -ER⁶].

1900 J. S. FARMER *Public School Word-Bk.* 102 *Greyers*, (Harrow) Grey flannel trousers. **1923** *Daily Mail* 27 June 8 The jacket and waistcoat may be worn with 'greyers' or white flannel trousers, thus providing all the sports clothes the average man needs. **1932** A. J. WORRALL *Eng. Idioms* 22 I'll wear my greys for tennis to-day as the ground is rather slippery. **1948** D. W. BALLANTYNE *Cunninghams* (1963) II. xxiii. 226 A couple of..boys, wearing sports coats, greys, and open-necked white shirts.

†**2.** *spec.* Grey fur; usually understood to be of badger skin. (Cf. sense 6, also *gra* GRO, and ON. *gráskinn, grávara.*) *Obs.*

a **1200**–*c* **1314** [see FAW *a.* 2]. *a* **1400** *Sir Perc.* 2272 And made the lady in to ga, In graye and in grene. **1436** *Pol. Poems* (Rolls) II. 171 Peltre-ware, and grey, pych, terre [etc.]. *a* **1450** *Knt. de la Tour* (1868) 9 A mantell furred with graie. **1460** *Lybeaus Disc.* 839 A veluwet mantyll gay, Pelured wyth grys and gray. *c* **1483** CAXTON *Dialogues* (E.E.T.S.) 46/21 A pylche of graye [F. *vne pelice de vaire*]. **1525** LD. BERNERS *Froiss.* II. ccii. [cxcviii.] 622 Gownes of sylke furred with Myneuere and gray. **1702** J. CHAMBERLAYNE *St. Gt. Brit.* I. III. ii. (1707) 256 Of Furrs, Filches, Grays, Jennets..40 Skins in a Timber.

3. A grey or subdued light; the cold, sunless light of the morning or evening twilight; esp. in phr. *the grey of the morning*.

1592 SHAKS. *Rom. & Jul.* III. v. 19 Yon gray is not the mornings eye. **1599** —— *Much Ado* v. iii. 27 The gentle day ..Dapples the drowsie East with spots of grey. **1674–91** RAY *S. & E.C. Words* 101 The Gray of the Morning; Break of day, and from thence till it be clear light. **1719** DE FOE *Crusoe* I. ii. (1840) 20 Our ship..was surprised in the grey of the morning. **1844** LD. HOUGHTON *Palm Leaves* 138, I saw a Shape dark-lined against the gray. **1845** LONGF. *To Driving Cloud* 30 In the gray of the day-break. **1884** W. C. SMITH *Kildrostan* 79 The sober grey of our dim Highland glens. **1892** W. PIKE *North. Canada* 78 The first grey of dawn being the favourite time of attack.

4. a. Grey colour. In *pl.* = shades of grey colour. Also *fig.*

1825 J. NICHOLSON *Operat. Mechanic* 753 Various shades of grey may be obtained. **1873** SYMONDS *Gr. Poets* xii. 404 The colour of the olive tree is delicate. Its pearly greys and softened greens in no wise interfere with the lustre. **1892** ZANGWILL *Childr. Ghetto* I. 16 To blur the vivid tints of the East into the uniform gray of English middle-class life. *a* **1907** F. J. THOMPSON *Works* (1913) III. 218 The Englishman says, 'Black's black—*furieusement* black; and white's white—*furieusement* white.' De Quincey saw many blacks, many whites, multitudinous greys. **1923** J. HERGESHEIMER *Bright Shawl* 21 He saw..the good on one side facing the bad on the other. There was no mingling of the ranks, no grey; simply, conveniently, black and white. **1948** *Amer. Sociol. Rev.* June 284 To disclose the blacks and imply the whites of a quality scale, the middle grays being largely lost.

b. with word prefixed, indicating some particular shade of grey, as ***dark, duffel, goose, lead grey***.

a **1693** AUBREY *Lives, Sir W. Petty* (1898) II. 145 His eies are a kind of goose-grey. **1796** STEDMAN *Surinam* xvii. 31 Those [parrots]..are rather of a lead-grey. **1817** T. L. PEACOCK *Melincourt* xxviii, Waistcoats of a duffel gray.

c. *Gunmaking.* A grey spot indicating a flaw.

1881 GREENER *Gun* 223 Before the introduction of the new mode of making gun-iron, it was a most difficult matter to obtain English barrels free from greys.

d. *in the grey*: unburnished.

1860 SIR E. BECKETT *Clocks & Watches* (ed. 4) 309 Earnshaw was the first watchmaker who had sense enough to set at defiance the vulgar and ignorant prejudice for 'high finish' of the non-acting surfaces, and to leave them 'in the grey', as it is called.

e. A grey-coloured pigment; usually with defining word prefixed, as ***aniline, Payne's grey***, etc.

1888 *Daily News* 9 Aug. 5/2 Naples yellow, Payne's grey, gamboge.

5. †**a.** A grey-haired person, an old man. *Obs.*

1374 CHAUCER *Troylus* IV. 99 (127) Tellyng his tale alwey, þis olde Greye, Humble in speche. *a* **1420** HOCCLEVE *De Reg. Princ.* 134 'I', quod this olde grey, ' Am here'. **1513** DOUGLAS *Æneis* II. ix. 6 The ald gray, all for nocht, to him tays His hawbrek.

b. A white-skinned person. *U.S. Black slang.* Cf. *adj.* 6 e.

1960 WENTWORTH & FLEXNER *Dict. Amer. Slang* 228 *Gray*, (derog.) a white person. **1963** in *Amer. Speech* (1964) XXXIX. 60 Beyond the ears of the greys. **1965** O. HARRINGTON in J. H. Clarke *Harlem* 90 The year was 1936, a bad year in most everybody's book. Ellis the cabdriver used to say that even the grays downtown were having it rough. **1966** *Publ. Amer. Dial. Soc.* *1964* XLII. 31 *Caucasian* ..gray.

c. A dull, anonymous, or 'faceless' person. Cf. *adj.* 5 b.

1967 *Observer* 17 Dec. 25/1 Let them..remember that many of the 'grey' citizens have been working for forty years or more for the forgiveness of enemies... The 'greys' would appreciate the co-operation of the bright ones in such activities. **1969** *Gandalf's Garden* VI. 11/1 *Greys*, those people whose minds have ossified and who have lost the wonder of living and the will to learn what it's all about. **1969** *It* 4–17 July 3/3 The whole scene is under the thumbs of the greys. Pretty well everywhere today the dead men, the square men and the greys are running things, calling the tune.

†**6.** A badger. *Obs.* (Cf. sense 2.)

α. **1432–50** tr. *Higden* (Rolls) VI. 205 Beverlay..the place or lake of bevers or of grayes. **1577** B. GOOGE *Heresbach's Husb.* (1586) 154 Sheepe and Goates..woulde soone be destroied by Woolfes, Foxes, Grayes, and other vermine. **1607** TOPSELL *Four-f. Beasts* (1658) 26 Of the Badger, otherwise called a Brocke, a Gray, or a Bauson. **1637** B. JONSON *Sad Sheph.* II. ii, This fine Smooth Bawsons Cub, the young Grice of a Gray. **1665** in *Sussex Archæol. Collect.* XIV. 247 To Catlin's maide for a Gray's hed £0 1*s.* 0*d.* **1686** BLOME *Gentl. Recreat.* II. 90 A Badger is known by several other Names, as a Gray, a Brock, [etc.].

β. **1413–22** *Hunting Rhymes* in *Rel. Ant.* I. 149 And .iij. other bestis..That ben neyther of venery ne chace..The grey is one therof with hyse slepy pace. **1423** JAS. I *Kingis Quair* clvi, There sawe I..the holsum grey for hortis. **1538** LELAND *Itin.* I. 113 There is a mighty stronge and usid Borow for Greys or Foxes. **1576** TURBERV. *Venerie* iii. 7 And kill at force, hart, hind, bucke, doe, foxe, grey and euery chace. **1616** SURFL. & MARKH. *Country Farme* 701 The Brocke or Badger, or as some call him the Grey, by reason of his colour.

7. A grey horse. Chiefly *pl.* and in phr. ***a pair of greys***.

[**1639**: cf. DAPPLE-GREY b.] **1760–72** H. BROOKE *Fool of Quality* (1809) IV. 159 A sumptuous coach proudly drawn by six German greys. **1789** GIBBON *Autobiogr.* (1896) 162 An handsome set of bays or greys. **1810** *Sporting Mag.* XXXV. 188 Several of the Four-in-hand Club..still adhere to their greys. **1813** HOGG *Queen's Wake* 149 When good Earl Walter rode the ring Upon his mettled gray. **1842** MACAULAY *Ess., Fredk. Gt.*, His English grey carried him many miles from the field. **1848** THACKERAY *Van. Fair* xxxvii, Mrs. Mantrap..drives her greys in the Park. **1861** WHYTE MELVILLE *Mkt. Harb.* 67 Leisure to..watch the roan putting on flesh, and the departure of the grey's cough.

8. *pl.* (in full **Scots Greys**). A regiment of dragoons raised in 1681 and called the Royal Regiment of Dragoons, now the 2nd Dragoons. *rare* in *sing.*

The regiment formerly wore a uniform of grey cloth. They are now mounted chiefly on grey chargers.

1751 *Phil. Trans.* XLVII. xxviii. 194 The Greys were cantoon'd in the village of Vucht. **1753** *Scots Mag.* June 306/1 A troop of Scots Greys arrived. **1875** KINGLAKE *Crimea* V. i. (1877) 122 The Inniskillinger and the Grey. **1881** TENNYSON *Charge Heavy Brig.* iii, Brave Inniskillens and Greys Whirling their sabres in circles of light! **1895** SIR E. WOOD *Cavalry Waterloo Camp.* v. 138 As the Scots Greys passed through the 92nd Regiment, each corps mutually cheered the other.

9. As a name for various animals.

†**a.** The GADWALL, *Anas strepera. Obs.*

'The synonym "Gray", given by Willughby and Ray, is doubtless derived from the general colour of the species' (Newton).

1678 RAY *Willughby's Ornith.* 374 The Gadwall or Gray.

b. A kind of fish; ? a GRILSE.

1686 RAY *Willughby's Ichthyogr.* I. xii. 23 *Salmo griseus.* The Gray. **1740** R. BROOKES *Art of Angling* I. v. 25 The Grey I take to be the same kind of Fish which in Scotland they call the Grey-Lord. In Magnitude it differs but little from the Salmon, but the Shape is very unlike..The body is everywhere stain'd with Grey or Ash-colour'd Spots. **1769** PENNANT *Zool.* III. 248 The Grey..We are uncertain whether this is not a meer variety of the salmon; but on the authority of Mr. Ray we describe them separate. **1818** TODD, *Gray*, a kind of salmon, having a gray back and sides; probably the same as the gilse.

c. A species of moth (see quot.).

1866 E. NEWMAN *Brit. Butterf. & Moths* 391 The Gray. (*Dianthœcia cæsia.*)

d. ***California grey***, the grey whale (see A. 8 b).

1884–5 *Riverside Nat. Hist.* (1888) V. 197 The California gray.

10. *slang.* (See quot.) [Perh. alluding to 'a pair of greys' (sense 7).]

1812 J. H. VAUX *Flash Dict.*, *Gray*, a half-penny, or other coin, having two heads or two tails, and fabricated for the use of gamblers. **1828** G. SMEETON *Doings in Lond.* 40 Breslaw could never have done more upon cards than he could do with a pair of 'grays'. **1851** in Mayhew *Lond. Labour* II. 120. **1868** *Temple Bar* XXIV. 539 The way they do it is to have a penny with two heads or two tails on it, which they call a 'grey'.

†**11.** *attrib.* and *Comb.* (sense 2 only) as ***grey merchant***; **grey cloak**, an alderman who has 'passed the Chair'; **greywork**, furriery; **grey-worker**, a furrier. *Obs.*

c **1483** CAXTON *Dialogues* (E.E.T.S.) 2/36 Of makers of greywerke. *Ibid.* 46/19 Vedast the graywerker Solde whiler to my lady A pylche of graye. **1542** *Act 33 Hen. VIII* c. 2. in Bolton *Stat. Irel.* (1621) 185 An Act for gray Merchants. **1557** *Order of Hospitalls* B ij b, xiiij of them to be Aldermen ..vj Graye clokes and viij callabre. *Ibid.* B iij, iij Alderman, whereof one shal be a graycloke.

grey (greɪ), *v.* Also **gray**. [f. GREY *a.*]

1. *intr.* To become or grow grey.

13.. *Gaw. & Gr. Knt.* 527 Al grayes þe gres, þat grene watz ere. **1878** *Scribner's Mag.* XVI. 332/2 The autumn seared and browned and grayed at last into winter. **1893** *Strand Mag.* VI. 283/2 The night began to grey. **1896** CROCKETT *Grey Man* v. 32 It was already greying for the dawn.

2. *trans.* To make grey.

1879 *Tinsley's Mag.* XXIV. 325 As some cloud-shadow swept across the valley, and grayed the greens. **1887** *Harper's Mag.* Aug. 454 The crumbling fence is grayed By the slow-creeping lichen.

3. †**a.** *intr.* Of a person: To become grey. **b.** *trans.* To cause (a person's hair) to become grey.

a **1618** SYLVESTER *Mem. Mortal.* II. xxix, In learning Socrates lives, grayes, and dyes. **1633** SHIRLEY *Bird in Cage* v. i. I 4 b, Canst thou..change but the complexion of one Hayre? Yet thou hast gray'd a thousand. **1810** *Assoc. Minstrels* 146 Ah tell me not thy locks are greyed. **1886** E. C. G. MURRAY *Yng. Widows* 29 Time may have grayed their hair. **1899** FIONA MACLEOD *Dominion Dreams* 175 He is a man whose hair has been greyed by years and sorrow.

4. *Photography.* **a.** *trans.* To give a dull surface to (glass): see quot. 1868. **b.** To give a mezzotint effect to (a photograph) by covering the negative, during printing, with such glass. **c.** *intr.* for *refl.* To assume a grey tint.

1868 M. C. LEA *Photogr.* iv. 45 The glass should, in fact, not be ground at all, but only 'grayed', that is, have its surface removed by rubbing with fine emery powder. **1891** *Anthony's Photogr. Bull.* IV. 251 The highest lights must not be allowed to 'gray' over.

Hence **greyed** (greɪd) *ppl. a.*, **'greying** *vbl. sb.* and *ppl. a.*

1819 G. SAMOUELLE *Entomol. Compend.* 327 The light.. may be lessened by placing..a piece of fine grayed glass between the object and the reflecting mirror. **1863** W. LANCASTER *Praeterita* 36 Singing under greying blue. **1890** *Anthony's Photogr. Bull.* III. 429 No print with grayed background..should be accepted. **1891** G. MEREDITH *One of our Conq.* I. xiv. 280 Barmby..quitted the forepart of the vessel at the first greying. **1895** HARDY in *Harper's Mag.* Apr. 730 His graying hair was curly. **1898** ZANGWILL *Dreamers Ghetto* xiii. 429 Girls footing it gleefully in the greying light.

grey-back, greyback ('greɪbæk).

1. *U.S. colloq.* A Confederate soldier in the American Civil War.

1864 *Daily Tel.* 7 July 3/4 The last thing he is likely to attempt is to send a solitary grayback or an army of gray-backs beyond the mountains. **1870** T. W. HIGGINSON *Army Life* vi. 152 Yonder loitering gray-back leading his horse to water. **1883** *Daily Tel.* 9 Feb. 5/4 The Confederate armies, during the great Civil War in America..were known..as 'greybacks'.

2. *U.S.* (See quot.) Cf. GREENBACK.

1897 GEN. H. PORTER in *Century Mag.* Aug. 593 The depreciation in the purchasing power of graybacks, as we call the rebel treasury notes, is so rapid.

3. *dial.* and *U.S. colloq.* A louse.

1864 *Daily Tel.* 17 Mar. 5/2 The darkies sat grinning and hunting in their rags for greybacks. **1864** SALA *ibid.* 22 Apr. 5/2 The attire of the Secesh partisans is.. infested.. by an insect sportively termed a 'greyback'. **1877** *Holderness Gloss.*

4. A name of various birds. **a.** The Hooded Crow, *Corvus cornix*. Also ***greyback crow***. **b.** *U.S.* The North American Knot, *Trigla canutus*. **c.** *dial.* and *U.S.* The scaup duck, *Fuligula marila*.

1888 G. TRUMBULL *Bird-names* 55 Another title at Chicago is *gray-back*, and certain gunners about Detroit prefer *black-neck* to.. 'blue-bill'. **1891** ATKINSON *Moorland Par.* 325 Once a grayback crow came. **1893** NEWTON *Dict. Birds*, *Greyback*, in England a common name of the Grey form of Crow, *Corvus cornix*; but in North America applied by gunners to the Knot. **1895** *East Angl. Gloss.*, *Grey-backs*, scaup ducks.

5. *U.S.* The grey whale (see GREY *a.* 8 b).

1884–5 *Riverside Nat. Hist.* (1888) V. 186 The gray whale has received many curious titles, such as 'hard-head', 'mussel-digger', 'devil-fish', and 'gray-back'.

6. *techn.* (See quot. Cf. GREY *sb.* 1 b.)

1876 J. PATON in *Encycl. Brit.* IV. 685/2 Between the central bowl [of a cylinder calico-printing machine] and the cloth to be printed there passes an endless band of cloth or blanket.. and a 'grey back' or web of unbleached calico, used to keep the blanket clean.

grey-backed ('greɪbækt), *a.* [f. GREY *a.* + BACK *sb.* + -ED[2].] Having a grey back. ***grey-backed crow*** = GREY-BACK 4 a.

1837 MACGILLIVRAY *Hist. Brit. Birds* I. 529 Grey-backed Crow. **1899** *Blackw. Mag.* Feb. 417/1 These grey-backed depredators [hoodies].

greybeard ('greɪbɪəd). Also graybeard.

1. A man with a grey beard; hence (often contemptuously) an old man.

1579–80 NORTH *Plutarch* (1676) 524 An old gray-beard. **1596** SHAKS. *Tam. Shr.* II. i. 340 *Gre.* Yongling thou canst not loue so deare as I. *Tra.* Gray-beard thy loue doth freeze. **1662** J. DAVIES tr. *Mandelslo's Trav.* 262 There are few gray-beards seen there, and few Christians reach 50. **1768** FOOTE *Devil on 2 Sticks* (1778) 23 It is I that couple.. girls and greybeards together. **1826** POLWHELE *Trad. & Recoll.* I. ii. 43 [She] was receiving homage at Bath from greybeards and from boys. **1886** BESANT *Childr. Gibeon* II. vi, Questions which have baffled all the grey-beards.

2. A large earthenware or stoneware jug or jar, used for holding spirits.

1788 G. WILSON *Collect. Songs.* 67 (Jam.) Whate'er he laid his fangs on, Be't hogshead, anker, grey-beard, pack. **1818** SCOTT *Hrt. Midl.* li, So long as her best greybeard of brandy was upon duty. **1866** *Cornh. Mag.* Mar. 355 Neither a mere jar, nor simply a basket, but one of those compounds of both, well known under the name of 'grey-beard', which are devoted to the conveyance of usque-baugh. **1885** J. H. MIDDLETON in *Encycl. Brit.* XIX. 631/1 Stoneware jug or 'greybeard'; Flemish ware, early 17th century. **1894** CROCKETT *Raiders* 150 There was not a farmer's grey-beard between the Lothians and the Solway filled with spirit that had done obeisance to King George.

3. ? = *grey-fish* (see GREY *a.* 8 b). Cf. GREYHEAD 2.

1769 *De Foe's Tour Gt. Brit.* (ed. 7) IV. 19 Pike, Scate, Greybeard, Mackerel.. Soles, Flukes.. are also caught.

4. A hydroid polyp which infests oyster-beds, *Sertularia argentea*.

In recent Dicts.

5. *attrib.* **greybeard lichen** (see quot. 1885).

1599 NASHE *Lenten Stuffe* 3 Those gray beard huddle-duddles.. were strooke with.. remorse. *a* **1634** RANDOLPH *Muse's Looking-Glass* II. iv, No, no, Asotus, trust grey-beard experience. **1770** GOLDSM. *Des. Vill.* 222 That house.. Where grey-beard mirth and smiling toil retir'd. **1780** COWPER *Progr. Err.* 342 Petronius!.. Thou.. Grey-beard corrupter of our listening youth. **1798** COLERIDGE *Anc. Mar.* I. iii, Unhand me, grey-beard loon! **1807–8** W. IRVING *Salmag.* xx. (1860) 450 This honest gray-beard custom.. handed down to us from our worthy Dutch ancestors. **1885** GOODALE *Physiol. Bot.* 191 The common graybeard lichen, *Usnea barbata*.

grey-bearded, *a.* (Stress variable.) [f. GREY *a.* + BEARD + -ED[2].] Having a grey beard; pertaining to or characteristic of a greybeard.

1597 *Pilgr. Parnass.* I. 10 Now, Philomusus, doe youre beardless years.. Urge mee to.. give gray-bearded counsell to youre age. **1674** N. FAIRFAX *Bulk & Selv.* 25 We.. speak no more wonders, than the grey bearded men, that have gone before us. **1750** JOHNSON *Rambler* No. 26 ¶7 To teach young men, who are too tame under representation, how grey-bearded insolence ought to be treated. **1818** R. PETERS in *J. Jay's Corr. & Public Papers* (1893) IV. 421 A pleasing delusion, which greybearded scrutiny.. should never extinguish. **1899** *Expositor* Feb. 131 We fancied them stately and grey-bearded.

† **greybitch.** *Obs.* Also 4 **graye bicche, grebytch,** 5 **grebyche,** 6 **grayebytche.** [f. *grey* (in GREYHOUND) + BITCH.] The female of the greyhound.

13.. *K. Alis.* 5394 Ac anon after that wonder, Comen tigres many hundre, Graye bicchen als it waren. **1398** TREVISA *Barth. De P.R.* XVIII. xxvi. (1495) 786 In bytches milke is founde many dayes tofore the whelpynge and soner in greybitches than in other. *c* **1420** *Chron. Vilod.* st. 222 Hym thou3t þ^t his greybyche lay hym beside. **1530** PALSGR. 155 *Leuriére*, a grayebytche.

grey-blue, *a.* and *sb.* **A.** *adj.* Of a blue colour tinged with grey. **B.** *sb.* A grey-blue colour.

1888 *Quiver* Sept. 827/1 Her keen grey-blue eyes. **1893** GUNTER *Miss Dividends* 263 He knows what those gray-blue lips mean. **1897** MARY KINGSLEY *W. Africa* 186 The more distant peaks were soft gray-blues and purple.

Hence **grey-blue** *v.*, to make greyish-blue in hue.

1834 *Blackw. Mag.* XXXV. 821 A hissing of red-hot iron, that loses none of its heat, though it grey-blues its colour.

greyce, variant of GRIS *a. Obs.*, grey.

greycing, var. GRACING *vbl. sb.*[2]

'grey-coat. One who wears grey clothing; *spec.* a Cumberland yeoman (see quots. 1837–66).

1644 VICARS *God in Mount* 200 A part of Colonell Ballards Grey-coats.. did most singular good service all this fight. **1675** *Hodge's Vis. for Monument* (1703) 128 in *Marvell's Wks.* (Grosart) I. 439 We'll part.. The spruce brib'd monsieurs from the true grey coats. **1837** *Penny Cycl.* VIII. 223/2 They.. wore kelt cloth, which was of a grey colour.. and hence the name of grey-coats which the Cumbrians received. **1866** *Reader* 20 Oct. 874 Many of the Cumberland yeomen still wear a plain home-spun grey cloth, hence their name of grey cootes.

b. *attrib.*: **Grey-coat Hospital**, a charity school, where the scholars were clothed in grey; **grey-coat parson** (see quot. *a* 1825, and next word).

1719 D'URFEY *Pills* III. 46 To Free-school.. My gray-coat Gransir put him. **1766** ENTICK *London* IV. 411 In Tothill-side is the Grey coat-hospital. *a* **1825** FORBY *Voc. E. Anglia*, *Grey coat parson*, an impropriator; or, the tenant who hires the tithes.

grey-coated, *a.* Having a grey coat; ***grey-coated parson*** (see quot. *a* 1825 in GREY-COAT b).

1592 SHAKS. *Rom. & Jul.* I. iv. 64 Her Waggoner, a small gray-coated Gnat. **1853** in *Cobbett's Rur. Rides* 647 *note*, A large holder of lay tithes: one of those to whom the author applied the name of 'grey-coated parson'. **1895** *Daily News* 9 Dec. 5/6 Detachments.. grey-coated and warmly clad.

greyers, *sb. pl.*: see GREY *sb.* 1 d.

grey-eyed, *a.* Having grey eyes.

1596 SPENSER *F.Q.* IV. xi. 48 The gray-eyde Doris. **1605** CAMDEN *Rem.*, *Names* 88 Our womens names are more gratious than their Rutilia, that is, Red-head: Cæsilla, that is, Grey-eyed. **1687** *Lond. Gaz.* No. 2272/4 A middle sized man.. Grey eyed, and speaks broad. **1716** *Royal Proclam.* 5 May *ibid.* No. 5431/1 Beetle-Browed, Grey-Eyed. **1813** PRICHARD *Phys. Hist. Man.* (1836) I. 227 Among the Romans a gray-eyed child was considered as something disgusting. **1871** PALGRAVE *Lyr. Poems* 16 A gray-eyed girl.

b. Applied poetically to the early morning.

1592 SHAKS. *Rom. & Jul.* II. iii. 1 The gray ey'd morne smiles on the frowning night. **1670** EACHARD *Cont. Clergy* 32 The grey-ey'd morn. **1720** GAY *Poems* (1745) I. 144 Soon as the grey-ey'd morning streaks the skies. **1830** TENNYSON *Mariana*, Till cold winds woke the gray-eyed morn About the lonely moated grange.

greyf, obs. form of GRIEF.

Grey friar. [See GREY *a.* 2.]

1. A member of the order of Franciscan or Minor friars, founded by St. Francis of Assisi in 1210 (see quot. 1838). *Grey Friars*, a convent of this order.

a **1310** in Wright *Lyric P.* 110 He leneþ on is forke ase a grey frere. *c* **1400** *Gamelyn* 529 Than seyde a gray frere, 'Allas! sire abbot' [etc.]. **1506** GUYLFORDE *Pilgr.* (Camden) 6 Saterdaye was the feeste of seynt Antony, whiche was a Grey Frere, and lyeth ryght fayre at the Grey Freres there. **1545** BRINKLOW *Compl.* (title), Roderyck Mors, somtyme a gray fryre. *a* **1578** LINDESAY (Pitscottie) *Chron. Scot.* (S.T.S.) I. 380 Scho wessit the blak freiris, the gray-freiris, the auld colledge and the new colledge. **1626** L. OWEN *Spec. Jesuit.* (1629) 17, I saw this Mason in his Gray-Friers-Frocke. **1838** *Penny Cycl.* X. 446/1 The followers of St. Francis were called Franciscans, Grey, or Minor Friars; the first name they had from their founder; the second from their grey clothing.

2. *pl. transf.* (See quot.)

1867 SMYTH *Sailor's Word-bk.*, *Grey-friars*, a name given to the oxen of Tuscany, with which the Mediterranean fleet was supplied.

greygle, greygo(y)le. *dial.* Also **grægle, greggle.** The bluebell or wild hyacinth (*Scilla nutans*). Also ***gramfer greygles***.

1844 BARNES *Poems Dorset Dial.*, Gloss., *Greygoyle.* **1848** —— (ed. 2), The wood-screen'd grægle's bell. **1851** *Dorset Gloss.*, *Greygole*, the bluebell. **1869** *N. & Q.* Ser. IV. IV. 345 When we came to some blue-bell squills (*Scilla nutans*).. I asked him [a Dorset boy] what their name was. Without any hesitation he answered.. 'Gramfer greygles'. **1886** T. HARDY *Mayor of Casterbr.* xx, She grew to talk of 'greggles' as 'wild hyacinths'.

grey goose. The greylag goose.

c **1000** *Ags. Voc.* in Wr.-Wülcker 259/3 *Canta* [? read *ganta*], græȝ gos. *c* **1050** *Ags. Voc.* ibid. 415/31 *Gans*, greȝe gos. **1885** SWAINSON *Prov. Names Birds* 147 Grey-lag goose (*Anser cinereus*).. Also called Grey goose. **1891** DOYLE *White Company* I. vi. 113 So we'll drink all together To.. the land where the grey goose flew.

b. *transf.* (See quot.)

1816 SCOTT *Bl. Dwarf* iv, In the name of wonder, what can he be doing there? 'Biggin a dry-stane dyke, I think, wi' the grey geese, as they ca' thae great loose stones'.

c. *attrib.* as ***grey-goose quill, weapon*** (a pen); ***grey-goose shaft, wing*** (an arrow).

1566 J. PARTRIDGE *Plasidas* 996 Some from towre with bow in hande the gray-goose wing do sende. **1644** HOWELL *Engl. Teares* (1645) 173 My next neighbour France (through whose bowels my gray-goose wing flew so oft). **1728** POPE *Dunc.* I. 198 Could Troy be sav'd by any single hand, This grey-goose weapon must have made her stand. **1781** C. JOHNSTON *John Juniper* II. 1 One of the keenest wits who ever wielded grey-goose quill. **1814** SCOTT *Ld. of Isles* VI. xxii, Forth whistling came the grey-goose wing.

grey-haired, *a.* (Stress variable.) Having grey hair; hence, old.

13.. *Evang. Nicod.* 1551 in *Archiv Stud. neu. Spr.* LIII. 420 Two grayhared men.. with þam mett. *a* **1400** *Pistill Susan* 339 þin hed is grei hored. **14..** *Sir Beues* 3322 (MS. M.) That ye thare not drede than Of Sabere, that grey-herud man. *c* **1440** *Promp. Parv.* 209/2 Grey heryd, *canus.* *a* **1649** DRUMM. OF HAWTH. *Poems* Wks. (1711) 37 If gray-hair'd Proteus songs the truth not miss. *a* **1706** EARL DORSET *Fr. Song paraphr.* 1 In gray-hair'd Celia's wither'd arms. **1801** SOUTHEY *Thalaba* VIII. xxxii, The grey-hair'd Sorceress stampt the ground. **1847** G. R. GLEIG *Waterloo* xxix. (ed. 2) 233 Many.. were grey-haired men and covered with the scars of old wounds.

b. *fig.* of things.

1611 BARKSTED *Hiren* xx. A vj. Alas faire Christian Saint.. So yong, and full of gray hair'd purity. **1622** H. SYDENHAM *Serm. Sol. Occ.* (1637) 8 A gray-hair'd custom of most times and places.

greyhead ('greɪhɛd).

1. A grey-headed person.

1702 STEELE *Funeral* V. i. 79 Else Boys will in your Presence lose their Fear, And laugh at the Grey-head they should revere. [But should not the reading be *grey head?*]

2. **a.** *Sc.* A kind of fish, prob. the grey-fish.

a **1692** A. SYMSON *Descr. Galloway* (1823) 25 Upon the coast of this parish are many sorts of white fish taken; one kind whereof is called by the inhabitants Greyheads.

b. A male sperm-whale, *Physeter catodon*, with grey markings on its head; cf. GREY-HEADED *a.* 4.

a **1889** C. M. SCAMMON (Cent. D.). **1908** *Westm. Gaz.* 28 Dec. 2/1 The right whale and the grayhead are gone.

3. = GREYBEARD 2.

1892 ROBSON in *Standard* 23 Nov. 3/3 'A grey head'.. was not a bottle, but a stone jar of whisky.

grey-headed, *a.* (Stress variable.)

1. Having a grey head of hair. *to be* or ***grow grey-headed in***, to grow old in, to have served in for a long period; hence, to be well versed or experienced in.

1535 COVERDALE *Ps.* lxx. 18 In myne olde age, when I am gray headed. **1644** VICARS *God in Mount* 75 The grey-headed.. Citizens of London. **1712** ADDISON *Spect.* No. 517 ¶2 Most of us are grown grey-headed in our dear master's service. **1813** LD. ELLENBOROUGH *Parl. Deb.* 22 Mar. in *Examiner* 29 Mar. 199/1 A man grey-headed in the law. **1843** MACAULAY *Lays Anc. Rome*, *Battle Regillus* ix, With boys, and with grey-headed men, To keep the walls of Rome.

transf. **1662** STILLINGFL. *Orig. Sacr.* I. vi. §5 Those snowy and gray headed Alps.

2. *fig.* Of things: **a.** Ancient, old; time-worn. **b.** Pertaining to old age, or to aged men.

1600 E. BLOUNT tr. *Conestaggio* A ij, To begin (after the common stampe of dedication) with a grai-headed Apophthegme. **1614** BP. HALL *Recoll. Treat.* 59 Heresie or abuse, if it be gray-headed, deserves sharper opposition. **1646** SIR T. BROWNE *Pseud. Ep.* III. i. 104 Which conceit is not the daughter of latter times, but an old and gray-headed errour, even in the dayes of Aristotle. **1652** BP. PATRICK *Funeral Serm.* in *J. Smith's Sel. Disc.* 526 By reason of his wisdom, experience, and gray-headed understanding. **1692** NORRIS *Curs. Refl.* 21 That grey-headed venerable Doctrine. **1753** *Adventurer* No. 25 ¶3 Love is beneath the dignity of grey-headed wisdom.

3. As an epithet of certain birds; esp. ***grey-headed duck***, the female of the Golden-eye (*Clangula glaucion*).

1747 G. EDWARDS *Nat. Hist. Birds* I. II. 127 *Picus, viridis, capite cinereo.* Grey-headed Green Wood-pecker. **1750** *Ibid.* II. III. 154 The Grey-Headed Duck. **1847** CRAIG, *Greyheaded-wagtail*, the bird *Budytes neglecta*, and *Motacilla flava* of Linnæus. **1885** SWAINSON *Prov. Names Birds* 160 Golden-eye (*Clangula glaucion*).. Grey-headed duck. Only applied to the female bird.

4. Of a male sperm whale; cf. GREYHEAD 2 b.

1839 T. BEALE *Nat. Hist. Sperm Whale* i. 31 Old 'bulls', as full-grown males are called by whalers, have generally a portion of grey on the nose immediately above the fore-part of the upper-jaw, and they are then said to be 'grey-headed'. **1874** C. M. SCAMMON *Marine Mammals N.W. Coast N. Amer.* viii. 75 Sperm Whale... The oldest males are frequently well-marked with gray about the nose, or upper portion of the head, and when this is indicated, they are called 'gray-headed'.

grey-hen ('greɪhɛn). The female of the Black Grouse (*Tetrao tetrix*), the heath-hen. (The male is called the BLACKCOCK.)

? **1427** in *Balfour's Practicks* (1754) 542 Wyld foulis, sic as pertrikis, pluveris, black cockis, gray hennis. **1618** *Naworth Househ. Bks.* (Surtees) 79, 2 gray hens. **1787** G. WHITE *Selborne* vi. (1789) 16 Within these last ten years one solitary grey hen was sprung by some beagles in beating for a hare. **1893** NEWTON *Dict. Birds* 393 *Tetrao tetrix*—the Blackcock and Greyhen, as the sexes are with us respectively called.

greyhound ('greɪhaʊnd). Forms: 1 **grīȝhund,** 3 **greahund,** 4–6 **grehound(e,** 5 **grehunde, grayhownd, -hund, grahounde, grawhond,** 5–6 **grehownde, greihound,** 6–7 **gray(e)-,**

greahound(e, 5–6 **greyhounde**, 6– **greyhound**. Cf. GREUND, GREWHOUND, GRIFHOUND. [OE. *griȝhund*, **grīeȝhund* (= ON. *greyhund-r*), f. **grīeȝ* (= ON. *grøy* neut., bitch:—OTeut. type **graujo*ᵐ) + *hund* dog, HOUND.

The etymology of the first element is unknown; it has no connexion with GREY *a*. or with GREW *a*., Greek, nor with *grey* = badger (GREY *sb*.).]

1. a. A variety of dog used in the chase, characterized by its long slender body, and long legs, by the keenness of its sight, and by its great speed in running.

It is not certain that the earlier examples always relate to the kind of dog now known by the name.

c **1000** *Ags. Voc.* in Wr.-Wülcker 276/3 *Unfer* [? read *Umber*], griȝhund. *a* **1225** *Ancr. R.* 332 Tristre is þer me sit mid þe greahundes forte kepen þe hearde. *c* **1330** R. BRUNNE *Chron. Wace* (Rolls) 11415 Somme gaf he hauberks, & somme grehoundes. *c* **1380** WYCLIF *Serm.* Sel. Wks. II. 359 And þus þes prelatis suen apostlis as gre-houndis suen an hare. **1480** CAXTON *Chron. Eng.* clxxxvi. 162 The forsayd dragon shold be ladde by an ylle grehounde. **1548** HALL *Chron., Rich. III*, 54 b, The fearefull hare never fledde faster before the gredy greyhound. **1555** EDEN *Decades* 134 They affyrme them to bee swifter then grehowndes. **1587** HARRISON *England* III. iv. in *Holinshed* I. 226 King Henry the fift..thought it a meere scofferie to pursue anie fallow deere with..greihounds. **1607** TOPSELL *Four-f. Beasts* (1658) 114 The Gray-hound or Grecian Dog. **1616** SURFL. & MARKH. *Country Farme* 673 Grey-hounds..are onely for the coursing of all sorts of wilde beastes by maine swiftnesse of foot. **1697** DRYDEN *Virg. Georg.* III. 804 The fearful Doe And flying Stag, amidst the Greyhounds go. **1781** W. BLANE *Ess. Hunting* Pref. (1788) 18 Arrian..proves that, in the time of Xenophon, Greyhounds were not known in Greece. **1814** SCOTT *Wav.* lxiii, Two grim and half-starved deer greyhounds. **1862** HUXLEY *Lect. Wrkg. Men* 110 It is a physiological peculiarity that leads the Greyhound to chase its prey by Sight.

fig. *a* **1649** DRUMM. OF HAWTH. *Poems* Wks. (1711) 27 The Nimrod fierce is death, His speedy gray-hounds are Lust, sickness, envy, care.

b. Applied with distinguishing prefix to different varieties, as ***Arabian, Highland, Irish, Italian, Persian, Russian, Scotch, Turkish greyhound***.

1743 H. WALPOLE *Lett.* (1846) I. 300, I really forget anything of an Italian greyhound for the Tesi. **1824** BEWICK *Hist. Quadrup.* (ed. 8) 340 The Irish Greyhound (*Canis Graius Hibernicus*, Ray..) Is the largest of the Dog Kind. **1837** *Penny Cycl.* IX. 57/2 The expression of the countenance [is] that of a coarse ill-natured Persian Greyhound. **1838** W. SCROPE *Deerstalking* xii. 260 The deerhound is known under the names of Irish wolfhound, Irish greyhound, Highland deerhound, and Scotch greyhound. **1848** MAUNDER *Treas. Nat. Hist.* 282/1 The Italian Greyhound is a small and very beautiful variety of the species. **1891** OUIDA in *N. Amer. Rev.* Sept. 316 The Siberian and the Persian greyhounds are one and the same breed.

c. ***harlequin greyhound*** = HARLEQUIN 2.

1750 COVENTRY *Pompey Litt.* I. v. (1785) 17/2 A harlequin greyhound, a spotted Dane.

2. The figure of a greyhound, used as a badge.

1763 CHURCHILL *Duellist* II. 262 Each, on his breast Mark'd with a Grey-hound, stood confest. [Poet. Wks. 1844 II. 33 *note, Carrington and his band of King's messengers; a silver greyhound, the emblem of dispatch, was then worn by these men as a distinctive badge of office when engaged in the execution of their duty.*]

3. *transf.* **a.** An ocean steamship specially built for great speed. More fully ***ocean greyhound***.

1887 *Sci. American* 1 Jan. 2/2 They [ships]..are so swift of foot, as to have already become formidable rivals to the English 'greyhounds'. **1891** *Engineer* 9 Oct. 301 The greyhounds of the Atlantic.

b. *Naut.* (See quot.)

1867 SMYTH *Sailor's Word-bk.*, *Greyhound*, a hammock with so little bedding as to be unfit for stowing in the nettings.

4. *attrib.* and *Comb.*, as ***greyhound-bitch, -fan, -kennel, -owner, make, -race, -racecourse, -track***; ***greyhound-like*** adj.; **greyhound fox** (see quot. 1774); **greyhound racing**, a sport in which a dummy hare propelled mechanically round a set track is pursued by greyhounds. Cf. GRACING *vbl. sb.*²

1711 SHAFTESB. *Charac.* (1737) III. 217 His hound or *greyhound-bitch who eats her puppys. **1946** R. GENDERS *Mod. Greyhound Racing* xiii. 134 One of the famous Wireless Rally/Erin Green litter so well known to *greyhound fans, he has been one of the finest sprinters this country has ever seen. **1774** GOLDSM. *Nat. Hist.* III. 332 There are only three varieties of this animal in Great Britain... The *grey-hound fox is the largest, tallest, and boldest... The mastiff fox is less... The cur fox is the least and most common. **1814** *Sporting Mag.* XLIV. 87 The hounds..unkennelled a remarkably large greyhound fox. **1946** R. GENDERS *Mod. Greyhound Racing* vi. 58 The breeder or keeper of *greyhound kennels. **1821** SOUTHEY in *Life* (1849) I. 35, I ..afterwards became the lean, lank, *greyhound-like creature that I have ever since continued. **1860** *All Year Round* No. 63. 298 The wolf..with a light greyhound-like form, which pursues deer. **1771** P. PARSONS *Newmarket* II. 87 What a thin slim figure it [a jockey] is!—very much of the *grey-hound make. **1927** 'LEVERET' *Greyhound Racing* iii. 12, I have been asked by several would-be *greyhound owners to find them dogs for track-racing purposes. **1926** *Manch. Guardian* 19 July 5/6 (Advt.), *Greyhound races. Belle Vue racecourse, Manchester. *Ibid.* 23 July 11/4 The *Greyhound Racecourse, Kirkmanshulme Lane, Gorton, applied for an occasional licence to sell intoxicating drink. **1933** E. C. ASH *Bk. Greyhound* (ed. 2) xii. 305 In the year 1876, two events took place,..one a swimming race between a man and a dog, which the dog won, and the other a Greyhound race after a mechanical hare. **1926** *Manch. Guardian* 26 July 9/4 Something of a novelty has been added to Manchester's odd collection of diversions by the opening of the new *greyhound racing track. **1928** R. KNOX *Footsteps at Lock* viii. 79 The conversation turned..on greyhound racing... One very old gentleman had to be convinced.. that it was the hare, not the hounds, which worked by electricity. **1949** H. E. CLARKE *Mod. Greyhound* ii. 16 In the early days of greyhound racing it was customary to bolster up the antipathy to the coursing animal by the argument that no dog from the coursing field had ever won a track classic. **1935** J. AGATE *More First Nights* (1937) 141 This category includes racecourses, *greyhound and dog tracks, [etc.]. **1946** R. GENDERS *Mod. Greyhound Racing* iii. 27 There has been little change in the construction of greyhound tracks since the first ones were opened. **1970** *Encycl. Brit.* VII. 555/1 All major tracks are members of the American Greyhound Track Operators association.

greyish (ˈgreɪɪʃ), *a.* Forms: 6–9 **grayish**, (6 **greiesh, graish**), 7– **greyish**. [f. GREY *a.* + -ISH.] Somewhat grey.

1562 A. BROOKE *Romeus & Juliet* (New Shaks. Soc.) 22 This barefoote fryer gyrt with cord his grayish weede. **1586** WARNER *Alb. Eng.* IV. xx. (1589) 86 An euen Nose, on either side Stood out a graish Eie. **1589** FLEMING *Virg. Georg.* IV. 72 The prophet [Proteus]..With great inforcement roll'd his flaminge eyes with greiesh sight [L. *lumine glauco*]. **1657** R. LIGON *Barbadoes* (1673) 9 Those of the second altitude.. had a grayish colour, as if covered with light and sandy earth. **1713** WARDER *True Amazons* (ed. 2) 36 Their Wings ..grow ragged, and somewhat greyish. **1814** SCOTT *Ld. of Isles* III. xxvii, Now over Coolin's eastern head The greyish light begins to spread. **1880** HUXLEY *Crayfish* i. 31 The young animal is of a greyish colour.

b. Of hair.

1611 COTGR., *Grisastre*, grayish, hoarie. **1663** COWLEY *Cutter Coleman St.* V. ii, A Beard a little greyish. **1774** GOLDSM. *Nat. Hist.* IV. vii. 194 The hair..also on the upper lip and chin, where it was greyish.

c. *Comb.*, qualifying the names of other colours, as ***greyish-black, blue, brown, green, white, yellow***, etc.; also ***greyish-looking*** adj.

1752 SIR J. HILL *Hist. Anim.* 259 The colour is a dusky greyish-brown. **1796** MORSE *Amer. Geog.* I. 357 Greyish blue marble. **1831** BREWSTER *Optics* vii. 70 The effect of all the colours when combined will be a greyish-white. **1843** PORTLOCK *Geol.* 211 Hypersthene..passes into a greyish-green diallage. **1873** RALFE *Phys. Chem.* 200 This..forms a greyish black precipitate. **1874** G. LAWSON *Dis. Eye* 37 A small..greyish-looking ulcer. **1888** *Athenæum* 10 Nov. 632/1 A little boy in a greyish-olive smock frock.

grey lag goose, ˈgreylag (goose). [Orig. three words (still often so written); the use of LAG *a.* is supposed to refer to the bird's habit of remaining longer in England than the other migratory species of the genus.] The common wild goose of Europe, *Anser cinereus* or *ferus*.

1713 RAY *Syn. Avium* 138 *Anser palustris noster*, Grey Lagg *dictus*. **1802** G. MONTAGU *Ornith. Dict.* (1833) 231 Grey Lag Goose—A name for the common Goose. **1891** *Daily News* 2 Feb. 5/3 In the north of Scotland, however, some grey-lags still breed.

greyle, obs. form of GRAIL¹.

greyling, obs. form of GRAYLING.

greyly, grayly (ˈgreɪlɪ), *adv.* [f. GREY *a.* + -LY².] With a grey hue or tinge. Also *fig.*

1818 KEATS *Endym.* I. 231 A hazy light Spread greyly eastward. **1831** LYTTON *Godolph.* 31 Ruins, that rose greyly ..from the green woods around it. **1870** MISS BROUGHTON *Red as Rose* II. xi. 246 Life..must be lived somewhere; it can be lived pleasurably nowhere. Then, why not unpleasurably, greyly, negatively, at Plas Berwyn? **1889** MRS. ALEXANDER *Crooked Path* III. i. 32 The lawyer..grew greyly pale.

greymin, variant of GRIMING *dial.*

greyn, obs. form of GRAIN, GREEN.

greyness, grayness (ˈgreɪnɪs). Also 5 **graynes**, 6 **graines**. [f. GREY *a.* + -NESS.] The state or quality of being grey; grey colour. Also *fig.*

1483 *Cath. Angl.* 162/2 A Graynes of hare, *canicies*. **1597** BROUGHTON *Epist. to Nobilitie* Wks. III. 569 Judah feared to bring his fathers graines to Scheol with sorrow. **1611** COTGR., *Gris*,..graynesse, or the colour gray. **1746** HARVEY *Flower Garden* (1818) 80 The grayness of the dawn decays gradually. **1855** BROWNING *Men & Women, Andrea del Sarto* 3 A common greyness silvers everything—All in a twilight. **1884** *Harper's Mag.* Jan. 211/2 Here was no shade, no weird grayness. **1898** FOTHERINGHAM *Stud. Browning* 416 He feels..the greyness of everything in his life and work.

greys, obs. form of GREASE.

grey squirrel. [GREY *a.* 1 and 8 b.] A common squirrel of the United States (*Sciurus carolinensis*), which was introduced into Europe in the late 19th century.

1674 J. JOSSELYN *Account Two Voy. New Eng.* 86 There are three sorts, the mouse squirril, the gray squirril, and the flying-squirril. **1781** T. PENNANT *Hist. Quadrupeds* II. 410 Grey Squirrel... *Sciurus cinereus* L. Inhabits the woods of North America, Peru, and Chili; are very numerous in North America; do incredible damage to the plantations of Mayz. **1804** in *Maryland Hist. Mag.* (1909) IV. 9 Squirrels in this neighborhood are of a deep black color..less in size than the grey squirrels of Maryland. **1831** J. J. AUDUBON *Ornith. Biogr.* I. 247 The Grey Squirrel..migrates in prodigious numbers. **1831** J. M. PECK *Guide Emigrants* 164 The grey and fox squirrels often do mischief in the corn fields. **1850** N. KINGSLEY *Diary* (1914) 105 In the afternoon went out with a gun for the first time, grey squirrels are quite plenty but too much water to hunt them. **1935** *Discovery* June 169/1 In North Leicestershire red and grey squirrels have been noticed inhabiting the same wood without coming into conflict, while in Northamptonshire the red squirrels had decreased before the few greys arrived. **1964** H. N. SOUTHERN *Handbk. Brit. Mammals* II. 275 Whereas in America Grey Squirrel is prized game animal, in British Isles regarded as forest pest. **1971** *Daily Tel.* 1 Dec. 8/6 By far the worst crime of the grey squirrel was its attacks on hardwood trees by stripping off the bark.

greystone, graystone (ˈgreɪstəʊn). *Min.* [f. GREY *a.* + STONE *sb.*] A grey volcanic rock, composed of feldspar (sometimes replaced by leucite or melilite), augite, or hornblende, and iron.

1815 W. PHILLIPS *Outl. Min. & Geol.* (1818) 151 Greystone according to Werner, is a mixture of white felspar and blackish hornblende. **1830** LYELL *Princ. Geol.* I. 396 But lavas of composition precisely intermediate occur, and from their colour have been called graystones.

greyth, greythly, obs. ff. GRAITH, GRADELY.

greyts, obs. pl. of GRIT *sb.*²

greyve, obs. form of GRIEVE *v.*

greywacke (ˈgreɪwækə). *Geol.* Also **graywacke, greywack**. [Anglicised form of GRAUWACKE.] A conglomerate or grit rock consisting of rounded pebbles and sand firmly united together; originally applied to various strata of the Silurian series. Also *attrib.*

1811 PINKERTON *Petral.* I. 293 Almost the whole of the mines in the Hartz are situated in greywack. **1813** BAKEWELL *Introd. Geol.* (1815) 106 Gray-wacke is nearly allied to clay-slate, and the finer kinds of gray-wacke-slate pass into clay-slate, and are not to be distinguished. **1833** LYELL *Princ. Geol.* III. 194 The fundamental rock of the Eifel is an ancient secondary sandstone and shale, to which the obscure and vague appellation of 'graywacke' has been given. **1834** H. S. BOASE *Prim. Geol.* 215 The greywacké..and cretaceous groups. **1849** MURCHISON *Siluria* viii. 172 From its southern margin..greywackès..rise from under the coal-fields. **1853** G. JOHNSTON *Nat. Hist. E. Bord.* I. 5 The greywacke and syenitic hills. **1895** A. HARKER *Petrol.* xvi. 193 The old term *greywacke* (Ger. Grauwacke) has been revived for a complex rock with grains of quartz, felspar, and other minerals and rocks united by a cement usually siliceous. **1939** *Amer. Jrnl. Sci.* CCXXXVII. 29 This is the direction of a marked change in the angle of slope of the hillside..which is inferred to mark the vertical or highly inclined outer margin of the granite at its contact with Silurian shales and greywackes. **1950** *N.Z. Jrnl. Agric.* Jan. 16/3 Sandy silts, silts, clays, and greywacke shingle have been deposited by the Waipawa and Tukituki Rivers. **1963** KRUMBEIN & SLOSS *Stratigr. & Sedimentation* (ed. 2) v. 171 Many Precambrian and early Paleozoic graywackes are partially metamorphosed. **1970** *Nature* 3 Jan. 57/2 They resemble 'gouge-channels' occurring in graded greywacke beds.

griat, obs. Kentish form of GREAT *a.*

ˈgribble¹. *Obs.* exc. *dial.* Also 6 **greble**, 7 **grible**. [? related to *grab*, current form in s.w. dial. of CRAB *sb.*² (cf. *grab-tree* in quot. 1578).]

a. A crab-tree or black-thorn; a stick made from either of these; also *attrib.* **b.** The stock of a crab (or other tree?) for grafting upon.

1578 LYTE *Dodoens* VI. xxx. 696 Roundish leaues, somwhat like the leaues of a gribble, grabbe tree, or wilding. **1591** PERCIVALL *Sp. Dict.*, *Gancho*, a sheeps crooke, knops in a greble staffe, braunches in a stags horne. *c* **1640** J. SMYTH *Hundred of Berkeley* (1885) III. 25 A grible, i.e. A crabstocke to graft vpon. **1825** JENNINGS *Observ. Dial. W. Eng.* 41 *Gribble*, a young apple-tree raised from seed. **1847–78** HALLIWELL, *Gribble*, a shoot from a tree; a short cutting from one. *West.* **1863** W. BARNES *Dorset Gloss.*, *Gribble* (diminutive of *grab*), a young crab-tree or black-thorn; or a knotty walking stick made of it. **1880** *E. Cornwall Gloss.*, *Gribble*, the young stock of a tree on which a graft is to be inserted.

gribble² (ˈgrɪb(ə)l). [Of obscure origin: ? cognate with GRUB *v.*] A small marine boring crustacean, *Limnoria terebrans*, resembling a wood-louse.

1838 E. MOORE in *Mag. Nat. Hist.* II. 207 Our harbour [Plymouth] is exposed to the attacks of a much more formidable enemy, the *Limnoria terebrans*, or gribble. **1884** *Stand. Nat. Hist.* II. 71 Many plans have been proposed for preventing the ravages of the gribble. **1895** *Daily News* 14 June 5/3 To protect the gutta percha insulation from the attack of a minute marine organism known as the 'gribble'.

gricche, obs. form of GRUTCH.

grice¹ (graɪs). *Obs.* exc. *Sc.* and *arch.* Forms: 3–6 **grise**, 4 **grys**, 4–7 **gryse**, 5–9 **gryce**, (7 **greece**), 7– **grice**. [a. ON. *gríss* (Sw., Da. *gris*) young pig, pig.]

1. A pig, *esp.* a young pig, a sucking pig; †*occas.* and *spec.* in *Her.*, a wild boar.

a **1225** *Ancr. R.* 204 Þe Suwe of ȝiuernesse, þet is, Glutunie, haueð pigges [*MSS. T., C.* grises] þus inemned. *c* **1325** *Gloss. W. de Bibbysw.* in Wright *Voc.* 174 *Porceus*, gryses. *c* **1375** *Sc. Leg. Saints, Blasius* 119, I pray þe þat sume helpe þu wil gyf me, þat, bot a gryse, had gud nane. *c* **1400** MAUNDEV. (Roxb.) ix. 36 Þe Sarzenes also bringes furth na grysez, ne þai ete na swyne flessch. *c* **1420** *Avow. Arth.* ii, Sir, ther walkes in my way A welle grim gryse. He is a balefulle bare. **1513** DOUGLAS *Æneis* III. vi. 72 A grete sow fereit of grysis thretty heid. **1536** BELLENDEN *Cron.*

Scot. (1821) II. 164 Ane swine that etis hir grisis, sal be stanit to deid. **1609** Skene *Reg. Maj.* 124 Na Castellane may enter within ane Burges house to slay his swyne, gryses, geise, or hennes. **1812** W. Tennant *Anster F.* iv. viii, As a swineherd puts in poke a grice. **1828–40** Berry *Encycl. Her.* I, *Grices*, young wild boars, but boars are sometimes called grices, and so blazoned in allusion to the bearer's name. **1899** J. Colville *Scott. Vernacular* 15 Beginning life as a grice, the pig when speaned became a shot.

Proverb. **1721** Kelly *Scot. Prov.* 62 Bring the Head of the Sow to the Tail of the Grice. That is, balance your Loss with your Gain. **1818** Scott *Rob Roy* xxiv, An' I am to lose by ye, I'se ne'er deny I hae won by ye mony a fair pund sterling. Sae, an' it come to the warst, I'se e'en lay the head o' the sow to the tail o' the grice.

b. The *sing.* form used as *pl.* or *collect.*

? On analogy of the plurals *mice, lice.*

1362 Langl. *P. Pl.* A. Prol. 105 Hote pies, hote! Goode gees and grys! *Ibid.* iv. 38 Bothe my gees and my grys his gadelynges fetten. *c* **1476** *Plumpton Corr.* 39 As for geese, grise, hennys, & copons, your said tenants may none keepe, but they are..stolen away by night. **1679** Blount *Anc. Tenures* 101 He is come thither to hunt, and catch his Lords Greese [*margin* 'Wild swyne'].

†**c.** *transf.* The young of a badger (see pig). *Obs. rare*$^{-1}$.

1637 B. Jonson *Sad Sheph.* ii. ii, This fine Smooth Bawsons Cub, the young grice of a Gray [etc.]. [**1863** Sala *Capt. Dangerous* II. vii. 225 They burrowed like so many Grice.]

†**2.** The flesh of a 'grice', pork. *Obs. rare*$^{-1}$.

c **1420** *Liber Cocorum* (1862) 54 Bothe grys and vele and rostyd motone.

†**grice**². *Obs.*$^{-0}$ [App. Cotgrave's assimilation of *grouse* to the F. *grièche* (:—L. type **Græcisca*, fem. of **Græciscus*: see Greekish), as in *poule, perdrix grièche*; erron. taken by some etymologists to be the original of grouse *sb.*¹]

1611 Cotgr., *Poule griesche*, a Moorehenne; the henne of the Grice, or Mooregame.

grice, obs. form of grece, steps.

grice, variant of gris *a. Obs.*, grey.

griceling ('graɪslɪŋ). *rare.* [f. grice¹ + -ling.] A little pig.

1782 Elphinston *Martial* i. xiv. 11 Soon as the mother fell, the gricelings flew.

grickischs, -isshe, obs. forms of Greekish.

grid (grɪd). [back-formation from gridiron.]

1. a. An arrangement of parallel bars with openings between them; a grating.

1839 Ure *Dict. Arts* 585 (Art. *Glass-making*) A is the pot, resting upon the arched grid *b a*, built of fire-bricks, whose apertures are wide enough to let the flames rise freely, and strike the bottom and sides of the vessel. *c* **1865** J. Wylde in *Circ. Sci.* I. 34/1 Air is admitted through openings or grids in the floor. **1879** *Cassell's Techn. Educ.* IV. 209/2 A circular enclosure formed by a grid of angular iron bars. **1884** *Health Exhib. Catal.* 27/1 An open earthen-ware channel, which conveys the drainage into a suitable grid placed outside the building.

b. *Electr.* (See quot. 1893.)

1884 F. Krohn tr. *Glaser de Cew's Magn.-& Dyn.-Electr. Mach.* 122 The red lead paste becomes very firmly gripped by the surrounding grid-work. **1893** Sloane *Stand. Electrical Dict.*, *Grid*, a lead plate perforated or ridged for use in a storage battery as the supporter of the active materials and in part as contributing thereto from its own substance. **1964** G. Smith *Storage Batteries* ii. 13 A grid consists of an outer frame with take-off lug and a central mesh or lattice of vertical and horizontal ribs. **1968** R. H. Bacon *Car* x. 136 If the battery is old, or subjected to repeated complete discharge and charge, the paste may fall away from the grid.

c. *Mining.* = griddle 3. (Funk's *Stand. Dict.*)

2. = gridiron 1.

1875 in Knight *Dict. Mech.* ['The Silver Grid' appears as the name of several restaurants in London.]

3. *Naut.* = gridiron 3 b.

1867 in Smyth *Sailor's Word-bk.* **1879** *Engineering* 7 Mar. 203/1 At high water the vessel is brought over the grid, and as soon as she is shored up the lifting commences.

4. *Theatr.* = gridiron 3 c. (Funk's *Stand. Dict.*)

1927 *Stage* 27 Oct. 17/6 Ask him [*sc.* the young actor] questions about the grid, the apron,..and he will be at sea. **1933** P. Godfrey *Back-Stage* iv. 43 Seventy feet above the stage-level is the grid from which the scenery is flown. **1959** A. S. Gillette *Stage Scenery* vii. 171 Hoisting cables run from the winches to dollies that may be shifted to any position on the grid.

5. *Electr.* **a.** Orig., a wire gauze or helix or a perforated plate between the filament and the anode of a thermionic valve, forming a third electrode to which a voltage can be applied to control or modulate the flow of electrons from the filament. Later extended to any electrode in a valve, gas discharge tube, or similar device, having one or more apertures for the passage of electrons or ions; *spec.* **control grid**, one that serves as a control electrode. Cf. *screen grid, suppressor grid.*

1907 *Electrical World* 30 Nov. 1034/1 In his talk, Dr. De Forest stated that many types of receivers are suitable for wireless Telephone work... However, the Audion receiver, especially in its latest form in which the antenna is joined to an isolated grid interposed between a tantalum filament and a platinum wing, gives perfect 'articulation'. **1919** R. Stanley *Text Bk. Wireless Telegr.* (new ed.) II. xi. 208 The output is controlled by the control grid, which is between the filament and the heavier grid anode beyond. **1923** E. W. Marchant *Radio Telegr.* iv. 52 When a grid is introduced into the valve, it may be used, not merely for rectifying signals.., but..for amplifying or increasing the strength of a signal. **1947** D. G. Fink *Radar Engin.* xi. 538 The potential on the control electrode (grid) controls the brightness of the spot. **1950** J. C. Slater *Microwave Electronics* xi. 279 For a relatively short accelerator, there may be few enough grids so that a considerable fraction of the ion beam penetrates all the grids. **1950** Rider & Uslan *Encycl. Cathode-Ray Oscill.* v. 86/1 Surrounding the cathode [of the electron gun] is a cylinder *G* which has a baffle containing a tiny aperture at its center... The baffle with its aperture is the actual control grid. **1959** *Chambers's Encycl.* XIV. 241/1 The two control grids in a frequency changer are usually the first and third from the cathode, the other grids being screens, accelerators and suppressors.

b. Freq. *attrib.* and *Comb.* (usu. in the sense *control grid*), as ***grid battery, condenser, potential, voltage***; **grid bias**, a steady, usu. negative, voltage applied to the control grid of a valve on which the signal voltage is superimposed; hence, the steady potential difference between the control gird and the cathode in the absence of a signal; **grid circuit**, the circuit connected between the grid and the cathode of a valve; **grid control**, control of the anode current, esp. the discharge in a gas discharge tube, by means of the grid voltage; so **grid-controlled** *a.*; **grid current**, the current flowing to the grid from outside the valve; **grid-dip meter** or **oscillator**, a calibrated valve oscillator used as a frequency meter, resonance of the tank circuit of the oscillator with the resonant circuit under test being indicated by a drop in the grid current of the valve; **grid leak (resistance)**, a high resistance connected between the grid and the cathode of a valve by which any excess charge on the grid can escape; **grid modulation**, modulation in which the modulating signal is applied to the grid of a valve in which the carrier is present.

1924 *Harmsworth's Wireless Encycl.* II. 1053/2 The *grid battery plays an important part in the operation of power-amplifying valves. **1926** S. O. Pearson *Dict. Wireless Terms*, *Grid bias. **1928** *Morning Post* 26 Jan. 13/4 When there are two stages of low frequency amplification a grid bias of negative 1½ volts is ample. **1968** *Listener* 20 June 800/3 There was endless trouble with grid-biases, valves, condensers, speakers. **1916** *Electrician* LXXVI. 798/2 Oscillations in the *grid circuit set up oscillations of similar character in the wing circuit of the audion. **1937** *Discovery* Feb. 54/1 A simple spherical electrode is connected with the grid circuit of a valve oscillator. **1916** *Electrician* LXXVI. 800/1 The radio frequency beats are then rectified by the audion to charge the grid and the *grid condenser, and this charge varies the electron current to produce an amplifying action on the current in the telephones. **1940** *Chambers's Techn. Dict.* 390/1 *Grid condenser*, a condenser connected between the grid and the cathode of a thermionic valve. **1921** L. B. Turner *Wireless Telegr.* vi. 91 (*heading*) *Grid control over anode circuit. **1952** W. G. Dow *Fund. Engin. Electronics* (ed. 2) xviii. 543 (*heading*) Grid control of current conduction in a thyratron. **1939** H. J. Reich *Theory & Appl. Electron Tubes* xi. 394 The time required for complete breakdown of *grid-controlled arc tubes is of the order of a few microseconds. **1962** Simpson & Richards *Junction Transistors* viii. 188 These devices show promise as solid state 'thyratrons'... They have the advantage over grid-controlled gas-tube rectifiers that they can be turned off more readily. **1919** *Radio Rev.* Dec. 144 The circuit..will be called the grid circuit, and the current flowing in it the *grid current. **1948** J. W. Gray in Valley & Wallman *Vacuum Tube Amplifiers* xi. 419 Positive grid current, caused by electrons flowing to the grid from the cathode, is much greater and much less erratic than the negative grid current. **1971** *Physics Bull.* Feb. 108/2 Conventional electrometer tubes have a minimum guaranteed grid current in the region of 10^{-15} A, somewhat large for a number of modern requirements. **1959** K. Henney *Radio Engin. Handbk.* (ed. 5) xiv. 11 *Grid-dip meters... The grid current of an oscillator will 'dip' slightly as the wavemeter is tuned through the operating frequency. **1962** Simpson & Richards *Junction Transistors* xiv. 355 It is possible to measure the input and output impedances [of the transistor] in such a case with the aid of a signal generator and a grid-dip meter. **1919** *Radio Rev.* Nov. 82, R is a large resistance which acts as a *grid leak, and should be chosen so as to keep the grids at a voltage found advantageous by trial. **1966** *McGraw-Hill Encycl. Sci. & Technol.* II. 184/1 There is always a small grid current flowing through the grid-leak resistor when cathode or fixed bias is used. **1924** F. H. Haynes *Amateur's Bk. Wireless Circuits* (ed. 2) 21 In another system of *grid modulation the microphone secondary is connected between the grid itself and the L.T. minus, with the grid condenser in the lead to the grid coil and this time not fitted with a leak. **1967** R. L. Shrader *Electronic Communication* (ed. 2) xvii. 348 Low audio power requirement is one of the advantages of grid modulation. **1916** *Electrician* LXXVI. 801/1 A point will finally be reached where the *grid potential is sufficiently reduced to allow the wing current to flow. **1918** *Wireless World* June 142 Up to the saturation currents for the gas space within the bulb, the change in plate current is approximately proportional to the *grid voltage.

6. a. A network of lines, esp. two series of regularly spaced lines crossing one another at right angles; *spec.* one provided on a map as a means of specifying the location of places and objects. Also ***grid finder, navigation, reference, sheet, system***; ***grid-like*** adj.

1918 in *Geogr. Jrnl.* (1919) LIII. 33 Doubtless the German was amused at the conservative Briton, who at first preferred to use a 'grid' of squares 1000 yards a side. **1922** *Encycl. Brit.* XXXII. 623/1 For the use of large scale maps in trench warfare..it must be possible to read off at sight the coördinates of any desired point from a 'grid' or network of lines printed on the map... For ease and accuracy of reference the 'grid' should be in squares. **1924** *Times Trade & Engin. Suppl.* 29 Nov. 241 Simplicity of reference is ensured by the use of a novel transparent grid sheet, ruled in squares and numbered to correspond with the grid numbers given in the Gazetteer. The use of this grid sheet enables the most obscure place to be found on the map in a moment. **1925** Close & Winterbotham *Text Bk. Topogr. Surveying* (ed. 3) 135 Some form of reference grid was found necessary by all combatants in the late war. *Ibid.* 136 To overprint his available maps with the appropriate grid. **1930** G. R. de Beer *Embryol. & Evol.* iv. 29 The comparison of one adult form with another can be made very instructive by inscribing the shape of one form on a grid-system of Cartesian co-ordinates. *Ibid.* 30 By a harmonious transformation of the grid, the skull of Hyracotherium can be distorted and made to resemble that of the horse. **1931** *Times Lit. Suppl.* 10 Sept. 674/4 This grid, which has the appearance of a transparent chessboard, can be made to appear at the same height as any object in the stereoscope picture. **1932** *Jrnl. R. Aeronaut. Soc.* XXXVI. 518 This template, often known as the grid finder, is placed on the photograph so that the line representing the apparent horizon coincides with the apparent horizon on the photograph. **1944** *Geogr. Rev.* XXXIV. 436 (*title*) Grid Navigation by Samuel Herrick. *Ibid.*, The introduction of a rectangular grid system and what is hereafter described as 'grid variation' makes it possible to navigate a straight line on any conformal..chart. **1946** R. J. C. Atkinson *Field Archaeol.* ii. 46 The interrupted grid system..enables a much larger area to be searched in a given time. **1950** *Mind* LIX. 302 The description..both suggests a kind of permanent grid-like world framework and denies it. **1954** M. Beresford *Lost Villages* viii. 270 Grid-references to the 1-inch Ordnance maps. **1958** *Listener* 13 Nov. 779/1 The first [major development in polar navigation] is the substitution of a rectangular 'grid' for the conventional graticule of parallels of latitude and meridians of longitude which converge at the Poles. This simple technique, which has been extensively developed since the war, is generally called 'grid navigation'. **1963** E. S. Wood *Collins Field Guide Archaeol.* iv. i. 306 A card index should be kept; one card for each find or site, showing details,..location, with grid reference. **1966** H. Williamson *Methods Bk. Design* (ed. 2) xiii. 211 The photographer places in the camera..a glass screen ruled with a rectangular grid of fine diagonal lines. **1971** D. Potter *Brit. Eliz. Stamps* xiv. 148 This tissue is first exposed behind a fine grid of horizontal and vertical lines.

b. *Building.* (See quot. 1935.) Also ***grid plan.***

1935 *Archit. Rev.* LXXVII. 65 The plan of the building conforms to a grid composed of rectangles of this proportion, measuring 2 ft. by 2 ft. 10 ins. **1964** J. S. Scott *Dict. Building* 153 *Grid plan*, a plan in which setting-out lines called grid lines coincide with the most important walls and other building components. Prefabricated buildings are usually designed to fit a grid plan.

c. *Motor Racing.* A pattern of lines painted on the track at the starting-point to indicate the position in which the cars are to line up (see also quot. 1971).

1951 C. A. N. May *Formula 3* x. 124 Imagine the feelings of young Jeremy Fry when..the engine stalled..and the white car was left on the grid. **1957** S. Moss *In Track of Speed* xiii. 161 On the first line of the starting grid were Fangio and myself on Mercedes and Ascari on a Lancia. **1966** *Publ. Amer. Dial. Soc. 1964* xlii. 5 *Grid*, area behind the starting line, usually painted in checked pattern. **1970** *Times* 8 May 9/2 The controversial qualifying race..would be to decide who should fill the last six places on the grid. *Ibid.*, The qualifying race will not take place and the grid will be decided on the fastest practice time. **1971** *Observer* 1 Aug. 19/3 The grid means the pattern of cars when stationary at the start—perhaps three cars on the first row of the grid, two on the second, and so on, the positions being allotted according to the best time you registered in the practice laps.

d. *Archit.* (See quots.) Also ***grid layout, plan, system.*** Cf. gridiron *sb.* 3 d.

1954 *Ann. Reg. 1953* 104 The Punjab's new capital at Chandigarh..was built on a grid system which separated fast traffic from slow and divided the city into 25 rectangular sectors. **1958** *Listener* 29 Nov. 826/1 The town is laid out on a grid plan. *Ibid.*, In spite of the imposed colonial grid, the landscaping tradition of the old country reasserts itself successfully. **1959** *Chambers's Encycl.* XIII. 703/2 Wherever land is approximately flat there has been a tendency to use the grid layout, by which a town is divided into 'blocks' of approximately equal size by streets at right-angles to each other. **1959** *Listener* 26 Mar. 542/2 He accepts, as indeed any architect today must accept, the rectangularities, the grid, the engineering forms, the big areas of glass that, for most people, *are* modern architecture. **1969** *Ibid.* 23 Jan. 98/1 Some of the factors blighting American cities (their ruthless grid-plan expansion, [etc.]).

e. *Phonetics.* 'A diagrammatic representation of approximate tongue-positions of average English vowels compared with those of cardinal vowels' (Daniel Jones).

1961 *Amer. Speech* XXXVI. 219 Daniel Jones's cardinal vowel grid is proposed as a more useful method of specifying vowel sounds in terms of auditory reference points. **1964** E. Palmer tr. *Martinet's Elem. Gen. Ling.* iii. 66 We can.. attempt to represent schematically the proportions of the system, by arranging in a 'grid' the sets of phonemes characterized by the same relevant feature.

7. A bicycle. *slang.*

1922 D. H. Lawrence *England, my England* 111 Oh, well! I wheel the grid, do I? **1943** *Coast to Coast 1942* 71 'I'll walk and wheel the grid, and if my dad's home he can drive out in the car to meet me.' 'Gosh, no!' you said. 'Here, you go on, on my grid, an' I'll do the walking.'

8. a. A network of high-voltage transmission lines and connections that supply electricity from a number of generating stations to various distribution centres in a country or a region, so that no consumer is dependent on a single station.

1926 *Public Opinion* 3 Apr. 331/2 The electrical 'grid' is absolutely necessary in the future just as our railway network has been in the past. **1930** *Times Financ. Rev.* 11 Feb. p. xxxiii/1 With transforming stations at the points most suitable for enabling the pool of electricity provided by the 'Grid' to be tapped for distribution throughout the area. **1955** *Times* 5 July p. ii/3 Water for the mill will be drawn from the Tarawera River at the rate of 10,000,000 gallons a day, while hydro-electric power will be supplied by the national grid. **1955** *Oxf. Jun. Encycl.* VIII. 191 Engineers in charge of the grid system meet this problem of changing demand by running the most efficient power stations continuously and by switching in the less efficient smaller stations as the demand increases. **1971** *Sci. Amer.* Sept. 47/3 Electric power can be transmitted as needed over grids of continental size.

b. Used of any network that serves a similar purpose for other services.

1943 *Times* 8 Dec. 5/5 Should not our leading water engineers be called upon by the Ministry of Reconstruction to report and prepare comprehensive plans for a national grid? **1960** *Economist* 15 Oct. 271/3 Total gasification (linked with a national high-pressure grid supplying industry direct and local systems with lean gas for enrichment to town gas), rather than carbonisation, offers the main opportunity. **1970** *Sci. Jrnl.* Aug. 82/1 [In Holland] a little over 80 per cent of the 13 million inhabitants..are connected to the gasgrid.

9. A strong open framework of iron fixed to the back of a motor car to hold luggage.

1928 *Evening News* 24 July 4/2 It can be carried on either luggage grid or running board. **1928** *Daily Mail* 25 July 1/5 All straps, loops, etc., which are necessary to fit to the grid of a car.

10. The field on which American football is played; hence loosely, American football. Also *attrib.* Cf. GRIDIRON *sb.* 3 e.

1928 *Chicago Tribune* 13 Dec. 25/8 (*headline*) Law..to lead Irish on Grid in 1929. **1968** *Globe & Mail* (Toronto) 15 Jan. 17/4 It was a satisfying triumph for the aging Packers, who showed their grid obituaries had been written prematurely. **1970** *New Yorker* 3 Oct. 34/1 You grid fans are just going to have to buckle down... Anybody who can't straighten out a plain old two-league, six-division distribution..probably isn't in shape.

Hence **grid** *v. trans.*, to cook on a gridiron.

1884 *J. Bull's Neighbour* xii. 90 Where is the Frenchwoman..who can cook a chop, grid a steak, [etc.]?

gridaline, obs. form of GRIDELIN.

gridded ('grɪdɪd), *pa. pple.* and *ppl. a.* [f. GRID + -ED[2].] Covered with, forming, or containing a grid (in various senses).

1926 *Blackw. Mag.* Dec. 774/2 A white screen, gridded and lettered, covered the wall. **1940** *Illustr. London News* CXCVII. 202 While fighters fly to the convoy's defence, women of the W.A.A.F. are moving counters and models of ships and other symbols with 'croupiers' rakes' to record all the information from various sources upon a big, gridded map. **1949** *Archit. Rev.* CV. 113/2 The pyramidal museum of the plastic arts is stratified from industrial art at the base, to a scattering of rare masterworks at the summit; each floor is gridded, the co-ordinates expressing respectively periods and schools. **1958** *Oxf. Univ. Gaz.* 10 Mar. 771/1 Other.. finds in Italy included..gridded layouts of roads. **1963** B. Fozard *Instrumentation Nucl. Reactors* ii. 18 The arrangement of a gridded chamber is shown. **1971** *Physics Bull.* June 346/1 Many experimenters choose to plot their data on the standard gridded graph paper.

griddle ('grɪd(ə)l), *sb.* Forms: 3 gredil(e, 4 gridele, -il, grydel, 5 gredel(le, -yl(e, grydele, -ell, -yl, gridel, griddyll, 8– griddle. [app. a. early OF. *gredil = greil, grail (mod.F. gril) masc., or *gredille = gradilie, greille (mod.F. grille) fem.: see GRILL *sb.*[4]

A Norman *grédil*, app. meaning 'gridiron', is quoted by Moisy from documents of the 16th c.; and an OF. *grediller* to scorch, crisp at a fire, survived until the 16th c. (when it was replaced by the altered form *grésiller*); but the relation of these to OF. *greil* is obscure.]

†**1. a.** = GRIDIRON 1. *Obs.*

1388 Wyclif *Exod.* xxvii. 4 And thou schalt make a brasun gridele [**1382** gredyrne, Vulg. *craticulam*] in the maner of a net. *c* **1400** *Destr. Troy* 13826 A Grydell full gay, gret-full of fiche. *c* **1420** *Liber Cocorum* (1862) 25 Take lampryaes and..rost hom on gredyl. *c* **1450** *Two Cookery-bks.* 114 Haddoke..yrosted on a gridel. **1746** *Exmoor Scolding* Gloss. (E.D.S.) 66 *Griddle*, a grid-iron.

†**b.** = GRIDIRON 1 b. *Obs.*

a **1225** *Ancr. R.* 122 Seint Lorens also iðolede þet te gredil hef him upwardes mid berninde gleden. *c* **1290** *S. Eng. Leg.* I. 208/269 Some op-on grediles of Ire i-rostede weren also. *Ibid.* 277/198 þe king het a-non þat Men him scholden op-on a strong gredile [*v.r.* gridire] do. **1447** Bokenham *Seyntys* (Roxb.) 107 Summe wyth forkys of yryn ful strong On the grydyl hir turnyd up and down. **1483** Caxton *Gold. Leg.* 249 b/1 He was..tormented uppon a gredyl of yron.

2. a. A circular iron plate upon which cakes are baked; also used for cooking grills, etc. Also *attrib.* = GIRDLE *sb.*[2]

1352 *Durham Acct. Rolls*, Grydel pro pane. **1812** W. Tennant *Anster F.* vi. liv, As would a hen leap on a fire-hot griddle. **1859** Jephson *Brittany* ii. 19 She poured upon a griddle..some batter. **1875** Le Fanu *Will. Die* i. 12 Sometimes we..made a hot cake, and baked it on the griddle. **1897** Mrs. W. M. Ramsay *Every Day Life Turkey* ii. 48 Large round scones..cooked..on an iron griddle. **1962** *Economist* 29 Dec. 1295/3 The latest [British Railways] idea is the 'griddle car'—..with a 'chef-conductor' grilling steaks and poaching eggs to order. **1963** *Daily Tel.* 8 Jan. 14/1 Meals cooked on the griddle in a matter of minutes may be taken back to seats in other parts of the train or eaten in the Griddle Car itself. **1968** *Times* 2 May 2/3 British Railways are to try out two new types of refreshment car, known respectively as a Griddle Buffet and a Lounge Buffet.

b. Gofer- or waffle-irons. *rare.*

1853 Kane *Grinnell Exp.* xxxiv. (1856) 306 Like a batter-cake between the two disks of a hot griddle.

3. *Mining.* A wire-bottomed sieve or screen.

1776 Pryce *Min. Cornub.* 233 A person near the Shaft.. sifts it [Ore] in a Griddle, or iron wire sieve. **1858** Simmonds *Dict. Trade*, *Griddle, Riddle*, a miner's wire-bottomed sieve for separating the ore from the halvans.

4. *attrib.* and *Comb.*, as †*griddle-sacrifice*, *griddle-ful*; *griddle-hot* adj.; **griddle-bread, -cake**, bread or cake baked on a griddle; †**griddle-iron** = sense 2.

1841 S. C. Hall *Ireland* II. 25 A few slices of *griddle bread. **1881** *Daily News* 26 Aug. 5/7 Cold mutton fat and griddle bread. **1783** Vallancey *Collect.* III. xii. 460 The good women are employed in making the *griddle cake. **1852** Mrs. Stowe *Uncle Tom's C.* xiii. 118 Mary stood at the stove, baking griddle-cakes. *Ibid.* iv. 19 De first *griddle-full of cakes. **1966** 'M. Renault' *Mask of Apollo* xv. 252 The streets were *griddle-hot and dusty. **1769** *De Foe's Tour Gt. Brit.* IV. 204 The *Gridle-Iron here is a thin Iron Plate.. about two Feet in Diameter. **1382** Wyclif *Lev.* ii. 7 If thin offryng shal be..for the *gredil sacrifice [Vulg. *sin autem de craticula fuerit sacrificium*], euen maner the tried flour shal be spreynt with oile.

griddle ('grɪd(ə)l), *v.*[1] [f. GRIDDLE *sb.*]

1. *trans.* To cook on a griddle.

c **1430** *Two Cookery-bks.* 40 Take Venyson or Bef, & leche & gredyl it vp broun. **1887** Besant *The World went* i. 6 He every day fried or griddled a great piece of beef-steak.

2. *Mining. to griddle out*: to screen ore with a griddle.

1776 Pryce *Min. Cornub.* i. iii. 62 Black Copper Ore..is generally griddled out and put to the pile for sale, as it rises from the Mine.

Hence **'griddling** *vbl. sb.*

1876 T. Hardy *Ethelberta* (1890) 358 I'll finish the griddling.

griddle ('grɪd(ə)l), *v.*[2] *slang. intr.* To sing in the streets as a beggar.

1851 Mayhew *Lond. Labour* (1861) I. 248 Another woman..whose husband had got a month for 'griddling in the main drag' (singing in the high street). **1877** Besant & Rice *Son of Vulc.* i. xii. 267 Cardiff Jack's never got so low as to be gridling on the main drag. **1892** *Daily News* 8 Feb. 7/2 They were singing a hymn, or what was better known in the begging fraternity as 'gridling'.

Hence **'griddler**, a street singer.

1859 in *Slang Dict.* **1888** Besant *Fifty Y. Ago* iv. 53 There are hymns in every collection which suit the Gridler.

†**griddled**, *a. Obs. rare*[−1]. In 3–4 grideld, griddeled. Only in *griddled frost*, hoar frost.

a **1300** *Cursor M.* 6520 Manna..fel fra lift sa gret plente, Als a grideld [*Fairf.* griddeled, *Gött.* rime] frost to se.

griddled ('grɪd(ə)ld), *ppl. a.* [f. GRIDDLE *v.* + -ED[1].] Fried or baked on a griddle.

1883 O'Donovan *Story Merv* xx. (1884) 225 The usual meal of griddled bread and weak tea.

griddly ('grɪdlɪ), *a. dial.* Also 8 gridly. [Cf. GRIDDLED *a.*[1]] Sandy, gritty.

1747 Hooson *Miner's Dict.* R 1 Sandy or gridly Gear. **1886** *Cheshire Gloss.*, *Griddly*, gritty.

†**gride**, *sb.*[1] *Obs.* [? A metathetic form of GIRD *sb.*[2] (sense 3).] A spasm of pain, a pang.

a **1400–50** *Alexander* 544 þe aire nowe & þe elementis ere evyn in þis tyme So trauailed out of temperoure & troubild of þat sone, þat makis þi grippis and þi gridis a grete dele þe kenere.

gride (graɪd), *sb.*[2] [f. GRIDE *v.*] A strident or grating sound.

1830–4 Whittier *Mogg Megone* iii. 1065 The gride of hatchets fiercely thrown On wigwam-log and tree and stone. **1880** L. Wallace *Ben-Hur* iv. vii, The trumpet, and the gride of the wheels, and the prospect of diversion excite me.

gride (graɪd), *v.* Chiefly *poet.* Also 5–6 **gryde**. Pa. pple. 5–7 **gride, gryde**. [metathetic form of GIRD *v.*[2], adopted by Spenser from Lydgate, and from Spenser by later writers. The mod. application of the word to sound is perh. due to a feeling of its echoic expressiveness, suggested by words like *grate*, *strident*, etc.]

1. *trans.* To pierce with a weapon; to wound; †also, to inflict (a wound) by piercing (*obs.*). Also with *away*. *Obs.* or *arch.*

a **1400–50** *Alexander* 2278 (Dublin MS.) He hym grydes [*Ashm. MS.* girdes] to þe grund, & þe gre wynnez. **1412–20** Lydg. *Chron. Troy* ii. xiv, To se her husband with large woundes depe Gryde through the body. **1579** Spenser *Sheph. Cal.* Feb. 4 The kene cold blowes through my beaten hyde, All as I were through the body gryde [*Gloss*, Gride, perced: an olde word much vsed of Lidgate]. **1590** —— *F.Q.* iii. i. 62 In minde to gride The loathed leachour. **1596** *Ibid.* iv. vi. 1 Such was the wound that Scudamour did gride. **1622** Drayton *Poly-olb.* xxii. 1491 With many a cruel wound [he] was through the body gride. **1647** H. More *Song of Soul* iii. App. lix, A stake should gride His stubborn heart. **1808** J. Barlow *Columb.* iii. 600 All gride the dying; all deface the dead. **1832** Motherwell *Ouglou's Onslaught* Poems 83 The steel grides their flank. **1842** Lytton *Zanoni* vii. xiii, The sharpness of grief cuts and grides away many of those bonds of infirmity.

absol. **1848** Lytton *Harold* vii. v, Famine marches each hour to gride and to slay.

fig. **1590** Spenser *F.Q.* ii. ix. 29 The wicked engine through false influence Past through his eies, and secretly did glyde Into his heart, which it did sorely gryde. **1647** H. More *Song of Soul* ii. i. ii. xxviii, Our own spirits gride With piercing wind in storming Winter tide, Contract themselves. **1830** W. Phillips *Mt. Sinai* ii. 62 Its murky wave Continuous closeth on the frequent gleam Of lurid hue that grides it.

2. *intr.* To pierce *through*. Now usually, To cut, scrape, or graze *along*, *through*, *up*, etc., with a strident, grating, or whizzing sound, or so as to cause intense rasping pain. Also, *to gride its way*.

1590 Spenser *F.Q.* ii. viii. 36 Through his thigh the mortall steele did gryde. *a* **1782** J. Scott *Amœbæan Eclog.* ii. 63 His keen sickle grides along the lands. **1818** Milman *Samor* 6 The keen scythes Gride through their iron harvest. **1843** *Blackw. Mag.* LIV. 16 A sword was now griding its way through my frame. **1858** Farrar *Eric* ii. xii. (1897) 363 The horrible rope fell on him, griding across his back. **1878** Stevenson *Inland Voy.* 102 Now, the river would approach the side, and run griding along the chalky base of the hill. **1880** L. Wallace *Ben-Hur* 158 Against the sides the hostile vessels yet crushed and grided.

3. *trans.* To clash or graze against with a strident sound; to cause to grate.

1821 Shelley *Prometh. Unb.* iii. i, Hear ye the thunder of the fiery wheels Griding the winds? **1850** Tennyson *In Mem.* cvii, The wood which grides and clangs Its leafless ribs and iron horns Together.

grideld: see GRIDDLED *a.*

gridelin ('grɪdəlɪn), *sb.* and *a.* Also 7 **grisdelin(e, greda-, gre(e)de-, grayde-, gridaline, gridilyon, grizelin.** [ad. F. *gridelin*, *gris-de-lin* 'grey of flax', flax-grey; Littré explains it as 'a colour partaking of white and red'.]

A. *sb.* The name of a colour, a pale purple or grey violet; sometimes, a pale red. **B.** *adj.* Having this colour.

c **1640** [Shirley] *Capt. Underwit* ii. ii. in Bullen *O. Pl.* II. 345 Shall I decipher my Colours to you now? Folimort is withered, Grisdelin [*ed.* **1649** ('*Country Capt.*', under the name of Dk. Newcastle) ii. i. 28 *reads* greedeline] is absent, and Isabella is beauty. **1652** H. Cogan tr. *Scudery's Ibrahim* ii. i. 10 The third..was in a wastcoat of gridilyon sattin. **1657** R. Ligon *Barbadoes* (1673) 83 Sky colour, and Orange tawny, Gridaline, and Gingeline, white and Philyamort. **1663** Killigrew *Parson's Wed.* ii. iii, His Love..fades like my Gredaline Petticote. **1665–76** Rea *Flora* 47 They are either red..or else sadder or paler violet, graydeline, or murey purple. **1685** Temple *Gardening* Wks. 1710 I. 184 The Burgundy [Grape] which is a Grizelin or Pale Red. **1688** R. Holme *Armoury* i. 13/2 Colours derived from Purple..Gredeline, pale Peach. **1698** *Phil. Trans.* XX. 465 The same vinous or Grisdeline Colour. **1712** tr. *Pomet's Hist. Drugs* I. 41 Large Gridelin Flowers mix'd with Purple. **1791** Hamilton *Berthollet's Dyeing* I. i. ii. iv. 199 Violets and gridelins of all shades. **1860** R. Macfarlane *Dyeing & Calico-pr.* ii. 47 A fine gridelin, bordering upon archil, is thereby obtained; but this color has no permanence.

griding ('graɪdɪŋ), *ppl. a.* [f. GRIDE *v.* + -ING[2].] That grides.

1. Piercing, wounding; cutting keenly and painfully through. *lit.* and *fig.*

1667 Milton *P.L.* vi. 329 So sore The griding sword with discontinuous wound Pass'd through him. **1782** Elphinston tr. *Martial* i. xxii. 35 For brawny necks the griding claw remains. *a* **1794** Sir W. Jones *Pindar's 1st Nemean Ode* 81 Griding anguish pierc'd his fluttering breast. **1812** W. Tennant *Anster F.* vi. xxix, Set their griding forks and knives to work. **1813** T. Busby *Lucretius* iii. 713 So swift the motion of the griding steel. *a* **1863** Thackeray *Character Sk.* (1872) 341 The griding excitement which thrills through every fibre of the soul. **1876** Farrar *Marlb. Serm.* xxvii. 270 He perished, as he deserved, by the pitiless, griding, contemptuous swords of those whom he had striven to seduce.

2. Grating, clashing; strident.

1740 Dyer *Ruins Rome* 462 The car..Which..dreadful roll'd its griding wheels Over the bloody war. **1830** Tennyson *Poems* 113 The heavy thunder's griding might. **1845** *Blackw. Mag.* LVIII. 679 A griding clash of steel and a shrill cry of agony. **1851** J. B. Hume *Poems early Years, Oct. Gales* 14 Oh, boist'rous sea! Oh griding gale!

gridiron ('grɪdaɪən), *sb.* Forms: α. 3–4 **gred-**, 4 **gridire**, 5 **gredyre, gerdyre.** β. 4 **gredyrne, gridirne**, 5 **grederne, -irne, -eyren, gredren, -yn, grydirne, -eyron, -eyorn**, 5–6 **gredyron**, 6 **-yern, -iren, gryderne, grede yron**, 6–7 **greediron(e, grediron**, 7 **gridyron**, 6– **gridiron.** γ. 6 *north.* **girdiron, -yrne, gerdyron, girde-, gyrd(e-iron.** [Of obscure formation. The earliest form *gredire* appears in the same text (*S. Eng. Leg.*) with *gredile* GRIDDLE, but it is not clear whether the change from *-ile* to *-ire* is phonetic, or due to popular etymology. The later forms, however, show that the *-ire* was at an early date identified with southern ME. *ire* = *iren* IRON (cf. *fur-ire* FIRE-IRON), the further development being parallel to that of ANDIRON, q.v.]

1. a. A cooking utensil formed of parallel bars of iron or other metal in a frame, usually supported on short legs, and used for broiling flesh or fish over a fire. †Also formerly, a girdle or griddle.

α. **14..** *Metr. Voc.* in Wr.-Wülcker 626/7 Gredyre, *craticula.*

β. **13..** *E.E. Allit. P.* B. 1277 þe gredirne & þe goblotes garnyst of syluer. **1382** Wyclif *Exod.* xxvii. 4 Thow shalt make..a brasun gredyrne [**1388** gridele, Coverdale gredyron, **1551** gredyern, **1611** grate or networke] in the manere of a nett. *c* **1450** *Two Cookery-bks.* 102 Kutte the chyne in ij. or in iij. peces, and roste him on a faire gredryn. **1482** *Paston Lett.* No. 867 III. 298 A gredeyren of sylver of Parysse towche, not gylt. **1485** *Naval Acc. Hen. VII* (1896) 51 Ketle hokes ij., Grydirnes j., fflesh hokes j. **1544** Phaer *Regim. Life* (1553) D iv b, Fyshe rosted vpon the gridiron. **1561** Hollybush *Hom. Apoth.* 6 Take the braynes of a hogge, rost the same vpon a grede yron. **1647** R. Stapylton *Juvenal* 211 Broil'd rashers, that on wide gridirons lay. **1749** Fielding *Tom Jones* x. iv, The said Chicken was then at Roost.., and required the several Ceremonies of catching, killing, and picking, before it was brought to the Grid-iron. *c* **1850** *Arab. Nts.* (Rtldg.) 621 Our gridiron is only fit to broil small fish.

γ. **1495** *Nav. Acc. Hen. VII* (1896) 260 Brasyn pottes brokyn..Gyrdeyrons Brokyn. **1528** *Test. Ebor.* (Surtees) V. 255 A girdyrne, xij d. **1557** *Richmond. Wills* (Surtees) 100 One old brandrethe, one gerdyron, one pare of tongs. **1599** *Acc. Bk.* in *Antiquary* XXXII. 243 A girde Iron.

b. A similar structure employed as an instrument of torture by fire.

As in the case of griddle, this is the connexion in which the word first appears in English.

α. *c* **1290** *S. Eng. Leg.* I. 344/154 Strong fuyr he lieth maken and gret, and a gredire þar-on sette. *c* **1305** *St. Cristopher* 202 in *E.E.P.* (1862) 65 þe king het þat me scholde anon vpe a gridire him do And roste him wiþ fur & pich. **1393** Langl. *P. Pl.* C. iii. 130 Laurens þe leuite lyggynge on þe gredire, Loked vp to oure lorde. **14..** *S. Eng. Leg.* (MS. Bodl. 779) in *Archiv Stud. neu. Spr.* LXXXII. 325/108 Vppon a gerdyre he let here to rosty.

β. **1483** Caxton *Gold. Leg.* 248/1 The mynystres..leyd hym stratched oute uppon a gredyron of yron. **1555** Eden *Decades* 39 A certeyne frame of woodde much lyke vnto a hurdle or grediren. **1613** Purchas *Pilgrimage* ix. xv. (1614) 913 The Nobles and commanders, they broiled on gridirons. **1631** R. Byfield *Doctr. Sabb.* 51 The wheele, greediron, racke and faggot. **1649** Jer. Taylor *Gt. Exemp.* iii. xv. 92 S. Laurence accounted the coals of his Gridiron but as a Julip. **1839–40** W. Irving *Wolfert's R.* (1855) 1 The gridiron of the blessed St. Lawrence. **1869** Lecky *Europ. Mor.* II. xi. 235 The devil was represented bound by red-hot chains on a burning gridiron.

2. *fig.* and in phrases. † ***the gridiron grumbles at the frying-pan***: cf. 'the pot calls the kettle black.' ***on the gridiron***: in a state of torment, persecution, or great uneasiness (cf. F. *être sur le gril*); so ***to lay*** (a person) ***on the gridiron.***

1590 Greene *Neuer too late* (1600) 114, I was so scorched on the grediron of affection, that I had no rest. **1660** Bp. Taylor *Duct. Dubit.* i. i. (1676) 15 He runs to weakness for excuse, and to sin for a comfort..and changes from side to side upon his grid-iron till the flesh drop from the bones on every side. **1672** R. Wild *Poet. Licen.* 27 The Calf at Bethel fears the Calf at Dan; The Gridiron grumbles at the Frying-pan. *a* **1734** North *Exam.* iii. vii. §30 (1740) 525 It was past Three before the Chief Justice heard that his Name was upon the Gridiron at Westminster. **1834** Macaulay in Trevelyan *Life & Lett.* (1878) I. 377 While London is a perfect gridiron, here am I, at 13° North from the equator, by a blazing wood fire, with my windows closed. **1859** W. Collins *Q. of Hearts* (1875) 11 When destiny has..heated his gridiron for him, he has nothing left to do..but to get up and sit on it. **1871** *Member for Paris* II. 9 He proceeded to do what is called in journalistic phrase 'laying a man on the gridiron', which means that he..served him up every day to the readers of the *Pavois*, skewered through and through with an epigram.

3. a. Applied to objects resembling or likened to a gridiron; †a grated weir or dam (*obs.*); a grating or grille; a network of pipes, lines, etc.; the United States flag, the stars and stripes.

1406–7 *Winchester College Acc. Roll*, In stip. j carpentarii facientis j gredyre ad introitum aquæ de Lurteborne. **1812** *Niles' Reg.* 12 Sept. 31/2 The masts from which they flew, went over the side, while Hull's four '*gridirons*' floated in the air triumphant. **1842–3** Grove *Corr. Phys. Forces* 58 Between this glass and the plate is a gridiron of silver wire. **1854** Ronalds & Richardson *Chem. Technol.* (ed. 2) I. 378 To this pipe are attached a number of arms formed of inch pipe, the whole forming a sort of gridiron. **1863** Miss Braddon *Eleanor's Vict.* (1878) I. i. 8 My father wore a silver gridiron in his button hole. **1866** E. A. Pollard *Southern Hist. War* II. 103 'It was,' says a Charleston paper, 'the identical "gridiron" carried from Fort Sumter in 1861.' **1869** Blackmore *Lorna D.* ii, He answered, in a whisper, through the gridiron of the gate. **1871** Schele de Vere *Americanisms* (1872) 258 Sailors laugh at it good-naturedly, and seeing it [*sc.* the Stars and Stripes] hoisted, say: 'There goes the gridiron.' **1892** *Harper's Mag.* Feb. 435/1 Chicago is criss-crossed by a gridiron of railway tracks. **1893** J. A. Barry *S. Brown's Bunyip* etc. 29 Run the gridiron half-mast, Mr. Stokes. **1893** Farmer *Slang, Gridiron*,..the bars on a cell window.

b. *Naut.* A heavy framework of beams in parallel open order (suggesting a gridiron) used to support a ship in dock. (So F. *gril.*)

1846 A. Young *Naut. Dict., Gridiron*, a frame formed of cross beams of wood, for laying a vessel upon in order to inspect or repair her at low water. **1863** *Q. Rev.* CXIV. 309 They raise a gridiron which is suspended between them at such a depth in the water as may be requisite to receive the vessel. **1896** *Daily News* 21 Dec. 2/1 A first-class gridiron, capable of taking vessels up to 300 feet long.

c. *Theatr.* A structure of planks erected above the stage and supporting the mechanism for the manipulation of drop-scenes, etc. (So F. *gril.*)

1886 H. S. Jennings *Stage Gossip* 69 The 'gridiron' is the name for a number of planks running at a great height above the stage from R. to L. **1887** *Standard* 13 Sept. 6/4 Did the magistrates inspect what is known as the 'gridiron'—the place immediately over the stage?

d. *Archit.* = grid 6 d. Usu. *attrib.*

1883 Ld. R. Gower *My Reminisc.* II. xxvii. 204 The formal and gridiron-like plan of the streets of this city. **1910** *Catal. Cities Exhib.* in P. Geddes *Cities in Evolution* (ed. 2) (1949) 167 The cities of the United States, with their monotonous gridiron-plans. **1938** *Oxoniensia* III. 85 Anything approaching a spider's web at the nucleus of an English town appears to be extremely rare, and apart from a few towns where the Roman street-plan influenced later development a proper gridiron system is uncommon in England. **1961** L. Mumford *City in History* xiv. 424 In the gridiron plan, as applied in the commercial city, no section or precinct was suitably planned for its specific function. *Ibid.* 425 The extension of the speculative gridiron and the public transportation system were the two main activities that gave dominance to capitalist forms in the growing cities of the nineteenth century. **1969** *Geography* LIV. 200 The grid-iron town plan of Ashburton.

e. = grid 10. Also *attrib.*

1896 *Daily News* 10 Dec. 3/4 The ground here is marked out by white lines..thus giving it the appearance of a gigantic gridiron—which, indeed, is the technical name applied to an American football field. **1900** *Dial. Notes* II. 39 *Gridiron*, foot-ball field. **1937** L. C. Douglas *Forgive us our Trespasses* vii. 126 He was gleefully welcomed by young Assistant Coach Roberts and the awkward assembly of prospective gridiron heroes. **1960** T. McLean *Kings of Rugby* 61 American, or gridiron, football. **1968** C. Drummond *Death & Leaping Ladies* i. 11 You can't just walk into a team like you can, say, in gridiron or soccer.

4. Short for *gridiron pendulum.*

1793 Sir G. Shuckburgh in *Phil. Trans.* LXXXIII. 88 The pendulum..is a compound gridiron composed of five rods.

5. Short for *gridiron manœuvre*, etc.: A naval manœuvre in which the paths taken by the vessels suggest the form of a gridiron.

1893 *Daily News* 26 June 6/1 In executing the 'gridiron' movement the vessels would at times be very close to each other. **1894** *Times* 30 July 8/1 The Admiral felt justified in twice putting it [the fleet] through the much-discussed evolution known as the 'gridiron'.

6. *attrib.* and *Comb.*: **gridiron-floor** = sense 3 c; **gridiron pendulum,** a compensation pendulum composed of parallel rods of different metals; **gridiron valve,** a sliding valve in which the cover and seat are both composed of parallel bars with spaces between them.

1881 L. Wagner *Pantomimes* 57 From the flies a ladder communicates with the *gridiron-floor, at the very roof of the stage, frequently at a height of sixty or seventy feet above the footlights. **1752** Ellicott in *Phil. Trans.* XLVII. 492–3 Your pendulum takes off the effect of heat and cold as well as either the *gridiron pendulum (as it is commonly called) or the quicksilver pendulum. **1854** J. Scoffern in *Orr's Circ. Sci., Chem.* 115 Another means of avoiding this source of error is the gridiron pendulum..—an invention of Harrison. **1867–77** G. F. Chambers *Astron.* viii. 771 Gridiron compensation pendulum. **1875** Knight *Dict. Mech.*, *Gridiron valve.*

'gridiron, *v.* [f. gridiron *sb.*] *trans.* To mark with parallel lines or a pattern suggesting the form of a gridiron; said *esp.* of railways with reference to their appearance on a map. Also *fig.*

1832 *Reg. Deb. Congress* 4 Apr. 2390 With this revenue we could gridiron our states with railroads. **1857** E. M. Whitty *Friends Bohemia* II. 34 Newland has been a blessing to the country..and gridironed the country with railways. **1867** Miss Braddon *Birds of Prey* v. ii. (1868) 246 A breakneck gallop across dreary fields gridironed with dykes and stone walls. **1887** Hissey *Holiday on Road* i. 17 Railways have gridironed the land all over. **1901** *Daily Chron.* 5 Apr. 5/2 He won the right to gridiron its hills with an electric system. **1914** *Chambers's Jrnl.* June 415/2 The Park is gridironed with its own railway system. **1932** R. Kipling *Limits & Renewals* 110 An open square, near by, eased the pressure before long. Here the Patrol broke into fours, and gridironed it, saluting the images of the Gods at each corner and in the centre.

Hence **'gridironing** *vbl. sb., N.Z.* (see quot. 1910); **'gridironer** *N.Z.*, one who practises gridironing.

1898 Morris *Austral Eng.* 176/1 *Gridironing*, a term used in the province of Canterbury, New Zealand. A man purchased land in the shape of a gridiron, knowing that nobody would take the intermediate strips, which later he could purchase at his leisure. **1910** Le Rossignol & Stewart *State Socialism in N.Z.* iii. 37 'Gridironing' consisted in buying a series of 20-acre sections so surveyed as to leave 19 acres unbought between each two sections bought; and as no one could buy less than 20 acres without going to auction, the alternating 19-acre sections were left to be occupied by the runholder. **1941** Baker *N.Z. Slang* iii. 26 Land was purchased in strips,..so that the intervening land was rendered useless to another prospective settler and might be bought at the gridironer's leisure.

grie, variant of gree *sb.*[1]

griebe, obs. form of grebe.

griece, variant of grece, steps.

grieced (griːst), *a. Her.* [f. *griece*, variant of grece + -ed[2].] = degraded *ppl. a.*[2]

griede, obs. form of greed *sb.*

grief (griːf), *sb.* Pl. griefs. Forms: 3–5 gref, 4–6 greffe, grefe, greve, 4–7 greef(e, (5 greyf, griff(e, 5–6 gryef(f, 6 greiff, 6–7 greif(e), (8 greaf), 5–7 griefe, 5– grief. Also *pl.* 4–6 greves, (5 -ys), 5–7 greeves, 6–7 greives, grieves. [a. OF. *grief, gref* masc., vbl. sb. f. *grever* to grieve. The form with *v* in the sing. may be from OF. *grieve, greve* fem., of the same etymology.]

†**1.** Hardship, suffering; a kind, or cause, of hardship or suffering. *Obs.*

a **1225** *Ancr. R.* 392 Ne muhte he mid lesse gref habben ared us? *a* **1300** *Cursor M.* 17228 Iesu..wit mi flexsli lust to fill forget i oft þine greues grill. **1382** Wyclif *1 Esdr.* ii. 29 To kingis greeues ben born in. *c* **1386** Chaucer *Shipman's T.* 127 Tel me of youre grief Parauenture I yow may in youre meschief Conseille or helpe. **1435** Misyn *Fire of Love* i. ix. 17 þe pore in body with hongyr, þirst, cald & nakydnes & oþer greuys of þis warld is noyed. *c* **1440** *Bone Flor.* 1245 Syr, ye muste wende home wyth me..Hyt schall turne yow to no grefe. *a* **1450** *Fysshynge w. Angle* (1883) 2 Suche grevys & meny oþer the hunter hapeth. *c* **1550** *Disc. Common Weal Eng.* (1893) 2 That gentlemen feele moste greef by this derthe. **1575** *Gamm. Gurton* v. i, If it be counted his fault, besides all his greeues When a poore man is spoyled, and beaten among theeues Then I confess my fault herein. **1616** W. Haig *Let.* in J. Russell *Haigs* vii. (1881) 156 Pardon a poor man much distracted with the grief of this place [the tolbooth]. **1722** De Foe *Plague* (1756) 182 Want of Breath, Fear, Anger, Vexation, and all the other Griefs attending such an injurious Treatment.

†**2. a.** Hurt, harm, mischief or injury done or caused by another; damaged inflicted or suffered; molestation, trouble, offence. *Obs.*

c **1330** R. Brunne *Chron.* (1810) 91 Neuer bifor in Wales was don so grete greue. **1340–70** *Alex. & Dind.* 50 Whan þei sien the seg wiþ so manye ryde, þei were agrisen of his grym, and wende gref tholie. **1390** Gower *Conf.* II. 324 His moder wiste well she might Do Tereus no more greve Than slee his child. *c* **1460** *Towneley Myst.* xii. 53 Cryst saue vs ffrom alle myschefys..ffrom those mens grefys That oft ar agans vs. **1475** *Bk. Noblesse* 7 To be venged for dammage or griefe done by another. **1513** Douglas *Æneis* xiii. i. 25 To implor forgifnes of all greiff. **1584** Powel *Lloyd's Cambria* 354 These be the greefes done by the Englishmen.

†**b.** A wrong or injury which is the subject of formal complaint or demand for redress; = grievance 1 b. Also, a document containing a formal statement of the grievance. *Obs.*

In quot. 1839 prob. a mere Gallicism.

c **1420** Lydg. *Assembly Gods* 47 That Diana and Neptunus myght haue audience To declare her greefe of the gret offence To theym done by Eolus, whereon they compleynyd. **1472** *Presentm. Juries* in *Surtees Misc.* (1888) 22 Thes are þe grefis þt xij men fendes defectyffe. **1502** Arnolde *Chron.* (1811) p. xvii, The answere by my Lorde of Wynchestere vnto ye greffe of my Lorde off Glocetyre. **1538** in *Vicary's Anat.* (1888) App. iii. 159 It ys agreed that the Wardeyns..shalbe here vpon tuysday next commyng, & there shewe theyre gryeff. **1596** Shaks. *1 Hen. IV*, iv. iii. 42 The King hath sent to know The nature of your Griefes. **1605** *Nottingham Rec.* IV. 274 A meetinge shalbe had here that the Burgesses may then prefer theyr greifes. *a* **1651** Calderwood *Hist. Kirk* (Wodrow Soc.) III. 725 The greeves which Secretary Walsingham presented to the King. [**1839** *Times* 30 Mar. in *Spirit Metrop. Conserv. Press* (1840) I. 126 For the settlement of more solid and lasting griefs between the nations, measures of corresponding magnitude and decision must be reasonably executed.]

†**3.** Gravity, grievousness (of an offence). *Obs.*

1494 Fabyan *Chron.* vii. ccxxx. 262 Some of the foresayde prysoners he put to deth, and some he dishereted, after ye grefe of theyr offense.

†**4. a.** Feeling of offence; displeasure, anger. *Obs.*

a **1300** *Cursor M.* 8405 (Cott.) þof salamon mi sun be yong He es wis and o redi tung, þat neuer serued grefe ne grame. *c* **1340** *Ibid.* 7663 (Trin.) And efte þe fend ful of greef Trauailed þe kyng to mischeef. *c* **1400** *Destr. Troy* 6440 For all the grefe of þo grekes, & þe grete þronge, Was no led might hym let, þof hom lothe were. **1513** Douglas *Æneis* i. i. 18 Is thair sic grief in hevinlie myndis hie? **1535** Bp. Shaxton *Let. to Cromwell* in Strype *Eccl. Mem.* I. App. lxi. 149 Yet perceive I right manifestly your grief towards me. *c* **1570** *Durham Depos.* (Surtees) 245 He spoke not thois wordes in any greiff, but rather in boorde. *c* **1573** *Ibid.* 261 Hard the said Rauffe caule the said Rosse slave in greiff.

†**b.** Phrases. ***to take in*** (***on, to***) ***grief***: to take offence at: see also agrief. ***to take grief with*** (a person): to be displeased with. ***without grief***: without being offended or annoyed; without grudging. *Obs.*

c **1300**, etc. [see agrief]. *c* **1325** *Deo Gratias* 35 in *E.E.P.* (1862) 125, I prey þe take hit nouht in greue. *c* **1340** *Cursor M.* 10967 (Laud) Zakarie seid with-outyn greve Thise tydyngges may I not leve. *c* **1400** *Gamelyn* 313 And seide ȝe be welcome with-out any greue. *c* **1420** *Sir Amadace* xxx, Gode Sirs, take noȝte on greue, For ȝe most noue take ȝour leue. *c* **1430** *Syr Tryam.* 119 That ys me wondur lefe, Wherefore taketh hyt to no grefe. **1548** Udall, etc. *Erasm. Par. Matt.* xiii. 36–43 Jesus without any griefe [L. *nihil gravatus*] declared it playnely. *a* **1553** —— *Royster D.* v. iv. (Arb.) 82, I beseech you, take with me no greefe: I did a true man's part, not wishyng your repreefe.

†**5. a.** A bodily injury or ailment; a morbid affection of any part of the body; a sore, wound; a blemish of the skin; a disease, sickness. *Obs.*

1398 Trevisa *Barth. De P.R.* v. lxiv. (1495) 182 Somtyme the greyffes of the skynne come of a cause that is wythin. **1481** Caxton *Myrr.* iii. x. 153 Nature may not suffre..the sodeyn agrauacions ne griefs, of whiche by theyr folyes they trauaylle nature. **1542** Boorde *Dyetary* xxxii. (1870) 295 For suche thynges causyth the grefe [epilepsy] to come the ofter. *c* **1550** Lloyd *Treas. Health* (1585) F viij, To put away the wrinkles out of the face and all other greefe. **1562** Turner *Baths* Pref., In the tyme of bathinge in certayne men certayn grefes and diseases aryse. **1567** Harman *Caveat* (1879) 55 Fayre skynned withoute anye spot or greffe. **1579** Lyte *Dodoens* i. lxx. 104 The seede..is good to be straked or applied unto hoate griefes of the joynts. **1606** Bryskett *Civ. Life* 5 Rather to preuent sicknesse, then for any present griefe, I had..begunne a course to take some physicke. **1691** WOOD *Ath. Oxon.* I. 392 Cancerous Vlcers also seise on this part (the Lipp) &c. This grief hastned the end of..Mr. Harriot. **1706** *Lond. Gaz.* No. 4209/4 Off Leg Joint above the Fetter-lock large, hard swell'd, old Grief. **1727** BRADLEY *Fam. Dict.* s.v. *Foul*, A Swelling and Grief like unto this, breeding between the Clees of the Cattle.

transf. **1570** DEE *Math. Pref.* 23 Theophrastus affirmed, that, by Musike, griefes and diseases of the Minde..might be cured.

†**b.** The seat of disease; the diseased part; the sore place. *Obs.*

1577 FRAMPTON *Joyfull News* II. (1596) 36 The Leaues of this Tabaco being laid hotte vpon the griefe..taketh away the paines therof. **1610** MARKHAM *Masterp.* II. cxxxi. 434 Mixe these with vinegar, and apply it to the griefe. **1624** CAPT. SMITH *Virginia* II. 34 For swellings..they vse small peeces of touchwood..which pricking on the griefe they burne close to the flesh.

†**6.** Physical pain or discomfort. *Obs.*

1509 BARCLAY *Shyp of Folys* (1570) 81 Clawe he his backe that feeleth itche of greue. **1544** PHAER *Regim. Life* (1553) F vij b, The griefe, which the pacient feleth in his backe. **1596** DALRYMPLE tr. *Leslie's Hist. Scot.* III. 184 Mair throuch sturt and dolour of mynd, than throuch greife of his woundes. **1608–33** BP. HALL *Medit.* (1851) 99 The tenderness of the part adds much to the grief. **1621** BURTON *Anat. Mel.* I. iii. II. ii, Hardnes and grief in the left Hypocondry.

7. a. Mental pain, distress, or sorrow. In mod. use in a more limited sense: Deep or violent sorrow, caused by loss or trouble; a keen or bitter feeling of regret for something lost, remorse for something done, or sorrow for mishap to oneself or others.

13.. *E.E. Allit. P.* A. 86 The adubbemente of þo downez dere Garten my goste al greffe for-ȝete. *c* **1350** *Will. Palerne* 2473 So glad was he þanne, þat na gref vnder god gayned to his ioye. *c* **1400** *Destr. Troy* 13957 Vlixes..With gronyng and greue gert hym to stynt. **1413** *Pilgr. Sowle* (Caxton 1483) IV. xx. 66 How may myn eyen..Restreyne them for to shewen by wepyng Myn hertes greef. **1554** COVERDALE *Hope Faithf.* xxxi. (1574) 221 Tediousnesse and grefe runneth customably with saturation or fulnesse. **1568** H. B. tr. *P. Martyr's Comm. Rom.* ix. 237 b, Griefe (as sayth Cicero..) is a dissease which vexeth the mind, and it is taken by reason of the euill which semeth to be already at hand, and to be present. **1592** SHAKS. *Rom. & Jul.* v. iii. 211 Griefe of my Sonnes exile hath stopt her breath. **1612** CHAPMAN *Widdowes T.* Plays 1873 III. 54 Then Grieues that sound so lowd, proue alwaies light. **1632** LITHGOW *Trav.* v. 198 Before my arrivall in Aleppo, the Caravan..was from thence departed, which bred no small griefe in my breast. **1657** AUSTEN *Fruit Trees* I. 5 He confesseth it with much greife. **1716** ADDISON *Drummer* II. i, There is a real grief and there is a methodical grief. **1756** BURKE *Subl. & B.* I. v, If the object of pleasure be..totally lost..a passion arises in the mind, which is called grief. **1760–72** H. BROOKE *Fool of Quality* (1809) II. 112 Mrs. Tirrel..was plentifully pouring forth her tears..for grief of having found him in that condition. **1817** BYRON *Manfred* I. i. 9 Grief should be the instructor of the wise. **1821** JOANNA BAILLIE *Basil* v. iii, Woman's grief is like a summer storm, Short as it violent is. **1883** OUIDA *Wanda* I. 36 Their father died of grief for his eldest son. **1888** F. HUME *Mad. Midas* I. i, He did not show much outward grief.

personified. **1822** B. CORNWALL *Flood of Thessaly* II. 281 Joy is slow believed, where grief hath lived Long a familiar.

b. A cause or subject of grief.

1535 COVERDALE *Prov.* xvii. 25 An vndiscrete sonne is a grefe [*so* **1611**] vnto his father. **1770** GOLDSM. *Des. Vill.* 57 A time there was, ere England's griefs began. **1886** RUSKIN *Præterita* I. v. 167 As fate would have it, they had the one grief of having no children.

8. a. Phr. *to come to grief*: to meet with disaster; (*Sporting*) to have a fall; to fail, prove abortive. So *to bring to grief*. Chiefly *colloq.*; somewhat rare in dignified use. Also *good* (or *great*) *grief!*, an exclamation indicating surprise, alarm, etc.

1850 THACKERAY *Pendennis* II. xxxvii. 364, I knew that your father had come to—to grief. You don't think it was—it was for your connexion I married you? **1854** —— *Newcomes* I. x. 107 We drove on to the Downs, and we were nearly coming to grief. **1857** KINGSLEY *Two Y. Ago* xxi, As for coming to grief,..we're on a good errand..and the devil himself can't harm us. **1862** T. SHORTER in *Weldon's Reg.* Aug. 4 A People's College..was founded at Nottingham, but speedily came to grief. **1873** *Punch* 25 Jan. 41/1 The third Empire..brought France to grief. **1883** BLACK *Shandon Bells* xxvii, He pointed out where the coal-smack had come to grief. **1885** J. MARTINEAU *Types Eth. Theory* I. 139 His logic came to grief. **1900** in *Eng. Dial. Dict.*, Good grief. **1924** *Dial. Notes* V. 268 Great grief. **1937** R. CHANDLER *Killer in Rain* (1964) 227 'Good grief,' De Spain said. 'He's up there right now.' **1957** 'N. CULOTTA' *They're Weird Mob* (1958) 180 'Do I ask your father for his daughter's hand?' 'Good grief no.' **1959** 'A. GILBERT' *Death takes Wife* xvii. 226 'Wonder if he expected this?' said the policeman grimly. And he called Crook at his home address. 'Good grief!' said Crook, when he heard. **1959** N. MARSH *False Scent* (1960) iv. 100 Great grief, I'd forgotten that gang!

b. *Sporting.* Accidents in steeplechasing or in the hunting-field. Also in *Golf* (see quot. 1897).

1891 *Sportsman* 28 Feb. (Farmer), The flag had scarcely fallen than the grief commenced. **1897** *Encycl. Sport* I. 472 *Grief*, when a player has played his ball into a hazard of any description he is said to be in grief. **1898** *St. James's Gaz.* 15 Nov. 6/1 [A pace sufficient] to test the condition of horses and their riders and to bring about a considerable amount of grief.

9. *attrib.* and *Comb.* **a.** simple attrib., as *grief-drop*. **b.** objective, as *grief-drinking* adj. **c.** instrumental, as *grief-bowed*, *-distraught*, *-dulled*, *-exhausted*, *-harmonized*, *-inspired*, *-oppressed*, *-rent*, *-ridden*, *-shot*, *-stricken*, *-worn* adjs. Also **grief-muscles**, a name given by Darwin to certain muscles concerned in the facial expression of grief; **grief therapy** (see quot.).

1839 MARY HOWITT *Marier's Pilgr.* XI. iii. 2 *Grief-bowed and labour-spent. **1844** MRS. BROWNING *Duchess May* lxiv, He in sooth is *grief-distraught. ? *c* **1600** *Distracted Emp.* II. i. in Bullen *O. Pl.* III. 203 Charactred on everye syde Of the *griefe drinkinge paper. **1838** ELIZA COOK *World* vii. 1 Though the eye may be dimmed with its *grief-drop awhile. *a* **1603** F. DAVISON in Farr *S.P. Eliz.* (1845) II. 319 My *grief-dull'd heart. **1768** C. SHAW *Address Nightingale* vi. 87 Till welcome death..Shall kindly stop my *grief-exhausted breath. **1827** HOOD *Hero & Leander* lxix, Though heretofore I have but set my voice To some long sighs, *grief-harmonized. **1764** *Oxford Sausage* 77 The *grief-inspired Muse. **1872** DARWIN *Emotions* vii. 185 Cases of Hypochondria, in which the *grief-muscles were persistently contracted. **1824** T. FENBY *Four Temperaments* IV. i, *Grief-oppressed, unhappy man. **1647** HERRICK *Hesperides* (1869) 419 To show a heart *grief-rent. **1891** SWINBURNE *Poems* (1904) II. 47 In that heart-stricken *grief-ridden time. **1607** SHAKS. *Cor.* v. i. 45 As a discontented Friend, *greefe-shot With his vnkindnesse. **1905** *Daily Chron.* 14 Aug. 5/5 The husband was sent for, but he was so *grief-stricken that he had to be removed. **1965** J. POLLITT *Depression & its Treatment* ii. 22 Similarly, in human affairs, bereavement occurring *during* a depressive illness is not followed by the normal process of forgetting, the patient remaining grief-stricken. **1963** J. MITFORD *Amer. Way Death* ii. 58 '*Grief therapy' is..commonly used by funeral men to describe the mental and emotional solace which, they claim, is achieved for the bereaved family as a result of being able to 'view' the embalmed and restored deceased. **1859** K. CORNWALLIS *New World* I. 202 He looked *grief-worn.

† **grief**, *a.* and *adv.* *Obs.* Forms: 3 greif, 4 grefe, greue, greeffe. [a. OF. *gref*:—L. *gravis* (also *grief*:—L. **grevis*, later form of *gravis*, influenced by *levis* light) heavy, GRAVE.]

A. *adj.* Grievous, grave; troublesome, oppressive; (of armour) ? formidable.

a **1300** *Cursor M.* 27986 þis sin..it es sua greif and god wit gan þat..it files þar it es don or said. **1303** R. BRUNNE *Handl. Synne* 10262 Here synne ys grefe þat bryngeþ a trew man on a þefe. *c* **1330** —— *Chron.* (1810) 138 If it so be, of Scotlond skape a thefe, & till Inglond fle, als a felon grefe. **1390** GOWER *Conf.* I. 166 For it is an unwise vengeaunce, Which to none other man is lefe, And is unto him selve grefe. *c* **1440** *Gaw. & Gol.* 1262 Lordis laught thair lancis..And graithit thame to the gait, in thair greif geir. **1520** *Caxton's Chron. Eng.* III. 21 b/1 Whiche worke he ended in 2 yere and 4 monethes and that with greve impedymentes.

B. *adv.* Grievously, excessively.

c **1400** *Destr. Troy* 3044 Hir nose..was nobly shapyn,.. Noght growen to grete ne to grefe smalle. *c* **1400** MAUNDEV. (Roxb.) xxiv. 112 He fell greeffe seke [F. *il cheust en maladie*] and feled wele þat he myght noȝt couer of þat sekeness.

grieffful ('gri:ffʊl), *a.* Forms: 4 greful, 5–7 greefull, 6–8 grieffull, (6 grefull, greffful, griefful(l, gre(e)fe-ful, griefeful(l, grievefull), 6, 9 griefful. [f. GRIEF *sb.* + -FUL.] Painful, sorrowful; †grievous.

a **1300** *Cursor M.* 13184 (Gött.) Bot þis dede was seld ful dere, þe mening ȝeit lastis bi ȝere, wid a greful [*Cott.* greithful] uengance. *c* **1489** CAXTON *Sonnes of Aymon* ix. 251 The wounde of Rycharde was soo greefull to see that it was pyte to beholde. *c* **1530** LD. BERNERS *Arth. Lyt. Bryt.* (1814) 20 It is grefull to me to leue your companye. **1561** NORTON & SACKV. *Gorboduc* I. i. (Shaks. Soc.) 97 And nowe the daie renewes my griefull plainte. **1602** MARSTON *Antonio's Rev.* II. iii, The most greefull, despairing, wretched [etc.]. *a* **1649** DRUMM. OF HAWTH. *Hist. Jas. III*, Wks. (1711) 42 To deliver this grief-full body to the rest of a desired grave. **1742** COLLINS *Ode to Fear* 27 The grief-full Muse address'd her infant tongue. **1868** BROWNING *Ring & Bk.* VI. 704 The same great, grave, griefful air. **1882** *Daily News* 21 Apr. 5/7 The stern reality of a griefful parting.

Hence **'grieffully** *adv.*

a **1400–50** *Alexander* 973 (Dublin MS.) And grettes for hym als grefully [*Ashm. MS.* greuously] as he hym gettyn hed. **1560** DAUS tr. *Sleidane's Comm.* 153 He is in dede very sory, but yet taketh the matter lesse greifefully, forasmuche as the thinge hath fortuned throughe another mans faulte, and not his.

[**griefhead.** Explained as: Sadness. Error for GREENHEAD[1], due to reading *grenehede* (Chaucer *Man of Law's T.* 65) as *greuehede* (taken to be f. *greue* GRIEF + *-hede* -HEAD).

1890 *Cent. Dict.*]

griefless ('gri:flɪs), *a.* [f. GRIEF *sb.* + -LESS.] Free from grief.

1552 HULOET, Griefeles or sorowles. **1566** GASCOIGNE *Iocasta* II. i, I graunte I can not grieflesse, well beholde My fathers pallace. **1843** *Tait's Mag.* X. 311 Unmurmuring, griefless, watching. **1847** S. DOBELL *Musing on a Victory*, Grand And griefless as a rich man's funeral. **1882** SWINBURNE *Tristram of Lyonesse* 6 The griefless ghost of grief.

Hence **'grieflessness**, griefless condition.

1571 GOLDING *Calvin on Ps.* xxxii. 3 Hee betokeneth not greeflesnesse or blockishnesse. **1574** tr. *Marlorat's Apocalips* 34 Greeflesnesse is thoughte too bee a signe of Desperatenesse. **1886** SIDGWICK *Outl. Hist. Ethics* ii. § 16. 81 The grieflessness which the sage was conceived to maintain amid the worst tortures.

† **'griefly**, *adv.* *Obs.* [f. GRIEF *a.* + -LY[2].] Grievously, 'sadly'.

1340–70 *Alisaunder* 490 Yee beene greefly bigo, but grace you falle. *Ibid.* 994 Whan I was greefly bigo with a grim people. **1577** T. KENDALL *Flowers of Epigr.* 20 By this my troublous toyle and grefe, and griefly pinchyng paine.

[**griefly**, *a.* Explained as: Indicative of grief. Error for *griesly* GRISLY *a.* (through misreading f for f).

[*a* **1586** SIDNEY *Arcadia* II. (1590) 165 b, Grisly [edd. 1629, 1633 griesly] Grones.] **1881** DAVIES *Suppl. Eng. Gloss.*, Griefly [quoting the above as 'griefly groans']. Hence in some later Dicts.]

† **'griefsome**, *a.* *Obs.* *rare*$^{-1}$. [f. GRIEF *sb.* + -SOME. Cf. GRIEVESOME.] Causing grief, distressing.

1635 HAYWARD tr. *Biondi's Banish'd Virgin* 209 He resolved..to get her thence to some other place lesse griefesome and lesse odious.

grieko, variant of GREGO.

grien, grienesse, obs. ff. GREEN, GREENNESS.

gries, obs. pl. of GREE *sb.*[1]

griese, -ly, obs. forms of GRECE, GRISLY.

grieshoch ('gri:ʃəx). *Sc.* Also **greeshoch, grieschoch.** [a. Gael. *griosach* embers, f. *grios*, *gris* heat.] 'Hot embers; properly those of peats or moss-fuel' (Jam.).

1802 SCOTT *Minstr. Scott. Bord.* I. Introd. 83 Gang a' to your beds, Sirs, and dinna put out the wee grieschoch (embers). **1818** —— *Hrt. Midl.* li, I saw the leaves the limmers had lain on, and the ashes of them; by the same token, there was a pit greeshoch purning yet. **1881** MISS LAFFAN in *Macm. Mag.* XLIV. 386 From the grieshoch, which was as she had left it that morning, she perceived the faintest possible glow.

griesly, obs. form of GRISLY, GRIZZLY.

griessing, obs. form of GRECING.

griest, obs. form of GRIST *sb.*[2]

griesy, variant of GRISY *Obs.*, grisly.

griet, obs. form of GREET *v.*[2], GRIT *sb.*[1]

† **'grievable**, *a.* *Obs.* [a. OF. *grevable*, f. *grever* to GRIEVE.] Causing grief or pain; distressing, hurtful, injurious.

1390 GOWER *Conf.* II. 11 There is a vice full grevable To him, which is therof coulpable. *c* **1440** ASHBY *Dict. Phil.* (E.E.T.S.) 92/1089 It is of goode and noble discrecion.. That can suffer aduer[si]tise greueable. **1483** CAXTON *Gold. Leg.* 426 b/2 The waye is to the right greueable by cause that thou knowest not the contreye. *c* **1500** *Melusine* xxiv. 192 Thinke you not that the thinge which is acustomed of long tyme be lesse greuable than that thing which is newly lerned?

grievance ('gri:vəns). Forms: 4–6 **grevaunce**, (5 **-awnce, -ons**), 4–7 **grevance**, (5 **-ans(e**, 7 **greevance**), 6– **grievance**. [a. OF. *grevance*, *grievance*, f. *grever* to harm, GRIEVE: see -ANCE.]

†**1.** The infliction of wrong or hardship on a person; injury, oppression; a cause or source of injury. *Obs.*

a **1300** *Cursor M.* 27823 (Cott. Galba) Couatyse es ane euil syn þat mikel greuance gers bygin. *c* **1386** CHAUCER *Melib.* ℙ520 If..a man of gretter myght and strengthe than thou art do thee grevaunce, studie and bisye thee rather to stille the same grevaunce, than for to venge thee. **1390** GOWER *Conf.* III. 34 The bodely delices alle..Unto the soule done grevaunce. *c* **1400** *Destr. Troy* 5034 And all giltes [ben] forgyffen & greuans of old. *c* **1440** *Promp. Parv.* 211/1 Grevawn[c]e, or offence, or trespace, *offensa, aggra[va]men.* **1523** LD. BERNERS *Froiss.* I. cclxxxvi. 427 The frenchmen kepte good company with their prisoners, and raunsomed them courtesly, without any greuaunce to them. **1609** BIBLE (Douay) *Song 3 Childr.* 27 The fire touched them not at al, nor payned them, nor did them anie grevance. **1641** *Protests Lords* I. 4 To the great and universal grievance of your people. **1684** H. MORE *Answ.* 190 To the much grievance and oppression of the people. **1720** POPE *Iliad* XXII. 159 The Wife with-held, the Treasure ill-detain'd (Cause of the War, and Grievance of the Land), With honourable Justice to restore. **1765** BLACKSTONE *Comm.* I. vii. 244 If the consequence of that exertion be manifestly to the grievance or dishonour of the kingdom. **1768** STERNE *Sent. Journ.* (1778) II. 127 (*Le Dimanche*) Happy people! that..sport away the weights of grievance which bow down the spirit of other nations.

†**2.** The state or fact of being oppressed, injured, or distressed; trouble, distress; suffering, pain. *Obs.*

a **1300** *Cursor M.* 23083 In mi greuance yee did me gode. **13..** *Seuyn Sag.* (W.) 2027 He..tolde hem alle his greuance. **1340** HAMPOLE *Pr. Consc.* 2753 þai sal haf a day þare Als mykel bitter payn or mare, Als a man mught thole here of penaunce A yhere and fele als mykel grevaunce. *c* **1386** CHAUCER *Frankl. T.* 213 Aurelius Hadde loued hire best of any creature..But neuere dorste he tellen hire his greuance. *a* **1420** HOCCLEVE *De Reg. Princ.* 1065 Povert hathe in hym self ynow grevaunce, Withouten that that man hym more purchace. **1422** tr. *Secreta Secret., Priv. Priv.* (E.E.T.S.) 196 Clothis, wodde, and colle..by the wych he myght escape wythout empeyrement the grevaunce of the wyntyr. *c* **1460** *Towneley Myst.* iii. 58 Sex hundreth yeris and od haue I..liffyd with grete grevance. *a* **1586** C'TESS PEMBROKE *Ps.* CXXI. iv, The moony vapours Shall not cast any mist to breed thy grevaunce. **1592** SHAKS. *Rom. & Jul.* I. i. 163 See where he comes..Ile know his greeuance, or be much denide.

3. A circumstance or state of things which is felt to be oppressive. In mod. use, a wrong or hardship (real or supposed) which is considered a legitimate ground of complaint; something to complain of.

1481 CAXTON *Myrr.* III. viii. 147 The fruytes..ben otherwhile sonner rype in one yere than in an other, and more assured of tempestes and other greuances. **1591** SHAKS. *Two Gent.* IV. iii. 37 Madam, I pitty much your grieuances. **1609** DANIEL *Civ. Wars* IV. lxxv, Future ill On present suffrings bruted to aryse, That farther grieuances ingender will. **1649** MILTON *Eikon.* v. Wks. (1847) 288/1 They undid nothing in the state but irregular and grinding courts, the maine grievances to be removed. **1661** BRAMHALL *Just Vind.* vii. 173 The hundred Grievances of the German Nation proposed to the Popes Legate. **1688** *Col. Rec. Pennsylv.* I. 226 As to ye Request of ye Assembly for Relief of Grievances. **1717** LADY M. W. MONTAGU *Let. to Abbé Conti* 17 May, The war is a general grievance upon the people. **1727** A. HAMILTON *New Acc. E. Ind.* II. xxxiii. 16 One Day meeting me on the Green near the Fort, he stopt me to relate his Grievances. **1795** BURKE *Corr.* (1844) IV. 310 It is a foolish language, adopted from the united Irish-men, that their grievances originate from England. **1839** KEIGHTLEY *Hist. Eng.* II. 42 They sent to the King a statement of their grievances. **1868** FREEMAN *Norm. Conq.* (1876) II. vii. 124 In an early state of society any kind of taxation is apt to be looked on as a grievance. **1882** A. W. WARD *Dickens* v. 112 The length of Chancery suits was a real public grievance. **1883** C. J. WILLS *Mod. Persia* 367 On being troubled by a pertinacious clergyman with many grievances.

†**4.** A disease, ailment, hurt. *Obs.*

1377 LANGL. *P. Pl.* B. XII. 61 Sapience..swelleth a mannes soule, Ac grace is a grasse therof The greuaunces to abate. *c* **1400** MAUNDEV. (Roxb.) viii. 32 Þai schuld neuer hafe swilke greuaunce ne disese of þam mare. *c* **1430** *Pilgr. Lyf Manhode* II. xxiv. (1869) 84 Al be it she hath no greuaunce, yet hath she displesaunce. **1578** LYTE *Dodoens* I. v. 11 Ulcers and grievances of the mouth. **1634** W. WOOD *New Eng. Prosp.* I. iii, Many that haue come infirme out of England, retaine their old grievances still. **1761** MRS. F. SHERIDAN *Sidney Bidulph* II. 279 The Bath surgeon.. declared it as his opinion, that the complaint might be removed without amputation, adding, that it was owing to wrong management that the grievance had gone so far.

†**5.** Displeasure, indignation, offence. *to take in* or *to grievance*, *to take grievance with*: to take offence at. *Obs.* (Cf. GRIEF *sb.* 4 b.)

c **1380** *Sir Ferumb.* 258 Charlys was in his greuance, stondyng among his feren. *c* **1400** *Ywaine & Gaw.* 126, I prai the tak to no grevance This kene karping of syr Kay. **1426** LYDG. *De Guil. Pilgr.* 10757 Grace dieu..Wych ys, sothly, evele apayd, And taketh gretly in greuaunce The maner off thy governaunce. **1523** SKELTON *Garl. Laurel* 1257 Yet sum there be therewith take grevaunce, And grudge thereat with frownyng countenaunce.

6. *attrib.* and *Comb.* **grievance-monger.**

1828 *Toronto Pub. Lib. MS. B 104* 41 Like William Lyon Mackenzie, he was a confirmed grievance-monger. **1860** *Sat. Rev.* IX. 304/2 They are the men who..hold grievance-meetings about the parson's surplice. **1890** *Spectator* 2 Aug., The grievance-mongers will gather together. **1896** *Tablet* 9 May 751 Those spoilt children of the State..are very busy just now in grievance-making. **1966** *Economist* 12 Nov. 647/2 Mrs Gandhi's government and party can hardly be considered blameless. What they have to do to meet the real grievances that the grievance-mongers exploit is, simply, to succeed.

Hence †ˈ**grievancer**, one who occasions a grievance; one who gives ground for complaint.

1655 FULLER *Ch. Hist.* XI. xvii. §4 ¶12 Now no day passed, wherein some petition was not presented..against the Bishops as grand grievancers.

grieve (griːv), *sb.* Forms: (sense 1) 1 grǽfa, 4 *Sc.* greff, 6, 8, greve, 7 greeve, 7–9 greave; *Sc.* (sense 2) 6 greif, greive, 8– grieve, (9 greeve). [The Sc. and northern *grieve* (*greve*) is the normal repr. of ONorthumb. *grǽfa* = WS. *ȝeréfa* (see REEVE). The later forms under 1 are literary adaptations of the OE. term, prob. under the influence of the northern word. Cf. GRAVE *sb.*^{3}]

1. a. A governor of a province, town, etc. Now only *Hist.* = SHERIFF. †**b.** = GRAVE *sb.*^{3} *Obs.*

a. *c* **950** *Lindisf. Gosp.* Matt. xxviii. 14 Gif ðis ȝehered bið from ðen groefa [*Rushw.* ȝeroefe] we ȝe-trewað him. —— Mark xv. 5 Se hælend..noht ȝeondsuarede suæ þætte þæt he woere awundrad se groefa [*Rushw.* groefa]. [*c* **1180** *Leg. Edw. Conf.* in Thorpe *Laws* I. 456 Greve autem nomen est potestatis; apud nos autem nichil melius videtur esse quam prefectura. Est enim multiplex nomen; greve enim dicitur de scira, de wapentagiis, de hundredo, de burgis, de villis.] *a* **1400** *Burgh Laws* xix. (*Sc. Stat.* I), þe borow greff [orig. *præpositus*]. **1629** DEKKER *Lond. Tempe* (Percy Soc.) 42 In the time of Edward Confessor, the chiefe ruler of the citty was called Reeve, Greeve, or Portreeve. **1708** *Termes de la Ley* 374 Greve, Præpositus, is a word of Authority and signifies as much as Comes or Vicecomes. **1844** LINGARD *Anglo-Sax. Ch.* (1845) II. xiv. 346 The instrument states.. that the bishop, with the aid of the greave or sheriff, should extirpate all heathenish superstitions.

b. **1537** *Par. Acc. Ecclesfield*, Boroyd off our ladye grevys to ye bell castyng, xx^{s}. Off ye same grevys to ye Organs, &c. vj^{s}. viij^{d}. **1607** in Morehouse *Kirkburton & Graveship of Holme* 137 Against which day the Greave did command all the inhabitants of Austonley to appear the tyme above said.

2. *Sc.* and *north.* The overseer, manager, or head-workman on a farm; a farm-bailiff. (See also quot. 1893.)

c **1480** HENRYSON in *Bannatyne MS.* (Hunter. Club) 151 This awstrene greif answerit angirly, For thy cramping thow salt baith cruke and cowre. **1513** DOUGLAS *Æneis* XIII. Prol. 161 Tyte on his hynis gaif the greif a cry, Awaik on fut, go till our husbandry. **1595** DUNCAN *App. Etymol.* (E.D.S.), *Magister, villæ vel pagi*, a greiue. **1721** KELLY *Scot. Prov.* 5 A good Grieve is better than an ill Worker. **1799** J. ROBERTSON *Agric. Perth* 361 There is a number of grieves, inspectors and overseers appointed in every little district. **1814** SCOTT *Diary* 6 Aug. in *Lockhart*, He has got a ploughman from Scotland who acts as grieve. **1842** H. STEPHENS *Bk. Farm* (1851) II. 611/2 The grieve's time may be fully occupied elsewhere. **1868** *Perthsh. Jrnl.* 18 June, The Grieve on Westhall will show the Farm. **1893** *Northumbld. Gloss.*, *Greeve, Grieve*, an overseer, an under-steward. It is generally applied to a resident agent who has charge of property in his locality.

grieve (griːv), *v.* Forms: 3–6 greve, (4 greven, grevye, grevi, greife), 4–5 gref, 4–6 grewe, 5 grevyn, grefe, 5–6 *Sc.* greif(f, 4–7 greeve, (7 grive), 6– grieve. [a. F. *grever*:—popular L. **grevāre* (see GRIEF *a.*) = class. L. *gravāre*, f. *gravis* heavy, GRAVE *a.*]

†**1.** *trans.* To press heavily upon, as a weight; to burden. Only in *pass.* *Obs.*

1340 *Ayenb.* 260 Nimeþ ye hede þet youre herten ne by ygreued ne y-charged of glotounie ne of dronkehede. **1382** WYCLIF *Matt.* xxvi. 43 And eftsone he came, and foonde hem slepynge; forsothe her eȝen weren greued. —— *1 Tim.* v. 16 If ony feithful man hath widewis, vndir mynistre he to hem, that the chirche be not greuyd.

†**b.** To make heavy. *Obs. rare*$^{-1}$.

1382 WYCLIF *1 Macc.* viii. 31 Whi hast thou greeuyd [L. *gravasti*] thy ȝock vpon oure freendis?

†**2.** Of persons: To harass, trouble, vex, gall by hostile action; to oppress; to do wrong, hurt, or harm to. *Obs.*

1297 R. GLOUC. (Rolls) 11815 Clerkes..þat hulde wiþ sir simon, he greuede manion. *a* **1300** *Cursor M.* 4076 (Gött.) Enuye þai had til him sua strang, þai soght him ay to greue with wrang. **1340** *Ayenb.* 39 Þe ualse playneres þet makeþ þe ualse bezechinges and zecheþ þe ualse..wytnesses..uor to greui oþren. **1377** LANGL. *P. Pl.* B. x. 204 Alle that lakketh vs or lyeth vs oure lorde techeth vs to louye And nouȝt to greuen hem that greueth vs. *c* **1400** MAUNDEV. (1839) xxi. 229 Als long as ȝee ben bounden to gedere..in Loue, in Trouthe, & in gode Accord no man schall ben of powere to greue ȝou. *a* **1450** *Knt. de la Tour* (1868) 101 To vse and kepe honeste lyf, and to loue and kepe in ryght his peple, and not greue them as Roboam dyd. *c* **1450** *Merlin* 186 Moche thei greved the hethen peple with alle theire power. **1512** *Act 4 Hen. VIII*, c. 1 §1 Nother pile blokhouse ne Bulwork is made to greve or annoye theym at their landyng. **1523** LD. BERNERS *Froiss.* I. xlvii. 68 The whiche garyson hadde greuyd sore the towne of Cambray. **1559** *Mirr. Mag., Owen Glendour* xiv, To greve our foe he quyckely to me sent Twelve thousand Frenchmen. **1616** R. C. *Times' Whistle* IV. 1506 What will he doe to thee, which seekst to grieve With an oppressours hand the innocent! **1651** HOBBES *Leviath.* I. iv. 13 Seeing nature hath armed living creatures, some with teeth, some with horns, and some with hands, to grieve an enemy, it is but an abuse of Speech, to grieve him with the tongue.

absol. *a* **1300** *Cursor M.* 7233 Þare es nan sa gret mai greif Als traitur dern and priue theif. **1393** LANGL. *P. Pl.* C. XII. 134 Loue is a lykynge thyng, and loth for to greue.

†**b.** Of non-personal agents: To bring trouble or harm to (a person); to cause damage to (a thing). *Obs.*

a **1300** *Cursor M.* 7072 Þat werre þat greued al bath ner and ferr. *c* **1330** R. BRUNNE *Chron.* (1810) 71 Our fredom that day for euer toke þe leue, For Harald it went away, his falshed did vs greue. **1390** GOWER *Conf.* II. 215 He shall wel finde his covetise Shall sore greve him ate laste. *c* **1440** *York Myst.* xxii. 54 Þer was neuere dede þat euere he dide þat greued hym warre. **1481** CAXTON *Myrr.* II. xxxi. 127 Adam was deceyued by thapple that he ete, whiche greued alle humayne lignage. **1542** *Lam. & Piteous Treat.* in *Harl. Misc.* (Malham) I. 235 That no tempeste of the see maye once vexe, greue, or trouble enye ship. **1574** tr. *Littleton's Tenures* 94 a, A disseisin and discent y^{t} is matter in dede shal not so grieve him y^{t} was disseised when he was out of the realme.

†**3.** To do bodily hurt or harm to (a person); to injure (a thing) materially. *Obs.*

1297 R. GLOUC. (Rolls) App. X. 6 Her liþ kenelm of his heuede bireued þat þoru his soster & þe stiward so was igreued. *c* **1340** *Cursor M.* 20960 (Fairf.) Þe nedder of venum þat was strange noȝt him greued wiþ hir stange. **1390** GOWER *Conf.* III. 115 There [i.e. Egypt] no stormy weder falleth, Which mighte greve man or beste. *c* **1420** *Pallad. on Husb.* IV. 24 Whan tyme is hoot, putte on hem [vines] softe at eue Good water oft, that they may ete and drinke, And bolde hem vppon hoot, that myght hem greue. **1483** CAXTON *Gold. Leg.* 213/1 She..lete make a strong poyson and gaf it to hir brother But god kepte hym y^{t} it neuer greuyd hym. *a* **1550** *Christis Kirke Gr.* xv, They girnit and lait gird with grainis, Ilk gossip uder grievit. **1610** GUILLIM *Heraldry* I. viii. 34 Alwaies (saith Sir John Froysard) by right of Armes a man ought to grieue his Enemy. **1810** SCOTT *Lady of L.* II. ix, The graceful foliage storms may reave, The noble stem they cannot grieve.

†**b.** *absol.* To be materially hurtful or harmful.

1398 TREVISA *Barth. De P.R.* VII. xviii. (1495) 235 Colde thynges greue, and heete helpe yf the teeres comen of outwarde cause. **1523** FITZHERB. *Husb.* §20 There be diuers maner of wedes, as thistyls, kedlokes, dockes..these be they that greue mooste. **1577** NORTHBROOKE *Dicing* (1843) 39 As manye things are necessarie and needefull in man's lyfe, so taking in excesse and out of season annoy and grieue much.

†**4.** To cause bodily discomfort or pain to (a person); to affect with pain or disease. *Obs.*

a **1225** *Ancr. R.* 422 Hwon ȝe beoð i-leten blod, ȝe ne schulen don no þing, þ eo þreo dawes, þet ou greue. *c* **1290** *S. Eng. Leg.* I. 105/147 Euere sat þis Maide stille; it [the torture] ne greuede hire no-þing. *a* **1300** *Cursor M.* 11734 Lauerd, þis es a mikel hete, It greues vs, it es sua grete. *Ibid.* 15657 Þair eien war greued sua wit grete. *c* **1375** *Sc. Leg. Saints, Paulus* 759 His breth hym grewit mar & mare. *c* **1400** MAUNDEV. (1839) ii. 11 That the Smelle scholde not greve men that wenten forby. *c* **1450** *St. Cuthbert* (Surtees) 4120 Þe same bolnyng þan him greued. **1483** CAXTON *Gold. Leg.* 70 b/1 He had so moche heere on his heed that it greuyd hym to bere. **1533** ELYOT *Cast. Helthe* (1541) 1 Helth..is the state of the body, wherein we be neyther greved with peyne, nor lette from doinge our necessary businesse. **1544** PHAER *Regim. Life* (1545) F vij, Somtymes it [the liver] is greued by bloud into [*read* in to] moche aboundance, or by cholerik humours. **1572** BOSSEWELL *Armourie* III. 17 This manner of Shooe..greueth not, or vexeth the wearer thereof on his feete. **1589** COGAN *Haven Health* cxciv. (1636) 177 Cholerick fumes, which both inflame the body and grieve the head. **1592** WEST *1st Pt. Symbol.* §102 A, Al maner of diseases, griefes and sorances wherewith the said H. is now infected, grieued or trobled in ye raines, bladder [etc.]. [**1781** COWPER *Conversat.* 600 A Christian's wit is inoffensive light, A beam that aids but never grieves the sight.]

absol. *a* **1450** *Knt. de la Tour* (1868) 13 It is a blessed thinge to faste, for the more harme it dothe the faster, the more is the merit..for, and the fast greued not, hit were not merit.

5. To affect with grief or deep sorrow. †Formerly, in wider sense: to vex, trouble, or oppress mentally; to cause pain, anxiety, or vexation to; to annoy.

a **1225** *Ancr. R.* 236 Ȝif þe ueonde mid fondunge greueð þe sore, þu greuest him hwon þu etstondest a þusend siðe more. *a* **1300** *Cursor M.* 2920 (Cott.) Abraham went him on þe morn To þat sted..And sagh þat [= what] can him sare greue. **1362** LANGL. *P. Pl.* A. v. 79 His grase and his good hap greueþ me ful sore. ? *a* **1400** *Morte Arth.* 2538 'Sir', sais syr Gawayne, 'so me Gode helpe! Siche glaue-rande gomes greues me bot lyttille!' *c* **1430** *Hymns Virg.* 72 Ȝouġþe staale from me; þat soore me greuis; Age steeleþ on me boþe day and nyȝte. **1525** LD. BERNERS *Froiss.* II. clx. [clvi.] 439 This synne greued greatly the conscience of the duke of Irelande. *a* **1533** —— *Huon* xcv. 309 Y^{e} losse of his good horse greuyth hym more than the losse of all his men. **1573** G. HARVEY *Letter-bk.* (Camden) 3, I had cause to be greeved at it. **1611** BIBLE *John* xxi. 17 Peter was grieued [Gr. ἐλυπήθη], because he said vnto him the third time, Louest thou me? —— *Eph.* iv. 30 Grieue not [Gr. μὴ λυπεῖτε] the holy Spirit of God. **1667** MILTON *P.L.* II. 887 Griev'd at his heart, when looking down he saw The whole Earth fill'd with violence. **1712** LADY M. W. MONTAGU *Lett.* (1861) I. 200 People are seldom very much grieved..at misfortunes they expect. **1747** DODDRIDGE *Life Col. Gardiner* 41 He was grieved to see human nature prostituted to such low and contemptible pursuits. **1833** HT. MARTINEAU *Charmed Sea* i. 6 The spirit of Taddeus was grieved as much by his sister's injustice as by his own remorse. **1841** LANE *Arab. Nts.* I. 74 He was grieved by the corrupt speech of his son.

With *adv.* **1860** PUSEY *Min. Proph.* 24 The Holy Spirit they have grieved away.

refl. *c* **1380** WYCLIF *Wks.* (1880) 372, I pray ȝou here þat ȝe greue ȝou not all-þouȝ I forȝete not liȝtly þe materialle swerde [etc.]. *c* **1500** *Debate Carpenter's Tools* 277 in Hazl. *E.P.P.* I. 89 And greue ȝou nothinge at this songe, Bot euer make mery ȝour selue amonge. **1530** PALSGR. 575/1, I greve my selfe more with the felowe than he is worthe.

b. *impers.* or *quasi-impers.* with subject *it* or a substantive clause.

c **1230** *Hali Meid.* 33 Ȝif þu him muche luuest & he let lutel to þe hit greueð þe. *a* **1300** *Cursor M.* 10443 (Gött.) It greuys me wonderly sare, I se þe leudy ma suilk care. ? **1370** *Robt. Cicyle* 61 Me grevyth noȝt. *c* **1380** *Sir Ferumb.* 262 Wel sore him greuede þat þe kyng was angred for ys sake. *c* **1430** *Syr Gener.* (Roxb.) 4130 To part from hir it wold him gref. **1530** PALSGR. 575/1 It greveth me to se hym in this case. **1590** SPENSER *F.Q.* II. x. 29 That nought him griev'd to beene from rule deposed downe. **1600** SHAKS. *A.Y.L.* v. ii. 22 Oh my deere Orlando, how it greeues me to see thee weare thy heart in a scarfe. **1611** BIBLE *Ruth* i. 13 It grieueth me much for your sakes, that the hand of the Lord is gone out against me. **1657** R. LIGON *Barbadoes* (1673) 84 Pare off the rinde, which is so beautiful, as it grieves us to rob the fruit of such an ornament. **1836** W. IRVING *Astoria* II. 163 Much did it grieve the friends of that gentleman to see him [etc.]. **1852** MRS. STOWE *Uncle Tom's C.* xxv. 239 It really grieves me to have you be so naughty.

†**6.** To make angry; to provoke to anger or resentment; to incense, offend. Also *pass.*, To be angry *with*. *Obs.*

a **1300** *Cursor M.* 1227 (Gött.) For þai him greued [*Cott.* warryed, *Fairf.* wraþet] wid þair dedis He þaim forsoke in all þair nedis. **13..** *E.E. Allit. P.* B. 302 Now god in nwy to Noe con speke, Wylde wrakful wordeȝ in his wylle greued. *c* **1340** *Cursor M.* 18317 (Trin.) Him to greue [*Gött.* greme] hit is ful grille. **1362** LANGL. *P. Pl.* A. VII. 216, 'I wolde not greue god', quod Pers, 'for al the gold on ground'. **1426** AUDELAY *Poems* 8 God and mon thou schalt never greve. *c* **1460** *Towneley Myst.* xxx. 128, I had leuer go to rome yei thryse on my fete Then forto grefe yonde grome,..he lokys full grisly. **1535** BP. SHAXTON *Let. to Cromwell* in Strype *Eccl. Mem.* I. App. lxi. 151 Be not greived with them that for christen love admonish you, and even pray for you. **1535** COVERDALE *Ps.* lxxvii[i]. 40 O how oft haue they greued him in the wyldernesse? How many a tyme haue they prouoked him in the deserte? [**1611** How oft did they prouoke him in the wildernesse: and grieue him in the desert. (The second vb. in the Heb. usually means 'to distress, afflict'.)]

impersonal. **1390** GOWER *Conf.* III. 246 It had hem greved Ayein a folk, which thanne hight The Gabiens.

†**b.** *refl.* To grow angry. *Obs.*

1377 LANGL. *P. Pl.* B. Prol. 139 Thanne greued hym a goliardeys a glotoun of wordes. *Ibid.* VII. 318 He greueth hym aȝeines god, and gruccheth aȝeines resoun.

†**7.** *intr.* To feel annoyance or anger. *Obs.*

a **1300** *Cursor M.* 5949 Quen pharaon sagh rest and stund, His hert wex gret and gan to greue. *c* **1350** *Parl. Three Ages* 182 This gome alle in graye greued with this wordes, And sayde, 'felowe..þou fonnes full ȝerne.' *Ibid.* 194.

8. To feel grief; to be mentally pained or distressed; to sorrow deeply. Const. *at*, *for*, *over*, or *to* with *inf.*, occas. with cognate obj.

13.. [see GRIEVING *vbl. sb.* 2]. **1598** TOFTE in *Shaks. C. Praise* 25 They seemde to grieve, but yet they felt no care. **1599** MARSTON *Sco. Villanie* III. viii. 214, I doe sadly grieue, and inly vexe, To viewe the base dishonour of our sexe. **1647–8** COTTERELL *Davila's Hist. Fr.* (1678) 10 They exceedingly grieved to see him so much fallen. **1667** MILTON *P.L.* XI. 754. **1684** *Contempl. State Man* II. iv.

(1699) 163 Let those grieve and be melancholy who have no hope of Heaven. **1816** BYRON *Childe Harold* III. 27 Grieving, if aught inanimate e'er grieves, Over the unreturning brave. **1819** SHELLEY *Cenci* IV. iv. 11, I grieve thus to distress you, but the Count Must answer charges of the gravest import. **1830** TENNYSON *Song*, '*A spirit haunts*' ii, My whole soul grieves At the moist rich smell of the rotting leaves. **1882** H. S. HOLLAND *Logic & Life* (1885) 119 We cannot grieve the holy grief that comes only to the pure in heart. **1884** PAE *Eustace* 22 He..grieved for the gentle young wife who had been taken from him.

transf. **1794** MRS. RADCLIFFE *Myst. Udolpho* i, The long-haunted bower, where the nightingale grieves. *a* **1861** T. WOOLNER *My Beautiful Lady* (1863) 58 To you the wind but sobs and grieves Wailing with the streaming leaves.

b. *trans.* To feel or show grief at or for; to regret deeply. *poet.*

1598 DRAYTON *Heroic. Ep.* xvi. 152 Sorrow doth utter what it still doth grieve. **1622** FLETCHER *Sea Voy.* I. i, Most miserable men, I greive their fortunes. **1676** DRYDEN *Aurengz.* IV. i. 1577 'Tis little to confess your Fate I grieve. **1718** PRIOR *Solomon* II. 46 Till from the Parian isle, and Libya's coast, The mountains grieve their hopes of marble lost. **1725** POPE *Odyss.* VII. 297 Howe'er the noble, suff'ring mind, may grieve Its load of anguish, and disdain to live. **1871** BROWNING *Balaustion* 530 Nor any clipt locks strew the vestibule, Though surely these drop when we grieve the dead.

grieve, var. GREAVE[1] *Obs.*; obs. f. GREAVE[2].

grieved (griːvd), *ppl. a.* [f. GRIEVE *v.* + -ED[1].]

†**1.** Harassed, troubled, oppressed. *Obs.*

1627 DRAYTON *Agincourt*, etc. 68 The greeued people thus their iudgements spend, Of these strange Actions what should be the end. **1682** (*title*) The Sad and Lamentable cry of Oppression and Cruelty in the City of Bristol. Relating to the persecution of certain dissenting protestants in some passages most notorious to the grieved inhabitants of the said City.

b. (Usu. following the sb.) = AGGRIEVED 2. ? *Obs.*

1621 ELSING *Debates Ho. Lords* App. (1870) 136 To restitucion of certaine persons greved. **1647** N. BACON *Disc. Govt. Eng.* I. xxiv. (1739) 41 In case of injustice or error, the party grieved had liberty of appeal. **1768** BLACKSTONE *Comm.* III. 160 The usual application of this forfeiture is either to the party grieved, or else to any of the king's subjects in general. **1818** CRUISE *Digest* (ed. 2) II. 60 The person grieved may relieve himself.

†**2.** Afflicted with pain or disease. *Obs.*

1577 *Vicary's Anat.* Ep. Ded. (1888) 8 Those poore and greeued creatures..do knowe the profite of this Art [Anatomy] to be manyfolde. **1590** BARROUGH *Meth. Phisick* 211 You must sprinckle the grieued place with old vineger and oile of roses mixed. **1612** WOODALL *Surg. Mate* Wks. (1653) 3 Use wine and hony to foment the grieved part. **1689** MOYLE *Sea Chyrurg.* II. xviii. 72 Foment the grieved part with hot *Spiritus vini Communis*.

†**3.** Irritated, incensed, made angry. *Obs.*

c **1340** *Cursor M.* 6537 (Trin.) So greued [*other texts* menged] he wex in his mode He myȝt saye euel ne gode. *c* **1400** *Sege Jerusalem* (E.E.T.S.) 31/553 As greued grif-founs þei girden in samen Spokly her speres. *c* **1440** *Promp. Parv.* 211/2 Grevyd, or a-greuyd yn wrethe, *aggravatus*.

4. Affected with grief; vexed, afflicted, troubled or distressed in mind.

1586 Q. ELIZ. in *Leycester Corr.* (Camden) 209 Your grievid and woundid mynd hath more nede of comfort then reproof. **1604** MIDDLETON *Witch* IV. i. (1778) 76 The grievedst lady that was ere be-sett With stormes of sorrowes, or wild rage of people. **1633** P. FLETCHER *Poet. Misc.* 130 Sleep grieved heart and now a little rest thee. **1667** MILTON *P.L.* IV. 28 Sometimes towards Eden..his grievd look he fixes sad. **1738** LILLO *Marina* II. i. 25 Her griev'd Sire Shall curse the cruel fates. **1835** LYTTON *Rienzi* I. i, I do not wonder you are too grieved to listen to reason now. **1896** *Daily News* 21 Apr. 6/6 The grieved mother suffered several strokes of apoplexy.

Hence **'grievedly** *adv.*, †**'grievedness.**

1571 GOLDING *Calvin on Ps.* li. 19 The spirit of greevednesse and the broken or sory hart. **1892** *Century Mag.* June 267 'Ain't that child to sleep yet?' she asked grievedly.

†**'grievement.** *Obs. nonce-wd.* In 7 grievment. [f. GRIEVE *v.* + -MENT.] A hurt, injury.

1708 T. WARD *Eng. Ref.* I. 92 His Battels won and great Atchievments, Wounds, Bruses, Bangs, and other Grievments.

griever ('griːvə(r)). [f. GRIEVE *v.* + -ER[1].]

†**1.** One who molests or troubles another; the causer of a grievance. *Obs.*

1598 FLORIO, *Grauatore*..a grieuer. **1625** TURNER *Let. to the Speaker* in Rushw. *Hist. Coll.* (1659) I. 219, I chose out some few, not because they were greater, or more known Grievances, but because they did seem to direct us to find out the Griever, or the first Cause. **1660** R. COKE *Power & Subj.* 207 If any feel himself grieved, molested or inquieted ..the same molesters, grievers or inquesters [*sic*]..have and incur, the pains and punishments contained in the statute.

2. A person or thing that grieves or distresses.

1641 HAMMOND *Chr. Oblig. Peace* vii. (1649) 173 There is not a sinne..a greater waster of conscience, griever and quencher of the spirit.

3. One who feels or shows grief.

1819 CRABBE *T. of Hall* xx. 287 Nor should romantic grievers thus complain. **1852** TUPPER *Proverb. Philos.* 363 Griever at neglect, hear me to my comfort.

4. One who has a grievance. *nonce-use.*

1830 GEN. P. THOMPSON *Exerc.* (1842) I. 253 But the grievers who are aggrieved by the grievances shall not adjourn or alter time or place of meeting.

grieveship ('griːvʃɪp). [f. GRIEVE *sb.* + -SHIP.] A district under the charge of a grieve.

1711 HEARNE *Collect.* (O.H.S.) III. 138 Clifton, a free Grieveship, within the Maner of Coningsbrough. **1883** *Longm. Mag.* Apr. 646 The sheriff, or highest county official, is really the shire grieve; and the county is a grieveship. **1897** J. C. HODGSON *Hist. Northumbld.* IV. 76 The grieveships, which are now seven in number, are in almost all respects similar to the townships of other parishes.

†**'grievesome,** *a. Obs.* [f. GRIEVE *v.* + -SOME. Cf. GRIEFSOME.] Distressing, painful. Hence **'grievesomeness.**

1568 H. BULLINGER tr. *P. Martyr's Comm. Rom.* ix. 237 b, Anye misfortune, that is not customable grieuesome [*printed* grieuosome] vnto vs. **1583** T. WATSON *Centurie of Loue* lxiv. (Arb.) 100 Layinge open the long continued grieuesomnes of his misery of Loue. *Ibid.* lxxxv. 121 With grieusome wars, with toyles, with storms betost.

grieving ('griːvɪŋ), *vbl. sb.* [f. GRIEVE *v.* + -ING[1].] The action of the vb. GRIEVE.

1. From *trans.* senses of the vb.: The act of causing grief, †oppressing, troubling, paining, etc. †Also, a painful affection of the body (*obs.*).

1375 BARBOUR *Bruce* VIII. 510 All the lafe..He tuk, and gaf thame dispending, And send thame hame, but mar greving. **1398** TREVISA *Barth. De P.R.* XVIII. ix. (1495) 759 The serpent Ophites hath as many manere of brennynges and greuynges as he hath speckles and colours. *Ibid.* XIX. xliv. 886 It bredith many greuynges in the body. *c* **1400** *Destr. Troy* 8535 Comaundand þat comly, as his kynd fader, By all hor goddes so gret, & greuyng of him, þat he fare shuld ne ferre, ne the feld entre. **1523** LD. BERNERS *Froiss.* I. ccccxxviii. 752 The noblemen and men of warre..to be payed their wages, without greuynge of any parte of the kynges treasar. **1617** HIERON *Wks.* II. 230 To the grieuing of the godly. **1867** FREEMAN *Norm. Conq.* (ed. 3) I. v. 297 There was nothing..but grieving of the folk and spending of money and emboldening of their foes.

2. From *intr.* senses: The act of feeling or showing grief, etc. †*to take in grieving*, to be displeased or angry (*obs.*).

13.. *E.E. Allit. P.* B. 159 Depe in my doungoun þer doel euer dwellez, Greuing, & gretyng, & gryspyng harde. *c* **1340** *Cursor M.* 8800 (Trin.) If we durst say ȝou sir kyng þat ȝe toke not in greuyng. **1633** P. FLETCHER *Elisa* II. x, A helplesse griefs sole joy is joylesse grieving. **1677** GILPIN *Demonol.* (1867) 450 To be under continual grievings because of miscarriages, so that other things of outward enjoyment cease to be pleasing. **1711** STEELE *Spect.* No. 95 ¶3 Tears shed without much Grieving. **1834** R. M. MCCHEYNE in *Mem.* (1872) I. 34 What a blessed thing it is to see the first grievings of the awakened spirit. **1862** G. MEREDITH *Mod. Love*, etc., *Juggling Jerry* iii, Easy to think that grieving's folly, When the hand's firm as driven stakes!

grieving ('griːvɪŋ), *ppl. a.* [f. GRIEVE *v.* + -ING[2].]

a. That causes grief, pain, or annoyance. **b.** That feels or expresses grief.

c **1450** tr. *De Imitatione* I. xxii. 28 All þese temporall godes biþ..more grevinge þan esynge, for þei are neuere had wiþoute besynes and drede. **1611** BIBLE *Ezek.* xxviii. 24 There shall be no more pricking briar vnto the house of Israel, nor any grieuing thorne. **1721** *Wodrow Corr.* (1843) II. 593 The ship went off sooner than I expected, which was not a little grieving to me. **1791** ANNA SEWARD *Lett.* (1811) III. 54 If not so grieving, it is more mortifying. **1807** CRABBE *Parish Reg.* III. 786 His grieving kin for Rodger's smiles applied. **1873** L. FERGUSON *Discourses* 10 Your spiritual condition is such as to be grieving to the Spirit.

Hence **'grievingly** *adv.*, in a grieving manner.

1613 SHAKS. *Hen. VIII*, I. i. 87 Greeuingly I thinke, the Peace betweene the French and vs, not valewes The Cost that did conclude it. **1891** F. M. WILSON *Primer on Browning* 125 She is leaving James Lee grievingly.

grievous ('griːvəs), *a.* Forms: 4-6 grevous, (4 -os, -es, 5 -ows, -ose, ? -ours, ? -est, 6 -us), 4 grefeous, 5 greivos, grewo(u)s, 6 greveous, 6-7 greevous, 7 (9 *dial.*) gr(i)vious, 6- grievous. Also 5 grawous, gravewis. [a. OF. *grevos*, *-(o)us*, *-eus*, f. *grever* to GRIEVE. With the forms *grawous*, *gravewis*, cf. OF. *graveus*, (rare), med.L. *gravōsus*, It. and Sp. *gravoso*.]

†**1. a.** Pressing heavily upon a person (or persons), burdensome, oppressive. In later use only of public burdens or grievances. *Obs.*

Such collocations as *grievous burden* survive in occasional use, but the adj. is apprehended in sense 5.

13.. *Barlam & Jos.* 167 ȝif þer any þing be þat greuous is to þe, & we togedir ben, þe lyȝter it schal be. **1382** WYCLIF *1 Kings* xii. 4 The moost greuous ȝok that he hath putte on to vs. —— *Matt.* xxiii. 23 Tho thingis that ben greuouser.. of the lawe. **1426** in *Surtees Misc.* (1888) 3 þe charge is to me full hevy and grevous. **1531** TINDALE *Exp. John* (1537) 74 Hys commaundementes are not greueous. **1550** LATIMER *Serm. at Stamford* I. 90 Christ came to bring us out of..a greater burthen and a more greeuouser burthen, the burthen of sinne. **1593** BILSON *Govt. Christ's Ch.* 322 Your discipline is farre greeuouser to the faithfull. **1611** BIBLE *1 Kings* xii. 4 Thy father made our yoke grieuous: now therefore, make thou the grieuous seruice of thy father.. lighter. **1663** MARVELL *Corr.* xlii. Wks. 1872-5 II. 91 A Committee is also inspecting all illegall patents, and grievous to the subject. **1666** *Ibid.* lii. II. 188 The committee have voted the Canary Company grievous, illegal, and a monopoly. **1765** T. HUTCHINSON *Hist. Mass.* I. iii. 35 Mr. Dudley's short administration was not very grievous. [**1849** MACAULAY *Hist. Eng.* vi. II. 90 The High Commission was generally regarded as the most grievous of the many grievances under which the nation laboured.]

†**b.** Of a task: Heavy, arduous, difficult. *Obs.*

1375 BARBOUR *Bruce* x. 636 Fra-thine vp wes grevousar To clym vp. *c* **1386** CHAUCER *Pars. T.* ¶529 And in as muche as thilke love is the moore greuous to perfourne, in so muche is the more gretter the merite. *a* **1450** *Paston Lett.* No. 75 I. 97 It will be right gravewis to him to heile of his hurt, he is so sore streken. **1477** EARL RIVERS (Caxton) *Dictes* 108 It is a greuos thing to conquere them [Royaumes], yet is it a more greuours & more chargeable to kepe them wel.

†**c.** Of penalties, punishment, indignation: Falling heavily upon one; heavy, severe. *Obs.*

1393 LANGL. *P. Pl.* C. XVII. 77 So for hus glotonye and grete synne he haþ a greuous penaunce. **1422** tr. *Secreta Secret., Priv. Priv.* (E.E.T.S.) 160 God ther-of toke greivos vengeaunce. **1548** UDALL, etc. *Erasm. Par. Matt.* xviii. 92 Let this be the greuousest punishment emong you. **1564** HAWARD *Eutropius* VII. 72 He woulde not lightlye punyshe anye..with anye greuouser penaltye then by banishment only. **1648** GAGE *West Ind.* iv. 12 Signifying..his own grievous indignation against me. **1659** D. PELL *Impr. Sea* 146 War is a thing that punishes men, with the greatest, and grievousest punishments that can bee.

†**d.** Of persons: Causing trouble or annoyance to others; oppressive. Of an assailant: Pressing hard *on*. *Obs.*

1382 WYCLIF *2 Cor.* xii. 14, I schal not be greuous [L. *gravis*] to ȝou. **1470-85** MALORY *Arthur* I. xiv, The Duke Eustace..and Kynge Claryaunce..were alweye greuous on Vlfyus. **1483** CAXTON *Gold. Leg.* 124/2 And as she that was besy and greuous to hym he said to her goo unto the holy man that is named Effraym. **1535** COVERDALE *Isa.* vii. 13 Is it not ynough for you, that ye be greuous vnto men, but ye must greue my God also? **1548** UDALL, etc. *Erasm. Par. Matt.* x. 62 Ye shall be grieuouse to no man with beggyng. **1586** J. HOOKER *Girald. Irel.* in *Holinshed* II. 8/1 To his owne people he was rough and greevous, and hatefull unto strangers. **1600** HAKLUYT *Voy.* III. 847, I do intreat you all to forgiue me in whatsoeuer I haue bin grieuous vnto you.

e. Of a complaint: Pressing heavily on the person complained of. (In later use merely intensive or associated with sense 5 or 6.)

1553 EDEN *Treat. Newe Ind.* (Arb.) 36 Mouinge greuous complayntes agaynst them before the King of Spaine. **1596** SHAKS. *1 Hen. IV*, II. iv. 487 The complaints I heare of thee, are grieuous. *a* **1715** BURNET *Own Time* (1724) I. 370 They raised a grievous outcry for the want of a National Synod to regulate our worship and government. **1871** MORLEY *Carlyle* (1878) 175 There is the same grievous complaint against the time and its men and its spirit.

2. a. Of things, events, accidents, etc.: Bringing serious trouble or discomfort; having injurious effects; †causing hurt or pain. (Now only with mixture of sense 5—'grievous to think of'—qualifying intensively a sb. denoting something painful or injurious.)

1340 HAMPOLE *Pr. Consc.* 1565 And þa, þat with swylk gyses God greves, Sall fall in many grevos myscheves. *c* **1374** CHAUCER *Boeth.* I. pr. iv. 8 (Camb. MS.) By-twixen wikked folkes and me han ben greuos descordes. **1535** COVERDALE *Heb.* xii. 11 No maner chatisynge for the present tyme semeth to be ioyous, but greuous [also **1611** and **1881**]. **1549** CHEKE *Hurt Sedit.* (1641) 43 Can we not look for a grievouser and perillouser danger then the plague is? **1604** T. WRIGHT *Passions* v. iv. 253 The greater perill, or grievouser evill incurred by the gift, encrease the goodnesse and valuation of the gift. **1612** WOODALL *Surg. Mate* Wks. (1653) 3 We see daily many grievous Fractures healed without it [the Trapan]. **1751** JORTIN *Serm.* (1771) I. iii. 43 We are there told that grievous inconveniences would follow such rigorous methods. **1864** D. G. MITCHELL *Sev. Stor.* 281 Emile was laboring under a grievous delusion. **1870** BRYANT *Iliad* I. I. 22 Wide-ruling Agamemnon may perceive How grievous was his folly.

†**b.** Hurtful or injurious *to* something. *Obs.*

1398 TREVISA *Barth. De P.R.* VI. v. (1495) 193 Chyldren desire thynges that is to theym contrary and greuous. *c* **1400** *Lanfranc's Cirurg.* 123 For colde ys most greuest to bonys & to pannycles þat beþ woundyde.

†**c.** Offensive to the senses; having a bad taste, smell, etc. *Obs.*

1578 LYTE *Dodoens* I. xxx. 43 It is also of a very grievous savour. **1752** J. LOUTHIAN *Form of Process* App. 277 The Sheriff is required to visit and inspect such Room, and to disallow or prohibit the Use of the same, in case it shall appear to be grievous or unhealthy.

†**d.** *loosely.* Excessively great or strong. *Obs.*

1632 LITHGOW *Trav.* IV. 153 And the forequarters and head they threw into a grievous fire. *Ibid.* v. 193 A great Torrent..that maketh a greivous noyse night and day.

3. a. Of a disease, wound, or pain: Causing great suffering or danger; acute, severe. Now *rare.*

c **1290** *S. Eng. Leg.* I. 100/5 On Dame Eutice cam a siknesse: swiþe greuous and long. Four ȝer he hadde gret pine. **1340** HAMPOLE *Pr. Consc.* 2910 And þat syght es a payn ful grevous; For þe devels er swa foul and ydous. *c* **1380** *Sir Ferumb.* 499 He hadde a greuous wounde. **1471** RIPLEY *Comp. Alch.* VI. xv. in Ashm. (1652) 164 Wyth grevose throwys. *c* **1485** *Digby Myst.* (1882) III. 293 Thes grevous peynes make me ner mad! **1552** *Bk. Com. Prayer, Prayer Plague*, Thys plague and greuouse sickenesse. **1667** MILTON *P.L.* x. 501 A world who would not purchase with a bruise, Or much more grievous pain? **1683** SALMON *Doron Med.* I. 2984 The Leprosy is a more grievious Disease. **1865** R. W. DALE *Jew. Temp.* v. (1877) 58 The sufferings of Christ were grievous. **1879** J. M. DUNCAN *Lect. Dis. Women* xxxiii. (1889) 273 The disease..is not considered grievous enough to secure a bed in the hospital.

b. *grievous bodily harm*, a legal term denoting a serious injury (see quot. 1959). Also *transf.*

1861 *Act 24 & 25 Vict.* c. 100 §20 Whosoever shall unlawfully and maliciously wound or inflict any grievous bodily Harm upon any other Person, either with or without any Weapon or Instrument, shall be guilty of a Misdemeanour. **1958** [see G.B.H., G III. f]. **1959** JOWITT *Dict. Eng. Law* I. 258/2 *Bodily harm*, any injury which is merely technical or trivial, as distinguished from the more serious injury termed 'actual bodily harm', or the still more serious injury termed 'grievous bodily harm'. **1968** *Listener*

11 July 62/2 The spectator whose heart lifts at the sight of Clark Graebner committing grievous bodily harm on a tennis ball is a fortunate man indeed.

4. Of a fault, crime, sin, etc.: Involving a grave degree of guilt, deserving heavy penalties. In later use chiefly with stronger sense: Atrocious, flagrant, heinous. Now only *arch.*

a **1300** *Cursor M.* 26451 A sin of vnkindnes..þat als greues es [*Fairf.* þat iiij sa mikil greuouse is] Als all his oþer sinnes ware. *c* **1380** WYCLIF *Serm.* Sel. Wks. II. 240 Of al synnes þat now ben þis is moost perelouse and grevous. **1395** *Remonstr. agst. Rom. Corrupt.* (1851) 14 Auarice and symonie ben greuosere synnis in him thanne is bodili fornicacioun. **1508** FISHER *7 Penit. Ps.* xxxviii. Wks. (1876) 57 Have we not commytted many more greuouser offences than these be? **1583** STUBBES *Anat. Abus.* II. (1882) 41 We see greeuous crimes, and flagicious facts..daily committed. **1601** [see GRIEVOUSLY 1 b]. *a* **1656** HALES *Gold. Rem.* (1688) 96 Those are the more heavier and grievouser sins of our Lives. **1683** *Col. Rec. Pennsylv.* I. 87 A Heynous and Grevious Crime. **1860** SALA *Lady Chesterf.* Pref. 4 This little book.. has from first to last one grievous artistic fault.

5. Causing mental pain or distress. Now with narrowed sense: Exciting grief or intense sorrow.

1297 R. GLOUC. (Rolls) 4140 At tyme of midniȝt of þe niȝt, him mette a greuous cas. Him þoȝte he sey a grislich bere [etc.]. *c* **1400** MAUNDEV. (1839) xxxix. 314, I..was assoyled of alle that lay in my Conscience, of many a dyverse grevous poynt. **1535** COVERDALE *2 Esdr.* v. 21 After seuen dayes it happened, that yᵉ thoughtes of my hert were very greuous vnto me agayne. **1547–8** *Ordre of Commvnion* (1548) Bj b, The remembraunce of them is greuous vnto vs. **1594** SHAKS. *Rich. III*, I. i. 141 That Newes is bad indeed..'Tis very greeuous to be thought vpon. **1692** PEPYS *Let.* 9 Jan., Diary (1879) VI. 172, I would have come at you the other night at St. Martin's on that grievous occasion, but could not. **1712** STEELE *Spect.* No. 472 ¶8 The Pleasures and Advantages of Sight being so great, the Loss must be very grievous. **1794** MRS. RADCLIFFE *Myst. Udolpho* xxx, It was so very grievous to her to think that [etc.]. **1833** HT. MARTINEAU *Brooke Farm* vii. 87 It was grievous to see in a short time how poorly they lived.

6. Full of grief; very sad or sorrowful. *rare.*

c **1374** CHAUCER *Boeth.* I. pr. i. 3 (Camb. MS.) And she, byholdynge my cheere, þat was..heuy and greuos of wepynge, compley[n]de..þat I shal seyen the perturbacyon of my thowht. **1590** MARLOWE *2nd Pt. Tamburl.* III. i. The heir of mighty Bajazeth..Revives the spirits of all true Turkish hearts, In grievous memory of his father's shame. **1657** R. LIGON *Barbadoes* (1673) 36 And when he sees you come with a knife..to kill him, he vapours out the grievousest sighs, that ever you heard any creature make. **1828** HAWTHORNE *Fanshawe* ix. (1879) 144 Women.. wearing a deep grievous expression of countenance. **1893** *Daily News* 9 Jan. 5/6 All the while the grievous mother stands by..and varies the dreary tale of pecuniary difficulty by telling [etc.].

7. quasi-*adv.*

1596 SHAKS. *1 Hen. IV*, IV. i. 17 He cannot come, my Lord He is greeuous sick.

Hence **'grievoushead** [-HEAD] = GRIEVOUSNESS.

13.. *Minor Poems fr. Vernon MS.* x. 47 Meur wiþ-outen greuoushed And Murie wiþ-outen wyldehed. **1496** *Dives & Paup.* (W. de W.) VI. xxiii. 271/2 Only god knoweth the greuoushede of dedely synne.

grievously ('gri:vəslɪ), *adv.* [f. GRIEVOUS *a.* + -LY².]

1. In such a way as to be oppressive, painful, or hurtful to the affairs, person, or feelings of any one; to an oppressive or injurious extent. (Chiefly used with words implying hurt, harm, wrong, etc., and hence tending to become merely intensive; cf. 2.)

1303 R. BRUNNE *Handl. Synne* 6736 Ne Lazare asked nat greuuslyke, But a fewe crummes for to pyke. **1340** HAMPOLE *Pr. Consc.* 4537 Þan sal he shew grete parsecucion And grevusly þam tourment. *c* **1380** WYCLIF *Sel. Wks.* III. 431 Al ȝif he semeþ grevousliche unkynde for þe tyme. *c* **1386** CHAUCER *Pars. T.* ¶773 This cursed synne anoyeth greuousliche hem that it haunten. **1472** *Presentm. Juries* in *Surtees Misc.* (1888) 22 Grefesly hurt hem of parell of his dethe. **1483** *Act. 1 Rich. III*, c. 6 §1 Much people coming to the said Fairs be grievously vexed and troubled by feigned Actions. **1503–4** *Act 19 Hen. VII*, c. 36 Preamble, Stanhop ..lay in wayte uppon the seid sir William and hym grevously wouneded and maymed. **1509** FISHER *Funeral Serm. C'tess Richmond* Wks. (1876) 300 The moost paynful crampes soo greuously vexynge her. **1611** BIBLE *Matt.* viii. 6 My seruant lieth at home sicke of the palsie, grieuously tormented. **1657** R. LIGON *Barbadoes* (1673) 21 The Inhabitants..were so grievously visited with the plague. **1751** JORTIN *Serm.* (1771) V. ii. 30 To punish the offender and to afflict him more grievously. **1870** BRYANT *Iliad* II. xv. 75 He had seen the Greeks Pressed grievously beside their fleet.

†**b.** Heavily; with a heavy penalty, at a heavy or high rate; for a large sum. *Obs.*

a **1340** HAMPOLE *Psalter* i. 6 Þai sall greuoslyere be dampned þan hethen men. *a* **1500** in Arnolde *Chron.* (1811) 211 Yf any man wer taken and conuicte of takyng of veneri he shalbe greuously redemed if he haue wherof he may be redeemed. **1583** GOLDING *Calvin on Deut.* lx. 361 Now then we shall not faile to be yᵉ grieuouslyer condemned if we forget our God. **1601** SHAKS. *Jul. C.* III. ii. 85 The Noble Brutus Hath told you Cæsar was Ambitious: If it were so it was a greeuous Fault, And greeuously hath Cæsar answer'd it. **1670** BLOUNT *Law Dict.* s.v. *Attaint*, He shall be imprisoned and grievously ransomed at the Kings Will.

2. In a great or serious degree; heavily, deeply, strongly, exceedingly, etc. (In early, and occas. in mod. use, with more or less suggestion of the etymological sense.)

1340 *Ayenb.* 47 Hy zeneȝeþ wel greuousliche. *c* **1385** CHAUCER *L.G.W.* Prol. 349 He ne hath nat doon so grevously a-mis. *c* **1400** MAUNDEV. (Roxb.) vi. 21 He had.. sworne so greuously þat he schuld bring it to swilke a state þat wymmen schuld mow wade ouer and noȝt wete þaire kneesse. *c* **1430** *Life St. Kath.* (1884) 25 And hym offendyth no thyng more greuously than whan man..ȝeueþ worshep of godhed to creatures vnresonable. **1531** TINDALE *Exp. John* (1537) 81 The Jewes..synned greueouslyer agaynst God. **1590** SPENSER *F.Q.* III. x. 2 He behind them stayd, Maulgre his host, who grudged grievously To house a guest that would be needes obayd. **1595** SHAKS. *John* IV. iii. 134, I do suspect thee very greeuously. **1704** SWIFT *T. Tub* Ded., Wks. 1760 I. 3, I grievously suspected a cheat. **1794** SIR W. JONES *Instit. Hindu Law* ii. §226 A spiritual and a natural father..are not to be treated with disrespect..though the student be grievously provoked. **1873** RUSKIN *Arrows Chace* (1880) II. 100, [I] shall be grievously busy tomorrow. **1894** H. DRUMMOND *Ascent Man* 56 The sociologist has grievously complained of late that he could get but little help from science.

3. In a deplorable manner, 'sadly', 'wofully'.

1742 WARBURTON *Wks.* (1811) XI. 197 But our Advocate, now grievously bemired, yet flounders on. **1827** POLLOK *Course T.* iv, The winds of heaven Display his nakedness to passers by, And grievously burlesque the human form. **1847–8** H. MILLER *First Impr.* xviii. (1857) 321 Melancholy banks of mud, here and there overtopped by thickets of grievously befouled sedges. **1875** JOWETT *Plato* (ed. 2) I. 477 How grievously was I disappointed! **1883** SIR T. MARTIN *Ld. Lyndhurst* v. 126 The Government erred grievously in doing little or nothing to redress these abuses.

†**4.** With expression of grief; bitterly, piteously, sorrowfully. *Obs.*

c **1400** *Lanfranc's Cirurg.* 120 Þei syke greuousleche, & a scharpe feuere falliþ. **1604** SHAKS. *Oth.* v. i. 53 What are you heere, that cry so greeuously?

†**5.** *to take grievously*: (*a*) to be incensed or angered at; (*b*) to be distressed or grieved at. (Cf. *take in grief, in grievance.*) *Obs.*

a **1533** FRITH *Bk. agst. Rastell* (1829) 211 More and Rochester..took the matter so grievously, that they could never be at quiet in their stomachs, until they had drunken his blood. **1548** UDALL, etc. *Erasm. Par. Mark* v. 35–43 The common sorte are wounte to take the death of young folkes much greuouslyer then of olde. **1552** EARL SHREWSBURY in Ellis *Orig. Lett.* Ser. II. III. 61 My wyffe taketh my doughter Lennoux deathe so grevouslie that she neither dothe nor can thincke of any thinge but of lamentinge.

grievousness ('gri:vəsnɪs). [f. GRIEVOUS *a.* + -NESS.] The quality or condition of being grievous, in various senses of the adj.

1303 R. BRUNNE *Handl. Synne* 719 Þyn oþys done hym more greuesnesse þan alle þe Iewys wykkednesse. *c* **1340** HAMPOLE *Prose Tr.* (1866) 3 This name Ihesu..dose away greuesnes of fleschely desyris. *c* **1400** *Lanfranc's Cirurg.* 322 Of þe greuousnes of þe rigboon whanne he is out of ioyncte. *c* **1440** *Promp. Parv.* 211/1 Grevawnce, or grevowsnesse, *gravamen.* **1509** HAWES *Past. Pleas.* XI. xxxvii, A gentyll burden wythout grevousnes. **1526** *Pilgr. Perf.* (W. de W. 1531) 254 b, Also the greuousnesse of this payne saynt Augustyn toucheth. **1562** TURNER *Herbal* II. 45 b, The apples of thys [Mandrage]..smell plesantly ioyned wᵗʰ a certayn greuousnes. *a* **1600** HOOKER *Eccl. Pol.* VIII. ix. §3 For the grievousness of sin is aggravated by the greatness of him that committeth it. **1611** BIBLE *Isa.* xxi. 15 The grieuousnesse of warre. **1682** NORRIS *Hierocles* 48 We first alleviate the grievousness of Events by right reasoning. *a* **1864** J. D BURNS *Serm.* in *Mem. & Rem.* (1869) 387 Affliction..would lose all the grievousness and smart which make affliction.

†**grievousty.** *Obs.* In 5 grevouste, -osetee. [f. GRIEVOUS + -TY.] Grievousness, heinousness.

c **1410** LOVE *Bonavent. Mirr.* xxxiv. 68 (Gibbs MS.) Also to schewe þe greuouste of synn in custome. *c* **1425** *Orolog. Sapient.* ii. in *Anglia* X. 342/38 Þou schalt gretelye weye þe grevosetee of þine sinnes.

grife, variant of GRYPH *Obs.*, griffin.

griff (grɪf), *sb.*¹ *north. dial.* Also grif. [Origin obscure.] A deep narrow valley or chasm. ? Cf. GRIFT *sb.*¹

1788 W. MARSHALL *Yorksh.* II. 333 *Griff*, a deep valley, with a rocky fissure-like chasm at the bottom. **1882** *Good Cheer* 33 The broken receding angles at the foot of the Grif. **1891** ATKINSON *Moorland Par.* 344 One of the small tributary becks..comes into the open air again in a wild little griff.

griff (grɪf), *sb.*² *Anglo-Indian.* [app. a shortening of the earlier GRIFFIN, q.v.] = GRIFFIN².

1829 *Bengalee* 260 Whilst a call Of 'Griff! ho Griff!' re-echoed like the yell Of foul tormentors, in some modern hell. **1860** *All Year Round* No. 55. 117 What an unsophisticated griff you must be! **1878** BESANT & RICE *Celia's Arb.* xxx. (1887) 225 There had been joking with a lot of 'griffs', young recruits just out from England.

Comb. **1853** W. D. ARNOLD *Oakfield* I. iii. 38 Cadets.. going up to that great griff depot, Oudapoor.

griff (grɪf), *sb.*³ *rare.* Also in Fr. form *griffe.* [a. F. *griffe.*] A claw.

1820 SHELLEY *Sensitive Pl.* III. 113 A Northern whirlwind, wandering about Like a wolf..Shook the boughs thus laden, and heavy, and stiff, And snapped them off with his rigid griff. **1848** LYTTON *Harold* VII. iv, My disgrace at being so clawed and mauled by its *griffes.* **1865** OUIDA *Strathmore* I. xii. 195 The pretty panther, how handsome she looks! She has merciless *griffes*, though.

griff (grɪf), *sb.*⁴ *Louisiana.* Also griffe, griffo(n, griffin. [Of obscure origin: Buffon (quoted by Littré) gives the word as *griffe.*] A type of mulatto (see quots.).

1850 LYELL *2nd Visit U.S.* II. 67 The auctioneer began to describe him as a fine griff (which means three parts black), twenty-four years old, and having many superior qualities. **1859** BARTLETT *Dict. Amer.*, *Griffin, griffe*, this word, like the French *griffone*, is constantly used in Louisiana, both in conversation and in print, for a mulatto, particularly the woman. **1886** *Syd. Soc. Lex.*, *Griff*, same as *Griffo. Griffo*, the produce of a negro and a mulatto, containing one fourth white blood, and three fourths black. *Griffon*, same as *Griffo.*

griff (grɪf), *sb.*⁵ *Weaving.* [Origin unknown.] A frame composed of horizontal bars employed in pattern-weaving. Also ***griff-frame.***

1860 *Ure's Dict. Arts* (ed. 5) III. 1005 A mechanical arrangement connected with the treddle, which raises or depresses the griff frame. **1875** KNIGHT *Dict. Mech.*, *Griff.*

griff (grɪf), *sb.*⁶ *slang.* [Shortened form of GRIFFIN⁴.] A tip; news; reliable information.

1891 N. GOULD *Double Event* (1892) iv. 22 'He's a Newmarketer, he is. Not up here for nothing, you bet. He's got the straight griff for something.'.. Ike had the 'straightest griff' he ever had in his life, and that was to mount *Iberia* for Sydney. **1945** *Finito! Po Valley Campaign* 30 The officer who broke off a stern argument..to inquire.. the latest 'griff' from a passing Tommy. **1948** A. BARON *From City, from Plough* vi. 49 'Is that the griff, Higgsy?'.. 'Have I ever given you a wrong tip?' **1961** WODEHOUSE *Service with Smile* v. 75 You can't come telling a man to go pinching pigs without giving him the griff about why he's doing it and who for. **1967** M. PROCTER *Exercise Hoodwink* xvii. 119 Somebody in the centre of things had 'given the griff' whenever there had been any to give. **1968** *Listener* 8 Feb. 167/1 He was to give us the approved line, the authorised version, the holy griff on what we were actually up to in Suez. **1968** J. WAINWRIGHT *Edge of Extinction* 104 The informant was saying: 'It's griff, guv. The real thing.'

griff (grɪf), *v. Anglo-Indian.* [f. GRIFF *sb.*²]

1829 *Bengalee* 263 He deem'd no sin To griff a heedless friend,—plain English,—take him in.

griff, obs. form of GRAFF *sb.*¹, GRIEF.

griffade (grɪ'feɪd). *Falconry.* [a. F. *griffade*, f. *griffe* claw.] A sudden seizure with the claws.

1852 R. F. BURTON *Falconry Valley Indus* v. 62 The 'malle-hawk' dug her talons with a griffade into his head.

griffaun (grɪ'fɔ:n). *Anglo-Irish.* Also 8 **graffane**, 9 **griffawn.** [a. Irish *grafán* 'a grubbing-ax' (O'Reilly), f. *grafaim* scrape, grub.] (See quot. 1780.) Hence **griffaun** *v.*

1780 A. YOUNG *Tour Irel.* II. 10 They..pare with an instrument they call a graffane, and the husbandry they call graffaning and burning. It is a very strong hoe with which they cut up the turf, rolling it up with their foot as they do it, and leaving it to dry in order to burn. **1885** *Evening News* 25 July 2/6 William struck Tom Sheehan on the head with the griffaun. **1892** JANE BARLOW *Irish Idylls* iii. 62 Larry was dealing a few superfluous pats with the flat of his broad griffawn.

griffe (grɪf). *Archit.* [Fr.: see GRIFF *sb.*³] A claw-shaped ornament carved at the angle of the square base of a column; a spur.

1875 *Encycl. Brit.* II. 465/1 *Griffe*, a French term for an ornament at the angles of the base of early pillars, for which we have no proper equivalent. It first consisted of a single leaf, which became more elaborate, and was, no doubt, the origin of the foliated bases. **1901** R. STURGIS *Dict. Archit.* II. 323/1 The griffe..is often used for elaborate ornamentation, being carved into vegetable or even animal form. **1905** F. BOND *Gothic Archit.* 455 Griffes are found in Roman work in a similar position... Pliny describes griffes of lizards and frogs. **1952** H. H. SAYLOR *Dict. Archit.* (1963) 79 *Griffe*, an ornamental form, somewhat like a claw, extending from the torus of a column base and lying on the four corners of the plinth.

griffe, obs. form of GRAFF *sb.*¹, *sb.*³, *v.*¹, GRIEF.

griffier, obs. form of GREFFIER.

griffin¹ ('grɪfɪn), **griffon, gryphon** ('grɪfən). Forms: α. 4–5 griffun, gryffoun(e, (5 -own), 5 griffoun(e, greffon, 5–7 gryffon, 5, 7–8 grifon, 6 gryfon, 6–7 griffion, 6 griffen, 7 gryffen, 4 griffyn, (5 grefyne, grifyn), 7–8 gryffin, 4– griffon, 6– griffin. β. 5, 7 griphon, (6 girphinne, *Sc.* grephoun), 6–7 griphin, 6–8 gryphin, 7, 9 gryphen, 5– gryphon. [a. OF. *grifoun*, F. *griffon* (OF. also *gripon*) = It. *grifone*, f. L. *grȳphus* (Mela) = *grȳps* (gen. *grȳphis*), a. Gr. γρύψ (gen. γρυπός).

In sense 2, and its comb. in 4, the regular modern spelling is *griffon*, in other senses usually *griffin*, though *gryphon* is used by many writers as having more dignified associations.]

1. A fabulous animal usually represented as having the head and wings of an eagle and the body and hind quarters of a lion.

By the Greeks they were believed to inhabit Scythia, and to keep jealous watch over the gold of that country.

13.. *K. Alis.* 496 The griffon of him was agast. *c* **1386** CHAUCER *Knt.'s T.* 1275 Lik a grifphon looked he aboute [*Lansd.*, *Corpus & Hengw. MSS.* griffon, *Cambr. MS.* grefoun]. *c* **1400** MAUNDEV. (Roxb.) xxix. 132 In þat land er many griffouns..þai hafe þe schappe of ane egle before, and behind þe schappe of a lyoun. *c* **1435** *Torr. Portugal* 1981 Frome a greffon he was refte. **1481** CAXTON *Myrr.* II. iv. 69 The gryffons wylde whiche haue bodyes of lyouns fleyng. **1567** MAPLET *Gr. Forest* 88 The Griphin is a Foule of plentifull and thicke fether, and foure footed withall. **1601**

CHESTER *Love's Mart., Dial.* clxviii, The Griffon is a bird rich-feathered, His head is like a Lion, and his flight Is like the Eagles. **1620** QUARLES *Feast for Wormes* Propos., The Horse and Gryphin shall together sleepe. **1667** MILTON *P.L.* II. 943 As when a Gryfon through the wilderness.. Pursues the Arimaspian, who by stealth Had from his wakeful custody purloind The guarded Gold. **1713** STEELE *Guardian* No. 60 ¶4 A learned controversy about the existence of griffins. **1716** LADY M. W. MONTAGU *Let. to Mrs. T. Thistlethwayte* 30 Aug., Among these relics they showed me a prodigious claw, set in gold, which they called the claw of a griffin. **1829** CARLYLE *Misc.* (1857) II. 61 A stony desert tenanted by Gryphons and Chimeras. *a* **1856** H. MILLER *Test. Rocks* iii. (1857) 142 The great dragons and griffins and 'laithly worms' of mediaeval legend. **1865** 'L. CARROLL' *Alice in Wonderland* ix. (1886) 138 They very soon came upon a Gryphon, lying fast asleep in the sun.

b. A representation or figure of a griffin, as in Heraldry, Sculpture, etc.

13.. *Coer de L.* 2963 Off red sendel were her baneres. With three gryffouns depaynted wel. ? *a* **1400** *Morte Arth.* 3870 Qwat gome was he this with the gaye armes, With þis gryffoune of golde. **1439** *E.E. Wills* (1882) 117 A Skochen of myn Armes.. and ij Greffons to bere hit vppe. **1460** *Lybeaus Disc.* 81 A scheld.. Wyth a gryffoun of say. **1552** *Inv. Bexley* in *Archæol. Cant.* VIII. 108 On cope of red with floures and griffens of gold. **1640** YORKE *Union Hon.* 119 A Griffin Sergeant Or. **1753** HOGARTH *Anal. Beauty* vi. 33 The griffin, a modern hiero-glyphic, signifying strength and swiftness. **1778** PENNANT *Tour in Wales* (1883) I. 88 The Britons.. put letters on them [coins], elephants and gryphons; things they were before unacquainted with. **1818** SCOTT *Hrt. Midl.* ix, The paw remained suspended in the air like the claw of a heraldic griffin. **1828–40** BERRY *Encycl. Her.* I, *Griffin Male*, in heraldry is represented without wings, having rays of gold issuing from various parts of the body. **1831** LANDOR *Ct. Julian* Wks. 1846 II. 514 Gryphens and Eagles, ivory and gold, Can add no clearness to the lamp above. **1863** MISS BRADDON *J. Marchmont* I. v. 82 Grim stone griffins surmount the terrace-steps. **1864** BOUTELL *Her. Hist. & Pop.* ix. 67 A gryphon is the dexter Supporter of the Duke of Cleveland.

2. A vulture; now = griffon-vulture (see 4).

1382 WYCLIF *Lev.* xi. 13 An egle, and a griffyn [Vulg. *gryphem*], and a merlyoun. —— *Deut.* xiv. 12 Egle, and griffun. **1609** BIBLE (Douay) *Lev.* xi. 13 The Eagle, and the griffon, and the osprey. **1873** TRISTRAM *Moab* vii. 131 The griffons circled and soared from their eyries. **1876** *Oxford Bible-Helps* 95 'Eagle' (Deut. xxxii. 11).. the.. griffon, great vulture. **1884–5** *Riverside Nat. Hist.* (1888) IV. 274 The griffin or fulvous vulture, *Gyps fulvus*.

3. *transf.* A grim-looking or extremely vigilant guardian. (Cf. *dragon*.)

1824 R. B. PEAKE *Amer. Abroad* I. ii, It [the larder] is always locked up by that she griffin with a bunch of keys.

4. *attrib.* and *Comb.*, as ***griffin-beaked***, ***-guarded***, ***-like***, ***-winged*** adjs.; **griffin's foot**, a surgical instrument, so called from its form; **griffon-vulture**, a vulture of the genus *Gyps*, esp. *G. fulvus*.

1875 W. MCILWRAITH *Guide Wigtownshire* 140 The *griffin-beaked galleys of the ancient Scandinavians. **1611** COTGR., *Pied de Griffon*, a *Griffons foot. **1750** *Mem. R. Acad. Surg. Paris* I. 162 The instruments hitherto used to raise the bones of the cranium depressed on the dura mater are.. the griffin's foot. **1842** TENNYSON *Audley Crt.* 14 The *griffin-guarded gates. **1641** MILTON *Reform.* I. (1851) 14 A corporalty of *griffonlike Promooters, and Apparitors. **1831** BENNETT *Gard. & Menag. Zool. Soc.* II. 97 The *Griffon Vulture. *Vultur fulvus.* **1833** SIR C. BELL *Hand* (1834) 78 If the griffon-vulture be frightened after his repast, he must disgorge, before he flies. **1884–5** *Riverside Nat. Hist.* (1888) IV. 275 The griffon-vulture, *Gyps fulvus*. **1610** HEALEY tr. *Vives on St. Aug. Citie of God* 686 Ausonius makes her [the Sphynx].. *griffin-winged.

griffin[2] (ˈɡrɪfɪn). *Anglo-Indian.* [Of uncertain origin: usually explained as a fig. use of prec., but there is no evidence for this.] A European newly arrived in India, and unaccustomed to Indian ways and peculiarities; a novice, newcomer, greenhorn.

1793 CHILD in Southey *Life Bell* (1844) I. 459 Wilks.. will .. lend you every assistance in forwarding these matters, in which.. you must, I presume, be a perfect griffin. **1794** H. BOYD *Ind. Observ.* No. 34 ¶5, I am little better than an unfledged Griffin, according to the fashionable phrase here [Madras]. **1807** J. JOHNSON *Oriental Voy.* 73 Every arrival from Europe.. as soon as he touches terra-firma is a griffin. **1816** 'QUIZ' *Grand Master* II. 30 *note*, Young men, immediately on their arrival in India, are termed griffins, and retain this honour until they are twelve months in the country. **1836** *Lett. fr. Madras* (1843) 38 Mrs. Staunton laughs at me, and calls me a 'griffin'.. (N.B. Griffin means a freshman or freshwoman in India.) **1883** LD. SALTOUN *Scraps* II. iv. 159 Utter greenhorns or griffins, as Indian phraseology has it.

griffin[3]. *U.S.* A mulatto: see GRIFF *sb.*[4]

griffin[4]. *slang.* [Origin unascertained.] A tip (in betting, etc.); a signal, hint. Cf. GRIFF *sb.*[6]

1889 *Cassell's Sat. Jrnl.* Jan. 305/3 Plank yourself at the corner to give the griffin (signal) if you hear or see owt. **1891** J. NEWMAN *Scamping Tricks* 95 When he wanted to give the chaps in the office the straight griffin, he used to say, 'Nelson's my guide.' **1912** A. N. LYONS *Clara* xxiv. 265 'This is the Straight Griffin, Fred,' said Mr. Cozenza: 'the absolute straight Tip.' **1966** F. SHAW et al. *Lern Yerself Scouse* 63 Let's give de fellers de griffin.

griffinage (ˈɡrɪfɪnɪdʒ). *Anglo-Indian.* [f. GRIFFIN[2] + -AGE.] The state of being a 'griffin'; one's first year in India.

1829 *Bengalee* 122 Subscription pack, Champagne tiffin parties, and other first claims on the griffinage of a civilian. **1840** E. E. NAPIER *Scenes & Sports For. Lands* II. vi. 197 A large detachment of recruits, who, like myself, all in their griffinage, had but lately landed at Madras. **1878** G. P. SANDERSON *Wild Beasts Ind.* xxii. 214 In the days of our griffinage.

griffinesque (ɡrɪfɪˈnɛsk). In 9 **gryphonesque**. [f. GRIFFIN[1] + -ESQUE.] Of the style of a griffin.

1849 LYTTON *Caxtons* XVIII. iii, Blanche had just one of those faces that.. might become gryphonesque, witch-like, and grim.

griffiness (ˈɡrɪfɪnɪs). [f. GRIFFIN[1] + -ESS.] A she-griffin.

1840 LYTTON *Pilgrims Rhine* xi. (1840) 142 Nothing could now appease the Griffiness, but his positive assurance that.. poor puss should be.. boiled for the Griffin's soup.

griffinhood (ˈɡrɪfɪnhʊd). *Anglo-Indian.* [f. GRIFFIN[2] + -HOOD.] = GRIFFINAGE.

1854 *Tait's Mag.* XXI. 135, I was not quite released from the swaddling bands of my griffin-hood. **1890** 'ROLF BOLDREWOOD' *Col. Reformer* (1891) 146 It is the ordinary early phase of griffinhood.

griffinish (ˈɡrɪfɪnɪʃ), *a.* [f. GRIFFIN[1] and [2] + -ISH.] **a.** Characteristic of a griffin. **b.** *Anglo-Indian.* Indicative of the 'griffin'. Hence **ˈgriffinishness**.

a **1845** HOOD *Ode to R. Wilson* xxiii, I feel None of that griffinish excess of zeal. **1850** *Benares Mag.* IV. 85 We were afraid of eliciting some remark on our griffinishness, if we gave utterance to such a reflection. **1860** *Biog. & Crit. fr. Times* 394 My griffinish wonder at the want of white faces.

griffinism (ˈɡrɪfɪnɪz(ə)m). [f. GRIFFIN[1] + -ISM.] Griffinish nature or characteristics.

1856 RUSKIN *Mod. Paint.* III. IV. viii. §20 The honest imagination gains everything; it has griffinism, and grace, and usefulness, all at once.

griffinship (ˈɡrɪfɪnʃɪp). *Anglo-Indian.* [f. GRIFFIN[2] + -SHIP.] The position of being a griffin; the time during which one is a griffin.

1816 'QUIZ' *Grand Master* IV. 76 The griffinship expired, he's sent, On duty from his regiment.

griffish (ˈɡrɪfɪʃ), *a. Anglo-Indian.* [f. GRIFF *sb.*[2] + -ISH.] Like a 'griff', inexperienced, 'green'.

1836 *Lett. fr. Madras* (1843) 53 (Y.) He was living with bad men, and saw that they thought him no better than themselves, but only more griffish.

griffo: see GRIFF *sb.*[4]

†**Griffon[1]**. *Obs. rare.* In 4 gri-, gryffo(u)n. [a. OF. *griffon, grifon*, app. connected with *griu* GREW.] A Greek.

13.. *K. Alis.* 3134 He sat, and pleyghed at the chesse, With o Griffoun of hethenesse. **13..** *Coer de L.* 1761 The French and Gryffons down rightes, Slew there our English knights. *c* **1350** *Will. Palerne* 1961 þe gryffouns þan gayli gonne stint atte cherche þe briȝt burde meliors to abide þere. [**1677** F. SANDFORD *General Hist. Eng.* 78 He offers up the rich Standard of Cursar King of Ciprus which he took among the spoils of the Griffons Camp. **1837** SIR F. PALGRAVE *Merch. & Friar* i. (1844) 24 Greeks.. who are called Griffons wherever Romance is spoken.]

griffon[2] (ˈɡrɪfən). [a. F. *griffon* 'chien anglais', by Littré identified with *griffon* GRIFFIN[1].] A species of coarse-haired dog, resembling a terrier. **Brussels griffon** (also **griffon Belge**, **Bruxelles** or **Bruxellois**), a small griffon of European origin, with a short nose, flat face, prominent eyes and reddish-brown hair.

1882 *Blackw. Mag.* Aug. 292 Austrian boarhounds and French griffons. **1897** *Times* 12 Apr. 12/1 Griffons cannot be fitted with a head-cage. **1898** *Daily News* 10 Feb. 6/6 Animals of foreign nationality such as Chows, Griffons, and merry little Schipperkes. **1898** *Dog Owners' Ann.* 63 (*heading*) Dog clubs... Griffon Bruxellois Club. **1900** C. H. LANE *All about Dogs* xiv. 269 *Griffons Bruxelles*, one of the most recent of all the breeds suitable as pets and companions and which has been very much 'boomed' the last few years. **1904** H. COMPTON *20th Cent. Dog* I. 119 In the Griffon Bruxellois you have the Captain Kettle of dogdom. *Ibid.* 120 The latest recruit.. is the Brussels griffon. **1922** [see AFFENPINSCHER]. **1945** C. L. B. HUBBARD *Observer's Bk. Dogs* 209 *Griffon Belge*, a variety of Griffon Bruxellois. **1948** —— *Dogs in Brit.* 293 Also known as the Brussels Griffon, the breed [*sc.* Griffon Bruxellois] is one of the smallest of terriers. **1963** B. VESEY-FITZGERALD *About Dogs* iv. 29 I believe that one can point to the ancestor of all the northern rough-haired Terriers: and that that is the Griffon Bruxellois.

griffon: see GRIFF *sb.*[4], GRIFFIN[1].

‖**griffonage** (grifɔnaʒ). [a. F. *griffonage*, f. *griffonner* to write badly, scrawl.] Scribble.

1832 MRS. F. TROLLOPE *Dom. Manners Amer.* xxxiv. (1839) 335 We hastened to pack up our 'trumpery'.. and among the rest, my six hundred pages of griffonage. **1834** MAR. EDGEWORTH *Helen* II. vii. 148 There was a heap of little crumpled bills which, with Felicie's griffonage, Helen had thrown into her table-drawer.

griffoun(e, obs. f. GRIFFIN[1]; var. GRIFFON[1].

†**grifhound**. *Obs.* Also gref-. [app. a var. of *grewhound*; cf. the current pronunciation of *lieutenant* (lɪfˈtɛnənt).] A greyhound.

13.. *K. Alis.* 5284 In a cheyne of golde tweie grifhoundes. **1422** tr. *Secreta Secret., Priv. Priv.* (E.E.T.S.) 174 Scipion hym chased as a grefhound dothe the Fox.

grift, *sb.*[1] *dial.* [? a. Du. *grift*; cf. GRIFF *sb.*[1]] (See quot. 1889.)

1851 *Jrnl. R. Agric. Soc.* XII. II. 313 The waters.. form the main drains for the low lands under the names of 'cloughs', 'eaus', 'fleets', and 'grifts'. **1889** *N.W. Linc. Gloss.*, *Grift*, a channel shaped out by water for itself; a runnel.

grift (grɪft), *sb.*[2] *U.S. slang.* [Perh. corruption of GRAFT *sb.*[5]] = GRAFT *sb.*[5]

1914 JACKSON & HELLYER *Vocab. Crim. Slang* 39 *Grift*,.. graft. **1929** D. HAMMETT *Dain Curse* (1930) iii. 21 'How's the literary grift go?' I asked. He looked at me sharply. **1931** W. FAULKNER *Sanctuary* xvi. 112 ' If you'll just promise to get the kid a good newspaper grift when he's big enough to make change,' he said. **1940** R. CHANDLER *Farewell My Lovely* xxxiii. 157 Hell, I thought he sold reefers. With the right protection behind him. But hell, that's a small-time racket. A peanut grift. **1961** J. F. JOHNSON *Man who sold Eiffel Tower* (1962) iv. 52 A good confidence man.. has to have what is known as 'grift sense'.

grift (grɪft), *v. U.S. slang.* [f. GRIFT *sb.*[2]] = GRAFT *v.*[4] So **ˈgrifting** *vbl. sb.* and *ppl. a.*

1915 G. BRONSON-HOWARD *God's Man* IV. iv. 263 Grifting ain't what it used to be. Fourteenth Street's got protection down to a system—a regular underworld tariff on larceny. **1926** *Flynn's* 31 Jan., *Grift*, to steal; to graft. **1940** *Amer. Speech* XV. 110/2 *Grift*, to work any profession included in the grift. **1955** *Publ. Amer. Dial. Soc.* XXIV. 144 Tim Bairdon used to grift with a buzzer on his vest. **1956** H. GOLD *Man who was not with It* (1965) ii. 10 Grifting troubadours, bonnie princes of con with ten-gallon hats. *Ibid.* 16 How long you been grifting?

grift(e, obs. form of GRAFT *sb.*[1] and *v.*[1]

grifter (ˈɡrɪftə(r)). *U.S. slang.* [f. GRIFT *sb.*[2] + -ER[1].] = GRAFTER[3].

1915 G. BRONSON-HOWARD *God's Man* III. iii. 213 Every time I pick up one of these here magazines.. I jest naturally seem to encounter a lot of junk... whenever I read about grifters or guns—always this 'master cracks-man' stuff,.. but when it comes to blasting an ordinary box I could kick my way into in my stocking feet, I read.. 'The burglar leaped lightly over the garden wall.' **1927** K. NICHOLSON *Barker* 149 *Grifter*, grafter. **1930** J. LAIT *Big House* i. 7 A card or dice cheater is a 'grifter'. **1955** *Publ. Amer. Dial. Soc.* XXIV. 98 A *grifter* denotes a pickpocket or *sneak thief*. The term.. has.. in recent years so generalized that it now includes all sorts of non-violent criminals. **1965** R. O'CONNOR *Jack London* I. i. 18 He lived off the horoscope trade until the World Fair of 1893 suggested a move to Chicago, as it did to thousands of other.. grifters.

grig (grɪg), *sb.*[1] Also 5 grege, 7 greg, grigg(e. [Of obscure origin. The identity of the word in the various senses is very doubtful, but Johnson's conjecture that it originally meant 'anything below the natural size' would plausibly account for all the uses. (Cf. GRIGGLES.)

Cf. also Sw. dial. *krik* (literary Sw. *kräk*) little animal, small child; Sc. *crick, crike*, ? a louse (Jam.); also CRICK *sb.*[4]]

†**1.** A diminutive person, a dwarf. [Perh. *transf.* from sense 3 (or 4, if the latter be genuine).] *Obs. rare.*

a **1400–50** *Alexander* 1753 Slike a dwinyng, a dwaȝe, & a dwerȝe as þi-selfe, A grub, a grege out of grace [*Dubl.* A grob, a grig out of grece]. **1629** MAXWELL tr. *Herodian* 209 Having.. scoft him, for that being such a low Grigge [Gr. μικρὸς ὢν, L. *tantulæ homo staturæ*], he would presume to personate such High and Mighty Heroes as Alexander and Achilles.

2. A short-legged hen. Also **grig-hen**. *Obs.* exc. *dial.*

1589 RIDER *Eng.-Lat. Dict.*, A Grigge or shorte legged henne, *gallinella, gallinula*. **1601** HOLLAND *Pliny* I. 300 A dwarfish kind of hens, (i. grig hens) that are extraordinarie little. **1721–1800** in BAILEY. **1847–78** in HALLIWELL. **1866** *Derbysh. Gloss.* in *Reliquary* VI. 160 *Grig*, a Bantam fowl.

3. A species of eel; a small or young eel (see quots.). Also more fully ***grig-eel***.

1611 COTGR., *Anguillette*, a Grig, or little Eele. **1629** GAULE *Holy Madn.* 130 Silly Grigge! Come out of thy Pond and Mud. **1653** WALTON *Angler* x. 192 The silver-Eele, and green or greenish Eel (with which the River of Thames abounds, and are called Gregs). **1688** R. HOLME *Armoury* II. 325/1 An eel first a Fausen, then a Grigg, or Snigg. **1726** *Dict. Rust.* (ed. 3) s.v. *Elver*, A sort of Griggs, or small Eels, which.. swim on top of the Water about Bristol. **1758** *Descr. Thames* 193 The Greenish, or Greg-Eel. **1769** PENNANT *Zool.* III. 114 There is another variety of this fish [the eel] known in the Thames by the name of Grigs, and about Oxford by that of Grigs or Gluts. **1883** G. C. DAVIES *Norfolk Broads* xxxi. (1884) 234 The grig is a yellowish eel, with a projecting underjaw.

b. *attrib.* in ***grig-weel*** (†also shortened *grig*), a basket-work trap for catching grigs.

1798 *Trans. Soc. Arts* XVI. 135 Used by the fishermen to make grigs, or twig tunnels, to catch eels and other fish. **1883** *Fisheries Exhib. Catal.* 57 Grig Weel. Lamprey Weel... Improved Eel Pot.

4. A grasshopper or cricket. *dial.*

The genuineness of this sense is doubtful, as the dialect glossaries containing it usually quote as their sole example the phrase 'merry as a grig' (see 5).

1847 HALLIWELL, *Grig*.. a cricket. *Var. dial.* **1855** TENNYSON *Brook* 54 The dry High-elbow'd grigs that leap in summer grass. **1869** *Lonsdale Gloss.*, *Grig*.. a cricket.

5. ***a merry*** (or †***mad***) ***grig*** (rarely without adj.): an extravagantly lively person, one who is full of frolic and jest. Also in phrase ***as merry*** (or ***lively***) ***as a grig***.

[Commonly associated with sense 4; but it is possible that sense 4 is itself merely an erroneous inference from the equivalence of the above phrases with 'a merry crick', 'merry as a cricket'; if so, the allusion in 'a merry grig' may originally have been to sense 3 or even to sense 2. The relation of *merry grig* to the earlier recorded synonym *merry Greek* is obscure; no doubt one of them must have been a perversion of the other, but the difference of recorded date is too slight to afford ground for saying that *merry Greek* is the original. The probability seems indeed rather on the other side, as it is not easy to explain why *Greek* should be used in this sense, for which there is no precedent in Fr. Cf. also GIG.]

1566 DRANT *Horace's Sat.* I. iii. B v b, A merry grigge, a iocande frende. **1589** *Hay any Work* 4 A company of merrie grigs you must think them to be. **1638** BROME *Antipodes* I. v. Wks. 1873 III. 245 Whilst I And my mad Grigs, my men can run at base. *a* **1652** —— *Eng. Moor* III. iii. ibid. II. 50 Ile to my Griggs Again; And there will find new mirth to stretch And laugh. **1728** VANBR. & CIB. *Prov. Husb.* I. ii, A very pretty, civil young woman truly, and the maids are the merriest grigs. *Ibid.* v. i, *Man.* I thought you had all supt at home last Night? *Sir Fran.* Why so we did—and all as merry as Grigs. **1758–65** GOLDSM. *Ess.* vi. Wks. (Globe) 304/1, I grew as merry as a grig, and laughed at every word that was spoken. **1810** *Splendid Follies* I. 176 She capered mighty consequentially, and yet she has no bold appearance; but that nation [the French] are such a set of grigs, I don't wonder at it. **1840** DICKENS *Old C. Shop* l, I shall be as merry as a grig among these gentry. **1847** ALB. SMITH *Chr. Tadpole* xviii. (1879) 161 Her aunt.. has turned as lively as a grig. **1863** MRS. C. CLARKE *Shaks. Char.* viii. 200 To such a man, this grig of a girl, ever on the alert for roguery,.. is an absolute abomination. **1868** GEO. ELIOT in Cross *Life* (1885) III. 65 When I was a young grig—not very full of hope about my woman's future.

†**b.** App. the designation of the members of some convivial society. (Perh. a different word.) *Obs.*

1810 CRABBE *Borough* Let. x. 349 Griggs and Gregorians here their meetings hold.

6. *slang.* A farthing; *pl.* money, cash, 'dibs'.

1656–7 *Burton's Diary* (1828) I. 335 The poor man.. sent to one Mr. Best.. to pay her 40*l.* to accommodate her for her journey home; but she having received the griggs set sail another way. *a* **1700** B. E. *Dict. Cant. Crew* s.v., Not a Grig did he tip me, not a Farthing wou'd he give me. **1747** W. HORSLEY *Fool* (1748) II. 129 When speaking of a Man without any Money in his Pocket, we say that he is not worth a Grig; that is, he has not wherewith to make himself merry. **1785** in GROSE *Dict. Vulg. Tongue.* **1839** H. AINSWORTH *Jack Sheppard* iii, He shall go through the whole course.. unless he comes down to the last grig.

grig (grɪg), *sb.*[2] *dial.* [a. W. *grug*, Cornish *grig* = Ir., Gael. *fraoch*:—OCeltic **vroiko-s.*] The common heath or heather, *Calluna vulgaris*; also, cross-leaved heath, *Erica Tetralix*.

1674–91 RAY *Collect. Words* 126 Grig; Salopiensibus Heath. **1692** *Act 4 Will. & Mary* c. 23 §9 Any Grig, Ling, Heath [etc.]. **1791** *Trans. Soc. Arts* IX. 78 With strong heath, grig, or ling, growing thereon. **1829** *Evans & Ruffy's Farmers Jrnl.* 14 Sept. 291 Digging stone, cutting grig, fern, and rushes. **1829** GLOVER *Hist. Derby* I. 113 *Erica vulgaris*, long grig or common heath. **1878** BRITTEN & HOLLAND *Plant-n.*, Grig, (2) *Erica Tetralix.*

grig (grɪg), *v.*[1] Now *Anglo-Irish* and *U.S.* Also 6 grigge. *trans.* To irritate, annoy.

1553 T. WILSON *Rhet.* 98 When we jest closely, and, with dissemblyng meanes, grigge our felowe. **1837** HALIBURTON *Clockm.* Ser. I. viii, That remark seemed to grig him a little. **1845** S. C. HALL *Whiteboy* xii. 108 The counsellor grigging me. **1855** HALIBURTON *Nat. & Hum. Nat.* I. vi. 173 That word superiors grigged me.

grig (grɪg), *v.*[2] Also 8 greg. [f. GRIG *sb.*[1] 3.] *intr.* To fish for grig. Hence '**grigging** *vbl. sb.*

1764 *Low Life* (ed. 3) 68 Getting ready their Carting Nets to go a Gregging. **1820–2** PYNE *Wine & Walnuts* (1824) II. vi. 53 The wharf.. was much frequented.. by parties who were fond of the eel-net, or grigging.

griggish ('grɪgɪʃ), *a.* [f. GRIG *sb.*[1] 5 + -ISH.] Merry.

1879 G. M. HOPKINS *Let.* 12 Feb. (1956) 153 The more griggish the piece [of music] the more we clapped it. **1882** —— *Let.* 20 Dec. (1955) 167, I seem to be in a griggish mood; it must be because holidays have begun.

griggles ('grɪg(ə)lz), *sb. pl.* [cf. GRIG *sb.*[1]] Small apples left on the tree by the gatherer. Hence '**griggling** *vbl. sb.*, collecting 'griggles'.

1826 in Hone *Every-day Bk.* II. 1270 The small apples are called *griggles*... Climbing boys.. commence griggling. *Ibid.* 1271 Their *griggling* perambulations. **1847** HALLIWELL, *Griggles*, small apples. In some cyder counties, boys who collect these after the principal ones are gathered, call it *griggling*. **1893** in *Wilts. Gloss.*

griggory, grigri: see GREEGREE.

†'**griggy**, *a. Obs.*[−1] [Origin and sense doubtful; ? f. GRIG *sb.*[2] (though this is recorded much later) + -Y.] ? Heathy, wild.

1597 *Pilgr. Parnass.* v. 577 But what doe youe twoo here, in this griggie barbarous cuntrie?

gright(e, obs. pa. t. of GRUTCH; obs. f. GRITH.

griging, griking, obs. forms of GREKING.

Grignard ('griːnjɑː(r)). *Chem.* The name of F. A. V. *Grignard* (1871–1935), French chemist, used *attrib.* and in the possessive to designate organometallic compounds of magnesium represented by the formula RMgX (where R is an organic radical and X a halogen), and the organic syntheses performed using such compounds; so ***Grignard('s) compound, reagent; Grignard('s) reaction.***

[**1902** *Jrnl. Chem. Soc.* LXXXII. I. 70 The following compounds have been obtained by Grignard's methods.] **1904** *Ibid.* LXXXV. 1666 (*heading*) The Grignard reaction applied to the esters of hydroxy-acids. *Ibid.* LXXXVI. I. 38 (*heading*) Nitric oxide and Grignard's reagent. **1936** *Discovery* May 162/2 Active organic substances (like organo-metallic compounds and the Grignard reagents) which are used as reagents, and the function of anionoid and kationoid reagents in ionic reactions are treated. **1964** N. G. CLARK *Mod. Org. Chem.* v. 69 When dissolved in dry ether, and treated with dry magnesium metal, alkyl halides combine to give alkylmagnesium halides or 'Grignard compounds'. **1966** PHILLIPS & WILLIAMS *Inorg. Chem.* II. xxvii. 331 Grignard reagents are also of quite general applicability in substitution reactions of metal halides.

Grignolino (griɲo'lino). Also **Grignoli.** [It.]

a. The name of an Italian wine grape grown in Piedmont. **b.** The red wine made from this grape.

1894 J. L. W. THUDICHUM *Treatise on Wines* xxv. 333 A number of red wines are made from the Grignoli grape, and named Grignolinos. **1935** SCHOONMAKER & MARVEL *Compl. Wine Bk.* v. 115 The vast bulk of Italian wine is still.. insufficiently standardized (out of a hundred bottles of Grignolino,.. two dozen may very well be unintentionally sparkling and the others still). **1958** A. L. SIMON *Dict. Wines* 86 *Grignolino*, a red wine of no great distinction but none the less greatly prized locally; it is made in various parts of Piedmont from Grignolino grapes. **1966** H. JOHNSON *Wine* 208 There is some better and higher-strength wine made of the Grignolino, but it is hard to find. **1970** *Guardian* 6 Mar. 9/5 Half a bottle of Grignolino, a *pétillant* red wine from Piedmont.

gri-gri, var. GREEGREE, GROO-GROO.

‖**grihastha** (griː'hæsθə). Also **gr̥(h)astha, grihast.** [Skr. *gr̥hastha*, married Brahman householder.] A Brahman in the second stage of life, which carries with it certain social obligations, as the duty to marry and have children.

1871 E. BALFOUR *Cycl. India* (ed. 2) II. 409 *Grihastha*, a hindu married householder. **1876** *Encycl. Brit.* IV. 204/2 The pious Brāhman.. was enjoined to pass through a succession of four orders or stages of life... [The second is] *grihastha*.. or householder. **1894** *19th Cent.* Aug. 281 One [story] that gained some credence with the grihasts was, that three natives.. saw headless beings. **1949** R. B. PANDEY *Hindu Saṁskāras* viii. 264 One who longs for imperishable heaven and happiness in this world, should uphold the Gr̥astha-Āśrama. **1964** *Religious Hinduism* x. 117 Fidelity to the ritual and social duties of the caste are the qualities of the *gr̥hastha*. **1969** *Indian Mus. Jrnl.* V. 79 [Music and dance] were the essential equipment of the training of a monk, a prince, a gr̥ihastha.

grike (graɪk). Also **gryke.** [north. dial.: see *Eng. Dial. Dict.*] A crack or slit in rock, a ravine in a hill-side; *spec.* in *Geol.*, a fissure between clints (CLINT *sb.* 1 b).

1781–1885 in *Eng. Dial. Dict.* **1902** LD. AVEBURY *Scenery of Eng.* 437 Bare surface of Carboniferous Lime-stone, near Shap, showing 'grikes' or widened joints. **1919** *Glasgow Herald* 26 Dec. 8 Rock which lay about the 'grike' in the crag face. **1925** [see CLINT *sb.* 1]. **1928** A. E. TRUEMAN *Scenery England & Wales* xi. 160 Wide, level stretches of bare light-coloured limestone, with the joint planes enlarged by the solvent action of rain so that wide, irregular chasms (known as clints or grikes) trench the surface. **1952, 1963** [see CLINT *sb.* 1].

grikisc, obs. form of GREEKISH.

†**grill**, *sb.*[1] *Obs.* Forms: 4–5 grille, gryll(e. [Related to GRILL *a.* and *v.*[1] Cf. MLG. *grille* hatred, anger.] **a.** Ill-will, vexation; harm, mischief. **b.** ? Fierceness, violence.

a. 13.. *Cristenemon & Jew* 297 in Horstm. *Altengl. Leg.* (1878) 207 Mete and drynke þei hedde at wille Wiþouten grucchyng or grille In trouþe tente þei þer tille And lafte al þat oþer. *c* **1400** *Melayne* 224 The Sowdane grauntis wele þer-till, þat tornede oure gudmen all to grill. *c* **1450** *Erle Tolous* 279 Lady he ys to us a foo,.. He hath done us grete grylle. *c* **1485** *E.E. Misc.* (Warton Club) 64 For thi tale thou mayst bere the blame away Of every syde with gram, and grille.

b. *c* **1450** *Guy Warw.* (C.) 11488 Ther come neuer man in þys hylle Thorow qweyntys nor þorow grylle, But yf the lorde hym hedur broght.

†**grill**, *sb.*[2] *Obs. rare.* [After Spenser's *Gryll*, which is ad. Gr. γρύλλος a pig.] A quasi-proper name for a person of low tastes or lazy habits.

[**1590** SPENSER *F.Q.* II. xii. 86 One.. That had an hog beene late, hight Grylle by name, Repyned greatly, and did him miscall That had from hoggish forme him brought to naturall. *Ibid.* 87 Let Gryll be Gryll, and have his hoggish minde.] **1597** *Pilgr. Parnass.* I. 83 Let lazie grill snorte till the midst of the day. **1597** BP. HALL *Sat.* II. ii. D i b, Let swinish Grill delight in dunghill clay. **1644** QUARLES *Whipper Whipt* Wks. (Grosart) I. 177/2 Grains are fitter for Grill, then Pearles.

grill (grɪl), *sb.*[3] [f. GRILL *v.*[2]]

1. Meat, fish, etc., broiled on a gridiron; a grilled dish. Also *fig.*

1766 ANSTEY *Bath Guide* (1767) 81 These are your true poetic fires That drest this sav'ry grill. **1844** J. T. HEWLETT *Parsons & W.* xxiv, He.. enjoyed himself over a grill and other relishes. **1849** ALB. SMITH *Pottleton Leg.* vii. 41 West, get breakfast ready: cutlets and grill; and [etc.].

2. Short for *grill-room.*

1896 *Westm. Gaz.* 2 Oct. 7/2 The big hall, where most people will dine.. below this there is a grill.

3. A turn or spell of grilling. In quot. *fig.*

1842 BARHAM *Ingol. Leg.* Ser. II. *Old Woman in Grey*, So that after a grill [in Purgatory].. She'd have rubb'd off old scores.

4. *attrib.*, as *grill-cook, -stove*; **grill-room**, a room in a restaurant in which chops, steaks, etc., are grilled; also more generally, an informal restaurant.

1883 'ANNIE THOMAS' *Mod. Housewife* 126, I learnt to treat kidneys.. and beefsteaks better than I have ever known them treated out of a public grill-room. **1884** *Health Exhib. Catal.* 66/1 Smokeless Grill Stove. **1892** *Encycl. Cookery* (ed. Garrett) I. 721 All good grill cooks employ tongs. **1910** *Bradshaw's Railway Guide* Apr. 1027 Midland Hotel, Bradford.. popular grill room and restaurant. **1931** J. BETJEMAN *Mount Zion* 19, I *wish* you'd seen the rag we had In the Grill Room at the Cri. **1957** *Encycl. Brit.* XIX. 229/2 Modern grill rooms are an even later offshoot of the hotels and restaurants... The grill room made no demand for dress.

grill (grɪl), *sb.*[4] [a. F. *gril* gridiron (OF. *gril(l, grail, greil*, gridiron, grating), masc. corresponding to *grille* fem. GRILLE, perh.:—pop. L. **graticulum* neut.] **1. a.** A gridiron.

1685 COTTON tr. *Montaigne* I. xxx. (1711) I. 291 They.. cleave it [hard wood] into Swords, and make Grills of it to broil their Meat. **1892** *Encycl. Cookery* (ed. Garrett) I. 720 The grill may be placed either over or before the fire.

b. In modern use: a gas burner (on a gas cooker), or a hot plate or a set of elements (on an electric cooker), which directs radiant heat downwards. Also *attrib.*

1907 *Yesterday's Shopping* (1969) 218/2 Gas stoves... The Talbot, hot plate and grill, fitted with 1 Reversible Grill Burner. **1908** *Installation News* II. 49/2 Three terminals are fitted on the grill, so that by suitable arrangement of these connections, half, three quarters, or the whole of the coils fitted are placed in circuit, and the degree of heat can thus be regulated. **1923** *Harmsworth's Househ. Encycl.* II. 1034/1 Extending under the whole surface of the grill, and resting on the upper surface of the oven, is a white enamelled tray. **1928** *Daily Mail Cookery Bk.* 113 In making toast under the grill, be careful to see that the grill-pan with gridiron is underneath. **1951** *Good Housek. Home Encycl.* 75/2 A solid rectangular plate called the grill boiler. **1961** *Which?* Oct. 248/1 A recent trend in cooker design has been to move the grills to eye level.

2. *to put on the grill*: to subject (a prisoner) to 'third degree' treatment. *U.S.* (Cf. GRILL *v.*[2])

1928 *Daily Express* 25 May 10/5 Mr. John Brown.. is arrested on a murder charge. He does not sound frank, so he is 'put on the grill'.

grill, *sb.*[5]: see GRILLE *sb.*

†**grill**, *a.* (*adv.*) *Obs.* Forms: 3–6 grill(e, 3–6 gril, 4 gryl, 4–5 grylle, 5 gryle, 6 gryll. [First in early ME.; cf. Du. *gril* (*grel*) fierce, angry, rough (of persons, weather, etc.), shrill (of sound), glaring (of colour), LG. *grel, grell* (in the same senses), MHG. *grel*, rough, angry, G. *grell* (of sounds and colours); also ON. *grellskapr*, spite. It is not certain, however, that the Eng. word corresponds in ablaut-grade with these, as it might equally well represent an OE. **grylle*; cf. GRILL *v.*[1]]

1. Of persons: Fierce, harsh, cruel.

c **1200** ORMIN 9881 Hæþenn follkess herrte Iss harrd.. & grimme, & grill. *Ibid.* 19859 Ȝho warrþ sone gramm & grill Ȝæn Sannt Johan Bapptisste. *a* **1300** *Cursor M.* 719 A-ganis godd wex he sa gril þat al his werk he wend to spil. *c* **1330** R. BRUNNE *Chron.* (1810) 92 Whan William had his wille of Scotland & of Wales, To riche men was he grille. *c* **1450** *Cov. Myst.* (Shaks. Soc.) 230 The Jewys ageyn the were grym & grylle. **1460** *Lybeaus Disc.* 1875 Swerdes they through out tho, Wyth herte grym and grylle. *a* **1529** SKELTON *E. Rummyng* 6 Tell you I chyll.. of a comely gryll, That dwelt on a hyll, But she is not gryll, For she is somewhat sage And well worne in age.

2. Of things, actions, language, etc.: Cruel, painful, bitter, severe, terrible, dreadful.

a **1300** *Cursor M.* 17228 Iesu.. Forget i oft þine greues grill. *Ibid.* 22690 þe dai fourtend sal be ful il, Til al þe werld it sal be gril. *a* **1310** in Wright *Lyric P.* xxxi. 91 Shalt thou never for mi love woundes thole grylle. *c* **1330** *Amis & Amil.* 1275 Tho wordes.. That were so gret and grille. ? *a* **1366** CHAUCER *Rom. Rose* 73 Whyl they han suffred cold so strong In wedres grille. *a* **1400** in *Pol. Rel. & L. Poems* 226 þis sper þat is so gril. *c* **1420** *Anturs of Arth.* 620 (Douce MS.) Ho gretes one Gaynour, with gronyng grille. **1570** LEVINS *Manip.* 123/47 Chil, cold, *algidus*. Gril, *idem.*

3. *adv.* Bitterly, cruelly.

c **1400** *St. Alexius* (Laud) 564 þai grete & groned grille. *c* **1460** *Towneley Myst.* xv. 99 Full gryle may I grete, My fomen and I mete.

†**grill**, *v.*[1] *Obs.* Forms: 1 gri(e)llan, 2–4 grulle(n, 4–5 grill(e, 5 gryll(e. [The ME. forms indicate an OE. **gryllan* (for which *grillan, griellan* may be incorrect spellings) perh. = MHG. *grüllen*, *grullen* to mock, scorn, and related to MHG. *grolle* (G. *groll*, Du. *grol*, LG. *grul*), hatred, illwill, G. and Du. *grollen* to be angry, to feel spite. Cf. however MHG. *grellen*, MDu. *grillen* to be angry, and, with senses 3 and 4, Du. *grillen* to shiver with cold, to shudder. The

relationship between the forms and senses of these words is not clear.]

1. *trans.* To provoke, annoy, irritate, offend.

c **897** K. ÆLFRED *Gregory's Past.* xl. 292 Ðeah hie nan mon mid laðe ne grett hie willað grillan [*Hatton MS.* griellan] oðre men. *a* **1200** *Body & Soul* in *Fragm. Ælfr. Gram.* (Phillips) 6 þeo teone..þe he heom sore [*printed* sorc] grulde. *c* **1250** *Hymn to God* 30 in *Trin. Coll. Hom.* 259 Fader for ȝif vs ure gult, & eke alle ure sunne Al swo we doð þe us habbeð igrulde. **13..** *Childh. Jesu* 1098 in Horstm. *Altengl. Leg.* (1875) 38 ȝif ich were in þat wille þat ich seide ouȝt him for to grulle, He wolde cuyþe on me is miȝht. *c* **1420** *Anturs of Arth.* 422 (Douce MS.) Þou has wonene hem in werre, with a wrange wille, And geuen hem to sir Gawayne, þat my hert grylles. ? *a* **1500** *Chester Pl.* iii. 46 Thy bydding, lord, I shall fulfill, And never more the greeve ne grill.

2. ? To cause to sound, to play, twang.

a **1250** *Owl & Night.* 142 He song so lude and so scharpe, Riȝt so me grulde schille harpe.

3. *impers.* **me grulleð** = I am afraid, I shudder.

a **1225** *Ancr. R.* 366 'Sore', cweð he, ure Louerd, 'me grulleð aȝean mine pine.'

4. *intr.* To be fearful, to tremble with fear, to shudder.

c **1420** *Anturs of Arth.* 632 (Douce MS.) The grones of sir Gawayne dos my hert grille. *c* **1450** *Erle Tolous* 165 Game ne gle lyked hym noght, So gretly can he grylle. *c* **1450** MYRC 780 Lete also þe belles knylle To make her hortes the mor grylle. ? *a* **1500** *Chester Pl.* iv. 340 Your stroke, father, wold I [Isaac] not seene, lest I against yt grill.

Hence †**'grilling** *vbl. sb.*, shivering, shuddering.

1398 TREVISA *Barth. De P.R.* VII. xxxvii. (1495), The seconde [sygne] tofore suche a [roted] feuer comyth gryllynge & colde. *Ibid.* xl, It [feuer Qartane] greuyth from the fourthe daye to the fourth daye wyth gryllynge & rysynge of heere into the pores fyrste.

grill (grɪl), *v.*[2] Also 7 gril. [a. F. *griller*, f. *gril* (*grille*) GRILL *sb.*[4]]

1. a. *trans.* To broil on a gridiron or similar apparatus over or before a fire.

1668 [see GRILLED below]. **1672** MARVELL *Reh. Transp.* Wks. 1776 II. 448 The..boyling of men in caldrons, grilling them on grid-irons, [etc.] were but a small part of the felicities of Julian's Empire. **1677** MIEGE *Dict. Angl.-Fr.*, To gril or broil on a gridiron, *griller.* **1708** *Yorksh. Racers* 9 The pale side boil'd, the other grill'd with bread. **1826** MARGRAVINE OF ANSPACH *Mem.* II. x. 283 He had obtained greater reputation at Court for grilling a beefsteak à l'Anglaise than the most artful minister ever obtained by his negotiations. **1858** LYTTON *What will he do?* IV. vii, The old woman..made his tea, grilled his chop, and..shared his meals. **1873** E. SMITH *Foods* 77 Sheep's head is boiled or grilled.

b. To scallop (oysters or shrimps).

1727–41 CHAMBERS *Cycl.* s.v. *Grillade*, To grill oysters is to put them into scallop-shells, season them[etc.]..stewing them half an hour on the fire, and browning them with a red-hot iron. Shrimps are grilled after the same manner. **1730–6** BAILEY (folio), To Grill Oisters, the same as scolloping them. **1747** MRS. GLASSE *Cookery* ix. 99 To Grill Shrimps.

c. *transf.* To torment with heat, to 'broil'.

1825 SCOTT *Fam. Lett.* 18 July, I can go round its [Dublin's] walls and number its palaces until I am grilled almost into a fever. **1844** E. FITZGERALD *Lett.* (1899) I. 134 Oh, Barton man! but I am grilled here. **1849** E. B. EASTWICK *Dry Leaves* 36, I landed at Sakkar, where destiny had resolved on grilling me till the 10th of November.

d. To subject to severe questioning.

1894 G. MEREDITH *Let.* 30 Nov. (1970) III. 1178 Henry Parkman promised she would refresh me with an account of her last visit to you. Not a sign of her since. She comes to-day and she shall be grilled. **1928** A. G. HAYS *Let Freedom Ring* 289 The three men were grilled about their movements on the day of the..attempted hold-up. **1932** E. WALLACE *When Gangs came to London* ii. 25 Some day I'll be grilling you, big boy, up at police headquarters. **1938** G. HEYER *Blunt Instrument* vii. 139 Why on earth did your Superintendent go and grill the poor girl? **1970** *Radio Times* 8 Oct. 11/1 Listeners will be able to 'grill' leading public figures over the air when *It's Your Line*, a new-style 'live' current affairs programme begins.

2. *intr.* To undergo broiling, to frizzle. Chiefly *fig.*

1842 BARHAM *Ingol. Leg.* Ser. II. *Smuggler's Leap*, I'd rather grill Than not come up with smuggler Bill. **1849** CURZON *Visits Monast.* 2 Malta..was cool in comparison to the fiery furnace in which we were at present grilling. **1883** J. HAWTHORNE *Dust* I. 277 The spleen which was doubtless grilling within him. **1878** STEVENSON *Inland Voy.* 57 The landlady..set some beef-steak to grill. **1886** —— *Treas. Isl.* v. xxii. 177 Walking in the cool shadow of the woods,..while I sat grilling.

Hence **grilled** *ppl. a.*, **'grilling** *vbl. sb.* and *ppl. a.* **grill room** [pun on sense of *grill-room* s.v. GRILL *sb.*[3] 4], a room in a police station where suspects are questioned.

1668 PEPYS *Diary* 26 Sept., I had two grilled pigeons. **1796** H. HUNTER tr. *St.-Pierre's Stud. Nat.* (1799) III. 750 Potatoes roasted on the embers, grilled bananas [etc.]. **1839** THACKERAY *Major Gahagan* i. (1887) 10 We landed..on a grilling hot day. *Ibid.* ii. 25 The drumstick of a grilled chicken. **1843** LEVER *J. Hinton* xxvii. (1878) 196 The grilled bone that browned upon the fire. **1849** E. B. EASTWICK *Dry Leaves* 140 Phúlaji and other grilling stations near the desert. **1915** KIPLING in *Nash's & Pall Mall Mag.* Oct. 137/1 'They had a court-martial on me.'.. 'We *did* give you rather a grilling.' **1930** 'E. QUEEN' *French Powder Mystery* xii. 86 Welles is on his way here—now we'll have arrests, interviews, grillings, reporters. **1931** O. K. FRAENKEL *Sacco-Vanzetti Case* 16 The defendants had upon arrest been subjected to heavy grilling regarding their radical beliefs. **1950** G. GREENE *Third Man* xv. 129 You were brought here for a grilling almost as soon as you got back into the Inner City. **1958** M. PROCTER *Man in Ambush* iii. 21 The 'grill room' was a place to make a suspect yearn desperately to see God's sunshine. **1967** —— *Rogue Running* x. 64 The two men went along to the 'grill room'... A C.I.D. clerk sat at the corner table.

†**grill,** *v.*[3] *Obs. rare*$^{-1}$. [ad. L. *gryllāre*, f. *gryllus* a cricket. Cf. GRYLLE.] *intr.* To chirp.

1688 R. HOLME *Armoury* II. 191/1 The Worm, or Locust, grilleth.

†**grill,** *v.*[4] *Obs. rare*$^{-1}$. *trans.* Of a horse: To wrinkle (the nostrils).

c **1489** CAXTON *Sonnes of Aymon* vii. 176 Thenne he [Bayard] grylled his nostrelles [orig. *il fronca les narines*], and bare his hede vp.

grill, *v.*[5]: see GRILLE.

†**gri'llade,** *sb.*[1] *Obs.* Also 7 **grilliade.** [a. F. *grillade*, f. *griller* to GRILL *v.*[2]]

1. Something grilled, a broiled dish.

1656–7 DAVENANT *Rutland Ho.* Dram. Wks. 1873 III. 226 Your pottages, carbonnades, grillades, ragouts. **1658** PHILLIPS, *Grilliade* (French), a kinde of meat broyled. **1725** BRADLEY *Fam. Dict.*, *Grillade*, a culinary Term, signifying in general Meat broiled upon a Grid-iron.

2. (See quot.)

1727–41 CHAMBERS *Cycl.*, *Grillade*, in cookery,..the browning of any dish, by rubbing a hot iron over it.

†**gri'llade,** *sb.*[2] *Obs. rare.* [? erron. for GRILLAGE by confusion with prec.] A grille or grating.

1727 S. SWITZER *Pract. Gardiner* X. lxxx. 424 On the top of the terrasses..there may be a little grillade of iron, or a low pallisadoe of wood, to keep them from coming up too near the house.

†**gri'llade,** *v. Obs.* Also **griliade.** [f. GRILLADE *sb.*[1]] *trans.* To grill or broil.

1727 BRADLEY *Fam. Dict.*, *Carbonading*, or *Grillading*, a Term in Cookery. **1733** *Revolution Politicks* II. 53 Had I but Power, I'd soon griliade their Bodies to save their Souls. **1762** GOLDSM. *Cit. W.* lxxxviii, I fancy a slice of this, nicely grilladed..would be very pretty eating.

grillage ('grɪlɪdʒ). [a. F. *grillage*, f. *grille* GRILLE *sb.*]

1. *Engineering.* A heavy framework of cross-timbering, sometimes resting upon the heads of piles, serving as a foundation for building on watery or treacherous soil.

1776 G. SEMPLE *Building in Water* 14 A Grillage of Oak, strong and well pinned. **1842** FRANCIS *Dict. Arts*, *Grillage*, a term applied to the sleepers or cross beams supporting a platform, upon which some erections are carried up, as piers in the case of marshes or watery soils, whereby an equal bearing is given to the foundation. **1862** *Daily Tel.* 6 May, By driving piles, on which a double grillage of timbers was laid, a foundation sufficiently firm was obtained. **1868** *Proc. Instit. Civ. Engin.* XXVII. 276 The grillage and foundation distribute this weight.

‖**2.** *Lace-making.* (See quot.)

1882 CAULFEILD & SAWARD *Dict. Needlework*, *Grillé*, *Grillage*, or *Gaze au Fuseau*, are terms especially applied to ornaments that have open spaces barred or grated across them.

grillatalpa, erron. variant of GRYLLOTALPA.

grille, grill (grɪl), *sb.* [a. F. *grille* grating, †gridiron, OF. *greille* gridiron:—pop. L. *graticula* (Du Cange; cf. It. *graticola*), class. L. *crātīcula*, f. *crātis* a hurdle, grating: cf. GRIDDLE. The distinction in Fr. between *grille* and *gril* (GRILL *sb.*[4]) appears to date from about the 16th c.]

1. a. A grating; an arrangement of parallel or cross bars, or structure of open metal-work, used to close an opening or separate one part of a room, etc. from another; *spec.* a grating in a door through which callers may be observed or answered without opening the door; the grating which separates visitors from the nuns in a convent-parlour; the screen in front of the Ladies' Gallery in the House of Commons; etc.

1686 BURNET *Trav.* iii. (1750) 141 They [nuns] receive much Company; but that which I saw was in a publick Room, in which there were many Grills for several Parlours, so that the Conversation is very confused;..there being a different Company at every Grill. **1712** J. JAMES tr. *Le Blond's Gardening* 19 The Walls may be pierced with Grills ..to continue the View. *Ibid.* 24 A large Cross-walk, terminated by Grills of Iron. **1848** B. WEBB *Cont. Eccles.* 22 Open grills were not uncommon in mediaeval times instead of close screens. **1862** *Illustr. Times* 6 Dec. 521 There between the lovers is the horrible 'grille' of the convent. **1862** SIR G. SCOTT *Glean. Westm. Abbey* (1863) 93 The splendid gilt-brass grille which surrounds the tomb of Henry VII. **1870** *Daily News* 22 July 2 The ladies were allowed to retain their places behind the grille. **1876** C. M. DAVIES *Unorth. Lond.* 193 Behind a grille were the places for the female congregation.

b. *spec.* Such a structure fixed in the body of a motor vehicle in front of the radiator, which it protects without preventing the flow of air over it. Freq. as *radiator grill(e).*

1930 *Motor* 7 Oct. 434 New radiator styles are noticeable everywhere... Many use a grille of wire or a pierced metal screen to place in front of the honeycomb. *Ibid.* 437 The polished grille now fitted to the Panhard-Levassor radiator. **1938** NEWTON & STEEDS *Motor Vehicle* (ed. 2) xv. 260 The plated external casing is merely a dummy, and in the great majority of cars takes the form of an ornamental grille or stone guard. **1962** *New Scientist* 22 Feb. 439 (Advt.), The wide-span grille shows the new car in an expansive mood. **1970** *Times* 4 June 18/7 Many car components..are now plastic moulding,..the..radiator grille, for example. **1971** *Daily Tel.* (Colour Suppl.) 22 Oct. 50/1 Fluorescent orange discs..were mounted on the front of a dark blue Mercedes, one each side of the grille.

†**2.** One of the bars in the visor of a helmet. *Obs.*

1661 MORGAN *Sph. Gentry* III. v. 45 Among the French they distinguish their degrees by the grills or bars on the helmet. *Ibid.*, The lower degree of three Grills the lawful heirs turn to the right side, and natural sons to the left.

3. *Real Tennis.* The square opening in the end wall on the hazard side of the court, adjacent to the main wall.

1727 BOYER *Dict. Fr.-Angl.*, *Grille de Tripot*, the Grille, or hazard at Tennis. *Faire un coup de Grille*, to strike a Ball into the Grill. **1816** *Encycl. Perth.* XXII. 220/2 The last thing on the right hand side is called the grill. **1878** J. MARSHALL *Ann. Tennis* 182 Whenever he can send the ball into the grille. **1888** —— in *Encycl. Brit.* XXIII. 179 At the further end of the court is the grille, a square opening adjacent to the main wall.

†**4.** In ornamental hydraulics (see quot.). *Obs.*

1712 J. JAMES tr. *Le Blond's Gardening* 214 Grills of Water are several Spouts in the same Line, standing in a long Bason very near one another.

5. *Pisciculture.* A wooden frame fitted with glass tubes, between which the fish-eggs lie during incubation.

1883 G. B. GOODE *Rev. Fish. Industr. U.S.* 17 The hatching-box used by Dr. Garlick, a simple rectangular trough, was soon replaced by the glass grill, introduced from Europe. **1885** *Chamb. Jrnl.* 558 These eggs hatched just seventy five days after they were laid down on the grilles.

6. A rectangular pattern of small dots impressed on some issues of postage stamps (see quot. 1962). Also *attrib.* Also **grilled** *ppl. a.*, **'grilling** *vbl. sb.*

1887 J. K. TIFFANY *Hist. Postage Stamps U.S.A.* 170 All these values were issued with a grille, of which there are several sizes. **1896** *New Eng. Mag.* Jan. 566/1 The grilling of the stamps was continued until 1872, when a new ink was used that could not be removed from the paper without injuring the stamps. **1916** F. J. MELVILLE *Postage Stamps in Making* 19 This grille embossing was applied to stamps of the United States between 1867 and 1873. *Ibid.*, The variety known as 'grilled all over'. **1929** K. B. STILES *Stamps* v. 78 In the year 1867 there was invented a metal roll with points, and these made grill impressions on certain stamps of the United States. *Ibid.* 81 To count the grill points, examine the reverse side of the stamp. *Ibid.*, Only one other country has ever issued grilled stamps..Peru. **1962** K. F. CHAPMAN *Stamp Collecting* 137 *Grille*, a pattern of tiny square dots impressed into the paper of several United States issues with a view to hindering the removal of cancellations. The grille broke the fibres of the paper and permitted the cancelling ink to penetrate the paper instead of remaining on the surface.

7. *attrib.*, as (sense 3) ***grille-penthouse, -wall,*** (sense 1) ***grille-work.***

1878 J. MARSHALL *Ann. Tennis* 157 *Grille-pent-house*, the pent-house above the wall which contains the grille. *Ibid.*, *Grille-wall*, the inner end-wall which contains the grille. **1896** *Daily News* 31 Mar. 3/7 The two locks and the iron grill-work which stood guard over Pitson's treasures.

grille, grill (grɪl), *v.* [f. GRILLE *sb.*, or ad. F. *griller* in same sense.] *trans.* To fit with a grille or grating. ***to grille off***: to fence off with a grille. Hence **grilled** *ppl. a.*

1848 B. WEBB *Cont. Eccles.* 139 The choir is grilled, and rigidly kept private by parcloses. *Ibid.* 553 The chapels are all grilled off. **1896** *Daily News* 14 Nov. 2/4 Its quaint rococo architecture, and heavy grilled mediæval windows.

‖**grillé** (grije). *Lace-making.* [F. *grillé*, f. *grille* grating.] (See quot.)

1882 CAULFEILD & SAWARD *Dict. Needlework*, *Grillé*, a lace term used..to distinguish the ornamental flower or pattern of lace from the ground surrounding it.

griller ('grɪlə(r)). [f. GRILL *v.*[2] + -ER[1].]

1. One who grills, a grill-cook.

1869 *Daily News* 14 July, 'It was against first principles', this lady told the military griller..to stick a knife into a steak when turning it.

2. A grilling apparatus (in a cooking stove).

1895 *Daily News* 25 Apr. 3/2 With a properly arranged griller, heated by electrical means, fully 65 per cent. of the heat energy was utilised in the meat.

grilles, grillez, obs. forms of GRILSE.

grilliade, variant of GRILLADE *sb.*[1] and *v. Obs.*

‖**grillo** ('grɪləʊ). [It. and Sp.: see GRYLLE.] A cricket.

1845 R. FORD *Hand-bk. Trav. Spain* I. 520 The Spaniards, like the ancients, delight in the *Grillo.* **1929** C. MACKENZIE *Gallipoli Mem.* xi. 189 A wonderful race it was with..the grillos shrilling far and wide across that moon-drenched island. **1949** E. POUND *Pisan Cantos* lxxviii. 67 Be welcome, O cricket my grillo, but you must not sing after taps.

†**'grilly,** *v. Obs. rare.* [a. F. *griller*; the *lly* is meant to give the sound of F. *ll.*] = GRILLE *v.*[2]

1678 BUTLER *Hud.* III. ii. 1526 W'are Grylly'd all at Temple Bar. *Ibid.* 1676 And rather save a Crippled piece Of all their crush'd and broken Members, Than have them Grillied on the Embers.

grilse (grɪls). Forms: *sing.* and *collective pl.* α. 5 **grill(e)s, grillez** (AF.), **grils(s, griles, girles, girlss,** 6 **grylse, grylss,** 5– **grilse.** β. 5 **girsilles,** 6 **grissillis.** γ. 5 ? **gulse,** 7 **gils,** 8–9 **gilse.** δ. *Anglo-Irish* 8–9 **grawls** (also *sing.* **graul**), 9 **graulse.** [Of unknown origin; the β forms have the appearance of being nearest to the original; cf. OF. *grisle* grey. The δ forms may perh. represent a Scandinavian synonym; cf. Sw. *grålax* (lit. grey salmon).] The name given to a young salmon on its first return to the river from the sea, and retained during the same year.

α. **1417** *Durham Acc. Rolls* (Surtees) I. 55 In 8 grills salsis ..4*s*. **1469** *Sc. Acts Jas. III*, c. 13 (1814) II. 96/2 Salmonde grilss and trowtis. **1482** *Rolls of Parlt.* VI. 221 Small fyssh called Grilles, not havyng the perfite lenght of a Samon. [**1482–3** *Act 22 Edw. IV*, c. 2 Le graund Salmon par soy mesme saunz mixture ovesqe icell dascuns grillez ou Salmons rumpez lez ventrez. Et que toutz petitz pessons appellez grillez soient pakkez par soy mesmez soulement saunz ascun mixtur.] **1494** *Acta Dom. Conc.* (1839) 345/1, ix barrellis of salmond & a barell of girlss ȝerly. **1495** *Act 11 Henry VII*, c. 23 The greate Salmon by it self without medeling of any Grilles..and that all small fisshe called Grilles should be packed by theym self only without any medlyng. **1527** *Extracts Aberd. Reg.* (1844) I. 120 Ane barrell of grylse. **1549** *Banff Burgh Court Bk.* 14 May in Cramond *Ann. Banff* (1896) I. 23 Personis sall not tak na kynd of fysche grylss and salmond at thair awne hand. **1609** SKENE *Reg. Maj., Stat. Robt. I.* 22 That na man take fisch or take Salmond or salmon Trouts, Grilsis, in forbidden time. **1824** SCOTT *Redgauntlet* Let. iv, One or two salmon, or grilses, as the smaller sort are termed. **1867** F. FRANCIS *Angling* ix. (1880) 309 The salmon's return to the river after spawning as a grilse. **1868** PEARD *Water-Farm.* v. 55 Three or four months later, the fish re-enter their own river as grilse, weighing from three to nine pounds each.

β. **1469** *Sc. Acts Jas. III.* (1597) c. 37 Salmond, Girsilles and trowtes. **1597** *Compt Buik D. Wedderburne* (S.H.S.) 98, I tynt xxj lib. on thame, they being all grissillis & he selling me thame for Salmond.

γ. **1493** *Extracts Aberd. Reg.* (1844) I. 49 Johannes Blak,.. d. barrel grilse..Johannes Thomsone, d. barrel gulse. **1612** *Naworth Househ. Bks.* (Surtees) 29 A salmon gils and iiij troutes. *c* **1817** HOGG *Tales & Sk.* I. 273 Shoal of gilses.

δ. **1726** *Nat. Hist. Irel.* 190 Those that escaped of the former years return with the young ones, and are called full salmons; whereas those of the same year are small, and are called grawls or half salmon. **1780** A. YOUNG *Tour Irel.* I. 141 The young salmon are called grawls. **1824** MACTAGGART *Gallovid. Encycl.*, *Graulse*, a young salmon. **1851** NEWLAND *Erne* 33 *note*, *Graul*, called in the north a grilse..a salmon that has made but one sea voyage. **1867** SMYTH *Sailor's Word-bk.*, *Grawls*.

b. *transf.* A child. *Anglo-Irish.*

1825 T. C. CROKER *Fairy Leg. S. Irel.* (1828) II. 236 Judy and myself and the poor little grawls will be turned out.

c. *attrib.*, as ***grilse-fly***, ***-rod***, ***-time***.

1769 PENNANT *Zool.* III. 242 The height of Gilse time. **1885** E. D. GERARD *Waters Hercules* xxiii, A grilse-fly. **1885** BLACK *Wh. Heather* iii, He..was rather proud that so slight a grilse-rod..should..have overmastered so big a beast.

Hence **'grilsing** *vbl. sb.*, the taking of grilse.

attrib. **1867** F. FRANCIS *Angling* ix. (1880) 339 A light grilsing weapon.

†**grim**, *sb. Obs.* Also **grym(e**. [f. GRIM *a.*; cf. Du. and MHG. *grim* (G. *grimm*) masc.; also OHG. *grimmî* (MHG. and M.Du. *grimme*) fem.] Grimness, fury, rage.

13.. *Sir Beues* 1880 (MS. A), Thus beginneth grim to growe. **1340–70** *Alex. & Dind.* 50 þei were a-grisen of his gryme & wende gref þolie. *c* **1400** *Destr. Troy* 7770 Then the grekes with grym there gedurt þere hertes. *c* **1400** *Ywaine & Gaw.* 1661 To him he stirt, with birful grim, His bow and arwes reft he him. *c* **1470** HARDING *Chron.* CXXXVIII. xiii, The Sarasyns also he slewe with muche gryme.

grim (grɪm), *a.* and *adv.* Forms: 1 **grim(m,** 3 **grimm,** 3–7 **grimme,** 4–5 **gryme,** 4–6 **grime, grym(me,** 3– **grim.** [OE. *grim(m)* = OFris. *grim*, OS. *grim* (Du. *grim*), OHG. and MHG. *grim* (G. *grimm*), ON. *grimmr* (Sw. *grym* harsh, Da. *grim* ugly). Ormin employs a disyllabic form *grimme*, corresponding to OHG. *grimmi*, MHG. *grimme*. The OTeut. root **grem-* is an ablaut-variant of **gram-*; see GRAME *a.*]

A. *adj.*

1. Of persons or animals: Fierce, cruel, savage or harsh in disposition or action. Also, in weaker sense, daring, determined, bold. Occas. const. *with*, *against*, or with dat. (Now merged in sense 4.)

Beowulf (Z.) 121 Wiht un-hælo grim ond grædiȝ ȝearo sona wæs reoc ond reþe. **971** *Blickl. Hom.* 63 Ne þearf he.. wenan..þæs freondes þe hine æfre of þæs grimman deofles ȝewealdum alesan mæȝe. *c* **1200** ORMIN 8246 He Wass ifell mann wiþþ alle..& grimme wiþþ þe leode. *a* **1225** *Ancr. R.* 280 He iseih hu ueole þe grimme wrastlare of helle breid up on his hupe. *c* **1290** *S. Eng. Leg.* I. 466/164 Giwes weren proute and grimme. *a* **1300** *Cursor M.* 11613 Iesus..lighted of his moder kne, And stod a-pon þaa bestes grim. **1387** TREVISA *Higden* (Rolls) I. 145 þe houndes of þat londe beeþ so greete, so grym, and stronge þat þey þroweþ doun boles and sleeþ lyouns. *c* **1430** *Hymns Virg.* 52 Quod Dauid, 'we spoken of oon so grym þat schulde breke þe brasen ȝatis'. *c* **1450** *Cov. Myst.* (Shaks. Soc.) 230 The Jewys ageyn the were grym & grylle. **1513** DOUGLAS *Æneis* III. ix. 108 And fer out fra my cavern did espy The gryme Ciclopes. **1624** CAPT. SMITH *Virginia* III. v. 55 The first people we saw were two grim and stout Salvages. **1635** SWAN *Spec. M.* viii. §2 (1643) 404 The shrill voice of this commanding fowl [the Cock], will keep in aw the grimme and fierce Lion. **1637** MILTON *Lycidas* 128 What the grim Woolf with privy paw Daily devours apace. [**1726–46** THOMSON *Winter* 394 Bony, and gaunt, and grim, Assembling wolves in raging troops descend.]

absol. *c* **1400** *Destr. Troy* 880 Hit [fyre] gird from the grym with so gret hete. *c* **1450** HOLLAND *Howlat* 369 He bure a lyon as lord..Of pure gold was the ground, quhar the grym hovit. **1535** LYNDESAY *Satyre* 4465 The feind ressaue that graceles grim!

†**b.** Fiercely angry. *Obs.*

971 *Blickl. Hom.* 25 He him æt his ende grim ȝeweorþeþ and hine ȝelædeþ on ece forwyrd. *c* **1205** LAY. 15566 þa wes swiðe grim Dinabuȝ touward Mærlin. **13..** *K. Alis.* 754 Now is the kyng wroth and grym, Who schal beo kyng after him. *c* **1330** R. BRUNNE *Chron.* (1810) 94 God is þe turned grym, Ouþer in word or dede has þou greued him. *c* **1375** *Sc. Leg. Saints, Adrian* 39 þar-at richt gryme wes þe king. *c* **1450** *St. Cuthbert* (Surtees) 5657 þe mare he besoght him ..þe langer he wax mare grym. **1535** COVERDALE *Zeph.* ii. 11 The Lorde shall be grymme vpon them, and destroye all the goddes in the londe.

2. Of personal actions, character, feelings, or utterances. **a.** Fierce, furious, cruel (*obs.* or *arch.*). **b.** In mod. use: Stern, unrelenting, merciless; resolute, uncompromising.

a **1000** *Byrhtnoth* 61 (Gr.) Us sceal ord and ecg ær ȝeseman, grim guðpleȝa, ær we gofol syllon. *c* **1200** ORMIN 672 Deofell iss..Off grimme & niþfull herrte. *c* **1205** LAY. 2283 Moni grimne reas..þolede ich on solde bi-foren Brutone. *a* **1225** *Ancr. R.* 100 þis is a cruel word, & a grim word mid alle. *a* **1300** *Cursor M.* 471 Again him gaf a batell grim. **13..** *Propr. Sanct.* (Vernon MS.) in *Archiv Stud. neu. Spr.* LXXXI. 304/101 þer he dronk wiþ wille grym Bitter atter and eke venym. **1387** TREVISA *Higden* (Rolls) VII. 335 Also þis Lanfrank tredede and bylad kyng William conquerour by an holy craft, nouȝt wiþ grym chidynge, but somtyme in good merþe. *c* **1400** *Melayne* 678 There was none oþer haylsynge Bot stowte wordes and grym. *c* **1460** *Launfal* 461 He smot to Launfal..Well sterne strokes, and well grym. **1535** COVERDALE *Nahum* i. 6 Who is able to abyde his grymme displeasure? **1605** SHAKS. *Macb.* v. ii. 4 Their deere causes Would to the bleeding and the grim Alarme Excite the mortified man. **1667** MILTON *P.L.* VI. 236 To.. open when, and when to close The ridges of grim Warr. **1678** BUNYAN *Pilgr.* I. 151 With a grim and surly voice he [Giant Despair] bid them awake. **1852** MRS. STOWE *Uncle Tom's C.* xv, She..sat with grim determination, up-right as a darning-needle stuck in a board. *a* **1853** ROBERTSON *Lect.* i. (1858) 95 An age of grim earnestness. **1863** GEO. ELIOT *Romola* lx, A man's own safety is a god that some-times makes very grim demands. **1865** KINGSLEY *Herew.* xix. 244 Then began a murder grim and great. **1877** MRS. OLIPHANT *Makers Flor.* xv. 377 The Forentines..prepared to do grim battle for their liberties. **1879** G. W. KITCHIN in *Encycl. Brit.* IX. 549/2 The King's bodyguard, on whom fell ever the grimmest of the fighting, suffered terribly.

3. Of pain, wounds, diseases, painful or destructive conditions: Cruel, terribly severe. Now only in weakened sense: cf. 2 b and 4 b.

c **900** tr. *Bæda's Hist.* I. xiv. (1890) 50 þa com..mycel wol & grim ofer þa ȝehwyrfdon modes men. **971** *Blickl. Hom.* 213 Wæs se winter..to þæs grim þæt maniȝ man his feorh for cyle ȝesealde. **11..** *O.E. Chron.* an. 1005 (Laud MS.) On þyssum ȝeare wæs se mycla hungor ȝeond Angelcynn swilce nan man ær ne ȝemunde swa grimne. *c* **1200** ORMIN 1442 Crist..Drah harrd & hefiȝ pine inoh þurrh fife grimme wundess. *c* **1300** *Havelok* 155 He..preyden Cristes hore, That he [wolde] turnen him Vt of that yuel that was so grim! *c* **1400** *Destr. Troy* 907 The dragon..gird him agayne with a grym noyse. *c* **1435** *Torr. Portugal* 981 Mo than fyfty had he slayne With gryme wounddes and sare. *c* **1450** MYRC 1561 For yef the synne be gret or grym. **1535** STEWART *Cron. Scot.* (1858) I. 303 Quhilk sall nocht schrink quhair nakit swardis ar drawin..Or for na grym wound other grym or grow. **1658** A. FOX tr. *Wurtz' Surg.* II. xiv. 110 Many times there is a grim anger in the Hand or Finger. **1667** MILTON *P.L.* II. 170 What if the breath that kindl'd those grim fires, Awak'd should blow them into sevenfold rage? *a* **1716** SOUTH *Serm.* (1744) IX. vi. 185 And then, whether it would not be the grimmest dispensation that ever befell him. **1814** SCOTT *Ld. of Isles* III. xxiii, Wind and weather wax'd so grim. **1865** DICKENS *Mut. Fr.* i. xiii, 'This is becoming grim', said Eugene in a low voice. **1871** R. ELLIS tr. *Catullus* xxi. 11 Now shall beauty to thirst be train'd or hunger's Grim necessity.

†**b.** Of weapons or destructive agencies: Cruel, formidable. ***to wend to the grim tooth***: to have recourse to harsh measures. *Obs.*

a **1225** *Ancr. R.* 218 [He] makeð him swuðe sterne, & went to þene grimme toð. **13..** *E.E. Allit. P.* B. 1553 Al hit frayes my flesche þe fyngres so grymme. *Ibid.* 1696 Ful grymme clawres þat were croked and kene. **13..** *Gaw. & Gr. Knt.* 2261 Gederez vp hys grymme tole, Gawayn to smyte. *c* **1384** CHAUCER *H. Fame* II. 33 With hys grym pawes strong ..Me..he hente. **1470–85** MALORY *Arthur* II. xv, Thenne kyng Pellam cauȝt in his hand a grym wepen.

4. Formidable in appearance or demeanour; of stern, forbidding or harsh aspect, suggesting a cruel or unbending disposition. †Also, in weaker sense, hard-featured, ugly.

1340 HAMPOLE *Pr. Consc.* 2250 þe devel þat es grisely and grym, Til hym come. *c* **1394** *P. Pl. Crede* 222 A greet cherl & a grym, growen as a tonne. *c* **1440** *Promp. Parv.* 212/1 Grym, or sterne.., *austerus, rigidus*. *c* **1450** *Merlin* 339 The Geaunte was so grym a figure that he was dredefull for to beholde. **1513** DOUGLAS *Æneis* V. i. 67 A beir skyn of Affrik aboun his weid, Full grym of luik, with dartes kene and rude. **1535** COVERDALE *Dan.* ii. 31 A greate ymage, whose fygure was maruelous greate, and his vysage grymme [Vulg. *terribilis*]. **1587** TURBERV. *Trag. T.* (1837) 31 Whose face was grimme, and he in blacke yclad. **1588** SHAKS. *L.L.L.* II. i. 256 Then was Venus like her mother, for her father is but grim. **1641** DENHAM *Sophy* IV. i, He..that dares to die, May laugh at the grim face of law. **1697** DRYDEN *Virg. Georg.* IV. 146 Like their grisly Prince appears his gloomy Race: Grim, ghastly, rugged. **1703** ROWE *Fair Penit.* V. i. 1720 How Pale he looks! How Grim with clotted Blood and those dead Eyes. **1794** MRS. RADCLIFFE *Myst. Udolpho* xxvi, It threw a stronger gleam upon the grim and sallow countenance of Barnardine. **1808** SCOTT *Marm.* III. xx, Norweyan warriors grim. *Ibid.* xxi, Vigil and fast had worn him grim. **1827** POLLOK *Course T.* VIII, On their grim features, now, The plain unvisored index of the soul. **1838** J. L. STEPHENS *Trav. Greece*, etc. 107/1 The commandant, a grim, gaunt-looking figure about fifty. **1862** BURTON *Bk. Hunter* 396 Grim and ghastly human figures.

b. of things personified, *esp.* of death. Phr. ***to hold on, cling,*** etc. ***like grim death***.

1590 SHAKS. *Com. Err.* v. i. 80 Moodie and dull melancholly Kinsman to grim and comfortlesse despaire. **1596** —— *Tam. Shr.* Induct. i. 35 Grim death, how foule and loath-some is thine image. **1635** QUARLES *Embl.* III. xi. (1718) 170 Mine eye Shall scorn grim death, although grim death stand by. *c* **1680** BEVERIDGE *Serm.* (1729) I. 249 Can we look grim death in the face? **1713** ADDISON *Cato* II. iv, Doubling the native horror of the war And making death more grim. **1816** SHELLEY *Alastor* 608 The very winds, Danger's grim playmates, on that precipice Slept. **1847** LADY G. BLOOMFIELD *Remin.* (1883) I. x. 263 There was nothing for it but to hold on like grim death, and be shaken to pieces. **1865** TROLLOPE *Belton Est.* ix. 101 People must eat and drink even when the grim monarch is in the house.

c. of looks or aspect.

1340 HAMPOLE *Pr. Consc.* 2233 Ful hydus sightes þai [the devils] sal shew hym þat his chere sal make grisly and grym. *c* **1450** *Merlin* 44 A man of a grym chere. **1564** HAWARD *Eutropius* II. 15 After they were dead keping stil theyr grim lokes. **1590** SPENSER *F.Q.* III. viii. 32 For shame, but more for feare of his grim sight, Downe in her lap she hid her face. **1602** MARSTON *Antonio's Rev.* III. v. Wks. 1856 I. 115, I will ..Outstare the terror of thy grimme aspect. **1697** EVELYN *Numism.* ix. 306 A grim and crabbed look. **1823** GALT *Entail* I. iii. 18 Tremendous forms, in warlike attitudes and with grim aspects. **1838** DICKENS *Nich. Nick.* xv, With a grim and ghastly stare. **1863** GEO. ELIOT *Romola* i, This city of yours turns a grim look on me just here.

d. *absol.* or quasi-*sb.* = GRIMNESS.

1845 CARLYLE *Cromwell* (1871) IV. 70 Faces settling into permanent grim.

5. *transf.* Of things, scenes, situations, etc.: Harsh or repellent of aspect; uninviting.

[**13..** *E.E. Allit. P.* A. 1069 þ e mone may þer of acroche no myȝte To spotty, ho is of body to grym.] **1820** SCOTT *Monast.* v, The very crags and scaurs seemed higher and grimmer. **1839** tr. *Lamartine's Trav. East* 78/1 On slopes, somewhat less grim, vine-plants are seen. **1860** HAWTHORNE *Marb. Faun* (1879) I. xxv. 252 In a grim old vaulted apartment. **1871** L. STEPHEN *Playgr. Europe* iii. (1894) 82 The great Oberland peaks..stand round in a grim circle. **1877** BLACK *Green Past.* xxxii. (1878) 260 We bade farewell to this gay haunt of pleasure and set out for grimmer latitudes.

b. *absol.* or quasi-*sb.*

1840 GALT *Demon Destiny*, etc. 73, I..often wonder'd in the grim of night, To what dread land the dead-man did invite.

6. Of stern or sinister import.

1873 OUIDA *Pascarèl* I. 4 A monarch yesterday, to-day a scape-goat, in grimmest ironic symbol of all human histories. **1889** JESSOPP *Coming of Friars* ii. 81 A saying that had a grim truth in it.

7. Of laughter, jests, humour: Stern, implying no relenting or softening. In recent use often: Dealing with ghastly or painful subjects.

1641 MILTON *Animadv.* Pref., Such a grim laughter, as may appear at the same time in an austere visage. **1823** SCOTT *Quentin D.* xxvi, One of those grim smiles, of which it was impossible to say, whether it meant good or harm. **1833** HT. MARTINEAU *Loom & Lugger* II. v. 106 Before the crowd had quite ended their grim pastime. **1850** CARLYLE *Latter-d. Pamph.* iv. 4 Our friend in grim banter would reply: 'Reform a Popedom,—hardly'. **1868** MILMAN *St. Paul's* xiv. 352 One of those grim pleasantries in which Oliver took delight. **1869** FREEMAN *Norm. Conq.* (1876) III. xii. 162 Mingled with all this there is a certain element of grim merriment.

8. *Comb.*, as ***grim-cheeked***, ***-faced***, ***-featured***, ***-looked***, ***-looking***, ***-visaged***, ***-whiskered*** adjs.; †***grim-sightedness***. Also †**grim-face** = GRIMACE *sb.*

1601 MARSTON *Pasquil & Kath.* II. 94 The siluer Ensigne of the *grimme-cheekt night. **1671** CROWNE *Juliana* I. 9 [*Stage direction*] Landlord squints, and makes *grim-faces. **1610** R. NICCOLS *Eng. Eliza* in *Mirr. Mag.* 863 Like the *grim-fac'd God of war. **1833** HT. MARTINEAU *Charmed Sea* v. 74 Groups of grim-faced miners. **1811** W. R. SPENCER *Poems* 121 He thinks his new porter, *grim-featur'd Suspicion. **1590** SHAKS. *Mids. N.* v. i. 171 O *grim look't night, o night with hue so blacke. **1844** LEVER *T. Burke* II. 166 A *grim-looking, hard-featured man. **1878** J. BULLER *40 Years N. Zealand* I. i. 24 This stormy and grim-looking islet. **1648** HEXHAM *Dutch Dict.* (1660), *Grim-sichtigheydt*, *Grim-sightednesse, Severitie, or Austere-lookes. **1594** SHAKS. *Rich. III*, I. i. 9 *Grim-visag'd Warre, hath smooth'd his wrinkled Front. **1848** BUCKLEY *Iliad* 191 A grim-visaged Gorgon. **1780** MICKLE *Let.* 15 Aug. in *Lit. Panorama* (1809) V. 1174 *Grim-whiskered soldiers, tearing children from their mothers and killing them.

B. *adv.* (OE. *grimme*) or quasi-*adv.* In a grim manner or mood; fiercely, savagely, horribly. In later use only ***to look grim***, where *grim* is perh. adjectival.

c **893** K. ALFRED *Oros.* I. ii. §1 Hy him æfter þæm grimme forguldon þone wiȝcræft þe hy æt him ȝeleornodon. *a* **1000** *Cædmon's Gen.* 1275 (Gr.) He..þohte forgripan gumcynne grimme and sare. *a* **1300** *Cursor M.* 14668 þai loked on him lath and grim. *a* **1300** *E.E. Psalter* civ. 18 Irne thurgh-yhode his saule ful grim. *c* **1330** R. BRUNNE *Chron.* (1810) 133 Whan þe fader wist þe sonne wild werre on him, I blame him not if him list turne ageyn fulle grim. *c* **1400** *Sowdone Bab.* 3129 He loked on her al grymme As he wode wroth wer. **14..** *Siege Jerusalem* (E.E.T.S.) 10/165 þer is no gome in þis [grounde] þat is grym wounded. *c* **1450** HOLLAND *Howlat* 53 He grat grysly grym, and gaif a gret ȝowle. **1596** SPENSER *F.Q.* IV. i. 50 So stood Sir Scudamour when this he heard,

Ne word he had to speake for great dismay, But lookt on Glauce grim. **1675** HOBBES *Odyss.* (1677) 293 Round about he lookt upon us grim.

b. *Comb.*, as *grim-blue, frowning, -grinning, -rising, -set, -white* adjs.

1592 SHAKS. *Ven. & Ad.* 155 Thus chides she Death, Grim-grinning ghost. **1786** BURNS *Addr. Edin.* v, Thy pond'rous wall and massy bar, Grim-rising o'er the rugged rock. **1831** CARLYLE *Sart. Res.* II. ix. (1838) 219 Round some Schreckhorn, as yet grim-blue, would the eddying vapour gather..in the clear sunbeam your Schreckhorn stood smiling grim-white. **1881** H. PHILLIPS tr. *Chamisso's Faust* 15 Steep, grim-frowning, rugged chasms. **1885** FITZPATRICK *Life T. N. Burke* I. 20 *note*, The grim-set, clenched aspect of the faces.

grim (grɪm), *v.* Also 6 **grimme**, *Sc.* **grym.** [In sense 1, ad. Du. or G. *grimmen* (OS. and OE. *grimman*), f. *grim(m* adj. GRIM. In sense 2, f. GRIM *a.*]

†**1.** *intr.* To be angry, look fierce. Const. *at, on, to. Obs.*

a **1400–50** *Alexander* 4653 Ne nothire gesse we vs godis ne grym at oure driȝtin. **1481** CAXTON *Reynard* (Arb.) 35 Thenne grimmed he, and was angry on me. **1484** —— *Curiall* 2 b, Now she lawheth to one and she grimmeth to other. **1530** PALSGR. 575/1, I grimme, I make a foule countenaunce, *je grongne.* **1535** [see GRIM *a.* 3]. [**1848** LYTTON *K. Arthur* VIII. lvi, Black from a brazen flag, with outstretched wings Grimmed the dread Raven of the Runic kings. *Note. Grimm'd*, from the verb *grimmen.*]

2. *trans.* To make grim or fierce; to cause to look grim; to give a grim look to.

1710 *Brit. Apollo* III. No. 26. 3/1 There Small-Cole one Cries..And looks Ugly and Grimm'd like a Witch. **1808** J. BARLOW *Columb.* III. 527 Grimm'd by the horrors of the dreadful night, The hosts woke fiercer for the promised fight. **1837** CARLYLE *Fr. Rev.* II. v. viii, Bailly and his Feuillants..had to withdraw.. into lurid half-light, grimmed by the shadow of that Red Flag of theirs. **1840** GALT *Demon of Destiny* II. 13 The sculptured effigies That grim the silence of chivalric aisles.

grimace (grɪˈmeɪs), *sb.* Also 7 **grimass(e.** [a. F. *grimace* (14th c.), of uncertain origin.]

1. A distortion of the countenance whether spontaneous or involuntary, expressive of some feeling (esp. annoyance, embarrassment, ill-humour or pain) or tending to excite laughter; a wry face. Phr. ***to make a grimace*** or ***grimaces.***

1651 HOBBES *Leviath.* I. vi. 27 Sudden Glory, is the passion which maketh those Grimaces called Laughter. **1668** T. ST. SERFE *Tarugo's Wiles* Epil., Say with an indifferent Grimasse, 'tis well enough for a Novice. **1678** BUTLER *Hud.* III. ii. 1004 With smart remarks of leering faces, And annotations of grimaces! **1786** MAD. D'ARBLAY *Diary* 11 Nov., [The] little heroine, making many involuntary grimaces, but resisting her evident inclination to cry. **1824** W. IRVING *T. Trav.* I. 97, I tried to laugh, but could only make a grimace. **1840** DICKENS *Old C. Shop* xi, Nor were the lawyer's smiles less terrible to her than Quilp's grimaces. **1874** L. STEPHEN *Hours in Library* (1892) I. vii. 258 He..chooses to..make grimaces before us, like an ordinary clown.

transf. **1841** W. SPALDING *Italy & It. Isl.* II. 357 His boldness of drawing sometimes produces exaggeration and grimace.

2. An affected expression of countenance. †Formerly in wider sense, applied contemptuously to any affected or exaggerated attitude or gesture of politeness.

1678 MARVELL *Growth Popery* Wks. 1875 IV. 336 To learn how to make the Plenipotentiary grimass for his Majesty's service. **1709** STEELE *Tatler* No. 38 ¶8 Take one of your Men of Business, he shall keep you half an Hour with your Hat off..till he has drawn a Crowd that observes you in this Grimace. **1711** ADDISON *Spect.* No. 69 ¶2 As I am not versed in the Modern Coptick, our Conferences go no further than a Bow and a Grimace. **1758** JOHNSON *Idler* No. 8 ¶12 Men who can bear at once the grimaces of the Gauls, and the howl of the Americans. **1860** GEO. ELIOT *Mill on Floss* VI. ix, The Miss Guests were much too well-bred to have any of the grimaces and affected tones that belong to pretentious vulgarity.

b. The employment of affected looks †or gestures. ? Now *rare.*

1686 DRYDEN *Ep. to H. Higden* 10 For posture, dress, grimace, and affectation, Though foes to sense, are harmless to the nation. **1712** ADDISON *Spect.* No. 305 ¶10 This Artist is to teach them how to nod judiciously, to shrug up their Shoulders in a dubious Case, to connive with either Eye, and in a Word, the whole Practice of *Political Grimace.* **1757** SMOLLETT *Reprisal* I. iii, A peacock in pride, in grimace a baboon. **1789** BELSHAM *Ess.* I. xiv. 270 What may be thought grace at Paris, at London may appear grimace. **1816** *Remarks Eng. Mann.* 58 We are too apt to consider as French grimace every deviation from our more reserved or churlish habits.

3. *fig.* Affectation, pretence, sham; †an instance of this. ? Now *rare.*

1655 *Nicholas Papers* (Camden) II. 184 They did veryly beleeue it would be a warr, what grimaces soeuer they made. **1672** DRYDEN *Marr. à la Mode* II. i. Wks. 1883 IV. 286, I..said nothing but *à d'autres, à d'autres*, and that it was all grimace, and would not pass upon me. **1715** tr. *C'tess D'Aunoy's Wks.* 83 Hypocrisie and Grimace seem'd to me the most unworthy of all Vices. **1739** CIBBER *Apol.* (1756) I. 22 All this my parade and grimace of philosophy. **1759** ROBERTSON *Hist. Scot.* (1817) II. III. 117 In all her violent declarations against Darnly, there was much more of grimace than reality. **1785** PALEY *Mor. Philos.* (1818) I. 359 He sees through the grimace of this counterfeited concern for virtue. **1818** JAS. MILL *Brit. India* II. v. ii. 384 He..treated the renewal of the title of Naib Subah..as idle grimace. **1832** MACAULAY *Mirabeau* Misc. Writ. (1889) 280 They had found it so easy to perform the grimace of piety, that it was natural for them to consider all piety as grimace. **1855** MOTLEY *Dutch Rep.* I. 543 The Prince..listened to all this commendation... He knew it to be pure grimace. **1891** F. HALL in *Nation* (N.Y.) LII. 297/2 Everything that had passed before me bore..the stamp of..grimace, hollowness, or histrionism.

grimace (grɪˈmeɪs), *v.* [f. GRIMACE *sb.*, or ad. F. *grimacer* (Cotgr. 1611).] *intr.* To distort the countenance; to make a wry face; †to put on an affected air. Also, *to grimace it.*

1762 GOLDSM. *Cit. W.* xcvi. ¶1 It is only clapping on a suit of sables, grimacing it for a few days, and all, soon forgotten, goes on as before. **1768** —— *Good-n. Man* Epil., He nods, they nod; he cringes, they grimace. **1826** SCOTT *Woodst.* v, I can grimace like a baboon. **1837** CARLYLE *Fr. Rev.* I. VII. iv, When so much goes grinning and grimacing as a lifeless Formality..here once more, if nowhere else, is a Sincerity and Reality. **1863** MARY HOWITT *F. Bremer's Greece* I. iii. 65 On one spot grimaces the winged lion of St. Mark's, the emblem of Venice. **1892** ZANGWILL *Childr. Ghetto* I. 188 Solomon stuck his tongue in his cheek, and grimaced.

Hence **gri'maced** *ppl. a.*, affected. *rare.*

1853 W. ANDERSON *Expos. Popery* (1878) 214 It is your grimaced priests and demure nuns who are most dexterous at the juggling of conscience.

grimacer (grɪˈmeɪsə(r)). [f. GRIMACE *v.* + -ER[1].] One who makes grimaces or distorts his face.

1810 *Sporting Mag.* XXXVI. 169 When the grimacers have distorted their flexible countenances. **1833** *Fraser's Mag.* VIII. 346 Such grimacers as Harley, or such actors as Power.

gri'macery. *rare*[−1]. [ad. F. *grimacerie*, f. *grimacer* GRIMACE *v.*; see -ERY.] The practice of using grimaces or affected gestures.

1863 G. H. CALVERT *Gentleman* vii. 94 Verbal courtesy, hat-in-hand grimacery.

grimacier (grɪˈmeɪsɪə(r)). [ad. F. *grimacier*, f. *grimacer* GRIMACE *v.*; see -IER.] = GRIMACER.

1815 T. MOORE *Mem.* (1856) VIII. 197 We ought to be like the grimacier at Astley's. **1820–2** PYNE *Wine & Walnuts* (1824) I. vi. 60 He was too much of a grimacier to be tolerated by the judges of good acting. **1864** *Daily Tel.* 18 July, We have lost the great grimacier [Grimaldi].

grimacing (grɪˈmeɪsɪŋ), *vbl. sb.* [f. GRIMACE *v.* + -ING[1].] The action of the verb GRIMACE.

1897 *Allbutt's Syst. Med.* III. 51 Genuine chorea, apart from mere grimacing..is very closely associated with the rheumatic state.

grimacing (grɪˈmeɪsɪŋ), *ppl. a.* [f. GRIMACE *v.* + -ING[2].] That grimaces.

1804 *Something Odd* I. 83 Cringing alacrity and grimacing volubility. **1844** L. S. COSTELLO *Béarn & Pyrenees* II. ix. 148 The sculpture of..the grimacing heads amongst the foliage. **1863** GEO. ELIOT *Romola* iv, Nello..cast a grimacing look of intelligence at the Greek.

Hence **gri'macingly** *adv.*

1854 *Tait's Mag.* XXI. 287 The Jew..winked grimacingly.

Grimaldi (grɪˈmældɪ). The name of the caves in Liguria, Italy, where the skeletons of a type of Upper Palæolithic man were found by Emile Rivière in 1872, used *attrib.* as in ***Grimaldi skull.*** Hence **Gri'maldian** *a.*, pertaining to or characteristic of Grimaldi man or of this culture.

1902 *Daily Chron.* 8 May 3/3 The Grimaldi Skulls. Dr. Verneau proposes to call the skulls by the name of Grimaldi, and I presume they will henceforth be so designated. **1932** *Antiquity* June 193 Various names, more particularly Creswellian and Grimaldian, have been given to this 'developed' Aurignacian [culture]. **1948** [see CRESWELLIAN *a.*]. **1958** F. E. ZEUNER *Dating Past* (ed. 4) 301 In the layers above, upper Aurignacian stone tools become abundant, and the bone tools rarer and atypical. For this Italian facies of the Upper Palaeolithic, Vaufrey adapted Rellini's term, Grimaldian.

grimalkin (grɪˈmælkɪn, -ˈmɔːlkɪn). [prob. f. GREY *a.* + MALKIN.] A name given to a cat; hence, a cat, *esp.* an old she-cat; *contemptuously* applied to a jealous or imperious old woman.

In quot. 1605 used as the name of a fiend.

[**1605** SHAKS. *Macb.* I. i. 9, I come, Gray-Malkin!] **1630** J. TAYLOR (Water P.) *Wks.* II. 114/1 Like Grimalkin Or a kinde needfull Vermin-coursing Cat. *Ibid.* 226/2, I list not write the bable praise Of Apes, or Owles, or Popinjaies Or of the Cat Grimalkin. **1703** J. PHILLIPS *Splendid Shilling* 74 Grimalkin to Domestic Vermine sworn An everlasting Foe. **1709** PRIOR *When Cat is Away* 18 Grimalkin far all cats outshone. **1789** G. WHITE *Selborne* lxxvi, That a poor little sucking leveret should be fostered..by a bloody grimalkin. **1798** CHARLOTTE SMITH *Yng. Philosopher* III. 15 The venerable old grimalkin had taken Louisa with her, and accompanied the married folks into Suffolk. **1826** DISRAELI *Viv. Grey* II. xvi, Like veritable Grimalkins, they [the Toadeys] fawn upon their victims previous to the festival. **1843** BORROW *Bible in Spain* 53 Growling to herself, something after the manner of an old grimalkin when disturbed.

attrib. *a* **1745** SWIFT *Dan Jackson's Picture* ii. 6 But still were wanting his grimalkin eyes, For which gray worsted stocking paint supplies. **1784** GIBBON *Misc. Wks.* (1814) II. 354 And now, my Lady, Let me approach your gentle, not grimalkin, presence, with deep remorse.

Hence **gri'malkined** *pa. pple.* (*nonce-wd.*), vexed by a 'grimalkin'.

1756 LD. CHESTERF. *World* No. 185 ¶2, I am not hen-pecked; I am not grimalkined; I have no Mrs. Freeman with her Italian airs; but I have a wife more troublesome than all three.

†**grimask.** *Obs. rare*[−1]. = GRIMACE.

1671 E. HOWARD *Womens Conquest* First Prol., What think you then, if I speak to all the Judges in the Pit by looks and grimasks? [Possibly only a misprint for *grimasses.*]

grimass(e, obs. form of GRIMACE.

†**grim'cundleʒc.** *Obs. rare*[−1]. [f. GRIM *sb.* + *-cund* (as in GODCUND, q.v.) + *-leʒc* -LAIK.] Grimness, fierceness.

c **1200** ORMIN 4706 þatt tu beo..þwerrt ut clene off grimm-cunndleȝȝc & þwerrt ut clene off braþþe.

grime (graɪm), *sb.* [= mod. Flemish *grijm* in the same sense (Kilian has *grijmsel*): cf. GRIME *v.*] Soot, smut, coal-dust, or other black particles, deposited upon or ingrained in some surface, esp. the human skin.

1590 SHAKS. *Com. Err.* III. ii. 106 She sweats a man may goe ouer-shoes in the grime of it. **1612** W. PARKES *Curtaine-Dr.* (1876) 24 Now will he..note it deepe with a pen of brasse, with the blackest grime and colour that can be deuised. **1728** WOODWARD *Cat. Fossils* II. 3 Collow is the word by which they denote black Grime of burnt Coals or Wood. **1740** SOMERVILLE *Hobbinol* III. 179 Her Legs unclean, Booted with Grime. **1850** CARLYLE *Latter-d. Pamph.* iv. 4 A wretched old kettle..consisting mainly now of foul grime and dust. **1870** BRYANT *Iliad* I. x. 330 Descending to the sea They washed from knees and neck and thighs the grime Of sweat. **1893** *Northumbld. Gloss., Grime*, the black ashes upon wood which are in a state between soot and charcoal. Any black smudge is called a grime mark. Lignite, or wood coal, is sometimes called grime.

fig. **1719** DE FOE *Crusoe* II. xvi. (1840) 324 The dirt and grime of human affairs. **1899** H. WRIGHT *Depopulation* 109 He forgot all the squalor of monotony, and the grime of grinding circumstances by which human life was surrounded.

grime (graɪm), *v.* Also 5 *Sc.* **grymme.** [Cf. mod. Flemish *grijmen*, Fris. *griemjen*, LG. *gremen, grêmen* to blacken, dirty; a MDu. **grimen* is assumed by Verwijs and Verdam. Cf. also *begremen, -griemen* (Kilian), to BEGRIME.] *trans.* To cover with grime, to blacken, befoul. Also fig. ***to grime the face of.*** (Cf. BEGRIME.)

c **1470** HENRYSON *Mor. Fab.* XI. (*Wolf & Sheep*) xvi, Than quhair the gait was grymmit he him brocht. **1483** *Cath. Angl.* 165/2 To Grime, *fuscare, fuliginare.* *a* **1592** H. SMITH *Wks.* (1866–7) I. 62 He seemeth like a collier which is grimed with his own coals. **1601** DENT *Pathw. Heaven* 67 The Apostle laieth out the great danger of this sinne [covetousness], and doth exceedingly grime the face of it. **1605** SHAKS. *Lear* II. iii. 9 My face Ile grime with filth. **1647** R. STAPYLTON *Juvenal* 237 Vulcan pour'd Nectar himself, and his own fingers scour'd, Grim'd in his Liparene work-house. **1730** SWIFT *Lady's Dressing-Room* 46 The Towels..With Dirt, and Sweat, and Ear-wax grim'd. **1806–7** J. BERESFORD *Miseries Hum. Life* (1826) VIII. ii, Letting your book fall into the ashes, so as to..rumple and grime the leaves. **1878** H. PHILLIPS *Poems fr. Sp. & Germ.* 18 A rudely cut inscription Grimed with dust of many a year.

†**b.** To smear, anoint. *Obs. rare*[−1].

c **1580** JEFFERIE *Bugbears* Epil. in *Archiv Stud. neu. Spr.* (1897), With amber greece he must be grymde, and such lyke costly geare.

grime, obs. form of GRIM.

grimed (graɪmd), *ppl. a.* [f. GRIME *v.* + -ED[1].] Blackened with grime; grimy.

1483 *Cath. Angl.* 165/2 Grimed, *fuscatus, fuliginatus.* **1493** *Will of Hilbrond* (Somerset Ho.), A Hekfeyr of grymed colo[r]. **1592** NASHE *P. Penilesse* (ed. 2) 6 b, A gray beard cut short to the stumps, as though it were grimde. **1819** CRABBE *T. of Hall* VIII. Wks. 1834 VI. 194 With hair uncomb'd, grimed face, and piteous look. **1841** J. L. STEPHENS *Centr. Amer.* (1854) 258 The smith's grimed face. **1896** A. MORRISON *Child Jago* 1 There rose from the foul earth and the grimed walls a close, mingled stink.

fig. **1815** W. H. IRELAND *Scribbleomania* 25 Panegyrists, Errant Knights! That whitewash one as grim'd as Nero.

griment, variant of GREEMENT, *Obs.*

†**'grimful,** *a. Obs.* Also 3 **grimfule,** 4 **grymfull.** [f. GRIM *sb.* or *a.* + -FUL.] Full of grimness; fierce, terrible.

a **1240** *Sawles Warde* in *Cott. Hom.* 253 To i seon eauer þe unseli gastes..biseon on hare grimfule ant grurefule nebbes ant heren hare rarunge. **13..** *Minor Poems fr. Vernon MS.* (E.E.T.S.) 443 Wyth gret and grymfull wrathe full sone Thei shull heryn a full hard dome. **1715** *Disc. on Death* 55 Never more shall dread Death's grimful frown.

grimgribber (ˈgrɪm,grɪbə(r)). Also 8–9 **grimgibber,** 9 **glimglibber.** In quot. 1722 the name of an imaginary estate, extemporized in a discussion between two sham counsel respecting a marriage settlement. Hence used by Tooke, Bentham, and later writers for: Legal or other technical jargon, learned gibberish. Also *attrib.*

Quot. 1835 is a direct allusion to Steele's use.

[**1722** STEELE *Consc. Lovers* III. i. (1723) 51 *Mrs. Seal.* The single Question is, whether the Intail is such, that my Cousin Sir Geoffry is necessary in this Affair? *Bram.* Yes, as to the Lordship of Tretriplet, but not as to the Messuage of Grimgibber.] **1786** J. H. TOOKE *Purley* 103 The grimgribber of Westminster-Hall is a more fertile..source of imposture than the abracadabra of magicians. *c* **1788** BENTHAM *Ch. of Eng. Catech. Exam.* (1868) 66 The..grimgribber of modern technical theology. **1802–12** ——

Ration. Judic. Evid. (1827) V. 344 The grimgibber, nonsensical reason..of the identity of the two persons. **1824** *New Monthly Mag.* X. 366 Medical writers, whose grimgribber is seldom much..read. **1828** *Edin. Rev.* XLVIII. 468 The law's grim-gribber. **1835** LADY LOUISA STUART *Introd. Anecdotes* in Ld. Wharncliffe *Lett. & Wks. of Lady M. W. Montagu* (1837) I. 18 Lord Dorchester..was very gracious to him, till the Grim-gribber part of the business—the portion and settlements—came under consideration.

griminess ('graɪmɪnɪs). [f. GRIMY *a.* + -NESS.] The quality or state of being grimy.

1650 H. MORE *Observ.* in *Enthus. Triumph.* (1656) 85 How the man is frighted into devotion by the smut and griminesse of his own imagination. **1854** HAWTHORNE *Eng. Note-bks.* (1883) II. 178 A great deal of dirt and griminess on the stone floor of the market-house. **1859** GEO. ELIOT *A. Bede* 13 Mr. Rann's leathern apron and subdued griminess can leave no one in any doubt that he is the village shoemaker.

griming ('graɪmɪŋ), *vbl. sb. dial.* A sprinkling.

a **1802** *Jamie Telfer* vii. in Child *Ballads* (1890) IV. 6 It was the gryming of a new-fa'n snaw. **1893** *Northumb. Gloss.*, *Greymin, Grimin, Gryming*, a sprinkling, a smirch.

†**grimleȝc.** *Obs. rare*$^{-1}$. [a. ON. *grimmleik-r*: see GRIM *a.* and -LAIK.] Grimness, cruelty.

c **1200** ORMIN 4719 þiss mahhte tredeþþ unnderrfot All grimmeleȝȝc & braþþe.

grimly ('grɪmlɪ), *a. Obs.* or *arch.* Also 5 *superl.* grimlokkest. [OE. *grimlic* (= MDu. *grimmelijc*, MHG. *grimmelich*, ON. *grimmligr*); see GRIM *a.* and -LY[1].] Grim-looking; grim in appearance or nature.

Beowulf (Z.) 3041 Wæs se leȝ-draca, grimlic gryre, gledum be-swæled. *c* **893** K. ÆLFRED *Oros.* I. ii. §2 Ða ȝewin wæron grimlicran þonne hy nu syn. *c* **1000** ÆLFRIC *Hom.* I. 454 Ðone grimlican garsecg. *c* **1205** LAY. 8176 Euielin þene brond igrap mid grimliche lechen. *c* **1275** *Moral Ode* 141 in *O.E. Misc.* 63 Swiþe grimlych stench þer is. *a* **1310** in Wright *Lyric P.* 111 The love of him us haveth ymaked sounde, Ant ycast the grimly gost to grounde. *c* **1380** *Sir Ferumb.* 1876 Ys berd was long, & al whyt hor; a was [a] grymly freke. *a* **1400** *Octouian* 1742 Doun he fyll deed to grounde, Gronynge fast with grymly wounde. *c* **1400** *Sowdone Bab.* 144 Ther londed many a grymlye gome. **1470–85** MALORY *Arthur* VIII. i, She had many grymly throwes. **1611** BEAUM. & FL. *Knt. Burn. Pestle* II. v, In came Margaret's grimly ghost, And stood at William's feet. *a* **1650** *Sir Aldingar* 73 in Furniv. *Percy Folio* I. 169, I dreamed the grype & a grimlie beast had carryed my crowne away. **1766** G. CANNING *Anti-Lucretius* I. 68 Canst thou, undaunted, meet the grimly king? **1783** JOHNSON *Let. to Mrs. Thrale* 20 Aug., I told her it was Johnson's grimly ghost. **1810** BENTHAM *Packing* (1821) 108 Behold! at the bed's feet a grimly spectre. **1863** BARING-GOULD *Iceland* xxi. 361 Hard by this a grimly abyss.

Hence '**grimliness**, the state of being grimly.

14.. *Chaucer's Parson's T.* ¶790 (Ch. Ch. MS.) Grymlynesse of the deueles [see GRIMNESS]. **1580** HOLLYBAND *Treas. Fr. Tong*, *Affreuseté*, sturdinesse, grimlinesse. **1898** *N. & Q.* 9th Ser. I. 445 Poetical licence, for the sake of intensifying the grimliness of the apparition.

grimly ('grɪmlɪ), *adv.* Forms: 1 grim-, grymlice (*compar.* grimlicor, *superl.* grimlicost), 3 grimliche, *Orm.* grimmeliȝ, 4 grimli, 4–6 **grymly**, 3– **grimly**. [OE. *grimlíce* (= OHG. *grimlîche*, *grimmelîcho*, MHG. *grimmelîche*, MDu. *grimmelike*, ON. *grimmliga*): see GRIM *a.* and -LY[2].]

1. In a grim fashion; with stern or cruel action, intention, or feelings; fiercely, cruelly; also, in mod. use, austerely, rigidly, uncompromisingly.

971 *Blickl. Hom.* 63 þam mannum sceolan þa deman grimlice styran. *a* **1000** *Martyrol.* (E.E.T.S.) 134 þa het se cyning þone hyra ealra grimlicost acwellan. *c* **1205** LAY. 1904 He..igrap hine bi þon gurdle & him grimliche heaf. *a* **1225** *Ancr. R.* 104 þi spus..spekeð swuð grimliche ȝif þu wendest vt. *a* **1300** *Cursor M.* 15832 Nu wit bastons þai him beft ful grimli to þe grund. *c* **1320** *Sir Tristr.* 2376 Vrgan to tristrem ran, And grimli þere þai gret. *c* **1400** *Destr. Troy* 10453 þes gird in full grymli with a grete ost. **1618** BOLTON *Florus* (1636) 261 How grimly they fought, the event sheweth. **1767** JAGO *Edge-Hill* IV. 493 Now Death, with hasty Stride, stalks o'er the Field, Grimly exulting in the bloody Fray. **1871** R. ELLIS *Catullus* lxiv. 355 So..shall.. Achilles, Charge Troy's children afield and fell them grimly with iron. **1881** FOWLER *Bacon* 198 Both of them [Bacon and Luther] were grimly in earnest.

†**2.** Dreadfully, frightfully, shockingly, terribly.

c **1200** ORMIN 4494 Baþe gilltenn grimmeliȝ. *a* **1240** *Ureisun* in *Cott. Hom.* 187 Mine sunnen habbeþ grimliche iwreþed me. *a* **1310** in Wright *Lyric P.* 112 His grene wounde so grimly conne blede. **13..** *E.E. Allit. P.* B. 1534 þer apered a paume..þat was grysly & gret, & grymly he wrytes. *c* **1420** *Anturs of Arth.* 163 (Thornton MS.), Nowe I am a grisely gaste, and grymly grane. **1460** *Lybeaus Disc.* 1632 Whan they togydere mette, Ayder yn other scheld hytte, Strokes grymly greete. *c* **1470** HENRY *Wallace* VII. 460 Sum grymly gret, quhill thar lyff dayes war gayne.

3. With a grim look or air: **a.** of persons.

1340 HAMPOLE *Pr. Consc.* 2226 Als wode lyons thai [the devils] sal than fare..And grymly gryn on hym and blere. *c* **1400** *Melayne* 1398 He hade no worde to speke agayne, Bot grymly stude lukande. **1450–70** *Golagros & Gaw.* 558 Gaudifeir and Galiot, in glemand steil wedis,..grymly thai ride. *c* **1489** CAXTON *Sonnes of Aymon* ii. 61 He loked grymly and fyersly in his vysage for grete wrath. **1535** COVERDALE *Esther* xv. 7 He lift vp his face..and loked grymly vpon her. **1606** SHAKS. *Ant. & Cl.* IV. xii. 5 The Auguries..looke grimly, And dare not speake their knowledge. **1635–56** COWLEY *Davideis* III. 23 Th' uncircumcis'd smil'd grimly with disdain. **1725** POPE *Odyss.* XXII. 39 Grimly frowning with a dreadful look. **1836** W. IRVING *Astoria* III. 243 The Indian warriors..shook their heads grimly. **1848** C. BRONTE *J. Eyre* xii. (1873) 115 [He] sprang to his saddle; grimacing grimly as he made the effort. **1856** MASSON *Ess.* vi. 235 That hard, austere man of letters..who receives you so grimly, [etc.].

b. *transf.* of things.

1602 MARSTON *Antonio's Rev.* IV. iii. Wks. 1856 I. 122 Death, hel more grimly stare Within my heart, then in your threatning browes. **1611** SHAKS. *Wint. T.* III. iii. 3 The skies looke grimly, And threaten present blusters. **1819** BYRON *Juan* II. xlix, The night..grimly darkled o'er the faces pale. **1870** BRYANT *Iliad* VI. I. 206 The horse-hair plume That grimly nodded from the lofty crest. **1890** *Times* 31 Jan. 9/2 Symbol of a grimly unsuccessful country.

c. So as to produce a grim appearance. *rare.*

?*a* **1366** CHAUCER *Rom. Rose* 161 Hir heed y-writhen was, y-wis, Ful grimly with a greet towayle. **1824** W. IRVING *T. Trav.* I. 45 The grimly painted portrait of her poor dear man. **1895** SIR H. MAXWELL *Duke of Brit.* i. 11 The faces of most were grimly tattooed.

grimm(e (grɪm). [a. F. *grimme* (Buffon 1764), ad. mod.L. (*Capra*) *grimmia*, the name given by Linnæus to a South-African antelope described by Herm. Nic. Grimm (1641–1711). The application to the coquetoon is due to misunderstanding.] A West-African antelope, the coquetoon.

1834 *Penny Cycl.* II. 82/1 The original grimm was brought from the Cape of Good Hope;..the animal at present under consideration..is an inhabitant of Sierra Leone and the coast of Guinea. **1855** OGILVIE, Suppl., *Grimm*, a species of antelope (*A. grimmia*). **1897** WEBSTER, *Grimme.*

[**grimmer:** spurious word in Dicts., arising from mistaken form of GIMMER.]

grimmish ('grɪmɪʃ), *a.* [f. GRIM *a.* + -ISH.] Somewhat grim.

1864 CARLYLE *Fredk. Gt.* IV. 142 A grimmish feeling against the Saxons. **1876** G. MEREDITH *Beauch. Career* II. iii. 40 The grimmish slyness of his uncle Everard's conspiracy.

Grimm's law: see LAW *sb.*[1] 17 c (*c*).

grimness ('grɪmnɪs). [f. GRIM *a.* + -NESS.] The quality or condition of being grim; fierceness; sternness; formidable aspect.

971 *Blickl. Hom.* 55 He [the devil] wile hit him mid grimnesse & mid yfele eall forȝyldan. *a* **1000** *Guthlac* 550 (Gr.) Cwædon cearfulle Criste laðe to Guðlace mid grimnysse. *c* **1050** *Voc.* in Wr.-Wülcker 341/8 *Atrocitas*, grimnes. *c* **1386** CHAUCER *Parson's T.* ¶790 (Ellesm. MS.) They shul han..sharpe hunger and thurst and grymnesse [*v.r.* grislines, grymlynesse] of deueles. *c* **1440** *Promp. Parv.* 212/2 Grymnesse, or horrybylnesse. **1563** GOLDING *Cæsar* I. (1565) 29 b, They were not able to abyde the grymnesse of their countenaunces. **1619** BP. J. KING *Thanksgiv. Serm.* 26 The grimness of her visage disguised, yet will it be fearefull enough. **1670** MILTON *Hist. Eng.* II. Wks. (1851) 60 That in the grimness of Death they might seem to eat their own flesh. **1787** GLOVER *Athenaid* XXX. 284 Whose ravell'd brow, and countenance of gloom, Present a lion's grimness. **1837** CARLYLE *Fr. Rev.* I. IV. iv, A sardonic grimness lies in that irreverend Reverence of Autun.

‖**grimoire** (grimwar). [Fr.; altered f. *grammaire* GRAMMAR.] A magician's manual for invoking demons, etc.

1849 W. H. AINSWORTH *Lancashire Witches* III. III. v. 201 A witch with a Bible! It should be a grimoire. **1891** A. E. WAITE *Occult Sciences* 55 The most noticeable feature of the Grimoires..is their utter futility. **1902** *Daily Chron.* 9 July 3/2 A monstrous brood of 'grimoires' and 'clavicles'. **1923** *Blackw. Mag.* Aug. 153/2 The curé's argument almost legitimised the *grimoire* as a commentary on the Bible. **1926** *Chambers's Jrnl.* July 460/1 The *grimoires* of the Middle Ages. **1945** M. SUMMERS *Witchcraft & Black Magic* v. 133 *The Grimoire of Pope Honorius* is pretended to be found in manuscript as early as the thirteenth century. **1967** *Punch* 6 Dec. 854/1 One could fill a library with grimoires, ghost stories, studies of occult phenomena.

grimp (grɪmp), *v. rare.* [ad. F. *grimper* to climb.] †**a.** *trans.* To cause to mount; to elevate, haul *up* (*obs.*). **b.** *intr.* To clamber, climb.

1684 *Bucaniers Amer.* II. (ed. 2) 13 Lolonois and his companions, not being able to grimp up the Baskets of Earth, were compelled to make use of an old stratagem. **1893** G. ALLEN *Scallywag* I. 44 How the little beasts grimp..such plucky little creatures, and so strong for their size!

grimpen ('grɪmpən). [Etym. uncertain.] ? A marshy area.

1902 A. CONAN DOYLE *Hound of Baskervilles* vii. 153 Life has become like that great Grimpen Mire, with little green patches everywhere into which one may sink and with no guide to point the track. **1940** T. S. ELIOT *East Coker* ii. 10 In a dark wood, in a bramble, On the edge of a grimpen, where is no secure foothold. **1968** W. S. BARING-GOULD *Annotated Sherlock Holmes* II. xxxvi. 47 As is well known, Watson's 'Great Grimpen Mire' is *Grimspound Bog*, three miles to the north and west of Widecombe-in-the-Moor.

†'**grimsir(e.** *Obs.* [f. GRIM *a.* + SIR, SIRE.] An austere, stern, morose or overbearing person.

[**1450–70** *Golagros & Gaw.* 86 With that come girdand in greif ane woundir grym sire.] *c* **1450** *Cov. Myst.* (Shaks. Soc.) 69 A grym-syre at domysday xal he be. **1601** HOLLAND *Pliny* II. 297 Tiberius Cæsar..was knowne for a grim sir, and the most unsociable..man in the world. **1603** FLORIO *Montaigne* III. v. (1632) 476 The Goddesse..with soft embrace, Of snow white arme, the grim-sire doth enchase. **1621** BURTON *Anat. Mel.* III. iii. I. ii, I have an old grim sire to my husband.

Grimston ('grɪmstən). The name of several towns and villages in eastern England (*spec.* Hanging Grimston, Yorks.), used *attrib.* to designate archæological remains found there, as ***Grimston ware***. Also **Grimston hybrid** (see quot. 1960).

1954 S. PIGGOTT *Neolithic Cultures* iv. 114 Fine carinated bowls typified by those from the Hanging Grimston long barrow..which may conveniently be called *Grimston ware*. **1960** P. H. REANEY *Orig. Eng. Place-Names* vii. 170 'Grimston hybrid' is a convenient term for place-names consisting of a Scandinavian personal-name compounded with OE *-tūn*, of which Grimston is particularly common. It derives from ON *Grímr*, ODa *Grim*.

Grim the Collier. [The name of a character in an Elizabethan play (modernized as 'Grim the Collier of Croydon' 1662).] A species of hawk-weed (*Hieracium aurantiacum*).

1629 PARKINSON *Paradisi* lxv. (1656) 300 The fittest English name we can give it, is Golden Mouse-eare..for the name of Grim the Collier, whereby it is called of many, is both idle and foolish. **1633** JOHNSON *Gerarde's Herbal* II. xxxvi. 305 Women, who keep it in gardens for noueltie sake, haue named it Grim the Colliar. **1713** J. PETIVER in *Phil. Trans.* XXVIII. 36 Golden Mousear, or Grim the Collier.

Grimthorpe ('grɪmθɔːp), *v.* [f. the name of Sir Edmund Beckett, first Lord *Grimthorpe* (1816–1905), whose restoration of St. Albans Cathedral, completed in 1904, aroused fierce criticism and controversy.] *trans.* To restore (an ancient building) with lavish expenditure rather than skill and fine taste.

1890 *Antiquary* Jan. 34 To this a keen and well-known Yorkshire ecclesiologist replied: 'Heaven forbid! the building might be grimthorped!' **1892** *Athenæum* 23 July 138/2 St. Albans and other great national fabrics that have been 'Grimthorped'. **1900** *Ibid.* 28 July 129/2 This is indeed grimthorping with a vengeance. **1909** *Daily Chron.* 9 July 6/6 The parish church, which despite of vigorous 'grimthorping' still shows a trace of its old Norman architecture.

grimy ('graɪmɪ), *a.* [f. GRIME *sb.* + -Y[1]; cf. Flem. *grijmig*.] **a.** Covered with grime; begrimed, black, dirty. Also, dark-complexioned, swarthy.

App. not in literary use during the 18th c. (cf. quot. 1848); Todd (1818) cites it from H. More.

1612 W. PARKES *Curtaine-Dr.* (1876) 62 Vulcan vowing in his grymy breast, His wiues dishonour shall inrich his chest. **1630** *Tinker of Turvey* 12 Grimy face, all smutted ore, His tann'd hide tough as wild boare. **1642** H. MORE *Song of Soul* I. III. vi, Foure grisly black-smiths..with stern grimy look do still avise Upon their works. **1840** DICKENS *Barn. Rudge* xxxvii, In his grimy hands he held a knotted stick. **1848** DE QUINCEY *Sortilege & Astrol.* Wks. 1890 XIII. 262 He returned; looking more lugubrious than ever—more grim—more grimy (if *grime* yields any such adjective). **1883** *Longm. Mag.* July 256 Most frequently the grimiest families are not the poorest.

Comb. **1861** SMILES *Engineers* (1862) III. 12 The keel is a tubby grimy looking craft.

b. *fig.* Unpleasant, mean. (Cf. quot. 1848 above.)

1833 DICKENS *Let.* ? 15 Apr. (1965) I. 19 The machinery is finished,..the Orchestra complete—and the manager *grimy*. **1834** —— *Let.* 3 Sept. (1965) I. 41 The grimy monotony of my every-day life. **1946** MEZZROW & WOLFE *Really Blues* 374 *Grimy*, sour, unpleasant.

grin, *sb.*[1] Forms: α. 1, 3–7, 9 **grin**, 1, 4–5, 9 **gryn**, 2–3 grun, 4 grine, 4–5 gryne, (5 grynde), 5–6 **grynne**, (6 grynn), 6 **grinne**, 7 **grinn**. β. 3–5 **grene**, 4–5 greene. γ. 4–6 **grenne**, 6 gren. [OE. *grin*, *gryn* fem. and neut. (also *giren* in *Vesp. Ps.*, cf. GIRN *sb.*[1]).

The evidence of metre seems to show that there were two distinct OE. forms, *grīn* neut. (pl. *grīnu*) and *grin* fem.; but the ME. and mod.E. words descend exclusively from the form with short vowel. The form *grīn*, standing alone, might be cogn. with GRANE and YARN, but the existence of a form with *ī* can hardly be reconciled with this.]

1. A snare for catching birds or animals, made of cord, hair, wire, or the like, with a running noose. *Obs.* exc. *dial.* or *arch.*

In the Bible of 1611 *grin* is found in certain passages (*Job* xviii. 9, *Ps.* cxl. 5, cxli, 9) where mod. edd. read *gin*. The altered reading is found in an edition printed at Cambridge in 1762; Cruden's *Conc.* 1737–69 retains the original reading.

α. *c* **825** *Vesp. Psalter* ix. 16 In grin ðissum..ȝegripen is fot heara. *c* **1000** *Ags. Ps.* (Th.) lxv. 10 þu us on grame..gryne gelæddest. *Ibid.* xc. 3 He me alysde of laðum grine. *c* **1200** *Trin. Coll. Hom.* 209 Ure fo fareð on hunteð and leið grune in a wilderne to henten þe deor þe wunieð þerinne. *a* **1225** *St. Marher.* 3 þe fuhel þe is fon i þe fuheleres grune. *a* **1250** *Owl & Night.* 1057 Thu were i-nime in one grine. **1398** TREVISA *Barth. De P.R.* xiv. lii. (Tollem. MS.), Also fouleres hiden ofte here grynnes [**1535** grennes] and here nettes. *c* **1440** *Jacob's Well* (E.E.T.S.) 250 Whanne a sparowe is takyn in a grynde. **1481** CAXTON *Reynard* (Arb.) 21 The preest..had sette a gryn..for he wold fayn haue take the foxe. **1579** TWYNE *Phisicke agst. Fort.* I. xc. 112 b, So doth the foule flie safe betweene the line and the grin. **1630** J. TAYLOR (Water P.) *Praise Hempseed* Wks. III. 64/2 All sorts of faire fowle.. Are with ingenuous jins, grins, nets and snares..oft taken vnwares. **1652** TRAPP *Comm. Esther* vii. 8 Made to stand upon snares or grinnes with iron teeth. **1671** M. BRUCE *Good News in Evil Times* (1708) 39 The Grins and Snares laid for them. **1879** MISS JACKSON *Shropsh. Word-bk.*, *Grin*, a snare, as for a hare or rabbit. **1894** F. S. ELLIS *Reynard* 58 The poor trapped beast At last broke from the gryn.

β. **1382** WYCLIF *Ps.* cxxxix. [cxl.] 5 Proude men hidden a grene to me. And cordis thei straȝten out in to a grene; by side the weie sclaunder thei putten to me. —— *Prov.* vii. 23 As if a brid heeȝe to the grene. **1387** TREVISA *Higden* (Rolls) II. 385 Maydens of Athene were compelled as it were to snarles and grenes [*printed* greues]. *c* **1420** *Pallad. on Husb.* IV. 164 A green another hath for hem [moles] ytilde: To take hem therwithal is not vnlike. **14..** *Voc.* in Wr.-Wülcker 591/42 *Laqueus*, a lace, a grene.

γ. *a* **1380** *Virg. Antioch* 360 in Horstm. *Altengl. Leg.* (1878) 31 Out of þat hous, as brid fro gren, Heo fleih awei and scaped þen. **1399** LANGL. *Rich. Redeles* II. 188 Lymed leues were leyde all abouȝte..With grennes of good heere. **1480** CAXTON *Chron. Eng.* ccxxviii. 239 He shal be hold and teyde with a grenne. **1549–62** STERNHOLD & H. *Ps.* cxxiv. 331 Euen as the bird out of the foulers grenne [*rimes with* then, men]. **1580** HOLLYBAND *Treas. Fr. Tong, Vn laqs*, a snare, a gren, a gin, a trap.

b. *fig.* or in fig. expressions.

c **1000** *Ags. Ps.* (Th.) xvii. 5 Deaðes grynu me ȝefengon. *c* **1200** *Trin. Coll. Hom.* 209 Liðere lahtres beð his grunen. **1340** *Ayenb.* 47 Hi ne heþ leme ine hire bodye þet ne is a gryn of þe dyeule. *c* **1450** tr. *De Imitatione* III. vii. 73 Bileue him not..þouȝ he ofte tymes tende to þe grynnes of deceite. **1529** MORE *Supplic. Souls* I. Wks. 313/2 Ye lyke good Christen people auoiding theyr false straines & grinnes, geue none eare to theyr haynous heresies. **1557** N. T. (Genev.) *Gal.* Argt., Men ought..not to haue their consciences snared into the grennes of mans traditions. **1610** G. FLETCHER *Christ's Vict.* II. xxix, Vnder that same baite a fearefull grin Was readie to intangle him in sinne. **1615** W. HULL *Mirr. Maiestie* 140 Rid me from fatall grins Of passions abused.

†**2. a.** A noose. **b.** A halter. *Obs.*

c **1000** *Ags. Gosp.* Matt. xxvii. 5 And he awearp þa scyllingas inon þæt templ & ferde & mid gryne [*v.r.* grine] hyne sylfne aheng. **1591** PERCIVALL *Sp. Dict., Dogal o cordel*, a cord, a rope,..a grin to hold a horse.

grin (grɪn), *sb.*[2] Also 8 grinn. [f. GRIN *v.*[2]; cf. GIRN *sb.*[2]] An act of grinning.

1635–56 COWLEY *Davideis* III. 564 He walks, and casts a deadly Grin about. *a* **1661** HOLYDAY *Juvenal* Pref. 3 A perpetual grin does rather anger than mend. **1711** ADDISON *Spect.* No. 173 ¶5 He shew'd twenty Teeth at a Grinn. *Ibid.*, They found he was Master only of the merry Grinn. **1718** LADY M. W. MONTAGU *Let. to Pope* Wks. 1837 II. 113 The French grin is equally remote from the chearful serenity of a smile, and the cordial mirth of an honest English horse-laugh. *a* **1729** CONGREVE *Of Pleasing* 30 Thersites..Attempts a Smile, and shocks you with a Grin. **1781** COWPER *Hope* 747 These move the censure and the illiberal grin Of fools that hate thee and delight in sin. **1818** MRS. SHELLEY *Frankenst.* xix. (1865) 231 A ghastly grin wrinkled his lips as he gazed on me. **1874** C. GEIKIE *Life in Woods* xviii. 310 He ended with a broad grin. **1884** SALA *Journ. due South* I. xxvi. (1887) 356 The gaunt hobbledehoy ..grinning a very unlovely grin.

transf. **1887** LOWELL *Old Eng. Dram.* (1892) 22 Like a belated masquerader going home under the broad grin of day.

b. ***on the*** (***broad*** or †***high***) ***grin***: grinning (openly and unmistakeably).

1738 SWIFT *Pol. Conversat.* i. 26 What! you would not have one be always on the high Grin. **1809** MALKIN *Gil Blas* I. viii. ¶3 They were all on the broad grin except myself. **1863** HAWTHORNE *Our Old Home* (1883) I. 283 A ring.. thickly gemmed around with faces, mostly on the broad grin. **1884** *Punch* 25 Oct. 196/2 He is perpetually on the grin.

grin, *v.*[1] *Obs.* exc. *dial.* Forms: 1 grinian, 4 grene, (9 green), 7, 9 grin. [f. GRIN *sb.*[1]; independently formed at different periods. Cf. GRANE *v.*] *trans.* To catch in a noose; to snare, ensnare; to choke, strangle.

a **850** *Kent. Glosses* in Wr.-Wülcker 59/9 *Inlaqueatus es*, ðu eart ȝegrinad. **1382** WYCLIF *Prov.* vii. 21 She grenede hym with manye woordis. —— *Isa.* viii. 15 Manye of hem shul.. ben to-brosid, and grened [Vulg. *irretientur*], and ben taken. *c* **1400** *Apol. Loll.* 51 It semiþ þat lewid men hiring prestis.. are grenid [*printed* greuid] in þe same synne. **1622** S. WARD *Woe to Drunkards* (1627) 18, I haue..heard of one that, hauing stolne a sheepe, and laying it downe vpon a stone to rest him, was grin'd and hang'd with the strugling of it about his necke. **1823** [see GRANE *v.*]. **1824** MACTAGGART *Gallovid. Encycl.*, *Grinning Hares*, the devilish art of setting gins..to hang hares. **1841** HARTSHORNE *Salop. Antiq.* 449 *Grin, v.*, to take hares or game by means of a running noose set in those particular parts of a hedge through which they are accustomed to pass. **1879** MISS JACKSON *Shropsh. Word-bk.*, *Grinned*, trapped in a 'grin'.

grin (grɪn), *v.*[2] Forms: *α.* 1 grennian, 3 grennen, 4–6 grenne, (5 grennyn), 6 gren. *β.* 4–5 gryn, 5–6 grynne, 7 grinne, 4– grin. [The OE. *grennian* (:—OTeut. type **granjôjan*) is cognate with OHG. *grennan* to mutter (MHG. *grennen* to grin):—OTeut. **granjan*; possibly related to **granâ* moustache. A root of identical form appears in OHG. *granôn* to grunt (MHG. *granen, grannen* to grunt, wail), ON. *grenja* to howl, OSw. *gränia* to roar, to gnash or show the teeth threateningly.

The mod.Eng. *grin* appears to be only a phonetic development, orig. northern, of the older *gren-* (cf. *glent* and *glint*, *hent* and *hint*), but it presents a remarkable contact of sense and form with a number of Teut. words belonging to a different ablaut-series: OHG. *grînan* str. vb. to distort the countenance, gnash the teeth, grin, weep profusely (MHG. *grînan*, mod.G. *greinen* wk.), mod.Du. *grijnen* (the mod.Icel. *grina* to stare, Sw. *grina*, Du. *grine* to grin, are perh. from LG.); further MHG. *grinnen* to gnash the teeth, MDu. *grinsen* (mod.Du. *grijnzen*), mod.G. *grinsen* to grin. There has probably been some associative influence between the two Teut. forms *gran-* and *grîn-*, the latter of which appears to be an extension of the root *gri-* of OE. *grima* mask. The vb. GIRN is a northern metathetic form of *grin*.]

1. *intr.* Of persons or animals: To draw back the lips and display the teeth:

a. generally, or as an indication of pain or †anger; † also ***to grin with the teeth***. Const. *at*, †*on*, †*upon*. Said also of the jaws or teeth.

a. a **1000** *Juliana* 596 He grennade and grisbitade. *a* **1050** *Liber Scintill.* lv. (1889) 172 Nelle þu grenniendum [L. *dissolutis*] welerum hleahter forðbringan. *a* **1225** *Ancr. R.* 212 Heo schulen ham sulf grennen & niuelen..iðe pine of helle. *c* **1290** *S. Eng. Leg.* I. 84/36 He grennede and femde touward hire. **13..** *Coer de L.* 3406 Lay every hed on a plater ..Upward hys vys, the teeth grennand. ? *a* **1366** CHAUCER *Rom. Rose* 156 Y-frounced foule was hir visage, And grenning for dispitous rage. *c* **1400** *Apoll. Loll.* 58 þe hound of wrechfulnes grenniþ wiþ his teþ. **1413** *Pilgr. Sowle* (Caxton) II. li. (1859) 53 This cruel Sathanas, that so fowle grenneth vppon me. *c* **1450** *Merlin* 667 The catte..grenned with his teth, and coveited the throte of the kynge. **1530** PALSGR. 574/2, I grenne, I make an yvell countenaunce, *je grongne*. **1539** BIBLE *Ps.* lix. 6 They grenne lyke a dogg. **1546** BALE *Eng. Votaries* II. (1550) 83 b, Grennyng vpon her lyke termagauntes in a playe. **1596** SPENSER *F.Q.* VI. xii. 27 And some of Tygres, that did seeme to gren And snar at all that ever passed by.

β. a **1300** *Cursor M.* 11878 (Gött.), He liftid vp his lathli chin, and felunli gan on þaim grin. **1340** HAMPOLE *Pr. Consc.* 7411 Ilk ane salle other hate dedly, And ilk ane gryn on other and cry. *c* **1400** *Rowland & O.* 1322 Whi grynnes thou nowe so one mee As thofe thou wolde mee byte? *c* **1450** *Mirour Saluacioun* 2630 Y[e] the Jewes..shuld..grynne on hym like beestes. **1592** SHAKS. *Ven. & Ad.* 460 As the wolfe doth grin before he barketh. **1596** SPENSER *F.Q.* V. iv. 37 Which when as Radigund there comming heard, Her heart for rage did grate, her teeth did grin. **1602** *2nd Pt. Return fr. Parnass.* V. iv. 2231 Nought can great Furor do, but barke and howle, And snarle and grin. **1629** GAULE *Holy Madn.* 210 Grinnes like a Dogge. **1697** DRYDEN *Æneid* VII. 927 The Teeth and gaping Jaws severely grin. **1713** ADDISON *Cato* IV. i. 52, I saw the hoary Traytor Grin in the Pangs of Death, and bite the Ground. *a* **1774** HARTE *Vision Death* 285 A skeleton..Whose loose teeth in their naked sockets shook, And grinn'd terrific. *c* **1800** H. K. WHITE *Gondoline* 258 The mouth it ghastly grinn'd. **1810** SCOTT *Lady of L.* I. xxvii, Here grins the wolf as when he died. **1840** LYTTON *Pilgr. Rhine* xi. 148 The Fox grinned with pain, and said nothing.

transf. and *fig.* **1447** BOKENHAM *Seyntys* (Horstm.) 23 My penne also gynnyth make obstacle..For I so ofte haue maad to grenne Hys snowte vp-on my thombys ende. *c* **1460** *Towneley Myst.* vii. 205 Then shall hell gape and gryn. **1647** SIR J. BIRKENHEAD *Assembly-man* in *Harl. Misc.* (1745) V. 97/1 His Sermon and Prayer grin at each other, the one is Presbyterian, the other Independent. **1698** FRYER *Acc. E. India & P.* 37 From this Point..a Dozen Guns more that grin upon Maderas.

b. by way of a forced or unnatural smile, or of the broad smile indicative of unrestrained or vulgar merriment, clownish embarrassment, stupid wonder or exultation, or the like. Const. *at*, *on*.

c **1480** *Yng. Childr. Bk.* 57 in *Babees Bk.*, Loke þou laughe not, nor grenne. *a* **1541** WYATT *Courtier's Life* 53 Grin when he laugheth. **1590** SPENSER *F.Q.* I. vi. 11 All..gently grenning, show a semblance glad To comfort her. **1621** WITHER *Motto* B 2 b, I cannot..grin When he causeles laughter doth begin. **1682** DRYDEN *Relig. Laici* Pref., Wks. (Globe) 190 The most saint-like of the party..grinned at it with a pious smile. **1742** YOUNG *Nt. Th.* VIII. 1311 Athens' fool Grinn'd from the port, on ev'ry sail his own. **1781** COWPER *Conversat.* 902 With rash and awkward force the chords he shakes And grins with wonder at the jar he makes. **1824** W. IRVING *T. Trav.* I. 285 They often grinned and capered with heavy hearts.

Phrase. **1840** DICKENS *Barn. Rudge* xxxix, He grinned from ear to ear at every word he said.

c. ***to grin for*** (a prize): in quot. in indirect passive. (Cf. GRINNING *vbl. sb.* b.)

1711 ADDISON *Spect.* No. 173 ¶2 A Gold Ring to be Grinn'd for by Men.

†**d.** quasi-*trans.* ***to grin the teeth***. *Obs.*

c **1430** *Syr Gener.* (Roxb.) 4916 He grenned his teth, and gan to swere. **1483** CAXTON *Gold. Leg.* 98 b/2 They wythsayde it in theyr hertes and grennyd theyr teeth ayenst hym. **1599** MINSHEU *Sp. Gram.* (1623) 8 Dogs, in grinning their teeth, when they would bite, sound this letter R. *a* **1700** DRYDEN *Cymon & Iphig.* 622 They neither could defend, nor can pursue; But grinn'd their teeth, and cast a helpless view.

e. with cognate object.

1667 MILTON *P.L.* II. 846 He [Satan] ceas'd, for both seemd highly pleasd, and Death Grinnd horrible a gastly smile. **1884** [see GRIN *sb.*[2]].

f. Of a coat of paint: to show *through* (an upper coat). Also used of other surfaces that exhibit gaps.

1854 A. E. BAKER *Gloss. Northants. Words* I. 291 You must undo your work, the stitches grin so. **1901** in *N. & Q.* 9th Ser. VIII. 225/2 The priming coat grins through the paint of the sashes. **1916** R. A. FREEMAN *Exploits of Danby Croker* vii. 145 When you have drilled the holes, you must put a drop of walnut stain in each, or else they 'grin'. **1966** *Times* 25 Apr. 13/1 Tufting can produce a wide range of fabric qualities,..though cheaper ones have a tendency to 'grin'.., that is, to show the backing through the all-too-sparse pile.

2. a. *trans.* To express by grinning.

1681 N. LEE in *Dryden's Wks.* 1701 III. p. vii, Even the Phanaticks..Bow in their own despite, and grin your Praise. **1732** LD. LANSDOWNE *Unnat. Flights Poetry* 62 He grins defiance at the gaping crowd. **1748** SMOLLETT *Rod. Rand.* (1812) I. 181 The surgeon grinned approbation. *a* **1822** SHELLEY *Devil* VI. 3 Grinning applause, he just showed them his claws. **1865** CARLYLE *Fredk. Gt.* XXI. iv. (1872) X. 13 You do not much mean this, Monsieur? You merely grin it from the teeth outward. **1894** *Outing* (U.S.) XXIV. 40/2 We grinned farewells.

b. *intr.* Of a feeling: To find expression by grinning. *nonce-use.*

1749 FIELDING *Tom Jones* XIV. x, The counterfeit Satisfaction which grinned in the features of the young one.

3. Phrases. ***to grin and abide, to grin and bear it***: to submit to one's fate with no other sign of impatience than a grin. ***to grin in a glass case*** (slang: see quot. 1785). ***to grin like a Cheshire cat*** (see CAT *sb.*[1] 13 f). ***to grin through a horse-collar*** (see HORSE-COLLAR).

1785 GROSE *Dict. Vulg. Tongue*, s.v., To grin in a glass case, to be anatomised for murder. **1794–6** E. DARWIN *Zoon.* (1802) II. 114 Thus we have a proverb where no help could be had in pain, 'to grin and abide'. *c* **1810** W. HICKEY *Mem.* (1960) viii. 132 Vexed at..the childishness of his behaviour, I answered, 'I recommend you to grin and bear it'—an expression used by sailors after a long continuance of bad weather. **1813** E. S. BARRETT *Heroine* III. xxxix. 151, I heard a sudden disturbance below; his lordship crying out 'Oh, what shall I do?' and Jerry bidding him 'grin and bear it'. **1859** GEO. ELIOT in M. Porter *Ann. Publishing House* (1898) III. ii. 51 'Adam Bede' flourishes, so I grins and bears it! **1870** MISS BRIDGMAN *Ro. Lynne* II. ix. 190, I must grin and bear it.

grinagog ('grɪnəgɒg). Now *dial.* Also 6 grinagod. [f. GRIN *v.*[2]; cf. *stareagog, turlygod.*] One who is always grinning.

1565 CALFHILL *Answ. Treat. Crosse* 45 Many of the diuels children, grinagods and such other. **1785** GROSE *Dict. Vulg. Tongue*, *Grinagog, the cat's unkle*, a foolish grinning fellow, one who grins without reason. *Mod.* (*Birmingham*) Stop your silly laughing, you grinagog!

grinch (grɪnʃ), *v.* [echoic; cf. F. *grincer.*] *intr.* To make a harsh grating noise.

1892 R. KIPLING *Barrack-r. Ballads* 126 It's woe to bend the stubborn back Above the grinching quern.

†**grinched**, *ppl. a.* *Obs. rare*[−1]. [? f. F. *grinche-r*, dial. form of *grincer* to gnash (the teeth) + -ED[1].] Of the teeth: Tightly closed, clenched.

1635 J. HAYWARD tr. *Biondi's Banish'd Virgin* 186 A long time hee lay motionlesse, with lither artirs, dead clouded eyes, grinched teeth, and grappled hands.

†**grincome.** *slang. Obs.* Also 7 grincam, -om, -um, grinkcome, grinkum. Also CRINKUM. Chiefly *pl.* A name for syphilis.

1608 MIDDLETON *Fam. Love* I. iii, 'A had a receipt for the grincomes in his hand. **1632** MARMION *Holland's Leaguer* IV. iii. Dram. Wks. (1875) 73, I have the grincums in my back. **1635** J. JONES *Adrasta* I. C 2, In a Nobleman 'tis abusive; no, in him the Sarpigo, in a Knight the Grincomes, in a Gentleman the Neopolitan scabb [etc.]. **1678** BUTLER *Hud.* III. i. 702 For Jealousie is but a kind Of Clap and Grincam of the Mind, The natural effect of Love.

grind (graɪnd), *sb.*[1] [f. GRIND *v.*[1] OE. had *ȝegrind* clashing of weapons.]

1. a. The action of grinding. *lit.* and *fig.*

c **1200** *Trin. Coll. Hom.* 183 Ðan þe sowle fundeð to faren ut of hire licame, hie..binimeð..toðen here grind, and tunge here speche. **1871** M. COLLINS *Mrq. & Merch.* I. vii. 218 Mud..churned into chaotic slush by..interminable grind of wheels. **1872** EARL PEMBROKE & G. H. KINGSLEY *S. Sea Bubbles* ix. 235, I felt a sudden shock, a terrible lurch, and long trembling grind. **1881** D. G. ROSSETTI *Bride's Prelude* Wks. 1886 I. 57 And cries I knew of hostile lords, And crash of spears and grind of swords. **1886** J. R. REES *Divers. Bk.-worm* ii. 61 One gets into an unnatural perspiration at the eternal grind of the barrel-organ.

†**b.** A set task of grinding. *Obs.*

1656 STANLEY *Hist. Philos.* IV. (1687) 151/2 The prison, where the common malefactors ground, and did their grind, and in pay of their labour, received two drachms.

c. *Cambridge.* (See quots. 1889 and 1950.)

1889 BARRÈRE & LELAND *Dict. Slang* I. 431/1 The ferry-boats at Chesterton, wound across by a winch and chain, 'to go over in the grind'. **1901** *Cambr. Rev.* 14 Nov. 76/1 Trinity Hall..had 50 yards to spare at the Red Grind. **1906** *Westm. Gaz.* 11 June 8/2 Besides Charon's, two other ferries—grinds, with chain from bank to bank. **1950** M. MARPLES *University Slang* 103 A chain-ferry at Chesterton near Cambridge was also known as the Grind, but it is not clear whether from its connection with walking or rowing, or from the effort required to operate it: later every ferry came to be so called.

d. The size of the particles of a powder, e.g. ground coffee.

1922 W. H. UKERS *All about Coffee* xxv. 401/1 A progressive coffee-packing house may have..a pulverizer for making a really fine grind. *Ibid.* 402/1 A mixture of a very fine with a coarse grind gives the best results in the cup. **1958** *Listener* 13 Feb. 299/1, I buy the grind [of coffee] I find suits my method of coffee-making best. *Ibid.* 299/2 The coarse grind [of coffee] gives the best results. **1959** *Gloss. Packaging Terms* (*B.S.I.*) 34 *Grind*, the size of the particles of which moulding powder is composed, generally graded according to the portions retained by different mesh sizes.

2. *colloq.* **a.** Steady hard work; labour of a monotonous kind, *esp.* close and hard study; an instance of this, a dull and laborious task.

1851 HALL *College Words*, *Grind*, an exaction; an oppressive action. Students speak of a very long lesson which they are required to learn, or of anything which is very unpleasant or difficult to perform as a *grind*. **1852** KINGSLEY in *Life* (1877) I. 349 We lost him [the fox] after sunset, after the fiercest grind I have had this nine years. **1857** HUGHES *Tom Brown* II. v, 'Come along, boys', cries East, always ready to leave the grind, as he called it. **1859** *Sat. Rev.* VII. 534/2 To a large proportion of students, both at our public schools and at the Universities, Latin and Greek are a mere grind. **1866** MRS. RIDDELL *Race for Wealth* II. xii. 250 Weary of the eternal work, of the everlasting grind, of the whirl of London life. **1884** H. SCOTT HOLLAND *Gd. Friday Addr.* 100 Poor women, slaving..to win..some few pennies by a long day's grind. **1887** T. B. REED *Dog with Bad Name* xix, 'Hadn't we better take overcoats?'..'Oh, no—they're a frightful grind to carry.'

b. (See quot. and cf. GRIND *v.* 8 b.)

1857 'C. BEDE' *Verdant Green* III. xi. 93 A medical student would have told him that a 'Grind' meant the reading up for an examination under the tuition of one who was familiarly termed 'a Grinder'—a process which Mr. Verdant Green's friends would phrase as 'Coaching' under 'a Coach'.

3. *Univ. slang.* **a.** A steeplechase; also, a walk taken for the sake of exercise, a 'constitutional'.

1857 'C. BEDE' *Verdant Green* III. xi. 93 To a University man, a Grind did not possess any reading signification, but a riding one. In fact, it was a steeple-chase, slightly varying in its details according to the college that patronised the pastime. **1860** *Slang Dict.* s.v., 'To take a grind' i.e. a walk, or constitutional, University. **1862** H. KINGSLEY *Ravenshoe* I. xiv. 173 The Christchurch grind had been slow, but the best that year. **1872** *Chamb. Jrnl.* 30 Mar. 194/2 The mighty gymnasiarch, the hero of a hundred 'grinds'. **1887** in M. Shearman *Athletics & Footb.* (Badm. Libr.) 41 It was the evening after the College Steeplechase (vulgarly called the 'College Grind'). **1896** GRAVES *Way abt. Oxfordsh.* 89 Just beyond, a turning to the left constitutes a part of the course of the famous 'Five miles grind' [A favourite walk at Oxford].

b. *U.S.* A hard student.

1893 W. K. POST *Harvard Stories* 11 Come now, old grind, do take a day off. **1896** in *Westm. Gaz.* 11 Aug. 8/1 He is neither a 'grind' nor a 'sport'. **1897** BARRÈRE & LELAND *Dict. Slang, Grind*,..a plodding student who keeps aloof from the usual sports and pastimes. **1908** R. L. DUNN *W. H. Taft* 210 He was keen to learn and if he had not been so lusty outside of the house, he would have been called a grind. **1951** S. LEWIS *World so Wide* viii. 90 He told himself that, with this conceited grind, there was no merit in even a boarding-house courtesy.

4. *slang.* (An act of) sexual intercourse. Also ***on the grind***.

1893 FARMER & HENLEY *Slang* III. 216/1 *On the grind*, said of incontinent persons of both sexes. Also of prostitutes. *c* **1912** D. H. LAWRENCE *Love among Haystacks* (1930) 26 'A good grind, eh?' said the tramp, nodding after the Fraülein. The men only half-understood him. **1969** J. WAINWRIGHT *Big Tickle* 112 A grind with a cheap scrubber?

5. The action of rotating the hips in a dance or the like. Cf. BUMP *sb.*[1] 1 f. *slang* (orig. *U.S.*).

1946, **1964** [see BUMP *sb.*[1] 1 f].

grind (grɪnd), *sb.*[2] *Orkney* and *Shetland dial.* [a. ON. (and Sw.) *grind* a barred gate.] 'A gate formed of horizontal bars, which enter at each end into hollows in two upright stakes, or in the adjoining walls' (Jam.).

1615 *Acts of Bailiary* in G. Barry *Orkney Isl.* (1805) 459 All grinds and slops on all highways shall be closed by all strangers that enter thereby. *a* **1733** *Shetland Acts* 6 in *Proc. Soc. Antiq. Scot.* (1892) XXVI. 197 That none big up accustomed grinds or passages through towns. **1814** SCOTT *Diary* 17 Aug. in *Lockhart*, The gates, or grinds, as they are here called, are usually of ship planks and timbers. **1845** *New Statist. Acc. Scot., Shetland* XV. 121 Every grind or gate is set open.

grind (graɪnd), *sb.*[3] *Naut.* [Origin obscure; cf. GRIND *v.*[3]; also *grinde*, obs. var. GROIN *sb.*[2]] 'A half-kink in a hempen cable' (Adm. Smyth).

1794 *Rigging & Seamanship* II. 288 A cable coiled against the sun will..have less grinds or kinks in it than a cable coiled with the sun.

‖**grind** (grɪnd), *sb.*[4] [Færöese; a single bottle-nose whale is called *grindahvalur*, whence Da. *grindehval*, Du. *grindewal*.

The word is commonly identified with *grind* gate, fence (GRIND *sb.*[2]), and is said to refer to the appearance presented by the school when swimming or resting on the surface of the sea. Others explain it as referring to the mode of capture, the whales being fenced or penned in by a line of boats.]

A collective term applied in the Færöes to the bottle-nose whale when it appears in large numbers. (App. used incorrectly in quot. 1883)

1883 *Fisheries Exhib. Catal.* 47 A Faroese 'Eight-man boat', fully equipped for the grind or chase of the..Bottle-nose Whale. **1885** *Sat. Rev.* 10 Oct. 475/1 The grind are not hunted out at sea like the larger whales. **1887** *Fisheries & Fish. Industries U.S.* (ed. Goode) II. 248 The fishermen of the Faroe Islands have been very successful in their captures ..of the 'grind-whale' or blackfish (*G*[*lobiocephalus*] *melas*). **1898** *Blackw. Mag.* Aug. 257 When the grind are sighted great excitement prevails throughout the islands.

grind (graɪnd), *v.*[1] Pa. t. and pple. **ground** (graʊnd). Forms: 1 **grindan**, 2–3 **grinden**, 4 **grynden**, (5 **-yn**), 4–5 **grynd**, 4–6 **grynde**, (6 **grynede?**), 5–7 **grynde**, 4– **grind**. 3 *sing. pres. ind.* 4 **grint**, **grynt**. *Pa. t.* 1–4 **grond**, (3 **gront?**), 6 **groond**, 7– **ground**; *pl.* 1 **grundon**, 3 **grunden**; also *weak* 6–9 **grinded**. *Pa. pple.* 4–5 **i-**, **ygrounde(n**, (4 **i-gronde**), **grownden**, (**-yn**, **-yne**), 4–6 **grounden**, (**-in**, **-yn**), **gronden**, (**-ine**, **-yn**), *Sc.* **grundin**, (**-yn**), 5–6 **grounde**, (6 **groond**, 7 **groune**, *Sc.* **grunde**), 6– **ground**; also *weak* 6–9 **grinded**, 7–8 **grounded**. [OE. *grindan* (*grǫnd*, *grundon*, **grunden*) str. vb. is cogn. w. Du. *grenden* (rare), *grinden* wk. vb. (cf. *grind*, *grint* sb., gravel, coarse meal); the pre-Teut. root **ghrendh-* is perh. represented in L. *frendĕre* to gnash the teeth, to bruise, pound. The word is wanting in the other Teut. langs., which have instead a verb cogn. with L. *molĕre*: see MEAL *sb.*]

1. *trans.* **a.** To reduce to small particles or powder by crushing between two hard surfaces; *esp.* to make (grain) into meal or flour in a mill. Freq. with adverbial or other complement denoting the result of the action, as *down*, *small*, *into dust*, *to pieces*, etc.

c **1000** ÆLFRIC *Gram.* (Z.) 168 *Molo*, ic grinde. *c* **1200** ORMIN 1486 þu..gaddresst swa þe clene corn..& grindesst itt, & cnedesst itt. *c* **1250** *Gen. & Ex.* 3339 To dust he it grunden and maden bread. **13..** *K. Alis.* 4431 (Laud MS.) Myllen miȝtten by þe blood Grynden corne as by þe flood. *c* **1374** CHAUCER *Former Age* 15 No man yit in the morter spices grond. *c* **1375** *Sc. Leg. Saints, Agatha* 94 It wes les maystry hard stanis to grynd..þane for to wryth agathis wil fra cryst. *c* **1420** *Pallad. on Husb.* I. 405 Lyme & grauel commixt ther on do glide, With marbul greet ygrounde & mixt with lyme. *c* **1450** *M.E. Med. Bk.* (Heinrich) 72 [Take] þe rote of horshelne & þe rote of comfyry..and grynde hem smale in a morter. **1568** in W. H. Turner *Select. Rec. Oxford* (1880) 326 Any corne or meale, ground or to be grynded. **1576** BAKER *Jewell of Health* 101 Lyme not quenched or slaked, joyned with the whites of egges, and grinded on a marble stone. **1613** PURCHAS *Pilgrimage* (1614) 650 They.. lay it [steeped millet] on a stone, and (as Painters their colours) grinde it with another stone, till it be dowe. **1662** H. STUBBE *Ind. Nectar* ii. 9 They grinded the nuts into a paste. **1697** DRYDEN *Virg. Georg.* II. 757 The Olives, ground in Mills, their Fatness boast. **1768** BOSWELL *Corsica* i. (ed. 2) 48 They even have them [chestnuts] grinded into flour. **1799** G. SMITH *Laboratory* I. 96 Grind them again, as painters do their colours. **1837** M. DONOVAN *Dom. Econ.* II. 345 The practice of keeping coffee roasted and ground.. seems to be injurious to its aroma. **1850** *Young's Patent* in *Law Times Rep.* X. 862/1 To each 100 gallons there is added 28lbs. of chalk, ground up with a little water into a thin paste. **1860** TYNDALL *Glac.* II. vii. 261 The glaciers..grind the mass beneath them to particles of all sizes.

b. Denoting the action of teeth, or apparatus having the same function; = to masticate. Also *fig.*

c **1200** *Trin. Coll. Hom.* 181 Teð hine grindeð. Tunge hine swoleȝeð. *a* **1225** *Ancr. R.* 70 þe two cheoken beoð þe two grinstones..Lokeð..þet ouwer cheoken ne grinden neuer bute soule uode. **1398** TREVISA *Barth. De P.R.* v. xx. (1495) 124 Quadrupli or keruers ben sharp in the endes and ben able to bruse and grynde harde metes. **1555** EDEN *Decades* 354 Foure teeth wherwith he eateth and gryndeth his meate. **1606** SHAKS. *Ant. & Cl.* III. v. 16 Then would thou hadst a paire of chaps no more, and throw betweene them all the food thou hast, they'le grinde the other. **1654** JER. TAYLOR *Real Pres.* 39 Christs flesh was sensually..to be handled by the Priests hands, to be broken and grinded by the teeth of the faithful. **1774** GOLDSM. *Nat. Hist.* (1776) VI. 382 The tortoise has..no teeth..only two bony ridges in the place, serrated and hard. These serve to gather and grind its food. **1836–9** TODD *Cycl. Anat.* II. 11/2 The three first stomachs being intended to macerate and grind it [food] down.

c. *transf.* and *fig.* (Cf. 2 and 3.)

1535 COVERDALE *Micah* iv. 13, I wil make thy horne yron, and thy clawes brasse, that thou mayest grynde [*A.V.* break in pieces] many people. **1583** BABINGTON *Commandm.* ix. (1637) 93 The denyall of it..grindeth his soule in sunder. **1587** FLEMING *Contn. Holinshed* III. 1354/1 He groond himselfe euen to his graue by mortification. **1640** FULLER *Joseph's Coat* 1 Cor. xi. 24 (1867) 58 All His bones were broken, that is, contrited and grinded with grief and sorrow. **1784** COWPER *Task* II. 362 He grinds divinity of other days Down into modern use. **1838** THIRLWALL *Greece* IV. xxviii. 30 It was..safer to let the Greeks grind each other down in a protracted conflict. **1842** TENNYSON *St. Sim. Styl.* 115 A grazing iron collar grinds my neck.

d. To force *out* by, or as by, grinding.

1790 J. B. MORETON *Mann. W. Ind.* 46 Describing the mill which grinds, or rather squeezes the juice out of the canes. **1801** NELSON in Nicolas *Disp.* (1846) VII. p. cciii, I went on board Sir Hyde this morning..I ground out something, but there was not that openness which I should have shown to my Second in Command.

e. *intr.* in quasi-passive sense, with adj. complement or adv.: To admit of being ground (fine, easily, etc.).

2. *fig.* **a.** (Cf. 1 c.) To crush, to oppress; to harass with exactions. Also with *down*, *to the dust*.

a **1626** BACON *Advice to Villiers* Wks. 1826 VI. 442 Some few merchants and tradesmen, under colour of furnishing the colony with necessaries, may not grind them so as shall always keep them in poverty. **1642** FULLER *Holy & Prof. St.* v. xix. 436 Much regretting that their Priviledges, Civil and Ecclesiasticall, were infringed, and they grinded with exactions against their Laws and Liberties. **1691** BAXTER *Nat. Ch.* xiii. 53 Landlords grinding their Poor Tenants. **1764** GOLDSM. *Trav.* 386 Laws grind the poor, and rich men rule the law. **1784** COWPER *Task* IV. 30 Is India free?..Or do we grind her still? **1833** HT. MARTINEAU *Manch. Strike* iii. 33 You are not the man to grind the poor. **1838** LYTTON *Leila* I. ii, Yet you suffer the Hebrews themselves..to be ground to the dust. **1872** YEATS *Growth Comm.* 249 By reforming the laws, and checking monopolies, he enabled the kingdom to pay its way without grinding the poor. **1883** S. C. HALL *Retrospect* II. 326 [He] had but one..excuse for grinding down the wretched peasantry.

b. In same sense: ***to grind the faces*** (occas. *face*) ***of***. A Hebraism.

1388 WYCLIF *Isa.* iii. 15 Whi al to-breken ȝe my puple, and grynden togidere the faces of pore men? **1608** BP. HALL *Recoll. Treat.* (1614) 609 They gave plentifull almes to the poore: wee in stead of filling their bellies, grinde their faces. **1659** HAMMOND *On Ps.* xcv. 5 When they oppress and grind the faces of the people and servants of God. **1791–1823** D'ISRAELI *Cur. Lit.* (1866) 306/1 Richelieu was grinding the face of the poor by exorbitant taxation. **1889** JESSOPP *Coming of Friars* ii. 88 The lord of the manor..might grind the faces of the poor while he ground their corn.

3. *fig.* **a.** To afflict, to torment; physically and mentally. Also *absol.* Now only *U.S.*, to annoy, vex.

absol. *c* **1350** *Med. MS.* in *Archæologia* XXX. 353 ȝif in mannys body vermys grynde Take mylfoly. **1610** SHAKS. *Temp.* IV. i. 259 Goe, charge my Goblins that they grinde their ioynts With dry Convultions. **1698** LISTER in *Phil. Trans.* XX. 246 A paining Grief towards the bottom of their Bellies, which did grind and torment them with Pain and Trouble. **1735** SOMERVILLE *Chase* III. 423 All the Pangs that grind thy Soul, In Rapture and in sweet Oblivion lost. **1879** HOWELLS *L. Aroostook* vii, After all, it does grind me to have lost that money!

b. *U.S.* (*College slang*). To satirize severely; make a jest of (*Cent. Dict.*).

c. *colloq.* To be a 'grind' (see GRIND *sb.*[1] 2) to, to fag.

1887 T. B. REED *Dog with Bad Name* xix, 'Will you come?' ..'I've never been up a mountain in winter before. We shall get a splendid view. Sure it won't grind you?'

4. To produce by grinding.

1382 WYCLIF *Isa.* xlvii. 2 Tac a grind ston, or queerne stoon, and grind me mele. *c* **1420** *Liber Cocorum* (1862) 14 Floure of ryce þou grynd also. **1535** COVERDALE *Isa.* xlvii. 2 Thou shalt bringe forth the querne, & grynede meel. **1624** HEYWOOD *Gunaik.* v. 255 There was meale that morning to be fetcht from the mill, which was grinded by that time. **1791** COWPER *Odyss.* xx. 145 With aching heart and trembling knees their meal Grinding continual. **1897** MRS. RAMSAY *Ev. Day Life Turkey* ii. 47 Each household grinds its own flour.

5. To wear down by friction so as to make sharp or smooth. **a.** To sharpen the edge or point of (a tool, a weapon). ***to have axes to grind***: see AXE *sb.*[1] 6. Also with complement, and ***up***.

13.. *K. Alis.* 5872 With his swerd, sharp y-grounde, He yaf many a dedly wounde. **1375** BARBOUR *Bruce* XII. 520 Axis that weill grundyn wer. *c* **1430** *Pilgr. Lyf Manhode* I. cxvii. (1869) 61 þe haubergeoun, which was of so strong a shap þat, for no wepene ygrounden, þer was neuere mayl ybroken. **1523** FITZHERB. *Husb.* §21 This hoke wolde be well steeled, and grounde sharpe. **1608** SHAKS. *Per.* I. ii. 58, I haue ground the Axe my selfe; Do you but strike the blowe. **1680** MOXON *Mech. Exerc.* xi. 193 The edges of these Flat Chissels are not ground to such a Basil as the Joyners Chissels are. **1697** DRYDEN *Virg. Georg.* III. 398 The bristled Boar..New grinds his arming Tusks. **1827** D. JOHNSON *Ind. Field Sports* 294 His tusks he is grinding to give us some play. **1840** DICKENS *Barn. Rudge* iv, I'll grind up all the tools.

fig. *c* **1586** C'TESS PEMBROKE *Ps.* LXIV. ii, For tongues they beare, not tongues, but swordes, So piercing sharp they have them ground. *c* **1600** SHAKS. *Sonn.* cx. 10 Mine appetite I neuer more will grin'de On newer proofe, to trie an older friend.

b. To smooth the surface of (glass, etc.) by friction. Also ***to grind in***: to smooth the surface of (a machine part) by moving it to and fro against the surface with which it is to fit or mate; *esp.* to make (a valve in a cylinder of an internal combustion engine) fit smoothly and tightly into its seat by rotating it to and fro against the seat with a suitable abrasive paste; occas. ***to grind*** (a valve) ***in*** or ***into*** or ***on to*** (its seat).

1641 FRENCH *Distill.* i. (1651) 6 The stopple of Glass ground very smooth. **1660** BOYLE *New Exp. Phys. Mech.* Proem 10 To the inward tapering Orifice of this Ring..are exquisitely ground the sides of the Brass stopple. **1678** BUTLER *Hud.* III. *Lady's Answ.* 229 How dull and rugged, ere 'tis ground And polish'd, looks a diamond? **1704** NEWTON *Opticks* I. (1721) 95 Good Workmen who can grind and polish Glasses truly spherical. **1832** G. R. PORTER *Porcelain & Gl.* 201 The labour bestowed in grinding and polishing their surfaces. **1837** WHITTOCK, etc. *Bk. Trades* (1842) 353 The Optician executes very little more of the work than fitting in the glasses, after these are grinded. **1888** *Sci. Amer.* 28 Apr. 258/2 To secure perfect smoothness in motion, each rack and pinion is 'ground in'. **1895** *Boy's Own Paper* XVII. 350/3 To make the valves fit tight you should grind them in their seating with a little fine emery and oil. **1903** R. J. MECREDY *Dict. Motoring* 281 New valves should also be ground on to their seatings. **1905** H. J. SPOONER *Motors & Motoring* 19 Grinding in valves is an operation that had better be left to the trained mechanic. **1916** J. E. HOMANS *Automobile Handbk.* xvii. 184 It is necessary in grinding a valve into its seat to place a ball of cotton waste.. into the port leading to the combustion space. **1924** A. W. JUDGE *Mod. Motor Cars* III. 297 It is usually necessary to grind in the valves whenever the cylinders are decarbonised. **1928** —— *Car Maintenance* 43 After replacing a ground-in valve. **1935** JELLEY & HARRISON *De Luxe Ford Handbk.* xii. 86 It is absolutely essential that each valve is ground into and assembled into the seat from which it was removed. *Ibid.* 87 It is always bad practice to grind in a badly pitted valve. **1950** A. W. JUDGE *Motor Vehicle Engine Servicing* iv. 55 The valve face..can readily be restored to its original condition by grinding with an abrasive paste on to its seating. **1962** 'S. ABBEY' *Motor-Car Maintenance* iv. 55 Sooner or later..it will be necessary to remove the cylinder head from the engine to allow.. the valves to be ground-in on their seatings. **1971** B. C. MACDONALD *Ford Cortina Repairs* i. 25 The next step is to grind-in the valves on their seats in the cylinder head.

fig. **1779** JOHNSON in *Boswell* 16 Apr., To be contradicted, in order to force you to talk, is mighty unpleasing. You shine, indeed; but it is by being ground.

†**c.** Used for: To file down (teeth). *Obs. rare.*

1625 BACON *Ess., Usury* (Arb.) 545 That the Tooth of Usurie be grinded, that it bite not too much.

6. a. *intr.* or *absol.* To perform the operation of grinding, esp. of preparing meal or flour from grain. Said also of a mill, etc.

c 950 *Lindisf. Gosp.* Matt. xxiv. 41 Tuu wif ȝegrundon on coernæ [*Rushw.* twa grindende æt cweorne]. *c* 1000 ÆLFRIC *Judg.* xvi. 21 þa Philistei..heton hine grindan æt hira handcwyrne. 1382 WYCLIF *Matt.* xxiv. 41 Two wymmen shulen be gryndynge in oo querne. *c* 1386 CHAUCER *Wife's Prol.* 389 Who so comth first to Mille, first grynt. *c* 1400 *Destr. Troy* 1604 Mylnes full mony, made for to grynde. *c* 1420 *Liber Cocorum* (1862) 27 Take persole, peletre an oyns, and grynde. 1625 BACON *Ess., Counsel* (Arb.) 321 But then it must be a Prudent King, such as is able to Grinde with a Hand-Mill. *a* 1632 G. HERBERT *Jacula Prudent.* 747 Gods Mill grinds slow but sure. 1671 MILTON *Samson* 35 To grind in Brazen Fetters under task With this Heav'n-gifted strength. 1825 J. NICHOLSON *Operat. Mechanic* 123 When one pair [of stones] only is wanted to grind. 1837 CARLYLE *Fr. Rev.* I. VII. vii, Millers shall grind, or do worse, while their millstones endure. 1846 LONGF. *Aphorisms fr. F. von Logau*, Though the mills of God grind slowly, yet they grind exceeding small.

b. *trans.* To work (a handmill) so as to grind meal, etc. In vulgar phrase ***to grind the coffee mill***: to imitate with the hand the action of grinding, by way of contempt (cf. GRINDER 8).

1894 J. T. FOWLER *Adamnan* Introd. 58 And at supper time each..used to grind the quern, but an angel ground for Colum-cille.

7. a. *intr.* To work as if grinding with a hand-mill; hence, to turn the handle of a barrel-organ.

1840 DICKENS *Old C. Shop* xviii, Meanwhile the dog in disgrace ground hard at the organ. 1866 [see BARREL-ORGAN]. 1872 CALVERLEY *Fly Leaves, On hearing an organ*, Tell me, Grinder, if thou grindest Always, always, out of tune. 1887 JESSOPP *Arcady* viii. 235 A half-starved organ grinder comes and delights my heart by grinding for half an hour.

b. quasi-*trans.* To produce (music) on a hurdy-gurdy or barrel-organ. Also with *out.*

1784 R. BAGE *Barham Downs* II. 197 One grinds music upon—I forget the name of the instrument; it is common enough in London. 1805 *European Mag.* XLVII. 256 Do, my good girls, grind me a pennyworth more of your music. 1868 HELPS *Realmah* xvii. (1869) 468 The polka which the organ-man was grinding out. 1883 *Eng. Illustr. Mag.* Nov. 91/1 Like a delicious tune ground too often on a barrel-organ.

8. *intr.* **a.** To work laboriously and steadily; to toil away at some monotonous task; *esp.* to study hard. Const. *at.* Also with *away, on.*

1855 BROWNING *Grammar. Funeral* 126 So, with the throttling hands of death at strife, Ground he at grammar. 1857 HUGHES *Tom Brown* II. iii. (1871) 260 What's the good of grinding on at this rate? 1872 *Chamb. Jrnl.* 30 Mar. 195/2 Whereas our fellows grind on the river, or in the gymnasium, at the very crisis of the mind. 1881 S. R. HOLE *Nice* i. 2 How often I thought of them when I was grinding at my Latin verses.

b. To ride in a steeplechase. (Cf. GRIND *sb.* 3.)

1857 LAWRENCE *Guy Livingst.* iii. 17 They..would grind over the Vale of the Evenlode..as gaily.. as over the Bullingdon hurdles.

c. To work hard at a subject of study under the direction of a tutor or 'grinder'.

1835 E. FORBES in Wilson & Geikie *Mem.* vi. 176, I am obliged to 'grind'..that is, undergo a private examination with an authorized teacher or tutor. 1849 BEHREND *Let.* in *N. & Q.* Ser. VIII. VII. 183, I was the only man of the 14 who had not been grinding in London, and one poor fellow was rejected who had been two sessions with a grinder. 1861 ALB. SMITH *Med. Student* 51 Jones himself has never paid, though he has been grinding some years. 1870 LOWELL *Among my Bks.* Ser. I. (1873) 308 After grinding with private-tutor Mylius the requisite time, Lessing entered the school of Camenz.

d. *trans.* To teach (a subject) in a steady laborious manner; also, to prepare (a pupil) in a subject.

1815 [see GRINDING *vbl. sb.*]. 1848 THACKERAY *Van. Fair* lvi, A pack of humbugs and quacks that weren't fit to get their living but by grinding Latin and Greek. 1859 WILSON & GEIKIE *Mem. E. Forbes* vi. 180 [Dr. Bennett] undertook to grind him in anatomy and physiology.

9. a. *intr.* To scrape or rub *on* or *against* something; to make a grating noise. Also, to work *into* or *through* by means of pressure and friction. Also with adv.

a 1000 *Riddles* (Exeter Bk.) xxxiii, Ic seah searo hweorfan, grindan wið greote, ȝiellende faran. *a* 1225 *Juliana* 56 (Royal MS.) Grisen him mahen þet sehen hu hit [a wheel] grond [*Bodl. MS.* gront] in hwet so hit rahte. 13.. *E.E. Allit. P.* A. 81 þe grauayl þat on grounde con grynde Wern precious perleȝ of oryente. *c* 1350 *Will. Palerne* 1242 þurth scheld & scholder þe sharpe spere grint. *Ibid.* 3443 þurth helm & hed hastili to þe brest it grint. 1781 ARCHER in *Nav. Chron.* XI. 291 Our poor Ship grinding, and crying out at every stroke. 1837 HT. MARTINEAU *Soc. Amer.* II. 26 We went aground, —grinding, grinding, till the ship trembled in every timber. 1855 TENNYSON *Maud* I. i. 42 The villainous centre-bits Grind on the wakeful ear in the hush of the moonless nights. 1856 KANE *Arctic Expl.* I. vii. 68 How gallantly her broken rocks have protected us from the rolling masses of ice that grind by her. 1924 GALSWORTHY *White Monkey* I. iii, A taxicab ground up.

b. *trans.* To rub (one thing) gratingly *against* or *upon* (another); to force *into* by grinding; also quasi-*trans.* to make (one's way) by grinding.

1644 DIGBY *Nat. Bodies* (1645) 343 He used to grind his hands against the walls..in so much, that they would run with blood. 1805 WORDSW. *Waggoner* III. 94 Yet here are we ..Grinding through rough and smooth our way. 1820 KEATS *Hyperion* II. 51 Upon the flint He ground severe his skull. 1837 T. HOOK *Jack Brag* xii, They ground their way, instep deep, over the shingles. 1873 *Sunday Mag.* Feb. 340 He..ground his heel into it as if it had been a viper.

10. †**a.** *intr.* To gnash *with the teeth.* Const. *at*

c 1000 *Ags. Ps.* (Spelman) xxxiv. [xxxv.] 19 [16] Hi grundon ofer me mid toðum heard. *c* 1340 *Cursor M.* 19434 (Trin.) Whenne he had hem tolde þe soþe þei bigon to grynde wiþ toþe. 1563-87 FOXE *A. & M.* (1596) 44/1 The Gentiles grinded and gnashed at the Christians with their teeth. 1581 *Confer.* I. (1584) F iv, The Deane of Paules.. grinded with his teeth for despite.

b. *trans.* To rub (the teeth) together with a grating sound. Const. *at.*

c 1340 [see GRINDING *vbl. sb.*] 1573 GOLDING *Calvin's Job* vii. 32 They that taste not of the mercie and grace that God sheweth to men, when he afflicteth them, must nedes grynd their teeth at him. 1697 DRYDEN *Virg. Georg.* III. 766 He grinds his Teeth In his own Flesh. 1761 SMOLLETT *Gil Blas* I. x. (1782) I. 53, I..grinded my teeth. 1820 SCOTT *Monast.* xxi, The knight changed colour and grinded his teeth with rage. 1865 KINGSLEY *Herew.* xix. 244 Hereward ground his teeth.

c. ***to grind out***: to utter (an oath or the like) while grinding the teeth.

1889 'ROLF BOLDREWOOD' *Robbery under Arms* xxix, He ground out a red-hot curse betwixt his teeth.

11. *intr.* and *trans.* To copulate (with). Hence **'grinding** *vbl. sb. slang.*

[1598 FLORIO *Worlde of Wordes* 210/2 *Macinio*, the grinding or greest. Also taken for carnall copulation.] 1647 *Ladies Parliament* sig. C 2, Digbies Lady takes it ill, that her Lord grinds not at her mill. 1811 *Lex. Balatronicum, To grind*, to have carnal knowledge of a woman. 1879-80 *Pearl* (1970) 258 A married man grinding another man's wife. 1928 D. H. LAWRENCE *Lady Chatterley* xiv. 243 She had to work the thing herself, grind her own coffee. 1966 I. JEFFERIES *House Surgeon* ix. 162 Rob, what do you think about grinding..? I know it's time-wasting but it's so difficult to do without it.

12. *Comb.*, as †**grind-jest** *a.*, that grinds a jest; **grind-organ**, a barrel-organ.

1598 E. GUILPIN *Skial.* (1878) 66 As soone disioynt His grind-iest chaps as hurt our credites. 1888 *Pall Mall G.* 9 Apr. 2/1 There was at Torquay the usual man with the grind-organ.

†**grind**, *v.*[2] *Obs.* In 4 (*Kentish*) **grend(en.** [OE. *gryndan* = OHG. *grunden*, MHG., G. *gründen*:—**grundjan*, f. *grund* GROUND *sb.*] *intr.* Of the sun, etc.: To set, go down.

c 1050 *Voc.* in Wr.-Wülcker 389/37 *Descendens*, gryndende. *c* 1315 SHOREHAM 137 The sonne and monne and many sterren By easte aryseth..By weste hy grendeth.. And cometh aȝen ther hy a-ryse.

grind, *v.*[3] *Naut.* [Cf. GRIND *sb.*[3]] (See quot.)

1794 *Rigging & Seamanship* II. 288 A cable generally grinds or kinks from more turns being forced into it..than it had when first made.

grindability (graɪndə'bɪlɪtɪ). [f. GRIND *v.*[1] + ABILITY.] The extent to which a material is readily ground or pulverized; susceptibility to grinding.

1932 *Trans. Amer. Soc. Mech. Engineers* LIV. Fuels & Steam Power 37/1 If accurate knowledge of the grindability and abrasive qualities of the coal could be determined..it would be of considerable help to the coal buyer. 1950 J. H. PERRY *Chem. Engineers' Handbk.* (ed. 3) XVI. 1114/2 In the case of grinding to No. 48 sieve fineness, values of 0·304 and 9·26 are reported as the grindabilities for petroleum coke and graphite, respectively. 1958 *Engineering* 21 Mar. 375/2 Investigations in the field of coke testing, coal 'grindability', and petrographical work. 1965 G. J. WILLIAMS *Econ. Geol. N.Z.* xvi. 245/1 Where possible the species of diatoms are named in this section as the shape affects the grindability of the material.

'grindable, *a. rare.* [f. GRIND *v.*[1] + -ABLE.] Capable of being ground.

1652 *Munim. Burgh Irvine* (1891) II. 75 The rest of all corns grindable. 1659 TORRIANO, *Macinabile*, grindable.

grinde, obs. form of GROIN *sb.*[2]

grinded ('graɪndɪd), *ppl. a.* [f. GRIND *v.*[1] + -ED[1].] = GROUND *ppl. a.*, in various senses.

1613 HAYWARD *Norm. Kings* 111 Many bagges of grinded gold were drawen out of riuers, wherein the Bishop had caused them for a time to be buried. 1624 QUARLES *Div. Poems, Job* vi. 37 The grinded Pris'ner heares not [there] the noyse, Nor harder threatnings of th' Oppressors voyce. 1661 LOVELL *Hist. Anim. & Min.* 150 Young Ducks fed with grinded malt are of good nourishment. 1697 DRYDEN *Virg. Georg.* I. 360 Let him..grinded Grain betwixt two Marbles turn. 1831 LYTTON *Godolph.* xv. 25 Instead of providing..for the amusement of the grinded labourer. 1841 —— *Nt. & Morn.* (1851) 141 He drew the words out, one by one, through his grinded teeth. 1867 MORRIS *Jason* xvi. 9 And every man had ready to his hand Sharp spear, and painted shield, and grinded sword.

†**'grinded**, *ppl. a.*[2] *Obs.* [f. *grind*, obs. form of GROIN *sb.*[3] + -ED[2].] = GROINED. Cf. *cross-grinded.*

1715 LEONI *Palladio's Archit.* (1721) I. 42 There are six different forms of Arches, viz., cross'd, flat, faciated, round, grinded [It. *a lunette*], and shell-like..The two last are but of a modern invention.

†**'grindel**, *a. Obs.* In 4 **gryndel.** [Of unknown origin; cf. ON. *grimd* fierceness, f. *grimm-r* GRIM *a.*] Fierce; angry.

13.. *E.E. Allit. P.* C. 524 Be noȝt so gryndel god man, bot go forth þy wayes. 13.. *Gaw. & Gr. Knt.* 2338 Bolde burne, on þis bent be not so gryndel.

Hence †**'grindellaik** [see -LAIK], fierceness, anger; †**'grindelly** *adv.*, in a fierce manner.

13.. *Gaw. & Gr. Knt.* 312 Your gryndel-layk, & your greme, & your grete wordes. *Ibid.* 2299 Ful gryndelly with greme þenne sayde.

grinder ('graɪndə(r)). [f. GRIND *v.*[1] + -ER[1].]

I. An instrument for grinding.

1. a. A molar tooth; hence *colloq.* or *jocularly* in *pl.*, the teeth generally.

1398 TREVISA *Barth. De P.R.* v. xx. (1495) 125 Some [teeth] hyght grynders, whyche..grynde alwaye as myl-stones the mete. 1528 PAYNEL *Salerne's Regim.* 2 A iv, The laste tethe: whiche be behynde them that we call the grynders. 1604 DRAYTON *Owl* 414 Whilst this base Slave his nastie Grinders drest. 1767 FRANKLIN *Lett.* Wks. 1887 IV. 24, I return you many thanks for the box of elephants' tusks and grinders. 1786 WOLCOT (P. Pindar) *Bozzy & Piozzi* (ed. 5) 41 Dear Doctor Johnson lov'd a leg of pork, And hearty on it, would his grinders work. 1819 MOORE *Tom Crib* (ed. 3) 23 With grinders dislodg'd, and with peepers both poach'd. 1834 MCMURTRIE *Cuvier's Anim. Kingd.* 95 The other ordinary Edentata have no grinders. 1887 BESANT *The World went* xxvi. 204 Sit down... It is a grinder, and will take a strong pull.

†**b.** (See quot.) *Obs.*

1799 CORSE in *Phil. Trans.* LXXXIX. 215 A grinder or case of teeth, in full grown elephants, is more than sufficient to fill one side of the mouth.

2. A machine for grinding (in various senses); the upper millstone or 'runner'; †a muller or pestle.

1688 R. HOLME *Armoury* III. 382/1 The Inamel Grinder ..is..an Agate Stone set in a Brass..socket with a wooden handle; it is to Grind..Inamels in a Flint Mortar. 1708 J. PHILIPS *Cyder* II. 54 For thy mill a sturdy post Cylindric, to support the grinder's weight. 1805 FORSYTH *Beauties Scotl.* II. 10 A Roman hand-mill..was discovered in working a quarry, from the top of which the grinder had dropped. 1860 *Eng. & For. Mining Gloss., Cornwall Terms, Grinder*, machinery for crushing the ores between iron cylinders or barrels. 1877 RAYMOND *Statist. Mines & Mining* 386 One man..tends the grinder.

transf. 1860 TYNDALL *Glaciers* I. xv. 99 The mighty grinder [glacier action] has rubbed off the pinnacles of the rocks.

†**3.** A muscle of the lower jaw. *Obs. rare*[−1].

1615 CROOKE *Body of Man* 757 The motion vpward is performed by the temporall muscle..; to the right hand and to the left by the first grinder called *Mansorius primus.*

II. A person who grinds.

4. a. One who grinds anything in a mill.

1483 *Cath. Angl.* 165/2 A Grinder, *molitor.* *c* 1515 *Cocke Lorell's B.* (Percy Soc.) 10 Stryngers, grynders, Arowe heders, maltemen, and corne mongers. 1611 BIBLE *Eccl.* xii. 3 *marg.*, The grinders faile, because they grind little. 1756 J. LLOYD in W. Thompson *R.N. Advoc.* (1757) 51, I have.. desired the Grinder not to pick his Mill so often. 1852 MRS. STOWE *Uncle Tom's C.* xxxii. 294 The mills were few in number compared with the grinders. 1892 *Labour Commission* Gloss., *Grinders*, men in the seed crushing industry who put the rolled seed under a pair of stones to be ground preparatory to being made hot.

b. One who grinds cutlery, tools, glass, etc.

1600 SURFLET *Country Farme* I. xii. 48 The durt found in the bottome of the troughes of cutlers or grinders. 1639 WOODALL *Wks.* Pref. (1653) 16 It is a base office belonging to meer Barbers and Grinders. 1665 *Phil. Trans.* I. 32 With very little or no trouble in fitting the Engine, and without much skill in the Grinder. 1811 BYRON *Hints fr. Horace* 485 I'll labour gratis at a grinder's wheel. 1839 URE *Dict. Arts* 591 This pyramidal muller, if small sized, bears at each of its angles of the upper face a peg or ball, which the grinders lay hold of in working it. 1870 READE *Put yourself*, etc. I. 177 The strike was over, the grinders poured into the works, and the grindstones revolved. 1892 *Labour Commission* Gloss., *Grinder*, the man who grinds the wire teeth of the card sharp.

c. A lithotritist.

1846 R. LISTON *Pract. Surg.* xii. (ed. 4) 500 If he fell into the hands of the professed grinder, no matter what the peculiarities of the case, he was as certain to be subjected to the boring or hammering processes.

5. a. One who prepares pupils for examination; a crammer.

[1710, etc.: cf. *gerund-grinder*, GERUND b.] 1813 MAR. EDGEWORTH *Patronage* iii. (1838) I. 49 Put him into the hands of a clever grinder or crammer, and they would soon cram the necessary portion of Latin and Greek into him. 1849 THACKERAY *Pendennis* v. (1863) 37 She sent me down here with a grinder: she wants me to cultivate my neglected genius. 1857 [see GRIND *sb.*[1] 2 b].

b. = GRIND *sb.*[1] 3 b.

1852 J. C. PATTESON *Let.* Aug. in C. M. Yonge *Life J. C. Patteson* (1874) I. iv. 116 The difficulty is great enough to discourage any but a real 'grinder' at such work. 1942 BERREY & VAN DEN BARK *Amer. Thes. Slang* §825.10 *Diligent student*.., grinder, grindstone, grub.

6. a. One who works under another. *rare.* **b.** One who makes others work under him at diminished wages; a 'sweater'.

1814 SCOTT *Let. to J. B. S. Morritt* 7 Jan. in *Lockhart*, A sort of grinder of mine, who assisted me in various ways. 1851 MAYHEW *Lond. Labour* (1861) II. 233 Grinders, or those who compel the workmen (through their necessities) to do the same amount of work for less than the ordinary wages.

7. A bird that makes a grinding noise: **a.** The dishwasher or flycatcher (*Sisura inquieta*) of Australia. **b.** The night-jar or goat-sucker (*Cent. Dict.*, given as 'local Eng.'; Swainson has only *scissor-grinder, razor-grinder*).

1848 J. GOULD *Birds Austral.* II. pl 87 *Seisura inquieta*, Restless Flycatcher..the Grinder of the Colonists of Swan River and New South Wales.

III. 8. *slang.* **a.** (See quot. 1837).

1837 DICKENS *Pickw.* xxxi, Mr. Jackson..applying his left thumb to the tip of his nose, worked a visionary coffee-mill with his right hand: thereby performing a very graceful piece of pantomine..which was familiarly denominated 'taking a grinder'. **1870** *Athenæum* 8 Jan. 57/2 He finds himself confronted by a..lightly-clad Indian, who salutes him with what street-boys term 'a grinder'.

b. *U.S.* (See quots.)

1954 WEBSTER Add., *Grinder*, a large sandwich made of two slabs of bread cut lengthwise from the loaf and containing ham, salami, or other meat, usually cheese, and pickle, tomato and lettuce, or other appetizers. **1967** *Amer. Speech* XLII. 287 *Grinder*,..one explanation offered..is that the consumer must be able to grind the diverse ingredients in his mouth.

9. *Radio.* An atmospheric disturbance of relatively long duration heard as a rumbling sound and probably caused by lightning.

1922, 1936 [see CLICK *sb.*[1] 1 b]. **1940** *Chambers's Techn. Dict.* 390/2 *Grinder*, a type of atmospheric disturbance.., best characterised by its name.

IV. 10. *Comb.*, †**grinder-tongue muscles**, those which work the lower jaw and tongue; **grinder's asthma, phthisis, rot** *Path.*, 'a lung disease produced by the mechanical irritation of the particles of steel and stone given off in the operation of grinding' (Webster, *Suppl.* 1879).

1615 CROOKE *Body of Man* 762 The second paire are called *Myloglossi* or the grinder-tongue Muscles. They arise ..from the sides of the lower iaw neare the roots of the grinding teeth. **1898** *Allbutt's Syst. Med.* V. 244 Grinders' rot.

grindery ('graɪndərɪ). [f. GRIND *v.*[1] + -ERY.]

1. Materials, tools, and appliances used by shoemakers, and other workers in leather.

Quot. 1805 makes it probable that the term was orig. applied only to the whetstone used by shoemakers; then perh. to the tools sharpened on it, and finally extended to other 'furnishings'.

1805 *Sporting Mag.* XXVI. 46 Whetstone pits.. From these..all the grindery—a term well known to the gentle craft of England—is supplied. **1851** H. MAYHEW *Lond. Labour* I. 362 There are..old and blind shoemakers, who sell a few articles of grindery to their shopmates. **1886** BESANT *Childr. Gibeon* II. ii, They deal in grindery.

b. *attrib.* and *Comb.*

1854 *Illustr. Lond. News* 5 Aug. 118 Occupations of the people..Grindery-dealer. **1858** SIMMONDS *Dict. Trade*, *Grindery-warehouse*, a shop where the materials and tools for shoemakers..are kept for sale.

2. A place for grinding tools, weapons, etc.

1884 (*Over shop window, Sevenoaks, Kent*), Grindery for knives. **1896** *Westm. Gaz.* 30 Jan. 2/1, I proceeded to the Grindery... I saw keen edges put to a couple of swords.

grinding ('graɪndɪŋ), *vbl. sb.* [f. GRIND *v.*[1] + -ING[1].]

1. The action of GRIND *v.*[1], in various senses.

1340 *Ayenb.* 265 þer is wop and grindinge of teþ. *c* **1440** *Promp. Parv.* 212/2 Gryndynge of a mylle, *molatura, multura.* *c* **1487** *Acc. Prioress of Pray* in *Monast. Angl.* (1821) III. 360 Item paid for helvyng of an ax and gryndyng of knyfe iij[d]. **1606** SHAKS. *Tr. & Cr.* I. i. 15 Hee that will haue a Cake out of the Wheate, must needes tarry the grinding. **1758** J. S. *Le Dran's Observ. Surg.* (1771) 78 A Grinding of the Teeth..attended each Dressing. **1815** KEBLE *Let. Coleridge* in *Memoir* (1869) iv. 63 Perhaps when Tom leaves Oxford..we may contrive some gainful grinding [*i.e.* tutorial] scheme between us. **1860** O. W. HOLMES *Prof. Breakf.-t.* viii. (Paterson) 163 The..grinding of the..gravel changes to a..rumble. **1883** STEVENSON *Treas. Isl.* v. xxii, A certain tossing of foliage and grinding of boughs.

2. *attrib.* and *Comb.* **a.** 'Adapted for, or connected with, grinding'; in names of apparatus, machinery, etc. used in various trades, as ***grinding-bed, -bench, -block, -clamp, -lathe, -machine, -mill, -pan, -slab, -slip, -vat***, etc.; also ***grinding-operation, -room, -season***. **b.** 'Suitable for being ground', as ***grinding-barley***, etc. **c.** Special comb., as †**grinding-barrow**, a knife-grinder's barrow; †**grinding-house**, a mill (tr. L. *pistrinum*); **grinding-money**, an allowance paid in certain trades to cover the time spent in sharpening tools; †**grinding-organ**, a barrel-organ; **grinding-wheel**, (*a*) a wheel adapted for grinding or polishing; (*b*) a building fitted up with water or steam power for grinding cutlery or tools.

1881 *Daily News* 23 Aug. 3/6 *Grinding barley was.. dearer by 1*s.* per quarter. **1780** JOHNSON in *Boswell* (1847) 661/2 He would bring home a *grinding barrow, which you see in every street in London. **1853** O. BYRNE *Artisan's Handbk.* 118 The machinery for driving the beam is fixed in a frame about six feet square and eighteen inches high, placed between the two *grinding-benches. **1875** KNIGHT *Dict. Mech.*, **Grinding-clamp*. **1598** BERNARD *Terence in Engl.* 226 The fellow is worthie to be put into the *grinding-house. **1796** MORSE *Amer. Geog.* I. 541 Two boring and *grinding-mills for gun-barrels. **1892** *Labour Commission* Gloss., s.v. *Money*, **Grinding-money*, the money paid in the barge-building industry for the time allowed for sharpening tools on leaving a job. **1846** R. LISTON *Pract. Surg.* xii. (ed. 4) 496 [Lithotomy] was done, as he said, with less pain than that attendant upon any of the *grinding operations. **1801** MRS. CROFTS *Salvador* I. 91 He added also a French horn, a clarionet, a *grinding organ, all which he kept continually playing. **1877** RAYMOND *Statist. Mines & Mining* 332 Large *grinding-pan, with capacity of eight tons of tailings daily. **1890** W. J. GORDON *Foundry* 130 We follow our guide to the *grinding-room, where this roughness is ground off. **1856** OLMSTED *Slave States* 668 During the last *grinding-season nearly every man, woman, and child on his plantation, including his overseer and himself, were at work fully eighteen hours a day. **1890** W. J. GORDON *Foundry* 131 Two long rows of *grinding-slabs. **1875** KNIGHT *Dict. Mech.*, **Grinding-slip*, a thin slab of oil-stone or hone to reach edges of tools which cannot be conveniently applied to the usual stone. **1791** W. JESSOP *Rep. Thames & Isis* 21 An old arch way next adjoining to the *Grinding Wheel. **1839** URE *Dict. Arts* 381 Grinding wheels or grinding mills are divided into a number of separate rooms.

'**grinding**, *ppl. a.* [f. GRIND *v.*[1] + -ING[2].]

1. That grinds. ***grinding tooth*** = GRINDER 1.

a **1000** *Laws Æthelbert* c. 11 (Schmid) ȝif man wið cyninges mæȝden-man ȝeliȝeð, I scillinga ȝebete. ȝif hio grindende þeowa sio, xxv scillinga ȝebete. **1653** R. SANDERS *Physiogn.* 226 To have the arms and grinding teeth ready and fit to do some action. *a* **1718** ROWE (J.), Shrinking sinews start, And smeary foam works o'er my grinding jaws. **1825** J. NICHOLSON *Operat. Mechanic* 143 The surface of the under grinding mill-stone. **1869** J. E. GRAY *Guide to Brit. Mus.* 2 Flying Foxes have blunt grinding teeth. **1878** L. P. MEREDITH *Teeth* 76 The tooth-brush should be applied.. from side to side on the grinding surfaces.

fig. **1884** *Athenæum* 16 Aug. 207/3 A yearly examination, frequently of a mechanical and grinding character.

b. Of sounds: Similar to that made by grinding; grating, strident.

1794–1804 BEWICK *Brit. Birds* I. 139 This bird..is best known by the lengthened, grinding, sibilous noise, which it makes. **1853** KANE *Grinnell Exp.* xlii. (1856) 386 You become conscious of a sharp, humming, grinding murmur.

2. Burdensome, crushing, exacting, oppressive. †Of a person: Extortionate.

1599 MARSTON *Sco. Villanie* II. vii 203 He that doth snort in fat-fed luxury, And gapes for some grinding Monopoly. **1649** MILTON *Eikon.* v. 44 They undid nothing in the State but irregular and grinding Courts. *a* **1703** BURKITT *On N.T., Matt.* ix. 9 Matthew, a grinding publican, is the man. **1818** SHELLEY *Rev. Islam* v. xxxii, The stress of grinding toil. **1844** LD. BROUGHAM *Brit. Const.* xvii. (1862) 280 A heavy excise or a grinding income-tax. **1845** S. AUSTIN *Ranke's Hist. Ref.* II. 267 The clergy were accused of..acts of grinding oppression.

3. Of pain, etc.: Excruciating, racking, wearing.

Also, in *Midwifery*, the distinctive epithet of the pains in the first stage of labour.

1581 FLAVEL *Meth. Grace* ix. 189 Are we glad when the grinding pains of the stone..are over? **1693** DRYDEN *Ovid's Met.* ix. *Iphis & Ianthe* 52 Now grinding pains proceed to bearing throes. **1831** R. W. EVANS *Rectory Valehead* v. (ed. 2) 79 Thou shalt with grinding wounds be gor'd. **1851** RAMSBOTHAM *Obstetric Med.* (ed. 3) 101 So long as the 'grinding pains' continue there is no chance of a speedy release. **1869** TROLLOPE *He Knew* xlv. (1878) 247 The grinding suspicion that he was to be kept in the dark.

Hence '**grindingly** *adv.*, in a grinding manner.

1828 SOUTHEY in *Q. Rev.* XXXVIII. 543 No other peasantry..is..so grievously and grindingly oppressed by the land-holders. **1889** A. T. PASK *Eyes Thames* 97 The poor Thames has been hardly served indeed in these grindingly practical times.

'**grinding-stone.** = GRINDSTONE.

c **1440** *Promp. Parv.* 212/2 Gryndyngstone, or myllestone, *molaris. Ibid.*, Gryndyngstone or grynstone, *mola.* **1677** R. CARY *Palæol. Chron.* II. I. ix. 119, I have whet..my Coulter at their Grinding-Stone. **1706** *Reflex. upon Ridicule* (1707) 298 A troublesome Creditor, that keeps your Nose to the Grinding-stone. **1816** J. SMITH *Panorama Sci. & Art* II. 828 Take fresh curds, and bruise the lumps on a grinding-stone. **1869** E. A. PARKES *Pract. Hygiene* (ed. 3) 98 The makers of grinding-stones suffer in the same way.

grindle[1]. *Obs.* exc. *dial.* A narrow ditch or drain. (Cf. GRINDLET.)

1463 *Bury Wills* (Camden) 31 There is vij acres lond lying by the hih weye toward the grendyll. **1587** GOLDING *De Mornay* xiv. (1617) 230 As who would say this present life were vnto it [the future life] but a narrow grindle. *a* **1825** FORBY *Voc. E. Anglia*, *Grindle*, a small and narrow drain for water. But *Drindle* is a better word. **1847** HALLIWELL, *Grindle*, a small drain. (Suffolk.)

†**grindle**[2]. *Obs. rare*[−1]. Some bird.

1610 W. FOLKINGHAM *Art of Survey* IV. iii. 83 Gray, Greene and Bastard Plover..Grindle, Skirwingle, Sea and Land Larkes.

grindle[3] (grɪnd(ə)l). *U.S.* [a. G. *gründel*, f. *grund* GROUND, bottom.] A name of the mud-fish (see quot.).

1884–5 *Riverside Nat. Hist.* (1888) III. 97 *Amia calva*, the bow-fin, mud-fish,..grindle, 'John A. Grindle', or lawyer, as it is variously termed.

grindle-coke, -colk. *dial.* [See next and COLK[1].] A worn-out grindstone.

1831 J. HOLLAND *Manuf. Metal* I. 291 A razor, being considerably concave on the sides, is wrought on a mere grindle coke, as it is called. **1847** HALLIWELL, *Grindle-coke*, a worn-down grindstone, sometimes used as a stool in the cottages of the poor. (North.) **1888** *Sheffield Gloss.*, *Grindel-colke*.

grindle stone. *Obs.* exc. *dial.* Also 3 **grindelstane**, 4 **gryndelston**, 5 **gryndylston, gryndulstone**, 6 **gryndel(l stone**, 7–8 **grindle stone**, 8 **grindel stone**, 9 *dial.* **grindlestun, grunnleston.** [prob. repr. OE. **grindelstán*, f. **grindel* (instrumental n., f. *grindan* to GRIND) + *stán* STONE.]

†**1.** = GRINDSTONE 1. *Obs.*

a **1225** *Ancr. R.* 332 þet no mon ne scholde twinnen þe two grindstones [*v.r.* grindelstanes].

2. = GRINDSTONE 2.

13.. *Gaw. & Gr. Knt.* 2202 Hit clatered in þe clyff..As one vpon a gryndelston hade grounden a syþe. ? *c* **1400** *Turnament Totenham* 262 in Hazl. *E.P.P.* III. 94 Ther was gryndulstones in gravy, And mylstones in mawmany. *a* **1500** *Burlesques* in *Rel. Ant.* I. 81 Mylnestons in mortrews have I sene bot fewe; Gryndylstons in grwell with tho blw brothes. **1633** B. JONSON *Love's Welcome at Welbeck*, [They] turn round like grindlestones, Which they dig out fro' the dells. **1675** J. SMITH *Chr. Relig. App.* II. 11 What Grindle-stone had that Architect to Sharpen his Tools upon. **1855** ROBINSON *Whitby Gloss.*, *Grunston* or *Grunnleston*, a grindstone. **1886** *Chester Gloss.* s.v., Lady-bird, lady-bird, fly away home; All thi childer are dead but one, And he lies under the grindlestun.

†**3.** A piece, or kind, of stone suitable for making grindstones. *Obs.*

1523 FITZHERB. *Surv.* 31 Those may be taken as mynes of tynne leed ore cole yronstonne freston mylne stones gryndell stones lymestonne. **1662** *Irish Acts* (1765) II. 408 Grindle stones the chaudler 1*l.* 10*s.* 0*d.* **1706** PHILLIPS (ed. Kersey), *Grindle-stone*, a Kind of whitish Greet, of which there are several sorts, some more rough, and others very smooth.

†**grindlet.** *Obs.* [Cf. GRINDLE[1].] (See quot.)

1674–91 RAY *S. & E.C. Words* 101 A *Grippe* or *Grindlet*; a small Drain, Ditch, or Gutter.

†**grindle-tail.** *Obs. rare*[−1]. [app. f. GRINDLE (STONE) + TAIL; cf. *trundle-tail*.] A kind of dog.

1621 FLETCHER *Isl. Princess* v. iii, They tosse our little habitations like whelps, Like grindle-tailes, with their heeles upward.

†**Grindle'tonian.** *Obs.* Also (?*erron.*) **Grundletonian.** [Origin not traced; there is a place in Yorkshire called *Grindleton*.] A member of a sect of Familists which arose in Yorkshire in the 17th century. Also as *adj.*

1641 LD. BROOKE *Disc. Nat. Episc.* II. vi. 93 The Family of Love, the Antinomians and Grindletonians. **1655** BAXTER *Conf. Faith* 3 The..shameful lives of those Libertines that lived in England before these late years of trouble, whereof both London, and the Grundletonians in York-shire..can give too full Testimony. *Ibid.*, *marg. note*, They were possessed with the spirit of the Grundletonians. **1661** E. PAGITT *Heresiog.* 115 The Grindletonian Familists.

grindstone ('graɪndstəʊn). Forms: 3–8 **grinstone**, 4–6 **gryn(e)stone**, (4 **gryn(d)stoon**), 5–7 **gryndston(e**, (5 **grynd(i)stan**, 6 **grindestone**, 8 **grinestone**, *Sc.* **grunstane**, 9 *dial.* **grinstwun**), 3– **grindstone.** [f. GRIND *v.* + STONE.]

†**1.** A millstone. *Obs.* (exc. in *nonce-use*).

a **1225** *Ancr. R.* 332 [see GRINDLE STONE 1]. **1382** WYCLIF *Deut.* xxiv. 6 Thow shalt not taak in stedde of a wed the nethermore and ouermore grynstoon. **1725** *Dict. Heraldry* 238 Upton tells us, this Cross is call'd *Molendinaris*, because it bears the upper Grindstone. **1820** SCOTT *Monast.* xv, It could not but strike the man of meal and grindstones, that [etc.].

2. A disc of stone of considerable thickness, revolving on an axle, and used for grinding, sharpening, or polishing.

1404 *Durham Acc. Rolls* (Surtees) 398, j gryndstan cum j axiltre de ferro. *c* **1475** *Pict. Voc.* in Wr.-Wülcker 768/25 *Hec acates*, a grynstone. **1573** TUSSER *Husb.* xvii. (1878) 36 A grinstone, a whetstone, a hatchet and bil, with hamer and english naile, sorted with skil. **1594** BLUNDEVIL *Exerc.* III. I. vi. (1636) 284 Suppose that you turne with your hand from East to West a Grind-stone, or some other turning wheele. **1624** CAPT. SMITH *Virginia* III. ii. 49 To send him two great gunnes, and a gryndstone. **1719** DE FOE *Crusoe* I. iv. (1840) 63 That most useful Thing called a Grindstone. **1759** GOLDSM. *Bee* No. 2 ¶12 Four yards of good lutestring wearing against the ground, like..knives on a grindstone. **1833** MARRYAT *P. Simple* (1863) 249 Sharpening their cutlasses at the grindstone. **1878** *Masque Poets* 95 And ground upon a huge grindstone His penknife, sharp and bright.

transf. and *fig.* **1654** HAMMOND *Fundamentals* xvi. 174 Literature..is the grindstone to sharpen the coulters, and to whet their natural faculties. **1771** SMOLLETT *Humph. Cl.* 24 Apr., Our aunt Tabitha acts upon him as a perpetual grindstone. **1860** DICKENS *Let.* 4 Oct., Now the preparations to get ahead..will tie me to the grindstone pretty tightly.

b. Phr. ***to hold*** (***keep, bring, put***) ***one's nose to the grindstone***: to get the mastery over another and treat him with harshness or severity, to grind down or oppress; also, in mod. use, to keep (oneself or another) continually engaged in hard and monotonous labour.

1532 FRITH *Mirr. to know Thyself* (1829) 273 This Text holdeth their noses so hard to the grindstone, that it clean disfigureth their faces. **1546** J. HEYWOOD *Prov.* (1867) 10, I shall to reueng former hurtis, Hold their noses to grinstone. **1647** WARD *Simp. Cobler* 46 *Salus Populi* suffer'd its nose to be held to the Grindstone, till it was almost ground to the grisles, and yet grew never the sharper. **1697** VANBRUGH *Relapse* v. iii, Let him be fetched in by the ears: I'll soon bring his nose to the grindstone. **1742** RICHARDSON *Pamela* III. 309 If they can make the Man stoop to the great Point, they'll hold his Nose to the Grindstone, never fear. **1786** BURNS *Ded. to G. Hamilton* 58 Be to the poor like onie whunstane, And haud their noses to the grunstane. **1828** *Lights & Shades* II. 13 People whose heads are a little up in the world, have no occasion to keep their nose to the grindstone. **1886** MISS TYTLER *Buried Diamonds* xxviii, His nose is not to be kept at the grindstone the whole year round.

3. A kind of stone suitable for making grindstones. Also ***grindstone grit***.

1703 MOXON *Mech. Exerc.* 61 Take a piece of Grin-stone or Whet-stone and rub hard upon your Work to take the black Scurf off it. **1858** H. G. NICHOLLS *Forest Dean* ii. 27 In A.D. 1637 a grant was made to Edward Terringham of 'all the mines of coal and quarries of grindstone within the Forest of Dean'. **1863** DANA *Man. Geol.* 73 *Grit, Grit-Rock*, a hard, gritty rock, consisting of sand and small pebbles, called also *millstone grit*, and *grindstone grit*, because used sometimes for grindstones.

grine, obs. form of GRIN *sb.*[1], GROIN *sb.*[2]

‖**gringo** (ˈgrɪŋgəʊ). [Mexican Sp.] Among Spanish Americans, a contemptuous name for an Englishman or an Anglo-American. Also *attrib.*

1849 J. W. AUDUBON *Western Jrnl.* (1906) 13 June 100 We were hooted and shouted at as we passed through, and called 'Gringoes'. **1871** *Republican Rev.* (Albuquerque, N.M.) 14 Jan. 2/2 Three Mexicans from Socorro.. calling her a *gringo* bitch, finally threw her on the body of her husband. **1876** *Congress. Record* 30 June 4310/1 Cortina has never failed to rouse the hatred of the Mexican population against the 'gringos'. **1884** *Harper's Mag.* Oct. 748/2 *Gringo*, a term of ridicule and obloquy applied to Americans throughout all Mexico. **1892** E. WHYMPER *Trav. Andes* xii. 227, I..left him..uncertain whether he had seen a vision or entertained a gringo. **1927** W. CATHER *Death comes for Archbishop* v. i. 135 Any European, except a Spaniard, was regarded as a gringo. **1933** A. HUXLEY *Let.* 24 Mar. (1969) 369 Annoying foreigners and especially white Gringoes is a national sport in Honduras. **1962** N. MAXWELL *Witch-Doctor's Apprentice* iii. 22 When he revived, he explained that cameras are known to be gringo machines emitting 'electricity' which hypnotizes the victim and robs him of his will. **1964** *Daily Tel.* 11 Jan. 1/1 Mobs conducting a 'gringo hunt' roamed the streets and looted homes of Americans living in Panama. **1969** J. MANDER *Static Soc.* iii. 95 It is unadorned *gringo* imperialism.

grinkcome, grinkum, vars. GRINCOME *Obs.*

grinn(e, obs. form of GRIN *v.*[1]

grinner (ˈgrɪnə(r)). [f. GRIN *v.*[2] + -ER[1].] One who grins, in senses of the vb.

c **1440** *Promp. Parv.* 210/1 Grennare, or he that grynnythe. **1594** CAREW *Huarte's Exam. Wits* vi. (1596) 85 This..maketh men blockish, sluggards, and grynnars, because they want imagination. **1694** *Poet Buffoon'd* 1 One Smiler and two hundred Grinners. **1713** STEELE *Guardian* No. 29 ¶5 We may range the several kinds of laughers under the following heads:..The Smilers. The Laughers. The Grinners. **1779** MAD. D'ARBLAY *Diary* 26 May. He went up to the biggest grinner, and shaking him violently by the shoulders, said [etc.]. **1868** BROWNING *Ring & Bk.* IV. 667 Whose first bleat..Will strike the grinners grave.

grinning (ˈgrɪnɪŋ), *vbl. sb.* [f. GRIN *v.*[2] + -ING[1].] The action of the vb. GRIN.

a **1225** *Ancr. R.* 212 Hwu þe ateliche deouel schal ȝet agesten ham mid his grimme grennunge. *c* **1450** *Bk. Curtasye* 29 in *Babees Bk.*, Grennynge & mowynge at þi table eschewe. **1530** PALSGR. 227/2 Grennyng, makyng of an yvell Countynaunce. **1579** LYLY *Euphues* (Arb) 116 In the one hir grinning will shew hir deformed. **1607** TOPSELL *Four-f. Beasts* (1658) 371 Turning himself with a scornful grinning, he fighteth with all his force against the Dogs. **1689** WOOD *Life* 30 Nov. (O.H.S.) III. 80 Grinning and rejoycing of phanatiques upon the news of the conspirators being bayl'd. **1711** ADDISON *Spect.* No. 173 ¶6 A great Master in the whole Art of Grinning. **1861** THACKERAY 4 *Georges* 85 The old poets have sung a hundred jolly ditties about great cudgel-playings, famous grinning through horse-collars..and morris-dances.

attrib. **1897** *Allbutt's Syst. Med.* II. 695 The contraction of the levatores anguli oris, which gives the grinning expression peculiar to tetanus.

b. *Comb.*, **grinning-match**, a competition in grinning or grimacing (see also HORSE-COLLAR).

1711 ADDISON *Spect.* No. 173 ¶5 An Account..of one of these Grinning-Matches. **1801** [see HORSE-COLLAR]. **1812** *Sporting Mag.* XL. 18 Mr. Shanks..contrived to assemble his customers with a grinning-match. **1827** HONE *Every-day Bk.* II. 675 Grinning matches, through a horse-collar.

grinning (ˈgrɪnɪŋ), *ppl. a.* [f. GRIN *v.*[2] + -ING[2].] That grins, in senses of the vb.

1413 *Pilgr. Sowle* (Caxton 1483) IV. xxx. 80 Hornes or grennyng teeth to aferen fooles. **1561** *Child Marriages* 117 She..callid hym 'grinninge thief'. **1596** SPENSER *F.Q.* IV. vii. 24 Seeming wondrous glad, That by his grenning laughter mote farre off be rad. **1596** SHAKS. *1 Hen. IV*, v. iii. 62, I like not such grinning honour as Sir Walter hath; give me life. **1599** MASSINGER, etc. *Old Law* III. ii, And I have a scurvy grinning laugh a' mine own. **1688** LD. DELAMER *Wks.* (1694) 75 To pinch your Servants bellies to make entertainments, is a piece of grinning honour. **1742** GRAY *Distant Prosp. Eton Coll.* 74 To bitter Scorn a sacrifice, And grinning Infamy. **1820** BYRON *Mar. Fal.* III. ii, O'er their shrine Sate grinning Ribaldry and sneering Scorn. **1853** KANE *Grinnell Exp.* xlvi. (1856) 423 No earthly covering masks the grinning rocks of Pröven.

Hence **ˈgrinningly** *adv.*

1755 in JOHNSON.

grinstone, obs. form of GRINDSTONE.

†**grinstool ball.** *Obs.* ? = STOOL-BALL.

1579 J. JONES *Preserv. Bodie & Soule* I. xi. 23 Other exercises, as riding, running easily at Bace, at grinstole ball, boules, riding on horseback..I wil omitte.

†**grint**, *v. Obs.* In 4 **grinte**, 5 **grynte**. *Pa. t.* 3–4 **grynte**, 5 **grint**; also 4 **gryntide**, 5 **grynted**. [app. an onomatopœic formation, suggested by GRIND, GRENT, GRUNT *vbs.*] **a.** *intr.* To grind or gnash the teeth; usually *to grint with the teeth.* Said also of the teeth. **b.** ? To grunt or groan.

a **1300** *S. Gregory* 722 in *Archiv Stud. neu. Spr.* LVII. 67 He was bore ouer his horse croupe þat he grynte as a bere. **13..** *S.E. Leg.* (MS. Bodl. 779) *ibid.* LXXXII. 418/95 Decie þo for wraþþe gan to grinte & grede. *c* **1386** CHAUCER *Sompn. T.* 453 He grynte with his teeth, so was he wrooth. *c* **1430** *Life St. Kath.* (1884) 53 þe tyraunt as a ranpynge lyon grynted wyth hys teeth. *c* **1430** *Pilgr. Lyf Manhode* II. xi. (1869) 79 And at euery woord..j sygh his teeth grynte. *c* **1475** *Partenay* 3267 Then sore he grint And strayined his teth apace. **1491** CAXTON *Vitas Patr.* (W. de W. 1495) II. 309 b/1 A lyon..began to grynte with his teeth & to crye.

Hence †**ˈgrinting** *vbl. sb.*

c **1386** CHAUCER *Pars. T.* ¶134 Ful of waymentynge and of gryntynge [*v.r.* gruntynge] of teeth. **1388** WYCLIF *Matt.* viii. 12 There schal be wepyng and grynting of teeth. *c* **1440** *Gesta Rom.* ii. 6 (Harl. MS.) He lay in a certeyne tyme by the fire in siȝyngis and gryntingis. *c* **1450** LONELICH *Grail* xii. 420 Ther was Sorwe & grynteng of teth Inowe.

†**ˈgrinter.** *Sc. Obs.* Also 5–6 **gryntar**, 6 ? **grainter.** [ad. F. *grenetier*, f. *grenette* dim. of *grain* or *graine*: see GRAIN *sb.*[1] and cf. GRANATOR.] One who has charge of a granary or grange. Also ***grinter-man.***

c **1450** HOLLAND *Howlat* 179 The Goule was a gryntar, The Suerthbak a sellerar. **1535** LYNDESAY *Satyre* 2495 Thir is my Grainter [*v.r.* Graniter] and my Chalmerlaine, And hes my gould and geir vnder thair cuiris. **1552** —— *Monarche* 4309 Thare Gryntaris, and thare Chamberlanis, With thare temporall Courtissianis. **1624** *Crt. Bk. Barony of Urie* (1892) 56 Alexander Fraser is admitit grinter man. **1683** *Bk. of Rec. Glamis* (1890) 7, I have given a factorie to David Lyon the grinter at Glammiss.

grintern (ˈgrɪntən). *dial.* [? from the source of GRINTER.] 'A compartment in a granary' (W. Barnes, *Dorset Dial.* 1863).

1898 T. HARDY *Wessex Poems* 157 Ye mid zell my favourite heifer, ye mid let the charlock grow, Foul the grinterns, give up thrift.

griot (ˈgriːəʊ). [a. Fr. (17th. cent.), of uncertain ulterior etym.] A member of a class of travelling poets, musicians, and entertainers in North and West Africa, whose duties include the recitation of tribal and family histories; an oral folk-historian or village story-teller, a praise-singer.

1820 tr. *G. Mollien's Trav. Interior Afr.* p. viii, Explanation of certain terms, employed in Africa... *Griot*, public singer. **1906** F. B. ARCHER *Gambia Colony* I. ii. 33 In most of the towns the head chiefs have a band of musicians and dancing women known as 'Griots'. **1935** G. GORER *Africa Dances* I. iv. 55 The griots form a special caste... They are outcasts... Griots are by tradition attached to families. **1968** M. A. KLEIN *Islam & Imperialism in Senegal* 10 The griots were the historians, the genealogists, the musicians, and the praise-sayers. **1978** J. UPDIKE *Coup* (1979) vii. 273 The one robe in which I would always be clothed, even in death, as long as the *griots* could sing my ancestry. **1983** *Spectator* 28 May 20/3 Charters was introduced to several griots, the troubadours of West Africa, who played for him on strange tribal versions of the fiddle, banjo and xylophone.

grip (grɪp), *sb.*[1] Forms: 1 **gripe, gripa**, 5–7 *Sc. pl.* **grippis**, 6–7 **grippe**, 8 **gripp**, 3– **grip**. [Two formations: (1) OE. *gripe* str. masc., grasp, clutch, corresp. to OHG. *grif-*, in comb. (MHG. *grif*, mod.G. *griff*) grasp, handle, claw, etc., ON. *grip-r* possession, property; (2) OE. *gripa* handful, sheaf; both f. root of GRIPE. ON. had also *grip* neut., grasp, clutch (Sw. *grepp*, Da. *greb*). In some senses, the sb. may be a mod. new formation from the vb. The instances of the word in the 15–17th centuries are chiefly Scotch, while examples in the 18th c. are very rare.]

1. a. Firm hold or grasp; the action of gripping, grasping, or clutching; esp. the tight or strained grasp of the hand upon an object (cf. HANDGRIP); also, grasping power.

Beowulf (Z.) 1148 Siþðan grimne gripe Guð-laf and Os-laf æfter sæ-siðe sorȝe mændon. *c* **1000** ÆLFRIC *Gloss.* in Wr.-Wülcker 158/16 *Pugillus*, se gripe ðære hand. *c* **1205** LAY. 15273 þa Hengest hine igrap mid grimmen his gripen. **1423** JAS. I *Kingis Q.* clxxi, 'Now hald thy grippis', quod sche, 'for thy tyme'. **1535** STEWART *Cron. Scot.* III. 414 Thir four ilkane out of his grippis flang. **1637–50** ROW *Hist. Kirk* (Wodrow Soc.) 331 Taking a grip of the table to help him-self up. *a* **1651** CALDERWOOD *Hist. Kirk* (1843) II. 314 Fadownside bendeth backe his middle finger, so that for paine he was forced to forgoe his grippe. **1820** SHELLEY *Vis. Sea* 44 Twin tigers..have driven..The deep grip of their claws through the vibrating plank. [Cf. I. 143 the gripe of the tiger.] **1828** SCOTT *Diary* 13 Jan. in *Lockhart*, Grip and accuracy of step have altogether failed me. **1840** DICKENS *Barn. Rudge* lix, He grasped a little hand that sought in vain to free itself from his grip. **1859** LANG *Wand. India* 263 The hawk..was just about to give the minar a blow and a grip. **1871** DIXON *Tower* III. i. 2 His grip on sword and rein was close and tight. **1871** L. STEPHEN *Playgr. Europe* vi. (1894) 147 The insecure grip of one toe on a slippery bit of ice. **1877** BLACK *Green Past.* xxx. (1878) 240 His hands keeping a tight grip of about a dozen umbrellas. **1885** *Athenæum* 23 May 661/1 The horrors of the bear's grip. **1897** *Allbutt's Syst. Med.* III. 86 In..rheumatoid arthritis the grip of the hands should be regularly measured. **1898** *Blackw. Mag.* Sept. 380/1 That tide had the grip of an ice-floe.

b. More particularly, of one hand grasping another; sometimes said with reference to the mode of grasping used as a means of mutual recognition by members of a secret society, such as the freemasons.

1785 BURNS *Addr. to Deil* xiv, Masons' mystic word and grip. **1820** SCOTT *Abbot* vii, Give us a grip of your hand, man, for auld lang syne. **1857** 'C. BEDE' *Verdant Green* III. x. 80 It all at once occurred to Billy to give him the masonic grip. **1860** TENNYSON *Sea Dreams* 159, I found a hard friend in his loose accounts, A loose one in the hard grip of his hand. **1888** *Encycl. Brit.* XXIII. 159/2 Good Templary is the freemasonry of temperance with ritual, passwords, grips, &c., closely modelled on those of the old secret societies.

c. Phr. ***at grips*** (= *at hand* (or *handy*) *grips*: see HANDGRIP 1): in close combat; hand to hand *with.* Similarly, ***to come to grips***: to come to close quarters. ***in grips***: in custody.

1640 RUTHERFORD *Lett.* ccxciv. (1894) 593 When ye come to grips with death, the king of terrors. **1818** SCOTT *Hrt. Midl.* xvii, You and I will..see him in grips, or we are done wi' him. **1857** HUGHES *Tom Brown* II. iii. (1871) 248 At grips with self and the devil. **1893** STEVENSON *Catriona* 43, I saw we were come to grips at last. **1895** *Sat. Rev.* 21 Sept. 366/2 The British farmer..is now at grips with world-wide competition.

†**d.** An opportunity for seizing. *Obs.*

c **1470** HENRY *Wallace* XI. 607 We may our grippis waill.

2. *fig.* **a.** Firm or tenacious hold, grasp, or control; power, mastery (now esp. associated with the idea of oppression or irresistible force). †Formerly also *pl.* as ***to fasten one's grips on, let go one's grips***, etc. Also ***to get*** (or ***take***) ***a grip on*** (oneself), ***to get to grips with*** (something).

1450–70 *Golagros & Gaw.* 347 In his grippis and ye gane, He wald ourcum yow ilkane. *Ibid.* 1169 Al the gretest Of gomys that grip has..Of baronis and burowis [etc.]. **1567** *Satir. Poems Reform.* v. 40 Gif ȝe lat ga that is in ȝour grippis. **1600** in Pitcairn *Crim. Trials* (Bannatyne Club) II. 283, I cair nocht for all the land I hew in this kingdome, incase I get a grip of Dirleton. **1604** DRAYTON *Owle* 1213 Let those weake Birds..Submit to those that are of grip and might. **1632** RUTHERFORD *Lett.* xxiv. (1894) 82 Loose your grips of them all [fears]. *a* **1732** T. BOSTON *Crook in Lot* (1805) 127 Fasten your grips on the other world, and let your grip of this go. **1832** J. W. CROKER in *C. Papers* 9 Nov., Promoting a subscription to purchase Abbotsford..out of the grip of creditors. **1865** DICKENS *Mut. Fr.* I. xv, The clutching old man had lost his grip on life. **1883** GILMOUR *Mongols* xviii. 213 Perhaps no other religion..holds its votaries clutched in such a paralysing grip. **1894** J. KNIGHT *Garrick* i. 7 The grip of poverty is everywhere apparent. **1895** *Harper's* Nov. 962/1 My dear boy, get a grip on yourself... I won't bite you. **1897** MARY KINGSLEY *W. Africa* 627 In the grip of malarial fever, on his way to the grave. **1898** J. CAIRD *Univ. Serm.* 94 The iron grip of long unresisted habits. **1929** W. FAULKNER *Sound & Fury* 174 My throat wouldn't quit trying to laugh, like retching after your stomach is empty. 'Whoa, now,' Anse said. 'Get a grip on yourself.' **1947** *Sci. News* IV. 7 They [*sc.* readers] have to translate his article into understandable language before they can get to grips with its actual subject matter. **1950** R. ACKLAND in *Plays of Year 1949* 611 Don't be such a foolish woman... Sit down and take a grip on yourself. **1955** *Times* 25 July 5/4 What we have now agreed makes it possible to get to grips with the twin problems of the unity of Germany and the security of Europe. **1967** S. BECKETT *No's Knife* 52 Come now, come now, he said, get a grip on yourself, be a man.

b. Intellectual or mental hold; power to apprehend or master a subject. ***to lose one's grip*** (cf. LOSE *v.*[1] 3 d).

[**1635** D. DICKSON *Hebr.* vi. 19–20 And nowe hee showeth the stabilitie of the grippe which the Believer taketh of these groundes, in the similitude of the grippe which a Shippes Ancre taketh, beeing casten on good ground.] **1861** THORNBURY *Turner* (1862) I. 309 His brain does not retain with the sure grip it once did. **1875** J. MILLER *First Fam'lies of Sierras* (1876) 246 Lost my 'grip'.., didn't have any 'snap' any more. **1884** *Pall Mall G.* 20 Feb. 4/1 It [a play] lacks colour, stamina, in short, the indefinable something known as 'grip'. **1885** *Manch. Exam.* 28 Jan. 3/4 An essay..singularly deficient both in intellectual grip and literary charm. **1894** DOYLE *Sherl. Holmes* 3, I have a grip of the essential facts of the case. **1894** 'MARK TWAIN' *Pudd'nhead Wilson* xx, Come, cheer up, old man; there's no use in losing your grip. **1968** *Times Lit. Suppl.* 8 Feb. 122/5 His work after the war shows a steady decline.., until he seems to have lost his grip altogether.

c. That quality in a beverage which gives it a 'hold' on the palate.

1892 WALSH *Tea* (Philad.) 98 The commoner grades [of Basket-fired tea] are..lacking in 'grip' and flavor. **1894** H. NISBET *Bush Girl's Rom.* 167 These Bush drinkers..had a decided leaning towards flavour and grip.

3. A seizure or twinge of pain; a spasm.

a **1400–50** *Alexander* 544 For þe aire nowe & þe elementis ere..So trauailid out of temperoure & troubild of þat sone, þat makis þi grippis and þi gridis a grete dele þe kenere. **1575** GASCOIGNE *Pr. Pleas. Kenilw.* (1821) 34, I feel great grips of grief, Which bruise my breast. *a* **1605** MONTGOMERIE *Misc. Poems* xlvii. 8 Sik gredie grippis I feell. **1786** BURNS *Sc. Drink* xix, Colic grips an' barkin hoast May kill us a'. **1840** LADY C. BURY *Hist. of Flirt* iv, 'Grips, Mr. Ellis! what sort of disorder is that?' 'A little hacking in my throat, which causes difficulty in breathing'.

4. As much as can be seized in the hand; a handful. ***to lie in grip***: (of corn) to lie as it is left by the reapers. *Obs.* exc. *dial.*

c **1000** *Sax. Leechd.* I. 136 Genim þysse ylcan wyrte godne gripan. *c* **1000** *Ags. Ps.* (Spelman) cxxvi[i]. 6 Berende gripan heora [*L. portantes manipulos suos*]. **1572** BOSSEWELL *Armorie* II. 19 Romulus..vsed Fasciculos fæni, that is to saie, a grippe or knitche of hay bound together at the ende of a long staffe. **1621** BP. R. MOUNTAGU *Diatribæ* Introd. 106 Tithe in Sheafe, in Shocke, in Grippe, in Ridge, or at the Lumpe. *Ibid.* II. 301 While it [Corne] lay in grip, or in shock, or in sheafe. **1722** LISLE *Husbandry* 178 The wheat after it is cut and lies in gripp, does not lie so exposed for the sun and wind to dry the gripps after being fogged with wet. **1739** J. TULL *Horse-Hoing Husb.* (1740) 213 To make up the Grips [of Barley or Oats] into little Heaps by Hands. **1805** R. W. DICKSON *Pract. Agric.* (1807) II. 193 They are usually reaped with the Sickle, and laid in thin grips or reaps. **1842** AKERMAN *Wilts. Gloss.* s.v., A grip of wheat is the handful grasped in reaping.

5. Something which grips or clips. **a.** *Sc.* An ear-ring. **b.** In various technical applications; *e.g.* a device on a cable car by which the car is attached to and freed from the cable; a tooth or hooked device on the barrel of a rifle, pistol, etc., to secure it to the stock while firing; the narrow part of the bore of a rifled cannon, immediately in front of the shot-chamber; in boat-construction (see quot. 1857). **c.** A hair-grip.

a **1800** *Bonny J. Seton* xiii. in Child *Ballads* (1890) IV. 53 They cutted the grips out o his ears, Took out the gowd signots. **1857** P. Colquhoun *Comp. Oarsman's Guide* 30 Knees are angular pieces of wood placed perpendicularly in various parts..but where lateral, they are termed grips, as 'transom grips'. **1881** Greener *Gun* 194 Lefaucheux's first gun had but a single grip,..leaving that part unsecured that received the greatest force of the explosion,..Many methods were tried to remedy this evil, one of the best being the double-grip action. **1886** *Pall Mall G.* 29 Sept. 6/2 Through this slit works the plate connecting the moving body above with what is termed the 'grip' on the cable beneath. **1887** J. Bucknall Smith *Cable or Rope Traction* 100 Immediately the cars are taken on to the road, the cable is pulled or guided into the 'grips'. **1960** C. Storr *Marianne & Mark* xi, 144, I want two cards of grips and a set of rollers.

6. That which is gripped or grasped. **a.** The handle of a sword; the part of the handle gripped by the hand.

1867 Smyth *Sailor's Word-bk.*, *Grip*, the handle of a sword. **1870** Morris *Earthly Par.* III. iv. 402 His blanched and unused hand Clutched the spoiled grip of his once trusty blade. **1884** Burton *Sword* vii. 124 The grip is the outer case of the tang. **1894** C. N. Robinson *Brit. Fleet* 509 All officers..were to have black grips to their swords.

b. In a rifle, pistol, etc.: that part of the stock which is held by the hand and is roughened to make the grasp firmer. (Cf. Du. *greep*.)

1881 Greener *Gun* 248 Good gun-stocks must be..straight in the grain at the grip and head of the gun. **1899** *Pall Mall Mag.* Jan. 136 My fingers touched the roughened horn of the grip [of the pistol].

c. The part of the handle in any implement covered with indiarubber, leather, etc. to make the grasp firmer. Also, the cover itself.

1886 *St. Nicholas Mag.* July 658 Holding the rod by the 'grip', the part of the butt wound with silk or rattan to assist the grasp. **1890** Hutchinson *Golf* (Badm. Libr.) 446 *Grip*, the part of the handle covered with leather by which the club is grasped. **1891** *Cyclist* 25 Feb. 153 The handles are brought well back, and fitted with elliptical horn grips.

7. *U.S.* A scene-shifter.

1888 *Scribner's Mag.* IV. 444/2 Meanwhile the 'grips', as the scene-shifters are called, have hold of the side scenes ready to shove them on. **1961** A. Berkman *Singers' Gloss. Show Business* 26 *Grip*, stage hand, especially one who works on the stage floor. **1965** J. von Sternberg *Fun Chinese Laundry* (1966) viii. 191 Grip and Property Man..$100. **1967** H. Harrison *Technicolor Time Machine* (1968) ix. 92 One of the grips brought out a baby spot and plugged it in for light.

8. *colloq.* Short for: **a.** *grip-car* (*U.S.*); **b.** GRIPSACK (orig. *U.S.*).

1879 *Chicago Tribune* 7 Mar. 9/5 At Cherokee I stepped from the train, took my 'grip', and began in earnest the life of a pilgrim. **1883** *Pall Mall G.* 11 Dec. 2/2 The word 'grip-sack'..contracted to 'grip', has come to be applied to other articles of luggage [than the hand-satchel]. *Ibid.* 'Will you take the grip?' is equivalent to 'Will you take the cable tramway?' **1894** *Outing* (U.S.) XXIV. 442/2, I..had stowed my guncase and grip where they would be least in the way. **1926** *Daily Colonist* (Victoria, B.C.) 14 July 5/6 Experienced travellers in all countries always take a bottle of ENO in their grip to offset changes of water and diet. **1928** W. Gillette *Astound. Crime Torrington Rd.* v. 282 'Want anything from the hotel—toilet articles—clothing—tobacco?' 'Thanks—I've got 'em outside in a grip.' **1960** J. Betjeman *Summoned by Bells* vii. 66 Clutching a leather grip Containing things for the first night of term. **1965** G. McInnes *Road to Gundagai* xii. 207, I toted my grip all the way back.

9. (See quot. 1916.) *Austral.*

1906 E. Dyson *Fact'ry 'Ands* xviii. 243, I had t' do it 'r resign me grip on ther spot. **1916** C. J. Dennis *Songs Sentimental Bloke* 123 *Grip*, occupation, employment. **1941** Baker *Dict. Austral. Slang* 32 *Grip*, a job, regular employment.

10. *attrib.* and *Comb.* (in some instances perh. of the stem of GRIP *v.*^{1}), as **grip-bag** = GRIPSACK; **grip-brake**, a brake worked by gripping with the hand; **grip-car** *U.S.*, a tramcar worked by means of a grip (see 5 b) on an endless cable driven by a stationary engine, a cable-car; **grip-grass** *dial.*, the plant Cleavers, *Galium Aparine*; **grip-knob**, a contrivance for holding an article when being turned in a lathe; **grip-lug**, a lug to grip or hold fast (a handle); **grip-man**, the man who manipulates the grip of a cable-car; **grip-pedal**, a pedal designed to prevent the foot from slipping; **grip-pulley**, (*a*) a form of grip on a cable-car using the principle of the pulley (Funk's *Stand. Dict.*); (*b*) (see quot. 1894); **grip-slot**, a slot in the track through and along which the shank of the gripping apparatus of a cable-car passes; **grip treadle**, an early name for *grip-pedal*.

1958 *Listener* 17 July 107/2 Take, if you can, an extra *grip-bag—a canvas one. **1963** T. Parker *Unknown Citizen* i. 22 In one hand he carried a blue grip-bag, like those sometimes used by airline passengers. **1885** *Cycl. Tour. Club Gaz.* IV. 136 The *grip brake in our 'Club' tandem. **1883** *Pall Mall G.* 11 Dec. 2/2 The appliances for attaching and detaching the cars from the cable being called the 'grip', and the car in which it is operated a '*grip-car'. **1889** *Advance* (Chicago) 7 Mar. 188 Whistles of engines..and the gong of grip-cars. **1862** C. P. Johnson *Useful Plants Gt. Brit.* 136 Our English word Cleavers,..and the Scotch '*Grip-grass', have been given from the same cause. **1833** J. Holland *Manuf. Metal* II. 135 The concentric circles of perforations, and the four grooves..admit of the insertion of *grip-knobs ..so that the article to be turned may be held in any situation. **1891** *Cyclist* 25 Feb. 153 A *grip-lug serves to secure the handlebar within the steering post. **1886** *Science* 24 Sept. 275 The driver, or *grip-man, then opened the valve admitting air to the engine. **1891** *Daily News* 13 June 2/3 Each car, being manned by a 'gripman' in front and a conductor behind. **1885** *Cycl. Tour Club Gaz.* IV. 309 Would not rat-trap or patent *grip pedals be safer than the feet-straps now in use? **1886** *Appleton's Ann. Cycl.* 122/2 It was not until 1870 that the first patent for a *grip-pulley was issued to Andrew S. Hallidie, of San Francisco. **1894** D. K. Clark *Tramways* (ed.2) 556 The clutch communicates the motion of the countershaft to the grip pulley, the pulley which moves the cable. **1887** J. Bucknall Smith *Cable or Rope Traction* 100, *bb* represents the '*grip slots'. **1881** *Advt.*, The fastest times on record will be made with..*grip treadles.

grip (grɪp), *sb.*^{2} Now *dial.* and in *Hunting* language. Forms: 4–6 **gryppe**, 5–7 **grippe**, 6 **grypp**, 7 **griphe**, 7–8 **gripp**, 4– **grip**. (See also GRIPE *sb.*^{2}) [ME. *grip*, OE. *gryp-e* (or *a*) wk. fem. (or masc.), cogn. w. *gréop* burrow ('cuniculus' Wr.-Wülcker 216/1), and MDu. *greppe*, *grippe*, MLG. *grüppe*; cf. GRIPPLE. The OE. *grép*, *grépe* (*grœ́pe*) burrow, trench (cogn. with GROOP) may have coalesced with this word; cf. the pronunciation of *sheep* as (ʃɪp) in many dialects.]

1. A small open furrow or ditch, esp. for carrying off water; a trench, drain.

a **1000** *Aldhelm Glosses, Brussels* (in Engl. Stud. IX. 505) *Grypan*, cloacæ, latrinæ. *c* **1300** *Havelok* 1924 Summe in gripes bi the her Drawen ware, and laten ther. *Ibid.* 2102 Þan birþe men casten hem in poles, Or in a grip, or in þe fen. **1398** Trevisa *Barth. De P.R.* xvii. cxviii. (1495) 682 Vine braunches bent downe in to a gryppe [*ed.* 1538 grip] of erthe. *c* **1400** *Destr. Troy* 1543 The walles vp wroght, wonder to se With grippes full grete was þe ground takon. *c* **1440** *Promp. Parv.* 212/2 Gryppe..where watur rennythe a-way in a londe..*aratiuncula*. **1579** *Mem. St. Giles's, Durham* (Surtees) 9 Payde..for castinge of the grypp aboute the pynfoalde. **1611** *N. Riding Rec.* (1884) I. 236 Making a ditch, hole, or griphe in the King's highway. **1625** Boyle in *Lismore Papers* (1886) II. 149 The parck or meddow without the gripp and walles of yoghall. *a* **1722** Lisle *Husb.* (1752) 207 The higher the stubble is left the gripps are thereby borne up the higher. **1784** Sir J. Cullum *Hist. Hawsted* iii. 171 A Grip, a shallow drain to carry water off the roads, ploughed fields, &c. **1844** J. T. Hewlett *Parsons & W.* liv, The long grass rotted on the banks and in the grips. **1864** Tennyson *North. Farmer* ii. viii, An' 'e ligs on 'is back i' the grip, wi' noän to lend 'im a shuvv. **1883** *Law Times* 1 Dec. 79/2 The owner of the estate caused the grass strips to be intersected by ditches called grips..for the purpose of draining the road. **1883** E. Pennell-Elmhirst *Cream Leicestersh.* 346 Your horse was sure to find his level in the first grip or ditch.

b. (See quot.)

1824 Mander *Derbysh. Miners' Gloss.*, *Grip*, a small narrow cavity in the Mine, or in a rocky or hilly place.

2. The gutter in a cowhouse. (Cf. GROOP.)

[*a* **1000**: cf. 1.] **1825** Brockett *N.C. Words*, *Grip*, *Gruap*, *Groop*, the space where the dung lies in a cow house, having double rows of stalls; that is, the opening or hollow between them. **1848** *Rural Cycl.* II. 531 *Grip*,..the urine gutter of a cow-house or a cattle-shed. **1891** Atkinson *Moorland Par.* 93 It was in the grip, but it would not win into the calves' pen.

3. *Comb.*, as **grip-yard** (see quot. 1882).

1593 *Manch. Crt. Leet Rec.* (1885) II. 85 Roberte Blomeley hath incroched vppon the Queenes hye waye in the Deanes-gate by makinge a grypyarde And A hedge. **1847** Halliwell, *Grip-yard*, a seat of green turf, supported by twisted boughs. *North.* **1882** *Lanc. Gloss.*, *Grip-yard*, *Grip-yort*, a platting of stakes and twisted boughs filled up with earth; generally made to confine a water-course, and occasionally to form artificial banks and seats in pleasure gardens.

grip (grɪp), *v.*^{1} Forms: 1 *Northumb.* **grioppa**, **ȝegrippia**, 5 *north.* **grep**, 4–6 **grippe**, **gryppe**, 7–9 *Sc.* **gripp**, 9 *Sc.* **grup**, 6– **grip**; also *pa. t.* (and *pa. pple.*) 3 **gripte**, 4–6 (8–9) **gript**; *Sc.* 4–5 **gryppet**, **-it**, **-yt**, 5–9 **grippet**; 4– **gripped**. [ONorthumb. *grippa* (corresp. to MHG. *gripfen*; cf. the synonymous OHG. *chripphan*, MHG. *kripfen*):—WGer. type **grippjan*, f. **gripi-z* GRIP *sb.*^{1}]

1. a. *trans.* To grasp or seize firmly or tightly with the hand; to seize with the mouth, claw, beak or other prehensile organ.

c **950** *Lindisf. Gosp.* Luke ix. 39 Heono gast ȝegrippde hine & ferlice clioppiað. *Ibid.* xxiii. 26 Miððy ȝelæddon hine ȝegrippedon sumne simon cyrinisce..& ȝeseton him þæt rod. —— John vii. 30 Sohton forðon hine to grioppanne [*Rushw.* ȝigripanne, *Ags. Gosp.* nimanne]. **1297** R. Glouc. (1724) 22 Corineus..sterede hym a non, And gripte [*MS.A.* kipte] þis geant. *c* **1350** *Will. Palerne* 744 He gript his mantel, as a weiȝh woful he wrapped him þer-inne. *c* **1430** *Chev. Assigne* 220 The grypte eyþur a staffe in here honde. *a* **1450** *Piers Fulham* in Hartshorne *Metr. T.* 118 Whan thow hym [an ele] grippist and wenest wele Too haue hym siker right as the list. *c* **1450** *St. Cuthbert* (Surtees) 6302 A serpent..His nek full sare it grepyd. **1500–20** Dunbar *Poems* xxxii. 29 He grippit hir abowt the west. **1513** Douglas *Æneis* iv. v. 85 Making his prayeris and gripping the alter. **1590** Spenser *F.Q.* i. i. 19 He grypt her gorge with so great paine. **1632** Lithgow *Trav.* x. 450 Gripping my throat to stop my crying. **1785** Burns *Halloween* vi, He grippet Nelly hard an' fast. **1861** Hughes *Tom Brown at Oxf.* vii. (1889) 60 His right arm behind his back, the hand gripping his left elbow. **1863** Ouida *Held in Bondage* 1 Our oars feathered..; the river foamed and flew as we gripped it. **1864** Burton *Scot Abr.* I. i. 55 The flag gripped in his teeth. **1867** F. Francis *Angling* v. (1880) 174 If he has gripped the weed in his mouth, as fish will do. **1873–4** Moggridge *Ants & Spiders* i. 42 Still the ants gripped their prey as firmly as ever. **1894** Crockett *Raiders* 70 He..held it [his weapon] gripped between his knees as he rowed.

†**b.** *to grip up*: to pull up forcibly. *Obs.*

c **1400** *Destr. Troy* 1377 The Grekes..Grippit vp the grounde, girdyn doun þe wallys. *Ibid.* 1784 Antenor..Grippit vp a gret sayle, glidis on þe water.

c. *transf.* Said of a disease.

1818 Scott *Fam. Lett.* 14 Jan., Mine old enemy the cramp grippet me by the pit of the stomach. **1852** Dickens *Bleak Ho.* xvi, The gout..grips him by both legs. **1884** Sala *Journ. due South* i. xii. (1887) 161 Asthma came down upon me like..armed men..and gripped me by the throat.

d. To place (one's hands) so that they hold each other or an object in a grip.

1907 *Smart Set* Jan. 32/2 She fell back in the chair and gripped her hands round the arms of it. *Ibid.* Feb. 24/1 He gripped his hands together and put the doubt behind him. **1910** E. M. Albanesi *For Love of Anne Lambart* 112 Anne's two cold hands gripped themselves together.

†**2. a.** *gen.* To seize, catch, lay hands upon; to obtain hold or possession of. Chiefly *Sc. Obs.*

c **1400** *Destr. Troy* 7114 The Troiens..Haue grippit the goodis. *c* **1470** Henry *Wallace* i. 170 No for the Pape thai wald no kyrkis forber, Bot gryppyt al be wiolence of war. **1500–20** Dunbar *Poems* lxvi. 37 The temporall stait to gryp and gather. *c* **1560** A. Scott *Poems* (S.T.S.) iv. 90 The moir digest and grave, The grydiar to grip it. **1724** Ramsay *Tea-t. Misc.* (1733) I. 34 The whillywha's will grip ye'r gear. **1825–80** Jamieson s.v., She's like the man's mare; she was ill to grip, and she wasna muckle worth when she was grippit. **1826** J. Wilson *Noct. Ambr.* Wks. 1855 I. 172, I gripped about a hundred and forty [hares] wi' the grews.

b. *spec.* To seize or encroach upon (land). *Sc.*

1602 *Min. Dunrossness Distr. Court* in Mill *Diary* (1889) 180 Airthour in Skelberie is fand to have grippit wrangouslie ane halff of ane rigg. **1632** in Barry *Orkney* (1805) App. 473 That no man gripp his neighbours lands under the paine of 10 *l.* Scots. *a* **1800** *Jamie Telfer* xii. in Child *Ballads* (1898) IV. 6 My lord may grip my vassal-lands.

3. a. *absol.* and *intr.* To take firm hold; to make a grasp or seizure: to get a grip. *lit.* and *fig.*

1375 Barbour *Bruce* i. 115 Had ȝe..consideryt his vsage, That gryppyt ay, but gayne-gevyng. **1567** *Gude & Godlie Ball.* (S.T.S.) 30 Thay gryp sa fast his geir to get. **1663** Blair *Autobiog.* iii. (1848) 56 The thumb in the hand is able to grip and hold against the four fingers. **1728** Ramsay *Gen. Mistake* 136 He..Jobs..extorses, cheats and grips, And no ae turn of gainfu' us'ry slips. **1730** T. Boston *Mem.* App. 436 Like a bird on the side of a wall gripping with its claws. **1821** Scott *Fam. Lett.* (1894) II. xvii. 111 Tell me if the boy ..can grip hard as a Scott should. **1867** Smyth *Sailor's Word-bk.*, *Grip*,..to hold, as 'the anchor grips'. **1894** *Times* 13 July 12/1 The gain was not made in fore-reaching, but in gripping closer to the wind.

†**b.** *to grip to*: to seize upon, take hold of (*lit.* and *fig.*) *north.* and *Sc. Obs.*

13.. *Gaw. & Gr. Knt.* 421 Gauan gripped to his ax & gederes hit on hyȝt. *c* **1400** *Destr. Troy* 931 Iason grippede graithly to a grym sworde. **1450–70** *Golagros & Gaw.* 530 He grippit to ane grete speir. *Ibid.* 1026 Gude schir Gawane Grippit to schir Gologras on the grund grene. *a* **1572** Knox *Hist. Ref.* Wks. 1846 II. 128 Some war licentious; some had greadelie gripped to the possessionis of the Kirk.

4. *trans.* To join firmly *to* something, as with a 'grip', grappling-iron, etc.

1886 *Science* 24 Sept. 275 Until the car is gripped to the moving cable, it must depend for its motive power on some other agent. **1887** Hall Caine *Deemster* xxvii. 170 We know your heart was gript to him with grapplins.

5. To close tightly, clench (the teeth, etc.). Also *intr.* for *refl.*

1861 J. Thomson *Ladies of Death* iii, He grips his teeth, or flings them words of scorn. **1898** G. W. Steevens in *Westm. Gaz.* 23 Sept. 7/3 Macdonald's jaws gripped and hardened as the flame spurted out again.

6. *fig.* To take hold upon (the mind, the emotions); to compel the attention and interest of (a reader, etc.).

1891 H. Herman *His Angel* 109 An indistinct remembrance dashed upon him and gripped his mind. **1894** H. Nisbet *Bush Girl's Rom.* 13 Charlotte Brontë and George Eliot—yes, she admired them both, but somehow they didn't grip her as Dickens did.

absol. **1894** *Forum* (U.S.) July 587 In other countries, where tradition has gripped more tightly for exclusion [of women from universities]. **1895** *Lit. World* Oct. 313/2 Even if the character..is slightly overdrawn the story grips.

7. (See quots. and cf. GRIP *sb.*^{1} 4.) *dial.*

a **1722** Lisle *Husb.* (1757) 405 To *Grip* or *Grip up*, to take up the wheat, and put it into sheaf. **1787** Grose *Prov. Gloss.*, *Grip*, to bind sheaves, Berks. **1888** in *Berksh. Gloss.*

8. *Austral. slang. absol.* To catch sheep (for the shearer). Cf. GRIPPER 2 b.

1886 C. Scott *Sheep-Farming* 137 One man can 'grip' for about ten or twelve clippers.

grip (grɪp), *v.*^{2} Now *dial.* Also GRIPE *v.*^{2} [f. GRIP *sb.*^{2}] *trans.* To make 'grips' or trenches in; to ditch, trench. Also, to dig (a trench, etc.).

1597 *Regul. Manor Scawby, Linc.* (*MS.*), That euery man doe suffyciently gryppe & trench ouer all his lands in Stauera bottom. **1601** in Stark *Hist. Gainsborough* (1817) 161 That every man gripp his lands in the corne fields. **1800** *Trans. Soc. Arts* XVIII. 110 The water furrows were opened by the plough..and finally gripped with the spade wherever it was necessary to a complete drainage. **1882** J. Evans in *Archæologia* XLVIII. 106 The objects..were found by a man while 'gripping' or cutting a deep narrow grip across the ground.

gripe (graɪp), *sb.*[1] [f. GRIPE *v.*[1] (The early examples may belong to GRIP *sb.*[1])]

1. a. The action of griping, clutching, grasping or seizing tenaciously, *esp.* with the hands, arms, claws, and the like. ***to come to gripes***: to come to close quarters *with* (cf. GRIP *sb.*[1] 1 c).

1393 LANGL. *P. Pl.* C. xx. 146 Al that the fyngres and the fust felen and touchen, Beo he greued with here gripe the holy gost let falle. *c* **1400** *Destr. Troy* 3761 Grete armys in the gripe, growen full rounde. **1583** STANYHURST *Æneis* III. (Arb.) 71 When I thee third tyme with grype more fiercelye [L. *maiore nisu*] dyd offer. **1599** SHAKS. *Hen. V*, IV. vi. 22 He ..raught me his hand, And with a feeble gripe, sayes [etc.]. **1613** HEYWOOD *Silver Age* III. i. Wks. 1874 III. 130 He chokes him with his gripes. **1644** MILTON *Educ.* Wks. 1738 I. 139 All the Locks and Gripes of Wrestling. **1647** W. BROWNE tr. *Gomberville's Polexander* III. ii. 62 Bellerophon could not avoid the coming to gripes with the Monster. **1672** DRYDEN *Marr. à la Mode* III. i. Wks. 1883 IV. 306 Like a weak dove under the falcon's gripe. **1718** PRIOR *Power* 442 The bear's rough gripe. **1762** FALCONER *Shipwr.* II. 355 The ropes, alas! a solid gripe deny. **1815** ELPHINSTONE *Acc. Cabul* (1842) I. 371 He..seized me by the arms with a rude gripe, and pressed me..to his breast. **1828** SCOTT *F.M. Perth* iv, Rescue me from the gripe of this iron-fisted.. clown. **1841–4** EMERSON *Ess.*, *History* Wks. (Bohn) I. 13 Antæus was suffocated by the gripe of Hercules.

transf. **1842** BROWNING *Pied Piper* vii, I heard a sound as of..putting apples..Into a cider-press's gripe.

b. *fig.* Grasp, hold, control, grip. †Formerly common in *pl.*

1387–8 T. USK *Test. Love* II. xi. (Skeat) l. 70 Vertue with ful gripe encloseth al these things. **1592** DEE *Comp. Rehears.* (Chetham Soc.) 35 Under the thraldome of the usurer's gripes. **1613** SHAKS. *Hen. VIII*, v. iii. 100, I take my cause Out of the gripes of cruell men. **1651–3** JER. TAYLOR *Serm. for Year* (1678) 225 To oppress his Tenants, and all that are within his gripe. **1735** SOMERVILLE *Chase* I. 111 The Gripe severe Of brazen-fisted Time. **1750** JOHNSON *Rambler* No. 80 ¶6 When we have..felt the gripe of the frost. **1780** BURKE *Sp. Bristol prev. Election* Wks. III. 368 As things wrung from you with your blood, by the cruel gripe of a rigid necessity. **1838** LYTTON *Leila* IV. iii, Not only did more than five hundred Jews perish in the dark and secret gripe of the grand inquisitor, but [etc.]. **1868** G. DUFF *Pol. Surv.* 64 Russia..has Bokhara within her gripe.

†**c.** *Phr.* (in fig. context). ***to lay, fasten a gripe on, upon***: to stretch forth a griping hand upon. ***to get a gripe of***: to secure a hold of. *Obs.*

a **1586** SIDNEY *Arcadia* v. (1598) 435 The Latines.. hauing..long gaped to deuoure Greece..were euen ready to lay an vniust gripe vpon it. **1583** A. KING tr. *Canisius' Catech.* 59 Be hop it [*sc.* the soul] gettis ane neirer gripe of ye guidnes of God. **1623** MASSINGER *Bondman* I. i. (1624) B 2 Ambitious Carthage, That to enlarge her Empire striues to fasten An vniust gripe on vs (that liue free Lords Of Syracusa). **1633** —— *Guardian* II. (1655) 32 May we not have a touch at Lawyers? *Claud.* By no means; they may To soon have a gripe at us. *a* **1639** WOTTON in *Reliq.* (1651) 488 You have left in him *illos aculeos* which you doe in all that (after the Scottish phrase) get but a gripe of you.

d. *Surg.* An act of compressing (e.g. an artery) with the fingers (cf. GRIPE *v.* 3 b, GRIPER 1). ***cutting on the gripe***: a mode of operating for the stone in which it is seized and held by the finger.

1676 WISEMAN *Surg.* VI. ii. 452 In stead of the Ligature.. they make a gripe, which gripe is commonly made by some Assistent who hath strength to do it. **1725** BRADLEY *Fam. Dict.* II. H iv/2 This Way is called Apparatus minor,..this we in England call Cutting upon the Gripe, and is the Method our Suters always cut by. **1739** S. SHARP *Surg.* xviii. 84 The most antient way of cutting for the Stone is that describ'd by Celsus, and known by the name of Cutting on the Gripe. **1886** in *Syd. Soc. Lex.*

e. *Mil.* ***at the gripe*** (see quot.).

1833 *Regul. Instr. Cavalry* I. 95 Raise the carbine with the right hand..and seize it with the left at the 'Gripe' (that is, with the full hand round the barrel and stock).

†**f.** The kind of sensation produced by an object when grasped. (Cf. FEEL *sb.* 5.) *Obs.*

1632 LITHGOW *Trav.* x. 495 The Calabrian silke, had never a better luster, and softer gripe, then [etc.].

2. *transf.* and *fig.* (cf. 1 b). **a.** The 'clutch' or 'pinch' of something painful. Formerly often in *pl.*: Spasms of pain, pangs of grief or affliction. Now *rare* or *Obs.*

a **1547** SURREY *Æneid* II. 288 New gripes of dred then pearse our trembling brestes. **1549–62** STERNHOLD & H. *Ps.* xxx. 6 Gripes of griefe and pangues full sore. **1613** PURCHAS *Pilgrimage* (1614) 156 More violently tortured with inward convulsions, and evill gripes, then by outward disease. **1667** MILTON *P.L.* XI. 264 Heart-strook with chilling gripe of sorrow. *a* **1716** SOUTH *Serm.* (1717) VI. 235 The secret Girds, and Gripes of a dissatisfied..Conscience! **1725** POPE *Odyss.* XVIII. 150 The gripes of poverty, and stings of care. **1751** JOHNSON *Rambler* No. 163 ¶3 The gripe of distress. **1840** THIRLWALL *Greece* VII. lvi. 200 The sharpest gripe of cold and hunger.

b. An intermittent spasmodic pain in the bowels. Usually *pl.*, colic pains.

1601 HOLLAND *Pliny* II. 331 If gripes come thick, they prescribe the ashes of Harts horn. **1611** COTGR., *Trenchaison*, a gripe or a wring, as of the Chollicke, &c. **1688** LUTTRELL *Diary* (1857) I. 443 The young prince hath been troubled with the gripes and had some fits. **1753** J. BARTLET *Gentl. Farriery* xiii. 121 The cholic or gripes in horses. **1766** [ANSTEY] *Bath Guide* iv. 2 My Time has been wretchedly spent With a Gripe or a Hickup wherever I went. **1806–7** J. BERESFORD *Miseries Hum. Life* (1826) xx. 250 Poor Margery's tripes Are the martyrs of gripes. **1812** COMBE *Picturesque* xxvi. 386 Swift has said..That he who daily smokes two pipes, The tooth-ache never has—nor gripes. **1846** J. BAXTER *Libr. Pract. Agric.* (ed. 4) I. 444 Excess of green food, sudden exposure to cold, are..occasional causes of gripes.

†**3.** The hand held in the position for grasping or clutching. *Obs.*

1555 PHILPOT In Coverdale *Lett. Mart.* (1564) 227 They went forth and wepte, sayth the Prophet: such shall come agayne hauing their gripes full of gladnes. **1577–87** HOLINSHED *Chron.* III. 939/1 God with a sparing hand reacheth out those things to the faithfull, which with full gripes he..powreth into the laps..of..epicures. **1644** BULWER *Chiron.* 102 The Fingers formed into a gripe or scratching posture. **1791** COWPER *Odyss.* XVII. 4 He seized his sturdy spear match'd to his gripe.

4. a. As much as can be grasped in the hand; a handful; also applied to other quantities (see quots.). *local.* (Cf. GRIP *sb.*[1] 4.)

1570 LEVINS *Manip.* 141/40 Yᵉ Gripe of a hand, *pugnus, manipulus.* **1573–80** BARET *Alv.* G. 559 A Gripe of corne in reaping, or so much hay or corne, as one with a pitchforke or hooke can take vp at a time. **1641** J. TRAPPE *Theol. Theol.* Ep. Ded., He once accepted..a gripe of goates-haire for an Oblation. **1656** W. D. tr. *Comenius' Gate Lat. Unl.* §335. 93 When it [corn] is shorn place it in gripes, and with rakes gather the gripes into sheaves. **1681** W. ROBERTSON *Phraseol. Gen.* (1693) 1124 We'l grasp all shortly in one gripe; *In unum quasi manipulum contrahemus.* *a* **1722** LISLE *Husb.* (1757) 405 *Gripe*, Armfull. **1794–1813** DAVIS *Agric. Wilts* 265 Reaping, done with a short crooked hook in handfuls, or gripes; laid down in gripe, when laid down in handfuls untied.

†**b.** A cluster (of grapes). *Obs.*

a **1400–50** *Alexander* 1347 A growen grape of a grype [*Dublin MS.* grope of a gripe] a grette & a rype.

5. Something which is griped or grasped. †**a.** A lute stop (*obs.*). **b.** The handle of an implement; the hilt of a sword; = GRIP *sb.*[1] 6.

1610 R. DOULAND *Var. Lute-lessons* B j b, By reason of many Gripes or stops (as you call them). **1748** F. SMITH *Voy. Disc.* I. 28 Their Paddle being double bladed, or two Paddles the Gripes or Handles sewed together, and the Blades one at each Extreme. **1775** WRAXALL *Tour North. Europe* 332 Round the gripe [of a sword] is a bandage of straps of leather crossed. **1793** W. HODGES *Trav. India* 3 The gripe of the sabre is too small for most European hands. **1846** H. TORRENS *Mil. Lit. & Hist.* I. 95 The lance was of a different description to ours, the staff of it resembling two elongated cones joined at their bases, at which point was the gripe.

6. *slang.* †**a.** (See quots. 1592, 1608). *Obs.* †**b.** A covetous person, a miser, a usurer. Also *Gripes* (as quasi-proper name). (? Sometimes with allusion to GRIPE *sb.*[3]) *Obs.*

1592 GREENE *Art Conny Catch.* II. 7 Certaine old sokers, which are lookers on, and listen for bets..are called Gripes. **1608** DEKKER *Belman Lond.* (ed. 2) F 3 He that Betteth is the Gripe. He that is cozened is the Vincent. **1621** BURTON *Anat. Mel.* III. iv. II. i. (1651) 691 Professed Usurers, meer Gripes. **1694** ECHARD *Plautus* Pref. a iij, Dos't think, Boy, we shall be able to squeeze out a swinging sum of Money of this old Gripes, to purchase our Freedom with? *a* **1700** B. E. *Dict. Cant. Crew*, *Gripe*,..an old Covetous Wretch: also a Banker, Money Scrivener, or Usurer.

c. A complaint; a grumble. *slang* (orig. *U.S.*).

1934 J. FARRELL *Studs Lonigan* (1936) III. xv. 341 The water was just right..and he took rhythmic strokes... It was like losing all the gripes that had been piling up within him. **1949** *Harper's* Jan. 61/1, I want to clear my desk of various matters, mostly gripes. **1954** *Chem. & Engin. News* 8 Mar., As a standard bearer in the cause of accurate nomenclature, you may be interested in one of my pet gripes. **1959** J. THURBER *Years with Ross* v. 76 Ingersoll was the main target of his gripes. **1964** S. M. MILLER in I. L. Horowitz *New Sociol.* 306 The 'gripes' of low-income neighborhood..are political issues.

7. Something which gripes or clutches.

a. †A claw (*obs.*); *pl.* pincers (*dial.*). †**b.** A device to secure a portcullis (*obs.*). **c.** = BRAKE *sb.*[7]

a. 1578 LYTE *Dodoens* III. lxxi. 413 Fashioned like gripes, or clawes, almost lyke the clawes of Wolfe. **1598** FLORIO, *Grifagno*, any bird that is rauenous, or that hath clawes or gripes. *Grifo, Griffo*, a griffon, a gripe, a clawe, a pounce. **1869** *Lonsdale Gloss.*, *Gripes*, a pair of wooden pincers with long handles for weeding corn.

b. 1587 HARRISON *England* II. ii. (1877) I. 45 One Roger builded the Castell of the Vies in the time of Henrie the first, taken in those daies for the strongest hold in England, as vnto whose gate there were regals and gripes for six or seven port cullises.

c. 1792 *Trans. Soc. Arts* X. 233 The gripe, or brake..and its lever. **1803** *Ibid.* XXI. 357 Preventing accidents to horses and carriages in going down hills by a gripe or clasp acting on the naves of the wheels. **1825** J. NICHOLSON *Operat. Mechanic* 140 The brake or gripe used in common windmills to stop their motion. **1875** KNIGHT *Dict. Mech.*, *Gripe*,..a brake applied to the wheel of a crane or derrick.

8. *Naut.* (See also GRIPE *sb.*[5]) *pl.* Lashings formed by an assemblage of ropes, etc., to secure a boat in its place on the deck; also, two broad bands passed respectively round the stem and stern of a boat hung in davits, to prevent swinging.

1762 FALCONER *Shipwr.* II. 102 The boats..are..with fastening gripes secured. **1832** MARRYAT *N. Forster* xxii, Some of the..men jumped into quarter-boats, and [cast] off the gripes and lashings. *c* **1860** H. STUART *Seaman's Catech.* 7 Pass the gripes, and see the falls clear for lowering. **1867** SMYTH *Sailor's Word-bk.* s.v., Gripes for a quarter boat.

9. *attrib.*, as (sense 2 b) ***gripe mixture, water.***

1728 E. SMITH *Compleat Housewife* (ed. 2) 231 *To make Gripe-water.* Take..Penny royal,..Coriander-seeds, Aniseeds, sweet Fennel-seeds, Carraway-seeds; bruise them all, and..sprinkle on them a quart of Brandy..distil it off.. drink it warm, and go to bed. **1891** *Star* 10 Dec. 2/7 A horse medicine known as gripe mixture. **1926** *Daily Colonist* (Victoria, B.C.) 3 July 4/6 (Advt.), The baby screamed day and night, having been slightly poisoned. I tried Woodward's Gripe Water when all else failed. **1953** E. TAYLOR *Sleeping Beauty* xiii. 198 The difficulties of obtaining the right brands of gripe-water, groats, or rusks.

gripe (graɪp), *sb.*[2] Dialectal variant of GRIP *sb.*[2]

1674 RAY *N.C. Words* 22 A Grip or Gripe: a little ditch or trench... This word is of general use all over England. **1796** *Ned Evans* I. 258 The hovel in which they were born was built in a ditch, the gripe of which formed two sides of it. **1839** *Ann. Reg.* 3 He saw a man at the other side of the hedge in the gripe. **1842** S. LOVER *Handy Andy* iii, It's a wide gripe, and the hedge is as thick as a wall.

†**gripe**, *sb.*[3] *Obs.* Forms: 3–4 **grip**, **gryp**, (4 **grypp**, 5 **grypp**, 6 **grippe**), 4–7 **grype**, 4–8 **gripe**. [ad. L. *grȳp-em, grȳph-em, grȳps* GRIFFIN, in med.L. used also for 'vulture'. Cf. OF. *grip* griffin, and ON. *grip-r* (Sw. *grip*, Da. *grib*) vulture; also OHG. *grîf*, *grîfo* (MHG. *grîf*, *grîfe*, mod.G. *greif*):—early Ger. **grîpo-z*, **grîpon-*, prob. from the Lat. See also GRYPH and GRAPE *sb.*[3]]

1. A griffin.

(In early instances perh. not clearly distinguished from sense 2.)

c **1205** LAY. 28062 þer ich isah gripes & grisliche fuȝeles. *c* **1290** *S. Eng. Leg.* I. 231/432 þare cam a gryp fleoinde, after heom in þe se..and fondede heom to sle. **13..** *K. Alis.* 5667 Addres with foure hedes and dragouns, Gripes, tygres, and lyouns. **1398** TREVISA *Barth. De P.R.* XVIII. lvi. (1495) 814 The grype is stronge enmye to horses and he takyth vp the horse and the man armyd, and grypes kepe the mountayns in the whiche ben gemmis and precious stones. **1483** CAXTON *Gold. Leg.* 396 b/2 A grete grype..assayled them & was lyke to haue destroyed them. **1559** W. CUNNINGHAM *Cosmogr. Glasse* 191 There are diverse straunge beastes bred in Asia, as Vnicornes,..Mercattes, Grippes. **1592** LYLY *Galathea* II. iii, Grypes make their nests of gold though their coates are feathers.

b. A figure or representation of a griffin.

1420 *E.E. Wills* (1882) 46 Also 1 bord mausure..wyth a prent in þe myddylle, and a grypp amyde. *a* **1650** *Sr. Lambewell* 105 in Furnivall *Percy Folio* I. 148 Vpon the topp a gripe stood, of shining gold.

2. A vulture.

a **1250** *XI Pains of Hell* 148 in *O.E. Misc.* (1872) 151 Gripes freteþ heore Mawen. *a* **1300** *Havelok* 572 þat him ne hauede grip or ern..þat wolde him dere. **1432–50** tr. *Higden* (Rolls) III. 57, vij gripes apperede firste to Remus. *c* **1440** *Promp. Parv.* 212/2 Grype, byrde, *vultur.* **1520** *Caxton's Chron. Eng.* III. 20/1 His faders deed bodye..he devyded to an hondred grypes lest he sholde ryde from dethe to lyfe. **1561** NORTON & SACKV. *Gorboduc* II. i. (Shaks. Soc.) 114 The hellish Prince adjudge my dampned Ghoste to Tantalus thirste..or cruell gripe to gnawe my growing harte. **1593** SHAKS. *Lucr.* 543 Like a white hind under the gripe's sharp claws. **1609** BIBLE (Douay) *Deut.* xiv. 12 The uncleane eate not: to witte, the eagle, the grype, and the osprey. **1630** J. TAYLOR (Water P.) *Wks.* II. 67/1 The Gripe no more on Titius guts should feed. **1672** JOSSELYN *New Eng. Rarities* 10 The Gripe, which is of two kinds, the one with a white Head, the other with a black Head, this we take for the Vulture. *a* **1767** *Sir Aldingar* xix. in Child *Ballads* (1885) II. 45/1, I dreamed a grype and a grimlie beast Had carryed my crowne away.

3. *Comb.*, as **gripe-foot**, the foot of a vessel made in the form of a griffin's claw; **gripe-shell** = GRIPE'S EGG.

1451 *Will of Kelyngholm* (Somerset Ho.), Vnum maser wiþ gripe fete. **15..** *Inv. Fountains Abb.* in Burton *Monast. Ebor.* (1758) 144 A grype-schill, with a covering, gilt.

†**gripe**, *sb.*[4] *Obs.* Also **grype**. [ad. obs. F. *grip* a pirate ship (Diez), It. *grippo* 'a little skiffe, or cock-boate' (Florio), perh. to be referred to F. *gripper* to seize (cf. Cotgr. s.v. *Grip*).] A vessel used in the Levant.

1506 GUYLFORDE *Pilgr.* (Camden) 76, iiij of vs Englyshe men..hyred vs a lytell grype, whiche we thoughte shulde have passed more redely with vs than the grete galye. **1548** HALL *Chron.*, *Hen. VIII*, 204 A vessell called a Gripe, and in her, 111. C. men. **1599** HAKLUYT *Voy.* II. 75 He brought fifteene vessels called Gripes, laden with wine.

gripe (graɪp), *sb.*[5] *Naut.* Also 6 **greepe**. [Orig. *greepe*, ad. Du. *greep*, but afterwards assimilated to GRIPE *sb.*[1]] The piece of timber terminating the keel at the forward extremity; sometimes taken as = FOREFOOT 2.

1580 H. SMITH in Hakluyt *Voy.* (1599) I. 449 This day by misfortune a piece of ice stroke of our greepe afore at two aforenoone. **1691** T. H[ALE] *Acc. New Invent.* 120 The false Stemm, Gripe, Keel, Stern-post, and Dead-rising. **1706** PHILLIPS (ed. Kersey), *Gripe*,..in Sea-Affairs, the Compass or Sharpness of a Ship's Stem under Water, especially towards the bottom of the Stem. **1711** W. SUTHERLAND *Shipbuild. Assist.* 62 A But left for the Gripe to join to. **1769** FALCONER *Dict. Marine* (1780) U 2 b, The gripe or fore-foot which unites the keel with the stem. **1830** HEDDERWICK *Nav. Arch.* 113, *Gripe*, the under part of the stem and cut-water. **1882** NARES *Seamanship* (ed. 6) 2 *Gripe*, a projection forward at the lowest part of the stem; by exposing a larger surface it prevents the foremost part of the ship, when sailing with the wind on the side, from being driven sideways away from the wind.

gripe (graɪp), *v.*[1] Forms: 1 **grípan**, 3–4 **gripen**, 4–7 **grype**, (6 **greep**), 4– **gripe**. *Pa. t.* 1 **gráp**, *pl.* **gripon**, 3 **grap**, **grop**, **græp**, *pl.* **gripen**, **grippen**, 3–4 **grep(e**, *pl.* **grepen**, 4– **griped**, (6 *Sc.* **-it**). *Pa. pple.* 1 **ȝegripen**, 2–4 **gripen**, 4 **igripen**, **grypen**, 4– **griped**. [A Com. Teut. str. verb: OE. *grípan* = OS. *grîpan* (MLG., MDu. *grîpen*, Du. *grijpen*),

OHG. *grîfan* (MHG. *grîfen*, Ger. *greifen*), ON. *gripa* (Sw. *gripa*, Da. *gribe*), Goth. *greipan*:—pre-Teut. *ghreib-: *ghroib-*, found in Lith. *grĕbti* to seize, *graibýti* to grope. (See GROPE *v.*) The wk. conjugation came in in the 14th c., and the str. forms became obsolete before the 15th c.]

†**1. a.** *intr.* To make a grasp or clutch, to seek to get a hold (*lit.* and *fig.*): in OE. const. *dat.* (sometimes accompanied by locative advb. phr.) or *genitive*, later with *to* (Sc. *til*), *towards, for, at, upon*; to grasp *at*; to seize *upon*. *Obs.*

Beowulf 1501 Grap þa toȝeanes, guðrinc ȝefeng atolan clommum. **971** *Blickl. Hom.* 211 þa fynd..heora gripende wæron, swa swa græðiȝ wulf. *a* **1000** *Cædmon's Gen.* 2063 (Gr.) Gripon unfæȝre under sceat werum scearpe garas. *a* **1250** *Prov. Alfred* 192 in *O.E. Misc.* (1872) 114 þanne schulle vre ifon to vre vouh gripen. **1393** LANGL. *P. Pl.* C. IV. 89 He gripeþ þer-for as grete as for þe grete treuthe. *c* **1430** *Pilgr. Lyf Manhode* I. v. (1869) 3 He gripede faste to þe knottes. *c* **1592** MARLOWE *Massacre Paris* III. iii. 1080 Upon whose heart may all the Furies gripe. **1596** DALRYMPLE tr. *Leslie's Hist. Scot.* II. 152 How greidilie men gripis til it, quhen anes it is offirit. **1608** SHAKS. *Per.* I. i. 49 [They] Gripe not at earthly ioyes as earst they did. **1615** ROWLANDS *Melancholie Knt.* 40 All gripe to get their owne. **1637** GILLESPIE *Eng. Pop. Cerem.* I. ix. 34 That which they gripe to in this Epistle, is, that Calvine..saith, *hoc tamen testatum esse volo.* **1657** CROMWELL *Sp.* 20 Apr. in *Carlyle*, I meant to gripe at the Government. **1727** J. WILLISON *Afflicted Man's Comp.* ii. (1850) 77 Faith gripes to the great Gospel promise of Salvation. **1810** SCOTT *Lady of L.* II. xxxiv, Their desperate hand Griped to the dagger. **1820** —— *Ivanhoe* v, His quivering fingers griped towards the handle of his sword.

†**b.** ***to gripe with***: to grapple with, come to close quarters with. *Obs.*

1377 LANGL. *P. Pl.* B. XVII. 202 Who so synneth in seynt spirit, it semeth that he greueth God, that he grypeth with [1393 ther he gripeth], and wolde his grace quenche. **1631** R. H. *Arraignm. Whole Creature* xiii. §1. 168 We will come (as in a Land, or Sea-fight) to grapple and gripe, with Vanities.

†**c.** Used for GROPE. *Obs.*

a **1598** ROLLOCK *Serm.* Wks. 1849 I. 460 We should gripe down to the heart from whence the prayers of the godly do flow.

2. *trans. gen.* To lay hold of, seize, catch, grasp; to get into one's power or possession. †In OE. and ME. also occas.: To take, receive. *Obs.* exc. *arch.*

a **900** *Kent Gloss.* in Wr.-Wülcker 57/9 *Ne capiaris*, ðet ðu ne sio gripen. *a* **1000** *Sal. & Sat.* 151 (Gr.) Hwilum flotan gripað. *a* **1225** *Leg. Kath.* 1969 Grure grap euch mon hwen he lokede þeron. *a* **1240** *Wohunge* in *Cott. Hom.* 273 Hare praie þat tai hefden grediliche gripen. *a* **1300** *E.E. Psalter* ix. 16 In þis snare..Gripen es þe fote ofe þa. **1362** LANGL. *P. Pl.* A. III. 235 Heo that gripeth heore ȝiftus. ?*a* **1366** CHAUCER *Rom. Rose* 204 Coveityse is ever wood To grypen other folkes good. *c* **1421** HOCCLEVE *Complaint* 265 Othar thinge the[n] woo may I none grype. **1551** ROBINSON tr. *More's Utop.* (Arb.) 167 Woldest thou gripe both gaine and pleasure? **1583** GOLDING *Calvin on Deut.* iii. 15 He whiche grypeth too much can hardly holde it. **1596** SHAKS. *1 Hen. IV*, v. i. 57 To gripe the generall sway into your hand. **1608** *Yorksh. Trag.* I. x, Let me entreat to speak with her, before The prison gripe me. **1670** BROOKS *Wks.* (1867) VI. 376 They greedily griped the possessions of the church. **1814** SCOTT *Wav.* xvii, We gripe nothing but a fat baillie of Perth.

absol. **1362** LANGL. *P. Pl.* A. III. 175 Thow hast hanged on my nekke enleue tymes; And eke i-gripen of my gold. ?*a* **1366** CHAUCER *Rom. Rose* 1156 Not Avarice..Was half to grype so ententyf, As Largesse is to yeve and spende.

3. a. To clutch, seize firmly, or grasp tightly with hand, paw, claw, or the like; to grip. Also said of the hand.

c **1200** ORMIN 8125 Mann grap þa þatt cnif himm fra. *c* **1205** LAY. 18027 Heo [the Irish] to-biliue & gripen heore cniues & of mid here breches. *c* **1275** *Ibid.* 21213 Cheldrich wid his ohte men leopen heom to horse and grepen [*c* **1205** igripen] hire wepne. *c* **1300** *Havelok* 1872 [He] grop an ore, and a long knif. **13..** *Sir Beues* (MS. A.) 2485 Be þe riȝt leg ȝhe him grep. *c* **1450** *Merlin* 9 She griped hir be the shulders, and put hir owt at the dore. **1530** PALSGR. 575/2 He that taketh to moche in his hande at ones grypeth it yll. **1608** D. T. *Ess. Pol. & Mor.* 69 *Par trop presser l'anguille, on la perd*, he that grypes an Eele too hard, is in danger to lose it. **1638** SIR T. HERBERT *Trav.* (ed. 2) 20 A bird..so strong as in her tallons can easily gripe and trusse up an Elephant. **1667** MILTON *P.L.* VI. 543 Let each..gripe fast his orbed Shield. **1719** DE FOE *Crusoe* II. ii. (1840) 32 One of her hands was clasped round the frame of a chair, and she griped it so hard that we could not easily make her let go. **1781** COWPER *Charity* 525 Conjecture gripes the victims in his paw. **1843** LYTTON *Last Bar.* VII. iii, Hilyard griped his dagger. *a* **1863** THACKERAY *Duval* vi. (1869) 78 When my mother lifted her hand, I..griped it so tight that I frightened her. **1866** ROGERS *Agric. & Prices* I. xxi. 534 So slender at the upper end that a man may easily gripe it.

transf. **1870** MORRIS *Earthly Par.* III. IV. 178 The hard frost griped all things bitterly.

b. *Surg.* (Cf. GRIPE *sb.*[1] 1 d).

1830 COOPER *Dict. Pract. Surg.* (ed. 6) 819 With the fingers the calculus was next griped.

†**c.** To enclose in a tight embrace, encircle tightly. *Obs.*

c **1400** *Siege Jerusalem* (E.E.T.S.) 73/1249 No gretter þan a grehounde, to grype in þe medil. *c* **1450** *Merlin* 655 He..griped him sore in his armes. **1525** LD. BERNERS *Froiss.* II. clxviii. [clxiv.] 468 They gryped fast their horses with their legges. **1548–77** VICARY *Anat.* vii. (1888) 49 The Adiutor bone..is..crooked, because it shoulde be the more habler to grype thinges. **1607** HEYWOOD *Wom. kilde w. Kindnesse* Wks. 1874 II. 107 With my full hand Ile gripe him to the heart. **1715–20** POPE *Iliad* XVIII. 644 The children, in whose arms are borne (Too short to gripe them) the brown sheaves of corn. **1758** J. KENNEDY *Curios. Wilton-Ho.* 41 Hercules wrestling with Antaeus; he only gripes him high from the Ground.

d. *absol.*

1597 A. M. tr. *Guillemeau's Fr. Chirurg.* 47/2 The property of the hande is to gripe and take houlde. **1611** SHAKS. *Cymb.* III. i. 40 We haue..many among vs, can gripe as hard as Cassibulan. **1723** *Flying Post* 11–13 Apr. in *Masonic Mag.* (1881) IX. 25 Examination of a Mason..To Gripe, is when you take a Brother by the right Hand and put your middle Finger to his Wrist, and he'll do so to you. **1741** H. BROOKE *Constantia* in Chalmers *Poets* (1810) XVII. 397/2 Struggling they gripe, they pull, they bend, they strain. **1817** COLERIDGE *Sibyll. Leaves, Three Graves*, At first She gently press'd her hand. Then harder, till her grasp at length Did gripe like a convulsion!

†**4.** To close (the fingers) tightly; to clench (the fist). *Obs. rare.*

a **1633** AUSTIN *Medit.* (1635) 137 Wee are borne the Children of wrath with our hands griped-close together. **1728** POPE *Dunc.* II. 210 Unlucky Welsted! thy unfeeling master, The more thou ticklest, gripes his fist the faster.

†**5.** *fig.* To lay hold of; to apprehend; to comprehend. *Obs. rare.*

a **1340** HAMPOLE *Psalter* ii. 12 Gripes disciplyne [Vulg. *apprehendite disciplinam*], leswhen lord wreth. **1674** N. FAIRFAX *Bulk & Selv.* 13 All the things we can gripe in our minds. *Ibid.* 137 It gripes within the bounds of its wide verge the restlesness that we are..justling with. **1742** YOUNG *Nt. Th.* VII. 1252 Can such a soul contract itself, to gripe A point of no dimension, of no weight?

6. To oppress by miserly or penurious treatment; to 'pinch', 'squeeze'. (Said also of poverty.)

1645 QUARLES *Sol. Recant.* v. 8 Seest thou..poor men grip'd beneath th' oppressours hand? *c* **1680** BEVERIDGE *Serm.* (1729) I. 198 All that oppress and gripe poor workmen in their prices. **1729** SAVAGE *Wanderer* iii. (1761) 49 For this, he grip'd the Poor, and Alms denied. **1735** DYCHE & PARDON *Dict.*, *Gripe*,..also to pinch, grind, or give a Person too little for their Wages or Goods. **18..** DICKENS *Repr. Pieces* (1866) 119 He feeds the poor baby when he himself is griped with want. *a* **1868** LD. BROUGHAM (Ogilv.), A disposition is everywhere exhibited by men in office to gripe and squeeze all submitted to their authority.

absol. **1694** F. BRAGGE *Disc. Parables* xiv. 459 How to gripe, and over-reach, and oppress, was the subject of their thoughts. **1755** *Man* No. 11. 2 Yet for this nonsensical end they will gripe, pinch, pilfer, cheat..renounce the conveniences, and almost the necessaries, of life. **1895** *Forum* (U.S.) Jan. 569 There is a little less sociability [in winter] and poverty gripes harder.

7. To grieve, afflict, distress.

1559 *Mirr. Mag., Mowbray's Banishm.* xxix, Grief gryped me so, I pyned awaye and dyed. **1567** DRANT *Horace, Art of Poetry* B vj, Those which inwardly with griefe Are gryped in their minde. **1593** SHAKS. *3 Hen. VI*, I. iv. 171 How inly Sorrow gripes his Soule. **1671** FLAVEL *Fount. Life* xxiii. 70 How sick was his conscience as soon as he had swallowed it! It grip'd him to the heart. **1871** B. TAYLOR *Faust* I. ix. 150 What ails thee? What is 't gripes thee, elf? A face like thine beheld I never. **1905** R. E. BEACH *Pardners* (1912) i. 29. It gripes me to hear a man cry. **1941** J. M. CAIN *Mildred Pierce* (1943) 88 What's griping him is that he can't do anything for the kids.

8. a. To affect with 'gripes'; to produce griping pains in. Now chiefly in pa. pple.: see GRIPED.

1611 COTGR., *Trenchaisonner*, to wring or gripe like the Cholicke, &c. **1619** H. HUTTON *Follies Anat.* (Percy Soc.) 12 The thought of To[bacco] his intrailes more doth gripe Then physicks art. **1668** CULPEPPER & COLE *Barthol. Anat.* I. xv. 39 Such persons fasting, are often griped in their Bellies. **1712** SWIFT *Jrnl. to Stella* 7 Jan., I..came home, because I was not very well, but a little griped. **1756** BROOKE in *Phil. Trans.* LI. 76 They were much griped, and purged more than 20 times in 24 hours. **1865** *Pall Mall G.* 20 Sept. 3/2 Anybody calling for champagne or claret at a place of public entertainment..is certain to be cheated, and..very likely to be griped.

b. *absol.* To produce pain in the bowels as if by constriction or contraction; to cause 'gripes'.

1702 SIR J. FLOYER in *Phil. Trans.* XXIII. 1171 Crato describes Sena as if it had *Viscidum quid*, by which it gripes. **1811** A. T. THOMSON *Lond. Disp.* (1818) 134 Scammony..is..apt to gripe. **1875** H. C. WOOD *Therap.* (1879) 464 Whenever senna is exhibited, an aromatic should be united with it, to lessen its tendency to gripe.

9. *Naut.* **a.** *trans.* To secure (a boat) with 'gripes'. (In *pa. pple.* only, also ***griped to***.)

1840 R. H. DANA *Bef. Mast* xxiv. 76 We got..the launch and pinnace hoisted, chocked and griped. **1867** SMYTH *Sailor's Word-bk.*, *Griped-to*, the situation of a boat when secured by gripes.

b. *intr.* Said of a ship which has a tendency to come up into the wind in spite of the helm, as when sailing close-hauled.

1627 CAPT. SMITH *Seaman's Gram.* xi. 53 Not [to] gripe..is when shee will not keepe a winde well. **1870** *Eng. Mech.* 25 Feb. 580/1 A cutter is sometimes apt to 'gripe'; that is, to turn its bowsprit suddenly up in the wind. **1879** THOMSON & TAIT *Nat. Phil.* I. I. §325 A steamer with sail..griping so badly with any after canvass that it is often impossible to steer.

10. *intr.* To complain, 'grouse'. So '**griping** *vbl. sb. slang* (orig. *U.S.*).

1932 *Amer. Speech* June 332 *Gripe*, to complain. **1934** F. SCOTT FITZGERALD *Tender is Night* II. i. 153 In some moods he griped at his own reasoning: Could I help it. **1940** *New Yorker* 21 Sept. 37 He got good and sore and griped. **1945** E. FORD *Larry Scott* v. 51 I've already told him that the newspaper game is a lousy business, so you can save your griping for somebody else. **1947** D. M. DAVIN *Gorse blooms Pale* 199 Old Snow was griping away about his girl turning him down. **1959** *Times Lit. Suppl.* 20 Nov. 678/1 Let us get the griping over quickly. **1963** *Time* 30 Aug. 18/2 Ike..griped publicly: 'There are too many of these generals who have all sorts of ideas.' **1967** *Boston Traveler* 27/2 People are always griping about kids hanging around and being at the wrong places at the wrong time.

11. *Comb.*, as **gripe-all**, a grasping, avaricious person; †**gripe-money, -penny**, a miser, niggard; †**gripe-stick** (see quot.).

1823 *New Monthly Mag.* VIII. 34 The city *gripeall who has amassed his million. **1611** COTGR., *Gripp'argent*, a *Gripe-money, or Catch-coyne. **1860** WORCESTER, **Gripe-penny*, a niggard, a miser. *Mackenzie.* **1706** PHILLIPS (ed. Kersey), *Tourniquet*, a Turn-Still: also the *Gripe-stick us'd by Surgeons..in cutting off an Arm, &c.

gripe (graɪp), *v.*[2] Dialectal variant of GRIP *v.*[2]

1597 *Stanford Churchw. Acc.* in *Antiquary* (1888) May 212 For gripinge the church acre j[d]. **1805** PRICE in *Ann. Agric.* XLIII. 123 [Land] must be cleared of the surface water by griping or under-draining. **1846** J. BAXTER *Libr. Pract. Agric.* (ed. 4) II. 315 In the following autumn, immediately after the drawing is completed, the plants left standing are to be worked well and deeply with the spade: this operation is generally termed griping. **1869** *Lonsdale Gloss.*, *Grip, Gripe*, to make shallow ditches or grips.

griped (graɪpt), *ppl. a.* [f. GRIPE *v.*[1] + -ED[1].] In senses of the vb. **a.** Grasped or gripped tenaciously. **b.** Of the fist, the jaws: Clenched. **c.** Pained in the bowels; affected with 'gripes'.

1583 STUBBES *Anat. Abuses* I. (1879) 184 To hit him vnder the short ribbes with their griped fists, and with their knees to catch him vpon the hip. **1590** SPENSER *F.Q.* I. xi. 41 From his cruell claw To reave by strength the griped gage away. **1695** BLACKMORE *Pr. Arth.* III. 47 The Earth's griped Bowels with Convulsions rack. **1753** J. BARTLET *Gentl. Farriery* xiv. 134 If..he appears griped and in pain, let this glyster be given. **1855** BROWNING *Protus* 56 The Smith's rough-hammered head. Great eye, gross jaw, and griped lips. **1897** *Allbutt's Syst. Med.* III. 750 [He] draws up his legs uneasily as if griped.

gripeful ('graɪpfʊl), *sb. rare.* [f. GRIPE *sb.*[1] + -FUL.] As much as can be grasped in the hand.

1727 BRADLEY *Fam. Dict.* s.v. *Bait*, A Gripe-full of Cummin, and a Handful of Aniseed.

gripeful ('graɪpfʊl), *a. rare.* [f. GRIPE *v.*[1] + -FUL.] Apt to 'gripe'; gripy.

1864 in WEBSTER. **1879** *Tinsley's Mag.* XXIV. 185 The most gripeful of all gripy wines.

†**gripe-handed**, *a. Obs. rare.* [Parasynthetic formation on the stem of GRIPE *v.*[1]] Close-fisted.

1698 SOUTH *Serm.* III. 96 Implying..that for a Man to be Gripe-handed and Clear-sighted too was Impossible.

gripell, obs. form of GRIPPLE.

†**gripen**, *ppl. a. Obs.* [Vulgar survival of the str. pa. pple. of GRIPE *v.*[1]] Of the fist: Clenched.

1706 VANBRUGH *Prov. Wife* IV. iii, I did but offer in mere civility to help her up the steps into our apartment,—and with her gripen fist (*Sir John Brute knocks him down*)—aye, just so, sir. **1790** MRS. WHEELER *Westmld. Dial.* (1821) 14 He up wie his gripin neaf an felt me owar.

griper ('graɪpə(r)). [f. GRIPE *v.*[1] + -ER[1].]

†**1.** One who grasps. *Obs.*

1676 WISEMAN *Surg.* VI. ii. 452 Suppose the uneasie posture, and the long griping tires the Griper.

2. One who oppresses people by extortionate or niggardly methods; an extortioner. Now *rare.*

1587 HARRISON *England* II. iii. (1877) I. 88 Our noble universities, whose lands some greedie gripers doo gape wide for. **1647** TRAPP *Comm. Matt.* ix. 9 They were great gripers, and exacted extremely upon the Jews. *a* **1700** B. E. *Dict. Cant. Crew*, *Gripe*, or *Griper*, an old Covetous Wretch. Also a Banker, Money Scrivener, or Usurer. **1823** in *Spirit Publ. Jrnls.* (1824) 533 Southey's sackbut tunes the praise of every Royal griper. **1865** DICKENS *Mut. Fr.* III. xiv, That foxey old grasper and griper.

†**3.** A person or thing that distresses or inflicts pain. *Obs.*

1573 TUSSER *Husb.* xxix. (1878) 68 Winter..a griper of all things and specially age. **1602** *Narcissus* (1893) 420 Love's a griper.

†**4.** An instrument of torture. *Obs.*

1598 FLORIO, *Catollo*, a tormenting instrument called a griper or pincher.

†**5.** A canine tooth. *Obs.*

1600 SURFLET *Country Farme* VII. xxxvii. 865 With pincers..break al the teeth of the neather iaw, wherein the great gripers stand.

†**6.** A griping medicine. *Obs.*

1766 [ANSTEY] *Bath Guide* iv. 82 Tho' I've taken a Griper I'll venture to peck at the Dory and Piper.

7. One who complains. *U.S. slang.* Cf. GRIPE *v.*[1] 10.

1937 *Amer. Speech* XII. 315/2 Radio lacks a word to describe the disgruntled listener... Griper is not precise enough. **1938** *Ibid.* XIII. 315/2 *Griper*, a customer that always finds fault.

†**gripe's egg.** *Obs.* Forms: 4 **grypesheye**, 5 **gripesei, -ey(e, gryppeshey**; 5 **gryp ey**, 5, 6 **gripes egg(e.** [GRIPE *sb.*[3]] A large egg (? an ostrich's) supposed to be that of a 'gripe'; a vessel shaped like this; an oval-shaped cup.

[**1390** GOWER *Conf.* I. 127 (Fairfax MS.) The Cuppe..was policed ek so clene That no signe of the Skulle was sene, But as it were a Gripes Ey.] **1391** *Will of Horbury* (Somerset Ho.), Ciphum vocat[um] Grypesheye. **1419** in *Test. Ebor.* I. 393 Alius ciphus vocatus a gryp ey. **1491** *Will of Vaughan* (Somerset Ho.), A gripes egg harnased with siluer. **1610** B. JONSON *Alch.* II. iii, Let the water in Glasse E. be feltred, And put into the Gripes egge.

† **griph.** *Obs.* In 7 gryphe; also in L. form griphus. [ad. L. *griphus*, a. Gr. γρῖφος fishing-basket, creel; dark saying, riddle. Cf. F. *griphe*.] A puzzling question; a riddle, enigma.

a **1652** J. SMITH *Sel. Disc.* iv. 71 That old gryphe or riddle of the Peripatetic school. *a* **1670** HACKET *Abp. Williams* II. (1692) 132 No Law or Practice directs the Subject to bring such Gryphes and Oracles, but plain, litteral, grammatical Notions of Libels to a Justice of Peace. **1678** CUDWORTH *Intell. Syst.* I. iv. §21. 388 That seemingly monstrous Paradox or puzzling Griphus of theirs [the Pythagoreans] that 'Numbers were the Causes and Principles of all things'. **1796** PEGGE *Anonym.* (1809) 418 A griphus or ænigma adduced by Tollius in his edition of Ausonius.

griph(e, variant of GRYPH, vulture. *Obs.*

griphin, -on, obs. forms of GRIFFIN[1].

griphite ('grɪfaɪt). *Min.* [f. Gr. γρῖφ-ος riddle (see quot. 1891) + -ITE[1].] A basic phosphate of manganese, sodium, calcium, iron, and aluminium occurring as dark brown or black masses.

1891 W. P. HEADDEN in *Amer. Jrnl. Sci.* CXLI. 416, I would propose to call this new phosphate Griphite, from *γριφος puzzle*, in allusion to its unusual and somewhat enigmatical composition. **1942** *Amer. Mineral.* XXVII. 452 Griphite is cubic and its structure is similar to that of garnets.

griping ('graɪpɪŋ), *vbl. sb.*[1] [f. GRIPE *v.*[1] + -ING[1].] The action of GRIPE *v.*[1] in various senses.

a **1300** *E.E. Psalter* cxlix. 6 Gripinges ofe swerde in þair hende. *c* **1440** *Promp. Parv.* 213/1 Grypynge wythe þe hande, or oþer lyke, *constrictio, compressio.* ?*c* **1440** STAUNTON *St. Patrick's Purgatory* (E.E.T.S.) 73 Bi þe help of þat woman and of myne owne grypyng, I steied vppon þat ladder. **1526** TINDALE *Matt.* iv. 24 They brought unto hym all sicke people, that were taken with divers diseases and gripinges. [So Coverdale, Geneva; **1611** torments.] **1607** HIERON *Wks.* I. 390 Rackings, enhaunsings, gripings, vsuries. **1610** R. DOULAND *Var. Lute-lessons* B 2 b *marg.*, For Griping of stops in B. *a* **1665** J. GOODWIN *Filled w. the Spirit* (1867) 237 Secret wringings and gripings and gnawings of conscience. **1709** MRS. MANLEY *Secr. Mem.* (1736) III. 190 Her Favourite Stauratius's Griping and Extortions. **1769** FALCONER *Dict. Marine* (1780), *Griping*..the inclination of a ship to run to windward of her course, particularly when she sails with the wind on her beam or quarter. **1822–34** *Good's Study Med.* (ed. 4) II. 185 Ventral gripings. **1840** DICKENS *Old C. Shop* xxxv, The tendency of her legal practice had been to fix her thoughts on small gains and gripings. **1898** P. MANSON *Trop. Diseases* xviii. 289 The leading symptoms of dysentery are those of inflammation of the great intestine—namely, griping, tenesmus, &c.

'**griping,** *vbl. sb.*[2] The action of GRIPE *v.*[2]

1805, 1846 [see GRIPE *v.*[2]].

griping ('graɪpɪŋ), *ppl. a.* [f. GRIPE *v.*[1] + -ING[2].]

1. That gripes, grasps, or clutches tightly. Also *fig.* of persons, their actions, etc.: Grasping, usurious, avaricious, 'squeezing'.

1573 L. LLOYD *Pilgr. Princes* (1586) 47 To auoid yᵉ griping pawes of a hungry Sparhaucke. **1587** HOLINSHED *Chron.* I. 71/1 Manie of them..were constrained to yeeld themselues into the griping hands of their enemies. **1658** *Whole Duty Man* xi. §9. 89 Extortion, and griping usury. **1697** DRYDEN *Æneid* VI. 303 He seiz'd the shining bough with griping hold. **1710** STEELE *Tatler* No. 223 ¶1 This Method of making Settlements was first invented by a griping Lawyer. **1846** J. BAXTER *Libr. Pract. Agric.* (ed. 4) I. p. xxxi, A griping landlord. **1855** MACAULAY *Hist. Eng.* xx. IV. 518 Oppressed by cruel and griping men in power.

absol. **1785** J. TRUSLER *Mod. Times* II. 57 The griping, the usurious, and the lawless.

2. Causing pain or distress, physical or mental; painful, distressing.

1568 T. HOWELL *Newe Sonets* (1879) 117 Through greeping griefe, and thought so sore opprest. **1577** T. KENDALL *Flowers Epigr.* S vj b, Oh grisly gripyng grief. **1645** QUARLES *Sol. Recant.* v. 68 The heart-corroding Fangs Of griping Care. **1666** BAXTER *Call to Unconverted* 225 O what a griping thought it will be..to think..That this was your own doing! **1897** P. WARING *Tales Old Regime* 97 The griping hunger, which might be gratified in a moment if they would.

3. Applied more or less *spec.* to spasmodic constricting pains in the bowels; having the pathological effect of 'gripes'; also, causing or producing 'gripes'.

1578 LYTE *Dodoens* I. xlix. 71 The same..swageth the gryping paynes of the belly. **1626** BACON *Sylva* §546–47 That Windinesse is Grosse, and Swelling; Not Sharpe or Griping. **1732** ARBUTHNOT *Rules of Diet* 351 It excites Vomiting, sharp griping Pains with wind in other Parts of the Bowels. **1822–34** *Good's Study Med.* (ed. 4) II. 254 The griping property of Castor oil. **1882** *Garden* 28 Oct. 381/2 The Griping Fruited Service. **1897** *Allbutt's Syst. Med.* III. 752 Each stool is preceded by griping pains in the belly.

Hence '**gripingly** *adv.*, '**gripingness**.

1626 BACON *Sylva* §65 Clisters also helpe, lest the Medicine stop in the Guts, and worke gripingly. **1640** DIGBY in *Lismore Papers* Ser. II. (1888) IV. 139 Thinges.. being wrested out of it, maketh it not onely be gripingly held, but [etc.]. **1683** KENNETT tr. *Erasm. on Folly* 80 Another with a Logic-fisted gripingness catches at and grasps all he can come within the reach of.

griple, variant of GRIPPLE *sb.*[2] *Obs.*

gripless ('grɪplɪs), *a. rare.* [f. GRIP *sb.*[1] + -LESS.] Having no grip or hold.

1606 BIRNIE *Kirk-Burial* (1833) 33 Builded upon the sandy foundation of three griplesse grounds. **1889** A. MUNRO *Siren Casket* 192 What means my Mary's gripless hand?

‖**grippe** (grip). Also (anglicized) grip. [Fr., vbl. sb. f. *gripper* to seize.] = INFLUENZA.

1776 J. JEKYLL *Corr.* (1894) 64 An epidemic cold seems to have spread itself from London to Barcelona. In passing through this kingdom [France], it has obtained the name of 'grippe'—a term significant enough from the nature of its attack on the throat. **1803** T. CAMPBELL *Let.* 27 Mar. in *Life & Lett.* (1849) I. 425 John has been dubbed Dr. Leyden, and the influenza has been called La grippe. **1834** J. FORBES *Laennec's Dis. Chest* (ed. 4) 193 The epidemic of 1803–4 (known by the name of *grippe*). **1890** LOWELL *Lett.* (1894) II. 441 Four of the weans have had the *grippe*. **1891** *Boston Daily Globe* 24 Mar. 5/1 The grip is with us again... This year the grip seems to have started in Chicago.

Hence ‖**grippé** *a.*, **gripped** *a.*, affected with the 'grippe'.

1890 W. BATESON *Let.* 16 Jan. in B. Bateson *W. Bateson* (1928) 40, I am glad to hear that you were so slightly '*grippé*' after all. **1892** *Contemp. Rev.* Aug. 233 The one whose bed was opposite to the gripped patient. *Ibid.* 235 A visitor arrived there gripped on Dec. 12, 1889. **1933** J. JOYCE *Let.* 18 Oct. (1966) III. 288, I..have to put it off, being slightly *grippé*.

grippe, obs. form of GRIP.

† **grippen,** *v. Obs.* [f. GRIPEN *ppl. a.*] *trans.* To clench (the fist).

1814 *Way to win Her* I. ii, You..grippening your fist for all the world like Madona the great boxer. *Ibid.* IV. i, She has such a trick of grippening her fist upon occasion.

gripper ('grɪpə(r)). [f. GRIP *v.*[1] + -ER[1].] One who or that which grips.

† **1.** *gen.* = GRIPER 1. *Obs. rare.*⁻¹

1570 LEVINS *Manip.* 74/24 A Gripper, *harpax*.

2. *spec.* **a.** 'In Ireland, a sheriff's officer; a bailiff' (Cassell 1884). **b.** *Austral. slang.* One who catches sheep for the shearers.

1886 C. SCOTT *Sheep-Farming* 137 The catcher or 'gripper' supplies the shearers with a fresh sheep as soon as he is finished with the former.

3. An implement used for gripping or clutching; a clutch or claw of any kind; any contrivance employed to seize or embrace an object.

1857 *Illustr. Lond. News* XXXI. 246/1 Conveying a discharge to the said cartridge, and thereby releasing a gripper, and detaining the cable from running away. **1870** L. SIMON in *Eng. Mech.* 4 Mar. 609/1 Grippers or fingers take hold of the cut end of the paper. **1871** *Amer. Encycl. Printing* (ed. Ringwalt), *Grippers*, the metal claws..which seize hold of the sheet of paper as it lies on the feeding-board. **1882** DREDGE, etc. *Electric Illumin.* I. 383 The actual work of liberating the catch or the gripper, and feeding the carbon, is effected by gravity. **1884** in J. Bucknall Smith *Cable or Rope Traction* 104 The carriages..shall always be attached by the gripper to the cable. **1886** *Textile Manufacturer* 15 June 288/2 On each carriage 112 to 224 iron tongs or grippers are placed at regular distances.

4. *attrib.*, as ***gripper edge, machine, mechanism.***

1871 *Amer. Encycl. Printing* (ed. Ringwalt), *Gripper Machines*, power-presses in which grippers, as contradistinguished from tapes, are used. **1892** *Pall Mall G.* 9 Dec. 4/1 By means of a gripper mechanism the driver of the car can reduce the speed to any rate desired. **1932** W. ATKINS *Art & Practice Printing* II. iv. 49 Turn the Cylinder forward until the gripper edge is in a position convenient for undoing the three screws. **1940** *Chambers's Techn. Dict.* 391/1 *Gripper edge*, the edge of a sheet of paper caught by the grippers when it is fed into a cylinder machine.

gripping ('grɪpɪŋ), *vbl. sb.*[1] [f. GRIP *v.*[1] + -ING[1].] The action of GRIP *v.*[1]; a taking firm grasp or hold (*lit.* and *fig.*); seizure.

1632 in Barry *Orkney* (1805) App. 473 Act 40 Anent Gripping of Lands. *a* **1658** J. DURHAM *Expos. Rev.* i. (1680) 15 There is most sensible footing and, so to speak, gripping to be gotten by looking to the Mediator. **1818** SCOTT *Hrt. Midl.* xlii, A neglect of the higher things that belong to salvation, and also a gripping unto the things of this world. **1898** *Daily News* 23 Sept. 6/5 The bruises caused..by gripping were recent.

b. *attrib.* (with reference to cable-traction).

1887 J. BUCKNALL SMITH *Cable or Rope Traction* 86 Advocating the Chicago type of grip..in preference to those provided with gripping wheels or rollers. *Ibid.* 99 The gripping apparatus provided upon the cars..is a device consisting of two movable jaws..which engage or release the cable at the will of the operator. **1899** J. PENNELL in *Fortn. Rev.* LXV. 121 The two gripping arms of the brake were applied by chains.

† **gripping,** *vbl. sb.*[2] *Obs.* In comb. **gripping-iron,** = *grooping-iron*, a carpenter's gouge.

a **1500** *Ortus Voc.* in *Promp. Parv.* 216 note, *Runcina est quoddam artificium fabri lignarii gracile et recurvum, quo cavantur tabule, et una alteri connectatur; Anglicè*, a gryppynge yron.

gripping ('grɪpɪŋ), *vbl. sb.*[3] [f. GRIP *v.*[2] + -ING[1].] = GRIPING *vbl. sb.*[2]

1852 WIGGINS *Embanking* 128 Gripping at 1½*d.* or 2*d.* per rod.

gripping ('grɪpɪŋ), *ppl. a.* [f. GRIP *v.*[1] + -ING[2].] That grips, clutches, clips, or grasps tightly.

1630 DRUMM. OF HAWTH. *Flowers Sion, Cypress Grove* 75 [Riches] are like to Thornes which laid on an open hand are easilie blowne away, and wound the closing and hard-gripping. **1741** MONRO *Anat. Nerves* (ed. 3) 20 The gripping Fingers stopt the Course of a Fluid. **1877** BLACK *Green Past.* xxxviii. (1878) 305 We were shod not in gripping felt but in goloshes of an enormous size.

fig. **1895** *Daily News* 20 Apr. 7/5 Death, he rejoiced to say, had only cost them 20*l.* in spite of the gripping winter. **1896** *Athenæum* 11 Apr. 487/1 There is..much that is genuine and gripping in the play.

Hence '**grippingly** *adv.*

1934 in WEBSTER. **1961** *John o' London's* 14 Dec. 664/1 It was grippingly well acted. **1969** *Daily Tel.* 5 Nov. 13/5 Nearly all the work's varied utterances were similarly well characterised by the Group, the clarinet solo..grippingly so if with a certain unauthorised licence.

gripple ('grɪp(ə)l), *sb.*[1] *Obs.* exc. *dial.* In 5 **gryppel, grippull.** [Parallel to mod.Du. *greppel, grippel, gruppel*, LG. *grüppel*:—WGer. **gruppilo-*; see GRIP *sb.*[2]] A small ditch or trench.

c **1440** *Promp. Parv.* 212/2 Gryppe, or a gryppel, where watur rennythe a-way in a londe, or watur forowe [*P.* a grippull], *aratiuncula.* *a* **1825** FORBY *Voc. E. Anglia*, *Grup, groop*, a trench, not amounting in breadth to a ditch. If narrower still it is a *grip*; if extremely narrow, a *gripple*.

† '**gripple,** *sb.*[2] *Obs. rare.* In 6 grypell, griple. [f. root of GRIP, GRIPE: cf. GRAPPLE *sb.*]

1. A hook to seize things with.

1530 PALSGR. 228/1 Grypell a hoke, *hauet*.

2. Grasp.

1596 SPENSER *F.Q.* v. ii. 14 Ne ever Artegall his griple strong For any thinge wold slacke, but still upon him hong.

'**gripple,** *a. Obs.* exc. *dial.* or *arch.* Also 1 gripul, 3 gripel, 6 gripell, grippel, *Sc.* grippill, 6–7 griple, 9 *Sc.* grippal. [OE. *gripul*, f. *grip-*, wk. root of *grīpan* GRIPE *v.*[1]]

1. Griping, niggardly, usurious.

a **1000** *Ags. Gloss.* in Wr.-Wülcker 198/39 *Capax, qui multum capit*, andȝetul, gripul, numul. *c* **1205** LAY. 7336 þu sulf ært swiðe gripel, þine gumen sunden ȝefere. **1565** GOLDING *Ovid's Met.* VII. (1603) 85 b, [She] upon receit thereof..Was turned to a bird, which yet of gold is gripple still. **1574** RICH *Mercury & Soldier* C ij b, The greatest cause that stirreth both these sortes [of Captaines] to seruice, as may be supposed, procedeth of one mocion, which is the gripell desyre they haue of Princes paye. **1589** WARNER *Alb. Eng.* v. xxvii, Grippel in workes, testy in words. **1590** SPENSER *F.Q.* I. iv. 31 He gnasht his teeth to see Those heapes of gold with griple Couetise. *a* **1677** BARROW *Serm.* Wks. 1716 I. 316 The gripple wretch who will bestow nothing on his poor brother. **1808** SCOTT *Marm.* VI. Introd., While gripple owners still refuse To others what they cannot use. **1814** —— *Wav.* lxvii, Nae body wad be sae grippal as to tak his geer after they had gi'en him a pardon. **1876** *Whitby Gloss.*, *Gripple*, avaricious. 'As gripple as sin'.

2. Gripping; tenacious.

1513 DOUGLAS *Æneis* XII. xii. 193 Amang the grippill rutis fast haldand. **1604** DRAYTON *Owle* 350 The gripple Vulture argues me too bold. **1880** W. WATSON *Prince's Quest* (1892) 61 Clutched with his gripple claws the Prince his prey.

3. *Comb.*, as ***gripple-handed, minded*** adjs.

1626 MIDDLETON *Anyth. for Quiet Life* I. i. 76 That a man of your estate should be so gripple-minded and repining at his wife's bounty! *a* **1632** T. TAYLOR *God's Judgem.* II. I. xix. (1642) 64 This gripple minded Prince. **1647** C. HARVEY *Sch. of Heart* (1778) 110, I was close and gripple-handed.

Hence '**grippleness,** avarice, greed, niggardliness; also, greedy desire (*to* do something).

1571 GOLDING *Calvin on Ps.* To Rdr. 8 Greedy grippelnesse of shameful gaine. **1655** GURNALL *Chr. in Arm.* I. x. §2. 290 A grippleness to save some of the stuff. **1660** HEXHAM *Dutch Dict.*, *Hebbigheyt*, Greedinesse, Gripplenesse, or Niggardlinesse. **1882** *W. Worc. Gloss.*, *Grippleness*, greed. ''E inna so bad off as 'e makes out, 'tis nowt but grippleness makes 'im live so near.'

† '**gripple,** *v. Obs.* [An alteration of GRAPPLE *v.*, ? influenced by GRIP *v.*[1]] = GRAPPLE *v.* in various senses. Hence '**grippled** *ppl. a.*, anchored; '**grippling** *vbl. sb.*, anchoring, mooring, *attrib.* in ***grippling chain.***

1591 H. SMITH *Serm. Usury* i. 3, I am glad that I haue any occasion to griple with this sinne, where it hath made so many spoyles. **1606** HEYWOOD *If you know not Me* II. Wks. 1874 I. 346 The distant corners of their gripled fleet. **1607** TOPSELL *Four-f. Beasts* (1658) 167 The root..is more then a man can well griple in his hand. **1630** WADSWORTH *Pilgr.* iv. 34 The Vice Admirall..prepared himselfe for to fight.. hanging his gripling chaine on the maine Mast.

grippy ('grɪpɪ), *a.* [f. GRIP *v.*[1] + -Y[1]. Cf. MDu. *gripich*, MLG. *gripech.*]

1. Having a tendency to be avaricious or parsimonious. *Sc.* and *north.*

1808 JAMIESON, *Grippy*, pron. gruppy, avaritious, as implying the idea of a disposition to take the advantage, S. **1822** GALT *Provost* xliii. 315 It may be, that standing now clear and free of the world, I had less incitement to be so grippy. **1825** BROCKETT *N.C. Words*, *Grippy*, mean, avaricious, hardly honest. **1860** RAMSAY *Remin.* Ser. I. (ed. 7) 88 A character noted for avarice or sharp looking to self interest, was termed 'grippy'. **1876** *Whitby Gloss.*, *Grippy*, inclined to cheat. **1882** *Edin. Rev.* Apr. 1525 A typical Scottish laird of the shrewdest and 'grippiest' order.

2. Tenacious.

1870 *Contemp. Rev.* XIV. 380 The tenacious, grippy clinging to traditionary usages.

3. Capable of holding the attention and interest of a spectator, reader, etc.

1921 *Pall Mall & Globe* 15 Nov. 2/3 With a little cutting-down, 'Wat Tyler' would make an entirely good and grippy little play.

Hence '**grippiness.**

1882 *Athenæum* 21 Jan. 88/1 A satire on the 'grippiness' that may have characterized the earlier lairds.

gripsack (ˈgrɪpsæk). *U.S. colloq.* [f. GRIP *v.*[1] + SACK.] A traveller's handbag.

1877 R. J. BURDETTE *Rise & Fall of Mustache* 59 If I was going to Europe, I would just rush into the house, put on a clean shirt, grab up my gripsack, and fly. **1883** *Pall Mall G.* 11 Dec. 2/2 The word 'grip-sack' has long been in use in America as a slang term for hand-satchel. **1889** 'MARK TWAIN' *Yankee at Crt. K. Arth.* xxiii. 255 Take your gripsack and get along. **1891** *19th Cent.* Oct. 588 They pack their grip-sacks and go off to Europe. **1909** W. J. LOCKE *Septimus* xiv. 213 Gives instant relief for blistered feet. Every mountaineer should carry it in his gripsack. **1911** *Daily Colonist* (Victoria, B.C.) 29 Apr. 3/1 This most refreshing, invigorating and purifying of Fruit Salts should be in..the gripsack of every tourist. **1926** CHESTERTON *Incredulity of Father Brown* i. 4 His grip-sack held in a steely grip. **1949** E. POUND *Pisan Cantos* lxxvii. 49 Preceded by a crash, i.e. by a Huge gripsack or satchel.

†**ˈgripulous**, *a. Obs.* Also gripo-. [app. f. GRIPPLE *a.* + -OUS, with spelling assimilated to that of adjs. in *-ulous.*] Grasping, avaricious. Hence **ˈgripulousness**. (Only in T. Adams.)

1614 T. ADAMS *Devils Banquet* 127 The labourers hyre cries in the gripolous Landlords hand. **1633** —— *Exp. 2 Peter* ii. 12 Gripulous avarice. *Ibid.* iii. 18 Liberality is *in medio* between gripulousness and profuseness.

gripy (ˈgraɪpɪ), *a.* [f. GRIPE *v.*[1] + -Y[1].] Tending to cause 'gripes'.

1879 [see GRIPEFUL *a.*].

grip-yard: see GRIP *sb.*[2]

Griqua (ˈgriːkwə), *sb.* and *a.* [Hottentot.] **A.** *sb.* One of a coloured people of mixed Hottentot and European descent inhabiting chiefly East and West Griqualand in the Cape Province of South Africa; = BASTARD *sb.* 1 b. **B.** *adj.* Of or pertaining to this people. Cf. COLOURED *ppl. a.* 2 b.

1731 G. MEDLEY tr. *Kolb's Pres. State Cape Good-Hope* I. vi. 78 Next to the Damaquas, lie the Gauros or Gauriquas. **1793** tr. *Thunberg's Trav.* I. 308 Gauriquas land extends more to the north-eastward: this is a very fine country, and abounds in grass. **1815** J. CAMPBELL *Trav. S. Afr.* (ed. 2) xiii. 162 The people were employed by one of the Griqua captains to watch his cattle. *Ibid.* 163 We partook together of the Lord's Supper, at which were present, Griquas, Hottentots, Dutch, English and Scotch. *Ibid.* xxvii. 349 The people in this part, being a mixed race, went by the name of Bastards; but having represented to the principal persons the offensiveness of the word to an English or Dutch ear, they resolved to assume some other name. On consulting among them-selves, they found the majority were descended from a person of the name of Griqua, and they resolved hereafter to be called Griquas. **1822** —— *Trav. S. Afr. 2nd Journey* I. xiii. 130, I marked the Hottentot, Caffre, Bushmen, Griqua, Namaqua, and Matchappee countries. **1833** J. PHILIP *Let.* May in D. J. Kotzé *Lett Amer. Missionaries* (1950) 30 Our missionary stations among the Griquas. **1839** F. OWEN *Diary* (1926) 149 Several Boers reside in the Griqua country. *Ibid.*, The Griqua or Hottentot language. **1848** H. H. METHUEN *Life in Wilderness* iii. 72 Thence we proceeded to the Griqua village of Ramah, and rejoined our waggons there. **1850** [see LAAGER *sb.*]. **1857** LIVINGSTONE *Missionary Trav. S. Afr.* v. 104 On crossing the Orange River we come into independent territory inhabited by Griquas and Bechuanas. By Griquas is meant any mixed race sprung from natives and Europeans. **1866** [see BASTARD *sb.* 1 b]. **1897** [see HOTTENTOT 2]. **1905** G. W. STOW *Native Races S. Afr.* xvii. 316 Among the old Hottentot tribes..was a clan..variously called Chariguriqua and Grigriqua... It was from this tribe the modern Griquas derived their name. **1958** L. VAN DER POST *Lost World of Kalahari* i. 24 Griqua robbers. **1970** *Cape Times* 28 Oct. 2/9 In it he tells how, during the second British occupation of the Cape, there lives a Griqua-Hottentot, by name Nossie.

Hence **ˈGriqualander**, an inhabitant of E. or W. Griqualand; a Griqua.

1897 A. J. BUTLER tr. *Ratzel's Hist. Mankind* II. III. 295 The term 'Griqualanders'..has become usual since the Griquas have..had a country of their own allotted them.

griqualandite (ˈgriːkwəlændaɪt). *Min.* [Named by Hepburn, 1887, from its locality, Griqualand.] A mineral consisting essentially of silica in a fibrous form, more or less impregnated with iron, forming the gem known as tiger eye.

1887 *Chem. News* LV. 240 *Griqualandite*, a pseudomorph of crocidolite.

†**gris**, *sb. Obs.* Forms: 3–6 gris(e, 4–5 grece, 4–6 grys(e, (4 griis, 5 grijs), 5 gryce. [a. OF. *gris* (14th c. in Godef.), subst. use of adj. *gris* (see GRIS *a.*). Cf. It. *grigio* homespun cloth, russet.] A kind of grey fur.

a **1300** *Cursor M.* 25466 Riche robe wit veir and grise. *c* **1320** *Sir Tristr.* 1220 Þai raft me fowe and griis, And þus wounded þai me. *c* **1375** *Sc. Leg. Saints, Jacobus (minor)* 764 Furryt wele in wayre & grece [*rime* dewice]. **1393** LANGL. *P. Pl.* C. XVII. 342 Both in grey and in grys And in gilt harneis. *c* **1400** *St. Alexius* 398 Pelured wiþ Ermyne & wiþ grijs. **1460** *Lybeaus Disc.* 838 A velowet mantyll gay, Pelvred wyth grys and gray, Sche caste abowte her swyre. **1481** CAXTON *Reynard* (Arb.) 65 He may were scarlet and gryse. **1523** LD. BERNERS *Froiss.* I. ccclxxxi. 640 They ar clothed in veluet and chamlet furred with grise. **1575** *How Merchande dyd Wyfe betray* 14 in Hazl. *E.P.P.* I. 197 Gownys of grete pryce, Furryd with menyuere and with gryse. [**1896** J. H. WYLIE *Hist. Hen. IV*, III. 469 A red jacket, with cap furred with gris.]

†**gris**, *a. Obs. rare.* In 4 **gris, grys, grice, 6 gres, grece, greyce.** [a. F. *gris* (= Pr., Sp., Pg. *gris*, It. *griso*), a. OHG. *grîs* (in mod.G. *greis*) = OS. *grîs* (Du. *grijs*), of unknown origin; a derivative is med.L. *griseus*, It. *grigio.*] Grey.

c **1386** CHAUCER *Can. Yeom. Prol.* 6 His hakeney, which þat was al pomely grys [*v.r.* gris, grice]. **1513** DOUGLAS *Æneis* Prol. 107 Sum grece [*v.r.* greyce, gres], sum gowlis, sum purpour.

gris, obs. form of GRASS.

grisaille (grɪˈzeɪl, or as Fr. grizɑj). *Painting.* [a. F. *grisaille*, f. *gris* grey (see prec.).] **a.** A method of decorative painting in grey monochrome to represent objects in relief (see quot. 1854); a work, *e.g.* a stained-glass window, executed according to this method. Also *fig.*

1848 B. WEBB *Sk. Cont. Eccles.* 9 In the Lady-chapel are some modern *grisailes* [sic]. **1849** RUSKIN *Sev. Lamps* ii. §14. 41 The roof of the Sistine chapel has much architectural design in grisaille mingled with the figures of its frescoes. **1854** FAIRHOLT *Dict. Art*, *Grisaille*,..a style of painting employed to represent solid bodies in relief, such as friezes, mouldings..bas-reliefs, &c., by means of grey tints. The objects represented are supposed to be white; the shadows which they project, and the lights..are properly depicted by ..various grey tints. **1897** L. F. DAY *Windows* 119 Early glass divides itself..into two classes: work in rich colour.. and work in 'grisaille', as it is called; that is to say, in which the glass is chiefly white or whitish, relieved only here and there by a line or a jewel of colour.

fig. **1937** R. STORRS *Orientations* ii. 38 As I look on my lines they seem, compared with what he was, the mere *grisaille* cartoon of some heroic Victorian radiance. **1965** *Listener* 4 Mar. 333/1 Schopenhauer was the first to admit his indebtedness to the French moralists, and the *grissaille* of his prose is relieved..by quotations not only from the French but [etc.].

b. *attrib.* or *adj.* Executed in grisaille.

1860 *Handbk. of Ludlow* (1865) 34 The windows were filled with grisaille glass. **1870** F. R. WILSON *Ch. Lindisf.* 29 The designs of the glass are all ornamental patterns on light grisaille grounds. **1897** L. F. DAY *Windows* 146 The best-known grisaille windows in England are the famous group of long lancets, ending the north transept of York Minster, which are known by the name of the Five Sisters. **1899** R. GLAZIER *Man. Hist. Ornament* 93 Painted Enamels were introduced and Limoges became the centre of this art, called late Limoges or Grisaille Enamel. **1968** *Medium Ævum* XXXVII. 63 One may not greatly admire..the 105 large grisaille pictures made by Jean Tavernier to illustrate the Brussels manuscript.

gris-amber: see AMBERGRIS.

grisard (ˈgrɪsəd), *a.* and *sb. rare.* [ad. F. *grisard*, f. *gris* grey: see -ARD.]

†**A.** *adj.* Greyish. *Obs.*

1607 TOPSELL *Four-f. Beasts* (1658) 27 Their [badgers'] skin is hard, but rough and rugged, their hair harsh and stubborn, of an intermingled grisard colour.

B. *sb.* A grey-haired man.

1880 BROWNING *Dram. Idylls* Ser. II. *Pietro* 25 Straight-way would the whileom youngster grow a grisard.

grisbate, -bet, -bite, etc., vars. GRISTBITE.

†**grise**, *a. Obs.* Also 3 **greis**, 5 **gryse.** [? Abstracted from GRISLY *a.*] Terrible; fearful.

a **1300** *Cursor M.* 18649 Wit his cri þat es sua grise [*Gött.* greis]. *Ibid.* 23249 Of helle..þe aghtand pine it es ful grise. **1460** *Lybeaus Disc.* 597 To fyght with bothe yn same Hyt wer no chyldes game, That beth so grymme and gryse. ? *a* **1500** *Ser J. Mandevelle* 59 in Hazl. *E.E.P.* I. 157 Or elles ..Depyst in helle in paynes grise Salbee our set.

†**grise**, *v. Obs.* Forms: 3–4 **grise-n**, 4 **-yn**, 4–5 **gryse, grise**, 5 **gryes**, 6 *Sc.* **gryis.** *Pa. t.* 4 **gros, grisede.** [ME. *grisen* str. vb. (later wk.):—OE. **grísan*, implied in *á-grísan* (recorded in pres. stem only: see AGRISE *v.*) = MDu., MLG. *grisen* (Du. *grijzen*, pa. t. *grees*, pa. pple. *gegrezen*); cf. MHG. *grisenlich* GRISLY.

The root **grīs-* is not found in Goth. or Scandinavian, nor is its equivalent found outside Teut. Possibly it may have originated by onomatopœic modification from the synonymous **greus-*, *grus-* (in OE. *grorn* sad, *begroren* terrified, *gryre* horror) which seems to be an extension of the root **greu-*, *grū-*: see GRUE *v.*]

1. *impers.* (*it*) *grises me*: I shudder with fear or horror, I tremble, am greatly afraid.

c **1200** *Trin. Coll. Hom.* 165 Of swilch mai grisen men. *a* **1225** *Ancr. R.* 366 'Sore', cweð he, ure Louerd, 'me grulleð [*MS. T.* grises] aȝean mine pine'. *a* **1225** *Juliana* 56 Grisen him mahte [*v.r.* mahen] þat sehe hu hit [þat axtreo] gront in to hwet se hit of rahte. *a* **1300** *Body & Soul* 96 in *Map's Poems*, A weyle sore may me grise. **1303** R. BRUNNE *Handl. Synne* 7875 Hyt was no wundyr þoȝ hym gros.

2. *intr.* To shudder or tremble with terror; to be full of horror, greatly afraid; = AGRISE 1.

a **1225** [see 1]. *a* **1300** *Cursor M.* 7983 To ger þam for him gru and grise Vm-thoght him gern on quatkin wise. *c* **1330** R. BRUNNE *Chron. Wace* (Rolls) 8532 His herte a-geyns hym gros & grew. *c* **1400** *Beryn* 2140 Of this petouse compleynt a mannys hert may grise. *c* **1450** *St. Cuthbert* (Surtees) 7222 Þe woman sho began to gryes. *c* **1460** *Towneley Myst.* iv. 254 When I look to hym, I gryse. **1513** DOUGLAS *Æneis* I. xii. 21 Albeit my spreit abhorris, and doith grise, Thairon for to remembir.

3. *trans.* To shudder at with terror or abhorrence; to dread, abhor, loathe; = AGRISE 2.

1382 WYCLIF *Judith* xvi. 12 The Persis grisiden hir stedefastnesse, and Medis hir hardynesse. —— *Wisdom* xii. 3 Tho olde dwelleris of thin holi lond, the which thou grisedist.

4. To terrify, affright; = AGRISE 5 a.

1501 DOUGLAS *Pal. Hon.* I. lxxi, Terribill thochtis oft my hart did gryis. **1513** —— *Æneis* VI. ii. 52 Virgyne, na kynd of pane may rise, Vnknaw to me, of new that may me grise. **1556–8** PHAER *Æneid* IV. K ij b, He warns me through my dreames, & me wt fearfull gost doth grise.

grise, var. GRIS *Obs.*; obs. f. GRASS, GRECE.

grisel, obs. form of GRIZEL, GRIZZLE *a.* and *sb.*[1]

griseli, -lich(e, -ly, obs. forms of GRISLY.

grisell(e, obs. form of GRIZZLE *a.* and *sb.*[1]

griseo- (ˈgrɪzɪəʊ), comb. form of med.L. *grīseus* grey, used in sense 'greyish', as *griseo-fuscous* adj.

1847 HARDY in *Proc. Berw. Nat. Club* II. No. 5. 247 Abdomen..thickly clothed above and beneath with griseo-fuscous pubescence.

griseofulvin (ˌgrɪzɪəʊˈfʌlvɪn). *Chem.* [f. mod.L. *griseofulv-um* (f. GRISEO- + L. *fulvus* reddish yellow), epithet of a species of *Penicillium*: see -IN[1].] An anti-fungal antibiotic, $C_{17}H_{17}O_6Cl$, produced by several species of mould of the genus *Penicillium* and used esp. in the treatment of ringworm.

1939 A. E. OXFORD et al. in *Biochem. Jrnl.* XXXIII. 240 The purpose of the present communication is to record observations on a hitherto undescribed chlorine-containing metabolic product of *P. griseo-fulvum* which has been isolated from the mycelium of this mould and for which the name griseofulvin is proposed. **1960** *N.Y. Times* 14 Aug. 77/3 The first few cases of improvement with griseofulvin therapy. **1968** J. H. BURN *Lect. Notes Pharmacol.* (ed. 9) 126 Ring worm (Tinea capitis) responds well to oral treatment with antibiotic Griseofulvin (also used for ringworm of glabrous skin which does not respond to fungicidal lotions or salves).

griseous (ˈgrɪzɪəs), *a.* [f. med.L. *grīse-us* (see GRIS *a.*) + -OUS.] Grey; *spec.* in *Zool.* and *Bot.*, bluish grey, pearl-grey. (For an aberrant use see quot. 1826.)

1819 G. SAMOUELLE *Entomol. Compend.* 221 *Pentatoma*.. Body griseous above. **1826** KIRBY & SP. *Entomol.* IV. 279 Griseous (*Griseus*), white mottled with black or brown. Ex. *Curculio nebulosus.* **1828** STARK *Elem. Nat. Hist.* I. 274 Tail-feathers wedge-shaped, griseous, spotted with black. **1847** HARDY in *Proc. Berw. Nat. Club* II. No. 5. 240 Abdomen.. griseous pubescent. **1893** *Contemp. Rev.* Aug. 294 French soil and notably French skies are griseous.

‖**grisette** (grɪˈzɛt). Also 8 **griset, grisset, grizette.** [a. F. *grisette*, f. *gris* grey: see -ETTE.]

1. An inferior grey dress fabric, formerly the common garb of working girls in France. (In quot. *attrib.*)

1700 T. BROWN, etc. tr. *Scarron's Com. Wks.* (1712) 2 His Doublet was a Griset-Coat.

2. A French girl or young woman of the working class, esp. one employed as a shop assistant or a seamstress.

1723 SWIFT *Stella at Wood-Park* 59 She vows she will no longer stay In lodgings, like a poor grizette. *a* **1745** —— (*title*) To Betty the Grisette. **1768** STERNE *Sent. Journ.* (1775) II. 116 (*Case Conscience*), In a few minutes the Grisset came in with her box of lace. **1815** *Sporting Mag.* XLVI. 128 The women of Paris of all ranks, grisettes as well as Duchesses. **1885** MISS BRADDON *Wyllard's Weird* I. i. 23 That pretty, neat appearance which one sees in French girls of a class just a little above the grisette.

attrib. **1803** MARY CHARLTON *Wife & Mistr.* IV. 29 A fellow..was scarcely able to vie with his valet-de-chambre in any expenditure upon his grisette adventures. **1844** LOUISA S. COSTELLO *Béarn* I. 335 The remarkable beauty of its young women of the grisette class.

3. A noctuid moth, *Acronycta strigosa.*

1869 NEWMAN *Brit. Moths* 253 The Grisette.

†**ˈgrisful**, *a. Obs.* [f. GRISE *v.* + -FUL.] Horrible; terrible. Hence †**ˈgrisfully** *adv.*

a **1300** *Signs bef. Judgem.* 16 in *E.E.P.* (1862) 8 Hit is iwrit in holi boke..þat no þing no man mai loke þat is so grisful forto drede. **1382** WYCLIF *Wisdom* xi. 19 Vnknowen bestes ..bringende forth smel of smoke, or puttende out grisful [**1388** hidouse] sparkes fro eȝen. *Ibid.* xvii. 3 Thei ben scatered, dredende grisfulli [**1388** hidousli].

grisgris: see GREEGREE.

grishop, variant of GRASSHOP *Obs.*

†**ˈgrisil**, *a. Obs.* In 5 **grysyl, -il.** [f. GRISE *v.*] Horrible; grisly.

c **1440** *Promp. Parv.* 213/2 Grysyl [*v.r.* grysil], *horridus.*

grisiliche, obs. form of GRISLY.

ˈgrising. pseudo-*arch.* [An accommodation of med.L. *grisengus*, used adjectively as the name of a fabric; prob. f. *gris* grey; cf. OF. *grisan*, explained by Godef. as a stuff of *Greek* orgin.] The name of some fabric.

[*c* **1112** *Laws Æthelred* IV. ii. §8 (Liebermann) Duos grisengos pannos. **1148–56** *Charter Vaudey Abb., Lincolnsh.* in Dugdale *Monast.* (1825) V. 490/1 Vestimenta autem dabunt mihi de griseng, vel halberget, et pellibus agninis; uxori autem meæ ad carius bluet, et pellibus similiter agninis. *a* **1200** *MS. Ashmole* 1285 fol. 231 Quidem griengis hoc est panniculis aerium colorem imitantibus vestiuntur.]

1865 KINGSLEY *Herew.* II. i. 10 Clothing..of grising or halbergit and lambs' skins.

†**grising**, *vbl. sb. Obs.* [f. GRISE *v.* + -ING[1].] Terror, horror, dread; loathing.

a **1225** *Ancr. R.* 190 Nere þet þing sulf grislich hwas scheadewe ȝe ne muhte nout for grislich [*MS. C.* grisung] biholden? **1382** WYCLIF *1 Chron.* xvii. 21 By his gretnesse & grysynges [**1388** dredis] he caste out nacyouns fro his face. *c* **1440** HYLTON *Scala Perf.* (W. de W. 1494) I. xlii, Also thou shalt fele a lothyng & a grysyng of thy self.

griskin (ˈgrɪskɪn). Also 8 grisking. [? f. *gris*, GRICE a pig + -KIN.] The lean part of the loin of a bacon pig. †Also formerly, the corresponding part of beef.

a **1700** B. E. *Dict. Cant. Crew, Griskins*, steaks off the Rump of Beef; also Pork-bones with some tho' not much Flesh on them. **1727** SWIFT *Circumcis. E. Curll* Wks. 1755 III. I. 165 To convince them of his christianity he called for a pork grisking. **1733** —— *Corr.* Wks. 1841 II. 717, I have a good deal of company to sup at my house upon beef griskins. **1747** MRS. GLASSE *Cookery* i. 4 The best Way to dress Pork Griskins is to roast them. **1761** MURPHY *Citizen* I. ii, Then he rocked the cradle, hush ho! hush ho!—then he twisted the griskin. **1820** LAMB *Elia* Ser. I. *Christ's Hosp.*, His hot plate of roast veal, or the more tempting griskin. **1880** JEFFERIES *Gt. Estate* ix. 199 He called at the butcher's ..and..got a little bit of griskin, or a chop.

transf. **1713** STEELE *Englishman* No. 40. 262 So many Drops of such a one's Milk, with a Griskin of St. Lawrence.

¶ *in griskins*: torn to rags.

1830 CARLETON *Traits Irish Peas.* (1843) I. 247 My feet by this time were absolutely in griskins.

†**grisle.** *Obs.* [f. GRISE *v.*] Horror; terror.

a **1225** *St. Marher.* 15 Ha moten..hare ahne deð ant drihtines munegin ilome, ant te grisle ant te grure þe bið et te dome. *a* **1240** *Sawles Warde* in *Cott. Hom.* 251 Wel ha i seoð ham to grisle ant to grure.

grisle, obs. form of GRISTLE, GRIZZLE.

grisled (ˈgrɪz(ə)ld), *a. Obs.* exc. *dial.* Also 4 griseled, 6 griseld. [f. GRISLE or GRISIL *a.* + -ED[2].] Awe-inspiring; horrible; grisly.

c **1340** *Cursor M.* 24081 (Fairf.) His face þat be-fore waas shene hit is now griseled [*other MSS.* grisli] on to sene. **1565** *Darius* (1860) 20 So griseld vpon him I did looke, As he had bene a very cooke. **1583** STANYHURST *Æneis* II. (Arb.) 50 Al we fle from sacrifice with sight so grisled afrighted. **1869** *Lonsdale Gloss.*, *Grisled*, grisly, frightful.

grisled, variant of GRIZZLED *a.*

grisley, -li(e. -lic, -lich(e, obs. ff. GRISLY.

†ˈ**grislihead.** *Obs.* In 4 gryselichhede, -lychhede. [f. GRISLY *a.* + -HEAD.] Grisliness.

a **1400** *Prymer* (1891) 88 Ther woneth euerelastynge gryselychhede. *c* **1430** *Pilgr. Lyf Manhode* IV. xxx. (1869) 192 My grete maace is cleped þe vengeaunce of god, and þe gryselichhede of helle.

grislik, obs. form of GRISLY.

grisliness (ˈgrɪzlɪnɪs). [f. GRISLY *a.* + -NESS.] The quality or condition of being grisly; horribleness, gruesomeness.

1340 HAMPOLE *Pr. Consc.* 2310 Ne swa sleygh payntur never nan was..þat couthe ymagyn of þair gryslynes. *c* **1386** CHAUCER *Pars. T.* ¶790 (*Harl. MS.*) þey schuln haue.. hunger and þurst and grislines of deueles þat schul alto-tere hem wiþout respit. [Cf. GRIMNESS.] *a* **1586** SIDNEY *Arcadia* III. (1622) 251 That ill agreeing musicke, which was beautified with the grislynesse of wounds [etc.]. **1591** FLORIO *2nd Fruites* 131 *G.* What, is she so loathsome? *L.* More than grislenes or hell it selfe. **1631** R. BOLTON *Comf. Affl. Consc.* 307 Hee..addes more grisselinesse to his many hatefull transgressions. **1867** HOWELLS *Ital. Journ.* 209 All the horrors for which we had come were then in perfect grisliness.

grisloker, -luker, obs. compar. ff. GRISLY.

grisly (ˈgrɪzlɪ), *a.* Now only *arch.* and *literary*. Forms: 2 grislic, 2–5 grislich, -lych, (3–4 *comp.* grisloker, -luker), 3–5 gryslich, -lych, 4–5 griselich(e, gryselich(e, -lyche, -ly, (4 grissiliche, grislik, greselich); 3 *Orm.* grissliȝ, 3 gresle, 4 greesly, 4–5 gresely(e, gresli, 5 gresly, griss(e)ly(e, 4–6 grysely(e, 4–7 grysly, 5 grysle, gryssly, 6 gryslie, greislie, greizlie, griesely, -lie, gryesly, 5–7 greisly, 6–7 grislie, grizely, 6–9 griesly, 8–9 grizly, (grizzly), 4– grisly. [Late OE. *grislic*; ultimately f. *gris-* wk. root of GRISE *v.* + *-lic*, -LY[1]; but the history is unknown.

Perh. aphetized from OE. *ongrislic*, **ongrisenlic* (implied in the adv. *ongrysenlice*), f. pa. pple. of **ongrísan*, synonymous with *ágrísan* AGRISE *v.* Cf. the continental Teut. synonyms MDu. *grezelijc* (from the weak form of the root), *griselijc*, mod.Du. *grijzelijk* (from the str. form); the quantity of the root-vowel in MHG. *grisenlich* is uncertain.]

1. Causing horror, terror, or extreme fear; horrible or terrible to behold or to hear; causing such feelings as are associated with thoughts of death and 'the other world', spectral appearances, and the like. In mod. use tending to a weaker sense: Causing uncanny or unpleasant feelings; of forbidding appearance; grim, ghastly.

a. of visible objects, their qualities, etc.

a **1150** *Passio B. Margaretæ* in Grein *Bibl. Angels. Prosa* (1889) III. 175 þær inn eode an grislic deofol. *c* **1200** *Vices & Virtues* (1888) 19 Eifulle dieulen, ðe bieð swa laðliche and swo grislich an to lokin. *c* **1200** ORMIN 3842 þohh þatt he grissliȝ deofell seo. *c* **1205** LAY. 28063 þer ich isah gripes & grisliche fuȝeles. *a* **1225** *Ancr. R.* 118 Bledinde mon is grislich & atelich ine monnes eihsihðe. *c* **1350** *Will. Palerne* 4935 Ac he haþ sent ȝou to socoure so grissliche an host. *c* **1386** CHAUCER *Monk's T.* 119 He slow the grisly boor. —— *Frankl. T.* 131 The grisly Rokkes blake. **1393** LANGL. *P. Pl.* C. XXI. 479 May no grysliche gost glyde þer hit shadeweþ. *c* **1450** *Merlin* 15 Ther was none othir women that durste norishe it but the modre, for it was so grysly to syght. **1513** DOUGLAS *Æneis* VI. iv. 4 Ane hiddouis hole, deip gapand and grisly. **1551** ROBINSON tr. *More's Utopia* I. (Arb.) 53 A man of greslie and sterne grauitie. **1579** SPENSER *Sheph. Cal.* Nov. 55 Vp grieslie ghostes. **1590** —— *F.Q.* I. v. 20 Griesly night, with visage deadly sad. **1607** HIERON *Wks.* I. 220 The griesly and ghastly countenance of approching death. **1629** MILTON *Nativity* 209 In vain with cymbals' ring They call the grisly king, In dismal dance about the furnace blue. **1684** EARL ROSCOMMON *Ess. Transl. Verse* 157 The Greisly Ferry-man of Hell. **1697** DRYDEN *Virg. Georg.* IV. 145 Like their grisly Prince appears his gloomy Race. **1788** W. BLANE *Hunt. Excurs.* 15 Our grisly enemy [an elephant] was overpowered by the number of bullets. **1807** WORDSW. *White Doe* I. 244 Look down, and see a griesly sight; A vault where the bodies are buried upright! **1841** W. SPALDING *Italy & It. Isl.* II. 198 Minos, transformed by the Florentine poet..into a strange and grisly shape. **1865** DICKENS *Mut. Fr.* I. xv, There was the old grisly four-post bedstead. **1867** EMERSON *May-Day* etc. Wks. (Bohn) III. 457 Hunted by Sorrow's grisly train. **1885** STEVENSON *Dynamiter* 132 The grisly shelter of a coffee-shop.

†**b.** of sounds. *Obs.*

c **1275** *Serving Christ* 28 in *O.E. Misc.* 91 þer is gronynge and grure and gryslich gle. *a* **1300** *Cursor M.* 18953 (Gött.) For þat farli sone war þai fus, And ran þaim til þe apostlis hus, All carpand of þat grisli crack. *a* **1385** CHAUCER *L.G.W.* 1219 *Dido*, The thundyr rorede with a gresely steuene. **14..** *Sir Beues* 2733 + 9 (MS. M.) He keste vp a gret yell That was grisselye as a thonder. **1552** LYNDESAY *Monarche* 5545 Gretand with mony gryslie grone. **1576** FLEMING *Panopl. Epist. Epit.* A iv b, Ætnaes..grieslie thundering. *a* **1586** SIDNEY *Arcadia* II. (1590) 165 b, With Dayly Diligence and Grisly Grones, he wan her affection.

c. of actions, occurrences, conditions; also *arch.* of threats, imprecations, etc.

c **1200** *Trin. Coll. Hom.* 5 þat loðeliche word and ateliche and grisliche..*Ite maledicti in ignem eternum.* [*a* **1240** *Lofsong* in *Cott. Hom.* 209 Mine sunnen þat ateliche beoð and grisliche i þine eih sihðe.] **1297** R. GLOUC. (Rolls) 11745 Grisloker weder þan it was ne miȝte anerþe be. **1340** *Ayenb.* 49 Vor asemoche ase þe zenne is more uoul and more grislich, þe more is worþ þe ssrifte. *c* **1375** *XI Pains of Hell* 33 in *O.E. Misc.* 211 Gret snow, gret yse, gret cold greslé. *c* **1385** CHAUCER *L.G.W.* 2238 *Philomela*, So gresely was his dede, That whan that I his foule storye rede, Mynne eyen wexe foule & sore also. *c* **1386** —— *Pard. T.* 380 Many a grisly ooth thanne han thay sworn, And Cristes blessed body thay to-rente. **14..** *Pol. Rel. & L. Poems* 240 Godes grisliche dom. **1494** FABYAN *Chron.* I. ccxxxii. (1533) 158 b, Gresely & cruel fyghte. **1583** STANYHURST *Æneis* III. (Arb.) 71, I viewd with wundring a grisly monsterus hazard. **1596** H. CLAPHAM *Briefe Bible* I. 58 No maruell, if so greislie a fall, put him from that sacred figuring Seate. **1826** SCOTT *Woodst.* ii, Grisly oaths suit ill with grey beards. **1850** HAWTHORNE *Scarlet L.* xii. (1879) 171 The like grisly sense of the humorous again stole in among the solemn phantoms of his thought. **1892** JESSOPP *Stud. Recluse* i. (1893) 25 The ground..teeming with the tangible memories of grisly conflict. **1892** E. GOSSE *Secr. Narcisse* i. 11 His griesly imagination and adroit hand as a modeller.

2. Ugly. *dial.*

[*a* **1300** *Cursor M.* 23620 þir sal be fair and dughti bath, þai sal be grisli and lath.] **1674–91** RAY *N.C. Words* 32 *Grisly*, ugly: from Grize, Swine. **1684** *Yorkesh. Dial.* 216 in *Specim. Eng. Dial.* 159, I wad this grisely Cat was hang'd, for me. **1684** J. LACY *Sir H. Buffoon* II. iii. Dram. Wks. (1875) 240 Ah, thou's an ill-favoured grizely-like fellow, that is sa. **1788** W. MARSHALL *Yorksh.* II. 333 *Grizely*..ugly in the extreme.

†**3.** Full of fear, inspired by fear. Also qualifying *fear, dread. Obs.*

c **1320** R. BRUNNE *Medit.* 101 Eche loked on ouþer with grysly ye, And seyd, 'lorde wheþer hyt be y?' *c* **1386** CHAUCER *Pars. T.* ¶103 Grisly drede that euere shal laste. *c* **1400** *St. Jeremie's 15 Tokens* (E.E.T.S.) 33 Allas! hou schull we þan ouercome þilk griselich fere, Whan vche seint schal aferde be oure lord crist to see þere? **1698** FRYER *Acc. E. India & P.* 23 Which made the Males leap out of their Cabins with the same grisly Look as if going to give up their last Accounts.

ˈ**grisly**, *adv. Obs.* exc. *arch.* [f. as prec. + -LY[2]. Cf. MDu. *griselike*, MLG. *grisliken.*] Horribly, terribly; grimly; so as to inspire terror.

c **1200** *Trin. Coll. Hom.* 61 Grisliche he us mid orde pilted. *a* **1225** *Juliana* 69 Te balefule beast..fen[g] on to..grist-beatien grisliche up o þis meoke meiden. **1297** R. GLOUC. (Rolls) 574 His ax..so grisliche he ssoc & vaste, þat þe king kwakede & is men. *a* **1300** *Cursor M.* 16182 (Cott.), I hope þat þai sal bath grisly bi-for him quake. **1387** TREVISA *Higden* (Rolls) I. 81 Satyri..grisliche and wonderliche i-schape. *c* **1394** *P.P. Crede* 585 Swiche a gome godes wordes grysliche gloseþ. *c* **1400** *Ywaine & Gaw.* 3843 The thoner grisely gan out-brest. *c* **1400** *Melayne* 1252 Grisely gronande. **1529** MORE *Dyal.* I. 20 a/2 She..was there..in face eyene loke & countenaunce so grysely chaunged..yt yt was a terryble syght to behold. **1563** BECON *Reliques of Rome* 245 There is nothing in al this world yt a Christen man or woman ought so griselich to dread, as for to falle into sinne. **1638–48** G. DANIEL *Eclog.* ii. 1 The North lookes grisly blacke. **1663** BULLOKAR, *Grisly*, abominably, gastly, fearfully. **1868** BROWNING *Ring & Bk.* VIII. 1714 *Læsa*, gashed griesly, *tam enormiter*.

grisly, obs. form of GRISTLY, GRIZZLY *a.* and *sb.*[1]

†ˈ**grisness.** *Obs.* Also 4 grise-, 5 grysnesse. [f. GRISE *a.* + -NESS.] Terror, horror, dread.

1398 TREVISA *Barth. De P.R.* VIII. i. (Tollem. MS.), The worlde is a place of trespas and of gilte..of grisnesse [*ed.* 1535 ferefulnes] and of schame. *Ibid.* XIV. li, Londe of wastynge and of grisenesse [*ed.* 1535 horrour]. **1422** tr. *Secreta Secret., Priv. Priv.* (E.E.T.S.) 153 Nero be-hilde his chylde, and grysnesse therof hadd, and hym merwelid of Suche an shape.

grisolet, obs. variant of CHRYSOLITE.

1672 BOYLE *Virtues of Gems* i. 44 Indian-Gems, particularly Grisolets. [**1750** tr. *Leonardus' Mirr. Stones* 109 Grisoletus, is the same as the Crisolete.]

†**grison**, *sb.*[1] *Obs.* [a. F. *grison*, f. *gris* grey.]

1. *grison stone* (= F. *peirre de grison*): a kind of freestone.

1653 URQUHART *Rabelais* II. xxix, Riflandouille or pudding-plunderer, who was armed *cap-a-pe* with grison stones.

2. 'A servant without livery, dressed in grey, for secret errands' (Hatz.-Darm.).

1693 SHADWELL *Volunteers* II. i. 14, I think I must keep a Secretary, I keep Grisons [*printed* Grifons] Fellows out of Livery, privately for nothing, but to carry Answers.

grison (ˈgrɪzən), *sb.*[2] [a. F. *grison*; app. the same word as prec. and next. (Both animals are grey.)]

1. A carnivorous quadruped of South America, *Galictis vittata*, belonging to the family *Mustelidæ*, and thus allied to the glutton and marten.

1796 STEDMAN *Surinam* II. xvii. 41 That animal mentioned by Mr. Allemand, in the Count de Buffon.. which he there calls the *grison* or grey-weazel...If this be the same animal (as I doubt not, and have therefore given it the name of the *crabbo-dago* or grison). **1838** *Penny Cycl.* XI. 485/1 The Grison, *Gulo vittatus* of Desmarest..and *Galictis vittata* of Bell. **1884** *Riverside Nat. Hist.* (1888) V. 397.

2. A South American monkey (see quot.).

1840 tr. *Cuvier's Anim. Kingd.* (1849) 61 The Caparo.. and the Grison (*Lagothrix canus* Geof.; *Gastromargas infumatus* Spix.)—Inhabitants of the interior of South America, said to be remarkable gluttons.

†**grison**, *a. Obs.* In 5 gresone. [a. F. *grison*, f. *gris* grey.] Grey.

1438 *Alexander the Great* (Bannatyne) 115 With lyart berd and hare gresone.

grison, obs. form of GRECING, stairs.

†**grisp**, *v. Obs.* [A mixture of GRIP and GRASP *vbs.*] *intr.* To grasp, to grope.

c **1420** LYDG. *Thebes* III. in *Chaucer's Wks.* (1561) 372 Upon the corps with a mortall face He fel atones, and gan it to embrace Sore to grispe, and agein vpsterte. **1532** MORE *Confut. Tindale* Wks. 553/1 He grisped and longe felt about here & ther in the darke.

grispatien, obs. form of GRISTBITE.

†ˈ**grisping**, *vbl. sb.*[1] *Obs.* [Contracted form of GRISTBITING.] Gnashing the teeth.

13.. *E.E. Allit. P.* B. 159 Depe in my doungoun þer doel euer dwellez, Greuing, & gretyng, & gryspyng harde of teþe.

†ˈ**grisping**, *vbl. sb.*[2] *Obs.* [Cf. GRASP *sb.* 4, GROPSING and dial. *grapslin.*] Twilight (morning or evening).

1580 LYLY *Euphues* (Arb.) 233 In the grisping of the euening. **1581** H. GOLDWELL *Brief Decl. Shews, Devices*, etc. B v, Rising according to his maner to walke in the mosse in the grisping of the day.

griss(e, obs. form of GRASS.

grissel(l, obs. ff. GRISTLE, GRIZEL, GRIZZLE.

grissely(e, -lly, obs. forms of GRISLY, GRISTLY.

grissens, dial. form of GRECING, stairs.

grissergan, variant of GRITHSERGEANT *Obs.*

grisset, obs. form of GRISETTE.

grissil(l, obs. form of GRIZEL.

grissiliche, obs. form of GRISLY.

‖**grissino** (grisˈsino). Pl. grissini. [It.] A crisp bread made in long slender sticks.

1851 LYTTON *My Novel* I. IV. xvii. 383 Crisp *grissins*,.. they make so pleasant a noise between one's teeth. **1906** S. BEATY-POWNALL *'Queen' Cookery Bks.* (ed. 2) XI. iii. 56 Abroad,..grissini are very popular. **1967** H. PORTER in *Coast to Coast 1965–6* 171 The School Matron and the Housekeeper had got crisper and leaner than *grissini*. **1969** A. LASKI *Dominant Fifth* i. 27 There [were]..sticks of celery and carrot and grissini to dip.

grissle, obs. form of GRISTLE.

grissliȝ, grissly, obs. forms of GRISLY.

†**grist**, *sb.*[1] *Obs.* Forms: 1 grist- (in comb.: see GRISTBITING), gyrst, 4 gryste. [OE. *grist-*, *gyrst*, cogn. w. OS. *grist-* in *gristgrimmo* gnashing of teeth; cf. OHG. *grisgrimmôn*, *grisgramôn* to gnash the teeth (MHG. *grisgimmen*, *-gramen*, *grustgramen*; G. *griesgramen* to sulk), MHG. *grisgram* gnashing of teeth (G. *griesgram* peevishness, peevish person, also as adj.). It is difficult, in spite of the resemblance of sense (cf.

'to *grind* the teeth'), to connect the word etymologically with GRIND *v.*; it may be cognate with OE. *gryrran*, *ȝeorran*, L. *hirrire* to snarl, or be purely onomatopœic.] Gnashing of teeth; hence, anger.

c1000 *Ags. Gloss.* in *Haupt's Zeitschr.* (1853) IX. 513 Gyrst, *stridor.* 13.. *E.E. Allit. P.* A. 465 Þy heued hatz nauþer greme ne gryste.

grist (grɪst), *sb.*^{2} Forms: 1 grist, 5–7 griste, gryste, ? 6 *Sc.* girst, 6–7 gr(e)est, greist, 7 griest, 8 griss, 5– grist. [OE. *grist*:—OTeut. type **grinstu-* (? *-to-*, *-ti-*), f. **grind-* GRIND *v.* The vowel was shortened in ME. as in *fist* from OE. *fýst.*]

†1. The action of grinding; an act or spell of grinding. *Obs.*

c1000 ÆLFRIC *Gloss.* in Wr.-Wülcker 141/3 *Molitura*, grist. c1050 *Voc.* ibid. 448/16 *Molitura*, grist. 1676 WORLIDGE *Cyder* (1691) 96 Some [mills] are so large that they grind half a hogshead at a grist.

2. a. Corn which is to be ground; also (with *pl.*) a batch of such corn.

c1430 [see b]. 1483 in *Eng. Gilds* (1870) 336 That all Dowers of the Cite.. grynd att the Cite-is myllis,.. as long as they mey have sufficiaunt grist. 1568 in W. H. Turner *Select. Rec. Oxford* 325 Every of the said bakers and brewers ..shall forfaite their griste and wheate malte so grounde. 1589 R. HARVEY *Pl. Perc.* (1590) 3 Thy late Customers.. haue brought greists to be ground. 1613–16 W. BROWNE *Brit. Past.* II. i, As a miller having ground his grist. 1670 G. H. *Hist. Cardinals* III. III. 297 The new Gabels, impos'd upon Grist, Wine.. Aqua-vitæ. 1744–50 W. ELLIS *Mod. Husbandm.* VI. III. 77 A griss of wheat to be sent to the mill. 1862 *Q. Rev.* Apr. 286 The grist which has been served out too damp for the miller. 1865 *Morn. Star* 13 Jan., They can purchase grists of their employers at 1s. per bushel under the market price of best wheat. 1896 L. ABBOTT *Chr. & Soc. Problems* iii. 87 His water-courses grind our grist for us.

b. *Proverbial* and *fig.*

c1430 *Hymns Virg.* 44 Oon wolde riflee us at hame, And gadere þe flour out of oure gryst. *Ibid.* 74 Þouȝ þou deye, þou schalt not be myste; Þou combrest boþe foo & frende, Þi mylle haþ grounde þi laste griste. 1598 T. BASTARD *Chrestoleros* (1882) 96 When pride like polling miller sits vpon, The bated gryst of poore religion. 1623 FLETCHER & ROWLEY *Maid in Mill* v. ii, Shall the sayles of my love stand still? Shall the grists of my hopes be unground? 1641 SYMONDS *Serm. Ho. Comm.* D iv b, They have put you to grinde their grist. 1674 *Camden's Rem., Proverbs* (1870) 334 The Horse that is next the Mill carries all the Grist. 1740 E. BAYNARD *Health* (ed. 6) 29 This grinds life's grist, yet takes small tole. 1820 SCOTT *Monast.* xiii, Ye might have had other grist to grind. 1840 HOOD *Kilmansegg, Fancy Ball* xxxiii, How little of praise or grist would have come To a mill with such a hopper! 1880 WEBB *Goethe's Faust* II. iv, Gratis he never grinds your grist.

c. Phrases. ***to bring grist to the (one's) mill***: to bring business to one's hands; to be a source of profit or advantage. ***all is grist that comes to his mill***: he turns everything to account.

1583 GOLDING *Calvin on Deut.* cxxiii. 755 There is no lykelihoode that those thinges will bring gryst to the mill. 1664 H. MORE *Myst. Iniq.* xx. 77 Such superstitious surmizes as these will indeed bring grist to the mill in plenty for them that infuse them into the heads of the people. 1726 AYLIFFE *Parergon* 210 The Computation of Degrees in.. Matrimonial Causes.. brings grist to the Mill by way of Dispensations. 1770 FOOTE *Lame Lover* I. Wks. 1799 II. 68 Well, let them go on, it brings grist to our mill. 1818 BYRON *To Murray* 25 Mar. v, Sermons to thy mill bring grist. 1838 DICKENS *Nich. Nick.* xxxiv, Meantime the fools bring grist to my mill, so let them live out their day. 1885 *Harper's Mag.* Feb. 397/1 It is all grist that comes to her mill.

d. *U.S.* A 'lot', number, or quantity (of).

1832 J. K. PAULDING *Westward Ho!* I. 77 There has been a mighty grist of rain lately up above. 1840 HALIBURTON *Clockm.* Ser. III. xviii, Some smart grists of rain has fell. 1848 J. F. COOPER *Bee-hunter* I. iii. 80 There's an onaccountable grist on 'em [bees]. 1852 *Traits Amer. Humour* I. xxvii. 305, I.. got pretty considerable soaked by a grist of rain. 1881 S. P. MCLEAN *Cape Cod Folks* xviii. 295 'Grists on 'em, this year!' he said. 'Heaps!' Aunt Patty responded. 1906 *Springfield* (Mass.) *Weekly Republ.* 8 Feb. 9 A good-sized grist of matters was presented in the House last week under suspension of the rules.

3. Corn that has been ground.

c1566 *Merie Tales* in *Skelton's Wks.* (1843) I. p. lxvii, The seruaunt, hauynge hys gryste, went home [from the mill]. 1629 CHAPMAN *Juvenal* 126 Hoary cantles of unboulted grist. c1640 GATAKER *Man* 235 (L.) The motion of a winde-mill driven with the winde, that maketh grist no longer than the winde bloweth upon it. 1700 TYRRELL *Hist. Eng.* II. 808, A Farthing Loaf of the whole Grist. 1784 COWPER *Task* VI. 108 Swallowing.. The total grist unsifted, husks and all. 1887 *Kentish Gloss.*, *Grist*, anything which has been ground —meal, flour.

4. Malt crushed or ground for brewing.

1822 IMISON *Sci. & Art* II. 155 The water rises upwards through the malt, or as it is called, the grist. 1836 *Penny Cycl.* V. 403/2 Many brewers prefer a fine grist. *Ibid.*, A circular sieve, called a separator, through which the grist passes from the millstones. 1844 T. WEBSTER *Encycl. Dom. Econ.* 574 *Grist*, malt that has been ground for mashing.

5. *attrib.* and *Comb.*, as ***grist-cart***, †***-corn***, ***-grinding***, ***-watermill***; **grist-mill**, a mill for grinding corn; so ***grist-miller***.

1893 *Newspaper Advt.*, Wanted, Man to Milk.. and occasionally go with *Grist Cart. 1623 *Althorp MS.* p. lii. in Simpkinson *Washingtons* App., Spent to the baker of *grist corne 169 qua. 1807 VANCOUVER *Agric. Devon* (1813) 149 The price of *grist-grinding.. is about 5*d.* per bushel for wheat; 4*d.* for barley; and 2*d.* for oats. 1602 CAREW *Cornwall* 266 Amongst other commodities afforded by the Sea, the Inhabitants make vse of diuers his creekes for *griste-milles. 1727 DUDLEY in *Phil. Trans.* XXXIV. 261 The Owner of it was a common Carter to a Grist-Mill. 1886 ELWORTHY *W. Somerset Word-bk.* s.v., The small mills for grinding people's own corn, all over the country side are always called grist-mills. 1879 *Cassell's Techn. Educ.* IV. 211/1 *Grist-millers, masons, maltsters. 1637 HARRISON *Surv. Manor Sheff.* in *Sheffield Gloss.* s.v., Item a *Greist water mill standing on the south of Owlerton greene.

grist (grɪst), *sb.*^{3} Also 8 girst. [? Connected with GIRD *v.*^{1}] The size or thickness of yarn or rope.

1733 P. LINDSAY *Interest Scot.* 20 A Certificate from the Master of the Work-house, bearing that he or she, the Bearer, is a sufficient Tradesman, or good Spinner of such a Staple or Girst of Cloath, or Yarn, &c. 1792 *Specif. Kelly's Patent* No. 1879. 5 These wheels are calculated according to the size or grist of the yarn. 1835 URE *Philos. Manuf.* 24 The lace-maker.. verifies the grist of all the thread he purchases. 1875 KNIGHT *Dict. Mech.* s.v., Common grist is a rope 3 inches in circumference, with twenty yarns in each of the three strands. 1882 PATON in *Encycl. Brit.* XIV. 666/2 The grist or quality of all fine yarns is estimated by the number of leas in a pound.

transf. a1774 FERGUSSON *Leith Races* Poems (1845) 32 Here is the true and faithfu' list O' noblemen and horses; Their eild, their weight, their height, their grist, That rin for plates or purses.

grist, *v.*^{1} *Obs.* exc. *dial.* [f. GRIST *sb.*^{1}] *intr.* To gnash or grind the teeth.

c1460 J. RUSSELL *Bk. Nurture* 301 Good son, þy tethe be not pikynge, gris[t]ynge, ne gnastynge. 1842 AKERMAN *Wilts. Gloss.*, *Grist*, *Griz*, to gnash and shew the teeth angrily. 1893 *Wiltsh. Gloss.*, *Grist*, *Griz*, to snarl and show the teeth as an angry dog or man. N.W.

grist, *v.*^{2} [f. GRIST *sb.*^{2}] *trans.* To grind (corn). Hence **ˈgristing** *vbl. sb.*, the action of grinding corn, or the result of this. Also **ˈgrister**, 'one who brings grain to be ground at a mill' (Jamieson 1825).

1825–80 JAMIESON, *Grist*, *v. a.* to grind corn. 1883 *Gentl. Mag.* Oct. 378 Riding to Trumpington Mill with the sack of College grain for the gristing. 1887 *Kentish Gloss.*, *Gristing*, *Grysting*, the flour which is got from the lease-wheat.

†**gristbite**, *sb. Obs.* In 3 gristbat. [OE. *gristbite*, **gristbát*, f. GRIST *sb.*^{1} + *bite*, *bát*, nouns of action f. *bítan* BITE *v.*] Gnashing of teeth.

c1205 LAY. 5189 Þer wes muchel gristbat.

gristbite, *v. Obs.* exc. *dial.* Forms: 1 gristbitian, -bittian, -bátian, 3 gristbeatien, -betien, grisbatien, -patien, 4 grisbite, -bate, 9 grisbet, grizbite. [OE. *gristbitian*, *-bátian*, f. *gristbite*, **gristbát*: see prec.] *intr.* To gnash the teeth.

c900 tr. *Bæda's Hist.* IV. ix. [xi.] (1890) 184 He.. ongon.. mid his toðum gristbitian. c950 *Lindisf. Gosp.* Mark ix. 18 Fæmeð & gristbitteð mið toðum [*Rushw.* grist-bites, *Ags. Gosp.* gristbitað, *Hatton* grist-byteð]. a1000 *Voc.* in Wr.-Wülcker 242/35 *Fremit*, gristbataþ. c1000 ÆLFRIC *Gram.* xxvi. (Z.) 157 *Strideo* oððe *strido*, ic cearciȝe oððe ic gristbitiȝe. a1225 *Ancr. R.* 326 On hwam ure Louerd weop, ase þe Gospel telleð, and grisbatede. a1225 *Juliana* 66 Swa þe reue gromede þat he grispatede aȝein [*Bodl. MS.* gristbetede]. *Ibid.* 69 [He].. feng on to feamin & gristbeatien [*Royal MS.* grispatien] grisliche up o þis meoke meiden. c1340 *Cursor M.* 19354 (Trin.) Þenne bigon þei.. wiþ her teeþ to grisbate [*v. rr.* gnast, gnaist(e)]. 1387 TREVISA *Higden* (Rolls) VII. 377 He gan to ligge and to fome, to grisbite and to grynde wiþ þe teeþ. 1847–78 HALLIWELL, *Grisbet*, to make a wry face. *Somerset.* 1866 THORNBURY *Greatheart* II. v. 61 Mrs. Tolpedden achieved a dashing cannon, and then gave a miss, at which she 'grisbetted', as Milly called it. 1890 *Gloucestersh. Gloss.*, *Grizbite*, to gnash the teeth.

†**gristbiting**, *vbl. sb. Obs.* Forms: 1 gristbiot(t)ung, -bittung, -bitung, -bátung, 2 grisbating, 3 gris(t)bat-, 4 grisbait-, -bayt-, grysbating(e, -yng(e, grysbitting. [OE. *gristbitung*, *-bátung*, f. *gristbitian*, *-bátian* (see prec.).] Gnashing of the teeth.

c950 *Lindisf. Gosp.* Matt. viii. 12 In ðyostrum wytmesto ðer bið wop and grist-biottung teða [*Rushw.* gristbatung, *Ags. & Hatton Gosp.* gristbitung]. 971 *Blickl. Hom.* 185 Þær biþ a wop & hrop & toþa gristbitung. c1175 *Lamb. Hom.* 33 A þer [in helle] is waning and graming and toþen grisbating. c1205 LAY. 1806 Al was heora gristbatinge al swa wilde bares eȝe. 1370–80 *XI Pains of Hell* 248 in *O.E. Misc.* 230 Goulyng, And grisbatyng of teþe. 1387 TREVISA *Higden* (Rolls) I. 11 Wiþ grisbaitinge, gruntynge, and whistelynge. a1450 in *Trevisa's Higden* (Rolls) VII. App. 501 He had ofte herde the voys and the grysbitting of thilke soules that beth delyvered by prayers and almes dedes of cristen men.

gristeli, -lly, -ly, obs. ff. GRISTLY, GRIZZLY *a.*

gristle (ˈgrɪs(ə)l), *sb.* Forms: 1– gristle, 4 grystil, -tyll, (grusle), 4–5 gristil, 5 grystyl(le, 6 gristel, -ell(e, -ill, grystell, gressell, 6–8 grissel(l, (7 crissel, cristle, grisle, 8 grissle). *β.* 5 *north.* girstelle, *Sc.* 6 girssill, 8 girsle. [O.E. *gristle* = OFris. *gristel*, *gristl*, *grestel*, *gerstel*, EFris. *grössel*, *grüssel*, MLG. *gristel*, MHG. *gruschel*; cogn. with OE. *grost* gristle (Leiden glosses); synonymous forms of similar sound are OHG. *c(h)rustula*, *-ila*, *crostila*, *-ela*, *-illa*; *chrustilîn*, *crustili* (MHG. *krostel*, *krossel*, *krosel*, *krustel*; also *kruspel*, *krospel*). The mutual relation of these forms, and the etymology, are obscure.]

1. A tough flexible tissue, of a whitish colour, in vertebrate animals; = CARTILAGE 1.

a700 *Epinal Gloss.* 174 *Cartilaga*,.. næsgristlae. a800 *Erfurt Gloss.* 350 *Cartilago*, naesgristle. c1000 ÆLFRIC *Gloss.* in Wr.-Wülcker 158/22 *Cartilago*, gristle. c1050 *Voc.* ibid. 414/1 *Gartilago*, gristle. 1398 TREVISA *Barth. De P.R.* v. lix. (1495) 175 Grystyll is tendernes of the bones and is callyd cartilago in latyn. c1440 *Promp. Parv.* 213/2 Grystylle of the nose, *cartilago.* 1483 *Cath. Angl.* 157/1 A Girstelle, *cartilago.* 1523 FITZHERB. *Husb.* §89 The hawe is a sorance in a horse eye, and is lyke gristell. 1589 COGAN *Haven Health* cxli. (1636) 142 The Eares are nothing else but gristill and skinne. 1615 CROOKE *Body of Man* 943 Very thin bones and gristle bound or vnited by Synchondrosis. a1711 KEN *Hymnotheo* Poet. Wks. 1721 III. 21 The soft spinal gristle of his back, He turns and winds. 1776–96 WITHERING *Brit. Plants* (ed. 3) II. 47 Leaves egg-spear-shaped.. serratures like gristle. 1802 PALEY *Nat. Theol.* viii. §3 The bones which work against each other, are tipped with gristle. 1843 CARPENTER *Anim. Phys.* 42 Another tissue of which cells form the principal part, is that termed cartilage or gristle.

b. *fig.* with reference to the gristly nature of the bones in infancy. ***in the gristle***: in an initiatory, unformed, or embryonic stage of existence.

1775 BURKE *Sp. Conc. Amer.* 18 A people who are still, as it were, in the gristle, and not yet hardened into the bone of manhood. 1865 *Morn. Star* 22 May, As yet, of course, this business is in the gristle. 1880 E. KIRKE *Garfield* 46 Talleyrand once said to the first Napoleon that 'the United States was a giant without bones'. Since that time our gristle has been rapidly hardening.

2. A structure or formation consisting of such tissue; a gristly part; = CARTILAGE 1 b. (Now rare in *pl.*)

a1240 *Sawles Warde* in *Cott. Hom.* 251 Tadden and froggen þe freoteð ham ut te ehnen ant te nease gristles. 13.. *Coer de L.* 2144 The emperour of evil trusle Carved off his nose by the grusle. c1325 *Gloss. W. de Bibbysw.* in Wright *Voc.* 145 *Un tendroun*, a gristel. c1400 *Lanfranc's Cirurg.* 23 A gristil is cold & drie, & is neischere þan a boon. a1533 LD. BERNERS *Huon* xlii. 140 Yᵉ grystell of his nose as grete as the mossell of an oxe. 1574 *Sc. Acts Jas. VI* (1814) III. 87 Gif thay happin tobe convicted, To be adiugeit tobe.. burnt throw the girssill of the rycht eare wᵗ ane het Irne. 1597 A. M. tr. *Guillemeau's Fr. Chirurg.* 13 b/2 The synnues, Tendones, and Cartilages or grissells. 1601 MUNDAY *Downf. Earl Huntington* III. iii. G j b, Is this a pawe.. To holde a tender hand in?.. Looke I pray, His armes are gristles. 1658 A. FOX *Wurtz' Surg.* II. xxv. 152 The bones and crissels of the Nose. 1747 MRS. GLASSE *Cookery* xii. 126 Take six Pounds of good Pork, free from Skin and Gristles, and Fat. 1820 SHELLEY *Œdipus* I. 63 To fill our colons With rich blood, or make brawn out of our gristles. 1822 SCOTT *Nigel* xxiii, We would slit it [the nose] up to the gristle.

†b. In various transf. senses: (see quots). *Obs.*

1533 ELYOT *Cast. Helthe* (1539) 31 b, The kernelles and gristell whiche are in the rootes, if they be welle digested they make nourishment. 1578 LYTE *Dodoens* III. xxv. 308 The best Ammoniacum.. pure and without shardes, splinters, or stonie gristels or gravell. *Ibid.* III. cxiv. 307 Galbanum is also a gumme or liquor.. and the best is gristel, or betwixt hard and soft. 1688 R. HOLME *Armoury* II. 85/1 The Gristle of the Walnut is that as lies between the two halves of the kernel, within the shell. 1785 BURNS *Ep. to J. Lapraik* 1 Apr. xxii, To conclude my lang epistle, As my auld pen's worn to the grissle.

c. *Sc.* The nose.

1790 A. WILSON *Ep. to E. Picken* Poet. Wks. (1846) 109 Whiles a glass to heet my gab, And snuff to smart my girsle.

†3. *fig.* A tender or delicate person. *Obs.*

a1553 UDALL *Royster D.* I. iv. (Arb.) 27 Ah sir, be good to hir, she is but a gristle, Ah sweete lambe and coney. 1591 LYLY *Endym.* v. ii. 73 *Sam.* We will helpe you to find a young ladie. *Top.* I love no grissels,.. I desire old matrons. 1623 MASSINGER *Bondman* I. ii, I am a gristle, and these spider fingers Will never hold a sword. a1652 BROME *Mad Couple* v. ii. (1653) G 6 b, Alas y'are but a grissell, Weake picking meat.

4. *attrib.*, as †***gristle-ring***; †**gristle-bone** = sense 2.

1398 TREVISA *Barth. De P.R.* v. xii. (1495) 116 Whan the voys of thayer smyte to the grystil-boon, there it is gretly holpe. c1400 *Lanfranc's Cirurg.* 148 In þe fore partie of þe brest þere is sett þe canne of þe lungis, þe which is compounned of gristil ryngis bounde togidere wiþ pannicleris ligamentis. c1440 *Promp. Parv.* 106/1 Cruschylbone, or grystylbone, *cartilago.* 1557–8 PHAER *Æneid* VII. T iij b, While the poyson.. gropes her gristlebones, and venim droppes her sences drinkes. 1886 *Pall Mall G.* 22 Oct. 11/1 Four other eighty thousands not yet reached manhood and womanhood, or gone beyond the gristle stage.

†**gristled** (ˈgrɪs(ə)ld), *a. Obs. rare*$^{-1}$. [f. GRISTLE *sb.* + -ED^{2}.] Formed into gristle.

1633 T. ADAMS *Exp. 2nd Peter* ii. 5 Infants who cannot speake or doe ill, whose flesh is but new quick'ned in the wombe, or bones scarce gristled out of the wombe.

gristly (ˈgrɪslɪ), *a.* Forms: *α.* 4, 7 grystly, 5 grustlye, gristeli, 6 -el(l)y, grisselye, 7 grissly, (gristlely), grisselly, 7–9 grisly, 6– gristly. *β.* *Sc.* 6 girsillie, 8 girslie. [f. GRISTLE *sb.* + -Y^{1}.]

1. Pertaining to, or of the nature of gristle; consisting or full of gristle; cartilaginous.

1398 TREVISA *Barth. De P.R.* v. xii. (1495) 116 The substaunce of the very ere is grystly. c1400 *Lanfranc's Cirurg.* 23 Þe eende of þe þrote bolle is gristeli [*v.r.* grustlye]. 1555 W. WATREMAN *Fardle Facions* I. vi. 102 When thei haue gnabeled of the softest and gristely partes with their tiethe. 1596 DALRYMPLE tr. *Leslie's Hist. Scot.* I. 30 His flesche was all girssillie bot of a trim taist. 1615 H. CROOKE *Body of Man* 379 A hard substance sometimes gristlely.. which in some Creatures.. is a very gristle. *Ibid.* 613 An vpper part which is immoueable and bony, and a lower, which is moueable and gristly. 1657 EVELYN *Diary* 19 Sept., Certaine grissly skinns curiously jointed, yet loose. 1796 MORSE *Amer. Geog.* I. 195 On his shoulders arises a large fleshy or grisly substance. 1797 M. BAILLIE *Morb. Anat.*

(1807) 144 The peritonæal covering of the stomach..has almost a gristly hardness. **1805** J. NICOL *Poems* I. 155 (Jam.) His girslie nose. **1863** LYELL *Antiq. Man* 14 The gristly parts have been gnawed off, as if by dogs. **1884** M. MACKENZIE *Dis. Throat & Nose* II. 176 A piece of gristly meat one inch in length.

†**b.** Having a cartilaginous skeleton, as some fishes. (See CARTILAGINOUS 1 b.) *Obs.*

1601 HOLLAND *Pliny* I. 333 Such fishes as wee called Cartilagineous and gristly. **1607** TOPSELL *Serpents* (1658) 682 It [a serpent] also beareth egges in her place of conception..which are there disposed in order, as in other living gristly creatures.

2. Having a texture resembling that of gristle, in toughness, etc.

1601 HOLLAND *Pliny* I. 378 The best Galbanum..is gristly and cleare withall. **1688** R. HOLME *Armoury* II. 115/2 Gristly seeds are thin skinny flat seeds. **1776–96** WITHERING *Brit. Plants* (ed. 3) I. 189 Cup 5 leaves and 5 angles, gristly. **1800** *Phil. Trans.* XC. 337 The gristly substance which forms the bulbs.

Hence **'gristliness** (Bailey vol. II, 1727).

gristole, variant of *grith-stool*: see GRITH *sb.* 7.

gristy ('grɪstɪ), *a. dial.* [? f. GRIST *sb.*[2] + -Y[1].] Gritty.

1676 J. BEAUMONT in *Phil. Trans.* XI. 729 A sort of ash-colour'd gristy Clay. *Ibid.* 732 In the Courses,..betwixt the clifts I find of these Plants growing up in the gristy clay. **1881** *I. of W. Gloss.*, *Gristy*, sandy; having hard particles.

†**grisy**, *a.*[1] *Obs.* Also 6 **grizy, grysie, griesy, -ie, gryesy,** 8 **greecy.** [f. GRISE *v.* + -Y[1]. In quot. 1590 the reading *grizy* may be a misprint.] Horrible; grim; grisly. Hence †**'grisyness.**

1382 WYCLIF *Gen.* xv. 12 Whanne the sunne was goon down, feer felle vpon Abram, and greet grisynes [**1388** hidousenesse, Vulg. *horror*] and derk assaileden hym. **1590** SPENSER *F.Q.* II. vi. 18 The slouthfull wave of that great griesy [*ed.* 1609 griesly] lake. *Ibid.* II. xi. 12 That fourth band..Was, as the rest, a grysie rablement. *Ibid.* III. xii. 19 A most faire dame, Led of two grysie villeins, th' one Despight, The other cleped Cruelty. **1590** SHAKS. *Mids. N.* v. i. 140 (Fo. 1 1623) This grizy [Qos. **1600** grizly] beast (which Lyon hight by name). *a* **1800** *Johnie Scot* in Child *Ballads* (1886) II. 390 Out they brought the Itilian, And a greecy ghost was he.

†**'grisy**, *a.*[2] *Obs.* Forms: 6 **griesie, gryesy,** 7 **grizie, grizy.** [app. f. GRIS *a.* + -Y[1].] Grey, grizzled.

1590 SPENSER *F.Q.* I. ix. 25 His griesie [*ed.* 1611 griesly] lockes, long growen and unbound. *Ibid.* III. i. 67 Earely, ere the grosse Earthes gryesy shade Was all disperst out of the firmament. **1603** KNOLLES *Hist. Turks* 874 His beard grizie [**1638** grizy], though not for age.

grit (grɪt), *sb.*[1] Forms: α. 1 **gréot,** 3, 5, 7, (9 *dial.*) **gret,** 3–4 **greot,** 4, (9 *dial.*) **greit,** 4, 7 **grett,** 4–8 **grete,** 4–9 **greet,** (5–7 **greete,** 7 **griet,** 8–9 *dial.* **grate**). β. 6 **grite, gryt,** 7– **grit.** [OE. *gréot* = OS. *griot*, OHG. *grioz* (MHG. *griez*, G. *griesz*), ON. *grjót* pebbles:—OTeut. **greuto*[m], str. neut.; a pre-Teut. root **ghreud-*: *ghrud-* appears in Lith. *grudżti* to crush, pound, Lettish *grauds* grain, OSl. *gruda* clod. The abnormal development of the vowel may be due to assimilation to GRIT *sb.*[2]]

1. a. *collect. sing.* Formerly: Sand, gravel, small stones. Now: Minute particles of stone or sand, as produced by attrition or disintegration.

α. *Beowulf* 3168 Forleton eorla ȝestreon eorðan healdan, gold on greote, þær hit nu ȝen lifað..unnyt. *a* **1000** *Cædmon's Gen.* 909 (Gr.) þu scealt greot etan þine lifdaȝas. *a* **1000** *Andreas* 425 (Gr.) Sand is ȝeblonden, grund wið greote. *a* **1300** *Cursor M.* 9938 (Cott.) Four strandes rinnes suete Thoru þat grauel and þat grett [*other MSS.* grete]. *c* **1320** *Sir Tristr.* 2501 He fond awele [*sc.* a well] ful gode Al white it was, þe grete. ? *a* **1500** *Chester Pl.* (Shaks. Soc.) I. 121 With grete gravill and greete I skoure an oulde pane. **1513** DOUGLAS *Æneis* XII. Prol. 55 The syluer scalyt fyschis on the greit Ourthwort cleir stremis sprynkland for the heyt. **1639** G. DANIEL *Ecclus.* xxv. 55 An Asscent straw'd wth a slippery greet. *a* **1650** *Dth. Robin Hood* 100 in Furnivall *Percy Folio* I. 56 There make me a full fayre graue of grauell & of greete. **1655** FULLER *Ch. Hist.* I. v. §30 Small Griet and Gravell may choak a man. **1869** *Lonsdale Gloss.*, *Gret*, fine gravel, sand. **1883** *Almondbury & Huddersf. Gloss.*, *Greet.* **1887** *S. Chesh. Gloss.*, *Greit.*

β. **1589** RIDER *Eng.-Lat. Dict.*, Grite, or duste of stones or mettal, *scobs.* **1618** E. ELTON *Compl. Sanct. Sinner* (1622) 239 Bread of deceit..afterwards it turnes to grit and grauell in his mouth. **1657** R. LIGON *Barbadoes* (1673) 37 Though we wash it never so well, yet the grit cracks in our teeth. **1747** MRS. GLASSE *Cookery* vi. 62 Take two or three Eels,..and wash them from Grit. **1845** *Florist's Jrnl.* 218 A considerable quantity of road grit. **1865** DICKENS *Mut. Fr.* II. xv, The City grit gets into the hair and eyes and skin.

¶ Used for GRIT *sb.*[2]

a **1225** *Ancr. R.* 70 Muche fol he were þe muhte, to his owene bihoue, hweðer se he wolde, grinden greot oðer hwete, ȝif he grunde þe greot & lefde þene hwete. 'Hwete is holi speche', ase Seint Anselme seið. Heo grint greot þe cheofled.

b. *fig.*, with reference to the unpleasant or injurious qualities of grit.

1876 LOWELL *Among my Bks.* Ser. II. 184 It gives you a shock of unpleasant surprise, a kind of grit, as when one's teeth close on a bit of gravel in a dish of strawberries and cream. **1884** J. S. BREWER *Hen. VIII*, I. 105 The Venetian ambassador, gleeful as a schoolboy when he could throw grit into Wolsey's bread, was not sorry at the opportunity of carrying him the tidings. **1890** *Spectator* 13 Dec., Every tax is a handful of grit thrown into the machinery of industrial wealth, and impairs its productive powers.

c. A particle of sand. *rare.*

1601 HOLLAND *Pliny* I. 314 If haply there doe arise a tempest..they [bees] catch up some little stonie greet to ballaise and poise themselves against the wind. **1890** ABNEY *Treat. Photogr.* (ed. 6) 56 Application of acid may dissolve the grits away.

2. a. Coarse sandstone, esp. of the kinds used for millstones and grindstones; gritstone.

α. *c* **1275** *Serving Christ* 67 in *O.E. Misc.* 92 Me graueþ þis gode in greote and in ston. **1391** *Mem. Ripon* (Surtees) III. 109 In xvj petris de grete emp. pro j herthe. *c* **1400** *Siege Jerusalem* (E.E.T.S.) 35/621 With grete stones of gret & of gray marble. **1587** HARRISON *England* III. ix. (1877) II. 64 These [whetstones] also are divided either into the hard griet, as the common that shoomakers use, or the soft griet called hones. **1678** HOBBES *Decam.* x. 123 The Stone of which are made Milstones, which Stone is here called Greet. **1731** LOWTHORP in *Phil. Trans.* Abr. I. viii. 588 The Portland stone is of a fine Chalky Greet, fit for all curious hewn and carved Work. **1747** HOOSON *Miner's Dict.* M, Shale, Chirts, Greet, &c. do produce very good Veins, and that last very well likewise.

β. **1710** *Brit. Apollo* III. No. 3. 2/1 A Grit or course free Stone. **1784** BELKNAP *Tour White Mts.* (1876) 20 Grindstones are found at Fryeburg and at Amariscogin, of a fine grit, and hard. **1833** LYELL *Princ. Geol.* III. 222 The lacustrine strata are composed of gravel, grit and micaceous sandstone. **1851** RICHARDSON *Geol.* (1855) 450 The upper beds consist of quartzose grits. **1874** DAWKINS *Cave Hunt.* ii. 25 The massive millstone grit of Derbyshire and Yorkshire. **1882** GEIKIE *Text Bk. Geol.* II. II. §6. 158 By an augmentation in the size of the grains, a sandstone may become a grit, or a pebbly conglomerate sandstone.

†**b.** Applied by J. Hill to a 'genus' of fossils.

1748 SIR J. HILL *Hist. Fossils* 569 Series III. Class IV. Order II. Genus I. Saburræ. Gritts. Fossils found in minute masses, forming together a kind of powder. *Ibid.*, The white stony Gritts..consisting of pure Spar.

3. Earth, soil, mould; †the ground, as ***under, in, on the greet.*** Now *Obs.* exc *dial.*

c **1250** *Gen. & Ex.* 3774 Erðe..opnede vnder ere fet; Held up neiðer ston ne gret. *a* **1300** *Cursor M.* 16923 Nu is þe croice grauen vnder greit, and iesus vnder stan. *c* **1330** *Amis & Amil.* 1530 Graven in grete so cold. **1393** LANGL. *P. Pl.* C. XIV. 23 As greyn that lyth in the greot and thorgh grace, atte laste, Spryngeth vp and spredeth. *c* **1400** *Melayne* 1252 Many a Sarazene lay on his bake,..Full Grisely gronande one the grete. ? *a* **1500** *Chester Pl.* (E.E.T.S.) 405 Take we the body of this sweet, and lay it low under the greet! **1601** HOLLAND *Pliny* I. 502 The blacke mould or grit. *a* **1722** LISLE *Husb.* (1752) 6 The side lands in the hill country are always the poorest, because the good grete, or mold, is washed down by the rain. **1813** [see 6 below]. **1880** *E. Cornwall Gloss.*, *Greet*, earth, soil.

4. The grain or texture of a stone, in respect of fineness, coarseness, etc.

1529 RASTELL *Pastyme, Hist. Brit.* (1811) 105 These stonis at Stonehenge be all of one gryt, without chaunge of colour, or vayne. **1601** HOLLAND *Pliny* II. 588 In this kind there be of a more free and softer grit. **1662** R. MATHEW *Unl. Alch.* lxxxix. 154 Let not the sand be either too sharp or too fine, but of a middle greet. **1694** S. FOLEY in *Phil. Trans.* XVIII. 171 Of a whitish Free-stone colour, but a finer closer gret. **1776** G. SEMPLE *Building in Water* 40 The Grit or Grain of it greatly resembled that of a Millstone. **1811** G. S. KEITH *Agric. Surv. Aberd.* 56 (Jam.) When they mean to split it, they begin by drawing a straight line along the stone in the direction of its grete. *a* **1835** RICKMAN *Archit.* App. (1848) 11 The ancient door is..of..a dark red sandstone of a strong grit.

fig. *c* **1630** RISDON *Surv. Devon* §114 (1810) 118 There..lived in this parish one Stone, who was of so hard a greete, that he lived to the age of one hundred and twenty years.

5. *colloq.* **a.** orig. *U.S. slang.* Firmness or solidity of character; indomitable spirit or pluck; stamina. ***to be clear, hard*** (etc.) ***grit***: to have genuine spirit or pluck. ***to be the grit***: to be the 'right sort', the genuine 'article'.

1825 J. NEAL *Bro. Jonathan* III. 386 Proper fellow he was too; 'cute enough, I tell you—sharp as a razor—clear grit. **1843** HALIBURTON *Attaché* II. i. 13 If he hadn't a had the clear grit in him, and showed his teeth and claws. **1861–2** THACKERAY *Adv. Philip* xxxi, If you were a chip of the old block you would be just what he called 'the grit'. **1863** HAWTHORNE *Our Old Home* (1883) I. 322 His main deficiency was a lack of grit. **1873–4** DIXON *Two Queens* III. XIII. ii. 12 John Fisher..had not lost his northern grit and twang. **1880** *Daily Tel.* 7 Oct., Our English lads are hard grit. **1892** *Times* 23 Apr. 7/1 Every appointment of the kind must be based wholly upon fitness and grit.

b. In Canadian politics, a Radical or Liberal. Formerly ***clear grit.***

1884 *Fortn. Rev.* May 592 There arose up [in Canada] a political party of a Radical persuasion, who were called Clear-Grits, and the Clear-Grits declared for the secularisation of the Clergy Reserves. **1887** GOLDWIN SMITH in *Contemp. Rev.* July 15 The names 'Tory' and 'Grit', by which they call each other, therefore, being free from meaning, are really more appropriate than Conservative and Liberal, by which they call themselves. *Ibid.*, Their leaders are more ready to accept baronetcies and knighthoods than the leaders of the Grits.

6. *attrib.* and *Comb.*, as ***grit-ashlar, -band, -bed, -country, -getter; grit-tempered*** adj.; **grit-berry**, a name for the genus *Comarostaphylis* (*Treas. Bot.* 1866); **grit-blasting** *vbl. sb.*, the use of a stream of abrasive particles directed at a surface to clean it and roughen it; hence (as a back-formation) **grit-blast** *v. trans.* and *absol.*; **grit-board** *dial.*, the earth-board of a plough; **grit-cell** = *stone-cell* (STONE *sb.* 20), SCLEREID; **grit-emery**, coarse emery; **grit-rock** = GRITSTONE.

1855 *Cornwall* (1862) 77 The 'best blue fine granite, or *grit-ashlar, for building sea-walls'. **1881** *Geol. Mag.* Nov. 488 The beds are traversed by a coarse cleavage dipping south, which usually ignores the hard *grit bands. **1890** *Jrnl. Geol. Soc.* XLVI. 496 The red slates with hard *grit beds south of Goodrington beach support a Triassic outlier. **1953** ARKELL & TOMKEIEFF *Eng. Rock Terms* 53/1 The original sense of 'gravelly' seems to be preserved in the local term Grit Bed used for the Melbourn Rock in the Middle Chalk of Kent and Sussex, which is a band of limestone with a hard nodular structure. **1962** *Flight International* LXXXII. 201/1 The finished spar would be *grit-blasted,.. principally in order to remove small amounts of metal under closely controlled conditions. **1964** *Financ. Times* 8 Sept. 11/4 The operator can safely grit-blast without having to dress in protective clothing. **1936** *Metals Handbk.* (Amer. Soc. Metals) 841 (*heading*) Cleaning metals by blast cleaning process (also known as sand blasting, *grit, and shot blasting). **1947** *Mettallurgia* Apr. 279/2 Such a cleaning process as grit blasting lowers the corrosion resistance of the alloys. **1963** *Times* 22 Apr. p. v/1 To make sure the zinc sticks the steel must be roughened by gritblasting immediately beforehand. **1813** T. DAVIS *Agric. Wilts* 263 **Grate board*, or bread Board—The mould or earth-board of a plough which turns the furrow; earth being frequently called grate. **1880** *E. Cornwall Gloss.*, *Greet-board*, the earth-board of a plough. **1900** B. D. JACKSON *Gloss. Bot. Terms* 115/2 **Grit-cell*, a sclerotic cell, as in the flesh of pears. **1960** W. B. R. LAIDLAW *Guide Brit. Hardwoods* 103 Fruit pear-shaped; with grit-cells. **1878** DAVIS & LEES *West Yorksh.* I. i. 14 The deep valleys in the *grit country usually have a stream at the bottom. **1884** F. J. BRITTEN *Watch & Clockm.* 101 *Grit or corn Emery used for sharpening cutting burnishers. **1854** *Illustr. Lond. News* 5 Aug. 118 Occupations of the people,..*Grit-getter. **1838** *Penny Cycl.* XI. 439/2 In the Carpathian mountains and in the Alps *grit-rocks with abundance of fuci (*grès des Carpathes*) represent the greensands of France and England. **1939** V. G. CHILDE *Dawn Europ. Civilization* (ed. 3) xii. 214 The 'classical' beaker..made of relatively fine *grit-tempered ware. **1839** STONEHOUSE *Axholme* 189 Mr. Wesley was buried in Epworth churchyard under a plain *grit tombstone, supported by brick-work.

grit (grɪt), *sb.*[2] Now only *pl.* and *dial.* Forms: α. *sing.* (rare) 1 **grytt,** 7 **gritt,** 8 **grit.** *pl.* 1 **grytta, gretta,** 3 *genitive* **gruttene,** 7 **gritts,** 7– **grits.** β. *pl.* 7 **gurts, gert** (see GIRT-BREW), 9 **girts.** γ. *pl.* 6– **greats,** (7 **greyts,** 7–8 **greets**). [OE. *grytt(e* str. and wk. fem., usually in pl. *grytta(n* = MLG., Du. *grutte* fem., OHG. *gruzzi* (MHG., G. *grütze*):—OTeut. type **grutjâ, grutjôn-*, f. Teut. root **greut-, graut-, grŭt-*, whence also GROATS (a synonym, usually regarded as a mere variant, of this word), and GRIT *sb.*[1]

This and the preceding sb. seem to have mutually influenced each other in form, whence the γ forms here and the β forms of GRIT *sb.*[1]]

†**1.** Bran, chaff, mill-dust. *Obs.*

a **700** *Epinal Gloss.* 823 *Pullis*, grytt. *c* **1000** ÆLFRIC *Gloss.* in Wr.-Wülcker 141/20 *Apludes* uel *cantabra*, hwæte gryttan. *c* **1000** *Sax. Leechd.* II. 220 þam mannum sceal man sellan..niwe beren mela oððe grytta. *a* **1100** *Ags. Voc.* in Wr.-Wülcker 330/33 *Furfures*, gretta. **11..** *Voc.* ibid. 505/13 *Polline*, gryttes. *a* **1225** *Ancr. R.* 186 þis is Godes heste, þet him is muchele leouere þen þet tu ete gruttene bread, oðer werie herde here.

2. Oats that have been husked but not ground (or only coarsely); coarse oatmeal.

This is the general use of the word, but its application varies and has varied in Eng. dialects; in America it is applied to other kinds of grain. (See quots.)

1579 LANGHAM *Gard. Health* (1633) 457 Otemeale Greyts. **1589** COGAN *Haven Health* vii. (1636) 31 Of the greats or groats..boiled in water with salt, they make a kind of meat. **1601** HOLLAND *Pliny* I. 559 In Gaule..they have a kind of fourmentie corn or gurts..named in their language Brance. **1615** MARKHAM *Eng. Housew.* II. viii. (1668) 178 The Greets or full Kernels will separate from the smaller oatmeal. *a* **1661** FULLER *Worthies, Linc.* II. (1662) 153 Gruel ..is wholsome Spoon-meat,..Water is the Matter, Grits the Form thereof. **1686** PLOT *Staffordsh.* 205 They are much smaller, without husk, and are indeed perfect gritts naturally, requiring no Mill to make them into Oatemeal. **1725** BRADLEY *Fam. Dict.* s.v. *Oat meal*, The bigger kind of Oat-Meal, which is call'd Greets, or Corn Oat-Meal. **1750** W. ELLIS *Country Housewife* 206 Whole greets boiled in water till they burst, and then mixt with butter. **1796** MRS. GLASSE *Cookery* xxi. 335 Grits [**1747** (ed. 1) grotes] once cut does better than oatmeal. **1811** A. T. THOMSON *Lond. Disp.* (1818) 68 Gruels, or decoctions of grits or of oatmeal, are excellent demulcents. **1847–78** HALLIWELL, *Girts*, oatmeal. *Var. dial.* **1884** KNIGHT *Dict. Mech.* Suppl., *Grits* (*Milling*), cracked fragments of wheat smaller than *groats*. **1886** *Syd. Soc. Lex.* s.v., In America, fine hominy is called grits, and wheat prepared in the same way is likewise so designated. **1938** M. K. RAWLINGS *Yearling* iii. 27 Breakfast was on the table... There were grits and gravy, hot cakes, and buttermilk. **1961** *Encounter* XVI. 20 Other eaters..were forking up eggs and grits. **1969** *New Yorker* 10 May 32/1 We stopped for scrambled eggs and grits in a little town in Alabama.

3. *attrib.*, as ***grit-gruel.*** See also GIRT-BREW.

1844 T. WEBSTER *Encycl. Dom. Econ.* 739 In the case of grits, this cuticle is entirely kept back, which accounts for the smoothness, as it is termed, of grit-gruel.

grit (grɪt), *sb.*[3] (Only in dicts.: see also GRYFF.) [? Repr. OE. *grytte* spider, which is found once as a gloss on *gongeweafre* (Vulgate *aranea*) in *Vesp. Ps.* lxxxix. 9.] A kind of crab.

1598 FLORIO, *Paguro*, a kind of creuis or crafish called a grit, a grampell, or a punger. **1658** PHILLIPS, *A Grit*, a kinde of fish, otherwise called a Grample fish. **1721** in BAILEY. **1847–78** HALLIWELL, *Grit*, the sea-crab. *Linc.* **1867** SMYTH *Sailor's Word-bk.*, *Gritt*, an east-country term for the sea-crab.

grit (grɪt), *v.* [f. GRIT *sb.*[1]]

1. *intr.* To produce a grating sound such as is caused by the crushing of grit; to move with such a grating noise.

1762 GOLDSM. *Cit. W.* xxx, The sanded floor that grits beneath the tread. **1810** *Splendid Follies* I. 191 The wheel gritted slowly along. **1834** M. SCOTT *Cruise Midge* (1859) 343 Several gigs and carriages of various descriptions gritted past us through the deep sand of the unpaved thoroughfares. **1847–78** HALLIWELL, *Grit*, to squeak or grunt. *Somerset.* **1851** LOWELL *Lett.* (1894) I. 216 A burnt stick that goes gritting, Grit, gritting o'er the canvas. **1859** MRS. GASKELL *Round Sofa* 250 He pulled a face as if he had heard a slate-pencil gritting against a slate.

2. *trans.* To cover with grit or sand.

1842 [see GRITTED *ppl. a.*]. **1899** *Blackw. Mag.* Feb. 421/2 His hands and gun all sand gritted with his labour of wall erection.

3. To cause to make a grating or 'gritty' sound.

1851 MRS. BROWNING *Casa Guidi W.* 131 Murmurously the ebbing waters grit The little pebbles.

4. **a.** To grind or grate (the teeth).

1797 JEFFERSON *Writings* (1903) I. 416 Mr. Adams,.. gritting his teeth, said [etc.]. **1840** *Southern Lit. Messenger* VI. 735/2 The duellist gritted his teeth as he cocked the gun a second time. **1848** LOWELL *Fable for Critics* Poet. Wks. 1890 III. 30 Just conceive how much harder your teeth you'd have gritted. **1887** F. R. STOCKTON *Borrowed Month* etc. 27, I gritted my teeth as I thought what a despicable thing it would be.

b. To utter with gritting of the teeth.

1900 *Daily News* 11 Oct. 3/1 The Boers have gritted it between their teeth, mingling it with sullen curses—for to the veldtsman the name [of J. Chamberlain] is as the name of a thing accursed. **1910** C. E. MULFORD *Hopalong Cassidy* i. 11 'I'll kill you some day, you whelp,' he gritted.

Hence **ˈgritted**, **ˈgritting** *ppl. adjs.*; **ˈgritting** *vbl. sb.*

1823 *Massachusetts Spy* 30 Apr. (Th.), The harmony arising from the filing of a saw, or the gritting of teeth. **1833** M. SCOTT *Tom Cringle* xviii. (1859) 504 Thundering them down again against the flint-hard coral spikes, with a loud gritting rumble. **1842** TENNYSON *Will Waterproof* 242 When.. thou shalt cease To pace the gritted floor. *a* **1849** POE *Tales & Sketches* (1852) 255, I could have sworn that it was the gritting of this vagabond's teeth. **1897** *Outing* (U.S.) XXX. 422/1 The gritted teeth, and the tension of the body, show what power this player has put into his shot. **1901** *Daily News* 13 Mar. 5/2 The gritting and corroding of tubes. **1908** *Westm. Gaz.* 14 Dec. 11/2 The Borough Council includes no less a sum than £2,000 for snow removal and the gritting of the roads. **1963** *Guardian* 21 Jan. 1/1 Todmorden local authority has a plough and gritting lorry out. **1963** *Times* 4 Feb. 6/6 Snow ploughs and gritting gangs worked throughout yesterday to clear 50,000 miles of snow-covered trunk roads. **1968** *Times* 26 Mar. 2/2 A big new road-gritting machine.

grit, obs. form of GRITH; Sc. f. GREAT.

grite, obs. form of GRIT *sb.*[1]; Sc. f. GREAT.

grith (grɪθ), *sb. Obs.* exc. *Hist.* Forms: α. 1–4 **griþ**, 3 **gryþ**, **gryt**, *Orm.* **griþþ**, 4 **grit**, **gryht**, **grid**, 4–5 **gryth**, 4–7 **grithe**, (5 **grythe**, **greth**, **gryethe**, **gryght(e)**, 3– **grith**. β. *Sc.* and *north.* 4–6, 9 **gyrth**, 4–9 **girth**, (5 **girthe**, 6 **gyrthe**, **gyrtht**). [OE. *griδ*, a. ON. *griδ* neut., orig. domicile, home; in pl., truce, peace, pardon; hence, sanctuary, asylum.]

† 1. Guaranteed security; protection, defence; safe conduct. *Obs.*

c **1000** *Laws of Cnut* I. c. 2 §1 in Schmid *Gesetze* 250 Ælc cirice is mid rihte on Cristes ageнum griδe, and ælc cristenman ah micele þearfe, þæt he on þam griδe micele mæδe wite, forþam Godes griδ is ealra griδa selost to ʒeearnianne and ʒeornost to healdenne, and þær nehst cyninges. *a* **1300** *Cursor M.* 492 þas oþer gastes þat fell him wiht þe quilk for-sok godds grith. *Ibid.* 7517 Ga þan.. in godds grith, þat he-self ai be þe with. *c* **1330** R. BRUNNE *Chron.* (1810) 34 Erles & barons þat wer in þe land, So wele were þei chastised, alle com tille his grith. *c* **1350** *Will. Palerne* 3899 Defende we vs douʒtili or we deiʒen sone; þer goþ non oþer griþ, it geineþ nouʒt to flene. *c* **1425** WYNTOUN *Cron.* VII. Prol. 27 Than suld I.. wyn, till succoure me fra blame, The gyrth of excusatyowne. *c* **1440** *York Myst.* xvii. 150 To come and goo I graunte yow grith. *c* **1450** MYRC 1693 Agayn enuye loue ys gryth. *c* **1450** *Robin Hood & Monk* lxxxvi. in Child *Ballads* (1888) III. 101/1, 'I gaf hem grith', seid oure kyng, 'Thorowout all mery Inglond'. **1568** in *Bannatyne MS.* (Hunter. Club) 59 Sen that fra God your grace cummis all, Fra your regrait ye gif him girth. *a* **1650** *Flodden Field* 266 in Furnivall *Percy Folio* I. 330 There shold neither be grith nor grace, but on a boughe he sholde be hanged.

2. *spec.* in *O.E. Law.* Security, peace, or protection guaranteed under particular limitations of time or place; as CHURCH-GRITH (OE. *ciric-griδ*), security within the precincts of a church; HAND-GRITH (OE. *hand-griδ*), protection under the king's hand; after the OE. period used without qualification = *church-grith* (occas. *kirkes grith*), sanctuary. *to take grith*: to take sanctuary; hence *gen.*, to take refuge or shelter.

a **1000**, *c* **1205** [see CHURCH-GRITH]. *c* **1000** *Laws of Æthelred* VIII. c. 1 in Schmid *Gesetze* 242 ʒif æfre æniʒ man .. Godes ciric-griδ swa abrece δæt he binnon ciric-waʒum man-slaʒa weorδe. *a* **1225** *Ancr. R.* 174 Understondeδ.. tet ʒe beoδ ivlowen to chirche griδe: uor nis non of ou þet nes sume chere Godes þeof. *a* **1300** Kirkes grith [see CHURCH-GRITH]. **1375** BARBOUR *Bruce* II. 44 He mysdid thar gretly, but wer, That gave na gyrth to the Awter. *c* **1470** HENRY *Wallace* VII. 1047 Thai.. To the kyrk rane, wend gyrth for till haiff tayne. **1480** CAXTON *Chron. Eng.* ccxxviii. (1482) 238 A Breton murthred a good wedowe.. and after this he toke the grith [*ed.* 1520 gyrthe] of holy chirche. **1519** *Sanctuar. Dunelm.* (Surtees) 86, I aske gyrth for Godsake and Saint Cuthbert's. **1549** *Compl. Scot.* xiv. 118 Thai gart pausanias seruitur pas to the tempil to tak gyrtht and protectione, as dois ane tresgressour. **1603** STOW *Surv.* xxxiv. 310, 5 of his fellowship.. took him [a souldier prisoner] from the Officer, brought him into sanctuary, at the west dore of S. Martins church, and tooke grithe of that place. **1828** SCOTT *F.M. Perth* x, Three or four men.. came this morning before daylight to ask the privilege of girth and sanctuary. **1872** E. W. ROBERTSON *Hist. Ess.* 178 The Grith that ranked next after that which was given ('from the king's own hand' was 'the grith which the ealderman and king's reeve give in the Assembly of the Five-Burghs'. **1892** *Edin. Rev.* July 223 Charles availing himself of the law of grith or sanctuary, went down to Holyrood.

3. *concr.* A place of protection; a sanctuary, asylum.

Some of the earlier examples may belong to sense 1.

a **1300** *Cursor M.* 1778 þe bestes ran þan to monetains.. Well went þai to þar haue grith. *Ibid.* 8829 þis tre þai tok þan o cipres, and did in wirscip and in pes, in þat hali temple grith. **1375** BARBOUR *Bruce* IV. 47 Ridin.. Throw Ross, rycht to the gyrth off Tayne. *c* **1460** *Towneley Myst.* xx. 320 The house that he gose to grith, ye shall folow and go hym with. **1513** DOUGLAS *Æneis* II. xii. 4 At the porchis or closter of Juno, Than all bot waist, thocht it was girth [L. *asylo*], stude.. wardanes tway. **1536** BELLENDEN *Cron. Scotl.* (1821) II. 310 Quhiterne, quhare ane girth is dedicat in the honour of Sanct Miriane. *a* **1557** *Diurn. Occurr.* (Bannatyne Club) 13 The saidis seruandis wer tane furth of the girth of Torphichin. **1567** *Gude & Godlie Ball.* (S.T.S.) 108 Thy gyrth is set in sicker place, For he sall saif the mychtfullie. **1596** DALRYMPLE tr. *Leslie's Hist. Scot.* IX. 219 Vinice, the commoune girth of al strangeris. **1609** SKENE *Reg. Maj.*, *Stat. Robt. II*, 49 He sall make securitie to the Schiref, anent that crime, before he pas furth of the immunitie, or girth, to the quhilk he did flie. **1774** PENNANT *Tour Scotl. in 1772*, 251 The precinct of these tombs.. enjoyed the privileges of a Girth or Sanctuary. **1828** SCOTT *F.M. Perth* iv, So they are safe in girth and sanctuary.

† 4. Peace (in the general sense). Often collocated in OE. and early ME. with *frith*, in later ME. with *peace*. *Obs.*

c **1000** *Battle of Maldon* 35 (Gr.) We willaδ wiδ þam golde griδ fæstnian. **11..** *O.E. Chron.* an. 1002 (Laud MS.) He þa þæs cynges worde & his witena griδ wiδ hi ʒesætte. *Ibid.* an. 1011 þonne nam man griδ, and friδ wiδ hi. *Ibid.* an. 1048 And ʒeaf se cyng Godes griδ and his fulne freondscipe on æʒδre healfe. *c* **1175** *Lamb. Hom.* 45 Griδ on eorδe, and griδ on hefene, and griδ bitwenen uwilc cristene monne. *Ibid.* 79 Ierusalem bitacneδ griþes sihþe. *c* **1200** ORMIN 3519 O þatt Keʒʒseress time, þatt held wiþþ mikell griþþ & friþþ Hiss kinedom onn eorþe. *c* **1205** LAY. 4035 þa aræste here vnfriδe, Ouer al me brac þene griδ. *c* **1300** *Havelok* 61 Michel was svich a king to preyse, That held so Englond in grith. *a* **1310** *Harrow. Hell* 124 (Harl. MS.) Y shal.. do þe to holde gryht [*other MSS.* griþ]. **13..** *Coer de L.* 2234 She grette Kyng Richard in peace and gryth. *c* **1330** *Arth. & Merl.* 4604 (Kölbing) He com.. to speke him wiþ Mani word of loue and griþ. *a* **1400** *Octouian* 1785 Yn France plenere pes Was cryde, and gryth. *c* **1450** *Cov. Myst.* (Shaks. Soc.) 7 This gle in grythe Is mater of myrthe. *c* **1460** *Towneley Myst.* ix. 54 Byd hym go hastely.. Amang youre folk.. your gyrth & peasse to cry.

† 5. Quarter (in battle), as in *to give grith*. *without(en grith*: no quarter being given; hence, without mercy, relentlessly. *Obs.*

a **1300** *Cursor M.* 5545 Al þe knau barns þat þai fand wit-outen grith þai suld þam sla. *Ibid.* 7261 þat hus he feld, gaf naman grith, And slogh his faas, him self þar with. **13..** *Arth. & Merl.* 1974 (Kölbing) Al, þat was þer ynne on lyue, Best and mon.. His brente doun, wiþ owte gryth. *c* **1340** *Cursor M.* 12055 (Fairf.) þai hate vs alle wiþ-oute griþ. *a* **1400** *Sir Perc.* 1648 Bad hym ther he his fo fande, To gyff hym no grythe. *c* **1410** *Sir Cleges* 293, J schall the bette euery leth, Hede and body, wythout greth. *c* **1470** HENRY *Wallace* IV. 660 He gat no gyrth for all his burnyst weid. *c* **1475** *Rauf Coilʒear* 836 Thair was na girth on the ground, quhill ane gaif the gaist.

6. *Sc.* The cessation of the criminal courts during Christmas time and certain other seasons, in accordance with the granting of the king's peace to criminals. (Cf. ON. *jóla-friδr*, Sw. *jula-friþer*, etc.)

c **1575** in *Balfour's Pract.* (1754) 279 Gif he haldis the court in time forbiddin and defendit be the law, that is to say, fra ʒule grith be proclamit, quhill efter the halie dayis.

7. *attrib.* and *Comb.*, as **grith-man**, a man, esp. a criminal, who has taken sanctuary; **grith-priest**, a priest who ministered to those who took sanctuary; **grith-rod** (see quot. 1875); **grith-place**, **-stool**, **-stone**, **-town**, a place, stool, etc. at which sanctuary was taken.

1342 in Rymer *Fœdera* (1708) V. 328 Assignavimus, Magnificum Principem.. Edwardum de Balliolo, Regem Scotiæ ad omnes Homines, vocatos *Grithmen. **1458** in *Ripon Ch. Acts* (Surtees) 72 Confugæ sive gyrthmanii, citati ad allegandum causas racionabiles quare non debent puniri canonice propter eorum perjuria. **1468** *Ibid.* 134 N. Y., gyrthman, citatus est. **1779** HAILES *Ann. Scotl.* II. 211 *note*, All persons who on account of felony had taken refuge in sanctuaries, were pardoned by royal proclamation, under condition of serving, at their own charges, in the army of Baliol (Fœdera, tom. V. p. 328). They are denominated *Grith-men*, i.e. *Girth-men*. **1388** WYCLIF *Deut.* xix. 3 That he that is exilid for mansleyng haue of ny3 [*one MS. adds* a *grith place] whidur he may escape. **1391** *Mem. Ripon* (Surtees) III. 105 Domini Johannis vocati le *Grithpreste. **1471** in *Ripon Ch. Acts* (Surtees) 151 Johannes Eksmyth, gyrthman, fecit finem [*MS.* funem] ijs., applicatum fabricæ ecclesiæ pro portacione le *gyrthrod. **1875** J. T. FOWLER *ibid.* 383 It appears that these [Gyrthrods] were staves with banners, carried before the feretory at Rogation-tide by the Girth-men. **1706** in PHILLIPS (ed. Kersey), *Grithstole (i.e. Seat of Peace), a Sanctuary, or place of Refuge for Malefactors. **1728–1800** BAILEY, *Gristole.* **1228** in *Mem. Ripon* (Surtees) I. 51 Infra.. locum qui vocatur *Grythstane. **1388** WYCLIF *Deut.* xix. 6 Lest.. the next kynesman.. pursue, and take hym, if the weie is lengere [*some MSS. add* fro the *grith toun], and smyte the lijf of hym which is not gilti of deeth.

† **grith**, *v. Obs.* Forms: 1 **griδian**, 3 **griþie(n**, *pa. pple.* **igreþid**, **igriδed**. [OE. *griδian*, f. *griδ* GRITH *sb.*]

1. *intr.* To make peace.

11.. *O.E. Chron.* an. 1016 (Laud MS.) Lundene waru griδede wiδ þone here. *c* **1205** LAY. 5551 þat folc of Cascuine þe noht nælden griδien.

2. *trans.* To give peace or protection to.

c **1000** *Laws of Æthelred* vi. c. 42 in Schmid *Gesetze* 234 þæt hi Godes cirican æʒhwar ʒeorne griδian and friδian. *c* **1205** LAY. 21908 We nefden nænne mon þe us wiδ heom mihten griδien. *c* **1275** *Ibid.* 10605 Ich ou wolle griþie.

grith, variant of GIRTH *sb.*

grithbreach. *Obs.* exc. *Hist.* Forms: see GRITH and BREACH. [OE. *griδ-bryce*, *-brice*, f. *griδ* GRITH + *bryce* BREACH. Cf. ON. *griδabrek.*]

1. Breach of the peace.

c **1000** *Laws of Æthelred* VIII. c. 4 in Schmid *Gesetze* 244 Bete man æfre ærest þone griδ-bryce into þare circan, be þam þe seo dæd si, and be þam þe þare circan mæδ si. **11..** *Laws of Hen. I*, c. 12 §2 ibid. 444 Haec [placita] emendantur C solidis: griþebreche, stretbreche, forestel, [etc.]. *a* **1250** *Owl & Night.* 1732 Hunke schal i-tide harm and schonde, ʒef ʒe doth grith-bruche on his londe. *c* **1250** *Gloss. Law Terms* in *Rel. Ant.* I. 33 Gridbriche, *pais enfrainte.* **1387** TREVISA *Higden* (Rolls) II. 95 Grythbruche, brekynge of pees. **1607** COWELL *Interpr.*, *Grithbreach*, is a breach of peace.

2. The penalty for breach of the peace.

c **1030** *Laws Cnut* II. c. 15 in Schmid *Gesetze* 278 And on Dena-laʒe he ah fyte-wita and fyrd-wita and griδ-bryce and ham-socne. **1290** *Rolls of Parlt.* I. 27/2 Cum sacha, soca, overstronde & streme, on wode & felde, tol, them, & gridbruch, hamsokne, murdrum & forestal. **1353** in Pote *Windsor Cas.* (1749) 122 [They should be.. discharged from] Grithbrech, Forstall, Homesoken, Blod-wite, Ward-mote. **1598** STOW *Surv. Lond.* 262 Sack and socke, Thole and The, Infangthefe and Grithbriche. **1844** LINGARD *Anglo-Sax. Ch.* (1858) II. App. 392 The grithbrice, the penalty for violating the peace of a church.

† **ˈgrithful**, *a. Obs.* [f. GRITH *sb.* + -FUL.] Peaceful. Hence † **ˈgrithfulness**, peacefulness.

c **1205** LAY. 9171 Kinbelin wes god king & griþful [*c* **1275** griþfol] þurh alle þing. *Ibid.* 12166 þa andswerede Gracien mid griδfulle worden. *a* **1225** *Ancr. R.* 406 Luue makeδ hire schir and griδful and cleane. *Ibid.* 416 Ne none wise ne mei heo beon Marie, mid griδfulnesse of heorte.

† **ˈgrithly**, *a.* and *adv. Obs.* [f. GRITH *sb.* + -LY[1], -LY[2].] **A.** *adj.* Peaceable. **B.** *adv.* Peaceably.

c **1205** LAY. 121 He griδliche spac. *c* **1205** *Ibid.* 445 And grete Pandrasum þaue king mid griþliche [*c* **1205** greiδlicre] speche.

† **grithsergeant.** *Obs.* In 3 *pl.* grissergans, grithsergeans, -serjauns. [f. GRITH *sb.* + SERGEANT.] An officer appointed to maintain the peace.

1293 *Year-bk 21 & 22 Edw. I* (Rolls) 49 Illis constituere servientes qui vocantur Grissergans [*Iter Roll* Grithserjauns]. *c* **1300** *Havelok* 267 Grith-sergeans, wit longe gleyues, To yemen wilde wodes and pathes Fro wicke men.

gritless (ˈgrɪtlɪs), *a. rare.* [f. GRIT *sb.*[1] + -LESS.] Having no 'grit' or solidity of character.

1892 *Contemp. Rev.* Jan. 17 The most impulsive, pliant, gritless race in Europe.

gritstone (ˈgrɪtstəʊn). In 6–8 usually **greet-**. [f. GRIT *sb.*[1] + STONE *sb.*] = GRIT *sb.*[1] 2.

1555 EDEN *Decades* 328 Albasans (which I thynke to be of that kynde which we caule the greete stone). **1652** FRENCH *Yorksh. Spa* i. 2 Hard greet-Stone (which broken in the middle doth oftentimes very much resemble Loaf-Sugar). **1761** *Nat. Hist.* in *Ann. Reg.* 100/2 The loose stones near the summit [of Ingleborough] the people call greet-stones. **1775** SIR E. BARRY *Observ. Wines* 412 The inhabitants on gret-stone are healthier than those on chalk. **1781** J. HUTTON *Tour to Caves* Gloss., *Greet-stones*, a sort of freestones. **1854** F. C. BAKEWELL *Geol.* 31 The lower portion of the hill is surrounded by shale and gritstone. **1885** *Law Rep.* 14 Q. Bench Div. 196 Gritstone.. taken in.. certain quarries in Fairfield.

attrib. **1789** J. PILKINGTON *View Derbysh.* I. 314 Those [sheep] upon gritstone being 3 pounds lighter than those upon limestone land. **1878** DAVIS & LEES *West Yorksh.* 14 The moors generally terminate westward in an abrupt gritstone escarpment.

grittily (ˈgrɪtɪlɪ), *adv.* [f. GRITTY *a.*[1] + -LY[2].] In a gritty manner; with a gritty sound.

1911 D. H. LAWRENCE *White Peacock* II. i, He marched me .. into the sanded passage of the little inn... As we tramped grittily down the passage, [etc.]. **1953** *New Statesman* 17 Oct. 462 One can see what a successful story Mr. Peake could have made out of it had he.. made his 'natural' characters grittily real.

grittiness (ˈgrɪtɪnɪs). [f. GRITTY *a.*[1] + -NESS.] The quality, state, or condition of being gritty.

1611 FLORIO, *Grezzaria*, grittinesse, ruggednesse. **1659** TORRIANO, *Arenosita*, sandinesse, grettinesse. **1707** *Curios. in Husb. & Gard.* 349 Wash them well to take away all the Grittiness. **1769** J. WALLIS *Nat. Hist. Northumbld.* I. iii. 33 It melts in the mouth, and has no disagreeable taste; pure, and free from grittiness. **1874** G. LAWSON *Dis. Eye* 14 A constant feeling of grittiness of the eye. **1875** H. C. Wood *Therap.* (1879) 459 Imparting to the teeth a sense of grittiness, due to the presence of great numbers of minute crystals of the oxalate of calcium. **1896** *Daily News* 15 Apr. 7/5 A hazel loam with some character of grittiness.

fig. **1898** F. Harrison in *19th Cent.* Sept. 376 Froude's English..has none of the artifices of Macaulay, nor the grimaces of Carlyle,..nor the grittiness of Hallam and Grote.

grittle ('grɪt(ə)l), *v. dial.* [? f. GRIT *sb.*[2]] *trans.* To break (corn) or grind it coarsely. Hence **'grittle** *sb.*, corn so treated.

1736 Bailey (folio), *Grittle*, to just break corn or but a little in the mill. **1894** *Times* 17 Sept. 8/4 A Hampshire farmer uses grittled wheat. **1895** *E. Angl. Gloss.*, *Grittle*, corn just broken or cracked. Oatmeal so done is called Grits or Grots.

grittum(e)lie, var. GREATUMLY *adv. Sc. Obs.*

gritty ('grɪtɪ), *a.*[1] Also 6–7 greetie, 7 grettie, -y, 7, 9 *dial.* greety. [f. GRIT *sb.*[1] + -Y.]

1. Of the nature of or resembling grit; containing, consisting of, or full of grit; sandy.

1598 Florio, *Renóso*, sandie, grauelly, greetie, full of grauell. **1610** W. Folkingham *Art of Survey* I. iii. 7 Base herbes, and rough sandy stone, denotate a leane greety sandie or grauelly ground. **1694** Falle *Jersey* ii. 60 The higher Grounds are gritty, gravelly, and some stony and rocky. **1726** Leoni *Alberti's Archit.* I. 35/1 Pit-sand..is of several kinds.., the carbuncly, and the gritty. *c* **1790** Imison *Sch. Art* II. 14 Permit it to stand about ten seconds of time, in order to let the gritty parts settle to the bottom. *a* **1806** S. Horsley *Serm.* II. 43 The grovelling posture and the gritty meal [of the serpent]. **1840** Dickens *Old C. Shop* xix, A four-horse carriage, dashing by, obscured all objects in the gritty cloud it raised. **1876** Page *Adv. Text-Bk. Geol.* xviii. 338 In Devon and Dorset a gritty bed with numerous fossils occurs towards the base of the chalk. **1860** Tristram *Gt. Sahara* xiii. 213 A strong..wind saturated the air with impalpable sand, till every pore of the body was gritty and irritated.

2. Full of or containing minute hard particles impairing the quality or condition of the substance which harbours them, or rendering it unpleasant.

1603 Florio *Montaigne* I. xx. (1632) 44 A fantasie conceived..by eating of some gretty peece of bread. **1671** H. M. tr. *Erasm. Colloq.* 491 They sopped that gritty bread in the wine that was made of very old Lees. **1795** *Rapin's Garden* 313 The worthless Thorn a valu'd Plum will bear, And what was gritty prove a melting Pear. **1806–7** J. Beresford *Miseries Hum. Life* (1826) III. xxxiii, Hitching your knife in the gritty flaws of a black-lead pencil. **1829** Landor *Imag. Conv.* Wks. 1846 II. 43 These young bakers make their bread very gritty. **1831** J. Davies *Manual Mat. Med.* 367 Of a dull and rough fracture, gritty under the teeth.

b. *fig.* of literary style, with allusion to the unpleasant quality of 'gritty' bread.

1882 J. C. Morison *Macaulay* 68 Alternate pages of extract and comment—generally rather dull and gritty. **1894** A. Birrell *Ess.* xi. 122 The style is gritty and the story far from exciting.

3. *U.S. colloq.* Having firmness of character or courage; full of determination or pluck.

1847 Robb *Squatter Life* 106 There never was a grittyer crowd congregated on that stream. **18..** Lowell *Standish* Poet. Wks. 1890 I. 222 My neighbor Buckingham Hath somewhat in him gritty, Some Pilgrim-stuff that hates all sham. **1891** *Century Mag.* Nov. 65 They were captured by a band of gritty frontiersmen under Sheriff Boswell.

†**gritty** ('grɪtɪ), *a.*[2] *Obs. Her.* In 5–6 **grytty**, 6 **grittie.** [Origin unknown; connexion with GRATE *sb.*[1] is suggested by the sense.] Of a field: Composed equally of a metal and a colour.

1486 *Bk. St. Albans, Her.* B v, Thre Cootarmuris grytty ther bene in armys. **1562** Leigh *Armorie* (1597) 76 After this furre, as many as are out of these orders aforesaid, shall be named of the colour and mettall they are of, and haue bin commonly called Grytty of Herehaughtes. **1586** Ferne *Blaz. Gentrie* 204 The first feeld that is Grittie, is, when as the feeld is checqued of two or more cullors. **1780** Edmondson *Her.* II. Gloss., *Grittie*, a term used by English writers to express the field when composed equally of metal and colour.

gritumlie, var. GREATUMLY *adv. Sc. Obs.*

grive, obs. form of GRIEVE *v.*

grivet ('grɪvɪt). [Of unknown origin; the L. specific name seems to be due to interpreting *grivet* as if f. F. *gris* grey + *vert* green.] A small greenish-grey monkey of north-east Africa (*Cercopithecus griseiviridis*); the tota.

1859 Wood *Nat. Hist.* I. 45 The Grivet, or Tota, as it is called by some writers, is of a sombre green colour. **1871–82** *Cassell's Nat. Hist.* I. 110 The Grivet Monkey.

grizbite, variant of GRISTBITE *v.*

grize, rare obs. form of GRECE, stairs.

Grizel ('grɪzəl). Also 6 Gressell, 6–7 Grissell, 7 Grissil(l, grizell, Grisel, 8–9 grizzle, 9 Grizzel. Later form of the proper name *Grisilde* (= *Griseldis*, *Griselda*), borne by the heroine of Chaucer's *Clerk's Tale* (adapted from a story of Petrarch's), who is the proverbial type of a meek, patient wife.

[*c* **1386** Chaucer *Clerk's T.* 1126 No wedded man so hardy be tassaille His wyves pacience, in hope to fynde Grisildes, for in certein he shal faille.] **1565–6** *Stationers' Reg.* (Arb.) I. 132 b, The songge of pacyente Gressell vnto hyr make. **1596** Shaks. *Tam. Shr.* II. i. 297 For patience shee will proue a second Grissell. **1624** Heywood *Captives* IV. i. in Bullen *O. Pl.* IV, Have patience woman, I have ben too longe a grizell. **1766** H. Brooke *Fool of Qual.* (1792) III. 192 He had married five shrews in succession, and made Grizels of every one of them before they died. **1797** Mrs. A. M. Bennett *Beggar Girl* (1813) III. 19 The pounds and pounds she paid the doctor was enough to make a grizzle fret. [*a* **1849** Mar. Edgeworth (*title*) The Modern Griselda. **1885** Brewer *Reader's Handbk.* s.v., Octavia, the wife of Mark Antony, and sister of Augustus, is called the 'patient Grizel of Roman story'.]

Hence **'grizel** *v. trans.*, to make a Grizel of.

a **1797** Mary Wollstonecr. *Posth. Wks.* (1798) II. 78, I had afterwards an opportunity of observing the treatment she had to endure, which grizzled her into patience.

grizeld, obs. form of GRIZZLED *a.*

grizelin, obs. form of GRIDELIN.

grizely, obs. form of GRISLY.

grizette, obs. form of GRISETTE.

grizle, obs. form of GRIZZLE *a.* and *sb.*[1], and *v.*[1]

grizly, variant of GRISLY, GRIZZLY.

grizy, variant of GRISY *a.*[1] and [2], *Obs.*

grizzel ('grɪz(ə)l), *adv.* [perh. back-formation from GRISLY.] Horribly.

1898 T. Hardy *Wessex Poems* 196 Yet I note the little chisel Of never-napping Time Defacing ghast and grizzel The blazon of my prime.

grizzle ('grɪz(ə)l), *a.* and *sb.*[1] Forms: 4, 7 **grisel**, 4–7 **-ell**, 5 **-elle**, **gresel**, **grysselle**, 6 **gresle**, **grysle**, 6–7 **gryselle**, **grissell**, 7–8 **grisle**, **grissel**, **grizle**, 7– **grizzle.** [a. OF. *grisel*, f. *gris*: see GRIS *a.*] **A.** *adj.* Of grey colour, grey, grizzled. †Formerly also, of a horse: Roan.

c **1425** *Thomas of Erceld.* 382 Stedis..baye and broun, grysselle [*v.r.* gresel] and graye. **1548** Hall *Chron.*, *Hen. VIII* (1809) 578 Weryng a Cote of Orange tawny on a horse cooler grysell, trottyng. **1570** Levins *Manip.* 147/37 Grysle coloure, *glauculus.* **1577–87** Holinshed *Chron.* (1807–8) IV. 694 The friers minors..whose apparell was grisell garments girded with cords full of knots. **1598** Sylvester *Du Bartas* II. ii. III. *Colonies* 40 The grissell Turtles..Dis-payer'd and parted, wander one by one. **1601** Holland *Pliny* II. 397 To preserue the haire from being gray and grisle. **1634–5** Brereton *Trav.* (Chetham) 151 A grissell gelding. **1706** *Lond. Gaz.* No. 4277/4 She is about 14 Hands and a half high, with a small grizle star in her Forehead. **1748** *Whitehall Evening Post* No. 405, Grey Breeches, and a light Grizzle Wig. **1808** J. P. Malcolm *Mann. & Cust. Lond.* 437 Light grizzle Ties [*i.e.* wigs] three guineas. **1832** J. Taylor *Rec. my Life* I. 331 An actor..had dressed himself like a doctor, with a large grizzle wig.

b. *Comb.*, as ***grizzle-headed***, **-*white*** adjs.; **grizzle-pate**, a grey-headed old man.

1880 Ouida *Moths* I. 18 Fräulein Schroder..was not beautiful to the eye, and was *grizzle-headed. **1797** Mary Robinson *Walsingham* II. 171 Sport your glass-blinkers, old *grizzle-pate! **1691** *Lond. Gaz.* No. 2631/4 Rid away.., a bay Mare about 14 hands,..two *grissell white patches on the Rump.

B. *sb.*

†**1.** A nickname for a grey-haired old man. *Obs.*

1390 Gower *Conf.* III. 356 That olde grisel is no fole. *c* **1393** Chaucer *Scogan* 35 But wel I wit þou wilt answere & seye 'Lo! olde grisel leste to ryme and pleye'. *a* **1420** Hoccleve *De Reg. Princ.* 401 This olde doted griselle holte him wise.

2. A grey animal; *esp.* a grey horse.

a **1620** *J. Armstrong's Last Goodnt.* xx. in Child *Ballads* (1889) III. 369 But little Musgrave, that was his foot-page, With his bonny grissell got away untain. *Ibid.* xxiii, Thou are welcome home, my bonny grisel! Full oft thou hast fed at the corn and hay. **1765** *Treat. Dom. Pigeons* 54 Blacks, black-grisles, black-splash'd, yellows, whites, duns.

3. Grey hair; a sprinkling of grey hairs.

1601 Shaks. *Twel. N.* v. i. 168 O thou dissembling Cub: what wilt thou be When time hath sow'd a grizzle on thy case? **1810** *Splendid Follies* I. 17 A broad frizzed toupée, well powdered to conceal the grizzles that occasionally peeped over her scarified cheek. **1851** Mayne Reid *Scalp Hunt.* xxiii, These parts [head and neck] were covered with a dirty grizzle of mixed hues.

b. A grey wig.

1755 *Connoisseur* No. 65 ¶9 His very grizzle is scarce orthodox. **1756** *Ibid.* No. 105 ¶2 Pudding-sleeves, starched bands, and feather-top grizzles. **1766** Anstey *Bath Guide* xi. 127 Emerg'd from his Grizzle, th' unfortunate Sprig Seems as if he was hunting all Night for his Wig. **1816** Scott *Antiq.* xvii, Sir Arthur's ramilies being the positive, his own bob-wig the comparative, and the overwhelming grizzle of the worthy clergyman figuring as the superlative.

4. Grey colour; the colour grey. †Formerly also: Light roan.

1611 Markham *Countr. Content.* I. xix. (1649) 105 Your Henne..must be of a right plume, as gray, grissel, speckt, or yellowish, black or brown is not amisse. **1706** in Phillips (ed. Kersey), *Grissel*, a light Rount, or light Flesh-Colour in Horses. **1893** Lydekker *Horns & Hoofs* 126 The legs are dark brown in front, and paler behind, with a whitish grizzle pervading their whole extent.

5. A second-class stock brick. (So called from its colour; cf. *grey stock*, GREY *a.* 8.)

1843 *Mech. Mag.* XXXIX. 192 The grizzles obtained a price midway between the two last named [stocks and places]. **1865** *Pall Mall G.* 19 Sept. 11/1 Here you may see a 'grizzle' and a 'malm-brick'. **1879** *Notes Build. Construct.* III. 105 Grizzle and Place bricks are underburnt. They are very weak.

grizzle ('grɪz(ə)l), *sb.*[2] [f. GRIZZLE *v.*[2]] **1.** One who grizzles or frets.

1893 Mrs. C. Praed *Outlaw & Lawmaker* III. 102 Lady Waveryng, however, was not a woman to fret vainly over the inevitable. Lord Waveryng was far more of a 'grizzle'.

2. A bout of grumbling or sulking; a peevish mood; a fretful effusion.

1900 in *Eng. Dial. Dict.* **1908** A. E. Lyons *Arthur's* I. ii. 12 At first I thought she was goin' to do a grizzle, but she turned round quick, with a kind of smile. **1923** U. L. Silberrad *Lett. J. Armiter* xi. §2, Opportunity to write a good long letter to make up for the short grizzle of last month. **1930** H. M. Tomlinson *All our Yesterdays* I. viii. 85 Out he went without saying good-bye.., which would have given any girl the grizzles.

grizzle ('grɪz(ə)l), *v.*[1] [f. GRIZZLE *a.* or back-formation from GRIZZLED *a.*]

1. *trans.* To render grey or grey-haired.

1740 Somerville *Hobbinol* II. 218 He spur'd his sober Steed, grizled with Age, And venerably dull. **1822** Byron *Werner* III. iv. 153 The grey Begins to grizzle the black hair of night. **1822** Scott *Nigel* xxii, The colour with which time had begun to grizzle her tresses. **1827** Clare *Sheph. Cal.* 4 Night Hastens to..grizzle o'er the chilly sky.

2. *intr.* To become grey or grey-haired.

1875 Lowell *Lett.* (1894) II. 151, I suppose you are a gray old boy by this time. I am just beginning to grizzle with the first hoar-frost. **1894** *Athenæum* 24 Nov. 705/1 [A Chinese sonneteer will allude] to the crow's-feet of wisdom around the first sonneteer's own eyes and the poetical grizzling of his own pigtail.

grizzle ('grɪz(ə)l), *v.*[2] *local.*

1. *intr.* To show the teeth; to grin or laugh, esp. mockingly.

1746 *Exmoor Scolding* 58 (E.D.S.) Tamzen and Thee be olweys..stivering or grizzling, tacking or busking. *Ibid.* Gloss., *To Grizzle*, to grin, or smile with a sort of Sneer. **1837** Mrs. Palmer *Devon. Dial.* 14 The ould man grizzled: No sure, lovy, zed he, I ne'er had the leastest inkling for such a thing. **1880** *W. Cornwall Gloss.* s.v., 'What's the g'eat bufflehead grizzling at?' 'He grizzled at me; he was as vexed as fire'.

2. To fret, sulk; to cry in a whining or whimpering fashion. Hence **'grizzling** *vbl. sb.* and *ppl. a.*

1842 *Catnach Ballad* in *Westm. Gaz.* 7 Apr. (1899) 2/2 Useless is our grumbling, our grizzling, or mumbling. **1867** E. Yates *Forlorn Hope* xxix. 392, I went abroad, and remained grizzling and feeding on my own heart for months. **1872** Miss Braddon *To Bitter End* I. xvi. 264 'If the locket's lost, it's lost', and there's no use in grizzling about it. **1887** *Kentish Gloss.* s.v., She's such a grizzling woman. **1889** 'Rolf Boldrewood' *Robbery under Arms* xxxiii, He'd sit grizzling and smoking by himself all day long. No getting a word out of him.

grizzle ('grɪz(ə)l), *v.*[3] *local.* [Origin unknown.] *trans.* and *intr.* To fry, frizzle, over-cook.

1900 in *Eng. Dial. Dict.* **1913** H. S. Walpole *Fortitude* I. viii. 98 Poor old man..nobody loves him..to hell with the lot of 'em..let 'em grizzle in hell fire. **1941** J. Cary *House of Children* 202 Four or five men surrounded the table,..eating and calling out to the girl not to grizzle the bacon.

grizzled ('grɪz(ə)ld), *a.* Also 5 **grecelled**, **griseld**, 6–7 **gryseld(e**, (6 **greistled**, 7 **grisseld**, **grizeld**, 8 **grizled**), 6–9 **grisled.** [f. GRIZZLE *a.* + -ED[2]. Cf. obs. F. *grisellé* (Palsgr.), on which the Eng. word might have been directly formed, but evidence is wanting.]

1. Grey, grizzly; now used almost exclusively of hair. Also (now *dial.*), roan-coloured.

1458 *Test. Ebor.* (Surtees) II. 216 A lytill grecelled nage. **1485** *Inv.* in *Ripon Ch. Acts* (Surtees) 372 Equus griseld. **1530** Palsgr. 314/1 Graye or gryselde, *grisellé.* **1595** *Nottingham Rec.* IV. 64 Et quarta est coloris grey greistled. **1607** Topsell *Four-f. Beasts* 103 Cats are of diuers colours, but for the most part gryseld, like to congealed yse. **1608** Shaks. *Per.* III. Prol. 47 The grisled North Disgorges such a tempest forth. **1611** Bible *Zech.* vi. 3 In the third charet white horses and in the fourth charet grisled and bay horses. **1660** *Trial Regic.* (1679) 273 The other had a grey grisled periwig hung down very low. **1728** Young *Love Fame* v. (1757) 137 Her grizzled locks assume a smirking grace. **1810** Scott *Lady of L.* III. iv, His grisled beard and matted hair. **1840** Dickens *Old C. Shop* iii, Such hair as he had, was of a grizzled black. **1876** T. Hardy *Ethelberta* (1890) 312 Ethelberta..entering the nave began to inspect the sallow monuments which lined the grizzled pile.

b. ***grizzled sandpiper***, ***skipper***: see the sbs.

2. Having grey hair.

1606 Shaks. *Ant. & Cl.* III. xiii. 17 To the Boy Cæsar send this grizled head. **1828** Scott *F.M. Perth* xxviii, Torquil of the Oak, a grizzled giant. **1877** Black *Green Past.* xi. (1878) 86 The only occupant of the yard was a grizzled and feeble old man. **1886** J. R. Rees *Pleas. Bk.-Worm* i. 22 With his serious old grizzled face he appears at the office.

grizzler ('grɪzlə(r)). *dial.* or *colloq.* [f. GRIZZLE *v.*[2] + -ER[1].] One who frets or grumbles.

1900 *Eng. Dial. Dict.* s.v. *Grizzle v.*[1] 2, If ever there was a grizzler she's the one. **1910** H. G. Wells *Mr. Polly* vi. 201 'I don't think I *could* abide a grizzler,' said Uncle Pentstemon. **1924** 'R. Dehan' *Pipers of Market Place* xvi. 153 She who scorned the women who cried as 'wimmickers' and 'grizzlers'.

†**'grizzlish**, *a. Obs. rare*[−1]. [f. GRIZZLE *a.* + -ISH.] Greyish.

1680 *Lond. Gaz.* No. 1529/4 A young Fox Hound Bitch, White, with one Grizlish broad spot on her left Shoulder.

grizzly ('grɪzlɪ), *a.* and *sb.*[1] Forms: 6 ? **gristelly**, 7–9 **grizly**, 7 **greisly**, **grisly**, 8 **griesly**, 9 **gresley**, **gristly**, **grizzlie**, 8– **grizzly**. [f. GRIZZLE *a.* + -Y.]

A. *adj.* **a.** Grey; greyish; grey-haired; grizzled.

1594 CAREW *Tasso* (1881) 74 A beard bigge, bushy, knotted gristelly. **1602** SHAKS. *Ham.* I. ii. 24 His Beard was grisly? **1626** BACON *Sylva* §851 Old Squirrels, that turne Grisly. **1694** J. WOOD in *Collect. Voy.* (1729) IV. II. 109 We ..came to an Anchor in eleven Fathom Water greisly Sand. **1748** RICHARDSON *Clarissa* (1811) VIII. xli. 158 Her matted griesly hair. **1770** G. WHITE *Selborne* xxviii. 79 The colour was a grizzly black. **1774** GOLDSM. *Nat. Hist.* (1776) III. 184 The colour of the body is grizly, and beset with bristles. **1840** DICKENS *Barn. R.* i, He had a grizzly jagged beard of some three weeks' date. **1843** LANDOR *Imag. Conv.* Wks. 1846 II. 213 A middle-aged gentleman, tall, round-shouldered, and..somewhat grizzly. **1864** LOWELL *Fireside Trav.* 274 Rojate, the next town,..grim and grizzly,.. looked drearier. **1868** MISS YONGE *Cameos* I. i. 10 He was an old grizzly warrior.

b. grizzly bear: a large and ferocious bear, *Ursus horribilis*, peculiar to the mountainous districts of western North America; also, the name of an American dance in which the hug and walk of a bear are imitated.

1807 P. GASS *Jrnl.* 221 The bears from which they get these skins are a harmless kind, and not so bold and ferocious as the grizly and brown bear. **1859** MARCY *Prairie Trav.* vii. 247 The grizzly bear is assuredly the monarch of the American forests. **1912** *Lit. Digest* 30 Mar. 656/2 Steps that would have ruled him off any cotillion floor in New York in these days of the ban on the grizzly-bear and kindred dances. **1928** F. SCOTT FITZGERALD in *Sat. Even. Post* 29 Sept. 118 They moved around the room, locked in the convulsive grip of the grizzly bear. **1959** M. T. WILLIAMS *Art of Jazz* (1960) xii. 109 The halls where they had so recently danced the Grizzly Bear and the Buzzard Lope to the music of the jazz bands.

c. ***grizzly king, queen***: the names of artificial flies for angling.

1894 *Outing* (U.S.) XXIV. 227/1 Bass flies of proved merit include the bob white, grizzly queen, grizzly king.

Hence **'grizzliness.** *rare*[−1].

1654 GAYTON *Pleas. Notes* III. xi. 152 The Don..like an Ape..shews himselfe to be descended from Hercules by the melan-pygitie (that is, the grizlinesse) of his posteriours.

B. *sb.* The grizzly bear.

1808 PIKE *Sources Mississ.* (1810) III. App. 7 North Mexico produces elk, deer, buffalo, cabrie, the gresley, black bear, and wild horses. **1859** J. G. WOOD *Nat. Hist.* I. 400 The Grizzly, or 'Ephraim' as the creature is familiarly termed by the hunters. **1879** MISS BIRD *Lady's Life Rocky Mts.* 18 A man..asked me if I were the English tourist who had 'happened on' a 'grizzlie' yesterday.

grizzly ('grɪzlɪ), *sb.*[2] *Mining. U.S.* A grating of parallel iron bars with interstices between to allow the finer material to fall into the sluices below while the larger stones are screened off.

1877 RAYMOND *Statist. Mines & Mining* 56 The *débris*.. is again caught up, the bowlders precipitated over a 'grizzly' into the cañon below [etc.]. **1879** *Encycl. Brit.* X. 746/1. **1881** RAYMOND *Mining Gloss.*, *Grizzly*, Pac[ific Coast], a grating to catch and throw out large stones from sluices.

grizzly, variant of GRISLY *a.*

†**gro.** *Obs.* Also 3–4 **gra.** [Properly the neut. of an adj., ad. ON. *grá-r*: see GREY *a.*]

1. A kind of fur. [Cf. MHG. *grâ.*]

c **1230** *Hali Meid.* 43 As ewel vnder grei as under grene and gra. *a* **1310** in Wright *Lyric P.* v. 26 Glad under gore in gro ant in grys. *c* **1325** *Metr. Hom.* 42 Es he nan of tha That er cled in gren and gra. *c* **1460** *Launfal* 237 Har manteles wer of grene felwet..Ipelvred with grys and gro.

2. An evil spirit. [Cf. ON. *grá-r* = spiteful.]

a **1225** *St. Marher.* 6 Ant tu, grisliche gra..þi mihte schal unmuchelin. *a* **1225** *Juliana* 53 Heo..of þat grisliche gra weren a-grisen swiðe.

groan (grəʊn), *sb.* Forms: 4–7 **grone**, (4 **gron**, 7 **groane**), 7– **groan**. *β. Sc.* 4–8 **grane**, (5 **grayne**). [f. GROAN *v.*] An act of groaning; a low vocal murmur, emitted involuntarily under pressure of pain or distress, or produced in voluntary simulation as an expression of strong disapprobation.

a **1300** *Cursor M.* 3731 Wit þis gaue ysaac a grane [*Gött., Trin.* grone]. *c* **1325** *Body & Soul* in *Map's Poems* (Camden) 343/1 As thing al seek hit ȝaf a gron. **1375** BARBOUR *Bruce* XIII. 35 Men herd nocht ellis bot granys & dyntis. *c* **1420** *Anturs of Arth.* 620 (Thornton MS.) Scho grete one dame Gaynour, with granes so grylle. *c* **1470** HENRY *Wallace* VII. 459 The peple..Rewmyd in reuth, with mony grysly grayne. **1500–20** DUNBAR *Poems* xxvi. 24 Thay gyrnd with hiddouss granis. **1581** MULCASTER *Positions* xxxv. (1887) 128 The pitifull grones, the lamentable shrikes. **1592** SHAKS. *Ven. & Ad.* 377 Loues deep grones I neuer shall regard. **1615** G. SANDYS *Trav.* 11 There was heard a great lamentation, accompanied with grones and skreeches. **1697** DRYDEN *Virg. Georg.* III. 353 Often he turns his Eyes, and, with a Groan, Surveys the pleasing Kingdoms, once his own. **1738** WESLEY *Psalms* VI. iv, Weary of my unanswer'd Groans,..I languish for Relief. **1796** MACNEILL *Waes of War* I. 74 'Wha this rudely wakes the sleeping?' Cried a voice wi' angry grane. **1828** SCOTT *F.M. Perth* xx, A low groan went through the assembly. **1846** LUNDIE *Mission. Life Samoa* xviii. 113 Groans of woe and tears of penitence were all around. **1872** DARWIN *Emotions* xii. 285 The North American Indians express astonishment by a groan. **1884** F. M. CRAWFORD *Rom. Singer* I. 8 His singing ended in a sort of groan.

b. attributed to inanimate objects.

1605 SHAKS. *Lear* III. ii. 47 Such groanes of roaring Winde, and Raine, I neuer Remember to haue heard. **1718** ROWE tr. *Lucan* 183 In hollow Groans the falling Winds complain. **1797** MRS. RADCLIFFE *Italian* i. (1826) 7 The pauses of silence succeeded each groan of the mountain.

c. *Comb.*, as ***groan-like*** adj.

1802 H. MARTIN *Helen of Glenross* II. 146 Her groan-like sighs..pierced my ears.

groan (grəʊn), *v.* Forms: 1 **gránian**, 2–3 **granien**, 3 **gronie, -y**, 4 **gronen**, 4–8 **grone**, (5 **gronne**, **gronyn**, 6 **groane**, 6– **groan**. *β. north.* and *Sc.* 4–6, 8–9 **grane**, 5 **grayn(e**, 6, 8 **grain**). [OE. *gránian*:—OTeut. type **grainôjan*, f. Teut. root **grai- gri-*, whence OHG. *grînan* mentioned s.v. GRIN *v.*[2]]

1. *intr.* To breathe with a deep-toned murmur; to utter a low deep sound expressive of grief or pain.

7.. *Blickl. Gloss.* in *Blickl. Hom.* 258/1 Granode *vel* asten, *rugiebam*. *c* **1000** *Ags. Ps.* (Th.) cv[i]. 20 [25], Ac hi granedan, and grame spræcan. *c* **1175** *Lamb. Hom.* 43 Summe þer graninde sikeð. *c* **1205** LAY. 25558 Swiðe he wes idræcched and granein [*read* granien, *c* **1275** gronie] agon. *c* **1230** *Hali Meid.* 47 To..greden ai & granen i þe eche grure of helle. **1297** R. GLOUC. (Rolls) 7813 King willam..bigan sone to grony & to febly al so. **1340** HAMPOLE *Pr. Consc.* 798 He is ofte seke and ay granand. *c* **1400** *Lay-Folks Mass-Bk.* App. iv. 325 þe Pope ful sore gon grone. *a* **1400–50** *Alexander* 1219 [He] Gers many grete syre grane & girdis þurȝe maillis. *c* **1470** HENRY *Wallace* VIII. 766 Within the dykys thai gert feill Sotheroun grayn. **1500–20** DUNBAR *Poems* lxxv. 19 My wame is of ȝour lufe sa fow, That as ane gaist I glour and grane. *a* **1550** *Christis Kirk Gr.* xviii, He grainit lyk ony gaist. **1697** DRYDEN *Virg. Georg.* I. 70 Produce the Plough, and yoke the sturdy Steer, And goad him till he groans beneath his Toil. **1753** J. BARTLET *Gentl. Farriery* viii. 74 He [a horse] coughs sharply by fits..and frequently groans with it. **1829** HOOD *Eug. Aram* xix, A dozen times I groan'd—the dead Had never groan'd but twice. **1888** MISS BRADDON *Fatal Three* I. vi, Greswold groaned aloud.

fig. *c* **1600** SHAKS. *Sonn.* cxxxiii. 1 Beshrew that heart that makes my heart to groane. **1607** —— *Timon* III ii. 83 Religion groans at it. **1737** WHISTON *Josephus, Hist.* III. viii. §4 Now may the laws of our forefathers well groan to purpose. **1833** J. H. NEWMAN *Arians* IV. iv. (1876) 350 The lively statement of Jerome: 'The whole world groaned in astonishment to find itself Arian'. **1878** BROWNING *La Saisiaz* 44 Needs there groan a world in anguish just to teach us sympathy?

b. Phr. ***to groan inwardly, in oneself, in the spirit,*** †***with the heart.***

a **1300** *Cursor M.* 17836 Wit al þair flesche þai quok onnan, And wit þair hertes can þai gran. **1535** COVERDALE *John* xi. 33 Whan Iesus sawe her wepe..he groned in the sprete. **1596** SPENSER *F.Q.* VI. iii. 11 He deepely sigh'd, and groaned inwardly. **1611** BIBLE *John* xi. 38 Iesus therefore againe groning in himselfe, commeth to the graue. **1747** P. DODDRIDGE *Life J. Gardiner* 21 He could not forbear groaning inwardly.

c. quasi-*trans.* To breathe (one's life, soul) *away* or *out* in groaning. Similarly, ***to groan one's heart out.***

1642 J. EATON *Honey-combe Free Justif.* 106 Christ groaned out his blood and life upon the Crosse. **1671** MILTON *P.L.* XI. 447 He fell, and deadly pale, Groand out his Soul with gushing blood effus'd. **1695** BLACKMORE *Pr. Arth.* II. 817 Stretcht on the cursed Tree his Body hangs, Groaning its Life away in dying Pangs. **1816** SCOTT *Antiq.* xii, I'se warrant I might grane my heart out or ony body wad gie me either a bane or a bodle.

d. To talk in a groaning voice, grumble.

1816 SCOTT *Old Mort.* xiv, The tane was aye graning about giving tribute to Cæsar.

e. attributed to inanimate objects.

1602 MARSTON *Ant. & Mel.* I. Wks. 1856 I. 17 The flintie rocks groand at his plaints. **1668** R. STEELE *Chr. Husbandm. Calling* viii. (1672) 207 The field groans that bears the grain which thou thus abusest. *a* **1774** FERGUSSON *Poems* (1845) 48 Would it no fret the hardest stane Beneath the Luckenbooths to grane? **1862** B. TAYLOR *Poet's Jrnl. 1st Eve., Symbol*, The forests fain would groan.

†**2.** *spec.* Of the buck: To utter its peculiar cry at rutting-time. (Cf. GROIN *v.* 1 b.) *Obs.*

1486 *Bk. St. Albans* E v, An hert belowys and a bucke gronys. **1576** TURBERV. *Venerie* 100 A hart belloweth, a Bucke groneth. **1686** BLOME *Gentl. Recr.* II. 76 A Hart Belloweth, a Buck Groaneth or Twateth.

3. *trans.* **a.** To utter with groans; with an exclamation or sentence as obj. Also with *out.*

1606 SHAKS. *Tr. & Cr.* III. i. 136 So dying loue liues still ..O ho grones out for ha ha ha. *a* **1716** SOUTH (J.), To sigh his griefs and groan his pains. **1785** BURNS *Death & Dr. Hornbook* xxiv, The creature grain'd an eldritch laugh. **1847** BUSHNELL *Chr. Nurt.* II. vii. (1861) 379 He [Christ] lives it [the truth], acts it forth, groans it in his Gethsemane. **1864** TENNYSON *Sea Dreams* 141 'No trifle', groan'd the husband.

†**b.** To bewail, lament. *Obs. rare.*

a **1762** LADY M. W. MONTAGU *Poems* (1785) 2 They groan the cruel load they're doom'd to bear. **1766** ELIZ. GRIFFITH *Lett. Henry & Frances* III. 113 The Sun hides its Face, for Grief; and the Winds groan her departure.

4. *intr.* To be oppressed or overburdened to the point of groaning. Const. *beneath, under, with.*

1613 PURCHAS *Pilgrimage* (1614) 71 Under which Turkish servitude it groned, till our dayes. **1634** SIR T. HERBERT *Trav.* 145 For above five hundred yeares Persia groaned under many Lords and Tyrants. **1711** ADDISON *Spect.* No. 163 ¶7 If the Afflictions we grone under be very heavy. **1742** YOUNG *Nt. Th.* II. 130 As Atlas groan'd The world beneath, we groan beneath an hour. **1748** *Anson's Voy.* II. xiv. 280 They might take a severe revenge for the barbarities they had groaned under for more than two ages. **1762** CHURCHILL *Ghost* I. 162 Modest merit..Is left in poverty to groan. **1818** JAS. MILL *Brit. India* II. v. iv. 428 The injustice under which he appeared to himself to groan. **1833** HT. MARTINEAU *Manch. Strike* iv. 50 Their interests demand the reductions under which we groan. *a* **1861** T. WOOLNER *My Beautiful Lady* (1863) 146 Groaning beneath a Despot.

b. attributed to inanimate objects (sometimes with mixture of sense 5).

1697 DRYDEN *Virg. Georg.* IV. 253 With labour'd Anvils Ætna groans below. **1732** BERKELEY *Alciphr.* v. §20 Those arguments, answers, defences, and replications which the press groans under. **1764** *Oxford Sausage* 191 The Chimnies blaze the Tables groan. **1789** JEFFERSON *Writ.* (1859) III. 10 The press groans with productions, which, in point of boldness, make an Englishman stare. **1821** SHELLEY *Hellas* 937 Come, feast! the board groans with the flesh of men. **1874** BLACKIE *Self-Cult.* 25 Though the library-shelves groan with books.

5. *transf.* To make a deep harsh sound resembling a groan.

1513 DOUGLAS *Æneis* VI. vi. 62 Vnder the paysand and the hevy charge Gan grane or geig ful fast the jonit barge. **1781** COWPER *Expostulation* 58 He heard the wheels..Groan heavily along the distant road. **1820** KEATS *St. Agnes* xli, The key turns, and the door upon its hinges groans. **1847** TENNYSON *Princ.* II. 451 The great organ almost burst his pipes, Groaning for power. **1853** KANE *Grinnell Exp.* xxii. (1856) 172 The ice is so driven in around us as to grate and groan against the sides of our little vessel. **1875** MCLAREN *Serm.* Ser. II. vii. 121 The swaying branches creak and groan.

6. To express earnest longing by groans; to yearn or long, as if with groans; hence *fig.* of things (cf. 4 b). Const. *for, to* with inf.

c **1560** A. SCOTT *Poems* (S.T.S.) xxxiv. 46 ȝe preiche, ȝe fleich, ȝe frane, ȝe grane ay quhill thay grant. **1601** SHAKS. *Jul. C.* III. i. 275 This foule deede shall smell aboue the earth With Carrion men, groaning for burial. **1608–9** in *Crt. & Times Jas. I* (1848) I. 88 It seems the gallows groans for him. *a* **1633** G. HERBERT *Temple, Ch.* Superl. 17 Nothing but holy, pure, and cleare, Or that which groneth to be so. **1643** [ANGIER] *Lanc. Vall. Achor* 10 It is now harvest time, our Corn..is in the field, ripe and groaning for the sickle. **1727** BOYER *Angl.-Fr. Dict.* s.v., The Gallows groans for him, *le Gibet l' attend avec impatience.* **1742** YOUNG *Nt. Th.* I. 257 How groaning hospitals eject their dead! What numbers groan for sad admission there!

7. *trans.* **a.** To express disapproval of by means of groans. **b.** ***to groan down***: to silence by means of groans.

1799 ANNA SEWARD *Lett.* (1811) V. 205 They would be hissed, groaned, and cat-called. **1861** *N.Y. Tribune* 19 Dec. (Cent.), Yesterday they met, as agreed upon, and, after groaning the Ward Committee, went to the mayor's office.

groaner ('grəʊnə(r)). [f. prec. + -ER[1].] **a.** One who groans; also *slang*, a thief who attends funerals or religious gatherings.

1795 POTTER *Dict. Cant.*, *Groaner and Sigher*, wretches hired by methodists and others to attend their meetings for the purposes of fraud. **1848** in *Duncombe's Sinks of Lond.* 109 *Groaners*, a sort of wretches who attend meetings, sighing and looking demure; in the meantime their pals pick the pockets of those persons who may be in the same pew with them. **1876** *Whitby Gloss.*, *A desperate greeaner*, a great complainer. **1884** A. FORBES *Chinese Gordon* ii. 66 The gunner non-coms. replied with groans. The most vehement groaner, a corporal, Gordon dragged out of the rank and had him shot on the spot.

b. A whistling buoy. *local U.S.*

1903 G. S. WASSON in *Century Mag.* 538/1 'These here plaguy bell-b'ys an' groaners is a ter'ble old nuisance, you!' exclaimed Cap'n Roundturn. **1941** T. S. ELIOT *Dry Salvages* 5 *Groaner*: a whistling buoy. *Ibid.* i. 8 The heaving groaner Rounded homewards..Measures time not our time. **1947** C. D. WHITE *Handbk. Sailing* xxii. 236 Effective at night in fog or low visibility, whistling buoys do not sound like a whistle but like a groan, and are called 'groaners' by seafaring men.

groanful ('grəʊnfʊl), *a. rare.* [f. GROAN *sb.* + -FUL.] Full of groans or groaning; lugubrious.

1590 SPENSER *F.Q.* II. xi. 42 Adowne he kest it with so puissant wrest, That backe againe it did alofte rebownd, And gave against his mother earth a gronefull sownd. **1855** SINGLETON *Virgil* I. 393 Gnashing with his teeth With groanful cry. **1879** G. MACDONALD *P. Faber* II. i. 9 All was to him gloomy, groanful, cold.

groaning ('grəʊnɪŋ), *vbl. sb.* [f. GROAN *v.* + -ING[1].]

1. The action of the vb. GROAN.

c **1000** ÆLFRIC *Hom.* I. 68 Wununga..on ðam ne ablinþ granung. *c* **1205** LAY. 17797 þer wes muchel waning heortne graning. *c* **1275** *Serving Christ* 28 in *O.E. Misc.* 91 þer is gronynge and grure. **1340** *Ayenb.* 264 þer is groinynge wyþ-oute ende. **1398** TREVISA *Barth. De P.R.* XII. vii. (1495) 417 A culuoure hath gronynge in stede of songe. *c* **1420** *Anturs of Arth.* 620 (Douce MS.) Ho gretes one Gaynour, with gronyng grylle. **1535** COVERDALE *Ps.* xxxvii[i]. 9 Lorde, thou knowest all my desyre, & my gronynge is not hyd from the. **1672** WILKINS *Nat. Relig.* 194 Our most secret thoughts and inward groanings are not hid from Him. **1727–41** CHAMBERS *Cycl.*, *Groaning*, in heraldry, a term used for the cry or noise of a buck. **1828** SCOTT *F.M. Perth* xxxii, I heard a groaning as of one in extreme pain. **1877** L. J. JENNINGS *Field Paths & Gr. Lanes* 39 The groaning and creaking of its branches..was a distressing sound to hear.

2. A lying-in. Now only *dial.*

1579 [see *groaning-time* in 3]. [**1602** SHAKS. *Ham.* III. ii. 259.] **1724** S. SEWALL *Diary* 9 Jan. (1882) III. 328 She came from a Groaning very cheerfull. **1744** *Trial Campbell Craig v. Earl Anglesey* 5 Was you ever at a Groaning before? I never was. **1781** S. PETERS *Hist. Connecticut* 234 At groanings there are always a little boy and a rattle-snake's skin, the latter of which prevents numbness and the cramp. **1895** *E. Angl. Gloss.*, *Groaning*, a lying-in.

3. *attrib.*, as ***groaning-time*** (sense 2); esp. of food and drink provided for attendants and visitors at a lying-in, as ***groaning-beer, -bread, -cake, -cheese, -drink, -malt, -pie***; **groaning-chair** (see quots. 1886 and 1893); so †***groaning-stool.***

1677 S. SEWALL *Diary* 16 Feb. (1878) I. 36 Brewed my Wives *Groaning Beer. **1893** *Northumbld. Gloss.*, **Groanin-breed*..is the cake provided on the occasion. *a* **1796** PEGGE *Derbicisms* Ser. II. 103 **Groaning-cake*, [cake] given to the assisting women, after the good woman is brought to bed. **1841** J. T. HEWLETT *Parish Clerk* I. 71 Caudle and groaning-cake were handed round. **1664** J. WILSON *Cheats* v. i. Dram. Wks. (1874) 86 Enter Boy with a glass and a *groaning chair. **1710** SWIFT *Baucis & Phil.* 85 The Groaning Chair began to crawl, Like a huge snail, along the wall. **1886** ELWORTHY *W. Somerset Word-bk., Groaning-Chair.* The large chair often found by bedsides. **1893** *Northumbld. Gloss., Groanin-chair*, the chair on which the matron is set after a child-birth to receive her gossips and friends. **1636** W. SAMPSON *Vow-breaker* IV. 1 H, Bring the *groaning cheece and all requisites. **1822** SCOTT *Nigel* iii, To taste a glass of aniseed, and a bit of the groaning cheese. **1743** *Annesley Ejectm. Trial* in Howell *St. Trials* (1813) XVII. 1153 Lord Altham said, deponent must dine with him, and come to drink some *groaning-drink, for that his wife was in labour. **1886** ELWORTHY *W. Somerset Word-bk., Groaning-drink*, ale brewed in anticipation of childbirth. *c* **1780** BURNS *Rantin' Dog* ii, Who will buy my *groanin' mawt? **1815** SCOTT *Guy M.* iii, Meg Merrilies descended to the kitchen to secure her share of the groaning malt. *c* **1626** *Dick of Devon.* IV. i. in Bullen *O.P.* II. 63 Midwives travell at night and are weary with eating *groaning pyes, and yet sleepe not. *a* **1668** DAVENANT *News fr. Plym.* IV. Dram. Wks. 1873 IV. 171 No matter who's the father, so I have work, And eat the groaning pie. **1596** NASHE *Saffron Walden* Wks. (Grosart) III. 196 Let him vnderstand, I more scorne it, than to haue so foule a iakes for my *groaning stole as hys mouth. **1579** NORTH *Plutarch* (1595) 11 When her *groning time was come..she [Ariadne] died..in labour. **1881** *I. of W. Gloss., Groanin time*, the time of a woman's accouchment.

groaning ('grəʊnɪŋ), *ppl. a.* [f. GROAN *v.* + -ING[2].] That groans, in senses of the vb.

1398 TREVISA *Barth. De P.R.* XII. xxxv. (1495) 434 The turture comyth in spryngynge time and warnyth of nouelte of tyme wyth gronynge voyce. **1597** R. BRUCE *Let.* in *Life* (Wodrow) 172 A taste of a groaning and broken spirit. **1603** SHAKS. *Meas. for M.* II. ii. 15 What shall be done, Sir, with the groaning Iuliet? Shee's very neere her howre. **1697** DRYDEN *Virg. Georg.* III. 291 The Courser..Inur'd the groaning Axle-tree to bear. **1735** SOMERVILLE *Chase* II. 56 Groaning Staddles bend beneath their Load. **1814** SCOTT *Wav.* xxx, Ye cut-lugged graning carles. **1878** STEVENSON *Inland Voy.* 170 The sweet groaning thunder of the organ. **1898** *Edin. Rev.* Oct. 417 The cattle ploughed or turned groaning waterwheels.

Proverb. **1546** J. HEYWOOD *Prov.* (1867) 49 A gronyng horse, and a gronyng wyfe, Neuer fayle their maister.

†**b.** ***groaning-board*** (see quot. 1673-4).

1673-4 GREW *Anat. Plants* III. II. vii. §7 (1682) 138 The Planks commonly called Groaning-Boards, lately exposed, as a kind of Prodigy..were of Elm. The Aer-Vessels of this Wood, being..more ample, than in any other Timber..upon the application of the Red-hot-Iron..every vessel became, as it were a little Wind-Pipe..a great many of these Pipes playing together, might make a kind of big or groaning noyse. **1710** STEELE & ADDISON *Tatler* No. 257 ¶2 There was an Organ, a Bagpipe, a Groaning-Board.

groaningly ('grəʊnɪŋlɪ), *adv.* [f. GROANING *ppl. a.* + -LY[2].] In a groaning manner.

1830 *Blackw. Mag.* XXVIII. 587 Neither better nor worse than prize poems generally are—that is groaningly stupid. **1834** LYTTON *Pompeii* III. x, The hag groaningly picked up the heavy purse. **1870** THORNBURY *Tour Eng.* II. xxxi. 293 They groaningly disclosed where they had hidden their money. **1887** S. CUMBERLAND *Queen's Highw. fr. Ocean to O.* 159 The train groaningly proceeds higher and higher.

groap(e, obs. form of GROPE.

groat (grəʊt, grɔːt). Forms: 4-6 **groot(e, grote,** 5-6 **grott(e,** 6 **grot, groate, grootte,** *Sc.* and *north.* **groit, groyt,** 6- **groat.** [a. MDu. *groot*, properly an elliptical use of the adj. etymologically = *great* (in the sense 'thick'); cf. MHG. *grôze pfenninge* 'thick pennies', GROSCHEN. The equivalent med.L. *grossus*, OF. *gros* (see GROSS *sb.*) occur earlier than the Teut. forms.

The pronunciation (grɔːt), for which compare (brɔːd) *broad*, is recognized by many Dicts., but is now old-fashioned.]

1. *Hist.* A denomination of coin (in med. Latin *grossus*, F. *gros*, It. *grosso*, MDu. *groot*) which was recognized from the 13th c. in various countries of Europe. Its standard seems to have been in the 14th c. theoretically one-eighth of an ounce of silver; but its actual intrinsic value varied greatly in different countries and at different periods. (The adoption of the Du. or Flemish form of the word into English shows that the 'groat' of the Low Countries had circulated here before a coin of that denomination was issued by the English sovereigns.) †***a shilling, pound of groats***: a Flemish money of account bearing the same proportion to the ordinary 'shilling' or 'pound' as the groat or 'thick penny' did to the ordinary penny.

1387 TREVISA *Higden* (Rolls) VI. 259 þe groot turoney is somwhat lasse worþy þan an Englische groote. *c* **1483** CAXTON *Dialogues* viii. 44 Qvyntyne the tollar Hath taken of me A pound of grotes [Fr. *vng liure de gros*] More than he ought to take Of right tolle. *a* **1500** *Sir Beues* 3472 (Pynson) Beuys gaue that man for his tydynge Of grotes twenty shelynge. **1542** RECORDE *Gr. Artes* K iij b, A flemmish grote is a litell aboue 3 farthynges englishe.

2. The English groat coined in 1351-2 was made equal to four pence. This ratio between the groat and the penny continued to be maintained; but owing to the progressive debasement of both coins, the 'old groats' which remained in circulation were valued at a higher rate (see quots. 1465, *c* 1483, also 1552 in b). The groat ceased to be issued for circulation in 1662, and was not afterwards coined under that name. The 'fourpence' (popularly 'fourpenny bit,' 'fourpenny piece'), which was issued from 1836 to 1856 (and since 1888 reissued for colonial circulation) was occasionally called a 'groat,' but the name was neither officially recognized nor commonly used. The Scottish fourpenny piece, first struck in 1358, is called a 'groat' (AF. *grote*) in an English Act of 1390, and this name was used in Scotland itself in the 15th c. Its value was already only 3*d.* English in 1373, and 2*d.* in 1390; later it fell much lower. In Ireland the groat was first struck in 1460. ***Harry groat*** (see HARRY 9). ***York groat*** (see quot. 1837).

[**1351** in Rymer *Fœdera* (1708) V. 709/1 Si avoms, par avis de nostre Conseil..ordene & fait faire Novele Monoie..d'Argent cest assavoir une Monoie, que serra appellee Un Gros, de la value de Quaters Esterlings.] **1362** LANGL. *P. Pl.* A. III. 133 Heo ȝeueth the jayler gold and grotes to-gedere. *c* **1386** CHAUCER *Pard. T.* 617 Ye, for a grote, vnbokele anon thy purs. **1444** *Pol. Poems* (Rolls) II. 220 A good be stille is offte weel wourth a groote. **1451** *Sc. Acts Jas. II* c. 1 At þar be strikin of the vnce of brynt siluer or bulȝeoun of þat fynes viij grottes. **1465** *Mann. & Househ. Exp.* (Roxb.) 492 My master payd hym..of old grotes, l.s. **1480** CAXTON *Chron. Eng.* ccxxix. 239 In the xxvi yere of his regne the kyng lete ordeyne and make his newe money..the peny, the grote of value of iiij pens, and the half grote of value of ii pens..but it was of lasse weight than the old sterlyng was by v shyllyng in the pounde. *c* **1483** —— *Dialogues* v. 17 The olde grotes of englond Which be worth v pens The newe be worth foure pens. **1494** FABYAN *Chron.* VII. 461 In this yere [24 Edw. III, 1351-2] also the kynge caused to be coyned grotes and halfegrotes, the whiche lacked of yᵉ weyghte of his former coyne. *ii.s.* vi.*d.* in a li. Troy. **1503** *Act 19 Hen. VII* c. 5 Coin of other Lands now current in this Realm for Groats, or for iv.*d.* being Silver. **1526** WRIOTHESLEY *Chron.* (1875) I. 15 This yeare [1526] in November, the Kinge enhaunsed his coyne..that is to saye, the riall at $11^s\ 3^d$, the angell $7^s\ 6^d$..allso he..valued an ownce sylver fyne sterlinge at $3^s\ 8^d$; and also made new grotes and halfe grotts after the rate. **1543** [see CHEKASYDE]. **1547** BOORDE *Introd. Knowl.* iii. (1870) 133 In Irlond they haue Irysh grotes, and harped grotes. **1578** LYTE *Dodoens* II. vi. 153 There commeth up white huskes, which be flat, rounde, and very large, of the quantitie of a groote, or Testerne. **1626** BERNARD *Isle of Man* (1627) 239 Two pence, yea a groate sometimes. **1700** DRYDEN *Cock & the Fox* 181, I dare lay a groat [*rime-word* lot]. **1712** ADDISON *Spect.* No. 295 ¶4 A Pin a Day, says our frugal Proverb, is a Groat a Year. **1714** GAY *Shepherd's Week, The Ditty* 106 With apron blue to dry her tears she sought, Then saw the cow well serv'd, and took a groat. **1786** BURNS *Earnest Cry & Prayer* ix, An' plunder'd o' her hindmost groat By gallows knaves. **1837** *Penny Cycl.* VII. 330 It was one of the charges against Wolsey, that he had put the cardinal's hat upon the king's money, as is seen upon his York groats and half-groats. **1849** JAMES *Woodman* iv, For the young lord at their head gave me a York groat. **1885** W. ROSS *Aberdour & Inchcolme* v. 144 A shearer would look askance at a groat dropped into the palm of his hand, as payment for a day's work.

†**b.** Used to translate Gr. δραχμή or L. *denarius.*

1526 TINDALE *Luke* xv. 9, I have founde the groate which I had loost. *c* **1550** CHEKE *Matt.* xx. 2 He agreed with yᵉ workmen for a groot a dai. [**1552** *Elyot's Dict., Didrachmum*, a siluer coyne, conteynyng .ii. Drachmas, euerie Drachma, beyng in value an old sterling groat, when eight went to the ounce.] **1563-87** FOXE *A. & M.* (1596) 257/1 Seeke the grote that is lost, of the unitie, I meane of faith. **1570** LEVINS *Manip.* 178/1 A grote, *drachma.*

†**c.** Taken as the type of a very small sum. *Obs.*

1513 DOUGLAS *Æneis* VI. v. 71 Than, at the last, to pas our in this boit Thay bene admit, and costis thaim not a groit. *a* **1605** MONTGOMERIE *Sonn.* xxi. 2 Except ȝour gouns, some hes not worth a grote. *a* **1704** T. BROWN *Sat. French King* Wks. 1730 I. 59 'Slife, I'll not take thy honour for a groat. **1749** CHESTERF. *Lett.* (1792) II. cxcviii. 244, I do not care a groat what it is, if [etc.].

†**d.** ***a cracked*** or ***slit groat***: referred to as the type of something worthless. *Obs.*

1600 DEKKER *Gent. Craft* i. (1862) 10 Peace you cracked groats. **1677** W. HUGHES *Man of Sin* II. ix. 145 Their Vulgar Catechismes leave wholly out the Second Commandement..These wicked Cheats, of the Tenth make Two. But 'tis a Slit Groat. **1679** PENN *Addr. Prot.* II. 156 The People..take all upon trust for their Souls, that would not trust an Arch-bishop about a Slit Groat.

†**3.** A point at cards, ? from the practice of using groats to score with. *Obs.*

1680 COTTON *Compl. Gamester* (ed. 2) 83 If either side are at eight Groats he hath the benefit of calling *Can-ye*, if he hath two Honours in his hand.

4. *attrib.*, as **groat-silver**, a customary gratuity of a groat.

1394-5 *Durham Acc. Rolls* (Surtees) I. 214 Hominibus de domo dei pro eorum grotsiluer, vjs. viij*d.* **1522-3** *Ibid.* 255, 15 fratr. et soror. de domo Dei pro eorum grotsiluer, cuilibet eorum 5*d.*, 6*s.* 3*d.*

groath, obs. form of GROWTH.

groats (grəʊts, grɔːts), *sb. pl.* Forms: (? 1 **grotan**), 5 **grotene,** 4-6, 8 **grotes,** 5-6 *Sc.* **grotis,** 4, 6-8 **grots, (6 groots),** 6-9 **grotts, (6 grottes),** 7- **groats.** [OE. **grotan* wk. pl., cogn. w. *grot* neut., fragment, particle (see GROT[1]), and with GRIT *sb.*[2], q.v. for other connexions.

The word first occurs in an interpolation written *c* 1200 on the margin of an 11th c. MS.; it is there spelt *gratan*, but as the passage is a blundered and half-modernized transcript from something of earlier date, there is little risk in correcting it to *grotan*, which is pre-supposed by the northern ME. forms. The OE. form is commonly cited as *grátan*, but this admits of no known etymology, and is irreconcilable with the phonetic history of the word.

With reference to the pronunciation cf. GROAT.]

1. Hulled, or hulled and crushed grain of various kinds, chiefly oats, but also wheat, barley, and †maize. ***embden groats***: crushed barley or oats.

? *a* **1100** [*MS. c* 1200] *Sax. Leechd.* III. 292 Nim atena grotan [*MS.* gratan]. [**1324-5** *Durham Acc. Rolls* (Surtees) I. 14 In Grotis emp. pro exitibus, 3*d.*] *c* **1358** *Ibid.* 561 In iiij bus. de grotes emp. pro coquina, iijs. vj*d.* *c* **1420** *Liber Cocorum* (1862) 47 Fyrst take porke, wele thou hit sethe With otene grotes, that ben so smethe. *Ibid.* 20 Ote grotis. *Ibid.* 48 Grynd hom..With grotene. *c* **1470** HENRYSON *Mor. Fab.* II. (*Town & C. Mouse*) xviii, Ane plait of grottis, and ane dische full of meill. **1508** KENNEDIE *Flyting w. Dunbar* 427 Fra Etrike Forest furthward..Thow beggit..cruddis, mele, grotis, grisis, and geis. **1601** HOLLAND *Pliny* I. 559 The people of Rome for three hundred years together, used no other food than the groats made of common Wheat. **1616** SURFL. & MARKH. *Country Farme* 556 As for the Groats, which is vsually called common or course Oat-meale, they are excellent to make porridge of all kinds. **1747** MRS. GLASSE *Cookery* xvi. 146 Grotes [**1796** Grits] once cut does better than Oatmeal. **1775** ROMANS *Florida* 121 To enumerate the vast variety of ways in employing this noble grain [maize] for food such as hommany, mush, groats,..would be too tedious. **1789** *Trans. Soc. Arts* II. 117, I think it very possible, by some such operation as making grotts, to clear away the husks. **1869** *Lonsdale Gloss., Groats*, always used along with the blood in the composition of black puddings; hence the proverb current in Lonsdale, 'Blood without groats is nowt', meaning that family without fortune is of no consequence.

b. Phr. (*Sc.*) ***to ken one's own groats in other folks' kail***: to know one's own handiwork. ***to give groats for pease, to gie (one) kail o' his ain groats***: to pay (a person) in his own coin.

1727 P. WALKER *Remark. Pass.* 3 *Worthies* 64 The Church excommunicated him, and he gave them Groats for Pease, he excommunicated them. **1819** RENNIE *St. Patrick* I. v. 76 He tell't..how keen ye war tae gie the warlocks kail o' their ain groats. **1861** RAMSAY *Remin.* Ser. II. 93 D'ye think, Sir, I dinna ken my ain groats in ither folk's kail?

†**2.** Naked oats. *Obs.*

1669 WORLIDGE *Syst. Agric.* (1681) 41 There is a new sort of Oats, or Groats growing like unto whole Oatmeal, without any Hulls; they grow near the City of Durham. **1725** in BRADLEY *Fam. Dict.* s.v. *Oats.*

3. *attrib.*, as ***groat-broth, chest, gruel***; †**groat-sugar**, coarse sugar.

1741 *Compl. Fam.-Piece* I. i. 44 Give the Child *Groat-broth sometimes. **1531** *Durham Bursar's Mem.* in *Charters*, etc. *Priory of Finchale* (Surtees 1837) Gloss. s.v. *Grots.* [Paid for a lock and key for] 'le *grot-chyst', [4*d.*]. **1844** T. WEBSTER *Encycl. Dom. Econ.* 945 Common *groat gruel—Wash three ounces of common groats, and [etc.]. **1743** *Lond. & Country Brew.* IV. (ed. 2) 330 Boil Half a Pound of *Groat Sugar in a Quart of Water.

†**'groatsworth.** *Obs.* [f. *groat's*, genitive of GROAT *sb.* + WORTH.] As much as is bought or sold for a groat. Also *fig.* a small amount.

1562 J. HEYWOOD *Prov. & Epigr.* (1867) 211, I would haue a groates worth of your seede. **1592** GREENE (*title*) Greens Groats-worth of Wit, bought with a Million of Repentaunce. **1600** ROWLANDS *Letting Humours Blood* VII. 82 Yet for a groates-worth makes him pay a shilling. **1678** BUTLER *Hud.* III. ii. 694 To gain one Groats-worth of Applause.

groave, var. GROOVE; obs. f. GROVE.

†**grob**, *v. Obs. rare*[−1]. [variant of GROPE *v.* Cf. GRUB.] *trans.* = GROPE *v.* 3.

1654 GAYTON *Pleas. Notes* III. ii. 73 The Don caught and grob'd her smock. [Cf. SHELTON *Don Quix.* III. ii. (1652) 30 Groped her smock.] **1876** *Whitby Gloss., Grob*, to probe; to dive into the pocket for change.

grobbe, obs. form of GRUB.

Grobian ('grəʊbɪən). [a. G. *grobian*, ad. med.L. *Grobiān-us*, name of an imaginary personage, often referred to by writers of the 15-16th c. in Germany as the type of boorishness, f. G. *grob* coarse, rude: see GRUFF.] A clownish, slovenly person. Also *attrib.* or as *adj.* Hence **'Grobianism.**

1609 DEKKER *Gull's Horn-bk.* To Rdr., This Tree of Guls..hath a relish of Grobianisme. **1611** COTGR., *Grobianisme*, Grobianisme, slouenlinesse. **1621** BURTON *Anat.* III. ii. III. i. (1624) 420 Let them be neuer so clownish,..Grobians and sluts, if once they be in loue, they will be most neat and spruce. **1654** GAYTON *Pleas. Notes* II. iii. 43 For handsomenesse of feeding..they had been very well all trained up in Grobians school. *Ibid.* III. ii. 74 He..utter'd Grobian returnes for the kinde entertainments of his friend Marius. **1706** PHILLIPS (ed. Kersey), *Grobian*..a slovenly ill-bred Fellow. **1855** KINGSLEY *Westw. Ho!* ii, He who is a Grobian in his own company will, sooner or later, become a

Grobian in that of his friends. **1881** A. LANG *Library* 48 All these slatternly practices..seem fine manly acts to the grobians who use them.

grobling, obs. form of GROVELLING.

groce, grocche, obs. forms of GROSS, GRUTCH.

grocer ('grəʊsə(r)). Forms: 4-6 **grosser**, 5-7 **groser**, 5 **grocere**, 6 **-ier**, 5- **grocer**. [ad. OF. *grossier*:—med.L. *grossārius*, f. *grossus* GROSS.]

†**1.** One who buys and sells in the gross, i.e. in large quantities, a wholesale dealer or merchant; also with mention of the article dealt in, e.g. fish. (The company of Grocers, said to have been incorporated in 1344, consisted of wholesale dealers in spices and foreign produce; hence prob. the later sense 2.) *Obs.*

[**1321** *Liber Cust.* in *Munim. Gildh.* (Rolls) II. I. 304 Qe ne soient grossours de vin ne taverners. **1363** *Act 37 Edw. III* c. 5 Les Marchauntz nomez grossers engrossent totes maneres des marchandises vendables.] **1427** in Heath *Grocers' Comp.* (1869) 4 In here tyme..was the furste stoon leyd of the Groceres Place in Conyhoope-lane in the Warde of Chepe. **14..** *Customs of Malton* in *Surtees Misc.* (1888) 63 It is ordanyd þ[t] no groser of fysche awe to cutt hys awn fysche. **1437** *Bury Wills* (Camden) 5 Ego Joħes Notyngh[a]m de Bury scī Eđi grocer. **1472** J. PASTON in *P. Lett.* No. 701 III. 56 There is a grosser dwellyng ryght over ayenst the well with ij boketts a lytyll fro Seynt Elens, hathe evyr hawkys to sell. **1541** *Act 33 Hen. VIII* c. 25 Thomas Pointes of London Grosser, occupieng the feate of marchandise in the partes beyonde the sea. **1689** RAVENHILL *Acc. Comp. Grocers* 1 The word Grocers was a term at first distinguishing Merchants of this Society, in opposition to Inferiour Retailers; for that they usually sold in gross Quantities by great Weights.

2. a. A trader who deals in spices, dried fruits, sugar, and, in general, all articles of domestic consumption except those that are considered the distinctive wares of some other class of tradesmen.

In 18-19th c. tea, coffee, and cocoa have become characteristic articles of the grocer's trade. Since 1860 many grocers hold licences to sell beer, wines, and spirits, in bottles.

1465 *Mann. & Househ. Exp.* (Roxb.) 299 He paid to the grocer in Fanchestrete for spycez, x. s. vj. d. *c* **1510** BARCLAY *Mirr. Gd. Manners* (1570) A ij, What should an Irenmonger meddle with Grocer's ware? **1578** LYTE *Dodoens* v. lxx. 635 A man shal..find it to be sold in the shops of the Apothecaries and Grossers. **1608** *Pennyless Parl.* in *Harl. Misc.* (Malh.) III. 76 The grocers are plentifully blessed, for their figs and raisins may allure fair lasses. **1725** WATTS *Logic* I. vi. §6 (1726) 108 A Grocer is a Man who buys and sells Sugar and Plums and Spices for Gain. **1845** JAMES *A. Neil* ii, A grocer, or rather general dealer. **1855** MACAULAY *Hist. Eng.* xxi. IV. 626 The grocer weighed out his currants.

b. ***grocers' itch***, a form of eczema incident to grocers and others who handle sugar.

1799 UNDERWOOD *Dis. Children* (ed. 4) I. 95 An eruption resembling the psora of the Greeks, or what is called amongst us the Grocer's-itch. **1822-29** *Good's Study Med.* V. 635 The local form is mostly produced by the use of irritant materials, constantly applied to the parts affected.. as sugar among the labourers in grocery warehouses, and lime among bricklayers. Whence this variety has been vulgarly called Grocers' Itch, or Bricklayers' Itch.

c. ***grocer's paper*** = *grocery-paper*.

1861 ROSSETTI *Let.* Jan. (1965) II. 392, I shall have it printed..on blue grocer's-paper. **1925** E., O. & S. SITWELL *Poor Young People* 59 And tied in a packet of blue grocer's paper.

d. ***grocer's Graves, port, sherry, wine***, cheap wine bought at a grocer's shop.

1931 W. HOLTBY *Poor Caroline* i. 21 The cultivation of a palate cannot be achieved on grocer's port. **1936** 'N. BLAKE' *Thou Shell of Death* i. 22 His idea of dinner is boiled mutton and grocer's Graves. *Ibid.* iii. 48 I've..met him..at a dinner at Christ Church..you know the sort of grocer's port they dish out there. **1940** GRAVES & HODGE *Long Week-End* xxiii. 399 Ordinary cheap grocer's wine. **1958** 'W. HAGGARD' *Slow Burner* iv. 72 Dublin glass..and grocers' sherry at best. **1960** J. MORRIS *Hired to Kill* III. xvi. 141 To that it bears about as much resemblance as does a bottle of the finest vintage claret to grocer's wine.

Hence (*nonce-wds.*) '**grocerdom**, the realm or world of grocers; '**groceress**, a female grocer; '**grocering**, the trade or occupation of a grocer; '**grocerly** *a.*, of or pertaining to the grocery trade; '**grocerwise** *adv.*, after the manner of a grocer.

1828 [see GRAZIERDOM]. **1854** *Chamb. Jrnl.* I. 226 Almost every man above the rank of a mere daily cultivator has a wife who is groceress, linen-draperess, butcheress, or confectioner. **1894** CROCKETT *Raiders* 52 It was him an' nae ither that pat my Jerry, that was aye a guid lad, past the grocering. *a* **1845** HOOD *T. Trumpet* xxxix, For some grocerly thieves Turn over new leaves, Without much amending their lives or their tea. **1898** ZANGWILL *Dreamers Ghetto* viii. 328 Biographers will weigh me grocer-wise as Kant weighed the Deity.

grocery ('grəʊsərɪ). Also 6-7 **grossery**. [f. GROCER *sb.* + -Y.]

1. a. *collect. sing.* The goods sold by a grocer. **b.** *pl.* Various sorts of such goods.

1436 *Libel Eng. Policy* in *Pol. Poems* (Rolls) II. 179 Wee bene ageyne charged wyth merceyre, Haburdasshere ware, and wyth grocerye. **1608** MIDDLETON *Fam. Love* II. iii, Our ladies in the court were but brown sugar candy, as gross as grocery to her. **1635** *Rec. Merchants Alnwick* in Gross *Gild Merch.* I. 130 Any sort of grosseries or maynchester [i.e. Manchester] wares. **1660** F. BROOKE tr. *Le Blanc's Trav.* 47 Confections, and preserves, of all sorts, spices, and all sorts of grocery come from China. **1740** WOODROOFE in *Hanway's Trav.* (1762) I. II. xvii. 75 Mosco supplies it with groceries. **1766** GOLDSM. *Vic. W.* xii, A deal box before him to bring home groceries in. **1830** CARLYLE *Misc.* (1857) II. 126 To get his groceries and dainties furnished gratis by his grandmother. **1865** BARING-GOULD *Werewolves* xiv. 245 She had been sent with a parcel of grocery to a cottage.

2. The trade of a grocer.

1689 RAVENHILL *Acc. Comp. Grocers* 1 Various ways of Dealing and Trading passed under the Denomination of Groceries. **1885** *Law Times* 16 May 47/1 In the present case the business of greengrocery was not auxiliary to that of grocery.

3. *slang.* †**a.** Small change (*obs.*). **b.** *pl.* (see quot. 1839). ***the grocery***: sugar.

a. 1721 BAILEY, *Grocery*,..small Money as Farthings and Half-Pence. **1812** J. H. VAUX *Flash Dict.*, *Grocery*, halfpence, or copper coin, in a collective sense. **1823** in *Grose's Dict. Vulg. Tongue* (ed. Egan), *Grocery*, halfpence. *Cant.*

b. 1839 LEVER *Harry Lorrequer* vi. 44 'Hand his lordship over the groceries'.—Thus he designated a square decanter, containing about two quarts of whisky, and a bowl heaped high with sugar. **1841** LYTTON *Nt. & Morn.* v. ii, A pint of brandy, my dear. Hot water and lots of the grocery.

4. *U.S.* **a.** A grocer's shop. **b.** A dram-shop.

a. 1828-32 in WEBSTER. **1853** LOWELL *Moosehead Jrnl.* Prose Wks. 1890 I. 9 We drove up to the grocery to leave and take a mail-bag. **1893** GUNTER *Miss Dividends* 272 A wedding breakfast..served in the grocery at the side of the track.

b. 1806 *Balance* (Hudson, N.Y.) 28 Jan. 31 (Th.), There are 174 licensed groceries in the city of Albany. **1830** *Jeffersonian* (Albany, N.Y.) 30 June (Th.), Wilson told the Sheriff to take the jury to a grocery, that he might treat them. **1846** W. T. PORTER *Quarter Race*, etc. 104 He went into his favourite grocery or drinking-house. **1847** RUXTON *Mexico*, etc. xxiii. 189 Every other house [in Santa Fé] was a grocery, as they call a gin and whisky shop. **1856** OLMSTED *Slave States* 73 [The word 'grocery'] in Virginia, means the same thing as in Ireland—a dram-shop. **1871** E. EGGLESTON *Hoosier Schoolmaster* (1872) xi. 99, I must a took a little too much at Welch's grocery. **1923** *Dial. Notes* V. 240 *Grocery*, a grocery store where liquor was sold. **1946** G. FOREMAN *Last Trek Indians* 201 The Missouri state line, all along which were placed the so-called 'groceries', which were nothing more than grog-shops.

5. *attrib.* and *Comb.*, as ***grocery-goods, -keeper*** (U.S.), ***-man*** (U.S.), ***-ration, -store(s), -ware(s), -warehouse***; **grocery-captain**, the captain of an East Indiaman; **grocery-paper**, the paper used in wrapping up grocery.

1816 'QUIZ' *Grand Master* I. 19 This *groc'ry captain now, forsooth, With voice infernal hails our youth. **1776** ADAM SMITH *W.N.* I. x. (1869) I. 118 It costs no more to bring *grocery goods to the great town than to the country village. **1839** *Indiana Ho. Repres. Jrnl.* 274 An act to be passed repealing the present law granting licence to *grocery keepers. **1872** 'P. V. NASBY' *Struggles* 112 The grocery-keepers are intimatin' that before long I must begin to pay for my licker. **1888** J. BRYCE *Amer. Commw.* II. II. xliii. 134 Grocery keepers, liquor dealers, insurance, vendors of patents. **1895** *Pop. Sci. Monthly* July 376 One [was] a *groceryman. **1883** *Life Mrs. Prentiss* ix. 282 Written on coarse brown *grocery paper. **1890** *19th Cent.* Nov. 833 Lord Wolseley has..on several occasions spoken in favour of a free *grocery ration. **1811** B. RUSH in *J. Adams' Wks.* (1854) IX. 637 *note*, To lessen the number of taverns and *grocery stores. **1875** W. MCILWRAITH *Guide Wigtownshire* 137 A little cluster of houses, including a grocery-store and a blacksmith's-shop. **1554** *Act 1 & 2 Ph. & M.* c. 7 §2 *Grocery Wares, Mercery Wares. **1706** PHILLIPS (ed. Kersey), Grocery, or Grocery-Ware. **1769** *Dublin Merc.* 16-19 Sept. 3/1 Thomas Frayne..has opened a *Grocery Ware-house.

groceteria (grəʊsə'tɪərɪə). *N. Amer.* Also **grocerteria**. [f. GROCERY, after CAFETERIA.] A grocery store in which customers serve themselves and pay the cashier as they leave.

1913 *Official Gazette* (U.S. Pat. Off.) 25 Mar. 1036/1 Lutey Bros., Butte, Montana. Filed Mar. 14, 1912. Groceteria. **1916** *Illustr. World* (Chicago) Jan. 655/1 In Pomona, California, a small grocery store has suddenly sprung into prominence..by adopting the 'wait-on-yourself' plan of cafeteria. A 'Groceteria' if you please. **1920** [see BOOTERY]. **1921** *Daily Colonist* (Victoria, B.C.) 24 Mar. 20/4 (Advt.), Groceteria Daily Bulletin. All Day Specials. **1921** *Dial. Notes* V. 112 *Grocerteria*, n. (gro-ser-ter'-ja; gro-ser-te-rî'-a; gro-se-tér-ja). Pronunciation varies. First pronunciation dominant in California; but second commoner here and there in West. **1925** *Canad. Labor Advocate* 18 Sept. 8/1 Kirkham's Grocerteria Ltd. the working man's store. **1935** *Words* Jan. 11/2 Some years ago in Oregon a self-service grocery opened under the sign 'Groceteria', evidently under the impression that the suffix '—teria' means 'serve yourself'. **1962** *Guardian* 30 Aug. 6/6 An American 'grocertaria' [*sic*], a sort of super super-market.

grochauite ('grɒxaʊaɪt). *Min.* [Named by Websky in 1873 (G. *grochauit*), from Grochau, Silesia, its locality.] A chlorite-like mineral occurring in small hexagonal crystals in serpentine.

1875 DANA *Min.* App. II. 25 Grochauite..Occurs mixed with a chromic spinel.

grochche, groche, -chge, -chi, obs. ff. GRUTCH.

grockle ('grɒk(ə)l). *dial.* and *slang.* [Origin uncertain.] A holiday-maker or tourist (esp. in southwest England); a summer visitor. Also *transf.* and *attrib.* (Mildly *disparaging.*) Cf. EMMET 1 b.

1964 *Films & Filming* Oct. 31 It concerns life's drifters who wend their way down to these resorts to make an easy living off the 'grockles' (holidaymakers) during the four months of the summer season. **1968** A. DIMENT *Gt. Spy Race* viii. 124 He hasn't had a bit since last summer's crop of grockle chicks. **1975** [see EMMET 1 b]. **1977** J. FOWLES *Daniel Martin* (1978) 405 He was townee, he..looked like one of the countless Midland and Northcountry grockles that invade the West every summer. **1978** 'J. GASH' *Gold from Gemini* vi. 52 A few people.., mostly grockles ([antique] dealers' slang: tourists, not necessarily foreign, derogatory). **1982** M. HINXMAN *Telephone never Tells* xx. 146 The Isle of Wight ferry from Portsmouth to Ryde was packed..with..holiday people known locally as grockles. **1984** *Listener* 20 Sept. 23/1 With the memory of my month in Devon receding, the grockles remain vivid, and the term grows more and more repellent to me. **1986** *Daily Tel.* 25 Aug. 12/2 The term 'Grockle' now commonly used in the South West to mean holidaymaker, has also given rise to the following descriptive expressions Grockle fodder (fish and chips), Grockle bait (the merchandise sold in gift and souvenir shops), and Grockle nests (camp sites).

grode, obs. pa. t. of GROW.

grodge, obs. form of GRUDGE.

grodgeons, obs. variant of GURGEONS.

Groenendael ('grœnəndeɪl). [f. the name of the town in Belgium where the breed was developed.] A black, smooth-coated Belgian sheepdog.

1925 *Kennel Gaz.* Aug. 706/2 (*heading*) Any other breed or variety..not classified... Groenendals. 4 Registrations. **1945** C. L. B. HUBBARD *Observer's Bk. Dogs* 80 The Groenendael Sheepdog was recognized as a pure breed by the Belgian Kennel Club in 1891. **1964** E. F. DALGLISH tr. *Schneider-Leyer's Dogs of World* xii. 132 The Groenendael and the Tervuren are popular in Belgium as watch and companion dogs. **1971** *Times* 28 June 24/6 (Advt.), Pedigree Groenendael (Belgian Shepherd) puppies.

groeve, obs. form of GROOVE.

grof, obs. Sc. form of GRUFF.

grof(e, obs. pa. t. GRAVE *v.*

grof(e, grofel, obs. forms of GROVE, GROVEL.

grofen, obs. Sc. pa. pple. of GROW.

groff, Sc. form of GRUFF.

groffe, obs. form of GROOF; obs. Sc. form of GRUFF.

groflins, -lyngis, var. GROVELLINGS *Obs.*

grog (grɒg), *sb.* Also 8 **grogg**. [Said to be short for GROGRAM, and to have been applied first as a personal nickname to Admiral Vernon, from the fact of his wearing a grogram cloak, and afterwards transferred to the mixture which he ordered to be served out instead of neat spirit.

Vernon's order, dated Aug. 1740, is still extant. The statement that he wore a grogram cloak, and was thence nicknamed 'Old Grog', first appears explicitly in Grose *Dict. Vulg. Tongue* 1796, but derives some support from Trotter's allusion in quot. 1781.]

1. a. A drink consisting of spirits (originally rum) and water. ***half and half grog***, a drink made of equal parts of spirits and water; ***seven-water grog***, a contemptuous name among sailors for very weak grog.

1770 [see GROGGY *a.* 1]. **1773** IVES *Voy. & Hist. Narr. India* 100 A common sailor..having just been served with a quantity of grog (arrack mixed with water), had his spirits.. much elated. **1781** TROTTER *Written on board the Berwick* in *N. & Q.* Ser. I. I. 168 A mighty bowl on deck he drew, And filled it to the brink; Such drank the Burford's gallant crew, And such the gods shall drink, The sacred robe which Vernon wore Was drenched within the same; And hence his virtues guard our shore, And Grog derives its name. **1794** SOUTHEY *Botany Bay* III. Poems II. 82 Thou wilt go without grog, Sam, to-morrow at dinner. **1823** BYRON *Island* II. xix, But such as wafts its cloud o'er grog or ale. **1835** MARRYAT *Jac. Faithf.* xii, Do put a little drop of stuff in mine—it's seven water grog. **1837** W. IRVING *Capt. Bonneville* (1849) 87 A free allowance of grog..soon put them in the most braggart spirits. **1876** JAS. GRANT *One of the '600'* xxvi. 207 It will still freeze half-and-half grog as hard as rock crystal. **1883** STEVENSON *Treas. Isl.* II. x, Double grog was going on the least excuse.

b. A social gathering at which grog is drunk.

1888 SIR M. MACKENZIE *Fredk. the Noble* xii. 228 A 'Grog' ..was held every evening in the Reading Room of the Hôtel Mediterranée.

c. *Austral.* and *N.Z. colloq.* Alcoholic liquor, including beer.

1946 *New Statesman* 23 Nov. 375/1 A 'Wowser' seeks to interfere with or limit the pleasure of others... Common types are the Grog Wowser, Sheila Wowser, Sunday Wowser, Cine-wowser. **1948** D. W. BALLANTYNE in *Landfall* II. 110 Taking the old man's car, and there'll be some grog. **1955** 'N. SHUTE' *Requiem for Wren* i. 9 The man was always on the grog, 'n your Dad gave them the sack. **1966** G. W. TURNER *Eng. Lang. in Austral. & N.Z.* vi. 130 Grog is still used as a general term for drink, including, or even especially beer.

2. A 'groggy' horse. (Cf. GROGGY 2.)

1818 *Sporting Mag.* II. 207 Pronouncing any horse a grog, that, although not absolutely lame, goes stiff in his joints.

3. (See quots.).
1879 *Cassell's Techn. Educ.* II. 158 With it [the clay for fire-bricks] is ground up a certain proportion of some refractory substance, such as previously burnt pottery ..'Grog', as it is termed, opens the pores of the clay. **1881** C. T. DAVIS *Manuf. Bricks & Tiles* etc. (1889) 110 The vitrifying ingredients usually added to the terra-cotta clays are pure white sand, old pottery, and fire-bricks finely pulverized, and clay previously burned, termed 'grog'.

4. *attrib.* and *Comb.*, as ***grog-bibber, -butt***; **grog-blossom**, a redness or pimple on the nose caused by excessive drinking (*acne rosacea*); hence ***grog-blossomed*** adj.; †**grog-den** *N.Z.* = GROGGERY (*obs.*); **grog-fight** (*slang*), a drinking-party (cf. *tea-fight*); †**grog-hole** *U.S.*, †**grog-shanty** *U.S.*, *Austral.*, and *N.Z.* = GROGGERY (*obs.* exc. *Hist.*); **grog-shop**, a dram-shop, public-house; also (*pugilistic slang*) the mouth.
1824 in *Spirit Publ. Jrnls.* (1825) 207 [It] was enough to anger the most sober *grog-bibber that ever tossed tumbler over lip. **1796** *Grose's Dict. Vulg. Tongue*, *Grog-blossom. **1822–34** *Good's Study Med.* (ed. 4) II. 56 The common name for these protuberances in Ireland is Grog-Blossoms. **1883** T. HARDY *Wessex Tales, Three Strangers* (1889) 13 A few grog-blossoms marked the neighbourhood of his nose. **1852** *Househ. Words* 23 Oct. 135 The ancient huntsman has transferred his stained scarlet frock and *grog-blossomed countenance to another master. **1863** *Cornh. Mag.* Feb., These gentlemen [master's assistants of a Man-of-war] have had to stand at the *grog-butt, and see the grog served out. **1840** *N.Z. Jrnl.* I. xvi. 198/2 Where a year ago only three *grog-dens warned the passer-by..not to land on the beach, a neat row of wooden houses..extends along the line at high water. **1865** *Slang Dict.*, *Grog-fight, a drinking party.—Military. **1876** R. M. JEPHSON *Girl he Left Behind* i, He had been having a 'grog-fight' in his room to celebrate the event. **1848** *Knickerbocker* XVIII. 521 He was busy about the village, penetrating every *grog-hole and gambling-alley. **1871** *Scribner's Monthly* I. 537 Grog-holes, billiard saloons ..were well patronized. **1869** *Auckland Punch* 163/1, I.. reached the *grog-shanty in safety. **1888** C. D. WARNER *On Horseback* (1896) 47 The woods were full of grog-shanties. **1963** A. LUBBOCK *Austral. Roundabout* 77 It consists of a weatherboard, tin-roofed grog-shanty. **1966** *Telegraph* (Brisbane) 7 Dec. 10/3 As Australia developed, pubs and drinking habits changed. The grog shanties were replaced by comfortable inns. **1790** J. B. MORETON *Mann. W. Ind.* 35 There are some good taverns,..also an incredible number of petty ones, called *grog shops. **1850** THACKERAY *Mr. & Mrs. Berry* i, Claret drawn in profusion from the gown-boy's grogshop. **1883** STEVENSON *Treas. Isl.* I. i, 'This is a handy cove', says he, 'and a pleasant grog-shop'.

grog (grɒg), *v.* [f. the sb.]
1. *intr.* To drink grog.
1833 J. JEKYLL *Corr.* (1894) 318 Captain Ross..has dined and grogged with messmate William at Windsor. **1886** *Tinsley's Mag.* July 53 [They] met, grogged, smoked and discussed the news of the day. **1887** S. SAMUELS *From Forecastle to Cabin* 193, I ordered all hands to grog and turn-in.
2. *trans.* To extract spirit from (an empty cask) by pouring hot water into it, and letting it stand.
1878 *Lincoln, Rutland, & Stamf. Mercury* 8 Mar. (D.), The defendants had 'grogged' the casks by putting in hot water, and thereby had extracted 15 gallons of proof spirit on which duty had not been paid. **1899** *N.B. Daily Mail* 20 Jan. 2 Some traders..'grogged' the empty cask and thus obtained some additional spirit from the wood, duty free.
3. ? *U.S.* To make (spirits) into grog by mixing with water (*Cent. Dict.*).

grogane, grogaram, -om, obs. ff. GROGRAM.

grogeraine, -am, etc., obs. ff. GROGRAM.

grog(g)e, obs. forms of GRUDGE *v.*

grogged (grɒgd), *ppl. a.* [f. GROG *sb.* and *v.* + -ED.]
1. a. Of persons: Overcome with grog; drunk. **b.** Of a spirit cask: Treated with hot water (see GROG *v.* 2); said also of the liquor thus obtained.
a. 1842 *Comic Almanack* Oct. 41 'Fined five bob' for being grogged.
b. 1898 *N.B. Daily Mail* 31 Dec. 5/2 A large number of grogged whisky casks. **1899** *Daily News* 21 Sept. 8/3 A cask containing grogged liquor.
2. Of a horse: = GROGGY 2.
1796 *Grose's Dict. Vulg. Tongue*, Grogged, a grogged horse; a foundered horse.

groggery ('grɒgərı). *U.S.* [f. GROG *sb.* + -ERY.] A low drinking-place; a grog-shop.
1822 J. A. QUITMAN *Let.* in J. H. Claiborne *Life of Quitman* (1860) 71 Consisting of warehouses, low taverns, groggeries, dens of prostitution, and gaming-houses. **1835** J. H. INGRAHAM *South West* II. 190 Wretched looking dwellings, occupied as 'groggeries' by free negroes. **1855** HALIBURTON *Nat. & Hum. Nat.* I. vi. 183, I know a town that's on the chart, that has only a court-house, a groggery, a jail, [etc.]. **1857** T. PARKER in J. Weiss *Life* I. 344 He has no society except the low Germans who frequent the groggery downstairs.
Comb. **1892** A. E. LEE *Hist. Columbus* (Ohio) II. 127 A groggery keeper..was implicated.

'**groggified**, *ppl. a. colloq.* [f. **groggify* vb. (f. GROGGY + -FY) + -ED¹.] Affected by grog; tipsy.
1796 in *Grose's Dict. Vulg. Tongue* s.v. *Grog*. **1828** *Sporting Mag.* XXIII. 184 The Shenies on their return home appeared as groggified from the effects of the fog. **1867** SMYTH *Sailor's Word-bk.*, Groggy or Groggified.

groggily ('grɒgılı), *adv.* [-LY².] In a groggy manner; shakily.
1897 KIPLING *Capt. Cour.* ii. 31 He stepped, rather groggily..to the cabin steps. **1927** *Daily Express* 2 May 11/3 The bull staggers groggily like a pugilist who has received a severe body blow. **1936** P. FLEMING *News from Tartary* I. iii. 196 Groggily, but full of hope..the little caravan picked its way through the marsh. **1958** J. COURAGE in C. K. Stead *N.Z. Short Stories* (1966) 33, I had..gone groggily down into..the main lounge. **1972** R. PERRY *Fall Guy* v. 89 Groggily I scrambled to my feet.

grogginess ('grɒgınıs). [f. GROGGY *a.* + -NESS.] The condition or state of being groggy.
1818 *Sporting Mag.* II. 171 Grogginess is a common term for fullness and swelling in the legs. **1831** YOUATT *Horse* xiii. 252 The peculiar knuckling over of the fetlock-joint, and tottering of the whole of the fore-leg, known by the name of *grogginess*, and which is so often seen in old and over-worked horses. **1849** STEPHENS *Bk. Farm* (ed. 2) I. 342/1 A single journey may produce lameness; it may give the horse spavin, or grogginess. **1884** *Sat. Rev.* 5 July 27/2 It is a breach of a warranty of soundness if the warranted horse suffers from grogginess.

grogging ('grɒgıŋ), *vbl. sb.* [-ING¹.] The process of extracting spirits from an empty cask by soaking the interior with hot water (see GROG *v.* 2).
1901 *Daily News* 5 Mar. 7/5 [A wine and spirit merchant] was fined £5 and costs for 'grogging'. **1902** *Daily Chron.* 18 Oct. 8/6 Many casks were found on the defendant's premises undergoing the process of grogging.

groggy ('grɒgı), *a.* [f. GROG *sb.* + -Y¹.]
1. Intoxicated. Also, characterized by drinking habits, bibulous.
1770 T. NORWORTH in *Gentl. Mag.* 559/2 [Eighty names for having drunk too much.] 25. Groggy; this is a West-Indian Phrase; Rum and Water, without sugar, being called Grogg. **1801** M. G. LEWIS *Sailor's T.* iii. in *Tales Wonder* I. xv. 82 Groggy last night, my luck was such, that overboard I slid. **1840** MARRYAT *Poor Jack* vi, He wasn't the least groggy. **1868** HAWTHORNE *Amer. Note-Bks.* (1879) II. 164 In his groggy..destitution.
2. *Farriery.* Of a horse: Having a disease or weakness in the forelegs, which causes a hobbling or tottering movement.
1828 *Sporting Mag.* XXII. 119 A rare shaped thoroughbred horse very groggy. **1838** J. STEWART *Stable Econ.* (ed. 2) 384 Long journeys, at a fast pace, will make almost any horse groggy. **1862** TROLLOPE *Orley Farm* I. xxviii. 222 [Of a horse] Rather groggy on his pins the next morning? **1879** E. K. BATES *Egyptian Bonds* I. vii. 142 Your steed looks a little groggy about the legs.
3. *slang.* Weakened in a fight, so as to stagger; hence, *gen.* shaky, tottering, unsteady.
1832 MARRYAT *Jac. Faithf.* iv, He was what is termed groggy, from the constant return of blows on the sides of the head. **1854** THACKERAY *Newcomes* I. 282 My poor old governor is exceedingly shaky, very groggy about the head. **1883** C. KEENE *Let.* in *Life* xi. (1892) 348 Rheumatism in my heel,..I'm groggy on my pins. **1888** *Sportsman* 28 Nov. (Farmer), Thompson, who had been growing groggy,.. began to force the fighting. **1894** *Pall Mall Mag.* Feb. 615 It [*sc.* a lay figure] was getting groggy at the joints.

‖**grognard** (grɔnjar). [Fr., lit. 'grumbler'. 'Nom donné aux soldats de la vieille garde sous le premier empire, et, en général, à un vieux soldat, le plus souvent en un sens favorable' (Littré).] A soldier of Napoleon's Old Guard. Also *transf.*, a veteran soldier.
1912 J. H. ROSE *Personality of Napoleon* iii. 68 He [*sc.* Napoleon] loved to talk with his Old Guard, asking them how long and where they had served... He it was who nicknamed them *les grognards*. **1945** G. B. SHAW *Geneva* (1946) 19 They did not receive him as the grognards of the Bourbon army received Napoleon on his return from Elba. **1959** *Spectator* 21 Aug. 218/3 No wonder some of the *grognards* of the Soviet old guard mumble that the Czechs have always had it too easy.

grogram ('grɒgrəm). Forms: 6–7 grogeram, -an(e, grogran(e, grograin(e, -ayn(e, grow-graine, 7–8 grogrein(e, -eyn, (7 grogane, grogaram, -arom, -eraine, -erin, -eron, -oram, -oran, grograme, -gran(t, -gren, -grum), 6– grogram. [ad. F. *gros grain* large or coarse grain.]
1. A coarse fabric of silk, of mohair and wool, or of these mixed with silk; often stiffened with gum. Cf. GROSGRAIN.
1562 *Wills & Inv. N.C.* (Surtees 1835) 200 Thre gounes one of grograyn, gardid wᵗ velvet. **c 1570** *Pride & Lowl.* (1841) 19 His upper stockes of sylken grogerane. **1593** DONNE *Sat.* IV. 86 Your only wearing is your Grogaram. **1598** B. JONSON *Ev. Man in Hum.* II. i, He shall ha' the grogran's, at the rate I told him. **1630** BRATHWAIT *Eng. Gentlem.* (1641) 125 Stampe and fret like gumm'd grogran. **1674** JEAKE *Arith.* (1696) 65, 1 Piece of Moccadoes and Lile Grograins. **1712** ADDISON *Spect.* No. 530 ¶4 [She] did more Execution upon me in Grogram, than the greatest Beauty.. had ever done in Brocade. **1752** CARTE *Hist. Eng.* III. 481 Instructing the English in the art of making sayes grogreins and other light stuffs. **1757** W. THOMPSON *Milkmaid* 34 The charmful Village-Maid, With Innocence and Grogram blest. **1823** SCOTT *Peveril* xi, But then there is..her Aunt, that wears eternal black grogram for that unlucky Colonel Christian.
transf. **1633** P. FLETCHER *Purple Isl.* VI. lxix, The Lily high her silver Grogram reares.
2. A garment made of grogram.
1633 FORD *Love's Sacr.* I. ii, Go, thou art as fretting as an old grogrum. **1767** *Char.* in *Ann. Reg.* 53/2 The doctor.. appeared in a greasy black grogram which he called his scholar's coat. **1807–8** W. IRVING *Salmag.* (1824) 32 No longer our fair ones their grograms display. **1867** OUIDA *C. Castlemaine* (1879) 9 Madam from the vicarage, in her grogram.
3. *attrib.*, as ***grogram apron, camlet, cassock-case, cloak, coat, doublet, gown, petticoat, silk, yarn.***
1810 *Splendid Follies* II. 4 Catching his spurs in her *grogram apron. **1582** *Rates Custom-ho.* C iv, *Grogram Chamlets the peece. **a 1658** CLEVELAND *Wks.* (1687) 290 A wretched Serge, or *grogane Cassock case. **1614** C. BROOKE *Will* in *Poems* (Grosart) 21 Unto my nephewe..I give my silk *Grograine cloake. **1861** READE *Cloister & H.* I. 284 A little grogram cloak over her shoulders. **1811** *Sporting Mag.* XXXVII. 131 The Admiral [Vernon] at that time wore a *grogram coat. **1628** BOYLE in *Lismore Papers* (1886) II. 263, I gaue..Wᵐ New..a *grogran dublet. **1605** CHAPMAN, etc. *Eastward Hoe* I. A 4, To line a *Grogarom gowne cleane thorough with veluet. **1859** GEO. ELIOT *A. Bede* 238 An excellent grogram gown. **1649** *Bury Wills* (Camden) 220 My watered grogerin gowne and watered *grogerin petticoate. **1582** *Rates Custom-ho.* C iv, *Grograin silk the yarde. **1638** L. ROBERTS *Map Commerce* I. 123 *Grograme yarne. **1662** *Stat. Irel.* (1765) II. 418 Grograin yarn, the small pound.. 2*s.* 6*d.* **1703** *Lond. Gaz.* No. 3931/3 Some Raw Silk and Grogram Yarn.

groiff, obs. Sc. form of GRUFF.

groigne, variant of GROIN *v.*¹ *Obs.*

groin (grɔın), *sb.*¹ *Obs.* exc. *dial.* Forms: α. 4–9 groyn(e, 6–7 groine, 6, 9 groon, (4 gryn, 5 grone, growne, grune, gruyn, 9 gruin), 4– groin. β. 5 gron(e)y. See also GRUNYIE. [ad. OF. *groign* (F. *groin*), Burgundian *groigno*, Pr. *groing, grong*, fem. *groingna*, It. *grugno*, OPg. *gruin*:—popular L. **grunnium*, f. L. *grunnīre* to grunt like a swine.]
†**1.** A grunting, grumble. *Obs.*
c 1374 CHAUCER *Troylus* I. 349 Yet yf she for other enchesoun, Be wrooth, þen shalt þow han a groyn a-noon. **c 1440** *Promp. Parv.* 214/1 Grony, magry. [*Ibid.* 319/2 Magry, vn-thanke, *vituperium, reprobacio.*]
2. The snout, *esp.* of a swine.
13.. *Sir Beues* 815 (MS. A) A spanne of þe groin be-forn Wiþ is swerd he haþ of schoren. **c 1386** CHAUCER *Pars. T.* ¶82 He..lykneth a fair womman, that is a fool of hire body, lyk to a ryng of gold that were in the groyn of a soughe. **c 1460** *Towneley Myst.* xii. 229, I haue here in my mayll.. two swyne gronys. **c 1475** *Partenay* 5875 The beres gret groin tho smote he vppon. **c 1490** *Promp. Parv.* 214/1 (MSS. K. & H.) Grony, *MS. S.* groney, *Rostrum porcinum*. **1583** GOLDING *Calvin on Deut.* cx. 676 The partie..shall but wring his mouth or rather his Groyne and steppe forth with a shamelesse foreheade to aske who accuseth him. **1600** THYNNE *Emblems* xxiii. 5 With wrootinge groyne, with [*sic*; *read* the] feirce and warlike bore Turnes vp and betters that bad lande before. **1703** THORESBY *Let. to Ray* (E.D.S.), *Groyn*, the groyn of a swine, the snout. **1869** *Lonsdale Gloss.*, *Groon*, the snout of a pig. **1882** *Lanc. Gloss.*, *Groyn*, a swine's snout.
†**b.** *contemptuously.* A face. *Obs.*
c 1460 *Towneley Myst.* xii. 432 Fayr fall thi growne. *Ibid.* xvi. 382 Haue at the, say I! take the ther a foyn!..haue at thi groyn An othere.
†**3.** *Naut.* ***the groin*** (***of Spain***) [an etymological perversion of the Spanish name *Coruña*]: a sailor's name for Corunna, a seaport on the N.W. of Spain. *Obs.*
1367 *Pol. Poems* (Rolls) I. 112 Vocatur Le Groyne; est in mare ut rostrum porci, ubi intraverunt terram. **c 1485** *Digby Myst.* (1882) I. 478 Here ys..wyn of gyldyr and of galles, þat made at þe groine, wyn of wyan and vernage, I seye also. **1489** *Barbour's Bruce* xx. 324 (Pinkerton 1790) III. 167 Betwix Cornwaill and Bretaynné He sailyt; and left the grune [*ed. Jamieson* grunye; *MS. Camb.* grund] off Spainye On northhalf hym. **1589** *Pappe w. Hatchet* B ij b, Did your Father die at the Groyne? **a 1700** B. E. *Dict. Cant. Crew*, *Groyne*, corruptly by the Tarrs for Coronna, a Seaport of Galicia. **1719** DE FOE *Crusoe* I. xix. (1840) 345 Pressed me earnestly not to go by sea, but either to go by land to the Groyne [etc.].

groin (grɔın), *sb.*² Forms: 4–6 grynd(e, (5 *erron.* ground, 6 grinde); 5–7 grine, gryne, groine, groyn(e, (5 grune), 6– groin. [orig. *grynde, grinde* of uncertain origin; connexion with GRAIN *sb.*² is excluded by the early form. The form *grine* appears in 1530, but did not finally displace *grind* until the last quarter of the 16th c., when it underwent corruption into *groin*, prob. through phonetic association with prec.
Prof. Skeat suggests that the original sense may have been a channel or depression (cf. 2), and that the word may be identical with OE. *grynde*, recorded only in the sense of 'abyss', but etymologically capable of meaning 'depression', 'valley' (:—prehist. **grundjo-*, f. **grundu-* GROUND; cf. G. *grund*, used dial. for 'valley'; also GRINDLE¹, GRINDLET).]
1. a. The fold or depression on either side of the body between the abdomen and the upper thigh. (In quot. 1541 *pl.* the inguinal glands.)
c 1400 *Lanfranc's Cirurg.* 41 If þe prickynge be in þe foot, anoynte þe grynde wiþ hoot comoun oile. *Ibid.* 226 Of an enpostym þat comeþ in iguine id est þe gryndis. **14..** *Voc.* in Wr.-Wülcker 589/39 *Inguen*, the grynde. **1483** CAXTON *Gold. Leg.* 330/2 He was..seke in his grynde of a pestilence botche. **c 1532** DU WES *Introd. Fr.* in *Palsgr.* 903 The grynes, *les aines*. **1541** COPLAND *Guydon's Quest. Chirurg.* K ij, What are the gryndes?.. They are the clensynge places of the lyuer, & are of Glandynous flesshe ordeyned to the bought of the thyghes. **1576** BAKER *Jewell of Health* 64 b, The water druncke twyse a daye..putteth away..harde swellings in the grynde. **1592** SHAKS. *Ven. & Ad.* clxxxv, The loving swine Sheathed, unawares, the tusk in his soft

groin. 1611 Cotgr., *Aines*, the grine, or groyne of man or woman. 1657 W. Coles *Adam in Eden* cxii. 160 The leaves ..laid warm on any botch happening in the Groin or share, doth dissolve and heal them. 1691 Wood *Ath. Oxon.* II. 49 The Keeper thrust his sword into his groyn. 1735 Somerville *Chase* III. 333 The ..angry Beast..at one sidelong Glance Rips up his Groin. 1804 Abernethy *Surg. Obs.* 53 A gland enlarged in the left groin. 1865 Dickens *Let.* 13 Nov., The man returned the compliment by kicking him in the groin. 1872 Baker *Nile Tribut.* v. 66 Two glands are situated in the groin.

†**b.** *fig.* Regarded as the seat of lust. *Obs.*

1625 B. Jonson *Staple of News* III. ii, Who can endure to see The fury of mens gullets, and their groines? 1636 —— *Discov., Impostura* Wks. (1640) 87 They set the signe of the Crosse over their outer doores, and sacrifice to their gut and their groyne in their inner Closets.

†**2.** A deep trench, or excavation. *Obs.*

1587 Holinshed *Chron.* (1808) IV. 851 He [Ferdinando Poins] vndertooke to make certeine groins or nocks, which at the hauens mouth should cause such a depth, as thereby the whole harborough should lie drie at a low water. 1587 Fleming *Contn. Holinshed* III. 545/1 There was one Juline appointed to attend vpon Poins his groins.

3. *Arch.* The edge formed by the intersection of two vaults. Also, the rib or fillet of stone or wood with which this is usually covered.

1725 Halfpenny *Art Sound Build.* 15 To find the Angle, or Mitre-Arch of a regular Groin. 1790 Pennant *London* 87 On the north outside, beyond the windows, are many marks of recesses, groins, arms, on the remains of some other room. 1812–16 J. Smith *Panorama Sci. & Art* I. 155 The shafts in front running up without stop to the roof, and from their capitals springing the groins. 1825 J. Nicholson *Operat. Mechanic* 568 In framing centres for groins, the boarding which forms the interior surface is supported by transverse ribs of timber. 1849 Freeman *Archit.* 246 In the earliest examples the groins are without ribs. 1860 Emerson *Cond. Life, Illusions* Wks. (Bohn) II. 441 The vaults and groins of the sparry cathedrals. 1861 Beresf. Hope *Eng. Cathedr. 19th C.* vi. 226 There [York Minster]..the whole space of the nave and choir was spanned with groins of wood.

transf. 1855 Holden *Hum. Osteol.* (1878) 135 Notice how the interior of the dome is strengthened by 'ribs' or 'groins' of bone, which run in the line of the principal sinuses.

4. A ring. *slang.*

1931 W. F. Brown in *Police Jrnl.* IV. 500 *Henry.* 'Did he get any sparkle?' *George.* 'Yes, a couple of kettles,..a lovely groin and a prop.' 1936 J. Curtis *Gilt Kid* v. 57 There was one [woman] with three groins on her fingers.

5. *attrib.* and *Comb.*, as (sense 1) ***groin gland***; (sense 3) ***groin-rib***; **groin-point, -vault** (see quots.).

1897 *Allbutt's Syst. Med.* II. 1074 The endemic forms of a group of diseases—including Chyluria, varicose *groin glands. 185. *Dict. Archit.*, **Groin point*, the name given by bricklayers to the arris or line of intersection of cross arches of vaulting executed in brickwork. 1823 P. Nicholson *Pract. Builder* 113 To find the diagonal or *groin-rib of a Vault. 1879 Sir G. Scott *Lect. Archit.* I. ii. 59 *Groin-ribs* —those narrow arches erected under the lines of the intersection of the vaults. 1825 J. Nicholson *Operat. Mechanic* 540 A **Groin vault*, is a complex vault, formed by the intersection of two solids, whose surfaces coincide with the intrados of the arches, and are not confined to the same heights.

†**groin**, *v.*[1] *Obs.* Forms: 4 groigne, 4–5 gronyn, 4–6 groine, 4–7 groyne, 5–6 grone, (6 groone), 5, 7 growne, 6, 9 groyn. [ad. OF. *grogni-r* (also with change of conjugation *grogner*, as in mod.Fr.) = Pr. *gronhir*, *gronir*, It. *grugnire* (also altered *grugnare*):—L. *grunnīre*.]

1. *intr.* Of animals: To grunt; to growl.

13.. *Gaw. & Gr. Knt.* 1442 For he watz b[este &] bor alþer grattest, [And eue]re quen he gronyed, þenne greued mony. *a* 1450 *Knt. de la Tour* (1868) 126 Of thaire nature thei growne and berke euermore, but gentille greyhoundes do not so. 1530 Palsgr. 917 A hogge groneth, *ung pourceau grongne.* *a* 1541 Wyatt *How to use the court* in *Tottel's Misc.* (Arb.) 91 For swine so groines In stye. 1596 Spenser *F.Q.* VI. xii. 27 Some were of dogs, that barked day and night,.. And some of beares, that groynd continually.

b. *esp.* of the buck: To utter its peculiar cry at rutting time. (Cf. groan *v.* 2.)

1496 *Bk. St. Albans, Hunting* d ij b, An harte belowyth and a bucke groynyth [1486 gronys] I fynde. 1576 Turberv. *Venerie* 238 A Bucke groyneth. 1610 Guillim *Heraldry* III. xiv. (1660) 166 A Buck growneth. 1688 R. Holme *Armoury* II. 134/1 A Buck when he sendeth forth his Cry, Groyneth or Growneth. 1711 Puckle *Club* (1817) 90 And [he] told us, that an hart bellows, a buck groyns.

2. *transf.* Of persons: To grumble, murmur.

a 1300 *Cursor M.* 13590 Quen þai had striued þam emel And groigned, cuth na resun find. *c* 1400 *Rom. Rose* 7049 Whether so that he loure or groine. *c* 1490 *Promp. Parv.* 214/1 (MS. K.) Gronyn, or grochyn,..*murmuro.* 1537 *St. Papers Hen. VIII*, I. 555 To see who wold groyne at their execution. 1583 Golding *Calvin on Deut.* cxxxvi. 837 It is not ynough for a man to keepe his wyfe in his house..and in the meane time hee groyne at hir, he spurne hir, hee beateth hir.

groin (grɔɪn), *v.*[2] *Arch.* [f. groin *sb.*[2]]

1. *trans.* To form into or furnish with groins; to build with groins.

1812–16 J. Smith *Panorama Sci. & Art* I. 150 The roof is often most delicately groined. 1848 Lowell *Launfal* Poet. Wks. 1890 I. 298 All night by the white stars' frosty gleams He groined his arches and matched his beams. 1869 *Daily News* 27 Apr., The roof..is groined throughout in pitch pine of unusually beautiful quality. 1879 Sir G. Scott *Lect. Archit* I. 57 The difficulty was how to groin these oblong bays.

2. *intr.* Of an arch, etc.: To spring as a groin.

1805 W. Close *West's Antiq. Furness* vi. 70 The vaulted roof that groined from those pillars. *Ibid.* 71 It is a single ribbed arch that groins from the wall.

groin: see groyne *sb.* and *v.*

groined (grɔɪnd), *ppl. a. Arch.* [f. groin *sb.*[2] and *v.*[2] + -ed.] Built or furnished with groins.

[1715: see grinded *ppl. a.*[1]] 1789 P. Smyth tr. *Aldrich's Archit.* 59 The middle sized rooms are of equal height with the others, with groined vaults. 1823 Rutter *Fonthill* 9 The ceiling is vaulted, and divided into two groined compartments. 1858 Hawthorne *Fr. & It. Jrnls.* II. 76 Two great pointed arches crossing one another in a groined roof.

†**groiner.** *Obs.*[−1] [f. groin *v.*[1] + -er[1].] A grumbler; a murmurer.

1382 Wyclif *Prov.* xxvi. 20 The groynere [L. *susurrone*] withdrawen, striues togidere resten.

groinery (ˈgrɔɪnərɪ). [f. groin *sb.*[2] + -ery.] Groins or groined work.

1880 L. Wallace *Ben-Hur* 225 If he looked up, it was to see the sky palely blue through the groinery of countless date-bearers, very patriarchs of their kind.

†**groining,** *vbl. sb.*[1] *Obs.* [f. groin *v.*[1] + -ing[1].] The action of groin *v.*[1] **a.** Grunting. **b.** Murmuring; muttering, discontent.

a. *c* 1440 *Promp. Parv.* 214/2 Groynynge of swyne, *grunnitus.* *a* 1529 Skelton *Agst. Garnesche* Wks. 1843 I. 118 Ȝour grontynge, your groinynge lyke a swyne.

b. *c* 1386 Chaucer *Knt.'s T.* 1602 The groynynge, and the pryuee empoysonyng. *c* 1440 *Promp. Parv.* 214/2 Gronyynge, or grutchynge, *murmur.* 1513 *Bk. Keruynge* in *Babees Bk.* 156 Than must ye reyse the vpper parte of yᵉ towell, & laye it with-out ony groynynge. 1591 R. Turnbull *Expos. Jas.* 202 When without grudging or groyning: muttering or murmuring: wee can pray as our Saviour teacheth.

groining (ˈgrɔɪnɪŋ), *vbl. sb.*[2] [f. groin *v.*[2] + -ing[1].] The action of groin *v.*[2] (sense 2); *concr.* the result of this, groined work, a groin or arrangement of groins.

a 1653 I. Jones in Leoni *Palladio's Archit.* (1742) I. 104 These Arches..are commonly called Groinings. 1845 Todd & Bowman *Phys. Anat.* I. 139 At this last situation two ribs, analogous to groinings in architecture, intersect each other. 1870 F. R. Wilson *Ch. Lindisf.* 119 The chancel has the original Norman groining.

†**groining,** *ppl. a. Obs.* [f. groin *v.*[1] + -ing[1].] **a.** That grunts or growls. **b.** That murmurs or grumbles. Hence ˈ**groiningly** *adv.*

1523 Skelton *Garl. Laurel* 1376 The Gruntyng and the groynninge of the gronnyng swyne. 1557–8 Phaer *Æneid* vii. S ij b, Both brystlyd groyning bores, & beares at mangers yelling yawle. *a* 1656 Bp. Hall *Rem. Wks.* (1660) 146 If we be ready..groyningly to repine at His correction, it showes we do not acknowledge him for our Father.

groise (grɔɪz). *Public School slang.* Also groize. [Perh. altered form of grease *sb.* 5 b.] **a.** A hard worker, a swot; one who curries favour. **b.** Hard work. So **groise** *v. intr.*, to work hard, to swot; to curry favour; ˈ**groiser,** ˈ**groising** *vbl. sb.*

1913 A. Lunn *Harrovians* ii. 37 'Are you a scholar?'.. 'Yes, in history.' 'Oh, then you'll probably be in our form,' said Cadby. 'I suppose you're a horrid little groise?' *Ibid.* 306 We all have to groise a lot harder than we used. *Ibid.* 307 The whole time-table's altered... They try and make groise more amusing. You can choose your own line of sweat much more. *Ibid.* 311 'What's the old place coming to?' 'It's in a very bad way, I'm afraid. Why, groising is in a fair way to becoming fashionable.' 'Oh rot! I say, rot! You'll be telling me next that a man's keener on getting some bally scholarship than on getting his fez.' 1936 'I. Hay' *Housemaster* 115 The School looked forward to it [*sc.* the Regatta] with strained anticipation from the first day of term,—oarsmen, cricketers, and groisers alike. 1940 M. Marples *Public School Slang* 130 *Groise*, to curry favour (Cheltenham, 1928+). *Ibid. Groize* (Uppingham, 1930+), one who is over-efficient—e.g. a corps groize is one who tries to gain favour by his efficiency in the O.T.C.

groiss, obs. form of gross.

groit, Sc. form of groat.

grok (grɒk), *v. U.S. slang.* Also **grock.** [Arbitrary formation by Heinlein (see quot. 1961).] **a.** *trans.* (also with obj. clause) To understand intuitively or by empathy; to establish rapport with. **b.** *intr.* To empathize or communicate sympathetically (with); also, to experience enjoyment.

1961 R. Heinlein *Stranger in Strange Land* iii. 18 Smith had been aware of the doctors but had grokked that their intentions were benign. *Ibid.* xxiv. 250 Now that he knew himself to be self he was free to grok ever closer to his brothers. 1968 T. Wolfe *Electric Kool-Aid Acid Test* vi. 86 Instead they are all rapping and grokking over the sound it made..as if they had synched into a never-before-heard thing, a unique thing. 1968 *Playboy* June 80 He met her at an acid-rock ball and she grokked him, this ultracool miss loaded with experience and bereft of emotion. 1969 *New Yorker* 15 Mar. 35, I was thinking we ought to get together somewhere, Mr. Zzyzbyzynsky, and grok about our problems. 1975 D. Lodge *Changing Places* iv. 137 Nestling earth couple would like to find water brothers to grock with in peace. 1984 *InfoWorld* 21 May 32 There isn't any software! Only different internal states of hardware. It's all hardware! It's a shame programmers don't grok that better.

Grolier (grolje, ˈgrəʊlɪə(r)). Name of a famous French book-collector, Jean *Grolier* de Servin, Vicomte d'Aiguisy (1479–1565), used *attrib.* to designate the interlacing geometrical designs which adorn the bindings of his books. Also *absol.*, a Grolier binding. So **Grolier Club** (see quot. 1960). Hence **Grolieˈresque** *a.* (also *absol.*).

1827 *Catal. Libr. T. Williams* 3 Extremely rare, beautiful copies in Grolier binding, red morocco. *Ibid.* 118 Green morocco, with insides most richly tooled in the Grolier style. 1880 J. W. Zaehnsdorf *Art of Bookbinding* p. xix, A centre block of Grolier. *Ibid.* xx, The Grolier bindings were bold. 1885 W. J. E. Crane *Bookbinding for Amateurs* xxi. 173 The pattern generally used was that of interlaced strapwork... Books so bound are often called 'Groliers'. *Ibid.* 175 Fig. 150 shows a side of an ancient book in the Grolier style. 1889 B. Quaritch *Coll. Facsim. Bookbinding* 25 The design is smaller in scale than that of the true Grolieresque. 1893 *Q. Rev.* July 196 The geometrical strapwork patterns known as Grolieresque were introduced into England in the time of Edward VI. *Ibid.* 199 Another small volume in a Grolier binding. 1896 B. Matthews *Book Bindings* v. i. 294 The Grolier Club is a gathering of those who love books for their external beauty. 1928 E. P. Goldschmidt *Gothic Bookbindings* I. 102 The earliest Groliers. 1936 *Times Lit. Suppl.* 13 June 493 The restrained geometric Grolieresque style was elaborated into the richer and more exuberant design which is described by the phrase *à la fanfare.* 1952 J. W. Carter *ABC for Bk. Collectors* 94 The Grolier Club of New York..has published many valuable exhibition catalogues and other bibliographical reference books. 1960 G. A. Glaister *Gloss. Bk.* 161/2 *Grolier Club*, a New York club for bibliophiles, founded in 1884. 1968 *Times Lit. Suppl.* 1 Feb. 116/2 The Grolier Club's *Gazette*, which has of late carried useful handlists of minor and major exhibitions. 1969 *Bodl. Libr. Rec.* VIII. 141 One (lot 18) is described as a 'Grolier binding'; while a number of others are described as 'Grolier style'.

†**groll.** *Obs.* Also grol. [a. Du. *grol* 'inconditus sermocinator, auctor sordidus, proletarius' (Kilian).] A foolish or superficial person; a gossip, a smatterer. (App. peculiar to Bastwick.)

1637 Bastwick *Litany* I. 8 See the parishioners be rich and plump as the grols said. *Ibid.* III. 21, I could be as voluminous as any man, and yet never take quotations at the second hand, as many grolls in this age doe.

Hence †ˈ**grollery** [Du. *grollerije*], folly. †ˈ**grollish** *a.*, foolish, senseless, superficial.

1637 Bastwick *Litany* I. 6 One can scarce keepe from laughter, to see the grollery of it. *Ibid.* 17 Such a multitude of trumperyes and grollish ceremonyes are brought in by the Prelats. *Ibid.* II. 26 Who had more policy in the paring of his nayles, then all the Grollish Polititians that are now extant. *Ibid.* III. 14, I am pretily well acquaynted with all their grolleries.

†**grolling,** *vbl. sb. Obs. rare*[−1]. [Echoic; cf. *groule*, gurl.] ? Rumbling.

1398 Trevisa *Barth. de P.R.* VI. xxi, Yf þe mete be to moche it..streccheþ þe stomak and bloweþ it and bredeþ grollynge and gnawynge in þe wombe.

grom, -andise, obs. ff. groom, gormandize.

gromaly, obs. form of gromwell.

gromatic (grəʊˈmætɪk), *a.* and *sb.* [ad. L. *grōmătic-us*, *grūm-*, f. *grōma*, *grūma* surveyor's measuring-rod.]

A. *adj.* Pertaining to land-surveying.

1873 Wagner tr. *Teuffel's Hist. Roman Lit.* II. 149 From the gromatic work [of Frontinus] we possess only explanatory excerpts. *Ibid.* 203 The gromatic writer Siculus Flaccus.

B. *sb.* **a.** *pl.* The art of land-surveying or castrametation. **b.** A writer on gromatics.

[1867 Burton *Hist. Scot.* I. ii. 79 A certain Hyginus, who calls himself a gromaticus or land-surveyor.] 1873 Wagner tr. *Teuffel's Hist. Roman Lit.* II. 147 We possess excerpts from a work on gromatics. *Ibid.* 204 Balbus is repeatedly quoted by the later gromatics.

†**groˈmatical,** *a. Obs.* [Formed as prec. + -al[1].] = prec. adj.

1610 Holland *Camden's Brit.* I. 255 Boetius and the Gromaticall Writers have made mention of such mounts. 1658 W. Burton *Comm. Antoninus' Itin.* 29 The Gromaticall Authors. 1718 Hearne *Reliq.* (1857) I. 406 The accounts given of the ancient Grumæ or Gromæ in the Gromatical writers.

gromble, obs. form of grumble.

grome, obs. var. grame *sb.*; obs. f. groom *sb.*[1]

gromel(l, obs. form of gromwell.

gromercy, -ersy, -essye, -esty, rare obs. forms of gramercy.

gromet, -it: see grummet.

gromil, -ill, -ille, obs. ff. gromwell.

gromme, var. grumme *v. Obs.*, to grumble.

gromwell (ˈgrɒmwəl). Forms: 4 gromyl(e, gromylyoun, 5 gromylle, -ille, grumelle, -eyle, 5–6 gromaly, -ely, 5–9 gromel(l, 6 grommel(l, -all, gremile, grumle, 6–7 grummel(l, grumble, 7 gromwel, grumell, 7–9 gromil(l, 7– gromwell. [a. OF. *gromil* (13th c. in Hatz.-Darm.), *gremil* (16th c.), mod.F. *grémil*, of doubtful origin. The form *gromwel(l* is late and the *w* is app. due to analogy with *speedwell*. See also GRAYMILL.

As to the possible origin of F. *gromil, grémil*, several suggestions have been made. Its derivation from *grānum milii* is impossible on account of the early form *gromil*, but the 15th c. variants *grinnil, grenil* perhaps exhibit some popular etymologizing approximation to *grain*. Hatz.-Darm. suggest that the second part is the word *mil* 'millet', while the first is of indeterminate origin.]

The common name for any of the plants of the genus *Lithospermum* (N.O. *Boraginaceæ*), characterized by hard stony seeds, which were formerly much used in medicine.

a **1310** in Wright *Lyric P.* v. 27 Ase gromyl in grene grene is the grone, Ase quibibe and comyn cud is in crone. **13..** *E.E. Allit. P.* A. 43 Gilofre, gyngure & gromylyoun. *a* **1387** *Sinon. Barthol.* (Anecd. Oxon.) 23 *Granum solis*, i. milium solis, i. gromil. *c* **1425** *Voc.* in Wr.-Wülcker 645/38 *Hec gensta*, gromylle. *c* **1450** *ME. Med. Bk.* (Heinrich) 75 *Ad lapidem* Take gromylle [*v.r.* gromel seed] & percil. **1589** COGAN *Haven Health* xxv. (1636) 46 Grummell is..not used in meats but in medicine, especially the seeds. **1621** BURTON *Anat. Mel.* II. iv. I. iii. (1651) 368 For the kidnies, grumell, parsly. **1741** *Compl. Fam.-Piece* I. iv. 243 Take Seeds of Smallage, Treacle Mustard, Gromwell and Parsley. **1851** S. JUDD *Margaret* I. xvi. 135 Yellow bent spikes of the gromwell. **1888** *Daily News* 14 June 5/1 The gromwell adds a touch of imperial purple.

b. Preceded by a defining word forming the designation of a particular species. **common gromwell**, *Lithospermum officinale*. **corn gromwell**, *L. arvense*, Bastard Alkanet. **purple** (or **creeping**) **gromwell**, *L. purpureo-cæruleum*. **c.** Applied also to the genus *Onosmodium* (**false gromwell**).

1578 LYTE *Dodoens* II. ciii. 289 The Gromell is of two sortes, one of the garden, the other wilde: and the garden Gromell also is of two sortes, great and small. **1597** GERARDE *Herbal* II. clxxx. §1. 486 The great Gromell hath long slender and hairie stalkes. **1657** W. COLES *Adam in Eden* ccxxv. 354 Great upright Gromel..is that which usually groweth in Gardens. **1804** *Med. Jrnl.* XII. 124 Bastard gromill, salern, corn gromwell, painting root, bastard Alkanet. **1837** MACGILLIVRAY *Withering's Brit. Plants* (ed. 4) 111 *L[ithospermum] officinale*. Common Gromwell. Graymill..*L. arvense*. Corn Gromwell..*L. purpuro-cæruleum*. Creeping or Purple Gromwell. **1894** *Times* 21 May 12/1 The tall-growing corn gromwell, or bastard alkanet.

d. *attrib.*, as *gromwell seed*; † **gromwell-gainer**, a 'skinflint', miser.

1588 J. HARVEY *Discoursive Probl. conc. Proph.* 70 Hath not euery vocation..yeelded some such counterprophets, and pennyfathers, very *gromelgainers? *c* **1400** tr. *Secreta Secret., Gov. Lordsh.* (E.E.T.S.) 77 Onoþer of Mede affermyd mekyl profyt to vse greynes melyens fastyng, þat er *Gromell sedes. *c* **1440** *Promp. Parv.* 213/2 Gromaly, herbe (gromely sede), *milium solis*. **1544** PHAER *Regim. Lyfe* (1553) B j b, A bagge of gromell sedes. **1553** *Respublica* I. i. 24 But to rake grumle sede Avaryce ys a Lone. **1573** TUSSER *Husb.* xlv. (1878) 97 Gromel seed, for the stone. **1694** E. FLOYD in *Phil. Trans.* XVIII. 46 Of the form and bigness of Gromwel-seeds.

grond, obs. pa. t. of GRIND *v.*[1]

grond(e, grondage, obs. ff. GROUND, -AGE.

gronddar, obs. form of GROUNDER.

gronden, -ine, -yn, obs. pa. pples. of GRIND *v.*

grondeswyle, obs. form of GROUNDSEL *sb.*[1]

grondsil, obs. form of GROUNDSEL *sb.*[2]

grone, var. GRANE, GROIN *v.*[1] *Obs.*; obs. f. GROAN.

grone, groney, obs. ff. GROIN *sb.*[1] and *v.*[1]

gronie, obs. form of GROAN *v.*

gronnard, gronne, obs. ff. GURNARD, GROAN.

gronsel, obs. form of GROUNDSEL *sb.*[2]

gront(e: see GRIND *v.*[1], GRUNT.

grony, obs. form of GROIN *sb.*[1], GROAN *v.*

groo, obs. form of GROW.

groof, grufe (gru:f), *sb.* and *adv. Obs.* exc. *Sc.* Forms: 4–5 gruf(f, 5–8 grouf(e, 8–9 groof, 5 gruffe, grouff(e, groffe, 5, 7 growffe, 6 growf(e, 6, 9 grufe; also with prefixed prep. 5 ogrufe, 7 a-groufe, agruif, 8 a grouf. [a. ON. *grúfa*, in phr. *á grúfu* (in sense 1) = Sw. dial. *å gruve*; the occurrence of *f* instead of the normal *v* is unexplained. Cf. GROVELING.]

1. In phr. *on grufe* (rarely *on the grufe*), later *agrufe, a-gruif*: face downwards, in a prone position, grovelling. *Sc.* and *north.*

c **1375** *Sc. Troy-bk.* II. 786 He ley before þe gret altere One gruff. ? *a* **1400** *Morte Arth.* 3850 Than Gawayne gyrde to þe gome, and one þe groffe fallis. *Ibid.* 3869 Qwat gome was he ..that es one growffe fallyne? *c* **1470** HENRY *Wallace* XI. 574 In angwyss greiff, on grouff so turned he. **1483** *Cath. Angl.* 259/1 Ogrufe, *supinvs*. **1500–20** DUNBAR *Poems* xi. 13 Ly all on grufe, befoir that hich grand Roy. **1513** DOUGLAS *Æneis* XI. iv. 24 He ruschis..And fell on grouf abuf deid Pallas beyr. **1535** STEWART *Cron. Scot.* 33258 Sum on groufe la granand on the grene. **1637–50** ROW *Hist. Kirk* (Wodrow Soc.) 460 Then [he] lay a-groufe upon his face, begins to poure out his heart to God. **1638** H. ADAMSON *Muses' Threnodie* (1774) 112 And some lay swelting in the slykie sand: Agruif lay some, others with eyes to skyes. *a* **1651** CALDERWOOD *Hist. Kirk* (Wodrow Soc.) III. 574 During the time of which prayer the Erle of Morton lay on growffe upon his face. **1719** RAMSAY *Fam. Ep.* Answ. ii. 20 Swith to Castalius' fountain-brink, Dad down a grouf, and take a drink.

2. *on one's grufe*: = sense 1. *Sc.*

1788 E. PICKEN *Poems* 127 Doun on their groof lay five or sax. **1826** J. WILSON *Noct. Ambr.* Wks. 1855 I. 293 Layin mysel doun a' my length on my grufe and elbow. **1887** J. SERVICE *Life & Recoll. Dr. Duguid* 245 Streekit on my grufe below some rowan tree.

3. as *adv.* (or *predicative adj.*) On the face, on the belly; prone. (Cf. Sw. dial. *ligga gruve*.)

c **1374** CHAUCER *Troylus* IV. 884 (912) She on here armes two Fil gruf, and gan to wepe pitously. *c* **1400** *Rom. Rose* 2561 Now dounward groffe, and now upright. *c* **1430** LYDG. *Compl. Bl. Knt.* xxiv, He thus lay in lamentacioun Gruffe on the grounde. *c* **1460** *Emare* 656 She was aferde of the See, And layde her gruf upon a tre. **1567** TURBERV. *Ovid's Ep.* 70 b, With toren tresse and lying groufe Upon my face.

groof, obs. form of GROOVE, GRUFF.

groo-groo, gru-gru ('gru:gru:). Also 8 groe-groe, 9 gri-gri, grou-grou. [? Native name.]

1. In the West Indies and South America, a name for two species of palm, *Astrocaryum aculeatum* and *Acrocomia sclerocarpa*.

1796, 1852 [see sense 2]. **1871** KINGSLEY *At Last* (1892) vii. 138 This [*Desmoncus*] furnishes the gri-gri-canes. **1885** LADY BRASSEY *The Trades* 128 The Groo-Groo palms (*Acrocomia*) we also saw for the first time on this occasion. **1892** MAR. NORTH *Recoll. Happy Life* I. 92 The principal palms on the hills were..'Mackaw-foot' and the 'Grou-grou'.

2. Usually *groo-groo worm*: The grub of the coleopterous insect *Calandra palmarum*.

1796 STEDMAN *Surinam* II. xvi. 22 Another negro also brought me a regale of groe-groe, or cabbage-tree worms, as they are called in Surinam. **1826** H. N. COLERIDGE *West Indies* 215 *note*, I have some doubts also of the admissibility of the Groo-groo worms. **1852** *Zoologist* X. 3662 The groogroo worm—so called because it is found in a species of palm vulgarly called the groogroo. **1883** IM THURN *Among Indians Guiana* 266 Gru-gru worm.

groom (gru:m), *sb.*[1] Forms: 3–5 grom, 3–7 grome, 5–6 grume, 5–7 groome, (5 groyme, 6 growme, grum), 6– groom. [Of difficult etymology. According to the evidence of the quots. 'boy, male child' seems to be the orig. sense. The word might conceivably represent an OE. **grōm*, f. root **grō-* of GROW *v.* + Teut. suff. *-mo-*. But there is no trace of the word in any Teut. lang.; MDu. and mod.Du. have *grom* fry of fish, offspring, (jocularly) children; an unauthenticated sense 'boy, child' is given by the lexicographers Kilian ('puer'), Mellema ('enfant, marmouset') and Hexham ('stripling or groome'); but this does not correspond phonologically. The relation, if any, between the Eng. or the Du. word and OF. *gromet* GRUMMET, is unascertained; but in AF. and Anglo-L. documents *gromet* and its latinized form *grometus* appear to be used for *groom* in the senses 3–5 below.

There appears to be no evidence for an OF. *gromme*; the *grommes* quoted by Du Cange is prob. for *gromez* pl. of *gromet*. The alleged ON. *grómr* or *gromr* 'man' has no other authority than its occurrence in the list of poetical appellations applicable to yeomen, in the 14th c. expansion of *Snorra Edda* (ed. 1848, II. 496) where it may be from ME.]

† **1.** A man-child, boy. *Obs.*

a **1225** *Ancr. R.* 442 Hire meiden mei, þauh, techen sum lutel meiden, þet were dute of forto leornen among gromes. *c* **1300** *Havelok* 790 Ich am now no grom; Ich am wel waxen. *c* **1300** *Beket* 148 Tho he com he fond his sone a god goinge grom. *c* **1300** *Proverbs Hending* xxxii, He fareþ so doþ þe luþer grom þat men euer beteþ on wiþ one smerte ȝerde. *a* **1330** *Syr Degarre* 242 The holi man..fond the cradel in the stede, He tok up the clothes anon, And biheld the litel grom. *c* **1330** *Arth. & Merl.* 980 (Kölbing) Sche childed a selcouþe grome. **1387** TREVISA *Higden* (Rolls) I. 359 Kynde, i-hurt and defouled by wykkedness of lyuynge bryngeþ forþ ..foule gromes and euel i-schape. **1675** COTTON *Burlesque upon B.* 146 To bring him Plums and Mackaroons, Which welcome are to such small Grooms.

2. A man, male person; in the pastoral poetry of 16–17th c. freq. applied to shepherds (cf. HERD-GROOM). Sometimes *contemptuous* = 'fellow'. *Obs.* exc. *arch.*

c **1330** *Florice & Bl.* 1088 (Hausknecht), I..fond bi hire an naked grom..I þoȝte to habbe iqueld hem boþe. *c* **1340** *Cursor M.* 17609 (Laud) Loke we yern how me might do þat dowghty grome [*Cott.* gum, *Gött., Trin.* gome] Ioseph of Aramaty to vs to come. *c* **1420** *Chron. Vilod.* (Horstm.) 3986 Stondyng in an heyron þere, an horribull foull grome. *c* **1460** *Towneley Myst.* xxx. 128, I had leuer go to rome; yei thryse, on my fete Then forto grefe yonde grome. *c* **1470** HENRY *Wallace* VI. 728 Mony groyme thai maid full sar agast. *c* **1485** *Digby Myst.* (1882) III. 489, I-wys ȝe seye soth, ȝe grom of blysse. *c* **1510** *Lytell geste of Robyn hode* (W. de W.) I. 16 There was no ynch of his body But it was worthe a grome. **1549** *Compl. Scot.* vi. 67, I sau mony landuart grumis pas to the corne land to laubir there rustical occupatione. *c* **1560** A. SCOTT *Poems* (S.T.S.) v. 15 In May gois gentill wemen gymmer, In gardynnis grene thair grumis to glaid. **1588** SHAKS. *Tit. A.* IV. ii. 164 The fields are neere, and you are gallant Groomes. **1590** GREENE *Neuer too late* Wks. (Grosart) VIII. 204 She was weary of the groomes [a shepherd] importunate fooleries. **1595** SPENSER *Col. Clout* 12 A iolly groome was he, As ever piped on an oaten reed. **1603** DRAYTON *Odes* v. 2 Let no barbarous Groome How brave soe'r he bee, Attempt to enter. **1610** FLETCHER *Faithf. Shepherdess* I. ii, The prime of our young Grooms, even the top Of all our lusty Shepherds! **1625** LISLE *Du Bartas, Noe* 1 The mighty Groome that led his flocke and heard From home to follow God, and sacrifiz'd his sonne. **1632** HEYWOOD *2nd Pt. Iron Age* v. i. Wks. 1874 III. 421 Can you find teares for such an abiect Groome, That had not for an husband one to shed? **1815** WORDSW. *White Doe Rylst.* I. 11 And, up among the moorlands, see What sprinklings of blithe company! Of lasses and of shepherd grooms.

3. A man of inferior position; a serving-man; a man-servant; a male attendant. *Obs.* exc. *arch.*

1297 R. GLOUC. (Rolls) 2214 Me may yse a bondemannes sone..& some gromes squiers & suþþe kniȝtes some. **13..** *K. Alis.* 7282 Ageyn heom come bothe lord and grom, For to here what tidyng They broughte. **13..** *Guy Warw.* (A.) 234 þai sett hem to mete anon, Erl, baroun, sweyn, and grom. *c* **1310** in *Pol. Songs* (Camd. 1839) 238 Gobelyn made is gerner Of gromene mawe. *c* **1340** *Cursor M.* 11610 (Laud) The gromys [*Cott.* suanis] tho bygan to cry. *c* **1384** CHAUCER *H. Fame* I. 206 That he shulde drenche Lorde and lady, grome and wenche Of al the Troian nacion. **14..** *Voc.* in Wr.-Wülcker 585/48 *Garcio*, a grome. *c* **1450** *St. Cuthbert* (Surtees) 4559 Bathe grete man and grome. *c* **1450** *Merlin* 510 The gromes toke the palfreys and lepte up and rode into the foreste. *c* **1532** DU WES *Introd. Fr.* in *Palsgr.* 909 Gromes of the kechin, *uarletz de cuisin*. **1596** SHAKS. *Tam. Shr.* IV. i. 128 You logger-headed and vnpollisht groomes, What? no attendance? **1605** —— *Macb.* II. ii. 50 Goe carry them [daggers], and smeare The sleepie Groomes with blood. *a* **1632** T. TAYLOR *God's Judgem.* II. vii. (1642) 102 Maximinus, a Groome of base and sordid condition, borne of needy Parents. *a* **1654** SELDEN *Table-T.* (Arb.) 62 Then all the Company Dance, Lord and Groom, Lady and Kitchen-Maid, no distinction. **1697** DRYDEN *Virg. Georg.* IV. 627 Seated on a Rock, A Shepherd's Groom Surveys his Ev'ning Flocks returning Home. **1725** POPE *Odyss.* XX. 221 Two grooms assistant bore the victims bound. **1865** KINGSLEY *Herew.* xviii. 228 Your nephew's lands are parted between grooms and scullions.

fig. **1612** DONNE *Progr. Soul, 2nd Anniv.* 85 Thinke then, my soule, that death is but a Groome Which brings a Taper to the outward roome.

4. The specific designation of several officers of the English Royal Household, chiefly members of the Lord Chamberlain's department: with defining prepositional phrases, as ***Groom of the (Privy, Great) Chamber, G. of the Stole, G. in waiting***, etc.; also † ***Groom of the Beds***, † ***G. of the Crossbows***.

1464 *Mann. & Househ. Exp.* (Roxb.) 159 Item, the same tyme..my mastyre to the gromys off chambre ffore reshis, xvj. d. **1502** *Priv. Purse Exp. Eliz. of York* (1830) 42 John Browne grome of the beddes. *Ibid.* 54 Elys Hilton grome of the robys. **1530** *Privy Purse Exp. Hen. VIII* (1827) 70 Giles grome of the Crosbowes. **1589** PUTTENHAM *Eng. Poesie* I. viii. (Arb.) 32 King Henry the 8...for a few Psalmes of Dauid turned into English meetre by Sternhold, made him groome of his priuy chamber. **1657** WOOD *Life* Sept. (O.H.S.) I. 227 One of the gromes of the bed-chamber to K. Charles I. **1685** EVELYN *Mrs. Godolphin* (1847) 8 The late Countess of Guilford, Groome of the Stoole of the late Queens Mother. **1731** *Gentl. Mag.* I. 35 Edward Williams, Esq.; made Groom of his Majesty's removing Ward-robe. **1818** CRUISE *Digest* (ed. 2) III. 143 Lord Rochfort being Groom of the Stole to His Majesty. **1844** DISRAELI *Coningsby* IV. vi, A groom of the chambers indicates the way to him. **1868** *Pall Mall G.* 23 July 5 Sir Henry was a Groom-in-Waiting to Her Majesty.

5. A servant who attends to horses. (Until 17th c. only a contextual use of sense 3; now the current sense.)

[**1340** *Ayenb.* 210 [Huo] þet mest heþ hors mest him fayleþ gromes and stablen. **1553** BALE *Vocacyon* 26 b, An horse grome of his came into my court one daye. **1553** BRENDE *Q. Curtius* VIII. 161 b, Thei..receiued the horses of the gromes of the stable. **1593** SHAKS. *Rich. II*, v. v. 72, I was a poore Groome of thy Stable (King) When thou wer't King.] **1667** MILTON *P.L.* v. 356 Thir rich Retinue long Of Horses led, and Grooms besmeared with Gold. **1718** LADY M. W. MONTAGU *Let. to Lady Rich* 16 Mar., My grooms are Arabs; my footmen french. **1780** COWPER *Progr. Err.* 95 Like a slain deer, the tumbrel brings him home, Unmissed but by his dogs and by his groom. **1802** WORDSW. *Sonn. to Liberty*, '*O Friend I know not*', Mean handywork of crafts-man, cook, Or groom. **1827** LYTTON *Pelham* viii, His groom was walking about his favourite saddle-horse. **1859** *Art Taming Horses* ix. 150 It is a fact..that a man does not ride any better for dressing like a groom.

6. Short for BRIDEGROOM. (Rare except in context with *bride*.)

1604 SHAKS. *Oth.* II. iii. 180 Friends all..In Quarter, and in termes like Bride, and Groome, Deuesting them for Bed. **1611** —— *Cymb.* III. vii. 70 Were you a woman, youth, I should woo hard, but be your Groome in honesty. **1700** DRYDEN *Cymon & Iph.* 540 By this the brides are waked, their grooms are dressed; All Rhodes is summoned to the nuptial feast. **1789** ANNA SEWARD *Lett.* (1811) II. 270 The bride and groom were so good as to call upon me. **1841** BROWNING *Pippa* Introd. 50 What care bride and groom Save for their dear selves? **1850** TENNYSON *In Mem.* Concl. 83 Drinking health to bride and groom We wish them store of happy days.

7. *attrib.* and *Comb.*, appositive, as ***groom-boy***, ***-falconer***, ***-fellow***, ***-garneter***, ***-purveyor***; † **groom-grubber** (*-grobber*), an officer in the royal household (see quots.).

1863 KINGSLEY *Water-B.* ii. 66 Among the lot was a little *groom-boy, a very little groom indeed. **1826** HOR. SMITH *Tor Hill* (1838) II. 82 The young *groom-falconer was out this morning with his goss-hawk. **1823** SCOTT *Peveril* vi, There are two lackeys..besides the other *groom fellow. *a* **1483** *Liber Niger* in *Househ. Ord.* (1790) 70 One *groome garnetour, to receive, to kepe, and to delyver the wheete comyng from the countries. **1526** *Ibid.* 234 That he doe cause the *Groome-Grobber to looke dayly to drawing out the lees of the Wyne spent. **1601** *Ibid.* 284 Groom Grubber ..His office is to see that the vessailes which come into the seller bee tight and full. **1641** *Negotiations Wolsey* v. 11 Thirteene Pages, two yeomen Purveyours, and a *groome Purveyor.

Hence (chiefly *nonce-wds.*) **'groomess**, a female groom (of the stole). **'groomish** *a.*, characteristic of a groom, like that of a groom; hence **'groomishly** *adv.* **'groomless** *a.*, having no groom. **'groomlet**, **'groomling**, a diminutive groom. **'groomship**, the office or condition of a groom.

1624 T. SCOTT *2nd Pt. Vox Populi* 11, I sold moreouer, the place of *Groomesse of her highnesse Stoole, to six seuerall English Ladyes. **1854** R. S. SURTEES *Handley Cross* (1898) I. 140 To smoke cigars, pick up a steeple-chaser, wear *groomish clothes. **1836** *New Monthly Mag.* XLVIII. 458 The tiger, though more *groomishly attired, is not less scrupulously exact. **1870** DISRAELI *Lothair* xxviii, St. Aldegonde..was lounging about on a rough Scandinavian cob..listless and *groomless. **1824–8** T. HOOK *Say. & Doings* (1836) 165 (Hoppe) *Groomlet. **1834** BECKFORD *Italy* II. 13 We were obliged to be escorted by grooms and *groomlings with candles and lanterns. **1880** MISS BRADDON *Just as I am* II. 230 The groomling in charge slumbered placidly in the bottom of the carriage, with the reins in his hands. **1691** WOOD *Ath. Oxon.* (1721) II. 1036 Silas Titus.. In the Year following [1679] did, with the consent of his Majesty, resign his *Gromeship. **1882** W. H. GRENFELL in *Standard* 2 Nov. 5/5 If I had been honoured by the offer of a non-Parliamentary Groomship.

groom (gruːm), *sb.*[2] *dial.* Also grom. [? A western variant of CROME, CROMB.] A forked stick used by thatchers.

1790 GROSE *Prov. Gloss.*, *Grom* or *Groom*, a forked stick used by thatchers for carrying the parcels of straw called helms. *Wiltsh.* **1847–89** in HALLIWELL. **1874** T. HARDY *Far fr. Madding Crowd* xxxvii, He had stuck his rick-rod, groom, or poignard into the stack.

groom (gruːm), *v.* [f. GROOM *sb.*[1]]

1. *trans.* To tend as a groom; to curry, feed, and generally attend to (a horse); to 'fettle'.

1809 MALKIN *Gil Blas* I. x. ¶1 We were obliged to groom them ourselves. **1847** TENNYSON *Princ.* v. 446 She's yet a colt..strongly groom'd and straitly curb'd. **1856** FROUDE *Hist. Eng.* (1858) I. iv. 310 Ostlers quarrelled over such questions as they groomed their masters' horses. **1878** BOSW. SMITH *Carthage* 237 The Numidian horses..soon recovered their condition when they were groomed day by day with the old wine of Italian vintages.

absol. **1900** *Blackw. Mag.* Feb. 223/1 If he understands horses and can groom tolerably, he despises gardening.

2. a. *transf.* To tend or attend to carefully; to give a neat, tidy, or 'smart' appearance to. Also *absol.* in ***to groom up***.

1843 HALIBURTON *Attaché* I. ii. 26 Here was to clean and groom up agin' till all was in its right shape. **1859** *Sat. Rev.* VII. 363/2 The very chair you sit on has to be groomed. **1861** *Our Eng. Home* 86 He had to repair his own buskins, mend the tables, and groom my lady's chamber. **1879** J. BURROUGHS *Locusts & W. Honey* (1884) 125 Sometimes a few underclouds will be combed and groomed by the winds ..as if for a race.

b. *fig.* To prepare as a political candidate; in extended use, to prepare or coach for a career, a sporting contest, etc. orig. *U.S.*

1887 *Courier-Jrnl.* (Louisville, Ky.) 3 May 4/5, I learn that Sam Hill, of Hartford, is being groomed for the temporary chairmanship of the Convention. **1903** J. HAWTHORNE *Hawthorne & his Circle* 264 Grover Cleveland was being groomed for his first Presidential term. **1922** WODEHOUSE *Clicking of Cuthbert* v. 115 A man whom the committee were grooming for the amateur championship. **1955** *Times* 15 June 12/3 He did not agree that Professor Dent..had groomed him (the witness) to become president in order to keep out an 'Iron Curtain' delegate. **1957** *Listener* 19 Sept. 416/1 Committing the same mistake as Bismarck in not grooming his successor. **1959** *Times* 26 Aug. 4/1 Swetman has been groomed to succeed him [*sc.* Evans] in the Test matches. **1964** C. CHAPLIN *Autobiogr.* xxv. 435, I was surprised that Mr. Hoover should remember, because at the time he had seemed intensely preoccupied with grooming himself for the White House. **1968** *Globe & Mail* (Toronto) 3 Feb. 25/2 The Music Canada School in Montreal, which grooms pop musicians.

3. *pass.* To be made a bridegroom. *nonce-use.*

1824 BYRON *Juan* xv. xxxix, It is an even chance That bridegrooms, after they are fairly groom'd, May retrograde a little in the dance Of marriage.

Hence **groomed** *ppl. a.* (chiefly qualified by adv.), **'grooming** *vbl. sb.*

1813 *Sporting Mag.* XLII. 54 Feeding, grooming, trimming and managing of most descriptions of the horse. **1852** DICKENS *Bleak Ho.* xxviii, The Honourable Bob Staples daily repeats..his favourite original remark that she is the best-groomed woman in the whole stud. **1859** JEPHSON *Brittany* iii. 29 The grooming was wretched, and I could see some of the horses eating the straw. **1896** EDITH THOMPSON in *Monthly Packet* Xmas No. 80 Radetzoff, with his..neatly trimmed moustache, smart and well-groomed.

groom, obs. form of GRUM *a.*

groomer ('gruːmə(r)). [f. GROOM *v.* + -ER[1].] An instrument for the mechanical grooming of horses (see quot.).

1884 KNIGHT *Dict. Mech.* Suppl., *Groomer*, an application of the flexible or jointed revolving shaft to rotate a brush used in the grooming of horses.

groomet: see GRUMMET.

groom-porter. *Obs.* exc. *Hist.*

1. An officer of the English Royal Household, abolished under George III; his principal functions, at least from the 16th c., were to regulate all matters connected with gaming within the precincts of the court, to furnish cards and dice, etc., and to decide disputes arising at play.

1502 *Privy Purse Exp. Eliz. of York* (1830) 35 George Hamerton grome porter. **1503–4** in *Ld. Treas. Acc. Scotl.* II. 337 Thomas Hallye, grome portair of the Quenis chamir. **1610** BEN JONSON *Alchemist* III. ii, They will set him Vpmost, at the Groom-Porter's, all the Christmasse; And, for the whole yeare through, at euery place Where there is play, present him with the Chayre. *a* **1654** SELDEN *Table-T.* (Arb.) 59 Though there be false Dice brought in at the Groom-Porters, and cheating offer'd, yet unless he allow the Cheating, and judge the Dice to be good, there may be hopes of fair play. **1678** OTWAY *Friendship in F.* I. i. Wks. 1728 I. 244, I ran to the Groom-Porter's last Night, and lost my Money. **1705** *Lond. Gaz.* No. 4095/3 Thomas Archer Esq. is appointed to be Groom-Porter to Her Majesty. **1716** LADY M. W. MONTAGU *Basset-Table* 99 At the groom-porter's, batter'd bullies play. **1898** *Daily News* 7 Nov. 4/5 From Christmas to Epiphany, the Groom Porter kept an open gambling-house for the Court.

transf. **1768** GOLDSM. *Good-n. Man* II. i, He had scarce talents to be groom-porter to an orange barrow.

fig. **1659** FULLER *App. Inj. Innoc.* (1840) 350, I appeal to the reader, whom I make groom-porter (termed by Mr. Camden, *aleatorum arbiter*), and let him judge who plays with false, who cogs, who slurs a dye.

2. *pl.* Loaded dice. (Cf. quot. 1654 in 1.)

1687 MIEGE *Gt. Fr. Dict.* II, Grumporters, heavy Dice, *de gros Dez.* **1847** in HALLIWELL.

Hence **groom-portership**, the office of groom-porter.

1620 in Rymer *Fœdera* (1707) XVII. 236 Wee..doe give and graunte unto..Clement Cotterell Esquior the Roome and Office of Groomeporter or Groome Portership within all and everie our Howse and Howses.

groomsman ('gruːmzmən). [f. *groom's*, genitive of GROOM *sb.*[1] + MAN, as a parallel form to BRIDESMAID, q.v.] A young man acting as friend or attendant on the bridegroom at a marriage, either alone (as 'best man') or as one of a company; = BRIDEMAN 2, BRIDESMAN.

1698 M. HENRY *Let.* 10 Oct. in *Thoresby's Corr.* I. 330, I tell Mr. Boyse he must let me have the honour of being his groomsman at his next journey to Leeds. **1861** S. LYSONS *Claudia & Pr.* 178 Then came the ceremony of carrying the brides over the threshold by the groomsmen. **1889** *John Bull* 2 Mar. 151/2 The bridegroom was attended by his brother ..as groomsman. **1899** *Daily News* 30 Nov. 5/1 The old custom of having groomsmen at a wedding was revived yesterday afternoon at the marriage of —— ..There were five bridesmaids..two pages, and nine groomsmen.

groomy ('gruːmɪ), *a.* [f. GROOM *sb.*[1] + -Y[1].] Pertaining to or characteristic of a groom; 'horsy'.

1852 R. S. SURTEES *Sponge's Sp. Tour* i. 3 Mr. Sponge's groomy gait and horsey propensities. **1881** *Cheq. Career* 247 A correct groomy costume—which means cord trousers, stick-up round collars, and a tweed jacket.

Comb. **1853** G. J. CAYLEY *Las Alforjas* II. 110 A most disreputable groomy-looking rogue.

groon, variant of GROIN *sb.*[1]

groond, obs. pa. pple. of GRIND *v.*[1]

groone, variant of GROIN *v.*[1] *Obs.*

groop (gruːp), *sb.* Now *dial.* Forms: 5 grope, groupe, growpe, 5, 7, 9 *dial.* grupe, 6–7 groope, 8–9 *Sc.* gruip, 9 grup, groop. [a. MDu. *groepe* (Du. *groep*) = OFris., LG. *grôpe*; cf. also Icel. *gróp* groove, Norw., Sw. *grop* hollow, cavity, Da. dial. *grob* ditch. Cf. GRIP *sb.*[2]

In some dialects the word is used interchangeably with GRIP *sb.*[2]]

1. The drain or gutter in a stable or cowhouse; = GRIP *sb.*[2] 2.

c **1440** *Promp. Parv.* 216/2 Growpe, where beestys, as nete, standyn..(*H.P.* groupe of a netys stall), *musitatorium.* **1483** *Cath. Angl.* 167/2 A Grupe, *minsorium.* **1664** GOULDMAN *Dict.*, A groope in stables and houses, *minthorium.* **1674–91** RAY *N.C. Words* (E.D.S.), Grupe, Groop, *lat[r]ina.* **17..** *Mucking o' Geordies Byre* in Whitelaw *Bk. Sc. Song* (1875) 221 The Mucking o' Geordies byre And shooling the gruip sae clean. **1825** BROCKETT *N.C. Words, Grip, Gruap, Groop*, the space where the dung lies in a cow house, having double rows of stalls; that is, the opening or hollow between them. **1899** J. COLVILLE *Scott. Vernacular* 15 The open trench or gruip made the byre unsavoury.

b. A small trench, ditch, open drain; = GRIP *sb.*[2] 1. (*dial.*) †Also *Mil.* a trench (*obs.*).

1556 J. HEYWOOD *Spider & F.* lvii. 129 Behold how euerie peece that lith there in groope Hath a spider gonner with redy fired mach. *a* **1825** FORBY *Voc. E. Anglia, Grup, groop*, a trench, not amounting in breadth to a ditch. If narrower still it is a *grip.* **1829** BROCKETT *N.C. Words* (ed. 2), *Grip* or *Groop*..also a small ditch or open drain in a field.

†2. A groove; a mortice. *Obs.* (Cf. GROOP *v.*)

c **1440** *Promp. Parv.* 216/2 Growpe, yn a boorde, *incastratura.* **1688** R. HOLME *Armoury* III. 108/1 To put in the round Boards fitted together into the Groop made to receive them.

†groop, *v. Obs.* Forms: 4 groupe, 5 grope, 5–6 growpe. [Cf. Icel. *grópa* to groove (in carpentry), Færöese *grópa* to dig (a hole).]

1. *trans.* To dig (a trench).

c **1330** R. BRUNNE *Chron. Wace* (Rolls) 8165 Sykes do ȝe graue & groupe. **14..** *Medulla* in *Cath. Angl.* 167 *note, Runco*, to wedyn or gropyn.

2. To groove, hollow out, incise. Also *absol.*

1412–20 LYDG. *Chron. Troy* II. xi, Such as coulde graue groupe or carue Or suche as were able for to serue With lime and stone for to reyse a wall. *c* **1440** *Promp. Parv.* 216/2 Growpyd, as boordys or oþer þyngys, *incastratus.* Growpyn wythe an yryn, as gravowrys, *runco* (K.P. *incastro*). **1530** PALSGR. 576/1, I growpe (Lydgate), sculpe or suche as coulde grave, groupe, or carve: this worde is nat used in comen spetche. **1638** A. READ *Treat. Chirurg.* vii. 52 [The] needles..ought to have good eyes, and well grooped, that they may receive the threads readily.

grooper. *Obs.*^−0^ In 5 gropare. [f. GROOP *v.* + -ER[1].] One who digs trenches.

14.. *Medulla* in *Cath. Angl.* 167 *note, Runcio*, a wedare or a gropare.

grooper, obs. form of GROUPER.

†'grooping, *vbl. sb. Obs.* [f. GROOP *v.* + -ING[1].] The action of the verb GROOP; grooving, gouging. Chiefly in *Comb.* **grooping-iron**, a kind of chisel or gouge; **grooping tool**, a cooper's tool for making 'groops'.

c **1440** *Promp. Parv.* 217/1 Grow(p)ynge or gravynge yryn, *runcina, scrophina.* **1453** *Mem. Ripon* (Surtees) III. 162 Et de 6*d.* solutis Ricardo Carvour et servienti suo pro gropyng mensal dicti Purpityll. **1475** *Pict. Voc.* in Wr.-Wülcker 807/29 *Hec strofina*, a gropyng-yryn. **1483** *Cath. Angl.* 167/2 A Grupynge yren, *runcina.* *a* **1500** *Debate Carpenter's Tools* 31 in Hazl. *E.P.P.* I. 80 The groping-iren than spake he: Compas, who hath greuyd the? **1688** R. HOLME *Armoury* III. 108/1 Grooping is the making of the Rigget at the two ends of the Barrel to hold the head in. *Ibid.* 318/1 This may be termed the Coopers Grooping Tool.

groos, obs. form of GROSS.

groose (gruːz), *v. Sc.* and *north.* Also 7 growze, 9 grooze, gruze. [app. a derivative of GRUE *v.*] *intr.* To shiver, shudder.

1674–91 RAY *N.C. Words* (E.D.S.), *Growze*, to be chill before the beginning of an ague-fit. **1806** SCOTT *Lett.* I. 63–4 This story makes me grouze whenever I think of it.

Hence **'groosing** *vbl. sb.*, **groose** *sb.*, shivering, a shivering fit.

1825–80 JAMIESON, *Gruzin, Groozin*, a shivering. **1825** SCOTT *Fam. Lett.* 25 Aug. (1894) II. 345, I own one felt a little gruse at a pass called Shanes Inn..where they cut an unfortunate Inspector of the Mail-Coaches..to pieces with scythes. **1861** SIR R. CHRISTISON *Let.* in *Life* (1886) II. xvi. 420 The consequence was horrid groozing with goose-skin, enduring for two hours. **1862** J. BROWN *Rab & his friends* 27 My patient had a sudden and long shivering, a 'groosin'', as she called it.

groose, obs. form of GROSS.

groot (gruːt), *sb. Obs.* exc. *dial.* Also 4–7 grut, 5 (9 *dial.*) grute, 7 grewt, 8 greut. [Related to OE. *grēot*, GRIT *sb.*[1], and GROUT *sb.*: but the precise nature of the relation is uncertain.] Mud, soil, earth.

13.. *Coer de L.* 4339 The toun dykes..wer..Ful off grut, no man myghte swymme. *c* **1440** *Promp. Parv.* 218/1 Grute [*MS. Harl.* 221 gurte, *other MSS.* grut], fylthe, *limus.* **1600** *Hosp. Inc. Fooles* 62 All the horse and cowes dung..in time of dearth that grut or riff-raffe woulde be good to make an Italian *torto* withal. **1671** *Phil. Trans.* VI. 2097 The earth, or Grewt. **1681** GREW *Musæum* III. §2 ii. 328 A sort of Tin Ore with its Grewt. **1776** PRYCE *Min. Cornub.* 322 *Greut* or *Grit*, a kind of fossil body, of sandy rough, hard, earthy, particles. **1827** D. JOHNSON *Indian Field Sports* 294 In Devonshire the word *groot* is used by all farmers..for dry earth. **1880** *W. Cornwall Gloss.*, *Grute, Greet*, coffee grounds, finely pulverised soil. **1891** *Hartland Gloss.*, *Grute*, loose earth, soil. *Grute-rest*, the *moal-board* (mould-board) of a *timbern-zole.*

Hence **'grooty** *a.*, muddy.

1848 S. CARTER *Midnt. Effusions* 192 The measureless solitudes shrubless and grooty.

groot (gruːt), *v.* See also GROUT *v.*[2] [app. f. GROOT *sb.* Cf. however *wroot*, ROOT *v.*] Of a hog: To grub up or 'muzzle' the ground. Hence **'grooting** *vbl. sb.*

1827 D. JOHNSON *Indian Field Sports* 247 Marks of their feet and grooting are visible in every moist place. *Note*, Grooting is..used by hog-hunters for the places where they have been muzzling the earth. **1834** MEDWIN *Angler in Wales* I. 109 Heaps of earth, and holes, where the hogs had been 'grooting'.

groote, obs. form of GROAT.

grooth, variant of GROWTH[2] *dial. Obs.*

grootte, obs. form of GROAT.

groove (gruːv), *sb.* Also 5 grofe, groof, 7 groeve, 7–9 grove, (7, 9 gruff, 9 groave, gruve). [ad. early mod.Du. *groeve* 'sulcus, fossa, scrobs', (Kilian), Du. *groef* = OLG. *gruova*, OHG. *gruoba*, MHG. *gruobe*, G. *grube* pit, hole, ditch, mine, fosse (in Anat.), ON. *gróf* pit, Goth. *grôba*, f.

OTeut. root *grôƀ-, graƀ- (see GRAVE *sb.*[1] and *v.*[1]).]

1. a. A mining shaft; a mine, pit. Now *dial.* †Also, in 15th c., a cave (*obs.*).

a **1400–50** *Alexander* 5394 Makis he gracis to his goddis & þan þe grofe entres. *a* **1483** *Mendip Laws* in Phelps *Hist. Somerset* VII. (1839) 6 Any man that doth begin to pitch or groof..must stand to the..waist in the same groof. **1631** *Star Chamb. Cases* (Camden) 91 Pulling the minors out of their groves by head and shoulders. **1666** LOCKE in Boyle *Hist. Air* (1692) xvii. 137, I rode to Minedeep, with an Intention to make use of it [a barometer] there, in one of the deepest Gruffs (for so they call their Pits) I could find. *a* **1698** W. BLUNDELL *Caval. Note Bk.* (1880) 251 The pits where lead is digged, in Derbyshire, are called grooves. **1747** HOOSON *Miner's Dict.* Kj, *Groove* [is] the Mine or Work that a Man is employ'd in, hence it is if a Question be asked, Where is Tom to day? He is gone to the Groove, he is at the Groove; sometimes it is used for the Shaft. **1797** W. G. MATON *West. Counties* II. 131 On Mendip they call their works *grooves*, and the miners *groovers*, which are terms that seem to be peculiar to this part of the country. **1825** J. JENNINGS *Observ. Dial. W. Eng.* 41 *Gruff*, a mine. *Gruffer, Gruffier*, a miner. **1829** J. HODGSON in J. Raine *Mem.* (1858) II. 157 The coal is worked by a grove of fair quality. **1873** *Swaledale Gloss.*, *Gruve*, a lead mine. *Gruver*, a lead miner. **1881** RAYMOND *Mining Gloss.*, *Groove* or *Grove*. 1. Derb. A mine.

b. = DRIFT *sb.* 15. *dial.*

1887 H. MILLER *Geol. Otterburn & Elsdon* 130 *Mouth-groves*, short levels, generally entering upon the crop of a coal. **1893** *Northumbld. Gloss.*, *Grove, Grove-hole, Mouth-grove*, an adit level driven in from the surface for coal or fire-clay. Sometimes this is called a *grove-hole*, but the common term is a drift.

2. a. A channel or hollow, cut by artificial means, in metal, wood, etc.; e.g. the spiral rifling of a gun, one of the air-passages leading from the wind-chest to the pipes of an organ, etc.

1659 LEAK *Waterwks.* 33 The Valves are marked with M, the Groves by E. **1664** EVELYN tr. *Freart's Archit.* 130 Excavated Channules, by our Workmen call'd Flutings and Groeves. **1680** MOXON *Mech. Exerc.* 187 This String is laid in the Groove made on the edge of the Wheel. **1688** R. HOLME *Armoury* III. 89/1 Grove of a Screw, is the hollow.. between the Thrids. **1752** W. & J. HALFPENNY *New Designs* IV. (1755) 4 Feather-edged Boards, not more than 8 Inches wide, including Lap, Grove, and Tongue. **1813** SCOTT *Trierm.* I. xv, Portcullis rose with crashing groan, Full harshly up its groove of stone. **1816** *Sporting Mag.* XLVIII. 191 The slide [in a gun] still works freely, no rust having been found on the groaves. **1839** URE *Dict. Arts* 882 He now forms the groove with a single stroke of a small file, dexterously applied, first to the one side of the needle, and then to the other. **1852** SEIDEL *Organ* 52 These partitions are called grooves..every groove holds exactly as much wind as is necessary to sound either a large or a small pipe. **1858** GREENER *Gunnery* 363 He formed a number of circular grooves on the cylindrical part of the bullet, in imitation of the feathers of an arrow.

b. *Theatr.* (See quot. 1886.)

1866 W. DAVIDGE *Footlight Flashes* xv. 150 The scenery is pushed back as far as it will go in the slides, or grooves, so called. **1881** G. DANIEL *Merry Eng.* 352 At this moment the scenes stuck fast in the grooves. **1886** *Stage Gossip* 69 The 'grooves' are the supports for the 'wings' and 'flats'. **1966** *Amer. N. & Q.* Sept. 13/2 Some promptbooks of the eighteenth century and most of those of the nineteenth show at the head of each scene..the number or numbers of the grooves in which the wings and shutters..are to stand.

c. The spiral cut in a gramophone record (earlier, in a phonograph cylinder) which forms the path for the needle.

1902 *Encycl. Brit.* XXXI. 679/1 In the first phonograph a spiral groove was cut on a brass drum fixed on a horizontal screw. *Ibid.*, The sharp edge of the needle ran in the middle of the spiral groove when the cylinder was rotated. *Ibid.* 680/1 The grooves on the cylinder are $\frac{1}{100}$ of an inch apart. **1931** B. BROWN *Talking Pictures* ix. 194 Examining an ordinary record we find the spiral grooves of very fine pitch somewhere about 100 to the inch. **1956**, etc. [see *fine-groove* (FINE *a.* D. 3)]. **1957** *Records & Recording* Nov. 20/1 It is these grooves which must be tracked with absolute accuracy by the pickup needle. **1958**, **1962** [see *coarse groove* (COARSE *a.* 7 c)].

3. A channel or furrow of natural formation.

a. *spec.* in *Anat.* and *Zool.*

1787 G. WHITE *Selborne* iii. 7 The alternate flutings or grooves and the curved form of my specimen. **1828** STARK *Elem. Nat. Hist.* II. 389 The fore part of the head is generally more membranaceous than the hind part,..with a longitudinal furrow on each side, or a groove to receive the antennæ. **1878** L. P. MEREDITH *Teeth* 157 A continuous groove across..the teeth near the gum. **1899** J. HUTCHINSON *Archives Surg.* X. 145 The parts [of the nails] which have received names, are the body, the root, the free edge, the sides, the lunula, the matrix or bed, and the groove.

b. *gen.*

a **1852** MACGILLIVRAY *Nat. Hist. Dee Side*, etc. (1855) 6 The groove or narrow valley in which the Dee flows. **1865** GEIKIE *Scen. & Geol. Scot.* iv. 80 Its rocks covered with ruts and grooves, running in long persistent lines.

4. *transf.* and *fig.* **a.** A 'channel' or routine of action or life. Often in depreciatory sense: A narrow, limited, undeviating course; a 'rut'.

1842 TENNYSON *Locksley Hall* 182 Let the great world spin for ever down the ringing grooves of change. **1868** HELPS *Realmah* iv. (1876) 58 His ideas were wont to travel rather in a groove. **1869** ROGERS *Pref. to Adam Smith's W.N.* I. 27 The whole course of legislation..had flowed in the same groove for centuries. **1871** L. STEPHEN *Playgr. Europe* viii. (1894) 174, I see that I am inevitably falling into the old groove. **1874** GREEN *Short Hist.* x. §4. 806 Labour was thus thrown out of its older grooves. **1882** BESANT *Revolt of Man* viii. (1883) 193 The conversation flowed in the accustomed grooves.

b. Phr. *in the* (or *a*) *groove* (cf. 2 c above) = GROOVY *a.* 3. Hence *groove* is used to mean: a style of playing jazz or similar music, esp. one that is 'swinging' or good; a time when jazz is played well; more widely, one's predilection or favourite style, = BAG *sb.* 1 d; something excellent or very satisfying. *slang* (orig. *U.S.*).

1932 *Melody Maker* Oct. 836/1 Having such a wonderful time which puts me in a groove. **1933** *Fortune* Aug. 90/2 The jazz musicians gave no grandstand performances; they simply got a great burn from playing in the groove. **1935** *Hot News* Sept. 17/1 The Boswells are not in the hot groove. **1936** *Rhythm* Apr. 27/2 His first chorus in the latter is really in the right groove, but he loses it completely in the next one. **1940** *Swing* Nov. 27 *Travelin'* has a sax-unison melody somewhat in the Tuxedo groove. **1946** B. TREADWELL *Big Book of Swing* 124/2 *In the groove*, everything going O.K. **1954** *Jive Jungle* 32 The all night 'grooves' began. **1957** M. MEZZROW in S. Traill *Concerning Jazz* 18 What we had played was so good I doubted if we could even get in that same groove again. **1958** G. LEA *Somewhere there's Music* iv. 35 Romance? No, bruz, that's not my groove. **1959** N. MAILER *Advts. for Myself* (1961) 296 If you as a cat are way out too, and we are in the same groove.., why then you say simply, 'I dig.' **1962** R. MANHEIM tr. *Grass's Tin Drum* III. 518 We made music, played ourselves into the groove. **1966** *Melody Maker* 15 Oct. 19 The rhythm team..developed a very propulsive rhythmic groove. **1967** *Ibid.* 16 Dec. 8 This is what makes the Indian one such a groove for me.

†**5.** A gardener's transplanting tool. *Obs.*

1725 BRADLEY *Fam. Dict.* s.v. *Orange Tree*, He must take away with his displanting Groove as much of the Earth as he can. **1726** *Dict. Rust.* (ed. 3), *Groove*, a Gardiners Tool for transplanting Flowers.

6. *attrib.* and *Comb.*, as ***groove-piece***; **groove-board**, in an organ (see quot.); **groove cast** *Geol.*, a ridge on the lower surface of a layer of sandstone corresponding to a groove on underlying mudstone; **groove-fellow**, one of a company of men working a mine or a section of it in partnership; **groove-going** *a.*, that travels 'in a groove', that keeps to one course; **groove-hole** *dial.* (see quot. 1893 in sense 1 b); **groove-like** *a.*, wanting in novelty or originality; **groove-locating unit**, a device that indicates the position of a stylus on a record as the record is played; **groove-roller** (see quot.)

1881 C. A. EDWARDS *Organs* 55 Where there is..not room for the entire sound board, or..for the larger pipes,..they are..supplied by means of grooves cut usually in the upper board or in a kind of second upper board called a *groove-board. **1948** R. R. SHROCK *Sequence in Layered Rocks* iv. 163 These interesting and puzzling ridges, here designated *groove casts, seem to represent sand fillings (casts) of rectilinear, V-shaped and U-shaped grooves existing in the upper few millimeters of the bottom sediment on which sand was deposited. **1963** KRUMBEIN & SLOSS *Stratigr. & Sedim.* (ed. 2) iv. 130 The upper right illustration shows groove casts, elongated parallel grooves or scratches oriented in the direction of current flow. **1829** *Glover's Hist. Derby* I. 74 Each person or company possessing their meer or meers in partnership (called *groove fellows). **1880** KINGLAKE *Crimea* VI. xi. 429 Under this discipline the *groove-going men winced in agony. **1902** *Daily Chron.* 5 July 8/3 There are commendations without end waiting for the linen frock that displays just a little originality, so *groove-like is the manifestation of that material as a general rule. **1908** *Westm. Gaz.* 4 June 10/3, I think the modern tendency is too groove-like. Once make a success as a Cockney or a love-sick maiden, and a Cockney or a love-sick maiden you will be to the end of time. **1941** *B.B.C. Gloss. Broadc. Terms* 14 **Groove-locating unit*, device forming part of a reproducing desk, and consisting of an arm carrying a pick-up, together with a pointer and scale to indicate the position of the needle on the record. **1962** A. NISBETT *Technique Sound Studio* viii. 145 BBC studios are equipped with record players which have optical groove-locating units. On these a mirror is fixed beneath the pivot and throws the image of a scale on to a ground-glass screen. **1825** J. NICHOLSON *Operat. Mechanic* 90 Iron *groove pieces or channels which are let into the stone-work of the side walls. **1867** SMYTH *Sailor's Word-bk.*, **Groove-rollers*, these are fixed in a groove of the tiller-sweep in large ships, to aid the tiller-ropes, and prevent friction.

groove (gruːv), *v.* Also 5 groof, 8 gruve. [f. GROOVE *sb.* Cf. Flem. *groeven* 'cælare, sculpere, cauare' (Kilian).]

1. *intr.* To sink a mining shaft; to mine. *dial.*

a **1483** [see GROOVE *sb.* 1]. **1892** [see GROOVING *vbl. sb.*[1]].

2. *trans.* To cut a groove or grooves in; to provide with grooves. (Also with *out.*) ***to groove into***: to fit into by means of a groove.

1686 PLOT *Staffordsh.* 174 If the plaister fall..out from between the Timber..for want of grooving it round within side before the plaister be laid on. **1688** R. HOLME *Armoury* III. 322/1 In these holes are threads of Screws grooved inwards. **1721** SWIFT *G. Nim-Dan-Dean's Answ. to Sheridan* 28 One letter still another locks, Each groov'd and dove-tail'd like a box. **1751** W. & J. HALFPENNY *New Designs Chinese Bridges* II. 8 The side Timbers and middle Pieces.. are gruv'd and bolted together. **1808** SHELLEY *Zastrozzi* i. Pr. Wks. 1888 I. 6 One end being grooved into the solid wall. **1848** BAILEY *Festus* ix. (1852) 115 You see yon wretched starved old man; his brow Grooved out with wrinkles. **1870** RUSKIN *Lect. Art* ii. 44 It may be possible to show the necessities of structure which groove the fangs..of the asp. **1899** *Edin. Rev.* Apr. 316 A metamorphic rock..rent by earthquakes, fissured, grooved, eroded.

3. To cut in the form of a groove or channel; to excavate (a channel). Also, to force *itself* along a channel.

1866 R. S. STORRS *Serm.* in *Nat. Preacher* (N.Y.), When the searching, scientific spirit awakens among men,..they.. hunt the records that are grooved upon rocks. **1881** SHAIRP *Asp. Poetry* v. 128 High-pitched imagination and vivid emotion tend..to groove for themselves channels of language which are peculiar and unique. **1883** *Century Mag.* XXVII. 146 The glacier moves silently,..grooving the record of its being on the world itself. **1890** H. M. STANLEY *Darkest Africa* II. xxviii. 259 The Rami-lulu [river] had eventually furrowed and grooved itself deeply through.

4. a. *pass.* and *intr.* To fit or be fitted as *into* a groove. *rare.*

1854 DE QUINCEY *War* Wks. IV. 271 Phenomena of chance growth, not..so grooved into the dark necessities of our nature, as we had all taken for granted. **1886** C. GIBBON *Clare of Claresmede* I. ix. 109 Sheldon adjoined Winston, and would groove into that estate nicely.

b. *fig.* To settle or be settled *into* (or *in*) a routine of work, habit, etc. Also with *down.*

1866 J. CONINGTON *Let.* 28 June in *Misc. Writ.* (1872) I. p. lvi, I am grooving down into work here. **1879** FROUDE *Cæsar* ii. 10 Morality thus engrained in the national character and grooved into habits of action creates strength, as nothing else creates it. **1922** A. S. M. HUTCHINSON *This Freedom* I. v, She found Anna grooved in the business of helping her mother in the house.

5. *intr.* To play jazz or similar music with 'swing'; to be 'in the groove' (see GROOVE *sb.* 4 b); to dance or listen *to* such music with great pleasure; hence, to make good progress or co-operate; to get on well *with* someone; to make love. Also *trans.*, to play (music) swingingly; to give pleasure to (a person). *slang* (orig. *U.S.*).

1935 *Vanity Fair* Nov. 38/1 That's the third date we've grooved half a dozen schmaltzy tunes. **1937** in *Amer. Speech* XII. 182/1 Men who can lay on sugar or groove it. **1945** 'DIZZY' GILLESPIE (*title of tune*) Groovin' high. **1959** *Esquire* Nov. 70 I, To groove someone means to provide them with enjoyment. Example: Her singing grooved me. **1960** *Melody Maker* 31 Dec. 11/5 (*record title*) Benny Golson 'Groovin' with Golson'. **1967** *Observer* (Colour Suppl.) 4 Dec. 28 *Groove*, make good progress, co-operate. **1967** *Melody Maker* 16 Dec. 10/7 The rhythm section..grooves along in true Basie manner. **1968** *Listener* 5 Sept. 306/3 The radio Peel is quiet, self-mocking, sardonic and scornful of the 'let's move and groove to this latest gas group from Croydon' school of presentation. **1970** *New Yorker* 14 May 34/2 Sad Arthur put away his boots and helmet..to stay in Nutley and groove with the fair Lambie. **1970** *Observer* 24 May 40/6 We're trying to get humanity to transcend its cultural limitations and groove with it.

grooved (gruːvd), *ppl. a.* [f. GROOVE *sb.* and *v.* + -ED.] Provided with or having a groove or grooves; furrowed; channelled; *spec.* in *Anat.*, *Zool.*, *Bot.*, *Archæol.*, and *techn.*

1793 MARTYN *Lang. Bot.*, *Furrowed*, fluted, or grooved Stem. *a* **1798** PENNANT *Zool.* (1812) IV. 307 The aperture [is] grooved at the margin. **1831** BREWSTER *Optics* xiv. 118, I discovered in almost every specimen a grooved structure, like the delicate texture of the skin at the top of an infant's finger. **1836** DUBOURG *Violin* ix. (1878) 274 The ordinary construction of the grooved violin. **1849** E. B. EASTWICK *Dry Leaves* 3 The deadly grooved rifle. **1871–82** *Cassell's Nat. Hist.* IV. 252 The Grooved Tortoise, *Testudo sulcata.* **1876** ROUTLEDGE *Discov.* 33 Passing the metal between grooved rollers. **1882** MISS HOPLEY *Snakes* 225 The last or back tooth of the maxillary bone is a grooved fang. **1888** S. HISLOP in *Life* viii. (1889) 231 Low-growing plants with grooved and jointed stems inhabited the marshes. **1936** *Proc. Prehist. Soc.* II. 197 Significant associations are few, but of these two..suggest that grooved-ware was contemporary with Neolithic B pottery. **1939** V. G. CHILDE *Dawn Europ. Civilization* (ed. 3) 338 Grooved—with broad incisions, not normally round-bottomed. **1967** *Antiquaries Jrnl.* XLVII. 169 The Grooved Ware obtained from Durrington is closely allied to that from Woodhenge.

grooveless ('gruːvlɪs), *a.* [f. GROOVE *sb.* + -LESS.] Having no grooves.

1855 *Illustr. Lond. News* 24 Nov. 615/4 Graduated grooveless needles. **1862** T. MORRALL *Needle-making* 22 A. Morrall preferred staying in England, and making an assortment of grooveless needles. **1886** *Homil. Rev.* (U.S.) Jan. 50 God launched our flying planet and sent it spinning round its grooveless orbit swifter than a cannon ball.

grooveling, -lyn, obs. forms of GROVELLING.

groover ('gruːvə(r)). Also 7 grover, 8 groaver, 9 grovier, gruver, gruffer. [f. GROOVE *v.* + -ER[1]. Cf. Du. *groever* 'cælator, sculptor' (Kilian).] One who or that which grooves.

1. A miner. Now *dial.*

1610 HOLLAND *Camden's Brit.* I. 581 A fire begunne by a candle..through the negligence of a grouer or digger. **1653** MANLOVE *Lead Mines* 119 To order grovers, make them pay their part, Joyn with their fellows, or their grove desert. **1693** G. POOLEY in *Phil. Trans.* XVII. 673 As to the finding out the Calamine,..the Groovers tell me there is no certainty at all, but that it is a meer Lottery. **1778** *Eng. Gazetteer* (ed. 2) s.v. *Matlock*, The only inhabitants are a few groavers, who dig for lead-ore. **1797**, **1825**, **1873** [see GROOVE *sb.*[1] 1]. **1824** MANDER *Derbysh. Miners' Gloss.* s.v. *Grove*, In Mendip, they call the Miner, a Grovier. **1893** *Northumbld. Gloss.*, *Grover*, a miner who works in an adit level or a lead mine.

2. A tool for making grooves: a gouge. *rare.*

1865 LUBBOCK *Preh. Times* 401 In the South the men have bows and arrows, harpoons,..snow-shovels, groovers [etc.].

3. *Comb.*: **groover-head**, an appliance for making grooves, attached to a wood-planing machine.

1884 in KNIGHT *Dict. Mech.* Suppl. **1892** *Mod. Mechanism* (ed. Benjamin) 387 A very desirable addition to grooving-machines is the solid expansion groover-head..which is arranged so that without removing or changing the cutters they will extend to double their width.

grooviness ('gru:vɪnɪs). *colloq.* [f. GROOVY *a.* + -NESS.] The condition of being 'groovy'; tendency to routine.

1867 *Pall Mall G.* 1 Apr. 2 The grooviness and insincerity of Western diplomacy and the opposition of Russia. **1887** *Monthly Packet* May 497 To extend one's work and interests is surely the best protection from narrowness and grooviness. **1892** *Blackw. Mag.* Sept. 409 Hard work unrelieved by competitive games is apt to produce 'grooviness'.

grooving ('gru:vɪŋ), *vbl. sb.*^{1} [f. GROOVE *v.* + -ING^1.] The action of the vb. GROOVE.

1. *dial.* Mining.

1892 *Daily News* 10 Mar. 5/1 There are men still living who remember the old mining days, when 'grooving' for calamine was the main occupation of the [Mendip] district.

2. a. The making or cutting of grooves in wood, etc. **b.** The formation of channels or furrows in the surface of rocks by glacial action. **c.** The result of the action; a groove or set of grooves. Also *fig.*

1728 R. MORRIS *Ess. Anc. Archit.* 81, I must just explain ..the foregoing Plate concerning Fluting or Grooving. **1823** P. NICHOLSON *Pract. Build.* 159 Grooving and Rebating consist in taking or abstracting a part which is every where of a rectangular section. **1846** E. FORBES in *Mem. Geol. Surv.* I. 345 This was the epoch of glaciers and icebergs, of boulders, and groovings, and scratches. **1850** MRS. BROWNING *Woman's Shortcomings* i, Her soul must slip Where the world has set the grooving. **1860** TYNDALL *Glac.* I. ii. 20 The laminated structure..always corresponded to the superficial grooving. **1877** W. THOMSON *Voy. Challenger* II. iv. 249 We can fully accept the grooving of rocks and the accumulation of moraines as complete evidence of a former existence of glacial conditions. **1883** L. OLIPHANT *Haïfa* (1887) 25 In the groovings of rocks upon which the sea now breaks. **1899** *Q. Rev.* July 159 The softer material would be blown through the barrel without taking the grooving—would *strip*, as it is technically called.

3. *attrib.*, as ***grooving-head, -hook, -plane, -saw, -tool.***

1678 MOXON *Mech. Exerc.* iv. 70 There are several other Plains in use among Joyners,..as,..the Grooving-plain, &c. **1681** *Ibid.* xi. 196 Of Grooving Hooks and Grooving Tools. **1825** J. NICHOLSON *Operat. Mechanic* 582 Others are occasionally used in forming any kind of prismatic surfaces, viz. rebating-planes, grooving-planes, &c. *a* **1877** KNIGHT *Dict. Mech.* III. 2033/2 List of sawing-machines invented and manufactured by him [*sc.* Gen. Sir Samuel Bentham].. previous to 1800... Double-grooving saws. **1882** R. GRIMSHAW *Suppl. to Grimshaw on Saws* 235 Fig. 322 shows a form of sectional grooving saw in which the action is gradual throughout the width of the cut. **1892** *Mod. Mechanism* (ed. Benjamin) 387 An expansion-gaining or grooving-head. **1915** *Saw in History* (Henry Disston & Sons) iii. 35 Grooving Saws, as the name indicates, are designed for cutting grooves of various widths and depths. **1940** *Chambers's Techn. Dict.* 391/1 *Grooving saw*, a circular saw which may be of the drunken type, used for cutting grooves. **1964** W. L. GOODMAN *Hist. Woodworking Tools* 155 (*caption*) Grooving Saws, dated 1771 and 1803.

†**'grooving,** *vbl. sb.*^{2} *Obs.* A variant (perh. only graphic) of GRUEING, shivering.

1637 BRIAN *Pisse-prophet* ii. (1679) 15 This party was taken in the manner of an Ague with a grooving in the back, and pain in the head. *Ibid.* iii. 45. **1638** A. READ *Chirurg.* xvii. 123 If a fever in these wounds doe appeare..with a cold and grooving, it is dangerous.

groovy ('gru:vɪ), *a.* [f. GROOVE *sb.* + -Y^1.]

1. Of or pertaining to a groove; resembling a groove.

1853 O. BYRNE *Artisan's Hand-bk.* 383 Its main purpose is to keep the surface of the ivory slightly lubricated, so that the rag may not hang to it and wear it into rings or groovy marks. **1966** *New Statesman* 29 Apr. 623/2 The flat tops.. are richly textured to resemble pieces of groovy mud.

2. *fig.* Having a tendency to run in 'grooves' (cf. GROOVE *sb.* 4). *colloq.*

1882 *Railway News* 12 Aug. 245/1 Railway managers are apt..to get a little 'groovy'. **1893** FARMER *Slang, Groovy*, settled in habit; limited in mind. **1896** *Blackw. Mag.* July 96 Schoolmasters as a class are extremely groovy.

3. Playing, or capable of playing, jazz or similar music brilliantly or easily; 'swinging'; appreciative of such music, 'hep', sophisticated; hence as a general term of commendation: excellent, very good. Cf. GROOVE *sb.* 4 b. *slang* (orig. *U.S.*).

1937 *Amer. Speech* XII. 46/2 *Groovey*, name applied to state of mind which is conducive to good playing. **1944** *Sat. Even. Post* 13 May 89/2 A boy or girl who is really 'groovy' is 'skate wacky' or a 'skate bug'. **1946** MEZZROW & WOLFE *Really Blues* 52 When he was groovy..he'd begin to play the blues on a beat-up guitar. **1948** *Cosmopolitan* Dec. 163/1 'I pitched a no-hit game last summer,' said Georgie. 'Hey, groovy,' said Sally. **1951** W. MORUM *Gabriel* II. vii. 225 The boys have a groovy number they want to put across. *Ibid.* viii. 243 It's damned silly to say that. Just because I was extemporising Bach—feeling a bit groovy. **1958** *Spectator* 11 July 67/2 That was a good record..cool and groovy. **1959** *Observer* 1 Nov. 7/7 To-morrow I'll tell him to go to hell, and what's so groovy is, he will. **1968** *Listener* 5 Sept. 307/1 There are a lot of guys going round with groovy hair-styles.

grooze, var. GROOSE *v. Sc.*, to shiver.

grop, obs. pa. t. of GRIPE *v.*^{1}

'gropable, *a. rare.* [f. GROPE *v.* + -ABLE.] That can be felt.

14.. *Medulla* in *Promp. Parv.* 214 *note, Palpalis*, gropeable. **1660** FISHER *Rustick's Alarm* Wks. (1679) 205 Thy Disputation..be it never so full of groapable darkness, even to thy Friends and Fellows..yet its laid up close.. within the linnen shrowd of a dark Language.

grope (grəʊp), *sb.*^{1} Also 1 gráp, 3 grap, 6 *Sc.* graip. [In sense 1, repr. OE. *gráp* (see GROPE *v.*); in sense 2, f. GROPE *v.*]

†**1.** Grasp; *fig.* grasp of a subject. *Obs.*

Beowulf 555 Me..fæste hæfde grim on grape. *c* **1000** *Guthlac* 407 Wæron hy reowe to ræsanne ȝifrum grapum. *a* **1225** *Leg. Kath.* 855 Esculapies creftes, & Galienes grapes [L. *sagacissimas latentium rerum inventiones*].

2. The action or an act of groping. *lit.* and *fig.*

1500–20 DUNBAR *Poems* liv. 7 Scho is..lyk a gangarall unto graip. **1894** *Kingdom* (Minneapolis) 20 Apr., The grope of a stricken soul. **1899** *Speaker* 2 Sept. 237/1 A step and a grope would tell me.

†**grope,** *sb.*^{2} *Obs.* A kind of nail.

[**1411** in Rogers *Agric. & Pr.* (1882) III. 546/3, 50 grope & 1 *c* clout nails.] **1425** in Kennett *Par. Antiq.* (1818) II. 253 In clavis carectat., gropys, et aliis ferramentis..xii sol. iv den. **1720** STRYPE *Stow's Surv. Lond.* (1754) II. v. x. 280 The length and breadth of the Gropes belonging to the wheels of the Carts.

grope (grəʊp), *v.* Forms: 1 grápian, 3 grapien, grapin, gropien, 4 gropen, (*pa. pple.* ygrope), 4–6, 9 *Sc.* and *north.* grape, 5 gropyn, groop(e, 5, 7 groppe, 6–8 groap(e, *Sc.* graip, 3– grope. [OE. *grápian* = OHG. *greiphôn, greifôn*:—OTeut. **graipôjan*, f. **graipâ* fem. (OE. *gráp* grasp, OHG. *greifa* fork = GRAIP), f. **graip-*, ablaut-var. of **grip-*, whence GRIP *sb.*^{1} and *v.*^{1}]

†**1.** *intr.* To use the hands in feeling, touching, or grasping; to handle or feel something. *Obs.*

Beowulf 2085 He mæȝnes rof min costode grapode ȝearofolm. *c* **825** *Vesp. Ps.* cxiii. 15 [cxv. 7] Honda habbað & ne grapiað. *a* **1000** *Riddles* xlvi. 3 Ic..on þæt banlease bryd grapode hyȝewlonc hondum. *c* **1205** LAY. 30269 He grapede an his nebbe he wende þat bledde. *c* **1325** *Old Age* in *E.E.P.* (1862) 149 Ihc ne mai no more grope vnder gore. **1382** WYCLIF *Wisd.* xv. 15 The maumetis of naciouns..to the whiche nouther siȝte of eȝen is to seen..ne fingris of hondis to gropen. *c* **1386** CHAUCER *Can. Yeom. Prol. & T.* 683 Look what ther is, put in thyn hand and grope. *c* **1440** HYLTON *Scala Perf.* (W. de W. 1494) I. lv, Now may þou grope [L. *palpare*] that this ymage is not nought. **1471** RIPLEY *Comp. Alch.* v. xliv. in Ashm. (1652) 159 Fyrst examyn, grope and taste. **1509** HAWES *Past. Pleas.* x. (Percy Soc.) 37 They grope over where is no felynge. **1568** *Gd. Counsel* 19 in *Kingis Q.* (S.T.S.) 52 Graip or thow slyd, and creip furth on the way.

2. To attempt to find something by feeling about as in the dark or as a blind person; to feel *for* (or *after*) something with the hand (or other tactile organ, *rarely* with an instrument); to feel about in order to find one's way.

971 *Blickl. Hom.* 151 Hie grapodan mid heora handum on þa eorþan, & nystan hwyder hie eodan. *c* **1000** ÆLFRIC *Deut.* xxviii. 29 þæt þu grapie on midne dæȝ, swa se blinda deð on þistrum. *c* **1386** CHAUCER *Reeve's T.* 302 She gropeth alwey forther with hir hond And foond the bed. *c* **1430–40** LYDG. *Bochas* III. vi. 16 With her handes for to fele his hede, And to grope after both his eares twayne. *c* **1440** *York Myst.* xlvi. 238 Go we groppe wher we graued hir, If we fynde ouȝte þat faire one in fere nowe. **1535** COVERDALE *Ruth* iii. 8 Now whan it was midnight, the man was afrayed, and groped aboute. **1565–73** *Durham Depos.* (Surtees) 211 Robson groped about his girdle for his key. **1660** F. BROOKE tr. *Le Blanc's Trav.* 11 Groaping with our hands in the sand. **1687** A. LOVELL tr. *Thevenot's Trav.* II. 121 A covered way that.. is..so dark, that one must groap along as they go in it. **1700** S. L. tr. *Fryke's Voy. E. Ind.* 96 [They] searched our Boat very narrowly, and then with their Hooks groped all round the outside. **1785** BURNS *Halloween* iv, They steek their een, an graip an' wale, For muckle anes and straight anes. **1792** J. BARLOW *Conspir. Kings* 82 Dim, like the day-struck owl, ye grope in light. **1838** DICKENS *Nich. Nick.* xv, Hats and bonnets having been groped for under the table. **1864** TENNYSON *Aylmer's F.* 821 He groped as blind, and seem'd Always about to fall.

b. Applied to the catching of fish, esp. trout, by feeling for them in the water. Const. *for*; also in *indirect pass.*

1603 SHAKS. *Meas. for M.* I. ii. 91 Groping for Trowts, in a peculiar River. **1678** BUNYAN *Pilgr.* Apol., Fish must be grop't for, and be tickled too. **1692** R. L'ESTRANGE *Fables* cxxxi. 121 A Boy was Groping for Eles, and layd his hand upon a Snake. **1834** LANDOR *Exam. Shaks.* Wks. 1846 II. 272 Every carp from pool, every bream from brook, will be groped for.

c. *fig.* To behave as if blind or in the dark; to search blindly, tentatively, or uncertainly (*for, after*); †to make a blind guess *at.*

c **1325** *Know thyself* 99 in *E.E.P.* (1862) 132 þi Concience schal þe saue and deme, Wheþer þat þou be ille or good, Grope aboute and take good ȝeme. *c* **1340** *Cursor M.* 13590 (Trin.) Whenne þei had stryuen as I telle þei groped & coude no cause fynde. *c* **1386** CHAUCER *Can. Yeom. Prol. & T.* 126 Ay we han good hope It for to doon, and after it we grope. **1558** KNOX *First Blast* (Arb.) 44 Greate wonder it is, that in so greate light of Goddes truthe, men list to grope and wander in darknes. **1589** *Pappe w. Hatchet* B ij b, It was well groapt at. **1594** T. B. *La Primaud. Fr. Acad.* II. Ep. Rdr., If they will but grope after Him, in whom we all liue, mooue, and haue our being. **1682** DRYDEN *Relig. Laici* 23 As blindly groped they for a future state. **1718** PRIOR *Solomon* I. 723 O wretched impotence of human mind! We..darkling grope, not knowing we are blind. **1779** JOHNSON 16 Apr. in *Boswell*, Mallet, I believe, never wrote a single line of his projected life of the Duke of Marlborough. He groped for materials, and thought of it. **1845** MAURICE *Mor. & Met. Philos.* in *Encycl. Metrop.* II. 600/1 The scientific principle which Parmenides had been groping after. **1850** TENNYSON *In Mem.* lv, I stretch lame hands of faith, and grope. **1867** FREEMAN *Norm. Conq.* (1876) I. App. 665 A minute knowledge which certainly cannot be got by the dull process of groping in the Chronicles. **1889** JESSOPP *Coming of Friars* vii. 325 The prophets had been groping after a formula which might be their strength.

d. ***to grope one's way***: to find one's way by feeling about or groping; to feel one's way; to proceed in a tentative manner. *lit.* and *fig.*

1580 BARET *Alv.* G 567 To proue, trie, or feele the way as he goeth: to grope the way. **1714** GAY *Trivia* III. 224 Hence wert thou doom'd in endless Night to stray Through Theban Streets, and cheerless groap thy Way. *c* **1789** GIBBON *Autobiographies* (1896) 227, I groped my way to the chappel and the communion-table by the dim light of my catechism. **1824** W. IRVING *T. Trav.* I. 93, I groped my way out of the room. **1838** DICKENS *O. Twist* xxviii, We..groped our way down stairs in the pitch dark. **1862** SIR B. BRODIE *Psychol. Inq.* II. i. 7 With our limited capacities, we are compelled..to grope our way as well as we can.

†**3.** *trans.* To touch with the hands; to examine by the touch; to handle, feel; to probe (a wound). Also, to take hold of, grasp, seize. *Obs.*

c **1000** ÆLFRIC *Hom.* II. 134 Se cuma his cneow grapode mid his halwendum handum. *a* **1225** *Ancr. R.* 378 Auh is for sum þet schal reden þis inouh reaðe, þet gropieð hire to softe noðeleas. *c* **1250** *Gen. & Ex.* 1544 Ysaac wende it were esau, for he grapte him and fond him ru. *a* **1300** *Cursor M.* 18694 Thomas..he lete To put his hand in at his side, Al for to grape his wond wide. *c* **1375** *Sc. Leg. Saints, Magdalena* 459 þe child cane..grape þe modyr pape, for fud to tak. **1387** TREVISA *Higden* (Rolls) III. 449 He by-clipped þe deed body and gropeþ the woundes. *c* **1440** *York Myst.* xlii. 57 Se þat I haue flessh and bone, Gropes me nowe. *c* **1450** *St. Cuthbert* (Surtees) 850 It [an animal] walde of him be graped and fedde. **1501** DOUGLAS *Pal. Hon.* I. lxviii, Oft I wald my hand behald to se Gif it alterit, and oft my visage graip. **1575** *Gamm. Gurton* III. iv, Ichould twenty pound your neele is in her throte! Grope her, ich say! Me thinkes ich feele it. **1597–8** BP. HALL *Sat.* II. iv. 10 Grope the pulse of euerie mangie wrest. **1641** J. SHUTE *Sarah & Hagar* (1649) 88 Those that grasp and grope all that they can pretend any right to..shall finde God blowe upon it, and make it uncomfortable. **1647** J. HALL *Poems* II. 98 They grope but Aire. **1730** SWIFT *Ladies Dressing-r.* 93 But Strephon, cautious, never meant The Bottom of the Pan to grope. **1738** JOHNSON *London* 151 Slaves that..Can Balbo's eloquence applaud, and swear He gropes his breeches with a monarch's air.

†**b.** in indecent sense. *Obs.*

13.. *Sir Beues* 3105 (MS. A.) þow gropedest þe wif aniȝt to lowe. *a* **1380** *St. Bernard* 133 in Horstm. *Altengl. Leg.* (1878) 43 Heo lay stille a luytel whil, þen heo groped him atte laste. **1664** WOOD *Life* 26 Jan., Kissed her and groped her and felt her brests.

c. To handle (poultry) in order to find whether they have eggs.

1590 NASHE *Almond for Parrat* 5 Groaping his owne hennes, like a Cotquean. **1611** COTGR., *Apprendre aux poissons à nager*, to teach fishes to swimme; (an idle, vaine, or needlesse labour) we say, to teach his grandame to grope ducks.

†**d.** To probe with an instrument. *Obs. rare*$^{-1}$.

1610 MARKHAM *Masterp.* II. xcv. 383 Then grope the hoofe with a paire of pinsons round about vntill you haue found the place grieued.

e. To search, rummage. *Obs.* exc. *Sc.*

1526 SKELTON *Magnyf.* 2258 Nay, I know well inough ye are bothe well handyd To grope a gardeuyaunce, though it be well bandyd. **1837** CARLYLE *Fr. Rev.* II. III. v, All men in black, spite of their Tickets of Entry, are clutched by the collar, and groped.

†**f.** *hyperbolically. Obs.*

a **1240** *Sawles Warde* in *Cott. Hom.* 251 Se þicke is þrinne þe posternesse þat me hire mei grapin. *a* **1300** *Cursor M.* 23242 Of helle..þe sext paine..es suilk mercknes men mai it grape. **1340** HAMPOLE *Pr. Consc.* 6566 Swa mykel myrknes, þat it may be graped, swa thik it es.

†**4.** *fig.* **a.** To apprehend as something palpable. Often with clause as obj. *Obs.*

13.. *K. Alis.* 6627 Monye buth theo merveilles of Ethiope, That Alisaundre hath y-grope. **1390** GOWER *Conf.* I. 205 This king hath spoke with the pope And tolde all that he couthe grope, What greveth in his conscience. *c* **1470** HARDING *Chron.* ccxlii. App. ix, Your nauy maye receaue vytayle in that countre, A longest the water of Foorth, as I can grope. **1584** FENNER *Def. Ministers* (1587) 70 Which meaning.., if he could not grope it by the purpose wee had in answering the first obiection: yet it was maruelous hee espyed it not by our words. *a* **1603** T. CARTWRIGHT *Confut. Rhem. N.T.* (1618) 561 This doctrin..is so evident that it is marvell that any can be so senceless as not to grope it. **1611** MIDDLETON & DEKKER *Roaring Girl* II. i, Thou'rt familiarly acquainted there, I grope that. **1617** COLLINS *Def. Bp. Ely* II. viii. 329 So notorious is the originall corruption of mankinde, that sense gropes it, and nature feeles it. **1642** ROGERS *Naaman* 350 When you might have felt and groped the Lord in his manifest providence.

†**b.** To take hold of (a person) mentally. *Obs.*

1602 MARSTON *Ant. & Mel.* v. Wks. 1856 I. 60 As I am a true knight, I feele honourable eloquence begin to grope mee alreadie.

†**c.** To make examination or trial of; to examine, sound, probe (a person, the conscience, etc.); to investigate (a matter). *Obs.*

a **1225** [see GROPING *vbl. sb.* (2nd quot.)]. *c* **1386** CHAUCER *Prol.* 646 Who so koulde in oothur thyng hym grope Thanne hadde he spent al his Philosophie. —— *Sompn. T.* 109 Thise curatz been ful negligent and slowe To grope tendrely a conscience. *c* **1440** *York Myst.* xxiii. 104, I rede we..grope þam how þis game is begonne. *c* **1450** MYRC 912 When he seyþ I con no more Freyne hym þus and grope hys sore [*i.e.* sin]. **1513** DOUGLAS *Æneis* I. Prol. 502 Gif I haue failȝeit, bald[l]y repruif my ryme, Bot first, I pray ȝou, grape the mater clene. **1523** SKELTON *Garl. Laurel* 617 Sume fayne themselfe..medelynge spyes, by craft to grope thy mynde.

1542–5 BRINKLOW *Lament.* 23 b, Prestes, as longe as they shall grope our partyculare synnes. **1557** N. T. (Genev.) *Acts* xxiv. *Contents*, Felix gropeth him, thinking to haue a bribe. **1596** DALRYMPLE tr. *Leslie's Hist. Scot.* v. 296 Fenela, quhome nature had formet to deceiue, grapet the kingis mynd. *a* **1651** CALDERWOOD *Hist. Kirk* (1843) II. 313 Davie gropped their mindes, how they were affected to the banished lords.

5. *to grope out*: to find by feeling about. Chiefly *fig.* To find by tentative effort; to search out.

1590 R. HITCHCOCK *Quintess. Wit* 17 So muche lesse we doo gather and groape out the trueth. **1647** TRAPP *Comm. 1 Cor.* i. 21 Not the Jews by their deep Doctours, nor the Gentiles by their wits and wizards..could grope out God. **1701** CIBBER *Love makes Man* IV. ii, At last I have grop'd out a Window, that will let me into the Secret. **1727** A. HAMILTON *New. Acc. E. Ind.* I. p. xxii, Our Duty..is..set before us in the brightest Light, while theirs is to be groped out by the dark Glimmerings of very fallible Reason. *c* **1820** *Houlston's Juvenile Tracts* No. 11 *Hold Up your Head* 12 He will grope it out, and brood over it. **1846** J. W. CROKER in *C. Papers* 4 Feb. (1884), You..enable me to grope out somewhat of the present posture of affairs. **1864** LOWELL *Fireside Trav.* 150, I..began to hack frozenly at a log which I groped out.

grope, obs. f. GROOP *sb.*; var. GROOP *v.*

groper (ˈgrəʊpə(r)). [f. GROPE *v.* + -ER[1].]
1. a. One who gropes, in various senses of the vb.

1567 DRANT *Horace's Ep.* I. xviii. F v, A groper after nouelties. **1693** EVELYN *De la Quint. Compl. Gard.* II. 86 Those Gropers, who, to gather one according to their Mind, will spoil a hundred by the violent impression of their Unskillful Thumb. **1760–72** H. BROOKE *Fool of Quality* (1809) III. 26 A substitute in the want of knowledge, a groper in the want of light. **1781** H. SWINBURNE *Crts. Europe Last Cent.* (1841) I. 379 A groper in politics, without sufficient steadiness or understanding to..carry through a great..plan. **1899** *Blackw. Mag.* Feb. 348/1 Thou groper after vainglory.

b. *slang.* A blind man; the blindfolded player in the game of blind-man's-buff.

a **1700** B. E. *Dict. Cant. Crew*, Gropers, blind Men. **1813** R. H. in *Examiner* 17 May 315/2 A man..nearly approached by the darkened groper.

2. *Naut.* *Channel groper, North Sea groper*: a cruiser stationed in the Channel or the North Sea.

1830 MARRYAT *King's Own* xiii, If he is an old channel groper, we shall have some difficulty. **1867** in SMYTH *Sailor's Word-bk.*

3. *Old slang.* A pocket.

1789 G. PARKER *Life's Painter* 130 *Gropers*, pockets.

4. A jocular appellation for a West Australian. So **'Groperland**, West Australia; also **'Groperlander**, a West Australian. Cf. *sand groper* (SAND *sb.*[2] 10).

1924 LAWRENCE & SKINNER *Boy in Bush* iii. 39 Western Australia is full of old prisoners, black fellers, and white ones too. The whites, born here, is called 'gropers', if you take me, sir. **1926** J. DOONE *Timely Tips for New Austral.*, *Groper*, a West Australian. **1941** BAKER *Dict. Austral. Slang* 33 *Groperland*, Western Australia. **1945** —— *Austral. Lang.* x. 186 *Western Australians*.., groperlanders. **1949** *Geogr. Mag.* Feb. 373 *Groper*, a Western Australian.

groper, var. GROUPER.

gropery (ˈgrəʊpərɪ). *nonce-wd.* [f. GROPE *v.* + -ERY.] The action of groping (in the dark).

1777 T. TWINING *Let. Dr. Burney* 16 June in *Country Clergym. 18th C.* (1882) 51 What the deuce, then, should make you shrink now, when almost all drudgery, and gropery, and pokery is over?

groping (ˈgrəʊpɪŋ), *vbl. sb.* [f. GROPE *v.* + -ING[1]. In OE. *grâpung*.] The action of the verb GROPE in its various senses; †in early use, touch, the sense of touch; *in groping*, to the touch (*obs.*).

c **1000** ÆLFRIC *Hom.* I. 234 Forðan ðurh his [*sc.* St. Thomas's] grapunge we sind ȝeleaffulle. *a* **1225** *Ancr. R.* 206 Mid luue speche, cos, unhende gropunges. *Ibid.* 314 Unneaðe, þauh a last, þuruh þen abbodes gropunge, he hit seide. *c* **1380** WYCLIF *Serm.* Sel. Wks. I. 249 þese [fyve] wittis ben clepid siȝte, and heering, smelling and taist, wiþ groping. **1398** TREVISA *Barth. De P.R.* III. xxi. (1495) 69 The wytte of gropynge. *Ibid.* XVII. lii. (Tollem. MS.), Ebenus..is playne and smoþe in gropynge. *c* **1440** *Jacob's Well* 219 Wyht mowth in kyssyng, wyth hand in gropyng. *c* **1560** A. SCOTT *Poems* (S.T.S.) iv. 52 Thair followis thingis thre To gar thame ga in gucking, Brasing, graping, and plucking. **1594** T. B. *La Primaud. Fr. Acad.* II. 549 Euery Spirit always searcheth after God as a blind man goeth by groaping. **1791** BURKE *App. Whigs* 84 They lost their way by groping about in the dark, and fumbling among rotten parchments and musty records. **1830** D'ISRAELI *Chas. I*, III. vii. 119 Feeling our way..in these cautious gropings after truth. **1847** HALLIWELL, *Groping*, (1) A mode of ascertaining whether geese or fowls have eggs. *Var. dial.* (2) A mode of catching trout by tickling them with the hands under rocks or banks. **1855** LYNCH *Rivulet* XL. i, Is life a groping and a guess, A vain cry in a wilderness? **1888** *Athenæum* 1 Dec. 739/1 The tentative mathematical gropings of the Egyptians and Phœnicians.

groping (ˈgrəʊpɪŋ), *ppl. a.* [f. GROPE *v.* + -ING[2].] That gropes, in senses of the vb.

13.. *E.E. Allit. P.* B. 591 He is þe gropande god. **1599** MARSTON *Sco. Villanie* I. iii. 184 Shall Curio streake his lims on his daies couch, In Sommer bower? and with bare groping touch Incense his lust? **1691** HARTCLIFFE *Virtues* 309 The groping World had so bewildred it self in an endless Maze of Errour. **1714** GAY *Trivia* II. 51 The groaping Blind direct. **1861** TULLOCH *Eng. Purit.* i. 75 Amidst its wild and groping earnestness, it sheds a vivid light upon the inward man.

absol. **1850** MRS. BROWNING *Poems* II. 168 Or, that a hundred of the groping Like himself had made one Homer.

gropingly (ˈgrəʊpɪŋlɪ), *adv.* [f. GROPING *ppl. a.* + -LY[2].] In a groping manner; as one feeling his way blindly or in the dark. *lit.* and *fig.*

1550–67 THOMAS *Ital. Gram., Dict.*, *Tentone*, gropyngly, as he that goeth in the derk. **1620** T. GRANGER *Div. Logike* 41 To our sences, whereby we attaine gropingly, and creepingly to some apprehension of the forme. **1660** tr. *Amyraldus' Treat. conc. Relig.* I. i. 4 This Divinity whom men have sought after, as it were, gropingly in all Ages. **1848** C. BRONTË *J. Eyre* xxxvii, He descended the one step, and advanced slowly and gropingly toward the grass plat. **1885** E. F. BYRNE *Entangled* I. I. xvi. 295 The fly..felt it gropingly with its antennæ.

gropple (ˈgrɒp(ə)l), *v. dial.* [var. of GRAPPLE *v.*, after GROPE.] *intr.* = GROPE *v.* 2 b.

1860 HUGHES *Tom Brown at Oxf.* xxx, Tom..had gone off to the brook to gropple in the bank for crawfish. *Ibid.* xlvii, Creeping brooks afforded good sport for small truants groppling about with their hands.

†**'gropsing.** *Obs.* [Cf. GRASP *sb.* 4 and GRISPING.] Twilight.

1606 in *Wilts Archæol. Mag.* XXII. 227 Both came unto the sayd Tryvatts howse in the gropsing of the yevening.

groroilite (grəʊˈrɔɪlaɪt). *Min.* [f. *Groroi* (see below) + -LITE. (Named by Berthier, 1832).] Earthy manganese, occurring in roundish masses, of a brownish-black colour with reddish-brown streaks; wad.

1844 DANA *Min.* (ed. 2) 444 The Groroilite of Berthier occurs in rounded pieces in sand and clay at Groroi, Cautern, and Vecdessos in France.

grorudite (ˈgrəʊrʊdaɪt). *Petrogr.* [a. G. *grorudite* (W. C. Brögger 1890, in *Zeitschr. f. Krystallogr.* XVI. I. 66), f. *Grorud*, name of a locality now included in the north-eastern part of the city of Oslo, Norway + -ITE[1].] (See quot. 1960.)

1896 J. F. KEMP *Handbk. Rocks* 140 *Grorudite*, Brögger's name for a porphyritic dike rock from Grorud, near Christiania, Norway. **1926** H. H. READ et al. *Geol. Strath Oykell* 72 The grorudites of the Loch Ailsh mass carry much less ægirine than the type grorudites of Norway. **1960** *Gloss. Geol.* (Amer. Geol. Inst.) (ed. 2) 131/1 *Grorudite*, a hypabyssal rock with trachytoid texture containing phenocrysts of alkalic feldspar and aegirine and much quartz.

gros, pa. t. GRISE *v. Obs.*

‖**gros** (gro), *a.* [Fr. (see GROSS *a.*).] Occurring in various French designations, as **gros bleu**, a dark blue used to paint china; **Gros Michel**, the West Indian banana; **gros point**, (*a*) (**de Venise**) a type of lace worked in bold relief, originally from Venice; (*b*) any of a variety of stitches employed in canvas embroidery; **gros sel**, coarse salt (in quot. 1917 *fig.*).

1870 LADY C. SCHREIBER *Jrnl.* 22 Feb. (1911) I. 74 Sèvres cups and saucers, gros bleu, with gold decoration. **1882** *Hamilton Sale Catal.* No. 495 A Gros-bleu and Gold Sevres Coffee-cup and Saucer. **1885** *Encycl. Brit.* XIX. 638/1 The chief colours [of Sèvres porcelain] are *gros bleu*, a very dark blue; *bleu du roi*, [etc.]. **1961** *Connoisseur New Guide Ant. Eng. Pott., Porc., & Glass* 57 The ground colours of Sèvres were also imitated, such as the 'gros bleu' (called 'mazarine' blue). **1970** *Times* 10 Mar. 7/2 (Advt.), Gros-bleu and blue-scale wares with floral and bird decoration. **1913** W. FAWCETT *Banana* i. 16 An improvement on the ordinary fruit occurred in Martinique, and eighty years ago M. Jean Francois Pouyat..was..sufficiently alive to its importance to introduce it into Jamaica. This variety..is known now as the Jamaican or Gros Michel banana. **1927** *Observer* 17 Apr. 7/1 The Gros Michel..which comes from Jamaica. **1951** *New Biol.* XI. 67 But, when it is a question of really large scale enterprise, *the* banana is the Gros Michel banana, sometimes known as the Jamaica banana. **1962** *Queensland Fruit & Veg. News* 11 Oct. 338/1 Bodles Altafort has good qualities, which are superior to those of Lacatan and Gros Michel. [**1390** [see POINT *sb.*[1] B. 5].] **1865** F. B. PALLISER *Hist. Lace* iv. 47 This is our Rose (raised) Venice point, the Gros Point de Venise, the Punto a rilievo, so highly prized and so extensively used for albs, collerettes, berthes, and costly decoration. **1882** *Encycl. Brit.* XIV. 186 Works of bold design done in relief are called 'gros point de Venise'. **1911** *Ibid.* XVI. (*caption*, facing p. 40), Jabot of needlepoint lace worked partly in relief, and usually known as 'gros point de Venise'. **1934** M. THOMAS *Dict. Embroidery Stitches* 110 *Gros point*, a term sometimes used when referring to certain Canvas Stitches worked over two or more horizontal threads of the canvas, such as the variations of Cross Stitch, Florentine Stitch and the Gobelin Stitches. **1958** *Observer* 20 July 9/1 What appears as gros-point embroidery worked with the greatest skill in the shape of birds, trees and flowers, proves to be a design woven into the silk fabric. **1962** *Victoria & Albert Mus. Internat. Art Treas. Exhib.* 9/1 A George I needlework winged armchair with upholstered adjustable back and loose cushion seat covered with floral gros-point needlework. **1968** *Times* 8 Feb. 8/8 Since beginning rehearsals..she has almost completed a chair cover in *gros point*. [**1849** THACKERAY *Pendennis* I. xxxiv. 340 He instantly related a funny story, seasoned with what the French call *gros sel*.] **1917** G. SAINTSBURY *Hist. Fr. Novel* I. viii. 169 There is no want of salt, though there is no (or very little) *gros sel* in the *Astrée*. **1935** M. MORPHY *Recipes of all Nations* 30 Sprinkle it with salt—the French always use 'gros sel', a very coarse salt, which gives an excellent flavour. **1958** *Spectator* 15 Aug. 222/2 The Maldon Crystal Salt Company's product is apparently the only *gros sel* sold in this country and is a 99.617 per cent. pure sea-water evaporation from the Blackwater estuary. **1967** *Sunday Times* (Colour Suppl.) 5 Mar. 42/1 That first purchase of *gros sel* for cooking.

gros(e, variant or obs. form of GROSS.

grosbeak (ˈgrəʊsbiːk). Also 8 gross-beak. [ad. F. *gros-bec*, f. *gros* large + *bec* beak.] A name given to a number of small birds having a large stout bill, chiefly of the families *Fringillidæ* and *Ploceidæ*. The common grosbeak is the hawfinch (*Coccothraustes vulgaris*). Other species are indicated by a defining word prefixed, as **green grosbeak** = GREENFINCH 1; **pine g.**, *Pinicola enucleator*; **cardinal g.** (see CARDINAL *sb.* 7); **grenadier g.** (see GRENADIER[2] 2 *a*); **sociable g.**, a South African weaver-bird, *Philhetærus socius*; also (in U.S.) **blue g.** (*Guiraca cærulea*), **evening g.** (*Hesperophona vespertina*), **rose-breasted g.** (*Hedymeles ludovicianus*).

1678 RAY *Willughby's Ornith.* 244 The common Grosbeak: *Coccothraustes vulgaris*. **1730** MORTIMER in *Phil. Trans.* XXXVI. 430 *Coccothraustes cærulea*, the blue Gross-Beak. *Coccothraustes purpurea*, the purple Gross-Beak. **1767** G. WHITE *Selborne* (1853) 364 Mr. B. shot a cock grosbeak which he had observed to haunt his garden. **1773** *Gentl. Mag.* XLIII. 220 The red-throated Gross-beak. **1810** A. WILSON in *Poems & Lit. Prose* (1876) I. 222 The blue grosbeak. **1850** R. G. CUMMING *Hunter's Life S. Afr.* (ed. 2) I. 233 Many of them [cameel-dorn trees] were inhabited by whole colonies of the social grosbeak. **1859** *Amer. Cycl.* III. 283/1 The pensile grosbeak swings its basket nest from a pendant twig over a running stream..The sociable grosbeaks unite in the construction of a large basket-like cluster of nests..in a single structure. **1882** *Century Mag.* June 210 Hear the grosbeak's whistle bold. **1884** ROE in *Harper's Mag.* Mar. 619/1 One of our most beautiful.. visitants is the pine grosbeak.

‖**groschen** (ˈgrəʊʃən). Also 7–8 groshen, (8 grosch). Pl. groschen; also 7–8 groshen(s, 8 grosches, 9 groschens. [G. *groschen* masc., altered form (not dim.) of MHG. *gros*, *grosse* = F. *gros*: see GROSS *sb.*[2]] Before the establishment of the present German monetary system, a small silver coin and money of account variously = $\frac{1}{24}$, $\frac{1}{30}$, or $\frac{1}{36}$ of a thaler.

1617 MORYSON *Itin.* I. 35 Here each man paid..seuen maria-groshen for meat. *c* **1622** J. TAYLOR (Water P.) *Wks.* (1630) I. 67/1 The Grosh, Potchandle, Stiuer, Doyte, and Sowse Compar'd with me, are all scarce worth a Lowse. **1753** HANWAY *Trav.* (1762) I. VII. lxxxviii. 407 They keep their accounts here in gilders, grosch and phennigen. **1756–7** tr. *Keysler's Trav.* (1760) IV. 305 Reckoning the quart of wine only at four groshens. **1823** W. IRVING *Life & Lett.* (1864) II. 149, I am let off for two dollars eight groschen fine. **1831** CARLYLE *Sart. Res.* (1858) 136 Their Flag..had you sold it at any market-cross, would not have brought above three groschen. **1892** ZANGWILL *Childr. Ghetto* II. 5 With our Groschen let us rebuild Jerusalem and our holy Temple.

‖**gros de Naples** (gro də nap(ə)l). [F. *gros* GROSS *a.*, used subst.] A heavy silk fabric, made originally at Naples. Also *attrib.* So ‖**gros de Tours**, a similar fabric orig. made at Tours.

1799 W. TOOKE *View Russian Emp.* III. 510 These manufactories..make taffety..gros-de-tour, velvet,..and various kinds of half-silks. **1828** *Lights & Shades* I. 239 Mrs. Gubbins had a new Gros-de-Naples silk bonnet and feathers. **1848** CLOUGH *Bothie* II. 90 We should soon see them abandon..gros-de-naples for plain lindsey-woolsey.

groser (ˈgrəʊzə(r)). *Obs.* exc. *Sc.* and *north.* Also 7, 9 grozer, 9 grosier. [ad. F. *groseille*, with substitution of *r* for final *l*.] A gooseberry. Also *attrib.*, as *groser-bush*.

1548 TURNER *Names of Herbes* 88 Vua crispa is also called Grossularia, in english a Groser bushe, a Goose-bery bush. **1615** LAWSON *Orch. & Gard.* III. iii. (1668) 3 Bushes bearing berries, as..Goose-berries or Grosers. **1674** JOSSELYN *Voy. New Eng.* 72 The Gooseberry-bush, the berry of which is called Grosers or thorn Grapes. **1833** *Gentl. Mag.* I. 597 A garden filled with grosier bushes. **1886** *Chesh. Gloss.*, *Grosier*. **1893** *Northumbld. Gloss.* s.v., An eager person is said to 'Jump like a cock at a grozer'.

groser: see GROCER, GROSSER[1].

groset (ˈgrəʊzɪt). *Sc.* Also 8–9 grozet, 9 grosert, grossart. [f. GROSER, by addition of excrescent *t*, and subsequent omission of *r*.] A gooseberry.

1786 BURNS *To a louse* 26 Ye set your nose out As plump and gray as onie grozet. **1824** SCOTT *Redgauntlet* Let. xiii, Saunders lap at the proposition, like a cock at a grossart. **1890** J. SERVICE *Thir Notandums* iii. 14 A chappin o' grozets. *attrib.* **1821** GALT *Annals Parish* xxviii. (1895) 178 Many ..had planted groset and berry bushes. **1823** *Blackw. Mag.* XIII. 367 His grozet eyes. **1895** *Cumnock News* 28 Jan. 5/7 Grozet Fair day. **1896** CROCKETT *Grey Man* xiv. 101 The garden..was full of groset bushes.

grosgrain (ˈgrəʊgreɪn, ‖grogrɛ̃). [Fr., = coarse grain; cf. GROGRAM.] Any of various corded fabrics. Hence **grosgrained** *a.* Also *fig.*

1869 *Rep. U.S. Commissioner Agric.* 290 Dress silks, *gros grains*, poplins, foulards, and pongees. **1897** *Sears, Roebuck Catal.* 408 Silk Watch Fobs... The Ribbons are of Fine Quality Black Gros Grained Silk. **1905** *Westm. Gaz.* 5 Aug. 10/2 Grosgrain is far better with alpaca than any shiny make of taffeta. **1927** *Daily Express* 14 Mar. 5 Two toned grosgrained ribbon. **1930** *Times* 17 Mar. 15/6 On the black grosgrain ribbon hat is a jewelled pin. **1932** F. L. WRIGHT

Autobiogr. III. 309 Every flat plane grosgrained like the sahuato itself. **1969** *Sears Catal.* Spring/Summer 18 Widely-brimmed Hat. Braid straw with grosgrain ribbon streamers.

grosh(en, obs. ff. GROSCHEN.

†**gross,** *sb.*[1] *Obs. rare*$^{-1}$. [ad. L. *grossus.*] A green fig; a young fig.

c **1420** *Pallad. on Husb.* IV. 633 And premature yf that the list enlonge Their grossis, whenne as grete as benys be So tacke hem of.

†**gross,** *sb.*[2] *Obs.* Also 7 **grosse,** (7 *pl.* **grooz**). [repr. F. *gros*, It. *grosso.*] A name for various foreign coins (historically representing the mediæval *grossus* or GROAT); e.g. the German GROSCHEN, and the Italian *grosso*, worth about 3*d.*

1638 L. ROBERTS *Map Comm.* clxxix. II. 104 Their Accounts are heere [at Antwerpe] kept by Livers, Sol and Deniers, which they terme Pounds, Shillings and Pence of grosses, 12. grosses making a Sold, and 20. Sold a Liver or pound Flemish. *Ibid.* clxxx. II. 111 A grosse is 6. deniers turnois. **1655** DIGGES *Compl. Ambass.* 96 Queen Maries.. Dowry [was] Three thousand pounds Flemish, after fourty grooz to the pound. **1673** *Necessity Maintain. Estab. Relig.* (ed. 5) 31 His Holiness..has valued the most horrid crimes at so easie rates as a few Grosses, or a Julio. **1686** *Lond. Gaz.* No. 2177/3 The Letters from Buda..tell us, That 1000 Hey-dukes who have three Gross a day..are daily at work. **1705** HICKERINGILL *Priest-cr.* II. i. 7 For keeping a Concubine (if a Priest) 7 Gross..but if a Lay-man keep a Miss, the price is—8 Gross. [*Ibid.* II. viii. 73 To keep a Wench—will cost you Eight Groats, or Seven Grosso's, if a Lay-Man.]

gross (grəʊs), *sb.*[3] Forms: 5 **groos,** 5, 7 **groce,** 6 **gros,** 6–7 **grosse,** 8–9 **grose,** 7– **gross.** [a. F. *grosse* (= Sp. *gruesa*, Pg., It. *grossa*), orig. the fem. of *gros* big, GROSS *a.*] Twelve dozen. Not found in *pl.*, the sing. being used with numerals. Also ***small gross***, in opposition to ***great gross*** = 12 gross (see GREAT *a.* 8 d).

1411 *Close Roll, 12 Hen. IV*, 26 Apr., [To export from England to Ireland] unum groos de poyntes. **1480** *Wardr. Acc. Edw. IV* (1830) 150 A groos pointes of sylk of divers colours. **1495–7** *Naval Acc. Hen. VII* (1896) 265 Bowes—cc; Strynges—v groce; Arowes—cccc sheffes. **1549** *Privy Council Acts* (1890) II. 348 Bowe stringes, xl gros. **1598** B. JONSON *Ev. Man in Hum.* III. i, Sure, he utters them [sonnets] then, by the grosse. **1630** J. TAYLOR (Water P.) *Superbiæ Flagellum* 36 Wks. 31/1 Fourteene groce of buttons and gold lace. **1660** *Act 12 Chas. II*, c. 4 Schedule s.v. *Bosses*, Bosses for Bridles the small groce, cont. 12 dozen *jl.* **1685** *Lond. Gaz.* No. 2001/4 A Groce of Gimp Lace mixt with Tincy, a Groce of Silk Buttons. **1719** DE FOE *Crusoe* I. ix. (1840) 153 A gross of tobacco-pipes. **1803** S. PEGGE *Anecd. Eng. Lang.* 261 We call twelve dozen; i.e. twelve multiplied by itself a gross or grose by tale. **1805** T. HARRAL *Scenes of Life* II. 63 A manufacturer of ghosts and monsters by the gross.

gross (grəʊs), *a.* and *sb.*[4] Forms: 5 **groos,** 5–7 **groce,** 5–8 **gros(e, grosse,** (6 **groose, grouse**), 6 *Sc.* **groiss,** 5– **gross.** [a. F. *gros*, fem. *grosse* big, thick, coarse (11th c. in Littré) = Pr. *gros*, Sp. *grueso*, Pg., It. *grosso*:—late L. *grossus* thick (freq. in the Vulgate). The word has developed in Eng. several senses not found in Fr.

The origin of the late L. word is unknown; chronology shows that it cannot be ad. OHG. *grôz* GREAT; there is no probability that it is cogn. w. the synonymous *crassus.*]

A. *adj.* **I.** With reference to bulk.

†**1. a.** Thick, stout, massive, big. *Obs.*

14.. LYDG. & BURGH *Secrees* 2660 With nekke to smal in proporcioun whoo be sene Is a fool..And ovir gross A lyeer detestable. **1516** *Life Bridget* in *Myrr. Our Ladye* p. lvii, Whiche fro hyr byrthe had a great grosse throte moche foule & dyfformyd. **1570** DEE *Math. Pref.*, It [Architecture] is but for building of a house, Pallace, Church, Forte, or such like, grosse workes. **1600** *Vestry Bks.* (Surtees) 132 For regestering the presentment into on grosse booke, iiij d. **1605** SHAKS. *Lear* IV. vi. 14 The Crowes and Choughes, that wing the midway ayre Shew scarce so grosse as Beetles. **1661** BOYLE *Spring of Air* (1682) 95 The particles of the Air (being so gross as not easily to pervade the Pores of the Bladder). **1667** MILTON *P.L.* VI. 552 With heavie pace the Foe Approaching gross and huge. **1687** DRYDEN *Hind & P.* III. 691 Your finger is more gross than the great monarch's loins. **1776** G. SEMPLE *Building in Water* 39 The Piers being extremely gross, increased the Rapidity of the Water between them. **1794** KIRWAN *Elem. Min.* (ed. 2) I. 21 The grains will appear distinct, small or gross, coarse or fine.

absol. **1624** WOTTON *Archit.* in *Reliq.* (1651) 229 The length thereof shall be six Diameters, of the grossest of the Pillar below.

b. Of a shoot or stalk: Thick, bulky. Now only (exc. *dial.*) with notion of abnormal growth: Luxuriant, rank.

1578 LYTE *Dodoens* I. xxvi. 39 Orpyne hath a round grosse brittell stem [F. *a la tige ronde et espesse*]. **1597** GERARDE *Herbal* I. cvi. § 1. 176 A thick soft grosse stalk. *a* **1682** SIR T. BROWNE *Tracts* (1684) 11 An extraordinary Cluster, made up of many depending upon one gross stalk. **1747** WESLEY *Prim. Physic* (1762) 112 Burn to ashes..the gross Stalks, on which the red Coleworts grow. **1863** WISE *New Forest* 283 *Gross*, often used in a good sense for luxuriant, and applied to the young green crops. **1881** MASTERS in *Encycl. Brit.* XII. 213/2 Strong-growing pears..are grafted on the quince stock in order to restrict their tendency to form 'gross' shoots. **1882** *Garden* 11 Mar. 169/1 Gross shoots and leaders only being tied in to check an uneven distribution of the sap.

†**c.** Of letters printed or written: Large. *Obs.*

c **1470** HENRY *Wallace* VII. 110 The fyrst writtyng was gross letteris off bras. The secound gold, the thrid was siluir scheyne. **1705** WANLEY in Hearne *Collect.* 4 Aug. (O.H.S.) I. 24 Y[e] King must have his Bible printed with a gross Letter. **1765** BLACKSTONE *Comm.* I. 182 The bill is then ordered to be engrossed, or written in a strong gross hand.

†**d.** ***gross meat*** [= F. *grosse viande*]: the flesh of large animals. (Cf. *gros chare* in CHARE *sb.*[4] 1.)

The expression was used also in a different sense: see 12.

c **1460** J. RUSSELL *Bk. Nurture* 461 The maner & forme of kervynge of metes þat byn groos, afftur my symplenes y haue shewed. **1477** NORTON *Ord. Alch.* vii. in Ashm. (1652) 103 Such heate, As Cookes make when they roast grosse Meate. **1697** tr. *C'tess D'Aunoy's Trav.* (1706) 46 When 'tis gross Meat, they fasten it to a String, and so let it hang on the Fire.

†**e.** Of a voice: Big, loud, deep. *Obs. rare*$^{-1}$.

1398 TREVISA *Barth. De P.R.* VI. xii. (1495) 196 Males haue a more gretter and grosser voys in all maner of kynde of beestes.

†**f.** *Hawking.* ***to fly gross***, i.e. at great birds.

1659 HOWELL *Vocab., Terms Arts* etc. iv, To fly grosse, viz. at great birds. **1677** COLES, *Fly gross* when hawks fly at great Birds, as Cranes.

2. Of persons or animals: **a.** Big-bodied, corpulent, burly. (Now only *dial.*) †***the Gross***: transl. of F. *le Gros* as an epithet of certain Frankish and French sovereigns. **b.** With mixture of other senses: Overfed, bloated with excess, unwholesomely or repulsively fat or corpulent. Hence said also of the 'habit of body'.

1577 NORTHBROOKE *Dicing* (1843) 40 Surfetting lyke a grosse and swollen Epicure. *a* **1578** LINDSAY (Pitscottie) *Chron. Scot.* I. 46 James..quho was callit gros because he was corpolent and growin of body. *Ibid.* 47 This James callit gros James. **1584** COGAN *Haven Health* cciii. 170 b, A man who was before verie grosse and fat..within a yeare or two became slender. **1596** SHAKS. *1 Hen. IV*, II. iv. 559 One of them is well knowne, my gracious Lord, a grosse fat man. **1609** BIBLE (Douay) *Deut.* xxxii. 15 The beloved was made grosse [Vulg. *incrassatus est*]. **1610** BP. CARLETON *Jurisd.* 196 Charles the grosse then Emperor. **1640** YORKE *Union Hon.* 7 Doing his homage for the same to Lewis the Grosse, king of France. **1732** ARBUTHNOT *Rules of Diet* 396 A full gross Habit of Body. **1744** ELIZA HEYWOOD *Female Spect.* (1748) I. 297 She had been observed, some months past, to be more gross than usual, and had affected to wear a loose dress. **1833** MARRYAT *P. Simple* (1863) 197 His gross habit of body rendered him very unfit for the climate. **1835** LONGF. *Outre-mer, Notary of Perigueux* (1851) 113 He was a gross, corpulent fellow, raised from a full-blooded Gascon breed. **1880** *W. Cornwall Gloss., Gross*, stout; big. 'A gross man'.

†**c.** Of a fruit: Full of pulp, large and succulent.

1578 LYTE *Dodoens* VI. xlii. 713 The sweete & grouse Peares [F. *les poyres douces et grasses*] are moystier and very little astringent.

†**3.** Of conspicuous magnitude; palpable, striking; plain, evident, obvious, easy to apprehend or understand. *Obs.*

c **1380** WYCLIF *Wks.* (1880) 408 Hoolynesse of lif techiþ rude men by groos ensaumple. **1551** ROBINSON tr. *More's Utop.* (Arb.) 128 They haue very few lawes: and the plainer and grosser that anye interpretation is: that they allowe as most iuste. **1586** EARL LEYCESTER in *Leyc. Corr.* (1844) 331 These things be so grosse as all men see them. **1596** SHAKS. *1 Hen. IV*, II. iv. 250 These Lyes are like the Father that begets them, grosse as a Mountaine, open, palpable. **1601** —— *All's Well* I. iii. 178 Now to all sence 'tis grosse You loue my sonne. **1638** FORD *Fancies* IV. i, Appear, Spadone! my proofs are pregnant and gross. **1690** DRYDEN *Don Sebastian* III. i, I might have marked it too: 'twas gross and palpable. *a* **1715** BURNET *Own Time* II. (1724) I. 212 Where he retracted all he had said, in so gross a manner, that [etc.]. **1727** DE FOE *Syst. Magic* I. i. (1840) 8 We should presently give him up for a Magician in the grossest acceptation of the word, and say, in short, that he deals with the Devil. **1793** SMEATON *Edystone L.* § 77 Which valediction, though in the gross sense, it might be said to contain little of Obligation.

quasi-*adv.* **1603** SHAKS. *Meas. for M.* II. iv. 82 To bee receiued plaine, Ile speake more grosse: Your Brother is to dye.

4. In concord with sbs. of evil import, and serving as an intensive of their meaning: Glaring, flagrant, monstrous.

a. with sbs. denoting vices, errors, faults, etc.

1581 J. BELL *Haddon's Answ. Osor.* 4 Or as though this your tedious quarell about this word Private did ought els, but bewray your grosse ignorance? **1597** HOOKER *Eccl. Pol.* V. iii. § 3 To capitall heresies lesse inclined, yet vnto grosse superstition, more. **1630** PRYNNE *Anti-Armin.* 125 We must make the effect more generall than its cause, which were a grosse absurdity. **1692** BENTLEY *Boyle Lect.* i. 10 The gross Folly and Stupidity of Atheists. **1709** BERKELEY *Theory of Vision* § 75 The gross blunders that ingenious men have been forced into. **1732** LAW *Serious C.* ii. (ed. 2) 16 So gross and prophane a Sin. **1781** J. MOORE *View Soc. It.* (1790) I. xxxix. 431 The grossest sophistry will pass on men's understandings. **1809–10** COLERIDGE *Friend* (1865) 134 The errors of the aristocratic party were full as gross and far less excusable. **1845** S. AUSTIN *Ranke's Hist. Ref.* III. 47 It is full of the grossest improbabilities. **1847** GROTE *Greece* II. xxvii. (1862) III. 41 An act of the grossest perfidy. **1880** C. R. MARKHAM *Peruv. Bark* ix. 88 They [plants]..all died through gross carelessness in their removal to Darjiling. **1884** CHURCH *Bacon* i. 26 Bacon is able..to show gross credulity and looseness of assertion on the part of the Roman Catholic advocate.

b. with personal designations.

1638 SIR T. HERBERT *Trav.* 302 The idolaters beyond all measure grosse Demonomists. **1817** G. S. FABER *Eight Dissert.* (1845) II. VI. iii. 30 No plea of conditionality..can save them from the charge of being gross impostors. **1869** TROLLOPE *He Knew* xx. (1878) 110 [He] had in his opinion made a gross fool of himself.

II. With reference to comprehensiveness.

†**5. a.** Of a denomination of value or weight: Relatively large; containing lower denominations. Of a mode of reckoning: Proceeding by large units. *Obs.*

1542 RECORDE *Gr. Artes* (1543) I viij b, That I call a grosse denomination, whiche doeth contayne vnder it manye other subtiller or smaller: as a pound in respect to shyllynges is a grosse denomination. **1680** H. MORE *Apocal. Apoc.* 123 The things foretold..are not to terminate on a year, but rather require that grosser numbring by Semitimes. **1682** SCARLETT *Exchanges* 115 Bills payable in currant Moneys out of Bank, must be paid in large (Gross) Moneys, and not in small pieces, as Stivers. **1801** A. RANKEN *Hist. France* I. I. v. 492 Corn and wine..may be bartered by the gross quantity.

†**b.** ***a hundred gross*** = 112 lb. or 1 cwt. ***fifty gross*** = 56 lb. or ½ cwt. *Obs.*

1659 WILLSFORD *Scales Comm.* 2 In all Commodities where a hundred gross is mentioned, it is 112 lb. **1762** ELIOT in *Phil. Trans.* LIII. 58 The barrs of iron which have hitherto been made of sand, and from fifty to fifty gross, hope in time to have them reach to seventy pounds weight each.

6. a. Entire, total, whole. Now only (opposed to *net*) of an amount, value, weight, number, or the like, before necessary deductions have been made. Also in advb. phrase †***gross sale***: by wholesale. ***gross reproduction rate***: a reproduction rate representing the average number of girls born to each woman of a population when deaths before the end of the child-bearing period are neglected, calculated from the average fertility rates of each age-group during the period considered.

1523 FITZHERB. *Husb.* § 36 And therfore he that byeth grosse sale, and retayleth, muste nedes be a wynner. —— *Surv.* xvii. (1539) 36 Cast togyther in one grosse some. **1571** DIGGES *Pantom.* P iv b, The producte is the grosse capacitie. **1600** SHAKS. *A.Y.L.* IV. i. 199 The most hollow louer..that may bee chosen out of the grosse band of the vnfaithfull. **1660** WILLSFORD *Scales Comm.* 23 The Tare..subtracted from the grosse weight. **1769** *Junius Lett.* vii. (1804) I. 45, I dare say you will not sell it either for a gross sum, or for an annuity upon lives. **1776** ADAM SMITH *W.N.* I. xi. (1869) I. 179 A sixth part of the gross produce may be reckoned the average rent of the tin mines of Cornwall. **1806** A. HUNTER *Culina* 138 The gross amount is one hundred and ninety-nine times. **1837** WHEWELL *Hist. Induct. Sci.* (1857) II. 229 Making a gross number of above 8000. **1849** MACAULAY *Hist. Eng.* iii. I. 388 The net receipt was little short of fifty thousand pounds..The gross receipt was about seventy thousand pounds. **1868** GLADSTONE *Juv. Mundi* v. (1869) 143 The gross figures of the chronology may be exaggerated. **1879** LUBBOCK *Addr. Pol. & Educ.* viii. 149 Over-insurance, insurance of gross-freight, and the law as regards seaworthiness on time policies. **1896** *Law Times* C. 508/1 The gross personal estate is sworn at £37,405..the net at £29,389. **1928** R. R. KUCZYNSKI *Balance Births & Deaths* I. ii. 25, 1·958 would then be what we may call the gross reproduction rate of Sweden in 1891–1900. **1945** *New Biol.* I. 42 A gross reproduction rate sustained at a level below 1·0 signifies that no reduction of mortality could save the community from eventual extinction. **1970** W. D. BORRIE *Growth & Control World Popul.* vi. 146 In terms of the gross reproduction rate there seems little danger of population decline among European peoples.

†**b.** Main, the great majority of. *Obs.*

1692 LUTTRELL *Brief Rel.* (1857) II. 502 Admirall Russell with the grosse fleet arrived at Torbay on Friday last. **1793** GIBBON *Misc. Wks.* (1814) III. 562 The gross mass of the laity..were more addicted to the exercises of the body than to those of the mind.

c. ***gross national product***, the total monetary value of all goods produced and services provided in a country during one year.

1947 J. F. DEWHURST *America's Needs & Resources* I. iv. 52/1 Gross national product represents the gross value of all the goods and services produced by business enterprises, including farmers, professional persons and other self-employed individuals. **1962** *Listener* 17 May 836/1 Economic growth is a purely materialistic concept. The rate of growth is usually defined as the rate of increase in gross national product or in gross national product per head, that is productivity, gross national product itself being the sum of all goods and services for which money changes hands. **1969** *Times* 12 Feb. 9/1 Although the gross national product (g.n.p.) may be increasing at about 4 per cent a year, it has to be shared out among a population growing at 2·5 per cent.

7. Concerned with large masses or outlines; general, opposed to *particular*. Now chiefly with reference to Anatomy or Pathology, opposed to *microscopic*. †***gross average*** = general average (see AVERAGE 4).

1433 LYDG. *St. Edmund* III. 927 Ingland hath suffryd this tribut ful terryble, Fond fauour noon, groos nor particuler. **1494** FABYAN *Chron.* VII. 437 All grose maters that concernyd the gouernaunce of his realme. **1702** BP. PATRICK *Josh.* xvi. 8 This is the inheritance of the tribe of Ephraim by their families.—A gross description of it. **1727–51** CHAMBERS *Cycl.* s.v. *Average*, For gross or common average to have place. **1748** HARTLEY *Observ. Man* I. ii. 141 To determine the Seat of the Pain within gross Limits. **1755** MAGENS *Insurances* I. 6 The Damage should not have been declared a gross Average, but a particular one on the Goods damaged. **1888** *Amer. Jrnl. Psychol.* I. 209 Anatomical results have a reputation for superior credibility, and it is a generally accepted idea that within the limits of gross anatomy the reputation is well grounded. **1897** *Allbutt's Syst. Med.* II. 849 A supposed drunken fit which may eventually turn out to be a state due to gross cerebral lesion.

III. With reference to density or consistency.

8. Dense, thick. (Often with mixture of the sense of branch IV.)

†**a.** of liquids, soils, and things generally. *Obs.*

1460–70 *Bk. Quintessence* I. 5 Lift vp þe glas as it stondith, and ȝe schal se in þickenes and cleernesse a difference bitwene þe quintam essenciam sublymed, and þe grose mater þat is in þe necke. **1533** Elyot *Cast. Helthe* I. (1541) 2 The urine redde & grosse. **1563** B. Googe *Eglogs* (Arb.) 90 And put my Plow, in grosse vntylled soyle. **1578** Lyte *Dodoens* III. x. 329 It cureth the blooddy flixe..being..dronken with some astringent liquor, as..grosse and thicke redde wine. **1608** Topsell *Serpents* (1658) 809 Beaten together with the grossest decoction of bitter Lupines. **1671** Salmon *Syn. Med.* III. xxiv. 454 *Staphsacre*, the seed is Emetick, and brings forth gross Flegm with violence. **1691** Ray *Creation* I. (1692) 38 The most subtile Body..may become as gross, and heavy, and stiff as Steel or Stone.

b. of air, vapour, darkness. *arch.* or *poet.*

a **1592** H. Smith *Wks.* (1867) II. 64 The darkness of Egypt, the which, as Moses saith, was so gross that it might be felt. **1660** Boyle *New Exp. Phys. Mech.* xvii. 124 The difference of the grosser English Air, and that of Italy and France. **1714** Pope *Rape of Lock* II. 83 Or suck the mists in grosser air below, Or dip their pinions in the painted bow. **1784** Cowper *Task* III. 495 Like a gross fog Bœotian rising fast. **1822** Shelley *Chas. I*, II. 450, I saw a grosse vapour hovering in a stinking ditch. **1839** Longf. *Celestial Pilot* 2 Through the gross vapours, Mars grows fiery red.

absol. **1850** Tennyson *In Mem.* xli, As flies the lighter thro' the gross.

c. said of things material or perceptible to the senses, as contrasted with what is spiritual, ethereal, or impalpable.

1509 Fisher *Funeral Serm. C'tess Richmond* Wks. (1876) 304 It [the body when it dieth] is so grosse that it occupyeth a rowme. **1530** Rastell *Bk. Purgat.* II. vi, The soule of man may use hys operacyon & properte wythout occupyenge of the grosse bodye. **1664** Power *Exp. Philos.* III. 155 Those grosser, and far more material, Effluviums, from Electrical and Aromatical Bodies. **1667** Milton *P.L.* VI. 661 Spirits of purest light, Purest at first, now gross by sinning grown. **1700** Dryden *Cymon & Iph.* 499 They gave you love to lighten up your mind, And purge the grosser parts. **1736** Butler *Anal.* I. i. Wks. 1874 I. 28 It does not appear..that the relation of this gross body to the reflecting being, is..necessary to thinking. **1831** Brewster *Newton* (1855) I. vi. 145 He supposes a subtle and elastic ether to pervade all gross bodies. **1841** Elphinstone *Hist. Ind.* I. 221 At birth, each soul is invested with a subtile body, which again is clad in a grosser body.

†**9.** 'Solid' in the geometrical sense; having three dimensions. *Obs. rare*⁻¹.

1571 Digges *Pantom.* III. Defin., Q, A Sphere is a grosse or solide body comprehended of one conuex Superficies.

†**10.** Of a body of armed men: Compact, solid.

1579 Fenton *Guicciard.* (1618) 289 The Almaines..casting themselues in a grosse squadron, their wiues in the middest, made a valiant defence for certaine houres. *a* **1608** Sir F. Vere *Comm.* (1657) 77 The enemy, seeing no grosse troop to follow them, began to take heart. **1667** Milton *P.L.* II. 570 Another part in Squadrons and gross Bands On bold adventure to discover wide That dismal World. **1670** Dryden *2nd Pt. Conq. Granada* III. i. Wks. 1883 IV. 162, I can, with few, their gross battalion face.

IV. With reference to texture or quality; coarse.

†**11. a.** Consisting of comparatively large parts or particles. Hence, in disparaging sense: Wanting in fineness or delicacy of texture, granulation, or outline. ***gross grinding***: that which leaves the substance in coarse particles. (Opposed to *fine*. Cf. coarse 2.) *Obs.*

1504 Atkynson tr. *De Imitatione* I. xxv. 178 They be porely fedde, content with vyle & grosse clothynge. **1525** Ld. Berners *Froiss.* II. ccxv. [ccxi.] 661 Many had no armure but their cootes of wadmoll, and course grose clothe. **1549** *Privy Council Acts* (1890) II. 350 Fine corne powder, ij last; gros [ditto]. **1584** Cogan *Haven Health* cxxvii. (1636) 126 Take a pound of good Cinamom, and beat it grosse. **1599** Hakluyt *Voy.* II. II. 131 We sounded and had 15 fadom water and grosse red sand. **1624** Wotton *Archit.* in *Reliq.* (1651) 291 That fine and delicate Sculptures be helped with Neerness, and Gross with distance. **1641** French *Distill.* iii. (1651) 78 With red hot gross powder of brick imbibe the water. **1727–46** Thomson *Summer* 888 The parent-sun himself.. the roseate bloom Of beauty blasting, gives the gloomy hue And feature gross. **1742** *Lond. & Country Brew.* I. (ed. 4) 72 A gross Grinding is best. **1756** Nugent *Gr. Tour* I. 40 Both men and women [Dutch] have the grossest shapes. **1769** *De Foe's Tour Gt. Brit.* II. 386 As the Stone is of a reddish, crumbling Kind..Time has made it look gross and rough. **1793** Smeaton *Edystone L.* §186, I afterwards added..tarras, or other gross matter.

†**b.** Of a file, whetstone, etc.: Coarse, rough. *Obs.*

1606 Chapman *Mons. D'Olive* Plays 1873 I. 237, I am ashamde of my selfe that euer I chusde such a Grosse-blocke to whet my wits on. **1658** tr. *Porta's Nat. Magic* x. ix. 264 Shave off the peal [of a Citron] with a gross Steal-File. **1680** Moxon *Mech. Exerc.* 221 Its sharp Edge scrapes or shaves off the little roughness the grosser Tools left upon the Work.

†**12. a.** Of articles of food, or commodities of any kind: Coarse, inferior, common. *Obs.*

1474 Caxton *Chesse* 64 Many fooles daigne not to vse grose metes of labourers. *c* **1530** *Pol. Rel. & L. Poems* 29 Feede thi howce with groce, & not with delycate meete. **1590** *Disc. conc. Sp. Invas.* in *Harl. Misc.* (Malh.) II. 157 Casting off the bulk of her, together with certain gross stuff therein, as..altogether unprofitable. **1622** Bacon *Hen. VII*, Mor. & Hist. Wks. (1860) 439 Ships of London merchants, fraught with some gross and slight wares. **1624** T. Scott *Eng. Sp. Pilgr.* viii. 78 This *grossura* is the same with that wee call grosse meat. *a* **1687** Petty *Pol. Arith.* i. (1691) 20 One sort of Vessels..for cheap gross Goods, another for..precious Commodities. **1719** De Foe *Crusoe* I. xii. (1840) 245 Dealing only in fish and oil, and such gross commodities. **1763** *Brit. Mag.* IV. 547 Nor matters it, the joint how coarse, or gross, Where a good stomach is the best of sauce.

b. Of diet: †(*a*) In early use, plain, not delicate; (*b*) in recent use, uncleanly or repulsive in quality. ***gross feeder***, one who feeds grossly; said *transf.* of plants.

1599 H. Buttes *Dyets drie Dinner* E vij b, Best in cold weather, for grosse and homely feeders. **1662** J. Davies tr. *Olearius' Voy. Ambass.* 85 The subjection in which they are born, and the grosse feeding they have..they are taught to be content with any thing. **1836** Lane *Mod. Egypt.* II. 347 Their diet is extremely gross. **1845** *Florist's Jrnl.* 57 All the cultivated alliaceous plants that I am acquainted with are what may be termed gross feeders. **1861** Whyte Melville *Mkt. Harb.* 32 'Well, sir', says I, 'the mare's a gross feeder'.

13. a. Lacking in delicacy of perception; dull, stupid. *Obs.* of persons, their opinions and utterances; *arch.* of faculties, after Matt. xiii. 15.

1526 *Pilgr. Perf.* (W. de W. 1531) 1 b, My wytte is grosse, my selfe rude, and my tonge very barbarouse. **1535** Coverdale *Matt.* xiii. 15 For yᵉ hert of this people is waxed grosse, & their eares are thick of hearinge. **1579** J. Lyly *Euphues* (Arb.) 170 Such grosse questions are to be aunswered with slender reasons. *c* **1580** Jefferie *Bugbears* I. ii. in *Archiv Stud. neu. Spr.* (1897) XCVIII. 309 Is his head so grosse, that you can bob him? **1602** T. Fitzherbert *Apol.* 38 Our aduersaries..shew themselues very grosse in that they seeke to abolish altogeather the vse of Images. *c* **1630** Milton *Arcades* 73 The heavenly tune, which none can hear Of human mould with grosse unpurged ear. **1662** J. Davies tr. *Olearius' Voy. Ambass.* 80 The opinion the Muscovites have of themselves..is sottish, gross, and impertinent. **1691** Ray *Creation* I. (1692) 45 Our Eyes and Senses..are too gross to discern the Curiosity of the Workmanship of Nature. **1727** De Foe *Syst. Magic* I. i. (1840) 10 Attempted by the grossest and dullest fancies on earth. **1774** Goldsm. *Nat. Hist.* (1776) II. 185 The grossest, and yet the most useful of all the senses, is that of feeling. **1823** Byron *Juan* VII. lxxvii, Suwarrow, who but saw things in the gross, Being much too gross to see them in detail. **1844** Whittier *Ezekiel* 105 Men..gross of ear, of vision dim.

†**b.** Of workmanship, method of proceeding, etc.: Rough, 'rough and ready'; clumsy. *Obs.*

1513 Douglas *Æneis* I. Prol. 312 My werk is mair obscure and gross. **1594** Plat *Jewell-ho.* I. 43 Hops..whose poles stand vpright after our ordenary and grosse manner. **1600** Dekker *Gentle Craft* Wks. 1873 I. 30 Fine ladies, my lads, commit their feet to our apparelling, put grosse worke to Hans. **1641** Wilkins *Math. Magic* II. iv. (1648) 173 But this would have been too grosse a way for so excellent an artificer. **1657** Austen *Fruit Trees* I. 11 Without which [Gardens] Buildings and Pallaces are but grosse handiworks.

†**c.** Wanting in clearness or definiteness; rough, approximate, general, indefinite. Of an instrument: Wanting in delicacy. *Obs.*

1534 More *On the Passion* Wks. 1320/1 Many a poore simple soule with a groce playne faythe. **1678** Dryden *All for Love* Pref., The crowd cannot be presumed to have more than a gross instinct, of what pleases or displeases them. **1684** R. Waller *Nat. Exper.* 7 This Instrument [a thermometer] is more gross then the rest. **1690** Locke *Hum. Und.* III. x. §22 Some gross and confus'd Conceptions Men indeed..have, to which they apply the common Words of their Language. **1748** *Anson's Voy.* II. v. 181 The gross estimations of heat and cold which every one makes from his own sensation. **1748** Hartley *Observ. Man* I. iii. 269 The First ascertains the Ideas belonging to Words and Phrases in a gross Manner. **1768** *Woman of Honor* II. 128 Mr. Salway ..not so much as knowing where he lived, but on a gross guess that it might be at his mother's, gave directions for his being carried thither. **1796** Kirwan *Elem. Min.* (ed. 2) I. Pref. 6 The gross indications of the unassisted senses. **1818** Cruise *Digest* (ed. 2) II. 467 The expression of not being assets is a gross expression.

14. a. Of persons: Rude, uninstructed, ignorant. Now *rare*.

1561 T. Norton *Calvin's Inst.* I. 19 Peter and John..all grosse vnlerned men, had learned nothing in mennes schole. **1563** *Homilies* II. *Agst. Idolatry* III. 67 b, The ignoraunt and grosse people. **1598** Barret *Theor. Warres* I. i. 5 Comparaisoned, as the Phisition Theorike to the grosse practitioner. **1613** Purchas *Pilgrimage* (1614) 712 The Inhabitants were so grosse before they were discovered, that they knew not the use of fire. **1833** S. Hoole *Discourses* v. 67 His studies confined to one single book, the law of a gross unlettered people. **1857** Buckle *Civiliz.* I. viii. 517 They easily gained over the ordinary citizens who were then a gross and uneducated body.

†**b.** Of a language, dialect: Rude, uncultivated. Of expressions: Unlearned, uncultured, untechnical.

1513 Douglas *Æneis* I. Prol. 43, I wald into my rurale wlgar gros, Write sum savoring of thi Eneados. **1589** R. Harvey *Pl. Perc.* 11 Vse a grosse tearme amongst huntsmen in chaze, you shall be leasht for your labor. **1638** F. Junius *Paint. Ancients* 248 He grew..to have..an eloquent tongue, without any affectation or grosse countrey termes. **1670–98** Lassels *Voy. Italy* Pref. 2 They spake but coarse Lombard language and gross Scotch. **1781** Gibbon *Decl. & F.* liii. III. 315 The vulgar dialect of the city was gross and barbarous.

15. Extremely coarse in behaviour or morals; brutally lacking in refinement or decency.

a. of persons.

c **1532** Du Wes *Introd. Fr.* in *Palsgr.* 1017 Grose folke of rude affection, dronkerdes..lubbers, knaves. *c* **1620** in Farr *S.P. Jas. I* (1848) 95 Love's a starre grosse hearts refining. **1642** Rogers *Naaman* 50 Rests upon his smooth civill bottome, that he is no grosse person. **1667** Milton *P.L.* I. 491 Belial..than whom a Spirit more lewd Fell not from Heaven, or more gross to love Vice for it self. **1693** Dryden *Juvenal* (1697) 161 Agamemnon's Wife Was a gross Butcher, with a bloody Knife. **1772** Burke *Corr.* (1844) I. 402 The Turks..grow more gross in the very native soil of civility and refinement. **1817** Moore *Lalla R.* (1824) 178 Beauty, curtain'd from the sight Of the gross world. **1874** Bancroft *Footpr. Time* i. 59 A people are debased and gross in proportion to their ignorance. **1881** Evans in *Sp. Com. 1 Cor.* Introd. 239 Society of high culture, but in morals lax, even gross.

absol. **1829** I. Taylor *Enthus.* ii (1867) 31 It will not be so with the gross and the uneducated.

b. of habits, language, pleasures, etc.

1588 Shaks. *L.L.L.* I. i. 29 The grosser manner of these worlds delights, He throwes vpon the grosse worlds baser slaues. **1651** Hobbes *Leviath.* I. viii. 38 The acquisition of the grosse pleasures of the Senses. **1725** De Foe *Voy. round World* (1840) 154 They have certainly gross ideas. **1777** Priestley *Philos. Necess.* 189 You will blush when you reflect a moment upon things so very gross as these. **1791** Boswell *Johnson* Jan. an. 1749, Some of them [Juvenal's Satires]..were too gross for imitation. **1838** E. Brown *Serm.* iv. 65 Some are under the dominion of the grosser lusts, as drunkenness and sensuality. *c* **1850** *Arab. Nts.* (Rtldg.) 400 He at length broke out in terms of the grossest abuse, and altogether unworthy a king. **1884** 'Rita' *Vivienne* I. i, Of life in its grosser, harsher phases Albert knew scarce anything.

16. *Comb.*: **a.** parasynthetic, as ***gross-bodied, -brained, -headed, -jawed, -lived, -mannered, -minded, -natured, -pated, -witted*** adjs.

1635 R. N. *Camden's Hist. Eliz.* II. an. 22. 207 A man exceeding *grosse-bodyed. **1696** tr. *Du Mont's Voy. Levant* 7, I willingly leave all those Gross-body'd Wines to the Germans. **1727** A. Hamilton *New Acc. E. Ind.* I. xxviii. 346 Their Trees are not so high nor gross bodied as those which grow on the Continent. **1877** Dowden *Shaks. Prim.* vi. 99 We know him to be a gross-bodied, self-indulgent old sinner. **1600** *Dr. Dodypoll* II. i. in Bullen *O. Pl.* III. 112 Asse that I was, dull, sencelesse, *grosse braynd fool. **1561** Hoby tr. *Castiglione's Courtyer* II. M b, They haue shewed themselues but *grosseheaded. **1642** Milton *Apol. Smect.* Wks. (1851) 256 The conceit that all who are not Prelaticall, are grosse-headed. **1812** J. Corry in *Mem. T. Moore* (1856) VIII. 131 The..*gross-hearted herd of Dublin. **1897** *Manch. Guardian* 13 Oct., *Gross-jawed and splendid humanity. **1597** A. M. tr. *Guillemeau's Fr. Chirurg.* 3/1 A thicke, and *grosse-lived man. **1853** Lynch *Self-Improv.* vi. 142 The ignorant and *gross-mannered. **1768–74** Tucker *Lt. Nat.* (1834) II. 424 The voluptuous, the debauched, the giddy, the *grossminded. **1552** T. Barnabe in Strype *Eccl. Mem.* II. App. E. 152 They of France accept us to be *grosse-natured people and covetous. **1611** Florio, *Grosso di pasta*, *grosse-pated. **1587** Golding *De Mornay* xxvi. 409 They make the counsell of the Aegyptians very *grossewitted, in casting themselues away so rashly.

b. quasi-adverbial and complementary, as ***gross-daubed, -fed, -ground, -living*** adjs.

1670 Dryden *2nd Pt. Conq. Granada* III. i, Marriage views the *gross-daubed landscape near. *a* **1743** Savage *Verse on Hill's Gideon* 52 Like *gross-fed spirits, sick in purer air, Their earthly souls by their dull taste disclose. **1653** Walton *Angler* I. x. 151 Sweet *gross-ground barley-malt. **1898** J. Caird *Univ. Addr.* 203 Her well-meaning but somewhat stupid and very *gross-living husband, George II.

B. quasi-*sb.* (the adj. used *absol.*) and *sb.*

†**1. by gross**: in large quantities, wholesale. *Obs.*

1500 *Galway Arch.* in *10th Rep. Hist. MSS. Comm.* App. v. 391 To sell the said warres..as well by grosse as retaylle. **1588** Shaks. *L.L.L.* v. ii. 319 We that sell by gross..Haue not the grace to grace it with such show. **1660** Willsford *Scales Comm.* 103 Merchandizes and all Commodities are sold either by number, weight, or measure, and those by gross or retail.

2. in gross, in the gross. [F. *en gros.*]

a. In a general way, generally, without going into particulars; in the main, on the whole. Cf. A. 7. Now *rare*.

1430–40 Lydg. *Bochas* VI. xi. (1554) 158 This tragedy of the great Pompey Declareth in grose the chief occasion. Why he and Cesar gan fyrst to werrey. **1591** Horsey *Trav.* (Hakl. Soc.) App. 296, I was..greevosly complayned of to hir Majesty in grose. **1596** Shaks. *Merch. V.* III. ii. 160 The full summe of me Is sum of nothing: which to terme in grosse, Is an vnlessoned girle. **1601** Holland *Pliny* I. 127 The measure of the sea coast..I wil expresse generally and in grosse. **1625** Burges *Pers. Tithes* 49 The former Statutes spake of them [Personal Tithes] only in Grosse; This declareth of what in particular they shall arise. **1681–6** J. Scott *Chr. Life* (1747) III. 631 It cannot be supposed that the God of Truth would approve any Doctrine in the gross, if any Part or Proposition of it had been false. **1682** Dryden *Relig. Laici* 322 The unlettered Christian, who believes in gross Plods on to Heaven and ne'er is at a loss. **1707** *Col. Rec. Pennsylv.* II. 370 He could very easily deny these articles in Gross. **1748** Hartley *Observ. Man* I. iii. 351 That Uncertainty and Confusion, to which Persons who take things merely in the gross, are liable. **1775** Burke *Sp. Conc. Amer.* Wks. III. 101 You cannot refuse in the gross, what you have so often acknowledged in detail. **1822** Hazlitt *Table-t.* Ser. II. iv. (1869) 107 We take things in the gross or in the detail, according to the occasion. **1874** Trench *Sacred Lat. Poetry* (ed. 3) Pref. 10 It is the duty of each successive age of the Church, as not to accept the past in the gross, so neither in the gross to reject it. **1899** *Daily News* 29 July 6/6 To take away in detail what seems to be given in the gross.

†**b.** In a body; 'en masse'. *Obs.*

1450–70 *Golagros & Gaw.* 1168 Heir ye ar gaderit in grosse, al the gretest Of gomys that grip has, vndir my gouernyng. **1614** Raleigh *Hist. World* II. (1634) 406 The army of Juda prest Abner in grosse, and brake him. **1647** Clarendon *Hist. Reb.* v. §139 At this first triumphant muster the members of both Houses appeared in gross. **1710** *Let.* in *Select. Harl. Misc.* (1793) 561 It was not safe..either to let the bill pass, or to have it rejected in gross.

†**c.** In bulk, in large quantities, on a large scale, wholesale: opposed to *by* (†*in*) *retail*. *Obs.*

1538 Fitzherb. *Just. Peas* 109 The But, Tone,..Barel or Roundelet to be sold in grosse. **1540–1** Elyot *Image Govt.* (1556) 60 b, Of suche straungers it was lefull to the Romaynes to bie in grosse, and retayle. **1646** H. Lawrence *Comm. Angells* 125 Love hath given all in grosse, and therefore can reteyne nothing in retayle. **1661** Cowley *Disc. Govt. O. Cromwell* in *Verses & Ess.* (1687) 73 Things that are too many to be number'd, and must only be weighed in gross. **1667** *Lond. Gaz.* No. 150/4 Renish Wines in Gross at 6*l.* the Ame, and 12*d.* the Quart by Retail. **1749** FIELDING *Tom Jones* XII. i, The learned world are . . imposed upon to buy a second time in fragments and by retail what they have already in gross. **1799** W. TOOKE *View Russian Emp.* III. 142 Nowhere . . is the fishery carried on so much in the gross as here. **1802–12** BENTHAM *Rat. Judic. Evid.* (1827) IV. 527 How inconsistent and absurd, to do away the mischief in retail, and, in the very self-same shape, leave it to remain in gross! **1818** BYRON *Beppo* viii, To bid their cook . . ride to the Strand, and buy in gross . . Ketchup, Soy, [etc.]

†**d.** In full; nothing being omitted or withheld. *Obs.*

1606 CHAPMAN *Mons. D'Olive* II. i. D 2, If youle deliuer me your mind in grosse Why so I shall expresse it as I can. **1641** PRYNNE *Antip.* To Rdr. 19 Behold the latter part in Epitome, till thou enjoy it in grosse. **1678** *Trans. Crt. Spain* 78 He came . . to tell me in gross what had been done. **1774** J. BRYANT *Mythol.* II. 479 Many writers have taken the account in gross.

e. *Law.* [med.L. *in grosso.*] Said of that which is absolute and independent, belonging to the person, and not to a manor; esp. in ***advowson, villain in gross. common in gross*** (see COMMON *sb.* 6).

a **1626** BACON *Max. & Uses Com. Law* i. (1636) 2 If I be seised of an advowson in grosse, and [etc.]. **1642** *Perkins' Prof. Bk.* i. §61. 28 A rent common in grosse, advowson in grosse and villeine in grosse can not be granted for yeares . . without deed. **1727–41** CHAMBERS *Cycl.* s.v. *Common*, Common in gross, is a liberty to have common alone, that is, without any land or tenement in another man's land. **1767** BLACKSTONE *Comm.* II. 93 Else they [villeins] were in gross, or at large, that is, annexed to the person of the lord, and transferrable by deed from one owner to another. **1818** CRUISE *Digest* (ed. 2) VI. 90 Such a will as in the present case, would be sufficient to pass a term in gross. **1844** WILLIAMS *Real Prop.* (1877) 340 Another important kind of separate incorporeal hereditament is an advowson in gross. **1891** SIR R. V. WILLIAMS in *Law Times' Rep.* LXV. 608/2 Such a right of property may have a legal existence as an easement in gross to the exclusion of the grantor.

†**f.** In solid form. *Obs.*

1748 *Earthquake Peru* i. 122 Among Minerals the Pyrites, both in Gross and in Vapour.

3. The gross or coarse part of anything; the dregs, dross. *Obs.* exc. *dial.*

1708 J. PHILIPS *Cyder* II. 316 And now thy Wine's transpicuous, purg'd from all It's earthy Gross. **1886** ELWORTHY *W. Somerset Word-bk.*, *Gross*, scum; dross of melting metals or other liquids.

†**4. a.** The greater part; the majority, the bulk. *Obs.*

1625 BACON *Ess. Viciss. Things* (Arb.) 571 Comets . . haue likewise Power and Effect, ouer the Grosse and Masse of Things. *c* **1645** [see GREGARIAN]. **1656** FINETT *For. Ambass.* 164 Intreating me to proceed with the grosse of his Traine. **1670** G. H. *Hist. Cardinals* II. III. 194 The gross of the quarrel was compos'd by the Treaty at Pisa. **1677** PLOT *Oxfordsh.* 99 The gross of the stone is somwhat whiter. *a* **1682** SIR T. BROWNE *Tracts* (1684) 132 So much still remaineth with us that it maketh the gross of our language. **1698** FRYER *Acc. E. India & P.* 177 Bamboos make the gross of the Woods. **1712** STEELE *Spect.* No. 502 ⁋3 The gross of an audience is composed of two sorts of people. **1726** BUTLER *Serm. Rolls Chap.* xiii. 261 It was doubtless intended, that Life should be very much a Pursuit to the Gross of Mankind. **1753** HANWAY *Trav.* (1762) I. III. xxxii. 140, I delivered the gross of my baggage to the hahdgee. *c* **1766** BURKE *Tracts Popery Laws* Wks. IX. 391 This denial of landed property to the gross of the people has this further evil effect.

b. *esp.* Of an army or fleet: The main body. *Obs.* exc. *arch.* Cf. A 6 b.

1600 DYMMOK *Ireland* (1843) 40 The Lord Lieutenant . . presented a charge to the rebells grosse of horse and foote. **1633** T. STAFFORD *Pac. Hib.* I. iii. (1810) 44 The grosse of the rebells left their standing in the plaine. **1666** PEPYS *Diary* 27 Sept., The gross of the French fleete are gone home again. **1691** DRYDEN *K. Arthur* I. Wks. 1884 VIII. 144 The Saxon gross begins to move. **1728** MORGAN *Algiers* I. iv. 158 His Horse immediately ran away full Speed and got back to the gross of the Army. **1865** CARLYLE *Fredk. Gt.* XVIII. ii. (1872) VII. 123 Schwerin, with the gross of the army, pushes into Mähren.

c. The sum, sum total; the whole. Now usu. (chiefly *U.S.*), the total amount earned or 'grossed' by a film, theatrical production, etc.

1579 SPENSER *Sheph. Cal.* Sept. 135 By much wrestling to leese the grosse. **1596** SHAKS. *Merch. V.* I. iii. 56, I cannot instantly raise vp the grosse Of full three thousand ducats. **1614** RALEIGH *Hist. World* II. (1634) 440 The grosse, and totall is not in that place set downe. **1625** BACON *Ess., Viciss. Things* (Arb.) 571 Comets, out of question, haue likewise Power and Effect ouer the Grosse and Masse of Things. **1728** PEMBERTON *Newton's Philos.* 9 One sort of genius dwells too much upon the gross and sum of things. **1930** F. SCOTT FITZGERALD in *Sat. Even. Post* 18 Jan. 109/1 A hit at the New Strand, a hit at the Prince of Wales, and the weekly grosses pouring in. **1969** GISH & PINCHOT *Lillian Gish* xii. 157 *The Birth of a Nation* has become the all-time money maker in film history. There have been so many black-market prints in circulation that no one will ever know its true gross.

†**5.** Chiefly *Mil.* A large body; a mass. *Obs.*

1617 MORYSON *Itin.* II. I. i. 36 Their foot are so unwilling to fight in battell or grosse. **1626** *Rayleigh's Ghost* 5 The use of the Sword, push of the Pike, bringing of Grosses bodie to bodie, [etc.]. **1646** CODRINGTON *Life Earl Essex* 31 Which caused our foot to unite themselves into one Grosse. **1651** DAVENANT *Gondibert* I. v. li, Every where where rallies made a gross He charged. *a* **1700** DRYDEN (J.), After they have separated themselves in many petty divisions, they rejoin one by one into a gross.

transf. **1666** DRYDEN *Ann. Mirab.* ccxxxiii, The fire, mean time, walks in a broader gross.

gross (grəʊs), *v.* Also 5 groce-n, -yn, groson, 6 gross(e, 5–6, 9 *dial.* grose, (6 groace, groce, 8 groze). [f. GROSS *a.*]

†**1.** With *up*: = ENGROSS 1. *Obs.*

1412–20 LYDG. *Chron. Troy* IV. xxxiv. (1513) Y v b, Vnto tyme that they were assuryd Of the ende grosyd [**1555** groced] vp in dede. **1525** LD. BERNERS *Froiss.* II. xliii. 136 When these letters were wryten and grosed vp in Frensshe and in Latyn, then they were redde before y^e kyng.

†**2. a.** With *up*: = ENGROSS 3, 4. *Obs.*

c **1440** *Promp. Parv.* 214/2 Groson, or grocyn vp, or take mony thyngys togedur, *ingrosso.* **1530** PALSGR. 575/2, I grosse, I take or heape up thynges a great, *je engrosse.* This man groseth up all the market. *c* **1550** BALE *K. Johan* (Camden) 3 Pore wydowys howsys ye grosse up by long prayers.

b. *absol.* (See quots.) *dial.*

1796 W. MARSHALL *Yorksh.* (ed. 2) II. 324 *Groze*, to save or lay up. **1855** ROBINSON *Whitby Gloss.*, *Grose*, to save or amass wealth.

†**3. a.** *intr.* To become gross or great; to increase, amount. **b.** *trans.* To render gross or coarse. *Obs.*

1548 FORREST *Pleas. Poesye* 96*/449 When they haue groaced vnto a some, Of scoarys or hundredis as they appoynte shall. **1635** HEYWOOD *Hierarch.* IV. 211 The subtile essence of the Angels . . was grossed in their fall Of courser temper than th' Origenall.

4. a. *trans.* To make a gross profit of; to earn a total of.

1884 *Harper's Mag.* Jan. 220/1 Captain . . Lawrence . . once 'grossed' $60,000. **1887** *Pall Mall G.* 18 Mar. 3/2 Having grossed over £4,000. **1936** WODEHOUSE *Laughing Gas* iv. 52 My last picture but one grossed twenty-two thousand there on the week. **1970** *Observer* 19 Apr. 9/3 The . . brokerage business brought him far more prestige than cash; specifically, it grossed something like $60,000 a year, but the firm's overhead was high.

b. With *up*: to count, add as part of the total; to treat (a payment) as if it were a larger taxable amount of the same net value. Hence **grossed** *ppl. a.*; '**grossing** *vbl. sb.*

1931 *Economist* 28 Feb. 456/2 This [tax] is charged . . on the 'grossed-up' dividend. **1954** *Times* 24 Feb. 12/4 When discussing M.P.s' emoluments we ought to gross-up the expectations of pension rights. **1959** *Economist* 11 Apr. 146/1 For that rare bird paying surtax at the top rate, the 'grossed up' yield on savings certificates earning £4 4s. od. tax free has fallen by over a third. **1969** *Times* 25 Jan. 2/3 Some estimates had been made by means of plain 'grossing-up'—a very loose way of computing.

gross(e, variant of GRUSH *v.*

grossart, variant of GROSET.

gross-beak, variant of GROSBEAK.

‖**grossdeutsch** ('grəʊsdɔɪtʃ), *a.* [G.] Pan-Germanic; referring to a Greater Germany, including Austria.

1946 A. J. P. TAYLOR *Course of Germ. Hist.* 8 The interplay of *Kleindeutsch* and *Grossdeutsch* programmes. **1959** *Listener* 21 May 902/1 The Germans as a whole reverted to *grossdeutsch* ambitions for the absorption of Austria and expansion at the expense of the Slav nations to their east. **1963** *Ibid.* 14 Mar. 469/1 Schuschnigg himself emerges as all too honest, but as so drugged by his *grossdeutsch* mysticism as to be politically quite incompetent.

grossen ('grəʊs(ə)n), *v.* [f. GROSS *a.* + -EN[5].] *trans.* To render gross or coarse.

1899 *Q. Rev.* Apr. 424 His coarsenesses have been vulgarised, his refinements grossened. **1947** *Penguin New Writing* XXIX. 10 This face . . had now become expanded and grossened.

'**grosser**[1]. *Obs.* exc. *dial.* Also 6, 9 **groser**, 8 **grozer.** [f. GROSS *v.* + -ER[1].] = ENGROSSER *sb.* 1.

1545 BRINKLOW *Compl.* xx. (1874) 49 All inclosars, grossers vp of fermys, extorcyonars, and oppressers of the common welth. **1796** W. MARSHALL *Yorksh.* (ed. 2) II. 324 *Grozer*, one who keeps money or other valuables long by him. **1855** ROBINSON *Whitby Gloss.*, *Groser*, a saver.

grosser[2] ('grəʊsə(r)). [f. GROSS *v.* + -ER[1].] A film, etc., that 'grosses' or brings in a sum of money: usually qualified by a defining word (*big*, etc.).

1959 N. MAILER *Advts. for Myself* (1961) 335 We've had approximately the same number of big box-office grossers and box-office duds. **1964** C. CHAPLIN *Autobiogr.* xxv. 432 *The Great Dictator* . . turned out to be the biggest grosser of all my pictures up to that time. **1966** *Listener* 15 Dec. 889/3 The gross last year of *Goldfinger* was £15,000,000. When the film is re-released it will almost certainly become the biggest grosser in the history of the cinema.

grosser, grossery, obs. ff. GROCER, GROCERY.

†'**grossful**, *a. Obs. rare*$^{-1}$. [irreg. f. GROSS *a.* + -FUL.] Full of grossness.

1613 CHAPMAN *Rev. Bussy D'Ambois* Plays 1873 II. 109 But let me heare My grossest faults, as grosse-full as they were.

grosshe, obs. variant of GRUSH *v.*

†'**grosshead.** *Obs.* Also 6–7 gros(e-, grosshead. [f. GROSS *a.* + HEAD.] A thick-headed person, a dullard.

1580 HOLLYBAND *Treas. Fr. Tong*, *Hinard*, a grose head. **1589** *Hay any Work* A iij, Non would be so groshead as to gather that I threatned him with blowes, and to deale by stafford law. **1589** WARNER *Alb. Eng.* VI. xxx. (1612) 148 The Groshead now and then, as hapt, a thred-bare terme lets drop. [**1598** BARCKLEY *Felic. Man* (1631) 467 Many simple and grosse heads [shall bee preferred] before the suitable and fine-witted.] **1606** *Crt. & Times Jas. I* (1848) I. 58 Thomas Symondes hath got an office in court, and is become the king's grosehead.

grossification (ˌgrəʊsɪfɪ'keɪʃən). *Bot.* [f. GROSS *a.* + -(I)FICATION.] (See quot. 1835.)

1835 LINDLEY *Introd. Bot.* (1848) I 364 The swelling of the ovary after fertilisation is termed grossification. **1860** in WORCESTER; and in mod. Dicts.

grossify ('grəʊsɪfaɪ), *v.* [f. GROSS *a* + -(I)FY.]

a. *trans.* To make gross or thick. **b.** *intr.* To become gross or thick (Ogilvie 1882).

†'**grossity.** *Obs.*$^{-0}$ [f. med.L. *grossilāt-em*, f. *grossus* GROSS: see -ITY. Cf. GROSTÉ.] Grossness. (Bailey vol. II, 1727.)

grossly ('grəʊslɪ), *adv.* [f. GROSS *a.* + -LY[2].] In a gross manner.

†**1.** Densely, thickly. *Obs.*

1561 HOLLYBUSH *Hom. Apoth.* 37 b, The same . . is specially good for them that are grosly stopped in the bladder. **1711** J. GREENWOOD *Eng. Gram.* 297 When we are about to pronounce *T*, if the breath goes out very grosly or thick, and as it were by a hole, the Greek *Θ* is formed . . that is the English *Th.*

†**2.** In a plain or obvious manner; palpably, plainly, obviously; in plain terms. *Obs.*

1526 TINDALE *Rom.* vi. 19, I wyll speake grossly because off the infirmitie off youre flesshe. **1601** SHAKS. *All's Well* I. iii. 184 Thine eies See it so grosely showne in thy behauiours, That in their kinde they speake it. **1632** *Star Chamb. Cases* (Camden) 169 He . . when he had donne this denyed it in substance as grossely as ever anie did. **1650** *Vind. Hammond's Addr.* §60 This is so grossely true, that 'tis pitty any longer to insist on it. **1675** BAXTER *Cath. Theol.* I. II. 7 You set up Free-will and Power more grossly in terms than I dare do. **1771** FLETCHER *Checks* I. iii. Wks. 1795 II. 41 Myriads of witnesses who have heard him preach, and thousands of printed sermons, . . will prove it grossly.

3. With terms of depreciative or evil import: Excessively, flagrantly. **a.** with adjs.

1618 E. ELTON *Compl. Sanct. Sinner* (1622) 414 Some that are grosly ignorant. **1632** SANDERSON *Serm.* 514 His ignorance therein was not grosly affected and wilfull. **1711** SHAFTESB. *Charac.* (1733) I. III. 283 A People who of all human Kind were the most grossly selfish. **1833** S. HOOLE *Discourses* xii. 151 The bulk of mankind are grossly deficient in duty. **1849** MACAULAY *Hist. Eng.* v. I. 526 A grossly calumnious paper. **1876** GEO. ELIOT *Dan. Der.* I. v, An extensive commentary on some melodic ideas not too grossly evident.

b. with verbs.

1594 HOOKER *Eccl. Pol.* IV. xii. §1 The weightiest exception . . is against such kind of ceremonies, as have been so grossly . . abused. **1647** CLARENDON *Hist. Reb.* v. §412 The Earl of Holland . . had . . grossly deceived him in other undertakings. **1682** SHEFFIELD (Dk. Buckhm.) *Ess. Poetry* 14 In many things they grosly fail. **1749** FIELDING *Tom Jones* IV. i, Bombast . . which Mr. Locke's blind man would not have grossly erred in likening to the sound of a trumpet. **1783** BURKE *Rep. Affairs Ind.* Wks. XI. 318 The care of the Nabob's education was grossly neglected. **1860** MOTLEY *Netherl.* (1868) I. i. 10 That compact had been grossly violated. **1870** DICKENS *E. Drood* viii, He insulted me most grossly. **1878** HUXLEY *Physiogr.* xix. 335 Its size is grossly exaggerated.

†**4.** Of grinding, pounding, etc.: Coarsely; opposed to *finely*. *Obs.*

1576 BAKER *Jewell of Health* 231 b, In which infuse your proper simple . . grosely brought to pouder. **1577** HARRISON *England* II. vi. (1877) I. 157 Some grinde the Malt somewhat groselie. **1615** MARKHAM *Eng. Housew.* II. ii. (1668) 75 Strawberry leaves, sorrel, spinage, grossely chopt together. **1620** VENNER *Via Recta* vi. 103 One pound of Cinnamon grossely beaten. **1670** W. SIMPSON *Hydrol. Ess.* 103 Marcasites of vitriol . . grosly pulverised. **1742** H. BAKER *Microsc.* II. ii. 71 Put common black Pepper, grossly bruised, into any open Vessel. **1823** P. NICHOLSON *Pract. Build.* 334 Baked earth, grossly powdered.

†**5.** Materially; opposed to *spiritually*. *Obs.*

1585 FETHERSTONE tr. *Calvin's Acts* i. 14 We do not eat his [Christ's] flesh grosly . . but he poureth vnto vs by the secret power of his spirit, his force and strength. **1596** SHAKS. *Merch. V.* v. i. 65 Such harmonie is in immortal soules, But whilst this muddy vesture of decay Doth grosly close it in, we cannot heare it. **1601** —— *Twel. N.* v. i. 244 A spirit I am indeed, But am in that dimension grossely clad, Which from the wombe I did participate.

6. †**a.** With want of clear perception, stupidly. *Obs.*

1526 FRITH *Disput. Purgatory* 170 Paul . . took not this word fire for material fire, as they grossly imagine. **1595** SHAKS. *John* III. i. 163 All the Kings of Christendom Are led so grossely by this medling Priest. **1615** G. SANDYS *Trav.* 218 Some write that Cyprus was so named . . of Cyrus, . . but grossly: for Cyrus lived sixe hundred yeares after Homer, by whom it was so named. **1712** *Spect.* No. 524 ⁋10 They grossly overlook that which the rules and laws of the place prescribe to them.

†**b.** Awkwardly, clumsily, unskilfully. *Obs.*

c **1550** *Robin Conscience* 264 in Hazl. *E.P.P.* III. 243 Yovr clothes uery grossely abovt yov do sit. **1598** SHAKS. *Merry W.* II. ii. 149 Let them say 'tis grossely done, so it bee fairely done, no matter. **1605** BACON *Adv. Learn.* I. iv. §12 (1873) 37 Artillery, sailing, printing, and the like, were grossly managed at the first. **1642** ROGERS *Naaman* 541 If thou goe to worke grossely with commands.

c. Roughly, sketchily; in a general way, generally, inexactly. *arch.*

1537 tr. *Latimer's Serm. to Clergy* B vij, This alonly I can say grosselye and as in a summe. **1545** ELYOT *Dict.*,

Adumbro.. Some do suppose that it signifieth, to trycke a thynge, or drawe it grossely, as paynters doo at the begynnyng. **1562** (*title*) Wigand's De Neutralibus et Mediis .. Grossly Englished, Jack of both sides. **1612** BREREWOOD *Lang. & Relig.* xxii. 198 Although Alvarez in his story of Æthiopia have related .. too grossly and boldly that [etc.]. **1671** SALMON *Syn. Med.* Introd. 3 Physical Precepts .. only grosly inform the Mind, how to .. Cure Diseases. **1697** T. SMITH *Voy. Constantinople* in *Misc. Cur.* (1708) III. 2 Three hours, which is grosly speaking the time of half a Tide. **1704** NEWTON *Optics* I. II. (1721) 108, I would be understood to speak not philosophically and properly, but grossly, and according to such conceptions as vulgar people .. would be apt to frame. **1722** WOLLASTON *Relig. Nat.* v. 81 The manner how we know not; or but grosly. **1775** JOHNSON *Western Isl.* 267 The rude speech of a barbarous people, who .. were content as they conceived grossly, to be grossly understood. **1806** SYD. SMITH *Sk. Moral Philos.* (1850) 357 Speaking very generally and grossly.

7. a. Indelicately, indecently. **b.** Of eating or drinking: Coarsely, without delicacy or refinement; to a rude excess.

1547 BOORDE *Introd. Knowl.* xiv. (1870) 160 They do fede grosly, and they wyll eate magots as fast as we wyll eate comfets. **1596** SHAKS. *Merch. V.* v. i. 266 Speak not so grossely. **1883** STEVENSON *Silverado Sq.* (1886) 17 Dinner-parties, where the guests drank grossly.

grossness ('grəʊsnɪs). [f. GROSS *a.* + -NESS.] The quality or condition of being gross.

†**1.** Bigness, bulkiness, size. *Obs.*

1494 FABYAN *Chron.* VII. ccxxx. 260 This Lewis .. was surnamed Lewys the Greate, for grossenesse of his body. **1606** SHAKS. *Tr. & Cr.* I. iii. 325 The purpose is perspicuous euen as substance, Whose grossenesse little characters summe up. **1638** F. JUNIUS *Paint. Ancients* 213 One found fault with the grossenesse of the nose: another with the length of the face. **1652** URQUHART *Jewel* Wks. (1834) 246 Garne .. for the height and grosseness of his person .. was elected King of Bucharia.

2. Exaggerated or flagrant character, enormity.

1575–85 SANDYS *Serm.* xiii. 220 Our Sauiour .. doth .. lay open the grosnesse of their fault. **1596** SHAKS. *Merch. V.* III. ii. 80 Hiding the grosenesse with faire ornament. *a* **1633** AUSTIN *Medit.* (1635) 166 The grossenesse of this Lie every Child may discover. **1807** G. CHALMERS *Caledonia* I. Pref. 5 Boece, and Buchanan .. went beyond these useful chroniclers, in the grossness of their fables. **1865** DICKENS *Mut. Fr.* III. v, The very grossness of this flattery.

3. Thickness, density, materiality, solidity. Also *concr.* or semi-*concr.*

1527 ANDREW *Brunswyke's Distyll. Waters* A j, The waters that there ben devyded from the grossenes of the herbes eche in his substance. **1590** SHAKS. *Mids. N.* III. i. 163, I will purge thy mortall grossenesse so, That thou shalt like an airie spirit go. **1627** DRAYTON *Batt. Aginc.* etc., *Moon-Calf* 168 A black cloud .. Whose foggy grosnesse so oppos'd the light, As it would turn the noone-sted into night. ? **1630** MILTON *On Time* 20 Then all this Earthy grosnes quit, Attir'd with Stars we shall for ever sit. **1644** DIGBY *Nat. Bodies* xxvii. 245 The element immediately next the earth in grossenesse is water. **1709** POPE *Ess. Crit.* 469 For envy'd Wit, like Sol eclips'd makes known Th' opposing body's grossness, not its own. **1807** KNOX & JEBB *Corr.* I. 358 An expert diver can see under water, but it must be cloudily, on account of the grossness of the medium.

fig. **1766** JOHNSON *Let. to W. Drummond* 13 Aug., This speculation may perhaps be thought more subtle than the grossness of real life will easily permit. **1842** TENNYSON *Locksley Hall* 48 The grossness of his nature will have weight to drag thee down.

†**b.** Thickness as a third dimension (*obs.*). **c.** Magnitude, with the implication of materiality.

1570 BILLINGSLEY *Euclid* I. def. xv. 3 A plaine figure, that is a figure without grossenes or thicknes. **1579** FULKE *Heskins' Parl.* 167 That body being so subtile .., was voyde of all grossenesse or thicknesse. **1862** F. HALL *Hindu Philos. Syst.* 121 Grossness is essential in order to perception.

4. Coarseness, want of fineness or refinement: **a.** of food, feeding, or material substances; **b.** of habits, ideas, speech, etc.

a. 1681 DRYDEN *Abs. & Achit.* 619 His Shrieval Board The Grossness of a City Feast abhorr'd. **1751** EARL ORRERY *Remarks Swift* (1752) 175 The grossness of our food, and .. our immoderate use of spirituous liquors. **1899** JOHN CAIRD *Fundamental Ideas of Christianity* II. x. 51 The vital energy of the plant transmutes into flower and fruit the grossness and foulness of the soil from which it springs.

b. 1563 *Homilies* II. *Places H. Script.* I. 160 Places that men are offended at for the homelynesse & grossenesse of speach. **1594** SHAKS. *Rich. III*, III. i. 46 Weigh it but with the grossenesse of this Age. **1667** (*title*) The most delectable History of Reynard the Fox .. purged from all grossness in phrase and matter. **1738** WARBURTON *Div. Legat.* III. vi. Wks. 1788 II. 198 To be bleached and purified from the grossness and pollution of their ideas. **1763** JOHNSON *Let. to Miss Reynolds* 27 Oct., I do not .. think the grossness of a ship very suitable to a lady. **1790** BURKE *Fr. Rev.* Wks. V. 150 That chastity of honour .. under which vice itself lost half its evil, by losing all its grossness. **1816** J. SCOTT *Vis. Paris* (ed. 5) 130 Grossness of conduct is the natural and becoming barrier that stands between virtue and vice. **1860** EMERSON *Cond. Life, Worship* Wks. (Bohn) II. 396 With these grossnesses, we complacently compare our own taste and decorum. **1885** *Manch. Exam.* 4 May 5/1 The .. desire to disguise the native grossness of their motives.

5. Want of instruction and enlightenment; dullness, stupidity.

1526 *Pilgr. Perf.* (W. de W. 1531) 228 b, Shall brynge with them theyr olde grosnes, heuynes & passibilite. **1552** LATIMER *Serm. Lincolnsh.* ix. (1562) 144 What a pacient man our sauior Christ was, which could so wel beare w[t] the grosenes of Iohns disciples. **1597** HOOKER *Eccl. Pol.* v. ii. § 1 They .. are .. for grosnesse of wit such, as they .. scarcely seeme to holde the place of humane being. **1626** BACON *Sylva* § 137 It were extreame Grossenesse to thinke .. that the Sound in Strings is made .. between the Hand and the String. **1638** F. JUNIUS *Paint. Ancients* 350 This was his grosnesse. As for the other more refined .. men, they knew well enough what difference there was. **1837** HT. MARTINEAU *Soc. Amer.* II. 59 Their intellectual torpor, their mental grossness, are melancholy to witness. **1857** KEBLE *Euchar. Adoration* 58 To bring men to that requires .. extreme grossness of understanding.

grossolite, corrupt form of CHRYSOLITE.

1523 SKELTON *Garl. Laurel* 466 With turkis and grossolitis enpauyd was the grounde.

‖**grosso modo** ('grɔsso 'mɔdo), *adv. phr.* [It.] Roughly, approximately.

1952 G. SARTON *Hist. Sci.* I. xvi. 405 There is a general agreement *grosso modo* on the following basis. **1961** *Amer. Speech* XXXVI. 219 Change of Formant 2 frequency of vowels in disyllables corresponds *grosso modo* to the change in tongue-alveolar distance. **1964** G. GERMANI in I. L. Horowitz *New Sociol.* 396 The first phase of disposability and mobilization may be followed by a second one of integration, which may, *grosso modo*, occur in different ways.

†**gross-table, grostable**, variant of *grasstable*, see GRASS *sb.* 14.

1663 GERBIER *Counsel* 87 The Base called gross-table, at the bottome of a building. *Ibid.* 89 For cleansing and setting again old work, as window stuff, grostable, water-table, cornish, quines.

grossu'laceous, *a. Bot. rare*[-0]. [f. mod.L. *Grossulāce-æ*, the gooseberry tribe + -OUS.] Belonging to the N.O. *Grossulaceæ* (now *Grossulariaceæ*).

1847 in CRAIG; hence in later Dicts.

grossular ('grɒsjʊlə(r)). *Min.* Also **-are.** [ad. mod.L. *grossulār-ia* (Werner in 1811), an application of the specific name of the gooseberry, in allusion to the colour of the stone.] A pale-green variety of garnet from Siberia, often called the gooseberry garnet.

[**1814** T. ALLAN *Min. Nomen.* 21 Garnet .. Olive Green. Grossularia.] **1819** W. PHILLIPS *Min.* (ed. 2) 24 Grossular .. occurs in the varieties of the dodecahedron. **1821** JAMESON *Min.* 224 Grossulare. [In Webster 1828–32, and later Dicts., which have the word also as an adj.]

grossu'larious, *a. rare*[-1]. [f. mod.L. *grossulāri-a* (see prec.) + -OUS.] Of the nature of, or resembling, the gooseberry.

1845 DON *Hortic.* in *Encycl. Metrop.* VI. 120* Grossularious Fruits.

grossularite ('grɒsjʊləraɪt). *Min.* [f. as prec. + -ITE.] = prec.

1847 in CRAIG. **1868** DANA *Min.* 267 Pale green .. garnets are not invariably grossularite.

'**grossy**, *a.* [f. GROSS *a.* + -Y[1].] †**a.** Somewhat gross (*obs.*). **b.** *dial.* (see quot. 1877).

1648–60 HEXHAM *Dutch Dict.*, *Grofachtigh*, Grossie, or Thickish. *a* **1661** FULLER *Worthies, Lincoln* (1662) II. 149 Wild-foule being more dainty and digestable than Tame of the same kind, as spending their Grossie humours with their Activity and constant Motion in Flying. **1877** *Holderness Gloss., Grossy*, .. green and vigorous (applied to vegetation); .. stout (applied to persons).

grost, obs. variant of *gorst*, GORSE.

14.. *Voc.* in Wr.-Wülcker 608/39 *Ruscus*, a grost, or furses.

grostable: see GROSS-TABLE.

†**grosté.** *Obs. rare.* [a. OF. *grosseté*:—med.L. *grossitāt-em* GROSSITY.] Grossness; in quots. *concr.* gross or thick parts.

1460–70 *Bk. Quintessence* I. 5 þat .. þe grosté of þe mater of þe watir descende dounward to þe necke. *Ibid.*, þe grosté schal abide byneþe in þe botme.

†**grot**[1]. *Obs.* Forms: 1–4 **grot**, 3–5 **grote**, (3 **greot**), 4 **grott(e.** [OE. *grot* str. neut., related by ablaut to *grêot* GRIT *sb.*[1], *grytt* GRIT *sb.*[2], *grút* GROUT: see also GROATS.] A fragment, particle, atom. *every grot* = every whit.

c **888** K. ÆLFRED *Boeth.* xxxv. § 1 Hu mæȝ þonne æniȝ man rihtwislice .. acsiȝan, ȝif he nan grot rihtwisnesse on him næfð. *a* **1225** *Ancr. R.* 260 Of al þe brode eorðe ne moste he habben a grot, forte deien uppon. *a* **1240** *Sawles Warde* in *Cott. Hom.* 251 Iteilede draken .. to cheoweð ham euch greot. *c* **1300** *Havelok* 472 Of bothen he karf on two here throtes, And sithen hem al to grotes. *a* **1330** *Roland & V.* 786 Now ich wot, ȝour cristen lawe eueri grot. *c* **1386** CHAUCER *Friar's Prol.* 28, I shal hym quiten euery grot. **1398** TREVISA *Barth. De P.R.* III. xli. (Tollem. MS.), Atthomis a litill þinge, as it were, of þe grotis in þe Sonne beme. **1399** LANGL. *Rich. Redeles* Prol. 35 Not to gruccchen a grott aȝeine godis sonde. *c* **1400** *St. Alexius* (Laud 622) 608 Ac on Ionas fel vche grot. *c* **1425** *Seven Sag.* (P.) 2071 Hys eyen, hys nose, and hys throte, Thay fyldan wit golde every grote.

†**grot**[2]. *Obs.* Also 4 **grate.** [a. ON. *grát-r*, cogn. w. *gráta*: see GROTE *v.*] Weeping, lamentation.

c **1250** *Gen. & Ex.* 1577 Grot sal bi-cumen, And wreche of iacob sal bi-numen. *Ibid.* 1978 Long grot and sorȝe is him bi-tid. *Ibid.* 2288, 3717. **13..** *St. Alexius* 570 in Horstm. *Altengl. Leg.* (1881) 187 His wife kome þan wiþ sorowfull late Wiþ goulinge & wiþ rewfull grate.

grot[3] (grɒt). Now only *poet.* Forms: 6–8 **grott(e**, 7 **grote**, 6– **grot.** [ad. F. *grotte*: see GROTTO.]

1. a. = GROTTO I.

1506 GUYLFORDE *Pilgr.* (Camden) 16 There we lay in the same grotte or caue Frydaye all day vpon the bare, stynkynge, stable grounde. **1598** FLORIO, *Grotta*, a grot, a cave, a den, a caverne. **1608** E. GRIMSTONE *Hist. France* (1611) 1030 To shew him his buildings, his Grots or Caues, and his Chases. **1647** JER. TAYLOR *Lib. Proph.* Ep. Ded. 23 They who for their security runne into grots and cellars. **1670–98** LASSELS *Voy. Italy* II. 186 Entring into the Grotte of Pausilipus we found it to be about forty foot high. **1680** MORDEN *Geog. Rect., Germany* (1685) 113 In his Palace or Castle of Heidelburg are divers things remarkable, viz. the Grotes and Water-works. **1702** W. J. *Bruyn's Voy. Levant* xxxvi. 143 Near those Buildings of everlasting continuance there are also some Grotts or Caves. **1753** JOHNSON *Adventurer* No. 108 ¶ 5 A natural grot shaded with myrtles. *a* **1755** SHENSTONE in Dodsley *Coll. Poems* (1755) IV. 351 Here in cool grot and mossy cell We rural fayes and faeries dwell. **1814** SCOTT *Lord of Isles* III. xxviii, Mermaid's alabaster grot. **1901** 'M. FRANKLIN' *My Brilliant Career* xxii. 192 She and Harold would rest while I did the honours of the fern grots to my companion. **1958** R. LIDDELL *Morea* II. i. 45 On the plain there is a spring of excellent water, which comes here underground from the grot of Hermes.

†**b.** A crypt under a church. *Obs.*

1658 J. BURBURY *Hist. Christina A. of Swedland* 441 Her Majesty, when she had ador'd the most holy Sacrament, went down into the grots below the Church. **1670–98** LASSELS *Voy. Italy* II. 28, I got leave to go down into the Grot under this Church.

2. = GROTTO 2.

1641 EVELYN *Diary* 19 Aug., We .. went to visit the Hoff, or Prince's Court, with the adjoining gardens full of .. grots, fountains, and artificial music. **1693** C. DRYDEN in *Dryden's Juvenal* (1697) 172 Lucan .. may lie at ease In costly Grotts, and marble Palaces. **1749** LADY LUXBOROUGH *Let. to Shenstone* 24 June, You may be secure in your grott from all intruders, and see your Shrubbery prosper unmolested. **1764** *Oxford Sausage* 60 Fresh Shade and Vale No more to visit, or vine-mantled Grot. *a* **1839** PRAED *Poems* (1864) II. 366 The Baron is blind to a beauteous day, If it beam in my Lady's grot. **1865** DICKENS *Mut. Fr.* I. iii, He opened a cool grot at the end of the yard.

grot[4] (grɒt). Abbrev. of GROTESQUE *sb.* 3.

1961 *SIA Jrnl.* Sept. 6/2 Typography .. is dominated by a particular sort of sans-serif letter, the 'grotesque'... It is useful to examine this dictatorship of the grot. **1964** L. DEIGHTON *Funeral in Berlin* i. 11 He sipped .. tea from an antique Meissen cup; around mine it said 'British Railways S.R.' in brown grot letters.

grot (grɒt), *a. slang.* Shortened form of GROTTY *a.*

1967 *Sun* 22 Feb. 6/6 [Teenage terms] *Grot*, from grotty, itself derived from grotesque. **1983** *Listener* 11 Aug. 14/1 What with grot hotels .. and general anxiety, I had not had what I would call a meal since leaving Khartoum. **1985** *Times* 3 Sept. 8/2 A new film can be 'totally brilliant' or 'totally grot'.

†**grote**, *v. Obs.* Also 4 **graten.** [a. ON. *gráta*: see GREET *v.*[2]] *trans.* and *intr.* To bewail; = GREET *v.*[2]

c **1250** *Gen. & Ex.* 1984 Ic sal liȝten til helle dale, And groten ðor min sunes bale. *c* **1300** *Havelok* 329 Of Goldeboru shul we nou laten, þat nouth ne blinneth forto graten. *Ibid.* 1390 He .. Siþen yede sore grotinde awey.

grote, obs. form of GROAT, GROATS.

†'**groten**, *v. Obs. rare*[-1]. [Of obscure origin; cf. *glut* and ME. *aglotye*. See also AGROTEN, INGROTEN.] *trans.* To glut.

c **1440** *Promp. Parv.* 215/1 Groton, or ingroton wythe mete or drynke, *ingurgito*.

†**grotes.** *Obs.*[-1]. [variant of CROTEY *sb.*] = CROTTELS.

c **1450** *ME. Med. Bk.* (Heinrich) 140 Take þe grotes of þe gose, and boile hem in vynegre [etc.].

grotesque (grəʊ'tɛsk), *sb.* and *a.* Forms: α. 6 **crotes(c)que**, 7 **crotesco, -ko.** β. 7–8 **grot(t)esc, -k(e, -q, grot(t)esco, -ko,** 7– **grotesque** [Orig. a. early mod.F. *crotesque* sb. fem., an adaptation (by assimilation to OF. *crote* = It. *grotta*) of It. *grottesca* 'a kinde of rugged vnpolished painters worke, anticke worke' (Florio 1598), 'anticke or landskip worke of Painters' (Florio 1611), an elliptical use (= *opera* or *pittura grottesca*) of the fem. of *grottesco* adj. f. *grotta*: see GROTTO and -ESQUE. (Cf. Sp., Pg. *grutesco*, an alteration of the It. word after Sp. Pg. *gruta* = It. *grotta*.) It is remarkable that Florio in both his Dicts. (1598 and 1611) has *crotesca* as an It. word, explained as 'antique, fretted, or carued worke'; this, if genuine, would seem to be a readoption from Fr. Before the end of the 16th c. the Fr. word was occasionally spelt *grotesque*, after the original It; this form was adopted into Eng. about 1640, and has been the prevailing form ever since. But early in the 17th c. writers acquainted with It. had introduced the masc. form of the adj., *crotesco*, which occurs as late as 1646; the more usual It. form *grotesco* appears as Eng. first in the 1632 edition of Florio's transl. of Montaigne, and did not become obsolete until the 18th c.

The etymological sense of *grottesca* would be 'painting appropriate to grottos'. The special sense is commonly explained by the statement that *grotte*, 'grottoes', was the popular name in Rome for the chambers of ancient buildings which had been revealed by excavations, and which contained those mural paintings that were the typical examples of 'grotesque'. (See *Voc. della Crusca*, s.v. *Grotta*, §iv.) Although this seems to be only a late conjecture, without any actual evidence, it appears to be intrinsically plausible.]

A. *sb.*

1. a. A kind of decorative painting or sculpture, consisting of representations of portions of human and animal forms, fantastically combined and interwoven with foliage and flowers.

1561 *Inv. R. Wardrobe* (1815) 130 Item, twa paintit broddis the ane of the muses and the uther of crotescque or conceptis. [**1624** WOTTON *Archit.* II. 97 Whether Grotesca (as the Italians) or Antique worke (as wee call it) should be receiued.] **1636** B. JONSON *Discov., De progres. picturæ* Wks. (1640) 113 He complaines of their painting Chimæras, by the vulgar unaptly called Grottesque. **1645** EVELYN *Mem.* (1857) I. 143 The foliage and grotesque about some of the compartments are admirable. **1658** W. SANDERSON *Graphice* 25, I would confine Grotesco only to Borders and Freezes. **1686** AGLIONBY *Painting Illustr.* Explan. Terms, Grotesk, is properly the Painting that is found under Ground in the Ruines of Rome. **1715** LEONI *Palladio's Archit.* (1742) I. 59 The Chambers..are all..painted in grotesque of a very fine Invention. **1762–71** H. WALPOLE *Vertue's Anecd. Paint.* (1786) I. 260 Don Julio Clovio, the celebrated limner, whose neatness and taste in grotesque were exquisite. **1823** P. NICHOLSON *Pract. Build.* Gloss. 586 *Grotesque*, the light, gay, and beautiful style of ornament, practised by the antient Romans in the decoration of their palaces, baths, villas, etc.

attrib. **1711** SHAFTESB. *Charac.* (1737) III. 6 'Tis the perfection of certain grotesque-painters, to keep as far from nature as possible. *a* **1744** POPE *Hor. Sat.* II. vi. 192 Grotesco roofs, and Stucco floors.

b. A work of art in this style. Chiefly *pl.*, figures or designs in grotesque; in popular language, figures or designs characterized by comic distortion or exaggeration. The Italian form **grottesco** (pl. **grotteschi**) is sometimes used.

1643 SIR T. BROWNE *Relig. Med.* I. §15 There are no Grotesques in nature. **1691** tr. *Emillianne's Frauds Romish Monks* 333 They expose to public view in the Streets..many infamous naked Pictures, and Grotesques, to cause laughter. **1746** W. HORSLEY *Fool* (1748) I. 141 The reigning Taste of the Age for Oddities, Monsters, Grotesques, Caricatura's, &c. **1756** BURKE *Subl. & B.* II. v, All the designs I have chanced to meet of the temptations of St. Anthony were rather a sort of odd, wild grotesques, than any thing capable of producing a serious passion. **1819** BYRON *Juan* I. xlvi, This [missal] all Kinds of grotesques illumined. **1856** RUSKIN *Mod. Paint.* III. IV. viii. §4 A fine grotesque is the expression, in a moment, by a series of symbols thrown together in bold and fearless connection, of truths which it would have taken a long time to express in any verbal way [etc.]. **1865** *Lond. Rev.* 23 Dec. 668/1 The ornamentalists of that period..revelled in their grotesques. **1893** LELAND *Mem.* II. 248 Adorned with fifteenth century grotesques. **1926** A. HUXLEY *Essays New & Old* 180 Very pretty little *grotteschi* in the Pompeian manner. **1934** *Burlington Mag.* Apr. 199/1 A certain type of symmetrical *grotteschi* design. **1958** 'M. INNES' *Long Farewell* 11, I like *grotteschi* on my walls. All these little nudes like amorous shrimps.

c. *fig.*

1644–7 CLEVELAND *Char. Lond. Diurn.* 28 A strange Grottesco this, the Church and States. **1710** STEELE *Tatler* No. 202 ¶2 This indeed is Ambition in Grotesque. **1889** *Spectator* 21 Dec., To Browning, life is a medley of grotesques, with a glowing horizon beyond it.

2. A clown, buffoon, or merry-andrew. [So in mod.Fr. (as masc. sb.).] Cf. ANTIC.

1864 SALA in *Daily Tel.* 18 Nov., The great grotesque himself will be in the grave. **1871** MORLEY *Voltaire* iii. (1872) 120 Some men of true genius seem only to make sure of fame by straining themselves into grotesques.

3. *Printing.* A square-cut letter without ceriph, THUS; formerly called *stone-letter*.

1875 SOUTHWARD *Dict. Typogr.*, *Grotesque*, the name of a peculiar fancy jobbing type.

B. *adj.*

1. *Arch.* Having the character of the work described in A. 1. (In some of the early instances the word may be the sb. used *attrib.*)

1603 FLORIO *Montaigne* I. xxvii. 89 Antike Boscage or Crotesko [*so also ed.* 1613; *ed.* 1632 *has* Grotesko] works, which are fantastical pictures, having no grace, but in the variety and strangenes of them. **1610** FOLKINGHAM *Art of Survey* II. vi. 58 Compartiments are Blankes or Figures bordered with Anticke Boscage or Crotesko-woorke. **1646** SIR T. BROWNE *Pseud. Ep.* III. xxiv. 170 As for Sea-horses..they are but Crotesco deliniations. **1664** EVELYN tr. *Freart's Parall. Archit.* 128 There are also Voluta's in the Corinthian and Compounded Capitels, but they consist rather of certain large Stalkes after a more Grotesco designe. *a* **1668** DAVENANT *Masque* Wks. (1673) 360 And in the midst was placed a large compartiment composed of Groteske work. **1687** BURNET *Trav.* ii. (1750) 100 They have built great Vaults and Porticos along the Rock, which are all made Grotesque. **1695** DRYDEN *Paral. Poet. & Paint.* 26 Grotesque painting is the just resemblance of this. **1841–4** EMERSON *Ess., Manners* Wks. (Bohn) I. 215 Let there be grotesque sculpture about the gates and offices of temples.

2. a. In a wider sense, of designs or forms: Characterized by distortion or unnatural combinations; fantastically extravagant; bizarre, †quaint. Also *transf.* of immaterial things, esp. of literary style.

1653 J. HALL *Paradoxes* 45 They..ought to bee accounted one of those Grotesco Maximes..that doe so disfigure and misguide the life of man. **1687** DRYDEN *Hind & P.* III. 1044 An hideous figure of their foes they drew, Nor lines, nor looks, nor shades, nor colours true; And this grotesque design expos'd to public view. **1709** STEELE *Tatler* No. 118 ¶6 You have employed your self more in Grotesque Figures, than in Beauties. **1718** LADY M. W. MONTAGU *Let. to Lady Rich* 10 Oct., These grotesque daubers give me a still higher esteem of..natural charms. **1728** MORGAN *Algiers* I. Pref. 25 Matters of so peregrine and grotesk a Nature as this [History]. **1762–5** H. WALPOLE *Vertue's Anecd. Paint.* (ed. 2) I. 118 Those Grotesque monsters..with which the spouts..of ancient buildings are decorated. **1820** HAZLITT *Lect. Dram. Lit.* 36 Our literature..is Gothic and grotesque.

absol. **1809** MALKIN *Gil Blas* XI. v. (Rtldg.) 404 He preferred the stately, or rather the grotesque in writing. **1851** RUSKIN *Stones Ven.* (1874) I. App. 367 The Northern love of what is called the Grotesque. **1888** *Pall Mall G.* 4 Apr. 11/1 The grotesque is a branch of the fantastic.

†b. Of landscape: Romantic, picturesquely irregular. *Obs.*

1667 MILTON *P.L.* IV. 136 A steep wilderness, whose hairie sides With thicket overgrown, grottesque and wilde, Access deni'd. *c* **1764** R. DODSLEY *Leasowes*, in *Shenstone's Wks.* II. (1777) 296 The more pleasing parts of this grotesque and hilly country.

3. Ludicrous from incongruity; fantastically absurd.

1747 *Gentl. Mag.* 374 A woman with her head peeping out of a sack, could hardly..make a more Grotesque figure. **1829** LYTTON *Devereux* II. v. 46 O'Carroll gave a grotesque sort of signal between a wink and a beckon. **1840** DICKENS *Old C. Shop* iii, But what added most to the grotesque expression of his face, was a ghastly smile. **1849** MACAULAY *Hist. Eng.* ii. I. 163 These peculiarities appeared far more grotesque in a faction which ruled a great empire. **1863** FR. A. KEMBLE *Resid. in Georgia* 58 You can conceive nothing more grotesque than the Sunday trim of the poor people. **1866** G. MACDONALD *Ann. Q. Neighb.* ix. (1878) 154 The most grotesque machine I ever saw that *did* something. **1870** R. W. DALE *Week-day Serm.* xii. 246 The grotesque doctrine that it is good for trade.

4. *Comb.*, as ***grotesque-minded*** adj.

1822 MOORE *Mem.* (1853) III. 347 Found there Beresford..a grotesque-minded person, very amusing.

Hence **gro'tesque** *v. trans.*, to give a grotesque form or appearance to; to caricature, travesty.

1875 BROWNING *Aristoph. Apol.* 432 After obscenity grotesqued so much It slunk away, revolted at itself. **1891** *Sat. Rev.* 19 Dec. 707/2 This is to grotesque Dante, not to translate him.

grotesquely (grəʊ'tɛsklɪ), *adv.* [f. GROTESQUE *a.* + -LY².] In a grotesque manner; with incongruous absurdity; fantastically, whimsically.

1740 H. WALPOLE *Ep. fr. Florence* 285 in Dodsley *Coll. Poems* (1755) III. 80 The wearied arms grotesquely deck the wall. **1814** SCOTT *Wav.* lxv, His absurdities..had appeared grotesquely ludicrous during his prosperity. **1818** FOSTER in *Life & Corr.* (1846) II. 26 Grotesquely-constructed sentences. **1829** LYTTON *Devereux* II. ii, A man of about the middle age, very grotesquely attired.

grotesqueness (grəʊ'tɛsknɪs). [f. GROTESQUE + -NESS.] The quality of being grotesque; incongruous absurdity. Also *concr.* *pl.* Grotesque objects.

1826 MISS MITFORD *Village* Ser. II. (1863) 329 His face, with all its grotesqueness, was infinitely pleasanter to look at than his figure. **1860** *Heads & Hats* 12 The women [temp. Edw. IV] wore absurdly high coiffures; and the men vied with them in their height, if not in their grotesqueness. **1883** J. HAWTHORNE in *Harper's Mag.* Nov. 926 1, I sauntered about the studio, taking note of the various beauties, grotesquenesses, and curiosities that it contained.

grotesquerie (grəʊ'tɛskərɪ). Also **grotesquery**. [as if a. F. **grotesquerie*, f. *grotesque* GROTESQUE.] Grotesque objects collectively; grotesque quality; a piece of grotesqueness.

1654–66 LD. ORRERY *Parthenissa* (1676) 517 In a large Compartiment composed of Groteskery were seen Sphynxes, Harpyes, the Claws of Lyons and Tygers, to evidence that within inhabited Mysteries and Riddles. **1862** R. TAYLOR *Home & Abr.* Ser II. II. 339 Where so much is beautiful, the occasional anomalies and grotesqueries of taste fail to offend you. **1877** 'H. A. PAGE' *De Quincy* I. v. 92 Casting a 'jet' of gentle humour over the grim grotesquerie of the situation. **1878** BAYNE *Purit. Rev.* iii. 59 The incidents..of waking existence are therein..tossed and heaped together as the materials of a wild grotesquerie. **1880** HOWELLS *Undisc. Country* xiii. 197 She showed her sense of degradation in the brutal grotesquery. **1885** *Manch. Exam.* 22 July 3/2 The inventive grotesquerie of his [Gustave Doré's] later work.

grotha, grothe, obs. ff. GROTTO, GROWTH¹.

grothite ('grəʊθaɪt). *Min.* [f. *Groth* the name of a German mineralogist + -ITE. Named by Dana 1867.] A variety of titanite containing yttrium.

1867 *Amer. Jrnl. Sci.* Ser. II. XLIV. 258 Grothite..Described as a variety of Titanite by Groth.

Grotian ('grəʊʃ(ɪ)ən), *a.* [See -AN.] Of or pertaining to the Dutch lawyer, statesman, and theologian Hugo *Grotius* (1583–1645), who founded the modern science of international law and propounded the 'governmental' view of the Atonement. Also as *sb.*, an adherent of the tenets or policies of Grotius; **'Grotianism**, the views or teaching of Grotius.

1864 W. G. T. SHEDD *Hist. Chr. Doctr.* II. 366 The Grotian soteriology. **1920** *Expositor* May 372 Jonathan Edwards the younger, went over to Grotianism, bag and baggage. *Ibid.* 373 Johnson had enunciated views of the doctrine [of the Atonement] which one can only characterize as strongly Grotian. **1934** J. LAIRD *Hobbes* III. vii. 255 Boëcler, a Grotian, was said to have counted Hobbes a great intellect who had gone astray by neglecting the classics.

grotis, grots, obs. ff. GROATS.

grotta, original form of GROTTO, q.v.

grotte, obs. form of GROAT, GROT.

grottes, obs. form of GROATS.

grottesc(o, -k(e, -ko, obs. ff. GROTESQUE.

grotto ('grɒtəʊ). Pl. grottos, grottoes. Forms: α. 7 **grotta**, (**grotha**); *pl.* **grotta's, grottas, grotha's**, (*erron.* **grottae**); β. (7 **groto**), 7– **grotto**; *pl.* 7–8 **grotto's**, 7– **grottos, grottoes**. [ad. It. *grotta* (for which Dante has also *grotto*) = OF. *crote, croute*, Pr. *crota*, Sp. and Pg. *gruta*:—pop.L. *crupta*, *grupta* (= literary L. *crypta*), ad. Gr. κρύπτη vault; f. κρυπτειν to hide. (The mod.F. *grotte* is from It.)]

1. A cave or cavern, esp. one which is picturesque, or which forms an agreeable retreat.

1617 COLLINS *Def. Bp. Ely* II. vi. 241 To bee respected and credited, afore your grottae, or your Cryptae. **1632** LITHGOW *Trav.* VI. 276 We arrived at a Cave,..and from the mouth of this delectable Grotto, gusheth forth a most delicious Fountaine. **1695** WOODWARD *Nat. Hist. Earth* I. (1723) 3 To inform my self of the present Condition of the Earth..as far as either Grotto's or other Natural Caverns..let me into it. **1774** GOLDSM. *Nat Hist.* (1776) I. 67 Of all the subterraneous caverns now known, the grotto of Antiparos is the most remarkable, as well for its extent, as for the beauty of its sparry incrustations. **1818** KEATS *Endym.* I. 459 Echoing grottoes, full of tumbling waves And moonlight. **1856** STANLEY *Sinai & Pal.* ii. (1858) 153 Partly perhaps the cause, partly the effect of this consecration of grottoes, began the caves of hermits. **1887** RUSKIN *Præterita* II. 89 The Dog's grotto with its floor a foot deep in poisoned air.

2. An excavation or structure made to imitate a rocky cave, often adorned with shell-work, etc., and serving as a place of recreation or a cool retreat.

1625 BACON *Ess., Building* (Arb.) 552 On the Vnder Story, towards the Garden, Let it be turned to a Grotta, or place of Shade, or Estiuation. **1644** EVELYN *Mem.* (1857) I. 56 A grotto or shell-house, on the summit of the hill. *c* **1645** HOWELL *Lett.* (1650) I. III. 92 The keeper of the house was very officious to shew him every room, with the garden, grotha's, and aqueducts. **1680** MORDEN *Geog. Rect., Germany* (1685) 119 There is nowhere to be seen fairer Rows of Orange-Trees, Grottas better contrived and beautified. **1791** *Gentl. Mag* 26/1 These seeds are sold at many shops in London, for ornamenting grottoes and shell-work. **1832** G. DOWNES *Lett. Cont. Countries* I. 283 Under the palace is a very curious and beautiful grotto of shell-work, with a mosaic floor. It consists of several chambers..adorned with statues.

transf. **1720** STRYPE *Stow's Surv.* (1754) II. VI. vi. 663/1 A small Grotto of trees most pleasant in the Summer season.

3. A structure of oyster-shells in the form of a grotto erected and exhibited by London street-boys on the 5th of August.

a **1845** [implied in *grottoing* below]. **1864** *Chambers' Bk. Days* II. 122. **1877** *Punch* 244 The Derby outing comes, like the 'grotter', only once a year.

4. *Comb.* as ***grotto-work***; ***grotto-like*** adj.

1782 COWPER *Poet, Oyster, & Sensit. Plant* 49 You, in your grotto-work enclosed, Complain of being thus exposed. **1840** MRS. NORTON *Dream* 39 There in a cool and grotto-like repose.

Hence **'grottoed** *ppl. a.*, ensconced in a grotto; also, formed into grottoes; **grotto'esque** *a.*, resembling a grotto; also *absol.*; **'grottoing** *vbl. sb.*, making grottos (sense 3).

Quot. 1863 illustrates a nonce *absol.* use.

a **1748** J. WARTON *Fashion* 21 in Dodsley *Coll. Poems* (1748) III. 275 Happy the grotto'd hermit with his pulse. *a* **1845** HOOD *Lost Heir* 76 And the threepence he'd got by grottoing was spent in plums. **1863** J. C. ATKINSON *Stanton Grange* 107 A massive piece of rock..supplying them with a kind of natural grotto-esque back to the recess. **1881** J. P. BRISCOE *Old Notts.* 123 Only a groto-esque [*sic*] summer house to the Castle when it was inhabited. **1892** LD. LYTTON *King Poppy* Prol. 301 Grey, gaunt, and silent as its grotto'd rock. **1955** S. SPENDER *Making of Poem* 101 Gilded Romanticism is atmosphere in the Ballad-makers, fancy in Shakespeare and the other Elizabethans, desperation in the Jacobeans, the grottoesque in Pope.

grotty ('grɒtɪ), *a. slang.* [Shortened form of GROTESQUE *a.* + -Y¹.] Unpleasant, dirty, nasty, ugly, etc.: a general term of disapproval.

1964 J. BURKE *Hard Day's Night* iv. 88 'I wouldn't be seen dead in them. They're dead grotty.' Marshall stared. 'Grotty?' 'Yeah—grotesque.' **1964** *Daily Mail* 18 Aug. 1/6, I felt dead grotty. **1964** *Sunday Times* 25 Oct. 22/5 A charming touchline companion called the [hockey] match 'grotty' which seemingly means disappointing. **1966** M. HASTINGS *Cork on Telly* ii. 29 I've been checking my tapes...They sound pretty grotty when they're scrambled. **1967** *House & Garden* Apr. 59/3 The house was a ruin—dirty, really grotty, but with obvious potential. **1970** *Times* 19 June 10/4 'I don't like the grotty old pub,' says Miss McCormick.

grou(e, grouff(e, obs. ff. GROW, GROOF.

grouan, variant of GROWAN.

grouch (graʊtʃ), *sb.* orig. *U.S.* [Var. of GRUTCH *sb.*] **1.** Grumbling; a complaint or grumble; a grumbling, sulky mood; a fit of ill temper or sulkiness.

1895 W. C. GORE in *Inlander* Nov. 66 *Grouch*, .. a fit of ill-humor. **1900** 'J. FLYNT' *Notes Itinerant Policeman* 160 They began to get a grouch on against the gay-cats that kep' comin' to their camps. **1903** *Harper's Bazaar* Oct. 947 No woman who comes down to her breakfast table with what her son frankly calls a 'grouch on' is grouchy to herself alone. **1905** *N.Y. Even. Post* 2 Sept. 4 We need still another breakfast food.. one that will take away matutinal grouch. **1906** B. VON HUTTEN *What became of Pam* I. ii, You are not going to spoil my birthday with one of your grouches. **1913** C. E. MULFORD *Coming of Cassidy* iii. 61 Longhorn.. felt savage elation at this opportunity to unload quite a cargo of accumulated grouches of various kinds and sizes. **1921** *Chambers's Jrnl.* Jan. 37/1 He was known there as the Englishman whom Providence had a grouch against. **1940** 'G. ORWELL' in *World Review* (1950) June 33 Part of his grouch was that he had tried to join the Air Force.. and always been put off. **1966** *Listener* 8 Sept. 355/3 The students were not demonstrating on behalf of a fashionable grouch.

2. A grumbler.

1900 *Yale Fun* 25. **1916** *Recruiter's Bulletin* (U.S.) Apr. 12/2 Why, even the old-fashioned grouch, The biggest in the land, With 29 years' service will On pay-day shake your hand. **1919** H. L. WILSON *Ma Pettengill* ii. 61 A fifty-five-year-old male grouch.. who had been snarling at everyone that came near him ever since the train left New York. **1923** *Public Opinion* 12 Oct. 361/1 Whether I thought myself a Gentleman or a Grouch.. is no part of this Parable. **1957** *Listener* 10 Oct. 581/1, I am probably a humourless old grouch. **1966** D. VARADAY *Gara-Yaka's Domain* x. 112 Had I been a gipsy palmist I might have paid more attention to the old grouch's lines of life and fate.

3. *Comb.* **grouch-bag** *U.S. slang*, a hidden pocket or a (draw-string) purse carried in a concealed manner for the hiding and storing of money, etc.; also, money saved and kept hidden.

1908 K. MCGAFFEY *Sorrows of Show Girl* xiii. 152, I have met gentlemen who threw the lid of their grouch bag in the gutter and didn't care if they ever found it again. **1914** JACKSON & HELLYER *Vocab. Criminal Slang* 39 *Grouch bag*, a place, as a pocket or receptacle, for concealing money or valuables; a reserve fund held in secret to the exclusion of fraternists. **1956** N. ALGREN *Walk on Wild Side* (1957) i. 17 Circus roustabouts.. took their money out of grouch-bags, pouches drawn by string, like tobacco pouches. **1960** B. KEATON *Wonderf. World of Slapstick* (1967) 24 Like every other woman in vaudeville she carried the act's cash in a grouch bag. This was a chamois purse which hung under her dress from a string round her neck. **1969** *Telegraph* (Brisbane) 6 Dec. 2/2 Groucho.. earned his nickname in poker games because he always carried his money in a 'grouch bag'.

grouch: see KURUS.

grouch (graʊtʃ), *v.* orig. *U.S.* [var. of GRUTCH *v.*] *intr.* To grumble. Also with words spoken as object.

1916 C. J. DENNIS *Moods of Ginger Mick* 133 *Grouch*, to mope; to grumble. **1925** H. L. FOSTER *Trop. Tramp Tourists* 137 The tourists.. all came back to the train at a painfully slow walk,.. and grouched all the way home. **1926** J. BLACK *You can't Win* viii. 90 'Everything's all right now, ain't it?' 'Oh, sure,' he grouched. 'Everything's all right—just like Denmark.' **1931** H. DE V. STACPOOLE *Pacific Gold* II. i. 99 'Now what *she* grouchin' about?' asked the Captain.

grouchy (ˈgraʊtʃɪ), *a.* orig. *U.S.* [f. GROUCH *sb.* or *v.* + -Y¹.] Grumbly, ill-tempered.

1895 W. C. GORE in *Inlander* Nov. 66 *Grouchy*, gloomily irritable; cross. **1902** *Daily Chron.* 25 Jan. 7/2 Thus we may learn which of them, in the opinion of his fellows, is.. the slouchiest, the biggest fusser, the 'grouchiest'. **1903** [see GROUCH *sb.* 1]. *a* **1910** 'O. HENRY' *Trimmed Lamp* (1916) 212 What's the matter, Andy, you are so solemn and grouchy to-night? **1915** *Times* 12 Apr. 10/1 The Germans are still pretty grouchy over their beating. Both sides begin firing on the slightest alarm. **1929** C. H. SMITH *Bridge of Life* i. 5 My maternal grandfather.. was a grouchy, crusty old fellow. **1932** H. J. MASSINGHAM *Wold without End* iii. 77 Father Hiems rallied from his swoon and was grouchy with snow-showers. **1942** E. PAUL *Narrow St.* xii. 90 Maggie, the unspeakable terrier beloved by the grouchy Madame Marie at the Caveau, took every advantage of her mistress's indulgence.

Hence **ˈgrouchily** *adv.*, **ˈgrouchiness**.

1906 H. GREEN *At Actors' Boarding House* 314 Ned was grouchily chopping ice and shooing flies away. **1923** R. D. PAINE *Comrades of Rolling Ocean* iii. 41 'They are all new to me,' grouchily replied Judson. **1925** C. E. MULFORD *Cottonwood Gulch* vi. 87 The second bar-tender, whose grouchiness was due to lack of proper sleep. **1930** *Time & Tide* 25 Apr. 529/2 He.. had decided—a trifle grouchily—to stay on and make the best of a bad job.

grouf(f)lings, variant of GROVELLINGS *Obs.*

grough, obs. form of GROW; variant of GRUFF.

grought, obs. form of GROWTH¹.

grouhund, obs. form of GREW-HOUND.

groul, groume, obs. ff. GROWL, GRUME.

groule: see GURL *v.*

groun, obs. f. *grown*, pa. pple. of GROW.

ground (graʊnd), *sb.* Forms: 1–5 (6– *Sc.*) grund, 4–6 grond, (5 gronnde), 4–7 grounde, 5 grownd(e, (5 grount, growende, 6 growinde, groune, 7 grown), 3– ground. [Com. Teut.: OE. *grund* str. masc. = OFris., OS. *grund* (MDu. *gront*, inflected *grond-*, Du. *grond*), OHG. *grunt*, *krunt* (MHG. *grunt*, *grund-*, G. *gruna*), Goth. **grundus* (cf. *grundu-waddjus* ground-wall, foundation, *afgrundiþa* abyss):—OTeut. **grundu-z*:—pre-Teut. **ghrn̥tú-s*; no cognates outside Teut. are known. The formal equivalent is not found in ON., which has however *grund* fem. (declined like the *-i-* stems), earth, plain, and a cognate type (Teut. **grunþo-*:—pre-Teut. *ghrn̥to-*) in *grunn-r*, *gruð-r* masc., bottom, *grunn-r* adj., shallow, *grunn* neut., shoal (Da. *grund* bottom, shallow, Sw. *grund* bottom, foundation, ground).]

I. The bottom; the lowest part or downward limit of anything.

†**1. a.** Of the sea, a well, ditch, etc., and of hell; rarely of heaven. (Cf. BOTTOM *sb.* 3.) *Obs.*

c **825** *Vesp. Psalter* lxiv. 8 Ðu ȝedroefes grund [L. *fundum*] sæs. *a* **1000** *Cædmon's Gen.* 345 (Gr.) Het hine þære sweartan helle grundes ȝyman. *c* **1175** *Lamb. Hom.* 19 He.. alesde us of helle grunde. *c* **1200** ORMIN 12059 Modiȝnesse, þatt warrp þe deofell.. Inntill þe grund off hellepitt. *c* **1275** *Luue Ron* 154 in *O.E. Misc.* 98 Hit is ymston of feor iboren, nys non betere vnder heouene grunde. **1340** HAMPOLE *Pr. Consc.* 7213 In þe grond of helle dongeoune þe hevedes of ȝynfulle salle be turned doune. *c* **1425** *Eng. Conq. Irel.* 12 He fel doun yn the grounde of þe dich. **1483** CAXTON *Gold. Leg.* 237 b/2 Thangel of our lord plunged them doun in the grounde of the see. **1535** COVERDALE *Job* xxxviii. 16 Camest thou euer in to the grounde of the see? **1637** RUTHERFORD *Lett.* (1862) I. 218 Cast Him.. into the ground of the Sea, He shall come up again.

†**b.** Of other things, esp. of a vessel or a wound (cf. BOTTOM *sb.* 1). Also in phrase *all to ground*: completely, thoroughly. *Obs.*

c **1205** LAY. 7779 þer mihten sitten in þon grunde [of the tower] cnihtes sixti hundred. *Ibid.* 21508 And duden heom alle clane into þan scipen grunde. *a* **1300** *K. Horn* 1197 Horn dronk of horn a stounde And þrew hys ryng to þe grounde [of the horn]. **13..** *Minor Poems fr. Vernon MS.* xxxvii. 814 þe leche clanseþ þe wounde: Clene in þe ground And leiþ salue a-boue. *c* **1305** *J. Iscariot* 118 in *E.E.P.* (1862) 110 Of oure louerdes god.. he stal al to grounde. *c* **1420** *Pallad. on Husb.* IX. 153 Decoct in bras yf grauel in the ground Noon leue, is preef that that licour is sound. *c* **1440** *Jacob's Well* 215 ȝe schul be þe ground of þis laddere in helle, be-cause ȝe be begynners of þat wrong! *c* **1500** *Lancelot* 2079 His dedly wound god helyth frome the ground. **1597** MONTGOMERIE *Cherrie & Slae* 1362 Quhyle we grip it [an ailment] to the grund. **1824** SCOTT *St. Ronan's* ix, I ken weel eneugh how a customer looks that's near the grund of the purse.

†**c.** *fig.* Of the heart: (cf. BOTTOM *sb.* 5 b). *Obs.*

c **1200** ORMIN 13286 Crist sahh all hiss herrtess grund. *c* **1290** *S.E. Leg.* I. 220/19 þis olde man riȝt of is heorte grounde Al weopinde he hem tolde ȝwat he hadde i-founde. *a* **1310** in Wright *Lyric P.* 81 Sone, y fele the dede stounde, The suert is at myn herte grounde. *c* **1440** *Jacob's Well* 170 In þe bothme, in þe ground, in þe depthe of þin herte. **1535** COVERDALE *Gen.* xliii. 30 The grounde of his hert was kyndled towarde his brother. **1611** BIBLE *Transl. Pref.* 7 Let vs rather blesse God from the ground of our heart. **1745** WESLEY *Wks.* (1872) I. 506 We praised God from the ground of the heart.

d. *Theol.* [repr. G. *grund* as used by 14th-c. mystics, notably Eckhart and Tauler.] (*a*) The divine essence or centre of the individual soul, in which mystic union lies. (*b*) Godhead as the source of all that is.

a **1400** *Book of Privy Counselling* (1944) 144/19 God, þi grounde & þi purete of spirit. **1865** J. H. STIRLING *Secret of Hegel* I. II. i. 235 Being is posited as Existence, and the Mediating agency of this Being as the Ground. **1899** W. R. INGE *Chr. Mysticism* i. 7 The curious doctrine which we find in the mystics of the Middle Ages, that there is at 'the apex of the mind' a spark which is consubstantial with the uncreated ground of the Deity. **1911** E. UNDERHILL *Mysticism* iii. 64 The point of contact between man's life and the divine life.. is called the Ground of the Soul, the foundation or basal stuff whence springs all spiritual life. **1945** A. HUXLEY *Time must have Stop* viii. 92 There was the ultimate all-embracing field—the Brahma of Sankara, the One of Plotinus, the Ground of Eckhart and Boehme. *Ibid.* xxx. 289 There is a Godhead or Ground, which is the unmanifested principle of all manifestation... The Ground is transcendent and immanent. **1945** —— *Perennial Philos.* (1946) ii. 29 The divine Ground of all existence is a spiritual Absolute, ineffable in terms of discursive thought, but.. susceptible of being directly experienced. **1949** P. TILLICH *Shaking of Foundations* vi. 47 The God Whom he cannot flee is the Ground of his being. **1950** W. R. TRASK tr. J. Bernhart in *Theologia Germanica* 95 What Plotinus had called the 'kentron' (center) of the soul, and Richard of St. Victor the 'height and inwardness of the spirit'..; what Bernard of Clairvaux called the 'point of the mind' (*acies mentis*), or again the 'spark' (*scintilla*) is now given a variety of German names and is indefatigably discussed and speculated upon. It is called the 'soul's essence' (*Wesen*), 'soul' (*Gemut*), ..'ground' (*Grund*)... These concepts are intended to designate that which God and man must have in common if a contact is to be established between them... The thing in which they [*sc.* individual mystics] agree is always the idea of the mystic function of the 'ground' of the soul. **1961** J. WALSH tr. *Dame Julian's Rev. Divine Love* lxii. 168 God.. is the Ground; he is the Substance. **1963** J. A. T. ROBINSON *Honest to God* iii. 45 (*heading*) The Ground of our Being.

2. a. The solid bottom or earth underlying the sea (†or other water). Now only *Naut.*, esp. in reference to soundings, or in phrase *to break ground*: to heave the anchor clear of the bottom.

Beowulf (Z.) 553 Hreo wæron yða.. Me to grunde ȝeteah fah feondscaða. *c* **1000** *Sal. & Sat.* 227 (Gr.) Dol bið se ðe gæð on deop wæter, se ðe.. mid fotum ne mæȝ grund ȝeræcan. *c* **1200** ORMIN 14861 All all swa summ þe sæ wass þær Dun till þe grund toworrpenn, Swa þatt teȝȝ o þe driȝȝe grund Wel sæȝhenn openn weȝȝe. *a* **1300** *Cursor M.* 1840 þat was no creatur in liue þat moght to grund or reche or riue. *Ibid.* 23198 Stang als men sais es vmstund Sua depe þat þar-on es na grund. **13..** *Seuyn Sag.* 885 (W.) To a fische-pole he come.. He lepe in and sanke to gronde. *c* **1400** MAUNDEV. (Roxb.) xxxiii. 148 As þai saile þai may.. see þe ground of þe see. *c* **1440** *Jacob's Well* xi. 75 Caste out of þi pytt þe stynkyng wose of pride, tyl þou fynde a syker ground & a clene. *c* **1485** *Digby Myst.* (1882) III. 1395 Lett fall an ankyr to grownd! *a* **1568** *Satir. Poems Reform.* xlvi. 393 Gif ȝe can nocht get the grund, Steir be the compas. **1596** SHAKS. *1 Hen. IV*, I. iii. 204 Diue into the bottome of the deepe, Where Fadome-line could neuer touch the ground. **1600** HAKLUYT *Voy.* III. 190 There is good ground and ankorage here: and you shall ride in three fathom water. **1611** MARKHAM *Countr. Content.* I. xiv. 93 If you Angle for him [Trout] at the ground.. the Menow is a good bayte. **1698** FRYER *Acc. E. India & P.* 1 The Ship then breaking Ground from Graves-End, to fall down to the Buoy in the Nore. **1712** W. ROGERS *Voy.* 50 We kept continual Soundings, and had always Ground from one League to ten off the Shore, from 20 to 50 Fathom Water. **1752** [see BREAK *v.* 44 d]. **1782** *Log of Albemarle* in Nicolas *Disp. Nelson* (1846) VII. p. v, With this depth and ground you may be sure you are without the Capes. **1807** J. JOHNSON *Oriental Voy.* 220 On the 5th the men of war.. broke ground, and steered past. **1867** SMYTH *Sailor's Word-bk.*, s.v., *To strike ground*, to obtain soundings.

fig. **1781** C. JOHNSTON *Hist. John Juniper* I. 80 His readers .. may have flattered themselves with hope of finding ground at last, after the pains of diving so deep for it.

b. The bottom at a point where the water becomes too shallow for a vessel, etc. to float. *to take* (*the*) ***ground***: to run ashore, to strand. *to* ***smell the ground*** (see quot. 1875).

1597 SHAKS. *2 Hen. IV*, IV. i. 17 Thus do the hopes we haue in him, touch ground, And dash themselves to pieces. **1830** LYELL *Princ. Geol.* I. 299 These masses [icebergs] may sometimes take the ground in great numbers. **1875** E. FITZ-GERALD *Lett.* (1889) I. 374, I.. fancy that I begin to 'smell the Ground', as Sailors say of the Ship that slackens speed as the Water shallows under her. **1880** *Times* 4 Aug. 12/4 The Laine, Russian barque,.. took the ground on the Somersetshire side. **1893** STEVENSON *Catriona* Summary p. viii, The *Covenant* took ground and sank off the coast of Mull. **1893** 'Q' *Delect. Duchy* 295 Miss.. Lear heard her brother's boat take ground on the narrow beach.

†**c.** ***on ground*** = AGROUND. *to set* or *run on* ***ground***: *fig.* to puzzle, nonplus (a person). Cf. 9 b.

1597 SHAKS. *2 Hen. IV*, IV. iv. 40 Like a Whale on ground. **1601** BP. ANDREWES *Serm.* (1843) V. 127 The Pharisees and Sadducees had no further end but to set Him on ground, and so to expose him to the contempt of the people. *a* **1642** SIR W. MONSON *Naval Tracts* VI. (1704) 522/1 The English.. may come on Ground. **1642** ROGERS *Naaman* 442 Will God heale, that man may be set on ground and bee convinced of his owne impotency. **1659** J. ARROWSMITH *Chain Princ.* 138 Whilest others run themselves on ground, and dispute it till their understandings be nonplust. **1667** *Lond. Gaz.* No. 217/4 The Ship called the Van Hoorn.. is on ground without the mouth of the Texell.

3. a. *pl.* The particles deposited by a liquid in the bottom of the vessel containing it; dregs, lees. †Also *sing.* a residuum, sediment.

a **1340** HAMPOLE *Psalter* lxiv. 9 Ill men sall drynke þe grundis of þe chalice. *c* **1450** *M.E. Med. Bk.* (Heinrich) 93 Streyne hit wel þorouȝ a caneuas, and do awey þe groundes of þe roses. **1601** HOLLAND *Pliny* II. 159 The grounds or dregs of the black oile oliue. **1625** HART *Anat. Ur.* viii. 98 Wheresoever there is a swim there is also a ground or residence. **1742** *Lond. & Country Brew.* I. (ed. 4) 53 The unwholesome Settlements or Grounds of the Beer. **1775** SHERIDAN *St. Patr. Day* II. iv, *Just.* Did you perceive anything in my chocolate cup..? *Ser.* Nothing,.. unless it was a little grounds. **1824** MACAULAY *Misc. Writ.* (1860) I. 141 [Telling fortunes] neither from the lines of a hand, nor the grounds of a teacup. **1860** *All Year Round* No. 42. 367 Cups of smoking black coffee (half grounds as the Turks drink it).

fig. **1629** RUTHERFORD *Lett.* (1862) I. 44 Fulfil with joy the remnant of the grounds and remainders of the afflictions of Christ in your body. **1642** HALES *Schism* 4 If so be you be *animo defæcato*, if you have cleared your self from froth and growns. **1672** MARVELL *Reh. Transp.* I. 185 How much another thing it is to hear him speak that hath cleared himself from froth and growns.

b. Refuse (of meal, wool, etc.). *rare.*

1629 CHAPMAN *Juvenal* 21 The mustiest grounds Of Barley-griest, bak'd purposely for hounds. **1653** WALTON *Angler* v. 117 You must be sure you want not.. the Peacocks feather, and grounds of such wool and crewel as will make the Grasshopper. **1808** JAMIESON, *Grounds*, the refuse of flax, left in dressing it.

II. Base, foundation.

†**4. a.** The solid base or foundation on which an edifice or other structure is raised. In early use *pl.* in the same sense (cf. *foundations*). *Obs.*

c **950** *Lindisf. Gosp.* Luke vi. 48 Gelic is [he] ðæm menn timbrende hus seðe delfæð.. & ȝesette ða grundas [L. *fundamenta*] ofer carr *vel* stan. *Ibid.* xiv. 29. *a* **1300** *E.E. Psalter* xvii. 8 Groundes ofe hilles todreued are. *Ibid.* 16 Groundes ofe ertheli werlde vn-hiled are. *a* **1300** *Cursor M.* 128 For þi þat na werc may stand Wit-outen grundwall to be lastand, þar for þis werc sal I fund Apon a selcuth stedfast grund. **1382** WYCLIF *Ezra* v. 16 Thilke Zazabazar cam, and sette the groundis of the temple of God in Jerusalem. **1423** JAS. I *Kingis Q.* cxxx, On him traist and call, That corner-stone and ground is of the wall. **1535** COVERDALE *1 Kings* vi. 15 Salomon.. buylded the walles.. from the grounde of yᵉ house vnto the rofe. **1581** *Satir. Poems Reform.* xliv. 35 As ȝour maisters grund is laid, Lyk do the vallis and bigging be. **1634** SIR T. HERBERT *Trav.* 57 There be but nineteene standing,.. howbeit the ruines and ground of fivescore more, are yet visible. **1715** LEONI *Palladio's Archit.* (1742) I. 88 The beams which make the ground or bottom of the Bridge.

b. The floor.

1847 WEBSTER, *Ground*, a floor or pavement. **1900** *Eng. Dial. Dict.*, Put the baby an the ground and let 'er craal. **1921** E. O'NEILL *Emperor Jones* (1925) I. 7 (*stage-direction*) Woman (seeing the uselessness of struggling, gives way to frantic terror, and sinks to the ground). **1937** A. CHRISTIE *Murder in Mews* i. 14 We.. forced the door open. Mrs. Allen was lying in a heap on the ground shot through the head. **1939** JOYCE *Finnegans Wake* 452 Pricking up ears to my phono on the ground and picking up airs from th'other over th'ether.

5. In various immaterial applications.

a. That on which a system, work, institution, art, or condition of things, is founded; the basis, foundation. Now somewhat *rare*.

a **1300** *Cursor M.* 19307 þat was to strenght þair trout[h] in grund. **1340** HAMPOLE *Pr. Consc.* 209 Mekenes, þat es grund of al vertus..On whilk al vertus may be sette fast. *c* **1374** CHAUCER *Troylus* II. 793 (842) As he þat is þe welle of worþinesse Of trouþe ground, myrour of goodlyhed. *c* **1400** *Destr. Troy* Prol. 80 How þe groundes first grew..Bothe of torfer and tene þat hom tide aftur. **1423** JAS. I *Kingis Q.* vi, And so the vertew of his ȝouth before Was in his age the ground of his delytis. *a* **1483** *Liber Niger* in *Househ. Ord.* (1790) 18 He ordeyned his groundes for household so sure that his greete hospitalitie dayly stode wurshypfully without decay xxxiii yeres. **1500–20** DUNBAR *Poems* xxvi. 56 Cuvatyce, Rute of all evill and grund of vyce. **1523** FITZHERB. *Surv.* Prol., For a grounde of this treatyse..I do take an olde statute named Extenta manerii as a principall grounde therof. **1596** SPENSER *F.Q.* VI. i. 1 Which of all goodly manners is the ground, And roote of civill conversation. **1611** BIBLE *Transl. Pref.* 4 The Edition of the Seuentie..was vsed by the Greeke fathers for the ground and foundation of their Commentaries. **1653** WALTON *Angler* iv. 110 These and the May-fly are the ground of all fly-Angling. **1674** PLAYFORD *Skill Musick* I. i. 1 The Gamut is the Ground of all Musick. **1867** MAURICE *Patriarchs & Lawg.* x. (1877) 198 The ground of the national existence was laid in sacrifice. **1870** JEVONS *Elem. Logic* xxvi. 219 Upon a similar ground rests all the vast body of certain knowledge.

†**b.** A fundamental principle; also *pl.* the elements or rudiments of any study or branch of knowledge. *Obs.*

1531 *Doctor & Student* Introd. 2, I wyll gladly shewe the as me thynketh what be the groundes of the lawe of Englande. **1574** tr. *Littleton's Tenures* 2 b, There is a ground in the law, that inheritance may..not lyneally ascend. **1592** DAVIES *Immort. Soul* I. x. (1714) 22 Marrying divers Principles and Grounds, Out of their Match, a true Conclusion brings. **1605** BACON *Adv. L.* II. i. §2 Let this ground therefore be laid that [etc.]. **1625** —— *Ess., Boldness* (Arb.) 519 Men that vndertake great Cures..but want the Grounds of Science. **1648** GAGE *West Ind.* xx. 160 And counselled me to learn the..language, (whereof I had already got some grounds). **1708** J. CHAMBERLAYNE *St. Gt. Brit.* II. III. x. (1743) 434 They have likewise a chaplain to instruct them in the grounds of learning. **1762** FOOTE *Orator* I. Wks. 1799 I. 195 Though he is the Poitier who teaches you the step and the grounds; yet I am the Gallini who gives you the air, and the grace of the minuet.

c. A circumstance on which an opinion, inference, argument, statement, or claim is founded, or which has given rise to an action, procedure, or mental feeling; a reason, motive. Often with additional implication: A valid reason, justifying motive, or what is alleged as such. ***on the ground of***: by reason of (some circumstance alleged in justification of a procedure). ***on*** (***public, religious,*** etc.) ***grounds***: for reasons of the nature specified.

c **1205** LAY. 3191 Al þis ilka ich wulle don; iseid ich habbe þene grund. *c* **1374** CHAUCER *Compl. Mars* 160–3 The grounde an cause of al my peyn..I wol reherse not for to haue redresse But to declare my grounde of heuynesse. **1395** *Remonstr. Rom. Corrup.* (1851) 20 Ambrose and Crisostom witnessen, with greet ground of holi writ and opin resoun, that confessioun to God sufficith to saluacioun. **1467** *Mann. & Househ. Exp.* (Roxb.) 171 He..saw his growende scholde be preved nowte, thanne he mad a new mater. **1535** COVERDALE *Isa.* xli. 21 Stonde at youre cause (saieth the Lorde) and bringe forth youre strongest grounde. **1592** SHAKS. *Rom. & Jul.* v. iii. 179 The true ground of all these piteous woes. **1599** H. BUTTES *Dyets drie Dinner* E iij, Chestnut, Chastnut: say some. I knowe not upon what ground. **1605** *Verstegan's Dec. Intell.*, Commend. Verses, To gratifie that nation is his ground To whom he thinks his best endeuours bound. **1642** FULLER *Holy & Prof. St.* IV. xx. 343 The beginnning of a rumour is sometimes all the ground thereof. **1657** P. HENRY *Diaries* (1882) 42 Hee refus'd; his grounds I know not. **1662** STILLINGFL. *Orig. Sacr.* II. iii. §6 Then all former ages have believed without sufficient ground for faith. **1671** M. BRUCE *Good News in Evil Times* (1708) 18 A great ground of Gladness. **1698** FRYER *Acc. E. India & P.* 340 On which ground it is, that their best Cities seldom have splendid Edifices..from..private Hands. **1703** MAUNDRELL *Journ. Jerus.* (1732) 126 The ground and reason of this tradition, I could not learn. **1732** LAW *Serious C.* xi. (ed. 2) 167 Let but any complaining, disquieted man tell you the ground of his uneasiness. **1775** SHERIDAN *Duenna* I. iii, That is to be the ground of my dismission. —— *Rivals* II. i, What grounds for apprehension? **1790** BURKE *Fr. Rev.* 19 There is ground enough for the opinion that all the kingdoms of Europe were, at a remote period, elective. **1796** —— *Regic. Peace* i. Wks. VIII. 201, I thought the insolent, unprovoked aggression..a good ground of war. **1856** FROUDE *Hist. Eng.* (1858) I. ii. 134 His desire was publicly urged on public grounds, and..thus only, the pope was at liberty to consider it. **1859** MILL *Liberty* ii. (1865) 21/2 He has no ground for preferring either opinion. **1868** J. H. BLUNT *Ref. Ch. Eng.* I. 283 The modern usurer will on such grounds leave his money to a hospital. **1875** JOWETT *Plato* (ed. 2) I. 233 Thus all ground of offence is taken away. **1876** GLADSTONE *Homeric Synchr.* 57, I am unable to perceive the grounds of the assumption. **1882** J. H. BLUNT *Ref. Ch. Eng.* II. 293 Ferrar was deprived..on the ground of his marriage. **1883** C. J. WILLS *Mod. Persia* 109 Whether or no this legend had any ground I cannot say. **1895** F. HALL *Two Trifles* iii, My grounds for doing so shall soon be stated explicitly.

6. The foundation or substratum on which other parts are overlaid, or on which they rest for support or display. In various technical uses:

a. The chief or underlying part in a composite textile fabric; a piece of cloth used as a basis for embroidery or decoration. In *Lace-making*: The meshes upon which the pattern is worked.

c **1386** CHAUCER Prol. 453 Hir couerchiefs ful fyne weren of ground I dorste swere they weyeden ten pound. **1480** *Wardr. Acc. Edw. IV* (1830) 116 Cloth of gold broched upon satyn ground. **1494** *Act 11 Hen. VII*, c. 27 They pluck off both the Nap and Cotton of the same Fustians, and break commonly both the Ground and Threads in sunder. **1667** DRYDEN *Maiden Queen* III. i. Wks. 1882 II. 455 No mortal hand so ignorant is found, To weave coarse work upon a precious ground. **1722** *Lond. Gaz.* No. 6068/8 A Suit of Double Ground, yellow and white, lined with a yellow Mantua Silk. **1779** SHERIDAN *Critic* I. i, Your occasional tropes and flowers suit the general coarseness of your style as tambour sprigs would a ground of linsey-woolsey. **1882** CAULFEILD & SAWARD *Dict. Needlework* (ed. 2), *Devonia Ground*, a ground used in Duchesse lace, and as a variety when making Honiton lace.

b. Any material surface, natural or prepared, which is taken as a basis for working upon: *esp.* in painting or decorative art, a main surface or first coating of colour, serving as a support for other colours or a background for designs; the prevailing or principal colour of any object, picture, etc.; that portion of a surface which is not coloured, decorated, or operated upon. Also *pl.*

1398 TREVISA *Barth. De P.R.* XIX. xi. (1495) 871 The meane coloures ben groundyd in none other colour better than in whyte, and the more whyte the grounde is the faster the colour cleuyth. **1593** SHAKS. *Lucr.* 1074 My sable ground of sin I will not paint. **1601** HOLLAND *Pliny* II. 621 The rest had need of a ground of Latton foile to giue them a lustre. **1625** N. CARPENTER *Geog. Del.* I. vii. (1635) 168 The Ground (in a Plaine-chart) is the space or Platforme wherein the Lines are to be inscribed. **1687** A. LOVELL tr. *Thevenot's Trav.* I. 200 All the Wall is painted in lovely Mosaick Work of Green, upon a Ground of fine Gold. **1799** G. SMITH *Laboratory* I. 347 When you begin to work, lay a thick ground against the ceiling or wall, with plaster. **1820** SCOTT *Monast.* xviii, The gems, being relieved and set off by the darker and more grave ground of the stuff, show like stars. **1839** URE *Dict. Arts* 921 Laying the grounds [of wall-paper] is done with earthy colours or coloured lakes thickened with size, and applied with brushes. **1860** RUSKIN *Mod. Paint.* V. VII. ii. 124 Seen in broken flakes on a deep purple ground of heavier cloud beyond. **1875** JOWETT *Plato* (ed. 2) III. 51 Dyers first prepare the white ground and then lay on the dye of purple.

fig. **1633** MARMION *Fine Companion* I. vii. Dram. Wks. (1875) 124 A man cannot discern the ground of their discourse for oaths. **1828** *Lights & Shades* II. 157 Cockneyism is a ground of native shallowness, mounted with pertness and conceit.

†**c.** *Mus.* The plain-song or melody on which a descant is raised. Also = *ground-bass*. *Obs.*

1592 R. D. *Hypnerotomachia* 19 A cunning Musition, who having devised his plaine grounde in right measure [etc.]. **1594** SHAKS. *Rich. III*, III. vii. 49 For on that ground Ile make a holy Descant. **1596** *Edward III*, II. i. 122 Ah, what a world of descant makes my soule Vpon this voluntarie ground of loue. **1633** B. JONSON *Love's Welcome at Welbeck*, Welcome is all our Song, is all our sound, The Treble part, the Tenor, and the Ground. **1670–98** LASSELS *Voy. Italy* II. 199 An untouched organ underneath the hill, plays soft ground to the Muses instruments. **1719** WATTS *Doxology*, *'Let God the Father live'*, Sinners from his free Love derive The Ground of all their Songs. **1811** BUSBY *Dict. Mus.* (ed. 3), *Ground*, the name given to a composition in which the bass, consisting of a few bars of independent notes, is perpetually repeated to a continually varying melody: as in Purcel's *Ground*, Pepusch's *Ground*, etc.

d. *Etching.* (See quots. 1727–41 and 1837.) Also ***etching-ground***. Cf. G. *ätzgrund*.

1727–41 CHAMBERS *Cycl.* s.v., Ground in Etching denotes a gummous composition, smeared over the surface of the metal to be etched; to prevent the aqua fortis from eating, or having effect, except in places where this *ground* is cut through, or pared off, with the points of needles. **1790** [see ETCHING]. **1821** CRAIG *Lect. Drawing* vii. 386 This ground must be made up into small balls. **1834** *Penny Cycl.* II. 203/1 (art. *Aquatinta*) He..formed a granulated surface on the plate, usually called a *ground*. **1837** *Ibid.* IX. 441 This etching-ground is a substance composed of wax, asphaltum, gum-mastic, resin, etc... The *laying of the ground*, as it is called, is thus effected [etc.]. *Ibid.* 442 The parts which are bitten-in enough are now to be covered with what is called *stopping-ground*, which is a mixture of lamp-black and Venice turpentine. **1885** *Chemist's Circular*, Holding the plate perfectly level, pour on the centre as much of the Liquid Ground as will freely flow over the entire surface.

e. *Carpentry.* (See quots.) Usually *pl.*

1823 P. NICHOLSON *Pract. Build.* 225 *Grounds.*—Pieces of wood concealed in a wall, to which the facings or finishings are attached. **1825** J. NICHOLSON *Operat. Mechanic* 593 Ground, or boxing-stile, grooved to receive the plastering. **1847** SMEATON *Builder's Man.* 248 *Grounds.*—Those pieces of wood imbedded in the plastering of walls, to which skirting and other joiner's finishings are attached. **1876** *Encycl. Brit.* IV. 492 Where the plasterer's work joins the grounds, they should have a small groove ploughed in the edge to form a key for the plaster.

†**f.** *pl.* (See quots.) *Obs.*

1664 EVELYN *Sylva* I. xvii. (1729) 79 Of the whitest part of the old Wood..is made the Grounds of our effeminate farined Gallants Sweet Powder. *a* **1700** B. E. *Dict. Cant. Crew*, *Chalk*, used in Powder by the Perfumers to mix with their Grounds. *Ibid.*, *Grounds*, unscented Hair Powder, made of Starch or Rice.

†**7.** The fundamental constituent or the essential part of any thing. *Obs.*

1580 FRAMPTON *Monardes' Two Med. agst. Venome* 123 b, Taking away the grounde, and evill qualitie, that the venomes doe infuse into the bodies. **1607** TOPSELL *Four-f. Beasts* (1658) 429 Our Musk is compounded of divers things, the ground whereof is the bloud of a little Beast. **1634** SIR T. HERBERT *Trav.* 149 Though the meat be particoloured, or party named. Yet the ground and meate is Pelo and no other. **1737** BRACKEN *Farriery Impr.* (1757) II. 14 The Ground of the Eye (as they call it) should be large and full..What they mean by the Ground of the Eye is the Pupil or Hole thro' the Iris and Uvea.

III. The surface of the earth, or a part of it.

8. a. The earth regarded as the surface upon which man and his surroundings naturally rest or move; freq. in prepositional phrases, as ***along, on, to the ground*** (†formerly also without the article), ***above*** or ***under ground***.

Beowulf (Z.) 2295 Hord-weard sohte ȝeorne æfter grunde, wolde guman findan. **971** *Blickl. Hom.* 221 Ða eodan hie eft to ðæm tune, & þæt ȝild ȝebræcan & ȝefyldan eal oþ grund. *c* **1200** ORMIN 9285 Illc an treo þatt..Ne bereþþ nohht god wasstme Shall bi þe grund beon hæwenn upp. *c* **1250** *Gen. & Ex.* 2640 Ðe child it warp dun to ðe grund. **1297** R. GLOUC. (Rolls) 2768 Wat is binuþe þe gronde, þat makeþ þat þe fondement ne stont none stounde. **1340** *Ayenb.* 246 Ase þet trau þet is ykarked mid frut, þe more hit bouȝ to þe grunde. *c* **1386** CHAUCER *Prioress' T.* 223 He fil al plat vp on the grounde. *c* **1430** *Syr Gener.* (Roxb.) 8738 Oon gaf him on the ere Such a clap with his fist That he thoo the ground kyst. *c* **1470** HENRY *Wallace* VI. 10 In Aperill quhen cleithit is..The abill grounde be wyrking off natur. **1513** DOUGLAS *Æneis* XII. Prol. 29 On the fertill skyrt lappis of the ground. **1571** HANMER *Chron. Irel.* (1633) 86 If any be much under grownd, the dampnesse of the earth takes away their lively colour. **1579** SPENSER *Sheph. Cal.* June 6 The simple ayre, the gentle warbling wynde..The grassye ground with daintye Daysies dight. **1590** —— *F.Q.* III. xii. 34 To ground He fell halfe dead. **1698** FRYER *Acc. E. India & P.* 43 Were the City again in the hands of the Moors, or even with the Ground, it were better for us. **1772** in G. White *Selborne* (1880) 126 After I left Sussex the tortoise retired into the ground under the hepatica. **1828** SCOTT *F.M. Perth* xiv, He looked on the ground while he answered her. **1888** MCCARTHY & PRAED *Ladies' Gallery* II. xi. 214 He stumbled ..and I came to the ground with him.

b. *fig.* in phr. † ***to bring to the ground***: to cast down, overthrow, overcome, subdue; ***to come*** (or ***go***) ***to the ground***: to be overcome; to perish; ***to fall to the ground***: (of schemes) to come to nothing, to be given up or abandoned; so ***to be dashed to the ground*** (of hopes); ***down to the ground***: completely, thoroughly, in every respect (*colloq.*); ***from the ground up*** (colloq., orig. *U.S.*), completely, entirely; 'down to the ground'; ***to get off the ground***, to make a successful start; ***on the ground***, in situ, on the spot.

c **1200** ORMIN 11773 þatt illke wise þatt Adam I Paradys wass fandedd, & brohht to grund. **1297** R. GLOUC. (Rolls) 1292 þis lond was ibroȝt þoru treson verst to grounde. *Ibid.* 7495 þus lo þe englisse folc vor noȝt to grounde com. *c* **1330** R. BRUNNE *Chron. Wace* (Rolls) 9888 Arthur..preyed hym of help a stounde, Or elles he scholde go to grounde. *c* **1400** *Destr. Troy* 9342 Hit greuys me full gretly, & to ground brynges. **1579** FULKE *Heskins' Parl.* 411 It must needes fall to the ground. **1587** GOLDING *De Mornay* xiv, Let such vanities passe and come to the groune. **1640** C. HARVEY *Church-gate* iii, He holds us up, whilst in him we are found: If once we fall from him, we go to ground. **1762–71** H. WALPOLE *Vertue's Anecd. Paint.* (1786) II. 106 It fell to the ground with the rest of the King's plans and attempts. **1849** E. E. NAPIER *Excurs. S. Africa* II, These poor fellows' hopes were suddenly dashed to the ground. **1856** EMERSON *Eng. Traits, Ability* Wks. (Bohn) II. 34 The strong survived, the weaker went to the ground. **1867** [see DOWN *adv.* 31]. **1878** MISS BRADDON *Clov. Foot* xlv, Some sea-coast city in South America would suit me down to the ground. **1894** DU MAURIER *Trilby* (1895) 421 He looks as if he could be trusted down to the ground. **1895** *Congress. Record* 6 Feb., App. 207/1 There never has been a time that a democratic administration has not been American from the ground up. **1910** W. M. RAINE *B. O'Connor* 52 We suited each other from the ground up. **1960** *Guardian* 25 Nov. 15/1 On-the-ground investigations. **1961** *New Statesman* 28 July 129/3 Intended as a half-way point of the Festival, at which audience and platform might fruitfully interact, it never got off the ground. **1963** *Listener* 10 Jan. 59/2 There is no longer any good reason why the young..American writer should undergo a European apprenticeship unless it be to satisfy his curiosity or to watch the operations of another literature on the ground. **1969** *Ibid.* 3 Apr. 469/1 It soon became evident ..that the history of contemporary music required reconsidering from the ground up. **1969** *Guardian* 4 July 5/5 If thefts continue, the future plans for the Crewe to Glasgow [railway] line can never really get off the ground.

c. Regarded as the place of burial. ***above ground***: unburied, alive. ***to bring, come to the ground*** (now only *dial.*): to bury, be buried.

c **1400** *Siege Troy* 1334 in *Archiv Stud. neu. Spr.* LXXII. 44 So doughty a body..That soo lowe is leyd in þe ground. ?*c* **1430** *St. Greg. Trental* in *Tundale's Vis.* (1843) 79 Sone to the gronde the con hor bere bryng And beryd hor. **1570** *Bury Wills* (Camden) 157 To see me honestly brought to the grownde. **1607** SHAKS. *Cor.* IV. i. 51 While I remaine aboue the ground, you shall Heare from me still. **1611** BIBLE *Gen.* iii. 19. **1694** ECHARD *Plautus* 208 I'll find out my Master, if he be above Ground, and bring him t'ye. **1858** HAWTHORNE *Fr. & It. Jrnls.* (1872) I. 19 Rachel, who died last week, and is still above ground. **1877** L. J. JENNINGS *Field Paths & Gr. Lanes* 28 Poor thing! it was only fourteen months afore she came to the ground.

d. The portion of the earth's surface on which a person or thing stands or moves; often *fig.* in phr. *to cut the ground from under one* or *one's feet.*

c **1530** *Interl. Beauties Women* A vi, Yet worship I the ground that thou gost on. **1809** MALKIN *Gil Blas* IV. i. ¶2, I took all possible pains to feel the ground under my feet, and to study the characters of the whole household. **1855** TROLLOPE *Warden* xi, The ground was cut from under her on every side. **1869** —— *He Knew* lxiii, Why should you have cut the ground away from your feet in that way? **1938** B. LUNN in 'H. Kingsmill' *Eng. Genius* 205 The Presbyterian divines were maddened by answers which cut the ground from institutional religion. **1962** *Christian Cent.* 18 July 886/2 In short, *Veterum Sapientia* has actually succeeded in cutting the ground from under the feet of the exponents of a living liturgy.

†**e.** The bare floor which constituted the pit of a theatre. *Obs.*

1614 B. JONSON *Barth. Fair* Induct., The understanding Gentlemen o' the Ground.

f. *Fox-hunting.* (*to run*) *to ground*: into a burrow or hole in the ground, 'to earth'. Cf. RUN *v.* 42 e. Also *to lie at ground. to go to ground*: also said of a dog. Also in other phrases, and *fig.* (of a person), to withdraw from public notice and live quietly or 'lie low'.

1797 *Monthly Mag.* III. 246 They soon found a fox, who ..saved himself by running to ground. **1801** DANIEL *Rural Sports* I. 90 In deep Snow, Foxes will lie at ground. *Ibid.* 91 When a Fox goes to ground, after a long chase..With respect to the digging of Foxes which hounds run to ground. **1860** G. D. PRENTICE *Prenticeana* 175 A Party of our friends ..chased a fox thirty-six hours. They actually 'ran the thing into the ground'. **1871** MRS. STOWE *My Wife & I* ix. 93 Show me up the weak points of those reformers; raise a laugh at those temperance men,—those religionists, who, like all us poor human trash, are running religion, and morals, and progress into the ground. **1900** *Daily News* 23 Oct. 6/2 The British infantrymen watched the race for shelter, their sporting spirit rising..above all racial hatred, and hailing with a 'gone to ground' whoop the final disappearance of the gun. **1905** LODER-SYMONDS & CROWDY *Hist. Old Berks Hunt* xv. 292 Hatford. Gorse, where they soon marked him [the fox] to ground. **1920** A. C. SMITH *Dog* 18 Strictly speaking..Airedales and bull terriers should not be classified among the terriers, both being much too big to go to ground. **1925** *Times* 7 Jan. 5/6 Sticking to their fox, the pace continued good to Chesterton, where he was marked to ground. **1930** 'SAPPER' *Finger of Fate* 265 It so happens that on occasions members of the fraternity [*sc.* snakes] go to ground in the bunches of fruit as they lie stacked beside the railway line. **1931** *Our Dogs* 23 Oct. 292/2 Working Terrier Dog..goes to ground to fox or badger, and stays. **1964** *Ann. Reg. 1963* 326 The four men 'went to ground', probably in Johannesburg. **1968** K. WEATHERLY *Roo Shooter* 39 When they found where a fox had been caught they would track it, sometimes for miles, and shoot it, but often the fox would go to ground and another trap was lost. **1968** *Times* 11 May 4/6 They are looking for a suburban villa where they can go to ground.

9. †**a.** The earth as contrasted with heaven. Chiefly in phr. *on* (*the*) *ground.* (In later use perh. not different from sense 8.) *Obs.*

a **1000** *Hymns* ix. 39 (Gr.) And we men cweðað on grunde her. **1362** LANGL. *P. Pl.* A. IX. 52 God saue þe from mischaunce, And ʒiue þe grace vppon grounde, In good lyf to ende. *a* **1400-50** *Alexander* 1964 All þe gracieux goddez þat þe ground viseten All er vndir my obedience. *c* **1460** *Towneley Myst.* xvi. 443 Ther goys none on grounde that has sich a wyght. **1611** SHAKS. *Cymb.* v. v. 146 A Nobler Sir, ne're liu'd 'Twixt sky and ground. **1616** B. JONSON *Devil an Ass* IV. i, There's not a finer Officer goes on ground. **1742** SHENSTONE *Schoolmistress* 72 And think, no doubt, she been the greatest wight on ground. **1883** R. W. DIXON *Mano* III. iii. 123 The truest gentleman that is on ground.

†**b.** The earth as distinguished from the sea; the dry land. Phr. *to lay on dry ground*: to floor, gravel (cf. 2 c). *Obs.*

a **1000** *Andreas* 747 (Gr.) þone, þe grund & sund, heofon & eorðan & hreo wæʒas..amearcode. *a* **1300** *K. Horn* 142 Of schip þe gon fonde An sette fot on grunde. **1519** *Interl. Four Elem.* (Percy Soc.) 40 But sir, if that a man sayle farre Upon the see, wyll than that starre Do there as on the grounde? **1590** SPENSER *F.Q.* I. iii. 32 The glad marchant that does vew from ground His ship farre come. **1599** NASHE *Lenten Stuffe* 50 Who this king should bee, beshackled theyr wits, and layd them a dry ground euery one. *a* **1649** DRUMM. OF HAWTH. *Poems* Wks. (1711) 13/2 Cannot believe..That other elements are to be found, Than is the water and this ball of ground. **1653** H. COGAN tr. *Pinto's Trav.* xix. 67 Then we unladed all her furniture..and set her on ground for to caulk her. **1697** DRYDEN *Æneid* x. 937 Too late young Turnus the delusion found, Far on the sea, still making from the ground.

10. With *a* and *pl.* †**a.** A region, land, country. *Obs. rare.*

Beowulf (Z.) 2073 Heofones ʒim glad ofer grundas. *a* **1000** *Widsith* 136 (Gr.) Swa scriþende ʒesceapum hweorfað gleomen gumena ʒeond grunda fela. *c* **1436** *Libel Eng. Policy* in *Pol. Poems* (Rolls) II. 188 In alle Cristendome Ys no grounde ne lond to Yreland lyche, So large, so gode. *Ibid.* 191 Kepe welle that grounde [Wales]. **1609** B. JONSON *Case is altered* I. i, *Onion*..though I haue no learning, yet I honour a scholer in any ground of the earth sir.

†**b.** A piece or parcel of land. *Obs.*

1548 UDALL, etc. *Erasm. Par. Matt.* xxvii. 7 And with that moneye they bought a ground of a certayne potter for godlye vses. **1565** COOPER *Thesaurus*, *Arborum contemplatione fundum comparare*, to bye a grounde for the trees that is in it. **1733** TULL *Horse-Hoing Husbandry* 23 When Part of a Ground has been better Till'd than the rest [etc.].

c. *pl.* An enclosed portion of land of considerable extent surrounding or attached to a dwelling-house or other building, serving chiefly for ornament or recreation. †Formerly in more general sense = lands, fields.

c **1460** *Towneley Myst.* xvi. 268 Markys, rentys, and powndys, Greatt castels & growndys. **1538** FITZHERB. *Just. Peas* 158 b, No person shall kepe..in his owne proper landes, nor in the possession, londes or groundes of any other..aboue the nombre of two thousande Shepe at one tyme. **1593** SHAKS. *2 Hen. VI*, IV. x. 36 Like a Theefe to come to rob my grounds; Climbing my walles inspight of me the Owner. **1678** BUNYAN *Pilgr.* I. 184 Giant Despair.. caught Christian and Hopeful asleep in his grounds. **1697** DRYDEN *Virg. Georg.* I. 141 His [labours] who ploughs across the furrowed grounds. *Ibid.* 194 No..marks nor bounds Distinguished acres of litigious grounds. **1751** JOHNSON *Rambler* No. 161 ¶2 Till he has learned the history of his grounds. **1806-7** J. BERESFORD *Miseries Hum. Life* (1826) II. xviii, After having cut down every foot of grass upon your grounds. **1837** DICKENS *Pickw.* xix, The Captain's house was a villa, and his land 'grounds', and it was all very high, and mighty, and great. **1855** PRESCOTT *Philip II*, iii. (1857) 243 Extensive grounds were also laid out around the palace, and a park was formed.

11. a. Area or distance on the face of the earth. (Usually without article, and most commonly depending on a word implying extent or partition.) Also *fig.* (cf. 4,5).

c **1400** *Destr. Troy* 12556 Naules..hade londes full long, & of leue brede, And the grettist of grise, of gronnde & of pepull. **1523** FITZHERB. *Husb.* §12 An acre of grounde..as moche grounde. **1576** FLEMING *Panopl. Epist.* Ded. ¶iij b, Anon, haveing gone a litle ground, mine eyes were fead with most delectable appearaunces. **1596** SHAKS. *Merch. V.* II. ii. 111, I will not rest till I haue run some ground. **1625** N. CARPENTER *Geog. Del.* II. xi. (1635) 185 That parcell of ground..has become the Salt Sea. **1667** PEPYS *Diary* 21 Apr., I have a mind to buy enough ground to build a coach-house and stable. *a* **1774** GOLDSM. tr. *Scarron's Com. Romance* (1775) II. 58 We travelled till night, and afterwards having gone a great deal more ground [etc.]. **1842** S. LOVER *Handy Andy* iii. 34, 'I bungle the loading of pistols! I that have stepped more ground than any man in the country!' **1860** TYNDALL *Glac.* I. xvii. 121 The glacier..takes up ground which belonged to it in former ages. **1900** *Pilot* 24 Mar. 110/2 Much of the ground covered in these expeditions is practically new to the modern European.

fig. **1727** A. HAMILTON *New Acc. E. Ind.* II. xlvii. 170 And thought that the Kings Refusal to make good their Demands, was a sufficient Piece of Ground to build their War on.

b. *esp.* in phr. *to break* (*new*) *ground*, to make progress in a new direction (see BREAK *v.* 44 c); *to gain, gather, get ground*: to advance, make progress; *lit.* and *fig.* (see GAIN *v.* 8, GATHER *v.* 9, GET *v.* 5 c); *to give ground*: to recede, retire (see GIVE *v.* 45); *to lose ground*: to fall back, decline (see LOSE *v.*); *to make* (*up*) *ground*, to make progress.

c **1436** *Libel Eng. Policy* in *Pol. Poems* (Rolls) II. 188 Wylde Yrishe so muche of grounde have gotyne There upon us. *Ibid.* 189 In that land..we lesse every yere More grounde and more. **1529** [see GET *v.* 5 c]. **1576** FLEMING *Panopl. Epist.* 254 To outrunne the ringleader, and thereby to gett ground. **1607** DEKKER *Sir T. Wyatt* Wks. 1873 III. 114 They come, no man giue ground..Be Englishmen and berd them to their faces. *c* **1645** HOWELL *Lett.* (1650) II. 3 To deal plainly with you, you have lost som ground at Court by it. **1687** A. LOVELL tr. *Thevenot's Trav.* I. 111 Though we beat and tack'd to and agen till the evening, we gained no ground. *a* **1776** R. JAMES *Dissert. Fevers* (1778) 53 He sweated profusely and the delirium began to give ground. **1804** W. TENNANT *Ind. Recreat.* (ed. 2) I. 39 A more independent spirit..is daily gaining ground among that class of men. **1873** BURTON *Hist. Scot.* VI. lxxiii. 354 They were steadily losing ground in the war. **1895** *Brewer's Dict. Phr. & Fable* 557/2 *To break ground*, to be the first to commence a project, etc.; to take the first step in an undertaking. **1906** H. C. WYLD *Hist. Study Mother Tongue* v. 94 Those tendencies..which are peculiar to the individual, and which are not shared by the community, will not gain ground, but will be eliminated. **1921** *Granta* 30 Nov., The local side again and again made ground galore with long kicks down wind. **1928** *Nation & Athenæum* 7 Jan. 537/2 Montesquieu..had been the first to break the new ground. **1931** F. L. ALLEN *Only Yesterday* ix. 229 Theodore Dreiser, Willa Cather,..the Imagists and exponents of free verse had been breaking new ground since before the war. **1932** *Sunday Express* 3 July 22/7 Udaipur is gradually making up ground on the colts in Butters' stable. **1954** G. D. H. COLE *Hist. Socialist Thought* II. xiii. 362 Communities breaking new ground were in constant danger of becoming the prey of fraudulent financiers and bankers. **1954** A. S. C. ROSS in *Neuphilologische Mitteilungen* LV. 45 *Posh* 'smart' is essentially non-U, but recently, it has gained ground among schoolboys of all classes. **1966** *Listener* 10 Mar. 345/2 I've had to break new ground in all directions in order to say them.

c. *to take ground*: to take up, or move into, a certain position. *lit.* and *fig.*

1700 [see 13 b]. **1818** JAS. MILL *Brit. India* II. v. v. 489 Uncertainty was at last removed, by his marching towards Arcot, and taking ground before it on the 21st of August. **1859** F. A. GRIFFITHS *Artil. Man.* (1862) 18 Take ground to the right (or left) in fours. **1883** *Harper's Mag.* Nov. 850/1 He took new ground..as to..painting.

d. *fig.* With allusion to a metaphorical 'travelling' or the like: Subject-matter, things that may be the object of study or discourse. Also *rarely* with *a*: A department of study.

1796 H. HUNTER *St. Pierre's Stud. Nat.* (1799) I. 12 His pupil had the courage to walk over the same ground after him. **1804** W. TENNANT *Ind. Recreat.* (ed. 2) I. 117 The learned Dr. Robertson has travelled partly over the same ground. **1842** S. LOVER *Handy Andy* xiii. 112 Mr. B... thought he had touched on forbidden ground. **1847** L. HUNT *Men, Women, & B.* I. i. 8 The more we know of any one ground of knowledge, the further we see into the general domains of intellect. **1933** H. L. ICKES *Diary* 12 Sept. (1953) I. 88 At eleven o'clock we had a meeting of the Public Works Board and we covered a great deal of ground.

12. Preceded by a descriptive or limiting adj., or an attributive sb.: Area or space having a specified extent or character, or adapted for a specified purpose. *lit.* and *fig.*

a. with *a* and *pl.* (Now only with attrib. sb. or with an adj. indicating relative position or change of level.)

c **1391** CHAUCER *Astrol.* II. §29 Lat thyn Astrolabie couch adoun evene up-on a smothe grond. **1535** COVERDALE *Exod.* iii. 5 The place where vpon thou stondest, is an wholy grounde. —— *Ps.* cvi[i]. 35 He maketh..water sprynges of a drye grounde. **1553** T. WILSON *Rhet.* (1580) 225, I feare none, because I stande uppon a saufe grounde. **1577** [see CORN-GROUND]. **1618** BOLTON *Florus* (1636) 79 Hee..did beate the enemy from a ground of advantage. **1662** GERBIER *Princ.* 14 On a low ground by the River side. **1707** FREIND *Peterborow's Cond. Sp.* 215 The Country..was full of little rising Grounds and Valleys. **1777** [see HUNTING-GROUND]. **1805** *Med. Jrnl.* XIV. 565 That our author may be able to meet Dr. Jackson..on equal grounds. **1855** PRESCOTT *Philip II*, I. I. viii. 108 A level ground, four leagues in breadth, lay between the armies. **1872** YEATS *Growth Comm.* 112 The fishing grounds of Portugal and England were used in common. **1894** J. T. FOWLER *Adamnan* Introd. 59 The spot was on a rising ground in a bend of the Foyle.

b. in generalized sense.

c **1436** *Libel Eng. Policy* in *Pol. Poems* (Rolls) II. 192 Lytelle wenythe the fole..What woo it were for alle this Englysshe grounde. **1508** KENNEDIE *Flyting w. Dunbar* 286 Out of Dumbar that theif he maid exyle, Unto Edward, and Inglis grund agane. **1533** FITZHERB. *Husb.* §6 In tough cley, and vpon hylly ground. **1580** SIDNEY *Ps.* XXVI. vi, I..Sett on plaine ground will thee Jehovah praise. **1601** SHAKS. *Jul. C.* III. i. 191 My credit now stands on such slippery ground. **1611** BIBLE *Exod.* iii. 5 [cf. 1535 Coverdale in a]. **1639** FULLER *Holy War* IV. xiv. (1647) 192 Though he stood on the lower ground in point of birth. **1781** COWPER *Friendship* 34 If..on forbidden ground..We sought without attaining. **1832** SHELLEY *Masque Anarchy* lxv, On some spot of English ground. **1853** TENNYSON *To E.L.* 10, I..track'd you still on classic ground. **1888** INGLIS *Tent Life Tigerland* 1 The best tiger-shooting ground in the world.

13. With reference to possessor or occupier, denoted by a genitive noun or possessive pronoun.

a. The portion of land forming the property (†or territory) of a person (†or people), or occupied by one as a tenant.

a **1400-50** *Alexander* 188 ʒour king sall..gett agayn his avyn gronde. *Ibid.* 1973 Miʒt þou þe marches of Messedoyne mayntene þi-selfe And gouerne bot þine awen gronde. *c* **1436** *Libel Eng. Policy* in *Pol. Poems* (Rolls) II. 188 Oure grounde there is a lytelle cornere To alle Yrelonde in trewe comparisone. **1533** *Presentm. Juries* in *Surtees Misc.* (1888) 34 That every man ryng his swyne, except they kepe theyme of theire owne growinde. **1548** FORREST *Pleas. Poesye* xix. 61 Hee [the farmer] cannot els lyue, so deeare is his grownde. **1598** SHAKS. *Merry W.* II. ii. 225 Like a fair house, built on another mans ground. **1787** COWPER *Let.* 30 Aug., Wks. (1876) 262 Mr. Throckmorton having long since put me in possession of all his ground, has now given me possession of his library. **1842** TENNYSON *Amphion* 75 'Tis in my neighbour's ground. **1855** —— *Maud* I. xxi. 1 Rivulet crossing my ground.

b. The space upon which a person, etc., takes his stand; the position maintained or defended by one; *esp.* in phrases *to hold, keep, maintain, stand, shift one's ground*; now usually *fig.* (sometimes with suggetion of 5 a).

1616 J. LANE *Contn. Sqr.'s T.* (Chaucer Soc.) ix. 176 He fightinge to maintaine Fregilia towne, they bearinge in to make his grown their grown. **1657** SPARROW *Bk. Com. Prayer* (1661) 239 The Church thereby keeping as it were her ground. **1657** R. LIGON *Barbadoes* (1673) 1 A friend, as willing to shift his ground as I, gave me an Overture which I accepted. **1700** DRYDEN *Flower & Leaf* 287 Drawn in two lines adverse they wheeled around, And in the middle meadow took their ground. **1707** *Lond. Gaz.* No. 4353/1 The Deserters..stood their Ground, and..fir'd on 'em. **1712** W. ROGERS *Voy.* 278 We can hardly keep our Ground against the Current. **1796** *Instr. & Reg. Cavalry* (1813) 221 The commanding officer turns on his own ground. **1801** STRUTT *Sports & Past.* I. i. 4 The sports of the field still maintained their ground. **1809** MALKIN *Gil Blas* II. vii. ¶24 She met me on my own ground. **1833** HT. MARTINEAU *Briery Creek* v. 113 Here the humblest slave might stand erect on the ground of his humanity. **1856** FROUDE *Hist. Eng.* (1858) I. i. 34 The government was strong enough to hold its ground. **1859** MILL *Liberty* iii. (1865) 43/2 It is not easy to see how it [Individuality] can stand its ground. **1881** JOWETT *Thucyd.* I. 197, I, like him taking the ground of future expediency, stoutly maintain the contrary position.

14. a. The particular space or area under consideration, or one used for some special purpose, *esp.* the scene of any contest, or meeting. *off the ground*: out of the way. *on the ground*: engaged in a duel.

c **1400** *Destr. Troy* 1174 A noumbur hoge Of Grekes were gedret & þe grounde hade. *Ibid.* 1352 The Troiens.. ffleddon in fere..When the Grekys hade the gre & the grounde wonen. *a* **1572** KNOX *Hist. Ref.* Wks. 1846 I. 115 Content to talk with the Governour, providit that the Cardinall and his cumpany war of the ground. **1601** SHAKS. *Jul. C.* IV. ii. 49 Bid our Commanders leade their charges off A little from this ground. **1678** DRYDEN & LEE *Œdipus* IV. Wks. 1883 VI. 213 I'm too well acquainted with the ground, Quite to forget it. **1816** SCOTT *Old Mort.* vi, Why came ye na hame when other folk left the grund? **1837** DICKENS *Pickw.* iv, There were sentries posted to keep the ground for the troops. **1837** THACKERAY *Ravenswing* vii, He has been 'on the ground' I don't know how many times. **1850** SCORESBY *Cheever's Whalem. Adv.* iii. (1859) 41 They had just arrived on the ground, and had not yet taken any whales. **1897** *Encycl. Sport* I. 72 (Bandy) *Ground*, a rectangular sheet of ice, measuring not more than 200 yds. × 100 yds. and not less than 100 × 50.

b. *Cricket*. (*a*) The space on which the game is played; (*b*) the space within which a player may lawfully stand while taking a particular part in the game; ***the, his,*** etc. ***ground*** (of a batsman) = the ground behind the popping-crease; (*c*) the paid staff of players attached to a club (also ***ground-staff***).

1718 in G. B. Buckley *Fresh Light on 18th Cent. Cricket* (1935) 2 Three of their men made an elopement and got off the ground without going in. **1733** in H. T. Waghorn *Cricket Scores* (1899) 6 There will be a line around the ground as usual, within which none but the gamesters are to be allowed. **1774** *Laws of Cricket* 8 The strikers need not keep within their ground till the Umpire has called *Play*. **1788** *Ibid.*, This rule is not meant..to prevent the bowler from filling up holes, watering his ground, or using sawdust, &c., when the ground is wet. **1850** 'BAT' *Cricketer's Man.* 78 The..players of 'the Ground'..act in the..capacity of..umpire. **1857** HUGHES *Tom Brown* II. viii, He is never in his ground, except when his wicket is down. **1880** J. LILLYWHITE *Cricketer's Ann.* 49 The ground staff for 1879 at Lord's consisted of [the twenty-two professional players named]. **1882** *Daily Tel.* 27 May, His colleague driving the ball into his wicket whilst he was just out of the ground. **1894** *Times* 23 Mar. 10/2 There are various additions to the ground staff... The list of 'the ground' is now as follows. **1955** T. H. PEAR *English Social Diff.* xi. 260 Boys of outstanding promise [at cricket] can receive coaching if they take jobs on a club ground-staff.

c. ***to have the ground on one's side***: to have the advantage of position (in a contest.)

1650 B. *Discolliminium* 1 He knows well that he hath gotten the ground and winde on his side, but I think I have the Sun on my back.

15. In technical uses. †**a.** (See quot.) *Obs.*

1753 CHAMBERS *Cycl. Supp.* s.v. *Bowling, Ground*, a bag or handkerchief laid down to mark where a bowl is to go.

b. *Telegraphy*. The contact of the conductor of an electric circuit with the earth; the escape of current resulting from this.

1870 F. L. POPE *Electr. Tel.* v. (1872) 63 The effect of a ground or escape is..to exhaust the batteries more rapidly. **1883** T. D. LOCKWOOD *Electr. Tel.* 138 If an accidental connection with the ground should occur, or, as it is technically said, a ground appears on the wires. **1893** in SLOANE *Electrical Dict.*

IV. 16. a. The soil of the earth. Also without article: Soil, earth, mould; now only in *Mining* (see quot. 1881) except with descriptive adj. Phr. ***to break ground*** (see BREAK *v.* 44).

a **1300** *Cursor M.* 6747 Theif hus brecand, or gruband grund. **1523** FITZHERB. *Husb.* §10 If the grounde be good, putte the more beanes to the pease. **1547** *Homilies* I. *Misery Mankind* I. (1859) 16 We may learn to know ourselves to be but ground, earth, and ashes. **1660** WILLSFORD *Scales Comm.* 196 This Trench (where the labourers first break ground). **1696** tr. *Du Mont's Voy. Levant* 131 There are no Woods in it by reason of the shallowness of the Ground. **1700** MOXON *Mech. Exerc.* I. 17 He ought to dig it deeper till he comes to firm ground; or if it proves to be loose, or made Ground [etc.] **1795** *Gentl. Mag.* 539/1 The extreme wetness of the ground had delayed the operation of the share. **1881** RAYMOND *Mining Gloss.*, *Ground*, the rock in which a vein is found; also, any given portion of the mineral deposit itself. **1884** *Public Opinion* 12 Sept. 338/1 The loose shale..has moved forward..and carried away both shafts..down to blue ground.

b. With *a* and *pl.* A kind or variety of soil. ? *Obs.*

1398 TREVISA *Barth. De P.R.* XVII. lxv. (1495) 642 Corne thryueth in one grounde and faylyth in a nother. **1523** FITZHERB. *Husb.* §2 There be many maner of groundes and soyles. Some whyte cley, somme redde cley [etc.]. **1542** BOORDE *Dyetary* iv. (1870) 238 Let hym make his fundacyon vpon a graualy grownde myxt with clay. **1583** STUBBES *Anat. Abus.* II. (1882) 44 They know exactly..what ground is best for euerie kinde of corne. **1626** BACON *Sylva* §409 In some Grounds which are strong, you shall haue a Raddish, &c. come in a Moneth. **1697** DRYDEN *Virg. Georg.* I. 80 This ground with Bacchus, that with Ceres, suits. **1787** WINTER *Syst. Husb.* 9 When a farmer cannot keep the produce of each ground separate.

V. *attrib.* and *Comb.*

17. General combinations. **a.** Simple attributive, locative and objective (senses I and III) as ***ground-bed***, ***-builder***, ***-clearance***, ***-end***, ***-fabric***, ***-feeder***, ***-herb***, ***-leaf***, ***-level***, ***-mark***, ***-nest***, ***-nester***, ***-pipe***, ***-soil***, ***-sward***, ***-tilth***, ***-whirl***; ***ground-building***, ***-deep***, ***-feeding***, ***-nesting***, ***-routing*** adjs.

1958 *Chambers's Techn. Dict.* Suppl. 1018/1 *Ground-based..radio duct. **1965** *Punch* 7 Apr. 506/2 A report just published by the National Academy of Sciences (counterpart of the Royal Society) surveys the requirements of 'ground-based' astronomy over the next ten years. **1615** G. SANDYS *Trav.* 88 Vntil rowzed from our *ground-beds by the report of the Cannon. **1859** *Amer. Cycl.* III. 282/1 The hawks are platform-builders, *ground-builders, occupants of hollow trees, &c. **1863** ATKINSON *Stanton Grange* 114, I think the mouse has the odds in an attack on a *ground-building bee's nest. **1959** *Motor Man.* (ed. 36) 4 The chassis frame cannot be lowered beyond a certain point without endangering the *ground clearance of the car. **1610** W. FOLKINGHAM *Art of Survey* I. iv. 9 The Goates of Angori are hung with shag *ground-deepe. **1523** FITZHERB. *Husb.* §15 The *grounde ende of a yonge asshe. **1938** *Burlington Mag.* Sept. 115/1 The loosely-woven linen *ground-fabric is entirely covered..with rich ornament. **1967** E. SHORT *Embroidery & Fabric Collage* i. 19 These all entail cutting away part of the ground fabric. **1887** *Encycl. Brit.* XXII. 611 Sturgeons are *ground-feeders. **1938** *Brit. Birds* XXXII. 222 An attempt to measure the frequency of association in the same fields of the more conspicuous *ground-feeding birds was made. **1859** DARWIN *Orig. Spec.* v. (1873) 108 the larger ground-feeding birds seldom take flight except to escape danger. **1626** BACON *Sylva* §530 To make the Herbe grow contrary to his Nature; As to make *Ground-Herbs rise in Heighth. **1851** MRS. BROWNING *Casa Guidi W.* I. 205 To let the *ground-leaves of the place confer A natural bowl. **1910** *Daily Chron.* 8 Mar. 1/6 The Parisian 'star', returning to her room at midnight, sees a strange object approaching her *ground-level windows from the garden. **1959** *Times* 22 Aug. 9/4 Being nearer to eye-level can be better appreciated than when at ground-level in the border or rockery. **1633** T. STAFFORD *Pac. Hib.* II. xiii. (1810) 368 That the Artillery might play as well by night as day himself did take and score out his *ground-markes. **1671** MILTON *P.R.* II. 280 And now the Herald Lark Left his *ground-nest. **1833** HT. MARTINEAU *Briery Creek* vi. 134 A lark sprang up from the ground-nest where she was sitting solitary. **1875** *Field & Forest* I. 10 It was a very neat structure, and looked to me as though the owner was habitually a '*ground-nester'. **1964** A. L. THOMSON *New Dict. Birds* 524/1 Other non-passerines may be broadly divided into ground-nesters, hole-nesters, and the builders of simple nests in trees. **1880** A. R. WALLACE *Isl. Life* 79 The seeds becoming attached to the plumage of *ground-nesting birds. **1664** EVELYN *Kal. Hort.* in *Sylva*, etc. (1729) 231 The Air *Ground-pipe, laid ..in the middle of the Floor. **1867** F. FRANCIS *Angling* i. (1880) 55 Barbel, which are a *ground-routing fish. **1822–34** *Good's Study Med.* (ed. 4) II. 645 The lowness and original swampiness of the *ground-soil. **1829** COLERIDGE *Garden of Boccaccio* 66, I..sit on the *ground-sward. **1553** GRIMALDE *Cicero's Offices* (1556) 59 For of all thinges whereoute anie gayne is sought, nothing is better than *ground tilth. *a* **1881** ROSSETTI *House of Life* iv, The *ground-whirl of the perished leaves of Hope.

b. attributive (sense II), often *quasi*-adjectival = 'fundamental', †'deep-seated', etc., as ***ground-basis***, ***-fact***, ***-faith***, ***-feature***, ***-form***, †***-harm***, †***-hate***, ***-idea***, ***-principle***, ***-quality***, ***-root***, ***-sense***, ***-thought***, ***-tint***, ***-tone***, etc.

Many of these formations are recent imitations of German compounds of *grund*, such as *grundform*, *grundgedanke*, *grundidee*, etc.

1920 T. P. NUNN *Education* 156 The function of the self-regarding sentiment is to exercise control over the 'objective' sentiments that form the *ground-basis of the self. **1905** *Spectator* 11 Mar. 353/1 The underlying *ground-fact of Russia, the inadequacy of her food-supply. **1871** R. H. HUTTON *Ess.* (1877) I. 37 In the absence of this *ground-faith. **1807** tr. *Goede's Trav. Eng.* II. 221 The *ground-features of his portrait must be natural. **1847** J. D. MORELL *Hist. View Philos.* (ed. 2) I. i. 118 The native construction of the intellectual faculty..contains all those *ground-forms of the understanding, by which knowledge from experience can be assimilated. **1879** J. A. H. MURRAY *Addr. Philol. Soc.* 611 From the ground-form—Ostyak *ma*, Samoyed *man*. **1881** *Amer. Jrnl. Math.* IV. 41 Tables of the ..Groundforms of the Binary Duodecimic. **1938** J. R. CARPENTER *Ecol. Gloss.*, *Ground form*, elementary form, as distinguished from growth form. *c* **1400** *Destr. Troy* 1431 A light wrathe..growes into *ground harme. *Ibid.* 1403 Thurgh vnhappe of þat kynde..Myche greuance shall groo & a *ground hate. **1865** *Sat. Rev.* 7 Jan. 16/1 Moulding his *ground-idea into a poetical whole. **1872** J. MORLEY *Voltaire* 299 When we come to the ground idea of the Essay on Manners. **1847** J. D. MORELL *Hist. View Philos.* (ed. 2) I. 3 The primary efforts of reason to get at the *ground principles of human knowledge were naturally weak and imperfect. **1873** M. ARNOLD *Lit. & Dogma* (1876) 89 This was the very ground-principle in Jesus Christ's teaching. **1897** HARDY *Well-Beloved* II. iii, Avice..had yet possessed a *ground-quality absent from her rivals. *Ibid.* III. vii, Pierston heard a voice below, the accents of a woman. They had a ground quality of familiarity, a superficial articulation of strangeness. *a* **1569** KINGESMYLL *Man's Est.* xi. (1580) 65 That this love might take a more *groundroote in our hartes. **1909** E. B. TITCHENER *Text-bk. Psychol.* I. 116 The sense of smell..is also a *ground-sense:..our own disregard of smell sensations is largely due to our assumption of the upright position. **1873** M. ARNOLD *Lit. & Dogma* (1876) 266 Righteousness is its *ground-thought. **1875** tr. *Vogel's Chem. Light* vii. 59 The painter indeed contents himself with three *ground tints—yellow, blue, and red. **1841–4** EMERSON *Ess.*, *Poet.* Wks. (Bohn) I. 157 We hear, through all the varied music, the *ground-tone of conventional life. **1874** H. R. REYNOLDS *John Bapt.* iii. §3. 199 David's psalms reveal the ground-tone and key-notes of Nathan's prophecies. **1909** *Westm. Gaz.* 8 Mar. 5/2 Her sash will repeat the ground-tone of her dress.

†**c.** With adjs. and pples. = 'to the bottom', hence 'completely, thoroughly, extremely', as ***ground-filled -hot***, ***-laden***, ***-stalwart***. (Cf. G. *grundfalsch*, etc.) *Obs.*

c **1205** LAY. 1088 þa scipen weoren igreþede, mid gode grund fulled. *Ibid.* 1106 Feower scipen greate þe weren grund ladene. *Ibid.* 5692 Ofte heo letten grund-hat læd gliden heom an heore hæfd. *c* **1300** *Havelok* 1025 þe ston was mikel, and ek greth,..Grund stalwrthe man he sholde be, þat mouthe liften it to his kne.

d. In Aviation, as ***ground alert***, ***attack***, ***boost***, ***control*** (landing, etc., by instrument direction from the ground; so ***ground control(led) approach*** (abbrev. *G.C.A.*), ***ground controller***); ***ground crew***, ***cushion***, ***defence***, ***effect***, ***engineer***, ***loop*** (so as vb.; also ***ground looping*** vbl. sb.); ***ground marker***, ***mechanic***, ***organization***, ***position***, ***resonance***, ***school***, ***speed***, ***staff***, ***stunt***, ***support***, ***troops***, ***wallah***; ***ground-based*** adj.; ***ground-straf(f)ing*** vbl. sb. (so, as a back-formation, ***ground-strafe*** v. trans., ***-strafer***); ***ground-to-air***, ***ground-to-ground***, used esp. as attrib. phrs.

1965 H. KAHN *On Escalation* 294 A *ground-alert bomber. **1917** 'CONTACT' *Airman's Outings* I. vii. 203 We shall see a great extension of *ground attacks by air cavalry. **1954** *Economist* 11 Sept. 11/1 In some countries..special aircraft for ground attack duties only have been developed. **1960** *Times* 23 Feb. 5/3 In the semi-active homing system a *ground-based radar illuminates the target. **1965** H. KAHN *On Escalation* ix. 171 Ground-based missiles. **1930** *Flight* 14 Mar. 305/2 Supercharging was the expression used to denote restoring the ground h.p. at some height, while *ground boost was used to get increased power at ground level. **1933** *Jrnl. R. Aeronaut. Soc.* XXXVII. 31 How would he suggest the air control and *ground control should be organised there? **1945** *Newsweek* 20 Aug. 42/3 GCA (Ground Control Approach) which permits blind landings of planes through overcast. **1969** *Listener* 1 May 596/1 He explained to ground control what was happening and ordered the crew to bail out. **1945** *Amer. Speech* XX. 309/2 GCA, *Ground Controlled Approach, Ground radar landing system. **1959** R. COLLIER *City that wouldn't Die* vii. 105 His navigator..was in minute-by-minute touch with the new G.C.I. (Ground Controlled Interception). **1958** *Listener* 21 Aug. 259/1 It is the *ground controllers' job to see that collisions do not happen. **1970** *Daily Tel.* 15 Apr. 1/7 Ground controllers..decided against a speed-up plan that would have brought Apollo 13 down by tomorrow night. **1934** *Sci. Amer.* Feb. 83 (*caption*) The *ground crew guiding the ship [*sc.* airship] into the hangar. **1940** *Flight* 7 Nov. *b*/2 The efficient devotion of ground crews and excellence of material is responsible for the trouble-free journeys made each night. **1952** *Ann. Reg. 1951* 109 The Government announced that pilots and ground crews had won 154 U.S. decorations. **1949** *Jrnl. R. Aeronaut. Soc.* LIII. 317/1 For take-off at altitude, a strong '*ground cushion' is an advantage. **1956** *N.Y. Times* 8 Jan. p. X 41/5 The issue revolves about a phenomenon peculiar to helicopters known as ground cushion effect. What it means is this: Up to ten or twelve feet off the ground, or over water, a helicopter receives added buoyancy by the packed mass of air churned downward from the overhead rotors. **1952** R. SHERBROOKE-WALKER *Khaki & Blue* i. 3 The problem became acute when '*Ground Defence' came along in the early days. **1935** *Jrnl. R. Aeronaut. Soc.* XXXIX. 277 The machine was a high wing monoplane and one would not expect much '*ground effect'. **1938** *Aeronaut. Res. Committee Rep. & Mem. No. 1865* 1 General formulae for.. corrections to ground effect have been obtained for wings of any span. **1959** *Observer* 18 Jan. 15/4 The principle on which the Hovercraft is built has a good deal in common with an infuriating phenomenon known to pilots as 'ground effect', which occurs when certain types of aircraft come in to land. Their closeness to the ground creates something akin to a pad of air on which the aircraft floats tantalisingly a foot or so above the runway instead of sinking to the ground. **1966** *Electronics* 17 Oct. 131 It would be carried on anything from a hydrofoil craft and a ground-effect machine, which rides over water and land on a cushion of air, to helicopters and pilotless drone aircraft. **1920** *Flight* 11 Nov. 1182/2 Under present arrangements, a machine is supposed to receive an inspection by a *ground engineer. **1928** *Daily Mail* 9 Aug. 7/1 Ground engineer of the London Aero Club. **1932** D. GARNETT *Rabbit in Air* I. 7 The ground engineer gave us pamphlets about the Flying Club. **1958** 'N. SHUTE' *Rainbow & Rose* i. 2 He had a ground engineer. **1921** *Flight* 5 May 315/2 The aeroplane has a tendency to *ground loop in landing or in taxying in a strong wind. **1928** *Daily Mail* 7 May 6/4 Ground Loops.—Touching the ground and rising again. **1959** F. D. ADAMS *Aeronaut. Dict.* 86/1 *Ground loop*, 1. a violent, whirling turn of an airplane while moving on the ground... 2. loosely, a nose-over. **1937** *Jrnl. R. Aeronaut. Soc.* XLI. 829 The author investigates some of the causes of so-called '*ground looping', i.e., the instability observed with certain machines when landing in a cross wind and which causes them to swing violently after touching ground. **1950** *Gloss. Aeronaut. Terms* (*B.S.I.*) I. 11 *Ground looping*, an uncontrollable violent turn of an aircraft while taxying, alighting or taking-off. **1944** *Times* 26 Apr. 4/1 A number of crews were bombing from a clear sky while others at the same moment were aiming at the *ground markers through the clouds. **1935** C. DAY LEWIS *Time to Dance* 57 But those hands have been always The *ground mechanics of our wide-wing pride. **1920** *Proc. Air Conference, London* 11 A problem of considerable difficulty is the *ground organisation for night flying. **1933** *Discovery* Dec. 367/1 All these difficulties could..be got over if there was a good ground organization and aircraft..to operate at such heights with multi-engines. **1951** *Gloss. Aeronaut. Terms* (B.S.I.) III. 7 **Ground position*, the position on the earth vertically below an aircraft. **1940** *Jrnl. Aeronaut. Sci.* Aug. 449/2 A series of high-speed motion pictures were taken of a turning rotor which was made to oscillate in *ground resonance. **1959** F. D. ADAMS *Aeronaut. Dict.* 86/1 *Ground resonance*, a self-excited, mechanical, potentially destructive vibration of a rotary-wing aircraft in operation on the ground or surface, involving a coupling between the motion of the rotor blades and the motion of the supporting structure or the motion of the aircraft as a whole on its landing gear. **1924** WEBSTER Addenda, **Ground school*, a school giving courses in aërodynamics, map-making, photography, etc., for aviators. **1917** *Blackw. Mag.* May 805/2 Our *ground speed was now a good deal greater than if we had travelled directly west. **1924** WEBSTER Addenda, *Ground speed*, the horizontal component of the velocity of an aircraft relative to the earth. **1928** C. F. S. GAMBLE *N. Sea Air Station* i, If there be no wind..a very much greater 'ground speed' has to be attained..before the machine will gain enough flying speed for the wings to take some load off the floats, and eventually enable the machine to 'take-off' from the surface of the sea. **1967** F. G. MERCER *Applied Aviation Sci.* viii. 48 An airplane flying eastward at a true airspeed..of 120 mph in still air, will have a ground speed exactly the same—120 mph. **1933** P. FLEMING *Brazilian Adv.* iv. 35 He..joined the *ground staff of an aerodrome there. **1957** R. W. ZANDVOORT et al. *Wartime English* 8 *Aircrew*,..a collective term for flying personnel, as opp. to ground staff. **1943** C. H. WARD-JACKSON *Piece of Cake* 35 **Ground-strafe*, to attack ground objectives. **1938** *Flight* 15 Sept. 222/2 The *ground-strafer's weapon should be..the light bomb. **1928** C. F. S. GAMBLE *N. Sea Air Station* iv, '*Ground-straffing' by low-flying machines. **1934** V. M. YEATES *Winged Victory* I. iii. 31 Unfortunately they were good machines for ground-strafing. They could dive straight down on anything, and when a few feet off the ground, go straight up again. **1941** *Times Weekly* 5 Feb. 8 In Libya..air activity was mainly confined to protective fighter patrols for our advancing troops and ground-strafing of the retreating enemy between Derna and Barce. **1943** HUNT & PRINGLE *Service Slang* 38 *Ground-strafing*, low-flying attack on transport or trenches; careless driving by servicemen. **1963** S. DOUGLAS *Years of Combat* viii. 194 Ground strafing

..had been a somewhat haphazard sort of business. **1917** 'Contact' *Airman's Outings* I. vii. 196 Fighting squadrons soon caught the craze for *ground stunts and carried it well beyond the lines. **1953** *Aero Digest* Oct. 37/3 An entire system of enemy destruction..includes a four-jet delta-wing supersonic bomber including its..reconnaissance, training, ground support and logistics systems. **1956** W. A. Heflin *U.S.A.F. Dict.* 238/2 **Ground support*, 1. either close air support or general air support. 2. the maintenance and care of flying equipment by the ground echelon. **1962** J. Glenn in *Into Orbit* 11, I flew..jets for sixty-three ground-support missions. **1967** *Technology Week* 20 Feb. 41/3 Design openings include development of..ground support equipment. **1920** *Flight* 10 June 624/1 Radio-Telephony.. *Procedure.*—Ground to air and *vice versa.* The following illustrates the procedure adopted for work between a *ground and an air station. **1945** *Aeroplane* 30 Nov. 619/2 An interesting point about the German development of air-to-air and *ground-to-air weapons was the way in which 'pukka' aircraft designers were brought in to design missiles. **1951** *Gloss. Aeronaut. Terms* (*B.S.I.*) III. 18 *Ground-to-air communication*, one-way communication from ground stations to aircraft. **1958** *Observer* 15 June 18/6 The Russians can be assumed to be building ground-to-air missiles that are every bit as good. **1920** *Flight* 10 June 624/2 Radio Telephony.. *Procedure.*—*Ground to ground. The following abbreviated procedure to be used between ground stations A and B. **1943** L. Cheshire *Bomber Pilot* 18 It was ground-to-ground tracer, firing east and so probably British. **1958** *Times* 11 Sept. 4/5 The huge Corporal ground-to-ground guided missile. **1941** *Flight* 6 Feb. 107/2 A Rhodesian squadron has been giving support to the *ground troops. **1925** Fraser & Gibbons *Soldier & Sailor Words* 112 **Ground wallah*, an Air Force term for a member of the R.A.F. whose duties were concerned with administrative, or office and aerodrome technical work.

18. a. Special combs.: **ground-air** (see quot.); **ground and lofty**, applied to acrobatic feats or performers on the ground and on a rope, etc.; also *transf.*; **ground-angling**, fishing with a weighted line without a float, bottom-fishing (*Dict. Rust.* 1704); similarly ***ground angler***; **ground-bailiff**, a superintendent or inspector of mines (Simmonds *Dict. Trade*, 1858); **ground ball** *Cricket* and *Baseball* = grounder 3c; **ground-bass** *Mus.*, a bass-passage of four or eight bars in length, constantly repeated with a varied melody and harmony (Stainer & Barrett, 1876); also *fig.*, an undercurrent; **ground-beam**, 'the sill of a frame' (*Cent. Dict.*); **ground-bowler** (see quot. 1934); **ground-breaking** *a.* (cf. break *v.* 44c *fig.*); **ground-bridge** *U.S.* (see quot.); **ground-bundle** *Anat.*, one of the bundles of nerve-fibres lying on either side of the grey matter of the spinal cord; **ground-cable**, that portion of a mooring-cable which is intended to lie on the sea-bottom; **ground chain** *Naut.* (see quot.); **ground-chamber**, a chamber on the ground-floor; **ground cloth**, (*a*) (see quot. 1919); (*b*) = *ground-sheet*; **ground-colour**, (*a*) a first coating of paint (cf. 6b); (*b*) the prevailing colour of any object, diversified with markings of other colours; **ground cover**, the plants covering the surface of the earth, esp., in horticulture, plants whose low, spreading habit of growth smothers weeds; so ***ground-coverer***; **ground-crab**, a kind of hoisting-apparatus used in mining (see quot.); **ground detector** *Electr.*, any instrument which is used to detect an accidental connection to earth in a circuit; †**ground-drawer**, **-drove**, (see quots.); †**ground-ebb**, low water; also as *adj.*, at low water; **ground-end** *Mining* (see quot.); **ground-fast** *a.*, firmly fixed in the ground; †also as *sb.*, that which holds a thing firm; **ground-fielding**, fielding or stopping a cricket-ball near the ground; **ground-fish**, a fish which lives at the bottom of the water; **ground-fishery, -fishing**, fishing with the bait at or near the bottom of the water; **ground-flat** = ground-floor; **ground force** *Mil.* = land force; also *attrib.*; **ground(-)frost**, a frost on the surface of the ground, or in the upper layer of the soil (see also quot. 1963); **ground-game**, game which lives on the ground, as hares and rabbits; **ground-grue** *dial.* = ground-ice; †**ground-hold**, the anchors of a vessel; †**ground-hop**, a leap from the ground, in quot *fig.*; **ground-itch** (see quot.); **ground-joint**, the joining of one stone or course in masonry with the ground or course immediately below; **ground-joist**, a joist supporting the ground floor of a building (*Dict. Archit.* 1851); **ground-keeper**, (*a*) *Cricket* = ground-man; (*b*) a root vegetable accidentally left in the ground during harvesting; **ground-landlord**, the owner of the land which is leased for building on; **ground-layer**, †(*a*) one who lays a foundation; (*b*) in *Pottery*, etc., the workman who lays the 'ground' (sense 6b); similarly ***ground-laying*** vbl. sb.; **ground level** *Physics* = *ground state*; (see also 17a above); **ground-mail** *Sc.*, payment for burying-ground; **ground-mass**, the compact basal part of an igneous rock, in which the distinctive crystals are imbedded; †**ground-measure**, ? a dance set to a 'ground' or ground-bass; **ground-moraine**, subglacial till, boulder-clay; also *attrib.*; **ground-net**, a trawl or drag-net (*Cent. Dict.*); **ground-niche**, a niche having its base on a level with the floor or ground (Chambers *Cycl.* 1741, s.v. *Niche*); **ground noise**, in sound reproduction, noise that is introduced by the recording medium (e.g. needle hiss on a gramophone record); **ground-note** *Mus.* (see quot. 1877); also *fig.*; **ground-officer**, one who has charge of the grounds and lands of an estate; †**ground-pillar**, a supporting pillar; **ground pin**, a main pin or beam in any structure; so †**ground-pinning**, underpinning; **ground-plane**, the horizontal plane of projection in perspective drawing; †**ground-planked** *a.*, ? having beds on the floor; **ground-plumbing** (see quot.); **ground-provisions**, root-crops suitable for food, as yams, potatoes, etc.; **ground return** *U.S.* = *earth-return* (a); **ground-room**, a room on the ground-floor; **ground-rope**, a rope by which the lower edge of a trawl is kept on the ground; **ground-row**, a row of gas-jets on the floor of a theatre-stage; **ground rule**, (*a*) *Sport*, a rule devised for a particular ground; (*b*) a basic principle; †**ground-salt**, a movement in the manege (see quot.); **ground-seine**, a form of seine or drag-net; **ground-sheet**, a waterproof sheet for spreading on the ground as a protection against damp; **ground-sluice** *sb.*, *Mining* (see quot. 1869); **ground-sluice** *v.*, to wash down earth by means of a stream of water; so **ground-sluicing** *vbl. sb.*; †**ground-smooth** *a.*, level with the ground; †**ground-sope** (= Du. *grond-sop*), dregs, sediment (quots. *c* 725 and 14.. are obscure, perh. mistranslations; Palsgrave's rendering may be an error); **ground-space**, the area of ground occupied by a structure; †**ground-stand**, a standing place in the pit of a theatre; **ground state** *Physics* [tr. G. *grundzustand*, lit. 'fundamental state'], the stationary state of lowest energy of a quantized system (as an atom or molecule); †**ground-statheling, -stathelness**, foundations; **ground station** *Radio*, a complex of buildings where radio and radar equipment is used in connection with aeronautical and aerospace projects; **ground-story** = ground-floor; **ground-strake** = garboard-strake (Smyth *Sailor's Word-bk.* 1867); **ground-stroke** *Lawn Tennis*, a stroke played near the ground, after the ball has hit the court; **ground-substance** *Phys.*, the homogeneous matrix in which the structural elements of a tissue are embedded; **ground-sweat** *slang*, the grave; ***to take a ground-sweat***, to lie in the grave; **ground-sype** (see quot.); **ground-table** *Arch.*, the plinth or projecting course resting on the foundation of a wall; an earth-table; **ground-tier**, (*a*) the lowest tier of goods in a vessel's hold (Young *Naut. Dict.* 1846); (*b*) the lowest range of boxes in a theatre; **ground-timbers**, the main timbers laid on the keel of a ship, floor-timbers; **ground-tissue** *Bot.*, the mass of cells separating the vascular bundles from each other and from the epidermis; †**ground-toiled** *a.*, field-working; **ground-torpedo**, a torpedo fixed to the ground or bottom of the sea; **ground-tow** (see quot. 1794 and cf. 3b above); †**ground-wart**, a small eminence resembling a wart; **ground-water, -ways** (see quots.); **ground wave**, the radio wave that passes from a transmitter to a receiver other than by reflection from the ionosphere, comprising one or more of the direct wave, the ground-reflected wave, and the surface-wave; also *attrib.*; †**ground-wind**, a wind blowing at the level of the sea; opposed to *rack-wind*; **ground wire** *Telegraphy* (*a*) (see quot. 1893); (*b*) *U.S.*, an earth wire, i.e. a wire that is connected to earth, either directly or through another earthed conductor (the usual sense); **ground-worm**, an earth-worm; **ground zero**, that part of the ground situated immediately under an exploding bomb, esp. an atomic one. Also ground-annual, ground-bait, ground-line, ground-man, etc.

1886 *Syd. Soc. Lex.*, **Ground air*, the air contained in the soil. This contains a large portion of carbonic acid gas due to the disintegration of organic substances. **1796** *Gazette of U.S.* (Philad.) 19 Nov. (Advt.) (Th.), *Ground and Lofty Tumbling [at the Pantheon, Philadelphia]. **1840** *Southern Lit. Messenger* VI. 386/1 He is an adept in the art of walking on his head, turning somersets, and ground and lofty tumbling generally. **1843** T. Weed *Let.* 19 July (1866) 108 A strolling company of 'Ground and Lofty' Tumblers. **1898** J. Hollingshead *Gaiety Chron.* viii. 330 The 'talented Cocksure family' in their celebrated ground and lofty performance. **1907** M. C. Harris *Tents of Wickedness* III. iv. 260 He has resigned his parish, left the ministry and bought a seat on the Stock Exchange. Isn't that ground and lofty tumbling? **1848** *Chambers' Inform. People* I. 683/2 Remarkably fine gut ought to be used by all *ground anglers. **1839** *Bell's Life* 13 Oct., It was for the umpire at the bowler's end to decide whether it was a '*ground' ball. **1851** J. Pycroft *Cricket Field* vii. 99 The toss, the tice, the half volley, the long hop, and ground balls. **1948** *P.C.C. Chron.* (Pasadena, Calif.) 7 May 4/5 Salter hit a hard ground ball to shortstop Bill Davis. **1699** Wanley in *Lett. Lit. Men* (Camden) 274 'Tis very like such a common *ground-Bass as this. **1955** A. L. Rowse *Expansion Eliz. Eng.* ii. 76 Their correspondence, their reports on the condition of their dioceses, always come back to this ground-bass. **1963** *Guardian* 20 Feb. 7/1 With rising unemployment, scarcer money, and a mutinous groundbass already discernible about the new rates householders will soon be called upon to pay, this could be a vintage year for bailiffs. **1968** *Listener* 23 May 657/3 These highlights apart, there is a ground bass of beatings, shootings and torture, all weltering in blood. **1874** *Baily's Mag.* June 225 The club has an efficient staff of *ground bowlers. **1891** W. G. Grace *Cricket* xi. 314 So pleased were the authorities of the M.C.C. with his [*sc.* W. Gunn's] first display at Lord's, that they made him the offer of a place as one of the ground-bowlers. **1934** W. J. Lewis *Lang. Cricket* 113 *Ground-bowler*, a professional bowler attached to a club as a member of its 'ground staff'. **1907** W. James *Let.* 6 Oct. (1920) II. 299, I am going to settle down to the composition of another small book, more original and *ground-breaking than anything I have yet put forth (!). **1965** *Language* XLI. 138 She has had to do groundbreaking work in establishing the phonological..correspondences between a number of foreign languages and Russian in the 16th and 17th centuries. **1859** Bartlett *Dict. Amer.*, **Ground Bridge*, the well-known corduroy road of the South, laid on the bed of a creek or other body of water, to render it fordable. **1893** H. Morris *Treat. Anat.* 781 The anterior *ground bundle appears to be continuous with the posterior longitudinal bundle.. The lateral ground bundle is a mixed tract. **1793** Smeaton *Edystone L.* §129 Our *ground cables for the sloop could not yet be got ready. **1883** *Man. Seamanship for Boys* 195 Q. What is *ground chain? A. A piece of small chain shackled to the anchor shackle,..of sufficient length to come through the hawse pipe when the anchor is high enough for catting. **1638** Sir T. Herbert *Trav.* (ed. 2) 169 The *ground chambers were large. **1886** Willis & Clark *Cambridge* I. 223 The first floor, as usual, overhangs the ground-chamber. **1919** W. B. Faraday *Gloss. Aeronaut. Terms* 54 **Ground cloth*, a floor covering, usually of canvas, placed on the ground under an envelope to protect it from damage. **1931** T. S. Stribling *Forge* xxiv. 204 The oilcloths were for raincoats or for ground cloths, or they could be propped up with sticks for tents. **1614** T. Jackson *Creed* II. 286 This conceit..serues as a *ground colour for disposing mens soules to take the sable dye of Hell. **1658–9** *Burton's Diary* (1828) III. 558 Do ..as Zeuxis did, who painted for eternity; which you can never do, unless your ground-colours be well laid. **1849** *Sk. Nat. Hist., Mammalia* III. 147 In adult specimens the ground-colour of the back is yellowish-white, with markings varying from dark gray to dusky black. **1860** Ruskin *Mod. Paint.* V. viii. iv. 192 The ground-colours then to be laid firmly... On this first colour, the second colours. **1904** W. H. Hudson *Green Mansions* vi. 72 A coral snake..its ground colour a brilliant vermilion. **1912** W. R. Ogilvie-Grant *Catal. Birds' Eggs Brit. Mus.* V. 105 The ground-colour varies from greyish-white to very pale greyish-green. **1970** H. E. Smith *Bantams* iii. 20 Females..should be chosen for clear ground colour. **1900** L. H. Bailey *Cycl. Amer. Hort.* II. 629/2 In suitable soil they [*sc.* Gaultherias] are apt to form a handsome, evergreen *ground-cover. **1906** *Westm. Gaz.* 31 May 4/2 As soon as the ground-cover was gone, the soil lost its moisture. **1946** *Nature* 13 July 71/1 Sparse ground-cover of herbs and dense undergrowth of hawthorn, bird-cherry, etc. **1970** G. S. Thomas *Plants for Ground-Cover* i. 3 Ground-cover can be of any height in nature or in the garden. *Ibid.* 4 The use of ground-cover plants may be the epitome of natural gardening. **1970** G. S. Thomas *Plants for Ground-Cover* p. xvii, Herbaceous plants..were limited to the stalwart clump-formers and the *ground-coverers. **1851** Greenwell *Coal-trade Terms Northumbld. & Durh.* 17 *Ground crabs are used in sinking, for lowering the sinking set of pumps as the pit is deepened. **1904** Swenson & Frankenfield *Testing Electro-Magn. Mach.* I. 36 Figure Q shows a General Electric *Ground Detector. **1958** *Van Nostrand's Sci. Encycl.* (ed. 3) 768/1 Lamp type ground detectors are used to a considerable extent on low-voltage circuits because they are reliable and cheap. **1597** A. M. tr. *Guillemeau's Fr. Chirurg.* 7b/1 If the bullet sticke faste in anye bone, we drawe him forth with that instrument which we call Extractor or *Grownde-drawer. *Ibid.* 13b/2 This Grounde-drawer is verye acute on his end, becaus the bullet might sticke fast therone. **1819** Rees *Cycl.*, **Ground drove*, in a Mine, is said of such parts as have been worked, or excavated for the ore or minerals. *a* **1420** Hoccleve *De Reg. Princ.* 669 God..whan þat his lust was, withdrow þe flood Of welþe, & at *grounde ebbe sette he me. *c* **1430** Lydg. *Min. Poems* (Percy Soc.) 50 The floode was passed and sodainly of newe A lowe ground ebbe was fast by the strond. *c* **1450** *St. Cuthbert* (Surtees) 6680 It may noȝt full wele be sene Bot when the se grounde eb bene. **1819** Rees *Cycl.*, **Ground-end*, of a Mine, signifies the forefield or foremost place of working, in the whole or footground. *c* **1680** Hickeringill *Hist. Whiggism* Wks. (1716) I. 25 He is *ground-fast and safe, that keeps to this certain Principle of Truth. **1720** D. Campbell in De Foe *Life* Ep. Ded. (1840) 15 In Yorkshire they kneel on a ground-fast stone, and say, All hail to the moon [etc.]. **1658** Hoole *Comenius' Vis. World* (1672) 173 The Nave is the ground-fast [L. *basis*] of the Wheel. **1891** Atkinson *Last Giant Killers* 215 Earth and sods and ground-fast rocks. **1884** I. Bligh in Lillywhite *Cricket Ann.* 5 Our *ground fielding was both brilliant and effective. **1856** Woodward *Mollusca* III. 426 Immense quantities of crustacea and shell-fish are taken with the trawl, as well as *ground-fish. **1883** E. P. Ramsay *Food Fishes N.S. Wales* 13 The Flathead is a ground-fish, but is found on a sandy bottom only. **1856** Woodward *Mollusca* III. 427 In North Britain an extensive *ground-fishery is conducted by means of long lines, often a mile in length. **1883** J. Rennie *Alph. Angling* 64 It requires a finer top for fly-fishing than for trolling or *ground-fishing. **1865** *Daily Tel.* 8 July, In the consulting-room on the *ground-flat. **1929** F. GIBBONS *Red Napoleon* ix. 222 The *ground forces were exposed constantly day and night to bomb and gas attacks from above. **1951** *Ann. Reg. 1950* 322 Our people's ground forces must be strengthened continuously so that they can defeat any aggression. **1959** *N.Z. Listener* 17 Apr. 6/3 The reduction in the ground forces of the United States and Britain impairs their ability to fight limited wars. **1965** H. KAHN *On Escalation* vi. 128 Tactical nuclear weapons were a relatively small part of the NATO ground-force structure. **1900** *Daily News* 12 Oct. 5/1 Towards night, the thermometer fell briskly, and it seemed probable that a sharp *ground frost would occur. **1958** HAYWARD & HARARI tr. *Pasternak's Dr. Zhivago* II. viii. 249 Probably there's still ground frost in the mornings. **1963** *Meteorol. Gloss.* (Met. Office) (ed. 4) 122 From 1906 to 1960, inclusive, the [British] Meteorological office practice was to record a 'ground frost' when the grass minimum thermometer reached 30°F or below... From 1 January 1961..no statistics have referred to 'ground frost'. The use of the term 'ground frost' in forecasts signifies a grass minimum temperature below 0°C (32°F). **1872** *Spectator* 5 Oct. 1262 To give the occupant a right to kill *ground-game (i.e., hares and rabbits). **1895** *Law Times* 13 July 255 The Ground Game Act, 1880. **1835** FARQUHARSON in *Phil. Trans.* CXXV. 330 [At Alford] they call it *ground-gru; gru being the term by which they designate snow saturated with, or swimming in water. **1596** SPENSER *F.Q.* VI. iv. 1 Like as a ship with dreadfull storme long tost, Having spent all her mastes and her *ground-hold. **1602** CAREW *Cornwall* 37 a, Nay thei [farms] are taken mostly at a *ground-hop, before they fall, for feare of comming too late. **1823** THACKER *Mil. Jrnl.* 177 Men infected with the *ground itch generated by laying on the ground. **1793** SMEATON *Edystone L.* §149 The *ground joint of the work with the rock. *Ibid.* §199 The ground joint, or under-bed of each stone. **1876** *Haygarth's Cricket Scores* v. 16 [G. H. Wright was engaged] on the Bramhall Ground, at Sheffield, where he still remains as *groundkeeper. **1938** *Nature* 17 Sept. 530/1 Future policy.. should aim at..the suppression of ground-keepers, always a fertile source of virus infection [in potatoes]. **1961** *New Scientist* 30 Mar. 795/3 The mild winter has also meant that more beet crowns, 'groundkeepers' (the beet missed by the lifting machines), and common weeds infected by the virus will have lasted through the winter. **1719** DE FOE *Crusoe* II. ii. (1840) 46 If they were *ground-landlords, he hoped if they built tenements on the land..they would..grant them a long lease. **1848** MILL *Pol. Econ.* v. iii. §6 (1876) 502 A tax on ground-rent, one would suppose, must fall on the ground-landlord. **1603** JAS. I *Sp. Parlt.* (1604) B, Hee was also the first *ground-layer of the other Peace. **1898** *Daily News* 8 June 2/5 Employed as a ground-layer at Stoke. **1884** C. T. DAVIS *Manuf. Bricks* etc. 89 In fine enamelling, *ground-laying is the first process. **1923** H. L. BROSE tr. *Sommerfeld's Atomic Struct. & Spectral Lines* vi. 325 In our diagram the absorption lines would have to be represented by arrows that start out from the natural or *ground level and are directed upwards. **1953** L. H. ALLER *Astrophysics* 25 The excitation potential in ev is the potential through which a bombarding electron must drop in order to acquire sufficient energy to excite an atom from the ground level to the level in question. **1818** SCOTT *Br. Lamm.* xvi, 'Reasonable charges?' said the sexton; 'ou, there's *grund-mail—and bell-siller..and the kist'. **1879** RUTLEY *Study Rocks* x. 168 In many cases felsite, or the *groundmass of porphyries, consists of a microscopically fine-grained aggregate. **1621** B. JONSON *Masque Augurs* A 4, Very sufficient Beares as any..and can dance..and play their owne tunes..the Beareward offers to play them with any Citie-Dancers, christned, for a *ground measure. **1863** A. C. RAMSAY *Phys. Geog.* xxiv. (1878) 395 *Ground-moraine matter, the *moraine profonde* of Swiss and French authors. **1880** A. R. WALLACE *Isl. Life* ix. 169 The ground-moraine, consisting of mud and imbedded stones. **1929** *Trans. Soc. Motion Picture Engin.* XIII. 53 **Ground noise*, any noise due to foreign matter or imperfections in or on the film arising during manufacture, processing or handling; does not include amplifier or photoelectric cell noises. **1938** *Motion Picture Sound Engin.* (Acad. Motion Pict. Arts & Sci.) iv. 44 Such a system..will differ from the ideal in several respects, one of which is the introduction of 'ground noise' during the recording process. **1942** *Electronic Engin.* XIV. 709 The fundamental failing of the disk is the fact that reproduction of the full frequency range recorded involves the production of atrocious scratch... We must not regard this ground noise as a defect altogether beyond improvement. **1877** STAINER *Harmony* vii. §77 The note on which a common chord is built..is called by some the Fundamental Bass, by others the Root or *Ground-note. **1878** *N. Amer. Rev.* CXXVI. 305 Seriousness is..the ground-note of his temperament. **1815** SCOTT *Guy M.* vii, Their asses were poinded by the *ground-officer when left in the plantations. *c* **1475** *Pict. Voc.* in Wr.-Wülcker 779/15 *Hec basys*, the *grownd-pelyr. **1632** VICARS *Æneid* II. 44 We..hack in twain The joyn'd crosse beams, and rais'd the *ground-pins main. *a* **1633** AUSTIN *Medit.* (1635) 284 The ground-Pins of this Cottage begin to faile. **1843** J. C. FRÉMONT *Exped.* (1845) 54 Our lodge had been planted, and, on account of the heat, the ground pins had been taken out, and the lower part slightly raised. **1507-8** in Willis & Clark *Cambridge* (1886) I. 415 Cronall laboranti circa facturam muri superioris coquine, et *grownde-pynnyng, et circa tegulacionem coquine. **1762** FORSTER in *Phil. Trans.* LII. 476 The ground-pinning of some houses, which had been burnt down. **1833** HERSCHEL *Astron.* viii. 271 The ecliptic is the plane to which an inhabitant of the earth most naturally refers the rest of the solar system, as a sort of *ground-plane. **1871** J. R. DICKSEE *Perspective* 32 *Ground plane*, the plane on which objects to be represented stand. **1632** LITHGOW *Trav.* VIII. 360, I stayed in a Spaniards house..who kept a roguish Taverne, and a *ground planked Hospitality. **1704** *Dict. Rust.*, **Ground-plumbing*, is to find out the depth of Water in fishing. **1827** O. W. ROBERTS *Central Amer.* 108 The raising of stock, and cultivation of *ground provisions. **1893** E. J. HOUSTON *Electr. Transmiss. Intell.* i. 9 The line wire or conductor may form what is technically known as a *ground-return circuit. *Ibid.* 10 This is..called a ground-return, because the ground acts as the return conductor. **1968** FINK & CARROLL *Stand. Handbk. Electr. Engin.* (ed. 10) xiv. 3 In d-c transmission ground return can be used as one conductor. This means that each separately insulated transmission conductor, together with the ground-return path, forms a separate electric circuit. **1662** J. DAVIES tr. *Olearius' Voy. Ambass.* 294 The *ground-rooms of the House. **1798** EDGEWORTH *Pract. Educ.* (1822) I. 342 Locked up in a ground-room. **1874** HOLDSWORTH *Deep-sea Fishing* i. 58 The curved lower margin of the mouth of the trawl is fastened to and protected by the '*ground rope'. This..answers the useful purpose of keeping the edge of the net on the ground. **1881** *Daily News* 28 Dec. 2/1 The light distributed about the stage from concealed 'battens' and '*ground rows'. **1890** H. C. PALMER *Stories of Base Ball Field* 70 In the olden days there was a *ground rule which only allowed two bases for a hit over this fence. **1953** *Manch. Guardian Weekly* 27 Aug. 1 Ground rules of American press-conferences. **1965** G. MCINNES *Road to Gundagai* vi. 104 His ground-rules were so elastic. **1967** M. MCLUHAN *Medium is Massage* 68 The groundrules, pervasive structure, and overall patterns of environments elude easy perception. **1614** MARKHAM *Cheap Husb.* I. ii. (1668) 23 To pass them about in *ground-salts, as by taking up his fore-Legs from the ground both together, and bringing his hinder Feet into their place. **1874** HOLDSWORTH *Deep-sea Fishing* iv. 157 Seans may be divided into three classes, namely, the sean proper,..the 'tuck-sean', and the '*ground or foot-sean'. **1907** *Daily Chron.* 15 Mar. 9/5 *Groundsheet (waterproof). **1928** *Daily Express* 12 May 5/5 Some of the motorists were having tea in the cars, and some had spread ground-sheets and cushions on the ground. **1959** S. CLARK *Puma's Claw* v. 65 We could not afford heavy luxuries like ..groundsheets. **1970** *Which?* May 132/1 The other half of the outer tent (the living room) does not have a groundsheet. **1869** R. B. SMYTH *Goldf. Victoria* 612 **Ground-sluice*, a channel cut in the bottom or bed-rock, into which the earth is conveyed by a stream of water. **1857** *Hutchings' Mag.* July 8/1 Among the more important operations connected with gold mining upon an extensive scale, is '*ground sluicing'. **1860** *Harper's Mag.* Apr. 612/2 Ground-sluicing accomplishes the same result..with the chance of obtaining from the upper earth some gold, which..would be lost by the first plan. **1862** J. G. WALKER *Jrnl. Voy. N.Z.* (1863) [1] Jan., We..watched a man ground-sluicing. **1865** V. PYKE *Goldfields Report* in *Appendices to Jrnls. House of Reps. N.Z.* C. IVA. 10 Of the various methods of working, that of ground sluicing is most universally adopted—a ground sluice being nothing more than a rectangular drain cut for a depth of about a foot into the surface soil. **1874** A. BATHGATE *Colonial Experiences* viii. 91 In Otago, the principal kind of mining is ground-sluicing..similar to the method of working for tin in Cornwall. **1879** ATCHERLEY *Boërland* 138 Our host took us to his workings, where he was ground-sluicing. *c* **1520** BARCLAY *Sallust's Jugurth* 71 a, Whan Marius came to any suche towne..he set fyre in them and brent them *grounde smothe. *c* **725** *Corpus Gloss.* (Hessels) C 186 *Cartilago*, *grundsopa. *c* **1440** *Promp. Parv.* 216/1 Growndesope of any lycoure..*fex, sedimen.* **14..** *Nominale* in Wr.-Wülcker 717/36 *Hoc suber, intima pars corticis, Hoc abdomen*, grundsope. **1530** PALSGR. 228/1 Grounde soppe in lycoure, *payn trempé.* **1866** *Chambers's Jrnl.* 18 Aug. 521/2 The houses..are large.., with very little accommodation, considering the *ground-space they occupy. **1908** *Westm. Gaz.* 28 Mar. 9/2 All citizens are users or consumers of air, water, ground-space. **1659** *Lady Alimony* I. iv, All our Galleries and *Ground-stands are long ago furnished. **1926** H. L. BROSE tr. *Sommerfeld's Three Lect. Atomic Physics* ii. 35 To every electron in its *ground state there belongs an original momentum $s = \frac{1}{2}$. **1946** *Nature* 26 Oct. 593/2 To evaluate *D* for a diatomic gas, it is necessary to examine the vibrational energy-levels of the ground-state. **1963** B. FOZARD *Instrumentation Nuclear Reactors* ii. 13 This is duly emitted as radiant energy as the excited electrons return to the ground state. *a* **1300** *E.E. Psalter* cxxxvi. 7 Vnto þe *grond-staþelnes [*v.r.* groun-staþelinge] in it. **1919** *Radio Rev.* Dec. 105 On aeroplanes, the problem of the reception of wireless signals is complicated... There is always so much noise that signals must be of much greater intensity than at *ground stations in order to be of any use. **1966** *Electronics* 14 Nov. 58 The ground station, which was publicly introduced Nov. 10 in Melbourne, Fla., is also behind schedule and running 40% over cost expectations. **1657** R. LIGON *Barbadoes* (1673) 103 You shall feel that heat above..in the *ground stories below, though your sieling be a foot thick. **1823** P. NICHOLSON *Pract. Build.* 307 Brick walls in the basement and ground-stories of buildings. **1895** H. W. W. WILBERFORCE *Lawn Tennis* 51 There are two ways in which a *ground-stroke may be taken, namely, at the top of the bound, and again quite late, when the ball is near the ground. **1970** *Times* 5 June 14/6 His services and ground strokes were hit to a good length. **1882** *Quain's Elem. Anat.* (ed. 9) II. 58 The *ground-substance, matrix or intercellular substance of the connective tissue. *a* **1700** B. E. *Dict. Cant. Crew*, **Grownd-Sweat*, a Grave. **1834** F. MAHONY *Father Prout's Rem.* (1836) II. 117 We waked him in clover, And sent him to take a ground-sweat. **1839** STONEHOUSE *Axholme* 25 The water..is not spring water, but merely what is termed a *ground sype, i.e. water filtering through from the surface. **1640** in Willis & Clark *Cambridge* (1886) I. 97 Plinth and *Ground-table for y[e] South Range. **1820** W. SCORESBY *Acc. Arctic Reg.* II. 305 The hold of the ship must be cleared of its superstructure of casks, until the '*ground-tier', or lowest stratum of casks, is exposed. **1627** CAPT. SMITH *Seaman's Gram.* ii. 2 Before you vse any plankes, they lay the Rungs, called floore timbers, or *ground timbers, thwart the keele. **1793** SMEATON *Edystone L.* §85 The interior ground timbers. **1881** HAMERSLY *Naval Encycl.*, *Ground-timber*, In making up the frame of a wooden ship, the timbers of the lower course are called ground-timbers. **1882** VINES *Sachs' Bot.* 482 A loose spongy parenchyma.. sharply defined from the firm compact *ground-tissue. **1895** J. R. GREEN *Man. Bot.* I. 329 A mass of cells which constitutes the ground or fundamental tissue. **1632** LITHGOW *Trav.* VIII. 359 Arabs, who falling downe from the Mountaines..upon the *ground toyled Moores [etc.]. **1878** *N. Amer. Rev.* CXXVII. 389 The *ground-torpedo is fired by a wire connected with a battery from the shore. **1669** J. COX in *St. Papers, Dom.* 574 The *ground tow sold to Mr. Gould is not fetched away. **1794** *Rigging & Seamanship* 54 *Ground-tow*, the loose hemp that comes from the sides of the hatchellers and spinners. **1568** C. WATSON *Polyb.* 68 This hill is straitly incompassed with stepe rocks, hauing a plain on y[e] very tippe..in y[e] midst there is a *ground wart, which serueth for y[e] watch-house. **1890** *Nature* 27 Nov. 94 Mr. Latham defines '*ground water' as all water found in the surface soil of the crust of the earth, except such as may be in combination with the materials forming the crust of the earth. **1927** E. V. APPLETON in *Wireless World* 5 Jan. 3/2 There is a very real difference between a *ground wave and an atmospheric wave if we consider the magnetic force in the wave as well as the electric wave. For a horizontally travelling ground wave, such as that which travels direct from transmitter to receiver, [etc.]. **1941** K. HENNEY *Radio Engin. Handbk.* (ed. 3) xv. 514 The signal..may have been propagated either by the ground wave, which travels along the earth's surface, or by the sky wave. **1943** F. E. TERMAN *Radio Engineers' Handbk.* x. 675 The surface wave.. represents the whole of the ground wave when both transmitting and receiving antennas are located at the surface of the earth. **1965** *BBC Handbk.* 115 The signals which carry domestic broadcasting programmes are usually designed to be received by ground-wave on medium and long waves. *Ibid.*, Ground-wave propagation of short waves is not feasible over long distances. **1711** W. SUTHERLAND *Shipbuilder's Assist.* 160 **Ground-ways*; large Pieces of Timber lying a-thwart the Bottom of a Dock, or Launch, to make the Foundation firm and substantial. **1867** SMYTH *Sailor's Word-bk.*, *Ground ways*, the large blocks and thick planks which support the cradle on which a ship is launched. Also, the foundation whereon a vessel is built. **1620** T. SCOTT *God & King* (1633) 16 It is for me to observe the *ground-winde, not the rack-winde. **1621** S. WARD *Jethro's Just. Peace* (1627), It is the ground-wind, not the rack-winde, that driues mils and ships. **1893** SLOANE *Stand. Electrical Dict.*, **Ground-wire*, a metaphorical term applied to the earth when used as a return circuit. **1922** J. C. WRIGHT *Automotive Repair* II. 208 If the ground wire is disconnected the generator will build up an excessive pressure within itself. **1966** *McGraw-Hill Encycl. Sci. & Technol.* XIV. 54/1 Lines built where severe thunderstorms are prevalent are equipped with overhead ground wires.. for intercepting the lightning stroke and leading it to ground at the nearest tower. **1599** A. M. *Gabelhouer's Bk. Physicke* 158/2 For the Dropsye. Take *groundewormes, choppe.. them smalle [etc.] **1830** CARLYLE *Misc.* (1857) II. 147 Fools that we are! To dig and bore like ground-worms. **1844** EMERSON *Lect. New Eng. Ref.* Wks. (Bohn) I. 259 Ground-worms, slugs, and mosquitos. **1946** *N.Y. Times* 7 July E10/1 The intense heat of the blast started fires as far as 3,500 feet from '*ground zero'. **1955** *Bull. Atomic Sci.* Sept. 255/1 There was no noticeable contamination even at ground zero at Hiroshima.

b. In names of animals (denoting generally, in regard to birds, those of terrestrial habits; in regard to other animals, those that burrow, or lie in holes or on the ground); as **ground-bear**, the common brown bear, *Ursus arctos* (Cassell, 1884); **ground-bee**, a bee that nests in the ground; **ground-beetle**, a general name for all beetles of the family *Carabidæ*; **ground-cuckoo**, a member of one of the four genera of *Neomorphinæ*, a subfamily of the *Cuculidæ*; **ground-dove**, a dove or pigeon of terrestrial habits, esp. of the genera *Chamæpelia* and *Geopelia* (cf. *ground-pigeon*); **ground-finch**, (*a*) a bird of Swainson's sub-family *Fringillinæ* or true finches; (*b*) an American finch of the genus *Pipilo* (*Cent. Dict.*); **ground-gudgeon**, the loach; **ground-hornbill**, the African genus *Bucorvus* (or *Bucorax*) of horn-bills; **ground-hornet**, a hornet that has its nest on the ground; **ground-lackey, -lark, -lizard, -mite** (see quots.); **ground-mouse** *U.S.*, a field mouse of the genus *Reithrodontomys*; **ground-parrakeet**, any bird of the genera *Geopsittacus* and *Pezoporus*; **ground-parrot**, (*a*) = prec.; (*b*) the Kakapo of New Zealand (*Strigops habroptilus*); **ground-pearl, -pig** (see quots.); **ground-pigeon**, a pigeon which passes most of its time on the ground; esp. one of the family *Gouridæ*; also = *ground-dove*; **ground-puppy** = HELLBENDER; **ground-rat** (see *ground-pig*); **ground rattler** *U.S.* (see quot. 1931); **ground-robin** *U.S.*, any of several small American buntings, esp. the most common one, *Pipilo erythrophthalmus*; see CHEEWINK; **ground-roller** (see quot. and ROLLER); **ground-scratcher**, a name for the *Rasores* or gallinaceous birds; **ground-seal**, a large species of seal; **ground-shark**, any species of shark that rarely comes to the surface, *esp.* the spinous shark (*Echinorrhinus spinosus*); **ground-sloth**, one of an extinct group of New World herbivorous mammals of the group *Edentata*, intermediate between the existing sloths and ant-eaters; **ground-snake** (see quots.); **ground-sparrow** *U.S.*, one of several sparrows of terrestrial habits, e.g. the grass-finch and savannah-sparrow (*Cent. Dict.*); **ground-spearing**, a fish (*Trachinocephalus myops*) found in the tropical parts of the Western Atlantic (1896 Jordan & Everman *Fishes Amer.* 296); **ground-spider**, any kind of spider that burrows or lives under stones; **ground-thrush**, (*a*) a thrush of the genus *Geocichla*; (*b*) a bird of the Australian genus *Cinclosoma*; (*c*) the pitta or ant-thrush; **ground-tit**, a small Californian bird (*Chamæa fasciata*), allied to the wrens and titmice; **ground-wasp**, a wasp that has its nest on the ground; **ground woodpecker**, a member of the family Picidæ that lives on the ground, esp. *Colaptes campestris* of South America and

Geocolaptes olivaceus of South Africa; **ground-wren**, (*a*) the willow wren, *Sylvia trochilus*; (*b*) = *ground-tit*. Also GROUND-BIRD, GROUND-HOG, GROUND-SQUIRREL.

1849 C. BRONTË *Shirley* xxv, The nest..of some *ground-bees, which had burrowed in the turf under an old cherry-tree. **1890** LD. LUGARD *Diary* 17 Apr. (1959) I. 195 Found ground bees' nest, and tried to dig it out, but it was some 16 inches down. **1848** *Rural Cycl.* II. 532 **Ground beetle*, a coleopterous insect, whose larva is found in corn-fields. **1883** *Cassell's Nat. Hist.* IV. 134 The Malays..capture ..*Ground Cuckoos. **1895** LYDEKKER *Nat. Hist.* IV. 11 The four genera of ground-cuckoos, all of which are terrestrial birds with powerful feet for running. **1792** MAR. RIDDELL *Voy. Madeira* 60 Five kinds of doves are natives of Antigua, of which the ramier and the *ground dove are the most beautiful. **1885** *Stand. Nat. Hist.* IV. 247 The ground-doves, little creatures which pass their time on the ground almost exclusively. **1837** W. SWAINSON *Birds* II. 122 The *Fringillinæ* may correctly be termed *ground finches; since, with scarcely an exception, they are all birds which habitually walk or hop in such situations. **1867** SMYTH *Sailor's Word-bk.*, *Ground-gudgeon, a little fish, the *Cobitis barbatula*. **1880-4** F. DAY *Fishes Gt. Brit. & Irel.* II. 204 The loach..ground-bait or ground-gudgeon, Northumberland. **1883** *Cassell's Nat. Hist.* III. 355 The *Ground Hornbills (*Bucorax*). These are an African form, of which there are two or three kinds. **1822** Z. HAWLEY *Tour* 95 (Th.), A nest of *ground hornets, concealed under the logway. **1888** INGLIS *Tent Life Tigerland* 68, I have known an elephant to bolt..through the attacks of wasps or ground hornets. **1869** E. NEWMAN *Brit. Moths* (1874) 42 The *Ground Lackey (*Bombyx castrensis*)..Very abundant in the Isle of Sheppey. **1848** *Zoologist* VI. 2290 The tree pipit is the '*ground lark'. **1849** *Ibid.* VII. 2354 The bunting is the 'ground lark'. **1792** MAR. RIDDELL *Voy. Madeira* 65 The *ground lizard is commonly of the colour of the earth on which it creeps. **1885** *Stand. Nat. Hist.* III. 432 *Ameiva dorsalis*, the ground lizard, is one of the most abundant lizards in Jamaica. **1839** J. BUEL *Farmer's Comp.* 99 Moles or *ground-mice cannot penetrate and find a shelter. **1883** *Harper's Mag.* Aug. 462/2 A storm of expletives that must have startled the ground-mice and the birds. **1847** CARPENTER *Zool.* §840 The *Trombidiæ*, or *Ground-Mites, are distinguished by having the palpi converted into raptorial organs. **1865** GOULD *Birds Austral.* II. 87 The *Ground-Parrakeet is diffused over the whole of the southern portions of Australia, including Tasmania. **1885** *Stand. Nat. Hist.* IV. 356 The crested ground-parakeet (*Callipsittacus novæ-hollandiæ*). **1794** G. SHAW *Zool. New Holland* 10 *Psittacus terrestris*. The *Ground Parrot. **1827** VIGORS & HORSFIELD in *Trans. Linn. Soc.* XV. 278 *Psittacus pulchellus*... The settlers call it Ground Parrot. **1885** *Stand. Nat. Hist.* IV. 351 The single genus *Geopsittacus*..is the ground-parrot of Southern and Western Australia. **1895** *Pop. Sci. Monthly* Apr. 776 The Kakapo of New Zealand..also known as the 'owl parrot' or 'ground parrot'. **1884** *Stand. Nat. Hist.* II. 218 Another [bug] is the curious '*Ground Pearl' of the Bahama Islands. It lives beneath the soil in crevices frequented by ants, and acquires a shell-like calcareous scaly covering. **1883** *Cassell's Nat. Hist.* III. 133 In Sierra Leone it [*Aulacodus Swinderianus*] is known as the Ground Rat, or *Ground Pig. **1885** *Challenger Rep.* I. II. 535 A little *Ground Pigeon (*Geopelia*), not much bigger than a sparrow. **1885** *Stand. Nat. Hist.* IV. 242 The *Gouridæ* comprises the great ground-pigeons..They are natives of the Papuan Archipelago. **1863** *Ground Puppy [see HELLBENDER]. **1908** *Daily Chron.* 29 Aug. 7/5 The red dog..jumped a *ground-rattler. **1931** R. L. DITMARS *Snakes of World* x. 105 The Pygmy Rattlesnake or 'Ground' Rattler, *Sistrurus miliarius*, seldom more than sixteen to twenty inches long, has a rattle so minute it would be unnoticed outside a distance of about eight feet. **1794** *Philos. Soc. Trans.* IV. 110 This bird was the chewink, or *ground robin. **1844** J. E. DE KAY *Zool. N.Y.* II. 172 (*heading*) The Chewink or Ground Robin. Pipilo Erythrophthalmus. *Ibid.*, This beautiful and unobtrusive little species is..known..under the name of Ground Robin. **1955** *Sci. News Let.* 23 Apr. 271 The towhee is a bird of many aliases. 'Ground robin' is a popular name, and justified by his deceptively robin-like appearance. **1883** *Cassell's Nat. Hist.* III. 364 In Madagascar..there are found the *Ground Rollers (*Atelornis*), extraordinary birds which live entirely on the ground, and only come out at dusk. **1840** BLYTH *Cuvier's Anim. Kingd.* (1849) 251 *Rasores* (*ground-scratchers)—the Poultry. **1868** R. BROWN in *Proc. Zool. Soc.* 427 The Grey Seal,..possibly this species may be confounded with the '*Ground-Seal'. **1880** *Standard* 20 May 3 The 'ground seal', the largest of all the species. **1833** MARRYAT *P. Simple* (1863) 217 There are several kinds of sharks, but the most dangerous are the great white shark and the *ground shark. **1885** *Stand. Nat. Hist.* III. 76 The sleeper shark *Somniosus microcephala*..By the fishermen it is known as ground-shark or gurry-shark. **1860** OWEN (*title*), Memoir on the Megatherium, or Giant *Ground-Sloth of America. **1896** *B.M. Guide Fossil Mammals* 69 The entire skeleton of the great extinct 'Ground Sloth'. **1885** *Stand. Nat. Hist.* III. 362 The genus *Carphophis* is very generally distributed; in the United States, the species *amœna*,..as the thunder, *ground, or worm-snake, is most familiar. *Ibid.* 363 The *Coronella australis*, or the Australian ground-snake. **1874** B. F. TAYLOR *World on Wheels* II. vii. 249 The *ground-sparrows build in its margins. **1882** *Vermont Agric. Rep.* VII. 67 The blue bird, cat bird, wren and ground sparrows are acknowledged beneficial. **1867** *Amer. Naturalist* Oct. 410 Some of the *ground spiders carry their eggs in a sack attached to the tip of their abdomen. **1880** 'SILVER & Co.' *S. Africa* (ed. 3) 179 One of the great ground spiders in the Karroo districts..has a body $2\frac{1}{2}$ inches long. **1869** GOULD *Birds Austral.* Suppl. 63 *Cinctosoma castaneothorax*,..this richly coloured and very distinct species of *Ground Thrush. **1881** *Brit. Mus. Catal. Birds* V. 147 The genus *Geocichla* comprises a well-defined group of forty Thrushes, which may be distinguished as Ground-Thrushes. **1885** *Stand. Nat. Hist.* IV. 467 The pittas, or ground-thrushes, are a group of insectivorous birds which inhabit the forests of the eastern tropics. *Ibid.* 506 The so-called *ground-tit, or perhaps better wren-tit (*Chamœa fasciata*)..has very little in common with the true tits. **1880** *New Virginians* I. 98 There is a small *ground-wasp, like the English wasp in shape and colour; and a very large ground-wasp, whose sting is very vicious. **1867** E. L. LAYARD *Birds S. Afr.* 238 The Sub-Family, Colaptinæ, or *Ground Woodpeckers, have the bill broad at the base. **1958** E. T. GILLIARD *Living Birds of World* 258/2 Tunnels of the Ground Woodpecker are often several feet deep. **1964** A. L. THOMSON *New Dict. Birds* 896/2 The 'ground woodpeckers' prefer stumps or rotten branches where many insects (especially ants) have their favourite haunts. **1839** MACGILLIVRAY *Brit. Birds* II. 371 Willow Wren. *Ground Wren.

c. In names of plants, generally denoting plants dwarfish in height and sometimes those of a trailing habit; **ground-archil**, *Lecanora parella*, a species of lichen used in dyeing (*Syd. Soc. Lex.* 1886); **ground-berry**, (*a*) *U.S.* = CHECKER-BERRY (*Cent. Dict.*); (*b*) *Austral.* (see quot.); **ground-birch**, ? the dwarf birch (see BIRCH 1 b); **ground-box**, *Buxus sempervirens*, the small variety used for edgings; **ground-cedar** (see quot.); **ground-cherry**, (*a*) the Dwarf Cherry, *Cerasus Chamæcerasus*; (*b*) an American plant of the genus *Physalis*; †**ground-chestnut** (see quot.); **ground-cistus**, *Rhododendron Chamæcistus* (Paxton *Bot. Dict.* 1840); **ground-cypress**, *Santolina Chamæcyparissus* (ibid.); **ground-elder**, a name for *Sambucus Ebulus*, *Angelica silvestris*, *Ægopodium Podagraria* (Britten & Holland *Plant-n.* 1879), and *Mercurialis perennis* (Paxton); **ground-enell** (see quot. 1879); **ground-fir** = GROUND-PINE (*Cent. Dict.*); **ground-flax**, the genus Camelina (Paxton); **ground flower**, a low-growing wild flower; †**ground-furze** = CAMMOCK; †**ground-hele** [ad. G. *grundheil*], *Veronica officinalis*; **ground-hemlock**, an American variety of the common yew, *Taxus baccata*; **ground-holly** = CHECKER-BERRY (*Syd. Soc. Lex.*); **ground-jasmine**, *Passerina Stelleri* (*Treas. Bot.* 1866); **ground-laurel**, the Trailing Arbutus (*Epigæa repens*) of North America; †**ground-myrtle**, Butcher's Broom (*Ruscus aculeatus*); **ground-needle**, *Erodium moschatum*; **ground-oak**, (*a*) an oak-sapling; (*b*) a species of dwarf-oak; **ground-plum, -rattan** (see quots.); †**ground-saligot**, *Tribulus terrestris*; **ground-sorrel** (see quot.); **ground-thistle**, the cardoon (*Cynara Carduncululus*); **ground-willow**, a dwarf willow; also *dial.* = *Polygonum amphibium* (Britten & Holland); **ground-yew** = CROWBERRY 1. Also GROUND-ASH, GROUND-IVY, GROUND-PINE.

1889 J. H. MAIDEN *Useful Pl. Australia* 8 *Astroloma humifusum*..and *A. pinifolium*..Commonly called '*Ground-berry'. **1885** FENN *This Man's Wife* in *Gd. Words* 61 A dozen bundles of clean-looking *ground-birch sticks. **1578** LYTE *Dodoens* VI. xxxii. 699 The smal Boxe is called..in Latine, *Humi Buxus*: that is to say, *Ground Boxe, or Dwarffe Boxe. **1836** *Backw. Canada* 120 A trailing plant bearing a near resemblance to the cedar, which..has..a claim to the name of *ground or creeping cedar. **1601** HOLLAND *Pliny* I. 448 Certain dwarfe Cherries..called *Chamecerasi* (*i.* *ground cherry-shrubs). **1859** BARTLETT *Dict. Amer.*, *Ground cherry* (Physalis),..sometimes called Winter Cherry. **1693** C. DRYDEN in *Dryden's Juvenal* vii. (1697) Notes 185 *Treuffles*, in English call'd *Ground-Chest-nuts, or Pignuts. **1597** GERARDE *Herbal* App., *Ground Enell is Venus combe. **1879** BRITTEN & HOLLAND *Plant-n.*, Ground Enell, *Scandix Pecten.* Hal. and Wr. print the name incorrectly *Ground-evil*. **1829** A. EATON *Man. Bot.* (ed. 5) 336 *Polygala polygama*, *ground flower. **1902** *Daily Chron.* 1 Apr. 2/1 At Easter there are but the ground-flowers. **1928** D. COTTRELL *Singing Gold* I. vi. 50 The cup-like tufts of the little white ground-flower, with the sweetest scent in all Australia. **1578** LYTE *Dodoens* VI. x. 669 Cammocke or *ground Furze hath many small, lythey, or weake branches. *Ibid.* I. xvii. 26 Paules Betony, Herbe Fluellyn, or Speede-well, *Ground-hele. **1807** F. PURSH *Jrnl. Bot. Excursion* 20 July (1869) 64 Here I found..taxus braccata or procumbens, calld *Ground Hemlock. **1834** J. J. AUDUBON *Ornithol. Biogr.* II. 170 The Ground Hemlock (*Taxus canadensis*), or Canadian Yew. **1848** *Rural Cycl.* II. 532 **Ground-jasmine*, an ornamental, evergreen, white-flowered, Siberian undershrub of the wild olive-tree family. It is regarded by some botanists as a Stellera, and by others as a sparrow-wort. **1814** J. BIGELOW *Florula Bostoniensis* 101 *Ground laurel..grows in woods. **1867** *Amer. Naturalist* May 154 In the books, this plant is known as the 'Epigea repens', but otherwise as the Trailing Arbutus, May Flower, and Ground Laurel. **1877** BRYANT *27th Mar.* 27 Within the woods Tufts of ground-laurel,..send their sweets Up to the chilly air. **1932** P. A. RYDBERG *Flora Prairies & Plains Cent. N. Amer.* 615 Epigaea L. Trailing Arbutus, Ground Laurel. **1601** HOLLAND *Pliny* II. 284 As for the herb Idæa, the leaues therof resemble those of *ground-Myrtle or Butchers broom. *a* **1400** *Med. MS.* Gloss. in *Archæol.* XXX. 409 *Ground Nedle. *Acus muscula.* **1633** JOHNSON *Gerarde's Herbal* App., Ground needle, *Geranium muscatum.* *a* **1723** *R. Hood & Little John* in Child *Ballads* (1888) III. 135 Then Robin Hood stept to a thicket of trees, And chose him a staff of *ground-oak. **1805** A. WILSON in *Poems & Lit. Prose* (1876) II. 144 Waving reeds and scrubby ground-oak grew Where stores and taverns now arrest the view. **1859** BARTLETT *Dict. Amer.*, **Ground Plum* (*Astragalus caryocarpus*), a plant growing on dry soil on the Mississippi River..The fruit, which is a pod, closely resembles a plum. **1823** CRABB *Technol. Dict.*, **Ground-ratan*, the *Rhapis flabelliformis.* **1866** *Treas. Bot.* 970/2 *Rhapis flabelliformis* is commonly called the Ground Rattan Palm, and is said to yield the walking-canes known by that name in this country. **1597** GERARDE *Herbal* Table Eng. Names, **Grounde Saligot*, that is Landcaltrops. **1775** CLAYTON in *Phil. Trans.* LXVI. 100 *Ground-sorrel every where [in the Falkland Islands] abounds in the greatest plenty;..the flower it produces is exactly like the wild rose which grows in the hedges in England. **1591** PERCIVALL *Sp. Dict.*, *Cepa cavalle*, *Ground thistle. **1875** CROLL *Climate & T.* xvi. 262 In a region where ..the *ground-willow and dwarf-birch have to struggle for existence. **1674** tr. *Scheffer's Lapland* 141 The thin leaved heath, that bears a Berry, which some call *ground Ewe.

ground (graʊnd), *v.* Forms: 3 grundien, 4 *north.* grund, 4-6 grounde, grownde, 5-6 gronde, (7 grownd), 5- ground. [ME. f. GROUND *sb.*; cf. MDu., Du. *gronden*, MSw. *grunda*. For OE. *gryndan* see GRIND *v.*[2]]

†**1.** *trans.* To lay the foundations of (a house, etc.); to found; to fix or establish firmly. *Obs.*

Chiefly in renderings or echoes of biblical passages.

a **1300** *E.E. Psalter* viii. 4 Þe mone and sternes..þat þou grounded to be swa. *a* **1300** *Cursor M.* 28853 Almus..es to þe sawl als a wall grunded ful fast and will noght fall. *a* **1340** HAMPOLE *Psalter* xxiii. 2 He abouen þe seas grundid it. **1450-1530** *Myrr. our Ladye* 86 The drye erthe hys handes hathe grounded. *c* **1460** *Towneley Myst.* viii. 90 Gret god, that all thys Warld began, and growndyd it in good degre. **1535** COVERDALE *Luke* vi. 48 That house..was grounded vpon yᵉ rocke. **1591** SPENSER *Virg. Gnat* 453 Th' Okes deep grounded in the earthly molde. **1627** P. FLETCHER *Locusts* IV. ii, Deep grounded on that Rocke most firmely stood.

fig. **1555** EDEN *Decades* 327 Grounded vppon the foundation of truth. **1684** *Contempl. State Man* I. iv. (1699) 45 How frail is all the Glory of the World, being Grounded upon so feeble a Foundation.

2. To set on a firm basis, to establish (an institution, a principle of action, belief, science, conclusion or argument), *on* some fact, circumstance, or authority.

a. const. *on*; also *in* (now only in *passive*).

c **1374** CHAUCER *Troylus* IV. 1644 (1672) Moral vertue grounded vpon trouþe. *c* **1380** WYCLIF *Wks.* (1880) 332 He can not grounde þis lawe in reson. *a* **1415** LYDG. *Temp. Glas* 1199 Lat no dispeire hindir þe with drede, But ay þi trust opon hir merci grovnd. **1539** *Act 31 Hen. VIII* c. 4 Actions of det..grounded vpon contract or specialties. **1581** NOWELL & DAY in *Confer.* I. (1584) D b, You ground the credit of S. James Epistle..vpon these Councils. **1639** WOODALL *Wks.* Pref. (1653) 5 Galen saith..all arts are grounded upon experience and reason. **1641** MILTON *Ch. Govt.* iv. Wks. (1851) 111 The impossibility of grounding Evangelick government in the imitation of the Jewish Priest-hood. **1674** tr. *Scheffer's Lapland* 74 They must necessarily have had some probabilities whereon they grounded their opinion. **1728** NEWTON *Chronol. Amended* ii. 252 Nechepsos ..invented Astrology, grounding it upon the aspects of the Planets. **1769** *Junius Lett.* xix. Postscr. 85 It is..the law of the land, grounded upon the clearest principles of reason and common sense. **1789** *Durnford & East's Reports* III. 467 The right of a seller to his goods, where he cannot receive payment for them, is grounded in conscience. **1838** THIRLWALL *Greece* II. 104 An oligarchy which grounded its political claims solely on superior wealth. **1875** HELPS *Ess.*, *Self-Discipline* 16 Self-discipline is grounded on self-knowledge. **1884** tr. *Lotze's Metaph.* 516 The nature and occurrence of these actions being..grounded in something external.

†**b.** *simply.*

c **1380** WYCLIF *Wks.* (1880) 362 Þis state or power is þe vicar of þe godheede as it may be growndid here. —— *Sel. Wks.* III. 342 Firste shulde þe fend grownde þat þis pope is Petris viker. *c* **1449** [see GROUNDABLE]. **1538** STARKEY *England* II. iii. 198 Wythout that ther ys no gud ordynance can be stablyschyd nor grondyd. **1580** SIDNEY *Ps.* xlii. v, Still my hope is grounded, That thy anger being spent, I by day thy love shall tast. **1603** FLORIO *Montaigne* II. xii. (1632) 32 Copernicus hath so well grounded this doctrine..that [etc.]. **1614** BP. HALL *Rem. Wks.* (1660) 28 We knew not wherein to insist, nor where to ground a complaint. **1621** ELSING *Debates Ho. Lords* (Camden) 15 Yf he confesse, we may ground our sentence. *a* **1628** F. GREVIL *Alaham* II. iv. Poems (1633) 35 How should I ground a faith, that faithlesse know Myselfe to be? **1650** T. B[AYLEY] *Worcester's Apoph.* 55 That is it they desire, and thence they would ground their quarrel. *a* **1677** HALE *Prim. Orig. Man.* I. ii. 50 But intellectual Reason hath to do with universals, and for the most part grounds and directs its Ratiocination by them. **1724** A. COLLINS *Gr. Chr. Relig.* 5 The Apostles ground and prove Christianity from the Old Testament.

c. In *pass.* with advs. Of conjectures, fears, etc.: To have a (good or bad) foundation.

1748 *Anson's Voy.* II. ix. 228 We afterwards found our suspicions..to be well grounded. **1765** BLACKSTONE *Comm.* I. i. 127 A fear of battery, or being beaten, though never so well grounded, is no duress. **1838** THIRLWALL *Greece* II. xvi. 322 Their suspicions and fears were not ill grounded.

†**3.** To establish, settle (a person in respect of his position, beliefs, etc.). Const. *in*, *of*. Also, in *pass.*, to be advanced (*in* years). *Obs.*

1382 WYCLIF *Hab.* i. 12 Thou groundidist [Vulg. *fundasti*] hym strong, that thou shuldist chastise. *c* **1400** *Destr. Troy* 7579 He is gret of degre, groundit of old. **1423** JAS. I *Kingis Q.* cxxxviii, Gif the hert be groundit ferm and stable In goddis law. *c* **1450** tr. *De Imitatione* III. viii. 75 If he be grounded in very mekenes & fulfilled wiþ dyvine charite. **1535** COVERDALE *Isa.* liv. 14 In rightuousnes shalt thou be grounded. *a* **1540** BARNES *Wks.* (1573) 326/2 They themselues are grounded onely of their owne sensuall mynde, hauyng no learnyng, nor reason for them. **1624** HEYWOOD *Gunaik.* IV. 205 Appolonia a virgin, but somewhat grounded in years. **1657** R. LIGON *Barbadoes* (1673) 56 Such a loss as this, is able to undo a Planter, that is not very well grounded.

refl. *c* **1400** *Apol. Loll.* 29 It is foly ani prest to presume him to haue euyn power wiþ ilk oþer, be for þat he may ground him in þe feiþ.

†**4. a.** *refl.* To rest or rely *upon*, esp. in argument. *Obs.*

1387 TREVISA *Higden* (Rolls) IV. 401 Som..fondith for to grounde hem uppon þe auctorite of Quintilianus. **1471** RIPLEY *Comp. Alch.* Admon. xii. in Ashm. (1652) 192

Uppon my wrytynge therfore to ground the be bold. **1494** FABYAN *Chron.* VI. clxxvi. 174 Antonyus, whiche groundeth hym vpon ye said Vyncent. *a* **1533** FRITH *Disput. Purgat.* (1829) 124 In solving this argument, he groundeth him on two lies at once. **1635** HAKEWILL *Apol.* v. vi. 340 Some.. grounding themselves upon those words, have beene so bold as to affirme [etc.]. **1802–12** BENTHAM *Rat Judic. Evid.* (1827) III. 625 The state of things on which the above question grounds itself is [etc.].

†**b.** *intr.* for *refl. Obs.*

1551 ROBINSON tr. *More's Utop.* II. (Arb.) 150 If herein they grounded vpon reason they would mock them. **1594** CAREW *Huarte's Exam. Wits* xi. (1596) 165 Graue and learned men..labour to deliuer their opinion, concealing the opinions whereon they ground. **1643** SIR T. BROWNE *Relig. Med.* II. §10, I say moreover, and I ground upon experience, that poisons contain within themselves their own antidotes. **1682** —— *Chr. Morals* iii. 22 He..wisely grounding upon true Christian expectations..will wholly fix upon what is to come.

5. *trans.* To instruct (a person) *in* the fundamental or elementary principles of any branch of study. ***to be grounded in***: to be (well or ill) acquainted with (a subject or science).

c **1386** CHAUCER *Prol.* 414 He was grounded in Astronomye. **1553** T. WILSON *Rhet.* 3 In all poynctes throughly grounded and acquainted with the preceptes. **1617** *Moryson Itin.* II. 47 Touching his studies..he came young and not well grounded from Oxford University. **1658** A. FOX *Wurtz' Surg.* II. viii. 73 He that is well grounded in Surgery will find Receipts enough in his daily practise. **1725** BERKELEY *Proposal* Wks. III. 217 To ground these young Americans thoroughly in religion. **1839** LD. BROUGHAM *Statesm. Geo. III, Horner* (ed. 2) 319 He was well grounded in the exacter sciences. **1861** HUGHES *Tom Brown at Oxf.* viii. (1889) 67, I grounded myself pretty well in Latin and Greek. **1884** L. J. JENNINGS in *Croker Papers* I. i. 27 He always sought to ground himself thoroughly in the facts [etc.].

6. Of a non-personal subject: To form or supply a basis, ground, or reason for (something). *rare.*

1667 PEPYS *Diary* 2 Sept., I did then desire to know what was the great matter that grounded his desire of the Chancellor's removal. *a* **1677** BARROW *Serm.* (1683) II. x. 141 Every attribute, every title, every relation of God doth ground an obligation. **1788** JEFFERSON *Writ.* (1859) II. 353 A single day's retard in which [the payment of interest] would ground a prejudice of long duration. **1875** POSTE *Gaius* III. Comm. (ed. 2) 444 A convention is statutory which derives validity from some statute, and grounds or destroys a right of action.

†**7.** To investigate thoroughly. *Obs.*

a **1529** SKELTON *Col. Cloute* 726 Some other man That.. can Well scrypture expounde, And hys textes grounde. **1597** A. M. tr. *Guillemeau's Fr. Chirurg.* 6/2 M. Paré hath verye learnedlye discussed, and, as it weare, grownded this questione, in his boockes of Chyrurgerye.

8. To furnish with a ground or basis for painting, embroidery, etc. (see GROUND *sb.* 6). Also ***to ground in***: in *Calico-printing*, to apply (a second colour or a mordant) to a piece of material already printed with the colour of the first block.

1398 TREVISA *Barth. De P.R.* XIX. xi. (1495) 871 The meane coloures ben groundyd in none other colour better than in whyte. **1581** *Act 23 Eliz.* c. 9 §3 No kynde of Clothe ..shall from henceforth bee mathered for a Blacke, excepte the same be firste grounded with Woade onelye. **1839** URE *Dict. Arts* 230 (Calico-printing) Ground-in the neutral reserve..Ground-in the topical colours at pleasure. *Ibid.* 921 Pieces [of wall-paper] intended to be satined, are grounded with fine Paris plaster. **1860** RUSKIN *Mod. Paint.* V. VIII. iv. 194 It is all the same to him whether he grounds a head..or whether he grounds the whole picture. **1862** MISS YONGE *C'tess Kate* ii. (1880) 31 Kate had a bunch of flowers, in Berlin wool, which she was supposed to be grounding.

9. a. To bring to the ground, knock down.

In quot. *c* 1205 there is app. some error in the text.

c **1205** LAY. 26553 þus we [? *insert* eou] scullen grundien, ȝif godd us wule fulsten! **1430–40** LYDG. *Bochas* II. ii. (1554) 121 a, Their aduersaries bete doune and grounded. *c* **1430** *Pilgr. Lyf Manhode* IV. xxxi. (1869) 193 Swich a strok he yaf me þat.. doun he hadde grounded me ne hadde my burdoun be. **1812** *Sporting Mag.* XXXIX. 187 Penton was ultimately grounded by a doubler on the left side. **1908** H. G. WELLS *War in Air* viii. 252 Not one third..succeeded in getting back to the mother airship. The rest were either smashed up or grounded. **1968** EAGLESON & MCKIE *Terminol. Austral. Nat. Football* II. 13 *Ground*, a variant for bring down, recorded by two informants.

†**b.** *fig.* To 'floor', 'gravel'. *Obs. rare.*

1597 TOFTE *Laura* in *Alba* (1880) Introd. 38 Tis a worke to ground the wisest Hed. **1598** SYLVESTER *Du Bartas* II. ii. I. *Ark* 330 Miracles, that ground Man's wrangling Reason and his Wits confound.

10. a. To place or set on the ground; to cause to touch the ground; to lay down. †Also, to bring down (a weapon).

? **1650** *Don Bellianis* 228 He..hoisted aloft his sword.. and grounded it with mighty force upon the Giants head. **1751** JOHNSON *Rambler* No. 96 ¶9 When once she had grounded her foot, neither gods nor men could force her to retire. **1751** PALTOCK *Peter Wilkins* II. xx. 255, I ordered my Bearers..to ground me just at the Foot of the Wood. **1773** J. DUNCOMBE *Surry Triumphant* xlvii, in R. Freeman *Kentish Poets* (1821) II, Ere the foe could ground his bat, His ardour Lewis quell'd. **1774** *Laws Cricket* in Lillywhite *Cricket Scores* I. 16 Except his bat be grounded within it [*i.e.* the popping-crease]... If..the wicket is struck down before his foot, hand, or bat, is grounded over the popping-crease. **1801** STRUTT *Sports & Past.* II. iii. 99 Before the striker is at home, or can ground his bat. **1879** *Boy's Own Paper* 18 Jan. 2/3 The players [at Rugby football] are scrambling to their feet, and waiting for the ball to be 'grounded'. **1884** *Mil. Engineering* I. II. 90 In grounding ladders, the men..lower the ladders gently on to the ground. **1899** *Westm. Gaz.* 10 Nov. 2/1 The Rules Committee have decided that..the [golf] club may be grounded.

b. ***to ground arms*** (Mil.): to lay one's arms upon the ground, *esp.* as an act of surrender.

1711 *Milit. & Sea Dict.* (ed. 4) I, s.v. *Straw*, A word of Command, to dismiss the Soldiers when they have grounded their Arms. **1802** JAMES *Milit. Dict.*, *Ground arms*, a word of command on which the soldiers lay down their arms upon the ground. This word of command has been exploded since the introduction of the new exercise. Soldiers are now ordered to *pile arms.* **1855** MACAULAY *Hist. Eng.* xiii. III. 325 Every burgher who should anywhere meet a person wearing the Macdonald tartan should ground arms, in token of submission. **1874** *Rifle Exerc.*, etc. 58 Ground Arms—Turn the rifle on the heel, lock to the rear, sink the body, bending both knees; and place the rifle flat on the ground. **1884** M. THORNHILL *Pers. Adv. Ind. Mutiny* ii. 13 Eventually the native officer ordered the guard to ground their arms, and allowed us to enter the office.

transf. **1711** ADDISON *Spect.* No. 102 ¶6 When the Fans are thus discharged, the Word of Command in course is to ground their Fans.

c. *Electr.* To connect with the earth as a conductor. Also *absol.* Chiefly *U.S.*

1881 *Operator* 15 June 218/1 Never, if possible, ground within a hundred feet of any place where an electric light wire is grounded. **1882** T. D. LOCKWOOD *Pract. Inf. Telephonists* 28 It is not well to ground on a plate of one metal at one end and another metal at the other. **1883** T. D. LOCKWOOD *Electr. Tel.* 138 If an accidental connection with the ground should occur..it is at once tested for by grounding the circuit at the office. **1892** *Pall Mall G.* 21 Mar. 7/3 One wire would be grounded. **1967** *Technology Week* 20 Feb. 35/1 A resistance inserted in the 'V's' effectively 'grounds' the antennas.

d. *intr.* To alight on the ground; to come to or strike the ground.

1751 PALTOCK *Peter Wilkins* II. xx. 261, I hovered over the City a considerable time, to be sure of grounding right. **1801** STRUTT *Sports & Past.* (1810) 100 [Trap-ball] He..is also out if he strikes the ball into the air and it is caught.. before it grounds. **1908** H. G. WELLS *War in Air* viii. 258 The *Zeppelin*..circled down and grounded in Prospect Park, in order to land the wounded.

e. To keep 'on the ground', prevent (an aircraft, pilot, etc.) from flying.

1931 *Vanity Fair* Nov. 78/1 A *flying ticket* is the pilot's license, which he holds until he is *grounded* by having the license cancelled. *a* **1940** F. SCOTT FITZGERALD *Last Tycoon* (1949) i. 6 The assistant pilot is always in uniform... I want to find out if we're going to be grounded in Nashville. **1940** *War Weekly* 2 Feb. 464/2 With catapults at an aerodrome, damage done by the enemy would not 'ground' all the aeroplanes in the hangars. **1944** *Flight* 20 July 61 That's young Begley. He's being grounded to-morrow! **1970** *Daily Tel.* 28 Apr. 1/8 Three..jets were grounded by mechanical faults and an accident.

11. a. *intr.* Of a vessel: To run ashore or aground; to strand. Const. *on.*

1624 CAPT. SMITH *Virginia* III. v. 59 Our bote..chansing to grownd vpon a many shoules lying in the entrances. **1748** *Anson's Voy.* II. iii. 146 She..grounded between two small Islands. **1814** SCOTT *Ld. of Isles* v. xiv, With that the boats approach'd the land, But Edward's grounded on the sand. **1868** E. EDWARDS *Raleigh* I. xxv. 615 The flagship had already grounded under circumstances of peril.

transf. **1850** SCORESBY *Cheever's Whalem. Adv.* ix. (1859) 116 The bow of the boat grounded on the body of the whale.

b. *trans.* To cause to run ashore. †Also *fig.* in *pass.* To be stuck fast, unable to help oneself.

1658 PHILLIPS, *To Ground a ship*, to bring her on the ground to be trimmed. **1704** J. LOGAN *Let. to W. Penn* 26 Mar. in *Mem. Hist. Soc. Pennsylv.* (1870) IX. 288 My life.. is not worth the living: I am grounded on all sides. **1712** W. ROGERS *Voy.* App. 16 If you water above in the River, do not ground your Boat. **1806** *Naval Chron.* XV. 388 Three of our ships seemed to be grounded.

12. a. *trans.* To lower (an anchor) to the bottom. **b.** *intr.* To sink to, or settle on, the bottom.

1632 LITHGOW *Trav.* VII. 329 Our Anchors being grounded, and our Boate ready to court the shoare, I bad farwell to all. **1739** LABELYE *Short Acc. Piers Westm. Br.* 30 We sunk the Caisson..to try how it sat and grounded. **1793** SMEATON *Edystone L.* §143 We proceeded lowering till our anchor was grounded. **1867** F. FRANCIS *Angling* ii. (1880) 69 The bait grounds too soon.

ground (graʊnd), *ppl. a.* See also GROUNDED *ppl. a.*², GROUNDEN. [pa. pple. of GRIND *v.*]

1. a. Reduced to fine particles by grinding or crushing.

1765 *Univ. Mag.* XXXVII. 320/2 Ground and powdered refined sugar. **1781** in D. Davis *Hist. Shopping* (1966) x. Pl. 11 Rice whole. Do. ground. **1818** *Art Preserv. Feet* 131 A cataplasm of oatmeal and ground linseed. **1839** URE *Dict. Arts* 225, 8 ounces of ground indigo. **1845** MCCULLOCH *Taxation* II. v. (1852) 230 The roots of chicory..when dried and ground, bear a strong resemblance to ground coffee. **1846** 'A LADY' *Jewish Man.* i. 2 Mix a little potatoe-flour, ground rice, or pounded vermicelli, in a little water. **1905** H. G. WELLS *Kipps* I. i. 15 Toke and cold ground-rice puddin' with plums. **1947** 'G. ORWELL' *Shooting Elephant* (1950) 165 Cold ground-rice pudding.

b. With advs., as ***ground-down*** (also *fig.*, exhausted), ***-up.***

1897 *Allbutt's Syst. Med.* III. 80 Synovia..mixed with ground-down particles of cartilage. **1899** *Outing* (U.S.) XXX. 171/1 A country of ground-up pebbles and water. **1911** J. MASEFIELD *Everlasting Mercy* 49 The ground-down starving man. **1946** S. SPENDER *European Witness* (1947) 32 The German soldiers now have the soulless ground-down expression as in carved-wood faces of Slav peasants.

2. a. Having the surface abraded or fashioned by grinding, esp. of joints, stoppers, etc. intended to fit closely.

1807 T. THOMSON *Chem.* (ed. 3) II. 41 Phials with ground stoppers. **1875** KNIGHT *Dict. Mech.*, *Ground-joint.* **1884** *Ibid.* Suppl., *Ground-cock.*

b. ***ground-down*** (sb.): the trade designation of a kind of needle (see quots.).

1862 T. MORRALL *Needle-making* 39 The Ground downs are..for tailors, and are shorter than the Short Sharps. **1880** *Plain Hints Needlework* 95 There are sharps, the ordinary long sewing-needles; ground downs, short and stumpy.

3. ***ground glass.*** †**a.** Glass which has its surface polished by grinding; plate glass (*obs.*). **b.** Glass which has had its transparency destroyed by grinding or other processes; also *attrib.*

1793 SMEATON *Edystone L.* Explan. Plate 6 The panes were of ground glass, on account of strength. **1823** P. NICHOLSON *Pract. Build.* 420. **1848** DICKENS *Dombey* xviii, The ground-glass windows are made more dim by shutters. **1869** TYNDALL *Notes Lect. Light* §103 If the screen be semi-transparent, say of ground glass or tracing-paper. **1885** HOWELLS *Silas Lapham* (1891) I. 7 He..pushed the ground-glass door shut.

4. ground wood (see quot. 1937).

1885 G. F. GREEN in Rattray & Mill *Forestry & Forest Products* xviii. 473 Ground wood was first used for paper-making about the year 1846, when it was manufactured by Keller. **1937** E. J. LABARRE *Dict. Paper* 119/1 *Ground wood*, wood pulp produced by grinding wood; another term for mechanical wood. **1955** *Times* 5 July p. ii/2 Some will be cut into lengths for the groundwood mill.

†**'groundable**, *a. Obs. rare*⁻¹. [f. GROUND *v.* + -ABLE.] Capable of being established or proved.

c **1449** PECOCK *Repr.* I. xx. 125 Doom of resoun and lawe of kinde and not Holi Scripture muste expresseli grounde this..if it be in eny wise groundable and leeful.

groundage ('graʊndɪdʒ). [f. GROUND *sb.* + -AGE.]

1. †**a.** Some kind of toll or tax. *Obs. rare*⁻¹.

c **1440** *Jacob's Well* 29 Alle þo, þat don men of holy cherche ..to paye toll, pyckage, murage, or grondage, panage or gwydage, for swyche godys as are noȝt led to feyres & markettes, be-cause of marchaundise.

b. A duty levied on vessels lying upon a shore or beach, or entering a port; *spec.* in the City of London (see quot. 1854).

1567 *St. Papers, Dom. Add. Eliz.* 26 Such as touch or lie upon the shore a time, pay that money (1*s.*) to the officers there as groundage. **1609** *Patent 7 Jas. I* in *Act 4 Geo. III*, c. 26 Preamble, Tolls, duties, anchorages, groundages, profits, commodities, advantages..and appurtenances whatsoever. **1728** JEAKES *Charters Cinque Ports* 57 *note*, Terrage, or Groundage, nothing to be paid for their Ships lying a Ground, or at Anchor in any of the King's Havens or Harbours. **1848** WHARTON *Law Lex.*, *Groundage*, a custom or tribute paid for the standing of a ship in port. **1854** *Fraser's Mag.* XLIX. 564 The groundage of corn is a duty of 6*d.* on every vessel with corn on board entering the port.

c. (See quot.)

1852 WIGGINS *Embanking* 138 In the cases of mines or quarries, the royalty, seignorage, or groundage varies according to circumstances, from one-eighth to..one twenty-fourth.

†**2.** Running aground, stranding. *Obs. rare*⁻¹.

1477 W. PEKOE in *Paston Lett.* No. 807 III. 211 Sche had never no wrekke nor growndage till withinne this xx wynter.

†**3.** The bottom, as suitable or otherwise for anchorage. *Obs. rare*⁻¹.

1637 T. MORTON *New Eng. Canaan* (1883) 122 The groundage is a sandy sleech, free from rockes to gaule Cables, but is good for anchorage.

†**4.** The right of occupying ground. *Obs. rare*⁻¹.

1721 *Lond. Gaz.* No. 5953/3 They shall have their Groundage..free, for such the two ensuing Fairs.

ground-annual. *Sc. Law.* 'A perpetual yearly duty payable upon land, and made a real burden upon it either by constitution or reservation' (Sheriff Æ. J. G. Mackay).

1551 *Sc. Acts Mary* (1814) II. 490/1 The ground annuall appeiris ay to be payit quha euer big the ground and fail-ȝeing thairof that the annuellar may recognosce the ground. **1597** SKENE *De Verb. Signif.* s.v. *Annuell*, [In Acts Mary 1551] mention is maid of ground annuell, few annuell, and top annuell, quhairof I haue red nathing in onie vther place: and am incertaine quhat they do signifie. **1874** *Act 37 & 38 Vict.* c. 94 §30 Securities by way of ground annual, whether redeemable or irredeemable. **1890** *Bell's Dict. Law Scotl.* (ed. 7) s.v., In the beginning of the seventeenth century, the Lords of Erection resigned their superiorities to the Crown, with the exception of the feu-duties, which the Crown had power to redeem on payment of a certain consideration. The consideration never having been paid, the power of redemption was renounced, and the feu-duty thus perpetually payable to the successor of a Lord of Erection is called a ground-annual.

ground-ash.

1. A young ash-plant; an ash sapling (see quot. 1707). Also *attrib.*

1664 EVELYN *Sylva* vi. 23 From these low Cuttings come our Ground-ashes, so much sought after for Arbours, Espaliers, and other Pole-Works. **1697** DRYDEN *Æneid* IX. 1003 A lance of tough ground ash the Trojan threw. **1707** MORTIMER *Husb.* I. (1708) 335 Some cut the young Ashes off about an Inch above the Ground, which causes them to make very large straight Shoots, which they call Ground-Ash. **1878** JEFFERIES *Gamekeeper at H.* i. 13 His ground-ash stick under his arm.

2. *dial.* **a.** The gout-weed, *Ægopodium Podagraria* (Withering *Brit. Plants* 1796) **b.** *Angelica sylvestris* (Johnston *Bot. East. Border* 1853).

'ground-bait.

1. † **a.** A bait used in bottom-fishing (*obs. rare*). **b.** A bait thrown to the bottom of the water in which it is intended to fish, in order to lure the fish thither. Also *fig.*

a. 1651 T. BARKER *Art of Angling* (1653) 1, I am indifferent where the wind standeth either with ground Bait or Menow, so that I can cast my Bait into the River. *Ibid.* 3, I am determined to Angle with the ground Baits and set my Tackles to my Rod.

b. 1655 WALTON *Angler* x. (1661) 174 The Ground-Bait. **1821** SCOTT *Kenilw.* iii, I expect not to catch the old jack till I have disposed my groundbaits handsomely. **1895** *Westm. Gaz.* 9 Dec. 2/1 Is a candidate entitled to lay.. ground-bait? In plainer terms, may he give subscriptions [etc.]. **1895** 'JOHN BICKERDYKE' *Sea Fishing* vi. 184 Then the ground-bait net will be found of great advantage.. Sink this [ground-bait] in a piece of netting, by means of stones, near the bottom, and fish close to it.

2. *Northumb.* The loach or groundling.

1867 in SMYTH *Sailor's Word-bk.* **1880-4** in F. DAY *Brit. Fishes* II. 204.

Hence **ground-bait** *v.*, to lay with ground-bait (also *fig.*); **ground-baiting** *vbl. sb.*

1840 BLAINE *Encycl. Rural Sports* 1031 It is the practice of all experienced anglers.. to groundbait the spots they intend to fish in. **1896** A. MORRISON *Child of Jago* 236 A large swindle, requiring much ground-baiting and preliminary out-lay. **1899** *Blackw. Mag.* June 977/1 He will have to 'ground-bait' the place heavily, if he wishes decent attendance.

ground-bird.

†**1.** Applied to a particular swan out of a 'game', or perh. more than one, possibly as being the due of the owner of the land. *Obs.*

1560 in W. H. Turner *Select. Rec. Oxford* (1880) 285 For uppyng the ground byrde in portemeade. **1562** *Ibid.* 304 Item, payed for a grounde byrd.. xijd. **1570** *Ibid.* 330 Payed for two growne burds. **1887** *Standard* 1 Aug. 5/2 The owner of the soil claimed one cygnet as 'the ground bird'.

2. A general name for any columbine, gallinaceous, grallatorial, or struthious bird.

1840 BLYTH *Cuvier's Anim. Kingd.* (1849) 251 The various groups of Ground-birds (as the vast majority of the foregoing extensive series may be appropriately denominated) fall into six principal divisions.

3. *U.S.* The grass-finch or ground-sparrow.

1856 BRYANT *Poems, Rivulet* iii, And the brown ground-bird, in thy glen Still chirps as merrily as then.

groundcel(l, obs. form of GROUNDSEL *sb.*[2]

ground-down: see GROUND *ppl. a.* 2 b.

grounded ('graʊndɪd), *ppl. a.*[1] [f. GROUND *v.* or *sb.* + -ED[1] or [2].]

1. a. Deeply or strongly founded; firmly fixed or established; resting upon a good basis. Chiefly *fig.* of immaterial things.

1548 GEST *Pr. Masse* in H. G. Dugdale *Life* (1840) App. i. 98 It is a grounded proufe of falshode. **1553** BRENDE *Q. Curtius* A iij, A stable and grounded wysedome. **1605** *Lond. Prodigal* v. i, To shake my grounded resolution. **1612** BACON *Ess., Empire* (Arb.) 298 Solide and grounded courses to keep them [dangers] aloofe. **1653** R. SANDERS *Physiogn.* b iij, So have I fortified this building with grounded pillars. **1783** BURKE *Affairs India* Wks. 1842 II. 9 A grounded apprehension of the ill effect.. of all strong marks of influence and favour. **1817** COLERIDGE *Biog. Lit.* I. x. 203 A grounded knowledge of the German language and literature. **1871** MORLEY *Voltaire* (1886) 5 The temperament which mistakes.. violent phrase for grounded conviction.

b. with advs.; esp. *well-*, *ill-grounded*.

1596 SPENSER *F.Q.* IV. iv. 1 Friendship.. Without regard of good, dyes like ill grounded seeds. **1634** SIR T. HERBERT *Trav.* 92 The King caused a.. large and deepe grounded Causey be built. **1648** GAGE *West Ind.* xx. 160 A good and well grounded knowledge of the tongues. **1662** GERBIER *Princ.* 14 Leaving to their Posterity to prop and redresse their ill grounded Buildings. **1724** DE FOE *Mem. Cavalier* (1840) 202 Had our counsels been.. ready and well grounded. **1777** WATSON *Philip II* (1793) II. XIII. 175 A well grounded apprehension.

†**2.** Of persons: Thoroughly instructed or proficient in some study; also, deeply imbued with certain principles. *Obs.*

1613 T. JACKSON *Creed* I. 315 Questions.. which would require a grounded scholers serious paines & long search. **1619** R. HARRIS *Drunkard's Cup* 26 A very iudicious Diuine, and grounded Text-man. **1666** E. MOUNTAGU in *12th Rep. Hist. MSS. Comm.* App. v. 8 If the young Lord was a strict and a grounded Papist there was some danger my Lady Dorothy might bee perverted. **1807** ANNA SEWARD in *Athenæum* 2 Mar. (1895) 282/1 Mr. Day, who was a grounded Greek scholar.

3. Of lace: Having the intervals of the pattern filled in with plain stitches. ? *Obs.*

1695 *Lond. Gaz.* No. 3101/4 A grounded Lace Nightrail. **1720** *Ibid.* No. 5881/3 A fine Valencia grounded laced Suit of Night Clothes. **1740** LADY HARTFORD *Lett.* I. lii. 226 Four fine laced Brussels heads—two looped and two grounded.

4. Having a ground of a specified colour.

1761 *Public Advertiser* 1 Jan., Dressed in a yellow grounded velvet. **1765** *Treat. Dom. Pigeons* 57 You may breed twenty light grounded ones for one deep ground. **1813** *Examiner* 12 Apr. 239/1 A red grounded frock.. was.. found. **1865** MRS. WHITNEY *Gayworthys* II. iii. 54 A simple white grounded lawn.

5. Having the ground applied or prepared.

1839 URE *Dict. Arts* 921 Spreading the piece [of wall-paper] upon the table with the grounded side uppermost.

6. a. Placed on, or brought into contact with, the ground. **b.** Forced aground, stranded.

1784 COWPER *Tiroc.* 308 To pitch the ball into the grounded hat, Or drive it devious with a dext'rous pat. **1862** DANA *Man. Geol.* v. 542 Stones in.. the under surface of a grounded [ice]berg. **1888** *Amer. Nat.* XXII. 230 As the grounded floebergs are forced up the shelving sea-bottoms [etc.].

7. *Electr.* Electrically connected with the ground, either directly or through another conductor; earthed. Chiefly *U.S.*

1889 *Daily News* 8 Nov. 5/8 An alternating current.. from a partially grounded wire. **1913** *Wireless World* I. 99/2 Grounded conductors, such as gas, steam, and water pipes. **1938** L. F. BLUME *Transformer Engin.* vii. 198 Grounded neutral power systems generally connect to ground through the neutral of a step-up delta-Y bank, located at the generating station. **1949** *Electronics* Aug. 120/2 The grounded-emitter arrangement [of a transistor circuit].. is analogous to a grounded-cathode tube circuit. **1971** *Sci. Amer.* Aug. 107/1 The charging current is measured with a microammeter in series with the grounded side of the coil.

8. Of an aeroplane, pilot, etc.: unable, or not allowed, to fly. Also *transf.* of sportsmen, etc., suspended, disqualified.

1939 in *Amer. Speech* (1955) XXX. 286 When a jockey is suspended or disqualified, he is said to be 'grounded'. **1942** T. RATTIGAN *Flare Path* II. ii. 140 And on my confidential report they'd put—grounded. Lack of moral fibre. **1942** *Amer. Speech* XVII. 103/2 *Grounded*, license revoked [of a truck-driver]. **1954** in *Amer. Speech* (1955) XXX. 286 'We're all grounded.' It took only another question or two to discover that for these youths 'grounded' meant not having the use of the family car. **1967** *Sunday Times* (Colour Suppl.) 10 Sept. 45/4 *Grounded*, stranded for lack of petrol. Borrowed from the R.A.F.

†**'grounded**, *ppl. a.*[2] *Obs.* [Incorrect var. of GROUNDEN *ppl. a.*] = GROUNDEN, GROUND.

1566 DRANT *Horace's Sat.* I. A 1 b, The maces keene, the grounded sworde, the Tucke, the targe, the sheilde. **1698** A. VAN LEEUWENHOEK in *Phil. Trans.* XX. 171 Two or more grounded Glasses.

groundedly ('graʊndɪdlɪ), *adv.* [f. GROUNDED *ppl. a.*[1] + -LY[2].] †In a grounded or well-established manner; fundamentally, deeply, thoroughly (*obs.*); with good reason. Now *rare.*

1546 BALE *Eng. Votaries* I. (1550) 7 b, Thys repeted he thryse after that.. to the intent it might be groundedlye marked. **1596** HARINGTON *Metam. Ajax* (1814) 95, I am.. groundedly studied in the reformation of Ajax. **1643** *Plain English* 8 That Accommodation can onely be safe in this Kingdome, which shall place the power of it in the hands of them that may be groundedly presum'd will use it for the preservation of it selfe. **1669** GALE *Crt. Gentiles* I. III. ii. 24 This, I conceive, may be groundedly concluded. **1674** ALLEN *Danger Enthusiasm* 26 That they might believe more groundedly and firmly. **1716** M. DAVIES *Athen. Brit.* III. *Crit. Hist.* 6 Both.. seem rather to be Seekers or Scepticks, than any ways groundedly satisfy'd in their tortur'd Consciences. *a* **1805** D. GILSON *Serm. Pract. Subj.* vii. (1807) 142 Elijah and Elisha were.. uninformed also we may groundedly suppose, of the precise manner and moment in which the former was to be taken from the earth. **1832** AUSTIN *Jurispr.* (1879) II. 1119 Those who are acquainted with.. the historical basis of the actual system, will acquire that actual system more readily as well as more groundedly. **1868** BROWNING *Ring & Bk.* XI. 948 Oh, how I wish some cold wise man Would.. pronounce on my desert Groundedly.

†**'groundedness.** *Obs. rare.* [f. as prec. + -NESS.] The quality or condition of being grounded or firmly established.

1601 DENT *Pathw. Heaven* 234, I iudge these to be most sound and infallible euidences of a mans saluation: Assured faith in the promises.. Groundednesse in the truth. *a* **1647** BOYLE *Autobiog.* Wks. 1772 I. p. xxiii, Philaretus derived from this anxiety the advantage of groundedness in his religion. [**1826** BENTHAM in *Westm. Rev.* VI. 454 In proof of its well-groundedness I call two witnesses.]

groundeles, obs. form of GROUNDLESS.

groundely, variant of GROUNDLY *a. Obs.*

†**'grounden**, *ppl. a. Obs.* Forms: see GRIND *v.*[1] [pa. pple. of GRIND *v.*[1]]

1. Of weapons: Sharpened by grinding.

a **1300** *Cursor M.* 21437 Scarp grunden knijf in hand he bar. *c* **1400** *Rowland & O.* 57 A Saraȝene.. With grymly growenden gare. *c* **1400** *Melayne* 1554 Full grym strokes he ouer þam satt, With growndyn speris and grym. *c* **1470** HENRY *Wallace* II. 64 The grounden suerd throuch out his cost it schar. **1513** DOUGLAS *Æneis* IV. iv. 41 His grundin dartis clattering by his syde. **1557** NORTH tr. *Gueuara's Diall Pr.* 258 b/2 You feare vs not with sharpe grounden swoordes and daggers. *a* **1650** *Death Robin Hood* 75 in Furnivall *Percy Folio* I. 55 Red Roger with a grounding glave thrust him through the milke white side.

2. Of substances: Ground, brayed, crushed.

13.. *Metr. Hom.* (Vernon MS.) in *Archiv Stud. neu. Spr.* LVII. 308 Summe smered hire Mouþ withoute with grounden Mustard. *c* **1386** CHAUCER *Can. Yeom. Prol. & T.* 222 Our Orpyment and sublymed Mercurie, Oure grounden litarge, [etc.]. *c* **1420** *Pallad. on Husb.* I. 1123 Grounden shellis dight With flour of lym. *c* **1430** *Two Cookery-bks.* 38 Take groundyn Porke, & knede it with Spicerye.

grounden, obs. pa. pple. of GRIND *v.*

grounder ('graʊndə(r)). Also 5 growndar, gronddar. [f. GROUND *v.* + -ER[1]. Cf. MDu. *grondere* (Du. *gronder*), G. *gründer*, MSw. and Sw. *grundare.*]

1. One who, or that which, founds, establishes, causes, etc.

14.. *Ave Reg. Celorum* in *Tundale's Vis.* (1843) 146 Heyle, gudly growndar of all grace! *c* **1449** PECOCK *Repr.* 79 Holi Scripture may not be ther of the Reuler bi cause He is not therof the Grounder. *c* **1485** *Digby Myst.* (1882) III. 326 ȝe worthy word, ȝe be gronddar of gladnesse. *c* **1530** L. COX *Rhet.* (1899) 53 Fayned fables of poetes (and fleyng tales of lyght fokes) ar, for the more parte, the grounders of fame and rumours. **1560** ROLLAND *Crt. Venus* III. 305 Grounder of euill, and na vertew hir neir.

2. One who does the grounding in the manufacture of wall-paper, or in other arts of design.

1878 MACLEOD *Hist. Dumbarton* III. 79 The merchants had the ordinary trade of the town supplemented.. by the Leven printers and grounders.

3. *colloq.* **a.** A catching the ground (in angling). **b.** A knock-down blow. **c.** In cricket and other games: A ball sent along the ground (Barrère & Leland).

1847 ALBERT SMITH in *Illustr. News* 12 July 374 The fish that I have caught I will not name Nor yet confess my bites have all been grounders. **1849** *Boy's Own Bk.* 69 Grounders and home tosses. **1862** J. PYCROFT *Cricket Tutor* 8 The old bat used to be heavy at the point—very requisite for picking up a Grounder. **1867** H. CHADWICK *Base Ball Player's Bk. Reference* 137 *A grounder*, a ball hit along the ground, either on a line or on a series of bounds. **1889** WESTGARTH *Austral. Progress* 171 Lifting him up, and giving him a heavy grounder on his back. **1927** *Daily Express* 27 May 13/7 Brown opened the scoring, receiving a fine pass from Dean and sending in a beautiful grounder from eighteen yards. **1932** J. T. FARRELL *Studs Lonigan* (1936) viii. 617 Studs watched the infield practice, the grounders slapped hard, cutting over the dirt, the ball snapped around from player to player. **1970** *Washington Post* 30 Sept. D1/7 A fielder's-choice grounder by Dave Nelson knocked in Mike Epstein.

groundesueli, -swele, obs. ff. GROUNDSEL *sb.*[1]

'ground-floor. The floor in a building which is more or less on a level with the ground outside.

1601 HOLLAND *Pliny* II. 597 In processe of time pauements were driuen out of ground-floores, and passed vp into chambers. **1669** in Willis & Clark *Cambridge* (1886) II. 557 Uppon the Groundfloore there shalbe five outward chambers. **1703** MOXON *Mech. Exerc.* 265 You may imagine this Design to be the Ground Floor, having no Cellar beneath it. **1760-72** tr. *Juan & Ulloa's Voy.* (ed. 3) I. 336 All the houses of note have a story; but the others only a ground floor. **1809** MALKIN *Gil Blas* IV. x. ¶5 A window on the ground-floor. **1845** FORD *Handbk. Spain* I. 25 The ground floor is a sort of common room for men and beasts. **1884** G. ALLEN *Philistia* I. 3 A large room on the ground floor of the tenement.

attrib. **1886** W. J. TUCKER *Life E. Europe* 102 A straggling ground-floor edifice. ? *c* **1890** W. H. CASMEY *Ventilation* 17 Eight drying machines in one ground-floor room. **1897** *Daily News* 10 June 7/1 The building will consist mainly of a ground floor storey.

b. *fig.* Also in phr. *to get* (or *be let*) *in on the ground-floor* orig. *U.S.*: 'to be allowed to share in a speculation on the same terms as the original promoters' (Farmer). Also in other similar expressions with wider meaning.

1864 BOWEN *Logic* vii. 225 The inductive truth-seeker is on the ground-floor of facts. **1872** T. TALMAGE *Abom. Mod. Society* 118 A select number go in on the 'ground floor'. **1878** *N. Amer. Rev.* CXXVII. 181 The ground-floor of material industry. **1901** MERWIN & WEBSTER *Calumet 'K'* xi. 211 Well then, we'll have to let you in on the ground floor. **1904** 'O. HENRY' *Cabbages & Kings* xii. 206 Says he's heard of the boom along this coast, and wants to get in on the ground floor. **1909** E. S. BARNETT *Dragnet* 12 To take advantage of this ground floor proposition Alexander and Company will have to give up its identity, and be a branch. **1916** J. BUCHAN *Greenmantle* xii. 159 The promoters are keeping it to themselves. They aren't taking in more than they can help on the ground-floor. **1930** W. S. MAUGHAM *Cakes & Ale* xiv. 167 It was out of the question then for Mrs. Barton Trafford to get in on the ground floor. She could only buy in the open market. **1939** J. B. PRIESTLEY *Johnson over Jordan* 57 Still plenty of good things if you know where to find 'em and get in on the ground floor. **1945** R. HARGREAVES *Enemy at Gate* 82 Spain bestirred herself to get in on the nearest thing she could find in the way of a ground floor, by declaring war on England in the June of [1779]. **1946** K. TENNANT *Lost Haven* (1947) xix. 319 It'd be a big thing, Alec.. You're in on this, in on the ground floor. **1958** *Spectator* 7 Feb. 169/1 It was thus comparatively easy to get in on the ground floor of the occasional project. **1966** A. LOOS *Girl like I* (1967) iii. 68 My problem was that, without realizing it, I was in on the ground floor of a sex revolution: the twentieth century's breakdown of romantic love between the sexes. **1968** *Globe & Mail* (Toronto) 3 Feb. 48/5 (Advt.), Surgical sales representative... Outstanding future—ground floor opportunity. **1970** *Observer* 1 Mar. 31/6 I'd get in on the ground floor and see it now if I were you.

c. The lower deck of a bus. *slang.*

1936 *Daily Herald* 5 Aug. 8/4 Here is a short list of busmen's slang phrases:.. *ground floor*, inside.

Hence **'ground-floored** *a.*, consisting of a ground-floor; one-storied.

1824 HEBER *Jrnl.* (1828) I. 326 A tavern, a large ground-floored house with excellent rooms.

ground-glass: see GROUND *ppl. a.*

ground-hog.

1. = AARD-VARK.

1840 tr. *Cuvier's Anim. Kingd.* 125 Only one species is known of this genus..which the Dutch colonists style the Ground Hog.

2. The American marmot (*Arctomys*).

1784 J. FILSON *Kentucke* 28 Nor are the animals common to other parts wanting, such as foxes,..ground-hogs, pole-cats, and oppossums. **1789** *Maryland Jrnl.* 13 Nov. (Advt.) (Th.), A Monack, or Ground-Hog, presented [to Peale's Museum] by Mr. Johnston. **1807** P. GASS *Jrnl.* ii. 25 Two of our hunters went out and killed an animal called a prarow, about the size of a ground hog. **1843** MARRYAT *M. Violet* II. 226 We had not met with one [buffalo], nor even with a ground-hog. **1859** BARTLETT *Dict. Amer., Woodchuck*, the ground hog, a rodent mammal of the marmot tribe. **1884** *Stand. Nat. Hist.* V. 122 The marmots proper, wood chucks, or ground-hogs are the largest and heaviest animals of the family [*Sciuridæ*].

3. A slang designation for various workmen whose occupation keeps them on the ground. Also *spec.* a caisson worker. *U.S.*

1926 *Amer. Speech* I. 651/2 *Ground hogs*, men who work in compressed air at caisson work. **1931** *Ibid.* VII. 48 'Tie men' who camp far out from the main camps are called 'Ground Hogs' or 'Pole Cats'. **1931** G. IRWIN *Amer. Tramp & Underworld Slang* 92 *Ground hog*, a rail-road brakeman. **1934** WEBSTER, *Ground hog*, a man who works under air pressure in caisson sinking or shield tunnelling. Called also sand hog. **1948** H. L. MENCKEN *Amer. Lang.* (Second Suppl.) xi. 713 A brakeman is a..ground-hog. *Ibid.* 718 A lineman's helper..who never leaves the ground is a..groundhog. **1960** WENTWORTH & FLEXNER *Dict. Amer. Slang, Ground-hog*, a pilot who does not like to fly. Early aviator use... A railroad brake-man.

4. *Comb.* **ground-hog case** *U.S.*, a desperate or urgent affair; **Gound-hog Day** *N. Amer.*, (see quots. 1871, 1948).

1885 C. A. SIRINGO *Texas Cow Boy* 125 Dangerous to cross. But the wagons being over made it a *ground hog case. **1897** KIPLING *Capt. Cour.* x. 234 'Ground-hog case,' said the Galway man. 'Badly lighted port, Danny.' **1927** *Amer. Speech* II. 356/1 [W. Virginia dial.], *Ground hog case*, something that has to be settled immediately. **1871** SCHELE DE VERE *Americanisms* 369 Candlemas is known as *Ground-hog Day, for on that day the ground-hog comes annually out of his hole, after a long winter nap, to look for his shadow. If he perceives it, he retires again to his burrow, which he does not leave for six weeks—weeks necessarily of stormy weather. But if he does not see his shadow, for lack of sunshine, he stays out of his hole till he can, and the weather is sure to become mild and pleasant. **1948** A. L. RAND *Mammals Eastern Rockies* 128 Groundhog day is February 2. Current belief has it that if on this day the groundhog sees its shadow, there will be 6 weeks more of winter; if it does not see its shadow, winter will be soon gone. **1965** *Kingston* (Ont.) *Whig-Standard* 2 Feb. 11/1 Today is groundhog day.

ground-ice. [Cf. Du. *grondijs*, G. *grundeis*.]

1. Ice formed at the bottom of the water; also called *anchor-ice* and *ground-grue*.

1694 *Acc. Sev. Late Voy.* II. (1711) 40 It looketh likest unto the Ground Ice of the Rivers in our country, or like unto Loaf-sugar. **1839** DOUGLAS in *Proc. Berw. Nat. Club* I. No. 7. 187 The frost, fixing on the shallow bottom, forms a ground-ice. **1856** KANE *Arct. Expl.* I. viii. 85 The ground-ice is forced in upon our stern. **1878** HUXLEY *Physiogr.* 153 This ground-ice is generally found in little masses clinging to stones and weeds.

2. (See quot.)

1838 *Penny Cycl.* XI. 459/1 The term ground-ice..has been sometimes given to the ice occasionally met with at certain depths in the ground in northern countries.

groundie swallow, -swally, dial. variants of GROUNDSEL *sb.*[1]

grounding (ˈgraʊndɪŋ), *vbl. sb.* [f. GROUND *v.* and *sb.* + -ING[1].]

1. The action of founding or establishing; foundation, establishment; chiefly in immaterial sense. Also quasi-*concr.* that on which something is grounded. Now *rare.*

c **1380** WYCLIF *Sel. Wks.* III. 353 And but þis grounding be in dede dremes and confermyngis ben nouȝt. **1395** *Remonstr. Rom. Corrup.* (1851) 67 Cristine men ben not holden for to bileve, withouten open groundinge of holi scripture. **1538** BALE *Thre Lawes* 2042 Of these..doubtles those lawes their groundynges take. **1597** MIDDLETON *Wisdom of Solomon* iii. 16 That tree whose root is sound, whose grounding strong. **1644** DIGBY *Mans Soul* (1645) 70 All the rest..would have no grounding nor fixednesse in the soule. **1898** J. BULLOCH *Centen. Mem. 1st Congreg. Ch. Aberdeen* i. 2 The important proposals he advanced were felt ..to be..well grounded. Their grounding lay in the religious condition of Scotland. **1899** J. CAIRD *Fundam. Ideas Xtianity* II. xvi. 176 [Anselm's] attempt to give speculative grounding to the relation between the.. sufferings of Christ and the remission of sins.

2. The act of instructing in elementary or fundamental principles; instruction of this kind.

1644 BP. HALL *Rem. Wks.* (1660) 104 Catechetical Sermons..for the grounding of Gods People in the principles of saving Doctrine. **1883** C. J. WILLS *Mod. Persia* 164 Euclid, Algebra, Latin, and French, in which, unlike the smattering of a middle-class school at home, a thorough grounding is given.

†**3.** *pl.* Grounds, sediment. *Obs.*

c **1420** *Liber Cocorum* (1862) 46 Þer in þou stepe white brede fayre..And voyde þy groundyngus for sonde.

4. The preparation or laying of a 'ground' in various arts and manufactures (see quots.). Also *grounding-in*, the application of the secondary colours in calico-printing.

1466 *Paston Lett.* No. 549. II. 266 For xxii yerdes and iii quarters of brod wythts, xxxiiiis. iiid. For grownedyng, iiis. iiiid. For dyeng, iiiis. **1839** URE *Dict. Mech.* 216 (Calico-printing) The grounding in, or re-entering, of the other colours is the next process. *Ibid.* 226 Topical Prussian blue for grounding. **1852** MORFIT *Tanning & Currying* (1853) 436 The laborious process of grounding, or frizing. **1877** *Sci. Amer.* XXXVII. 223 The first process undergone [in the manufacture of wall-paper] is termed 'Grounding' and the object is to give the paper the requisite body to enable it to receive the colored pattern. **1885** WATT *Leather Manuf.* 326 When dry they [i.e. dyed skins] are again seasoned with water, to prepare them for grounding, which operation is performed by scraping the flesh side with the 'moon-knife'.

b. The ground of any fabric.

1882 CAULFEILD & SAWARD *Dict. Needlework* (ed. 2) 231 The colour of a background or the 'grounding' of a piece of embroidery should be selected with a view to showing off the colours of the design.

5. a. The action of laying a ship aground for examination, repairs, etc. **b.** The action or an act of running aground, stranding.

1691 T. H[ALE] *Acc. New Invent.* 42 An opportunity of Grounding or Docking. **1769** FALCONER *Dict. Marine, Grounding*, the act of laying a ship ashore, in order to bream or repair her. It is also applied to running aground accidentally when under sail, or driving in a tempest. **1840** *Evid. Hull Docks Comm.* 70 *Q.* Is any inconvenience experienced by sloops? *A.* Yes, by grounding. **1856** KANE *Arct. Expl.* I. vi. 61 If she will bear the frequent groundings that we must look for. **1885** *Act 48 & 49 Vict.* c. 36. §3 Any right of navigation, anchoring, grounding, [etc.].

6. *attrib.*, as ***grounding-blue***; **grounding-machine**, a machine for grounding in the manufacture of wall-paper; **grounding-tool**, in mezzotint engraving, the tool with which the plate is roughened.

c **1790** IMISON *Sch. Art* II. 50 For the shades use a small grounding-tool. **1821** CRAIG *Lect. Drawing* vii. 411 The more the ground is scraped away,..the coarser and more evident is the granulation made by the grounding tool. **1839** URE *Dict. Arts* 225 This plan..is nearly superseded by the following grounding blue. *Ibid.* 226 Topical grounding blue for the cylinder press. **1877** *Sci. Amer.* XXXVII. 223 The grounding machine is represented in Fig. 1. While passing over a roller the paper is covered with a mixture of so called Jersey clay.

grounding (ˈgraʊndɪŋ), *ppl. a.* [f. as prec. + -ING[2].] That grounds (in senses of the vb.).

a **1641** BP. MOUNTAGU *Acts & Mon.* (1642) 117 The literall sense of Scriptures, is the prime, principall and grounding sense, but not the sole or onely sense. **1875** J. VEITCH *Lucretius* 56 Postulating a grounding and surrounding visible universe. **1876** S. LANIER *Poems* (1884) 130 'Lay down your arms, damned Rebels!' But never a grounding gun is heard.

groundis walle, obs. form of GROUNDSEL *sb.*[1]

ground-ivy.

1. a. The herb ale-hoof, *Nepeta Glechoma* or *Glechoma hederacea*, a common labiate plant having bluish-purple flowers and kidney-shaped leaves. †**b.** The periwinkle, *Vinca minor* (*obs. rare*$^{-1}$).

These plants have no obvious resemblance to ivy, but were classed by the older botanists as *hedera* on account of their creeping stems.

[*c* **1350** *Med. MS.* 864 in *Archæol.* XXX. 376 Parwynke.. Men calle it þe juy of grownde. Anoþer erbe is callyd soo, þ[t] we callyn tun-hoo.] *c* **1400** in Henslow *Med. Wks. 14th C.* (1899) 42 Take grounde-suylie and groundyuy and weybrede and stampe hem to-gedre. *c* **1450** *ME. Med. Bk.* (Heinrich) 200 3yf þou mow not haue alle þese erbes, tak ground yuy alone. **1578** LYTE *Dodoens* III. I. 389 Grounde Iuye hath many square tender stalkes growing foorth from a roote full of thveddes. **1597** GERARD *Herbal* II. ccc. 705 *Hedera terrestris*..in English ground Iuie, Alehoof [etc.]. **1616** SURFL. & MARKH. *Country Farme* 207 Ground Iuie groweth likewise in a moist and shadowed place. **1676** BEAL in *Phil. Trans.* XI. 587 Ale-hoof, or Ground-Ivy, famous for dispatching the maturation of Ale and Beer. **1712** tr. *Pomet's Hist. Drugs* I. 31 It runs upon the Ground, after the manner of Ground-Ivy. **1845** LINDLEY *School Bot.* (1862) 96 *N[epeta] Glechoma* (Ground Ivy)... A popular country remedy for colds.

attrib. **1734** MRS. DELANY in *Life & Corr.* (1861) I. 453 Your cough not gone yet?—I beg you will drink asses milk and ground ivy tea.

†**2.** The barren trailing ivy (*Hedera Helix*).

1597 GERARD *Herbal* II. ccci. 708 Creeping or barren Iuie is called..in English ground Iuie.

†**3.** The ground-pine (*Ajuga Chamæpitys*). *Obs.* [App. *ivy* is here a corruption of *ive*: see HERB IVE.]

1640 PARKINSON *Theat. Bot.* 284 It [*Chamæpitys*] is called in English Ground Pine, and Ground Ivie after the Latine word *Iva*.

groundless (ˈgraʊndlɪs), *a.* Forms: 1 **grundléas**, 4 **groundlyas**, 4–5 **groundeles**, 5 **growndles**, 6– **groundless**, (7 **-lesse**). [OE. *grundléas*, f. *grund* GROUND *sb.* + *-léas* -LESS. Cf. MDu. and Du. *grondeloos*, MHG. *gruntlôs* (G. *grundlos*), MSw. and Sw. *grundlös*.]

†**1.** Bottomless, unfathomable. *lit.* and *fig.* *Obs.*

c **888** K. ÆLFRED *Boeth.* vii. §4 Sio grundlease swelᵹend hæfð swiðe mæneᵹu westu holu on to gadrianne. *c* **1315** SHOREHAM *Poems* 154 Godes domes beth A groundlyas pet. **13..** *E.E. Allit. P.* C. 310 All the gotez of þy guferes, & groundelez powlez. *c* **1450** tr. *De Imitatione* III. xv. 83 O hov deply I owe to submitte myself under þi depe groundeles iuggementes, lorde. **1605** SYLVESTER *Du Bartas* II. iii. I. *Vocation* 393 Shallowest Foords to ground-less gulfs doe change.

2. Destitute of foundation, authority, or support; having no real cause or reason; unfounded.

1620 T. GRANGER *Div. Logike* 331 Groundleese imaginations, and vaine confidences. **1651** BAXTER *Inf. Bapt.* 77 A groundless fiction that cannot be proved. **1719** YOUNG *Revenge* III. i, 'Twas your mistake, and groundless are your fears. **1776** ADAM SMITH *W.N.* I. xi. (1869) I. 199 This notion..seems to be altogether groundless. **1838** THIRLWALL *Greece* IV. xxxiii. 319 This report proved as groundless as the message of Ariaeus. **1849** E. E. NAPIER *Excurs. S. Africa* II. 168, I came to the conclusion that their murmurs were not entirely groundless.

groundlessly (ˈgraʊndlɪslɪ), *adv.* [f. prec. + -LY[2].] Without grounds; without adequate reason or cause.

1645 PAGITT *Heresiogr.* (1661) 177 Surely both you and others do it very groundlessly and presumptuously. **1682** TATE *Abs. & Achit.* 699 Seduc'd by these we groundlessly complain. **1735** E. CURL in *Pope's Lett.* I. Suppl. 22 You groundlessly imagine I have attempted to betray you to Mr. Pope. **1834** J. BROWN *Lett. Sanctification* I. 194 It is groundlessly, therefore, that any souls stand off from Jesus Christ. **1865** DICKENS *Mut. Fr.* I. vi, Of her father's being groundlessly suspected, she felt sure.

groundlessness (ˈgraʊndlɪsnɪs). [f. as prec. + -NESS.] The quality of being groundless, or without foundation; want of adequate reason.

1661 BOYLE *Style of Script.* 42 Such examining Readers, as are rational enough to discern the groundlesnesse of one part of the Doctrine. **1755** CARTE *Hist. Eng.* IV. 123 The groundlessness of their clamours. **1817** *Edin. Rev.* XXIX. 114 The groundlessness of their former pleas. **1856** FROUDE *Hist. Eng.* (1858) I. iii. 192 No proof of the groundlessness of the original charge availed..till they had paid for their deliverance.

ground-line. [Cf. Du. *grondlijn*, G. and Sw. *grundlinie* (in senses 2 and 3).]

1. A line used for bottom-fishing. ? *Obs.*

a **1450** *Fysshynge w. angle* (1883) 22 Ye may angle to hym at all tymys with a grownde lyne. **1704** *Dict. Rust.* s.v. *Ground-angling*, The Morning and Evening are the chiefest seasons for the ground Line for Trout.

2. *Geom.* †**a.** The base upon which a diagram is constructed (*obs.*). **b.** (See quot. 1857).

1551 RECORDE *Pathw. Knowl.* I. Defin., When one line lyeth flatte (whiche is named the ground line) and an other commeth downe on it, and is called a perpendiculer. **1571** DIGGES *Pantom.* I. iii. Cj, Measure out the like length in the perpendiculare..beginning from the ground line. **1659** WILLSFORD *Scales Comm.* 118 Let fall a Perpendicular.. upon the Basis or ground-line. **1857** W. BINNS *Treat. Orthogr. Project.* i. (1862) 2 The vertical and horizontal planes are generally divided by a line called the ground line, or intersecting line of the two planes of projection.

3. *pl.* Outlines (*lit.* and *fig.*).

1624 WOTTON *Archit.* I. 65 Let no man..setle his Fancie vpon a draught of the Worke in paper..much less vpon a bare Plant thereof, as they call the Schiographia or Ground lines. **1858** J. MARTINEAU *Stud. Chr.* 150 We owe to the deeper Evangelical spirit..the ground-lines of an Ethical philosophy.

groundling (ˈgraʊndlɪŋ). [f. GROUND *sb.* + -LING. Cf. MDu. *grundelinck* (Du. *grondeling*), MHG. *grundelinc* (G. *gründling*) gudgeon.]

1. A name given to various small fishes which live at the bottom of the water, *esp.* a gudgeon or loach.

1601 HOLLAND *Pliny* I. 265 As the Apuæ which are the groundlings..[come] of the fome of the sea. **1611** COTGR., *Loche de mer*, a little fish..; some call it a sea Groundling. *Lochette*, a Groundling, or small-bearded Loach. **1655** MOUFET & BENNET *Health's Improv.* (1746) 274 Groundlings are also a kind of Gudgeons never lying from the Ground, freckled as it were on each Side with seven or eight Spots. **1769** PENNANT *Zool.* III. 237 The loche is found in several of our small rivers, keeping at the bottom of the gravel, and is on that account, in some places, called the Groundling. **1802–3** tr. *Pallas's Trav.* (1812) II. 461 The mountain-streams..also afford a small kind of barbel, the groundling. **1840** tr. *Cuvier's Anim. Kingd.* 314 *Cobitis tænia*, the Groundling..is the smallest of the species inhabiting the smaller running waters, and lurking under stones.

2. a. A plant that creeps on the ground or is of low growth.

1822 BEWICK *Mem.* 256 A profusion of wild-flowers.. which peep out amongst the creeping groundlings. **1827** in Hone *Every-day Bk.* II. 893 Towering up from among the low groundlings that..surround it, [grows] the stately fox-glove.

b. An animal that lives on the ground.

1874 WOOD *Nat. Hist.* 6 It is a remarkable fact that the Chimpansees are groundlings, and are not accustomed to habitual residence among the branches of trees.

c. *nonce-use.* Said of a person (see quot.).

1822 LAMB *Elia* Ser. I. *Decay of Beggars*, A man, who used to glide his comely upper half over the pavements of London, wheeling along..upon a machine of wood..The accident which brought him low took place in the riots of 1780, and he has been a groundling so long.

d. A person on the ground, as opposed to an airman, passenger in an aircraft, etc.

1940 *Manch. Guardian Weekly* 25 Oct. 304/1 Of the R.A.F.'s courage and skill it would be almost presumptuous for any mere groundling to speak. **1966** M. R. D. FOOT *SOE in France* iv. 81 The groundlings assumed, wrongly, that the aircraft had accidentally dropped a couple of small bombs. **1969** *Daily Tel.* 13 Sept. 10 An occasional crash [of an aeroplane] may be expected, possibly involving the death of 500 passengers and an unpredictable number of groundlings. *Ibid.* 15 Nov. 22/6 The giant Saturn 5 rocket

..sent the lunarnauts soaring up into a blue sky hidden from groundlings by heavy clouds.

3. A frequenter of the 'ground' or pit of a theatre; hence, a spectator (reader, etc.) of average or inferior tastes, an uncritical or unrefined person. (Only in literary use, as a reminiscence of Shakespeare's phrase, and sometimes app. associated with the more general sense of 'ground'.)

1602 SHAKS. *Ham.* III. ii. 12 O it offends mee to the Soule, to see a robustious Pery-wig-pated Fellow, teare a Passion to tatters, to verie ragges, to split the eares of the Groundlings. **1609** DEKKER *Guls Horne-bk.* vi. 28 Your Groundling and Gallery-Commoner buyes his sport by the penny. **1659** *Lady Alimony* I. iv, The Groundlings within the yard grow infinitely unruly. **1762** CHURCHILL *Ghost* IV. Poems I. 322 The minds of Groundlings to enflame. **1829** LYTTON *Devereux* II. i, But how do you like sharing the mirth of the groundlings? **1873** SYMONDS *Grk. Poets* vi. 183 The soliloquies of Hamlet..must have been lost upon the groundlings of Elizabeth's days. **1900** H. W. SMYTH *Grk. Melic Poets* p. lvii, The dithyramb was meretricious art and appealed to the taste of the groundlings.

†**4.** One of humble rank; one of base breeding or sentiments. *Obs. rare.*

1622 FLETCHER *Prophetess* I. iii, We tilers may deserve to be senators,..For we were born three stories high; no base ones, None of your groundlings, master. **1630** BRATHWAIT *Eng. Gentl.* (1641) 31 Here you shall see One unmeasurably haughtie, scorning to converse with these Groundlins (for so it pleases him to tearme his inferiours). *Ibid.* 56 These whose erected minds are removed from the refuse and rubbish of earth (which our base Groundlins so much toyl for).

5. *attrib.* or as *adj.*

1825 LAMB *Reflect. in Pillory*, That domicile for groundling rogues and base earth kissing varlets [the stocks]. **1829** SOUTHEY *O. Newman* II. Poet. Wks. X. 285 Grunts And strives with stubborn neck and groundling snout. **1885** J. S. STALLYBRASS tr. *Hehn's Wand. Plants & Anim.* 94 It must have been a mere groundling sucker.

†**'groundly**, *a. Obs.* Forms: 3 **grund(e)lich, -like,** 5 **groundli, -ly,** 5–6 **groundely.** [f. GROUND *sb.* + -LY[1]. Cf. MSw *grundeliker* (Sw. *grundlig*), G. *grundlich*] **a.** Well-founded or established, solid, firm. Of instruction: Thorough. **b.** Thoroughly instructed or educated.

c **1205** LAY. 15813 Ich habbe bigunnen a weorc mid grund-liche stre[n]gðe. *c* **1300** *Havelok* 2013 Þe burgeys þat þer bi stode þore Grundlike and grete oþes swore,..þat was soth, þat bernard tolde. *c* **1449** PECOCK *Repr.* 78 Trowing.. that thei han noon or litle nede to groundli clerkis. *Ibid.* 90 Profound and groundli scoling in logik. **1494** FABYAN *Chron.* VI. clxiii. 156 Withoute defyaunce or groundly cause of warre. **1524** WOLSEY in *St. Papers Hen. VIII*, VI. 278 The good introductions persuasions and groundly reasons made unto His Holynes. **1548** UDALL, etc. *Erasm. Par. Luke* Pref. 8 After a more exacte and groundely sorte.

†**'groundly**, *adv. Obs.* Forms: 3 **grundliche, -like,** 4–5 **groundli,** 5 **growndly,** (6 **-lie**), 5–6 **groundely,** (6 **growndely**), 5– **groundly.** [f. GROUND *sb.* + -LY[2]. Cf. OHG. *chruntlichô*, MSw. *grundelika* (Sw. *grundligt*).] In a well-founded, firmly established, deep-seated or fundamental manner; in relation to the ground or root; thoroughly, profoundly.

c **1205** LAY. 9783 Cnihtes heom gereden, grundliche feire. *a* **1225** *Juliana* 69 Þe reue..bigon to cwakien, se grundliche him gromede. *c* **1300** *Havelok* 651 Hauelok anon bigan to ete Grundlike, and was ful blipe. **1395** *Remonstr. Rom. Corrup.* 140 Grosted seith groundli al this. **1435** MISYN *Fire of Love* I. xxviii. 60 Vse we slike rewle þat fleschly desire groundly ma be restrenyd. *c* **1449** PECOCK *Repr.* I. xvii. 101 Noone othere argumentis han place forto groundli and fundamentali schewe and proue [etc.]. **1515** BARCLAY *Egloges* III. (1570) Cij/2 Men groundly learned, in Latin commoning. **1538** STARKEY *England* I. ii. 29 When the opynyon ys waueryng and not groundly set. **1581** W. STAFFORD *Exam. Compl.* ii. (1876) 55 They bee farre wide from the trueth, as men that doe not consider the thinge groundly. **1602** WARNER *Alb. Eng.* Epit. (1612) 366 Hence may groundly be said deriued our best and still experienced Method wherein we now execute lawes.

ground-man: see GROUNDSMAN.

†**'groundment.** *Obs.* [f. GROUND *v.* + -MENT.] Foundation, origin.

?*a* **1412** LYDGATE *Two Merchants* 307 Yif of colre he [fever] take his groundement.

ground-nut. [Cf. Du. *grondnoot*, in sense 1.]

1. One of the small farinaceous edible tubers of the wild bean (*Apios tuberosa*), a climbing plant of North America; also, the plant producing these.

1636 in M. A. Green *Springfield, Mass.* (1888) 12 They shall..have liberty to take Fish and Deer, groundnuts, walnuts, akornes. **1765** T. HUTCHINSON *Hist. Mass.* I. ii. 301 The Indians coold come at the ground-nuts, which seem to have been all their provision. **1854** THOREAU *Walden* xiii. 257, I discovered the ground-nut (*Apios tuberosa*) on its string—the potato of the aborigines. **1865** PARKMAN *Champlain* vii. (1875) 274 Biencourt and his followers were ..digging ground-nuts.

2. The pea-nut or ground-pea (*Arachis hypogæa*), largely cultivated in the West Indies and West Africa, the fruit of which is a pod ripening under ground.

1769 WATSON in *Phil. Trans.* LIX. 379 They..are the produce of a plant..much cultivated in the Southern colonies, and in our American sugar islands, where they are called ground nuts, or ground pease. **1775** ROMANS *Florida* 131 The ground nut also introduced by the Blacks from Guinea, is next after this for its easy cultivation. **1863** *Wand. West Afr.* I. 184 The commerce of the place consists principally of the ground nut [etc.].

attrib. **1839** URE *Dict. Arts* 895 Ground-nut oil. **1887** MOLONEY *Forestry W. Afr.* 54 The finest ground-nut oil is used as a substitute for and mixture with olive. *Ibid.* 57 The ground-nut industry.

3. The earth-nut (*Bunium flexuosum*).

1653 CULPEPER *Eng. Physitian* 64 They are called Earth-Nuts, Earth-Chestnuts, Ground-Nuts, [etc.]. **1879** [see EARTH-NUT 1].

ground-pea. [GROUND *sb.* 18 c.] = GROUND-NUT 1 and 2.

1769 [see GROUND-NUT 2]. **1796** B. HAWKINS *Let.* 2 Dec. in *Georgia Hist. Soc. Coll.* (1916) IX. 21 They made beans, ground peas, cymblins. **1823** E. JAMES *Long's Exped. Rocky Mts.* I. 200 The squaws..are often necessitated to dig the pomme de terre..and to scratch the groundpea. **1854** *Florida Plant. Rec.* 115, I have picked 80 bushels of ground peas. **1893** *Jrnl. Amer. Folklore* V. 95 *Arachis hypogæa*, ground-peas. *Ibid.* VI. 140 *Apios tuberosa*, ground-pea. **1946** *Publ. Amer. Dial. Soc.* v. 24 *Ground peas*, peanuts.

ground-pine.

1. The herbaceous plant *Ajuga Chamæpitys*; said to be named from its resinous smell.

1551 TURNER *Herbal* I. I vj b, Grounde pyne, the leaues dronken seuen dayes in wyne hele the Iaundes. **1578** LYTE *Dodoens* I. xviii. 28 In English also Chamæpitys, Ground Pyne, Herbe Iue, Forget me not. **1597** GERARDE *Herbal* II. clxxxv. §1. 497 There be diuers sortes of Ground Pines growing neere vnto the sea. **1657** W. COLES *Adam in Eden* cccxviii. 591 The Common Ground-pine groweth low, seldome rising to be above the height of an hand-breadth. **1718** QUINCY *Compl. Disp.* 122 Ground-Pine, flowers in July and August. **1861** MISS PRATT *Flower. Pl.* IV. 177 This plant is well called Ground Pine, as its narrow leaves look like a tuft of foliage taken from the pine-tree.

2. The club moss (*Lycopodium clavatum*) or other species of *Lycopodium*.

1847 EMERSON *Poems, Each & All* Wks. (Bohn) I. 400 The ground-pine curled its pretty wreath, Running over the club-moss burrs. **1880** *Libr. Univ. Knowl.* (U.S.) VII. 123 Ground-pine, the popular name of the *lycopodium clavatum*, an evergreen vine sometimes three yards long.

ground-plan. [Cf. Du. *grondplan*, Sw. *grundplan*.]

1. The representation on a plane of the arrangement, divisions, etc., of a building or other structure, at the ground-level.

1731 W. HALFPENNY *Perspective* 23 To draw the Perspective Elevation of the Stage..Draw the Ground-Plan ..by the Rule laid down in the foregoing Example. **1870** EMERSON *Soc. & Solit.* xi. 235 It is the dulness of the multitude that they cannot see the house, in the ground-plan. **1877** RAYMOND *Statist. Mines & Mining* 383 There are three of these furnaces, which are marked D in the ground-plan.

2. *fig.* The outline, general plan or basis upon which any work is constructed or composed.

1831 CARLYLE *Sart. Res.* III. viii, Did the Maker take them into His counsel; that they read His groundplan of the incomprehensible All? **1840** HOOD *Up Rhine* Pref. 1 The following work was constructed, partly on the ground-plan of Humphrey Clinker. **1873** SYMONDS *Grk. Poets* viii. 254 It was the purpose of Aristophanes to keep his serious ground-plan concealed.

†**ground-plat.** *Obs.* = GROUND-PLOT.

1570 DEE *Math. Pref.*, I will give you the Groundplatt of my whole discourse, in a Table annexed. **1571** DIGGES *Pantom.* I. xxxii. K ij, Measure..howe hyghe the grounde platte of the Castell is aboue the leuell right lyne of the fountayne. **1665** MANLEY *Grotius' Low C. Warres* 293 He burned the Town,..yet he seemed to maintain the Ground-plat thereof. **1769** *De Foe's Tour Gt. Brit.* III. 178 There is a great Resemblance between the Ground-plat of Lincoln, and that of Canterbury.

ground-plate. [Cf. Du. *grondplaat*, G. *grundplatte*.]

1. The lowest horizontal timber in a framing; a ground-sill.

1663 GERBIER *Counsel* 67 Ground plates nine inches one way. **1679** MOXON *Mech. Exerc.* I. 135 Plates..lying on the Foundation, are called Ground-plates. **1823** P. NICHOLSON *Pract. Build.* 225 Ground-Plate or Sill.—The lowest plate of a wooden building for supporting the principal and other posts.

2. a. A bed-plate carrying railway sleepers or ties (Knight *Dict. Mech.* 1875).

b. A piece of flattened metal on which anything is fixed, as in a spectroscope.

1871 tr. *Schellen's Spectr. Anal.* xxvii. 94 Of the prisms,.. the first only is fastened to the ground-plate PP.

c. *Electr.* A metal plate sunk in the ground and connecting an electric current with the earth.

1875 in KNIGHT *Dict. Mech.* **1893** in SLOANE *Stand. Electr. Dict.*

3. *Anat.* (See quot.)

1882 *Quain's Anat.* (ed. 9) II. 65 According to Klein.. each connective tissue corpuscle is composed of two distinct substances: (*a*) a hyaline plate—ground-plate—which contains the oval nucleus..; and (*b*) a second substance.

ground-plot.

1. The plot or portion of ground occupied or covered by a building, etc.; foundation. ? *Obs.*

1580 SIDNEY *Ps.* XI. iii, That in building they begunn With ground-plotts fall, shall be undunn. **1624** WOTTON *Elem. Archit.* I. 26, I haue sayd nothing of..Pyling of the Ground-plot..when we build vpon a moist or marshy soile. **1679** MOXON *Mech. Exerc.* I. 130 Suppose your Ground-plot be a Long-square, 50 Foot in length, and 20 Foot wide: This Ground-plot will contain in its length two good Rooms, and a Yard behind it 10 Foot long. **1856** KANE *Arct. Expl.* I. ii. 28 The tide, as it rises, converts a part of the ground-plot into a temporary island.

fig. **1834** LANDOR *Exam. Shaks.* Wks. 1846 II. 284/1 The foolishest dolts are the ground-plot of the most wit.

†**2.** = GROUND-PLAN 1. *Obs.*

1563 SHUTE *Archit.* B iij b, How to cast your ground plotte, wherin you must deuide all your seuerall places of offices. **1663** GERBIER *Counsel* g j a, Nor are the lines for the ground plots of Houses to serve for Castles in the Aire. **1691** *Lond. Gaz.* No. 2651/4 A large Parchment Writing containing two Skins, with a Ground-Plot annex'd to it.

†**3.** = GROUND-PLAN 2. *Obs.*

1581 SIDNEY *Apol. Poetrie* (Arb.) 52 They schal vse the narration, but as an imaginative groundplot of a profitable inuention. **1594** CAREW *Huarte's Exam. Wits* i. (1596) 23 All that which Galen writeth in..his booke is the ground-plot of this my Treatise. **1677** *Govt. Venice* 1 An Epitome of the whole History, and..a Scheme or Ground-plot to my Work. **1794** MATHIAS *Pursuits Lit.* (1798) 243 Method was all; yet would he seldom write: He fear'd the ground-plot wrong, or—out of sight.

ground-rent. [Cf. Du. *grondrente*, G. *grundrente*.] The rent paid to the owner of land which is let for building upon. Also *U.S.* (see quot. 1856).

1667 PRIMATT *City & C. Build.* 35 Fifty pounds per ann. is but a reasonable ground-rent for a House that will cost five hundred pounds..and yield one hundred pounds per annum. **1682** N. O. *Boileau's Lutrin* IV. 292 Fifty Marks a year in Ground-Rents. **1701** *Lond. Gaz.* No. 3712/4 The Ground Rent [is] but 10s. per Annum. **1776** ADAM SMITH *W.N.* v. ii. (1869) II. 436 Ground rents are a still more proper subject of taxation than the rent of houses. **1834** *West Ind. Sketch Bk.* II. 158 A great convenience..to the tenants, in all questions of ground-rent. **1856** BOUVIER *Law Dict.*, *Ground rent*, in Pennsylvania this term is used to signify a perpetual rent issuing out of some real estate. **1863** FAWCETT *Pol. Econ.* II. vii. (1876) 621 The occupier of a house pays a ground-rent to the owner of the land.

†**b.** A piece of land rented for building on. *Obs.*

1714 GAY *Shepherd's Week*, Proeme, As a London mason, who calculateth his work for a term of years, when he buildeth with old materials upon a ground-rent that is not his own, which soon turneth to rubbish and ruins.

ground-sea. A heavy sea in which large waves rise and dash upon the coast without apparent cause.

a **1642** SIR W. MONSON *Naval Tracts* II. (1704) 247/2 He met with so great a Storm and Ground Seas. **1756** PRINCE in *Phil. Trans.* XLIX. 642 A rumbling noise was heard, like that which usually precedes what the sailors call a ground-sea. **1835** R. S. HAWKER *Prose Wks.* (1893) 28 On, through the ground-sea, shove! **1865** *Englishm. Mag.* Oct. 296 A heavy ground-sea.

groundsel ('graʊndsəl), *sb.*[1] Forms: α. 1 **gundæsuelʒ(i)æ, gundesuilʒe, grundeswel(i)ʒe, -swyliʒe,** 2 **-swulie,** 3 **-swilie, -swylie,** 4 **grounswili,** 5 **groundeswele, -sueli, grondeswyle, groundis walle,** 6 **grundeswell, groundswel(l,** 6–7 **grownswell, grunswel(l,** (9 *dial.* **groundie-, grundy-swallow, swally, grinning-swallow,** etc.). β. 6 **grounsel,** 6–8 **groundsell,** 6– **groundsel.** γ. 6–7 **grunsell,** 7 (9 *dial.*) **grunsel,** (9 *dial.* **grinsel**). [OE. *gundæswelʒ(i)æ* (7th c.), *grundeswyliʒe* (10th c.); of difficult etymology.

Unless the word be corruptly adopted from some foreign language, the second element must be connected with *swelʒan* to swallow, absorb. The earliest recorded form *gundæswelʒiæ* has the appearance of being f. *gund* pus (see GOUND); the resulting sense 'pus-absorber' is plausible, as the chopped leaves of the plant are still (in country places) used in poultices for reducing abscesses. If this be the true etymology, the form *grundeswyliʒe*, whence the mod. word is descended, must be due to popular etymology, the word being associated with *grund* GROUND *sb.*, as if meaning 'ground-swallower', with reference to the rapid spread of the weed. There is, however, an unexplained difficulty in the form of the first element (*gundæ-* instead of the normal *gund-*); and it cannot be positively affirmed that the form without the *r* is not a mistake, as the three glossaries in which it occurs are too closely related to be considered independent witnesses.]

1. Any plant belonging to the genus *Senecio* (N.O. *Compositæ*), esp. *S. vulgaris* ('common groundsel'), a common European weed, which is given as food to cage-birds and was formerly largely used for medical purposes.

α. *a* **700** *Epinal Gloss.* 976 *Senecen*, gundaesuelʒiae [*Erfurt Gloss.* gundaeswelʒe]. *c* **725** *Corpus Gloss.* 1850 *Senecen*, gundesuilʒe. *c* **1000** *Sax. Leechd.* I. 180 Ðeos wyrt ðe man senecio, & oðrum naman grundeswyliʒe nemneð. *Ibid.* II. 124 Genim grunde swelʒean þe on eorþan weaxeþ. *c* **1250** *Voc.* in Wr.-Wülcker 558/12 *Iregerontis*..grundeswilie. *a* **1387** *Sinon. Barthol.* (Anecd. Oxon.) 39 *Senecio*.. grounswili. *c* **1400** in Henslow *Med. Wks. 14th C.* (1899) 9 Nyme horshouue, groundesueli, ysope [etc.]. *c* **1450** *ME. Med. Bk.* (Heinrich) 135 Take grounde swele & daysyes..þe two deel of groundeswele, þe þridde part of daysyes. *c* **1460** *Receipts* in *Rel. Ant.* I. 324 Take groundis walle that ys senchion. **1538** TURNER *Libellus*, Grundeswell, Grunswell, *Senecio*. **1578** LYTE *Dodoens* V. xvii. 570 The great Groundswel hath rough whitish leaves. **1600** SURFLET *Countrie Farme* II. xlii. 276 Groundswell groweth in euery ground, and without any great care. **1608** TOPSELL *Serpents* (1658) 815 Marcellus..addeth further groundswell, and the tender tops of the box-tree. **1688** R. HOLME *Armoury* II. 60/1 Grunswel, or Groundsel. **1808–25** JAMIESON,

Groundie-swallow, groundsel. **1893** *Northumbld. Gloss.*, *Grundy-swallow*.

β. **1562** TURNER *Herbal* II. 132 Senecio is named..in English groundsel. **1597** GERARDE *Herbal* II. xxv. §1. 216 The stalke of Groundsell is round. **1676** T. GLOVER in *Phil. Trans.* XI. 629 There grow wild in the Woods, Plantane of all sorts, Groundsel [etc.]. **1747** WESLEY *Prim. Physic* (1762) 29 Take a Handful of Groundsell. **1830** MACGILLIVRAY *Withering's Brit. Plants* (1837) 319 S[*enecio*] *viscosus*. Stinking Groundsel... *S. lividus*. Green-scaled Groundsel. .. *S. Sylvaticus*. Mountain Groundsel. **1838** DICKENS *O. Twist* xxxii, Fresh groundsel, too, for Miss Maylie's birds. **1871** H. MACMILLAN *True Vine* vii. (1872) 286 In the garden, the chickweed and the groundsel disfigure the beds of lilies and roses.

γ. **1594** PLAT *Jewell-ho.* III. 27 Some commend a handfull of grunsell sodden in the aforesaide ale. **1657** W. COLES *Adam in Eden* cl. 228 The Latines call it Senecio..It is called in English Groundsell or Grunsell. **1688** R. HOLME *Armoury* II. 89/2 Like Grunsel or a Succory leaf. **1886** *Chester Gloss.*, *Grinsel*, groundsel. **1887** *Suppl. Jamieson*, *Grunsel*, the common pron. of groundsel.

2. *Comb.*: **groundsel-tree**, a North American shrub, *Baccharis halimifolia*.

1741 *Compl. Fam.-Piece* II. iii. 412 You have also the black Hellebore now in Flower, with the Spurge Laurel, Virginian Groundsel Tree. **1796** C. MARSHALL *Garden.* xix. (1813) 336 Groundsel tree, or ploughman's spikenard, must have a snug situation.

groundsel (ˈgraʊndsəl), *sb.*[2], **ground-sill** (ˈgraʊndsɪl). Forms: 5 **gronsel, grondsil, grounselle, grownsel, -celle,** 5–6 **groundsille,** 5–7 **grownsell,** 6 **grunsell, grounsyll,** 6–7 **groundsyll, -cell, grounde sill,** 6–8 **groundsell,** 7 **-cel, grunsill** (also 9) **-sel,** 7–8 **grundsil(l, groundsil,** (9 **grounsel),** 6– **groundsel, -sill.** [First in ME.; app. f. GROUND *sb.* + SILL, but the earliest examples already show the second element reduced in form to a mere termination.]

1. A timber serving as a foundation to carry a superstructure, esp. a wooden building; the lowest member of a wooden framework; a ground-plate; hence, the foundation or lowest part of any structure. Now *rare* exc. in technical use.

[**1406–7** *Winchester College Acc. Roll*, In stipendiis ij positorum ponencium lez gronsell domus stauri.] **1433** LYDG. *St. Edmund* III. 1205 Oon at the grownsel [*v.r.* growncelle] lowe gan to myne. **1463** *Bury Wills* (Camden) 15 No stoon to be steryd of my graue, but a pet to be maad vnder the ground sille ther my lady Schardelowe was wont to sitte. **1486** *Nottingham Rec.* III. 253 For a grondsill of tymber. **1532** MORE *Confut. Tindale* Wks. 473/2 He sheweth himself as wise, as one that lest hys rotten house should fall, wold..pull vp yᵉ groundsel to vndershore the sides with the same. **1556** J. HEYWOOD *Spider & F.* iii. 16 No parte hath rest From roofe to groundsill. **1589** PUTTENHAM *Eng. Poesie* III. xix. (Arb.) 230 They first vndermined the groundsills, they beate downe the walles. **1611** R. FENTON *Usury* II. vii. 64 If they find the foundation or groundcels vnsound, they haue great reason to suspect the building. **1658** GURNALL *Chr. in Arm.* II. 37 The House must needs be in danger, when the groundsels are loosened. **1739** LABELYE *Short Acc. Piers Westm. Bridge* 17 The Ground-cills, or Bottom-pieces of these Frames. **1793** SMEATON *Edystone L.* Contents 13 The Groundsel of the Lantern applied and fitted to the Stone work. **1837** CARLYLE *Fr. Rev.* I. v. vi, Patriotism rushes in..from grunsel up to ridge-tile, through all rooms and passages. **1851** *Archit. Publ. Soc. Dict.* s.v. *Ground-plate*, After the fire of London it became usual to set the posts that carry the bressumer of a shop front on a ground sill. **1869** R. B. SMYTH *Gold-f. Victoria* 612 *Groundsill* is that part of a drive-set of timber which is laid on the floor of a drive.

transf. **1837** MEDWIN in *Fraser's Mag.* XVI. 232 Tear the firm-set groundsel of the world Up from its roots.

b. *fig.* The foundation on which something (immaterial) is built up; an underlying principle.

1604 EDMONDS *Observ. Cæsar's Comm.* 2 The basis and groundsill of all militarie architecture. **1609** BP. W. BARLOW *Answ. Nameless Cath.* 322 An Heresie subuerting the maine ground-cel of our Religion. **1627** HAKEWILL *Apol.* III. iv. §1 The barley-corne the grownsell as it were and simplest principle of measures. **1705** HICKERINGILL *Priestcr.* II. iii. 39 The two main Groundsels of Priest-Craft's Antichristian Throne, is Avarice and Ambition.

2. The lower framing-timber of a door; a door-sill, threshold. †Also, a window-sill.

1523 LD. BERNERS *Froiss.* I. lv. 77 They made them to fall downe on the grounsyll of the gate. **1576** FLEMING *Panopl. Epist.* 319 My threshold is even worn away, with the feete of right worshipful..men, that..thinke not scorne to step over and treade upon my groundcell. *a* **1632** G. HERBERT *Jacula Prud.* 295 The groundsell speakes not save what it heard at the hinges. **1679** MOXON *Mech. Exerc.* I. 148 If the Window-Frame stands on a Timber-house, the Head and Groundsell are sometimes Tennanted into the Posts of the Carcass. **1709** *Brit. Apollo* II. No. 33. 3/2 Here prostrating low as the Groundsil. **1726** LEONI *Alberti's Archit.* I. 16/2 Doors..shou'd be of the heighth of the Diagonal of a Square whereof the Groundsell is one of the Sides. **1864** LOWELL *Fireside Trav.* 288 The groundsel, side-posts, and lintel of a barn-door.

3. *attrib.*, as ***groundsel-bar, -edge, -plot***.

1625 LISLE *Du Bartas, Noe* 96 Of the meanest townes to lay the grundsill plot. **1667** MILTON *P.L.* I. 457 Head and hands lopt off In his own Temple, on the grunsel edge, Where he fell flat. [**1700** ADDISON *3rd Æneid* 77 He dash't and broke 'em on the grundsil edge.] **1793** SMEATON *Edystone L.* 196 The Ground-sil bars of wrought iron.

†**ˈgroundsel, ˈgroundsill,** *v.* [f. prec. sb.] *trans.* To lay the foundation or threshold of.

1486 *Nottingham Rec.* III. 255 For stonne and for ground-sillyng..of þe same bothes. *c* **1535** in *Yorksh. Archæol. Jrnl.* (1886) IX. 322 A howse..growncellyd wᵗ stone. **1635** QUARLES *Embl.* v. xiv. 298 The milder glaunces sparkled on the Ground, And grunsild ev'ry doore with Diamond. **1651** *Rec. Dedham, Mass.* (1892) III. 188 Ye Carpenters account that did groundcell the Meetinghouse.

fig. **1657** REEVE *God's Plea* 99 They..groundsell their estates with damages, roof them with detriments.

Hence **ˈgroundselling** *vbl. sb.*

1579 *Nottingham Rec.* IV. 182 For makyng of the chymney at the Fre Scole, and grounselyng of alle the house. **1589–1617** RIDER *Dict.*, *Substructio*, ..an vnderpinning, or groundsilling of an house, or making of a foundation vnder. **1623–4** *Nottingham Rec.* IV. 388 Workmanshippe for planckinge, grondsellinge [etc.].

groundsman. Also 8–9 **ground-man.**

a. A labourer employed to dig out or work on the ground, an excavator. **b.** One who is employed to keep in order a ground or grounds, esp. a cricket ground.

a. 1785 J. PHILLIPS *Treat. Inland Navig.* 39 Two hundred and fifty ground-men, and fifty carpenters. **1837** WHITTOCK, etc. *Bk. Trades* (1842) 197 To the 'ground-men' as they are called, the digging is let, at per cubic yard, according to the nature of the soil to be excavated.

b. 1886 *Standard* 27 May 8/4 Wages of gardeners, groundsmen, and gamekeeper. **1887** M. SHEARMAN *Athletics & Footb.* (Badm. Libr.) 79 The ground-man of the L.A.C. **1895** *Daily News* 1 Jan. 7/3 The ground-men worked hard on the wicket.

ground-squirrel.

1. A terrestrial squirrel-like rodent: **a.** of the genus *Tamias*; esp. the chipmuck (*T. striatus*) of the U.S.; **b.** of the genus *Spermophilus*; = GOPHER *sb.*[1] 2.

1772 FORSTER in *Phil. Trans.* LXII. 378 This creature is called a ground squirrel, at Churchill fort. **1791** W. BARTRAM *Carolina* 284 The ground squirrel, or little striped squirrel of Pennsylvania. **1859** BARTLETT *Dict. Amer.*, *Ground squirrel*, a name sometimes erroneously given to the striped and spotted prairie squirrel (*Spermophilus tredecimlineatus*). **1883** *Cassell's Nat. Hist.* III. 91 The true Ground Squirrels (*Tamias*) are distinguished from the rest of the Squirrels (*Sciurinæ*), and approach the Marmots. **1884** *Stand. Nat. Hist.* V. 125 The numerous species of Ground-squirrels (*Spermophilus*). *Ibid.* 126 The Ground-squirrels proper or Chipmunks (*Tamias*),—a small genus comprising some of the prettiest and most familiar representatives of the family. **1898** P. MANSON *Trop. Diseases* xvi. 269 The ground squirrel (*Spermophilus guttatus*).

2. An African squirrel of the genus *Xerus*.

1867 SCLATER in *Proc. Zool. Soc.* 817 Seven Ground-squirrels (*Xerus getulus*) from..Morocco.

ground-stone. [Cf. Du. *grondsteen*, G. *grundstein*, Sw. *grundsten*.] A foundation-stone. Chiefly *Sc.* and *fig.*

a **1000** *Voc.* in Wr.-Wülcker 203/34 *Cementa, i. petre*, grundstanas. **1567** *Gude & Godlie Ball.* (S.T.S.) 201 Land and money..Quhilk is the ground staine of thair quier, And nete of all thair pryde. **1591** R. BRUCE *Serm.* (Wodrow Soc.) 298 It may remain a sure foundation and Ground-stone to us. **1637** RUTHERFORD *Lett.* lxxxii. (1894) 171 Try upon what ground-stone ye have builded. **1871** ROSSETTI *Ave* 12 Poems 41 Thou headstone of humanity, Ground-stone of the great Mystery.

groundswel(l, obs. form of GROUNDSEL *sb.*[1]

ground-swell. A deep swell or heavy rolling of the sea, the result of a distant storm or seismic disturbance.

1818 SCOTT *Hrt. Midl.* iii, The agitation of the waters, called by sailors the ground-swell. **1840** R. H. DANA *Bef. Mast* i. 2 The vessel..rolled with the heavy ground swell. **1877** BLACK *Green Past.* xxviii. (1878) 221 Crashing its way through the rolling waves of a heavy ground-swell.

b. *fig.* Usually with reference to mental or political agitation.

1817 COLERIDGE *Zapolya* I. Wks. IV. 219 It is the ground-swell of a teeming instinct. **1856** R. A. VAUGHAN *Mystics* (1860) I. 91 The religious world was rocking still with the groundswell that followed those stormy synods. **1870** LOWELL *Among my Bks.* Ser. I. (1873) 219 The deep-raking, ground-swell of passion, as we see it in the sarcasm of Lear.

groundsyll, obs. form of GROUNDSEL *sb.*[2]

ground-tackle. [Cf. Du. *grondtakel*, G. *grundtackelage*.] A general name for all ropes, cables, anchors, or other tackle made use of in anchoring, mooring, or kedging a vessel.

1556 J. INCENT in Hakluyt *Voy.* (1599) I. 286 The said ship being beaten from her ground tackles, was driuen vpon the rocks. **1600** J. JANE *Ibid.* III. 848 To put into the Streights, wee durst not for lacke of ground-tackle. *a* **1642** SIR W. MONSON *Naval Tracts* III. (1704) 375/2 Never Ships ..were better fitted with Ground Tackle. **1742** WOODROOFE in Hanway *Trav.* (1762) I. II. xvii. 77 With such ships, by the help of good ground tackle, they navigate the Caspian. **1859** J. S. MANSFIELD in *Merc. Marine Mag.* (1860) VII. 15 The ground tackle seems..to have been free from objection.

So **ground-tackling** (in same sense).

1600 J. JANE in Hakluyt *Voy.* III. 843 Wee haue no sailes, no victuals, no ground-tackling, no cordage. **1710** *Lond. Gaz.* No. 4703/4 Cordage and Ground-Tackling very good. **1798** CAPT. BERRY in Nicolas *Disp. Nelson* (1845) III. 66 The dismasted Prize..is badly off for ground tackling.

†**ground-wall.** *Obs.* Forms: see GROUND and WALL.

1. The lower portion of a wall or building: a foundation. Also *transf.* and *fig.*

c **1000** *Ags. Gosp.* Luke vi. 48 He ys ȝelic timbriendum men his hus, se..hys grundweall ofer þæne stan asette. *c* **1000** ÆLFRIC *Gram.* (Z.) 289 Se cræft is ealra boclicra cræfta ordfruma and grundweall. *c* **1200** ORMIN 13372 Crist iss stan to ben grunndwall Off all hiss hallȝhe temmple. *a* **1225** *Juliana* 72 Lokeð þat te heouenlich lauerd beo grundwal of al þat ȝe wurcheð. *c* **1275** *Luue Ron* 124 in *O.E. Misc.* 97 Ne may no Mynur hire [? hit] vnderwrote ne neuer false þene grundwal. *a* **1300** *Cursor M.* 2242 Tua and sexti fathum brad Was þe grundwall þat þai made. *Ibid.* 8424 Lere o clerge well he sal, þat es o wisdom þe grundwall. *c* **1330** R. BRUNNE *Chron.* (1810) 210 A castelle he þouht to reise, He cast þe groundwalle þik. **1392–3** *Mem. Ripon* (Surtees) 114 In salar. iij cementariorum operant. super j Grundewall ibidem per iiij dies, 5s. [From other passages, this app. means: The plinth of masonry in a half timber building.] *c* **1425** *Voc.* in Wr.-Wülcker 667/11 *Hoe fundum*, growndwalle.

attrib. *a* **1755** *Edom o' Gordon* xii. in Child *Ballads* III. 433/2 Why pow [= pull] ye out my ground-wa-stane, Lets in the reek to me?

2. A retaining wall (see quot.).

1712 J. JAMES tr. *Le Blond's Gardening* 206 The Wall.. from the Bottom of the Digging, to the Level of the Ground above..is called the Ground-Wall, because it is built only to resist the Pressure of the Ground about it.

Hence †**ground-waller,** one who builds a ground wall.

1477 *Order* in *York Myst.* (1885) Introd. 21 *note*, Erthe wallers, pavers, dykers, ground wallers with erthe.

ˈgroundward, *adv.* and *a.* [See -WARD.]

A. *adv.* Towards the ground. †In early use, *to the groundward* (see TOWARD). Now *rare*.

1562 LEIGH *Armorie* (1597) 24 A Target..with three corners, two aboue his face, and one beneath to the ground-ward. **1583** STANYHURST *Æneis* II. (Arb.) 60 Hee fel to the groundward. **1599** H. BUTTES *Dyets drie Dinner* F iv b, The top now bowing to the ground-ward. **1620** SHELTON *Quix.* III. xxx. 211 He hung..with his Mouth and Breast to the Groundward. **1855** BROWNING *Andrea del Sarto* 83 Their.. works drop groundward.

B. *adj.* Turned or inclined towards the ground.

1878 *Masque Poets* 28 With groundward brow and quivering limb They come, the slaves that are to die.

So **ˈgroundwards** *adv.*

1885 LADY BURTON *Arab. Nts.* (1887) III. 70 Ali bowed his head groundwards awhile.

groundwork (ˈgraʊndwɜːk). [Cf. MDu. *grontwerck* (Du. *grondwerk*), G. *grundwerk*.]

1. a. The solid base on which an edifice or other structure is built; foundation. Now *rare*.

c **1550** CHEKE *Matt.* xxv. 34 Sins yᵉ groundworkes of yᵉ world weer laied. **1562** PILKINGTON *Expos. Abdyas* 49 Thei could not pearce the hard stones of the grounde worke, beinge so many, harde, depe, and stronge. **1591** SPENSER *Vis. Bellay* 99 A riuer swift, whose fomy billowes Did wash the ground-work of an old great wall. **1611** TOURNEUR *Ath. Trag.* v. i. Wks. 1878 I. 136 Like the falling noise of some great building when the ground-worke breakes. **1662** J. DAVIES tr. *Mandelslo's Trav.* 5 The Ground-work of it [Cyrus's Palace] is twenty two Geometrical feet in height. **1776** G. SEMPLE *Building in Water* 139 The first Course of the Ground-work. **1891** ATKINSON *Last of Giant Killers* 96 They..had dug out the foundations, and got the ground-work laid.

b. *fig.* The basis or foundation of something immaterial.

1557 N.T. (Geneva) Ep. *iv, The Lord Iesvs, which was the groundeworke and substance therof. **1605** TIMME *Quersit.* II. ii. 108 The groundworke and beginnings of medicine depend upon them. **1631** GOUGE *God's Arrows* iii. §33. 243 God's promises are the most proper ground-worke of faith. **1711** ADDISON *Spect.* No. 62 ¶8 No Thought can be valuable, of which good Sense is not the Ground-work. **1774** JEFFERSON *Autobiog.* Wks. 1859 I. App. 139 These.. still form the basis or groundwork of the Common law. **1818** SCOTT *Rob Roy* i, Some things..I must recall to your memory, because..they afford the ground-work of my destiny. **1856** STANLEY *Sinai & Pal.* xiii. (1858) 433 A ground-work of historical and geographical fact. **1878** BOSW. SMITH *Carthage* 61 The grand moral qualities which formed the groundwork of the Roman character.

†**2.** = GROUND-PLAN. *Obs.*

1574 R. SCOT *Hop Gard.* (1578) 48 The grounde worke hereof is so set out here, that anye Carpenter will easily frame the whole house by the same fygure.

3. a. The body or foundation on which other parts are overlaid, or on which they rest for display, as in embroidery work, painting, and the like.

1655 GURNALL *Chr. in Arm.* verse 15. x. (1669) 147/1 In needle-work, the sad ground-work is laid before the beautiful colours. **1662** J. DAVIES tr. *Olearius' Voy. Ambass.* 276 Cushions of flower'd Satin, the ground-work thereof Gold and Silver. **1693** DRYDEN *Ovid's Met.* I. 220 A way there is, in Heavn's expanded plain Which..mortals, by the name of milky, know. The ground-work is of stars. **1875** KNIGHT *Dict. Mech.*, *Ground-work*, the base color on which the painting is performed. **1892** E. REEVES *Homeward Bound* 221 Where there was fine embroidery or other work the effect was spoilt by..common material for ground-work.

b. The principal ingredient in anything. *rare*.

1822 LAMB *Elia* Ser. I. *Praise Chimneysweepers*, There is a composition, the ground-work of which I have understood to be the sweet wood yclept sassafras.

4. †**a.** Working in earth (*obs.*). **b.** (See quot. 1875.)

1655 MOUFFET & BENNET *Health's Improv.* (1746) 292, I permit unto true Labourers and Workmen to feed often.. if their Work be Ground-Work or very toilsome. **1875** KNIGHT *Dict. Mech., Ground-work*, the preparation of ground for the foundation of a structure, or giving it the required contour for any other purpose.

5. *Cricket.* = *ground-fielding* (GROUND *sb.* 18).

1898 K. S. RANJITSINHJI *With Stoddart's Team* (ed. 4) iv. 79 The catching of the team was far better than the ground work. **1905** *Westm. Gaz.* 19 Sept. 3/1 The ground-work was always splendid, and the throwing a joy to behold.

6. *Boxing* and *Judo*. Physical exercises performed by a sportsman whilst lying on the ground.

1906 MIYAKE & TANI *Game of Ju-Jitsu* (ed. 2) vi. 40 Ground-work cannot be described as systematically as standing work... Ju-jitsu ground-work is merely the proper use of the legs. **1948** D. S. LISTER *Boxing* 24 Gymnasium training..consists of..top work, ground work and, of course, boxing. **1954** E. DOMINY *Teach Yourself Judo* vii. 77 Groundwork ability is seldom related to the ability of the judoka with the standing up side of the sport.

So †**groundwork** *v. trans.*, to lay the foundations of, to found (*nonce-wd.*).

c **1550** CHEKE *Matt.* vii. 25 It fel not for it was ground-wrought on a rock. *Ibid.* xiii. 35 Thinges hiden sins yᵉ world was groundwrought.

groundy ('graʊndɪ), *a. rare.* [f. GROUND + -Y[1]. Cf. Du. *grondig*, G. *grundig*.] †**a.** ? Gritty, sandy (*obs.*). **b.** Containing grounds or sediment.

1602 *Narcissus* (1893) 199 Rest a little on the groundy gravell. **1892** W. J. CLUTTERBUCK *Ceylon & Borneo* xxvi. 213 Some of the groundiest coffee it has ever been my fortune to encounter.

groune, obs. form of GROUND *sb.*

grounsel(le, etc. obs. ff. GROUNDSEL *sb.*[1], sb.[2]

grount, obs. form of GROUND *sb.*

grounye, var. GRUNYIE *Sc. Obs.*, snout.

group (gruːp), *sb.* Also 8–9 groupe, (8 grouppe). [ad. F. *groupe*, ad. It. *gruppo* group; cf. *groppo* knot, *groppa* crupper of a horse, Sp. *grupo*, *gorupo*, *grupa*, knot, cluster, group, Pg. *garupa* crupper; prob. like F. *croupe*, Pr. *cropa* crupper, adapted from Teut. **kroppo*-: see CROP. The etymological sense would appear to be 'lump' or 'mass'. In Eng. the artistic senses came earliest, and the wider use was at first chiefly transferred.]

1. *spec.* **a.** *Fine Art.* An assemblage of (two or more) figures or objects forming in combination either a complete design, or a distinct portion of a design.

1686 [see GRUPPO]. **1695** DRYDEN *Du Fresnoy's Art Paint.* 20 The Figures in the Grouppes ought not to be like each other in their Motions, any more than in their Parts. **1710** STEELE *Tatler* No. 194 ¶15 The beautiful Grouppe of Figures in the Corner of the Temple. **1713** —— *Guardian* No. 21 ¶5 The Huddle Group of those who stand most distant. **1756–7** tr. *Keysler's Trav.* (1760) III. 94 A very pretty marble groupe by Cosmo, of the virgin Mary with the child Jesus in her arms, and John the Baptist kissing his feet. **1796** MORSE *Amer. Geog.* II. 557 Besides the temple are various images and groupes..cut in the stone. **1833** MISS MITFORD in L'Estrange *Life* (1870) III. i. 2 They even work groups of figures in tent stitch for screens. **1848** MRS. JAMESON *Sacr. & Leg. Art* (1850) 100 The group in one corner, of a child starting from a dog, is admired for its truth. *fig.* **1816** F. H. NAYLOR *Hist. Germany* II. xxv. 524 It has so often been my task to delineate scenes of bloodshed and desolation, that it is hardly possible any longer to transpose the groupe, or vary the colours.

b. *Mus.* (See quots.)

[**1674**, etc.: see GRUPPO.] **1727–51** CHAMBERS *Cycl.* s.v., In music, a Group is one of the kinds of diminutions of long notes, which in the writing forms a sort of group, or cluster. The group usually consists of four crotchets, quavers, or semiquavers, tied together, at the discretion of the composer. **1876** STAINER & BARRETT *Dict. Mus. Terms, Group*, (1) a series of notes, of small time-value, grouped together; a division or run. (2) The method of setting out band parts in score.

c. *Arch.* (See quot.)

1731 BAILEY vol. II, *Group*, in Architecture, a term used of columns, as they say, a group of columns, when there are three or four columns joined together on the same pedestal.

d. A set of letters used in coding.

1911 *Encycl. Brit.* XXV. 72/2 Each word or 'group' sent by the Morse code must be 'answered' before the sender passes on to another... All cipher 'groups' are repeated *en bloc*. **1916** T. E. LAWRENCE *Lett.* (1938) 211, I don't suppose my wire of conditions in Feisul's camp will get through for some days yet, as it is a long one of about 400 groups. **1966** M. R. D. FOOT *SOE in France* ix. 241 A suspicious-minded staff officer noticed both coded telegrams had the same number of groups.

2. *gen.* An assemblage of persons, animals, or material things, standing near together, so as to form a collective unity; a knot (of people), a cluster (of things). In early use the word often conveys a notion of confused aggregation, which in recent use is not implied.

a. of persons.

1748 CHESTERF. *Lett.* (1792) II. cxlvii. 117 You will find, in every groupe of company two principal figures, viz. the fine Lady, and the fine Gentleman. **1769** MRS. BROOKE *Emily Montague* (1784) IV. cxciii. 44 Were you here.. we should be the happiest groupe on the globe. **1803** E. HAY *Insurr. Wexford* 134 As the different groupes thus collected were perceived by the yeomanry, these pursued and cut them down. **1826** J. F. COOPER *Mohicans* (1829) II. vi. 85 They stood, clustered in a dark and savage groupe. **1863** GEO. ELIOT *Romola* i, The notary turned and left the group with a look of indignant contempt. **1897** *Cavalry Tactics* xii. 61 To compare the merits of the two systems taught in textbooks, viz. the cordon or continuous line, and the method of cossack posts or groups.

b. of things, *esp.* natural objects.

1736 BOLINGBROKE *Patriot.* (1749) 236 Nothing was to be seen but a confused groupe of mis-shapen, and imperfect forms. **1759** B. MARTIN *Nat. Hist. Eng.* I. *Cornwall* 4 It consists of a groupe of Rocks. **1807** G. CHALMERS *Caledonia* I. I. ii. 72 *note*, Smaller Carns, scattered, at different distances, generally in groupes of eight, or ten together. **1830** HERSCHEL *Stud. Nat. Phil.* 240 The accidental fracture of a fine groupe of crystals. **1841** W. SPALDING *Italy & It. Isl.* I. 318 Elba..belongs to the group of Corsica and Sardinia. **1848** W. H. BARTLETT *Egypt to Pal.* xv. (1879) 319 Two or three large mountain groups were in sight. **1851** CARPENTER *Man. Phys.* (ed. 2) 424 The Pancreas..presents itself in the condition of a group of prolonged follicles. **1872** RAYMOND *Statist. Mines & Mining* 131 The lodes referred to compose the westerly group. **1885** LEUDESDORF *Cremona's Proj. Geom.* 149 The same is therefore true of the groups of points in which these pencils are cut by the transversal.

c. *spec.* A group of hits made by a series of shots fired at a target; = *shot group*.

1911 *Encycl. Brit.* XXVI. 419/2 The position of his shot group with reference to the bull's-eye does not matter; if his group is comprised within a 6 or 12-inch ring (at 100 yards range) he is passed on to more advanced practices at service targets. **1913** A. G. FULTON *Notes on Rifle Shooting* 27 If the rifle gradually or suddenly..changes to a lower or higher group, there is no doubt that some adjustment is necessary to the bands or fore-ends. **1958** J. A. BARLOW *Elem. Rifle Shooting* (ed. 5) i. 4 When the firer is satisfied that the rifle is maintaining a good group under these conditions, a more severe test must be applied, since some rifles shoot very nicely when cold, but tend to throw a more scattered group when hot.

3. A number of persons or things regarded as forming a unity on account of any kind of mutual or common relation, or classed together on account of a certain degree of similarity.

a. of persons.

1782 W. COWPER *Poems* I. 6 But where, good Sir, do you confine your kings? There—said his guide, the groupe is full in view. **1807** [see FAMILY *sb.* 9a]. **1809–10** COLERIDGE *Friend* (1837) III. 187 As the modes of error are endless, the hundred forms of polytheism had each its groupe of partizans. **1872** BAGEHOT *Physics & Pol.* (1876) 213 Man can only make progress in co-operative groups. **1891** *Speaker* 11 July 36/1 Any group of 50,000 citizens will thus be able to force the Federal Chambers to deal with any matter. **1935** HUXLEY & HADDON *We Europeans* iii. 104 It follows that practically all human groups are of decidedly mixed origin. **1970** E. D. CHAPPLE *Culture & Biological Man* xv. 307 During the struggle, life crises occur and, afterward, rites of passage..are necessary mediators to re-establish the equilibrium of the group.

b. of things.

At Oxford University the subjects of the Final (Pass) examination for the degree of B.A. are classified into 'groups', called respectively 'Group A', 'Group B', etc. Hence 'to read for groups' is colloquially used for 'to study with a view to taking a pass degree'.

1729 SAVAGE *Wanderer* ii. 200 A Mirror in one Hand collective shows, Varied and multiplied, that Group of Woes. **1748** HARTLEY *Observ. Man* I. iii. 381 The Power of recollecting a large Groupe of Words. **1852** DISRAELI *Sel. Sp.* (1882) I. 419 The question naturally divided itself into several groups—if I may use a word now familiar to us. **1871** RUSKIN *Fors Clav.* I. i. 3 We begin to-day another group of ten years, not in happy circumstances. **1892** WESTCOTT *Gospel of Life* 101 Natural groups of religions and natural groups of languages are generally coincident. **1899** *Speaker* 16 Dec. 289/2 No better text-book could be given to a young man intent upon taking his groups in the Oxford Schools.

c. Specific senses in *Chem.*: (i) In qualitative analysis, a set of ions or radicals the presence of at least one of which in a presumed mixture of compounds can be ascertained by a single test specific for that set, provided that a standard procedure is followed; *esp.* any such set of the more usual cations which are precipitated from solution together in the course of analysis.

1843 J. L. BULLOCK tr. *Fresenius's Elem. Instr. Chem. Anal.* I. iii. 77 To teach the relation of the various bodies to reagents, it is usual..to treat of the substances individually ..and to point out their characteristic reactions. I have, however,..deemed it more judicious..to collect into groups those substances which are in many respects analogous. *Ibid.* 82 The solutions of the salts of the alkaline earths are ..not precipitated by sulphuretted hydrogen,..but alkaline carbonates and phosphates do precipitate them. This relation distinguishes the oxides of the second group [*sc.* barytes, strontian, lime, magnesia] from those of the first [*sc.* potash, soda, ammonia]. *Ibid.* II. ii. 257 If, therefore, we add to our solution..Hydrochloric acid, we remove from the solution the metallic oxides of the first section of the fifth group. **1869** HARCOURT & MADAN *Exercises Pract. Chem.* 250 The chlorides, iodides, nitrates, &c. are also classed together in one group, as having the common property of not being precipitated from aqueous solutions by barium chloride. **1888** A. H. SEXTON *Outl. Qual. Anal.* II. 24 The metals..are classified for analytical purposes into six groups —not according to their natural affinities, but according to their behaviour with certain reagents. The number of divisions adopted, and the exact lines of demarcation vary. **1938** *Thorpe's Dict. Appl. Chem.* (ed. 4) II. 551/1 The filtrate from the foregoing sulphides should be examined thoroughly as to the complete precipitation of all metals of analytical Group II. **1957** H. HOLNESS *Adv. Inorg. Qual. Anal.* 35 The case of platinum appearing in this Group of elements is of some interest for it is only precipitated here when selenium is present as well.

(ii) One of the sets of elements which show some similarity in chemical and physical properties and which are commonly represented in a column of the periodic table.

Nine groups are now recognized, numbered O–VIII, which represent the eight groups of Mendeleev's revised periodic table (1871) with the addition of the noble gases. Groups I–VII are each divided into two sub-groups in which the similarity in properties is more marked.

[**1863** J. A. R. NEWLANDS in *Chem. News* 7 Feb. 71 Many chemists..have..pointed out some very interesting relations between the equivalents of bodies belonging to the same natural family or group. *Ibid.*, Group I. Metals of the alkalies:—Lithium, 7; sodium, 23; potassium, 39; rubidium, 85; cæsium, 123; thallium, 204... Group II. Metals of the alkaline earths:—Magnesium, 12; calcium, 20; strontium, 43·8; barium, 68·5... Group VII.—Nitrogen, 14; phosphorus, 31; arsenic, 75; osmium, 99·6; antimony, 120·3; bismuth, 213... Group XI.—Mercury, 100; lead, 103·7; silver, 108.] **1871** H. E. ROSCOE *Less. Elem. Chem.* (new ed.) xxv. 278 We have the carbon group, the nitrogen group,.. that of the alkaline metals, and that of the metals of the alkaline earths. **1922** J. W. MELLOR *Inorg. & Theoret. Chem.* I. vi. 258 The valency of the elements shows a peculiar relation, for the maximum valency rises from 1 to 8 in passing along a given series from the first to the last group. **1950** N. V. SIDGWICK *Chem. Elements* I. 11 Hydrogen..was one of the chief problems of the original Periodic Table, since it has close affinities both with the alkali metals of Group I and with the halogens of Group VII. **1952** T. MOELLER *Inorg. Chem.* xix. 859 The sulfides of the Group IIb elements are water insoluble. **1959** R. A. SMITH *Semiconductors* iii. 61 (*heading*) Energy levels of group III or group V impurities in group IV semiconductors. **1963** J. HICKS *Compreh. Chem.* xiii. 247 Elements in the same group usually have the same valency.

(iii) Any combination of atoms (usually composed of more than one element) which, being recognizable in a number of compounds and persisting through a series of chemical changes, is regarded as a distinct entity.

1869 HARCOURT & MADAN *Exercises in Pract. Chem.* I. v. 140 In many cases a group of two or more elements appears to be more easily detached from a substance than the individual elements; the substance, like a crystal, cleaving more easily in some directions than in others. **1894** G. S. NEWTH *Text-bk. Inorg. Chem.* iv. 22 It is some-times necessary to represent the presence in a molecule of certain groups of atoms, groups which seem to hold together, and often to function as a single atom. **1962** D. H. CALAM in A. Pirie *Lens Metabolism Rel. Cataract* 439 At the low pH employed, only strongly acidic groups remain charged, most of the carboxyl groups are unionized.

d. One of the constituent bodies of the (*Oxford*) *Group(s) Movement* (or *Oxford Group*), a religious revivalist movement brought from America to England in 1921 by Frank Buchman, characterized by the 'sharing' of personal problems by groups. Hence '**Grouper**, '**Groupist**, a member of the movement; '**Groupism**, the principles of the movement; '**groupy** *a.* (used disparagingly). Cf. BUCHMANISM, *Moral Rearmament* s.v. MORAL *a.* 7f.

[**1923** H. BEGBIE *Life Changers* iv. 101 A group soon formed in his room of men who really longed for spiritual life... F.B. [*sc.* Frank Buchman]..sent him over to Oxford ..to begin there a similar work of personal religion.] **1928** *Isis* 16 May 1/1 Attendance at several of them [*sc.* meetings] is a preliminary step to admission to a 'group'—a gathering of perhaps four or five friends... Here..souls are laid bare by hysterical confession, and with a fervour which no longer pretends to be religious the tenets of the doctrine are discussed. *Ibid.* 25/1 Buchmanism, to give the Group its popular name, bases the whole of Christianity on four points —Honesty, Unselfishness, Purity and Love. *Ibid.* 24 May 34/1 In three of the Societies, no group meetings had been held. **1931** *A Group Speaks* iii. 100 What I owe to the Cambridge Group can never be estimated. **1932** A. J. RUSSELL *For Sinners Only* viii. 109 The well-dressed Doctor of Divinity..founder of the Oxford Group. *Ibid.* 116 A kindly and fruitful worker in the Oxford Group Movement. *Ibid.* 118 The Thursday night Group meeting. **1933** H. H. HENSON *Oxford Groups* 7 Religion—unless all the masters of the spiritual life throughout Christian history are mistaken —is not quite so cheerful a matter as these gay, almost uproarious teams of missioning Groupists affirm. *Ibid.* 9 A religious system like Groupism, which appears to be mainly adapted to the needs of adolescents, can hardly have much staying power. *Ibid.* 15, I have read as many publications of the Groups Movement as I could. *Ibid.* 24 The movement commonly designated, though rather misleadingly, 'The Oxford Group Movement', of which the founder and director is an American Lutheran minister named Frank Buchman. **1934** R. MACAULAY *Going Abroad* v. 49 The next thing will be..you'll go groupy. *Ibid.* xx. 160 The eyes of the Oxford Groupers brightened. *Ibid.* xxiv. 201 A cheerful company—the four Groupers. *Ibid.* xxix. 252 There is a book the Groupists all seem to recommend and like called *Inspired Children.* **1937** W. H. AUDEN in Auden & MacNeice *Lett. fr. Iceland* xiii. 203, I am no Grouper, I will never share With any prig. **1937** F. T. JESSE *Act of God* xiii. 163 'Oxford Groupers?' said Erskine vaguely. 'Oh yes. They're harmless people, I believe, though rather bright and jolly.' **1939** *Times* 7 Mar. 15/5 Again, not by any means all of our youth are represented by those who frequent mass meetings, 'go all groupy', and discuss with great emotion topics on which, by the nature of things, they can be but very inadequately informed. **1940** GRAVES & HODGE *Long Week-end* xii. 205 One of the Groupist songs. **1959** *Chambers's Encycl.* VI. 604/1 The organization in Great Britain was incorporated in 1939 as the Oxford Group... Its object is to 'change lives' by the power of Christ. *Ibid.*, The Cambridge Group Movement, no longer in existence, was a fellowship of young methodists which in the 1930s adopted many of the principles and methods of the Buchmanite movement in a less extreme form. **1961** [see BUCHMANISM].

e. An air-fleet or division of an air-fleet; *spec.* one in the Royal Air Force.

1922 *Times* 15 Feb. 14/5 The Officer Commanding Irak Group is directly responsible to the Air Ministry for the command and administration of the Air Force units located in Irak. **1939** *War Illustr.* 29 Dec. 538/2 A Squadron in the R.A.F...is the basic tactical unit, a number of Squadrons forming a Wing, so many Wings a Group, and so to the Command. **1942** T. RATTIGAN *Flare Path* I. 114 Been a bit of a muck-up at Group. *Maudie.* What's Group? *Dusty.* Group headquarters. Where the orders come from. **1959** *Chambers's Encycl.* I. 189/1 The main formations of the R.A.F. are the flight, the squadron, the wing and the group.

f. An ensemble of popular musicians; = *pop group*.

1958 in *Conc. Oxf. Dict.* Add., Skiffle group. **1964** *Gramophone Pop. Record Catal.* (Artist Section) Dec. 44/1 *Barron-Knights, The...* Call up the groups. Medley. **1967** *Melody Maker* 27 May 9 Groups who are going to give us action. **1967** *Listener* 20 July 80/1 It is an eye to detail.. which keeps the group on its toes.

g. Any of several international committees having common economic interests, as ***Group of Five***, consisting of financial representatives of the five major non-Communist economic powers of Great Britain, the United States, Japan, West Germany, and France; ***Group of 77*** (see quot. 1968); ***Group of Ten***, consisting of ten of the main industrial member nations of the IMF, which have undertaken to lend the Fund money when necessary in order to bolster the international monetary system. Cf. G III.

1963 *Internat. Financial News Survey* (IMF) 11 Oct. XV. 351/1 The following statement was issued on October 2 on behalf of the 'Group of Ten' members of the International Monetary Fund. **1964** *Ann. Reg. 1963* 472 A fresh initiative ..was taken by the 'Group of Ten'—the governments which had banded together in a mutual credit arrangement..to supplement the resources of The International Monetary Fund. **1968** B. GOSOVIC in *Internat. Conciliation* May DLXVIII. 14 There are three distinct sets of actors in UNCTAD: the Group of 77, composed of developing countries; the B Group, composed of Western developed states; and the D Group, composed of the socialist countries of Eastern Europe. The Group of 77 was never constituted formally, but the Joint Declaration of the Developing Countries at the 1963 session of the General Assembly can be considered as the Group's official appearance, and the Joint Declaration of the Seventy-Seven Developing Countries made at the conclusion of the Geneva Conference as its first birthday. **1977** *Economist* 26 Nov. 92/1 The *Group of 5* is made up of the largest economies (United States, Japan, West Germany, France, Britain). **1983** *Listener* 27 Jan. 5/1 The principle of self-determination, though enshrined in the UN Charter, is subordinated by the Group of 77 (the Third World) and the Communist powers to the spirit of anti-colonialism. **1986** *Times* 20 Jan. 21/1 The Group of Five finance ministers of the biggest industrial market economies..have been meeting at No 11, Downing Street. **1986** Group of Ten [see *G10* s.v. G III f].

4. a. *esp.* in scientific classification. Chiefly used as an indefinite term for any classificatory division whatever its relative rank (so, e.g., in *Zoology*), though in various branches of natural science attempts have been made to appropriate the term to some one particular grade of classification.

In *Botany*, e.g., Lindley applied the word to a grade intermediate in comprehension between *alliance* and *sub-class*; but in a later work he discarded this use.

1826 KIRBY & SP. *Entomol.* IV. 390, I would..propose the following primary and subordinate divisions of an Order: 1. Suborder; 2. Section..8. Genus; 9. Subgenus. I would further propose that each of these successive groups should have a name always terminating alike. **1826** [see AXINE]. **1859** DARWIN *Orig. Spec.* ii. (1873) 47 The forms of life throughout the universe become divided into groups subordinate to groups. **1859** *Amer. Cycl.* III. 282/1 The mining birds compose a very large group, belonging to nearly every order, and having no other common peculiarity. **1892** GARDINER *Student's Hist. Eng.* 5 A group of races sometimes known as the Aryan group.

b. In *Stratigraphy*: formerly, any of various categories into which rocks were classified and which would now correspond to the following modern geological time units: (i) Period (in some systems also Epoch); (ii) Age; (iii) Era. (iv) In modern use: a stratigraphic unit consisting of two or more formations.

(i) **1830** H. T. DE LA BECHE *Geol. Notes* p. xxxv, The superior stratified or fossiliferous rocks are divided into groups. *Ibid.* p. xxxvi, Group 3. (Supercretaceous)... Group 4. (Cretaceous). **1838** C. LYELL *Elem. Geol.* xiii. 281, I proposed to give short technical names to these four groups [*sc.* Eocene, Miocene, Older Pliocene, Newer Pliocene], or the periods to which they respectively belonged. **1893** *Jrnl. Geol.* I. 187 De la Beche..carries out the system more completely, calling the first, or superior order, Supercretaceous group, and applying the terms Cretaceous, Oölitic and Red sandstone to three groups into which he divides the second order, and giving the third the name Carboniferous group.

(ii) **1883** G. K. GILBERT in *Nature* XXVII. 261 The term ..group, which by the..Bologna Congress was made more comprehensive than system, is by Geikie used as the equivalent of stage. **1912** A. J. JUKES-BROWNE *Student's Handbk. Stratigr. Geol.* (ed. 2) i. 11 Systems are divided into sections or formations... These sections are again divided into stages or groups.., and these again are often divisible into zones.

(iii) **1883** [see sense (ii)]. **1898** *Jrnl. Geol.* VI. 353 The terms, Group, System, Series, Stage, and the correlative time-divisions, Era, Period, Epoch, Age, are to my mind very satisfactory. **1927** LAKE & RASTALL *Text-bk. Geol.* (ed. 4) xvi. 299 In this way the rocks of the earth's crust have been divided into four great divisions, which are often known as groups. The groups are subdivided into systems, the systems into series, and the series into stages.

(iv) **1933** *Bull. Geol. Soc. Amer.* XLIV. 429 Article 2. The following divisions or units of rocks are recognized:..(3) Group, a local or provincial subdivision of a system, based on lithologic features. It is usually less than a standard series and contains two or more formations. **1963** KRUMBEIN & SLOSS *Stratigr. & Sedim.* (ed. 2) ii. 33 Two or more successive formations, related by lithology or by position with reference to unconformities, may be assembled as a group.

5. *Math.* **a.** Orig., a set or system of operations so constituted that the product of any number of these operations is always itself a member of the 'group'. Now more generally defined as: A set of elements, together with a single-valued associative binary operation, which is closed with respect to the operation and contains an inverse for each element and an identity element. (Except for the property of being closed these properties were formerly tacitly assumed.) [The sense is due to E. Galois, who used F. *groupe* (*Bull. d. Sciences math., astron.*, etc. (1830) XIII. 435).]

1854 CAYLEY *Math. Papers* (1889) II. 124 A set of symbols 1, α, β,..all of them different, and such that the product of any two of them..or the product of any one of them into itself, belongs to the set, is said to be a group. *Note.* The idea of a group as applied to permutations or substitutions is due to Galois. **1893** FORSYTH *Theory Functions* 610 The Fuchsian groups conserve a line, the axis of x, or a circle, the fundamental circle; the Kleinian groups do not conserve such a line or circle, common to the group. **1907** M. BÔCHER *Introd. Higher Algebra* vi. 82 The positive and negative integers with zero form a group if the rule of combination is addition... These same elements, however, do not form a group if the rule of combination is multiplication,..since zero has no reciprocal. **1941** BIRKHOFF & MACLANE *Surv. Mod. Algebra* vi. 130 A group whose operation satisfies the commutative law is called a 'commutative' or 'Abelian' group. **1958** SYKES & BELL tr. *Landau & Lifshitz's Quantum Mech.* xii. 317 The set of all symmetry transformations for a given body is called its symmetry transformation group (or simply its symmetry group). **1965** PATTERSON & RUTHERFORD *Elem. Abstract Algebra* ii. 31 Any element of a group S can be expressed in one and only one way in the form $a \wedge x$, where a is a fixed element of the group. **1969** A. P. CRACKNELL *Crystals* ii. 65 All the operations of this type, combinations of a point-group operation and a lattice translation are said to make up a space group, and it is really a space group which is needed to describe the symmetry of a real crystal.

b. group theory, a branch of algebra concerned with the properties of groups and their applications, esp. in mathematical physics (e.g. to the investigation of symmetries in physical systems).

1898 *Proc. Calif. Acad. Sci.* (ser. 3: Maths-Physics) I. IV. 29 In the application of group theory to problems of geometry and analysis, simple groups play the fundamental rôle. **1919** F. CAJORI *Hist. Math.* (ed. 2) 335 A line-geometry and kinematics are elaborated, partly by the use of group theory, which are carried over to non-Euclidean spaces. **1965** J. C. DAVIS *Adv. Physical Chem.* iii. 75 The student of quantum mechanics and spectroscopy will find the structure of group theory beautiful and its utility exciting.

6. *attrib.* and *Comb.*, as ***group-burial***, ***-firing***, ***-formation***, ***-name***, ***-photograph***, ***-portrait***, ***-system***, ***-table***; **Group Areas Act** (see quots.); **group captain**, a rank in the Royal Air Force equivalent to colonel in the army; **group dialect**, distinctive language used by members of a group sharing the same occupation or interests; so **group language**; **group-flashing**, the repeated emission of a set group or pattern of flashes by a lighthouse; also *attrib.*; **group genitive** (see quot. 1957); **group language** (see *group dialect* above); **group (life) assurance** or **insurance** (see quot. 1927); **group-marriage**, a primitive form of familial relationship hypothesized by some anthropologists in which certain groups within a tribe were considered husbands and wives; also *transf.*; **group-order** *Naut.* (see quot.); **group-person**, a person belonging to or drawn from a special set of people; **group practice**, a medical practice in which several doctors are associated; **group-rate**, a rate of railway fare applicable to each one of a group of stations; **group-spring**, *U.S.*, a car-spring, composed of several spiral springs in a nest; **group velocity**, the speed at which the energy of a wave or wave-group travels: so called because if the sinusoidal components of a wave-group do not differ greatly in frequency, the group-velocity is the speed at which the group as a whole travels; **group-verb** (see quots.); **group-wise** *adv.*, (performed) by groups; **group-word** (see quot.); **group work** (see quots.).

1952 L. MARQUARD *Peoples & Policies S. Afr.* vii. 152 In 1950 the *Group Areas Act was passed empowering the Government to declare any area a group area for Coloured, European, African, or Asian. **1957** *Encycl. Brit.* XXII. 426/2 The Group Areas act of 1950 was one of a series of acts which sought to implement Smuts's Natives Land act of 1913, which checked the penetration of natives into European areas and vice versa. **1920** H. DOUGHARTY *Pension, Endowment, Life Assurance* xi. 52 The following features of *Group Assurance are common to practically all Group Policies—1. The insurance is effected by the employer on the lives of his employees. **1932** *Times* 12 Feb. 11/1 The significance of this unique *group-burial must remain a mystery. **1920** *Group captain [see *air officer*, AIR *sb.*[1] B. III. 3]. **1922** *Man. Seamanship* I. i. 11 Marks of Rank. .. R.A.F... Group Captain. R.N... Captain. **1923** *Daily Mail* 13 Feb. 9 Group-captain in the Air Force. **1934** PRIEBSCH & COLLINSON *German Lang.* II. v. 260 We propose to use the term '*group dialects' as the equivalents of the German *Sondersprachen* and French *Langues spéciales*. The word contrasts with 'regional dialects'. **1959** I. & P. OPIE *Lore & Lang. Schoolch.* viii. 152 'Pax' is group dialect not regional dialect. **1896** *Daily News* 6 Aug. 7/2 The garrison *group-firing competition at a moving target proceeded in the afternoon. **1891** A. G. FINDLAY *Lighthouses of World* Add. facing p. 32, Its [*sc.* electric light's] range, definition, and, where a distinctive character is employed as **Group-Flashing*, its unmistakable superiority to all other modes of Illumination, pronounce its excellence and pre-eminence. **1911** *Encycl. Brit.* XVI. 629/1 The 12 lens panels are arranged in groups of two, thus producing a group flashing light. **1958** R. DE KERCHOVE *Internat. Maritime Dict.* (ed. 2) 310/2 *Group flashing light*, a light showing at regular intervals a group of two or more flashes. **1894** O. JESPERSEN *Progress in Lang.* viii. 306 It will not be easy to lay down fully definite and comprehensive rules for determining in which cases the *group genitive is allowable and in which the *s* has to be affixed to each member. **1927** *Rev. Eng. Studies* Oct. 438 There are other practical problems of syntax... One might instance the Split Infinitive, and the modern development of the group genitive. **1957** R. W. ZANDVOORT *Handbk. Eng. Gram.* II. 91 The genitive-suffix is always added to the last element of a word-group: *the Prince of Wales's birthday*, *Miss Mansfield's wedding*. This is known as the group-genitive. **1934** PRIEBSCH & COLLINSON *German Lang.* II. v. 262 Like all *group languages student slang has a number of different designations for the people and things most familiar in student life. **1964** C. BARBER *Present-Day Eng.* iii. 68 The importance of a special group-language in promoting feelings of cohesion can easily be seen. **1913** *Craftsman* Sept. 652/1 A new and progressive form of life insurance has recently been developed, which is of interest to every employer of labor and every employee. '*Group insurance' it is called, and by its means an employer is able to insure the lives of those who work for him at a much less cost than would be possible if each employee were to become individually insured. **1928** *Daily Mail* 25 July 19/5 Group Insurance came into existence only seventeen years ago and it took seven years for all companies to accumulate as much Group Life Assurance as this one contract. **1964** G. L. COHEN *What's Wrong with Hospitals?* v. 103 Nor do large firms relish the idea of highly paid men frittering hours away: hence the marked spread of professional and industrial group insurance. **1920** H. DOUGHARTY *Pension, Endowment, Life Assurance* xi. 51 *Group Life Assurance, introduced by an American Life Office some four years ago, is a non-contributory system of Staff Life Assurance. **1927** B. C. HOSKINS *Insurance Lex.* 105 Group Life Assurance. —Under this contract groups or numbers of lives are assured instead of individuals. **1880** *Group marriage [see MARRIAGE 1 d]. **1899** A. H. KEANE *Man Past & Present* v. 153 Here it is necessary to distinguish carefully between *class*-marriages and the so-called 'communal' or 'group' marriages. **1906** *Westm. Gaz.* 13 Aug. 10/1 Dr. J. W. Gregory, in his 'Dead Heart of Australia'..includes them [*sc.* the Aborigines] in the same race-group as ourselves.. and reminds us that their system of 'group marriage' was prevalent in Britain at the time of Julius Cæsar's invasion. **1921** E. WESTERMARCK *Hist. Human Marriage* (ed. 5) I. vii. 268 Even if it were worth while inventing such a society in the interest of the cherished institution of group marriage, it would be impossible to find mothers who were equally ignorant of their chldren as the children were of their mothers. *Ibid.* III. xxxi. 260 Nor can the hypothesis that it [*sc.* the classificatory system] is an indication of group-marriage or sexual communism be accepted as even probably correct. **1937** R. H. LOWIE *Hist. Ethnol. Theory* viii. 88 Morgan had suggested a stage of group-marriage. **1957** AUDEN & KALLMAN *Magic Flute* 60 Whether they live in air-borne nylon cubes, Practise group-marriage or are fed through tubes. **1902** *Folk-Lore* XIII. 386 It appears to me that *group-names may, originally, have been imposed *from without*. **1935** *Discovery* Sept. 253/1 *Arya* has been used.. as a religious group-name, to distinguish the worshippers of the gods of the Brahmans from the worshippers of certain other Indian deities. **1968** *Times* 13 Mar. 11/5 Surnames are group names which subdivide the Johns and Jameses into.. Smiths,..&c. **1882** NARES *Seamanship* (ed. 6) 114 A fleet is said to be in *group order when the ships composing each group are so placed as to be able at once to assume group formation in whatever manner the fleet may be disposed, with the ships in line. **1898** MAITLAND *Township & Boro.* 15 Oxford and Cambridge are peopled by '*group-persons'. **1918** W. OWEN *Let.* c 9 June (1967) 558 Preserve me from.. plush chairs, *group-photographs, flowers under glass-shades. **1935** J. JOYCE *Let.* 18 Jan. (1966) III. 342 Send me a group photograph like the last lovely one we had taken. **1937** H. READ *Art & Society* iv. 171 There had grown up in Holland..a custom of commissioning group-portraits—just as we still commission group-photographs of..wedding parties—and Rembrandt was not above undertaking such a commission. **1942** *Lancet* 19 Sept. 345/1 *Group practice was defined here as referring to general practitioner practice only. **1947** *Jrnl. Amer. Med. Assoc.* 6 Dec. 904/1 (*heading*) Medical group practice in the United States. **1954** S. TAYLOR *Good General Practice* iv. 90 It is useful to begin by testing the hypothesis that group practice is inherently better than individual practice. *Ibid.* 93 True group practice is comparatively rare. **1958** *New Statesman* 18 Oct. 530/2 The development of health centres and group practice has been much too slow, and the education of general practitioners barely touches on..social medicine and thus offers no training for over two-thirds of their future work. **1961** *Brit. Med. Dict.* 1152/1 *Group practice*, the co-operation of several medical practitioners, usually in partnership, for the diagnosis of and treatment of patients. Frequently, one partner specializes in medicine, another in surgery, etc. **1968** *Guardian* 6 May 7/2 There are strong incentives to form group practices. **1888** *Act 51 & 52 Vict.* c. 25 §29 Provided that the distances shall not be unreasonable, and that the *group rates charged and the places grouped together shall not be such as to create an undue preference. **1897** *Cavalry Tactics* xii. 62 The cossack post, or *group system, consists in placing small detached posts, of a double or single vedette, with reliefs, commanded by a n.-c. officer, on all avenues of approach from the enemy. **1866** ODLING *Anim. Chem.* 35 As shown in the *group-tables to which I have already adverted. **1887** *Proc. Inst. Mech. Engin.* Aug. 426 Calculate out the result from the law that the *group-velocity is half the wave-velocity—the velocity of a group of waves at sea is half the velocity of the individual waves. **1948** MOTT & SNEDDON *Wave Mech. & its Applications* i. 24 The group and wave velocities are equal only if the wave velocity is independent of frequency (as for light in a vacuum). **1892** H. SWEET *New Eng. Gram.* I. 138 We may regard *pass-by* and *run-across* in such constructions as *group-verbs, logically equivalent to such simple transitive verbs as *pass* and *cross* in *he passed the house, he crossed the road.* **1924** H. E. PALMER *Gram. Spoken Eng.* II. 169 Some adverbs are so intimately associated with verbs that such combinations may be considered as group-verbs. **1963** F. T. VISSER *Hist. Syntax* I. iv. 407 Prepositional object after such group-verbs as *break in upon, look out for.* **1901** E. A. ROSS *Social Control* 29 The fittest to survive when the competition is man-wise, may be eliminated when the competition is *group-wise. **1953** C. E. BAZELL *Linguistic Form* vi. 73 (Type *queen of France's son*). This abnormality led to the whole group (e.g. *queen of France*) being taken as a word, albeit of a special kind ('*group-word'). **1941** J. S. HUXLEY *Uniqueness of Man* xi. 233 We may distinguish such [joint] work from true *group work, using the term group in the sense of a body of people pooling their different knowledges and skills to cope with quantitatively differentiated problems. **1958** *Times* 6 Sept. 10/2 Another attractive group-work is the huge 'Wise Man' (Hornsey High School). **1959** *Gloss. Terms Work Study (B.S.I.)* 24 *Group work*, work done by a number of workers in close association, each worker contributing towards a completed unit of production. **1970** *New Society* 5 Mar. 401/1 Social group work is a tool to solve external problems and is based on activity, discussion and again action.

b. *Social Sciences.* In many *Combs.* in which *group* means 'a group of people, esp. a social group or community', as ***group-action***, ***-analysis***, ***-attitude***, ***-behaviour***, ***-centred*** adj., ***-characteristic***, ***-conflict***, ***-consciousness***, ***-counselling***, ***-counsellor***, ***-discussion***, ***dynamics***, ***-experience***, ***-feeling***, ***-interest***, ***-life***, ***-living***, ***-loyalty***, ***-mate***, ***-membership***, ***-memory***, ***-mentality***, ***-migration***, ***-mind***, ***-norm***, ***-organization***, ***-person***, ***-personality***, ***psychiatry***, ***-psychologist***, ***psychology***, ***psychotherapy***, ***-sentiment***, ***-solidarity***, ***spirit***, ***status***, ***survival***, ***theory***, ***therapy***, ***-think***, ***-thinking***, ***-type***, ***-will***.

1931 *Times Lit. Suppl.* 20 Aug. 635/1 The work of Mr. Edmund Selous on *group-action in bird flocks recently reviewed by us. **1943** *Mind* LII. 228 The term 'I' could be said to be a sociological term, because it designates a class of group-actions. **1927** D. H. LAWRENCE *Let.* 3 Aug. (1932) 687, I must come and be present at your *group-analysis work one day. **1943** H. READ *Educ. through Art* vi. 198 Therefore, for the Freudian method of individual analysis, Dr. Burrow substitutes a method of group analysis, by which he does not mean an analysis of the group, but a 'phyletic principle of observation', that is to say, group activities which involve the group's analysis of any one of its component individuals. **1937** C. M. ARENSBERG *Irish Countryman* 116 For we are dealing.. with *group-attitudes reciprocally held. **1920** E. D. MARTIN *Behavior of Crowds* iv. 79 We would sit in chapel and hear a wrathful president denounce our *group behavior as 'boorishness and hoodlumism'. **1927** G. A. DE LAGUNA *Speech* xiv. 261 The adaptation of group-behaviour to the situation. **1959** *Times Lit. Suppl.* 27 Mar. 181/2 It is to cover.. biological reproduction, dynamic psychology, group-behaviour patterns, and so on. **1951** *Jrnl. Abnormal & Soc. Psychol.* XLVI. 521/1 This study is concerned with the effects of two contrasting group-leadership techniques—*group-centered ..and leader-centered. **1958** W. J. H. SPROTT *Human Groups* ix. 144 'Group-centred' ones [*sc.* groups], in which interaction was encouraged. **1944** KOESTLER in *Horizon* Mar. 162 Historically, it is.. the 'aspiration to independent thinking' which provides the only valid *group-characteristic of the intelligentsia. **1954** H. GIBBS *Background to Bitterness* 8 Nevertheless, the country contains many who fear that future *group-conflicts or racial conflict may occur within the next decade. **1915** A. HUXLEY *Let.* Dec. (1969) 87 All the men who are running the *Palatine*, who are infused with the Palatinate *group-consciousness, which is a good group-consciousness, are good men. **1951** R. FIRTH *Elem. Social Organiz.* iii. 115 In their own social and ceremonial life they display a strong group consciousness. **1957** H. READ *Tenth Muse* xxxi. 277 This quality may sometimes be due to some kind of collective intuition—the working of several minds to a common conception; the spontaneous overflow of a group consciousness. **1950** HAHN & MACLEAN *Gen. Clin. Counseling* i. 11 To talk of '*group counseling' and to imply that it is similar in structure and outcomes to one-to-one clinical counseling is as silly as talking about 'group courtship'. **1959** *News Chron.* 4 Dec. 7/5 Describing the experiment, known as 'group counselling', as 'the most important thing to happen in penology for a very long time', the report stresses that the discussions were spontaneous and wide. **1961** 'C. H. ROLPH' *Common Sense about Crime* ix. 144 In prisons and Borstals what is now called Group Counselling is now being developed... The technique in its modern form.. began at San Quentin prison in California. *Ibid.* 145 Selected members of the.. staff at San Quentin.. were doing the work of *group counsellors. **1912** C. H. COOLEY *Social Organiz.* (ed. 2) iii. 24 As regards play, I might.. multiply illustrations of the universality and spontaneity of the *group discussion and coöperation to which it gives rise. **1963** A. HERON *Towards Quaker View of Sex* v. 44 They may.. feel it necessary to initiate group discussion on sexual matters. **1953** A. K. C. OTTAWAY *Educ. & Society* 13 *Group dynamics is an excellent example of a subject which overlaps with sociology and psychology. **1959** G. D. MITCHELL *Sociol.* i. 23 This modern micro-sociological development, often called group dynamics. **1941** *Mind* L. 395 The members participating in a family meal round the same table share, each in his own way, in the *group-experience of eating together. **1945** A. L. ROWSE *Eng. Spirit* 46 Patriotism is a form of *group-feeling. **1904** *Group-interest [see COMMUNITARY *a.*]. **1931** A. L. ROWSE *Politics & Younger Generation* 232 The basic factors in society are the impersonal *blocs* of group-interest. **1902** *Amer. Jrnl. Sociol.* VIII. II. 189 In the case of the dyad and triad configurations, we had to do with that inner *group-life, with all its differences, syntheses, and antitheses. **1913** J. N. FIGGIS *Churches in Mod. State* 226 Facts so tremendous as the complex group-life which is to most of us more than the State. **1941** *Mind* L. 396 The group-life of the rural parish. **1951** *Essays in Criticism* I. 1 The literary problem must not be divorced from the problems of *group-living, in the widest sense, that lie behind it. **1958** HAYWARD & HARARI tr. *Pasternak's Dr. Zhivago* i. 18 It is always a sign of mediocrity in people when they herd together, whether their *group loyalty is to Solovyev or to Kant or Marx. **1927** *Mod. Philol.* XXV. 213 Successive actions of his *group-mates (parents, etc.).. 'condition' him to the social habits. **1949** M. MEAD *Male & Female* x. 205 He will very likely live longer than his more active group-mates. **1950** T. H. MARSHALL *Citizenship & Social Class* 105 My consciousness of age.. does not take the form of a feeling of *group-membership. **1923** J. S. HUXLEY *Ess. Biologist* i. 52 What may be called the '*group-memory'—the power of storing and rendering knowledge available. **1965** *Listener* 30 Sept. 491/1 Group memory.. is no more than the transmittal to many people of the memory of one man or a few men, repeated many times over. **1920** B. RUSSELL *Pract. & Theory Bolshevism* I. i. 19 The *group-mentality that Communism requires. **1960** P. H. REANEY *Orig. Eng. Place-Names* 103 This evidence of somewhat extensive *group migration is a matter of some importance to the historian and student of dialect. *a* **1899** D. G. BRINTON *Basis of Social Relations* (1902) I. ii. 28 The actual existence of the *group-mind can no more be denied than the constant inter-relation between it and the individual mind. **1960** *Times Lit. Suppl.* 20 May 323/4 We know that men may lose their individual identities.. by music and rhetoric, and that (as the careers of Dr. Goebbels and Senator McCarthy have shown) this state of group-mind can be stretched out over long periods. **1936** M. SHERIF *Psychol. Soc. Norms* vi. 105 If the leader changes his norm after the *group norm is settled he may cease thereupon to be followed. **1958** R. K. MERTON *Soc. Theory* 317 Departures from the strict definitions of group-norms. **1913** L. T. HOBHOUSE *Development & Purpose* x. 186 *Group-organisation becomes a system of peace and, on the whole, co-operation. **1940** H. READ *Annals of Innocence & Experience* III. 210 Such a society.. would give the individual the greatest degree of liberty consistent with a group organization. **1915** E. BARKER *Polit. Thought in England* 175 Permanent groups are themselves persons, *group-persons, with a group-will of their own. **1934** —— tr. *Gierke's Natural Law & Theory of Soc.* I. III. i. 81 In his [*sc.* Hobbes's] theory of corporations, as in his theory of the State, the central conception is that of the unity of *group-personality. **1942** L. B. NAMIER *Conflicts* 91 As members of a group-personality most people enjoy greater freedom from moral scruples and inhibitions. **1944** *Horizon* Jan. 79 Dr. Maxwell Jones, who is experimenting in *group-psychiatry. **1969** E. MCGIRR *Entry of Death* vi. 114 An interest in group psychiatry. **1933** H. G. WELLS *Shape of Things to Come* III. §5. 291 The new economists on the one hand and the *group psychologists on the other. **1920** W. MCDOUGALL *Group Mind* 8 *Group Psychology has, first, to establish the general principles of group life. **1949** KOESTLER *Insight & Outlook* xiii. 194 Its demonstrable connections with the phenomena of projection,.. group psychology, and so on. **1938** P. SCHILDER *Psychotherapy* x. 197, I shall try here to give a detailed description of a method of *group psychotherapy which I have employed.. in the out-patient department of Bellevue Hospital. **1948** *Sci. News* VIII. 106 Group psychotherapy.. implies that a group of patients is treated together rather than individually. **1970** *New Society* 5 Mar. 401/1 Group psychotherapy is based on '"free floating discussion"', the equivalent in the group of '"free association"' in the one-to-one psycho-analytic process'. **1935** HUXLEY & HADDON *We Europeans* i. 12 For the moment we will refer to the sentiment which animates tribal and national units alike, by the non-committal phrase '*group sentiment'. **1927** G. A. DE LAGUNA *Speech* xviii. 318 The importance of the celebration of tribal deeds in fostering *group-solidarity. **1951** M. MCLUHAN *Mech. Bride* 10/1 A very able person may often choose to freeze or anesthetize large areas of his mind and experience for the sake of.. the pleasures of group solidarity. **1920** W. MCDOUGALL *Group Mind* 63 The *group spirit, the idea of the group with the sentiment of devotion to the group developed in the minds of all its members. **1934** R. BENEDICT *Patterns of Culture* (1935) iv. 103 It [*sc.* initiation] makes the children valuable by giving them *group status. **1946** *Mind* LV. 45 It is quite possible that the community will develop a philosophical view that serves the end of *group survival. For example, this is what appears to be happening very rapidly in South Africa among the Afrikaans-speaking community ('the Dutch'). **1916** C. C. J. WEBB (*title*) *Group theories of religion and the individual. **1943** S. R. SLAVSON (*title*) An introduction to *group therapy. **1948** *Sci. News* VIII. 107 The first recorded use of group therapy was the experiment of Dr. J. H. Pratt in Boston [in 1905]. **1957** A. HUXLEY *Let.* 18 Nov. (1969) 830 Group therapy.. I personally wd try, if I got into a state of psychological distress. **1970** *Daily Tel.* 18 May 4/8 Group therapy is to be tried as a means of curbing bad driving in New York State under a three-year experimental plan to be started on June 1. **1959** *Sunday Times* 22 Nov. 9/6 The *group-think that is one of Chelsea's strongest assets, is also a source of weakness. **1969** D. E. WESTLAKE *Up your Banners* (1970) xxxvii. 266 If ever I'd seen a document that was the result of group-think, that was it. **1923** J. MACCURDY *Probl. Dynamic Psychol.* xxi. 324 This rationalization tendency points to the fact that we dislike the thought of not forming our own opinions and that there is some antagonism between individual, intellectual activity and acceptance of '*group thinking'. **1933** 'R. WEST' *St. Augustine* i. 18 This led inevitably to comic fatuities of the sort that Gibbon loved to mock, and to the depreciation of thought by the hasty and facile processes inevitable in group-thinking. **1903** E. A. ROSS in *Amer. Jrnl. Sociol.* VIII. 762 The hundred interlacing groups into which men combine, are the proper subject of study. This.. conception ..excuses us from showing.. how a *group-type or a group-will arises. **1939** V. A. DEMANT *Religious Prospect* iii. 66 Politics rapidly loses its character as the corporate attempt to embody a Natural Law and becomes increasingly a conflict of bare *group-wills.

group (gruːp), *v.* [f. the sb. Cf. F. *grouper*.]

1. a. *trans.* To make a group of, to form into a group; to place in a group *with* (something). Also ***to group together***.

Johnson 1755 gives the sense 'to put into a croud, to huddle together'. This meaning, if it existed, is now obs.; cf. GROUP *sb.* 2.

1754 FOOTE *Knights* Pref., Nor can I claim any other merit than grouping them together. *a* **1785** W. WHITEHEAD *On the Improvements at Nuneham* 29 Who thinn'd, and who group'd, and who scatter'd those trees. **1810** SCOTT *Lady of L.* I. xii, Fox-glove and night-shade, side by side, Grouped their dark hues with every stain, The weather-beaten rocks retain. **1853** KINGSLEY *Hypatia* xxii. 280 Peitho and the Graces retired a few steps, and grouped themselves with the Cyclops. **1855** BAIN *Senses & Int.* III. ii. §23 (1864) 500 We thus group in the mind a number of things not lying together in nature. **1894** J. T. FOWLER *Adamnan* Introd. 38 Scattered huts or cells grouped around a church or oratory.

b. *intr.* for *refl.* To form a group or part of a group; to gather in a group or groups.

1801 SOUTHEY *Thalaba* III. xxi, Home-birds, grouping at Oneiza's call. **1823** H. RAVELIN *Lucubrations* 349 The blazing watch fire, throwing its red glare upon the swarthy figures which danced or grouped in indolence around it. **1897** *19th Cent.* Aug. 218 Lord Tennyson when among us grouped with these.

2. a. *trans.* To dispose (colours, figures, etc.) with due regard to their mutual relations and subordination so as to form a harmonious whole. Also with *about*, *together*.

1718 PRIOR *Solomon* Pref., The difficulty lies in drawing and disposing, or (as the painters term it) in grouping such a multitude of different objects. **1753** HOGARTH *Anal. Beauty* 1 Almost every figure in them (how oddly soever they may seem to be group'd together). **1774** GOLDSM. *Nat. Hist.* (1776) IV. 116 Nature.. groupes her pictures. **1829** SCOTT *Let. to Earl Elgin* 20 Jan. in *Lockhart*, Six figures will form too many for a sculptor to group to advantage. **1848** DICKENS *Dombey* xxxi, Mrs. Miff, and Mr. Sownds the Beadle, group the party in their proper places at the altar rails. **1871** L. STEPHEN *Playgr. Europe* iii. (1894) 70 The architecture of nature displays.. such exquisite powers of grouping the various elements of beauty. **1889** GUNTER *That Frenchman* xvi, These hackmen.. are grouped about in picturesque attitudes.

b. *intr.* for *refl.*

1820 W. TAYLOR in *Monthly Rev.* XCIII. 64 Massinger is so much more modern than the other writers noticed in this lecture, that they do not groupe well together. **1871** FREEMAN *Norm. Conq.* (1876) IV. xviii. 211 The proud polygonal keep of the fortress still groups well with the soaring towers.

3. a. *trans.* To arrange in groups with reference to the presence of some common feature or property; to classify.

1862 H. SPENCER *First Princ.* II. i. §37 (1875) 131 Science concerns itself with the co-existences and sequences among phenomena; grouping these at first into generalizations of a low order [etc.]. **1869** MRS. SOMERVILLE *Molec. Sci.* I. i. 15 However numerous the crystalline forms assumed by substances.. may be, they are all capable of being grouped into geometrical systems. **1875** MANNING *Mission H. Ghost* xiii. 368 Having defined its doctrines, it assembles them and groups them together.

b. *Med.* To assign to a particular blood group; to determine the blood group of.

1936 *Brit. Med. Jrnl.* 28 Mar. 651/2 The patient's blood should in any case be grouped, so that an immediate transfusion may be given later if necessary. **1968** PASSMORE & ROBSON *Compan. Med. Stud.* I. xxvi. 19/2 With improved laboratory techniques and increased care in grouping and cross matching the blood of both patient and donor, reactions are now uncommon.

4. *intr.* Of shots from a fire-arm: to cluster about a point on the target; to form a compact shot group. Also, of a fire-arm or the firer: to fire shots which do this (*trans.* and *intr.*).

1900 W. W. GREENER *Sharpshooting* v. 84 Having learned so to shoot that all shots group closely, proceed by altering the sights to get the groups centrally placed upon the bull's-eye. **1911** *Encycl. Brit.* XXVI. 419/2 The use of the bull's-eye to-day is to teach the soldier to shoot uniformly, that is, to 'group' his shots closely. **1913** A. G. FULTON *Notes on Rifle Shooting* 28 It is often difficult to account for some beginners grouping right away and others proving almost hopeless. **1958** J. A. BARLOW *Elem. Rifle Shooting* (ed. 5) i. 2 The one and only essential in any rifle for competition purposes is that it should group within a certain predetermined maximum.

†**groupade.** *Obs.* Early variant of CROUPADE. (Cf. It. *groppata*.)

1656 BLOUNT *Glossogr.*, *Groupade.* **1671** SKINNER *Etym. Ling. Angl.* IV, *Grouppade*, a kind [of] Curvet in Horsmanship.

groupage (ˈgruːpɪdʒ). [f. GROUP *v.* + -AGE. Cf. F. *groupage*.] The arrangement of objects in a group or groups.

1850 B. TAYLOR *Eldorado* viii. (1862) 70 Whichever way I looked, my eye met the same enchanting groupage of the oaks. **1864** W. T. FOX *Skin Dis.* 23. **1887** W. G. PALGRAVE *Ulysses* 102 The cowed attitudes of the labourers, their groupage, in bands, each presided over by an official twice the ordinary human size.

grouped (gruːpt), *ppl. a.* [f. GROUP *v.* + -ED[1].] Arranged or situated in a group or groups, clustered; said both of material and immaterial things. ***grouped column, pillar***, etc. (see quots. and GROUP *sb.* 1 c). ***grouped rates*** = ***group rates*** (see GROUP *sb.* 6).

1702 W. J. *Bruyn's Voy. Levant* liv. 209 By Grouped Pillars are to be understood those large ones composed of several other small ones, which are united to each other, or rather one Massy Pillar, which in appearance seems to have the others fastned to it. **1770** FOOTE *Lame Lover* Prol., Wks. 1799 II. 53 If the group'd figures false connexions show. **1805–17** R. JAMESON *Char. Min.* (ed. 3) 176 Another accident, extremely common, is the manner in which grouped crystals are inserted into each other. **1851** RUSKIN *Stones Ven.* I. i. §28 Perhaps two or three pine trunks, used for a single pillar, gave the first idea of the grouped shaft. **1859** GWILT *Archit.* (ed. 4) Gloss., *Grouped Columns or Pilasters*, a term used to denote three, four or more columns placed upon the same pedestal. **1875** WHITNEY *Life Lang.* ii. 24 The non-identity and incommensurability of its shaped and grouped ideas. **1890** SAINTSBURY *Ess. Eng. Lit.* 20 The three parts of 'The Parish Register', the twenty-four Letters of 'The Borough', some of which have single, and others grouped subjects. **1897** *Daily News* 21 May 8/4 Through grouped rates from Paddington and its group of stations to Southampton Town, Southampton West, and adjacent places on the South Western line. **1899** J. HUTCHINSON *Archives Surg.* X. 182 They are a form of grouped papillomata.

grouper (ˈgruːpə(r)). Also 7–8 grooper, 8- groper, 9 gruper, garope, garrupa, garoup(h)a. [ad. Pg. *garupa*, ? repr. some S. American name.]

1. One of several species of the genus *Epinephelus* of serranoid fishes, inhabiting West Indian waters and the Mexican gulf and used extensively for food. The chief species are the Red G. (*E. morio*) and Black G. (*E. nigritus*). In California, the name is applied also to rock-fish (*Sebastichthys*).

1697 DAMPIER *Voy.* (1729) I. 91 The Rock-Fish is called by Sea-men a Grooper.. It is rounder than the Snapper, of a dark brown Colour. **1748** *Anson's Voy.* II. i. 125 We caught ..cavallies, gropers, large breams [at Juan Fernandez]. **1775** ROMANS *Florida* App. 7 At this place there is vast abundance and variety of fish..particularly groopers. **1805** T. LINDLEY *Voy. Brasil* (1808) 216 A large fish of the Salmon species (*garope*), which they sell for the Bahia market. **1829** MARRYAT *F. Mildmay* xiii, Of these, the best is the red grouper. **1833** M. SCOTT *Tom Cringle* xv. (1859) 365 Up came a beautiful black grouper about four pounds weight. **1885** LADY BRASSEY *The Trades* 314 The black and white striped gropers, supposed to be the best fish for the table in the West Indies. **1897** *Outing* (U.S.) XXIX. 231/2 The grouper, or 'gruper', or 'garoupha'.

attrib. **1883** G. B. GOODE *Fish. Industr. U.S.* 21 On the shoals of the Gulf of Mexico the red snapper and grouper fisheries are yearly increasing in value.

2. *Austral.* and *N.Z.* (usu. in the form *groper.*) **a.** A name for several types of fish, esp. a percoid fish of the genus *Oligorus*.

α. **1865** *Morning Star* 26 May, A Queensland paper says that a large fish called a grouper was caught off the coast there. It was 7 ft. long, 6 ft. in circumference at its thickest part, and its head weighed 80 lb.

β. **1878** P. THOMSON in *Trans. N.Z. Inst.* XI. 383 The Hapuku, or Groper, was in pretty regular supply. **1898** MORRIS *Austral Eng.*, *Groper*,..in Queensland, *Oligorus terræ-reginæ*, Ramsay; in New Zealand, *O. gigas*..a large marine species. **1908** E. J. BANFIELD *Confess. Beachcomber* I. iv. 152 Blacks..are..fearful of the monstrous groper (*Promicrops itaiara*), which lying inert among the coral blocks and boulders of the Barrier Reef, bolts anything. **1947** I. L. IDRIESS *Isles of Despair* xxxv. 234 'What was it?' Talalulu laughed. 'Groper,' she answered. 'Old man devil of the sea. You would hardly have made one mouthful for him, Gi'Om.' She was right. For a giant groper is known to have bitten a man in half. **1953** *Landfall* VII. 174 Where they sailed the groper fled. **1957** A. W. PARROTT *Sea Angler's Fishes N.Z.* 69 The Groper or Hapuka is well known throughout New Zealand. **1965** *Austral. Encycl.* IV. 396/1 *Groper*, a name applied in Australia to several distinct types of fish, including the southern gropers (*Achoerodus*), which are discussed under wrasses; the Queensland groper (*Promicrops lanceolatus*) and various species of *Epinephelus* ..and the New Zealand groper (*Polyprionum oxygeneios*).

b. ***blue groper***: a labroid fish, *Cossyphus gouldii*.

1880 INGLIS *Austral. Cousins* 300 The blue-groper still affords pretty fair winter sport. **1883** E. P. RAMSAY *Food Fishes N.S. Wales* 24 (Fish. Exhib. Publ.) The blue groper (*Cossyphus gouldii*), a valuable and delicious fish..often 20 to 30 lbs. in weight. **1962** L. WEDLICK *Fishing in Australia* IV. 159 The blue groper is occasionally caught on offshore reefs.

3. *local U.S.* The triple-tail or flasher, *Lobotes surinamensis*.

grouper: see GROUP *sb.* 3 d.

groupie (ˈgruːpɪ). **1.** *R.A.F. slang.* Short for *group captain* (GROUP *sb.* 6).

1943 in C. H. WARD-JACKSON *Piece of Cake* 35. **1952** M. TRIPP *Faith is Windsock* iv. 74 'Oh sergeant, don't leave us for a moment,' said Groupie acidly. **1966** *Listener* 21 Apr. 589/3 There is a horrible Cyclops of a groupie. **1968** I. LAMBOT *Queen dies First* xii. 84 Groupie's a devil for the girls.

2. Also **groupy**. [GROUP *sb.* 3 f.] (See quots. 1967 and 1970.)

1967 *Sun* 22 Feb. 6/6 (Teenage terms) *Groupy*, a girl who follows the pop groups. **1969** *Examiner* (San Francisco) 29 Jan. 39 'The Groupies'—girls who chase boys in the rock groups—are now getting so way out in their adulation that the whole mess warrants a federal investigation. **1969** *Private Eye* 10 Oct. 2/1 (Advt.), Read the sensational story, in her own words, of Katie a nineteen-year-old Groupie, as she 'pulls' from pop group to pop group. **1970** *Times* 15 Sept. 5/3 His defence described the sisters as 'groupies', girls who deliberately provoke sexual relations with pop stars.

grouping (ˈgruːpɪŋ), *vbl. sb.* [f. as GROUPER + -ING[1].] **a.** The action of placing in groups, a manner in which things are grouped.

1748 *Anson's Voy.* III. x. 412 Their painters..rarely succeeding..in the grouping of large compositions. **1813** *Examiner* 26 Apr. 266/1 Faculties of combination and grouping, equal to those of Newton. **1822** MISS MITFORD in L'Estrange *Life* (1870) II. vii. 144 He [Lord Byron] has no spirit of dialogue—no beauty in his groupings. **1851** MAYNE REID *Scalp Hunt.* xxxv. 270 Mountains, whose tops shot heavenward in fantastic forms and groupings. **1869** J. MARTINEAU *Ess.* II. 149 The grouping of its objects..is materially changed. **1883** *Law Times* 10 Nov. 21/1 A similar effect is produced by the grouping of counties for the purposes of an assize. **1902** *Encycl. Brit.* XXX. 256/1 One of the most useful distinctions for lighthouses consists in the grouping of two or more flashes separated by short intervals of darkness, the group being succeeded by a longer eclipse. **1931** *Economist* 15 Aug. 315/2 This shows that the position of the railways, when 'grouping' was achieved in 1923, was particularly difficult. **1958** J. A. BARLOW *Elem. Rifle Shooting* (ed. 5) i. 2 Provided it [*sc.* a rifle] satisfies grouping requirements, anything else about it that may not be quite up to standard can be altered or rectified quite easily. *Ibid.* 5, I..tested it [*sc.* a rifle]..and found that its grouping powers had more or less vanished. **1959** *Times Lit. Suppl.* 17 July 423/1 Our new international, continental groupings clash. Inside the same religion, political philosophy, or system of thought there are bitter clashes.

b. = ***blood grouping*** (BLOOD *sb.* 21).

1907 *Jrnl. Infectious Dis.* IV. 298 The exceptions to Landsteiner's grouping are given in heavy type. *Ibid.* 299 There is no striking alteration in the agglutinative grouping of the blood of persons suffering with various diseases. **1921** *Jrnl. Immunol.* VI. 363 In 1908 while working on the relation of the isoagglutination to blood transfusion, I noticed that the groupings were hereditary. **1957** *Encycl. Brit.* XI. 495/2 In the ABO system, which is very important in blood transfusion, there are four classes of individuals, O, A, B and AB, the grouping being based on certain agglutination reactions. **1968** 'C. AIRD' *Henrietta Who?* xvi. 152 'I've done a grouping.' 'Yes, doctor?' 'The girl's group O.'

Groupism, Groupist: see GROUP *sb.* 3 d.

groupist (ˈgruːpɪst). [f. GROUP *sb.* + -IST.] An adherent of a 'group' or section of a political party.

1895 *19th Cent.* Apr. 568 The Groupist in him will give place to the partisan.

grouplet (ˈgruːplɪt). [f. GROUP *sb.* + -LET.] A little group.

1837 CARLYLE *Fr. Rev.* I. IV. ii, Which organic groups, again, hold smaller organic grouplets.

groupment (ˈgruːpmənt). [f. GROUP *v.* + -MENT.] **a.** A group. **b.** The action of placing in groups.

1887 A. M. BROWN *Contrib. Animal Alkaloids* 87 It corresponds to two molecules of kreatinine, plus the CNH groupment. **1933** *Burlington Mag.* Mar. 144/1 A student needs these for purposes of groupment and comparison. **1953** *Britannica Bk. of Year* 639/1 *Groupment*, a national [U.S.] military unit of 1,300 men.

groupy: see GROUP *sb.* 3 d; GROUPIE 2.

grouse (graʊs), *sb.*[1] Forms: 6–7 **grows**, (?**grewes**), 7–9 **grous**, (7 **groose**, 8 **groust** (?), **grouss, growse**), 7- **grouse**. [Of unknown origin; it is uncertain whether the 16th c. form *grows* is a sing. (used *collect.*) or the pl. of **grow*; in the latter case cf. Giraldus Cambrensis (*c* 1210) *Topogr. Hib.* Opera (Rolls) V. 47 'gallinæ campestres, quas vulgariter *grutas* vocant'.

The suggestion that *grouse* is a spurious singular evolved to match the supposed plural *grice* appears to be inadmissible. GRICE[2] (= grouse) occurs only once, and is in that instance neither plural nor collective; moreover, it may be merely a mistaken recollection of Cotgrave's, due to the suggestion of *F. griesche*. *Grouse* occurs nearly a century earlier, and first as a pl. or collective.]

1. a. In scientific use, any of the gallinaceous birds having feathered feet (the family *Tetraonidæ* of many naturalists, of which the largest genera are *Tetrao* and *Lagopus*). **b.** In popular use, restricted almost entirely to the reddish-coloured game bird of the British Islands, *Lagopus* (formerly *Tetrao*) *scoticus*, more particularly called **Red Grouse**, and also commonly known as Moor Fowl or Moor Game.

Besides the Red Grouse, the most important British varieties are: **Black G.**, *Tetrao tetrix*, Black Game or Heath Fowl, the male being called BLACKCOCK and the female GREY-HEN. **Wood** or **Great G.**, the capercailye, *Tetrao urogallus*. **White G.**, *Lagopus mutus*, the ptarmigan, locally called also *Rock Grouse*. Other European and American varieties are: **Canada G.**, *Canace* or *Dendragapus canadensis*, called also *Spotted Grouse*. **Dusky G.**, *Canace* or *Dendragapus obscurus*. **Pinnated G.**, *Cupidonia cupido*. **Ruffed G.**, *Bonasa umbellus*; another species is the HAZEL-GROUSE, *B. silvestris*. **Sage G.**, *Centrocercus urophasianus*. **Sharp-tailed G.**, a grouse of the genus *Pediœcetes*.

1531 *Househ. Ord.* in *Archæol.* III. 157 [Among fowl for the tables are crocards, winders, runners, grows, and peions]. *a* **1547** in *Househ. Ord.* (1790) 220 Prices of all kindes of Poultry-stuff..Grewes 14*d.* **1603** *Act 1 Jas. I*, c. 27 § 1 Any Phesant Partridge..Ducke Teale Wigeon Grouse Heathcocke Moregame [etc.]. **1611** COTGR., *Francoule*;..as *Francolin*; or (as some imagine) our Moore-game, or Grouse. **1674** JOSSELYN *Voy. New Eng.* 99 They are indeed a sort of Partridges called Grooses. **1678** RAY *Willughby's Ornith.* 173 The Heathcock or Black game or Grous, called by Turner the Morehen. **1725** SWIFT *Receipt to Stella* Wks. 1755 IV. I. 43 The squires in scorn will fly the house For better game, and look for grouse. **1766** PENNANT *Zool.* (1768) I. 205 The *Francolino* is not the same with our grous. **1769** *De Foe's Tour Gt. Brit.* IV. 244 Partridge, Groust, Plover..and Snipes. **1772** J. R. FORSTER in *Phil. Trans.* LXII. 397, 1. The great Cock of the Wood, *Tetrao Urogallus* Linn... 3. The Spotted Grous, *T. Canadensis*, *T. Canace*. 4. The Ruffed Grous, *T. Umbellus*. 5. The Shoulder-knot Grous, *T. Togatus*. **1773** *Ibid.* LXIII. 229 The common Grous..is well known to be a bird of most excellent flavour. **1790** BURNS *Elegy M. Henderson* vii, Ye grouss that crap the heather bud. **1801** SOUTHEY *Thalaba* XI. xxiii, From yonder pines they hear The clatter of the Grouse's wings. **1808** PIKE *Sources Mississ.* (1810) 44 Killed nothing but five prairie hens..this bird I took to be the same as grouse. **1828** STARK *Elem. Nat. Hist.* I. 277 *Tetrao lagopus*, Lin. Ptarmigan or White Grous. **1893** *Westm. Gaz.* 1 Apr. 6/1 The prairie chickens (sharp-tailed grouse) meet every morning at grey dawn in companies of from six to twenty. **1894** *Outing* (U.S.) XXIV. 385/1 The pinnated grouse, or prairie chicken. **1900** *Longman's Mag.* Mar. 447 Colonel Dasent went off to shoot grouse.

c. Applied to birds of the genera *Syrrhaptes* and *Pterocles*, the SAND-GROUSE, q.v., formerly referred to the genus *Tetrao*.

1772 J. R. FORSTER in *Phil. Trans.* LXII. 397 The Pyrenæan Grous, *T[etrao] Alchata*, Linn.

d. The flesh of the bird.

1786 WOLCOT (P. Pindar) *Bozzy & Piozzi* I. Wks. 1816 I. 258 With ev'ry rarity she fill'd her house, And gave the doctor, for his dinner, grouse. **1899** PHIL. ROBINSON in *Contemp. Rev.* Dec. 794, I saw a scrap of grouse thrown to a pug.

†**2.** Used as a term of contempt. *Obs. rare*[−1].

1633 B. JONSON *Tale Tub* II. i, Look to 't, young grouse.

3. *attrib.* and *Comb.*, as ***grouse-butt, -chick, -cock, -disease, -drive, -dung, -hackle, -land, -moor, -pie, -protector, -shooter, -sledge***; ***grouse-breeding, -shooting, -stalking*** vbl. sbs.; **grouse-berry** *U.S.*, the blueberry, *Vaccinium scoparium*; cf. DEER-BERRY; **grouse-pigeon**, the sand-grouse.

1804 A. F. M. WILLICH *Domestic Encycl.* III. 150/2 It is called Canadian Gaultheria, or Mountain Tea, *Grouse-berry, Deer-berry, Ground-ivy. **1932** P. A. RYDBERG *Flora Prairies & Plains Cent. N. Amer.* 618 *V[accinium] scoparium*... Grouse-berry. **1898** *Daily News* 20 Dec. 7/3 As he walked with his guests over his sheep feeding and *grouse-breeding estate. **1904** *Westm. Gaz.* 26 Aug. 3/1 One of the unfailing topics that come up..for debate..is the mental attitude of the driven grouse towards the *grouse-butt. The opinion of the good men of old, who were in their prime in the beginning of the grouse-driving, [etc.]. **1888** *Pall Mall G.* 11 Aug. 5/2 The young *grouse-chicks. **1860** G. H. K. in *Vac. Tour.* 138 Scrambling upwards along the bed of the burn, startling the *grousecock. **1884** W. C. SMITH *Kildrostan* 63 And the grouse-cock gaily crowing Fears not either dog or gun. **1884** *St. James's Gaz.* 22 Aug. 7/1 Mr. Speedy discusses the question of *grouse-disease at considerable length. **1882** *Society* 21 Oct. 19/1 The setting out for a deer-drive or a *grouse-drive is romantic. **1904** *grouse-driving [see *grouse-butt*]. **1933** *Times Lit. Suppl.* 16 Mar. 175/4 The no less difficult art of grouse-driving on a Yorkshire moor. **1867** F. FRANCIS *Angling* vi. (1880) 244 The *Grouse Hackle, a capital hot-weather fly. **1897** *Daily Chron.* 22 July 4/5 The *grouse lands of Ireland. **1863** KINGSLEY *Water-Bab.* iv. 131 He smelt..the wafts of heather honey off the *grouse-moor far above. **1770** E. MONTAGU *Let.* 31 Aug. in *Private Corr. David Garrick* (1831) I. 395, I shall endeavour to send you a *grouse pie. **1861** MRS. BEETON *Bk. Househ. Managem.* 516 (*heading*) Grouse pie. **1931** H. NICOLSON *Diary* 26 Sept. (1966) 92 We have..grouse-pie and mushrooms. **1895** *Mountain, Moor & Loch* 93 Little rattling squares of tin hang at intervals along the telegraph wires, and particularly at the opening of glens. These are known as '*grouse protectors', and are hung thus in order that their noise in the wind may warn the grouse of the existence of a danger. **1832** *Chambers's Edinb. Jrnl.* I. 186/3 A neat little mountain inn, much frequented.. by fishers and *grouse-shooters. **1860** G. H. K. in *Vac. Tour.* 126 The blue hare..is a..plague both to the sheep-farmer..and the grouse-shooter. **1785** G. A. BELLAMY *Apology for Life* (ed. 2) I. 163 *Grouse shooting claimed his attention in Autumn, and hunting in winter. **1814** SCOTT *Wav.* vi, The diversion of grouse-shooting upon his moors in Perthshire. **1897** *Allbutt's Syst. Med.* III. 251 Some quiet grouse-shooting or deer-stalking resort in the Highlands of Scotland. **1892** SIR R. PAYNE-GALLWEY in *Field* 14 May 733/2 *Grouse Sledge. [Contains] a receptacle for the grouse, cartridge bags, &c. **1893** J. WATSON *Confess. Poacher* 122 *Grouse stalking is fascinating sport, done from behind an old moorland horse.

grouse (graʊs), *sb.*[2] *slang.* [f. GROUSE *v.*[2]] A grumble or complaint: a reason for grumbling.

1918 W. OWEN *Let.* 17 July (1967) 564 I'll make my grouse. Why didn't you come to Scarborough for a few days? *Ibid.* 15 Oct. 585 The Parcel came all right; my only grouse is that it was too big. **1923** *Pictorial Weekly* CXIX. 127/1 A Transfer 'Grouse'. **1927** *Daily Express* 27 Apr. 3/1, I cannot understand the point of view of the hanging committee... I have no grouse against them. I am not an Academician, but I do not agree with their choice. *Ibid.* 5 Oct. 3/4 The 'moan' of a Gun Room is the naval version of an Army 'grouse'.

grouse (graʊs), *v.*[1] [f. GROUSE *sb.*[1]] *intr.* To shoot grouse. Also *transf.* (cf. *snipe* vb.).

c **1798** HOPE in R. R. Madden *Lit. Rem. United Irishmen* (1887) 100 In Wexford and Wicklow 'tis said That Orange for Croppies went grousing. **1802** [see GROUSING *vbl. sb.*]. **1824** *Mirror* III. 151/1 A gentleman, residing near Cader Idris, while grousing in that neighbourhood [etc.].

grouse (graʊs, gruːs), *v.*[2] *Army slang.* Also grouce. [Origin unknown. The word has a curious resemblance to Norman Fr. dial. *groucer* = OF. *groucier, grousser*: see GRUTCH.] *intr.* To grumble.

1887 KIPLING *From Sea to Sea* (1899) II. 396 That's the only thing as 'ill make the Blue Lights stop grousin' and stiffin'... 'Grousing' is sulking, and 'stiffin'' is using unparliamentary language. **1892** R. KIPLING *Barrack-r. Ballads* 47 If you're cast for fatigue by a sergeant unkind, Don't grouse like a woman, nor crack on, nor blind. **1896** *Daily News* 2 July 9/1 The camels groused and gurgled afar off. **1897** *Chamb. Jrnl.* 86 It cannot be said with truth that British soldiers never grumble or 'grouce' as they call it.

grouse (graʊs), *a. Austral.* and *N.Z. slang.* Formerly also grouce. [Origin unknown.] Excellent, very good.

[**1938** PARTRIDGE *Dict. Slang* (ed. 2) Add. 1000/2 *The grouse.* (Only predicatively.) Very good: Australian cant: C.20. Origin?] **1941** BAKER *Dict. Austral. Slang* 33 *Grouce, grouse,* good, excellent. **1944** L. GLASSOP *We were Rats* I. i. 5 You know them two grouse sheilas we've got the meet on with tomorrer night? **1947** D. M. DAVIN *Gorse blooms Pale* 200 An Iti bint, a real grouse brush she was, with bonzer black eyes. **1963** *Australasian Post* 14 Mar. 51/2 'Real good, Knobs... How about you?' 'Extra grouse.' **1968** *Telegraph* (Brisbane) 1 May 24/3 (*heading*) Grouse slang guide.

grouse, obs. form of GROSS.

grouseless (ˈgraʊslɪs), *a.* [f. GROUSE *sb.*[1] + -LESS.] Having no grouse.

1869 *Daily News* 23 June, Upon the edge of a grouseless moor. **1880** *Punch* 28 Aug. 96/1 The Twelfth gone and past, not a bang at the grouse! I.. pity the sorrows of grouseless M.P.'s.

grouser[1] (ˈgraʊsə(r)). [f. GROUSE *v.*[1] + -ER[1].] One who goes grousing; a grouse-shooter.

1865 E. YATES *Business of Pleasure* I. 186 The manufacturing gentry.. are tremendously keen grousers.

grouser[2] (ˈgraʊsə(r)). *Hydraulics.* [Origin unknown.] An iron-pointed pile or timber attached to a boat or other floating object as a means of anchorage or of keeping the object in position.

1876 *Rep. Chief of Engineers* II. II. 403 (in Knight *Dict. Mech.* Suppl.). **1884** EISSLER *Mod. High Explosives* III. vii. 329 To overcome the motion of the waves, and the current, they are provided with a submarine contrivance (spuds, grousers), which reaches to the bottom of the river.

grouser[3] (ˈgraʊsə(r)). [f. GROUSE *v.*[2] + -ER[1].] One who grumbles or complains.

1885 J. B. PATTERSON *Life in Ranks* 120 Impossible to do anything at all entirely to the satisfaction of a certain class of individuals... This.. body of men is commonly designated by their.. comrades as the 'grousers'.

grouseward, -wards (ˈgraʊswəd, -wədz), *adv.* [See -WARD(S.] In the direction of grouse.

1853 A. H. CLOUGH *Lett. & Rem.* (1865) 263 The Commons are off grousewards, and scarcely anyone remains to ask one to dinner or anything else. **1895** *Daily Tel.* 13 Aug. 5/4 He was certainly not 'grouseward' bent.

grousing (ˈgraʊsɪŋ), *vbl. sb.* [f. GROUSE *v.*[1] + -ING[1].] The action of GROUSE *v.*[1]; grouse-shooting.

1771–72 *Batchelor* (1773) I. 134 Are you fond of grousing, my lord? I'll show you fine sport this season in my neighbourhood. **1802** R. L. & MAR. EDGEWORTH *Irish Bulls* xvi. 292 He had in former times gone out a grousing, near Cork, with our hero. **1880** MRS. L. B. WALFORD *Troublesome Dau.* I. ii. 34 Nearly every August found him in Scotland, either for the salmon-fishing or the grousing.

attrib. **1860** LD. PALMERSTON in *Daily News* (1895) 27 Apr. 6/4 The Speaker, who has not been quite well, grows as impatient as any official who has hired a grousing moor and cannot get to it.

grousome, obs. form of GRUESOME.

grousy (ˈgraʊsɪ), *a.* [f. GROUSE *sb.*[1] + -Y[1].] Abounding in grouse.

1830 *Blackw. Mag.* XXVIII. 585 The stony regions.. melt away into miles of the grousey heather. **1879** *Daily News* 12 Aug. 5/1 So vast an expanse of 'grousey' land, so many heather-coloured valleys.

grout (graʊt), *sb.*[1] [OE. *grút* str. fem. (declined as consonant-stem, dative *grýt*), corresponding to MDu. *grute, gruit* coarse meal, peeled barley or rye, malt, flavouring for beer, yeast (mod.Du. *gruit* dregs), MHG. *grûȥ* masc. and fem., grain, small beer; related to GRIT *sb.*[1], GRIT *sb.*[2], GROATS.]

1. Coarse meal, peeled grain. In *pl.* = GROATS. Now *rare.*

c **725** *Corpus Gloss.* 1619 *Pollinis,* gruiit [?gruut]. **835** *Charter* in *O.E. Texts* 448, L ambra maltes, VI ambra gruta, & III weȝa spices & ceses. *c* **1000** *Sax. Leechd.* II. 342 Gif he [wenn] sie men on cneowe oþþe on oþrum lime wyrc clam of surre riȝenre grut oððe daȝe. **11..** *Voc.* in Wr.-Wülcker 549/3 *Furfures,* gruta. **1601** HOLLAND *Pliny* II. 46 If their stalkes or stemmes bee stamped with drie grout or Barley meale. **1624** CAPT. SMITH *Virginia* II. 29 The groutes and peeces of the cornes remaining, by fanning.. away the branne, they boyle 3 or 4 houres with water. **1723** *Pres. State Russia* I. 56 Each Farm being taxed a certain Measure of Corn, Grout and Oatmeal. **1744–50** W. ELLIS *Mod. Husbandm.* V. I. 129 It [wheat].. kerned only half way, so that it was as thin as grouts. **1896** *Allbutt's Syst. Med.* I. 441 The making of gruel by mixing the fine oatmeal or grouts into a smooth paste.

2. The infusion of malt before it is fermented, and during the process of fermentation. Also, small beer. *Obs.* exc. *dial.*

c **1000** *Sax. Leechd.* III. 42 Genim.. æȝes þæt hwite and ealde grut. **1589** *Tri. Love & Fortune* I. (Roxb. Club) 90 The olde wife, when her ale would not come, Thrust a fire brand in the groute. **1593** 'FOULFACE' *Bacchus Bountie* C 2b, Goody Goodale.. deliuered to Bacchvs a iack full of groute, or a sack full of hops. **1671** SKINNER *Etym. Ling. Angl., Grout,..* Condimentum cerevisiæ, Mustum cerevisiæ. **1674** RAY *N.C. Words* 22 *Grout,* wort of the last running... Ale before it be fully brewed or sod, new Ale. It signifies also millet. *c* **1700** KENNETT (Halliw.), In Leicestershire, the liquor with malt infused for ale or beer, before it is fully boiled, is called grout, and before it is tunned up in the vessel is called wort. **1727** *Vin. Britan.* 29 The worst small Beer, if that wretched Stuff called Grout, deserve the name. **1853** SOYER *Pantroph.* 302 When the brewer was satisfied that the grout was properly ripened, he poured it forth into the copper. **1888** *Sheffield Gloss., Growte,* small beer, made after the strong beer is brewed.

†**b.** App. (= MDu. *grute*) some plant used as a flavouring for beer before the introduction of hops.

14.. *Nom.* in Wr.-Wülcker 725/26 *Hoc idromellum,* growtt. *Hoc ciromellum,* wort. **14..** *Voc.* ibid. 562/27 *Agromellum,* growt. *c* **1440** *Promp. Parv.* 217/1 Growte for ale, *granomellum.* *c* **1475** *Pict. Voc.* in Wr.-Wülcker 772/12 *Hoc ciromellum,* growte. **1483** *Cath. Angl.* 166/1 Growte, *idromellum, agromellum, Acromellum, granomellum.* **1530** PALSGR. 228/1 Grout that serveth to brewyng, in Fraunce is none used. **1671** [see 2].

3. A kind of coarse porridge made from whole meal. ? *Obs.*

[Possibly another word, ad. Norw. *graut,* Da. *grød,* Sw. *gröt* (:—ON. *graut-r.*]

1587 MASCALL *Govt. Cattle* (1627) 280 Some doe seethe it with water, and make it thicke like grout. **1692** W. KING *Acc. Denmark* 33 The Danes make their so much talkt of grout, that resembles the English Hasty pudding. **1708** W. KING *Art Cookery* v, As for Grout it is an old Danish dish. **1710** E. WARD *Vulgus Brit.* XII. 139 These.. rave till grown as Piping Hot, As the dull Grout o'er which they sot. **1748** F. SMITH *Voy. Disc.* I. 122 Feeding on Grout, which is Oatmeal, boiled to a Thickness, sweetened with Molossus. **1753** HANWAY *Trav.* (1762) II. I. x. 54 The animal food which our common people eat, is incomparably more strengthening than their fish, cheese, milk, and grout. **1779–81** JOHNSON *L.P., Dryden* (1839) I. 238 Never was Dutch grout such clogging, thick, indigestible stuff. **1793** WOLCOT (P. Pindar) *Ep. to Pope* 4 Wks. 1816 II. 405 France .. Knocks the poor growling German o'er the snout, And threatens hard the man of cheese and grout.

4. Sediment; dregs; lees; grounds.

1697 DRYDEN *Virg. Georg.* IV. 239 Sweet Honey some condense, some purge the Grout. **1739** 'R. BULL' tr. *Dedekindus' Grobianus* III. iv. 222 The Mug may have some sedimental Grout. **1855** DICKENS *Dorrit* v, The ceilings were so fantastically clouded by smoke and dust, that old women might have told fortunes in them, better than in grouts of tea. **1870** ROSSETTI *Dante at Verona* lii, Wherefore should we turn the grout In a drained cup? **1876** *Mid-Yorksh. Gloss., Grout,* sediment of a coarse nature, such as the particles left in a tea-cup.

5. *attrib.,* as (sense 3) ***grout-pot.***

a **1734** NORTH *Lives* (1826) II. 342 They.. went all hands to the grout-pot and bread-basket.

grout (graʊt), *sb.*[2] [Possibly a use of prec.; but cf. F. *grouter* (16th c.), mod.Limousin patois *greuta* to grout a wall (Godef.).] Thin fluid mortar, which is poured into the interstices of masonry and wood-work.

1638 PENKETHMAN *Artach.* G 4b, For Growt and furning 3d. oq. **1793** SMEATON *Edystone L.* §199 Pouring in liquid mortar, commonly called Grout, in so fluid a state, as to run into every cavity and crevice. **1793** SIR G. SHUCKBURGH in *Phil. Trans.* LXXXIII. 87 *note,* The bricks of this arch were laid dry, and then grout, consisting of gravel and hot lime, was poured upon them. **1796** W. MARSHALL *W. England* II. 297 Liquid Coating, of cement poured into the wall, in a state of grout. **1825** J. NICHOLSON *Operat. Mechanic* 532 *Grout,..* a cement containing a larger proportion of water than the common mortar. **1839** STONEHOUSE *Axholme* 22 The powder is.. mixed with water to the consistency of that thin mortar which is called grout. **1861** SMILES *Engineers* II. 37 It was.. settled to use the finest grout for the intervals between the upright or side joints of the dovetailed part of the work. **1883** *West. Daily Press* 22 Oct., It is built of material resembling concrete or grout.

b. *attrib.,* as ***grout-floor, -work.***

1840 HOWITT *Visits Remark. Places* Ser. I. 224 The walls are of strong grout-work, about four feet thick. **1884** *Harper's Mag.* LXIX. 437 A casing of stone.. covered the rubble and grout work. **1895** L. H. BAILEY *Horticulturist's Rule-bk.* (ed. 3) 92 To secure a good grout or cement floor.

[**grout** *sb.*[3] Explained as: A kind of wild apple. Error due to misinterpretation of *agromelum* (quasi *agriomelum,* Gr. ἀγριόμηλον wild apple), which occurs in glosses as a synonym of *idromelum,* etc. (see GROUT *sb.*[1] 2b).

1755 JOHNSON, *Grout..*3. A kind of wild apple (*Agriomelum,* Latin.)]

grout (graʊt), *v.*[1] [f. GROUT *sb.*[2]] *trans.* To fill up or finish with 'grout' or liquid mortar; to cement. Also with *in.*

1838 F. W. SIMMS *Public Wks. Gt. Brit.* 60 The whole of the brickwork was well grouted every course. **1840** *Jrnl. R. Agric. Soc.* I. IV. 360 These carriers down the slopes are pitched with strong limestone, and grouted with lime and water. **1880** J. LOMAS *Alkali Trade* 162 The sole itself must be of 9-in. bricks, laid dry on end, and 'grouted in' with a thin mixture of finely ground fireclay and water.

fig. **1863** W. PHILLIPS *Speeches* xxiii. 508 It was grouted and dove-tailed into the foundation of the state. **1877** *Tinsley's Mag.* XXI. 29 That self-reliance which makes men, builds up colonies, and cements and 'grouts in' the foundations of States.

Hence ˈ**grouted** *ppl. a.*

1844 TUPPER *Crock of G.* ii. 11 Four bare rubble walls enclosing a grouted floor. **1888** C. KERRY in *Jrnl. Derbysh. Archæol. Soc.* X. 21 A large block of grouted rubble.

grout (graʊt), *v.*[2] [Variant of GROOT *v.*]

1. *intr.* Of a pig: To 'muzzle' or turn up the ground with the snout. Also *transf.* and *fig.*

a **1723** D'URFEY *Eng. Stage Italianized* iv. (1727) 10 A great Herd of Swine, grouting among the Acorns. **1834** BECKFORD *Italy* II. 365 Wandering flocks of sheep, goats and swine, which rout, and grout, and nibble uncontrolled and unmolested. **1877** BLACKMORE *Cripps* xlix, A pig or two grouting in the tufted grass. **1907** C. E. RYDER *Bede Papers* xi. 170 Modern science.. with pickaxe and spade grouting at the immemorial roots of her tree of life. *a* **1941** V. WOOLF *Captain's Death Bed* (1950) 31 He went off.. to grout for fossils. **1951** N. ANNAN *L. Stephen* iv. 136 Jowett.. encouraged his undergraduates to grout among the pearls that he cast before them and select whichever they regarded valuable. **1956** J. MASTERS *Bugles & Tiger* 240 The tribesmen could have walked in anywhere while we grouted around in the soup [i.e. liquid mud] for our rifles and machine-guns.

2. *trans.* To turn *up* with the snout.

1877 BLACKMORE *Cripps* xlix, Here comes that old pig again! If he could only grout up that board.

grout (graʊt), *v.*[3] *U.S. intr.* To grumble, sulk.

1848 LOWELL *Biglow P.* Poems 1890 II. 111 Ez long 'z the people git their rattle, Wut is there fer 'm to grout about?

grouth, obs. form of GROWTH[1].

†**grout-head.** *Obs.* Also 6 growthed. [f. GROUT *sb.,* taken as the type of something big and coarse; cf. *pudding-head.* In 2 there is confusion with *great*; perh. the sound recalled the Du. *groot.*]

1. A blockhead, thickhead, dunce.

1550 BALE *Eng. Votaries* II. E iij, So daintye mouthed were these greasye grout heades. **1573** TUSSER *Husb.* li. (1878) 115 Though sleeping one hower refresheth his song, yet trust not hob growthed for sleeping too long. **1597–8** W. HAUGHTON *Englishm. for money* IV. i. (1616) F 4, Then, theres not onely a growte head, but an Asse also. **1599** NASHE *Lenten Stuffe* 39 Those Turbanto grout-heads, that hang all men by the throates on Iron hookes. **1611** COTGR. s.v. *Gros, Il a vne grosse teste,* he is a verie blockhead, grouthead, ioulthead. **1649** *Woodstock Scuffle* xlviii. in Scott *Woodst.* App. i, The old parsons.. are out-driv'n; Their colledges dispos'd, and livings, To grout-heads.

2. A big head; a person with a big head.

a **1627** MIDDLETON & ROWLEY *Sp. Gipsy* IV. i. (1653) G, We no Camells have to shew, nor Elephant with growte head. **1706** PHILLIPS (ed. Kersey), *Grout-head,* one that has a great-head.

Hence †**grout-headry,** stupidity.

1600 *Hosp. Incur. Fooles* A iv b, This is no two-penie matter, nor no triuiall gridiron grout-headrie.

grout-headed, *a. Obs.* or *dial.* [f. as prec.: see HEADED.] Thick-headed, stupid.

1578 FLORIO *1st Fruites* 58 b, Alwayes there were, are, and I beleeve wyl be certaine groutheaded, yl manered, and to say better, envious. **1593** 'FOULFACE' *Bacchus Bountie* A 4, The groutheaded Græcians, especiallie the annointed Achiues, I meane the Beziladistes. **1607** WALKINGTON *Opt. Glass* xii. (1664) 125 Stoically visaged, like Grout-headed Arcesilaus. **1694** MOTTEUX *Rabelais* v. xix. (1737) 83 We are a silly sort of Grout-headed Lobcocks. **1847–78** HALLIWELL, *Groutheaded,* stupidly noisy. *Sussex.* Also, large or great-headed, stupid.

grouting (ˈgraʊtɪŋ), *vbl. sb.*[1] [f. GROUT *v.*[1] + -ING[1].] The action of GROUT *v.*[1]; filling of chinks, etc. with 'grout'; chiefly *concr.* the material used in this operation.

1793 SMEATON *Edystone L.* §199 The best method of grouting. **1812–16** J. SMITH *Panorama Sci. & Art* I. 188 The interstices [may be] filled and wedged up, by pouring in lime putty, plaster of Paris, grouting, or any other convenient material. **1853** PHILLIPS *Rivers Yorksh.* ix. 248 The body thus placed was covered by a grouting of lime. **1882** D. K. CLARK *Tramways* Suppl. xix, 164 All spaces.. are to be filled with gravel and macadam, and thoroughly rammed before the final grouting of the paving. **1894** *East. Daily Press* 11 June 5/2 The holes might be filled up with grouting or cement.

grouting (ˈgraʊtɪŋ), *vbl. sb.*[2] [f. GROUT *v.*[2] + -ING[1].] The action of GROUT *v.*[2] (in quot. *fig.*).

1961 M. KELLY *Spoilt Kill* ii. 36 By a bit of discreet grouting in the cupboards.. I've found it.

†**groutnoll.** *Obs.* Forms: 6 growte-, groutnowle, 6–7 groutnoll, (7 -nold, growtnoll, grutnol). [f. GROUT *sb.*[1] + NOLL.] = GROUT-HEAD.

1578 WHETSTONE *2nd Pt. Promos & Cass.* III. ii, Growtenowle, come to the King. **1580** HOLLYBAND *Treas.*

Fr. Tong, Lourdault, a loute, a lob, a groutnoll. **1600** SURFLET *Countrie Farme* vi. xxii. 779 The seede of drunkards becommeth dead and fruitlesse, and their children block-headed groutnolles. **1611** BEAUM. & FL. *Knt. Burn. Pestle* II. iii, That same Dwarfe's a pretty boy, but the Squire's a grout-nold. **1653** URQUHART *Rabelais* I. xxv, Noddie meacocks, blockish grutnols, doddi-pol-jolt-heads. **1658** CLEVELAND *Rustic Rampant* Wks. (1687) 459 The other Growtnolls of the Neighbourhood.. wait for them.

grouty (ˈgraʊtɪ), *a.*[1] *dial.* [f. GROUT *sb.*[1] + -Y[1].] **a.** Muddy, dirty. **b.** Of the sky, weather: Thundery.

1744–50 W. ELLIS *Mod. Husbandm.* III. II. 74 Many have wondered how the Cattle could drink such grouty, black, stinking Water. **1868** ATKINSON *Cleveland Gloss.*, *Grouty*, soiled, dirty-looking, begrimed. **1876** *Whitby Gloss.*, *Grouty*, full of sediment. **1893** *Wiltsh. Gloss.*, *Grouty*, of the sky, thundering, threatening rain. It looks 'ter'ble grouty' in summer when thunder clouds are coming up.

grouty (ˈgraʊtɪ), *a.*[2] *U.S.* [f. GROUT *v.*[3] + -Y[1]] Sulky, cross, ill-tempered. Hence **ˈgroutiness.**

1836 LOWELL *Lett.* (1894) I. i. 11 Been quite 'grouty' all the vacation: 'black as Erebus'. **1881** *Pennsylv. Sch. Jrnl.* XXXII. 57 As grouty and glum as if he pondered the wrongs of his race for the last two centuries. **1895** *Columbus* (Ohio) *Disp.* 23 May 9/4 He can take a passenger's groutiness for what it is worth.

grouue, grouwe, obs. forms of GROW *v.*

grouze (graʊz), *v. dial.* Also **growze**, ? GRUSE. [? Echoic.] *trans.* To devour or munch with a crunching sound. Also with *up*.

[*a* **1225**: see GRUSE *v.*] **1624** SANDERSON *Twelve Serm.* (1637) 461 Like Swine under the Oakes, we grouze up the Ake-cornes,.. and when we have done, lie wrouting, and thrusting our noses in the earth for more. **1877** *N.W. Linc. Gloss.* s.v., I can't abide him, he growzes his meat like a pig. **1887** *S. Cheshire Gloss.*, *Grouze*, to munch, e.g. walnuts or anything else of which the crunching sound can be heard during the process. Thus we might speak of pigs grouzing raw potatoes.

grovayr, variant of GROVER *Obs.*

grove (grəʊv). Forms: 1–2 **gráf**, 4 **grof(e**, 6 *Sc.* **grave, grawe**, 6–7 **groave**, 2– **grove.** [OE. *gráf* masc. and neut.:—prehistoric **graibo-*. Cf. GREAVE *sb.*[1]

The word is not found in any other Teut. lang., and no Teut. or even Indogermanic root seems to be known to which it can plausibly be referred.]

1. A small wood; a group of trees affording shade or forming avenues or walks, occurring naturally or planted for a special purpose.

Groves were commonly planted by heathen peoples in honour of deities to serve as places of worship or for the reception of images. Cf. 2 a.

889 *Grant* in Birch *Cartul. Sax.* II. 199 Heo hæbbe ðа wudu-raeddenne in ðæm wuda ðe ða ceorlas brucaþ & ec ic hire lete to þæt ceorla graf. *c* **1205** LAY. 469 Al swa þat wilde swin: þæt wroteð ȝeond þan grouen. [**1249–52** *Visit. Ch. belong. St. Paul's Cathedr.* (Camden 1895) 13 Tenentes de ecclesia de Heubrege. Johannes Gobbe j acra et reddit vj *d* .. Johannes ad portam j parvam grovam et reddit iiij *d* sed grova destructa est.] *a* **1250** *Owl & Night.* 380 He.. hupth and stard suthe cove, And secheth pathes to the grove. **1387** TREVISA *Higden* (Rolls) VII. 11 Eueriche grove schoon wiþ horten treen and oþer tren ful of fruyt. *c* **1400** *Destr. Troy* 13557 Þan se þai besyde.. A grete herte in a grove. *c* **1500** *Lancelot* 2481 The birdis may them hiding in the grawis Wel frome the halk. **1513** DOUGLAS *Æneis* IV. ii. 46 Scho skipping furth.. Gan throw the forrest fast and gravis glyde. *Ibid.* XII. Prol. 190 In gresy gravis wandrand by spring wellis. **1590** SHAKS. *Mids. N.* III. i. 390, I,.. like a Forrester, the groues may tread. **1629** SIR W. MUIR *True Crucifix* 1262 Such vncouth flames made men the Temple leaue Worship to Images in groaues to giue. **1735** SOMERVILLE *Chase* III. 478 Proud Monarch of the Groves, whose clashing Beam His Rivals aw'd. **1770** GOLDSM. *Des. Vill.* 361 The breezy covert of the warbling grove. **1838** THIRLWALL *Greece* IV. xxxiv. 358 The temple stood in a grove of fruit trees. **1856** STANLEY *Sinai & Pal.* vii. 301 The forest.. was a vast grove of majestic palms.

b. *transf.* and *fig.*

1667 MILTON *P.L.* IV. 982 When a field Of Ceres ripe for harvest waving bends Her bearded Grove of ears. *Ibid.* VII. 404 Through Groves Of Coral. [**1671** —— *P.R.* IV. 244 The olive-grove of Academe, Plato's retirement.] **1715–20** POPE *Iliad* II. 182 The moving host appears, With nodding plumes and groves of waving spears. **1793** WORDSW. *Old Cumbld. Beggar* 120 They who live Sheltered, and flourish in a little grove Of their own kindred. **1821** SHELLEY *Prometh. Unb.* IV. 404 Labour, and pain, and grief, in life's green grove Sport like tame beasts. **1849** ROBERTSON *Serm.* Ser. I. viii. (1866) 142 The groves of Athenian literature. **1849** THACKERAY *Pendennis* I. xviii. 166 Into this certainly not the least snugly sheltered arbour among the groves of Academe, Pen now found his way. **1889** RUSKIN *Præterita* III. 49 The sunset shining down a long street through a grove of bayonets.

¶**2.** In Eng. versions of the Bible, e.g. Coverdale's and the Authorized, an erroneous rendering, following the Septuagint and the Vulgate: **a.** of Heb. *Ashērāh*, which is now understood as the name of a goddess or of a pillar serving as an idol.

1535 COVERDALE *1 Kings* xviii. 19 The foure hundreth and fiftye prophetes of Baal, and the foure hundreth prophetes of yᵉ groue, which eate at Iesabels table. **1611** BIBLE *2 Kings* xxi. 7 He set a grauen image of the grove [COVERD. groue Idol, Vulg. *idolum luci*, *R.V.* of Asherah, *marg.* or obelisk] that he had made, in the house. **1853** MAURICE *Proph. & Kings* vii. 108 The prophets of the grove were building their own power upon the degradation of the multitudes whom they drew after them.

b. of Heb. *ēshel* (R.V. 'tamarisk tree').

1535 COVERDALE *1 Sam.* xxii. 6 Whyle Saul dwelt at Gibea vnder a groue in Rama. **1611** BIBLE *Gen.* xxi. 33 And Abraham planted a groue [*marg.* Or, Tree, COVERD. trees, Vulg. *nemus*] in Beer-sheba.

3. *attrib.* and *Comb.*, as ***grove idol*** (see 2), ***-pine, -spirit, -tree, -worship; grove-encircled, -like*** adjs.; †**grove-crop**, a grove; **grove-dock**, *Rumex Nemolapathum* (Paxton *Bot. Dict.* 1840); **grove-snail** (see quot.).

1583 STANYHURST *Æneis* I. (Arb.) 32 In towns myd center theare sprouted a *groauecrop, in arbours Greene weede thick shaded. **1831** CARLYLE *Sart. Res.* I. v, A mystic *grove-encircled shrine. **1535** COVERDALE *2 Kings* xxi. 7 A *groue Idol also which he had made, set he in the house. **1864** TENNYSON *Aylmer's F.* 510 That old oak.. Once *grovelike, each huge arm a tree. **1873** *Atlas of Michigan* Pref. 20 Some varieties of '*grove' pine are found on a lighter soil. **1861** HULME tr. *Moquin-Tandon* II. III. 174 The Wood snail, *Helix Sylvatica*, Drap., and the *Grove snail, *H. Nemoralis*, Linn. **1827** STEUART *Planter's G.* (1828) 353 The adjoining space.. is massed up with *Grove Trees and Underwood. **1845** A. DUNCAN *Discourses* 387 Abraham worshipped under an oak or in a grove.. We shall thus be able to account for.. the origin of *grove-worship.

Hence **ˈgroveless** *a.*, devoid of groves.

1835 *Blackw. Mag.* XXXVII. 686 Even were her shore-hills silvan no more—groveless the bases of all her remoter mountains. **1873** MᶜARTHUR in *Harp Renfrewsh.* 391 These groveless banks, those ruined walls.

grove, var. GROOVE; obs. pa. t. of GRAVE *v.*[1]

groved (grəʊvd), *ppl. a.* [f. GROVE + -ED[2].] Having groves; planted with groves. Also of a bird: 'Embowered' in a grove.

1827 G. DARLEY *Sylvia* 43 Like waters trembling in their fountain-cell at hearing the groved nightingale. **1876** MRS. WHITNEY *Sights & Ins.* xxxv. 336 A beautiful height, groved with chestnut.

grovel (ˈgrɒv(ə)l), *v.* Also 6 **grovell.** [Back-formation from GROVELLING *adv.*, apprehended as a pr. pple.]

1. *intr.* To lie prone or with the face downwards; to move with the body prostrate upon the ground; ***to grovel in the dust*** or ***dirt*** (fig.): to humble oneself, perform an act of humiliation.

1593 SHAKS. *2 Hen. VI*, I. ii. 9 Gaze on, and grouell on thy face. **1634** SIR T. HERBERT *Trav.* 8 [Idols] They ceremoniously kneele and bow unto, groveling then upon the Earth, they throw dust on their faces. **1671** MILTON *Samson* 141 Old warriors turn'd Their plated backs under his heel, Or groveling soil'd their crested helmets in the dust. **1700** ADDISON *Æneid* III. Misc. Wks. 1726 I. 58 Thunder-struck Enceladus Groveling beneath the incumbent mountain's weight Lyes stretch'd supine. **1725** POPE *Odyss.* VIII. 575 Close to his breast she grovels on the ground. **1839** TENNYSON in *Mem.* (1897) I. 171 She was grovelling on the floor in an extremity of fear. **1865** DICKENS *Mut. Fr.* III. xiv, Am I to grovel in the dust for him to walk over? **1867** TROLLOPE *Chron. Barset* II. liii. 105 She is not such a paragon that a man should condescend to grovel in the dirt for her. **1882** J. H. BLUNT *Ref. Ch. Eng.* II. 211 The Parliament.. grovelled in the dust at the Cardinal's feet.

b. *fig.*

1605 BP. HALL *Medit. & Vows* I. §33 Every worldling is an hypocrite, for while his face naturally lookes upward.. his hart grovels beneath on the earth. **1655** MOUFET & BENNET *Health's Improv.* (1746) 378 Through surfeiting we live groveling and groping after base Delights, as Hogs do for Acorns. **1719** WATTS *Hymn*, '*Come, holy Spirit, Heav'nly Dove*', Look how we grovel here below. **1751** JOHNSON *Rambler* No. 147 ⁋9 A wretch doomed to grovel in obscurity for want of assurance. **1828** D'ISRAELI *Chas. I*, I. viii. 272 The vindictive Laud grovelled in a meaner and more cruel victory. **1875** JOWETT *Plato* (ed. 2) IV. 280 The philosophy of Berkeley.. is still grovelling on the level of sense.

c. quasi-*trans.* with *out*.

1790 *By-stander* 7 If neglected, they grovel out their day, and vanish at night like a vapour.

2. *causal.* To lay prone on the ground. *rare*$^{-1}$.

1843 E. JONES *Sens. & Event* 25 [He] grovelleth on the ground His naked flesh.

Hence **ˈgrovel** *sb.*, the action of grovelling; **ˈgrovelled** *ppl. a.*, humiliated, debased.

a **1845** HOOD *Lamia* i. 73 If you could see How this poor figure once was marred and villified, How grovelled and debased. **1892** *Black & White* 19 Mar. 366/1 The only possible attitude is a grovel.

†**ˈgroveling.** *Obs. rare*$^{-1}$. [f. GROVEL *v.* + -ING[3] (or perh. subst. use of GROVELLING *a.*).] A groveller.

1708 *Brit. Apollo* No. 68. 2/1 Of Aspiring Creatures it makes us Grovelings.

groveller, groveler (ˈgrɒv(ə)lə(r)). [f. GROVEL *v.* + -ER[1].] One who grovels; chiefly *fig.*

1779–81 JOHNSON *L.P.*, *Milton* (1790) I. 185 Among this lagging race of frosty grovellers he might still have risen into eminence by producing something which they should not willingly let die. **1835** J. H. NEWMAN *Par. Serm.* (1836) II. iv. 55 What are we but.. grovellers who are creeping on to heaven? **1840** DICKENS *Barn. Rudge* xiii, Mere worms and grovellers as we are!

grovelling, groveling (ˈgrɒv(ə)lɪŋ), *vbl. sb.* [f. GROVEL *v.* + -ING[1].] The action of the verb GROVEL; *lit.* and *fig.*

1611 FLORIO, *Trabocco*, a downe-fall, a groueling on the ground. **1634** SIR T. HERBERT *Trav.* 153 Mahomet.. perswaded them.. that his groveling and foming (a disease much troubling him) was caused by [etc.]. **1726** BROOME *To Mr. Pope, on his Wks.* 62 Sink, without groveling; without rashness, rise. **1874** L. STEPHEN *Hours in Library* (1892) II. iv. 132 This lavish splendour.. implies no grovelling before the ordinary British duke.

grovelling, groveling (ˈgrɒv(ə)lɪŋ), *a.* (*ppl. a.*) [Orig. an attributive use of GROVELLING *adv.*; subsequently apprehended as pr. pple. of GROVEL *v.*]

1. Having the face or belly towards or on the ground; prone. (Said esp. of the lower animals.)

1538 H. MEDWALL *Interlude Nature* (1896) 41/90 All other bestys as thyngys vnworthy To behold therth wyth grouelyng countenaunce. **1565** COOPER *Thesaurus* s.v. *Abijcio*, Nature hath made beastes bent or grouelynge with their heades downewarde to their foode. **1634** MILTON *Comus* 53 Circe.. Whose charmed Cup Whoever tasted, lost his upright shape, And downward fell into a groveling Swine. *a* **1680** BUTLER *Rem.* (1759) II. 18 Nature gave Man an erect Figure, to raise him above the groveling Condition of.. the Beasts. **1738** WESLEY *Psalms* CXLVII. x, While groveling Beasts attempt his Praise In hoarser Harmony. **1803** LEYDEN *Scenes Infancy* III. 331 The grovelling monster long Blew the shrill hiss.

b. Applied to a low-growing plant.

1750 G. HUGHES *Barbadoes* Pref. 6 A pompous stile would ill fit.. the description of a grovelling plant. *Ibid.* 127 It is but a grovelling, prickly, uncouth tree.

2. *transf.* and *fig.* Of persons, qualities, conditions, etc.: Abject, base, low, mean, sordid.

1608 SYLVESTER tr. *Odet de la Noue's Paradox agst. Libertie* Wks. (1621) 644 Our groueling earth-desires. **1633** G. HERBERT *Temple, Pearl* iv, Not my groveling wit, But thy silk twist let down from heav'n to me, Did.. teach me, how by it To climbe to thee. **1664** POWER *Exp. Philos.* III. 192 You.. may be well placed in a rank specifically different from the rest of groveling Humanity. **1697** DRYDEN *Virg. Georg.* III. 13 New ways I must attempt, my groveling Name To raise aloft, and wing my Flight to Fame. **1711** ADDISON *Spect.* No. 58 ⁋1 One who had written a Treatise upon the Sublime in a low groveling Stile. **1749** FIELDING *Tom Jones* XVII. iv, I cannot bear your groveling temper; you have none of the blood of the Westerns in you. **1821** BYRON *Cain* I. i. 289 That is a grovelling wish. **1826** SCOTT *Woodst.* ii, The ploughman Desborough—as grovelling a clown as is in England. **1827** KEBLE *Chr. Y.*, *Easter Eve*, Lift on high Thy grovelling soul. **1835** THIRLWALL *Greece* I. i. 13 The Bœotians sank into a depth of groveling sensuality. *a* **1862** BUCKLE *Misc. Wks.* (1872) I. 195 Some of the most powerful minds were still corrupted by foolish and grovelling superstition.

absol. **1797** GODWIN *Enquirer* I. viii. 75 The groveling and feeble-hearted are consequently discouraged.

Hence **ˈgrovellingly**, †**ˈgrovellingwise** *advs.*, in a grovelling manner.

1548–67 THOMAS *Ital. Dict.*, *Istraboccheuola*, fallyng grouelynglie. **1561** T. NORTON *Calvin's Inst.* I. 51 Where all other liuing creatures do grouellingwise behold the ground. **1898** *Westm. Gaz.* 14 Feb. 3/1 His wife.. is grovellingly apologetic.

grovelling, groveling (ˈgrɒv(ə)lɪŋ), *adv. Obs.* or *arch.*; but see GROVELLING *a.* Forms: 4–6 **grovelyng(e**, 5– **groveling**, 6– **grovelling**, (5 **grovelinge, groflyng, -eling**, 6 **grovellynge, gruffelyng, grooveling, -lyn**, 7 **grovelong, grobling**); *north.* and *Sc.* 5 **grufelynge, growflyng, growelynge**, 6 **grufling, gruling.** [ME. *grovelynge*, north. *grufelynge*, f. GROOF, GRUFE + -LING[2]. After the verb GROVEL had come into general use the adv. began to be restricted to uses in which it could be apprehended as the pres. pple. used predicatively.] Face downward; in or to a prone or prostrate position.

13.. *E.E. Allit. P.* A. 1119 Þise alder men quen he aproched, Grouelyng to his fete þay felle. **1413** *Pilgr. Sowle* (Caxton) II. xliii. (1859) 49 Sathanas was fallen grouelinge gretyng and cryenge with a lothely voys, byholding doune in to erthe. **1470–85** MALORY *Arthur* IV. viii, Sir launcelot lepte vpon hym, and pulled hym grouelyng doune. **1483** CAXTON *Gold. Leg.* 79/2 They were trobled and tremblyng fyl doun groflyng on theyr faces upon the ground. **1483** *Cath. Angl.* 166/2 Grufelynge [*MS. A.* Growflyng], *supinus*. **1513** DOUGLAS *Æneis* III. ix. 37 Gruling on his kneis, He lappit me fast by baith the theis. **1542** BOORDE *Dyetary* E ij, To slepe grouellynge vpon the stomacke and bely is not good. *c* **1560** A. SCOTT *Poems* (S.T.S.) xxxvi. 3 Soir mornyng, grufling on my face. **1598** HAKLUYT *Voy.* I. 54 In regarde of the great winde we were constrained to lye groueling on the earth. **1601** HOLLAND *Pliny* I. 165 The dead corps of a man floteth on the water with the face vpward, but contrariwise women swim groveling. *Ibid.* II. 408 Some.. lay themselues grouelong with their chinnes touching the ground. **1631** J. ROUS *Diary* (Camden) 60[She] fell grobling (her armes being foulded) at the head of a payre of staires. **1665** MANLEY *Grotius' Low C. Warres* 886 A Bullet.. broke and tore off his left Thigh, and threw him groveling. **1706** PHILLIPS (ed. Kersey) s.v., Among Hunters a Deer is said To feed groveling when she feeds upon her Belly, being tir'd with the Chace. **1855** KINGSLEY *Heroes* IV. 138 The bull fell grovelling on his knees. **1869** FREEMAN *Norm. Conq.* (1876) III. xi. 42 The Earl of the West Saxons bowed himself to the ground, and lay grovelling.

transf. **1713** DERHAM *Phys.-Theol.* 10 *note*, Flat Fishes, as Soles, Plaise, &c. which lie always grovelling at the bottom.

fig. *a* **1674** CLARENDON *Hist. Reb.* XIII. §119 The royal and loyal party lay grovelling and prostrate after the defeat at Worcester.

†**b.** Horizontally. *Obs. rare*$^{-1}$.

1562 TURNER *Herbal* II. 74 b, The moste parte [of date stones] haue a nauel in the myddes of theyr bellies. And from that place commeth first furthe yᵗ it diuideth it self into a roote. It is best to saw it grouelyng.

'grovellings, *adv. Obs.* exc. *dial.* Forms: 3–5 **groveling(e)s**, 5 **grovelonges**, 5–6 **grovelynges**, **(-ys)**; *north.* 3 **gruflinges**, 5 **groflyngis**; *Sc.* 5 **grulingis**, 6 **gruf(e)lingis**, **-lyngis**, **gruff(il)lingis**, **grouf(f)lings**, **groflins**; 9 *dial.* **grubblings**. [f. as prec. + -LINGS.] = prec.

a **1300** *Cursor M.* 11760 Al þair idels in a stund Grouelings fel vnto þe grund. *Ibid.* 17709 þai fell.. Gruflinges dun to erth plate. *a* **1400–50** *Alexander* 5276 þe pilars ware of purfire polischt & hewen, With gomes grouelings of gold. *c* **1420** *Anturs of Arth.* (Camden) xlvii, Alle grouelonges in grounde. **1450–70** *Golagros & Gaw.* 1024 Schir Gologras graithly can ga Grulingis to erd. *c* **1460** *Towneley Myst.* iv. 203 Therfor groflyngis thou shall be layde, That when I stryke thou shal not se. **1513** DOUGLAS *Æneis* III. ii. 52 We plat law gruffillingis on the erd. **1535** STEWART *Cron. Scot.* II. 96 Richt mony als la gruflingis on the grund, In thair bodie buir mony bludie wound. **1570** *Henry's Wallace* XI. 172 Grouflings to ground. *a* **1578** LINDESAY (Pitscottie) *Chron. Scot.* (S.T.S.) I. 258 He maid him lyttill reverence.. bot leinitt doune groufflingis on the dask befoir him. *a* **1825** FORBY *Voc. E. Anglia, Grubblings*, Phr. 'to lie grubblings', i.e. grovelling, with the face downwards.

transf. **1562** TURNER *Herbal* II. 75 If ye will sow Dates lay them all grouelynges toward the grounde.

†**grover.** *Obs.* Also 4 **grovayr.** [a. OF. *gros vair*, lit. 'large vair' (opp. to *menu vair*: see MINIVER and VAIR).] A kind of fur.

1310–11 *Durham Acc. Rolls* (Surtees) 507 In 13 fururis de Grouayr empt., 40s. ?*c* **1325** *Earth* ix. in *E.E.P.* (1862) 151 We.. þat weriþ grouer and groy, and schrud so schene. [**1799** STRUTT *Dress & Habits* IV. i. II. 138 The furs.. which adorned the garments of the nobility, are distinguished by several appellations; as *gros vair*, *minever*, *pennevaire*, and sometimes simply *vair*.]

grover, obs. form of GROOVER.

groves, dial. form of GREAVES.

†**grovet.** *Obs.* Also 6 **grovette**, 8 **grovett.** [f. GROVE + -ET[1].] A little grove.

In OE. charters a form *grafet(t* occurs, which is commonly read as *grǣfet*, and explained as 'trench'. If it be *grǽfet* f. *gráf* GROVE (and so identical with the present word) the suffix is not orig. diminutive.

1504 *Will of Gurdon* (Somerset Ho.), Pastures woodes groves & grovettes. **1538** LELAND *Itin.* V. 95 In Hegge Rowes and Grovettes is meately good Plenti of Wood. **1547** *Mem. Ripon* (Surtees) III. 59 Un' grovett' bosci continente ij acras. **1607** NORDEN *Surv. Dial.* 240 What if a man were desirous to make a little grouet, where now no kind of such plantes doe grow? **1612** BEAUMONT *Masque Inner Temple* (1613) B 3 b, A Hill..with diuers boscages and Grouets vpon the steepe or hanging grounds thereof. **1736** LEWIS *Isle Tenet* (ed. 2) 115 A grovett of Oaks.

grovier, dial. form of GROOVER, miner.

grovy ('grəʊvɪ), *a.* Also 6–7 **grovie**, 9 **grovey.** [f. GROVE + -Y.] Of, pertaining to, or resembling a grove; abounding in groves; situated in a grove.

1594 WILLOBIE *Avisa* (1880) 24 Old Asues grandame is restor'd; Her grouie Caues are new refin'd. **1606** J. RAYNOLDS *Dolarney's Prim.* (1880) 61 Where Philomele, the weary time beguiles, In grouie shades. **1620–55** I. JONES *Stone-Heng* (1725) 60 See where Diana's grovy Temple stands. *Ibid.*, Vitruvius calls her grovy [L. *nemorensis*] Diana. **1699** DAMPIER *Voy.* (1729) II. I. 45 In the dry Season these grovy dwellings are very pleasant. **1834** J. WILSON in *Blackw. Mag.* XXXV. 17 One grovey wilderness of.. trees. **1890** *Century Mag.* Aug. 488/2 The eye ranges far up over the green grovy floor between the mighty walls.

grovy, obs. form of GRAVY.

†**grow**, *sb. Obs.* [f. GROW *v.*] The process or result of growing; growth.

1536 *Act 28 Hen. VIII* c. 17 in Bolton *Stat. Irel.* (1621) 141 Conveying of the wooll of the grow of this land out of the same, is one of the greatest occasions of the idlenesse of the people. **1590** GREENE *Mourn. Garm.* (1616) K 1 b, The tallest Cedars haue the fairest growe. **1768** ROSS *Helenore, Rock & Wee Pickle Tow* 62 I'll gar my ain Tammie gae down to the how, An' cut me a rock of a widdershines grow, Of good rantry-tree to carrie my tow.

grow (grəʊ), *v.* Pa. t. **grew** (gruː, grjuː). Pa. pple. **grown** (grəʊn). Forms: 1 **grówan**, (*3rd sing. pres.* **gréwð**), 3–7 **growe**, (3 **greowen**, 4 **grewen**), 4–5 **grow(e)yn**, *Sc.* and *north.* **groy**, 4, 6 **grou(e**, (5 **grawe**, **grew**, **gr(o)uwe**, **grw**, *Sc.* and *north.* **grofe**, **groyf**, **grufe**, **groo**, 7 **grough**), 5– **grow.** *Pa. t.* 1 **gréow**, 3 **greowe**, 3–4, 6 **greu**, 4 **gru**, 4–5 **greue**, 4–7 **grewe**, 5 **grue**, 4– **grew**; *weak forms*: 4 **growide**, **grouuede**, 4–5 **groued**, 5 **grewed**, **growyd**, 5–6 **gro(w)de**, 6 **grode**, 5 (8–9 *dial.* and *vulgar*) **growed.** *Pa. pple.* 4 *Sc.* **growine**, 4, 6 **groun(e**, 4–7 **growe(n**, 5 **grow**, **groyn**, *Sc.* and *north.* **grofen**, **growane**, **-yn**, 6 *Sc.* **-in**, 6–7 **growne**, 6– **grown**; also 5 **i-**, **ygrowe(n**; *weak form*: 5, (9 *dial.* and *vulgar* **growed**). [OE. *grówan*, pa. t. *gréow*, pa. pple. *grówen*, corresp. to OFris. *growa*, *groia*, MDu. *groeyen*, *groyen*, usually wk., once with pa. t. *griu*, (Du. *groeien* wk.), OHG. *gruoan*, only in pres. stem, (MHG. *grüejen* wk.), ON. *gróa*, pa. t. *grera* on analogy of *róa* to ROW, (Sw. *gro*, Da. *groe* wk.), f. OTeut. root *grô-* (see GRASS).

With the 15th c. northern forms with *f*, cf. Sc. *rufe* for *roo*, a. ON. *ró* rest.]

I. Intransitive senses. (In early use always conjugated with *be*, and still so conjugated when a state or result is implied.)

†**1. a.** Of a plant: To manifest vigorous life; to put forth foliage, flourish, be green. Also of land: To be verdant, produce vegetation. Often associated with BLOW *v.*[2] *Obs.*

c **725** *Corpus Gloss.* 2138 *Viresceret*, greouue. *c* **888** K. ÆLFRED *Boeth.* xxxiii. §5 (Sedgefield), Seo eorðe.. grewð & blewð & westmas bringð. *a* **1000** *Ags. Gloss.* in Wr.-Wülcker 243/32 *Frondescere*, growen. *c* **1000** *Riddles* xxxv. 9 (Gr.) Læteð hio þa wlitigan [wyrte].. blowan & growan. *c* **1200** [see BLOW *v.*[2] 1]. *c* **1205** LAY. 2014 Bi-heold he þene wode hu he bleou, Bi-heold he þæt corn hu hit greu. *c* **1340** *Cursor M.* 384 (Fairf.) þe dry þe erþe calde þat kynge, and bad hit grow and frute forþ bringe. *a* **1400** *Pistill of Susan* 67 Heo greyþed hir til hir gardyn, þat growed so grene.

†**b.** *fig.* To flourish. *Obs.*

a **1000** *Cædmon's Gen.* 88 (Gr.) Him on laste sett wuldorspedum weliȝ wide stodan, ȝifum growende on godes rice.

2. a. In weaker sense: To have vegetative life; to undergo the process of development characteristic of living plants. Hence also, to exist as a living plant in a specified habitat, or with specified characteristics of form, habit, etc.

a **1000** *Boeth. Metr.* xxix. 69 Se milda metod.. fet eall þætte groweð Wæstmas on weorolde. *c* **1205** LAY. 8697 Hasles þer greowen. *a* **1300** *Cursor M.* 385 Alkin things grouand sere.. in þam self þaire seding bere. *c* **1300** *Childh. Jesu* 987 In one felde þare nouȝt ne grev er bote gras wilde. **1419** in *Surtees Misc.* (1888) 14 The herbage that grewys apon the mote. *c* **1536** in *Ballads fr. MSS.* (1872) I. 410 Alone on the Toppe þer growde A brere. **1597** GERARDE *Herbal* II. ii. (1633) 234 The Chadlock groweth.. among corn. **1634** SIR T. HERBERT *Trav.* 209 The Palmeto.. growes like the Date or Coco-tree save that her boughes are more large and round. **1660** F. BROOKE tr. *Le Blanc's Trav.* 324 This Pepper.. growes in a shell, though without prickles. **1697** DRYDEN *Virg. Georg.* IV. 181 Green Beds of Parsley near the River grow. **1762** FALCONER *Shipwr.* I. 492 Not fairer grows the lily of the vale, Whose bosom opens to the vernal gale. **1796** H. HUNTER tr. *St. Pierre's Stud. Nat.* (1779) I. 246 You may judge.. what must have been the height of the tree as it grew, when a cutting of it had such dimensions. **1808–80** JAMIESON s.v. *Catchrogue*, Generally growing in hedges, it tears the clothes of one who attempts to break through. **1842** TENNYSON *Amphion* 83 [They] show you slips of all that grows From England to Van Diemen. **1871** R. ELLIS tr. *Catullus* lxii. 49 A lone lorn vine in a bare field sorrily growing.

b. *transf.* †(*a*) Of minerals (cf. 6 c): To be native in a certain situation (*obs.*); (*b*) *jocularly*, of other things.

c **1400** MAUNDEV. (1839) ix. 99 Fro Jerico, a 3 Myle, is the dede see. Aboute that see growethe moche Alom and of Alkatran. *c* **1540** tr. *Pol. Verg. Eng. Hist.* (Camden) I. 24 Iron allso growethe in the costes bordering on the sea, thowghe nothing plentuoslie. **1580** LYLY *Euphues* (Arb.) 439 They want no Tinne nor Leade, there groweth Yron, Steele and Copper, and what not. **1613** T. MILLES tr. *Mexia's Treas. Anc. & Mod. Times* 699/1 There groweth not any Mettall in Moscovia. **1632** LITHGOW *Trav.* VI. 274 The doores [of stone].. in that same place where they grew they are squared. **1674** tr. *Scheffer's Lapland* 143 That mettals grow in Lapland.. is only a conjecture of the Antients, and there is no certainty of it. **1748** H. WALPOLE *Lett.* (ed. 1846) II. 222 The yacht is not big enough to convey all the tables and chairs and conveniences that he [Duke of Newcastle] trails along with him, and which he seems to think don't grow out of England.

c. *Naut.* (See quot. 1780.)

1780 FALCONER *Dict. Marine*, *Growing*, implies the direction of the cable from the ship towards the anchors; as, the cable grows on the starboard-bow, i.e. stretches out forwards towards the starboard, or right side. **1794** *Rigging & Seamanship* II. 251* The cable grows on the starboard bow.

3. With advs. or preps., forming phrases primarily indicating incidental results of vegetative development, but chiefly used *transf.* or *fig.*

a. To become by degrees ineradicably fixed *into*, vitally or indissolubly united *to* (†*with*) something, as by the process of growth. So *to grow into one*, *to grow together*: to coalesce, become united.

1593 SHAKS. *Rich. II*, v. iii. 30 For euer may my knees grow to the earth,.. Vnlesse a Pardon, ere I rise, or speake. **1606** —— *Ant. & Cl.* I. v. 32 Great Pompey Would stand and make his eyes grow in my brow. **1613** —— *Hen. VIII*, I. i. 10, I.. Beheld them when they lighted, how they clung In their Embracement, as they grew together. **1631** SHIRLEY *Love's Cruelty* IV. ii, *Hip.* The more you vex the more we grow together In honour and chaste love. **1640** —— *Doubtful Heir* III. i, And I will say 'tis virtue, and that yet Your heart may grow with mine. **1668** CULPEPPER & COLE *Barthol. Anat.* I. xix. 50 The Ureters are commonly two in Number, on each side one, sometimes two, and sometimes more, yet al growing into one before their Insertion. **1818** BYRON *Ch. Har.* IV. cxxxviii, We become a part of what has been, And grow unto the spot. *a* **1822** SHELLEY *Invocat. Misery* 45 Clasp me till our hearts be grown Like two lovers into one. **1842** TENNYSON *St. Sim. Styl.* 206 'Tis gone; 'tis here again; the crown! the crown; So now 'tis fitted on and grows to me. **1859** —— *Lynette* 139 The Queen.. sought.. To break him from the intent to which he grew.

†**b.** Hence, *to grow to*: to be an organic or integral part of. *Obs.*

1597 SHAKS. *2 Hen. IV*, I. ii. 100 *Ser.* I pray you (Sir) then set your Knighthood and your Souldier-ship aside. *Fal.* I lay aside that which growes to me? **1601** HOLLAND *Pliny* I. 62 In time past it [Sicily] grewe to the Brutians countrey [L. *Bruttio agro cohaerens*], but soone after by the gushing of the sea between, it was plucked from it.

†**c.** *to grow out*: to become obliterated by growth. *Obs. rare.*

1716 *Lond. Gaz.* No. 5457/4 With an (I) and a (G) clipt on his Buttock, but almost grown out.

4. a. With especial reference to the beginning of vegetable life. Of seeds: To germinate. Of plants: To spring up, be produced.

a **900** *Kent. Gloss.* in Wr.-Wülcker 69/7 *Germinabunt*, growað. *c* **1000** *Ags. Gosp.* Mark iv. 27 Swylce man wurpe god sæd on his land.. And þæt sæd growe and wexe þonne he nat. *a* **1225** *Ancr. R.* 404 O sond ne groweð no god, and bitocneð idel; and idel acoaldeð & acwencheð þis fur. *a* **1250** *Owl & Night.* 1202 Ich wat ȝef cornes schule growe. *a* **1300** *Cursor M.* 1140 In-sted o þi noþer sede, Ne sal þe groue bot thorne and wede. *Ibid.* 1262 Of our sin Moght na gres groue siþen þar-in. *c* **1420** LYDG. *Thebes* III. in *Chaucer's Wks.* (1561) 377/2 For seld in felds groweth any corne But if some wede spryng vp there emong. *c* **1460** *Towneley Myst.* xix. 54, I thank the, lord, that thi sede sawes Emong mankynde to groyf so sone. *c* **1560** A. SCOTT *Poems* (S.T.S.) ii. 77 Als gude the tre had nevir growin Quhairof my speir wes maid. **1660** F. BROOKE tr. *Le Blanc's Trav.* 324 Sugar-canes grow without planting. **1685** BAXTER *Paraphr. N.T.* Mark iv. 26–7 Man soweth, but God blesseth it; and we see it not grow, but see that it hath grown. **1842** TENNYSON *Amphion* 80 Methods of transplanting trees To look as if they grew there.

b. Of the grains of corn in the sheaf, etc.: To sprout, 'chit'. Also with *out.*

1575 *Durham Depos.* (Surtees) 202 This last harvest when the corne was growen. **1740** J. TULL *Horse-Hoing Husb.* 261 Wheat.. grow'd, plow'd in, or otherwise spoiled, is in no Danger [from Rooks]. **1783** BARKER in *Phil. Trans.* LXXIII. 244 From the coolness of the season, and the unripeness of the barley, very little of it grew. *Mod.* The onions in the cellar have begun to grow. The potatoes have grown out.

c. Of fruit, wine, etc.: To be produced by vegetative processes.

a **1300** *Cursor M.* 6895 Almandes was groun þar-on. **1340–70** *Alex. & Dind.* 123 Grete grouuede frut on þe grene braunchus. *c* **1350** *Will. Palerne* 1809 Bolaces & blake-beries þat on breres growen. *c* **1410** *Sir Cleges* 201 What manere of beryse may this be That grovyn this tyme of yere? *c* **1460** FORTESCUE *Abs. & Lim. Mon.* xi. (1885) 135 The vth parte of thair graynes, and of all oþer thynge that growed to thaim yerely off þe erthe. **1526** *Pilgr. Perf.* (W. de W. 1531) 108 b, No meruayle though of that grene blade growe no whete or good corne. **1526** TINDALE *Matt.* xxi. 19 Never frute growe on the hence forwardes. **1547** BOORDE *Introd. Knowl.* i. (1870) 118 They haue no wines growing within the realme. **1599** H. BUTTES *Dyets drie Dinner* D 8 It growes of an Almond-tree-Imp, inserted to a Mastick stock. **1667** MILTON *P.L.* IX. 776 Here grows.. this Fruit Divine, Fair to the Eye. **1725** POPE *Odyss.* VII. 157 The same mild season gives the.. fruits to grow. **1839** URE *Dict. Arts* s.v. *Kermes*, Pliny says.. that there grew upon the oak in Africa.. a small excrescence like a bird.

d. *transf.* Of animals and their parts.

1435 MISYN *Fire of Love* II. ix. 95 Brode horns and in gretnes horribyll of here wroyght that grw not ther on ther hedis tha sett. **1604** SHAKS. *Oth.* I. iii. 145 Men whose heads Grew beneath their shoulders. **1632** LITHGOW *Trav.* VII. 326 Their [flying Fishes'] finnes.. grow from their backe, as feathred wings doe from Fowles. **1667** MILTON *P.L.* X. 244 Methinks I feel new strength within me rise, Wings growing. **1677** N. COX *Gentl. Recreat.* I. (1706) 78 Horns only grow upon the Male. **1866** B. TAYLOR *Palm & Pine Poems* 268 The child that from their meeting grew.

5. *fig.* **a.** Of immaterial things: To spring up, come into existence as by natural process; to arise, originate, be developed as from a germ; to issue or spring naturally as from a stock.

Beowulf 1718 Him on ferhþe greow breosthord blodreow. *c* **1320** *Sir Tristr.* 1273 In warld was non so wiis Of craft þat men knewe Wiþ outen sir tramtris þat al games of grewe On grounde. **1390** GOWER *Conf.* I. 21 Where lawe lacketh errour groweth. **1400–10** CLANVOWE *Cuckow & Night.* 32 Of that longing cometh hevinesse, And therof groweth ofte greet seknesse. **1430–40** LYDG. *Bochas* III. i. 54 (1494) k i, For out of wronge may growe no prowesse. *c* **1460** *Towneley Myst.* viii. 326 What, dwyll! is grevance grofen agayn? **1473** WARKW. *Chron.* (Camden) 22 Lo, what myschef groys aftir insurreccion! **1534** MORE *On the Passion* Wks. 1276/1 God suffered the contagion of the selfe same infeccion, to stretche vnto himselfe to, and thereof to growe hys destruccion. **1572** J. JONES *Bathes of Bath* Ep. Ded. 4 Against such accidents as growe by reason of hote bathes. **1604** E. G[RIMSTONE] *D'Acosta's Hist. Indies* I. xx. 64 Heerevpon groweth a difficultie, which troubleth me much. **1667** MILTON *P.L.* XII. 400 The penaltie to thy transgression due And due to theirs which out of thine will grow. **1712** ADDISON *Spect.* No. 267 ¶5 The Parts of it [Paradise Lost].. grow out of one another in the most natural Order. **1847** TENNYSON *Princ.* III. 61 How grew this feud betwixt the right and left? **1855** —— *Maud* III. vi. 3 As months ran on and rumour of battle grew. **1875** JOWETT *Plato* (ed. 2) III. 432 The States are as the men are; they grow out of human characters.

†**b.** *to grow to*: to arise or come into existence to the benefit or injury of (a person, etc.). Also *absol.* with omission of *to*. *Obs.* (Cf. ACCRUE *v.* 1, 2.)

the law of growing-to [= AF. *dreit de accres*]: reversion, escheat.

[**1382** WYCLIF *Luke* xii. 18, I schal gedere alle things that growen to me [L. *quæ nata sunt mihi*] and alle my goodis.] **1390** GOWER *Conf.* III. 12 For the fortune of every chaunce After the goddes purveaunce To man it groweth from above. *c* **1450** *Bp. Grossetest's Househ. Stat.* in *Babees Bk.* (1868) 331 No worshippe therby growythe to the lorde. *c* **1460** *Towneley Myst.* iii. 463 Then begynnys to grufe to us mery chere. *c* **1460** FORTESCUE *Abs. & Lim. Mon.* ix (1885) 130 Ther mought therby groue perell to his estate. *a* **1483** *Liber Niger* in *Househ. Ord.* (1790) 47 Cloathing to be taken of the issue and profitts growing to the kinge. **1551** ROBINSON tr. *More's Utop.* I. (Arb.) 41 Reuenues and profytes that were wont to grow to theyr fore-fathers. **1587** LADY STAFFORD in *Collect.* (O.H.S.) I. 210 Nor [shall] any hinderaunce growe to theim by this demize. **1592** West *1st Pt. Symbol.* §42 A, A Particuler estate which is onelie a Chattell.. groweth either by the act of the parties, or by the law. **1598** Manwood *Lawes Forest* xvi. §10 (1615) 117 The forfeiture, that doth grow unto the king, onely for the keeping of mastiues within a forest unexpeditated. **1605** Verstegan *Dec. Intell.* vi. (1628) 162 Canutus, vpon the law of growing-too.. tooke vpon him the possession of the whole Realme.

6. Of living bodies generally: To increase gradually in size by natural development. (In OE. said of plants only, the usual word, both with reference to plants and animals, being *weaxan* WAX *v.*)

a. of plants. Also ***to grow away***, to develop (well).

c **888** K. Ælfred *Boeth.* xxxiv. § 10 (Sedgefield), Hwy ne meaht þu onȝitan.. þæt eall se dæl se ðe þæs treowes on twelf monðum ȝewexð, þæt he onȝinð of þæm wyrtrumum & swa upweardes grewð oð ðone stemn? *c* **1400** Maundev. (1839) x. 117 The Hed smot in to the Eerthe and wax grene and is growed to a gret Tree. **1585** T. Washington tr. *Nicholay's Voy.* ii. iii. 33 Great bushes, and wilde brambles, which in process of time.. were so growen and multiplyed. **1593** Shaks. *Rich. III*, ii. iv. 13 Great Weeds do grow apace. **1624** Quarles *Sion's Sonn.* xiii. 1 How can my thriving Plants refuse to grow Thus quickned with so sweet a Sun as thou? **1719** De Foe *Crusoe* i. viii. (1840) 140 When it [corn] was growing and grown. **1883** H. Drummond *Nat. Law in Spir. W.* iv. (1884) 128 The living organism grows, the dead crystal increases. **1933** *Jrnl. R. Hort. Soc.* LVIII. 99 When .. the requisite number of shoots are growing away well. **1961** *Listener* 10 Aug. 222/2 All Talisman plants will be small and behind all other varieties, but they grow away to produce good crops without any difficulty.

fig. **1414** Brampton *Penit. Ps.* (1842) 13 My gylt is growyn over myn heed. **1599** Daniel *Ep. Octavia to M. Antonius* li, Words still with my increasing sorrows grough.

b. Of human beings, and animals generally, their limbs, hair, nails, etc. (when said of human beings, the word refers usually to stature).

The pa. pple. is used (now only *arch.* or U.S.) in the sense of 'grown up'; see 13 and GROWN-UP *ppl. a.*

a **1300** *Cursor M.* 10596 Godd wald sco greu and clamb on hei. **1382** Wyclif *Gen.* xxi. 8 The child growide. *c* **1400** Maundev. (1839) xxxi. 311 To make hem [nails] growen alle weys to ben as longe as men may. **1412–20** Lydg. *Chron. Troy* i. v, Well growe on heyght & of good stature. *c* **1450** Holland *Howlat* lxviii, And I sall gar thaim [fedders] samyn be To growe or I ga. **1486** *Bk. St. Albans* c. ij, Vnto tyme hir sercell be full groyn. **1548** Hall *Chron., Edw. IV*, 234 He was a goodly fayre and a beautefull Prince, beginninge a littel to growe in flesh. **1585** T. Washington tr. *Nicholay's Voy.* iii. iii. 73 b, They do not suffer their beards too grow but above the lips. **1611** Bible *Ruth* i. 13 If I should haue a husband also to night, and should also beare sonnes: Would ye tary for them till they were growen? **1613** Purchas *Pilgrimage* (1614) 648 The King keepeth his daughters when they are growne, for wives. **1634** Milton *Comus* 378 She plumes her feathers, and lets grow her wings. **1638** Sir T. Herbert *Trav.* (ed. 2) 322 [Elephants] grow till fifteen, in that time mounting to foure and twenty foote. **1774** Goldsm. *Nat. Hist.* (1776) III. 228 Young elephants.. he [the lion] often attacks before their trunk is yet grown. **1847** Marryat *Childr. N. Forest* iv, Edward, you must not think of showing yourself.. until you are grown out of memory. **1889** J. A. F. Maitland in *Dict. Nat. Biog.* XVIII. 407/2 (John Field), The awkward English youth.. grown out of his clothes to such an extent that [etc.]. **1890** V. Roseborough *Reign Reason* in *Century Mag.* July 349 And now her children were both grown, and her bad days past.

transf. **1847** Tennyson *Princ.* vi. 144 She.. arose.. Once more thro' all her height, and o'er him grew Tall as a figure lengthen'd on the sand When the tide ebbs in sunshine.

c. Formerly said of minerals. (Cf. 2 b.)

1695 Woodward *Nat. Hist. Earth* iv. (1723) 215 The Metalls.. which are lodged in the perpendicular Intervalls of the Strata do still grow (to speak in the Mineralists Phrase), or receive additional Increase from the Corpuscles. **1877** Huxley *Anat. Inv. Anim.* Introd. 2 In the well-known aphorism of Linnæus [*Lapides crescunt*..] the word 'grow', as applied to stones, signifies a totally different process from what is called 'growth' in plants and animals.

7. a. Of things material or immaterial: To increase gradually in magnitude, quantity, or degree.

1382 Wyclif *Exod.* i. 20 The puple growide, and was coumfortid greetli. *c* **1450** *Mirour Saluacioun* 1377 That stone.. in [= into] a grete mowntaigne grewe. **1482** *Monk of Evesham* (Arb.) 61 Her lyfe of thys world.. in the whyche her synnys and mysdedys encresyn and growyn to her perdycyon and destruccyon. **1573** *Satir. Poems Reform.* xlii. 600 The Kirk.. Had growin vntill ane greiter strenth. **1597** Shaks. *2 Hen. IV*, i. iii. 10 Our present Musters grow vpon the File To fiue and twenty thousand men of choice. **1617** Moryson *Itin.* i. 126 The Potters of old dwelt there.. whereupon a heape grew to a Hill, and a Hill to a Mount. **1697** Dryden *Virg. Georg.* iii. 723 During th' Autumnal Heats th' Infection Grew. **1718** Prior *Solomon* i. 523 New moons may grow or wane, may set or rise. **1784** Cowper *Task* iv. 151 The needle plies its busy task, The pattern grows. **1849** Tennyson *In Mem.* Prol. 25 Let knowledge grow from more to more. **1852** —— *Wellington* 16 Let the long long procession go, And let the sorrowing crowd about it grow. **1879** Froude *Cæsar* ix. 98 They grew at last into a thousand sail, divided into squadrons.

†**b.** Of the sea: To swell. Also ***to grow high***.

1600 E. Blount tr. *Conestaggio* 296 The seas growing high he came with them to Lisbone. *a* **1618** Raleigh *Royal Navy* (1650) 14 Maryners.. who.. are used to the tumbling and rowling of ships from side to side, when the Sea is never so little growne. *Ibid.* 35 If any stormes arise, or the Sea grow so high as that the Kettle cannot Boyle in the Fore-castles.

c. ***to grow down***. (*a*) To extend downwards. (*b*) To become less in height or in size; also ***to grow downwards***. †(*c*) Of the sea: To subside.

1523 Fitzherb. *Husb.* §100 Morfounde.. wyll growe downe, and waxe whyte, and cromely lyke a pomis. **1530** Palsgr. 576/1, I growe downwardes, as an aged thing dothe that boweth, or stoupeth downwardes, *je me decline. Ibid.*, I growe downeward: I waxe lesse, or drawe towardes myn ende, *je decroys.* **1748** F. Smith *Voy. Disc.* i. 15 The Wind .. in the Evening towards Eight was less, and the Sea grew down. **1847–78** Halliwell s.v., To grow downward, i.e. to get smaller, a common phrase in the provinces.

8. a. To increase in some specified quality or property; sometimes with more or less notion of progress toward maturity. Const. *in*, †*of*.

c **1375** Barbour *Bruce* xix. 638 Ane host.. That ilk day growis of mycht. *c* **1470** Henry *Wallace* iii. 45 Adam, eldest, was growand in curage. **1526** *Pilgr. Perf.* (W. de W. 1531) 12 b, Whom God almyghty.. protected.. vnto they were growen in the knowlege of the fayth of God. **1526** Tindale *2 Pet.* iii. 18 Growe in grace, and in the knowledge off oure lorde and saveoure Jesus Christ. **1576** Fleming *Panopl. Epist.* 126 As I grow in hope day by day, through sundrie reportes. **1667** Milton *P.L.* xii. 351 They.. In mean estate live moderate, till grown In wealth and multitude, factious they grow.

†**b.** To rise by degrees *to* (a position of eminence). *Obs.*

1622 Bacon *Hen. VII*, 140 The King.. was growne to such an height of Reputation for cunning and Policie. **1651** Fuller *Abel Rediv., Fox* 381 It may seeme strange.. that he grew to no place of more honour. *a* **1674** Clarendon *Surv. Leviath.* (1676) 146 The Clergy was grown to a wonderful power over the People.

9. ***to grow on*** or ***upon*** (a person, etc.): **a.** To increase so as to be more troublesome to. Now only of a business or the like, ***to grow upon*** one's *hands*. †**b.** To gain ground upon (an enemy or rival). †**c.** To come to take liberties with (a superior), to presume upon, take advantage of (kindness, etc.). **d.** Of an affection, feeling: To acquire more and more influence over (a person). Hence, in recent use, of an object of contemplation: To gain more and more of (a person's) liking or admiration.

a. 1603 Bp. Hall *Serm.* v. 9 How shamefully is this latter vice [drunkenness], especially, grown upon us with time! **1636** Denham *Destr. Troy* 410 Then their numbers swell, And grow upon us. **1667** *Decay Chr. Piety* xviii. 397 Divisions have come to grow upon us,.. by neglect of practick duties. **1711** Shaftesb. *Charac.* (1737) III. Misc. ii. i. 61 This.. is of a kind apt enough to grow upon our hands. **1774** Burke *Sp. Amer. Tax.* 12 The disgrace, and the necessity of yielding, both of them, grow upon you every hour of your delay. **1860** Reade *Cloister & H.* lxv, From that hour another phase of his misery began; and grew upon him.

b. 1603 Knolles *Hist. Turks* (1621) 817 The Christians still growing upon them both in number and strength. **1650** Cromwell *Let.* 2 Apr. in *Carlyle* (1850) II. 323 We hope.. still to grow upon the Enemy. *a* **1687** Petty *Pol. Arith.* Pref. (1691) a ij, The Hollanders are at our heels, in the race of Naval Power; the French grow too fast upon both.

c. 1600 Shaks. *A.Y.L.* i. i. 91 Is it euen so, begin you to grow vpon me? **1723** *True Briton* xxxiii. ¶1 Having in my last Letter taken Notice by what Steps the Quakers have grown upon the Indulgence of the Government, 'till they have procur'd for themselves Privileges.. beyond what much better Subjects.. could obtain. **1741** Richardson *Pamela* I. 35, I thought her humble, and one that would not grow upon my Favours, or the Notice I took of her.

d. 1712 Addison *Spect.* No. 447 ¶2 The Love of a retired or busy life will grow upon a Man insensibly. **1796** Jane Austen *Pride & Prej.* vi. (1813) 16 Miss Bennet's pleasing manners grew on the good-will of Mrs. Hurst. **1798** Ferriar *Illustr. Sterne* i. 3 Particular attachments grow upon us. **1831** Macaulay in Trevelyan *Life* (1876) I. 174, I feel the whole character of the place growing upon me. **1883** W. H. Rideing in *Harper's Mag.* July 168/2 Hampstead grows on one, and improves with acquaintance.

10. a. To advance in age (*obs.* or *arch.*). †**b.** ***to grow on*** (of a season, time, etc.): To advance, make progress.

a. *c* **1477** Caxton *Jason* 67 b, Whan they were growen to age he deliuered to them his landes to gouerne. **1635** R.N. *Camden's Hist. Eliz.* i. vi. 54 A man well grown in yeeres. **1715** Pope *Iliad* I., *Ess. Homer* 24 As he grew forward in Years, he was train'd up to Learning.

b. 1603 Knolles *Hist. Turks* (1621) 287 For Winter was now growne on. **1615** Bedwell *Moham. Imp.* i. §39 The night growen on. *a* **1625** Beaum. & Fl. *Knt. Malta* ii. iii, Ye know my businesse, I must leave ye Sir, My houre grows on a pace. **1655** *Theophania* vi. 182 The winter growing on, for the present [he] desisted from any further enterprise. **1695** Earl Essex *Lett.* (1770) 265, I see such multitudes of perplexities growing on.

11. a. To come or pass by degrees *into*, *to* (rarely †*from*) some state or condition. Also const. *to* with *inf.* Now *rare*.

1450–70 *Golagras & Gaw.* 960 Golagras at Gawyne in sic ane grief grew, As lyoune, for falt of fude, faught on the fold. *c* **1460** Fortescue *Abs. & Lim. Mon.* x. (1885) 133 Ther shulde non off hem growe to be like vnto hym. *c* **1560** R. Morice in *Lett. Lit. Men* (Camden) 26 Specially grown into the Kynges favor by my Lorde Cranmers commendacion. *c* **1590** Marlowe *Faust.* xiv. Belike he is grown into some sickness by being over-solitary. **1596** Harington *Metam. Ajax* (1814) 14 We grew to be friends. **1613** Shaks. *Hen. VIII*, iii. i. 161 Consider.. How you may hurt your selfe: I, vtterly Grow from the Kings Acquaintance, by this Carriage. **1616** Sir F. Kingsmill in *Lismore Papers* (1887) Ser. ii. II. 18 Much dowting I shall growe into a Consumption. **1654** Whitlock *Zootomia* 95 It is no Paradox (such an Olla podrida are we grown to) to say, we cannot see Audience for Preachers, nor Patients for Physitians. *c* **1665** Mrs. Hutchinson *Mem. Col. Hutchinson* 10 Growing into a familiarity with Sir George Carew. **1726** Leoni *Alberti's Archit.* I. 31/1 The Cement all dissolves, and the Wall grows to be all of a piece. **1762–71** H. Walpole *Vertue's Anecd. Paint.* (1786) I. 234 His works growing into esteem, he was much employed by the merchants in painting portraits. **1825** Lamb *Elia* Ser. II. *Superannuated Man*, I grow into gentility perceptibly. **1867** Trollope *Chron. Barset* II. lvi. 124 He grew to be somewhat ashamed of himself.

b. To develop gradually. Const. *to. arch.*

1530 Palsgr. 576/1 This mater will grow to a scabbe, *or de ceste chose en prendra mal.* **1535** Coverdale *Ruth* iii. 18 Abyde my doughter, tyll thou se what yͤ matter wil growe to. **1548–9** (Mar.) *Bk. Com. Prayer, Of Ceremonies*, They [ceremonies] grewe dayly to more and more abuses. **1598** Shaks. *Merry W.* i. i. 79 If matters grow to your likings. **1601** F. Godwin *Bps. of Eng.* (1610) 216 Before the matter could grow to a full conclusion, it was otherwise ended. **1850** Tennyson *In Mem.* lxxi. 11 The days that grow to something strange.

†**c.** To come by degrees *to*, *upon*; to arrive at, draw to (an agreement, conclusion, point, etc.). Also with *on*. *Obs.*

c **1589** *Theses Martinianæ* 28 To growe to a point with you. **1590** Shaks. *Mids. N.* i. ii. 10 Say what the play treats on: then read the names of the Actors: and so grow on to a point. **1594** Plat *Jewell-ho.* i. 55 To force the sopeboilers to growe to composition with them. **1603** Knolles *Hist. Turks* (1621) 72 K. Richard.. thought it best to grow to some good end with Saladin. **1616** Capt. Smith *Descr. New Eng.* 52 But Chambers and Minter grew upon tearmes they would not. **1624** Massinger *Parl. Love* ii. ii, Stay, best Madam, I am growing to a period. **1634** Sir T. Herbert *Trav.* 160 So soone as hee was buried, they grew among themselves to an immediate difference.

12. To become or come to be by degrees, sometimes with inclusion of the literal sense of increase of magnitude or quantity.

a. with adj. or (*arch.*) sb. as complement.

a **1300** *Cursor M.* 6941 Þar þai [sc. wandes] gru, ne less ne mare, Bot euer als þai forwit ware. **1340–70** *Alex. & Dind.* 252 Emperour alixandre egrest of princis, þat is grimmest igrowe and grettest of kingus. *c* **1440** *Promp. Parv.* 215/1 Growe ballyd, *calvesco*. Growe blake, *nigresco*. **1506** Guylforde *Pilgr.* (Camden) 61 The wynde grewe so contraryous vnto vs. **1615** J. Stephens *Satyr. Ess.* 245 Hee will grow frends with any man, that serves his stomacke. **1657** R. Ligon *Barbadoes* (1673) 61 When it grew dark, they lighted upon.. the ship. **1679–88** *Secr. Serv. Money Chas. II & Jas. II* (Camden) 11 To Sir John Poulett, in part of 25ˡⁱ for a quarter to grow due at Lady Day next, upon 100ˡⁱ per ann. **1701** De Foe *True-born Eng.* 17 Here they grew quickly Lords and Gentlemen. **1712** Steele *Spect.* No. 263 ¶1 There are so few who can grow old with a good Grace. **1748** *Anson's Voy.* ii. xii. 266 Turtle now grew scarce, and we met with none in this harbour. **1784** Cowper *Task* ii. 713 Learning grew Beneath his care a thriving vigorous plant. **1820** W. Irving *Sketch-Bk.* I. 55 Time grew worse and worse with Rip Van Winkle as years rolled on. **1842** Tennyson *Gardener's Dau.* 5 We grew The fable of the city where we dwelt. **1874** Green *Short Hist.* iv. §5. 198 The Jews grew wealthy enough to acquire estates.

b. with advb. or adjectival phr. formed with a preposition. Now *rare*.

1555 Eden *Decades* 61 So variable and vnconstant is the nature of man, that he soone groweth owte of vse, becommeth insolente and vnmindful of benefites. **1578** Lyte *Dodoens* v. xliii. 609 Albeit it be nowe growen out of knowledge, yet we have thought it good to describe the same. **1597** Bacon *Coulers Good & Evill* x. (Arb.) 153 The decay of a man's estate seemes to be most touched in the degree when he first growes behinde. **1632** Lithgow *Trav.* vi. 250 This Temple afterward growing in decay. **1646** J. Hall *Horæ Vac.* 145 Wrestling seemes to grow out of use; tis of ancient standing. **1666** Pepys *Diary* 25 June, Mrs. Pen carried us to two gardens at Hackny (which I every day grow more and more in love with). **1724** De Foe *Mem. Cavalier* (1840) 256 The soldiers grew.. out of all discipline.

†**c.** To come to pass, to happen. *Obs. rare*⁻¹.

1614 Raleigh *Hist. World* II. v. iii. §21. 492 Hence it partly grew, that the Carthaginians were so earnest in pressing Hannibal to fight.

13. grow up.

a. To advance to or towards maturity. Of persons, esp. in pa. pple.; cf. GROWN UP *ppl. a.*

1535 Coverdale *Ruth* i. 13 Though I shulde saye: I hope this night to take an huszbande & to brynge forth children, yet coulde ye not tary till they were growne vp. —— *1 Sam.* ii. 26 The childe Samuel wente and grewe up, & was accepted of the Lorde & of men. **1712** Budgell *Spect.* No. 313 ¶16 As soon as they were grown up to be Men. **1809** Malkin *Gil Blas* ii. vii. ¶1 When he saw me grown up to the age of fifteen. **1833** Ht. Martineau *Loom & Lugger* i. i. 6 If he did not mean the girls to grow up the greatest gossips in the neighbourhood. **1875** Jowett *Plato* (ed. 2) I. 188 His children, one of whom is growing up.

b. Of plants: To emerge from the soil, spring up; also, to grow to full size.

1611 Bible *Exod.* ix. 32 The wheat and the rye were not smitten: for they were not growen vp. **1840** Hawthorne *Biog. Sketches, Mrs. Hutchinson* (1879) 173 The beams of the roof still wear the rugged bark with which they grew up in the forest.

c. Of a custom, state of things, etc.: To arise gradually, come into existence.

1596 Spenser *State Irel.* Wks. (Globe) 649/1 To suffer an evill to growe up, which he might timely have kept under. **1654** tr. *Scudery's Curia Pol.* 15 When.. a particular accident grows up against a Prince, or State, it may suffice that the heads of some chief offenders be sacrificed to a reparation. **1847** Tennyson *Princ.* iv. 291 Thus a noble scheme Grew up from seed we two long since had sown. **1847** Grote *Greece* ii. xlvii. (1862) IV. 187 A dispute grew up respecting the city of Epidamnus. **1885** Sir C. S. C. Bowen in *Law Rep.* 29 Ch. Div. 295 A practice had grown up, which it was too late to disturb.

†**d.** To become gradually closed in the process of growth. *Obs.*

1653 WALTON *Angler* vii. 153 The Frogs mouth grows up and he continues so for at least six months without eating.

e. To be sensible, mature; freq. *imp.*

1951 [see CHRIS(S)AKE]. **1959** A. WESKER *Chicken Soup with Barley* in E. M. Browne *New Eng. Dramatists* II. ii. 212 Oh, grow up, Ronnie. You should know that by now. **1967** G. NORTH *Sgt. Cluff & Day of Reckoning* xx. 181 'The Abbot who shirked his obligations hasn't lived!' 'Grow up!' **1969** 'A. GILBERT' *Missing from Home* v. 55 You're surely never on that old game. You want to grow up, Dad. **1971** D. DEVINE *Dead Trouble* ii. 17 That was Dorothy's constant refrain: 'Grow up, Nev!'..He'd show her who was immature.

II. Transitive senses.

14. *causative.* To cause to grow.

a. To produce (plants, wool, etc.) by cultivation.

1774 J. CAMPBELL *Pol. Surv. Brit.* II. 652 They likewise grow some Rice and Tobacco, which is sent through Virginia. **1801** GABRIELLI *Mysterious Husband* III. 8, I grow my own corn, make my own bread, cheese, and butter. **1828** *Life Planter Jamaica* (ed. 2) 55 As we grow only a certain quantity of Indian corn, be sparing of it. **1842** BISCHOFF *Woollen Manuf.* II. 149 We had the Duke of Norfolk's wool, grown in Norfolk. **1849** MACAULAY *Hist. Eng.* iii. I. 314 The whole quantity of wheat, rye, barley, oats, and beans then annually grown in the kingdom, was somewhat less than ten millions of quarters.

b. Of land, etc.: To produce; to bring forth.

1847 MARRYAT *Childr. N. Forest* v, My garden will then grow more potatoes. **1876** OUIDA *Winter City* i. 3 Toy trees, that are cropped as soon as they presume to grow a leaf. **1885** *Manch. Exam.* 13 June 5/3 The depressions, which are of course warmer..than the plateaus, grow Indian corn, millet, and wheat.

fig. **1825** A. W. FONBLANQUE in *Westm. Rev.* IV. 380 He seems to have flattered himself [that his mind] would, without sowing, grow knowledge.

c. Of persons and animals: To let grow on the body.

1819 SOUTHEY *Lett.* (1856) III. 146 Have the geese and ganders entered into a resolution to grow no more quills? **1860** RAWLINSON *Herodotus* VIII. civ. IV. 348 When a mischance is about to befall any of their neighbours within a certain time, the priestess of Minerva in their city grows a long beard. **1897** MAX PEMBERTON in *Windsor Mag.* Jan. 265/2 It was obvious that he was about to grow a beard.

d. To cause to develop *into*.

1811 A. BELL in Southey *Life* (1844) II. 300 It requires a length of time to grow the boys, now on his foundation, into men.

†**e.** To cause to increase, to enlarge. *Obs.*$^{-1}$

1481 CAXTON *Godfrey* clxix. 250 Whan dauid had regned vii. yere in Ebron he grewe [F. *creut*] and amended moche this cyte [Jerusalem].

f. *Cryst.* To bring about the formation of (a crystal); to cause (a crystal) to increase in size.

1911 [implied in GROWN *ppl. a.* 1 b]. **1915** *Amer. Jrnl. Sci.* CLXXXIX. 567 We can, by proper treatment, grow crystals that are nearly symmetrical and complete in their parts. **1950** *Sci. News* XV. 55 We start with our spherical crystal and grow it into a larger crystal by depositing more atoms on it. **1971** *Sci. Amer.* May 130/2 Diamonds are best grown from a solution of carbon in a molten metal such as nickel.

g. *to grow on*, to keep (seedling plants) in suitable situations or conditions as they develop to maturity.

1947 R. P. FAULKNER *Commercial Hort.* xix. 134 They [*sc.* cinerarias] should then be transferred to cooler conditions, and may eventually be grown on in frames. **1971** L. N. & V. L. FLAWN *Gardening under Glass* xvii. 208 In March move [the Cape primroses] into 5 or 6 in. pots and grow on in a cool temperature.

15. *passive.* Of land, etc.: To be covered with a growth of something. Also with *over*. So †*to be grown about* (i.e. surrounded by a growth), *to be grown up* (i.e. crowded with a growth).

These uses seem to have arisen partly from the indirect passive of phrases like *to grow over*, and partly from the intransitive perfect conjugated with *be*.

*c*1470 HENRY *Wallace* VI. 716 That bog..Growyn owr with reyss. **1565** COOPER *Thesaurus, Circunlita musco saxa*, ..growen about with mosse. **1611** BIBLE *Prov.* xxiv. 31 It was all growen ouer with thornes. **1613** PURCHAS *Pilgrimage* (1614) 539 This Iland is throughly growne with Woods. **1720** DE FOE *Capt. Singleton* v. (1840) 90 The country held verdant, well grown with trees. **1748** *Anson's Voy.* II. iii. 142 The country in the neighbourhood was so grown up with wood,..that it appeared impracticable to penetrate it. **1842** S. LOVER *Handy Andy* xv, Its banks sedgy and thickly grown with flaggers and bulrushes. *a*1885 U. S. GRANT *Mem.* I. xx. 277 The field was grown up with corn so tall as to cut off the view.

transf. **1612** BREREWOOD *Lang. & Relig.* v. 38 Italy in that long time being grown well with their seed and posterity.

grow, obs. of GRUE *v.*[1]

growable ('grəʊəb(ə)l), *a.* [f. GROW *v.* + -ABLE.] Capable of being grown or cultivated.

1881 *American* III. 100 Cotton proved growable on a large scale in Georgia. **1882** *Garden* 3 June 380/3 This fine plant seems with us only growable well in the imported state.

growan ('grəʊən). *Cornish dial.* Also **grouan**. [Cornish **growan* (= Bret. *grouan*) gravel, f. Cornish *grou*: see GRAVEL *sb.*] A soft decomposed granite, overlying the veins of tin in Cornwall. *hard growan*: granite or moorstone.

1753 CHAMBERS *Cycl. Supp.*, *Growan*, a word used by the miners in Cornwall to express a sort of coarse and gritty stone, which they are usually obliged to dig through before they come at the veins of ore. **1778** PRYCE *Min. Cornub.* 73 Soft Grouan..can scarcely be called a Stone; for it is rather a sandy or priany Stratum of Moorstone gravel... It generally lies at the extremities of the Moorstone Stratum, or hard Grouan. **1855** *Cornwall* (1862) 75 A decomposition of the rock [granite], more particularly of the felspar in it, which gradually pulverizes it to a 'soft growan'.

attrib. **1768** *Cookworthy's Patent* in Smiles *J. Wedgwood* xv. (1894) 177 A kind of porcelain composed of moor-stone or growan and growan clay. **1824** HITCHINS & DREW *Cornwall* I. xiii. §4. 564 The black growan soil consists of a thin stratum of light black earth..the detritus of the granite or growan. **1894** SMILES *J. Wedgwood* xv. 169 The Porcelain or Growan Clay was suitable for many purposes for which the Staffordshire Clays were unsuitable.

growane, obs. Sc. pa. pple. of GROW.

growat, obs. Sc. form of CRUET.

1542 *Inv. R. Wardr.* (1815) 58 Item, twa growattis.

growde, obs. pa. t. of GROW.

growe, obs. form of GROW, GRUE *v.*[1]

growed, obs. and dial. pa. t. and pple. of GROW.

growel(le, obs. forms of GRUEL.

growelynge, obs. Sc. form of GROVELLING.

growen, obs. inf. and pa. pple. of GROW.

growende, obs. form of GROUND *sb.*

grower ('grəʊə(r)). [f. GROW *v.* + -ER[1].]

1. Of a plant (usually with adj. having advb. force): One that grows (in the specified way).

1562 J. HEYWOOD *Prov. & Epigr.* (1867) 212 Ye..pining graffes, great growers as can bee. **1674** N. FAIRFAX *Bulk & Selv.* 128 The waxings and sproutings forth, which are found in all growers. **1758** ELLIS in *Phil. Trans.* L. 442 Many people, who have been in North America, agree, that it is but a slow grower there. **1796** C. MARSHALL *Garden.* xix. (1813) 333 The balm of Gilead and hemlock sorts [of pine] are the lowest growers. **1854** S. THOMSON *Wild Fl.* III. (ed. 4) 293 The sea-kale, a grower in the sand. **1878** *R. Thompson's Gardener's Assist.* 694 *Eupatorium*, a useful genus of tall..composite plants; remarkably free growers.

b. 'The lower part of a growing thorn used in making hedges, a thick limb of a thorn hedge' (*E. Dial. Dict.*).

1829 *Sporting Mag.* XXIV. 54 A strong grower catching his knee, he is displaced from his saddle. **1892** 'RUSTICUS EXPECTANS' in *Field* 26 Mar. LXXIX. 436/3 Mr. C—— fell at the first fence, being swept off by a grower.

2. Of a person: One who grows (produce).

*a*1687 PETTY *Pol. Arith.* x. (1691) 113 The growers of Commodities, do commonly trust them to such Merchants or Factors. **1776** ADAM SMITH *W.N.* III. iv. (1869) I. 410 Its rude produce being charged with less carriage, the traders could pay the growers a better price for it. **1787** MARSHALL *Norfolk* (1795) II. 380 *Growers*, farmers. *Great growers*, capital farmers. **1817** *Parl. Debates* 784 A..petition.. signed by..respectable growers of wool in the county of Essex. **1873** C. ROBINSON *N.S. Wales* 19 Other growers state the yield to be at 60 tons [of sugar] for first crop.

groweth, obs. form of GROWTH[1].

growf(f)e, obs. forms of GROOF.

growflyng, obs. Sc. form of GROVELLING *adv.*

growge, obs. variant of GRUDGE.

grow-graine, obs. form of GROGRAM.

growide, obs. pa. t. of GROW.

growinde, obs. form of GROUND *sb.*

growing ('grəʊɪŋ), *vbl. sb.* [f. GROW *v.* + -ING[1].]

1. The action of the vb. GROW.

a. in intransitive senses. (Also with *up*.)

*c*1380 WYCLIF *Sel. Wks.* III. 347 þei [Apostles].. traveliden more bisili to growyng & profiting of þe Chirche. **1398** TREVISA *Barth. De P.R.* v. xxx. (1495) 140 The growyng and feding of nayles is lyke to the growynge of here. **1549** COVERDALE, etc. *Erasm. Par. 1 Pet.* 7 The ghospels doctryne hath his principles, it hath his infancy,.. it hath also his farther growinges. **1642** FULLER *Holy & Prof. St.* IV. x. 288 Thus a Saint of God, like an oke, may be cut down in a moment; but how many years was he a growing! **1719** DE FOE *Crusoe* I. vi. (1840) 105 The growing up of the corn. **1818** *Art Preserv. Feet* 182 A nail which bends down-wards and grows in that position, produces one species of what is commonly called 'growing into the flesh'. **1862** H. SPENCER *First Princ.* II. iv. §53 (1875) 174 A growing up to the recognition of certain truths. **1869** MORRIS *Earthly Par.* II. 210 In the orchard hangs aloft The purple fig, a-growing soft. *Mod.* 'All a-blowing, all a-growing' (London flower-seller's cry).

b. in transitive senses.

1889 *Daily News* 21 Jan. 5/4 Trial growings of new sorts, side by side with established varieties.

†**2. a.** Growth; the faculty, period, or process of growth. Rarely *pl.* *Obs.*

1390 GOWER *Conf.* I. 35 Man of soule resonable..lich to beste he hath feling And lich to tres he hath growing. *c*1430 *Hymns Virg.* 19 Wiþ trees and gras þou ȝaf us growinge. **1523** FITZHERB. *Husb.* §127 If the hedge be of x. or xii. yeres growing syth it was first set. **1560-1** *Bk. Discipline Ch. Scot.* (1621) Pref., To consider the different conditions of the Kirk in her infancie, in her growing and in her ripe age.

†**b.** *concr.* A growth, a crop. *Obs.*

1549 COVERDALE, etc. *Erasm. Par. 1 Cor.* xi. 13-16 To whome [womanne] of nature is gyuen a more thicke and more large growyng of heare, than to the manne. **1722** WODROW *Ch. Hist.* III. iii. II. 76 His Master took from him Nine Cows..with all the Crop and Growing of that Year.

†**3.** In nonce-uses: **a.** Interest on money advanced. **b.** Advance, progress. *Obs.*

1483 CAXTON *Gold. Leg.* 431 b/1 To paye or yelde to them theyr usure or growyng. **1611** SHAKS. *Wint. T.* IV. i. 16 Your patience this allowing, I turne my glasse, and giue my Scene such growing As you had slept betweene.

†**4.** *growing-to*: see GROW *v.* 5 b.

5. *attrib.* and *Comb.*, as ***growing-age***, ***-period***, ***-place***, ***-region***, ***-season***, ***-time***; **growing-cell**, a microscope-slide on which minute objects are kept growing in water; **growing-on**, the cultivating of seedlings, the breeding of young chicks, etc., to maturity or full size; **growing pains** (see quot. 1886); also *fig.*; **growing point** (see quot.); also *fig.*; **growing season**, the season when rainfall and temperature permit plants to grow; **growing-slide** = *growing-cell*; **growing stock** *Forestry*, the total quantity of trees in an area; **growing weather**, weather adapted to further the growth of plants; **growing zone**, the region of an annelid worm in which growth or regeneration is initiated.

Growing weather might belong to GROWING *ppl. a.* (cf. quot. 1782 there).

1881 H. JAMES *Portr. Lady* xxi, A plain muslin gown, too short for the wearer, and denoting that she was at the so called '*growing' age. **1867** J. HOGG *Microsc.* I. iii. 198 *Growing-cells. **1960** *Farmer & Stockbreeder* 15 Mar. 150/2 A new popular system for *growing-on from 8 to 10 weeks to laying stage. **1960** *Jrnl. R. Hort. Soc.* LXXXV. 89 Cost can also be reduced by purchasing small specimens and growing on. **1962** J. N. WINBURNE *Dict. Agric.* 354/2 *Growing-on-house*, a greenhouse used for growing potted plants from the small plant stage to maturity. **1810** COLERIDGE *Notes & Lect.* (1874) 79 In the third [class], as indicating a greater energy..yet still with some of the *growing-pains, and the awkwardness of growth—I place —Troilus and Cressida [etc.]. **1886** *Syd. Soc. Lex.*, *Growing pains*, the neuralgic pains in the limbs which are not uncommon in young persons during the period of growth. **1915** A. HUXLEY *Let.* Oct. (1969) 80 Germany seems to be like..a new growing country, swelled with its own pride, filled by its growing pains with an immense folie de grandeur. **1923** J. M. MURRY *Pencillings* 70 The struggles of a generation towards complete rationality..are growing pains. **1896** *Allbutt's Syst. Med.* I. 162 New formation and regeneration are continually taking place during life, even after completion of the *growing period. **1551** TURNER *Herbal* I. A iv b, Pliny writeth of the *growyng place of this herbe thus..This groweth in the sea. **1835** J. LINDLEY *Introd. Bot.* (ed. 2) I. ii. 56 They [*sc.* the leaf-buds] consist of scales imbricated over each other..and surrounding a minute cellular axis, or *growing point. **1880** S. H. VINES tr. *Prantl's Elem. Textbk. Bot.* ii. 64 The growing end or apex of an organ, such as a root or a stem, is called the growing-point (*punctum vegetationis*). **1882** VINES *Sachs' Bot.* 138 The terminal portion of an organ with permanent apical growth, consisting entirely of primary meristem, is termed the *Growing Point* or 'Punctum Vegetationis'. **1948** *Mind* LVII. 103, I shall..indicate what seem to me the growing points in his theory. **1959** *Listener* 15 Jan. 108/2 Muir..had truly perceived where lay the growing-point of poetry in our time. **1962** *Punch* 28 Feb. 343/2 Secondary Modern..is undoubtedly one of the 'growing points' in English education. **1927** HALDANE & HUXLEY *Animal Biol.* xii. 282 This *growing-region often continues active throughout life. **1958** BROCKLEHURST & WARD *Gen. School Biol.* 146 (*caption*) Growing region of a root. **1845** *Florist's Jrnl.* 61 We advise a decided difference in the supply at the *growing season and afterwards. **1924** W. S. JONES *Timbers* i. 5 The process [of tissue growth] continues throughout the growing season. **1957** G. E. HUTCHINSON *Treat. Limnol.* I. vii. 526 The incidence of small lakes may increase the growing season for crops. **1856** W. B. CARPENTER *Microscope* 144 A small addition may be conveniently made to the glass stage-plate, which adapts it for use as a *Growing-slide. **1889** W. SCHLICH *Man. Forestry* I. I. i. 15 The capital employed in forestry consists principally of the soil and the *growing stock of wood. **1967** D. R. JOHNSTON et al. *Forest Planning* xviii. 287 The level of the growing stock is clearly an important factor in thinning. **14..** *Nom.* in Wr.-Wülcker 736/41 *Hoc ver*, *groyngtyme. *c*1440 LYDG. *Secrees* 1301 The growyng tyme and the yong sonne; I mene the sesoun whan veer is be gonne. **1794** *Trans. Soc. Arts* XII. 137 The first *growing weather in March and April. **1921** *Phil. Trans. R. Soc.* B. CCXI. 145 There were behind this four segments with setæ, one without setæ and a *growing zone. **1952** *Biol. Rev.* XXVII. 408 The posterior residual growing zone itself grows progressively more slowly.

growing ('grəʊɪŋ), *ppl. a.* [f. GROW *v.* + -ING[2].] That grows, in senses of the vb. (Also with *up*.) ***growing pay, wages*** (see quot. 1867).

*a*900 *Kent. Gloss.* in Wr.-Wülcker 66/23 *Uirens folium*, growende leaf. *a*1000 *Cædmon's Gen.* 890 (Gr.) Hwæt druȝe þu, dohtor..growendra ȝifa. *c*1587 *Let. All Souls' Coll.* in *Collect.* (O.H.S.) I. 211 Expences, which..are to be defrayed by our woodes as by a growinge treasure. **1590** SPENSER *F.Q.* III. ii. 46 If thou may with reason yet represse The growing evill, ere it strength have gott. **1631** WEEVER *Anc. Funeral Mon.* 18 Hewne and framed out of the rocke or growing stone. **1703** ROWE *Ulyss.* v. i. 1878 Each moment brings the growing Danger nearer. **1744-50** W. ELLIS *Mod. Husbandm.* VIII. I. 44 The great Stones that we call growing Stones, composed of vast Numbers of small Pebbles that lie in little Cells or Holes. **1782** BARKER in *Phil. Trans.* LXXII. 282 Soon after April came in, the weather was fine and growing, sometimes showery. **1783** BURKE *Rep. Affairs Ind.* Wks. XI. 278 This receipt of sums of money, under colour of gift, seemed a growing evil. **1804** NELSON in Nicholas *Disp.* (1846) VI. 126 You are to inquire whether blame is to be attached to any individual for the said loss, in order that it may be charged against his growing wages. **1859** HELPS *Friends in C.* Ser. II. To Rdr. 3 The growing practice of maintaining large standing armies in times of peace. **1863** LYELL *Antiq. Man* 31 It seems..to have been surrounded by growing trees. **1867** SMYTH *Sailor's Word-bk., Growing pay*, that which succeeds the dead-horse, or pay in prospect. **1868** HELPS *Realmah* v. (1869) 87 He has growing up boys to deal with. **1889** BURDON-SANDERSON in *Nature* 26 Sept. 523 A growing organism is not the same to-day as it was yesterday.

Hence **'growingly** *adv.*, increasingly; **'growingness** *rare*, the characteristic quality of a growing plant; in quot. *fig.*

1758 S. HAYWARD *Serm.* Introd. 10 He seems to have been growingly solicitous to advance the interest of religion. **1869** I. BURNS *Life W. C. Burns* iv. (1870) 85 The result was seen in a growingly heightened tone of moral and religious life. **1872** *Contemp. Rev.* XIX. 211 Every one..must have been growingly persuaded that its investigations were destined to bring out results of deep interest. **1894** *Sat. Rev.* 3 Mar. 231 There is a rapid fresh growingness in it [a novel].

growl (graʊl), *sb.* [f. GROWL *v.*[3]]

1. a. An act of growling; a low angry guttural sound uttered by an animal.

1727 GAY *Fables* I. xliii. 32 Let him the lion first control, And still the tiger's famished growl. **1774** GOLDSM. *Nat. Hist.* (1776) III. 225 When enraged he has a different growl, which is short, broken, and reiterated. **1843** MACAULAY *Lays Anc. Rome, Virginia* 222 The growl of a fierce watch-dog but half-aroused from sleep. **1884** *Manch. Exam.* 7 Oct. 5/7 The lowing of the kine, the growls of the camels.

fig. **1849** MACAULAY *Hist. Eng.* v. II. 609 The general voice of the kingdom, however, effectually drowned the growl of this hateful faction.

b. *transf.* Of cannon, an earthquake, thunder, etc.: A rumble.

1833 J. MARTINEAU *Ess., Rev. & Addr.* (1890) I. 10 All was quiet on the surface, not a growl was heard, not a vibration felt. **1859** HELPS *Friends in C.* Ser. II. II. ii. 41 The solemn growl of philosophic thunder. **1899** *Q. Rev.* Apr. 429 The distant growl of cannon.

2. An expression of anger or dissatisfaction uttered by human beings.

1821 LAMB *Elia* Ser. I. *Old Benchers I.T.*, Many a sarcastic growl did the latter cast out. **1853** KINGSLEY *Hypatia* xvi, An ominous growl rose from the mob of monks. **1884** S. J. REID *Life Syd. Smith* xiii. 342 The muttered growl with which the eclipsed poet relieved his overcharged feelings.

3. In Jazz, a deep rasping sound made on a wind instrument. Also *attrib.*

1935 *Hot News* Aug. 18/3 He used the non-pressure method common to most white players, producing a tone.. with just a suggestion of a growl. **1946** R. BLESH *Shining Trumpets* (1949) II. xii. 280 Here, too, is the growl trumpet, an atmospheric part of the tissue paper jungle in which the band was then ensconced. **1959** 'F. NEWTON' *Jazz Scene* vii. 122 Bubber Miley (1902–32) pioneered the systematic use of the mute and the 'growl'. **1961** *Times* 20 May 11/4 The art of 'growl' trumpet playing has declined so much over the years.

†**growl**, *v.*[1] *Obs. rare*$^{-1}$. [ad. MDu. *growelen, gruwelen* used impersonally in same sense.]

impers. ***it growls me***: I have a feeling of terror or horror.

1481 CAXTON *Reynard* (Arb.) 78 That ther sholde..suche wrake be taken therof that hym myght growle that ever he sawe hym.

†**growl**, *v.*[2] *Obs. rare*$^{-1}$. [ad. F. *grouiller* in the same sense.] *intr.* To swarm.

1542 UDALL *Erasm. Apoph.* 158 He dyed of lyce contynually growlyng out of his fleshe as Scylla and Herode didde.

growl (graʊl), *v.*[3] Also 8 groul. [Prob. an echoic formation; cf. GURL *v.*

Exc. for the one instance under 1 a, and one instance of the vbl. sb. GROLLING, the word has not been found before the 17th c. The continuity of the word is doubtful; it may however have been preserved in some dialect. Walter de Bibbysworth (13th c.) uses AF. *growler* as the distinctive verb for the cry of the crane (*grwe*), and *grouler, groullier* occurs in OF. and mod. north-east Fr. with the sense 'to grumble, scold'. The latter appears to be adopted from Teut.; cf. MDu., Du., LG., MHG., mod.G. *grollen* to growl, to sulk, nurse wrath: see GRILL *v.*[1]]

1. *intr.* †**a.** Of the bowels: To rumble; = GURL *v. Obs. rare*$^{-1}$. (Cf. GROLLING *vbl. sb.*)

c **1380** WYCLIF *Serm.* in *Sel. Wks.* II. 249 (MS.I) As a mete ..not defied..makiþ mannis bodi to groule [*other MSS.* gurle].

b. Of an animal: To utter a low guttural sound, expressive of rising anger.

a **1667** SKINNER *Etym. Angl.* (1671), *To Growl*, à Teut. *Groll*..*Grollen.* **1705** [see GROWLING *ppl. a.*]. **1719** DE FOE *Crusoe* I. ii, He started up growling at first, but finding his Leg broke fell down again, and then got up upon three Legs, and gave the most hideous Roar that ever I heard. **1783** COWPER *Let.* 17 June, Wks. (1876) 135 A surly mastiff will bear perhaps to be stroked, though he will growl even under that operation. **1836** W. IRVING *Astoria* II. 106 The bear.. turned, reared, showed his teeth, and growled. **1859** TENNYSON *Enid* 1411 He fears To lose his bone, and lays his foot upon it Gnawing and growling.

fig. **1848** W. H. KELLY tr. *L. Blanc's Hist. Ten Y.* I. 72 England was growling; Canning was showing his teeth. **1899** A. LANG in *Longm. Mag.* July 281 The cat..growled to keep them away, just as newspapers growl at foreign nations.

c. *transf.* Of thunder, etc.: To rumble.

1727–46 THOMSON *Summer* 1134 At first, heard solemn o'er the verge of heaven, The tempest growls. **1805** WORDSW. *Waggoner* I. 152 The thunder had begun to growl. **1833** M. SCOTT *Tom Cringle* xvi. (1859) 446 A strong murmuring noise like the rushing of many waters growled amongst the ranks. **1864** SKEAT *Uhland's Poems* 242 Low growls the distant thunder. **1958** *Spectator* 15 Aug. 225/2 The bulldozers of the New Towns growl nearer. **1970** *Observer* (Colour Suppl.) 15 Feb. 24/1 The big jets of Qantas and BOAC growl in and out daily on their way round the world.

2. Of persons: **a.** *intr.* To murmur angrily.

1707 *Reflex. upon Ridicule* 328 He Growls, he Rages, he Swears. **1714** GAY *What d'ye call it* Prelim. Scene, He would rave..about a foolish flower'd Handkerchief!—and then he would groul so manfully. **1782** MAD. D'ARBLAY *Diary* Dec., Though he pretended to growl, he was evidently delighted. **1822** W. IRVING *Braceb. Hall* (1823) I. 103 One of those who eat and growl, and keep the waiter on the trot. **1857** HOLLAND *Bay Path* v. 69 He's no business to growl and talk about money.

b. *trans.* To utter or express with a growl or in a growling manner: with simple sb., quoted words, or clause as obj. Also with *out.*

1758 JOHNSON *Idler* No. 53 ¶12 She growls out her discontent. **1784** COWPER *Task* VI. 376 Each animal.. growled defiance in such angry sort, As [etc.]. **1828** SCOTT *F.M. Perth* xxiii, Bonthron was silent for an instant, then growled out,—'He is too mighty for me to name'. **1847** TENNYSON *Princ.* v. 199 Here he reach'd White hands of farewell to my sire, who growl'd An answer. **1876** E. JENKINS *Blot on Queen's H.* 17 A few of the waiters there growled that they were obliged to play second-fiddle. **1880** L. STEPHEN *Pope* iv. 81 Dennis..continued to growl out criticisms against the triumphant poet.

3. *intr.* Of a wind instrument: to make a low, rasping sound. Of a musician: to make such a sound on an instrument. Also *trans.*, to play (music) in a growling manner.

1935 N. E. WILLIAMS *His Hi de Highness of Ho de Ho* 35 Even white musicians will say 'growl it' to a trumpet player when they are asking him to play it 'lowdown' or 'dirty'. **1935** *Hot News* Apr. 19/1 He has the dirtiest tones imaginable, using his hand in front of the bell to produce a unique growling effect. *Ibid.* Aug. 6/2 Only a trumpeter who can growl well is necessary. **1935** *Metronome* Nov. 25/3 A trumpet..growls really effectively for a change. **1955** DUKE ELLINGTON in Shapiro & Hentoff *Hear Me Talkin' to Ya* xii. 195 Everybody told him he'd have to use a plunger and growl all night long.

Hence (*nonce-wds.*) **'growlsome** *a.*, inclined to growl; **'growly** *a.*, resembling a growl.

1882 L. KEITH *Alasnam's Lady* I. 149 You are not as growlsome as some men I know. **1893** MARY E. HULLAH *My Aunt Const. Jane* iii. 91 A gruff growly voice.

growler ('graʊlə(r)). [f. GROWL *v.*[3] + -ER[1].]

1. One who or something which growls.

1753 *World* No. 7. 38 If these Growlers..would content themselves with giving repeated histories of their own ill-fortunes. **1840** DICKENS *Barn. Rudge* xxxiv, Haven't you slept enough, growler? **1867** SMYTH *Sailor's Word-bk., Growlers*, smart, but sometimes all-jaw seamen, who have seen some service, but indulge in invectives against restrictive regulations, rendering them undesirable men. **1880** *Harper's Mag.* LX. 622 But the routs and the revelry were no more agreeable to loyalist growlers like Judge Jones than to the patriots.

2. *slang* or *colloq.* A four-wheeled cab.

1865 M. COLLINS *Who is Heir?* II. 231 His servant Norris followed with his baggage in a 'growler'. **1888** J. PAYN *Myst. Mirbridge* II. xxii. 111 A splended footman..called for a four-wheeled cab..; it was the most debauched-looking 'growler' that ever was seen.

3. The name of certain fishes. **a.** A species of black-bass (see quot.). **b.** The grunt or pig-fish (*Cent. Dict.*).

1880 GÜNTHER *Fishes* 393 One species from the fresh waters of the United States (*Grystes salmonoides*)..is known by the name of 'Growler'.

4. *U.S. slang.* A vessel in which beer is fetched. ***to rush the growler*** (see quot. 1888).

1888 *N.Y. Herald* 29 July (Farmer), The employment by hands in a number of factories of boys and girls, under ten and thirteen years, to fetch beer for them, or in other words to rush the growler.

5. A compact mass of floating ice, smaller than a 'bergy bit', but of such a size that waves do not quite break over its top; a small iceberg.

1912 *Standard* 4 May 7/7 He thought the distinction between icebergs and growlers was that the growler was an iceberg with very little protruding above the water. **1922** JOYCE *Ulysses* 609, I seen icebergs plenty, growlers. **1934** *Geogr. Jrnl.* LXXXIII. 393 The faces [of the glaciers] break away in small pieces making brash and growlers common around the islands. **1958** *New Scientist* 10 July 359/1 As it weathers away, a berg becomes known as a 'bergy bit'.., and finally a 'growler' (when almost awash).

6. *Electr.* An electromagnet with two poles designed to receive an armature, used for testing the windings for short circuits.

If a short circuit exists in the armature coils its presence is indicated by a 'growling' noise.

1922 J. C. WRIGHT *Automotive Repair* II. 73 For making tests showing the general conditions of an armature, an instrument commonly known as a 'growler' is desirable. **1951** H. COTTON in P. Kemp *Electr. Engin.* II. 30 The growler is applied to the armature as shown..and a thin steel rule held to the teeth at a distance equal to the coil pitch away from the centre line. **1961** K. WILKINSON *Armatures & Field Coils* v. 104 The growler is a very simple and extremely valuable piece of test equipment.

7. *dial.* and *slang.* A dog. (In quot. 1822 *fig.*)

1822 'REAL PADDY' *Real Life Ireland* xii. 264 All the blackguards backed the growler. **1959** I. & P. OPIE *Lore & Lang. Schoolch.* ix. 154 Barker or growler.

growlery ('graʊlərɪ). [f. GROWL *v.*[3] + -ERY.]

1. Growling, rumbling, or grumbling.

1830 *Blackw. Mag.* XXVII. 588 At first a low muttering is heard—a sort of mountain growlery. **1833** *Fraser's Mag.* VII. 706 The round-about, hubble-bubble, rumfustianish ..roly-poly growlery of style [of Carlyle].

2. (After Dickens's use in *Bleak House.*) A place to 'growl' in; jocularly applied to a person's private sitting room. (Cf. *boudoir* and *den.*)

1852 DICKENS *Bleak Ho.* viii, 'Sit down, my dear', said Mr. Jarndyce; 'this, you must know, is the Growlery. When I am out of humour I come and growl here'. **1883** 'MAX O'RELL' *John Bull* x. 85 Every Englishman has his boudoir ..He calls this place his growlery, a name having the same meaning as our boudoir. **1887** G. MACDONALD *Home Again* ix. 68 Lady Tremaine received him in what she called her growlery.

growling ('graʊlɪŋ), *vbl. sb.* [f. GROWL *v.*[3] + -ING[1].] The action of GROWL *v.*[3]

1752 MRS. DELANY *Let. to Mrs. Dewes* in *Life & Corr.* 131 Many impatiences, disappointments, grumblings and growlings have they cost. **1807** *Med. Jrnl.* XVII. 185 The voice is hoarse and sometimes resembles the growling of a dog. **1834** R. M. MCCHEYNE in *Mem.* (1872) 467 The increasing growling of the thunder. **1899** *Blackw. Mag.* May 796/1 The deep growling of the great bears..could always be heard.

growling ('graʊlɪŋ), *ppl. a.* [f. GROWL *v.*[3] + -ING[2].] That growls.

1705 VANBRUGH *Confed.* II. i, A Husband is a growling animal. **1735** SOMERVILLE *Chase* I. 154 Soon as the growling Pack with eager Joy Have lapp'd their smoaking Viands. **1825** J. NICHOLSON *Operat. Mechanic* 370 Sufficiently loud to produce the most horrible growling sound which can be conceived. **1867** R. W. DALE *Week-day Serm.* v. 123 Growling thunder and pelting rain.

Hence **'growlingly** *adv.*, in a growling manner.

1803 *Med. Jrnl.* X. 176 The nurse..will once or twice at most growlingly remove it. **1889** *Chamb. Jrnl.* 14 Sept. 583/2, 'I'm worried', returned Snelling growlingly.

growly ('graʊlɪ), *a.* [f. GROWL *sb.* or *v.*[3] + -Y[1].] Resembling a growl.

1920 GALSWORTHY *In Chancery* I. vii, Val, uttering a growly sound, followed her. **1954** *Time* 25 Oct. 74 Terry plays some pretty, growly trumpet.

†**growme.** *Obs.* In some edd. of Bailey's *Dict.* erroneously **grown.** [Perh. the same word as GROOM *sb.*[2]] (See quots.)

1601 *Act 43 Eliz.* c. 10 §2 No persone or persons..shall have keepe or use any manner of Wrinche Ringehead Growme Rope or other Engine to stretche or straine any roughe and unwroughte Woollen Clothe [etc.]. **1607** COWEL *Interpr., Growme*, anno 43 E. ca. 10. seemeth to be an engine to stretch wollen cloth withall after it is wouen.

Growmore ('grəʊmɔə(r)). [f. GROW *v.* + MORE *adv.*] Formerly ***National Growmore.*** A non-proprietary name for a standard preparation of garden (esp. vegetable) fertilizer first marketed during the war of 1939–45 (see quot. 1975).

1944 *Pop. Gardening* 25 Nov. p. viii/4 (Advt.), National Growmore fertiliser 28lbs 7/6. **1955** *Ibid.* 12 Nov. 1627 (Advt.), National Growmore Fertiliser. **1975** *Handyman Which?* Nov. 155/1 If buying lots of different fertilisers is too much bother you may want to use Growmore (formerly National Growmore)—a standard formulation of seven per cent nitrogen, seven per cent phosphate and seven per cent potash—for nearly all your plants. **1986** *Gardening from Which?* Mar. 60/1 If you grow a lot of leafy vegetables, buy some Growmore.

grown (grəʊn), *ppl. a.* [Pa. pple. of GROW *v.*, q.v. for forms.]

1. a. Advanced in growth; increased in size, degree, etc.

1340–70 *Alex. & Dind.* 133 Eueri grene growe tre þat on þe ground spronge Hadde bremliche a brid þe braunchus alofte. **1605** SHAKS. *Macb.* III. iv. 29 There the growne Serpent lyes, the Worme that's fled. **1616** *Rich Cabinet* 124b, Reason teacheth the Gardner to cut his growne herbes, and not pull them vp by the rootes. **1692** LOCKE *Educ.* §37 This is now so grown a Vice, and has so great Supports, that I know not whether it do not put in for the Name of Vertue.

b. Of a crystal: produced by growing (GROW *v.* 14 f).

1911 *Encycl. Brit.* VII. 584/1 The pitted and cavernous faces of artificially grown crystals of sodium chloride and of bismuth are..a result of rapid growth. **1962** SIMPSON & RICHARDS *Junction Transistors* iii. 46 The manufacture of *n-p-n* grown-junction transistors. **1966** *McGraw-Hill Encycl. Sci. & Technol.* VII. 318/2 There are several variations of the grown-junction technique. The simplest consists of successively adding different types of impurities to the melt from which the semiconductor crystal is being grown.

2. Arrived at maturity; grown-up. See also FULL-GROWN. †***grown years***: mature, ripe years.

For examples of the predicative use, see GROW *v.* 6 b.

1645 J. COTTON *Way Ch. New. Eng.* 9 The Lords Supper, whereto persons of growner yeares, and fit to examine themselves, are invited. **1690** LOCKE *Educ.* §12, I saw lately a Pair of China Shoes, which I was told were for a grown Woman.., they would scarce have been big enough for one of our little Girls. **1734** tr. *Rollin's Anc. Hist.* (1827) I. Pref. 39 The grown and robust men. **1787** 'G. GAMBADO' *Acad. Horsemen* (1809) 14 Instructions to grown horsemen. **1823** SCOTT in *N. & Q.* Ser. IX. (1898) I. 264/1 They are really fitter for grown people than for children. **1894** BARING-GOULD *Kitty Alone* II. 91, I wish I had..never cared for you as a child, never watched over you as a grown girl.

3. Of the sea: Swollen, running high.

1600 HAKLUYT *Voy.* (1810) III. 500 We found the winde so boystrous and contrary, and the sea so growen. **1730**

CAPT. W. WRIGLESWORTH *MS. Log-bk. of the 'Lyell'* 4 May, A very hollow grown Sea from the N.W. **1867** SMYTH *Sailor's Word-bk.*, *Grown-sea*, when the waves have full influence of a gale.

4. Of corn: That has sprouted in the ear after reaching maturity.

1699 *Poor Man's Plea* 11 The Corn being ill cur'd, was wet, and grown, and soft, and what not. **1750** W. ELLIS *Country Housew.* 8 What we call grown Wheat, in Hertfordshire, is that which is damaged in the Field by extra-ordinary wet Weather..then..for want of a free Air and Sun the Kernels grow and sprout before the Wheat is fit to be reaped. **1886** T. HARDY *Mayor of Casterbr.* v, If anybody will tell me how to turn grown wheat into wholesome wheat.

Hence **'grownness**, the state or condition of being (over-)grown.

a **1578** LINDESAY (Pitscottie) *Chron. Scot.* (S.T.S.) I. 47 He thocht ewer to haue excusit him self for his grownes and unhabilietie. **1747** *Mem. Nutrebian Court* II. 98 From his low stature, and thick growness [*sic*], she stiled him, The little great captain of the rabble.

grown, obs. form of GROUND *sb.*

grown, erron. form of GROWME *Obs.*

growncelle, obs. form of GROUNDSEL *sb.*[2]

grownd, obs. form of GROUND.

grownd(e, var. of (or mistake for) *grewnd* GREUND *Obs.*, greyhound.

1473 SIR J. PASTON in *Past. Lett.* No. 732 III. 102 As for the brace of growndes.

growne, obs. variant of GROIN.

grownsel(l, **-swell**, obs. forms of GROUNDSEL.

grownte, rare obs. form of GRANT *v.*

grown-up, *ppl. a.* and *sb.* [See GROW *v.* 13.]

A. *ppl. a.* **1.** Having reached the age of maturity; adult.

1633 MASSINGER *Guardian* v. iv, Denying A grown-up maid the modest conversation Of men. **1789** MRS. PIOZZI *Journ. France* I. 103 She had her three grown-up sons standing round her. **1798** MALTHUS *Popul.* (1817) II. 25 Labour appropriate to grown-up persons. **1849** SIR G. C. LEWIS *Lett.* (1870) 209 In politics they seem to be nothing but a set of grown-up children.

2. Befitting, suitable to, characteristic of, an adult; sensible, worthwhile.

1852 C. M. YONGE *Two Guardians* vi. 93 As to books, all the real good grown-up ones are down in Mr. Lyddell's library where no one can get at them. **1907** E. WHARTON *Fruit of Tree* xxv. 382 Gravely measuring Cicely's milk in to a 'grown-up' teacup. **1958** *Sunday Express* 22 June 15/4 This film somehow manages to be memorable, moving, and outstandingly grown-up. **1960** *Times* 17 May 3/7 It is also capable of undertaking long journeys at 'grown-up' average speeds. **1964** V. NABOKOV *Defence* x. 164 It was impossible to express his recollections in words—there simply were no grown-up words for his childish impressions.

B. *sb.* A grown-up person; an adult.

1813 JANE AUSTEN *Lett.* (1884) II. 208 They bring Isabella and one of the grown-ups. **1865** DICKENS *Mut. Fr.* II. i, No children for me. Give me grown-ups. **1892** FURNIVALL *Hoccleve's Min. Poems* I. Forewords 48 'May we children have the boat all to ourselves? None of you grown-ups'. *attrib.* **1799** HAN. MORE *Fem. Educ.* (ed. 4) I. 166 The approach of her first grown up ball. **1870** MISS BRIDGMAN *Ro. Lynne* II. xiii. 283, I may wear grown-up dresses in future.

Hence **grown-up-dom**; **grown-up-ness.**

1862 MRS. SPEID *Last Years Ind.* 7 Rejoicing in their strength and grown-up-ness. **1871** G. M. HOPKINS *Let.* 25 Apr. (1938) 41 There was such a youngladyship and grownupdom about the address. **1900** *Westm. Gaz.* 7 July 2/1 They will say a conventional 'Thank you'..; the manners of youth being..superior to those of grown-up-dom. **1925** 'R. CROMPTON' *Still—William* v. 85 He seemed to them to be free of all the drawbacks that usually accompany the state of grown-upness. **1944** 'G. ORWELL' *Crit. Ess.* (1951) 154 The grown-upness, the lack of surprise or denunciation, the pity and irony with which the story is told, show the advantage, when one is handling a theme of this kind, of being a European. **1969** *Daily Tel.* 2 May 17 Most parents really want their children to grow up and become successful adults. But many find it hard to accept the onset of grown-upness soon enough.

grows(e, obs. form of GROUSE.

growsome ('grəʊsəm), *a. dial.* [f. GROW *v.* + -SOME.] **a.** Of an animal: Apt to grow. **b.** Of the weather: Favourable to growth. Hence †'**growsomeness.**

1579 J. JONES *Preserv. Bodie & Soule* I. xviii. 32 A great helpe vnto growsomnesse, largenesse, and talnesse. **1863** (*Staffordsh. Cottager*), Our pig is such a growsome little thing; it will eat anything. **1877** *N.W. Linc. Gloss.* s.v., 'It's growsome weather noo'.

growsome, obs. form of GRUESOME.

growt, obs. form of GROUT.

growth[1] (grəʊθ). Also 6 grothe, groweth, 6–7 grouth, (7 groath, grought). [f. GROW *v.* + -TH[1]. ON. had *gróðr* (genit. *gróðrar*) and *gróðe* wk. masc.]

1. a. The action, process or manner of growing; both in material and immaterial senses; vegetative development; increase.

1587 GOLDING *De Mornay* viii. 117 Should we rather graunt an euerlasting ignorance in man, than a kynd of youthfulnesse which hath learned things according to the growths thereof in ages? **1593** SHAKS. *Lucr.* 1062 This bastard graff shall never come to growth. **1599** HAKLUYT *Voy.* To Rdr. **1 b, The beginnings, antiquities, and growth of the classical and warrelike shipping of this Island. **1604** SHAKS. *Oth.* v. ii. 14 When I haue pluck'd thy Rose, I can-not giue it vitall growth againe, It needs must wither. **1615** CHAPMAN *Odyss.* x. 101 [My men] worse did beare Their growing labours; that they causd their grought [*rime-wd.* thought], By selfe-willd follies. **1653** HOLCROFT *Procopius* I. 19 The saltness of the water hindring the grouth of any thing but salt. **1662** *Bk. Com. Prayer* Pref., The growth of Anabaptism. **1667** PEPYS *Diary* 18 May, My wife whose growth in musique do begin to please me mightily. **1677** TEMPLE *Ess. Gout* Wks. 1720 I. 137 In preventing the growth of this Disease, where it is but new. *a* **1682** SIR T. BROWNE *Tracts* 7 Ivy being of no swift growth. **1719** DE FOE *Crusoe* II. iii, The growth of the trees and hedges. **1781** COWPER *Charity* 578 Exuberant is the shadow it supplies, Its fruit on earth, its growth above the skies. **1848** tr. *Regnault's Elem. Treat. Crystallogr.* 59 Sometimes the crystal assumes the form shewn... The growth of the crystal, perpendicularly to the horizontal faces, has been almost nothing. **1851** CARPENTER *Man. Phys.* (ed. 2) 23 Plants obtain the chief materials of their growth from water and carbonic acid. **1860** TYNDALL *Glac.* II. ix. 269 The snow which falls upon the glacier proper can contribute nothing to its growth or permanence. **1870** YEATS *Nat. Hist. Comm.* 93 Barley, oats, and rye may be measured in their daily growth. **1873** *Weale's Dict. Terms* (ed. 4) *Growth of water*, in mining, the accumulation of water in the levels of a mine. **1875** JOWETT *Plato* (ed. 2) IV. 276 Simultaneous with their [the faculties'] growth in man a growth of language must be supposed. **1891** *Speaker* 2 May 534/1 The growth of education and the spread of scientific training. **1911** *Encycl. Brit.* VII. 583/2 When crystals are aggregated together, and so interfere with each other's growth, special structures.. often result. **1962** F. C. PHILLIPS *Smith's Gemstones* (ed. 13) ii. 39 Natural crystals frequently depart from..ideally symmetrical growth and show instead a variable degree of distortion.

b. *of* (such or such) ***growth***: having a specified place of origin or production. Said primarily of vegetable products, hence *transf.* of immaterial things.

1657 *Burton's Diary* (1828) I. 325 Resolved, that for every ton of wine, not of the growth of Spain, there be paid 6*l.* **1684** *Col. Rec. Pennsylv.* I. 108 To ad to yᵉ same bill, not being of the natural groath of the province. **1700** DRYDEN *Fables* Pref., *D 1 b, I had thought for the Honour of our Nation..that this Story was of English Growth, and Chaucer's own. **1781** COWPER *Truth* 515 Is virtue then, unless of Christian growth, Mere fallacy, or foolishness, or both? **1822** LAMB *Elia* Ser. I. *Artif. Comedy*, Affection's depth and wedded faith are not of the growth of that soil. **1879** JAS. GRANT in *Cassell's Techn. Educ.* IV. 95/1 Specimens of plants, most of which were of foreign growth.

c. *spec.* in *Economics.* See also sense 5 (*growth area*, *industry*, etc.).

1952 W. W. ROSTOW *Process Econ. Growth* (1953) iv. 81 Growth is defined as a relation between the rates of increase in capital and the working force,..and in population,..such that *per capita* output (not necessarily consumption) is rising. **1965** H. WILSON in *Oxf. Times* 3 Dec. 16/2, I am now fighting a losing battle on another word I dislike—growth—which had a certain medical and agricultural connotation. 'Economic growth involves more purposeful work than leaving it to nature.'

d. A crop or yield as used in a classification of (esp. the best) vineyards to indicate the quality of the wine produced there. Cf. CRU.

1707 [see CLARET *sb.*[2] (*a.*) 1 b]. **1715** *Lond. Gaz.* No. 5378/4, 200 Hogsheads of Claret, the best Growths in France. **1851** C. REDDING *Hist. Mod. Wines* (ed. 3) vi. 170 The first growths of Medoc are scarcely ever sent to England in a perfect state. **1862**, etc. [see CRU]. **1920** G. SAINTSBURY *Notes on Cellar-bk.* iv. 53 It was customary..to lay down.. hogsheads of the best reputed first or second growths. **1964** *Harper's Bazaar* Dec. 60/2 A claret of a bourgeois growth and a moderate price. **1965** A. SICHEL *Penguin Bk. Wines* 135 The sixty-two best red wines were classified in 1855 by an official committee into five 'growths' or '*crus*', known collectively as the Classed Growths, or *Crus Classés*. **1970** *Times* 18 Apr. p. vii/2 First it showed how exaggerated is the importance which some attach to the words 'Great Classed Growth'.

2. Stage in the process of growing; size or stature attained by growing. *Obs.* exc. in ***full growth.***

1557 *Tottel's Misc.* 128 A graffe of so small grothe. **1597** SHAKS. *2 Hen. IV*, I. ii. 180 A Wassell-Candle, my Lord; all Tallow: if I did say of wax, my growth would approue the truth. **1599** H. BUTTES *Dyets drie Dinner* I v b, Swines Flesh. Nor olde, nor thinne; but of a full groweth. **1638** SIR T. HERBERT *Trav.* (ed. 2) 322 The Elephant is for growth and understanding chiefest, of unreasonable Animalls. **1662** J. DAVIES tr. *Mandelslo's Trav.* 147 Serpents..of so extraordinary a growth, that there are Serpents have swallowed children and sheep intire. **1672** PETTY *Pol. Anat.* (1691) 54 An Ox is come to its full growth at 6 years old. **1678** DRYDEN *All for Love* IV. i, Men are but Children of a larger growth. *a* **1732** GAY *Acis & Galatea* II. 13 Bring me a hundred Reeds of decent Growth, To make a Pipe for my capacious Mouth. **1781** COWPER *Truth* 115 Pride has attained its most luxuriant growth, And poisoned every virtue in them both. **1841–71** T. R. JONES *Anim. Kingd.* (ed. 4) 453 Between the shell and the exterior of the body, where they remain until the embryo attains its full growth.

3. The process of causing or assisting to grow; production by cultivation. Chiefly qualified by possessive pronoun. Also, the process of growing crystals: see GROW *v.* 14 f.

1663 BUTLER *Hud.* I. ii. 130 Chiron, the four-legg'd Bard, hath both A Beard and Tayl of his own Growth. **1697** DRYDEN *Virg. Georg.* Ded. (*ad fin.*), The happy Old Coricyan..whose Fruits and Salads..were all of his own growth, and his own Plantation. **1726** SHELVOCKE *Voy. round World* (1757) 116 Every family has all the necessaries of life of its own growth and produce. **1890** 'ROLF BOLDREWOOD' *Col. Reformer* (1891) 214 A yeoman class.. could use these great levels for the growth of certain semi-tropical crops. **1950** *Sci. News* XV. 56 A typical example of its use is..for the growth of metal crystals. **1962** SIMPSON & RICHARDS *Junction Transistors* iii. 40 Crystal growth by zone melting. *Ibid.*, Floating-zone crystal growth. The floating-zone refining process may also be used for the production of single crystals.

4. *concr.* **a.** That which grows or has grown; produce, product; said both of material and immaterial things.

1580 *Lease* in *Collect.* (O.H.S.) I. 236 Those their woods underwoods growths shawes. **1671** TEMPLE *Ess. Const. & Interests Empire* Wks. 1731 I. 89 The State of Holland, in point both of Riches and Strength, is the most prodigious Growth that has been seen in the World. **1764** GOLDSM. *Trav.* 126 Man seems the only growth that dwindles here. **1861** M. PATTISON *Ess.* (1889) I. 32 If any one part of the English system rather than another could be claimed as a modern growth, it is her foreign policy. **1873** W. M. THOMSON *Land & Bk.* xiv. 199 Some of our missionary band..have counted the growths (as we Western people call the annual concentric circles) for a few inches into the trunk of the oldest cedars. **1876** E. MELLOR *Priesth.* ii. 73 Sacerdotalism was a growth traceable to a concurrence of influences..some of which were wholly innocent. **1885** U. S. GRANT *Mem.* I. xx. 273 Marshy ground covered with a heavy growth of timber. **1890** *Daily News* 14 Oct. 2/3 Hops contracted for some time previous to the picking of the growth.

b. *Path.* Often *spec.* a morbid formation.

1847 TODD *Cycl. Anat.* IV. 125/1 The property of infiltration has been ascribed to other Growths besides Cancer. **1899** J. HUTCHINSON *Archives Surg.* X. 182 His head was covered with papillomatosis growths in various stages.

5. *attrib.* and *Comb.*, as ***growth-condition***, ***-control***, ***-direction***, ***-hormone***, ***-measurer***, ***-phase***, ***-policy***, ***-rate***, ***-ratio***, ***-regulation***, ***-target***; ***growth-controlling***, ***-inducing***, ***-influencing***, ***-inhibiting***, ***-making***, ***-promoting***, ***-regulating***, ***-retarding***, ***-seeking***, ***-stimulating*** ppl. adjs.; **growth area**, an area designated for economic growth; **growth company**, a company (sense 7) that has expanded, or is likely to expand, more than the average; **growth curve**, a line drawn so as to represent growth diagrammatically by showing how some quantity like size, weight, or numbers varies with time; **growth factor** *Biol.*, any substance required by an organism in minute amounts in order to maintain its growth; **growth-form** (see quot. 1960); **growth-gradient** *Biol.*, a continuous variation in the rate of growth along an axis of an organism, limb, etc.; †**growth-halfpenny** (see quot.); **growth industry**, an industry which has been, or is in process of, developing at a faster rate than other industries; **growth leader**, an investment stock with much past and potential growth; **growth-line** *Phys.*, a line indicating a stage of growth; **growth-man**, a person who advocates a policy of economic growth; hence **growthmanship**, such a policy; **growth point**, (*a*) = *growth area*; (*b*) = *growing point*; **growth potential**, (*a*) potentiality of growth in living matter; (*b*) potentiality of economic growth; **growth regulator**, an organic substance, such as a hormone, vitamin, or auxin, which regulates growth; **growth ring**, the layer of wood added to a tree during one growing season; cf. *annual ring* (s.v. ANNUAL *a.* and *sb.* A. 1 c; RING *sb.*[1] 7 c); **growth stock** (see quot. 1965); **growth zone**, (*a*) = *growing-region*; (*b*) = *growth area*; (*c*) = *growing zone.*

1963 *Daily Tel.* 5 Dec. 14/2 The conception of '*growth areas' is new. **1966** *Listener* 2 June 788/2 The Humber estuary is already one of the most significant economic growth areas in the country. **1959** T. E. & D. L. BABSON *Investing for Successful Future* xii. 157 Listed..are a few outstanding *growth companies, with the length of their business lives. **1969** *Times* 8 Jan. 23/2 It has been the growth company par excellence. **1890** *Daily News* 12 Sept. 5/3 Grave men of science who are investigating..the *growth conditions of fish in Scottish waters. **1964** *New Statesman* 20 Mar. 468/3 Calves..injected with *growth-control substances. **1922** *Times Lit. Suppl.* 27 Apr. 279/1 A *growth-controlling principle which he named tethelin. **1916** *Jrnl. Biol. Chem.* XXIV. 368 In the *growth curves the dots represent the actually determined weights. **1946** *Nature* 5 Oct. 462/1 Fischer describes the sigmoid growth-curve of the culture, its limiting size, shape-regulation, and power of true reconstitutive regeneration. **1916** *Ibid.* 1 June 290/2 The word 'tropism', first used to indicate the *growth-direction of plant-members under the influence of some stimulus. **1928** *Biochem. Jrnl.* XXII. 790 There is, therefore, no justification for calling vitamin B_2 a '*growth factor' in contradistinction to vitamin B_1. **1937** Growth factor [see BIOTIN]. **1964** WAGNER & FOLKERS *Vitamins & Coenzymes* i. 5 The antiberiberi factor, designated vitamin B, was later found to contain both a heat labile antiberiberi factor and a thermostable growth factor. **1887** H. E. F. GARNSEY tr. *De Bary's Fungi* i. 2 Both [forms] are *growth-forms (Wuchsformen) comparable with those growth-forms in the higher plants which are known as the tree, shrub and herb. **1909** GROOM & BALFOUR tr. *Warming's Oecol. Plants* ii. 4 In 1884, Warming, having in view the North-European

Spermophyta, gave a general survey of growth-forms which he arranged in fourteen chief groups with many sub-groups, based upon morphological and biological characters. **1960** N. POLUNIN *Introd. Plant Geogr.* iii. 92 The 'life-form' or 'growth-form' of a plant is the form which its vegetative body produces as a result of all the life-processes, including those that are affected by the environment within the plant's life-time and are not heritable. **1929** *Nature* 15 June 910/1 (*heading*) *Growth-gradients and the axial relations of the body. **1932** J. S. HUXLEY *Probl. Rel. Growth* iii. 80 It was found that there existed within the limb what we may call a growth-gradient. **1956** C. H. WADDINGTON *Princ. Embryol.* xiii. 292 It appears probable that there is a single continuous growth gradient with its high point towards the feet, falling off as one goes higher up the body. **1676** COLES, **Growth half-peny*, paid (in some places) for tythe of every fat beast, Ox and other unfruitfull cattel. So PHILLIPS (ed. Kersey) 1706, and BAILEY 1736–92. **1924** T. B. ROBERTSON *Princ. Biochem.* (ed. 2) xx. 579 Such catalyzers being distributed by the circulation and operating as *growth-hormones. **1953** Growth hormone [see ACROMEGALY]. **1969** *Times* 25 Mar. 12/7 When growth hormone is injected into young rabbits the fleas are induced to copulate. **1961** L. MARTIN *Clin. Endocrinol.* (ed. 3) i. 5 Insulin itself, when combined with a high carbohydrate diet, has also been shown to have some *growth-inducing effect. **1957** *Economist* 7 Sept. 778/2 The pattern of growth in Britain's biggest *growth industry.. is not a balanced one. **1961** *Times* 30 May 13/6 Publishing is judged to be a 'growth' industry. **1966** *Listener* 15 Sept. 397/3 Only one laird preferred to keep his moor for private use... The grouse shooting agent's view was rather different — his is a growth industry. **1918** *Nature* 21 Feb. 484/2 The *growth-influencing substance 'Tethelin', which Prof. Robertson had isolated from the anterior lobe of the pituitary body. **1922** *Jrnl. Exper. Med.* XXXV. 647 (*heading*) Heat and *growth-inhibiting action of serum. **1946** *Nature* 10 Aug. 200/2 The antibiotic substances present in these extracts had a marked growth-inhibiting effect both on litter-decomposing and mycorrhiza-forming fungi. **1967** *N.Y. Times* (Internat. Ed.) 11–12 Feb. 9/6 The *growth leaders with phenomenal rises are now well known stocks to all investors. **1857** GOSSE *Creation* 218 On each of the scutal valves in this individual I can count about 260 *growth-lines. **1922** *Chambers's Jrnl.* Dec. 875/1 The natives.. chew it from boyhood, and attach great importance to it as a *growth-making agent. **1961** *Britannica Bk. Year* 537/2 From commerce and organization generally came *growthman, one favouring a policy of expansion, and growthmanship, the fixing of specific economic goals. **1964** *New Statesman* 3 Apr. 539/1 Political growthmen. **1966** *Ibid.* 18 Nov. 748/2 It is well-fed public opinion which presents the growthman with his chief problem. **1960** *Times* 18 Aug. 9/2 Both parties advocate a higher rate of economic growth (though not long ago Mr. Nixon was deriding '*growthmanship'). **1961** C. CLARK (*title*) Growthmanship. **1967** *Economist* 26 Aug. 733/1 'Growthmanship'.. has dominated economic policy-making throughout Europe since the end of the second world war. **1924** J. A. THOMSON *Science Old & New* xxxvi. 206 *Growth-measures (auxanometers). **1915** P. GEDDES *Cities in Evolution* xvii. 361 Our synoptic vision of the city, for each and all of its *growth-phases, thus ranges through region to homes, and back again. **1932** J. S. HUXLEY *Prob. Rel. Growth* i. 8 The weights of chela and rest-of-body.. over the earlier and longer growth-phase. **1963** *Economist* 11 May 520/2 Turning many more people to new houses at new or refreshed *growth points. **1968** *Listener* 4 Jan. 8/3 His energy and intellectual passion place him at the growth-point of English study to-day. **1960** *Encounter* Oct. 11/2 *Growth-policies in relatively young economies like China. **1932** J. S. HUXLEY *Probl. Rel. Growth* i. 40 The distribution of *growth-potential in different regions. **1958** *Listener* 13 Nov. 792/2 He regards any repression of demand below the growth potential as a development that would aggravate a rise in the cost of living [etc.]. **1968** *Globe & Mail* (Toronto) 17 Feb. B6 (Advt.), Growth potential is strong due to the enthusiastic management support this position enjoys. **1914** *Jrnl. Biol. Chem.* XIX. 248 The *growth promoting substance was transferred from the butter fat to the olive oil by the procedure described. **1926** J. S. HUXLEY *Ess. Pop. Sci.* viii. 90 More growth-promoting proteins. **1966** *Economist* 11 June 1206/1 Strategy for growth—specifically the question of growth-promoting industries—is treated by Perroux (France). **1927** *Biol. Abstr.* I. 547/2 A quantitative analysis of the *growth-rate of the chick embryo. **1930** R. A. FISHER *Genet. Theory Nat. Selection* 45 The vital statistics of an organism in relation to its environment provide a means of determining a measure of the relative growth-rate of the population. **1932** J. S. HUXLEY *Probl. Rel. Growth* i. 3 The relative growth-rates of.. various parts [of the body]. **1970** P. R. & A. H. EHRLICH *Population, Resources, Environment* x. 243 The population of Europe is growing at considerably less than 1 percent per year... Only Albania, Rumania, and Iceland have growth rates that exceed 1·2 percent. **1924** J. S. HUXLEY in *Nature* 20 Dec. 895 Constant differential *growth-ratios and their significance. **1929** *Biol. Bull.* LVII. 176 *Growth regulating substances in echinoderm larvæ. **1948** *New Biol.* V. 47 'Growth regulating substances'.. will inhibit, increase, or otherwise alter.. the subsequent growth of the plants. **1956** *Nature* 4 Feb. 201/1 Pigments, weed-killers, insecticides and plant growth-regulating substances. **1927** HALDANE & HUXLEY *Animal Biol.* viii. 165 Sometimes *growth-regulation breaks down, and the cells of some part of the body grow too quickly, causing a tumour. **1936** G. S. AVERY tr. *Jensen's Growth Hormones in Plants* i. 3 Plant-growth substances, i.e., *Wuchsstoffe*, have been referred to by various workers as growth hormones, *growth regulators, growth enzymes, phytohormones, and auxins. **1954** *Plant Physiol.* XXIX. 307 The term *growth regulator*, as recommended here, includes the auxins, but it is broader, and it encompasses other regulators that may modify growth. **1969** SALISBURY & ROSS *Plant Physiol.* xx. 444/2 Synthetic growth regulators often mimic the effects of naturally occurring growth regulators (including hormones) or interfere with their actions. **1930** *Biol. Abstr.* IV. 351/1 It is concluded that a *growth-retarding substance has not been found. **1932** J. S. HUXLEY *Probl. Rel. Growth* vi. 188 A much greater growth-retarding effect. **1907** D. P. PENHALLOW *Man. N. Amer. Gymnosperms* ii. 24 In proceeding to a study of the transverse section the first feature to which attention is naturally directed is the *growth ring. **1937** *Discovery* Apr. 98/1 The largest of the Sequoias of California, estimated by growth-rings to exceed 3,500 years of life. **1960** N. POLUNIN *Introd. Plant Geogr.* i. 13 Where cells of different sizes are produced at different seasons, annual 'growth-rings' are formed which may easily be seen in most timbers. **1966** *Times* 28 Feb. (Canada Suppl.) p. iv/1 *Growth-seeking industries. **1914** *Jrnl. Biol. Chem.* XIX. 246 (*heading*) *Growth-stimulating substance in butter fat. **1957** *Economist* 9 Feb. 490/2 Undistributed income.. has been transmuted into capital... Hence the investor's emphasis on '*growth' stocks. **1965** J. L. HANSON *Dict. Econ.* 209/1 *'Growth' stock*, a stock or share which can be expected to appreciate in value in the future, the policy of the directors of the company being to plough back each year a considerable portion of the profits for the purposes of expansion. **1969** *Times* 13 Jan. 11/3 This is a growth stock yielding only about 2 per cent, and no investment adviser would advocate putting that proportion of their total worth into that kind of investment. **1962** *Listener* 8 Mar. 400/2 The question of labour costs cannot be excluded from any realistic discussion of a specific industrial *growth-target. **1927** HALDANE & HUXLEY *Animal Biol.* xii. 282 A *growth-zone near the hind-end. **1963** *Daily Tel.* 15 Nov. 27/1 The three main centres of expansion in the growth zone. **1967** P. A. MEGLITSCH *Invert. Zool.* xiv. 636/1 During metamorphosis, this part of the [annelid] larva grows very rapidly; it may be termed the growth zone.

Hence **'growthful** *a.*, full of growth; capable of growing; **'growthless** *a.*, having no growth, destitute of growth; †**'growthsome** *a.*, productive, fertile.

1610 W. FOLKINGHAM *Art of Survey* I. x. 32 The Tilthe.. growes so growthsome that it yeeldes an after-math. **1674** N. FAIRFAX *Bulk & Selv.* 186 You cannot dig many spades in mold or growthsom earth, before you come at a dead soyl. **1824** in *Harp of Renfrewsh.* (1873) Ser. II. 97 From its growthless tree I'd dangle like the bell. **1849** J. HAMILTON *Mem. Lady Colquhoun* ii. (1850) 58 We see how much more growthful is a lowly commencement, if genuine. **1879** J. TODHUNTER *Alcestis* 108 A weak, sad, cowering, joyless, growthless shade. **1882** *Amer. Missioary* Dec. 372 The church work.. has been steady, growthful, and encouraging.

†**growth**[2]. *dial. Obs.* Also 6 **grath**, 8 **grooth**. [a. ? ON. **gráð-r* corresponding to OE. *græd* 'ulva'.] (See quot. 1507–8.)

1507–8 in Boyle *Hist. Hedon* (1895) p. c, Inter le Halff ebbe mark in le Grath meter in Humbr'. [*Ibid.* Gloss. p. ccxvii, 'Grath meter(e), growth meter. Growth is the name used in the Humber district for the foreshore lying between the river embankment and highwater mark, because covered by a growth of coarse grass. A 'meter' is a mark or boundary.] **1741** *MS. Court Roll, Burstwick* (*York*), Pasture in Newforth and in the Grooth in Preston. **1773** *Preston Incl. Act* 22 The salt end of a certain piece of ground.. called the hay marsh, lying between the New Bank and the River Humber, together with the growths thereunto belonging.

growthy ('grəʊθɪ), *a. local.* [f. GROWTH *sb.* + -Y[1].] **a.** Promoting growth. **b.** Of good growth; capable of growing to a large size.

a. 1768 ROSS *Helenore* (1789) 65 And now the sun to the hill-heads gan speal, Spreading on trees and plants a growthy heal. **1812** SOUTER *Agric. Surv. Banffs.* App. 59 Sandy fields,.. being.. warm and growthy, soon entertain the communications of the dung. **1888** *Scot. Leader* 3 May 2 [At Edinburgh.] We have had a week of good 'growthy' weather, which has given a new appearance to the country.

b. 1868 ATKINSON *Cleveland Gloss.*, *Growthy*,.. luxuriant ..; of vegetables, growing crops, etc. **1884** *West. Morn. News* 9 Aug. 1/5 The Bullocks are good growthy Devons. **1886** C. SCOTT *Sheep-Farming* 166 Such [lambs] are not desirable, and neither are those that do not appear to be growthy.

growyd, -yn: see GROW *v.*

growze, obs. form of GROOSE *v.*, to shiver.

groy, groyf, obs. Sc. and north. f. GROW.

†**groyl**, *v. Obs. rare*[−1]. [? ad. F. *grouiller* to move, swarm.] *intr.* To move, make one's way.

1583 STANYHURST *Æneis* III. (Arb.) 92 His tusk grimlye gnashing, in seas far waltred, he groyleth [L. *graditur*].

So †**groyl** *sb.*, ? one who is always on the move.

1583 STANYHURST *Æneis* IV. (Arb.) 100 Fame the groyl vngentil, then whom none swifter is extant.

groyn, obs. pa. pple. of GROW *v.*

groyn(e), obs. variant of GROIN.

groyne (grɔɪn), *sb.* Also 9 **groin**, **groyn**. [Of obscure origin: perh. identical with GROIN *sb.*[1]; cf. the use of OF. *groin* (lit. 'snout') in the sense of a projection of rock, promontory.] A framework of timber, or now sometimes a low broad wall of concrete or masonry run out into the sea, for the purpose of arresting the washed-up sand and shingle and thus raising a barrier against the encroachment of the sea.

1582 *Calendar State Papers* (1865) 44 A groyne to be made for the defense of the pier [at Dover]. **1593–5** NORDEN *Spec. Brit., M'sex* I. Prepar. 22 Greenwich.. rather it is Groynewich, a towne neere or vpon the Groyne: for a Groyne it is that is made for a defence against the force of water. **1808** *Ann. Reg.* 128 Their new groynes do not project far enough into the sea. **1872** LYELL *Princ. Geol.* I. II. xx. 533 Since the Point of Dungeness has advanced, forming a great natural groin, it intercepts the shingle which formerly travelled eastward, and was accumulated by artificial groins at Hythe. **1887** E. J. GOODMAN *Too Curious* xvi, Where the huge timber piles of a groyne intersected a portion of the beach.

transf. **1872** DIXON *Switzers* iv. 33 A groyne of slabs and stones is thrown along the higher rim, but slantwise from the alpine scarp (as we in England groyne the sea), to turn all floods of rain and rolling earth and stones aside.

groyne (grɔɪn), *v.* [f. prec.] *trans.* **a.** To build groynes or breakwaters against the sea. **b.** To furnish with groynes or breakwaters.

1872 [see GROYNE *sb.* (*transf.*)]. **1889** *Sussex Daily News* 4 June 3/3 The first thing necessary is to build up a protecting wall.. and then groyne the beach.

groyning ('grɔɪnɪŋ), *vbl. sb.* [f. GROYNE *v.* + -ING[1].] The building of groynes; an arrangement or system of groynes.

1867 SMYTH *Sailor's Word-bk.*, *Groining*, a peculiar mode of submarine embankment; a quay run out transversely to the shore. **1889** *Sussex Daily News* 4 June 3/3 Wherever groyning stopped it ceased to have any protecting influence.

groyt, obs. form of GROAT.

groze, grozer, var. ff. GROSS *v.*, GROSER.

grozet: see GROSET.

†**'grozier.** *Obs.* In 4–5 **groser**, 7 **grosier**. [In F. *grésoir*, *grugeoir*, f. *gréser* (17th c. *groizer*), *gruger* to trim (glass), to break with the teeth, a. Du. *gruizen* (see next). The Eng. word may be formed on a vb. **groze* adapted from the Du. word.] = GROZING-IRON 1.

1404 *Durham Acc. Rolls* (Surtees) 397 In custodia Vitriarii ..4 grosers. **1688** R. HOLME *Armoury* III. ix. 385/1 A Double Grosier, and a Stoping Knife all in one peece. **1847** [see next].

grozing-iron ('grəʊzɪŋ 'aɪən). Also **grosing-**. [Formed after Du. *gruisijzer*, f. *gruis-* stem of *gruizen* to trim glass, to crush, f. *gruis* fragments.]

†**1.** A tool in the form of nippers formerly used by glaziers in cutting glass. *Obs.*

1688 R. HOLME *Armoury* III. ix. 384/2 An Instrument used by the Glasiers, being a Working or Stopping Knife at one end, and a Nipper at the other, and is termed a Knife, and Grosing Iron conjoined in one. **1823** P. NICHOLSON *Pract. Build.* 422 Glaziers formerly cut their glass out with an instrument called a grozing-iron. **1847** *Gloss. Heraldry*, *Grater*, or Glaziers' nippers, called also Grazier [? *mistake for* Grozier], and Grosing-iron: a tool used by glaziers and borne by their company. **1847** C. WINSTON *Anc. Glass Painting* I. 27 The pieces of glass were.. reduced to the exact shape required, by chipping away their edges with an iron hook, called in Theophilus 'grosiarum ferrum', and at the present day a grozing iron.

2. An iron tool terminating in a bulb, which, when heated, is used for smoothing the solder joints of lead pipes.

1825 J. NICHOLSON *Operat. Mechanic* 629 These grozing-irons are of several sizes, generally about twelve inches in length. **1847** SMEATON *Builder's Man.* 132 The solder employed by the plumber.. is run into the joint in a liquefied state; after which it is smoothed down by a grozing-iron heated almost to redness.

gru: see GRUE.

grub (grʌb), *sb.* Forms: 5 **grobbe**, **grubbe**, 7 **grubb**, 6– **grub**. [? f. GRUB *v.*]

1. The larva of an insect, esp. of a beetle; a caterpillar, maggot; also (now *dial.*), a worm.

c **1420** *Pallad. on Husb.* VII. 63 Benys.. vpplucked sone, maad clene, and sette vp wel refrigerate, ffrom grobbis saaf wol kepe vp their estate. **1486** *Bk. St. Albans* A iv, If the frounce be wex as greete as a note Than ther is a grubbe ther in. ? *a* **1500** *Chester Pl.* (E.E.T.S.) vii. 227 The dirte is so deepe.. and the grubbs thereon doe creepe. **1592** SHAKS. *Rom. & Jul.* v. iii. 126 What Torch is yond that vainley lends his light To grubs, and eyelesse Sculles? **1607** —— *Cor.* v. iv. 11–12 There is differency between a Grub & a Butterfly; yet your Butterfly was a Grub. *a* **1653** G. DANIEL *Idyll* iii. 169 The World's an Ant-hill, and the little Grubbs Stocke themselves warme. **1664** POWER *Exp. Philos.* I. 28 That Spumeous froth or dew which.. we call Cuckow-Spittle,.. in which you shall always find a little Grub, or Animal. **1669** *Phil. Trans.* IV. 914 He affirms, that Timber-trees fell'd, when the wind is in the West,.. will keep them free from grubs, (as they call it) i.e. from being worm-eaten. **1688** R. HOLME *Armoury* II. 204/1 The Grub is a general term for the smaller worms that breed in the Earth. **1774** GOLDSM. *Nat. Hist.* (1776) VIII. 63 The history of grubs changing into their corresponding winged animals. **1784** COWPER *Task* v. 90 The very rooks and daws forsake the fields, Where neither grub, nor root, nor earth-nut, now Repays their labour more. **1796** C. MARSHALL *Garden.* xv. (1813) 242 Those lettuces in the open ground are often destroyed by grubs lurking about the roots. **1859** R. THOMPSON *Gardener's Assist.* 571 The grub of another insect (*Byturus tomentosus*) is very frequently found in the fruit. **1883** *Encycl. Amer.* I. 138/2 The White Grub (*Lachnosterna fusca* Froh.).. is the larva of the well-known 'May-bug' or 'June-bug'. **1887** *S. Cheshire Gloss.*, *Grub*, any kind of worm except the largest.

fig. **1837** MACAULAY *Ess.*, *Bacon* (1880) 356 He was now in a chrysalis state, putting off the worm and putting on the dragon-fly, a kind of intermediate grub between sycophant and oppressor. **1840** DICKENS *Barn. Rudge* xl, He.. knelt down a grub, and rose a butterfly. John Chester, Esquire, was knighted and became Sir John.

2. *contemptuous.* †**a.** A short, dwarfish fellow.

a **1400–50** *Alexander* 1753 And slike a dwinyng, a dwaȝe, & a dwerȝe as þi-selfe, A grub [*Dubl. MS.* grob], a grege out of grace. **1602** CAREW *Cornwall* 63 John Romaine, a short clownish grub, would beare the whole carkase of an oxe, and yet neuer tugged with him. **1611** COTGR., *Rabougri*,.. a grub, counterfeit, short or short-necked crooke-backe. **1706** PHILLIPS (ed. Kersey), *Grub*, a Dwarf, or short Fellow.

b. A person of mean abilities, a dull industrious drudge, a literary hack; in recent use, a person of slovenly attire and unpleasant manners.

1653 URQUHART *Rabelais* I. Prol. 6 So saith a Turlupin or a new start-up grub of my books. **1748** SMOLLETT *Rod. Rand.* xxx. (1804) 198 This miserable grub [the captain's clerk] who had been an attorney's boy. **1771** —— *Humph. Cl.* 10 June, A dull author generally distinguishes himself by some oddity or extravagance. For this reason, I fancy that an assembly of Grubs must be very diverting. **1796** MARY ROBINSON *Angelina* I. 71 Is it not a scandal to humanity that such an illiterate grub as Sir Edward should feed on all the luxuries of life? **1838** DE QUINCEY *Shaks.* Wks. (1863) XV. 7 Mr. Nahum Tate:—This poor grub of literature. **1896** DU MAURIER *Martian* (1898) 390 Clubs have a way of blackballing grubs—especially grubs that are out of the common grubby.

†**c.** ? A money-grubber. *Obs.* [Cf. Du. dial. (Gelderland) *grobbe* in the same sense.]

a **1681** J. LACY *Sauny the Scot* IV. (1698) 31 'Tis the Old Grub, Woodall. What shall we do with him?

d. *dial.* A small dirty child.

a **1845** HOOD *Clubs* iii, The Cook's a hasher—nothing more—The Children noisy grubs. **1888** *Berksh. Gloss.* s.v., A dirty little child is called 'a young grub'.

e. *U.S.* A hard-reading student.

1847 D. A. WELLS & S. H. DAVIS *Sk. Williams College* 76 A man must not be ashamed to be called a 'grub' in college, if he would shine in the world. **1851** B. H. HALL *College Words*, *Grub*, a hard student. Williams College.

†**3. a.** (See quot. 1706 and cf. *maggot.*) *Obs.*

1681 FLATMAN *Heraclitus Ridens* No. 42 (1713) II. 22, I thought my Song might have removed your Grubs; but I see some Marks still of Melancholy upon you. **1706** PHILLIPS (ed. Kersey), *Grub*,..a capricious Humour or Whimsey.

b. Phr. ***to ride grub, be up a grub*** (dial.): to be sulky or bad-tempered. (Cf. GRUBBY 4.)

1785 GROSE *Dict. Vulg. Tongue* s.v., To ride grub, to be sullen or out of temper. **1840** SPURDENS *Suppl. to Forby* (1858) 20 'To be up a grub', 'to ride grub', is to be out of temper, morose. [Cf. **1847-78** HALLIWELL s.v., The grubs bite him hard, i.e. he is sulky. *East.*]

4. (See quots.)

1731 BAILEY vol. II, *Grubbs*..a kind of white, unctuous, little pimples or tumours, rising on the face, chiefly on the *Alæ* of the nose. **1833** in *Cycl. Pract. Med.* I. 27/2 They [pimples of *acne folliculiaris*] are commonly known by the name of..grubs.

5. *Cricket.* A ball bowled along the ground.

1870 *Baily's Mag. Sports* Aug. 355 Nor did we ever before see a species of underhand bowling, known to schoolboys as 'grubs', made use of in the crack match of the year. **1882** *Australians in England* 92 The latter bowls left-handed 'grubs' of the most pronounced description. **1894** ASTLEY 50 *Years Life* I. 63 We had a private who could bowl fast left-hand grubs. **1896** *Blackw. Mag.* Apr. 581 Abe Hollo well bowled really good grubs on occasion.

6. *slang.* **a.** Food or provender of any kind. Colloq. phrs.: ***grub up!***, the food is ready; time to eat!; ***lovely grub***, good food; also *transf.*

1659 *Anc. Poems, Ball.*, etc. (Percy Soc.) 22 Let's joyne together; I'le pass my word this night Shall yield us grub, before the morning light. **1691** *Pol. Ballads* (1860) II. 20 This weasel..to get him some grub,..and a little good bub. **1781** G. PARKER *View Society* I. xxii. 171 How did you procure your Grub and Bub? **1813** COL. HAWKER *Diary* (1893) I. 68 The boys..finished the evening with some prime grub, swizzle, and singing. **1833** MARRYAT *P. Simple* (1863) 147 How you'll relish your grub by and by! **1880** E. FITZGERALD *Lett.* (1889) I. 456, I and my Reader Boy were going into the Pantry for some grub. **1889** 'ROLF BOLDREWOOD' *Robbery under Arms* (1890) 177 We had brought some grub with us and a bottle of grog. **1953** 'R. GORDON' *Doctor at Sea* xiv. 165 All the way down—*Miss, Miss, Miss.* Lovely grub! **1957** E. TAYLOR *Angel* v. i. 220 We're here, madam. Grub up! **1959** I. & P. OPIE *Lore & Lang. Schoolch.* ix. 161 Cries of jubilation include..Lovely grub!

b. A feed.

1857 HUGHES *Tom Brown* I. vii, Twice as good a grub as we should have got in the hall.

7. *U.S.* A root left in the ground after clearing.

1788 WASHINGTON *Diary* 20 Feb. (1925) III. 306 At Muddy hole they were..taking up grubs in the Winter fallow of No. 4. **1825** J. LORAIN *Pract. Husb.* 334 The Yankee farmer first chops the fallen timber, then scalps off the grubs level with the ground. **1839** C. M. KIRKLAND *New Home* xx. 133 Grubs are, in western parlance, the gnarled roots of small trees and shrubs. **1875** KNIGHT *Dict. Mech.*, *Grubber*, a machine or tool to pull *grubs*; that is, stumps and roots of bushes, saplings, and small trees. **1888** *Sci. Amer.* 21 Apr. 247 The John Cornelius Grub and Stump Puller.

8. *attrib.* and *Comb.*, as (sense 1) ***grub-destroyer, -destroying, -hunter, -hunting, -skin; grub-like*** adj.; (sense 6) ***grub-box, -shop, -wagon***; **grub-kick** *Rugby Football*, = GRUBBER 6; hence as *v. intr.*; **grub-plank** *U.S.*, 'refuse plank used in fastening together the parts of a lumber-raft' (*Cent. Dict.*); **grub-screw**, a screw without a head but with a recess at one end to receive a screwdriver or key; **grub-stake** *U.S. Mining slang*, 'the outfit, provisions, etc. furnished to a prospector on condition of participating in the profits of any find he may make; a lay-out' (*Ibid.*); also *transf.*; hence ***grub-stake*** vb. trans., to furnish with grub-stake; also *transf.*; **grub-staker**, a prospector who is supplied with a grub-stake, or the supplier of a grub-stake; **grub-worm** = sense 1, also *contemptuous*.

1887 FARRELL *How He Died* 68 There's not much in the *grub-box, but I've never turned a man off without a feed. **1894** R. B. SHARPE *Handbk. Birds Gt. Brit.* (1896) I. 26 Its [the starling's] good deeds as a *grub-destroyer are apt to be forgotten. **1863** ATKINSON *Stanton Grange* 78 Anybody would have mentioned the sparrow as a worker at *grub-destroying. **1797** WOLCOT (P. Pindar) *Ode to Sir J. Banks* Wks. 1812 III. 459 The King of Men May make the Knight a *grub-hunter agen And bid him mind his butterflies and hammer. **1870** LOWELL *Among my Bks.* Ser. I (1873) 320 The regular occupation of *grub-hunting is as tame and wearisome as another. **1951** *Rugger* Dec. 5 He uses the *grub kick so much favoured by Northern Union players. **1959** *Times* 6 Mar. 16/2 Elliot and Patterson engineered a try at the posts for the latter from a grub kick by Horrocks-Taylor. **1960** *Times* 4 Jan. 4/3 Tolson grub-kicked ahead. **1882-34** *Good's Study Med.* (ed. 4) II. 54 A *grub-like concretion of mucus. **1874** LUBBOCK *Orig. & Met. Ins.* i. 18 Apod grub-like larvae. **1903** *Jrnl. Inst. Electr. Engin.* XXXII. 384 It is ..becoming quite common..to fasten the armature connection to the commutator segment by means of steel *grub screws. **1930** *Engineering* 26 Dec. 815/2 The terminals ..are fixed by a grub screw. **1840** THACKERAY *Barber Cox* in *Comic Almanack* 25 'That's the *grub-shop', said my lord, 'where we young gentlemen wot has money buys our wittles, and them young gentlemen wot has none, goes tick'. **1849** HARE *Serm.* II. 76 You are not to..furl up your wings, and wrap yourself up in your cast-off *grub-skin. **1863** H. EDGAR *Jrnl.* 27 May in *Montana Hist. Soc. Contrib.* (1900) III. 138 'A *grub stake is what we are after' was our watchword all day, and it is one hundred and fifty dollars in good dust. **1885** BUTTERWORTH *Zig-zag Journ. West. States* 309 What is roughly termed a 'grub stake'. **1895** *Forum* (N.Y.) June 475 The prospector with his led horse, loaded with grub-stake, blankets, pick, and pan. **1932** *Atlantic Monthly* Mar. 322/1 The farmer realizes the..plight of the out-of-work who..is left without a grub-stake between himself and hunger. **1947** V. PALMER *Golconda* ii. 10 We'd been out for six months on a grubstake from the store here, looking for mica. **1957** *Times* 12 Nov. (Canada Suppl.) p. xi/4 The prospector can no longer look forward to making his fortune with a 'grubstake' of a few hundred dollars. **1968** R. M. PATTERSON *Finlay's River* 96 On the Ingenika itself three prospectors were making at least a good grubstake: they finally took out seventy ounces of gold. **1879** *Chicago Tribune* 15 May 9/6 Judge Pendery, a former Congressman, politician, and lawyer, has been *grubstaking a party of miners who were digging a shaft down near the base of the hill. **1890** GUNTER *Miss Nobody* ix. 100 He grub-staked us and we used to work on the Tillie mine together. **1919** W. A. FRASER *Bulldog Carney* 38 I'm goin' to grubstake you,.. leave you rations for three days. **1937** PARTRIDGE *Dict. Slang* 358/1 *Grub-stake*, to give (an author) money to keep him going while he writes a book. **1947** L. HASTINGS *Dragons are Extra* i. 30 Grub-staked by some optimistic colleague in town, they could be found at every wayside pub. **1959** *Economist* 21 Mar. 1073/2 For over seven years, from 1951, soon after the Korean outbreak, until mid-1958, the federal government in effect 'grubstaked' owners of promising deposits of strategic minerals. **1965** G. MCINNES *Road to Gundagai* x. 176 A..dentist whose son Ian..had been grubstaked to Wembley *hors concours.* **1880** A. A. HAYES *New Colorado* (1881) vii. 107 Here does the whilom *grub-staker and present millionaire purchase his corner lot. **1897** A. C. HARRIS *Alaska & Klondike Gold Fields* 444 A grub-staker is a man who wants someone to stake him with grub, and 'grub' is Klondike for beans, bacon and tea. **1898** J. GRINNELL *Gold Hunting in Alaska* (1901) xii. 45 We may have to foot it home just like..prodigal sons who have wasted their substance and that of our grub-stakers in 'riotous living'. **1926** *Glasgow Herald* 8 Mar. 10 But the grub-staker who is financed by some wealthy man and will share his discoveries with his backer, is in the fortunate position of having enough money to avoid the dangerous trail. **1969** *Daily Colonist* (Victoria, B.C.) 27 Nov. 9/4 The telegram recalled the chamber had recommended..that the prospector and grubstaker tax exemption be maintained in its present form. **1891** *Fur, Fin & Feather* Mar. 150 They take with them a *grub wagon and ten saddle horses, and expect to be absent four months. **1920** J. M. HUNTER *Trail Drivers of Texas* 69 We were two miles from the grub wagon. **1752** SMART *Hilliad* I. 115 Moths, mites, and maggots, fleas (a numerous crew), And gnats and *grub-worms crowded on his view. **1807-8** W. IRVING *Salmag.* (1824) 134 Giblet was as arrant a grub-worm as ever crawled. **1849** C. BRONTË *Shirley* v, My grub-worm is always a straitened, struggling, careworn tradesman. **1966** *Publ. Amer. Dial. Soc.* XLV. 14 *Grubworm*, the larva of the Green June Beetle.

Hence **grubbed** *a.*, infested with grubs; **grubbing** *vbl. sb.*, infestation by grubs.

1843 *Jrnl. R. Agric. Soc.* IV. I. 125 When turnips have what is termed a 'grubbed' appearance, it has been attributed to the larvæ of these little beetles. **1844** STEPHENS *Bk. of Farm* II. 591 They [the grub larvæ] attack different kinds of corn, especially oats, the effects of grubbing in which are well known to every farmer. *Ibid.* 592 Every loose turf clod on a grubbed field of oats.

†**grub**, *a.* *Obs. rare*$^{-1}$. = GRUBBY *a.* 3.

1717 D'URFEY *Pills* (1719) II. 315 The Taylor with grub Beard and Crimson Nose.

grub (grʌb), *v.* Forms: (4 groube), 4-5 grobbe, 4-6 grube, grubbe, 6- grub. [Perh. repr. OE. **grybban*:—prehistoric **grubbjan*, f. OTeut. **grub-* ablaut-variant of **grab-* to dig, GRAVE *v.*^{1}; cf. ON. *gryfja* wk. fem. pit, hole, OHG. *grubilôn* to dig, search (mod.G. *grübeln* to pursue over-subtle meditations), MDu. *grobben* (once) to scrape together (money), Du. *grobbelen* to root, feel about for something. For the phonology cf. *stub* repr. OE. *stybb*, *shrub* repr. OE. *scrybb*.]

1. *trans.* To dig superficially; to break up the surface of (the ground); to clear (ground) of roots and stumps. Also with *up*. Said *occas.* of animals 'rooting'.

a **1300** *Cursor M.* 6747 Theif hus brecand, or gruband grund. **1572** *Lament. L. Scotl.* in *Sc. Poems 16th C.* II. 251 Ze suld your ground grube with simplicitie. **1603** FLORIO *Montaigne* III. xiii. 635 As the ground the more it is crumbled, broken, and deepely remoued or grubbed vp, becommeth so much more fertile. **1653** H. COGAN tr. *Pinto's Trav.* xxxi. 122 These serve to manure grounds that are newly grubb'd. **1698** FROGER *Voy.* 126 Since the Island has been grubbed up, they have begun to grow more healthy. **1786** BURNS *Bard's Epit.*, Whether thy soul Soars fancy's flights beyond the pole, Or darkling grubs this earthly hole. **1798** MALTHUS *Popul.* (1817) I. 165 Vast tracts of land lay in their original uncultivated state, having never been grubbed up or cleared. **1827** MONTGOMERY *Pelican Isl.* VI. 275 Like the swine That grubb'd the turf. **1840** BARHAM *Ingol. Leg.* Ser. I. *Spectre Tappington*, Some workmen employed in grubbing an old plantation. **1869** MRS. MEREDITH *Tasman. Mem.* 10 A bit of land all grubbed and clear'd too. **1878** BROWNING *Poets Croisic* 11 Batz whose Saxons grub The ground for crystals.

†**2.** To dig round the roots of (a plant). *Obs.*

1387-8 T. USK *Test. Love* I. v. (Skeat) I. 92 See now how, seven yere passed and more, have I graffed and grubed a vyne; and with al the wayes that I coude I sought to a fede me of the grape. **1513** DOUGLAS *Æneis* XIII. ix. 76 Saturne.. Tawcht thame to grub the wines,..and saw the cornys, and 3ok the cart.

3. To dig up by the roots, to root up, uproot: *esp.* with *up*, less commonly *out*. Also *transf.* and *fig.*

1555-8 PHAER *Æneid* II. E iv, Like as on the mountayn top, some auncient oke to fall The plowmen with their axes strong do striue, and twibles tall To grubbe, and round about hath hewd. **1558** BP. WATSON *Sev. Sacram.* xviii. 113 Wyth good hope of pardon, the roote of Desperation beyng cleane grubbed oute. **1609** HOLLAND *Amm. Marcell.* XXX. xi. 394 Papyrius chaunced to espie a shrub hard by, and caused it to be grubbed up. **1613** SHAKS. *Hen. VIII*, V. i. 23 The fruite she goes with I pray for heartily..but for the Stocke ..I wish it grubb'd vp now. **1640** SHIRLEY *St. Patrick* IV. ii, We will redeem our rashness, By grubbing up these Christians, that begin To infect us and our kingdom. **1658-9** *Burton's Diary* (1828) III. 321 Commonwealth was a good title, but grubbed up by the title of Chief Magistrate. **1664** EVELYN *Sylva* iii. §13 (1679) 23 The very stumps of Oak, especially that part which is dry,..being well grubb'd, is many times worth the pains and charge, for sundry rare, and hard works. *a* **1697** AUBREY *Nat. Hist. Surrey* (1719) III. 328 A kind of Stony Coal..he found by grubbing up the Roots of an old Oak. **1719** D'URFEY *Pills* II. 165 A Country Bumpkin that Trees did grub. **1807** E. S. BARRETT *Rising Sun* II. 86 To lay the axe to the root of decency, and to grub up morality. **1819** CRABBE *T. of Hall* IV. 81 Look at that land, —you find not there a weed, We grub the roots, and suffer none to seed. **1831** MACAULAY *Hampden* Ess. (1889) 203 The mutilated defenders of liberty..manfully presented the stumps of their ears to be grubbed out by the hangman's knife. **1881** WHITEHEAD *Hops* 8 Modern hop-planters have remorselessly grubbed the male plants. **1888** INGLIS *Tent Life Tigerland* 140 Jungles..in which the huge grey tusker grunts suspiciously as he grubs up his meal of roots.

†**b.** To pluck out (hair) by the roots. Also *absol.*

c **1320** R. BRUNNE *Medit.* 972 My body y 3ave to men smytyng And also my chekes to men grubbyng. **1633** T. ADAMS *Exp. 2 Peter* i. 16 Yet I would not have men..to grub their beards, yea, their very chins.

4. With *up*, *out*: To extract by digging. Also *transf.* and *fig.*

c **1374** CHAUCER *Former Age* 29 To grobbe vp metal lurkynge in dirkenesse. **1840** COBBETT *Advt. Fr. Gram.*, I had learnt French without a master. I had grubbed it out, bit by bit. **1842** MOTLEY *Corr.* (1889) I. iv. 102, I..began grubbing up antiquities. **1842** S. LOVER *Handy Andy* i. 16 He pulled forth his hand which had been grubbing up his prizes from the bottom of his pocket.

†**5.** ? To 'dig' (something) into a surface. *Obs.*

1607 DEKKER *Westw. Hoe* II. i, *Iusti.* She leanes somewhat too hard vppon her pen yet. *Hony.* Then she grubs her pen. *Iusti.* Its but my paines to mend the neb agen.

6. *intr.* To dig. In recent use, connoting the idea of mean or grovellingly laborious occupation.

a **1350** *Finding Cross* 267 in Horstm. *Altengl. Leg.* (1881) 60 Fast grubed þai þore obout; So depe þai grubbed & so fast, Thre crosses fand þai at þe last. *c* **1380** WYCLIF *Serm.* Sel. Wks. II. 208 Crist, gardener of þis vine3erde, grubbide inne and dongide it. *c* **1400** *Sege Jerusalem* (E.E.T.S.) 64/1108 With mynours & masouns; myne þey bygonne, Grobben faste vndir þe grounde. *c* **1440** *Promp. Parv.* 217/1 Grubbyn' yn the erthe, *fodico.* *c* **1460** FORTESCUE *Abs. & Lim. Mon.* iii. (1885) 114 Thai be arted bi necessite so to wacch, labour, and grubbe in the ground for thair sustenaunce, that their nature is much wastid. **1794** MATHIAS *Purs. Lit.* (1798) 256, I look for no pasture in the fields of Ministers or of Booksellers: nor would I be turned out..to grub and delve in Mr. Pitt's Straw-yard. **1800** ADDISON *Amer. Law* 294 McInnes sent a man to this place who grubbed a week. **1864** MRS. A. GATTY *Parables fr. Nat.* Ser. IV. 6 Many were the hours he had spent..grubbing in the old black soil. **1886** STEVENSON *Kidnapped* xv. (1888) 137, I met plenty of people, grubbing in little miserable fields.

b. *transf.* Of animals: To root, search for something in the earth, etc.

1647 TRAPP *Comm. Mark* ix. 46 Having worms ever grubbing and gnawing upon the entrails. **1845** ALB. SMITH *Fort. Scatterg. Fam.* xlii. (1887) 138 [He] was..making the animal crawl upon its knees after him, with its nose grubbing in the sawdust. **1862** MISS YONGE *C'tess Kate* ix. (1880) 96 A hole that looked as if an old hen had been grubbing in it. **1867** F. FRANCIS *Angling* iii. (1880) 79 The carp..might be seen rolling and grubbing all around the hook.

7. *transf.* and *fig.* To search in an undignified, abject, or grovelling manner; to rummage.

1800 COLQUHOUN *Comm. Thames* ii. 67 These miserable beings..grub in the River at low water for old Ropes, Metals, &c. **1837** *Lett. fr. Madras* (1843) 97 Coleoptera are more scarce, as I cannot grub for them myself for fear of centipedes. **1847** EMERSON *Repr. Men, Swedenborg* Wks. (Bohn) I. 314 Such a boy..goes grubbing into mines and mountains,..to find images fit for..his versatile..brain. **1855** E. FORBES *Lit. Papers* xi. 280 [They] were too absorbed in the delights of their own peculiar pursuits to think of grubbing for lucre. **1884** A. LANG in *Century Mag.* Jan. 325/2 Grubbing among Roman remains and relics. **1886** MALLOCK *Old Order Changes* II. 50 Meanwhile, however, he had been grubbing about in his bag. **1895** C. R. B. BARRETT *Survey* ii. 58 Grubbing about in the oldest..part of the building, I found..four pieces of Norman..moulding.

8. Chiefly with *on, along, away*: To lead a meanly plodding or grovelling existence; to live laboriously or ploddingly, to toil, 'fag'.

1735 DYCHE & PARDON *Dict.*, *Grub*..to go on in a mean, servile, covetous, nasty Way or Manner of Living. **1766** [ANSTEY] *Bath Guide* viii. 33 We may grub on with-out it through Life, I suppose. **1809** MRS. MITFORD in L'Estrange *Friendships Miss M.* (1882) I. Introd. 18, I must grub away all the evening to get it accomplished. **1852** DICKENS *Bleak Ho.* v, We both grub on in a muddle. **1862** G. MEREDITH *Mod. Love*, etc. *Juggling Jerry* x, I, lass, have lived no gipsy, flaunting Finery, while his poor help-mate grubs. **1868** LOWELL *Lett.* (1894) I. 401, I was grubbing away at an article for the *North American*. **1894** 'J. S. WINTER' *Red-coats* 10 This sort of thing isn't living—it's only grubbing along from day to day. **1895** *E. Angl. Gloss.*, *Grub*, to pick up a living in mean, haphazard ways.

9. [? f. the sb.] *slang*. **a.** To take 'grub' or food; to feed, eat. Also ***to grub it***.

1725 *New Canting Dict.*, *Grub*,..to Eat, to Dine, &c. **1839** DISRAELI *Corr. w. Sister* (1886) 121, I found some twenty-five gentlemen grubbing in solemn silence. **1848** THACKERAY *Van. Fair* lxiv, Come away into the supper-room..seeing those nobs grubbing away has made me peckish too. **1893** R. KIPLING *Many Invent.* 32, I was grubbing on fowls and boiled corn.

b. *trans.* To provide with 'grub' or food. *slang*.

1812 J. H. VAUX *Flash Dict.* s.v., To grub a person, is to diet him, or find him in victuals. **1837** DICKENS *Pickw.* xxii, The red-nosed man warn't by no means the sort of person you'd like to grub by contract. **1883** *Daily Tel.* 18 May 3/1 They are not bound to grub you.

10. *Cock-fighters' slang*. (See quot.)

1706 PHILLIPS (ed. Kersey), *Grubbing a Cock*, a cutting off the Cock's Feathers under the Wings.

11. *Comb.* (the vb.-stem used *attrib.*), as **grub-axe** (corruptly †*grubbage*), **-hoe, -hook**, implements used in grubbing up roots, stumps, etc.; **grub-fell** *v. trans.*, to bring down (a tree) by cutting at the root; **grub-saw**, a hand-saw used for sawing marble slabs into strips.

1611 COTGR. *Aigre*, a kind of *Grub-axe, or instrument wherewith roots, and shrubs are plucked up. **1669** WORLIDGE *Syst. Agric.* 271 *Grubbage*, see *Mattock*. **1706** PHILLIPS (ed. Kersey), *Grubbage* or *Grub-ax*, a Tool to grub up Roots of Trees, Weeds, etc. **1878** JEFFERIES *Gamekeeper at H.* iv. 72 Strong spades and grub-axes for rooting out a lost ferret. **1894** *Times* 11 Sept. 16/7 Every tree should be '*grub-felled'—that is, taken up by the roots. **1787** W. MARSHALL *Norfolk* (1795) II. 381 **Grub-felling*, the common method of taking down timber trees. **1884** KNIGHT *Dict. Mech.* Suppl., **Grub Hoe*, **Grub Hook*. **1853** O. BYRNE *Handbk. Artisan* 92 The cutting is effected with smaller blades, called *grub-saws.

Hence **grubbed** *ppl. a.*

1826 MISS MITFORD *Village* Ser. II. (1863) 414 The excellent double hedge-row of grubbed wood.

Grub-, (in comb. ***Grub-Pegasus***,) used as equivalent to GRUB-STREET (sense 2).

1715 *Swift's Real Diary* Ded. (D.), Nor could I mount my Pad for a Day's journey, but strait some paultry poet, astride his Grub-Pegasus, wrote at me, or rode, and sent his Hue and Cry after me.

Grubæan: see GRUBEAN.

grubbage: see *grub-axe* s.v. GRUB *v.* 11.

grubbed, *ppl. a.*: see under GRUB *sb.* and *v.*

grubber ('grʌbə(r)). [f. GRUB *v.* + -ER[1].]

1. One who grubs, *lit.* and *fig.*; a digger; a searcher among ruins and the like; a laborious worker.

13.. *St. Erkenwolde* 41 in Horstm. *Altengl. Leg.* (1881) 267 Mony grubber in grete þe grounde for to seche. *c* **1440** *Promp. Parv.* 217/1 Grubbare in þe erthe, or oþer thynggys (*H.* grovblare, *P.* growblar), *fossor, confossor, fossatrix*. **1776** S. J. PRATT *Pupil of Pleasure* I. 33 Homespun soon discovered himself to be a grubber in books. **1825** SCOTT *Fam. Lett.* 17 Sept. (1894) II. xxiii. 346 You are so capital a grubber that I have little doubt you will light upon it sooner or later. **1849** MISS MULOCK *Ogilvies* xxviii. (1875) 209 The hard-working grubbers in science. **1882** F. J. FURNIVALL *E.E. Wills* Ded. 9, I, or some grubber of like kind. **1892** *Daily News* 26 May 3/1 It is time to see the grubbers at work. We reach 'the face'—that is to say, the parts where the hewers and blasters of the rock are at work.

2. An implement for grubbing, breaking up ground, uprooting stumps or weeds, etc.

1598 FLORIO, *Arpago*..a rake, a harrow, a grubber. **1831** SIR J. SINCLAIR *Corr.* II. 157 The scarrifier or grubber, for pulverizing the soil. **1848** *Chambers' Inform.* I. 487/2 The common Scotch grubber resembles a strong harrow frame, running upon four wheels and guided like a plough. **1861** *Times* 10 Oct., The bean stubble is broken up by Tennant's grubber and the wheat lightly ploughed in. **1886** ELWORTHY *W. Somerset Word-bk.*, *Grubber*, a tool for rooting—a combination of axe and mattock. **1911** *Encycl. Brit.* VII. 618/2 *Cultivator*, also called scuffler, scarifier or grubber. **1940** *Chambers's Techn. Dict.* 392/2 *Grubber*, a heavy type of cultivator in which the teeth are set rigidly in a frame. **1950** *N.Z. Jrnl. Agric.* Feb. 271/2 The aim should be to secure a seed-bed with a rubbly surface and with the fine soil worked to the bottom through frequent use of grubber and harrows.

3. One who gets together wealth by sordid or contemptible methods. Now usually ***money-grubber***. [Cf. Du. *grobber* money-grubber.]

1578 T. WHITE *Serm. at Paul's Cross* 58 Such grubbers there bee whiche grynde the faces of the poore.

4. **a.** An eater, a feeder. **b.** *slang*. (See quot. 1940.) **c.** Food.

1838 'P. PRY' *Oddities London Life* I. 235 She chucks ony von tater at me, and a bit of meat vot aint of no use to sitch a heavy grubber as I am. **1861** HUGHES *Tom Brown at Oxf.* vi. (1889) 50, I like to see a fellow an honest grubber at breakfast and dinner. **1861** DICKENS *Gt. Expect.* III. 9 'I'm a heavy grubber, dear boy', he said, as a polite kind of apology when he had made an end of his meal. **1940** M. MARPLES *Publ. School Slang* 91 *Grubber*, tuck-shop..tuck-box. **1959** I. & P. OPIE *Lore & Lang. Schoolch.* ix. 163 Food in general is referred to as 'bait'.., 'grub', or 'grubber'.

5. *Cricket*. = GRUB *sb.* 5.

1837 *Bell's Life* 15 Oct. 4/1 The Catapulta..was capable of..giving a home toss or a grubber. **1924** LAWRENCE & SKINNER *Boy in Bush* 116 Ross..sent down a sulky grubber. **1963** *Times* 23 May 4/1 Constable was undermined by a 'grubber'.

6. In full ***grubber kick***. In *Rugby Football*, a forward kick of the ball along the ground. Hence **grubber-kick** *v. intr.*, to make a grubber kick.

1950 *Adam* (Sydney) Feb. 29 If it wasn't Sullivan's boot winning kicking duels, it was Parkin's grubber-kicks. **1956** V. JENKINS *Lions Rampant* xiii. 199 This time Ulyate put through a grubber kick from fly-half which Cameron failed to gather. **1958** *N.Z. Listener* 18 July 6/4 He tried grubber kicking. All right, if they're going to grubber kick there's only one thing to do. **1960** *Sunday Times* 27 Nov. 20/1 From a set scrum, Lockyer fed Kirkpatrick, going right, and he put a grubber kick between Rogers and D. Bebb.

grubbery ('grʌbərɪ). [f. GRUB *sb.* or *v.* + -ERY.]

†1. A room for hard work or study. ? *Obs. rare*[−1].

1791 MAD. D'ARBLAY *Let. Dr. Burney* 8 Oct. in *Diary* V. 260 The great grubbery will be in nice order for you, as well as the little; both have..many accessions of new books.

2. *slang*. **a.** Food, 'grub'; also, a (public) meal. **b.** A place where one 'grubs' or takes food.

1823 'J. BEE' *Slang* 91 *A grubbery*, a cook's-shop. **1831** TRELAWNY *Adv. Younger Son* lxiii, A nice little cabin there ..with grubbery, free of rent and taxes. *Ibid.* lxxiii, You seem not very well found in the grubbery line. **1837** *Boston Herald* 31 Jan. 4/2 The out-and-out speech of Lord Spencer at the late grubbery. **1889** BARRIÈRE & LELAND *Dict. Slang*, *Grubbery* (popular), an eating-house.

3. Something grubbed or dug out; an excavation.

1887 TUER & FAGAN *1st Yr. Silken Reign* viii. 164 Brunel's Thames Tunnel..this damp and sombre grubbery.

4. Grovelling or sordid way of life. *rare*[−1].

1891 SYMONDS in H. F. Brown *Biog.* (1895) II. 336 Let us not allow ourselves to be submerged in passion or our love to lapse in grubbery.

grubbing ('grʌbɪŋ), *vbl. sb.*[1] [f. GRUB *v.* + -ING[1].] The action of the verb GRUB.

1. Digging; the uprooting of stumps of trees, etc.; the clearing of ground of trees, weeds, and the like.

c **1440** *Promp. Parv.* 217/1 Grubynge (*H.* grublyng, *P.* growblinge), *confossio*. *c* **1460** FORTESCUE *Abs. & Lim. Mon.* xiii. (1885) 141 In grobbyng and stokkyng off treis, busses, and groves. **1598** FLORIO, *Estirpatione*..an extirpation, a rooting out, a grubbing. **1639** HORN & ROB. *Gate Lang. Unl.* xvii. §205 By delving, or grubbing, the cunny, or rabbet, maketh burrowes. **1725** BRADLEY *Fam. Dict.*, *Grubbing*, a Term used in Agriculture, and signifies the clearing of Ground of Stubs, &c. **1861** MUSGRAVE *By-roads* 287 The grubbing-up of twenty or thirty acres of wood.

2. *fig.* Close search or investigation; plodding work, laborious study.

1831 CARLYLE in *Westm. Rev.* XV. 21 Antiquaries..in their Blackletter stubbing and grubbing. **1838** MACAULAY *Ess.*, *Temple* (1889) 436 No grubbing among old state-papers will ever bring to light any document which will shake these facts. **1849** H. ROGERS *Ess.* (1874) II. vi. 308 The indefatigable grubbings and gropings of the literary antiquary.

3. *slang*. Eating, feeding; *concr.* food, 'grub'.

1819 MOORE *Tom Crib* (ed. 3) 28 What with snoozing, high grubbing, and guzzling like Cloe. **1819** *Sporting Mag.* V. 125 There's an end of all good grubbing. **1867** W. H. L. TESTER *Poems* 132 They're first rate grubbin for the poor.

†4. Some trick formerly practised among college students. *Obs.*

1679 *2nd Reg. Bk. Magd. Coll. Camb.* 370 in *5th Rep. Hist. MSS. Comm.* (1876) 483/2 Those sottish and even savage tricks of grubbing, salting, mustarding, and yᵉ like. *c* **1720** SWIFT *Tripos* Wks. 1824 VI. 239 His bedfellow dreams of grubbins all night.

5. *attrib.* and *Comb.*, as ***grubbing-axe***, †*-fork*, *-hoe*, †*-hook*, *-instrument*, *-mattock*, †*-tool* (cf. the corresp. combs. of GRUB *v.*); **grubbing-iron**, †(*a*) a kind of chisel or gouge; (*b*) *dial.* 'an iron instrument for grubbing up thistles' (*Sheffield Gloss.* 1888); **grubbing-machine**, a tool used in gunnery; also (sense 3) ***grubbing-hall***.

1585 HIGINS tr. *Junius' Nomenclator* 265 *Bidens*..a deluing toole with two teeth, wherewith yᵉ earth is opened in such places as the plough cannot pearse: some call it a *grubbing axe. **1611** COTGR., *Houë fourchuë*, a grubbing ax; or forked pickax. **1859** R. THOMPSON *Gardener's Assist.* 123 Mattock, or Grubbing-axe. **1611** COTGR., *Bisnoire*, a *grubbing forke, or grubbing axe. **1897** BARRIÈRE & LELAND *Dict. Slang*, **Grubbing hall* (Winchester), the hall in which college 'men' take their meals. **1891** *Auckland Star* 1 Oct. 1/6 *Grubbing and Dutch Hoes. **1896** P. A. BRUCE *Econ. Hist. Virginia* I. 463 There were several kinds of this implement [*sc.* the hoe], the hilling, the weeding, and the grubbing. **1603** HOLLAND *Plutarch's Mor.* 163 When he would rid the ground of some wilde bushes and fruitlesse plants, he laieth at them mainely with his *grubbing hooke or mattocke. **1719** LONDON & WISE *Compl. Gard.* 319 Where the closeness of the Plants to one another will permit us to use only *grubbing Instruments. *c* **1440** *Promp. Parv.* 217/2 *Grubbynge yryn of gravowrys, *supra in* formowre. **1869** *Lonsdale Gloss.*, **Grubbin-mattock*, an instrument or tool to grub roots or trees with. **1591** PERCIVALL *Sp. Dict.*, *Roçador*, a *grubbing toole.

grubbing, *vbl. sb.*[2]: see under GRUB *sb.*

grubbing ('grʌbɪŋ), *ppl. a.* [f. GRUB *v.* + -ING[2].] That grubs. *lit.* and *fig.*

1765 C. SMART *Phædrus* II. iv. (Bohn) 490 That grubbing Swine Still works the tree to overset. **1838** DICKENS *Nich. Nick.* xvi, Poor grubbing devils of authors. **1882** W. B. WEEDEN *Soc. Law Labor* 257 The slave, the serf, the grubbing laborer..have been released from..fetters.

grubble ('grʌb(ə)l), *v.* [variant of GRABBLE *v.*, influenced by GRUB *v.* Du. has *grobbelen* synonymous with *grabbelen*.]

†1. *intr.* and *trans.* To grope. ***to grubble up***: to scrape together. *Obs.*

a **1690** E. HOPKINS *Regeneration* (1694) 28 Being now deprived of the Image of God, the Soul grubbles here below. **1690** DRYDEN *Don Sebast.* I. i. (1692) 8 Let me rowl and grubble thee. *a* **1700** —— *Ovid's Amours* I. iv. 73 There I will be, and there we cannot miss, Perhaps to grubble, or at least to kiss. **1712** STEELE *Spect.* No. 444 ¶4 He looked at the Fish, then at the Fiddle, still grubling in his Pockets,..then altered his Mind as to Farthings and gave my Friend a Silver Sixpence. **1719** D'URFEY *Pills* I. 353, I'll grubble all my Jokes up to Delight ye. *Ibid.* II. 329 And Foreign *Sol fa* grubbles up the Pence.

2. *intr.* = GRUB *v.* 6b. *rare*.

1867 G. MACDONALD *Poems* 265 The limping, cheating plover Not upon an elm tree hover, But prefer in fields to grubble With the partridge.

Hence **'grubble** *sb.*, *rare*, an act of 'grubbling'.

1852 *Tait's Mag.* XIX. 336 The cherubs hungry come from play, Dirt-pies and gutter grubbles.

†**grubbler**. *Obs.* or *arch.* Also 5 **groublare, growblar**. [Altered form of GRUBBER.] = GRUBBER 1.

c **1440** [see GRUBBER 1]. **1813** W. TAYLOR in *Monthly Rev.* LXXII. 283 That which not the parish-clerk, but the conversation of the neighbourhood, might have supplied, is too commonly left to the sagacity of grubblers yet unborn.

†**grubbling**, *vbl. sb. Obs.* In 5 **growblinge**, 5–6 **grublyng**. [Altered form of GRUBBING.]

1. Digging, grubbing.

c **1440** [see GRUBBING *vbl. sb.* 1].

2. In comb. ***grubbling iron***, a 'grubbing-iron'.

1530 PALSGR. 222/1 Formour or grublyng yron.

grubblings, dial. form of GROVELLINGS *adv.*

grubby ('grʌbɪ), *a.* [f. GRUB *sb.* + -Y.]

1. **a.** Infested with grubs. **b.** Of the nature of a grub or larva.

1725 BRADLEY *Fam. Dict.* s.v. *Tree*, Reject those trees.. that are knotty and appear to be grubby. **1852** *Househ. Words* 23 Oct. 138 Divesting themselves of the grubby or chrysalis-like covering of great-coats and wrap-rascals.

2. Stunted, dwarfish. (Cf. GRUB *sb.* 2a.) Now *dial.*

1611 COTGR., *Rabougri*, growne crooked, and low;..mis-growne, grubbie, dried up. *Ibid.*, *Ratatiné*, grubbie, shrunke in, thick and short. **1712** J. JAMES tr. *Le Blond's Gardening* 11 Observe, if there are great Trees near, whether they grow crooked, ill-shap'd, and grubby. **1886** *Chesh. Gloss.*, *Grubby*, small, poor, stunted.

3. Dirty, grimy; also slovenly and underbred.

a **1845** HOOD *Black Job* vi, They look'd so ugly in their sable hides: So dark, so dingy, like a grubby lot Of sooty sweeps. **1855** *Chamb. Jrnl.* III. 105 The lint..is sure to suffer;..it is sure to become foul, and, as it is technically termed, 'grubby'. **1859** F. E. PAGET *Curate of Cumberworth*, etc. 227 A pack of grubby children in a frowzy school. **1861** SALA *Dutch Pict.* xxi. 330 That shabby, grubby, ill-smelling old street. **1893** G. ALLEN *Scallywag* I. 153, I like Mr. Thistleton..he's quite nice, of course, and there's nothing grubby about him.

4. *dial.* (See quot. and cf. GRUB *sb.* 3.)

1841 HARTSHORNE *Salop. Antiq.* 450 Grubby, testy, ill-tempered, peevish.

Hence **'grubbiness**, grubby or grimy condition.

1866 *Morn. Star* 20 Aug. 4/6 Their face in a condition of grubbiness.

†**Grubean**, *a. jocular. Obs.* Also **Grubæan, Grubbean**. [f. GRUB(-STREET) + *-ean*, after *Sabean*, etc.] Of or belonging to Grub-street.

1704 SWIFT *T. Tub* I. (1709) 30 The Grubaean sages have always chosen to convey their precepts..shut up within the Vehicles of types and fables. **1759** DILWORTH *Pope* 39 The overt acts of the Grubean sowers of poetic sedition. **1795** *Chron.* in *Ann. Reg.* 6 A Grubean elegy. **1803** *Spirit Publ. Jrnls.* (1804) VII. 33 The Grubean sages have exalted their society, in point of fame, above all societies.

‖**Grübelsucht** ('gry:bəlzʊxt). *Psychiatry.* [Ger., f. *grübeln* to brood + *sucht* mania.] A form of obsession in which even the simplest facts are compulsively queried.

1876 *Mind* I. 413 Under the name *Grübelsucht*, Griesinger ..described three examples of a peculiar mental condition, characterised by continuous uncontrollable questionings as to the origin and causes of things great and small. **1885** W. JAMES in *Mind* X. 37 It would practically be a case of *Grübelsucht*, if a ruffian were assaulting and drubbing my body, to spend much time in subtle speculation. **1909** W. F. ROBERTSON tr. *Tanzi's Textbk. Mental Dis.* v. 150 Some cannot cease from putting to themselves metaphysical and insoluble problems. This constitutes interrogative obsession, the obsession of the why, or *Grübelsucht*.

grubhood (ˈgrʌbhʊd). [f. GRUB *sb.* + -HOOD.] The condition of a grub or larva.

1859 W. S. COLEMAN *Woodlands* (1866) 75 [He] feeds the last days of his grubhood upon the nutty pips. **1859** SALA *Tw. round Clock* (1861) 105 Yonder broken-winged butterfly, relapsing..into a state of grubhood again.

Grub-street (ˈgrʌbstriːt).

1. *orig.* The name of a street near Moorfields in London (now Milton-street), 'much inhabited by writers of small histories, dictionaries, and temporary poems' (J.); hence used allusively for the tribe of mean and needy authors, or literary hacks.

1630 J. TAYLOR (Water P.) *Wks.* II. 2/1 When strait I might descry, The Quintescence of Grubstreet, well distild Through Cripplegate in a contagious Map. **1689** SHADWELL *Bury F.* v. 56 The very Spirit of Grubstreet Reigns in you. **1712** ARBUTHNOT *John Bull* Pref., O Grubstreet! thou fruitful Nursery of tow'ring Genius's! **1809** BYRON *Eng. Bards & Sc. Reviewers* 547 Long, long beneath that hospitable roof Shall Grub-street dine, while duns are kept aloof. **1870** EMERSON *Soc. & Solit.*, *Books* Wks. (Bohn) III. 80 Now and then, by rarest luck, in some foolish Grub Street is the gem we want.

2. *attrib.* or as *adj.* Pertaining to, emanating from, or characteristic of Grub-street; of the nature of literary hack-work; *rarely*, like a needy scribbler.

1648 *Mercurius Fidelicus* (*Thomasson Tracts* B.M.) CCCLXXXIV. No. 32. 6 The Grub-street pamphleteer. **1672** MARVELL *Reh. Transp.* I. 26 Grubstreet and Polemical Divinity. *a* **1700** B. E. *Dict. Cant. Crew*, *Grub street News*, false, Forg'd. **1710** SWIFT *Tatler* No. 230 ¶2 Till of late Years, a Grubstreet Book was always bound in Sheep-skin. **1760** *Voy. W. O. G. Vaughan* I. 129 Grub-street Quill-drivers. **1785** GROSE *Dict. Vulg. Tongue* s.v., A Grub-street writer means a hackney author, who manufactures books for the booksellers. **1856** LOWELL *Lett.* (1894) I. 276 At present I am perfectly Grubstreet, but then I have the pleasure of earning every penny I spend. *a* **1860** MACAULAY *Hist. Eng.* xxiii. (1889) II. 644 Nor was it only in Grub Street tracts that such reflections were to be found.

Hence **Grubstreetian** *sb.*, **Grubstreetonian** *a.* (*nonce-wds.*).

c **1721** *Misc. Lett. Mist's Jrnl.* (1722) II. 303 Ha, ha, ha, all the Judges sit upon the Grub-Streetians! *Ibid.* 321 Any able Grubstreetian. **1805** *Spirit Publ. Jrnls.* (1806) IX. 245 A Ballad in the Style Grubstreetonian.

grucche, obs. form of GRUTCH.

†ˈ**grucchild**. *Obs. rare*⁻¹. [f. *grucche* GRUTCH *v.* + *-ild* fem. suffix, as in ONorthumb. *fœreld* female relative, *néhebýrild* female neighbour, ME. *begenild*, *beggild*, *cheapild*, *fostrild*, *motild*, *totild*.

The origin of the suffix is obscure; the suggestion that it is derived from *-hild* as a frequent terminal element in female names can hardly be right, on account of the umlaut in the ONorthumbrian examples. Perh. it may represent a Teut. fem. agent-suffix *-iþljâ*.]

A (female) grumbler.

a **1225** *Ancr. R.* 108 Heo is a grucchild [*MS. C.* grucinde, *MS. T.* grucchere], & ful itowen.

gruch(e, **grudche**, obs. forms of GRUTCH.

grudge (grʌdʒ), *sb.* Forms: see the verb. [f. GRUDGE *v.*, or variant of GRUTCH *sb.*]

†**1.** Murmur, murmuring, grumbling; discontent, dissatisfaction; reluctance, unwillingness. *Obs.*

1477 MARG. PASTON in *P. Lett.* No. 801 III. 197 For syche grwgys and other causys, I am ryght sory that the graunte is knowyn that I have mad, with ought it myght take effect. **1484** RICH. III in Ellis *Orig. Lett.* Ser. III. I. 104 The gret clamor grugge and complainte which our liege people of this our Royᵐᵉ have made of and upon the coigne of silver made in our lande of Irland. **1518** in W. H. Turner *Select. Rec. Oxford* (1880) 19 Ther shold ensew grogis and murmures amongst the kyngis subgects. **1526** TINDALE *Acts* vi. 1 There arose a grodge amonge the grekes agaynste the ebrues. **1533** MORE *Answ. Poysoned Bk.* Wks. 1092/2 That they shulde eat his fleshe and drincke his bloud after their owne carnal vnderstandinge, but yet in another fourme, to put awaye all grudge of stomacke. *c* **1555** HARPSFIELD *Divorce Hen. VIII* (Camden) 193 They declare what murmur and grudge was in England. **1611** B. JONSON *Catiline* III. i, That still your counsell of me be approu'd; Both by your selues, and those to whom you haue, With grudge, prefer'd me.

†**2.** 'Murmuring' of the conscience; uneasiness or disturbance of mind; scruple, doubt, misgiving. Also, an instance of this. *Obs.*

1483 *Vulgaria abs Terentio* 7 b, There is oon grugge or dout that maketh me euyll at ese [L. *vnus scrupulus restat*]. **1531** *Dial. on Laws Eng.* I. xxxii. (1638) 56 Without any scruple or grudge of Conscience. **1540** MORYSINE *Vives' Introd. Wysd.* C v, We must be content, that in our conscience, we fele our selves void of secret gruge and unquietnes. **1558** BP. WATSON *Sev. Sacram.* xxi. 134 God gaue hym grudge in his conscience agaynste hys sinne. **1598** BARRET *Theor. Warres* I. ii. 11 Is it no grudge to the souldiers conscience to fight against them?

3. a. Ill-will or resentment due to some special cause, as a personal injury, the superiority of an opponent or rival, or the like. *Obs.* (exc. as in b).

1477 EARL RIVERS (Caxton) *Dictes* 17 b, The lesse grugge ye haue, the more ye fle from malice and wikkedenesse. **1494** FABYAN *Chron.* VII. 435 He wanne of them as moche grudge & hatred as he to fore hadde loue & good wyll. **1513** MORE in Grafton *Chron.* (1568) II. 768 To the great grudge of all men and high displeasure of God. **1533** —— *Debell. Salem* Wks. 1016/1 He might dyffame all the temporall ministers too, and bryng them in grudge & obloquie of the people. **1579** LYLY *Euphues* (Arb.) 88 Although he were moved with inward grudge yet he wisely repressed his anger. **1590** SPENSER *F.Q.* III. iv. 61 Heavy looke..that plaine In him bewraid great grudge, and maltalent. **1635** R. N. *Camden's Hist. Eliz.* I. ii. 23 Queen Elizabeth bare..secret grudge against her. **1722** SEWEL *Hist. Quakers* (1795) I. Pref. 21 This hath raised envy, grudge, and malice against them. **1784** COWPER *Task* v. 203 They plough'd, and sow'd, And reap'd their plenty without grudge or strife. **1878** BROWNING *La Saisiaz* 57 There is no such grudge in God as scared the ancient Greek.

b. A particular instance of this feeling: const. *against* (a person); also freq. in phr. ***to have a g. against***, (†*to*, †*at*), ***to bear***, ***owe*** (a person) ***a g.***, etc.

1531 ELYOT *Gov.* II. ix. (1883) II. 102 The people called Dores..wolde aduenge their olde grudges agayne the Atheniensis. **1581** SAVILE *Tacitus' Hist.* II. v. (1591) 55 They laid grudges aside [L. *positis odiis*]. *a* **1586** SIDNEY *Arcadia* II. (1622) 201 Public affairs were mingled with private grudges. **1601** F. GODWIN *Bps. of Eng.* 169 The Conqueror ..hauing a priuate grudge at Stigand. **1603** R. JOHNSON *Kingd. & Commw.* 75 The Countes of Maunsfielt have a grudge to the house of Saxony. **1611** BIBLE *Mark* vi. 19 Herodias had a quarrel [*marg.* inward grudge] against him. **1657** *North's Plutarch*, *Add. Lives* (1676) 4 The Arians.. bore Athanasius a grudge. **1678** DRYDEN *Kind Keeper* II. i. Dram. Wks. 1725 IV. 312, I have a grudge to him, for the Privilege of his Sex. **1767** T. HUTCHINSON *Hist. Mass.* II. iii. 282 There was a private grudge against him. **1830** CUNNINGHAM *Brit. Paint.* II. 244 He went on his errand with a grudge. **1849** MACAULAY *Hist. Eng.* vi. II. 40 He had ..an old grudge to stimulate his zeal. **1871** DIXON *Tower* III. xxvii. 306 He nursed some grudge against the Duke. **1876** MOZLEY *Univ. Serm.* x. (1877) 204 Men of this character pursue a grudge unceasingly, and never forget or forgive.

†**4.** = GRUDGING *vbl. sb.* 2. *Obs.*

1562 TURNER *Herbal* II. 20 b, If any grudge of the same disease chance to rise againe. **1584** COGAN *Haven Health* ccxiii. (1636) 225 [He] was never vexed with any sickness.. except the grudge of a fever of one day. **1678** R. L'ESTRANGE *Seneca's Mor.* (1702) 106 They are past the Hazard of a Relapse, but they have still the Grudges of a Disease.

†**5.** Injury, injurious influence or effect. *Obs. rare.*

1491 *Act 7 Hen. VII*, c. 10 It was ordeyned..that the said Statute..shuld be adnulled..to the grete prejudice grugge singler hurte and jeoperdie of all your seid true lieges. **1641** MILTON *Reform.* II. (1851) 69 This our shaken Monarchy, that now lies labouring under her throwes, and struggling against the grudges of more dreadfull Calamities.

6. *Comb.*, as ***grudge-bearing*** adj.; **grudge fight**, a fight based on personal antipathy; also *fig.*

1611 COTGR., *Maling*, malignant, ill-willie, grudge-bearing. **1927** *Daily Express* 19 July 3/4 It is a 'grudge fight', ..and it is clear that Stalin is trying to expel Trotsky..from the Central Committee of the Communist Party. *Ibid.* 22 Sept. 2//5 It may be that the interchange of letters between the Dempsey and Tunney camps has convinced the sporting public that this will be a 'grudge fight'. **1964** J. HALE (*title*) The grudge fight.

grudge (grʌdʒ), *v.* Forms: 5–6 gruge, grugge, groge, 6–7 grudg, (5 grwge, grughe, grogge, growge, 6 grodge, groudge), 5– grudge. [Altered form of GRUTCH *v.*; possibly influenced by GREGGE, *agregge*, AGGREGE; cf. AGGRUDGE (*aggroggynge*, *aggrugged*) synonymous with AGGRIEVE.]

†**1.** *intr.* To murmur; to utter complaints murmuringly; to grumble, complain; to be discontented or dissatisfied. *Obs.*

1461 *Paston Lett.* No. 404 II. 30 They grudge and sey, how that the kyng resayvith sych..as haff be his gret eanemyes. **1470** FORTESCUE *Articles* in *Abs. & Lim. Mon.* (1885) App. B. 349 Somme man..shal mowe obtayne gretter rewardis than thei have disserved, and yit grugge, seying they haue to litill. **1502** ATKYNSON tr. *De Imitatione* I. ix. 159 They haue therin peyne, and lyghtly gruges [*earlier version* gretchin, *v.r.* gruccheth]. **1535** COVERDALE *Ps.* ii. 1 Why do the Heithen grudge? why do the people ymagyn vayne thinges? **1540–1** ELYOT *Image Gov.* (1556) 89 b, Not with standynge all this tourment..he never grudged. **1552** LATIMER *Serm. St. John Evang. Day* (1584) 284, I woulde not haue you in any wise to grudge or murmure because ye lack houses. **1600** HOLLAND *Livy* IV. i. (1609) 139 The Volscians and Æquians grudged and muttered for the fortifying of Verrugo. **1611** BIBLE *Ps.* lix. 15 Let them wander vp and downe for meate, and grudge if they be not satisfied. *a* **1632** T. TAYLOR *God's Judgem.* I. II. x. (1642) 207 The Cardinall..on his death bed, murmured and grudged.

†**b.** Const. *against*, earlier also *with* (chiefly, a person); *at*, *of* (chiefly, a thing). *Obs.*

c **1450** *Cov. Myst.* (Shaks. Soc.) 228 Thus for to grugge ageyns Godys myght, Aȝens hyȝ God ȝe do offens. **1483** *Presentm. Juries* in *Surtees Misc.* (1888) 29 The comyns gretly grughis ther wythe þᵗ ther is non as ther was wont to be. **1494** FABYAN *Chron.* VII. ccxxiii. 248 He toke vpon hym ..to rule in suche wyse, as the Kynge grudged with his doynge. *a* **1529** SKELTON *Sp. Parrot* 435 Grocers were grugyd at and groyned at but late. **1535** COVERDALE *Mark* xiv. 5 And they grudged against her. **1538** STARKEY *England* I. iii. 82 The temporalty grugyth agayn the spiritualty, the commyns agayne the nobullys. **1582–8** *Hist. Jas. VI* (1804) 98 The people of the countrey grudget heavilie at the promotion of this Regent. **1597** HOOKER *Eccl. Pol.* v. xvii. §2 Nor is there cause why the guilty..should grudge or complain of injustice. **1612** T. TAYLOR *Comm. Titus* ii. 9 That too ordinarie a sinne of seruants, when as they priuatly mutter and grudge against the commandments and corrections of their masters and mistresses. **1679** HARBY *Key Script.* I. 10 Nor let any grudg at this brief Digress. *a* **1720** SHEFFIELD (Dk. Buckhm.) *Wks.* (1753) II. 260 What! shall we too..Like children, grudge at one another's play-things? **1820** BROWN *Hist. Brit. Ch.* I. xi. 345 Stillingfleet.. grudged at the late toleration.

†**c.** with *clause* expressing the cause.

1561 T. NORTON *Calvin's Inst.* I. 47 Many perhaps do grudge, that the Scripture doth not..set forth that fall and the cause..therof. **1621** DONNE *Serm.* xv. 148 Neither grudge that thou goest, nor that worse stay. **1642** ROGERS *Naaman* 304 How ready..to grudge..that the heat of the day lyes upon them more then others. **1760** BEATTIE *Virg. Past.* II. 49 Nor grudge, Alexis, that the rural pipe So oft hath stain'd the roses of thy lip.

†**d.** ***to grudge a thought***: to think an envious thought. *Obs.*

1591 SHAKS. *1 Hen. VI*, III. i. 176 So perish they, That grudge one thought against your Maiesty.

2. *trans.* To be unwilling to give, grant, or allow (something); to begrudge. Also with *infinitive* as obj.

c **1500** *Three Kings' Sons* 110 For the symplesse & pouert of his persone, he gruggid the lesse his delieueraunce. **1549** COVERDALE, etc. *Erasm. Par. Jas.* 32 Shall his faythe auaile him, that at Goddes commaundement grudgeth to geue a cote to hys neyghbour that staruethe for colde. **1596** *Edward III*, III. iv. F 4 b, The garrison of Genoaes..weary with their march, Grudging to be soddenly imployd. **1614** BP. HALL *Recoll. Treat.* 415 What if God had called mee to heaven; would you have grudged my departure? **1618** J. BULLOKER in Farr *S.P. Jas. I* (1848) 291 His owne disciples, too, that sate at bord, Do grudge such cost bestow'd vpon their Lord. **1687** A. LOVELL tr. *Thevenot's Trav.* I. 268 The English are very good Sea-men..never grudging their labour. **1711** ADDISON *Spect.* No. 10 ¶6, I hope these my gentle Readers ..will not grudge throwing away a Quarter of an Hour in a Day on this Paper. **1755** YOUNG *Centaur* v. Wks. 1757 IV. 236 Shall we grudge to pay half that pains for an eternity? **1758** JOHNSON *Idler* No. 80 ¶4 [She] tells how she grudges every moment of delay. **1830** D'ISRAELI *Chas. I*, III. ix. 198 Some..were jealous to obtain the distinction of a royal visit, though they grudged the cost. **1845** MᶜCULLOCH *Taxation* II. ii. (1852) 169 The duties on spirits and tobacco..are paid without being grudged. **1846** KEBLE *Lyra Innoc.* (1873) 158 Why should we grudge the hour of prayer? **1848** B'NESS BUNSEN in Hare *Life* (1879) II. iii. 120, I grudge your being disturbed in the composure you had re-conquered. **1873** BROWNING *Red Cott. Nt.-cap* 199 And as with body, so proceed with soul: Nor less discerningly..grudge To play the doctor.

b. Const. *to* or *dat.*

1639 FULLER *Holy War* v. iii. (1640) 233 The world.. never grudged them great wages who did good work. **1697** DRYDEN *Virg. Georg.* I. 677 Long the Gods..Have grudg'd thee, Cæsar, to the World below. **1719** YOUNG *Busiris* II. i, I'd grudge her beauties to the gods that gave them. **1855** MACAULAY *Hist. Eng.* xv. III. 508 Even zealous Royalists might not have grudged the old Republican a grave in his native soil. **1871** R. ELLIS tr. *Catullus* lxiv. 170 Thus to my utmost need chance..Grudges an ear. **1873** HELPS *Anim. & Mast.* iii. (1875) 63, I don't grudge these people their pleasures.

†**3.** *trans.* To envy (a person). Also *intr.* To be envious. *Obs. rare.*

1587 GASCOIGNE *Wks.*, *Pr. Pleas. Kenilw.* A v, Whose graces make the Gods to grudge, me thinkes it should be shee. *a* **1661** FULLER *Worthies* (1840) III. 376 No good man will grudge him under this title, who shall seriously peruse this his epitaph.

†**4.** *trans.* To trouble or vex mentally: said either of something which grieves the conscience or of the conscience distressing a person. Also *impers. Obs.*

1483 *Nottingham Rec.* II. 393 On thyng in especyalle gruggyd theyr consyens. **1488** *Will of Sir E. Shea* (Somerset Ho.), My conscience gruggeth me that I wronged hym. **1534** MORE *Let. to Marg. Roper* Wks. 1429/1, I woulde not declare any speciall part of that othe that grudged my conscience. **1535** *Goodly Primer*, *Chr. Instruct. Childr.*, Call to your mind what offence..chiefliest grudgeth your conscience. **1619** JER. DYKE *Counterpoyson* (1620) 22 Oh how it grudges the wretch to spare God so much time! *Ibid.* 50 It would have grudged him farre more to haue seene them hang from yeare to yeare.

absol. or *intr.* *c* **1460** G. ASHBY *Poems* III. 895 To do ayeinste conscience in suche guise, Whiche shal frete and gruge in your soule & mynde. **1558** BP. WATSON *Sev. Sacram.* xxi. 134 He stopped hys eares, and woulde not suffer hys conscience to grudge, nor shewe hym hys offences.

†**5.** *pass.* and *intr.* To be seized *with* a disease; to have the first touch or access of a fever. *Obs.* (Cf. GRUDGE *sb.* 4, GRUDGING *vbl. sb.* 2.)

1494 FABYAN *Chron.* VI. clxv. 160 He was grudgyd with a feuoure; for remedye whereof, he toke a pocion of a physycion Iewe. **1530** PALSGR. 575/2, I groudge, as one doth that hath a groudgyng of the axes, *je frilonne*... Me thynke his axes cometh upon hym, for he groudgeth all redy. **1549** CHALONER *Erasm. on Folly* H j a, Who maie auant him selfe to do wiseli, and not to be grudged with some spyce of madnesse [L. *quique non aliquo insaniæ genere teneatur*].

†**b.** *intr.* To chatter with the teeth (? as in ague). *Obs. rare*⁻¹.

c **1440** CAPGRAVE *Life St. Kath.* v. 1309 There is noon that it seeth But for feer he gruggeth with his teeth.

†**6.** *trans.* To load, cram [? for *gregge*, *aggrege*].

1642 ROGERS *Naaman* 532 Hee shall choke them with their owne morsells, and grudge them therewith till they come out at their nostrills.

Hence **grudged** *ppl. a.*

1549 CHALONER *Erasm. on Folly* G ij a, They fele not what a twitching turment it is to have a grudged conscience. *c* **1636** *Strafford Papers* I. 210 Nobility is such a grudged and envied piece of monarchy. **1853** KANE *Grinnell Exp.* xlvii. (1856) 442 A grudged ration of seal's meat.

†**ˈgrudgeable**, *a. Obs. rare*$^{-0}$. [f. GRUDGE *v.* + -ABLE.] That may be complained of.

1570 LEVINS *Manip.* 3/4 Grudgeable, *murmurabilis*.

grudgeful (ˈgrʌdʒfʊl), *a. rare.* [f. GRUDGE *sb.* + -FUL.] Full of resentment or rancour; resentful.

1596 SPENSER *F.Q.* IV. viii. 28 The hag did scold And rayle at them with grudgefull discontent. **1632** VICARS *Æneid* II. 49 Grudgefull Greeks. **1877** BLACKIE *Wise Men* 86 The full-eyed spouse of Zeus Grudgeful that Troy no bloodier bane should brook. **1893** STEVENSON *Catriona* xv. 182 These red-shank's are unco grudgeful.

Hence **ˈgrudgefully** *adv.*

1882 H. E. MERIVALE *Faucit of B.* III. II. xv. 95 She laughed with a real enjoyment which Guy rather grudgefully envied her.

grudgekin (ˈgrʌdʒkɪn). *nonce-wd.* [f. GRUDGE *sb.* + -KIN.] A little grudge.

1860–1 THACKERAY *Lovel* iii, Some twaddler against whom I have a grudgekin.

grudgement (ˈgrʌdʒmənt). *rare*$^{-1}$. [f. GRUDGE *v.* + -MENT.] Envy, resentment.

1845 BROWNING *Flight Duchess* xv. 289 A little plait of hair ..which at my breast I wear, Ever did (rather to Jacynth's grudgment), And ever shall, till the Day of Judgment.

grudgeons, obs. form of GURGEONS.

grudger[1] (ˈgrʌdʒə(r)). [f. GRUDGE *v.* + -ER[1].] One who grudges or murmurs; one who cherishes ill-will, resentment, or envy.

1552 HULOET, Grudger, *malignans, zelotes.* **1606** FORD *Fame's Mem.* Wks. 1869 III. 307 Of all his foes, backbiters, grudgers fear'd. **1631** MABBE *Celestina* VI. 74 Murmurers, grudgers of my good, repiners of my prosperity. **1898** *Westm. Gaz.* 26 Jan. 2/1 The grudgers, ever ready to interfere with other folk's innocent pleasures.

So **ˈgrudgery** [see -ERY], grudging.

1889 *Spectator* 23 Nov., He expressed himself with a vulgar grudgery of rank that suggested dislike to all superiority.

†**grudger**[2]. *Obs. rare.* [f. GRUDGE *v.* + -ER[4], the AF. ending as in *trover, user*, etc.] Complaint, dissatisfaction.

1467 *Paston Lett.* No. 575 II. 306, I trost..that he nothyr hath ne shall have cause of grudger by my defaut, for I can not understand ony cause of grudger.

grudging (ˈgrʌdʒɪŋ), *vbl. sb.* [f. GRUDGE *v.* + -ING[1].]

1. The action of the verb GRUDGE: †**a.** Murmuring, grumbling, complaint. **b.** Reluctant or unwilling action. **c.** The cherishing of ill-will, resentment, or envy.

c **1420** LYDG. *Assembly Gods* 217 What pyne or greef ye for me prouyde, Without any grogyng I shall hit abyde. **1477** EARL RIVERS (Caxton) *Dictes* 17 b, Holde you content with that, that ought to suffise you, and so ye shal not haue no gruggyng. **1547** *Homilies* I. *Obedience* III. (1859) 115 She gladly, without any excuse or grudging, for conscience sake did take that cold..winter journey. **1587** GOLDING *De Mornay* xxiv. (1617) 411 Wherefore languished hee fortie yeers in the wildernesse among a thousand grudgings. **1601** BP. W. BARLOW *Serm. Paules Crosse* 20 Grudging marres charitie. **1655** FULLER *Ch. Hist.* IX. viii. §12 The Grudgings which began to grow betwixt Secular Priests and Iesuits. **1712** STEELE *Spect.* No. 268 ¶3 Who without grudging allow whatever is prudent and convenient. **1783** BURKE *Rep. Affairs India* Wks. XI. 50 The export of so much silver was sometimes a subject of grudging and uneasiness in Europe. **1866** MRS. CARLYLE *Lett.* III. 321 No appearance of envy or grudging in anybody. **1876** B'NESS BUNSEN in Hare *Life* (1879) II. viii. 466 The gift of God is granted without stint or grudging.

†**2.** An access or slight symptom of an approaching illness, or a trace remaining of a previous one; a 'touch' (of an ailment, pain, etc.). *Obs.*

c **1440** *Promp. Parv.* 217/2 Grudgynge of sekenesse, *submurmur.* **1548** RECORDE *Urin. Physick* viii. (1651) 46 There goeth with it some spices and grudgings of the Ague. **1588** DEE *Diary* (Camden) 28, June 19th, I had a grudging of the ague. **1606** HOLLAND *Sueton.* 251 Some light motions and grudgings of his sicknesse. **1619** FLETCHER *M. Thomas* II. i, A grudging caus'd by th' alteration Of air, may hang upon me. *a* **1643** W. CARTWRIGHT *Ordinary* IV. iv, When did you Feel the first grudging on 't? 'tis not broke out In any place. **1672** DRYDEN *2nd Pt. Conq. Granada* IV. iii, The grudging of my ague yet remains. **1710** T. FULLER *Pharm. Extemp.* 127 As soon as ever any grudging of the Fit a coming is perceived. *a* **1796** PEGGE *Derbicisms* Ser. II. 103 (E.D.S.) *Grudging*, 'a grudging of pain', a spice or small degree of it, a tendency to it.

fig. **1613** BEAUM. & FL. *Honest Man's Fortune* V. iii, Now have I A kinde a grudging of a beating on me, I fear my hot fit.

†**3.** Inward disquiet or vexation. (Cf. GRUDGE *sb.* 2.)

1450–1530 *Myrr. our Ladye* 44 Theyre spyrytes ar dryuen from quyetnes of deuocyon into anguysshe & paynefull grudginges. **1601** DENT *Pathw. Heaven* 242 When such little grudgings are felt in the soule.

†**4.** A secret longing, wish, or inclination. *Obs.*

1625 B. JONSON *Staple of N.* I. ii, I'd faine be doing some good..I feele a grudging Of bounty, and I would not long lye fallow. **1682** DRYDEN *Medal* 58 Ev'n in the most sincere advice he gave He had a grudging still to be a knave. **1694** CONGREVE *Double-Dealer* III. v, Nay, I don't despair; but still she has a grudging to you.

grudging (ˈgrʌdʒɪŋ), *ppl. a.* [-ING[2].] That grudges; †complaining, repining (*obs.*); unwilling, reluctant; resentful, envying.

a **1533** FRITH *Disput. Purgat.* (1829) 119 If I..pay albeit mine heart be never so grudging & evil-willing yet have I fulfilled the law. **1590** SPENSER *F.Q.* I. ii. 19 [In death] his grudging ghost did strive With the fraile flesh. **1634** MILTON *Comus* 725 We should serve him as a grudging master. **1874** GREEN *Short Hist.* ix. §4. 629 His industry earned the grudging praise of his enemies. **1889** JESSOPP *Coming of Friars* i. 40 A certain grudging provincialism is observable in the East Anglian character.

grudgingly (ˈgrʌdʒɪŋlɪ), *adv.* [f. GRUDGING *ppl. a.* + -LY[2].] In a grudging manner; unwillingly, reluctantly; with stint or reluctance.

1549 COVERDALE, etc. *Erasm. Par. 1 Pet.* iv. 7–11 Let him that hath substaunce..bestowe vnto them that haue nede, not grudgingly nether with murmuryng, but gladly and chearefully. **1644** BP. HALL *Rem. Wks* (1660) 138 The one doth it cheerfully and willingly; the other grudgingly and repiningly. **1781** COWPER *Charity* 218 Trouble is grudgingly and hardly brooked While life's sublimest joys are overlooked. **1828** D'ISRAELI *Chas. I*, II. xii. 314 The reluctant civilities so grudgingly accorded by the Monarch. **1879** TROLLOPE *Cousin Henry* xxiv. 276, I had nothing to do but to obey his orders. But I did it most grudgingly.

grudgingness (ˈgrʌdʒɪŋnɪs). [f. as prec. + -NESS.] The condition or quality of being grudging, unwilling, reluctant, or stinting.

1820 L. HUNT *Indicator* No. 51 (1822) I. 404 A jealous grudgingness. **1876** GEO. ELIOT *Dan. Der.* lxiv, Nothing grates on me more than that posthumous grudgingness towards a wife.

grudgin(g)s, -ions, var. or obs. f. GURGEONS.

†**grue**, *sb.*[1] *Obs.* Also 4 **grwe**, 5 **grew**, 5, 9 *Sc.* **gru**. [Commonly taken to be a. OF. *gru* meal, grain (see GRUEL); but there is no trace in OF. of the sense 'particle'.

The phrase 'not a grue' has a curious resemblance to the Gr. οὐδὲ γρῦ, adopted by the Latin comedians as *ne gry quidem* (see GRY); but it is difficult to see how this could have come into ME. and mod.Sc. use.]

With negatives: ***not a (one) grue, no grue***: not an atom, not a whit.

13.. *Gaw. & Gr. Knt.* 2251, I schal gruch þe no grwe. **13..** *St. Erkenwald* 319 in Horstm. *Altengl. Leg.* (1887) 273, I folwe þe in þe fader nome & his fre childes & of þe gracious holy goste—& not one grue lenger. *a* **1400–50** *Alexander* 3270 We had bene drawen..into disspaire clene, And of þe godness of god noȝt a grew [*Dublin MS.* dele] traisted. *a* **1420** HOCCLEVE *De Reg. Princ.* 1939 Where as þer is but smal or naght a gru. **1825–80** JAMIESON, *Gru*, a particle, an atom. *No a gru of meal*, not a particle of meal..He has na a gru of sense.

grue (gruː), *sb.*[2] *rare.* In 6 gru. [ad. L. *gru-em*, *grus* crane, or a. F. *grue*.] A crane.

1595–6 BUREL *Pilgr.* in J. Watson *Collect. Poems* (1706) II. 27 The Gru befoir me thair appeirs, Quhois legs wer lang and syde.

†**grue**, *sb.*[3] *dial. Obs.* [? a. OF. *gru* meal: see GRUEL.] A kind of meal cake made in Cheshire.

1655 MOUFET & BENNET *Health's Improv.* xxiv. 233 Had Galen seen the Oaten Cakes of the North; the Janocks of Lancashire..and the Grues of Cheshire, he would have confessed that Oates and Oatmeal are..meat..for tall, fair and strong men.

grue (gruː), *sb.*[4] *Sc.* Also grou. [f. GRUE *v.*[1]] The action of GRUE *v.*[1]; shivering, shuddering; a shiver, shudder.

1820 *Edinb. Mag.* May 423 A seikenan' grou cam ower my heart, I swarf't amang his hands. **1867** N. MACLEOD *Starling* xiii, The Sergeant experienced what is called in Scotland a grue—the sort of shiver one feels in a nightmare. **1899** *Daily News* 9 Nov. 8/6 Her new book..lacks nothing by which to give its readers a 'grue'.

grue (gruː), *sb.*[5] *north. dial.* Also gru, grew. ? Ice in flakes, or detached pieces.

1835 FARQUHARSON in *Phil. Trans.* CXXV. 330 [see *ground-grue* in GROUND *sb.* 18]. *Ibid.* 333 At this rapid, the whole bottom..was covered with silvery gru. *Ibid.* 334 A number of pieces of loose gru. **1839** DOUGLAS in *Proc. Berw. Nat. Club* I. No. 7. 185 An immense quantity of *grew*, incompact ice, floated down. *Ibid.* 187 The frost..catching the light floating grew, makes a chance of obstruction. **1891** *Scott. Leader* 3 Feb. 7/1 The 'grue' floating down the Tweed.

grue (gruː), *v.*[1] *Sc.* and *north. dial.* Forms: 3–4 **gru**, 4–7 **grow**, 5, 9 **grue**, 6 **grou**, 5–6, 9 **growe**. *pa. t.* 4 **grew**, **greuyt**, 4–5 **growyt**, **-it**. [Not recorded in OE. or ON.; cognate with the synonymous OHG. *in-grûên* (MHG. *grûwen*, mod.G. *grauen*), Du. *gruwen*, Da. *grue* OSw. *grwa gröywa* (mod.Sw. *grufva* now only refl. to grieve).]

1. *intr.* To feel terror or horror, shudder, tremble; quake; to shrink from something; to be troubled in heart.

a **1300** *Cursor M.* 7983 Dauid..thoght on his fas philistiens, Gladli wald he þam confund, To ger þam for him gru [*Fairf.* grow] and grise. *c* **1330** R. BRUNNE *Chron. Wace* (Rolls) 8532 His herte a-geyns hym gros & grew. **1375** BARBOUR *Bruce* XVII. 686 Thair hertis than begouth till grow. *Ibid.* XX. 517 At tresoune growyt [so *M.S. E.*; *MS. C.* grevit, *ed.* 1616 groowed] he so gretly, That na tratour mycht be hym by. *c* **1450** HOLLAND *Howlat* xxxv, To James Lord Dowglas thow the gre gaif, To ga with the kingis hart; thairwith he nocht growit. **1513** DOUGLAS *Æneis* XII. xiii. 110 [Scho] Can fle, and flaf, and maid hym for to grow. **1674** RAY *N.C. Words* 23, 'I grow', I am troubled. **1819** W. TENNANT *Papistry Storm'd* (1827) 142 Garrin' Sir Freir growe in his skin Wi' ane prophetic dreid. **1893** STEVENSON *Catriona* 14, I begin to grue at the sound of it.

b. Of the body: To shiver, shudder.

c **1470** HENRYSON *Mor. Fab.* VIII. (*Preach. Swallow*) xxvi, My flesche growis, my bodie quaikis all. *a* **1605** MONTGOMERIE *Sonn.* iv. 7 It garis my body grou, To tell it nou. **1824** SCOTT *Redgauntlet* Let. xi, He..said things that garr'd folk's flesh grue.

¶**c.** To thrill.

a **1849** H. COLERIDGE *Poems* (1850) II. 276 His every member grueing with delight.

†**2.** *impers. it grues me*: I shudder, tremble, quake; I shrink from something. *Obs.*

1375 BARBOUR *Bruce* XV. 541 Swa with his fayis dred wes he That thame grevit till heir his name. *c* **1460** *Play Sacram.* 155 To do agen thy entent yt shuld grue me yll.

†**grue**, *v.*[2] *Obs.* [f. GRUE *sb.*[2]] *intr.* Of a crane: To utter its characteristic cry.

1688 R. HOLME *Armoury* II. 310/2 The Crane grueth.

grue: see GREW.

grueful (ˈgruːfʊl), *a. rare*$^{-1}$. [f. GRUE *v.*[1] + -FUL.] Fearful, horror-struck.

1880 BLACK *White Wings* xxxvii, He returned—somewhat grueful— his hair wild,—his face wet.

grueing (ˈgruːɪŋ), *vbl. sb. Sc.* Forms: 4 **growyng**, **greuyng**, 6 **gruwing**, 7 **groouing**, 8 **gruing**. [f. GRUE *v.*[1] + -ING[1].] The action of GRUE *v.*[1]; shuddering; horror.

1375 BARBOUR *Bruce* XIX. 555, I wat nocht quhat may tyd vs heir; Bot a richt gret growyng [so *MS. E.*; *MS.C.* grevyng, *ed.* 1616 groouing] me tais. **1595** DUNCAN *App. Etymol.* (E.D.S.), *Horror*, gruwing, or feare..*Rigor*, stiffness or gruwing. **1732** ARBUTHNOT *Rules of Diet* 353 A chilliness or Gruing affects the Body.

gruel (ˈgruːəl), *sb.* Forms: 4 **gruwel**, 4–5 **growel**, **-ell(e**, 4–6 **grewel**, 4–7 **gruell**, 5 **grewylle**, **grewl**, **-el(l)e**, **gruelle**, ? **gravelle**, 5– **gruel**. [a. OF. *gruel* (12th c. in Littré), mod.F. *gruau* ground grain, flour, gruel, for **grueau*, *gruyau*:—med.L. **grūtellum*, dim. of *grūtum* of Teut. origin: cf. OE. *grút* GROUT.]

1. Fine flour, meal, or other farinaceous substance. *Obs.* or *dial.*

[**1311** in *Charters*, etc. *Priory Finchale* (Surtees) p. iv, De gruell' sufficientia usque Pascham.] *c* **1330** [see 5 below]. **14..** *Nom.* in Wr.-Wülcker 740/31 *Hec polenta*, grewylle. **1544** PHAER *Regim. Life* (1553) H v b, It is good to vse grewel, clene barley [etc.]. **1847–78** HALLIWELL, *Gruel*, same as Grudgings.

2. A light, liquid food (chiefly used as an article of diet for invalids) made by boiling oatmeal (or occas. some other farinaceous subtance) in water or milk, sometimes with the addition of other ingredients, as butter, sugar, spices, onions, etc. ***Grantham gruel*** (see quot. 1818). See also WATER-GRUEL.

1362 LANGL. *P. Pl.* A. VII. 169 A bolleful of gruwel. *c* **1400** tr. *Lanfranc's Cirurg.* 13 He schal ete for his mete growel maad of otemele, eiþir of barli mele wiþ almaundis. *c* **1450** *ME. Med. Bk.* (Heinrich) 77 Take otenmele & cow mylke and make grewel. **1514** BARCLAY *Cyt. & Uplondyshm.* (Percy Soc.) 3 Sethynge some grewell & sterynge the pulment Of peese or frument. **1551** TURNER *Herbal* I. L iv, Beane of Egypt..is good..taken wyth beane mele after the maner of grewelle. **1611** COTGR., *Orgée*, barlie gruell. **1634** J. TAYLOR (Water P.) *Gt. Eater Kent* 12 His appetite..neuer ..needed the assistance of cawdle, iulep, alebery, cullise, grewell, or stewd-broth. **1688** R. HOLME *Armoury* III. 82/2 Grewel, is a kind of Broth made only of Water, Grotes brused and Currans, some add Mace, sweet Herbs, Butter and Eggs and Sugar: some call it Pottage Gruel. **1728** YOUNG *Love Fame* v. Wks. (1757) 123 Cooling gruel, and composing tea. **1791** W. NICHOLSON tr. *Chaptal's Elem. Chem.* (1800) III. 102 The Icelanders obtain a very delicate gruel with the fecula of the lichen Icelandicus. **1815** JANE AUSTEN *Emma* I. xii, A basin of nice smooth gruel, thin but not too thin. **1818** SCOTT *Hrt. Midl.* xxix, Thou wilt get naething at night save Grantham gruel, nine grots and a gallon of water. **1869** J. MARTINEAU *Ess.* II. 28 A sinful preference of roast mutton over gruel.

transf. **1605** SHAKS. *Macb.* IV. i. 32 Make the Grewell thicke, and slab. **1842** BARHAM *Ingol. Leg.* Ser. II. *St. Medard*, And he hurl'd it straight At the Saint's bald pate, To knock out 'the gruel he call'd his brains'.

Prov. *c* **1374** CHAUCER *Troylus* III. 662 (711) So thriue I this nyght shal I make it wel, Or casten al þe Growel in þe fyre.

†**3.** Broth or pottage of oatmeal in which chopped meat has been boiled. Commonly ***gruel forced*** (***aforced, enforced***), ***gruel*** (***of***) ***force***, or ***gruel of beef***, etc. Similarly ***gruel of almonds***. *Obs.*

? *c* **1390** *Form of Cury* (1780) 12 For to make grewel forced. Take grewel, and do to the fyre with gode flessh, and seeþ it well. **14..** *Noble Bk. Cookry* (1882) 88 To mak grewelle enforced tak mary bones and freche brothe and mak grewelle and draw them throughe a strener, then tak [etc.]. *c* **1420** *Liber Cocorum* (1862) 14 Gruel of Almondes. Take almondes unblanchid and bray hom sone, Put ote mele to.. And grynde alle sammen. *Ibid.* 20 Gruel of Porke. *Ibid.* 47 For gruel of fors. Fyrst take porke, wele þou hit sethe With otene grotes. *c* **1430** *Two Cookery-bks.* 6 Gruelle a-forsydde. *c* **1450** *Ibid.* 70 Growelle fforce. Take Growell y-made of ffresh beef. *c* **1460** J. RUSSELL *Bk. Nurture* 519 Growelle of force Gravelle of beeff or motoun, haue ye no care. **1513** *Bk. Keruynge* in *Babees Bk.* 273 Tansey is good, hote wortes, or gruell of befe or of motton is good. **1552** HULOET, Grewell, forced or stewed broth, *offella.* **1565** COOPER *Thesaurus, Pulmentaris cibus*, chopped meate made with pottage or broth: forced gruell. **1601** HOLLAND *Pliny* II. 63 If a thicke grewell or sew be made thereof,.. it cureth the pleurisie or paines of the sides.

4. Phr. ***to have*** or ***get one's gruel***: to receive one's punishment, to get killed. So ***to take one's gruel, to give*** (a person) ***his gruel.*** *colloq.*

1797 MARY ROBINSON *Walsingham* IV. 26 My pupil talked of nothing but of returning to Devizes, to 'give the ostler his gruel' for having taken him in. **1815** SCOTT *Guy M.* xxviii, He gathered.. that they expressed great indignation against some individual. 'He shall have his gruel', said one. **1823** BYRON *Juan* XI. xvi, I've got my gruel! **1851** KINGSLEY *Yeast* viii, They've done for me, Paul. Old Harry's got his gruel. **1898** DOYLE *Trag. Korosko* 192 What have we to hope for? We may just as well take our gruel.

5. *attrib.*, as ***gruel-dish, -meal, -pot, -sieve***; **gruel-tree** *dial.* (see quot.).

c **1330** *Durham Acc. Rolls* 525 In iij cribris empt. pro granario et uno Growell seue et I Colour pro pistrina. **14..** in *Rel. Ant.* I. 82 He fell doun.. into a gruell potte. *Ibid.* 83 These iij kyngus ete but of wone gruell dysche. **1649** G. DANIEL *Trinarch., Hen. V*, cccxlvi, 'Tis a strange Gutt, that for a Gruell Meale Resigns her Birthright. **1825-80** JAMIESON, *Gruel-tree*, the stick used for stirring the porridge.

gruel ('gruːəl), *v.* [f. GRUEL *sb.*]

1. *trans.* To exhaust or disable; to 'punish'. (Cf. GRUEL *sb.* 4.)

1850 KINGSLEY *Alt. Locke* xii, Wadham ran up by the side of that first Trinity yesterday, and he said that they were as well gruelled as so many posters, before they got to the stile. **1877** *Punch* 24 Mar. 129 The Crews were drinking each other's healths, in the vain attempt of each to gruel the other before the race.

2. *nonce-use.* To feed with gruel.

1804 tr. *La Marteliere's Three Gil Blas* I. 69 You see.. a man who has been confined to his bed a fortnight, consequently well plaistered and gruelled. **1892** *Longm. Mag.* July 319, I had better halt and gruel my exhausted mount.

grueller ('gruːələ(r)). [f. GRUEL *sb.* and *v.* + -ER[1].]

†**1.** One who feeds on gruel; a name given to a particular set of Oxford students in 17th c. *Obs.*

1691 WOOD *Ath. Oxon.* II. 616 He.. and other students.. feeding on thin broth, made of Oatmeal and water only, they were commonly called Grewellers. **1708** HEARNE *Collect.* 8 Oct. (O.H.S.) II. 140 Here they had Prayers, and this deform'd old Maid [Elizabeth Hampton].. made them water Gruell, whence they were call'd the sect of yᵉ Gruellers.

2. *colloq.* A poser, settler, floorer. (Cf. GRUEL *v.* 1.)

1856 KINGSLEY *Let. T. Hughes* in *Alt. Locke* (1881) I. Pref. Mem. 65 But this £25 of his is a grueller.

gruelling ('gruːəlɪŋ), *vbl. sb. colloq.* [f. GRUEL *v.* + -ING[1].] The action of the vb. GRUEL; 'punishing', defeat, esp. in an athletic contest.

1882 *Society* 14 Oct. 22/2 After the consistent gruelling he received.. it is very probable that he will run all the better for being a bit above himself. **1892** H. COX *Coursing* (Badm. Libr.) 19 Misterton had a rare gruelling in his first course, and was put out by Devastation next round.

gruelling ('gruːəlɪŋ), *ppl. a. colloq.* [f. GRUEL *v.* + -ING[2].] That 'gruels'; exhausting, 'punishing'.

1852 J. F. BATEMAN *Aquatic Notes* v. 70 Their rivals [in a boat-race].. were pulling a very quick and 'gruelling' stroke. **1891** *Sportsman* 8 July 8/4 After a gruelling finish, Magdalen just struggled home by two feet amidst great excitement. **1894** ASTLEY *Fifty Years Life* II. viii. 131 What gruelling courses I have seen on Snail Down.

gruellous ('gruːələs), *a. rare*⁻¹. [f. GRUEL *sb.* + -OUS.] Resembling gruel; gruelly.

1862 'C. BEDE' *College Life* 74 Mr. Percival Wylde was lying back upon his pillows, apparently engaged in sipping the gruellous compound.

gruelly ('gruːəlɪ), *a.* [f. GRUEL *sb.* + -Y[1].] Of the nature of or resembling gruel.

1838 A. B. GRANVILLE *Spas Germ.* 283 It assumes a gruelly appearance. **1868** F. E. PAGET *Lucretia* xi. 47 It was no longer literature, but literary *pap*, soft, and passing into a gruelly consistency. **1872** EARL PEMBROKE & G. H. KINGSLEY *S. Sea Bubbles* viii. 216 She squeezed about half a tumbler-full of the gruelly fluid into it.

gruenlingite, var. GRÜNLINGITE.

gruesome ('gruːsəm), *a. literary* and *dial.* Forms: 6, 8 growsome, 8 grousome, groosome, 9 (grausome), grewsome, gruesome. [f. GRUE *v.*[1] + -SOME. Cf. MDu. *grou-, grusaem*, Du. *gruwzaam* = MHG. *grû(we)sam* (G. *grausam*), horrible, cruel, fierce, inhuman.

App. introduced into literary use by Scott. The spelling *gruesome* did not become well established until after 1850; *grewsome* is still occasionally used. Lytton's *grausome* is after G. *grausam* (cf. GRAULY).]

1. Inspiring fear, awe, or horror; such as to cause one to shudder with fear; fearful, horrible; grisly.

1570 LEVINS *Manip.* 162/10 Growsome, *horridus.* **1781** J. HUTTON *Tour to Caves* 90 *Growsome*, ugly, disagreeable. **1785** BURNS *Halloween* xxiii, He takes a swirlie, auld moss-oak, For some black, grousome carlin. **1816** SCOTT *Old Mort.* xli, He's as grave and grewsome an auld Dutchman as e'er I saw. **1848** LYTTON *K. Arthur* v. xlix, With many a grausome shape unutterable, Limn'd were the cavernous sepulchral walls. **1855** BROWNING *Lover's Quarrel* v, He has taken a bride To his gruesome side. **1857** HUGHES *Tom Brown* I. i, A grewsome sound between a moan and a roar. **1874** B. HARTE *Wan Lee*, The dim, mysterious half-light of the cellar falling in a gruesome way upon the misshapen bulk of a Chinese deity. **1877** A. B. EDWARDS *Up Nile* xxi. 649 It is like a feverish sleep, troubled by gruesome dreams. **1891** *Chamb. Jrnl.* 4 Apr. 219 A few broken, leafless, doddered stumps of trees.. help to give the dark chill marsh a more gruesome and uncanny aspect.

Comb. **1878** BESANT & RICE *Celia's Arb.* xxxii. (1887) 235 It was a gruesome-looking shadow, with high back and head thrust forward.

2. Full of or inspired by fear. *rare.*

1869 BLACKMORE *Lorna D.* vii, These trees and pools.. are making a gruesome coward of thee. **1880** H. JAMES *Hawthorne* 87 Some of his companions.. took.. rather a gruesome view of his want of articulate enthusiasm.

Hence **'gruesomely** *adv.*, **'gruesomeness.**

1886 *Pall Mall G.* 30 Sept. 2/2 Mr. Matthews, with much of Poe's ingenuity, has a touch, too, of Poe's gruesomeness. **1893** *Columbus Dispatch* (Ohio) 26 Jan., The wind whistles and moans among them grewsomely.

gruf, obs. form of GROOF.

grufe, rare obs. pa. t. GRAVE *v.*[1]; var. GROOF.

grufe, obs. Sc. and north. f. GROW.

grufelingis, -lynge: see GROVELLINGS, -ING.

gruff (grʌf), *a.* and *sb.* Forms: *Sc.* 6 groiff, grof, groffe, 8 groof, 9 grouff, 6- groff, 7- gruff, (9 grough). [app. a. Du. or LG. *grof = OHG. *girob, grob*, MHG. *gerop, grop*, mod.G. *grob*, of uncertain origin. Some scholars have regarded it as f. *ga-* prefix (OE. *ȝe-*: see Y-) + WGer. **hruƀ-* wk. grade of the root of OE. *hréof* rough, scabby.

Possibly the Du. or LG. word was introduced in commercial use.]

A. *adj.*

1. Coarse, coarse-grained; containing coarse or rough particles. *Obs.* exc. *Sc.* and *techn.*

1533 GAU *Richt Vay* (1888) 66 Our body is alsua oncleyne and foul and groiff. **1563** WINȜET *Four Scoir Thre Quest.* Wks. 1888 I. 114 Sklate, thak, and grof stanis, rottin tymmir and siklyke. **1565** *Extracts Aberd. Reg.* (1844) I. 360 Tuentie stanis of groff pulder. **1572** *Satir. Poems Reform.* xxiii. 339 Seing ȝe and ȝour wairs gros and grof [*rime* of]. **1596** DALRYMPLE tr. *Leslie's Hist. Scot.* I. 94 A groffe seck spred undir thame. **1743** J. WILLIAMSON in *Scenes & Leg. N. Scot.* (1889) 382 And now the broken clouds fall down In groff rain from on high. **1800** WELLESLEY in Owen *Desp.* 712 The ..purchase of sugar and other gruff goods. **1801** *Naval Chron.* VI. 427 She.. is engaged.. to proceed to.. Bengal, for a cargo of gruff goods. **1880** *Jamieson's Dict.*, *Groff*,.. 3. Thick, large, coarse; as, *groff meal*, large-grained meal. **1881** GREENER *Gun* 308 In a large vat.. is placed two tons of grough saltpetre. *Ibid.* 309 The grough sulphur.

b. Of immaterial things: Rude, gross, unpolished. Also said of a guess = 'rough'. *Sc.*

1681 COLVIL *Whigs Supplic.* (1751) 19 To speak in terms more groff, It [his head] was just like a sugar-loaf. **16..** in J. Watson *Collect. Poems* (1706) I. 67 Now have ye heard the Tragedy.. though it be both Groff and Rude, And of all Eloquence denude. **1825-80** JAMIESON s.v. *Groff*, 'A grouff guess', i.e., a rough or inaccurate calculation, or conjecture. **1875** G. MACDONALD *Malcolm* II. iii. 39 That's no rizzon 'at I sudna hae a groff guiss at her.

†**2.** Of a surface: Rough, rugged. *Obs. rare*⁻¹.

1697 *Phil. Trans.* XIX. 598 We were in danger of losing our Cable and Anchor; the Ground, where we rode.. being somewhat gruff.

3. Rough, surly, or sour in aspect or manner; said also of appearances.

1690-1 [Implied in GRUFFNESS]. **1706** *Reflex. upon Ridicule* 95 One man's air gruffer than another. **1706** PHILLIPS (ed. Kersey), *Gruff*, or *Grum*, grim-fac'd, sower-look'd, dogged, surly. **1726** LEONI *Alberti's Archit.* II. 51/1 Their gruff beards, and stern countenances. **1728** RAMSAY *Last Speech Miser* xi, My looks were groff and sour. **1777** CHARLOTTE BURNEY *Jrnl.* in *Mad. D'Arblay's Diary*, He turned to me with one of the gruffest of his lion looks. **1849** JAMES *Woodman* viii, He seemed as gruff as a large Church-bell. **1862** SALA *Accepted Addr.* 93 Her papa was a gruff religionist. **1863** SPEKE *Discov. Nile* p. xxiv, The gruff hippopotamus is as widespread as any. **1887** FRITH *Autobiog.* I. vii. 70 Under a somewhat gruff manner there beat a warm and tender heart.

b. Of the voice and speech, implying the utterance of hoarse or guttural sounds.

a **1712** W. KING *Skillet* 35 After some gruff muttering with himself. **1838** DICKENS *Nich. Nick.* ii, Sounds of gruff voices practising vocal music. **1877** BLACK *Green Past.* xxv, 'Ay' said the elder man, with gruff emphasis. **1878** BROWNING *Poets Croisic* Ep. 18 'Love' comes aptly in when gruff grows his singing. **1887** R. N. CAREY *Uncle Max* vii. 58 He gave a gruff little laugh.

c. quasi-*adv.*

1841 D'ISRAELI *Amen. Lit.* (1867) 676 They spoke gruff and short, affecting brevity of words.

4. *Comb.*, as ***gruff-speaking*** (cf. 3 b), ***-voiced*** adjs.

1814 *Love, Honor, & Interest* I. i, Old frosty-faced, gruff-speaking Vanderclufe. **1885** J. K. JEROME *On the Stage* 57 That gruff-voiced officer passed the order on to his men.

B. *sb.*

1. a. *Pharmacy.* (See quot.) **b.** *Mining.* (*pl.*) 'The worst pieces rejected in the manufacture of black-lead pots' (*Weale's Dict. Terms* 1873).

1853 DUNGLISON *Med. Lex.* (ed. 9), *Gruff*,.. In pharmacy, the coarse residue, which will not pass through the sieve in pulverization.

2. A quarrel, 'tiff'. ? *local U.S.*

1857 HOLLAND *Bay Path* v. 64 He was weak with the softening influences of the morning and never 'felt so little up to a gruff' as he did at the time he met Cubel. *Ibid.* xii. 137 You and I never had a gruff, but I don't stand any o' that sort o' nonsense.

gruff (grʌf), *v.* Now *dial.* [f. GRUFF *a.*]

1. † **a.** *trans.* To treat gruffly or surlily (*obs.*). **b.** To drive *away* by gruff behaviour (*rare*⁻¹).

1706 *Reflex. upon Ridicule* 197 Those that have no complaisance for you, but gruff you upon your good successes. **1847** MRS. GORE *Cast. in Air* xii, On the very day we so inexcusably gruffed you away from the Elms.

2. *intr.* To grunt, snore. *dial.*

1855 in ROBINSON *Whitby Gloss.* **1876** *Mid-Yorksh. Gloss.*, *Gruff*, to snore, in a short, noisy manner; to grunt.

gruff, -er, dial. forms of GROOVE, -ER.

gruff(e, obs. form of GROOF.

gruffelyng, obs. form of GROVELLING *adv.*

gruffillingis, obs. Sc. variant of GROVELLINGS.

gruffiness ('grʌfɪnɪs). [f. GRUFFY *a.* + -NESS.] Gruffness.

1865 MISS BRADDON *Sir Jasper* I. ii. 24 The stereotyped gruffiness and brutality of the misanthrope.

gruffish ('grʌfɪʃ), *a.* [f. GRUFF *a.* + -ISH.] Somewhat gruff. Also quasi-*adv.*

1812 G. COLMAN *Poet. Vagaries* (1818) 13 His voice had broken to a gruffish squeak. **1836** DICKENS *Sk. Boz* (1837) II. 3 A short elderly gentleman with a gruffish voice. **1855** MRS. GASKELL *North & S.* xi, If father's at home, and speaks a bit gruffish.

grufflingis, obs. Sc. variant of GROVELLINGS.

gruffly ('grʌflɪ), *adv.* [f. GRUFF *a.* + -LY[2].] In a gruff manner, with a gruff voice.

1700 DRYDEN *Pal. & Arcite* II. 613 Gruffly looked the god. **1775** SHERIDAN *St. Patr. Day* (L.), Can ye swear well? Gruffly, Gruffly. Handle a Frenchman? Roughly, Roughly. **1848** C. BRONTE *J. Eyre* xiii. (1873) 121 'Who talks of cadeaux?' said he gruffly: 'did you expect a present, Miss Eyre?' **1849** JAMES *Woodman* vi, 'Every one knows his own business best', said Arden gruffly.

gruffness ('grʌfnɪs). [f. GRUFF *a.* + -NESS.] The condition or quality of being gruff.

1690-1 in *Ep. Corr. Atterbury* (1783) I. 17 No gruffness, I beseech you; use them civilly, and stick to your point. **1799** in *Spirit Publ. Jrnls.* (1800) III. 135, I pray that your gruffness aside may be laid, While you deign to partake of our prog. **1856** EMERSON *Eng. Traits, Char.* Wks. (Bohn) II. 58 You shall find in the common people [of England] a surly indifference, sometimes gruffness and ill temper. **1880** VERN. LEE *Stud. Italy* IV. ii. 154 He.. began to treat his clerk with the most insulting gruffness.

†**'gruffy**, *a.* and *sb. Obs.* [f. GRUFF *a.* + -Y.]

A. *adj.* = GRUFF *a.* **B.** *sb.* A nickname for a gruff person, a 'cross patch'.

1790 J. WILLIAMS *Shrove Tuesday* (1794) 8 Teach gruffy Cerberus to dance *pas russe.* **1802** MARY CHARLTON *Wife & Mistress* I. xii. 273 He ['cross Lord John'] don't vally what he says to young or old, man or woman—its all the same to old gruffy!

grufling, gruflinges, vars. GROVELLING, -INGS.

gruft (grʌft). *local.* Particles of soil which are washed up by rain among the grass.

1803 E. HARRISON *Rot in Sheep* in *Ann. Agric.* XL. 529 A gruft which adheres to the grass in wet weather. *Ibid.* 530 By beating rains.. particles of the soil, or the gruft, as it is called, will be washed among the grass.

Hence **grufted** ('grʌftɪd) *ppl. a.*, begrimed, dirty.

1880 TENNYSON *Village Wife* vii, An' 'is nöase sa grufted wi' snuff es it couldn't be scroob'd awäay. **1886** *S.W. Linc. Gloss.* s.v., His hands are grufted up.

grugings, obs. form of GURGEONS.

gru-gru: see GROO-GROO.

gruiform ('gruːɪfɔːrm), *a.* [f. L. *grus, grui-*, crane + -FORM.] Resembling the crane.

1875 PARKER in *Encycl. Brit.* III. 699 *note*, The Cariama is .. a low, gruiform, rapacious bird.

gruling(is, obs. Sc. var. of GROVELLING, -INGS.

grulle, variant of GRILL *v.*[1] *Obs.*

grum (grʌm), *a.* Also 8 groom. [First recorded in the 17th c., when it appears suddenly in very frequent use; it was prob. a new formation due to blended reminiscence of words like *grim, glum, gruff, grumble.* Cf. Da. *grum* cruel.] Of persons, and their aspect and mode of speaking: Gloomy, morose, surly; = GLUM *a.* 1.

1640 LD. KYNALMEAKY in *Lismore Papers* Ser. II. (1888) IV. 146 The King replyed nothing but Look'd very grum. 1670 COTTON *Espernon* III. IX. 465 Retaining a kind of a grum reservedness in the rest of his Actions. 1704 *Lond. Gaz.* No. 4030/4 There is lately come to Colchester.. a tall Man,.. grum countenance. 1734 FIELDING *Old Man* 1010/1 Oh, dear Papa! don't look so grum. 1764 T. BRYDGES *Homer Travest.* (1797) I. 83 He silence broke, And with so grum an accent spoke, Those people that the circle stood in, Fancy'd his mouth was full of pudding. 1781 ARCHER in *Naval Chron.* XI. 284 An old grum fellow of a sailor. 1845 W. E. FRYE tr. *Oehlenschl. Gods* 20 Then thus replied with accent grum The god to heroes dear. 1861 L. L. NOBLE *Icebergs* xiv. 68 Shy and grum at first, but presently talkative enough.

†b. *dial.* Of the voice: Gruff, harsh, and deep in tone. *Obs.*

1744 ALMOND in *Phil. Trans.* XLIII. 250 His Voice, like a Man's, very groom.

grumble ('grʌmb(ə)l), *sb.* [f. GRUMBLE *v.*]

1. An act of grumbling; a murmur, of discontent or dissatisfaction; a subdued utterance of complaint. Of an animal: A low growl. Of thunder: A rumble.

1623 W. SCLATER *Tythes* 57 Least the little grumble of Conscience be calmed with that parcell of your opinion. 1636 BRATHWAIT *Roman Emperors* To Rdr., I.. referre me to thine impartiality, who (if thou art a good fellow) wilt accept a bit with a friend without grumbles. 1682 FLATMAN *Heraclitus Ridens* (1713) II. 193, I heard sometimes a deep hollow grumble, like the noise of a Stone ratling down a Well. 1724 *Wodrow Corr.* (1843) III. 124 When this came to be known there was a considerable grumble. 1840 HOOD *Up Rhine* 173 The Hound at his feet gave a grumble. 1884 *Cycl. Tour. Club Gaz.* Mar. 82/1 The only regret or grumble that we heard expressed. 1893 CROCKETT *Stickit Minister* 36 Efter a show o' hands, an' a bit grummle, they juist did that. 1899 *Blackw. Mag.* Feb. 348/2 The thunder.. fading at last to a distant grumble.

2. *the grumbles*: ill-humour, vented in grumbling. (Used *jocularly*, as if the name of a malady.)

1861 F. W. ROBINSON *No Church* II. 78 Pity it isn't catching, like the measles, or that opposite affair, which we all can show—the grumbles. 1869 SPURGEON *J. Ploughm. Talk* 23 Keep out of the way of a man who has the complaint called the grumbles. 1897 MARY KINGSLEY *W. Africa* ix. 167 Before we reach Njole I recognise my crew have got the grumbles, and at once inquire into the reason.

3. *slang.* [Shortened from *grumble and grunt*, rhyming slang for *cunt.*] = CRUMPET 4 c.

1962 E. BROCK *Little White God* v. 68 There's this copper ..and he puts away a local tea-leaf. And this tea-leaf's old woman's a fair bit of grumble. 1966 *Melody Maker* 30 July 8/5 American visitors are invariably delighted by references to birds, scrubbers, grumble.

grumble ('grʌmb(ə)l), *v.* Also 6 gromble. [Proximate source uncertain: cf. F. *grommeler* to mutter between the teeth, Du. *grommelen*, f. *grommen* to rumble, growl (cf. GRUMME *v.*), G. *grummeln* to rumble.]

1. *intr.* a. Of persons and animals: To utter dull inarticulate sounds; to mutter, mumble, murmur; to growl faintly.

1596 SHAKS. *Tam. Shr.* IV. i. 170 You heedlesse iolt-heads, and vnmanner'd slaues, What, do you grumble? Ile be with you straight. 1605 —— *Lear* III. iv. 43 *Kent.* Giue me thy hand, who's there? *Foole.* A spirite, a spirite, he sayes his name's poore Tom. *Kent.* What art thou that dost grumble there i'th' straw? Come forth. 1611 FLORIO, *Grugnare*, to grunt or grumble as a hog. *a*1700 DRYDEN (J.), The Lion.. with sullen pleasure, grumbles o'er his prey. 1735 SOMERVILLE *Chase* III. 599 The disappointed, hungry Pack Retire submiss, and grumbling quit their Prey. 1870 MORRIS *Earthly Par.* II. III. 354 Goodly store Of honey that the bees had grumbled o'er In clover fields of Kent.

b. Of thunder, a drum, etc.: To rumble, esp. faintly or as from a distance.

1621 FLETCHER *Pilgrim* III. iii, Didst thou never see a Drum: Canst thou make this grumble? *a*1704 T. BROWN *Sat. Fr. King* Wks. 1730 I. 60 In fine, the Government may do its will, But I'm afraid my guts will grumble still. 1708 ROWE *Royal Convert* III. Wks. (1766) 39 Like a storm That gathers black upon the frowning sky And grumbles in the wind. 1746–7 HERVEY *Medit.* (1818) 177 Ye Thunders, that awfully grumbling in the distant clouds, seem to meditate indignation. 1864 HAWTHORNE *Amer. Note-Bks.* (1879) II. 226 The wind.. grumbles past the angle of the house. 1865 M. ARNOLD *Ess. Crit.* i. (1875) 33 The echoes of the storm which was then raised I still from time to time hear grumbling round me.

2. To utter murmurs expressive of discontent; hence *gen.*, to complain. Const. *about*, *at*, *over*, occas. *for* (a desired object), with *inf.*, or *clause*.

*a*1586 SIDNEY *Arcadia* III. (1590) 301 b, A countenance still formed to smiling before him.. and grumbling behind him, at any of his commaundements. 1603 HOLLAND *Plutarch's Mor.* 506 Upon which unmeasurable and incessant toile, many died, and all were wery, and grumbled thereat. 1632 LITHGOW *Trav.* VII. 316 What.. doe you grumble for Wine, having the Water of Nylus to drinke. 1646 ABP. MAXWELL *Burd. Issach.* in *Phenix* (1708) II. 301 The best.. Subjects grumbled exceedingly to see their Prince so abus'd. 1650 BULWER *Anthropomet.* 10 Philoxones, that grumbled at Nature for the shortnesse of his Neck. 1701 DE FOE *True-born Eng., Britannia* 85 Wise Men affirm it is the English way, Never to Grumble till they come to pay. 1717 PRIOR *Alma* III. 425 L'Avare, not using half his store, Still grumbles that he has no more. 1779–81 JOHNSON *L.P., Pope* Wks. IV. 56 Many more grumbled in secret. 1843 *Penny Cycl.* XXVII. 134/2 He grumbled on about having sacrificed himself to his principles. 1849 THACKERAY *Pendennis* (1850) II. 93 Pendennis, in reality, suffered it very equanimously; but in words.. grumbled over it not a little. 1865 TROLLOPE *Belton Est.* xv. 170 He was always grumbling about his food. 1883 H. SPENCER in *Contemp. Rev.* XLIII. 5 The English are remarked on for their tendency to grumble in such cases.

quasi-*trans.* *a*1661 FULLER *Worthies* (1840) III. 503 He grumbled out the rest of his life in visible discontentment. 1810 *Splendid Follies* III. 163 Immerged in such ruminations, she grumbled herself to sleep.

3. *trans.* a. To express or utter with mumbling, muttering, or complaining. Also with *out*.

1824 in *Spirit Publ. Jrnls.* (1825) 285 He.. grumbled out good night, and departed to his domus. 1852 MRS. STOWE *Uncle Tom's C.* iii, At first he only scolded and grumbled these things. 1894 C. H. SIMPKINSON *Life Laud* vii. 124 Lord Brooke and the Puritan leaders might grumble out the hope that all the cathedrals.. would soon be demolished.

†b. *causative.* To cause to grumble or rumble. *Obs. rare.*

1690 R. CROMWELL in *Eng. Hist. Rev.* (1898) XIII. 102 Taxes grumble the gizards of many.

Hence **'grumbled** *ppl. a.*

1786 WOLCOT (P. Pindar) *Bozzy & Piozzi* I. Wks. 1816 I. 268 That actually surpass'd in tone and grace The grumbled ditties of his fav'rite base.

grumble, obs. form of GROMWELL.

†grumbledory. *Obs. rare*⁻¹. [Alteration of *drumbledory*, after GRUMBLE *v.*]

1599 [see GIGANTOMACHIZE].

grumbler ('grʌmblə(r)). Also 7 **grumler**. [f. GRUMBLE *v.* + -ER¹.]

1. One who grumbles; one who is given to utterances of discontent or dissatisfaction.

1633 J. DONE *Hist. Septuagint* 114 His people.. were not .. Grumlers at their paynestaking or unwilling to their Commaunders. 1724 SWIFT *Drapier Demolished* Wks. 1762 X. 355 If I made them [the Halfpence] of Silver, it would be the same Thing to this Grumbler. *a*1791 BEATTIE *Ep. to Blacklock* 9 Peace to the grumblers of an envious age. 1836 HOR. SMITH *Tin Trump.* (1876) 187 Grumblers.. excite but little sympathy. 1883 *Durham Univ. Jrnl.* 2 July 115 For are we not a nation of grumblers?

2. A name for the GURNARD.

[1759 tr. *Adanson's Voy. Senegal*, etc. 215 These strugglings are.. attended with a hollow rumbling noise, which has given it the name of grondin, or grumbler, whereby it is known on this coast.] 1867 in SMYTH *Sailor's Word-bk.*

grumbles, pl. f. GRUMMEL *Obs.*, mud, dregs.

grumblesome ('grʌmb(ə)lsəm), *a.* [f. GRUMBLE *sb.* + -SOME *suffix*¹.] Grumbling, complaining.

1925 *Brit. Weekly* 9 July 333/1 It doesn't lose its temper when you lose the way: it doesn't get tired and grumblesome. 1940 BLUNDEN *Poems 1930–40* 193 The gold-chained bee.. seemed inclined, though grumblesome, To pass the time of day. 1950 *Publ. Amer. Dial. Soc.* XIV. 33 *Grumblesome*, irritable, complaining.

grumbletonian (grʌmb(ə)l'təʊnɪən). [f. GRUMBLE *v.*, in imitation of *Muggletonian* and *Grindletonian*, names of religious sects in the 17th c.]

†1. A contemptuous designation applied in the latter part of the 17th c. to the members of the so-called 'Country Party' in English politics, who were accused by the 'Court party' of being actuated by dissatisfied personal ambition; hence in later times applied to supporters of the Opposition.

1690 *Andros Tracts* I. 206 The great Sect of Grumbletonians in the Countrey whom nothing will satisfie. 1721 RAMSAY *Prospect Plenty* v, Straight a grumbletonian appears. *a*1791 GROSE *Olio* (1796) 3 With respect to politics, I am a staunch Opposition-man and Grumbletonian. 1838 *Fraser's Mag.* XVIII. 379 Quite as cracked as any grumbletonian could possibly be. 1855 MACAULAY *Hist. Eng.* xix. IV. 299 Those who were sometimes nicknamed the Grumbletonians and sometimes honoured with the appellation of the Country party.

attrib. 1690 DRYDEN *Amphitryon* I, No more of your grumbletonian morals, brother; there's preferment coming. 1705 E. WARD *Hud. Rediv.* I. i. 19 All the Grumbletonian Throng Did with such Violence rush along. 1731 *Gentl. Mag.* I. 345 Last Saturday one of the Grumbletonian Writers stole the Hint.

2. A grumbler.

1773 GOLDSM. *Stoops to Conq.* I. ii, Father-in-law has been calling me whelp and hound this half year. Now, if I pleased I could be so revenged upon the old grumbletonian. 1806 R. CUMBERLAND *Mem.* (1807) I. 181 The sullenness of a Grumbletonian. 1864 *Auld Ayr* 77 Her old grumbletonian of a husband.

transf. 1830 *Blackw. Mag.* XXVII. 423/1 Playing on that eternal grumbletonian, the unhappy violoncello.

grumbling ('grʌmblɪŋ), *vbl. sb.* [f. GRUMBLE *v.* + -ING¹.] The action of the vb. GRUMBLE; a low rumbling sound; a murmuring, a subdued utterance of discontent.

1610 SHAKS. *Temp.* I. ii. 249, I have done thee worthy service.. without or Grudge or Grumblings. 1645 CHAS. I *Let. to his Wife* 4 May in *Ludlow's Mem.* (1699) III. 260 Wherefore I thought fit to put my Nephew Rupert in that Place; which will both save me Charge, and stop other Mens Grumblings. 1674 PLAYFORD *Skill Mus.* I. v. 20 When you come to your highest Note you may reach it without Squeaking, and your lowest Note without Grumbling. 1767 HAMILTON in *Phil. Trans.* LVII. 200 We heard most dreadful inward grumblings, rattling of stones, and hissing. 1803 *Med. Jrnl.* X. 501 Grumbling and contraction of the bowels. 1809 PINKNEY *Trav. France* 253 And after.. some grumbling we procured them [horses], and departed. 1855 MACAULAY *Hist. Eng.* xviii. IV. 214 There was still some grumbling about ecclesiastical questions. 1884 *Athenæum* 2 Aug. 139/3 [Southern Italy] is no land of comfort which the British paterfamilias should choose for the field of his annual grumbling at the foreigner. 1897 *Outing* (U.S.) XXX. 116/1 The grumbling of frogs along the shore.

grumbling ('grʌmblɪŋ), *ppl. a.* [f. as prec. + -ING².] That grumbles, in various senses. Of persons: Querulous, discontented.

1596 SHAKS. *Tam. Shrew* III. ii. 155 A grumlling [*sic*] groome. 1635 QUARLES *Embl.* III. xi. 166 Thou.. That through the deeps gav'st grumbling Isr'ell way. 1654 *Nicholas Papers* (Camden) II. 95 The Parisians are exeeding grumbling and the taxes promised to be abated are augmented. 1658 J. JONES *Ovid's Ibis* 45 One viol set in tune and hanged in a room with others, being touched, the rest do sympathize with a grumbling sound. 1764 WESLEY *Jrnl.* 13 Jan. (1827) III. 153 Three or four grumbling men. 1795 MARIA EDGEWORTH *Lett. Lit. Ladies* (1799) 111 If each bee were content in his cell, there could be no grumbling hive. 1840 R. H. DANA *Bef. Mast* xxxiv. 131 Low grumbling thunder was heard. 1935 J. C. THOMSON *Appendicitis* 21 If he [the surgeon] is to keep his death-rate low.. he must operate in many normal conditions, but he must have a good excuse... Hence we have the 'grumbling appendix'. 1966 *Lancet* 10 Dec. 1308/2 If interaction is responsible for, say, a 'grumbling' appendix, the removal of the appendix will also remove the symptoms.

Hence **'grumblingly** *adv.*, in a grumbling manner; †mumblingly (*obs.*).

1685 E. BROWNE *Trav. Europe* (ed. 2) 156 The Common & Country people seemed to speak grumblingly. 1836 E. HOWARD *R. Reefer* xxxiii, Who viewed the West India station.. grumblingly. 1861 HUGHES *Tom Brown at Oxf.* iv. (1889) 32 The men.. grumblingly confessed that he was a first-rate coxswain. 1886 W. J. TUCKER *Life E. Europe* 398 He.. will grumblingly throw well-weighed coppers into the collecting gipsy's plate.

grumblous ('grʌmbləs), *a.* *nonce-wd.* [f. GRUMBLE *sb.* + -OUS.] Full of grumbles.

1889 C. EDWARDES *Sardinia* 377 His grumblous appeals to all the saints.

grumbly ('grʌmblɪ), *a. colloq.* [f. GRUMBLE *sb.* + -Y¹.] Resembling a grumble; inclined to grumble.

1858 CARLYLE *Fredk. Gt.* VII. v, Pious auroral memories from the Past Ages, instead of grumbly dusty provocations from the present. *Ibid.* xx. v, The population there is rather disposed to be grumbly on its once heroic Fabius. 1897 *Advance* (Chicago) 23 Dec. 910/2, I used to.. feel real grumbly, and compare my lot with other folk's lots.

grume (gruːm). Also 6 groume. [ad. late L. *grūmus* little heap, hillock; cf. obs. F. *grume* 'a knot, bunch, cluster; clutter' (Cotgr.), mod.F. *grumeau* clot, It. *grumo* lump, clot.]

†1. A lump. *Obs.*

1555 EDEN *Decades* 145 Emonge those groumes of rude or natyue golde there was one founde of the weyghte of two Castellans.

2. *Med.* A clot of blood; blood in a clotted or viscous condition. Also, any viscous fluid or mass of fluid.

1619 JER. DYKE *Caveat* (1620) 16 In loue to him who, in loue to vs, shed not sweat, but sweat grumes of bloud. *a*1684 N. HODGES *Acc. Plague* (1721) 115 Blood.. will after some stagnation run for the most part into Grume. 1718 QUINCY *Compl. Disp.* 92 It is accounted very penetrating, and therefore good in all Grumes and Coagulation. 1756 C. LUCAS *Ess. Waters* I. 143 The solid contents coalesced in grumes or a kind of roundish granules. 1782 W. HEBERDEN *Comm.* xvi. (1806) 88 A little grume of blood often forms the nucleus of a stone. 1808 J. BARLOW *Columb.* v. 480 His blood-stain'd limbs drip carnage as he strides, And taint with gory grume the staggering tides. 1822–34 *Good's Study Med.* (ed. 4) I. 649 Repeated tides of dark granulated grume, like the grounds of chocolate, are ejected by the mouth. 1886 in *Syd. Soc. Lex.*

grume, obs. form of GROOM.

†grume'faction. *Obs. rare*⁻¹. [ad. mod.L. *grumefactiōn-em*, f. *grumefacĕre*, f. L. *grūm-us* GRUME + *facĕre* to make.] The formation of a grume or clot of blood.

1684 tr. *Bonet's Merc. Compit.* XIX. 745 The very grumefaction supposes I. Blood extravasated.

grumell, obs. form of GROMWELL.

†gru'mescence. *Obs. rare*⁻¹. [ad. mod.L. *grūmescentia*, f. *grūmescent-em*: see next.] Tendency to form clots.

1684 tr. *Bonet's Merc. Compit.* XIX. 760 Things that take away grumescence or clodding, and resolve coagulation.

†gru'mescent, *a.* *Obs. rare*⁻¹. [ad. mod.L. *grūmescent-em*, pres. pple. of *grūmescĕre* to form clots, to coagulate, f. *grūmus* GRUME.] Having a tendency to coagulate.

1684 tr. *Bonet's Merc. Compit.* VIII. 274 These Acids.. coagulate a Bloud too fluid, and attenuate it, when grumescent.

grumet, variant of GRUMMET¹.

grumle, obs. form of GROMWELL.

grumler, obs. form of GRUMBLER.

'grumly, *a. dial.* ? = GUMLY *a.*

1826 *Sir P. Spens* x. in Child *Ballads* (1885) II. 22/2 Till cold and watry grew the wind, And grumly grew the sea. 1892 STRANG *Earth Fiend* I. xii, The tearfu' sky mak's grumly brooks O'er a' the land.

'grumly, *adv.* [f. GRUM *a.* + -LY².] Sullenly, morosely.

1727 BAILEY vol. II, *Grumly*, grimly. 1755 in JOHNSON. 1827 J. F. COOPER *Red Rover* iii, 'Any fool knowd it,' returned Scipio grumly. 1854 H. H. RILEY *Puddleford* 92 (Th.), Mr. Bird very grumly said he'd better hold on. 1880 G. W. CABLE *Grandissimes* vi. 41 'Um-hum,' he said grumly.

†**grumme**, *v.* Also 6 gromme. [Cf. Du. *grommen* of similar meaning.] *intr.* To grumble.

*c*1430 *Pilgr. Lyf Manhode* II. xi. (1869) 79 Wherof the cherl was no thing wel apayed; For alwey he grummede, and alwey shook his chyn. 1579 TOMSON *Calvin's Serm. Tim.* 1047/1 They gromme against it as wilde beastes.

'grummel. *Obs.* exc. *dial.* Also (*pl.*) 6 grommelles, 7 grumbles. [Cf. Sw. *grummel* in same sense.] Mud, dregs, sediment. *lit.* and *fig.* (In the Peak of Derbyshire still used, as is the Sw. word, for 'coffee-grounds'.)

1558–80 WARDE tr. *Alexis' Secr.* I. VI. 105 a, That first and cheefly it [earth for casting] be fine and small, and in no wise rough, or full of grommelles. 1614 BP. COWPER *Dikaiologie* 83 Let the auncient wals of our Church-gouernment stand, where they be decaied, let them be repaired, not with sand and grummell of promiscuall regiment. 1637 SANDERSON *Serm.* II. 81 The grumbles and mud of their impatience and discontent beginneth to appear.

grummel(l, obs. form of GROMWELL.

grummet¹ ('grʌmɪt). *Obs.* exc. *Hist.* and *dial.* Forms: 3, 6–9 gromet, 6 groomet, 6, 8 grumet, 8 grummet. [a. OF. *gromet*, *groumet*, servant, valet, shop-boy, wine-merchant's assistant (see GOURMET) = Sp. *grumete* ship's-boy.

In Anglo-Latin documents down to the 16th c. the word *grometus*, a latinization of AF. *gromet*, is frequently used in the sense of GROOM. Whether there is any etymological connexion between F. *gromet* and Eng. *groom* is at present uncertain.]

1. A ship's boy; a cabin-boy; the boy required to form part of the crew of every ship formerly provided by the Cinque Ports.

[1229 in Jeakes *Charters Cinque Ports* (1728) 25 *note*, Servicia inde debita Domino Regi, xxi naves, & in qualibet nave xxi homines, cum uno gartione qui dicitur gromet.] 1570–6 LAMBARDE *Peramb. Kent* (1826) 110 Hasting shall finde 21. ships, in everie ship 21. men, and a garcion, or boye, which is called a gromet. 1591 PERCIVALL *Sp. Dict.*, *Grumete*, a grumet of a ship, a ship boy. 1717 tr. *Frezier's Voy. S. Sea* 198 Sixteen Grummets. 1763 SIR T. S. JANSSEN *Smuggling Laid Open* 285 The Gromets is an Establishment which was formerly in the Navy; they are meant to be young Fellows of about Eighteen, who were never at Sea, to breed up as Seamen. 1894 C. N. ROBINSON *Brit. Fleet* 207 The average ship's company [in 13th c.] was twenty-four..a 'rector' or master, 'constable' or boatswain, twenty-one seamen, and a boy or 'gromet'.

2. *dial.* 'An awkward boy' (*Sussex Gloss.* 1875).

1894 JACKSON *Southward Ho* I. 251 (E.D.D.), I knowed anuder pore chap, a grummut as had na wurk.

grummet², grommet ('grʌmɪt). Chiefly *Naut.* and *Mil.* Also 7 gromit, 8–9 -et. [ad. F. *gromette* (15th c. in Hatz.-Darm.), now *gourmette* curb of a bridle, f. *gourmer* to curb, of unknown origin.]

1. A ring or wreath of rope, *spec.* one consisting of a single strand laid three times round. **a.** One of those used to secure the upper edge of a sail to its stay. **b.** A ring of rope used as a substitute for a rowlock in a boat. (Also applied to an eyelet of metal serving the same purpose.) **c.** A wad for keeping the shot steady in the bore when firing at a depression. **d.** In other connexions: see quots. **e.** A washer used to insulate electric conductors passing through a hole in a conducting material. **f.** A stiffener used inside a Service cap.

a. 1626 CAPT. SMITH *Accid. Yng. Sea-men* 12 Grummets, and staples for all yards. 1627 —— *Seaman's Gram.* v. 25 Caskets are..small ropes..made fast to the gromits or rings upon the yards. 1644 MANWAYRING *Sea-mans Dict.*, *Grommets* are little rings which are made fast to the upper-side of the yard, with staples, which are driven into the yard; which have no other use but to tie and make fast the Casketts into them. 1769 FALCONER *Dict. Marine* (1780), *Bague*, a small grommet, or wreath fixed in the eye-let hole in a sail. 1877 W. THOMSON *Voy. Challenger* I. ii. 114 Because our education has been sadly neglected in the matter of cringles and toggles and grummets.

b. 1802 *Trans. Soc. Arts* XX. 289 With iron tholes and rope grommets. 1833 MARRYAT *P. Simple* (1863) 249 The oars of the boats were fitted to pull with grummets upon iron thole-pins. 1883 *Fisheries Exhib. Catal.* 46 Six-oared yawl.. pulled with one thole-pin..and a grummet.

c. 1828 J. M. SPEARMAN *Brit. Gunner* Notes 16 By discarding the pincers, and applying grummets or wood bottoms to the shells in lieu of them. 1861 *Times* 7 June 5/3 The grummets fit the bore of the gun exactly and act as wads, allowing the base of the shell to rest in close contact with the charge.

d. 1775 FALCK *Day's Diving Vessel* 26 When I had taken my proper land-marks, I secured my sweep with a grummet. 1869 SIR E. REED *Shipbuild.* xxi. 467 In order to prevent leakage through the bolt-holes, hempen grummets saturated with paint are placed between the nuts and the plating. 1875 BEDFORD *Sailor's Pocket Bk.* viii. (ed. 2) 283 The ends of the whip should be made fast to the grummets on the sides of the life buoy. 1888 CLARK RUSSELL *Death Ship* III. 244, I discovered a rope grummet or hempen hook fastened to the larboard horn. 1892 *Edin. Rev.* Apr. 479 A thick grummet of rope round his loins.

transf. 1881 CLARK RUSSELL *Ocean Free Lance* II. iv. 193 Round the horizon was stretched what sailors would call a 'grummet' of sooty vapour.

e. 1942 *Electronic Engin.* XV. 303 The power cord should have been threaded through that grommet first. 1959 *B.S.I. News* June 10/2 Tiny grommets for aircraft instruments.

f. 1953 J. MASEFIELD *Conway* (ed. 2) III. 164 Next term, arriving back with no grommet in my cap as an 'old hand', and promptly being told to put it back. 1956 W. A. HEFLIN *U.S.A.F. Dict.* 236/2 *Grommet*, a ring-like device of rubber, roll cloth, or metal used inside the top of the service cap to keep it tightly stretched.

2. *attrib.* and *Comb.*: **grummet-hole**, a hole bound by a ring of rope; **grummet-iron**, a toggle-iron (*Cent. Dict.*); **grummet strop**, a strop made like a grummet; **grummet-wad** (see quot.: = 1 c).

1856 KANE *Arct. Expl.* I. xviii. 218 To run the tent-poles through *grummet-holes in the canvas. *c*1860 H. STUART *Seaman's Catech.* 30 How do you make a *grummet strop? 1867 SMYTH *Sailor's Word-bk.*, *Grommet-wad, a ring made of 1½ or 2 inch rope, having attached to it two cross-pieces or diameters of the same material; it acts by the ends of these pieces biting on the interior of the bore of the gun.

grumness ('grʌmnɪs). [f. GRUM *a.* + -NESS.] The quality of being 'grum'.

1675 WYCHERLEY *Country Wife* I. (1675) 11 Well, Jack, by thy long absence from the Town, the grumness of thy countenance, and the slovenlyness of thy habit; I shou'd give thee joy, shou'd I not, of Marriage? 1842 J. F. COOPER *Jack o' Lantern* I. 155 The English peculiarity of grumness.

grumose (gruː'məʊs), *a. rare*⁻⁰. [ad. mod.L. **grūmōs-us* GRUMOUS: see -OSE.] = GRUMOUS 3.

1753 CHAMBERS *Cycl. Supp.*, *Grumose Roots* are those which are composed of several small knobs, such as those of the anemones, and of the little celandine. 1840 PAXTON *Bot. Dict.*, *Grumose*, clubbed, knotted.

†**gru'mosity.** *Obs. rare*⁻⁰. [ad. mod.L. **grūmōsitās*, f. **grūmōs-us*: see next.] (See quot.)

1658 PHILLIPS, *Grumosity*, a curdling of any liquid substance into a thick masse or clod. 1721 BAILEY, *Grumosity*, Fulness of Clods or Lumps.

grumous ('gruːməs), *a.* [ad. mod.L. **grūmōs-us*, f. *grūmus* GRUME: see -OUS.]

1. Containing, consisting of, or resembling grume; clotted; thick, viscid. **a.** of blood.

1665 *Phil. Trans.* I. 86 The Kidneys filled with a kind of grumous blood. 1733 CHEYNE *Eng. Malady* II. i. §5 (1734) 119 When the globular and grumous Part [of the Blood] is in a far greater Proportion than the Serum. 1805 *Med. Jrnl.* XIV. 489 Extravasated blood, partly fluid and partly grumous. 1822–34 *Good's Study Med.* (ed. 4) I. 655 Grumous or granular blood, let loose from the liver, stomack, or some other digestive organ. 1872 F. G. THOMAS *Dis. Women* (ed. 3) 471 He..cut into a tumor behind the uterus and gave exit to a large amount of black, grumous blood.

b. of other fluids.

1665 NEEDHAM *Medela Medic.* 412 The offending matter is grown grumous, curdled or gellied. 1736 BAILEY *Housh. Dict.* 129 The scalding the vessel..stirs up the grumous resinous and oily part of the wood. 1756 C. LUCAS *Ess. Waters* I. 104 Soaps..soon after separate into grumous coagulations. 1852 TH. ROSS *Humboldt's Trav.* II. xvi. 53 *note*, The substance which falls down in grumous and filamentous clots is not pure caoutchouc. 1874 COOKE *Fungi* 41 The minute sooty spores are developed either on delicate threads or in compacted cells, arising first from a sort of semi-gelatinous, grumous stroma. 1890 *Lancet* 3 May 957/2 The appendix on examination, after removal, was found to contain a dark grumous fluid.

2. *transf.* Of diseases, appearances, etc.: Characterized or caused by grume.

1779 JOHNSON *Let. to Mrs. Thrale* 5 Oct., That Mr. Thrale's disorder, whether grumous or serous, must be cured by bleeding. 1801 *Med. Jrnl.* V. 258 A grumous dark appearance like to a slight extravasation. 1802 PALEY *Nat. Theol.* xxiii. 467 A small grumous tumour. 1843 *Blackw. Mag.* LIII. 806 Flies and wasps, which no flapping will keep off from his [the thunny's] grumous liver. 1849 SIEVEKING *Rokitansky's Pathol. Anat.* II. 85 The contents of the intestine are of a..fetid, flocculent and grumous character.

3. *Bot.* Of roots, etc.: Consisting or formed of clustered grains; granulated.

1688 R. HOLME *Armoury* II. 116/1 Grumous or knotty kernelly roots, fastned to one head. 1830 LINDLEY *Nat. Syst. Bot.* 74 Seeds extremely minute (their nucleus consisting of a mass of grumous matter). 1863 BERKELEY *Brit. Mosses* iii. 9 The spores of Mosses..consist of a grumous mass.

Hence **'grumousness**, grumous condition.

1676 WISEMAN *Surg.* I. xiv. 65 The cause of which may be referred either to the coagulation of the Serum, or grumousness of the Bloud.

grump (grʌmp), *sb.* [? Suggested by GRUNT, with ending imitative of an inarticulate exclamation of displeasure; cf. GRUMPH *v.*]

†**1.** ***humps and grumps***: slights and snubs.

1727 DE FOE *Protest. Monast.* 4 Under many Hardships and Restrictions, many Humps and Grumps. 1760 GRAY *Lett.* Wks. 1884 III. 40 We attribute it to a miff about the garter, and some other humps and grumps that he has received.

2. *pl.* The sulks; a fit of ill-humour.

1844 C. RIDLEY *Let.* 6 Oct. in *Life & Lett.* (1958) xiv. 173 Wells has ceased to be under the dominion of the grumps. 1868 L. M. ALCOTT *Little Women* (1871) iv. 41 Hannah had the grumps, for being up late. Never did suit her. 1873 W. CORY *Lett. & Jrnls.* (1897) 360 D. got into wretched grumps, but got out of them.

3. A gruff, grumpy, or ill-humoured person. *colloq.*

1900 *Eng. Dial. Dict.*, *Grump* (pl.), a surly person. 1947 P. BENNETT *Varmints* 225 The grumps who secretly did a little charity. 1959 I. & P. OPIE *Lore & Lang. Schoolch.* x. 186 In Fife 'grump' and 'peenger' apply more to people who are snivelling and fretful than openly sobbing. 1959 T. GRIFFITH *Waist-high Culture* (1960) iii. 36, I called on an affectionate grump known throughout the journalism department as 'Pa' Kennedy. 1970 *New Yorker* 12 Sept. 39/1 Oh, you are the world's worst grump.

grump (grʌmp), *v.* [Cf. prec. and GLUMP *v.*] *intr.* To sulk.

1875 FENN *Both Sides Mirror* i, Instead of stopping grumping here at home.

grumph (grʌmf), *sb. Sc.* [f. GRUMPH *v.*] A grunt, whether from an animal or a human being.

1737 RAMSAY *Sc. Prov.* (1797) 23 Better thole a grumph than a sumph. 1814 *Saxon & Gael* I. v. 42 He drew a long sigh or rather grumph, through his nose, while he shook his head and said, 'O Jane! Jane! ye was aye a dour kimmer!' 1821 *Blackw. Mag.* IX. 137 Loud was the grumph and grumble from hog-stye. 1827 SCOTT *Jrnl.* 10 Apr., What can be expected of a sow but a grumph?

grumph (grʌmf), *v. Sc.* [Echoic, with suggestion from GRUNT. Cf. GRUMP.] *intr.* To grunt; said both of animals and human beings. Also quasi-*trans.*, to utter with a grunt, to grunt out.

1807 J. STAGG *Poems* 8 The breydegroom grumph'd agreed. 1821–30 LD. COCKBURN *Mem.* 326 He stopped, and grumphed. 1862 HISLOP *Prov. Scot.* 36 Better speak bauldly out than aye be grumphin'. 1896 CROCKETT *Grey Man* xii. 84 The loathly sow..lay..grunting and grumphing most filthily.

grumphie ('grʌmfɪ). Chiefly *Sc.* Also 9 grumphy. [f. GRUMPH *v.* + -IE.] A quasi-proper name for the pig.

1785 BURNS *Halloween* xxi, She trotted thro' them a'; An' wha was it but Grumphie. 1824 MACTAGGART *Gallovid. Encycl.* 212 Wi' his mouth fu' o' strae, He to his den will gae; Grumphie is a prophet, wat weather we will hae. 1834 M. SCOTT *Cruise Midge* (1836) II. vi. 206 A black hand.. protruded every now and then, to give grumphy..a good crack over the skull. 1842 J. AITON *Domest. Econ.* (1857) 230 If he find grumphy so lazy, that nothing but a stroke will raise him.

grumphy ('grʌmfɪ), *a.* [Cf. GRUMPH *v.*] = GRUMPY.

1846 MRS. GORE *Eng. Charac.* 95 Conviviality only renders him grumphier and grumphier.

grumpish ('grʌmpɪʃ), *a.* [f. GRUMP *sb.* + -ISH.] = GRUMPY.

1797 MRS. A. M. BENNETT *Beggar Girl* (1813) V. 242 Our stuart is as grumpish as an old hound. 1805 in *Spirit Publ. Jrnls.* (1806) IX. 314 Diddle..was sure it was a grouse or a woodcock, it looked so grey and so grumpish. 1840 MRS. F. TROLLOPE *M. Armstrong* I. vi. 158 If you blubber or look grumpish, I'll have you strapped ten times over. 1897 BARING-GOULD *Bladys* xii. 143 She is grumpish and the world is well rid of such baggage.

grumpy ('grʌmpɪ), *a.* [f. GRUMP *sb.* + -Y¹.] Surly, ill-tempered.

1778 MISS BURNEY *Evelina* (1784) II. ix. 68 You were so grumpy you would not let me. 1824 MISS MITFORD *Village* Ser. I. (1863) 160 The grumpy gentleman in the opposite corner. 1858 R. S. SURTEES *Ask Mamma* xv. 53 His lordship was very grumpy all that evening. 1870 RAMSAY *Remin.* (ed. 18) p. xxxii, A..short and grumpy manner. 1887 FRITH *Autobiog.* (1888) III. 66, I found the old engraver somewhat grumpy.

absol. 1849 E. E. NAPIER *Excurs. S. Africa* II. 241 Never mind, old grumpy; sleep away.

Hence **'grumpily** *adv.*, **'grumpiness**.

1835 E. FITZGERALD *Lett.* (1889) I. 28 [Tennyson's] little humours and grumpinesses were so droll, that I was always laughing. 1882 L. KEITH *Alasnam's Lady* II. 274, I wish you would speak less grumpily to Philippa. 1890 BESANT *Armorel of Lyonesse* I. 154 The grumpiness which he showed on the way back.

†**'grumulous**, *a. Obs.* [f. L. *grūmul-us*, dim. of *grūm-us* GRUME + -OUS.] = GRUMOUS *a.* 1.

1758 J. S. *Le Dran's Observ. Surg.* (1771) 269 The Cystis ..evacuated a thick grumulous Lympha.

grun, obs. form of GRIN *sb.*¹

grünauite ('gryːnaʊaɪt). *Min.* [Named by Nicol, 1849, from its locality *Grünau* in Rhenish Prussia: see -ITE.] Native sulphide of nickel and bismuth of a silver grey colour.

1849 NICOL *Min.* 458 Grünauite..occurs granular and disseminated. 1868 DANA *Min.* (ed. 5) 47 Grünauite.. Isometric..Cleavage octahedral.

grunch (grʌnʃ), *v. Sc. Obs.* exc. *arch.* Also 6 grunsch, 6, 9 gruntch. [Perh. a modification of GRUTCH *v.*, influenced by GRUNT.] *intr.* To grumble, express discontent. Const. *at.* Also with *inf.* To grudge, to object.

14.. *Dietary* 15 in *Barbour's Bruce* (E.E.T.S.) 538 Mek in troubill, glad in pouerte..Neuir grunching, bot mery lik thi degre. 1513 DOUGLAS *Æneis* VIII. Prol. 165 As I grunchit at this grum, and glysnyt about. *Ibid.* x. xi. 61 Quhilk be thy wordis of fatale destane Now grunschis thou to give or to conceid. *c* **1560** A. SCOTT *Poems* (S.T.S.) xxxiv. 92 For, haif ane bismeir baggis, ȝe grunche no^t at hir grunȝe. **1616** *Barbour's Bruce* (ed. Hart) 24 And gif his keeper oft grunches [*MSS.* gruchys] Looke that thou take him magre his.

b. quasi-*trans.* with cognate obj.: To utter grumblingly; to grumble out.

1819 W. TENNANT *Papistry Storm'd* (1827) 55 His drone did gruntch sae dour a sound, Black Pluto heard it underground.

Hence **'grunching** *vbl. sb.* and *ppl. a.* Also **'gruncher**, one who 'grunches' or grumbles; in quot. a nickname.

1498 *Barbour's Bruce* XVI. 9 (*MS.C.*) And he hym levit with a grunching [*MS.E.* gruching]. *c* **1470** HENRYSON *Mor. Fab.* II. (*Cock & Fox*) xxii, To-gidder all but grunching furth ye glide. **1535** STEWART *Cron. Scot.* III. 171 With grunschand luke quhen scho [Fortoun] lykis to greif. *c* **1560** A. SCOTT *Poems* (S.T.S.) xxxiii. 14 Sturt, angir, grunching, yre, and greif. **1892** *Macm. Mag.* Dec. 128 One of the contemporaries of my own bright days was known as 'the Gruncher'. *Ibid.* 129, I vow and declare that grunching was no spontaneous growth in my nature.

grund, obs. pa. t. GRIND *v.*; obs. f. GROUND.

grundel ('grʌndəl). Also 5 grundyl. [f. *grund* GROUND *sb.* + -EL[1]. Cf. MDu., Du. *grondel*, G. *grundel*; also GRINDLE.] A fish; = GROUNDLING 1.

14.. *Voc.* in Wr.-Wülcker 584/42 *Fringulus*, a grundyl. **1753** CHAMBERS *Cycl. Supp.*, *Grundel*, or *Grundling*, in zoology, a name used by some for the common loach or locho, a small freshwater fish, known among writers by the names of cobitis and fundulus.

grundelich, grundelike, vars. GROUNDLY.

grundeswell, -swulie, -swylie, obs. ff. GROUNDSEL *sb.*[1]

grundien, obs. form of GROUND *v.*

grundlich, grundlike, vars. GROUNDLY.

grundsil(l, obs. form of GROUNDSEL *sb.*[2]

†**'grundy**[1]. *Obs. rare*[−1]. [? a. Du. *grundje*, *grontje*, groundling.] A designation applied to a short person.

1570 FOXE *A. & M.* (ed. 2) II. 2307/2 Of some he [John Vander Warfe, of Andwerpe] was called..Shildpad..for that he beyng a short grundy and of litle stature, did ryde commonly with a great broad hat.

grundy[2] ('grʌndɪ). [? Echoic: see quot. 1840.] Granulated pig-iron.

1840 D. MUSHET *Papers Iron & Steel* 12 Fifty years ago this process of granulation was carried on at the Cyfarthia iron works to some extent. The iron so obtained was called grundy, from the noise produced by the revolution of a large horizontal stone, placed in the water-pit, on which the iron fell in its descent. **1881** in Raymond *Mining Gloss.*

Grundy[3] ('grʌndɪ). The surname of an imaginary personage (*Mrs. Grundy*) who is proverbially referred to as a personification of the tyranny of social opinion in matters of conventional propriety.

In Morton's play *Speed the Plough* (1798), Dame Ashfield is represented as constantly fearing to give occasion for the sneers of her neighbour, Mrs. Grundy. Her frequent question 'What will Mrs. Grundy say?' became proverbial (prob. with especial reference to the passage quoted below) as expressing the attitude of those who regard the disapproval of society as the worst of evils.

1798 T. MORTON *Speed the Plough* II. iii. (1801) 29 *Dame Ashfield.* If shame should come to the poor child [her daughter]—I say, Tummas, what would Mrs. Grundy say then? *Farmer Ashfield.* Dom Mrs. Grundy; what wou'd my poor wold heart zay? **1813** *Examiner* 15 Mar. 170/2 What will Mrs. Grundy say? *a* **1845** HOOD *Open Question* i, Now, really, this appears the common case Of putting too much Sabbath into Sunday—But what is your opinion, Mrs. Grundy? **1857** LOCKER *Lond. Lyrics* (1874) 102 And many are afraid of God—And more of Mrs. Grundy. **1896** *Daily News* 26 Oct. 6/3 Without the smallest regard for the Grundy tribe in office or out of it. **1899** MISS BROUGHTON *Game & Candle* 129 You do not mean to imply..that Mrs. Grundy is going to interpose between you and me?

Hence **'Grundified** *ppl. a.*, arranged according to the ideas of Mrs. Grundy; **'Grundyish** *a.*, prudish; **'Grundyism**, the principles of Mrs. Grundy, conventionalism; **'Grundyist, 'Grundyite**, a stickler for propriety.

1836 *Backw. Canada* 270 Having shaken off the trammels of Grundyism, we laugh at..those who voluntarily forge afresh and hug their chains. **1845** TENNYSON in *Mem.* (1897) I. 227 Us poor devils, whom the Grundyites would not only not remunerate, but kick out of society as barely respectable. **1883** 'WANDERER' *Notes Caucasus* vi. 149 Unfit, in this Grundyish age, for print. **1889** *Jrnl. Educ.* 1 June 282/1 Perhaps, after all, our rules were but a set of conventional observations; our system but a sort of grammatical grundyism. **1890** T. HARDY in *New Rev.* Jan. 19, Unreal and meretricious, but dear to the Grundyist and subscriber. **1893** LADY BURTON *Life R. F. Burton* II. 258 The usual small worries and Grundified conventions that form the cab-shafts of domestic life in civilization.

grundyn, obs. Sc. pa. pple. of GRIND *v.*

grundy-swallow, -swally, dial. variants of GROUNDSEL *sb.*[1]

grune, obs. form of GROIN.

grünerite ('gryːnəraɪt). *Min.* [Named in German (*grünerit*) by Kenngott, 1853, after E. L. Grüner, who first described it: see -ITE.] A variety of hornblende, of silky lustre and brown colour, containing much iron.

1861 BRISTOW *Gloss. Min.* 168 *Grünerite*, a pure iron augite. **1868** DANA *Min.* (ed. 5) 234 Grünerite: Asbestiform or lamellar-fibrous.

grunge (grʌndʒ). *U.S. slang.* [See next.] A general term of disparagement for someone or something that is repugnant or odious, unpleasant, or dull; also, dirt, grime. Also *attrib.*

1965 *N.Y. Times* 27 Dec. 20/7 A difficult date is an 'octopus', a dull one a 'grunge' and an untidy one a 'dip' or a 'spook'. **1967** *Wentworth & Flexner's Dict. Amer. Slang* Suppl. 688/1 *Grunge, grunch, n.*, a dull or boring person. **1968–70** *Current Slang* (Univ. S. Dakota) III–IV. 62 *Grunge*, a bad, unpleasant thing, especially food.—University of Kentucky. **1973** *New Yorker* 19 Nov. 234/2 Your average American rock-and-roll fan can stand the Dolls' brand of high-strung urban grunge only if it comes from somewhere besides New York—preferably England. **1977** *Amer. Speech 1975* L. 60 *Grunge*, filthy substance. 'There's grunge in the bottom of my Dr. Pepper bottle!' **1983** *Computerworld* 18 July 6/3 In the programming stage, Telon saved 'a lot of the "grunge" work of writing call programs for IMS/DC', Serovy explained. **1986** *Washington Post* 19 Jan. D4/2 Most bands would fall headlong into cliché when dishing out the sort of overdriven guitar grunge served up in 'Don't You Go Walking'.

grungy ('grʌndʒɪ), *a. slang* (chiefly *N. Amer.*). [App. arbitrary formation, after *grubby*, *dingy*, etc.: cf. prec. and GUNGY *a.*] Grimy, dirty; hence, of poor quality, unappealing; unpleasant, bad; untidy.

1965 *N.Y. Times* 15 Jan. 41/2 Liquor flows freely, jokes are the 'grungiest', fun and games abound. **1968–70** *Current Slang* (Univ. S. Dakota) III–IV. 62 *Grungy*, bad, dirty, ugly, (like ugly day).—College students, both sexes, Minnesota. **1970** *Washington Post* 30 Sept. B14/1 The shopping center may be new, but the store will have the same grungy merchandise. **1974** A. LURIE *War between Tates* (1977) i. 31 She wouldn't admit she was pissed at being turned out of Her Own Living-Room, and how grungy we left the kitchen. **1976** *New Yorker* 8 Mar. 58/1 Some of the grungy details he adds are good. **1983** *Sunday Times* (Colour Suppl.) 30 Oct. 57/2 In 1973, 47th Street Photo moved one block east to its current location, a grungy walk-up at 67 West 47th Street. **1985** *Dirt Bike* Mar. 19/3, I would like to know who made those blasted white pants so popular—mine are splattered with oil specks and other grungy stains.

Hence **'grunginess**, the quality or state of being grimy, unpleasant, or 'grungy'.

1978 *Fanfare* (Toronto) 31 May 3 The Inheritance, with its emphasis on the grunginess of human nature..was probably seen as somewhat scandalous in Catholic Italy. **1986** *New Yorker* 27 Jan. 86/2 Harry Dean Stanton has the right tequila-swigging grunginess (except for his sparkling-white teeth).

grunion ('grʌnjən). [Prob. ad. Sp. *gruñón* grunter.] A small Californian marine fish, *Leuresthes tenuis*, which comes ashore to spawn.

1917 *Overland Monthly* Dec. 529/1 Of all the peculiar fish of which the southern coast of California boasts, the Grunyon is the most peculiar, on account of its phenomenal manner of spawning. **1919** *Fish Bulletin* (Calif. Fish & Game Commission) 15 July 3 At Long Beach no name other than 'grunion' is ever heard, although one gleans from scientific works such names as 'silver-sides' and 'little-smelt'. **1927** *Glasgow Herald* 17 Sept. 4 A very striking rhythm is exhibited by a Californian smelt, called the Grunion. *Ibid.*, This is a very adaptive rhythm that works out profitably for the race of grunions. **1932** M. MILLER *I cover Waterfront* 112 The spring tides, which accompany the full and the dark of the moon, are the time-tables by which the grunion runs can be predicted. **1965** A. J. MCCLANE *Standard Fishing Encycl.* 167/1 The grunion come completely out of the water to spawn in moist beach sand at which time they are caught by hand.

grünlingite ('grʏnlɪŋgaɪt). *Min.* Also **gruenlingite**. [ad. G. *grünlingit* (Muthmann & Schröder 1897, in *Zeitschr. f. Kryst.* XXIX. 145), f. the name of F. *Grünling*, formerly keeper of the mineral collection of the Univ. of Munich: see -ITE[1].] A sulphide and telluride of bismuth, similar to or identical with joseite, which occurs in steel-grey lamellar masses.

1898 *Jrnl. Chem. Soc.* LXXIV. II. 78 A tellurium mineral from Cumberland... This new mineral is named grünlingite. **1941** *Amer. Mineral.* XXVI. 200 The pattern is identical with that given by joseite.., 'grünlingite'..from Carrock Fells, Cumberland (type locality), and 'oruetite'. **1944** C. PALACHE et al. *Dana's Syst. Min.* (ed. 7) I. 165 The relation of gruenlingite to joseite is uncertain. **1950** *Mineral. Abstr.* XI. 112 Results..for joseite, grünlingite, a new mineral Bi_6TeS_4, and seleniferous cosalite, all from Rézbánya [in Rumania].

grunnleston, dial. form of GRINDLE STONE.

†**grunny**, *v. Obs.* Variant of GROIN *v.*[1]

c **1340** *Ayenb.* 67 He beginþ to grochi betuene his teþ and grunny [Fr. *il comence a murmurer et gromeler*].

grunsch, obs. form of GRUNCH *v.*

grunsel, variant of GROUNDSEL *sb.*[1] and *sb.*[2]

grunsell, -sill, obs. f. GROUNDSEL *sb.*[1] and *sb.*[2]

grunstane, Sc. form of GRINDSTONE.

†**grunstein.** *Min. Obs.* Also 8 **grunsten**. [a. G. *grünstein* = Sw. *grönsten*.] = GREENSTONE 1. ? A mineral, compounded of siderite and mica. Also *attrib.*

1796 KIRWAN *Elem. Min.* (ed. 2) I. 343 Of the binary aggregates of the Granitic kind. M. Werner..denotes only the aggregate of hornblende and felspar, or mica, by the name of Grunsten. **1811** PINKERTON *Petral.* I. 7 Grunstein porphyry, the green porphyry of the ancients, and grunstein slate. *Ibid.* 12 The real grunstein of the Swedes is a mixture of siderite and mica, sometimes with particles of quartz.

grunswel(l, obs. form of GROUNDSEL *sb.*[1]

grunt (grʌnt), *sb.* [f. GRUNT *v.*]

1. The characteristic low gruff sound made by a hog; a similar sound uttered by other animals.

1615 CHAPMAN *Odyss.* x. 324 Swines snowts, swines bodies, tooke they, bristles, grunts. **1697** DRYDEN *Æneid* VII. 20 The Grunts of Bristled Boars. **1820** SHELLEY *Œdipus* I. i. 95 Let me hear Their everlasting grunts and whines no more! **1859** DICKENS *T. Two Cities* II. v, With a deprecatory grunt, the jackal again complied. **1894** A. ROBERTSON *Nuggets*, etc. 68 What can ye expec' frae a pig but a grunt.

2. a. A similar sound, uttered by a human being; sometimes expressive of approbation, or the opposite. †In early use, a groan.

1553 BRENDE *Q. Curtius* x. 214 b, But he had not so sone dronke of Hercules cuppe, but that he gaue a grunte as thoughe he had bene striken to the harte. **1567** TURBERV. *Ovid's Ep.*, *Hypermnestra to Lynceus* 43 When..round about I heard Of dying men the grunts. **1774–77** COOK *Voy. S. Pole*, etc. III. viii. II. 107 Two or three old men..giving a kind of grunt, significant, as I thought, of approbation. **1829** LYTTON *Devereux* II. iv, They raised the fallen watchman, who, after three or four grunts, began slowly to recover himself. **1865** CARLYLE *Fredk. Gt.* IV. viii. (1872) II 16 The Britannic Majesty gave some grunt of acquiescence. **1899** *Blackw. Mag.* Oct. 453/1 He emitted only a sulky grunt.

transf. **1879** H. DRUMMOND in *Life* (1899) 162 [The geyser] gave a grunt and then threw up a little water.

b. *U.S. slang.* An infantry soldier.

1969 I. KEMP *Brit. G.I. in Vietnam* v. 106 The sound of..engines, among the most welcome of all music to the average infantryman—or 'grunt', as we were impolitely called—in Vietnam. **1970** *Times* 28 May 7/5 These luckless victims of the American military machine are known as 'grunts', a name said to be derived from their way of complaining as they trudge along the jungle trails.

3. a. A name for American fishes of the genus *Hæmulon* and allied species (as *Orthopristis chrysopterus*). So called from the noise they make when taken.

Apparently not connected with Du. *gront*, *grunt*, which is a shortened form of *grondel* GRUNDEL, and denotes a different fish (*Cyprinus gobio*).

1713 RAY *Synopsis Piscium* 96 The Gray Grunt. **1725** SLOANE *Jamaica* II. 291 Gray-Grunt. It was taken at Old Harbour. **1734** MORTIMER in *Phil. Trans.* XXXVIII. 316 *Perca marina capite striato.* The Grunt. **1792** MAR. RIDDELL *Voy. Madeira* 69 The cobler-fish, the king-fish..the grunt, and the flying gurnard. **1884–5** *Riverside Nat. Hist.* (1888) III. 218 Grunt, pig-fish, and red-mouth, are the principal common names of the species of *Hæmulon*..Another fish, also called grunt and pig-fish..is the *Orthopristis chrysopterus.* **1885** C. F. HOLDER *Marvels Anim. Life* 176 Grunts that opened their wide mouths in audible protest.

b. An English fish, ? the perch.

1851 MRS. BROWNING *Casa Guidi W.* 78 The pool in front Wherein the hill-stream trout are cast to wait The beatific vision, and the grunt Used at refectory, keeps its weedy state. **1880** *Antrim & Down Gloss.*, *Grunt*, a fish, the perch.

grunt (grʌnt), *v.* Forms: 1 grunnettan, 3, 5 grunten, 4–5 grunte, 5 gronte, grunton, 6 grunte, 6– grunt. *Pa. t.* 3 gronte, grunte, 4 grunt(e, 5– grunted. [OE. *grunnettan* (= OHG., mod.G. *grunzen*), freq. of *grunian* (cf. MHG. *grunnen*) to grunt, an echoic formation parallel with L. *grunnire*.]

1. *intr.* Of a hog: To utter its characteristic low gruff sound. Also of other animals and of persons (with conscious allusion to the pig): To utter a sound resembling this.

c **725** *Corpus Gloss.* (Hessels) G. 173 *Grunnire*, grunnettan. **1297** R. GLOUC. (Rolls) 4233 He vemde & grunte & stod aȝen as it were a strong bor. **1398** TREVISA *Barth. De P.R.* XVIII. lxv. (1495) 820 The olde lyon resyth woodly on men and oonly gruntyth on wymmen, and resyth selde on chyldren but in grete hungre. *c* **1400** MAUNDEV. (1839) xxvii. 274 In that Desert ben many wylde men..thei gronten, as Pygges. *c* **1440** CAPGRAVE *Life St. Kath.* IV. 1481 Eke your goddis arn not soo goode as swyn—Thei can noȝt grunten whan hem eyleth ought. **1530** PALSGR. 576/2, I grunte, as a horse dothe whan he his spored. **1593** NASHE *Christ's T.* (1613) 101 As the Hogge is still grunting, digging, and wrooting in the mucke, so [etc.]. **1633** P. FLETCHER *Purple Is.* VII. lxxxiii, Still did hunt..In his deep trough for swill..Gryll could but grunt. *a* **1740** TICKELL *Ep. to Gentl. Avignon* 104 Thy brinded boars may slumber undismay'd, Or grunt secure beneath the chestnut shade. **1768** BEATTIE *Minstrel* I. lvi, Sneak with the scoundrel fox, or grunt with glutton swine. **1820** W. IRVING *Sketch Bk.* II. 365 Sleek unwieldly porkers were grunting in the repose and abundance of their pens. **1831** [see GRUNTER[1] 1 b]. **1865** LECKY *Ration.* I. 66 He told how an aged minister had been interrupted..by a devil who was grunting behind him like a pig. **1893** EARL DUNMORE *Pamirs* II. 192 Yaks grunted after the manner of their kind.

†**b.** To groan. *Obs.*

1340–70 *Alisaunder* 388 For greefe of hur grim stroke grunt full many. **1494** FABYAN *Chron.* v. ciii. 78 Many knyghts vpon bothe parties lay slayne & gruntynge vpon the erthe. **1535** W. MARSHALL tr. *Menandrinus' Def. Peace*, To Bk., Those persones, I wareunt, aswell pleased shall be all. As wood Rome shall grunte, at the rubbynge on the gall. **1602** SHAKS. *Ham.* III. i. 77 Who would these Fardles beare To grunt and sweat vnder a weary life?

2. To utter a similar sound, expressive of discontent, dissent, effort, fatigue, etc.; to grumble, murmur.

c **1325** *Body & Soul* 104 in *Map's Poems* (Camden) 341 The bodi grunte and gon to seye, Gost, thou hast the wrong i-wis. **1548** UDALL, etc. *Erasm. Par. Luke* v. 21–6 The Phariseis, they grunte and murmour, and haue enuy at hym. **1577–87** HOLINSHED *Chron.* III. 1156/1 Wherat Sir Henrie Benefield grunted, and was highlie offended. **1647** TRAPP *Comm. Matt.* vi. 5 [Saul] grunts against himself because he [God] handles him nat after his own mind. **1705** HICKERINGILL *Priest-cr.* IV. (1721) 230 Not *Priest-craft* and *Superstition*, not grunting and groaning, and looking surly, and sighing. **1804** A. WILSON in *Poems & Lit. Prose* (1876) I. 114 Isaac grunting and lagging behind. **1890** HALL CAINE *Bondman* II. ii, A pace or two behind came Chalse.. grunting hoarsely in his husky throat.

b. *trans.* To utter or express with a grunt; to breathe *out* with a grunt.

1613 PURCHAS *Pilgrimage* (1614) 331 A Bore..there fell downe dead of a wound which they gave him, grunting out his last gaspe. **1786** BURNS *Ordination* xi, Learning, with his Greekish face, Grunts out some Latin ditty. **1787** —— *Ded. G. Hamilton* 63 Grunt up a solemn lengthen'd groan. **1840** DICKENS *Old C. Shop* xv, Grunting their monotonous grumblings as they prowled about. **1875** BUCKLAND *Log-bk.* 100 He only grunted his gratitude.

†**3. a.** *trans.* To grind (the teeth). **b.** *intr.* To grind *with* the teeth. *Obs.* (Cf. GRIND, GRINT.)

13.. *Coer de L.* 2107 He grunte his teeth. **1426** LYDG. *De Guil. Pilgr.* 10470 Grucchynge, he grunte wyth hys teth. **1483** CAXTON *Gold. Leg.* 331 b/1 She..lost her speche & foomyd atte mouth lyke a bore & grunted her teeth to gydre merueylously.

gruntch, variant of GRUNCH *v.*

grunter[1] ('grʌntə(r)). [f. GRUNT *v.* + -ER[1].]

1. An animal or person that grunts; *esp.* a pig.

c **1440** *Promp. Parv.* 217/2 Gruntare, *grunnitor*. **1591** PERCIVALL *Sp. Dict.*, *Grunidor*, a grunter. **1641** BROME *Joviall Crew* II. (1652) F 3, Here's Grunter and Bleater, with Tib of the Butt'ry. **1785** GROSE *Dict. Vulg. Tongue*, *Grunter's gig*, a smoaked hog's face. **1798** BLOOMFIELD *Farmer's Boy, Summer* 248 Whose [the Gander's] nibbling warfare on the grunter's side, Is welcome pleasure to his bristly hide. **1820** SCOTT *Ivanhoe* i, Collecting the refractory grunters. **1847** TENNYSON *Princ.* v. 26 **1853** HICKIE tr. *Aristoph.* (1887) I. 33 For how much shall I buy your little grunters of you? **1889** FARRAR *Lives Fathers* II. xii. 348 Jerome has no name for him but the 'grunter'.

b. (See quots.)

1831 YOUATT *Horse* x. 196 Every horse violently exercised on a full stomach, or when overloaded with fat, will grunt very much like a hog..But there are some horses who will at all times utter this sound, if suddenly touched with the whip or spur. They are called grunters, and should be avoided. **1888** W. WILLIAMS *Princ. Vet. Med.* (ed. 5) 553 If a horse when struck at or suddenly moved, emits, during expiration, a grunting sound, it is called a 'grunter'.

2. Used as a name for various fishes making a grunting noise; cf. GRUNT *sb.* 3.

1726 SHELVOCK *Voy. round World* 55 All their bays and creeks are well stock'd with mullets, large rays, grunters, cavallies, and drum-fish. **1859** BARTLETT *Dict. Amer.*, *Grunter*, one of the popular names of the fish called by naturalists the Banded Drum.

3. *slang.* **a.** A shilling (? *obs.*) or a sixpence. **b.** A policeman.

a. 1785 GROSE *Dict. Vulg. Tongue*, *Grunter*, a shilling. **1858** A. MAYHEW *Paved with Gold* III. iii. 267 One of the men..had only taken three 'twelvers' and a 'grunter'.

b. 1823 EGAN *Grose's Dict. Vulg. Tongue*, *Grunters*, traps, officers of justice.

grunter[2] ('grʌntə(r)). (See quot.)

1858 SIMMONDS *Dict. Trade*, *Grunter*, an iron rod bent like a hook, used by iron founders. **1875** in KNIGHT *Dict. Mech.*

Grunth, var. GRANTH.

gruntil(l, obs. form of GRUNTLE *sb.* and *v.*

grunting ('grʌntɪŋ), *vbl. sb.* [f. GRUNT *v.* + -ING[1].] The action of the vb. GRUNT; the uttering of a grunt; groaning.

13.. *Childh. Jesus* 378 in *Archiv Stud. neu. Spr.* LXXIV. 332 Vn-to the owenne þane gare þay gaa, And thare-Ine herde þay gronntynge grete [of pigs]. *c* **1430** *Hymns Virg.* 83 Mi modir for me suffride sorewe With gruntyngis gril & siȝinge sare. **1494** FABYAN *Chron.* VII. ccxxxii. 266 The crye of the enemyes..noyse of trumpettys, and gruntynge of horsysse, approchyd and smote together. *c* **1560** VERON (*title*), A Fruteful treatise of predestination..against the swynyshe gruntinge of the Epicures and Atheystes of oure time. **1577–87** HOLINSHED *Chron. Scot.* 230 Nothing was heard but grunting and groning of people. **1620** MIDDLETON *Chaste Maid* I. ii, When she lies in, As now she's even upon the point of grunting, A lady lies not in like her [etc.]. **1646** SIR T. BROWNE *Pseud. Ep.* III. i. 107 Pliny and divers since affirme, that Elephants are terrified, and make away upon the grunting of Swine. **1774** GOLDSM. *Nat. Hist.* (1776) IV. 289 A peculiar cry, somewhat a mixture between the grunting of a hog, and the bellowing of a calf. **1820** SHELLEY *Œdipus* II. ii. 40 For God's sake stop the grunting of those pigs! **1876** GREEN *Stray Stud.* 215 But murmurings and gruntings broke idly against the old abbot's imperious will. **1894** BARING-GOULD *Kitty Alone* III. 80 With random gruntings of the violoncello.

†**b.** = GRINDING (of teeth). *Obs.*

1388 WYCLIF *Luke* xiii. 28 There schal be wepyng and gruntyng [**1382** beting to gidere] of teeth.

'grunting, *ppl. a.* [-ING[2].] That grunts.

1633 P. FLETCHER *Purpl. Isl.* XI. xlii, There lies the grunting swine. **1697** DRYDEN *Æneid* VII. 786 Here Pluto pants for breath from out his cell And opens wide the grunting jaws of hell. **1704** SWIFT *T. Tub* (1709) 137 A lazy, an impatient and a grunting reader. **1727** *Philip Quarll* 101 To save his Money, and to be ridd of a grunting Companion. **1817** BYRON *Beppo* xliv, Like our harsh northern whistling, grunting guttural. **1828** *Lights & Shades* II. 123 A grunting hog, with a rope tied to his left leg. **1863** ATKINSON *Stanton Grange* 20 The odd, uncouth, grunting coo of the stock-dove was heard.

b. Special collocations: †**grunting-cheat** *slang*, a pig; **grunting-ox**, the yak, *Poëphagus grunniens* (*Cent. Dict.*); **grunting-peck** *slang*, pork.

1567 HARMAN *Caveat* 86 She hath a Cacling chete, a grunting chete, ruff Pecke, cassan, and popplarr of yarum. **1622** FLETCHER *Beggar's Bush* v. i, Or surprising a boor's ken for grunting-cheats. *a* **1700** B. E. *Dict. Cant. Crew*, *Grunting-Peeck*, Pork. **1836** SMITH *Individual* (Farmer), 'The Thieves' Chaunt'. But dearer to me Sue's kisses far, Than Grunting Peck or other grub are.

Hence **'gruntingly** *adv.*, in a grunting manner.

1611 COTGR., *Murmurantement*, murmuringly, mutteringly, gruntingly. **1829** LYTTON *Disowned* 17 In earnest admiration of two pigs, which marched, gruntingly, towards him. **1837** *New Monthly Mag.* L. 415 James.. gruntingly breathed, and snuffingly said.

gruntle ('grʌnt(ə)l), *sb. Sc.* Also 6–8 **gruntill**, 9 **grunkle**. [f. GRUNTLE *v.*]

1. The snout of a pig, or other animal.

1535 LYNDESAY *Satyre* 2109 Heir is ane relict..The gruntill of Sanct Antonis sow, Quhilk buir his haly bell. *a* **1557** *Diurn. Occurr.* (Bannatyne Club) 235 Xiij grysis, off the quhilkis, thair wes ane a monstoure. It haid the gruntill thairof in the heich of the heed. **1596** DALRYMPLE tr. *Leslie's Hist. Scot.* I. 123 Slay out of hand a swyne that eites the corne, or wt the gruntle casting vp the tilet ground. **1824** J. TELFER in Whitelaw *Bk. Sc. Ballads* (1875) 460/2 The stinkan brocke Shotte up hir gruntle to see. **1844** JACK *Hist. St. Monance* iv. 36 [The pig] presented its ominous grunkle full in his view.

b. *transf.* The face of a man, etc. (Cf. MUZZLE.)

1508 DUNBAR *Flyting w. Kennedie* 127 The gallowis gaipis efter thy graceles gruntill. **1786** BURNS *Sc. Drink* xvii, May ..gouts torment him inch by inch, Wha twists his gruntle wi' a glunch O' sour disdain, Out owre a glass o' whisky punch Wi' honest men. **1819** W. TENNANT *Papistry Storm'd* (1827) 50 Some Papists said it was the Deil; Na, na; it was some better chiel; I ken his grunkle unca weil.

2. A little grunt; a subdued grunting sound.

1697 W. CLELAND *Poems* 92 He threw a gruntle, hands did fold, [etc.]. *a* **1774** FERGUSON *Poems* (1807) 262 Can lintie's music be compar'd Wi' gruntles frae the City Guard? **1785** BURNS *Halloween* xix, Presently he hears a squeak, And then a grane and gruntle.

gruntle ('grʌnt(ə)l), *v.* Also 5 **gruntil.** [f. GRUNT *v.* with dim. or frequentative ending -LE.]

1. *intr.* To utter a little or low grunt. Said of swine, occas. of other animals; *rarely* of persons. Const. *against*, *at*. *Obs.* exc. *dial.*

c **1400** MAUNDEV. (Roxb.) xxx. 135 Þai..spekez noȝt, bot gruntils as swyne duse. **15..** *Gyre-Carling* 20 in Laing *Anc. Pop. Poetry* 275 The Carling schup hir in ane sow, and is hir gaitis gane Gruntlyng our the Greik sie. **1603** DEKKER *Batchelars Banq.* Wks. (Grosart) I. 161 She..seemes on a suddaine to awake from a sound sleepe, gruntling and nusling under the sheets. **1605** Z. JONES tr. *Loyer's Specters* 11 Shee growing enraged, made so filthy a noyse and gruntled so horribly against him. **1679** DRYDEN *Tr. & Cr.* IV. ii, So, so; the boars begin to gruntle at one another: set up your bristles now, o' both sides. **1688** R. HOLME *Armoury* II. 134/2 An Elke, when he sendeth forth his Cry, gruntleth. **1735** SOMERVILLE *Chase* IV. 338 By Circe's Charms To Swine transform'd, ran gruntling thro' the Groves. **1777** *Justification* 29 The tythe-pig gruntles in the vicar's ear. **1855** ROBINSON *Whitby Gloss.*, To *Gruntle*, to grunt in a low or murmuring tone, as a sickly cow.

transf. **1793** BERESFORD in *Looker-on* (1794) II. No. 54. 313 Oft hearing the sow-gelder's horn..Through the long street gruntling far.

2. To grumble, murmur, complain.

1589 R. BRUCE *Serm.* (1843) 166 It becomes us not to have our hearts here gruntling upon this earth. **1601** DENT *Pathw. Heaven* 213 He cannot indure that we should gruntle against him with stubborne sullennesse. **1687** MIEGE *Gt. Fr. Dict.* II. s.v., She does nothing but gruntle. **1876** 'P. PYPER' *Mr. Gray & Neighb.* II. 138 There's some on 'em..is gruntling over it above a bit.

Hence **'gruntler** *rare*⁻¹, a grumbler.

1893 *Standard* 2 Sept. 3/2 If they were gruntlers, the chief gruntler was the Secretary of State for War.

gruntled ('grʌnt(ə)ld), *ppl. a.* [Back-formation f. DISGRUNTLED *a.*] Pleased, satisfied, contented.

1938 WODEHOUSE *Code of Woosters* i. 9 He spoke with a certain what-is-it in his voice, and I could see that, if not actually disgruntled, he was far from being gruntled. **1962** C. ROHAN *Delinquents* 76 Come on, Brownie darling, be gruntled. **1966** *New Statesman* 11 Nov. 693/2 An action against a barrister for negligence..would open the door to every disgruntled client. Now gruntled clients are rare in the criminal courts. **1967** E. MCGIRR *Hearse with Horses* i. 17 The Agency has a nice file of gruntled exes who have found their talents in a great variety of jobs.

gruntling ('grʌntlɪŋ), *sb.* [f. GRUNT *v.* + -LING.] A little grunter, a young pig.

1686 *Bk. Boys & Girls* 32 (Halliw.) But come, my gruntling, when thou art full fed, Forth to the butchers stall thou must be led. **1780** *Gentl. Mag.* Apr. 193/2 The good fruit for me, the mean for my slave, The worst you design my gruntlings shall have. **1823** *Blackw. Mag.* XIII. 90 The ..gambols of a litter of sucking gruntlings. **1834** BECKFORD *Italy* II. 134 Calves, turkeys, and gruntlings, which had long been fattening..for this solemn occasion.

gruntling ('grʌntlɪŋ), *vbl. sb.* [f. GRUNTLE *v.* + -ING[1].] The action of the verb GRUNTLE.

1607 TOPSELL *Four-f. Beasts* 327 He vttereth a voice like the gruntling of a Swine. **1611** MIDDLETON *Roaring Girl* v. i. Wks. 1885 IV. 130 The gruntling of five hundred hogs coming from Rumford market. **1819** W. TENNANT *Papistry Storm'd* (1827) 55 Sae what wi' gruntlin', what wi' squealin', The causey-stanes were maist set reelin'. **1824** *Blackw. Mag.* XVI. 89 Don't make a hoggish gruntling as you drink. **1834** BECKFORD *Italy* II. 173 After a deal of adulatory complimentation..for which they got nothing in return but rebuffs and gruntling.

gruntling ('grʌntlɪŋ), *ppl. a.* [f. as prec. + -ING[2].] That gruntles.

15.. tr. *Martial* III. lviii. 158 (MS.) The gruntling swine follow the house-wife's feete. **1607** TOPSELL *Four-f. Beasts* (1658) 156 The gruntling clamour or cry of hogs. **1679** EARL ROCHESTER *Epigr. Ld. All-pride* 12 in *Roxb. Ballads* (1883) IV. 567 So Swine for nasty meat to dunghills run, And toss their gruntling Snouts up when they've done. **1896** CROCKETT *Grey Man* xii. 86 Nothing loath to get away from gruntling horror on the hill-top.

†**'grunyie.** Chiefly *Sc. Obs.* Also 6 **grounye, grunȝe**, 7 **grunȝie**, 8–9 **grunzie.** Variant of GROIN *sb.*[1], snout.

1500 DUNBAR *Flyting w. Kennedie* 123 Fy skolderit skyn, thou art bot skyre and skrumple; For he that rostit Lawarance had thy grunȝe. **1552** HULOET, Grystle or grounye of a Swyne, *probossis*. *c* **1560** A. SCOTT *Poems* (S.T.S.) xxxiv. 92 Ȝe grunche not at hir grunȝe. *a* **1605** MONTGOMERIE *Flyting w. Polwart* 88 Ȝour gryses grunȝie is gracelesse and gowked. **1792** BURNS *Willie's Wife* iv, Willie's wife is nae sae trig, She dights her grunzie wi' a hushion. **1892** AINSLIE *Pilgr. Land of Burns* 182 What..Should been a Christian face, I vow, It kyth'd the grunzie o' a Jew!

gruper, variant of GROUPER.

‖**gruppetto** (grup'pɛtto). *Mus.* Also **grupetto.** Pl. **gruppetti, gruppettos.** [It., dim. of *gruppo* turn.] = TURN *sb.* 5.

1842 J. F. WARNER *Univ. Dict. Mus. Terms* p. xliv/2 *Groppo*, *Gruppo*, *Gruppetto*.—These terms..are rather indefinitely employed in music to denote, in general, every species of musical ornament which consists of several small notes. **1950** G. B. SHAW *How to Become Mus. Critic* (1960) 330 Where we fall short is in *roulades*, shakes, and *gruppettos*, which many of our singers simply cannot sing at all. **1958** *Times* 3 Nov. 14/4 Small *grupetti* were sometimes taken in one bow, but mostly it was the single stroke to the single note. **1959** *Listener* 29 Jan. 228/1 She sang the Queen of Night's aria..her *gruppetti* being..'bang on'.

‖**'gruppo.** *Obs.* Also in anglicized form **grup(p.** [It.: see GROUP.] = GROUP 1, 1 b.

1674 PLAYFORD *Skill Mus.* I. (ed. 7) 38 Those excellent Graces and Ornaments..which we call Trills, Grupps. *Ibid.* 47 The Trill and the Grup. *Ibid.*, Gruppo or Double Relish. **1686** AGLIONBY *Painting Illustr.*, Expl. Terms, *Gruppo* is a Knot of Figures together, either in the middle or sides of a piece of Painting. Carache would not allow above three Gruppos..for any Piece. **1688** R. HOLME *Armoury* III. 159/2 Trills and Gruppo's.

†**'grure** (-y-). *Obs.* [OE. *gryre* (= OS. *gruri*), f. *grus-*, wk. root of *gréosan* to frighten.] Fright, terror; something frightful, fearful agony.

Beowulf (Z.) 1282 Wæs se gryre læssa. *c* **900** tr. *Bæda's Hist.* IV. xxvii[i]. (1890) 364 In ðæm tunum..þa ðe..oðrum on gryre wæron to neosienne. *a* **1000** *Cædmon's Exod.* 489 (Gr.) He maneȝum ȝesceod ȝyllende gryre. *a* **1225** *Leg. Kath.* 1968 Þat alle þat hit bihaldeð schulen grure habben. *c* **1230** *Hali Meid.* 47 Greden ai, & granen, iþe eche grure of helle. *a* **1240** *Lofsong* in *Cott. Hom.* 205 Ich bide þe..bi his deaðfule grure, and bi his blodie swote.

†**'grureful**, *a.* [f. prec. + -FUL.] Awful, terrible. Hence †**'grurefulliche** *adv.*, terribly.

a **1225** *Ancr. R.* 306 Þet grisliche word & grureful ouer alle, 'Ite maledicti in ignem eternum'. *Ibid.* 320 Hu grurefulliche God sulf þreateð þe þuruh Naum þe prophete. *a* **1240** *Wohunge* in *Cott. Hom.* 271 Hwuch of ham [deueles] swa is lest laðeliche and grureful?

†**gruse, 'grusel**, *v. Obs. rare*⁻¹. In 3 **gruselien.** [Cf. Du. *gruizen*, *gruizelen*, LG. *grüsen grüsseln*, Sc. dial. *gruse*, *gruzzle*, Eng. dial. *grouze*.] *trans.* To munch.

a **1225** *Ancr. R.* 428 Bitweonen mele ne gruselie [*MS. T.* gruse] ȝe nout nouðer frut, ne oðerhwat.

grush, grushie (grʌʃ, 'grʌʃɪ), *a. Sc.* Healthy, thriving.

1786 BURNS *Twa Dogs* 112 The dearest comfort o' their lives, Their grushie weans an' faithfu' wives. **1811** A. SCOTT *Poems* 91 (Jam.) An' treads the vale o' humble life Wi' five grush bairnies an' a wife. **1879** R. ADAMSON *Lays Leisure Hours* 89 Grushy growing weeds.

grush (grʌʃ), *v. Obs.* exc. *arch.* Also 5 **gross(h)e, grusshe**, 9 **gruss.** [variant of CRUSH.] *trans.* To

crush; †to make a deep wound in; to gash. Also †*intr.* for *refl.* To crumble; so **'grushing** *ppl. a.*
c1400 *Destr. Troy* 9482 He..Gird þurgh þe gret vayne, grusshet the necke. c1420 *Pallad. on Husb.* I. 59 Al chalk or grauel grosshyng in thyn honde. *Ibid.* 357 Grossing grauel finest wol be fonde [L. *quæ compressa manu edit stridores*]. 1819 W. Tennant *Papistry Storm'd* (1827) 173 To gruss him down intill a graff. 1871 Waddell *Scot. Ps.* lviii. 6 Grush the lang teeth o' the lyouns, O Lord.

grusle, obs. form of GRISTLE.

†**'grusnen**, *v. Obs. rare*$^{-1}$. [f. **grus-*; see GRURE.] *intr.* To cry out with fright.
c1250 *Gen. & Ex.* 481 Caim unwarde it [arwe] underfeng, Grusnede, and strekede, and starf wið-ðan.

grusome, obs. form of GRUESOME.

gruss, variant of GRUSH *v.*

grustlye, obs. form of GRISTLY.

†**grutch**, *sb. Obs.* [f. GRUTCH *v.*]
1. Complaint; = GRUDGE *sb.* 1.
c1400 *Beryn* 2408 I wold have..outid all yeur chaffare without[en] gruch or groun. c1460 Fortescue *Abs. & Lim. Mon.* xx. (1885) 157 They that opteyne nat that they desire shal have thanne litel coloure of grucche, considryng that they lak it by the discrecioun of þe kynges counseil. 1553 *Primer, Prayer in Adversity* V ij b, That I maye without murmur or grutch paciently beare this thy fatherly chastisement. 1556 Abp. Parker *Ps.* xxxix, At last I spake wyth murmuryng grutch.
2. = GRUDGE *sb.* 2.
1509 Barclay *Shyp of Folys* (1570) 62 Sinne alway threatneth vnto the doer payne And grutche of conscience.
3. = GRUDGE *sb.* 3.
1540-1 Elyot *Image Gov.* 47 Quenchyng the good opinion and loue that all men had toward me, and changeyng it to a fervent grutche and hatred. 1637 G. Daniel *Genius this Isle* 542 Would you Looke Vpon that Splendour with or frowne or grutch? 1663 Butler *Hud.* I. i. 357 Foes..To whom he bore so fell a grutch He ne'er gave quarter to any such. a1687 Cotton *Poet. Wks.* (1765) 8 So hard it is, where an old Grutch is, To get out of a Woman's Clutches. 1898 A. Nicholas *Idyl of Wabash* 36 There'd been some old grutch atween him an' Bill.
4. The condition of a thing which is refused or given grudgingly; want, lack, scarcity. *rare*$^{-1}$.
1815 *Hist. J. Decastro & bro. Bat* II. 197 Too much is worse than grutch: it is the frugal use of pleasure that gives us pleasure.

grutch (grʌtʃ), *v. Obs.* exc. *dial.* or *arch.* Forms: α. 3 **gruce**, 3-4 **gruchche**, 3-5 **grucche**, 3-6 **gruche**, 4 **grochi**, **grouche**, **grochge**, 4-5 **groche**, **grocche**, **grochche**, 4-6 **grutche**, 5 **gruch**, **grosschen**, 5-6 **grotche**, **grudche**, 6 *Sc.* **gruich**, 6- **grutch**. *Pa. t.* 3-6 **gruched**, etc., 6- **grutched**; also 4 **gruȝt**, 5 **growht**. β. 4 **grychche**, 5 **gre(t)che**, **grychge**, **gricche**, **gryche**. *Pa. t.* 4-5 **gricched**, etc.; also 5 **griht**, **gright**. γ. 5 **gurche**. (See also GRUDGE *v.*) [a. OF. *groucier, groucher, grocier, grocher, grucer, gruchier*, to murmur, grumble (whence med.L. *groussare*), of unknown origin.]
1. *intr.* To murmur, complain, repine; = GRUDGE *v.* 1.
α. a1225 *Ancr. R.* 186 Ne wrekie ȝe nout ou seluen, ne ne grucche ȝe nout. c1250 *Kent. Serm.* in *O.E. Misc.* 34 Hedden here euerich ane peny: þo wenden hi more habbe: þo gruchchede hi a-menges hem. 1303 R. Brunne *Handl. Synne* 1084 Ȝyf..þou wylt nat bleþly þarto By þy wyl, but euer gruchande [F. *groinant*]. 1340 *Ayenb.* 67 He beginþ to grochi betuene his teþ and grunny. 1387 Trevisa *Higden* (Rolls) IV. 137 He made places of socour for pore men, forto sese þe peple þat grucched [*v. rr.* grochgede, grutchyde] for þe oponynge of þe sepulcre. 1389 in *Eng. Gilds* (1870) 91 If he grucche, he shal pay ij^d. c1400 Maundev. (1839) v. 57 The People grucched, for thei fownden no thing to drynke. a1420 Hoccleve *De Reg. Princ.* 1060 Shuldest thow grucche and thyne annoye bewepe? c1460 *Emare* 669 And ever she lay and growht. c1460 *Towneley Myst.* xix. 104 Whethere that he will saue or spyll, I shall not gruch in no degre. 1531 *Dial. Laws Eng.* II. xlviii. (1638) 152 The appellants would grutch and think them [the Judges] partiall. 1587 Turberv. *Trag. T.* (1837) 94 Rough handed Surgeons make the patient grutch. 1590 Spenser *F.Q.* II. ii. 34 Both did at their second sister grutch And inly grieve. 1624 Quarles *Job* VIII. med. xlvi, If we receive for one halfe day, as much As they that toyle till Evening, shall we grutch? 1647 Crashaw *Music's Duel* 91 They seem to grutch And murmur in a buzzing din. 1679 Penn *Addr. Prot.* II. iii. (1692) 100 To be Stewards of our External Substance for the Good of Mankind..not Grutching.
β. ?a1400 *Morte Arth.* 2557 Syr Gawayne was grevede, and grychgide [*printed* grythgide] fulle sore. c1450 tr. *De Imitatione* I. ix. 10 þei haue peyne, & sone & liȝtly gretchin [*v.r.* grucchcth].
b. Const. *against, with; of, at.*
α. a1240 *Wohunge* in *Cott. Hom.* 275 Aȝaines al þe woh and te schame þat tu þoledest.. neauer ne opnedes ti muð to grucchen aȝaines. 1303 R. Brunne *Handl. Synne* 3493 Hyt ys grete pryde Grucchyng wyþ God. c1380 Wyclif *Serm.* Sel. Wks. I. 7 His peple shal be saved, algif preestis grutchen þere agen. 1382 —— *John* vi. 41 Jewis grucchiden of him, for he hadde seyd, I am breed that cam doun fro heuene. 1390 Gower *Conf.* I. 84, I grucche sore Of some thinges that she doth. 1432 *Paston Lett.* No. 18 I. 33 The whiche..shul causen him, more and more to grucche with chastising. 1531 Elyot *Gov.* I. iii, His gouernance..is to the people more tollerable, and they therwith the lasse grutch. 1548 Udall, etc. *Erasm. Par., Matt.* xxvi. 116 [They] murmured and grutched at the costes and expenses. 1549-62 Sternhold & H. *Ps.* cvi. 16 At Moses they did grutch. 1595 Hunnis *Joseph* 2 In all things that he saide or did against him sore they grutch. a1677 Barrow *Serm.* Wks. 1716 III. 33 Can we grutch at any kind of service..when the Son of God was put to the hardest tasks?
β. c1400 *Destr. Troy* 9367 Toax, the tore kyng..Gright with the gret & agayne stode. c1420 *Anturs of Arth.* xli, Gawayne greches [*Ireland MS.* grechut] þerwith, and gremed ful sare.
c. with *clause.*
c1380 Wyclif *Sel. Wks.* III. 359 Grutche we not þat many men þenken ful hevy wiþ þis sentence. a1637 B. Jonson *Underwoods, To Chas. I. & Q. Mary Epigr. Consol.*, Do not grutch That the Almighty's Will to you is such. 1655 Fuller *Ch. Hist.* v. v. §21 Grutching much, that K. Henry the substance, and more, that Cromwell, His shadow, should assume so high a Title to himself.
d. said of the conscience. (Cf. GRUDGE *v.* 5.)
1508 Fisher *7 Penit. Ps.* xxxviii. Wks. (1876) 59 The conscyence alwaye pryccheth and grutcheth ayenst synnes euyl commytted.
2. *trans.* To be reluctant to give or allow (something); to begrudge; = GRUDGE *v.* 2. (The quots. in brackets may be *intr.*)
[1340-70 *Alex. & Dind.* 770 Wheþur þei graunte hit or gruche þei greuen ȝou ofte. 1375 Barbour *Bruce* II. 123 Gyff his ȝhemar oucht gruchys [*ed.* 1616 grunches]. c1400 *Rom. Rose* 6465 If that prelats grucchen it.] c1418 *Pol. Poems* (Rolls) II. 246 What unkyndly gost Shuld greve that God grucchede nouȝt! 1513 Douglas *Æneis* III. vi. 77 The nedis nocht to gruich [*ed.* 1553 grudche], in tyme to cum, The gnawing of ȝour tabillis every crum. 1613 Wither *Abuses Stript* I. v. Juvenilia (1633) 34 Foes I have some, whose lives I do not grutch. 1672 Crowne *Chas. VIII.* v. Dram. Wks. 1873 I. 201 Grutch not the love thy widow to him bears. 1719 De Foe *Crusoe* I. ix. 150 Who grutches pains that have their deliverance in view?
absol. 13.. *E.E. Allit. P.* B. 810 Þay hym graunted to go & gruȝt no lenger.
b. with *infinitive object.*
c1375 *Sc. Leg. Saints, Cosme & Damyane* 107 Gyf þai gruchit to do sa. c1400 *Destr. Troy* 9315 If he gright with the grekes to graunt hom his helpe. c1440 *York Myst.* xxxii. 243 He grucchis noȝt to graunte his gilte. a1553 Udall *Royster D.* IV. v. (Arb.) 67 At my first sending to come ye neuer grutch. 1663 Butler *Hud.* I. iii. 219 Who would grutch to spend his Bloud in His Honour's Cause? a1677 Barrow *Serm.* (1687) I. xiii. 191 One would think, that a man of sense should grutch to lend his ears..to such putid stuff.
c. Const. *dat.* or *to.*
α. a1300 *Cursor M.* 13263 Þair heling groched he þam noght. 13.. *E.E. Allit. P.* B. 1347 Þay gruchen him his grace to gremen his hert. c1400 *Destr. Troy* 9956 Neuer the grete for to grutche..All his lust & his lykyng. 1546 Phaer *Bk. Childr.* (1553) A ij b, Why grutche they phisicke to come forth in Englishe. 1626 Middleton *Anyth. Quiet Life* IV. i. 130 The angry woman, methought, grutched us our victuals. 1677 Crowne *1st Pt. Destr. Jerusalem* Ded., I am sure they will not grutch you the few flowers that a poor poet brings to strew in your way. 1700 Congreve *Way of World* IV. ii, S'heart, an you grutch me your liquor, make a bill.
β. c1400 *Destr. Troy* 7072 Hit shalbe gricchit hym þat grace in his grete nede. ?a1500 *Chester Pl.* II. 392 Gright they bene that grace. *Ibid.* 397 Against mankinde..To whom grace cleane is gright.
absol. ?a1500 *Chester Pl.* (Shaks. Soc.) II. 6 Lose them [the asses] bringe them heither anon Yf anye man gryche you as you gone..Saye that I will ride therone.
3. *intr.* (app.) To be stinted. *rare*$^{-1}$.
c1530 *Interl. Beauties Women* A iv, But for ye shall not dispayr I assure you No labour nor dylygens in me shall gruch.
4. To make a jarring or grating sound.
1493 *Festivall* (W. de W. 1515) 70 b, They..grutched with theyr tethe for angre. 1509 Barclay *Shyp of Folys* (1570) 54 Still grutching like vnto the frogges sounde.

†**'grutcher.** *Obs.* [f. GRUTCH *v.* + -ER^1.] A murmurer, grumbler, complainer.
a1225 *Ancr. R.* 108 Heo is a grucchid [*MS. T.* grucchere], & ful itowen. 1382 Wyclif *Ecclus.* v. 17 To the priue gruchere..hate, and enemyte, and strife. —— *Jude* 16 Thes ben grucchers pleynynge. c1440 *Promp. Parv.* 217/2 Grutchare (*MS. K.* gruchar), *murmurator, murmuratrix.* 1483 *Cath. Angl.* 166/2 A Grucher (*MS. A.* Grochere), *murmurator, susurro.*

grutching ('grʌtʃɪŋ), *vbl. sb. Obs.* exc. *arch.* and *dial.* Forms: see GRUTCH *v.* [f. GRUTCH *v.* + -ING^1.] The action of the verb GRUTCH; murmuring, complaining; murmur, complaint, reluctance.
a1225 *Ancr. R.* 114 Grucchunge of bitter & of sur heorte is him surre & bitture. c1250 *Gen. & Ex.* 3332 Quad moyses,.. 'Ille gruching is ȝu for-bead'. 13.. *E.E. Allit. P.* C. 53 What grayþed me þe grychchyng bot grame more seche? 1340 *Ayenb.* 67 Of grochinge, þet is of him þet ne dar naȝt ansuerie. 1375 Barbour *Bruce* XVI. 9 He hym levit with a gruching. 1422 tr. *Secreta Secret., Priv. Priv.* 188 Amonestynge recewe thou gladly, and reprowynge wythout wrath or gurchynge. c1450 Lonelich *Merlin* 476 (Kölbing) Loke thow love..thy neyghbour with owten grochcheng. 1502 *Ord. Crysten Men* (W. de W. 1506) III. iii. 144 Wyth grutchynge they gyue an halfe peny or a peny unto Ihesu cryst. 1645 *Arraignm. Persecution* 4 It divideth their Powers one against another, and in themselves occasioneth murmurings, grutchings, and repinings. 1683 Tryon *Way to Health* 432 There being no Grutching, Envying or Contention amongst them. 1847 L. Hunt *Jar Honey* ii. 17 Scylla hath words, but words well-stored with grutching. 1892 Stevenson *Vailima Lett.* (1895) 241 The rest is grunting and grutching.
b. Of the conscience. *rare*$^{-1}$.
c1450 tr. *De Imitatione* I. xx. 25 Grucching of conscience & dispersion of herte.
†**c.** = GRUDGING *vbl. sb.* 2.
1621 B. Jonson *Gipsies Met.* (near end), Or from any Gowtes least grutching. Blesse the Sov'raigne, and his touching.

†**'grutching**, *ppl. a. Obs.* [f. GRUTCH *v.* + -ING^2.] Grumbling, complaining; reluctant.
a1225 *Ancr. R.* 108 (MS. C.) Ha is grucinde and dangerus, and arueð forto paiȝen. ?a1400 *Morte Arth.* 1076 He gapede, he groned faste, with grucchande latez. 1490 Caxton *How to die* 6 Many ther be that ben Impacyent & grutchynge. c1520 *Mayd Emlyn* 183 in Hazl. *E.P.P.* IV. 89 She answered hym With wordes grotchynge. 1712 *Spect.* No. 292 ¶4 A grutching uncommunicative Disposition.
Hence †**'grutchingly** *adv.*
1340 *Ayenb.* 193 More likeþ..to god an alfpeny þet a poure yefþ gledliche..þanne a riche man yeaue an hondred marc grochindeliche and mid zorȝe of herte. 1382 Wyclif *Ecclus.* xii. 19 Many thingus grucchendeli whistrende [Vulg. *multa susurrans*]. c1400 *Trojan War* II. 1641 in Horstm. *Barbour's Leg.* II. 275/1 Thaime grauntede wes Half gruchandly.

grutnol, variant of GROUTNOLL *Obs.*

gruve, -er, obs. and dial. ff. GROOVE, -ER.

gruwe, obs. form of GROW.

‖**Gruyère** (gruːˈjɛə(r); Fr. gryjɛr). [The name of a town in Switzerland, used *attrib.* in 'Gruyère cheese', also with omission of 'cheese'.] A cheese made of cows' milk, of firm consistence, containing numerous cavities.
[1775 T. Blaikie *Diary Scotch Gardener* 7 June (1931) 39 This is the Mountaine that furneshes a vast quantity of cheese to France under the name of fromage du Gruyere.] 1802 W. Dyott *Diary* 28 June (1907) Got excellent trout and good Gruyère cheese and also good wine. 1822 L. Simond *Trav. Switzerland* I. 22 Great quantities of cheese are made here in imitation of Gruyère cheese. 1826 Scott *Diary* 14 June in *Lockhart*, Bought a little bit of Gruyère cheese, instead of our dame's choke-dog concern. 1827 B. Disraeli *Vivian Grey* VI. vi. 204 The Prince..contented himself for the present with assisting his Gruyère with one of the very fine-looking cucumbers. 1845 Gresley *Frank's First Trip* 210 You must manage to eat gruyère with your dessert on this side the Channel. 1871 M. Collins *Mrq. & Merch.* III. iv. 130 Gruyère and celery. 1897 *Allbutt's Syst. Med.* III. 206 The brain tissue may contain cavities which have been aptly compared with those met with in Gruyère cheese.

gruyn, obs. form of GROIN *sb.*^{1}, snout.

gruze, variant of GROOSE *v. Sc.*, to shiver.

grw, grwge, obs. forms of GROW, GRUDGE.

†**gry**, *sb. Obs.* [a. L. *gry* (in Plautus *Most.* I. iii. 67 where recent edd. have γρῦ), a. Gr. γρῦ occurring in the phrase οὐδὲ γρῦ, and explained by the lexicographers as meaning (1) the grunt of a pig, (2) the dirt under the nail; hence the veriest trifle.] The smallest unit in Locke's proposed decimal system of linear measurement, being the tenth of a line, the hundredth of an inch, and the thousandth of a ('philosophical') foot.
[1623 W. Sclater *Tythes* 148 To this you ne gry; you loue to euade, not to answere.] 1679 Locke *Let. to Boyle* B.'s Wks. 1772 VI. 541 The longest..was three inches and nine grys long, and one inch seven lines in girt. 1690 —— *Hum. Underst.* IV. x. §10 A Globe, Cube, Cone, Prism, Cylinder, &c., whose Diameters are but 1000000th part of a Gry. 1813 E. S. Barrett *Heroine* (1815) To Rdr. xiv, The work has every fault which must convict it..but which will leave it not the ninety-ninth part of a gry the worse.

†**gry**, *v. Obs.*$^{-1}$ *intr.* ? To rage, roar.
1594 Carew *Tasso* ii. (1881) 34 The hearing this doth force the Tyrant gry, With threatfull sound.

gry-: see GRI-.

gryce, var. GRIS, fur, *Obs.*; var. GRICE^1.

grychche, gryche, -chge, obs. ff. GRUTCH *v.*

gryderne, -eyorn, etc., obs. ff. GRIDIRON.

†**grye**, *v. Obs. rare*$^{-1}$. [? related to GRUE *v.*^{1}] *intr.* ? To shudder, feel horror.
13.. *Gaw. & Gr. Knt.* 2370 So agreued for greme he gryed with-inne.

gryesy, variant of GRISY *a. Obs.*

gryethe, obs. variant of GRITH *Obs.* exc. *Hist.*

gryf, obs. form of GRAFF.

†**gryfely**, *a. Obs. rare.* [? Shortening of *grufeling*, GROVELING.] Prone, groveling.
a1450 *Le Morte Arth.* 2912 Ouer the sadylle downe he wente, And gryfely gronyd vpon the ground.

[**gryff.** Perh. a misprint for *grytt*, GRIT *sb.*^{3}
1608 Topsell *Serpents* 312 Tarentinus [saith] that the Sea-fish called Gryff, or Grample, doth greedily devour them [worms].]

gryffar(e, gryffe, obs. ff. GRAFFER, GRAFF.

gryft, obs. form of GRAFT *sb.*^{1}

gryght(e, obs. variant of GRITH *Obs.* exc. *Hist.*

grygynge, obs. form of GREKING, dawn.

gryht, obs. form of GRITH.

gryis, Sc. var. GRISE *v. Obs.*

gryking, obs. form of GREKING, dawn.

†**grylle.** *Obs. rare.* [ad. L. *gryllus* a cricket or grasshopper, a. Gr. γρύλλος.] A cricket.
1555 EDEN *Decades* 115 Baskets full of gressehoppers, grylles, crabbes or crefysshes..all well dryed and salted.

gryllotalpa (ˌgrɪləʊˈtælpə). Also 8 **grillatalpa.** [f. L. *gryllo-*, comb. f. of *gryllus* a cricket + *talpa* a mole.] The mole-cricket.
[**1706** PHILLIPS (ed. Kersey), *Gryllo-talpa.*] **1791** WOLCOT (P. Pindar) *Lousiad* III. 167 Bats shriek'd, and grillatalpas join'd the sound. **1815** *Hist. J. Decastro & bro. Bat* II. 325 His clothes were full of beetles, bats, lizards, gryllotalpas and scolopendras that crawled all over him.

gryn, obs. variant of GROIN *sb.*[1], snout.

grynd(e, obs. form of GRIND *v.*[1], GROIN *sb.*[2]

gryne, obs. form of GREEN, GROIN *sb.*[2]

grypanian (grɪˈpeɪnɪən), *a. Ornith.* [f. mod.L. *grypani-um (rostrum)*, a. Gr. γρυπάνιος bowed by age, f. γρυπός curved.] (See quot.)
1879 R. B. SHARPE *Brit. Mus. Catal. Birds* IV. 6 Bill notched or grypanian (Illiger), i.e. with the culmen nearly straight, bent at the end in an arched curve, acuminate, generally incised at the sides.

grype: see GRIPE.

grypesheye, variant of GRIPE'S EGG *Obs.*

†**gryph(e.** *Obs.* Also 6 **griph(e.** [A perversion of GRIPE, after L. *grȳphus*: see GRIFFIN.]
1. A griffin.
1398 TREVISA *Barth. De P.R.* XVI. lii. (1495) 571 Gryphes kepe this stone [Iaspis] as they done Smaragdus. *c* **1425** WYNTON *Cron.* I. x. 576 Gryphys [*v.r.* grypis] gret nerhande thaim ar And dragownys. **1579** TWYNE *Phisicke agst. Fort.* II. Ep. Ded. 154a, What strange..conflictes doth..desire of golde raise vp betweene the people Arimaspi and the Gryphes?
2. A vulture. Also *fig.*
1563-87 FOXE *A. & M.* (1596) 81/1 The griph with talen, the dog with his tooth. **1574** HELLOWES *Gueuara's Fam. Ep.* (1577) 197 They did eate a griphe in potage, and a Goose in pickle. **1584** R. SCOT *Discov. Witchcr.* XI. xiii. (1886) 162 Plinie reporteth that griphes flie alwaies to the place of slaughter. **1586** J. HOOKER *Girald. Irel.* in *Holinshed* II. 43/1 Argent three griphs or geires gules crowned gold: this griph or geire is a kind of an eagle.

gryphen, -in: see GRIFFIN[1].

gryphite (ˈgrɪfaɪt). *Min.* [ad. mod.L. *grȳphītes*, f. L. *grȳph-us*: see GRIFFIN + -ITE.] A fossil oyster-shell of the genus *Gryphæa.* (Cf. CROWSTONE.)
[**1753** CHAMBERS *Cycl. Supp.*, *Gryphites*, in natural history, the name of a very common fossile shell.] **1796** KIRWAN *Elem. Min.* (ed. 2) I. 81 It [Compact Limestone] frequently abounds with impressions or petrifactions of..pectinites, gryphites, mytulites, &c. **1811** PINKERTON *Petral.* I. 481 Gryphites..enter into the composition of the singular calcareous chain of the Pyrenees. **1872** W. S. SYMONDS *Rec. Rocks* ix. 327 A fine section of Lower Lias, with numerous gryphites and other characteristic fossils.
attrib. **1833** LYELL *Elem. Geol.* (1865) 415 The name of Gryphite limestone has sometimes been applied to the lias.

gryphon, -esque: see GRIFFIN, -ESQUE.

gryppeshey, variant of GRIPE'S EGG *Obs.*

grys, obs. var. GRICE[1]; var. GRIS *sb.* and *a.*

†ˈ**grysande**, *a. Sc. Obs.* [f. GRISE grey; cf. Of. *grisan*, med.L. *grisengus.*] Greyish.
a **1400** *Burgh Laws* xlii. (*Sc. Stat.* I.), þe clathing sall be of a hew grysande or quhyte [L. Vestimentum sit unius coloris scilicet grisii vel albi].

grysbok (ˈgraɪsbɒk). Also 9 **greisbok.** [ad. Du. *grijsbok*, f. *grijs* GREY + *bok* BUCK.] A small grey South African antelope (*Antilope melanotis*).
1786 SPARRMAN *Voy. Cape G.H.* II. 224 The grys-bok is of a greyish colour, with black ears, and a large black spot round the eyes. **1859** WOOD *Nat. Hist.* I. 643 The Grys-bok ..is a native of Southern Africa [etc.]. **1885** W. GRESWELL in *Macm. Mag.* Feb. 280/1 The little greisbok that has continually been nibbling his vines. **1897** *Encycl. Sport* I. 39 The Bushbucks..Grysbuck (*Nanotragus melanotis*) are small antelopes, which [etc.].

gryscysme, obs. form of GRÆCISM.

gryse, obs. var. GRECE, GRICE[1]; var. GRIS, GRISE *Obs.*

gryselich(e, -lyche, -ly(e, obs. ff. GRISLY.

gryselle, obs. form of GRIZZLE.

grysie, variant of GRISY *a. Obs.*

†ˈ**grysomyle, ˈgrysmolle.** *Obs.* [ad. OF. *grisomole*, also *crisomole*, *-mile*, ad. L. *chrȳsomēlum*, a. Gr. χρυσόμηλον, f. χρυσός gold + μῆλον apple.] Some gold-coloured fruit; the Greek name seems to mean either an apricot or a quince.
c **1485** *E.E. Misc.* (Warton Club) 70 The same graffyng may be understond of an grysmolle tre; that is better than a peche. *c* **1550** LLOYD *Treas. Health* (1585) C vij, Oyle of grysomyle taketh alwaye all impedimentes of the tonge.

grysope, variant of GRASSHOP *Obs.*

gryt, gryt-, Sc. ff. GREAT, GREAT-.

†**G-sol-re-ut.** *Mus. Obs.* The note G, sung to the syllable *sol*, *re*, or *ut*, according as it occurred in one or other of the hexachords to which it belonged; the upper G of the bass.
c **1325** *Song* in *Rel. Ant.* I. 292 Qwan ilke note til other lepes and makes hem a-sawt, That we calles a moyson in gesolreutȝ en hawt. *c* **1400** *Beryn* 1837 The hoost made an hidouse cry, in gesolreut the haut. **1596** *Pathw. to Mus.* A iv b, Note also that what is vnder G *sol re vt*, the same is vnder *Gamma-vt*, and what is aboue E *la mi*, the same is aboue ee *la.* **1609** DOULAND *Ornith. Microl.* 32 The tuning of the lesser Psalmes out of Csolfaut, and of the greater out of Gsolreut, is this. **1674** PLAYFORD *Skill Mus.* II. 112 For the Tuning of your Violin..the Bass or fourth string is called G sol re ut.

G string. 1. *Mus.* [G 2, STRING *sb.* 3.] (See quot. 1876.)
1831 T. L. PEACOCK in *Examiner* 12 June 374/1 The real magic is..the surpassing beauty of the effect. It is the same with his [*sc.* Paganini's] performance on the single string (the fourth, or G string), as with his performance on four. **1876** STAINER & BARRETT *Dict. Mus. Terms, G string*, the name of the first string on the double bass, the third on the violoncello, viola, and guitar, and the fourth on the violin. **1884** W. HOE *Dict. Fiddles* s.v. *Strings*, To preserve strings in good condition they should be kept in a tin box... This prevents the G string from shrinking in the heat of the summer. **1961** A. BAINES *Mus. Instruments* vi. 110 Originally all four strings were of gut, but early in the eighteenth century some players began to use a G string wound with silver or copper wire to improve its speaking properties. **1964** *Conc. Oxf. Dict. Mus.* 242/2 *G string* (violin), the lowest string, with a rich tone.
2. (Usu. hyphenated.) Also **gee-string. a.** A loin-cloth or breech-cloth, or the string supporting this, worn by American Indians, etc.
1878 J. H. BEADLE *Western Wilds* xvi. 249 Around each boy's waist is the tight 'geestring', from which a single strip of cloth runs between the limbs from front to back. **1885** *Rep. Indian Affairs* 179 The more industrious, intelligent, and independent [Indians]..dress partially in civilized clothing and invariably stick to the blanket, leggins, and geestring. **1891** *Harper's Mag.* Dec. 36/2 Some of the boys wore only 'G-strings' (as, for some reason, the breech-clout is commonly called on the prairie). **1907** S. E. WHITE *Arizona Nights* I. ix. 163 These Yuma Indians..were a peaceful, fine-looking lot, without a thing on but a gee-string. **1913** C. E. MULFORD *Coming of Cassidy* iv. 67 'It's a G-string an' a medicine-bag..' cried Dad from the harness-shop.
b. A similar piece of material worn by showgirls, strip-tease artists, etc.
1936 J. DOS PASSOS *Big Money* 488 One of the girls..wiggled her geestring at him. **1939** A. HUXLEY *After Many a Summer* I. xii. 168 It had happened, but quite unwillingly ..at Congo Club with nothing on but a G-string and some talcum powder. **1951** I. SHAW *Troubled Air* xxii. 377 What I know about politics you could put in a chorus girl's g-string and it wouldn't raise a lump. **1960** V. H. GIELGUD *To Bed at Noon* I. ix. 61 Her costume consisted of two tinsel stars and a G-string.

G-suit, g-suit (ˈdʒiːs(j)uːt). [f. *g* as a symbol for the acceleration due to gravity.] A garment designed to enable a person to withstand high accelerations; also, a similar garment used in surgical operations. Cf. ANTI-G *a.*
1945 *Aeroplane* 12 Jan. 44/2 Many experiments..have been conducted..and success has now been accomplished with the United States Berger G-suit, used by operational fighter pilots. **1952** A. COPPEL in Bleiler & Dikty *Best Sci. Fiction Stories* 4th Ser. (1955) 92 There was pain in the vice-like grip of the g-suit as it banged hard against his flesh. **1956** L. MALLAN *Men, Rockets & Space* 295 *G-suit*, a protective costume designed so that expanding air bladders increase pressure against the body as acceleration increases. **1956** *Jrnl. Amer. Med. Assoc.* 22 Sept. 275/2 The increased venous filling that the g-suit creates decreases the possibility of air embolism during operations with the patient in this position. **1962** J. GLENN et al. *Into Orbit* 244 *G suit* is a garment worn by pilots which contains inflatable bags positioned over various parts of the body. When the pilot is subjected to abnormally high G forces, the bags inflate automatically and prevent his blood from draining from one area of his body and pooling in another.

guaba, obs. form of GUAVA.

‖**guaca** (ˈgwɑːkə). [Quichua *huaca*; according to Tschudi *Kechua-Wb.* (1853) a vague term for any object of religious reverence.] A general term for objects connected with the religious worship of the Incas, as idols, temples, grave-mounds, etc.
1604 E. G[RIMSTONE] *D'Acosta's Hist. Indies* v. ii. 332 In this first kind of idolatry [worship of natural objects] they have exceeded in Peru, and they properly cal it *Guaca. Ibid.* v. v. 340 They shewd me..a little hill or great mount of sand, which was the chiefe Idoll or *Guaca* of the Antients. *Ibid.* v. xii. 359 In every Province of Peru, there was one principall *Guaca*, or house of adoration. **1613** PURCHAS *Pilgrimage* (1614) 878 This Guaca (so they called their Idols and Temples) was Generall to all the Indians of Peru. **1748** *Earthquake Peru* Pref. 8 In their Guaca's (the Indian Word for Sepulchre)..they always buried great quantities of Gold. **1777** ROBERTSON *Hist. Amer.* II. VII. 321 The Guacas, or mounds of earth, with which they covered the bodies of the dead.

‖**guacamole** (gwakaˈmole, gwɑːkəˈməʊlɪ). [Amer. Sp. *guacamole*, ad. Nahuatl *ahuacamolli*, f. *ahuacatl* avocado + *molli* sauce.] A Mexican dish made from avocado pears mixed with onions, tomatoes, chili peppers, and seasoning.
1920 W. POPENOE *Man. Tropical & Subtropical Fruits* ii. 23 In the tropics, the fruit is added to soups at the time of serving; mashed with onions and lemon juice to form the delectable *guacamole* of Cuba and Mexico. **1943** I. S. ROMBAUER *Joy of Cooking* (rev. ed.) 38/1 (*heading*) Avocado Spread (Guacamole). **1956** C. SPRY *Cook Bk.* i. 13 There is one particularly delicious cocktail savoury, Guacamole, which one serves in this country only when avocado pears can be bought inexpensively. **1966** *Listener* 4 Aug. 164/2 A piquant *guacamole*, a paste of avocado pear seasoned with tomatoes, onions, coriander, and..chilli peppers. **1969** E. STEWART *Heads* (1970) 18 A bowl of tortillas and chilli with guacamole. **1970** *Good Housek. Cooking for Company* III. 121 *Guacamole*, a Mexican dish that's good to start a meal.

‖**guacharo** (ˈgwɑːtʃərəʊ). [Sp. *guácharo*, of S. Amer. origin.] A nocturnal bird, *Steatornis caripensis*, of South America and Trinidad, valued for its oil; the oil-bird. Also *attrib.*
1830 W. COOLEY *Marit. & Inland Discov.* (1846) III. v. xvii. 252 The Guacharo is of the size of our fowls, of a dark bluish grey plumage, and resembling in its manners both the goat-sucker and the alpine crow. **1838** *Penny Cycl.* XI. 462/1 The use of the Guacharo oil is very antient. *Ibid.* 462/2 [Among the Indians] 'to go and join the Guacharoes' means to rejoin their fathers—in short, to die. **1893** NEWTON *Dict. Birds* 395 The hard, indigestible seeds swallowed by the Guacharo are found in quantities on the floor and the ledges of the caverns it frequents.

guacho, incorrect spelling of GAUCHO.

‖**guaco** (ˈgwɑːkəʊ). [Sp.-American.] **1.** The name given in tropical America to *Mikania Guaco*, *Aristolochia anguicida*, and other plants used as an antidote to snake-bites. Also, the medicinal substance obtained from the plant. Hence ˈ**guaconize** *v. trans.*, to treat with guaco.
1822-34 *Good's Study Med.* (ed. 4) III. 301 *note*, The guaco, a vegetable matter employed in South America as an antidote for the bite of serpents, has been strongly recommended as an antidote for hydrophobia. **1853** SEEMAN in *Hooker's Jrnl. Bot.* V. 76 Remarks on Guaco-plants... The natives informed him that they had 'guaconized' themselves, *i.e.* taken Guaco.
2. The Rocky Mountain bee plant, *Cleome serrulata*; also, the pigment made from it and used by the Pueblo Indians for decorating pottery. *U.S.*
1844 J. GREGG *Commerce Prairies* I. 278 This kind of crockery..is often fancifully painted with colored earths and the juice of a plant called *guaco*, which brightens by burning. **1936** *Burlington Mag.* Nov. 241/2 The use of 'guaco' to bind the glaze. **1956** A. O. SHEPARD *Ceramics for Archeologist* i. 33 Before firing, the paint, which is called *guaco*, is a dark olive-green.

guaco, var. HUACO.

guacum, obs. form of GUAIACUM.

guadalcazarite (gwɑːdəlˈkæzəraɪt). *Min.* [f. *Guadalcazar*, a town in Mexico, + -ITE. (It was named first *Guadalcazite* by Adam in 1869.)] Sulphide of mercury containing a little zinc.
1875 DANA *Min.* App. ii. 25 Guadalcazarite.

Guadalupe (ˌgwɑːdəˈluːp, ˌgwadaˈlupe). The name of a Mexican island off the coast of California, used *attrib.* in the names of plants found wild there, as **Guadalupe palm**, *Erythea edulis*, an ornamental palm bearing edible pulpy fruit.
1895 'F. FRANCESCHI' *Santa Barbara Exotic Flora* 11 More plentiful still and represented by large specimens, is Erythea Edulis, the Guadalupe Palm. **1969** T. H. EVERETT *Living Trees of World* 77/1 Among those [species] that exceed 20 feet in height [is]..the Guadalupe palm.

guag (gwæg). *Mining.* [Cornish; = Welsh *gwag* empty, cogn. w. L. *vacuus.*] A Cornish term for: An old working.
1778 PRYCE *Min. Cornub.* 322 Tinners holeing into a place which has been wrought before, call it 'Holeing in Guag'. **1860** *Eng. & For. Mining Gloss., Cornwall Terms, Guag*, a place that has been wrought before for tin.

guage, obs. form of GAGE, variant of GAUGE.

guaiac (ˈgwaɪæk). Also 7 **guajack, guaic,** 9 **guiac.** [ad. mod.L. GUAIAC-UM. Cf. F. *gaïac, gayac* (1532 Rabelais).] **a.** = GUAIACUM 2, 3.
1558 WARDE tr. *Alexis' Secr.* I. (1559) 5 The barke of Lignum Sanctum called Guaiac. **1604** E. G[RIMSTONE] *D'Acosta's Hist. Indies* IV. xxix. 288 The wood of Guayac, which they call *Lignum sanctum*, or Indian wood..is as heavie as yron. **1638** A. READ *Chirurg.* xi. 81 The decoction of guajack is good, used in stead of ordinarie drink. **1661** HICKERINGILL *Jamaica* 22 Medicinal Drugs, as..Gum Guaic. **1727-51** CHAMBERS *Cycl.* s.v., The wood guaiac is extremely hard and heavy. **1811** A. T. THOMSON *Lond. Disp.* (1818) 188 The wood of guaiacum is inodorous... The resin, or guaiac, has a fragrant odour, with scarcely any taste. **1875** H. C. WOOD *Therap.* (1879) 538 Guaiac, as an emmenagogue, is much less stimulating than cantharides.
b. *attrib.*, as *guaiac-resin*, *-tree*, *-wood*; **guaiac test**, a test for the absence of blood from the urine or fæces involving guaiac as a reagent.

1727–51 CHAMBERS *Cycl.* s.v., The guaiac-tree is of the height of our walnut-tree. **1767** MONRO in *Phil. Trans.* LVII. 504, I had some guaiac wood. **1838** *Penny Cycl.* XI. 463/2 Genuine guaiac-wood is destitute of smell, but if rubbed, and still more if set on fire, it evolves an agreeable aromatic odour. *Ibid.*, Guaiac resin exudes spontaneously, or in consequence of incisions. **1894** GOULD *Illustr. Dict. Med.* 1479/1 Guaiac-test. Blood. **1897** *Allbutt's Syst. Med.* IV. 730 A pastil containing 2 grs. of guaiac resin, &c. **1904** C. H. BEDFORD *Clin. Handbk. Urine Anal.* (ed. 2) 72 The Guaiac test is an exceedingly delicate one. **1953** J. C. TODD et al. *Clin. Diagnosis* (ed. 12) iv. 326 The benzidine test.. is similar to the guaiac test and has the same fallacies, but is distinctly more sensitive.

guaiacene ('gwaɪəsiːn). *Chem.* [f. GUAIAC(UM + -ENE. Cf. F. *gaïacène.*] A light colourless oil, obtained by the dry distillation of guaiacum resin.

1844 WATTS *Dict. Chem.* II. 945. **1886** in *Syd. Soc. Lex.*

guaiacic (gwaɪ'æsɪk), *a. Chem.* [f. GUAIAC(UM + -IC. Cf. F. *gaïacique.*] ***guaiacic acid***, $C_6H_8O_3$, a substance obtained by Thierry from guaiacum resin and wood (*Syd. Soc. Lex.*).

1884 HOBLYN *Dict. Med., Guaiacic acid.*

guaiacin ('gwaɪəsɪn). *Chem.* Also -ine. [f. GUAIAC(UM + -IN.] A non-nitrogenous vegetable principle discovered in the wood and bark of the *Guaiacum officinale*, having a sharp acrid taste.

An earlier word *guaiacine* occurs in Timme's *Quersitanus* I. xiii. kj b (1605), where 'salt of guaiacine' renders the L. *sal guaiacinus* (app. = GUAIACUM 2).

1830 LINDLEY *Nat. Syst. Bot.* 137 All the Guaiacums.. contain a particular matter often designated as resin.. but which is now considered a distinct substance, called Guaiacine. **1875** H. C. WOOD *Therap.* (1879) 423 Landerer asserts that he has found in it a peculiar crystallizable substance which he calls guaiacin.

guaiacol ('gwaɪəkɒl). *Chem.* [f. GUAIAC(UM + -OL.] A phenol contained in wood tar, and also obtained in the dry distillation of guaiacum resin.

1864 WATTS *Dict. Chem.* II. 946 *Guaiacol*,.. Produced, together with guaiacene and pyroguaiacin, by the dry distillation of guaiac resin. **1898** *Allbutt's Syst. Med.* V. 45 Among the tar derivatives [may be specially mentioned] creosote and guaiacol.

‖**guaiacum** ('gwaɪəkəm). Forms: 6 guaicum, guiacan, 6–7 guaiacan, 7 guacum, gwacum, gwakin, 7–8 guajacum, 6– guiacum, guaiacum. [mod.L., ad. Sp. *guayaco*, *guayacan*, of native Haytian origin.]

1. A genus of trees and shrubs (N.O. *Zygophyllaceæ*), native to the West Indies and the warmer parts of America; a tree of this genus, esp. *Guaiacum officinale* and *G. sanctum.*

1553 EDEN *Treat. Newe Ind.* (Arb.) 40 The wood of Guiacum, otherwyse called *Lignum Sanctum*, wherewith dyuerse diseases are healed by the order of the newe dyete. **1626** BACON *Sylva* §456 Some Hot Trees, as Turpentine, Mastick-Tree, Guaiacum, Iuniper, &c. **1712** tr. *Pomet's Hist. Drugs* I. 66 Guajacum.. is a Tree the Size of a common Walnut Tree. **1792** MAR. RIDDELL *Voy. Madeira* 90 The guiacum, or *lignum vitae*, is found here. The bark is white and gummy, the leaves winged, the blossoms of a beautiful violet colour, and the berries are used as bitters.

2. The hard and heavy brownish-green wood of *G. officinale* and *G. sanctum*, used in medicine; lignum vitæ.

1533 T. PAYNELL tr. *Hutten's De Morbo Gall.* vi. 11 Yet hath this woode Guaiacum alwayes bene there vsed. **1580** FRAMPTON tr. *Monardes* 10 b, The Guiacan that is called the wood of the Indias. **1671** SALMON *Syn. Med.* III. xxii. 423 The Oak; the salt expells Urine and gravel; the wood is of like use as Guajacum. **1744** BERKELEY *Siris* §47 Guaiacum, and other medicinal woods. **1876** ELLEN FREWER tr. *J. Verne's Adv. 3 Eng. & 3 Russians* iii. 32 They had laid in a good stock of ebony and guaiacum.

3. A resin obtained from the tree; also, the drug prepared from it. Also ***gum guaiacum.***

1553 in Lodge *Illustr. Brit. Hist.* (1791) I. xxii. 165 He told me that his Matie taketh Guaiacum, & is far better now than he was a xii dayes sins. **1605** B. JONSON *Volpone* II. i, Ne yet, of guacum one small stick, sir, Nor Raymond Lollies great elixir. **1636** DAVENANT *Witts* IV. i. Dram. Wks. 1872 II. 188 His Afflicted female.. feeds him with beds of guacum For his salad, and pulp of salsa for His bread. **1663** BOYLE *Usef. Exp. Nat. Philos.* II. App. 386 Some of our eminentist English Doctors.. have not scrupled of late years to use the strong and fetid chymical oyles of Amber and Guajacum. **1686** *Lond. Gaz.* No. 2186/1, 12 Thousand Quintals of Cakau of Caracas and Gwakin. **1741** *Compl. Family-Piece* I. i. 20 Take Gum-Guaiacum 1 Ounce. **1756** C. LUCAS *Ess. Waters* I. 47 Oils of guajacum, box, &c... are found heavier than water. **1813** J. THOMSON *Lect. Inflam.* 199 The guaiacum, sarsaparilla, [etc.].. have all been supposed to be useful in the cure of scrophula.

4. *attrib.*, as ***guaiacum-bark***, ***-lozenge***, ***-potion***, ***-resin***, ***-test***, ***-tree***, ***-wood.***

1596 BURROUGH *Meth. Phisick* (ed. 3) 375 The guaiacum potion is wont sometimes to worke that effect. **1605** TIMME *Quersit.* I. xiii. 65 The Boxe, the Oake, Guaiacan Tree, and such like. **1812** J. SMYTH *Pract. Customs* (1821) 40 Guiacum Bark. **1876** GROSS *Dis. Bladder* 31 The guaiacum test of Dr. Day. **1879** *St. George's Hosp. Rep.* IX. 599 Guaiacum lozenges.

guaiaretic (gwaɪə'rɛtɪk), *a. Chem.* [f. GUAIA(C + Gr. ῥητ-ίνη resin + -IC, after G. *guajakharzsäure* guaiac resin acid (H. Hlasiwetz 1861, in *Ann. d. Chem. und Pharm.* CXIX. 267).] ***guaiaretic acid***: a white compound, $C_{20}H_{24}O_4$, found in gum guaiacum. So **guai'aretate**, a salt of this acid.

1866 H. WATTS tr. *Gmelin's Hand-bk. Chem.* XVII. 243 Guaiaretic acid dissolves very slightly in cold or warm ammonia-water. **1892** *Photogr. Ann.* II. 73 Guaiaretic Acid, .. when freshly prepared, is soluble in alcohol, ether, [etc.]. *Ibid.*, Addition of small quantities of colouring matters.. to the guaiaretic acid or guaiaretates. **1964** *Jrnl. Chem. Soc.* 4011 Fractionation of the resin, by solvents, pyrolysis, etc., resulted in numerous products. Outstanding among these is the dihydric phenol, guaiaretic acid, readily isolated as its sparingly soluble sodium salt.

‖**guajira** (gwə'hɪərə). Also guajiro. [Cuban Sp.] The music of a Cuban peasant dance whose rhythm shifts from $\frac{6}{8}$ to $\frac{3}{4}$ time.

1923 *Blackw. Mag.* Nov. 711/1 A traveller could sing soleares and guajiras which I could accompany. **1947** A. EINSTEIN *Mus. Romantic Era* xvii. 331 Pieces characteristic of the South, with musical impulses from the slums of New Orleans, from Cuba and Brazil.. habaneras, tangos, *guajiros.* **1956** [see GUARACHA].

‖**guajiro** (gwə'hɪərəʊ). [Cuban-Sp. *guajiro* rustic, rural.] A Cuban agricultural worker.

1901 *U.S. Bur. of Statistics (Treasury Dept.) Monthly Summary of Commerce & Finance* Oct. 1352 The 'estancieros', as well as those who are engaged in stock raising, are known in the country under the name of 'guajiros'. **1937** E. HEMINGWAY *To have & have Not* III. x. 164 We want to end the slavery of the *guajiros*, you know, the peasants. **1961** *New Left Rev.* May–June 6/2 Consumer goods have been priced down drastically to place them within reach of the poorest *guajiro.* **1965** H. JOHNSON *Bay of Pigs* 18 From Fidel Castro to the humblest *guajiro* toiling in the fields, everyone talked about it.

guall, guam, obs. forms of GALL *v.*[1], YAM.

Guam (gwɑːm). [The name of the largest island of the Marianas.] Phr. ***to clear out, sail for Guam***: to sail 'for some port unknown'.

1881 *Times* 23 June 4/5 Having.. docked the steamer.. they cleared out 'for Guam'. **1898** *Westm. Gaz.* 7 Dec. 12/1 Sailed for Guam.

guan (gwɑːn). Also 8 quan, 9 guam. [prob. a native name.] One of a family or subfamily (*Pelopinæ*, Newton) of gallinaceous birds of South America, allied to the curassows.

1743 G. EDWARDS *Nat. Hist.* I. 13 The Quan or Guan, so called in the West Indies.. is a little bigger than a common Hen. **1827** O. W. ROBERTS *Centr. Amer.* 228 He fired at three guams, each as large as a turkey-cock. **1852** TH. ROSS *Humboldt's Trav.* II. xxiv. 444 Large birds, a guan (*pava de monte*) for instance, or a curassao (*alector*), when wounded in the thigh, die in two or three minutes. **1895** C. DIXON in *Fortn. Rev.* Apr. 645 The Cracidæ or curassows and guans, with fifty-three species.

guana ('gwɑːnə). Forms: 7 guiana, 7–9 guano, 8 gauna, gwana; also (*anglicized*) 7 gwane, gwayn, 8 guane. [variant of IGUANA.]

1. The IGUANA, a large arboreal lizard of the West Indies and South America.

1607 G. PERCY in Purchas *Pilgrims* (1625) IV. 1686 We also killed Guanas, in fashion of a Serpent, & speckled like a Toade vnder the belly. **1624** CAPT. SMITH *Virginia* III. i. 42 With a lothsome beast like a Crocodil, called a Gwayn.. we daily feasted. **1748** *Anson's Voy.* II. xi. 267 The animals we met with on shore [at Chequetan] were principally guanos, with which the country abounds, and which are by some reckoned delicious food. **1763** W. ROBINSON in W. Roberts *Nat. Hist. Florida* 100 [List of animals] The guane. **1792** MAR. RIDDELL *Voy. Madeira* 63 The guana is of various colours; but most commonly it is either brown, green, or blue. **1834** M. SCOTT *Cruise Midge* (1859) 287 Look at these two guanas chasing each other up that tree.

2. *Austral.*, *Anglo-Indian*, etc. Any large lizard, e.g. *Sphenodon punctatum* (*Hatteria punctata*) of New Zealand. Cf. GOANNA.

1802 G. BARRINGTON *Hist. N. S. Wales* viii. 285 Among other reptiles were found some brown guanoes. **1864** J. ROGERS *New Rush* I. 6 The shy Guana climbs a tree in fear. **1883** 'EHA' *Tribes on my Frontier* 36 The large Monitor which Europeans in India generally call an iguana, sometimes a guano!

guana, variant of GUANO.

‖**guanaco** (gwə'nɑːkəʊ). Also 7 guanco, guianaco, guinaco, 7–9 huanaco, 8 guanico, -aca, 9 -acho. [Quichua *huanaco*, *huanacu.*] A South American mammal, *Auchenia huanaco*, a kind of wild llama producing a reddish brown wool.

1604 E. G[RIMSTONE] *D'Acosta's Hist. Indies* I. xxi. 70 There are few of those beastes, which at Peru they call Guancos. *Ibid.* III. xx. 185 There are also of those beasts which they call Guanacos and Pacos, which are sheepe. **1670** NARBOROUGH *Jrnl.* in *Acc. Sev. Late Voy.* I. (1711) 98 There are many Ostriches in the plain Lands, and Guianacoes, which are the Beasts that bear the red Wool, whereof Hats are made in England. **1725** DE FOE *Voy. round World* (1840) 304 We.. saw guinacoes, or Peruvian sheep, as big as small mules. **1773** J. HAWKESWORTH *Voy.* I. 15 Guanicoes.. resemble our deer, but are much larger, the height of some not being less than thirteen hands. **1811** W. WALTON *Peruv. Sheep* 83 The Huanaco or Guanaco of the Spaniards.. is the largest of the two species of wild Peruvian sheep.

attrib. **1811** W. WALTON *Peruv. Sheep* 84 Horse hides and Guanaco skins. *Ibid.* 167 Guanaco wool is obtained from the wild animal of that name. **1865** LUBBOCK *Preh. Times* vii. (1869) 234 On the east coast, the natives.. have guanaco cloaks.

guanajuatite (gwɑːnə'hwɑːtaɪt). *Min.* [f. *Guanajuat-o*, the name of a city and state in central Mexico + -ITE[1]: see quot. 1877.] A bluish-grey selenide of bismuth, Bi_2Se_3, often containing a high proportion of sulphur.

1877 *Amer. Jrnl. Sci. & Arts* CXIII. 319 It seems, however, that the same mineral was at first named *guanajuatite* by Fernandez, who described it in full in the Guanajuato paper, 'La República' for July 13th, 1873. The latter name should consequently be accepted instead of the name frenzelite. **1967** *Mineral. Abstr.* XVIII. 281/2 The rare bismuth selenide, guanajuatite, is recorded associated with native gold.

guanamine ('gwænəmaɪn). *Chem.* Also -in. [f. GUAN-O + AMINE.] (See quot. 1881.)

1881 H. WATTS in *Nature* XXV. 148 The Guanamines.. a series of bases discovered by Nencki in 1874 and 1876, and formed by the action of heat on the guanidine salts of the fatty acids. **1899** CAGNEY tr. *R. von Jaksch's Clin. Diagnosis* vi. (ed. 4) 239 *note*, The characteristic pointed rhomboids of the guanamin of isobutyric acid.

guanase ('gwɑːneɪz, -s). *Biochem.* [a. G. *guanase* (Jones & Partridge 1904, in *Hoppe-Seyler's Zeitschr. f. physiol. Chem.* XLII. 347), f. GUAN(INE + -ASE.] An enzyme that hydrolyses guanine to xanthine and ammonia; guanine aminohydrolase, guanine deaminase.

1904 *Jrnl. Chem. Soc.* LXXXVI. I. 838 Fresh pancreas, when subjected to autolysis, does not yield adenine or guanine, and guanine which is added is transformed into xanthine within 3 days. The enzyme present in pancreas which induces this change is termed Guanase. **1967** *Biochem. Jrnl.* CIV. 634/1 Guanase (guanine aminohydrolase, EC 3.5.4.3) was of special interest as guanine is metabolically a precursor of xanthine and is thus indirectly a source of uric acid.

guanay ('gwɑːneɪ). [ad. Amer. Sp. *guanae*, prob. from Quechua.] The Peruvian cormorant, *Phalacrocorax bougainvillei.*

1860 *Times* 17 Dec. 7 The guanaes or cormorants and other allied tribes of birds which deposit guano must have existed thousands of years before man. **1925** R. C. MURPHY *Bird Islands of Peru* iv. 73 The range of the guanay is restricted to coastwise waters along the arid, western shores of South America. **1968** B. NELSON *Galapagos* xvi. 272 Guanays are heavy birds, none too well endowed for getting off the ground and landing again. **1971** *Islander* (Victoria, B.C.) 25 July 3/1 The guanay cormorant of South America has poured millions into the Peruvian economy.

Guanche ('gwɑːntʃeɪ). Also **Guancho.** [Sp.] One of the aboriginal inhabitants of the Canary Islands, who were absorbed by the Spanish on their conquest of the islands in the fifteenth century. Also, the language of the Guanches.

1599 T. NICOLS in Hakluyt *Voy.* (ed. 2) II. II. 5 These people were called Guanches, naturally they spake another language cleane contrary to the Canarians. **1797** *Encycl. Brit.* IV. 81/1 The inhabitants are chiefly Spaniards; though there are some of the first people remaining, whom they call Guanches, who are somewhat civilized by their intercourse with the Spaniards. **1814** H. M. WILLIAMS tr. *Humboldt's Trav.* I. 117 Santa Cruz, the Annaza of the Guanches, is a neat town, with a population of 8000 souls. **1876** *Encycl. Brit.* IV. 796/1 Many of the Guanches fell in opposing the Spanish invasion. **1884** tr. *De Candolle's Orig. Cultiv. Plants* 320 It is not known whether the Guanchos (the Berber people of the Canaries) knew the bean. **1890** J. G. FRAZER *Golden Bough* I. i. 19 In times of drought the Guanches of Teneriffe led their sheep to sacred ground. **1939** L. H. GRAY *Foundations of Lang.* 366 To these [dialects] must be added the *Guanche* of the Canary Islands, which became extinct in the seventeenth century.

guanethidine (gwə'nɛθɪdiːn). *Pharm.* [f. GUANIDINE, by insertion of ETH(YL.] A drug, 2-(octahydro-1-azocinyl)-ethyl guanidine, used to reduce blood pressure.

1959 *Jrnl. Amer. Med. Assoc.* 11 July 1265/1 The former has been given the generic name guanethidine by the manufacturer. **1959** *Lancet* 12 Dec. 1048/2 The hypotensive action of guanethidine appears to be due to selective blockade of the sympathetic nervous system. **1970** *Jrnl. Pharmacol. & Exper. Therap.* CLXXIII. 166/1 Reserpine and guanethidine prevented the glandular enlargement induced by papain or amputation.

guango ('gwæŋgəʊ). [a. Amer. Sp. *guango*, prob. from Quechua.] The Jamaican name for an ornamental tree, *Samanea saman*, of the family Leguminosæ, the pods of which are used as cattle fodder; also called *rain-tree* (s.v. RAIN *sb.*[1]) and SAMAN.

1886 E. D. M. HOOPER *Rep. Forests of Jamaica* 31 Guango, Pithecolobium (Inga) saman. **1920** FAWCETT & RENDLE *Flora of Jamaica* IV. 152 Guango... The wood is hard and ornamental, but cross-grained and difficult to saw. **1956** J. HEARNE *Stranger at Gate* vii. 55 Under the guango tree Tom and Joshua.. were saddling the ponies. **1963** ROBERTSON & GOODING *Bot. for Caribbean* xxiii. 183 Guango, Saman or Rain Tree—*Enterolobium saman.* This is a large, spreading tree, a native of Central and South America, naturalised or cultivated throughout the West Indies. **1971** H. D. CARBERRY in J. Figueroa *Caribbean Voices* I. 25 Also there are the days when the leaves fade from off guango trees.

guanidine ('gwænɪdɪn). *Chem.* Also -in. [Modified from GUANINE.] A strongly alkaline base, CN_3H_5, formed by the oxidation of guanin.

1864 WATTS *Dict. Chem.* II. 949 *Guanidine*... An organic base discovered and investigated by Strecker..It is produced..by the action of hypochlorous acid on guanine. **1899** CAGNEY tr. *R. von Jaksch's Clin. Diagnosis* vi. (ed. 4) 239 *note*, Carbonate of guanidin.

Hence **guani'dinic** *a.*, in ***carbo-guanidinic acid***.

1866 ODLING *Anim. Chem.* vi. 139 Biuret..may be regarded as carbo-guanidinic acid.

guanidino- (ˌgwɑːnɪ'diːnəʊ). *Chem.* Combining form of GUANIDINE. So ***guanidino acid, group***, etc.

1910 *Jrnl. Chem. Soc.* XCVIII. I. 825 The guanidino-butyric acid which crystallises out is purified by conversion into the hydrochloride. **1951** *Jrnl. Amer. Chem. Soc.* LXXXIII. 1870/1 The basic nature of the guanidino group indicated that it might also be a specific site for water absorption. **1952** E. H. RODD *Chem. Carbon Compounds* I. xiv. 932 Guanidino acids. This group includes the biologically important compounds creatine and arginine. **1965** P. A. S. SMITH *Chem. Open-Chain Org. Nitrogen Compounds* I. vi. 277 The prefix 'guanidino', for $H_2NC(=NH)NH-$, is used in cases where naming the substituent on guanidine would be awkward or would misplace the desired emphasis; e.g. guanidinoacetic acid, $H_2NC(=NH)NHCH_2COOH$.

guanido- ('gwɑːnɪdəʊ). *Chem.* = prec. So ***guanido group***.

1874 *Jrnl. Chem. Soc.* XXVII. 906 Guanido-dibenzoic acid. **1951** *Chem. Abstr.* XLV. 3433 (*heading*) Participation of the guanido group of arginine in the gelling of gelatin. **1967** CANTAROW & SCHEPARTZ *Biochem.* (ed. 4) xxi. 579 In the first reaction, the amidine group of arginine is transferred to glycine, forming guanidoacetate (glycocyamine) and ornithine.

guaniferous (gwə'nɪfərəs), *a.* [f. GUAN(O) + -(I)FEROUS.] Producing guano.

1844 *Jrnl. R. Agric. Soc.* V. I. 288 The guaniferous islands.

guanine ('gwɑːniːn). *Chem.* Formerly also -in. [f. GUAN(O + -INE.] A white amorphous substance obtained abundantly from guano, forming a constituent of the excrement of birds, and found in the liver, pancreas, and other parts of animals.

1850 FOWNES *Chem.* (ed. 3) 499 Guano also contains a peculiar substance called guanine, which closely corresponds with xanthic oxide. **1859** *New Syd. Soc. Year-bk.* 93 Scherer detected guanin in the pancreas of the ox. **1889** GEDDES & THOMSON *Evol. Sex* 23 Guanin, so abundant on the skin of fishes and some other animals. **1952** *New Biol.* XIII. 75 This same silvery sheen, due to the deposition of crystals of guanine in the skin, also appears in the rainbow trout of Michigan streams. **1966** *New Scientist* 24 Nov. 424/1 These are the four main genetic 'code letters' or bases adenine, guanine, thymine and cytosine.

guanize ('gwɑːnaɪz), *v.* [f. GUAN(O + -IZE.] *trans.* To treat with guano. Hence **'guanized** *ppl. a.*

1843 J. A. SMITH *Product. Farming* (ed. 2) 81 Comparing it with patches not guanised, the produce of the former may, without exaggeration, be stated to be double. *Ibid.* 83 The growth of the guanised rye was uniformly good.

guano ('gwɑːnəʊ, gjuː'ænəʊ), *sb.* Also 8–9 **guana**. [Sp. *guano*, S. Amer. Sp. *huano*, ad. Quichua *huanu* dung.]

1. A natural manure found in great abundance on some sea-coasts, esp. on the Chincha and other islands about Peru, consisting of the excrement of sea-fowl.

1604 E. G[RIMSTONE] *D'Acosta's Hist. Indies* IV. xxxvii. 311 They are heapes of dung of sea-fowle..They cal this dung Guano. **1669** EARL SANDWICH tr. *Barba's Art Metals* 16 It is called Guano (*i.e.* Dung), not because it is the Dung of Sea-fowls (as many would have it understood), but because of its admirable vertue in making ploughed ground fertile. **1726** SHELVOCKE *Voy. round World* (1757) 170 Cormorants dung, which the Spaniards call Guana. **1846** J. BAXTER *Libr. Pract. Agric.* (ed. 4) II. 346 The seed was drilled in with 2 cwt. guano, and a cart load of mould mixed together per acre. **1876** PAGE *Adv. Text-Bk. Geol.* xx. 430 The guano of the Pacific and other tropical islets, so valuable as manure.

fig. **1860** EMERSON *Cond. Life, Fate* Wks. (Bohn) II. 314 The German and Irish millions, like the Negro, have a great deal of guano in their destiny. **1870** 'OUIDA' *Held in Bondage* 16, I find soda-water and brandy the best guano for the cultivation of my intellect.

2. *transf.* Artificial manure, esp. that made from fish, called more fully ***fish-manure*** or ***fish-guano***.

1844 EMERSON *Lect., Yng. Amer.* Wks. (Bohn) II. 301 Agricultural chemistry..offering by means of a tea-spoonful of artificial guano, to turn a sandbank into corn. **1883** *Fisheries Exhib. Catal.* 202 Fertilizers in the preparation of which fish are used, including Menhaden guano, crude and ground, guano made from fish skins, and from fish heads and bones. **1888** *Pall Mall G.* 30 Aug. 2/2 Converting the bottle-nosed whale into patent guano.

3. A general name for sea-birds which produce guano. ? *Obs.* [This is in Sp. *guanae*, pl. *guanaes*: cf. GUANAY.]

1697 DAMPIER *Voy.* I. 101 [They] found multitudes of Guanoes, and Land-turtle or Tortoise, and named them the Gallapago's Islands. **1726** SHELVOCKE *Voy. round World* (1757) 190 Isles Lobos... Here are also plenty of Guanoes and carrion-crows. **1760–72** tr. *Juan & Ulloa's Voy.* (ed. 3) II. 104 Innumerable flights of birds with which all those islands abound and commonly called Guanoes..; many of them are indeed alcatraces, a kind of gull, though all comprehended under the generical name of Guanoes.

4. *attrib.*, as ***guano-island, -manure, -water***.

1844 *Catholic Weekly Instructor* 64 It is said, more than 300 vessels from Liverpool are engaged in the guano-manure trade. **1851** *Beck's Florist* 199 Guano-water improves wonderfully the colour of the flowers and the general health of the plants. **1858** *Cycl. Commerce* (ed. Homans) 899 The claim of the Peruvians to the exclusive possession of the guano islands.

Hence **'guano** *v. trans.*, to fertilize with guano. Also *fig.*

1847 DISRAELI *Tancred* II. ix, Lady Constance..having guanoed her mind by reading French novels, had a variety of conclusions on all social topics. **1856** OLMSTED *Slave States* 43 The ground is..again guanoed, two hundred weight to the acre. **1865** *Spectator* 18 Feb. 176 He announced that he intended to guano the public mind.

guano, variant of GUANA.

guanophore ('gwɑːnəfɔə(r)). *Zool.* [a. G. *guanophore* (W. J. Schmidt 1912, in *Zeitschr. f. wissenschaftl. Zool.* CI. 188), f. GUAN(INE + -O + -PHORE.] A chromatophore containing crystals of guanine, found in the skin of fishes and reptiles; cf. IRIDOCYTE, LEUCOPHORE.

1924 L. T. HOGBEN *Pigment. Effector Syst.* 24 In the skin of the Chameleon there are present, immediately below the epidermis, cells charged with yellow pigment..described as guanophores. **1960** FOX & VEVERS *Nature of Animal Colours* x. 150 When guanophores are overlain by a reddish carotenoid pigment a golden hue results. **1963** M. FINGERMAN *Control of Chromatophores* i. 4 Cells that contain guanine or guanine-like substances are called guanophores.

guanosine ('gwɑːnəsiːn). *Chem.* Formerly also -in. [ad. G. *guanosin* (Levene & Jacobs 1909, in *Ber. d. Deut. Chem. Ges.* XLII. 2470), f. GUANINE, by insertion of -OS(E[2].] A nucleoside, $C_{10}H_{13}N_5O_5$, which yields guanine and ribose on hydrolysis and is itself a hydrolysis product of ribonucleic acid.

1909 *Chem. Abstr.* III. 2562 Guaninepentoside, $C_{10}H_{13}O_5N_5.2H_2O$, termed 'guanosin' by the authors. **1968** A. WHITE et al. *Princ. Biochem.* (ed. 4) xlix. 1035 Guanosine is directly utilized for pteridine synthesis.

guanylic (gwɑː'nɪlɪk), *a.* *Chem.* [tr. G. *guanylsäure* guanylic acid (I. Bang 1898, in *Hoppe-Seyler's Zeitschr. f. physiol. Chem.* XXVI. 136), f. GUAN(INE + -YL + -IC.] ***guanylic acid***: a nucleotide, $C_{10}H_{14}N_5O_8P$, which is a constituent of ribonucleic acid; guanosine monophosphate.

1899 *Jrnl. Chem. Soc.* LXXVI. I. 180 Nine-tenths of the nitrogen originally present in guanylic acid is obtained, after hydrolysis, in the form of guanine. **1969** *Times* 25 Aug. 4/8 In the genetic code three guanylic acid units are..the code for glycine.

guar (gwɑː(r)). [a. Hindi *guar.*] **1.** An Indian plant, *Cyamopsis tetragonoloba* (*psoralioides*), of the family Leguminosæ, which tolerates drought and is grown as a vegetable, fodder crop, and green manure, and as a source of guar gum.

[**1832** W. CAREY *Roxburgh's Flora Indica* III. 317 Goor-chikurkai..is an annual esculent plant, much cultivated in the gardens of the natives on the coast of Coromandel.] **1882** DUTHIE & FULLER *Field & Garden Crops* II. 24 Guár is grown in these Provinces for two very different purposes, —as a vegetable for human consumption, and as a pulse for horses and cattle. **1908** G. WATT *Commercial Prod. India* 449 Gúar is specially suitable as a green manure or green fodder crop. **1948** *Chem. Industries* Jan. 60/3 As a consequence of the demand for a gum such as may be obtained from guar, General Mills undertook large scale agricultural production of the plant. **1965** R. R. AGARWAL *Soil Fertility in India* vii. 157 Cowpea (*Vigna catjang*), guar (*Cyamopsis psoralioides*)..are examples of other leguminous plants that are used as green manures.

2. Commercial guar gum.

1945 *Paper Mill News* 8 Dec. 52/1 It is intended to explore the possibilities of tub sizing with converted guar. **1952** J. P. CASEY *Pulp & Paper* I. vii. 406 When added dry at the beater, guar acts as a strong cementing agent which greatly increases the strength of the paper. **1966** *Kirk-Othmer Encycl. Chem. Technol.* (ed. 2) X. 750 Guar solutions can be gelled by the addition of small amounts of borax.

3. *attrib.*, as ***guar seed***; **guar flour**, commercial guar gum; **guar gum**, a fine greyish-white powder obtained by grinding the endosperm of guar seeds and used in the food, paper, and other industries; also, the polysaccharide that is the main constituent of this.

1945 *Sat. Even. Post* 30 June (Back cover), Science has found that guar seeds contain a gum which has..dozens of important uses. **1946** *Progress thru Research* (General Mills, Inc.) Fall 6/2 (*caption*) This experimental mill..produces guar flour for development research and commercial evaluation. **1950** *Jrnl. Amer. Chem. Soc.* LXXII. 4634/1 Guar gum extracted from the endosperm of guar seed is a galactomannan polysaccharide in which the ratio of D-mannose to D-galactose is 2:1. **1959** SMITH & MONTGOMERY *Chem. Plant Gums* xii. 325 The polysaccharide in guar flour, as the crude, powdered gum is sometimes called, contains 84 per cent of D-mannose and 16 per cent D-galactose... The crude guar gum..may contain 1 to 5 per cent protein. **1969** *Encycl. Polymer Sci. & Technol.* XI. 404 Guar seeds have been the source of large quantities of industrial gum.

‖**guara**[1] ('gwɑːrə). [mod.L., a. Tupi *guará*. *Guirá* in Tupi is simply = 'bird', but the description in quot. 1796 relates to the guara.]

An American bird, the Scarlet Ibis, *Eudocimus ruber*.

1678 RAY *Willughby's Ornith.* 296 The Brazilian Guara of Marggrave..is a Land and Water-fowl, of the bigness of the Spoon-bill..It feeds upon fish and flesh, water always added. **1688** R. HOLME *Armoury* II. 260/2 The Guara..It is of some Authors called an Indian Curlew. **1753** CHAMBERS *Cycl. Supp.*, *Guara*, in zoology, the name of a Brasilian bird, called by Clusius, *Numenius Indicus*, or the *Indian Curlew*.. It is all over of a fine gay red, only that the long-wing feathers are tipped with black at their extremities. [**1796** MORSE *Amer. Geog.* I. 745 The guira famous for often changing its colour, being first black, then ash-coloured, next white, afterwards scarlet, and last of all crimson.]

‖**guara**[2] ('gwɑːrə). Also aguara. [Tupi *jagoára* 'dog, ounce' (Dias); cf. JAGUAR.] A large-maned wild dog of S. America, *Canis jubatus*.

1884–5 *Stand. Nat. Hist.* (1888) V. 416 Largest and fiercest of the South American species is the Guara (*Canis jubatus*), which has a mane, and outwardly presents some resemblance to the hyena... The name of Aguara or Guara appears to be an imitation of its loud cry 'gou-a-a'.

‖**guaracha** (gwa'ratʃa). Also *erron.* **guaracia**. [Sp. (Velasquez *Sp. Dict.* 1878).] 'A lively Spanish dance in $\frac{3}{8}$ or $\frac{3}{4}$ time, usually accompanied on the guitar by the dancer himself' (Stainer & Barrett 1876). Also, the music to which it is danced.

1828 MOORE *Say, what shall we dance?* i. 8 Shall we..To the light Bolero's measures move? Or choose the Guaracia's languishing lay? **1956** M. STEARNS *Story of Jazz* (1957) iii. 26 Of the native Cuban dances, the Habanera, Guajira, Punto, and Guaracha contain strong Spanish elements. **1958** E. BORNEMAN in P. Gammond *Decca Bk. Jazz* xxi. 270 The music of the Machito band..boiled down to two types: (1) Afros, rumbas, guarachas, congas, sones and boleros, with jazz trumpets, jazz tenor and alto-saxophones improvising against the Cuban rhythms; (2) jazz numbers of the sort..written for Chick Webb. **1962** J. STEWART tr. *Cousseau's Death Miss Cunningham* I. 58 To the raucous sound of a *guaracha*, Indian women..were dancing.

guarache, var. HUARACHE.

‖**guarana** (gwə'rɑːnə). [Tupi *guaraná.*] A Brazilian shrub, *Paullinia sorbilis*; a paste prepared from the seeds of this shrub, which is used for food and medicine. Also ***guarana-bread, -paste***.

1838 T. THOMSON *Chem. Org. Bodies* 291 Guaranina. This substance was discovered by Theod. Martius, in the *guarana*. **1861** *New Syd. Soc. Year-bk.* 459 The author has employed guarana paste in numerous cases of hemicrania. **1876** HARLEY *Mat. Med.* (ed. 6) 707 Guarana. The seeds of this plant furnish the Guarana bread so highly esteemed by the natives of Brazil.

†**guarand**. *Obs.* Also 7 garand, -end. [? ad. F. *garant*: see GUARANTEE *sb.*] = GUARANTEE *sb.* 1.

1674 TEMPLE *Let. to King* 30 Nov., Wks. 1720 II. 316, I said, Your Majesty having been the Author and Guarand of the Peace at Aix..could with ill Grace propose any thing to France beyond those Terms. **1687** BURNET *Reply to Varillas* 86 He cites again Florimond for his Garand. **1702** *Lond. Gaz.* No. 3812/3 The King and the Cardinal Primate shall write to the Emperor, and the other Guarands of the Peace of Oliva.

Guarani ('gwɑːrəniː). Also **Guarany**. [Sp.]

1. One of the main divisions of Tupi-Guarani, a family of South American Indian languages; also, a speaker of one of these languages. Also *attrib.* or as *adj.* Cf. TUPI-GUARANI.

1797 *Encycl. Brit.* XIII. 730/1 The Guaranies resolved to quit their settlements in the neighbourhood of the Portuguese, and to remove into the province of Paraguay. **1840** *Penny Cycl.* XVII. 226/1 The Guaranis compose the bulk of the population [of Paraguay]. **1875** *Encycl. Brit.* I. 702/1 The supposition..that the Guarani tribes are the remnants of a once powerful and united people, is scarcely admissible. **1885** *Ibid.* XVIII. 244/2 The inhabitants of Paraguay are mainly Guaranis or halfbreeds with a strong proportion of Guarani blood. **1900** *Fortn. Rev.* Jan. 79 There the women speak nothing but the Guarany language, and the men use only Guarany in talking to them, whereas among themselves the men always speak Spanish. **1947** *Whitaker's Almanack* 939/1 Most of the inhabitants are bi-lingual, speaking Guarani (the language of the extinct tribe of Indian inhabitants at the time of the Spanish occupation) and Spanish. **1959** *Times* 1 June (Lat. Amer. Suppl.) p. ii/2 Guaraní is still the language of many people.

2. (With lower-case initial.) The currency unit of Paraguay, consisting of 100 centimos, introduced in 1943.

1943 *Economist* 6 Nov. 624/2 The guarani will replace the 'peso fuerte' at the rate of 1 guarani for 100 pesos. **1947** *Whitaker's Almanack* 939/1 From November 4, 1943, a new currency unit (*Guarani*, plural *Guaranies*) symbolised by a crossed G, replaced the *Peso Fuerte* at the rate of 1 *Guarani* = 100 *Pesos*, and 1·75 *Guaranies* = 1 Gold *Peso*.

guaranin (gwə'rɑːnɪn). *Chem.* Also 9 -ina, -ine. [f. GUARAN(A + -IN.] A crystalline principle contained in guarana, and regarded by some as identical with caffeine.

1838 [see GUARANA]. **1841** BRANDE *Chem.* 1230/2 Guaranin [obtained] from the fruit of the *Paullinia sorbilis*, by Martius. **1880** *Libr. Univ. Knowl.* (U.S.) VII. 134 The essential crystallizable principle is said to be identical with caffeine, but has received the name of guaranine.

guarantee (gærən'tiː), *sb.* Also 7 **garante**, 9 **guarrantee**. [The early form *garanté* (sense 1) is perh. a. Sp. *garante* = F. *garant*, OF. *guarant*, *warant* (whence WARRANT *sb.*). The later development *guarantee* (with which cf. *grandee* from Sp. *grande*) was subsequently misused for GUARANTY, being perh. taken as a semi-phonetic adoption of F. *garantie*; hence senses 2 and 3 below. Sense 4 should perh. be regarded as a distinct word; it may however be viewed as a perversion of the meaning of the word, produced by identifying the ending with -EE[1] of legal terms.]

1. A person or party that makes a guaranty or gives a security; a guaranteeing party.

1679 PENN *Addr. Prot.* II. v. (1692) 139 As if he..could be their Garanté, in t'other World, they become very insolicitous of any further search here. **1683** *Apol. Prot. France* v. 68 That promise, of which our King was the Garante. **1710** *Lond. Gaz.* No. 4713/1 The second complained of the Violation of the Treaty..of which..the King of Prussia was a Guarantee. *a* **1715** BURNET *Own Time* IV. (1724) 663 Pursuant to an article of the treaty of Nimeguen, of which the King of England was the guarantee. **1724** SWIFT *Drapier's Lett.* Wks. 1755 V. II. 92, I will not venture to be your guarantee. **1753** *Scots Mag.* Jan. 8/2 His allies should be guarantees. **1796** MORSE *Amer. Geog.* II. 63 They are the sole trustees, guarantees, and managers of the national bank. **1819** R. CHAPMAN *Jas. V*, 123 The emperor ..was guarantee of the treaty of marriage betwixt her and the elector. **1855** MILMAN *Lat. Chr.* XI. v. (1864) VI. 450 He even threatened the King of England with interdict, if, as guarantee of the treaty, he should enforce its forfeitures. **1860** WOOLSEY *Introd. Internat. Law* §105 (1875) 129 If he guarantees a debt, and the payment is refused, he is not bound to make it good; for in this, according to Vattel, lies the difference between a surety and a guarantee. **1871** BLACKIE *Four Phases* I. 151 He stood guarantee that I should remain and wait the result of the trial.

2. The act of guaranteeing or giving a security; = GUARANTY *sb.* 1.

1786 BURKE *Charges agst. W. Hastings* Wks. 1813 (4°) VI. 692 Taking occasion from a late application of Fyzoola Khân for the Company's guarantee. **1806** WELLINGTON in Owen *Wellesley's Desp.* (1877) p. civ, This very act of guarantee has always been considered important in India. **1832** HT. MARTINEAU *Ella of Gar.* vii. 88 The laird was willing to enter into the proposed guarantee. **1845** S. AUSTIN *Ranke's Hist. Ref.* III. 341 At length, having received sufficient guarantee, he assented. **1883** STEVENSON *Silverado Sq.* 17 This I relate as I heard it, without guarantee. **1886** *Law Times* LXXXII. 94/2 A material alleviation of the strictness with which contracts of guarantee are enforced.

3. Something given or existing as security, e.g. for fulfilment of an engagement or conditions; = GUARANTY *sb.* 3.

1832 LEWIS *Use & Ab. Pol. Terms* xi. 95 Good education is no guarantee. **1836** LONGF. in *Life* (1891) I. 227 Your love for literary labor is a sure guarantee of success. **1856** KANE *Arct. Expl.* II. viii. 90 This announcement was received as a guarantee of their personal safety. **1860** W. COLLINS *Wom. White* i. ix. 46 My situation in life was considered a guarantee. **1876** MOZLEY *Univ. Serm.* iv. 75 Our Lord anticipates the time when active zeal for Himself will be no guarantee. **1894** H. DRUMMOND *Ascent Man* 390 Sacred and happy homes..are the surest guarantees for the moral progress of a nation.

4. A person to whom a guaranty is given: the correlative of *guarantor*.

1853 J. BOUVIER *Law Dict. U.S.* (1856) s.v., The guarantee is entitled to receive payment, in the first place, from the debtor, and secondly, from the guarantor. **1875** POSTE *Gaius* III. Comm. (ed. 2) 403 Guarantors are relieved by the guarantee being compelled, if one is ready to pay the whole, to sell him the debt of the others.

5. *attrib.*: **guarantee fund**, a sum of money pledged as a contingent indemnity for future loss; **guarantee society** (see quot. 1858).

1844 H. H. WILSON *Brit. India* III. 508 The President of the Board announced to the Court, their consent to extend the amount of the Guarantee Fund to two millions. **1858** SIMMONDS *Dict. Trade, Guarantee Societies*, certain joint-stock companies, which, upon payment of an agreed premium, guarantee to the employer the honesty of a person employed, or, at least, undertake to make good any defalcations in his accounts. **1879** MCCARTHY *Own Times* II. xxi. 107 A guarantee fund of two hundred thousand pounds was very soon obtained. **1891** *Pall Mall G.* 14 Oct. 7/1 The guarantee arrangement made with certain of the Australasian colonies for testing the effect of a 4*s.* rate to Australia. **1897** *Westm. Gaz.* 21 April 7/3 He has decided to give up the country [*sc.* hunting it] unless a guarantee subscription of £2,000 a year is forthcoming.

Hence **guaran'teeship**.

1715 M. DAVIES *Athen. Brit.* I. 227 Its Catholick Union scarce ever going any further than the Politick Point of Tolerating one another under the Papal Guaranteeship.

guarantee (gærən'tiː), *v.* [f. GUARANTEE *sb.*]

1. *trans.* To be a guarantee, warrant, or surety for; *spec.* to undertake with respect to (a contract, the performance of a legal act, etc.) that it shall be duly carried out; to make oneself responsible for the genuineness of (an article); *hence*, to assure the existence or persistence of; to set on a secure basis.

1791 BURKE *Th. Fr. Affairs* Wks. 1802 IV. 22 Publick treaties made under the sanction, and some of them guaranteed by the Sovereign Powers of other nations. **18..** LD. BROUGHAM (Ogilvie), By the treaty of alliance she guaranteed the Polish constitution in a secret article. **1860** WOOLSEY *Introd. Internat. Law* §105 (1875) 128 Thus, the treaty of Teschen..which was guaranteed by Russia, renewed the treaties of Westphalia. **1860** [see GUARANTEE *sb.* 1]. **1865** KINGSLEY *Herew.* xvii, If he would but guarantee the Danish laws..to all north of the Watling street. **1868** FREEMAN *Norm. Conq.* (1876) II. ix. 432 It is a more difficult question whether Harold's succession was at all guaranteed. **1874** SAYCE *Compar. Philol.* i. 55 Written languages guarantee a systematic pronunciation. **1876** L. STEPHEN *Eng. Thought 18th C.* I. 17 The intellectual activity of the acuter intellects, however feeble may be its immediate influence, is the great force which stimulates and guarantees every advance of the race.

b. with *inf.* or *obj. clause*: To engage to do something; to warrant or ensure that something will happen or has happened.

1820 KEATS *Lamia* I. 339 Her beauty..while it smote, still guaranteed to save. **1858** J. B. NORTON *Topics* 153, I will undertake to guarantee, that a mass of oppression and injustice..has been wrought under colour of these Acts. **1862** STANLEY *Jew. Ch.* (1877) I. v. 107 Here is a case of that precision which guarantees to us that the spot was once well known. **1884** PAE *Eustace* 84 I'll guarantee that he'll never return to Bengurry.

2. To secure the possession of (something) *to* a person, etc.

1838 PRESCOTT *Ferd. & Is.* I. ii. I. 162 Eager to anticipate the possession of Navarre, which had been guaranteed to them on their father's decease. **1845** S. AUSTIN *Ranke's Hist. Ref.* III. 553 Liberty to follow the Confession of Augsburg..was guaranteed to the city for its six parish churches. **1860** MOTLEY *Netherl.* (1868) I. iii. 71 In that case he promised..to guarantee to the Prince the earldoms of Holland and Zeeland. **1899** FINDLAY in *Expositor* Feb. 87 Christ guarantees to the faith of His brethren..a true quittance and defence from sin.

3. To secure (a person or thing) *against* or *from* (risk, injury, etc.); to secure *in* (the possession of anything).

1804 WELLESLEY in Owen *Desp.* (1877) 451 The British Government was pledged..to guarantee them against all exactions. **1820** A. RANKEN *Hist. France* VIII. i. §1. 25 The protestant states were now acknowledged and guaranteed in their full rights and privileges. **1832** HT. MARTINEAU *Ella of Gar.* vii. 88 Angus was strongly disposed to make the attempt, if he could be guaranteed from loss. **1859** MILL *Liberty* i. 9 On condition of being guaranteed more or less efficaciously against his tyranny.

absol. **1823** T. MOORE *Mem.* (1853) IV. 62 He could not guarantee against the folly of people in prosecuting.

Hence **guaran'teed**, **guaran'teeing** *ppl. adjs.*

1876 *Daily News* 3 Nov. 7/5 The mighty shield of guaranteeing Europe will defend our territorial integrity and our national rights. **1882** *Macm. Mag.* XLVI. 256, I vote the abolition of the guarantees and of the guaranteed. **1892** *Labour Commission* Gloss., *Guaranteed men*, men employed by a contractor, and having regular wages. **1895** A. J. WILSON *Gloss. Terms Stock Exch.*, *Guaranteed stocks*, Stocks the interest of which is guaranteed by a Government or company are thus described. **1931** *Economist* 24 Jan. 163/1 The remaining proposals involve the cancellation of the present agreements as to the guaranteed day and guaranteed week, overtime on a daily basis, [etc.]. **1939** *Monthly Labor Rev.* (U.S.) Apr. 914 Guaranteed annual wage encouraged by Fair Labor Standards Act. Interpretation..of the Fair Labor Standards Act, 1938.. has opened the way for growth of the policy of guaranteed annual wages in industry. **1941** ALLEY & HALL *Farmer in N.Z.* iv. 113 The Primary Produce Marketing Act 1936.. originated the principle of the guaranteed price, which may be summarised as the principle of a state guarantee of a definite price each season to dairy farmers for their butter and cheese and the taking over by the state of the responsibility for marketing these products overseas. **1958** *N.Z. News* 29 July 2/2 The Dairy Board flatly rejected the Government's proposed guaranteed price for butterfat which reduced the return to the farmer by 12 per cent. and upwards. **1964** *Lebende Sprachen* IX. 100/2 *Guaranteed bonds* are backed by the guaranty of another company. **1970** *Times* 11 Mar. 14/4 A memorandum of March, 1948, headed 'Guaranteed week', stated that where workmen regularly worked, say, a six-day week, they should be entitled to a six-day guarantee.

guarantor (gærən'tɔː(r)). [Formed after GUARANTEE, by substitution of -OR for the correlative -EE[1].] One who makes or gives a guaranty or security.

1853 J. BOUVIER *Law Dict. U.S.* (1856) s.v., A guarantor differs from a surety in this, that the former cannot be sued until a failure on the part of the principal, when sued; while the latter may be sued at the same time with the principal. **1862** *Sat. Rev.* XIII. 651/1 It is said that a regular army of 60,000 visitors a-day will relieve the guarantors; and already on the Derby Day 50,000 were in the building. **1874** MOTLEY *Barneveld* II. xvi. 206 He intended.. to maintain the Treaty of Truce of which his Majesty had been one of the guarantors. **1875** POSTE *Gaius* III. Comm. (ed. 2) 405 A surety or guarantor of a debt may require the creditor to proceed against the principal first. **1893** GLADSTONE *Sp. Ho. Com.* 13 Feb., I want to know..who will be the effective guarantor that this remainder will not also vanish?

Hence **guaran'torship**, the position or function of a guarantor.

1885 *Times* 13 June 13 Guarantorships to a large amount are already volunteered as a nucleus to the guarantee fund.

guaranty ('gærəntɪ), *sb.* Also 7 **garranty**, **-ie**, **guarranty**. [ad. AF. *guarantie* (also *warantie*, WARRANTY), f. *guarant*, *warant* (see WARRANT).]

1. The action or an act of securing, warranting, or guaranteeing; security, warranty; *spec.* a written undertaking made by a person (called the *guarantor*) to be answerable for the payment of a debt or the performance of an obligation by another person, who is in the first instance liable to such payment or obligation.

1592 *Expos. Terms Law* 103 Garrantie of charters is a writ, & it lyeth where any deede is made that comprehendeth a clause of warrantie..and if the tenant be impleaded by a stranger..then [etc.]. *Ibid.* 106 *Garrantie*, is when one is bound to an other which hath land, to warrant yᵉ land to him. **1665** TEMPLE *Let. to Dk. Ormond* Wks. 1731 II. 25 We have some Ground of Complaint, seeing the Emperor's Name among all the other Princes in the Guarranty of the Munster Peace. **1678** MARVELL *Growth Popery* Wks. 1875 IV. 266 His Majesty..continued to solicit other princes..to come into the guaranty of this treaty. **1681** LUTTRELL *Brief Rel.* (1857) I. 151 The league of guaranty is said to advance apace. **1682** *Ibid.* I. 166 The ratifications of the treaty of guaranty between the King of Sweden and the states generall are exchanged. **1725-6** BOLINGBROKE *Study Hist.* vii. (1752) 226 They consented to give Spain an act of guaranty for securing the execution of the treaty. **1753** HANWAY *Trav.* (1762) II. IX. ii. 217 This article concludes with a reciprocal guaranty of the provinces of Persia. **1792** *Anecd. W. Pitt* I. iv. 74 Our guaranty of the pragmatic sanction was an effect of that enmity. *a* **1850** CALHOUN *Wks.* I. 334 The guaranty of a republican form of government. **1860** MOTLEY *Netherl.* (1868) I. vi. 302 They are to ask assistance in men and money upon a mere taliter qualiter guaranty. **1860** WOOLSEY *Introd. Internat. Law* §105 (1875) 127 Treaties of guaranty..are especially accessory stipulations, sometimes incorporated in the main instrument, and sometimes appended to it, in which a third power promises to give aid to one of the treaty-making powers, in case certain specific rights—all or a part of those conveyed to him in the instrument—are violated by the other party. **1867** FREEMAN *Norm. Conq.* (1876) I. iii. 91 To give a guaranty for his good behaviour. **1874** GREEN *Short Hist.* ix. §10. 715 England alone showed herself true to her guaranty of the Austrian Succession. **1875** POSTE *Gaius* III. Comm. (ed. 2) 405 The most noticeable rule of English law respecting the contract of guaranty is that it must be in writing.

†**2.** A person who gives a guaranty (sense 1) or 'undertakes to see stipulations performed' (J.). *Obs.*

1684 *Scanderbeg Rediv.* vi. 152 Offering him very good Termes, for the performance of which he would be Guaranty. **1692** SOUTH *Serm.* (1697) I. 560 God..is the great Guaranty for the Peace, Order, and good Behaviour of Mankind.

3. Something which secures or guarantees the existence or persistence of a thing; a ground or basis of security.

1697 *Let. Necess. Land Force* 2 Yet the best Guaranty of a Peace, is a good Force to maintain it. **1754** RICHARDSON *Grandison* (1781) IV. vii. 67, I have no doubt of overcoming her unhappy Mother, by making her husband's interest a guaranty for her..good behaviour to her child. **1855** PRESCOTT *Philip II*, I. I. viii. 116 Four or five places of importance..were to be held as guaranties by the French king. **1867** FREEMAN *Norm. Conq.* (1876) I. iv. 151 Requiring baptism and nominal homage as guaranties for peace. **1871** *Ibid.* IV. xvii. 4 The consecration of William by the Northumbrian Primate might be looked on as some sort of guaranty..for the obedience of his province.

guaranty ('gærəntɪ), *v.* Now *rare*, superseded by GUARANTEE *v.* Also 8 **guarranty**. [f. the sb.]

1. *trans.* = GUARANTEE *v.* 1.

1753 *Scots Mag.* Jan. 8/2 Her allies should engage to guaranty the tranquillity of the north. **1775** JOHNSON *Tax. no Tyr.* 58 They talk of their pretended immunities guarrantied by the plighted faith of Government. **1779-81** —— *Fredk. Gt.* Wks. IV. 545 He was ready to guaranty all the German Dominions of the House of Austria. **1786** BURKE *W. Hastings* Wks. 1813 (4°) VI. 693 His..request of the Company's guarantying his treaty with the Vizier. **1857** R. TOMES *Amer. in Japan* xiii. 301 That friendly intercourse with the Japanese which was guarantied by the compact solemnly entered into between Japan and the United States. *a* **1861** MRS. BROWNING *Bianca* iii, God's Ever guaranties this Now. **1875** POSTE *Gaius* III. Comm. (ed. 2) 402 The fidejussor may be employed to guaranty any obligation.

2. = GUARANTEE *v.* 2.

1796 MORSE *Amer. Geog.* II. 289 The respective districts which they had allotted for and guarantied to each other.

3. = GUARANTEE *v.* 3. Also, to secure (a person) in the possession of something.

1732 *Gentl. Mag.* II. 945 The Establishment of an Indivisibility, and Primogeniture in Favour of the eldest Arch-dutchess, guaranty'd *contra quoscunque*. **1783** BURKE *Rep. Affairs India* Wks. 1813 (8°) XI. 265 The allowances made by the Company to the Presidents of Bengal were abundantly sufficient to guaranty them against any thing like a necessity for giving into that pernicious practice. **1786** —— *W. Hastings* ibid. XII. 94 Who..did not only guaranty him in the possession of what he then actually held, but engaged to restore all the other territories.

Hence '**guarantied** *ppl. a.*

1786 BURKE *W. Hastings* Wks. 1813 (4°) VI. 697 To exact a due observance of the guarantied treaty.

‖**guarapo** (gwa'rapo). [Peruvian.] A drink made from the fermented juice of the sugar-cane.

1760-72 tr. *Juan & Ulloa's Voy.* (ed. 3) I. 304 The guarapo..is nothing more than the juice of the cane, as it flows from the mill, and afterwards suffered to ferment. **1852** TH. ROSS *Humboldt's Trav.* I. xv. 483.

‖**guarauna** (gwə'raʊnə). [Guarani; app. a compound of GUARA.] A bird of the genus *Aramus*; the courlan or limpkin.

1678 RAY *Willughby's Ornith.* 292 The Brasilian Guarauna of Marggrave. **1688** R. HOLME *Armoury* II. 248/2 The Brisilian Guarauna. It hath a long bill a little inclining downwards..It is in form like the Woodcock. **1753** CHAMBERS *Cycl. Supp.*, *Guarauna*, in zoology, the name of a small Brasilian bird common in watery places, and of the size of our snipe. **1895** C. DIXON in *Fortn. Rev.* Apr. 645 Such peculiar forms as the hoazin..the two guaraunas.

guard (gɑːd), *sb.* Forms: 4–7 **garde**, 5–6 *Sc.* **gaird(e**, 6–7 **gard, guarde**, 6– **guard**. [a. or ad. F. *garde*, earlier also *guarde* (= It., Sp. *guarda*):—Rom. **guarda*, a. OTeut. **wardâ*. (Cf. WARD.)]

†**1. a.** Keeping, guardianship, custody, ward. ***to take guard***: to take care. *Obs.*

1426 LYDG. *De Guil. Pilgr.* 8793 She is a tresourere Off konnyng & of sciencys, And off all Experyencys That be commyttyd to hyr garde. *c* **1440** *Partonope* 768 Of the contree he taketh grete garde. **1579** TOMSON *Calvin's Serm. Tim.* 22/1 That we may walke as it were in the garde of our God, fearing nothing in the middest of all daungers. **1590** SHAKS. *Com. Err.* V. i. 149 Anon I wot not, by what strong escape He broke from those that had the guard of him. **1606** —— *Ant. & Cl.* V. ii. 67 For the Queene, Ile take her to my Guard. **1636** E. DACRES tr. *Machiavel's Disc. Livy* I. 23 To which of these two more safely may be intrusted the Guard of liberty. *a* **1711** KEN *Hymnarium* Poet. Wks. 1721 II. 101 O may the Angel to my Guard assign'd, Contract a sacred Friendship with my Mind.

†**b.** *spec.* in *Law. Obs.*

1607 COWEL *Interpr.* s.v. *Gard*, It..hath diuers applications..sometime to a writte touching wardshippe. Which writs are of three sorts: one called a right of guard or ward, in French, *droit de gard.* **1641** *Termes de la Ley* 173 *Gard* is when an Infant whose Ancestour held by Knights Service is in the ward or keeping of the Lord of whom those lands were holden. **1706** PHILLIPS (ed. Kersey), *Gard* or *Guard*..In a Law-sense Guardianship or Management of Children under Age or Idiots... *Writ of Gard or Ward*, a Writ relating to Guardianship or Wardship.

2. Protection, defence. *Obs.* or *arch.*

1576 FLEMING *Panopl. Epist.* 24 Al provinces and places of guard were shaken. **1590** SPENSER *F.Q.* III. ii. 21 Such was the glassy globe that Merlin made, And gave unto king Ryence for his gard, That never foes his kingdome might invade. **1614** BP. HALL *Recoll. Treat.* 58 When I see so strong a guard of providence over him. **1634** MILTON *Comus* 42, I was dispatcht for their defence, and guard. **1680** MORDEN *Geog. Rect.* (1685) 204 Turin..a place very important for the Guard of Italy and fortified with a strong Citadell. **1781** GIBBON *Decl. & F.* xvii. II. 45 The rivals who contended for the possession of the Roman world, had withdrawn the greatest part of their forces from the guard of the general frontier. **1814** CARY *Dante, Par.* VIII. 88 Ask the guard of braver arms. **1844** H. H. WILSON *Brit. India* II. 357 The Raja marched from Nagpur on the 3rd of May, under the guard of one wing of the 22nd Bengal N.I.

3. a. *Sword-exercise, Boxing*, etc. A posture of defence; hence, the weapons or arms in such a posture. ***at open guard***: in a position which leaves the swordsman open to attack.

1596 B. JONSON *Ev. Man in Hum.* I. iv, Twine your bodie more about, that you may fall to a more sweet, comely, gentlemanlike guard. **1602** SHAKS. *Ham.* IV. vii. 102 (2nd Qo. 1604) The Scrimures of their nation, He swore had neither motion, guard, nor eye, If you oppos'd them. **1649** FULLER *Just Man's Funeral* 7 This makes them lie at an open guard, not fencing. **1655** GURNALL *Chr. in Arm.* I. iv. (1669) 42/2 He is a weak Fencer that lays his Soul at open Guard to be stabbed and wounded with guilt, while he is lifting up his hands to save a broken head. **1692** SIR W. HOPE *Fencing-Master* (ed. 2) 4 A Guard is a posture which a Man putteth his body into for the better defending of himself from his Adversaries thrusts or blowes. **1802** C. JAMES *Milit. Dict.* s.v., The word *guard* is seldom applied among small swordsmen to any position but those of carte and tierce; the other motions of defence are stiled parades. *Ibid.* s.v. *Broadsword*, The principal guards with the broad sword are: The *inside guard* (similar to carte in fencing)..The *outside guard* (resembling tierce)..The *medium guard*, which is a position between the inside and outside guard..The *hanging guard* (similar to prime and seconde)..The *St. George's guard*, which protects the head. **1833** *Regul. Instr. Cavalry* I. 123 The Files engage on the 'Inside Guard', change to the 'Outside Guard'. *Ibid.* 126 It is good practice to put them through the 'Guards' and 'Points'. **1840** DICKENS *Old C. Shop* lvi, Mr. Swiveller performed..the broad-sword exercise with all the cuts and guards complete. **1897** *Encycl. Sport* I. 144 There are four chief guards to one or other of which the swordsman should constantly return after an interchange of blows, and these are known as Engaging Guards.

b. *Cricket.* The position in which the bat is held to defend the wicket; esp. in ***to give, take guard***.

1843 'WYKEHAMIST' *Pract. Hints Cricket* 4 Let the player first obtain guard..for the middle stump. **1868** Box *Theory & Pract. Cricket* 111 To prevent any unfair confusion to the batsman by allowing such [delivery] as would throw him off his given guard. **1877** —— *Eng. Game of Cricket* xxvi. 451 A batsman often applies to the umpire for guard, i.e. to know which stump or stumps his bat is defending.

4. a. The condition or fact of guarding, protecting, or standing on the defensive; watch; *esp.* in ***to keep guard***. Hence, the special service of watching performed by a soldier or sailor.

1596 SPENSER *F.Q.* VI. x. 43 When faire Pastorell Into this place was brought and kept with gard Of griesly theeves. **1601** SHAKS. *All's Well* III. v. 76 She is arm'd for him, and keepes her guard In honestest defence. **1602** —— *Ham.* I. i. 10 *Barn.* Haue you had quiet Guard? *Fran.* Not a Mouse stirring. **1625** BACON *Ess., Cunning* (Arb.) 441 Which serueth.. to keepe themselues more in Guard. **1640** tr. *Verdere's Rom. Rom.* I. 104 They boorded the Pagans ship all three together, leaving their Squires in guard of their bark. **1667** MILTON *P.L.* VI. 412 Michaël and his Angels..plac'd in Guard thir Watches round. **1706** PHILLIPS (ed. Kersey), *Guard*, or *Gard*,..in the Art of War the Duty performed by a Body of Men, to secure all with watchfulness against the Attempts or Surprizes of an Enemy. **1712** W. ROGERS *Voy.* 249 The Inhabitants kept Guard on their Walls. **1726** SHELVOCKE *Voy. round World* (1757) 197 One of the quarter-deck guns..being mounted at our guard, was fired at sun-set. **1833** HT. MARTINEAU *Loom & Lugger* I. v. 79 The eldest boy was directed to keep guard at the entrance of the closet. **1835** *Hoyle's Games* 336 (*Chess*) Play your men in guard of one another, so that if any be taken, the enemy may also be captured by that which guarded yours. **1867** SMYTH *Sailor's Word-bk.* s.v. *Guard-ship*, The officer of the guard is accountable to the admiral for all transactions on the water during his guard. **1876** T. HARDY *Ethelberta* (1890) 154 It was characteristic of Ethelberta's jealous motherly guard over her young sisters that [etc.].

†**b.** A post of observation. *Obs.*

c **1500** *Melusine* xxiv. 168–9 Thenne made the captayn fyre to be putte high vpon the garde for manere of token.. soone after fyre was made fro garde to garde, that knowleche was therof thrugh all the royalme.

5. a. on or **upon one's guard, on guard** (†formerly also ***upon one's*** or ***the guards, upon a guard***): in a position of defence, on the defensive; (*a*) with reference to fencing and sentry duty; hence (*b*) *generally*. ***to stand, be, lie upon one's guard***: to be watchful, cautious, or vigilant, to take care; so ***to put, set*** (a person) ***on*** (***his***) ***guard***. Const. *against, for*. [Cf. F. *sur ses gardes* and *en garde*.]

1577 *St. Aug. Manual* (Longm.) 42, I will..stand upon my gard, and with wakyng eyes will I sing in my hart. **1610** SHAKS. *Temp.* II. i. 321 'Tis best we stand vpon our guard. *a* **1635** NAUNTON *Fragm. Reg.* (Arb.) 29 Sussex was thought much the honester man, and far the better souldier: but he lay too open on his guard. **1647** N. BACON *Disc. Govt. Eng.* I. (1739) 202 Both or one of them were ever upon the guard, to keep out that which was without. **1653** HOLCROFT *Procopius* I. 23 He sent direction..if they heard that the Enemie was entred at any other part, not to succour, but to continue upon their guards. *a* **1674** CLARENDON *Hist. Reb.* xv. §80 The Soldiers which were upon the Guards in some out-Forts. **1683** D. A. *Art Converse* 108 In Disputes relating to Religion be upon your Guards. **1700** DRYDEN *Pal. & Arcite* II. 73 For this the wise are ever on their Guard. **1701** W. WOTTON *Hist. Rome* 327 The Intelligence ..set him upon his Guard. *a* **1704** R. L'ESTRANGE (J.), It is wisdom to keep ourselves upon a guard. **1712** POPE *Spect.* No. 408 ¶ 5 In like manner should the Reason be perpetually on its Guard against the Passions. **1809** ROLAND *Fencing* 1 On the Position of the Body for being on Guard. **1845** McCULLOCH *Taxation* Introd. (1852) 10 We must be on our guard against the abuse of this doctrine. **1875** JOWETT *Plato* (ed. 2) V. 67 No one can be on his guard against that of which he has no experience. **1888** BRYCE *Amer. Commw.* II. liii. 341 Every sensible man feels in himself the struggle between these two tendencies, and is on his guard not to yield wholly to either.

b. off one's guard: in or into a defenceless condition or a condition in which one is easily surprised by an attack.

1682 DRYDEN & LEE *Duke of Guise* I. iii, Or at the court among my enemies, To be, as I am here, quite off my guard, Would make me such another thing as Crillon. **1692** R. L'ESTRANGE *Fables* ccxxxv. 205 Temerity puts a Man off his Guard. **1777** WATSON *Philip II* (1839) 371 They had not been put entirely off their guard. **1856** READE *Never too Late to Mend* ii, Isaac Levi caught both faces off their guard. **1885** *Law Rep.* 29 Ch. Div. 797 The agent throws me off my guard..and I therefore do not employ an independent valuer.

†**c. out of (one's) guard** = *off* (*one's*) *guard*. *Obs.* [Cf. F. *hors de garde*.]

1601 SHAKS. *Twel. N.* I. v. 93 Looke you now, he's out of his gard already vnles you laugh and minister occasion to him, he is gag'd. **1685** DRYDEN *Thren. Augus.* 17 The thunder-clap..took us unprepared and out of guard.

6. †**a.** Caution, precaution (*obs.*). **b.** (with *pl.*) A precaution (now *rare*).

1597 SHAKS. *Lover's Compl.* 298 There my white stole of chastity I daft, Shooke off my sober gardes, and ciuill feares. **1625** BACON *Ess., Plantations* (Arb.) 534 Vse them iustly, and gratiously, with sufficient guard neuerthelesse. **1707** ATTERBURY *Vind. Doctr. Funeral Serm. T. Bennet* 28 Where ..they have express'd themselves with (at least) as few Guards and Restrictions as I have done. **1741** RICHARDSON *Pamela* (1883) I. 163 For the poor gentleman has no guard, no caution at all. **1769** BURKE *Late St. Nat.* Wks. 1842 I. 112 On what other idea are all our prohibitions, regulations, guards, penalties, and forfeitures, framed? **1790** —— *Fr. Rev.* 38 All this guard..serves to shew the spirit of caution which predominated in the national councils. **1875** SEARS *Serm. Chr. Life* 7 The guards, the warnings, the denunciations interposed throughout the old Bible.

7. a. One who keeps, protects, or defends; a protector, defender; *spec.* one of a guard (sense 9), a sentry, sentinel; a warder in a prison or other place of detention (chiefly *U.S.*). Also with preceding sb. denoting the object defended, as COASTGUARD, *telegraph guard*, etc.

1412 *Extracts Aberd. Reg.* (1844) I. 389 Ilke man duelland in the burgh..sal stand gaird, and [etc.]. **1474** CAXTON *Chesse* III. vii. 55b, The gardes and kepars of cytees ben signefied by the .vii. pawn which stondeth in the lyfte side to fore the knyght. **1483** —— *Gold. Leg.* 259 b/1 Saynt Iohan euangelist..as kepar and garde of so noble vyrgyn. **1590** SPENSER *F.Q.* I. iii. 43 Her faithfull gard remov'd, her hope dismaid, Her selfe a yielded pray to save or spill. **1591** SHAKS. *1 Hen. VI*, I. ii. 127 Fight till the last gaspe: Ile be your guard. **1598** BARRET *Theor. Warres* IV. ii. 104 He is to ..consult..with them touching the placing of the gards and Sentinels. **1606** SHAKS. *Tr. & Cr.* IV. iv. 130 Though the great bulke Achilles be thy guard. *a* **1715** BURNET *Own Time* IV. (1724) I. 660 Such as endeavoured to make their escape, and were seized, (for guards and secret agents were spread along the whole roads and frontier of France). **1780** COWPER *Table T.* 135 Guards, mechanically formed in ranks, Playing, at beat of drum, their martial pranks. **1819** SHELLEY *Cenci* V. ii. 20 Guards, there, Lead forth the prisoners. **1871** B. TAYLOR *Faust* (1875) I. xxv. 208 Thy cries will wake the guards, and they will seize thee! **1889** in *Cent. Dict.* **1907** J. LONDON *White Fang* 299 During Jim Hall's third term in prison he encountered a guard that was almost as great a beast as he. **1936** *S.P.E. Tract* XLV. 190 Why has American practice decided in favour of..guard rather than warder? **1952** *Manch. Guardian Weekly* 15 May 4 The guard knew they would do it and retreated. **1968** *Times* 11 Mar. 4/2 There were rumours that some of the men had threatened to decapitate a guard every 40 minutes.

b. The man who has the general charge and control of a stage coach or a railway train.

Originally an armed man charged with the duty of protecting a mail-coach against robbery; hence the designation.

1788 *Gentl. Mag.* LVIII. I. 558 A King's officer..stopped the mail-coach from Dover, and demanded of the guard the key of the trunk on which he sat. **1790** *Act 30 Geo. III.* c. 36 §5 If any Person..travelling as a Guard to any Stage Coach ..shall fire off the Arms he is entrusted with..otherwise than for the Defence of such Coach [he shall be fined 20*s.*]. **1792** THOS. PENNANT *Let. to a memb. Parlt.* 16 These guards shoot at dogs, hogs, sheep, and poultry, as they pass the road ..to the great terror and danger of the inhabitants. **1837** *Penny Cycl.* VII. 280/2 s.v. *Coach*, The guard is the servant of the Post-office. **1842** DICKENS *Amer. Notes* I. iv. 147 The conductor or check-taker, or guard..wears no uniform. **1863** G. MEREDITH *Let.* 27 Apr. (1970) I. 200 On Tuesday next, my little recovered rosy man will journey down, alone, by that train... The Guard will be bribed to keep eye on him. **1864** *Law Times Rep.* X. 719/2 A guard in the employ of the railway company. **1871** M. COLLINS *Mrq. & Merch.* I. iv. 141 Another guard came up the platform. **1893** PEEL *Spen Valley* 277 In the winter [*c* 1820] the guard carried a blunderbuss for protection in a box near him.

c. *Freemasonry.* See quots. (Cf. GUARDIAN 1 d.)

a **1843** R. CARLILE *Man. Freemasonry* I. 1 The next in order to the Master is the Senior Warden, then the Junior Warden, Senior Deacon, and Junior Deacon; lastly an Inner Guard and Tylers, or Door Keepers, the one inside, the other out. **1870** *Text-bk. Freemasonry* Introd. 7 The Inner Guard..and Tyler act as doorkeepers, the first-named acts as inside, and the last outside, armed with a drawn sword.

d. *U.S. Football.* Either of the two players (called the ***right*** and ***left guard*** respectively) that are stationed one on each side of the 'centre-rush'. Also in *Basketball*, either of the two players who are chiefly responsible for the marking of opposing forwards.

1897 *Encycl. Sport* I. 426 To the immediate right of the snap-back is the 'right-guard'..The 'left-guard', 'left-tackle', and 'left-end' complete the line on the other side. **1905** *Official Basket Ball Rules* 30 The position of the guard is the most difficult and unsatisfactory place in the team... He is expected to prevent his opponent from throwing a goal, and that without making a foul himself. **1929** *Encycl. Brit.* III. 182/2 The players are divided into three groups, forwards, centres and guards. **1961** J. S. SALAK *Dict. Amer. Sports* 207 *Guard*, a defensive player in basketball and football.

8. *pl.* (Freq. with capital initial.) The household troops of the English army, consisting of the FOOT-GUARDS, the HORSE-GUARDS (1 b), and the LIFE-GUARDS. Also applied, by extension, to the (orig. seven) regiments of heavy cavalry known as the Dragoon Guards (as distinguished from the Dragoons).

[**1661, 1675**, etc.: see FOOT-GUARDS, HORSE-GUARDS.] *a* **1674** CLARENDON *Hist. Reb.* xv. §68 The King [in 1656].. resolved to raise one regiment of guards, the command whereof he gave to the lord Wentworth. **1682** DRYDEN *Prol. to 'Loyal Brother'* 13 The Critic all our troops of friends discards: Just so the Whigg wou'd fain pull down the Guards. **1708** *Lond. Gaz.* No. 4421/7 He..was seen in Fleet-street with the Guards. **1806** J. S. SURR *Winter in London* (ed. 3) I. 18 An ensign in the guards. **1831** J. JEKYLL *Corr.* (1894) 266 Old parson Cholmondely, then in the Guards, ran away at the battle of Dettingen. **1863** KINGLAKE *Crimea* II. 351 The brigade of Guards will be destroyed; ought it not to fall back?

9. a. A body of persons, esp. soldiers (†also *occas.* ships) engaged to preserve a person or place from injury or attack, to act as an escort, or keep watch over prisoners: with reference to military sentry duty, freq. in phr. ***to mount, relieve*** (†***the***) ***guard***. (See also *advance guard* (ADVANCE *sb.* V), BODYGUARD, GRANDGUARD 2, *main guard*, REARGUARD, etc., and cf. CORPS-DE-GARDE, GARDE-DU-CORPS.) ***guard of honour***: a body of soldiers, sailors, policemen, etc. appointed to receive a royal or other person of distinction and to attend at state ceremonials. ***Yeomen of the Guard***: see YEOMAN.

1494 FABYAN *Chron.* V. lxxxi. 58 [He] founde to haue aboute the Kyngs parsone an hondreth Pictes, or, after some, Scottes, the whiche he ordeyned for a Garde for the Kynges parsone. **1532** *Fortescue's Abs. & Lim. Mon.* vi. (1714) 43 The secund Ordynarye charge, is the payment of the Wags and Fees of the Kyngs grete Officers, his Courts, his Counceil, his Garde, and other Servaunts. **1535** STEWART *Cron. Scot.* II. 118 Quhair ȝoung Constans that tyme faucht with his gaird, He brocht with him out of Armorica. **1568** GRAFTON *Chron.* II. 389 The king reteyned unto him a gard of Archers of Chesshire. **1596** DALRYMPLE tr. *Leslie's Hist. Scot.* VII. 36 King Chairlis VI...elected an(e) band of Scotis horsemen; quhilke commounlie was calit the Scotis gaird of armes. **1611** BIBLE *2 Kings* xxv. 20 Nebuzaradan captaine of the guard tooke these, and brought them to the king of Babylon. **1650** *Nicholas Papers* (Camden) 183 There was a Guard of 100 Souldiers sett to keepe all manner of persons whatsoever from coming to speake wth his Lo^{P}. **1671** [see BEEF-EATER 2]. **1687** A. LOVELL tr. *Thevenot's Trav.* I. 258 These Sangrack Beys mount the Guard by turns. **1687** MIEGE *Gt. Fr. Dict.* II. s.v., To come off from the Guard, *descendre la Garde.* **1691** LUTTRELL

Brief Rel. (1857) II. 294 Our fleet for the winter guard is to consist of 33 men of war. **1700** S. L. tr. *Fryke's Voy. E. Ind.* 248 Two Dutch Soldiers that had absented themselves from the Guard two days, ran the Gauntlet. **1797** MRS. RADCLIFFE *Italian* xvii, Vivaldi perceived that the guard was changed. **1802** C. JAMES *Milit. Dict.* s.v., As soon as they have taken post, fronting their respective guards, the word of command will be given—'Officers and non-commissioned officers—to your guards—March! Halt! Front!' 'Officers and non-commissioned officers, inspect your guards!' **1840** DICKENS *Barn. Rudge* 4 Some say that Lord George Gordon had been sent under a strong guard to the tower. **1884** *Mil. Engineering* (ed. 3) I. II. 15 The guard of the trenches is divided into two bodies—1. The main body. 2. The reserve. **1887** *Spectator* 13 Aug. 1097 A company of this regiment was guard of honour to the Empress Eugenie.

b. *transf.* and *fig.*

1548 P. NICOLS 12 *Spyes* (1553) D v, Some there be that perceive the Pope and his garde have led us blindly this many yeeres into a shamefull confusion of our faith. **1549** CHALONER *Erasm. on Folly* D b, But (Lorde) what.. inconueniences.. woulde not commonly happen.. were not now with flaterie now with daliance.. (all of my garde [L. *satellitium*] I warrant you) boeth propped up and nourished. **1613** PURCHAS *Pilgrimage* (1614) 764 As if they had beene the infernall guard, comming with Cerberus to welcome Proserpina to her Palace. **1834** J. BROWN *Lett. Sanctif.* v. 289 A powerful though unseen guard of angels continually surrounds him. **1848** DICKENS *Dombey* vii, The perseverance with which she walked out of Princess's Place to fetch this baby and its nurse, and walked back with them, and walked home with them again, and continually mounted guard over them. **1850** H. MELVILLE *White Jacket* I. iii. 10 Hearty old members of the Old Guard; grim sea grenadiers. **1852** J. A. QUITMAN *Let.* 20 Feb. in J. F. H. Claiborne *Life of Quitman* (1860) II. xvii. 164 What shall we of the strict state-rights school, what shall the 'Old Guard' do? **1894** A. FORBES in *Daily News* 27 Nov. 6/5 Gradually are thinning the ranks of the 'Old Guard' of war correspondents. **1902** A. BENNETT *Anna of Five Towns* ii. 28 Tellwright belonged by birth to the Old Guard of Methodism; there was in his family a tradition of holy valour for the pure doctrine. **1954** N. COWARD *Future Indefinite* IV. 183 The old guard however ..sang some of the vintage Maori songs. **1965** N. GULBENKIAN *Pantaraxia* viii. 151, I am a member of the Old Guard. 'Leave my gloves?.. Not on your life! I was sent home [from court] twenty-five years ago for not having them.' **1968** *Listener* 25 July 102/1 There is.. another reason for the angry panic among the Old Guard in Warsaw.

†**c.** ***body of guard*** = CORPS DE GARDE. *Obs.*

1579 DIGGES *Stratiot.* 91 These little bodies of gard or watch.

10. Something which guards, defends, or protects; a protection, defence. *lit.* and *fig.*

1606 SHAKS. *Tr. & Cr.* v. ii. 54 There is betweene my will, and all offences A guard of patience. **1608** —— *Per.* II. iv. 15 Though This King was great, His greatnesse was no gard To barre heauens shaft. **1691** NORRIS *Pract. Disc.* 310 We need no other Guard.. against Sin.. than these Three Words well considered, God is Present. **1696** BLACKMORE *Pr. Arthur* VI. (1714) 197 Their Hands a woven Guard of Osier saves, In which they fix their Hazel Weapon's End. **1713** DERHAM *Phys.-Theol.* IV. xii. (1714) 221 Feathers are.. to Birds.. not only a good guard against Wet and Cold.. but also most commodious for their Flight. **1732** POPE *Ess. Man* II. 162 Reason is here no guide, but still a guard. **1756** BURKE *Vind. Nat. Soc.* Wks. I. 47 The nicest and best studied behaviour was not a sufficient guard for a man of great capacity. **1780** COWPER *Table T.* 66 Keep Vice restrained behind a double guard. **1821** JOANNA BAILLIE *Metr. Leg., Wallace* lxxxi. 11 The dark brown water.. lashed the margin's flinty guard. **1822-34** *Good's Study Med.* (ed. 4) I. 487 It is.. necessary to watch its [squill's] effects upon the kidneys and intestinal canal and to attemper it with opium or some other guard. **1856** EMERSON *Eng. Traits, Aristocr.* Wks. (Bohn) II. 83 Every one who has tasted the delight of friendship, will respect every social guard which our manners can establish.. to secure from the intrusion of.. distasteful people.

b. *spec.* in *Card-playing.* (See quots.)

1885 R. A. PROCTOR *How to play Whist* 241 A third best card generally requires *two* guards. **1932** H. PHILLIPS *Week-End Probl. Bk.* 299 He will lead through South's guard in Hearts. **1936** E. CULBERTSON *Contract Bridge Complete* xxxviii. 423 A card which accompanies a higher card of the same suit is called a *guard*. **1960** *Times* 7 Dec. 16/7, I was sure that my little partner had a guard in the suit.

11. a. An ornamental border or trimming on a garment. *Obs.* exc. *Hist.* or *arch.*

(The original notion may have been that of a binding to keep the edge of the cloth from fraying.)

a **1529** SKELTON *Mann. World* 9 So many gardes worne, Jagged and al to-torne.. Sawe I never. **1535** COVERDALE *Num.* xv. 38 Speake to the children of Israel & saye vnto them yᵗ they make them gardes vpon yᵉ quarters of their garmentes. *c* **1550** *Disc. Common Weal Eng.* (1893) 83 When oure gentlemen went simply and oure servingemen plainly, with out cut or garde, bearinge the hevie sworde and bucler, on theire thighes, in steade of cuttes and gardes, and light daunsinge swordes. **1601** HOLLAND *Pliny* II. 459 A Senatour was distinguisht from the Gentlemen.. by his coat embrodered with broad gards and studs of purple. **1603** *Const. & Canons Eccl.* lxxiv, Priests' Cloaks, without gards, welts, long Buttons, or cuts. **1610** *Histrio-m.* III. 248 Out on these velvet gards, and black-lac'd sleeves. **1631** JORDEN *Nat. Bathes* Ded. (1669) 4 A plain sute of our Country Cloath, without welt or gard. **1637** DAVENANT *Brit. Triumph.* Dram. Wks. 1872 II. 267 A young man in a rich habit down to his knees with a large guard of purple about the skirt. **1707** CHAMBERLAYNE *St. Gt. Brit.* III. iii. 275 He [a Baron] hath two Guards or Doublings on his Mantle. **1766** PORNY *Heraldry* Gloss. (1777), *Guard*, term used by some Heralds to signify the Doubling of the Mantle of the Nobility.

b. *fig.* Chiefly in phrase ***without welt or gard.***

1581 SIDNEY *Apol. Poetrie* (Arb.) 59 Who reades Plutarchs eyther historie or philosophy, shall finde, hee trymmeth.. theyr garments, With gards of Poesie. **1588** SHAKS. *L.L.L.* IV. iii. 58 O Rimes are gards on wanton Cupids hose. **1594** NASHE *Unfort. Trav.* 4 A plaine ale-house without welt or gard of anie iuybush. **1641** BP. HALL *Answ. Vind. Smectymnuus* 95 The words are plaine, without either welt, or gard. **1660** FULLER *Mixt Contempl.* xxxiii. 299, I am a Protestant without wealt [*mod. ed.* wealth], or gard. **1692** STEELE in Spurgeon *Treas. Dav.* Ps. xviii. 25 Jacob was a plain man without welt or gard.

†**c.** *transf.* A stripe, band of colour. *Obs.*

1579 T. STEVENS *Let.* in *Hakluyt's Voy.* (1589) 161 These [Tuberones] haue waiting on them 6. or 7. smal fishes.. with gardes blew and greene round about their bodies, like comely seruing men. **1613** PURCHAS *Pilgrimage* (1614) 558 The Zebra.. resembling a Horse.. all over-laid with partie coloured Laces, and guards, from head to Taile.

†**12.** *Astr. pl.* The two stars of the constellation of the Lesser Bear known astronomically as Beta and Gamma respectively; also ***guards of the pole.*** Applied also to the two 'pointers' of the Great Bear. *Obs.*

1574 BOURNE *Regiment for Sea* 34 You may knowe it by.. the Starres rounde about the Pole, as Charles Wayne and the Guardes. **1594** BLUNDEVIL *Exerc.* VII. Introd. (1636) 649 All these instruments serue to little purpose, vnlesse you know also the North star, with his guards. *Ibid.* VII. xxvi. 687 The two guardes or pointers of Charles Waine. **1604** SHAKS. *Oth.* II. i. 15 The winde-shak'd-Surge, with high and monstrous Maine Seemes to cast water on the burning Beare, And quench the Guards of th' euer-fixed Pole. **1674** MOXON *Tutor Astron.* (ed. 3) 209 The two stars that are in the shoulders of the *Bear*, are called the *Guards*,.. because they are diligently to be looked unto, in regard of the their singular use which they have in Navigation. **1783** R. TURNER *View Heavens* (1798) 56 The two foremost of the square lie almost in a right line with the Pole-star, and are called the Guards or Pointers. **1819** T. WHITING *Syst. Astron.* (1828) 28 *Guards*, a name that has been sometimes applied to the two stars nearest the North Pole.

†**13.** The amnion or 'caul'. *Obs.*

1611 FLORIO, *Guardia*,.. also the gard that infoulds a child in the mothers wombe.

†**14.** *Hunting.* (See quot.) [F. *gardes.*] *Obs.*

1576, 1616 [see GARD[2]]. **1849** H. AINSWORTH *Lanc. Witches* III. viii, [Of a boar.] The toes being round and thick.. and the guards, or dew-claws, great and open.

15. *Curling.* (See quot. 1878.)

1849 *Chambers' Inform.* II. 650/2 Each man is warned by his respective friends to plant, if possible, an excellent guard —dislodge this stone, and cover that [etc.]. **1878** 'CAPT. CRAWLEY' *Football*, etc. 127 (*Curling*) A stone is said to guard when it lies in a line between the player and the tee, with another stone belonging to the same side within it; a guard may also lie on any other part of the ice beyond the hog-score, on a similar principle. **1897** *Encycl. Sport* I. 264 (Curling) *Guard*, (1) a stone that lies in a direct line before another.

16. A contrivance of metal, wood, or other material, made for the protection of an object from injury, to prevent accidents by falling, etc.; orig. in many cases used with a prefixed word indicating the position or nature of the protecting contrivance, e.g. *fire-guard, trigger-guard*, etc. **a.** *gen.* (In several instances a defining word is more usually found prefixed, as *leg-guard, mud-guard, step-guard, watch-guard*, etc.) **b.** The part of the hilt of a sword that protects the hand, often of curious workmanship or elaborate design. **c.** (See quot.) **d.** A piece of metal designed for the protection of the trigger of a gun. **e.** *pl.* The wards of a lock. **f.** = *fire-guard* (see FIRE *sb.* 5). **g.** *Archery.* = BRACER[2]. **h.** *Railway.* An iron placed in front of a locomotive engine to catch and remove obstacles; *U.S.* a cow-catcher. **i.** (See quot. 1842.) **j.** A lateral extension of the deck of a steamboat beyond the lines of the hull so as to overhang the water. **k.** (See quot.) **l.** A welt or reinforcing slip of paper inserted between the leaves of a book, as a scrap-book, catalogue, etc., for the attachment of additional leaves. **m.** (See quot.) **n.** *Conch.* In cephalopods, a calcareous structure enveloping the apex of the phragmacone; the rostrum. **o.** (See quot.) **p.** A protector worn on various parts of the body by cricketers or other sportsmen.

a. 1774 PENNANT *Tour Scotl.* in 1772, 107 The two principal doors have their grated guards. **1827** STEUART *Planter's G.* (1828) 310 The Guards generally in use for protecting Trees, are well known; hurdles and cordage of different kinds; three-cornered, four-cornered, and circular palings, and the like. **1871** COLBURN *Loco. Engin.* v. 133/2 The axle boxes of the driving axle are guided vertically by suitable guides, or axle guards. **1875** KNIGHT *Dict. Mech.*, *Guard*.. 6. (*Fire-arms*).. *b.* A safety-lock of a fowling-piece to prevent the accidental dropping of the hammer. *c.* A nipple-shield to protect the little tube which receives the percussion-cap. 7. A bow or wire around a lantern to protect the glass. **1884** *Ibid.* Suppl., *Guard*, a fence, fender, screen, canopy, etc., as the case may be:—A dash-board, or step-guard in cars. A grating to a window to preserve it from blows. **1884** *Health Exhib. Catal.* 128/1 Model of Safety Drum Guard. *Ibid.* 131/1 Hygrometer.. of lever action bearing on five horsehair lines, which are exposed to atmospheric influences through guards of spiral wire. **1900** *Daily News* 19 Feb. 6/3 The starboard propeller guard of the Bat is smashed off.

b. 1596 DALRYMPLE tr. *Leslie's Hist. Scot.* VII. 123 A singular sword with scheith and gairdis of gold, sett in precious stanes. **1662** J. DAVIES tr. *Mandelslo's Trav.* 16 A kind of broad sword, whereof the hilt is very large, but without any guard. **1687** A. LOVELL tr. *Thevenot's Trav.* III. 43 The Guard is very plain; commonly no more but a handle of Iron, with a cross Bar of the same underneath the Pummel ..that the Sword may not slip out of their Hands. **1728** P. WALKER *Peden* Pref. (1827) 33 What Handles the Swords had whether small or Three barred, or Highland-guards. **1815** ELPHINSTONE *Acc. Caubul* (1842) I. 353 The sword is of the Persian form.. The hilt resembles our own, except that it has no guard for the fingers. **1856** WHYTE MELVILLE *Kate Cov.* (1882) 23/1 The silver-mounted guard of a rapier. **1898** *Century Mag.* Jan. 392/1 The guard [of the sword] was a coiled serpent of exquisite workmanship.

c. 1892 SIMMONDS *Dict. Trade* Suppl., *Guards*, protections to a book.

d. 1687 MIEGE *Gt. Fr. Dict.* II. s.v. *Gard*, The gard of a Gun, *sougarde de Fusil*. **1753** HANWAY *Trav.* (1762) I. III. xxxvi. 163 This accident was occasioned by one of my servants.. touching the trigger, which in very few Persian muskets has any guard. **1874** *Rifle Exerc.*, etc. 40 Seize the guard with the forefinger and thumb of the right hand.. the remaining fingers under the hammer.

e. 1677 MOXON *Mech. Exerc.* 21 There are several Inventions in Locks, I mean in the making and contriving their Wards or Guards. **1878** *Technol. Dict., Eng.-Ger.-Fr.* (ed. 3), *Guards*, wards of a lock.

f. 1845 DE QUINCEY *Autobiog. Sk.* Wks. 1853 I. 13 As my three sisters with myself sat by the firelight round the guard of our nursery.

g. 1853 'C. BEDE' *Verdant Green* I. xi, A fancy-wood bow, with arrows, belt, quiver, guard, tips, tassels, and grease-pot. **1860** HUGHES *Tom Brown at Oxf.* xxx, 'You must string my bow', she said, handing it to him, as she buckled on her guard.

h. 1838 D. STEVENSON *Civil Engin. N. Amer.* 260 To.. render railway travelling more safe, an apparatus called a 'guard' has been very generally introduced. **1866** *Morn. Star* 16 Mar. 6/1 The number-taker.. saw the body of a man impaled on the iron guards in front of the engine. **1897** *Westm. Gaz.* 20 May 9/3 Death was due to fracture of the skull, the guard of the engine having struck the man's head.

i. 1840 H. S. TANNER *Canals & Railr. U.S.* 111 High water guard 5 to 6 feet. Working guard 3 to 4 feet. **1842** FRANCIS, *Dict. Arts, Guards*, in engineering, upright pieces of wood, iron, or stone, fastened to the lock gates of a canal, the corners of a street, and similar situations, to prevent the passage of barges in the one place, and waggons in the other, from injuring the parts flush with, or near to the guard.

j. 1829 T. FLINT *George Mason* 140 Madam Mason was.. sitting on the guards of the boat. **1850** LYELL *2nd Visit U.S.* II. 47 The other [door] leads out to the guard, as they call it, a long balcony or gallery, covered with a shade or verandah, which passes round the whole boat. **1855** OGILVIE Suppl., *Guards of a steam-boat*, a widening of the deck by a frame-work of strong timbers, which curve out on each side to the paddle-wheels, and protect them and the shaft against collisions with wharfs and other boats. **1897** *Daily News* 28 Sept. 6/6 Each boat that comes up the river is loaded to the guards with railway supplies for Wardner.

k. 1881 RAYMOND *Mining Gloss.*, *Guard*, a support in front of a roll-train to guide the bar into the groove, sometimes called a side-guide.

l. 1708 *Brit. Apollo* No. 1. 4/1 Any Persons, upon directing their Letters to the Printer superscrib'd, for the *British Apollo*, may have this Paper brought to their Houses .. Likewise the Books of Guards neatly bound to keep 'em in, at two Shillings a piece. **1747** SPENCE *Polymetes* Direct. Binder, Plate 9, 18, 24, & 34; to be done with guards. **1882** P. FITZGERALD *Recreat. Lit. Man* (1883) 250 When the guards have been filled and the volume begins to bulge. *Ibid.* 274 Special books with guards.. for pasting into. **1896** *Times* 29 Feb. 10/3 It has been arranged for the book to be issued.. with 'guards' at the end for additional leaves.

m. 1860 R. FOWLER *Med. Voc.*, *Guard*, a thickly folded cloth, or other article, placed upon a bed so as to guard it from the discharges of parturition, or of any disease.

n. 1851-6 WOODWARD *Mollusca* 74 The phragmocone of the belemnite.. is usually eccentric, its apex being nearest to the ventral side of the guard. **1877** HUXLEY *Anat. Inv. Anim.* viii. 542 A straight phragmocone is enclosed within a more or less conical calcified laminated structure, the guard or rostrum.

o. 1875 KNIGHT *Dict. Mech.*, *Guard*, a light frame in which the nuts of bolts fit to prevent their unscrewing by the vibration of the engine.

p. 1889 in *Cent. Dict.* **1906** A. E. KNIGHT *Compl. Cricketer* ii. 49 Many players and most wicket-keepers wear additional guards for the more delicate parts of the body. **1939-40** *Army & Navy Stores Catal.* 811/3 Football shin guards. *Ibid.* 812/3 The 'Stopem' hockey leg-guard.

17. †**a.** Short for GUARD-ROOM or GUARD-HOUSE. *Obs.*

1613 PURCHAS *Pilgrimage* (1614) 549 The Court hath three guards, betweene each of which is a great greene. **1714** RAMSAY *Elegy J. Cowper* 47 John quietly put them in the guard To learn mair sense. **1773** FERGUSSON *Poems* (1807) 257 Pleys that bring him to the guard, And eke the council chaumir, Wi' shame that day.

b. Short for *guard-finger, -lock, -rail*, etc.

1875 KNIGHT *Dict. Mech.*, s.v.

18. *attrib.* and *Comb.*, as ***guard-dress, -duty, -mounting, -parade, -sloop, -soldier, -squadron; guard-like*** adj.; **guard action** *Horology*, ? the action connected with a guard-pin; **guard band** (*a*) *Telecommunications*, one of the frequency bands on either side of a communication band which serve to protect it from interference from adjacent communication bands; (*b*) a strip separating neighbouring recording tracks on magnetic tape; **guard-board**, (*a*) = CHAIN-WALE, CHANNEL *sb.*[2] (Smyth *Sailor's Word-bk.* 1867); (*b*) a board designed to prevent objects from falling on to workmen engaged in building; **guard-bolt** (see quot.); **guard book**, (*a*) a blank book, furnished with guards (sense 16 l), for the reception of pasted scraps, invoices, newspaper cuttings, etc.; (*b*) see quot. 1867; **guard-brush**, on an electric railway, a metallic brush by means of which the current is conveyed to the motor; **guard-cell** *Bot.*, one of the two cells that embrace the stomata of plants; **guard-chain**, (*a*) a chain used to secure something, esp. a part of the dress or personal equipment, as a watch, brooch, or bracelet; (*b*) a chain used as a protection; also *fig.*; **guard-chamber** = GUARD-ROOM; **guard-changing** *vbl. sb.*, the action of changing the guard, esp. at St. James's and Buckingham Palace; **guard-coat**, a coat worn by a soldier of the Guards; **guard-coffer**, an external framework for the protection of the coffer or casing surrounding a concrete foundation; †**guard-cot** *Anglo-Indian*, a charpoy occupied by a soldier in the intervals of sentry duty; **guard cradle** (see quot. 1924); †**guard-dagger**, ? a dagger with a guard; in quot. *attrib.* of the shape of a certain cut of 'whiskers' (i.e. moustaches); **guard-detail**, 'men from a company, regiment, etc. detailed from guard duty' (Webster, 1890); **guard dog**, a watch-dog; **guard-finger**, 'one of the teeth projecting forward from the cutter-bar of a harvester, and through which the knife plays' (1875 Knight *Dict. Mech.*); **guard-flag**, 'in a squadron, a flag indicating the ship whose turn it is to perform the duty of a guard-ship' (*Cent. Dict.*); **guard-foot** , the foot of a contrivance, which acts also as a guard; **guard hair** = OVERHAIR; **guard-horn**, the horn used by the guard of a coach; **guard-iron**, (*a*) *Naut.* (see quot. 1769); (*b*) = 16 h; **guard-lace**, a kind of figured lace; **guard-leaf**, one of the leaves which separate the closely-packed blossoms on the stem of a double hollyhock; **guard-lock** (see quots.); **guard-log** *Austral.*, a piece of timber laid on a road to keep the traffic on and off certain portions; **guard net** = *guard cradle*; **guard-petal** = *guard-leaf*; **guard-pile**, a pile placed as a protection in front of a quay or other structure; a fender or fender-pile (cf. 16 i); **guard-pin**, (*a*) *Horology* (see quot. 1884); (*b*) in a rifle, the pin by which the guard (sense 16 d) is attached; **guard-plate**, (*a*) in an electrometer = *guard-ring*; (*b*) 'the plate which closes the opening in front of a cupola furnace, to whose iron casing it is attached by staples' (1875 Knight *Dict. Mech.*); **guard-polyp** *Zool.*, a zooid modified to serve a defensive function, as in the nematophore of a cœlenterate, a machopolyp; **guard-report** (see quot.); **guard-ring**, (*a*) a finger ring worn to keep another from slipping off; a keeper; (*b*) *Electr.* (see quot. 1893); †**guard-star** (see sense 12 above); **guard-stone**, one of a row of stones placed to keep vehicles off the sidewalk; **guard-stops**, the two points placed one on each side of a numeral, letter, figure, etc.; **guard's van**, the railway coach or compartment occupied by a guard; **guard tent**, 'one of the tents occupied by a military guard when the command is in the field or in camp' (*Cent. Dict.*); **guard tube**, (*a*) (see quot. 1893; (*b*) a cylindrical conductor surrounding part of a wire anode (in an ionization chamber or proportional counter) which modifies the shape of the electric field and makes the sensitive volume of the chamber more clearly defined; (*c*) one of a series of ionization chambers placed so as to surround a weakly radioactive source and the chambers used to detect its radiation, and connected so as to prevent radiation from other sources from being counted (see quot. 1964); **guard wire** (see quot. 1941). Also GUARD-BOAT, GUARD-HOUSE, GUARD-ROOM, GUARD-SHIP.

1884 F. J. BRITTEN *Watch & Clockm.* 89 *Double Roller Escapement*, a variety of the Lever Escapement, in which a separate roller is used for the *guard action. **1956** W. C. MICHELS *Internat. Dict. Physics* 79/1 Interference *guard bands. **1958** H. G. M. SPRATT *Magn. Tape Recording* viii. 219 The centre 0·05 in. wide strip is left as a guard band and reduces the possibilities of cross-talk. **1960** J. L. BERNSTEIN *Video Tape Recording* v. 91 When a signal track slips off the playback gap so that ⅓ of the gap length is covered by a guard band, the noise level increases by 3 db. **1960** M. S. KIVER *F-M Simplified* (ed. 3) i. 8 Each station..is assigned a bandwidth of 200 kc. Of this 200-kc bandwidth, 150 (±75) kc is to be employed for the modulation and the remaining 50 (±25) kc is to function as a guardband. **1898** *Daily News* 22 Mar. 2/5 Evidence was given that *guard boards were put up immediately after the accident. **1884** KNIGHT *Dict. Mech.* Suppl., **Guard Bolt*, a flat-headed screw-bolt, fully counter-sunk, for fastening the guards of mowing machines to the bars. **1839** J. ROMILLY *Diary* 8 May (1967) 169 Pasted docum^ts^ in *Guard Book all the Ev^s^. **1867** SMYTH *Sailor's Word-bk.*, *Guard-book*, report of guard; a copy of which is delivered at the admiral's office by the officer of the last guard. Also, a full set of his accounts kept by a warrant-officer for the purpose of passing them. **1881** *Bookseller's Catal.*, *Guard Book*—Twenty-two inches square, containing 68 leaves of stout drawing paper. **1891** *Daily News* 28 Oct. 2/7 In respect of this he had searched the guard-book, and could find no trace of the transfer of this share. **1903** *Daily Chron.* 18 Nov. 8/6 Book Sewers wanted, used to guardbooks and scrap-books. **1907** *Westm. Gaz.* 9 Dec. 7/2 He also produced the 'transfer guard-book'. **1933** D. L. SAYERS *Murder must Advertise* i. 18 He propped up the Dairyfields guard-book before him, and fell to studying his predecessor's masterpieces on the subject of Green Pastures Margarine. **1961** T. LANDAU *Encycl. Librarianship* (ed. 2) 158/2 *Guard book catalogue*, a catalogue in book form (bound or loose-leaf), the entries being..made on slips and pasted on blank pages. **1888** *Science* 21 Dec. 302/1 The current is conveyed from the *guard-brushes and the wheels to the motor, and through the other rail to the ground [on an electric railway]. **1875** BENNETT & DYER *Sachs' Bot.* 88 We have a cell surrounded by several cells formed in this manner, which afterwards forms the two *guard-cells (as in Crassulaceæ, Begoniaceæ, Cruciferæ). **1832** F. TROLLOPE *Dom. Manners* II. xxx. 211 [His] toilet was equally studied; eye-glass, *guard-chain, nothing was omitted. **1837** DICKENS *Pickw.* liv. 591 Very little watches and very large guard chains. **1838** DICKENS *O. Twist* ix, The merry old gentleman; placing..a watch in his waistcoat pocket, with a guard-chain round his neck. **1846** MRS. GORE *Eng. Charac.* (1852) 101 In a velvet waistcoat and gilt guard-chain. **1860** PIESSE *Lab. Chem. Wonders* 7 It [Gunpowder] is the guard-chain and strong bolt which keep the barbarian thief from entering the precincts of the peaceful and industrious. **1894** A. MORRISON *Tales Mean Streets* 280 Old Jack sat on the guard-chain of a flowery grave. **1896** *Daily Tel.* 19 Mar. 8/3 The guard-chain of Waterloo Pier. **1611** BIBLE *1 Kings* xiv. 28 The guard..brought them backe into the *guard-chamber. **1707** *Lond. Gaz.* No. 4334/5 When they had ascended to the Guard-Chamber, they were receiv'd there by the Captain of the Yeomen of the Guard. **1788** H. WALPOLE *Remin.* iii. 32 The yeomen in the guard-chamber pointed their halberds at my breast. **1904** *Daily Chron.* 30 May 8/2 The minor formalities of *guard-changing are completed. **1907** *Westm. Gaz.* 12 Nov. 9/1 The ceremony of guard-changing in the quadrangle. **1924** S. R. ROGET *Dict. Electr. Terms* 102/1 **Guard cradle or net*, an earthed network of wires placed under overhead conductors at points where danger might be produced by their falling. **1940** *Chambers's Techn. Dict.* 393/1 *Guard cradle*, a network of wires serving the same purpose as a guard wire. Also called guard net. **1711** STEELE *Spect.* No. 88 ⁋4 Coming down a tavern-stairs in his master's fine *guard-coat..he met the colonel coming up with other company. **1776** G. SEMPLE *Building in Water* 131 To secure the Coffer or Coffers more effectually, you may environ and secure them with double or single *Guard-coffers. *c* **1813** MRS. SHERWOOD *Stories Ch. Catech.* xi. 86 Three or four men, who sat talking together upon a *guard-cot, just out at the door in the verandah. **1786** *Pogonologia* 80 There were Spanish, Turkish, *guard-dagger, &c. whiskers. **1796** WINDHAM *Speeches Parl.* 25 Apr. (1812) I. 287 The dogs that worry sheep are pointers, hounds, lurchers, *guard-dogs, &c. **1967** 'M. HUNTER' *Cambridgeshire Disaster* v. 31 The double chainlink fencing and the *guard dogs. **1971** B. CALLISON *Plague of Sailors* 7 Ancillary boards stated..: Unrestricted guard dog operation do not pass this point. **1832** G. DOWNES *Lett. Cont. Countries* I. 141 An old Vienna *Guard-dress. **1862** T. W. HIGGINSON *Army Life Black Reg.* (1870) 28 *Guard duty is an admirable school for this. **1894** *Outing* (U.S.) XXIV. 314/1 There should be no time devoted to company drills in camp, or to teaching the rudiments of guard duty. **1879** THOMSON & TAIT *Nat. Phil.* I. I. §168 One or two *guard feet, not to touch the plane except in case of accident, ought to be added to give a broad enough base for safety. **1913** J. W. JONES *Furs Farming in Canada* iv. 96 Mammals which have a short, fine, soft coat of fur through which grows hair, usually of greater length, variously called overfur, water-fur, *guard-hair, are known as fur-bearers. **1921** *Daily Colonist* (Victoria, B.C.) 9 Oct. 19/4 The fur of the muskrat..is very much like the beaver's fur..having two kinds—the long, coarse guard hairs and the soft undercoat. **1930** M. DE LA ROCHE *Finch's Fortune* xxiii. 303 It was growing into a rugged animal of good girth, the glossy black of its pelt shading to blue-black, the silver bands on the guard hairs bright as polished metal. **1966** *Times* 25 Apr. 13/1 Simulated..furs..now..have..'guard-hair'. **1829** T. HOOK *Bank to Barnes* 42, I was prevented from examining other objects by the *guard-horn. **1769** FALCONER *Dict. Marine*, **Guard-irons*, certain curved or arched bars of iron placed over the ornamental figures, on a ship's head or quarter, to defend them from the impression of some other ship when they lie close to, or rub against each other. **1802** J. PERROTT in *Naval Chron.* VII. 349, I saw him taking hold of the guard-iron. **1877** M. REYNOLDS *Loco.-Engine Driving* 100 He also stepped over to his own side of the engine foot-plate, and he had scarcely been there fifteen seconds when something was struck by the buffer-beam or guard-iron of the engine. **1804** *Trans. Soc. Arts* XXII. 234 A Loom that makes the satin *guard lace, or any other figured lace. **1849** *Beck's Florist* 276 The new and superior varieties have a semi-spherical flower exceedingly double, with closely serried petals, and a flat regular *guard-leaf. **1608** CHAPMAN *Byron's Conspir.* Plays 1873 II. 201 Pitch him from him with such *guardlike strength. **1815** *Niles' Weekly Reg.* IX. 44/2 The boat, having entered the *guard lock, went through the new canal. **1840** H. S. TANNER *Canals & Railr. U.S.* 250 *Guard lock*, in canalling, is employed in maintaining the level of a canal, by preventing the encroachment of water from rivers, lakes, &c., when elevated beyond the prescribed level. **1875** KNIGHT *Dict. Mech.*, *Guard-lock* (Hydraulic Engineering), a *tide-lock*, forming a communication between a basin and tide-water. **1890** 'ROLF BOLDREWOOD' *Col. Reformer* (1891) 128 We may do it yet,..if we can clear those cursed *guard-logs near the bottom. **1844** *Regul. & Ord. Army* 158 In *Guard Mounting Order, the Great Coat is to be folded and carried flat, the top being in a line with the bottom of the Coat Collar. *Ibid.* 261 All Grenadier and Fusilier Regiments are, when marching in quick time, upon occasions of Guard-mounting, Parade or Review, to march to the *Grenadier's March.* **1861** G. F. BERKELEY *Sportsm. W. Prairies* xiv. 233, I attended guard-mounting and with Major Wassells inspected the barrack-rooms and arms. **1924**, **1940** *Guard net [see *guard cradle*]. **1828** J. M. SPEARMAN *Brit. Gunner* (ed. 2) 97 From the quarter *guard parade to the line of parade of the Battalion..62 yards. **1851** *Beck's Florist* Oct. 237 This is a rosy-pink flower, full, and well formed, with just sufficient *guard-petal and no more. **1739** LABELYE *Short Acc. Piers Westm. Bridge* 19 The Use of these Fenders, or *Guard-Piles, was to secure the Works from the approach of Barges, and other large Vessels. **1879** *Cassell's Techn. Educ.* IV. 369/1 Passing on to the driving plane and repelling the pallet, would thereby press the *guard-pin against the edge of the roller. **1881** GREENER *Gun* 262 To take to pieces a breech-loader..first remove the fore-end and barrels; then..turn out the side-pins, and remove the locks and hammers together; next turn out the guard-pins, and remove the bow or guard. **1884** F. J. BRITTEN *Watch & Clockm.* 115 *Guard Pin, Safety Pin*, a pin in the lever escapement that prevents the pallets leaving the escape wheel when the hands of the watch are turned back. **1873** MAXWELL *Electr. & Magn.* §201 The interval between the disk and the *guard-plate may be regarded as a circular groove of infinite depth. **1888** ROLLESTON & JACKSON *Anim. Life* (ed. 2) 758 The structures known as nematophores, sarcothecae, *guard-polypes or macho-polypes. **1872–6** VOYLE & STEVENSON *Milit. Dict.*, **Guard report*, a report sent in by the relieved officer to the officer commanding, detailing a statement of duties peformed by his guard while on duty. **1817** M. EDGEWORTH *Harrington* I. xvii. 462 She never wore Sir Josseline's ring, without putting on.. another,..which she called her *guard ring, a ring which being tighter than Sir Josseline's, kept it safe on her finger. **1873** MAXWELL *Electr. & Magn.* §201 A plane disk.. surrounded by a large plane plate called a Guard-ring with a circular aperture..concentric with the disk. **1893** SLOANE *Electr. Dict.*, *Guard Ring*, an annular horizontal surface surrounding the balanced disc in the absolute electrometer. **1708** *Lond. Gaz.* No. 4459/1, 14 Sail of Brigantines and Sloops,..under Convoy of the Duke of Anjou's *Guard Sloop, of betwixt 70 and 80 Men. **1739** *Encour. Sea-f. People* 35 Capt. Coleby..fought the Guard-Sloop. **1601** HOLLAND *Pliny* I. 166 Iunius Valens a captaine, pensioner or centurion of the *gard-souldiers about Augustus Cæsar. **1850** GROTE *Greece* II. lxiii. VIII. 143 *note*, Although watch had been enjoined to them (i.e. to the Peloponnesian *guard-squadron at Abydos). **1690** LEYBOURN *Curs. Math.* 693 Then find the Point of the Compass, that the *Guard-Star is upon, in the first..Column of the Table. **1865** PARKMAN *Champlain* v. 257 His foot upon a *guard-stone, he thrust his head and shoulders into the coach. **1878** *Technol. Dict., Eng.-Ger.-Fr.* (ed. 3), Guard-stone (Build., Roads, etc.). *Der Prellstein, Borne.* **1866** FURNIVALL *Pref. to Stacions of Rome* (E.E.T.S. 1867) 6 Here..it is, and printed with all its metrical points, and *guard-stops on each side of figures and single letters. **1848** E. BRYANT *California* iv. 52 They were greatly alarmed when brought to the *guard tent, expecting immediate punishment. **1893** SLOANE *Electr. Dict.*, **Guard Tube*, a metal tube surrounding a dry pile used with a quadrant electrometer, or other electrometers of that type. **1951** *Rev. Sci. Instr.* XXII. 38/1 The best possible insulation of the collecting electrode is required, and..the use of earthed guard tubes to protect the wire is generally a necessity. **1958** H. ETHERINGTON *Nuclear Engin. Handbk.* v. 14 End effects will involve regions of non-uniform *A* and of uncertain limits of the counting volume unless 'guard tubes' or field-shaping features are employed. **1963** B. FOZARD *Instrumentation Nuclear Reactors* v. 60 Counting work of this kind requires the use of anticoincidence circuits and guard tubes. **1964** R. D. RUSK *Introd. Atomic & Nucl. Physics* (ed. 2) xiii. 308 The surrounding ring of guard tubes is connected in anticoincidence with the counting tubes that are near the source. A cosmic ray passing through one of the counting tubes would not be counted because it would first have to pass through one of the anticoincident guard tubes. **1881** *Guard van [see *van boy* (VAN *sb.*³ 3)]. **1916** W. OWEN *Let.* 29 Dec. (1967) 417 Train was wickedly late. I travelled in Guard's van. **1902** *Jrnl. Inst. Electr. Engin.* XXXI. 91 Probably the most efficient safeguard at present is *earthed* *guard wire put up in accordance with Post Office regulations. **1920** R. E. NEALE *Whittaker's Electr. Engin. Pocket-bk.* (ed. 4) 579 Earthed guard wires..must be erected, at a minimum height of 2′ above the trolley wires, where telephone and telegraph wires cross the latter. **1941** S. R. ROGET *Dict. Electr. Terms* (ed. 4) 156/2 *Guard wire*, an earthed wire, above an overhead line, to catch other wires which may fall accidentally across the line, and to ensure their being earthed before coming into contact with the line to be protected.

guard (gɑːd), *v.* Also 6–8 gard(e, (in sense 7, 6 *pa. pple.* gard, 9 gard), *Sc.* gaird, 7 guaird. [f. GUARD *sb.*, or ad. F. *garder*, earlier *guarder* (= It. *guardare*, Sp. *guardar*):—Rom. **guardare*, a. OTeut. **wardôn*, f. **wardâ*: see WARD, GUARD *sbs.*]

1. a. *trans.* To keep in safety from injury or attack; to stand guard or sentinel over; to keep (a door, etc.) so as to prevent entrance or exit; to take care of, protect, defend. (With material and immaterial objects.) †Also with *in*.

1583 STANYHURST *Æneis* III. (Arb.) 81 King Helenus, with a crowding coompanye garded. **1593** SHAKS. *Lucr.* 626 Draw not thy sword to gard iniquitie. **1597** —— *2 Hen. IV*, IV. v. 145 There is your Crowne, And he that weares the Crowne immortally, Long guard it yours. **1598** BARRET *Theor. Warres* IV. ii. 105 The companies which haue the ward, are alwayes to sallie to gard the trenches. **1608** DAY *Hum. out of Br.* v. i. (1881) 69 Guard in my safety with a ring of steele, And marke how proudly heele demeane reuenge. **1617** SIR W. MURE *Misc. Poems* xxi. 55 Heavens..did thy royall grandeur guaird. *a* **1657** —— *Ps.* cxxi. 8 He guaird thee shal about. **1667** MILTON *P.L.* II. 1033 Except whom God and good Angels guard by special grace. **1687** A. LOVELL tr. *Thevenot's Trav.* II. 143 Two men, each holding a Pike, as if they Guarded these Doors. **1742** H. WALPOLE *Lett.* (1846) I. 239 The King of Poland is guarding all the avenues of Saxony. **1749** FIELDING *Tom Jones* XII. xiv, Jones stood with his sword drawn in his hand to guard the poor fellow. **1780** COWPER *Table T.* 315 Let active laws apply the needful curb To guard the peace that riot would disturb. **1838** THIRLWALL *Greece* III. 149 He was to guard the entrance of the Corinthian gulf. *Ibid.* V. 47 They were so negligently guarded, that..they contrived to make themselves masters of the fortress. **1859** TENNYSON *Elaine* 4 Elaine..High in her chamber up a tower to the east Guarded the sacred shield of Lancelot. **1883** C. J. WILLS *Mod. Persia* 376 Peacocks are..supposed only to be kept by royalty;..the privilege of keeping them is zealously guarded. **1898** J. ARCH *Story of Life* xv. 369 You may just as well expect the cat to guard the cream.

refl. **1606** SHAKS. *Tr. & Cr.* IV. v. 253 Henceforth guard thee well. **1781** COWPER *Anti-Thelyph.* 189 Guard thee well, expect no feigned attack; And guard beside the sorceress at thy back!

b. said of impersonal objects.

1593 SHAKS. *Lucr.* 493, I thinke the honie garded with a sting. *a* **1625** BEAUM. & FL. *Bloody Bro.* IV. i, Mercy becomes a Prince, and guards him best. **1667** MILTON *P.L.* XI. 122 Of a sword the flame Wide-waving..to..guard all passage to the Tree of Life. **1698** FRYER *Acc. E. India & P.* 40 A Coat of Armour over it like an Hedg-hogs, guards its weighty Fruit. **1725** BERKELEY *Proposal* etc. Wks. III. 222 Two narrow entrances, both well guarded by forts. **1794** MRS. RADCLIFFE *Myst. Udolpho* xxv, The place is guarded enough by the high walls of the castle and the east turret. **1830** TENNYSON *Recoll. Arab. Nts.* 23 Where clear-stemm'd platans guard The outlet [of a stream]. **1876** J. PARKER *Paracl.* I. ii. 15 Every moment of the Jew's time, and every act of the Jew's life, was guarded by a regulation.

c. To protect or defend *from, against.* Also *refl.*

1593 SHAKS. *2 Hen. VI*, III. i. 249 To guard the Chicken from a hungry Kyte. **1697** DAMPIER *Voy.* I. 8 They will guard them-selves from Arrows, tho they come very thick. **1711** ADDISON *Spect.* No. 162 ¶4 One would take more than ordinary Care to guard ones self against this particular Imperfection [inconstancy], because it is that which our Nature very strongly inclines us to. **1838** LYTTON *Calderon* v, By guarding him from all friendships save with those whose affection to myself I can trust. **1852** TENNYSON *Wellington* 68 Guarding realms and kings from shame. **1855** —— *Maud* I. vi. 60 Myself from myself I guard.

d. To attend, accompany, or escort (*to* a place) as a guard. *arch.*

1597 SHAKS. *2 Hen. IV*, IV. ii. 122 Some guard these Traitors to the Block of Death. **1613** PURCHAS *Pilgrimage* (1614) 434 A triple Sunne, attended and guarded with a double Rainbow. **1697** S. SEWALL *Diary* 6 Oct. (1878) I. 461 Came between 12. and 1. to the Townh. Chamber and Guarded the Governour and Council to the Anchor. **1702** *Ibid.* 11 June (1879) II. 59 Just about dark Troops Guarded the Govr. to Roxbury. *a* **1732** GAY *Town Eclog., Friday* 18 in *Lady M.W. Montagu's Poet. Wks.* (1768) 36 No more..shall..white-glov'd beaus encroach In crowds behind, to guard me to my coach. **1850** TENNYSON *In Mem.* xvii. 12 My blessing, like a line of light, Is on the waters day and night, And like a beacon guards thee home.

2. To provide with safeguards; to secure from misunderstanding or abuse by explanations or stipulations; *Med.*, to render the action of (a drug) safe by administering correctives along with it.

1726 BROOME *On Odyss.* xxiv. V. 261 It is not easy to guard the doctrine of Homer from such unhappy consequences. **1891** *Law Times* XC. 462/2 The judges carefully guarded themselves from being supposed to lay down any new rule. **1900** J. HUTCHINSON *Archives Surgery* XI. No. 41, I give it [*sc.* mercury] in small, frequently repeated doses, well guarded with opium.

†**3.** To find out or ascertain by watching. *Obs.*

1597 MONTGOMERIE *Cherrie & Slae* 1351 First gaird the grund of all his grief, Quhat sicknes ȝe suspect.

4. To keep watch over, to prevent from exceeding bounds; to keep in check, control (thoughts, utterance).

1742 YOUNG *Nt. Th.* II. 95 Guard well thy Thought; our Thoughts are heard in Heav'n. **1759** STERNE *Tr. Shandy* II. i, No doubt my uncle Toby had great command of himself, and could guard appearances, I believe, as well as most men. **1768** H. WALPOLE *Hist. Doubts* 112 This..would make his testimony most suspicious, even if he had guarded his work within the rules of probability. **1780** COWPER *Table T.* 83 Guard what you say: the patriotic tribe Will sneer, and charge you with a bribe. **1885** BIBLE (R.V.) *Prov.* xiii. 3 He that guardeth his mouth keepeth his life.

†**5.** To parry (a blow); to ward *off. Obs.*

1661 BRAMHALL *Just Vind.* ii. 20 We did not judge him, or punish him,..but only defended ourselves, by guarding his blowes, and repelling his injuries. **1695** COLLIER *Ess.* II. (1697) 112 There are few but may Shine in their own Orb..; so far at least as to guard off Contempt, and secure a moderate Repute.

6. *Sporting colloq.*

1893 *Daily News* 8 May 2/2 The list of disasters caused by starting Siffleuse and putting T. Loates up, without guarding the favourite. **1897** *Encycl. Sport* I. 209 *Guarding*—When two or more greyhounds are entered in a stake, the *bona fide* property of the same owner, the order of running is altered, so that they may meet other greyhounds, should they come together.

7. To ornament (a garment, etc.) with 'guards'; to trim, as with braid, lace, velvet, etc.; also *transf.*, to stripe. *occas.* with *about.*

1500 in Furnivall *Ballads fr. MSS.* I. 456 Hys hosen shalbe freshely gard Wyth colours ii or thre. *a* **1529** SKELTON *Bowge of Crt.* 508 His hode all pounsed and garded lyke a cage. **1530** PALSGR. 560/2 Some men garde their cootes for plesure, but I garde my hose for profyte. **1585** T. WASHINGTON tr. *Nicholay's Voy.* II. iii. 37 Gownes or coates of velvet..which they gard about with broad bands of velvet. **1606** HOLLAND *Sueton.* Annot. 2 This purple Robe bordered, called Prætexta, was..embrodered..or garded about with purple. **1613** PURCHAS *Pilgrimage* (1614) 712 Sharkes..which had other six or seven smaller fishes, garded with blew and greene, attending. **1665–76** REA *Flora* (ed. 2) 93 The flowers are of a pale blush colour, with small and sharp pointed leaves, which become striped, and garded with a dark sad purple. **1707** CHAMBERLAYNE *St. Gt. Brit.* II. xiv. 183 These wear Scarlet Coats down to the Knee, and Scarlet Breeches, both richly guarded with black Velvet. **1826** SCOTT *Woodst.* xxx. III. 159 A boy, in an orange-tawney doublet,..guarded with blue worsted lace. **1884** J. PAYNE *Tales fr. Arabic* I. 61 On the mule's back was a litter of gold-inwoven brocade, garded about with an embroidered band set with gold and jewels.

fig. **1595** SHAKS. *John* IV. ii. 10 To guard a Title, that was rich before; To gilde refined Gold. **1599** —— *Much Ado* I. i. 288 The body of your discourse is sometime guarded with fragments, and the guardes are but slightly basted on neither. **1655** FULLER *Ch. Hist.* II. ii. §26 He brought in a Religion spun with a Courser Threed, though garded with a Finer Trimming.

punningly. **1624** HEYWOOD *Captives* III. ii. in Bullen *O. Pl.* IV, We will see his fooles coat guarded, ey and reguarded too from slipping out of our fingers.

8. a. *intr.* To be on one's guard; to stand on guard or as a sentinel; to take up or maintain a position of defence (with direct or indirect reference to fencing).

1590 SHAKS. *Com. Err.* V. i. 185 Come stand by me, feare nothing: guard with Halberds. **1593** —— *2 Hen. VI*, V. ii. 33 Feare frames disorder, and disorder wounds Where it should guard. **1607** —— *Cor.* V. ii. 2, 1 *Wat.* Stay: whence are you. 2 *Wat.* Stand, and go backe. *Me.* You guard like men. **1695** COLLIER *Ess.* II. (1697) 69 There are other nice..Cases in which a Man must Guard, if he intends to keep Fair with the World, and turn the Penny. **1802** JAMES *Milit. Dict.* s.v., Prepare to Guard, in the cavalry sword exercise. **1860** O. W. HOLMES *Meet. Nat. Sanitary Assoc.* 51 To guard is better than to heal,—The shield is nobler than the spear! **1892** E. REEVES *Homeward Bound* 208 Apparently imitating English fencing, they occasionally struck and guarded in the different positions.

b. *to guard against*: to take up a position of defence with regard to, to take precautions against. Also with *indirect pass.*

1725 WATTS *Logic* I. iv. §1 (1726) 46 To guard against such Mistakes..it is necessary to acquaint our selves a little with Words and Terms. **1769** *Junius Lett.* xviii. 81 Laws..are intended to guard against what men may do, not to trust to what they will do. **1818** CRUISE *Digest* (ed. 2) I. 464 The great danger of parol declarations, against which the statute was intended to guard. **1832** HT. MARTINEAU *Demerara* ii. 17, I do not see at present how we are to guard against hurricanes. **1874** GREEN *Short Hist.* iii. §2. 120 He had guarded jealously against any revolt of the baronage. **1883** A. ROBERTS *O.T. Revision* ii. 29 This is a fallacy to be most carefully guarded against in dealing with all Biblical questions.

9. *Curling.* **a.** *trans.* To 'cover' or defend (a stone) by planting one in a line between it and oneself. Also *absol.* **b.** *intr.* Said of a stone so planted to defend a partner's stone. Applied also to a similar stroke of play in *Bowls* (see GUARDING *vbl. sb.* 3).

1685 *Lintoun Green* (1817) 38 (E.D.D.) To draw, guard, strike, or wick he tries. **1786** BURNS *Tam Samson's El.* 26 He was the king o' a' the Core, To guard, or draw, or wick a bore. **1840** BLAINE *Rur. Sports* 118 The object of the next in order is to guard the stone of his partner, or to strike off that of his antagonist. **1878** 'CAPT. CRAWLEY' *Football* etc. 127 (*Curling*) A stone is said to guard when it lies in a line between the player and the tee, with another stone belonging to the same side within it. **1897** *Encycl. Sport* I. 258 (Curling) The Stone played..must be over the Hog, but must not touch the Stone to be guarded.

10. *Chess.* (*trans.*) To support a piece or pawn with another.

1761 HOYLE *Ess. Chess* 53 You are to observe this Rule, not to guard your Pawn, unless [etc.]. **1835** *Hoyle's Games* 338 Never guard an inferior piece or pawn with a better, if you can do it with a pawn.

11. *Bookbinding.* **a.** To supply (a guard book) with guards. **b.** To attach (a leaf or plate) to a guard. (Funk's *Stand. Dict.*)

12. *Cricket.* To defend, protect, or cover (the wicket). (Cf. GUARD *sb.* 3 b.)

c **1742** J. LOVE *Cricket* III. 20 Now the two mightiest of the fainting Host..With pow'rful Skill, their threat'ned Wickets guard. **1851** J. PYCROFT *Cricket Field* vii. 117 Yet few, very few, every play as upright as they might play, and that even to guard their three stumps.

‖**guarda-** ('gwarda), stem of It. *guardare* and Sp. *guardar* to GUARD, used in several combinations (*Obs.* exc. *Hist.*), as ‖**,guarda-ca'ballo**, a guard in charge of horses; ‖**,guarda-'damas**, duenna of the Queen's maids-in-waiting; ‖**'guard(a)-in'fante**, a farthingale or hoop; ‖**,guarda-'roba** = WARDROBE. See also GUARDA-COSTA.

1808 PIKE *Sources Mississ.* III. (1810) 256 We..came..to a horse range of the marquis's, where he had four of his soldiers as a *guarda caballo. **1662** EVELYN *Diary* 2 June, Now saw I her Portuguese ladies, and the *Guarda-damas, or Mother of her Maids. *Ibid.* 30 May, A traine of Portuguese ladies in their monstrous fardingals or *guard-infantas. **1670** LASSELS *Voy. Italy* I. 96, I found all the great Ladies here to go like the Donnas of Spain, in Guardinfantas, that is, in horrible overgrown Fartingals of whalebone. **1602** *Archpriest. Controv.* (Camden) II. 28 His *guarda robe had none but riche ones. **1612** in *Crt. & Times Jas. I* (1848) I. 183 Having withdrawn himself into his guarda roba. **1823** LADY MORGAN *Salvator Rosa* I. ii. 46 Vesuvius blazed over the faded frescoes of the dilapidated *guarda-roba.*

guardable ('gɑːdəb(ə)l), *a.* [f. GUARD *v.* + -ABLE.] Capable of being guarded.

1608 E. GRIMSTONE *Hist. France* (1611) 659 Places ill guarded, or not guardable. **1618** SIR R. WILLIAMS *Low Countries* 58 This place was guardable without batterie.

‖**guarda-costa** ('gɑːdə 'kɒstə, Sp. 'gwarda-). Also 8 **guard de costa, guarda-coasta.** [Sp.; f. GUARDA- + Sp. *costa* COAST.] A Spanish vessel used for the protection of the coast; a custom-house cutter.

1731 *Gentl. Mag.* I. 218 Admiral Stewart having received orders to cruize upon the Spaniards, as well Merchant Ships as Guard de Costas. **1742** FIELDING *J. Andrews* II. xvii, I was attacked by one of those cursed guarda-costas who took our ships before the beginning of the war. **1760–72** tr. *Juan & Ulloa's Voy.* (ed. 3) I. 39 While the galleons, guarda costas, or other Spanish ships are here. **1817** P. MOORE in *Parl. Debates* 1797 Slave-dealing, which..might..be stopped more easily by a few vessels in the nature of *guarda costas.* **1845** FORD *Handbk. Spain* I. 227 Swarming with privateers in war-time, and with *guarda costas* or preventive-service cutters in peace. **1876** BANCROFT *Hist. U.S.* IV. xl. 153.

†**'guardage.** *Obs. rare.* Also 7 **gardage.** [f. GUARD *v.* + -AGE.] Keeping, guardianship.

1604 SHAKS. *Oth.* I. ii. 70 Whether a Maid, so tender, Faire, and Happie,..Would euer haue..Run from her Guardage to the sootie bosome, Of such a thing as thou. *a* **1621** BEAUM. & FL. *Thierry & Theod.* V. i, You see this cardicue, the last, and the only quintessence of 50 Crowns, distill'd in the limbeck of your gardage.

†**'guardance.** *Obs. rare*$^{-1}$. In 7 **gardance.** [f. GUARD *v.* + -ANCE]. = prec.

1591 *Troub. Raigne K. John* (1611) 46 If at last nephew thou yeeld thy selfe Into the gardance of thine vncle Iohn, Thou shalt be used as becomes a Prince.

guardant ('gɑːdənt), *a.* and *sb.* Also 6–9 **gardant,** (6–7 **-ante**). [a. F. *gardant*, pres. pple. of *garder* to GUARD.]

A. *adj.*

1. Guarding protecting, watching; on guard.

[**1574** ? Implied in GARDANTLY *adv.*] **1609** HEYWOOD *Brit. Troy* xv. 83 For young Askanius he his left hand spares, In his right hand his guardant sword he shakes. **1816** SOUTHEY *Lay Laureate, Dream* 19, Guardant before his feet a Lion lay. **1851** R. H. STODDARD *Castle in Air* ii. 37 My rivers flow beyond, with guardant ranks Of silver-liveried poplars on their banks.

2. *Her.* Of a beast: Having the full face towards the spectator. (Cf. AFFRONTEE and GAZE *sb.* 3 b.) Also *fig.*

1572 BOSSEWELL *Armorie* II. 44 b, A Lyon Passante, Gardante, betwene three keies d'Or. **1610** GUILLIM *Heraldry* III. xv. (1611) 140 This Lion passant seemeth to goe with more confidence and resolution, but the gardant with more vigilance and circumspection. **1641** BROME *Jovial Crew* II. (1652) E, Couchant and Passant, Guardant, Rampant Beggars. **1790** PENNANT *Lond.* 392 It was a vast house, and, in the time of Stow, distinguished by the arms of England, at that time three leopards passant, guardant, and two angels the supporters, cut on stone. **1828–40** [see GAZE *sb.* 3 b]. **1864** BOUTELL *Her. Hist. & Pop.* xix. §8 (ed. 3) 331 A lion statant guardant or.

B. *sb.* A keeper, guardian, protector.

1591 SHAKS. *1 Hen. VI*, IV. vii. 9 When my angry Guardant stood alone, Tendring my ruine, and assayl'd of none. **1592** WYRLEY *Armorie* 153 [He] bode within the towne as gardant of the same. **1607** SHAKS. *Cor.* v. ii. 67 You shall perceiue, that a Iacke gardant cannot office me from my son Coriolanus. **1616** J. LANE *Cont. Sqr.'s T.* xi. 248 Th' marshallers, gardantes, and tipp staves. *a* **1632** T. TAYLOR *God's Judgem.* I. II. xli. (1642) 372 One of his owne nephews (being his over-seer and gardant for bringing up).

guard-boat ('gɑːdbəʊt).

a. A boat appointed to row the rounds among the ships of war in a harbour, to observe that their officers keep a good look-out. **b.** A boat employed by harbour authorities to enforce quarantine or custom-house regulations.

1696 *Lond. Gaz.* No. 3078/2 The Guard Boat belonging to His Majesty's Garison of Tinmouth Castle. **1758** J. BLAKE *Plan Mar. Syst.* 4 By rowing round the ship, during the night, in a guard-boat, as is done by the officers of the customs with regard to homeward bound Indiamen. **1772–84** COOK *Voy.* (1790) I. 19 They attempted to go on shore, but were stopped by the guard-boat. **1833** HT. MARTINEAU *Cinnamon & Pearls* i. 2 The guard-boat might as well have been empty for any opposition that it offered to the approach of the raft. **1878** *N. Amer. Rev.* CXXVII. 384 To run the gauntlet of the guard-boats.

†**guard-cock.** *Obs.* Corruption of GARDE-CAUT, itself a corruption of F. *garde-corde.*

1706 PHILLIPS (ed. Kersey), *Gardecaut*, or *Gard-du-cord*, ..otherwise call'd *Gard-du-gut*, and Guard-cock.

†**guard-corps.** *Obs.* = GARDE-DU-CORPS, bodyguard.

1583 T. STOCKER *Civ. Warres Lowe C.* II. 58 a, Our people had..greevously wounded his guarde corpes, and put his Souldiers to flight.

guarded ('gɑːdɪd), *ppl. a.* [f. GUARD *v.* or *sb.* + -ED.]

1. a. Defended, protected, watched; having a guard or sentinel. In *Fencing* (hence *fig.*, quot. 1821), protected by the 'guard'.

1570 LEVINS *Manip.* 49/24 Guarded, *communitus.* **1637** MILTON *Lycidas* 161 Where the great Vision of the guarded mount Looks toward Namancos and Bayona's hold. **1667** —— *P.L.* II. 945 Who by stealth Had from his wakeful custody purloined The guarded gold. **1781** COWPER *Conversat.* 556 Truth divine for ever stands secure, Its head as guarded as its base is sure. **1810** SCOTT *Lady of L.* IV. xvi, What! said he nought..Of guarded pass? **1821** SHELLEY *Adonais* xii, The breath Which gave it strength to pierce the guarded wit. **1838** THIRLWALL *Greece* II. 167 The fortress was surprised on its strongest and least guarded side.

absol. **1749** FIELDING *Tom Jones* VII. xiv, By a strange reverse of fortune, the guard became the guarded. **1887** *Pall*

Mall G. 16 Aug. 10/1 The number of the guard depended on the character of the guarded.

b. *Curling.* (See GUARD *v.* 9.)

1685 *Lintoun Green* (1817) 38 (E.D.D.) Roaring up the rink he flies The guarded tee to clear.

c. *Surgery.* (See quot. 1884.)

1883 MARTIN & MOALE *Vertebr. Dissect.* II. 145 Find the duct of the pancreas, through which pass a guarded bristle into the duodenum. **1884** KNIGHT *Dict. Mech.* Suppl., *Guarded Instrument* (*Surgical*), said of an instrument the point or cutting edge of which is concealed or guarded during introduction, and uncovered when at the place where it is to become effective.

d. *Card-playing.* Said of a card, esp. the next to the highest of a suit, when it is protected (in the same hand) by a lower card of the suit.

1742 HOYLE *Whist* iv. 34 Do not throw away any of that Suit, even to keep a King or Queen guarded. **1821** J. BURNEY *Essay on Game of Whist* 20 If you have the queen in sequence, guarded with a small card. **1863** 'CAVENDISH' *Whist* (ed. 5) 19 When a player holds the second best card guarded, he is said to have a *minor tenace*, or an *imperfect minor tenace*. *Ibid.* 37 In trumps, if king or queen is turned up, and it is only singly guarded (i.e. if you have only one other trump), it is generally best to put the turn-up on second hand. **1876** 'CAPT. CRAWLEY' *Card-players' Man.* 44 With 'king singly guarded'—that is, with king and only one other card, play your king boldly.

e. *Chess.* (See GUARD *v.* 10.)

1835 *Hoyle's Games* 337 Take care that no guarded pawn of your adversary's fork two of your pieces.

2. Surrounded by a guard of reserve or restraint; on one's guard; hence, esp. of a person's behaviour, speech, etc.: Careful; prudent; cautious.

1709 STEELE *Tatler* No. 79 ¶1 Be guarded against giving or receiving little Provocations. **1728** GAY *Begg. Op.* II. x, Learn to be more guarded. **1772** *Junius Lett.* lxviii. 335 The charge..brought against you is expressed in terms guarded and well considered. **1802** MAR. EDGEWORTH *Moral T.* (1816) I. vii. 43 If you were upon your trial for life or death ..you could not look more resolutely guarded. **1816** BYRON *Ch. Har.* III. x, Secure in guarded coldness. **1837** HT. MARTINEAU *Soc. Amer.* II. 81 The government has preserved a cool and guarded tone throughout. **1849** MACAULAY *Hist. Eng.* vii. II. 360 Their language was so guarded that nothing was gained by the examination. *a* **1859** *Ibid.* xxiii. (1861) V. 106 Portland made a courteous but guarded answer. **1897** *Allbutt's Syst. Med.* IV. 790 In people over forty..limitation of the affection to one [vocal] cord..should lead to a guarded prognosis.

3. a. Ornamented, as with lace, braid, embroidery, etc.; trimmed; tricked out; having 'guards' or trimmings (in 17th c. often *allusively*). *Obs.* exc. *Hist.* and *spec.* in *Her.* of a garment: Trimmed or turned up with some material.

1509–10 *Act 1 Hen. VIII*, c. 14 §1 No servyng manne waytyng uppon his Maister..were eny garded Hose. **1583** STUBBES *Anat. Abus.* II. (1882) 108 Ministers, that flaunt it out in their saten doblets,..garded gownes, cloakes, and the like. **1599** MARSTON *Sco. Villanie* II. vii. 204 Would not some head..Sweare yon same Damaske-coat, yon garded man Were some graue sober Cato Vtican? **1606** DAY *Ile of Guls* V. i. H 3 b, *Man.* I am no knight, I am Manasses, they made a plaine foole. *Dam.* The onely were [*i.e.* wear] for the guarded [*printed* gaurded] foole is out of request. **1609** *Ev. Woman in Hum.* II. i. in Bullen *O. Pl.* IV, I grieve to see this double garded age, all side-coate, all foole. **1626** MASSINGER *Rom. Actor* I. i, The most censorious of our Roman gentrie, Nay, of the guarded robe, the Senators. **1628** FORD *Lover's Mel.* I. ii, In stead of a fine guarded Page, We haue got him A boy, trickt vp in neat and handsome Fashion. **1655** FULLER *Ch. Hist.* x. v. 89 Besides, the Place was proper not for the plain but guarded Gown. **1834** PLANCHÉ *Brit. Costume* 274 Large Gallic or Venetian hosen, slashed, quilted, stuffed, and guarded (or laced), were worn as before. **1868** CUSSANS *Her.* (1893) 129.

†**b.** Of a flower: Having a border or stripe of colour. *Obs.*

1688 R. HOLME *Armoury* II. 115/1 Edged, as Flower leaves often are..of which there are several terms, as edged, striped or streaked, garded, [etc.]. **1779** SHERIDAN *Critic* II. ii, The striped carnation and the guarded rose.

4. Of a book: Having guards. (See GUARD *sb.* 16 l.)

1888 JACOBI *Printer's Voc.* s.v., Books are said to be 'guarded' when the plates are mounted or sewn on guards instead of being stitched or pasted in the ordinary way. **1889** H. B. WHEATLEY *How to Catal.* iii. 71 The slips are lightly pasted down into guarded volumes.

guardedly ('gɑːdɪdlɪ), *adv.* [f. GUARDED *ppl. a.* + -LY².] In a guarded manner; in guarded language; cautiously.

1784 SHERIDAN *Life Swift* 243 It obliquely pointed out the true object of their resentment; but this so guardedly, that it was impossible to make any serious charge against the Author of his having such a design. **1856** KANE *Arct. Expl.* II. vi. 72, I am acting very guardedly with them, I cannot punish till I have the evidence of an overt act. **1883** SIR W. V. FIELD in *Law Rep.* 11 Q. Bench Div. 765 The Act.. dealing very guardedly with the common law right..to prefer a bill before a grand jury. **1887** *Manch. Exam.* 7 Feb. 5/3 This desire was guardedly stated and carefully fenced about with conditions.

guardedness ('gɑːdɪdnɪs). [f. GUARDED *ppl. a.* + -NESS.] The quality of being guarded (in speech, behaviour, etc.); cautiousness.

1807 W. TAYLOR in *Monthly Mag.* XXIV. 331 Lessing.. tries what his rules permit.. with a guardedness which would not be expected from his tolerance. **1838** DICKENS *Nich. Nick.* li, How he had baffled the said Ralph by extreme guardedness of manner and ingenuity of speech. **1895** F. HALL *Two Trifles* 8 What..have all my painstaking guardedness and scrupulous exactness..stood me in stead?

guardee (gɑː'diː). [f. GUARD *sb.* 8 + -EE².] A familiar name for a guardsman, esp. as a type of smartness and elegance. Also *attrib.* or as quasi-*adj.*

1904 KIPLING *Traffics & Discov.* 281 That old chap..is an ex-Guardee. That's why he's saluting in slow time. **1931** BROPHY & PARTRIDGE *Songs & Slang 1914–18* (ed. 3) 213 *Guardsman's wriggle*, exaggerated salute affected by the Guards. Variants, 'tickling his ear', 'Guardee wriggle'. **1932** 'A. BRIDGE' *Peking Picnic* xv. 184 Music, of which Touchy, for all his rather Guardee appearance, was passionately fond. **1937** *Oxford Mag.* 6 May 565 Blow the trumpet! Guardee tramp it! **1939** J. CARY *Mr. Johnson* 151 He hollows his back like a guardee.

guarder ('gɑːdə(r)). [f. GUARD *v.* + -ER¹.]

1. One who or that which guards, *lit.* and *fig.*; a keeper, watcher, protector, guardian, warder, guard.

1542 UDALL tr. *Erasm. Apophth.* II. 264 b, Vsyng theim not as kepers but as seruauntes and garders of his bodie. **1578** BANISTER *Hist. Man* VIII. 98 The Nerues..beyng therfore rightly iudged the diligent messengers and garders of the brayne. **1589** GREENE *Menaphon* (Arb.) 46 Thus sate poore Menaphon..keeping his teeth garders of his stomacke, and his eyes watchmen of his loues. **1603** FLORIO *Montaigne* (1634) 392 They were pursued by the guarders and Souldiers of the Port. **1625** FLETCHER *Noble Gent.* I. i, Groomes and pages, chamber-maides and garders. **1628** in Rushw. *Hist. Coll.* (1659) I. 551 The Kings heart is the best guarder of his own promise. **1753** J. SCOTT *Epidemic Mortality* 11 When the bold guarders of the house shall shake, And, pain'd, their station at the door forsake. **1840** BROWNING *Sordello* VI. 448 With guarders row on row, Gay swarms of varletry that come and go.

2. ? A contrivance to prevent a (church) bell from swinging over.

1583 in Picton *L'pool Munic. Rec.* (1883) I. 98 Garder & Clevicorde. **1684** *Vestry Bks.* (Surtees) 253 For a garder for the bells, 1*s.* 6*d.*

guard-fish, variant of GARFISH.

guardful ('gɑːdfʊl), *a.* Now *rare* or *dial.* [f. GUARD *sb.* + -FUL.] Watchful; careful. Hence '**guardfully** *adv.*, carefully.

c **1611** CHAPMAN *Iliad* I. 441 O thou Fautour of Chrysa, whose fair hands doth guardfully dispose Celestial Cilla. **1749** A. HILL *Merope* I. ii, I, mean while, Watch, with a guardful Eye, these Murd'rers Motions. **1830** H. ANGELO *Remin.* I. 209 An injunction to be guardful of these had been given to the people. **1876** J. ELLIS *Caesar in Egypt* 36 Dost thou frown? Was it not well?—nay, blame me guardfully. **1887** *S. Chesh. Gloss.*, *Guardful*, careful.

guard-house ('gɑːdhaʊs).

a. A building for the accommodation of a (military) guard. **b.** A building in which prisoners are detained under guard.

1592 *Extracts Aberd. Reg.* (1848) II. 76 Ilk persone.. being warnit to the wache to cum theirto to the gaird hous. **1698** FRYER *Acc. E. India & P.* 67 The English have a pretty Custom-house and Guard-house. **1712** W. ROGERS *Voy.* 43 They have also a Guard-house, where there are about 20 Men commanded by the Governour, a Lieutenant, and Ensign. **1818** SCOTT *Hrt. Midl.* iii, The Captain proceeded to withdraw his men towards their guard-house in the High Street. **1825** JEFFERSON *Autobiog.* Wks. 1859 I. 87 They collected the next day, burnt ten or twelve guard-houses, killed two or three of the guards [etc.]. **1875** JOWETT *Plato* (ed. 2) III. 698 There were guard-houses at intervals for the body-guard.

‖**guardia civil** ('gwarðja θi'vil). Pl. **guardias civiles.** [Sp., = civil guard.] A force formed in Spain in 1844 to take over police duties from the military, and chiefly responsible for public order and safety. Also *ellipt.*

1846 R. FORD *Gatherings from Spain* xiii. 149 The alcalde, the muleteer, the guardia, and all who have shared in the booty. *Ibid.* xvi. 188 The mounted guards, who are now stationed in towns, and by whom the roads are regularly patrolled..are called *guardias civiles*. **1946** G. MILLAR *Horned Pigeon* xxiii. 416 They had found no sign of the *Guardia Civil*. **1955** J. THOMAS *No Banners* iii. 26 On the Pyrenees Franco's *guardias civiles* blocked the roads into Spain. **1966** M. CATTO *Bird on Wing* x. 153 The *Guardia Civil* shouted again, raising his rifle.

guardian ('gɑːdɪən). Forms: α. 5 gardyene, 5–6 gardeyn, 5–8 -ein, (6 -aine, -ayne, -en, guarden, 7 gardeine). β. 5–7 gardian, (6 -iane, -ien), 6– guardian. [a. AF. *gardein* (1275), OF. *g(u)arden*, earlier *-enc*, nom. sing. and acc. pl. *guardens*, *-ains* (12th c.), f. *garde* GUARD *sb.* or perh. a. Teut. **warding-*, f. *wardâ* WARD *sb.* + *-ing*: see -ING³. The assimilation of the ending to the suffix *-ien*, which has given the mod.F. *gardien*, dates from the 14th c., while the appearance of the corresponding *-ian* in the Eng. word is evidenced from the 15th c. Cf. Pr. *gardian*, Sp. *guardian*, It. *guardiano*, and see WARDEN.]

1. One who guards, protects, or preserves; a keeper, defender; 'one to whom the care and preservation of any thing is committed' (J.); sometimes = *guardian angel*. Applied also *occas.* to impersonal objects.

c **1477** CAXTON *Jason* 87 b, She retorned into her chamber wher was but one auncient lady her gardyene or maystresse. **1494** FABYAN *Chron.* VI. clxxx. 177 Foure knyghtes, whiche were called gardeyns of her corps, were slayne fast by her. *Ibid.* VII. 365 From that yere..were al custodyes & gardeyns, and no mayres: & who tho that was than constable of the Toure of London, was also custos of the cytie. *a* **1547** SURREY *Æneid* II. (1557) D ij, In the void porches Phenix, Ulisses eke, Sterne guardens stood watching of the spoile. **1598** W. PHILLIPS *Linschoten's Disc. Voy.* I. iii. 4 The Guardian, that is the quarter master hath 1400 reyes the month. **1605** SHAKS. *Macb.* II iv. 35 The Sacred Store-house of his Predecessors, And Guardian of their Bones. **1605** BACON *Adv. Learn.* II. Ded. to King §9 (1872) 79 Readers in sciences are indeed the guardians of the stores and provisions of sciences. **1667** MILTON *P.L.* III. 512 The Stairs were such as whereon Jacob saw Angels ascending and descending, bands Of Guardians bright. *a* **1711** KEN *E. Hymn* Wks. (1838) 438 O may my Guardian while I sleep, Close to my bed his vigils keep. **1767** JUNIUS *Lett.* xiv. 59 The attorney-general is *ex officio* the Guardian of liberty. **1856** FROUDE *Hist. Eng.* (1858) I. iii. 189 The clergy were the guardians of morality. **1875** JOWETT *Plato* (ed. 2) V. 10 Plato ..explains the manner in which guardians of the law..are to be appointed. **1883** C. J. WILLS *Mod. Persia* 277 The dervish who usually acts as guardian to the tomb.

b. † ***Guardian of the Peace***: an earlier name for a 'Justice of the Peace'. ***Guardian of the Spiritualities***, ***G. of the Temporalities***: see those words. ***Guardian of the Poor*** (often simply *Guardian*): one of a board elected to administer the poor laws in a particular parish or district.

[**1330** *Act 4 Edw. III*, c. 5 Et eient les Justices, assignez a la deliverance des gaoles poair a deliverer les gaoles de ceux qi serront enditez devant les gardeins de la pees.] **1417** LD. FURNIVAL in Ellis *Orig. Lett.* Ser. II. I. 61 The Gardeins of the spirituallities of Ardmaghe. **1581** LAMBARDE *Eiren.* I. ii. (1588) 9 The Gardeins of the Peace (who afterward obtained the name of Iustices of the Peace). **1764** BURN *Poor Laws* 183 Twelve persons residing in each district, of a certain estate in land, to be guardians of the district. **1782** *Act 22 Geo. III*, c. 83 §2 The Visitor, Guardian, and Governor of such Poor House. *Ibid.* §7 It shall and may be lawful for two Justices of the Peace..to appoint one of the Persons so recommended to be Guardian of the Poor for each of such Parishes. **1783–94** BLAKE *Songs Innoc.*, *Holy Thursday* 11 Beneath them sit the aged men, wise guardians of the poor. **1834** *Act 4 & 5 Will. IV*, c. 76 §38 A Board of Guardians of the Poor for such Union shall be constituted and chosen, and the Workhouse or Workhouses of such Union shall be governed, and the Relief of the Poor in such Union shall be administered, by such Board of Guardians. **1857** TOULMIN SMITH *Parish* 166 'Guardians' may exist either for single parishes, or for groups of parishes joined in 'Unions'. **1876** FAWCETT *Pol. Econ.* IV. v. (ed. 5) 598 The Manchester guardians have lately made able-bodied paupers grind corn by hand. **1876** FREEMAN *Norm. Conq.* V. xxv. 549 A reform of a generation back entrusted the care of the poor..to Boards of Guardians.

c. (See quot.)

1727–41 CHAMBERS *Cycl.* s.v., In the order of the garter, the officer who in other military orders is called grand-master, is called the sovereign guardian of the order.

d. In an Oddfellows' lodge, ***Inner*** and ***Outer Guardian***. (Cf. GUARD *sb.* 7 c.)

1879 *Man. Oddfellowship* 141 The lodge is properly arranged, and the inner door opened wide; the Grand Marshal, with white baton trimmed with scarlet, approaches the Inner Guardian from without.

2. *spec.* in *Law.* One who has or is by law entitled to the custody of the person or property (or both) of an infant, an idiot, or other person legally incapable of managing his own affairs; a tutor. (The correlative of *ward*.)

1513 MORE *Rich. III*, Wks. 50/2 Syth he hath nothing by discent holden by knightes seruice, the law maketh his mother his gardaine. **1561** T. NORTON *Calvin's Inst.* (1634) Table Contents, The old Church is compared to an heire under age, which is governed by Gardians. **1599** SHAKS. *Much Ado* II. iii. 174, I am sorry for her, as I haue iust cause, being her Vncle, and her Guardian. **1611** BIBLE *Transl. Pref.* 2 A wastefull Prince, that had neede of a Guardian, or ouerseer. **1628** COKE *On Litt.* I. 135 b, When an Ideot doth sue or defend, he shall not appeare by Gardeine or Procheine Amy. **1700** PRIDEAUX *Lett.* (Camden) 195 Mr Walpole, who was guardian to ye Lord Townshend. **1758** JOHNSON *Idler* No. 6 ¶10 She only ran away from her guardians. **1765** BLACKSTONE *Comm.* I. xvii. 379 The guardian with us performs the office of both the tutor and curator. **1818** CRUISE *Digest* (ed. 2) III. 429 The possession of the mother as guardian, gave actual possession to the son. **1859** W. COLLINS *Q. of Hearts* (1875) 5, I knew perfectly well that I should hear myself appointed guardian, and executor with his brother, of this young lady.

b. ***guardian in chivalry***: the guardian of a minor holding by knight service. (†Rarely ***g. in knight service***.) ***guardian in socage***: the guardian of a tenant in socage. ***guardian by nature***: the father, with respect to his tutelage of the heir apparent or heiress presumptive. ***guardian for nurture***: the father, and, after his death the mother, until the minor has reached the age of 14. (These four were classed together as guardians *by the common law*.) ***guardian by custom*** or ***customary guardian***: an officer, corporation, etc. having by local custom a legal right to exercise guardianship. ***guardian by election***: a guardian chosen by an infant who would otherwise have none. (See also quot. 1823.) ***guardian ad litem*** (see quot. 1838).

1565 COOPER *Thesaurus*, *Curatores dicuntur qui pupillis loco tutorum dantur.* Gardians in socage, or they that haue the charge and custodie of wardes or other under yeres of discretion. **1574** tr. *Littleton's Tenures* 10 b, The childes mother entrethe in the remnant, and it occupieth as garden or warden in socage. **1628** COKE *On Litt.* I. 85 There is Gardeine in right in Chiualrie, and Gardeine in Deede in

Chiualrie. *Ibid.* 88 b, There are three manner of Gardeinships, viz. by the Common Law, by the Statute Law, and Custome. By the Common Law there are foure manner of Gardians, viz. Gardein in Chiualrie.. Gardein by nature.. Gardein in Socage.. Gardein per cause de nurture. **1642** tr. *Perkins' Prof. Bk.* i. §60. 28 Gardien in Knight Service of the bodie and land may grant the wardship of the land without deed. **1654** *Sheppard's Crt.-Keepers Guide* 112 A Gardeine in Chivalry that hath a Manor of the Wards may make Copyhold Estates. **1660** R. COKE *Power & Subj.* 83 Guardian in Chivalry may give or sell to another the Guardianship of his Ward; but Guardian in Socage cannot, for his is *delegata potestas.* **1660** *Act 12 Car. II*, c. 24 §8 Every person or persons claiming the custody or tuition of such childe or children as Guardian in soccage or otherwise. **1765** BLACKSTONE *Comm.* I. 449 Of the several species of guardians, the first are guardians by nature: viz. the father and (in some cases) the mother of the child.. There are also guardians for nurture which are of course the father, or.. mother, till the infant attains the age of fourteen years. *Ibid.* 462 These guardians in socage, like those for nurture, continue only till the minor is fourteen years of age. **1820** GIFFORD *Compl. Eng. Lawyer* III. xii. (ed. 5) 387 Guardians are of six kinds:—1. Guardians by nature; 2. Guardians by nurture; 3. Guardians in socage; 4. Guardians by testament; 5. Guardians by custom of particular places; 6. Guardians by election of the infant. **1823** CRABB *Technol. Dict.* s.v., *Guardian by statute*, or *testamentary guardian*, one appointed according to the statute of 12 Car. 2, c. 24... *Guardian by appointment*, is either of the Lord Chancellor or the Ecclesiastical Court. **1838** *Penny Cycl.* XI. 465/1 All courts ..have power to appoint a guardian *ad litem*, that is, to defend a prosecution or suit instituted by or against an infant.

†**3.** In various official titles in which the form WARDEN is now prevalent. *Obs.*

1495 *Act 11 Hen. VII*, c. 35 Preamble, His Lyeutenaunte of Ireland and Gardeyn of the.. Marches. **1529** RASTELL *Pastyme* (1811) 195 Ryse Meridocke rebellyd agaynst the kynge's Gardeyn of his Castels in Wales. **1571** *Act 13 Eliz.* c. 10 §2 Master or Gardian of anye Hospitall. **1581** LAMBARDE *Eiren.* III. ii. (1588) 337 The writ *de homine Replegiando* to be directed to the garden of a Forest. **1632** *Star Chamb. Cases* (Camden) 109 Lord Gardein of the Cinque Portes. **1867** SMYTH *Sailor's Word-bk.*, *Guardian of the Cinque Ports*, otherwise *lord-warden.*

4. The superior of a Franciscan convent. [L. *custos.*]

1466 *Paston Lett.* No. 549 II. 266 Item, to xxiii. susters of Normandys, with the gardian, eche of them iiiid., and the gardian viiid. **1727-41** CHAMBERS *Cycl.* s.v., In the convents of Franciscans, the officer is called guardian, who in the rest is called superior. **1883** *Catholic Dict.* (1885) 356/2 Fr. John Perez de Marchena, guardian of a convent near Seville.. a learned cosmographer.

5. *pl.* = GUARD *sb.* 12. ? *Obs.*

1555 EDEN *Decades* 38 The gardens of the north pole were owte of syght. **1879** PROCTOR *New Star Atlas* 16 The course of the pair of stars (called 'the Guardians of the Pole') belonging to the Little Bear is also shown by arrows.

6. *attrib.* and *Comb.*, as ***guardian election***; **guardian-cell** = *guard-cell.*

1880 GRAY *Struct. Bot.* iii. §4. 89 The stomata.. consist usually of a pair of cells (called *guardian-cells), with an opening between them. **1885** GOODALE *Physiol. Bot.* (1892) 377 The cellulose film is produced almost simultaneously throughout the whole extent of the mother-cell, which is cut into two guardian-cells, forming a stoma. **1898** *Daily News* 23 Feb 6/5 The question of a Saturday poll at the forthcoming *guardian elections.

b. *attrib.* passing into adj. with sense 'protecting, tutelary.' **guardian-angel**, an angel conceived as watching over or protecting a particular person or place; also *transf.*

1610 HEALEY *St. Aug. Citie of God* 125 Your great guardian-gods bore all this unmoved. *a* **1631** DONNE *Relique* 26 Difference of sex no more wee knew, Then our Guardian Angells doe. **1697** DRYDEN *Virg. Georg.* I. 670 Mother Earth, Goddess unmov'd! whose Guardian Arms extend O'er Thuscan Tiber's Course, and Roman Tow'rs defend. *a* **1711** KEN *Hymns Festiv.* Poet. Wks. 1721 I. 384 Bless'd Angels,.. Your Guardian cares bestow. **1711** SHAFTESB. *Charac.* (1737) I. 168 We have each of us a dæmon, genius, angel, or guardian-spirit. **1725** POPE *Odyss.* III. 481 Distinguish'd care of guardian Deities! **1760** FOOTE *Minor* I. Wks. 1799 I. 239 Then will I step in, like his guardian-angel, and snatch him from perdition. **1764** GOLDSM. *Trav.* 12 Round his dwelling guardian saints attend. **1780** COWPER *2nd Poem Burn. Ld. Mansfield's Libr.*, They.. blessed the guardian care that kept His sacred head from harm. **1810** SCOTT *Lady of L.* I. xvii, The Guardian Naiad of the strand. **1834** J. H. NEWMAN *Par. Serm.* (1837) I. xx. 311 His guardian friends now long departed. **1847** L. HUNT *Jar Honey* xii. (1848) 161 The goddess Proserpina, when she was the guardian angel of Sicily. **1864** PUSEY *Lect. Daniel* v. 257 Then followed the Guardian-promise to the house of Jehu. *Ibid.* viii. 523 Each Christian at least is, from childhood, assigned to the care of his own guardian angel.

†**'guardianage.** *Obs. rare.* Also guardenage. [f. GUARDIAN + -AGE.] Guardianship.

1600 HOLLAND *Livy* XLII. xix. (1609) 1126 To take the charge of publicke tuition, and as it were the guardianage of him. **1601** —— *Pliny* I. 184 His yonger brother.. had recommended his daughter to his tuition and guardenage.

†**'guardiance.** *Obs.* Also 6 gardience. [f. as if GUARDIANT: see -ANCE.] Guardianship.

1560 DAUS tr. *Sleidane's Comm.* 250 Themperoure knoweth, how we commytted the prouince taken, to gardience. **1598** I. D. tr. *Loys Le Roy's Aristot. Polit.* 140 The Aduocators, to whome the guardiance and defence of the lawes is cheefly committed. *c* **1611** CHAPMAN *Iliad* XXII. 436 A soft bed, a careful nurse's arms Took him to guardiance. **1633** BP. HALL. *Medit. Love Christ* §8 To secure my soul.. by the guardiance of thy blessed angels.

'guardiancy. *rare*$^{-1}$. [f. GUARDIAN + -CY.] Guardianship.

1865 CARLYLE *Fredk. Gt.* XV. xi. (1872) VI. 78, I must have Silesia again.. Or would you have us administer it under the guardiancy of Prussia?

†**'guardianer.** *Obs. rare.* Also 6 **gardeiner, -eaner.** [f. GUARDIAN + -ER[1].] A guardian.

1595 *Wills & Inv. N.C.* (Surtees 1860) 253 My brother-in-lawe, whom I maik gardeiner, to have the full governance of hym, his landes, &c... I do ordaine.. my brother-in-lawe to be gardeaner and governore of.. my children. **1626** MIDDLETON *Women Beware Wom.* I. ii, A poulterer's wife made a great complaint Of you last night to your guardianer.

guardianess ('gɑːdɪənɪs). [f. GUARDIAN + -ESS.] A female guardian or tutor.

1614 BEAUM. & FL. *Wit at Sev. Weap.* I. i, I've yet a neece to wed, over whose steps I have plac'st a trusty watchful Gardinesse. **1622** CALLIS *Stat. Sewers* (1647) 201 Gardianesses in Chivalry. *a* **1693** *Urquhart's Rabelais* III. xxxi. 262 The Goddess of Wisdom, Tutress, and Guardianess of such as are.. studious. **1751** ELIZA HEYWOOD *Betsy Thoughtless* I. 33 Have you been so closely watched by your guardian and guardianesses here? **1754** RICHARDSON *Grandison* (1810) VI. liii. 359 She is my guardianess, may I say? Is there such a word? **1891** MISS C. MITFORD in *J. M.'s Lett. & Rem.* 23 She had been selected by the Lord Chancellor as guardianess to one of his wealthy female wards.

guardianize ('gɑːdɪənaɪz), *v. rare*$^{-0}$. [f. GUARDIAN + -IZE.] *intr.* 'To act the part of a guardian' (Ogilvie).

guardianless ('gɑːdɪənlɪs), *a.* [f. GUARDIAN + -LESS.] Having no guardian.

1604 MARSTON *Malcont.* III. ii, A Lady gardianlesse, Left to the push of all allurement. **1676** WYCHERLEY *Pl. Dealer* III. i, I'll bring my Action of Detinue or Trover. But first I'll try to find out this Guardianless, graceless Villain. **1758** COOPER *Call Aristippus* 102 A like regard the British Loves To me their future poet bore, Nor left me guardianless alone. **1838** BULWER *Lady of Lyons* V. ii, Thy youth will not be guardianless.

guardianly ('gɑːdɪənlɪ), *a. rare.* [f. GUARDIAN + -LY[1].] Pertaining to or characteristic of a guardian.

1872 *Anteros* xxxii. 271 Affecting still to take a guardianly interest in the former's welfare. **1890** *Harper's Mag.* Aug. 407/1 An uncle with strongly developed guardianly instincts.

guardianship ('gɑːdɪənʃɪp). [f. GUARDIAN + -SHIP.] The condition or fact of being a guardian; the office or position of guardian.

a. *spec.* (Legal) tutelage.

1553 GRIMALDE *Cicero's Offices* I. (1558) 38 Like as garden-shyppe [L. *tutela*] even so government of the common weale ought to be used to the profit of them to whom it is committed. **1577-87** HOLINSHED *Chron.* III. 467/1 Euerie heire being in the gardianship of anie lord, when he is growne to be one and twentie yeares of age, ought presentlie to inioy the inheritance left him by his father. **1622** CALLIS *Stat. Sewers* (1647) 49 If a Garden assign to a woman more dower then she ought to have, and then grant his Gardenship over, [etc.]. **1651** G. W. tr. *Cowel's Inst.* 18 The Guardianship of wards is double, one by vertue of the common, the other of the Statute Law. **1765** BLACKSTONE *Comm.* I. xvii. 452 Among the antient Greeks and Romans women were never of age, but subject to perpetual guardianship. **1838** *Penny Cycl.* XI. 464/2 Guardianship in chivalry is now abolished by the statute 12 Car. II, c. 24. **1875** POSTE *Gaius* I. Comm. (ed. 2) 121 Guardianship in Socage occurs when lands descend upon a minor, and devolves by the Common law upon those of his next of blood upon whom the inheritance cannot descend.

b. *gen.* Keeping, protection, guard.

1646 H. LAWRENCE *Comm. Angells* 21 Some consider whether the Angell keepers doe ever leave men or no with whose Guardianship they are betrusted. **1652** NEEDHAM tr. *Selden's Mare Cl.* 244 The same Dominion, the same Victorie, and the same Guardianship or Protection alwaies both of the British Tethys, or Sea, and the Isle it self. *a* **1715** BURNET *Own Time* (1724) I. 809 In the case of lunaticks, the right still remained in him: Only the guardianship, or the exercise of it, was to be lodged with a Prince Regent. **1814** JANE AUSTEN *Mansf. Park* (1851) 59, I cannot call that situation nothing.. which has the guardianship of religion and morals. **1837** W. IRVING *Capt. Bonneville* III. 261 Passing days and nights under the calm guardianship of the laws. **1856** KANE *Arct. Expl.* II. viii. 88, I left him under the guardianship of Mr. Bonsall's weapon.

†**'guardiant.** *Obs. rare.* [A mixture of GUARDIAN and GUARDANT. Cf. *guardiance.*] A guardian.

1618 WITHER *Motto, Nec Careo* Wks. (1633) 536, I want no Guard, or Coate of Musket proofe; My Innocence is guardiant strong enough. **1635** A. STAFFORD *Fem. Glory* (1869) 122 Joseph.. who as before had been a guardiant of her.

guarding ('gɑːdɪŋ), *vbl. sb.* [f. GUARD *v.* + -ING[1].]

1. The action of the vb. GUARD; protection; guardianship.

1551 UDALL *Erasm. Par. Luke* xi. 1-4 Vnder the tuicion and guarding [**1548** wardyng] of their heauenly father. **1577-87** HOLINSHED *Chron.* III. 887/2 A castell ancientlie vsed by the kings of Aragon for the garding of great personages. **1817** J. SCOTT *Paris Revisit.* (ed. 4) 329 The guarding of the Louvre was committed by turns to the British and Austrians, while this process lasted. **1877** *Daily News* 30 Nov. 5/5 Our only care was the guarding of the valleys by which our flank could be turned.

2. *concr.* A trimming of braid, lace, etc. *Obs.* exc. *Hist.*

1538 STARKEY *England* I. iii. 80 The new devysys of gardyng and faggyng of mennys apparayle. **1608** MACHIN *Dumb Knt.* I. i, Crownes, garlands, gardins, and what not. **1869** MRS. PALLISER *Lace* xxii. 258 The London apprentices had adopted the white stitching and garding as a decoration for their collars.

3. *Curling* and *Bowls.* (See GUARD *v.* 9.)

1897 *Encycl. Sport* I. 128 The aim of every player is to get his bowls.. nearer to the jack than his opponent, and immense variety is afforded by 'drawing', 'guarding' a shot or a road, 'trailing' a jack [etc.]. *Ibid.* 129 *Blocking* (also *Guarding* and *Obstructing*), playing a bowl so that it shall come to rest between the next player and the jack, or any bowl at which he may wish to aim.

guarding ('gɑːdɪŋ), *ppl. a.* [f. GUARD *v.* + -ING[2].] That guards or protects.

1819 CRABBE *T. of Hall* I, So good a cause was only to be kept by guarding laws. **1895** *Daily News* 1 Feb. 6/7 The little book.. has a guarding flap. **1897** MARY KINGSLEY *W. Africa* 176 The Adoomas left and fled to the French authority at Njole and remained under its guarding shadow until the French came up and chastised the Fans.

Hence **'guardingly** *adv.*

1821 *Examiner* 142/1 St. Peter.. has a sword guardingly, as he stands up against a tree 'in a disturbed sleep'.

guardless ('gɑːdlɪs), *a.* [f. GUARD *sb.* + -LESS.]

1. Having no guard; undefended, unprotected; destitute of safeguards.

c **1611** CHAPMAN *Iliad* V. 146 His flocks left guardless. **1621** LADY M. WROTH *Urania* 67 Fortune and your power, hath left me guardlesse. **1692** SOUTH *Serm.* (1697) I. 324 A rich Land, guardless and undefended. **1715** M. DAVIES *Athen. Brit.* I. 241 Ever looking upon the self-guiding Spirit to be guardless and dangerous. **1725** POPE *Odyss.* XXII. 43 To your lust and spoil a guardless prey. **1819** CRABBE *T. of Hall* VIII, Watching long the now confiding maid, He thought her guardless, and grew less afraid.

2. Off one's guard; incautious.

1654 GATAKER *Disc. Apol.* 2 His, as groundless, so still deserted, and least guardless, assertion. **1849** LYTTON *K. Arthur* VIII. v, The lone, unconscious, guardless modesty.

3. Of a sword: Having no guard.

1882 O'DONOVAN *Merv Oasis* I. ii. 30 The Georgian.. with.. guardless Caucasian sabre. **1887** T. STEVENS *Around the World* I. xvii. 404 They are armed with Circassian guardless swords and flint-lock horse-pistols.

'guardman. ? *Obs.* = GUARDSMAN 1, 2.

1756 W. TOLDERVY *Two Orphans* III. 83 This brought a watchman; but Copper, being more than a match for a couple of these sort of guard-men [etc.]. **1815** MRS. M. PILKINGTON *Celebrity* I. 212 They kept a coach for the convenience of their brother's family, into which lady Beauchamp resolved to push the young guard-man.

guardo ('gɑːdəʊ). *U.S.* [Arbitrarily f. GUARDSHIP + *-o*, simulating Sp. words.] A receiving-ship for enlisted men who are to be drafted to sea-going vessels. Chiefly *attrib.* and *Comb.*

1834 W. N. GLASCOCK *Naval Sketch-bk.* 2nd Ser. I. 232 Why, bless ye, some o' your *guardo*-chaps come over you now with the pride o' their pratin' schoolmaster. *a* **1846** J. A. GARDNER *Recoll.* (1906) 116 A droll old guardo midshipman. **1850** H. MELVILLE *White Jacket* II. xxvi. 168 Familiarity with the *guardo-moves*.. of a frigate. **1909** *Cent. Dict. Suppl.*, *Guardo-move*, a trick played upon a landsman on a receiving-ship.

guardon(e, obs. form of GUERDON.

guard-rail ('gɑːdreɪl).

1. A hand- or other rail for the purpose of guarding against accidents by falling, being caught in machinery, etc.

Naut. (*a*) A hand-rail on the paddle box bridge of a steam-vessel. (*b*) A breast rail on the break of the poop. (*c*) A safety rail round a hatch-way (1875 Knight *Dict. Mech.*).

1860 *Merc. Marine Mag.* VII. 218 The guard-rail.. had been heightened. **1894** *Outing* (U.S.) July 250/1 Hanging upon the upright posts were a barometer, a thermometer, and the Professor's banjo. There was also a small mariner's compass let into the guard-rail.

2. *Railways.* (See quot. 1875.)

1875 KNIGHT *Dict. Mech.*, *Guard-rail*, a short rail placed on the inside of a main rail, so as to keep a wheel on the track by pressing against the inside of the flange of the wheel. It is used when there is a short break in the continuity of the other rail, as in switches and crossings. A *safety, side*, or *wing* rail. **1888** *Engineer* LXV. 295/1 The trestle had.. no guard-rails.

Hence **guard-rail** *v.*, to furnish with a guard-rail.

1891 R. KIPLING *City Dreadf. Nt.* 67 Our machinery is fenced and guard-railed as much as possible, and these men don't get caught up by the belting.

guard-room ('gɑːdruːm). **a.** A room for the accommodation of a (military) guard. **b.** A room in which prisoners are guarded.

1762 GOLDSM. *Cit. W.* cxviii, They at length arrived at the palace-gate, and after waiting half an hour, were admitted into the guard-room. **1772-84** COOK *Voy.* (1790) I. 24 In the guard-room are stationed the Viceroy's body-guard, who are relieved every morning between eight and nine. **1826** SCOTT *Diary* 2 Nov. in *Lockhart*, In the guard room were the heroes of la Vendée. **1829** W. IRVING *Granada* (1850) 42 The guard-room was a scene rather of massacre than combat. **1844** *Regul. & Ord. Army* 264 The Officers and Non-Commissioned Officers are responsible that no drinking, swearing, gaming, or other irregularity, is allowed in the Guard-Room.

attrib. **1818** LADY CHARLEVILLE in *Lady Morgan's Autobiog.* (1859) 244 A corrupt, disorganised, uneducated mass of ardent-minded guard-room youths.

guardship[1] (ˈgɑːdʃɪp). *rare.* [f. GUARD *sb.* + -SHIP.] The condition or position of a guard or guardian; guardianship.

1624 MASSINGER *Parl. Love* I. v, But wherefore come you in divided troops, As if the mistresses would not accept Their servants' guardship. *a* **1626** BACON *Max. & Uses* (1636) 60 *marg.*, The third part must descend to the heire to answer Guardship [*corresponds to* Wardship *of the text*]. **1730** SWIFT *Panegyrick on Dean* Wks. 1755 IV. I. 137 Under whose wise and careful guardship I now despise fatigue and hardship. *c* **1817** HOGG *Tales & Sk.* V. 141, I have with sore travail procured a guardship of your life.

guard-ship[2], **guardship** (ˈgɑːdʃɪp).

a. A vessel of war appointed to protect a harbour and to superintend its marine affairs, and to receive seamen until they are able to join their ships. **b.** 'The ship (of the squadron) having guard-duty for the day' (Funk's *Stand. Dict.*).

1689 WOOD *Life* 1 Oct., Colonel Thomas Wilford, late commander of the guardship at Chatham. **1696** *Baker's Chron.* 756 While our Guard-Ships were remote at Sea, they [the Hollanders] arrived at the mouth of the River Medway. **1697–9** DAMPIER *Voy.* II. 164 To secure that Trade, they had a Guardship lying there. **1753** *Scots Mag.* Jan. 47/2 Eighteen men of war are put into commission as guard-ships. **1806** A. DUNCAN *Nelson* 179 The Goliath was stationed at Portsmouth as a guard-ship. **1833** MARRYAT *P. Simple* (1863) 86, I was sent on board of the guard-ship, where I remained about ten days, and then was sent round to join this frigate. **1836** —— *Midsh. Easy* xxxv, I will procure his discharge as soon as I arrive, and send him on board the guard-ship till I obtain it. **1876** BANCROFT *Hist. U.S.* V. xx. 569 Prescott.. had his quarters at a lonely farm-house.. with.. no protection but a sentry and the guard-ship in the bay.

guardsman (ˈgɑːdzmən). [In sense 1, f. *guard's*, genitive of GUARD *sb.*: cf. *draughtsman*, *headsman*. In sense 2, f. *Guards* pl: see GUARD *sb.* 8. Cf. GUARDMAN.]

1. A man who acts as a guard; a member of a guard. Also *fig.*, a guardian (*rare*$^{-1}$).

a **1854** H. REED *Lect. Brit. Poets* Ess. i. (1857) 357 So far as literature is concerned, we are by our calling guardsmen of English rights and English merits. **1870** BRYANT *Iliad* I. x. 306 Com'st then to find One of the guardsmen or a comrade? **1877** FRASER *Wigtown* 54 (E.D.D.) It was the duty of the guardsman to fire his gun, and thus alarm the inhabitants. **1879** FARRAR *St. Paul* II. 425 The necessity of his being coupled to guardsman after guardsman, day after day and night after night.

2. A soldier (usually, an officer) of the guards or household troops of the English army.

1817 [see HORSE-GUARDSMAN]. **1823** BYRON *Juan* XIII. lxxxviii, There was Jack Jargon, the gigantic guardsman. **1844** DISRAELI *Coningsby* IV. xiv, A young guardsman who was then a guest at the Castle, and who had been in garrison in Ireland. **1876** GEO. ELIOT *Dan. Der.* III. xxii, Tannhäuser, one suspects, was a knight of ill-furnished imagination, hardly of larger discourse than a heavy Guardsman.

guardy (ˈgɑːdɪ). *colloq.* Also **guardie**. Shortened form of GUARDIAN.

1833 J. ROMILLY *Diary* 15 Jan. (1967) 26 Box from Manchester containing wedding cake from Williams (Ackers' guardian): suppose Guardy's daughter has entrapped the wealthy heir. **1858** A. MAYHEW *Paved with Gold* I. i. 33 When he and the other little ones were allowed.. to go out for a walk.. he would call every well dressed man that passed 'a guardy'. **1924** GALSWORTHY *Old English* I. i, You *are* an awful boy! Guardy, he really is too awful.

‖**guariba** (gwɑːˈriːbə). [Native Brazilian.] The Howling Monkey. (Cf. ALOUATTE, ARAGUATO.)

[**1693** RAY *Syn. Quad.* 153 *Guariba* Brasiliensibus Marcgr.] **1753** CHAMBERS *Cycl. Supp.*, *Guariba*,.. the name of a species of monkey found in the West-Indies. **1774** GOLDSM. *Nat. Hist.* (1862) I. VII. i. 508 The Warine, or the Brazilian Guariba. This monkey is as large as a fox. **1876** K. JOHNSTON in *Encycl. Brit.* IV. 227/2 The largest [monkeys] belong to the genus *Stentor*, including the guaribas or howling monkeys.

guarinite (ˈgwærɪnaɪt). *Min.* [Named by Guiscardi, 1858, after G. *Guarini*: see -ITE.] Silicotitanate of calcium, found in small yellowish crystals.

1859 *Amer. Jrnl. Sci.* Ser. II. XXVIII. 142 Guarinite, after Prof. G. Guarini, of Naples. **1869** PHILLIPS *Vesuv.* x. 300 Guarinite in ejected blocks, with prisms of hornblende.

†ˈ**guarish**, *v.* *Obs.* Also 5 garissh, -ysshe, guarisshe, -yshe, -ysse, gwerysshe. See also WARISH. [f. OF. *g(u)ariss-*, pres. stem of *g(u)arir*, modF. *guérir* = OSp., OPg. *guarir*:—OTeut. **warjan* in Goth. *warjan*, OHG. *giweren-*, *biwerjan* to protect, defend.]

1. *trans.* To cure, heal. (Frequent in Caxton.)

1474 CAXTON *Chesse* III. v. (1860) Hj b, Alle thys maner of peple.. that haue the charge for to make hoole and guarisshe alle maner of maladyes and Infirmytees. **1483** —— *G. de la Tour* F vij b, That it wold plese hym to hele and gwerysshe her. **1590** SPENSER *F.Q.* III. v. 41 Daily she dressed him, and did the best, His grievous hurt to guarish, that she might. **1596** *Ibid.* IV. iii. 29 All his wounds, and all his bruses guarisht.

2. *intr.* for *pass.* To recover. Const. *of*.

1489 CAXTON *Faytes of A.* III. xxi. 219 We putte caas that he beynge in prison shulde gwarisshe of his sicknesse.

†ˈ**guarisher.** *Obs.*$^{-1}$ In 5 guarysshour. [f. GUARISH *v.* + -ER[1].] A healer or curer.

1474 CAXTON *Chesse* III. v. (1860) Hj b, They.. myght better be callyd bouchers thenne helars or guarysshours of woundes and sores.

guarison, rare obs. form of GARRISON.

guarland, obs. form of GARLAND.

Guarnerius (gwɑːˈnɪərɪəs). Also **Joseph Guarnerius; Guarn(i)eri.** The name of a family of famous Italian violin- and violoncello-makers of Cremona of the seventeenth and eighteenth centuries, used to designate a violin or violoncello made by a member of this family. (Cf. JOSEPH.)

1866 J. PEARCE *Violins & Violin Makers* 130 Fifty years ago, a Guarnerius of the best time might have been bought for £50 that will now command £500. **1875** G. HART *Violin* 96 A 'Joseph Guarnerius' for one hundred and fifty guineas! **1898** H. R. HAWEIS *Old Violins* 217 It was no more a Guarnerius than a Strad. [**1902** *Grove's Dict. Mus.* IV. 284/2 A full-sized Stradivari or Giuseppe Guarnieri.] **1905** O. RACSTER *Chats on Violoncellos* (1908) iv. 164 Another violoncello by the redoubtable Andreas.. was found.. six months after the sale of Mr Gillot's Guarnerius. **1923** *Weekly Dispatch* 18 Feb. 2 A new violin alongside his old Guarnerius. **1971** *Daily Mail* 19 Jan. 6/4 A Del Gesu Guarnerius made in 1743.

guarrent, obs. form of GARRON[1].

guarri (ˈgwarɪ). *S. Afr.* Also **ghwarrie, guarry, guerrie, gwarri(e, quarri.** [Kaffir *um Gwali.*] Any one of several trees or shrubs of the genus *Euclea*, esp. *E. undulata* or *E. lanceolata*; the fruit of these trees or shrubs. Also *attrib.*

1789 W. PATERSON *Narr. Journeys Country of Hottentots* 43 The ground is covered with shrubs about four feet high, called by the natives Guerrie, a species of Royena. **1793** tr. *Thunberg's Trav.* I. 202 The berries of the Guarri bush (*Euclea undulata*) had a sweet taste, and were eaten by the Hottentots. **1801** J. BARROW *Trav. S. Afr.* I. iii. 149 The *guerrie bosch*, apparently a species of rhus. **1843** J. C. CHASE *Cape of Good Hope* II. 152 The wild fruits, indigenous to the country, are also incredibly numerous.. Among these are the wild grape (*Vitis Capensis*),.. quarri (*Euclea undulata*) [etc.]. **1866** LINDLEY & MOORE *Treas. Bot.* s.v. *Euclea*, The fruit is globular, fleshy, and juicy, sometimes as large as a cherry. Those of many of the species, known by the colonists as Guarry, are eaten. **1897** S. J. DU TOIT *Rhodesia* 32 Various kinds of sweet grass and small shrubs, varied with very good large bush and trees, as 'quarri', &c. **1913** PETTMAN *Africanderisms*, *Guarri honey*, a very pale honey in much esteem in the Riversdale District, obtained by the bees from *Royena sp. Guarri tea*, this is made by the Hottentots from the leave of *Euclea lanceolata*. **1939** E. N. MARAIS *My Friends the Baboons* iv. 42 Near the sleeping-place there was, in a corner of the rocks, a large gwarrie-bush. **1966** E. PALMER *Plains of Camdeboo* xvii. 271 They made vinegar from the little fruits of the gwarri tree.

†ˈ**guary.** *Obs.* Also 5 garye. [Cornish *guare* (in full *guare mirakel*), cogn. with Welsh *chwareu* to play.] An ancient Cornish miracle play.

c **1460** *Emare* 1032 Thys ys on of Brytayne layes, That was used by olde dayes, Men callys playn the garye. **1602** CAREW *Cornwall* I. (1723) 71 b, The Guary miracle, in English, a miracle-play, is a kinde of Enterlude, compiled in Cornish out of some scripture history, with that grossenes, which accompanied the Romanes *vetus Comedia*. *Ibid.* 72 A great deale more sport and laughter, then 20 such Guaries could haue afforded.

guaryson, variant of GUERISON *Obs.*

‖**guasa** (ˈgwɑːsə). The West-Indian jew-fish.

1884–5 *Riverside Nat. Hist.* (1888) III. 224 The jew-fish, guasa or warsaw (*Promicrops itaira*).

guast, obs. Sc. form of GUEST.

Guatemalan (gwɑːtɪˈmɑːlən, ˈgwæt-), *sb.* and *a.* Also **Guateˈmalian** and (no longer current) **Guatelˈmalan.** [f. *Guatemala* + -AN.] **A.** *sb.* A native or inhabitant of Guatemala, the most northern republic of Central America, bordering on Mexico. **B.** *adj.* Of or pertaining to Guatemala. Also **Guateˈmaltec(an)** [Sp. *guatemaltecano*].

1823 *Gentl. Mag.* XCIII. II. 636/2 The kingdom of Guatemala.. has since separated, and the Guatemalans have established themselves as a sovereign State. **1831** J. BELL *Syst. Geog.* V. 617 The Guatelmalans declared themselves independent. **1877** BODDAM-WHETHAM *Across Cent. Amer.* 19 The kind-hearted Guatemaltecans have a custom of driving out to the plain to meet expected friends. **1880** *Encycl. Brit.* XI. 240/1 Singing-birds are commonly kept in the Guatemalian houses. **1888** *New Princeton Rev.* May 356 Zaldivar transmitted a series of despatches misrepresenting the situation, and appealing for protection against Guatemalan tyranny. **1902** *Encycl. Brit.* XXIX. 151/1 A Guatemalan company. **1920** *Glasgow Herald* 7 Apr. 10 Ayutla, on the Guatemalian border. **1927** *Blackw. Mag.* Aug. 173/1 This map, the work of a well-known Guatemalan engineer. **1932** *Times Lit. Suppl.* 24 Nov. 869/3 Harassed by Guatamaltec Jacks-in-office. **1972** *Buenos Aires Herald* 3 Feb. 7/6 The British troops issue was put to the juridical committee by the Guatemalan delegate.

‖**guava** (ˈgwɑːvə). Forms: 6 ? guannaba, 6–7 guiava, 6, 8 guaiava, 7 goyave, guavar, -ee, -er, guayava, -avo, guiave, -avo, guayva, gwave, 8 goava, gojavu, goyava, -avier, guaba, guavo, guayabo, guyava, gwavah, (9 gauva), 7– guava. [Sp. *guayaba*, *-abo*, presumably a. some S. American or W. Indian name.]

1. A tree of the myrtaceous genus *Psidium* of tropical America, esp. *P. Guayava* (now naturalized in many tropical countries), which yields a fruit of an acid flavour, used to make jelly, etc.

white guava, *Psidium pyriferum*. **red guava**, *P. pomiferum*. **mountain guava**, *P. montanum*. Also **black guava**, *Guettarda argentea*, a rubiaceous tree of Jamaica, having a black, globose, pulpy fruit (*Cent. Dict.*).

1555 EDEN *Decades* 81 They noorysshe a tree which they caule *Guaiaua* [printed *Guaiana*], that beareth a frute much resemblynge the kynde of citrons which are commonly cauled limones, of taste sumwhat sharpe myxt with swetenes. **1604** E. G[RIMSTONE] tr. *D'Acosta's Hist. Indies* IV. xxiv. 277 The Guayavos be other trees which commonly carry an ill fruite. **1660** HICKERINGILL *Jamaica* (1661) 12 Nature hath stor'd it.. with Oranges, Lymes.. Guavars. **1748** *Earthquake Peru* iii. 209 There as those of the Caribbee Islands, as Ananas, Guayavas. **1756** P. BROWNE *Jamaica* 239 The Mountain Guava. This is one of the largest trees in the woods of Jamaica. **1760–72** tr. *Juan & Ulloa's Voy.* (ed. 3) I. 48 Besides these trees, here are also the tamarind, the medlar, the sapote, the papayo, the guayabo,.. and several others. **1859** R. THOMPSON *Gardener's Assist.* 33 Musas, Granadillas, Guavas, or other tropical plants bearing fruit, should be watered occasionally with manure water.

2. The fruit of the guava-tree.

1555 EDEN *Decades* 45 The fruite cauled *Guannaba* vnknowen vnto vs, and sumwhat lyke vnto a quynse. **1577** FRAMPTON tr. *Monardes* 90 b, They brought from the firme lande the seede of the fruite.. whiche they call guiauas. **1600** HAKLUYT *Voy.* (1810) III. 583 Feeding on nothing but roots, and Guiauos, a fruit like figs. **1626** P. NICHOLS *Sir F. Drake Revived* (1628) 50 Sundry sorts of fruits.. Mammeas, Guyauas [etc.]. **1657** R. LIGON *Barbadoes* (1673) 71 The Guaver grows on a Tree, bodied and leav'd like a Cherry-tree.. the fruit of the bigness of a small Lemon, and near that colour. **1698** FROGER *Voy.* 61 The Goyave is somewhat bigger than a Nut; Its Pulp is red, very stony, and of the Taste of a Peach. **1706** PHILLIPS (ed. Kersey), *Goyavier*, a sort of Fruit growing in the West-Indies. **1796** STEDMAN *Surinam* II. xvi. 4 There are two species of guava; that which is the sweetest has the smallest quantity of seeds. **1879** MRS. A. E. JAMES *Ind. Househ. Managem.* 58 Guavas are only eatable when preserved or in jellies.

3. *attrib.*, as ***guava-bush***, ***-fruit***, ***-jelly***, ***-plantation***, ***-tree***; **guava-apple** = 2; **guavafly-catcher**, *Turdus analis* (Cassell, 1884).

1866 MARY B. CLARKE *Mosses fr. a Rolling Stone* 120 Where the *guava-apple ripens. **1792** MAR. RIDDELL *Voy. Madeira* 101 The *psidium pomiferum*, or *guava bush. **1697** DAMPIER *Voy.* I. 222 The *Guava Fruit grows on a hard scrubbed Shrub. **1848** THACKERAY *Van. Fair* lv. Cayenne pepper, hot pickles, *guava jelly, and colonial produce. **1834** M. SCOTT *Cruise Midge* (1859) 400 A narrow bridle-path.. led us through a *guava plantation. **1630** CAPT. SMITH *Trav. & Adv.* xxvi. 56 *Gwane [sic] trees beare a fruit so bigge as a Peare, good and wholsome. **1697** DAMPIER *Voy.* (1699) II. II. 107 The N.W. part of it is full of Guaver Trees of the largest variety. **1819** BOWDICH *Mission Ashantee* I. ii. 15 Richly varied with palm, banana, plantain, and guava trees.

[**guay.** Originally in *cheval guay*, rep. F. *cheval gai*, a heraldic term for a horse without harness, misinterpreted as in quots.

1725 COATS *Dict. Her.* (1739), *Guay*, as *Cheval guay*, is a Horse rearing, and standing on his hinder Legs. **1730–6** in BAILEY (fol.). **1828–40** in BERRY *Encycl. Her.* I. **1830** ROBSON *Brit. Herald*, *Guay*, or *Cheval Guay*, a horse in the position of rearing, or standing on its hind legs.]

guayaquillite (gwaɪəˈkɪlaɪt). *Min.* Also **guya-.** [Named by Johnston, 1838, from Guayaquil in S. America, its locality.] A fossil resin of pale yellow colour.

1838 *Phil. Mag.* Ser. III. XIII. 329 Guyaquillite. **1868** DANA *Min.* (ed. 5) 745 Guyaquillite.. Yields easily to the knife, and may be rubbed to powder.

guayava, -avo, guayva, obs. ff. GUAVA.

guayule (gwaɪˈuːliː, ‖hwaɪˈuli). [a. Amer. Sp. *guayule*, f. Nahuatl *cuauhuli.*] A silver-leaved shrub, *Parthenium argentatum*, of the family Compositæ, native to northern Mexico and adjacent parts of Texas, formerly cultivated as the source of a type of rubber; also, the rubber produced from the plant.

1906 *Bull. Imper. Inst.* IV. 114 The Guayule rubber of Mexico. *Ibid.*, The Guayule plant. *Ibid.* 115 The Guayule is found at altitudes ranging from 3,000 to 5,600 feet. **1926** P. C. STANDLEY *Trees & Shrubs of Mexico* v. 1520 The guayule rubber plant is one of the most important members of the Mexican flora. **1939** J. STEINBECK *Grapes of Wrath* ix. 102 Remember a fella wanted us to put in that rubber bush they call guayule. **1944** *Bot. Gaz.* CVI. 198/1 The experiments indicate that substances unfavorable to the growth of guayule plants emanate from the roots of actively growing plants of this species [*sc.* guayule]. **1964** F. O'ROURKE *Mule for Marquesa* 72 The distant green of deceptively deadly ocotillo savannahs, filled with the scorched grey of candelilla and guayule. **1969** A. S. CRAIG *Dict. Rubber Technol.* 75 Intensive research, started in 1942, has not succeeded in making guayule competitive with *Hevea* rubber, and since 1962 there has been no commercial production.

‖ˈ**guazil.** *Obs. rare*$^{-1}$. = ALGUAZIL.

1665 R. HEAD *Eng. Rogue* I. lxviii. (1874) 422 This made him haste to the Guazil or Judge.

guazu (gwɑːˈsuː, ˈgwɑːzuː). [a. Guarani *guaçú* deer.] The South American marsh-deer, *Blastoceros dichotomus*. Also **guazapuco, guazubira, guazu-pita**, etc. (formerly regarded as comprising more than one species; see quots.).

1837 *Penny Cycl.* VIII. 361/2 The Guazapuco deer, *Mazama paludosa* of Smith, *Cervus paludosus* of Desmarest and Lichtenstein. *Ibid.*, The Guazu-bira, *Cervus nemorivagus* of Lichtenstein... Locality the same as that of the Guazu-pita. **1838** W. P. HUNTER tr. *Azara's Nat. Hist. Quadrupeds of Paraguay* II. 126 The Guaranese denominate all deer *Guazu*. *Ibid.* 130 Guazupucu signifies *large deer*... We caught..two female of the guazupucu deer. *Ibid.* 145 The fourth species is universally called Guazubira; and its skin is held in high repute, for gloves. *Ibid.*, It was stated that the guazupita is met with in New Spain. **1850** *Proc. Zool. Soc.* XVIII. 237 Blastoceros paludosus. The Guazupuco... Inhabits the Brazils. **1871** C. KINGSLEY *At Last* x, A little brown guazu-pita fawn. **1898** R. LYDEKKER *Deer of all Lands* xii. 282 (*heading*) The Guazu Group—Sub-Genus Blastoceros. *Ibid.* 286 He [*sc.* Illiger] refers to the gouzoupoucou of Azara, which is the present species.

guazuti (gwɑːsuːˈtiː, gwaˈzuːtiː). [a. Guarani *guaçuti* white deer.] The brown and white South American pampas deer, *Ozotoceros* (or *Blastoceros*) *bezoarticus*.

1837 *Penny Cycl.* VIII. 361/2 The Guazuti of D'Azara. **1838** W. P. HUNTER tr. *Azara's Nat. Hist. Quadrupeds of Paraguay* II. 135 Guazuti, the name given to this species by the Guaranese, signifies *white deer*..others call it guazay. **1850** *Proc. Zool. Soc.* XVIII. 237 Blastoceros campestris. The Mazame or Guazuti. **1898** R. LYDEKKER *Deer of all Lands* xii. 291 In certain parts of Brazil this deer [*sc.* the pampas deer] is known as the guazuti.

‖**guazzo.** [It.] = GOUACHE.

1722 J. RICHARDSON *Statues Italy* 158 There are in the Apartments of this Palace some single Boys of *Guido Reni* in *Guazzo* under Glasses. **1854** FAIRHOLT *Dict. Art, Guazzo*, a hard and durable kind of distemper painting used by the ancients, the vehicle or medium consisting of egg, rum, or glue, which resists the action of damp of all kinds, and preserves the colours very completely.

gub (gʌb), *sb.* [Cf. GAB *sb.*[4], of which this may be a corruption or local variant.

The passage quoted seems to be the sole authority for this word, which appears in some recent Dicts., but is unknown to several mechanicians who have been consulted.]

A projection on the back of a wheel for engaging the loops of an endless chain or rope.

1839 URE *Dict. Arts* 1072 (*Rope making.*) A wheel with gubs at the back of it, over which the endless rope passes and gives motion to the machinery of the carriage.. The speed may be regulated..by the diameter of the circle formed by the gubs on the wheel.

gubbahawn (ˈgʌbəhɔːn). *rare*[−1]. [? a. Irish *gobagán* 'dog-fish'.] Some small fish.

1857 KINGSLEY *Two Y. Ago* xiii, When you can't catch salmon, you catch trout, and when you can't catch trout, you'll whip on the shallow for poor little gubbahawns.

gubbe, obs. form of GOB *sb.*[1]

‖**gubber.** *Obs.* [Conjectured by Yule to represent Pers. *dīnār-i-gabr*, 'money of the infidel': see GUEBRE.] 'Some kind of gold ducat or sequin' (Y.).

1711 C. LOCKYER *Trade India* vii. 201 They have Venetians, Gubbers, Muggerbees, and Pagodas. *Ibid.* viii. 242 When a Parcel of Venetian Ducats are mixt with others, the whole goes by the Name of Chequeens at Surat, but when they are separated, one sort is call'd Venetians, and all the others, Gubbers indifferently. **1752** T. BROOKS *Weights & Meas. E. Indies* (1766) 5 Gold and Silver Weights. 100 Venetian Duccats 11 oz. 0 dw. 5 Gr. 100 Gubbers at a Medium 10 oz. 17 dw. 12 Gr.

gubber-tush (ˈgʌbətʌʃ). *Obs.* exc. *dial.* [The first element is obscure: cf. GOBBER-TOOTH.] 'A large projecting tooth' (*Sheffield Gloss.* 1888). Hence †**gubber-tushed** *a.*, having large projecting teeth.

1621 BURTON *Anat. Mel.* III. ii. IV. i. (ed. 1651) 519 Every Lover admires his Mistress, though she have..a nose like a promontory, gubber-tushed, rotten teeth [etc.]. **1688** R. HOLME *Armoury* II. 427/1 Gubber Tushed is when teeth stand out, and not in order.

gubbin (ˈgʌbɪn). *Mining.* [? A variant of GOBBIN, though prob. connected with GUBBINS.] A kind of ironstone. Also ***gubbin bat*** (BAT *sb.*[2] 12), ***iron(stone)***.

1712 H. BELLERS in *Phil. Trans.* XXVII. 542 A black fissile Substance, called the Gublin-Bat [*sic*]. *Ibid.* A hard blackish Iron Oar, with white spots in it, called the Gublin Iron-Stone [*sic*]. **1847–8** H. MILLER *First Impr.* v. (1857) 70 A specimen..known to the miners as the 'gubbin iron'. **1860** W. WHITE *Wrekin* xxvi. 271 'Newmine', 'gubbins', 'blue-flats', and 'black-jacks'. **1881** RAYMOND *Mining Gloss., Gubbin*, a kind of ironstone.

gubbins (ˈgʌbɪnz), *sb. pl.* Also **gubbings**. Rarely *sing.* [var. of GOBBON.]

1. Fragments, esp. of fish; fish-parings. In later use (also const. *sing.*), trash; anything of little value; a gadget, thingummy. In *sing.*, a fragment. Also *fig.* and *attrib.*

1553 *Respublica* I. i. 40 in Brandl *Dramas* (1898) 286 The skimmynges, the gubbins of booties and praies. **1599** NASHE *Lenten Stuffe* 73 Hough you hungerstarued gubbins, or offalles of men, how thriue you? **1630** J. TAYLOR (Water P.) *Wks.* II. 165 To be a Laundres, imports onely to wash or dresse Lawne, which is as much impeachment as to cal..a Fishmonger, a seller of Gubbins. *Ibid.* III. 64/2 All that they could buy, or sell, or barter, Would scarce be worth a Gubbin once a quarter. **1677** MIEGE *Fr. Dict.*, Gubbings, the parings of haberdine, *coupures ou rongnures de poisson*. **1696** PHILLIPS, A *Gubbin* (old word), a fragment. **1721–1800** BAILEY, *Gubbins*, Fragments; the Parings of Haberdine, Codfish, &c. **1754** in Hone *Every-day Bk.* (1827) II. 827 Cold provisions..by a cant name he usually called 'his gubbins'. **1918** P. MACGILL *Glenmornan* v. 106 That gubbin iv land was at one time nothin' but a bare rock. **1925** FRASER & GIBBONS *Soldier & Sailor Words* 112 *Gubbins*, mere stuff. Trash. Anything of no value—*e.g.*, 'That's only gubbins, all rot!' Also, personal effects—*e.g.*, 'See after my gubbins, will you?' **1944** *Amer. Speech* XIX. 280 A *gubbins* is used to describe almost any part of the equipment of a plane, with about the same meaning as *gadget*. **1958** I. BROWN *Words our Time* 60 You can save more petrol by how you drive than with the gubbinses now floating around. **1965** *Sunday Times* (Colour Suppl.) 5 Dec. 16 Many machines flying have a vast illicit complement of rivets, nails, nuts, bolts, torches, pliers and half-eaten sandwiches. .. One of the modern test pilot's less enviable jobs is to fly new aircraft upside down and try to catch the gubbins as it hurtles past his face. **1968** *New Scientist* 3 Oct. 8/2 Behind that again is the engine and propeller, the fuel tank and various bits of 'gubbins'.

2. a. A contemptuous name formerly given to the inhabitants of a district near Brent Tor on the edge of Dartmoor, who are said to have been absolute savages. *Obs.* exc. *Hist.*

a **1661** FULLER *Worthies, Devonshire* I. (1662) 248 The Gubbings (so now I dare call them secured by distance) which one of more valour durst not do to their Face.. The Gubbings-Land is a Scythia within England, and they pure Heathens therein. **1836** MRS. BRAY *Descr. Tamar & Tavy* I. Let. xiv. 253 Even at the present day, the term Gubbins is well known in the vicinity.. They still have the reputation of having been a wild and almost savage race. **1887** *Cornh. Mag.* Nov. 508 The race of 'Gubbins', as Fuller calls them, may die out. **1900** *Scott. N. & Q.* Mar. 139/1 Those Welsh bandits recall the Dartmoor 'Gubbins' or 'gubbings' familiar to readers of Westward Ho.

b. *colloq.* A fool, a duffer.

1916 E. F. BENSON *David Blaize* vii. 124 'Silly gubbins,' she said. **1955** 'E. C. R. LORAC' *Ask a Policeman* ii. 25 If we only get these old gubbinses out I could let the rooms proper. **1957** [see BATTER *sb.*[4]].

Gubbio (ˈgʊbɪəʊ). The name of a city in northern Italy, used *attrib.* to designate mojolica made there in the sixteenth century, particularly a ruby-lustred majolica made by Giorgio Andreoli.

1857 J. MARRYAT *Hist. Pott. & Porcelain* (ed. 2) ii. 24 The Gubbio ware unites in some degree the qualities of the mezza majolica and fine majolica; its prismatic glaze has never been surpassed. **1885** *Encycl. Brit.* XIX. 626/2 The early Pesaro and Gubbio ware. *Ibid.* 627/2 The pictured wares of Urbino sometimes have the Gubbio lustre colours. **1942** *Burlington Mag.* June 156/2 Several pieces of Italian Maiolica,..a Gubbio dish by Maestro Giorgio, signed and dated 1522.

gubble (ˈgʌb(ə)l), *v.* [Echoic.] *intr.* To make the sound rendered by 'gub': a verb formed to imitate an inarticulate sound.

1904 H. F. DAY *Kin o' Ktaadn* 88 Like molasses gubblin' out of a bung-hole. **1929** A. MASON *Swansea Dan* 199 The ocean plunked and gubbled as if in a nightmare. **1944** L. A. G. STRONG *All fall Down* 22 If you'd have the goodness to let me finish, instead of praying and gubbling.

gubbon, variant of GOBBON. *Obs.*

†**gubern**, *v. Obs. rare*[−1]. [ad. L. *gubern-āre* to GOVERN.] *trans.* To govern.

1500–20 DUNBAR *Poems* lxxxv. 11 ȝerne ws, guberne, wirgin matern, of reuth both rute and ryne.

†**ˈgubernacle.** *Obs. rare*[−1]. In 6 *Sc.* -akle. [ad. L. *gubernāc(u)lum* (see next).] A rudder.

1513 DOUGLAS *Æneis* VI. v. 112 The helmstok, or gubernakle of tre, Quhairwith I reulit our cours throw the se.

‖**gubernaculum** (gjuːbəˈnækjʊləm). Pl. gubernacula. [L. *gubernāculum*, f. *gubernāre* to steer, rule, govern.] Applied to several animal and vegetable structures which are used for steering (e.g. in flight), or for regulating the (embryonic) development or course of an organ.

†**a.** ? The elytron of a coleopterous insect. **b.** *Anat.* In the male human fœtus, a fibrous cord connecting the testis with the scrotum and drawing it down as the fœtus grows. **c.** *Odontology.* 'The solid pedicle of fibrous tissue which connects the dental sac of the permanent teeth with the gum in the early stage of their development' (*Syd. Soc. Lex.* 1886) **d.** *Zool.* (See quot. 1871.) Also, 'the posterior trailing flagellum of a biflagellate infusorian, used for steering' (*Cent. Dict.*).

a. 1661 LOVELL *Hist. Anim. & Min.* Introd., Locusts make a noise by rubbing themselves with their gubernacula. **b. 1786** HUNTER *Observ. Anim. Œcon.* Wks. 1837 IV. 7 A substance..which at present I shall call the ligament, or gubernaculum testis, because it connects the testis with the scrotum, and seems to direct its course through the rings of the abdominal muscles. **1842** E. WILSON *Anat. Vade M.* (ed. 2) 573 The Gubernaculum is a soft and conical cord. **c. 1841** tr. *Cruveilhier's Descr. Anat.* II. 241 The influence exerted by the iter dentis and gubernaculum upon the direction of the permanent teeth is by no means constant. **1876** C. S. TOMES *Dental Anat.* 135 The gubernacula of the front permanent tooth sacs. **d. 1871** ALLMAN *Gymnoblastic Hydroids* p. xvi, Gubernaculum.., a common sack-like membrane which surrounds the generative buds within the gonangium, and aids in directing them or their contents towards the orifice of the gonangium. **1880–81** SAVILLE KENT *Man. Infusoria* I. 434 [In Anisonema] The posterior flagellum, or gubernaculum, trailing in the rear.

Hence **guberˈnacular** *a.*, of or pertaining to a gubernaculum.

1871 ALLMAN *Gymnoblastic Hydroids* 51 Gonophores in various stages of development, all surrounded by the gubernacular membrane. **1882** *Quain's Elem. Anat.* II. 908 There is likewise a fibrous structure attached inferiorly to the lower part of the scrotum, and surrounding the peritoneal pouch above, which may be distinguished as the gubernacular cord. **1886** *Syd. Soc. Lex., Gubernacular sac.*

†**gubernance.** *Obs.* Also 5 -aunce. [f. L. *gubernant-em*, pres. pple. of *gubernāre* to GOVERN, after GOVERNANCE.] Governance, government.

1455 *Test. Ebor.* (Surtees) II. 215, I will that my moder dame Jane of Boynton have the reule and gubernaunce of all my landes, tenements. **1550** in Strype *Eccl. Mem.* (1721) II. xxxiii. 273 The gubernance of all the king's tenants and subjects within the said manor and hundred, inhabitant.

†**gubernate**, *v. Obs. rare*[−0]. [ad. L. *gubernāt-*, ppl. stem of *gubernāre* to GOVERN.] *trans.* To govern.

1623 in COCKERAM.

gubernation (gjuːbəˈneɪʃən). Now *rare.* [a. obs. F. *gubernation*, or ad. L. *gubernātiōn-em*, n. of action f. *gubernāre* to steer, rule, GOVERN.] The act or fact of governing, guiding, or controlling; guidance, government.

1432–50 tr. *Higden* (Rolls) IV. 33 These men be the lxx[ti] interpretatores, whiche instructe lawe and psalmes of the cognicion of oon God, and gubernacion of theire realme. *c* **1485** *Digby Myst.* (1882) III. 200 Yf we hem gett onder ower gubernacyon. **1502** *Ord. Crysten Men* (W. de W. 1506) I. vi. 51 Appereth clerely that the creacyon and gubernacyon of all the worlde procedeth of all the blyssed trynyte. **1560** *Wills & Inv. N.C.* (*Surtees* 1835) 191, I will that my said brother xp'ofor ffenne [have] the gubernac'on and custodie of the said xl[s]. a pece, amownting to the sume of vj[l]. duringe the minorities of the thre childeren. **1574** HELLOWES *Gueuara's Fam. Ep.* (1577) 150 If you will gouerne this Earledome verie well, begin the gubernation in your selfe. **1635** F. WHITE *Sabbath* Ep. Ded. 12 The adversaries of the Prelacie contend, that Episcopall gubernation is prohibited by Christ. **1653** GATAKER *Vind. Annot. Jer.* 97 There was no suspition of a supernatural gubernation or direction. **1741** WATTS *Improv. Mind* I. xvi. §1 There is little or nothing in the government of the kingdoms of nature, and grace, but what is..employed as a medium or conscious instrument of this extensive gubernation. **1851** G. S. FABER *Many Mansions* (1862) 317 They ascend in the scale of orderly gubernation.

b. *attrib.* in ***gubernation money*** (Sc.).

1837 *Evid. taken bef. Commissioners Univ. Scotl.* II. 496 [Payments made out of Snell's charity] To ten exhibitioners ..£1333 6*s.* 8*d.* The master of Balliol for gubernation money £31 15*s.* 0*d.*

Hence **guberˈnational** *a. rare*, pertaining to government.

1863 RUSSELL *Diary North & South* I. 168 Another gubernational dignitary laconically replied to the demand for so many thousand soldiers, 'Nary one'.

gubernative (ˈgjuːbənətɪv), *a.* Now *rare.* [ad. L. **gubernātīv-us*, f. *gubernāre*, to GOVERN. Cf. obs. F. *gubernatif*.] Of or pertaining to government; having the function of governing.

1387–8 T. USK *Test. Love* I. vi. (Skeat) I. 120 Feoble witted people, that haue none insight of gubernatife prudence. **1653** GAUDEN *Hierasp.* 268 The power of proving and ordeyning Presbyters,..of rebuking.. excommunicating, silencing and restoring (all Acts gubernative). **1660** R. SHERINGHAM *King's Suprem. Asserted* viii. (1682) 94 Having the gubernative, and executive power in their hands. *a* **1670** HACKET *Abp. Williams* I. (1692) 39 Real and gubernative wisdom. **1677** GALE *Crt. Gentiles* IV. 473 If it be so, that this gubernative dispositive Mind doth thus dispose althings. **1853** G. S. FABER *Revival Fr. Emperorship* 11 The Territorial Roman Empire and the Gubernative Roman Emperorship were, each alike, a strict Unit. **1897** *Columbus Disp.* (Ohio) 12 Oct. 1/8 The action of the Spanish authorities in Cuba was a gubernative measure.

Hence **ˈgubernatively** *adv.*

1853 G. S. FABER *Revival Fr. Emperorship* 22 The Imperial Head..is the Head, either gubernatively, or feudally, or reputedly, of the legally one empire.

gubernator (ˈgjuːbəneɪtə(r)). *rare.* [a. L. *gubernātor*, agent-n. f. *gubernāre*, *gubernāt-*, to GOVERN.] A ruler, governor.

1522 J. CLERK in Ellis *Orig. Lett.* Ser. III. I. 304 Who is in Spayne, and chief gubernator there vnder the Emperor. **1623** COCKERAM, *Gubernatour*, hee which governeth. **1678** GALE *Crt. Gentiles* III. 5 The wise Creator and Gubernator of althings. **1886** W. J. TUCKER *Life E. Europe* 281 Whenever our freedom was called into question, or our rights trespassed upon..by our Woiwodes or Gubernators to whom was intrusted the administration of the principality.

gubernatorial (ˌgjuːbərnəˈtɔərɪəl), *a.* Chiefly *U.S.* [f. L. *gubernātor* (see prec.), perh. through an assumed **gubernātōri-us*: see -IAL, -AL[1].] Of or pertaining to a governor (esp. one holding this as an official title) or government.

1734 *N. Jersey Archives* (1894) XI. 368 The Governor in his gubernatorial Capacity. **1809** W. IRVING *Knickerb.* (1861) 113 Wilhelmus Kieft, who, in 1634, ascended the gubernatorial chair (to borrow a favourite though clumsy appellation of modern phraseologists), was of a lofty descent. **1845** STOCQUELER *Handbk. Brit. India* (1854) 43 A mass of gubernatorial machinery for British India. **1852** HAWTHORNE *Blithedale Rom.* xxii. (1885) 214 The old gubernatorial residence. **1882** *St. James's Gaz.* 15 Nov. 6 Leaving important dependencies of the crown to drift along for months together under some hastily improvised gubernatorial direction. **1888** BRYCE *Amer. Commw.* II. xlix. 250 Even in colonial days there was a tendency to substitute popular for gubernatorial nomination.

b. Of or pertaining to 'the governor', i.e. one's father.

1825 DISRAELI in *Scott's Fam. Lett.* (1894) II. 423, I have had a view of the gubernatorial article, and I must say..it was never equalled. [Refers to an article written by his father.] **1880** H. JAMES *Portr. Lady* v, His mother, on the other hand, was paternal, and even, according to the slang of the day, gubernatorial.

'gubernatory, *a. rare*⁻¹. [ad. L. type **gubernātōri-us*: see prec. and -ORY.] Concerned with governing.

1866 *Elgin & Cathedral Guide* iv. 222 Chastity is at best only negative and gubernatory.

‖**guber'natrix.** *Obs.* Also in anglicized form **gubernatrice.** [L. fem. of *gubernator.*] She that governs or rules. Also *appositively* = Governing, gubernative.

1556 *Extracts Aberd. Reg.* (1844) I. 300 The quenis grace, regint and gubernatrice of the realme. **1623** COCKERAM, *Gubernatrix*, shee which ruleth. **1632** LITHGOW *Trav.* x. 471 Behold the powerfull majesty of Gods mother,..and sole Gubernatrix of the earth. **1677** GALE *Crt. Gentiles* IV. 388 If it be so, that the gubernatrix and dispositrix Mind do thus dispose althings.

gublett, obs. form of GIBLET.

†**guck,** *sb. Sc. Obs.* [Of obscure origin; cf. GECK, GOWK.] A foolish saying.

1596 DALRYMPLE tr. *Leslie's Hist. Scot.* x. 471 Another writeng sensles, ful of Gukis and Glaikis.

†**guck,** *v. Sc. Obs.* [f. prec. sb.] *intr.* To play the fool. Hence †**gucking** *vbl. sb.*

c **1560** A. SCOTT *Poems* (S.T.S.) iv. 52 Thair followis thingis thre, To gar thame ga in gucking. **1603** *Philotus* iv, I lauch to sie ane auld Carle gucke.

†**gucked,** *ppl. a.* Chiefly *Sc. Obs.* Also 5 **guked, gukkit,** 5–6 **gukit,** 6 **guckit,** 7 **gok't.** [f. GUCK *sb.* or *v.*; cf. GOWKED.] Foolish; silly.

c **1450** HOLLAND *Howlat* lxiv, In come twa flyrand fulis.. The Tuchet and the gukkit Golk. *c* **1470** HENRYSON *Mor. Fab.* v. (Parl. Beasts) xvi, The gukit gait, the selie scheip, the swyne. ? *a* **1500** *Peebles to Play* iii, Scho was so guckit and so gend, That day ane byt scho eit nocht. **1500–20** DUNBAR *Poems* xiv. 16 So mony guckit clerkis. *Ibid.* lxxv. 10 He wes townysche, peirt, and gukit. **1596** DALRYMPLE tr. *Leslie's Hist. Scot.* x. 397 Thair gukit, vnwyse, and glaiket preichings. **1632** B. JONSON *Magn. Lady* III. iv, Nay, looke how the man stands, as he were gok't!

Hence †**'guckedly** *adv.*

1589 R. BRUCE *Serm.* (1843) 146 There is nothing quherein nature places her honour mair guckedly nor in privie revengement.

†**'guckry.** *Sc. Obs.* Also 6 **gukrie.** [f. GUCK *sb.* + -RY.] Foolishness, folly.

1596 DALRYMPLE tr. *Leslie's Hist. Scot.* x. 414 ȝour former deidis, full of gukrie and dafrie. **1603** *Philotus* ciii, I trow that all the warld euin, Sall at ȝour guckrie geck.

†**gud.** *Obs.* Also **Gudd.** Deformation of GOD (see etymological note and sense 13).

1678 OTWAY *Friendship in F.* II. i. Wks. 1728 I. 265 Uh gud; murder! I had rather you had offer'd me a Toad. *a* **1726** VANBRUGH *Journ. to Lond.* II. i. (1735) 28 *La. Ara.* Gud soons! **1727** BOYER *Dict. Angl.-Fr.*, Gudds-bob (A Comical Oath)..*Ventre Saint-gris.*

guddle, *v.*¹ *Obs.* exc. *dial.* [Echoic; cf. GUTTLE *v.*]

†**1.** *intr.* To gargle. *Obs.*

1584 COGAN *Haven Health* i. (1636) 7 With the same [cold water]..you may gargarize or guddle in your Throate.

2. To guzzle.

1825 J. JENNINGS *Observ. Dial. W. Eng.* 41 *Guddle*, to drink much and greedily. **1867** *Jim an' Nell* 61 in *Spec. Eng. Dial.* (E.D.S.) 34 Tis ninnyhammer's work, I zay, To graunge an' guddle all tha day, Being gude things be sent 'e.

guddle ('gʌd(ə)l), *v.*² *Sc.*

1. *trans.* To catch (fish) with the hands, by groping under the stones or banks of a stream.

1818 HOGG *Brownie of Bodsbeck* II. 167, I guddle them [fish] in aneath the stanes. **1897** C. M. CAMPBELL *Deilie Jock* 268 We waded in the burn and guddled some fine trout. **1951** F. S. CHAPMAN *Mem. Mountaineer* I. i. 10 About this time I learned the art of poaching... I learned to 'guddle' trout. **1955** 'M. INNES' *Man from Sea* vi. 66 You and a friend had been guddling Lord Urquhart's trout.

fig. **1893** *Nat. Observer* 25 Nov. 33/2 He dished M. Constans and 'guddled' the Moderates by electioneering addresses hinting at religious toleration.

2. *intr.* To grope for fish in this manner.

1881 *Blackw. Mag.* July 108 We would be plunging down the water like otter-hounds, guddling for the trout under the tree roots and beneath the stones. **1886** STEVENSON *Kidnapped* xxi. 202 Stripped to the waist and groping about or (as they say) guddling for these fish. **1966** J. CAIRD *Perturbing Spirit* xix. 204 He went about on his own, guddling in the burns, bird's-nesting.

Hence **'guddling** *vbl. sb.*

1818 HOGG *Brownie of Bodsbeck* II. 170 'So this is what you call gumping?' 'Yes, sir, this is gumphing, or guddling, ony o' them ye like to ca't'. **1895** *Daily News* 18 July 5/2 Horrible to say, Mr. Graham gives instructions for tickling trout, otherwise guddling, or gumping.

guddler ('gʌdlə(r)). Chiefly *Sc.* [f. GUDDLE *v.*² + -ER¹.] One who guddles for fish.

1880 in JAMIESON *Dict. Sc. Lang.* **1919** G. RAE *'Tween Clyde & Tweed* 72, I close my een, and a' is seen, The burn edge, and the guddler's play. **1928** *Daily Express* 4 Aug. 4/6 The guddler has his chance. **1940** J. BUCHAN *Memory Hold-the-Door* 304, I was an expert 'guddler', scooping up trout from below stones in the channel.

gude, Sc. and north. form of GOOD.

See also GOD (etymological note).

gudeing, Sc. form of GOODING.

1577–95 *Descr. Isles Scotl.* in Skene *Celtic Scot.* (1880) III. App. 435 With less gudeing [*i.e.* manuring] or labour.

Gudermannian (gju:də'mænɪən), *a.* and *sb. Math.* [f. the name of *Gudermann*, a German mathematician who first investigated these functions.] **A.** *adj.* Applied (by Cayley) to the function (denoted by the letters *gd*) defined by the equation $x = \log \tan (\frac{1}{4}\pi + \frac{1}{2} \text{gd}\, x)$. **B.** *sb.* A Gudermannian function.

The circular functions of the Gudermannian of any quantity correspond to the hyperbolic functions of that quantity (e.g. tan gd x = sinh x, etc.).

1876 CAYLEY *Elliptic Functions* 56 The Gudermannian. *Ibid.*, Instead of the general function am *u*, we have the gudermannian gd *u*, giving rise to the two functions sin gd *u* and cos gd *u*, or say sg *u* and cg *u*. **1888** GREENHILL *Chapter Integral Calculus* 28 The Gudermannian function connects the circular and hyperbolic functions.

gudge (gʌdʒ), *v.* Now *Sc. intr.* 'To eat ravenously or too much, to be gluttonous' (Jam.).

1735 SEWEL *Dutch Dict.*, *Uyt gulpen*, to Gudge, guggle; also, to Vomit.

gudgeon ('gʌdʒən), *sb.*¹ Forms: 5 **gogen, (-eorn), -yn, gojon(e, gojoun, -une,** 6 **gogeon, -ion, gougeon, gojen,** 6–7 **gudgin, -ion,** 7 **gougin,** ? **goojon,** 6– **gudgeon.** [ME. *gojon, gogen*, a. F. *goujon* (14th c. in Littré):—L. *gōbiōn-em, gōbio*, by-form of *gōbius* GOBY. Cf. It. *gobione.*]

1. A small European fresh-water fish (*Gobio fluviatilis*), much used for bait.

c **1425** *Voc.* in Wr.-Wülcker 642/20 *Hic gobio*, gojune. *c* **1430** *Two Cookery-bks.* 60 Goions fryid. *a* **1450** *Fysshynge w. angle* (1883) 15 Ye schall angle..for the wexen Roche the bleke and the gogyn & þe Roffe with a lynne of ii herys. *c* **1481** CAXTON *Dialogues* iv. 12 Loches, gogeorns. **1558** *Act 1 Eliz.* c. 17 §4 Places where Smelts, Loches, Minnies, Bulheads, Gudgions or Eels, have been used to be taken. **1570** LEVINS *Manip.* 163/34 A Gogeon, fish, *gobio.* **1620** VENNER *Via Recta* iv. 81 The Gudgion, and other such little fishes are of pleasant taste. **1622** PEACHAM *Compl. Gent.* xxi. (1634) 254 The Gudgin, Roch and Dace, which are Fish of eager bite, and soonest deceived. **1651–7** T. BARKER *Art of Angling* (1820) 38 The greedy Gudgeon doth love the Gild taile. **1653** WALTON *Angler* xi. 203 The Gudgion is an excellent fish to eat. **1727** SWIFT *Art Polit. Lying* Wks. 1755 III. I. 120 When there is too great a quantity of worms, it is hard to catch gudgeons. **1736** BAILEY *Househ. Dict.* 535 Gudgeons must be scaled, gutted and washed, then floured and put into the hot lard. **1780** COWPER *Progr. Err.* 483 Minnows and gudgeons gorge the unwholesome food. **1802** BINGLEY *Anim. Biog.* (1813) III. 82 The food of the Gudgeon consists of aquatic plants, worms, the larvae of water insects and the spawn of fish. **1873** G. C. DAVIES *Mount. & Mere* xi. 91 Gudgeons had to be caught for bait.

†**b.** Applied to fishes of the genus *Gobius* or family *Gobiidæ*: see GOBY. ***sea gudgeon***, the Black Goby or Rock-fish. *Obs.*

1584 COGAN *Haven Health* clxxvii. (1636) 163 Gogion..is found as well in the sea as in fresh waters. **1661** LOVELL *Hist. Anim. & Min.* 205 Sea Gudgions, called Paganelli, and by some Sea Cobs, are a most sound, light, wholesome, and nourishing meat. **1769** PENNANT *Zool.* III. 175 The Black Goby... Sea Gudgeon. Rock-fish. *Ibid.* 308 Aristotle mentions the gudgeon in two places; once as a river fish, and again as a species that was gregarious: in a third place he describes it as a sea fish. **1774** GOLDSM. *Nat. Hist.* (1776) VI. 307 The Gobius or Gudgeon.

2. *fig.* **a.** One that will bite at any bait or swallow anything: a credulous, gullible person.

1584 R. SCOT *Discov. Witchcr.* XII. xvi (1886) 208 They would doo no harme, were it not to make fooles, and catch gudgins. **1657** HAWKE *Killing is M.* 51 They will not swallow this Impostors principles of knavery, which none but fools and gudgeons will. **1701** CIBBER *Love Makes Man* I. i. (1705) 8 Did ever two old Gudgeons swallow so Greedily? **1727–8** MRS. PENDARVES *Let. to Mrs. A. Granville* in *Mrs. Delany's Life & Corr.* 165 You are a mere wag, sister, to think London ladies such gudgeons as to bite at anything. **1786** WOLCOT (P. Pindar) *Bozzy & Piozzi* II. 11 In vain at glory gudgeon Boswell snaps. **1809** W. IRVING *Knickb.* I. iv. (1849) 53 A conjecture..too tempting not to be immediately snapped at by the gudgeons of learning. **1839** in *Spirit Metrop. Conserv. Press* (1840) I. 141 The stupid gudgeons who swallowed the Hanover lie in 1837.

b. A bait, something swallowed greedily or credulously: in phr. ***to gape for gudgeons, to swallow a gudgeon, to give a gudgeon.***

1579 LYLY *Euphues* (Arb.) 97 But what fish so euer you be, you haue made both me and Philautus to swallow a Gudgen. **1581** PETTIE *Guazzo's Civ. Conv.* I. (1586) 42 b, To force us to beleeve that which is false, which is nothing else but to give us a gudgin, and flout us. **1586** J. HOOKER *Girald. Irel.* in *Holinshed* II. 91/2 Doo you thinke that James was so mad, as to gape for gogions, or so ungratious, as to sell his truth for a piece of Ireland? **1598** FLORIO, *Sciarpellone*, a grosse ly, an vnluckie tale, as we say a gudgeon or lying for the whetstone. **1606** *Sir G. Goosecappe* I. iii. in Bullen *O. Pl.* III. 21 Here's a most sweet Gudgeon swallowed, is there not? **1607** WALKINGTON *Opt. Glass* Ep. Rdr. 2, I know right well thou usest not to gape after gougins. **1620** SHELTON *Quix.* IV. xxix. 221 The Gullings and Gudgeons that he had given him. **1665** J. WEBB *Stone-Heng* (1725) 122 Readers would never be induced to swallow such a Gudgeon, as that seven-penny Men should be fed with Venison. **1892** *Nat. Observer* 23 July 235/1 It has educated Hodge into an increased readiness to gorge any gudgeon that may be offered him.

3. *attrib.* and *Comb.*, as in ***gudgeon-dole, -fish, -fishing, -gift, -prince, -rake, -swim.*** Also ***gudgeon-like*** adj.

1599 NASHE *Lenten Stuffe* 61, I haue distributed *gudgeon dole amongst them, as God's plenty, as any stripling of my slender portion of witte farre or neere. **1611** FLORIO, *Ghiozzo*,..some take it for a *Gudgeon-fish. **1727–41** CHAMBERS *Cycl.* s.v. *Fishing*, *Gudgeon-Fishing. **1889** 'J. BICKERDYKE' *Bk. All-round Angler* I. 99 The Thames method of *Gudgeon-fishing. **1557** *Tottel's Misc.* (Arb.) 156 The fisher man doth count no care, To cast hys nets to wracke or wast, And in reward of eche mans share A *gogen gift is much imbrast. **1792** WOLCOT (P. Pindar) *Ep. to Sir W. Hamilton* Wks. 1812 III. 188 *Gudgeon-like prepared to bite. *a* **1704** T. BROWN *Praise Poverty* Wks. (1730) I. 90 This is a bait they often throw out to such *gudgeon-princes as will nibble at it. **1787** BEST *Angling* (ed. 2) 59 When you angle for them, be provided with a *gudgeon-rake, with which rake the ground every ten minutes which gathers them together. **1889** 'J. BICKERDYKE' *Bk. All-round Angler* I. 99 By the side of the *gudgeon-swim.

gudgeon ('gʌdʒən), *sb.*² Forms: 5 **goggyn, gogion, gogoyne, gudyon, gugeoune, goyvn,** 5–6 **gogeon, gojon(e,** 6 **gog(g)in, gogon, -yn(e, goudgen, gudging, gugen, -yne, gujen,** 7 **gudgin, gug(g)ion,** 7–8 **gudgion,** 8–9 **googing,** 6– **gudgeon.** [a. OF. *gojon, goujon, gougon* (12–13th c. in Hatz.-Darm.); perh. an application of prec. sb., though connexion has been suggested with F. *gond* hinge (cf. the 14th c. form *goignon*).]

1. A pivot, usually of metal, fixed on or let into the end of a beam, spindle, axle, etc., and on which a wheel turns, a bell swings, or the like; in recent use more widely applied to various kinds of journals and similar parts of machinery.

1400 *Churchw. Acc. Wigtoft, Linc.* (Nichols 1797) 195 Payd to ed. Smyth, for a gudyon and kays. **1408** *Durham Acc. Roll* in *Eng. Hist. Rev.* XIV. 518 Soluta..pro..ii gogoynes ferri..emptis pro fine del axeltre rotae aquaticae. *c* **1440** *Promp. Parv.* 201/2 Goione of a poleyn (*MS. Harl.* 2274 goyvn off a polene) *vertibulum*, C.F. *cardo.* **1555** *Richmond. Wills* (Surtees) 86 Item a gogon for a possenet, jd. **1555** *Ludlow Churchw. Acc.* (Camden) 62 For mendynge gugyne, and settynge upright the secound belle..xijd. **1587–8** in Swayne *Sarum Churchw. Acc.* (1896) 136 Mending of a Goudgen of the great bell. **1634** J. BATE *Myst. Nat. & Art* (1654) 52 The gudgins of this wheel must be set to turn in strong brasse sockets. **1688** R. HOLME *Armoury* III. 462/1 The Guggions, great Iron pins put in the Head stock, for the Bell to turn with. **1762** FRANKLIN *Lett.* Wks. 1887 III. 202 The spindle, which is of hard iron,..is made to turn on brass gudgeons at each end. **1787** WINTER *Syst. Husb.* 296 Iron plates, in which the gudgeons of the fore wheel are placed. **1805** BREWSTER in *Ferguson's Lect.* I. 82 *note*, The extremities of an axle or spindle..are called gudgeons when the wheels are large. **1825** J. NICHOLSON *Operat. Mechanic* 47 The gudgeons of a water-wheel should never rest on the wall of the building. It shakes it. **1839** URE *Dict. Arts* 750 The gudgeons..move in brass bushes fixed upon iron supports. **1884** BLACKMORE *Tommy Upm.* I. 275 He would lend them a spare wheel-barrow, if they would put new gudgeons in.

2. The ring or 'eye' in the 'heel' of a gate which turns on the hook or pintle in the gate-post.

1496 *Nottingham Rec.* III. 291 For a gogion to þe Town Hall dore. **1737** BRACKEN *Farriery Impr.* (1756) I. 353 In the same Manner as we fix the Gudgeons of a Door in Stone, by melting Lead into the Cavities. **1886** in *Cheshire Gloss.*

3. *Naut.* **a.** A metal socket in which the pintle of a rudder turns. **b.** One of 'the notches made in the carrick-bits for receiving the metal bushes wherein the spindle of a windlass works' (Smyth *Sailor's Word-bk.* 1867).

1558 W. TOWRSON in Hakluyt *Voy.* (1589) 124 Our pinnesse broke one of the gudgeons of her rudder. **1626** CAPT. SMITH *Accid. Yng. Sea-men* 3 The Carpenter..is to haue the..rudder-irons called pintels and gudgions. **1723** *Lond. Gaz.* No. 6222/5 The Middle Gudgeon of her Rudder broken off. **1769** FALCONER *Dict. Marine* (1780), *Googings*, ..certain clamps of iron bolted on the stern-post of a ship, whereon to hang the rudder, and keep it steady. **1815** *Hist. J. Decastro* I. 313 Madam Stickleback..turned round in it [her bed] as if Madam Stickleback's body moved upon a gudgeon and pintle exactly in the middle of her bed. **1874** THEARLE *Naval Archit.* 77 Sometimes the braces or gudgeons for the rudder are forged to the post.

†**4.** ? A wedge or block (of metal). *Obs.*

14.. *Siege Jerusalem* 26/467 A which of white seluere; wal[w]ynde þer-ynne On four goions of gold, þat hit fram grounde bar. **1488** *Inv.* in Tytler *Hist. Scot.* (1864) II. 393 Item a grete gugeoune of gold.

5. A metallic pin used for securing together two blocks or slabs of stone, etc.

1873 SPON *Workshop Rec.* Ser. I. 387/2 Marble workers mount and fasten their works upon plaster mixed with a third-part of dust... These are joined together by cramps and gudgeons of iron and copper.

6. *attrib.*, as ***gudgeon end, -pin, -plate.***

1839 A. BYWATER *Sheffield Dial.* 26 Dustah kno what sooat on a thing 't north powl is, Jerra? *J.* Hah sloik e doo. Its't gudgen end o 't world axeltree, wot sticks aht. **1879** *Man. Artillery Exerc.* III. §7. 101, 6 and 7 hand the gun roller to No. 1, who places it in the lower steps of the gudgeon plates. **1891** *Times* 12 Oct. 10/6 Previous to leaving the persistent heating and scoring of her gudgeon-pins had been effectually overcome by the substitution of wrought-iron case-hardened pins for the original ones made of steel.

gudgeon ('gʌdʒən), *v.* [f. GUDGEON *sb.*[1]] **a.** *intr.* To play the gudgeon (see quot. 1785). **b.** *trans.* To cheat, defraud *of*, delude *into*.

1785 GROSE *Dict. Vulg. Tongue, Gudgeon*, to swallow the bait, or fall into a trap, from the fish of that name which is easily taken. **1787** *Generous Attachment* I. 197 Mr. and Mrs. Angle.. will have the satisfaction of seeing.. every person in Bath gudgeoned into an idea of their importance. **1826** SCOTT *Woodst.* xvi, To be.. gudgeoned of the opportunities which had been given you.

†**gudget.** *Sc. Obs.* Also 6 **gudiate, gudgett.** [ad. F. *goujat.*] A camp-follower; hence, a person of menial or low type. (See also GOUJAT.)

1581 *Satir. Poems Reform.* xliv. 159 Thair sleikit tungis ar sua veil creischit indeid, Better gudgettis ar not of Scotland borne. **1584** *Let. to Nobles* in J. Melvill *Diary* (Wodrow Soc.) 179 Slaves and gudiates serving thairunto. **1595** DUNCAN *App. Etymol.* (E.D.S.), *Calo*, a gudget, or burden-bearer. *a* **1598** ROLLOCK *Wks.* (Wodrow Soc.) II. iii. 39 Whether thou be a captain, or a single soldier, or a gudget, beware to be in evil company. **1603** *Philotus* lxxxiv, Unwomanlie in sik ane wyse, As gudget for to gang. *a* **1651** CALDERWOOD *Hist. Kirk* (Wodrow Soc.) III. 87 Slue a poor gudget.. in a trench.

gudgin, -ing, -ion, obs. forms of GUDGEON.

gudlene, -lyne, -lyng, obs. Sc. ff. GULDEN.

gudmundite ('gʊdmʊndaɪt). *Min.* [ad. G. *gudmundit* (K. Johannson 1928, in *Zeitschr. f. Krist.* LXVIII. 87), f. *Gudmundstorp*, name of a locality near Sala, Västmanland, Sweden + -ITE[1].] A rare greyish-white antimonide-sulphide of iron, FeSbS, related to arsenopyrite.

1928 *Chem. Abstr.* XXII. 4411 Gudmundite is a new mineral belonging to the marcasite group. **1959** *Mineral. Mag.* XXXII. 133 The apparent rarity of gudmundite may be due solely to the failure of many geologists to distinguish it from arsenopyrite.

gudyon, obs. form of GUDGEON *sb.*[2]

†**gue**[1]. *Obs.* [ad. F. *gueux* beggar.] A rogue.

1612 J. WEBSTER *White Devil* F 4 Pretious gue. Weel neuer part. **1658** BRATHWAIT *Honest Ghost* 232 Diligent search was made all there about, But my ingenious gue had got him out Before this inquisition.

¶ **blind gue**: app. ad. Ger. *blinde kuh*, blind-man's buff.

1604 *Meeting of Gallants* B 3 b, For blinde Gue you know has six-pence at the least for groping in the Darke.

gue[2] (gjuː). *Shetland.* [? repr. ON. *gígja* (in oblique cases *gígju*; the second *g* was pronounced (ɣ)) = MHG. *gîge*, mod.G. *geige*, fiddle.] A musical instrument (see quot. 1809) formerly used in Shetland (Jam.).

1809 A. EDMONSTONE *Zetland* II. 60 Before violins were introduced, the musicians performed on an instrument called a gue, which appears to have had some similarity to a violin, but had only two strings of horse hair, and was played upon in the same manner as a violoncello. **1822** SCOTT *Pirate* xv, A knocking at the door of the mansion, with the sound of the *Gue* and the *Langspiel*, announced, by their tinkling chime, the arrival of fresh revellers.

guean, variant of GEAN.

Guebre ('giːbə(r), 'geɪbə(r)). Forms: 8 **geber**, 9 **gheber, -ir, -re, gueber**, 7- **guebre**. [a. F. *guèbre*, ad. Pers. *gabr*. Cf. GIAOUR.] An adherent of the ancient Persian religion; a Zoroastrian, fire-worshipper, Parsee.

[**1662** J. DAVIES tr. *Olearius' Voy. Ambass.* VI. 302 A certain people called Kebber, that is to say, Infidels, from the Turkish word *Kiaphir*, which signifies a Renegat.] **1687** A. LOVELL tr. *Thevenot's Trav.* III. 57 There are a great many Parses or Guebres there, but they are poor. **1753** HANWAY *Trav.* (1762) I. IV. lvii. 263 This object of devotion to the Gebers, lies about ten English miles north-east by east from the city of Baku. **1834** MEDWIN *Angler in Wales* II. 298 And Ghebres too.. Best of idolaters, who worship fire. **1871** TYLOR *Prim. Cult.* II., 256 In general, this name of Ghebers is applied to the Zoroastrians or Parsis. **1884** J. PAYNE *Tales fr. Arabic* II. 36 *note, Nawous*, a sort of overground well or turricle of masonry,.. on which the Gueber's body is placed for devoration by the birds.

attrib. **1817** MOORE *Lalla R., Fire-Worshippers* 191 The Gheber belt that round him clung.

Hence †**'Guebrish** *a.*, belonging to the Guebres.

1687 A. LOVELL tr. *Thevenot's Trav.* II. 110 The Guebrish women have their Faces all naked, and never cover them.

guegaw, guegaye, obs. forms of GEWGAW.

guejarite ('giːdʒəraɪt). *Min.* [f. *Guejar* (in Sp. pronounced ge'xar), a district of Andalusia: see -ITE. Named by Cumenge, 1879.] Sulphantimonide of copper, found in orthorhombic crystals of a steel-grey colour.

1880 *Min. Mag.* IV. 64 Guejarite is.. isomorphous with Wolfsbergite.

gueld(e, obs. form of GELD *v.*[1]

guelder rose ('gɛldərəʊz). Forms: 6 **gelders**, 7 **gilder**, 7-8 **gelder**, 8 **guilder, gueldre**, 9 **guelder**. Also 7-8 **gelderland rose**. [Named from *Guelders* (a town in Prussia, on the borders of Holland) or *Guelderland* (a province of Holland, formerly a German duchy of which Guelders was the capital); so Du. *Geldersche roos*, G. *Gelderische rose*, F. *rose de Gueldre*, It. *rosa di Gueldra*, Sp. *rosa de Gueldres*.] The plant *Viburnum Opulus*, esp. the cultivated form, bearing globular bunches of white flowers; the snowball-tree. Also, the flower of this plant.

1597 GERARDE *Herbal* III. lxxii. 1237 The Rose Elder is called in Latine *Sambucus Rosea*, and *Sambucus aquatica*.. in English Gelders Rose, and Rose Elder. **1653** PLAT *Gard. Eden* 150 So of the tree that beareth a white flower as big as a rose, called the Gelderland-rose. **1688** R. HOLME *Armoury* II. 103/1 Gilder rose, or Marsh Elder,.. the flowers.. being set many together in a round tuft or ball on the top of the young branches. **1796** C. MARSHALL *Garden.* xix. (1798) 307 Gueldre rose, often called snow-ball tree. **1816** SCOTT *Fam. Lett.* 23 Dec. (1894) I. 388 A strange secluded ravine full of old thorn trees, hazels, guelder roses, willows, and so forth. **1824** MISS MITFORD *Village* Ser. I (1863) 148 Guelder-roses, pionies, tulips, stocks—hanging down like chandeliers among the dancers. **1855** BROWNING *Lovers' Quarrel* xviii, Heaps of the guelder-rose. **1882** *Garden* 3 June 391/3 Boughs of Guelder Rose.

gueles, obs. form of GULES.

Guelph (gwɛlf). Also 6-9 **Guelf**. [ad. It. *Guelfo*, med.L. *Guelphus*, ad. MHG. *Welf*, the name of the founder and of several successive chiefs of the princely family (hence commonly known in history as the *Guelphs*) which is represented in modern times by the ducal house of Brunswick and the present dynasty of Great Britain and Ireland. The name *Welf* is said to have been used as a war-cry at the battle of Weinsberg in 1140 by the partisans of Henry the Lion, duke of Bavaria, who belonged to this family, and fought against the Emperor Conrad III; hence it is believed to have been adopted in Italy as a name for the adversaries of the Hohenstauffen emperors, and later for the anti-imperialist party in Italian politics. Cf. GHIBELLINE.] A member of one of the two great parties in mediæval Italian politics, characterized chiefly by supporting the popes against the emperors. (Cf. GHIBELLINE.)

1579 E. K. *Gloss. Spenser's Sheph. Cal.* June 25 All Italy was distraict into the Factions of the Guelfes and Gibelins. *a* **1649** DRUMM. OF HAWTH. *Prophecy* Wks. (1711) 181 Thence arose the Guelfs and Gibellines, Imperialists against papists, and the universal war turned in a thousand petit wars and deadly fewds. **1711** ADDISON *Spect.* No. 125 ¶7 Italy was long torn in Pieces by the Guelfes and Gibellines. **1841** W. SPALDING *Italy & It. Isl.* II. 172 A sedition of the Ghibellines, which gave the ruling Guelfs a reason or pretence for banishing the heads of the defeated faction. **1855** MOTLEY *Corr.* (1889) I. vi. 184 The Church party, the Guelphs, were in reality a phalanx of intellectual opposition to imperial and brutal dominion.

attrib. **1847** LD. LINDSAY *Chr. Art* I. p. ccxii, Sympathy with the Guelph or classic element.

Hence †**'Guelphian** *a.* and *sb.* = GUELPHIC, GUELPH; **'Guelphish** *a.* = GUELPHIC; **'Guelphism**, the politics of the Guelphs; adherence to the party of the Guelphs.

1641 R. BROOKE *Eng. Episc.* II. vi. 89 Betweene 1215 and 1294 was that great Faction betweene the Guelfians and Gibelines. **1651** HOWELL *Surv. Venice* 28 The Cittie being heated with indignation by the persuasions of som Guelphian Agents. **1660** BURNEY *Κέρδ. Δῶρον* (1661) 133 There is none of your Garagantes will terrifie a King, nor the Guelphish faction. **1851** GALLENGA *Italy* i. 4 It never originated anything, save only disorganising Guelphism. *Ibid.* 31 Gioberti.. whose prophecies about the plenitude of the times, to be brought about by an Italian league, or Guelphish bond [etc.].

Guelphic ('gwɛlfɪk), *a.* Also **Guelfic**. [f. GUELPH + -IC.]

1. Of or pertaining to the Guelph faction.

1851 GALLENGA *Italy* 293 Ancona, and Rome, have shown not a little of the stubborn valour of the Guelphic burgesses of old. **1872** LOWELL *Dante* Prose Wks. 1890 IV. 130 The family of Dante had been Guelphic. **1896** TOUT *Edw. I*, iv. 70 The barefaced partisanship of a series of fiercely Guelfic popes.

2. Of or pertaining to the Guelph family.

1823 CRABB *Technol. Dict., Guelphic Order*, a new military order of Hanover, instituted in 1815, entitled the Royal Hanoverian Guelphic Order. **1838** *Murray's Hand-Bk. N. Germ.* 345 The Schloss, or old castle, formerly a residence of the Guelphic ancestors of the Royal Family of England, is turned into a magazine. *a* **1861** T. WOOLNER *My Beautiful Lady* (1863) 138 Then through the Guelphic line.

guelsought, obs. var. GULESOUGHT, jaundice.

guelt, var. GELD, money; obs. f. GILT *sb.*[2]

guelt, obs. form of GELT *ppl. a.*

1653 R. SANDERS *Physiogn.* 170 Those that have no beard, like guelt men, are of an ill nature.

guelye, variant of GULY *a. Obs.*

guemal ('gweɪməl). Also **gemul, guemul, huemal, huemul**. [Amer. Sp., ad. native name.] A small Andean deer of the species *Hippocamelus bicolor* or *H. antisensis*, having the antlers simply forked.

1808 R. ALSOP tr. *Molina's Geogr. Nat. & Civil Hist. Chili* I. iv. 226 The *guemul*, or *huemul* (equus bisulcus) is an animal which I have classed with the horse, although it ought to form a separate genus in consequence of its hoofs being divided. **1850** *Proc. Zool. Soc.* XVIII. 236 The female Gemul in the British Museum and in Lord Derby's Museum at Knowsley is considerably larger, and has the legs thicker, than the Siberian Ahu. **1875** *Proc. Zool. Soc.* 44 The Huemul is found in the Andes on either side from Magellan to near Santiago. **1898** R. LYDEKKER *Deer of all Lands* xii. 297 Ancient travellers in Chili brought reports of a cloven-hoofed animal known to the natives as guemal, or huemal. **1966** *Punch* 25 May 775/3 Chile should also be all right with its *huemal*, an elusive furciferine deer.

‖**guenon** (gənɔ̃). [Fr., of unknown origin.] 'The French name for a group of monkeys belonging to the antient continent and its islands, the type of which may be considered to be the Green Monkey, *Cercocebus sabæus*' (*Penny Cycl.*).

1838 *Penny Cycl.* XI. 468/2 The true Guenons comprise the genera *Cercopithecus* and *Cercocebus* of Geoffroy. **1871-82** *Cassell's Nat. Hist.* I. 103 The.. odd gestures of these Monkeys have given to them the name of Guenons.

Comb. **1897** *Q. Rev.* Oct. 397 There are in Africa about a dozen species of Guenon-like monkeys.

guep, variant of GUP *int. Obs.*

guepard ('gɛpəd). Also **gepard**. [a. F. *guepard* (Buffon); acc. to Hatz.-Darm. a corruption of Eng. *leopard*.] **a.** = CHEETAH. (In mod. Dicts.) **b.** A kind of leopard, the *Cynailurus guttata*.

1882 *Athenæum* 4 Mar. 286 The Marquis Antinori.. says that the natives [of Shoa] distinguish clearly between the true leopard, the gepard [*Cynailurus guttata*] and *Pardus varius*.

guerdon ('gɜːdən), *sb.* Now *poet.* and *rhetorical.* Forms: 4 **gerdo(u)n**, 4-6 **guerdone, -oun**, (4 **gardwyne, gwerddoun**, 5 **gerdonne**), 5-6 **gardo(u)n, guardon(e**, 5-7 **gwerdon(e**, (6 *Sc.* **gwairdoun**), 4- **guerdon**. [a. OF. *guerdon, gueredon, guedredon*, Pr. *guazardon* (for *guadardon*), *guiardon, guierdon*, Sp. *galardon*, Pg. *galardão*, It. *guiderdone*:—med.L. *widerdonum*, repr. (by assimilation of *d* and *l*) OHG. *widarlôn* = OE. *wiðerléan*, f. *wiðer* again + *léan* payment.] A reward, requital, or recompense.

? *a* **1366** CHAUCER *Rom. Rose* 1516 He quitte him wel his guerdon there. **1401** *Pol. Poems* (Rolls) II. 112 For thi grete labour thi gardoun thou shalt gete. *c* **1450** *Mirour Saluacioun* 4194 Who littel wanne was lesse mede taken hym for his gerdonne. **1483** CAXTON *Gold. Leg.* 85 b/2, I requyre of the Juste and debonayr gwerdon and reward. **1508** KENNEDIE *Flyting w. Dunbar* 422 Traistand to haue of his magnificence Guerdoun [*v.r.* Gwairdoun], reward, and benefice bedene. **1559** *Mirr. Mag., Dk. Glocester* xxix, Blood axeth blood as guerdon dewe. **1599** SHAKS. *Much Ado* v. iii. 5 Death in guerdon of her wrong Giues her fame which neuer dies. **1633** P. FLETCHER *Pisc. Ecl.* II. vii, My fish (the guerdon of my toil and pain) He causelesse seaz'd. **1653** H. COGAN tr. *Pinto's Trav.* xxxii. (1663) 127 That so falling into the hands of the Ministers of his Justice, we might receive the guerdon of our wicked works. **1684** *Scanderberg Rediv.* i. 3 Sovereignty.. is there the sole Guerdon or Reward of superlative Merit. **1751** G. WEST *Education* I. iii. 7 The Guerdons of bold Strength and swift Activity. **1781** COWPER *Charity* 293 Verse, like the laurel, its immortal meed, Should be the guerdon of a noble deed. **1813** SCOTT *Trierm.* II. xx, As at her word his sword he draws, His fairest guerdon her applause. **1859** TENNYSON *Enid* 1072 Take A horse and arms for guerdon; choose the best. **1862** NEALE *Hymns East. Ch.* 89 If I find Him, if I follow, What His guerdon here? 'Many a sorrow, many a labour, Many a tear'. **1884** J. PAYN *Some Lit. Recoll.* 240 Such guerdon as the novelist does receive is gained very pleasantly and accompanied by many charming circumstances.

guerdon ('gɜːdən), *v.* Now *poet.* and *rhetorical.* Forms: 4 **guerdone, -oun**, 4-5 **gerdon**, 5 **gardon**, 6 **gwerdon**, 5- **guerdon**. Also *pa. pple.* 4 **iguerdonned, ygerdoned**. [a. OF. *guer(e)doner*, f. *guer(e)don*: see prec. sb.]

1. *trans.* To reward, recompense.

c **1374** CHAUCER *Boeth.* v. pr. iii. 122 (Camb. MS.) þat is to seyn þat shrewes ben punyshed or ellys þat goode foolk ben ygerdonyd. *c* **1386** —— *Pars. T.* ¶209 The glorie of heuene with which god shal gerdone a man for hise goode dedes. *a* **1420** HOCCLEVE *De Reg. Princ.* 819 He hathe for my longe servise Guerdonede me. **1483** CAXTON *Cato* A iv, Thou mayst guerdon them that haue so wel done to the yf they haue nede and necessyte. *c* **1530** LD. BERNERS *Arth. Lyt. Bryt.* (1814) 417 She may right wel guerdon hym for hys seruice. *c* **1572** GASCOIGNE *Fruites Warre* (1831) 215 And bad me bide till his abilitie Might better gwerdon my fidelitie. **1607** HEYWOOD *Faire Maid* Wks. 1874 II. 68 Confusion guerdon his base villainie. *c* **1650** *Don Bellianis*

35, I pray the Almighty Lord that hath delivered us from so great danger and perill to guerdon you for it. **1820** T. MITCHELL *Aristoph.* I. 48 Death must guerdon deeds so bold. **1847** TENNYSON *Princ.* I. 201 Him we gave a costly bribe To guerdon silence. **1885** *Evangel. Mag.* Dec. 435 The father can guerdon his child.

absol. **1859** NEALE *Rhythm Bern. de Morlaix* (1864) 28 The Lamb is ever near thee,.. The Crown is He to guerdon, The Buckler to protect.

2. To give as a reward. *rare*⁻¹.

1881 H. PHILLIPS tr. *Chamisso's Faust* 17, I guerdon thee the prize which thou hast won.

Hence **'guerdoned** *ppl. a.*, given as a reward; **'guerdoning** *vbl. sb.*, the action of the vb. GUERDON; reward. Also **'guerdonable** *a.*, that may be guerdoned; **'guerdoner**, one who guerdons.

*c***1374** CHAUCER *Boeth.* IV. pr. vii. 112 (Camb. MS.) Fortune is yeuen eyther by cause of gerdonynge or ellys of excersisinge of good folk or ellis by cause to punnyssen. *c***1400** *Rom. Rose* 2380 In love, free yeven thing Requyrith a gret guerdoning. **1530** LYNDESAY *Test. Papyngo* 1006 The guerdonyng of ȝour Courticience, Is sum cause of thir gret Enormyteis. **1606** FORD *Fame's Mem.* Wks. 1889 III. 301 To get a guerdon'd favour for his hire. **1646** BUCK *Rich. III*, 75 Finding it as well guerdonable, as gratefull, to publish their Libels. *Ibid.*, Explic. of dark words, *Guerdonable*, worthy of reward. **1881** ROSSETTI *House of Life, Sonn.* xxxiii, And Venus Victrix to my heart doth bring Herself, the Helen of her guerdoning.

† **'guerdonize**, *v. Obs.* [f. GUERDON *sb.* + -IZE.] *trans.* To bestow a guerdon upon, to reward.

1594 J. DICKENSON *Arisbas* (1878) 77 On sea-washt rockes, reward from arte would plucke, And guerdonize desert with direst lucke. **1606** J. RAYNOLDS *Dolarney's Prim.* (1880) 57 What trophe rare, what wreath or Coronet, Can guerdonize, your meriting desert. **16..** M. PARKER *Hist. Arthur C*, He [Arthur] bethought him how he might in some manner guerdonize their incomparable worth with some honourable Order of Knights.

guerdonless ('gɜːdənlɪs), *a.* [f. GUERDON *sb.* + -LESS.] Without guerdon; not receiving, *occas.* not bestowing, a guerdon.

?*c***1400** LYDG. *Æsop's Fab.* iv. 53 Takyng theyr service and labour to theyr vse Gwerdounles to make theym to travaile. **1470–85** MALORY *Arthur* x. lxxxvi, Yet had I neuer reward nor bounte of her the dayes of my lyf and yet haue I ben her knight gwerdonles. **1604** MIDDLETON *F. Hubburd's Tales* Wks. (Bullen) VIII. 51 Most guerdonless sir, pinching patron. **1881** W. WILKINS *Songs of Study* 214 Ride far by coast and city, An envoy guerdonless.

guerdoun, obs. form of GUERDON.

‖**guereza** ('gɛrɪzə). [? African.] An Ethiopian monkey (*Colobus guereza*) with long hair and a bushy tail.

1859 WOOD *Nat. Hist.* I. 43 The beautifully adorned Guereza. **1884–5** *Riverside Nat. Hist.* (1888) V. 520 The guereza is found in the mountainous parts of Abyssinia.

guéridon ('gɛrɪdən, ‖geridɔ̃). [Fr.] A small ornamental table or stand, usually ornately carved.

1853 C. BRONTË *Villette* xliii. 329 In one corner appeared a guéridon with a marble top, and upon it a work-box. **1938** *Burlington Mag.* May 227/1 Candlesticks.. could be placed on 'guéridons', nowadays usually called 'torchères'. **1955** *Times* 7 July 5/7 £340 for a pair of early Georgian carved gilt and painted wood *guéridon*, resting on carved tripods terminating in claw-and-ball feet (4 ft. high). **1967** M. WARD *Du Barry Inheritance* xii. 184 The Empress Josephine ..particularly cherished the Sèvres porcelain guéridon.

†**guerie, guierie.** *Obs. rare.* [? For *gery, f. GERE + dim. suffix -Y. Cf. GERY *a.*] A sudden access of passion; = GERE.

1542 UDALL *Erasm. Apoph.* I. *Diogenes* § 112 p v b, Because this pangue or guierie [L. *hic affectus*] of loue dooeth especially..possesse suche persones as been altogether drouned in idlenesse. *Ibid.* II. *Cicero* § 6 Q iij, One yᵗ could none other but folowe euery soodain guerie or pangue that shotte in his braine [L. *affectibus seruiens*].

guerilla: see GUERRILLA.

†**guerison.** *Obs.* Also 5 guaryson, 6 guerysone. [a. OF. *guarisun* (F. *guérison*), f. OF. *guarir* (F. *guérir*) to cure.] Cure; healing.

1484 CAXTON *Fables of Auian* 13 The stroke of a tongue is Incurable and withoute guaryson. *a***1577** GASCOIGNE *Ferd. Ieronimi* Wks. (1587) Yj, In receiving that guerison at your hands, I have beene constreined to fall into an extasie. [**1777** EARL CARLISLE in J. H. Jesse *G. Selwyn & Contemp.* (1844) III. 218 You will be able to converse upon a subject which it will be necessary for your *guérison* not to keep to yourself.]

guérite (gerit). *Mil.* [a. F. *guérite*: see GARRET *sb.*¹] A turret or box of wood or stone for the accommodation of a sentry; a sentinel's box.

1706 in PHILLIPS (ed. Kersey). **1717** tr. *Frezier's Voy. S. Sea* 93 There is a little Redan, or indented Work..with a Guerite, or Sentinel's Box. **1841** JAMES *Brigand* vi, He stopped at the entrance of one of those little guerites, or watch towers.

guerkin, obs. form of GHERKIN.

1735 LADY BROWNLOWE in *Swift's Lett.* (1768) IV. 91 The cucumbers are not larger than guerkins.

guern, obs. form of GIRN *v.*¹

Guernsey ('gɜːnzɪ). Also 6 Garnesie, Garnsey, 7 Gernsey. The name of one of the Channel Islands.

1. Used *attributively* in the following: **Guernsey coat, frock, shirt** = sense 2 a; **Guernsey eyestone** (see quot.); †**Guernsey flower, lily**, a ? Japanese or S. African plant (*Nerine Sarniensis*) with handsome lily-like flowers, naturalized on the island of Guernsey; **Guernsey lizard** (see quot.); **Guernsey partridge**, the red-legged partridge, *Perdix* or *Caccabis rufa*; **Guernsey violet**, the *Matthiola incana* (Britten & Holland *Plant-n.*).

1859 EMERSON *Sp. Burns Cent. Boston* Wks. 1884 XI. 367 The poet..of poor men, of gray hodden, and the *guernsey coat. **1886** *Syd. Soc. Lex.*, *Guernsey eyestone, the operculum of *Turbo pullus*. **1677** LADY CHAWORTH in *12th Rep. Hist. MSS. Comm.* App. v. 30 The scarlet *Gernsey flower is in great fame but they will not prosper scarce one in twenty of them. **1832** *Chambers's Edin. Jrnl.* I. 307/2 Before any of his associates had entered the cabin, he had secreted his prize under his *Guernsey frock. **1840** R. H. DANA *Bef. Mast* xxxiii. 126 Our south-westers, thick boots, Guernsey frocks, and other accompaniments of bad weather. **1856** [see FROCK *sb.* 3 c]. **1664** EVELYN *Kal. Hort.* (1729) 201 The Narcissus of Japan (or *Guernsey Lilly). **1764** GRAY in *Corr. w. N. Nicholls* (1843) 57 Guernsey lilies bloom in every window. **1792** MAR. RIDDELL *Voy. Madeira* 94 The *lilia jacoboea*, or Guernsey lily, is one of the most beautiful flowers indigenous in this island [Antigua]. **1838** *Penny Cycl.* XI. 470/2 The Guernsey lily, a species of the amaryllis, is a native of Japan. **1895** AMHERST *Garden.* 282 The Guernsey lily (*Nerine sarniensis*) which was said to have grown in Guernsey from bulbs washed ashore from a wreck of a ship from Japan about 1659. **1769** PENNANT *Zool.* (1776) III. 21 Related to this species [Scaly lizard] is the *Guernsey lizard, which we are informed has been propagated in England from some originally brought from that island. **1802** MONTAGU *Ornith. Dict.*, Partridge-Guernsey ..*Guernsey Partridge..Why this should be called Guernsey Partridge we cannot imagine..It is also..called ..Red-legged Partridge. **1835** DICKENS *Sk. Boz* II. 184 Two or three fellows in great rough trousers and *Guernsey shirts. **1874** M. C. *Explorers* 53 So you have come to make your fame With pick-axe, in a Guernsey-shirt. **1578** LYTE *Dodoens* II. iv. 152 The greater sorte is called in English *Garnesie Violets, white Gillofer, and Stocke Gillofer. **1597** GERARDE *Herbal* II. cxiv. §4. 373 The Stocke Gilloflower is called..in English..Garnsey Violet, and Castle Gilloflower.

2. In senses originally elliptical.

a. A thick, knitted, closely-fitting vest or shirt, generally made of blue wool, worn by seamen. Also *Austral.*, a coloured shirt worn by Austral. Rules players; so ***to get*** (or ***draw***) ***a guernsey***, to be selected (for a team); *transf.*, to be invited, to succeed.

1839 *Bell's Life* 16 June 3/5 The Etonian crew were dressed in white guernseys, with pale blue facings; rosette, sky blue. **1845** *Ainsworth's Mag.* VII. 499 An amateur boatman..in a Fez cap, striped Guernsey. **1851** MAYHEW *Lond. Labour* I. 66 The sailors in their striped guernseys. **1861** MUSGRAVE *By-roads* 170 Villers Bretonneaux [was] celebrated, from an early period, for its manufacture of.. socks, caps, waistcoats, and jackets or Guernseys. **1887** HALL CAINE *Deemster* ix. 61 There was Dan in his guernsey on the deck of his boat. **1963** *Times* 5 June 5/4 The flying gold guernsies of the Australians lit the gloomy arena with their explosive action. **1966** BAKER *Austral. Lang.* (ed. 2) xix. 392 *Get a guernsey* (succeed or be selected, from football). *Ibid.* xxi. 428 Success: get (or draw) a guernsey. **1969** *Australian* 24 May 17/3 Goold..wears either a hacking jacket or a football guernsey with easy grace.

b. One of a breed of cattle of the Channel Islands.

1834 YOUATT *Cattle* iii. 30 Mr. King recommends the addition of one Guernsey to every dozen country-cows. **1890** *Daily News* 24 June 6/1 There are 169 Jerseys and 81 Guernseys in the show.

†**guerpe, guerpish**, *v. Obs.* [ad. OF. *guerpir* (or the lengthened stem *guerpiss-*) to throw away, f. the Teutonic stem represented in Eng. by WARP.] *trans.* To abandon, forsake.

1483 CAXTON *G. de la Tour* cxxix. L viij b, They shalle not gwerpysshe or leue eche other for none other better or worse. **1646** J. COOKE *Vind. Law* 33 The learned Serjeants ..shall guerpe and abandon the cause.

†**guerre**, *sb. Obs.* Also 5 gwerre, 6 guerr. [a. F. *guerre* = ONF. *werre* WAR.] War.

1432–50 tr. *Higden* (Rolls) VIII. 283 From that tyme guerres began to cease in Wales. *Ibid.* 307 A knyȝhte of Lancastreshire movede gwerre..ageyne Thomas of Lancastre his lorde. **1491** *Act Hen. VII*, c. 23 Preamble, Richard White..traitrously levyed guerre ayen our seid Souvereign Lord. **1539** *St. Papers Hen. VIII*, III. 141, I am enfourmed that the King of Skottes wilnat that any of his men goo out of the countrey, in feare of the guerr of Ingland.

Hence **guerre** *v. Obs. intr.*, to wage war.

1432–50 tr. *Higden* (Rolls) II. 321 Men of Ethioppe guerrenge ageyn men of Egipte. **1616** BULLOKAR, *Guerring*, Brawling [also in COCKERAM 1623].

guerrilla, guerilla (gɛ'rɪlə, gə'rɪlə). [a. Sp. *guerrilla*, dim. of *guerra* war. With the form *guerilla* cf. F. *guérilla*.]

1. An irregular war carried on by small bodies of men acting independently. Now somewhat *rare*.

1819 SYD. SMITH *Wks.* (1859) I. 255/2 A succession of village guerrillas;—an internecive war between the gamekeepers and marauders of game. **1837** W. IRVING *Capt. Bonneville* III. 254 To avoid being involved in these guerillas. **1851** MAYNE REID *Scalp Hunt.* xvii. 121, I was offered the command of this strange guerilla. **1862** RUSSELL in *Times* 18 Mar., Arkansas is now the theatre of a large guerilla.

2. One engaged in such warfare.

1809 WELLINGTON in Gurw. *Desp.* (1835) V. 9, I have recommended to the Junta to set..the Guerrillas to work towards Madrid. **1840** E. E. NAPIER *Scenes & Sp. For. Lands* I. iii. 54 We might easily have..been mistaken for.. a party of guerillas. **1887** *Edin. Rev.* Jan. 127 A swift and skilful guerilla. **1900** *Daily News* 9 June 4/6 A nation of farmers is not the material of which guerrillas have usually been made.

fig. **1861** J. PYCROFT *Ways & Words* 333 The mere skirmishers and guerillas of literature.

3. *attrib.* passing into *adj.*, esp. in ***guerrilla war*** (= sense 1).

1811 SCOTT *Don Roderick* xlix, The Guerilla band Came like night's tempest, and avenged the land. **1814** SOUTHEY in Robberds *Mem. W. Taylor* II. 428 Somewhat afraid of my old Guerrilla friends upon the road. **1843** PRESCOTT *Mexico* I. ii. (1864) 16 Making use of ambuscades, sudden surprises, and the light skirmish of guerilla warfare. **1860** W. G. CLARKE in *Vac. Tour.* 67 Garibaldi..is..a master of the 'dodges'..which are required in guerilla war. **1865** MAFFEI *Brigand Life* II. 41 He was forced to become, not a guerilla leader, but a highway captain. **1881** HUXLEY *Sci. & Culture* i. 3 It must be admitted to be somewhat of a guerilla force, composed largely of irregulars.

fig. **1843** THACKERAY *Irish Sk.-bk.* II. xvii. 318 A doubtful, lazy, dirty family vassal—a guerilla footman. **1863** OUIDA *Held in Bondage* 135 My guerilla life suits me better than my fashionable one. **1898** W. M. RAMSAY *Was Christ born in Bethlehem?* i. 8 The commentary on Luke then degenerates into a guerilla warfare against him.

Hence **gue'rrillaism**, the principles and practice of guerrilla warfare; **gue'rrillist** = GUERRILLA 2; **gue'rrillaship** = GUERRILLAISM; **guerri'llesque** *a.*, proper or habitual to a guerrilla.

1864 SALA in *Daily Tel.* 22 Apr. 5/2 This is the guerillesque formula. **1865** *Even. Stand.* 19 May, Owing to the unsettled state of affairs in the new empire, the prevalence of guerillaism, &c., these precautions, which have a military air, are considered quite necessary. **1889** A. H. DRYSDALE *Hist. Presbyt. Eng.* II. iii. 206 This mode of controversial guerillaship was not of long duration.

‖**guerrillero, guerillero** (gɛrɪ'leɪərəʊ, geri'ʎero). [a. Sp. *guerrillero*, f. *guerrilla*.] = GUERRILLA 2.

1832 SOUTHEY *Penins. War* III. 474 It is the only instance of any man who had acquired celebrity as a Guerrillero becoming a traitor. **1845** FORD *Handbk. Spain* I. 323 During the war the French were continually baffled by these Highland *Guerilleros*.

attrib. **1898** *Blackw. Mag.* Apr. 550/2 A parish priest was one of the guerillero leaders.

Guesdist ('geɪdɪst). [f. name of Jules *Guesde* (1845–1922), French political leader + -IST.] A follower of the principles of revolutionary Marxism advocated by Guesde. So **'Guesdism**, the policy or principles of the Guesdists.

1886 'ALB' *Living Paris & France* 337 The Marxists or Guesdists form the next considerable revolutionary party. **1901** *Daily Chron.* 25 May 5/4 The only true Socialists, the Guesdists. **1927** H. W. LAIDLER *Hist. Socialist Thought* xxii. 357 Guesdist's Revolutionary Program... The party of Guesde emphasized its revolutionary and Marxian character. **1940** D. W. BROGAN *Devel. Mod. France* VI. iii. 295 Blanquism, Broussism, Anarchism..all divided with Guesdism the allegiance of the French workers. *Ibid.*, Electorally, the Possibilists naturally did better than the less practical Guesdists. **1966** COLLINS & MITCHELL tr. *Braunthal's Hist. of International* xvi. 197 The Guesdists, at loggerheads with the Possibilists from the beginning, boycotted the congresses called by their rivals.

guess (gɛs), *sb.* Forms: 4–7 gesse, (5 ges, 6 gease), 6 *Sc.* gaiss, 6–7 guesse, 6–8 ghesse, 6– guess. [f. GUESS *v.*; cf. MDu. *gisse* (Du. *gis*).]

1. The action of guessing; an act of guessing, a conjecture, rough estimate; a supposition based on uncertain grounds. ***by guess***: at haphazard, by rough estimation instead of calculation or measurement; by conjecture, without having proofs; †also ***at, in, up, upon guess***; ***by guess and by God*** (or ***Godfrey***) (*slang*, orig. *Naval*): (to steer) at hazard without a set course or without the guidance of landmarks; † ***after*** (***by, to***) ***my guess***: as I estimate; † ***without guess***: assuredly; † ***the guess of the hand***: a rough estimate of the weight of something taken into the hand; ***my guess is*** or ***it is my guess***: I am tolerably sure; ***to miss one's guess*** (U.S.), to be wrong in one's assumption; ***you have another guess coming***: you are mistaken; ***your guess is as good as mine***: a phrase used to indicate uncertainty about facts or circumstances or about the outcome of a set of events; ***anybody's guess*** (see ANYBODY 3); ***anyone's guess*** (see ANY 8 c).

*c***1330** R. BRUNNE *Chron.* (1810) 321 Þe kynge's oste at gesse in þe Est mad lardere, Of tounes & hamelesse, of granges & garner. **1377** LANGL. *P. Pl.* B. v. 421, I nam nouȝte shryuen some tyme but if sekenesse it make, Nouȝt tweies in two ȝere and thanne vp gesse I schryue me. **1390** GOWER *Conf.* III. 211 For if a king shall upon gesse Withoute verray cause drede, He may be liche to that I rede. *c***1400** *Rom. Rose* 2817 Thy Ioye shal double, withoute gesse, Whan thou thenkist on hir semlinesse. *a***1400–50**

Alexander 3552 If gomes be gouerners of gods þan mai þi gesse worth. *c* **1430** LYDG. *Min. Poems* (Percy Soc.) 58 To keep trewe weight, and selle peper by gesse..it accordith nought. *c* **1460** *Towneley Myst.* xii. 439 Then must we go eest after my ges. **1529** MORE *Dyaloge* IV. Wks. 281/1 We maye haue also a greate gesse therat. *a* **1553** UDALL *Royster D.* II. i. (Arb.) 33, I bring hir a ring, with a token in a cloute, And by all gesse, this same is hir house out of doute. *c* **1560** A. SCOTT *Poems* (S.T.S.) xxxiii. 24 Thow lychtleis all trew properteis Off luve express, And markis quhair nevir styme thow seis, Bot hittis be gaiss. *a* **1586** SIDNEY *Sonn.* in *Arcadia*, etc. (1629) 529 Passing all ghesse, whence into me should fly So mazde a masse. **1587** FLEMING *Contn. Holinshed* III. 988/2 Soone after (by gesse) fiue of the clock [etc.]. *c* **1600** SHAKS. *Sonn.* lxix, They looke into the beauty of thy mind, And that in guesse they measure by thy deeds. **1601** —— *Jul. C.* II. i. 3, I cannot, by the progresse of the Starres, Giue guesse how neere to day. **1605** —— *Lear* V. i. 52 Heere is the guesse of their [the enemy's] true strength and Forces. **1607** TOPSELL *Four-f. Beasts* (1658) 555 Being only weighed by the guess of the hand, it seemeth much heavier. **1642** FULLER *Holy & Prof. St.* III. xxiii. 217 The Fame is antedated..being related at guesse before 'twas acted. **1647** H. MORE *Song of Soul* I. II. xlviii, 'Tis ghesse, not full perswasion. **1656** H. PHILLIPS *Purch. Patt.* (1676) 46 By which you may have some ghess of the other rates. **1660** BOYLE *New Exp. Phys. Mech.* xiii. 87 A small Receiver, capable of containing (by guess) about a pound and a half of Water. **1698** FRYER *Acc. E. India & P.* 304 Trees, not so long liv'd as elsewhere, if by the decayed Trunks any guess may be made. **1708** SWIFT *Death Partridge* Wks. 1755 II. I. 158 Mr. Bickerstaff spoke altogether by guess, and knew no more what will happen this year, than I did myself. **1718** PRIOR *Knowledge* 740, I confess, That human science is uncertain guess. **1719** DE FOE *Crusoe* I. viii, By my Guess it could not be less than Fifteen or Twenty Leagues off. **1736** BUTLER *Anal.* II. vii. 331 Mere guess, supposition and possibility, when opposed to historical evidence, prove nothing. **1751** R. PALTOCK *P. Wilkins* (1884) I. x. 101, I was, to my guess, five weeks in the vault or cavern. **1773** GOLDSM. *Stoops to Conq.* v. Wks. (Globe) 673/1 By my guess we should come upon Crackskull common. **1781** COWPER *Let.* 23 Apr., Wks. (1876) 68 It is worth while to send you a riddle You make such a variety of guesses. **1827** SCOTT *Jrnl.* (1890) I. 394, I have a guess the best gamecocks would call a truce if a handful or two of oats were scattered among them. **1842** W. ARNOT *Mem. J. Halley* v. 304 Every effort of indolence to do a thing by guess..was sure to meet with an instant reproof. **1846** POE *N.P. Willis* Wks. 1864 III. 28 All this must be considered as mere guess on my part. **1871** TYNDALL *Fragm. Sci.* (1879) II. xiii. 294 The inductive guess precedes experiment. **1879** BROWNING *Ivan Ivanovitch* 99 No care to guide old Droug, he knows his way by guess, Once start him on the old road. **1884** tr. *Lotze's Logic* 344 The discovery of an universal law is always a guess on the part of the imagination, made possible by a knowledge of facts. **1909** [see GODFREY[2]]. **1916** T. WOLFE *Let.* Sept. (1958) 4, I hope I will do well in all my studies and my guess is I'll have to 'bone' on math. **1921** *Sat. Rev.* 21 May 413/2 Governor Miller, who is responsible for the new legislation, seems to have missed his guess, if he means business. **1930** J. C. RANSOM *God without Thunder* xi. 231 It is my guess, in brief, that the scientists, with their Tables No. 2, hope to have, in the first place, a means of predicting Tables No. 1. **1931** W. G. CARR (*title*) By Guess and by God. **1931** R. GRAVES *Poems 1926–30* 41 He lurches here and there by guess And God and hope and hopelessness. **1935** *Punch* 3 July 12/2 If you think I am fool enough to be hoodwinked.., you have another guess coming. **1936** M. DE LA ROCHE *Whiteoak Harvest* xviii. 199 You're wot I calls a well-plucked 'un... *And*, w'en you're older, an overdose of sex appeal, or I miss my guess. [**1939** A. DERLETH *Let.* 29 Dec. in *N. & Q.* (1965) July 268/2 My guess, naturally, is the latter—but I would value a letter from you setting down your own convictions.] **1939** C. DAY LEWIS *Child of Misfortune* III. vi. 337 If you think that's your doing.. you've got another guess coming. **1939** L. BAIRD *Waste Heritage* xxii. 310 Your guess is as good as mine. **1943** N. BALCHIN *Small Back Room* xii. 135 'The question is, what will happen then?'..'Your guess is as good as mine.' **1951** M. KENNEDY *Lucy Carmichael* II. v. 130 'Who's going to get in?'..'Your guess is as good as mine.' **1957** E. WHATE *Press on Regardless* i. 10 We drove by guess and by God, and the rest of that journey is best left to the obscurity which shrouded it at the time. **1958** I. MURDOCH *Bell* xx. 246 My guess is that once you start to fight you'll know you can't stay with Paul. **1965** F. L. UTLEY in Bessinger & Creed *Medieval & Linguistic Stud.* 308 If I don't go down into history as the martyr President I miss my guess. **1967** *Observer* 30 Apr. 29/3 Will bloomers and shorts catch on? My guess is that they will. **1967** M. PROCTER *Exercise Hoodwink* vi. 47 'Did he give you the impression of being honest.' Evans allowed himself a shrug. 'Your guess is as good as mine, sir.' **1969** *New Yorker* 12 Apr. 121/1 It is not certain that there are any moonquakes, though Dr. Latham says he will miss his guess if the passive seismic experiment records none.

2. *attrib.* and *Comb.*, as ***guess-aim, -monger***.

1863 ATKINSON *Stanton Grange* 266 Taking the best guess-aim I could. **1892** SKEAT in *N. & Q.* Ser. VIII. I. 10 The day of the etymological guess-mongers will be gone for ever.

¶**3.** The expressions ANOTHERGUESS, OTHERGUESS, etc., in which *-guess* is a corruption of *-gates*, have given rise to phrases in which *guess* appears as an attributive sb. or adj., with the sense 'kind of'.

1825 *Blackw. Mag.* XVIII. 43/2 Oho! is it so indeed?.. why, then, that's a different guess-story altogether, shipmate. **1834** *Fraser's Mag.* X. 668 Every one..knows what guess-sort of wiseacre France gave birth to in the person of that algebraical gentleman. **1843** HALIBURTON *Attaché* II. xiii. 265 Not look at a woman?..why, what sort of a guess world would this be without petticoats? **1898** *Blackw. Mag.* Mar. 423 He had no guess-idea of what bemused his vision.

guess (gɛs), *a. dial.* Also guest, guessed. [Cf. LG. *güst* of the same meanings.] Of a cow or ewe: Barren; temporarily barren (see quots.). Also, not yielding milk.

1736 PEGGE *Kenticisms* 31 (E.D.S.), *Guess-cow*, a barren cow. **1744–50** W. ELLIS *Mod. Husbandm.* III. I. 103 Guess-Cows..are those that did not stand to their Bulling last Year. **1750** —— *Country Housew.* 29 They [Cows] are not always in Milk, as being in Calf, or that they go, what we in Hertfordshire call, guess, or dry. **1845** *Jrnl. R. Agric. Soc.* VI. II. 363, I get far fewer 'guest' or barren ewes. **1855** MORTON *Cycl. Agric.* II. 723 *Guessed ewes* (Lin.), not seasonably in lamb.

guess (gɛs), *v.* Pa. t. and pa. pple. **guessed** (gɛst). Forms: 4 gesce, gese, gessen, 4–7 gess(e, 5 gessyn, 5–7 ges, (6 geasse), 6–7 guesse, 6–8 ghess(e, 6– guess. *Pa. t.* and *pa. pple.* (contracted forms) 4–5 gest, 6 ghest, 6–8 guest. [ME. *gessen*, cognate with the synonymous MLG., MDu. and mod.Du., Fris. *gissen* (MDu. also *gessen*, NFris. *gezzen, gedsen*), MSw. *gissa, gitza*, Sw. *gissa*, MDa. *gidze, gitse, getze*, Da. *gisse*; mod.Icel. has a derivative form *gizka*.

The relation between the various forms is obscure. According to Tamm *Svenskt Etym. Ordb.* the Scandinavian forms are adopted from LG. *gissen*, a phonetic alteration of *gessen* (cf. LG. *hissen*, var. of *hessen*, a. HG. *hetzen* to hunt). It seems, however, more probable that the Sw. and Da. forms are native, as the Eng. word can hardly be referred to any other than a Scandinavian source. The word cannot well descend from an OE. form = LG. *gissen*, as the initial would then have been *y* (ME. 3). The only remaining possibility would be that it was adopted from continental LG., but there is nothing in the nature of the meaning to account for its having come from that source in or before the early 14th c. The forms may represent one, or prob. more than one, of the OTeut. types **gitisôjan*, **gatisôjan*, **gessôjan*, **gissjan*; in any case the word is a derivative of the root of GET *v.*; cf. ON. *geta* v., to get, guess, *geta* wk. fem. a guess.

In the 14th c. the word was the usual rendering of L. *æstimare*, the influence of which probably affected some of the early senses.]

1. a. *trans.* To form an approximate judgement of (size, amount, number, distance, etc.) without actual measurement or calculation; to estimate. Sometimes with clause as *obj.*

c **1340** HAMPOLE *Pr. Consc.* 7672 Fra þe poynt of þe erthe tille Saturnus þe heghest planete may be gesced þus. ?*a* **1366** CHAUCER *Rom. Rose* 1115 No man coude preyse or gesse Of hem the valewe or richesse. **1382** WYCLIF *1 Kings* iii. 8 A puple without eende, that may not be noumbred and gessid, for multitude. **1390** GOWER *Conf.* II. 207 Great richesse Wel more than they couthen gesse. *a* **1400–50** *Alexander* 5512 Þare was a mi3ti montayne at to þe mone semed He gessis it gaynir to god þan to þe grounde vndire. **1413** *Pilgr. Sowle* (Caxton) v. v. (1859) 76 The gretenes therof ne couthe I not gesse, nor acounte. **1660** *Trial Regic.* 191, I saw this person standing within a Pike or two length as I can guesse it. **1674** JOSSELYN *Voy. New Eng.* 258 As near as can be ghessed. **1726** G. ROBERTS *Four Years Voy.* 162 That they who had Life..could nothing nigh measure or guess Time as that [glass] did. **1776** *Trial of Nundocomar* 39/1 How many people do you guess might follow you to Hougly, expecting employment? **1804** W. TENNANT *Ind. Recreat.* II. 38 Boiled down to a proper consistence, which they guess by the eye, and by the touch. **1841** ELPHINSTONE *Hist. Ind.* I. 207 A statue..cut out of a rock, which has been guessed at different heights. **1860** TYNDALL *Glac.* II. x. 277 The eye being liable to be grossly deceived in guessing the direction of a perpendicular.

absol. c **1330** R. BRUNNE *Chron.* (1810) 205 The ferth day formest next Palmesonenday, þe tyme, as I gest, R. 3ede to play. *c* **1386** CHAUCER *Knt.'s T.* 1735 So euene were [they] chosen for to gesse. —— *Frankl. T.* 684 Mo than a thousand stories as I gesse Koude I now telle. *c* **1391** —— *Astrol.* II. §40, I..sette the point of A in the wex on my label as, euene as y kowde gesse ouer the Ecliptik lyne. **1605** SHAKS. *Oth.* I. iii. 36 The Ottamites..Haue there inioynted them with an after Fleete. *1 Sen.* I, so I thought: how many, as you guesse? **1712** W. ROGERS *Voy.* 103 It lay as near as we could guess ENE. and WSW. **1757** WASHINGTON *Let.* Writ. 1889 I. 478 Our present strength, I guess, is about seven hundred.

†**b.** With numbers. *to guess*: approximately, 'or thereabouts'. *Obs.*

c **1330** R. BRUNNE *Chron.* (1810) 150 Þer duellid R. schip þre daies to gesse. **1375** BARBOUR *Bruce* XIV. 270 Thai war, to gess, fiffty thousand.

†**c.** To add (an ingredient) without exact measurement. *Obs.*

c **1420** *Pallad. on Husb.* XI. 385, iij piluls of cupresse, Or leef of box an hondful, therto gesse.

†**2.** *intr.* To take aim (const. *to*). Also, to purpose, aim, direct oneself *to* do something. *Obs.*

13.. *Coer de L.* 4482 When the Crystene myght draw hem tylle, To shete the arweblasteres hem dresse, And the archeres to hem gesse. ?*c* **1320** *K. Horn* (*Harl. MS.*, ed. Ritson) 1187 Horn..seide he wolde gesse [*older texts* agesce, agesse] To aryve at Westnesse. **1530** PALSGR. 561/2, I gesse, I mente or ayme to hytte a thynge that I shote or throwe at, *je esme*.

†**3.** *trans.* To esteem, account, reckon: with obj. and complement. *Obs.*

c **1340** HAMPOLE *Pr. Consc.* 3934 Þan es a day of pardon to gesce Mare worthy þan alle þis worldis riches. *c* **1380** WYCLIF *Serm.* Sel. Wks. II. 229 Poul..biddiþ..bi oure life þat man have mater to gesse us as mynystris of God. **1382** —— *Matt.* xi. 16 To whom shal I gesse this generacioun lichy? —— *Mark* xv. 28 The prophecie is fulfild that seith, And he is gesside, or ordeyned, with wickide men. *a* **1400** *Prymer* (E.E.T.S.) 64 Gessist þou it worþi to opene þin i3en on siche a man? *a* **1400–50** *Alexander* 4495 3e..gesse wele as many gods as growis in him membris.

†**4.** To think, judge, suppose; with clause as obj. *Obs.* (Cf. sense 6.)

c **1380** WYCLIF *Wks.* (1880) 422 As we gessen þat þis man þat holdiþ wel cristis lawe is a leme of hooly chirche,.. So we gessen of an-oþer man þat reuersiþ cristis lawe, þat he is a leme of þe fend. —— *Acts* viii. 20 Thou gessidist the 3ifte of God for to be had..by money. **1388** —— *Jer.* xxiii. 23 Gessist thou [Vulg. *putasne*] whether Y am God of ni3, seith the Lord, and not God afer? *a* **1400** *Prymer* (E.E.T.S.) 64 Gessist þou not [Vulg. *putasne*] þat a deed man schal lyue a3en? *c* **1400** *Apol. Loll.* 48 Hector Thebanus..wen he went to vse philosophie at Athenis, he kest a wey a gret peise of gold; he gessid þat he mi3t not haue to gidre, riches & vertu. *a* **1400–50** *Alexander* 2905 Þe Persyns..gesses him to be gode for glori of his wedis.

5. To form an opinion or hypothesis respecting (some unknown state of facts), either at random or from indications admittedly uncertain; to conjecture. Const. *by, from.*

a. with clause or indirect question as obj.; also with obj. and inf., and with advs. *so, otherwise*, in lieu of clause.

1390 GOWER *Conf.* I. 103 For I can nought my selfe gesse, Which is the best unto my chois. **1398** TREVISA *Barth. De P.R.* XVI. lxxxvii. (1495) 583 The stone smaragdus helpyth them that vse to dyuyne and gesse what shal befall. *a* **1400–50** *Alexander* 2071 And wele he geses be þe graynes 3oure gomes ere fele. *c* **1425** LYDG. *Assembly of Gods* 1386, I trow, as I gesse, At Vertu hys castell ye may soone hym fynde. **1530** PALSGR. 561/2 Gesse what we were talkynge of afore you came in a dores. **1555–8** PHAER *Æneid* I. Bj, I gesse Some goddesse thou art, and Phebus bright thy brother is. *a* **1605** MONTGOMERIE *Sonn.* xxiii. 2 If gentle blude ingendrit be by baggis, Then culd I ges vho wer a gentle Jhone. **1653** H. COGAN tr. *Pinto's Trav.* x. 30 One amongst them, whom we guessed to be the chiefest of them. **1680** OTWAY *Orphan* IV. i. (1691) 37 *Acast.* And went your Maid to bed too? *Mon.* My Lord, I guess so. **1709** HEARNE *Collect.* (O.H.S.) II. 277, I guess it to have been a Piece of the Chapell. **1723** R. MILLAR *Hist. Propagat. Chr.* II. VIII. 367 We may ghess what sort of Christians these Popish Proselytes were. **1741** MIDDLETON *Cicero* II. VII. 93 At present we can onely guess rather than know what Caesar will do. **1774** GOLDSM. *Nat. Hist.* (1776) VI. 135 What it is can employ them all the day is not easy to guess. *a* **1806** BP. HORSLEY *Serm.* (1811) 292 They were effected by what you might the least guess to be the instruments of Providence. **1838** LYTTON *Alice* 5 You would scarcely have guessed, from her appearance, that she was more than seven or eight and twenty. **1879** B. TAYLOR *Stud. Germ. Lit.* 101 We may guess when its growth began.

b. with *simple object*.

?**1513** MORE *Rich. III* Wks. (1557) 57/1 Whose iugement semeth me somwhat like, as though men should gesse ye bewty of one longe before departed. **1591** SPENSER *Ruines Rome* v, O Rome! thee let him see, In case thy greatnes he can gesse in harte. **1592** GREENE *Upst. Courtier* F 2, You may gesse the inward mind by the outward apparel. **1603** KNOLLES *Hist. Turks* (1621) 707 Some ghessing one thing and some another. **1654** WHITLOCK *Zootomia* 67 His Water ..cleer like Well-water, insomuch as I could never have guest a burning Feaver. **1673** DRYDEN *Amboyna* IV. iii, This I guess, but saw it not because I came too late. **1694** —— *Love Triumph.* III. i, Beware: for by my own I guess your passion. **1817** CHALMERS *Astron. Disc.* i. (1852) 24 We may guess with plausibility what we cannot anticipate with confidence. **1844** MRS. BROWNING *Rom. Page* xvi, I..little guessed the end.

†**c.** with *obj.* and complement. *Obs.*

1605 KYD *1st Pt. Jeronimo* B 3 b, Spaines choyce embassador..for soe I gesse thee. **1632** RANDOLPH *Jealous Lovers* III. vii, Your boy? I should have guess'd him for your father. **1633** MASSINGER *Guardian* III. v, Yet by your language, I ghess you a Gentleman. **1667** MILTON *P.L.* v. 290 For on som message high they guessd him bound.

d. *absol.* and *ellipt.*, chiefly in parenthetic use. (The early examples may possibly belong to 4.)

1340 HAMPOLE *Pr. Consc.* 1136 Yhernyng of eghe, als I can gese Falles to worldes rychese. *c* **1460** ROS *La Belle Dame* 173 in *Pol. Rel. & L. Poems* 57 In hir failed nothyng, as I koude gesse. *c* **1520** *Interl. Beauties Women* A ij b, Thys lute is out of tune now as I ges. **1562** *Nottingham Rec.* IV. 128 Sheryffz off cetyes ar, I ges, for eleccion and for retornes. **1591** SHAKS. *1 Hen. VI*, II. v. 60 Discouer more at large what cause that was, For I am ignorant, and cannot guesse. **1599** H. BUTTES *Dyets drie Dinner* H iij, Carot, that is, redde roote: as some Antiquaries gesse. **1600** SHAKS. *A.Y.L.* II. iv. 24 *Sil.* Oh Corin, that thou knew'st how I do loue her. *Cor.* I partly guesse: for I haue lou'd ere now. **1632** MASSINGER *Emperor East* III. iii, *Theod.* Whither went shee? speake. *Phil.* As they ghesse, to the lawrel groue. **1737** GRAY *Let.* Wks. 1884 II. 12 You..will prefer a picture of still life to the realities of a noisy one, and as I guess, will imitate what you prefer. **1818** SHELLEY *Marenghi* xii, He went Alone, as you may guess, to banishment. **1819** —— *Julian & Maddalo* 535 He had store Of friends and fortune once, as we could guess From his nice habits and his gentleness.

6. *I guess*: sometimes used, with playful moderation of statement, in reference to what the speaker regards as a fact or a secure inference. Hence *colloq.*, orig. in the northern U.S. (sometimes with omission of the pronoun) = 'I am pretty sure'.

1692 LOCKE *Educ.* § 28 Once in Four and Twenty Hours, I think, is enough; and no Body, I guess, will think it too much. *Ibid.* §59 If this were constantly observ'd, I guess there would be little need of blows or chiding. *c* **1698** —— *Cond. Underst.* IV. xii. §10 Beyond this I fear our talents reach not, nor are our faculties, as I guess, able to advance. **1776** R. KING in *Life & Corr.* (1894) I. 23, I guess the pious Elder would as lieve tarry where he is. **1778** FRANKLIN *Let.* Wks. 1889 VI. 195, I write this letter to you, notwithstanding; (which I think I can convey in a less mysterious manner, and guess it may come to your hands). **1814** BYRON *Diary* 8 Apr., 'I guess now' (as the Yankees say), that he will yet play them a pass. **1818** SCOTT *Hrt. Midl.* xxxviii, I guess..you winna be the waur o' a glass of the right Rosa Solis. **1826** —— *Jrnl.* (1890) I. 85, I guess (as Mathews makes his Yankees say) that we shall not be troubled with visitors, and I calculate that I will not go out at all. **1830** GALT *Lawrie T.* III. ix. (1849) 114, I guess Squire

Lawrie talks too much. **1843** HALIBURTON *Attaché* I. ii. 23 What on airth shall I do?—guess, I'll strap my rasor. **1848** LOWELL *Biglow P.* Poems 1890 II. 126 Thet kin' o talk I guess you'll find'll answer to a charm. **1885** HOWELLS *Silas Lapham* II. xxii, I guess those English parties have gone back on Rogers. **1916** A. HUXLEY *Let.* 21 Jan. (1969) 89 Say, kiddo, guess you're between the Devil and the W.C. **1927** M. DE LA ROCHE *Jalna* xv. 165, I guess I've just the right amount of brains for that. **1938** R. D. FINLAYSON *Brown Man's Burden* 46 Py korry she cost the Pakeha thousands *and* thousands of pounds I guess. **1946** K. TENNANT *Lost Haven* (1968) i. 19, I guess it was a bandicoot, or else an ole swamp wallaby that died in the lonely scrub. **1959** M. CALLAGHAN in R. Weaver *Canad. Short Stories* 2nd Ser. (1968) 5 There's no harm in you talking to Mother if you want to, I guess.

7. a. *intr.* To form conjectures. (†Const. *of*.) *to* ***guess at***: to attempt to estimate conjecturally; to hazard a random or insufficiently founded opinion about; to attempt to solve or discover by conjecture.

a **1400** *Plowman's T.* 170 In hir sentence..They willen gesse in hir gay hall. *a* **1586** SIDNEY *Arcadia* I. (1590) 14 More then the letter I haue not to ghesse by. *Ibid.* III. 333 b, Philoclea..ghessed somewhat at Zelmanes mind. **1593** SHAKS. *Lucr.* 1238 Their gentle sex to weepe are often willing, Greeuing themselues to gesse at others smarts. **1605** —— *Macb.* IV. iii. 203 *Rosse.* Let not your eares dispise my tongue for euer, Which shall possess them with the heauiest sound That euer yet they heard. *Macd.* Humh: I guesse at it. **1606** —— *Ant. & Cl.* III. iii. 29 Guesse at her yeares, I prythee. **1613** PURCHAS *Pilgrimage* (1614) 63 Wisards, which by conjectures and casting of lots did ghesse of things to come. **1625** —— *Pilgrims* II. 1480 He is on his birthday.. yearely weighed and account kept therof by his Physicians, thereby ghessing at his bodily estate. **1641** WILKINS *Math. Magick* I. xvii. (1648) 127 From the understanding of which, you may the better ghesse at the nature of the rest. **1711** LADY M. W. MONTAGU *Let. to Mrs. Hewet* Lett. 1887 I. 31 By what fine gentlemen write, you know, it is not easy to guess at what they mean. **1748** *Anson's Voy.* II. vi. 202 The total amount..can only be rudely guessed at. **1806–7** J. BERESFORD *Miseries Hum. Life* (1826) III. xxxviii, Vain endeavours to guess at a riddle. **1818** SHELLEY *Rosalind & Helen* 1181 There was a change, but spare to guess, Nor let that moment's hope be told. **1878** BROWNING *La Saisiaz* 23 Would I shirk assurance on each point whereat I can but guess—Does the soul survive the body? [etc.].

b. In phr. *to keep* (a person) ***guessing***: to keep in a state of uncertainty. *colloq.* (orig. *U.S.*).

1896 ADE *Artie* v. 41 When your old college chum gets that letter it'll keep him guessin' where to begin on it. **1905** *Springfield* (Mass.) *Weekly Republ.* 24 Nov. 1 More doubt is now thrown upon the question whether he will go to Washington at all. The governor seems determined to keep us guessing. **1924** A. C. MACLAREN *Cricket Old & New* xii. 116 A. G. Steel..putting the ball where he liked and keeping the batsman guessing all the time. [**1927** M. A. NOBLE *Those 'Ashes'* 175 Mailey..varied his pace splendidly and had everyone guessing.] **1930** H. ZINK *City Bosses in U.S.* 23 Murphy proceeded with considerable caution, sometimes withdrawing from a position, sometimes forcing it, and altogether keeping his opponents guessing what he would do next. **1955** L. P. HARTLEY *Perfect Woman* xiii. 124 She always tries to keep me guessing.

8. *trans.* 'To conjecture rightly' (J.); to hit upon the answer to (a question), the solution of (a riddle, †a parable); to discover by conjecture, divine. †Also with *out*.

1548 UDALL, etc. *Erasm. Par. Matt.* xv. 15–20 Out of one [parable] to haue diuined and gessed [**1552** geassed] another. **1563–83** FOXE *A. & M.* II. 1786/2 Wolfe..partly gessing which Ambassadour he ment. **1636** E. DACRES tr. *Machiavel's Disc. Livy* II. 535 Because it is hard to attaine to that knowledge, he deserves the greater commendations, who takes such a course, that he ghesses it out. *a* **1718** PENN in *Pa. Hist. Soc. Mem.* I. 205 Thomas Lurting may guess the man. *c* **1718** PRIOR *Beauty, A Riddle* 37 Your riddle is not hard to read: I guess it. **1783** GOUV. MORRIS in Sparks *Life & Writ.* (1832) I. 250, I do not pretend to guess precisely their sentiments. **1847** BUSHNELL *Chr. Nurt.* II. vi. (1861) 347 But which is worse..it is not difficult, I think, to guess. **1884** CHILD *Ballads* I. 418/1 Choose comrades that can guess riddles.

absol. **1603** SHAKS. *Meas. for M.* IV. iv. 8 Why meet him at the gates and re[de]liuer our authorities there? *Esc.* I ghesse not. **1840** DICKENS *Barn. Rudge* vi, Sure enough it's Barnaby—how did you guess?

Hence **guessed** (-*at*), *ppl. a.*

1832 R. H. FROUDE *Rem.* (1838) I. 253, I have observed one thing, and one only, in favour of my guessed-at theory. **1917** J. MASEFIELD *Lollingdon Downs* 61 The discoverer scans..the guessed-at satellite. **1930** AUDEN *Poems* 26 Areas ..Whose guessed at wonders would be worth alleging.

guess, variant of CHESS *sb.*[2]

1631 MARKHAM *Countr. Content.* I. xvi. (ed. 4) 99 There is no better way to take him than by setting Roddes drest with water Lime, and set shoring on the edge of the water, one guess [*ed.* 1614 crosse] or row ouer another.

guess(e, obs. pl. form of GUEST.

guessable (ˈgɛsəb(ə)l), *a.* [f. GUESS *v.* + -ABLE.] That can be guessed.

1828 DISRAELI *Voyage Capt. Popanilla* iii. 16 My plots are not of that extremely guessable nature. **1865** CARLYLE *Fredk. Gt.* VI. iv. (1872) II. 166 Without date to it:—the guessable date is about two years hence. **1881** *Spectator* 19 Mar. 373 The uncertain, and at most only guessable store of forces at work in human nature. **1890** *Sat. Rev.* 22 Nov. 581/2 Within, if not exactly measurable, at least guessable, distance.

guessen, dial. form of GESTEN *v. Obs.*

guesser (ˈgɛsə(r)). Also 5 **gessare**, 6 **gesser**. [f. GUESS *v.* + -ER[1].] One who guesses.

c **1440** *Promp. Parv.* 190/2 Gessare (*K.* or a soposare), *estimator*. **1580** HOLLYBAND *Treas. Fr. Tong, Vn devin*, a soothsayer, a gesser. **1651** HOBBES *Leviath.* I. iii. 10 The best guesser, he that is most versed and studied in the matters he guesses at. **1671** H. M. tr. *Erasm. Colloq.* 115 You shall be ..the guessers of my dream. **1754** RICHARDSON *Grandison* (1781) III. xxx. 355 You are a strange guesser. **1833** T. HOOK *Widow & Marquess* vii, French physicians are, if possible, worse guessers than English ones. **1881** *Nation* (N.Y.) XXXII. 316 For in these a guesser would be correct exactly half the time.

guessing (ˈgɛsɪŋ), *vbl. sb.* [f. GUESS *v.* + -ING[1].] The action of the vb. GUESS; an instance of this, a conjecture, prognostication. †***without guessing***: beyond estimation, incalculably.

1340 *Ayenb.* 268 More hy byeþ glede wyþ -oute gessynge of godes holynesse þanne of his oȝene and of alle oþre myd hym. **1387** TREVISA *Higden* (Rolls) II. 59 William, þat hadde nouȝt i-seie þat Brittisshe book, wroot so..by his owne gessynge. *c* **1440** *Promp. Parv.* 190/2 Gessynge (*K.* or wenyn), *estimacio*. **1535** COVERDALE *Ezek.* xiii. 22 Therfore shal ye spie out no more vanyte, nor prophecie youre owne gessinges. *a* **1643** W. CARTWRIGHT *Birth Dk. York* 31 The Forehead, Eye, and Lip, poor humble Parts, Too shallow for resemblance, show the Arts Of private guessings. **1692** BENTLEY *Boyle Lect.* vi. 182 Beyond the possibility of good guessing. *a* **1715** BURNET *Own Time* (1724) I. 18 Some.. probable guessings which they delivered as prophecies. **1875** JOWETT *Plato* (ed. 2) I. 263 A sort of guessing or divination which rests on no knowledge of causes. **1887** *Athenæum* 12 Nov. 632/3 We expect something more from an historian than happy guessing.

b. *attrib.* and *Comb.* ***guessing game***, a parlour game in which much of the playing consists of guessing; also *transf.*

1654 WHITLOCK *Zootomia* 548 All writ by Prophane, or Sacred Pen-men may be tearmed guessing Discoveries..in comparison of the Experiment of dying. **1711** *C.M. Lett. to Curat* 82 And upon this he imploys his Guessing Faculty. **1727** BOYER *Dict. Angl.-Fr.* s.v., Physick is but a guessing Science. **1889** W. C. BROWNELL *French Traits* iii. 98 The French intelligence seems to have almost no frivolous side. The different varieties of mental arithmetic, guessing-games, puzzles, puns, spiritualism, theosophy, fanaticisms, have no attractions for it. **1936** E. S. GARDNER *Case of Stuttering Bishop* (1937) viii. 122 If you want to waste your time playing guessing games with me, that's your funeral. **1938** D. KINCAID *Brit. Social Life in India* ix. 254 After dinner..there would be guessing games and competitions. **1941** E. BOWEN *Look at all those Roses* 125 Juvenile parties ..when guessing games could be played. **1955** I. FLEMING *Moonraker* xiv. 139, I can't spend all the morning playing guessing games. **1966** 'R. STANDISH' *Widow Hack* xiv. 153, I played a little guessing game in an effort to divine in advance what Madeleine's next move would be. **1969** I. & P. OPIE *Children's Games* ii. 108 Popular at the beginning of the century, was the guessing game 'Dead Men, Dark Scenery'.

guessing (ˈgɛsɪŋ), *ppl. a.* [f. GUESS *v.* + -ING[2].] That guesses; that does things by guess-work. Hence **ˈguessingly** *adv.*, in a guessing manner; by guess-work or conjecture.

1605 SHAKS. *Lear* III. vii. 47, I haue a Letter guessingly set downe. *a* **1668** DAVENANT *Philosopher's Disquis.* Wks. (1673) 326 A Guide..Who guessingly her progress doth begin. **1703** T. N. *City & C. Purchaser* 86 According to their way of Working by Guess..these Guessing Workmen too often guess wrong, and commit many Faults. **1827** G. S. FABER *Orig. Expiatory Sacrifice* 32 If piacular sacrifice anterior to the promulgation of the Law can be shown to have not originated from a guessing superstition. **1850** A. GRAY *Lett.* (1893) 367, I dislike to take the time to study out laboriously and guessingly..these things which are mostly well known to botanists.

†**ˈguessive,** *a. Obs. rare*$^{-1}$. [f. GUESS *sb.* + -IVE.] Of the nature of a guess; conjectural.

1628 FELTHAM *Resolves* [II.] I. xcvi. 302 The guessiue interpretations of dim-ey'd Man.

guess-rope: see GUEST-ROPE.

guesstimate (ˈgɛstɪmət), *sb.* orig. *U.S.* Also **guestimate**. [f. GUESS *sb.* + ES)TIMATE *sb.*] An estimate which is based on both guesswork and reasoning.

1936 *N.Y. Times* 22 Dec., 'Guesstimates' is the word frequently used by the statisticians and population experts. **1943** *N.Y. Times* 19 July 4/6 Many Americans..think the Axis..will be defeated in less than two years. Intangibles.. might make this popular 'guestimate' close to correct. **1948** *Jrnl. R. Aeronaut. Soc.* LII. 614/2 The former is a firm figure which arises in fact. The latter is an arbitrary 'guesstimate'. **1957** R. WATSON-WATT *Three Steps to Victory* liii. 316 This mixture of estimates and guestimates comes out better than we deserve, for the Opana clock was very unlikely to agree with whatever clocks and watches were consulted in the aircraft and in Pearl Harbor. **1967** *New Scientist* 24 Aug. 373/2 Faced with engineering problems of this magnitude, £20 million is likely to prove as elusive a 'guesstimate' as the original figure for Concord. **1970** *Daily Tel.* 1 Oct. 19 (Advt.), £1000 tax free clear profit. .. This is proved performance—not an optimistic guesstimate.

Hence **ˈguesstimate** (-eɪt) *v. trans.* and *intr.*, **guesstiˈmation**, **ˈguesstimator**.

1937 D. C. T. BENNETT *Compl. Air Navigator* v. 152 'Guess-timation' is an art in navigation which should not generally be encouraged. **1942** BERREY & VAN DEN BARK *Amer. Thes. Slang* §179.5 *Guesstimate*, blend of 'guess' and 'estimate'. **1943** in *Amer. Speech* (1944) XIX. 149/2 At no time in the past has so much depended upon the correct guesstimation of the tactical requirements of the future. **1948** *Elks Mag.* Oct. 11 One conservative guesstimator predicts 375,000 [television] sets in the country by January 1. **1950** *Jrnl. R. Aeronaut. Soc.* LIV. 175/1 50,000 lb...he had arrived at by a bit of 'guesstimating'. **1969** *Daily Tel.* (Colour Suppl.) 31 Jan. 32/3 The experts can 'guesstimate' how much gas is there [*sc.* under the North Sea], but there is no sure way of telling.

guess-warp (ˈgɛswɔːp). *Naut.* Also 5 **gyes-**, 9 **ges-**, **guest-warp**. [The first element is of doubtful origin: see quot. 1862 (sense 1) and GUEST-ROPE (GUESS-ROPE); the second is WARP *sb.*]

1. 'A rope carried to a distant object, in order to warp a vessel towards it, or to make fast a boat' (Smyth *Sailor's Word-bk.*). By some writers applied to any rope used to attach a boat astern of a vessel.

1495–7 *Naval Acc. Hen. VII* (1896) 272 Bote roppes for the seid Shippes Grete bote, ij. Gyes warpes, j. Boy ropes, vij. **1730** CAPT. W. WRIGLESWORTH *MS. Log-bk. of the 'Lyell'* 15 July, At 3 made a Guess Warp, with the Stream Cable and a 7 Inch Hawser bent to the Stream Anchor. **1840** R. H. DANA *Bef. Mast.* xiv. 33 The boats are..made fast astern, or out to the swinging-booms, by ges-warps. **1862** NARES *Seamanship* (ed. 2) 87 In laying out a guesswarp, the whole hawser is taken in the boat, and the end is brought back to the ship, the distance being 'guessed'.

2. = GUEST-ROPE 2. Also *attrib.* in ***guess-warp boom*** (see quot. 1867).

1833 MARRYAT *P. Simple* viii, Oblige me by underrunning the guess-warp. **1867** SMYTH *Sailor's Word-bk.*, *Guest-warp boom*, a swinging span (lower studding boom) rigged from the ship's side with a warp for boats to ride by. **1875** BEDFORD *Sailor's Pocket Bk.* vii. (ed. 2) 260 A 'guess warp' is to be stretched alongside each ship's sides for boats whilst loading, to ride by.

ˈguess-work. [f. GUESS *sb.*] Procedure consisting in or based on guessing, as opposed to knowledge, reasoning, or methodical investigation.

1725 N. ROBINSON *Th. Physick* 238 To believe, there is no Certainty in the Principles of Physick, and that all Practice is mere Guess-work and Empiricism. **1768–74** TUCKER *Lt. Nat.* (1834) II. 322 It were mere guess-work to say what was their belief of the gods and a future state. **1818** BYRON *Ep. Murray* iii, The pompous rascallion, Who don't speak Italian Nor French, must have scribbled by guesswork. **1846** GROTE *Greece* I. xvi. I. 585 The one process as well as the other was interpretative guesswork. **1879** L. CAMPBELL *Sophocles* I. Pref. 29 A piece of more or less clumsy guess-work on the part of the scribe. **1889** 'ROLF BOLDREWOOD' *Robbery under Arms* xx, We had been riding all night from track to track, sometimes steering by guesswork.

guest (gɛst), *sb.* Forms: 1 **ȝiest, ȝist, ȝyst, ȝæst, ȝest**, 2–5 **gist(e**, 2–6 **gest(e**, 3–4 **gust(e**, 4–7 **ghest(e**, 5–6 **geest**, (6 **geast(e, gehaste**), 6 **gueste**, 6–7 **ghuest**, (7 *Sc.* **guast**), 6– **guest**. Also *pl.* 6 **gess**, 6–7 **gesse, guess**, 7 **guesse**. [Com. Teut.: OE. *ȝiest* (*ȝist, ȝyst*), *ȝæst*, Anglian (also in Ælfric) *ȝęst* (? or *gęst*), = OS. (MDu., Du., LG.), OHG. (MHG., mod.G.) *gast*, ON. *gęst-r* (Sw. *gäst*, Da. *gjæst*), Goth. *gast-s*:—OTeut. **gasti-z*:—WAryan **ghosti-s*, represented also by L. *hostis*, orig. 'stranger', in classical use 'enemy' (whence the compound **hosti-pot-*, contracted *hospit-*, *hospes* guest, host) and by OSl. *gostĭ* guest, friend. According to Brugmann, the synonymous Gr. *ξ-ένος* is from **gh's-*, wk. grade of the root **ghos-* represented in the Teut. word.

According to phonetic law as at present understood, the initial consonant in the OE. word must have had a palatal pronunciation, which would normally yield ME. *ȝ*, mod.Eng. *y*. No forms with *ȝ* or *y* are, however, known to exist; the abnormal guttural pronunciation is usually explained as due to the influence of ON. *gest-r*; but the occurrence of hybrid forms like *gist*, *gust* (Y) in the S.W. dialects of the 13th c. is hard to account for on this supposition.]

1. a. One who is entertained at the house or table of another.

Beowulf 1800 Reste hine ða rumheort..ȝæst inne swæf. *a* **1000** *Cædmon's Gen.* 2455 þæt hie behæfdon..Loth mid ȝiestum. *c* **1020** *Rule St. Benet* lvi. (Logeman) 94 *Hospites*, ȝystes. **1154** *O.E. Chron.* an. 1137 (Laud MS.) Martin abbot ..fand te munekes & te ȝestes al þæt heom behoued. *c* **1200** *Trin. Coll. Hom.* 165 Nis nower non trewðe, for nis þe gist siker of þe husebonde ne noðer of oðer. *c* **1250** *Gen. & Ex.* 1070 Loth hem bead his doȝtres two, for to friðen hise geste swo. *c* **1297** R. GLOUC. (Rolls) 5787 He sed a wel hey word among is gustes [*v.rr.* gistes, gestes] echon. *c* **1340** *Cursor M.* 14086 (Fairf.) Suche a geste come neuer vn-to þaire hous to rest. **1393** LANGL. *P. Pl.* C. XI. 179 Herodes þe daffe ȝaf hus douhter..þe hefde Of þe blessyde baptiste by-fore alle hus gustes. **1431** *Eng. Gilds* (1870) 277 The alderman schal haue ..to his drynk & for his geestys .j. Galone of ale. **1474** CAXTON *Chesse* 115 They coueyte not to haue the goodes of theyr ghestes. *c* **1475** *Rauf Coilȝear* 104 Schir ȝe ar welcome hame, And ȝour Gaist baith. **1566** DRANT *Horace's Sat.* IV. H, If..thou shouldst..sauce thy meate with foystie oyles, thy gesse woulde the disdaine. **1592** SHAKS. *Rom. & Jul.* I. ii. 21 This night I hold an old accustom'd Feast, Whereto I haue inuited many a Guest. **1648** GAGE *West Ind.* xiv. 90 The Indians intreated us to bee their guesse at dinner. **1690** NORRIS *Beatitudes* (1694) I. 164 He does not..take up his Residence and be a familiar Ghest, til [etc.]. **1733** MRS. H. PRATT in *Swift's Lett.* (1768) IV. 55, I wish I had a house in some measure worthy to entertain a guest that should be so welcome to me. **1814** SCOTT *Ld. of Isles* I. xx, For if a hope of safety rest, 'Tis on the sacred name of guest. 1861 M. PATTISON *Ess.* (1889) I. 45 A stone-vaulted kitchen, where dinner could be dressed for an army of guests. 1883 C. J. WILLS *Mod. Persia* 243, I agreed..to be the guest of my patient.

Proverb. 1546 J. HEYWOOD *Prov.* (1867) 17 An vnbydden geast knoweth not where to syt.

b. *transf.* and *fig.* esp. A person or thing personified that comes and is entertained, or is viewed as coming and being entertained.

c 1000 *Whale* 29 (Gr.) Đonne semninga on sealtne wæȝ mid þa noþe niþer ȝewiteþ garsecges ȝæst. a 1300 *Cursor M.* 9873 Bot godd, sin he wald sua be gest, In clene sted al most he rest. 1340 *Ayenb.* 249 Huanne þe gate of þe mouþe is open, þe gest of zenne geþ in li3[t]liche. 1393 LANGL. *P. Pl.* C. XVI. 199 Mynstralcie can ich nat muche bote make men murye, As a waffrer with waffres and welcome godes gistes. 14.. *Ecce Aucilla Domini* in *Tundale's Vis.* (1843) 141 God will be borne within thi brest Then seyde tho meydon full myldely To me he schall be a welcom geste. c 1420 *Pallad. on Husb.* I. 574 With iiii or v Of thrusshis tamed, putte hem in this mewe To do disport among this gestis newe. 1551 P'CESS ELIZ. in Ellis *Orig. Lett.* Ser. I. II. 163 To hire of your siknes is unpleasant to me..I understande it is your olde gest that is wont oft to viset you. 1592 SHAKS. *Ven. & Ad.* 449 Lest iealousie, that sower vnwelcome guest, Should by his stealing in disturbe the feast. 1606 G. W[ODCOCKE] *Justine* 136 b, The bodies of these inhabitants do well away with these two vnwelcom guests, hunger and paine. 1629 SIR W. MURE *Trve Crvcifixe* 680 Graves backe to light their sleeping guasts doe send. 1633 R. S. tr. *Drexelius' Nicetas* 109 That poore yong man became the guest of hogges. 1654 WHITLOCK *Zootomia* 69 Feavers, the guests (though unwelcome) of the Veines and Arteries. 1691 E. TAYLOR *Behmen's Theos. Philos.* Incarnation 332, I have so evil a ghest in me. 1713 DERHAM *Phys.-Theol.* I. iii. 23 Snow; which although an irksom Guest, yet hath its great Uses. a 1800 COWPER *Ode to Peace* 1 Come, peace of mind, delightful guest! 1814 CARY *Dante, Par.* XI. 13, I thus gloriously Was raised aloft, and made the guest of heaven.

c. Phr. *be my guest*: you are welcome to (something); do as you wish.

1955 *Amer. Speech* XXX. 302 *Be my guest*, used when someone asks for something: 'Join me' or 'Go right ahead'. 1962 D. MAYO *Island of Sin* xiii. 118 Rum? Scotch? Bourbon? Be my guest. 1965 *New Statesman* 14 May 760/3 'Did you say something, man?' the face asked. I took a deep breath..and then I address the face. 'Not a thing, brother,' I reply, 'not a thing. Be my guest.' 1967 J. GARDNER *Madrigal* i. 18 Mostyn gestured towards the telephone. 'Be my guest,' said the Chief. 1968 D. FRANCIS *Forfeit* iv. 55 'Goodnight, honey.' 'Thanks for everything.' 'Be my guest.' 1969 B. MALAMUD *Pictures Fidelman* 159 'Do you mind if I get on top?' she asked. 'It's hard to breathe since I had my illness.' 'Be my guest.'

†**2. a.** A stranger. *Obs.*

c 950 *Lindisf. Gosp.* Matt. xxv. 36 Gest ic wæs and ȝe somnadon meh. a 1000 *Riddles* xvi. 10 (Gr.) Hwonne ȝæst cume to durum minum him biþ deað witod. c 1175 *Lamb. Hom.* 109 Mon mei wurchen elmessan on ete and on wete.. and þet mon gistas underuo. 1340 HAMPOLE *Pr. Consc.* 1374 Na syker wonnyng-sted here haf we,.. For as gestes we here soiourne. c 1374 CHAUCER *Troylus* II. 1062 (1111) Ther is right now y-come in to towne a geste A Grick espie. c 1450 tr. *De Imitatione* I. xxiii. 32 Kepe þiself as a pilgrime & a geste upon þe erþe. 1578 LYTE *Dodoens* III. ix. 327 Chiron.. being received as a ghest or straunger in Hercules house or lodging.

b. *transf.* An object considered as an omen of the coming of a stranger. *local.*

1727 BOYER *Angl.-Fr. Dict.* s.v., There's a Guest in your Candle, *il y a des nouvelles à vôtre chandelle.* 1807 HOGG *Mtn. Bard* note vi. Poet. Wks. 1838 II. 331 If a feather, a straw, or any such thing, be observed hanging at a dog's nose or beard, they call that a guest, and are sure of the approach of a stranger.

3. a. A temporary inmate of an hotel, inn, or boarding house.

c 1290 *S. Eng. Leg.* I. 361/62 Hostiler he was þare i-mad gistes to onder-fonge. c 1449 PECOCK *Repr.* III. ii. 284 An oosteler seith to his gist. 1533 MORE *Debell. Salem* Wks. 991/2 He fareth lo lyke a geste, yt maketh hys rekening himselfe without hys hoste. 1591 SHAKS. *Two Gent.* IV. ii. 26 *Ho.* Now, my yong guest; me thinks your' allycholly; I pray you why is it? *Iu.* Marry (mine Host) because I cannot be merry. 1607 MIDDLETON *Phoenix* I. iii, Sirrah, what guess does this inn hold now? 1631 T. POWELL *Tom All Trades* (1876) 141 The Ostlers of Holborne had more than ordinary care to lay up theyr Ghuests bootes. 1774 GOLDSM. *Retal.* 4 If our landlord supplies us with beef and with fish Let each guest bring himself, and he brings the best dish. 1845 FORD *Handbk. Spain* I. 24 'Let no man', said Apuleius, 'think that he is the mere guest of his landlord'. 1860 TYNDALL *Glac.* I. xxiii. 165, I was the only guest at the hotel.

b. An occasional performer, one not belonging to the regular company in a theatre, etc.

1900 W. A. ELLIS tr. *Glasenapp's Life R. Wagner* I. vii. 259 She..appeared four times as 'guest' at the theatre.., playing Preziosa, Maria Stuart, [etc.]. 1901 *Athenæum* 27 Apr. 539/2 In addition to the artists of the Hofoper, 'guests' from Frankfort, Wiesbaden,..and Vienna will take part in the performances.

4. A man, fellow, 'customer'. *Obs.* exc. *dial.*

c 1394 [see GLEIM *sb.* 2]. a 1400-50 *Alexander* 460 Þou has ragid..with vnryd gestis. a 1440 *Sir Degrev.* 1195 He was the sternest gest ffro heven to helle! 1470-85 MALORY *Arthur* VI. vii, Yonder is a shrewde gest sayd syre Madore de la port therfore haue here ones at hym. 1869 *Lonsdale Gloss.*, *Guest*, a creature or person. 'An ill guest' = a bad-looking fellow.

5. A parasite animal or vegetable. Also *guest-fly*.

1864 COBBOLD *Entozoa* v. 232 In the case of the adult worm, the happiest cures are readily affected by the expulsion of the 'guest', but as regards the larvæ the case is very different. 1887 *Jrnl. Soc. Arts* 29 Sept. 913/1 When the fungus dies, the invaded and malformed part also generally dies, and the plant is further injured by contact of the healthy tissue with the decaying tissue and all its eventual guests and products.

6. *attrib.* and *Comb.* **a.** simple attrib., as *guest-quarters*, *-ranch*, *-register*. **b.** appositive, as *guest-cavalier*, *-friend* [cf. G. *gastfreund*], *-justice*; (sense 3 b) *guest actor*, *actress*, *artist* (so as v. intr.), *conductor* (so, as a back-formation, *guest-conduct* vb.), *critic*, *producer*, *soloist*, *speaker*, *star* (so as v. intr.). **c.** objective, as †*guest-caller*, *-inviter*. Also **guest-(gall-)fly** (see INQUILINE 2); **guest-gift**, a gift presented to a guest at parting; **guest-hall**, a hall or room for the reception of guests; **guest-line** = GUEST-ROPE; **guest-master**, in a monastery, a monk whose duty it is to entertain guests = HOSTELER 1; **guest-moth**, an inquiline moth; **guest-night**, the night on which guests are entertained at a club, college, etc.; **guest-present** = *guest-gift*; **guest-psalm** (see quot.); †**guest-right**, ? what is due to a guest; **guest-rite(s**, a rite or rites to be observed in entertaining a guest (cf. *guest-right*); **guest-room** = GUEST-CHAMBER; **guest-size** *a.*, of a size (usually smaller than the 'regular' size) suitable for a guest; †**guest-stable**, a stable for the horses belonging to guests; **guest-towel**, a small hand-towel intended for visitors' use. See also GUEST-CHAMBER, GUEST-HOUSE.

1961 BOWMAN & BALL *Theatre Lang.* 164 **Guest actor*, a distinguished actor playing temporarily with a repertory or stock company. 1910 *Busy Man's Mag.* Jan. 26 (*caption*) Miss George has abandoned her regular season to become '*guest actress' at the New Theatre. 1934 A. HASKELL *Balletomania* ix. 183 She appeared for him again many times, but only as a *guest-artist during the London seasons. 1942 BERREY & VAN DEN BARK *Amer. Thes. Slang* §619.7 *Guest-artist*, to appear as a guest performer. 1959 *Listener* 19 Mar. 512/3 A guest artist from the Royal Swedish Ballet. 1552 LATIMER *Serm. Lincolnsh.* i. (1562) 60 Than we must know how the *gest callers behaued them selues; and then howe the gestes behaued themselues towardes them that called them. 1598 SHAKS. *Merry W.* II. i. 221 Hast thou no suit against my Knight? my *guest-Caualeire? 1933 *Sat. Even. Post* 7 Jan. 15/3 (*caption*) William Mengelberg, who has served as *guest conductor for many of the leading philharmonic orchestras. 1945 *Time* 16 Apr. 58/3 He will guest-conduct the Minneapolis Symphony. 1968 *London Symphony Orch. Programme Bk.* 7 Mar. 3 At this period he began to make appearances as a guest conductor with most of the important orchestras in Europe. 1925 *New Yorker* 14 Mar. 20/2 Ernest Newman, *guest critic of the *Evening Post*, packs up his troubles and returns to London. 1879, 1884 *Guest-flies, guest-gall-flies [see INQUILINE 2]. a 1873 LYTTON *Pausanias* 181 Child, I bid thee welcome my *guest-friend, Antagoras of Chios. 1874 MAHAFFY *Soc. Life Greece* iii. 47 The Homeric heroes readily give away the gifts of respected guest friends. 1884 J. PAYNE *Tales fr. Arabic* II. 130 This is my *guest-gift to thee. c 1325 *Lai le Freine* 257 The abbesse and the nonnes alle, Fair him gret in the *gest-halle. 1870 MORRIS *Earthly Par.* II. III. 206 They sat within the city's great guest-hall. 1863 M. BRYDIE *Tableau fr. Geol.* 35 The feast-preparer and the *guest-inviter. 1598 SHAKS. *Merry W.* II. iii. 59 Pardon, *Guest-Iustice. 1926 *Blackw. Mag.* May 624/2 As the *Carmania* came down she took the force of wind and sea off the boat so that those in her were able to grab the *guest-lines and hold the boat against the ship's sides. 1860 *Luck Ladysmede* (1862) II. 102 He dismissed him courteously, with directions to his *guest-master for his due entertainment. 1897 *Westm. Gaz.* 18 Mar. 10/1, I paid a visit to a monastery of the Silent Monks of La Trappe, and I was shown over the grounds by the Guestmaster. 1885 A. EDWARDS *Girton Girl* I. xiv. 283 The usual *guest-night at mess. 1894 *Westm. Gaz.* 29 Aug. 3/2 On guest nights at the Savage Club in London he is a welcome guest. 1968 *Times* 11 Dec. 13/8 Guest night in the officers' mess and the bellicosity of sergeants. 1898 *Q. Rev.* July 99 Imported as merchandize or *guest-presents. 1958 *Times* 7 Oct. 5/5 The Belgrade Theatre director's hope to have *guest-producers working in Coventry. 1898 J. ROBERTSON *Poetry & Relig. Psalms* viii. 201 Psalms which have not inappropriately been termed '*guest' psalms. The chief of these are xv., xxiv. 1-6, xxvii. 1-6 and xxiii... From being a worshipper, the psalmist comes to think of himself as a guest. 1856 EMERSON *Eng. Traits, Race* Wks. (Bohn) II. 26 This the king calls going into *guest-quarters. 1932 *Bull. Arizona Agric. Exper. Station* CXLI. 2 Unclassified. Land owned and operated by the State or a public agency, *guest ranches, private estates, forest products. 1968 *Punch* 31 Jan. 174/3 A ritzy guest-ranch overlooking Santa Barbara. 1926 E. HEMINGWAY *Torrents of Spring* (1933) 58, I..demanded to see the *guest-register. 1615 CHAPMAN *Odyss.* XVIII. 88 Ile see thy *guest-right paide Thou here art come In my protection. c 1611 —— *Iliad* XVIII. 365 Haste Charis, and appose Some daintie *guest-rites to our friend. 1648 HERRICK *Hesper.* (1844) II. 49 No comer to thy roof his guest-rite wants. 1838 S. BELLAMY *Betrayal* 177 How of the guest-rites paid Unto their presence? 1638 WHITING *Hist. Albino & Bell.* 131 There was but one *guest-roome, Hangd with a pentice cloath spoke age enough. 1809 R. CUMBERLAND *John De Lancaster* I. 175 The practice of introducing noisy children and prattling nurses into the guest-room. 1862 H. MARRYAT *Year in Sweden* II. 398 He rolled into the guest-room a tun. 1928 *Daily Mail* 25 July 16/6 The sample box containing two *guest-size tablets of Erasmic. 1942 'R. CROMPTON' *William carries On* i. 38 Lemon soap. Guest size. 1951 in M. McLuhan *Mech. Bride* 47/2 We'll send you a guest-size tube absolutely free. 1962 *Melody Maker* 7 July 10/4 The full..bands have already agreed to appear for no fee, as have *guest soloists Terry Lightfoot..and Mike Cotton. 1959 *Listener* 26 Mar. 569/1 The debate..at which Professor A. J. Ayer was the *guest speaker. 1942 BERREY & VAN DEN BARK *Amer. Thes. Slang* §619.7 **Guest-star*, to appear as a guest performer. 1951 L. HOBSON *Celebrity* (1953) xiii. 206 Kitterley had begun to guest-star on just about every radio programme on the air. 1957 WEBSTER, Guest artist or guest star. 1471-2 *Durham Acc. Rolls* (Surtees) 644 Pro punctuacione..super le *Geststable. 1921 *Daily Colonist* (Victoria, B.C.) 6 Apr. 4/5 (Advt.), Huckaback *Guest Towels in a very fine quality; offered at a snap price. 1922 S. LEWIS *Babbitt* i. 6 He wiped his face on the guest-towel.., a pansy-embroidered trifle. 1967 'K. O'HARA' *Unknown Man* vi. 55 Giving..attention ..to the match of James's guest-towels and the serving of James's dinners.

guest (gɛst), *v.* Also 4 **gest**, 5 *pa. pple.* **gest.** [f. GUEST *sb.*]

1. *trans.* To make a guest of; to receive as a guest; to entertain, lodge; to put up (a horse). Also *fig.*

c 1330 R. BRUNNE *Chron.* (1810) 160 In tentis R. rested alle þat ilk nyght, His men wer wele gested with brede, wyne & light. c 1450 *St. Cuthbert* (Surtees) 5186 Some were febill ..And had nede to be gest. *Ibid.* 5392 Monkes horse to gest he had no fors In a hyrne of his Innes. 1494 FABYAN *Chron.* VI. clxxxvi. 186 The..vilayne..whiche slewe his lorde vnder colour of byddyng or gestynge hym in his howse. a 1603 T. CARTWRIGHT *Confut. Rhem. N.T.* (1618) 655 They so farre regarded the outward person..that in guesting certaine to their houses, they preferred the wicked rich unto the goodly poore. 1605 SYLVESTER *Du Bartas* II. iii. *Abraham* I. *Vocation* 1148 O Hosts, what know you, whether ..When you suppose to feast men at your Table, You guest God's Angels in Men's habit hid? 1839 BAILEY *Festus* xix. (1848) 48/1 Every thought and atom of thy being, Shall guest His glory. 1884 J. PARKER *Apost. Life* III. 236 The great, big soul that guests the angel of joy. 1893 *Yorksh. Post* 27 Sept. 4/2 Many delegates will find themselves guested by hospitable, good people.

2. *intr.* To be, or to become, a guest; to be entertained; to lodge. *rare.*

1615 CHAPMAN *Odyss.* I. 627 Tell me, best of princes, who he was That guested here so late? 1654 Z. COKE *Logick* Ep. Ded. (1657) A vj b, Then shal..the World venerate each of you..As a little Deity guesting in a body of flesh. 1804 SOUTHEY *Lett.* (1856) I. 270, I shall be very glad to see Rickman,..with whom I shall guest.

3. To appear as a guest or as a guest artist, etc. orig. *U.S.*

1936 H. L. MENCKEN *Amer. Lang.* (ed. 4) XI. ii. 586 *To guest*, to appear as a guest. 1942 BERREY & VAN DEN BARK *Amer. Thes. Slang* §593.18 *Guest*, to appear as a guest artist. 1943 in *Amer. Speech* (1944) XIX. 102 Many stars guest on the program. 1959 *Spectator* 3 July 9/1 Stars from one company 'guesting' with the other. 1965 *Melody Maker* 10 July 10/4 Ian Carr guested with the Roy Budd Trio..on Saturday.

Hence †'**guested** *ppl. a.*, frequented by guests. Also '**guester**, one who makes a guest of another; an entertainer, host (*rare*).

1577 VALLANS *Tale 2 Swannes* in *Leland's Itin.* (1759) V. p. xi, This was done least that undecently They should passe by the guested towne of Ware. 1702 *Lond. Gaz.* No. 3809/8 The George Inn at Leeds is to be Let, with very good Stables,..and very well Guested. 1890 MORRIS in *Eng. Illustr. Mag.* July 765 My guester amongst the foemen, my fellow-farer and shipmate.

guest, obs. pa. t. and pple. of GUESS.

†**guestan**, *a. Obs. rare*[-1]. In 6 **ghestan**. [? f. GUEST *sb.* + -AN.] ? Suitable for guests.

1555 W. WATREMAN *Fardle Facions* App. 326 To take part of suche ghestan commodities as God hath giuen ye, for the time of yere.

'**guest-ˌchamber.** A room used for the lodging or entertainment of a guest.

1526 TINDALE *Luke* xxii. 11 Where is the gest chamber, where I shall eate myne ester lambe wyth my dissciples? a 1656 USSHER *Ann.* an. 4037 (1658) 835 He sends Peter and John into the City, telling them that..they should find a guest-chamber ready furnished by the good man of the house. 1732 LEDIARD *Sethos* II. VIII. 213, I will conduct you to the guest-chamber, where you may repose yourself. 1879 FARRAR *St. Paul* (1883) 169 The guest-chambers which were attached to Jewish synagogues.

fig. 1686 HORNECK *Crucif. Jesus* xxii. 635 How often.. hath thy great Master attempted to enter into thy heart and to make that his guest-chamber!

guesten ('gɛst(ə)n). *arch.* Also 5 **geston**, 6 **gestyn**, 9 **guestern.** [OF uncertain origin; it may stand for GUESTING *vbl. sb.* or for ME. **gestene* gen. pl. of GUEST *sb.*, or it may represent the stem of GESTEN *v.*] *attrib.* in **guesten chamber**, **guesten hall**, = *guest-chamber*, *-hall*.

1488 *Will of Kyrkeby* (Somerset Ho.), The Geston Chambyrs. 1502 *Will of Moore* (ibid.), Gestyn chamber. 1838 BRITTON *Dict. Arch.* etc., *Guest-hall*, *Guestern-hall*, a large apartment annexed to a monastery..destined for the reception..of pilgrims, or visitors. 1864 KING *Cathedrals, Worcester* 233 The Guesten Hall formed part of the deanery until 1862. 1870 MORRIS *Earthly Par.* I. I. 307 To this town or that we took our way, Or in some abbey's guesten-chamber lay.

guesten, later form of GESTEN *v. Obs.*

1817 SCOTT *Harold* IV. xiv, Whoever shall guesten these chambers within.

guest house. [OE. *ȝiest-hús* = Du. *gasthuis*, G. *gasthaus*: see GUEST *sb.* and HOUSE.]

†**1.** An inn. *Obs.*

c 1000 *Apollonius* (1834) 18 Gan we secean ure ȝesthus. a 1100 *Ags. Voc.* in Wr.-Wülcker 337/8 *Hospitium*, ȝæsthus. c 1200 ORMIN 7040 Gode menness herrtess..sinndenn þatt haliȝhe gessthus þatt crist iss borenn inne.

2. a. A house or apartment for the reception or entertainment of strangers or guests. Also *attrib.*

c 1000 *Ags. Gosp.* Mark xiv. 14 Hwar is min ȝyst-hus [COVERDALE gest house, *A.V.* guest chamber]? c 1450 *St. Cuthbert* (Surtees) 2364 þe thak of his gest house rygg. 1633 T. STAFFORD *Pac. Hib.* II. xiii. (1810) 369 That.. had bin in the Ghest-house amongst them. 1844 LINGARD *Anglo-Sax. Ch.* (1858) I. vii. 312 One day a Scot from Connaught.. was received at the guest house. 1870 MORRIS *Earthly Par.* I. I. 309 Yet is it still the tale I then heard told Within the guest-house of that minster-close. 1883 C. J. WILLS *Mod. Persia* 357 Put up in the guest-house of the shrine.

†**b.** A hospital, a poorhouse. *Obs.*

1617 MORYSON *Itin.* II. II ii. 171 At Corke we haue prouided a guesthouse for them [the sicke and hurt men]. 1641 BROME *Joviall Crew* IV. i. Wks. 1873 III. 413 He keeps a Guest-house for all Beggars, far and neer.

fig. 1600 *Hosp. Incur. Fooles* 24 In obscuritie and holes, in this darksome Guest-house of their madnes.

3. A house for the reception of paying guests.

1925 *Daily Tel.* 13 May 19/4 For Sale, Guest House, South London. 1953 E. TAYLOR *Sleeping Beauty* i. 11 That house on the cliff is a guest-house, is it?

guestimate, var. GUESSTIMATE.

'guesting, *vbl. sb. Obs.* exc. *arch.* and *dial.* [f. GUEST *v.* + -ING¹.] The action of the vb. GUEST; entertainment, lodging.

a 1300 *Floriz & Bl.* 125 For his niȝtes gestinge He ȝaf his oste an hundred schillinge. a 1300 *Cursor M.* 11443 þai toke þair gesting in þe tun. 14.. *Sir Beues* 3173 (MS. M.) All he bad to his gestynge. 1529 MORE *Suppl. Soulys* Wks. 304 The gesting of the best pore man and most gracious gest that ever was gested in this worlde [Our Lord]. 16.. *K. Arthur & K. Cornw.* xvii. in Child *Ballads* (1884) I. 284/2 Pray him for.. one ghesting and two meales meate. 1846 BROCKETT *Gloss. N.C. Words* (ed. 3), Guesting, an hospitable welcome—a warm reception. [Edd. 1825 and 1829 have *Guestning*.] 1876 MORRIS *Sigurd* I. 37 It were all too ill a deed In reward for the wood-wight's guesting to betray him in his need.

†**'guestive**, *a. Obs. rare*⁻¹. [f. GUEST *sb.* + -IVE.] Pertaining to or suitable for guests.

1615 CHAPMAN *Odyss.* XVI. 88 If she shall.. take fit care, For all such guests as there seek guestive fare.

guestless ('gɛstlɪs), *a.* [f. GUEST *sb.* + -LESS.] Having no guests. Sometimes as a translation of Gr. ἄξενος, inhospitable.

1598 J. DICKENSON *Greene in Conc.* (1878) 138 More deafe .. then are the wrack-rich Libique rocks, or the guestlesse ship-swalowing Sirtes, to the cries of dying marriners. 1806 W. TAYLOR in *Ann. Rev.* IV. 266 The Black Sea has deservedly been named 'the guestless', the inhospitable. 1883 J. PAYN *Thicker than Water* II. xix. 20 The long table stretched before the guestless chairman like a coffin.

guestling¹ ('gɛstlɪŋ). Also 9 gestling. [App. connected with GUEST *sb.* There is a place named *Guestling* near Hastings.] The name of an assembly of representatives of the corporations of the Cinque Ports, formerly held annually.

1629 in Boys *Sandwich* (1792) 749 The ancient assemblies of brotherhood and guestling. 1683 *Addr. fr. Cinque-Ports* in *Lond. Gaz.* No. 1857/2 The humble Address of the Mayors, Bayliffs [etc.] of the Cinque-Ports.. Assembled at a Brotherhood and Guestling holden at New Romeney. 1771 *Gentl. Mag.* XLI. 332 To represent that Corporation [Sandwich] at a general meeting of the Cinque Ports, two antient towns, and their Members, called the Brotherhood and Guestling. 1888 BURROWS *Cinque Ports* 177-8 The Guestling consisted of the Mayor (formerly the Bailiff), two jurats, and two commoners from each of the seven Corporate Members of the Ports, to which in modern times was added Deal. When both sets of representatives were assembled they were called a 'Brotherhood and Guestling'. 1891 J. SIMSON *Historic Thanet* 30 The books recording the proceedings of the Brotherhoods and Guestlings of the Cinque Ports are still extant.

guestling² ('gɛstlɪŋ). [f. GUEST *sb.* + -LING.] A young guest.

1855 BAILEY *Mystic* 141 The fay-queen.. Came forthright to greet her crownèd spouse, and royal guestling there. 1876 MOTLEY *Corr.* 18 Aug. II. 393 The *déjuner dinatoire* was worthy of the imperial guestling.

†**'guestly**, *a. Obs.* In 7 ghestly. [f. GUEST *sb.* + -LY¹.] Suitable for guests; hospitable.

1636 N. WALLINGTON in *Ann. Dubrensia* (1877) 31 A Towne for Gods on Earth t' have lodged in, Hadst thou not .. made it ghestly for so great a power.

†**'guestred**. *Obs.* In 6 gestred. [f. GUEST *sb.* + -RED.] The position or standing of a guest.

1573 TWYNNE *Æneid* x. Ee iv b, Tables which in gestred wise He first approcht.

'guest-rope, 'guess-rope. Also 7 gest-, ghest-rope. [The first element is of doubtful form and origin; it has been referred to GUEST *sb.* ('a rope to assist guests in coming on board'; but this suits sense 2 only) and to GUESS *sb.* (cf. quot. 1862 s.v. GUESS-WARP).]

1. A second rope, fastened to a boat in tow, to keep it steady.

1623 J. TAYLOR (Water P.) *Praise Hemp-seed* 10 The boighrope, boatrope, guestrope [etc.]. 1626 CAPT. SMITH *Accid. Yng. Sea-men* 14 The boy rope, guest rope, the cat rope [etc.]. 1627 —— *Seaman's Gram.* vi. 28 The Ghest rope is added to the Boat rope when shee is towed at the ships sterne, to keepe her from shearing. 1644 SIR H. MANWAYRING *Sea-man's Dict.* s.v. *Bluff*, The Roape by which it [a long boate] is towed at the Ships sterne, is called the Boate roape, to which, to keepe the boate from sheering, we adde an other, which we call a Gest-roape. 1711 W. SUTHERLAND *Shipbuilder's Assist.* 113 The Guess-rope, which is also made fast to the Boat to keep her directly in the Wake of the Ship. 1769 FALCONER *Dict. Marine* (1780), *Hale à bord*, the boat-rope, or guess-rope of a boat's moorings. 1875 KNIGHT *Dict. Mech.*, *Guest-rope*, the rope by which a boat is kept steady while in tow.

2. A stout rope slung outside a vessel fore and aft, formerly also fastened to the end of a boom, to give a hold for boats coming alongside.

1794 *Rigging & Seamanship* I. 172 *Guest-rope* is fastened to an eye-bolt in the ship's side, and to the outer end of a boom projecting from the ship's side, by guys, to keep the boats clear off the sides. 1848 G. BIDDLECOMBE *Art Rigging* 27.

guestship ('gɛstʃɪp). [f. GUEST *sb.* + -SHIP.] The condition or position of being a guest.

1868 GLADSTONE *Juv. Mundi* vi. (1869) 169 It was in every way fit, then, that he [Euphetes] should continue to be united by the ties of guestship with the lord of Elis. 1886 *Homilet. Rev.* (U.S.) May 440 In guestship with the poor. 1893 *Harper's Mag.* LXXXVII. 104/1 Glorious days of honoured guestship.

[**guest-taker**, in some Dicts. erroneous form of *gist-taker*.]

'guestwise, *sb.* and *adv.* [f. GUEST *sb.* + -WISE.]

†**A.** *sb.* ***in, on, a guestwise***: as a guest. *Obs.*

1548 UDALL, etc. *Erasm. Par. Acts* vii. 1-5 Ouer broughte he him in gestwyse and as a straunger. 1561-6 *Child Marriages* 43 Was never at Hatton but for a night or two in a year on gestwise. 1563 GOLDING *Cæsar* (1565) 241 Familiaritye that had bene privatly betwene them, by reason of resortinge a guestwyse one to another. 1641 BROME *Joviall Crew* IV. i. Wks. 1873 III. 413 As a Friend or stranger, in Guest-wise, you are welcome to it.

B. *adv.* After the manner of a guest or stranger.

1590 SHAKS. *Mids. N.* III. ii. 171 My heart to her, but as guest-wise sojourn'd, And now to Helen it is home return'd, There to remaine. 1610 HOLLAND *Camden's Brit.* I. 359 Being entertained guest-wise by Sir Walter Clifford. 1642 T. LECHFORD *Plain Dealing* (1867) 119 He is a Sachem, whose wife hath her cleane spoons in a chest, for some chief English men, when they come guest wise to the wigwam. a 1714 M. HENRY *Wks.* (ed. Fullarton) II. 722 If he will please to come guestwise.. he shall be welcome.

†‖**guetre**. *Obs.* [F. *guêtre*: see GAITER *sb.*¹] = GAITER *sb.*¹ I.

1760-72 tr. *Juan & Ulloa's Voy.* (ed. 3) I. 195 We had provided ourselves with guetres, and muschito cloths. 1794 T. COXE *View U.S.* 121 Eight millions of pairs of boots, shoes, half boots, guetres, slippers, clogs, and goloshes, are annually consumed in or exported from the United States.

‖**Gueux** (gø), *sb. pl. Hist.* Also 7-8 geuses, 8 gheus. [F. *gueux*, pl. of *gueux* ragamuffin, beggar.] A name first given in contempt to the Protestant nobles who opposed Margaret of Parma, Regent of the Netherlands, and afterwards adopted by various bodies of Dutch and Flemish partisans in the wars with the Spaniards in the 16th c.

1624 BEDELL *Lett.* x. 133 Yet these people were neither *Geuses* nor *Caluinists*. 1665 *Surv. Aff. Netherl.*, Those of Flanders about Liberty of Religion, carried on in a most Tumultuous and Riotous manner, by a Rabble of *Geux* or Beggars, as my Lord Barlement called them. 1706 in PHILLIPS (ed. Kersey). 1735 BAILEY, *Gheus*. 1756 NUGENT *Gr. Tour* I. 155 Soon after the *water-gueux*, or malcontents under the earl of March, took possession of the Briel.

Guevarism ('geɪvərɪz(ə)m). [f. *Guevara* + -ISM.] The fashion of literary style resulting from imitation of the Spanish writer Ant. de Guevara (1490-1544). So **'Guevarist**, a writer whose style is characterized by Guevarism.

According to many modern critics, EUPHUISM is essentially a development of Guevarism.

1883 S. L. LEE in *Athenæum* 14 July 50/1 Most probably this 'envoy' in praise of Guevarism was written by Sir Francis Bryan. *Ibid.* 18 Aug. 205/3 Mr. Lee, as it seems to me, has misrepresented Dr. Landmann's views.. in his attempt to show that he has been the first critic to appreciate the true *rôle* of the earlier English Guevarists in the development of the Euphuistic style. *Ibid.*, My business was rather with Lyly than with the history of Guevarism in England.

gufa ('gu:fə). Also gufar. [Arab., f. *quffa* basket.] A round boat, made from straw and palm branches, found in Mesopotamia since ancient times.

1914 R. MEINERTZHAGEN *Army Diary* 30 Jan. (1960) 65 Fortunately we were surrounded by gufas into which we quickly transferred our belongings and ourselves. 1919 *Chambers's Jrnl.* Jan. 23/2 Moored behind the *mahailas* are two strings of the up-river *gufars*. 1925 *Countries of World* IV. 2729/2 The 'gufas', the round cauldron-shaped coracles of the Tigris and Euphrates are the oldest river-craft in existence. 1951 A. CHRISTIE *They came to Baghdad* xii. 111 A *gufa*, the primitive craft of the Tigris.

†**guff**¹. *Obs.* [Cf. Fr. dial. *gofe*, *goffe*, thick, swollen, clumsy.] A chub. (See CHUB I.)

1655 MOUFET & BENNET *Health's Improv.* (1746) 274 Guffs.. are a kind of jolt-headed Gudgeons.

guff² (gʌf). [Echoic. Cf. Norw. dial. *gufs* puff of wind, *guffa* to blow softly.]

1. A puff, whiff.

1825-80 JAMIESON, *Guff*, a savour; generally used in relation to the sense of smelling, and to what is unpleasant. 1864 R. PAUL *Let.* in *Mem.* xviii. (1872) 296 A guff of Highland air from this very enjoyable place.

2. *slang.* (orig. *U.S.*). Empty talk, nonsense, 'stuff', 'blather'.

1888 *Scribner's Mag.* Aug. 219/1, I tell you all this talk is guff, and it just comes down to the money. 1889 *Sportsman* 19 Jan. (Farmer), He can have the newspapers to him-self, and with that windbag Mitchell fill them with guff and nonsense. 1897 *Sat. Rev.* 12 June 657/1 Histrionic guff and bugaboo, instead of fine acting. a 1911 D. G. PHILLIPS *Susan Lenox* (1917) II. vi. 161 Don't listen to their guff about wanting to see you again... There's nothing in it. 1930 G. B. SHAW *Apple Cart* II. 78 You cant run them [*sc.* power stations] on patriotic songs.. and guff and bugaboo. 1936 'F. O'Connor' *Bones of Contention* 187, I never thought .. that my Tom had such ould guff in him. 1959 *Encounter* Aug. 64/1 All that guff in *Look Back in Anger* about how there are no causes left to die for. 1966 J. DOS PASSOS *Best of Times* (1968) iv. 144 Whether it was politics or literary work or painting he [*sc.* Hemingway] would take the guff out of a situation with a wellplaced fourletter word. 1966 *Crescendo* Jan. 32/1 The sleeve-notes give us a lot of guff about getting with it and so on and tell us nothing constructive.

guff, variant of GOFF².

guffaw (gʌ'fɔ:), *sb.* orig. *Sc.* Also 8 *Sc.* gaffa(w, 9 guffaugh, *Sc.* guffaa, guffa'. [Echoic; cf. the related vb. and GAWF *sb. Sc.*] A burst of coarse laughter; a loud or boisterous laugh.

1720 RAMSAY *Wealth* 121 Syne circling wheels the flattering gaffaw, As well they may, he gars their beards wag a'. 1728 —— *Fables, Caterpillar & Ant* 28 The airy Ant syne turn'd awa, And left him with a proud gaffa. 1816 SCOTT *Antiq.* xxxv, That silly fliskmahoy.. has.. done naething but laugh and greet, the skirl at the tail o' guffa', for twa days successfully. 1821 *Blackw. Mag.* VIII. 619 The fidging Prentices, their elbows claw, And speak their triumph in a loud guffãã. *Ibid.* X. 572/2 Horse laughter, and loud gaffaws. 1840 BARHAM *Ingol. Leg.* Ser. I. *Spectre of Tapp.*, At the last he burst out into an absolute 'guffaw'. 1865 LIVINGSTONE *Zambesi* xxiv. 503 It is no senseless loud guffaw. 1887 BROWNING *Parleyings* I. *With Bernard de Mandeville* iv. 10 This friend—(Whose groan I hear, with guffaugh at the end Disposing of mock-melancholy). 1891 E. W. GOSSE *Gossip in Library* xx. 260 There was a general guffaw of laughter.

fig. 18.. D. JERROLD in Smiles *Self-Help* xi. (1859) 268, The world will get tired.. of this eternal guffaw about all things.

guffaw (gʌ'fɔ:), *v.* orig. *Sc.* Also *Sc.* 8-9 **gaffaw**, 9 **gaffaa.** [Echoic; cf. the related sb. and GAWF *v. Sc.*] *intr.* To laugh loudly or boisterously; to laugh coarsely or harshly.

1721 RAMSAY *Petit. to Whin-Bush Club* 12 To bend wi' ye and spend wi' ye An evening, and gaffaw. 1819 W. TENNANT *Papistry Storm'd* (1827) 19 They Gaffaw and smirkle in their play. 1821 CARLYLE *Early Lett.* (1886) I. 362, I have been dining and *gaffaaing* with one Nichol, a Mathematical Teacher here. 1832-53 VEDDER in *Whistle-binkie* (Scot. Songs) Ser. III. 83 M'Rory guffaw'd like a laughing 'hyenar'. 1860 SALA *Lady Chesterf.* 31 How men grin and guffaw behind her back. 1879 BROWNING *Ned Bratts* 254 'It comes of heat and beer!'—hark how he guffaws plain!

b. *trans.* To say with a guffaw; to express by means of a guffaw.

1865 J. HATTON *Bitter Sweets* viii, Mat shrugged his shoulders and guffawed his satisfaction. 1893 GUNTER *Miss Dividends* 130 'Reckon he's down on your card a few times more', he guffaws.

Hence **gu'ffawing** *vbl. sb.* and *ppl. a.*, **gu'ffawingly** *adv.*

1822 *Blackw. Mag.* XII. 790 Sydney Smith has turned the laugh against the Bishop most triumphantly and guffawingly. 1826 J. WILSON *Noct. Ambr.* Wks. 1855 I. 47 Glorious guffawing all night and immeasurable murder all day. 1894 BLACKMORE *Perlycross* 425 You guffawing jackanapes.

guffer ('gʌfə(r)). A Scotch name for the Viviparous Blenny (*Zoarces viviparus*). Also ***guffer-eel***.

1684 SIBBALD *Scot. Illustr.* II. III. 25 *Mustela Vivipara, nostratibus*, the Guffer, *quibusdam* Eelpout. 1710 —— *Hist. Fife* (1803) 121 Mustela vivipara Shonfeldi; our fishers call it the Guffer. 1810 P. NEILL *Fishes Firth of Forth*, etc. 8 (Jam.) Viviparous Blenny... Here this species sometimes gets the name of Eelpout and Guffer. 1836 YARRELL *Brit. Fishes* I. 243. 1883 *Fisheries Exhib. Catal.* 357 Long Line for catching.. Guffer-eel (*Zoarces viviparus*).

guffin ('gʌfɪn). *dial.* and *slang.* A stupid, clumsy person.

1862 *Dial. Leeds* Gloss., *Guffin*, one who, from timidity, commits gross blunders, and is awkward in movement, with a spice of dulness to boot. 1866 SLEIGH *Derbysh. Gloss.* in *Reliquary* VI. 160 *Guffin*, a fool. 1882 MISS BRADDON *Mt. Royal* III. i. 16 The little guffin didn't notice which.

guffy ('gʌfɪ). A sailor's name for a soldier.

1882 CLARK RUSSELL *My Shipm. Louise* I. vii. 147 There aint an oncleanlier man than the guffy. 1883 —— *Sailor's Lang.*, *Guffy*, a soldier.

guga(u, gugaw(e, gugay, obs. ff. GEWGAW.

1659 *Lady Alimony* II. ii. B 4 What may that gaudy gugay Lady be?

guga ('gu:gə). *Sc.* Also goug. [Gael.] A young gannet.

c 1840 N. MACKENZIE in J. B. Mackenzie *Episode Life Rev. N. Mackenzie at St. Kilda* (1911) iii. 47 When it [*sc.* the young gannet] is about a month old it is called 'guga', and looks like a young white lamb. 1897 H. A. MACPHERSON *Hist. Fowling* xxii. 207 Before the young Solan-Geese, which they call *Goug*, fly off, they are larger than the mothers, and excessively fat. **1938** *Brit. Birds* XXXI. 292 A party of men..undertake the unpleasant voyage to Sula Sgeir and stay there a few days, taking all the gugas, or nestling Gannets, they can. **1953** *Scotsman* 13 Aug., Eight Ness men..are spending 14 days on the uninhabited rocky islet of Sulisgeir,..killing and salting the young of the gannet known locally as the 'guga'.

guge, gugement, obs. ff. JUDGE, JUDGEMENT.

‖**gugelhupf** (ˈguːg(ə)lhʊpf). Also **guglhupf.** [Ger. dial. var. of KUGELHUPF.] = KUGELHUPF.
1936 M. MORPHY *Recipes of All Nations* 316 *Wiener Gugelhupf*... This cake is also made in Alsace and Germany, but the Viennese claim it as one of their national cakes. **1954** G. BEER *Austrian Cooking* 163 A *Guglhupf* really does taste better when baked in its proper 'setting'. *Ibid.*, On the Continent *Guglhupf* forms are generally available in copper. **1965** M. STEWART *Airs above Ground* xi. 141 You wouldn't say no to some really nice *Gugelhupf*, would you? **1967** *House & Garden* Apr. 85/3 A *gugelhupf* mould (a deep ring mould for making a traditional Austrian sponge-like cake in).

gugelle: see GAZELLE.

gugen, gugeoune, obs. forms of GUDGEON.

†**gugg,** *v. Obs. rare.* Also **gugge.** [? Onomatopœic: cf. GAG *v.*² 2.] *trans.* To wound, gall.
1633 D. R[OGERS] *Treat. Sacram.* II. 127, I cast arrowes and darts into the flesh of the Lord Jesus, in sport! But now they gugg me! **1642** —— *Naaman* 223 We doe but gugge and tire most men with our preaching of selfe-deniall and faith. *Ibid.* 257 This error of thine will gugge the to the quicke.

Guggenheim (ˈguːgənhaɪm, ˈgʊg-). [f. the John Simon *Guggenheim* Memorial Foundation, established in 1925 by Simon Guggenheim (1867–1941), American senator.] Designating a grant for advanced study and research provided by the Guggenheim Foundation. Also *ellipt.*
1930 H. CRANE *Let.* 21 Nov. (1965) 358, I have applied for a Guggenheim Scholarship (which would give me a year's study and creative freedom abroad). **1931** *Ibid.* 379 My father's will left modest provisions for me, but they are as good as an annual Guggenheim, anyway. **1934** H. MILLER *Tropic of Cancer* (1948) 220 Artists who had a little money, Guggenheim prize men, etc. **1956** O. NASH *Good Intentions* 74 He had won a Nobel award and a Pulitzer Prize, A Guggenheim and a leg on the Davis Cup. **1958** *Times Lit. Suppl.* 24 Jan. 37/4 Has not 'He's on his fourth Guggenheim' become part of the life story of many a quondam rebel or of his nominal successors?

guggion, obs. form of GUDGEON *sb.*²

guggle (ˈgʌg(ə)l), *sb.* [f. GUGGLE *v.*¹]
1. a. *slang* and *dial.* The windpipe. †**b.** The epiglottis. *Obs.*
1680 *Tom & Will* 36 in *Roxb. Ballads* (1881) IV. 200 Men were to come..Out of Utope, to cut and slice Protestant Guggles all in a Trice. **1688** R. HOLME *Armoury* II. 382/1 The Epiglottis, or after tongue; it is..called the Flap or Guggle. **1896** *Warwicksh. Gloss.*, *Guggle*, the windpipe, trachea.
2. A guggling sound (see GUGGLE *v.*¹).
1821 CLARE *Vill. Minstr.* II. 32 The guggles and groans The water made passing the pebbles. **1857** LIVINGSTONE *Trav.* (1861) 120 We heard human-like voices..with splash and guggle, as if rare fun were going on. **1860** RUSSELL *Diary India* I. xiii. 211 The slow guggle of the natives' hubble-bubbles..breaks the lazy repose.

guggle (ˈgʌg(ə)l), *v.*¹ Also *rarely* **goggle.** [Echoic; cf. GURGLE *v.*]
1. *intr.* To make a sound like that made by liquid pouring from a small-necked bottle. (Said chiefly of persons, with reference to speech or laughter.)
1611 COTGR., *Glouglouter*, to guggle, to sound like a narrow mouthed pot, or strait neckt bottle, when it is emptied. **1748** RICHARDSON *Clarissa* (1811) VI. lxvi. 305 Something rose in my throat..which made me for a moment, guggle, as it were, for speech. **1848** THACKERAY *Van. Fair* xxviii, Dobbin..fell back in the crowd, crowing and sputtering until he reached a safe distance, when he exploded..with shrieks of yelling laughter..'Hwhat's that gawky guggling about?' said Mrs. O'Dowd. **1894** HALL CAIN *Manxman* 27 Guggling, chuckling, crowing, panting ..she danced on the flags of the kitchen.
2. To flow *forth* with a guggling sound. Also *fig.*
1755 *Gentl. Mag.* XXV. 326 Nor much lov'd Languedoc, that guggles forth From mouth of long-neck'd bottle. **1885** A. MUNRO *Siren Casket* 241 'Browst' as keen as e'er Had guggled from a cask. **1885** *Manch. Exam.* 22 July 5/2 The moment a deputation addresses him on any topic out flies the cork and his sympathies goggle forth.
3. *trans.* To bring *up* or pour *forth* with a guggling sound. *lit.* and *fig.*
1731 MORTIMER in *Phil. Trans.* XXXVII. 172 We poured a little Milk into his Throat, which at first he could not swallow, but guggled it up again. **1831** *Fraser's Mag.* IV. 163 On he labours..whooping and gasping..guggling forth an excellent speech all the time.

guggle (ˈgʌg(ə)l), *v.*² *Obs.* exc. *dial.* [? Suggested by GULL and JUGGLE.] *trans.* To deceive, cheat.
1617 S. COLLINS *Def. Bp. Elie* I. 107 Anicetus, a pretie name too, to guggle Baronius, yet resisted by Polycarpus. **1847** HALLIWELL, *Guggle*,..(2) To gull, or cheat. *North.*

gugglet: see GOGLET¹.

guggling (ˈgʌg(ə)lɪŋ), *vbl. sb.* [f. GUGGLE *v.*¹ + -ING¹.] The action of the vb. GUGGLE¹.
1668 WILKINS *Real Char.* II. ix. §4. 244. **1765** *Treat. Dom. Pigeons* 133 Not unlike the guggling of a bottle of water, when poured out. **1827** HOR. SMITH *Tor Hill* (1838) I. 6 The calm guggling and poppling of the waves as they were parted by the piles. **1854** THACKERAY *Newcomes* I. 120 Guggling of wine into the decanter.

ˈ**guggling,** *ppl. a.* [f. GUGGLE *v.*¹ + -ING².] That guggles, in the senses of the verb.
1764 *Nat. Hist.* in *Ann. Reg.* 99/2 The water..making a guggling noise. **1819** *Blackw. Mag.* IV. 728 From his gob the guggling claret gush'd. **1831** LARDNER *Pneumat.* iv. 277 The peculiar guggling noise which is produced in decanting wine. **1837** CARLYLE *Fr. Rev.* II. IV. iv, Till all France is ruffled,—roughened up (metaphorically speaking) into one enormous..red guggling Turkey Cock!

gugion, obs. form of GUDGEON *sb.*²

guglet: see GOGLET¹.

‖**guglio** (ˈguːljəʊ, ˈguʎʎo). Pl. **guglio(e)s.** Also 7 **guglia, gulio.** [It. *guglia*, aphetic var. *aguglia* needle.] An obelisk, 'needle'.
1644 EVELYN *Diary* 7 Nov., A vast broaken gulio, or obelisq. **1670** LASSELS *Voy. Italy* II. 27 In the midst of this Piazza stands the famous *Guglia*; which was brought out of Ægypt in the time of the old Romans. **1722** J. RICHARDSON *Statues*, etc. *Italy* 108 Upon this Rock..on a Pedestal of near 17 Foot is put the Guglio, which is almost 60 Foot high, on which is a Cross. **1740** LADY POMFRET *Lett.* I. xlviii. 205 Public ornaments—such as pillars, guglios, horsemen in brass. *Ibid.* II. 96 Two guglioes.

‖**guhr** (guːr). *Min.* See also GUR. [Ger. dial.; lit. 'ferment', related to *gähren* to ferment: see YEAST.] A loose earthy deposit from water found in the cavities of rocks.
[1686, **1753**: see GUR.] **1770** ENGESTROM tr. *Cronstedt's Mineral.* xiv. 23 Gypseous Earth properly so called, *Guhr*. **1839** URE *Dict. Arts* 185 Guhr, lac-lunæ, and fossil meal. **1852** TH. ROSS tr. *Humboldt's Trav.* I. ii. 78 *note*, The siliceous *gurh* [sic] of the volcanoes of the Isle of France.

guiac, -an, -ol, -um: see GUAIAC, etc.

Guianese (giːəˈniːz), *a.* and *sb.* [f. *Guiana* + -ESE.] **A.** *adj.* Of or pertaining to Guiana, a tropical region in north-eastern South America. **B.** *sb.* An inhabitant of the region of Guiana; also in collective sense. So **Guianan** (giːˈɑːnən), *a.*; **Guiˈanian** *a.* and *sb.* (See also GUYANESE *a.* and *sb.*)
1600 RALEIGH *Discoverie of Guiana* in Hakluyt *Voy.* III. 636 Those Guianians..are marvellous great drunkards. *Ibid.* 641 The poore Guianian, betrayed on all sides, was delivered to the campe-master of Berreo. **1869** *Month* Feb. 191 The Chief varieties of native Guianese now seen are the Arawaks, Acawoios, Waraus, and the Caribs. **1879** J. G. WOOD in C. Waterton *Wand. S. Amer.* (ed. 6) 478 The European and Guianan types of the human frame. *Ibid.* 479 The Guianan type of female beauty. **1881** C. D. DANCE (*title*) Chapters from a Guianese log-book. **1883** H. V. P. BRONKHURST *Colony of Brit. Guyana* p. vii, My numerous English and West Indian and Guyanian friends. **1888** RODWAY & WATT *Chron. Hist. Guiana* i. 11 Martinez sought for and obtained permission to depart, a number of Guianians being deputed to conduct him to the Orinoco. **1896** J. RODWAY *West Indies & Spanish Main* 44 These were Guianians, who had never before seen a white man. **1954** G. DURRELL *3 Singles to Adv.* ii. 43 A Guianian sand reef may be of great botanical and zoological interest, but it is a most exhausting place to cross in a hurry. **1960** *Guardian* 9 Apr. 2/1 Guianese leaders complain of threats at London conference. **1964** M. DICKSON *World Elsewhere* iv. 147 The Guianese are naturally hospitable. *Ibid.* 148 The Guianese staff at the school.

guib (gwɪb). Also 8 **guiba.** The harnessed antelope of West Africa. *Tragelaphus scriptus.*
1774 GOLDSM. *Nat. Hist.* III. iii. 81 The third that may be mentioned, he [Buffon] calls the Guiba. It resembles the gazelles in every particular, except in the colour of the belly, which..is of a deep brown. **1834** *Penny Cycl.* II. 78/2 The Guib (*Antilope scripta*, Pallas) has the same general characters of the boshbok. (In recent Dicts.)

Guibeline, variant of GHIBELLINE.

‖**guichet** (giʃe). [Fr.] A wicket, grating, or hatch, *spec.* one through which tickets are issued.
1839 THACKERAY in *Corsair* (N.Y.) 26 Oct. 521/2 The porter closes the *guichet* behind us. **1848** H. GREVILLE *Diary* (1883) 280 Hundreds of prisoners have been shut up. In the Church of L'Assomption..they are fed through a guichet. **1907** *Westm. Gaz.* 22 July 3/1 The *Bigliettaio*, ducking his gold-braided cap through the guichet, triumphantly gave us a ticket. **1926** 'C. BARRY' *Detective's Holiday* 131 The post-mistress herself came to the guichet. **1931** H. G. WELLS *Work, Wealth & Happiness of Mankind* (1932) ix. 381 Within are the familiar bank desks and counters with their brass rails and guichets. **1961** *Times* 6 Nov. 11/4 Not everybody is a *guichet* user. Some there are so insulated from the bustle of life that they would not go to a theatre or a football match unless someone provided them with a ticket in advance.

Guickwar, Guicowar, varr. GAEKWAR.

guid, Sc. form of GOOD.

guidable (ˈgaɪdəb(ə)l), *a.* [f. GUIDE *v.* + -ABLE.] Capable of being guided.
1676 SPRAT *Serm. bef. King* (1677) 11 All the true followers of Christ should endeavour to obtain a submissive and guidable spirit. **1689** HICKERINGILL *Ceremony-Monger Wks.* 1716 II. 502 The Flock are not guideable by such a Novice. **1737** BRACKEN *Farriery Impr.* (1757) II. 132 This Sort may be tamed, and made guidable. **1815** JANE AUSTEN *Emma* III. ix, An easy, guidable man, to be persuaded into anything. **1836** L. HUNT in *New Monthly Mag.* XLVIII. 60 Balloons shall be equally safe and guidable. **1872** BAGEHOT *Physics & Pol.* (1876) 219 The comparatively gentle and guidable thing which we now call human nature.

guidage (ˈgaɪdɪdʒ). Also 5 **gwydage.** [a. OF. *guidage*. In sense 2, f. GUIDE *v.* + -AGE.]
†**1.** *Old Law.* A fee or tax paid for guidance (see quots.). *Obs.*
c **1440** *Jacob's Well* 29 To paye toll..panage or gwydage, for swyche godys as are noȝt led to feyres & markettes, be-cause of marchaundise. **1607** COWELL *Interpr.*, *Guydage* is that which is given for safe conduct through a strange territorie. **1800** W. CHAPMAN *Witham & Welland* 32 The proprietor of the Inn..claimed an exclusive privilege of guidage over the Wash.
2. The action of guiding, guidance. *rare*⁻¹.
1805 SOUTHEY *Madoc* II. x, Bedew Mexitli's altar with your blood, And go beneath his guidage.

guidame, Sc. var. GOOD-DAME, grandmother.
1596 DALRYMPLE tr. *Leslie's Hist. Scot.* x. 456 The Quene had maid residence with her Guidame Duiches of Guise.

guidance (ˈgaɪdəns). [f. GUIDE *v.* + -ANCE.]
1. The action of guiding; guiding or directing agency; leadership, direction.
a. with reference to a journey or movement.
1590 SPENSER *F.Q.* III. iv. 6 So forth she rode..Following the guydance of her blinded guest. **1788** GIBBON *Decl. & F.* I. (1846) V. 17 They steered by the guidance of the stars. **1835** URE *Philos. Manuf.* 219 Mounting the heckles, and carrying them along the chainway by the guidance of parallel bars. **1860** TYNDALL *Glac.* I. xi. 74 We trusted to our own muscles to make good any mistake in the way of guidance. **1870** BRYANT *Iliad* I. VI. 199 At Lycia he arrived Under the favoring guidance of the gods.
(*b*) *spec.* in *Astronautics.*
1962 F. I. ORDWAY et al. *Basic Astronautics* p. vii, High-thrust space carrier vehicles with accurate guidance systems. **1969** *Sunday Times* 13 July 13/2 *Guidance system*, the system which measures and evaluates flight information, correlates this with target data, converts the results into the conditions necessary to achieve the desired flight path and communicates this data in the form of commands to the flight control system. **1970** *Guardian* 18 Apr. 1/1 Guidance control officers reported..that it had gone well, putting the spacecraft within a hundredth of the 6.5 re-entry angle.
fig. **1725** POPE *Odyss.* VIII. 423 Wisdom's sacred guidance he pursues. **1871** MORLEY *Voltaire* (1886) 11 It was time to trust firmly to the free understanding of men for guidance in the voyage after truth.
b. with reference to conduct or procedure.
1538 BALE *Thre Lawes* 50 For gydaunce of mankynde. **1672** T. DUNING in *Essex Papers* (Camden) I. 39 Yʳ Excellenc..whose influenc we must have to sho, and imploring the guidanc and blessing of God on yʳs. **1775** BURKE *Corr.* (1844) II. 72 God and nature never made them to think or to act without guidance and direction. **1804** W. TENNANT *Ind. Recreat.* (ed. 2) I. 331 Whose elevated rank.. gave him in a great measure the guidance of fashion. **1849** MACAULAY *Hist. Eng.* vi. II. 3 Instructions..for the guidance of his son. **1858** FROUDE *Hist. Eng.* III. xvii. 496 An English sovereign could know no guidance but the existing law. **1865** BUSHNELL *Vicar. Sacr.* iv. (1866) 55 Angels..ministering unseen, where they may, in warnings and secret guidances. **1874** GREEN *Short Hist.* vii. §4. 375 The Huguenots..had become a formidable party under the guidance of the Admiral Coligny.
c. With reference to problems and advice relating to education, marriage, careers, etc. Also *attrib.*
1927, etc. [see *child guidance*, CHILD *sb.* 22]. **1935**, etc. [see *marriage guidance*, MARRIAGE 8]. **1947** ERICKSON & SMITH *Organ. & Admin. Guidance Services* viii. 207 The administrator should recognize the necessity for beginning the guidance program at a point consistent with its existing stage of development. The nature and amount of guidance training present among staff members and the facilities that the school has for proceeding with the extension and refinement of guidance services must be considered. **1951** M. MCLUHAN *Mech. Bride* 42/1 Vocational-guidance investigation has turned up the curious fact that executives ..do show an aptitude for words. **1957** *Encycl. Brit.* XII. 295/2 The primary problem of vocational guidance is, given a person, to find the most suitable occupation. **1967** *Medium Ævum* XXXVI. 144 Benoit and Guido..characterized him [*sc.* Calkas] as the guidance counsellor. **1968** *Lancet* 9 Mar. 518/2, 41% [of medical students] acknowledged that they had been given guidance about sexual difficulties unrelated to marriage.
2. quasi-*concr.* Something which guides or leads.
1712 J. JAMES tr. *Le Blond's Gardening* 40 Walks..are as so many Guidances and Means to conduct us throughout a Garden. **1840** CARLYLE *Heroes* (1858) 304 The Writer of a Book..wanders like a wild Ishmaelite, in a world of which he is as the spiritual light, either the guidance or the misguidance! **1899** *Expositor* Nov. 405 We have..a great picture of His attitude towards the other religions of the world and therein a guidance for ourselves.

†ˈ**guidant.** *Obs. rare.* Also 5 **gydant.** [f. GUIDE *v.* + -ANT.]
a. One who guides. **b.** Guidance, guiding.
1495 *Act 11 Hen. VII*, c. 64 Preamble, The same persones ..were adherentis assistencis..gydantis. **1691** WOOD *Ath.*

Oxon. II. 557 To persue a success in villany and rebellion was to follow the guidant of providential dispensations.

guide (gaɪd), *sb.* Forms: 4-6 **gyde, guyde,** 5-6 **gide,** (5 **gydde**), 6 **gyd,** *Sc.* **gyid, gwyd(e,** (**gwide**), 7 **guid,** 6- **guide.** [a. F. *guide*, orig. fem., now masc. (exc. in the pl. *guides* reins), an altered form (first recorded in 14th c.) of the earlier OF. *guie* (see GUY *sb.*[1]) = Pr., It. *guida*, Sp., Pg. *guia*:—Com. Rom. **guida*, vbl. noun f. *guidare*: see GUY *v.*[1] The *d* of the Fr. word is due to the influence of Pr. or It. forms.]

I. One who guides.

1. a. One who leads or shows the way, esp. to a traveller in a strange country; *spec.* one who is hired to conduct a traveller or tourist (e.g. over a mountain, through a forest, or over a city or building) and to point out objects of interest.

1362 LANGL. *P. Pl.* A. VIII. 1 This weore a wikked wei bote hose hedde a gyde, That mihte folwen us vch a fote forte that we come there. **1377** *Ibid.* B. XV. 428 Hem..that the heigh weye shulde teche, And be gyde, and go bifore as a good baneoure. *c* **1425** *Eng. Conq. Irel.* 84 The lydder gyddes that hym shold lode, slowe hy[m]. **1463** *Mann. & Househ. Exp.* (Roxb.) 227 Item, ffor a gyde ovyr the Wayssche the sayd day, ij.d. **1535** COVERDALE *Acts* i. 16 Iudas which was a gyde of them that toke Iesus. **1585** T. WASHINGTON tr. *Nicholay's Voy.* IV. x. 122 He which is the guide goeth before mounted on a cammel. **1644** MILTON *Educ.* Wks. 1738 I. 140 To ride out in companies with prudent and staid guides to all the quarters of the Land. **1766** GOLDSM. *Vic. W.* iii, As the floods were not yet subsided, we were obliged to hire a guide, who trotted on before. **1791** MRS. RADCLIFFE *Rom. Forest.* i, La Motte wished at first to take a guide. **1806** FELTHAM *Guide Watering Places* 27 A Guide shall not demand more than 1s. for each time of bathing. **1838** *Murray's Hand-bk. N. Germ.* 192 A driver..who will serve as a guide, and be able to give some information about the inns and country through which he has to pass. **1860** TYNDALL *Glac.* I. iii. 23, I sought to obtain a guide at Kaltebrunnen.

b. *transf.* and *fig.*

1599 DAVIES *Nosce teipsum* 42 Here are they [*sc.* eyes] guides, which do the Body leade; Which else would stumble in eternall night. **1667** MILTON *P.L.* XII. 647 The World was all before them..and Providence thir guide. **1795-1814** WORDSW. *Excursion* v. 741 My feet and hands at length became Guides better than mine eyes.

†**c.** A director or wielder (of a weapon). *Obs.*

c **1381** CHAUCER *Parl. Foules* 136 Thorw me men gon.. Onto the mortal strokis of the spere Of whiche disdayn & daunger is the gyde.

†**d.** One who controls the movements of an animal or a flock; a driver, keeper. *Obs. rare.*

1687 A. LOVELL tr. *Thevenot's Trav.* III. 22 Each Elephant had his Guide sitting upon his Neck. **1697** DRYDEN *Virg. Georg.* IV. 780 Bulls..Which on Lycæus graze without a Guide.

2. a. *Mil.* One employed or forced to accompany an invading army, in order to show the way, give information about the enemy's country, position, etc.

c **1540** *Order in Battayll* B 7 He muste haue guydes that knowe the countrye. **1802** C. JAMES *Milit. Dict.*, *Guides*, are generally the country people in the neighbourhood where the army encamps: they are to give you intelligence concerning the country [etc.].

b. *pl.* In certain armies, men formed into companies for guiding and reconnoitring service. (See quots.)

1802 JAMES *Milit. Dict.* s.v., *Corps des guides*, The corps of guides. This body was originally formed in France in the year 1756. **1820** RANKEN *Hist. France* VIII. vii. 408 The captain general of his majesty's guides. **1876** VOYLE & STEVENSON *Milit. Dict.* (ed. 3) 173 In the Indian army the name of 'Guides' is given to a regiment of cavalry and infantry attached to the Punjab frontier force. It was raised by the late Sir Henry Lawrence, chiefly with the view to the men acting as scouts. **1892** R. KIPLING *East & West* 9 in *Barrack-r. Ballads* (ed. 2) 76 Then up and spoke the Colonel's son that led a troop of the Guides.

c. One of the two officers of a company, called respectively the ***right*** and ***left guide***, who superintend the movements of the company, and mark the pivots, formations, etc. in military evolutions. Also a vessel by the movements of which the others are guided in the manœuvres of a fleet.

1870 *Field Exerc. Infantry* II. vi. 59 The commander of the company will be termed 'the captain', the senior subaltern, 'the right guide', and the junior subaltern 'the left guide'. *Ibid.* 68 On the word *Advance*, the guide will select points to march on. **1899** *Daily News* 21 July 10/3 The meaning of the term 'Guide of the Fleet' will now be apparent. The Europa is the only vessel which has nothing to do except go straight ahead on the course set by the Admiral, all the others depending upon her.

d. (Usu. with capital initial.) A girl aged between about 10 and 16 who is a member of the Girl Guides Association, an organization of girls, established in 1910, corresponding to the Boy Scouts. In full (formerly) ***Girl Guide.*** Also *attrib.* and *Comb.*, as ***Guide camp, -mistress,*** etc.

1909 *Boy Scouts' Headquarters' Gaz.* Nov. 12/1 (*heading*) The scheme for 'Girl Guides'. *Ibid.* 12/2 Each Guide must be able to describe the..flower..and must be able to draw its outline. *Ibid.* 13/1 Where it is desired to start 'Girl Guides' it would be best for ladies interested to form a Committee. **1916** [see BROWNIE[1] 2]. **1916** *Daily Colonist* (Victoria, B.C.) 23 July 4/5 While he was in that part of the grounds he happened to notice Guide-mistress Miss Leighton in the crowd. He greeted her again, telling her how well he thought the Girl Guides had marched. **1924** A. D. SEDGWICK *Little French Girl* I. v, Alix heard of a Women's Institute, of Boy Scouts and Girl Guides. **1932** H. NICOLSON *Public Faces* viii. 213 She entered, swinging her hips a little with what Shorland had once called her girl-guide gait. **1941** J. S. HUXLEY *Uniqueness of Man* xii. 253 A girl-guide organizer. **1962** *Guardian* 21 Mar. 6/7 The elder children will..go to Guide camps. **1969** *Policy, Organisation & Rules of Girl Guides Assoc.* (ed. 33) 40 A Brownie Guide, Guide, or Ranger Guide may belong to only one Unit but may be attached to another. **1971** *Guider* Oct. 363 May I please make a further appeal..for all Guiders to make sure that their Brownies, Guides and Rangers know all about their respective section magazines.

(*b*) Hence **Guider**, an adult leader in the Girl Guide movement (in full formerly ***Girl Guider***; now ***Brownie Guider, Guide Guider***, or ***Ranger Guider***); **Guide's honour**, the oath taken by a Girl Guide, used as a protestation of honour and sincerity; also *transf.* in jocular use; **girl-guidey, -guidish** *adjs.*, pertaining to, or typical of, a Girl Guide; **guiding** *vbl. sb.*, the activities practised by Girl Guides (cf. SCOUTING *vbl. sb.*[1] 1 b).

1912 A. BADEN-POWELL *Handbk. Girl Guides* i. 38 A Guide's Honour is to be trusted. If a Guide says 'On my honour it is so', that means that it *is* so just as if she had taken a most solemn oath. **1924** A. KINDERSLEY *Guiding Bk.* 7 It is these things, then, that poets have always sung and writers celebrated, and it is to them once more that we have looked ..to help with this true explanation of Guiding. **1931** E. M. R. BURGESS *Girl Guide Bk. Ideas* 3 It is an inspiring thought that throughout the British Empire there are Guides and Guiders like ourselves. **1944** *Times* 5 May 7/2 Guiders, Rangers, Guides and Brownies continued to render valuable war service. **1953** K. TENNANT *Joyful Condemned* xv. 135 If there was a fat, thumping falsehood to be propped up, 'Guide's Honour' was always promptly evoked. **1959** Guide's honour [see BROWNIE[1] 2]. **1960** J. BETJEMAN *Summoned by Bells* iv. 37 She came, a woman of the open air, Swarthy and in Girl-Guide-y sort of clothes. **1962** A. LEJEUNE *Duel in Shadows* vii. 96 'You must keep this to yourself.' 'My dear man,' she protested. 'Professional ethics. Guide's honour.' **1963** *Listener* 10 Jan. 96/3 If occasionally girl-guidish, she has a sharp eye. **1963** I. FLEMING *On H.M. Secret Service* x. 106 The girls all seemed to share a certain basic, girl-guidish simplicity. **1966** *Listener* 20 Oct. 571/3 They see Scouting (and Guiding) as a unique medium for this 'social education'. **1968** *Even. Standard* 23 Oct. 15 (*heading*) Former Girl Guider jailed for contempt. **1969** *Policy, Organisation & Rules of Girl Guides Assoc.* (ed. 33) 42 The Guide Guider and the Assistant Guide Guider are the adult leaders of the Company. *Ibid.*, All Units..are known officially as Ranger Guide Service Units, their members as Ranger Guides, and their Guiders as Ranger Guiders.

3. a. One who directs a person in his ways or conduct; an adviser; †a ruler, leader, governor.

c **1385** CHAUCER *L.G.W.* Prol. 94 Be ye my gyde and lady souereyne. *c* **1400** *Destr. Troy* 4053 Agamynon the gret, was gide of hom all, Leder of þo lordis. *c* **1450** *Merlin* 524 Now God be his gide for his grete pite. **1526** *Pilgr. Perf.* (W. de W. 1531) 2 Seynge the holy lyfe and examples of vertue in theyr gydes or leaders. **1594** HOOKER *Eccl. Pol.* I. iii. §4 Who the guide of nature, but only the God of nature? **1597** *Ibid.* V. lxxviii. §1 They subject to the principal guides and leaders of their own order, and they all in obedience under the high priest. **1696** PHILLIPS, *Guide*,..a director of Youth. **1711** SHAFTESB. *Charac.* (1733) I. iii. 169 He could be enobled to become our Adviser and Guide. **1769** ROBERTSON *Chas. V*, VI. Wks. 1813 VI. 110 They were the spiritual guides of almost every person eminent for rank or power. **1806** FELTHAM *Guide Watering Places* 24 Persons of delicate constitutions are frequently recommended by their medical guides to use the bath in the evening. **1859** TENNYSON *Vivien* 879 The course of life that seem'd so flowery to me With you for guide and master.

b. *transf.* of things.

14.. *That Pes may Stond* in *Tundale's Vis.* (1843) 155 Wolde we be trewe..And lett not falsdom be owre gyde. **1641** MILTON *Animadv.* iv. Wks. (1847) 65/1 Open your eyes to the light of grace, a better guide than Nature. **1683** PETTUS *Fleta Min.* I. (1686) Ded., I..make my publick Acknowledgements that it may be a Guid to other mens Contentments. **1736** BUTLER *Anal.* Introd., Wks. 1874 I. 3 To us, probability is the very guide of life. **1756** C. LUCAS *Ess. Waters* III. 271 Let experiments then and facts be our guides. **1842** TENNYSON *Locksley Hall* 95 They were dangerous guides, the feelings. **1880** GLENNY *Year's Work in Garden* viii. 208 Our selection may be looked upon as a trustworthy guide. **1884** A. R. PENNINGTON *Wiclif* ix. 286 Scripture is our guide even in matters of ecclesiastical usage.

c. *Spiritualism.* = CONTROL *sb.* 4 b.

1856 *Spiritual Herald* July 191 Annie passed into the trance, and said: I can see my guide now, my own guide. **1885** *Cent. Mag.* XXX. 381/2, I can't seem to do anything in these days, now that I no longer have a Guide. **1957** J. S. HUXLEY *Relig. without Revelation* i. 19 The so-called 'controls' or 'guides' of mediums... It is considered *de rigueur* for a professional medium to be under control by a spirit guide.

4. In the titles of books: **a.** A book of instruction or information for beginners or novices (in an art, etc.).

1617 MINSHEU *Ductor* (title-p.), The Gvide Into Tongves. **1660** F. BROOKE tr. *Le Blanc's Trav.* a iv, Mr. Thomas Coopers Art of Giving, or a Guide to Charity, in Octavo. **1667** R. H. (*title*) The Guide in Controversies. **1780** *Newgate Cal.* V. 146 *note*, One little pamphlet, called 'The Lover's New Guide'. **1879** MRS. A. E. JAMES *Ind. Househ. Managem.* 54, I should advise a 'David's Household and Commercial Guide'.

b. A book of information on places or objects of interest in a locality, city, building, etc.; a guidebook.

1759 (*title*) The New Oxford Guide; or, Companion through the University. **1766** [ANSTEY] (*title*) The New Bath Guide. **1781** (*title*) The Cheltenham Guide: or, useful companion, in a journey..to the Cheltenham Spa. **1824** BYRON *Juan* XVI. l, Once she was seen reading the 'Bath Guide'. **1833** L. RITCHIE *Wand. by Loire* 183 On entering a great city, a stranger usually [visits] the booksellers' shops, in search of some descriptive guide which may assist him in exploring.

fig. **1882** MISS BRADDON *Mt. Royal* I. vi. 147 He was a walking guide, a living hand-book to fashionable London.

II. Something that guides.

5. *gen.*

1700 S. L. tr. *Fryke's Voy. E. Ind.* 19 The directions they gave from the Shore, was a great guide to those poor people who were still in the Sea. **1721** PERRY *Daggenh. Breach* 51 Any sort of Timber work..cannot bed close, and must be a guide to Leakage. **1749** F. SMITH *Voy. Disc.* II. 322 Concealing the true Reason that they [Charts] might be no Guides to others.

6. a. *Mechanics.* Something which serves to steady or direct the motion of a thing, and upon, through, or against which it moves, slides, or is conducted in the required direction; *esp.* a bar, rod, etc. which guides or 'bears' machinery having reciprocating motion; often in *pl.*; *spec.* in the *Steam engine*, the rods on which the cross-head of the piston slides; also called ***cross-head guides*** (see CROSS-HEAD *sb.* 1); in *Mining*, the bars or rails which guide the cage up and down the shaft. Also (see quot. 1844).

1763-6 W. LEWIS *Comm. Phil Techn.* 57 [Wire-drawing.] Directed by means of a small conical hole in a piece of iron, called a guide. **1825** J. NICHOLSON *Operat. Mechanic* 427 Each spinner splices his thread, and throws it on the nearest guide, to keep it out of the way, and to conduct it to the winding-machine. **1839** URE *Dict. Arts* 500 If flax..be passed into the machine..through a guide..and be conducted [etc.]. **1844** W. BARNES *Poems Dorset Dial.* Gloss., *Guides* of a waggon, felly-pieces or arcs of circles fastened on the fore axle as a bearing for the bed of the waggon when it locks. **1846** HOLTZAPFFEL *Turning* II. 597 There is a guide to prevent the lateral displacement of the edges. **1869** R. B. SMYTH *Goldf. Victoria* 612 The distance between each couple of guides is just sufficient to admit of a cage working up and down between them. **1879** THOMSON & TAIT *Nat. Phil.* I. I. §424 The nut, if prevented by fixed guides from rotating, will move in the direction of the common axis. **1881** RAYMOND *Mining Gloss.*, *Guides*, the holes in a cross-beam through which the stems of the stamps in a stamp-mill rise and fall. **1894** *Outing* (U.S.) XXIV. 227/1 A useful rod for fly-fishing..may be equipped with either rings and keepers or standing guides. **1896** R. KIPLING *Seven Seas* 43 The rod's return whings glimmerin' through the guides.

b. Something which guides a tool or the work operated upon; *spec.*, in *Oval-turning* (see quots. 1680, 1877); in *Iron-rolling* (see quot. 1881); in *Surgery*, a director; in *Boring* (see quot. 1883).

1680 MOXON *Mech. Exerc.* xiv. 236 For then as the Treddle-Wheel carries the Axis about, the Guide being firmly fastned upon the Axis, comes also about; and having the Groove of the Guide-pulley set against the outer edge of the Guide, as the..small Diameter of the Guide comes to the Guide-pulley, the small Diameter of the Work is Formed; and as the great Diameter of the Guide comes to the Guide-pulley, the great Diameter of the Work is formed. **1812-16** J. SMITH *Panorama Sci. & Art* I. 72 At the end of the mandrel..there is a screw..the thread of which is like that intended to be made. Upon this screw, called the guide, is fitted a piece of wood. **1839** URE *Dict. Arts* 860 A ledge or guide..to conduct the metal and to regulate the breadth of the piece to be cut off. **1874** THEARLE *Naval Archit.* 354 A guide being placed upon the drill. **1877** KNIGHT *Dict. Mech.* 1984/1 If an oval or elliptical pattern be required, it may be obtained by means of an eccentric guide or ring of brass fastened to the puppet of the lathe. **1881** RAYMOND *Mining Gloss.*, In a rolling-mill a *guide* is a wedge-shaped piece held in the groove of a roll to prevent the sticking of the bar by peeling it out of the groove. **1883** GRESLEY *Gloss. Coalmining* s.v., Guides..A boring-rod having an enlargement or wings fitted to it to suit the size of the borehole for steadying the rods when a considerable depth has been attained. **1892** POWELL *Southward's Pract. Print.* 426 *Setting the Guides*.. Having ascertained these places, and marked them with a pencil, affix guides (which serve the place of the pins in the tympan of the hand press). These are also called 'gauges' and 'lay marks'. **1898** P. MANSON *Trop. Diseases* xxiii. 372 These tubes he introduces by means of a special guide.

7. Something which marks a position or serves to guide the eye.

1875 SOUTHWARD *Dict Typogr.*, *Guide*, a piece of heavy rule or lead, balanced by a light cord and a quotation, laid upon the copy to assist the compositor in keeping the connexion. **1875** KNIGHT *Dict. Mech.*, *Guide*, a pile driven to mark a site.

8. *Mus.* = DUX 2.

1753 CHAMBERS *Cycl. Supp.*, *Guida*, in the Italian music, the guide, or leading voice or instrument, in fugues. **1846** BUCHANAN *Technol. Dict.*, *Guide* in music, the leading part in a canon or fugue.

9. *Mining.* A cross-course or -vein.

1874 J. H. COLLINS *Metal Mining* 27 In St. Just, the cross veins are known as trawns, or guides.

10. *dial.* A sinew or tendon. (Cf. GUIDER 5.)

1881 in *Leicestersh. Gloss.* **1893** *Northumbld. Gloss.* s.v., 'The guide's off'—that is, the tendon is dislocated.

11. *Electr.* A linear structure (as a pair of wires or a waveguide) or a surface along or over which an electromagnetic wave is propagated and to which it is confined. Now usu. short for WAVEGUIDE.

1893 O. HEAVISIDE *Electromagnetic Theory* I. iv. 399 When waves are left to themselves in ether without the presence of conductors, they expand and dissipate themselves... To prevent this we require conducting guides or leads..as a pair of parallel wires. **1902** *Encycl. Brit.* XXXIII. 215/1 The effects of the resistance of the guides are very complicated in general. **1936** *Bell Syst. Techn. Jrnl.* XV. 284 Extremely high-frequency waves may be transmitted from one point to another, through specially constructed wave guides. The guide..may be a hollow copper pipe. **1947** W. H. Watson *Physical Princ. Wave Guide Transmission* p. v, A dielectric cylinder may also be used to guide electromagnetic waves of sufficiently high frequency and is usually called a dielectric guide. **1962** Corson & Lorrain *Introd. Electromagnetic Waves* xii. 424 The guide wave length..is longer than the free space wave length.

III. 12. The action of the vb. guide, in various senses; direction; conduct; guidance. Now *rare.*

1500–20 Dunbar *Poems* lxxi. 37 Of gyd and gouirnance we ar all solitair. **1570** *Satir. Poems Reform.* x. 288 My Lords the Duke and Hereis baith Wer put in waird..Quhair thay are zit..And will be quhill sum men get ye gyde. **1602–3** Sir E. Stanhope *Will* in Willis & Clark *Cambridge* (1886) II. 672, I comende..this Famous Colledge..to the guide and governement of the most holie and Blessed Trinitie. **1607** Shaks. *Timon* i. i. 252 Pray entertaine them, giue them guide to vs. **1615** Chapman *Odyss.* xvii. 273 A man renown'd For guard of goats, which now he had in guide. **1649** Jer. Taylor *Gt. Exemp.* Disc. vii. §3 Whether we come ..by the guide of an angel or the conduct of Moses. **1857–8** Sears *Athan.* vii. 64 Under the guide of these principles.. the Bible pneumatology stands before us clear. **1887** *S. Chesh. Gloss., Guide,* guidance. 'That mon dunna sem to have much guide on his hoss'.

IV. *attrib.* and *Comb.*

13. Simple attrib., as †*guide-text*; chiefly in the names of technical appliances and parts of machinery (see senses 6, 7), as ***guide-bar, -blade, -chain, -curve, -eye, -face, -frame, -framing, -groove, -iron, -ledge, -line, -piece, -pile, -pin, -plate, -rail, -ring, -rod, -roller, -stick, -timbers, -wire.***

1839 Ure *Dict. Arts* 846 Small upright *guide-bars or rods for one of the corves. **1860** W. Cullen *Constr. Turbine* 8 By means of curved *guide blades the quantity and direction of water are regulated and guided into the radiating passages of the wheel. **1865** I. T. F. Turner *Slate Quarries* 8 Chains..which..as they guide the course of the loads, are termed *guide-chains. **1853** Glynn *Power Water* 43 The pressure of the water is directed by the vanes or *guide-curves of the upper wheel into the buckets of the lower one. **1839** Ure *Dict. Arts* 1240 The yarn..finally proceeds obliquely downwards..after traversing the *guide-eye. **1900** P. N. Hasluck *Mod. Eng. Handy-bk.* 59 The *guide-faces may be got up with a file. **1901** P. Marshall *Metal Working Tools* 44 A rising and falling *guide-frame. **1936** Guide-frame [see *all-welded* adj. (all- III. 13)]. **1900** *Engineering Mag.* XIX. 781/1 The *Guide-Framing of Gasholders. **1903** *Brit. & Col. Printer* 19 Nov. 12/2 The ends slide in parallel guide-grooves. **1888** *Lockwood's Dict. Mech. Engin.,* **Guide Iron,* a piece of iron rod,..which being put to the contour of a curved pattern pipe, becomes a guide by which the core maker strickles up its core without requiring a core-box. **1839** Ure *Dict. Arts* 922 The oblong brush with *guide ledges is dipped into them [long, narrow colour-pans] across the whole of the parallel row at once. **1881** Young *Every Man his own Mechanic* §375 It is better..in making any saw-cut of considerable length, to mark the *guide-line on its surface with the line and reel. **1839** Ure *Dict. Arts* 1293 The *guide pieces connected with the axletrees. **1791** R. Mylne *2nd Rep. Thames & Isis* 11 At the upper End of it [the Pen], four *Guide Piles are wanting. **1825** J. Nicholson *Operat. Mechanic* 428 The *guide pins are..driven into the beam. **1839** Ure *Dict. Arts* 922 *Paper-hangings.—Printing.* Each block carries small pin points fixed at its corners to guide the workman in the insertion of the figure exactly in its place. An expert hand places these guide pins so that their marks are covered..by the impression of the next block. **1888** *Lockwood's Dict. Mech. Engin., Ramps,* or **Guide Plates,*.. clip the rails, and are provided with flat helical extensions against which the wagon wheels slide up to the rail. **1889** G. Findlay *Eng. Railway* 104 Cross pieces connecting the axle-box guide plates. **1839** Ure *Dict. Arts* 501 The heckle bars..are..supported at their ends by fixed horizontal *guide rails, on which they slide. **1882** Ogilvie, *Guide-rail,* in *railways,* an additional rail placed midway between the two ordinary rails of the track, and employed in connection with devices on the engine or carriages to keep a train from leaving the track in curves, crossings, or steep gradients. **1883** *Century Mag.* July 378/1 He rove the line through the *guide-rings [of a fishing-rod]. **1839** Ure *Dict. Arts* 1287 These..should slide freely on their *guide-rods. **1860** *All Year Round* No. 55. 103 Baskets that would rarely be dangerous if they were caged and supplied with proper guide-rods. **1880** *Encycl. Brit.* XI. 425 The 'Hercules' [hammer], a ponderous mass of iron attached to a vertical guide rod. **1839** Ure *Dict. Arts* 221 It [the endless felt] is led over a *guide roller. **1759** Pullein in *Phil. Trans.* LI. 22 To change the position of the silk thread, that it might not always fall on the same part of the reel, the *guidestick was introduced. **1641** J. Jackson *True Evang. T.* ii. 140 According to the two former *guid-texts of 2 Tim. 3. 16, & Rom. 15. 4. **1882** *Rep. to Ho. Repr. Prec. Met. U.S.* 591 The frame of the cage has clips which extend upon each side of the *guide timbers. **1825** J. Nicholson *Operat. Mechanic* 399 *Guide-wires for the threads to pass over.

14. Special comb.: **guide-block,** a 'block' or piece of metal which slides between or upon guides or guide-bars; **guide-board,** a board erected at a fork in a road, for the direction of travellers; **guide card** (see quot. 1923); **guide coat** (see quot. 1953); **guide dog,** a dog trained to lead the blind; **guide-feather** = cock-feather (*Cent. Dict.*); **guide fossil** (see quots.); **guide-law,** (see quot.); **guide letter** (see quot. 1960); **guide-line,** (*a*) a line used as a guide, a guiding line; also *fig.*; (*b*) = *guide-rope* (*c*); **guide mill** (see quot. 1892); **guide number** *Photogr.* (see quot. 1962); **guide-pulley** (*a*) *Oval-turning,* a pulley by means of which motion is communicated to the guide (sense 6 b); (*b*) a pulley over which a band or cord is passed, where its course is altered or where it needs support; **guide-rope,** †(*a*) = guy *sb.*[1] 2; (*b*) a small rope attached to an object to be raised or lowered by a crane or pulley, in order to guide it; (*c*) *Aeronautics,* a long rope hung from a balloon or small airship so as to trail along the ground and to preserve altitude automatically by the drag of the rope without loss of ballast or gas; also, one of a number of ropes used to steady an airship before flight; hence **guide-rope** *v. intr.,* to use a guide-rope; **guide-screw,** a screw-thread in a screw-cutting lathe which regulates the thread of the screw being cut; **guide seam** *Coal-mining* (see quot.); **guide stone,** a stone set up by the wayside to direct travellers; **guide-tackle,** a rope secured to the top of a pole, etc., to steady it; **guide vane** *Aeronaut.* (see quot. 1962); **guide-way,** a groove, track, or 'way' along which a thing is moved or run in the required direction; **guide-wheel,** a wheel used to guide a moving structure or vehicle.

1871 Colburn *Locomotive Engin.* v. 128/2 A pair of *guide blocks. **1881** Greener *Gun* 127 The breech-piece..is furnished with a guide-block on its upper surface, which works between the two lips of the shoe. **1810** M. V. H. Dwight *Journey to Ohio* 27 Oct. (1912) 13 Soon after we cross'd the mountain, we took a wrong road, owing to the neglect of those whose duty it is to erect *guide boards. **1872** Plumer *Short Serm.* 38 The guide went a little way to the one side and there he found one of the guide-boards, which were in the shape of a cross. **1895** *Century Mag.* Aug. 561/2 He came to a fork in the road where there was no guide-board. **1923** H. A. Maddox *Dict. Stationery* 35 **Guide cards,* a segment of the card index and vertical filing system. Guide cards, or guiders, are stiff manilla cards, usually in distinctive colourings and provided with projecting tabs.. and the purpose of the cards is to act as dividers, or indicators. **1969** R. L. Collison *Indexes & Indexing* (ed. 3) i. 27 In the case of 5 in. by 3 in. cards, suitably printed guide cards of this description can be purchased,..and there are also larger sets of guide cards which can break up the sequence into any number of parts. **1930** *Motor Body Building* May 105/1 **Guide coat,* the staining coat put on top of the filling as a guide to rubbing down. **1937** *Times* 13 Apr. p. xiii/1 The various stages.., therefore, are as follows:—First coat of primer, or foundation coat; first, second, third, and fourth coat of oil filler; guide coat for rubbing down; oil filler, [etc.]. **1953** *Gloss. Paint Terms (B.S.I.)* 8 *Guide coat,* a very thin coat of loosely bound paint applied over a continuous coating of surfacer or filler, prior to rubbing down... It serves as a guide to the operator in producing a smooth surface. **1932** *Proc. World Conference on Work for Blind 1931* 183 (*caption*) *Guide dogs for the blind. **1944** D. Hartwell *Dogs against Darkness* 7 The modern guide dog provided by the Guide Dogs for the Blind Association is of the very greatest use. *Ibid.* 161 The majority of Guide Dogs in England are now types of British sheep-dogs. **1960** *News Chron.* 13 Jan. 5/6 Margaret Barber, 21, blind since she was six, was promised a guide dog. **1867** *Q. Jrnl. Geol. Soc.* XXIII. p. xlviii, The various divisions.. were to be recognized in all countries by special *guide-fossils. **1909** *Cent. Dict.* Suppl., *Guide-fossil,* a fossil species regarded as specially characteristic of a given geological formation, horizon, or fauna. **1914** Schuchert & Barrell in *Amer. Jrnl. Sci.* 4th Ser. XXXVIII. 6 In the chronologic correlation of the stratified rocks most dependence is put upon a few species, known as 'guide fossils', together with the collateral evidence of associated forms. These guide fossils may be represented by many or few individuals. **1957** Dunbar & Rodgers *Princ. Stratigr.* xvi. 279/1 A good guide fossil should have relatively wide geographic distribution and limited stratigraphic range. **1961** J. Challinor *Dict. Geol.* 97/1 *Guide fossil,* a species (or genus) or fossil useful as a guide to stratigraphical horizon or to the conditions under which the organism lived. **1605** Verstegan *Dec. Intell.* v. (1628) 137 There remaines yet a tole called *Guid-law, which is paid for cattell at Bowdumbar, a Gate of the City so called, and was first granted for the payment of guides. **1931** A. F. Johnson *Decorative Initial Letters* 6 Zainer's first outline initials were probably intended as *guide-letters for the rubricator. **1960** G. A. Glaister *Gloss. Bk.* 162 *Guide letters,* small letters inserted in the otherwise blank space left for an illuminated, historiated, or rubricated capital to be executed by hand after a work had been printed: a feature of early printed books and still earlier manuscripts. **1785** A. Ellicott in C. V. Mathews *A. Ellicott* (1908) 44 My Brother Joseph at Present runs the *guide Line for the choppers. **1846** *Illustr. London News* 30 May 356/1 The difficulty,..of getting a fulcrum..without which all attempts at steering an aëronaut machine must be failures, Mr. Green meets by the adoption of the guide-line, as he calls a rope about 1000 feet long. **1867** *All Year Round* XVIII. 452/1 In hauling in his guide-line, lest it should entangle itself with a factory chimney. **1881** Guide-line [see guide *sb.* 13]. **1931** *Times* 27 Aug. 13/6 The coast..serves as a guide-line to their destinations. **1948** A. Toynbee *Civilization on Trial* 4 The national history of England itself as the principal guide-line. **1952** A. Grimble *Pattern of Islands* 161 Tekirei and Mautake first drew guide-lines on my arms with stretched strings, which they dipped in their tattooing dye. **1963** *Listener* 7 Mar. 404/2 Today, in an age of religious doubt, the moral guide-lines are less obvious than they were. **1964** I. L. Horowitz *New Sociol.* 37 The past offers guidelines (not mandates) to the present and future. **1825** J. Nicholson *Operat. Mechanic* 428 One of the guide pullies for the endless rope. **1892** *Labour Commission* Gloss. s.v. *Mills,* **Guide mills,* the mills in which is finished small merchant iron. **1904** J. W. Hall in Harbord & Hall *Metallurgy of Steel* xvi. 311 The term 'guide mill' is reserved for mills in which the bar could not be properly entered with the workmen's tongs, and must have a guide to hold the bar on edge when it is being entered. **1948** A. L. M. Sowerby *Dict. Photogr.* (ed. 17) 317 s.v. *Flash bulbs,* The figures given are *guide-numbers; by dividing these by the distance.. between object and flash the stop to be used is given directly. **1959** L. A. Mannheim *Successful Flash Photogr.* 44 Guide numbers vary with film speed. **1962** M. L. Haselgrove *Photographer's Dict.* 120 Manufacturers of flash bulbs specify a guide number for each bulb to be used in conjunction with a given shutter speed and given film. This ..simplifies the matter of determining what aperture to use to obtain the correct exposure for any given subject at a known distance from the flash bulb. **1680** *Guide-pulley [see 6 b]. **13..** *E.E. Allit. P.C.* 105 Gederen to þe *gyde ropes, þe grete cloþ falles. **1729** Desaguliers in *Phil. Trans.* XXXVI. 195 A small Rope, call'd the Guide-Rope, is fasten'd to the Weight. **1838** M. Mason *Aeronautica* 23 An incident connected with the use of this guide-rope. **1848** *Chambers's Jrnl.* 6 May 301/2 Mr. Green as a substitute, uses a long rope, called the 'guide-rope'. **1897** *Strand Mag.* XIII. 227/2 One rope (the guide-rope) is securely tied to this crow-bar, and then thrown on the cliff. **1903** *Ibid.* 27 June 476/2 A life-saving kite. The kite carries a guide-rope. **1904** *Pall Mall Mag.* XXXII. 20 One can guide-rope in the centre of Paris. **1905** *Spectator* 11 Mar. 371/1, I hopped over the trees of the Bois..and guide-roped down the Avenue des Champs Elysées to my door at the corner of the Rue Washington. **1928** *Daily Express* 12 Oct. 2/2 Four hundred sinewy fists released their hold on the guide-ropes that still leashed the mammoth [Zeppelin] to earth. **1812–16** J. Smith *Panorama Sci. & Art* I. 73 A concave screw in the end of the mandrel, to which any variety of convex or *guide screws may then be alternately attached. **1863** Smiles *Indust. Biog.* 240 He made a turning-lathe with a sliding mandrill, and guide-screws, for cutting screws, furnished also with the means for correcting guide-screws. **1867** W. W. Smyth *Coal & Coal-mining* 79 There are here no less than 117 seams..of coal..They are now recognised and mapped over the entire district by the aid of three or four *guide-seams of special character and persistence. **1762** J. Hall Stevenson *Crazy Tales* 41 Guides as blind as a *guide-stone. **1665** J. Webb *Stone-Heng* (1725) 214 A Pair of Shears..having *Guide-Tackles, Blocks and Shivers. **1941** *Illustr. London News* 28 June 827/1 (*caption*) At Langley Field, Virginia, U.S.A., where these powerful *guide-vanes direct the air in pressure wind-tunnels. **1962** *Gloss. Aeronaut. Terms (B.S.I.)* iv. 15 *Guide vanes,* a cascade of fixed vanes which guide the fluid stream round the bends in the passages of a wind tunnel. **1876** J. S. Ingram *Centenn. Exposition* ix. 270 Both the upper and lower *guide-ways were adjustable for keeping the saw in line whenever required by the settling of floors. **1887** *Sci. Amer.* 9 July 18/2 The tool carriage..is adapted to slide on guideways on the main frame [of an automatic wood-turning lathe]. **1890** W. J. Gordon *Foundry* 111 Thence it passes on to a guideway in the floor, which runs it off on to a measuring-stage. **1966** *Electronics* 14 Nov. 16 Seifert will analyze such problems as propulsion, guideway, communications and control. **1969** *Times* 16 Apr. 11/6 The dual mode vehicle..is driven normally at either end of its journey, but..automation takes over once it runs on the 'automated guideway'. *Ibid.,* The automated guideway system has been under study..for some 18 months. **1840** *Mag. Sci.* 29 Aug. 173/2 Have it [*sc.* a tricycle] upon three wheels, the first of them a *guide wheel. **1847** *Patent Jrnl.* III. 471/1 The next feature is the provision of safety guide-wheels [on a locomotive engine]. **1885** *Marine Engineer* 1 July 91/2 The guide-wheel supports the 'bag' of the bucket chain. **1909** *Westm. Gaz.* 22 July 5/2 The pilot must be careful to hold the guide-wheel so as to maintain this position.

guide (gaɪd), *v.* Forms: 4–5 **gide,** 4–6 **gyd(e,** (6 **gid),** 5–6 **guyde,** 4, 6– **guide.** [a. F. *guide-r* (recorded from 14th c.), an altered form (influenced by Pr. *guidar* or It. *guidare*) of the older *guier,* whence guy *v.*[1] Cf. prec. sb.]

1. a. *trans.* To act as guide to; to go with or before for the purpose of leading the way: said of persons, of God, Providence, and of impersonal agents, such as stars, light, etc. Also ***to guide the way*** (cf. *lead*). Also *refl.*

c **1374** Chaucer *Troylus* ii. 1055 What maner wyndes gydeth yow now here. *Ibid.* v. 322 And god Mercurye of me now woful wrecche, The soule gide. *c* **1386** —— *Clerk's T.* 776 He on his wy is goon..In riche array this mayden for to gyde. *a* **1400–50** *Alexander* 5387 Nowe aires furth oure conquirour & candoile him gidis. *c* **1440** *Generydes* 116 And to this place he gidyd yow the weye. **1463** *Mann. & Househ. Exp.* (Roxb.) 227 Item, govyn to Thomas Barkere ys brothyr, for gydyng the weye, iiij[d]. **1502** in *Ld. Treas. Acc. Scotl.* (1900) II. 151 Item, to the man that gydit the King quhen he passit to Dunbertane, ij[s]. **1535** Coverdale *Luke* i. 79 That he might geue light..to gyde oure fete in to the waye of peace. **1598** Shaks. *Merry W.* v. v. 83 And twenty glow-wormes shall our Lanthornes bee To guide our Measure round about the Tree. **1610** —— *Temp.* v. i. 105 Some heauenly power guide vs Out of this fearefull Country. **1613** Purchas *Pilgrimage* (1614) 723 The gold in stone will runne as small as a pin or thread, and meeting with a hollow place, filleth it, and so guideth the Miner by thicke and thinne. **1661** Boyle *Style of Script.* (1675) 20 The known rocks and shelves do as well guide the sea-men as the pole-star. **1725** Pope *Odyss.* x. 595 How shall I tread..The dark descent, and who shall guide the way? **1794** Mrs. Radcliffe *Myst. Udolpho* i, Till moon-light steals down.. and chequers all the ground, and guides them to the bower. **1820** Shelley *Cloud* 22 Over earth and ocean, with gentle motion This pilot is guiding me. **1860** Tyndall *Glac.* i. xviii. 122 The slopes..and precipices, which were to guide us. **1865** M. C. Harris *Christine* iii, Moving cautiously upon the ice..he..lay down, guiding himself by his hands alone. **1868** Geo. Eliot *Sp. Gipsy* iv. 228 The stars will guide us back. **1870** Bryant *Iliad* I. i. 5 He Had guided Ilium-ward the ships of Greece. **1888** Mrs. H. Ward *Robt. Elsmere* i. viii. 231 And refusing all help, she guided herself out of the room. **1894** J. T. Fowler *Adamnan* Introd. 28 God guided him to the ship. **1907** *Smart Set* Mar. 128 He guided himself cautiously with his left arm stretched out against the object of quest.

b. To direct the course of (a vehicle, tool, physical action, etc.).

c **1460** HENRYSON *Test. Cresseid* 205 As king, royall he raid upon his chair, The quhilk Phaeton gydit sum-tyme unricht. **1562** WINȜET *Cert. Tractates* i. Wks. 1888 I. 3 Ane schip..gydit..be sleuthfull marinaris and sleipand sterismen. **1588** SHAKS. *Tit. A.* IV. i. 75 Heauen guide thy pen to print thy sorrowes plaine. **1613** PURCHAS *Pilgrimage* (1614) 35 Lamech was blinde, and by the direction of Tubalcaine his sonne guiding his hand slew Caine. **1651** HOBBES *Leviath.* I. iii. 8 As water upon a plain Table is drawn which way any one part of it is guided by the finger. **1782** COWPER *Expostulat.* 437 Unless a zeal for virtue guide the blow. **1805** SOUTHEY *Madoc* II. xxvii, Still with steady hand Guiding the death-blow on. **1807** CRABBE *Par. Reg.* II. 298 How strange that men Who guide the plough, should fail to guide the pen. **1839** URE *Dict. Arts* 1284 A small hole ..to receive and guide one thread.

†**c.** To keep *from* by guidance. *Obs.*

c **1560** A. SCOTT *Poems* xxxvi. 57 Lord God, deliuer me, and gyd Frome schedding blude.

d. *Electr.* To serve as a guide for (an electromagnetic wave); so ***guided wave***. Cf. GUIDE *sb.* 11.

1893 O. HEAVISIDE *Electromagnetic Theory* I. iv. 368 If we abolish the fictitious magnetic conductivity throughout the medium traversed by the waves we should, to have distortionless transmission, also abolish the electric conductivity. This is only to be attained by using wires of no resistance to guide the waves through a non-conducting medium. **1902** *Encycl. Brit.* XXXIII. 214/2 The use of conductors will now be seen partly. They serve to *guide* a wave along from place to place without loss, and with a limited amount of energy. **1925** A. M. MORSE *Radio: Beam & Broadcast* iii. 66 [He] enunciated the theory that a 'Heaviside Layer' was unneccessary, since all radio waves were guided by the earth, which was the real conductor; just as was the wire, in guided-wave telephony or telegraphy. **1936** *Bell Syst. Techn. Jrnl.* XV. 285 It is possible to reduce the size of the guiding structure for a given frequency by the use of a suitable dielectric. *Ibid.* 312 In the ordinary type of guided-wave systems..the guiding conductors form two sides of a circuit in which equal and opposite currents flow. **1947** [see GUIDE *sb.* 11]. **1962** CORSON & LORRAIN *Introd. Electromagnetic Waves* xii. 429 In the process of guiding electromagnetic waves conductors waste part of the wave energy in the form of Joule losses. This is because the guided waves always induce electric currents in the conductors.

2. *fig.* and in immaterial senses: To lead or direct in a course of action, in the formation of opinions, etc.; to determine the course or direction of (events, etc.).

a. of persons or agents.

a **1400-50** *Alexander* 4425 Þus..ere ȝe..to þe way of wickidnes be warlaȝes gidid. **1447** BOKENHAM *Seyntys* (Roxb.) 37 Whil that grace Of God the guydyth thou mayst not mys. **1477** EARL RIVERS (Caxton) *Dictes* 64 If he gouerne hym self euyll, by liklyhode right so wyl he guyde the. **1526** *Pilgr. Perf.* (W. de W. 1531) 20 Grace is the moost sure safeconducte to gyde man through the troubles of this worlde. **1596** SPENSER *State Irel.* Wks. (Globe) 652/1, I will ..make myne eyes..my schoole-master, to guide my understanding to judge of your plott. **1597** HOOKER *Eccl. Pol.* v. x. §1 Being taught, led, and guided by his spirit. **1608** SHAKS. *Per.* III. ii. 111 Her relapse is mortal. Come, come; And Æsculapius guide us! **1611** BIBLE *John* xvi. 13 The Spirit of trueth..wil guide you into all trueth. **1662** *Bk. Com. Prayer, Prayer Ember Week*, So guide and govern the minds of thy servants. *a* **1716** SOUTH *Serm.* (J.), Whosoever has a faithful friend to guide him in the dark passages of life. **1788** SIR W. JONES *Charge Gr. Jury* 4 Dec. Wks. 1799 III. 26 So as to..guide your judgement in finding or rejecting the several bills. **1898** T. ADAMSON *Stud. Mind in Christ* xi. 278 The Saviour guided events sympathetically.

b. of indications, principles, motives, etc.

a **1547** SURREY *Æneid* II. (1557) B iij, Amid the flame and armes ran I in preasse: As furie guided me. **1602** MARSTON *Antonio's Rev.* II. v. Wks. 1856 I. 103 Confusion and black murder guides The organs of my spirit. *a* **1695** KETTLEWELL (J.), When nothing but the interest of this world guides men. **1834** *West Ind. Sketch Bk.* II. 26 It is preposterous for him to be guided too rigidly by the recommendations of others. **1844** DISRAELI *Coningsby* VI. ii, The fine taste which has guided the vast expenditure. **1848** R. I. WILBERFORCE *Incarn. our Lord* iv. (1852) 90 Our Lord's true perception of the real evils of man's nature..guided the general course of His sympathy. **1863** H. COX *Instit.* III. v. 656 The Secretary of State..has been guided by the reports of the Board.

c. *refl.* To conduct oneself or 'get along' (in a specified manner); †to manage one's affairs (*obs.*). Cf. GUY *v.*[1] 3 b. †Similarly, ***to guide one's ways***.

14.. *Sir Beues* 2974 (MS. M.) That in ffrenche couth hym selfe guyde. **1491** *Act 7 Hen. VII*, c. 20 Preamble, The seid Edmond is not of sufficient discrecion to gyde himself and his lyvelode. **1500-20** DUNBAR *Poems* xx. 8 He rewlis weill, that weill him self can gyd. **1535** COVERDALE *2 Chron.* xxvii. 6 He gyded his wayes before the Lorde his God. [**1759** GOLDSM. *Pol. Learn.* viii, For while so well able to direct others, how incapable is he frequently found of guiding himself!] **1816** SCOTT *Old Mort.* xxxix, He..formed the resolution of guiding himself by the circumstances in which he might discover the object of his quest. **1874** J. W. DRAPER *Hist. Conflict Relig. & Sci.* 136 He guides himself by past as well as by present impressions. **1877** *N.W. Linc. Gloss.*, *Guide one's self*, to behave well.

†**3. a.** To lead or command (an army, etc.). *Obs.*

c **1374** CHAUCER *Troylus* I. 183 This Troilus as he was wont to gyde His yonge knyghtes ladde hem vp and doun. *c* **1450** *Merlin* 151 The thirde warde lede the kynge Boors of Gannes, that full wele cowde hem guyde. **1514** BARCLAY *Cyt. & Uplondyshm.* (Percy Soc.) 12 Unto the thyrde he gave such dygnyte, To guyde an army. **1548** HALL *Chron., Edw. IV* (an. 22) (1550) 54 b, The lefte wyng was guyded by the lorde Fitz Hewe.

†**b.** To lead and tend (a flock). *Obs.*

1551 CROWLEY *Pleas. & Pain* 317 You that woulde nedis take in hande To guyde my flocke, as shepheardis shoulde, Only to possesse rent and land. **1611** BIBLE *Ps.* lxxviii. 52 [He] guided them in the wildernesse like a flocke. **1615** *Vestry Bks.* (Surtees) 68 The stock of sheepe..to be fedd and guided winter and sommer.

4. a. To conduct the affairs of (a household, state, etc.).

1390 GOWER *Conf.* III. 183 The people for to guide and lede, Which is the charge of his kinghede. **1535** COVERDALE *1 Tim.* v. 14, I wil therfore that the yonger wemen mary, beare children, gyde the house. **1540-41** ELYOT *Image Gov.* 7 Moyses..was by almightie God chosen to guyde and rule his people. **1662** *Bk. Com. Prayer, Pr. for all Conditions of Men*, We pray for the good estate of the Catholick Church; that it may be so guided and governed by thy good Spirit that [etc.]. **1693** DRYDEN *Ovid's Met.* xv. *Pythag. Philos.* 1 A king is sought to guide the growing State.

b. To manage (money or other property, a process, an affair). Also *absol.* Now *Sc.*

1465 MARG. PASTON in *P. Lett.* No. 529 II. 241 He is ryght ille plesyd that the mater was so gydyt. **1500-20** DUNBAR *Poems* xix. 28 Evill he gydes ȝone man trewlie; Lo! be his claithis it may be sene. **1514** *Extracts Aberd. Reg.* (1844) I. 92 To be masteris of thar artalery, and to gid and keipe thar powder and wayr quarteris. **1526** SKELTON *Magnyf.* 1466 For a memory, Make indentures howe ye and I shal gyde. **1529** MORE *Dyaloge* I. Wks. 151/2 Which affeccion whoso happeth to haue geuen him, is very fortunate, if he with grace & mekenes gyde it well. **1586** T. B. *La Primaud. Fr. Acad.* I. (1594) 46 Being delivered from the care of house-keeping and of guiding his goods. **1637** RUTHERFORD *Lett.* cclvi. (1894) 503 So that I have not the right art of guiding Christ; for there is art and wisdom required in guiding of Christ's love aright when we have gotten it. **1721** KELLY *Scot. Prov.* 63 Better guide well, as work sore. And indeed good Management will very much excuse hard Labour. **1781** BURNS *My Nanie, O* vi, My riches a' 's my penny fee An' I maun guide it cannie. **1816** SCOTT *Antiq.* xxvi, Them that sells the goods guide the purse—them that guide the purse rule the house. **1824** MISS FERRIER *Inher.* lix, I didn't believe she had one [a cook] that..knew how to guide a sheep's head and trotters.

5. *trans.* To treat or use (a person) in a specified manner. *Sc.* and *north. dial.*

1768 ROSS *Helenore* (1789) 69 Our ain lads..guided them right cankerdly and snell. **1785** FORBES *Dominie Deposed* in *Poems Buchan Dial.* II. 43 Had you been there to hear and see The manner how they guided me. **1822** SCOTT *Nigel* xxxv, There are few,..either of fools or of wise men, ken how to guide a woman. **1893** *Northumbld. Gloss., Guide*, to treat, to use. 'Weel guided.' 'Badly guided.'

'guide-book. A book for the guidance of strangers or visitors in a district, town, building, etc., giving a description of the roads, places, or objects of interest to be found there. Also *fig.*

1814 J. MAYNE *Jrnl.* 25 Oct. (1909) x. 164 At Mr. Vasi's we purchased his guide-book, which is considered the best of its kind. **1823** BYRON *Juan* XI. xxiii, I..do not choose to encroach Upon the Guide-book's privilege. **1845** M. PATTISON *Ess.* (1889) I. 10 That boundless plain of Languedoc, convicted of all guide-books of being arid, brown, and wholly uninteresting. *a* **1846** B. R. HAYDON *Autobiogr.* (1927) ix. 135, I mean my Life, if possible, to be a guide book to youth. **1862** BURTON *Bk. Hunter* II. 116 In any district of country not desecrated by the tourist's guide-books. **1935** T. S. ELIOT *Murder in Cathedral* ii. 86 The sanctity shall not depart from it..though sightseers come with guide-books looking over it.

attrib. and *Comb.* **1866** J. MACGREGOR *Thousand Miles in Rob Roy Canoe* i. 8 In his guide-book route,..from town to town. **1887** HISSEY *Holiday on Road* 4 Guide-book-lauded spots. **1889** *Spectator* 14 Dec. 849 The somewhat depressing 'guide-book' style.

guide-booky ('gaɪd,bʊkɪ), *a.* [f. GUIDE-BOOK + -Y[1].] Resembling or characteristic of (that of) a guide-book; having the style of a guide-book. Also **'guide-,bookishly** *adv.*

1878 A. MACKENNAL in D. Macfadyen *Life & Lett.* (1905) 72 This talk is a little guide-booky. **1882** W. H. RUSSELL *Hesperothen* I. 165 There are, I am told, nearly one hundred churches—to be guide-bookishly accurate, ninety-six—in Cleveland. **1895** *Academy* 23 Mar. 251/3 The guide-booky lines on p. 222 of the same volume.

guided ('gaɪdɪd), *ppl. a.* [f. GUIDE *v.* + -ED[1].]

a. Directed or led by guidance; *spec.* of a tour: accompanied by a guide, having a guide in charge.

1857 H. R. REYNOLDS in *Life* vi. (1898) 140, I was.. prepared to accept the decision..as a rightly guided one. **1882** *19th Cent.* XII. 131 It is difficult, indeed, for the guider ..to avoid giving hints..to the guided one. **1909** *Daily Chron.* 6 Sept. 4/6 On a guided ascent. **1969** *New Yorker* 30 Aug. 30/1 There is a very good museum... There are guided tours. **1970** *Ibid.* 12 Sept. 31/1 We were taken to see it [*sc.* Lenin's body] as part of a guided tour.

b. Of weapons: operating by remote control or as directed by equipment carried in the weapon, as ***guided bomb, missile, rocket, weapon***.

1945 *Newsweek* 27 Aug. 25/1 The 'guided missile'—a rocket projectile that can be aimed accurately over great distances. **1948** J. STEINBECK *Russ. Jrnl.* (1949) i. 3 Experiments with atomic weapons and guided missiles. **1952** *Ann. Reg. 1951* 96 United Kingdom experts attended tests of rockets and guided weapons at the Woomera range. **1954** *Economist* 11 Sept. 12/3 *Guided*, containing electronic control mechanisms, designed to seek out the target. Capable of altering course during flight. **1954** K. W. GATLAND *Devel. Guided Missile* (ed. 2) v. 130 A guided bomb of this type need have no inherent propulsion unit. It will leave the bomber in the normal way... The task of the bomb-aimer will then be to guide the weapon by remote radio-control. **1954** *Ann. Reg. 1953* 6 In the field of armament research..work on guided rockets had been intensified. **1955** *Times* 30 June 7/4 Probably few people know that the first guided missile was designed and made in Great Britain. It was the invention of Mr. A. M. Low, developed by him in the course of the war of 1914-18. **1956** *Nature* 7 Apr. 636/1 The first guided-weapons trial ship should be in operation next summer. **1958** *Daily Mail* 30 June 2/6 The guided-missile ship..will be in Greek or Dodecanese ports. **1958** 'N. BLAKE' *Penknife in my Heart* i. 20 Swift and frantic as a volley of guided missiles out of control. **1965** M. SPARK *Mandelbaum Gate* i. 12 The State of Israel had that day sent up its first guided rocket.

guidee (gaɪ'di:). [f. GUIDE *v.* + -EE[1].] One who is guided.

1922 *Chambers's Jrnl.* Apr. 250/2 A 'guide'..who only started duties after the 'guidee' had made himself acquainted with his guider. **1934** J. B. PRIESTLEY *Eng. Journey* 220, I am probably too conceited and dogmatic a person myself to make a good guidee. To be at ease, I ought to be doing the guiding.

guideless ('gaɪdlɪs), *a.* [f. GUIDE *sb.* + -LESS.]

1. Without a guide to show the way. †Of a ship: Without a steersman.

1557 NORTH tr. *Gueuara's Diall Pr.* 262 b/2 Not seing y[e] wherilpole, guidles I entred in the rashnes of my youth. **1598** J. DICKENSON *Greene in Conc.* (1878) 151 Some guidelesse Pinnace in a storme. **1611** SPEED *Hist. Gt. Brit.* IX. xxiv. §210. 861 The greatest of their Galliasses..lost her Rudder, so that guidelesse she droue with the tyde vpon a shelue in the shoare of Callis. **1665** DRYDEN *Ind. Emperor* II. i. Dram. Wks. 1725 I. 345 Empty Shades..Which guideless in those dark Dominions stray. **1703** POPE *Thebais* 105 Deprived of eyes, Guideless I wander. **1855** *Tait's Mag.* XXII. 544 A flat, guideless waste. **1856** RUSKIN *Mod. Paint.* III. IV. i. §1 A traveller..who had to recommence an interrupted journey in a guideless country.

2. Without a guide or director; without a controller or ruler.

1561 NORTON & SACKV. *Gorboduc* V. ii. (1590) G ij b, Thus leaue this guideles realme an open pray To endlesse stormes. **1611** SPEED *Hist. Gt. Brit.* VI. xxxvi. §1. 136 The now guidelesse Army of Rome, occupied only in spoile and mutiny, their Leaders in faction. **1616-61** HOLYDAY *Persius* 304 Whether is the fittest guard..for a young guideless ward? **1635-56** COWLEY *Davideis* IV. 243 Where e're his Guidless Passion leads his Will. **1662** DRYDEN *Astræa Redux* 12 Th' ambitious Swede..To his now guideless kingdom peace bequeath'd. **1725** POPE *Odyss.* II. 219 His guide-less youth, if thy experienc'd age Mislead. **1728** R. MORRIS *Ess. Anc. Archit.* 27 Their guideless, ungrounded, and thoughtless Fancies. **1827** HARE *Guesses* (1859) 457 The poor guideless Heathens. **1869** RUSKIN *Q. of Air* §158 Helpless and guideless, he indulges his idiosyncracies till they change into insanities.

Hence **'guidelessness,** guideless condition.

1850 KINGSLEY *Alt. Locke* ii. (1879) 28 Hast thou too to fight with poverty and guidelessness?

†**'guidement.** *Obs.* In 6 guidment. Guidance; rule; direction.

a **1578** LINDESAY (Pitscottie) *Chron. Scot.* (1728) 172 The Government and Guidment of his Country. **1592** WYRLEY *Armorie* 120 He..Sendeth for me, as chiefetaine to attend His wars by guidment of my prooued skill.

'guide-post. A post with a direction-board affixed, set up for the guidance of travellers, *e.g.* at the fork of a road; a finger-post. Also *transf.* and *fig.*

1761 L. STERNE *Tr. Shandy* III. xxiii. 90 Wherever.. three several roads meet..set up a guide-post in the centre of them. **1774** BURKE *Amer. Tax.* 46 Great men are the guide-posts and land-marks in the state. **1812** COMBE *Picturesque* 11, A guide-post rose within his view. **1856** R. A. VAUGHAN *Mystics* I. Pref. 7 To distinguish between the genuine and the spurious in their opinion or their life, is to erect a guide-post on the very road we have ourselves to tread. **1872** JENKINSON *Guide Eng. Lakes* (1879) 121 Enter the road at the point where a guide-post directs to Langdale. **1873** TRISTRAM *Moab* vii. 125 In this treeless land a fair-sized terebinth..was a conspicuous guide-post. **1940** [see AUDIENCE 7 d]. **1967** *Times Rev. Industry* Feb. 16/1 Our prices and incomes board is an attempt to apply the experience of the USA in using guide posts to influence increases in wages and prices.

Hence **guide-post** *v. nonce-wd.*, to furnish with a guide-post. In quot. *fig.*

1890 *Blackw. Mag.* CXLVII. 264/1 The ancient well-trodden path of womankind, fenced and guide-posted, is.. the best.

guider ('gaɪdə(r)). Forms: 5-6 **gyder,** (5 **gydoure, gidour**), 6 **gider, guyder,** (**gidar,** *Sc.* **gydar(e, gydear, gydder,** 7 **guidor**), 6- **guider.** [f. GUIDE *v.* + -ER[1]. Cf. OF. *guideur* guide.]

1. One who guides, in various senses of the vb. Formerly often used as equivalent to GUIDE *sb.*; now *rare*, to express mere agency apart from official function.

a. One who leads, or points out the way to (others); one who directs the course of (a vehicle, ship, etc.); †one who wields (a weapon).

c **1475** *Partenay* 4105 After in laughter saide to hys Gidour [etc.]. *a* **1533** LD. BERNERS *Huon* clvi. 597 Then Huon.. entered into the lytel shyppe and saluted the gyder therof. **1535** STEWART *Cron. Scot.* 3011 Send..Gydaris rycht gude, that culd thame convoy Fra all perrell. *c* **1550** *Order in Battayll* C, When he wyll battayle, lette it be secretlye done, that the guyders knowe it not. **1548** UDALL, etc. *Par. Erasm. John* ix. 39-41 They professe themselues teachers of the people, y[t] is, gyders of the blynde. *a* **1586** SIDNEY *Arcadia* III. (1590) 267 b, Some launces, according to the mettall they mett, and skill of the guider, did staine themselues in bloud. **1607** SHAKS. *Cor.* I. vii. 7 Our Guider come, to th' Roman

Campe conduct vs. **1611** SPEED *Hist. Gt. Brit.* IX. v. (1623) 489 The Disherited were the Guiders of an other [Squadron]. *a* **1718** PARNELL *Deborah* 84 Nine hundred chariots roll along, Expert their guiders, and their horses strong. **1810** SCOTT *Lady of L.* I. xvii, A Damsel guider of its way, A little skiff shot from the bay.

†**b.** *spec.* A man stationed on shore to signal to fishermen the direction taken by a shoal of herrings or pilchards; a balker or conder. *Obs.*

1603 *Act 1 Jas. I*, c. 23 Diuers persons within the said counties [Somerset, Devon, and Cornwall] called.. Directors or Guidors..haue vsed to watch..vpon the high Hilles and Grounds neere adioyning the Sea-Coasts for the giving Notice to the Fishermen.

c. One who directs the conduct or actions of (a person), or the affairs of (a state, household, etc.).

c **1400** *Sowdone Bab.* 163 Seinte Poule be oure gydoure. **1461** *Rolls of Parlt.* V. 464 The gyders and leders of the noble Reame of Englond. **15..** *Sir Tryam.* 1530 in Utterson *E. Pop. Poet.* (1817) I. 69 My knyght Syr Roger he dyde slo, That my gyder sholde haue bene. **1513** DOUGLAS *Æneis* V. x. 3 Eneas..Epitides to hym hes callit sone, Maister and gydar of Ascanyus ȝong. **1542** *Extracts Aberd. Reg.* (1844) I. 185 The haill consell..ordanis Androw Luk to be gyder of the said artillierie. **1588** A. KING tr. *Canisius' Catech.* Deuot Prayers 34 Vouchesaif to send, o lord, thyne halie angel..to be the guyder of our lyf. *c* **1610** *Women Saints* 206 She chose greate Macrina for the keeper and guider of her widdowhood. **1619** VISCOUNT DONCASTER in *Eng. & Germ.* (Camden) 196 The Baron de Rupa is at the present a chiefe guider among them. **1650** WELDON *Crt. Jas. I*, 10 This Sir George Hewme being the only man that was the Guider of the King. **1685** SOUTH *12 Serm.* (1697) I. 358 [He] had great reason to acknowledge..Providence for the Guider of his Hand. **1808** SCOTT *Marm.* IV. xxxii, God is the guider of the field, He breaks the champion's spear and shield. **1832** GEN. P. THOMPSON in *Westm. Rev.* XVI. 299 They were the only people to guide the guiders. **1883** *Congregationalist* Sept. 771 The would-be guider of the world.

†**d.** *fig.* of things personified. *Obs.*

c **1530** *Hickscorner* in Manly *Spec. Pre-Shaks. Drama* I. 403 Let Trouth..Be your guyder. **1556** J. HEYWOOD *Spider & F.* xxxvii. 34 Where reason and equalnesse be giders. **1639** GLAPTHORNE *Poems 22* (*Epithalamium*), With that immaculate guider of her Youth, Rose-colour'd Modestie.

†**e.** In 16–17th c. the title of the head officer of certain charitable institutions. *Obs.*

1578–9 *Cal. MSS. Hatfield Ho.* (1888) II. 237 Protection for the Poor House of Waltham Cross, granted to George Philipp, guider, to gather in Middx. and Essex. **1603** in F. Blomefield *Hist. Norfolk* (1745) II. 605–6 The office, place, and room, of the Guide and Guidership of S. Stephen's Hospital by Norwich, void by the death of John Bellmy, late Guider deceased.

2. Something which guides: **a.** see quot. 1825 and GUIDE *sb.* 6 b; **b.** a front or steering-wheel of a bicycle.

1825 J. NICHOLSON *Operat. Mechanic* 397 The threads are guided by passing through wire eyes..The guiders are in constant motion, and lay the threads regularly upon the reel. **1886** *Cyclist* 6 Oct. 1324/1 We expect to see the small steering-wheel give way to the large one, and guiders of 24 in. to 30 in. lead the way.

c. *dial.* A sinew, tendon. (Cf. GUIDE *sb.* 10.)

1824 *Craven Gloss.*, *Guiders*, tendons. **1886** *S.W. Linc. Gloss.* s.v., 'He has strained his guiders'.

Hence **'guidership**, the office of guider; guidance.

1603 [see GUIDER 1 e]. **1849** ALB. SMITH *Pottleton Leg.* 177 The old coach..was confided once more to the guidership of old Will Turret.

†**'guideress.** *Obs.* Also 6 guidres, 6–7 guidress(e. [f. GUIDER + -ESS.] A female who guides, a conductress; a female ruler or director; an instructress.

c **1374** CHAUCER *Boeth.* IV. pr. i. 85 (Camb. MS.) Thow art gyderesse of verrey lyht. **1413** *Pilgr. Sowle* (Caxton) I. xxii. (1859) 24, I, Grace..In erthe alowe, to be theyr guydresse That lyte the redy weyes for to lerne, In pilgrymage him selff to gouerne. **1549** CHALONER *Erasm. on Folly* P iv a, Fortune hirselfe, the guidresse of all worldly chaunces. **1624** HEYWOOD *Gunaik.* II. 63 Euterpe is..said to be delighted in all sorts of pipes and wind instruments, and to be both their inventresse and guidresse. *c* **1650** *Don Bellianis* 201 The blind guidress of the round revolving wheeled chance.

†**guides.** *Obs.* Also 6 gwidege. [Corruptly ad. med.L. *guidegi*, ad. Arab. *widāj*.] The jugular vein.

c **1400** *Lanfranc's Cirurg.* II. iii. 149 þer ben ij. greete veynes þat ben clepid organice or ellis guydes. **1548–77** VICARY *Anat.* vi. (1888) 48 The great Veines which ramefie by the sydes of the necke to the vpper part of the head, is of some men called Gwidege, & of others *Vena organices.* **1597** A. M. tr. *Guillemeau's Fr. Chirurg.* xij b/2 The Iugulare or organicke vayne, of the Arabians called Guides. *Ibid.* 29 b/2 The ninth [vein] is lyinge in the necke, and is called the Iugularis vayne, and of the Arabians, Gvides.

guideship ('gaɪdʃɪp). *Sc.* [f. GUIDE *sb.* + -SHIP.]

1. The office of guide or ruler.

a **1578** LINDESAY (Pitscottie) *Chron. Scot.* (S.T.S.) I. 284 [They] desyrit him for to come to resaue the autorietie and gydeschip of the contrie. **1843** CARLYLE *Past & Pr.* IV. i. 325 A spiritual Guideship, a practical Governorship..have established themselves.

2. The exercise of the office of guide. †**a.** Guidance, leading (*obs.*). **b.** Treatment, usage.

a **1693** *Urquhart's Rabelais* III. xliv. 362 He did..submit himself to the Conduct and Guideship of the blessed Spirit. **1882** W. ALEXANDER *Life Ain Flk.* 18 (E.D.D.) He cudna expeckit better guideship though he hed been ane o' oor nain faimily.

guidguid ('gwɪdgwɪd). Also hued-hued, huet-huet. [Probably echoic: cf. GUIT-GUIT.] A ground-dwelling South American bird, *Pteroptochos tarnii*, belonging to the tapaculo group.

1845 [see BARKING *ppl. a.*[1] 2 b]. **1912** BRABOURNE & CHUBB *Birds S. Amer.* I. 183 Hylactes..tarnii... Tarn's Barking-bird. Hued-hued; Guid-guid. **1932** C. E. HELLMAYR *Birds of Chile* 215 The 'Hued-hued' is a common bird in southern Chile..and ranges across the Andes to the extreme western section of Rio Negro and Chubut. **1964** A. L. THOMSON *New Dict. Birds* 806/2 The Huet-huet *Pteroptochos tarnii* has the upper parts and foreneck very dark brown.

guiding ('gaɪdɪŋ), *vbl. sb.* [f. GUIDE *v.* + -ING[1].]

1. The action of the verb GUIDE in various senses; leading or showing the way; administration, management, command; guidance, governance, direction.

c **1425** LYDG. *Assembly of Gods* 59, I..Ouer all desertys, forestes and chases, Haue take the guydyng. **1462** *Paston Lett.* No. 453 II. 104 The gidyng and governaunce of the Barge of Yermouthe. **1477** EARL RIVERS (Caxton) *Dictes* 64 Take hede of the guydyng of him that thou axes conseyle of. *c* **1500** *Three Kings Sons* 139 As to the guydyng of your warres, they se neither rewle nor ordenaunce. **1523** LD. BERNERS *Froiss.* I. cxviii. 141 Y[e] seneshall..rode byways couert about y[e] towne by gidyng of the spye. **1529** *Extracts Aberd. Reg.* (1844) I. 122 For the rewill and gydin of thair skuill. **1583** *Leg. Bp. St. Androis* 954 in *Satir. Poems Reform.* xlv, Sa oft as I misvsit my sell, In guyding of the giftis of grace. **1592** WYRLEY *Armorie, Chandos* 46 Charles, duke of Romandie had second guiding. **1596** DALRYMPLE tr. *Leslie's Hist. Scot.* VII. 14 Throuch..his gydeng, Scotland was now at a gude poynte. **1609** *Vestry Bks.* (Surtees) 155 a, Paid to Thomas Carr and Richard Bilsburie for guideing of the windowes for 5 daies..vj s. viij d. **1637** SANDERSON *Serm.* II. 87 For the better guiding of those that are desirous of this learning. **1888** C. DENT in *Chambers' Encycl.* I. 192 (art. *Alps*) It must be borne in mind that guiding too is an art.

†**b.** (See quot. Cf. GUIDAGE 1.) *Obs. rare*$^{-1}$.

1681 W. ROBERTSON *Phraseol. Gen.* (1693) 693 Guidings, i.e. money given for false guidance and conduct.

†**2.** The conducting or ruling of oneself, behaviour, conduct; *pl.* doings, 'goings-on'. Chiefly *Sc. Obs.*

c **1460** G. ASHBY *Dicta Philos.* 177 Poems 51 A kynge sholde knowe al his owne seruantes, Their rule, ther gidyng and condicion. **1500–20** DUNBAR *Poems* xix. 41, I wald my gyding war diwysit; Gif I spend littill I am despysit. **1508** —— *Tua mariit wemen* 451 Wise women has wayis, and wonderfull gydingis. **1567** *Satir. Poems Reform.* vii. 215 God maid hir paine aggre with hir guyding. **1572** *Ibid.* xxxiv. 12 Thair lyfis and guydingis ar detest.

3. *attrib.*, as ***guiding-rod***, ***-staff***; **guiding-stick**, an artist's mahl stick.

1607 DEKKER *Whore Babylon* Wks. 1873 II. 270 On each leader Bestowe a guiding-staffe. **1857** W. SMITH *Thorndale* v. iii, Clarence..steps out from behind his easel, and with his guiding-stick in his hand by way of wand, unveils to me the programme of the Future. **1885** E. C. AGASSIZ *Life Louis Agassiz* II. 614 Nemesis wields rather a guiding-rod than a scourge.

guiding ('gaɪdɪŋ), *ppl. a.* [f. GUIDE *v.* + -ING[2].]

a. That guides, in the senses of the vb.

1601 SHAKS. *All's Well* II. iii. 111, I giue Me and my seruice..Into your guiding power. **1671** MILTON *Samson* 1 A little onward lend thy guiding hand To these dark steps. *a* **1691** FLAVEL *Sea-Deliverances* (1754) 166 The guiding usefulness of it [the sun] to us. **176.** COWPER *To Miss Macartney* 95 So may your guiding angel give Whate'er you wish or love. **1856** BAGEHOT *Coll. Works* (1965) I. 362 When we had learned the great landmarks, understood the guiding-stars, we might amuse ourselves with small points. **1865** DICKENS *Mut. Fr.* I. vii, It being one of Wegg's guiding rules in life. **1875** JOWETT *Plato* (ed. 2) III. 97 Good is to become the guiding principle of politics. **1899** LECKY *Map of Life* xvii. 328 The great guiding landmarks of a wise life. **1900** *Q. Rev.* Jan. 73 He [Goethe] has been a sort of guiding star to them. **1961** A. O. J. COCKSHUT *Imagination of Charles Dickens* x. 141 Here Dickens's sense of the superiority of life to fact, which is the guiding star of the novel, up to this point, seems ironically to have deserted him. **1962** *Daily Tel.* 11 Jan. 1/1 'Guiding light' on pay rises. *Ibid.*, A 'guiding light' figure, about 2½ per cent., which unions and employers would be expected to accept.

b. *Coal-mining.* ***guiding-bed*** (see quot.).

1883 GRESLEY *Gloss. Coal-mining, Guiding Bed*, a thin band or seam of coal, &c., in a nip leading to the regular seam on either side of it.

c. ***guiding telescope***: a visual telescope fixed rigidly to a photographic telescope so that the latter may be 'guided' manually to follow the course of a star, etc., kept under observation during an exposure.

1897 A. H. MILES *Concise Knowl. Astron.* II. xv. 195 In the guiding telescope are two spider threads at right angles to each other, and it is by constantly keeping the image of a star at the intersection of these 'wires' that the operator ensures the images remaining in a constant position upon the sensitive plate. **1945** DIMITROFF & BAKER *Telescopes & Accessories* vii. 252 It is not advisable to use as a guiding telescope one whose aperture is less than one half of that used in the photographic telescope. **1959** T. RACKHAM *Astron. Photogr. at Telescope* iv. 68 It has long been the custom to mount a short focal length wide aperture camera on a larger telescope of greater focal length and, using the latter as a guiding telescope, make long exposures at the night sky. **1959** *Listener* 22 Jan. 162/1 The 50-inch reflector does not possess a separate guiding telescope.

guidlin(g, obs. Sc. form of GULDEN.

guidon ('gaɪdən). Forms: 6 guyd home, guyd(e)home, 7 guid(e)home, (6 guydion, guidone, guydone, 7 guidhim), 6–7 guydon, 6– guidon. [a. F. *guidon*, ad. It. *guidone*, perh. connected with *guida* GUIDE *sb.* (Cf. GETON.)

Some of the 16th c. forms are due to popular etymology, the word being interpreted as if it were F. **guide-homme* guider of men (cf. the 18th c. F. *guid'âne* 'guide-ass', handbook for the ignorant).]

1. A flag or pennant, broad at the end next the staff and forked or pointed at the other. It is the standard now used by dragoon regiments.

In U.S., a flag borne by a troop of cavalry or mounted battery; also used as a marking or signalling flag.

1548 HALL *Chron., Hen. VIII* (1809) 551 Sir Ihon Peche had his guyd home taken and diuers of his men hurt. *Ibid.* 830 After them followed the Dromes & fyffes and immediatly after them a Guydon of the Armes of the citie. **1577–87** HOLINSHED *Chron.* III. 1215/1 His lordship..with his owne standard, and the lord of Hunnesdons guidon, marched forward. **1598** BARRET *Theor. Warres* V. ii. 143 In their middle troupes is the Guidon placed. **1602** SEGAR *Hon. Mil. & Civ.* II. x. 69 The King or Generall shall cause the Points of his Pennon or Guydon to be rent off. **1603** DRAYTON *Bar. Wars* II. xxiv, The Noble Percy..With a bright Cressant in his Guidehome came. **1615** G. SANDYS *Trav.* 84 The Greeke kings then With guidons trail'd on earth, led forth their men In seven troupes. **1685** F. SPENCE tr. *Varillas' Ho. Medicis* 372 He was seen as a Knight of Rhodes carrying the great Guidon of St. John of Jerusalem. **1687** A. LOVELL tr. *Thevenot's Trav.* I. 160 Every Trooper having a green Guidon on the top of his Pike. **1722** *Lond. Gaz.* No. 6084/4 The Guidon on a Lance. **1844** *Regul. & Ord. Army* 10 The Guidons of Regiments of Dragoons are to be of Silk. **1863** KINGLAKE *Crimea* II. 250 Marshal St. Arnaud, whose guidon was seen coming towards our lines. **1890** ELIZ. B. CUSTER *Following the Guidon* Pref. 13 The present cavalry guidon is a small United States flag sharply swallow-tailed, and mounted on a standard with a metal point so that it can be thrust into the ground when in use as a marker.

attrib. **1581** SAVILE *Tacitus' Hist.* III. xvii. (1591) 124 With his lance he [Antonius] ranne thorow a guidon bearer.

b. 'The flag of a guild or fraternity' (Webster 1864).

2. An officer who carries such a standard.

1591 SPARRY tr. *Cattan's Geomancie* (1599) 41 Of many it is called the Guidon or Ensigne-bearer of the times. **1622** F. MARKHAM *Bk. War* III. i. 83 The Cornet or Guydon is the same that the Ensigne on foot is. **1658** PHILLIPS, *Guidon*, a Cornet of Argolatiers that serve on hors-back with Petronels. **1699** LUTTRELL *Brief Rel.* (1857) IV. 521 The lord Lovelace is made guidon of the horse guards. **1728** MORGAN *Algiers* II. v. 300 The Turkish Horse pursued them..killing the guidon, or Standard-bearer. **1779** G. SMITH *Milit. Dict.*, *Guidon*, an officer in troops of horse-guards who ranks as Major. **1880** O'FLANAGAN *Munster Circuit* 3 He had his Captain, and Guidon, and Trumpeter.

†**3.** A company, troop. *Obs.*

1560 DAUS tr. *Sleidane's Comm.* 226 Eyght guydons of horsemen. **1610** HOLLAND *Camden's Brit.* I. 76 The Count ..had..two guidons of horsemen.

4. *Mus.* A direct.

1811 BUSBY *Dict. Mus.* (ed. 3). **1825** DANNELEY *Encycl. Mus.*

Guidonian (gwɪ'dəʊnɪən), *a. Mus.* [f. *Guidon-*, taken as the stem of *Guido* (see below) + -IAN.] Of or pertaining to the Italian musician Guido d'Arezzo (11th c.), the reputed inventor of the system of hexachords. ***Guidonian hand*** (see quot. 1811).

1721 A. MALCOLM *Treat. Mus.* xiv. 558 Thus far go the Improvements of Guido Aretinus, and what is called the Guidonian System. **1811** BUSBY *Dict. Mus.* (ed. 3), *Guidonian hand*, the figure of the left-hand with the syllabic signs of the intervals of the three hexachords, instituted by Guido, marked on the joints of the fingers. **1889** W. S. ROCKSTRO in Grove *Dict. Mus.* IV. 660 The Harmonic or Guidonian Hand.

guierie: see GUERIE.

guigaw, obs. form of GEWGAW.

‖**guige** (giʒ). *Hist.* Also 5 gyge. [ME. *gyge*, a. OF. *guige*, which has been re-adopted by recent antiquaries.] (See quot. 1834.)

c **1386** [perh. implied in GIGGE *v.*]. *c* **1450** *Merlin* 195 He.. kyutte the gyge of the shelde with all the arme so that he dide it falle in-to the felde. *Ibid.* 496 He smote Pindolus on the sholdre that he kutte the gige that the shelde henge by. **1834** PLANCHÉ *Brit. Costume* 61 These shields [*temp.* William Conq.], besides the holders..had a long strip of leather which went round the neck and formed an additional support for it..This extra strap was called the guige. **1864** BOUTELL *Heraldry Hist. & Pop.* xvii. 277 An imperial eagle holds in his beak the guige of the shield. **1878** J. MACKINTOSH *Hist. Civiliz. Scot.* I. IV. 272 It is suspended in front of the body by a guige.

Guignet's green ('giːɲeɪz griːn). [f. the name of C. E. *Guignet* (b. 1829), French chemist, who discovered and patented it in 1859.] A green pigment, consisting chiefly or wholly of hydrated chromic oxide, which gives a bright, transparent, very fast colour and is used esp. in high-quality paints and printing inks; = VIRIDIAN.

1862 C. O'NEILL *Dict. Calico Printing* 52/2 A pigment green, which is an oxide of chromium,..known as Guignets' [*sic*] green, is obtained by making an intimate mixture of about three parts of boracic acid with one part of bichromate. **1876** *Encycl. Brit.* IV. 51/1 A very beautiful pigment, now much used in calico-printing, under the name of Guignet's green, is a borate of chromium. **1920** F. A MASON tr. *von Georgievics's Text-bk. Dye Chem.* (ed. 2) 541

Frequently Guignet's Green itself is termed Permanent Green when used for chromolithography, bank-note printing, etc. though not in calico printing. **1967** *Introd. Paint Technol.* (Oil & Colour Chemists' Assoc.) (ed. 2) v. 93 The hydrated oxide (Viridian or Guignet's Green) is bright but transparent.

Guignol (giɲɔl, giːˈnjɒl). [see GRAND GUIGNOL.] **a.** = GRAND GUIGNOL. **b.** A Punch and Judy show. Hence **guigno'lesque** *a.* and *sb.*

1882 G. MEREDITH *Let.* 8 Sept. (1970) II. 671, I think you would have been impressed by the Guignol, or rather by an episode in the career of Polichinelle. **1919** G. B. SHAW *Great Catherine* Pref. 114 They were great sentimental comedians, these Peters, Elizabeths and Catherines who played their Tsarships as eccentric character parts... Catherine kept this vast Guignol Theatre open for nearly half a century. **1923** J. M. MURRAY *Pencillings* 205 Molière's attitude to life 'reminds him too often of the attitude of *Punch*'—not the famous figure of Guignol, I imagine, but our own comic weekly. **1935** *Punch* 17 Apr. 440/1, I think the truth is that here are three clever portraits woven into a length of strong Guignol with the ends left loose. **1953** J. Y. COUSTEAU *Silent World* 26 Inspired by the camera he enacted fantasies. He leaned down dramatically and clutched a red starfish to his breast. We 'filmed' long sequences of his underwater *guignol.* **1957** *Listener* 18 July 101/1 The Roman ghost in a Senecan shroud stalked through the guignolesque sensationalism of the minor Jacobeans. *Ibid.* 3 Oct. 513/1 Guignol, the French Punch and Judy shows. **1964** C. WILDMAN tr. E. Ionesco in *Listener* 24 Dec. 1002/1 *Ionesco*: I was in the gardens of the Tuileries or the Luxembourg, and I saw the *Guignol. Wildman*: Punch and Judy! They are violent too! *Ionesco*: Indeed. After that, I've always sought the guignolesque, in other words, an extremely schematic, simplified, elemental and caricatural type of theatre... A kind of theatre very close to Jarry. In *Ubu-Roi*, Jarry wrote a play which is guignolesque.

guild, gild (gɪld). Forms: α. 1 **ȝyld, ȝild, ȝeȝyld,** 3–4 **ȝild,** 4–6 **yelde,** 5 **ȝeld,** 5–6 **yeld,** 6 **yeald,** 7 **yeelde,** 8 *dial.* **yild-.** β. 4–6 **gyld(e,** 4–7 **gilde,** 5 **gyylde, geld-,** 6 **gelde, gyeld, guilde, guylde,** 5– **gild,** 7– **guild.** [Several distinct formations from the same Teut. root have here coalesced. (1) The forms within initial 3, *y* prob. represent mainly OE. *ȝild, ȝyld,* (*ȝield*) str. neut., recorded only twice in this sense, but frequent in the senses 'payment, compensation, offering, sacrifice, worship, idol'; corresp. to OFris. *geld, ield* money, OS. *geld* payment, sacrifice, reward, OHG. *gelt* payment, offering, tribute, money (Du., G. *geld,* money), ON. *giald* payment, Goth. *gild* tribute:—OTeut. **geldo*m. (2) OE. had also *ȝeȝyld* str. neut., where the prefix *ȝe-* (see Y- *prefix*) expresses the notion of combined or collective action. This has not been found later than OE., but as the prefix *ȝe-* regularly disappeared in substantives (cf. *reeve*) its representative in the 14th c. would coincide with that of the simple *ȝyld.* (3) The pronunciation with (g) must be due to adoption of, or influence from, the ON. *gildi* str. neut. guild, guild-feast, banquet, also payment, value (Sw. *gille,* Da. *gilde* guild):—OTeut. **gildjo*m.

In continental Teut. the sense of 'guild' was expressed by a fourth formation from the same root, repr. OTeut. type **gildjôn-* wk. fem., and occurring as MLG., MDu. *gilde* fem. and neut. (Du *gild*), whence mod.G. *gilde*; in Carolingian Latin the word appears as *geldonia, gildonia,* explained by *confraternitas*; the later med.Lat. form is *gilda*; OF. had *gilde, ghelde, gheude, jode,* etc., in the senses 'guild, band of foot-soldiers.'

The root **geld-* in these derivatives is prob. to be taken in the sense 'to pay, contribute', so that the sb. would primarily mean an association of persons contributing money for some common object. As, however, the root also means 'to sacrifice, worship', some have supposed that guilds were so called as being combinations for religious purposes, heathen or Christian.

The sense 'member of a guild, guild-brother', was expressed by OE. *ȝylda* and *ȝeȝylda,* MLG. *gilde* wk. masc.; the Teut. word appears in med.L. as *gildō* (also *congildō, congilda*), and in OF. *gelde, geldon* (with many variants), one of a company (*gelde*) of foot-soldiers.]

1. A confraternity, brotherhood, or association formed for the mutual aid and protection of its members, or for the prosecution of some common purpose.

a. *Primarily* applied to associations of mediæval origin.

The guilds mentioned in OE. pre-Conquest documents fulfilled much the same functions as modern burial and benefit societies, but their objects included the providing of masses for the souls of deceased members, and the payment of *wergild* in cases of justifiable homicide. They had always originally a strong religious element in their constitution. Their meetings were app. usually convivial (cf. ON. *gildi* banquet, GUILD-ALE, and quot. *a* 1109 below). In later times the guilds of this 'social-religious' type underwent development in various directions; some becoming purely religious confraternities, while others acquired secular rights and privileges, eventually developing into municipal corporations.

The ***guild of merchants, merchant guild*** (or ***guild merchant,*** late OE. *cēapmanna ȝild*), an incorporated society of the merchants of a town or city, having exclusive rights of trading within the town, is an institution which in England has not been found before the Conquest; on the Continent the name and thing were older. In many English towns, and in the royal burghs of Scotland, the merchant guild became the governing body of the town; in Scotland the name of 'guild' is still preserved (cf. *dean of guild* s.v. DEAN).

The ***trade guilds,*** which in England come into prominence in the 14th c., were associations of persons exercising the same craft, formed for the purpose of protecting and promoting their common interests. In some towns the representatives of these bodies superseded the older organizations as the municipal authority. The trade guilds are historically represented in London by the Livery Companies, but these are not ordinarily known as guilds, and retain little of their original functions. The trade guilds of mediæval Europe closely resemble the ancient Roman *collegia,* with which they may perh. have been historically connected.

? *a* **1000** *Abbotsbury Charter* in Kemble *Cod. Dipl.* IV. 279 Forðan ðe we for his lufon þis ȝeȝyld ȝegaderodon. *a* **1109** in Gross *Gild Merch.* (1890) II. 37 Ðis beoð þa ȝehworfe betwux ðan hirede æt Xrescircean and þan cnihtan on Cantwareberig of ceapmanne ȝilde. Se heap on ceapmanne ȝilde let [etc.]. *a* **1109** ANSELM *Epist.* II. vi, De domno Henrico, qui camerarius fuit, audio quia in multis inordinate se agit, et maxime in bibendo; ita ut in Gildis cum ebriosis bibat, et cum eis inebrietur. *a* **1189** *Charter of Hen. II to Lincoln* in Rymer *Fœdera* (1816) I. 40 Sciatis me concessisse civibus meis Lincolniae omnes libertates, & consuetudines, & leges suas, quas habuerunt tempore Edwardi & Willelmi, & Henrici, Regum Angliæ, & gildam suam mercatoriam de hominibus civitatis & de aliis mercatoribus comitatus, sicut illam habuerunt tempore prædictorum antecessorum nostrorum, Regum Angliæ melius & liberius. **1190** *Charter of Rich. I to Winchester* ibid. 50 Sciatis nos concessisse civibus nostris Wintoniae de gilda mercatorum, quod nullus eorum placitet extra muros civitatis Wintoniae de ullo placito preter placita de tenuris exterioribus, exceptis monetariis & ministris nostris. *c* **1205** LAY. 32001 Ʒilden he gon rere. *c* **1330** R. BRUNNE *Chron. Wace* (Rolls) 14746 Þey hadde wel leuere.. Þat þe lond were in partis leyd Þan þe Anglys of þe out ildes Schulde be chef of alle þer gyldes. **1389** in *Eng. Gilds* (1870) 19 Alle ye bretheren & sisteren of yis gilde shul comen togeder to ye paroche chirche. *Ibid.* 37 Þe ordenaunces of þe gilde of Carpenteris. *c* **1430** LYDG. *Min. Poems* (1840) 207 Let mellerys and bakerys gadre hem a gilde. **1442** *Extracts Aberd. Reg.* (1844) I. 397 It was statut and ordanit be the brethir of gilde, that [etc.]. **1467** in *Eng. Gilds* (1870) 377 Also it ys ordeyned by this present yeld, that [etc.]. **1544** *Supplic. Hen. VIII* (1871) 42 Prestes of gyldes and of fraternytees. **1600** HOLLAND *Livy* v. lii. (1609) 213 Thereto we have ordeined and founded a new Guild or Fraternitie. **1726** MADOX *Firma Burgi* 24 The Religious Gilds were founded chiefly for Devotion and Almsdeeds; the Secular chiefly for Trade and Almsdeeds. *Ibid.* 26 Anciently, a Gild either Religious or Secular could not legally be set-up without the Kings Licence. **1838** PRESCOTT *Ferd. & Is.* Introd. (1846) I. 25 The several crafts, whose members were incorporated into guilds. **1873** L. O. PIKE *Hist. Crime* I. 178 There were at least as early as the twelfth century guilds of weavers in London, Oxford, York [etc.]. **1874** GREEN *Short Hist.* i §1. 5 Industry was checked by a system of trade guilds which confined each occupation to an hereditary caste.

b. Used in the names of various modern associations, with more or less notion of imitating the mediæval guilds in their object, spirit, or constitution.

1827 HONE *Every-day Bk.* II. 670 In 1817 colonel.. Mason.. established a guild or festival for rural sports. **1876** (*title*) Guild of the Holy Cross, Holywell. Constitution, Rules & Office. **1877** RUSKIN *Fors Clav.* VII. 231, I have written to our solicitors that they may register us under the title of St. George's Guild. **1890** (*title*) Transactions of the Guild & School of Handicraft. **1895** *Whitaker's Almanack* 283/1 Church Choir Guild. *Ibid.* 286/1 Guild of Organists. *Ibid.* 289/2 Teachers' Guild of Great Britain and Ireland. **1900** *Offic. Year-bk. Ch. Eng.* 116 The Church and Stage Guild.. is a Society for getting rid of the prejudices of religious people against the stage.

c. *transf.* A company or fellowship of any kind.

1630 B. JONSON *Chloridia* A 4 Cupid hath ta'ne offence of late At all the Gods, that he was so deserted, Not to be call'd into their Guild But slightly pass'd by, as a child. **1728** POPE *Dunc.* II. 250 When the long-ear'd milky mothers.. For their defrauded, absent foals.. make A moan so loud, that all the guild awake. **1817** COLERIDGE *Biog. Lit.* 68 Their names had never been enrolled in the guilds of the learned. **1871** B. TAYLOR *Faust* (1875) II. II. iii. 122, I like her best of all the guild of Sibyls.

†**2.** The place of meeting of a guild. Also, the building in which a religious guild or fraternity lived.

? *a* **1000** *Abbotsbury Charter* in Kemble *Cod. Dipl.* IV. 278 Se ȝylda þe oðerne misgret innan ȝylde.. ȝebete he [etc.]. **1546** *Suppl. Poor Commons* (1871) 75 Building of abayse, churches, chauntries, gyldes. **1590** SPENSER *F.Q.* II. vii. 43 The rowme was large and wyde, As it some gyeld or solemne temple weare. **1602** WARNER *Alb. Eng.* XII. lxxiii. (1612) 301 The Capitol, where wont their Guild to bee. **1609** SKENE *Reg. Mag., Stat. Gild* 142 Gif any of our brether does wrang or injurie be word to ane other brother.. in comming to the Gild. **1644** EVELYN *Mem.* (1857) I. 109 Halls and guilds (as we call them) of sundry companies.

¶**3.** Used to render OE. *ȝielda* guild-brother.

1605 VERSTEGAN *Dec. Intell.* viii. (1628) 258 For shortnes of speech a Gild brother was also called a Gild.

4. *attrib.* and *Comb.*, as ***guild-bell, -court, -day, -due, -house, -land, -man, -master, -order, -priest, -rent, -silver, -steward;*** **guild-mercatory** [ad. med.L. *gilda mercatoria*], **guild merchant** [MERCHANT *a.*] (see 1 a); **guild-rent,** rent payable to the Crown by a guild; **guild-socialism,** an economic system by which the profits, resources, and methods of each industry are to be controlled by a council of its members, on the model of mediæval guilds; so **guild socialist; guild-wine,** ? wine drunk at festivals of the guild; **guild-wite,** a fine levied by a guild. Also GUILD-ALE, GUILD-BROTHER, GUILD-HALL.

1555 *Ludlow Churchw. Acc.* (Camden) 61 The claper of the *yeld belle. **1870** BRENTANO *Gilds* 97 The citizens.. mustered at the call of the Gild-bell. **1449** *Extracts Aberd. Reg.* (1844) I. 402 At he inquir and accuse sic forstalling ilke xv daiis in the *gilde courte. **1525** *Ibid.* 112 The haill toun.. on the gild curt day, all in ane voce.. obleist thame [etc.]. **1583** in W. Maitland *Hist. Edin.* (1753) 233 The Dene of Gild may assemble his Brether and Counsell in their Gild Courts. **1827** in E. H. Barker *Parriana* (1828) I. 245 The *Guild-day.. is a high day at Norwich. **1849** ROCK *Ch. of Fathers* II. 403 Regularly paying his *gild-dues for the space of seven years. **1870** *Eng. Gilds* Introd. 33 They met in good fellowship at the *Gild-house. **1752** CARTE *Hist. Eng.* III. 215 Their *guild-lands should be restored to them. **1896** *Westm. Gaz.* 31 Oct. 1/2 The preacher.. held up Nehemiah to the *guildmen as an admirable specimen of a Church reformer. **1782** PENNANT *Journ. Chester to Lond.* 114 It [Lichfield] was originally governed by a guild and *guild-master. **1656** D. KING *Vale Royal, Chester* II. 157 Before the said City had any Charter they.. enjoyed a *Guild Mercatory. **1862** DOBSON & HARLAND *Hist. Preston Guild* 72 The original grant of a Guild mercatory, with Hanse, &c., seems to have been made by Henry II. **1467** in *Eng. Gilds* (1870) 376 Ordinaunces.. made.. by hole assent of the citesens inhabitantes in the Cyte of Worcester, at their *yeld marchaunt. **1682** *Lond. Gaz.* No. 1743/4 The Guild-Merchant for the Borough of Preston. **1706** PHILLIPS (ed. Kersey), *Gild-Merchant,* a Privilege whereby Merchants may hold Pleas of Land among themselves. **1844** STEPHEN *Blackstone* III. 190 These persons were also authorized to have a guild merchant. **1873** L. O. PIKE *Hist. Crime* I. 64 The guild merchant.. is difficult to distinguish from the town-corporation. **1890** GROSS *Gild Merch.* II. 201 The companies then have their *guild-orders sealed. **1849** ROCK *Ch. Fathers* II. 340 This done, the *gild-priest arose. **1670** *Act 22 Chas. II,* c. 6 §1 Fee-Farme Rents,.. Chauntry Rents, Rents reserved, *Guild Rents, Pensions [etc.]. **1890** GROSS *Gild Merch.* I. 195 The 'customa mercatorum', called '*gild-silver', at Henley. **1912** *New Age* 10 Oct. 560/2 Unless we can prove the practicality of *Guild Socialism, and so attract the practical man, we admit that we are preparing for a moral catastrophe. **1913** C. BOOTH *Industr. Unrest* 16 The Guild Socialists in England occupy middle ground between Syndicalist and Socialist. *Ibid.* 21 Syndicalism, Guild Socialism, and State Socialism hold no terms with each other. **1915** D. H. LAWRENCE *Let.* 27 Dec. (1932) 300 That is why we are *bound* to get something like Guild-Socialism in the long run. **1919** G. D. H. COLE *Guild Socialism* (1920) 4 The desire of the Guild Socialist is.. to convert the Socialist Movement as well as the Trade Union Movement to its point of view. *Ibid.* 5, I do not pretend.. that Guild Socialism is the right way for all the peoples of the world to tackle their economic problems. **1930** *Times Lit. Suppl.* 26 June 521/3 Back to nature is his [*sc.* the reformer's] cry, back to the land,.. back to the Middle Ages and guild-socialism. **1952** V. A. DEMANT *Religion & Decl. Capitalism* ii. 54 The condemnation of proletarianism was taken up later by the Guild Socialists who numbered many churchmen and who unsuccessfully sought to divert British labour from state collectivism to the recovery of authentic artisan status through industrial corporations. **1696** *Lond. Gaz.* No. 3175/3 The *Guild-Stewards, Burgesses, and other the Inhabitants of the Borough of Calne. **1597** *Extracts Aberd. Reg.* (1848) II. 155 Of ilk ane, four pundis for his *gild wyne. **1870** *Eng. Gilds* 185 If it is found by his bretheren that he had no guest, but stayed at home through idleness, he shall be in the '*Gildwyt' of half a bushel of barley. **1890** GROSS *Gild Merch.* I. 195 The 'gildwite', extorted by the gild of Lincoln from merchants passing near that city.

guild, obs. f. GILD *v.*[1] and [2], and of GOLD[2].

guildable: see GILDABLE.

†**guild-ale.** *Obs.* [OE. **ȝield-ealo*; cf. *bride-ale,* BRIDAL.] (See quots.)

1240 *Synod of Worcester* xxxviii. in Du Cange s.v. *Gild-ales,* Ne intersint [clerici] ludis inhonestis, nec sustineant ludos fieri di Rege et Regina.. nec Gildales inhonestas. **1706** PHILLIPS (ed. Kersey), *Gildale,* a Compotation or Drinking-Match, when every one paid his Club or Share.

†**'guildate,** *v. Obs. rare.* [f. GUILD + -ATE[3].] *trans.* To combine or form into a guild.

1726 MADOX *Firma Burgi* 27 Peradventure, from these Secular Gilds.. sprang the method or practice of gildating and embodying whole Towns. *Ibid.* 200 He.. used a certain Trade or Craft called Lynnenweverscraft, which was never incorporated or gildated.

guild-brother. A member of a guild.

1382 in *Eng. Gilds* (1870) 57 Ye den xal.. warnen alle ye gylde breyeren yt ben in toune. *c* **1470** HENRYSON *Mor. Fab.* 172 in *Anglia* IX. 348 The vther mous.. Was gild-brother and maid ane fre burges. **1583** in W. Maitland *Hist. Edin.* (1753) 233 Alsweill Craftsmen as Merchands sall be receivit and admittit Gild-brother. **1690** *Def. Dr. G. Walker* 12 Collonel.. Walker.. is admitted and received Burgess and Gild-Brother of the foresaid City of Glasgow. **1771** SMOLLETT *Humph. Cl.* 8 Aug., The 'good town of Edinburgh', of which we are become free denizens and guild brothers. **1828** SCOTT *F.M. Perth* xx, Those who occupied the higher seats were merchants, that is, guild brethren. **1872** E. W. ROBERTSON *Hist. Ess.* 154 The Guild-brethren instead of the kindred, became responsible for the wergild.

guilde, obs. variant of GOLD[2].

guilder (ˈgɪldə(r)). Forms: 5 **guldren,** 6 **gild(e)r(e)n, gylder, gelder,** 6–8 **gilder,** 7– **guilder.** [An English corrupted pronunciation of Du. *gulden*: see GULDEN.] **a.** A gold coin formerly current in the Netherlands and parts of Germany. **b.** A Dutch silver coin, worth in 1900 about 1*s.* 8*d.* English.

c **1481** CAXTON *Dialogues* v. 17 Rynnysh guldrens. **1542** UDALL *Erasm. Apoph.* 197 b, The same for euery good verse that he made should receiue a philippes gildren. **1547** BOORDE *Introd. Knowl.* xi. 153 In gold they haue Clemers gylders and golden gilders, and gelders arerys. **1590** SHAKS. *Com. Err.* IV. i. 4, I am bound To Persia, and want Gilders for my voyage. **1622** FLETCHER *Burning Bush* I. ii, Two hundred chests, valued by you At thirty thousand Gilders. **1691** LOCKE *Money* Wks. 1727 II. 46 Guilders is the Denomination that in Holland they usually compute by, and make their Contracts in. **1709** ADDISON *Tatler* No. 20 ¶7 Tradesmen, who, after their Day's Work is over, earn about a Gilder a Night by personating Kings and Generals. **1756-7** tr. *Keysler's Trav.* (1760) IV. 121 The hire and keeping of a horse from Trieste to Fiume comes to three Rhenish guilders. **1777** WATSON *Philip II* (1839) 265 The damage..was estimated at six hundred thousand guilders. **1842** BROWNING *Pied Piper* ix, A thousand guilders! The Mayor looked blue. **1872** YEATS *Growth Comm.* 368 The gold guilders coined in the fourteenth century in Hungary and the Rhine regions.

guilder rose, obs. form of GUELDER ROSE.

guild-hall. (Stress level or variable.) Forms: see GUILD and HALL. The hall in which a guild met. From its use as a meeting-place for the town and corporation often synonymous with 'town-hall'; *spec.* (spelt *Guildhall*), the hall of the Corporation of the City of London, used for municipal meetings, state banquets, etc.

?*a* **1000** in Kemble *Cod. Dipl.* IV. 277 Orcy hæfð ȝeȝyfen þæ ȝeȝyld healle..þam ȝyldscipe to aȝenne. **1382** in *10th Rep. Hist. MSS. Comm.* App. v. 292 In the Gyldhal of the citie of Watirforde. *c* **1386** CHAUCER *Prol.* 370 Wel semed ech of hem a fair burgeys To sitten in a yeldehalle on a deys. *a* **1400** *Pistill of Susan* 293 Aȝein to þe ȝild-halle [*v.rr.* geld-, gilde-, gylde-halle] þe gomes vn-greiþ. **1467** in *Eng. Gilds* (1870) 387 Also, that no maner persone pleye at the pame or at tenys, withyn the yeld halle of the seid cite. **1530** WRIOTHESLEY *Chron.* (1875) I. 16 There dyned in the Guylde hall at the said feast the Lorde Chauncellor. **1556** *Chron. Gr. Friars* (Camden) 85 Condemnyd at the yeldehalle for hye tresone. **1594** SHAKS. *Rich. III*, III. v. 73 The Maior towards Guild-Hall hyes him in all poste. **1598** STOW *Surv.* 217 William Hariot Draper Mayor 1481. gave 40. pound to the making of two louers in the said Guildhal. **1629** MAXWELL tr. *Herodian* (1635) 135 All the Citizens, utterly forsaking Iulian, assembled in the Guild-hall [*margin* συνέδριον] by command of the Consuls. **1728** POPE *Dunc.* I. 270 This the Great Mother dearer held than all..her own Guildhall. **1765** BLACKSTONE *Comm.* I. 473 Their place of meeting is frequently called the Gild-hall. **1797** *Encycl. Brit.* X. 243/1 The lord-mayor elect..is soon after presented to the lord-chancellor..; and on the 9th of November following is sworn into the office of mayor at Guildhall. **1830** H. THOMAS *City of London* I. 423 At the northern extremity of King Street in Guildhall yard, the north side of which is occupied by the principal front of the Guildhall or common hall of the corporation of London. **1873** L. O. PIKE *Hist. Crime* I. 64 The Guild-hall of the burgesses of Dover. **1965** C. TRENT *Greater London* xvi. 264 The rebuilding of the City is far from complete but the skyline has changed out of all recognition since 1945... The Guildhall has been rebuilt, many new fine blocks of offices have appeared.

guildic ('gɪldɪk), *a.* [f. GUILD *sb.* + -IC.] Of or pertaining to a guild.

1881 G. S. HALL *German Culture* 39 It [the Passion Play] is eminently national, although it is animated by the old guildic local spirit.

†**'guildive.** *Obs. rare*⁻¹. [Fr.; it has been said to be a corruption of the Eng. West-Indian name *kill-devil*.] (See quot.)

1698 FROGER *Voy.* 58 Canes, of which the finest sugar is made; and also a kind of very strong Brandy, which we call Guildive.

guildry ('gɪldrɪ). *Sc.* Also 6 gildrie, 9 gildry. [f. GUILD + -RY.]

1. The municipal corporation of any one of the royal burghs of Scotland, historically representing the ancient Guild Merchant.

1583 in W. Maitland *Hist. Edin.* (1753) 233 Conforme to the ancient Laws of the Gildrie, and Priviledges theirof. **1775** L. SHAW *Hist. Moray* (1827) 240 Earl Thomas.. confirmed King Alexander's charter of Guildry. **1815** *Chron.* in *Ann. Reg.* 88/2 The Fraternity of Guildry of Dumfernline. **1823** SCOTT *Quentin D.* xxi, Could I get some of the tight lads of our guildry together. **1836** *Penny Cycl.* V. 221/1 The guildry which appears in Scotland to have always designated properly an association of merchants. **1890** GROSS *Gild Merch.* I. 202 The Gild Merchant or Gildry of Scotch towns first comes to view in the reign of David I. **1897** LD. ROSEBERY in *Observer* 10 Oct. 5/4 The Guildry of Stirling..might then be called an unreformed corporation.

†**2.** The privilege of being a member of the guild.

1583 in W. Maitland *Hist. Edin.* (1753) 234 The Dewtie payit to the Dean of Gild for his Burgeship or Gildrie, which is Twenty Punds for his Burgeship, and Fourtie Pund for his Gildrie.

guildship ('gɪldʃɪp). [OE. *ȝieldscipe*: see GUILD and -SHIP.]

1. = GUILD I.

a **1000** *Canons of Edgar* c. 9 Þæt nan preosta oðrum ne ætdo ænig þara þinga þe him to-ȝebiriȝe ne on his mynstre ne on his scrift-scipe ne on his ȝildscipe. *a* **1000** in Thorpe *Diplomat.* (1865) 608/30 An ȝildscipe is ȝegaderod on Wudeburȝ lande. **1835** SOAMES *Anglo-Sax. Ch.* 282 The Guild-ship, as every such confederacy was vernacularly called, proposed an interchange of masses for the benefit of each other. **1849** ROCK *Ch. of Fathers* II. vii. 397 This loaf was offered by two brethren of the gildship. **1870** *Eng. Gilds* Introd. 17 Ordinances for the keeping up of social duties in the Gilds, or Gild-ships as they are called, of London.

2. The status and privileges of a guildsman, membership of a guild.

1844 LINGARD *Anglo-Sax. Ch.* (1858) II. ix. 57 The more celebrated monasteries offered Guildships of a superior description. **1870** *Eng. Gilds* 183 Whoever will not obey the judgement of the bretheren shall lose his gildship. **1890** GROSS *Gild Merch.* I. 62 The relation of the gildship to burgess-ship.

guildsman ('gɪldzmən). [f. *guild's*, genitive of GUILD + MAN; cf. *craftsman, tradesman.*] A member of a guild. So **'guildswoman** (*nonce-wd.*).

1873 L. O. PIKE *Hist. Crime* I. 378 A guildsman of the latter kind. **1877** RUSKIN *Fors Clav.* VII. No. 80. 231 The members of the Guild shall be called St. George's Guildsmen and Guildswomen. **1891** F. A. HIBBERT *Eng. Gilds* 156 There could no longer be any invidious distinction between freemen and non-freemen..gildsmen and tensers.

guile (gaɪl), *sb.* Forms: 3-6 gile, 3-7 gyle, (4 gil, *Sc.* ghyle, gule), 4-5 gyl, 5 gyll(e, (gilee), 5-6 guyle, 4- guile. [a. OF. *guile* = Pr. *guila*, Pg. *guilha*; presumably of Teut. origin, but no certain etymon is known, as the late OE. *wīl*, occurring only once, may itself be adopted from Fr., and ON. *vél* seems to be inadmissible for phonetic reasons. See WILE *sb.*]

1. Insidious cunning, deceit, treachery.

†*without guile*: in ME. poetry a formula = 'sooth to say'. *a* **1225** *Ancr. R.* 202 Much gile is iðe uoxe. **1297** R. GLOUC. (Rolls) 6332 Hii fondede mid alle gile to do þis luþer dede. **13..** *K. Alis.* 1427 The thridde day, withoute gyle, He aryved at Cysile. **1380** WYCLIF *Wks.* (1880) 387 Neþir was eny gyle founden in his mouþe. **1435** MISYN *Fire of Love* II. ix. 92 Gyl to fulfyll in ther frendys tha schame nott. *c* **1470** HENRY *Wallace* VI. 630 Than rais thai wp, for Wallace dredyt gyll. **1535** COVERDALE *Ps.* xxxii. 2 Blessed is the man, vnto whom the Lorde imputeth no synne, in whose sprete there is no gyle. *a* **1547** SURREY *On Wyatt* 24 With vertue fraught, reposed, voyd of gyle. **1596** DALRYMPLE tr. *Leslie's Hist. Scot.* I. 104 Thay rusche fordward with al thair force vpon the ennimie, nathir throuch fraud and gyle, bot strenth and armes. **1671** MILTON *Samson* 989 Jael, who with inhospitable guile, Smote Sisera sleeping through the Temples nail'd. **1741** RICHARDSON *Pamela* (1824) I. 57 No guile appearing in them, but rather a face of grief. **1813** H. & J. SMITH *Horace in Lond.* 30 Unpractised in a woman's guile, Thou think'st [etc.]. *a* **1834** COLERIDGE *Poems* (1862) 16 Tender, serene and all devoid of guile, Soft is her soul, and sleeping infant's smile. **1852** TENNYSON *Death Wellington* 134 Pure as he from taint of craven guile. **1868** FREEMAN *Norman Conq.* (1876) II. vii. 106 Who nevertheless shrank from the fouler wickedness of slaying a kinsman by guile.

†**2.** With *a* and *pl.* An instance of this; a deceit, stratagem, trick, wile. *Obs.*

a **1225** *Ancr. R.* 12 And don al þet oðer & leten þis nis bute a trukunge & a fals gile. **1297** R. GLOUC. (Rolls) 11151 He let someni an hundred, & þer he hente an gile. **1340** *Ayenb.* 39 To þise zenne belongeþ al þet barat alle ualshedes and alle gyles þet comeþ in plait. *a* **1400** *Sir Perc.* 1034 He was bythoghte of a gyle. **1543** GRAFTON *Contn. Harding* 453 He made towardes hym; and that it should not bee thought to bee a made guyle, sette his hoost in araye as though he would fight. **1545** BRINKLOW *Compl.* 17 How many gyles and suttylteys be there, to auoyde and escape the seruyng the kyngs wrytt. **1609** BIBLE (Douay) *Ps.* xxxvii. 13 They.. spake vanities: and meditated guiles al the day. **1657** AUSTEN *Fruit Trees* I. 139 That they may be caught and taken as by a spirituall guile. **1671** MILTON *P.R.* II. 391, I..count thy specious gifts no gifts but guiles. **1728-46** THOMSON *Spring* 380 While yet the dark-broun water aids the guile, To tempt the trout. **1767** W. L. LEWIS *Statius' Thebaid* IX. 212 Halys she shews to carry on the Guile.

3. *Comb.*: †**guile-bones**, a boys' game ? similar to DIBS; †**guile-man**, one who deals in 'guiles', a deceiver; †**guile-shares**, cheating shares; division of spoils, or shares of wreckage (*Kent. Gloss.*).

1606 *N. Riding Rec.* (1883) I. 49 Walter Parkhurst presented for keping Guile-bones or Ten-bones and other unlawfull games at his house. **1613** W. BROWNE *Sheph. Pipe* I. (1614) C6 Thus wretchedly (lo!) this guile-man dyde. **1723** LEWIS *Isle Tenet* 22 Nothing sure can be more vile and base than under pretence of assisting the distressed Masters [of stranded vessels], and saving theirs and the Merchants goods, to convert them to their own use, by making what they call guile shares.

guile (gaɪl), *v. Obs.* or *arch.* Forms: 3-4 gilen, gylen, 4-5 gile, gyle, 5 gylyn, (4 gily, 5 gyll, 6 guylen), 4- guile. [a. OF. *guile-r* (= Pr. *guilar*), f. *guile* GUILE *sb.* Cf. WILE *v.*] *trans.* To beguile; to deceive.

a **1225** *Ancr. R.* 74 Ȝif eni weneð þat beo religius, & ne bridleð nout his tunge, his religiun is fals; he gileð his heorte. **1303** R. BRUNNE *Handl. Synne* 362 Manyon trowyn on here wylys. And many tymes þe pye hem gylys. **1377** LANG. *P. Pl.* B. xx. 124 With glosynges and with gabbynges he gyled þe peple. **1390** GOWER *Conf.* III. 47 For often he that will beguile Is guiled with the same guile. *c* **1425** *Seven Sag.* (P.) 989 Thorugh thy false clerkis sevene Thou wylt by gylled, by Good in heven! **1468** *Medulla Gram.* in *Cath. Angl.* 156 *note*, *Prestigio*, to tregetyn or gylyn. **1590** SPENSER *F.Q.* III. ix. 7 Who wotes not, that womans subtiltyes Can guylen Argus, when she list misdonne? **1821** LIDDLE *Poems* 13 (E.D.D.) At last he knew he was guil'd long By that false tyrant's wily tongue. **1854** H. MILLER *Sch. & Schm.* (1858) 387 Its tones can guile the dark and lonesome day.

guile, variant of GULE *sb.*², GYLE.

†**guiled**, *ppl. a. Obs.* [f. GUILE *v.* and *sb.* + -ED.] **a.** Beguiled; deceived. In quot. *absol.* **b.** Full of guile; treacherous.

c **1400** *Rom. Rose* 6824, I..Robbe both robbed and robbours, And gyle gyled and gylours. **1596** SHAKS. *Merch. V.* III. ii. 97 Thus ornament is but the guiled shore To a most dangerous sea.

guile-fat, obs. variant of GYLE-FAT.

guileful ('gaɪlfʊl), *a.* Now only *literary.* [f. GUILE *sb.* + -FUL.] Full of guile; deceitful, treacherous.

13.. *K. Alis.* 444 Swithe blithe was Olimpias Of Neptanabus gileful has. *c* **1380** *Antecrist* in Todd 3 *Treat. Wyclif* 116 A noþer gyelful persecucioun is don bi eritykis and false breþeren. **1382** WYCLIF *Hosea* vii. 16 Thei ben maad as a gyleful bowe. *c* **1449** PECOCK *Repr.* II. iii. 151 Thei ben double and gileful. **1480** CAXTON *Descr. Brit.* 50 Turgesius deyde by gylefull wyles of women. **1508** FISHER *7 Penit. Ps.* cxlii. Wks. (1876) 258 His enemyes which haue layde in his waye gylefull baytes. **1591** SHAKS. *1 Hen. VI*, I. i. 77 By guilefull faire words, Peace may be obtayn'd. **1594** CAREW *Huarte's Exam. Wits* xi. (1596) 166 All men will know that he relied upon guilefull reasons. **1610** G. FLETCHER *Christ's Vict.* II. lx, Thus sought the dire Enchauntresse in his minde Her guilefull bayt to haue embosomed. **1633** P. FLETCHER *Purple Isl.* XI. xxvii, He whets her wrath with many a guilefull word. **1700** DRYDEN *Fable, Pythagorean Philos.* 141 Nor needed fish the guileful hooks to fear. **1763** SIR W. JONES *Caissa* Poems (1777) 139 Each guileful snare, and subtle art he tries. **1776** MICKLE tr. *Camoens' Lusiad* II. 94 The God..in the town his guileful rage employed. **1813** HOGG *Queen's Wake* 234 Woe to the guileful friend who lied! **1879** BUTCHER & LANG *Odyss.* 135 Guileful Circe of Aia would have stayed me in her halls.

guilefully ('gaɪlfʊlɪ), *adv.* [f. GUILEFUL + -LY².] In a guileful manner; artfully, deceitfully; treacherously.

1388 WYCLIF *Ps.* v. 11 Thei diden gilefuli with her tungis. **1450-1530** *Myrr. our Ladye* 231 The fende, whyche hathe gylefully made all subgecte to the lordeshyp of his cruelte. **1573** TUSSER *Husb.* xxxv. (1878) 83 If yee deale guilefully, parson will dreue. **1604** PARSONS *3rd Pt. Three Convers. Eng., Relat. Trial* 107 He had guilfully patched togeather two different sentences of that epistle. **1667** MILTON *P.L.* IX. 655 To whom the Tempter guilefully repli'd. *a* **1711** KEN *Edmund* Poet. Wks. 1721 II. 115 Loose probable Opinions he selects, And his Intention guilefully directs. **1825** COLERIDGE *Aids Refl.* Aph. xxxii. 18 He who speaks guilefully contrary to his inward conviction and knowledge.

guilefulness ('gaɪlfʊlnɪs). [f. GUILEFUL + -NESS.] The quality of being guileful; deceitfulness; treachery.

1388 WYCLIF *Ecclus.* xxxvii. 3 A! the worste presumpcioun, whereof art thou maad to hile drie malice, and the gilefulnesse thereof? **1556** ABP. PARKER *Ps.* lvi. 160 They put theyr hope, by guilefulnes and craft, to scape away. **1583** GOLDING *Calvin on Deut.* xxxix. 235 He wil not haue them defiled by guilefulnes. **1609** BIBLE (Douay) *Jer.* xiv. 14 Lying vision, and deceitful divination, guilfulnes, and the seduction of their owne hart they prophecie unto you.

guileless ('gaɪllɪs), *a.* [f. GUILE *sb.* + -LESS.] Devoid of guile.

1728-46 THOMSON *Spring* 362 The plain ox, That harmless, honest, guileless animal. *a* **1763** SHENSTONE *Elegies* xxvi. 23, I chas'd the guileless daughters of the plain, Nor dropt the chace, till Jessy was my prey. **1810** SCOTT *Lady of L.* I. xix, Than every freeborn glance confessed The guileless movements of her breast. **1844** R. M. McCHEYNE in *Mem.* i. (1872) 18 The golden days of guileless youth. **1880** W. S. PLUMER in Spurgeon *Treas. Dav.* Ps. cxix. 1-8 True piety is..guileless, unspotted from the world.

Comb. *a* **1834** COLERIDGE *Notes & Lect.* (1874) 254 Cassio's full guileless-hearted wishes for the safety..of Othello.

Hence **'guilelessly** *adv.*, **'guilelessness**.

1727 BAILEY vol. II, *Guilelesness..Guilelesly.* **1819** SHELLEY *Cenci* IV. iv. 183 The truth of things..written on a brow of guilelessness. **1844** H. ROGERS *Ess.* (1860) III. 113 The simplicity, innocence, and guilelessness of child-hood. **1870** SPURGEON *Treas. Dav.* Ps. xxxv. 7 Traps..into which they have fallen as guilelessly as beasts which stumble into concealed pits.

†**'guiler.** *Obs.* Forms: 4 gilowre, guilour, gylor, gyulere, 4-5 giler(e, -our(e, 4-6 gylour(e, guiler, 5 gyler, gyllor, 6 guyler. [ad. OF. *guilleor, gileor, gyllour*, f. *guil(l)er, giler*: see GUILE *v.*] A beguiler; a deceiver.

1303 R. BRUNNE *Handl. Synne* 5975 Hyt semeþ þou art a gylour, And coueytous, and trechour. *c* **1380** WYCLIF *Serm.* Sel. Wks. I. 129 We þenken on þat þis gilour saide whan he was on lyve. *c* **1430** *Hymns Virg.* 44 Neewe gilours wolde waite us schame. *c* **1460** *Towneley Myst.* xiii. 713 The fals gyler of teyn now goys he begylde. **1570** *Satir. Poems Reform.* xviii. 75 Wo to thay Gylouris of godlynes denude! **1590** SPENSER *F.Q.* II. vii. 64 He..So goodly did beguile the Guyler of his pray.

'guilery. *Obs.* exc. *dial.* Forms: 4 gelori, gilerie, gill(e)ry, gilri, -ye, gyl(e)ry(e, 4-5 gil(e)ry, gylory, 9 *dial.* gil(l)ery. [ad. OF. *gillerie*, f. *guiler*: see GUILE *v.*]

1. Deception, deceit, cheating, trickery.

1303 R. BRUNNE *Handl. Synne* 6611 Hyt ys a tokene of felunnye To weyte hym wyþ swych gylrye. *c* **1340** HAMPOLE *Prose Tr.* (1866) 11 Here es forbodene gillery of weghte. *c* **1375** *Sc. Leg. Saints, George* 732, I persawe wele þi gilry euir-ilke dele, þat þu wald lede me yddir quhare. **1426** in *Surtees Misc.* (1888) 10 Wyth outen any gylory, fraude, or deceyt. *c* **1440** *York Myst.* xxxvii. 160 He leuys with gaudis and with gilery. **1863** MRS. TOOGOOD *Yorksh. Dial.*, Take care, there's a good deal of gillery about him.

2. With *a* and *pl.* An instance of deceit, an act of treachery, a trick.

c **1330** R. BRUNNE *Chron.* (1810) 215 It was a gilery. *a* **1340** HAMPOLE *Psalter* ix. 25 When he suffirs him or any oþer come til honures & riches thorgh gilrys & syn. **1483** *Cath. Angl.* 156/1 A Gillry (*A.* Gylery), *prestigium.*

† **'guilesome,** *a. Obs.* In 4 gilesum. [f. GUILE *sb.* + -SOME.] Full of guile; deceitful, false.

1382 WYCLIF *Isa.* x. 6 To a folc gilesum I shal senden hym.

guilfat: see GYLEFAT.

† **'guiling,** *vbl. sb. Obs.* [f. GUILE *v.* + -ING[1].] Deceit; cunning.

13.. *K. Alis.* 3475 There caste Alisaunder the kyng For to aspye Daries gylyng. *c* **1400** *R. Glouc. Chron.* (Rolls) App. XX. 59 þe king of scotlond al mid grete gilinge Seide he wolde come in pes & gistny mid þe kinge. *c* **1430** *Hymns Virg.* 105 Leue alle fals mesuris & al gilinge.

† **'guilingly,** *adv. Obs.* [f. **guiling*, ppl. a. of GUILE *v.* + -LY[2].] In the manner of one who deceives; with guile; deceitfully.

1382 WYCLIF *Gen.* xxvii. 35 Thi brothir com gilyngliche, and took thi blissyng. —— *Prov.* xi. 13 Who goth gilendeli, shewith.. priue thingus.

guill, Sc. variant of GULE *sb.*[1] *Obs.*

‖ **guillaume** (gijom). [Fr., a use of the proper name (= William).] A rabbet-plane.

1885 *Spons' Mech. Own Bk.* 378 The ends are.. worked to the gauge marks with an iron guillaume. *Ibid.*, The checks are worked out with fillester and guillaume planes. **1964** W. L. GOODMAN *Hist. Woodworking Tools* 106 Félibien's plate gives several types of *guillaume* or rabbet plane.

guillem ('gɪləm). Also 7 guillam, -iam, gwylim. [app. a. Welsh *Gwilym* = William. Cf. GUILLEMOT.] = GUILLEMOT.

1603 OWEN *Pembrokesh.* (1891) 131 The gwylim. **1668** WILKINS *Real Char.* II. viii. §4. 155 Guillam. **1674** RAY *Collect. Words, Water Fowl* 92 The Guilliam, Cuillem or Kiddaw: *Lomwia insula Ferræ.* **1867** SMYTH *Sailor's Word-bk.*, *Guillem*, a sea-fowl. **1885** SWAINSON *Prov. Names Birds* 217.

'guillemin. *Hist.* Also 3 gilmin. [a. OF. *Guillemin*, f. *Guillelme* (mod. *Guillaume*) William; for the suffix see -INE[1].] A hermit of the order founded in the 12th c. by disciples of St. William.

The reference to their habit in the quot. indicates that they wore a grey hood like the Franciscans and a black gown like the early Dominicans.

a **1300** *Sat. People Kildare* vii. in *E.E.P.* (1862) 153 Hail be ȝe gilmins wiþ ȝur blake gunes ȝe leuith ȝe wildirnis and filliþ þe tiuns Menur wiþ-oute and prechour wiþ-inne. **1844** LOUISA S. COSTELLO *Béarn* I. 135 Orders of hermit monks rose up in every quarter, bearing his name of Guillemins.

guillemot ('gɪlɪmɒt). [a. F. *guillemot* (1555 in Hatz.-Darm.), app. a derivative of the name *Guillaume* = William. Cf. GUILLEM and WILLOCK.] The name of several species of sea birds of the genus *Alca* or *Uria*; esp. *Uria* or *Alca troile*, the Common or Foolish Guillemot, and *Uria grylle*, the Black Guillemot.

1678 RAY *Willughby's Ornith.* 324 The Bird called.. by those of Northumberland and Durham a Guillemot or Sea hen. **1766** PENNANT *Zool.* (1768) II. 517 The black Guillemot.. [is] found on the Bass-isle in Scotland. **1774** GOLDSM. *Nat. Hist.* III. 256 The frequent chatter of the Guillemot. **1828** STARK *Elem. Nat. Hist.* I. 326 The Guillemots, like the Divers, inhabit the northern seas, are little fitted for moving on land, and seldom venture on shore except in breeding time. **1849** KINGSLEY *N. Devon* in *Misc.* II. 305 Some unseen guillemot would give a startled squeak. **1859** ATKINSON *Walks & Talks* (1892) 328 Guillemots, or willocks, as they are locally [Yorkshire] called. **1883** BLACK in *Harper's Mag.* Dec. 70/1 The soft 'Kurroo! kurroo!' of the .. guillemots. **1893** NEWTON *Dict. Birds* 399 The commmon or Foolish.. Guillemot of both sides of the Atlantic is replaced further northward by.. the *Alca arra* or *Alca bruennichi* of ornithologists.

guillevat, variant (in Dicts.) of GYLEFAT.

guillevine: see KEELIVINE.

guilliam, obs. form of GUILLEM.

Guillian ('gɪlɪən). [f. F. *Guill-aume* + -IAN.] An adherent of William III.

1690 D'URFEY *Collin's Walk* III. 99 Grave Bishops, Barons, Baronets, The Guillians, and the Jacobites.

guilloche (gɪ'ləʊʃ, Fr. gijoʃ), *sb. Arch.* [a. or ad. F. *guillochis* the ornament itself or *guilloche* the tool with which it is made.] 'An ornament in the form of two or more bands or strings twisting over each other, so as to repeat the same figure, in a continued series, by the spiral returning of the bands' (Gwilt *Encycl. Archit.* 1842). See also GALACE, GOLOSE.

1857 BIRCH *Anc. Pottery* (1858) I. 128 Not only are there fine architectural ornaments,—such as the guilloche, rosettes, leaves and flowers [etc.]. **1883** A. DOBSON in *Eng. Illustr. Mag.* 83/1 The ceiling.. is painted black, partly gilded, and divided into panels by bands, ornamented with a guilloche.

attrib. **1865** TYLOR *Early Hist. Man.* ix. 272 The interlaced, or guilloche ornaments, on the early Scottish crosses. **1884** W. WRIGHT *Empire Hittites* 145 Along the base of the stone, below the feet, runs a single band of the guilloche pattern. **1893** *Westm. Gaz.* 17 Feb. 6/1 This portion.. is marked off by a guilloche border running from end to end.

guilloche (gɪ'ləʊʃ), *v.* [ad. F. *guillocher.*] *trans.* To decorate with intersecting curved lines, or with any pattern composed of curved lines. Hence **gui'lloched** *ppl. a.*

1883 MOLLETT *Dict. Art & Archæol., Guilloched*, waved or engine-turned.

guillochee (gɪləʊ'ʃiː), *v.* [f. F. *guillochis* sb., with semi-anglicized spelling.] *trans.* To decorate with guilloches. Hence **guillo'cheeing** *vbl. sb.* (in quot. *attrib.*).

1886 *Pop. Sci. Monthly* July 349 A charming effect is produced at the Neuwelt houses by means of a guillocheeing machine in which an engraver's tool is drawn in regularly massed lines over the slowly revolving vase.

guillotinade (ˌgɪlətɪ'neɪd). [ad. F. *guillotinade* (Dupré, 1801), f. *guillotine*: see next and -ADE.] An execution by means of the guillotine.

1835 MACAULAY *Sir J. Mackintosh* Ess. (1850) 312 Then came commotion, proscription.. civil war, foreign war, revolutionary tribunals, guillotinades.

guillotine ('gɪlətiːn, gɪlə'tiːn), *sb.* [a. F. *guillotine*, f. *Guillotin*, the name of a physician at whose suggestion the instrument was employed in 1789.]

1. An instrument used in France (esp. during the Revolution) for beheading, consisting of a heavy knife blade sliding between grooved posts. Also, execution by this instrument.

1793 *Ann. Reg.* 278 At half past 12 the guillotine severed her head from her body. **1819** BYRON *Juan* I. cxxix, One makes new noses, one a guillotine. **1848** W. H. KELLY tr. *Le Blanc's Hist. Ten Y.* II. 417 Alibaud was condemned to the guillotine. **1877** E. B. HAMLEY *Voltaire* xxvi. 202 The violent overturning of the old monarchy, the proscriptions, the massacres, the guillotine—these would have received no countenance from him.

transf. and *fig.* **1800** HURDIS *Fav. Village* 137 The monarch daffodil uprears his head, Nor dreads the guillotine of the keen gale. **1802** *Let.* 14 May in *Papers Twining Fam.* (1887) Ser. II. 243 A neat silver guillotine, to cut off the heads of asparagus. **1815** J. ADAMS *Wks.* (1856) X. 122 Down would fall the guillotine of a negative upon the neck of poor Muhlenberg. **1884** *Graphic* 1 Nov. 446/2 Cayenne is so malarious that transportation thither used to be styled 'the dry guillotine'.

2. The name of various instruments acting in a similar manner: **a.** *Surg.*, an instrument for excising the tonsil or uvula and for other surgical operations. **b.** (See quots.) **c.** A machine for cutting the edges of books, paper, straw, etc.

a. **1866** J. M. SIMS *Notes Uterine Surg.* iii. 224 But I think I have at last hit upon something better [than the curved scissors] which I would term the uterine guillotine. **1880** M. MACKENZIE *Dis. Throat & Nose* I. 321 Abscission may be performed by means of knives, scissors, guillotines, or écraseurs. **1886** in *Syd. Soc. Lex.*

b. **1881** RAYMOND *Mining Gloss.*, *Guillotine*, a machine for breaking iron with a falling weight. **1892** *Labour Commission* Gloss., *Guillotines*, machines used in the iron and steel industry for cutting square blocks of steel to a certain length.

c. **1883** *Scotsman* 9 May 11/7 Valuable Printing Plant.. Two Guillotines. **1896** *Advt.*, Printers.—Wanted, young man as Machine Man... One with knowledge of guillotine preferred.

3. a. *U.S.* (See quot. 1883.) **b.** A method of shortening the discussion on a bill in parliament, by fixing a day when the Committee stage must close.

1850 N. HAWTHORNE *Scarlet Letter* 56 Keeping up the metaphor of the political guillotine, [etc.]. **1883** *Encycl. Amer.* I. 200/1 The axe, or rather the guillotine, is made to represent the dismissal of Government officials upon the coming in of a new President, or in case of some grave complication, and the victims are said to be beheaded. **1893** *Boston* (Mass.) *Jrnl.* 20 Mar. 1/2 The Post-Office Guillotine Working Rapidly. **1893** *Scotsman* 28 June 6 Let us suppose that the Government have resolved to adopt the guillotine. **1893** *Westm. Gaz.* 30 June 2/2 The Coercion Bill (1887) was allowed 15 days in Committee before the application of the guillotine.

4. a. *attrib.*, as ***guillotine-massacre***, ***-process***; (sense 3 b) ***guillotine closure***, ***motion***, ***resolution***, ***time***; **guillotine-cravat**, a fashion of cravat current during the French revolution; **guillotine-cutter** = 2 c; **guillotine-instrument** *Surg.* = 2 a; **guillotine-window** [F. *fenêtre à guillotine*], an ordinary sash window, jocularly so called from the fact that the sashes slide in grooves.

1909 *Westm. Gaz.* 14 May 2/2 Let it be understood.. that the *guillotine closure will not be used, however prolonged the sittings may be. **1927** *Daily Express* 10 May 2/7 To introduce the guillotine or kangaroo method of closure. **1880** VERN. LEE *Stud. Italy* iii. 225 Italy had become cosmopolitan and eclectic, borrowing top boots, *guillotine cravats, and Grecian sandals. **1884** KNIGHT *Dict. Mech.* Supp., *Guillotine instrument. **1796** BP. WATSON *Apol. Bible* i. (1799) 6, I cannot, with you, attribute the *guillotine-massacres to that cause. **1946** *Ann. Reg. 1945* 94 The *guillotine motion in Standing Committee should take the form of naming the date by which the Bill should be reported. **1958** *Ann. Reg. 1957* 7 A 'guillotine' motion for its [*sc.* the Bill's] acceleration was moved and carried. **1893** *Daily News* 10 June 3/8 There might be an objection to applying the *guillotine process to the Bill as a whole. **1927** *Daily Tel.* 10 May 12/3 The Government will bring in a '*guillotine' resolution. **1968** *Globe & Mail* (Toronto) 3 Feb. 3/4 (*heading*) *Guillotine time only days away as broadcasting debate goes on. **1898** *Daily News* 28 Feb. 4/7 The French laugh at our '*guillotine windows', and greatly prefer their own, which open inwards.

b. guillotine shears, a form of shearing machine having a stationary lower blade and used chiefly for cutting metal sheet and strip.

1884 W. H. GREENWOOD *Steel & Iron* xvi. 348 A form of powerful guillotine shears. **1967** *Times Rev. Industry* Feb. 96/2 The Swedish company's range of hydraulic press brakes and guillotine shears.

Hence **guillotinism**, execution by means of the guillotine; **guillotinist**, one who favours execution by the guillotine.

1793 *Poetry* in *Ann. Reg.* 404 Lo! I who erst.. Disclos'd the secrets of the Royal House, And sang the Guillotinism of —a louse! **1796** BURKE *Regic. Peace* iv. Wks. IX. 11 The humane guillotinists of Bourdeaux.

guillotine ('gɪlətiːn, gɪlə'tiːn), *v.* [ad. F. *guillotine-r*, f. *guillotine* GUILLOTINE *sb.*]

1. *trans.* To behead by the guillotine.

1794 *Chron.* in *Ann. Reg.* 10 May (1799) 14/2 Guillotined at Paris, madame Elizabeth, sister of the late king of France. **1810** *Q. Rev.* Nov. 464 Our late philosophers (for we believe they are most of them guillotined). **1837** CARLYLE *Fr. Rev.* III. VII. ii, They have suffered much: their friends guillotined; their pleasures.. ruthlessly repressed. **1880** OUIDA *Moths* I. 146 You could fancy her going to be guillotined in old lace like Marie-Antoinette.

transf. and *fig.* **1804** FESSENDEN *Democr.* (1806) I. 121 And guillotine the reputation Of every good man in the nation. **1832** G. DOWNES *Lett. Cont. Countries* I. 39 The view.. includes some hills, with vineyards guillotined after the French manner. **1887** *Pall Mall G.* 3 Sept. 3/1 Mr. Calmour has a short and easy way with dissyllables which refuse to fit into his verse. He simply guillotines them, thus: 'And redbreasts fearless 'proach the door'.

2. In various applied senses. **a.** To cut (the edges of a book) with a guillotine. **b.** To cut short discussion upon (a bill, a clause).

1893 *Times* 1 June 9/5 To fix a date for guillotining each clause in succession. **1896** *Daily News* 23 Mar. 8/6 Only the cheaper books are sewn by machinery.. the better volumes being sewn with silk by hand. Then the edges are guillotined.

Hence **guillotined** *ppl. a.* (also *absol.*); **ˌguilloti'neer, guillotiner**, one who guillotines; **guillo'tinement** [so in Fr.], execution by the guillotine.

1796 *Times* 1 Aug. in J. Ashton *Old Times* (1885) 322 The widows of twenty guillotined poor souls. **1832** *Blackw. Mag.* XXXII. 275 They.. would rather be the guillotined than the guillotiners. **1837** DICKENS *Pickw.* xl, The vehicle was not exactly a gig.. nor a guillotined cabriolet. **1837** CARLYLE *Fr. Rev.* III. VII. ii, Bewildered by long terror, perturbations and guillotinement. **1890** *Longm. Mag.* Aug. 359 These were would-be guillotiners, now to be guillotined in their turn! **1897** *Expositor's Grk. Test.* I. 164/1 Even persecutors and guillotineers get weary of their savage work.

guillotining ('gɪlətiːnɪŋ, gɪlə'tiːnɪŋ), *vbl. sb.* [f. GUILLOTINE *v.* + -ING[1].] The action of the vb. GUILLOTINE.

1794 in *Spirit Publ. Jrnls.* (1799) I. 331 Confusions, uproars, commitments, guillotinings, &c. **1799** COLERIDGE *Lett.* (1895) I. 329 Guillotining is too republican a death for such reptiles. **1859** SALA *Tw. round Clock* (1861) 304 We have had.. no confiscations, no deportations, and no guillotinings.

attrib. **1837** THACKERAY *Carlyle's Fr. Rev.*, His.. guillotining system had its hour. **1893** *Times* 1 June 9/5 Cutting short the discussion on.. the remaining clauses of the Bill by what is known as the 'guillotining' process.

guilour, variant of GUILER *Obs.*

† **'guilous,** *a. Obs.* In 4 gilous(e, 4–5 gylous. [f. *gile*, GUILE *sb.* + -OUS.] Guileful.

1382 WYCLIF *2 Cor.* xi. 13 Forwhi suche false apostlis ben trecherous, or gylous work men, transfigurynge hem into apostlis. **1496** *Dives & Paup.* (W. de W.) v. v. 202/2 The gylous tonge, that is called in latyn *lingua dolosa.*

Hence † **'guilously** *adv.*, guilefully.

c **1425** *St. Mary of Oignies* I. ix. in *Anglia* VIII. 143/16 þat sly enmy.. warned hym also gylously of sum good dedys þat hee shulde do. **1496** *Dives & Paup.* (W. de W.) v. v. 202/2 Ioab gylously sloughe the noble prynce Amasam.

guilt (gɪlt), *sb.* Forms: 1 gylt, *irreg.* gielt, 1, 2, 4 gelt, 2–5 gult(e, 2–6 gilt, 2–7 gylt(e, 3 *Orm.* gillt, 3–5 gilte, 4 gelte, 4, 6 guilte, (gelthe, gylthe), 6– guilt. [OE. *gylt* str. masc.:—prehistoric type **gulti-z*; related to next vb.

No equivalent forms are known in the other Teut. langs. The connection commonly assumed with the OTeut. root **geld-*, *gald-*, *guld-*, to pay, YIELD, is inadmissible phonologically, and its apparent plausibility with regard to sense disappears on examination. From the fact that OE. *gylt* renders L. *debitum* in the Lord's Prayer and in Matt. xviii. 27, and that *is gyltiȝ* renders *debet* in Matt. xxiii. 18, it has been inferred that the sb. had a primary sense 'debt', of which there seems to be no real evidence, though OE. *scyld*, G. *schuld*, have developed the sense of 'guilt' from that of 'debt'.]

† **1.** A failure of duty, delinquency; offence, crime, sin. *Obs.* (Cf. 5 b.)

971 *Blickl. Hom.* 193 þonne onfoþ hie forȝifnesse ealra heora gylta æt urum Drihtne. *a* **1000** *Kentish Ps.* I. 39 (Gr.) Geltas ȝeclansa, þa ðe ic on aldre æfre ȝefremede. *c* **1000** *Ags. Gosp.* Matt. vi. 12 Forgyf us ure gyltas [*c* **1160** *Hatton* geltas]. *c* **1050** *Byrhtferth's Handboc* in *Anglia* VIII. 320 þæt we ne ȝefremmon gylta æniȝne. *a* **1175** *Cott. Hom.* 223 Se lichame is deadlic þurh adames gylt. *c* **1200** Ormin 15873 Iff þeȝȝ muȝhenn turrnenn hemm To betenn þeȝȝre gilltess. **12..** *Paternoster* in *Rel. Ant.* I. 282 Forȝif us oure gultes. *c* **1250** *Gen. & Ex.* 2409 So ðinked euerilc wis man..ðe of adames gilte muneð. **1340** *Ayenb.* 15 þe ten hornes of þe beste betokneþ þe geltes of þe ten hestes of our lhorde. *a* **1400-50** *Alexander* 3213 (Dublin MS.) þat Sloghen so þair souerent þat neuer þaim gilt made. **1401** *Pol. Poems* (Rolls) II. 39 For which gilts and defaults it were worthy that the order..were fordone.

†**2.** Responsibility for an action or event; the 'fault' *of* (some person). (In OE. const. genitive.)

11.. *O.E. Chron.* an. 1048 (Laud. MS.) Eustatius hæfde ȝecydd þam cynge þet hit sceolde beon mare gylt þære burhwaru þonne his. **1377** Langl. *P. Pl.* B. xiii. 257 It is for men ben nouȝt worthy To haue the grace of god and no gylte of the pope. *c* **1380** *Sir Ferumb.* 317 If þe sarsyn ouercompþ [*sic*] him þare certis ȝe bereþ þe gilt. **1390** Gower *Conf.* II. 122 She taketh upon her self the gilt. *a* **1400-50** *Alexander* 2384 It was þe gilt all of þe gome & noȝt of þe gud lord. **1671** Mrs. Behn *Forc'd Marriage* I. i, I shall grow angry, and believe your pride Would put the guilt off on your modesty.

†**3.** Desert (*of* a penalty); *esp.* in phrase ***without guilt***, without having done anything to deserve one's fate, innocently. *Obs.*

c **1275** *Passion our Lord* 342 in *O.E. Misc.* 47 Nenne gult of deþe ich on hym i-seo. **1393** Langl. *P. Pl.* C. v. 75 Withoute gult, god wot gat ich thys scathe. *c* **1400** Maundev. (Roxb.) xv. 67 Godd þan had done agayne his riȝtwisnesse for to suffer swilk ane innocent die withouten gilt. *c* **1430** *Life St. Kath.* (1884) 51 Seynge þat þe kepers scholde haue be turmented wyth oute gylte. **1535** Stewart *Cron. Scot.* 39904 He fand ane subtill wyle, But ony gilt how he suld them begyle. *a* **1625** Boys *Wks.* (1629-30) 268 Shee.. abideth vnder the wrath of God, horror of conscience, guilt of death and hell.

4. The fact of having committed, or of being guilty of, some specified or implied offence; guiltiness. †Formerly (now *poet.*) const. *of.*

c **1330** R. Brunne *Chron.* (1810) 129 If a clerke men founde in his lond þat reft, þorgh slauhter or wounde, or þorgh oþer theft, Men suld schewe his guilte in þe courte of lay. **1387** Trevisa *Higden* (Rolls) VI. 165 Iustinianus Cesar was prived of þe ioye of his kyngdom for gilt of mysbyleve. *c* **1450** Myrc 1100 Hast thow forsake þyn owne gult, And on a-noþer þe blame I-pult? **1622** Bacon *Hen. VII* 196 It was neither guilt of Crime, nor reason of State, that could quench the Enuie that was vpon the King for this Execution. *a* **1715** Burnet *Own Time* iv. (1724) I. 636 He in his deposition said somewhat that brought Sir Hugh Cambell and his son under the guilt of treason. **1833** Tennyson *Lady Clara Vere de V.* 43 The guilt of blood is at your door. **1844** H. H. Wilson *Brit. India* III. 324 Positive proof of his guilt could not be adduced. **1891** *Speaker* 2 May 532/2 He has put the believers in the guilt of Richard III in a dilemma.

5. a. The state (meriting condemnation and reproach of conscience) of having wilfully committed crime or heinous moral offence; criminality, great culpability.

c **1510** More *Picus* Wks. 32 Spare vs wretches, and washe awaye our gilt, That we be not by thy iuste anger spilt. **1596** Spenser *F.Q.* v. v. 48 That his guilt the greater may appeare ..I will a while with his first folly beare. **1654** Hammond *Fundamentals* xvi. 167 These..are taken away, the possibility of guilt, and the possibility of innocence. **1709** Steele *Tatler* No. 35 ⁋1 Several of my intimate Friends are in the Guilt. **1737** Whiston *Josephus, Antiq.* Dissert. ii, Most of which seem to have had no other peculiar guilt upon them than that common to soldiers in war. **1757** Smollett *Reprisal* Prol., No guilt attends a fact involuntary. **1785** Burke *Corr.* (1844) III. 39 Guilt resides in the intention. **1813** Byron *Giaour* 1243 But Heaven in wrath would turn away, If Guilt should for the guiltless pray. **1828** Scott *F.M. Perth* xiii, She never saw the child of her love stand before her doubly dishonoured, by guilt and by falsehood. **1876** Mozley *Univ. Serm.* viii. 176 Guilt is the direct consequence of a crime having been committed.

b. (With *a* and *pl.*) An instance, kind, or degree of guilt. *rare.*

1500-20 Dunbar *Poems* ix. 135 Of every gilt, and wicket govirnance, I cry The mercy, and lasar to repent. **1605** Shaks. *Lear* iii. ii. 57 Close pent-vp guilts, Riue your concealing Continents. **1679** *Gentl. Call.* Pref. §8 'Twas amongst the Jews a Capital Guilt to curse a Parent. **1685** South *Serm.* (1843) II. xvii. 281 The pardon of a guilt (too big for the common measures of pardon). **1702** Rowe *Tamerl.* v. i. 2115 Nor has my Soul One unrepented Guilt upon remembrance. **1711** Steele *Spect.* No. 139 ⁋1 Rapine, Murder, and all the Guilts that attend War when it is unjust. **1864** H. H. Brownell *War Lyrics* (1866) 21 Ah ever..In the crash of falling crime Some lesser guilt must share.

c. Conduct involving guilt; heinous sin or crime.

1729 Butler *Serm.* Wks. 1874 II. 127 It [self-deceit] is itself the greatest of all guilt in proportion to the degree it prevails. **1780** *Newgate Cal.* V. 120 The life of this man seems to have been one chain of guilt from the cradle to the gallows. **1819** Byron *Juan* ii. cxxvii, He was a Greek, and on his isle had built..A very handsome house from out his guilt.

¶ **d.** Misused for 'sense of guilt'.

1690-1 Tillotson *Serm.* xxxviii. (1735) I. 355 Guilt being nothing else but trouble arising in our minds, from a consciousness of having done contrary to what we are verily perswaded was our Duty. **1932** *Brit. Jrnl. Psychol.* Apr. 377 The author considers that all individuals nourish large numbers of fads, fancies, hypothetical and unreal 'guilts'. **1966** *Listener* 10 Mar. 341/2 If he [*sc.* a child] does take something that he knows is not his property, and if you detect him at it you will often find guilt written all over his face.

6. a. In legal use: The state of being regarded as justly liable to penalty. *rare.*

1765 Blackstone *Comm.* Introd. §2. 46 Here it is impossible that the party could foresee that an action, innocent when it was done, should be afterwards converted to guilt by a subsequent law. **1858** J. Kent *Comm. Amer. Law* (ed. 9) I. 157 If a ship has contracted guilt by a breach of blockade, the offence is not discharged until the end of the voyage.

b. Phr. ***guilt by association*** (see quot. 1964).

1941 Z. Chafee *Free Speech in U.S.* (1942) xi. 359 The doctrine of guilt by association is abhorrent enough in the criminal and deportation fields without being extended into the relation between lawyer and client. **1960** *Listener* 3 Mar. 415/1 He introduced those concepts of guilt by association and guilt by intention which have always been a feature of political trials and disputes in Russia. **1964** Gould & Kolb *Dict. Soc. Sci.* 298/2 Another form of legal usage comprehends the idea of guilt by association or guilt attaching to an individual through his relation or connection with a group of persons who are charged with a violation of a legally established line of conduct.

7. *attrib.* and *Comb.*, as ***guilt-feeling, -sense; guilt-born, -concealing, -formed, -free, -haunted, -imbrued, -laden, -reeking, -ridden, -sick, -stained, -stricken, -won*** adjs. Also **guilt-complex** (see complex *sb.* 3), a mental obsession with the idea of having done wrong; †**guiltwite** [OE. *wíte* penalty], penalty for commission of crime.

1813 Scott *Rokeby* iii. xiv, *Guilt-born Excess the goblet drain'd. **1927** Henderson & Gillespie *Text-bk. Psychiatry* ix. 198 *Guilt complexes..also lead to compensating phantasies. **1929** A. Adler *Probl. Neurosis* vi. 84 The complicated state of self-accusation and repentance at the same time, which we call a guilt complex, which is always a superiority-striving on the useless side of life. **1960** Koestler *Lotus & Robot* 276 Auden's *mea culpa*..might serve as a motto for the Western guilt complex towards Asia. **1730-46** Thomson *Autumn* 1174 Beneath the cloud of *guilt-concealing night. **1951** —— *Age of Longing* i. i. 25 We can only achieve a constructive attitude if we rid ourselves of fallacious *guilt-feelings about the past. **1963** A. Heron *Towards Quaker View of Sex* ii. 18 Without the special guilt-feelings which her upbringing has so often laid on the girl, man and maid are..on equal terms. **1830** Scott *Demonol.* x. 364, I cannot forbear giving you another instance of a *guilt-formed phantom. **1960** Koestler *Lotus & Robot* ii. viii. 198 The permitted, and therefore *guilt-free, pleasure of saké and concubinage. **1952** S. Spender *Shelley* 11 His friendship with Hogg now entered a new and perhaps *guilt-haunted phase. **1845** Hirst *Poems* 69 Others, sweet and dove-like;—others, regal:—Others, *guilt-imbrued. **1944** *Mind* LIII. 847 The repressed *guilt-laden hatred, originally felt towards the mother for checking a certain impulse, may be extended or diverted to that impulse itself. **1951** S. Spender *World within World* 31, I was intensely self-conscious, guilt-laden, undisciplined, curious, inspired, and naïve. **1811** Shelley *Tear* ii. 4 Patriotism red with his *guilt-reeking gore. **1960** Koestler *Lotus & Robot* 280, I accepted it as a truism, as most *guilt-ridden Westerners do. **1959** *Times Lit. Suppl.* 16 Jan. 37/1 Unless the distinction is clearly made and recognized between objective and subjective guilt (between 'guilt' and '*guilt-sense'), the significance of the former may all too easily escape the attention of the analyst. *a* **1625** Beaum. & Fl. *Custom Country* iv. i, A *guilt-sick conscience. *a* **1822** Shelley *Posth. Fragm. Marg. Nicholson* 82 At the orphan's sigh.. Totters the fabric of thy *guilt-stained throne. **1899** E. M. Aveling tr. *Marx's Secret Diplomatic Hist. 18th Cent.* v. 74 Whether we consider her [*sc.* Russia's] power..as the mere vision of the *guilt-stricken consciences of the European peoples—the question remains the same. **964** in Birch *Cart. Sax.* (1893) III. 379 Debitum transgressionis et penam delicti quæ Anglice dicitur Ofersæwnesse et *Gyltwyte. **1387** Trevisa *Higden* (Rolls) II. 95 Gultwite amendes for trespas. **1607** Cowell *Interpr.*, Gultwit. **1706** Phillips (ed. Kersey), *Gyltwite..Gultwit* (Sax. Law-Term).

†**guilt**, *v. Obs.* Forms: 1 gyltan, 2-3 gulten (y), *Orm.* gilltenn, 4 gilte(n, 4-5 gilt, 5-6 gylte, 6 guilt. *Pa. t.* 2-4 gulte, 3-5 gilte, 4 gilted, -id, 5 gylted. *Pa. pple.* 2 igult, 4-6 gilt, 5 gult, 5 gilted, 6 guilted. [OE. *gyltan*:—prehistoric type **gultjan*; related to prec. sb.]

1. *intr.* To commit an offence or trespass, to sin.

c **825**, *c* **897**, *c* **1000** [see guilting *ppl. a.*]. *c* **1020** *Rule St. Benet.* vi. (Logeman) 25 Ic sæde ic ȝehealde weȝas mine þæt ic na gylte on minre tungan. *c* **1175** *Lamb. Hom.* 83 þa com þes Mon, he nefre ne gulte. *a* **1200** *Moral Ode* 27 Al to lome ich habbe igult a werke and o worde often. *a* **1250** *Owl & Night.* 1521 Ther-fore the were gulte That leof is over wummon to pulte. **1340-70** *Alex. & Dind.* 550 Michel gilte ȝe, gome, bi ȝour godus falce. *a* **1400-50** *Alexander* 472 þou has giltid, bot noȝt gretly. **1530** Palsgr. 566/1, I gylte, I faulte or commyt a trespasse (Lydgate).

b. Const. *against*, rarely *to* (a person, a law). Also with *dat.* of person, and *acc.* of thing (neuter pron.).

c **1200** Ormin 5142 Godd itt te forrbedeþþ To gilltenn ohht onȝæness himm. **1340-70** *Alex. & Dind.* 384 We ne gilte noht god no no gome here. **1393** Langl. *P. Pl.* C. viii. 151 Alle thuse rybaudes that repenten hem sore, That euere thei gulte aȝens the. **1398** Trevisa *Barth. De P.R.* xiv. xxviii. (Tollem. MS.), In þoo mawmetes Salomon trespasid and giltid his owne God. *a* **1400-50** *Alexander* 2430 þare as he gilt me agayns & I him gradid haue. **1414** Brampton *Penit. Ps.* xxvi. (Percy Soc.) 10 Graunte me grace..Thi lawe to understande..That I nevere gylte aȝens itt. **1423** Jas. I *Kingis Q.* xxxviii, Quhat haue I gilt to him or doon offense, That I am thrall, and birdis gone at large? *c* **1450** Lonelich *Grail* l. 658 Why hast þou thus here now wrowht, with goddis peple that Gylted the nowht? *c* **1500** *Lancelot* 699 Qwhat haue y gilt, allace! or qwhat deseruit?

2. [f. the sb.] *trans.* To render guilty. In quot. *refl.*

1553 Grimalde *Cicero's Offices* iii. (1558) 121 Hath he then guilted himself of murder?

guilt, obs. form of gilt *sb.* and *v.*

guilt(e, -ed, obs. ff. gilt, gilted *ppl. adjs.*

†**'guilter.** *Obs.* Also 3 gultare, 4 gilter. [f. guilt *v.* + -er[1].] An offender, transgressor.

12.. *Paternoster* in *Rel. Ant.* I. 282 Forȝif us oure gultes, also we forȝifet oure gultare. **1382** Wyclif *Isa.* i. 28 He shal to-trede the hydous gilteres and the synneres togidere.

†**'guiltful**, *a. Obs.* [f. guilt *sb.* + -ful.] Full of guilt; guilty; heinous. Hence †**'guiltfully** *adv.*

c **1375** *Sc. Leg. Saints, Andrea* 103 Wikit women, þou þolis þus Ill, for þou..has consawit giltfully. **1655** R. Capel in Spurgeon *Treas. Dav.* Ps. cxix. 36 Worldliness is a most guiltful sin in respect of God. **1675** Walker etc. *Paraph. St. Paul* 22 Prohibition..making it more guilt-full. **1791** Learmont *Poems* 15 (E.D.D.) The lady heard the guiltfou tale Wi' mickle dole an' dread.

guilt-head, obs. form of gilt-head.

guiltily ('gɪltɪlɪ), *adv.* [f. guilty *a.* + -ly[2].] In a guilty manner or condition; like one that is guilty.

1594 Shaks. *Rich. III*, v. iii. 146 Bloody and guilty: guiltily awake, And in a bloody Battell end thy dayes. **1662** *Jesuits' Reasons* (1675) 104 Who have guiltily provoked..the Sanguinary Laws. **1843** Carlyle *Past & Pr.* iv. iii, Our friends of China, who guiltily refused to trade. **1873** Black *Pr. Thule* v. 69 Consciousness that he had been guiltily remiss.

guiltiness ('gɪltɪnɪs). [f. guilty *a.* + -ness.] The condition, quality, or state of being guilty; criminality, culpability; an instance of this; also, consciousness of guilt. Const. *of.*

c **1375** *Sc. Leg. Saints, Thomas* 172 Of giltines þe schame Is generit, & of It þe blame. **1535** Coverdale *John* xix. 6 Take ye him & crucifye him for I fynde no giltynesse in him. **1601** Sir W. Cornwallis *Disc. Seneca* (1631) 10 Too much doubt argueth too much guiltinesse. **1676** Allen *Address Nonconf.* 97 A guiltiness of a great Schism in the Church, and consequently of the many sad effects of it. *a* **1740** Waterland *Wks.* (1823) VI. 286 Arguments against Christianity, be they serious or ludicrous, are indifferently (not always in the same degree, or with the same guiltiness) attempts to subvert Christianity, and are consequently to be punished. **1752** J. Louthian *Form of Process* (ed. 2) 89 His Guiltiness of the Crime libelled against him. *a* **1834** Lamb *Misc. Wks.* (1871) 469 False surmises of her guiltiness. **1849** Stovel *Introd. to Canne's Necess.* 6 The loss of truth by neglect, whatever the present inducement, must ever before God be attended with inexcusable guiltiness.

†**'guilting**, *ppl. a. Obs.* Chiefly OE. In 1 **gyltend**, 4 **giltend**. [f. guilt *v.* + -ing[2].] That offends or trespasses. In quots. *absol.*

c **825** *Vesp. Psalter* xxiv. 8 Swoete & reht dryten fore ðissum aee ȝesette gyltendum in weȝe. *c* **897** K. Ælfred *Gregory's Past.* xxi. 166 Ðara gyltendra scylda. *c* **1000** *Ags. Gosp.* Matt. vi. 12 Forgyf us ure gyltas, swa swa we forgyfað urum gyltendum. **1382** Wyclif *Job* ix. 28, I shamede alle my werkis, witende that thou shuldist not spare to the giltende.

†**'guiltist.** *Obs. rare*[−1]. [f. guilt *sb.* + -ist.] A guilty person; an offender.

1693 W. Freke *Art War* vi. 252 Only the Principal Guiltists among Your Enemy ought to suffer Death.

guiltless ('gɪltlɪs), *a.* Forms: see guilt *sb.* [Late OE. *gyltléas*, f. *gylt* guilt + *-léas* -less.]

1. Free from guilt; innocent. Const. *of*, †*from.*

c **1200** *Vices & Virtues* (1888) 133 Hande on hande nis naht ðe euele man gylt-leas. *c* **1200** Ormin 1977 ȝho, þatt all wass gilltelæs. **1297** R. Glouc. (Rolls) 6707 þe erl godwin.. Let þis giltelese men sette al arewe. *c* **1340** *Cursor M.* 16406 (Trin.) Alle ȝe se he seide þat I am giltles of his lyue. **1382** Wyclif *Matt.* xxvii. 24, I am innocent or giltlesse, fro the blood of this iust man. *c* **1460** *Towneley Myst.* xv. 207 And thus gyltles [I] shall be arayde. **1548** Hall *Chron., Rich. III*, 8 b, The cause of the destruction of manye gyltles persones. **1590** Spenser *F.Q.* i. viii. 36 All the floore..With blood of guiltlesse babes..Defiled was. **1647** Cowley *Mistr., Concealment* i, So handsomly the thing contrive, That she may guiltless of it live. **1713** Berkeley *Guardian* No. 62 ⁋3 The cheapness of puerile delights, the guiltless joy they leave upon the mind. **1750** Gray *Elegy* xv, Some Cromwell, guiltless of his country's blood. **1853** Grote *Greece* ii. lxxxiv. XI. 189 Upon their guiltless heads fell all the terrors of retaliation for the enormities of the despot.

quasi-*advb.* **1542** Udall *Erasm. Apoph.* ii. 291 a, He was ..through enuie & falsely surmised accusacions, guiltelesse condemned & putte to death.

b. *absol.* or quasi-*sb.* Now only with *the.*

c **1200** *Trin. Coll. Hom.* 105 þe unbileffulle man werpeð his aȝen gilt uppe þe giltelese. *a* **1300** *Cursor M.* 11554 He made oon ordinaunce in hiȝe þat mony gultles shulde diȝe. **13..** *E.E. Allit. P.* A. 668 Hit is a dom þat neuer god gaue, þat euer þe gyltlez schulde be schente. *c* **1450** *St. Cuthbert* (Surtees) 5152 Bathe giltles and als gylty. **1484** Caxton *Fables of Alfonce* i Ye shold do grete synne yf ye dyd put this Innocent and gyltles to dethe. **1769** Blackstone *Comm.* iv. xxvii. 336 In consequence of a notion that God would always interpose miraculously to vindicate the guiltless.

†**c.** *transf.* Of things, places, etc.: Free from the stain of crime. Const. *of. Obs.*

1602 Marston *Ant. & Mel.* iv. Wks. 1856 I. 46 Was ever Prince..Left shipwrackt, banisht, on more guiltlesse ground? **1652** Benlowes *Theoph.* xii. lxxii, We there, on grassie tufted Tapistries In guiltlesse shades, by full hair'd trees..view natures ants and bees. **1725** Pope *Odyss.* xi. 658 Though spears in iron tempests rain'd around, Yet innnocent they play'd, and guiltless of a wound. **1784** Cowper *Task* iii. 698 That dissipated minds..Should seek the guiltless joys that I describe.

†**2.** *nonce-uses.* **a.** Free from penalty, scot free. **b.** Undeserved. *Obs.*

1579 LYLY *Euphues* (Arb.) 90 God, who permitteth no guile to be guiltlesse, will shortly requite this injury. **1602** MARSTON *Antonio's Rev.* IV. iii. Wks. 1856 I. 126 Have I liv'd to see his ventures blurd With guiltlesse blots?

3. Having no acquaintance, dealings, or familiarity with, no experience or use of (something). Const. *of*. (Cf. INNOCENT 2 c and GUILTY 2 c.)

1667 MILTON *P.L.* IX. 392 Not as shee with Bow and Quiver armd, But with such Gardning Tools as Art yet rude, Guiltless of fire had formd. **1693** DRYDEN *Ovid's Met.* I. 132 The teeming earth, yet guiltless of the plough, And unprovok'd, did fruitful stores allow. *a* **1763** SHENSTONE *Elegies* i. 15 Guiltless of disguise. **1862** *Atlantic Monthly* Sept. 338/2 Gabriel was..reported..to be guiltless of the alphabet. **1874** LISLE CARR *Jud. Gwynne* I. i. 1 Distinguishing it from other farm-houses, which were guiltless of that special ornamentation.

guiltlessly ('gɪltlɪslɪ), *adv.* [f. prec. + -LY².] In a guiltless manner; without guilt.

1548 UDALL, etc. *Erasm. Par. 1 Pet.* i. 1–2 Whom the rageing crueltie of them, which hated the name of Christe, hathe giltelesly dryuen out of the places where their fathers dwelt before them. **1612** T. TAYLOR *Comm. Titus* ii. 13 The trifling vse of the name of God and Christ, the which no man shall guiltelessely lift vp in vaine. **1870** RUSKIN *Lect. Art* i. 27 It is not possible..for any, guiltlessly, to pass their days in a succession of pleasures.

guiltlessness ('gɪltlɪsnɪs). [f. GUILTLESS *a.* + -NESS.] The condition, quality, or state of being guiltless; innocence.

1571 GOLDING *Calvin on Ps.* iv. 2 If at any tyme our giltlessenesse appeere not before the world. **1650** HOBBES *De Corp. Pol.* 23 When Justice is taken for Guiltlesnesse, the Actions are just, and yet not alwayes the Man. **1681** T. FLATMAN *Heraclitus Ridens* (1713) II. 30 If the Declaration of a Grand Jury..cannot convince the World of the guiltlessness of any Man, what can? **1813** SIR S. ROMILLY *Speech Parl.* 5 Mar., The guiltlessness of the Princess of Wales was established. **1877** MISS YONGE *Cameos* III. vii. 58 These preposterous charges almost show the real guiltlessness of the veteran on whom national hatred had fixed.

guilty ('gɪltɪ), *a.* Forms: 1 gyltiȝ, 2 geltiȝ, 2–4 gelty, 3–4 gulti (y), 4 gelti(f, gilt-, guiltif(e, gylti, -if, -yf, 4–5 gulty, 4–6 gilti, gylty, 5 gillty, giltyf, 5–6 giltie, gyltie, 6 giltye, gylté, 7 guiltie, 6– guilty. [OE. *gyltiȝ*: see GUILT *sb.* and -Y¹. Some ME. forms are due to association of the suffix with *-if*, -IVE.]

1. That has offended or been in fault; delinquent, criminal. Now in stronger sense: That has incurred guilt; deserving punishment and moral reprobation; culpable. Often *absol.*

c **1000** *Ags. Gosp.* Matt. xxiii 18 Swa hwylc swa swereþ on þære offrunge þe ofer þæt weofud ys se ys gyltiȝ [*Hatton Gosp.* geltiȝ, Vulg. *debet*]. *a* **1175** *Cott. Hom.* 239 þan seied ham god þe gelty mannen ȝe seneȝeden [etc.]. *a* **1240** *Lofsong* in *Cott. Hom* 205 Ich icnowe me gulti and creie þe leafdi merci. **13..** *Seuyn Sag.* (W.) 856 Thourgth the conseil of hiis wif, He sloughth his greihond nowt geltif. **13..** *E.E. Allit. P.* A. 688 þe gyltyf may contryssyoun hente & be þurȝ mercy to grace þryȝt. *c* **1380** WYCLIF *Wks.* (1880) 9 þei ben ..most gyltif of alle. *c* **1400** *Rom. Rose* 6394 Penaunce..for my sinne Which that I fond me gilty inne. *c* **1400** *Gamelyn* 822 We wil sle þe giltif and late þe tother goo. **1638** FORD *Lady's Trial* IV. i, Tis the guilty trembles At horrors, not the innocent. **1712** W. ROGERS *Voy.* 12 We put ten of the Mutineers in Irons... Others less guilty I punish'd and discharg'd. **1781** COWPER *Anti-Thelypth.* 188 The guiltiest still are ever least ashamed. **1814** CALHOUN *Speech* 25 Feb., Wks. 1864 II. 92, I know not which to pronounce the most guilty: the nation that inflicts a wrong, or that which quietly submits to it. **1820** BYRON *Mar. Fal.* I. i, And secret as the grave to which they doom The guilty. **1870** R. W. DALE *Week-day Serm.* vi. 127 To pardon the guiltiest.

b. *transf.* of the instrument with which, or the scene where, a crime is committed; or the like.

1588 SHAKS. *Tit. A.* v. ii. 184 This one Hand yet is left, to cut your throats, Whil'st that Lauinia tweene her stumps doth hold: The Bason that receiues your guilty blood. **1590** —— *Com. Err.* IV. iv. 66 Vpon me the guiltie doores were shut. **1629** MILTON *Nativity* 39 Only with speeches fair She woo's the gentle Air To hide her guilty front with innocent Snow. **1709** MRS. MANLEY *Secr. Mem.* (1736) III. 264 Had he..not have gone to the guilty Rendezvous. **1780** COWPER *Table T.* 450 The storms that overset the joys of life, Are but His rods to scourge a guilty land. **1821** BYRON *Cain* III. i. 397 He hangs his guilty head. *a* **1854** H. REED *Lect. Brit. Poets* iv. (1857) 123 Perceiving that the barge was steering to the traitor's gate, she refused to enter that guilty portal.

2. That has committed a particular offence or crime, or is justly chargeable with a particular fault. Const. *of*.

1297 R. GLOUC. (Rolls) 6898 Holdeþ hom gulti of þe dede & lateþ..in strong prison be ydo. *c* **1380** WYCLIF *Sel. Wks.* III. 289 Gilti of schedyng þerof [þe blood of Jesus Crist]. **1414** BRAMPTON *Penit. Ps.* lxxi. (Percy Soc.) 27 Thowȝ thou be gylty of synnes sevene. **1450** LOMNER in *Paston Lett.* No. 93 I. 125 He was arreyned..upon the appechementes..and fonde gylty. **1590** SHAKS. *Com. Err.* III. ii. 168 Least my selfe be guilty to selfe wrong, Ile stop mine eares against the Mermaids song. **1593** —— *2 Hen. VI*, III. ii. 17 We intend to try his Grace to day, If he be guiltie. **1613** PURCHAS *Pilgrimage* (1614) 112 In some cases of homicide the guiltie person was put in a little-ease prison. **1676** tr. *Guillatiere's Voy. Athens* 46 They are guilty of very foul mistakes. **1681** *Trial S. Colledge* 6 You must plead to the Court, Guilty or not Guilty. **1710** BERKELEY *Princ. Hum. Knowl.* I. §91 [We] are guilty of no innovation in that respect. **1769** BLACKSTONE *Comm.* IV. xxvii. 338 One cannot but be astonished at the folly and impiety of pronouncing a man guilty, unless he was cleared by a miracle. **1792** *Anecd. W. Pitt* III. xxxix. 39, I charge the Ministers with the highest crimes that men in their stations can be guilty of. **1818** CRUISE *Digest* (ed.2) II. 392 The heir at law..had been guilty of breach of trust. **1859** LANG *Wand. India* 381 Well, plead Not guilty, and you will have it. **1884** LD. ESHER in *Law Times Rep.* LXXIII. 616/2 *note*, The deceased was also guilty of negligence or of want of reasonable care contributing to the accident. **1884** SIR S. ST. JOHN *Hayti* iii. 86 The first and last chief who was ever guilty of so unaccountable a weakness. **1894** *Solicitors' Jrnl.* XXXIX. 2/2 The..report..must state that fraud has been committed, though the guilty person need not be specified.

†**b.** *absol.* as *sb.* The person who is guilty. *Obs.*

1550 W. LYNNE *Carion's Cron.* 231 b, Therupon was the gyltye fastned aboute the necke with an yron coller..and then a fyer made..and so the Gylty roasted tyll he dyed. **1611** SPEED *Hist. Gt. Brit.* IX. xv. §56. 644 Yet at length was that Castle enforced to surrender vpon composition of life, excepting the guilties of Burgundies death. **1700** DRYDEN *Cock & Fox* 287 Oft a speedier pain the guilty feels.

c. In playful or ironical use.

1588 SHAKS. *L.L.L.* I. ii. 116 *Brag.* Is there not a ballet Boy, of the King and the Begger? *Boy.* The world was very guilty of such a Ballet some three ages since. **1648** SYMMONS *Vind. K. Chas.* 15 These Papers might have been Evidences of Truth and of Loyalty too had the Surprizers of them been guilty of these vertues. *a* **1661** FULLER *Worthies* (1840) III. 65 He died not guilty of much wealth. **1673** *Ladies Call.* II. iii. §23 The World is apt enough to malicious errors..but 'tis seldom guilty of the charitative. *a* **1704** T. BROWN *Persius' Sat.* I. Wks. 1730 I. 54 For read his trifles, and scarce in one line You'll find him guilty of the least design. **1717** BERKELEY *Jrnl. Tour Italy* 27 Jan., Wks. 1871 IV. 551 Church of the Carmelites..in the front a little diamond work, which they are sometimes guilty of. **1784** COWPER *Task* II. 12 He finds his fellow guilty of a skin Not coloured like his own.

†**3.** ***guilty of*** (rarely *to*): culpably responsible for (a result); to blame for the loss or destruction of (something). *Obs.*

a **1225** *Ancr. R.* 58 Heo is gulti of þe bestes deaðe. **1395** PURVEY *Remonstr.* (1851) 34 Ye ben giltif of alle, and cause of here dampnacioun. *Ibid.* 139 He that takith gouernance of a ship in great tempest to a man vnkunnynge, is gilti of al the ship, and alle thingis conteynid therynne. **1532** FRITH *Mirr.* ii. Wks. (1573) 87 Or els are they in ieoperdie to perishe at euery pit, and the eye giltie of their destruction for withdrawing her office from them. **1535** COVERDALE *1 Sam.* xxii. 22, I am giltye of the soules of thy fathers house. **1611** SHAKS. *Wint. T.* IV. iv. 549 Th' vnthought-on accident is guiltie To what we wildely do. **1628** MILTON *Vac. Exerc.* 96 Severn swift, guilty of Maiden's death. **1648** BOYLE *Seraph. Love* (1660) 24 It was..a want of Discretion, that was guilty of their faults. **1700** DRYDEN *Pal. & Arc.* III. 815 With mortal hatred I pursued his life, Nor he nor you were guilty of the strife. *a* **1715** BURNET *Own Time* I. (1724) I. 40 The preachers..cried out against all that were for moderate proceedings, as guilty of the blood that had been shed.

†**4.** Deserving *of*, liable *to* (a penalty). Also bound to the performance *of* (a vow) = L. *reus voti*. *Obs.*

c **1380** WYCLIF *Wks.* (1880) 10 þei ben..gylti of dampnacion. **1382** —— *Matt.* xxvi. 67 He is gilty of deth. [So **1611**; *R.V.* worthy.] *c* **1430** *Life St. Kath.* (1884) 42 And wyth sotel sleyghtes maken hem gylty to þe peynes of helle. *c* **1440** *Jacob's Well* 98 He schal be gylty to þe doom. **1577** VAUTROUILLIER *Luther on Ep. Gal.* 72 By doing good works thou shalt be made worthie of eternall life: but by beleuing in Christ thou shalt be made culpable and giltie of eternal death. **1607** HIERON *Wks.* I. 328 The sinne of nature.. maketh vs guiltie of the wrath of God. *a* **1648** LD. HERBERT *Life Hen. VIII* (1683) 420 A Man..guilty of the highest punishment. **1700** DRYDEN *Pal. & Arc.* I. 427 Some pray from prison to be freed; and come, When guilty of their vows, to fall at home.

5. Of actions or conditions: Involving guilt, culpable, criminal.

1591 SHAKS. *1 Hen. VI*, II. iv. 94 His Trespas yet liues guiltie in thy blood. **1700** DRYDEN *Fables, Cinyras & Myrrha* 263 Ill she presag'd, and yet pursu'd her lust, For guilty pleasures give a double gust. **1784** COWPER *Task* III. 70 Let her pass, and charioted along In guilty splendour, shake the public ways. **1871** MACDUFF *Mem. Patmos* vii. 85 These Laodiceans were living in guilty self-deception.

6. Of the conscience, mind, etc.: Laden with guilt, haunted by the recollection of crime.

1593 SHAKS. *3 Hen. VI.* v. vi. 11 Suspition alwayes haunts the guilty minde. **1660** F. BROOKE tr. *Le Blanc's Trav.* 28 He was in great fear during the tempest, because of his guilty conscience. **1693** T. CREECH in *Dryden's Juvenal* (1697) 335 Not sharp Revenge, not Hell it self can find A fiercer Torment than a Guilty Mind. **1821** SHELLEY *Hellas* 731 Revenge, and Wrong, bring forth their kind: The foul cubs like their parents are; Their den is in the guilty mind. **1871** E. F. BURR *Ad Fidem* iii. 53 Our minds dark, because they are guilty.

b. Of feelings, etc.: Prompted by sense of guilt.

1593 SHAKS. *Lucr.* 1482 Let guiltlesse soules be freed from guilty woe. **1641** MILTON *Ch. Govt.* v. Wks. (1851) 114 Their own guilty carriage protests they doe feare. **1667** —— *P.L.* IX. 1058 Naked left To guilty Shame. **1813** SCOTT *Rokeby* II. xxiii, In Wycliffe's conscious eye appear A guilty hope, a guilty fear.

†**7.** Conscious, cognizant, privy. Also ***guilty to oneself*** = L. *conscius sibi*. Const. *of*, *to*. *Obs.*

1599 HAKLUYT *Voy.* II. I. 7 Being guilty vnto himselfe of the murther of his kinseman Bruno..he trauailed vnto Ierusalem. **1599** B. JONSON *Cynthia's Rev.* III. ii, Ile giue out ..that I know the time, and place where he stole it, though my soule bee guiltie of no such thing. **1605** BP. HALL *Medit. & Vows* II. §4 The Elephant, that being guilty to his deformity, he cannot abide to look on his owne face in the water, but seeks..muddy channels. **1607** TOPSELL *Four-f. Beasts* (1658) 373 The Lion went away guilty of his hurt. **1613** PURCHAS *Pilgrimage* (1614) 301 Not to suffer the Alcoran..to be read..of every one; guilty of the absurdities therein contained. **1633** J. ADAMS *Exp. 2 Peter* ii. 1 Like an old courtesan, guilty of her own witheredness. **1651** N. BACON *Disc. Govt. Eng.* II. xxxvi. (1739) 162 In truth they were guilty oftentimes to themselves, that they were not within the degrees. **1685** DRYDEN *Theocritus Idyll* xxiii. *Despairing Lover* 54 Farewell..ye stones And threshold guilty of my midnight moans. **1690–1** TILLOTSON *Serm.* xxxviii. (1735) I. 359 When we are not guilty to our selves that we have deserv'd them [persecutions] from men.

8. *Comb.*

1604 SHAKS. *Oth.* III. iii. 39, I cannot thinke it That he would steale away so guilty-like, Seeing your comming. **1642** J. EATON *Honey-combe Free Justif.* 251 Guiltie-making sinne. **1860** THACKERAY *Round. Papers, On being found out* 130 This wrath of the guilty-conscienced Sachs.

Hence †'**guiltyship**, guiltiness.

1557 N. T. (Genev.) *Rom.* v. 18 Lykewyse then as by the offence of one, giltiship came on all men to condemnation.

†'**guily**, *a.* *Obs.* In 5 gyly. [f. GUILE *sb.* + -Y¹.] Full of guile; deceitful, wily.

c **1430** LYDG. *Min. Poems* (Percy Soc.) 36 Thou wenest wel but she is ful gyly,—Thou art deceyvd whanne thou best gynnest to trust. **1515** BARCLAY *Egloges* I. (1570) A ij b/2 Then let not, Cornix, playnly to say the troth, Let scabbed clawe, and gyly men be wroth. [**1849** J. WILSON *Christopher under Canvass* in *Blackw. Mag.* LXVI. 630 Richard himself is not more wily—guily—smily—and oily.]

‖**guimauve** (gimov). Also gummauve. [Fr.] The marsh-mallow, *Althæa officinalis*; also, the medicinal preparation made from its root.

1812 J. STOKES *Bot. Mat. Med.* III. 531 Marsh Mallow... Guimauve. **1857** A. HENFREY *Elem. Bot.* II. 245 The ordinary properties of this Order [*sc.* Malvaceæ] depend on the abundance of a bland mucilage, especially in the roots, as in the Marsh-mallow (the French *Guimauve*). **1866** LINDLEY & MOORE *Treas. Bot.* I. 46/2 The roots [of marshmallow] are much used, especially in France, under the name of Guimauve, to form demulcent drinks. **1870** J. D. HOOKER *Student's Flora* 71 Marsh-mallow, Guimauve. [**1880** BENTLEY & TRIMEN *Medicinal Plants* I. 35 A favourite preparation in France is the *pâte de guimauve*.] **1895** *Army & Navy Co-op. Soc. Price List* 15 Sept. 702 Guimauve Pastilles. **1900** in *N. & Q.* (1959) CCIV. 418/2 Medicated and other Lozenges, Jujubes, Pastilles, Drops and Gummauves. **1950** R. C. WREN *Potter's Cycl. Bot. Drugs* (ed. 6) 228 Marshmallow... Syn.—Mallards, Guimauve, Schloss Tea.

guimbard ('gɪmbɑːd). [ad. F. *guimbarde*, of unknown origin.] A jew's-harp.

[**1825** DANNELEY *Encycl. Mus.*, *Guimbarde*, the Jews'-harp.] **1830** MAUNDER *Treas. Knowl.* 1, *Guimbard*, a musical instrument; the Jews' harp. And in recent Dicts.

guimp, variant of GIMP *sb.*¹

guimpe (‖gɛ̃p, gɪmp). Also **guimp.** [Fr.; cf. GIMP *sb.*², WIMPLE *sb.*] A chemisette coming high up the throat; an under-blouse designed to be worn with a low-necked frock.

1850 Guimpe bouillonné [see ENTREDEUX]. **1889** in *Cent. Dict.* **1909** *Westm. Gaz.* 15 Feb. 5/3 Some of the high corselet bodices permit of nothing more than a small guimpe with sleeves. *Ibid.* 3 June 8/3 The corsage is finished with a guimpe of white spotted net. **1931** F. HURST *Back St.* III. xxxi. 276 Remaking last year's blouse into this year's guimp. **1957** M. B. PICKEN *Fashion Dict.* 155/2 *Guimpe*,.. 1. Short blouse, often with sleeves. Usually worn with a pinafore type of dress... 2. Chemisette or yoke with high, standing collar. Worn about 1910 to fill in neck-line when low-necked dresses were introduced.

guind, guine, obs. ff. of GEAN, wild cherry.

1803 J. LEYDEN *Scenes Infancy* iv. 73 The guine.

†'**guindall.** *Obs.* Also 7 **gyndall.** [a. OF. *guindal* (mod.F. *guindeau*), f. *guinder*, f. Teut. root *wind-*: see WIND *v.*] A windlass.

1628 R. NORTON *Gunner* li. 118 The Guindall or Windlas, is a conuenient inuention, to mount a peece of Ordnance. *Ibid.* liv. 123 Gyndall.

Guinea ('gɪnɪ). Forms: 7 (gennie), gin(n)ey, ginnie, -y, guinnea, -(e)y, gynny, 7–8 guiney, -ie, guyny, 7– guinea. [The geographical name appears first in Pg. as *Guiné* (hence Sp. *Guiné*, F. *Guinée*); its origin is unknown.]

I. 1. a. The European name of a portion of the West Coast of Africa, extending from Sierra Leone to Benin, used *attrib.* and *Comb.* in the following:

(In several instances the name is used loosely for West Africa or for some far-off or unknown country.)

Guinea aloe, amomum, cloth, drill, hairworm, pea, stuff; **Guinea bird**, (*a*) a guinea-hen or guinea-fowl (also *fig.*); (*b*) *jocularly*, a native African; **Guinea corn** (also with small *g*), DURRA or Indian millet, *Sorghum vulgare*; **Guinea cubebs**, *Piper Afzelii* (Syd. Soc. Lex. 1886); **Guinea current** (see quot.); **Guinea deer**, the CHEVROTAIN; †**Guinea duck**, the Muscovy duck; **Guinea goose**, the Chinese goose or swan-goose, *Anser* or *Cygnopsis cygnoides*; **Guinea grains**, grains of Paradise (Simmonds *Dict. Trade* 1858); **Guinea grass** (also with small *g*), a tall-growing fodder-grass of tropical Africa, *Panicum maximum*; **Guinea green**, same as acid-green, a bright greenish yellow (*Cent. Dict.*); **Guinea hog**, the river-pig of Guinea, *Potamochœrus pictus* (by Marcgraf

1648 called *Porcus guineensis*); **Guinea merchant**, one who trades with Guinea; hence, a slave-dealer; †**Guinea negro** or **nigger** = GUINEA-MAN 3 (*obs.*); also *ellipt.*; **Guinea (oil) palm**, *Elais guineensis* (Syd. Soc. Lex. 1886); **Guinea peach**, a strong climbing shrub of western tropical Africa, *Sarcocephalus esculentus* (N.O. *Rubiaceæ*), yielding a fruit resembling a peach (Loudon *Encycl. Plants* 1829); †**Guinea peacock, piece** (see quots.); **Guinea plum**, the plum-like fruit of a large West African tree, *Parinarium excelsum* (Loudon 1829); **Guinea pods**, the fruit of *Capsicum frutescens* (Syd. Soc. Lex. 1886); **Guinea ship**, (*a*) a ship trading to Guinea, a slave-ship; (*b*) a sailor's name for a floating medusa, *Physalia pelagica* (Cassell); **Guinea sorrel**, *Hibiscus sabdariffa* (Syd. Soc. Lex. 1886); **Guinea trader** = *Guinea merchant*; **Guinea weed**, *Petiveria alliacea* (*Treas. Bot.* 1866); †**Guinea wheat** (also with small *g*), an old name of Indian corn; †**Guinea wood** = RED-WOOD. Also GUINEA-COCK, -HEN, etc.

1759 tr. *Adanson's Voy. Senegal* 201 The *Guinea aloe, of which the negroes..make very good ropes. **1886** *Syd. Soc. Lex.*, Large-seeded *Guinea amomum, the *Amomum macrospermum*. **1637** POCKLINGTON *Altar Chr.* 52 It is a world to see, what pert *Gynny Birds their Gossips are. **1792** MAR. RIDDELL *Voy. Madeira* 60 The turkey, the African Guinea bird, and the quail, are found here. **1826** H. N. COLERIDGE *West Indies* 263 'Ki', retorted my Guinea bird. **1886** YULE & BURNELL *Hobson-Jobson*, *Guinea cloths, *Guinea stuffs*. Apparently these were piece-goods bought in India to be used in the West African trade. **1697** DAMPIER *Voy.* (1698) I. iii. 48 The Indians are Husband-men, and plant Maiz and *Guinea Corn. **1759** tr. *Adanson's Voy. Senegal* 69 At that time they [*sc.* the fields] were covered with a large kind of millet, called *guiar-natt*, or Guinea corn. **1775** ROMANS *Florida* 84 They cultivate for bread..two varieties of that species of *Panicum* vulgarly called guinea corn. **1834** R. H. FROUDE *Rem.* (1838) I. 343 The guinea-corn grows near fifteen feet high. **1875** BEDFORD *Sailor's Pocket Bk.* iv. (ed. 2) 105 The *Guinea Current is a stream current, running to the Eastward, along that part of the African coast comprised chiefly between Cape Roxo and the Bight of Biafra; extending Southward to the 3rd and 2nd parallels of North latitude. **1752** SIR J. HILL *Hist. Anim.* 579 The *Guinea-deer. **1774** GOLDSM. *Nat. Hist.* (1776) III. 240 The Chevrotain, or Guinea deer. **1644, 1652** *Ginnie, Ginney Drill [see DRILL *sb.*[3]]. **1602** CAREW *Cornwall* 24 b, Of tame Birds, Cornwall hath Doues, Geese,..*Ginney duckes. **1688** R. HOLME *Armoury* II. 299/2 The Guinny Duck..is by some Authors called a Cairo-Duck; of others a Muscovy-Duck. **1879** NEWTON in *Encycl. Brit.* X. 778/2 The largest living Goose is that called the Chinese, *Guinea, or Swan-Goose, *Cygnopsis cygnoides*. **1756** P. BROWNE *Jamaica* 366 *Guinea Grass..is frequently cultivated, to supply stabled and working cattle with food. **1834** *West Ind. Sketch Bk.* II. 9 *note*, The accidental introduction of the Guinea-grass into Jamaica in 1744. **1834** M. SCOTT *Cruise Midge* xx. (1836) 330 The faces of them [*sc.* hills] being covered with guinea-grass pieces. **1885** LADY BRASSEY *The Trades* 262 Mixed with this vegetation in large quantities was Guinea-grass. **1857** tr. *Küchenmeister's Man. Hum. Parasites* (Syd. Soc.) I. 398 By the English [it is known as] the *Guinea hair-worm. **1788** *Guinea hog [see HOG *sb.*[1] 3]. **1719** T. GORDON *Cordial Low Spirits* I. 214 You may as well argue with a *Guiney Merchant against the Selling of Slaves. **1748** in *Amer. Speech* (1952) XXVII. 283 Run-Away, a likely well-made *Guiney Negro Man, named Toney. **1789** S. LOW *Politician Outwitted* III. i, He talks as crooked as a Guinea niger. **1823** J. F. COOPER *Pioneers* xxx, One of them Guineas down in the kitchen there. **1856** P. CARTWRIGHT *Autobiogr.* 192 (De Vere), If he don't get his soul converted God will damn him as quick as he would a Guinea Negro. **1861** J. R. LOWELL *Biglow P.* 2nd Ser. i. 183 'Tain't quite hendy to pass off one o' your six-foot Guineas. **1896** J. G. WILLIAMS *Ole Plantation* Pref., I remember hearing the old plantation negroes before the war speak of one as a 'Gullah nigger' and another as a 'Guinea nigger'. **1567** G. FENNER in Hakluyt *Voy.* (1589) 148 Certain peason called *Guinie peason. **1698** FROGER *Voy.* 33 The *Guinee Peacock, which others call the Imperial, or the Lady, is black, and almost of the bigness of a Turkey. **1838** *Penny Cycl.* XI. 480/2 **Guinea pepper*, the seeds of two species of Amomum, found on the west coast of Africa, within the tropics; the one, *A. grana Paradisi*, the other *A. grandiflorum*. **1804** *Ann. Rev.* II. 29/1 The Moors are paid for their gum in pieces of calico dyed blue, called *guinea-pieces; they are seven or eight ells long, and half an ell wide. .. The Moors instantly ascertain whether a guinea-piece is fabricated in France or India, by the smell. **1855** MACAULAY *Hist. Eng.* vii. III. 161 They were crowded together like slaves in a *Guinea ship. **1813** W. MILBURN *Orient. Comm.* I. 289 *Guinea stuffs, 4½ yards each [per ton] 1200 [pieces]. **1756** *Guinea trader (see GUINEA-MAN 2). **1598** FLORIO, *Brena*, a kind of *ginnie or turkie wheate. **1610** GUILLIM *Heraldry* III. iii. (1611) 112 He beareth Azure, three eares of Ginny Wheate louped and bladed or. **1688** R. HOLME *Armoury* II. 56/2 Ginny Wheat..is also termed Indian, or Turky Wheat. **1722** *Act* in *Lond. Gaz.* No. 6040/7 Red Wood or *Guinea Wood the Hundred Weight,..one Pound ten Shillings.

b. A derogatory term for an immigrant of Italian or Spanish origin, or one of similar appearance. Also **ginny, guinny.** *U.S. slang.*

1896 *Dial. Notes* I. 418 *Guinea*, an Italian. **1897** F. MOSS *Amer. Metropolis* III. viii. 113 Boys and girls together, we would sing and waltz, While the 'Ginnie' played the organ on the sidewalks of New York. **1910** *Sat. Even. Post* 3 Sept. 18/1 Almost every Ginny..or Dutchman who lands in New York has..the address of some..cheap hotel. **1927** J. BARBICAN *Confess. Rum-runner* iv. 54 Tell that squint-eyed guinea to throw the mud-hook overboard. **1932** D. RUNYON *Guys & Dolls* x. 221 A bomb such as these Guineas like to chuck at people they do not like, especially Guineas from Chicago. **1934** J. O'HARA *Appointment in Samarra* (1935) ii. 53 Tony Murascho, who up to that time had been known only as a tough little guinny, was matched to fight a preliminary bout at McGovern's Hall.

†**2.** Short for GUINEA-FOWL, GUINEA-HEN. *Obs.*

1620 VENNER *Via Recta* iii. 58, Ginnies; or Turkies. **1647** A. ROSS *Myst. Poet.* xiv. (1675) 357 She was called Penelope, from the gennies or turky hens, named Meleagrides and Penelope, for they fed her, being an infant. [**1661** LOVELL *Hist. Anim. & Min.* Introd., The Cock and hen, patavine, Turcick, Persick, Scottish, Indian and Ginnie.]

II. (With lower-case initial.) The coin so called, or its value.

3. a. An English gold coin, not coined since 1813, first struck in 1663 with the nominal value of 20*s.*, but from 1717 until its disappearance circulating as legal tender at the rate of 21*s.* ***double guinea***: a coin equal in value to two guineas. ***spade guinea***: a guinea of the pattern coined 1787–1800, so called from the form of the escutcheon on the reverse.

In 1663 the Royal Mint was authorized to coin gold pieces of the value of 20*s.* 'in the name and for the use of the Company of Royal Adventurers of England trading with Africa'; these pieces were to bear for distinction the figure of a little elephant, and 44½ of them were to contain 1 lb. troy of 'our Crowne gold'. The 20*s.* pieces of the African company received the popular name of *guineas* almost as soon as they were issued, as being intended for use in the Guinea trade, and made of gold from Guinea; and the name was extended to later coins of the same intrinsic value. As silver was the sole standard till 1816, the value of the guinea was from the first subject to market fluctuations, according to the condition of the silver coin, which became so bad that the guinea rose as high as 30*s.* in 1695. In Dec. 1717 it was fixed at 21*s.*, after which it underwent no further alteration. The latest coinage of guineas took place in 1813; the *sovereign*, of the value of 20*s.*, was first issued in 1817.

1664 EVELYN *Diary* 9 Mar., Now it was that the fine new-milled coin, both of white money and guineas, was established. **1666** PEPYS *Diary* 29 Oct., My goldsmith..tells me that ginnys, which I bought 2,000 of not long ago, and cost me but 18½*d.* change, will now cost me 22*d.*; and but very few to be had at any price. **1673** MARVELL *Reh. Transp.* II. 19 The great little Animal was on a sudden turn'd so yellow, and grown withall so unwieldy that he might have past currant for the Elephant upon a Guinny. **1686–7** in Wood *Life* (1848) 247 *note*, I give to my dearest child y[e] Lady Shuttleworth..a gilt box wth 30 gynnyes in it. **1700** A. HAIG in J. RUSSELL *Haigs* xi. (1881) 336 Zerubabell got from me..a guinie, which is to be at 23 shillings starling and 6 penies. **1706** *Lond. Gaz.* No. 4208/3 Lost,..a..Purse, with 3 Five-Guinea Pieces, 3 double Guineas. *a* **1734** NORTH *Exam.* II. iv. §55 (1740) 259 The Duke gave him twenty Guineys to hire him to kill the King. **1777** SHERIDAN *Trip Scarb.* I. i, Can you give me change for a guinea? **1832** BABBAGE *Econ. Manuf.* xiv. (ed. 3) 124 The great step, that of abolishing the guinea, has already been taken without any inconvenience.

b. Proverbial phr. (Cf. *guinea-gold.*)

1727 GAY *Beggar's Opera* I. v. (1729) 7 A wife's like a guinea in gold.

4. A sum of money equal to the value of this coin. In present use, a name for the sum of £1.05 (21/-).

The guinea is the ordinary unit for a professional fee and for a subscription to a society or institution; the prices obtained for works of art, racehorses, and sometimes landed property, are also stated in guineas. Otherwise the word is now only occasionally used.

1688 in *Ellis Corr.* (1829) II. 186 The Royal African Company have lately a dividend of ten guineas per cent. **1699** G. HICKES in *Lett. Lit. Men* (Camden) 283 Its prime cost will at least be a guiney. **1732** FIELDING *Miser* III. iii, A turkey..which..may be bought for a guinea, or thereabouts. **1767** A. YOUNG *Farmer's Lett. to People* 49 To regard a guinea raised by cultivation as materially different in value to us from a guinea raised by any other trade. **1778** in *Boswell's Johnson* 3 Apr., I have been looking at this famous antique dog..valued at a thousand guineas. **1818** LADY MORGAN *Autobiog.* (1859) 47 A..shawl..for five guineas. **1883** *Whitaker's Almanack* 362 Winners of Races 1863–82. Derby, Oaks, St. Leger, 2,000 Guineas, 1,000 Guineas. **1884** H. SMART *Post to Finish* vii, It's a guinea to a gooseberry on Sam. **1885** *Act 48 Vict.* c. 16 §16 Such substitutes..shall be paid at the rate of seven guineas per day.

5. a. *attrib.* and *Comb.*, as ***guinea-stamp***; ***guinea-fed*** adj.; **guinea-boat** (see quot.); **guinea-corps** (see quot. 1810 s.v. GUINEA TRADE); **guinea-dropper**, one who cheats by dropping counterfeit guineas; **guinea-edge** (see quot.); **guinea-gold**, †(*a*) *collect.* guineas; (*b*) gold of which guineas were coined, gold of 22 carats; (*c*) *adj.*, of the colour of a gold guinea; **guinea-table**, ? a gaming-table, where the stake is a guinea; **guinea-wedge**, ?

1867 SMYTH *Sailor's Word-bk.*, **Guinea-boat*, a fast-rowing galley, of former times, expressly built for smuggling gold across the Channel, in use at Deal. **1710** PALMER *Proverbs* 209 'Tis astonishing that a young gentleman, bred five or six years in our own universities, shou'd, at his first coming to London, be drawn in by *guinea-droppers. **1712** GAY *Trivia* III. 249 Who now the Guinea-Dropper's Bait regards, Trick'd by the Sharper's Dice or Juggler's Cards? **1890** ZAEHNSDORF *Art Bookbinding* 176 **Guinea-edge*, a roll with a pattern similar to the edge of an old guinea. **1810** BENTHAM *Art of Packing* (1821) 175 *note*, Inconvenient to a *guinea-fed juryman to attend oftener than the Act requires! **1671** *Lond. Gaz.* No. 599/4 On Wednesday the second of August, there went away from his Masters house..a young man by name John Kirke..with a considerable summ in *Guiny-Gold. **1938** M. K. RAWLINGS *Yearling* xi. 110 The river shone in the late sunlight, Guinea-gold, like the bright flowers. **1966** E. PALMER *Plains of Camdeboo* xiii. 220 They [*sc.* cobras] must just have sloughed their old skins, for they shone as if fresh minted. Often they are brown or yellow, sometimes a guinea-gold or this handsome red-gold. **1795** BURNS *For a' That* 7 The rank is but the *guinea stamp; The man's the gowd for a' that. **1811** L. M. HAWKINS *C'tess & Gertr.* II. 57 She will go to the *guinea-table..rather than not play. **17..** MRS. DELANY in *Life & Corr.* (1861) III. 251 He has given me some very pretty *guinea wedges.

b. quasi-*adj.* Priced at or amounting to a guinea.

1742 ? PITT *Sp. Ho. Comm.* in *Anecd.*, etc. (1797) I. iv. 79 The most stupid serjeant at law that ever spoke for a guinea fee. **1742** H. WALPOLE *Lett.* (1846) I. 188 Twice a-week there are to be [in Ranelagh-gardens] ridottos, at guinea tickets, for which you are to have a supper and music. **1801** C. LAMB in C. Kegan Paul *W. Godwin* (1876) II. 87 Leave him to take guinea-and-a-half lodgings with mama in Leghorn. **1897** *Daily News* 15 June 8/5 Most of the business has been in the guinea and two guinea seats.

†**guinea-cock.** *Obs.* The male of the guinea-fowl; the guinea-fowl (earlier called *turkey-cock*).

1577 B. GOOGE *Heresbach's Husb.* IV. (1586) 166, I would faine learne the right ordring of their outlandish Birds, called Ginny Cocks, and Turky Cockes...before the yeere of our Lorde .1530. they were not seen with us. **1599** HAKLUYT *Voy.* II. II. 108 We found in this place..great plentie of partriges, Guiniecocks, and other wilde foules. **1599** H. BUTTES *Dyets drie Dinner* K v, The Ginny-Cocke was first brought out of Numidia, into Italy. **1601** HOLLAND *Pliny* I. 332 We haue written alreadie of the Ginny or Turky cocks and hens, vpon whom Nature hath bestowed a folding crest.

guinead, obs. form of GWYNIAD.

'guinea-fowl. [Imported from Guinea in 16th c.; cf. F. *poule de la Guinée* (Belon 1555).] A gallinaceous bird of the genus *Numida*, esp. *N. Meleagris*, which is a common domestic fowl in Europe. It has slate-coloured plumage with white spots.

[**1655** MOUFET & BENNET *Health's Improv.* (1746) 166 There are some which lately brought hither certain chequer'd Hens and Cocks out of New Guinea, spoted white and black like a Barber's Apron, whose Flesh is like to the Flesh of Turkies.] **1788** J. MATHEWS *Voy. Sierra-leone* 48 It is..surprising that the Guinea fowls, which are real natives of the country..should be neglected by them. **1802** BINGLEY *Anim. Biog.* (1813) II. 249 The common guinea-fowl. **1862** H. KINGSLEY *Ravenshoe* lii, Some guinea-fowl were noisily preparing for roost.

'guinea-hen.

†**1.** The turkey-hen or turkey. *Obs.*

1578 LYTE *Dodoens* II. lii. 214 With white and blacke spots, lyke to the feathers of the Turkie or Ginny hen. **1588** R. PARKE tr. *Mendoza's Hist. China* 322 Ginny hennes, otherwise called Turkey cockes, and in Spanish Pauos. **1601** HOLLAND *Pliny* I. 296 The Ginnie or Turkey hens in a part of Africke called Numidia, be in great request. *a* **1637** B. JONSON *Horace's Country Life* 53 The Ginny-hen Could not goe downe my belly then More sweet than Olives. **1669** WORLIDGE *Syst. Agric.* (1681) 176 Turkeys, or Ginney-hens, or Cocks, are a melancholy Fowl. **1698** FRYER *Acc. E. India & P.* 21 Fowls for Game they have several, the best of which is the Guinney Hen.

2. The guinea-fowl, or the female of the same.

1599 H. BUTTES *Dyets drie Dinner* K iv, The Græcians call these foules Meleagridae:..For (they say) Meleagers Sisters were transformed into Ginny-hens. **1703** DAMPIER *Voy.* III. 23 Guinea-Hens; which the Natives of these Islands call *Gallena Pintada*, or the Painted Hen. **1781** PENNANT in *Phil. Trans.* LXXI. 76 The Guinea hens have long been imported into Britain. **1855** TENNYSON *Brook* 126 He praised his hens, his geese, his guinea-hens.

†**b.** *slang.* A courtezan, prostitute. *Obs.*

1604 SHAKS. *Oth.* I. iii. 317 Ere I would say, I would drowne my selfe for the loue of a Gynney Hen, I would change my Humanity with a Baboone. **1639** GLAPTHORNE *Alb. Wallenstein* III. iii, Yonder's the cock oth' game, About to tred yon ginny hen, they'r billing. **1708** *Brit. Apollo* No. 90. 2/2 You in an Honourable Amour,..cannot bear a little Cackling from a Guinea Hen!

3. *Comb.*, as **guinea-hen flower**, the fritillary, *Fritillaria Meleagris*; **guinea-hen weed**, a West Indian herb, the *Petiveria alliacea*.

1597 GERARDE *Herbal* I. lxxix. 122 The checkered Daffodill or Ginny hen flower, hath..flowers..checkered most strangely. **1629** PARKINSON *Paradisi* vii. 44, I leaue to eueryone their owne will to call it in English eyther Fritillaria, as it is called of most, or the checkerd Daffodill, or the Ginnee Hen flower, or, as I doe, the checkerd Lilly. **1829** LOUDON *Encycl. Plants* 297 *Petiveria*..is thought..to be coveted by Guinea-hens, and hence its vulgar name of Guinea-hen weed. **1866** *Treas. Bot.* 556/1 Guinea-hen flower, *Fritillaria meleagris*.

Guinea-man ('gɪnɪmən).

1. A vessel trading to the coast of Guinea; hence, a slave-ship. *Obs.* exc. *Hist.*

c **1695** J. MILLER *Descr. New York* (1843) 37 On board a small Guineaman. **1773** *Gentl. Mag.* XLIII. 46 A ship belonging to Liverpool, with 350 slaves on board, was lately carried into Barbadoes by another Guineaman, after a smart engagement. **1800** CAPT. CUNNINGHAM in *Naval Chron.* IV. 417 The *Dick* Guineaman, of Liverpool. **1834** M. SCOTT *Cruise Midge* i. (1836) 6 The bars of the various African rivers where the contraband Guineamen were in the habit of lurking. **1881** CLARK RUSSELL *Ocean Free Lance* II. iv. 167 With the hope of netting one of the numerous contraband Guineamen crossing the Atlantic for the Spanish Main.

†**2.** A Guinea merchant. *Obs. rare.*

1756 SPENCE *Anecd.* (1858) 281 Mr. Pope was with Sir Godfrey Kneller one day, when his nephew, a Guinea trader, came in. ' Nephew, (said Sir Godfrey,) you have the honour of seeing the two greatest men in the world'. 'I don't know how great you may be, (said the Guinea-man), but I don't like your looks: I have often bought a man, much better than both of you together, all muscles and bones, for ten guineas'.

3. A native of Guinea.

1830 CAPT. H. CROW *Mem.* 168 Convinced me that there were more untruths said of Guineamen than any other class of people. **1846** MRS. GORE *Eng. Charac.* (1852) 92 Dissimilar in aspect and aspirations as a Guineaman and a Hindoo. **1866** WHITTIER *Marg. Smith's Jrnl.* Prose Wks. 1889 I. 14 His skin was swarthy, not black like a Moor or Guinea-man, but of a color not unlike that of tarnished copper coin.

4. (With small *g.*) *nonce-uses.* One who earns guinea fees (as a juryman); also, a subscriber of a guinea per annum to a society.

1810 [see GUINEA TRADER]. **1818** BENTHAM *Ch. Eng.* 232 This impertinently intruding guinea-man at Sion-College.

Guinean ('gɪniːən), *a.* and *sb.* Also 6 **Guynean.** [f. GUINEA + -AN.] **A.** *adj.* Of or pertaining to Guinea. **B.** *sb.* An inhabitant of Guinea.

1589 J. HAWKINS *Voy. Coast of Guinea* in Hakluyt *Voy.* 525 Their foode..passeth all other Guyneans for kine. **1607** TOPSELL *Foure-f. Beasts* 705 The Tatus, or Gvinean Beast ..is brought..out of the new-found world, and out of Guinia. **1650** BULWER *Anthropomet.* 112 The Guineans take their meat torne in peeces with the thre midmost fingers. **1875** A. NEWTON in *Encycl. Brit.* III. 758/2 Beginning on the West Coast, where the Libyan Subregion stops, we have another Subregion, the 'Guinean', comprising the seaboard from Sierra Leone to somewhere about Angola. **1893** —— *Dict. Birds* 350 This 'Guinean' Province occupies what is commonly called the 'West Coast' of Africa. **1963** *Daily Tel.* 14 Feb. 16/1 The teacher, Miss Svetlana Ushakova, 30, offended the ambassador by fraternising with Guineans. **1963** *Guardian* 11 Mar. 9/3 All Guinean francs held abroad were yesterday declared valueless, to combat currency trafficking and the circulation of counterfeit money. **1970** *Times* 6 May 10/6 She wears a striking brown and gold Guinean warrior's hat.

Guinea pepper. **a.** An early name for Cayenne pepper. **b.** (See quot. 1839.)

1597 GERARDE *Herbal* II. lxvi. 293 Guinie pepper hath the taste of pepper, but not the power or vertue. **1620** MELTON *Astrolog.* 40 Hee flung Ginny-Pepper in the Hangmans eyes as he came to put the noose ouer his necke. **1626** BACON *Sylva* §922 It hath beene a Practice to burne a Pepper, they call Ginny-Pepper; Which hath such a strong Spirit, that it prouoketh a Continuall Sneezing, in those that are in the Roome. **1678** BUTLER *Hud.* III. i. 320 And choak with Fumes of Guiny-Pepper. **1705** BOSMAN *Guinea* 305 *Guinea Pepper* ..grows on Shrubs in red Shells or Husks. **1794** MARTYN *Rousseau's Bot.* xvi. 202 Capsicum or Guinea Pepper, is also of this lurid order. **1832** *Veg. Subst. Food* 313 The Guinea Pepper..introduced into England, from India, so early as 1548. **1839** *Penny Cycl.* XI. 480/2 *Guinea pepper*, the seeds of two species of Amomum, found on the west coast of Africa, within the tropics; the one *Amomum grana Paradisi*, the other, *Amomum grandiflorum*. They are powerfully aromatic, stimulant, and cordial.

guinea-pig ('gɪnɪpɪg). [Perh. the animal was thought to resemble the young of the Guinea Hog (*Potamochœrus*); or the name *Guinea* may have been applied loosely, as in some other instances, as a designation for an unknown distant country. Confusion with *Guiana* seems unlikely.]

1. a. A rodent mammal (*Cavia Cobaya*) of the genus *Cavia*, originating in S. America, but now widely distributed in a half-domesticated state.

The term is applied dialectally to the wood-louse, and in Cornwall to the small white cowrie.

1664 POWER *Exp. Philos.* I. 16 You may see them [Cheese Mites]..like so many Ginny-Pigs, munching and chewing the cud. **1673** C. BROWN *Trav. Germany*, etc. (1677) 109 Some odde dishes at their Tables; as Guiny-pigs, divers sorts of Snails, and Tortoises. **1713** STEELE *Guardian* No. 106. ¶4 These were driven off at last by a Lap-dog, who was succeeded by a Guiney pig. **1774** GOLDSM. *Nat. Hist.* (1776) IV. 72 The mouse being..the most timid of all quadrupedes, except the guinea-pig. **1806** HATCHETT in *Phil. Trans.* XCVI. 378 The same chemist found that the urine of the guinea-pig deposited carbonat of lime. **1881** BESANT & RICE *Chapl. of Fleet* II. xvii, There isn't a mouse in all Epsom can be muter, or a guinea-pig dumber.

b. A person or thing used like a guinea-pig as the subject of an experiment.

[**1913** G. B. SHAW *Quintessence of Ibsenism Now Completed* 135 The..folly which sees in the child nothing more than the vivisector sees in a guinea pig: something to experiment on with a view to rearranging the world.] **1920** U. SINCLAIR *Brass Check* xviii. 102 Say to yourself that Upton Sinclair is a guinea-pig. **1923** H. G. WELLS *Men Like Gods* 180 And may I ask..the nature of this *treatment* of yours, these experiments of which we are to be the—guinea pigs, so to speak? Is it to be anything in the nature of a vaccination? **1955** *Times* 15 June 5/3 The corporation are also guinea-pigs, because it is hoped that decisions arising out of these cases will save a great amount of public money and trouble, and provide a guide in law and principle which may go a long way in aiding other cases. **1955** R. BANNISTER *First Four Minutes* 119 In some of my experiments I used other athletes as guinea pigs. **1961** *Times* 24 May 13/6 Something of a guinea-pig, the ship has demonstrated its value. **1970** *Daily Tel.* 13 Oct. 19/5 'You can't detect any difference unless you know it's synthetic material,' one guinea-pig commented yesterday.

2. *Naut.* **a.** A midshipman in the East Indian service. **b.** An inefficient seaman.

1747 *Adv. Kidnapped Orphan* 69 He sent his nephew, at the age of fourteen, on a voyage as a Guinea-pig. **1748** SMOLLETT *Rod. Rand.* xxiv, A brave fellow as ever crackt bisket;—none of your guinea pigs. **1840** MARRYAT *Poor Jack* xxvi, The midshipmen, or guinea pigs, as they are called. **1867** SMYTH *Sailor's Word-Bk.*, *Guinea-pigs*, the younger midshipmen of an Indiaman.

3. In various jocular or contemptuous applications with allusions to the coin. **a.** One who receives the fee of a guinea; e.g. a medical man, a director of a public company (see quot. 1895), a clergyman doing duty for another, etc. **b.** (See quot.)

a. 1821 COMBE *Wife* IV. (1869) 347 'Oh! oh!' cried Pat, 'how my hand itches, Thou guinea pig [a 'vet.'], in boots and breeches, To trounce thee well'. **1855** SMEDLEY *H. Coverdale* xxxvii, That ailment ['heart-ache'] which defies those guinea-pigs, 'the faculty'. **1858** *Chamb. Jrnl.* 1 May 279/2 Whenever the court sits..the guinea-pigs [jurymen] sit along with it. **1871** *Temple Bar* XXXI. 320 'Guinea pigs,' the pleasant name for those gentlemen of more rank than means..who have a guinea and a copious lunch when they attend board meetings. **1891** S. MOSTYN *Curatica* 18 The Vicar has managed by himself, with occasional help from guinea-pigs. **1895** A. J. WILSON *Gloss. Terms Stock Exch.* s.v., A man who lives by getting himself placed upon the Boards of a number of companies whose business he can have neither the time nor the qualifications to assist in directing, is a 'guinea pig'.

attrib. **1887** *Standard* 12 May, We..have here the 'guinea pig' Director in all his pristine simplicity. **1909** *Daily Chron.* 18 Jan. 4/6 Greedy manufacturers..have already laid their plans for large commercial trusts with their 'expenses'-paid Members of Parliament, purchased Press and guinea-pig peers. **1930** *Economist* 9 Aug. 284/2 A large number of the 'bubble' company boards of the 1928 boom were packed with guinea-pig directors.

b. 1860 FAIRHOLT *Costume* (ed. 2) 328 Those who persevered in the fashion [of wearing hair-powder] paid one guinea a year for the privilege, hence the jesters nicknamed them *guinea-pigs*.

c. An evacuee or billetee in the war of 1939–45. *colloq.*

1939 *Daily Dispatch* 10 Oct., We are known here [West of England] as the *guinea-pigs*..and we are being treated locally like those tailless rodents. **1940** *Manch. Evening News* 16 July, I toured a part of Manchester in which every other house seems to be teeming with *guinea-pigs*, the nickname for the men [*sc.* soldiers] because the billeting allowances are about a guinea. **1941** *New Statesman* 30 Aug. 218/3 Guinea Pig—Evacuated civil servant.

Hence **guinea-pigging** *vbl. sb.*, the practice of acting as director of a company for the sake of the guinea fees; also of acting as clerical substitute (or, rarely, engaging the services of one); **guinea-pig** *v. intr.*, to act as the subject of an experiment; also *trans.*, to use (a person) thus.

1887 *Ch. Times* 14 Jan. 26/4 The Rector..preferred guinea-pigging once a Sunday to being present at his post twice a day. **1890** J. HATTON *By order Czar* (1891) 125 A unanimity of belief in joint-stock enterprises that makes guinea-pigging a positive virtue. **1894** WILKINS & VIVIAN *Green bay tree* I. 7 By 'guinea-pigging', floating Companies, and other means. **1955** *Times* 20 June 9/4 He..might like to spend a 'holiday' at Salisbury, guinea pigging for the Common Cold Research Unit. **1961** *Time* (Atlantic ed.) 3 Mar. 19 [The astronauts] were guinea-pigged into hot chambers.

Guinea trade. [In sense 1 from GUINEA I, in 2 from GUINEA II.]

†**1.** The trade with Guinea.

1673 DRYDEN *Amboyna* Prol. 9 They shall have all..The Straits, the Guinea trade, the herrings too, Nay to preserve them, they shall pickle you.

2. *jocularly.* The taking of guinea fees.

1808 in *Bentham's Art Packing* (1821) 190 Deeply concerned and interested in the Guinea Trade. **1810** BENTHAM *Art Packing* (1821) 33 The corps being termed the Guinea corps; the members of it collectively Guineamen; and it taken separately, this or that one is familiarly spoken of as being concerned and interested in the Guinea trade.

Guinea worm. A parasitic nematoid worm (*Filaria medinensis*) frequent in many parts of Guinea, whence the name; it is long and thread-like, of a white colour, inhabiting the human skin, esp. of the lower extremities, where its presence causes painful suppuration. Also, the disease occasioned by its presence.

1699 DAMPIER *Voy.* II. II. 89 Guinea Worms are very frequent in some Places of the West Indies. **1799** W. G. BROWNE *Trav. Africa & Syria* xxi. 326 The disease called the Guinea Worm is known..by the same name [*Fertît*]. **1833** BAIRD in *Proc. Berw. Nat. Club* I. No. 1. 24 The Guinea-worm, which is a species of Filaria. **1872** W. AITKIN *Sci. Med.* (ed. 6) I. 138 The Guinea worm is essentially a tropical parasite.

attrib. **1898** P. MANSON *Trop. Diseases* xxxiii. 517 Lately ..a French naval surgeon, has introduced a system of managing guinea-worm cases which bids fair to shorten treatment.

†**guinet.** *Obs.* [? ad. F. *guinot.*] A small bird, ? a chaffinch.

1725 BRADLEY *Fam. Dict.* s.v. *Plover*, When some Guinets get into your Nets, which are Birds a little bigger than Larks.

guingam, obs. form of GINGHAM.

‖**guinguette**[1] (gɛ̃gɛt). [Fr., of unknown origin.] A suburban cabaret; a place of entertainment of a rather low class, for drinking and dancing.

1779 KEATE *Sketches fr. Nat.* (ed. 2) II. 68 Any of the guingettes about Paris. **1818** LADY MORGAN *Autobiog.* (1859) 64 Oh! England, if you would only have guinguettes where '*on danse tous les jours*', instead of drinking porter and gin. **1839** W. CHAMBERS *Tour Belgium* 77/1 The small village of Laeken..contains a number of guinguettes, or taverns with public gardens. **1885** D. HANNAY in *Mag. of Art* Sept. 448/2 Tearing up an old garden with its fountains to put a guinguette in place thereof.

Hence **guingettize** *v. intr.*, to dance as at a guinguette (*nonce-wd.*).

1840 DISRAELI in *Corr. w. Sister* 15 Aug., There was a temporary room for the ball, which was in itself a blunder, as anybody can guingettise and princes give balls because they have palaces.

‖**guinguette**[2] (gɛ̃gɛt). [Fr.] A two-wheeled vehicle without a hood; a gig.

1852 THACKERAY *Esmond* II. xiii, The king drove thither in Marshal Villar's own guinguette.

Guinness ('gɪnɪs). [Family name.] The proprietary name of a brand of stout manufactured by the firm of Guinness; a bottle or glass of this. Also *Comb.*, as ***Guinness-coloured*** adj.

1836 DICKENS *Sk. Boz* I. 190 A large hamper of Guinness's stout. *Ibid.* 191 Taking..a draught of Guinness. **1842** BARHAM *Ingol. Leg.* 2nd Ser. 79 With a three-corner'd Sandwich, and *soupçon* of 'Guinness's'. **1897** *Sat. Rev.* 2 Jan. 2/1 An Irishman drinking his Guinness with uncharacteristic quietude in a London 'pub'. **1922** G. SAINTSBURY *Scrap Bk.* viii. 33 You can't see the stones for the Guinness-coloured foam. **1928** H. JENKINS *Stiffsons* iv. 118 Oh! for some fish and chips and a bottle of Guinness. **1930** [see *black velvet*, BLACK *a.* 19].

guin(n)iad, obs. form of GWYNIAD.

guipp, variant of GUP *int. Obs.*

‖**guipure** (gipyr). [Fr., f. *guiper* to cover with silk, etc., ad. Teut. *wîp-*, represented by G. *weifen* to turn, Goth. *weipan* to crown.]

1. A kind of lace (see quot. 1869).

1843 MRS. ROMER *Rhone*, etc. II. 14 These exquisite mouldings produce the effect of costly guipure laid over coloured satin. **1869** MRS. PALLISER *Lace* iii. (ed. 2) 34 The term guipure is now so extensively applied it is difficult to give a limit to its meaning. We can only define it as lace where the flowers are either joined by 'brides', or large coarse stitches, or lace that has no ground at all. **1883** *Truth* 31 May 769/2 The latter being covered with a piece of old Venetian guipure.

attrib. **1844** LADY G. FULLERTON *Ellen Middleton* (1854) II. xiv. 149 A berthe of the richest Guipure old lace. **1850** *Harper's Mag.* I. 288 An embroidery of lace imitating guipure royal. **1891** *Times* 5 Oct. 4/2 Some laces in the guipure style are also selling. **1899** *Daily News* 19 Aug. 7/5 Puffings of yellow chiffon, with a pair of guipure wings.

2. A kind of gimp.

1864 in WEBSTER. **1890** *Daily News* 20 June 6/4 The bodice was pink silk, with trimming of black guipure; the sleeves being also pink with guipure let in. **1893** *Times* 8 July 12/2 Finished with white guipure and ribands.

guira ('gwaɪərə). [Amer. Sp., f. Tupi *guira* bird.] In full ***guira cuckoo***. A non-parasitic cuckoo, *Guira guira*, found in eastern tropical South America.

1866 *Proc. Zool. Soc.* 79 Guira Cuckoo (*Guira piririgua*). One of these birds during the early part of the summer dropped or laid an egg on the ground in the aviary. **1867** *Ibid.* 585 When alarmed it [*sc. Opisthocomus cristatus*] throws up its crest in exactly the same manner as the Guira. **1889** P. L. SCLATER *Argentine Ornith.* II. 32 The Guira Cuckoo is about sixteen inches long, has red eyes and blue feet, and an orange-red beak. **1904** *Westm. Gaz.* 13 May 12/1 The guira lays blue eggs covered with a network of chalky matter. **1957** M. H. MITCHELL *Observ. Birds S.E. Brazil* 93 Guira Cuckoos are odd-looking birds, with their shaggy heads, very long tails..and baleful yellow eyes. *Ibid.* 94 The voice of the Guira is louder and the calls more varied.

guird, guirlande, obs. ff. GIRD, GARLAND.

‖**guiro** ('gwaɪrəʊ). Also †**guira.** [Sp., gourd.] A musical instrument consisting usu. of a gourd with a serrated surface, the rubbing of which produces a rasping sound.

1898 E. H. HAWLEY in *Amer. Anthropologist* XI. 344 An instrument of this class which has seemed to be confined to the West Indies..is called the *guira*, and is made of a gourd varying in size in different instruments... In the hand of a native *guira* player a wonderful rhythmic sound comes from this dried..shell. **1914** F. MORRIS *Catal. Crosby Brown Coll. Mus. Instr.* II. II. 183 In..Cuba the *maruga*..is rubbed with pieces of wire. The *guiro*, still another form, is made of a long-necked gourd with lines cut in the surface while the gourd is still green. The scraper is a small stick. **1934** S. R. NELSON *All about Jazz* vii. 166 The Guiro is a native vegetable which is scraped with a fork of two prongs, or, alternatively, struck with a pair of xylophone sticks. **1944** W. APEL *Harvard Dict. Mus.* 566/2 Primitive instruments such as..the guiro (a serrated gourd scraped with a stick), have been used by Prokofiev..and Stravinsky. **1961** A. BAINES *Mus. Instruments* i. 27 Scrapers have survived into modern times, for instance in the folk music of Venezuela, where the *guiro* or *charrasca* is made from a bull's horn, or in the rumba bands of Cuba and the fashionable Western world which use a scraping gourd, also known as *guiro*. **1966** *Crescendo* Dec. 27/1 The rest of the front-line thump tambourines, click claves, scratch guiros or shake maraccas.

guis, obs. Sc. form of GOOSE.

guisan, obs. form of GUISIAN.

†'**Guisard**, *sb.*[1] *Obs.* Also 7 guyzard. [a. F. *guisard*, f. (*duc de*) *Guise.*] A partisan of the Guise faction in France in the 16th c. (In the

first quot. app. used with allusion to the name of *Guy* Fawkes.)

1607 DEKKER *Knts. Conjur.* (1842) 54 Factious guyzards, that lay trains of sedition to blow vp the common-wealth. **1681** DRYDEN *Medal* Ep. Whigs, The Holy League of the French Guisards. **1683** —— *Vind. Dk. Guise* 32 The three Estates were at that time compos'd generally of Guisards, factious, hot-headed, rebellious, interressed men.

guisard ('gaɪzəd), *sb.*[2] Chiefly *Sc.* Forms: 7 **guyz-, gyzard, 7-9 gysart, 8 guisart, gysard, 9 guizard, -art, 8- guisard.** [f. GUISE *v.* + -ARD.]

One who goes about in a fantastic guise or dress; a masquerader, a mummer. See also GUISER.

1626 *Presbyt. Rec. Lanark* in *Annals Lesmahagow* (1864) 149 Wm Weir pyper to the gysarts of Lesmohego. **1696** in Maidment *Sc. Pasquils* (1868) 307 Thou would terrify the Souterkines, More than a gyzard in black sheep skines. **1755** R. FORBES *Ajax' Sp., Jrnl. fr. Lond.* 28 The third was an auld wizen'd, haave coloured carlen, a sad gysard indeed, an' as baul' as ony ettercap. **1770** DALRYMPLE in *Bannatyne Poems* Notes 286 The exhibitions of gysarts are still known in Scotland, being the same with the Christmas mommery of the English. **1805** J. NICOL *Poems* I. 29 (Jam.) Whan gloamin gray comes frae the east, Through a' the gysarts venture; In sarks an' paper helmets drest. **1854** KEDDIE *Phemie Millar* III. 191 It is not Christmas to be looking out for guisards. **1869** MRS. GORDON *Life Sir D. Brewster* xii. 182 Apparitions of tall bearded guisards into quiet families. **1893** *Northumbld. Gloss.*, *Guizard, Guizart, Guizer*, a masquerader, a mummer.

Hence **'guisard** *v. intr.*, to act as a guisard, to masquerade. (Only in vbl. sb.)

1815 SCOTT *Guy M.* xxxvi, They hae taen Yule before it comes and gaun a-guisarding.

guisard, obs. form of GIZZARD.

guisarme, variant of GISARME.

guise (gaɪz), *sb.* Forms: 3-6 **gise**, 3-7 **guyse**, 4-8 **gyse**, 5-6 **gys**, 6 **geyse, gyze**, *Sc.* **gyis(s, gyss**, 6-7 **guize**, 4- **guise**. [a. OF. and F. *guise*, = Pr., It. *guisa*, of Teut. origin; cf. OHG. *wîsa* (G. *weise*), OE. *wîse* WISE *sb.*]

†**1.** Manner, method, way; fashion, style. Rarely *pl. Obs.*

13.. *K. Alis.* 6988 Tho thou myghtest, in mony gyse, Y-seo solas and game arise. **1340** HAMPOLE *Pr. Consc.* 1572 Þat may be knawen bi sere gyse. *c* **1380** WYCLIF *Wks.* (1880) 186 Many newe gises of pride and worldly vanyte. *c* **1400** *Rom. Rose* 4292 She knew ech wrenche and every gyse Of love. *c* **1420** *Pallad. on Husb.* II. 68 To wede ek cornys drie, is no good gise. **1456** *How Wise Man taught Son* 143 in Hazl. *E.P.P.* I. 175 Louys awe ys the best gyse, My sone, to make thy wyfe aferde. **1513** DOUGLAS *Æneis* I. Prol. 156 The thre first bukis he [Caxton] hes ourhippit quyte, Salfand ane litle twiching Polidorus,.. And that full sympillie on his awin gyse. **1523** FITZHERB. *Husb.* §35 In some countreys.. they do fan theyr corne, the whiche is a verye good gise. **1568** *Hist. Jacob & Esau* v. x. G iij, Jacob must be aduanced in any wyse; But I shall one day handle him of the new guise. **1596** SPENSER *F.Q.* IV. x. 6 On stately pillours fram'd after the Doricke guize. **1637** RUTHERFORD *Lett.* (1862) I. 258 Follow not the guises of this sinful world. **1644** MILTON *Areop.* (Arb.) 37 A military roughnes, resembling most of the Lacedæmonian guise. **1670** EACHARD *Cont. Clergy* 28 Thinking, that whatsoever is written.. must be beyond the guise of common speech. **1714** GAY *Sheph. Week* Proeme, No poet.. hath hit on the right simple Eclogue after the true ancient guise of Theocritus. **1728** MORGAN *Algiers* I. Pref. 24 The Introduction or Epitome of the Country I treat of is ..in no guise what I first intended. **1765** H. WALPOLE *Otranto* v. (1798) 80 He began in artful guise to sound the Marquis. **1782** COWPER *Gilpin* xliii, And thus unto the Calender In merry guise he spoke.

b. With mixture of sense 5.

1820 BYRON *Mar. Fal.* I. ii. 163 Sneering nobles, in more polish'd guise, Whisper'd the tale. **1864** *Social Sci. Rev.* 266 To learn in how varied a guise, shell and shot.. do their work.

†**2.** Appointed, usual, or characteristic manner; custom, habit, practice; the 'ways' (of a country). *Obs.* Very common in the 16th and first half of the 17th c.

13.. *Seuyn Sag.* (W.) 246 Thai weren wedded bi commun dome, Anon in the gise of Rome. *c* **1400** *Sowdone Bab.* 1932 'Sir' she saide, 'drinke to me, As the Gyse is of my londe.' *c* **1440** *Generydes* 2974 As the Costom was, after ther gise, They beryed hym in honorabill wise. **1494** *Househ. Ord.* (1790) 112 As for the voyde after meate the guise hath been thus. **1513** DOUGLAS *Æneis* v. ii. 71 Eftir thair payane ryte and gise. **1528** SIR F. BRYAN *Let to Hen. VIII* in Froude *Hist. Eng.* (ed. 2) I. 138 He knew the gyze of England as well as few men did. **1536** BELLENDEN *Cron. Scot.* (1821) I. 18 As is the gise of the gentil lioun. **1578** TIMME *Calvin on Gen.* 26 As is the guise of rash and fickle headed men. *a* **1592** H. SMITH *Serm.* (1637) 557 This hath beene alwayes the guise of the wicked, to use the smoothest speech when they intend most mischiefe. *a* **1605** MONTGOMERIE *Misc. Poems* xxxviii. 11 All such rites as wes the guyse, They made that grit god sacrifyce. **1660** H. MORE *Myst. Godl.* v. xiv. 168 The Apostles and Martyrs highly complemented according to the ancient guize of the Pagan Ceremonies. **1725** POPE *Odyss.* XIV. 65 It never was our guise To slight the poor, or aught humane despise.

†**3.** Manner of carrying oneself; behaviour, carriage, conduct, course of life. *Obs.*

1303 R. BRUNNE *Handl. Synne* 3329 Shal grace come neuere yn þat lande þere men haue swyche gyse yn hande. *c* **1315** SHOREHAM 52 Wanne he [the prest] y-ordred hys, Hym falth an holy gyse. **1422** tr. *Secreta Secret., Priv. Priv.* 158 Suche byth the vyse manys gyse and his maneris. *c* **1450** *Cov. Myst.* (Shaks. Soc.) 118 Thou hast begownne a synfulle gyse. *a* **1529** SKELTON *P. Sparowe* 1251 It were no gentle gyse This treatyse to despyse. **1540** HYRDE tr. *Vives' Instr. Chr. Wom.* (1592) Q ij, Thou art a foole to looke after that I should name thee for a wife, when thou usest not wives guise. **1549-62** STERNHOLD & H. *Ps.* xxxvii. 8 Their wicked steps avoyd and flie, and follow not their guise. *a* **1639** W. WHATELEY *Prototypes* II. xxxi. (1640) 119 See here the guise of a carnall earthly-minded man. **1667** MILTON *P.L.* XI. 576 By thir guise Just men they seemd. *a* **1670** SPALDING *Troub. Chas. I* (Bannatyne Club) II. 260 This goukit gys wes begun be our baillie to schow his love to the good caus. **1813** HOGG *Queen's Wake* 229 That morning found rough Tushilaw In all the father's guise appear.

4. Style or fashion of attire or personal adornment; condition with regard to dress; attire, costume, garb. Now only *arch.* in phrases such as ***in the guise of...***, in ***lowly (festive,*** etc.), ***guise.*** †***new guise*** (advb. phr.): in the new fashion.

c **1275** LAY. 19641 Six cnihtes.. in pore men guyse. **1303** R. BRUNNE *Handl. Synne* 3215 þey.. leue crystyn mennys acyse And haunte alle þe newe gyse. **13..** *Coer de L.* 593 All in palmeres gyse The holy land for to devyse. *c* **1440** *Generydes* 5272 He mett in his viage A pore palmer, goth in sympill gise. *a* **1450** *Knt. de la Tour* (1868) 29 Faire doughtres, y praie you that ye be not the furst to take new shappes and gises of array. *c* **1450** *Merlin* xxiii. 420 Theire heer longe waxen, in gise of maydenes and tressed at theire bakkes. *a* **1529** SKELTON *E. Rummyng* 74 With clothes vpon her hed.. Wrythen in wonder wyse, After the Sarasyns gyse. *a* **1555** LYNDESAY *Tragedy* 359 Ane Tailȝeour quhilk hes fosterit bene in france, That can mak garmentis on the gayest gyse. **1583** GREENE *Mamillia* II. (1593) H, Vp fro the wast like a man, new guise to be casde in a dublet. **1612** T. TAYLOR *Comm. Titus* i. 15 When men or women weare strange fashions and guises. **1682** BUNYAN *Holy War* 8 To ..sit down against Mansoul, in their now ragged and beggarly guise. **1726** GAY *Butterfly & Snail* 32 In base, in sordid guise array'd. **1822** BYRON *Werner* III. i 231 Thou know me? in this guise Thou canst not know me. **1878** M. A. BROWN *Nadeschda* 17 The joyous prince will fall to us, Therefore all appear in festive guise.

¶**b.** *concr.* Apparel, clothes. *rare.*

1796-7 COLERIDGE *Raven* 24 Soon came a woodman in leathern guise. **1870** MORRIS *Earthly Par.* II. iii. 350 She watched his men do on their riding guise.

5. External appearance, aspect, semblance.

1340 *Ayenb.* 158 He comþ ine gyse of angle and ssseweþ þet guod uor to draȝe to kueade. **1390** GOWER *Conf.* I. 133 Anone his olde guise chaunge He woll. *c* **1450** *Merlin* xxi. 377 Ye shull se me.. in so many gises that I will not be knowe of no man. *a* **1533** LD. BERNERS *Huon* xxxv. 111 Thou trauesyd ye grete waues in gyse of a meruelous beest. *a* **1698** TEMPLE *Health & Long Life* Wks. 1720 I. 283 Both [diseases] were thought to appear in many various Guises. **1781** COWPER *Expost.* 87 He.. In form a man, in dignity a God, Came, not expected in that humble guise. **1833** N. ARNOTT *Physics* (ed. 5) II. 138 Calling forth the hidden spirit of combustion in some new or less familiar guise. **1847** EMERSON *Poems* (1857) 25 In the parlor sits Some figure of noble guise. **1870** M. CONWAY *Earthw. Pilgr.* xxiii. 271 Old carvings represent a fox in the guise of a priest preaching to a flock of geese. **1891** SMILES *J. Murray* I. iii. 69 Mr. Murray grew more particular as to the guise of the books which he issued.

b. *fig.* and in immaterial sense.

a **1677** BARROW *Serm.* Wks. 1716 II. 23 The Gospel cometh under trial in a guise no-wise plausible or advantageous to human conceit. **1708** SWIFT *Sent. Ch. Eng.-Man* Misc. (1711) 121 Some, who under the Guise of Religion, Sacrificed so many Thousand Lives to their own Ambition. **1773** MRS. CHAPONE *Improv. Mind* (1774) I. 109 He will put on the guise of benevolence. **1818** MRS. SHELLEY *Frankenst.* xvii. (1865) 211, I clothed my desires under the guise of wishing to travel. **1849** MACAULAY *Hist. Eng.* i. I. 20 Blessings in the guise of disasters. **1868** FREEMAN *Norm. Conq.* (1876) II. vii. 91 He was able to interfere in English affairs in the guise of a deliverer. **1868** E. EDWARDS *Ralegh* I. ii. 28 A large armament was almost ready to sail.. under the guise of a.. merely mercantile enterprise. **1894** HALL CAINE *Manxman* VI. iii. 364 An evil thought in the guise of a pious one took possession of Philip.

c. In bad sense: Assumed appearance, pretence.

1662 R. MATHEW *Unl. Alch.* xxi. 13 A bold Woman came to me without any guise or colour, and told me plainly how it was with him. **1731** *Gentl. Mag.* I. 373 Plausibleness and Guises are inseparable from Courts. **1829** I. TAYLOR *Enthus.* iv. (1867) 97 In the enigma.. there is given, under a guise, some special mark which [etc.]. **1895** *Presbyterian* (Sydney) 14 Sept. 5/1 (*Suppl.*), A miserably weak and cowardly guise to hide their real intentions.

†**6.** *Sc.* A disguise, a mask. Also, a dance or performance in disguises or masks; a masquerade, a show. Also in phrase ***to turn the guise***: to change the parts in a play. *lit.* and *fig. Obs.*

1500-20 DUNBAR *Poems* xxvi. 10 He bad gallandis ga graith a gyiss. *Ibid.* 26 Heilie harlottis on hawtane wyiss Come in with mony sindrie gyiss. **1580** J. MELVILL *Diary* (Wodrow Soc.) 81 The gentilmen of the countrey about had a gyse and farce to play before the King. *a* **1605** POLWART *Flyting w. Montgomerie* 50 Blaide, blecke thee, to bring in a gyse. **1629** SIR W. MURE *Trve Crvcifixe* 449 Dumbe Doctors ..did devise, Guyses to gaze on, showes men's soules to feed. **1712-26** GIDEON *Guthrie* (1900) 11 Finding the gyse turned, the Lords of the Congregation prevailing, and the laws upon their syd. **1787** A. SHIRREFS *Poems* (1790) 109 It's in your power, my Bess, to turn the guise. **1801** BEATTIE *Parings* (1873) 27 (E.D.D.), I'll shortly gar you turn the guize.

7. *Comb.*, as **guise-dancer** *dial.* = GUISER.

1846 'J. TRENOODLE' *Spec. Dial.* 53 (E.D.D.), And tould us how a giz-daunce was to door. **1893** Q. [COUCH] *Delectable Duchy* 339 When the mummers, guise-dancers, and darkey-parties were dressing up.

guise (gaɪz), *v.* Also 4-5 **gyse**, 6 **guize, gys.** [f. GUISE *sb.*]

1. *trans.* To attire, attire fantastically; dress, equip, 'get up'. Also in immaterial sense. *arch.*

a **1400** *Relig. Pieces fr. Thornton MS.* 92 Þan þou gysed the gerne, and gafe þe to goo Tyll Ephesyne. *c* **1430** *Syr Tryam.* 660 When they harde of these tythandys, They gysed them fulle gay. **1618** SIR W. MURE *Dido & Aeneas* II. 417 His curled head with Phrygian mytre guised. **1796** T. TOWNSHEND *Poems* 20 Guised just like her true love swain. **1821** JOANNA BAILLIE *Metr. Leg.*, *Wallace* xix. 12 In that deceitful seeming guised. **1849** ROCK *Ch. of Fathers* III. ix. 220 Bands of children guised as Holy Innocents. **1882** *Society* 16 Dec. 5/2 The pawns.. will be guised as choristers.

†**b.** To prepare, get up (an eatable). *Obs.*

1604 PARSON *3rd Pt. Three Convers. Eng.* 143 The same Coleworts sodden againe, but guised after another fashion.

†**c.** To shape, assimilate *to* (such or such a guise). *Obs. rare*$^{-1}$.

1605 SYLVESTER *Du Bartas* II. iii. I. *Vocation* 192 To guise our selves (like counterfeiting Ape) To th' guise of Men that are but Men in shape.

2. To disguise. *Obs.* exc. *dial.*

a **1510** DOUGLAS *K. Hart* II. 70 Len me thy cloke, to gys me for ane quhyle. **1893** *Northumbld. Gloss.*, A man of notoriously dirty appearance asked his wife, 'Hoo mun a gize mesel?' 'Wesh thee fyess', was the prompt reply.

3. *intr.* To go about in disguise, or in masquerade dress. Chiefly *Sc.* and *north.*

1876 *Mid-Yorksh. Gloss.*, *Guise*, to masquerade. **1884** *Gd. Words* Nov. 747/1 The youths of Lerwick, attired in fantastic dresses, go 'guising' about the towns. **1891** *N. & Q.* XI. 82 [The phrase] is not an appropriate one in the mouth of the Duke when he is guising as a monk.

Hence **guised** *ppl. a.*

1662 GREENHALGH in Ellis *Orig. Lett.* Ser. II. IV. 10 Hooded, guized, veiled Jews, and my own plain bare self amongst them. *a* **1851** JOANNA BAILLIE (Ogilvie), Then like a guised band, that for a while Has mimick'd forth a sad and gloomy tale.

guisely, variant of GUISILY *Obs.*

guiser ('gaɪzə(r)). Chiefly *Sc.* and *north.* Forms: 5 **gyser**, 5, 8 **gysar**, 6 **gysour**, 9 **guisar, -or, guizer, guyser, guiser.** [f. GUISE *v.* + -ER[1].] One who guises (see GUISE *v.* 3); a masquerader, a mummer. (Cf. GUISARD, GEEZER.)

1488 *Ld. Treas. Acc. Scotl.* (1877) I. 93 Item, in Lannerik, to dansaris and gysaris, xxxvis. **1572** *Satir. Poems Reform.* xxxviii. 14 For gysours, deuysours, the Guysianis ar gude. *a* **1586** SIR R. MAITLAND in Pinkerton *M. Poems* (1786) 298, I saw no gysars all this yeir, Bot—kirkmen cled lyk men of weir. **1864** BURTON *Scot. Abr.* I. v. 309 Those who thus go a-masking on New Year's eve.. are called.. guizers. **1880** T. HARDY *Return Native* 124 The guisers themselves.. could not afford to offend those by whose assistance they so largely profited.

Hence **'guiser** *v. intr.*, to act as a mummer, to go masquerading; cf. GUISARD *v.*

1907 D. H. LAWRENCE in *Notts. Guardian* 7 Dec. 17/2 Hey, we're going to the Mill guysering. **1932** J. M. E. SAXBY *Trad. Lore* 77 On Hallowe'en the Grüliks went a-guisaring.

guiserne, obs. form of GIZZERN.

Guisian ('gi:zɪən), *a.* and *sb.* Also 6 **guisan, guysian.** [f. F. (*duc de*) *Guise* + -IAN.]

A. *adj.* Of or pertaining to the duke of Guise, or his family or faction.

1579 J. STUBBES *Gaping Gulf* E v b, This prince can not but.. be great with the Guysian duke. **1643** PRYNNE *Sov. Power Parl.* App. 35 The Guisian Popish faction, being the strongest party. **1828-40** TYTLER *Hist. Scot.* (1864) III. 144 The skilfulness of Guisian diplomacy.

B. *sb.* = GUISARD[1].

1562 CECIL *Let.* 16 July in M.A.S. Hume *Gt. Ld. Burghley* (1898) 129 Continue your wryting to putt the Quene's Majesty in remembrance of her peril if the Guisans prosper. **1642** MILTON *Apol. Smect.* Wks. 1738 I. 111 To give the watch-word like a Guisian of Paris to a mutiny or massacre. **1897** D. H. FLEMING *Mary Q. Scots* viii. 88 A marriage.. which the Guisians take for concluded.

†**'guisily**, *adv. Obs.* In 4 **gisely**, 5 **gisily.** [f. GUISE *sb.* + -(I)LY.] Handsomely; ingeniously, skilfully.

13.. *Orfeo* (Zielke) 297 Kniȝtes and levedis com daunceing In queynt atire gisely, Queynt pas and softly. *c* **1420** *Pallad. on Husb.* III. 409 A Spaynald taught me wonder gisily To graffe, and baad me theron not deuyne.

guising ('gaɪzɪŋ), *vbl. sb.* [f. GUISE *v.* + -ING[1].] The action of the vb. GUISE. †**a.** Assumption of a certain guise or character (*obs.*). **b.** *dial.* Masquerading, mummering. Also *attrib.*

1563 WINȜET *Wks.* (1890) II. 42 The Sone of God become nocht the persoun of a man in substance, bot, be a certane apperand gysing and conuersation, finȝeit the samin. **1822** BEWICK *Mem.* 26 The man who personated the devil.. was going 'a guising'. **1837** CARLYLE *Fr. Rev.* II. I. ix, Your Christmas Guisings.. were a considerable something.

attrib. **1852** *Whistle-Binkie* (Scot. Songs) (1890) I. 43 In a guizing excursion he sung some verses.

guispin, variant of GISPIN *Obs.*

guiss, obs. Sc. form of GOOSE.

guissell, misspelling for *juissell*, obs. f. JUSSEL.

guisserne, obs. form of GIZZERN.

†**guissette**, bad form for CUISSET.

a **1548** HALL *Chron., Edw. IV* (1550) 12 Some had..the guissettes..droped & gutted with red.

guitar (gɪˈtɑː(r)), *sb.* Forms: 7 ghittar, gitarr(e, gittar(r, gotire, guittarre, 7–8 guitarre, 7–9 guittar, 8 guitare, 7– guitar. Also in Spanish, and quasi-Spanish or Italian form, 7, 9 guitarra, 7 guittara, 9 ghitarra. [a. Sp. *guitarra*, and its mod.F. adaptation *guitare* (Pr. *guitara*, It. *chitarra*), a. Gr. κιθάρα. The word had been adopted in classical L. as *'cithara*, whence It. *cetera*, *cetra*, Pr. *cidra*, OHG. *cithara*, mod.G. *zither*, mod.F. *cithare*, Eng. *cither*. See also CITOLE, GITTERN.] **a.** A musical instrument of the lute class, with six strings, which are twanged with the right hand, and a handle or finger-board provided with frets for stopping the notes with the left hand.

1621 B. JONSON *Gipsies Metamorph.* (1640) 51 Give me my *Guittara*, and room for our Chiefe. **1648** GAGE *West Ind.* viii. 23 Tuning his Guitarra and singing to us some verses. **1668** H. MORE *Div. Dial.* III. i. (1713) 180 Sometimes with a careless stroke I brush the Gittar. **1683** *Lond. Gaz.* No. 1862/8 A little Gittar, wrought with Ivory and Ebony on the back. **1700** ASTRY tr. *Saavedra-Faxardo* II. 99 So delicate, like a Guitarre, that it won't bear the fingers. **1766** GOLDSM. *Vic. W.* v, Mr. Thornhill..then took up the guitar himself. **1806–7** J. BERESFORD *Miseries Hum. Life* (1826) XVI. 90 The dead, lumpish, tubby, tones of the fourth and fifth strings of the guittar. **1820** C. R. MATURIN *Melmoth* (1892) III. xxviii. 117 Their ghitarras might be disposed of. **1842** BARHAM *Ingol. Leg.* Ser. II. *Sir Rupert the Fearless*, Full sweetly she sang to a sparkling guitar With silver cords. **1866** ENGEL *Nat. Mus.* ix. 350 The guitarra..is still to be found..among the Arabs in Tunis. **1879** STAINER *Music of Bible* 57 It is difficult to determine when the cithara had so far departed from the form of a lyre as to become a guitar.

fig. **1685** CROWNE *Sir C. Nice* II. Dram. Wks. 1874 III. 276 Oh! no, madam, he's the general guitar o' the town, inlay'd with every thing women fancy. **1710** *Brit. Apollo* II. No. 101. 3/2 Where is this Hatchet-fac'd Gittar?

b. *attrib.* and *Comb.*, as ***guitar-box***, ***-case***, ***-man***, ***-master***, ***-picker***, ***-picking***, ***-player***, ***-playing***; **guitar-fish**, a ray belonging to the family Rhinobatidæ; **guitar-plant**, a Tasmanian shrub, *Lomatia tinctoria* (Morris *Austral-Eng.*).

1859 LANG *Wand. India* 296 Here are the coolies returning! I can make out my guitar-box on the head of one man. **1657** J. VERNEY *Let.* 13 Jan. in M. M. Verney *Mem.* (1894) III. x. 365 You left your gittarre Case att Bremers. **1834** DICKENS *Sk. Boz* (1836) I. 152 Parasols, guitar-cases; and parcels of all imaginable shapes. **1848** *Knickerbocker* XVIII. 225 Mr. Thwackit..took his guitar-case in one hand and his double barreled fowling-piece in the other. **1959** *Sears, Roebuck Catal.* Spring & Summer 889/1 Popular-priced guitar cases. **1905** D. S. JORDAN *Guide to Study of Fishes* I. xxx. 550 The Rhinobatidæ (guitar-fishes) are long-bodied, shovel-nosed rays, with strong tails... The numerous species abound in all warm seas. **1963** D. G. STEAD *Sharks & Rays Austral. Seas* xv. 138 We come to a division of rays, almost all of which would be classed as Shovelnoses by Australian fishermen coming in contact with them, and known in America and elsewhere as Guitar-fishes. **1705** VANBRUGH *Confed.* II. 17 Her Guitar Master is with her. *Clar.* Psha, she's taken up with her impertinent Guitar Man. **1951** E. PAUL *Springtime in Paris* xi. 203 For many years, while the French were learning about jazz, no Frenchman except possibly Django Reinhardt, the guitar picker, could play it. **1959** 'F. NEWTON' *Jazz Scene* v. 78 The 'urban blues singers' circuits'..served by the guitar-pickers and itinerant piano players. **1956** M. STEARNS *Story Jazz* (1957) xv. 169 The guitar-picking colleagues of Huddie Ledbetter. **1834** LANDOR *Wks.* (1846) II. 289/2 They seem but whistlers and guitar-players compared to a full-cheeked trumpeter. **1898** ZANGWILL *Dreamers Ghetto* iv. 166 A guitar-playing gallant of Madrid.

guitar (gɪˈtɑː(r)), *v.* [f. GUITAR *sb.*] **a.** *intr.* To play the guitar. Hence **guiˈtarring** *vbl. sb.* **b.** *trans.* To serenade with a guitar.

a. *c* **1817** BYRON *To T. Moore*, Guitarring and strumming, Oh Thomas Moore! **1827** G. DARLEY *Sylvia* 138 Soft flutists, and sweet serenaders Guitarring o'er the level green. **1852** MRS. SMYTHIES *Bride Elect* xiii, Go and see what all this guitarring and serenading is about.

b. **1840** LADY C. BURY *Hist. of Flirt* viii, Guitaring silly girls as Thelwal did.

guitarist (gɪˈtɑːrɪst). Also 8 guittarist. [f. GUITAR *sb.* + -IST. Cf. Sp. *guitarrista*.] One who plays the guitar.

1770 *Acc. Bks.* in *Ann. Reg.* 244/2 The guittarist happens to have a good voice. **1846** LONGF. in *Life* (1891) II. 61 Call upon Camillo Sivori, the celebrated violinist, and his companion De' Ferranti, 'guitarist to his majesty the *Roi des Belges*'. **1882** *Athenæum* 10 June 738/2 The..woman..dancing with the wildest passion to the fierce music of the castanet players and the guitarist.

guitermanite (gɪˈtɜːmənaɪt). *Min.* [Named by Hillebrand, 1885, after *Guiterman*, its discoverer: see -ITE.] Sulph-arsenide of lead of a bluish-grey colour, and metallic lustre.

1885 *Geol. Surv. U.S.* Bulletin xx. 105 The mineral appears to be new to science, and a name, Guitermanite, is proposed.

guit-guit (gwɪt gwɪt). [Echoic.

Given by Hernandez (1615 *Rer. Med. Nov. Hisp. Thes.*) as the native American name of a bird which he describes as being no larger than a wren, green, and so courageous as to attack the raven. His description is repeated (after Nieremberg in 1635) by Ray (*Willughby's Ornith.* App. 1678) whence the Eng. currency of the name. The identification of the bird meant by Hernandez is uncertain.]

(See quot.)

1893 NEWTON *Dict. Birds* 401 Guit-guit, a name, presumably in imitation of the cry of a bird, used almost indefinitely for any species of the Neotropical genera *Cæreba*, *Dacnis* and their allies.

guive, obs. form of GYVE.

guiver, var. GYVER.

guizard, -art, variants of GUISARD *sb.*[2]

guize, obs. form of GUISE.

guizen, variant of GIZZEN *v.*

1674–91 RAY *N.C. Words*, *Guizen'd, adj.* Spoken of tubs or barrels that leak through drought.

Gujarati (guːdʒəˈrɑːtɪ), *sb.* and *a.* Also Gujarathi, Gujerati, Gurjarati, Guzarat(h)i, Guzatta, Guzerattee, etc. [Hind., f. *Gujarāt* (Skr. *Gurjarā*).] **A.** *sb.* A native or inhabitant of Gujarat, a state in Western India; a speaker of the Gujarati language; this language. **B.** *adj.* Of or pertaining to the state of Gujarat, its inhabitants, or its language.

c **1607** in Birdwood & Foster *1st Let. Bk. of E. India Co. 1600–19* (1893) 85 And alsoe the Guzarette do saile in the Portugalls shipps in euery parte of the East Indies. **1615** T. ROE *Jrnl.* 24 Aug. (1899) I. 31, 12 of his priuat Guard, hiered Gusaratts, some with Turkish bowes, some with Pistolls. *Ibid.* 37 Besides all the Cloth he and his people weare are stuffes and Callicoes of Suratt, which Guseratts bring. **1808** R. DRUMMOND (*title*) Illustrations of the grammatical parts of the Guzerattee, Mahratta, and English languages. **1835** J. BIRD tr. *Ali Mohammed Khan's Pol. & Stat. Hist. Gujarát* III. x. 413 They advanced to battle... Muzaffir..was accompanied by a great crowd of Gujarátis and Rájpúts. **1838** *Penny Cycl.* XII. 227/2 *Gurjaratí*, or *Guzeratí*, spoken in Gujerat, and along the coast as far as Bombay. **1925** A. HUXLEY *Let.* 4 Oct. (1969) 254 Somebody recited a poem in Gujarati, chanting lugubriously. **1927** *United Free Church Miss. Rec.* May 220/1 The programme..was a mixture of English, Marathi, and Gujerathi things. **1931** *Times Lit. Suppl.* 3 Dec. 983/1 An adept in the Gujarati tongue. **1936** *Ibid.* 18 Jan. 57/4 The Gujarati writers became inspired by Scott, Byron, Mill, and especially Shakespeare. **1937** L. BROMFIELD *Rains Came* I. iv. 26 That's what is the matter with Gandhi—besides being a Gujerati by race and a Bunya by caste. **1964** E. HUXLEY *Back Street New Worlds* vii. 76 There's been a lively demand for teachers with a knowledge of Urdu, Gujerati, Punjabi, Hindi and other Asian tongues. **1969** *Sunday Standard* (Bombay) 3 Aug. (Magazine Section) p. i/5 The modern Gujarati stage is about two decades old. **1970** H. R. F. KEATING *Inspector Ghote breaks Egg* iv. 41 His appearance..marked him not as a native of the place but as a Gujarati.

guked, gukit, vars. GUCKED *ppl. a. Obs.*

gukgo, guk-guk, obs. Sc. forms of CUCKOO.

gukkit, variant of GUCKED *ppl. a. Obs.*

gukkow, obs. Sc. form of CUCKOO.

‖**gul** (gʊl). [Pers. *gul*.] The Persian word for 'rose'; made familiar by Byron's use of the expression 'gardens of gul'.

1813 BYRON *Bride Abydos* I. 8 Where the light wings of Zephyr, oppressed with perfume, Wax faint o'er the gardens of Gúl in her bloom. *a* **1845** HOOD *Kilmansegg, Birth* vi, While Margaret..In a garden of Gul reposes—Poor Peggy hawks nosegays from street to street, Till..She hates the smell of roses! **1874** RUSKIN *Fors Clav.* xlvi. (1896) II. 459 Hear this you new-gilded Miss Kilmanseggs with your gardens of Gul.

gul, obs. form of GULL.

‖**gula** (ˈgjuːlə). [L. *gula* throat (hence, appetite).]

†**1. a.** The external throat. **b.** The gullet, or that which answers to it in the lower animals. *Obs.*

c **1400** *Lanfranc's Cirurg.* 148 In þe fore partie of þe necke þere is gula, þe which þat strecchiþ from þe chyn down to þe forke of þe brest. **1661** LOVELL *Hist. Anim. & Min.* Introd. b 8 Neere to the mouth is a venter, like the craw of birds, after which is the gula, to which the intestine is joyned, which is single.

2. *Ent.* 'The chitinous plate which supports the submentum in many Insecta' (*Syd. Soc. Lex.*).

1826 KIRBY & SP. *Entomol.* III. 367 *Gula* (the gula), the lower part of the neck. **1877** HUXLEY *Anat. Inv. Anim.* vii. 403 The part called gula which in many insects is a large plate confluent with the epicranium above and supporting the submentum anteriorly.

gula: see GOLA.

gular (ˈgjuːlə(r)), *a.* (*sb.*) [f. GULA (in sense 2 f. L. *gula*) + -AR.]

1. Of, pertaining to, or situated upon the gula.

1828 STARK *Elem. Nat. Hist.* I. 349 A gular pouch in the greater number. **18..** RIDGWAY in Coues *Birds N.W.* (1874) 287 Allowing the red of the gular patch to touch, for quite a distance, the white stripe beneath the eye. **1882** CATH. HOPLEY *Snakes* 67 The egg comes in contact with certain 'gular teeth', which then break the shell without any loss of the contents to the feeder. **1892** W. H. HUDSON *Natur. La Plata* 249 A large number of species have a bright or nearly bright gular spot.

2. *nonce-use.* Concerned with the appetite; devoted to good eating.

1854 *Fraser's Mag.* XLIX. 104 The second..was..the founder of a gular academy, distinguishing himself by his treatise *de opsoniis et condimentis*.

3. *ellipt.* as *sb.* A gular plate beneath the throat of a serpent or a fish.

1884–5 *Stand. Nat. Hist.* (1888) III. 350 Posterior to the mental, and lying between the infralabials, are the submentals and gulars.

gulardous: see under GOLIARD.

gulaund. [Icel. *gulönd*, f. *gul-r* yellow + *önd* (formerly written *aund*) duck.] The Icelandic name of the Goosander; cited by Pennant, *Arctic Zool.* (1784) II. 572; and thence copied into Eng. Dicts.

†**gulch**, *sb.*[1] *Obs.* [f. GULCH *v.*[1]] A glutton or drunkard.

1601 B. JONSON *Poetaster* III. iv, You'll see vs then, you will, Gulch, you will? **1607** BREWER *Lingua* v. xvi, You muddy gulche, darst looke me in the face? **1611** COTGR., *Engorgeur*, a rauener, glutton, gulch, ingorger.

gulch (gʌl(t)ʃ), *sb.*[2] *Obs.* exc. *dial.* Also **gulsh.** [f. GULCH *v.*[2]] A heavy fall. Used adverbially in ***to come down gulch.***

1671 ECHARD *Observ. Answ. Cont. Clergy* 39 Then he has me most cruelly upon the Hip, and brings me over with a most deadly Gulsh. *a* **1825** FORBY *Voc. E. Anglia*, *Gulsh*,..a heavy fall. **1839** *J. Noakes & Mary Styles* 12 (E.D.S. No. 76), I dorn't think I cud clime it now,..I shudn't warsley loike to troy, For gulch cum down I shud.

gulch (gʌl(t)ʃ), *sb.*[3] *U.S.* [? Connected with GULCH *v.*[1]]

1. a. A narrow and deep ravine, with steep sides, marking the course of a torrent; esp. one containing a deposit of gold.

1832 A. EARLE *Narr. Res. N.Z.* 1 May (1966) 220 From the Peak..to the sea shore, the earth is cut into gullies... The settlers call these ravines gultches. **1850** B. TAYLOR *Eldorado* ix. (1862) 87 The word gulch..denotes a mountain ravine..steep, abrupt, and inaccessible. **1888** BRYCE *Amer. Commw.* III. xc. 224 A crowd of men who..will scatter again as soon as..the gold in the gulch is exhausted. **1964** F. O'ROURKE *Mule for Marquesa* (1967) x. 124 The canyon..became..a mere gulch with fifty-foot walls that debouched ingloriously into the gap.

b. *transf.* 'A long, narrow, deep depression of the sea bottom' (*Cent. Dict.*).

2. *attrib.*, as ***gulch-diggings***, ***-gold***, ***-man***, ***-mine***, ***-miner***, ***-mining***, ***-washing***.

1859 *San Francisco Bulletin* 5 May 1/2 The gulch diggings are..paying well for the labor expended. **1876** R. W. RAYMOND *Statistics of Mines* VIII. 297 The production of gulch-gold on and below Spanish Bar has amounted..to $80,000. **1869** A. K. MCCLURE *Rocky Mtns.* 210 (Th.), The unfortunate politician is 'corraled' by the mountaineers, the gulchmen, or the settlers. **1866** *Beadle's Monthly* Oct. 279/1 The diggings yielded very richly..but, like most gulch mines, were soon exhausted. **1877** BLACK *Green Past.* xiii, The gulch and placer mines..were giving a fair yield. **1867** J. F. MELINE *2000 Miles on Horseback* 63 The gulch miner has been here in all his pristine strength and glory. **1867** *Harper's Mag.* June 11/2 We..passed over a creek which had been brought by an artificial ditch for gulch-mining purposes. **1876** R. W. RAYMOND *Statistics of Mines* VIII. 186 The gold comes from the gulch-washings in Indian district near the Eagle Mine.

gulch, *v.*[1] *Obs.* exc. *dial.* Also 9 *dial.* **gulge, gulsh.** [Echoic; cf. Ger. dial. *gulken*, Norw. *gulka*, Sw. dial. *gölka*. Derbyshire and Devonshire have a form *gulk*.]

1. *trans.* To swallow or devour greedily. Also with *down*, *in*, *up*.

a **1225** *Ancr. R.* 240 Heo drinkeð þene drunch..ne iueleð heo it neuer, auh gulcheð in ȝiuerliche. **1611** FLORIO, *Ingorgare*, to engurgle, to gargarize, to gulch. **1653** URQUHART *Rabelais* I. iv. 23 They should be all of them gulched up. **1890** *Gloucester Gloss.*, *Gulch*, to gulp, swallow greedily.

b. *Comb.*, †**gulchcup**, one who drains the cup greedily, a tosspot.

a **1225** *Ancr. R.* 216 Ʒif þe gulchecuppe weallinde bres to drincken, & ȝeot in his wide þrote þet he aswelte wiðinnen.

†**2.** ***to gulch out***: to vomit. *lit.* and *fig. Obs.*

a **1225** *Ancr. R.* 88 þe uorme..gulcheð al ut someð þet þe attri heorte sent up to þe tunge. *Ibid.* 206 Gulche hit ut ine schrifte, utterliche, ase heo hit dude, þeo þet iveleð hire schuldi.

gulch (gʌl(t)ʃ), *v.*[2] *dial.* [app. echoic.] *intr.* To fall or plunge heavily. **b.** *trans.* To fall heavily upon.

1821 CLARE *Vill. Minstr.* I. 207 Ne'er an axe was heard to sound, Or a tree's fall gulsh'd the ground. *Ibid.* II. 190 The splashings..Of fly-bit cattle gulshing in the brook.

gulch (gʌl(t)ʃ), *v.*[3] [f. GULCH *sb.*[3]]

1. *trans.* To drag (wood) down a gulch.

1877 RAYMOND *Statist. Mines & Mining* 28 Cutting and gulching 50 cords of wood, at $2.50 per cord.

2. *intr.* To dig (for gold) in a gulch.

1879 H. DRUMMOND in *Life* (1899) 157 A hundred prospectors gulching for gold and silver.

gulch, variant of CULCH.

1882 *Standard* 26 Sept. 2/2 The oyster dredgers are glad to give sixpence or sevenpence a bushel for them as 'gulch', to lay down to catch the 'spat'.

† **'gulchin.** *Obs. rare*$^{-0}$. [dim. of GULCH *sb.*[1]] A little glutton.

1671 SKINNER *Etymol. Ling. Angl.* 1, A Gulchin, q. d. a Gulekin (i.e.) parvus Gulo. **1677** MIEGE *Dict. Angl.-Fr.*, Gulchin, *un petit glouton*. [Hence in later Dicts.]

† **'gulchingly,** *adv. Obs.* [f. *gulching*, pr. pple. of GULCH *v.*[1] + -LY[2].] Greedily, voraciously.

1598 FLORIO, *Borreuolmente*, stuffingly, fully, gulchingly.

'gulchy, *a. Obs.* exc. *dial.* [f. GULCH *sb.*[1] + -Y[1].] Coarsely fat; corpulent.

1598 FLORIO, *Croio*, foule, fat, greasie, gulchie. **1808–80** JAMIESON, *Gulschy*, gross, thick; applied to the form of the body. **1895** *E. Angl. Gloss.*, *Gulsky*, corpulent and gross.

guld, variant of GOLD[2], marigold.

‖**gulden** ('gʊldən). Forms: 6– gulden, (6 guylden, gylden, 7 guilding); *Sc.* 6 gudlyne, -lyng, guidlin(g, 6–7 gudlene. [Ger., Du. *gulden* (also G. *gülden*), strictly an adj. = of gold, golden, cogn. w. OE. *gylden* GILDEN *a.*] † **a.** A gold coin, *spec.* one of various obsolete gold coins of Germany and the Netherlands (*obs.*). **b.** The name was subsequently transferred to a silver coin, the value of which differed in various countries and at various periods; it survives in Holland (= GUILDER).

In recent use the plural is commonly *gulden* as in Ger.

15.. *Aberd. Reg.* (Jam.), He gave hyme in kepyng tua vnicornis & ane Philipis gudlene. *Ibid.* XVII. (Jam.) The soum of fyw gudlyngis. **1528** ROY *Rede me* (Arb.) 40 He spendeth many a gulden To hange morther and bren The masses aduersaries. **1535** COVERDALE *2 Kings* v. 5 He..toke with him ten hundreth weighte of syluer, and sixe thousande guldens [**1611** pieces of gold]. **1535** LYNDESAY *Satyre* 4170 Gold Smythis fair-well!.. To mix, set ȝe nocht by twa preinis, Fyne Ducat gold with hard Gudlingis. *a* **1540** BARNES *Wks.* (1573) 330/1 These two men did gather.. within yᵉ space of ij. moneths...xx. M. guyldens. **1587** JAS. VI *Let. to Winȝet* in *W.'s Wks.* (1890) II. App. p. xxv, The sowme of sevin scoir fyve guidlins. **1617** MORYSON *Itin.* I. 285 Most reckonings of Germany are made by common siluer guldens..these Guldens are..neere the value of three shillings foure pence English... The Gold Rhenish Guldens of Germany are almost of the same standard with the Crowne Gold of England. **1645** *Sc. Acts Chas. I* (1814) VI. 163/2 Granted for payment of the Gudlines, Silver-work, and others publick debts. *a* **1652** BROME *Eng. Moor* IV. i. Wks. 1873 II. 51 Here at this Inne abide, and wait my coming. Be careful of my guildings. **1756–7** tr. *Keysler's Trav.* (1760) III. 311 The duke of Modena..proposed to some persons in Germany a loan of two hundred thousand guldens on a mortgage of the territory of Mirandola. **1845** S. AUSTIN *Ranke's Hist. Ref.* I. 97 The general grant of 100,000 gulden. **1865** *Pall Mall G.* 3 July 1/1 The Reichsrath was obliged to vote a supply of thirteen millions of guldens. **1898** *Q. Rev.* July 8 Reuchlin..was nominated..with a hundred gold gulden as salary.

attrib. **1873** OUIDA *Pascarel* I. 66 He was delighted to sell it for 12 gulden notes to a German Jew dealer.

† **guldenhead.** *Obs.* [? a. ON. *gullenhǫfðe, lit. 'goldenhead'.] The puffin, *Fratercula arctica.*

1676 WILLUGHBY *Ornith.* 244 *Anas Artica* [i.e. the Puffin] ..*Wallis..Meridionalibus circa* Tenby *oppidum* Guldenhead, Bottle-nose and Helegug.

guldren, obs. form of GUILDER.

guldsoch, obs. Sc. f. GULESOUGHT, jaundice.

† **gule,** *sb.*[1] *Obs.* Also 6 *Sc.* guill. [ad. L. *gula.*] **1.** The gullet.

1659 GAUDEN *Tears Ch. Eng.* III. xix. 323 There are.. gules so gluttonous..that they can swallow down goodly Cathedrals. **1750** W. DODD *Poems* (1767) 32 Her thirsty gule.

b. *Arch.* The 'neck' of a column.

1706 PHILLIPS (ed. Kersey), *Gorge, Gule*, or *Neck*,..the narrowest part of the Dorick and Tuscan Capitals, lying between the Astragal..and the Annulets.

2. Gluttony.

1390 GOWER *Conf.* III. 1 This vice, which so out of reule Hath set us all, is cleped gule. **1535** STEWART *Cron. Scot.* (1856) II. 228 He wes the first with glutony and guill That euir begouth to mak sic feist in ȝule.

gule (gju:l), *sb.*[2] [a. OF. *gule, goule*, med.L. *gula Augusti.*

The ulterior etymology is unknown. The Welsh form is *gwyl Awst* (*gwyl* festival, believed to be a. L. *vigilia* VIGIL), but as the med.L. and OF. terms were in continental use, this must be a mere popular etymology. The conjecture that *gula* is a corruption of 'Dies Sancti Petri ad vincula' is very unlikely, nor is it clear how it can be identified with the Lat. *gula* 'throat'.]

the Gule of August: Lammas Day, Aug. 1.

[*c* **1300** P. DE LANGTOFT *Chron.* (Rolls) I. 450 Le duk Robert les sayse, et of sa compaynye Iour de goul [*v.r.* gule] de Aust à Portesmue applye.] **1543** tr. *Act 47 Edw. III*, c. 1 If any cloth be put to sale after the gule of August. **1628** COKE *On Litt.* 180 From the feast of Easter, vntil the gule of August, (that is, the first of August). **1783** VALLANCEY *Collect. de Rebus Hibern.* III. 468 Of the Gule of August; or, Lammas day. **1899** NORA HOPPER in *Westm. Gaz.* 1 Aug. 10/1 Every bird on forest bough Sings for Gule of August now.

† **gule,** *v. Obs. rare.* [f. *gule* GULES.] *trans.* To stain or dye gules or red.

1609 HEYWOOD *Brit. Troy* VIII. viii. 171 Achilles durst not looke on Hector when He guld his Siluer armes in Greekish bloud. **1632** —— *2nd Pt. Iron Age* I. i. Wks. 1874 III. 357 Till Hecub's reuerent lockes Be gul'd in slaughter.

gule, variant of GOLD[2], marigold.

gule, Sc. var. GOLEE *Obs.*; obs. Sc. f. GUILE.

gule ffatt, obs. forms of GYLE, GYLE-FAT.

gulekin: see GULCHIN (quot. 1671).

guleravage, variant of GILRAVAGE.

gules (gju:lz), *sb.* and *a.* orig. and chiefly *Her.* Forms: 4 goulez, gowlez, gwlis, 4–5 goules, gowles, -is, 4–6 gowlys, 5 gols, goulis, -ys, 5–6 gull(e)s, 6 gewles, gowlles, gullis, 7 geulles, gueles, gueules, 6– gules. Also 6 guele, 7 gule. [ad. OF. *goules, gueules* (F. *gueules*) = med.L. *gulæ* pl., ermine dyed red.

The ulterior etymology is disputed: the word coincides in form with the pl. of the Fr. and med.Lat. word for 'throat'. If the heraldic sense be the original, the allusion may be to the colour of the open mouth of a heraldic beast. It seems more likely, however, that the heraldic use is transferred from the sense 'red ermine', in which case the word may represent some oriental name; but the suggestion of derivation from Pers. *gul*, rose (Hatz.-Darm.), is very improbable.]

A. *sb.* Red, as one of the heraldic colours; in engraving represented by vertical lines. Hence *poet.* and *rhetorically*, the colour red in general.

13.. *Gaw. & Gr. Knt.* 619 Then þay schewed hym þe schelde, þat was of schyr goulez. *c* **1375** *Sc. Leg. Saints, George* 922 Berand þe scheld of siluir schene of gwlis. *a* **1400–50** *Alexander* 4819 Quare all þe gronde was of gols [L. *cujus terra erat valde rubicunda*]. *c* **1440** *York Myst.* xvi. 19 þan glorius gulles þat gayer [is] þan golde. *c* **1475** *Rauf Coilȝear* 669 Gowlis glitterand full gay, glemand in grene. **1535** STEWART *Cron. Scot.* (1858) I. 203 With goldin gullis glitterand as the gleid. **1587** FLEMING *Contn. Holinshed* III. 1341/2 Banners of gewles beaten with the armes of Antwerpe. **1603** DRAYTON *Bar. Wars* II. xxiv, In his white Cornet, Verdon doth display A fret of Gueles. **1651** CLEVELAND *Poems* 26 Or parboyl'd Lobsters, where there joyntly rules The fading Sables, and the coming Gules. **1708** J. PHILIPS *Cyder* II. 293 The showery arch, With listed colours gay, ore, azure, gules. **1820** KEATS *Eve St. Agnes* xxv, The wintry moon..threw warm gules on Madeline's fair breast. **1856** R. A. VAUGHAN *Mystics* (1860) I. 10 Painted shapes of gules and azure.

B. quasi-*adj.* and *adj.* Red in colour. (In most instances properly an attributive use of the sb.; usually placed after the word which it qualifies.)

1503–4 in *Trevelyan Papers* (Camden) 7 The armys off Carminow, Garter seth, yᵗ sholde be gevyne wᵗ a labell of iij poyntts gulls. *a* **1533** LD. BERNERS *Huon* xxxii. 99 His shylde, wherin was purtruyed .iii. crosses gowlles. **1562** LEIGH *Armorie* (1597) 5 b, In colour neither red nor Sanguine, but is the verie vermilion it selfe, for that is right Geule. **1607** SHAKS. *Timon* IV. iii. 59 Follow thy Drumme, With mans blood paint the ground Gules, Gules. **1650** B. *Discolliminium* 46 My Complexion, a Sable Sanguine, with a few Gule drops about my Nose. *a* **1678** MARVELL *Unfort. Lover* 64 Wks. 1726 I. 59 In a Field Sable a Lover Gules. **1790** BURNS *Ep. to R. Graham* xiv, The Magna Charta flag ..All deadly gules its bearing. **1820** SHELLEY *Œdipus* I. 144 Their arms are seven bulls in a field gules. **1864** BOUTELL *Her. Hist. & Pop.* xv. 186 In the Calais Roll these mullets are blazoned gules. **1871** J. HAY *Pike County Ballads* (1880) 152 With silken mantles blushing angry gules.

'gulesought. *Obs.* exc. *Sc.* Forms: 5 gowyl sowght, 6 guelsought, gulesought; *Sc.* 6 gulset, guldsoch, 6–7 gulsoch, 7 gulsogh, 8–9 gulsach, 9 gulschoch. [f. *gule*, GULL *a.*, yellow + SOUGHT (OE. *suht*, ON. **soht, sótt*) sickness; = ON. *gulusótt*, Sw., Da. *gulsot*: cf. G. *gelbsucht*, Du. *geelzucht*. (The OE. name was *ȝeolu ádl*.)] Jaundice.

14.. *Nom.* in Wr.-Wülcker 709/5 *Hec glaucoma*, the gowyl sowght. **15..** *Rowllis Cursing* 54 in Laing *Anc. Pop. Poetry* 212 The panefull gravell and the gutt, The gulsoch that they nevir be but. **1549** *Compl. Scot.* vi. 67 Sourakkis, that vas gude for the blac gulset. **1551** TURNER *Herbal* I. A v b, The broth..heleth the Jawndes or gulesouyht. **1562** *Ibid.* II. 73 The brothe of Osyris dronken is good agaynst yᵉ ianndes or guel sought. **1595** DUNCAN *App. Etymol.* (E.D.S.), *Aurigo*, the guldsoch; *morbus Regius.* **1673** WEDDERBURN *Voc.* (Jam.), *Icterus*, the gulsogh. **1755** FORBES *Ajax' Sp.*, etc. 34, I wis never very brouden'd upo' swine's flesh, sin my mither gae me a forlethie o't, 'at maist hae gi'en me the gulsach. **1825–80** JAMIESON, *Gulschoch Gulsach.*

gulet, obs. form of GULLET.

gulf (gʌlf), *sb.* Forms: 4, 8 golf, 5–6 goulf(e, (6 gowlfe), 5–7 gulfe, (6 gulfre), 6–7 gulphe, 7–9 gulph, 7– gulf. [ad. OF. and F. *golfe* (sense 1; in senses 2, 3, and 4 the Fr. word is *gouffre*), ad. Pr., It., Sp., Pg. *golfo*, ad. late Gr. κόλφος, from class. Gr. κόλπος, lit. 'bosom', hence 'bay, gulf' (= L. *sinus*), and 'hollow of the waves, depth of the sea'. Cf. MDu. *golf, golve*, Du. *golf, gulp*, MHG., G. *golf.*]

I. 1. *Geog.* A portion of the sea partially enclosed by a more or less extensive sweep of the coast; often taking its name from the adjoining land.

The distinction between *gulf* and *bay* is not always clearly marked, but in general a *bay* is wider in proportion to its amount of recession than a *gulf*; the latter term is applied to long land-locked portions of sea opening through a strait, which are never called *bays*.

c **1400** MAUNDEV. (1839) v. 54 The See Adryatyk, that is clept the Goulf of Venyse. *c* **1477** CAXTON *Jason* 84 b, Argos hadde brought his ship in this goulf or arme of the See. **1527** R. THORNE in Hakluyt *Voy.* (1589) 254 The coast making a gulfe where is the riuer of Ganges. **1553** EDEN *Treat. Newe Ind.* (Arb.) 33 He commaunded that certayn shippes should searche the goulfes on euerye syde. **1604** E. G[RIMSTONE] *D'Acosta's Hist. Indies* III. iv. 128 The gulph of Yegues or of Mares, is variable, being beaten with divers windes. **1667** MILTON *P.L.* XI. 833 Down the great River to the op'ning Gulf. **1766** *Phil. Trans.* LVI. 43, I say nothing of the marine productions of this golf. **1781** GIBBON *Decl. & F.* xvii. II. 7 They leave on the left a deep gulf, at the bottom of which Nicomedia was seated, the imperial residence of Diocletian. **1840** THIRLWALL *Greece* liv. VII. 53 The gulph he had seen appeared to him..important as a naval station. **1868** G. DUFF *Pol. Surv.* 171 The gulf which runs so deep into the western side of the island.

II. A deep hollow, chasm, abyss.

2. A profound depth (in a river, the ocean); the deep. *poet.*

13.. *E.E. Allit. P.* A. 607 Gotez of golf þat neuer charde. **1580** SIDNEY *Ps.* XVIII. v, The gulphes of waters then were through their chanells seen. **1620** GRANGER *Div. Logike* 155 The heavenly lamps doe fall into the gulfe. **1715–20** POPE *Iliad* XXI. 229 From the bottom of his gulphs profound, Scamander spoke. **1784** COWPER *Task* I. 268 We pass a gulph in which the willows dip their pendent boughs. **1836** *Johnsoniana* I. 44 O'er the ice as o'er pleasure you lightly should glide; Both have gulphs which their flattering surfaces hide. **1846** LANDOR *Hellenics* Wks. II. 486 Some isle Hath surely risen from the gulphs profound. **1847** EMERSON *Poems* (1857) 60 Gulfs of sweetness without bound. **1870** BRYANT *Iliad* v. 496 Slippery cliffs arise Close to deep gulfs.

b. *transf.* with reference to the air.

1712 BLACKMORE *Creation* I. 92 Nothing check'd their flight, but gulphs of air. **1727** PITT *Job* xxv. 20 Down thro' the Gulphs of undulating Air. **1863** LONGF. *Wayside Inn* I. *Falcon of Ser Federigo* 42 The headlong plunge through eddying gulfs of air.

† **c.** ***to shoot the gulf***: a phrase used in various figurative applications. (If De Foe's statement be well founded, the phrase must originally have belonged to sense 2.)

c **1645** HOWELL *Lett.* (1650) II. 40 Your last you sent me was from Genoa, where you write that..'Husbands get their wives with child a hundred miles off'... In Venice..also such things are done by proxy, while the husband is abroad upon the Gallies, ther be others that shoot his *gulf* at home. **1725** DE FOE *Voy. round World* (1840) 16 Such a mighty and valuable thing also was the passing this strait (the Straits of Magellan) that Sir Francis Drake's going through it gave birth to that famous old wives' saying viz., that Sir Francis Drake shot the gulf;..as if there had been but one gulf in the world. **1752** YOUNG *Brothers* V. i. 1757 II. 281 For me, it matters not; but oh! the prince—When he had shot the gulph of his despair.

3. An absorbing eddy; a whirlpool. In later use chiefly *fig.*, that which devours or swallows up anything. (Blending with 4 b.)

1538 ELYOT *Dict.*, *Gurges*, a swallowe or depe pyll in a water, or a goulfe. **1567** TURBERV. *Epit.*, etc. 26 b, Hast thou not read in Bookes of fell Charybdis Goulfe? **1599** SHAKS. *Hen. V*, II. iv. 10 England his approaches makes as fierce, As Waters to the sucking of a Gulfe. **1612** BP. HALL *Serm.* 64 The Scribes and Pharisees..devoured but widows houses ..; but these gulfs of men, whole Churches. **1627–77** FELTHAM *Resolves* II. xlii. 241 He throws his Interest into a Gulph, that trusts it in such hands as have been formerly the Shipwrack of others. **1633** MARMION *Fine Companion* II. iv. Dram. Wks. (1875) 137 Here is the gulph that swallows all my land: And to this desperate whirlpit am I reeling. **1659** R. BROUGH *Pres. Schism* 529 To devour all persons and things..in one gulph. **1751** JOHNSON *Rambler* No. 167 ¶6 And whirl round the gulph before they sink. **1755** H. WALPOLE *Corr.* (1837) III. cclxvii. 105 Don't go and imagine that £1,200,000 was all sunk in the gulph of Madame Pompadour. **1825** BENTHAM *Ration. Rew.* 283 Large cities..are the gulphs..in which the population of the country is lost. **1834** *West Ind. Sketch Bk.* I. 248 Whose mind had been wrecked in the gulf of dim oblivion.

b. Often applied to a voracious appetite.

1566 ADLINGTON *Apuleius* 51 Whether thou wilt remaine with the serpent and in the ende to be swallowed up into the gowlfe of his bodie. **1579** SPENSER *Sheph. Cal.* Sept. 185 A wicked Wolfe, That with many a Lambe had glutted his gulfe. **1605** SHAKS. *Macb.* IV. i. 23 Maw and Gulfe Of the rauin'd salt Sea sharke. **1658** ROWLAND *Moufet's Theat. Ins.* 1077 In a dearth, or rather want of provision, they [Pismires] fight desperately for food,..and the lesser of them will rebell against the greater, (as being the greater gulphs of the Common-wealth.) **1819** SHELLEY *Cyclops* 343 Your gaping gulf, and your gullet wide.

4. A yawning chasm or abyss; an opening in the earth produced by an earthquake or volcanic action; a vast ravine or gorge. ***a fiery gulf, gulf of fire***: an abyss full of flame.

a **1533** LD. BERNERS *Gold. Bk. M. Aurel.* (1559) C c, We go suerlie ouer the bridge, and yet we will goe an other waie: and though the same way be sure, yet we will aduenture into the gulfe. **1563** *Mirr. Mag.* Induct. xxxi, A deadly gulfe where nought but rubbishe growes. **1590** SPENSER *F.Q.* I. v. 31 They..brought the heavy corse..To yawning gulfe of deepe Avernus hole. **1604** E. G[RIMSTONE] *D'Acosta's Hist. Indies* I. i. 3 Epicurus..holdeth, that on the other part of the earth, there is nothing but a chaos and infinite gulph. **1607** SHAKS. *Cor.* III. ii. 91 Thou hadst rather Follow thine Enemie in a fierie Gulfe. **1667** MILTON *P.L.* VI. 53 The Gulf of Tartarus, which..opens wide His fiery Chaos. **1697** POTTER *Antiq. Greece* II. xv. (1715) 331 A Gulf being open at Rome, Curtius leap'd into it to appease the angry Gods. **1713** YOUNG *Last Day* II. 106 A yawning gulph, and fiends on every side, Serene they view. **1774** GOLDSM. *Nat. Hist.* (1776) I. 90 [Volcanoes] A gulph two miles over, and so deep that no bottom can be seen. **1781** COWPER *Hope* 457 In the gulphs of her Cornubian mines. **1814** SOUTHEY *Roderick* I. 108 Gulphs of fire opening beneath his feet. **1830** LYELL *Princ. Geol.* I. 334 A gulph opened between the little town of Tripergola..and the baths in its suburbs.

b. *fig.* (Often coincident with fig. use of 3.)

1581 MULCASTER *Positions* xxxvi. (1887) 135 To haue so many gaping for preferment, as no goulfe hath stoore enough to suffise. **1652** C. B. STAPYLTON *Herodian* 140 The Globe of Earth and Sea..was not able to fill this Gvlph [a man's ambition or greed]. **1656** SANDERSON *Serm.* (1689) 65 The gulph of despair. **1715** DE FOE *Fam. Instruct.* I. i. (1841) I. 20 To recover sinful Men from the gulf of death. **1751** JOHNSON *Rambler* No. 146 ¶8 Pushing his predecessors into the gulph of obscurity. **1765** H. WALPOLE *Otranto* i. (1798) 21, I will follow thee to the gulph of perdition. **1780** COWPER *Table T.* 463 They frolic it along..Down to the gulph, from which is no return. **1833** L. RITCHIE *Wand. by Loire* 157 Buried ages rise again from the gulf of time. **1868** FARRAR *Silence & V.* i. (1875) 16 The whole universe becomes a gulf of silence. **1894** *Athenæum* 14 Apr. 471/3 A sum insufficient to fill up the gulf of his debts.

c. (After Luke xvi. 26.) A wide interval, an impassable gap, serving as a means of eternal separation.

1557 N. T. (Genev.) *Luke* xvi. 26 Betwene you and vs there is a great gulfe [χάσμα] set. **1774** FLETCHER *Ess. Truth* Wks. 1795 IV. 106 An immense gulph is fixed between them, and the Christian faith. **1849** ROBERTSON *Serm.* Ser. I. xii. (1866) 197 The Advent of Christ is the gulf which separates ancient from modern history. **1881** BP. A. P. FORBES *Explan. 39 Art.* i. (ed. 4) 12 Between such a God and an Infinite Intelligence there is a gulph fixed.

5. *University slang.* **a.** *Cambridge.* The position of those candidates for mathematical honours who fail to obtain a place in the list, but are allowed the ordinary degree. **b.** *Oxford.* The list of those who fail to obtain honours, yet are allowed to take a 'pass'.

1827 *Seven Yrs. at Cambridge* II. 60 The determination I had now formed of cutting honours, by quietly sitting down in the Gulph. **1852** BRISTED *Five Yrs. in Eng. Univ.* (ed. 2) 205 Some ten or fifteen men just on the line..are put into the 'gulf', as it is popularly called (the Examiners' phrase is 'Degrees allowed').

†**6.** [f. GULF *v.*] **a.** An act of swallowing. *lit.* and *fig.* **b.** What is gulfed or swallowed; a draught. (Cf. GULP *sb.*[1])

1638 SIR T. HERBERT *Trav.* (ed. 2) 323 Their mouths are very wide, at one gulph able to swallow horse or man. **1667** DRYDEN *Temp.* III. iii, Element! meer Element! as I live. It was a cold Gulph, such as this, which kill'd my famous Predecessor. **1771** SMOLLETT *Humph. Cl.* 28 Apr., It..requires a strong gulph of faith to make it go down.

7. *Mining.* A large deposit of ore in a lode.

1778 PRYCE *Min. Cornub.* 322 *Gulph of Ore.* Where a Lode throws up very great quantities of Ore and proves lasting and good in depth they say, 'They have a Gulph of Ore'. **1849** in *Weale's Dict. Terms.*

III. 8. *attrib.* and *Comb.*, as ***gulf-fishery***, ***-tide***; ***gulf-encrimsoning***, ***-indented*** adjs.; ***gulf-wards*** adv.; also †**gulf-breasted** *a.*, having a breast or mind as deep as a gulf; **gulf-dream**, a dream of drowning in, or falling into, a gulf; †**gulf-eating** *a.*, full of eddies; **gulf-separation**, a separation as if by a gulf; **Gulf State**, one of the States on the Gulf of Mexico; †**gulf-stomached** *a.*, (of a river) having deep eddies. Also GULF STREAM, GULF-WEED.

1598 E. GUILPIN *Skial.* (1878) 52 *Gulfe-brested is he, silent, and profound. **1813** SHELLEY *Q. Mab* IX. 175 The transient *gulph-dream of a startling sleep. *c* **1611** CHAPMAN *Iliad* XXI. 2 The goodly swelling channel of the flood, *Gulf-eating Xanthus [Ξάνθου δινήεντος]. **1847** EMERSON *Poems* (1857) 45 The *gulf-encrimsoning shells. **1883** L. Z. JONCAS *Fish. Canada* 20 (Fish. Exhib. Publ.) They..have almost a monopoly of the *gulf fishery trade. **1808** J. BARLOW *Columb.* I. 313 Sultry Mobile's *gulph-indented shore. **1871** R. B. VAUGHAN *Thomas of Aquin* II. 855 This *gulf separation..and this intimate connection in the creative act. **1863** W. PHILLIPS *Speeches* xvii. 389 The *Gulf States will monopolize all the offices. *c* **1611** CHAPMAN *Iliad* XXI. 311 Afraid lest that *gulf-stomach'd Flood [ποταμὸς βαθυδίνης] would satiate his desire On great Achilles. **1897** *Outing* (U.S.) XXIX. 440/1 A..sluggish stream, flowing up or down, according to the governing *gulf-tide. **1855** BAILEY *Mystic* 114 He who, where Hidekkel *gulfwards darts, Ruled with an absolute crown.

gulf (gʌlf), *v.* Also 6–9 **gulph**, (6 **golph**). [f. GULF *sb.*]

†**1.** *intr.* To rush along like a gulf or whirlpool; to eddy, swirl. *Obs.*

1538 LELAND *Itin.* V. 80 It standeth as it were betwixt to pointing Hillettes betwene the wich the Severn Se gulfith. **1549** CHEKE *Hurt Sedit.* (1569) D ij, Doe ye not see how many bottomlesse whirlepooles of mischiefe ye be golpht withal? **1591** SPENSER *Virg. Gnat* 542 Deep Charybdis gulphing in and out. **1658** FRANCK *North. Mem.* (1694) 91 A rapid and peremptory River, that gulphs forth of the Bowels of Loemon, replenished with Trout.

2. *trans.* To swallow like a gulf, or as in a gulf; to engulf. Also with *down*, *in*, *up*. *lit.* and *fig.*

1807 J. HALL *Trav. Scot.* I. 306 Some little birds were flying after a cuckoo and gulphing up his faeces as it dropped from him. **1817** BYRON *Manfred* I. ii. 6 It hath no power upon the past, and for The future, till the past be gulf'd in darkness. **1818** KEATS *Endym.* III. 351 Some friendly monster..Has div'd to its foundations, gulph'd it down. **1822** SHELLEY *To Jane, Recoll.* v, Each [pool] seemed as 'twere a little sky Gulphed in a world below. **1877** TENNYSON *Harold* II. ii, Why, let the earth rive, gulf in These cursed Normans. **1879** STEVENSON *Trav. Cevennes* (1895) 221 A yawning valley, gulfed in blackness.

3. In various nonce-uses: **a.** To plunge (oneself) *into* as into a gulf; to precipitate oneself, rush headlong. **b.** To form gulfs or indentations in. **c.** To separate *from* by a gulf or chasm.

1680 HICKERINGILL *Meroz* 8 Like men in a Shipwrack..that leap into the Sea for fear of Drowning, we gulf'd our selves into more Arbitrary Government, Tyranny and Popery. **1808** J. BARLOW *Columb.* I. 551 And hoarse resounding, gulphing wide the shore, Dread Laurence labors with tremendous roar. **1891** C. JAMES *Rom. Rigmarole* 121 The week gulfing me from meeting her again.

4. *University slang.* **a.** *trans.* To place the name of (an undergraduate) in the 'gulf' (see GULF *sb.* 5). **b.** *intr. to gulf it*: to get or be contented with a place in the 'gulf'.

1827 *Seven Yrs. at Cambridge* II. 61, I therefore 'Gulphed it'. **1831** DARWIN in *Life & Lett.* (1887) I. 184 Cameron is gulfed, together with other three Trinity scholars. **1857** 'C. BEDE' *Verdant Green* III. xi, I am not going to let them gulph me a second time. **1876** TREVELYAN *Macaulay* ii. (1881) 61 His name did not grace the list. In short..Macaulay was gulfed. **1895** L. J. TROTTER *Life Marq. Dalhousie* i. 10 Instead of 'gulfing' him with the herd of mere passmen, they marked their sense of his merits by granting him an honorary fourth class.

¶**5.** Used for GULP *v.* (Cf. GULF *sb.* 6.)

1650 BULWER *Anthropomet.* xi. 114, I saw a Porter..drink..without ever so much as once gulphing. *Ibid.*, He had been among the Malabars, where if he should have gulphed or have drunk any otherwise, he might have had his throat cut.

Hence **gulfed** (gʌlft) *ppl. a.* (see sense 4 a).

1852 BRISTED *Five Yrs. in Eng. Univ.* (ed. 2) 205 A gulfed Scholar of Trinity did not lose his Scholarship.

gulfing ('gʌlfɪŋ), *vbl. sb.* [f. GULF *v.* + -ING[1].] The action of plunging or sinking in a gulf.

1818 KEATS *Endym.* III. 659, I beheld the wreck; The final gulphing; the poor struggling souls.

gulfing ('gʌlfɪŋ), *ppl. a.* [f. GULF *v.* + -ING[2].] That gulfs, in senses of the vb.

1813 SCOTT *Trierm.* II. xxiv, Like the shrill sea-bird's wailing scream, Heard o'er the whirlpool's gulfing stream. **1821** CLARE *Vill. Minstr.* I. 88 Boughs..That overhang some gulphing brook. **1842** TUPPER *Proverb. Philos.* Ser. II. 182 Neither congealing of the grave, nor gulphing waters of the firmament..shall avail.

Gulf Stream, Gulf-Stream. *Geog.* A great oceanic current of warm water, that issues from the Gulf of Mexico and runs parallel to the American coast as far as Newfoundland, and thence in the direction of Europe. The name is sometimes given to a similar current in the Pacific, along the shore of Japan.

1775 ADAIR *Amer. Ind.* 371 He..proceeded..afterwards, along the gulph-stream of Mexico. **1796** T. TWINING *Trav. Amer.* (1894) 21 These signs denoted our arrival in the great current called by navigators the 'Gulf Stream'. **1812** SIR H. DAVY *Chem. Philos.* 72 The warmth of the Gulf Stream is felt a thousand miles from its source. **1833** TENNYSON *Early Sonn.* iii, The warm gulf-stream of Florida Floats far away into the Northern seas The lavish growths of southern Mexico. **1860** G. H. K. in *Vac. Tour* 124 Sutherland is..warm enough, thanks to the gulf-stream, to suit the roller and the Bohemian waxwing. **1875** BEDFORD *Sailor's Pocket Bk.* iv. (ed. 2) 103 The water of the Gulf Stream is a deep indigo blue in colour.

fig. **1859** *Autobiog. Beggar Boy* 16 Few are able, after entering the gulf-stream of dissipation, to check their headlong career. **1865** LOWELL *New Eng. Two Cent. Ago* Prose Wks. 1890 II. 8 Truly there is a tide in the affairs of men, but there is no gulf-stream setting forever in one direction.

b. *attrib.* **Gulf-Stream weed** = next.

1884 *Public Opinion* 3 Oct. 426/1 Among them is the Gulf Stream weed, so often talked of by travellers.

gulf-weed. A species of sea-weed (*Sargassum bacciferum* of the sub-order *Fucaceæ*) found in the Gulf Stream, the Sargasso Sea, and elsewhere; characterized by having a number of berry-like air-vessels. The name is sometimes given to another species (*S. vulgare*).

1674 JOSSELYN *Voy. New Eng.* 40 We met with abundance of Sea-weeds called Gulf-weed coming out of the Bay of Mexico. **1708** *Brit. Apollo* No. 86. 1/2 Weed (called by the Mariners Gulf Weed). **1835–6** TODD *Cycl. Anat.* I. 520/1 Floating Sargasso or gulf-weed of the Equator.

gulfy ('gʌlfɪ), *a. poet.* Forms: 6 **gulffy**, 6–9 **gulfie**, **-ye**, 7 **gulphie**, 8–9 **gulphy**, 9 **gulfy**. [f. GULF *sb.* + -Y[1].]

1. Full of eddies or whirlpools. Also, whirlpool-like.

1594 CAREW *Tasso* IV. v. 141 There thousands vncleane Harpyes might you vew,..And gulffy Scillaes an huge barcking crew. **1598** CHAPMAN *Iliad* II. 538 Well built ships ..To passe the gulffy purple Sea. **1628** MILTON *Vac. Exerc.* 92 Rivers, arise; whether thou be the Son, Of utmost Tweed, or Oose, or gulphie Dun. **1715–20** POPE *Iliad* II. 1071 Where gulphy Xanthus foams along the fields. **1792** E. DARWIN *Bot. Gard.* I. 49 The cliffs of Orkney's gulphy coast. **1856** AIRD *Poet. Wks.* 69 He sate and eyed The gulfy eddyings of the woolly smoke.

2. †**a.** *fig.* Deep as an abyss; abysmal (*obs.*). **b.** Full of hollows or depths.

1607 WALKINGTON *Opt. Glass* 154 The gulfye bottome of despaire. **1737** BROOKE *Tasso* II. 641 One step alone 'twixt triumph and defeat, The gulphy ruin and the towery height. **1791** COWPER *Iliad* XXI. 447 Into his gulphy channel rush'd The refluent flood. **1808** J. BARLOW *Columb.* IV. 371 The waves..scoop that gulphy bed. **1839** STONEHOUSE *Axholme* 309 A narrow, miry, and gulphy lane. **1871** G. MACDONALD *Wks. Fancy & Imag., Parable* 106 The well-pleased stars Threw quivering smiles across the gulfy skies.

fig. **1879** G. MACDONALD *Sir Gibbie* I. xi. 161 The cracks, crannies, and gulfy faults of our belief.

gulion, variant of GOLION *Obs.*

†**gulist.** *Obs.* [f. L. *gula* gullet, appetite, gluttony + -IST.] One who pampers his appetite; a glutton.

1632 J. FEATLY *Hon. Chast.* 12 The gluttonous satiety of our swelling gulists argues their necessity of offending by forgetfulnes.

gulix ('gju:lɪks). Also 8 **guilix**. [f. Du. *Gulik*, the town of Juliers.] A kind of fine linen. Also *attrib.*

1696 J. F. *Merch. Wareho. laid open* 17 Gulix..being the most proper of any for fine Shifts or Sheets. *Ibid.* 18 A sort of Holland we call small thred..scarcely to be known from Gulix. **1727–41** CHAMBERS *Cycl.* s.v. *Holland*, Guilix Holland is very white and fine, and is chiefly used for shirts. **1880** *Plain Hints* 89 That for shirting, commonly called gulix Holland, one yard wide.

gull (gʌl), *sb.*[1] Forms: 5–6 **gulle**, 7 **gul**, 5– **gull**; *Sc.* 5 **goule**, 6–7 **goul**, 7 **gow**. [Perh. a. Welsh *gŵylan*, Cornish *guilan* = Breton *goelann* (whence F. *goëland*), OIr. *foilenn* (mod.Ir. *faoileann*):—OCeltic **voilenno-*; cf. Breton *goelaff* to weep.] **a.** Any long-winged, web-footed bird of the family *Laridæ* and sub-family *Larinæ*, which contains several genera, *Larus* being the largest. In popular use the name is of much wider application, including the Terns and Skuas.

The Gulls are mostly marine birds and are distributed all over the world; their characteristic colour is white with a mantle varying from pearl-grey to dark-slate colour or black, the bill being usually bright-coloured; their cry is harsh or shrill.

The **common gull** is *Larus canus*, called otherwise ***sea-mew***, ***sea-gull***, and ***green-billed gull***. Other species are similarly distinguished by defining words indicating colour, appearance, habitat, etc., as ***grey***, ***hooded***, ***hovering***, ***long-billed***, ***Pacific***, ***red-legged***, ***white-headed***, ***white-winged***, etc.; also **black** or **black-toed g.**, the SKUA; **greater black-backed g.**, *Larus marinus*, called locally also ***carrion***, ***goose***, or WAGEL ***gull***, †by Willughby ***great black and white gull***; **lesser black-backed g.**, *L. fuscus*; **black-headed g.**, *L. ridibundus*, called also ***brown-headed***, ***laughing***, ***red-legged***, or PEEWIT ***gull***; **cloven-footed g.**, the common Black Tern; **glaucous g.**, *Larus glaucus*, the BURGOMASTER; **herring g.**, *L. argentatus*, called also ***silvery gull***; **ivory g.**, a small arctic gull of pure white colour with black legs, *L. eburneus*, *Pagophila eburnea*, or *Gavia alba*; **little g.**, *Larus minutus*; **ring-billed g.**, one of the commonest gulls of the U.S., *L. delawarensis*; **rosy, roseate** or **Ross's g.**, *Rhodostethia rosea*, called also ***wedge-tailed gull***; **Sabine's g.**, *Xema sabinii*, a fork-tailed gull common chiefly in arctic America and Siberia. Also *ice-gull*, s.v. ICE *sb.* 8 and KITTIWAKE *gull.*

c **1430** *Two Cookery-bks.* 62 Le .ij. cours..Pyions. Ve[n]ysoun Rostyd. Gullys. Curlew. *c* **1450** HOLLAND *Howlat* 179 The Se Mawis war monkis, the blak and the quhyte, The Goule was a Gryntar. **1573–80** BARET *Alv.* G 627 A *Gull*, a common name to sundrie birds of the sea, as a Cormorant &c., *Mergus*. **1601** HOLLAND *Pliny* I. 287 As touching the Guls or Sea-cobs, they build in rockes. **1655** MOUFET & BENNET *Health's Improv.* (1746) 194 *Gulones Albi & Cinerei.* White Gulls, Grey Gulls, and Black Gulls (commonly termed by the Name of Plungers and Water-crows). **1673** WEDDERBURN *Voc.* 14 (Jam.) *Gavia*, a gow. **1674** RAY *Collect. Words, Water Fowl* 93 The Herring-gull or greatest ash-coloured Mew: *Larus cinereus maximus*. **1678** —— *Willughby's Ornith.* 344 The great black and white Gull: *Larus ingens marinus Clusii. Ibid.* 354 Aldrovands cloven-footed Gull, with longer Wings. **1766** PENNANT *Zool.* (1768) II. 424 Common Gull. This is the most numerous of the genus. It breeds on the ledges of the cliffs that impend over the sea. **1839** SELBY in *Proc. Berw. Nat. Club* I. No. 7. 189 *Larus minutus* (little gull) near Embleton. **1839** *Penny Cycl.* XIII. 335/1 *Xema ridibundus*,..This bird is the..Laughing Gull, Pewit or Black-cap, Sea Crow and Mire Crow of the Modern British. **1865** GOSSE *Land & Sea* (1874) 36 The kittiwake, the smallest of the gulls that can be properly called indigenous to our shores. **1876** DAVIS *Polaris Exped.* App. 679 Saw several eider-ducks and ivory and burgomeister gulls. **1885** *Stand. Nat. Hist.* (1888) IV. 79 Ross's Gull (*Rhodostethia rosea*), or the wedge-tailed gull, as it is also called, on account of the form of its tail. *Ibid.* 81 The dazzling white ivory-gull (*Gavia alba*)..the fork-tailed gulls, constituting the genus *Xema*.

b. *allusively.*

1550 CROWLEY *Way to Wealth* A 3 b, Men that would haue all in their owne handes..Cormerauntes, gredye gulles; yea, men that would eate vp menne, women, and chyldren, are the causes of Sedition! **1628** WITHER *Brit. Rememb.* Pref. 137 As, our Gull, A bird much found among the Worshipfull.

c. *attrib.* and *Comb.*, as ***gull-kind***, ***-land***, ***rookery***; ***gull-like*** adj.; **gull-billed tern**, *Sterna anglica*; **gull-maw** (†Sc. *goul mau*), the Greater Black-backed Gull; **gull-teaser**, a bird that torments gulls, as a tern or jaeger; **gull wing**, (*a*) an aeroplane wing of which the short inner section slants upwards from the fuselage, and the longer outer section is approximately horizontal; (*b*) of a car door (used *attrib.*): opening upwards from the body of the car.

1813 G. MONTAGU *Ornith. Dict.* Suppl. y^a–^b, The new species which, from the shape of the bill, is denominated the *Gull-billed Tern..as it has originated in England we have added the more scientific name of *Sterna Anglica.* **1851** *Zoologist* IX. 3235 A fine adult male specimen of the gull-billed tern. **1668** WILKINS *Real Char.* II. v. §9. 155 The *Gull-kind, being much upon the wing as Swallows, commonly of an ash colour;..having red bill and legs, with a forked train. **1774** GOLDSM. *Nat. Hist.* III. vii. VI. 77 It is to such shores as these that the whole tribe of the gull-kind resort. **1899** *Academy* 8 Apr. 408/2 Throwing bread to the sea-gulls, she says, 'In *gull-land they don't like bread, but it's a point of honour to catch it'. **1895** P. H. EMERSON *Birds, etc. Norf. Broadland* l. 146 The danger signal is either a peculiar *gull-like noise, 'Kēo, kēo', or a 'Quah, quah'. **1549** *Compl. Scot.* vi. 39 The suannis murnit, be cause the gray *goul mau pronosticat ane storme. **1885** SWAINSON *Prov. Names Birds* 208 Greater Black-backed Gull..Also called..Gull maw—*i.e.* mew (East Lothian). **1885** *Stand. Nat. Hist.* (1888) IV. 78 The fascinating view of a *gull rookery with its ceaseless uproar. **1802** G. MONTAGU *Ornith. Dict.* (1833) 508 Common Tern, *Sterna hirundo*..*Gull-teazer. **1932** *Aviation* Jan. 39/3 The machine is a wire-braced monoplane of the *gull-wing type designed primarily to afford the widest possible angle of vision for both pilot and observer. **1934** *Flight* 15 Feb. 156 The 'gull' wings of the earlier type have been dispensed with. **1957** *Motor Body* Apr. 8/1 This was a streamlined design with..the gull wing or butterfly wing door. **1966** N. FREELING *King of Rainy Country* 122 We had a new sports car—you remember the first three-hundred SL—with the gullwing doors. **1967** C. H. BARNES *Shorts Aircraft* 421 The new craft was a very elegant and efficient gull-wing cantilever monoplane. **1969** *Daily Tel.* (Colour Suppl.) 17 Oct. 71/3 The gull-wing door is likely to be seen more widely in future as a new breed of low-slung sports two-seaters is developed.

gull (gʌl), *sb.*[2] Now *dial.* Also 4 goll, 6–7 gulle, 7 gul. [Prob. a subst. use of GULL *a.* yellow.] An unfledged bird, *esp.* a gosling.

1382 WYCLIF *Deut.* xxii. 6 A nest of briddis..and the moder to the bryddis [*MS. Bodl.* 959 gollis] or to the eyren aboue sittynge. **1596** SHAKS. *1 Hen. IV*, v. i. 60 As that vngentle gull the Cuckowes Bird, Vseth the Sparrow. **1607** —— *Timon* II. i. 31, I do feare When euery Feather stickes in his owne wing, Lord Timon will be left a naked Gull, Which flashes now a Phœnix. **1882** *W. Worcestersh. Gloss.*, *Gull*, a young goose. **1896** *Warwicksh. Gloss.*, *Gull*, an unfledged gosling.

gull (gʌl), *sb.*[3] Also 6–7 gulle, 7 gul. [Of doubtful and perh. mixed origin; sense 1 would be natural as a transferred use of GULL *sb.*[2], but it is also possible that the sb. may be f. GULL *v.*[3] to delude, and that this vb. may be an application of GULL *v.*[1] 2 to gorge, 'cram'.]

1. A credulous person; one easily imposed upon; a dupe, simpleton, fool. †*to grope a gull*: to swindle an unsuspecting person: cf. *to pluck a pigeon*, †*a finch.*

1594 NASHE *Terrors Nt.* Wks. (Grosart) III. 257 Liues there anie such slowe yce-braind beefe-witted gull. **1594** SHAKS. *Rich. III*, I. iii. 328 Clarence, who I indeede haue cast in darknesse, I do beweepe to many simple Gulles, Namely to Derby, Hastings, Buckingham. **1601** ? MARSTON *Pasquil & Kath.* I. 323 He..will not sticke to spend some twentie pound To grope a gull. **1616** R. C. *Times' Whistle* v. 2217 In these dayes hee's deemd a very gull That cannot take Tobacco. *a* **1622** DAVIES *Epigr.* Poems 1876 II. 9 To define a Gull in termes precise—A Gull is he which seemes, and is not, wise. **1645** MILTON *Colast.* Wks. (1851) 356 His very touching ought that is lerned, soiles it, and lays him still more and more open a conspicuous gull. **1748** SMOLLETT *Rod. Rand.* (1812) I. 359 If I had been such a gull..I would without more ado tuck myself up. **1811** WELLINGTON in Gurw. *Desp.* (1838) VII. 511 It is as well to let him believe that we are good natured gulls who will easily swallow. **1838** DICKENS *Nich. Nick.* xix, 'Done!' cried the noble gull. 'Within ten minutes'. **1885** STEVENSON *Dynamiter* 60 He perceived by what..unmanly fear of ridicule he had been brought down to be the gull of this intriguer.

†**2.** [From the vb.] A trick, deception, fraud; a false report. *Obs.*

1599 SHAKS. *Much Ado* II. iii. 123, I should thinke this a gull, but that the white-bearded fellow speakes it. **1604** (*title*), Pasquil's Jests,..whereunto is added a dozen of Gulles, Pretty and Pleasant to drive away the tediousness of a winter's evening. **1619** LUSHINGTON *Repet. Serm.* in *Phenix* (1708) II. 477 They say there was no such matter as the Resurrection, 'twas but a gull put upon the World by his Disciples. **1642** FULLER *Holy & Prof. St.* IV. xvi. 324 If gulls and rumours from his Countrey be raised on purpose to amuse our Embassadour. *a* **1668** DAVENANT *News from Plymouth* IV. Dram. Wks. 1873 IV. 169 For the gull Your Seawit put upon me, I have taken A full revenge.

3. *slang.* A trickster, cheat, impostor.

a **1700** B. E. *Dict. Cant. Crew*, *Gull*, a cheat. **1825** C. M. WESTMACOTT *Eng. Spy* I. 161 You'll excuse me, sir, but as you are fresh, take care to avoid the gulls. (*Note*), *Gulls*, knowing ones who are always on the look out for freshmen.

4. *attrib.* and *Comb.*, as ***gull-catcher***, ***-catching***, ***-gallant***; †**gull-finch**, a playful amplification of *gull* = 'simpleton', with reference to the bird of that name: cf. also *to pluck a finch*; **gull-groper**, one who 'gropes a gull' (see 1); **gull-sharper** (see quot.).

1601 SHAKS. *Twel. N.* II. v. 204 Heere comes my noble *gull catcher. **1823** *Spirit Publ. Jrnls.* (1824) 63 Taking in the 'deep ones' quite in the *gull-catching style. **1604** T. M. *Black Bk.* C 3 Delicate Knaues..that diue into Deedes and Writings of Landes, left to young *Gull-finches, poysoning the true sence and intent of them. **1630** J. TAYLOR (Water P.) *Wks.* II. 71/2 For 'tis concluded 'mongst the wizards all, To make thee Master of Gul-finches hall. **1613** PURCHAS *Pilgrimage* IX. ii. 826 The *gull-gallants of our dayes, to whom I could wish..that they would leave this vsurped Gallantrie to those true owners, and resume spirits truly English. **1602** DEKKER *Satiromastix* Wks. 1873 I. 201 Ile shake the *gull-groper out of his tan'd skinne. *a* **1700** B. E. *Dict. Cant. Crew*, *Gull-groper*, a Bystander that Lends Money to the Gamesters. **1826** J. WILSON *Noct. Ambr.* Wks. 1855 I. 185 The he, or the she, or the it, that..gangs out to glower like a gawpus at a Gallic gull-grupper. **1867** SMYTH *Sailor's Word-bk.*, **Gull-sharper*, one who preys upon Johnny Raws.

gull (gʌl), *sb.*[4] Also 5 golle, 5–6 gulle, 6–7 gul. [? Variant of GOOL, GOLE *sb.*[2]]

†**1.** The throat, gullet. *Obs.*

1412–20 LYDG. *Chron. Troy* I. vi, That as fast as he seeth theim [the bulles] gape Into theyr golles that he the lycour caste. **1490** CAXTON *Eneydos* x. 39 Neptunus..his grete gulle or throte wyde opene redy to swolowe..alle thooste. **1543** TRAHERON *Vigo's Chirurg.* I. iv. 6 There ben in the throte two Conduyctes. Of whiche by one the meate and drincke passe, descendynge in to the stomake, and is called Meri or Oisophagus, in Englishe the Gulle. **1663** GERBIER *Counsel* 32 The Freese, Gul or Throat.

†**b.** *transf.* A 'mouth', an orifice.

1545 RAYNOLD *Byrth Mankynde* I. xii. (1634) 43 In the inner face of the bladder, there be set before the mouth or gull of the conduits certaine little skinny flappes.

2. A breach or fissure made by a torrent; a gully, chasm; a channel made by a stream. *Obs.* exc. *dial.*

1553 BRENDE *Q. Curtius* v. 25 Their passage was suddenly stopped by a great gull made with the violence of the streams. **1673** RAY *Journ. Low C.* 275 Great channels, like Gulls made by suddain torrents and land-floods. **1692** —— *Dissol. World* iii. (1732) 24 The mighty Gulls and Channels in the Sides thereof [*sc.* a mountain]. **1769** *De Foe's Tour Gt. Brit.* III. 143 A Brook..running from those Gulls and Deeps between the Hills. **1792** S. IRELAND *Views Thames* II. 55 About the shallows or gulls, the water is beautifully transparent. **1852** WIGGINS *Embanking* 51 Currents will be formed by the disturbed action of the tide, 'gulls' (pits) will be formed [etc.].

†**gull**, *sb.*[5] *Obs.* [Cf. Du. *gul* (16th c. *gulle*) small codfish.] A fish not fully grown; also, a kind of gudgeon.

1495 *Act 11 Hen. VII*, c. 23 If the..fisshe shuld be well and truly packed, that is to sey, the tale fisshe by theym selfe and the small fissh called Gulles by them self. **1655** MOUFET & BENNET *Health's Improv.* (1746) 274 Gulls..are a kind of jolt-headed Gudgeons.

b. *Comb.*, **gull-fish**, the coal-fish, *Merlangus carbonarius*; **gull-head** = BULL-HEAD 1.

1583 *Rates Custom-ho.* C iv, Gulfish the barrel vi.*s.* viii.*d.* **1611** FLORIO, *Ghiozzo*, a Gul-head, a Millers-thumbe, a Curfish, or a Bull-head. Some take it for a Gudgeon-fish. **1663** *Act 15 Chas. II*, c. 7 §14 [Duties.] For Cod-fish the Barrell five shillings..For Gull fish the Barrell Two shillings. **1759** tr. *Adanson's Voy. Senegal* 178 There you might see pilchards, rock-fish, mullets or gull-fish of different sorts; mole-bats, with other fishes very little known.

†**gull**, *a. Obs.* Also 4 gowle, 5 gulle, 6 goule, *Sc.* gule, 8 gool. [a. ON. *gul-r* (Da., Sw. *gul*) yellow.] Yellow, pale.

13.. *Evang. Nicod.* 70 in *Archiv. Stud. neu. Spr.* LIII. 392 þe Iewes..wex all full gull and grene. **1398** TREVISA *Barth. De P.R.* XII. Introd. (Tollem. MS.), þe egle is sore greuid and heren wynges wexen white, and heren clawes gowle [**1582** goule] and feble [L. *et ebetant ungues ejus et debilitantur*]. **1483** *Cath. Angl.* 168/1 Gulle, *pallidus, lividus & cetera; vbi*, wanne. **1508** DUNBAR *Flyting w. Kennedie* 52 Evill farit and dryit..Lyke as the gleddis had on thy gulesnowt dynd. ? *a* **1600** *Hist. Sir Egeir*, etc. (1711) 4 Thou was full blyth, and light of late:..And thou art now both gool and green.

Hence †'**gullness**, paleness.

a **1300** *E.E. Psalter* lxvii. 14 In golnes [*v.r.* gulnes] of gold to se.

†**gull**, *v.*[1] *Obs.* Also 6 gool. [? f. GULL *sb.*[4] Cf. Du. *gullen* 'absorbere, ingurgitare, vorare' (Kilian) and obs. F. *engouler.*]

1. *trans.* To swallow, guzzle; *transf.* and *fig.* to devour voraciously. Also with *in*, *up*.

1530 PALSGR. 576/2, I gulle in drinke, as great drinkers do, *je engoulle.* **1553** BRENDE *Q. Curtius* VII. 133 b, Suche as had gulled in gredely the water that thei gote. **1607** C. LEVER *Crucifix* xiii, O you that gull the poyson'd cup of pleasure. **1645** *Arraignm. Persecution* in Prynne *Discov. Prodig. Blazing-Stars* 19 To gull up and devour more at one meale, then would make a feast for Bel and the Dragon. **1674** JOSSELYN *Voy. New Eng.* 211 They are roystering and gulling in wine with a dear felicity.

fig. **1624** MIDDLETON *Game at Chess* IV. ii, The swallow of my conscience Hath but a narrow passage;..If I had got seven thousand pounds by offices, And gull'd down that, the bore would have been bigger.

b. *absol.* or *intr.*

1541 R. COPLAND *Guydon's Quest. Chirurg.* M iij, People gullyng, fraungyng, and dronkerdes. **1567** FENTON *Trag. Disc.* 4 (5) b, The heate of the wine wherein they goolled. **1583** STUBBES *Anat. Abuses* I. (1879) 107 Swilling, gulling, & carowsing from one to another. **1618** BRETON *Crt. & Country* (Grosart) 6/2 They..drinke and gull, laugh and be fat.

2. *trans.* To gorge. Also *refl.*

1583 STANYHURST *Æneis* III. (Arb.) 77 With ramd cramd garbadge, theire gorges draftye be gulled. **1604** T. WRIGHT *Passions* v. §4. 274 Let us gull ourselves with eating and quaffing.

gull (gʌl), *v.*[2] Now *dial.* and *techn.* Also 9 *dial.* goal. [f. GULL *sb.*[4]]

1. *trans.* Of water: To make channels or ruts in, to hollow out; to sweep *away*, wear *down.*

1577 B. GOOGE *Heresbach's Husb.* I. 44 They gull [*printed* gult] and marre the grounde with the deepe sincking of their feete treading in the Grasse and breaking the Rootes. **1587** HARRISON *England* I. xix. (1877) III. 148 [They] doo utterlie neglect to dich and scowre their draines and watercourses, for better avoidance of the winter waters..whereby the streets doo grow to be much more gulled than before. **1642** ROGERS *Naaman* 502 As the sea tydes gull down the bankes. **1721** PERRY *Daggenh. Breach* 105 An Accident that gull'd away the Earth in such manner, that was very near obliging me to cut down..my Dam. **1776** G. SEMPLE *Building in Water* 20 The Water..continued to sap and gull the Frames every Flood. **1876** in *N.W. Linc. Gloss.* (1889) s.v. *Goal*, Th' rats hes maade a hoäle thrif th' bank, an' when Taacey taks in a tide, th' watter goäls it awaay. **1895** *E. Angl. Gloss.*, The bank has been gulled down by the freshes.

b. *gen.* of other things.

1796 W. FELTON *Carriages* (1801) II. Suppl. 108 That part of the bottom plate of the perch, against which it wears, after much use, is gulled. **1805** W. HUNTER in *Naval Chron.* XIII. 40 One..shell came so near us as to gull our whale. **1857** P. COLQUHOUN *Oarsman's Guide* 30 The upper filling, which, when worn, is said to be gulled.

c. *absol.* or *intr.*

1587 HARRISON *England* I. x. 31 Then breaketh there out another creeke from the maine sea, about Auant hauen, which gulleth vp almost to Portbridge. **1676** EVELYN in Aubrey *Nat. Hist. Surrey* (1719) I. Pref. 3 In the Cart-Roats, where the Rains have gull'd. **1721** PERRY *Daggenh. Breach* 5 The Water then gull'd to such a depth..that there was no Remedy found for the mastery of it. **1739** LABELYE *Short Acc. Piers Westm. Bridge* 61 The Piers..will always be in danger of the Water gulling underneath, and carrying away the Ground.

2. *intr.* To become worn away or hollowed out.

1763–6 W. LEWIS *Comm. Phil. Techn.* 227 The collars in which the axes of the rolls turned at each end, wore or gulled so fast, that the pressure continually diminished.

gull (gʌl), *v.*[3] Also 7 gul. [Related to GULL *sb.*[3], but it is uncertain whether as derivative or as source; in the latter case, this verb may be a transferred use of GULL *v.*[1]; cf. similar uses of *stuff*, *cram*; this supposition is favoured by some early examples, e.g. quot. *c* 1600 in sense 1.]

1. *trans.* To make a gull of; to dupe, cheat, befool, 'take in', deceive. Also *absol.*, to practise cheating.

a **1550** *Hye Way to Spyttel Ho.* 427 in Hazl. *E.P.P.* IV. 45 They..do but gull, and folow beggery, Feynyng true doyng by ypocrysy. **1593** NASHE *Christ's T.* 91 Cleanly coyned eyes, which some pleasant sportiue wittes haue deuised, to gull them most groselie. *c* **1600** SHAKS. *Sonn.* lxxxvi, That affable familiar ghost Which nightly gulls him with intelligence. **1602** *2nd Pt. Return fr. Parnass.* I. iv. 435 With those shreds of French..weele gull the world, that hath in estimation forraine Phisitians. **1613** PURCHAS *Pilgrimage* (1614) 271 In the night time by some fire-workes in the steeple, they would have gulled the credulous people with opinion of miracle. **1624** QUARLES *Job* VIII. xvi, See, how deceits Gull thee with golden fruit. **1635** FOXE & JAMES *Voy. N.W.* (Hakluyt Soc.) 443 Guld with the false Sea Cards or fabulous reports of strangers. **1655** FULLER *Ch. Hist.* VI. ii. *Civil Benefits Abbeys* §1 People in those daies..would never have been gulled into so long a toleration..of them. **1701** DE FOE *True-born Eng.*, *His fine Speech* 90 Not doubting I could gull the Government. **1808** SCOTT *Fam. Lett.* (1894) I. iv. 126, I care not for rewards..Neither is it easy to gull me with these fair promises. **1824** W. IRVING *T. Trav.* II. 47 Nothing is so easy as to gull the public, if you only set up a prodigy. *a* **1849** POE *Quacks of Helicon* Wks. 1864 IV. 412 The pertinacity of the effort to gull. **1861** *Times* 23 Aug., Gulled by this statement into the belief that [etc.]. **1880** HOWELLS *Undisc. Country* iii. 54 You are perfectly safe to go on and gull imbeciles to the end of time, for all I care.

†**2.** To deprive *of* by trickery or deception; to cheat *out of*. *Obs.*

1610 B. JONSON *Alch.* v. iv, Hast thou gull'd her of her Iewels or her Bracelets? **1691** WOOD *Ath. Oxon.* II. 74 The Presbyterians had been gull'd of their King by the Independents. **1722** DE FOE *Plague* (1840) 35 These unperforming creatures had gulled them of their money. **1783** POTT *Chirurg. Wks.* II. 188 The poor and credulous are gulled out of what little money they can spare.

gull, dial. var. GOLD[2], marigold.

gullable ('gʌləb(ə)l), *a.* [f. GULL *v.*[3] + -ABLE.] = GULLIBLE. Hence **gulla'bility**, **'gullableness** = GULLIBILITY.

1818 SCOTT *Rob Roy* xxiv, I am in certain things the most gullable and malleable of mortals. **1822** JEFFERSON *Writ.* (1830) IV. 360 With such persons, gullability, which they call faith, takes the helm from the hand of reason. **1830** *Fraser's Mag.* I. 319 The gullableness of fools. **1840–1** THACKERAY *Charac. Sk.*, *Fashionable Authoress*, The most gullable of publics.

†**'gullage.** *Obs.* [f. GULL *v.*[3] + -AGE.] Deception, cajolery.

1605 B. JONSON *Volpone* v. ix, Had you no quirk, To auoide gullage, Sir, by such a creature? **1611** CHAPMAN *May Day* Wks. 1873 II. 347 The deere gullage of my sweete heart mistress.

Gullah ('gʌlə). *U.S.* Also Golla, Goolah. [Conjectured to be either a shortening of *Angola*, or from a Liberian group of tribes known as Golas.] Used *attrib.* or *absol.* to designate Negroes living on the sea-islands and tide-water coastline of South Carolina and Georgia, and the dialect spoken by them.

1739 *South-Carolina Gaz.* 12 May 2/2 Run away a short well set Negro Man, named Golla Harry. **1822** *Account Late Intended Insurrection among Blacks of this City* (Corporation of Charleston) 22 These disclosures..were obtained from Harry Haig (whose confession and subsequent testimony went to implicate a corps of Gullah or Angola negroes). **1835** W. G. SIMMS *Partisan* 224 To their arts the Gullah and the Ebo negroes..added their spells and magic in no stinted quantities. **1838** *Southern Lit. Messenger* IV. 641/1 The etymology of all which terms..is quite as untraceable as that of any terms in the Goolah negro dialect. **1896** J. G. WILLIAMS *Ole Plantation* Pref. p. v, The older ones of that set of negroes..speak as pure Gullah as their grandfathers... They seem to have been scarcely affected in their low-country Gullah speech [etc.]. **1908** *S. Atlantic Q.* Oct. 339 The vocabulary of our *Gullah* patois is..five times as great. *Ibid.*, To some *Gullah* remains a closed book. **1931** E. LINKLATER *Juan in Amer.* II. vii. 111 They spoke mostly in the argot of Naples, with here and there a little Czech, Finnish, Gullah, and Yiddish. **1957** W. C. HANDY *Father of Blues* viii. 116 A humourous Negro custom that could be traced to the Gullahs and from them all the way back to Africa. **1969** *Times* 19 July 9/5 Gullah is a form of creolized English taken to the United States by slaves from West Africa,..rather than a regular dialect of black American English.

gulled (gʌld), *ppl. a.*^{1} [f. GULL *v.*^{2} + -ED^{1}.] Hollowed out.

1821 CLARE *Vill. Minstr.* I. 57 How he..would..Bend o'er gull'd holes where stood his trees, and sigh. *Ibid.* 111 Rut-gull'd lanes. *Ibid.* II. 101 It [a brook] rests collected in some gulled hole Scoop'd by the sudden floods.

gulled (gʌld), *ppl. a.*^{2} [f. GULL *v.*^{3} + -ED^{1}.] Duped, deceived, befooled.

1642 H. MORE *Song of Soul* I. II. cxi, That melting love which doth so please Her gulled soul. **1738** JOHNSON *London* 121 The gull'd conqueror receives the chain. **1811** LAMB *Guy Faux* Misc. Wks. (1871) 371 The simplicity of the gulled editor. **1812** H. & J. SMITH *Rej. Addr.* 21 An independent wish to open the eyes of this gulled people. **1859** HELPS *Friends in C.* Ser. II. II. x. 205, I am a gulled and swindled individual.

†**'guller**^{1}. *Obs.* In 7 gullar. [f. GULL *v.*^{1} + -ER^{1}.] A guzzler, glutton.

1604 T. WRIGHT *Passions* IV. ii. §2. 128 Great feasters and gullars cannot but be subiect to many vices.

†**'guller**^{2}. *Obs.* [f. GULL *v.*^{3} + -ER^{1}.] One who dupes or befools; a cheat.

1602 *How Choose Good Wife* v. iii, He was a great guller, his name I take to be Fuller. **1605** CHAPMAN *All Fools* v. i. Wks. 1873 I. 174 This Gull to him And to his fellow Guller, shall become More bitter then their baiting of my humour. **1611** COTGR., *Enjauleur*, a beguiler..; guller, a foisting companion..cousening mate.

guller, variant of GOLLAR *v. Sc.*

gullery^{1} ('gʌlərɪ). *Obs.* or *arch.* [f. GULL *v.*^{3} + -ERY.] Deception, trickery, imposture; an instance of this, a deception, trick.

1598 E. GUILPIN *Skial.* (1878) 4 Such as Hermaphroditize these poore times With wicked scald iests, extreame gullerie. **1598** B. JONSON *Ev. Man in Hum.* III. v, For your greene wound, your Balsamum, and your St. John's woort are all mere gulleries. **1621** BURTON *Anat. Mel.* I. ii. IV. iv, Leo Decimus took an extraordinary delight in humoring of silly fellowes, and to put gulleries upon them. **1638** FORD *Fancies* v. i, Spadone Confessed it was a gullery put on Secco. *a* **1680** BUTLER *Rem.* (1759) II. 315 Law..puts a thousand Tricks and Gulleries upon him. **1681** H. MORE *Let.* I in *Glanvill's Sadducismus*, The marvellous weakness and gullerie of Mr. Webster's Display of Witchcraft. **1691** HARTCLIFFE *Virtues* 269 Those Mountebanks in Religion, who by fair Stories, and specious Gulleries, wheedle men out of their Sense and Reason. **1821** SCOTT *Kenilw.* xx, Do you think..that you may put any gullery you will on me?

gullery^{2} ('gʌlərɪ). [f. GULL *sb.*^{1} + -ERY.] A haunt or breeding-place of gulls.

1833 SELBY *Illustr. Brit. Ornith.* II. 510 These breeding places, or gulleries [*printed* galleries], are sometimes at a considerable distance from the sea. **1839** *Penny Cycl.* XIII. 335/1 The Gullery (or summer resort of the species) produced a revenue of from 50*l.* to 80*l.* to the proprietor. **1853** *Chamb. Jrnl.* XX. 237 There used to be a 'gullery', as a colony of sea-gulls is called, at Norbury. **1873** G. C. DAVIES *Mount. & Mere* v. 35 With one last long look, we bade adieu to Scoulton Gullery.

gulles, obs. form of GULES, red.

gullet ('gʌlɪt), *sb.* Forms: 4–5 golet, 5 -ett, goolet, 5–6 golette, 6 goulet, gulet, 7 golit, gollet, gullit(t, 6– gullet. [a. OF. *golet, goulet (1358 in Hatz.-Darm.), dim. of *gole, goule*, mod.F. *gueule*:—L. *gula* throat. Cf. GULL *sb.*^{4}]

1. The passage in the neck of an animal by which food and drink pass from the mouth to the stomach; the œsophagus.

c **1380** WYCLIF *Wks.* (1880) 200 þis glotonye & dronkenesse makiþ men to loue more here bely & here golet þan god almyȝtty. *c* **1386** CHAUCER *Pard. T.* 215 Out of the harde bones knokke they The mary, for they caste noght a wey That may go thurgh the golet soft and swoote. *c* **1450** *Two Cookery-bks.* 116 Folde the necke a-boute the spite, and putt the hede ynne att the golet as a crane. **1491** CAXTON *Vitas Patr.* (W. de W. 1495) I. li. 108 That she maye be deliuered from the golette of the dragon. **1548–77** VICARY *Anat.* v. (1888) 43 The Uuila is a member..hanging downe from the ende of the Pallet ouer the goulet of the throte. **1555** ABP. PARKER *Ps.* lxxiii, Their gullets feele no thurst. **1615** CROOKE *Body of Man* 629 The Tongue helpeth the Diglutition by turning the meate ouer it towards the Gullet. *c* **1700** B. E. *Dict. Cant. Crew, Gullet*, a Derisory Term for the Throat, from *Gula*. *a* **1715** BURNET *Own Time* (1724) I. 553 His throat cut, so that both the jugulars and the gullet were cut. **1813** SCOTT *Trierm.* III. xxiii, Through gullet and through spinal bone, The trenchant blade had sheerly gone. **1831** R. KNOX *Cloquet's Anat.* 603 The Œsophagus or Gullet (*Gula*). **1897** *Allbutt's Syst. Med.* III. 366 It [thrush] may attack the whole length of the gullet.

transf. and *fig.* **1890** W. J. GORDON *Foundry* 13 Twelve barrow-loads altogether—are thrown on the conical furnace-lid,..and down slips the mouthful into the gullet of fire. **1893** F. ADAMS *New Egypt* 165 This morsel of your Egypt shall disappear down that vast and unappeasable gullet of our Empire.

b. *loosely*. The throat, neck.

1646 EVELYN *Diary* (1889) I. 240 A goodly sort of people, having monstrous gullets, or wens of flesh growing to their throats. **1725** SWIFT *Upright Judge* Wks. 1755 IV. I. 63 He cut his weazon at the altar; I keep my gullet for the halter. **1826** SCOTT *Woodst.* v, What if I had rewarded your melody by a ball in the gullet?

†**2.** A piece of armour for the neck; the part of a hood which envelops the neck. *Obs.*

? *a* **1400** *Morte Arth.* 1772 Throwghe golet and gorgere he hurtez hym ewyne! **1426** LYDG. *De Guil. Pilgr.* 12862 By the goolet off myn hood The beste goth. *c* **1450** *Robin H. & Monk* xlix. in Child *Ballads* (1888) III. 99/1 Be þe golett of þe hode John pulled þe munke down.

b. 'The lower end of a horse-collar, around which passes the choke-strap, and the breast-strap which supports the pole of a carriage' (Knight *Dict. Mech.* 1875).

3. A water channel; a narrow, deep passage through which a stream flows; a strait, estuary, river mouth, etc. Now *local*.

1515 in W. H. Turner *Select. Rec. Oxford* 13 The same..felowes..do stopp uppe the comyn golette next the saide College. **1552** T. BARNABE in Ellis *Orig. Lett.* Ser. II. II. 202 Yt is the verye gulfe, gulet, and mouthe of the See. **1601** HOLLAND *Pliny* I. 50 Many haue called those Streights of Gibralter, The entrie of the Mediterranean Sea. Of both sides of this gullet, neere vnto it, are two mountaines set as frontiers and rampiers to keepe all in. **1604** E. GRIMSTONE *Hist. Siege Ostend* 2 The Sea..hath opened a new gollet or Port. **1665** MANLEY *Grotius' Low C. Warres* 703 Out of the Estuary or Gollet, which we said flowed on another part, by digging a little on the Shore, a Channel was made. **1685** *Lond. Gaz.* No. 2061/4 The Gullet under the said Draw-Bridge (commonly called the Draw-Bridge Lock) will be stopped up all the month of September next. **1725** DE FOE *Voy. round World* (1840) 261 Gold which they had picked up in the hill or gullet where the water trickled down from the rocks. **1865** CARLYLE *Fredk. Gt.* XV. xiii. (1872) VI. 113 Yonder, sure enough;..deep gullet and swampy brook in front of him. **1869** BLACKMORE *Lorna D.* iii, John lay on the ground by a barrow of heather, where a little gullet was. **1886** *Act 49 Vict.* c. 17 §6 The Commission may..repair any bridge, arch, or gullett.

4. a. A gorge, defile, pass; a gully or ravine; a narrow passage. ? *Obs.* or *dial.*

1600 HOLLAND *Livy* IX. xiv. (1609) 322 The straight gullets [L. *furculas*] of Caudium. **1601** —— *Pliny* I. 67 Augusta Prætoria, of the Salassi, neer vnto the two-fold gullets or passages of the Alpes, to wit, Graija and Peninæ. **1644** DIGBY *Nat. Bodies* xv. (1658) 162 A high castle, standing in a gullet in the course of the wind. **1644** —— *Mans Soul* (1645) Concl. 120 The straight passage, and narrow gullet, through which thou strivest (my soule)..to make thy selfe away. **1648** NETHERSOLE *Problems* II. 7 The Romans Army was shut up fast..at the Caudine Gullets. **1737** *Gaudent. di Lucca* 156 The vast Falls and Gullets, which are seen on the Skirts of all the Mountains of the World. **1798** ANNA SEWARD *Lett.* (1811) V. 155 These houses are to form an handsome approach to the west front of our cathedral..extending down the gullet, which will be widened to admit carriages to pass each other. **1887** HALL CAINE *Deemster* xxxiii. 218 Davy fled..along the rocky causeway to a gullet under the Giant's Grave.

b. A long narrow piece of land. *dial.*

a **1553** *Ludlow Muniments* in Wright *Dict. Provinc.* (1857) s.v., And the residewe beinge xx. li. lyeth in sundrye gullettes in severall townes and shers. **1887** *S. Cheshire Gloss.*, *Gullet*, (1) a long, narrow piece of land.

c. *Mining.* 'An opening in the strata' (Raymond *Mining Gloss.* 1881).

1830 BUDDLE in *Trans. Nat. Hist. Soc. Northumb. & Durh.* I. 186 (E.D.D.) Sandstone roofs (in a mine) are subject to fissures of various sizes and extent, called threads and gullets by the colliers—the larger ones being called gullets. **1860** *Eng. & For. Mining Gloss.*, *Newcastle Terms.*

†**5.** The flue of a chimney. *Obs.*

1715 tr. *Pancirollus' Rerum Mem.* I. II. vi. 80 That we call a Chimney, which, as a Pipe or Gullet, receives the aspiring Smoke, and conveys it safely out of the House. **1672** LEONI *Alberti's Archit.* I. 15/2 The Gullets as we may call them of Chimneys.

6. (See quots.)

1864 WEBSTER, *Gullet*,..A concave cut made in the teeth of some saw-blades. **1875** KNIGHT *Dict. Mech.*, *Gullet*,..a hollow cut away in front of each saw-tooth, in continuation of the face, on alternate sides of the blade. Such saws are known as gullet-saws or brier-tooth saws.

7. *attrib.* and *Comb.*, as **gullet-bridge**, ? a bridge with a very low arch forming a narrow channel for water; **gullet-fancier**, a gourmet; †**gullet-lurker** (see quot.); †**gullet-nail**, some kind of large nail; **gullet-pipe** = sense 1; **gullet-saw** (see sense 6, quot. 1875); **gullet-tooth** (see quot.).

1896 *Edin. Rev.* Apr. 372 Old fashioned *gullet-bridges, which dam up the flood-waters. **1805** LAMB *Lett.* (1888) I. 211 Brawn was a noble thought. It is not every common *gullet-fancier that can properly esteem it..Its gusto is of that hidden sort. **1615** CROOKE *Body of Man* 771 The two Long Muscles which are seated in the forepart of the Neck vnder the Gullet, wherefore they are also called the vnder *Gullet-lurkers. [**1418** in Rogers *Agric. & Prices* III. 448/1 Tingle nail ½m. @ 1/4 *Gullet nail ½m. @ 1/4.] *c* **1520** *Mem. Ripon* (Surtees) III. 206 Item pro gullet nayles, 2*d.* **1836–48** B. D. WALSH *Aristoph., Knights* I. iii, [He] should moisten his *gulletpipe free at her expense. **1875** KNIGHT *Dict. Mech.*, **Gullet-saw* [see 6]. *Ibid.*, **Gullet-tooth*, a form of saw-tooth.

gullet ('gʌlɪt), *v.* [f. GULLET *sb.* (sense 6).] *trans.* To make 'gullets' in (a saw).

1875 [see GULLETING *vbl. sb.*^{2} 1]. **1888** *Lockwood's Dict. Mech. Engin.* s.v., Most circular and pit saws are gulleted, and the dust runs away with greater freedom from such saws.

gulleter ('gʌlɪtə(r)). [f. GULLET *sb.* + -ER^{1}. (Cf. GULLETING *vbl. sb.*^{2} 2.)] A gulleting-stick.

1883 *Fisheries Exhib. Catal.* 195 Bait-boxes, creels, gulleters, clearing rings..and other miscellaneous articles used by anglers.

†**'gulleting**, *vbl. sb.*^{1} *Obs.* [f. GULLET *sb.* + -ING^{1}.] Swallowing, guzzling; = GULLING *vbl. sb.*^{1} Also with *down*.

1633 HART *Diet of Diseased* I. xxviii. 129 After this gulleting downe of strong drinke, there insueth surfetting. **1651** WITTIE *Primrose's Pop. Err.* II. xii. 119 Too much gulleting..of hot drinks.

gulleting ('gʌlɪtɪŋ), *vbl. sb.*^{2} [f. GULLET *sb.* or *v.* + -ING^{1}.]

1. Making 'gullets' in saws; in *Comb.*, as *gulleting-file*, *-press*.

1875 KNIGHT *Dict. Mech.*, *Gulleting press*, a press for punching or gulleting saw-blades. **1888** *Lockwood's Dict. Mech. Engin.*, *Gulleting*, the deepening of the roots of the teeth of circular and gullet saws.

2. *U.S.* In Comb. **gulleting-stick**, 'a stick, notched at one end, used to extract a hook from a fish's mouth' (*Cent. Dict.*). Cf. GULLETER.

3. *Shipbuilding.* (See quot. 1869.)

1869 SIR E. REED *Shipbuild.* iv. 56 The groove or gulleting on the after side of the rudder post to receive the rudder was obtained by riveting on a solid piece of iron with a hollow in it. **1874** THEARLE *Naval Archit.* 66 The fore piece *D*,..is fitted to receive the gulleting *E, E*.

gullibility (gʌlɪ'bɪlɪtɪ). [App. an alteration of CULLIBILITY, after GULL *v.*^{3}

'A low expression, sometimes used for *cullibility*' (Todd 1818).]

The quality of being gullible.

1793 LD. AUCKLAND *Corr.* (1861) II. 505 He [Dumouriez]..by favour of the Duke of Brunswick's gullibility, gets considerable credit. **1809** N. SLONE in *Europ. Mag.* Jan. 18/2 This gentleman..entertained the House with a long descant upon the *gullibility* of the English nation..our future lexicographers will be much indebted to him for sanctioning a word so well calculated to enrich our language. **1826** SYD. SMITH *Wks.* (1859) II. 86/2 He had sounded the gullibility of the world; knew the precise current value of pretension [etc.]. **1831** CARLYLE *Sart. Res.* (1858) 69 In Education, Polity, Religion,..probably Imposture is of sanative, anodyne nature, and man's Gullibility not his worst blessing. **1874** BURNAND *My Time* xxxix. 442 [He] practised on the gullibility of..undergraduates.

gullible ('gʌlɪb(ə)l), *a.* [f. GULL *v.*^{3} + -IBLE; historically it seems to have been a back-formation from prec. Cf. GULLABLE.] Capable of being gulled or duped; easily cheated, befooled. Also *absol.*

1825 CARLYLE *Schiller* II. 104 The king of quacks, the renowned Cagliostro,..harrowing up the souls of the curious and gullible of all ranks..by various thaumaturgic feats. **1831** —— *Sart. Res.* (1858) 68 Gullible, however, by fit apparatus, all Publics are; and gulled, with the most surprising profit. **1860** GEN. P. THOMPSON *Audi Alt.* III. cxli. 121 Another fallacy..by which the gullible among the English are to be kept in awe. **1879** GEO. ELIOT *Theo. Such* xvii. 305 The very fishes of our rivers, gullible as they look.

Hence **'gullibly** *adv.*

1877 *Tinsley's Mag.* XXXI. 657 Mrs. Tittle was gullibly open to flattery.

gullied ('gʌlɪd), *ppl. a.* [f. GULLY *v.* + -ED^{1}.] Hollowed out, worn away. *lit.* and *fig.*

1794 WASHINGTON *Writ.* (1892) XIII. 16 To recover my land from the gullied and exhausted state into which it has..been thrown for some years back. **1799** *Ibid.* (1893) XIV. 227 The washed and gullied parts of this field should be levelled. **1844** LD. COCKBURN *Jrnl.* II. 61 A bare, deeply gullied throat.

†**gullified**, *ppl. a. Obs. rare*$^{-1}$. [f. *gullify (f. GULL *sb.*^{3} + -(I)FY) + -ED^{1}.] Made a gull or dupe of; gulled.

1624 GEE *Foot out of Snare* vii. 54 To the great admiration of the stupid, gullifyed, Romanizing beholders.

†**gulling**, *vbl. sb.*^{1} *Obs.* [f. GULL *v.*^{1} + -ING^{1}.] The action of GULL *v.*^{1}; swallowing, guzzling; hence, gormandizing, gluttonous feasting.

1543 BECON *Policy War* Wks. 1564 I. 136 What drynkyng, gullyng, quaffyng, & superfluous banketing do they vse! **1549** LATIMER *Serm. bef. Edw. VI*, vi. Tiiij, They were wonte to goo a brode in the fyeldes a shootynge, but nowe it is turned in to glossing, gullyng, and whoringe wythin the housse. **1604** T. WRIGHT *Passions* IV. i. 186 If men talke of meat and drinke, of gulling and feasting..such persons, for most part, addict themselves to gluttonie. **1615** G. SANDYS *Trav.* II. 124, I could not but obserue their gulling in of wine with a deare felicitie.

gulling ('gʌlɪŋ), *vbl. sb.*^{2} [f. GULL *v.*^{2} + -ING^{1}.] The action of GULL *v.*^{2}; wearing away or hollowing out effected by the action of running water or other means.

1565 GOLDING *Ovid's Met.* XV. (1593) 353 Hilles by force of gulling oft haue into sea beene worne. **1577** B. GOOGE

Heresbach's Husb. (1586) 45 Let them [meadows] be kept from gulling and trampling of cattel. **1715** KERSEY, *Gulling*, when the pin of a Block or Pully eats into the Shiver, or the Yard into the Mast. **1739** LABELYE *Short Acc. Piers Westm. Bridge* 61 The Gulling of a River..is nearly in Proportion to the Velocity of the Stream. **1744–50** W. ELLIS *Mod. Husbandm.* III. I. 166 Sudden damage [to roads]..by the wash of rain and the gulling of wheels. **1842** GWILT *Encycl. Archit.* 691 Gulling of the paper from the point of the compasses.

'gulling, *vbl. sb.*^{3} [f. GULL *v.*^{3} + -ING^1.] The action of GULL *v.*^{3}; cheating, deception.

1600 ROWLANDS *Lett. Humours Blood* I. 47 Wealthy Chuffes Worth gulling. **1621** BURTON *Anat. Mel.* I. II. IV. iv, What company soeuer they come in, they will be..putting gulleries of some or other, till they haue made by their humoring and gulling, *ex stulto insanum*. **1634** CANNE *Necess. Separ.* (1849) 257 A mere gulling and mocking of the world.

†**gulling** ('gʌlɪŋ), *ppl. a.*^{1} *Obs.* [f. GULL *v.*^{1} + -ING^2.] Guzzling; voracious. Also *transf.*

1579 *Remedy Lawlesse Loue* (Roxb.) c i, The drunkarde loues..To powre the wine into his gulling gut. **1604** T. WRIGHT *Passions* IV. ii. §2. 129 Such men, in the heat of their gulling feasts ouershoot themselues extreamely.

'gulling ('gʌlɪŋ), *ppl. a.*^{2} [f. GULL *v.*^{3} + -ING^2.] That gulls or deceives; cheating, deceptive.

? **1595** DAVIES (*title*) Gullinge Sonnets, in *Poems* (Grosart) I. 51. **1614** JACKSON *Creed* II. 57 To collect a gulling sence from such. **1866** GEO. ELIOT *F. Holt* (1868) 54 Those absurd medicines and gulling advertisements.

gullion ('gʌljən). *dial.* [Origin unknown; cf. *cullion*.] A mean worthless wretch.

1825–80 in JAMIESON. **1829** BROCKETT *N.C. Words* (ed. 2), *Gullion*, a mean wretch. It is also a term for a drunkard. *a* **1845** HOOD *Craniology* iii, No kind there was of human pumpkin, But at its bumps it had a bumpkin; Down to the very lowest gullion And oiliest scull of oily scullion.

gullis, obs. Sc. form of GULES, red.

gullish ('gʌlɪʃ), *a.* [f. GULL *sb.*^{3} + -ISH.] Of the nature of a gull; foolish, simple.

1598 FLORIO, *Dissitio*, foolish, gullish, lubbarly, shallowe witted. **1613** JACKSON *Creed* I. 304 As if some gullish Gentleman..should draw his pedigree from Adams great grandfather. **1621** BURTON *Anat. Mel.* III. iv. I. ii. (1651) 649 The gullish commonalty. **1845** DISRAELI *Sybil* (1863) 33 The gullish multitude studied the daily reports with grave interest. **1885** *Truth* 11 June 933/1 The loudly-expressed confidence of the gullish herd who went for Kingwood.

gullit(t, obs. form of GULLET.

†**'gullop**, *v. Obs. rare*$^{-1}$. *trans.* To belch *up*.

1642 H. MORE *Song of Soul* II. App. xcviii, The burning bowels of this wasting ball Shall gullop up great flakes of rolling fire.

†**'gullowing**, *ppl. a. Obs.*$^{-1}$ [f. *gullow (? f. GULL *v.*^{1}, perh. after *swallow*) + -ING^2.] Guzzling.

1598 R. BERNARD tr. *Terence, Andria* I. (1629) 12/2 *O cloacam edacem et bibacem* O thou deuouring and gullowing panch of a glutton.

gulls, obs. form of GULES, red.

gully ('gʌlɪ), *sb.*^{1} Also gulley. [Prob. an alteration of GULLET, or a phonetic adoption of its original (F. *goulet*).]

†**1.** The gullet. *Obs.*

1538 ELYOT *Dict.*, *Gurgulio*, the gully or gargylle of the throote or throote bolle. **1552** HULOET, Gullet, gullye or gargle of the throte.

2. a. A channel or ravine worn in the earth by the action of water, esp. in a mountain or hill side.

1657 R. LIGON *Barbadoes* (1673) 49 There were many gullies in the way, which were impassable. **1670** *Rec. Providence* (U.S.) (1892) I. 15 Eighty Ackors of this land beginning betweene two Gulleys which Jshu into the aforsaid west River. **1725** DE FOE *Voy. round World* (1840) 258 Gulleys made by the water. **1784** BELKNAP *Tour White Mts.* (1876) 14 *note*, The N.W. wind blows it [snow] over the tops of the mountains, and drives it into the long deep vallies or gullies. **1794** S. WILLIAMS *Vermont* 124 Fossil shells.. have been found on the sides, or rather in the gullies of the mountains. **1813** SCOTT *Trierm.* I. x, Torrents, down the gullies flung, Join'd the rude river that brawl'd on. **1816** —— *Old Mort.* xv, Bare hills of dark heath, intersected by deep gullies. **1865** LIVINGSTONE *Zambesi* xxiv. 494 The mountain torrents had worn gullies some thirty or forty feet deep. **1868** STANLEY *Westm. Abb.* i. 5 The Walebrook.. rushed with such violence down its gulley. **1879** JEFFERIES *Wild Life in S. Co.* 49 Ascending the steep sides of these gullys. **1883** STEVENSON *Silverado Sq.* (1886) 53 A wild, red, strong gully in the mountains.

b. *transf.* A furrow, groove.

1803 HATCHETT in *Phil. Trans.* XCIII. 143, I found..that little furrows or gullies were soon worn in them.

c. In extended meaning (see quots. 1871 and 1966). *Austral.* and *N.Z.*

1840 F. MATHEW *Founding of N.Z.* (1940) ii. 48 Crossing a deep and broken gully, the sides of which are so precipitous that [etc.]. **1840** *N.Z. Jrnl.* XIX. 245/1 The timber grows principally in the gullies between the hills and mountains. **1846** C. ROWCROFT *Bushranger of Van Diemen's Land* I. xi. 109 By this time they had descended into a deep and narrow gulley. **1856** *Richmond-Atkinson Papers* I. v. 218 Colson asked Hinde £300 for his 37½ acres of gulley. **1862** H. C. KENDALL *Poems* 17 The gums in the gully stand gloomy and stark. **1871** C. L. MONEY *Knocking about in N.Z.* i. 9 'Gully' means nothing more than a strip of ground lying between two hills, and having a 'creek' flowing down its centre. **1875** WOOD & LAPHAM *Waiting for Mail* 16 The terrible blasts that rushed down the narrow gully, as if through a funnel. **1908** E. J. BANFIELD *Confessions of Beachcomber* I. i. 16 *Pandanus aquaticus* marks the courses and curves of some of the gullies. **1911** C. E. W. BEAN *'Dreadnought' of Darling* xxvii. 230 For six months they had to live in this little gully—as barren as a stone quarry and not unlike it to look at. **1930** L. G. D. ACLAND *Early Canterbury Runs* iv. 66 Harper's Homestead was on the property which belonged to Mrs. Dunlop, but further up the gully than the present house. **1938** R. D. FINLAYSON *Brown Man's Burden* 63 They were winding along the side of a deep gully. **1966** G. W. TURNER *Eng. Lang. Austral. & N.Z.* iii. 57 The word *valley* has fallen from use in Australia and is not very common in New Zealand except in a few place-names. It is replaced by *gully*.

d. *Cricket.* The fielding position between point and the slips; the fieldsman in this position. Also (Austral.) ***gully-slip***.

1920 G. L. JESSOP in P. F. Warner *Cricket* 165 The position which has been favoured in recent years by fast bowlers, whenever signs of the wicket bumping have been apparent, namely, 'the gully'. **1921** P. F. WARNER *My Cricketing Life* xii. 229 He [*sc.* A. O. Jones] was, indeed, quite exceptional as a fieldsman in any position, but especially in the slips and at short third man, or in the 'gully', as it is called nowadays. **1927** *Observer* 19 June 25/1 Macaulay fell to a dazzling left-hand catch high up in the gully by Kidd. **1954** J. H. FINGLETON *Ashes crown Year* 43 Morris..found himself caught high at gully-slip. **1955** *Times* 12 July 12/4 Ralph was indeed unlucky, for Arnold with good intentions of not wasting time, cut him straight into gully's hands, when exit followed entry. *Ibid.* 15 July 3/3 At 252 Insole was caught in the gully slashing at Titmus. **1970** [see EDGE *v.*^{1} 7].

3. A narrow and deep artificial watercourse; a deep gutter, drain, or sink.

1789 G. WHITE *Selborne* xviii. (1853) 78 The gulleys that were cut for watering the meadows. **1882** *Worc. Exhib. Catal.* iii. 16 Large street gullies. **1883** *Times* 21 Aug. 6/3 The watering of the streets and flushing of the gullies.

4. *attrib.*, as (sense 2) ***gully-bottom***; (sense 3) ***gully-emptier***, ***-grate***, ***-grating***, ***-trap***, ***-wind***; **gully-drain** (see quot.; hence ***gully-drainage***, ***gully-drain*** vb.); **gully erosion**, the erosion of soil by rain-water forming channels; **gully-hole**, the opening from the street into a drain or sewer; **gully-raker** *Austral.*, (*a*) a cattle-thief; (*b*) a cattle-whip; so **gully-raking**, cattle-thieving; **gully-squall** *Naut.*, a violent gust of wind from the mountain ravines of Central America; **gully-washer** *U.S.*, a heavy downpour.

1917 J. MASEFIELD *Old Front Line* 49 He..tunnelled long living rooms, both above and below the *gully-bottom. **1965** F. SARGESON *Mem. Peon* iv. 58 Finally you reached the gully-bottom. **1850** CARLYLE *Latter-d. Pamph.* iii. 17 The very *gully-drains. **1851–61** MAYHEW *Lond. Labour* II. 398 The Gully-drain is a drain generally of earthen-ware piping, curving from the side of the street to an opening in the top or side of the sewer, and is the means of communication between the sewer and the gully-hole. *Ibid.* 399 The old street channels for *gully drainage. *Ibid.* 401 Taking only 1200 miles of public way as *gully-drained. **1929** *Even. News* 18 Nov. 16/4 Following a collision between an L.C.C. tramcar and a Fulham Borough Council *gulley-emptier in the Fulham Palace-road, S.W., to-day, passengers in the tramcar received a showerbath from the contents of the gulley-emptier, which poured into the tramcar. **1928** *Proc. 1st. Internat. Congr. Soil Sci.* VI. 755 That phase of normal *gully erosion which gradually cuts out V-shaped ravines usually not excessively deep. **1937** E. J. RUSSELL *Soil Conditions & Plant Growth* (ed. 7) viii. 579 The erosion takes two forms: sheet erosion, which goes on slowly and evenly over a large area, and gulley erosion, which is more localised and washes out the soil into great gulleys or ravines. **1861** FLO. NIGHTINGALE *Nursing* 20 Water-closet, sink, or *gully-grate. **1905** *Daily Chron.* 7 Aug. 6/5 Volumes of steam issued through the *gully grating. **1726** KERSEY, **Gully-Hole*, a Place at the Grate or Entrance of the Street-Canals for a Passage into the Common Shore. **1746** *Brit. Mag.* 346 The Water is let down out of the Street, by what we call the Gully-Hole. **1762** *Gentl. Mag.* 154 Mrs. Myltystre was hanged, and thrown into the gully-hole to rot. **1885–8** FAGGE & PYE-SMITH *Princ. Med.* (ed. 2) I. 192 The boys from that house were in the habit of playing every day in a yard, in which there were gully-holes leading from the sewer. **1847** *Settlers & Convicts* xii. 261 This practice derives its name from the circumstances of cattle straying.. into the bush..and breeding there..the *gully-rakers eventually driving them out and branding [them]..with their own brands. **1881** A. C. GRANT *Bush Life Queensld.* iv. (1882) 30 The driver appealing occasionally to some bullock or other by name, following up his admonition by a sweeping cut of his 'gully-raker'. **1847** *Settlers & Convicts* xii. 253 By a process technically called '*gully-raking', he had quadrupled the little herd his father gave him. **1867** SMYTH *Sailor's Word-bk.*, **Gully squall.* Well known off Tropical America in the Pacific, particularly abreast of the lakes of Leon, Nicaragua, &c. **1892** T. B. F. EMINSON *Epid. Pneumonia Scotter* 36 The sewer..had been opened to put down a *gully-trap. **1903** J. FOX *Little Shepherd* iv. 59 Send us, not a gentle sizzle-sozzle, but a sod-soaker, a *gully-washer. Give us a tide, O Lord! **1961** *Amer. Speech* XXXVI. 153 An old farmer looked at the threatening sky.. and said, 'It's goin' to be a gully washer and a chunk floater.' **1969** *Daily Progress* (Charlottesville, Va.) 22 Aug. 4/6 Other two-word names for a heavy rain [are]..gully-washer, [etc.]. **1869** E. A. PARKES *Pract. Hygiene* (ed. 3) 315 When there are marsh or *gully winds to be avoided.

gully ('gʌlɪ), *sb.*^{2} *Sc.* and *north.* Also 8 **gooly**, 9 **gulley**. [Of obscure etymology; Brockett's conjecture (quot. 1825) seems not impossible, though sense 1 of GULLY *sb.*^{1} is scantily authenticated.] A large knife. (The sense given in quot. 1653, if it existed, is obsolete.)

1582 A. MELVILLE in W. Morison *Melville* (1898) v. 46 [Spoke of the King's claim to spiritual authority as a 'bludie gullie' thrust into the Commonwealth]. **1653** URQUHART *Rabelais* I. xxvii. 129 Can you tell with what instruments they did it? with faire gullies [*printed* gullics], which are little hulchback't demi-knives, the iron toole whereof is two inches long, and the wooden handle one inch thick, and three inches in length, wherewith the little boyes in our countrey cut ripe walnuts in two. [The description is in the orig.; the Fr. word is *gouet*.] **1674–91** RAY *N.C. Words* 135 A Gully, a large household Knife. **1719** RAMSAY *Fam. Epist.* Answ. iii. 12 Had he [Julius Cæsar] 'midst his glories sheath'd his gooly, And kiss'd his wife. **1785** BURNS *Death & Dr. Hornbook* ix, I red ye weel, tak care o' skaith, See there 's a gully! **1818** SCOTT *Hrt. Midl.* xvii, Folk kill wi' the tongue as weel as wi' the hand—wi' the word as weel as wi' the gulley! **1824** —— *St. Ronan's* xiv, The poor simple bairn ..had nae mair knowledge of the wickedness of human nature than a calf has of a flesher's gully. **1825** BROCKETT *N.C. Words*, *Gulley*, a large knife used in farm houses, principally to cut bread, cheese, &c. for the family. Perhaps originally a butcher's, for the gullet. **1883** STEVENSON *Treas. Isl.* v. xxiii, I..took out my gully...and cut one strand after another.

b. *attrib.*, as ***gully-knife***.

1725 *Willie Winkie's Test.* in Whitelaw *Bk. Sc. Song* (1875) 540/1 A gullie-knife and a horse-wand. **1876** SMILES *Sc. Natur.* vi. (ed. 4) 102 He had neither his gun, nor even his gully knife with him.

gully ('gʌlɪ), *sb.*^{3} Also **gulley**. An iron tram-plate or -rail.

1800 *Trans. Soc. Arts* XVIII. 271 These waggon-ways are supplied with iron rails, or gullies, laid on sleepers. **1841** BREES *Gloss. Civil Engin.*, *Gullies*, a term sometimes applied to iron tram-plates or rails.

gully ('gʌlɪ), *v.* [f. GULLY *sb.*^{1}] *trans.* To make gullies or deep channels in; to form (channels) by the action of water. Also with *out*. Hence **'gullying** *vbl. sb.*

1775 H. KNOX in Sparks *Corr. Amer. Rev.* (1853) I. 87 Without sledding, the roads are so much gullied, that it will be impossible to move a step. **1787** M. CUTLER in *Life, Jrnls. & Corr.* (1888) I. 245 The road in many places was gullied several feet deep in this stone. **1848** BUCKLEY *Iliad* 43 The wintry torrent had broken away part of the road, and gullied the whole place. **1862** DANA *Man. Geol.* iii. 604 Turf protects earthy slopes from the action of rills that would gully out a bare surface. **1882** *Harper's Mag.* Dec. 7 Stripped of soil and gullied by the action of rapid water. **1897** *Outing* (U.S.) XXX. 164/1 The current had gullied out deep holes around the big bowlders. **1928** *Proc. 1st. Internat. Congr. Soil Sci.* VI. 755 The same general class of wide-spread carving-out of the soil material or deep gullying that characterizes the devastation of Memphis. **1958** *New Biol.* XXV. 51 The flooding in Devon was associated with gullying and soil erosion and much of upland Britain is scarred with gullies similar to those formed so dramatically in 1953. **1963** D. W. & E. E. HUMPHRIES tr. *Termier's Erosion & Sedimentation* i. 20 In contrast, the equatorial climate which is constantly hot and humid tends to remove soil by gullying.

gully-gully ('gʌlɪgʌlɪ). Also **gulli-gulli**. [Of unknown origin.] A conjuror's catch-word. So **gully-gully man**, in Egypt, esp. at Port Said, a conjuror who works with live chickens.

1930 E. WAUGH *Labels* iii. 69 [At Port Said] a conjuror came and did tricks for us with live chickens. These are called 'gully-gully men' because of their chatter. They are the worst possible conjurors but excellent comedians. They squat on the ground, making odd clucking noises in their throats and smiling happily, and proceed with the minimum of deception to pop things in and out of their voluminous sleeves. *Ibid.* 70 A little Arab girl..who had taught herself to imitate them perfectly..used not to bother about the conjuring at all, but would scramble from table to table in the cafés, saying, 'Gully-gully', and taking a chicken in and out of a little cloth bag. **1955** A. ROSS *Australia 55* 24 The decks were deserted, the gulli-gulli men departed. **1960** *Spectator* 15 July 95/3 The 'gully-gully' men ply between Port Said and Suez, boarding the ships and giving performances on deck at advertised times. **1962** D. J. ENRIGHT *Addictions* IV. 67 (*title*) I was a gulli-gulli man's chicken. **1969** J. R. D. TATA in *Assoc. Chambers Comm. & Industr. India Golden Jubilee Commem. Vol.* 74 A belief that all you had to do to create..large industry was to produce the money, order the plant, build the sheds, advertise for posts and 'presto, gully-gully!', you had production and sales following automatically.

†**'gully-gut**. *Obs.* Also 6–7 **gulligut(te**, 7 **gully-guts**. [f. GULL *v.*^{1} + GUT, prob. after GREEDY-GUT(S.)] A glutton, gormandizer.

1542 UDALL *Erasm. Apoph.* 119 The bealyes of gully-guttes (that can naught dooe, but eate & drynke, and slepe). **1548** ELYOT *Dict.*, *Lurco*..a deuourer of his owne substaunce, a gullygutte. **1599** NASHE *Lenten Stuffe* 5 [Vessels] nothing behinde in number with the inuincible Spanish Armada, though they were not such Gargantuan boystrous gulligutts as they. *a* **1625** BOYS *Wks.* (1629) 368 Christ ommitted the Gluttons name... Wherefore seeing Christ hath not expressed this Gully-guts name for so many good reasons, it [etc.]. **1629** CHAPMAN *Juvenal* 219 The gully-gut (Aledius) cries O Lybia, keep with thee thy wheats and ryes, And ease thy ouen, sending these supplies. **1694** MOTTEUX *Rabelais* IV. xl, Gully Guts.

b. *attrib.* or as *adj.*

1583 STANYHURST *Æneis* III. (Arb.) 77 Thee gulligut harpeys. **1653** URQUHART *Rabelais* I. Prol., A certaine gulligut Fryer.

Hence †**'gulligutted** *a.*, gluttonous.

1694 MOTTEUX *Rabelais* IV. xxxii, Gulligutted Dunces of the Cowl. *Ibid.* lix, Lozelly Gulligutted Gastrolaters.

‖**gulo** (ˈgjuːləʊ). Also 7 **gulon**. [L., 'glutton', f. *gula* gullet, throat, gluttony.] Formerly, the glutton, *Gulo luscus*: now, the name of the genus to which this animal belongs.

1607 TOPSELL *Four-f. Beasts* (1658) 205 Of the Gulon. This Beast was not known by the Ancients, but hath been since discovered in the Northern parts of the World. **1635** SWAN *Spec. M.* (1670) 435 The Gulon or Jerf is a beast in the North parts of Swetia. **1674** tr. *Scheffer's Lapland* 134 It [the Glutton] is called by the Swedes, *Jerff*, by the Germans, *Wildfras*:..the Gulo doth not only infest wild Beasts, but tame..and Water creatures too. **1836** J. F. DAVIS *Chinese* II. 342 A dentition resembling that of *gulo* or *mustela*.

gulose (ˈgjuːləʊz, -s). *Chem.* [a. G. *gulose* (Fischer & Piloty 1891, in *Ber. d. Deut. Chem. Ges.* XXIV. 521), f. GLUCOSE by omission and transposition of letters.] An artificial hexose sugar, $C_6H_{10}O_6$, which is stereoisomeric with glucose.

1891 *Jrnl. Chem. Soc.* LX. I. 677 The authors..call..the corresponding sugar gulose. **1963** K. MAYER tr. *Staněk's Monosaccharides* ii. 31 D-Glucose (6) and L-gulose (10) form the same dicarboxylic acid.

gulosity (gjuːˈlɒsɪtɪ). Now *rare*. Also 6 *Sc.* **gelocitie**. [ad. late L. *gulōsitāt-em*, f. *gulōs-us* (see next).] Gluttony, greediness, voracity.

a **1500** *Bernard. cura rei fam.* (E.E.T.S.) 70 Infekyt with gulosite. **1528** PAYNEL *Salerne's Regim.* R, This disease chanceth many tymes to swyne through theyr gulosite. **1535** STEWART *Cron. Scot.* (1858) I. 91 He gaif him alway to gelocitie, To fleschlie lust and foull faminitie. **1646** SIR T. BROWNE *Pseud. Ep.* IV. x. 202 They are very temperate, seldome..erring in gulosity or superfluity of meats. **1791** BOSWELL *Johnson* 5 Aug. an. 1763 The 206th number of his *Rambler* is a masterly essay against gulosity. **1837** CARLYLE *Fr. Rev.* I. II. viii, Corruption among the lofty and the low, gulosity, credulity, imbecility. **1865** *Pall Mall G.* 14 Dec. 10/1 He chuckled over his sensuality in such an unsuspiciousness of moral candour, and with such an intensity of relish, that you almost envied his gulosity.

†ˈ**gulous**, *a. Obs. rare*⁻¹. [ad. L. *gulōs-us*, f. *gula* gullet, gluttony.] Gluttonous.

1657 TOMLINSON *Renou's Disp.* 471* The Romans.. invented..a thousand gulous provocations.

gulp (gʌlp), *sb.*[1] Also 6–7 **gulpe**, 7–8 **gulph**, 8 *Sc.* **gowp**. [f. GULP *v.* Cf. Du. *gulp* stream or flush of water, large draught of liquid.]

1. The action or an act of gulping or swallowing in large portions.

1568 *Hist. Jacob & Esau* II. iii, I at the ladell got a goulpe or a licke. **1625–6** PURCHAS *Pilgrims* II. 1540 They give the accused to drinke saying that if hee bee innocent he shall drink it off at one gulp without any stay. **1807** *Med. Jrnl.* XVII. 345 He succeeded in getting down, at a single gulp, the small quantity of liquid he had taken into his mouth. **1837** MRS. CARLYLE *Lett.* I. 64 Dissolving it in a tumbler of water and swallowing it all at one gulp. **1870** LOWELL *Study Wind.* 8 [The robin] eats with a relishing gulp not inferior to Dr. Johnson's.

b. *trans.* and *fig.*

1610 BEAUM. & FL. *Scornf. Lady* I. i, He hath suck'd in ten thousand pounds worth of my land more than he paid for, at a gulp. **1669** WOODHEAD *St. Teresa* I. xxii. 147 All those joys which she [the soul] took, came to her but by sups, and gulps. **1726** DE FOE *Hist. Devil* (1840) I. vi. 72 Hell received them all at a gulp. **1758** A. MURPHY *Upholsterer* II. (1763) 27 *Quid.* What, and will the People believe that now? *Pamph.* Believe it!—believe any thing,—no Swallow like a true-born Englishman's..they give a Gulp,—and down it goes. **1876** LOWELL *Among my Bks.* Ser. II. 171 The sweetness of the verse enables the fancy, by a slight gulp, to swallow without solution the problem of being in two places at the same time.

c. Capacity for gulping; 'swallow'. *rare*⁻¹.

1837 CARLYLE *Fr. Rev.* III. I. vi, Here too is a Swallower of Formulas; of still wider gulp than Mirabeau.

d. An effort to swallow; the noise caused by this; a choke.

1873 HOLLAND *A. Bonnic.* v. 83 He gave a convulsive gulp as if his heart had risen to his throat and he were struggling to keep it down. **1887** R. BUCHANAN *Heir of Linne* i, The smith, with a great gulp in his throat, threw a handful of coppers into the singer's hat.

2. As much as is swallowed at a gulp; a mouthful.

1611 COTGR., *Goulette de vin*, a gulpe, mouthfull, or small quantitie of wine. **1637** G. DANIEL *Genius this Isle* 171 Goblets of blood he Qvaffes; and everie Gulpe Steam's in his cankred throte. **1700** DRYDEN *Fables, Ceyx & Alcyone* 222 As oft as he can catch a gulp of air And peep above the seas, he names the fair. **1755** SMOLLETT *Quix.* (1803) IV. 112 He was fain to break his fast with a little conserve, and four gulps of cold water. **1862** TYNDALL *Mountaineer.* vi. 55 He had..a gulp of wine, which mightily refreshed him. **1865** DICKENS *Mut. Fr.* III. vii, 'I was down at the water-side', said Venus,..taking another gulp of tea.

†**gulp**, *sb.*[2] *Obs. rare*⁻¹. [? ad. Sp. *golpe* blow.] ? Impact, shock.

1598 BARRET *Theor. Warres* v. i. 124 To resist and beare of the blow and gulpe of the artillery.

gulp (gʌlp), *v.* Forms: 5 **gulpe**, **golpe**, 6 **goulpe**, 9 *Sc.* **gowp**, 6– **gulp**. [Echoic; cf. Du. *gulpen* to swallow, guzzle, to issue in streams; also GLOBBE, GLOFF, GLOP *v.*[2], GLOUP; also MSw. *glup* throat, *glupsk* voracious, Sw. dial. *glapa* to gulp down.]

1. *trans.* To swallow in large draughts or morsels hastily or with greediness. Chiefly with *down*, †formerly also *in*, *up*.

14.. *Langland's P. Pl.* A. v. 191 (MSS. T. and U.) Y-gulpid, y-golped [see GLOUP *v.*]. **1542** UDALL *Erasm. Apoph.* 119 Charybdis..after a litle tyme, casteth vp again whatsoeuer it goulped in before. **1583** GOLDING *Calvin on Deut.* clxvii. 1036 Although hee powre in neuer so much wyne, yet is he neuer filled but doeth still gulp it vp without ende of drinking. **1735** SOMERVILLE *Chase* I. 182 With greedy Joy Gulp down the flying Wave. **1784** COWPER *Task* v. 269 Inflated and astrut with self conceit He gulps the windy diet. **1822–34** *Good's Study Med.* (ed. 4) III. 282 The convulsive spasms about the throat obliged her to gulp what she swallowed. **1842** THACKERAY *Fitz-Boodle's Conf.*, *Ottilia* i, Several tumblers of punch..I had gulped down without saying a word. **1843** LE FEVRE *Life Trav. Phys.* II. II. v. 220 The Russians..rise from table..before the last mouthful is well gulped down. **1890** *Anthony's Photogr. Bull.* III. 256 The big fishes gulping the little ones.

b. *absol.*

1714 GAY *Trivia* II. 191, I..See them puff off the froth, and gulp amain, While with dry tongue I lick my lips in vain. **1740** GARRICK *Lying Valet* I. Wks. 1798 I. 34 Nothing, while honour sticks in your throat: do gulp, master, and down with it. **1787** MAD. D'ARBLAY *Diary* Nov., I gulped as well as I could at dinner. **1867** TROLLOPE *Chron. Barset* I. xxxii. 267 She could only gulp at it, and swallow it.

2. *transf.* and *fig.* Chiefly ***to gulp down***: **a.** To swallow up, devour, take in. (Also with *up*.)

a **1625** BEAUM. & FL. *Wit without M.* I. ii, *Lance.* Has he devour'd you too? *Fran.* Has gulped me downe, Lance. *Lance.* Left you no meanes to study. *Fran.* Not a farthing: Dispatcht my poore annuity, I thanke him. *a* **1754** FIELDING *Voy. Lisbon* Wks. 1784 X. 259 The old man.. glibly gulped down the whole narrative. **1796** H. HUNTER tr. *St.-Pierre's Stud. Nat.* (1799) I. 318 So many brooks and springs..collected from every quarter, to be gulped up in one great navigable canal. **1816** SCOTT *Antiq.* v, The worthy knight fairly gulped down the oaths. **1899** *Westm. Gaz.* 21 Aug. 6/1 Gulping down any scheme of vain promise.

b. To keep in or 'stifle' by a process analogous to swallowing. (Also with *in*, *back*.)

1644 QUARLES *Barnabas & B.* i, Gulp downe care in frolique cups of liberall Wine. **1778** MAD. D'ARBLAY *Diary* Sept., [As] reproaches and expostulations..can do no good, I gulp them down. *c* **1793** LD. BULKELY in *G. Rose's Diaries* (1860) I. 131, I gulped in the grievance. **1839–40** W. IRVING *Wolfert's R.* (1855) 193, I felt my heart swell in my throat; but I gulped it back to its place. **1869** TROLLOPE *He Knew* xxviii. (1878) 157 [She] had gulped down her sobs and was resolved to be firm.

3. *intr.* To gasp or choke when or as when drinking large draughts of liquid.

1530 PALSGR. 573/2, I goulpe, as drinke dothe in ones throte that drinketh hastely, *je crocque*..and *je engoule.* **1790** COWPER *Let.* 11 May, He is ever gulping, as if swallowing somewhat that would hardly pass. **1840** MARRYAT *Olla Podr.* 304 She gulped when she looked at it, and..cried herself to sleep. **1840** BARHAM *Ingol. Leg.* Ser. I. *Bagman's Dog*, Poor Blogg went on ducking and bobbing, Sneezing out the salt water, and gulping and sobbing. **1894** *Outing* (U.S.) XXXIV. 140/2 Tom gasps apologies, opens his mouth to comment, but only gulps.

gulper (ˈgʌlpə(r)). [f. GULP *v.* + -ER[1].] One who gulps or swallows greedily.

1660 HEXHAM *Dutch Dict.*, *Gulper*, a Gulper, a Drunkard, or a Quaffer. **1836** *Fraser's Mag.* XIII. 195 It will be.. swallowed by that most open-throated of flummery gulpers.

gulph, obs. form of GULF, GULP.

gulpin (ˈgʌlpɪn). [f. GULP *v.*; perh. in the comb. *gulp in*.] One who will swallow anything; a credulous person, a simpleton; *Naut.*, a marine.

1802 MCEVOY in *Naval Chron.* VII. 50 There might be a few gulpins who would fire. **1867** SMYTH *Sailor's Word-bk.*, *Gulpin*, an awkward soldier; a weak credulous fellow. **1867** *N. & Q.* Ser. III. XII. 78/1 A marine was called a gulpin by the sailors; that is a person who would swallow anything told him. **1886** BESANT *The World went* II. xxix. 308 Go, then, for a brace of gulpins!

gulping (ˈgʌlpɪŋ), *vbl. sb.* [f. GULP *v.* + -ING[1].] The action of the verb GULP; swallowing in gulps; †guzzling, gormandizing (*obs.*); the noise made in swallowing large quantities; choking.

c **1394** *P. Pl. Crede* 92 Glotony is her God wiþ g[l]oppyng [*MS. B.* golping] of drynk. **1530** PALSGR. 573/2 Take hede of this glouton what a goulpynge he maketh as he drinketh. **1579** FULKE *Heskins' Parl.* 306 Hee spake of a..spirituall manner of eating his bodie, and drinking his bloud..and not of a swallowing or gulping in of the same at our mouth. **1586** J. HOOKER *Girald. Irel.* in *Holinshed* II. 113/2 He was.. much giuen to excessiue gulping and surfetting. **1733** CHEYNE *Eng. Malady* II. ix. §6 (1734) 213 Symptoms exceedingly troublesome in Vapours,..to wit, Choaking and Gulping. **1880** MISS BIRD *Japan* I. 276 It is proper to show appreciation of a repast by noisy gulpings, and much gurgling and drawing-in of breath.

gulping (ˈgʌlpɪŋ), *ppl. a.* [f. GULP *v.* + -ING[2].] That gulps; characterized by gulping.

1865 BARING-GOULD *Werewolves* vii. 88 Strange gulping bursts of fiendlike merriment from the strange boy. **1871** NAPHEYS *Prev. & Cure Dis.* II. i. 375 To swallow in a gulping manner.

Hence ˈ**gulpingly** *adv.*, with a gulp.

1705 HICKERINGILL *Priest-cr.* II. vii. 69 He'll swallow any thing, and as many Sacraments as (he swallows) Oaths gulpingly. *Ibid.* viii. 75 That so much Nonsence..should.. be so gulpingly swallowed by an unthinking World.

gulpy (ˈgʌlpɪ), *a.* [f. GULP *sb.* or *v.* + -Y.] Marked by gulps or choking.

1860 *All Year Round* No. 65. 353 The..neighbour.. delivered his dialogue with a glazed eye and an impaired and gulpy utterance. **1892** W. S. GILBERT *Foggerty's Fairy* 193 The poor little drab made many gulpy attempts to keep the tears down.

gulravage, obs. form of GILRAVAGE.

gulsach, -schoch, -set, -soch, Sc. forms of GULESOUGHT, jaundice.

gulsh, variant of GULCH.

gult, obs. form of GILT *ppl. a.*

gult(e, gulti(f, -y: see GUILT, GUILTY.

†ˈ**guly**, *a. Obs. Her.* Also 7 **guelye**. [f. GULE-S + -Y.] Of the colour gules or red.

1592 WYRLEY *Armorie, Chandos* 41 Sir Richard Stafford in gold shield did beare A gulie Cheuron and blew Labell faire. *c* **1600** THYNNE *Emblems & Epigr.* (1876) 38 And whye the guelye arme in midst of Sheild is placed. **1610** GUILLIM *Heraldry* I. v. (1611) 18 Guly sheild..Wrapt with dent-bordure siluer-shining. **1641** MILTON *Reform.* II. (1851) 54 To reare the horrid Standard of those fatall guly Dragons for so unworthy a purpose.

gulyardy, obs. f. GOLIARDY (s.v. GOLIARD).

gulyas, var. GOULASH.

gum (gʌm), *sb.*[1] Forms: 1 **góma**, 3–5 **gome**, 5–6 **gomme**, **gume**, 5–7 **goom(e**, 6 **gowme**, **gummb**, 6–7 **gumme**, 7 **gombe**, **gumb**, **gumm**, 7– **gum**. [OE. *góma* wk. masc., corresponds to OHG. *guomo* (MHG. *guome*), and (apart from difference of declension) to ON. *góm-r* palate. The vowel in these forms seems to represent a pre-Teut. long diphthong *ōu*; cf. the synonyms (app. related by ablaut) OHG. *giumo*, *goumo* (MHG. *goume*, mod.G. *gaumen*). Outside Teut. the Lith. *gomurỹs* 'palate' has been compared; the word may belong to the OAryan root **gheu-*, *ghŏu-* to yawn, whence Gr. χάος, χαῦνος.

The normal pronunciation (guːm) (cf. *loom*) still survives in dialects.]

†**1.** Used in OE. and early ME. *sing.* or *pl.* indifferently for the inside of the mouth or throat.

c **825** *Vesp. Psalter* lxviii[i]. 4 Ic won cleopiende hase ȝewordne werun goman mine. *a* **1000** *Riddles* xli. 58 (Gr.) Ic eom on goman ȝena swetra, þonne [etc.]. *c* **1000** *Sax. Leechd.* I. 264 Wið þæs muþes & þæra gomena fulnysse..ȝenim [etc.]. *c* **1200** *Vices & Virtues* (1888) 119 We notieð on gomes [*printed* ȝomes] alles kennes attre of dieule. [**1535** COVERDALE *Ps.* xxi. 15 My tunge cleueth to my goomes.]

2. a. *pl. collect.* The firm fleshy integument of the jaws and bases of the teeth; also said of the toothless jaw and its integument. Also *sing.*, the portion of the integument attached to a single tooth.

1398 TREVISA *Barth. De P.R.* v. xvi. (1495) 122 Yf the gomes ben corrupt thenne [etc.]. *c* **1440** *Promp. Parv.* 202/1 Gome yn mannys mowthe (*S.* goomys), *gingiva.* *c* **1470** HENRYSON *Mor. Fab.* v. (*Parl. Beasts*) xxxiii, With that the meir gird him vpoun the gumis [*rimes with* presumis]. **1527** ANDREW *Brunswyke's Distyll. Waters* B iij b, The same water ..is good for..payne in the gommes. **1555** EDEN *Decades* 161 From the vppermoste parte of the lyppe euen vnto the nethermoste parte of the gumme. **1578** BANISTER *Hist. Man* I. 5 The callositie of the Gowmes serueth some men instead of teeth. **1610** BEAUM. & FL. *Scornf. Lady* III. i, Marry come vp my gentleman, are your gummes growne so tender they cannot bite? *a* **1656** BP. HALL *Rem. Wks.* (1660) 189 The canker from a scarce sensible begining consumes the gummes. **1711** SHAFTESB. *Charac.* (1733) I. iii. 288 Operations of the active Tongue on the passive Gum or Palat. **1747** WESLEY *Prim. Physic* (1762) 52 Keep a little Stick Liquorice between the Cheek and the Gums. **1814** LADY COLQUHOUN in *Mem.* ii. (1849) 44 The gum was still painful when exposed to the air. **1850** LYELL *2nd Visit U.S.* II. 118 Alligators' teeth..set in silver for infants..to rub against their gums when cutting their teeth. **1876** TOMES *Dental Anat.* 98 The gum is continuous with the mucous membrane of the inside of the lips. **1883** *19th Cent.* May 759 A rough outline of the Man of the Future with his bald scalp and empty gums.

†**b.** = *gum-tooth* (see 5). *Obs.*

c **1420** *Pallad. on Husb.* IV. 883 Er yeeris sixe out goth the gomes stronge [L. *molares superiores cadunt*].

3. *slang.* Impertinent talk, chatter, 'jaw'.

1751 SMOLLETT *Per. Pic.* xvi. I. 115 Pshaw! brother, there's no occasion to bowss out so much unnecessary gum. **1785** GROSE *Dict. Vulg. Tongue* s.v., Come let us have no more of your gum. **1824** R. B. PEAKE *Americans Abroad* i. 1 Come, none of your gum—now you are but an underlin'.

4. = GUMMER[1] b. (*Cent. Dict.*)

5. *attrib.* and *Comb.*, as ***gum-bleeding***, ***-lancet***; ***gum-chewed*** adj.; **gum-didder** *nonce-wd.*, the quivering or shivering of the gums (cf. DIDDER *v.*); **gum-digger** *Austral.* and *N.Z. slang*, a dentist; so **gum-digging** *vbl. sb.*; **gum-ridge**, the ridge of gum behind the upper teeth; **gum-ring**, a child's teething-ring; **gum-rubber**, something for a child to rub its gums on; **gum-shield** *Boxing* (see quot. 1954); †**gum-stake** *nonce-wd.*, a tooth; **gum-stick** = *gum-rubber*; **gum-tickler** *U.S.* (see quots.); **gum-tooth**, a molar tooth; **gumwork** *Dentistry* (see quot. 1969). Also GUMBOIL.

1897 *Allbutt's Syst. Med.* III. 461 Hæmorrhages, such as nose-bleeding, *gum-bleeding, and bloodshot eye. **1922** JOYCE *Ulysses* 364 Chap in the Burton today spitting back *gumchewed gristle. **1653** URQUHART *Rabelais* II. vii. 40 The teeth-chatter or *gum-didder of lubberly lusks. **1941** BAKER *Dict. Austral. Slang* 33 **Gumdigger*, a dentist. **1932** A. S. BRUCE *Early Days of Canterbury* xii. 135 Purdie the Dentist..was..among the leading practitioners in the somewhat primitive days of the art of '*gum digging'. **1784** M. UNDERWOOD *Dis. Children* (1799) I. 188 When it is found necessary to lance the gums..it should always be done effectually with a proper *gum-lancet. **1938** I. GOLDBERG *Wonder of Words* ix. 179 A consonant is called palato-alveolar because it is made by the palate and the gums... This term is applied, among other things, to the teeth sockets, or the *gum-ridge. **1965** W. S. ALLEN *Vox Latina* i. 13 An alveolar articulation (in which the tongue makes contact with the gum-ridge behind the upper teeth rather than with the teeth themselves). **1856** F. S. COZZENS *Sparrowgr. Papers* x. 138 It..sat up rigidly in its mother's lap, twirling its thumbs and cutting its teeth without a *gum-ring. **1708** PRIOR *Mice* 103 Stockings, shoes, to grace the bantling;..add to these the fine *gum-rubber. **1954** F. C. AVIS *Boxing Ref. Dict.* 50 **Gum shield*, a soft pad worn in the mouth by boxers to protect their teeth and gums during a contest. **1959** *Times* 27 Aug. 3/7 In the eighth [round] Erskine's gumshield went skidding across the canvas. **1963** *Times* 7 Feb. 3/6 He took a hammering and had his gum-shield knocked loose. **1671** CROWNE *Juliana* III. Dram. Wks. 1873 I. 71 Shaver o' shin-bones, drawer of *gum-stakes. **1789** W. BUCHAN *Dom. Med.* (1790) 17 A crust of bread is the best *gum-stick. **1810** J. LAMBERT *Trav. N. Amer.* (1813) II. 299 A *gum-tickler is a gill of spirits, generally rum, taken fasting. **1814** *Q. Rev.* X. 521 Of dram-drinking [in the States] there are different stages... The first drop..is called a gum-tickler. **1865** DICKENS *Mut. Fr.* IV. iii, Will you mix it [rum], Mr. Wegg?..I think not, sir..I prefer to take it in the form of a Gum-Tickler. **1535** COVERDALE *Judg.* xv. 19 Then God opened a *gome-tothe [Vulg. *dentem molarem*] in ye chekebone [of the ass]. *c* **1550** LLOYD *Treas. Health* (1585) A v, Children are payned with..ytchinge of the gummes, & espicially in the growyng of the gumme teethe. *a* **1872** B. HARTE *Notes by Flood & Field* I. Wks. 127 It was like pulling gum-teeth to get the money from you even then. **1878** L. P. MEREDITH *Teeth* 225 To wait until the gums have shrunk..sufficiently to allow gum-teeth to be inserted without being too prominent. **1881** P. H. AUSTEN *Harris's Princ. & Pract. Dentistry* (ed. 10) IV. xiii. 633 It [*sc.* platinum] is also the only metal used in a remarkably beautiful style of work known as the Continuous Gum Work. **1940** J. OSBORNE *Dental Mechanics* viii. 88 The absence of the anterior gumwork has a serious effect upon the retention of the denture in the mouth. **1969** *Gloss. Terms Dentistry* (*B.S.I.*) 84 *Gumwork*, that part of the denture which replaces lost natural gum and alveolar process.

gum (gʌm), *sb.*[2] Forms: 4–5 gomme, (5 gom), 4–7 gumme, (5 gume, 6 gumb(e, 7 gumm), 6–7 goom(e, (6 goume), 4– gum. [a. OF. *gomme* = Pr., Sp. *goma*, Pg., It. *gomma*:—popular L. *gumma* = class. L. *gummi*, *cummi*, a. Gr. κόμμι.]

1. a. A viscid secretion issuing from certain trees and shrubs, which hardens in drying but is usually soluble in cold or hot water, in this respect differing from resin. Occas. in wider use, including resins (cf. 2).

c **1385** CHAUCER *L.G.W.* Prol. 109 As for to speke of gomme or erbe or tre. **1387** TREVISA *Higden* (Rolls) I. 101 Herbes groweþ þeron, þat droppeþ gom. *c* **1400** MAUNDEV. (1839) iv. 22 Out of hem [Trees] comethe Gomme, as it were of Plombtrees or of Cherietrees. *c* **1400** *Three Kings Cologne* 44 Hit droppeþ downe oute of certeyn trees in maner of gumme. **1513** DOUGLAS *Æneis* VI. iii. 98 The gvm or glew.. Is wont to seme ȝallow on the grane new. **1573** TUSSER *Husb.* xxxiii. (1878) 75 All trees that beare goom set now as they coom. **1591** SPENSER *Virg. Gnat* 669 The Spartan Mirtle, whence sweet gumb does flowe. **1613** PURCHAS *Pilgrimage* (1614) 507 Lac is a strange drug, made by certaine winged Pismires of the gumme of trees. **1631** JORDEN *Nat. Bathes* vi. (1669) 40 We use the word Gum in a more general sense, comprehending under it all Rosins, Turpentines, Pitches, &c. **1697** DRYDEN *Virg. Georg.* IV. 236 With Dew, Narcissus Leaves, and clammy Gum. **1805** *Med. Jrnl.* XIV. 266 There is a great resemblance between the physical properties of animal mucus and vegetable gum. **1867** MOLONEY *Forestry W. Afr.* 122 From the Gold Coast the export of gum (fossilized resin)..is trifling. **1878** BROWNING *La Saisiaz* 7 To heal and coat with amber gum the sloe-tree's gash. **1894** *Outing* (U.S.) XXIII. 391/2 The seams are usually payed with melted spruce gum, which effectually prevents leakage.

b. with *a* and *pl.* as denoting a kind of gum.

a **1300** *Cursor M.* 11501 (Gött.) It [rekels] es a gum þat cummes of firr. **1513** *Act 5 Hen. VIII*, c. 4 Preamble, Divers Strangers..dry calander Worsteds with Gums, Oils, and Presses. **1538** WRIOTHESLEY *Chron.* (1875) I. 90 Yt was noe bloude, but hony clarified and coloured with saffron, and lyinge lyke a goume. **1631** GOUGE *God's Arrows* I. xxv. 36 *Stacte*, a gumme that distils out of Myrrhe, or Cinamon. **1802** *Med. Jrnl.* 391 Opium is composed of a gum, a resin [etc.]. **1870** YEATS *Nat. Hist. Comm.* 225 Gums are soluble in water, but not in alcohol.

c. This substance dried and used in the arts, e.g. to stiffen linen, as a mucilage, etc. Hence *fig.*, stiffness.

1456 *Tintinhull Churchw. Acc.* (Som. Rec. Soc.) 187 It. in gume pro eisdem libris..j[d]. **1505** *Carpenters' Acc.* in T. Sharp *Cov. Myst.* (1825) 189 Rosyn & gome to þe same viijd. **1621** ELSING *Debates Ho. Lords* (Camden) 34 Shewes the washing by them, who washed away the gum. **1827** FARADAY *Chem. Manip.* v. 158 Gum, when pulverized should be kept perfectly dry. **1876** GEO. ELIOT *Dan. Der.* vi, The necessary gum and consistence of a substantial personality.

d. *U.S.* Short for *chewing-gum* (see CHEWING *vbl. sb.* 3).

1842 *Spirit of Times* (Phila.) 11 Apr. (Th.), [She] asked me if I didn't want A piece of gum to chaw. **1915** J. WEBSTER *Dear Enemy* (1916) 273 A painted yellow-haired thing who chewed gum like a cow. **1936** R. E. SHERWOOD *Idiot's Delight* I. 36 You've got to hoard your gum here in Europe.

e. *British gum* (see BRITISH 5).

f. The viscid or waxy substance which surrounds the filaments of silk in its natural state.

1774 in *Trans. Amer. Philos. Soc.* II. (1786) 352 The substance which forms the silk, is in their stomach, which is very long; wound up as it were on two spindles and surrounded with a gum, commonly yellow, sometimes white, not often greenish. **1825** J. NICHOLSON *Oper. Mech.* 399 The silk being now spun, is put into a boiler filled with hot water, into which is put a small quantity of soap, in order to divest the silk of its gum. **1835** URE *Philos. Manuf.* vi. 248 Marabout... Being white as it comes from the worm, it takes the purest and most delicate shades of colour at once, without the discharge of its gum. **1887** *Encycl. Brit.* XXII. 61/2 The natural gum of the cocoons which holds the filaments together. *Ibid.* 64/2 It has long been the practice to dye some dark silks 'in the gum'. **1959** *Chambers's Encycl.* XII. 555/1 After the first boiling the silk is hydro-extracted which removes the dirt and the bulk of the gum.

g. A mixture, of which gelatine is a main ingredient, from which a hard sweetmeat is made in a mould; a sweetmeat made of this.

1827 W. A. JARRIN *Italian Confect.* (ed. 3) xxvi. 220 Pastilles, Mille-Fleurs are made with fine gum paste, of different colours. **1868** L. M. ALCOTT *Little Women* vii. 101 Mr. Davis..had succeeded in banishing gum. **1894** E. SKUSE *Compl. Confect.* 103 There is a quantity of goods sold as French, American, German, &c., gums, all more or less a mixture of the genuine article, with gelatine, farina, &c. **1921** *Dict. Occup. Terms* (1927) §434 *Starch hand* (male), ..*gum boiler*; weighs on scales, or, measures by means of measuring glass, ingredients for gums, mainly gelatine and butter;..pours the mixture, known as 'gum' or 'boil', when boiled, into trays or moulds. **1950** C. T. WILLIAMS *Chocolate & Confect.* xiv. 172 Excessive stirring in any form of gum, pastille or jelly is to be discouraged, since granulation readily occurs. **1962** *Which?* Sept. 283/1 Rowntree's Fruit Gums (tube).

h. *ellipt.* for KAURI *gum*.

1839 J. D. LANG *N.Z. in 1839* 59 This gum has recently been sold in some quantity..to the Americans who manufacture it into varnish. **1887** *Col. & Indian Exhib.*, *Rep. Col. Sect.* 287 The ordinary gum of commerce is the semi-fossilized turpentine of the [Kauri pine] tree. **1906** *Macm. Mag.* Apr. 478 Not having caught on to the feel of the gum.

i. The substance whose presence causes a ropy condition in wine.

1888 *Encycl. Brit.* XXIV. 603/2 It sometimes happens that wine becomes viscous and forms threads when poured from the bottle. This mischief, which is caused by the development of a foreign ferment, can be cured by the judicious addition of a solution of tannin, which precipitates the 'gum'.

j. A non-volatile solid or semi-solid substance apt to be deposited by some petroleum products when stored for long periods or heated, and formed by the oxidation of certain of their constituents; it varies in nature from a soft, sticky mass to a hard, resinous layer.

1922 *Rep. Investigations U.S. Bur. Mines* No. 2394. 4 A study of the gums that develop spontaneously when cracked gasoline is stored. **1926** *Industr. & Engin. Chem.* Nov. 1198/2 Gum formation in gasoline claimed public notice when cracked gasoline began to be widely marketed. **1935** NASH & HOWES *Princ. Motor Fuel Prep. & Applic.* II. xiii. 105 The formation of gum in motor fuels..can lead to the seizure of inlet valves in their guides. **1944** M. VAN WINKLE *Aviation Gasoline Manuf.* vii. 206 The addition of certain gum inhibitors to all grades of aviation gasoline is permitted. **1967** W. A. GRUSE *Motor Fuels* iii. 68 One type of instability, troublesome twenty-five years ago, and still occurring occasionally when storage conditions are bad or when a very unstable stock is employed, is the development of gum content in gasoline.

†**2.** (Chiefly *pl.*) Products of this kind employed as drugs or perfumes, or for burning as incense. *Obs.*

1382 WYCLIF *Jer.* viii. 22 Whether gumme is not in Galaad, or a leche is not there? **1393** LANGL. *P. Pl.* C. III. 236 Spicers to hym speke..For he..knoweþ meny gommes. **1412–20** LYDG. *Chron. Troy* II. xvii, From the heade down unto her foote With sondry gommes..She is ennoynte. **1551** ROBINSON tr. *More's Utop.* II. (Arb.) 95 They burne swete gummes and spices or perfumes. **1559** W. CUNNINGHAM *Cosmogr. Glasse* 191 Divers aromaticall spices, and Gummes. **1667** MILTON *P.L.* XI. 327 Altars I would reare..and thereon Offer sweet smelling Gumms. *a* **1711** KEN *Hymns Evang.* Poet. Wks. 1721 I. 47 The Gumms which Sacred Rites consume, We bring. **1780** BURKE *Sp. Secur. Indep. Parlt.* Wks. III. 278 To embalm a carcass not worth an ounce of the gums that are used to preserve it.

3. With qualification.

a. In the names of various mucilaginous or resinous products, prefixed to a substantive or followed by an adjective, e.g. *gum acacia*, *ammoniac*, *copal*, *elemi*, *guaiacum*, *lac*, *ladanum*, *olibanum*, *sandarac*, *tragacanth*, for which see the second member; **gum accroides** = ACCAROID; **gum-arabic** (see ARABIC 2); **gum benjamin** (see BENJAMIN[1] 1); **gum-dammar** (see DAMMAR); **gum-dragon** = TRAGACANTH (see DRAGON[2]); **gum-juniper** = SANDARAC; **gum-kino** (see KINO[1] 1); **gum-senegal** or † **-senega**, a variety of gum-arabic, named from the locality where it is obtained. Also ***chagual gum*** (see quot. 1880); ***sonora gum***, resin obtained from the creosote-bush.

c **1400** *Lanfranc's Cirurg.* 49 Take frank encense, mastik, mirre, dragagantum, gumme arabik. **1718** MRS. MARY EALES *Receipts* 70 Make it up to a stiff Paste with Gum-Dragon well steept. **1759** ELLIS in *Phil. Trans.* LI. 208 Some of them were smeared several times over with gum senega. **1770** COOK *Jrnl.* 1 May (1893) 245 We found 2 Sorts of Gum, one sort of which is like Gum Dragon. **1830** Gum kino [see KINO[1] 1]. **1844** HOBLYN *Dict. Med.*, *Gum juniper*, a concrete resin which exudes in white tears from the *Juniperus Communis*. It has been called *sandarach*,.. Reduced to powder it is called *pounce*, which prevents ink from sinking into paper. **1851** *Illustr. Catal. Gt. Exhib.* IV. I. 997 Gum kino, from the blue gum-tree, the stringy bark, and other *Eucalypti*. **1851–9** Gum benjamin [see BENJAMIN[1] 1]. **1858** CARPENTER *Veg. Phys.* §346 Gum Senegal is similar to gum Arabic, being obtained from a kind of Acacia differing very little from that which yields the latter. **1868** WATTS *Dict. Chem.*, *Sonora gum*, a kind of lac produced by the puncture of a coccus in *Mimosa cerifera*, a tree growing in Mexico. **1869** A. R. WALLACE *Malay Archip.* II. 8 Tortoise-shell, rattan gum-dammer, and other valuable products. **1880** *Encycl. Brit.* XI. 275/2 Chagual gum, a new variety brought from St. Iago de Chili, resembles gum senegal. **1908** W. SCHLICH *Man. Forestry* (ed. 3) V. 730 Gum-kino, a bright red, astringent gum-resin ..from India and Ceylon. **1909** WEBSTER, Gum accroides. **1922** JOYCE *Ulysses* 502 Pellets of new bread with fennygreek and gumbenjamin. **1930** *Discovery* Aug. 260/2 A coating of red ochre and then..another of gum damar boiled in oil. **1937** Gum accroides [see ACCAROID].

b. gum elastic [after F. *gomme elastique*], india-rubber, caoutchouc (also *elastic-gum*: see ELASTIC); rarely applied to gutta percha. Hence **gum-elastical** *a.* (*nonce-wd.*), resembling india-rubber.

1800 SOUTHEY *Lett.* (1856) I. 90 A stretch of belief which requires a more gum-elastical faith than Heaven has allotted me. **1807** PEPYS in *Phil. Trans.* XCVII. 250 A small gum elastic bottle B. **1845** in *Proc. Amer. Phil. Soc.* IV. 221 Specimens of the manufacture of Gum-elastic goods. **1851** FORBES *Veg. World* II. p. vi †/2 The Isonandra gutta, the source of the gum-elastic, known as gutta-percha.

c. gum ivy, † **gum of ivy**: the inspissated juice of the stem of the ivy.

c **1550** LLOYD *Treas. Health* (1585) G ij, Fyl the hollowe tooth with the gum of Iuy it will take away the toothe ache. **1576** BAKER *Jewell of Health* 130 b, He tooke of Galbanum one pounde, of gumme yvie three ounces. **1653** WALTON *Angler* vii. 157 Dissolve Gum of Ivie in Oyle of Spike, and therewith annoint your dead bait for a Pike. **1712** tr. *Pomet's Hist. Drugs* I. 75 This is that which some Druggists..sell for Gum Ivy. **1787** in BEST *Angling* (ed. 2) 71. **1859** ATKINSON *Walks & Talks* (1892) 3, I was trying to get gum-ivy, which an old fishing book I had said was a famous thing to anoint the baits with.

4. The sticky secretion that collects in the inner corner of the eye. (Either a sense *transf.* from 1, or connected with GUM *sb.*[3])

1599 SHAKS. *Hen. V*, IV. ii. 48 The gumme downe roping from their pale-dead eyes. **1740** E. BAYNARD *Health* (ed. 6) 16 When sleep does first desert you, rise; Next, wash the gum from off your eyes. **1886** in *Syd. Soc. Lex.*

5. a. Short for GUM-TREE. Also preceded by various defining epithets, as ***black***, ***blue***, ***white***, ***mountain***, ***spotted***, etc. ***gum*** (see also at first word).

1802 D. COLLINS *Acc. N.S. Wales* II. xix. 235 The blue gum, she-oak, and cherry tree of Port Jackson were commonly here. **1820** J. OXLEY *Jrnl. Exped. Australia* 102 A few diminutive gums being the only timber to be seen. **1833** C. STURT *South. Australia* I. iii. 118 The cypresses became mixed with casuarina, box, and mountain-gum. *Ibid.* II. viii. 236 Eucalypti were the general timber on the ranges; one species..resembling strongly the black-butted gum, was remarkable for a scent peculiar to its bark. **1846** J. L. STOKES *Discov. Australia* II. iv. 132 York gum... Abundant in York—on good soil. *Ibid.* xii. 387 The trees, which grew only in the valleys, were small kinds of banksia, wattles, and drooping gums. **1847** F. W. L. LEICHHARDT *Jrnl. Overland Exped. Austral.* 6 The prevailing timber trees are Bastard box,..and the Flooded Gum. *Ibid.* i. 11 Ironbark ridges here and there with spotted gum..diversified the sameness. *Ibid.* 283 On the small flats, the apple-gum grew. **1848** T. L. MITCHELL *Trop. Australia* 107 A small group of trees of the yellow gum, a species of eucalyptus growing only on the poor sandy soil near Botany Bay. **1852** MRS. C. MEREDITH *My Home in Tasmania* I. xi. 169 A kind of *Eucalyptus*, with long drooping leaves, called the 'Weeping Gum', is the most elegant of the family. **1864** J. S. MOORE *Spring Life Lyrics* 114 Amid grand old gums, dark cedars and pines. **1868** *Rep. U.S. Commissioner Agric.* (1869) 281 Some of the plants from which bees gather honey..black-gum (*Nyssa multiflora*). **1887** *Col. & Indian Exhib., Rep. Col. Sect.* 420 Other noble trees, as the Blue, White, Red, Swamp, Water-rooted and Manna-drooping Gums. **1889** Cider Gum [see SUGAR *sb.* 5]. **1893** *Australasian* 5 Aug. 252/4 The bark of the salmon gum approaches in colour to a rich golden brown. **1893** *Sydney Morning Herald* 19 Aug. 7/1 Here are no straight and lofty trees, but sprawling cinnamon gums. **1894** H. NISBET *Bush Girl's Rom.* 34 A gaseous haziness, making the leafage of the gums look bluer than ever they were. **1930** BILLIS & KENYON *Pastures New* viii. 123 The trees were very pretty, being a kind of weeping gum. **1947** I. L. IDRIESS *Isles of Despair* vii. 44 Horn Island, with its stunted gums and cabbage-tree palms.

b. *U.S.* A log, usually cut from a gum-tree, hollowed out and adapted to serve as a beehive, a water-trough, or a well-curb. Cf. *bee-gum*.

1817 J. BRADBURY *Trav. Amer.* 286 *note*, Any portion so cut off is called a gum, a name probably arising from the almost exclusive application of the gum tree to these purposes. **1844** GOSSE in *Zoologist* II. 607 A 'gum' or square box to hive the swarm for domestication. *a* **1864** GESNER *Coal, Petrol.*, etc. (1865) 33 When the soil is not deep, a circular excavation is made down to the rock bed, and a hollow log, or 'gum', as it is called, is placed in it on one end. **1879** J. BURROUGHS *Locusts & W. Honey* 29 No hive seems to please them as well as a section of a hollow tree—'gums'—as they are called in the South and West where the sweet gum grows.

6. *U.S. colloq.* Short for *elastic gum*, i.e. india-rubber; *occas.* an india-rubber garment. Also *pl.* Goloshes. See *gum-boots, -shoes* in 9.

1859 BARTLETT *Dict. Amer.*, *Gum*...2 India-rubber. Hence the plural *Gums* is often applied to India-rubber shoes. **1870** R. G. WHITE *Words & their Uses* Pref. (1881), 'Where is Emily?'.. 'O, Emily is outside cleaning her gums on the mat'.

7. A disease in fruit trees consisting in a morbid secretion of gum.

1721 in BAILEY. **1727–41** CHAMBERS *Cycl.*, *Gum*, among gardeners, is a disease incident to fruit trees, of the stone kind. **1802** W. FORSYTH *Fruit Trees* v. (1824) 83 Wherever the knife is applied, it is sure to bring on the gum. **1852** *Beck's Florist* 147 It [a kind of cherry] is very subject to gum and canker.

8. *attrib.* and *Comb.*: **a.** simple attributive, as (sense 1) ***gum-forest, -furnace, -pot, -trade, -vessel***; (sense 5) ***gum-bough, -leaf, -log, -swamp, -timber, -tip, -trunk***; (sense 6) ***gum-catheter***; **b.** objective, as (sense 1) ***gum-bearing, -yielding*** adjs.; **c.** instrumental, as (sense 4) ***gum-glued*** adj.; (sense 5) ***gum-shadowed, -shrouded*** adjs.; **d.** similative, as ***gum-like*** adj.

1775 BRUCE in *Phil. Trans.* LXV. 415 There is another *gum-bearing tree. **1890** *Melbourne Argus* 2 Aug. 4/3 Make a bit of a shelter..with..*gum-boughs. **1884** M. MACKENZIE *Dis. Throat & Nose* II. 226 A *gum catheter would then be passed..into the stomach. **1804** *Ann. Rev.* II. 29/2 The Moors..encamp themselves round the *gum-forest of Zaara. **1839** URE *Dict. Arts* 1266 Then lay the fire in the *gum-furnace. **1682** O. N. tr. *Boileau's Lutrin* IV. 14 His Pages starting at the sudden Noyse, Began to bustle, rubbing their *gum-glew'd Eyes. **1874** TROLLOPE *Harry Heathcote* i. 2 When the *gum leaves crackle..before Christmas, there won't be a blade of grass by the end of February. **1894** H. NISBET *Bush Girl's Rom.* 204 Making a soft bed of gum leaves. **1966** 'J. HACKSTON' *Father clears Out* 182 They might have chewed the moss off old fences and, at a pinch, say, taken on the gum-leaves. **1841** BRANDE *Chem.* 1078 When the solutions are evaporated, uncrystallizable *gum-like compounds remain. **1836** D. CROCKETT *Exploits & Adv. Texas* 82 (Th.), A chap just about as rough hewn as if he had been cut out of a *gum log with a broad axe. **1868** W. L. CARLETON *Austral. Nts.* 1 To see the gum-log flaming bright Its welcome beacon. **1875** BENNETT & DYER *Sachs' Bot.* 77 The origin of resin and *gum passages depends on the formation of intercellular passages with a peculiar development of the cells which bound them. **1839** URE *Dict. Arts* 1266 The *gum-pot is now to be set upon the brick-stand. **1862** H. C. KENDALL *Poems* 134 The *gum-shadowed glen. **1890** 'ROLF BOLDREWOOD' *Col. Reformer* (1891) 201 Camped by the edge of the long black *gum-shrouded lagoon. **1816** *Sporting Mag.* XLVIII. 244 Mrs. Ratley was riding across the *Gum-swamp in North Carolina. **1828** P. CUNNINGHAM *N.S. Wales* (ed. 3) II. 107 Our *gum timber being as durable and as well adapted to ship-building as the teak. **1955** *Sci. News Let.* 12 Mar. 168/2 In 1952 it was discovered the koalas had eaten nearly all their food supplies and were in danger of starving to death. The public rushed to the rescue with carloads of *gum-tips. **1839** in *Spirit Metropol. Conserv. Press* (1840) II. 328 The *gum trade, on the western coast of Africa. **1894** H. NISBET *Bush Girl's Rom.* 151 *Gum-trunks instead of the homelike trees. **1804** *Ann. Rev.* II. 29/1 A large wooden tub, containing about 2000 lbs. weight,..is fixed on the deck of the *gum-vessels. **1887** MOLONEY *Forestry W. Afr.* 128 Other *gum-yielding Acacias.

9. a. Special comb.: **gum-animal**, the Senegal galago (see quot.); **gum-bichromate** *Photogr.*, designating a process of printing on paper coated with a mixture of pigment, gum-arabic, and potassium bichromate; also designating a print so produced; **gum-boiler**, one who boils certain sweetmeat mixtures; **'gum-booted** *a.*, wearing gum-boots; **gum-boots** orig. *U.S.*, boots made of 'gum' or india-rubber; **gum-bucket** *Naval slang*, a smoker's pipe; **gum-chewer**, one who chews chewing-gum; so **gum-chewing** *vbl. sb.* and *ppl. a.*; **gum-digger**, one who digs for KAURI gum; **gum-digging**, the occupation of a gum-digger; **gum-drop** *U.S.*, a preparation of sweetened gum, used as a confection and in pharmacy; **gum-field**, an area where Kauri gum may be found; **gum-flowers** *Sc.*, artificial flowers; also *attrib.*; **gum-game** *U.S. slang*, a trick or dodge; **gum-hole** *N.Z.*, the hole a gum-digger sinks; **gum-land** *N.Z.*, land where kauri gum is found; **gum-nut** *Austral.*, the hardened flower-cup of *Eucalyptus gummifera*; **gum-paper**, paper gummed on one side; **gum-platinum** *Photogr.* (see quots.); **gum-seal**, an impression of a seal taken on softened gum; **gum-shake** (see SHAKE *sb.*[1] 9); **gum-shoe** *U.S.*, (*a*) (in *pl.*) goloshes: cf. *gum-boots*; (*b*) *fig.* (*U.S. colloq.*), used *attrib.* to describe something done stealthily; hence, a detective; hence **gum-shoe** *v. intr.* (*colloq.*, orig. *U.S.*), to move or act with stealth as if wearing gum-shoes; **gum silk**, silk from which the natural gum has not been removed; **gum-spear** *N.Z.*, a spear used in probing soil for kauri gum; **gum-sucker** *Austral.*, (*a*) a native Australian (esp. a Victorian) or Tasmanian; (*b*) a fool or simpleton; †**gum-taffeta** = *gummed taffeta*; **gum-water**, a solution of gum-arabic in water; **gum-wood**, the wood of the gum-tree; the tree itself; also *attrib.*; **gum-worker** *Photogr.*, one who makes prints by any of the processes, such as the gum-bichromate process, in which gum-arabic is used.

1840 BLYTH *Cuvier's Anim. Kingd.* (1849) 65 The Senegal Galago (*Galago Senegalensis*, Geof.)..is known as the *Gum animal of Senegal, from its feeding much on that production. **1897** WALL *Dict. Photogr.* (ed. 7) 117 The *gum-bichromate or photo-aquatint process. **1900** *Daily News* 1 Oct. 7/4 A striking profile done in red by the gum-bichromate process. **1919** *Brit. Jrnl. Photogr. Alm.* 252 In the gum-bichromate process, also termed aquatint or photo-aquatint. **1962** M. R. HASELGROVE *Photographer's Dict.* 124 *Gum bichromate prints.* These are made by a nearly obsolete process, but are luckily still to be seen in our major exhibitions. **1921** *Gum boiler [see 1 g]. **1930** BLUNDEN *De Bello Germanico* 10 The unshaven, clay-cased, and *gum-booted one. **1960** *News Chron.* 27 Apr. 1/7 Gum-booted searchers waded in the shallows. **1850** E. CHRISTMAN *One Man's Gold* (1930) 119, I put on my long *gum boots and waded through the water. **1875** WOOD & LAPHAM *Waiting for Mail* 112 The long indiarubber 'gum' boots..that he worked in at the claim. **1897** *Daily News* 10 July 8/4 Without the assistance of 'gum' boots or dust-defying gaiters. **1917** 'CONTACT' *Airman's Outings* 220 A bus lands and taxies to a shed. From it descends the Squadron Commander, who, with gum-boots and a warm coat over his pyjamas, has been 'trying the air'. **1921** *Daily Colonist* (Victoria, B.C.) 28 Oct. 20/3 (Advt.), Men's pure gum boots, with red soles, hip length $6.95. **1962** *Lancet* 15 Dec. 1272/1 Twice a day I put on my gumboots to go out to feed [chickens]. **1970** *Times* 10 Feb. 1/7 More than 200 policemen in gumboots..drained ponds and dragged the stream. **1893** *Funk's Stand. Dict.*, *Gum bucket*, a tobacco pipe. **1917** 'TAFFRAIL' *Sub* viii. §2. 204 'The Bloke' was an inveterate smoker. I never remember seeing him off duty without a 'gum-bucket', as he called it, in his mouth. **1919** 'ETIENNE' *Strange Tales from Fleet* 143 Mr. Smith, revived by the cocoa and soothed by the pipe, known as the 'gum-bucket' to his pals. **1850** S. JUDD *R. Edney* 158 There are the *Gum-chewers,—all backlotters; and vulgar. **1938** I. KUHN *Assigned to Adventure* v. 51 His conviction that the gum-chewers relish stories about the upper classes. **1889** *Sunday Opinion* (Pueblo, Colo.) 14 July 4/5 The careful observer can not fail to note the growing prevalency of *gum chewing. **1907** *Daily Chron.* 29 July 5/2 The gum-chewing habit. **1960** D. STOREY *This Sporting Life* I. ii. 31 The other gum-chewing player. **1961** *Encounter* Apr. 24/1 Local hot-rodders and their gum-chewing molls. **1967** *Coast to Coast 1965–6* 101 He became the victim of their gum-chewing..inattention. **1884** C. F. GORDON CUMMING in *Century Mag.* XXVII. 924 A large class of men, both Maori and European, known as *gum-diggers. *c* **1858** in *Richmond-Atkinson Papers* (1960) I. 437 Of the kauri gum diggers 9/10ths are furnished by this tribe. **1871** *Evening Post* (Wellington, N.Z.) 4 Jan. 2/3 A gum-digger named Denis McManus, has been burned to death at Riverhead, Auckland. **1921** *N.Z. Jrnl. Agric.* 20 May 260 To break in these lands one must first face the legacy left by the gum-digger. **1965** G. J. WILLIAMS *Econ. Geol. N.Z.* ii. 14/1 Coal had been discovered by gum-diggers near Kawakawa in Northland in 1861. **1871** *McLean Papers* XXXVII. 72 (MS.), Paora Toki..is gone *gum-digging up the Thames. **1879** J. GREY *His Island Home* IV. 34 A great many of the natives abandoned their kaingas and went gum-digging, when that article brought a high price. **1892** *Star* 13 July 1/8 He picked up a precarious livelihood by gum-digging. **1860** *North-West* (Port Townsend, Wash.) 5 July 3/3 Candies, *gum drops, mottoes. **1864** SALA in *Daily Tel.* 30 Mar., The soldiers spending their abundant greenbacks ..in fig and gum-drops. **1880** W. SENIOR *Travel & Trout in Antipodes* II. ii. 182 The *gum-fields..indicate that the fine forests have disappeared at an alarming rate. **1886** *N. Zealand Herald* 28 May 5/5 Praying that the gumfields.. should be opened during the winter season. **1756** MRS. CALDERWOOD *Jrnl.* (1884) 316 A crown of *gum-flowers, which was afterwards put on her. **1821** GALT *Ann. Parish* xii. (1895) 86 There was she painted like a Jezebel, with gum-flowers on her head. **1829** CARLYLE *Misc.* (1857) I. 276 Broken Italian gumflowers. **1864** BROWNING in *Mem. Tennyson* (1897) II. i. 16 As if they want seed in a gum-flower manufactory. **1840** in *Amer. Speech* (1941) XVI. 299 I've come the *gum game over you. **1872** E. EGGLESTON *Hoosier Schoolmaster* xiv. 118 Now, looky here... You don't come no gum games over me. **1885** *Lisbon* (Dak.) *Star* 18 Sept., They tried the gum-game on me down in Pennsylvania..but I came out ahead. **1882** W. D. HAY *Brighter Britain!* II. i. 17 Rich *gum-holes here and there. **1900** *N.Z. Illustr. Mag.* III. 205/1 Each man sinks his own gumhole where he strikes the first gum. **1882** W. D. HAY *Brighter Britain!* II. i. 16 On our farm and in the surrounding bush, though these are distinctly not *gum-lands. **1900** *N.Z. Illustr. Mag.* III. 203/1 Here, then, on this gumland is where the old Kauri forests grew. **1950** *N.Z. Jrnl. Agric.* June 535/1 Gumland soils vary in type from peat, on some of the flats, through light to medium clay loams, to heavy clay soils. **1936** F. D. DAVISON *Children of Dark People* x. 143 They'd tell the *gum-nuts and they would drop to the ground and tell the grass. **1965** *Austral. Encycl.* III. 406/1 When stamens fall and the young seeds [of *Eucalyptus gummifera*] are fertilized, the flower-cup hardens into a woody capsule ('gum-nut') which opens..to shed the seed. **1965** M. SHADBOLT *Among Cinders* xx. 189 Gum-nuts. There might be a few scattered round. **1898** *Westm. Gaz.* 4 Mar. 5/3 An extremely thin slip of *gum paper inserted along the inside edge. **1918** *Photo-Miniature* XV. Mar. (Gloss.), **Gum-platinum process*—of first making a light print on platinum paper, then coating the print with sensitive gum mixture and reprinting from the same negative. **1919** *Brit. Jrnl. Photogr. Alm.* 252 *Gum-platinum* is a compound process, in which a pale print on platinum paper is coated with the sensitive gum mixture, and a second (pigment) image produced by re-printing under the same negative. **1826** MISS MITFORD *Village* Ser. II. (1863) 281 The most trifling womanly occupations—making *gum-seals, imitating cameos. **1887** *Col. & Indian Exhib., Rep. Col. Sect.* 427 These are all large trees..—some are a little liable to *gum-shakes. **1863** P. S. DAVIS *Young Parson* 12 A little boy who wore his father's *gum shoes in dry weather. **1872** *Morn. Post* 9 Jan. (Farmer) Forbidding him..to leave his gum-shoes in her hall. **1904** 'H. MCHUGH' *I'm from Missouri* iii. 44 It seemed that every voter in the community quit work and gum-shoed after the Two Candidates. **1904** *Omaha Bee* 24 Oct. 4 No gumshoe democratic campaign in Nebraska. **1906** A. H. LEWIS *Confess. Detective* 198 You're d'gum-shoe guy I was waitin' fer... It was Inspector Val tells me to lay for you. **1907** *Springfield* (Mass.) *Weekly Republ.* 4 Apr. 2 He..was forced to accomplish his ends by main strength rather than by gum-shoe methods. **1908** J. M. SULLIVAN *Crim. Slang* 11 *Gumshoe worker*, a private detective; a spotter. **1913** H. A. FRANCK *Zone Policeman 88* 159 But the 'gum shoe' naturally cannot twirl a police club. **1927** D. HAMMETT in *Black Mask* Nov. 21/2 He..looked me up and down, growled: 'So you're a lousy gum-shoe.' **1930** J. K. WINKLER *J. Pierpont Morgan* 264 That eminent political gum-shoe artist. **1951** J. CANNAN *And All I Learned* ix. 140 A seventeenth-century President of Trinity who *gum-shoed round the college gardens carrying a whip. **1930** *Publishers' Weekly* 8 Feb. 718 Under the present obscene book law the vice crusader..goes *gum-shoeing around from one bookseller to another. **1954** 'N. BLAKE' *Whisper in Gloom* iv. 58 What *were* you doing, gum-shoeing around Mr. Gray's premises? **1962** *Spectator* 1 June 728/3 Ross MacDonald..is a thoroughly competent detective-story writer, specialising in West Coast private-eye stories. In *The Wycherly Woman*..his gumshoe hero Archer searches for a missing student. **1885** *Encycl. Brit.* (1887) XXII. 64/1 Sugar is known to have been used for adulterating and loading *gum silk for a very long time. **1873** J. E. TINNE *Wonderland of Antipodes* 54, I saw them at work with their *gum-spears. **1888** P. W. BARLOW *Kaipara* xix. 147 A gum-digger's outfit..consists of a spade, a gum-spear and a piece of sacking... The gum-spear is a four-sided rod of steel, about four feet long, and pointed at one end. **1906** *Macm. Mag.* Apr. 478 A green hand of a gummy, that hadn't quite got the trick of it yet, went poking around that very cabbage-tree with his gum-spear. **1855** W. HOWITT *Two Y. Victoria* I. 24 Too 'cute to be bitten twice by the over 'cute '*gum-suckers', as the native Victorians are called. **1887** *All Year Round* 30 July 67/2 A 'gum-sucker' is a native of Tasmania, and owes his elegant nickname to the abundance of gum-trees in the Tasmanian forests. **1936** W. LAWSON *When Cobb and Co. was King* xii. 223 Some men.. called them 'gumsuckers', and a few other things. **1941** BAKER *Dict. Austral. Slang* 33 Gumsucker. **1738** SWIFT *Pol. Convers.* Wks. 1778 X. 236 Faith, you have made her fret like *gum-taffety. **1761** STERNE *Tr. Shandy* III. iv, You are so fortunate a fellow, as to have had your jerkin made of a gum-taffeta, and the body-lining to it, of a sarcenet or thin persian. **1639** ROBERTS *Compleat Canonier* (1672) 46 With a chalk line, dipt in *Gum-water. **1759** COLEBROOKE in *Phil. Trans.* LI. 43 A ground was laid..with levigated chalk mixed with gum water. **1869** SEMPLE *Diphtheria* 155 Injections of gum-water were passed into the trachea. **1683** PENN *Wks.* (1782) IV. 302 The trees of most note, are.. poplar, *gumwood, hickery. **1897** P. WARUNG *Tales Old Regime* 133 Blocks of pine or gum-wood. **1898** *Westm. Gaz.* 28 June 10/1, I tried..grafting on gumwood stocks. **1908** *Westm. Gaz.* 3 Oct. 14/2 Some photographers now classify themselves as *gum-workers, oil-workers, and so forth.

b. In names of plants yielding gum: **gum-cistus**, one of the shrubs of the genus *Cistus* which yield ladanum; **gum-plant**, a plant of the genus *Grindelia*, which is covered with a viscid secretion; **gum-succory**, (*a*) *Chondrilla juncea*; also, the gum produced from it; (*b*) *Lactuca perennis*; **gum-thistle**, *Onopordium acanthium*. Also GUM-TREE.

1688 R. HOLME *Armoury* II. 110/1 The *Gum Cistus hath ..a clammy sweet moisture called Gum Laudanum. **1824** MISS MITFORD *Village* Ser. I. (1863) 73 A flower almost as transitory as the gum cistus. **1858** G. MACDONALD *Phantastes* xix. 225 The gum-cistus..drops every night all the blossoms that the day brings forth. **1548** TURNER *Names of Herbes* 26 Chondrilla... It maye be named in englishe Ryshe Succory or *gum Succory because it hath a clammy humour in it. **1551** —— *Herbal* I. Kj, The leaues & the stalke of gume succory haue the poour for to degest. **1756** WATSON in *Phil. Trans.* XLIX. 845 The least wild Lettuce, or Dwarf Gum-Succory. **1548** TURNER *Names of Herbes* 8 Acanthium. .. I thynke it maye be called in englishe..*gum thistle.. because it is gummy. **1656** RIDGLEY *Pract. Physick* 311 He strewed..the powder of Gum Thistle very safely, upon Ulcers with rottenness of the Bones.

gum, *sb.*[3] See RED-GUM and WHITE-GUM.

†**gum**, *sb.*[4] *Sc. Obs.* Mist, vapour.

1513 DOUGLAS *Æneis* VII. Prol. 131 Wyth cloudy gum and rak ourquhelmyt the air. *Ibid.* XIII. Prol. 31 The gummys rysis, doun fallis the donk rym.

†**gum**, *sb.*[5] *Obs. rare*$^{-1}$. Also 6 **gomme**. = GUMMA. ?Also Comb. ***gum-galled*** adj.

1558 WARDE tr. *Alexis' Secr.* 13 b, A verie goodly secrete for the gommes [It. *gomme*] or burgeons that remaine of the great Pockes. **1693** *Sc. Presbyt. Eloquence* (1738) 139 That filthy Bitch, that gumgall'd Whore, the Whore of Babylon.

gum (gʌm), *sb.*[6] *dial.* and *vulgar.* [Deformation of GOD. Cf. GOM.] In phr. ***by*** (or ***my***) ***gum*** = by (or my) God. Also **gummie, gummy**.

c **1815** J. K. PAULDING *Bucktails* (1847) II. 34 By gum, that's jist what I want you to tell me, I swow. **1827** T. HOOD *Works* (1862) I. 311 But Hunks still ask'd to see the tooth, And swore by gum! he had not drawn it. **1832** W. STEPHENSON *Gateshead Local Poems* 100 Aw said let's ken what a' this means, By gum to hear't aw's weary. **1845** S. JUDD *Margaret* I. xvi. 139 'Gummy!' retorted the woman. 'He has been a talkin' about me.' **1857** 'C. BEDE' *Verdant Green* III. x, My gum, Giglamps! you'll be the death of me some fine day. **1887** H. SMART *Cleverly won* i. 10 Newmarket Heath may make you shiver, but, by gum! it gives you an appetite. **1894** BLACKMORE *Perlycross* 194 Got you there, Sergeant; by gum, I did! **1932** W. L. GRAFF *Lang.* 283 The name of God is avoided and gives way to such substitutes as

Jove,..gory, gummie. **1970** *Private Eye* 22 May 16 By gum, it must be visiting day up at hall.

gum (gʌm), *sb.*⁷ *Mining* (orig. *Sc.*). [Origin uncertain; perh. related to CULM¹, COOM *sb.*¹] Coal dust, fine coal; now esp. that produced by a coal-cutting machine.

1790–1925 in *Scottish Nat. Dict.* **1883** GRESLEY *Gloss. Coal-M.* 125 *Gum*, free-burning small slack or duff. **1938** *Colliery Engin.* Mar. 81/2 The amount of gum left in the bottom of the cut never exceeded ¾ in. in thickness. **1964** V. SHIFFER tr. *Shevyakov's Mining of Mineral Deposits* xi. 236 To prevent the formation of gum and dust, the combine is furnished with a spraying device.

b. *Comb.*, as ***gum-flinger, -loader, -thrower.***

1940 *Trans. Inst. Mining Engin.* May 53 Mechanical devices which trap the broken material brought out by the cutter-chain..have been given such names as jud cleaners, ..gummers, and gum loaders. **1956** E. MASON *Deputy's Man.* II. xxxiv. 501 The same machine can be equipped with a 'gum flinger'. **1960** SHEPHERD & WITHERS *Mech. Cutting & Loading of Coal* v. 75 'Gum-throwers'..take up the cuttings from the chain and eject them into the goaf.

So **'gummer³**, a man or a machine that clears away the fine coal and small bits of debris, etc., from under a coal-cutting machine.

1921 *Dict. Occup. Terms* (1927) §042 *Gummer*,..rakes small coal or stone by means of long-handled flat shovel.. out of groove cut by coal cutting machine, and loads into tubs or throws back into goaf. **1940** *Trans. Inst. Mining Engin.* May 54 Except in special cases, undercutting coal-cutters will be fitted with gummers as standard practice in the future. **1959** *New Scientist* 23 July 102/3 Beneath the cutting head is a 'gummer'—a paddle-bladed scraper which removes all the small coal from under the machine. **1959** G. D. MITCHELL *Sociol.* III. viii. 136 Four gummers, who clean out the undercut.

gum (gʌm), *v.*¹ Forms: 5 gomme, 5, 7 gumme, 7– gum. [f. GUM *sb.*²]

†**1.** *trans.* To treat with aromatic gums, as in flavouring wine or embalming a corpse. *Obs.*

1419 *Proclam.* in Riley *Lond. Mem.* (1868) 672 William Horold, Couper..gummyd and rasyd two buttes with diuers gummes. **1470–85** MALORY *Arthur* v. viii, Noble men whome the kynge dyd do bawme and gomme with many good gommes aromatyk.

2. To stiffen with gum; to coat or smear with or as with gum.

1610 B. JONSON *Alch.* I. i, Ile gumme your silkes With good strong water, an' you come. **1638** SIR T. HERBERT *Trav.* (ed. 2) 239 They register..his acts..in Cædar Tablets, gum'd with Cynabre. **1683** BURNET tr. *More's Utopia* (1684) 75 They use also in their Windows, a thin linnen Cloth, that is..oiled or gummed. **1896** *Indianapolis Typogr. Jrnl.* 16 Nov. 392 A new method of gumming paper.

3. To fasten, or fix in position with gum or some sticky substance. Also with *down, together, up*.

1592 KYD *Sp. Trag.* (1602) I 3 Thy eies are gum'd with teares, thy cheekes are wan. **1636** B. JONSON *Discov., De mollibus et effœminatis* (1641) 110 Bleaching their hands at Mid-night, gumming, and bridling their beards. **1655** GURNALL *Chr. in Arm.* x. 209/2 The doubting Christians eye of faith, is..gumm'd up with unbelieving fears. **1656** *Artif. Handsom.* 176 Scandalised at Ladies powdering, curling, and gumming their haire. **1776–96** WITHERING *Brit. Plants* (ed. 3) III. 775 When dried and gummed on paper, they [leafits] form an acute angle with the stalk. **1874** G. LAWSON *Dis. Eye* 145 If the lids become gummed together. **1876** F. E. TROLLOPE *Charming Fellow* I. iv. 46 Little rings of hair gummed down all over her forehead. **1880** *Standard* 15 Dec., Shilling deposits can be made by means of penny stamps gummed on forms.

4. *intr.* Of a fruit tree: To exude gum as a morbid secretion. Cf. GUM *sb.*² 7.

1794 *Trans. Soc. Arts* XII. 207 Several of the cherries [trees] were much gummed. **1802** *Ibid.* XX. 173 To prevent the cherry tree from gumming. **1837** *Penny Cycl.* VII. 41/1 When planted in stiff and wet soils it [the cherry] grows slowly, gums very much, and falls into a state of incurable bad health.

5. ? *U.S.* **a.** To become gummous. **b.** 'To become clogged or stiffened by some gummy substance, as inspissated oil; as, a machine will gum up from disuse' (*Cent. Dict.*). Also with *up*.

1874 RAYMOND *6th Rep. Mines* 509 The oil solidifies or gums, and clogs the holes. **1929** *Motor World* 24 May 328/2 The valves of car engines have always exhibited a tendency to 'gum-up' under certain conditions. **1931** *Carnegie Scholarship Mem.* XX. 96 The most unsatisfactory material in this respect was copper, which drew rather badly with all the lubricants tried, and seemed to 'gum up' in the die very readily.

c. *trans. fig.* To interfere with the smooth running of (something); to spoil, wreck. Chiefly with *up*. Freq. in phr. ***to gum the game, to gum (up) the works.*** orig. *U.S.*

1901 *Yale Fun* 27 (Weingarten), The plot that was gummed. **1911** L. J. VANCE *Cynthia* 174 You've just about gummed things up good and plenty, that's what you've done. **1915** *Dial. Notes* IV. 222 *Gum the game*, delay the game. 'Jack's tactics were to gum the game.' **1920** WODEHOUSE *Coming of Bill* I. v. 60 It sure would get my goat ..to have the old man gum the game for them. **1932** —— *Hot Water* xi. 181 When it comes to you horning into this joint and aiming to gum the works for me..well, that's something else again. **1932** KIPLING *Limits & Renewals* 281 The main point, as I read it, is that it makes one—not so much think—Research is gummed up with thinking—as imagine a bit. **1936** J. DOS PASSOS *Big Money* 263, I hope it wasn't me gummed the game. **1938** G. HEYER *Blunt Instrument* ix. 174 Helen's getting mixed up in it gummed up the works. **1948** 'M. WESTMACOTT' *Rose & Yew Tree* xxii. 183 She hasn't gummed up the works after all. What a relief that will be to her. **1964** *Listener* 8 Oct. 548/2 Their Land Commission—far from providing more and cheaper houses, would..gum up house-building.

6. *trans.* To cheat, delude, humbug. *U.S. slang.* [Said to originate from the opossum's eluding the huntsman in the foliage of a gum-tree.]

1840 *Frankfort* (Ky.) *Commonwealth* 20 Oct., You are always right as a book and nobody can gum you. In short, you are O.K. **1848** LOWELL *Biglow P.* Poems 1890 II. 144 You can't gum me, I tell ye now, an' so you need n't try. **1859** SALA *Tw. round Clock* (1861) 232, I began to think..he was quizzing me—'gumming' is the proper Transatlantic colloquialism. **1875** *Chamb. Jrnl.* 25 Sept. 611/1 Now don't you try to gum me.

gum (gʌm), *v.*² *U.S.* [f. GUM *sb.*¹] *trans.* To deepen and enlarge the spaces between the teeth of (a worn saw). See GUMMER¹.

1777 W. DUNBAR in E. O. Rowland *Life W. Dunbar* (1930) 41 Begun to gum one of our old saws, having unfortunately broke one of the new ones by the fall of a Log. **1859** BARTLETT *Dict. Amer., To Gum a Saw*, to punch out and give the set to the teeth of a saw, by means of a machine called a *gummer*. The phrase alludes to the growth of the teeth from the gums. **1887** *Sci. Amer.* 26 Feb. 130 The operation of gumming saws with an emery wheel.

gum, variant of GOME¹ *Obs.*

gumashins, var. *gamashins*: see GAMASH.

1830 GALT *Lawrie T.* I. ii, A decent..carlin, that could turn coats and shape gumashins.

gumb, obs. form of GUM *sb.*¹ and *sb.*²

gumba, gumbay, obs. forms of GOOMBAY.

Gumban ('gʌmbən), *a.* [f. Kikuyu *Gumba*, name of a race of diminutive people believed to have been former inhabitants of Kikuyu country.] Of or pertaining to a late Stone Age culture of East Africa. Also *absol.*

1931 L. S. B. LEAKEY *Stone Age Cultures Kenya Colony* xi. 243 In attempting to discuss the relation of the Gumban to cultures in other parts of the world..it should be noted here that the name of this culture has been derived from a Kikuyu term which is applied to-day primarily to a semi-mythical race of small people... In using the word for this culture, I am not referring to this, its primary meaning, but to its present more usual meaning, that is in reference to any people who preceded the Kikuyu. From the moment that I first started excavations, old Kikuyus who visited the camp used to talk of my 'search for the Gumba', and when thinking of a name for this comparatively recent culture the word Gumban seemed to be not inappropriate. **1931** *Times Lit. Suppl.* 20 Aug. 627/2 Coming to the Kenya cultures after the Aurignacian, Mr. Leakey believes that in one of the latest, the Gumban, we may have evidence 'of the contact of a late Stone Age people with one of the early civilizations of the world'. **1957** G. CLARK *Archaeol. & Society* (ed. 3) v. 166 Faience beads..were found with a burial at Nakuru in Kenya associated with the so-called Gumban A culture of sub-Neolithic type. **1959** *Chambers's Encycl.* I. 143/2 The best known of the East African neolithic cultures are the Gumban and Njoroan of Kenya described by Leakey. The Gumban is characterized by stone bowls, pestles and mortars, saddle querns and pottery with rolled-cord decoration and lugs.

gümbelite ('gʏmbəlaɪt). *Min.* [ad. G. *gümbelit* (F. von Kobell 1870, in *Sitzungsber. d. königl. bayer. Akad. d. Wissensch.* I. 294), f. the name of C. W. von *Gümbel* (1823–1898), German geologist: see -ITE¹.] A magnesium-containing variety of hydromuscovite.

1871 *Jrnl. Chem. Soc.* XXIV. 325 (*heading*) Gümbelite, a new mineral. **1962** W. A. DEER et al. *Rock-forming Minerals* III. 15 A fibrous magnesium-bearing hydromuscovite called gümbelite was investigated by Aruja (1944). Its formula is approximately (K, $H_2O)_2(Al_3Mg)$ $Si_6Al_2O_{18}(OH)_6$ and it crystallizes in the ZM_1 polymorph.

†**gumble.** *Obs. rare*⁻¹. A cheek-bone.

1688 R. HOLME *Armoury* II. 153/1 Bones in a Horse.. Inferiour Gumbles or Cheek-bones 2.

†**gumble-stool.** *Obs.* [Origin doubtful: cf. prec. with GUM *sb.*¹ 3.] A cucking-stool. Also †**gum-stool** (perh. from GUM *sb.*¹ 3).

1623 in Noake *Worc. in Olden Time* (1849) 110 For carrying of several women upon the gum stoole. **1653** BAXTER *Worc. Petit.* 35 That silly women shall be dipt over head in a Gumble-stool for scolding. **1655** —— *Quaker Catech.* 25, I desire of you that you will not put me by with Gumble-stool Rhetorick in stead of Answers.

gumbo ('gʌmbəʊ). *U.S.* Also gombo. [Negro patois; 'from the Angolan *kingombo*, the *ki-* being the usual Bantu prefix, and *-ngombo* the real word' (J. Platt, jun., in *Athenæum*, Sep. 1, 1900); Marcgraf 1648 writes *quingombo*.]

1. a. A colloquial name for the okra plant or its pods (*Hibiscus esculentus*). Also *attrib.* **b.** A soup thickened with the mucilaginous pods of this plant. Also ***gumbo soup.***

1805 J. F. WATSON in *Amer. Pioneer* (1843) II. 233 Shrimps are much eaten here; also a dish called *gumbo*. This last is made of every eatable substance, and especially of those shrimps which can be caught at any time. **1813** *Cramer's Alman. 1814* (Pittsburgh) 55 Beyond our usual dinner [we had]..gumbo soup. **1845** *Bangor* (Maine) *Mercury*, At St. Peter's [Ill.] there is a large commerce carried on between the whites and redskins, for heads and whiskey, in exchange for skins and gumbo. **1859** BARTLETT *Dict. Amer., Gombo*, or *Gumbo*, 1. the Southern name for what is called at the North, Okra, the pod of the *Hibiscus esculentus*. 2. In the southern States, a soup in which this plant enters largely as an ingredient. **1864** SALA in *Daily Tel.* 13 Oct., The three gentlemen..eating gombo soup. **1880** N. H. BISHOP *4 Mths. Sneak-Box* 205 The mild-eyed Louisiana Indian woman with her sack of gumbo spread out before her. **1883** *Harper's Mag.* Aug. 463/2, I should like mutton broth and gumbo every day. **1884** *Health Exhib. Catal.* 158/2 Gombo Fruits. **1893** LELAND *Mem.* I. 57 Terrapins and soft-shell crabs, gumbo,..peaches, venison. **1957** H. CROOME *Forgotten Place* 95 [An] affable American brigadier who told her that the hot and tasty stuff they were eating was gumbo. **1970** *New Yorker* 10 Jan. 62/1 (Advt.), You'll want to try—Crawfish Gumbo—a kind of spicy bouillabaisse.

2. a. *Geol.* 'The stratified portion of the lower till of the Mississippi valley' (Funk's *Stand. Dict.*). **b.** *colloq. Western U.S.* The mud of the prairies. Also ***gumbo mud.***

1881 *Chicago Times* 16 Apr., Such a thing as hard-pan, bed rock near the surface or gumbo is not found here [i.e. in Nebraska]. **1891** C. ROBERTS *Adrift Amer.* 27 The soil here is largely mixed with a kind of blue clay, locally known as 'gumbo'. **1894** *Century Mag.* Jan. 453/1 Gumbo is..the clay of Northern Wyoming. When wet, it is the blackest, stickiest..mud that exists on earth. **1897** *Outing* (U.S.) XXIX. 491/2 Only when in gumbo mud did we find our wheels to be a hindrance.

3. A patois spoken by Blacks and Creoles in the French West Indies, Louisiana, Bourbon, and Mauritius. Also *attrib.* [? A different word.]

1838 E. FLAGG *Far West* II. 36 A spirited colloquy ensued in the patois of these old hamlets—a species of gumbo-French. **1882** SALA *Amer. Revis.* (1883) II. v. 65 The coloured people [in New Orleans] who gabble a wondrous salmagundi of a patois, made up of French, Spanish, and indigenous African, which is known as 'Gumbo'. *Ibid.* vi. 74 Were the verb 'boumer' as an equivalent for to 'boom', admitted into the vocabulary of 'Gumbo' French. **1891** E. WAKEFIELD *Wisdom of Gumbo* in *19th Cent.* XXX. 575 Gombo is a mere phonetic burlesque of French, interlarded with African words.

gumboil ('gʌmbɔɪl). Also gumbile. [f. GUM *sb.*¹ + BOIL *sb.*¹] An inflammatory swelling or small abscess on the gum.

1753 N. TORRIANO *Gangr. Sore Throat* 63 Abscesses in the Mouth and Gums (called Gum-boils). **1828** LOWELL *Lett.* (1894) I. 6, I have got the ague together with a gum-bile. **1866** LIVINGSTONE *Last Jrnls.* (1873) I. i. 3 The Sultan had toothache, and a gumboil.

gumbo-limbo ('gʌmbəʊ'lɪmbəʊ). [f. GUMBO + second element of unknown origin.] A gum-yielding timber tree, *Bursera simaruba*, found in Florida, Central America, and the West Indies.

1837 J. L. WILLIAMS *Terr. of Florida* 98 Gum Elemi.—Called by the inhabitants, Gumbo-limbo, is a large spreading tree, with a smooth brown bark. **1890** H. M. FIELD *Bright Skies* v. 70 Perhaps some old savage..has been punished for his cruelty by being turned into that gumbo-limbo tree. **1908** N. L. BRITTON *N. Amer. Trees* 584 Gumbo Limbo, known also as Bitter-wood, Paradise tree, and on the Bahama islands as Ash, inhabits southern Florida, the Bahamas and Jamaica. **1924** J. A. THOMSON *Science Old & New* v. 27 The gumbolimbo, which exudes fragrant balsam when it is wounded. **1964** GLEASON & CRONQUIST *Nat. Geogr. Plants* xxii. 340 (*caption*) Gumbo limbo in a hammock on Big Pine Key, Florida.

gumboodge, -bouge, obs. forms of GAMBOGE.

gumbotil ('gʌmbəʊtɪl). *Geol.* [f. GUMBO + TIL(L *sb.*²] A leached grey clay, very sticky when wet and very hard when dry, found extensively in Iowa and neighbouring states.

1916 G. F. KAY in *Science* 3 Nov. 638/1 It is now proposed that the somewhat indefinite term 'gumbo' be no longer used for these super-drift clays, but that the name 'gumbotil' be used. **1957** J. K. CHARLESWORTH *Quaternary Era* II. xxxvii. 967 The gumbotils have often been regarded as loesses.

gumby, var. GOOMBAY.

gume, var. GOME¹ *Obs.*; obs. f. GUM *sb.*¹ and *sb.*²

gumfiate ('gʌmfieɪt), *v.* *nonce-wd.* [ad. It. *gonfiat-o*, pa. pple. of *gonfiare* = F. *gonfler*:—L. *conflāre*, f. *con-* together + *flāre* to blow.] *trans.* To puff up, cause to swell.

1820 GALT *Ayrshire Legatees* in *Blackw. Mag.* VIII. 18 The inflamed gout of polemical controversy..had gumfiated every mental joint and member of that zealous prop of the Relief Kirk.

gumfolly. ? Corrupt var. *cumphorie*, COMFREY.

1610 MARKHAM *Masterp.* I. lxxviii. 163 Seeth it in the iuyce of Gumfolly.

gum-gum ('gʌmgʌm). Also 8 gum-gumma, 8–9 gom-gom. [Presumably from some Malay dialect. Cf. GONG-GONG.] A hollow iron bowl, which is struck with an iron or wooden stick; a series of the same, varying in size and tone.

1700 S. L. tr. *Fryke's Voy. E. Ind.* 244 Their warlike Musick is an Instrument made of Mettle, called Gum-Gum, much in the Nature of our Drums. **1774** JOEL COLLIER [J. Bicknal] *Mus. Trav.* (1775) 56 Playing a warlike measure with his gom-gom. **1800** CHARLOTTE SMITH *Solit. Wanderer* (1801) I. 326 The conchs and gomgoms of the Maroons suddenly broke the silence of the night. **1836–9** DICKENS *Sk. Boz, Tales* vii. *Steam Excurs.*, 'What is a gum-gum?' eagerly enquired several young ladies.

gumlah ('gʌmlə). *India*. Also gumla. [Hind. *gamlā*.] An earthenware water-jar.

1834 H. Caunter *Oriental Ann.* ix. 114, I had seen her as she occasionally repaired to the river to replenish her gumlahs. **1837** T. Bacon *First Impr. Hindostan* II. xii. 415, I caught sight of the large *gumla* (earthern jar, containing about eighteen gallons) filled with water. **1892** H. D. Inglis *Tent Life* 285 Encasing his head in a great wide-mouthed *gumla*, or earthen pot.

gumless ('gʌmlɪs), *a.* [f. gum *sb.*[1] + -less.] Having no gums.

1790 J. Williams *Shrove Tuesday* (1794) 33 Ah! rattle not your gumless fangs at me, Thou King of terrors.

†**gumly** ('gʌmlɪ), *a. Sc. Obs.* [Cf. *gum(m)le* v., 'to render turbid' (Jam., with fig. quot. from Galt).] Muddy, turbid.

1786 Burns *Brigs Ayr* 126 Then down ye'll hurl.. And dash the gumlie jaups up to the pouring skies. **1804** Tarras *Poems* 71 Wae worth ye, webster Tam, what's this That I see gaupin gumlie?

gumm, obs. form of gum *sb.*[1] and *sb.*[2]

‖**gumma** ('gʌmə). *Path.* Pl. gummas, gummata. [mod.L. *gumma* (neut.), f. L. *gummi* gum *sb.*[2]] A tumour usually of syphilitic origin, so called from the gummy nature of its contents.

1722 Quincy *Lex. Physico-Med.* (ed. 2), *Gummata*. Strumous tumours are sometimes thus called from the Resemblance of their Contents to gummous Substances. **1861** Bumstead *Ven. Dis.* (1879) 610 In the central portion of the gumma the vessels are very small. **1873** T. H. Green *Introd. Pathol.* (ed. 2) 234 The gummata were formerly regarded as non-inflammatory neoplasms. **1897** *Allbutt's Syst. Med.* IV. 808 Gummas, before breaking down, are sometimes seen as smooth, red or yellowish defined swellings.

†**gummage** ('gʌmɪdʒ). *Obs.* [f. gum *sb.*[2] + -age.] Production of gum.

1610 W. Folkingham *Art of Survey* i. vi. 13 What Trees, Plants, Shrubs: what Fruitage, Mastage, Gummage.

gummate ('gʌmeɪt), *a. Chem.* [f. gumm-ic + -ate[4].] A salt of gummic acid.

1826 Henry *Elem. Chem.* II. 193 The supposition that the gummate of lead is composed of two atoms of oxide of lead and one of gum.

gummatous ('gʌmətəs), *a. Path.* [f. mod.L. *gummat-* gumma + -ous.] Of the nature of or resembling a gumma. ***gummatous tumour*** = gumma.

1684 tr. *Bonet's Merc. Compit.* x. 356 If there be gummatous Tumours.. Sarsa is proper. **1745** Amyand in *Phil. Trans.* XLIII. 296 She had a gummatous Swelling.. on the right Arm. **1861** Bumstead *Ven. Dis.* (1879) 594 Gummatous ulcers.. are always upon the upper surface of the tongue. **1897** *Allbutt's Syst. Med.* IV. 190 The development of gummatous tissue.

gummauve, var. guimauve.

gummb, obs. form of gum *sb.*[1]

gumme, obs. form of gum *sb.*[1], *sb.*[2], and *v.*[1]

gummed (gʌmd), *ppl. a.* [f. gum *sb.*[2] or *v.*[1] + -ed.] †**a.** Spread with aromatic gums. **b.** Stiffened with gum; coated or smeared with gum. Also *fig.* **c.** Of a pigment: Mixed with gum.

c **1450** *ME. Med. Bk.* (Heinrich) 172 A gommed clout [*v.rr.* gummit clowte, gomed cloth]. **1596** Shaks. *1 Hen. IV*, ii. ii. 2, I haue remoued Falstafs Horse, and he frets like a gum'd Veluet. **1632** Shirley *Ball* iv. i. Wks. 1833 III. 56 How now, gumm'd Taffeta? **1664** Evelyn *Diary* 22 June, Pictures of men and countries, rarely painted on a sort of gummed calico. **1713** *Gentl. Instructed* (ed. 5) 420 We hate the stiff and gumm'd Deportment of the Italian. **1799** G. Smith *Laboratory* II. 79 Mix a little gummed colour in a large shell. **1807** *Med. Jrnl.* XVII. 408 A small bandage of gummed silk, applied over the closed eye-lids. **1864** Lowell *Fireside Trav.* 113 A badly-gummed postage-stamp. **1898** *Daily News* 23 Sept. 5/4 Could the stamp be applied unless over some gummed slips? **1937** E. J. Labarre *Dict. Paper* 154/2 Gummed paper, also termed adhesive (U.S.A.), is any kind of paper gummed on one or both sides. **1962** F. T. Day *Introd. to Paper* 116 *Gummed tape*, Kraft paper in brown or colours, glued and dried.

gummed (gʌmd), *a.*[2] [f. gum *sb.*[1] + -ed[2].] Provided with gums (of a certain kind).

a **1529** Skelton *E. Rummyng* 40 A man would haue pytty To se how she is gumbed, Fyngered and thumbed. **1806** *Sporting Mag.* XXVII. 140 Be sure they [cocks] are sound that they be hard gummed.

gummer[1] ('gʌmə(r)). *U.S.* [f. gum *v.*[2] + -er[1].] **a.** A workman who enlarges the spaces between the teeth of a saw. **b.** A machine for this purpose.

1859 [see gum *v.*[2]]. **1887** *Sci. Amer.* 26 Feb. 130 Emery vulcanite saw gummer.

gummer[2] ('gʌmə(r)). [f. gum *v.*[1] + -er[1].] One who gums (in various technical uses).

1881 *Instr. Census Clerks* (1885) 82 Envelope Maker:.. Gummer, Cementer. **1902** *Daily Chron.* 24 July 9/4 Pattern-Card Mounters, Cutters and Gummers wanted. **1905** *Ibid.* 11 Aug. 10/6 Envelope Hand Gummers, also fountain gummers. **1921** *Dict. Occup. Terms* (1927) §549 *Gummer* (bookbinder's); applies gum to back of books,.. also gums edge of illustration pages, etc. for insertion in books. **1960** M. Spark *Ballad of Peckham Rye* i. 11 Raymond Lowther, packer, Lucille Potter, gummer.

gummer[3]: see gum *sb.*[7]

gummic ('gʌmɪk), *a. Chem.* [f. L. *gumm-i* gum *sb.*[2] + -ic.] ***gummic acid***: an acid obtained from gum = *Arabic acid* (see Arabic *a.* 2).

1838 T. Thomson *Chem. Org. Bodies* 157 Gummic acid was discovered by M. Simonin about the year 1830. **1880** *Encycl. Brit.* XI. 275/2 Gummic acid.

Gummidge ('gʌmɪdʒ). The name of a peevish, self-pitying, and pessimistic widow in Dickens's novel 'David Copperfield' (1850), used to describe a person of such a nature, or their complaints. Also *attrib.* Hence '**gummidge** *v. intr.*; '**gummidging** *ppl. a.*; '**gummagy**, '**Gummidgey** *adjs.*

1873 A. Helps *Animals & their Masters* viii. 191 There is a great deal of what I call 'Gummidge' talked in the world, and very unreasonable talk it is. **1889** A. Lang in *Longman's Mag.* May 111 One might do very well in the Transvaal if one did not 'gummidge'. **1889** Barrère & Leland *Dict. Slang* I. 437 To be *gummagy*, to be of a snarling, scolding disposition. **1895** *Westm. Gaz.* 14 Jan. 7/1 What good is there in merely Gummidgeing on like this? **1916** *Daily Colonist* (Victoria, B.C.) 20 July 9/7 (*heading*) A Nation of Gummidges. **1918** *Best Short Stories 1917* 209 At twenty-seven Jo had been the dutiful, hard-working son.. of a widowed and gummidging mother. **1927** *Sunday Express* 1 May 12/3 The Gummidge chorus is never silent. **1928** D. H. Lawrence *Let.* 9 Mar. (1962) II. 1042 It's true I've felt rather Gummidgey and 'low' and disheartened these last two years.

gummiferous (gʌ'mɪfərəs), *a.* [f. L. *gummi* gum *sb.*[2] + -ferous.] Producing gum.

1683-4 Robinson in *Phil. Trans.* XXIX. 475 Balsamiferous, Gummiferous, and Saccharine Plants.

gumminess ('gʌmɪnɪs). [f. gummy *a.*[1] and *a.*[2] + -ness.] The quality or condition of being gummy, in various senses. Also quasi-*concr.*, something gummy, a gummy concretion.

1600 Surflet *Country Farm* i. xii. 59 To take away the filthines or gummines of the eies. **1665** R. Kephale *Medela Pestil.* 61 Their gumminess excludeth infectious air. **1676** Wiseman *Surg.* viii. iv. 33 One.. came to me.. with a gumminess on the tendons reaching to his fingers. **1726** Leoni *Alberti's Archit.* I. 31/1 Ancient Aqueducts, whose Mouths, having contracted a kind of Gumminess, have seem'd incrusted all over with Stone. **1761** Sterne *Tr. Shandy* III. iv, Had there been the least gumminess in my lining, by Heaven! it had all of it, long ago, been frayed and fretted to a thread. **1801** W. Heberden *Comm.* lvi. (1806) 326 Accompanied with wateriness, or gumminess, where the tears are not supplied faster. **1825** J. Nicholson *Operat. Mechanic* 394 The thread should have lost part of its heat and gumminess before it touches the bars of the reel.

gumming ('gʌmɪŋ), *vbl. sb.*[1] [f. gum *v.*[1] + -ing[1].] The action of gum *v.*[1] in various senses.

1. The action †of treating with aromatic gums (*obs.*); the action of fastening or smearing with gum; *spec.* the action of applying gum-water to a lithographic stone.

1419 *Proclam.* in Riley *Lond. Mem.* (1868) 672 To have a lykly manere taste and smell to the drynkyng of Romeney, thurgh þe gummyng and rasyng aboue seyd. **1580** Hollyband *Treas. Fr. Tong*, *Gommement*, a gumming. **1687** A. Lovell tr. *Thevenot's Trav.* i. 137 The Face.. will not admit of Gumming so well as the other parts of the Body. **1688** R. Holme *Armoury* iii. 97/1 Gumming.. is to rub the in-side of the Bed-Tick with.. Gum.., to keep Feathers from coming through it.

2. a. The process (in fruit trees) of giving out a morbid exudation of gum; (in the eyelids) of becoming fastened *together* with gum; (in oils) of acquiring a gum-like consistence.

1703 tr. *H. van Oosten's Dutch Gardener* v. xii. 284 The common Ailments that the Orange-Trees are subject to in these Countries, are, Gumming, growing Yellow,.. and Changing. **1859** R. Thompson *Gardener's Assist.* 535 The latter [suckers or layers] are comparatively weak, and apt to cause gumming. **1874** G. Lawson *Dis. Eye* 3 The tarsal edges of the lids should be anointed at night.. to prevent their gumming together. **1892** *Garden* 27 Aug. 180 Much wood [of cherry trees] being lost through gumming and canker. **1931** in *New Biol.* (1953) XV. 38 Malformations of nuts, such as occur in gumming.. were found to be physiological diseases.

b. The deposition of gum by petroleum products (see gum *sb.*[2] 1 j); the clogging of an engine as a result of this. Also ***gumming-up***.

1915 *Jrnl. Inst. Petroleum Technologists* I. 179 Any oil which was to be used satisfactorily in a motor-car must naturally have the terpene products removed, otherwise gumming took place, and the valves became clogged. **1927** *Daily Express* 15 July 9 The total absence of 'gumming-up' of piston rings. **1935** *Nature* 14 Sept. 413/1 Even the schoolboy and his sister talk glibly of anti-knock and gumming. **1942** A. W. Judge *Automobile Eng.* (ed. 4) vii. 307 Important claims in regard to non-oxidising, gumming and sludging tendencies have been made for such oils. **1961** G. Claxton *Benzoles* xiv. 705 The extensive use of cracked petrols for blending purposes.. has drawn attention to the important problem of the gumming of internal-combustion engines when run on fuels containing unsaturateds.

gumming ('gʌmɪŋ), *vbl. sb.*[2] *Mining.* [f. gum *sb.*[7] + -ing[1].] **a.** The clearing away of the fine coal and debris from the groove or undercut made by a coal-cutting machine. Also *attrib.*

1934 Webster, Gumming spade. **1938** *Colliery Engin.* Mar. 81/1 The operation of 'gumming' or 'scuffling' out the kerf in the track of the coalcutter is at best a brutal and ineffective business. **1958** A. Nelson *Methods of Working* xiii. 156 Coal-cutters are now provided with efficient automatic gumming devices. **1960** J. Sinclair *Winning Coal* vi. 167 Gummers are provided as a substitute for a man with a gumming shovel.

b. *pl.* = gum *sb.*[7]

1938 *Colliery Engin.* Sept. 293/2 The gummings brought out by the cutter chain are received in this spiral and delivered on the goaf side of the machine. **1956** E. Mason *Deputy's Man.* I. xviii. 254 The smalls produced by the picks are termed kirvings, gummings or cuttings. **1958** A. Nelson *Methods of Working* xiii. 158 Various appliances have been designed to trap the gummings from the cutter-chain and in this way the dust clouds are considerably reduced. **1959** G. D. Mitchell *Sociol.* iii. viii. 136 The first shift is concerned with.. clearing out the 'gummings'.

gummite ('gʌmaɪt). *Min.* [Named by Dana in 1868, f. L. *gumm-i* gum *sb.*[2] + -ite.] A hydrate of uranium of reddish-yellow colour, and resembling gum.

1868 Dana *Min.* (ed. 5) 179 Gummite.. looking much like gum. **1892** —— *Min.* 893 Gummite is also abundant at the Flat-Rock mine.

gummose (gʌ'məʊs), *a.*[1] [ad. L. *gummōs-us*: see gummous and -ose.] = gummous.

1678 R. R[ussell] *Geber* iv. vi. 250 Grind clear and gummose Sulphurvive to a most subtile Powder. **1702** Sir J. Floyer in *Phil. Trans.* XXIII. 1171 The Leaves of Liquorish feel gummose. **1743** tr. *Heister's Surg.* 372 When the Eyelids are glued together by a gummose and inspissated Matter.

gummose (gʌ'məʊs), *a.*[2] *Path.* [f. gumma + -ose.] = gummatous.

1869 *New Syd. Soc. Bienn. Retrosp.* 346 Dr. Hippel describes a gummose tumour involving all the coats of the eye... A microscopic examination by Prof. Neumann, determined it to be a gummose syphilitic growth.

gummosis (gʌ'məʊsɪs). *Bot.* [mod.L., f. L. *gumm-i* gum *sb.*[2] + -osis.] The pathological production and exudation of gum by trees; *spec.* a disease of fruit trees marked by this process. (Cf. gumming *vbl. sb.* 2).

1882 *Gardeners' Chron.* 23 Sept. 396/2 The bacterial slime spreads, together with the sap-current, through the xylem, or woody part of the vascular bundles, and consequently infects the whole plant... The gum-disease (gummosis) of our stone-fruit trees might be explained in like manner. **1887** H. M. Ward tr. *Sachs's Lect. Physiol. Plants* xi. 180 Such gum-reservoirs are distinguished from the cases of proper Gummosis, where large groups of tissue in the older organs are changed into basorin and other kinds of gum. **1911** *Ann. Bot.* XXV. 108 Gummosis is a fairly common phenomenon in the vegetable kingdom. **1951** *Dict. Gardening* (R. Hort. Soc.) II. 936/2 In gummosis the tree is in ill health and even small shoots show the exudation of gum. **1970** W. H. Smith *Tree Path.* xiii. 129 Both canker types are characterized by exudation or gummosis (leakage of fairly viscous sap) during wet weather in the spring.

gummosity (gʌ'mɒsɪtɪ). [ad. L. **gummōsitāt-em*, f. *gummōs-us* gummous.] The quality of being gummous. †In *Alchemy*, a quality or condition of which metals were supposed to be capable.

1651 Biggs *New Disp.* ¶97 The gummosity of herbs. **1678** R. R[ussell] *Geber* iii. ii. iii. viii. 230 Among Bodies wanting the compleatment of Perfection, Jupiter [tin] most slowly flowreth its Gummosity. **1707** Floyer *Physic. Pulse-Watch* 265 The crudity and mucilaginous Gummosity [depends] on a deficient Pulse.

†**b.** *concr.* A gummy substance, deposit, concretion, etc. *Obs.*

c **1400** *Lanfranc's Cirurg.* 344 This gummosite þat is clepid.. olibanum. **1655** *Let.* in Hartlib *Ref. Commw. Bees* 39 Fewer [bees] can be kept, if they must seek their Wax out of the Gummosity of some floures. **1683** Salmon *Doron Med.* ii. v. 395/1 [It] mollifies and dissolves all hard knobs, & gummossities upon the joynts of the Fingers.

gummous ('gʌməs), *a.*[1] [ad. L. *gummōsus*, f. *gummi* gum *sb.*[2]: see -ous. Cf. F. *gommeux*.]

1. Of the nature of gum, gum-like.

1669 W. Simpson *Hydrol. Chym.* 185 Barthius.. concludes this gummous liquor to be the reguline parts of antimony. **1676** Boyle in *Phil. Trans.* XI. 802 Resinous or Gummous substance, that looked like high colour'd Amber. **1699** J. Woodward *ibid.* XXI. 209 Hence come our Mannas, our Honies, and other Gummous Exsudations of Vegetables. **1812** J. Smyth *Pract. of Customs* (1821) 152 Manna is a gummous substance, obtained by the incision of various sorts of trees. **1822-34** *Good's Study Med.* (ed. 4) IV. 346 To which we may add gummous blood, viscid mucous [etc.].

fig. **1767** Sterne *Tr. Shandy* IX. xiii, The thoughts rise heavily and pass gummous through my pen.

†**2.** Of a plant or tree: Abounding in or yielding gum; = gummy 2.

1693 J. Clayton *Acc. Virginia* in *Misc. Curios.* (1708) III. 306 If a Gummous Plant or Tree, that grows low,.. it abounds with acid Spirits.

Hence '**gummousness**.

1666 J. H. *Treat. Gt. Antidote* 4 Set it in an ash Furnace, with a gentle heat till the ingredients be fully dissolved, and the bitterness and gummousness be fully gone.

gummous ('gʌməs), *a.*[2] *Path.* [f. mod.L. GUMMA + -OUS.] = GUMMATOUS.

1588 J. READ *Compend. Method* 61 b, When ther are hard gummous tumors, as nodes or swellings, or pains or vlcers. **1861** BUMSTEAD *Ven. Dis.* (1879) 646 But sometimes gummatous infiltration supervenes, constituting a gummous meningitis. **1897** *Allbutt's Syst. Med.* II. 279 Ulcers, gummous tumours, and so on.

gummy ('gʌmɪ), *a.*[1] Forms: 6–7 gummie, (7 goomie, gommie), 4– gummy. [f. GUM *sb.*[2] + -Y[1].]

1. Of the nature of gum; gum-like, sticky, viscid.

1398 TREVISA *Barth. De P.R.* XVII. lxxviii. (1495) 651 The beste kynde of gutta..semyth yf it be broke shynynge wythin and gummy. *a* **1520** SKELTON *E. Rummyng* 25 Her lewde lyppes twayne They slauer, men sayne, Lyke a ropye rayne, A gummy glayre. **1575** TURBERV. *Faulconrie* 275 The gummie fatte of a fygge. **1601** HOLLAND *Pliny* I. 313 Of this gummie and glutinous substance they frame also their dores and entries which are wide and large. **1646** SIR T. BROWNE *Pseud. Ep.* II. i. 51 Gummy resinous bodies, Masticke, Camphire, and Storax. **1649** T. STANLEY *Europa*, etc. 29 Myrrha..darts The gummy Jewells of her weeping tree. **1677** PLOT *Oxfordsh.* 168 Especially if they have a more gummy juice. **1727** BRADLEY *Fam. Dict.* s.v. *Aloes*, Aloes.. fortifies the Stomach by its Gummy Substance. **1789** *Trans. Soc. Arts* (ed. 2) II. 116 A black gummy matter it contains. **1818** KEATS *Endym.* I. 229 And gummy frankincense was sparkling bright 'Neath smothering parsley. **1830** HERSCHEL *Stud. Nat. Phil.* III. i. (1851) 234 Those cases of near approach to the solid state which obtain in viscid or gummy liquids. **1890** SARA DUNCAN *Social Departure* 372 Their [mummies'] wide mouths stuffed with gummy drugs.

2. a. Abounding in gum. †***gummy thistle***: the gum-thistle (see GUM *sb.*[2] 9 b).

c **1420** *Pallad. on Husb.* XI. 222 This obseruance is to be kept, seith he, In chiritreen and alle that gummy be. **1589** FLEMING *Virg. Bucol.* VII. 27 Heere is a herth and gummy wood, heer's fire good store alwaies. **1598** FLORIO, *Euforbio*, Euphorbium, or gummie thistle. **1604** E. G[RIMSTONE] *D'Acosta's Hist. Indies* V. viii. 350 Then set they fire vnto it, increasing it still with goomie wood. **1667** MILTON *P.L.* X. 1076 The slant Lightning, whose thwart flame driv'n down Kindles the gummie bark of Firr or Pine. **1732** *Gentl. Mag.* II. 670 The gummy Pine. **1834** AIRD *Nebuchadnezzar* III. 32 Of gummy pine she bore a waving brand. **1869** ALDRICH *Story Bad Boy* 62 There are..ancient turtles wandering about that gummy woodland.

b. Of a process: Attended with the production of gum.

1884 BOWER & SCOTT *De Bary's Phaner.* 543 Starting-points of the gummy disorganisation.

3. Suffused with or exuding gum, or a gum-like substance. **a.** Of the eyes.

1580 HOLLYBAND *Treas. Fr. Tong*, *Erraillé*, which hath the eies gummie. **1693** DRYDEN *Persius* (1697) 437 The yawning Youth..Then rubs his gummy Eyes. **1720** SWIFT *Progr. Beauty* 15 Crack'd lips, foul teeth, and gummy eyes. **1759** *State Paper* in *Ann. Reg.* 252/1 His eyes..are gummy particularly his left eye.

b. Of the buds, etc. of plants and trees.

1776–96 WITHERING *Brit. Plants* (ed. 3) II. 21 Helmet of the blossom gummy. **1833** TENNYSON *Poems* 36, I came and lay Beneath those gummy chestnutbuds. **1870** HOOKER *Stud. Flora* 197 *Linosyris vulgaris*..involucre gummy.

†**c.** *transf.* Sticky, soiled, dirty. *Obs.*

1641 SIR W. MURE *Counterbuff* 274 Our inlightened King ..Through clear, not gommie spectacles shall see. **1720** GAY *Poems* (1745) II. 22 The wit..Whose gummy hat no scarlet plumes adorn.

d. Used as a derogatory epithet of varying application.

1907 [see BACK- A. 3]. **1909** J. R. WARE *Passing Eng.* 148/2 *Gummy composer*, old and insipid. **1928** S. VINES *Humours Unreconciled* xi. 143 'Oh, for the wings——' Mendelssohn is pretty gummy; how'd that do? **1936** E. M. FORSTER *Abinger Harvest* 139 He [*sc.* T. E. Lawrence] called the style gummy.

4. Said esp. of the ankles and legs: As if charged with lumps of gum; puffy, swollen.

1737 BRACKEN *Farriery Impr.* (1757) II. 40 The great Sinew behind should be large and a good way from the Bone ..otherwise he is what we call gummy in this particular Part. **1784** J. BARRY in *Lect. Paint.* iii. (1848) 148 The legs not only want beauty, but are even gummy and ill-formed. **1797–1802** G. COLMAN *Br. Grins, Low Ambition* xx, Blear-eyed, baker-kneed, and gummy. **1819** *Blackw. Mag.* V. 539 No man with short, chubby, flat-soled feet, and gummy ancles, is naturally inclined to run for a wager. **1824** W. IRVING *T. Trav.* II. 21 He had grown thickset and rather gummy. **1870** MISS BRIDGMAN *Ro. Lynne* II. viii. 164 *My* ankles ain't 'gummy'.

5. *Comb.*, as ***gummy-eyed***, ***-legged***, ***-like*** adjs.

1737 BRACKEN *Farriery Impr.* (1757) II. 172 There are some gummy-leg'd Horse very apt to the Grease and Scratches. **1849** D. CAMPBELL *Inorg. Chem.* 272 The acid thrown down by ammonia, ignited, is in gummy-like masses. **1911** R. BROOKE *Poems* 33 Oft she weeps, gummy-eyed and impotent. **1960** C. DAY LEWIS *Buried Day* viii. 162 Stumbling out of the cinema, gummy-eyed from an afternoon's session with Greta Garbo.

gummy ('gʌmɪ), *a.*[2] *Path.* [f. GUMMA + -Y.] = GUMMATOUS.

1861 BUMSTEAD *Ven. Dis.* (1879) 622 Gummy tumors of the larynx are much more common than has been supposed. **1873** T. H. GREEN *Introd. Pathol.* 234 Gummy growths frequently originate in the fibrous septa.

gummy ('gʌmɪ), *a.*[3] [f. GUM *sb.*[1] + -Y[1].] Toothless. Hence **'gummily** *adv.*

1906 E. DYSON *Fact'ry 'Ands* iii. 29 Sarah was a large.. woman..with..a gummy smile. **1947** 'A. P. GASKELL' *Big Game* 94 An old crone came out..smiling gummily. **1970** *Daily Tel.* 15 July 14 So great is the demand for false teeth among our gummy tots that in many cases they may have to wait for a year or so before being fitted up.

gummy ('gʌmɪ), *sb.*[1] [f. GUM *sb.*[1] + -Y[6].]

1. The Australian name for *Mustelus antarcticus*, a small shark found in the Pacific Ocean. In full ***gummy shark***.

1893 *Funk's Stand. Dict.*, Gummy, a galeoid shark. **1898** MORRIS *Austral. Eng.* 185/2 *Gummy*, name given to a shark of Victorian and Tasmanian waters, *Mustelus antarcticus* Günth., and called *Hound*..in New South Wales, Victoria and New Zealand. The word *Gummy* is said to come from the small numerous teeth, arranged like a pavement, so different from the sharp erect teeth of most other sharks. **1933** *Bulletin* (Sydney) 31 May 17/1 All sharks are said to be excellent eating, but the usual variety retailed as snapper or Murray cod are the small crustacean-eaters known as 'gummies' in the trade. **1963** D. G. STEAD *Sharks & Rays Austral. Seas* x. 108 The name of Gummy is applied to it because of the rhombic, pavement-like teeth, which, at a passing glance into the fish's mouth, give the impression of toothless gums. **1965** G. MCINNES *Road to Gundagai* iii. 47 All we caught was a gummy shark.

2. A sheep that has lost, or is losing, its teeth. *Austral.* and *N.Z.*

1910 H. JACKSON in *Golden Fleece* 92, I have seen scores of ewes, not 'gummies' either, cutting fleeces of pocket handkerchief dimensions. **1933** L. ACLAND in *Press* (Christchurch, N.Z.) 21 Oct. 15/7 *Gummy*, an old sheep that has lost its teeth. **1933** *Bulletin* (Sydney) 6 Sept. 24/1 One young breeding ewe is worth three old 'gummies'. **1965** J. S. GUNN *Terminol. Shearing Indust.* i. 27 When the sheep's teeth are beginning to decline it is called a 'faulty mouth' or 'failing mouth'. This is the stage before 'broken mouth', after which it becomes a 'gummy'.

gummy ('gʌmɪ), *sb.*[2] *N.Z. colloq.* [f. GUM *sb.*[2] 1 h + -Y[6].] A gum-digger.

1906 *Macm. Mag.* Apr. 476 We soon were giving those gummies a hand to get some tucker ready.

gump (gʌmp), *sb.*[1] *dial.* and *U.S.* Also **gumph**. A foolish person, a dolt.

1825 JAMIESON Suppl., *Gump*, a numscull; a term most generally applied to a female, conveying the idea of great stupidity. **1825** J. NEAL *Bro. Jonathan* II. xv. 42 He's..sort of a naiteral too, I guess; rather a gump, hey? **1848** LOWELL *Biglow P.* Poems 1890 II. 47 An' it makes a handy sum, tu, Any gump could larn by heart. **1866–1930** in *Sc. Nat. Dict.* **1883** F. R. STOCKTON *Rudder Grange* vii. 97 'Get down, gump', said Pomona, and down she scrambled. **1888** *Advance* (Chicago) 21 June 387 Molly,..has that great gump been making love to you? **1920** R. MACAULAY *Potterism* VI. i. 209, I never know whether to believe Clare; she's such a gumph. **1945** 'A. GILBERT' *Don't open Door* xv. 124 She might do her best to attract attention—any girl who wasn't a complete gumph would.

gump (gʌmp), *sb.*[2] *U.S. slang.* [Perh. the same word as *sb.*[1]] A chicken.

1914 JACKSON & HELLYER *Vocab. Crim. Slang* 39 *Gump*,.. a chicken; a fowl. **1926** J. BLACK *You can't Win* vi. 64 'I've got a gump in my bindle.'..He unrolled his blankets and produced a live chicken, big and fat. **1931** 'D. STIFF' *Milk & Honey Route* 193 While 'Slippery Slim' and 'Bashful Tim' Croaked gumps for our menu. **1934** *Amer. Ballads & Folk Songs* (1960) i. 24 Not even a shack to beg for a lump, Or a hen-house to frisk for a single gump. **1960** WENTWORTH & FLEXNER *Dict. Amer. Slang* 234/2 *Gump*, a chicken; esp. a live chicken that can be stolen to provide a meal... Because chickens are considered among the most foolish of creatures.

gump (gʌmp), *sb.*[3] Also **gumph**. Abbrev. of GUMPTION 1.

1920 *Chambers's Jrnl.* 13 Mar. 233/1 If they weren't so sure of getting me, they would have had the gump to wait a few days till the court adjourns. **1946** 'S. RUSSELL' *To Bed with Grand Music* iii. 44 Any impertinent stranger who had the gumph to ask her out. **1968** K. BIRD *Smash a Glass Image* i. 10 A phoney who hasn't the gump to feed and exercise properly.

gump (gʌmp), *v. Sc.* and *north.* Also **gumph**. **a.** *intr.* To grope with the hands, *esp.* to grope after fish. **b.** *trans.* To catch (fish) by groping. Also with *out*. Hence **'gumping** *vbl. sb.*

1811 A. SCOTT *Poems* 113 (Jam.) When I to ope the seal had gumpit, For vera joy the board I thumpit. **1818** HOGG *Brownie Bodsbeck*, etc. II. 168 Give me a specimen how you gump the fish?.. If ye'll gang wi' me..I'll let ye see gumping to perfection. *Ibid.* 170 Gumphing [see GUDDLING *vbl. sb.*]. **1870** W. BROCKIE in W. S. Crockett *Minstrelsy of Merse* (1893) 169 Ye never gumpt in a burn for trout. **1881** J. YOUNGER *Autobiog.* xiii, There I gumped out half a stone of speckled trouts.

gumpheon ('gʌmfiən). *Sc.* Also 9 **gumphion**. [Corruption of GONFALON or GONFANON.] A funeral banner.

a **1725** A. NISBET *Heraldry* (1742) II. IV. xiv. 151 Next followed the little gumpheon carried upright. *Ibid.*, Then the great gumpheon or mort-head charged as afore-said. **1815** SCOTT *Guy M.* xxxvii, Gumphions of tarnished white crape.

'gumple-,foisted, *a. Sc.* Sulky, out of temper.

(Cf. Sc. *gumple-face* 'downcast countenance', *gumple-faced* 'chap-fallen': see *Eng. Dial. Dict.*)

1824 SCOTT *Redgauntlet* ch. vii, Ye are gumple-foisted wi' me.

gumption ('gʌm(p)ʃən). *colloq.* Also **gumshion**. [Orig. Sc.; cf. *rum-*, *rumble-gumption*.]

1. Common sense, mother wit, shrewdness. Also, initiative, enterprise, 'drive'.

1719 RAMSAY *Fam. Epist.* ii. 52 'Tis sma presumption To say they're but unlearned clarks, And want the gumption. **1785** in GROSE *Dict. Vulg. Tongue*. **1786** ANDREWS in *Europ. Mag.* IX. 210 Why this here fellow here, who writes that there, Has no more gumption than my founder'd mare. *c* **1812** SIR C. NAPIER in W. N. Bruce *Life* ii. (1885) 76 It is ..rapid movement that gives cavalry value, the application of which requires gumption in the commander. **1817** LAMB *Lett.* (1888) II. 2 There'd be many a damn let Fly At my presumption, If I should try, Being a fellow of no gumption. **1819** J. LAWRENCE in *Monthly Mag.* XLVII. 312 A dangerous farrago of holy gumshion. **1825** J. T. BROCKETT *Gloss. N. Country Words* 87 *Gumshon, gumption*, common sense, combined with energy. **1832** LYTTON *Eugene A.* I. ix, One does not have gumption till one has been properly cheated. **1844** J. SLICK *High Life N.Y.* II. 134 Sez she, 'Jonathan, what *du* you mean?' My heart riz, it was the only sign of gumption she had made for a hull day. **1862** C. F. BROWNE *A. Ward his Book* 213, I like..your enterprise, gumpshun, [etc.]. **1889** 'ROLF BOLDREWOOD' *Robbery under Arms* xvii, If they..show pluck and gumption they..get promoted. **1903** M. E. FREEMAN *Six Trees* 193 Ain't you got any gumption, no snap at all? **1941** J. STREET *In my Father's House* ix. 170 Me and Papa and Mama kissed Teenie and then she just stood there looking at Woodie. Papa said, 'Buss her one, boy. Ain't you got no gumption?'

2. *Painting.* **a.** (See quot. 1825.) ? *Obs.* **b.** A vehicle for colour.

1813 SCOTT *Triermain* ii. 2 Interlude, This thicket, for their gumption fit, May furnish such a happy bit. **1825** JAMIESON *Suppl.* s.v. *Gumption*, In a note on this article, Sir W. Scott remarks, that 'painters call the art of preparing colours their gumption'.

b. 1854 FAIRHOLT *Dict. Art*, *Gumption*, this elegant and expressive name is applied to a nostrum much in request by painters in search of the supposed 'lost medium' of the old masters..The formula for preparing this medium gives a mixture of drying linseed oil and mastic varnish, which gelatinises; or simple linseed oil and sugar of lead. **1859** GULLICK & TIMBS *Paint.* 205 They [various vehicles] are called 'Meguilps' from their inventor; one variety receives the name of 'Gumtion'.

Hence **'gumptionless** *a.*, without gumption, senseless.

1823 GALT *Entail* xxii. 78 Come awa, ye gumshionless cuif. **1861** R. QUIN *Heather Lintie* (1866) 147 Gumptionless whinings.

gumptious ('gʌm(p)ʃəs), *a.* [f. GUMPTION: see -OUS.] Possessed of gumption, or common sense. Also, clever, vain, self-important [by association with BUMPTIOUS].

[**1823** E. MOOR *Suffolk Words* 158 *Gumshus*, quarrelsome, offensive, obstinate.] **1853** LYTTON *My Novel* I. IV. xii. 320 When I say that sum un is gumptious, I mean..sum un who does not think small beer of hisself. **1860** F. & J. GREENWOOD *Under Cloud* I. iii. 68 You are a gumptious old ooman, you are! Tarrible smaart! **1875** W. D. PARISH *Dict. Sussex Dial.* (1957) 52 *Gumptious*, smart. **1877** BARTLETT *Dict. Americanisms* 271 *Gumptious*, one who has a good opinion of himself; a 'knowing one'.

gumpus ('gʌmpəs). *Sc.* = GUMP *sb.*[1]

1825 LOCKHART in *Scott's Fam. Lett.* (1894) II. 297 Put that [portmanteau] in your mouth, you gumpus. **1825–80** in JAMIESON.

'gum-rash = RED-GUM.

1822–34 *Good's Study Med.* (ed. 4) IV. 422 *Exormia Strophulus*, Gum-rash.

gum resin, gum-'resin. [f. GUM *sb.*[2] + RESIN.] A vegetable secretion consisting of resin mixed with gum or mucilage; e.g. ammoniac, euphorbium, gamboge, etc.

1712 tr. *Pomet's Hist. Drugs* I. 64 It is a Gum-Rosin, said, by some, to come from the same Tree with the Chio Turpentine. **1800** HENRY *Epit. Chem.* (1808) 280 Gum-resins, along with resin, have an admixture of extractive matter. **1861** MISS PRATT *Flower Pl.* V. 2 The gum resin, or Euphorbium of the chemist, is procured from three species of Spurge. **1884** BOWER & SCOTT *De Bary's Phaner.* 136 The term gum-resin is used to indicate..the mixture of watery and resinous secretions, which is milky when fresh.

Hence **gum-'resinous** *a.*, of the nature of a gum resin.

1830 LINDLEY *Nat. Syst. Bot.* 46 The species all abound in a viscid, yellow, acrid, and purgative gum-resinous juice resembling Gamboge.

gum-stool: see GUMBLE-STOOL.

'gum-tree. [f. GUM *sb.*[2] + TREE.]

1. Any tree that exudes gum: *spec.* **a.** Any tree of the genus EUCALYPTUS; **b.** Various species of the N. American genus *Nyssa*; **c.** *Sweet gum tree* of the U.S., *Liquidambar styraciflua*.

1676 T. GLOVER in *Phil. Trans.* XI. 628 There is likewise black Walnut,..Dogwood,..Gum-tree,..with several others. **1756** P. BROWNE *Jamaica* 338 The Gum Tree.. yields a great quantity of resin,..which serves for the boiling house lamps. **1798** MALTHUS *Popul.* (1878) 14 Found in the body of the dwarf gum-tree. **1846** J. L. STOKES *Discov. Australia* II. iii. 108 The silvery stems of the never-failing gum-trees. **1870** WILSON *Austral. Songs* 140 The gum-trees ghastly shadows downward threw.

attrib. **1852** G. C. MUNDY *Our Antipodes* (1857) 4 The leaden tint of the gum-tree foliage.

2. Phrases. ***to be up a gum-tree***: to be in great difficulties. Cf. TREE *sb.* ***'possum up a gum-tree***: the title of a song or dance. (*Austral.*) ***he has seen his last gum-tree*** = it is all up with him.

1829 in *Amer. Speech* (1965) XL. 131 Dere's possum up de gum tree. **1837** THACKERAY *Ravenswing* vii, 'Possum up a gum-tree, eh? **1840** HALIBURTON *Clockm.* Ser. III. xxi, Many's the time I have danced 'Possum up a gum tree' at a quiltin' frolic or huskin' party. **1926** D. L. SAYERS *Clouds of Witness* iii. 86 S'long as they're in his trousers pocket you're up a gum-tree. **1927** *Daily Express* 15 July 1/4 Captain Lancaster cannot obtain any information, and, as he says, he is 'up a gum tree'. **1959** *Encounter* Nov. 60/2 Until somebody solves the problem of an English idiom we're going to be up a gum-tree.

Hence **'gum-treed** *a.*, grown with gum-trees.

1883 P. S. ROBINSON *Sinners & Saints* 309 Modesta, a queer, wide-streeted, gum-treed place.

Gumza, var. GAMZA.

gun (gʌn), *sb.* Forms: 4–6 gonne, gounne, gunne, 5 gowne, gune, 6 gon(e, gonn, goon(ne, *Sc.* gown, 5– gun. [ME. *gunne, gonne* (riming with *sonne* = sun); hence already in 14–15th c. the word was adopted as Welsh *gwn*, Irish (also Sc. Gaelic) *gunna*, Anglo-L. *gonna, gunna*.

With regard to the ultimate etymology, a suggestion has been made by Prof. Skeat that ME. *gunne* may represent a hypocoristic form of a Scandinavian female name compounded with *Gunn-*. This conjecture receives a strong confirmation from the fact (communicated to us by Mr. W. H. Stevenson) that an account of munitions at Windsor Castle in 1330–1 (Exchequer Accts. Q.R. Bundle 18, no. 34, Pub. Rec. Office) mentions 'una magna balista de cornu quæ vocatur Domina Gunilda'. There are other instances of the practice of bestowing female personal names on engines of war; but there was no distinguished lady named Gunilda (= ON. *Gunnhild-r*; spelt *Gunnild* in Havelok) in the 14th c., and it seems highly probable that this use of the name may have come down from Scandinavian times, when its exceedingly appropriate etymology would be understood (both *gunn-r* and *hild-r* mean 'war'). If *Gunnhildr*, as is likely, was a name frequently given to *ballistæ* and the like, it would naturally, on the introduction of gunpowder, be given also to cannon. Indeed, there is some appearance of evidence that an explosive engine was actually called by this name many years before the earliest recorded instance of the use of gunpowder in warfare. The 'song against the retinues of the great people' in *Pol. Songs* (Camden) 237, which must have been written in the reign of Edw. II, contains the following passage:—'The gedelynges were gedered *Of gonnylde gnoste*; Palefreiours ant pages, Ant boyes with boste, Alle weren y-haht Of an horse þoste'. The correct translation of this passage, which has hitherto been unexplained, seems to be as follows:—'The lackeys were gathered out of Gunnild's spark [OE. *gnást*: see GNAST *sb.*]; the grooms and pages, the varlets with their boasting, all were hatched of a horse's dung'. According to analogy, the regular 'pet-name' in ON. for *Gunnhild-r* would be **Gunna*, which would give *Gunne* in ME.; Rietz *Sv. dial.-lex.*, mentions *Gunne* as a female Christian name still surviving in Swedish country districts. (In Iceland *Gunna* is now common, but it is taken to stand for *Guðrún*.)

The other suggestions that have been made as to the origin of the word are obviously unsatisfactory. The assumed OF. **mangonne*, of which *gonne* has been supposed to be a shortening, is wrongly inferred from *mangonneau* MANGONEL, and is not philologically possible, unless as a back-formation. The F. *gonne*, large cask, does not occur before the 16th c., and is regarded by Littré as adopted from the Eng. *gun*. The conjecture that ME. *gunne* is of echoic origin perh. involves no impossibility, but it has no positive support, and little intrinsic probability.]

I. The weapon.

1. a. A weapon consisting essentially of a metal tube (massive enough to require to be mounted on a carriage or a fixed substructure) from which heavy missiles are thrown by the force of gunpowder, or (in later use) by explosive force of any kind; a piece of ordnance, cannon, 'great gun'.

1339 in Riley *Lond. Mem.* (1868) 205 Item, in Camera Gildaulæ sunt sex Instrumenta de latone, vocitata Gonnes, et quinque roleres ad eadem. Item, peletæ de plumbo pro eisdem Instrumentis, quæ ponderant iiii^c libræ et dimidium. Item, xxxii libræ de pulvere pro dictis Instrumentis. **1346** in *Archæologia* XXXII. 381 Et eidem Thomæ de Roldeston, per manus Willielmi de Stanes, ad opus ipsius Regis pro gunnis suis ix^c xii. lib. sal petræ [etc.]. **1365–70** *Exchequer Accts. Q.R.* Bundle 395 No. 1 (P.R.O.), ix. gunnes de cupro [received at the Tower]..ij. magna gunnes de cupro [in King's private wardrobe]..ij. gunnes magna de cupro et ix. gunnes parva de cupro [sent to constable of the king's castle in the Isle of Sheppey]. *c* **1370** J. ARDERNE *Practica* (MS. Sloane) in *Promp. Parv.* 219 Cest poudre vault à gettere pelottes de fer, ou de plom, ou d'areyne, oue vn instrument qe l'em appelle gonne. *c* **1384** CHAUCER *H. Fame* III. 553 Went this foule trumpes soun As swifte as pelet out of gonne Whan fire is in the poudre ronne. **1393** LANGL. *P. Pl.* C. XXI. 293 Setteþ bowes of brake and brasene gonnes, And sheteþ out shot ynowh. **1404** *Durham. Acc. Rolls* (Surtees) 395 Item unum gun cum pulvere pro guerra. **1450–70** *Golagros & Gaw.* 464 Gapand gunnys of brase..That maid ful gret dyn. *c* **1470** HENRY *Wallace* X. 816 We may nocht fle fra ʒon barge wait I weill, Weyll stuft thai ar with gun and ganʒe [*so ed.* 1570; *MS.* gwn ganʒe] off steill. **1473** WARKW. *Chron.* (Camden) 8 The Kynge.. losyde his gonnys of ordynaunce uppone them. **1532** MORE *Confut. Tindale* Wks. 469/1 Except Tyndall tell vs that Adam prynted bokes, and made glasses, and shotte gunnes too. *a* **1542** WYATT in *Tottell's Misc.* (Arb.) 54 The furious goonne..When that the boule is rammed in to sone: And that the flame cannot part from the fire, Crackes in sunder. *a* **1578** LINDESAY (Pitscottie) *Chron. Scot.* Ded. (S.T.S.) I. 8 This roy of gret renowne vas murdreit be ane misforttunit gown. **1687** A. LOVELL tr. *Thevenot's Trav.* I. 272 She carried then fourteen Guns, and had about two hundred Men on board. **1692** *Capt. Smith's Seaman's Gram.* II. xviii. 128 Gunners do allow three Ounces of Powder for every hundred Weight of Metal in Iron Guns: and Four Ounces.. in Brass Guns. **1712** W. ROGERS *Voy.* 14 A Frigate built Ship of 22 Guns. **1841** ELPHINSTONE *Hist. Ind.* II. 407 He mounted a battery of ten guns on a high and solid mound of earth. **1852** TENNYSON *Death Wellington* 97 He that gain'd a hundred fights, Nor ever lost an English gun. **1858** GREENER *Gunnery* 60 The guns of the British nation may be divided into four classes—Park, or Field artillery, Siege guns, or battering train, garrison guns, and marine artillery. **1859** F. A. GRIFFITHS *Artil. Man.* (1862) 50 A Gun (Smooth bore) is divided into five parts, which are named Cascable, First re-inforce, Second re-inforce, Chase, Muzzle. **1884** *Times* (weekly ed.) 7 Mar. 6/1 The guns of the Royal Artillery were..admirably served.

b. Guns are fired in honour of persons and events, at festivities, and as signals; in the navy, ***morning*** and ***evening gun***, 'warning-pieces' fired at morning and evening respectively; hence taken to indicate the times at which these guns are fired.

1556 *Chron. Gr. Friars* (Camden) 51 The xx^ti day of the same monyth after came in the lorde amrelle of France un to Grenwych with xiiij. goodly gallys, and many other sheppes, and there was shotte many gonnys. *Ibid.* 62 On Bartylmew evyne was shott dyvers goonnes at the gattes in London. **1627** CAPT. SMITH *Seaman's Gram.* xiii. 61 Giue them three gunnes for their funerals. **1634, 1660, 1694, 1836** [see GIVE *v.* 14 c]. **1687** A. LOVELL tr. *Thevenot's Trav.* I. 271 We put out English Colours, which they saluted with a Gun without shot. **1712** S. SEWALL *Diary* 8 Mar. (1879) II. 339 Many Healths were drunk, and Guns fired at drinking them. **1748** *Anson's Voy.* II. iii. 145 It being represented to him that.. the evening gun might possibly discover him..he was prevailed upon to omit it for the future. **1899** SIR A. WEST *Recoll.* I. vi. 206 A damaged elbow..did not prevent my sleeping till the morning gun.

c. *fig.*

1535 LATIMER *Serm.* (1584) 2 What great peeces [*sc.* of ordnance] hath he [the devil] had of Bishoppes of Rome, which haue destroyed whole Citties and countries, and haue slayne and brent many! what great Guns were those! **1651** CLEVELAND *Poems* 41 You're doubly free From the great Guns, and squibbing Poetry. **1820** LADY GRANVILLE *Lett.* (1894) I. 188 Great oratorical guns are to be fired to-day. **1888** A. T. PIERSON *Evangelistic Work* xi. 107 Sydney Smith trailed the guns of his satire against the 'nest of consecrated cobblers'. **1893** *19th Cent.* Feb. 193 The Government could not of course run away from their guns.

†**2.** In the 15th c. used somewhat vaguely for a large engine of war, often translating words meaning 'mangonel, ballista, battering-ram'. *Obs.*

The commonly cited example in *K. Alis.* 3268 is due to the scribe of the 15th c. Lincoln's Inn MS., the reading in MS. Laud 622 being *gynnes*.

c **1400** *Rom. Rose* 4176 They ne dredde noon assaut Of ginne, gunne, nor skaffaut. *c* **1400** *Melayne* 1288 With dartis kenely owte þay caste, Bothe with myghte & mayne, With gownnes & with grete stones. Graythe gounnes stoppede those gones [? = gomes, 'men'] With peletes vs to payne. *a* **1400–50** *Alexander* 2227 Sum with gunnes of þe grekis girdis vp stanes. **1432–50** tr. *Higden* (Rolls) IV. 429 Vespasian trowblede the wall sore with gunnes and with oper engynes [L. *ictu arietis*]. **14..** *Voc.* in Wr.-Wülcker 594/35 *Mangonale*, a mangnel, or a gunne. *c* **1489** CAXTON *Blanchardyn* xli. 152 He made gounes & other engynes to be caste ayenste the walles. **1494** FABYAN *Chron.* VI. cciii. 213 The walles of the castell fyll without stroke of gunne or other engyne. **1534** WHITINTON *Tullyes Offices* I. (1540) 17 The gones [L. *aries*] beare downe the walls yet they are to be receyved. [*a* **1654** SELDEN *Table-T.* (Arb.) 65 The word Gun was in use in England for an Engine to cast a thing from a man, long before there was any Gun-powder found out.]

3. a. (Originally HAND-GUN.) Any portable fire-arm, except the pistol; a musket, fowling-piece, rifle, etc. (Quot. 1495 may belong to sense 1.)

1409 *Excheq. Accts. Q.R.* Bundle 44 No. 17 (P.R.O.), iij. canons de ferro ove v. chambres, un handgone. **1446**, etc. [see HANDGUN]. **1495** *Act 11 Hen. VII*, c. 64 Preamble, Armours Defensives, as..Hauberts Curesses Gonnes Speres Mare-spikis. *a* **1568** ASCHAM *Scholem.* (Arb.) 64 To plaie at all weapones; to shote faire in bow, or surelie in gon. **1674** tr. *Scheffer's Lapland* 98 They use Guns, which they.. with a great deal of superstition enchaunt that they should never miss. **1794** MRS. RADCLIFFE *Myst. Udolpho* iii, His gun was slung across his shoulders. **1876** BESANT & RICE *Gold. Butterfly* Prol. i, Both men carried guns. **1897** BUTLER, etc. *Hist. Birds* IV. 65 A long single-barrelled gun called the 'goose-gun'.

b. A pistol or revolver. orig. *U.S.*

1744 A. HAMILTON *Itin.* (1907) 150 'Then surely you had needs ride with guns' (meaning my pistols). **1851** R. GLISAN *Jrnl. Army Life* (1874) 80 He might..not fire unless his gun has a revolving chamber with more than one load. **1890** *Harper's Mag.* Dec. 160/2 That six-shooter you gave Pete was such a pretty gun I couldn't resist when Pete offered to swap. **1902** C. HYNE *Mr. Horrocks Purser* 56 Then he made a great fuss and pulled out a gun. **1948** *This Week Mag.* 9 Oct. 22/2 Police believe that if more people carried guns, murders and suicides would zoom. **1971** *Daily Tel.* 26 Oct. 1 The dockers had been unloading a cargo of 72 tea chests containing pistols brought from Rotterdam... The discovery of the guns led to an immediate alert.

c. Any of various devices for discharging missiles or substances through a tube, as by the expansive force of compressed air; usually with defining word, as AIR-GUN, *blow-gun*, *Flit gun*, *grease-gun*, POP-GUN 1, SPRING-GUN 2 (which see).

1895 *Montgomery Ward Catal.* 261/1 The best Insect Powder Gun in the market in which to use insect powder. **1930** *Engineering* 31 Jan. 126/1 The Webb concrete gun has been used by the city's day labour gangs in lining operations. **1937** *Times* 13 Apr. p. iii/3 As many as 3,000 gallons of cellulose preparations are mixed each week, so that 1,000 car bodies can receive colour sprayed from 120 'guns'. **1938** F. D. SHARPE *Sharpe of Flying Squad* xxi. 227 The drug used was in a liquid form and one of the gang possessed a 'gun' loaded with it. He sprayed this dope at the favourites [at horse-racing]. **1968** *Times* 29 Apr. 2/7 The 'gun' is a new way of giving injections without puncturing the skin. It uses a fine but very powerful jet to penetrate the skin. *Ibid.* 27 May 25/2 The company has developed a new tear gas gun.

d. *spec.* in *Athletics*. The starting pistol; hence, the start of a race.

1900 [see NEEDLE *sb.* 12 b]. **1925** T. E. JONES *Track & Field* 18 Keep the mind concentrated on the gun. **1959** *Times* 23 Apr. 16/6 Smith..took the lead from the gun.

e. A hypodermic syringe used by drug addicts. *U.S. slang.*

1904 *San Francisco Chron. Suppl.* 30 Oct. 4/1, I..reached out my hand for my master, the little syringe, called the 'gun', which always lay ready at my bedside for the early morning 'shot'. **1923** N. ANDERSON *Hobo* vii. 102 One type of dope fiend is the Junkie. He uses a 'gun' or needle to inject morphine or heroin. **1926** MAINES & GRANT *Wise-Crack Dict.* 8 *Gun-toter*, user of a hypodermic needle. **1933** *Amer. Speech* VIII. 27/2 The hypodermic needle and its accessories used for the injection of narcotics are called the gun or artillery. **1955** *U.S. Senate Hearings* (1956) VIII. 4164 *Gun, dropper*, a syringe.

f. = *electron gun* (ELECTRON² 2 b). Also *attrib.*, as ***gun electrode***.

1933 *Electronics* Dec. 333/1 We shall now consider the gun. **1953** AMOS & BIRKINSHAW *Telev. Engin.* I. iv. 52 In cathode-ray tube guns the beam strikes the gun electrodes and releases secondary electrons from them. **1961** G. MILLERSON *Technique Telev. Production* ii. 19 A small gun in the camera-tube generates a continuous beam of electrical particles (electrons). **1971** *Physics Bull.* Oct. 590/1 It offered the advantages of..a colour tube with a single gun.

†**4.** A missile hurled from an engine of war. *Obs.*

c **1385** CHAUCER *L.G.W.* 637 *Cleopatra*, With grysely soun out goth the grete gonne, And heterly they hurtelyn al atonys, ffrom the top doun comyth the grete stonys. *c* **1420** *Avow. Arth.* lxv, There come fliand a gunne And lemet as the leuyn.

5. *transf.* **a.** One who carries a gun, one of a shooting party.

1818 KEATS *Let.* [29?] Dec. (1958) II. 18, I went.. shooting on the heath... There were as many guns..as Birds. **1822** VISCOUNTESS ANSON *Let.* 5 Nov. in *Creevey Papers* (1903) II. ii. 52, 780 head of game were killed by 10 guns. **1870** H. MEADE *Ride New Zealand* 284 Five guns went before breakfast, and brought back 107 [pigeons]. **1886** *Shooting* (Badm. Libr. 1895) 145 Where birds are plentiful much delay may be avoided by providing at least as many retrievers as there are 'guns'. **1897** *Pall Mall Mag.* Nov. 402 The irritable gun..stamps his foot impatiently. **1970** *Courier-Mail* (Brisbane) 13 Aug. 4/9 The price of being a 'gun'—the name for the shooter—is almost prohibitively high.

b. An artilleryman, a gunner.

1896 R. KIPLING *Seven Seas* 200 There was no one like 'im, 'Orse or Foot Nor any o' the Guns I knew. **1898** *Pall Mall Mag.* Sept. 97 The guns are cool, precise and nerveless.

c. *pl.* = gunnery-lieutenant. *Naval slang.*

1916 'TAFFRAIL' *Carry On* 25 The first lieutenant..is 'Jimmy the One'; the gunnery and torpedo lieutenants, the 'Gunnery Jack' and 'Torpedo Jack' respectively, but, to their messmates in the wardroom, these three officers, with the officer borne for navigation duties, are usually 'Number One', 'Guns', 'Torps' and 'Pilot'. **1925** FRASER & GIBBONS *Soldier & Sailor Words*, *Gunnery Jack* (also *Guns*), the Gunnery Lieutenant on board ship. **1962** W. GRANVILLE *Dict. Sailors' Slang* 57 *Guns*, wardroom nickname and vocative for the gunnery officer.

d. = GUN-MAN 1. *U.S.*

1931 C. W. WILLEMSE in *Detective Fiction Weekly* 15 Aug. 123/1 Hey, cap, there's a 'gun' outside. Wants to see you. **1958** R. CHANDLER *Playback* xxiii. 182 Goble was beaten up ..tonight—by a hired gun named Richard Harvest. **1965** T. CAPOTE *In Cold Blood* (1966) iv. 275 He was always talking about..making his living as a hired gun.

6. Phrases.

a. ***as a gun***, used as an intensive or superlative expression = perfectly, absolutely, *esp.* in (***as***) ***sure as a gun***: beyond all question, to a dead certainty.

1622 FLETCHER *Prophetess* I. iii, You are right, master, Right as a gun. **1655** J. SMITH *Musarum Deliciæ* 79 But when he thought her as sure as a gun She set up her taile and away she run. **1681** DRYDEN *Sp. Friar* III. ii, As sure as a gun, now, father Dominic has been spawning this young slender antichrist. *a* **1700** B. E. *Dict. Cant. Crew*, *As sure as a Gun*, or Cock-sure. **1733** FIELDING *Intrig. Chambermaid* I. i. Wks. 1882 IX. 396 'Tis as pure, and as sure, and secure as a gun, The young lover's business is happily done. **1764** FOOTE *Mayor of G.* I. Wks. 1799 I. 174 Gad's my life, sure as a gun that's her voice. **1864** HAWTHORNE *S. Felton* (1883) 389 You will kill yourself, sure as a gun! **1881** *Century Mag.* XXIII. 45/2 Hello! where is that boy? Gone, as sure as guns.

b. ***to stand*** or ***stick to one's gun***(***s***: to maintain one's position, not to flinch or retire before an attack.

1841 S. WARREN *Ten Thous. a Yr.* vi. 198 Titmouse, though greatly alarmed, stood to his gun pretty steadily. **1881** MRS. RIDDELL *Myst. Palace Gard.* i. 10 He stuck to his guns. **1899** MRS. ALEXANDER *Brown, V.C.* 259 An animated colloquy ensued. Manvers stuck to his guns.

c. ***son of a gun***, a somewhat depreciatory term for 'man, fellow'. (See quot. 1867.)

1708 *Brit. Apollo* No. 43. 3/2 You'r a Son of a Gun. **1840** BARHAM *Ingol. Leg.*, *Cynotaph* (*note*), We heard the rough voice of a son of a gun Of a watchman, 'One o'clock!' bawling. **1849** THACKERAY *Pendennis* lx, What a happy feller I once thought you, and what a miserable son of a gun you really are! **1867** SMYTH *Sailor's Word-bk.*, *Son of a gun*, an epithet conveying contempt in a slight degree, and originally applied to boys born afloat, when women were permitted to accompany their husbands to sea; one admiral declared he literally was thus cradled, under the breast of a gun-carriage. **1883** *Harper's Mag.* Oct. 759/2 Thou lubberly, duck-legged son of a gun.

d. ***to carry*** (or ***hold***) (***big***) ***guns***: to be in a position of strength or power; ***to have*** (or ***carry***) ***the guns for***: to have the ability for (something).

[**1732** T. FULLER *Gnomologia* no. 1824, He carries too big a Gun for me; I must not engage him.] **1867** G. MEREDITH

Let. 13 Dec. (1970) I. 364 We carry big but immoveable guns, and the work you can supply will be heartily acceptable. **1887** S. BUTLER *Notebks.* (1912) xvi. 256 This gentleman had a decided manner and carried quite as many guns as the two barristers. **1930** *Times* 25 Mar. 17/3 The Chancellor—whose.. concern is to make the two ends of his Budget meet—necessarily carries the biggest guns. **1939** A. POWELL *What's become of Waring* iv. 106 But do you really think I carry the guns?.. I shouldn't like to think that I was not going to do him justice. **1961** I. MURDOCH *Severed Head* xii. 104 'Why she should have followed it up beats me.' 'You didn't ask her?'.. 'Of course not! As I told you, she carries too many guns.' **1961** *Times* 8 Nov. 18/7 Miss Catherine Lacy has not the vocal guns for the part of Clytemnestra. **1963** *Times* 26 Feb. 3/5 It was Rangers and Celtic who held the biggest guns.

e. *to beat* (or *jump*) *the gun*: in Athletics, to make a false start; hence *fig.*, to act before the permitted or agreed time.

[**1905** S. CROWTHER *Rowing & Track Athletics* 302 False starts were rarely penalized.. and so shiftless were the starters and officials that 'beating the pistol' was one of the tricks which less sportsmanlike runners constantly practised.] **1933** C. LITTLEFIELD *Track & Field Athletics* 31 Do not learn how to try to beat the gun. **1936** WODEHOUSE *Laughing Gas* xxii. 239 Acting swiftly, I did a backwards leap of about five feet six. It was the manœuvre which is known in America as beating the gun. **1942** BERREY & VAN DEN BARK *Amer. Thes. Slang* §59 *Jump the gun*, to make a false start. **1951** *Economist* 24 Nov. 1258/1 Col. Hanley, judge-advocate of the Eighth Army in Korea, first jumped the gun with statistics. **1955** R. BANNISTER *First Four Minutes* 20 It seemed so unnecessary to beat the gun in a race that would last for 3¾ minutes. **1958** *Economist* 1 Nov. 391/1 The Prime Minister has jumped the gun by announcing that it will take the form of government advances to building societies. **1960** *Guardian* 7 Nov. 8/4 Both candidates jumped the traditional gun of Labour Day.

f. Used in *pl.* and contrasted with *butter* to describe a government policy in which the necessity for military expansion is weighed against the importance of social and economic development.

1936 *Times* 18 Jan. 12/3 Speaking on Germany's rearmament Dr. Goebbels said:—We can well do without butter, but not without guns, because butter could not help us if we were to be attacked one day. Some people say there is a world conscience which is the League of Nations,.. but I prefer to rely on guns. **1937** *Daily Herald* 15 Jan. 2/5 A scheme to dissuade Hitler from his 'guns rather than butter' policy. **1938** 'G. ORWELL' *Let.* 26 May in *Coll. Essays* (1968) I. 331 In every country.. the supposed necessity to prepare for war is being systematically used to prevent every kind of social advance. It goes without saying that this happens in the Fascist countries, but 'guns before butter' also rules in the democracies. **1968** *Sat. Rev.* 23 Nov. 32/1 The incredible American economy has such unprecedented wealth that it can afford both guns and butter. **1968** *Guardian* 4 Dec. 8/2 The wars in the Yemen and against Israel have added economic depression to endemic poverty. Is it the beginning of a 'guns or butter' argument in Egypt?

g. *at gunpoint*: threatened by a gun.

1958 *Globe & Mail* (Toronto) 4 June 1/5 Baskar was charged after two men robbed cab driver Benjamin Katz.. of $25 at gunpoint. **1962** *Times* 3 May 17/3 Three escaping criminals.. board a lightship and order the crew at gunpoint to help them reach shore.

h. *to give the gun* (see GIVE *v.* 14 c).

7. great gun. a. A fire-arm of the larger kind which requires to be mounted for firing; a piece of ordnance, a cannon. (Distinguished from *small guns*, under which appellation were included muskets, rifles, etc.; the terms are now obsolete.) Also *big gun*.

1408 ? TREVISA tr. *Vegetius' Art of War* IV. xxii. (Roy. MS. 18 A. XII) in *Promp. Parv.* 219 Grete gonnes that shete now a daies stones of so grete peyse that no walle may withstonde them; as hathe be wele shewede bothe in the Northe cuntre, and eke in the werres of Wales. **1528** T. MAGNUS in *St. Papers* (1836) IV. 325, 5 gret gonnes of brasse called cannons. **1556** *Chron. Gr. Friars* (Camden) 60 That same tyme all the gattes of the citte of London was layed with grett gonnes with-in the citte warte. **1659** D. PELL *Impr. Sea* 256 The crack of a great Gun. **1660** WILLSFORD *Scales Comm.* 196 A Mount or Platform is to be raised for battery, on which the great guns are to be mounted. **1662** J. DAVIES tr. *Olearius' Voy. Ambass.* 5 They were receiv'd with the shooting off the great Guns. **1684** S. G. *Angl. Spec.* 807 The Manufactures are great Guns, made of the Iron in this County. *a* **1715** BURNET *Own Time* (1734) II. 1. 59 He sent for some more Ammunition, and some great Guns. **1849** MACAULAY *Hist. Eng.* v. I. 611 There would have been much difficulty in dragging the great guns to the place where the battle was raging. **1886** [see GATLING]. **1900** J. RALPH *Towards Pretoria* xii. 153 Our big guns were painted like the ruddy earth, and our Maxims were wrapped in canvas great-coats. **1915** A. D. GILLESPIE *Let.* 11 July (1916) 231 Some big guns were firing on our right.., making a horrid noise.

b. A person of distinction or importance; one who is great or eminent in anything. Also *big gun*.

1815 LADY GRANVILLE *Lett.* (1894) I. 71 None of the great guns were at Madame de Coligny's. **1825** SCOTT *Fam. Lett.* (1894) II. 234 A worthy clergyman, one of the great guns, as they call them. **1834** *Knickerbocker* III. 439 The big guns of the nation are there. **1843** HALIBURTON *Attaché* I. xv. 265 The great guns, and big bugs. **1858** R. S. SURTEES *Ask Mamma* lvii. 258 Sir Moses being the great gun of the evening, of course timed himself to arrive becomingly late. **1867** DICKENS *Let.* 29 Mar. (1880) II. 26 The colleges mustered in full force from the biggest guns to the smallest. **1870** BLAINE *Encycl. Rur. Sport* (ed. 3) §4075 Great guns in the pugilistic ring. **1880** DISRAELI *Endym.* xl, I do not despair of its being done. But what I want is some big guns to do it. **1958** *Times Lit. Suppl.* 14 Feb. 83/1 We must now brace ourselves to receive broadsides from the great guns of science and technology. **1966** B. KIMENYE *Kalasanda Revisited* 41 Mrs. Lutaya's set absolutely refused to accept this high-handed ruling, preferring to remain large fish in their own small pond, rather than compete with the big guns of Gumbi and Male villages.

c. *to blow great guns*: to blow with great violence, to blow a violent gale. Also *to blow guns*.

1829 COL. HAWKER *Diary* (1893) I. 353 It blew great guns. **1833** A. CONSTABLE *Let.* 15 Feb. in *J. Constable's Corr.* (1962) 273 It rains every night & the wind has blown guns. **1840** DICKENS *Barn. Rudge* xxxiii, It blows great guns indeed. There'll be many a crash in the forest to-night. **1883** C. J. WILLS *Mod. Persia* 389 At sunset, as is usual at this place, it blew great guns. **1920** 'K. MANSFIELD' *Let.* 7 Oct. (1928) II. 50 It's blowing guns to-day.

d. *great guns!* used as an exclamation.

1884 'MARK TWAIN' *Huck. Finn* xiii. 115 Great guns! is *he* her uncle? **1895** *Pall Mall Mag.* Aug. p. xxxvi, But great guns! is a man obliged to blurt out everything he honestly thinks?

e. Phr. *to go great guns*: to have a run of success, to advance (rapidly) towards success.

1913 *Field* 3 May 849/3 A moment later Louvois shot out, passed Sanquhar and Fairy King, and going great guns.. beat the favourite by a head. **1958** *Times* 26 Sept. 19/2 Local partisanship will no doubt run high between Bristol, who are going great guns so far, and their old.. rivals Gloucester. **1971** *Times* 16 Jan. 16/8 Arsenal, going great guns in their functional, efficient way, must see the league title within their sights.

II. Transferred uses.

8. *Mining.* (See quots.) ? *Obs.*

1747 HOOSON *Miner's Dict.*, *Gun of Wood*, the same with a hollow Plug. **1753** CHAMBERS *Cycl. Supp.*, *Gun* is also a name given by the miners, to an instrument used in cleaving rocks with gunpowder. It is an iron cylinder.. having.. a hole drilled through it to communicate with the inside of the hole in the rock.

9. *slang* and *dial.* A flagon (of ale). *to be in the gun* (see quot. 1785.) [Cf. GOAN, GAWN.] ? *Obs.*

1645 EVELYN *Diary* (1889) I. 220 Captain Powell.. invited me on board,.. where we had a dinner of English powdered beef and other good meat, with store of wine and great guns, as the manner is. **1674** RAY *N.C. Words* 23 A *Gun*, a great flagon of Ale sold for 3^d. or 4^d. *a* **1700** B. E. *Dict. Cant. Crew*, s.v. *Gun, In the Gun*, Drunk. **1729** THEOBALD in Nichols *Illustr. Lit. Hist.* (1817) II. 246, I think there is a vehicle in the University, which they call a 'Gun of Ale'. **1785** GROSE *Dict. Vulg. Tongue* s.v., He's *In the Gun*, he is drunk, perhaps from an allusion to a vessel called a gun, used for ale in the universities.

10. *slang* or *jocular.* A tobacco pipe.

1708 E. COOK *Sot-weed Factor* (1865) 5 Out our Landlord pulls a Pouch,.. and straight begun To load with Weed his Indian Gun. *a* **1848** KERR *Maggie o' the Moss*, etc. (1891) 93 We each filled our 'gun' with the best Glasgow spun [tobacco].

11. *Glass-manuf.* (See quot.)

1889 *Encycl. Brit.* X. 662 (Plate Glass) The breadth of the plate.. is determined within the limits of the table by the two sides of the 'gun', an apparatus consisting of two plates of cast-metal, placed in front of the roller, and bolted together by cross bars at a distance apart which can be easily altered and adjusted according to the breadth of plate the apparatus is intended to control.

†**12.** *slang.* (See quot. and cf. GUNNER 7.) *Obs.*

1720 SPILLER in *Anti-Theatre* No. 13 ¶8 Robinson Crusoe.. has distinguished himself by many strange and unaccountable stories, which your smart fellows in conversation are pleased to call guns.

13. *slang.* A thief; also 'rascal', 'beggar'.

1858 A. MAYHEW *Paved w. Gold* II. i. 70, I tell you you ain't a-going to make a gun (thief) of this here young flat. **1863** in W. B. Jerrold *Signals Distress* 9 A year or two's practice in the delicate profession of a 'gun' (a pickpocket). **1890** 'ROLF BOLDREWOOD' *Col. Reformer* (1891) 219 He.. was always scraping the run bare as he could for fat stock, and let these old guns have their fling till he'd got time to.. clear em all out. **1894** A. MORRISON *Tales Mean Streets* 255 Circumstances had always been against Scuddy Lond, the gun. The word gun.. is a friendly synonym for thief.

14. In full *gun shearer*. An expert sheep-shearer. *Austral.* and *N.Z.*

1898 *Bulletin* (Sydney) 17 Dec., *Gun*.. generally speaking a man who can shear over 200 a day. **1947** P. NEWTON *Wayleggo* (1949) iii. 39 There I saw some of our greatest gun (fast) shearers in action. **1952** J. CLEARY *Sundowners* iii. 121 A 'gun' shearer, a crack man, was always welcome in a team. **1956** G. BOWEN *Wool Away!* (ed. 2) iii. 24 While perhaps this may be all right for odd 'guns' it is not a good practice for the majority of shearers or learners. **1970** *Tel.* (Brisbane) 18 Feb. 5/1 (*heading*) 'Gun' shearer only 11.

15. *Surfing slang.* A large heavy surfboard used for riding big waves.

1963 *Pix* 28 Sept. 62/1 *Big Gun*, big surfboard for heavy surfs. **1965** FARRELLY & MCGREGOR *This Surfing Life* vi. 69, I haven't a gun board myself. For the Australian surf that I call big.. the board I use is just a long hot-dog board. **1969** *Surfer* IX. vi. 57 Aipa rides the first wave, a long green wall, accelerating his gun to tremendous velocity across the face of the wave. **1970** *Surf '70* (N.Z.) 44/2 While in Hawaii I had two boards. They were an 8 ft 9 in 'hot-dog' and a 9 ft 6 in tracker type gun.

III. Combinations.

16. General relations: **a.** simple attrib., as ***gun-action***, ***-battery***, ***-belt***, ***-bore***, ***-breeching***, ***-butt***, ***-cart***, ***-cattle***, ***company***, ***-crew***, ***-cupboard***, ***-detachment***, ***draught***, ***drug*** (DRUG *sb.*²), ***emplacement***, ***factory***, ***-flash***, ***-founder***, ***-foundry***, ***-gear***, ***-guard***, ***† hammer***, ***† hoy***, ***-licence***, ***-line***, ***-match***, ***mounting***, ***-mouth***, ***-nipple***, ***-nostril***, ***-park***, ***† peck***, ***-position***, ***quoin***, ***-rack***, ***-range***, ***roller***, ***-ship***, ***-shop***, ***-sight***, ***-stand***, ***-steel***, ***† tampion***, ***-team***, ***-trade***, ***-trial***, ***-wad***, ***-wadding***, ***-wharf***, ***wheel***, ***-yard***.

1897 *B'ham Weekly Post* 8 May 4/6 Richard Hill, *gun-action filer. **1816** H. CLARKE *Hist. War* I. 319/2 The mortar and *gun-batteries of the enemy. **1918** E. S. FARROW *Dict. Mil. Terms*, *Gun Battery*, a defense constructed of earth faced with green sods or fascines, sometimes of gabions filled with earth. **1965** *Times Lit. Suppl.* 25 Nov. 1048 A.. cop who wears his *gunbelt in bed. **1806** HUTTON *Course Math.* II. 345 The whole length of the *gunbore. **1833** J. HOLLAND *Manuf. Metal* II. 105 A *gun-breeching till of late years, was what it still remains in muskets used in the army, simply a plug screwed into the end of the barrel. **1891** KIPLING *Light that Failed* ii, To drag down the slayer till he could be knocked on the head by some avenging *gun-butt. **1932** W. FAULKNER *Light in August* (1933) xi. 228 A hand more apt for a rope or a gunbutt.. than a pen. **1898** *Century Mag.* Apr. 928/2 [He] most ingeniously ran his *gun-cart far into the surf in the wake of a receding wave. **1846** H. TORRENS *Rem. Mil. Lit. & Hist.* I. 107 *note*, The breed of *gun cattle has much degenerated of late years. **1897** *Outing* (U.S.) XXX. 282/1 The two *gun companies were transferred to the infantry arm of the service. **1863** T. W. HIGGINSON *Army Life* (1870) 92 Even among the *gun-crews, not a man was hurt. **1892** W. W. GREENER *Breech-Loader* 180 If.. a dust-proof *gun-cupboard, it will last longer. **1860** *Man. Artill. Exerc.* II. 22 The medium 12-pounder requires two *gun detachments. **1918** E. S. FARROW *Dict. Mil. Terms* s.v., The cannoneers assigned to the service of a single gun, formed in double rank, constitute a gun detachment. **1846** H. TORRENS *Rem. Mil. Lit. & Hist.* I. 107 *note*, The bullock, useful as he is for heavy *gun draft in this country. **1879** *Man. Artil. Exerc.* 583 The 7-inch R.M.L. gun of 7 tons may be transported by land.. by heavy *gun drug for 25 tons. *Ibid.* 84 The roads, or lines of communication between the gun park and various *gun emplacements. **1780** in *Cal. Virginia St. Papers* I. 372 The warrant for Six thousand pounds on account of the *Gun Factory. **1812** *Niles' Reg.* III. 60/2 Messrs. Coggswell and Hosford are erecting a gun factory in Albany. **1876** VOYLE & STEVENSON *Milit. Dict.* (ed. 3) s.v., Elswick.. was formerly an adjunct of the Royal Gun Factory. **1950** J. BUSSELL *Puppets & I* iv. 85 *Gun flashes (made with wickless cigarette-lighters) denote the start of a battle. **1957** M. K. JOSEPH *I'll soldier no More* (1958) ix. 170 Over to the left, gunflashes lit the sky. **1549** *Privy Council Acts* (1890) II. 287 To Giles Pacquet, *gonfounder, towardes the making of certeyne peces of brasse. **1628** R. NORTON *Gunner* 44 That all his Gunne-founders should thenceforth cast all Cannons of 18 Dyametres of their Bores in length. **1688** CAPT. J. S. *Fortification* 132 By this a Gun-Founder may cast Guns, according to demand. **1870** *Daily News* 21 Oct., Bourges.. having an arsenal and *gunfoundries. **1867** SMYTH *Sailor's Word-bk.*, **Gun-gear*, everything pertaining to its handling. **1883** CLARK RUSSELL *Sailors' Lang.*, *Gun-gear*, left-handed rope used for securing cannons on board ship. **1896** A. AUSTIN *Jameson's Ride* ii, If sound be our sword, and saddle, And gun-gear. **1897** S. L. HINDE *Congo Arabs* 124 The officer had the rearguard and more particularly the *gunguard under supervision. **1485** *Naval Acc. Hen. VII* (1896) 50 *Gonne hamers.. iij. **1726** *Lond. Gaz.* No. 6454/2 A *Gun Hoy of the Burthen of 70 Tons. **1886** W. W. FOWLER *Year with Birds* 9 The *gun-licence and its own rapid flight give it a fair chance of escape. **1921** *Daily Colonist* (Victoria, B.C.) 1 Oct. 9/4 For not having his gun licence on his person, W. Whitta was fined $10 and costs. **1965** A. NICOL *Truly Married Woman* 92 He had not bothered to apply for a gun licence. **1945** *Diamond Track* (Army Board, N.Z.) 25/2 The defensive power of an anti-tank *gun-line. **1968** *Sunday Truth* (Brisbane) 11 Aug. 2/1 HMAS Hobart has won an American 'fleet citation' for action.. while on gunline duty off the Vietnam coast. **1644** NYE *Gunnery* (1647) Title-p., The art of Gunnery. Wherein is described the true way to make *Gun-match, [etc.]. **1799** G. SMITH *Laboratory* I. 17 With quick match.. or with gun match, they fire them. **1892** *Labour Commission* Gloss., **Gun mountings*, the framework upon which the guns on a vessel are mounted, that is the carriages with their fittings and fixtures. **1659** D. PELL *Impr. Sea* Proœm B vj, I may say of these mens *Gun-mouthes, Out of these Gun-mouthes go burning lamps,.. and sparks of fire leap out of their *Gun-nostrils [cf. Job xli. 19]. **1857** LIVINGSTONE *Trav.* xv. 280 The powder in the *gun-nipples cannot be kept dry. **1769** *De Foe's Tour Gt. Brit.* I. 136 On the East or Lower-part of the Town, is the Gun-yard, commonly called the Park, or the *Gun-park, where is a prodigious Quantity of Cannon of all Sorts for the Ships of War. **1879** [see *gun emplacement*]. **1940** 'GUN BUSTER' *Return via Dunkirk* I. ii. 27 Guides dashed off to meet the column and lead it to the gun-parks and vehicle-parks already selected. **1943** *Roof over Britain* 25 The guns are spaced around the sides of the gun park, with the command post at the centre. **1497** *Naval Acc. Hen. VII* (1896) 72 Gonne hamurs iij, *Gonne pekkes viij. **1901** 'LINESMAN' *Words by Eyewitness* (1902) 73 From the *gun-position one could look down upon line upon line of trenches. **1879** *Man. Artil. Exerc.* 98, 4 and 5 scotch the wheels with the *gun quoins. **1799** *Sporting Mag.* XIV. 107 One of the hooks in the *gun-rack caught the trigger. **1838** J. MCDONALD *Biogr. Sk. N. Massie* 38 His gun-rack was examined, and there hung his rifle and his pouch in their usual place. **1969** *Daily Colonist* (Victoria, B.C.) 19 Dec. 9/7 (Advt.), Wooden Gun Rack. A favorite gift for the hunter in the family. **1856** KANE *Arctic Expl.* I. xxvii. 356 If I am fortunate enough to stalk within *gun-range. **1879** *Man. Artil. Exerc.* 96 The special *gun roller, when in use, rests on two gudgeon plates fitted to the cheeks of the overbank or top carriage. **1841** L. M. CHILD *Lett. New York* viii. 59 You probably recollect that he built a large *gun-ship for the Turkish Sultan. **1898** P. H. COLOMB in *Nat. Rev.* Aug. 842 That fighting ships—that is, gun-ships—should no longer be supplied, as at present universally, with torpedoes. **1865** *Atlantic Monthly* XV. 717 The better class of work-men had gone.. to private *gun-shops in the North. **1893** M. BEERBOHM *Let.* 13 Aug. (1964) 47 The window of a gun-shop. **1940** *Illustr. London News* CXCVII. 22 (*caption*) Ranks of guns—some of them of the largest calibres—in this British gun-shop betoken good supplies of these naval weapons. **1867** SMYTH *Sailor's Word-bk.*, **Gun-sight*. **1856** KANE *Arct. Expl.* II. viii. 89, I jumped at once to the *gun-stand. **1891** *Pall Mall G.* 30 May 7/1 *Gun-steel in this country is subjected to the severest tests. **1485** *Naval Acc. Henry VII* (1896) 69 *Gonne Tampyons. **1897** *Cavalry*

Tactics xvi. 112 If the attack succeeds, the guns must be carried off or disabled; the easiest way for the former would be to utilise the *gun-team horses. **1908** *Westm. Gaz.* 30 Oct. 3/2 Horses..capable of drawing weight at the pace required in a gun-team. **1833** J. HOLLAND *Manuf. Metal* II. 94 The Birmingham *gun-trade. **1898** *Engineering Mag.* XVI. 112/1 Krupp's *gun-trial grounds. **1876** VOYLE & STEVENSON *Milit. Dict.* (ed. 3) 457 *Gun wads are stated to have no effect on the velocity of the ball. **1858** SIMMONDS *Dict. Trade*, **Gun-wadding*, circular pieces of card-board, cloth, felt, and chemically prepared substances, used to keep down the charge of ball or shot, &c. in a gun. **1769** FALCONER *Dict. Marine* (1780), *Arcenal de marine*, a royal dock-yard, together with its warren or *gun-wharf. **1890** W. J. GORDON *Foundry* 110 The guns at the Portsmouth gun-wharf. **1879** *Man. Artil. Exerc.* 95 Scotch the *gun wheels with handspikes. **1769** *Gun-yard [see *gun-park*].

b. objective, as ***gun-bearer***, ***-boring***, ***-carrying***, ***-fighting***, ***-firing***, ***-forger***, ***-forging***, ***-handling***, ***-pulling***, ***-testing***, ***-toter***, ***-toting***, etc. **c.** instrumental, as ***gun-battle***, ***-fight***, ***-murder***; ***gun-armed***, ***-equipped***, ***mounted*** adjs.

1938 *19th Cent.* Feb. 198 Germany had but few submarines, and of these not many were *gun-armed. **1945** *Everybody's Digest* Aug. 89 A *gun battle used to bring a puncher out 'a-smokin''. **1967** *Listener* 13 Apr. 486/1 In Aden, British troops and extremists fight gun battle. **1883** G. ALLEN in *Knowl.* 18 Aug. 97/1 Their [rabbits'] hereditary foe, man, the possible hunter and probable *gun-bearer. **1837** CARLYLE *Fr. Rev.* III. VI. i, This Thing, called La Révolution, which..hangs over France, noyading, fusillading, fighting, *gun-boring. **1896** *Daily News* 4 Nov. 7/2 The *gun-carrying power of the torpedo vessels. **1897** *Ibid.* 8 Mar. 5/2 Another silent host of hooded, shrouded, and *gun-equipped warriors. **1659** D. PELL *Impr. Sea* Prooem B ij b, *Gun-fighting Ships. *Ibid.* B v b, Great roaring *Gun-fights. **1848** CLOUGH *Let.* 22 May, Poems & Prose Rem. (1869) I. 125 The perpetual *gun-firing gave me a head-ache. **1694** *Lond. Gaz.* No. 3008/4 Whoever gives notice of him to Mr. John Parmiter, *Gun forger,..shall have a Guinea. **1659** D. PELL *Impr. Sea* Prooem B v, These are the *Gun-handling and Canon-firing Lads of the World. **1846** H. TORRENS *Rem. Mil. Lit. & Hist.* I. 107 We, too, have our war chariots, *gun-mounted. **1853** KANE *Grinnell Exp.* xxxvi. (1856) 332 My old hostility to *gun-murder was forgotten. **1909** 'O. HENRY' *Roads of Destiny* xvi. 271 The by-standers asserted that it was met by the most beautiful exhibition of lightning *gun-pulling ever witnessed in the Southwest. **1898** *Westm. Gaz.* 14 Feb. 7/3 Orders have been issued for a *gun-testing party to be despatched from the Sheerness School of Gunnery. **1925** O. P. WHITE *Them was Days* 120 This opened up the field for the renegade white man..the *gun-toter, [etc.]. **1948** *Sat. Rev.* 28 Aug. 37/1 His steps were the measured pace of a gun toter. **1912** I. COBB *Back Home* 293, I reckon none of you young fellows.. can remember when this wasn't a *gun-toting country down here? **1969** *Listener* 23 Jan. 103/3 One can imagine the sight of the gun-toting..in all the Westerns, joined together as one fusillade.

d. Forming, with a prefixed numeral, an adjectival compound qualifying *ship*, *frigate*, etc.

1748 J. LIND *Lett. Navy* ii. (1757) 95 That every captain of a forty gun ship..have a power to hold a court martial. **1769** FALCONER *Dict. Marine* (1780) U 2 b, A seventy-four gun ship. **1807–8** SYD. SMITH *Plymley's Lett.* Wks. 1859 II. 165/1 Three forty-gun frigates landed 1100 men under Humbert. **1832** MARRYAT *N. Forster* xxxiv, I..married a couple on board of a..ten-gun brig.

17. Special combs.: **gun apron** (see quot.); **gun-barrel** (see BARREL *sb.* 7); also *transf.* and comb. ***gun-barrel grinder***, ***maker***, ***prover***; **gun-beam** (see quot.); **gun-brig**, a two-masted ship of war, now obsolete; **gun-bright** (see quot.); **gun-brush**, a cylindrical or conical brush for cleaning the bore of a gun; **gun bus** [BUS *sb.*^{2} 2 b (a)] (see quot. 1925); **gun-camera** (see quot. 1948); **gun captain**, the captain of the crew of a ship's gun; **gun-carriage** (see CARRIAGE 27); **gun-case**, a case for holding a gun; also *colloq.* a name for a judge's tippet; **gun-chamber** (see quot. 1867); **gun club**, the name of a fabric design, freq. used in tweeds, consisting of large checks superimposed over small ones; **gun cruiser**, the same as CRUISER; **gun-crutch** (see quot.); **gun-dog**, a dog trained to accompany the 'guns'; †**gun dust**, the metallic dust produced in the boring of cannon; **gun-fight** *U.S. colloq.*, a fight with revolvers, a shooting affray; **gun-fighter**, one who frequently participates in gun-fights; also *fig.*; **gun-fire**, (*a*) the firing of a gun or guns; *Naut.* and *Mil.* the time at which the morning or evening gun is fired; *spec.* rapid firing in which each gun acts independently and fires as rapidly as it can be loaded; also *fig.*; (*b*) *Army slang*, an early morning cup of tea served out to troops before going on first parade; **gun flint** (see FLINT *sb.* 2 b); **gun-fodder** = *cannon-fodder*; **gun-harpoon**, a harpoon fired from a gun instead of being thrown by hand; **gun hoop**, one of the coiled or forged steel envelopes shrunk on the central tube of a modern cannon; **gun-house**, a shelter for the protection of a gun and the gunner in action; **gun-how**, **gun-howitzer** (see quot. 1942); **gun-iron**, (*a*) the iron used in the manufacture of guns; (*b*) a gun-harpoon (*Cent. Dict.*); **gun-lance**, see LANCE *sb.*^{1} 2; **gun-layer**, one who aims or lays a gun; hence ***gun-laying*** vbl. sb.; **gun-lift**, a hoisting arrangement for mounting and dismounting cannon (Wilhelm *Mil. Dict.* 1881); **gun microphone**, a moving-coil microphone having a number of parallel tubes of different length in front of the diaphragm to increase its directional property; **gun moll** *U.S. slang*, a female thief (cf. sense 13); an armed woman; **gun-money**, (*a*) = GUNNAGE; (*b*) money coined (by James II in Ireland) from the metal of old guns (see quot. 1853); **gun-paper** (see quot.); **gun-pendulum**, (*a*) 'a device employed to determine the initial velocity of projectiles by means of the recoil of the gun' (Hamersly *Naval Encycl.* 1881); (*b*) 'a pendulous box with sand-bags to receive the impact of a ball fired from a gun or cannon, and used to determine the strength of powder' (Knight *Dict. Mech.* 1875); **gun-pit**, (*a*) *Fortif.*, an excavation made to receive guns for protection against the enemy's fire; (*b*) 'a pit for receiving the mold used in casting a gun, or for receiving the tube or jacket in assembling a built-up gun' (*Cent. Dict.*); (*c*) in a fighting aeroplane, the compartment for a gun and gunner; **gun-plane**, a fighting aeroplane armed with a gun or guns; **gun-pointer** = *gun-layer*; **gun-port**, a port-hole for a gun; **gun-portion**, (see quot. 1876); **gun-power**, the number and strength of guns available in any given place or circumstances; **gun-range**, (*a*) the range of a gun's fire; (*b*) a place where gun-firing is practised; **gun-reach** = *gun-range* (a); **gun-rest**, (see quot. 1898); also, a wall-fixture for portable fire-arms, a gun-rack; **gun-runner** *colloq.*, one engaged in **gun-running**, the practice of illegally conveying fire-arms and ammunition into a country; **gun-sawdust**, an explosive made, in a similar way to guncotton, by steeping sawdust in nitric and sulphuric acids; **gun-searcher** (see quot.); **(helicopter) gunship**, a heavily armed helicopter; **gun-sight** (see SIGHT *sb.*^{1} 14 b); hence **gun-sighting** *vbl. sb.*; **gun-site**, an emplacement, usually fortified, for guns; †**gun-sleeved** *a.*, having gun-shaped sleeves; **gun-slide**, in naval guns, 'the chassis on which the top-carriage carrying the gun slides in recoiling' (*Cent. Dict.*); **gun-sling** (see quot.); also, a sling for carrying a portable fire-arm; **gun-slinger** = GUN-MAN 1; hence **gun-slinging** *vbl. sb.*; **gun-spaniel**, a spaniel that has been trained to accompany gunners; **gun-stick**, a ramrod, rammer; **gun-tackle**, (*a*) *Naut.* in full, ***gun-tackle-purchase***, 'a tackle composed of a rope rove through two single blocks' (Smyth); also attrib. *gun-tackle block*; (*b*) an arrangement of blocks and ropes for moving guns; †**gun-trap**, a trap which when touched discharges a firearm; **gun turret** (see quot. 1959); **gun-vessel**, ? a small ship of war; **gun washings**, the water in which a gun has been washed; **gun-well**, in a submarine, the sunk compartment for a gun; **gun-work**, (*a*) any labour performed in connexion with ordnance, its production, inspection, or the like; (*b*) shooting with a gun or rifle; **gun-worker**, one who works in a gun-foundry.

1876 VOYLE & STEVENSON *Milit. Dict.* (ed. 3), *Aprons*, **Gun*, covers for the protection of the vent and tangent blocks of guns against rain and dirt. **1789** (*title*) An Essay on Shooting, containing the various Methods of Forging, Boring, and Dressing *Gun Barrels. **1822–34** *Good's Study Med.* (ed. 4) I. 466 Edge-tool and gun-barrel grinders. **1858** GREENER *Gunnery* 291 It cannot be too often repeated, that a gun barrel is a spring, to all intents and purposes. **1858** SIMMONDS *Dict. Trade*, *Gun barrel maker*..*Gun barrel prover*. **1864** S. HIBBERD *Rose Bk.* 245 Gun-Barrel Budding. *Ibid.* 246 Bud it there at once just under one of the leaf-rings, 'gun-barrel' fashion. **1904** *Westm. Gaz.* 19 Jan. 10/1 The recent gun-barrel fight in Birmingham. **1907** 'ARTIFEX' & 'OPIFEX' *Causes of Decay in Brit. Industry* ii. 25 Gun-barrel welding is one of the handicrafts lost to Birmingham.., whilst it is thriving in Belgium. **1961** C. H. DOUGLAS-TODD *Pop. Whippet* 53 If she has no spring of ribs, a gun-barrel front and so on..do *not* regard her as a foundation brood bitch. **1970** *New Yorker* 22 Aug. 67/1 The children's kind of blindness was identified as tunnel, or gun-barrel, vision—a constriction of the visual fields. **1898** *Encycl. Sport* II. 168 (Punt shooting), **Gun-beam*, the principal beam in the fore deck, which supports the main weight of the gun in its crutch. **1801** NELSON in Nicolas *Disp.* (1845) IV. 314 Captain Rose..volunteered his services to direct the *Gun-brigs. **1833** MARRYAT *P. Simple* (1863) 123 Our gun-brigs, a sort of vessel that will certainly d—n the inventor to all eternity. **1918** E. S. FARROW *Dict. Mil. Terms*, **Gun-bright*, Dutch rush (*equisetum hyemale*) much used in scouring gun barrels. **1799** *Memoirs Med. Soc. Lond.* V. 407 (*heading*) Case of a *Gun Brush penetrating the Cranium. **1874** KEMMIS *Treat. Mil. Carriages* 171 Gun brushes are used for cleaning the bores of M.L.R. guns, the heads are conical in form. **1919** BLACKBURN & NEWBY *All about Aircraft* 63 The Vickers' '*Gun Bus'..having a Gnome engine. **1925** FRASER & GIBBONS *Soldier & Sailor Words* 112 *Gun-bus*, Air Force slang for a gun-carrying aeroplane. Specifically applied to the first Vickers' 'pusher' machine, the first aeroplane specially built to carry a machine-gun. **1970** R. JOHNSTON *Black Camels* xii. 183 Out on the flanks, four of Kassim's gun buses were standing by. **1921** *Flight* XIII. 414/1 Dealing with the *gun-camera, he said airmen were trained to aim and 'fire' with the gun, and the camera, which was attached, showed what part of their opponent they were actually on when they 'fired'. **1948** A. L. M. SOWERBY *Dict. Photogr.* (ed. 17) 356 *Gun camera*, a camera attached to a gun, usually in a fighter aeroplane, and operated when the trigger of the gun is pulled. These cameras were introduced during the war of 1914–18 for use in training fighter-pilots. **1901** *Westm. Gaz.* 27 June 8/1 The *gun captain and layer. **1769** FALCONER *Dict. Marine* (1780), *Cheville a œilettes d'affût*, the eye-bolts of the *gun-carriages. **1879** *Cassell's Techn. Educ.* III. 309 Two gunners sit immediately behind the horses, on the front of the gun-carriage. **1690** S. NILES *Indian Wars* in *Mass. Hist. Soc. Coll.* (4th Ser.) V. 275 We took two guns,..*gun-cases and four canoes. **1839** C. SINCLAIR *Holiday House* xv. 333, I observed a gun-case in the saloon. **1848** MRS. GASKELL *Mary Barton* II. v. 70 Having abstracted the paper, and bullets, &c., she saw a woollen gun-case, made of that sort of striped horse-cloth you must have seen a thousand times appropriated to such a purpose. **1857** THOREAU *Maine W.* (1894) 368 Polis picked up a gun-case of blue broadcloth. **1877** MRS. FORRESTER *Mignon* I. 22 The only indication that its owner is a votary of 'le sport', is the neat mahogany gun-case fastened to the wall. **1895** *Westm. Gaz.* 6 Aug. 3/1 The tippet or 'gun-case' of scarlet cloth from the right shoulder to the left side, held in by the sash or girdle. **1485** *Naval Acc. Hen. VII* (1896) 38 *Gonne chambres iiij ix. **1867** SMYTH *Sailor's Word-bk.*, *Gun-chambers*. In early artillery a movable chamber with a handle like a paterero, used in loading at the breech. In more recent times the name has been used for the small portable mortars for firing salutes in the parks. **1939** M. B. PICKEN *Lang. Fashion* 25/1 **Gun club check*, check design used frequently in tweeds, consisting of large check over smaller one. **1967** *Guardian* 7 Sept. 4/3 Pattern and colour in trousers are 'in', Tattersalls, gunclubs, dice checks, overchecks and stripes to blend with jackets. **1884** R. D. WHITE in *Pall Mall G.* 13 Nov. 5/1 Of *gun cruisers we should have at least one for every station, and two or three in reserve. **1898** *Encycl. Sport* II. 168 (Punt shooting), **Gun-crutch*, the spur in which the gun rests on the gunbeam. **1744** W. ELLIS *Mod. Husb.* VI. I. 184 The Dog.. which, you said, was a *Gun-dog and Setter. **1908** *Westm. Gaz.* 5 Mar. 9/3 The most handsome of all English gundogs. **1959** *Elizabethan* July 12/2 The *haute-école* of gundog training demands an intricate relationship of understanding between man and dog. **1703** T. N. *City & C. Purchaser* 135 Earthen-floors are commonly made..of Lime, and Brook-sand, and *Gundust, or Anvil-dust from the Forge. *Ibid.* 207 A Gallon of Boreing (or Gun) Dust. **1898** *McClure's Mag.* Feb. 380 You don't mean there is going to be a *gun-fight? **1907** S. E. WHITE *Arizona Nights* II. ii. 252 I'll go yore little old gunfight to a finish. **1961** K. REISZ *Technique Film Editing* (ed. 9) ii. 75 The gun-fight is simply presented in to-and-fro reaction shots. **1894** *Midwinter Appeal* (San Francisco) 27 Jan. 2/3 The *gun-fighters rushed up with cocked revolvers and ordered him to halt. **1910** J. HART *Vigilante Girl* xxvii. 374 This man Hawke is a gun-fighter, and as cool and courageous as Tower can be. **1950** *Manch. Guardian Weekly* 17 Aug. 7/3 All 'Westerns' are..strict observers of a moral and social code—..But 'The Gunfighter' goes much farther in moral lecturing. **1964** D. F. DOWD in I. L. Horowitz *New Sociol.* 59 To become..an intellectual gunfighter. **1801** MARIA LADY NUGENT 30 Oct. in *Jrnl. Voyage..Jamaica 1801–1805* (1839) I. ii. 83 Up at *gun-fire. **1814** T. E. HOOK *Let.* 24 Mar. in A. Mathews *Mem. Charles Mathews* (1838) II. xii. 269 Always up by gun-fire, five o'clock. **1823** CRABB *Technol. Dict.* s.v., *Gun-fire*, the time at which the morning or evening gun is fired. **1833** MARRYAT *P. Simple* (1863) 110, I will give you leave to go to-morrow morning and stay till gun-fire. **1870** *Daily News* 13 Oct. 5/5 This same shell disturbed a hare, which.. scampered across the battlefield right in a line with the gun fire. **1898** P. H. COLOMB in *Nat. Rev.* Aug. 841 Quite possibly an English admiral would have risked the dangers of navigation rather than the dangers of gun-fire. **1912** S. E. BURROW *Friend or Foe* x. 125 In the prayer-room they gathered at noon day by day for their 'Gun-fire', and around the Word had the most helpful fellowship. **1916** 'BOYD CABLE' *Action Front* 210 The gunners..will tell you how they stretched themselves to the call for 'gun-fire'. **1919** *War Slang* in *Athenæum* 18 July 632/2 'Gun fire' for early morning tea. **1926** *Times* 1 Jan. 13/3 After a sharp exchange of gunfire the massive tanks of the new property legislation have rolled over the last ditch. **1928** *Daily Mail* 31 July 13/1 A typical day in the life of a Territorial in camp..is as follows: 6 a.m. Réveillé. 6.30 'Gunfire' (morning tea and biscuits), [etc.]. **1940** 'GUN BUSTER' *Return via Dunkirk* II. xvii. 201 'Dawn just breaking, sir,' he affirmed, shoving into my hand a mug of hot 'gunfire'. **1951** M. MCLUHAN *Mech. Bride* 137/2 One has only to listen to the tense gunfire delivery of radio sports announcers to understand this. **1746** COOKE in *Hanway's Trav.* (1762) I. IV. liv. 253 The Tartars offered them two large loaves of bread, in exchange for a *gun flint. **1827** FARADAY *Chem. Manip.* iii. 71 A gun-flint is convenient for scratching on the surface of glass. **1900** *Westm. Gaz.* 9 July 2/1 Exceedingly useful in the capacity of *gun-fodder and stop-gap. **1925** P. GIBBS *Unchanging Quest* xxvii. 207 From historic houses..these boys of ours came as gun-fodder. **1941** KOESTLER *Scum* ix. 47 To fight against its enemies at home, instead of serving as gun-fodder for their purposes. **1867** SMYTH *Sailor's Word-bk.*, **Gun-harpoon*. **1891** *Daily News* 26 May 2/6 The exhibit, which consists of a hollow forging (technically known as a *gun hoop)..is 23 feet long, and weighs 34 tons. **1893** LLOYD & HADCOCK *Artillery* v. 109 The firer..looks along the sights above the roof of the shield or *gun-house. **1940** *Illustr. London News* 16 Mar. 345 (*caption*) Here we give some photographs of the new 25-pdr. '*gun-how,'—the outstanding artillery novelty of the war. **1942** J. T. GORMAN *Mod. Weapons War* iv. 80 Guns and howitzers, as separate weapons, have been largely superseded by a single, all-purposes 'Gun-How', combining the long range of guns with a howitzer's greater weight of fire. **1940** *Illustr. London News* 20 Jan. 75/1 This drawing shows a *gun-howitzer—a weapon unknown in the World War, but of increasing importance in recent years—in the development of which British artillerymen have played a leading part. **1881** GREENER *Gun* 257 All the iron for gun-work..is of a superior quality to that to be generally obtained, and is known as *gun-iron. **1901** *Westm. Gaz.* 27 June 8/1 Acting Bombardier Mullen, the *gun captain and layer, had a truly marvellous escape. **1906** *Daily Chron.* 13 Aug. 5/7 While carrying out gunlayers' tests with the six-inch guns. **1938** C. Day Lewis *Overtures to Death* 47 Brisk at their intricate batteries the German gun-layers go About death's business. **1909** *Westm. Gaz.* 26 July 7/2 (*heading*) Remarkable *gun-laying tests. [**1941** W. Abbot *Handbk. Broadcasting* (ed. 2) i. 8 Two interesting microphones are the machine-gun and the parabolic. The machine-gun accessory..consists of a series of tubes strapped together through which sound is conveyed to a dynamic microphone which fits into the end.] **1962** A. Nisbett *Technique Sound Studio* i. 23 A '*gun' microphone..is sufficiently directional to pinpoint surfaces which cause echoes in concert halls. **1967** *Punch* 25 Jan. 132/2 The camera-team..trained their directional gun-microphones on guilty couples. **1908** J. M. Sullivan *Criminal Slang* 2 *A *gun-moll*, a woman thief. **1910** *National Police Gaz.* (U.S.) 31 Dec. 3/1 When the professional woman thief, who is known to the denizens of the underworld as a gun moll is arrested and taken back to the office, she is searched thoroughly. **1928** M. C. Sharpe *Chicago May* 286 Gun Molls, women who steal from men in the street, or carry guns. **1949** Koestler *Promise & Fulfilment* II. v. 279 Fierce-looking Yemenite gun-molls, Sephardi beauties. **1712** *Lond. Gaz.* No. 5019/4 Rewards of *Gun-money for the said Service. **1853** Humphreys *Coin-Coll. Man.* II. 511 The base silver money struck..by James II., in 1689..principally from some brass cannon, from which they took the name of gun-money; but they were composed of a mixture of metals, in which silver formed a small proportion. **1867** Smyth *Sailor's Word-bk.*, *Gun and head money*, given to the captors of an enemy's ship of war destroyed, or deserted, in fight. It was formerly assumed to be about £1000 per gun. **1853** Faraday *Lect. Non-metallic Elem.* i. 110 Other forms of lignine or woody tissue may be made to assume the peculiar condition of gun-cotton by similar treatment. Thus we may have gun-sawdust, and what may be termed *gun-paper. **1867** Smyth *Sailor's Word-bk.*, **Gun-pendulum*. See *Ballistic Pendulum*. **1883** Mackinlay *Text-bk. Gunnery* 146 The gun-pendulum has lately been occasionally used in experiments to find the recoil of small arms. **1877** M. Prior in *Daily News* 1 Oct., We..saw the Russians building *gun pits and shelter trenches for our next attack. **1884** *Mil. Engineering* (ed. 3) I. II. 8 Field artillery positions protected by breast-works and gun-pits. **1928** C. F. S. Gamble *N. Sea Air Station* xii, The German officer..standing in the after gun-pit. **1915** *Times* 4 Oct. 8/4 Our *gunplanes carried out during the night a bombardment of the German lines. **1915** W. E. Dommett *Aeroplanes & Airships* vi. 75 What has latterly been described as a battleplane or gunplane..does not yet exist in very great numbers. **1904** *Collier's* 16 July 15 As the breech-blocks close with a snap the *gun-pointer bends over his sights. **1918** *Chambers's Jrnl.* Dec. 839/1 This time the gun-pointer, having overcome his pardonable excitement, aimed true. **1769** Falconer *Dict. Marine* (1780) U 2 b, The *gun-ports of the lower deck. **1894** *Daily News* 22 Aug. 5/6 An officer on board the steamer Islam..denies that the portholes were ever meant for gun-ports, being intended for the readier discharge of cargo into lighters. **1876** Voyle & Stevenson *Milit. Dict.* (ed. 3), **Gun Portion*, in fortification, is half the merlon on each side of the gun, that is to say, 9 feet on one side of the embrasure and 9 feet on the other. **1884** *Mil. Engineering* (ed. 3) I. II. 44 The gun-portion parties, consisting of as many parties as there are guns, are distributed on their tasks by their respective N.C.O.'s. **1890** G. S. Clarke *Fortification* xiii. 176 The actual *gun power of the broadside iron-clads. **1928** *Daily Tel.* 11 Sept. 12/4 A division today lacks the tank-power and the gun-power necessary for it to strike as a whole. **1940** W. S. Churchill *Into Battle* (1941) 244 None of the British ships..was..affected in gun-power or mobility. **1852** tr. *Görgei's My Life in Hung.* I. 398 At the distance of three or four *gun-ranges from the Monostor. *Ibid.* II. xix. 182 They were..far out of gun-range of our trenches. **1856** Gun-range [see gun *sb.* 16 a]. **1904** *Daily Chron.* 21 Nov. 5/2 The gun-range at Brassact, near Antwerp. **1954** W. Faulkner *Fable* (1955) 283 As soon as they can get us up in gun-range again. **1825** C. Waterton *Wand. S. Amer.* 118 Almost out of *gun reach. **1918** W. Beebe *Jungle Peace* xi, Within gun-reach in front of me. **1898** *Encycl. Sport* II. 168 (Punt shooting), **Gun-rest*, a flat wooden support for the barrel of the gun. It has a long handle, enabling the fowler to regulate the elevation of the gun. **1925** A. S. M. Hutchinson *One Increasing Purpose* III. xv, Pike-rests... Not gun-rests; they are too far apart for that. **1899** *Athenæum* 21 Oct. 551/1 Isaacs, the *gun-runner, has good points as a man. **1883** *Standard* 21 Mar. 3/2 Two Europeans ..were arrested in the act of *gun-running on the Pondoland frontier. **1853** *Gun-sawdust [see *gun-paper*]. **1867** Smyth *Sailor's Word-bk.*, **Gun-searcher*, an iron instrument with several sharp-pointed prongs and a wooden handle: it is used to find whether the bore is honey-combed. **1968** *Times* 3 Feb. 8/3 Helicopter '*gunships' armed with machine-guns accounted for most of the toll. **1969** I. Kemp *Brit. G.I. in Vietnam* iii. 63, I saw two Huey gun-ships—assault helicopters—swooping down towards us... I listened gratefully to the whoosh of its [*sc.* the leading gun-ship's] 2.75 inch rockets and the stutter of its M60 machine guns. **1969** *Australian* 7 June 2/7 Other RAAF gunships remained overhead until the crew were lifted out. **1867** *Gun-sight [see gun *sb.* 16 a]. **1908** *Westm. Gaz.* 17 Sept. 5/1 It was discovered that all the gunsights in the ship had been removed. **1941** C. Morgan *Empty Room* i. 10 'Bomb-sights and the Paramounts.' 'The what?' 'That's what I call the fighter gunsights.' **1905** *Daily Chron.* 5 Apr. 8/5 *Gun-sighting platforms. **1943** *Hutchinson's Pict. Hist. War* 17 Feb.-11 May 43 (*caption*) A Bofors anti-aircraft gun manned by men of the U.S. Army at a *gun-site situated on the coast of Algeria. **1944** *Times* 3 Feb. 6/1 At the beginning of this year the American gunners took over a gunsite on London's outskirts. **1786** *Coalman's Courtsh. Creel-Wife's Dau.* (ed. 20) 6 No less than a *gun sleev'd linen sark on him. **1812** *Niles' Reg.* II. 131/1 The purveyor of public supplies advertises for..25000 *gun slings. **1867** Smyth *Sailor's Word-bk.*, *Gun-slings*, long rope grommets used for hoisting in and mounting them. **1907** *Yesterday's Shopping* (1969) 653/2 Gun and Rifle Slings. Webbing—3/9. **1953** in Wentworth & Flexner *Dict. Amer. Slang* (1960) 236/1 The *gun-slinger will spend..his life behind bars. **1960** *Spectator* 4 Mar. 321 Yet another brutalised gun-slinger. **1967** *Boston Sunday Herald* 7 May *Show Guide* 2/4 (*caption*) The gunslinger..comes to town, cigar between teeth, his prowess with a gun for sale. **1944** R. F. Adams *Western Words* (1945) 70/1 **Gun slinging*, slang for the act of shooting. **1958** *Church Times* 12 Sept. 3/1 The EOKA boycott is resented even more than the EOKA gun-slinging, for it affects every single citizen. **1754** *Ess. Manning Fleet* 39 Every Greyhound, Pointer, Setter, and *Gun-Spaniel. **1589** *Nottingham Rec.* (1889) IV. 227 For iiij *gunstickes and twoe drumme stickes xvjd. **1746** Miles in *Phil. Trans.* XLIV. 32 The Sulphur, tho' of a great Thickness round the said Gun-stick, could by no means be excited to any tolerable Degree. **1859** Bartlett *Dict. Amer.*, *Gun stick*, a ramrod. Western. **1795** R. Dodd *Rep. Hartlepool* 16 Merely knowing the management of a *gun-tackle. **1858** Simmonds *Dict. Trade*, *Gun-tackle*, the blocks and pulleys of a gun-carriage affixed to the side of a ship, by which it is run in and out of the port-hole. **1859** F. A. Griffiths *Artil. Man.* (1862) 108 'A gun tackle' increases the effect of the power threefold. **1882** Nares *Seamanship* (ed. 6) 55 Gun tackle purchase. Two double blocks, each fitted with a hook. **1891** Stevenson & L. Osbourne *Wrecker* (1892) 217 The decks were washed down..and a gun-tackle purchase rigged, before the boat arrived. **1898** P. H. Colomb *Mem. Sir A.C. Key* 350 That the strops of the gun-tackle blocks should henceforth be of wire instead of hemp. **1749** F. Smith *Voy. Disc.* II. 3 These *Gun Traps are usually set under some Bank Side, or in a Hollow Way. **1916** *Flying* (Aero Club of America) Jan. 820/1 The Sturtevant Battleplane is a biplane of tractor type built with remarkable simplicity and.. attention to efficiency. There are many novel features, including the steel construction, the placing of *gun turrets on either side of the central body. **1919** A. Klemin *Text-bk. Aeronaut. Engin.* 175 Pilot forward machine gun firing through propeller. Passenger in rear with circular gun-turret. **1935** *Jrnl. R. Aeronaut. Soc.* XXXIX. 988 In the case of rotatable gun turrets for aircraft, it is proposed to provide a removable top so as to allow the gunner to escape in case of emergency. **1959** J. L. Nayler *Dict. Aeronaut. Engin.* 125 *Gun turret*, a gun position in an aircraft under the control of an air-gunner... Modern gun turrets are power-operated, equipped with gyro gun-sights and often radar ranged and fired automatically. **1800** *Med. Jrnl.* III. 238 A sailor belonging to a *gun-vessel. **1835** *Westm. Rev.* XXIII. Advt. to No. xlv. 8 A free government is like a gun-vessel, with its gun amidships. **1898** P. Manson *Trop. Diseases* vii. 134 The skin [in Yellow Fever] is said to emit a peculiar odour like *gun washings. **1915** *Illustr. London News* CXLVI. 234/1 The deck of a German submarine with the hatch of the *gun-well open. **1858** Greener *Gunnery* 183 This iron is sold to the *gun-work forgers. **1889** *Century Dict.* s.v., An officer detailed upon gun-work exclusively. **1899** *Westm. Gaz.* 15 Sept. 2/1 M. Foà's record of his gun-work amongst the big game of Central Africa. **1905** *Spectator* 4 Mar. 311/2 A meeting of *gun-workers..held at Birmingham on Monday.

gun (gʌn), *v.* Inflected **gunned, gunning.** [f. gun *sb.*]

1. *trans.* †**a.** To provide with guns. (See also gunned *a.*) *Obs.* †**b.** To assail or fight with guns. *Obs.*

[**1659**: see gunned.] *a* **1679** Earl Orrery *Guzman* iii, I cannot chuse but laugh to think how I shall gun the Oviedo's and Pirracco's. **1698** Vanbrugh *2nd Pt. Æsop* i, They gilded her, and painted her, and rigg'd and gunn'd her, and so sent her a privateering.

c. *Stock Exchange.* (See quot.)

1870 J. K. Medbery *Men & Myst. Wall St.* 136 Gunning a stock, is to use every art to produce a 'break', when it is known that a certain house is heavily supplied, and would be unable to resist an attack.

d. To shoot (a person). Also with *up. U.S. colloq.*

1898 H. S. Canfield *Maid of Frontier* 83 I'll gun you if you do that again. **1916** H. L. Wilson *Somewhere in Red Gap* i. 35 Wilfred went pasty, indeed, thinking his host was going to gun him. **1923** L. J. Vance *Baroque* xxvii. 178 If you don't want to have your Fiancy gunned up without notice by some wild-eyed wop. **1934** R. Chandler in *Black Mask* Oct. 36/1 Canales had no motive to gun Lou, unless it got back the money.

e. *Forestry.* (See quot. 1957.)

1905 *Terms Forestry & Logging* 39 *Gun*, to aim a tree in felling it. In the case of very large, brittle trees, such as redwood, a sighting device (gunning stick) is used. **1957** *Brit. Commonw. Forest Terminol.* II. 88 *Gun*, in felling, to select the direction in which a tree should fall.

2. *intr.* To shoot with a gun; hence, to make war. *to gun for*: to shoot for, to go in search of with a gun; also, to go after or in search of; to seek to attack, harm, or destroy (someone). Phrase *to go gunning*, in which the participial form represents historically *a-gunning* (see gunning *vbl. sb.* and -ing[2]). Chiefly *U.S.*

a **1622** Sir R. Hawkins *Observ.* §10 (1622) 19 Which is a bad custome received and vsed of many ignorant persons presently to gun at all whatsoever they discover, before they speake with them. **1622** Drayton *Poly-olb.* xxiii. (1748) 355 Forc'd by some yelping cute to give the greyhounds view, Which are at length let slip when gunning out they go. **1767** *N. Eng. Hist. & Gen. Register* (1860) XIV. 47 All Persons coming to gun on said Island after Game. **1779** D. Gookin *Ibid.* (1862) XVI. 29 Our men went out this day gunning, saw deer and wild Turkey, killed none. **1839** Marryat *Diary Amer.* Ser. I. II. 102, I was hardly twelve years old, and had never been allowed to go out gunning. **1865** U. S. Grant in *Century Mag.* (1889) Nov. 146/2 The whole captures since the army started out gunning, will amount to not less than twelve thousand men and probably fifty pieces of artillery. **1888** *Century Mag.* Mar. 780/1 The guards.. used..to gun for prisoners' heads..after the fashion of boys after squirrels. **1893** W. K. Post *Harvard Stories* 188 That bull Mick Shreedy is gunning for me just at present. **1903** *N.Y. Times* 29 Sept. 1 Others talked of mysterious influences that had been 'gunning' for financiers of prominence. **1922** *Daily Mail* 5 Dec. 9 Observing that the Company's statement is not a denial of the assertion that it is 'gunning' for the Mesopotamian oilfields claimed by the heirs of Abdul Hamid. **1930** 'E. Queen' *French Powder Mystery* xix. 171 Mr. Trask has been gunning for Bernice [with a view to marriage] for over a year. **1936** Wodehouse *Laughing Gas* xviii. 198 Nice little bit of luck, finding her like that... Matter of fact, I wasn't gunning for her at all, really. I came to get that notebook. **1950** G. Greene *Third Man* iii. 31 I'm gunning..for Colonel Callaghan. **1955** *Times* 16 June 12/2 You found when you came back from Oslo that for other reasons the Communist Party was 'gunning' for Mr. Frankel? **1958** *Observer* 10 Aug. 3/2 Last week American commentators were gunning for Mr. Dulles ('too busy, too tired, too discouraged, too stale,' said Walter Lippmann..). **1960** C. Day Lewis *Buried Day* ix. 204, I felt that 'They' were gunning for me again.

3. *trans.* To look at closely, to examine.

1819 J. H. Vaux *Mem.* II. 179 To *gun* anything is to look at or examine it. **1859** G. W. Matsell *Vocabulum* 39/2 The copper gunned me as if he was fly to my mug. **1946** Mezzrow & Wolfe *Really Blues* xii. 223 They wanted to be ..alert and keen-sighted.., gunning everything.

4. = *to give the gun* (give *v.* 14 c). Hence **gunned** *ppl. a.*

1930 *Amer. Speech* V. 290 *Gun the motor*, accelerate the motor [of an aircraft]. **1941** N. Alley *I Witness* 308 We gunned into an easy takeoff. **1943** R. Chandler *Lady in Lake* (1944) xxxiv. 180 Degarno let the clutch in and gunned the motor and hit forty in the first block and a half. **1965** G. McInnes *Road to Gundagai* xiii. 224 Dad's favourite manoeuvre..was to..gun the bike roaring down the front path. *Ibid.* xv. 274 A car door crashing shut and a terrific gunning of the motor. **1967** 'J. Cross' *To Hell for Half-a-Crown* i. 13 The car went by, with the heavy roar of the gunned motor. **1968** P. Durst *Badge of Infamy* xvi. 171 He gunned the Volkswagen and fell in behind.

gun, pa. t. of gin *v.*[1]

‖**guna** ('gʊnə), *sb.* Also goon. [Skr. *guṇa*.] **1.** In *Sanskrit Grammar*, the middle grade of an ablaut-series of vowels; by the native Indian grammarians viewed as produced from the weak grade by the prefixing of the vowel *ă*; the process of raising a vowel to the middle grade. Hence sometimes used in Indo-germanic comparative grammar for the *ĕ*-grade of the o:ĕ:ŏ series. Also *attrib.*

1804 Carey *Skr. Gr.* 12 The vowel which would otherwise take goon. **1835** Wollaston *Skr. Gr.* 5 The change is called Guna. **1841** H. H. Wilson *Skr. Gram.* (1847) 7 The purport of the terms Guṇa and Vṛiddhi. *Ibid.*, The Guṇa and Vṛiddhi representatives. **1866** Max Müller *Skr. Gram.* 11 The corresponding Guṇa-vowel.

2. In the Sankhya philosophy of India, any one of the three dominating principles of nature.

1862 Vijnana Bhikshu *Sankhya-Sára* 6 S'ankara's own definition is in these words: 'The reflecting, that the *gunas*, —goodness, passion, and darkness,—are objects of my perception, [etc.]'. **1875** M. Monier-Williams *Indian Wisdom* 67 The dominance of one or other of the three Gunas, goodness, passion, or darkness. **1962** Brahmacharini Usha *Ramakrishna-Vedanta Wordbk.* 34 Man's mood and character vary according to the predominating guna. **1968** *Jrnl. Mus. Acad. Madras* XXXIX. 25 An exposition of Rama's *Gunas* as depicted by Tyagaraja.

Hence **'guna** *v. trans.*, to gunate.

1862 T. Clark *Compar. Gram.* §117. 80 The four classes ..are distinguished..by the use or omission of guna... The First Class both gunaes and accents the root vowel... The Sixth Class does not guna the root vowel.

gunal, obs. form of gunwale.

gunarchy: see gynarchy.

gunate ('gʊneɪt), *v.* [f. guna + -ate[3].] *trans.* In *Sanskrit Grammar*, to subject to the change known as guna. Hence **gu'nated** *ppl. a.*; **gu'nation**, the process of gunating or condition of being gunated.

1864 M. Williams *Skr. Gram.* 24 The vowels of roots cannot be gunated or vriddhied. *Ibid.* 25 The practice of gunating vowels is not peculiar to Sanskrit alone. **1868** tr. *Benfey's Skr. Gram.* (ed. 2) 34 *note*, A long or short radical *i, u, ṛi*, is generally gunated, if final. **1879** Whitney *Skr. Gram.* 104 The abl. and gen. masc. and fem. have regularly ..the ending *s* with gunated vowel before it. **1882** Ogilvie, *Gunate..Gunation.*

gun-boat, gunboat ('gʌnbəʊt).

1. a. A boat or small vessel of light draft carrying one or more guns of large calibre; any small vessel fitted for carrying guns.

1793 Craufurd in *Ld. Auckland's Corr.* (1862) III. 117 The enemy were masters of the shore, and entirely commanded it by their gunboats. **1797** Nelson in Nicolas *Disp.* (1845) II. 404 The Spaniards having sent out a great number of Mortar Gun-boats and armed Launches. **1836** Marryat *Midsh. Easy* xiii, A small convoy..under the protection of two gun-boats. **1880** McCarthy *Own Times* III. xlii. 264 Four of the gunboats were almost immediately disabled.

attrib. **1804** Larwood *No Gun Boats* 25 A forest of Gun-boat-masts. *Ibid.* 40 This is the reception destined for the Gun Boat Armada. **1874** Bancroft *Footpr. Time* xxvi. 664 A second unsuccessful gunboat attack.

b. *gunboat diplomacy*, diplomacy supported by the use, or threatened use, of military force.

1927 *U.S. Naval Inst. Proc.* Feb. 234 It has been said that the days of 'gunboat diplomacy' in China are over. **1960** *Daily Tel.* 2 Sept. 12/2 'Gun-boat' diplomacy has long and properly disappeared. **1961** *Ibid.* 6 July 1 The Iraqi delegate called the British action in Kuwait 'gunboat diplomacy at its worst'. **1969** *Times* 3 Mar. 23/4 (Advt.), There's nothing to regret about the passing of gunboat diplomacy.

2. *local U.S. Coal-mining.* 'A self-dumping box on wheels, used for raising coal on slopes, and holding three or four tons of coal' (*Cent. Dict.*).

3. Usu. in *pl.* Large shoes or feet. *U.S. slang.*
1870 D. MACRAE *Americans at Home* I. 68 Most of the people wear rubbers over their boots—gunboats as they sometimes call them from their size. **1919** *Dialect Notes* V. 69 *Gunboats*, the feet. 'Keep your *gunboats* out of my way.' **1932** J. FARRELL *Studs Lonigan* (1936) I. ii. 22 Reardon nodded as he shifted his weight from the right to the left gunboat. **1939** *Amer. Speech* XIV. 90 *Gun boats*, big shoes. **1951** in Wentworth & Flexner *Dict. Amer. Slang* (1960) 235 He brought some of the [size 14 EE] gunboats with him from the states, but they wore out.

gun-cotton (ˈgʌnˌkɒt(ə)n). A highly explosive compound discovered in 1846 by Schönbein, and prepared by steeping cotton in nitric and sulphuric acids, formerly much used for blasting, but now almost superseded by dynamite.
Chemically, gun-cotton is one of a series of nitrates of cellulose differing in composition and properties according to the strength of acid used and the period of digestion. From other members of the series are obtained the products celluloid and collodion. See also PYROXYLIN.
1846 *Mech. Mag.* 3 Oct. 330 The last and most curious experiment was the explosion of a piece of the gun cotton when placed upon loose gunpowder. **1846** COL. HAWKER *Diary* (1893) II. 269 (31 Oct.) Went to see Mr. Charles Lancaster, after his miraculous escape in firing the new gun cotton. **1846** *Ann. Reg.* 203 The interest of scientific men and of the public has been strongly excited by the discovery by Professor Schönbein of an explosive compound..called Gun Cotton. **1847** FARADAY in B. Jones *Life* (1870) 237, I do not talk about gun-cotton, because I think you will let me know when anything philosophical or important turns up respecting it. **1875** DARWIN *Insectiv. Pl.* vi. 125 Gun Cotton which consists of cellulose with the hydrogen replaced by nitrogen. **1894** *Times* 31 Jan. 3/2 [Dr. Odling said] 'Guncotton' was most commonly used to express the least soluble form, and there was a broad distinction between collodion cotton and guncotton.
attrib. **1876** *Daily News* 30 Nov. 3/5 The short, sudden crack of a gun-cotton detonation.

gundalo, obs. form of GONDOLA.

gunde, variant of GOUND *Obs.*

gun-deck. *Naut.* A deck which carries guns; *esp.* in an old-fashioned ship of the line, the lowest of the decks on which guns are placed. Also *attrib.*
1677 *Lond. Gaz.* No. 1250/2 The English soon obliged them to quit their Upper-deck, and betake themselves to their Gun-deck. **1687** *Ibid.* No. 2251/4 Could we have played our whole Gun-Deck Fire. **1691** *Ibid.* No. 2690/4 The *St. David* is now got up so far, that her Gun Deck is dry at Low Water. **1691** T. H[ALE] *Acc. New Invent.* 125 Having found..the distance of Trunnions of the Guns from the Gun-deck..to determine the place of the Gun-deck. **1769** FALCONER *Dict. Marine* (1780) Ll. 4b, The gun-deck..is flush without cabins or bulk-heads. *Ibid.*, *Gun-room*, an appartment on the after end of the lower, or gun-deck, of a ship of war. **1897** MARY KINGSLEY *W. Africa* 427 On her gun deck is the hospital, on the main deck the officers' quarters and the exercise ground for the sailors.

gundelet, -olet, obs. forms of GONDOLET.

gundelo(e, -ow, -ilo(w, obs. ff. GONDOLA.

‖**gundi** (ˈgʌndɪ). [Tripolitan Arabic (? orig. Berber); Lyon writes it in Arab. characters *qundī*; in Tripoli the letter *qāf* is pronounced (g).] A kind of rat, *Ctenodactylus massoni.*
1781 PENNANT *Quadrupeds* II. 405 Gundi Marmot.. Inhabits Barbary. **1821** LYON *Trav. N. Africa* i. 31, I [sallied forth] with my gun in search of animals called Gundy [etc.]. **1884** *Stand. Nat. Hist.* V. 92 The gundi is about the size of a large *Arvicola*. **1895** LYDEKKER *Nat. Hist.* III. 155.

gundola, -dolo: see GONDOLA.

gundy, variant of GOUNDY *a. Obs.*

gundy, var. GOONDIE.

†**gundy-gut.** *Obs.* A fat paunch; *pl.* a gluttonous, voracious person. (Cf. GREEDIGUT(S.)
a **1700** B. E. *Dict. Cant. Crew*, *Gundigutts*, a fat pursy Fellow. **1712** ARBUTHNOT *John Bull* III. ii, They gave one another nick-names: she called him gundy-guts. **1718** OZELL *Tournefort's Voy.* I. 156 Bacchus sits quite o' top of the Basso Relievo with Asses ears and a huge gundy gut. **1764** T. BRYDGES *Homer Travest.* (1797) II. 292 Slice after slice you'll see him cut, And stuff within his gundy gut.

gunfainun, -fan(o)un, obs. vars. GONFANON.

gunfaneur, variant of GONFANEUR *Obs.*

‖**gunge**[1], **gunj** (gʌndʒ). Also 8 **gunja**. [a. Pers. *ganj* a magazine, granary.] A market.
1776 *Trial of Nundocomar* 93/1 On a terrass, up stairs, there is an upper room, where Gungabissen lives: on the outside of that, there is a gunja, where we sat. **1794** BURKE *Sp. agst. W. Hastings* Wks. XV. 365 By employing military men..as masters of markets and of gunges. **1800** *Asiat. Ann. Reg., Misc. Tracts* 290/1 The town of Bopaul is extensive... On the outside is a large gunge, with streets wide and straight. **1848** STOCQUELER *Orient. Interp., Gunjes*, grain-markets.

gunge[2] (gʌndʒ). *slang.* [Of uncertain origin; perh. associated with GOO, GRUNGE, GUNK, etc.] A sticky or viscid mass; any messy or clogging substance, esp. one considered otherwise unidentifiable. Also, general rubbish, clutter, filth.
1969 *Sunday Times* 7 Dec. (Business News) 35/7 Recently the Birkenheads received an export order for a rather special type of..er, well, gunge. This was for lissage, which is also known as English Ground Flake, mixed with linseed oil. **1970** PARTRIDGE *Dict. Slang* Suppl. 1181/1 *Gunge*, grease; oily dirt, the opposite of *clag*, dry dirt: engineers': since ca. 1940. (D. F. Wharton, Oct. 24, 1965.) **1973** *Amat. Photographer* 3 Jan. 33/3, I use a soft bristle brush and pure soap to really get the gunge out of the grooves [of a gramophone record]. **1977** *Times Lit. Suppl.* 6 May 547/1 Handed down like the recipe for some regional gunge from one bad cook to the next. **1979** *New Scientist* 11 Jan. 93/2 They call this solid material tholin (after the Greek word for muddy), but it seems likely that chemists will continue to call this rather familiar material 'gunge'. **1985** *Listener* 30 May 37/1 Adam and Eve emerge from a transportable saucer of murky gunge.

Hence as *v. trans.*, to clog (something) *up*, as with a sticky or messy substance; also *intr.*, to become obstructed or clogged *up*.
1976 NICHOLS & ARMSTRONG *Workers Divided* I. 68 They could be involved in very heavy physical work when, inevitably, this particular plant 'gunged up'. **1977** *Sounds* 1 Jan. 20/4 A few academic 'experts' know *something* about the short-term effects of sniffing, but aren't too sure about exactly *how* it gunges up the body.

gung ho (gʌŋ həʊ). Also **kung-hou**. [Chin. *kung* work + *ho* together.] A slogan adopted in the war of 1939–1945 by the United States Marines under General E. Carlson (1896–1947); hence as *adj.*: enthusiastic, eager, zealous.
1942 *Times Mag.* (New York) 8 Nov. 13/4 Borrowing an idea from China, Carlson frequently has what he calls 'kung-hou' meetings... Problems are threshed out and orders explained. **1943** *Life* 20 Sept. 58, I [*sc.* E. Carlson] told them of the motto of the Chinese Co-operatives, *Gung Ho*. It means Work Together... My motto caught on and they began to call themselves the *Gung Ho* Battalion. **1959** *She* May 21/3 All would be *gung ho* (in favour) of declaring him a *fungus* (musty character). **1967** R. M. STERN *Kessler Legacy* (1968) xvi. 143 In those days he was very gung ho for National Socialism and the pan-Germanic grandeur it was going to produce. **1968** M. LOCKWOOD *Accessory* (1969) ii. 59 I've always thought of you as being—I don't know, full steam ahead about life. Not gung-ho exactly, but—well always ready to manage and organize things. **1969** I. KEMP *British G.I. in Vietnam* iii. 49 He..was one of the most 'gung-ho' (exceptionally keen to be personally involved in combat) characters I ever met. **1970** *Times* 28 May 7/5 Today's grunts are noticeably different from those who filled the enthusiastic 'Gung-ho' units of a few years back.

gungy (ˈgʌndʒɪ), *a. slang.* Also **gungey**. [f. GUNGE + -Y[1].] Of a sticky or messy consistency; mucky, greasy, slimy. Also, second-rate, spoilt.
1962 S. RAVEN *Close of Play* xv. 188 Hugo started to lift the ball. This policy was rewarded by five sixes (two of them at least rather gungy ones) in three overs. **1971** *Frendz* 21 May 13 Country of Origin/Grade. Nepali, second Quality. .. Dope, Texture and quality. Very soft, pliable gungy & strong smelling. **1973** 'D. HALLIDAY' *Dolly & Starry Bird* xiv. 208 Then I remembered the pool and stepped sideways beside Di's gungy flask of sun lotion. **1976** *Observer* (Colour Suppl.) 12 Dec. 12/2 (Advt.), The soap is gungy and so greasy that you can't get it off your hands after you've washed. **1979** TOWLER & COXON *Fate Anglican Clergy* v. 126 Perhaps the most common piece of theological college argot is the word 'topos' to refer to lavatories, but..other terms enjoyed wide currency in the 1960s, such as 'Moab' (wash-place)..'prot' and 'protty' (Low Church)..'crud' and 'gungey' (second-rate, inferior, spoiled). **1985** *Spectator* 18 May 39/3 If you're in the mood for something gungey, there's certainly something here for you: chicken stuffed with lamb served with a port sauce.

gunhil(l, obs. form of GUNWALE.

†ˈ**gun-hole.** *Obs.*
1. An embrasure; a port-hole for a gun.
1532 *Extracts Aberd. Reg.* (1844) I. 145 Ane blokhouise.. with gunhollis and duris of aistlar. **1687** A. LOVELL tr. *Thevenot's Trav.* I. 274 Seven or eight great Gun-holes two foot above the Water, by which the Guns play level with the surface of it. **1705** BOSMAN *Guinea* 27 We had no Doors to most of our Gun-holes.

2. *attrib.* in **gunhole angel, groat**, coins.
Not known in the Coin Department of the British Museum. Mr. Barclay V. Head suggests that *goonhole*, *gunhoill*, may be corruptions of some foreign proper name.
a **1577** GASCOIGNE *Flowers* (1587) 32 Hick, Hob and Dick ..Have many times more goonhole grotes in store..than hee. **1598** *Extracts Aberd. Reg.* (1848) II. 165 'The prices of gold and syluer proclamit at Edinburgh..1598'..The harie ducatt 7 *lib.* 5*s.* 0*d.* The gunhoill angell 5 *lib.* 2*s.* 0*d.* The angell nobill 5 *lib.* 5*s.* 0*d.*

gunibri, gunibry, varr. GIMBRI.

gunite (ˈgʌnaɪt). *Build.* Also **gunnite**. [f. GUN *sb.* + -ITE[1] 4 a.] A mixture of cement, sand, and water applied through a hose. Also *attrib.*
1914 C. WEBER in *Jrnl. Western Soc. Engineers* Mar. 278 The product of the Cement Gun is called 'Gunite' in order to distinguish it from the ordinary cement stucco or plaster work, and for the reason that the material develops qualities which put it in a class all by itself. Gunite is usually a cement mortar composed of about one part of Portland cement and three parts of coarse, sharp sand passing through a ⅜ in. screen. **1930** *Engineering* 21 Mar. 368/3 The upstream face of the domes was covered with a layer of gunite, 1½ in. thick, reinforced with wire mesh. **1962** *Ibid.* 12 Jan. 52/1 The arduous conditions imposed on the hosing of cement guns has led to the development of an improved form of gunite hose. **1970** *Telegraph* (Brisbane) 30 Jan. 18/2 Swimming pools..built to the highest engineering standards of concrete and steel, using the latest gunnite spray methods.

gunj, variant of GUNGE.

gunja, variant of GANJA; obs. f. GUNGE.

gunk (gʌŋk). orig. *U.S.* **1. a.** [Proprietary term.] (See quots. 1948 and 1970.)
1932 *Official Gaz.* (U.S. Pat. Off.) 23 Aug. 864/1 A. F. Curran Co.,..Gunk. For Liquid Soaps and Liquid Cleaners for Hard Surfaced Materials or Articles. **1948** MENCKEN *Amer. Lang.* Suppl. I. v. 347 *Gunk*, a self-emulsifying colloidal detergent solvent... Launched by the Curran Corporation, Malden, Mass., in 1932. **1969** J. LEASOR *They don't make them like that any More* i. 14, I.. poured Gunk all over the engine to freshen it up. **1970** *UK Trade Names* 221/1 Gunk—degreasing compound—Bennett (Hyde) Ltd, Boston Mills, Hyde, Cheshire.

b. Any of a variety of viscous or liquid substances. *slang.*
1949 in Wentworth & Flexner *Dict. Amer. Slang* (1960) 235/2 You can actually see the gook and gunk that drains out with your [motor] oil. **1950** R. STARNES *Another Mug for Bier* (1952) xx. 82, I smeared additional gunk on my eye. **1958** C. C. ADAMS *Space Flight* iii. 84 Work has also been carried on with jelly and related propellants, sometimes affectionately known as 'gunk'. **1958** I. ASIMOV *Whiff of Death* (1968) v. 46 Foster referred to the useless materials prepared by side-reactions in the course of a synthesis as 'gunk'. **1959** *N.Y. Times* 30 May 2/1 Its openings have been washed with a black preservative 'gunk'. **1965** *Guardian* 19 Aug. 6/5 'Gunk' is..a crude rubber which he moulds on to costumes. **1966** C. HENRY *Third Twin* v. 66 Too much eye gunk and lipstick—that sort of girl.

2. A derogatory term for a person. *slang.*
1964 *Publ. Amer. Dial. Soc.* XLII. 30 Chinaman, Jap.. gunk. **1968** P. MARLOWE *Hire me Hearse* vi. 88 A couple of gunks who used to be bouncers at the 'Golden Pagoda'. **1968** J. D. MACDONALD *Pale Grey for Guilt* (1969) vi. 74 It was a drag to listen big-eyed to that tired gunk and say Oh and Ahh.

3. *Comb.* **gunk-hole** *colloq.*, a small cove or fishing hamlet.
1908 G. S. WASSON *Home from Sea* x. 317, I rec'lect well hearing of her call it nothing only a dead-and-alive little two-cent gunk-hole of a place. **1927** G. BRADFORD *Gloss. Sea Terms* 78/1 *Gunk hole*, a small narrow channel dangerous to navigate owing to current and to numerous rocks and ledges. **1958** K. M. WELLS *Cruising Georgian Bay* 94 And then you may cruise back to your hidden gunk hole near the inlet entrance and enjoy peace.

gunless (ˈgʌnlɪs), *a.* [f. GUN *sb.* + -LESS.] Without a gun; having no gun.
1867 H. KINGSLEY in *Fortn. Rev.* Nov. 555 It would seem incredible that a tried officer..should be foiled by a few almost gunless savages. **1893** W. H. HUDSON *Patagonia* 143 How a field naturalist spends his days gunless in the woods.

gun-lock (ˈgʌnlɒk). That part of the mechanism of a gun by which the charge is exploded. (See LOCK *sb.*) **b.** *attrib.*, as ***gun-lock hammer, maker, screw, spring.***
1731 *Gentl. Mag.* I. 265 They [*i.e.* Spaniards] treated her [*i.e.* a ship's] men barbarously, torturing their Fingers with Gunlock-Screws, and lighted Matches. **1771** H. WALPOLE *Vertue's Anecd. Paint.* (1782) IV. 219 Carving and graving for snuff-boxes, gun-locks, and in mother of pearl. **1795** R. DODD *Rep. Hartlepool* 16 The breaching gun-lock, on ship-board, is infinitely superior to any fire-match. **1814** *Sporting Mag.* XLIV. 150 John Bradford, a gun-lock maker. **1827** J. F. COOPER *Prairie* I. i. 21 The ticking of gun-locks was heard. **1875** KNIGHT *Dict. Mech.*, *Gun-lock Hammer*, the cock or striker of a fire-arm lock. **1894** *Outing* (U.S.) XXIV. 443/2 A gun-lock spring.

gunmaker (ˈgʌnmeɪkə(r)). One who makes or manufactures guns.
1385–6 *Durham Acc. Rolls* (Surtees) 390 Item Joh'i Gonmaker, ex præcepto d'ni Prioris, iijs. iiijd. **1597** in *Compt. Bk. D. Wedderburne* (S.H.S. 1898) 82 Sauld to John Traill and William Lowis wyffis gunmakeris twa boundis lynt. **1816** *Sporting Mag.* XLVII. 237 Our gun-makers, whose superiority over those in every other country..is universally acknowledged. **1849** MACAULAY *Hist. Eng.* viii. II. 441 All the gunmakers of Utrecht were found too few to execute the orders for pistols and muskets. **1858** GREENER *Gunnery* 229 *note*, Barrel welders, borers, lock-filers, &c., are not technically gun-makers: the latter are those workmen who, having barrels, locks, wood for stock, &c., make them into a gun. It has been customary to say gunsmiths; but this appellation can be applied to the worker in iron only.

So ˈ**gunmaking**, the manufacture of guns.
1846 GREENER *Sci. Gunnery* Pref. 7 Gun-making should be to the sportsman a matter of peculiar interest. **1858** —— *Gunnery* 171 The gunmaking profession.

gun-man, gunman (ˈgʌnmən).
1. One who is armed with a gun; one who shoots with a gun. (Formerly applied esp. to North American Indian warriors.) Also *fig.*
1624 GATAKER *Transubst.* 62 A gun-man (it may be) today, and a pike-man to morrow. **1685** COTTON tr. *Montaigne* II. 530 Gun-men of great ability and no common virtue. **1761** *Descr. S. Carolina* 60 The Cherokees..have about Three Thousand Gun-Men. **1791** W. BARTRAM *Carolina* 388 It is said they are able to muster five hundred gun-men or warriors. **1888** *Pall Mall G.* 19 May 6 H...is not only a

penman, but a gunman, a rodman, and a horseman. **1903** *N.Y. Sun* 23 Nov. 1 A notorious outlaw and one of the most expert gun men of the West. **1913** *Industrial Worker* (Spokane, Wash.) 3 July, Last evening one of the gunmen of the A.C.M. Co. came to the jail and tried to get a blacksmith out of here. **1921** *Daily Colonist* (Victoria, B.C.) 15 Oct. 4/7 The gunman who yesterday was foiled in his attempt to rob the Bank of Hamilton, robbed the Union Bank today. **1931** *Star* 8 May 6/2 Lord Hailsham is rapidly making a name for himself in the House of Lords as a gunman of debate. **1946** KOESTLER *Thieves in Night* xiv. 277 He seems to regard him as a kind of gunman-messiah. **1972** *Daily Tel.* 13 Jan. 1 The Army said five IRA gunmen were shot and injured during the two-and-a-half-hour battle.

2. One who has to do with guns or is engaged in their manufacture.

1881 GREENER *Gun* 270 The strikes of the gunmen in Birmingham during the Crimean War.

Hence **'gunmanship**, the status, performance, or practice of a gunman.

1925 L. O'FLAHERTY *Informer* vi. 78 We can imagine him perfecting himself in the arts of gunmanship. **1959** I. JEFFERIES *13 Days* ii. 29 We would practice academic gunmanship... The idea was to jerk the gun and fire it off like a rattle. **1965** *Economist* 20 Feb. 791/1 Just how serious was London's recent outbreak of criminal gun-manship?

'gun-metal. **1.** A bronze formerly much used for cannon; now, a common term for alloys of copper and tin (or zinc).

1541 *Act 33 Hen. VIII*, c. 7 §1 No person..should.. conuey anie brasse..laten, bell metall, gun metall, ne shroffe metal into..partes beyonde the sea. **1693** T. POVEY in *Phil. Trans.* XVII. 736 About 20*l.* of Lead is usually put into 100*l.* of Pot-metal; but about 6*l.* is sufficient to put into 100*l.* of Gun-metal. **1776** ADAM SMITH *W.N.* IV. viii. (1869) II. 240 The exportation of unmanufactured brass, of what is called gun-metal, bell-metal, and shroff-metal, still continues to be prohibited. **1824** TREDGOLD *Ess. Cast Iron* 114 A cast bar of the alloy of copper and tin commonly called gunmetal. **1854** J. SCOFFERN in *Orr's Circ. Sci., Chem.* 492 Gun-metal is an alloy of eleven parts tin and one hundred of copper. **1858** GREENER *Gunnery* 61 Gun metal, technically so called, is a compound of copper and tin, in the proportion of five, eight, and ten pounds of the latter to 100 pounds of the former. **1881** RAYMOND *Mining Gloss.* s.v., Aich's metal and some other gun-metals contain zinc and iron but no tin. **1887** D. A. LOW *Machine Draw.* (1892) 80 Alloys consisting of copper and tin are called bronze or gun-metal.

attrib. **1879** *Man. Artil. Exerc.* 168 Attach the gun-metal plates to it by screws supplied.

2. A colour resembling that of gun-metal, a dull bluish-grey.

1905 *Daily Chron.* 12 July 6/7 Gun-metal coloured taffeta. **1923** *Daily Mail* 8 Oct. 1/2 In Gun Metal, Shoe Grey and Black. **1931** *Daily Tel.* 21 May 6/3 A train of gun-metal chiffon. **1952** C. DAY LEWIS tr. *Virgil's Aeneid* II. 42 Its angrily-rearing head, its gun-metal neck.

Gunn (gʌn). [The name of John Battiscombe *Gunn* (b. 1928), physicist, who first observed the effect in 1963.] ***Gunn effect***: a phenomenon observed in certain semiconductors (as gallium arsenide and indium phosphide), in which a (constant) electric field greater than some threshold value applied between opposite faces of a thin piece of the material results in an oscillatory electric current with a frequency in the microwave region. So ***Gunn diode***: a semiconductor diode in which the Gunn effect is produced.

1964 H. KROEMER in *Proc. IEEE* LII. 1736/1 Gunn (1) has recently discovered a new kind of current oscillations at microwave frequencies, in *n*-type GaAs and InP... The purpose of this correspondence is to point out that most..of the known properties of the Gunn effect can be explained, at least quantitatively, if [etc.]. **1966** *Ibid.* LIV. 1480/2 Oscillations covering 4 Gc/s to 31 Gc/s from a single Gunn diode. **1969** *New Scientist* 4 Dec. 511/2 A solid-state microwave source—a Gunn diode—is used as part of a low-cost electron spin resonance (ESR) experimental system. **1971** I. J. KAMPEL *Semiconductors* xix. 198 Devices such as the Gunn-effect diode considerably extend the range of the electromagnetic spectrum in which we can control and generate frequencies.

gunnage ('gʌnɪdʒ). [f. GUN *sb.* + -AGE.] **a.** The money distributed among the captors of a ship, assigned in proportion to the number of guns on the captured ship. ? *Obs.* **b.** 'The number of guns in a ship-of-war' (Ogilvie 1855).

1703 *Lond. Gaz.* No. 3959/3 He will..pay..their just Proportion due to each of them for Gunnage and Tunnage of the said Ship. **1705** *Ibid.* No. 4186/8 The Officers and Companies of Her Majesty's Ship Orford will..be paid their Proportion of Gunnage and Tunnage of the Ship Hazardous, a French Man of War.

gunnal, obs. form of GUNWALE.

gunne, obs. pa. t. of GIN *v.*[1]; obs. form of GUN.

gunned (gʌnd), *a.* [f. GUN *sb.* + -ED[2].] Furnished with guns: chiefly qualified by advs., as ***heavily, lightly, powerfully gunned*** = having heavy, etc. guns.

1659 D. PELL *Impr. Sea* 177 *note*, To fight against all the Navies, and Gunn'd Armadoes in the world. *Ibid.* 555 *note*, Many a ship that is well rigged,..manned, and gunned. **1666** *Lond. Gaz.* No. 66/1 His ships were all of them old, and neither man'd nor gun'd. **1727** A. HAMILTON *New Acc. E. Ind.* I. ii. 19 He was attacked by three French Ships, each gunn'd and mann'd as well as he. **1804** NELSON in Nicolas *Disp.* (1846) VI. 282 The Schooner is far too heavily gunned. **1865** *Cornh. Mag.* Aug. 223 That company of men ..shooting-coated, gunned, and belted. **1897** C. BIGHAM *With Turkish Army Thessaly* iii. 22 Artillery..was excellently horsed and gunned, but poorly trained.

gunnel ('gʌnəl). [Of unknown origin; Ray regarded it as Cornish.] A small, eel-shaped marine fish, *Centronotus* or *Murænoides gunnellus*, common in British waters; the butter-fish. Also ***spotted gunnel***.

1686 WILLUGHBY & RAY *Hist. Pisc.* 115 Gunnellus Cornubiensium, nonnullis Butterfish. **1740** R. BROOKES *Art of Angling* II. xviii. 123 The Butter-Fish or Gunnel..sometimes attains the length of six Inches..is taken frequently on the Cornish Coast. **1828** J. FLEMING *Brit. Anim.* 207 *Gunnellus vulgaris*, Common Gunnel..*G. viviparus*, Viviparous Gunnel. **1836** YARRELL *Brit. Fishes* I. 239 The Spotted Gunnel, or Butterfish..is sufficiently distinguished from the true Blennies by its dorsal fin..and by its elongated, slender, and compressed body. **1863** WOOD *Nat. Hist.* III. 291 The Butter-fish, Swordick, or Spotted Gunnel (*Centronotus gunellus*), belongs to this family [*sc.* of the Blennies].

gunnel: see GUNWALE.

gunnelly, obs. variant of GOONHILLY.

gunnen, obs. pa. t. and pple. of GIN *v.*[1]

gunner ('gʌnə(r)). Forms: 4-6 **gonner**, 5-6 **gunnar(e**, (6 **goonner**, **gunner**), *Sc.* **gounar, guner**, 5- **gunner**. [ME. *gonner, gunner*, f. *gunne* GUN, after AF. analogies: see -ER[2].]

1. a. One whose office it is to work a cannon. In the British army, now the designation of all privates of artillery except the 'drivers'. In 15th c. Eng.-Latin glossaries it is often rendered by L. words meaning 'one who works a mangonel' or the like: cf. GUN *sb.* (In 16th c. sometimes = HANDGUNNER; cf. sense 4.)

1344 *Househ. Ord.* (1790) 4 Marynors Armorers Artellers Gonners. **1347** [CAMDEN *Rem. Artillarie* (1623) 208 cites 'gunnarij' as receiving pay at the siege of Calais]. **1401** *Pol. Poems* (Rolls) II. 58 The devel is ȝour duke, and pride berith the baner; wraththe is ȝoure gunner, envie is ȝour archer. **1412-20** LYDG. *Chron. Troy* II. xviii, Their gonners standyng at corners with this also, and caste of wylde fyre. *c* **1440** *Promp. Parv.* 219/1 Gunnare, or he þat swagythe a gunne, *petrarius, mangonalius*. **1483** *Cath. Angl.* 168/2 A Gunner, *fundilabarius, fundibalista*. **1489** CAXTON *Faytes of A.* II. xxx. I vij, Item for the gonners shal be appoynted L Carpenters and tuenty labores. **1495** *Naval Acc. Hen. VII* (1896) 195 Gonners hamers of Iron—xij. **1549** *Compl. Scot.* vi. 41 Gunnaris, cum heir & stand by ȝour artailzee, euyrie gunnar til his auen quartar. **1577-87** HOLINSHED *Chron.* III. 823/1 In the towne of Lisle was a noise that three gunners with hand guns should have slaine the king. *a* **1578** LINDESAY (Pitscottie) *Chron. Scot.* (S.T.S.) I. 228 [He] caussit his gounaris to charge his arteillzerie. **1598** BARRET *Theor. Warres* v. iii. 133 With euery peece of Ordinance.. there ought to go two or three Gunners. **1599** SHAKS. *Hen. V*, III. Prol. 32 The nimble gunner with lynstock now the devilish cannon touches. **1600** R. CAWDREY *Treasurie* 606 Gunners winke with the left eye, that they may leuell more truely. **1626** CAPT. SMITH *Accid. Yng. Sea-men* 24 Gunners spunge your Ordinances. **1766** ENTICK *London* IV. 339 Four quarter gunners, and forty warders. **1808** SCOTT *Marm.* I. ix, The gunner held his linstock yare. **1868** KINGLAKE *Crimea* (1877) III. i. 193 The gunner got their range. **1893** FORBES-MITCHELL *Remin. Gt. Mutiny* 72 Middleton's battery..dashed forward with loud cheers, the drivers waving their whips and the gunners their caps.

b. In the navy, a warrant officer who has special charge of the battery, small arms, magazine, and ordnance stores.

1495 *Naval Acc. Hen. VII* (1896) 220 To the maister lxvj[s] viij[d] the purser xl[s] the Boteswayne xl[s] Steward xxx[s] & the Gonner xxxvij[s] vj[d]. **1610** SHAKS. *Temp.* II. ii. 49 The Master, the Swabber, the Boate-swaine & I; The Gunner, and his Mate. *a* **1642** SIR W. MONSON *Naval Tracts* III. (1704) 342/2 A principal thing in a Gunner at Sea is to be a good Helms-Man, and to call to him at Helm to Loof. **1719** DE FOE *Crusoe* II. x. (1840) 232 This man they called captain was the gunner only. **1815** A. BURN *Mem.* (1816) I. 16 The boatswain, gunner and carpenter, my messmate and myself, got together. *c* **1860** H. STUART *Seaman's Catech.* 79 The oldest and most experienced men in the ship are usually selected for gunners.

c. ***Master gunner***: the chief gunner in charge of ordnance and ammunition, formerly *spec.* an officer under the Crown, the name still being retained as an honorary title conferred on distinguished soldiers; also, in more recent use, a warrant officer in the Royal Artillery who has charge of the stores and equipment in a fortification or other armed place.

a **1548** HALL *Chron., Hen. VIII* (1550) 41 b, Than oute brast the ordinaunce..and the Master gonner of the Englishe parte slew the Master gonner of Scotlande. **1598** W. PHILLIPS *Linschoten* I. iii. 5 One Master gunner, and eight vnder him, haue each man a different pay. **1627** CAPT. SMITH *Seaman's Gram.* viii. 34 The Master Gunner hath the charge of the ordnance, and shot, powder, match, ladles, spunges, wormes, cartrages, armes and fire-workes; and the rest of the Gunners..to receive their charge from him. **1647** L. HAWARD *Charges Crown Rev.* 21 Master Gunner of England: Fee, *per diem* 2.s. 6.d. **1679-88** *Secr. Serv. Money Chas. & Jas.* (Camden) 95 To Thomas Silver, master gunner at Whitehall, for himself and the rest of the gunners of Whitehall, bounty to them..20*l.* **1802** C. JAMES *Mil. Dict.*, *Master gunner*, in a ship of war, an officer appointed to take charge of the artillery and ammunition aboard, and to teach the men the exercise of the great guns. **1876** VOYLE & STEVENSON *Mil. Dict.* **1880** TENNYSON *Revenge* xi, Sink me the ship, Master Gunner. **1904** *Standard* 20 Dec. 5/3 Field Marshal Earl Roberts, V.C., K.G., has been appointed Master Gunner of St. James's Park. **1918** E. S. FARROW *Dict. Mil. Terms, Master Gunner*... In the United States, an enlisted specialist of the non-commissioned staff Coast Artillery Corps, who is assigned to duty as assistant to the Artillery Engineer in connection with the preparation of charts, maps, drawings, range tables, etc., in a coast defense command. **1966** *Chambers's Encycl.* VI. 667/1 Master-gunners are warrant-officers of artillery, generally placed in charge of one or more forts.

d. *fig.*

1657 COKAINE *Obstin. Lady* I. i. Dram. Wks. (1874) 29 The young gunner, Mr. Cupid, has somewhat tam'd me. **1698** FARQUHAR *Love & Bottle* I. Wks. 1892 I. 25 That little pimping Cupid is a blind gunner. **1706-7** —— *Beaux Strat.* IV. i, O, Sister, I'm but a young Gunner, I shall be afraid to shoot, for fear the Piece should recoil.

e. A member of an aircraft crew who operates a gun. Cf. *aerial gunner* s.v. AERIAL *a.* 5, *air-gunner* s.v. AIR *sb.*[1] B. III. 3.

[**1910** C. C. TURNER *Aerial Navig.* xv. 211 Swift must be the aerial gunner's calculation.] **1918** E. MIDDLETON *Glorious Exploits of Air* (*caption*, facing p. 240) He dived to 500 feet, thus enabling his gunner, 1st A.M. Donald, to open heavy fire on them. **1919** BLACKBURN & NEWBY *All about Aircraft* 25 To be efficient a gunner must have a good eye. **1935** C. G. BURGE *Complete Bk. Aviation* 168/2 Many interesting developments have been designed to protect the gunner from the air pressure when flying at these high speeds. **1968** *Encycl. Brit.* X. 1037/1 To assist the gunner in manual aiming, a movable wind vane type of gun sight, calibrated and designed to compensate for the forward motion of the gunner's own aircraft, is often placed on the forward end of the gun barrel.

2. In phraseological uses with the possessive case: ***gunner's coin***, a wedge of metal used to raise a cannon or mortar to the desired elevation; ***gunner's daughter***, a jocular name amongst seamen for the gun to which sailors were 'married', i.e. lashed, to receive punishment; ***gunner's gang***, the men under the direct superintendence of the gunner (Hamersly *Naval Encycl.* 1881); ***gunner's handspike***, one shorter and flatter than the ordinary handspike, and shod with iron at the point (Smyth *Sailor's Word-bk.* 1867); ***gunner's ladle*** (see LADLE); ***gunner's mate***, a petty officer of a ship appointed to assist the gunner; ***gunner's pendulum*** (see quot.); ***gunner's piece***, the fragment of a burst gun which flies upward (Hamersly); ***gunner's quadrant*** (see QUADRANT); ***gunner's ring, rule, ruler, scale*** (see quots.); ***gunner's tailor***, 'an old rating for the man who made the cartridge bags' (Smyth).

1779 FORREST *Voy. N. Guinea* 257 The island from the S.W. appears like a wedge, or what seamen call a *gunner's coin. **1821** BYRON in Moore *Lett.* (1833) III. 139 As.. Captain Whitby..used to say to his seamen (when 'married to the *gunner's daughter')—'two dozen, and let you off easy'. **1824** SCOTT *Redgauntlet* xiv, I was punished,..—made to kiss..the gunner's daughter. **1833** MARRYAT *P. Simple* xxxii, I'll marry some of you young gentlemen to the gunner's daughter. **1769** FALCONER *Dict. Marine* (1780) *Chargeoir*,..a *gunner's ladle. **1708** *R. Proclam.* in *Lond. Gaz.* No. 4440/1 The Midshipmen, Carpenters Mates, Boatswains Mates, *Gunners Mates. **1719** DE FOE *Crusoe* II. xi. (1840) 234 A gunner's mate on board an English East India ship. **1876** VOYLE & STEVENSON *Milit. Dict.* (ed. 3), **Pendulum, Gunner's*—consists of an upright frame of wood, having a cross-arm attached to it, from which a pendulum is suspended, vibrating seconds..It is used to measure the time of flight of a mortar shell. **1628** R. NORTON *Gunner* xxxii. 95 The *Gunners Quadrant. **1692** *Capt. Smith's Seaman's Gram.* II. iii. 92 A Gunner's Quadrant to level, elevate, or depress his Gun. **1898** *N. & Q.* 15 Oct. 309/2 The 'gunner's quadrant' was a quadrant with a ruler attached and also a plumb-line; the end of the ruler was inserted in the muzzle of the gun, and the plumb-line cutting the lines on the quadrant marked the proper degrees of elevation. **1866** *Chamb. Jrnl.* No. 28. 229 That peculiar wreath of smoke, apparent when a gun has been greased at the muzzle, and known as the '*gunner's ring'. **1692** *Capt. Smith's Seaman's Gram.* II. xxiv. 129 This *Gunner's Rule was invented. A *Gunner's Ruler, for the Elevating of any Piece of Ordnance to any degree of Mounture. **1628** R. NORTON *Gunner* xxxi. 94 My *Gunners Scale is to be made in Brasse..And in Wood. **1688** R. HOLME *Armoury* III. ix. 375/2 A Gunners Scale, one side being divided into inches, quarters and halfquarters, with a Gunners Quadrant described upon it; the other having the names of all sorts of Ordnance.

3. One who makes or attends to guns; a gunmaker, gunsmith. *Obs.* exc. *dial.*

1463 *Mann. & Househ. Exp.* (Roxb.) 225 My masters gonner..schalle haue euery weke xij.*d.*, and mete, and drynke, and beddynge. *c* **1515** *Cocke Lorell's B.* (Percy Soc.) 11 Gouners, maryners, and shypmaysters. **1555** *Acc.* in T. Sharp *Cov. Myst.* (1825) 193 Payd to xvij gonnarys lxijs. iiij*d.* **1556** *Ibid.*, xiiij gonnars and a lakye lixs. **1880** *Antrim & Down Gloss.*, *Gunner*, a workman who repairs fire-arms; a gun-smith.

4. One who shoots with a sporting gun or fowling piece; one who goes shooting game. (Sometimes used contemptuously in contradistinction to *sportsman*.)

1753 *Scots Mag.* Mar. 144/1 A gunner met them in the vale. **1755** *Gentl. Mag.* XXV. 392 Corn..beat down by pointers, spaniels, gunners, &c. going over it before it be cut. **1794** MRS. PIOZZI *Synon.* I. 292 Partridge fall at every stroke of the gunner. **1814** COL. HAWKER *Diary* (1893) I. 92 These gunners..literally make a merit of their wasteful expenditure of ammunition. **1843** *Zoologist* I. 13 The swallows are sadly persecuted by strolling gunners from the town. **1878** *Daily News* 24 Oct. 6/4 These birds are very seldom trapped in nets, caught with birdlime, or killed by gunners. **1890** SIR S. BAKER *Wild Beasts* I. Pref. 7 A vast gulf separates the true sportsman from the merciless gunner... The gunner is the curse of the nineteenth century; his one idea is to use his gun, his love is slaughter, indiscriminate and boundless.

5. ***big gunner, handgunner***, etc.: one who attends to a big gun, a handgun, etc. ***horse gunner***: a member of the Royal Horse Artillery.

1530 [see HANDGUNNER]. **1896** R. KIPLING *Seven Seas* 206 'Orse Gunner listen to my Song. **1897** LD. ROBERTS *41 Yrs. India* ii. (1898) 7 A fixed resolve to leave no stone unturned in the endeavour to become a horse gunner. **1898** *Encycl. Sport* II. 168 *Gunner*, term applied to the man who works the big gun aboard a double punt; aboard a single, often styled a 'big gunner'. **1931** *Geogr. Jrnl.* LXXVIII. 121 Two other officers, one a Sapper and one a Gunner—I believe I ought to say one of the Royal Engineers, one of the Royal Artillery.

6. With number prefixed: A vessel carrying (so many) guns.

1829 MARRYAT *F. Mildmay* xx, That there is..not less than a forty-four gunner. **1897** *Westm. Gaz.* 22 July 10/1 The design of the ship is that of a thirty-gunner of the sixteenth century.

†**7.** *slang*. (See quot. 1709 s.v. GUNSTER.) *Obs.*

8. *dial.* in certain applications of obscure origin. [Perh. unconnected words.] **a.** The Sea Bream, *Pagellus centrodontus*. **b.** The Great Northern Diver, *Colymbus glacialis*.

a. 1859 YARRELL *Brit. Fishes* II. 149 At Antrim it [the Sea Bream] is called Murranroe and Barwin, and on the north-west coast *Gunner*. **1880-4** F. DAY *Brit. Fishes* I. 37.

b. 1837 *Penny Cycl.* IX. 37/2 *Colymbus glacialis*..is provincially called..*Gunner* and *Greater Doucker*. **1863** H. G. ADAMS *Feathered Fam.* 252 The Ring-necked Loon (*Colymbus glacialis*), sometimes called the..Gunner.

9. *attrib.*, as ***gunner-like*** adv.; **gunner-fluke** *Sc.*, the turbot; †**gunner-room** = GUN-ROOM 1.

1628 R. NORTON *Gunner* xxxviii. 101 How to loade a Peece of Ordnance Gunner-like. **1676** W. ROW *Contn. Blair's Autobiog.* x. (1848) 229 Mr. Hutchison persuaded him to come up only to the gunner-room. **1710** SIBBALD *Hist. Fife & Kinross* (1803) 119 *Rhombus aculeatus Rondeletii*: our fishers call it, the Gunner Flook. **1884** A. FORBES *Chinese Gordon* ii. 49 The gunner non-coms. replied with groans.

Hence †**'gunnered** *ppl. a.*, trained in gunnery; **'gunneress**, a female gunner; **'gunnership**, the position of gunner.

1628 J. BUTLER in R. Norton *Gunner* A 4, Expert Gunnered Engineers. **1836** *Boston, Lincoln*, etc. *Herald* 23 Feb. 4/2 The gunner-ship of Dover Castle, which is now vacant, is in the gift of the Duke of Wellington. **1837** CARLYLE *Fr. Rev.* I. VII. v, The seized cannon are yoked with seized cart-horses: brown-locked Demoiselle Théroigne, with pike and helmet, sits there as gunneress.

gunnera ('gʌnərə, gʌ'nɪərə). *Bot.* [mod.L. (Linnæus *Mantissa Plantarum* (1767) 16), f. the name of J. E. *Gunnerus* (1718–73), Norwegian bishop and botanist.] A plant of the genus so called, esp. *G. manicata*, cultivated for its large ornamental leaves; cf. *prickly rhubarb* (s.v. PRICKLY *a.*).

1789 W. AITON *Hortus Kewensis* III. 304 Marsh Mary-gold-leav'd Gunnera. **1823** *Curtis's Bot. Mag.* L. 2376 (*heading*) Cape Gunnera. **1900** W. G. BAKER in W. D. Drury *Bk. Gardening* xx. 891 Conspicuous among water-side plants that are valued chiefly for their ornamental foliage are the giant Gunneras. **1930** *Times Lit. Suppl.* 18 Dec. 1079/2 We find bilberry, ling and woody night-shade included, but not guelder-rose nor gunnera. **1961** *Amateur Gardening* 23 Dec. 2 From the water garden we could take a stalk or two of the giant gunnera.

gunnery ('gʌnərɪ). Also 7 (rare) gunry. [f. GUN + -ERY.]

1. The science and art of constructing and managing guns, esp. large military and naval guns.

1605 CAMDEN *Rem.* (1629) 104 Archerie..now dispossessed by gunnery, how iustly let other iudge. **1626** CAPT. SMITH *Accid. Yng. Sea-men* 33 Master Burnes Arte of gunry. **1676** T. BINNING (*title*) A Light to the Art of Gunnery. **1778** *Phil. Trans.* LXVIII. 52 The knowledge of this velocity is of the utmost consequence in gunnery. **1885** *Act 48 & 49 Vict.* c. 36 (*title*) A School of Gunnery. **1897** LD. ROBERTS *41 Yrs. India* lxvii. (1898) 528 A great advance was made in gunnery.

2. The firing of guns; the use of guns for sporting purposes; = GUNNING *vbl. sb.* 2.

1816 *Gentl. Mag.* LXXXVI. I. 109 This bright amusement may challenge the preference of most kinds of gunnery. **1824** MISS MITFORD *Village* Ser. I. (1863) 98 They are..crying the 'Harvest Home' in a chorus before which.. the song, the scolding, the gunnery fade away and become faint echoes. **1869** *Echo* 9 Oct., The never-ending gunnery of..idle scamps, who go out valiantly to destroy linnets.

3. *concr.* Guns collectively.

1497 *Extracts Aberd. Reg.* (1844) I. 61 With horsis, gunrye, artailzerie, and ail vther defensabile wapinnis. **1881** MISS BRADDON *Asph.* III. 129 They went into the arsenal, where a funny old man in a blue blouse showed them ancient and modern gunnery.

†**4.** A place where instruction is given in the use of guns. *Obs. rare.*

1732 E. FORREST *Hogarth's Tour* 9 Paid at the gunnery and dock, 1s. 6d.

5. (See quot.)

1892 *Labour Commission* Gloss., *Gunnery*, work done by shipwrights in connection with guns and their stowage, &c.

6. *attrib.*, as ***gunnery-course, -drill, duty***; **gunnery jack** *Naval slang*, a gunnery-lieutenant; **gunnery-lieutenant**, 'one who, having obtained a warrant from a gunnery-ship, is eligible to large ships to assist specially in supervising the gunnery duties' (Smyth *Sailor's Word-bk.* 1867); **gunnery-ship**, a ship fitted for training men in the practice of gunnery.

1870 *Echo* 11 Nov., The gunnery ship Cambridge. **1886** *Pall Mall G.* 11 Sept. 11/1 The next day or two are employed..in carrying out the various gunnery drills and firing the great guns at a target. **1894** *Daily News* 7 Apr. 6/2 A gunnery course will be held on H.M.S. Cambridge, for retired officers of the Royal Navy. **1904** KIPLING *Traffics & Discov.* 53 The Gunner mops up a heathenish large detail for some hanky-panky in the magazines, an' led 'em off along with our Gunnery Jack. **1908** *Daily Chron.* 5 Oct. 4/6 A smarter man than Gunnery Jack is not to be found in the services. **1925** [see GUN *sb.* 5 c].

gunnies ('gʌnɪs). *Cornwall.* Also (in Dicts.) gunnis(s. A crevice in a mine or lode; 'the vacant space left where the lode has been removed' (Raymond); hence (app.) taken as a measure of breadth or width. (By some recent writers used as *pl.*)

1778 PRYCE *Min. Cornub.* 168 A Gunnies, or hollows of a Mine filled with water. *Ibid.* 322 Gunnies means breadth or width. A single Gunnies is three feet wide; a Gunnies and a half is four feet and a half; and a double Gunnies is six feet wide. [**1858** SIMMONDS *Dict. Trade, Gurmies*. Hence in some recent Dicts. *Gurmie*.] **1860** *Eng. & For. Mining Gloss., Cornwall, Gunnies*, levels or workings. **1875** J. H. COLLINS *Metal Mining* 44 Stuff may be brought from the surface to fill in the vacant spaces or 'gunnies'.

gunning ('gʌnɪŋ), *vbl. sb.* [f. GUN *sb.* and *v.* + -ING[1].]

1. The practice or art of firing guns; gunnery.

1570 DEE *Math. Pref.* 36 The record, where the occasion and order generall, of Gunning, is first discoursed of.

2. a. Shooting with a gun; esp. the act or practice of hunting game with guns.

1624 FLETCHER *Rule a Wife* I. ii, There is lesse danger in 't then gunning, Sanchio, Though we be shot sometimes the shot 's not mortall. **1655** SIR J. MENNIS & J. SMITH *Musarum Deliciæ* 83 When there were shows of gunning and blows. **1726** T. SMITH *Jrnl.* (1849) 45 There has been the best gunning here this winter than has been for some years past. **1774** GOLDSM. *Nat. Hist.* (1776) V. 119 In the earlier times, the art of gunning was but little practised, and the hawk then was valuable. **1816** SCOTT *Antiq.* xxii, He has had gunning and pistoling enough to serve him one while, I should think. **1846** COL. HAWKER *Diary* (1893) II. 265 My punts were all newly done up for gunning. **1851** THOREAU *Autumn* (1894) 63 Farming is an amusement which has lasted him longer than gunning or fishing. **1882** SALA *Amer. Revis.* (1885) 394 The sport which Western men call 'gunning'.

b. (*to go* or *be*) ***a-gunning***.

1689 *Depos. Cast. York* (Surtees) 294 Edward Shaftoe.. goeing out into Gunnerton moores a gunning. **1734** in B. Peirce *Hist. Harvard Univ.* (1833) App. 141 No Under-graduate..shall go a gunning, fishing, or scating over deep waters, without leave from the President or one of the Tutors. **1825** J. NEAL *Bro. Jonathan* I. 104 What luck a' gunnin'? **1829** GEN. P. THOMPSON *Exerc.* (1842) I. 172 Who is to be foolish enough to 'go out a gunning' upon the strength of two campaigns? **1857** THOREAU *Maine W.* (1894) 174 Such of my acquaintances as love to write verses and go a-gunning.

3. Provision of guns. *rare.*

1675 MARVELL *Let. to Corporat. Hull* clxxii. Wks. 1776 I. 263 They differed concerning the ward ships; some insisting, that thereby was ment also rigging and gunning. **1917** H. MACFALL *Germany at Bay* (1918) 210 The enormous gunning and munitionment of the Germans made trench warfare a costly affair for such as had it not.

4. *attrib.* and *Comb.*, as ***gunning-boat, -feat, -hut, -matter, -party, -prowess, -punt, -shout*** (see quot. 1847); **gunning-stick**, a device used by lumbermen in guiding the falling of a tree.

1562 BULLEYN *Bk. Simples* 72, I will..leaue Gunning matters to the Men of Warre. **1819** COL. HAWKER *Diary* (1893) I. 170 The gunning huts and straw decoy birds. **1851** *Zoologist* IX. 3055 A gunner here [Weymouth] was telling me of his gunning feats. **1847** HALLIWELL, *Gunning-boat*, a light and narrow boat in which the fenmen pursue the flocks of wild fowl along their narrow drains. Also called a *gunning-shout*. **1860** C. DURFEE *Hist. Williams College* 72 Accidentally shot dead, on a gunning party. **1863** FR. A. KEMBLE *Resid. in Georgia* 20 The robin redbreast..is not safe from the gunning prowess of the..sportsmen. **1883** G. C. DAVIES *Norfolk Broads* xix. 139 A gunning punt, with a couple of single-barrelled guns lying ready loaded in it. **1905** Gunning-stick [see GUN *v.* 1 e].

gunning ('gʌnɪŋ), *ppl. a. rare.* [f. GUN *v.* + -ING[2].] That shoots with a gun.

1883 F. A. WALKER *Pol. Econ.* 449 The lower elements of society, the gunning fishing tribe.

gunnist ('gʌnɪst). *rare.* [f. GUN *sb.* + -IST.] A gunner.

1894 *Blackw. Mag.* Sept. 388 Mr. Oudh the gunnist was satisfied with the moderate bags of quail that came to him in the ordinary course.

gunny ('gʌnɪ). Also 8 goney. [a. Hindi and Mahratti *gōn, gōnī*:—Skr. *gōṇī* sack.] **a.** A coarse material used chiefly for sacking and made from the fibres of jute or (in some parts) from sunn-hemp; a sack of this material.

1711 C. LOCKYER *Acc. Trade Ind.* 244 When Sugar is pack'd in double Goneys, the outer Bag is always valued in Contract at 1 or 1½ Shahee. **1727** A. HAMILTON *New Acc. E. Ind.* II. xxxiii. 17 Gunnies, which are much in use in Persia for embaling Goods. **1869** ROGERS in *Adam Smith's W.N.* I. I. x. 122 *note*, Almost every person in Hindostan Spins and Weaves Jute fibre into a coarse cloth called gunny. **1871** NAPHEYS *Prev. & Cure Dis.* III. iv. 725 Pack them in large gunnies. **1897** WILLIS *Flower. Pl.* II. 109 Corchorus olitorius [etc.]..furnish the chief supply of the valuable fibre jute or gunny.

b. *attrib.*, as ***gunny-bag, -bagging, -carpet, -cloth, -fibre, -sack, -sacking***.

1764 *Account of Expences* 5 Sept. in J. Long *Select. Unpubl. Rec. Bengal* (1869) I. 384 Baskets, gunny bags, and dubbers. **1798** WELLINGTON *Suppl. Desp.* (1858) I. 101 Shot carried on the backs of bullocks in gunny bags. **1800** *Asiatic Ann. Reg., Chron.* 2/2 Upon removing some gunny-bags that were stowed close to the lazaretto. **1856** OLMSTED *Slave States* 630 A curtain or screen, of gunny-bagging. **1858** J. S. HOMANS *Cycl. Commerce* 919/1 In 1841–42 there were exported from Calcutta..95,412 pieces of gunny cloth. **1862** W. S. EBEY *Diary* 6 July in *Pacific Northwest Q.* (1943) XXXIV. 42 To look at the claims on the hill. They are on the rime rock & prospect very fine, as much as a dollar to the gunny sack. **1872** OLIVER *Elem. Bot.* II. 153 In India it [Jute] is used for making rice and sugar bags, called Gunny-bags. **1879** H. KING in *Scribner's Mag.* Nov. 133/1 The sunlight.. changed the gunny carpet to cloth of gold. **1882** *Rep. to Ho. Repr. Prec. Met. U.S.* 73 A stream of water..keeps the pulp in continual motion and passes off through another double set of sluices lined with coarse gunny sacks. **1890** 'R. BOLDREWOOD' *Col. Reformer* (1891) 349 I've ridden many a mile..with nothing but an old gunny-bag to sit on. **1960** 'A. BURGESS' *Doctor is Sick* 166 He had brought with him a gunny sack which he emptied on to the floor—more fruit and vegetables. **1965** G. MCINNES *Road to Gundagai* ix. 142 Across the opening hung gunny-sacking.

gunny, dial. variant of GOUNDY *a. Obs.*

gunphanun, obs. variant of GONFANON.

'gun-play. orig. *U.S.* [GUN *sb.* 3 b.] The use of fire-arms; a shooting affray; skill in shooting.

1897 *Typogr. Jrnl.* Jan., The talk of 'gun-plays' at the Federation Convention..is without a germ of truth. **1899** ADE *Doc. Horne* vi. 57 So you made good with the gun-play did you. **1904** *N.Y. Even. Post* 7 Nov. 1 The feud has been the cause of several assaults and gunplays in Chinatown. **1913** C. E. MULFORD *Coming of Cassidy* ii. 30 I've heard so much about Bradley's gun-play that I'm some curious. **1928** *Sunday Dispatch* 22 July 9/3 Other charges of gunplay were made against the officer. **1956** *Times Lit. Suppl.* 9 Nov., Years of disorder and lightly controlled gun-play. **1958** *Listener* 9 Oct. 553/1 Perhaps gunplay and fisticuffs are as formal a part of the 'western' as blood and bodies are of the detective novel.

gunpowder ('gʌnpaʊdə(r)). Forms: 5 gonepowder, gonnepou(l)dre, -powdre, etc., gun-, gonpoudre, gonnpouldre, gounne pouldre, gonnepoder, gonn(e) powther, gunepoudir, gounpouder, etc., 6 gonepother, *Sc.* gun puldir, 6–7 gunnepouder, 6– gunpowder, 7– gun-powder. [f. GUN *sb.* + POWDER *sb.*]

1. a. An explosive mixture of saltpetre, sulphur, and charcoal, chiefly used in discharging projectiles from guns and for blasting.

[*a* **1387** *Brev. Bartholomæi* (Anecd. Oxon., Mediæval, I. I. 3), Pulvis pro instrumento illo bellico sive diabolico quod vulgaliter dicitur gunne.] **1411** *Indenture in Excheq. Accts.* Q. R. Bdle. 44, no. 17 (P.R.O.), Une petit barell' de gonpouder. [Misdated 1338 by Nicolas *Royal Navy* II. 476 App.] **1414** in Rymer *Fœdera* (1709) IX. 160 Aliquod Gunpoudre versus Partes exteras, in Portu prædicto. **1446** in *Archæologia* XXII. 63 Bought ij hand-gunnes de ere iiijs. Item, gonepowder iiijs. **1464** *Mann. & Househ. Exp.* (Roxb.) 160 Item, payd ffor xij. li. gonnepowdyr..xij.s. **1485** *Naval Acc. Hen. VII* (1896) 13 For ij barrelles Gonnepowdre. **1533** MORE *Apol.* xxxiv. Wks. 898/1 If he founde a corner of his neighbours house burning, he wold of greate loue and polycye lay on fagottes and gun-powder to put out the fyre. **1549** *Compl. Scot.* vi. 42 The reik, smeuk, and the stink of the gun puldir. **1555** *Acc.* in T. Sharp *Cov. Myst.* (1825) 193 Payd for xij li of gonepother xijs. vjd. **1599** SHAKS. *Hen. V*, IV. vii. 188, I doe know Fluellen valiant, And toucht with Choler, hot as Gunpowder. **1692** *Capt. Smith's Seaman's Gram.* II. v. 93 Gunpowder, as it is made in this Age, is compounded of Saltpetre six parts, and of Brimstone and Charcoal of each one part. **1797** *Phil. Trans.* LXXXVII. 290 The best gunpowder..is composed of 70 parts (in weight) of nitre, 18 parts of sulphur, and 16 parts of charcoal. **1827** CARLYLE *Misc.* (1857) I. 22 The three great elements of modern civilization, Gunpowder, Printing, and the Protestant Religion. **1846** GREENER *Sci. Gunnery* 69 Gunpowder is a lever if exploded on a solid base, if not, its effects become limited in proportion.

b. ***white gunpowder***: a name given to various explosives of recent invention; (*a*) (see quot. 1875); (*b*) a blasting mixture made of chlorate of potash, potassium ferrocyanide, and sugar.

1875 *Ure's Dict. Arts* II. 767 Schultze's White Gunpowder is a tri-nitro-cellulose, prepared from sawdust.

c. with reference to tattooing.

1715 *Lond. Gaz.* No. 5363/4 His Name on his right Hand in Gunpowder D. W. **1718** LADY M. W. MONTAGU *Let. to Abbé Conti* 31 July, The women have their arms..and their necks and faces, adorned with..various sorts of figures impressed by gunpowder. **1791** J. IRELAND *Hogarth Illustr.* I. 226, I think it is probable that these gunpowder initials are merely the marks of a woman of the lowest rank, and most infamous description.

d. *fig.*

1681 FLAVEL *Meth. Grace* xxviii. 474 Christian, thou knowest thou carriest gunpowder about thee; desire those that carry fire to keep at a distance from thee. **1900** *Speaker* 24 Mar. 674/1 Such mischievous words are just the sort of match to kindle the gunpowder of mob violence.

2. (In full, *gunpowder tea.*) A fine kind of green tea, each leaf of which is rolled up, so that it has a granular appearance.

1771 J. R. FORSTER tr. *Osbeck's Voy.* I. 250 Tio-te is rolled up like pease... A smaller kind is called Gunpowder tea. **1795** Æ. ANDERSON *Brit. Embass. China* 186 The shrub which bears what is called the Imperial and gunpowder teas. **1832** *Veg. Subst. Food* 379 Gunpowder tea is made of tender green leaves. **1839** THACKERAY *Major Gahagan* vi, 'Is it bohay tay or souchong tay that you'd like?'..'Any tea you like'... 'What do you say, then, to some prime gunpowder?' **1886** *Daily News* 24 Dec. 2/6 Tea.—Ping Suey gunpowder.

†3. *slang.* Some fiery drink. *Obs.*

1765 W. TOLDERVY *Hist. Two Orphans* II. 112 Tape, glim, rushlight, white port, rasher of bacon, gunpowder, slug, wild-fire, knock-me-down, and strip-me naked. *Ibid.* II. 118 Come, here's t'ye, in a glass of gunpowder.

4. a. *attrib.* and *Comb.*, as ***gunpowder-blue, flash, grinder, -law, -maker, match, mill, -pocket, -smoke, -squib, train, works***; ***gunpowder-blackened*** adj.; also **gunpowder cake**, gunpowder in a cake or mass, *i.e.* before it is corned; **gunpowder-engine**, a gas-engine in which the movement of the piston is produced by the evolution of gas resulting from the combustion of gunpowder (Knight *Dict. Mech.* 1875); **gunpowder-hammer**, a pile-driving machine worked by the explosion of gunpowder (*Ibid.*); **gunpowder-paper**, paper spread with an explosive compound and rolled up into the form of a cartridge (*Ibid.* Suppl. 1884); **gunpowder-press**, a press for compacting mill-cake into hard cake preparatory to granulation (Knight, 1875); †**gunpowder spot**, a 'beauty spot' produced by means of gunpowder (see quot. 1718 in 1 c); **gunpowder tea** (see 2); **gunpowder weed** *S. Afr.*, a name for *Silene gallica*, a plant having small black seeds.

1894 *Westm. Gaz.* 25 June 2/2 Lefebvre wishes to wash his *gunpowder-blackened hands. **1890** *Daily News* 21 Oct. 2/1 *Gunpowder-blue velvet. **1839** URE *Dict. Arts* 630 The mill for grinding *gunpowder cake. **1621** BURTON *Anat. Mel.* III. ii. VI. iii. (1651) 559 Burning lust is but a flash, a *gunpowder flash. **1719** D'URFEY *Pills* IV. 199 The next that came by, was a *Gun-powder grinder. **1614** T. ADAMS *Devil's Banquet* 2 Lawes..enacted in the vault of darkenesse; like those vnder the Parliament-house; *Gunpowder-lawes, fit for the Justices of Hell. **1550** *Acts Privy Council* (1891) III. 50, xx^{li} to Charles Wolman, *gonne powther maker. **1627** CAPT. SMITH *Seaman's Gram.* xii. 57 Giue fire by a *Gunpowder match, to preuent traines to the powder chest. **1642** WOOD *Life* (O.H.S.) I. 74 The *gunpowder myll was at Osney where the fulling myll stood. **1777** T. TWINING *to Burney* 16 June in Louisa Twining *Country Clergym. 18th Cent.* (1882) 51 With *gunpowder pockets under his armpits ready for the partridges in September. **1838** DICKENS *O. Twist* xxx, A couple of men catch one moment's glimpse of a boy, in the midst of *gunpowder-smoke. **1681** OTWAY *Soldier's Fort.* IV. i. Wks. 1728 I. 382 *Gun-pouder Spots and Moles. **1708** WILSON, etc. *Petronius Arbiter* 207 Fine Gentlemen in the Boxes, with their Patches, Gunpowder-spots, and Tooth-pickers. **1660** FISHER *Rustick's Alarm* Wks. (1679) 94 [They] threw Stones and *Gunpowder-squibs that fired among us. **1611** RICH *Honest. Age* (Percy Soc.) 45 These diuelish practises, of poysons, of pistoles, of stabbing kniues, and of *gunnepouder traynes. **1860** HARVEY & SONDER *Flora Capensis* I. 127 *Silene gallica*... This is the '*Gunpowder-weed' of the colonists; its black seeds resembling powder. **1897** EDMONDS & MARLOTH *Elem. Bot. S. Afr.* xvii. 139 *Silene*... Several species of Campion, also the so-called 'Gunpowder Weed' (*S. gallica*). **1926** J. B. DAVY *Man. Fl. Plants Transvaal* I. 149 S[ilene] gallica... Gunpowder weed... The black seeds resemble grains of gunpowder, hence the vern. [*sic*] name. **1946** M. WILMAN *Check List Fl. Plants Griqualand W.* 16 S[ilene] gallica..an increasingly frequent weed; September. *Gunpowder weed.* **1839** URE *Dict. Arts* 621 The Royal *Gunpowder Works at Waltham Abbey.

b. **Gunpowder plot**: the plot to blow up the Houses of Parliament on Nov. 5, 1605, while the King and Lords and Commons were assembled there. (So ***gunpowder conspiracy, treason, traitor***, etc.) †**Gunpowder (treason) day**: Nov. 5.

1611–12 in Swayne *Sarum Churchw. Acc.* (1896) 161 Ringinge..on the daie of the Gunpowder treasonn. **1613** *MS. Acc. St. John's Hosp., Canterb.*, For the ryngers on the goonpouder daye. **1626** *Raleigh's Ghost* 38 And to this I call vp the plot of all plots..the Gun-pouder conspiracie. **1630** WADSWORTH *Pilgr.* vii. 62 There is one Sir Edward Bainham, who was a grand complotter of the Gunpowder treason. **1654** WHITLOCK *Zootomia* 279 Even Gunpowder Enormities and Desolation did blow up all as at one crack. **1659** O. WALKER *Oratory* 61 The Earl of Northamptons speech against the gun-powder-Traitors. **1685** EVELYN *Diary* 5 Nov., It being the first Gunpowder Conspiracy anniversary that had ben kept now these 80 yeares. **1705** HEARNE *Collect.* 6 Nov. (O.H.S.) I. 66 Yesterday being Gunpowder treason 'twas observed more than it us'd to be at Lond. *a* **1715** BURNET *Own Time* III. (1724) I. 596 The fifth of November, being gunpowder treason day. **1796** J. CAULFIELD (*title*) The History of the Gunpowder plot. **1855** RUSKIN in Collingwood *Life* I. 194 Am going to press..on Gunpowder Plot day. **1897** S. R. GARDINER *Gunpowder Plot* i. 7 Was Salisbury such an idiot as to inform his 'domestic gentleman' that he had made up his mind to invent Gunpowder Plot?

5. *attrib.* passing into *adj.* a. *fig.* Explosive as gunpowder; easily fired or inflamed.

1596 SHAKS. *1 Hen. IV*, V. iv. 123, I am affraide of this Gun-powder Percy though he be dead. **1604** T. M. *Black Bk.* D 4, Such Gunne-powder Oathes they were, that I wonder how the Seeling held together. **1625** BP. MOUNTAGU *App. Cæsar.* II. i. 112 Men of moving violent, Quicksilver, Gunpowder spirits. **1814** SCOTT *Wav.* lii, Would you have him peace-maker general between all the gunpowder Highlanders in the army?

b. Of a bluish colour like gunpowder.

1817 COLERIDGE *Biog. Lit.* I. 169 The lank, black, twine-like hair,..cut in a straight line along the black stubble of his thin gunpowder eye brows.

Hence **'gunpowderous, 'gunpowdery** *adjs.*, pertaining to or characteristic of gunpowder; of the bluish colour of gunpowder; *fig.* fiery, easily fired, inflamed, or irritated.

1868 *Pall Mall G.* 18 Nov. 3 It [the poetry] is gunpowdery to an intense degree. **1870** DICKENS *E. Drood* vi, His philanthropy was of that gunpowderous sort that the difference between it and animosity was hard to determine. **1871** M. LEGRAND *Cambridge Freshm.* 168 There was a very gunpowdery atmosphere in the room when Mrs. Cribb came in. 'They're been lettin' off fireworks or something..', she said. **1872** *Daily News* 20 July, Brought up amid gunpowdery scenes of this kind..is it to be wondered at that the young Maurice de MacMahon should have started in the army as a Legitimist fire-eater of the fiercest kind? **1889** *Catholic Househ.* 2 Nov. 3/2 To give gunpowdery battle to the Pope and all his satellites. **1897** *Westm. Gaz.* 29 Dec. 5/1 Among these were a good many stage folk—you could tell them by their gunpowdery chins.

†**'gunpowdered**, *a. Obs.* [+ -ED[2].]

1. Charged with gunpowder.

1560 WHITEHORNE *Ord. Souldiours* (1588) 46 Vnto euery one of which [fireworks], must bee put a peece of a gunpoudred match.

b. *fig.* Readily inflamed or excited.

1604 T. WRIGHT *Passions* I. i. 6 Lest, by casting forth a sparke of fire, his gun-powdred minde of a sodayne be inflamed. **1622** BP. ABERNETHY *Phys. for Soule* (1630) 293 That fervent, gunpowdered and sudden anger.

2. Begrimed with gunpowder.

1702 FARQUHAR *Inconstant* I. ii, We..saw peeping over a parcel of scarecrow, olive-coloured, gunpowdered fellows, as ugly as the devil.

gun-room ('gʌnruːm).

1. In large ships of war, a compartment orig. occupied by the gunner and his mates, but now fitted up for the accommodation of the junior officers; in smaller vessels, that used as a mess-room by the lieutenants.

1626 CAPT. SMITH *Accid. Yng. Sea-men* 11 About the Gun-roome, the Tiller, the rudder, the pintels, the gudgions. *a* **1642** SIR W. MONSON *Naval Tracts* III. (1704) 360/2 The upper Gun-Room..is used for a Store-Room, Lodgings. **1673** DRYDEN *Amboyna* III. iii, Oh, now it begins, and the gun-room grows hot, Ply it with culverin and with small shot. **1711** W. SUTHERLAND *Shipbuilder's Assist.* 36 Upon the lower Gun-deck in Men of War there is an Apartment for the Gunner, called the Gun-room; it is for fitting and securing all his small Stores. **1720** DE FOE *Capt. Singleton* xi. (1840) 200 The gunner of the ship..secured himself in the gun-room. **1833** MARRYAT *P. Simple* (1863) 44 The first lieutenant had asked me to dine in the gun-room. **1884** PAE *Eustace* 86 You forget..that I shall be in the gun-room, and he in the forecastle.

Proverb. **1697** VANBRUGH *Relapse* III. iii, I'm afraid we shall find a great job on't. Pray Heaven that old rogue Coupler han't sent us to fetch milk out of the gunroom.

b. *attrib.*, as ***gun-room bulkhead, gossip, gun, hour, officer, steward***; **gun-room ports**, stern ports cut through the gun-room in a frigate (Hamersly *Naval Encycl.* 1881).

1712 W. ROGERS *Voy.* 27 We struck two of our Gun-room Guns into the Hold. **1748** *Anson's Voy.* I. iii. 32 They lowered down a bucket out of the cabbin-window, into which the gunner, out of one of the gun-room ports, put a quantity of pistol cartridges. **1825** H. B. GASCOIGNE *Nav. Fame* 61 The Gunroom hour to dine is long since past. **1855** SIR A. WEST *Recoll.* (1899) I. vi. 212 The gunroom officers had asked us to dinner. **1895** *Westm. Gaz.* 6 Nov. 3/2 The Doctor's cabin was next to the gun-room bulkhead. **1898** *Daily News* 9 Nov. 6/3 They..talk the most knowing gun-room gossip.

2. A room in which guns are kept.

1773 GOLDSM. *Stoops to Conq.* II. i, Your worship must not tell the story of Ould Grouse in the gun-room. **1883** BLACK *Shandon Bells* xxvi, It is like the place too—the gun-room even, and the stuffed birds.

gunry, rare obs. form of GUNNERY.

gunsel ('gʌnsəl). *U.S. slang.* Also **gonsil, gunshel, gun(t)zel.** [ad. Yiddish *genzel*, f. G. *gänslein* gosling, little goose.] **1.** A (naïve) youth; a tramp's young companion, male lover; a homosexual youth.

1914 JACKSON & HELLYER *Vocab. Criminal Slang* 40 *Gunshel*, current amongst yeggs chiefly. A boy; a youth; a neophyte of trampdom. **1923** N. ANDERSON *Hobo* vii. 101 *Gonsil*, youth not yet adopted by jocker. **1927** *Amer. Speech* II. 387/2 Men can be observed traveling with boys... The boy has many names,—punk, gazooney, guntzel and bronc. Punk, guntzel and gazooney are also used to refer to any sort of green lad. **1929** D. HAMMETT in *Black Mask* Nov. 43/1 Keep that gunsel away from me while you're making up your mind. **1931** G. IRWIN *Amer. Tramp & Underworld Slang* 88 *Gonsil*, a young tramp, not yet taken in hand and bent to his will by an older man. A boy. A passive male homosexual, usually a youth or younger man. Also gunsel. **1946** MENCKEN *Amer. Lang.* xi. 582 The tramp..carries a boy with him, to rustle food for him and serve him otherwise ..the boy is a punk,..guntzel. *Ibid.* 584 Gonov, which means a thief to thieves, means a fool on the carnival lot, and the same meaning is given to guntzel, which means, in the jungles, the boy companion of a tramp.

2. [as if f. GUN *sb.*] An informer, a criminal, a gunman.

1950 H. E. GOLDIN *Dict. Amer. Underworld Lingo* 89/1 *Gunzel*,..(by extension) an informer, a weasel, an unscrupulous person. **1951** *New Yorker* 3 Mar. 26/3 Scores of hoodlums, gunsels, informers. **1959** G. FISHER *Hospitality for Murder* xix. 151 Bruce thought he'd never make a reliable gunsel. **1964** W. MARKFIELD *To Early Grave* (1965) vi. 109 After all, didn't Ben Gurion himself hand her a blank cheque, she should have what to hire a couple gunsels? **1965** J. WAINWRIGHT *Web of Silence* 34 The voice said: '..This is a gun—and it's silenced. Okay?'..I tried to work out what sort of a voice the gunsel had.

gun-shot ('gʌnʃɒt). Forms: see GUN *sb.*; also 5 **gonnes shott.**

1. Shot fired from a gun or cannon; †also the shooting of guns. Now *rare.*

1471 *Arriv. Edw. IV* (Camden) 29 [They] were sore annoyed in the place where they were, as well with gonnes-shott as with shot of arrows. **1494** FABYAN *Chron.* VII. 450 [He] assaylyd this sayde shyppe on euery parte & bette hir w^t gunneshot & hir men w^t hayle shot. **1497** *Naval Acc. Hen. VII* (1896) 104 Gonneshot of Iren..Ston..leed. **1530** PALSGR. 889 To expresse the sounde of gonne shotte, I fynde tip tap, sip sap. **1553** in Strype *Eccl. Mem.* III. App. iii. 5 And have solemnised the said proclamation with bonfires gunshots. **1563** T. GALE *Antidot.* Pref., When as I hadde finished my..Treatise of woundes made wyth Gonneshotte. **1607** TOPSELL *Hist. Four-f. Beasts* (1658) 383 Whensoever they are hunted with Dogs, they run directly to the woods or to the next trees, wherein they are killed by gun-shot. **1613** PURCHAS *Pilgrimage* (1614) 269 With shouting, singing, hallowing, gun-shot and fire-workes all that night. **1632** SHERWOOD, Gun-shot, *arquebusade*; *canonnade.* **1855** MACAULAY *Hist. Eng.* xi. III. 39 Gun-shots were wildly fired in all directions.

b. *fig.*

1551 ROBINSON tr. *More's Utop.* To P. Giles (1895) 10 Beynge..sauffe, and, as sayth the proverbe, out of all daunger of gonneshotte. **1575** GASCOIGNE *Good Morrow* 64 As with gonnes we kill the Crowe For spoyling our releefe, The Deuill so must we ouerthrowe, With gonshote of beleefe. **1577** VAUTROUILLIER *Luther on Ep. Gal.* 19 With such gun-shot and artillerie must the Papacie be destroyed. **1581** J. BELL *Haddon's Answ. Osor.* 305 Being supported by the Popes authoritie, and armed with the gunneshotte of his excommunication. **1634** WITHER *Emblemes* 112 The gunshot of a slanderous tongue may smite.

c. *Her.* = PELLET, OGRESS. (Cf. GUNSTONE 2.)

1828 in BERRY *Encycl. Her.*

2. The range of a gun or cannon; the distance to which a shot can be effectively thrown from a gun. Chiefly ***out of, within gunshot.***

1532 MORE *Confut. Tindale* Wks. 366/1 Prouiding alwai that your selfes y^e chief captaines..stand and loke vpon sure and safe a syde halfe out of al gunshot. **1540** CRANMER *Bible* Prol., They sytte farre from the strokes of battayll, and farre out of gonneshoute, and therfore they be but seldome wounded. **1631** MABBE *Celestina* (1894) xi. 191 Hee is out of gun-shot, that rings the bell to the battell. **1676** S. SEWALL *Diary* 1 July (1878) I. 14 Mr. Hezekiah Willet slain by the Naragansets, a little more than a Gun-shot off from his house. **1696** *Lond. Gaz.* No. 3219/2 On the 20th appeared..21 French Galleys.., who Anchored out of Gun Shot. **1748** *Anson's Voy.* II. v. 171 [They] perceived a light, which they chased, till they arrived within gun-shot. **1805** SIR E. BERRY in Nicolas *Disp. Nelson* (1846) VII. 117 *note*, The Three-decker was within gun-shot of us at day-break. **1845** JAMES *A. Neil* vi, They were half across the Meadows, about half a gun-shot from the alders. **1879** JEFFERIES *Amateur Poacher* iii. 51 They [mallards] were always out of gunshot.

†b. *transf.* and *fig.* ***within, out of, past, beyond (the) gunshot (of)***: within, beyond reach (of); within, out of the sphere of influence (of).

1556 J. HEYWOOD *Spider & F.* lxv. 77 Marching toward the copweb, within goon shot. **1571** GOLDING *Calvin on Ps.* xxxv. 8 They..feare nothing, as though they were quite out of all gonneshot. **1593** NASHE *Christ's T.* 76 They might haue..lyu'd out of gunshot of misery. **1612** T. TAYLOR *Comm. Titus* ii. 12 If he can..liue out of the gunshot of the lawe. **1642** ROGERS *Naaman* 459 Set me beyond gun-shot of all corruptions. **1678** BUNYAN *Pilgr.* I. (1879) 81 You are not yet out of the gun-shot of the Devil. **1687** DRYDEN *Hind & P.* Pref. 1 Those who are come over to the Royal Party are consequently suppos'd to be out of Gunshot.

¶3. A pistol.

1663 BUTLER *Hud.* I. ii. 776 With hasty rage he snatch'd His Gun-shot that in holsters watch'd.

4. *attrib.* and *Comb.*, as ***gunshot-distance, -fracture, -wound.***

1672 WISEMAN *Wounds* II. 1 Great hath been the Contention amongst the Learned about fire and venom in Gun-shot-wounds. **1835–6** TODD *Cycl. Anat.* I. 227/1 Gun-shot wounds..are not often followed by hæmorrhage. **1837** W. IRVING *Capt. Bonneville* (1849) 207 The rider.. discovered an Indian fort within gunshot distance. **1842** ABDY *Water Cure* (1843) 109 His success in treating gun-shot wounds with cold water was most remarkable. **1879** *St. George's Hosp. Rep.* IX. 399 Gunshot fracture of the humerus.

gun-shy ('gʌnʃaɪ), *a.* Afraid of a gun; frightened at the report of a gun: said *esp.* of a sporting dog.

1884 SPEEDY *Sport* iv. 50 The first birds shot at over a gun-shy dog should certainly be killed. **1893** S. BONSAL *Morocco* 210 The Shereefian soldiers are far too gunshy to attack an armed foe. **1893** SELOUS *Trav. S.E. Africa* 16 Another..though an excellent horse for a journey, was so gun shy I could do nothing with him. **1894** *Field* 9 June 818/2 The first time I took the dog out he was inclined to be gun shy. **1938** C. DAY LEWIS *Overtures to Death* 59 He was gun-shy, Hating all quarrels. **1957** R. CAMPBELL *Portugal* 116 The gun-shy poets of the 'left wing'.

Hence **'gunshyness**, the condition of being gun-shy.

1890 *Q. Rev.* Oct. 427 Gunshyness [in dogs] is one of the worst difficulties with which sportsmen have to contend. **1960** C. DAY LEWIS *Buried Day* v. 91 What caused this gun-shyness, I have no idea.

gunsman ('gʌnzmən). *rare.* [f. *gun's*, genitive of GUN + MAN: cf. *marksman.*] = GUNMAN I.

1766 in W. Smith *Bouquet's Exped.* (1868) 156 In this list their warriors or gunsmen are 1180, and their inhabitants about 6000. **1775** ADAIR *Amer. Ind.* 281 The outmost boundaries of the colony, where commonly the best gunsmen reside. *a* **1849** J. C. MANGAN *Poems* (1859) 351 Gunsman and dragoon.

gunsmith ('gʌnsmɪθ).

1. One whose occupation it is to make and repair small fire-arms.

1588 in *Compt. Bk. D. Wedderburne* (S.H.S., 1898) 82 *note*, [William Low, gunsmith, son of James Low, smith, was entered in the Burgess Roll 30th Sept. 1588]. **1647** HAWARD *Crown Rev.* 21 Gun-smith: Fee, 6d. *per diem.* **1671** DRYDEN *Evening's Love* Pref. a 4 b, The employment of a Poet is like that of a curious Gunsmith, or Watchmaker. **1781** *Phil. Trans.* LXXI. 230 Wogdon, one of the most famous gunsmiths in London. **1858** [see GUNMAKER]. **1861** *Times* 21 Aug., Gunsmiths making or repairing rifles.

2. *slang.* A thief.

1869 *Temple Bar* XXV. 213 He.. returned to his old trade of 'gunsmith', gunning being the slang term for thieving.

Hence **'gunsmithery**, the trade of a gunsmith, the making of small arms; also, the place where the work of a gunsmith is carried on.

1847 in CRAIG. **1896** *Westm. Gaz.* 30 Jan. 2/1 The Government gun-smitheries.

†**'gunster.** *slang* (? or *nonce-wd.*). *Obs.* [f. GUN *sb.* + -STER.] (See quot.)

1709 STEELE *Tatler* No. 88 ¶2 The words Gunner and Gunster are not to be used promiscuously.. Those who recount strange Accidents and Circumstances which have no Manner of Foundation in Truth, when they design to do Mischief are comprehended under the Appellation of Gunners, when they endeavour only to surprise and entertain, they are distinguished by the Name of Gunsters. .. The Gunner is destructive, and hated; the Gunster innocent, and laughed at. *Ibid.* ¶9 Come we now to the Gunsters. This Race of Engineers deals altogether in Wind-Guns, which by recoiling often, knock down those who discharge them, without hurting any body else. **1727** BOYER *Fr. Dict.*, Gunster (a Cracker, or bouncing Fellow), *un Bavard.*

gun-stock ('gʌnstɒk). The wooden stock or support to which the barrel of a gun is attached; †a rest or support on which to place a cannon on board ship.

1495–7 *Naval Acc. Hen. VII* (1896) 246 Also payed in lykewith to John Keyte for xx. Elmyn tres price the pece xij[d] ..of hym so bought & apon makyng of Gonne stokkes for Gonnes belongyng to the seid ship. **1591** PERCIVALL *Sp. Dict.*, *Vaqueta*..a gunne stocke. **1725** BRADLEY *Fam. Dict.* s.v. *Walnut Tree*, The Timber is..used for Gunstocks, Coach-wheels, and the bodies of Coaches. **1748** *Anson's Voy.* II. v. 179 The Commodore ordered..a swivel gun-stock to be fixed in the bow both of the barge and pinnace. **1835** GREENER *Gun* 144 Walnut has for many years been considered the most handsome and the best wood for gun-stocks. **1899** *Blackw. Mag.* Aug. 175/1 The least tap on a gun-stock was carried a great distance.

Comb. **1689** *Ann. Albany* (1850) II. 112 Jan Nack, trader and gunstockmaker.

Hence **'gun-stocker**, one who fits the stocks of guns to the barrels; **'gun-stocking**, the fitting of gun-stocks.

In recent Dicts.

†**'gunstone.** *Obs.* [f. GUN *sb.* + STONE *sb.*]

1. A stone used for the shot of a cannon or gun; a cannon-ball; a bullet.

1432–50 tr. *Higden* (Rolls) IV. 455 He was sleyne with a gunneston [L. *ictu fundibali*]. *c* **1440** *Jacob's Well* 267 þe vyolence of a gunne or of an engyne-ston is qwenchyd, whan softe erthe or softe thyng is sett þer-ȝens. **1530** PALSGR. 680, I neuer sawe gonne stone skyppe on that facyon. *Ibid.* 739/2, I am stryken with a gonne stone, I am but deed. **1563–87** FOXE *A. & M.* (1596) 1948/2 Having at one siege no lesse then three thousand bullets and gunstones flying upon them. **1573** TUSSER *Husb.* x. (1878) 20 Make gunstone and arrow shew who is within. **1599** SHAKS. *Hen. V*, I. ii. 282 This Mocke of his Hath turn'd his balles to Gun-stones. **1605** B. JONSON *Volpone* v. v, That I could shoote mine eies at him like gun-stones. **1681** W. ROBERTSON *Phraseol. Gen.* (1693) 693 A Gun-stone or pellet. **1808** J. BARLOW *Columb.* VII. 702 Shells rain before him..Crags, gunstones, balls o'erturn the tented ground.

Comb. **1578** *Househ. Ord.* (1790) 254 Guneston maker fee per diem..o. o. 8. **1647** HAWARD *Crown Rev.* 21 Gun-stone maker: Fee *per diem*, 12. d.

2. *Her.* = PELLET, OGRESS. (Cf. GUN-SHOT I c.)

1486 *Bk. St. Albans, Her.* B iv b, Oglys be calde in armys gonestonys. **1688** R. HOLME *Armoury* I. 61/1 He beareth Argent 3 Ogresses. These are also termed Pellets, and do resemble bullets for Guns, and are often termed Gun-stones, or Bullets. **1766** PORNY *Heraldry* (1777) Dict., *Pellets*, the name given to the Black Roundlets, by English Heralds alone..these are also denominated in English by the apellations of Ogresses and Gunstones. **1847** *Gloss. Her.* 244.

Gunter ('gʌntə(r)). [The name of a distinguished English mathematician, Edmund Gunter (1581–1626). The phrase 'according to Gunter' is current in the U.S. in the same sense as the English 'according to Cocker' (Farmer *Americanisms* 1889).]

1. In the name of several mathematical instruments improved or invented by Gunter. ***Gunter's chain***: the chain of 4 poles' length now in general use for land-surveying (see CHAIN *sb.* 9). ***Gunter's line***: a logarithmic line on Gunter's scale used for performing mechanically the operations of multiplication and division; also called ***Gunter's proportion. Gunter's quadrant***: an apparatus for finding the hour of the day, the azimuth, etc. ***Gunter's rule, scale*** = 1 b.

1679 MOXON *Math. Dict.*, *Gunter's Chain, Quadrant, Rule, Scale*, and *Sector*, all useful Mathematical Instruments, invented or much improved by..Mr. Edmund Gunter..and from him bearing their names. **1688** J. BROWN, The Description and Use of the Carpenters-Rule, together with the Use of the Line of Numbers commonly called Gunter's-Line, applyed to the measuring of all superficies and solids. **1701** T. TUTTELL *Descr. Math. Instr.*, *Gunter's Quadrant*,..made in Wood or Brass, Curiously contrived to find the Hour..and Azimuth, and most Propositions of the Globe; also, the Height of Trees, Steeples, &c. **1706** PHILLIPS (ed. Kersey), *Gunter's Line*, the common Line of Numbers first invented by Mr. Edmund Gunter, and so well known that it needs no Description. **1727–41** CHAMBERS *Cycl.*, *Gunter's Line*, called also *line of lines*, and *line of numbers*. **1750** FRANKLIN *Opinions & Conject.* Wks. 1887 II. 186 Two pieces of thick looking-glass, as broad as a gunter's scale, and six inches long. **1801** [see CHAIN *sb.* 9]. **1890** *Dict. Nat. Biog.* XXXIII. 350 Gunter's admirable rule of proportion, now called the line of numbers ('Gunter's Line' and 'Gunter's Proportion'), and other lines laid down by it were fitted in the scale, which ever since has been called 'Gunter's Scale'.

b. Short for ***Gunter's scale***: A flat rule, two feet long, marked on one side with scales of equal parts, of chords, sines, tangents, etc., and on the other side with scales of the logarithms of those parts; much used for the mechanical solution of problems in surveying and navigation.

1706 PHILLIPS (ed. Kersey), *Gunter's-Scale*, commonly call'd *The Gunter* by Seamen. **1727–41** CHAMBERS *Cycl.*, *Gunter's scale*, also called by navigators absolutely *the Gunter*.. The same lines are also occasionally laid down on rulers to slide by each other; hence called *sliding Gunters*. **1886** *Dict. Nat. Biog.* VI. 225/2 Brandreth, T. S...had previously [to 1821] invented his logometer, or ten-foot gunter. **1890** *Ibid.* XXXIII. 350 In these tables [*sc.* of Artificial Sines and Tangents] Gunter applied to navigation and other branches of mathematics his admirable rule 'the Gunter', on which were inscribed the logarithmic lines for numbers, sines, and tangents of arches.

2. *Naut.* Applied to a method of rigging in which the topmast slides up and down the lower mast on rings or hoops; a mast so rigged or a sail attached to such a mast (more fully *sliding-gunter*). [So called from its resemblance to a 'sliding Gunter'; see quot. 1727–41 under 1 b.]

1794 *Rigging & Seamanship* I. 136 *Boat's Latteen Sail*... This sail, when the head of it (then called the fore-leech) is laced to a mast and topmast, is called a sliding-gunter-sail; the topmast being made to slide down the mast by means of hoops. *Ibid.* 229 Ship's Pinnaces..sometimes..rig with a sliding-gunter, like houarios. *Ibid.* 238 These sails are called sliding-gunters, and used in the English navy's pinnaces and barges. **1857** P. COLQUHOUN *Oarsman's Guide* 23 Three sorts of sails,—the spreet, the gunter, and the lug. **1867** SMYTH *Sailor's Word-bk.*, *Sliding Gunters*, masts fitted for getting up and down with facility abaft the mast; generally used for kites, as royals, skysails, and the like. **1875** BEDFORD *Sailor's Pocket Bk.* vi. (ed. 2) 227 Boats rigged with two sliding gunters are the best suited for cruising purposes. **1894** *Outing* (U.S.) XXIV. 35/1 The rig was a sliding gunter mainsail. *Ibid.* 148/2 The sliding gunter rig,..the mast is in two pieces, the topmast sliding up and down the lower mast on two wrought-iron rings or travelers.

guntz (gʌnts). *slang.* [Perh. f. Yiddish *gants* whole, f. G. *ganze* whole, entirety.] 'The whole lot, the whole way' (Partridge, *Dict. Slang* Suppl., 1961).

1958 F. NORMAN *Bang to Rights* III. 137 This time I went the guntz and blaged her for a grand. **1960** *News Chron.* 16 Feb. 6/3 This bird Barbara Windsor, who's had the real guntz from the audience on opening night—cheers, encores, the lot. **1967** J. MORGAN *Involved* 147 You don't want a pay-day, you boys are asking for the guntz.

gunwale, gunnel ('gʌnəl). Forms: α. 5 gonne walle, 7 gunwayle, -waile, (8 gun-wall), 8– gunwale, (9 gunwhale). β. 7 gun(n)al, 8– gunnel. γ. 7–8 gunhil(l. [f. GUN *sb.* + WALE, the gunwale having formerly served to support the guns (cf. quot. 1697 in β). The usual spelling is still *gunwale*, though the pronunciation ('gʌnweɪl) is, at least in Great Britain, never used by persons acquainted with nautical or boating matters.] The upper edge of a ship's side; in large vessels, the uppermost planking, which covers the timber-heads and reaches from the quarter-deck to the forecastle on either side; in small craft, a piece of timber extending round the top side of the hull.

α. **1466** *Mann. & Househ. Exp.* (Roxb.) 205 For tymbre for colers of the maste, and gonne walles, xx. *d.* **1626** CAPT. SMITH *Accid. Yng. Sea-men* 11 The wayst-boords, the gunwayle, stations for the nettings. **1627** —— *Seaman's Gram.* ii. 6 The sides and Deckes are wrought till you come at the Gunwaile, which is the vpmost waile. **1727** A. HAMILTON *New Acc. E. Ind.* II. xlv. 147 The Assailants.. when they got as high as the Gun-wall or Gunnel, were at a Loss how to get over the Netting. **1800** CAPT. MILNE in *Naval Chron.* IV. 421 Brass swivels on the gunwhale. **1833** MARRYAT *P. Simple* (1863) 325 She..proved to be a brigantine laden up to her gunwale, which was not above a foot out of the water. **1865** LIVINGSTONE *Zambesi* xvi. 329 Our canoes were not a foot above the water at the gunwales. **1868** MISS YONGE *Cameos* (1877) I. vi. 41 Horses were led into the ships, the shields hung round the gunwale, and the warriors crowded in. **1875** BEDFORD *Sailor's Pocket Bk.* vi. (ed. 2) 226 Cutters and pinnaces should have from 6 to 8 inches added to their gunwale forward. **1880** DIXON *Windsor* III. iii. 25 More than once her gunwale had been under water.

attrib. **1773** COOK *1st Voy.* II. x. (1842) I. 194 The gun-wale boards were..frequently carved in a grotesque taste.

β. **1697** DAMPIER *Voy.* (1729) I. 400 A very pretty neat Vessel..had about 40 men all armed..and some guns, that went with a Swivel upon their Gunnal. **1699** *Ibid.* III. 14 The first [ropes] going athwart from Gunnal to Gunnal. **1719** DE FOE *Crusoe* I. xvi. (1840) 287 Friday..set him down softly upon the side or gunnel of the Canoe. **1757** ROBERTSON in *Phil. Trans.* L. 34 As he was stepping on the gunnel, he fell over-board. **1833** MARRYAT *P. Simple* (1863) 103 The wind had caught the sails; and the ship..careened over to her gunnel with its force. **1834** MEDWIN *Angler in Wales* II. 23, I was never tired (when I leaned over the gunnel of the boat) in watching the fish. **1878** *N. Amer. Rev.* CXXVII. 384 Mitrailleuses and field-pieces were mounted on the gunnels.

γ. **1693** R. LYDE *Retaking 'Friend's Adv.'* 22, I kept up the Topsail, till at last the Wind in the Showers did put the Gunhil of the Ship in the Water. **1711** in A. Duncan *Mariner's Chron.* (1805) III. 292 Cutting away the vessel's gunhill.

b. Phrases. ***gunwale to*** (rarely †*in*): with the gunwale on a level with the water; also *transf.* ***gunwale under***: with the gunwale submerged.

[**1717** tr. *Frezier's Voy. S. Sea* 34 With such dreadful.. Gusts, that they brought the Gunwale to, under two Courses reef'd.] **1748** *Anson's Voy.* I. viii. 77 The ship rolling incessantly gunwale to. **1751** SMOLLETT *Per. Pic.* (1779) IV. civ. 339 He rolled himself almost gunwale to, at every motion of his horse. **1769** FALCONER *Dict. Marine* (1780) D dd 4, *Gunnel-in*, or *gunnel-to*. **1830** MARRYAT *King's Own* liii, She rolled gunwale under. **1833** M. SCOTT *Tom Cringle* (1862) 260 We continued to roll gunwale under, dipping the main yardarm into the water every now and then. **1873** G. C. DAVIES *Mount. & Mere* xvi. 141 She shot across gunwale under.

c. *transf.* The top plank of a hoarding.

1865 KINGSLEY *Herew.* II. ix. 150 At last one scaling ladder was planted upon the bodies of the dead, and hooked firmly on the gunwale of the hoarding.

gunyah ('gʌnjə). Also 9 gun(n)eah, guneeah, gun(n)ya, gunyer, -yia, -yio, guniar. [Native Australian.] A native Australian hut. (Cf. HUMPY and GIBBER.)

[**1798** D. COLLINS *Acc. Eng. Colony N.S. Wales*, *Aboriginal Voc. Port Jackson* I. 610 *Go-nie*, a hut.] **1820** J. OXLEY *Jrnl. Exped. Australia* 117 He [the native] threw down..the little bark guneah which had sheltered him and his family during the night. **1847** L. LEICHHARDT *Jrnl. Overland Exped.* ix. 290 We saw a very interesting camping place of the natives, containing several two-storied gunyas. **1848** H. W. HAYGARTH *Recoll. Bush Life Austral.* x. 105 Comfortably sleeping in an adjacent 'gunyio', or camp. *Ibid.* xii. 132 Perhaps the most primitive boat in the world: like the 'gunyio's', or huts, of the aborigines, it is built in a few minutes. **1870** WILSON *Austral. Songs* 140 From the gunyahs 'neath the headland Curled the smoke. **1890** 'ROLF BOLDREWOOD' *Squatter's Dream* xiv. 157 For two pins I'd put a match in every gunyah on the place.

gunyang ('gʌnjæŋ). *Bot.* [Native name.] An Australian shrub, *Solanum laciniatum* or *S. vescum*, which bears edible orange fruits; cf. *kangaroo apple* (*s.v.* KANGAROO *sb.* 4 b).

1867 W. WOOLLS *Contrib. Flora Austral.* 125 The native name of this fruit is 'gunyang'. **1874** LINDLEY & MOORE *Treas. Bot.* Suppl., Gunyang, *Solanum vescum*, known by this name in Victoria, where the native tribes collect its fruits eagerly as an article of food. **1888** D. MACDONALD *Gum Boughs* 222 A dwarfed ti-tree, clinging low about the ground, like the gunyang or kangaroo apple. **1911** W. R. GUILFOYLE *Austral. Plants* 334 *Solanum aviculare* 'Kangaroo Apple'. 'Bulli Bulli', or 'Gunyang' (herbaceous shrub, 6 to 8 ft.). **1965** *Austral. Encycl.* VIII. 196/1 *S*[*olanum*] *aviculare*, ranging almost across the temperate part of the continent..is the kangaroo apple—called *gunyang* by former Victorian aborigines and *poro-poro* or *kohoho* by the Maoris.

Günz (gʏnts). *Geol.* The name of a tributary of the Danube in southern Germany, adopted by A. Penck (in Penck & Brückner *Die Alpen im Eiszeitalter* (1901) I. I. 110) and used *attrib.* to designate the first Pleistocene glaciation in the Alps. Also *absol.*

1910 *Zeitschr. f. Gletscherkunde* IV. 244 The two older, known as Günz and Mindel, are separated from each other by a long interval of deglaciation. *Ibid.* 251 The Günz drift is almost completely covered by later glacial deposits. **1923** A. L. KROEBER *Anthropol.* ii. 21 The period of the stratum is generally considered early Pleistocene, possibly approximately contemporary with the first or Günz glaciation of Europe—nearly a million years ago. **1970** I. CORNWALL *Ice Ages* iii. 62 The North American correlative of European Günz was generally supposed to be the Nebraskan glaciation.

guos, obs. form of GOOSE.

‖**gup** (gʌp), *sb. Anglo-Indian.* [a. Hindustani *gup.*] Gossip. Also in general *colloq.* use with the sense: silly talk, blather, nonsense.

c **1806** MRS. SHERWOOD in *Life* xxi. (1847) 357 No other amusement than hearing 'the gup gup', or gossip of the place where they may happen to be. **1848** J. H. STOCQUELER *Oriental Interpreter* 94/2 *Gup*, or *Gup-shup*, the origin of *gossip*, to which, in India, it bears the closest possible affinity. **1868** F. MARRYAT (*title*) 'Gup'. Sketches of Anglo-Indian Life and Character. **1882** MRS. CROKER *Proper Pride* I. iv. 71 This occurrence was related.. as one of the items of local 'gup'. **1883** —— *Pretty Miss Neville* II. xvi. 23 Passing friends.. related the local 'gup'. **1884** *Manch. Exam.* 11 Nov. 8/2 The story.. rests on pure bazaar 'gup', as they say in India. **1924** GALSWORTHY *White Monkey* II. i, The usual 'gup' over the dividend. **1927** *Punch* 30 Mar. 340/3 Need I give the jury any more of this gup? **1942** S. HOPE *Sea Breezes* 36 With little to do except drink sherbert and listen to the gup—gossip, which, incidentally, they didn't understand. **1962** 'W. HAGGARD' *Unquiet Sleep* v. 41 The gup in the business is that Hassertons have agreed.

†**gup**, *int. Obs.* Also 6 goppe, guppe, 7 g'up, guipp, guep. [? Contracted from *go up*; cf. GIP *int.*] **a.** A cry of anger or chiding addressed to a horse. **b.** An exclamation of derision, remonstrance, or surprise; often coupled with *marry*.

a **1529** SKELTON *Dyuers Balettys* ii. 17 Spur vp at the hynder gyrth, with, Gup, morell, gup. —— *Poems agst. Garnesche* ii. 36 Gup, gorbellyd Godfrey, gup, Garnysche, gaudy fole. **1538** BALE *Thre Lawes* 962 Goppe with a vengeaunce, how comest thu so aloft? **1546** J. HEYWOOD *Prov.* (1867) 43 Gup with a galde backe gill, come vp to supper. **1598** E. GUILPIN *Skial.* (1878) 44 Mary and gup! haue I then lost my cap? **1604** DEKKER *Honest Wh.* viii. Wks. 1873 II. 50 Mary gup, are you growne so holy? **1622** MABBE tr. *Aleman's Guzman d'Alf.* I. 101 Marry g'up with a murraine. **1631** P. FLETCHER *Sicelides* Poems (Grosart) III. 80 Modestie? marry guipp: these are your modest creatures! **1682** T. FLATMAN *Heraclitus Ridens* (1713) II. No. 56. 99 Marry guep! how tender-credited our Friend is!

guppy[1] ('gʌpɪ). [f. the name of R. J. L. *Guppy*, a Trinidad clergyman who sent the first recorded specimen to the British Museum, used as the specific epithet in *Gerardinus guppyi* (A. Günther *Catal. Fishes Brit. Mus.* (1866) VI. 353), the name used when the fish was first described.] A small fish, *Lebistes reticulatus*, originally from the West Indies, well suited for the aquarium. Cf. MILLION 2 c.

1925 *Aquatic Life* Nov. 110/2 The following are live-bearing tropicals:.. Guppy (Lebistes reticulatus). Males small and brilliantly colored. **1927** A. E. HODGE *Tropical Aquarium-Fishes* v. 75 One of the best known of the Killifishes.. is the Guppy, or Rainbow Fish (*Lebistes Reticulatus*) commonly known as 'Millions'. **1950** O. NASH *Family Reunion* (1951) 71 Seals have puppies, But guppies just have little guppies. **1962** *Listener* 22 Nov. 852/2, I got some guppies—hardy little rainbow-coloured fish.

guppy[2] ('gʌpɪ). orig. *U.S.* [f. *g*reater *u*nderwater *p*ropulsive *p*ower + -Y[6].] A submarine which has been streamlined and equipped with a schnorkel. Also *attrib.* Hence **guppy** *v. trans.*, to streamline (a submarine).

1948 *Sci. News Let.* 27 Mar. 200/3 Called the 'Guppy' program, the alterations involve streamlining the hulls of the fleet submarines by reducing the size of their superstructures and by removing deck guns and other topside appendages to cut down on under-water resistance. **1948** *News* (Birmingham, Alabama) 13 Oct. 12/6 However, the Tigrone was not streamlined into the high speed 'guppy' class with which the Navy is experimenting. **1949** *Jane's Fighting Ships 1949–50* 380 *Pickerell* [U.S. Navy] is of the new 'Guppy' (Greater Underwater Propulsive Power) design and is equipped with the latest devices. *Ibid.*, *Cutlass*, *Sea Leopard*, *Sirago* converted to 'guppy-schnorkel'. **1959** *Jane's Fighting Ships 1959–60* 44 The boats in this class which have not been 'guppied'.

Gupta ('gʊptə), *a.* and *sb.* [f. *Chandragupta*, name of the founder of the dynasty.] **A.** *adj.* Of or pertaining to a dynasty which ruled in north India from the fourth to the sixth century A.D. **B.** *sb.* A member of this dynasty. Hence **'Guptan** *a.*

[**1845** *Encycl. Metropolitana* XVI. 354/2 Four families of the Vaïdyas were raised by the same Prince to the rank of Culínas; their family names are Séna, Mallíca, Datta, and Gupta.] **1871** E. BALFOUR *Cycl. India* (ed. 2) II. 440/2 The following is a table of the Gupta kings. *Ibid.*, 'Elder Guptas'. **1880** *Encycl. Brit.* XIII. 120/2 All the Gupta inscriptions are dated in the *Gupta-kála*, the Gupta era, the epoch of which has long been and still remains a subject of dispute. *Ibid.*, After the Sáhs come the Guptas of Kanauj, a dynasty which must not be confounded with the Maurya dynasty. **1939** A. J. TOYNBEE *Study Hist.* VI. 193 A Guptan 'Indian Summer'.. was followed.. by the blight of an irruption of Eurasian Nomads. **1947** AUDEN *Age of Anxiety* (1948) v. 103 The Ghuzz, the Guptas, the gloomy Krimchaks. **1963** *Times* 12 Feb. 12/4 A fifth century A.D. Gupta sandstone carving. **1969** *Sunday Statesman* (Calcutta) (Mag. Sect.) 27 July p. i/5 The most prolific period of Hindu art, from the Gupta age to the mediaeval times, saw the rapid development of sculptural ornamentation.

†**gur.** *Min. Obs.* [a. med.L. *gur*, perh. a. G. *guhr* ferment (used by later mineralogists with different sense: see GUHR).] (See quots.)

1686 PLOT *Staffordsh.* 160, I take it to be the Gur of the Adeptists, i.e. the matter of Metalls before it be coagulated into a Metallic form... It might be the Gur of Lead. [**1739** BROMELL *Mineralogia* vi. 6 En sådan silfwahaltig hwit bergmiölk eller *gur metallicum* utflöt åhr 1696.] **1753** CHAMBERS *Cycl. Supp.*, *Gur*, a word used to express a fluid matter looking like milk, but reduced sometimes, by evaporation, to the consistence of honey, and appearing in form of a white sediment. It always contains more or less silver, and is common in the mines of Sweden, and in some other places.

gur, variant of GOOR, a coarse Indian sugar.

gurab, obs. form of GRAB *sb.*[1]

gurah, var. GURRAH[2].

gural, var. GORAL.

Guran ('guːrən). One of a people of Kurdistan; also, the language of this people. Also as *adj.*

1882 *Encycl. Brit.* XIV. 157/2 The Gurán dialect.. which is spoken throughout Ardelán and Kirmánsháhán. *Ibid.* 158/1 The Guráns have for a long period abandoned nomadic habits. **1912** E. B. SOANE *To Mesopotamia & Kurdistan* x. 218 There was even a special court language, the graceful and euphonious Guran dialect, an ancient Persian tongue. *Ibid.* 224 Those who took protection under the Guran tribe, and have become Guran in name, were the Qadir Mir Waisi.. and the Gurgkaish. *Ibid.* xvi. 382 The Gurans ruled with great power from their old capital at Gahwara. **1948** A. SAFRASTIAN *Kurds & Kurdistan* vi. 89 The many tribes which bear the general denomination of Guran.

gurchen, rare obs. form of GHERKIN.

gurd, obs. form of GIRD, GOURD[1].

gurdel, -il, obs. forms of GIRDLE *sb.*[1]

gurdfish, variant of GARFISH.

gurdle, dial. variant GIRDLE *sb.*[2]

‖**gurdwara** (gɜːd'wɑːrə). [Punjabi *gurduārā*, f. Skr. *guru* teacher + *dvāra* door.] A Sikh temple.

1909 M. A. MACAULIFFE *Sikh Religion* I. i. 47 A temple at a place visited by a Guru is now called Gurdwāra. **1924** *Glasgow Herald* 15 Apr. 9 The [Sikh] community have numerous temples or shrines called gurdwaras. **1954** J. MASTERS *Bhowani Junction* II. xxvii. 228 This bare square temple, the Sikh gurdwara.

†**gure**, *a. Obs.* Also 3 girre. [f. OE. *gor* GORE.] In phr. *on* (*a*) *gure blode*: in or with gore. Cf. A-GORE-BLOOD and GORE-BLOOD 2.

a **1225** *Juliana* 28 Euch dunt defde into hire liche þat ha al biȝet on gure blode. *a* **1240** *Wohunge* in *Cott. Hom.* 281 Al þi blisfule bodi streamed on a Girre blod.

gurfish, variant of GARFISH.

gurge (gɜːdʒ), *sb. rare.* Also gorge. [ad. L. *gurges* abyss, whirlpool.] A whirlpool (*lit.* and *fig.*); *Her.* = GURGES b.

1667 MILTON *P.L.* XII. 41 The Plain, wherein a black bituminous gurge Boiles out from under ground, the mouth of Hell. **1730–6** BAILEY (folio), *Gurge*, a Whirl-Pool. **1820** KEATS *Hyperion* II. 28 Horribly convulsed With sanguine, feverous, boiling gurge of pulse. **1868** CUSSANS *Her.* vii. (1882) 116 *Gorge*, or *Gurge*,.. a whirlpool... This Charge covers the entire Field, and is blazoned Argent and Azure. **1893** M. FIELD *Underneath Bough* 9 Life's a tortured, booming gurge.

gurge (gɜːdʒ), *v.* [f. L. *gurges* whirlpool.]

†**1.** *trans.* To turn into a whirlpool.

1523 LD. BERNERS *Froiss.* I. i. 1 All great ryuers are gurged.. of diuers surges and sprynges of water.

2. *intr.* To make a whirlpool, to swirl, surge. Also **'gurging** *ppl. a.*

1578 *Mirr. Mag.*, *Sigebert* xiv, In gurging gulfe of these such surging seas. **1893** *Daily News* 28 Jan. 3/1 The water rises up one gurging mass of white foam. **1897** F. THOMPSON *New Poems* 73 At all gates the clangours gurge in, God's paludament lightens, see!

gurgeon ('gɜːdʒən). [perh. related to GURJUN.] *gurgeon-stopper*, a hardwood tree, *Eugenia buxifolia*, found in Florida and the West Indies; cf. STOPPER *sb.* 8.

1884 [see STOPPER *sb.* 8]. **1908** N. L. BRITTON *N. Amer. Trees* 724 Spanish Stopper—*Eugenia buxifolia*... Also called Gurgeon stopper; this small tree or shrub of the West Indies enters our area in southern peninsular Florida and the Keys. **1921** C. S. SARGENT *Man. Trees of N. Amer.* (ed. 2) 771 *Eugenia buxifolia* Willd. Gurgeon Stopper. Spanish Stopper.

gurgeons ('gɜːdʒənz), *sb. pl.* Now *dial.* Forms: α. 5– gurgeons, (7 gurgin, 7–8 gurgians, 8 -ins, 9 -ens). β. 7 grudgeons, -ions, -ins, grugings, 9 grudgings, 7– grodgeons. [Cf. F. *grugeons* lumps of crystalline sugar in brown sugar, formerly also (in Cotgr.) 'the smallest or most writhen fruit on a tree'; connected with *gruger* to crunch.] Coarse meal; the coarse refuse from flour; pollards.

α. *a* **1483** *Liber Niger* in *Househ. Ord.* (1790) 69 Not to boult it [the flour] soe sore uppon the gurgeones of branne. **1577** HARRISON *England* II. vi. (1877) I. 154 The bran (usuallie called gurgeons or pollard). **1688** R. HOLME *Armoury* III. 317/1 Bakers Terms in their Art. Gurgin, or Bran. **1706** PHILLIPS (ed. Kersey), *Pityron*, Bran, Gurgeons, the refuse of Ground Wheat. **1787** WINTER *Syst. Husb.* 229 Gurgians, which is nearly, if not equally as nutritive as barley-meal, and much cheaper. **1844** W. BARNES *Poems Dorset Dial.* Gloss., *Gurgens*, pollard, coarse flour. **1855** MORTON *Cycl. Agric.* II. 724/2 Meal.. is separated into flour .. seconds, middlings, and even thirds; then blues, boxings, sharps, gurgeons, scuftings, pollards.. and bran.

β. **1601** HOLLAND *Pliny* I. 564 Courser grodgeons for brown bread. **1611** COTGR., *Annone*,.. meslin, or grudgins; the corne whereof browne bread is made for the meynie. **1623** FLETCHER & ROWLEY *Maid of Mill* III. iii, You that can deal with G[r]udgins and coarse floure. **1655** MOUFET & BENNET *Health's Improv.* (1746) 339 Bread mingled of Meal and Grudgins. **1847–78** HALLIWELL, *Grudgings*, pollard; fine bran. *North.* **1881** *Leicestersh. Gloss.* s.v. *Meal*, Sharps or grudgeons.

gurges ('gɜːdʒiːz). Also 7 gorges, 9 *dial.* gurgise. [a. L. *gurges* whirlpool.] A whirlpool, gulf; *dial.* a pool, pond.

1664 COTTON *Scarron.* I. 19 Here a Boat kicking on the Surges, And there one sinking in a Gurges. **1668** *Phil. Trans.* III. 633 There may be a very Low Ebb, though no High-Spring, which they terme an Out-let or Gurges of the Sea. **1875** *Sussex Gloss.*, *Gurgise*, a fish-pool; lake or pond.

b. *Her.* A charge consisting of a spiral of two narrow bands, intended to represent a whirlpool, and blazoned argent and azure.

1661 MORGAN *Sph. Gentry* 19 A Gurges, or Whirlpoole proper, by the name of Gorges, here the Field is not named at all, by reason it doth fill up all the vacuity of the Field, and is always Azure and Argent, the proper colour of water. **1823** in CRABB *Technol. Dict.*

gurgitate, *v.* [f. L. *gurgitāt-*, ppl. stem of *gurgitāre*: see next.] †**a.** = INGURGITATE *v.* 1. *Obs. rare*$^{-0}$.

1656 BLOUNT *Glossogr.*, *Gurgitate*, to swallow or devoure.

b. = INGURGITATE *v.* 2 b. Also *fig.*

1907 A. QUILLER-COUCH *Major Vigoureux* xxiv. 242 The ledge looked full upon the Mermaid's Rock, and upon the heave of black water surging past it to gurgitate between the narrowing walls of rock. **1963** *Evening Standard* 12 Nov. 18/3 The memoranda ceaselessly gurgitated by government departments.

gurgitation (gɜːdʒɪ'teɪʃən). [ad. late L. **gurgitātiōn-em*, n. of action f. *gurgitāre* to engulf (*gurgitātus* 'gorged', in Du Cange), f. *gurgit-*, *gurges* whirlpool. Cf. *ingurgitation*, *regurgitation*.]

†**1.** Swallowing; guzzling; = INGURGITATION.

1542 BOORDE *Dyetary* ix. (1870) 250 A surfet is taken as well by gurgytacyons or to moche drynkynge, as it is taken by epulacyon. **1658** PHILLIPS, *Gurgitation*, an ingulphing, or swallowing up.

2. Surging or whirling up and down; ebullient motion.

1864 SPENCER *Illust. of Progress* 417 The distribution of crude nutriment is by slow gurgitations and regurgitations. **1879** H. JAMES *Confidence* ix, The gurgitation of the waves grew deeper to his ear. **1881** GEIKIE *Geol. Sk.* in *Macm. Mag.* Oct. 431 The water sank in the funnel, and the same restless gurgitation was resumed.

gurgiting ('gɜːdʒɪtɪŋ), *vbl. sb. Falconry.* [f. L. *gurgit-āre* (taken in sense of *ingurgitāre* to gorge): see prec.] (See quots.)

1615 LATHAM *Falconry* Terms, *Gurgiting* is when a Hawke is stuft or suffocated with any thing, be it meat or otherwise. **1686** BLOME *Gentl. Recreat.* II. 62 Gurgiping [*sic*; hence prob. the corrupt forms *Gurgipting*, *gurgypting*, in 18th c. Dictionaries]. **1891** HARTING *Bibl. Accipitr.* 223 *Gurgiting*, choking with too large a mouthful.

†**gurgitive**, *a. Obs. rare*$^{-0}$. [irregularly f. L. *gurgit-*, *gurges* whirlpool.] 'Belonging to a Gulph or stream' (Blount *Glossogr.* 1656).

gurgle ('gɜːg(ə)l), *sb.* [f. GURGLE *v.* Cf. the parallel forms cited there.]

†**1.** = GARGLE *sb.* 1. *Obs.*

1562 BULLEYN *Def. agst. Sickness*, *Compounds* (1579) 35 b, A Gargarizme or washing Gurgle, for the Mouth and Throate.

2. The action or an act of gurgling; the noise made by liquid escaping intermittently from a vessel, of a stream flowing over a stony bed, etc.

1757 W. THOMPSON *Bower* 26 Flow, flow, thou Crystall-Rill, With tinkling gurgles fill The Mazes of the Grove. **1831** CARLYLE *Sart. Res.* (1858) 9 A gurgle of innumerable emptying bumpers. **1860** TYNDALL *Glac.* I. viii. 59 Streams .. plunged into the depths of the ice, flowed under it with hollow gurgle. **1879** R. H. ELLIOT *Written on Forehead* I. 119 The gurgle made by the pebbles of the shingle as they roll ceaselessly to and fro. **1897** BLACKMORE in *Blackw. Mag.* Sept. 362 The light itself seemed to come in gurgles.

b. A guttural sound such as is produced by irregular emission of air from the throat, gargling, or the like.

1862 SHIRLEY *Nugæ Crit.* vi. 239 The rich gurgle of the peesweet. **1865** CARLYLE *Fredk. Gt.* VI. ii. (1872) II. 140 He .. gasped some gurgle of a sound like 'Osnabrück'. **1869** TROLLOPE *He knew* xxiv. (1878) 136 There came a faint sound as of an hysterical sob, and then a gurgle in the throat.

gurgle (ˈgɜːg(ə)l), *v.* Also 6 gurgull. [Parallel forms are Du., MLG. *gorgelen*, G. *gurgeln* (Sw. *gurgla*, Da. *gurgle*, prob. from LG.) to gargle, and It. *gorgogliare* to gargle, bubble up, boil, rattle, Pg. *gurgulhar* to gush out, bubble, perh.:—L. **gurguliāre*, f. *gurgulio* gullet, which appears to be the origin of the cogn. sbs. Du. *gorgel*, OHG. *gurgulâ* (MHG., G. *gurgel*) and Pr. *gorgolh*. Whether the Eng. word is a direct adaptation of any of those vbs. or is a native echoic formation is not clear. Cf. GARGLE, GUGGLE.]

† **1.** *intr.* = GARGLE *v. Obs.*

1562 BULLEYN *Def. agst. Sickness, Compounds* (1579) 35 b, *marg.* A gargarizme to gurgull in the mouth and throate. **1611** FLORIO, *Gargareggiare*, to gargarize, to gurgle.

2. Of water or other liquid: To flow in a broken irregular current, with intermittent low noises, as water from a bottle, or a stream among stones.

[? **1635**: see GURL *v.* 2.] **1713** ROWE *Lady Jane Grey* II. i. Wks. (1720) 33 Neverceasing Waters.. That purl and gurgle o'er their Sands for ever. **1789** BURNS *To Mary in Heaven* iii, Ayr gurgling kiss'd his pebbled shore. **1821** KEATS *Isabella* xxvii, Where Arno's stream Gurgles through straighten'd banks. **1840** DICKENS *Barn. Rudge* lix, He..sent the wine gurgling down his throat. **1894** SALA *London up to Date* ii. 32 Rare hocks that gurgle in the glass when poured out.

b. *transf.* To make a noise as of liquid issuing from a bottle, bubbling, or the like; to utter intermittent guttural sounds.

1779 MASON *Eng. Garden* III. 487 She will plain, and gurgle, as she goes, As does the widow'd ring-dove. **1857-8** SEARS *Athan.* II. xi. 240 Paul is so full of this thought, that, whenever he touches upon the theme, his language gurgles from his lips. **1880** JEFFERIES *Gt. Estate* vii. 133 The cuckoo began to lose his voice; he gurgled and gasped, and cried 'cuck—kuk—kwai—kash'. **1892** *Sunday Mag.* June 425/1 Baby is lying in mother's lap, crooling and gurgling.

3. *trans.* To utter with gurgling sounds. Also, *to gurgle down*: to swallow with a gurgle.

1814 CARY *Dante, Inf.* VII. 128 Such dolorous strain they gurgle in their throats. **1825** C. M. WESTMACOTT *Eng. Spy* I. 314 Gurgling down the glutinous calipash. **1831** CARLYLE *Sart. Res.* I. iii, He gurgled-out his pursy chuckle of a cough-laugh. **1854** THACKERAY *Newcomes* I. ix. 96 'A mother's bl-l-essings go with you', gurgled the lady. **1865** J. THOMSON *Sunday up River* XI. iii, When your voice has gurgled the last sweet note.

gurglet (ˈgɜːglɪt). *rare.* [f. GURGLE *sb.* + -ET[1].] A tiny whirlpool.

1796 *Mod. Gulliver's Trav.* 9 Thou mayest be carried about like a float on a fishing-line, the whirligig of every gurglet in the stream.

gurglet, variant of GOGLET[1].

gurgling (ˈgɜːglɪŋ), *vbl. sb.* [f. GURGLE *v.* + -ING[1].] The action of the vb. GURGLE; the noisy intermittent flowing of liquid as from a narrow-necked bottle, etc.

1814 SOUTHEY *Roderick* Poet. Wks. 1838 IX. 52 The constant fall Of water its perpetual gurgling made. **1847** ALB. SMITH *Chr. Tadpole* xii. (1879) 112 In the gurgling of tall bottles..there is much music. **1876** *Trans. Clinical Soc.* IX. 192 The act of swallowing was imperfectly done, the patient taking cautious sips, and there being pharyngeal gurgling. **1880** GILBERT *Pirates Penzance* II, He loves to hear the little brook a-gurgling. **1883** C. J. WILLS *Mod. Persia* 226 Camels have a habit of gurgling.

gurgling (ˈgɜːglɪŋ), *ppl. a.* [f. as prec. + -ING[2].] That gurgles; emitting a sound as of bubbling liquid or purling water; characterized by gurgling.

1596 ? SPENSER *Thestylis* 3 Gurgling sound Of Liffies tumbling streames. **1614** SYLVESTER *Bethulia's Rescue* V. 15 By some River's side Or gurgling Brook. **1631** MABBE tr. *De Rojas' Celestina* (1894) xix. 266 Harken to the gurgling waters of this fountaine. **1725** POPE *Odyss.* XII. 361 Where a fountain's gurgling waters play, They rush to land. **1764** J. G. COOPER *Tomb Shaks.* 12 The nightingale..ceas'd to float The gurgling notes of her melodious woe. **1844** DUFTON *Deafness* 79 On throwing air into the tympanum through the Eustachian tube, a distinct gurgling noise was heard. **1847** J. WILSON *Chr. North* (1857) I. 152 He pours the gurgling brandy down his throat. **1855** LONGF. *Hiaw.* VIII. 94 Whirled the birch-canoe in circles, Round and round in gurgling eddies. **1897** *Allbutt's Syst. Med.* III. 838 Rumbling and gurgling sounds in the abdomen.

Hence **ˈgurglingly** *adv.*, with a gurgle.

1895 MAR. CORELLI *Sorrows Satan* ix. (ed. 6) 103 'Murder!' he whispered gurglingly.

gurgly (ˈgɜːglɪ), *a. rare.* [f. GURGLE *sb.* + -Y.] Characterized by gurgling.

1894 R. KIPLING *Jungle Bk.* 199 A gurgly rumbly voice.

† **gurgolion.** *Obs. rare*[−1]. [ad. L. *gurgulio*, *-ōnem*, var. of *curculio* weevil.] A weevil.

c **1420** *Pallad. on Husb.* I. 485 This maner craft wol hold out of thi whete Gurgolions and other noyis bestis.

gurgoyl(e, variant of GARGOYLE.

† **gurgulation.** [ad. med.L. **gurgulatiōn-em* (whence OF. *gurgulacion*), f. *gurgulāre* (of echoic formation) to gurgle.] Rumbling in the bowels.

c **1400** *Lanfranc's Cirurg.* 268 Whanne þou touchist it [siphac] wiþ þi fyngir, it wole goon yn aȝen. & sumtyme it wole come aȝen, & it wole make noon gurgulacioun. **1542** BOORDE *Dyetary* xii. (1870) 267 It [milk] is not good for them the whiche haue gurgulations in the bely. **1649** BULWER *Pathomyot.* II. ii. 128 A little retraction of the Midriff without the manifest act of Gurgulation.

gurgulet, obs. form of GOGLET[1].

‖ **gurˈgulio.** *Obs.* [L., = gullet, windpipe.] The gullet; *transf.* appetite for food.

1630 RANDOLPH *Aristippus* Wks. (1875) 32 His palate is lost, and with it his gurgulio. **1651** ——, etc. *Hey for Honesty* II. iv. ibid. 414 I'll cut your throats, and slit your impudent gurgulios.

gurgull, obs. form of GURGLE *v.*

gurhofite (ˈgɜːhəʊfaɪt). *Min.* [Named *Gurhofian* by Karsten, 1807; this was altered by Jameson to *Gurhofite*; from *Gurhof* in Austria, its locality; see -ITE.] A variety of dolomite containing more than the normal amount of calcium.

[**1814** T. ALLAN *Min. Nomen.* 26 Gurhofian.] **1816** R. JAMESON *Min.* (ed. 2) II. 112 Gurhofite. Gurhofian, Karsten. **1892** DANA *Min.* 273 Gurhofian, or gurhofite; snow-white and subtranslucent.

Gurian (ˈgʊərɪən), *sb.* and *a.* **A.** *sb.* One of a Caucasian race, inhabiting Tiflis, closely related to the Georgians. **B.** *adj.* Of or pertaining to this race, or the region in which they live.

1876 *Encycl. Brit.* V. 257/2 The Gurians, a small people occupying the strip of land between the Rion and the mountains on the south, which form the frontier between Russia and Turkey. **1882** R. BROWN *Peoples of World* V. i. 22 Like all the Georgians, the Gurian is fond of music. **1906** *Daily Chron.* 9 Aug. 3/1 The Gurians are the..most warlike ..of the Georgians. **1932** W. E. D. ALLEN *Hist. Georgian People* v. 50 Many more were the sea-ports, towns and castles of the Colchian-Lazic basin..inland to Petra, a Roman stronghold under the Gurian hills. *Ibid.* xviii. 208 The debris of their army was cut to pieces in the Gurian forests. *Ibid.* 210 In Imereti Solomon the Great, after a disastrous defeat at the hands of the Turks and Gurians, had died recently in Kutais (23rd April, 1782). **1963** C. TOUMANOFF *Stud. Chr. Caucasian Hist.* 269 The Imeretian house of Mik'elaje (1850) and the Gurian house of T'avdgirije (1850) appear to be of Bagratid..origin.

gurjun (ˈgɜːdʒən). Also gurjan, gurjon.

The native name for a large tree of the East Indies and Philippine Islands, *Dipterocarpus alatus*, from which and other species of *Dipterocarpus* a viscid balsamic liquid is obtained, called ***gurjun balsam*** or ***gurjun oil***, used as a varnish and medicinally.

1858 SIMMONDS *Dict. Trade*, *Gurjun*, an oleo-resin; a thin balsam or wood oil. **1876** HARLEY *Mat. Med.* (ed. 6) 702 Gurjun balsam resembles copaiba balsam. **1889** *Tablet* 16 Feb. 273/1 The gurjun oil which I brought is making a manifest difference in his [Father Damien's] face and hands. **1892** *Blackw. Mag.* Sept. 384 The gray-stemmed gurjuns gleam like spectres. **1897** *Allbutt's Syst. Med.* II. 76 Hillis speaks well of the gurjon oil treatment. **1957** J. H. WILLIAMS *Spotted Deer* xi. 143 The two main species of which we were in search were gurjan and padauk... In others [*sc.* areas] [were] evergreen broad-leaved gurjan forests.

Hence **gurjunic** (gɜːˈdʒuːnɪk) *a.*, in ***gurjunic acid*** (see quots.).

1876 HARLEY *Mat. Med.* (ed. 6) 702 The resin contains a little crystallisable gurgunic [*sic*] acid C_{44} H_{68} O_8, which appears to be a hydrate of abietinic acid. **1886** *Syd. Soc. Lex.*, *Gurjunic acid*, C_{34} H_{64} O_5 + 3 H_2 O. A crystalline substance contained in the transparent semi-fluid resin left after the distillation of the volatile oil from gurjun balsam.

gurk (gɜːk), *v. colloq.* [Echoic.] To belch. Hence **ˈgurking** *vbl. sb.* and *ppl. a.*

1923 in MANCHON *Le Slang* 146. **1946** B. MARSHALL *George Brown's Schooldays* 34 Belching and gurking with ghoulish glee. **1948** C. FRY *Thor with Angels* 7 Spit some words at me instead, and gurk Away your grudge. **1954** G. DURRELL *Bafut Beagles* iii. 56 The loudest and most awesome gurking noises I have heard from a squirrel. **1966** *New Statesman* 10 June 839/2 They grunted and gurked with an unconcern that amazed me.

gurk (gɜːk), *sb. colloq.* [See prec.] A belch.

1932 N. MITFORD *Christmas Pudding* x. 151 That's right, darling, have a good gurk. *Ibid.* 153 The silence was broken by a shattering gurk from Elspeth Paula. **1961** G. DURRELL *Whispering Land* iii. 75 It was not an accidental gurk, the minute breach of good manners that we are all liable to at times. This was a premeditated, rich and prolonged belch, with all the fervour of the Orient in it. **1962** C. MIDDLETON *Torse 3* II. 38 A too hard sniff culminates in a sly gurk.

Gurkha (ˈgʊəkə). Also Ghoorka, Ghorkha, Ghurka, Goork(h)a. A member of one of the dominant races of Nepal, of Hindu descent and Sanskritic speech, and especially famous for prowess in fighting. Also *attrib.*

1811 W. KIRKPATRICK *Account Kingdom Nepaul* App. I. 339 The Goorkha envoy proposed, that, as they could not stop the circulation of the base coin with which they had been supplied, they should, at least, establish a just rate of exchange. **1822** (*title*) Military Sketches of the Goorka War, in India, in the years 1814, 1815, 1816. **1836** *Penny Cycl.* VI. 65/1 It was clearly established by the Ghorkhas..that the village of Butool had never rightly formed part of the dominions of Oude. **1848** [see BHUTANESE *sb.* and *a.*]. **1848** J. D. HOOKER in L. Huxley *Life J.D.H.* (1918) I. 269 The Goorkha Sepoys are immense fellows, stout and brawny. **1875** *Encycl. Brit.* II. 590/1 The four Ghoorka regiments, enlisted from Nepaul. **1905** *New Internat. Encycl.* IX. 388 In physique the Gurkha is very short and stout. **1914** G. B. SHAW in *New Statesman* (Suppl.) 14 Nov., A Ghoorka's religious conscience is respected: an Englishman's is insulted and outraged. **1952** MORIN & SMITH tr. *Herzog's Annapurna* ii. 30 For many years he had served as an officer in Gurkha battalions, crack units of the British Army. **1964** *Ann. Reg. 1963* 358 Great concern was caused..by the.. decision to reduce the size of the Brigade of Gurkhas.

Gurkhali (gʊəˈkɑːlɪ). **a.** *pl.* The Gurkhas. **b.** The language spoken by this people.

1884 *Encycl. Brit.* XVII. 341/2 The Ghōrkhālis use Parbatiya, a modern dialect of Sanskrit. **1911** *Ibid.* XIX. 379/2 The Gurkhalis (Gurkhas or Ghurkhas) are descendants of the Brahmans and Rajputs who were driven out of Hindostan. *Ibid.*, The Gurkhalis and western tribes use Khas [language]. *Ibid.* XX. 453/1 Khas-kura is also called Gōrkhālī, or the language of the Gurkhas. **1953** J. MASTERS *Lotus & Wind* xii. 168 Jagbir would have guessed that the Muralevs could not recognize Gurkhali when they heard it. **1956** —— *Bugles & Tiger* 131 At evening in my tent I studied Gurkali with the Jemadar head clerk.

gurl (gɜːl), *sb.* Now *Sc.* [Cf. GURL *v.*] A growl; boisterous or rough weather.

1755 J. SHEBBEARE *Lydia* (1769) I. 85 A voice that was rather a gurl, like an old hound gnawing a bone, than a human sound. **1790** A. WILSON in *Poems & Lit. Prose* (1876) II. 84 Poor starvin' dogs Glower fierce wi' hungry gurle. **1826** GALT *Last of Lairds* iv. 32 He had a pleasure..in gripping me by the coat-neck, and shaking me wi' a gurl. **1880** in D. H. Edwards *Mod. Sc. Poets* I. 325 He's houfft till the gurl gaed past.

gurl, *a. Sc.* Also 6 gurll, gourl. [Cf. GURL *v.*; also GRILL *a.*] Of weather: Boisterous, rough.

1513 DOUGLAS *Æneis* VII. Prol. 58 For gurll [*v.r.* gourl] weddir growyt bestis haire. **1719** RAMSAY *Fam. Ep.* Answ. iii. 27 When northern blasts the ocean shurl, And gars the heights and hows look gurl.

gurl (gɜːl), *v.* Now *Sc.* Also 4 gurle. [Echoic; cf. GROLLING, GROWL.]

1. *intr.* To rumble, growl; (of the wind) to roar, howl.

c **1380** WYCLIF *Serm.* Sel. Wks. II. 249 As a mete in a man, þat is not defied bifore, makiþ mannis bodi to gurle [*v.r.* groule]. **1587** MASCALL *Govt. Cattle* (1627) 62 The gurling or rumbling in the belly, and noyse in his guts. **1791** A. WILSON *Pack* in *Poems & Lit. Prose* (1876) II. 33 Fearfu' winds loud gurled. **1832-53** J. BALLANTINE in *Whistle-Binkie* (Scot. Songs) Ser. II. 90 Whaur the rain fa's in floods, an' the wind gurls chill. **1885** *Standard* 2 Apr. 5/2 They [*sc.* otter-dogs] 'gurl' and fight amongst themselves.

† **2.** = GURGLE *v.* 2. *Obs. rare*[−1].

But perh. *gurled* is a misprint for *gurgled*; if so this is the earliest instance of GURGLE *v.* 2.

1635 J. HAYWARD tr. *Biondi's Banish'd Virgin* 28 The blood that at thy appearing gurled out of this wound, both convicts thee, and requires at my hands Iustice.

gurle, obs. form of GIRL.

‖ **gurlet** (ˈgɜːlɪt). [F. *gurlet*, *grelet*.] 'A pickaxe with one sharp point and one cutting-edge' (Knight *Dict. Mech.* 1875).

gurly (ˈgɜːlɪ), *a. Sc.* [f. GURL *sb.* or *v.* + -Y.]

1. Boisterous, stormy, rough.

1718 RAMSAY *Edinburgh's Addr. to Country* 3 Bare fields and gurly skies Make rural scenes ungrateful to the eyes. *a* **1803** *Sir P. Spens* xiv. in Child *Ballads* (1885) II. 26/2 When the lift grew dark, and the wind blew loud, And gurly grew the sea. **1854** H. MILLER *Sch. & Schm.* ii. (1857) 27 When gurly breezes blow. **1882** G. MACDONALD *Castle Warlock* xx. (1883) 122 It's a gurly nicht; no a pinch o' licht, an' the win' blawin' like deevils. **1893** CROCKETT *Stickit Minister* 125 It was gurly weather.

2. Surly, cross, ill-humoured.

1721 RAMSAY *Cupid thrown into the South-Sea* 13 The god look'd gurly. **1813** HOGG *Queen's Wake* 77 Gurly James, and his baronis braw. **1896** STEVENSON *Weir of Hermiston* viii. 246 Ye'll have to look in the gurly face o'm.

gurmand, obs. form of GOURMAND.

† **gurmander**, *v. Obs. rare*[−0]. [app. irreg. a. F. *gourmander* (the inf. form) or f. GOURMANDER] = GOURMAND *v.*

1570 LEVINS *Manip.* 83/22 To Gurmander, *abligurire*.

gurmandize, etc., obs. forms of GORMANDIZE.

[**gurmie**, spurious word in Dicts.: see GUNNIES.]

gurmond, obs. form of GOURMAND.

Gurmukhi (ˈgʊəmʊkɪ). Also Gurumukhi. [Punjabi, f. Skr. *guru* teacher + *mukha* mouth.] The alphabet used for writing the Punjabi language; also, the language of the Punjab. Also *attrib.* or as *adj.*

1888 M. H. COURT in *Hist. of Sikhs* p. iv, I..have added a reverse index in English to enable a word to be easily found, if required, in translating English into Gurmukhí. At the commencement of the grammar, I have given the alphabet in the Gurmukhí character. **1907** G. A. GRIERSON in *Imp. Gazetteer India* (ed. 3) I. 369 An improved, and legible, form of Landā is known as Gurmukhī. This was invented about three hundred years ago for writing the Sikh scriptures, and is now the character in ordinary use for printing. **1909** *Westm. Gaz.* 22 Feb. 7/3 A seditious letter has been sent from England, written in Gurumukhi, the language of the Sacred Scriptures of the Sikhs. **1937** *Scrutiny* Mar. 447 In the Punjab..only 3 and ·4 per cent. of the candidates for Matriculation answered their history papers in Hindi and Gurmukhi respectively. **1948** D. DIRINGER *Alphabet* 378 The Gurmukhi script seems to be a polished form of the Landa character. **1971** *Illustr. Weekly India* 11 Apr. 37/1 At Lahore, some time ago, Punjabi in the Gurmukhi script was demanded and introduced as a part of the University syllabus.

gurmundist: see GOURMANDIST.

gurnard ('gɜːnəd), **gurnet** ('gɜːnɪt). Forms: α. 4- gurnard; also 5 gurnade, 5-6 gornard(e, 6 gurnerd, -arde, 6-7 gournard(e, 8 gronnard. β. 7 gournet, -it, 7, 9 gurnet, 8 *Sc.* girnot, 9 gurnett. [Prob. a. some variant of F. *grognard* grumbler (13th c. in Hatz.-Darm.), f. *grogner* to grunt (see GROIN *v.*¹); of cognate etymology are OF. *gournaux* pl. (1320 Du Cange s.v. *Gornus*) early mod.F. *grougnaut, gronau, gournauld, gourneau* (Cotgr., who gives the two first as 'Languedoc'), and perh. F. *grenaut* 'some large-headed fish' (Littré). For the sense cf. F. *grondin* gurnard, f. *gronder* to grunt; also G. *knurrhahn, knurrfisch* gurnard, f. *knurren* to grumble.]

1. One of the marine fishes of the genus *Trigla* or family *Triglidæ*, characterized by a large spiny head with mailed cheeks and three free pectoral rays.

The chief species are distinguished respectively as *grey, red* (otherwise *cuckoo-*), *lineated, streaked, French* (or *rock-*), *sapphirine*, and *shining* (or *long-finned*) *gurnard*.

α. **1314** in *Wardr. Acc. Edw. II*, 21/12, 4 gurnards, 12*d.* **14..** *Ordin. & Reg. Roy. Househ.* (1790) 449 Therwith brem de mere, and gurnade, and crabbes, and crevyse. **1467** *Mann. & Househ. Exp.* (Roxb.) 391 Davy..seithe he paid.. for a gurnard, iiij.*d.* *a* **1500** *Piers of Fullham* 18 in Hazl. *E.P.P.* II. 3 In stede of sturgen or lamprons, he drawyth vp a gurnerd or gogeons. *c* **1532** DU WES *Introd. Fr.* in *Palsgr.* 913 Gournardes, *tumbes*. **1620** VENNER *Via Recta* iv. 73 The Gurnard..some are red, and some grey. *a* **1672** WILLUGHBY *Icthyogr.* (1686) Table S 2 *Cuculus griseus*, gray Gurnard. *Ibid., Cuculus* Salv., Red Gurnard or Rochet. **1694** FALLE *Jersey* ii. 76 Another [fish] of a perfect blood Colour, with a Head and Throat almost as big as the rest of the Body; our Fishermen call it Gronnard, from the grunting Noise it makes. **1769** *De Foe's Tour Gt. Brit.* III. 341 The Gronnard is so called from its grunting Noise, when taken. **1836** YARRELL *Brit. Fishes* I. 40 The trivial names of *cuculus* and Cuckoo Gurnard are said to have been appropriated to this species [*Trigla cuculus*] on account of the similarity of the sound which issues from this fish, when taken out of the waters, to the note of the well-known bird. *Ibid.* 41 The Sapphirine Gurnard. *Trigla hirundo. Ibid.* 46 The Streaked Gurnard, French Gurnard, and Rock Gurnard. *Trigla lineata.* **1849** KINGSLEY *N. Devon* Misc. II. 278 To dine off gurnards of my own catching—excellent fish, despised by deluded Cockneys. **1895** 'J. BICKERDYKE' *Sea Fishing* xiii. 413 Grey Gurnard, or Hard-heads (*Trigla gurnardus*). **1898** MORRIS *Austral Eng.* s.v., The original word Gurnard is retained in New Zealand, and applied to the new species *Trigla kumu*.

β. **1611** FLORIO, *Grincio*..a Gournet, a Rotchet, or red fish. **1615** MARKHAM *Eng. Housew.* (1660) 67 Thus may you ..stew Roches, Gurnets, or almost any sea fish or fresh fish. **1682** WHELER *Journ. Greece* IV. 292 Barbouni, which I take to be the same with our Gournits. **1795** *Statist. Acc. Scotl., Argylesh.* XIV. 175 Laith, codling, seth, girnot, rock-fish. **1838** DR. JOHNSTON in *Proc. Berw. Nat. Club* I. No. 6. 170 The Gurnett or Crooner. **1843** *Q. Rev.* Sept. 477 Turbot, cod, ling..gurnet..and shad, abound on the coasts of Clare.

†**b.** *soused gurnet*: a term of opprobrium. *gurnet's head*: used allusively with reference to the disproportionate size of the fish's head. *Obs.*

1596 SHAKS. *Hen. IV*, IV. ii. 12 If I be not asham'd of my Souldiers, I am a sowc't-Gurnet. **1599** MARSTON *Sco. Villanie* II. vi. 200 His guts are in his braines, huge Iobbernoule, Right Gurnets-head, the rest without a soule. **1606** *Wily Beguiled* Prol. A 2 b, Out, you soust gurnet.

2. Applied, with qualifications, to certain allied genera. **a.** *yellow gurnard*, the gemmeous dragonet, *Callionymus lyra*. **b.** *bearded g.*, the red mullet, *Mullus barbatus*. **c.** *mailed* or *armed g.*, a fish of the family *Peristediidæ*. **d.** *flying g.*, a flying fish of the family *Cephalacanthidæ* or *Dactylopteridæ*: see also quots. 1882 and 1898.

1704 TYSON in *Phil. Trans.* XXIV. 1749, I shall take Liberty to call it the Yellow Gurnard. *Ibid.* 1750 In the hinder Fin of the Back of the Yellow Gurnard there were nine Radij; in the Red Gurnard fourteen. **1802-3** tr. *Pallas's Trav.* (1812) II. 463 The bearded gurnard. **1836** YARRELL *Brit. Fishes* I. 67 Armed Gurnard, Mailed Gurnard, Malarmat, *Peristedion Malarmat. Ibid.* I. 297 Yellow Gurnard. **1882** OGILVIE, s.v., The flying gurnard is the *T[rigla] volitans*, which inhabits the Mediterranean, Atlantic, and Indian seas. **1898** MORRIS *Austral Eng.* s.v., The Flying Gurnet is *Trigla polyommata*..family *Cottidæ*.

gurne, dial. form of GIRN.

gurnell, obs. form of GIRNEL *Sc.*

1612 *Inv. Dean Castle* in A. McKay *Hist. Kilmarnock* 308 Twa meikill meill gurnells of aick.

gurnet, variant of GARNET⁴, GURNARD.

gurnetty ('gɜːnɪtɪ), *a. rare.* [f. *gurnet* GURNARD + -Y¹.] Resembling a gurnard.

1872 EARL PEMBROKE & G. H. KINGSLEY *S. Sea Bubbles* v. 121 Amongst the flocks were divers very gurnetty specimens, the motion of whose pectorals was not nearly as pronounced as in the real flying-fish.

†'**gurnipper.** *New England. Obs.* [Cf. GALLINIPPER.] (See quots.)

1634 W. WOOD *New Eng. Prosp.* I. xi. (1865) 51 A Gurnipper..is a small blacke fly no bigger than a flea. **1674** JOSSELYN *Voy. New Eng.* 122 There is another sort of fly called a Gurnipper that are like our horse-flyes, and will bite desperately.

gurolite, variant of GYROLITE.

gurr (gʌr), *sb. Sc.* [Echoic; cf. GARRE *v.*] A growl, snarl. So **gurr** *v. intr.*, to growl, snarl.

1814 *Edin. Correspondent* 15 Dec. (Jam.), The gurr of a dog as if turning sheep. **1834** PRINGLE *Afr. Sk.* Proem 79 The panther round the folded flocks With stifled gurr is prowling. **1859** J. BROWN *Rab & F.* (1862) 34 He was aye gur gurrin'.

‖**gurrah**¹ ('gʌrə). *Anglo-Indian.* [Hindi *gāṛhā.*] A kind of plain coarse India muslin.

1727 A. HAMILTON *New Acc. E. Ind.* I. xxxii. 393 These manufactories are of..Silk, and Silk and Cotton Romals, Gurrahs and Lungies. **1858** in SIMMONDS *Dict. Trade.*

gurrah² ('gʌrə). Also **gurah.** [Hind. *ghaṛa*, Skr. *ghaṭa.*] An earthen jar.

1828 G. C. MUNDY *Jrnl.* 22 Mar. in *Pen & Pencil Sketches* (1832) iii. 137 The Rajah sent..sixty gurrahs (earthen vessels holding a gallon) of sugar candy and sweetmeats. **1864** J. A. GRANT *Walk across Africa* 41 With a gourd cup they drew water from their wells and filled it into earthen 'gurahs', similar to those in India. *Ibid.* 67 A few earthen jars, made like the Indian 'gurrah', for boiling vegetables or their stirabout. **1895** B. M. CROKER *Village Tales* (1896) 153 He..had been flung in the dust, like a broken gurrah.

gurrell, mod. dial. form of GORREL.

gurrie, obs. form of GHURRY.

gurry¹ ('gʌrɪ). Now *dial.* Also 6 gyrre, 7 gurrie. Diarrhœa.

1523 FITZHERB. *Husb.* §70 But ye can not gyue your draught oxe to moche meate, excepte it be the aftermath.. for that wyll cause hym to haue the gyrre. **1601** HOLLAND *Pliny* I. 399 The leafe also is as venimous as the graine, yet otherwhiles there ensueth thereof a fluxe and gurrie of the belly, which saves..life. *Ibid.* II. 41 Either the leafe or the seed of Siler..staies the gurrie or running out of the belly in 4 footed beasts. **1679** COLES, A gurry, *alvus concita.* **1881** *Leicestersh. Gloss.* s.v., I had a such a gurry on me as if I hadn't eaten nothink of a fortnit.

gurry² ('gʌrɪ). *local.* A hand-barrow; a small car or sledge.

1777 *Horæ Subsecivæ* (E.D.D.). **1848** C. A. JOHNS *Week at Lizard* 52 The men are employed in carrying the fish in 'gurries' (hand-barrows) to the cellar. **1855** MORTON *Cycl. Agric.* II. 723/3 *Gurry* (Devon), a thing for carrying apples, carried by two men. **1881** *Times* 19 Jan. 10/6 Large catches of sprats landed at St. Ives, the catches ranging up to 30 gurries per boat.

b. *Comb.* **gurry-butt** *dial.*, a dung-sledge.

1796 W. MARSHALL *W. England* I. 121 The 'Gurry-butt', or dung sledge, of Devonshire, is a sort of sliding cart or barrow; usually of a size proper to be drawn by one horse. **1834** *Brit. Husb.* I. 167 For carrying hay, straw, faggots, &c., a kind of car..called..gurry-butt, in Devonshire. **1867** in *Spec. Eng. Dial.* (1891) 36 My ould asneger 'll do vor put Into a little gurry-butt.

‖**gurry**³ ('gʌrɪ). *Anglo-Indian.* [Hindustani *gaṛhī*, f. *gaṛh* a hill fort.] A small native Indian fort.

[**1698** FRYER *Acc. E. India & P.* 129 This Gur or Hill is reckoned four Course up. *Ibid.* 144 Their Fortified Gurs or Castles. *Ibid.* 165 Strong Gurrs, or Fastnesses upon the Mountains.] **1786** BURKE *W. Hastings* Wks. 1813 (4⁰) VI. 429 The Zemindars in four Pergunnahs are so refractory as to have fortified themselves in their Gurries. **1825** W. HAMILTON *Handbk. Terms, Gurry* in the East Indies, a native fortification, generally consisting of a wall flanked with towers. **1858** in SIMMONDS *Dict. Trade.*

gurry⁴ ('gʌrɪ). Chiefly *U.S. Whale-fishing.* The refuse from 'cutting-in' and 'boiling out' a whale. Also, fish-offal. **b.** *Comb.*, **gurry-shark** (see quot. 1885).

1850 SCORESBY *Cheever's Whalem. Adv.* xiii. (1859) 183 Gurry is the term by which they call the combined water, oil, and dirt that 'cutting-in' a whale leaves on deck and below. **1885** *Stand. Nat. Hist.* III. 76 The sleeper shark *Somniosus microcephala*..By the fishermen it is known as ground-shark or gurry-shark, the word 'gurry' being a local term for fish offal.

Hence **gurry** *v. trans.*, to foul with fish-offal. (*Cent. Dict.*)

gurry⁵ ('gʌrɪ). [Etym. unknown.] *gurry sore*, a kind of boil.

1897 KIPLING *Capt. Cour.* v. 106 The affliction of gurry-sores being the mark of the caste that claimed him. *Ibid.* 118 Uncle Salters had a gurry-sore on his palm. **1950** C. S. FORESTER *Mr. Midshipman Hornblower* 109 Boils—gurry sores—blains—all the plagues of Egypt.

gurry, obs. form of GHURRY.

gurse, variant of GIRSE *Obs.*, girth.

14.. *Voc.* in Wr.-Wülcker 572/42 *Cingulum*, gurse.

gurt (gɜːt). *dial.* [? a. AF. *gort*: see GORCE. The word occurs in Fr. dialects (Beauce) with the sense of trench, conduit (see Godef. s.v. *gort*).] A trench or gutter, *esp.* in *Mining.*

1633 T. STAFFORD *Pac. Hib.* III. vi. (1810) 549 By reason of a Gurt or Cleft Rock, made by the Sea. **1671** *Phil. Trans.* VI. 2098 A heat, Gurt, or Trench. **1778** PRYCE *Min. Cornub.* 322 *Gurt*, a fret or channel made by great rain or floods in a highway; also a channel to carry off water from one place to another for dressing of Copper Ore, Tin or the like. **1842-71** G. P. R. PULMAN *Rustic Sk.* 100 The dykes or drains in Colyford Marsh are called 'gurts'—synonymous with 'rhines' in the Somersetshire Levels.

gurt, dial. form of GREAT.

gurtcher, var. GERTCHA.

gurth, obs. form of GIRTH.

gurts, obs. dial. pl. of GRIT *sb.*²

guru ('gʊruː, gʊ'ruː). Also 7, 9 goru, 9 gooroo. [a. Hindi *guru*, Hindustani *gurū* a teacher, priest; Skr. *guru* orig. an adj. 'weighty, grave, dignified'.] A Hindu spiritual teacher or head of a religious sect. Also in gen. or trivial use: an influential teacher; a mentor; a pundit.

1613 PURCHAS *Pilgrimage* (1614) 500 They have others which they call Gurupi, learned Priests. *Ibid.* (1626) 520 A famous Prophet of the Ethnikes, named Goru. **1810** T. WILLIAMSON *E. Ind. Vade Mecum* II. 317 Persons of this class often keep little schools..and then are designated gooroos. **1811** MRS. SHERWOOD *Henry & Bearer* 32 So much was he afraid of offending his gooroo. **1826** W. B. HOCKLEY *Pandurang Hàri* III. xii. 347 He was in want of a gùrù, a religious instructor, to his household. **1832** G. C. MUNDY *Pen & Pencil Sk. Ind.* I. 184 Its founder, a holy goru. **1867** DIXON *New Amer.* I. xxxi. 330 Except the guru of Bombay, no priest on earth has so large a power [etc.]. **1877** H. P. BLAVATSKY *Isis Unveiled* II. ii. 114 It is in the presence of his instructor, the guru..that he is suddenly placed face to face with the unknown *presence.* **1884** in *1st Rep. Comm. Soc. Psychical Research* (1885) 58 A letter.. being opened it was found to contain a distinct order from my Guru that I should stop at Calcutta. **1940** H. G. WELLS *Babes in Darkling Wood* III. i. 245, I ask you, Stella, as your teacher, as your Guru, so to speak, not to say a word more about it. **1949** KOESTLER *God that Failed* 40 My self-confidence as a *Guru* had gone. **1957** *Sunday Times* 12 May 9/3, I learnt to love French poetry from it, a schoolboy in a class of one, with my guru Mr de Solgé. **1967** *New Scientist* 14 Sept. 559/1 Marshall McLuhan is (or is about to be turned into) one of those gurus whom the United States hungers for more than most nations. **1968** *Times* 4 Oct. 11/5 In what was obviously intended to be a sneering reference, the Prime Minister in his facile glibness..described Mr. Enoch Powell as 'the guru of Wolverhampton'. **1969** *Eve's Weekly* (Bombay) 20 Dec. 11/4 Hannah Sahney, the chief instructress for the Indian Airlines' hostesses, is a guru to many of her young trainees.

b. *Comb.* **guru jacket**, a high-necked jacket fastened at the front by a vertical row of many small buttons; also *ellipt.*

1966 *Vogue* Nov. 21/2 Most colourful man's shop, Testa's ..newest here—the *guru* jacket in brilliant red, blue or white silk or wool buttoned up high Chinese style. **1968** *Guardian* 29 Aug. 5/4 The tailors began it all three years ago with the 'guru' jacket,..the guru with its high neckband notched at the throat and its multiple buttons.

Hence **guruship** [see -SHIP].

1848 H. H. WILSON *Wks.* (1862) II. 128 Their ninth Guru ..was publicly put to death in 1675..at the instigation of a competitor for the Guruship. **1885** F. HALL in *Nation* (N.Y.) XLI. 120/1 The four divided between them the Guruship of the new superstition..from 1504 till 1581.

guru, variant of GOUROU.

gusche, obs. form of GUSH *v.*

guse, obs. and Sc. form of GOOSE.

gusestards: see GUSTARD.

gush (gʌʃ), *sb.* [f. GUSH *v.*]

1. The action or an act of gushing; a copious or sudden emission of fluid; a rush (of water, blood, tears); *concr.* a quantity of fluid so emitted; a torrent of water, a flood of tears, etc.

c **1682** P. WALKER in Napier *Life Viscount Dundee* (1859) I. I. 157 When I saw his blood run, I wished that all the blood of the Lord's..enemies in Scotland had been in his veins;..I would have rejoiced to have seen it all gone out with a gush. **1712** STEELE *Spect.* No. 468 ⁋8 Giving him.. one Gush of Tears, for so many Bursts of Laughter. **1753** BORLASE in *Phil. Trans.* XLVIII. 92 It fell as several separate balls of fire; but upon the house as a large gush, or torrent. **1834** M. SCOTT *Cruise Midge* (1859) 326 The.. gushes from the rudder swirl..astern mellifluously. **1835-6** TODD *Cycl. Anat.* I. 238/2 The blood..never flows with a gush or per saltum. **1841** CATLIN *N. Amer. Ind.* (1844) II. xxxii. 4 Pardon this gush from a stranger's eyes. **1851** MAYNE REID *Scalp Hunt.* xl. 313 A red gush spurted over the garments of the Indian. **1885-6** SPURGEON *Treas. Dav.* Ps. cxlv. 6-7 A song fresh, free, constant, joyous, refreshing, abundant, like the gush of a spring.

b. The rustling sound of wind among trees.

1866 G. MACDONALD *Ann. Q. Neighb.* xii. (1878) 243 It [the wind] rose with a slow gush in the trees.

2. *transf.* and *fig.* A sudden and violent outbreak; a 'burst'. **a.** Of physical phenomena: A gust or rush of wind (now *dial.*); a burst (of light, heat, sound); a burst (of bloom).

1704 *Collect. Voy.* (Churchill) III. 649/2 Violent gushes of Wind. **1821** CLARE *Vill. Minstr.* II. 16 Till bursting off it [a damm'd brook] plopt, In running gushes of wild murmuring groans. *a* **1825** FORBY *Voc. E. Anglia, Gush*, a gust of wind. **1840** DICKENS *Barn. Rudge* lxxii, The host of that tavern approached in a gush of cheerful light to help them to dismount. **1849** RUSKIN *Sev. Lamps* vi. §1. 162 A blue gush of violets, and cowslip bells in sunny places. **1851** D. G. MITCHELL *Fresh Glean.* Wks. (1864) 323 A faint gush of a distant bugle-note came up over the evening air. **1871** TYNDALL *Fragm. Sci.* (1879) I. ii. 54 A gush of invisible radiant heat. **1892** *Garden* 27 Aug. 196 This is about the first gush of bloom.

b. Of feeling and its expression, of action, condition, etc.

1715–20 POPE *Iliad* XXIV. 638 Each by turns indulged the gush of woe. **1812** LANDOR *Count Julian* Wks. 1846 II. 512 The troubled dreams and deafening gush of youth. **1856** EMERSON *Eng. Traits, Char.* Wks. (Bohn) II. 59 The Saxon melancholy in the vulgar rich and poor appears as gushes of ill-humour. **1874** L. STEPHEN *Hours in Library* (1892) I. iii. 110 There are more frequent gushes of sustained rhetoric. **1878** BROWNING *Poets Croisic* 105 Gush on gush of praise.

c. *colloq.* A whiff, smell.

1838 DICKENS *Old C. Shop* vii, The gush of tobacco came from the shop. **1859** SALA *Gas-light & D.* iv. 43 A gush of fish, stale and fresh, stretches across Thames Street.

d. *U.S. colloq.* (See quot.)

1859 BARTLETT *Dict. Amer.*, *Gush*, a great abundance. A Texan would say, 'We have got a gush of peaches in our neck of the woods'.

3. *colloq.* Objectionably effusive or sentimental display of feeling, esp. in verbal expression.

1866 *Sat. Rev.* 4 Aug. 137/2 Some romantic nonsense, born of gush and the circulating library. **1869** *Daily News* 14 Dec., The book altogether is silly, and full of gush and twaddle. **1872** O. W. HOLMES *Poet Breakf.-t.* v. (1885) 124 He didn't go in 'for sentiment... Gush was played out'.

gush (gʌʃ), *v.* Forms: 4–5 **gosshe, gusche,** 6 **gus(s)he, guszhe, gousshe, gowshe,** 6– **gush.** [ME. *gosshe, gusche*; as the word is wanting in OE. and the other Teut. langs., there is nothing to forbid the supposition that it originated onomatopœically in ME. If it be of pre-English origin, it must app. be a derivative with suffix *k* or *sk* from the wk. grade of one of the Teut. roots **geut-* or **geus-* (see below), in which case its echoic expressiveness would be an accidental development.

The current but phonologically untenable view is that the word is an adoption of some one of the Scandinavian or LG. words representing the Teut. root **geus-* (:*gaus-*: *gŭs-*), several of which closely resemble it in sound and sense; cf., for instance, ON. *gjósa* str. vb., to spurt, gush, mod.Icel. *gusa* a gush, *gusa* wk. vb., to gush, MDu. *goysen* (Du. dial. *guisen, guizen, goezen*), Du. *gutsen, gudsen* to gush. The root **geus-* (which does not occur in OE.) is usually regarded as derived from pre-Teut. **gheud-* (Teut. **geut-*, OE. *géotan* to pour: see YETE *v.*, also GOTE, GUT) + suffix *t*, according to the phonetic law by which a dental + *t* became in OTeut. *ss*, simplified after a long vowel or diphthong to *s*; the wk. form *gus-* with single *s* being developed analogically.]

1. *intr.* 'To flow or rush out with violence' (J.); to issue suddenly or in copious streams, as water or other fluid when released from confinement, blood from a wound, etc. Freq. with *down, in, forth, out, up.*

?*a* **1400** *Morte Arth.* 1130 Bothe þe guttez and the gorre guschez owte at ones. *c* **1400** *Destr. Troy* 1607 The water.. Gosshet through Godardys & other grete vautes. **1535** COVERDALE *Ps.* lxxvii[i]. 16 He brought waters out of the stony rocke, so that they gusshed out like the ryuers. —— *Acts* i. 18 [He] hanged himself, and brast a sunder in the myddes, and all his bowels guszhed out. **1585** T. WASHINGTON tr. *Nicholay's Voy.* II. xii. 47 The blacke and Euxine Sea.. gusheth out through the mouth of her wyth great vyolence intoo the Sea Ponticque. **1590** SPENSER *F.Q.* I. i. 24 A streame of cole-black blood forth gushed from her corse. **1644** EVELYN *Diary* 7 Nov., In the nave of the church gushes a fountain. *a* **1691** BOYLE *Hist. Air* (1692) 176 Very exuberant springs.. issuing from the tops of most of the other mountains, gushing out in great spouts. **1727** S. SWITZER *Pract. Gard.* II. vii. 57 The air gushes in with too great violence. **1728** POPE *Dunc.* I. 211 Then gush'd the tears. **1820** W. IRVING *Sketch Bk.* I. 52 He could not speak, but the tears gushed into his eyes. **1838** THIRLWALL *Greece* II. xv. 284 A hot sulphureous spring gushes up in a copious stream. **1853** KANE *Grinnell Exp.* xxvii. (1856) 220 A cloud of vapor gushes out at every chink. **1860** TYNDALL *Glac.* I. xxiii. 161 The rain at length began to gush in torrents.

¶**b.** Taken as an echoic word.

1530 PALSGR. 573/2, I gowshe, I make a noyse, as water dothe that cometh hastely out... Herke howe this water goussheth with strykynge agaynst the stones: *escoutez comment ceste eaue bruyt*, or *grondelle en heurtant contre ces pierres*.

2. *transf.* and *fig.* To issue, emanate, or be emitted copiously. Often directly *fig.*

1586 J. HOOKER *Girald. Irel.* in *Holinshed* II. 82/2 To stop vp the spring, from whense all the enuious suspicions gushed. **1638** F. JUNIUS *Paint. of Ancients* 16 Their Poems gushing forth as out of a plentifull water-spring. *a* **1718** ROWE *Royal Convert* IV. i. Wks. (1720) 61 The native Greatness of my Spirit fails, Thus melts, and thus runs gushing thro' my Eyes. **1732** POPE *Ess. Man* I. 134 For me, Health gushes from a thousand springs. **1826** MRS. BROWNING *Ess. Mind*, Wisdom's music from thy lips hath gush'd. **1852** HAWTHORNE *Wonder-Bk., Paradise Children* (1879) 90 Sweet voices of children,.. gushing out in merry laughter. **1856** BRYANT *Poems, Antiq. Freedom* ii, Wavy tresses gushing from the cap. **1860** KINGSLEY *Misc.* I. 366 As for his tenderness.. it gushes forth toward every creature. **1860** TYNDALL *Glac.* I. xviii. 125 The sunlight gushed down upon the heights.

3. Of a person, parts of the body, etc.: To have a copious flow of blood, tears, etc.; also with *out, forth.* Const. *with,* †*of, in, into* (tears, blood, etc.).

1530 PALSGR. 573/2 Sodaynly his nose gousshed out of blood. **1535** COVERDALE *Ps.* cxviii. [cxix.] 136 Myne eyes gusshe out with water. **1561** *Hist. Jacob & 12 Sons* (Collier) 24 She.. smit her nose that gushed all in blood. **1612** N. FIELD *Woman is a Weathercock* I. ii. C4b, Gush eyes, thumpe hand, swell heart, Buttons flie open. *a* **1617** P. BAYNE *Lectures* (1634) 249 Whose eyes would not have gushed out? **1631** WEEVER *Anc. Funeral Mon.* 254 Gushing out with teares, he said [etc.]. **1741** RICHARDSON *Pamela* (1883) I. 335 My dear father, not able to contain himself,.. gushed out into a flood of tears. **1811** *Ora & Juliet* IV. 63 His nose gushed out with blood. **1821** KEATS *Isabella* xvi, Why were they proud? Because their marble founts Gush'd with more pride than do a wretch's tears? *a* **1845** HOOD *Desert-Born* xvii, My nostrils gush'd, and thrice my teeth had bitten through my tongue. **1874** L. STEPHEN *Hours in Library* (1892) I. vii. 238 He.. suddenly gushed forth in streams of wondrous eloquence.

4. *trans.* 'To emit in a copious effusion' (J.). Also with *out.*

1553 BRADFORD *Serm. Repent.* (1574) Eivb, We haue gushed out this geare more aboundantly in word and deede. *c* **1575** FULKE *Confut. Doctrine Purgatory* (1577) 367 He gusheth out nothing but bragging and faceing. **1635** HEYLYN *Hist. Sabbath* (1636) II. 216 It [*sc.* a cake] gushed out blood. *a* **1656** BP. HALL *Rem. Wks.* (1660) 107 Davids eyes gusht out rivers of waters. **1756** MASON *Ode to Memory* 16 Poems (1764) 17 Else vainly soft.. would flow The soothing sadness of thy warbled woe:.. Vainly.. The vine gush nectar, and the virgin bloom. **1821** KEATS *Isabella* xv, His ears gush'd blood. **1859** *Blackw. Mag.* Sept. 255/2 Marble wash-hand basins gushing water mysteriously at the touching of a spring. **1898** G. MEREDITH *Odes Fr. Hist.* 76 They were Ready to gush the flood of vain regret.

5. *intr.* (*colloq.*) To act with impulse or effusiveness of manner; to give verbal expression to feelings or opinions in an over-effusive, exaggerated, or sentimental fashion. Also *trans.* with quoted words as obj.

1864 WEBSTER, *Gush*.. 2. To act with a sudden and rapid impulse. **1873** MISS BROUGHTON *Nancy* I. 91, I go to bed, feeling rather small, as one who has gushed, and whose gush has not been welcome to the recipient. **1883** MISS BRADDON *Gold. Calf* vii, 'Yes, and you saw much of each other, and you became heart-friends', gushed Miss Wolf. **1887** RUSKIN *Præterita* II. 119 There were few things he [Turner] hated more than hearing people gush about particular drawings.

gush (gʌʃ), *adv.* [f. GUSH *v.*] With a gush. In quots. quasi-*int.* as an echoic word.

1608 TOURNEUR *Rev. Trag.* v. i. Wks. 1878 II. 132 He that dyes drunke falls into hell fire like a Bucket o' water, gush, gush! *a* **1845** HOOD *Compass* x, When, gush! a flood of brine came down The sky-light—quite a fountain.

gusher (ˈgʌʃə(r)). [f. GUSH *v.* + -ER[1].] One who or that which gushes.

1. One who is over-effusive or sentimental in the expression of opinion or feeling.

1864 E. YATES *Broken to Harness* vi, The enthusiastic gusher who flings his or herself upon our necks, and insists upon sharing our sorrow. **1882** MISS BRADDON *Mt. Royal* I. viii. 234 'That is too lovely', urged the gusher. **1892** *Chamb. Jrnl.* 7 May 292/1 You are no impulsive gusher.

2. orig. *U.S.* A gas-well or oil-well from which the material flows profusely without pumping. Also *fig.* and *transf.*

1886 *Pall Mall G.* 13 Oct. 6/1 Tagieff's 'gusher' beats out and out every previous record in the oil regions of the two hemispheres. **1892** *Harper's Mag.* May 906/2 In South Dakota.. there are already more than 50 high-pressure wells or 'gushers' as they call them there. **1930** *Times Lit. Suppl.* 24 July 608/2 Mr. Thomas Wolfe's novel.. might be called a 'gusher'; for Mr. Wolfe's words come spouting up with all the force of a subterranean flood.. breaking through the overlying strata of repression. **1934** DYLAN THOMAS *18 Poems* 30 Nor fenced, nor staked, the gushers of the sky Spout to the rod. **1936** I. L. IDRIESS *Cattle King* xxiv. 214 He dreamt of artesian bores. Out in the 'dry belt' a few both private and government 'gushers' had now been struck. **1959** C. OGBURN *Marauders* (1960) vii. 223 A PFC.. awakened at first light by a gusher from a mule towering above him from which he was protected by the fortuitous interposition of a log. **1970** *Times* (Canada Suppl.) p. iv/3 Only a few weeks ago Imperial Oil of Canada said cautiously they had found a gusher with considerable promise, the first oil strike in the Canadian North-West Territories.

gushet, Sc. form of GUSSET.

gushily (ˈgʌʃɪlɪ), *adv.* [f. GUSHY *a.* + -LY[2].] In a gushy manner, gushingly.

1921 W. DE MORGAN *Old Man's Youth* xxiii. 211 Our visitor gushily asked what the dear boy was saying.

gushiness (ˈgʌʃɪnɪs). [f. GUSHY *a.* + -NESS.] Violent or copious outflow; effusiveness.

1856 *Punch* 5 Jan. 7/1 We presume that it is a similar spirit of economy that has recently reduced one of the Trafalgar Fountains from the exuberant gushiness of a ginger-beer bottle, to the slow, uncertain trickling of a watering-pot. **1937** 'C. CAUDWELL' *Illusion & Reality* 240 We get the leaping and gushiness of 'spring' in poetry's use of it as a word for the idea 'season', but we do not get the fountain or the jump.

gushing (ˈgʌʃɪŋ), *vbl. sb.* [f. GUSH *v.* + -ING[1].]

1. Violent or copious outflow of water, tears, blood, etc. Also with *forth, out.*

c **1380** WYCLIF *Sel. Wks.* III. 437 As ȝif hevene of oon cloude sende gushyng of watir & ouerflowede som erþe. **1562** TURNER *Herbal* II. 170 The gussing out of blood of the nose. **1601** HOLLAND *Pliny* I. 62 By the gushing of the sea between, it was plucked from it, and left a Firth. *a* **1750** A. HILL *Reconciliation* Wks. 1753 III. 59 As I rais'd my eyes, their balls struck fire, And watery gushings wept the rash desire. **1832** TENNYSON *Lotos-Eaters* 31 To him the gushing of the wave Far far away did seem to mourn and rave On alien shores. *a* **1835** MRS. HEMANS *Dreaming Child* Poems (1875) 458 First gushings of the strong, dark rivers flow. *fig.* **1800** WORDSW. *Brothers* 407 A gushing from his heart, that took away The power of speech. **1840** R. M. MCCHEYNE in *Mem.* (1872) 363 The gushings of affection.

2. *colloq.* Extravagant display of feeling or sentiment.

1852 *Punch* 17 July 39/1 The Colonel vehemently condemned the bran new Bribery Act; and with his philanthropic gushings, the Colonel has good, benevolent cause for reprobation of the measure. **1884** W. JAMES *Coll. Essays & Rev.* (1920) 262 The sentimentalist is so constructed that 'gushing' is his or her normal mode of expression. **1890** *Athenæum* 8 Mar. 302/3 The story would be nothing without all the gushing between the brothers.

gushing (ˈgʌʃɪŋ), *ppl. a.* [f. GUSH *v.* + -ING[2].] That gushes.

1. Flowing or issuing with violence or in copious streams.

1583 STANYHURST *Æneis* II. (Arb.) 60 And liefe with the gushing bloodshed to the gods he released. **1590** SPENSER *F.Q.* I. xi. 22 A gushing river of blacke gory blood. **1640** LITHGOW (*title*), The Gushing Teares of Godly Sorrow. **1667** MILTON *P.L.* XI. 447 He fell, and deadly pale Groand out his Soul with gushing blood effus'd. *c* **1709** PRIOR *Callimachus' Hymn to Jupiter* 36 Adown the mount the gushing torrent ran. **1832** W. IRVING *Alhambra* I. 72 Her gushing fountains and perennial streams. **1840** DICKENS *Barn. Rudge* lxxviii, 'Yes, triumph', she cried, with her whole heart and soul in her earnest voice and gushing tears. **1869** PHILLIPS *Vesuv.* iii. 92 The fluid mass no longer issued in a continual and gushing stream.

2. Emitting fluid copiously. *rare.*

1717 POPE *Eloisa* 35 My gushing eyes o'erflow. **1725** —— *Odyss.* v. 413 From his nostrils wide, And gushing mouth, effused the briny tide. **1815** *Hortensia* v. v, Fled is her spirit thro' the gushing wound.

3. *transf.* Teeming.

1819 BYRON *Juan* I. 124 When the showering grapes In Bacchanal profusion reel to earth Purple and gushing. **1823** —— *Island* I. ii, The gushing fruits that nature gave untill'd.

4. *fig.* **a.** Effusive, overflowing, displaying or manifesting itself impulsively.

1807 WORDSW. *White Doe* VII. 111 By her gushing thoughts subdued She melted into tears. **1838** LYTTON *Alice* 51 The gushing fondness.. which should have characterised the love of such a mother to such a child. **1856** MRS. CARLYLE *Lett.* II. 297 Never such gushing affluence of imagery!

b. In depreciatory sense: Given to or characterized by 'gush', marked by effusive display of feeling or sentiment. *colloq.*

1859 E. FITZBALL *35 Yrs. Dram. Author's Life* II. 77 The gushing young ladies.. in possession of some of our theatres. **1864** *Fraser's Mag.* Nov. 627 Donald did not belong to what, in the slang of translated Cockneys, is called the Gushing School. **1865** MISS BRADDON *Only a Clod* i. 8 A gushing damsel of thirty-five. **1877** BLACK *Green Past.* xviii, To hear the confessions of this gushing young creature. **1878** SEELEY *Stein* III. 37 The Emperor Alexander.. was received with a gushing speech by the Superintendent Gusevius.

Hence **ˈgushingly** *adv.*, **ˈgushingness.**

1818 BYRON *Ch. Har.* IV. lxxi, Parent of rivers, which flow gushingly. **1859** *Sat. Rev.* 19 Feb. 220/2 This is.. in some degree attributable to her gushingness. **1865** MISS BRADDON *Sir Jasper* xiv, The gushingly spontaneous trifler she was wont to be. **1870** R. B. BROUGH *Marston Lynch* ii. 13 She seizes [him].. gushingly, by the arm. **1871** M. COLLINS *Mrq. & Merch.* II. viii. 223 Young ladies had.. been apt to show themselves gushingly affectionate.

gushy (ˈgʌʃɪ), *a.* [f. GUSH *sb.* + -Y[1].] Inclined to, or characterized by, 'gush'.

1845 *Punch* 12 Apr. 169/1 There is a gushy vivacity in the manner of telling the pleasant fact, that 'in the afternoon the Grand Duchess visited her daughter the Marchioness of Douglas'. **1880** 'MARK TWAIN' *Tramp Abroad* (App. D) 613 A mere rhythmical, gushy euphuism. **1893** *Strand Mag.* VI. 627/2 Not one of these inscriptions can be characterized as gushy or foolishly sentimental.

gusing, Sc. form of *goosing* (s.v. GOOSE *v.*).

gusle (ˈgʊslə). Also **gusla, gustlé, guszla, guzla.** [Serbian.] A bowed stringed musical instrument found in the Balkans, usually having only a single string, and used chiefly to accompany and support the chanting of the epic poems of the southern Slavs.

1869 H. F. TOZER *Highl. Turkey* I. 265 The national instrument.. is the guzla... In shape it is like an elongated pear cut in half, and it is something between a guitar and a violin. **1874** C. ENGEL *Descr. Catal. Mus. Instr. S. Kensington Museum* 204 This species of violin somewhat resembles the guszla which has been in use by most of the Slavonic tribes in Europe from an early period. **1880** *Grove's Dict. Mus.* I. 642 *Guzla*, a kind of rebab, a bow instrument with one string only, used in Illyria. **1922** D. H. LOW *Ballads Marko Kraljević* p. xxxvi, He then makes ready his gusle which in shape bears a rough resemblance to a mandolin. **1930** *Contemp. Rev.* Feb. 225 The gustlé player is the Serbian equivalent of the Saxon harpist. **1941** 'R. WEST' *Black Lamb* (1942) I. 313 A male gipsy who sang and played the gusla. **1969** *Observer* 26 Jan. 32/5 This was the residence of Petar Petrovic Njegos II.., prince, crack shot, player of the *gusle* (the Montenegrin lute) and author.

So **ˈguslar** (pl. *guslari*), one who plays the gusle; a singer of traditional epic poems.

1891 E. S. HARTLAND *Sci. Fairy Tales* i. 16 A viol having only one string accompanies the passages in verse..; and a similar instrument seems to be used.. among the orthodox Guslars of Bosnia and Herzegovina. **1908** *Daily Chron.* 29 July 4/4 A blind guslar, playing the gusla. **1922** D. H. Low

Ballads Marko Kraljević p. xix, If the Turkish dominion had endured a century or two longer, the separate ballads of the Kossovo cycle chanted by the Serbian guslari, would have fused together. *Ibid.*, The bard or guslar is often blind. **1923** *Glasgow Herald* 13 June 7 The wandering minstrels or guslari. **1930** *Harvard Stud. Class. Philol.* XLI. 79 There is too little known about the making of the early poetry in hexameters for us to liken the Singers to the Serbian Guslars without more ado, or to make of Homer a Singer like any other.

gusle, obs. form of GUZZLE *v.*

gusli (ˈgʊslɪ). [a. Russ. *gúsli.*] A Russian musical instrument resembling a zither.

1897 J. S. SHEDLOCK tr. *Riemann's Dict. Mus.* 314/1 Gusli (*Gussel*), Russian stringed-instrument, a kind of zither. **1910** *Encycl. Brit.* XII. 733/2 Among the Russians, the gusli is.. a kind of psaltery having five or more strings stretched across a flat, shallow sound-chest in the shape of a wing. **1959** *Listener* 9 Apr. 647/2 He [*sc.* Prokofiev] uses saxophones to imitate the sounds of the Russian *gusli.* **1961** A. BAINES *Mus. Instruments* 206 A true psaltery of medieval vintage survives in Russia in certain forms of *gusli*, much used by ballad singers formerly.

gusling, obs. form of GOSLING.

c **1475** *Pict. Voc.* in Wr.-Wülcker 760/35 *Hic ancerulus*, a guslyng.

guss (gʌs). *local.* (See quots.)

1883 GRESLEY *Gloss. Coal-m.*, *Guss* (Bristol Coal-field), a short piece of rope by which a boy draws a tram or sled in a pit. **1928** *Daily Tel.* 21 Aug. 13/2 A gentleman stated that he had seen in a newspaper an illustration of a 'guss', taken from a book dated 1842. **1928** *Times* 4 Oct. 11/4 The guss is a girdle fitted around the waist of boys who pull coal in 'putts' or sledges in the Somerset mines.

guss, obs. Sc. form of GOOSE.

gusschelle, var. JUSSEL *Obs.*

gussel, obs. form of GUZZLE *v.*

gusset (ˈgʌsɪt). Forms: 5-7 **gussett(e, 6 gossette, 8 gussit, 7 gousset** (also 9 *Hist.* in sense 1), 5- **gusset.** *β. Sc.* 5, 9 **guschet**, 7, 9 **gushet**, 8 **gooshet.** [a. OF. *gouchet*, *gousset* (13th c. in Hatz.-Darm.), app. f. *gousse* shell of nuts, etc. = It. *guscio.*]

1. In a suit of mail, a piece of flexible material introduced to fill up a space at the joints between two adjacent pieces of mail.

1412-20 LYDG. *Chron. Troy* III. xxii. (1513) N ij b, A payre gussettes on a pety cote. *c* **1470** HENRY *Wallace* II. 63 A rycht straik Wallace him gat that tyd: In at the guschet brymly he him bar. **1497** *Will of Sympson* (Somerset Ho.), A pair of gussettes a folde & a Standard of Mayle. **1500** *Nottingham Rec.* III. 72, i jak, i peyr de gossettes. **1653** URQUHART *Rabelais* I. xlii. 137 The gussets of his armour under the arm-pits. **1824** MEYRICK *Anc. Armour* II. 104 Instead of gussets to protect the armpits, circular plates are attached by points which are tied at their centre. **1874** BOUTELL *Arms & Arm.* x. 197 Goussets of mail were worn at the joints.

2. A triangular piece of material let into a garment to strengthen or to enlarge some part, esp. in order to afford ease in movement. † ***scent of gusset***: smell of the armpits.

c **1570** *Pride & Lowl.* (1841) 35 The woman and the wench were clad in russet.. worne so very neere, That ye might see cleane through both sleeve and gusset The naked skinne. **1580** HOLLYBAND *Treas. Fr. Tong, Gousset.. d'vne chemise*, ..the gusset of a shirte. **1688** R. HOLME *Armoury* I. 108/2 Gusset, a thing belonging to a Shirt or Shift. **1690** EVELYN *Mund. Muliebr.* 9 Essence rare..to repel, When Scent of Gousset does rebel. **1723** *Lond. Gaz.* No. 6150/3 A white great Coat,..with two Gussits in the Shoulder-Seam. **1843** HOOD *Song Shirt* iii, Seam, and gusset, and band, Band, and gusset, and seam. **1878** LADY HERBERT tr. *Hübner's Ramble* II. vi. 350 The gussets of his waistcoat. **1880** *Plain Hints Needlework* 63 The neck gusset of a gentleman's shirt is sometimes made the shape of an isosceles triangle.

b. The 'clock' of a stocking. *Sc.*

1685 *Lintoun Green* (1817) 12 (E.D.D.) He'd flame-like gushets, to his thighs Half up, on stockings blue. **1724** RAMSAY *Generous Gent.* ii, Silken hose with gooshets fine.

c. *pl.* The flexible sides of a pair of bellows. **d.** An elastic insertion in the side of a boot.

1861 *Our Eng. Home* 130 The gussets [of bellows in the 16th c.] fastened with trefoil bullion-headed nails, were made of scarlet velvet. **1881** *Daily News* 17 Jan. 3/3 The inquiry for gussets shows no improvement.

3. *transf.* A triangular piece of land.

1650 FULLER *Pisgah* I. 34 Which gore, or gusset of ground, was called Apherema, that is, a thing taken away, because parted from Samaria, and pieced to Judea. [**1667** in N. MITCHELL *Hist. Bridgewater* (Mass.) (1840) 69 A piece of common land between the lots in form like a gussett.] **1825-80** JAMIESON, *A guschet o' land*, a narrow intervening stripe; a small triangular piece of land interposed between two other properties. [**1871** ALEXANDER *Johnny Gibb* xlii, A gushetie o' finer lan' there is not upo' the place.]

4. *Her.* An abatement formed by a line drawn from the dexter or sinister chief to a central point from which the line is continued perpendicularly to the base of the escutcheon. (Cf. GORE *sb.*[2] 4.)

1562 LEIGH *Armorie* (1597) 72 b, Hee beareth Argent, two Gussets Sable..If he be too letcherous, the Gusset on the right side: If he commit Idolatrie to Bacchus, then the gusset on the left side. **1610** GUILLIM *Heraldry* I. viii. (1660) 45. **1661** MORGAN *Sph. Gentry* II. vii. 78 The gusset was proper for Reuben.

5. *techn.* A 'bracket' or angular piece of iron fixed at the angles of a structure to give strength or firmness.

18.. W. FAIRBAIRN in Ure *Dict. Arts* (1853) I. 213 Gussets, when used, should be placed in lines diverging from the centre of the boilers, and made as long as the position of the flues and other circumstances in the construction will admit. **1879** W. H. WHITE in *Cassell's Techn. Educ.* IV. 363/2 The principal transverse frames are made up of 'gusset' or 'bracket'-plates instead of plates lightened by holes.

6. *attrib.*, as ***gusset-armour***; **gusset (bracket) -plate, stay** = sense 5; **gusset needle** *Knitting*, one of the two side needles used in knitting the foot of a stocking.

1653 URQUHART *Rabelais* II. xxvii. 173 *Gushet-armour for the armpits. **1869** SIR E. REED *Shipbuild.* i. 13 All that was done to her was to refasten the *gusset bracket-plates at her beam ends. **1885** *Bazaar* 30 Mar. 332/1 When the left hand side *gusset needle is reached knit the eighteen stitches that were picked up from the side. **1883** *Philol. Soc. Trans.* Monthly Abstr. 21 Dec. III. iv, **Gusset-plate*, in girder-work, from gusset in needlework. **1887** D. A. LOW *Machine Draw.* (1892) 12 One form of boiler stay, called a '*gusset stay'... The stay or gusset plate is ⅝ of an inch thick.

Hence **ˈgusseted** *a.*, having a gusset or gussets; **ˈgusseting** *vbl. sb.*, insertion or making of gussets; also *concr.*, a gusset.

1883 *Daily News* 24 Sept. 2/6 Gussettings are as much neglected as ever; and only a revolution in fashion in the character of boots worn can effect any substantial revival. **1883** *Washington Evening Star* 31 Oct. 3/6 The gusseted feet [of stockings] in colors. **1888** BESANT *Fifty Y. Ago* vi. 91 Everybody knew that every girl in the place was always making, mending, cutting-out, basting, gusseting, trimming, turning, and contriving.

gussie[1] (ˈgʌsɪ). *Sc.* and *north.* Also 9 **goossy, guisie, gissy, geassy.** [Cf. Norw. *gosse* pig (Aasen).] A pig, swine. † ***the gussis croo***, i.e. the pig-stye, used jocularly as if the name of a constellation.

15.. *King Berdok* 3 in Laing *Anc. Pop. Poetry* 269 Quhen Phebus rang in sing of Capricorn And the mvne wes past the gussis cro. **1818** HOGG *Brownie Bodsbeck*, etc. II. 331 She didna only change me intil an ill-faurd he-sow, but guidit me shamefully ill a' the time I was a goossy. **1893** *Northumbld. Gloss.*, *Geassy*, a pig. **1895** CROCKETT *Men of Moss Hags* 172 A great fat gussie o' a loon they ca' Jock Webster.

gussie[2] (ˈgʌsɪ). *Austral. slang.* [dim. of the name *Augustus.*] An effeminate man.

1901 M. FRANKLIN *My Brilliant Career* xi. 94 I'm not a booby that will fall in love with every gussie I see. **1941** BAKER *Dict. Austral. Slang* 33 *Gussie*, an effeminate or affected man.

gussing, obs. form of GUSHING.

gussy (ˈgʌsɪ), *v. slang.* [Cf. GUSSIE[2].] With *up*: to smarten up. Hence **ˈgussied** *ppl. a.*; **ˈgussy** *a.*

1940 M. MARPLES *Public School Slang* 126 Gussy: of over-dressed persons. **1952** in WENTWORTH & FLEXNER *Dict. Amer. Slang* (1960) 236 When I get all gussied up, somebody says, 'Pull in your pot!' **1959** M. CHAMBERLIN *Dear Friends & Darling Romans* (1960) iv. 41 The French have gussied up their Riviera, so you can't see the foliage for the freaks. **1960** J. KIRKWOOD *There must be Pony* (1961) viii. 65 She was all gussied up..she looked very attractive. **1963** *Spectator* 1 Mar. 260 Dressy, not to say gussied-up. **1970** M. G. EBERHART *El Rancho Rio* (1971) iii. 23 'You're really all gussied up... Coast slang for dressed up,' she explained.

gust (gʌst), *sb.*[1] Also 6 **guste.** [app. a. ON. *gust-r*, related to *gjósa* to gush or *gjóta* to pour (see YETE *v.*). The late appearance of the word, however, causes some difficulty. Possibly it may have been preserved in nautical or dialectal use.]

1. a. A sudden violent rush or blast of wind; †formerly often in less restricted sense, a wind-storm, a whirlwind.

1588 SHAKS. *Tit. A.* v. iii. 69 A flight of Fowle, Scattred by windes and high tempestuous gusts. *c* **1600** —— *Sonn.* xiii, The stormy gusts of winters day. **1612** DEKKER *If it be not good* Wks. 1873 III. 293 A blacke Gust is comming: vp a-low-there hey: A young-man vp toth Top-mast-head, and looke-out. **1643** HOWELL *Parables reflecting on Times* 15 An Haraucana, that Indian gust. **1694** *Acc. Sev. Late Voy.* I. 157 A great gust of Wind at N.W. with Rain. *a* **1715** BURNET *Own Time* II. (1724) I. 110 By some easterly gusts the ship was cast away near Berwick. **1748** *Anson's Voy.* III. v. 334 A sudden gust of wind brought home our anchor. **1756** FRANKLIN in *Phil. Trans.* LV. 187 Hence gusts after heats, and hurricanes in hot climates. **1823** SCOTT *Peveril* xx, The wind..began to rise in gusts from the north-west. **1836** MACGILLIVRAY tr. *Humboldt's Trav.* x. 124 The gust accompanied by thunder returned periodically. **1843** LEVER *J. Hinton* ii, The wind swept in long and moaning gusts along the bleak pier. **1893** *Law Times* XCV. 104/2 On the day of the occurrence the wind was somewhat strong, coming in gusts.

b. A burst or gush (of water or rain).

1610 W. FOLKINGHAM *Art of Survey* I. x. 33 Land-flouds, fatte Riuers and Gusts of water. **1697** DRYDEN *Æneid* v. 19 What Gusts of Weather from yon gathering Cloud. **1817** COLERIDGE *Sibyll. Leaves* (1862) 170 The gust pelting on the out-house shed Makes the cock shrilly in the rainstorm crow. **1841** JAMES *Brigand* ii, The heavy rain dashed in gusts against the clattering casements. **1870** DICKENS *E. Drood* ii, The giant elm-trees as they shed a gust of tears.

c. A burst (of fire), a puff (of smoke); a burst (of sound).

1674 tr. *Martiniere's Voy. N. Countries* 136 To see..new gusts of Fire and Ashes break out. **1811** PINKERTON *Petral.* II. 552 Gusts of smoke..escape. **1849** MITCHELL *Battle Summer* (1852) 269 His words come to distant quarters of the hall only in feeble gusts of sound. **1894** HALL CAINE *Manxman* III. xi. 166 The voice of Pete came in gusts through the floor.

2. *fig.* Chiefly with conscious reference to the literal sense and retention of literal language; also *gen.*, a burst, outbreak, outburst.

1611 SPEED *Hist. Gt. Brit.* IX. xvii. §6. 675 The brute of which gust blowne into stout Warwickes eare. **1639** G. DANIEL *Ecclus.* xii. 16 The gust of Sin, may Stir a Surly tiding, In Seas pacificke. **1681** FLAVEL *Meth. Grace* xxviii. 486 O remember what a fearful thou art in the gusts of temptation. *a* **1704** T. BROWN *Beauties* Wks. 1730 I. 44 Gusts of pleasure hurry thro' my veins. **1705** *Double Welcome* xiv. 2 You fly On Gusts of Hope, and Wings of Victory. **1715-20** POPE *Odyss.* IV. 249 A gust of grief began to rise. **1783** BURKE *East Ind. Bill* Wks. IV. 77 When the first little sudden gust of passion against these gentlemen was spent. **1789** MAD. D'ARBLAY *Diary* 3 Aug., They..were received with the most violent gusts of joy and huzzas. **1807** CRABBE *Par. Reg.* III. 913 How and from whence these gusts of grace will blow. **1852** ROBERTSON *Serm.* Ser. III. xviii. 235 Tossed by a thousand gusts of unholy passion.

3. *attrib.* and *Comb.*, as (sense 1) ***gust alleviator***, ***effect***, ***load***, ***recorder***, ***response***, ***spectrum***, ***tunnel***; ***gust-flying*** vbl. sb.; ***gust-moved*** adj.

1947 *Shell Aviation News* CXII. 20/3 'Gust alleviators' as fitted to certain new British aircraft will provide some protection to passengers but even assuming these can relieve 50% of the gust effect, they will still only provide the same 'ride comfort' at 320 m.p.h. as one now gets in the D.C.3 at 160 m.p.h. **1919** A. KLEMIN *Text-bk. Aeronaut. Engin.* xix. 234 It is also clear from the above that the gust effects are most important, when the speed of the machine is lowest. **1922** *Flight* XIV. 659/2 At any rate, the mere trying should teach us quite a lot about air currents around hills, quite apart from the, as yet untouched, problem of real 'gust-flying', in which sudden changes in velocity of the wind itself are made use of. **1955** *Sci. News Let.* 1 Jan. 9/2 The accumulated effects of repeated, but mostly moderate, structural loads—normally gust loads—could sometimes cause failures of the primary structure before the airplane attains a reasonable service life. **1959** J. L. NAYLER *Dict. Aeronaut. Engin.* 125 *Gust loads*, the loads on an aircraft structure due to gusts. **1870** MORRIS *Earthly Par.* II. III. 111 The waving of her gust-moved hair. **1955** *Sci. News Let.* 24 Sept. 197/1 Fifty gust recorders. **1965** *Economist* 20 Feb. 733/2 This aircraft now has to have very low gust response to keep the crew functioning. **1935** *Jrnl. R. Aeronaut. Soc.* XXXIX. 372 It seemed..that if the gust spectra were extended to include the short period changes, some very large ordinates would be added to the curves. **1939** *Ibid.* XLIII. 784 To assist in answering these questions an apparatus, known as the 'gust tunnel' has been developed, in which it is possible to determine experimentally the reaction of suitably scaled dynamic models in controlled artificial gusts.

gust (gʌst), *sb.*[2] Now *arch.* [ad. L. *gust-us* taste; cf. GOÛT, GUSTO.] = TASTE, in various senses.

1. The sense or faculty of taste; †*occas.* an act of tasting or of satisfying the appetite.

c **1430** *Pilgr. Lyf Manhode* III. xli. (1869) 157 What thing, quod j, is guste? It is that, quod she, bi whiche passeth al that j swelwe. **1638** SIR T. HERBERT *Trav.* (ed. 2) 297 The fruit is somewhat unpleasant at first gust. **1638** G. SANDYS *Paraph. Job* (1648) 10 Oh can unseas'ned cates the gust invite? **1646** SIR T. BROWNE *Pseud. Ep.* VII. xiv. 367 Aristotle.. accuseth Philoxenus of sensuality, for the greater pleasure of gust desiring the neck of a Crane. **1670** J. BEALE in *Phil. Trans.* V. 1156 We call in the Testimony of the Gust..to prove the asperous..Particles in some Liquors. **1672** DRYDEN *Assignation* III. iii, I hate to snatch a morsel of Love, and so away: I am for a Set-meal, where I may enjoy my full Gust.

transf. **1696** SOUTHERNE *Oroonoko* II. iii, Such sweets, as best can entertain The gust of all the senses. **1893** W. WATSON *Excurs. in Criticism* 22 If any reader is so unfortunate as to find that a prolonged familiarity with Shakespeare begets at last a somewhat blunted sensibility to the master's supreme power, a remedy is at hand by which his palate may recover its gust.

†**2.** Individual taste, liking, or inclination. *Obs.*

c **1600** SHAKS. *Sonn.* cxiv, Mine eie well knowes what with his gust is greeing. *a* **1663** SANDERSON *Pref. to Ussher's Power Princes* (1683) 7 Condited to the gust and palate of the Publisher. **1664** H. MORE *Myst. Iniq.* 223 Types or Parables accommodate to the Conceit and Gust of the Vulgar. **1670** COTTON *Espernon* III. x. 526 This resolution was not for the gust of the Court. **1691** WOOD *Ath. Oxon.* II. 581 He preached..before the Commons, but..little to their gust and liking. **1707** in Hearne *Collect.* (O.H.S.) II. 46 'Tis with great satisfaction I learn y[t] y[e] Icon of y[e] Shield was so much to y[e] Gust of a Gentleman of your Learning. **1719** DE FOE *Crusoe* I. viii, My very Desires alter'd, my Affections changed their Gusts. **1732** *Gentl. Mag.* II. 965 Beauty may win the Eye, and satisfy the present Gust or Appetite. **1732** POPE *Ess. Man* I. 117 Destroy all Creatures for thy sport or gust, Yet cry, If Man's unhappy, God's unjust.

†**3.** Æsthetic or artistic taste, sense, or perception. *Obs. rare.*

1706 *Art of Painting* (1744) 335 He had a good gust in designing. **1715** M. DAVIES *Athen. Brit.* I. 14 All who have the least Tincture or Gust in Solid Erudition. **1716** *Ibid.* II. 161 Dedicated to him who is said to have had the best tast and most gust in such old Church-Collects.

4. Keen relish, appreciation, or enjoyment, esp. as displayed in speech or action.

1635 J. HAYWARD tr. *Biondi's Banish'd Virg.* 160 Wherein [*sc.* reading] she consumed her houres with a gust that exceeded her age and sex. **1660** JER. TAYLOR *Worthy Commun.* I. v. 102 Let no man judge..of the prosperitie..of his service in this ministerie by any sensible relish, by the gust and deliciousness which he sometimes perceives. **1667** MILTON *P.L.* x. 567 They, fondly thinking to allay Their appetite with gust, instead of Fruit Chewed bitter Ashes. **1693** DRYDEN *Juvenal* vi. (1697) 119 Such Lust Their Kisses have, and come with such a Gust. **1725** DE FOE *Voy. round World* (1840) 325 In this gust of their greedy appetite, they considered not where they were. **1734** WATTS *Reliq. Juv.* (1789) 111 O the shameful gust and relish that some people find in reproach and slander! **1776** JOHNSON in *Boswell* 26 Mar., A woman who gets the command of money for the first time upon her marriage, has such a gust in spending it, that she throws it away with great profusion. **1780** COWPER *Table T.* 240 He drinks his simple beverage with a gust. **1817** LAMB *Lett.* (1888) II. 3 Now could you expect her To take much gust In long speeches, With her tongue as dry as dust. **1820** SCOTT *Ivanhoe* xli, The more pampered burgess and guild-brother was eating his morsel with gust. **1831** LYTTON *Godolph.* xxxv, He tasted the sweets of companionship with more gust than he had yet done. **1869** F. W. NEWMAN *Misc.* 282 Michelet, who sees England in Carthage, reviles her with great gust.

b. Const. *of*, *for*, occas. *to*, *after*, *in*, esp. in phr. ***to have a gust of***: to have a liking or relish for, or keen appreciation of.

1627–77 FELTHAM *Resolves* II. xxxiv. 228 When..the gust of pleasure which help'd him to mispend his Youth, through time and languid Age shall be blunted and dull. **1658** JER. TAYLOR in *Evelyn's Mem.* (1857) III. 105, I perceive your relish and gust of the things of the world goes off continually. **1660** BOYLE *New Exp. Phys. Mech.* Pref. 17 If you have a true gust for the Book you read. **1683** KENNETT tr. *Erasm. on Folly* (1709) 26 There are others that have no gust in this sort of pleasure. **1691** E. TAYLOR *Behmen's Theos. Philos.* 188 It takes away the desire, gust or lust after them. **1702** *Eng. Theophrast.* 312 There's a gust of liberty in the following of a man's humours. **1708** HEARNE *Collect.* (O.H.S.) II. 120 A great obstructer of real Learning, and no true friend to any that have a gust for it. **1724** DE FOE *Mem. Cavalier* (1840) 30, I had no gust to antiquities. **1769** J. WALLIS *Nat. Hist. Northumbld.* I. Pref. 8 Such as have a gust for anything Roman. **1777** JOHNSON in *Boswell* 20 Sept., Why, Sir, I never knew any one who had such a gust for London as you have.

†**5.** Liking felt by others for oneself; favour. *Obs. rare.*

1654 H. L'ESTRANGE *Chas. I* (1655) 65 Ambitious by some meritorious service to earn a better gust, or correct the universal odium against him.

6. Savour or flavour (of food, etc.).

1536 BELLENDEN *Cron. Scot.* (1821) I. p. xxxvii, In this crag growis ane richt delicius herbe; and, quhen it is transportit..it is of litill sapor or gust. **1627–77** FELTHAM *Resolves* II. xv. 190 Like a draught of pleasant poyson, the gust is gone. **1669** WORLIDGE *Syst. Agric.* iii. §4 (1681) 122 Fruit..grafted on stocks of another contrary nature, much debaseth the Gust of the Fruit. **1699** EVELYN *Acetaria* 4 Herbs..eaten with..Oyl, Salt, &c. to give them a grateful Gust and Vehicle. **1743** *London & Country Brew.* II. (ed. 2) 101 That smooth Gust and pleasant Taste to the Palate, which, after a proper Age in the Malt-liquor, every Drinker enjoys both in Mouth and Body. **1821** LAMB *Elia* Ser. I. *Grace bef. Meat*, The whole vegetable tribe have lost their gust with me. Only I stick to asparagus. **1854–6** PATMORE *Angel in Ho.* I. I. vi. (1879) 70 Ever her chaste and noble air Gave to love's feast its choicest gust.

b. Pleasing taste or gratifying flavour; relish (as of something eaten or drunk).

1649 JER. TAYLOR *Gt. Exemp.* II. Ad sect. xii. 96 When we long for Manna and follow Christ for loaves, not of a low and terrestrial gust, but of that bread which came down from heaven. **1653** H. COGAN tr. *Pinto's Trav.* vi. 16 [He] sware ..never to eat either fruit, salt, or any other thing, that might bring the least gust to his palate. *a* **1677** HALE *Prim. Orig. Man.* IV. viii. 375 Sensual Goods have their proper gust and relish with him. **1679** PENN *Addr. Prot.* I. 18 'Tis the Taste, the Gust, the Relish, that makes the Victuals go down. **1681** GLANVILL *Sadducismus* 50 That things of gust and relish must be judg'd by the sentient and vital faculties. **1841** D'ISRAELI *Amen. Lit.* (1867) 7 The discussion is not yet obsolete, and it may still offer all the gust of novelty.

†**7.** A taste, an experience of something; also, a foretaste. *Obs.*

1658 GURNALL *Chr. in Arm.* II. 439 The Spirit, who is sent from Heaven to..give them some sweet gust of it, by shedding abroad the sense of it in their souls. **1672** *Mede's Life* in *Wks.* 25 A Gust of the powers of the world to come. **1675** tr. *Machiavelli's Prince* vii. (1883) 47 By giving them a gust of their future felicity. **1682** SIR T. BROWNE *Chr. Mor.* III. §22 In seventy or eighty years, a man may have a deep gust of the world. **1698** FRYER *Acc. E. India & P.* 69 Happy ..those, and only those, brought hither in their Nonage, before they have a Gust of our Albion.

gust (gʌst), *v.*^{1} Now only *Sc.* [f. GUST *sb.*^{2} or ad.L. *gustāre*, f. *gust-us* GUST *sb.*^{2}]

1. *trans.* To taste; to relish. Also *absol.* (or *intr.*).

c **1430** *Pilgr. Lyf Manhode* III. xli. (1869) 157 As michel or more as þe guste may gusten. *a* **1500** *Ratis Raving* II. 40 [Wisdom is] swetar..and of mare lust Than erdly thing that man may gust. **1536** BELLENDEN *Cron. Scot.* (1821) I. p. xli, Ane beist or fowll that hes nocht gustit of this meit. **1570** BUCHANAN *Admonitioun* Wks. (1892) 24 Having anys gustit how gude fischeing it is in drumly Watter. **1609** SKENE *Reg. Maj.* 150 The taisters of aill..are not reddie to taist or guste the aill, sa oft as the browsters hes tunned it. **1631** R. H. *Arraignm. Whole Creature* i. 2 The hungry soule sweetly gusts againe the same Spirituall cates, as did sometimes the hearers of Saint Peter. **1647** R. L'ESTRANGE *Beaum. & Fl. Plays*, The Palate of this age gusts nothing High. *a* **1657** R. LOVEDAY *Lett.* (1663) 189 That so many judicious palats should gust a piece so insipid.

2. ***to gust the mouth***, or ***the gab***: to give a relish to the palate. *Sc.*

c **1470** HENRYSON *Mor. Fab.* II. (*Town & C. Mouse*) xviii, Ane quhite candill..In steid of spyce to gust thair mouth with all. *a* **1774** FERGUSSON *Cauler Oysters* Poems (1845) 8 He's nae ill bodden, That gusts his gab wi' oyster-sauce. *a* **1801** R. GALE *Elegy Pudding Lizzie* Wks. 181 She had the knack sae weel, To gust the gab o' ony chiel. **1858** M. PORTEOUS *Souter Johnny* 13 He..took care..to..fill the jinglin' stoups wi' mair To gust their mou'.

gust (gʌst), *v.*^{2} [f. GUST *sb.*^{1}] *intr. to gust up*: to rise in gusts or bursts; also without *up*, to blow in gusts. Also *fig.*

1813 COLERIDGE *Lett.* (1895) 608 The Pride, like the bottom-swell of our lake, gusts up again. **1899** J. M. FALKNER *Moonfleet* xi, The wind came gusting round the corner. **1927** *Chambers's Jrnl.* 312/2 The wind was gusting. **1960** I. SHAW *Two Weeks in Another Town* v. 77 Jack.. remembered what Delaney had looked like gusting into the dressing-room. **1963** *Times* 13 May 4/4 An exciting final, fought out in winds that gusted to more than 30 knots. **1964** N. FREELING *Double-Barrel* v. 146 An erratic wind..gusted at me from all quarters.

gust, obs. form of GUEST *sb.*

gustable ('gʌstəb(ə)l), *a.* and *sb.* Now *rare.* [ad. late L. *gustābilis*, f. *gustāre* to taste: see GUST *v.*^{1} and -ABLE.]

A. *adj.*

1. That can be tasted, tasteable; also, having a pleasant taste, appetizing.

1480 CAXTON *Ovid's Met.* xv. iii, Mylk, hony & herbes gustable. **1601–2** FULBECKE *1st Pt. Parall.* 15 If the thing that is sold bee liquide and gustable, and the buyer doth taste of it. **1615** G. SANDYS *Trav.* II. 127 Of so many thousand wels..this only affoordeth gustable waters. **1713** DERHAM *Phys.-Theol.* v. viii. (1714) 316 A Gustable thing seen or smelt, excites the Appetite. **1838** *New Monthly Mag.* LIII. 557 Oysters have furnished food, both mental and gustable, to the wag. **1870** A. L. ADAMS *Nile Valley & Malta* 36 The removal of the skin adds apparently to the gustable qualities of these birds.

2. Of qualities: Perceptible by the sense of taste. Of perceptions: Gustatory.

1657 TOMLINSON *Renou's Disp.* 33 Some [qualities] are tangible..others gustable. **1661** GLANVILL *Van. Dogm.* vii. 67 A blind man cannot conceive colours, but either as some audible, gustable, odoriferous or tactile qualities. *c* **1705** BP. BERKELEY in Fraser *Life* (1871) 476 Gustable and olefactible perceptions. **1855** H. SPENCER *Princ. Psychol.* III. vi. (1870) I. 333 The higher animals perceive an increased number of gustable differences.

B. *sb.* A thing that can be tasted; an article of food.

1642 H. MORE *Song of Soul* II. ii. II. iv, The touch acknowledgeth no gustables; The tast no fragrant smell or stinking sent. *a* **1652** J. SMITH *Sel. Disc.* IV. iii. (1821) 87 Should we judge of gustables by our taste. **1838** A. B. GRANVILLE *Spas Germany* 85 What gastronome..can hope to partake of the tithe part of this long list of gustables? **1895** *Outing* (U.S.) Oct. 28/1 A table that literally cries aloud with its weight of gustables.

†**gustard.** *Sc. Obs.* Also 7 *pl.* **gusestards.** [Etymologizing alteration of OSTARDE or BUSTARD, by substitution of GOOSE for the first syllable.] A bustard.

1536 BELLENDEN *Cron. Scot.* (1821) I. p. xlii, Beside thir thre uncouth kind of fowlis, is ane uthir kind of fowlis in the Mers, mair uncouth, namit gustardis; als mekle as ane swan. **1596** DALRYMPLE tr. *Leslie's Hist. Scot.* I. 39 Ane foul.. quhilke the Gustarde commonlie thay cal. **1655** MOUFET & BENNET *Health's Improv.* (1746) 174 Bistards or Bustards, so called for their slow Pace and heavy flying; or as the Scots term them Gusestards; that is to say, Slow Geese.

gustation (gʌ'steɪʃən). [ad. L. *gustātiōn-em*, n. of action f. *gustāre* to taste, GUST *v.*^{1}] The action or faculty of tasting; taste.

1599 A. M. tr. *Gabelhouer's Bk. Physicke* 106/1 Mixe it with Suger, because it mighte be the more delectable of gustation. **1615** H. CROOKE *Body of Man* 631 This heape of Glandules..groweth to the roote of the Tongue that it might continually be moistned, for without moisture there can be no Gustation. **1646** SIR T. BROWNE *Pseud. Ep.* VII. xiv. 367 The Gullet and conveying parts..which partake not of the nerves of gustation or appertaining unto sapor. **1737** BRACKEN *Farriery Impr.* (1756) I. 197 Man..ransacks both the Indies for hot fiery Spices to satisfy his most unreasonable Gustation. **1841–71** T. R. JONES *Anim. Kingd.* (ed. 4) 732 The whole interior of the mouth is..from its construction, little adapted to gustation. **1846** SIR W. HAMILTON *Dissert.* in *Reid's Wks.* 828 While Gustation expresses the act of what is able to taste, the act of that capable of being tasted is nameless. **1873** A. FLINT *Nerv. Syst.* i. 16 The special senses, such as sight, audition, olfaction, and gustation.

fig. **1658** SIR T. BROWNE *Hydriot.* v. 83 If any have been so happy as truly to understand..gustation of God.

gustative ('gʌstətɪv), *a.* [f. L. *gustāre*: see prec. and -ATIVE.] Having the function of tasting; also, concerned with tasting, gustatory.

1620 VENNER *Via Recta* vii. 108 That may be said to be hot or cold, &c. in the first degree, which is but slenderly perceiued of the gustatiue sense. **1698** FRYER *Acc. E. India & P.* 182 A dulcid Sapor that imposes upon the Imagination and Gustative Faculty a Fancy that it relishes of any Fruit a man likes. **1865** MILL *Exam. Hamilton* 484 In the case of the rhubarb, the object itself was of a nature to disturb the gustative faculty. **1876** BERNSTEIN *Five Senses* 300 Neither the chemical nor gustative properties of these compounds are separated by sharply defined limits. **1880** LE CONTE *Sight* 10 The..gustative nerve.

Hence **'gustativeness**, gustative quality, taste.

1827 *Blackw. Mag.* XXI. 787 The organ of gustativeness enormously developed. **1875** MASSON *Wordsw.* etc. 176 He goes on to describe the nectarine in language that would reawaken gustativeness in the oldest fruiterer.

gustatory ('gʌstətərɪ), *a.* (*sb.*) [f. L. *gustāt-*, ppl. stem of *gustāre* to taste + -ORY (cf. *gustātōrium* antepast).] **A.** *adj.* Pertaining to or concerned with tasting or the sense of taste. ***gustatory nerve*** (Anat.): the lingual nerve upon which the sense of taste depends.

1684 tr. *Bonet's Merc. Compit.* IX. 324 Some thing.. gratefull to the palate, for there the Gustatory faculty is placed. **1712** tr. *Pomet's Hist. Drugs* I. 57 The Edges or Points of the Acid penetrate the pores of the gustatory Nerve. **1741** MONRO *Anat. Nerves* (ed. 3) 54 Some have thought this Nerve..to be the proper gustatory Nerve. **1768–74** TUCKER *Lt. Nat.* (1834) I. 388 The..gustatory papillæ of the tongue. **1835–6** TODD *Cycl. Anat.* I. 311/1 The gustatory sense is very imperfectly enjoyed in birds. **1872** HUXLEY *Phys.* xi. 264 One branch containing sensory fibres, supplies the front of the tongue and is often spoken of as the gustatory. **1872** DARWIN *Emotions* xiii. 344 When we actually taste sour fruit, an impression is sent through the gustatory nerves to a certain part of the sensorium. **1882** *Standard* 23 Aug. 5/1 Apart from its aesthetic and gustatory aspects, Cookery deserves..profound consideration.

†**B.** *sb.* 'A place where men were wont to banquet' (Blount *Glossogr.* 1670). *Obs.*

Hence ˌ**gusta'torial** *a.*

1937 F. M. FORD *Let.* 27 Sept. (1965) 284 For unless he will come to the rescue of our Western civilisations, in things gustatorial, what will become of us?

Gustavian (gʌ'steɪvɪən), *a.* [f. the name *Gustavus*: see -IAN.] Of or pertaining to the reign of any of the Swedish kings named Gustavus, *spec.* of Gustavus III (1771–1792) and Gustavus IV (1792–1809); used esp. with reference to the literature of the period.

1884 R. B. ANDERSON tr. *Horn's Lit. Scand. North* III. v. 356 The poets of the Gustavian period form two groups according to the prevalence, respectively, of the French and the national element. **1887** *Encycl. Brit.* XXII. 757/1 The excellent lyrical poet Frans Mikael Franzén..and a belated academician Johan David Valerius..fill up the space between the Gustavian period and the domination of romantic ideas from Germany. **1951** E. BREDSDORFF et al. *Introd. Scandinavian Lit.* iv. 80 Like the Gustavian Classicists, she handled her technique skilfully and unobtrusively. **1961** A. GUSTAFSON *Hist. Swedish Lit.* v. 135 Seldom if ever in literary history has a monarch's name more appropriately been attached to a literary period than those two or three decades in late eighteenth-century Swedish literature which it is customary to call 'The Gustavian Era'. *Ibid.* 145 Thorild and Lidner..proved to be anything but Gustavian in their literary tastes.

guste, obs. form of GUEST *sb.*

gusted ('gʌstɪd), *a.* [f. GUST *sb.*^{2} + -ED^2.] Having (a particular) taste; -flavoured, -tasted.

1535 COVERDALE *Wisd.* xvi. 20 Thou hast..sent them bred ready from heauen..beynge very pleasant & well gusted. *a* **1774** FERGUSSON *Poems* (1807) 307 You cock your nose Against my sweetly-gusted cordial dose.

†**guster.** *Sc. Obs.* In 7 **gustar.** [f. GUST *v.* + -ER^1.] A (professional or official) taster.

1609 SKENE *Reg. Maj.* Table 63 Gustars or taisters of Aill.

gustful ('gʌstfʊl), *a.*^{1} *Obs.* exc. *arch.* [f. GUST *sb.*^{2} + -FUL.]

1. Full of 'gust' or flavour; pleasant to the taste, tasty.

c **1645** HOWELL *Lett.* (1650) II. lv. 73 A famous composition..call'd Chiffi..which they throw into water to make it gustful. **1671** *Phil. Trans.* VI. 2146 A dull and insipid Apple is made more gustful by being grafted on the stock of the harshest Crab. **1709** WATTS *Horæ Lyr.* Pref., A distempered appetite will chew coals and sand and pronounce it gustful. **1828** *Blackw. Mag.* XXIII. 595 All the eatables were highly gustful.

b. Characterized by relish or zest.

1789 D. DAVIDSON *Seasons* 141 The flocks..roun the hay-stack Crowding, pluck the stalks O' withered bent, wi' gustfu' hungry bite.

2. *fig.* Pleasant to the mind or feelings.

c **1645** HOWELL *Lett.* (1650) II. 4 The base suds which vice useth to leave behind it, makes vertue afterward far more gustful. **1661** HARTLIB in *J. Worthington's Diary* (Chetham Soc.) I. 304, I should send him the book itself so exceeding gustful it is to my palate. **1699** CIBBER *Xerxes* I, Eternal Springs of Love, and gustful Joy Shall feed my ravish'd Sense. **1778** *Arminian Mag.* I. 91 Gustful and ready flow'd his song.

Hence **'gustfully** *adv.*, **'gustfulness.**

1659 HAMMOND *On Ps.* xix. 10 Most eagerly pursued and gustfully injoyed by us. **1665** BOYLE *Occas. Refl.* VI. iii, Whilst I saw such persons so gustfully swallow these extoll'd Fishes. *a* **1677** BARROW *Serm.* (1686) III. xix. 217 His divertisements and recreations have a lively gustfulness. **1891** STEVENSON & L. OSBOURNE *Wrecker* (1892) 76 Gustfully ordering and greedily consuming imaginary meals.

gustful ('gʌstfʊl), *a.*^{2} *rare.* [f. GUST *sb.*^{1} + -FUL.] Gusty.

1825 *Blackw. Mag.* XVII. 488 By some chance leaf Upturn'd, or gustful wind at evening's hour.

gustily ('gʌstɪlɪ), *adv.*^{1} [f. GUSTY *a.*^{1} + -LY^2.] In or with gusts, in sudden violent blasts.

1824 GALT *Rothelan* I. II. xvi. 294 The wind came gustily from the north. **1850** MRS. BROWNING *Isabel's Child* xv, Gustily blows the wind. **1871** R. ELLIS *Catullus* lxiv. 68 Not for silky tiara nor amice gustily floating Recks she at all any more.

gustily (ˈgʌstɪlɪ), *adv.*[2] *Sc.* [f. GUSTY *a.*[2] + -LY[2].] In a 'gusty' manner; with taste or gusto.

1819 W. TENNANT *Papistry Storm'd* (1827) 67 There he took hole like a rabbit, And denner'd gustily with th' Abbot. **1832** *Fraser's Mag.* VI. 151 How roundly and gustily, and with what sportsmanlike precision, the matter is set forth!

gustiness (ˈgʌstɪnɪs). [f. GUSTY *a.*[1] + -NESS.] The condition or quality of being gusty.

1901 *Westm. Gaz.* 20 June 10/1 The everlasting gustiness for which the Maoriland capital is famed. **1920** *Times Lit. Suppl.* 9 Sept. 586/1 From the point of view of construction his stories are..irregular, but for sheer gustiness they are hard to equal. **1946** G. MILLAR *Horned Pigeon* ix. 128 Binns ..thought all Italians were 'dirty people', and he could hate Garibaldi with fresh gustiness. **1957** G. E. HUTCHINSON *Treat. Limnol.* I. v. 275 The roughness of the water surface and gustiness of the wind.

†**gusting**, *vbl. sb.*[1] *Obs.* [f. GUST *v.*[1] + -ING[1].] Tasting.

c **1532** DU WES *Introd. Fr.* in *Palsgr.* 1055 By smelyng, goustyng & tastyng.

gusting (ˈgʌstɪŋ), *vbl. sb.*[2] [f. GUST *sb.*[1] + -ING[1].] Blowing in gusts.

1893 STEVENSON in *To-day* 11 Nov. 5/2 He lay there.. exposed to the gusting of the wind.

†ˈ**gustless**, *a. Obs.* [f. GUST *sb.*[2] + -LESS.]

1. Tasteless, insipid.

1597 MONTGOMERIE *Cherrie & Slae* 876 ȝour gustless jests. **1671** *True Nonconf.* 350 They greatly aggravat these jejune and gustless Methods. *a* **1682** SIR T. BROWNE *Tracts* 13 No gustless or unsatisfying Offal. **1695** J. SAGE *Cyprianic Age* Wks. 1847 II. 80 Is power such a gustless thing?

2. Having no sense of taste or appetite.

1766 NICOL *Poems* 16 (E.D.D.) From gustless gabs that cannot taste of love.

‖**gusto** (ˈgʌstəʊ). [It. 'taste' = Fr. GOÛT:—L. *gustus* taste. Cf. GUST *sb.*[2]] = TASTE, in various senses.

1. Individual or particular liking, relish, or fondness. Const. *for* (†*in*, †*of*).

1647 BOYLE in Birch *Life* Wks. 1772 I. p. xliv, Which [tobacco] tho' at first sucked in with reluctance barely to please the company, men afterwards find a gusto in, and are unable to leave off. **1651** *Life Father Sarpi* (1676) 67 He being but a young man himself, and one that did not abhor the ordinary gustoes of his Age. **1672** WYCHERLEY *Love in Wood* I. ii, Why should you force wine upon us? We are not all of your gusto. **1695** DRYDEN *Du Fresnoy's Art of Painting* 16 A Posture therefore must be chosen according to their gusto. **1715** tr. *C'tess D'Aunois' Wks.* 519 He had a particular Gusto for those sort of Performances. **1727** POPE, etc. *Art of Sinking* 73 Men of a nice and foppish gusto, whom after all it is almost impossible to please. **1851** H. MAYO *Truths Pop. Superstit.* (ed. 2) 2, I had planned going to a play to enjoy again the full gusto of scenic illusion. **1852** JERDAN *Autobiog.* II. xiii. 162 He had a grand gusto for the society he liked. **1899** *Q. Rev.* Apr. 491 Some allowance must be made for different gustos.

2. Keen relish or enjoyment displayed in speech or action; zest.

Becomes very common from the beginning of the 19th c.

1629 J. M. tr. *Fonseca's Devout Contempl.* 190 More are the fumes & vapours that ascend vp from beneath [Hell], than those gustos, & contents which descend from aboue [Heauen]. **1656** EARL MONM. *Advt. fr. Parnass.* 198 Base beetles which spent their lives with much gusto amidst the filth of excrements. **1665** PEPYS *Diary* 5 Nov., He read me, though with too much gusto, some little poems of his own. **1687** CONGREVE *Old Bach.* I. i, It adds gusto to an amour. **1727** A. HAMILTON *New Acc. E. Ind.* I. p. xiv, The Taste of those Times relished all he presented with a very good Gusto. **1808** SCOTT *Let. to T. Scott* 19 Nov., We have been both dining and supping upon them [herrings] with great gusto. **1866** GEO. ELIOT *F. Holt* II. xxxi. 258 The second Tory joke was performed with much gusto. **1874** L. STEPHEN *Hours in Library* (1892) I. ii. 88 [He] seems to have thrown himself with special gusto into the character. **1892** STEVENSON *Across the Plains* 310 No secret element of gusto warms up the sermon.

3. *Art.* Style in which a work of art is executed; artistic style; *occas.* prevailing or fashionable style in matters of taste. Often with qualification, as *great* (= It. *gran gusto*), *high*, *noble*.

1662 EVELYN *Chalcogr.* iii. Misc. Writ. (1805) 273 They used to carve out letters and other figures..but it was yet so rude, and their gusto so depraved, that [etc.]. **1706** *Art of Painting* (1744) 18 In Painting, the grand Gusto, the Sublime, and the Marvellous are one and the same thing. **1712** J. JAMES tr. *Le Blond's Gardening* 2 The Designs..are of very mean Gusto. **1747** *Gentl. Mag.* 374 Yours [*i.e.* petticoats] are plain, which is after the grand gusto in structures of every kind. **1761** STERNE *Tr. Shandy* III. xii, There is something of a hardness in his manner..but then there is such a greatness of gusto! **1822** LAMB *Elia* Ser. I. *Acting of Munden*, The gusto of Munden antiquates and ennobles what it touches. **1824** HAZLITT *Sk. Picture-Galleries Eng.* 92 We should think that in the gusto of form and a noble freedom of outline, Michael Angelo could hardly have surpassed this figure. **1847** CRAIG s.v. *Grand*, *Grand gusto*, in Painting, a term used to express that there is something very great and extraordinary in a picture, and calculated both to please and surprise.

†**4.** Æsthetic appreciation or perception. *Obs. rare.*

1663 GERBIER *Counsel* 106 The husband (after all his paines and Vexations) if he can turn all things to the best, will have (as the Italian saith) a sound gusto. **1711** SHAFTESB. *Charac.* III. iii. (1737) II. 430 Another, who has no Gusto of either sort, believes all those they call Virtuosi to be half-distracted.

†**5.** Flavour or savour (of food, etc.). *Obs. rare.*

1713 DERHAM *Phys.-Theol.* III. iv. 84 All sorts of pleasant Gusto's to gratify the Taste and Appetite of the most luxurious. *Ibid.* IV. i. 8 The Pleasures of delightful Odours and relishing Gusto's.

gusty (ˈgʌstɪ), *a.*[1] [f. GUST *sb.*[1] + -Y.]

1. Of wind: Blowing in gusts or sudden violent blasts. Of weather, etc.: Marked by gusts or squalls of wind; fitfully windy or stormy.

1600 HAKLUYT *Voy.* III. 845 Wee had great store of snowe, with some gustie weather. **1602** MARSTON *Ant. & Mel.* I. Wks. 1856 I. 16 Gustie flawes strook up the very heeles Of our maine mast. **1798** SOUTHEY *Ld. William* Poems VI. 35 The tempest, as its sudden swell, In gusty howlings came. **1819** CRABBE *T. of Hall* IV. Wks. 1834 VI. 83 One gusty day, now stormy and now still. **1833** HT. MARTINEAU *Loom & Lugger* I. v. 91 You have no chance out of doors on a gusty night. **1891** E. PEACOCK *N. Brendon* II. 2 The gusty rain dashed fiercely at intervals on the window panes.

b. Of physical features and other objects: Blown upon, tossed, or disturbed by gusts of wind.

1725 POPE *Odyss.* XIX. 217 From Malea's gusty cape his navy drove To bright Lucina's fane. **1818** KEATS *Endym.* II. 853 The gusty deep. **1820** —— *Eve St. Agnes* xl, The long carpets rose along the gusty floor. **1832** TENNYSON *Mariana* 52 In the white curtain, to and fro, She saw the gusty shadow sway. **1852** M. ARNOLD *Empedocles* I. ii, The gods..bade the winds through space impel the gusty toy.

c. Emitting air or wind in gusts.

1832 *Blackw. Mag.* XXXI. 321 Their gusty nostrils blew Steams of thick vapour. **1844** L. HUNT *Poems* 162 Ever and anon there roll'd The gusty organ.

2. *fig.* Given to or marked by sudden bursts of feeling or fitful action; (of action, etc.) coming in fits or bursts.

1690 NORRIS *Beatitudes* (1694) I. 232 In a warm gusty fit of Devotion. **1855** LONGF. *Hiaw.* II. 221 Hearing still the gusty laughter. **1862** MERIVALE *Rom. Emp.* (1865) III. xxiii. 77 As an experienced officer he knew the gusty passions of the veterans. **1870** THORNBURY *Tour Eng.* II. xx. 61 The quarrelsome Montagues and Capulets of those gusty days. **1870** R. W. DALE *Week-day Serm.* viii. 155 The gusty temper of the disputants. **1871** R. ELLIS *Catullus* xliv. 13 Whereat a cold chill, soon a gusty cough in fits Shook, shook me ever.

gusty (ˈgʌstɪ), *a.*[2] Chiefly *Sc.* [f. GUST *sb.*[2] + -Y.] Tasty, savoury, appetizing.

1721 RAMSAY *Prospect Plenty* 67 The rantin Germans, Russians, and the Poles, Shall feast with pleasure on our gusty sholes. **1786** BURNS *Sc. Drink* ix, Just a wee drap sp'ritual burn in, An' gusty sucker. **1802** LAMB *J. Woodvil* III, These high and gusty relishes of life. **1854** *Fraser's Mag.* XLIX. 105 'Cock-a-leekie', one of the most gusty of Scotch dishes.

gut (gʌt), *sb.* Forms: 1 *pl.* guttas, 3–5 gotte, 4–7 gutte, 5 gowt, gute, 5–8 gutt, 4– gut. [OE. *guttas* str. masc. pl.; the vowel seems to point to a prehistoric type **guttu-* (:—pre-Teut. **ghudnú-*), f. the root of Goth. *giutan*, OHG. *giozzan* (G. *gieszen*), OE. *ȝéotan* to pour: see YETE *v.*]

1. *collect. pl.* **a.** The contents of the abdominal cavity; the bowels, entrails. Formerly, but not now, in dignified use with reference to man.

†In biblical language sometimes *fig.* = 'bowels', 'inward parts'.

a **1000** *O.E. Gloss.* 198 in *Mone's Quellen und Forschungen* (1830) 333 *Viscerum receptacula*, guttas, innoþas, and fengcas [*read* and-fengcas]. **1297** R. GLOUC. (Rolls) 10806 On him smot..In aboute þe fondement..& so vp toward þe gottes. *a* **1300** *E.E. Psalter* l. 12 Clene hert make in me, God, and trewe, And right gaste in mi guttes newe. **13..** *K. Alis.* 4469 Of some theo gottes hongyn oute. **1393** LANGL. *P. Pl.* C. VII. 398 Hus guttes gonne godely as two gredy sowes. *c* **1440** *Anc. Cookery* in *Househ. Ord.* (1790) 440 Take the gottes of the goose..and scrape hom clene. **1480** CAXTON *Chron. Eng.* xcvii. 77 They caste on hym the guttes of reyghes and of fissh. **1580** SIDNEY *Ps.* XXXI. v, My eyes, my guts, yea my soule, grief doth wast. **1596** SHAKS. *1 Hen. IV*, II. iv. 285 Falstaffe, you caried your Guts away..nimbly. *a* **1605** MONTGOMERIE *Misc. Poems* v. 11 My guttis ar grippit so with grief, It eitis me vp in yre. **1664** CHAS. II in Julia Cartwright *Henrietta of Orleans* (1894) 176 Poor Oneale.. died this afternoon of an ulser in his guts. **1692** LOCKE *Educ.* 26 The Peristaltick motion of the guts. **1707** FLOYER *Physic. Pulse-Watch* 286 The more acrid any Purge is, the more it irritates the Guts. *a* **1715** BURNET *Own Time* (1724) I. 633 Yet he had not pierced his guts; So his wounds were not mortal. **1764** GRAINGER *Sugar-Cane* II. 75 *note*, They.. are..foul feeders, many of them greedily devouring the raw guts of fowls. **1846** GROTE *Greece* (1869) I. 62 On the one side he placed the flesh and guts..on the other he put the bones enveloped in fat. **1853** KANE *Grinnell Exp.* xxvi. (1856) 215 Half the guts, the spleen, and the pluck of my seal.

b. Phrases. †*to have one's guts about one's ears* (a hyperbolical threat); †(*to grieve*) *to the guts*: deeply, to the very soul; *to have* (a person's) *guts for garters* (a hyperbolical threat); *to hate* (a person's) *guts*: to dislike (a person) intensely; *to sweat* (or *work*) *one's guts out*: to work extremely hard.

a **1592** R. GREENE *Sc. Hist. James Fourth* (1598) III. ii, Ile make garters of thy guttes, Thou villaine. **1601** B. JONSON *Cynthia's Rev.* IV. iii, Sir, I will garter my hose with your guttes. **1658–9** *Burton's Diary* (1828) III. 108 They said our guts should be about our ears if we did not vote it. **1663** BUTLER *Hud.* I. ii. 894 It griev'd him to the guts, that they.. Shou'd offer such inhuman wrong. **1714** J. WALKER *Sufferings Clergy* II. 341/2 He hoped to have the Parson's Guts to Garter his Hose with. **1918** *Wine, Women & War* (1926) 140 R— decided on different way, so did it all over again. Great boy, R—. Hate his guts! **1925** F. SCOTT FITZGERALD *Great Gatsby* (1926) i. 9 There were men at New Haven who had hated his guts. **1930** W. S. MAUGHAM *Breadwinner* II. 101 God knows, it's been an uphill job, but I've done my best. I've just sweated my guts out. **1932** N. COWARD *Words & Music* in *Play Parade* (1939) II. 111 We have to work our guts out...We have to hop and bustle. **1933** *Cornh. Mag.* Mar. 698 I'll 'ave yer guts fer garters. **1935** AUDEN & ISHERWOOD *Dog beneath Skin* II. v, One o' these dys I'll 'ave 'is guts fer garters. **1936** N. COWARD *To-Night at 8.30* II. 31 You know perfectly well I hate Freda's guts. **1937** 'G. ORWELL' *England Your England* (1953) 191 It is brought home to you, at least while you are watching, that it is only because miners sweat their guts out that superior persons can remain superior. **1938** G. GREENE *Brighton Rock* VII. viii. 338 He hates her guts. **1945** WODEHOUSE *Let.* 22 May in *Performing Flea* (1953) 126 The entire personnel of the cast sweat their guts out..and then the studio discovers that it doesn't own the rights to the novel. **1959** *Listener* 24 Sept. 495/3 Those who (to use a colloquial phrase that does justice to feelings, especially in war time) 'hated his guts'. **1967** *Guardian* 29 Dec. 6/3 Resentment in Service quarters is now focusing on Mr Healey... But those who are demanding his guts for garters are making a mistake.

c. *transf.* The inside, internal fittings, contents of anything. Also *fig.* (*slang* or *colloq.*) substantial contents, 'something in' a thing; so †*to have guts in one's brains*.

1663 BUTLER *Hud.* iii. 1091 Truly that is no Hard Matter for a Man to do, That has but any Guts in 's Brains. **1694** MOTTEUX *Rabelais* v. Prol. (1737) 53 One without Guts in his Brains, whose Cockloft is unfurnish'd. *a* **1704** T. BROWN *Wks.* (1730) I. 278 His brother boars, I presume, will have more guts in their brains for the future than to pick a quarrel with such as preserve their lives. **1751** R. PALTOCK *P. Wilkins* xii. (1883) 39/2 Well, thinks I, what if I have lost my gourds, I have gained experience. I will dry them next time with the guts in. **1863** P. BARRY *Dockyard Econ.* 130 The whole 'guts' of the ships had besides to be torn out for the passage of the shaft. **1892** R. L. STEVENSON *Lett.* (1899) II. 276, I..can almost always get a happy day out of Marion Crawford—*ce n'est pas toujours la guerre*, but it's got life to it and guts, and it moves. **1897** BARRÈRE & LELAND *Dict. Slang*, *Guts*..(Artists), 'no guts in it'. The expression is pretty general, but it is more specially used by artists to announce their opinion that there is nothing in a picture.

d. *pl.* Energy, verve, staying power; courage, force of character. *colloq.*

Cf. dial. phr. *to have neither gut nor gall* (1887 in E.D.D.).

1893 FARMER *Slang* s.v., Put your guts into it.. = Row the very best you can. He (or it) has no guts in him (or it) = He (or it) is a common rotter. **1900** G. SWIFT *Somerley* 85 If you have what are, at Cambridge, vulgarly but expressively called 'guts'. **1924** W. M. RAINE *Troubled Waters* ii. 22 It's about your size to send a skull-and-crossbones threat through the mail, but I notice you haven't the guts to sign it. **1924** R. KEABLE *Recompence* i. 9 Can't you dig me out a chap with some guts, who has learned to rough it? **1933** J. C. POWYS *Glastonbury Romance* xxii. 713, I think, if you haven't the guts to act like a man in the matter, you ought to leave this girl alone. **1955** *Times* 30 Aug. 5/2 That policeman had plenty of guts. I have been informed that the policeman was not seriously hurt.

2. A particular portion of the lower alimentary canal between the pylorus and the anus; = INTESTINE: often preceded by a defining adjective, the higher portion being named *little*, *small*, †*subtle*, the lower *great*, *large*. †*fat gut* (= F. *gras boyau*, Cotgr.), the rectum (also ***arse-gut***; ***right-gut***: see the prefixed words). †***hungry gut*** (see HUNGRY *a.* 4), the jejunum. Also BLIND GUT, the cæcum; *transf.* a cul-de-sac.

a. *sing.*

13.. *E.E. Allit. P.* C 280 Þenne he [Ionas] lurkkes & laytes ..In vche a nok of his nauel, but nowhere he fyndez No rest ..bot ramelande myre, In wych gut so euer he gotz. **1398** TREVISA *Barth. De P.R.* v. xlii. (1495) 158 The thyrde lytyll gutte is callyd in latyn secundo simul unum. **14..** *Nom.* in Wr.-Wülcker 678/11 *Hic lien*,..a longe gute. **1486** *Bk. St. Albans* b vij b, Putt it in a small gut of a Capon. **1530** PALSGR. 228/1 Gutte, a bowell, *boyau*. **1722** QUINCY *Lex. Physico-Med.* (ed. 2) 224 There is very much Fat about its [i.e. the rectum's] external side, for which reason it is called the Fat-Gut. **1789** W. BUCHAN *Dom. Med.* (1790) 599 The operator ..must with his fingers artfully conduct the gut in by the same aperture through which it came out. **1806** FORSYTH *Beauties Scotl.* IV. 415 The harbour [of Aberdeen] lies at the bottom of the eminence on which it stands, and is a blind gut, into which the tide flows, bending in a curved form. **1830** R. KNOX *Beclard's Anat.* 89 He..supposes it to be absorbed by the large gut. **1889** J. M. DUNCAN *Lect. Dis. Wom.* xiv. (ed. 4) 96 They [fæces] may lie in any part of the great gut. **1897** HUGHES *Mediterr. Fever* iii. 153 The involvement of the large gut.

b. *pl.*

1398 TREVISA *Barth. De P.R.* v. xlii. (1495) 158, vj pryncypall guttes, thre of theym ben subtyll..and thre aren grete. *c* **1420** *Liber Cocorum* (1862) 9 Skoure tho guttus with salt ichon. **1601** HOLLAND *Pliny* I. 342 Next to the bag of the Stomacke, men and sheepe have the small guts, called Lactes. **1707** FLOYER *Physic. Pulse-Watch* 25, I injected into the small Guts of a Cow..a sufficient quantity of Water to fill them. **1722** QUINCY *Lex. Physico-Med.* (ed. 2) 223 The third and last of the small Guts is the Ilium... The thick and great Guts are the Cæcum, Colon, and Rectum. **1813** J. THOMSON *Lect. Inflam.* 93 A solution of this substance injected into the great guts of a dog.

c. In generalized sense.

1803 *Med. Jrnl.* X. 34 The portion of gut was about the size of a walnut. **1813** J. THOMSON *Lect. Inflam.* 211 The portion of gut which had been strangulated was found considerably inflamed. **1879** *St. George's Hosp. Rep.* IX. 295 A knuckle of much congested gut.

d. Extended to the whole of the alimentary canal or its lower portion.

*c***1460** J. RUSSELL *Bk. Nurture* 607 Make clene þe place also þat ye calle his gowt. **1553** UDALL *Geminus' Anat.* A ii/1 The seconde portion of the gutte is called *Ieiunum*, or the hungry gutte, because he is euermore emptye. **1713** WARDER *True Amazons* (ed. 2) 5 [Speaking of bees.] In the hinder parts there is a Gut. **1811** A. T. THOMSON *Lond. Disp.* (1818) 403 Sheathing the rectum in cases of abrasion, and inflammation of the gut. **1842** A. COMBE *Physiol. Digestion* (ed. 4) 132 The pylorus..opens and allows it to pass into the gut. **1878** BELL tr. *Gegenbaur's Comp. Anat.* 36 The inner germinal layer [is] the foundation of the gut or enteron. **1893** NEWTON *Dict. Birds* 137 The intestine, or gut proper, begins at the pyloric end of the stomach and ends at the cloaca.

e. *attrib.* †**small-gut man**, a fencer who can pierce the small guts.

*a***1625** FLETCHER *Love's Pilgr.* IV. ii, Is there Ever a good heartist, or a member percer, or a Small-gut man left?

†**f.** *transf.* Applied to the shoots or bine of hops. *Obs. rare.* (Cf. GUT *v.* 1 b.)

1573 TUSSER *Husb.* xxxviii. (1878) 91 From hop long gut away go cut... Sharpe knife to cut superfluous gut.

g. In machine sheep-shearing, a flexible shaft which conveys the power from an overhead source to the shearer's handpiece. *Austral.* and *N.Z.*

1956 G. BOWEN *Wool Away!* (ed. 2) viii. 100 The correct length of a gut is shown when, with the long and short gut connected, they hang so that the short gut swings just clear of the floor. **1965** J. S. GUNN *Terminol. Shearing Industry* II. 35 The tube is a casing down which runs a flexible driving shaft known as the 'gut'.

h. *fig.* Used, chiefly *attrib.*, of an issue, question, etc.: basic, fundamental; also, of a reaction: instinctive and emotional rather than rational.

1964 *Economist* 17 Oct. 261/3 For Harold Wilson it was a carefully planned campaign:..the neo-Kennedyism combined with a concentration on gut issues. **1968** *Guardian* 26 Sept. 10/3 The three nights of rioting that followed his murder were an immediate gut reaction. **1969** *Times* 22 July p. ii/3 The moon programme..was a gut issue, as even the less enthusiastic realized. **1969** *Daily Tel.* 14 Nov. 5/2 When we [*sc.* the Americans] first went into space, we had no idea how much it was going to benefit the economy. We went in as a gut reaction to the Soviet challenge. **1970** *Win* 15 June 4/1 There are some gut questions the pacifist must face. *Ibid.*, Really, the questions are too gut for us. **1971** *Listener* 19 Aug. 223/2 Most people's reaction to the *Oz* trial and sentences has been what one might call a gut-reaction—whether of shock or satisfaction.

i. Phr. ***to bust*** (or ***rupture***) ***a gut***: to exert oneself, to make a great effort. *colloq.*

1912 *Dialect Notes* III. 572 *Bust a gut*,..to make a supreme effort. 'Just bust a gut now and see if we can't lift this log.' **1968** C. DRUMMOND *Death & Leaping Ladies* i. 23 'I'll be back in twenty minutes.'..'Don't bust a gut,' advised Miss Winkelbaum, 'the hussies will be late.' **1970** J. PORTER *Rather Common Sort of Crime* xiii. 154 If Mack'd been some fat, respectable, middle-aged old bastard, the cops'd've bust a gut nicking somebody fer croaking him. **1970** W. SMITH *Gold Mine* xiii. 36 'Huh!' Popeye checked his watch. 'Two hours forty to get down, you don't reckon to rupture a gut do you?'

3. a. *sing.* and *pl.* Put for the belly or stomach, *esp.* as the seat of appetite or gluttony. Now *dial.* and *vulgar.* ***gut and ga'*** (gall) (*Sc.*): the whole contents of the stomach.

1362 LANGL. *P. Pl.* A. XI. 44 Thei..demeth god in-to the gorge whon heore gottus follen. **1393** *Ibid.* C. II. 34 Al is noȝt good to þe gost þat þe gut askeþ. **1535** TINDALE *Tracy's Test.* 13 Dame Avarice, with as greedy a gut..as the best. **1557** GRIMALDE in *Tottel's Misc.* (Arb.) 120 Lions..Whose greedy gutts the gnawing hoonger pricks. **1616** R. C. *Times' Whistle* II. 772 To putt Scraps twice runne over, in thy half starvd gutt. **1621** BURTON *Anat. Mel.* I. ii. II. ii. (1651) 72 Gluttony kills more than the sword,..this al-devouring and murdering gut. **1644** BP. HALL *Rem. Wks.* (1660) 101 That had learn'd to govern his Tongue, his Gut, his concupiscence; these three. **1693** *Dryden's Juvenal* iv. (1697) 77 For his own Gut he bought the stately Fish. **1726** GAY *Fables* II. iii. 96 Here ev'ry day he cram'd his guts. **1768** ROSS *Helenore* (1789) 56 Gut and ga' she keest with braking strange. **1790** A. WILSON in *Poems & Lit. Prose* (1876) II. 244 An inn's thy temple, and thy God thy guts.

b. *pl.* A corpulent or gluttonous person.

[**1550**, etc.: cf. GREEDY-GUT(S.)] **1596** SHAKS. *1 Hen. IV*, II. iv. 251 Thou Clay-brayn'd Guts. *a***1700** B. E. *Dict. Cant. Crew*, *Gutts*, a very fat, gross Person. **1869** R. LYTTON *Orval* 177 March, march, old guts! This is a lazy lord. **1896** *Warwicksh. Gloss.*, *Guts*, a glutton. **1959** I. & P. OPIE *Lore & Lang. Schoolch.* ix. 168 The unfortunate fat boy..is known as..guts, [etc.].

4. The intestines of animals employed for various purposes. **a.** *pl.* As food: = OFFAL. Phrase: ***not fit to carry guts to a bear.***

1602 *Narcissus* (1893) 284 O thou that pickest wisdome out of guttes. **1692** L'ESTRANGE *Fables* cxxxv. 124 Wee, the Kings Officers, crys the Fellow that carrys Guts to the Bears. **1840** MARRYAT *Poor Jack* xxviii, Well, if I'm a bear, you ar'n't fit to carry guts to a bear.

b. As an envelope for black puddings, sausages, etc.

1598 *Epulario* iij b, Take guts well washed and made clean, and fill them with the meat. **1819** *Sporting Mag.* V. 32 In Suffolk, black puddings made in guts are called links.

c. For making violin strings; hence, †*pl.* the strings themselves (*obs.*). In mod. use *sing.* as the name of a material. (Cf. CATGUT.)

1611 MIDDLETON & DEKKER *Roaring Girl* IV. i. 80 Heere take this viall, runne vpon the guts, And end thy quarrell singing. **1626** BACON *Sylva* §280 A Viall should haue..the Strings of Guts mounted vpon a Bridge, as in Ordinary Vialls. *a***1774** GOLDSM. *Surv. Exper. Philos.* (1776) II. 190 On this side [of the Eolian lyre] are seven strings of very fine gut. **1883** [see *gut-spinning* in sense 8].

d. *sing.* The silken fibre obtained from the intestines of the silkworm. (In full *silkworm gut*, *silk-gut*.) Chiefly used in the making of fishing tackle.

The worm, when about to spin, is killed and put into vinegar, then pulled in two, and the 'gut' is drawn out to a thin thread and dried.

1834 MEDWIN *Angler in Wales* I. 16 Where I procured some hanks of gut..My fishing companions did not know that each filum of gut is a drawn-out silkworm just before it is about to weave its cocoon. **1839** URE *Dict. Arts* 1115 Silkworm gut, for angling. **1867** F. FRANCIS *Angling* xiii. (1880) 462 Tying threads of gut together for lines. **1875** 'STONEHENGE' *Brit. Sports* I. v. II. §1. 309 It is generally made of pieces of gut, knotted together, and altogether comprising a length of from three to eight feet. **1899** *Speaker* 9 Sept. 260/2 At every cast the gut had fallen upon the water like a streak of lightning.

5. A narrow passage. **a.** A channel or run of water, a branch of a stream; a sound, strait.

1538 LELAND *Itin.* (1711) II. 13 Ethelwolde, Abbate of Abbingdon..did clerely renovate and augmentid this Abbay, digging and caussing a gut to cum out of Isis by force to serve and purge thoffices of thabbay. **1587** *Harl. MS.* 167 lf. 104 We riding (on ship) in a narrow gutt, the place yealding no better. **1628** DIGBY *Voy. Mediterr.* (1868) 9 The gutt of sea being here but narrow. **1703** J. LOGAN in *Pa. Hist. Soc. Mem.* IX. 223, I now design to keep her floating in a dock or gut. **1766** J. BARTRAM *Jrnl.* 4 Feb. in Stork *Acc. E. Florida* 61 Near the Store was a deep gut with a middling stream of water, which headed about a quarter of a mile up in the pine-lands. **1767** DALRYMPLE in *Phil. Trans.* LVII. 395 These banks are..often..divided by a narrow gut, without bottom. **1830** LYELL *Princ. Geol.* (1875) I. II. xx. 497 Coming up with her..in the middle of the gut, between Tarifa and Tangier. **1855** B. TAYLOR *Home & Abr.* Ser. I. xxii. (1880) 271 A gut between the rocks..conducts to the sea. **1887** T. N. PAGE in *Scribner's Mag.* I. 414/2 The trail ..terminated..in a gut of the swamp.

b. As a local designation; e.g. the Gut of Canso, the Gut of Gibraltar; also, a street in Valletta, Malta. (At Oxford and Cambridge) ***the Gut***: a bend of the river in the racing-course.

1716 B. CHURCH *Hist. Philip's War* (1867) II. 162 They had orders to go directly for Port Royal Gut. **1746** *Acc. French Settlem. N. Amer.* 9 There are three ways of getting into this great river:..the third is thro' the Gut of Canseau. **1770** WASHINGTON *Writ.* (1889) II. 316 The Old Town Gut was so high as to wet us in crossing it. **1793** SMEATON *Edystone L.* §102 The seamen thought it not safe to go into the Gut that night,..that the entrance or exit from the Gut might be impracticable or dangerous. **1829** MARRYAT *F. Mildmay* v, We could not..get out of the Gut of Gibraltar. **1862** H. KINGSLEY *Ravenshoe* I. xiv. 173 Pembroke had won the fours, very much in consequence of Worcester having gone round the flag, and on being made to row again, of fouling them in the gut. **1889** *Christ's Coll. Mag.* 77 The third night Queens' fell an easy prey in the Gut. **1948** PARTRIDGE et al. *Dict. Forces' Slang* 89 *The Gut*, a notorious street in Malta. **1970** 'ZENO' *Grab* iii. 25 Strait Street, Valetta, better known as the Gut, the centre of Malta's red light district. **1970** M. BUTTERWORTH *Vanishing Act* x. 108 Mosta dome and the Città Notabile, the trashy souvenir shops of Kingsway..and the honky tonk dives of the Gut.

c. On land: A narrow passage between two declivities; hence, a narrow passage or lane of any kind.

1615 G. SANDYS *Trav.* 188 North of it, in a gut of the hill was the fish-poole of Siloe. **1703** MAUNDRELL *Journ. Jerus.* (1732) 134 We enter'd into a narrow Gut, between two steep rocky Mountains. **1762–71** H. WALPOLE *Vertue's Anecd. Paint.* (1786) IV. 265 Before you arrived at these, you passed a narrow gut between two stone terrasses, that rose above your head. **1809** PINKNEY *Trav. France* 256 A stony channel or gut which was..cut out to ease the ascent. **1873** *Sat. Rev.* 5 Apr. 447/2 The prospective widening of the narrow gut of Whitehall. **1893** R. KIPLING in E. Gosse *Quest. at Issue* 261 A hundred fires sparkle in the gut of the pass. **1896** *Daily News* 20 July 7/3 The narrow valley gut of old Knightsbridge will be widened. *Ibid.* 26 Dec. 3/2 The signal-box in this narrow gut of traffic.

6. a. †A gutter along the eaves of a house (*obs.*); *dial.* The eaves (of a stack).

1703 T. N. *City & C. Purchaser* 211 Guts to save Water under the Eves of a House. **1855** MORTON *Cycl. Agric.* II. 723 *Gut* (Essex), the eaves of a stack.

†**b.** An outflow. *Obs.* Cf. GOUT[2].

1565 GOLDING *Ovid's Met.* XI. (1593) 262 His head to put Full underneath the foming spout where greatest was the gut.

7. (See quot.)

1853 *Archit. Publ. Soc. Dict.*, *Gut*, a term used in parts of Scotland for a sash bar.

8. *attrib.* and *Comb.*, as ***gut-dresser, -fat, -link, -rope, -string, -substitute,*** †***-vein, -wall***; also ***guts-box; gut-dressing, -spinning*** vbl. sbs.; ***gut(s)-griping*** vbl. sb. and ppl. a.; ***gut-open*** adj.; **gut-belting**, lathe or machine belting made of catgut (Knight *Dict. Mech.* 1875); **gut-bread**, sweetbread, pancreas; **gut-bucket** *slang* (orig. U.S.), a primitive, unsophisticated brand of jazz (see also quot. 1939); cf. BARREL-HOUSE 2; also *attrib.*; †**gut-bursten**, abdominal hernia; **gut-foundered** *a.*, (*a*) on the point of starvation (now *dial.*); †(*b*) affected with hernia; †**gut-head**, one who is stupid from over-feeding; **gut-hook**, a coupling hook and eye for round gut belts (Knight); **gut-house** = *gutting-house*; **gut-led** *a.*, ? ruled by one's appetite; **gut-length**, a length of silkworm gut; †**gut-matter**, something pertaining to bodily nourishment or appetite; †**gut-monger**, one whose chief concern is his 'gut' or belly; †**gut-pudding**, a sausage; **gut-rot** *colloq.*, unwholesome or unpalatable liquor or food (cf. ROT-GUT); **guts-ache** *colloq.* = STOMACH-ACHE; **gut-scraper**, a humorous or derisive term for a violin-player; **gut-scrapery**, an establishment where guts are scraped and cleaned; †**gut-seam** *Sc.*, fat of the intestines, lard; **gut-shoot** *v. trans. slang*, to shoot in the guts; so **gut-shot** *sb.* and *ppl. a.*; **gut-vexer** = *gut-scraper*; **gut-way**, ? a passage over a gut or watercourse; **gut-weed**, *Sonchus arvensis* (Britten & Holland *Plant-n.* 1879); †**gut-worm**, an intestinal worm.

1893 *Brit. Med. Jrnl.* 15 Apr. 812/2 The pancreas is vulgarly termed the '*gutbread'..and is the article which would be supplied in the great majority of cases by butchers asked for sweetbread. **1929** *N.Y. Age* 8 June 7/6 Using a mute, occasionally a small megaphone inserted at the bell of his trumpet, he [*sc.* Louis Armstrong] eschews the tin pail, hat, plunger and other devices of the '*gut bucket' player. **1934** *Melody Maker* 10 Feb. 5/1, I urge some good black-and-tan gutbucket records with Hawkins. **1938** *Manch. Guardian Weekly* 2 Sept. 188/3 Sometimes they play 'boogie-woogie'..sometimes 'gutbucket' (unrefined). **1939** RAMSEY & SMITH *Jazzmen* 12 From barrel-houses and honkey-tonks came many of the descriptive words which were applied to the music played in them; such as..'gut-bucket', referring originally to the bucket which caught drippings or 'gutterings' from the barrels, later to the unrestrained brand of music that was played by small bands in the dives. **1951** W. MORUM *Gabriel* II. viii. 239 Jake's suggestion of another two hours session of dance music at a gut-bucket joint in Piccadilly. **1607** TOPSELL *Four-f. Beasts* (1658) 307 First you shall understand, that the *Gut-bursten, and Flank-bursten, doth proceed both of one cause, that is to say, by means that the skin, called before Peritoneum, is either sore strained, or else broken. **1852** MORFIT *Tanning & Currying* (1853) 536 The workshop of the *gut-dresser. **1885** A. WATT *Leather Manuf.* 393 The art of *gut-dressing. **1847** *Rep. U.S. Comm. Patents* (1848) 527 The slaughterers formerly got the *gut fat for the whole of the labor thus described. **1895** *Daily News* 13 Dec. 8/1 Weights of fat, gut-fat, and trimmings. **1647** WARD *Simp. Cobler* 27, I can make my selfe sicke..with comparing the dazling splender wherewith our Gentle-women were imbellished in some former habits, with the *gut-foundred goosdom, wherewith they are now surcingled and debauched. *a***1658** CLEVELAND *Count. Com. Man* (1677) 100 The clamorous Mutiny of a Gut-foundred Garrison. **1691** J. WILSON *Belphegor* III. iv, *Cris.* But now she 'as beaten me to mash. *Min.* And made me mere gut-founder'd. *a***1700** B. E. *Dict. Cant. Crew*, *Gut-foundred*, exceeding Hungry. **1876** *Whitby Gloss.*, *Gut-founder'd*, diseased from the effects of hunger. **1606** SHAKS. *Tr. & Cr.* v. i. 21 The rotten diseases of the South, *guts-griping Ruptures, Catarres [etc.]. **1679** DRYDEN *Tr. & Cr.* IV. ii, The rotten diseases of the south, gut-gripings, ruptures, catarrhs, loads of gravel in the back ..and the like. *a***1704** T. BROWN in R. L'Estrange *Colloq. Erasm.* (1711) 351 That he might not lose a drop of this Gut-griping stuff. **1629** GAULE *Holy Madn.* 328 A very *Gut-head, he hath Asses' Eares direct. **1780** YOUNG *Tour Irel.* I. 231 Four to carry from *gut-house to curing-house. **1682** N. O. *Boileau's Lutrin* IV. 227 Nor was it Reason that the *gut-led Fops Should spend their Tongues, who could not use their Chops. **1863** ATKINSON *Stanton Grange* 173 Re-tie every knot, the same way as you tie your *gut-links. **1549** COVERDALE, etc. *Erasm. Par. Cor.* 32 At this souper is represented the misterie of christian concorde, no bealy, nor *gut matter. **1655** R. YOUNGE *Agst. Drunkards* 4 These drunken drones, these *gut-mongers. **1935** L. MACNEICE *Poems* 64 The town-dweller like a rabbit in a greengrocer's ..Hangs by the heels *gut-open against the fog. **1697** *Verdicts Virg. & Homer* v. 18 Homer compares Ulysses turning in his bed,..to a *Gut-pudding or Sawsage broyling on a Gridiron. **1722** QUINCY *Lex. Physico-Med.* (ed. 2) 12 Allentoies..in many Brutes is in the Shape of a Gut-Pudding. **1847** SMEATON *Builder's Man.* 205 Balistæ, catapultæ, and scorpions, in whose frames are holes for the passage of the homotona, which are strained by *gut-ropes attached to windlasses worked by hand-spikes. **1916** A. H. MACKLIN in A. Lansing *Endurance* (1959) v. vi. 217 '*Gut Rot, 1916'..served only to turn most of us teetotallers for life. **1938** S. BECKETT *Murphy* 83 The customer..was paying for his gutrot ten times what it cost to produce. **1941** BAKER *Austral. Slang* 33 Gutrot, unhealthy-looking food or strong drink. **1965** F. SARGESON *Mem. Peon* ii. 32 The garish-looking sweet stuff he made his living from... 'I make a dishonest living by trading in gutrot.' **1818** KEATS *Let.* 13 July (1958) I. 324 Cant!..It is enough to give a spirit the *guts-ache. **1934** BLUNDEN *Mind's Eye* 145 Don't eat that, Jack; it'll give you the Guts'-Ache. **1946** K. TENNANT *Lost Haven* (1947) vi. 89 'Ar,' Launce said contemptuously. 'You got a guts-ache or you're coming out in boils.' **1940** DYLAN THOMAS *Portrait of Artist* 133 He'd put his hand down in the *guts-box and bring you out a rat with its neck broken clean as a match for the price of a glass of beer. **1719** D'URFEY *Pills* II. 218 Strike up drowsie *Gut-scrapers. **1785** BURNS *Jolly Beggars* vi. 2 Her charms had struck a sturdy Caird, As well as poor Gut-scraper. **1854** *Q. Rev.* XCV. 282 Triperies, bone-boiling-houses, *gut-scraperies. **1606** BIRNIE *Kirk-Buriall* (1833) 4 The Greke and Romane did burne their dead; the Indean with *Got-seame did besmeare. **1878** C. HALLOCK *Amer. Club List & Sportsman's Gloss.* p. v, **Gut-shot*, hit in the belly; wounded, but not disabled. **1935** E. HEMINGWAY *Green Hills Africa* (1936) II. iii. 103 I'm afraid I gut-shot him. *Ibid.* 114 It looked, now, like a gut shot or one through the paunch. **1960** B. CRUMP *Good Keen Man* 33 He came to the door and shouted into the frosty dark that he'd gut-shoot the first of us to come near the hut. *Ibid.* 50 Phillip was as slow as a gut-shot pig and started yelling as soon as he lost sight of me through the bush. **1883** HALDANE *Workshop Receipts* Ser. II. 319/2 *Gut-spinning is the twisting of prepared gut into cord of various diameter for various purposes—i.e. for ordinary catgut, for use in machinery, and for fiddle-strings. **1659** TORRIANO, *Nérvi sonóri*, *gut-strings for Instruments. *a***1691** BOYLE

Hist. Air (1692) 33 This hygroscope.. is made by fastning to the upper end of a piece of gut-string.. a very light index. **1892** *Daily News* 6 Aug. 8/6 A Manufactory of Gut-Strings requires a really experienced and pushing man. **1939** 'G. ORWELL' *Coming up for Air* II. iv. 87 Even now I could give you all the details about *gut-substitute and gimp and Limerick hooks. **1615** CROOKE *Body of Man* 99 The second is called *Intestinalis* or the *Gut-veine. **1640** *Wizard* (MS. play) (N.), Get out of my sight, you unlucky *gut-vexers. **1897** *Allbutt's Syst. Med.* III. 606 When the intestine is healthy the bacillus coli communis has little disposition to escape through the *gut-wall. **1898** *Westm. Gaz.* 24 June 5/1 The standards were 25 ft. long at the '*gutway'. **1658** ROWLAND *Moufet's Theat. Ins.* 1106 The Arabians call them Emicar.. the Germans Spulworm, Bauchworm, the English *Gutworm.

gut (gʌt), *v.* Also 4 gotte, 5 gutton. [f. GUT *sb.*]

1. a. *trans.* To take out the guts of (fish); to eviscerate.

13.. *Metr. Hom.* (Vernon MS.) in *Archiv Stud. neu. Spr.* LVII. 315 Oþur while wesch he dissches And oþur while he gotted fissches. *c* **1440** *Promp. Parv.* 220/1 Gutton, *exentero.* **1596** DALRYMPLE tr. *Leslie's Hist. Scot.* I. 41 Quhen now thay [herrings] ar gutted, and the meltis takne out, thay ar sa leine that thay ar nocht to be compared with the rest. **1599** H. BUTTES *Dyets drie Dinner* L vii b, Carpe.. Lay it scaled and gutted sixe houres in salt. **1677** *Compleat Servant-Maid* 80 Wash your Eels and gut them. **1726** G. ROBERTS *Four Years Voy.* 263 In the Evening they us'd to gut, split, and salt what they caught. **1769** MRS. RAFFALD *Eng. Housekpr.* (1799) 33 Scale, gut, and wash your herrings. **1823** GALT *Entail* I. xxxvi. 317, I redde you to consider weel what ye're doing, and gut nae fish till ye catch them. **1861** MRS. BEETON *Housh. Managem.* (1880) 139 Take the herrings, cut off the heads, and gut them.

absol. **1842** J. WILSON *Voy. Scotl.* II. 161 In hiring servants it is by no means unusual for the latter to stipulate for leave to gut during a certain number of days, as a perquisite beyond their usual termly wages.

†**b.** To clear (a hop plant) of superfluous 'gut' or shoots. *Obs. rare.* (Cf. GUT *sb.* 2 f.)

1573 TUSSER *Husb.* xlvi. (1878) 98 Hop rootes.. well gutted and pared, the better they proue.

2. a. *transf.* To clear out the contents or inside of; to empty thoroughly; *esp.* to remove or destroy the internal fittings of (a building, etc.). Const. *of.* Now freq. used *pass.* and of destruction by fire.

1688 LUTTRELL *Brief Rel.* (1857) I. 486 The 11th, in the evening, the mobile gott together, and went to the popish chappel in Lincolns Inn Feilds, and perfectly gutted the same. **1693** DRYDEN *Juvenal* x. 246 A troop of Cut-Throat Guards were sent, to seize The Rich Mens Goods, and gut their Palaces. **1720** DE FOE *Capt. Singleton* xii. (1840) 216 We took an Arabian junk.. We gutted him of the pearl. **1780** *Gentl. Mag.* L. 313/2 The public-office in Bow-Street, and Sir John Fielding's dwelling-house adjoining, were gutted, as their [the rioters'] phrase was, and the whole contents committed to the flames. **1781** SMEATHMAN in *Phil. Trans.* LXXI. 177 While some are employed in gutting the posts, others ascend from them, entering a rafter or some other part of the roof. **1819** MOORE *Tom Crib* (ed. 3) 1 Whether diddling your subjects or gutting their fobs. **1848** THACKERAY *Bk. Snobs* xxvi, Stripes.. proceeded to gut my portmanteau and to lay out the black kerseymeres.. and other polite articles of evening costume. **1855** BROWNING *Holy-Cross Day* x, The hand.. Which gutted my purse, would throttle my creed. **1869** PHILLIPS *Vesuv.* vii. 174 Five times within the last hundred years the cone of Vesuvius has been gutted by explosive eruptions. **1873** L. FERGUSON *Discourses* Pref. 5 A thatched hut had been gutted and fitted up with seats. **1903** *Westm. Gaz.* 25 Aug. 8/2 The farmhouse and out-buildings were completely gutted. **1968** *Bucks Examiner* 3 May 1 (*heading*) Furniture factory gutted.

b. *fig.* In various applications; *esp.* to get out the essential contents of (a book); to extract all the important passages of (a book) in a review or abridgement.

1714 ADDISON *Spect.* No. 567 ¶4 This way of Writing was first of all introduced by T-m Br-wn, of facetious Memory, who, after having gutted a proper Name of all its intermediate Vowels, used to plant it in his Works, and make as free with it as he pleased. **1847** DISRAELI *Tancred* II. vii, As for the other guests, the peerage was gutted. **1868** *Pall Mall G.* 2 Dec. 3 We have not yet calculated how many of the victories of Mr. Disraeli's friends have been due to Mr. Disraeli's skilful manipulation of details in redividing the counties and in gutting them. **1888** *Ibid.* 6 Oct. 3/1 Now suppose Messrs. Longman issued a sixpenny edition of the book, properly 'gutted' (as the newspaper phrase is). **1897** W. T. STEAD in *Daily News* 13 June 6/4, I am never better pleased than when I see my books well 'gutted'—to use the expressive but somewhat vulgar term.

3. *intr.* To cram the guts; to eat greedily, to gormandize. *vulgar.* (Cf. dial. *guts* vb.)

1616 R. C. *Times' Whistle* VI. 2393 'Tis safest gutting at a loafe begunne. **1633** [see GUTTING *vbl. sb.* 3]. **1893** in FARMER *Slang.*

†**4.** *trans.* To make channels or ruts in (ground); to 'gutter'. *Obs.*

1557 TUSSER *100 Points Husb.* xxvii, Or winter doe come, while the weather is good: for gutting thy grounde, get the home with thy wood.

gut, obs. form of GOUT *sb.*[1]

gutah, variant of GUTTA *sb.*[2]

gutcher, obs. form of GOODSIRE *Sc.*

gute, obs. form of GOUT *sb.*[1], GUT *sb.*

†**'gutefestre** (y). *Obs. rare*$^{-1}$. [f. ME. **gute* (ü), OE. *gyte* (= OHG. *guz*) a pouring, f. wk. root of *ȝéotan* to pour (see YETE *v.*) + *festre* FESTER.] ? A running ulcer.

a **1225** *Ancr. R.* 328 Edmodnesse is iliche þeos kointe narloz þet scheaweð forð hore gutefestre & hore vlowinde cweisen.

gutful ('gʌtfʊl). *dial.* and *slang.* Also **gutsful.** [f. GUT *sb.* + -FUL.] = BELLY-FUL.

1900 *Eng. Dial. Dict.* II. 768/1 He's hungry when he's got a gutful (he is very stingy). **1932** N. LINDSAY *Cautious Amorist* xvi. 226 Let me have some fun out of you to prove it's not a gutsful of grunts you are. **1960** I. CROSS *Backward Sex* vi. 118 I've just had a gutful, and want to have hell scared out of her. **1965** M. SHADBOLT *Among Cinders* ii. 13 He said he'd had a gutsful of the bush when he was younger. **1970** *Daily Tel.* (Colour Suppl.) 15 May 7/2 Lately, we have had a 'gutful' of the permissiveness that seems to tolerate violence against the police.

gutherooned, variant of GADROONED.

1817 D. HUGHSON *Walks thro. Lond.* 66 The architect.. has introduced Corinthian columns, fluted and gutherooned.

guthorne, variant of GITTERN.

†**guth-strength.** *Obs. rare*$^{-1}$. [f. OE. *gúð* = ON. *guð-r, gunn-r* war.] ? Warlike strength.

c **1205** LAY. 1595 Corineus him geinde to mid his guð strencðe.

Gutian ('gu:tɪən), *sb.* and *a.*

A. *sb.* A member of a mountain people who lived *c* 2500–2000 B.C. in the area of the Tigris and the Euphrates. **B.** *adj.* Of or pertaining to this people.

[**1882** *Encycl. Brit.* XIV. 159/2 We now find that at the dawn of history the mountains overhanging Assyria were held by a people named *Gútú*, a title which signified 'a warrior'.] **1928** V. G. CHILDE *Most Anc. East* i. 19 The Gutians, the Kassites, the Chaldæans and the Persians. **1929** C. J. GADD *Hist. & Monuments of Ur* iii. 99 Throughout all the years filled by the end of the Agade dynasty and the Gutian tyranny hardly anything is known concerning the fortunes of Ur. **1960** tr. *S. Moscati's Face of Ancient Orient* ii. 25 Then the Gutians, savage people from the East, spread destruction far and wide, and earn themselves the name of 'mountain dragons' (about 2150–2050 B.C.). **1971** W. W. HALLO in *Reallexikon der Assyriologie* 716/2 By the end of the Old Babylonian period, the term 'Gutian' was of little more than vague geographic or ethnic significance. *Ibid.* 719/1 The earliest contemporary references to Gutium.. seem to place it, or persons designated as Gutians, in the mid-Euphrates area, in company with Amorites... In the Old Babylonian period, persons identified as Gutian, or bearing 'Gutian' names are attested throughout northern Mesopotamia and Assyria.

'gutless, *a.* [f. GUT *sb.* + -LESS.] †**a.** Having no guts; disembowelled. *Obs.*

1605 SYLVESTER *Du Bartas* II. iii. III. *Law* 643 When the Falcon.. shall.. make on the sense-less ground The gut-less Quar, once, twice, or thrice, rebound. **1606** BIRNIE *Kirk-Buriall* (1833) 4 The Gerrens, a Schithian sect, after exinteration bespyced their gutlesse goodsirs. **1621** G. SANDYS *Ovid's Met.* XII. (1626) 247 He bounds, and on the earth his bowels trailes;.. and with a gutlesse bellie dies.

b. Lacking in energy, courage, or determination. Also **gutsless.**

1915 E. POUND in *Lett. J. Joyce* (1966) II. 364 Gutless Oxford graduates. **1927** D. H. LAWRENCE *Let.* 19 May in E. & A. Brewster *D. H. Lawrence* (1934) 133 The rest [at an art exhibition] piffle... So old-fashioned and timid and gutsless. **1929** W. J. LOCKE *Ancestor Jorico* x, Dr. Chepstow firmly refused to allow the convalescent and.. gutless Nicholas to venture a second time. **1930** G. M. SANDERS *Burnt Man* xv. 175 He was thinking that the man before him was a poor gutless creature after all, and that he had been foolish to suppose either of his sisters would ever be attracted to him. **1941** L. A. G. STRONG *Bay* ix. 228 Now you see what a gutless poor worm I am. **1969** *Daily Tel.* 16 May 18 The housing situation in North Kensington has been created by a short-sighted and gutless national housing policy.

Hence **'gutlessness,** lack of determination.

1936 R. LEHMANN *Weather in Streets* II. 245 Isn't it [*sc.* psycho-analysis] an excuse for gutlessness?

†**'gutlet.** *Obs. rare*$^{-1}$. [f. GUT *sb.* + -LET.] A small gut, or something resembling it; hence, a case or involucre (of a vein).

1615 CROOKE *Body of Man* II. xi. (1631) 82 A Membrane called the Gut-let.

gutling ('gʌtlɪŋ). *Obs.* exc. *dial.* [f. GUT *sb.* + -LING.] A great eater; a glutton.

1592 GREENE *Groats W. Wit* Ep. Ded., The bestiall gutlings of this fulsome feeding age. **1621** SANDERSON *Serm.* I. 195 The poets.. made themselves bitterly merry with descanting upon.. the fat paunches of these lasie gutlings. **1681** W. ROBERTSON *Phraseol. Gen.* (1693) 542 Verry belly-gods, Gutlings. **1883** *Almondbury & Huddersf. Gloss.*, *Gutling*, a great eater; a guttler.

Gutnish ('gʊtnɪʃ), *sb.* and *a.* [ad. G. *gutnisch.*]

A. *sb.* An East Norse dialect spoken on the island of Gotland. **B.** *adj.* Of or pertaining to the island of Gotland or its inhabitants.

1892 J. WRIGHT *Primer Gothic Lang.* 1 *East Norse*, including Swedish, Gutnish, and Danish. **1908** J. & E. M. WRIGHT *O.E. Gram.* 2 Old Norse.. is sub-divided into two groups: (a) East Norse, including Swedish, Gutnish, and Danish; (b) West Norse. **1927** E. V. GORDON *Introd. O. Norse* 177 The Gutnish laws.. state that after the 'bride-mass' is sung, 'the wedding shall be drunk for two days with all the folk'. **1934** PRIEBSCH & COLLINSON *German Lang.* ii. 28 East Norse split up into Swedish, which now includes a peculiar dialect—Gutnish—spoken on the island of Gotland, and Danish.

guts (gʌts), *v. colloq.* [Cf. GUT *v.* 3.] To eat greedily, to gormandize. (See *E.D.D.*)

1903 S. MACPLOWTER *Mrs. McCraw* 28 Ef ye hedna kep' us in sae lang, wi' yer haivers, A wid hae been hame tae keep her frae gutsin'. **1934** B. PENTON *Landtakers* (1935) vii. 50 Did ye not guts up a dollop of that jumbuck I drove off.. last week. **1943** K. TENNANT *Ride on, Stranger* iii. 24 'Gutsing again, Briscoe?' she reproved. **1956** B. W. ALDISS in *Pick of Today's Short Stories* 28 In the lunch hour, while I gutsed a bun in the background, we were sometimes quite crowded. **1967** D. PINNER *Ritual* xvii. 164 They gutsed the food without chewing.

gutser ('gʌtsə(r)). *dial.*, *Austral.*, *N.Z.*, and *colloq.* Also **gutzer.** [f. *guts* (GUT *sb.* 3) + -ER[1].] A heavy fall. Esp. in *fig.* phr. *come (fetch,* etc.) *a gutser*, come a cropper, make a mistake; *Air Force slang* (in concr. use), to crash.

1918 *Chrons. N.Z.E.F.* 21 June 221/1 The tenderfoot and Zambuk, Working madly in the trenches, Comes a 'gutzer' in those trenches, And is taught to take a rumble. **1919** *War Slang* in *Athenæum* 8 Aug. 728/1 A 'gutser' is the last straw. **1925** FRASER & GIBBONS *Soldier & Sailor Words* 113 *To come a gutzer*, to 'crash' or fall badly. (Ordinarily an Air Force term with reference to an aeroplane.) Also used generally. To get into serious trouble, *e.g.*, 'He's before a court martial and looks like coming a gutzer.' 'Gutzer' is pre-war slang, and an old term among Scottish boys for falling flat on the water in diving, instead of making a clean header. **1933** *Bulletin* (Sydney) 6 Sept. 9/2, I work for the dole in a gutser gang, shovelling bits of coast.. the down-and-out brigade. **1936** M. FRANKLIN *All that Swagger* xl. 317 The banks will fetch old Robert a gutser one of these days. **1941** D. MASTERS *So Few* xxx. 335 The starboard Heinkel turned straight into.. McKellar's stream of bullets and got what is known in the service as a 'gutser'. **1957** I. CROSS *God Boy* (1958) xii. 98 The back wheel slid in some loose gravel. Down he went again in another beautiful gutzer. **1960** B. CRUMP *Good Keen Man* 111, I came one or two gutsers myself, and once, when I was carrying Flynn through a gorge below the forks, I got out of control.

gutsy ('gʌtsɪ), *a.* Also **gutsey, gutzy.** [f. *guts* (GUT *sb.* 3) + -Y.] **1.** Greedy, voracious. orig. *Sc.*

1803 T. CAMPBELL *Let.* 2 Mar. in W. Beattie *Life & Lett. T. Campbell* (1849) I. 456 A John-Bull song.. to the chorus of 'Gooseberry tarts'. Gutsy proud people—we sing songs in Scotland about her nature and love!.. but here, there is no song but 'Roast Beef', or 'Gooseberry Tarts'! **1829** J. WILSON in *Blackwood's Edin. Mag.* XXV. 392 There's nae denying that maist o' them's gutsy. **1893** R. L. STEVENSON *Catriona* xxx, Ye muckle, gutsey hash, here's a Scots boot to your English hurdies. **1893–4** R. O. HESLOP *Northumberland Words* II. 350 *Gutsy, gutty*, gluttonous, fond of his belly. **1902** *Daily Chron.* 27 Mar. 3/1 An inspector having got from a class that a cow was a graminiverous and a tiger a carniverous animal, went on to ask what an animal that eats everything, both grass and flesh, would be. 'A gutsy beast,' was the reply. **1946** B. MARSHALL *George Brown's Schooldays* 23 Half a rissole was quite enough for a gutsy young sod like him.

2. Tough, spirited, courageous; possessing or requiring 'guts' (GUT *sb.* 1 d).

1893 in FARMER & HENLEY *Slang* III. 237/2. **1936** *Amer. Speech* XI. 101/1 Gutsy folk do not care for much pussyfooting. **1937** S. O'FAOLAIN in *John o' London's* 12 Mar. 984/3 *Kit Brandon* is the life-story of a woman gangster, a regular tornado, a passionate, lawless 'gutsy' young girl from the mountains. **1951** E. COXHEAD *One Green Bottle* vii. 190 She took him up one of the horrid, gutsy little Cribin climbs. **1964** *Punch* 9 Sept. 372/1 The following gutsy alternative. **1970** *New Yorker* 3 Oct. 36/3 He would.. sing out if a tune came along that was of his persuasion—something gutsy like 'Onward, Christian Soldiers'.

Hence **'gutsily** *adv.*, gluttonously (1825 in Jamieson's *Sc. Dict.*; 1898 in *E.D.D.*); **'gutsiness,** (*a*) greediness, gluttony (1825 in Jamieson; 1898 in *E.D.D.*); (*b*) energy, spirit; courage.

1893 FARMER & HENLEY *Slang* III. 237/2 Gutsiness. **1959** *Times* 1 Apr. 5/4 Israel audiences like and admire a play if it shows the qualities they most respect: directness.. 'gutsyness'. **1969** *Guardian* 7 July 9/4 His brilliance, his intellect, his gutsiness. **1970** *Ibid.* 31 Mar. 8/2 Tilson's work.. has always been gutsily vulgar.

gutt, obs. form of GOUT *sb.*[1], GUT.

‖**gutta**[1] ('gʌtə). *Pl.* **guttæ** ('gʌti:). [L. *gutta* a drop. Cf. GOUT *sb.*[1]]

1. a. *Pharmacy* and *Path.* A drop. In prescriptions *gt*, pl. *gtt.* (Cf. GOUT *sb.*[1] 5 b.)

1562 BULLEYN *Dial. Sorenes & Chir.* 45 b, This will make a singular good water, drope one gutta or drop upon the grounde. **1866** *Syd. Soc. Lex.*, *Gutta*, a drop of any liquid matter; a minim, or the sixtieth part of a fluid drachm.

b. In mod.Lat. names of diseases: **gutta opaca,** cataract; **gutta rosacea, rosea, rubea** (see quots. and cf. *gout rose*, GOUT *sb.*[1] 2); † **gutta sciatica** = SCIATICA; **gutta serena** = AMAUROSIS; also *fig.*

1847 CRAIG s.v. *Gutta*, In Pathology, **gutta opaca*, cataract. *c* **1400** *Lanfranc's Cirurg.* 190 *Gutta rosacea, þat is a passioun þat turneþ þe skyn of a mannys face out of his propur colour and makiþ þe face reed. **1753** CHAMBERS *Cycl. Supp.*, *Butiga*, is an inflammation of the whole face, otherwise called *gutta rosacea*. **1398** TREVISA *Barth. De P.R.* VII. lxv. (1495) 282 The Infeccyon that hyghte **Gutta rosea* y[e] enfectyth y[e] face wyth smale pymples and comyth of gleymy & blody and coleryk humours that ben bitwene the skynne & the flesshe. **1541** R. COPLAND *Guydon's Quest. Chirurg.* Y j, The gutta rosa. **1886** *Syd. Soc. Lex.*, **Gutta rubea*, = *Gutta rosacea*. **1398** TREVISA *Barth. De P.R.* VII.

lvii. (1495) 271 In the euyl callyd *gutta sciatica the ache stretcheth fro the haunche in to the legges and anone to the hele and also anone to the lytill too. **1657** *Gutta serena [see AMAUROSIS]. **1665** SIR T. HERBERT *Trav.* (1677) 337 [He] hath his eyes open, but sees no otherwise than if a gutta serena, or heated Steel, had deprived the optique. **1807** G. GREGORY *Dict. Arts & Sci.* I. 230/3 The causes of blindness are various; proceeding from cataracts, gutta serena's, &c. **1834** YOUATT *Cattle* 293 Gutta serena, or palsy of the optic nerve..is a disease of rare occurrence among cattle. **1876** T. HARDY *Madding Crowd* liii, She was in a state of mental gutta serena.

c. *Arch.* = DROP 10 b.

1563 SHUTE *Archit.* C iij b, Geue Subtenia, and Gutta, pendante.. the sixte part of a modulus to their height and that part deuide vnto .4. partes, Geue 3. vnto Gutta pendant being .6. in number. **1688** R. HOLME *Armoury* III. 112/1 *Gutta*, are Drops, or square pieces, or things like Bells, cut on the Frize, to set out the work. **1806** DALLAWAY *Observ. Eng. Archit.* 162 In the temples of Ægina [etc.] the guttæ retain their position. **1850** LEITCH tr. *C.O. Müller's Anc. Art* §282 (ed. 2) 312 Guttæ in a continued row without triglyphs were not perfectly rare in antiquity.

attrib. **1851** PENROSE *Athen. Arch.*, Gloss., *Guttæ tablets*, the square tablets under the architrave band from which the guttæ or drops appear as though suspended. **1852** *Dict. Arch.* (Arch. Publ. Soc.), *Guttæ* band, the listel from which the guttæ seem to hang.

d. *Her.* = GOUTTE.

1868 CUSSANS *Her.* iv. (1893) 75 Guttæ, or Gouttes, as their name implies, are drops, and, like the Roundles, are distinguished by their Tinctures.

†**2.** A kind of gum. In 18th c. = GAMBOGE; also ***gutta gamandra, gutta gamba***. Obs.

1398 TREVISA *Barth. De P.R.* XVII. lxxviii. (1495) 651 Gutta ryght as Galbanum is the droppyng of a certen tree ather herbe and hyght also Armoniacum. **1693** *Phil. Trans.* XVII. 685 *Ponna*, distilling a Substance like the *Gutta Gamba* or *Gummi Gotte*. **1706** PHILLIPS (ed. Kersey), *Gutta Gamandra*, or *Gutta Gamba*, a kind of harden'd Juice or Gum, brought from the East Indies. **1712** tr. *Pomet's Hist. Drugs* I. 178 Gum Gutta, or Gutta Gamba, Gamboge, or Peruvian Gum, is a Gum that flows from the Trunk of a creeping Plant. *Ibid.* 179 Lastly the Pills of gutta gamandra ..borrow their names from it.

3. A drop-like marking on an insect's wing.

1826 KIRBY & SPENCE *Introd. Ent.* IV. xlvi. 285 Gutta... A roundish dot, intermediate in size between an *atom* and a *macula*.. Linné..has employed the term *Gutta* for a white or yellow spot in a darker ground, and *Pustula* for a red spot in a black ground. We thought one term sufficient to express spots bigger than atoms. **1906** J. B. SMITH *Explan. Terms Ent.* 59 *Gutta*, a light spot on a dark ground. **1913** N. K. JARDINE *Dict. Ent.* 91 Gutta.—A light spot upon a light ground, *viz.*, white upon yellow; a roundish dot of colour, intermediate in size between an atom and a macula. **1937** J. R. DE LA TORRE-BUENO *Gloss. Ent.* 121 *Gutta*, a roundish colored dot.

gutta[2] (ˈgʌtə). Also gu(t)tah. [ad. Malay *getah* a gum, exudation, or inspissated juice, whence mod.L. *gutta*, assimilated to GUTTA[1].]

1. a. Short for GUTTA-PERCHA.

1852 CRAWFURD *Malay Dict.* 136 *Pârcha*, name of the forest tree which yields some of the guttah of commerce. **1882** DE WINDT *Equator* 39 A firm trading in gutta, gold-dust, and diamonds.

attrib. **1853** URE *Dict. Arts* (ed. 4) I. 983 The vaccine virus transmitted in the gutta capsules.

b. A gutta-percha golf ball, a gutty.

1857 H. B. FARNIE *Golfer's Man.* 11 The first flight of 'Guttas' was hailed with a burst of joy financial by everyone except the old monopolists of the feather manufacture. **1858** *Chambers's Jrnl.* 4 Sept. 157/2 He seizes his sand-iron.. and, with a skilful jerk behind his ball, frees it..and taking his long spoon—a wooden-headed club..Jones drives forth his gutta from its not too favourably lying position. **1881** R. FORGAN *Golfer's Handbk.* 5 The 'guttas' speedily became popular. *Ibid.* 36 The 'gutta' ball..was still far from perfect. **1905** A. S. CUNNINGHAM *Rambles in Scoonie & Wemyss* 99 He and his brother were credited with devising the hand hammering of balls, which led to the ultimate marking of guttas.

2. In the Malay names of various substances resembling gutta-percha, mostly containing the name of the tree from which they are derived, as ***gutta-rambong, -singgarip, -sundek, -taban***; **gutta-jelutong** (or **-joolatong**), a substitute for rubber obtained from any one of several apocynaceous trees of Malaysia and Indonesia of the genus *Dyera*, spec. *D. costulata*; **gutta-shea, -trap** (see quots. 1858, 1887).

1858 *Cycl. Commerce* (ed. Homans), *Gutta Trap*, a substance allied to gutta percha and caoutchouc..It is the inspissated juice of an artocarpus. **1887** MOLONEY *Forestry W. Afr.* 379 A substance somewhat resembling gutta-percha is found in Shea Butter, and is called Gutta-Shea. **1897** WILLIS *Flower. Pl.* II. 287 Payena Leerii..yields a good gutta percha..known as Gutta Sundek. **1897** C. P. G. SCOTT *Malayan Words* 55 The present gutta-percha of commerce is said to be all or mostly obtained from other trees, and is called by the natives accordingly getah taban, getah rambong, getah sundi, getah gerih, etc. **1904** *Electr. World & Engin.* 18 June 1150 (Cent. D. Suppl.), Importations of 'gutta-joolatong',..which is used in certain industries as a substitute for india rubber. **1927** C. R. TOOTHAKER *Commercial Raw Materials* 207 There are several substances similar to gutta-percha obtained from the milky juices of trees in the East Indies. Gutta-jelutong (jelatong), or pontianak,..is the most important.

3. *Chem.* A white amorphous substance, the principal constituent of gutta-percha.

1864 WATTS *Dict. Chem.* II. 961 Pure gutta is a hydro-carbon isomeric with oil of turpentine, $C^{10} H^{16}$.

guttable (ˈgʌtəb(ə)l), *a. rare.* [f. GUT *v.* + -ABLE. (? Formed in imitation of GUSTABLE.)] That may be 'gutted' or guzzled: in quot. as *sb.*

1735 T. S[HERIDAN] in *Swift's Wks.* (1778) XVII. 312, I have..too much plenty of guttables; if we had agreeable companions as plenty as woodcocks, ducks, snipes..this would be a paradise.

gutta-percha (ˌgʌtəˈpɜːtʃə). Also -pertscha. [ad. Malay *getah percha*, f. *getah* GUTTA[2] + *percha* the name of the tree (sense 2), lit. 'the gum of percha'.]

1. The inspissated juice of various trees found chiefly in the Malayan archipelago (see sense 2), now extensively used in the arts.

1845 *Athenæum* 337 The Secretary described the substance called 'gutta percha'. **1852** CRAWFURD *Malay Dict.* 50, *Gâtah-pârcha*, the inspissated juice of the pârcha tree, *Isonandra gutta* of Sir William Hooker; the guttah-percha of commerce. **1858** CARPENTER *Veg. Phys.* §335 A substance, closely resembling Indian-rubber, has lately excited considerable interest, and, under the name of Gutta Pertscha, is now brought into the markets of Europe in considerable quantities. **1870** EMERSON *Soc. & Solit.*, *Work & Days* Wks. (Bohn) III. 65 No sooner is the electric telegraph devised, than gutta-percha, the very material it requires, is found. **1890** H. DRUMMOND in *Life* xv. (1899) 388 Blue star-fish like gutta-percha.

2. (Short for *gutta-percha tree*: see 3.) One of the trees that yield this juice, esp. *Isonandra* (or *Dichopsia*) *Gutta* (N.O. *Euphorbiaceæ*).

1860 L. OLIPHANT *Elgin's Mission China* I. 27 Among them [Singapore trees] are the ebony, sapan, and eagle wood, but more valuable than all the gutta-percha. **1876** HARLEY *Mat. Med.* (ed. 6) 671 Gutta-Percha is a handsome ever-green tree, native of Borneo, Sumatra, and others of the East India Islands.

3. *attrib.* and *Comb.*, as ***gutta-percha-joint, -jointing, -merchant, -sheeting, -tree, -tube***; ***gutta-percha-covered*** adj.; **gutta-percha-tissue**, 'gutta-percha in a very thin leaf, used as a waterproof covering to dressings to prevent evaporation' (*Syd. Soc. Lex.* 1886); **gutta-percha-wire** *Telegraphy*, wire covered with gutta-percha.

1876 PREECE & SIVEWRIGHT *Telegraphy* 236 *Gutta-percha-covered wire. *Ibid.* 241 The mean faults in *gutta percha joints..are [etc.]. *Ibid.* 236 Patience is another virtue in *gutta percha jointing, especially in the open air. **1851** in *Illustr. Lond. News* 5 Aug. (1854) 118 Occupations of the people..*Gutta-percha merchant. **1876** PREECE & SIVEWRIGHT *Telegraphy* 239 The *gutta percha sheeting, as supplied to jointers, should be cut into strips four inches wide. **1898** P. MANSON *Trop. Diseases* i. 30 Take one of the strips of *gutta-percha tissue. **1845** STOCQUELER *Handbk. Brit. India* (1854) 367 The *gutta-percha tree..is entitled to rank as a new genus. **1873** RALFE *Phys. Chem.* 182 The chambers communicate with each other, and into each of which the fluid potass is passed by means of *gutta percha tubes. **1876** PREECE & SIVEWRIGHT *Telegraphy* 235 Out-of-door jointing of *gutta percha wires.

guttate (ˈgʌteɪt), *a.* [ad. L. *guttāt-us* speckled, spotted, f. *gutta* drop.] In the form of drops; furnished with drops, spotted as if by drops.

1826 KIRBY & SP. *Entomol.* IV. 285 Guttate,..sprinkled with guttæ. **1876** RUSKIN *Deucalion* I. xi. 196 The silica..is stuck together just as if it had fallen in drops, which is what I mean by calling Hyalite characteristically 'guttate'. **1887** W. PHILLIPS *Brit. Discomycetes* 415 *Guttate, Guttulate*, furnished with one or more spherical drops; synonym for nucleate.

guttated (gʌˈteɪtɪd), *a.* [ad. L. *guttāt-us* (see prec.) + -ED[1].] Spread about as if in drops or spots.

1727 in BAILEY vol. II. **1822-34** *Good's Study Med.* (ed. 4) IV. 458 In the first or Guttated Variety the patches very seldom extend to the size of a six-pence.

‖**guttatim** (gʌˈteɪtɪm), *adv.* [L. = 'by drops', f. *gutta* drop.] Drop by drop.

1694 SALMON *Bate's Dispens.* (1713) 395/2 Give Fire gradation..so will the Mercury run guttatim into the Recipient. **1727-41** CHAMBERS *Cycl.* s.v. *Guttus*, To take the wine, and sprinkle it, guttatim, drop by drop, upon the victim. **1878** T. BRYANT *Pract. Surg.* (1879) II. 55 Tincture of galls, added guttatim to the urine. **1886** in *Syd. Soc. Lex.*

guttation (gʌˈteɪʃən). *Bot.* [a. G. *guttation* (A. Burgerstein 1887, in *Verh. Zool.-bot. Ges. Wien* XXXVII. 692), f. L. *gutta* drop + -TION.] The exudation of liquid from a plant, esp. from hydathodes in the leaves or from fungal mycelia.

1889 in *Cent. Dict.* **1900** A. J. EWART tr. *Pfeffer's Physiol. Plants* I. vi. 253 Burgerstein uses the special term 'Guttation' when the water escapes through water-pores. **1909** GROOM & BALFOUR tr. *Warming's Oecology of Plants* xxix. 101 Not only in the tropical rain-forest, but also in the temperate countries, are there many plants, especially herbs, exhibiting the phenomenon of guttation. **1932** FULLER & CONARD tr. *Braun-Blanquet's Plant Sociol.* v. 127 Guttation is especially common in warm, moist, tropical forests. **1966** F. M. IRVINE tr. *Lundegårdh's Plant Physiol.* vi. 296 In some trees and in many herbs the active xylem stream usually leaks through the hydathodes or in other ways if transpiration is restricted; this is the guttation phenomenon. Guttation occurs in almost all plants.

‖**gutté** (guteɪ), *a. Her.* Forms: 6 guttie, 7-8 gutte, 7-9 guttee, 9 goutté, goutty, guttée, gutty, 7- gutté. [AF. *gutté* (= F. *goutté*):—L. *guttātus* GUTTATE.] Besprinkled with drops; frequently in AF. phrases, as *gutté de larmes*, *de sang*, etc. ***gutté reversed***: charged with drops having the bulb or globe upwards.

1572 BOSSEWELL *Armorie* II. 88, I mynde here to speake but of the droppes vpon the said Crosse, being blazed Guttie. **1610** GUILLIM *Heraldry* III. xi. (1660) 152 This bearing is called Gutte de Larmes..because they represent Drops of Teares falling. **1655** M. CARTER *Hon. Rediv.* (1660) 157 You are to blazon them differently according to the Colour, as, if Sanguine, then Gutte de Sang. **1727-41** CHAMBERS *Cycl.*, *Gutty*, or *Gutte*, in Heraldry, is when a thing is represented as charged or sprinkled with drops. **1811** *Naval Chron.* XXV. 274 A bear, passant, argent, guttee de sang. **1828-40** BERRY *Encycl. Her.* I, *Gutté reversed.* **1838** *Penny Cycl.* XII. 143/2 When the field, charge, or supporter is covered with goutes, or drops, it is called *gutty*; and if of gold or yellow, *gutty d'or* [etc.]. **1864** BOUTELL *Her. Hist. & Pop.* xxi. §2 (ed. 3) 358 Gu., a bend or, guttée-de-poix, between two mullets arg., pierced of the field.

gutte, obs. form of GOUT *sb.*[1]

†ˈ**gutted**, *a. Her. Obs.* [Anglicized f. GUTTÉ.] = GUTTÉ.

a **1548** HALL *Chron.*, *Edw. IV* (1550) 12 Some had..the guissettes..droped & gutted with red.

gutted (ˈgʌtɪd), *ppl. a.* [f. GUT *v.* + -ED[1].] In senses of the vb.

1842 J. WILSON *Voy. Scotl.* II. 158 While one is filling a basket with her gutted fish. **1862** H. MARRYAT *Year in Sweden* II. 241 We pass by gutted towers, four stories high. **1897** *Daily News* 27 Dec. 5/5 It was some time, however, before the gutted house could be entered.

guttee, variant of GUTTÉ *Her.*

gutter (ˈgʌtə(r)), *sb.*[1] Forms: 3-5 **goter**, 4 **godere, gooter, gotur, guter**, 4-5 **gotere**, 5 **gotyr, guttyr, gutur**, 5-6 **guttur**, 5-7 **guttar, gutture**, 6 **gotter, gutt(e)re**, *Sc.* **gutar, guttour**, 4- **gutter**. [a. OF. *gutiere* (12th c. in Littré), *goutiere* (13th c.), mod.F. *gouttière* fem. (= Pr., Sp. *gotera*, Pg. *goteira*), also OF. *gou(t)tier* masc. (1325 in Godef.), f. *goutte* drop (see GOUT *sb.*[1]).]

†**1. a.** A watercourse, natural or artificial; in later use, a small brook or channel. In 14-15th c. often used to render L. *stillicidium* (shower), *catarractes* (cataract, deluge), etc. *Obs.*

a **1300** *E.E. Psalter* lxxi[i]. 6 He sat douncome..Als goters droppand þe erthe ogaine. **1382** WYCLIF *Gen.* viii. 2 The wellys of the see and the goterys of heuene ben closid. **1387** TREVISA *Higden* (Rolls) I. 181 þe ryuer Danubius..is..i-ladde in to dyuerse places of þe cite by goteres [L. *canalibus*] vnder erþe. **1398** —— *Barth. De P.R.* XIII. xvi. (Tollem. MS.), To renewe and refresche pondes fresche water is lad and brouȝte by goderes [**1495** gutters] condites and pipes. *c* **1440** *Promp. Parv.* 206/1 Gotere vndyr þe grownde, *cataduppa, cataracta.* *c* **1475** *Pict. Voc.* in Wr.-Wülcker 799/44 *Hic gurges*, a gotyr. **1551** TURNER *Herbal* I. B vij b, Henbayne..groweth..about guttures and ditches. **1591** SYLVESTER *Du Bartas* I. ii. 564 Some standing Lake Which neighbour Mountains with their gutters make. **1601** HOLLAND *Pliny* I. 137 He [Tigris] takes his way vnder the earth through certain blinde gutters. **1675** *Providence* (Rhode Isl.) *Rec.* (1893) IV. 39 On ye East sid of a little gutter on ye south side of a swompe. **1785** BURNS *Holy Fair* vii, Swankies young, in braw braid-claith, Are springin owre the gutters. **1797** B. TRUMBULL *Hist. Connecticut* I. 24 In the low lands, on the banks of the rivers, by the brooks and gutters, there was a variety and plenty of grapes. **1855** THOREAU *Cape Cod* iii. (1894) 40 We crossed a brook.. called Jeremiah's Gutter.

b. A furrow or track made by running water.

1586 D. ROWLAND tr. *H. de Mendoza's Lazarillo* (1677) D 2 a, A great wide Gutter which the raine had made. **1637** RUTHERFORD *Lett.* cxxxviii. (1894) 267 Prisoners of hope must run to Christ, with the gutters that tears have made on their cheeks. **1704** ADDISON *Italy* (1705) 164 The rude Prospects of many Rocks rising one above another, of the deep Gutters worn in the Sides of 'em by the Torrents of Rain [etc.]. **1859** GEO. ELIOT *A. Bede* v, There had been some heavy storms of rain, and the water lay in deep gutters on the sides of the gravel-walks.

c. *Austral. gold-mining.* The lower part of the channel of an old river of the Tertiary period containing auriferous deposits.

1856 S. DAVISON *Let.* 13 Aug. in W. B. Clarke *Res. S. Gold Fields N.S.W.* (1860) iv. 50 Pebble-covered local gold in evenly-spread beds or linear troughs of leads or gutters. **1864** J. ROGERS *New Rush* 55 Duffers are so common And golden gutters rare. **1888** F. HUME *Mad. Midas* I. i, The gutter proved remunerative enough to keep the mine going, and pay all the men.

2. A shallow trough fixed under the eaves of a roof, or a channel running between two sloping roofs, to carry off the rain-water.

1354 *Mem. Ripon* (Surtees) III. 92 In mercede j hominis mundantis guteres circa ecclesiam pro ij vicibus 6*d.* **1382** WYCLIF *2 Sam.* v. 8 The goters of the hows eues. **1472** *Mem. Ripon* (Surtees) III. 246, 12*d.* solut. pro reparacione unius guttur plumb. cameræ. **1522** *Churchw. Acc. St. Giles, Reading* 16 Paid to the plumer for metal to Sowder the gutters iij[s] iiij[d]. **1657** R. LIGON *Barbadoes* (1673) 29 Water they save likewise from their houses, by gutters at the eves, which carry it down to cisterns. **1789** P. SMYTH tr. *Aldrich's Archit.* (1818) 85 Experience has taught men to carry off the droppings from their shelving roofs by placing gutters in them. **1823** P. NICHOLSON *Pract. Build.* 220 Bridged Gutters—Gutters made with boards, supported below with bearers, and covered over with lead. **1861** DUTTON COOK *P. Foster's D.* iii, Dax's window opened on to a gutter.

3. a. A hollowed channel running at the side or (less commonly) along the middle of a street, to carry away the surface water.

1408 *Durham Acc. Roll* in *Eng. Hist. Rev.* XIV. 517 Soluta..laborariis..facientibus unam gutteram lapideam et illam in dicto Watergate ponentibus. **1449–50** *Durham Acc. Rolls* (Surtees) 276 Pro emendacione et le pavyng j gutter juxta capellam, iijs. iiij*d.* **1553** in Halliwell *Shaks.* (1887) II. 141 That every tenaunt do scour and kep cleane ther gutteres or dyches in the same lane. **1615** J. STEPHENS *Satyr. Ess.* 165 Hee cannot doe so much good as a Fellow that sweepes gutters. **1622** CALLIS *Stat. Sewers* (1647) 58 A Gutter is of a less size, and of a narrower passage and current then a Sewer is; and as I take it, a Gutter is the diminutive of a Sewer. **1712** ADDISON *Spect.* No. 317 ¶9 Went to the Club. Like to have faln into a Gutter. **1834** *West Ind. Sketch Bk.* II. 2 Flagstones which slope from the houses towards the middle of the streets to form a gutter. **1840** BARHAM *Ingol. Leg.* Ser. I. *Cynotaph, note,* All bare and exposed to the midnight dews Reclined in a gutter we found him. **1898** ZANGWILL *Dreamers Ghetto* iv. 128 The gutters run blood.

b. *fig.* Taken as the typical haunt of persons, esp. children, of low birth or breeding.

c **1846** W. E. FORSTER in T. W. Reid *Life* (1888) I. vi. 169, I would strive..to get the children of the working classes out of the gutter, by educating them. **1882** MISS BRADDON *Mt. Royal* I. iii. 95 The women I have cared for in days gone by have hardly got over their early affinity with the gutter. **1886** BESANT *Childr. Gibeon* I. i, To take a girl out of the gutter and pretend that she is a lady. **1890** HALL CAINE *Bondman* II. i, If he came to die in the gutter, who should say that it had not served him right? **1896** F. HALL in *Nation* (N.Y.) LXII. 234/2 Slang of the slums and the gutter.

c. A channel forming a receptacle for dirt or filth; a sink. *lit.* and *fig.* Now *dial.*

c **1440** *Promp. Parv.* 206/2 Gotere, *ad purgandum feces coquine.* *a* **1533** LD. BERNERS *Gold. Bk. M. Aurel.* Let. ii. (1536) 102 Thou Rome shalte be the syncke and gutter of the fylthynes of Asye. **1601** CORNWALLIS *Ess.* II. xxix. (1631) 36 A true thing out of the gutter of a false throat can hardly escape corrupting. **1718** T. GORDON *Cordial Low Spirits* 30 Girding it 'till you have quite stopped up the Gutter through which the aforesaid excrements issue. *a* **1825** FORBY *Voc. E. Anglia, Gutter, Gutter-hole,* a sink or kennel. The general sense of gutter is a passage for water particularly, but not exclusively, from the roofs of houses. But with us the idea of filth is inseparable from it.

d. Mud, filth. Chiefly *Sc.* (only *pl.*).

1785 R. FORBES *Poems Buchan Dial.* 28 Sae smear'd wi' gutters was his buik, He stinket in his hide. *a* **1825** FORBY *Voc. E. Anglia, Gutter-slush, gutter,* kennel dirt. 'She fell down in the street, and her clothes were all over nothing but gutter.' **1866** MITCHELL *Hist. Montrose* xxii. 162 She quenched his oratory with a mouthful of gutters.

4. A shallow trough or open conduit or pipe for the outflow of fluid.

1657 R. LIGON *Barbadoes* (1673) 90 Under the rollers, there is a receiver..into which the liquor falls, and..runs under ground in a Pipe or gutter of lead. **1757** A. COOPER *Distiller* I. xvi. (1760) 74 By placing in the middle of the tub a wooden Pipe or Gutter. **1800** tr. *Lagrange's Chem.* I. 417 Sometimes the trunk of a fir-tree, hollowed out, so as to form a kind of gutter, is placed in an inclined position. **1872** ELLACOMBE *Bell of Ch.* in *Ch. Bells Devon* i. 204 The fused metal is carried at once from the furnace to the pit by means of a series of gutters.

†5. a. A groove or elongated hollow in an animal or vegetable body. *Obs.* in gen. sense.

1553 UDALL *Geminus' Anat.* Biij b/2 Thys concauite or dyche or gutter [of the Nose]. **1578** LYTE *Dodoens* VI. xl. 709 A rough harde stone, full of creastes and gutters, within whiche is a kernell lyke an Almonde. **1607** TOPSELL *Four-f. Beasts* (1658) 331 All which veins are easie enough to know, because that every one lyeth in a little gutter. **1607** MARKHAM *Caval.* II. (1617) 8 His buttocke round, plumpe, and full, without either gutter or deuision of ioynts. **1616** READ *Descr. Body Man* 20 The sinus of the gutture of the arme receiuing the cubit. **1712** tr. *Pomet's Hist. Drugs* I. 42 These Seeds are separated from one another by Leaves folded into a Gutter.

†b. *spec. Venery.* One of the grooves in the 'beam' of a hart's 'head'. *Obs.*

1576 TURBERV. *Venerie* 53 The thing that beareth the Antliers, Royals, and toppes, ought to be called the beame, and the little clyffes or streakes therein are called gutters. *a* **1700** B. E. *Dict. Cant. Crew, Gutters,* the little Streak in a Deer's Beam.

c. *Ent.* Applied to certain folds on the hinder wings of lepidoptera.

1828 STARK *Elem. Nat. Hist.* II. 360 Internal margin of the lower wings arched and projecting over the abdomen to form a gutter.

6. A groove or channel of artificial formation. Now only *techn.*

1555 EDEN *Decades* 159 They are curiously buylded with many pleasaunt diuises as turrettes, portals, gutters. **1594** PLAT *Jewell-ho.* III. 23 A pistoll..hauing eight gutters somewhat deepe in the inside of the barrell. **1611** COTGR., *Coulisse d'un arbaleste,* the hollow furrow wherein the arrow lyes; we call it, the gutter, or chace. **1659** WILLSFORD *Scales Comm., Archit.* 31 The Dorick order,..this Column..more adorned then the last, to which some adde Flutings, or gutters. **1682** *Lond. Gaz.* No. 1684/4 A black brown Gelding..three Gutters cut in his Hoof. **1833** J. HOLLAND *Manuf. Metal* II. 106 The workman..ploughs out the gutter for the lodgment of the barrel [of a gun]. **1861** WYNTER *Soc. Bees* 187 The stamping shop, where girls, with inconceivable rapidity, place each wire beneath a die, and stamp exactly in the middle thereof two eyes, and two channels, or gutters as they are termed. **1888** *Sheffield Gloss., Gutter,* a hollow or groove running down the centre of a knife spring.

7. In *Printing* = *gutter-stick* (see 8). Also in *Bookbinding,* 'the white space between the pages of a book' (Barrère and Leland *Slang,* 1889).

1841 SAVAGE *Dict. Printing* s.v., We now mean by the term Gutter, the piece of furniture that separates two adjoining pages in a chase, as in an octavo that between pages 1 and 16, in a duodecimo that between pages 1 and 24 and so on. **1888** JACOBI *Printers' Voc., Gutter,* the 'back' margin or furniture of a sheet. This is the part of a sheet which when folded falls in the back of the book.

8. a. *attrib.* and *Comb.*, as ***gutter-boy, -brat, -canal, channel, -girl, -hole, -level, -lout, -mongrel, -snippet, spout, stone, -sweeping, water, waterway, work; gutter-bred, -draggled, -gorging, -grubbing, -like*** adjs.; ***gutter-wise*** adv.; **gutter-bearer**, 'the sort of joist upon which the boarding for a gutter is laid' (*Dict. Archit.* 1852); **gutter-bird**, the sparrow, hence *fig.*, a disreputable person; **gutter-board**, a board forming the foundation on which is laid the lining-material forming the gutter itself; **gutter-child**, a child such as haunts the street gutters, one of low birth or breeding; **gutter-crawling** *vbl. sb.*, the action of driving a car, etc., slowly along a road close to the pavement and attempting to entice into it women, esp. prostitutes (cf. *kerb-crawling*); **gutter-drift** = sense 1 c; **gutter-flag** *Austral.* (see quot.); **gutter-flanged** *a.*, having a flange shaped like a gutter; **†gutter lane** *slang,* the throat, gullet; **gutter-ledge** *Naut.* (see quot.); **gutter-man**, (*a*) a street vendor of cheap jewellery, fancy articles, toys, etc.; (*b*) (*U.S.*) *Logging,* one who removes underbrush, fallen trees, and other obstacles in making a gutter road; (*c*) one who cleans out the gutters of buildings; **†gutter-master**, (presumably) one who cleans out gutters; hence ***gutter-mastership***; **gutter-member** *Arch.*, a member made by decorating the outside face of a gutter with regularly spaced ornaments; **gutter-merchant** = *gutter-man*; **gutter plane**, a moulding-plane with a semi-cylindrical sole used in planing out gutters (Knight *Dict. Mech.* Suppl. 1884); **gutter-plate** *Ship-building* (see quots.); **gutter road**, the path or track followed in skidding logs (*Terms Foresty & Logging,* 1905); **gutter-snippet**, app. meant as a dim. of GUTTER-SNIPE; **gutter-sparrow** = *gutter-bird*; **gutter-splint**, a splint moulded to the shape of the limb; **gutter-stall**, the stall of a gutter-man; **gutter-stick** *Printing,* one of the pieces of furniture which separate pages in a form; **gutter-tree**, the Wild Cornel or Dogwood, *Cornus sanguinea* (*Syd. Soc. Lex.*); **gutter-way**, (*a*) = GUTTER *sb.*[1] 2; (*b*) = *gutter waterway*; **†gutter window**, ? a window opening on to a gutter. Also GUTTER-BLOOD, -SNIPE, -TILE, etc.

1896 *Westm. Gaz.* 18 Feb. 5/2 They seem to bear the same relation to ordinary dogs as the lowest *gutter-bird does to a respectable man. **1899** *Ibid.* 14 Mar. 2/3 The sparrow has a strong idea in his impudent little head that everything belongs to him... This..will not do for such a refined city as Boston, and so the fiat has gone forth against the little gutter bird. **1703** T. N. *City & C. Purchaser* 162 In these Plain-tile-gutters, there is a *Gutter-board laid which raises them. **1852** *Dict. Archit., Gutter-board.* **1901** G. K. CHESTERTON *Defendant* 15 We rate the *gutter-boys for their immorality. **1962** K. ORVIS *Damned & Destroyed* xii. 80 He was a *gutter-brat. **1877** RUSKIN *Fors Clav.* VII. lxxvi. 108 Any young *gutter-bred black-guard. **1946** KOESTLER *Thieves in Night* I. iii. 23 The *gutter-canal that ran along the middle of the street as the serpent's inverted spine. **1564–78** BULLEYN *Dial. agst. Pest.* (1886) 45 *Gutter chanilles uncleane kept. **1870** *Public Opinion* 16 July 57 It is not these *gutter children alone for whom compulsion is wanted. **1890** 'ROLF BOLDREWOOD' *Miner's Right* (1899) 102/2 There were no poor in rags, no houseless women, no aged paupers, no gutter children, no street boys, no out-casts. **1948** MENCKEN *Amer. Lang.* Suppl. I. vi. 504 *Gutter-crawling is practised by mashers who run close to the sidewalk, hoping to pick up light-headed girls. **1968** *Courier-Mail* (Brisbane) 30 Nov. 3/5 Thirty-five men were fined..on 'guttercrawling' charges... The charges, under an Act promulgated last December alleged the men 'loitered either to be accosted by a prostitute or for the purpose of inviting or soliciting any female to prostitute herself for pecuniary reward'. **1894** DU MAURIER *Trilby* I. 95 Her sordid, mercenary, little *gutter-draggled soul. **1887** H. H. HOWORTH *Mammoth & Flood* 372 Numerous remains of vegetation, we are told, occur in the *gutter-drift in Victoria. **1869** R. B. SMYTH *Goldf. Victoria* 612 *Gutter-flags—Flags fixed on the surface to denote where the course of gutter or lead underground has been discovered. **1869** SIR E. REED *Shipbuild.* ii. 20 To roll the *gutter-flanged plate to the required form. **1909** *Daily Chron.* 13 Nov. 3/1 A devoted priest, a noble *gutter-girl,..—these are Mrs. Baillie Saunders's stock-in-trade. **1598** SYLVESTER *Du Bartas* II. i. I. *Eden* 116 *Gutter-gorging durty muds. **1795** COLERIDGE *Lett.* (1895) 148 O God! that such a mind should fall in love with that low, dirty, *gutter-grubbing trull, Worldly Prudence! **1819** *Blackw. Mag.* V. 636 Who having dined abroad, returning late, Besplash your stockings in the *gutter-hole. *a* **1825** FORBY *Voc. E. Anglia, Gutter, Gutter-hole,* a sink or kennel. **1684** S. G. *Angl. Speculum* 483 All goeth down *Gutter-lane (a small lane in the City). Appliable to great Gluttons and Drunkards. *a* **1700** B. E. *Dict. Cant. Crew, Suit and Cloak, good store of..Liquor,* let down Gutter-lane. **1769–80** FALCONER *Dict. Marine,* **Gutter-ledge,* a cross bar laid along the middle of a large hatchway in some vessels, to support the covers, and enable them the better to sustain any weighty body. **1880** *Victorian Rev.* 2 Feb. 656 The gutters had virtually sucked them dry, and had left no gold worth having above the *gutter-level. **1776** E. MENDES DA COSTA *Conchol.* v. 117 The scoop (sinus) is the hollowed, or *gutter-like process placed side-ways of the beak, and lower down on the very lip. **1926** D. H. LAWRENCE *Plumed Serp.* i. 8 A real *gutter-lout came to look at their counterslips. **1892** *Pall Mall G.* 8 Apr. 6/1 For the past week the *gutter-men have been driving a brisk trade in Boat Race favours. **1904** *Dialect Notes* II. 397 *Gutterman,* a term used in logging camps. **1921** *Dict. Occup. Terms* (1927) §970 *Roofman; gutterman;* sweeps roofs and removes dirt and other obstruction from guttering, rain pipes, etc., of large buildings. **1607** MARSTON *What you will* III. i, Francisco Soranzo and perfumer and muscat, and *gutter maister. *Ibid.*, If I make you not loose your office of *gutter Maister-ship, and you bee Skauenger next yeare well. **1896** *Daily News* 4 Aug. 3/4 Fine weather brings people out, and enables the '*gutter merchant' to display his stock-in-trade. *a* **1930** D. H. LAWRENCE *Phoenix* (1936) 21 Not fit to be trusted with any dog but a *gutter-mongrel. **1869** SIR E. REED *Shipbuild.* i. 10 The *gutter-plates on the top of the floors, forming the flat central keelson. **1874** THEARLE *Naval Archit.* 72 It has been a common practice to place no longitudinal tie between the outer keel and the longitudinal combination of plates and angle irons on the top of the floors, known as the gutter plate and keelson. **1891** R. KIPLING *Light that failed* viii, She's a dissolute little scarecrow,—a *gutter-snippet and nothing more. **1931** S. BECKETT *Proust* 61 But he does not proceed pari passu with ..the Parnassians to the ineffable gutter-snippets of François Coppée. **1890** *Tablet* 20 Dec. 961 He denounced his late comrades as *gutter-sparrows. **1919** W. DEEPING *Second Youth* xxiv. 203 At his ease in a long cane chair, his left arm still in a *gutter-splint. **1957** *Encycl. Brit.* IX. 577/2 Aluminium gutter splints are of value in some cases [of fracture] on account of their malleability and translucence to X-rays. **1647** SANDERSON *Serm.* (1681) II. 201 Would any wise man..trust to a *gutter-spout to quench his thirst, when he might go to a spring? **1839** LONGF. *Hyperion* IV. iii, Then the whole scene changed, and he thought himself a monk's-head on a gutter-spout. **1889** A. T. PASK *Eyes Thames* 166 Let us look again at the butcher's shop, and then at the *gutter stalls. **1683** MOXON *Printing* §8. 29 *Gutter-sticks..are used to set between Pages on either side the Crosses... They have a Groove, or Gutter laid on the upper side of them, as well that the Water may drain away when the Form is Washed or Rinced, as that they should not Print, when through the tenderness of the Tinpan, the Plattin presses it and the Paper lower than ordinary. **1530** PALSGR. 228/1 *Guttar stone. **1954** W. FAULKNER *Fable* (1955) 26 The African regiment recruited from the prison- and *gutter-sweepings of Europe. **1730** A. GORDON *Maffei's Amphith.* 361 A lesser Conduit..carried the *Gutter-Water of several Streets. **1874** THEARLE *Naval Archit.* 123 In some cases, a *gutter waterway is fitted on the inside of the stanchions, the wood waterway being between the side plating and gutter waterway. **1908** *Daily Chron.* 19 Aug. 3/4 Choked *gutter-ways, creepers stuffed with unsightly straw ..induced him..to order that the sparrow nests should be removed from the walls and eaves of his house. **1923** *Man. Seamanship* II. 280 To drain water from the decks.. scuppers are fitted... These are led from the gutter-ways. **1620** J. DOUGHTY in *Lismore Papers* (1887) Ser. II. II. 263 When he was in his howse [he] gote out att a *gutter window and soe escaped. **1679** BEDLOE *Popish Plot* 24 They ran together out at the Gutter-window. **1657** W. COLES *Adam in Eden* xvii. 35 A..peece of soft wax, made a little hollow, *gutter-wise. **1611** COTGR., *Caneleure,*..*gutter-worke (in stone, or timber).

b. *attrib.* passing into *adj.* Brought up in or appropriate to the gutter; of a low or disreputable character. (Freq. in *gutter press, gutter journalism,* etc.)

1849 J. O. O'CONNELL *Recoll. Parl. Career* I. v. 104 Feargus O'Connor carried the election..he was everywhere and everything;—speechifier,..gutter-agent, mob leader. **1851** D. JERROLD *St. Giles* vii. 64 Could any of his gutter companions boast such greatness? **1884** VICE-ADM. MAXSE in *Pall Mall G.* 4 Mar. 2/1 All the gutter epithets which have been coined to express baffled malice and impotence. **1888** *Sat. Rev.* 20 Oct. 450/2 Evident..to any person who..has had some experience of the ways of gutter journalism. *Ibid.*, The gutter journalist. **1889** *Ibid.* 16 Nov. 549/1 Mr. Conybeare had, according to a gutter journal, charged Sir Edward with saying..that [etc.]. **1889** SWINBURNE *Study B. Jonson* 70 The accents of some gutter gaolbird. **1890** *Times* 12 Mar. 5/1 The gutter language used by the Portuguese Republican Press. **1892** SWINBURNE *Stud. Prose & Poet.* (1894) 235 The gutter slang of those reactionary dis-unionists. **1899** *Times* (weekly ed.) 520/2 The gutter Press of Paris. **1900** J. LONDON *Let.* 1 Oct. (1966) 112 How different from the gutter attack of Robert Buchanan on Kipling and Besant! **1940** 'G. ORWELL' *Inside Whale* 126 There is no clear reason why every adventure story should necessarily be mixed up with snobbishness and gutter patriotism. **1941** AUDEN *New Year Let.* I. 24 Conscious *Catullus,* who made all His gutter-language musical. **1953** *Manch. Guardian Weekly* 10 Dec. 4/4 Mr. Truman, a graduate of the Pendergast school of gutter politics, called the Red issue a 'red herring'. **1955** J. THOMAS *No Banners* xviii. 165 He found himself cursing under his breath, using foul Cockney gutter-slang that normally would have appalled him. **1957** 'P. QUENTIN' *Suspicious Circ.* viii. 87 One of..those terrible gutter magazines which make fortunes unearthing people's private lives. **1958** WODEHOUSE *Cocktail Time* v. 45 To..sell this information to the gutter press for what it will fetch. **1959** *Daily Tel.* 9 Apr. 22/4 One of the cheapest forms of gutter electioneering.

gutter ('gʌtə(r)), *sb.*[2] [f. GUT *v.* + -ER[1].] One who guts.

1. One employed in disembowelling fish or animals. Also *fig.*

1780 YOUNG *Tour Irel.* I. 148, Fishermen 90, Gutters 40. **1851** C. CIST *Sk. Cincinnati* 280 Here the animal falls into the hands of the gutter who tears out the inside, stripping at the rate of three hogs to the minute. **1854** MILLER *Sch. & Schm.* (1858) 43 Bevies of young women employed as gutters. **1883** *Chamb. Jrnl.* 310 The wives and daughters [of the fishermen] are gutters or packers or salters. **1963** *Guardian* 18 Sept. 10/6 Is it possible that..there is a clever summary in the last few pages..making the document easy work for an accomplished 'gutter' which I feel sure Mr Wilson is?

2. One who guts buildings.

a **1734** NORTH *Exam.* II. iv. §93 (1740) 277 He was a great Inquisitor of Priests and Jesuits, and Gutter (as the Term was for Stripping) of Popish Chapels.

gutter ('gʌtə(r)), *v.* [f. GUTTER *sb.*[1]]

1. a. *trans.* To make gutters in; to furnish with gutters; to channel or furrow with streams, tears, or the like.

1387 *Charters St. Giles* (1859) p. x, Alswa betwene the chapellis, guteryt with hewyn stane to cast the watir owte, and to save the werc fro the watir. **1634–5** BRERETON *Trav.* (Chetham Soc.) 149 There is meadow land and bog, which being guttered ditched and drained..will be good and rich meadow. **1638** SANDYS *Job* xvi. 33 My cheeks are gutterd with my fretting teares. **1640** BP. H. KING *Serm.* 51 Her wrinckled face, guttered with the Teares of her decay. **1697** DRYDEN *Virg. Georg.* IV. 418 A narrow Flooring, gutter'd, wall'd, and til'd. **1712** J. JAMES tr. *Le Blond's Gardening* 41 To discharge the Wet that might otherwise gutter the Walks. **1796** *Trans. Soc. Arts* XIV. 122 The field..has been remarkably well drained and guttered. **1832** J. HODGSON in J. Raine *Mem.* (1858) II. 269 Steps..once neatly fluted but now guttered by the weather. **1893** *Wiltsh. Gloss.*, *Gutter*, to drain land with open drains.

†**b.** To carry off (water) by means of gutters.

c **1420** *Pallad. on Husb.* XII. 289 Transplauntynge hem is best at yeeris too, So gutteryng [so *MS. Bodl.*] the water from hem shelue; Yf water stonde on hem, they beth fordo.

2. *intr.* Of water: To form gutters or gullies.

1632 LITHGOW *Trav.* VI. 282 The Brooke Cedron (which guttereth through the valley). **1670** NARBOROUGH in *Acc. Sev. Late Voy.* I. (1694) 69, I looked very carefully in Gullies, and places where Water had guttered.

3. To flow in streams, to stream *down*.

1583 STANYHURST *Æneis* IV. (Arb.) 111 His mynd vnuariant doth stand, tears vaynelye doe gutter. **1622** MABBE tr. *Aleman's Guzman d'Alf.* I. 72 That abundance of teares which fell guttering downe his cheekes. **1697** DRYDEN *Virg. Æn.* V. 261 Their lab'ring sides Are swell'd, and Sweat runs gutt'ring down in Tides. **1699** GARTH *Dispens.* V. Wks. (1771) 75 Tears of amber guttered down his cheeks. **1863** HAWTHORNE *Our Old Home* (1883) I. 331 You may see the young housewife, before the shower is ended, letting the raindrops gutter down her visage. **1863** WHYTE MELVILLE *Gladiators* III. 287 They must be fond of gold who can catch it by handfuls, guttering down like this in streams of fire. **1891** E. PHILLPOTTS *Folly & Fresh Air* vii. 117 A little stream that guttered down the hill-side.

†**4.** *trans.* To discharge in streams. *Obs. rare.*

a **1618** SYLVESTER *Job* III. 346 My waies were bath'd in butter And Rocks about mee Rolls of Oyle did gutter. **1622** MABBE tr. *Aleman's Guzman d'Alf.* II. 191 Darke and thicke clouds..guttered downe vpon vs huge and great drops of raine.

5. *intr.* Of a candle: To melt away rapidly by its becoming channelled on one side and the tallow or wax pouring down; to sweal. Also with *down*, *out*. (The chief current sense.)

1706 PHILLIPS (ed. Kersey), To *Gutter*, to sweal, or run, as a candle sometimes does. **1753** *Phil. Trans.* XLVIII. 236 The external coat, thus made, prevents them from guttering. **1840** DICKENS *Barn. Rudge* lv, The candles flickered and guttered down. **1875** HOWELLS *Foregone Concl.* iv. 149 A crown of..red formed upon the..wick, which toppled over in the socket and guttered out with a sharp hiss.

quasi-*trans.* **1891** BARING-GOULD *Troubadour-Land* vi. 68 My candle..guttered itself in no time into the tray of the candlestick.

transf. **1869** G. MEREDITH *Let.* 27 Dec. (1970) I. 409, I have turned Wendell Phillips like a drenching fireman's hose on a parson, and made him sputter and gutter and go to his wife to trim his wick. **1872** T. HARDY *Under Greenwood Tree* I. vii, With..a nose guttering like a candle. **1917** T. S. ELIOT *Prufrock* 22 My self-possession flares up for a second... My self-possession gutters; we are really in the dark.

6. *to gutter along*: to drag existence along 'in the gutter'. *nonce-use.*

1883 P. S. ROBINSON *Sinners & Saints* 44 They might have guttered along in helpless poverty..till old age found them in a workhouse.

gutteral, obs. form of GUTTURAL.

gutter-blood ('gʌtəblʌd). *Sc.* A base-born or low-bred person; one of the rabble.

1818 SCOTT *Hrt. Midl.* xviii, The gutter-bloods! and deil a gentleman amang them. **1825–80** in JAMIESON. **1868** E. YATES *Rock Ahead* III. vii, A dozen young gutter-bloods, street-boys, would have been round him in a moment.

Hence '**gutter-blooded** *a.*, base-born.

1829 SCOTT *Anne of G.* xiii, The gift he hath for chastising the gutter-blooded citizens of a free town.

guttered ('gʌtəd), *ppl. a.* [f. GUTTER *sb.*[1] and *v.* + -ED.]

1. Furrowed; grooved; fluted; gullied.

1562 TURNER *Herbal* II. 88 Euery lefe [of the Pine tree] is ..furrowed or guttered as sum kynde of yong grasse is. **1604** SHAKS. *Oth.* II. i. 69 The gutter'd Rockes, and Congregated Sands. **1662** GERBIER *Princ.* (1665) 5 The Guttered Colombs. **1678** YOUNG *Serm. at Whitehall* 29 Dec. 24 We will not advert the Gutter'd Cheeks, and Passionate Mournings..of the Primitive Penitents. **1696** DERHAM *Artificial Clock-m.* 3 The guttered Wheel, with Iron spikes at the bottom, in which the line of ordinary House-Clocks doth run, is called the Pully. **1730–46** THOMSON *Autumn* 816 The gutter'd rocks and mazy-running clefts. **1884** *Harper's Mag.* Nov. 850/2 Jehan and Pierre have greased guttered boards, which they slip under the keel. **1895** *Outing* (U.S.) XXVII. 202/1 Skate blades deeply grooved, or 'guttered', as it is termed.

2. Of a candle (see GUTTER *v.* 5).

1860 GEO. ELLIOT *Mill on Fl.* I. viii, Looking as irrelevant to the daylight as a last night's guttered candle. **1863** W. LANCASTER *Praeterita* 38 We have not much more light to spend, Two guttered ends of tallow.

3. Furnished with or having gutters.

1797 HOLCROFT tr. *Stolberg's Trav.* (ed. 2) III. lxxi. 76 The guttered pent-houses..are large.

guttering ('gʌtərɪŋ), *vbl. sb.* [f. GUTTER *sb.*[1] and *v.* + -ING[1].]

1. Trenching, draining. Also *attrib.* Now *dial.*

c **1420** *Pallad. on Husb.* VI. 60 Now as the treen beth cladde in her estate ffor gutteryng to hewe is and to hent. **1789** *Trans. Soc. Arts* VII. 63, I procured a draining or guttering plough. **1883** in *West Somerset Gloss.*

2. a. The construction of gutters.

1703 T. N. *City & C. Purchaser* 163 *Guttering*, In Carpentry, is commonly done by the Lineal Foot. **1825** J. NICHOLSON *Operat. Mechanic* 635 Sheet-lead used in roofing and guttering is commonly between 7 and 12 lbs. to the square foot.

b. *concr.* The material used for gutters; gutters collectively. Also *U.S. Mining* (see quot. 1883).

1703 T. N. *City & C. Purchaser* 98 Lintelling, Guttering, Cornish..&c. at so much per Foot. **1883** GRESLEY *Gloss. Coal Mining*, *Guttering* (Pa.), a channel or pipe cut along the side of a pit shaft to conduct the water not tubbed back into a lodge or sump. **1886** *Daily News* 28 Dec. 6/1 Numerous houses were stripped of their guttering.

3. The making of grooves or furrows: **a.** as a process in manufacture; **b.** as an accidental result.

1833 J. HOLLAND *Manuf. Metal* II. 359 During the foregoing operations the needles have severally become more or less crooked, especially in the guttering by hand. **1877** *Const. & Manuf. Ordnance* xii. 299 Scoring or guttering was caused by the rush of gas round the projectile. **1934** *Jrnl. R. Aeronaut. Soc.* XXXVIII. 326 This raises the working temperature of the former and may eventually cause 'blow past' of the gases when the valve should normally be closed, finally leading to valve burning or 'guttering'. **1948** *Shell Aviation News* CXIX. 17/2 The condition of the valve face was good, and there were no signs of definite guttering or blow-by.

4. Of a candle (see GUTTER *v.* 5); also *concr.* the melted tallow or wax which runs down.

1784–9 M. MADAN *Persius* (1795) 159 *note*, They stuck up candles or lamps, in their windows..and by their flaring and guttering they made the frames of the windows on which they stood all over grease. **1888** BURGON *Lives 12 Gd. Men* II. xi. 316 The guttering from the wax candle..invaded his plate.

guttering ('gʌtərɪŋ), *ppl. a.* [f. GUTTER *v.* + -ING[2].] That gutters.

1697 DRYDEN *Virg. Æn.* III. 871 From his bor'd Eye the gutt'ring Blood he laves. **1862** G. P. SCROPE *Volcanos* 68 A run of wax or tallow in a 'guttering' candle. **1896** A. MORRISON *Child of the Jago* 10 A little heap of guttering grease, not long ago a candle.

gutterling ('gʌtəlɪŋ). [f. GUTTER *sb.*[1] + -LING.] One bred in a gutter; one of the 'lower orders'. Also *attrib.* = GUTTER *sb.*[1] 8 b.

1846 MRS. GORE *Sk. Eng. Charac.* (1852) 115 After a week's experience as a gutterling of the fashionable world. **1896** *B'ham Weekly Post* 21 Mar. 4/8, I hate this gutterling assault on..a true poet, who has given us of his best.

gutter-snipe ('gʌtəsnaɪp). Cf. *gutter-bird*.

1. a. *dial.* The common snipe, *Gallinago cælestis* (*Northumbld. Gloss.* 1893). **b.** The common American or Wilson's snipe, *Gallinago wilsoni* or *delicata*.

(Mr. W. H. Patterson writes from Belfast that he has known the word 'Guttery-snipe' in Ireland since 1850, but it is not in common use; a synonym is *mire snipe*.)

1874 R. RIDGWAY *Birds Ill.* in *Annals Lyceum N.Y.* X. 383 *G[allinago] gallinaria*..var. *Wilsonii*..Common Snipe; Gutter Snipe; English Snipe.

2. a. A gatherer of refuse, such as rags and paper, from street gutters.

1869 *Echo* 11 Feb., One of the female gutter-snipes who gain a precarious living by hunting for 'unconsidered trifles' in the streets of Paris. **1898** *N.B. Daily Mail* 24 Sept. 2 It is about twelve years since I first scraped an acquaintance with the Glasgow guttersnipe.

b. A child brought up 'in the gutter'; one of the lowest class; an urchin. Also *attrib.* and as *adj.*

c **1869** 'MARK TWAIN' *Sk. New & Old* (1875) 70 Unfurl yourselves under my banner, noble savages, illustrious guttersnipes. **1882** L. WINGFIELD *Gehenna* II. iii. 71 This fellow, born and bred a guttersnipe, was exceedingly romantic. **1884** *Century Mag.* XXVIII. 557 The gutter-snipes and Arabs of the streets of Gravesend. **1907** *Daily Chron.* 17 May 3/6 Harry Lauder, in his Glasgow gutter-snipe character. **1961** *Encounter* Mar. 72/1 The guttersnipe ecstasies of [Henry Miller's *Tropic of*] *Capricorn*.

c. (See quot. 1877.) *U.S.*

1857 UNDERHILL & THOMSON *Elephant Club* 57 He belongs to a class of beings in New York..known by the ornithological appelation of 'gutter-snipes'. **1870** J. K. MEDBERY *Men & Myst. Wall St.* 136 Gutter snipes. Curbstone brokers. **1877** BARTLETT *Dict. Amer.* (ed. 4), *Gutter-snipes*, a Wall Street term for brokers who do business chiefly on the sidewalk or in the street, and who are not members of the Stock Exchange. **1942** BERREY & VAN DEN BARK *Amer. Thes. Slang* §563/4 *Guttersnipe*, one who operates in a curb market.

3. *Printing.* (*U.S.*) (See quot.)

1871 *Amer. Encycl. Printing* (ed. Ringwalt), *Gutter-snipe*, a small and narrow printed bill or poster, which is usually pasted on curbstones.

'**gutter-tile.** A tile used in the construction of gutters, or to line the 'valleys' of a roof.

1477 *Act 17 Edw. IV*, c. 4 Pleintile..thaktile, roftile, ou crestile, cornertile & guttertile. *a* **1680** BUTLER *Rem.* (1759) I. 92 Puss, wrapt warm in his own native Furs, Dreamt softly of as soft and warm Amours, Of making Galantry in Gutter-tiles. **1703** MOXON *Mech. Exerc.* 240 These Gutter Tiles are in length ten Inches and an half. **1842–59** GWILT *Archit.* II. ii. x. (ed. 4) 505 Gutter tiles..are now rarely used, their place having been long since supplied by lead. **1852** *Dict. Archit.*, *Gutter tile*, besides being applied to the valley tile which has a conical form, this name has been given to Eaves tiles with one end turned up so as to form a trough.

guttery ('gʌtərɪ), *sb.* [f. GUT *v.* + -ERY.] The place for gutting (fish).

1842 J. WILSON *Voy. Scotl.* II. 153 Herring guttery.

guttery ('gʌtərɪ), *a.* [f. GUTTER *sb.*[1] + -Y[1].]

1. Of corn: Grooved, channelled.

1744–50 W. ELLIS *Mod. Husbandm.* IV. IV. 128 If [wheat] is cut too soon..the Kernel will be somewhat shriveled and guttery. **1813** BATCHELOR *Agric.* 371 (E.D.D.) The corns of cancer wheat are commonly thin and guttery.

2. Miry, muddy. (Cf. GUTTER *sb.*[1] 2 d.) ? *dial.*

1808–80 JAMIESON s.v., A guttery road. **1874** E. A. FREEMAN in W. R. W. Stephens *Life & Lett.* (1895) II. 85 Streets guttery, stony, filthy. **1895** H. CALLAN *Clyde to Jordan* ix. 97 The streets are narrow, stony, broken and guttery.

'**gut-tide.** *Obs.* or *dial.* Also 8 gutties. [An alteration of *good tide* (see GOOD A. 8 c); perh. a mere phonetic development, though association with GUT *sb.* would inevitably suggest itself.] Shrove Tuesday; also *gen.*, a time of feasting.

[**1547**: see GOOD A. 8 c.] **1608** MIDDLETON *Fam. Love* IV. i. 47 At what time wert thou bound, Club! at Guttide, Hollantide, or Candletide? **1631** J. BURGES *Answ. Rejoined* 323 [He] is content to impute to Hester, Mordecai, and all the Iewes, the decreeing of a Gut-tide, rather then of an holy Festivall. **1797** F. LEIGHTON *Let. to J. Boucher* 25 Apr. (MS.), You will be pleased to add to your Shropshire words ..Gutties Day—Shrove Tuesday—evidently from the Guts. **1820** [see GOOD A. 8 c]. **1847** HALLIWELL, *Guttide.* **1887** *S. Cheshire Gloss.*, *Guttit*, Shrovetide; lit. Good tide. *Guttit Tuesday* is the name for Shrove Tuesday.

gut-tie ('gʌttaɪ). *local.* Also 8 guttie. [f. GUT *sb.* + TIE *sb.*] An abdominal disease in cattle.

1794 J. CLARK *Agric. Surv. Heref.* 76 The distemper is here called the Guttie. When it had once seized on an ox, it was considered as incurable. **1794** J. HARRIS *ibid.* 77 This stricture, or guttie, as it is called. **1834** YOUATT *Cattle* 490 Various abdominal diseases ensue, and, among the rest, the *cords* or *gut-tie*.

guttie, obs. f. GUTTÉ; var. GUTTY *sb.*

guttifer ('gʌtɪfə(r)). *Bot.* [ad. mod.L. *guttifera* (sc. *planta*), f. *gutta* drop (see GUTTA and -FEROUS). Cf. F. *guttifère*.] A plant that exudes gum or resin; a plant of the order *Guttiferæ*.

1846 LINDLEY *Veg. Kingd.* 400 Order CXLIV. *Clusiaceæ* —Guttifers.

guttiferous (gʌ'tɪfərəs), *a.* [f. as prec.: see -FEROUS.] Yielding gum or resinous substances; pertaining to N.O. *Guttiferæ*, of trees and shrubs remarkable for their abounding in a resinous sap.

1847 in CRAIG.

So **gu'ttiferal** *a.*, used by Lindley as the distinctive epithet of an 'alliance' including the order *Guttiferæ*; *sb.* A plant belonging to this 'alliance'.

1846 LINDLEY *Veg. Kingd.* 392 *Guttiferales*—the Guttiferal Alliance. *Ibid.*, It is in this respect indeed that Guttiferals principally differ from Sapindals. *Ibid.* 400 Guttiferal Exogens.

guttiform ('gʌtɪfɔːm), *a.* [f. L. *gutta* drop (GUTTA *sb.*[1], GOUT *sb.*[1]) + -(I)FORM.] Having the form of a drop; drop-shaped.

1874 COUES *Birds N.W.* 126 The markings below have a short, broad, guttiform character. **1883** *Nature* XXVII. 231 Their guttiform surface can be explained by the drops of the milky juice.

†'**gutting**, *sb. Obs.* [? f. *Göttingen*, name of a town in Hanover.] Some kind of canvas.

1640 in Entick *London* II. 167 Gutting and spruce canvas drillinges pack. **1812** J. SMYTH *Pract. of Customs* (1821) 135 Packing Canvass, Guttings, Spruce, Elbing, or Queenborough Canvass.

gutting ('gʌtɪŋ), *vbl. sb.* [f. GUT *v.* + -ING[1].] The action of the vb. GUT.

1. The eviscerating of fish. Also *attrib.*, as ***gutting-board, -house, -knife.***

1615 E. S. *Brit. Buss* in Arb. *Garner* III. 642 Six Gutting knives, at fourpence..0 2 0. **1736** J. LEWIS *Isle Tenet* 34 The Gutting-Knife. **1780** YOUNG *Tour Irel.* I. 231 Over the gutting-house is a hoop store. **1832** HT. MARTINEAU *Weal & Woe* i. 2 Girls were employed in gutting. **1842** J. WILSON *Voy. Scotl.* II. 161 They [women] never appear except around the gutting board in otherwise than rather trim array.

b. *concr.* What is removed from a fish in the process of evisceration.

1899 *Blackw. Mag.* Feb. 336/1 The peelings and guttings, the very offal and scour of the broth are flung further.

2. The clearing out of the contents of a building.
1690 DRYDEN *Don Sebastian* IV. iii, Your breaking open and gutting of houses. **1809** WELLINGTON in Gurw. *Desp.* (1837) IV. 471, I shall be very much obliged to you if you will let me know any cause that may have come to your knowledge for the desertion by its inhabitants, and plunder, even to gutting, of Cardigos.
fig. **1891** *Times* 13 Oct. 8/2 The gutting of the treasury of its net profits in order to pay and to parade an enormous dividend.

†**3.** Guzzling; gormandizing. *Obs.*
1633 AMES *Agst. Cerem.* II. 316 Heer the Rejoynder.. accuseth him of making it a Guttide; As if no Civill day of rejoycing could be without Gutting.

†ˈ**guttish,** *a. Obs. rare*$^{-1}$. [f. GUT *sb.* + -ISH.] Gluttonous.
1567 *Triall Treas.* (1850) 16 What guttish gredinesse the horeson can teache!

†**guttle,** *sb. Obs. rare*$^{-1}$. [f. GUTTLE *v.*] What one consumes gluttonously.
1784–9 M. MADAN *Persius* (1795) 141 Nor swallow with your guttle mercurial spittle.

guttle (ˈgʌt(ə)l), *v.* [? f. GUT *sb.*, after *guzzle.*]
1. *intr.* To eat voraciously; to gormandize.
1654 GAYTON *Pleas. Notes Don Quix.* II. iii. 42 Sancho durst not gormandize, and guttle and guzzle too.. under his Master's nose. **1675** COTTON *Scoffer Scoft* 24 Or swill and guttle every day With Nectar and Ambrosia. **1739** 'R. BULL' tr. *Dedekindus' Grobianus* 178 Such Praise inspires with a diviner Lust Your Friends, who guttle with a greater Gust. **1764** CHURCHILL *Times* Poems 1769 II. 258 Luxury sat guttling at the helm From meal to meal. **1815** W. H. IRELAND *Scribbleomania* 190 [A] stone trough, whence the swine us'd to guttle. **1893** VIZETELLY *Glances Back* I. xv. 300 A position which he utilised to guttle and guzzle in good company.
2. *trans.* To devour or swallow greedily. Also with *up, down.*
1685 [H. MORE] *Reflect. on Baxter* 9 He.. was not edified by the reading, or rather gutling up so many Books as he has hastily read. **1692** R. L'ESTRANGE *Fables* ccccxxxviii. 415 He Guttled 'em up, and Scalt his Chops. **1739** 'R. BULL' tr. *Dedekindus' Grobianus* 138, I constantly regarding her Advice, Have safely guttled whatsoe'er is nice. **1764** T. BRYDGES *Homer Travest.* (1797) II. 118 To.. guttle down six pound of turtle. **1827** *Mirror* II. 87/1 The gross appetite of the Iroquois and Tonopinambos, who guttle down their enemies out of absolute spite. **1844** THACKERAY *Crit. Rev.* Wks. 1886 XXIII. 207 Cleopatra's page guttling the figs in the basket which had brought the asp. **1853** F. HALL in *Ledlie's Misc.* II. 168 Guttling their beef and guzzling their beer.

guttler (ˈgʌtlə(r)). [f. GUTTLE *v.* + -ER^{1}.] One who guttles; a glutton; a gormandizer.
[*a* **1700** B. E. *Dict. Cant. Crew*, Rum-hopper, tip us.. a Boozing-cheat of Rum-gutlers.. Drawer, fill us.. a Bottle of the best Canary.] **1732** (*title*) Truth in Rhyme, to suit the time, or the Parish Guttlers, a Merry Poem. **1788** WOLCOT (P. Pindar) *Bro. Peter to Bro. Tom*, etc. 41 Plymouth town .. Where wandering gutlers, wandering gutlers meet. **1834** *Westm. Rev.* XXI. 399 The thing is done every day, and is good parish guttler's law. **1887** BROWNING *Parley. w. Cert. People* (1889) 247 In debauchery's guild Admitted prime guttler and guzzler.

guttlesome (ˈgʌt(ə)lsəm), *a. rare.* [f. GUTTLE *v.* + -SOME.] Gluttonous.
1861 *Sat. Rev.* 2 Feb. 115/2 The dying words of that guttlesome parson were, 'Oh, those horrid dinners, but for them I should have been saved'.

guttling (ˈgʌtlɪŋ), *vbl. sb.* [f. GUTTLE *v.* + -ING^{1}.] The action of the vb. GUTTLE; gormandizing.
1731 *Gentl. Mag.* I. 103 Depredations by guttling and tippling, junketting, gossiping, gaming, &c. are to be all item'd to the government. **1848** THACKERAY *Bk. Snobs* xxvi, Who.. dine for the mere purpose of guttling. *a* **1894** STEVENSON *St. Ives* (1898) 236 Here you will find no guttling nor gormandising.

guttling (ˈgʌtlɪŋ), *ppl. a.* [f. GUTTLE *v.* + -ING^{2}.] That guttles; gormandizing, guzzling.
1653 P. FLETCHER *Purple Isl.* VII. lxxx, With Methos, Gluttonie, his gutling brother, Twinne parallels, drawn from the self same line. *a* **1700** B. E. *Dict. Cant. Crew* s.v., *A Gutling Fellow*, a great Eater. **1799** *Monthly Mag.* July 446/2 The greasy bearded, gutling blades of Mother Madcap. **1845** THACKERAY *Xmas Bks.* (1872) 35 What a contempt they must have for the guttling crowd to whom they minister.

Guttman scale (ˈgʌtmən). *Psychol.* and *Sociol.* [f. the name of L. *Guttman* (b. 1916), American psychologist.] A type of scale used to measure and assess mental attitudes and properties (see quot. 1970).
1950 S. A. STOUFFER et al. *Measurement & Prediction* IV. i. 5 The perfect Guttman scale is not likely to be found in practice, but satisfactory approximations to it are not so rare as some critics of the early papers describing it have implied. **1968** J. WHITING in Lindzey & Aronson *Handbk. Soc. Psychol.* (ed. 2) II. xvii. 714 Guttman scales have been used effectively in a number of cross-cultural studies. **1969** *Computers & Humanities* III. 144 [They] have used Guttman scale analysis to measure attitudes of congressmen and senators about roll call votes between 1830 and 1860. **1970** G. A. & A. G. THEODORSON *Mod. Dict. Sociol.* 181 *Guttman scale*, a cumulative scale designed.. to determine whether the items can be arranged along a single continuum of increasing intensity. When a series of items (attitudes) forms a Guttman scale, acceptance of any item on the scale indicates acceptance of all the items below it.

†ˈ**guttorous,** *a. Obs. rare*$^{-0}$. [For *gutturous, ad. L. *gutturōs-us* goitred, f. GUTTUR.] 'Having a wide throat' (Cockeram, 1623).

†ˈ**guttose,** *a. Obs. rare*$^{-0}$. [ad. L. type **guttōs-us*, f. *gutta* drop: see -OSE.] 'Full of Drops' (Bailey vol. II, 1727).

‖**guttula** (ˈgʌtjʊlə). *Nat. Hist.* [L. *guttula* a little drop, dim. of *gutta* a drop.] A small drop-shaped spot.
1887 W. PHILLIPS *Brit. Discomycetes* 14 Sporidia furnished with two large guttulæ.

guttular (ˈgʌtjʊlə(r)), *a.* [f. prec. + -AR.] Spotted.
1811 PINKERTON *Petral.* II. 135 Red guttular marble of Campan.

guttulate (ˈgʌtjʊleɪt), *a. Nat. Hist.* [f. L. *guttul-a* a little drop + -ATE^{2}.] Having drops or spots; also with prefixed numeral indicating the number of spots.
1887 [see GUTTATE]. **1887** W. PHILLIPS *Brit. Discomycetes* 23 Sporidia 8, fusiform, curved, 3-guttulate.

guttule (ˈgʌtjʊl). [Anglicized form of GUTTULA.] A small drop.
1886 in *Syd. Soc. Lex.*

†ˈ**guttulous,** *a. Obs.* [f. GUTTULA + -OUS.] Taking the form of or occurring in small drops.
1646 SIR T. BROWNE *Pseud. Ep.* IV. viii. 198 From a partiall or guttulous irrigation, to conclude a totall descension. **1651** BIGGS *New Disp.* ¶ 241 A kind of guttulous distillation.

‖**guttur** (ˈgʌtə(r)). Also 6 gutter. [L. = throat.] The throat; used rarely in technical applications. Also *attrib.*, in †*guttur-neck.*
1562 TURNER *Herbal* II. 3 The rootes of the femall ferne taken wyth honye.. dryue brode wormes oute of the gutter. **1649** LOVELACE *Poems* 53 [To an Ostrich.] Snakes through thy guttur-neck hisse all the day, Then on thy Iron Messe at supper feed'st. **1864** MAX MÜLLER *Sci. Lang.* Ser. II. 151 The letters which we commonly call gutturals, k, g, have nothing to do with the guttur, but with the root of the tongue and the soft palate. **1872** COUES *Key N. Amer. Birds* (1884) 96 The front of the neck has been needlessly subdivided, .. *Guttur* is a term sometimes used to include gula and jugulum together; it is simply equivalent to 'throat', as just defined.

guttur, obs. form of GUTTER.

guttural (ˈgʌtərəl), *a.* and *sb.* Also 6–7 **gutturall,** 7 **gutteral.** [ad. mod.L. *gutturāl-is*, f. *guttur* (see prec.): see -AL^{1}. Cf. F. *guttural.*]
A. *adj.* Of or pertaining to the throat.
guttural artery, the same as thyroid artery. ***g. canal, duct***, the Eustachian tube. ***g. cartilage***, the arytenoid cartilage. ***g. fossa***, 'the central portion of the middle division in the external base of the skull' (Cassell). ***g. glands***, the same as pharyngeal glands. ***g. hernia*** = GOITRE. ***g. pouch***, one of 'two large air-sacs lying side by side in the median plane of the pharynx of the horse and allied animals' (*Syd. Soc. Lex.* 1886).
1625 USSHER *Answ. Jesuit* 68 The gutturall eating and drinking of the body and bloud of Christ. **1694** MOTTEUX *Rabelais* IV. xxxiv. (1737) 142 It no more open'd its guttural Trap-door. **1716** M. DAVIES *Athen. Brit.* II. 354 Cephalick and Guttural Distempers. **1747** tr. *Astruc's Fevers* 315 A dry and obstinate cough, which we may call guttural, because the patient feels more pain in the throat during his cough, than in any other part. **1831** R. KNOX *Cloquet's Anat.* 67 The first, or Sphenoidal Edge.. is divided into two laminæ, (*alæ vomeris*), which enter into the grooves on the guttural aspect of the sphenoid bone. **1836–9** TODD *Cycl. Anat.* II. 550/1 The guttural orifice of the Eustachian tube. **1872** MIVART *Elem. Anat.* iii. 131 Sometimes, as in the Crocodile and Great Ant Eater, this guttural part of the basis cranii is nearly concealed by the immense extension of the palate.
b. Of sounds or utterance: Produced in the throat.
By non-phoneticians any mode of pronunciation which is harsh or grating in effect is often supposed to be 'guttural'; with this notion the designation is popularly applied by Englishmen to the German *ch*, but not to *k* or *g*, though technically it belongs equally to them. As a technical term of phonetics, the word was first used to denote the Hebrew spirant consonants א, ה, ח, ע; it is now commonly applied (inaccurately, if its etymological sense be regarded to the sounds formed by the back of the tongue and the palate, as (k, g, x, ɣ, ŋ).
1594 T. B. *La Primaud. Fr. Acad.* II. 87 The Hebrewes name their letters, some gutturall, because they are pronounced more in the throat: others, dentall, because a man cannot wel pronounce them without the teeth. *c* **1620** A. HUME *Brit. Tongue* I. vii, A labial letter can not symboliz a guttural syllab. **1642** HOWELL *For. Trav.* (Arb.) 52 A gutturall pronunciation is an infallible badge of an ancient language. **1668** WILKINS *Real Char.* III. xi. 364 The Vowel (y) is wholly Guttural, being an emission of the breath from the throat, without any particular motion of the tongue or lips. **1756** NUGENT *Gr. Tour* III. 348 That guttural pronunciation, so disagreeable in the Florentines. **1840** R. H. DANA *Bef. Mast* xiii. 31 Their language is extremely guttural. **1863** GEO. ELIOT *Romola* i, The deep guttural sounds of the speaker were scarcely intelligible to the newly-waked.. listener. **1867** A. J. ELLIS *E.E. Pronunc.* I. iii. 191 The guttural nasal seems to have been the regular pronunciation of *ng* in English. **1898** J. CAIRD *Univ. Addresses* 349 An articulation thick and guttural.
Hence ˈ**gutturalness,** gutturality (Bailey vol. II, 1727).

B. *sb.* A guttural sound; *occas.*, guttural utterance.
1696 WHISTON *Theory Earth* II. (1722) 166 The first letter being such a guttural as could not well be pronounced by the Greeks. **1719** DE FOE *Crusoe* II. viii, His speech was.. all gutturals. **1816** SCOTT *Antiq.* iii, Giving each guttural the true Anglo-Saxon enunciation. **1834** MEDWIN *Angler in Wales* I. 133 Our [Welsh] language being full of harsh consonants and gutturals. **1877** MISS YONGE *Cameos* II. xiv. 132 The Portuguese.. despise the Spanish gutturals as Moorish abominations. **1888** *Pall Mall G.* 19 May 2/1 Occasionally the choir would cease their singing, and in deep guttural a black-bearded priest would chant some verses. **1889** JESSOPP *Coming of Friars* i. 29 The rabble of Cologne.. grumbling out their grating gutturals.

gutturalism (ˈgʌtərəlɪz(ə)m). [f. prec. + -ISM.] Guttural quality or characteristics.
1871–3 EARLE *Philol. Eng. Tongue* § 166 The desire to reassert the languishing gutturalism of H and of R. **1876** DOUSE *Grimm's L.* §33. 70 The purer forms of Low German have preserved the gutturalism, dentalism and labialism of the several Spirants down to the present moment.

gutturality (gʌtəˈrælɪtɪ). [f. as prec. + -ITY.] Guttural nature, character, or condition.
1770 BARETTI *Journ. Lond. to Genoa* III. lvii. 11 The Spanish language.. has some soft gutturality. **1796** SEWARD *Anecd.* IV. 495 His voice discovered something of that gutturality for which Mr. Garrick's was distinguished. **1824** *Westm. Rev.* II. 162 The *ch*, by which χ was rendered, seems to mark a gutturality and aspiration. **1871–3** EARLE *Philol. Eng. Tongue* §181 *Gh* was a reinforcement of the old gutturality of *h.*

gutturalize (ˈgʌtərəlaɪz), *v.* [f. as prec. + -IZE.]
1. *trans.* To pronounce or utter gutturally.
a **1860** *Gentl. Mag.* (cited in Worcester), To gutturalize strange tongues. **1823** *Blackw. Mag.* XIV. 427 Some grazier .. gutturalizes something pastoral out of George Thomson's Collection of Scottish Songs. **1832** WILSON *ibid.* XXXI. 266 The green goose gutturalizes 'Reform! Reform!'
2. To render (a sound) guttural in character.
1863 LEPSIUS *Standard Alphabet* (ed. 2) 58 The thick emphatic sound, which they transmit to the following vowels in gutturalising them. **1874** SWEET *Hist. Eng. Sounds* 74 These words are *children* and *milk*, in both of which the *i* has been gutturalized and labialized into *u* by the *l.*
Hence ˈ**gutturalized** *ppl. a.*; **gutturaliˈzation.**
1863 LEPSIUS *Standard Alphabet* (ed. 2) 56 Another formation of vowels, which we might call Gutturalisation. *Ibid.* 57 In the Arabic this gutturalisation of the vowels is distinctly heard. **1877** SWEET *Hand-bk. Phonetics* 15 A muffled gutturalised front vowel.

gutturally (ˈgʌtərəlɪ), *adv.* [f. GUTTURAL + -LY^{2}.] In a guttural manner; with a guttural sound or utterance. †In quot. 1659 = (app.) Indistinctly.
1659 C. NOBLE *Mod. Answ. to Immod. Queries* 7 He speaks more plainly there, what he says here but gutterally, and leaves to conjecture his meaning. **1774** D. JONES *Jrnl.* (1865) 61 The (ch) is pronounced gutturally as Welsh or old Scotch. **1826** *Blackw. Mag.* XX. 416 Ardchin-chrocan, the somewhat gutturally-sounding proper name of the abode. **1859** JEPHSON *Brittany* viii. 125 The *ch* in all these words is pronounced as in German, or even more gutturally.

†**gutturine,** *a. Obs. rare*$^{-1}$. [f. GUTTUR + -INE.] Pertaining to the throat.
1692 RAY *Dissol. World* 89 The Bronchocele or gutturine tumour [*marg.* Swoln Throats].

gutturize (ˈgʌtəraɪz), *v. nonce-wd.* [f. GUTTUR + -IZE.] *trans.* To enunciate gutturally.
1832 COLERIDGE *Table-t.* 7 July, That grand word—Death —for which the Germans gutturize a sound that puts you in mind of nothing but a loathsome toad.

gutturniform (gʌˈtɜːnɪfɔːm), *a.* [f. L. *gutturnium* narrow-necked pitcher + -FORM.] (See quot.)
1886 *Syd. Soc. Lex.*, *Gutturniform*, of or belonging to, or resembling, a water pitcher. Formerly applied to the arytenoid cartilage.

gutturo- (ˈgʌtərəʊ), taken as comb. form of L. *guttur* throat; in terms of *Anat.* and *Physiol.* = pertaining to the throat (and some other part), as ***gutturo-maxillary*** (= relating to the throat and the jaw), ***gutturo-palatine***, ***gutturo-tetanic*** (hence ***gutturo-tetany***); in *Phonetics* = 'guttural and..', as in ***gutturo-labial*** (= guttural and labial), ***-nasal***, †***-palatial*** (= *-palatal*), ***-sibilant.***
1786 SPARRMAN *Voy. Cape G.H.* II. 278 The gutturo-palatial sounds of the Hottentot language. **1871** *Public Sch. Lat. Gram.* 7 N is gutturo-nasal when it precedes *g*, *c*, or *q.* **1876** DOUSE *Grimm's L.* lv. 135 The representative of this gutturo-sibilant is invariably a pure *k.* **1881** *Academy* 19 Feb. 139 Latin *kw* (*qv*), a guttural followed by a gutturo-labial. **1886** *Syd. Soc. Lex.*, *Gutturo-palatine nerve*, the posterior palatine nerve. *Ibid.*, *Gutturo-tetanic stammering*, Colombat's term for the form of stammering which is produced by spasmodic contraction of the throat. Same as *Gutturo-tetany.*

guttus (ˈgʌtəs). *Class. Archæol.* Pl. -ti. [L.] A narrow-necked cruet or oil-flask.
1842 A. RICH in W. Smith *Dict. Gr. & Roman Antiq.* 141/2 Oil.. was dropped upon it from a small vessel called *guttus*, which had a narrow neck, so as to discharge its contents drop by drop, from whence the name is taken. **1883** J. W. MOLLETT *Illustr. Dict. Art & Archæol.* 163 *Guttus*,..

a vessel with a very narrow neck and mouth, by means of which liquids could be poured out drop by drop; whence its name. **1921** *Brit. Mus. Return* 61 Guttus of early Italian red-figure style.

gutty (ˈgʌtɪ), *sb.* *Golfers' slang.* [f. GUTTA[2] + -Y.] A gutta-percha ball. In full ***gutty ball***.

1881 A. WARDROP *Poems* 106 He's speel'd up tae the dresser heid, To get his gutty ba'. **1890** HUTCHINSON *Golf* (Badm. Libr.) iii. 70 We may make a brief comparison of these three balls, taking the ordinary 'gutty', which is the mean, as the standard. **1893** FARMER *Slang, Guttie*. **1902** *Daily Chron.* 9 Dec. 9/3 He advised them to select the 'gutty' ball only, as the best ball for golf. **1924** C. J. H. TOLLEY *Mod. Golfer* 64 Thousands to-day would not be playing the game if the 'gutty' ball remained the official ball of to-day.

gutty (ˈgʌtɪ), *a.* [f. GUT *sb.*[1] + -Y[1].]

1. Corpulent, pot-bellied. Chiefly *Sc.*

1785 BURNS *3rd Ep. to Lapraik* 45 Till ye forget ye're auld an' gutty [*usually printed* gatty]. **1818** SCOTT *Rob Roy* xxii, Ta filthy gutty hallions, tat they are. **1887** J. SERVICE *Life Dr. Duguid* 227 A gutty wee chiel that gaed aboot the toon wi' knee-breeks on.

2. *Jazz slang.* Earthy, primitive.

1939 in R. S. Gold *Jazz Lexicon* (1964) 133 Buster Bailey's reaction can be felt in the 'gutty' clarinet tones he uses. **1955** L. FEATHER *Encycl. Jazz* vii. 160 Higginbotham was..the supreme trombone stylist of the gutty, forceful school in the '30s. **1958** *Esquire* Feb. 35/2 You feel it in a beat, in jazzy..or a good gutty rock number. **1958** P. GAMMOND *Decca Bk. Jazz* vi. 80 The 1940 recordings.. serve as good examples of Freeman's gutty, swinging tenor[-saxophone] style.

3. = GUTSY *a.* 2.

1953 in WENTWORTH & FLEXNER *Dict. Amer. Slang* 236/2 Here Come the Guttiest Guys of All. **1960** *News Chron.* 30 June 6/4, I can get gutty characters to play at last.

gutty, variant of GUTTÉ *Her.*

gutwort (ˈgʌtwɜːt). ? *Obs.* [f. GUT *sb.*[1] + WORT.] The plant *Globularia Alypum*, a violent purgative, found in Southern Europe and Africa.

1597 GERARDE *Herbal* II. cxxxii. §2. 408 Tartonraire, called in English Gutwoort, which groweth by the sea. **1611** COTGR., *Tarton-raire*, gutwort; a beautifull, and extreamly purging French shrub. **1688** R. HOLME *Armoury* II. 93/2 The herb Gutwort, or trouble Belly, grows in branches with white hoary leaves.

guv (gʌv). Also **guvner, guv'ner, guvnor, guv'nor** (ˈgʌvnə(r)). Spellings representing vulgar or colloq. pronunciations of GOVERNOR.

1852 *Punch* 2 Oct. 152/1 (*caption*) Coster (to extremely genteel person). 'I say, Guvner, give us a hist with this 'ere bilin' o' greens!' **1866** [see GOVERNOR 7 c]. **1890** *Punch* 15 Mar. 123/1 Yes, you're right, Guv, this *is* dirty fun and dreary. **1895** *Ibid.* 17 Aug. 77/1 Guv wos in it all the while. **1959** I. & P. OPIE *Lore & Lang. Schoolch.* xvii. 362 The headmaster may be known as 'The Gaffer', 'The Guv'nor', or 'The Boss'. **1960** *Observer* 24 Jan. 5/2 Sometimes the peterman finds his own jobs and acts as guvnor of his own team. *Ibid.*, The guvnor of a team of active criminals. **1968** *Listener* 15 Aug. 210/1 You can be sure that if somebody calls you 'mister' on the railways he doesn't like you. The term of endearment is 'guv'nor'.

guvacine (ˈgjuːvəsiːn). *Chem.* [ad. G. *guvacin* (E. Jahns 1891, in *Ber. d. Deut. Chem. Ges.* XXIV. 2615), f. Skr. *guvāka* betel-nut tree, areca + -INE[5].] A white crystalline alkaloid, $C_6H_9NO_2$, obtained from the areca nut.

1891 *Jrnl. Chem. Soc.* LX. II. 1520 The examination of larger quantities of material has led to the discovery of a fifth alkaloïd in areca nut. This has been termed guvacine, from guvaca, the Indian name for the areca palm. **1946** *Jrnl. Amer. Chem. Soc.* LXVIII. 1053/1 The white solid remaining undissolved..was guvacine hydrochloride. **1970** R. K. HILL in S. W. Pelletier *Chem. Alkaloids* xiv. 411 The parent member of this family [*sc.* the areca alkaloids] is an amino acid guvacine, $C_6H_9O_2N$... Guvacine is a secondary amine, is optically inactive and nonresolvable.

guv'ner, -or: see GUV.

guy (gaɪ), *sb.*[1] Forms: 4–5 **gye**, 5, 9 *Sc.* **gy**, 6 *Sc.* **guye**, 7 **guie**, 7– **guy**. [a. OF. *gui-s* (obj. case *guion*), also *guie* = Pr., Sp., Pg. *guia*, It. *guida* (see GUIDE *sb.*); the two Rom. types **guido(n* and **guida* (etymologically fem., but masc. as a designation of men) are verbal sbs. f. *guidare*: see GUIDE *v.*]

†**1.** A guide; a conductor or leader. *Obs. rare.*

c **1350** *Will. Palerne* 2727 þan hiȝed þei hem to þe hauen.. as þe werwolf hem wissed þat was al here gye. *Ibid.* 2849 þe herte & þe hinde þere þanne hem hed sone, as þe werwolf hem wissed þat ay was here gye. *c* **1470** HENRY *Wallace* IX. 684 Bath Forth and Tay thai left and passyt by On the north cost, [gud] Guthrie was thar gy. **1500–20** DUNBAR *Poems* lxxxviii. 53 London..Thy famous Maire..is exampler, loode-ster, and guye.

2. a. Chiefly *Naut.* A rope used to guide and steady a thing which is being hoisted or lowered; also, a rope, chain, rod, etc. to secure or steady anything liable to shift its position or to be carried away, as the mast, funnel, etc. of a vessel, a derrick, a suspension-bridge, etc.

lazy guy, 'a small tackle or rope to prevent the spanker-boom from swaying about in fine weather' (Smyth *Sailor's Word-bk.* 1867). *travelling guy* (see quot. 1846).

1623 J. TAYLOR (Water P.) *Praise Hemp-seed* 10 Shrowds, ratlings, lanyards, tackles, lifts, and guies. **1626** CAPT. SMITH *Accid. Yng. Sea-men* 16 Sheeps feet is..a guie in staying the tackles when they are charged with goods. **1627** —— *Seaman's Gram.* v. 20 A Guy..is a rope brought to it from the foremast, to keepe the weight vpon it steady. **1711** W. SUTHERLAND *Shipbuilder's Assist.* 113 The Guy of the winding Tackle. **1755** *Phil. Trans.* XLIX. 352 His Majesty's ship the Gosport was..well-stay'd by guys and hawsers. **1816** SCOTT *Antiq.* viii, The experienced seaman had let down with the chair another line, which, being attached to it, and held by the persons beneath, might serve by way of gy. **1846** YOUNG *Naut. Dict.* s.v., There are sometimes also guys attached to the jib-traveller, which get the name of travelling guys. **1863** BARING-GOULD *Iceland* 105 Drive the [tent-] pegs home and stretch the guys. **1875** BEDFORD *Sailor's Pocket Bk.* v. (ed. 2) 173 A broken oar is driven into the sand, and supported by guys of spun yarn. **1882** NARES *Seamanship* (ed. 6) 207 If the wind is light, get a lazy guy on the spanker boom. **1897** *Westm. Gaz.* 24 Nov. 9/1 About six o'clock the funnel guy was carried away.

b. *Naut. slang.* Phrase ***to clap a guy on***: to put a stop to; to 'stow'.

1814 *Sailors' Return* II. vi, I..request you will join us at dinner, if you'll only clap a guy on your low lingo.

3. *attrib.* and *Comb.* (in sense 2), as ***guy-chain, -crane, -line, -peg, -rope, -tackle***; also **guy rein**, a guiding or leading rein; **guy-rod**, a rod used in place of a guy-rope.

1793 SMEATON *Edystone L.* §254 *note*, The shears were kept upright, and were managed, by two strong guy (or guide) ropes. **1861** *Man. Artil. Exerc.* 175 As soon as the centre of each tent is marked by a peg, 4 guy pegs are driven to the front, rear, right and left. **1866** SIR T. SEATON *Cadet to Colonel* I. 19 From a strong ring in the deck, near the head of the boat, ran a guy rope. **1869** *Daily News* 12 June, A gentleman leading a beautiful child by a guy rein. He is mounted on a superb bay, his little companion on a cream-coloured pony. **1879** *Man. Artil. Exerc.* 640 For guy tackles likely to be wetted with salt water tarred cordage should be used. **1879** R. S. BALL in *Cassell's Techn. Educ.* I. 208 In a crane which is often used for quarrying and other rough purposes, and which is sometimes called a guy crane, there are two stays. **1903** A. ADAMS *Log of Cowboy* x. 152 We took a guy line from the wagon and snubbed it to a tree. **1903** *Electr. World & Engin.* 31 Oct. 711 (Cent. D. Suppl.), Guy-rods are 8 ft. × ⅝ in., provided with an eye at one end. **1910** N. HAWKINS *Electr. Dict., Guy Rod Bands*, bands by which a guy rod is attached to a telegraph pole. **1928** *Daily Express* 7 Apr. 5/5 Drive in the remaining pegs and attach and true up the remaining guylines.

guy (gaɪ), *sb.*[2] Pl. **guys**.

1. a. An effigy of Guy Fawkes traditionally burnt on the evening of November the Fifth, usu. with a display of fireworks. Also in full ***Guy Fawkes***.

Guys were formerly paraded about in the streets on the anniversary of the 'Gunpowder Plot' (Nov. 5). They are now more frequently exhibited by children collecting money for fireworks during the days preceding Nov. 5.

The figure is habited in grotesquely ragged and ill-assorted garments (whence sense 2), and was formerly accompanied by other similar effigies (representing unpopular persons), to which the name of 'guys' is often given by extension.

1806 W. BURRELL in *Lett. C. K. Sharpe* (1888) I. 277 A month ago there was neither shape nor make in me... No guy ever matched me. **1825** HONE *Every-day Bk.* I. 1430 Formerly an old cocked hat was the reigning fashion for a 'Guy'. **1861** C. M. YONGE *Young Step-Mother* xxix. 442 'There's Guy Fawkes,' cried Albinia, as a procession of scare-crows were borne on chairs amid thunders of acclamation. **1867** TROLLOPE *Chron. Barset* II. lx. 175 What are you doing there, dressed up in that way like a guy? **1868** DICKENS *Uncomm. Trav.* xxi, Once on a fifth of November I found a 'Guy' trusted to take care of himself there, while his proprietors had gone to dinner. **1968** *Listener* 7 Nov. 606 I'm afraid Simon is rather burnt. It was so dark some of the children thought he was the guy. **1970** R. GARRETT *Run Down* iv. 95 It was the first Saturday of November. There were dozens of Guy Fawkes of varying merit lined along each street.

b. ***Guy Fawkes day (night)***, 5 Nov., the anniversary of the 'Gunpowder plot'. Also *ellipt.*

1825 W. HONE *Every-day Bk.* 1430/2 'Guy Fawkes-day', or, as they as often call it, 'Pope-day', is a holiday, and.., on account of its festivous enjoyment, is the greatest holiday of the season. **1833** J. ROMILLY *Diary* 5 Nov. (1967) I. 41 Webb (the W. merchant's) long dull son dined in hall with me being Guy Fawkes day. **1913** C. MACKENZIE *Sinister St.* I. iv. 63 Suddenly he heard the cry, 'Remember, remember the Fifth of November..,' and, almost before he had time to realize it was the dreaded Guy Fawkes, a band of..boys.. held close to the window a nodding Guy. **1970** *Times* 4 Nov. 2/2 The reserves of stamina the [fire]men have to build up for Guy Fawkes night each year.

2. A person of grotesque appearance, esp. with reference to dress; a 'fright'.

1836 *Lett. fr. Madras* (1843) 9 The gentlemen are all 'rigged Tropical',..grisly Guys some of them turn out! **1861** HUGHES *Tom Brown at Oxf.* xxvi. (1889) 246 He was such an old guy in his dress. **1880** *Daily Tel.* 15 Oct., We have far too many sculptured 'Guys' in the metropolis. **1893** VIZETELLY *Glances back* I. ii. 33 Little boys..were dressed up to look the greatest of guys.

attrib. **1875** R. F. BURTON *Gorilla L.* II. 145 He appeared habited in the usual guy style: a gaudy fancy helmet [etc.].

3. *slang.* **a.** A dark lantern. ? *Obs.*

1811 *Lex. Balatronicum* s.v., Stow the guy: conceal the lanthorn.

b. An act of decamping or running off 'on the sly'. ***to give the guy to***: to run away from, 'give the slip to'. Also ***to do a guy***.

1889 *Sporting Times* 3 Aug. 5/5 (Farmer) A cheerful guy to Waterloo was the game. **1897** [see GUY *v.*[4]]. **1898** *Daily News* 8 Sept. 2/3 'He's done a guy'... The Coroner—Done a what? Witness—Done a guy; 'bunked'. **1899** *Blackw. Mag.* Sept. 378/1 Don't think to give us the guy. **1925** N. VENNER *Imperfect Impostor* xiii. 221 He's just picked me up out of the road with a sprained ankle, or very near it, bandaged me up like a medical student, and brought me home. Then he wants to do a guy at the front door. **1954** N. BALCHIN *Last Recoll. Uncle Charles* iii. 43 It was..not so very surprising that he should 'do a guy', as they put it locally, with his employers' money.

c. (See quot.)

1835 *Tait's Mag.* II. 451 These crimps are Jews; there are a few Christians who profess the same commercial faith, and they are called *guys*. These crimps and guys prey like sharks on the unfortunate sailors.

d. A man, fellow. orig. *U.S.*

The earliest examples may be influenced by sense 2.

1847 *Swell's Night Guide* 41, I can't tonight, for I am going to be seduced by a rich old Guy. **1863** C. READE *Hard Cash* III. xiii. 270, I wouldn't speak to you in the street for fear of disgracing you; I am such a poor little guy to be addressing a gentleman like you. **1876** L. C. BARRAUD 15 Oct. in E. M. Barraud *Story of Family* (1967) xi. 133 The little children are such cures, and the nurses seem to go out with the master and mistress. The little boys look great guys. **1896** ADE *Artie* i. 3 You guys must think I'm a quitter. **1898** *Milwaukee Sentinel* 22 Jan. 4/7, I s'pose you got a Bible you'll let a guy look into. **1904** *Cincinnati Commercial Tribune* 29 June 4 Mr. Bryan is a hefty guy when it comes to Democratic conventions and the platforms thereof. **1928** D. H. LAWRENCE in *T.P.'s & Cassell's Weekly* 7 July 333/3, I say to Mother: *Show* me somebody happy, then! And she shows me some guy, or some bright young thing, and gets mad when I say: See the pretty monkey! **1931** R. CAMPBELL *Georgiad* I. 16 These are the guys that find the world forlorn And wish (correctly) they had not been born. **1931** D. RUNYON (*title*) Guys and Dolls. **1932** E. WILSON *Devil take Hindmost* xi. 114 The literary guys are taking public matters more seriously. **1951** AUDEN *Nones* (1952) 62 Thou shalt not be on friendly terms With guys in advertising firms. **1966** WODEHOUSE *Plum Pie* i. 32 All the other places..had been full of guys and dolls standing bumper to bumper.

Hence **ˈguydom**, the state of being a guy.

1882 BERESF. HOPE *Brandreths* I. i. 3 He could not deny a woman's right to refuse to make a guy of herself, as she understood guydom.

†**guy**, *v.*[1] *Obs.* Forms: 4–5 **gye, guye**, 4 **gie**, 4–5 **guie**, 4–6 **gy**, (5 *Sc.* **ghy**), 4–7 **guy**. [a. OF. *guie-r* (superseded in later Fr. by *guider*: see GUIDE) = Pr., Sp., It. *guiar*, It. *guidare*; prob. of Teut. origin, from some form of the root of Goth. and OE. *witan* to know (see WIT *v.*); cf. Goth. *fairweitjan* to spy.]

1. *trans.* To conduct or lead on the way; = GUIDE *v.* 1; to direct the course of (a vehicle, an instrument, etc.).

1362 LANGL. *P. Pl.* A. II. 162 Gyle was for-goere and gyede hem alle. *c* **1374** CHAUCER *Anel. & Arc.* 6 (Harl.) Yow fiers god of armes..Be present and my song contynne and guy. *c* **1384** —— *H. Fame* II. 435 (Fairf.) Whan..Pheton wolde lede Algate hys Fader carte, and gye. **14..** HOCCLEVE *Ad Beatam Virg.* 49 Vn-to my soules helthe thow me gye! **1447** BOKENHAM *Seyntys* (Roxb.) 37 He gan hym forth hye Up on his jurne fully trostyng That the grace of god shuld hym riht gye. *c* **1470** HARDING *Chron.* CXXXVIII. ix, Two hundred he kept, that ship to guie To Acres. *c* **1470** HENRY *Wallace* IX. 1881 Gydis thai chessyt, fra strenthis thaim to ghy. **1513** DOUGLAS *Æneis* II. Prol. 18 Thyne is the cure my wofull pen to gy. **1600** FAIRFAX *Tasso* X. ix, A writhen staffe his steps vnstable guies.

absol. *c* **1440** *Generydes* 2049 The formest warde All redy for to gye The kyng of Turkey had in gouernance.

2. To command (an army, etc.); to govern, rule (a country); to administer, manage (affairs, an office). Cf. GUIDE *v.* 3, 4.

c **1330** R. BRUNNE *Chron.* (1810) 92 Eustace of Ferers þat oste suld guye. *c* **1400** *Rowland & O.* 254 We will oure batells guy, And rape vs for to ryde Agayne þ[e] Emperour. *a* **1420** HOCCLEVE *De Reg. Princ.* 4842 A kyng..most don his diligence His peple for to gye by prudence. *c* **1425** *Seven Sag.* (P.) 5 Deocclivius, Al the londe hadde to gye. **1500–20** DUNBAR *Poems* viii. 6 Thy men of weir to governe and to gy. **1600** FAIRFAX *Tasso* I. lxiii, This band late heards and flocks that guied.

3. To control or direct (a person or his actions); = GUIDE *v.* 2. (Said of persons; also of immaterial things.)

13.. *Sir Beues* 364 (MS. A), I schel þe sende..a riche erl, þat schel þe gie And teche þe of corteisie In þe ȝouþe. *c* **1386** CHAUCER *Knt.'s T.* 1928 An Iuppiter so wys my soule gye To speken of a seruant proprely. *a* **1420** HOCCLEVE *De Reg. Princ.* 1335 Mesure is good; let hir þe gye and lede. **1422** tr. *Secreta Secret., Priv. Priv.* 138 Guy al thy thoghtis al tyme to do well. *a* **1510** DOUGLAS *K. Hart* I. 20 Nature had lymmit folk, for thair rewarde, This gudlie king to governe and to gy.

b. *refl.* To conduct or rule (oneself). Cf. GUIDE *v.* 2 c.

c **1325** *Song of Yesterday* 35 in *E.E.P.* (1862) 134 A syker ground who wol him gy I rede he þenke on ȝusterday. *c* **1380** *Sir Ferumb.* 1610 How schulle we now ous selue gye now ous lackeþ our hed? **1410** HOCCLEVE *Ball. to H. Somer* 34 Paie your lagh as dooth an othir wight, þat by mesure rulith him, and gyeth. **1430–40** LYDG. *Bochas* I. xii. (1544) 24 He yaue them lawes wherby they should them gye.

guy (gaɪ), *v.*[2] [f. GUY *sb.*[1] (sense 2).] *trans.* To fasten or secure with a guy or with guys. Also with *down, out, up*, etc. Chiefly *Naut.* Also *transf.*

1712 W. ROGERS *Voy.* App. 18 You must anchor near the Shore, and an Hawser on Shore to guy your Ship. **1840** R. H. DANA *Bef. Mast* xxiii. 70 The swinging booms were then guyed out. **1861** *Morn. Chron.* 20 Aug. (Crystal Palace Co. Advt.), It is essential the rope [of M. Blondin] should be well strained and guyed. **1882** NARES *Seamanship* (ed. 6) 71 It is

. . necessary to guy it down by a rope. **1886** T. Hardy *Mayor of Casterbr.* II. xvi. 224 Settles . . guyed to the ceiling . . by cords . . for stability. **1888** *Harper's Mag.* Apr. 711 As the Japanese have no bridge on the nose worth speaking of, the ponderous optical helps must be guyed in by cables of twine slung round the ears.

guy (gaɪ), *v.*[3] [f. guy *sb.*[2]]

1. a. *intr.* To carry an effigy of Guy Fawkes about the streets on Guy Fawkes' day. **b.** *trans.* To exhibit (a person) in effigy.

1851–61 Mayhew *Lond. Labour* III. 72, I always used to spend the money I got guying on myself. **1894** *Daily Tel.* 6 Nov. 5/3 The cavalcade gave the organisers the opportunity of 'guying' various faddists.

2. *trans.* (Originally *Theatrical slang.*) To make an object of ridicule or derisive wit, to ridicule by innuendo; to trifle with a theatrical part. Also *to guy at.*

1854 A. C. Mowatt *Autobiogr. Actress* xv. 227 Good gracious! the audience will guy you! . . 'Guy me? What do you mean by *guy*?' . . 'Why, laugh at you, to be sure—and *chaff* you!' **1872** 'Mark Twain' *Innoc. Abr.* xxvi. 203 The Roman street-boy who . . guyed the gladiators from the dizzy gallery. **1885** J. K. Jerome *On the Stage* 151, I particularly remember . . being 'guyed' on one occasion. . . The stage manager insisted on my wearing a most outrageous costume. I knew it would be laughed at. **1890** *Lit. World* 11 July 20 Mr. Burnand does not set himself to guy the book. **1890** Doyle *Sign of Four* vii. (ed. 3) 116 I'm guyed at by the children. **1890** J. Jefferson *Autobiogr.* 219 With all this at stake, some wanton actor deliberately 'guys' his part and overturns the patient care of his comrade. **1893** *Scribner's Mag.* Sept. 384/2 She and Edith Merry had been studying Anglo-Saxon together, and he had guyed them both about it, calling them blue-stockings. **1895** W. Archer *Theatr. World of 1894* xliii. 287 Larking and guying on the stage are my abhorrence. **1898** J. Hollingshead *Gaiety Chron.* x. 414 The actors, I am bound to say, treated this curious fossil of dramatic protection with more than proper respect, and did not 'guy' the parts allotted to them. **1906** *Daily Chron.* 31 Oct. 5/5 We must make an end of that disgusting blunder of guying them [*sc.* arrested suffragettes] up in hideous prison uniforms. **1963** *Times* 27 May 8/2 Francoise Sagan, British phlegmatism and many other picturesque aspects of contemporary life in the 1960s are gently but tellingly guyed by Mr. Kohout. **1970** G. Greer *Female Eunuch* 328 Vociferous women are guyed in the press.

Hence **'guying** *vbl. sb.*

1885 J. K. Jerome *On the Stage* 152 'Guying' is . . indulged in only by the silliest portion of the audience.

guy (gaɪ), *v.*[4] *slang.* [f. guy *sb.*[2] (sense 3 b).] *intr.* To go off, run away. Also with *off.*

1879 J. W. Horsley in *Macm. Mag.* XL. 500/2, I planned with another boy to guy (run away). **1897** *Daily News* 7 June 3/5 Prisoner . . 'done a guy'. . . He did what? Witness—He 'guyed' off. **1938** F. D. Sharpe *Sharpe of Flying Squad* xxvi. 263 Jack, guy for your b—— life. The Squad are here and they're pinching *everybody.* **1963** *Times* 15 Feb. 4/7 Hurry up, I have had to do a chap, we will have to guy out of here.

† **'guyage.** *Obs. rare.* In 5 gwyage. [a. OF. *guyage*, f. *guie* guy *sb.*[1]: see -age.] = guidage 1.

c **1425** *MS. Cott. Claud.* A. 2 lf. 124b, Alle þat vnrythefully settyth tallages vppon men of holy chirche, as podage, gwyage, or any oþur vnskylful thraldam.

guyan, obs. form of gean, wild cherry.

1578 Lyte *Dodoens* vi. l. 723 The Guyan or sweete Cherries.

Guyanese (gaɪə'ni:z), *a.* and *sb.* [f. *Guyana* + -ese.] **A.** *adj.* Of or pertaining to Guyana, formerly British Guiana. **B.** *sb.* A native or inhabitant of Guyana; also in collective sense. So **Gu'yanan.** Cf. Guianese.

1965 *New Statesman* 26 Nov. 814/1 If UDI had been proclaimed by Adenis or Guyanans, can anyone deny we would have sent in troops immediately? **1966** 'A. York' *Eliminator* vii. 131 The Guyanese police and us parted company. **1966** *Listener* 2 June 781/1 The uncertainties facing the Guyanese people as they acquire independence. *Ibid.* 781/2 Most Guyanese acquired a fairly uniform central culture. **1968** *Times* 10 Feb. 4/3 Five out of six Guyanese live in villages. **1969** *Daily Tel.* 11 Nov. 1/7 Sir David, first Guyanese Governor-General of Guyana, was leaving the West Indian Club. **1971** *Jamaican Weekly Gleaner* 3 Nov. 24/1 A Jamaican, a Trinidadian and two Guyanese women.

guyd(e)home, obs. form of guidon.

guydi, obs. form of giddy *a.*

guydion, -done, obs. forms of guidon.

guylden, obs. form of gulden.

guynny, obs. form of Guinea.

guyot ('gi:jəʊ). *Oceanogr.* [f. the name of the Swiss geographer A. H. *Guyot* (1807–84).] A flat-topped, submarine mountain; a kind of sea-mount.

1946 H. H. Hess in *Amer. Jrnl. Sci.* CCXLIV. 772 In discussing these submerged flat-topped peaks which rise from the normal ocean floor, the writer will henceforth call them 'guyots' after the 19th century geographer, Arnold Guyot. **1959** *New Scientist* 1 Jan. 14/3 These 'tablemounts' (or 'guyots', if one prefers to use the non-descriptive term of the discoverer, Prof. H. Hess of Princeton) must be deep-drowned ancient islands. **1962** *Ibid.* 12 Apr. 11/2 The deep flat-topped sea-mounts or guyots which are such a typical feature of the Pacific. **1970** *Sci. Amer.* Feb. 36 (*caption*) Mount Asmara . . resembles the numerous guyots, or submerged oceanic mountains, whose level summits are usually attributed to wave erosion.

† **guyour.** *Obs.* Also 4 gyour, 4–5 giour(e. [a. OF. *guyour, guieor*, agent-n. f. *guier* guy *v.*[1]] = guider.

13.. *K. Alis.* 7244 For his gwiuris [*printed* gwinris; *MS. Bodl.* gyoures] me han bytraied. *c* **1330** R. Brunne *Chron.* (1810) 6 Adelard of Westsex was kyng of þe Empire, Of Noreis & Surreis, guyour of ilk schire. —— *Chron. Wace* (Rolls) 3379 þey chose gyours þe contre knew. **1340–70** *Alex. & Dind.* 703 ȝe holde hin [appolin] giour ful good & god of þe handus. **1377** Langl. *P. Pl.* B. xx. 71 Conscience that kepere was and gyoure Ouer kynde Crystene and cardynale vertues. **1401** *Pol. Poems* (Rolls) II. 109 Ne were God the giour, and kept the stern, . . al schulde wende to wrak.

guysard, obs. form of gizzard.

guysarme, variant of gisarme.

† **guysyer,** obs. variant of gizzard, in quots. = 'liver'; see gizzard 3.

1491 Caxton *Vitas Patr.* (W. de W. 1495) ii. 312 a/1, I was strongly persecuted of the guyser in soo moche that I coude not praye to god. *Ibid.*, He put his honde in me & drewe out my guysyer & toke awaye my maladye.

guyton, guytorne, variants of geton. *Obs.*

1460 *Will Oldhall* (Somerset Ho.), Pynnons baners & Guytons.

guytrash, guyzard, vars. gytrash, guisard.

guyver, var. gyver.

‖**guz** (gʌz). *Indian.* Also 7 guzz, 9 gudge. [Hindustani and Pers. *gaz.*] A measure of length (see quot. 1875).

1698 Fryer *Acc. E. India & P.* 206 Corne and Measure in Ratag. The Guzz is 28 Inches ⅝. 5 Guzz is 4 Yards. *Ibid.* 211 Persia. 37½ Inches, 1 Guz for Cloath, &c. 27 Inches 1 Guz for Carpets, Silk, Fine Stuff, &c. **1800** *Asiat. Ann. Reg., Misc. Tracts* 237/1 The image is in an erect posture, and his feet measure ten guz in length. **1875** Bedford *Sailor's Pocket Bk.* ix. (ed. 2) 323 Guz (average) = 36 English Inches, at Madras = 33, Bombay = 27.

guze (gju:z). *Her.* [Of obscure origin; Cotgr. 1611 has *guses* as a Fr. word, with the same gloss as in quot. 1562.] A roundle of a sanguine tint.

1562 Leigh *Armorie* (1597) 88 The field Or, ix Guzes, iij, iij, and iij. The meaning wherof is the ball of the eye, and is so blazed, although it be sanguin of colour. **1610** Guillim *Heraldry* iv. xix. (1611) 226 If they [Roundles] be . . Sanguine . . They are reckoned . . Guzes. **1882** Cussans *Her.* iv. (ed. 3) 74.

guzla, var. gusle.

guzzle ('gʌz(ə)l), *sb.* Also 7 gozel(l. [? f. the vb.]

1. A gutter, drain. Also *fig. Obs.* exc. *dial.*

1598 Florio, *Solchi*, furrowes . . Also gullets or gozels of water. *Ibid.*, *Traghetto*, a ferrie, a passage, a foarde, a gozell ouer, or from shore to shore. **1599** Marston *Sco. Villanie* ii. vii. 203 Mean'st thou . . That sinke of filth, that guzzle most impure? What he? **1619** R. Harris *Drunkard's Cup* 12 Such as . . lie tumbling in their owne vomite, and sleeping in a guzle. **1619** W. Whateley *God's Husb.* i. (1622) 50 The filthy stinking guzzle of Original sinne. **1654** Trapp *Comm. Ps.* li. 2 Though a Swine be washed never so clean . . she will be ready to wallow in the next guzzle. **1659** Torriano, *Rigagno*, any little . . gutter or gozel of water drawn by art into some field or garden. **1695** Kennett *Par. Antiq.* Gloss. s.v. *Carecta*, *Carr* a gutter is in Lincolnshire a Gool, in Kent a Guzzle, in Wiltshire a Gushill, and Gooshill. **1825** Britton *Beauties Wilts* III. 374 *Guzzle*, a filthy drain, or the filth of a drain. **1888** *Berksh. Gloss.*, *Guzzle*, the hole for slops outside cottages.

attrib. **1599** Marston *Sco. Villanie* i. Proem 171 Quake guzzell dogs, that liue on putred slime.

2. Drink, liquor.

a **1704** T. Brown *Wks.* (1730) II. 180 Where [have you] squander'd away the tiresom minutes of your evening leisure, over seal'd Winchesters of three-penny guzzle? **1709** *Rambl. Fuddle-Cups* 16 Drink Porters Guzzle much oftner than Claret. **1788** Wolcot (P. Pindar) *P.'s Pension* Wks. 1816 I. 414 Lo, for a little meat and guzzle, This sneaking cur, too, takes the muzzle. **1893** Kennard *Diogenes' Sandals* xi. (ed. 2) 178 Then they'd sell ye 'guzzle' for next to nothin'.

3. A bout of excessive eating and drinking; a debauch.

1836 M. Scott *Cruise Midge* xviii. 285 About the time supper was announced . . and just before the guzzle began. **1898** *N.B. Daily Mail* 28 Oct. 3 He opposed the freedom of the city to Mr. C—— on account of the inevitable 'guzzle' thereafter.

4. *dial.* The throat.

1659 *Lond. Chanticleers* xi. 25 A single one [*sc.* a cord] I believe wou'd spoile your drinking, 'twou'd ty up your guzle. **1885** Mucklebackit *Rhymes* 39 (E.D.D.) This kingly dog His lugs down pendin' to his guzzle. **18..** *Oldham Recruit* (E.D.D.), I put my foot in his ribs, and my fingers in the guzzel of his neck.

5. *attrib.*, as **guzzle-guts,** a glutton.

1959 I. & P. Opie *Lore & Lang. Schoolch.* ix. 167 They call him [*sc.* a greedy-guts] . . guzzle-guts. **1968** *Gloss. Brit. Argot* (Paramount Pictures), *Guzzle-guts*, glutton.

guzzle ('gʌz(ə)l), *v.* Forms: 6 gussel, 6–8 guzle, 7 gusle, gousle, guzzel, 7– guzzle. [? a. OF. *gosiller* (recorded in the sense 'to vomit', also 'to chatter'), connected with *gosier* 'throat'.]

1. *trans.* To swallow (liquor, *rarely* food) greedily or to excess. Also with *down, up.*

1583 Golding *Calvin on Deut.* li, Wyne which they gussel and quaffe vp without measure or reason. **1609** W. M. *Man in Moone* (1857) 90 He hath . . gusled downe his throate more then Cleopatra quaffed in a bravado to Mark Anthonie. **1687** T. Brown *Saints in Uproar* Wks. 1730 I. 80 How many gallons have you guzzled for your morning's draught? **1692** Tryon *Good House-w.* xix. 175 Men and Women addict themselves . . to guzzle down the Richest Wines daily. **1711** Ramsay *Elegy on M. Johnston* 22 We guzl'd Scuds Till we cou'd scarce . . Cast off our duds. **1808** C. K. Sharpe *Corr.* (1888) I. 336 How it annoyed me to behold Belvidera [Mrs. Siddons] guzzle boiled beef and mustard, swill streams of porter [etc.]. **1826** Disraeli *Viv. Grey* ii. viii, Guzzling his venison pasties. **1841** Thackeray *Mem. Gormand.* Wks. 1886 XXIII. 350 It is absurd to be guzzling wine at fifteen francs a bottle.

transf. **1638** Rawley tr. *Bacon's Life & Death* (1650) 28 The Spirits are to be put into such a temperament, and degree of activity; That they should not (as He saith) Drink or Guzzle the juyces of the Body, but Sip them onely.

2. To consume or dissipate (time, money, etc.) in guzzling. With *away, down.*

1653 Manton *Exp. James* v. 5 It is prodigious in poor men to guzzle and drink away their days. **1658** Gurnall *Chr. in Arm.* verse 14 x. §2 (1669) 42/2 He that should save his money from guzling it down his throat. **1726** Amherst *Terræ Fil.* i. 4 To see the virtuous munificence of founders . . guzzled down in hogsheads of wine. *c* **1797** *Chronicle* in *Spirit Publ. Jrnls.* (1799) I. 356, I do not mean you should guzzle away all that large stock of money. **1895** 'Rosemary' *Under the Chilterns* 188 An' 'ere's me an' the children in rags . . an' you guzzlin' away down at the public wot should go to put cloes on their backs.

3. *intr.* To drink largely or greedily, to 'swill'.

1579–80 North *Plutarch* (1595) 880 They . . passed away the night in guzling and drinking drunk. **1618** E. Elton *Compl. Sanct. Sinner* (1622) 240 Many sit guzzeling in the ale-house. **1647** Trapp *Comm. Eph.* v. 4 Some men as ducks have their noses alwaies guzling in the gutter of obscene talk. **1784** Cowper *Task* iv. 473 There sit, . . guzzling deep, the boor, The lackey, and the groom. **1793** Wolcot (P. Pindar) *Ep. to the Pope* Wks. 1812 III. 208 In vice's drunken Cup for ever guzzling. **1855** Macaulay *Hist. Eng.* xv. III. 519 If he chose to shoot and guzzle at his country seat when important business was under consideration at Westminster.

4. *trans.* To seize by the throat, choke, throttle; to strangle, kill. (Cf. guzzle *sb.* 4.) *slang* and *dial.*

1885 F. Gordon *Pyotshaw* 318 *Guzzle*, to choke violently. **1916** Joyce *Portrait of Artist* (1917) iv. 195 Duck him! Guzzle him now, Towser! **1931** D. Runyon *Guys & Dolls* (1932) 186 He will be safe from being guzzled by some of Black Mike's or Benny's guys. **1960** *Observer* 17 July 9/8 'Can't you . . guzzle your friends, Hugh?' . . North of the Border it [*sc.* the word 'guzzle'] does not mean to stuff oneself: apparently it means to gag.

Hence **'guzzledom** *nonce-wd.*

1895 A. Nutt in K. Meyer *Voy. Bran* I. 207 A marvellous land of Cockayne, of gorging guzzledom, of bursting fatness.

guzzler ('gʌzlə(r)). [f. guzzle *v.* + -er[1].] One who guzzles, in the senses of the verb.

a **1704** T. Brown *Wks.* (1708) III. 144 Being an eternal Guzzler of Wine. **1731** Mrs. Pendarves *Let. to Mrs. A. Granville* in *Mrs. Delany's Life & Corr.* I. 309 There was a supper ordered . . and vast profusion of meat and drink, which you may be sure has gained the hearts of all guzzlers. **1852** Hawthorne *Tanglewood T., Circe's Palace* (1879) 138 These two-and-twenty guzzlers . . ate and drank.

guzzling ('gʌzlɪŋ), *vbl. sb.* [f. guzzle *v.* + -ing[1].] The action of the vb. guzzle.

1642 Rogers *Naaman* 392 [They] spend their time in guzling and drinking. **1711** E. Ward *Vulgus Brit.* ix. 99 By their Guzling and Neglect of Work . . They lose their Business. **1865** Dickens *Mut. Fr.* iii. x, Swine at least fatten on their guzzling. **1883** G. W. Curtis in *Harper's Mag.* Dec. 4/2 Christmas . . was all guzzling and gobbling.

guzzling ('gʌzlɪŋ), *ppl. a.* Also 7 gousling. [+ -ing[2].] That guzzles, in the senses of the verb; hence, drunken, gluttonous, greedy.

1637 R. Humphrey tr. *St. Ambrose* i. 137 The vndrainable draught of the gousling drunkards. **1714** Gay *Sheph. Week* v. 64 To fat the guzzling Hogs with Floods of Whey. **1827** Syd. Smith *Wks.* (1867) II. 133 There is something shocking in the greedy, growling, guzzling monopoly of such a blessing. **1840** Barham *Ingol. Leg* Ser. iii. *J. Jarvis's Wig*, The beer, you guzzling wretch!—what beer? **1852** Jerdan *Autobiog.* II. xii. 142 A quiet, large, guzzling native of the Emerald Isle. **1863** Whyte Melville *Gladiators* I. 94 He was busy . . with the eager, guzzling avidity of a pig.

gwacum, obs. form of guaiacum.

gwairdoun, obs. Sc. form of guerdon.

gwakin, obs. form of guaiacum.

gwan, g'wan (gwɑ:n). *U.S.* and *Irish dial.* pronunciation of *go on* (esp. go *v.* 86 j).

1906 C. E. Mulford in *Outing* Apr. 75/2 'Where'd he get you, Fat?' asked Hopalong. 'G'wan, don't get funny, son,' replied Skinny. **1924** *Dialect Notes* V. 269 *Gwan* (= 'go on'). **1968** 'N. Blake' *Private Wound* vii. 96 G'wan, Harry. Give him a kiss. He deserves it. **1970** M. Kenyon *100,000 Welcomes* xxii. 154 G'wan onto it! Anyone wantin' to interfere wid yous'd have to be hard up!

gwane, gwayn, obs. ff. guana, the Iguana.

gwarri, var. GUARRI.

gwash. Anglicized form of GOUACHE, q.v.
1830 H. ANGELO *Remin.* I. 202 What on the Continent is denominated *gwash*, or painting in body water-colours. *Ibid.* 203 In oil, in crayon, and in gwash.

gwely ('gwɛlɪ). [Welsh.] **a.** A social unit that was once traditional in Wales, consisting of four generations of one family in which the great-grandfather, the head of the group, had proprietary right over its landed property. **b.** The land held by the members of such a group.
1889 H. LEWIS *Anc. Laws Wales* iv. 81 There was..a family or *gwely*, then a joint family sprung from or including three generations of ancestors. *Ibid.* vi. 167 Gavell is often used interchangeably with *wele*, which meant the holding of a family (gwely). **1895** F. SEEBOHM *Tribal Syst. Wales* i. 9 We shall see..that the *wele* or *gwely* was, strictly speaking, rather the family or kindred occupying the hamlet than the hamlet itself. **1900** RHYS & BRYNMOR-JONES *Welsh People* vi. 195 The rights of the chief of household..and the lands in the occupation of himself and other members of his household were termed his *gwely*. *Ibid.* 197 There was no re-division of the ancestor's *gwely* after the second cousins had divided it. **1907** H. M. CHADWICK *Origin Eng. Nation* xii. 324 In some laws,..we find..evidence for a system similar to that of the Welsh gwely. **1951** *Trans. Anglesey Antiq. Soc. & Field Club* 35 The local unit was the 'gwely', a specific area of land held, semi-communally, by a group of relatives. *Ibid.* 36 After the Edwardian conquest, new factors reinforced those already at work... Even within the *gwely* itself, the individual tribesman of initiative could often buy up the portions of his less fortunate or less energetic kinsmen. **1968** *Encycl. Brit.* XXIII. 156/2 A movement toward more stationary settlement among freemen slowly spread..over the whole country, splitting the *maenor* into smaller township units (*trefs*)..and laying the foundations of the hamlets and clanlands (*gwelys*).

Gwentian ('gwɛntɪən), *sb.* and *a.* [f. the name *Gwent* + -IAN.] **A.** *sb.* **a.** An inhabitant of Gwent in Monmouthshire, historically a Welsh principality. **b.** The dialect of this region. **B.** *adj.* Of or pertaining to Gwent.
1831 S. LEWIS *Topogr. Dict. England* III. 318/2 The attempts of the Anglo-Saxon sovereigns to subjugate Wales were opposed by the Gwentians with extraordinary courage, insomuch that they do not appear to have been completely conquered during the Anglo-Saxon period. **1841** A. OWEN *Anc. Laws & Institutes of Wales* p. vi, The Laws and Institutes of Wales are here given in six parts: the three first of these are the Venedotian, the Dimetian, and the Gwentian Codes. *Ibid.* p. vii, The Gwentian Code.. contains an account of territorial divisions peculiar to Gwent. **1901** *Daily Chron.* 16 Oct. 3/2 The Gwentian bowmen were famous. **1911** J. E. LLOYD *Hist. Wales* I. x. 342 The Gwentian Code..appears to be also a compilation, to be ascribed, perhaps, to Morgeneu and his son Cyfnerth, who are mentioned as the authors. **1913** J. M. JONES *Welsh Gram.* 8 Gwentian, the dialect of Gwent and Morgannwg, or South East Wales.

gwerddoun, gwerdon(e, obs. ff. GUERDON.

gwerpysshe: see GUERPE, GUERPISH.

gwerre, variant of GUERRE *Obs.*, war.

gwidege, var. GUIDES *Obs.*, the jugular vein.

gwine (gwaɪn). Also **gwyn(e)**. Representing *dial.* pronunciation of GOING *pres. pple.* (GO *v.* A. 7).
1831 R. LOWER *Tom Cladpole's Jurney* XLII. 14 He said he must be gwyn. **1881** H. & C. R. SMITH *Isle of Wight Words* 50, I be gwine zoo vast as I can. **1882** 'MARK TWAIN' *Lett. to Publishers* 4 Mar. (1967) 152 I's gwyne to sen' you de stuff. **1896** *Longman's Mag.* Dec. 155 As I wur gwine up street, zo I looked in. **1908** *Sears, Roebuck Catal.* 200/1 Vocal Quartettes... I'se Gwine Back to Dixie (coon song). **1932** *Amer. Speech* VII. 178 By de time a'-wee was gwine tek de 'tart again, me foot get soak. **1950** *Publ. Amer. Dial. Soc.* XIV. 34 Whar you gwine? **1969** 'J. MORRIS' *Fever Grass* ii. 19 One day police gwine hol' you.

gwinead, -iad, obs. forms of GWYNIAD.

gwis, obs. Sc. form of GOOSE.

gwyage, variant of GUYAGE *Obs.*, guidage.

gwylim, variant of GUILLEM.

gwyniad ('gwɪnɪæd). Forms: 7 **guinead**, 7–9 **guiniad**, (8 **guinniad**, 9 **gwynniad**), 8–9 **gwiniad**, 9 **gwinead**, 8– **gywniad**. [a. Welsh *gwyniad*, f. *gwyn* white.] A fish of the salmon or trout kind (*Coregonus Pennantii*) with white flesh, found in lakes, esp. in Bala lake on the Dee.
1611 SPEED *Theat. Gt. Brit.* (1614) 117/2 The fish called guinead bred in that meare [Bala lake] never is seene in the river Dee. **1769** *De Foe's Tour Gt. Brit.* (ed. 7) II. 381 A Fish ..called Gwiniad or fresh-water Whiting. **1807** SIR R. C. HOARE *Tour Irel.* 224 The pollen..is the same as..the gwyniad of Bala lake in north Wales. **1861** *Act 24 & 25 Vict.* c. 109 §4 All migratory fish of the genus salmon, whether known by the names..white trout, sewin, buntling, guiniad, ..or by any other local name. **1884** G. F. BRAITHWAITE *Salmonidæ Westmorld.* ii. 5 The gwyniad or fresh water herring.
attrib. **1883** *Fisheries Exhib. Catal.* 365 Gwyniad Seine.. Gwyniad Net.

gy, Sc. var. GUY *sb.*[1]; var. GUY *v.*[1] *Obs.*

gy-, in words of Greek etymology, is in this Dictionary marked to be pronounced with (dʒ), in accordance with the general principle that in words of Gr. derivation (but latinized spelling) Eng. pronunciation follows the rule of the Romanic langs. for the 'softening' of *c* and *g*. The pronunciation (dʒ) is now practically universal in the case of those words beginning with *gy-* that have much colloquial currency (*gymnasium, gymnast, gymnastic*). Most scientific words of Greek etymology beginning with *gyn-* are now usually pronounced with (g) rather than (dʒ); in particular *gynæcology* and its derivatives are in general use with this pronunciation.
The orthoepists of the 18th c. (Sheridan, Nares, Walker) advocate the 'soft' pronunciation in *gymnastic*, but admit that prevailing usage may be against them. All the pronouncing Dicts. of the 19th c. have (dʒ) throughout, exc. Enfield, Jameson, and Cassell's Encyclopædic Dict.; the last-named restricts the 'hard *g*' to those terms of science and of classical antiquities 'which have not passed, and probably will not pass, into general use'.

gyal, variant of GAYAL.

gyand, -ane, -a(u)nt(e, etc., obs. ff. GIANT.

gyb(b)ate, obs. form of GIBBET *sb.*[1]

gybbe, variant of GIB *sb.*[2] *Obs.*; obs. f. JIB.

gybe, *sb.*[1] *Thieves' slang.* ? *Obs.* [Of unknown origin.] (See quot. 1673.)
1561 AWDELAY *Frat. Vacab.* 5 He useth to make counterfaite licences which they call Gybes. **1673** R. HEAD *Canting Acad.* 78 They have alwaies a Counterfeit Pass or License which they call a Gybe. **1818** SCOTT *Hrt. Midl.* xxv, He knows my gybe as well as the jark of e'er a queer cuffin in England—and there's rogue's Latin for you.

gybe (dʒaɪb), *sb.*[2] *Naut.* [f. next vb.; cf. Du. *gijp* (in 17th c. *gijb*), of the same meaning; also 'a boom'.] An act of gybing.
1880 *Boy's Own Bk.* 314 *Jibe*, the act of bringing over the sail from one side of the vessel to the other. **1884** *Sat. Rev.* 31 May 714/2 She beguiled the tedium of the run by gybing all standing..her main-boom went outside the strop on the second or third gybe.

gybe (dʒaɪb), *v. Naut.* Forms: 7 **gibe**, 8–9 **jibe**, 7– **gybe**. See also JIB *v.* [app. a. Du. *gijben* (now *gijpen*); but the initial (dʒ) is unexplained. Cf. G. *gieben, giepen* (from Du. or LG.), Da. *gibbe*, Sw. *gippa, gipa*.]
1. a. *intr.* Of a fore-and-aft sail or its boom: To swing from one side of the vessel to the other.
1693 *Minutes Prov. Counc. Pennsylv.* I. (1852) 377 Ned Burch..brought the saill to gybe. **1699** DICKENSON *Jrnl. Trav.* 2 Our Master being on the Quarter-Deck, our Boom-gibing knocked him down. [**1719**: DEFOE uses *gib*; see JIB *v.*] **1873** G. C. DAVIES *Mount. & Mere* xvi. 133 When the sails gybed one could hear the deep, thunderlike flaps of the brown canvas. **1885** 'NASEBY' *Oaks & Birches* I. 188 The mainsail had no boom, therefore it was more likely to jibe.
b. *trans.* To cause (a fore-and-aft sail) to swing from one side of the vessel to the other.
[**1776, 1834**, etc.: see JIB *v.*] **1899** *Daily News* 4 Oct. 3/2 Columbia..gybed her mainsail to port.
2. *intr.* To alter the course of a boat when the wind is aft so that her boom-sails gybe. Said also of the boat itself; also ***to gybe over***. Also *trans.* with the boat as object; also, to sail round (any object) by gybing.
1693 *Minutes Prov. Counc. Pennsylv.* I. (1852) 376 They gybed, and the boom knock't the sd. Mr. overboard. **1769** FALCONER *Dict. Marine* (1780), *Changer les voiles*, to shift the sails; to brace about; to jibe. **1856** OLMSTED *Slave States* 143 Belaying jib-sheet, he came aft, and put helm up to wear round. Just as he jibed, came another flaw from the southeast. **1868** *Daily News* 27 Aug., The Oimara was striving well to over-take the leaders, preparatory to gybing round the Noman's Fort. **1881** *Times* 3 Jan. 10/2 Mr. P. was looking out for a bird he had wounded, when the boat was gybed. Messrs. H. and P. lost their balance, and the boat capsized. **1889** H. M. DOUGHTY *Friesland Meres* 273 Having to gybe, the shock of the sail coming over..would have been considered dangerous. **1896** *Dundee Advertiser* 11 July 8 The Vigilant held out to gybe the mark. **1897** MARY KINGSLEY *W. Africa* 383 Eveke..lets her gybe, and I get knocked into the bottom of the boat by the boom. **1899** *N.B. Daily Mail* 9 Oct. 4 Shamrock took in her spinnaker and gybed over.
Hence **'gybing** *vbl. sb.*, the action of the verb.
1769 FALCONER *Dict. Marine* (1776), *Gybing*, the act of shifting any boom-sail from one side of the mast to the other. **1872** *Daily News* 12 Aug., A seaman, told to 'stand by' the preventive back stay in readiness for gybing, had let it go. **1963** *Times* 31 May 5/1 Inexorably, Shadow sailed past to leeward, where there was still some wind and, though Wildfire did at last get moving again, Shadow was ahead at the gybing mark.

gybe, var. JIBE *v.*
1959 *Economist* 14 Feb. 612/1 A..fall in export deliveries ..which gybes a little oddly with official trade figures.

gyb(e)let(t, gyblot, obs. forms of GIBLET.

gybot, erron. form of GIGOT[1].
1597 *Bk. Cookerie* E ij b, How to rost a Gybot of mutton.

gybrish, obs. form of GIBBERISH.

gybyt(te, obs. form of GIBBET *sb.*

gyddy, gydi(e, obs. forms of GIDDY.

gydya, variant of GIDDEA.

gye, obs. f. GUY *sb.*[1]; var. GUY *v.*[1] *Obs.*

gyeld, gyer, obs. ff. GUILD *sb.*, JEER.

†**'gyesite.** *Obs. rare*[−1]. [ad. med.L. *giezīta* (St. Bernard), f. *Giezi*, the L. (Vulg.) form of Heb. גיחזי Gehazi. Cf. the deriv. GIESETRYE.] One who commits the sin of Gehazi (2 Kings v), i.e. who asks or accepts money in return for spiritual things.
1426 LYDG. *De Guil. Pilgr.* (E.E.T.S.) 18024 The byggyng is called symony..They that it sell for gret or lyt Bene y-called Gyesite.

gyes warp, obs. form of GUESS-WARP.

gyf(fe, gyffe-gaffe, obs. ff. GIF *conj.*, GIFF-GAFF.

gyge, var. GIG *sb.*[3], ? a squeaking noise.

gygelot, gygge, obs. ff. GIGLET, GIG *sb.*[1]

gygget, gygot, obs. forms of GIGOT[1].

gyglot, gygyll, obs. ff. GIGLET, GIGGLE *v.*[1]

gyl, obs. form of GUILE.

gylat, variant of GILLOT *Obs.*

gyld, obs. form of GILD, GUILD.

gylden, gylder: see GILDEN, GULDEN, GUILDER.

gyldyn, obs. f. GILD *v.*[1]; var. GILDEN *a. Obs.*

gyle (gaɪl). *Brewing.* Forms: 5 **gyyl, gyylde**, 5–6 **gyl**, 5–8 **gile**, 6 **guyle**, *Sc.* **geill**, 7 **gaile, gial-, gule**, 7–9 **gail, guile**, 8 **gil**, 8–9 **gaal**, 9 **garl, geyle, guil-(vat)**, 4– **gyle**. [a. Du. *gijl*, earlier *ghijl* 'chylus, cremor cereuisiæ' (Kilian), connected with *gijlen* to ferment. Of obscure origin; Franck suggests that it may be related to *geil* luxuriant in growth; see GOLE *a.* Cf. F. *guiller* (of beer) to ferment, work off the yeast.]
1. A brewing; the quantity of beer or ale brewed at one time.
1594 PLAT *Jewell-ho.* III. 17 A double or treble quantitie of hoppes to an ordinary guile of Strong Beere. **1704** *Lond. Gaz.* No. 4028/4 Several Guiles of Drink brewed by one Brisca Coburn, Brewer. **1730** SWIFT *Panegyrick on Dean* 330 Teach Dennis how to stir the guile. **1839** URE *Dict. Arts* 101 Two coolers are indispensable when we make two kinds of beer from the same brewing, and even in single brewings, called gyles, if small beer is to be made. **1844** T. WEBSTER *Encycl. Dom. Econ.* 574 *Entire gyle*, when there is only one kind of beer from the same malt. *Party gyles*, a name used by the excise for making two kinds of beer from one malt. **1872** *Trans. R.I.B.A.* 107 Striking one of the old lucifer matches over a tun, is sufficient to give the whole gyle a flavour of sulphur.
2. Wort in process of fermentation.
*c***1440** *Promp. Parv.* 193/2 *Gyylde*, or newe ale (*MSS. K.* gile, *H.* gyyl, *S.* gyle of nw ale, *Pynson* gyle), *celium, vel celia.* **1756** C. LUCAS *Ess. Waters* II. 21 Quantities of must or gile or wort are fermenting. **1860** *Cornh. Mag.* II. 97, I have nothing better to offer you, than the skimmings of skimmed milk, and the gyle of thrice-brewed malt. **1871** *Q. Rev.* CXXXI. 401 As soon as the wort is sufficiently cool, it is run off into a vessel, called a fermenting tun or square; a quantity of yeast is then mixed with it, it begins to ferment, and is called a gyle.
3. A 'gyle-tun'.
1836 *Penny Cycl.* V. 404/1 The next operation, that of fermentation, is carried on in a vessel called a gyle, or fermenting tun, which is either of a square or round shape. **1875** in KNIGHT *Dict. Mech.*
4. *attrib.* and *Comb.*: **gyle-dish**, a funnel for pouring liquor into casks; †**gyle-house**, the place where the gyle was set to cool; †**gyle-tub**, **gyle-tun** = GYLE-FAT; †**gyle-wort** (see quot.), ? = GROUT *sb.*[1] 2 b.
1674 RAY *N.C. Words* 20 The *Gail or Guile-dish; the Tun dish. **1334–5** *Durh. Acc. Rolls* 525 Carpentar, pro opere de *Gylhous bracine, 13 *li.* 12*s.* 10*d.* **1498** *Nottingham Rec.* III. 297 Ye bakhows; ye gylhows. **1567** *Wills & Inv. N.C.* (Surtees 1835) 279 It'm In The Gile Howse one gile fatt, ij tubbes. **1662** LAMONT *Diary* (Maitld. Club) 151 Johne Rattray..being in the garden yearde, sneding tries on the north dyke, ouer against the coall-stabell, for the gyle-house. **1568** *Gile tub [see GYLE-FAT]. **1596** in *Unton Inv.* (1841) 3 In the Brewehowse.—Item..one gyle tubbe. **1743** *Lond. & Country Brew.* II. (ed. 2) 119 Set it in the *Guile-Tun, till it gathers a Head, which must be skimmed off. **1839** URE *Dict. Arts* 102 These fermenting tuns are commonly called gyle-tuns, or working tuns, and are either square or circular. **1565** COOPER *Thesaurus*, *Chelid[on]ium minus*, the herbe called *gylewoorte.

gyle, obs. form of GUILE.

gyle-fat. *Obs.* exc. *dial.* Forms: see GYLE and FAT *sb.*[1] The vat in which the wort is left to ferment.

1341 *Test. Ebor.* (Surtees) I. 2 Duas parvas cunas [*sic.*: *read* cuuas] quæ vocantur gylefatts. **1483** *Cath. Angl.* 155/2 A Gilefatte, *acromellarium.* **1496** *Nottingham Rec.* III. 44 Unum gylefatte cum coopertorio et unum pully. **1533** *Extracts Aberd. Reg.* (1844) I. 451 Ane brew fatt, ane geill fat, ane flesch fatt [etc.]. **1568** *Wills & Inv. N.C.* (Surtees 1835) 282 In ye Brewhouse. One gile tub, one maskin tub, and one gilefatt. **1674–90** RAY *N.C. Words* 39 *The Gaile or Guile-Fat*, the Vat in which the Beer is wrought up. **1727** BRADLEY *Fam. Dict.* s.v. *Brewhouse*, The Mash-Fat should be ever near to the Head, the Cooler near to the Mash-Fat, and the Guile-Fat under the Cooler. **1764** T. BRYDGES *Homer Travest.* (1797) II. 105 Though her guts and mazzard Work'd like a guile-fat. **1788** W. MARSHALL *Yorksh.* II. 330 *Gaalfat, Guilefat*, the vat in which new ale is set to ferment; also the liquor fermenting. **1869** *Lonsdale Gloss.*, *Gailfat.*

gyle-ker. *Obs.* exc. *dial.* In 6 gelker, 7 gailclear, 8 galkeer, 8–9 galker, gailker. [f. GYLE + KIER (a. ON. *ker* tub).] A tub or other vessel for holding wort; also, the liquor contained therein.

1573 *Lanc. & Chesh. Wills* (Chetham Soc.) III. 60 One mashtowinbe [*sic*] two gelkers and two lyttel turnells. **1674** RAY *N.C. Words* 20 *Gail-clear*, a Tub for wort. *c* **1746** J. COLLIER (Tim Bobbin) *View Lanc. Dial.* Wks. (1862) 53 [He] wawtit him o'er into th' Galkeer. **1775** J. WATSON *Halifax* 538 *Gailker*, a Vessel to work new drink in; or the drink itself. **1857** J. SCHOLES *Jaunt to see Queen* 22 (Lanc. Gloss.) Some o' thir own brewin wur browt eawt, ut aw believe coom fro under th' galker, fur it wur onkomon fresh o' berm.

gylen, gyler, -ery(e: see GUILE *v.*, GUILER, -ERY.

†'**gyling,** *vbl. sb. Obs.* Also 5 yilyng, 6 yailing. [f. GYLE + -ING[1].] Only *attrib.*, in ***gyling-house, -ker, -tub, -fat***, = gyle-house, etc.

1411 in *Charters*, etc. *Priory Finchale* (Surtees) p. clvii, In primis, iij lebetes magnæ et iiij parvæ in le gylnghous [*sic*]. **1420** *Inv.* in *Lincoln Ch. Acc. Bk.* A. 2. 30. lf. 69, 2 gilyng tubbes. *c* **1440** *Inv.* in *Camden Misc.* (1895) IX. p. xviii, Unum meschfatte, unum yilyngfatte. **1573** *Inv.* in *Lanc. & Chesh. Wills* (Chetham Soc. 1884) 64 A yailing keare xij[d]. **1583** *Wills & Inv. N.C.* (Surtees 1860) 77, j guylinge fatte.

gyll(e, obs. form of GILL, GUILE.

gyllofer, -fre, -fyr, obs. ff. GILLYFLOWER.

gyllor, gyllot, vars. GUILER, GILLOT *Obs.*

gylmyr, obs. form of GIMMER[2].

gylofre, obs. form of GILLYFLOWER.

gylo(u)r, -ory, -ous, var. GUILER, -ERY, -OUS.

gylt, obs. pa. pple. GILD *v.*[1]; obs. f. GUILT.

gylté, -i(e, -if, -y(f, obs. forms of GUILTY.

gym, obs. form of GIM *a.*, smart, spruce.

gym (dʒɪm). Colloq. abbreviation of GYMNASIUM or GYMNASTIC(S. Also *attrib.*, as ***gym-dress, -slip, -tunic*** (these also *spec.* of a schoolgirl's garment not primarily for use in the gymnasium); ***gym-knickers, -mistress, -shoe,*** etc.

1871 L. H. BAGG *Four Yrs. at Yale* i. 45 *Gym*, abbreviation for *gymnasium.* **1887** H. BAUMANN *Londinismen* 70/2 *Gym-shoes* (statt gymnastic-shoes) Schulsprache: Turnschuhe. **1888** *Boy's Own Paper* Summer No. 38/3 If you'll come round to the Gym. after, I'll show you. **1889** BARRÈRE & LELAND *Dict. Slang*, *Gymcad* (Royal Military Academy), a gymnasium instructor. **1891** H. S. HOLLAND in S. Paget *Mem.* (1921) 198 We had a superb exhibition in the gym. **1907** *Daily Chron.* 27 Nov. 3/3 The 'gym.' practices. **1922** JOYCE *Ulysses* 520 If you do tremble in anticipation of heel discipline to be inflicted in gym costume. **1926** F. M. FORD *Man could stand Up* I. i. 17 Five foot four in her gym shoes. **1930** *Cambridge Daily News* 25 Sept. 3/4 Gym slips should not be washed. **1932** D. C. MINTER *Mod. Needlecraft* 252 Gym Knickers.. 1¼ to 1½ yards blue or brown drill, nurse cloth or serge. **1936** *Daily Sketch* 9 Mar. 11/2 When a girl leaves school.. she throws away.. her hockey sticks and her gym tunic. **1944** A. THIRKELL *Headmistress* iv. 79 Going to a physical culture college to learn to be gym and games mistresses. **1947** DYLAN THOMAS *Let.* 20 May (1966) 307 She thumped the hot Florence pavements.. elbowing the droll Florentines from her gym-knickered way. **1949** 'G. ORWELL' *Nineteen Eighty-Four* I. 34 A youngish woman.. dressed in tunic and gym-shoes. **1949** D. SMITH *I capture Castle* I. iv. 41 My school gym-dress has a lot of life in it yet. **1961** M. SPARK *Prime of Miss Jean Brodie* ii. 24 Rose Stanley was pulling threads from the girdle of her gym tunic. **1967** H. W. SUTHERLAND *Magnie* iv. 64 That bloody gym dress with the black cotton stockings—and that old school hat. **1969** *Listener* 8 May 640/3 Yes, I've got a recollection of Barbara in a gym slip at Bradford Grammar School. **1970** D. CLARK *Deadly Pattern* vi. 145 One or two of the girls were married almost before they could get out of their gym knickers.

gymbal, gymblett, var. GIMBAL, GIMLET *sb.*[2]

gymbure, -byre, obs. forms of GIMMER[2].

gymell, gymelot, obs. ff. GIMMAL, GIMLET *sb.*[1]

gymew(e, -ey, vars. GEMEW, GEMOW *Obs.*

1413 *St. Mary Ottery Acc. Roll* in G. Oliver *Monast. Exon.* (1846) 280 Pro duobus gymeys emptis pro ostio campanilis 6[d].

gymitrie, obs. form of GEOMETRY.

gymkhana (dʒɪm'kɑːnə). Orig. *Anglo-Indian.* [Said to be a refashioning, by assimilation of the first syllable to that of *gymnastics*, of Hindustani *gend-khāna* 'ball-house', the name given to a racquet-court.] 'A place of public resort at a station, where the needful facilities for athletics and games of sorts are provided' (Y.). Hence (esp. in European use), an athletic sports display. Now *spec.* a meeting at which horses and their riders take part in games and contests; also a competition designed to test driving skill. Also *attrib.*, as ***gymkhana club, meeting.***

1861 ['The first use of it that we can trace is (on the authority of Major John Trotter) at Rurki in 1861, when a gymkhana was instituted there'.—Y.] **1877** *Pioneer Mail* 3 Nov. (Y.), Their proposals are that the Cricket Club should include in their programme the games, etc., proposed by the promoters of a gymkhana Club. **1890** *Blackw. Mag.* Dec. 755/2 We intended to have a gymkhana meeting in the afternoon. **1896** *Daily Tel.* 21 Aug. 5 The Duke and Duchess.. were present.. at a bicycle gymkhana in the grounds. **1900** N. NEWNHAM-DAVIS *Transvaal under Q.* 30 The race-meeting only differed from the gymkhanas in the fact that we had stewards for the former. **1933** A. BLEWITT *Ponies & Children* viii. 120 Nowadays gymkhanas have become very much the fashion. **1955** *Times* 20 Aug. 3/1 Miss Valerie Engelmann is leading by five points from Miss Pat Moss in the gymkhana points competition which is proving a popular feature of this show. **1966** *Publ. Amer. Dial. Soc. 1964* XLII. 5 *Gymkhana*, a tight, low speed sports car competition, in which only one car at a time runs a course. **1970** G. WHEATLEY *Let's start Riding* xxiv. 164 Gymkhanas can be great fun and there are many different events and games for which one can enter, if one has a fast, handy pony.

gymlet(t, -ley, -locke, -lot(te: see GIMLET.

gymmal(l, variant of GIMMAL.

gymmar, -er, obs. forms of GIMMER[2].

gymmew, variant of GEMEW *Obs.*

†**gymnade.** *Obs. rare*$^{-1}$. [ad. Gr. γυμναδ-, γυμνάς trained, exercised, as sb. gymnasium.] = GYMNASIUM.

1677 GALE *Crt. Gentiles* III. 77 Γυμναζειν properly signifies to exercise in the Gymnade.

gymnadenia (dʒɪmnə'diːnɪə). [mod.L. (see quot. 1813), f. Gr. γυμνός naked, bare + ἀδεν-, ἀδήν gland + -IA.] A terrestrial orchid of the genus so called, which includes *G. conopsea*, the fragrant orchid, native to Britain.

1813 R. BROWN in W. Aiton *Hortus Kewensis* (ed. 2) V. 191 Fragrant Gymnadenia. *Nat.* of Britain. *Fl.* June and July. **1856** W. A. BROMFIELD *Flora Vectensis* 479 Fragrant Gymnadenia.. not very general. [**1905** LD. AVEBURY *Notes on Life Hist. Brit. Flowering Plants* 405 This genus [sc. *Habenaria*], in which Gymnadenia is generally included, hardly seems to me to be sufficiently distinct from Orchis.] **1926** G. C. DRUCE *Flora Bucks.* 334 It is somewhat remarkable that the *Gymnadenia* should flourish not only on bare chalk slopes but also in wet bogs. **1965** A. D. HAWKES *Encycl. Cult. Orchids* 234/1 Most of the Gymnadenias, because of their habitat in temperate areas, require rather cool temperatures at all times.

gymnanthous: see GYMNO-.

†**gymnase.** *Obs. rare*$^{-1}$. [ad. L. GYMNASIUM.] = GYMNASIUM.

1598 GRENEWEY *Tacitus' Ann.* XV. v. (1622) 228 The Gymnase burnt [*below* Gymnasium].

gymnasial (dʒɪm'neɪzɪəl), *a.* [f. GYMNASI-UM + -AL[1].] Of or pertaining to the Continental gymnasia or similar educational establishments.

1852 BLACKIE *Stud. Lang.* 19, I would have this science.. taught.. during the last three years of the Gymnasial course. **1868** *Fortn. Rev.* Dec. 626 In Germany, the study [of philosophy] of late, practically, has vanished from the general or gymnasial course. **1883** *Edin. Rev.* Jan. 7 The defects of the gymnasial training.. in Germany.

gymnasiarch (dʒɪm'neɪzɪɑːk). [ad. L. *gymnasiarch-us* and *gymnasiarch-a*, a. Gr. γυμνασίαρχ-ος and γυμνασιάρχ-ης, f. γυμνάσιον GYMNASIUM + -αρχος, -αρχης ruling.]

1. *Gr. Antiq.* An Athenian official whose duty was to superintend athletic schools and games.

[**1579–80** NORTH *Plutarch* (1676) 410 When they had him amongst them, they chose him Gymnasiarchus, to say, a master of exercises of youth.] **1658** PHILLIPS, *Gymnasiarch* (Greek), the chief governour of a *Gymnase* which is a place for all manner of exercise, both of minde and body. **1673** *Lady's Call.* I. i. §8 [It] was thought so indecent in Carneades.. that the Gymnasiarch reproved him for it. **1727** LARDNER *Wks.* (1838) I. 196 The Jews refusing to use oil prepared by other people, the gymnasiarchs gave them a certain prescribed piece of money instead of the oil. **1862** MERIVALE *Rom. Emp.* (1865) III. xxviii. 296 To take his seat as gymnasiarch, or director of the public amusements.

b. *transf.* A leader among athletes.

1825 CLIAS *Gymnastics* I Before he gives his book to the press, this gymnasiarch has manifested a desire to conciliate the suffrages of several learned men. **1826** *Blackw. Mag.* XX. 130/2 Of all modern gymnasiarchs, Captain Clias is *facile princeps.* **1872** *Chamb. Jrnl.* 30 Mar. 194/2 Joe Rullock, the mighty gymnasiarch.

2. A governor of a school, college, or academy; a head instructor.

1682 WHELER *Journ. Greece* I. 56 Seleucus.. was Gymnasiarch, or chief Governour of the Schools. **1772** NUGENT tr. *Hist. Fr. Gerund* I. 92 Having been the first member of the celebrated college of St. Froylan.. he came in time to be the gymnasiarc or chief tutor. **1836** SIR W. HAMILTON *Discuss.*, *Study Math.* (1852) 283 Wolf.. as gymnasiarch and professor. **1884** SIR A. GRANT *University Edin.* I. ii. 85 The Gymnasiarch is to be learned in Theology.

So **gym'nasiarchy** [ad. Gr. γυμνασιαρχί-α], the office or function of gymnasiarch.

1836 LYTTON *Athens* (1837) II. 461 The Gymnasiarchy or charge of providing for the expence of the torch race. **1847** GROTE *Greece* II. xi. III. 163 Unpaid functions such as the trierarchy, choregy, gymnasiarchy.. were distributed in some way or other between the three classes.

gymnasiast (dʒɪm'neɪzɪæst). [As if ad. Gr. *γυμνασιαστ-ής, f. γυμνάσιον GYMNASIUM: in sense 1, after G. *gymnasiast.*]

1. A student in a (Continental) gymnasium.

1828 SIR W. NAPIER *Penins. War* III. iii. I. 316 Secret societies.. under the name of Tugenbunde, Gymnasiasts, and other denominations. **1882** *Pop. Sci. Monthly* XXI. 443 We have been told that the gymnasiast soon does as well as the real-scholar in the laboratory. **1886** *Athenæum* 27 Mar. 433/3 The 'gymnasiasts' in Amsterdam.. performed the 'Antigone' of Sophocles in the original.

2. A gymnast.

1857 'C. BEDE' *Verdant Green* III. xii, The vaulting-horse on whose wooden back the gymnasiast sprang at a bound. **1858** MAYHEW *Upper Rhine* v. §2 (1860) 265 A few years ago a professional gymnasiast sprang from bank to bank.

gymnasic (dʒɪm'neɪzɪk), *a. rare.* [f. GYMNASIUM + -IC.] Pertaining to the gymnasium (sense 2).

1831 CARLYLE *Sart. Res.* II. iii. (1871) 71 Over his Gymnasic and Academic years the Professor by no means lingers so lyrical and joyful as over his childhood.

gymnasium (dʒɪm'neɪzɪəm). Pl. **gymnasia, gymnasiums.** [L., a. Gr. γυμνάσιον, f. γυμνάζειν to train, exercise, lit. to train naked, f. γυμνός (γυμνάς) naked.]

1. A place or building for practice of or instruction in athletic exercises; a gymnastic school.

1598 GRENEWEY *Tacitus' Ann.* XIV. xii. (1622) 214 A place of all kinde of exercise called Gymnasium was dedicated by Nero. **1601** HOLLAND *Pliny* II. 490 Their yong men.. did exercise naked in their publick wrestling places, thereupon called Gym[n]asia. **1629** MAXWELL tr. *Herodian* I. 42 He [Cleander] also erected a stately Gymnasium [*marg. note* An Actiuity Court], and a publike Bathe. **1704** F. FULLER *Med. Gymn.* (1711) 225 Galen.. inveighs against the Athletick and other violent Practices of the Gymnasium. **1806** HUGHSON *London* III. 321 It [Moorfields] was likewise the great Gymnasium of our capital, the resort of boxers, runners, and foot-ball players, and every manly recreation. **1861** *Times* 23 July, Gymnasia are to be.. established at Chatham, Portsmouth.. and.. other important military stations. **1875** A. R. HOPE *My School-boy Fr.* 230 We climbed down the ladder of the gymnasium.

transf. *a* **1832** [see GYMNASTIC B. 2b]. **1861** C. READE *Cloister & Hearth* xciii, I fear they would have conducted him to that unpopular gymnasium, the gallows. **1887** *Times* (weekly ed.) 19 Aug. 4/1 The masts.. should be removed; they are only an expensive and very troublesome gymnasium.

attrib. **1895–6** *Cal. University Nebraska* 133 The object of the gymnasium work is to provide muscular exercise and recreation for brain workers. **1899** *Daily News* 23 Dec. 6/2 The foremost experts upon.. gymnasium construction.

2. † **a.** *gen.* A high school, college, or academy (*obs.*); **b.** *spec.* in Germany and other Continental countries, a school of the highest grade designed to prepare students for the universities. Now often pronounced as a Ger. word (gʏm'naːzɪʊm).

1691 WOOD *Ath. Oxon.* I. 337 He went to Amsterdam.. where.. he became Rector of the learned Academy or Gymnasium. **1758** JOHNSON *Idler* No. 33 ¶27 Cambridge and Oxford.. surpass.. the gymnasia of foreign countries. **1831** CARLYLE *Sart. Res.* (1858) 62 My Schoolmaster.. pronounced.. that I must be sent to the Gymnasium, and one day to the University. **1838** PRESCOTT *Ferd. & Is.* (1846) I. viii. 366 Colleges, academies, and gymnasiums springing up spontaneously.. in the most obscure villages. **1886** W. J. TUCKER *Life E. Europe* 64 The Gymnasium prepares the scholar during eight years of hard study for the university.

gymnast ('dʒɪmnæst). [ad. Gr. γυμναστ-ής trainer of professional athletes, f. γυμνάζειν (see prec.). Cf. F. *gymnaste* (Rabelais).] One skilled in gymnastic exercises; a gymnastic expert.

1594 R. ASHLEY tr. *Loys le Roy's Interch. Var. Things* 29 b, Gymnasts, pedotribes, athletes.. for the exercise of the bodie. **1653** URQUHART *Rabelais* I. xxiii, A young Gentleman of Touraine, named the Esquire Gymnast, who taught him the Art of riding. **1871** NAPHEYS *Prev. & Cure Dis.* I. vi. 168 Brilliant gymnasts are notoriously short-lived. **1883** STEVENSON *Treas. Isl.* III. xiv, Leaping back a yard.. with the speed and security of a trained gymnast.

gymnastic (dʒɪm'næstɪk), *a.* and *sb.* [ad. L. *gymnastic-us*, a. Gr. γυμναστικ-ός pertaining to or skilled in bodily exercises (subst. ἡ γυμναστικ-ή gymnastics), f. γυμνάζειν (see GYMNASIUM). Cf. F. *gymnastique* (14th c. in Oresme).]

A. *adj.* **1. a.** Pertaining to or connected with athletic exercises of the body; concerned with gymnastics (see B. 2).

1574 NEWTON *Health Mag.* Pref. 2 Gymnasticke Arte which is the trade of exercising men in feates of Activitie. **1704** F. FULLER *Med. Gymn.* (1711) 99 A most easie Natural Gymnastick Course. **1776** GIBBON *Decl. & F.* (1869) I. xviii. 483 He excelled in the gymnastic arts of leaping and running. **1839** THIRLWALL *Greece* II. 50 The state seems to have interfered, to compel his attendance at the gymnastic schools. **1855** H. SPENCER *Princ. Psychol.* (1872) I. II. iii. 204 The gymnastic feat of raising the body up a ladder hand over hand.

b. Characterized by or exhibiting positions of the body assumed in gymnastics. *rare.*

1850 LEITCH tr. *C.O. Müller's Anc. Art* §120 (ed. 2) 91 The art of modelling brazen statues of athletes.. was raised ..to the most perfect representation of beautiful gymnastic figures.

c. Physically active, athletic. *rare.*

1784 COWPER *Task* II. 591 A form not now gymnastic as of yore.

d. Of the initial letter of an illuminated manuscript: decorated with human figures, etc., which are portrayed climbing like gymnasts round the letter.

1945 F. WORMALD in *Archæologia* XCI. 127 These initials are composed of animals, monsters, and human figures, who clamber all over the framework of the letter as if using it as a kind of gymnastic appliance... In the Canterbury MSS. this gymnastic method is carried to extreme lengths. *Ibid.* 130 The Durham artists had some knowledge of the continental 'gymnastic' initial so popular at Canterbury. **1946** —— *Survival Anglo-Saxon Illumin.* 9 Another new type of English initial..is the so-called 'gymnastic' style, where animals and creatures clamber all over the frame of the initial rather in the manner of acrobats. This type was rare in England before the Conquest, but is found in the Durham MSS. and is an outstanding characteristic of Canterbury illumination of about the year 1100. **1952** D. T. RICE *Eng. Art 871–1100* vii. 216 The B of the Beatus page is in keeping with late Saxon developments, for in addition to the usual scroll-work, a number of little figures appear clambering amongst the stems; Wormald has aptly termed this the 'gymnastic' style. **1954** M. RICHERT *Painting in Britain: Middle Ages* iii. 66 The wholesale introduction of such human figures into the initial..decorative, 'gymnastic' figures. **1970** *Anglo-Saxon Illumination in Oxf. Libr.* 7 Initial 'þ'. Two dragons and a gymnastic figure make up the initial.

2. *fig.* 'Pertaining to disciplinary exercises for the intellect' (Webster, 1864).

1710 SHAFTESB. *Adv. Author* I. ii. 36 And here it is that our Sovereign Remedy and Gymnastick Method of Soliloquy takes its Rise. **1779** GIBBON *Misc. Wks.* (1814) IV. 612 He may learn from Jerom the difference of the gymnastic and dogmatic styles.

¶ **3.** = GYMNASIAL.

1802 ACERBI *Trav.* I. 139 The Swedish gentlemen are seldom contented with what may be called a scholastic, or a gymnastic education.

B. *sb.* **1. a.** *sing.* [= Gr. ἡ (τέχνη) γυμναστική.] = 2.

[**1581** MULCASTER *Positions* xxxv. (1887) 129 This term Gymnastice, which emplyeth in name, and professeth in deede the arte of exercise.] **1598** J. D. tr. *Loys Le Roy's Arist. Pol.* 204 They haue..more esteemed gymnasticke, which is the vse of bodily exercises, then musick. **1734** tr. *Rollin's Anc. Hist.* (1827) I. 71 The art by which they formed themselves for these encounters was called Gymnastic. **1875** JOWETT *Plato* (ed. 2) III. 40 Good gymnastic which will give health to the body. **1881** MAHAFFY *Old Grk. Educ.* iv. 38 The master of gymnastic.

b. *fig.*

1797 HOLCROFT tr. *Stolberg's Trav.* (ed. 2) III. lxxvii. 173 This music included both poetry and dancing. It was the gymnastic of the soul. **1838** SIR W. HAMILTON in *Reid's Wks.* (1842) II. 701/2 *note*, Mathematical study is the very worst gymnastic of the intellect. **1882** J. C. MORISON *Macaulay* i. 9 A course of what at Oxford is technically called 'science', would have been an invaluable gymnastic for Macaulay.

2. *pl.* **gymnastics** [see -ICS, -IC 2]. **a.** The practice of athletic exercises for the development of the body, now esp. of such exercises as are performed in a building set apart for them with special apparatus.

1652 EVELYN *State France* Misc. Writ. (1805) 84 Academies dedicated chiefly to this discipline, and other martial gymnastiques. **1825** HONE *Every-day Bk.* I. 1316 Gymnastics..have not until lately been practised. **1865** E. W. JACKSON (*title*) Gymnastics for the Fingers and Wrist. **1867** J. HOWARD (*title*) Gymnasts and Gymnastics. **1876** GRANT *Burgh Sch. Scotl.* II. v. 180 Gymnastics have become one of the institutions of the country.

b. *fig.*

a **1832** BENTHAM *Deontol.* (1834) II. 266 Efficient benevolence in action may be considered the gymnastics of the mind, or the field in which it is displayed, the mental gymnasium. **1841–4** EMERSON *Ess., Art* Wks. (Bohn) I. 148 Painting and sculpture are the gymnastics of the eye. **1854** —— *Lett. & Soc. Aims, Poet. & Imag.* ibid. III. 144, I think Hindoo books the best gymnastics for the mind. **1883** PROCTOR in *Knowl.* July 59/2 All who prefer singing to musical gymnastics. **1905** R. BROUGHTON *Waif's Progress* xxviii. 308 It seemed an impossible feat in mental gymnastics to..wrench his thoughts away. **1957** C. L. WRENN *Word & Symbol* (1967) 193 Will the deliberate ordinariness of dramatic language of *The Confidential Clerk* come any nearer to bringing poetry to the people than the stirring mental and verbal gymnastics of Mr. Christopher Fry? **1966** P. MOLONEY *Plea for Mersey* 25 These verbal gymnastics are heard in England elsewhere than in Liverpool.

†**c.** A treatise on athletic exercises. *Obs.*

1646 SIR T. BROWNE *Pseud. Ep.* III. i. 105 Mercurialis in his Gymnasticks justly makes standing one kinde of exercise.

†**3.** An authority on gymnastics. *Obs. rare.*

1572 J. JONES *Bathes Buckstone* 13 b, Diuers gymnastickes inuentinge other innumerable differences of frications, wan great prayse. **1623** COCKERAM *Gymnasticke*, a teacher of the Wrastling Science.

4. A gymnastic feat. *rare.*

1860 READE *Cloister & H.* x. (1896) 33 Giles' claws seized the side of the bed, and he returned to his place by one undivided gymnastic. **1907** 'MARK TWAIN' in *N. Amer. Rev.* 15 May 4 When he had been teaching me twice a day for three weeks I introduced a new gymnastic—one that he had never seen before.

Hence †**gym'nasticer**, one who trains others in gymnastic exercises; **gym'nasticate, gym'nasticize** *nonce-vbs. intr.*, to practise gymnastic exercises.

1574 NEWTON *Health Mag.* Pref. 2 Sithens Conservation and Preservation belonge either to the Gymnasticer or els to the Phisition. **1827** *Mirror* II. 274/2 Attendance at courts, gymnasticating, dumb-belling, and dancing-mastering, will not put quicksilver into a man's neck. **1828** A. HARE in *Macm. Mag.* XLIV. 358 Make Arthur ride hard and shoot often, and, in short, gymnasticise in every possible manner.

gymnastical (dʒɪm'næstɪkəl), *a.* [f. as prec. + -AL¹.] = prec. A.

1581 MULCASTER *Positions* xxxv. (1887) 129 What so euer concerneth the whole Gymnasticall and exercising argument. **1598** J. D. tr. *Loys Le Roy's Arist. Pol.* 349 There is appointed a magistrate..for gimnasticall and musicall games. **1817** BYRON *Beppo* iii, Harlequins and clowns, with feats gymnastical.

gymnastically (dʒɪm'næstɪkəlɪ), *adv. rare.* [f. as prec. + -LY².] In a gymnastic manner; in respect of gymnastics.

1646 SIR T. BROWNE *Pseud. Ep.* IV. v. 191 Such as..are not gymnastically composed; nor actively use those parts. **1890** *Jrnl. Educ.* 1 Feb. 98/2 Of greater value gymnastically.

gymnaxony, gymnetrous: see GYMNO-.

gymnemic (dʒɪm'ni:mɪk, -'nɛmɪk), *a. Chem.* [f. mod.L. *Gymnem-a*, name of an asclepiadaceous genus, f. Gr. γυμ-νός naked + νῆμ-α thread + -IC.] ***gymnemic acid***: an impure substance which is obtained from the leaves of *Gymnema sylvestre* and is believed to be the cause of the temporary loss of the ability to taste sweetness and bitterness which results when leaves of this plant are chewed.

1887 D. HOOPER in *Nature* 14 Apr. 566/2 The body just described has the characteristics of an organic acid related in some particulars to chrysophanic acid, but having some distinctly peculiar reactions, and possessing the anti-saccharine property ascribed to the leaves. I propose to call it Gymnemic acid. **1958** *Jrnl. Indian Chem. Soc.* XXXV. 650 It is also not certain whether the amorphous substance, described as gymnemic acid..by Hooper is a single substance or not. Further, Hooper's claim that gymnemic acid constituted the anti-saccharine principle of the leaves has been challenged.

gymnic ('dʒɪmnɪk), *a.* and *sb.* Now *rare.* [ad. L. *gymnic-us*, a. Gr. γυμνικ-ός pertaining to bodily exercises, f. γυμνός naked: see -IC. Freq. in the 17th c., when *gymnastic* had not yet a recognized standing. Cf. F. *gymnique* (1542 in Hatz.-Darm.).]

A. *adj.* = GYMNASTIC *a.* 1.

1601 HOLLAND *Pliny* II. 537 One who had obtained the victorie at the publique Gymnick exercises of actiuitie. *a* **1656** USSHER *Ann.* (1658) 225 Alexander..exhibited gymnick pastimes and exercises. **1671** MILTON *Samson* 1324 Have they not Sword-players, and ev'ry sort of Gymnic Artists, Wrestlers, Riders, Runners, Juglers and Dancers? **1778** APTHORPE *Preval. Chr.* 362 The seventh day, the gymnic games were celebrated by naked combatants. **1846** GROTE *Greece* I. iv. (1862) I. 76 The remaining daughters.. were given in marriage to the victors in a gymnic contest. **1862** MERIVALE *Rom. Emp.* (1865) III. xxviii. 329 Octavius instituted a gymnic and musical festival, with the designation of the Actian games.

B. *sb. pl.* **gymnics**: = *gymnastics* (see GYMNASTIC *sb.* 2).

1621 BURTON *Anat. Mel.* II. ii. II. i. (1676) 152/2 Others.. of a cold and dry constitution cannot sustaine those gymnicks without great hurt done to their own bodies. **1765** STERNE *Tr. Shandy* VIII. xxxiii, Provided it would not impair thy strength,..which these gymnics inordinately taken are apt to do. **1835** *Fraser's Mag.* XI. 536 Not only in the execution of particular gymnics, but in his histrionic performance generally.

†**'gymnical**, *a. Obs.* [f. as prec. + -AL¹.] = GYMNIC, GYMNASTIC *adjs.*

1576 FLEMING *Panopl. Epist.* 187 Such as be winners in Gymnicall games. **1697** POTTER *Antiq. Greece* I. xxvi. (1715) 152 They shall be instructed in the Gymnical exercises. **1737** WHISTON *Josephus, Antiq.* XIV. viii. §5 This present of a crown shall be proclaimed..in the..Gymnical shews.

gymnite ('dʒɪmnaɪt). *Min.* [Named by Thomson, 1843, from γυμν-ός naked, bare, in allusion to the name of its locality, Bare Hills, Maryland: see -ITE.] A synonym of DEWEYLITE.

1843 *Phil. Mag.* Ser. III. XXII. 191 'Gymnite'. **1868** in Dana *Min.* (ed. 5) 469.

gymno- (dʒɪmnə), before a vowel **gymn-**, comb. form of Gr. γυμνό-ς naked, bare, chiefly in technical terms of Botany, Biology, and Zoology (the more important are given as main-words): **gymnanthous** (dʒɪm'nænθəs) *a. Bot.* [Gr. ἄνθ-ος flower + -OUS], having naked flowers, wanting both calyx and corolla. **gymnaxony** (dʒɪm'næksənɪ) *Bot.* [Gr. ἄξων axis + -Y], a rare condition in flowers, in which the placenta protrudes through the ovary (R. Brown *Man. Bot.* 1874, Gloss.). **gymnetrous** (dʒɪm'ni:trəs) *a. Ichthyol.* [Gr. ἦτρ-ον abdomen + -OUS], 'having a naked or smooth belly; applied to those fishes which have no anal fins' (*Syd. Soc. Lex.* 1886). **gymnoblastic** (-'blɑ:stɪk, -æ-) *a. Zool.* [Gr. βλαστός (see -BLAST)], having the nutritive or generative buds unprotected by an external receptacle (hydrotheca or gonangium); so **gymno'blastous** *a.* (*Syd. Soc. Lex.*). **gymnobranchiate** (-'bræŋkɪət) *Zool.* [Gr. βράγχια *pl.*, gills] *adj.*, belonging to the *Gymnobranchiata*, a group of gastropods having naked gills; *sb.* an animal of this group (*Cent. Dict.* 1889). **gymnoceratous** (-'sɛrətəs) *a. Ent.* [Gr. κερατ-, κέρας horn], belonging to the *Gymnocerata*, a group of heteropterous insects having exposed antennæ (*ibid.*). ‖**gymnocyta** (-'saɪtə), **-cyte** (-saɪt) *Biol.* [Gr. κύτος cell], 'Häckel's term for a naked or wall-less cytode having a nucleus' (*Syd. Soc. Lex.*). **gymnocytode** (-'saɪtəʊd) *Biol.* [CYTODE], 'Häckel's term for a cytode without a proper cell wall and nucleus' (*ibid.*). **gymnodont** ('dʒɪmnədɒnt) *Ichthyol.* [Gr. ὀδοντ-, ὀδούς tooth] *adj.*, belonging to the *Gymnodontes*, a group of plectognath fishes having the jaw prolonged into a beak covered with a dental plate; *sb.* a fish belonging to this group. **gymnogen** ('dʒɪmnədʒən) *Bot.* [see -GEN] = GYMNOSPERM. **gymnogenous** (dʒɪm'nɒdʒɪnəs) *a. Bot.* [see -GENOUS] = GYMNOSPERMOUS (Cassell 1884). **gymnogram** ('dʒɪmnəgræm) *Bot.* [Gr. γραμμή line, mark], a fern of the genus *Gymnogramme* or *-gramma*, having the lines of spore-cases on the lower side of the frond uncovered. **gymnogynous** (dʒɪm'nɒdʒɪnəs) *a. Bot.* [see -GYNOUS], having a naked ovary (*Treas. Bot.* 1866). **gymnolæmatous** (-'li:mətəs) *a. Zool.* [Gr. λαιμός throat, gullet], belonging to the *Gymnolæmata*, a division of Polyzoa having no epistome or valve to close down upon the mouth. **gymnomerous** (-'mɪərəs) *a. Zool.* [Gr. μηρ-ός thigh], pertaining to the *Gymnomera*, a division of cladocerous crustaceans (*Cent. Dict.*). †**gymnomono'spermous** *a. Bot.* [Gr. μόνο-ς alone, one-, σπέρμ-α seed], having the seeds single and naked. **gymnomyxine** (-'mɪksaɪn) *a. Zool.* [Gr. μύξ-α slime], pertaining to the *Gymnomyxa*, a low grade of Polyzoa which are naked or not corticate (*Cent. Dict.*). **gymnophthalmate** (ˌdʒɪmnɒf'θælmət), **gymn-oph'thalmatous, gymnoph'thalmic, gymn-oph'thalmous** *adjs. Zool.* [Gr. ὀφθαλμός eye], belonging to the *Gymnophthalmata* or naked-eyed medusæ. †**gymnopoly'spermous** *a. Bot.* [Gr. πολύ-ς much, many, σπέρμ-α seed]: see quot. and cf. *gymnotetraspermous* (below). **gymnopterous** (-'ɒptərəs) *a. Ent.* [Gr. πτέρ-ον wing], having naked wings, without hairs or scales; having sheathless wings (*Cent. Dict.*). **gymnorhinal** (-'raɪnəl) *a. Ornith.* [Gr. ῥῖν-, ῥίς nostril], having naked or unfeathered nostrils (*ibid.*). **gymnosomate** (-'səʊmət), **-'somatous, -'somous** *adjs. Zool.* [Gr. σῶμ-α, σωματ- body], pertaining to the *Gymnosomata*, an order of pteropods having a naked body. **gymnospore** ('dʒɪmnəspɔə(r)) *Bot.* [SPORE], a naked spore; so **gym'nosporous**, having uncovered spores (Cassell, 1884). **gymnotetraspermous** (-tɛtrə'spɜ:məs) *a. Bot.* [Gr. τετρα- four, σπέρμ-α seed]: see quots. **gymnotocous** (-'ɒtəkəs) *a. Zool.* [Gr. τόκ-ος bringing-forth, offspring], having the genital products uncovered, as certain hydroids (*Cent. Dict.*). **gymnozoidal** (-'zəʊɪdəl) *a. Zool.* [Gr. ζῷ-ον animal: see -ID³], pertaining to the *Gymnozoida*, a section of Infusoria in Saville Kent's classification.

1880 GRAY *Struct. Bot.* 413/2 *Gymnanthous. Naked flowered. **1871** ALLMAN (*title*) A Monograph of the *Gymnoblastic or Tubularian Hydroids. **1876** MACALISTER *Anim. Morphology* I. 5 A naked cytode is called a *gymnocytode..a naked cell is a *gymnocyte. **1842** BRANDE *Dict. Sci.* etc., *Gymnodonts, *Gymnodontes*, the name of the family of Plectognathic fishes. **1846** LINDLEY *Veg. Kingd.* 4 Exogens have been broken up into 1. Exogens proper, or those having an ovary, style, and stigma; and 2. *Gymnogens, which have neither. **1861** SIR W. J. HOOKER

Brit. Ferns Pl. 1 *Gymnogramme leptophylla*..Small Annual *Gymnogram. **1864** T. Moore *Brit. Ferns* 35 The Gymnogram. This plant belongs to a family of which nearly all the species are tropical. **1875** Blake *Zool.* 329 It is called phylactolæmatous, as opposed to marine *gymnolæmatous. **1760** Jas. Lee *Introd. Bot.* II. vi. (1765) 85 Such as have an imbricated amentum and are *gymnomonospermous. **1870** Nicholson *Man. Zool.* I. 84 *note*, The old sub-class of the Acalephæ contained the *Gymnophthalmate Medusæ (= the Discophora) and the Steganophthalmate Medusæ. [**1870** Nicholson *Man. Zool.* Gloss., *Gymnophthalmata*, applied by Edward Forbes to those Medusæ in which the eye-specks at the margin of the disc are unprotected. The division is now abandoned.] **1871** Allman *Gymnoblastic Hydroids* 80 McCrady divides the *gymnophthalmatous or hydroid medusæ into the 'endostomata' and the 'exostomata'. *Ibid.* 2 The so-called naked-eyed or *gymnophthalmic Medusæ. **1879** Rossiter *Dict. Sci. Terms*, **Gymnophthalmous*, naked-eyed. **1730-6** Bailey (folio), **Gymnopolyspermous Plants*, such as bear two naked Seeds inclosed in a Calyx, without any Seed-Vessel. **1885** Ray Lankester in *Encycl. Brit.* XIX. 837 The naked protoplasmic particles that issue from such coated spores, or are formed directly by the rapid fission of the parent Protozoon..are termed '*gymnospores'. **1730-6** Bailey (folio), **Gymnotetraspermous Plants*, such as have four naked Seeds inclosed in a Calyx, without any Seed-Vessel. **1866** *Treas. Bot.* 560/2 *Gymnotetraspermous*, having such a four-lobed ovary as is found in labiates, which was formerly thought to consist of four naked seeds. **1880-1** Saville Kent *Man. Infusoria* I. 329 The independent or *Gymnozoidal section of the collared Flagellata or Discostomata.

gymno'biblism. *rare.* [f. Gr. γυμνό-ς naked + Bible + -ism.] The opinion that the bare text of the Bible, 'without note or comment', may be safely put before the unlearned as a sufficient guide to religious truth. So **gymno'biblical** *a.*, pertaining to, or holding, this opinion; **gymno'biblist**, a believer in 'gymnobiblism'.

1826 Bp. Jebb in C. Forster *Corr.* (1834) II. 539 As to distributing the Bible, gymno-biblism is less in fashion than it was. **1834** C. Forster *Life Bp. Jebb* ii. (1836) 88 Assailed ..on the one hand, by the gymnobiblical protestant, and, on the other hand, by the priest-governed Romanist. **1844** W. H. Mill *Serm. Tempt. Christ* Notes 155 Those whom the late Bishop Jebb and Mr. Knox term Gymnobiblists.

gymnocarpous (dʒɪmnəˈkɑːpəs), *a. Bot.* [f. Gr. γυμνόκαρπ-ος (f. γυμνό-ς naked, bare + καρπός fruit) + -ous.] Having a naked fruit; applied to those lichens in which the apothecia are open or expanded, or to a fructification of this character.

1856 W. L. Lindsay *Brit. Lichens* 70 They then find their way to the surface of the thalamium in gymnocarpous species. **1867** J. Hogg *Microsc.* II. i. 305 The Gymnocarpous Lichens. **1882** Vines *Sachs' Bot.* 306 The fertile hyphæ may..grow towards the exterior and form the spores at the surface, when the fructification is said to be gymnocarpous.

gymnogene (ˈdʒɪmnədʒiːn). [ad. mod.L. *Gymnogenys*, lit. naked-chinned, f. Gr. γυμνό-ς naked + γένυς chin; Temminck's specific name for the bird (*Falco g.*), afterwards used as a generic name by Lesson.] A book-name for an African hawk, *Polyboroides typicus* or *P. capensis*.

1875-84 R. B. Sharpe *Layard's Birds S. Africa* 9 *Polyboroides typicus.* Banded Gymnogene.

†**gym'nologize**, *v. Obs.*[−0] [ad. med.L. *gymnologizāre* (f. γυμνό-ς naked + λόγος speech), explained '*nude loqui*' by J. de Janua.] *intr.* 'To dispute naked, like an Indian philosopher' (Bailey vol. II, 1727).

gymnopædic (dʒɪmnəˈpiːdɪk), *a. Gr. Antiq.* [ad. Gr. γυμνοπαιδικός, f. γυμνό-ς naked + παιδ-, παῖς boy.] The distinctive epithet of the dances or other exercises performed by naked boys at public festivals.

1850 Leitch tr. *C. O. Müller's Anc. Art* (ed. 2) §77 *note* 2 The gymnopaedic, hyporchematic, and other kinds of orchestics were already cultivated in a highly artistic manner.

gymnosoph (ˈdʒɪmnəsɒf). *rare.* [As if ad. Gr. *γυμνόσοφος, after φιλόσοφος (see philosopher); cf. next.] = next.

a **1834** Coleridge *Lit. Rem.* (1839) IV. 282 To have the battle fairly fought out, Spinoza, or a Bhuddist, or a Burmese Gymnosoph, should be challenged.

gymnosophist (dʒɪmˈnɒsəfɪst). Also 5 *pl.* **genosophis**, 6-7 **gimnosophist**. [ad. L. (pl.) *gymnosophist-æ*, ad. Gr. γυμνοσοφισταί, f. γυμνό-ς naked + σοφιστής sophist. Cf. F. *gymnosophiste* (15-16th c. in Godefroy *Compl.*).] One of a sect of ancient Hindu philosophers of ascetic habits (known to the Greeks through the reports of the companions of Alexander), who wore little or no clothing, denied themselves flesh meat, and gave themselves up to mystical contemplation. Also *occas.* allusively, an ascetic or mystic.

a **1400-50** *Alexander* 4022 Ermets..A progenie of pore men þat neuir pride hauntis, And ȝit þe gentill genosophis þam in þe gest callis. **1576** Fleming *Panopl. Epist.* 349 The custome of the Gymnosophistes of India. **1590** Greene *Neuer too late* (1600) 6, I am not a Gimnosophist to iangle at euery sophisticall obiection. **1630** J. Taylor (Water P.) *Wit & Mirth* Wks. II. 193/1 Shamrooke, a famous Scithian Gimnosophist. *a* **1640** Massinger *Very Woman* III. v, The Curate..that great Philosopher, He that found out a Pudding had two ends; That learned Clerk, that notable Gymnosophist. **1786** *Pogonologia* 13 The Gymnosophists were particularly attentive to their beards. **1873** Symonds *Gk. Poets* ii. 53 There is no need to suppose that Empedocles visited the East and learned the secrets of Gymnosophists. **1882** Stevenson *Fam. Stud.* 171 Part gymnosophist part backwoodsman.

So **gymnosophy** (dʒɪmˈnɒsəfɪ), the doctrine or system of gymnosophists.

1826 Good *Bk. Nat.* (1834) I. 6 The Greeks, themselves ..seem..to have become acquainted with it as a branch of gymnosophy.

†**gymnoso'phistal.** *Obs. rare*[−1]. [f. gymnosophist + -al[1].] = gymnosophist.

1579 J. Jones *Preserv. Bodie & Soule* I. xliv. 115 Not regarding the words of..the Chaldean Prophetes, or rather Mathematists and Gymnosophistals.

†**gymnosophistian.** *Obs. rare*[−1]. In 4 **genosophistien.** [f. as prec. + -ian.] = gymnosophist.

1340-70 *Alex. & Dind.* 11 þe proude genosophistiens were þe gomus called; Now is þat name to mene þe nakid wise. *Ibid.* 23 þe gentil genosophistiens þat goode were of witte.

gymnosperm (ˈdʒɪmnəspɜːm). *Bot.* [ad. mod.L. *gymnosperm-us*, ad. Gr. γυμνόσπερμ-ος, f. γυμνό-ς naked + σπέρμ-α seed, sperm. Cf. F. *gymnosperme*.] A plant which has naked seeds, as the pine, hemlock fir, etc.; one of the *Gymnospermæ*, a class of exogenous plants so characterized, embracing the orders *Cycadaceæ*, *Coniferæ*, and *Gnetaceæ*.

[**1682** Ray *Method. Plant.* (1733) 193 Gymnosperma planta. Quæ semen nudum fert. **1830** Lindley *Nat. Syst. Bot.* 245 Gymnospermæ are known from all other Vasculares by the vessels of their wood having large apparent perforations.] **1838** *Penny Cycl.* XI. 510/1 *Gymnosperms*, one of the five divisions under which the vegetable kingdom is now classified. **1863** Lyell *Antiq. Man* xx. 398 The gymnosperms or coniferous and cycadeous plants abound in all strata. **1885** Goodale *Physiol. Bot.* (1892) 288 Certain Gymnosperms..develop a bright green color in the deepest darkness.

gymnospermous (dʒɪmnəˈspɜːməs), *a. Bot.* [f. mod.L. *gymnosperm-us* (see prec.) + -ous.] Naked-seeded; applied to those plants, e.g. conifers, in which the seeds are not provided with a seed-vessel; belonging to the class *Gymnospermæ*.

1727 in Bailey vol. II. **1760** J. Lee *Introd. Bot.* II. v. (1765) 84 Such as have irregular Corollæ, and the Fruit gymnospermous. **1880** Gray *Struct. Bot.* vi. §7. 268 Gymnospermous..plants are so named because the ovules ..are fertilized by direct application of the pollen.

So **gymno'spermal** (*Cent. Dict.*), **gymno'spermic** (*Syd. Soc. Lex.* 1886) *adjs.*, in the same sense. **gymno'spermy**, the attribute of being gymnospermous.

1890 Garnsey *Sachs' Hist. Bot.* I. iii. 142 Thus one of the most remarkable facts in vegetation, the gymnospermy of the Conifers and Cycads, was for the first time established [by Robert Brown, 1825].

gymnostomous (dʒɪmˈnɒstəməs), *a. Bot.* [f. Gr. γυμνό-ς naked + στόμ-α mouth.] Naked-mouthed; applied to those mosses in which the mouth of the sporangium has no peristome.

1861 Bentley *Man. Bot.* 377 When the mouth is naked, the Mosses in which such a sporangium is found are called gymnostomous or naked-mouthed. **1875** Bennett & Dyer *Sachs' Bot.* 331 If the peristome is wanting, the theca is said to be gymnostomous. **1881** Spruce in *Jrnl. Bot.* X. No. 217. 13 The capsule was gymnostomous.

So **gymnostomatous** (-ˈstɒmətəs) *a.*, in the same sense (*Syd. Soc. Lex.* 1886).

gymnote (ˈdʒɪmnəʊt). [Anglicized form of next.] A fish of the genus *Gymnotus*.

1819 *Pantologia* V, s.v. *Gymnotus*..1. *G. electricus.* Electric eel or gymnote... 2. *G. albifrons.* White-shouldered gymnote... 3. *G. carapo.* American gymnote.

‖**gymnotus** (dʒɪmˈnəʊtəs). Pl. **gymnoti** (dʒɪmˈnəʊtaɪ). [mod.L. (Linnæus 1748), for *gymnonōtus, f. Gr. γυμνό-ς naked + νῶτον back, with allusion to the absence of dorsal fins.] A freshwater eel-like fish of South America, *Electrophorus* (formerly *Gymnotus*) *electricus*, capable of giving an electric shock; an electric eel.

1775 Williamson in *Phil. Trans.* LXV. 95, I am induced to believe, that the gymnotus has powers greatly superior to ..those of the torpedo. **1834** *Nat. Philos.* III. *Phys. Geog.* 50/2 (U.K.S) The temperature of the waters in which the gymnoti habitually live, is from 78 to 80 degrees. **1854** Badham *Halieut.* 407 The gymnotus belongs to a small electric coterie composed of five individuals.

gymow(e, variant of gemew *Obs.*

gympe, variant of jimp, jest.

gympie (ˈgɪmpɪ). *Austral.* [Native name.] An evergreen shrub, *Laportea moroides*, which belongs to the nettle family, Urticaceæ, and has leaves covered with stinging hairs.

1895 A. Meston *Geogr. Hist. Queensland* 55 Gympie. The Mary River blacks' name for the stinging tree. **1911** W. R. Guilfoyle *Austral. Plants* 233 *Laportea moroides* 'Gympie Nettle Tree' or 'Mulberry Nettle Tree' (evergreen shrub, reputed poisonous and injurious to stock, 15 to 20 ft.). **1934** *Bulletin* (Sydney) 15 Aug. 21/2 Strangely enough, the weed is nearly always found near the gympie-gympie trees, and is easily identified by its narrow curled leaves on a pink stalk. **1963** W. V. Macfarlane in Keegan & Macfarlane *Venomous & Poisonous Anim. Pacific* I. 31 In the eastern rain forests of northern New South Wales and Queensland, *L[aportea] gigas* becomes a tree 30-40 m high and the Gympie bush, *L. moroides*, grows only 6-8 m. **1965** *Austral. Encycl.* IV. 406/2 In 1868 the name [Nashville] was altered to Gympie, an aboriginal term for the stinging trees found in the district.

gyn, variant of gin *sb.*[1]

gynae (ˈgaɪnɪ). Also **gynie**. Colloq. abbreviation of gynæcological *a.* and gynæcology.

1942 Berrey & Van den Bark *Amer. Thes. Slang* §534/1 *Gynae*, gynaecology. **1960** J. Grant *Come again, Nurse* xxiv. 158 Sister Judgeson on Gynie Theatre was a sweet middle-aged woman. **1962** G. Butler *Coffin in Oxford* ix. 123 'I'm over in Gynae now,' said the nurse. **1964** G. L. Cohen *What's Wrong with Hospitals?* iv. 75 'We didn't come across any horrors,' said Dr. Duncum..'unless you count adolescent girls in gynae wards.'

gynæcandrical: see gynæco-.

‖**gynæceum** (dʒaɪ-, dʒɪnɪˈsiːəm, g-). Also 7 **gynegium**, 8-9 **-eceum, -ecæum**, 9 **-ecium, -æcium**. [L. *gynæcēum, -īum*, a. Gr. γυναικεῖον, f. γυναικ-, γυνή woman.]

1. *Gr.* and *Rom. Antiq.* The women's apartments in a household; any building set apart for women.

1723 R. Millar *Propagat. Chr.* II. ix. 553 Their Gynecæum for young Gentlewomen taught at the expense of their parents. **1832** Gell *Pompeiana* I. viii. 151 A gynecæum or apartment for the women and children. **1847** Tennyson *Princ.* III. 262 Women, up till this Cramp'd under worse than South-Sea-isle taboo, Dwarfs of the gynæceum. **1848** Lytton *Harold* I. i, The lararium was deserted; the gynæcium was still, as in the Roman time, the favoured apartment of the female portion of the household. **1879** Farrar *St. Paul* (1883) 131 The degradation of the harem and the narrowness of the gynæceum.

†**b.** Under the Roman Empire: A textile manufactory. *Obs.*

1610 Holland *Camden's Brit.* I. 77 The Procurator of the Gynegium of Draperie in Britaine, in which the clothes of the Prince and souldiers were woven. **1781** Gibbon *Decl. & F.* xvii. II. 56 We had a treasury-chest in London, and a gyneceum or manufacture at Winchester.

2. *Bot.* The female organs of a flower, collectively. Now usually spelt **gynœcium**, having been supposed to be from Gr. οἰκίον house; under the influence of this notion androecium has been formed as its correlative.

1832 Lindley *Introd. Bot.* I. ii. §10. 138 The last organ to enumerate in the flower is..the *female system* or gynæceum of Röper..usually called the *pistillum.* **1858** A. Gray *Lett.* (1893) 449 When you speak of ovary in Clematis leave us to gather, from the context, whether you mean, (1) the whole gynæcium; (2) a separate pistil; or, (3) the ovuliferous portion of a pistil. **1875** Bennett & Dyer *Sachs' Bot.* 477 In *Althæa rosea*..the filaments form a membranous closed tube which completely envelopes the gynæceum. **1880** Gray *Struct. Bot.* vi. §1. 165 The aggregate stamens of a flower have been called the Andrœcium; the pistils, the Gynœcium. **1897** Willis *Fl. Plants & Ferns* I. 59 The rest of the flower is hypogynous (below the gynœceum or carpellary portion).

gynæcian, *a. rare*[−1]. Also **gynecian** (in mod. Dicts.). [f. Gr. γυναικ-, γυνή woman + -ian.] Pertaining or relating to women.

1640 tr. *Ferrand's Love Melanch.* 331 Moderne Physitians prescribe Fasting and Abstinence to Melancholy Lovers: as likewise doe all Gynæcian writers, to Women that are [etc.].

gynæcic (dʒaɪˈniːsɪk, g-), *a. Med.* Also **gynecic**. [ad. Gr. γυναικικ-ός, f. γυναικ-, γυνή woman.] Relating to diseases peculiar to women.

1878 J. H. Aveling (*title*) The Influence of Posture on Women in Gynecic and Obstetric Practice.

gynæco- (ˌgaɪnɪkə, dʒaɪ-, gaɪˈniːkə), also (esp. *U.S.*) **gyneco-**, repr. Gr. γυναικο-, comb. form of γυνή woman, female, as in: †**gynæ'candrical** *a.* [Gr. ἀνδρ-, ἀνήρ man], common to men and women. **gynæcocœnic** (-ˈsiːnɪk) *a.* [Gr. κοιν-ός common], having women in common. **gynæcoid** *a.* (see gyne). **gynæcolatry** (-ˈɒlətrɪ) [Gr. λατρεία: see -latry], woman-worship. **gynæcomasty** (-ˈmæstɪ) *Physiol.* [Gr. μαστ-ός breast: cf. Gr. γυναικόμασθος (Galen) and mod.L. *gynæcomastum*], the condition of a man's breasts in which they are as large as a woman's and functionally active; also in mod.L. form **gynæco'mastia. gynæco'mazia** [Gr. μαζός var. μαστός breast], gynæcomastia. **gynæcomorphous** (-ˈmɔːfəs) *a.* [Gr. μορφ-ή shape], having the form or characters of a female. †ˈ**gynæconome** [Gr. γυναικονόμος: see -NOMOUS], one of a board of magistrates at Athens which was formed to maintain manners among women; so **gynæˈconomist**, in the same sense. ˈ**gynæcophore** (-fɔə(r)) *Zool.* [Gr. -φόρος bearing], in certain invertebrate animals, as some trematodes, a receptacle in the male in which the female is borne, a gynæcophoric canal; hence **gynæcoˈphoric** (-ˈfɒrɪk) *a.* **gynæcophysiˈology** (-fɪzɪˈɒlədʒɪ), the PHYSIOLOGY of the female generative organs.

1684 I. MATHER in *Academy* 3 Feb. (1900) 102/1 *Gynecandrical Dancing, or that which is commonly called Mixt or Promiscuous Dancing of Men and Women together. **1822** SHELLEY *Chas. I*, II. 366 A commonwealth like Gonzalo's in the play, *Gynæcocœnic and pantisocratic. **1888** *Universal Rev.* Sept. 23 That fatal *gynæcolatry which rules all social and domestic life across the Channel. **1881** *Index-Cat. Surg.-Gen. U.S.* II. 421/2 (*title*) On the male mammary glands, and on *gynaecomastia. **1904** *Lancet* 26 Mar. 865/2 This was not so marked a case of gynæcomastia as in Case 1. **1962** *Lancet* 29 Dec. 1358/1 Gynæcomastia in the male may be associated with an abnormality of œstrogen production or metabolism. **1873** H. SPENCER *Stud. Social.* Notes (1874) 421 The mammæ of men will, under special excitation, yield milk: there are various cases of *gynæcomasty on record, and in famines infants whose mothers have died have been thus saved. **1850** J. BIRKETT *Dis. Breast* 254 *Gynecomazia..signifies a development of the mammary organ in the male which more or less resembles the form of that of the female. **1923** W. H. EVANS *Dis. Breast* xliii. 473 The secretion of milk by the breasts of men is, however, by no means confined to those with Gynæcomazia. **1865** *Reader* No. 142. 326/2 A *gynæcomorphous male of Fidonia Atomaria. **1594** *Mirr. Policy* (1599) 207 At Rome their Censors had such like aucthoritie and charge, as the *Gyneconomes at Athens. **1753** L. M. tr. *Du Boscq's Accomplish'd Woman* II. 121 Hesychius saith there were judges appointed particularly for this purpose, who were called *Gynæconomists. **1877** HUXLEY *Anat. Inv. Anim.* iv. 202 The formidable Bilharzia, the male of which is the larger and retains the female in a *gynæcophore. **1881** PACKARD *Zool.* 152 A canal or passage in the male formed by the infolding of the edges of the concave side of the body called a gynæcophore. **1885** W. ROBERTS *Urin. & Renal Dis.* III. xiii. (ed. 4) 648 The male [of *Bilharzia Hæmatobia*] is..provided with a *gynæcophoric canal. **1828** M. RYAN *Man. Midwifery* 19 *Gynæcophysiology, or uses of the female organs of generation.

gynæcocracy (ˌgaɪ-, dʒaɪ-, dʒɪnɪˈkɒkrəsɪ, g-). Also 7 **ginæcocratie**, 8-9 **gynecocracy**. [ad. Gr. γυναικοκρατία (Aristotle, Plutarch), f. γυναικ(ο)-, γυνή woman + -κρατία -CRACY. Cf. F. *gynécocratie* (16th c. in Hatz.-Darm.).] Government by a woman or women; female rule or mastery; *depreciatingly*, petticoat government.

1612 SELDEN *Drayton's Poly-olb.* xvii. Notes 276 Gynæcocracie. **1614** —— *Titles Hon.* II. i. 176 Goropius vndertakes a coniecture of the first cause which excluded Ginæcocratie (or female succession and gouernment) among them. **1660** R. COKE *Power & Subj.* 100 That God has owned Gynæcocraty..is evident in Deborah. **1692** WASHINGTON tr. *Milton's Def. Pop.* vii. 169 What if it would overthrow a Gynæcocracy too? **1788** H. CLARKE *School Candidates* (1877) 9 That there should be permitted such an abuse of power in the world, as either a public or domestic Gynecocracy! **1816** SCOTT *Antiq.* xxvi. *note*, In the fishing villages on the Firths of Forth and Tay..the government is gynecocracy. **1886** *Temple Bar* LXXVIII. 509 That social gynæcocracy for which France is famous.

Hence **gynæcoˈcratic**, **-ˈcratical** *adjs.*, pertaining to gynæcocracy or female government; **gyˈnecocrat**, an upholder of or adherent to gynecocratic government.

1856 F. E. PAGET *Owlet Owlst.* 201 Can you tell me the meaning of Gynecocratical? **1877** R. MARTINEAU tr. *Goldziher's Hebrew Mythol.* iv. 76 A theory of the history of civilisation usually called the Gynæcocratic. **1878** *Fraser's Mag.* XVII. 649 The rare respect for the proprietary rights of women in which Strabo saw a token of gynæcocratic barbarism. **1893** F. HALL in *Nation* (N.Y.) LVI. 68/3 The unalloyed natives of Kocch Behar are so far gone as gynecocrats that all their property is vested in the women.

gynæcological (ˌgaɪniːkəˈlɒdʒɪkəl, dʒaɪ-, dʒɪ-), *a.* [f. as next + -IC + -AL[1].] Pertaining or relating to gynæcology.

1876 (*title*) Transactions of the [American] Gynecological Society. **1879** *Cornh. Mag.* June 699 The gynæcological professor should be a man pledged to all the dogmas of the Women's Enfranchisement creed. **1879** J. M. DUNCAN *Lect. Dis. Wom.* ii. (1889) 4 Gynæcological investigations are.. chiefly carried out in the hypogastric region. **1884** *Health Exhib. Catal.* 104/1 Patent Surgical Couch for gynaecological and obstetric examinations and general operations.

Hence **gynæcoˈlogically** *adv.*, in accordance with the science of gynæcology.

1885 G. H. TAYLOR *Pelv. & Hern. Therap.* 116 Hyperaemia, which..is gynaecologically known by a multitude of other names.

gynæcologist (ˌgaɪnɪˈkɒlədʒɪst, dʒaɪ-, dʒɪ-). [f. next + -IST.] An expert in gynæcology.

1872 F. G. THOMAS *Dis. Women* 41 Gynæcologists ranged themselves into two parties. **1879** J. M. DUNCAN *Lect. Dis. Wom.* xxviii. (1889) 230 Many of the greatest gynæcologists say that these abscesses never should be opened.

gynæcology (ˌgaɪnɪˈkɒlədʒɪ, dʒaɪ-, dʒɪ-). Also **gynecology**. [f. GYNÆCO- + -LOGY.] That department of medical science which treats of the functions and diseases peculiar to women. Also *loosely*, the science of womankind.

1847 in CRAIG. **1867** *New Syd. Soc. Retrosp.* 368 Gynæcology, embracing the Physiology and Pathology of the non-pregnant state. **1883** HART & BARBOUR (*title*) Manual of Gynecology. **1885** *Jrnl. Educ.* 1 June 256 He.. was theoretically an adept in gynæcology—the science of womankind.

‖**gynæconitis** (gaɪniːkəʊˈnaɪtɪs, dʒaɪ-, dʒɪ-). [L., a. Gr. γυναικωνῖτις, f. γυναικ-, γυνή woman.]

1. The women's apartments in a household; = GYNÆCEUM 1.

1855 R. F. BURTON *El-Medinah* II. xv. 47, I often saw parties of women mount the stairs to the Gynæconitis.

2. The women's gallery in a church.

1850 NEALE *East. Ch.* I. I. 206 The women's gallery, or gynæconitis, formed an important part of the earlier Byzantine churches. **1865** *Sat. Rev.* 11 Feb. 182 The triforium is used throughout as a gynækonitis, or women's gallery, running round three sides of the church.

gynander (dʒaɪˈnændə(r), g-). [ad. Gr. γύνανδρος (see GYNANDROUS).]

1. A woman with male characteristics. *rare*[−1].

1888 *Scribner's Mag.* May 631/2 An emasculated type, product of short-haired women and long-haired men, gynanders and androgynes.

2. A plant of the class *Gynandria*.

1828-32 WEBSTER, *Gynander*, in botany, a plant whose stamens are inserted in the pistil.

gynandrian (dʒaɪ-, dʒɪˈnændrɪən, g-), *a.* [f. mod.L. *Gynandria* (Linnæus), f. Gr. γυν-ή + ἀνδρ-, ἀνήρ (see GYNANDROUS) + -IAN.] Pertaining to the Linnæan class *Gynandria*, which consists of plants characterized by gynandrous flowers.

1828-32 WEBSTER *Gynandrian*, having stamens inserted in the pistil.

gynandro- (dʒaɪ-, dʒɪˈnændrəʊ, g-), comb. form of Gr. γύνανδρος (see GYNANDROUS) in some modern scientific terms. **gyˈnandromorph**, an individual which exhibits gynandromorphism. **gynandroˈmorphic** *a.* = *gynandromorphous* adj. **gynandromorphism** (-ˈmɔːfɪz(ə)m) *Ent.*, the condition of being gynandromorphous. **gynandromorphous** (-ˈmɔːfəs) *a.* [Gr. μορφή shape, form], having both male and female characters; applied to some few insects which appear to have both male and female markings on the body. **gyˈnandrophore** (-fɔə(r)) *Bot.*, a gonophore which bears both the stamens and the pistil.

1897 WEBSTER, Gynandromorph. **1903** *Bull. Amer. Mus. Nat. Hist.* XIX. 648 A single incipient colony..was found to contain about twenty workers, a few worker cocoons, and a *gynandromorph. **1968** M. W. STRICKBERGER *Genetics* xxi. 468 Gynandromorphs differ from intersexes in the sense that gynandromorphs are obviously mosaic. **1894** W. BATESON *Study of Variation* 68 *Gynandromorphic insects, in which the characters of the whole or part of one side of the body, wings and antennæ, are male, while those of the other side are female. **1950** B. P. SONNENBLICK in M. Demerec *Biol. Drosophila* ii. 90 A wide assortment of gynandromorphic patterns can result. **1843** HUMPHREYS *Brit. Moths* I. 8 That so many instances of *Gynandromorphism have been observed in individuals of this species. **1867** *Athenæum* No. 2089. 616/3 Two *gynandromorphous insects. **1878** MASTERS *Henfrey's Bot.* 271 The *gynandrophore bearing the stamens and ovary.

gynandrous (dʒaɪ-, dʒɪˈnændrəs, g-), *a. Bot.* [f. Gr. γύνανδρ-ος (recorded in the sense 'of doubtful sex') + -OUS: cf. GYNO- and -ANDROUS.] Applied to those flowers and plants in which the stamens and pistil are united in one column, as in orchids; said also of the stamens.

1807 J. E. SMITH *Phys. Bot.* 462 The rest of the Order are in no sense gynandrous. **1830** LINDLEY *Nat. Syst. Bot.* 189 [Stylidieæ.] Nearly allied both to Campanulaceæ and Goodenoviæ, from both of which they are distinguished by their gynandrous stamens. **1870** HOOKER *Stud. Flora* p. xvii, Aristolochieæ..Stamens 6-12, epigynous or gynandrous. **1897** WILLIS *Flower. Pl.* I. 77 The stamens may be epipetalous or gynandrous.

gynantherous: see GYNO-.

gynarchy (ˈdʒaɪnɑːkɪ, g-). Also 6-8 **gunarchy**. [f. Gr. γυν-ή woman + -αρχία, ἀρχή rule.] Government by a woman or women.

1577-87 HOLINSHED *Chron.* I. 13/2 The gunarchie of queene Cordeilla. **1660** R. COKE *Power & Subj.* 101 That in Gynarchy the wife is not subject, but superior to her husband. **1758** CHESTERF. *Lett.* (1792) IV. cccl. 159, I have always some hopes of a change under a Gunarchy; where whim and humour commonly prevail. **1890** *Blackw. Mag.* CXLVII. 264/2 So will you best help to maintain..the true gynarchy.

gynbred, obs. form of GINGERBREAD.

gyndal, var. GUINDALL *Obs.*, windlass.

gyne (dʒaɪn). *Ent.* [ad. Gr. γυνή woman.] The fertile female in a colony of social insects, esp. a queen ant. Hence ˈ**gynæcoid** *a.* [see GYNÆCO- and -OID], showing some characteristics of this type of insect.

[**1905** tr. *E. Wasmann's Compar. Stud. Psychol. Ants* iv. 164 Intermediate forms between females and worker ants.. female-like workers, which I have named pseudo-females (pseudogynes).] **1907** *Bull. Amer. Mus. Nat. Hist.* XXIII. 54 The *female* (gynē), or queen, is the more highly specialized sex among ants and is characterized, as a rule, by her large stature and the more uniform development of her organs. **1915** H. ST. J. K. DONISTHORPE *Brit. Ants* 38 The female (*gyne*), queen, or α-female, is the most highly specialized sex. **1907** *Bull. Amer. Mus. Nat. Hist.* XXIII. 24 Wasmann's 'gynæcoid workers', which are merely workers whose ovaries contain mature eggs. **1933** W. M. WHEELER *Colony-founding among Ants* 132 He cites the development of fertile gynaecoid workers and the rearing of substitution queens in ant and termite colonies that have lost their mother. **1953** *Q. Rev. Biol.* XXVIII. 145/1 *Ergatogyne.* Individuals falling along the allometric progression connecting the queen and worker castes, ranging from subapterous forms with queen-like alitrunks to slightly gynecoid workers.

gynec-: see GYNÆC-.

gynee (ˈgaɪniː). Also **gaini, ghinee.** [Hindi (related to *go* cow *sb.*[1]).] One of a small variety of Indian cattle.

1829 J. SHIPP *Mem.* III. v. 132, I found that the said tiger had feasted on a more delicate morsel,—a nice little ghinee, a small cow. **1832** F. PARKS *Jrnl.* 1 Dec. in *Wand. Pilgrim* (1850) I. xxii. 251 We have become great farmers, having sown our crop of oats, and are building outhouses to receive some thirty-four dwarf cows and oxen (gynees), which are to be fed up for the table. **1873** H. BLOCHMANN tr. *Abul Fazl 'Allami's Ain i Akbari* I. 149 There is also a species of oxen, called *gaini*, small..but very beautiful.

gynegium, obs. form of GYNÆCEUM.

gyneocracy (dʒaɪ-, dʒɪnɪˈɒkrəsɪ, g-). *rare.* Also 7 **gynœcratie, (gyneiocracie).** [f. Gr. γυνή woman + -(O)CRACY.] Incorrect form for GYNÆCOCRACY.

1611 SPEED *Hist. Gt. Brit.* IX. xii. §47 The..law..which they call the Salick, by the which the French exclude Gyneiocracie [*in list of 'Faults escaped' altered to* Gynœocratie], or Womens Gouernement in chiefe. **1869** MRS. LYNN LINTON *Ourselves* 176 In the gyneocracy of the future,—that new moral world which is to be under woman's undivided sway. **1881** L. H. MORGAN *Contrib. Amer. Ethnol.* 66 The mother-right and gyneocracy among the Iroquois.

gyng, variant of GING *Obs.*

gyngangre, obs. form of GINGER.

†**gyngawdry, -awtre.** *Cookery. Obs.* Also **-audre, -autrey.** A dish prepared with the livers of certain fishes.

?*c* **1390** *Form of Cury* No. 94 (1780) 47 Gyngawdry. Take the Powche and the Lyuour of haddok codlyng and hake. *c* **1430** *Two Cookery-bks.* 15 Gyngaudre.—Take þe Lyuerys of Codlyngys, Haddok, Elys, or þe Hake hed, or Freysshe Mylwell hedys, þe Pouches, & þe Lyuerys, an sethe hem in fayre Water [etc.]. *c* **1450** *Ibid.* 94 Gyngautrey. **14..** in Warner *Antiq. Culin.* (1791) 70 Gyngawtre. Take the pake of the lyver of hake or of codlynge, or of hadok, and parboyle hit well.

gynge, variant of GING *Obs.*

gyngebrede, obs. form of GINGERBREAD.

gynger, -evere, -ure, -yvre, obs. ff. GINGER.

gyngle, obs. form of JINGLE.

gynglimos, obs. form of GINGLYMUS.

gyngour, obs. form of GINGER.

gynie, var. GYNÆ.

gyniolatry (dʒaɪ-, dʒɪnɪˈɒlətrɪ, g-). [Badly f. Gr. γυνή woman + -(O)LATRY.] Adoration of or excessive devotion to women. So **gyneˈolater**, an adorer of women.

1876 LOWELL *Among my Bks.* Ser. II. 36 The sentimental gyniolatry of chivalry, which was at best but skin-deep, is lifted in Beatrice to an ideal and universal plane. **1890** *Harper's Mag.* Oct. 757/2 He was become a gyneolater.

gynny, obs. form of GUINEA.

gyno- (gaɪnə, dʒaɪ-, dʒɪ-), before a vowel **gyn-** (gaɪn), reduced form of GYNÆCO-, used chiefly in botanical terms with the meaning 'pistil', 'ovary' (the more important are given as main-words): **gynantherous** (-ˈænθərəs) *a. Bot.* [ANTHER]: see quot. **gynocardic** (-ˈkɑːdɪk) *a. Chem.* [f. mod.L. *Gynocardia* (Gr. καρδία heart), a genus of the N.O. *Bixaceæ*], in ***gynocardic acid***, the supposed active principle of

Chaulmugra oil, which is produced by the plant *Gynocardia odorata*. **gynodiœcious** (-daɪ'iːʃ(ɪ)əs) *a. Bot.* [DIŒCIOUS], having perfect and female flowers on different plants; so **gynodiœcism** (-daɪ'iːsɪz(ə)m), the condition of being gynodiœcious. **gynodiœcy** (-daɪ'iːsɪ), gynodiœcism. **gynomonœcious** (-mɒ'niːʃ(ɪ)əs) *a. Bot.* [MONŒCIOUS], having both perfect and female flowers on the same plant. **gynomonœcism** (-mɒ'niːsɪz(ə)m), the condition of being gynomonœcious. **gynomonœcy** (-mɒ'niːsɪ), gynomonœcism. **gynophagite** (-'ɒfədʒaɪt) [Gr. -φαγ-ος eating + -ITE] *humorous nonce-wd.*, a woman-eater. †**gyno'philian, gy'nophilous** *adjs.* [Gr. -φιλος loving], woman-loving. **gyno'phobia**, fear of women. **gynoplastic** (-'plæstɪk) *a. Phys.* [PLASTIC], 'relating to the closing of unnatural openings in the female organs of generation, or to the opening of closed or dilatation of contracted natural openings of the same organs' (*Syd. Soc. Lex.* 1886). **'gynospore** = MEGASPORE. ‖**gynostegium** (-'stiːdʒɪəm) *Bot.* [Gr. στέγη roof], the sheath of a gynæceum. ‖**gynostemium** (-'stiːmɪəm) *Bot.* [Gr. στῆμων thread, stamen], the column consisting of the united stamens and pistil, as in the orchis.

1874 R. BROWN *Man. Bot.* Gloss., *Gynantherous, an abnormal condition of the flower in which the stamens are converted into pistils. **1897** *Allbutt's Syst. Med.* II. 76 The active principle of the oil [sc. chaulmoogra oil], *gynocardic acid, has also been prescribed internally by Besnier and others. **1877** DARWIN *Forms of Fl.* 298 The species now to be considered consist of hermaphrodites and females without males..which I have called *gynodiœcious. **1880** GRAY *Struct. Bot.* vi. §3. 191 Gyno-diœcious, where the flowers on separate individuals are some hermaphrodite and some female, but none male only. **1881** H. MÜLLER in *Nature* XXIII. 337 Stellaria glauca..is gynodiœcious. **1897** WILLIS *Flower. Pl.* I. 89 This is termed *gynodioecism and is common also in Caryophyllaceae..and other plants. **1940** *Nature* 30 Mar. 486/2 *Gynodiœcy should not be confused with unisexuality. **1956** *Evolution* X. 115 (*heading*) The genetics and evolution of gynodioecy. **1877** DARWIN *Diff. Forms Flowers* 12 Other species..bear on the same plant hermaphrodite and female flowers; and these might be called *gyno-monœcious, if a name were desirable for them. **1881** H. MÜLLER in *Nature* XXIII. 337 Syringa Persica..is gynomonœcious. **1897** WILLIS *Flower. Pl.* II. 97 The most common case is *gynomonoecism, the ray-florets being ♀, the disc ☿. **1963** DAVIS & HEYWOOD *Princ. Angiosperm Taxon.* xi. 369 Gynomonoecism where female and hermaphrodite flowers co-exist on the same plant. **1949** DARLINGTON & MATHER *Elem. Genetics* 394 *Gynomonoecy, the condition of plant individuals, or of species having individuals, which bear both female (*i.e.* male sterile) and hermaphrodite flowers. **1853** LYTTON *My Novel* III. xxii, He preys upon the weaker sex, and is a *Gynophagite. **1647** R. BACON *Cyprian Acad.* A ij b, My *Gynophilian or amorous infant. **1623** COCKERAM, **Gynophilous*, a louer of women. **1886** O. W. HOLMES *Mortal Antipathy* xix. 231 If we give it a name, we shall have to apply the term **Gynophobia*, or Fear of Woman. **1886** *Academy* 16 Jan. 37 A man.. has become afflicted with gynophobia. **1940** HINSIE & SHATZKY *Psychiatric Dict.* 245 *Gynophobia*, morbid fear of women. **1900** B. D. JACKSON *Gloss. Bot. Terms* 309/2 **Gynospore*.., formerly suggested for macrospore, that is, a Megaspore. **1937** *Sci. Proc. R. Dublin Soc.* XXI. 457 The development of several gynospores, supernumerary prothalli, lateral pollen tubes and lateral archegonia;..all seem to give the redwood an unique position. **1964** PRIESTLEY & SCOTT *Introd. Bot.* (ed. 4) xxxvi. 590 Alternative and more non-committal terms are indeed already proposed, viz...gynospore, or female spore, for the embryo sac. **1880** GRAY *Struct. Bot.* 414/1 *Gynostegium, a sheath or covering of the gynoecium, of whatever nature. **1861** BENTLEY *Man. Bot.* 256 The column is..termed the *gynostemium, and the flowers are said to be gynandrous. **1880** C. & F. DARWIN *Movem. Pl.* 226 The circumnutation of the gynostemium of Stylidium..is highly remarkable, and apparently aids in the fertilisation of the flowers.

gynobase ('dʒaɪn-, 'dʒɪnəbeɪs, g-). *Bot.* Also in mod.L. form **gynobasis.** [f. GYNO- + BASE.] The flat or conical enlargement of the receptacle of a flower supporting the gynæceum.

1830 LINDLEY *Nat. Syst. Bot.* 136 Carpella equal in number to the petals, lying upon an enlarged, tumid, fleshy disk (the gynobase). **1832** —— *Introd. Bot.* I. ii. §9. 137 Gynobasis. **1849** CARPENTER *Veg. Phys.* 414 The seed-vessel, when ripe, splits into four valves, leaving the thick hard gynobase in the centre.

Hence **gynobasic** (dʒaɪ-, dʒɪnə'beɪsɪk) *a.*, pertaining to or having a gynobase; ***gynobasic style***, one rising from the base of the ovary. Also **gynobaseous** (-'beɪsɪəs) *a. rare.*

1836 LINDLEY *Nat. Syst. Bot.* (ed. 2) 128 No Gynobaseous order has more than 5 carpels, except accidentally. Euphorbiaceæ, which are much more like gynobasic plants [etc.]. **1861** BENTLEY *Man. Bot.* 289 The ovary is said to be gyno-basic. **1872** OLIVER *Elem. Bot.* II. 212 The style springing from the centre and base of the lobes of the ovary, termed gynobasic. **1897** WILLIS *Flower. Pl.* I. 77 The style usually crowns the ovary but is sometimes lateral, basal or gynobasic.

gynocracy (dʒaɪ-, dʒɪ'nɒkrəsɪ, g-). [f. GYNO- + -CRACY.] = GYNÆCOCRACY; also quasi-*concr.*, women as the ruling class.

1728 POPE *Let. to Swift* S.'s Wks. 1761 VIII. 75, I am told the Gynocracy are of opinion, that they want no better writers than Cibber and the British journalist. **1822** SCOTT *Nigel* xvii, Oligarchy, limited monarchy, and even gynocracy. **1824** BYRON *Juan* XVI. lii, But wear the newest mantle of hypocrisy, On pain of much displeasing the gynocracy. **1864** *Macm. Mag.* July 219 From a gynocracy.. heaven save us and all Christian communities!

So **gyno'cratic** *a.* = GYNÆCOCRATIC.

1847 *Fraser's Mag.* XXXVI. 15 Hers was not a popular form of gynocratic government. **1861** HULME tr. *Moquin-Tandon* II. III. 198 Linnæus terms the government [of bees] a gynocratic republic.

‖**gynœcium**, the usual but incorrect form of GYNÆCEUM 2, *Bot.*

gynogenesis (gaɪnəʊ'dʒɛnɪsɪs). *Zool.* [f. GYNO- + -GENESIS.] Reproduction in which the development of the embryo occurs as a result of the penetration of an ovum by a sperm but does not involve the nuclear material of the latter.

1925 E. B. WILSON *Cell* (ed. 3) v. 460 In a nearly related phenomenon, which may be called gynogenesis, the sperm penetrates (and in some cases activates) the egg but otherwise takes no part in the processes of development. **1952** BOYD & HAMILTON in A. S. Parkes *Marshall's Physiol. Reprod.* (ed. 3) II. xiv. 42 Gynogenesis may occur to a limited degree in mammals as the result of irradiation of the semen. **1969** R. F. CHAPMAN *Insects* xix. 380 An unusual type of thelytoky, known as gynogenesis, occurs in the form *mobilis* of *Ptinus clavipes* (Coleoptera). The form *mobilis* exists only as triploid females which reproduce parthenogenetically, but the development of eggs is triggered by healthy sperm of *P. clavipes* or, less successfully, of *P. pusillus.*

Hence **gynoge'netic** *a.*

1925 E. B. WILSON *Cell* (ed. 3) v. 463 The conclusion seems probable..that even in such (presumably) diploid larvæ development is gynogenetic, the diploid number having been restored by a doubling of the maternal haploid group. **1964** L. B. RUSSELL in C. Pavan et al. *Mammalian Cytogenetics* 64 Ultraviolet irradiation of spermatozoa can destroy the paternally contributed chromatin without affecting the activating function of the sperm and thus lead to gynogenetic haploids.

gynophore ('dʒaɪn-, 'dʒɪnəfɔə(r), g-). [f. GYNO- + Gr. -φορ-ος bearing. Cf. F. *gynophore.*]

1. *Bot.* The pedicel or stalk which in some flowers supports the ovary.

1821 S. F. GRAY *Nat. Arrangem. Pl.* I. 159 It is sometimes difficult to distinguish between the gynophore and the nectary. **1832** LINDLEY *Introd. Bot.* II. ii. §10. 139 Sometimes the ovarium..is seated upon a long stalk... This stalk is often called the thecaphore or gynophore. **1871** H. MACMILLAN *True Vine* ii. (1872) 64 The central gynophore [of the Passion flower], bearing the stamens and pistil, was the pillar of the cross. **1880** C. & F. DARWIN *Movem. Pl.* 225 The gynophore of *Arachis hypogæa.*

2. *Zool.* One of the branches bearing the female gonophores in certain Hydrozoa.

1861 J. R. GREENE *Coelent.* 45 When male and female gonophores differ externally in form, the special terms 'androphore' and 'gynophore' are employed to distinguish them. **1877** HUXLEY *Anat. Inv. Anim.* 143 The groups of male and female gonophores are borne upon separate branches of the gonoblastidium (androphores and gynophores).

†**gynour.** *Sc. Obs.* [Aphetic form of *engynour* (see ENGINEER *sb.* and cf. GIN *sb.*[1]).] One who manages engines of war.

1375 BARBOUR *Bruce* XVII. 690 The gynour than gert bend in hy the gyne. [Cf. l. 682 engynour, *v.r.* gynour.]

-gynous (dʒɪnəs), *Bot. suffix* forming adjs., f. mod.L. *-gyn-us* (a. Gr. -γυνος adj. termination, f. γυν-ή woman, female) + -OUS; used as = 'having ...female organs or pistils', as in ***monogynous*** having one pistil, ***tetragynous*** having four pistils, etc., ***androgynous*** having stamens and pistils on the same flower or same plant. (Cf. -ANDROUS.)

gynypre, obs. form of JUNIPER.

gyo, variant of GEO, *dial.*, a gully, creek.

1878 R. DICK *Baker of Thurso* viii. 81 And roll along the gyoes far inland.

gyour, variant of GUYOUR *Obs.*

gyp (dʒɪp), *sb.*[1] (and *a.*) Also 8 jip, 9 gip. [perh. short for GIPSY or for GIPPO[1] 2.]

1. a. At Cambridge and Durham, a college servant, esp. one who attends on one or more undergraduates. In the first quot. the meaning appears to be somewhat different.

1750 DODD *Poems* (1767) 31 No more the jolly Jips..carol out their songs. *Note.* Are an idle useful set of hangers on the college, who procure ale, pence &c., by running errands, and doing little services for their masters. **1799** *Spirit Publ. Jrnls.* (1800) III. 216 The College Gyps, of high illustrious worth, With all the dishes in long order go. **1803** *Gradus ad Cantab.* (1824) 128 To avoid..gate-bills he will be out at night as late as he pleases..climb over the College walls, and fee his Gyp well. **1805** H. K. WHITE in *Rem.* (1819) I. 209 My bed-maker, whom we call a gyp, from a Greek word signifying a vulture, runs away with everything he can lay his hands on. **1822** SCOTT *Nigel* xvi, No scout in Oxford, no gip in Cambridge ever matched him in speed and intelligence. **1839–40** THACKERAY *Catherine* viii, I was a gyp at Cambridge. **1894** WILKINS & VIVIAN *Green Bay Tree* I. 234 The spiritual destitution of bedmakers and gyps.

b. *attrib.* **gyp-room**, a room where the gyps keep table furniture, etc.

1871 M. LEGRAND *Camb. Freshm.* 210 He fetched the.. reviving beverage from the gyp-room. **1886** WILLIS & CLARK *Cambridge* I. 624 The cloister..was cut off to supply a gyp-room.

2. *U.S. slang.* A thief.

1889 in *Century Dict.*

3. A fraudulent action; a swindle. Also as *adj.* Cf. GYP *v.* orig. *U.S.*

1914 JACKSON & HELLYER *Vocab. Criminal Slang* 41 *Gyp*, ..the act of short-changing; a defrauding by substitution; an action that belies a professed sincerity. **1930** 'A. ARMSTRONG' *Taxi* xvi. 220 The non-combine cabs..are referred to as 'gyp' taxis, which implies mingled piracy and deceit. **1967** *Boston Sunday Globe* 23 Apr. B61/2 Some are good, but gyps abound. Authorities report..phony practices.

gyp (dʒɪp), *sb.*[2] *U.S.* [? Short for *Gypsy*, GIPSY used as a proper name for a bitch.] A bitch.

1878 C. HALLOCK *Amer. Club List & Sportsman's Gloss.* p. v, *Gyp*, the young female pup. **1890** J. COOKE in G. O. Shields *Big Game N. Amer.* 148 Old Tige had filled up on the first Deer's inwards. He looked like a gyp, and near her time. **1895** A. HUNTER in *Outing* (U.S.) XXVII. 75/2 One of the pack—a long-limbed gyp named Queen..covered with black pitch-like mud.

gyp (dʒɪp), *sb.*[3] *dial.* or *colloq.* Also gip, jip. [App. contraction of GEE-UP, which is used in dial. as sb.] ***to give*** (a person) ***gyp***: to punish, thrash, treat roughly; to hurt, give pain.

1893 *Funk's Stand. Dict.*, *To give one gyp*, to make one smart for anything done. **1898** in B. KIRKBY *Lakeland Words.* **1902** *Eng. Dial. Dict.* s.v. *Jip*, Ah'll gi'e tha jip... 'Ah gav' it jip Ah can tell tha,' said of beating a carpet soundly with a stick in each hand. **1910** 'G. B. LANCASTER' *Jim of Ranges* xi. 212 'Jim Kyneton's a good man, and this is giving him particular gyp if I know anything of good men,' he [Jack West] said. **1915** 'BOYD CABLE' *Between Lines* 19 We'll give 'em gyp if they try it. **1917** P. MACGILL *Brown Brethren* xii. 170 A cramp in my guts!..Gawd, it isn't 'arf giving me gyp! **1936** WODEHOUSE *Laughing Gas* iv. 46 If you knew what gyp those shoes were giving me that night. **1966** I. JEFFERIES *House Surgeon* viii. 155, I should think his tum is giving him gip.

gyp (dʒɪp), *v.* orig. *U.S.* Also gip. [Cf. GYP *sb.*[1] 3.] To cheat, trick, swindle.

1889 in *Cent. Dict.* **1914** JACKSON & HELLYER *Vocab. Criminal Slang* 41 *Gyp*.., to flim-flam; to cheat by means of guile and manual dexterity... 'Gyp this boob with a deuce.' **1925** F. SCOTT FITZGERALD *Great Gatsby* (1926) ii. 42 We had over twelve hundred dollars when we started, but we got gyped out of it all in two days. **1930** D. BYRNE *Golden Goat* xiii. 106 Dariano had gipped the Greek Government during the war of millions in contracts. **1932** J. DOS PASSOS *1919* 55 American dollars went pretty far if you knew enough not to let 'em gyp you. **1935** WODEHOUSE *Luck of Bodkins* xiv. 156 A suspicion was growing with him that..he had been gypped. **1962** *Punch* 28 Feb. 356/2 If he..thinks the conductor is trying to gyp him..he..need only look at the fares table. **1965** R. HOWARD tr. *S. de Beauvoir's Force of Circumstance* 658 Turning an incredulous gaze toward that young and credulous girl, I realize with stupor how much I was gypped.

gyp, variant of GIP *v.*; GIP *int. Obs.*

gypcer, gypcyere, obs. variants of GIPSER.

gype, -ell, variant of GIPE, GIPEL *Obs.*, a tunic.

gypo(u)n, obs. variant of GIPON.

gyppe, variant of GIP *int. Obs.*

gyppie, gyp(p)o, gyppy, varr. GIPPY.

gyps (dʒɪps). Also 4 ? *pl.* gipsis, 5 gipse, 8 gypse. [Anglicized form of GYPSUM. Cf. F. *gypse*, G. *gips.*] = GYPSUM.

1398 TREVISA *Barth. De P.R.* XV. lvii. (1495) 509 In the grounde abowte Parys is a manere stone that hyght Gipsis. *c* **1420** *Pallad. on Husb.* XI. 383 Or gipse, or askes twey cotuls no wronge Thy wynes doth. **1756** P. BROWNE *Jamaica* 46 The gypse..is commonly found of some regular form approaching upon the rhomboide. **1774** *Projects* in *Ann. Reg.* 108/1 To coalesce and set as readily as our gypses and plasters. **1834** *Brit. Husb.* I. 439 *Gyps* is calcareous earth saturated with vitriolic acid. **1862** H. MARRYAT *Year in Sweden* II. 144 Coffered ceilings of gyps are triumphs of the plasterer's art.

attrib. **1862** H. MARRYAT *Year in Sweden* II. 141 The Wrangel Grafchor is a fine specimen of northern gyps-work.

gypsa, obs. plural of GYPSUM.

†**gyp'sation.** *Obs. rare*$^{-0}$. [as if ad. L. **gypsātiōn-em*, n. of action f. *gypsāre* GYPSE *v.*] The action or process of plastering with gypsum; pargetting.

1656–81 in BLOUNT *Glossogr.* **1676** in COLES.

gypse (dʒɪps), *v.* Also 5 gipse. [In sense a. ad. L. *gypsā-re*, f. *gypsum* (see GYPSUM *sb.*); in sense b. f. GYPS.] †**a.** *trans.* To close or plaster down with gypsum (*obs.*). **b.** To dress (a field) with gypsum; only in **gypsed** (dʒɪpst), *ppl. a.*

c **1420** *Pallad. on Husb.* XI. 477 So gipse hit vp, and kepe hit for thyn age. *Ibid.* 524 Now gipse hit fast. **1850** *Jrnl. R. Agric. Soc.* XI. II. 434 The gypsed clover becomes a good crop, while the ungypsed clover is burnt up by the drought.

gypsees, obs. pl. of GIPSY.

gypseous ('dʒɪpsɪəs), *a.* [f. late L. *gypse-us* (f. *gypsum*) + -OUS. Cf. GYPSOUS.]

1. Resembling or having the qualities of gypsum.

1661 LOVELL *Hist. Anim. & Min.* 437 Of phlegme... If gypseous, by nodous swellings. **1710** T. FULLER *Pharm. Extemp.* 278 And these [Expectorators]..cast purulent and gypseous Matter out of the Bronchia. **1782** *Phil. Trans.* LXXII. 323 This clay..contains no gypseous matter. **1796** W. MARSHALL *W. England* I. 16, I was led to the idea, that they [crystals of quartz] were of a gypseous nature.

2. Containing or consisting mainly of gypsum.

1771 BP. WATSON *Chem. Ess.* (1787) V. 127 Gypseous alabasters, plaster stone [etc.]. **1778** WOULFE in *Phil. Trans.* LXIX. 14 Heavy spars, commonly called selenitical or gypseous spars. **1830** LYELL *Princ. Geol.* (1875) I. I. vi. 111 The gypseous red marl of Aix, in Provence. **1849** MURCHISON *Siluria* xiii. 311 It is flanked by the Ural Mountains, gypseous limestones form the base. **1862** DANA *Man. Geol.* 247 Variegated gypseous marls. **1880** *Libr. Univ. Knowl.* (U.S.) XII. 478 The peculiar color [of the Red River] is attributed to the red clay of the gypseous formation ..of its bed.

gypsiferous (dʒɪp'sɪfərəs), *a.* [f. GYPS-UM + -(I)FEROUS. Cf. F. *gypsifère*.] Yielding or containing gypsum.

1847 in CRAIG. **1849** MURCHISON *Siluria* xviii. 444 The gypsiferous and salt-bearing formation of the Upper Silurian. **1862** RAWLINSON *Anc. Mon.* I. i. 236 The soil too is often gypsiferous.

† **'gypsine**, *a. Obs. rare*⁻¹. [f. GYPS-UM + -INE.] = GYPSEOUS.

1695 *Phil. Trans.* XIX. 151 It makes a glittering shew, being built of Gypsine Stone, or Rock-Ising-glass, resembling alabaster. **1753** in CHAMBERS *Cycl. Supp.*

gypsion, gypsire: see GIPSY, GIPSER.

gypsography (dʒɪp'sɒgrəfɪ). *rare.* [f. Gr. γύψο-ς gypsum + γραφία -GRAPHY.] The art or practice of engraving on gypsum or on plaster of Paris.

1840 *Mech. Mag.* XXXII. 256 Gypsography—This is the new title bestowed on the process..heretofore styled metallic relief engraving. **1845** *Athenæum* 11 Jan. 41 We were made acquainted with Gypsography and Glyphography.

gypsophila (dʒɪp'sɒfɪlə). *Bot.* [mod.L. (Linnæus *Dissertatio Botanica, qua Nova Plantarum Genera* (1751) no. 1103), f. Gr. γύψος chalk + φίλος loving.] A member of the genus of herbs so called, belonging to the family Caryophyllaceæ and bearing small delicate flowers in panicles.

1771 R. WESTON *Universal Botanist* II. 373 Tall Siberian White Gypsophila. **1810** *Curtis's Bot. Mag.* XXXI. 1281 (*heading*) Trailing Gypsophila. **1909** *Daily Mirror* 13 Aug. 7/4 The graceful gypsophila (chalk plant). **1970** C. LLOYD *Well-Tempered Garden* ii. 63 Dianthus and gypsophilas should not be kept under close conditions a day longer than is necessary for rooting them.

gypsophilous (dʒɪp'sɒfɪləs), *a. Ecol.* [See prec. and -OUS.] Of a plant: thriving on a soil rich in gypsum; formerly used in reference to limestone soils (cf. CALCICOLOUS *a.*).

1902 F. E. CLEMENTS in *Botanische Jahrbücher* XXXI. LXX. 14 *Gypsophytia*,..limestone plant formations; gypsophyta, limestone plants; gypsophilus, dwelling on limestone. **1932** FULLER & CONARD tr. *Braun-Blanquet's Plant Sociol.* vi. 186 On the high Algerian plateau the gypsophilous plants form an upper zone of scanty vegetation bordering some schotts at Le Kreider. **1941** *Jrnl. Arnold Arboretum* XXII. 154 Several gypsophilous species confined to Texas and New Mexico have also been included. **1966** *Madroño* XVIII. 185 (*heading*) Two gypsophilous species of Muhlenbergia.

gypsous ('dʒɪpsəs), *a.* [f. GYPS-UM + -OUS. Cf. F. *gypseux*.] = GYPSEOUS 1 and 2.

1655 FULLER *Hist. Camb.* 129 An exhalation in moist weather out of Gipsous or plaisterly ground. **1811** PINKERTON *Petral.* I. 501 The statues of the superb mausoleum..are of gypsous alabaster. **1852** TH. ROSS *Humboldt's Trav.* III. xxxii. 394 Nothing..proves the independence of those arenaceous and gypsous soils.

gypsum ('dʒɪpsəm), *sb. Min. Pl.* 8 **gypsa**, 8–9 **gypsums**. [a. L. *gypsum*, ad. Gr. γύψος chalk, gypsum.] Hydrous calcium sulphate, the mineral from which plaster of Paris is made.

[**1387** TREVISA *Higden* (Rolls) I. 271 Bysides Parys is greet plente of a manere stoon þat hatte gypsus.] **1646** SIR T. BROWNE *Pseud. Ep.* II. v. 92 Gypsum layed up in the earth the space of 80 yeeres. **1662** EVELYN *Chalcogr.* (1769) 33 Figures in..gypsum. **1759** W. CULLEN *Let.* in *Life* (1832) I. 127 Are the talcs and gypsums different in their Composition. **1776** WOULFE in *Phil. Trans.* LXVI. 610 The Bolognian stone and other such spars, as well as the gypsa, are decomposed by fixed alkalies. *a* **1817** T. DWIGHT *Trav. New Eng.* etc. (1821) II. 343 Lands, dressed with gypsum, have been equally favourable to wheat. **1860** TYNDALL *Glac.* II. xxxi. 409 The prism presented the appearance of a crystal of gypsum. **1871** ROSCOE *Elem. Chem.* 218 Gypsum when moderately heated loses its water, and is then called plaster of Paris.

attrib. **1823** BUCKLAND *Reliq. Diluv.* 169 Ancient and modern bones occur mixed together only in the gypsum cavities. **1849** *Sk. Nat. Hist., Mammalia* III. 95 The gypsum-quarries near Paris. **1862** *Proc. Amer. Phil. Soc.* IX. 33 These gypsum deposits have no geological connection with the coal.

gypsum ('dʒɪpsəm), *v.* [f. GYPSUM *sb.*] *trans.* To dress (land or a crop) with gypsum.

1819 *Commun. Board Agric.* 521 The whole field..was again gypsumed at the rate of four bushels per acre. **1834** *Brit. Husb.* I. 323 Cattle show..a remarkable predilection for clover which has been gypsumed.

Hence **'gypsumed** *ppl. a.*

1841 *Jrnl. R. Agric. Soc.* II. I. 111 The comparative produce of the gypsumed over not gypsumed land is very great. **1849** J. F. JOHNSTON *Exper. Agric.* 120 On wheat, after gypsumed clover.

gypsy, alternative form of GIPSY.

gyptian, gyraff(a, obs. ff. GIPSY, GIRAFFE.

gyral ('dʒaɪərəl), *a.* [f. GYRE or GYR-US *sb.* + -AL[1].] **a.** Moving in a circle or spiral; whirling, gyratory. **b.** Pertaining to a gyrus or gyri (see GYRUS). Hence **'gyrally** *adv.*, in a gyral manner; in a circular form or arrangement.

1750 G. HUGHES *Barbadoes* 204 The flower consists of five pale-white leaves gyrally incircling one another. **1827** *Blackw. Mag.* XXI. 791 We were not seen stoitering gyrally away up-hill. **1828–32** WEBSTER, *Gyral*, whirling, moving in a circular form.

gyrant ('dʒaɪərənt), *a. rare*⁻¹. In 9 **girant**. [ad. L. *gȳrant-em*, pres. pple. of *gȳrāre* to move in a circle.] Having a circular or spiral course.

1844 MRS. BROWNING *Drama Exile* Poems 1850 I. 35, I wound in girant orbits.

gyrate ('dʒaɪərət), *a.* [ad. L. *gȳrāt-us* rounded, pa. pple. of *gȳrāre*: see GYRE *v.*] Arranged in rings or convolutions. In *Botany* = CIRCINATE; also, see quot. 1836.

1830 LINDLEY *Nat. Syst. Bot.* 245 The peculiar gyrate vernation of the leaves of Cycadeæ. **1836** *Penny Cycl.* V. 253/1 *Gyrate*, see *Circinate*. Also, surrounded by an elastic ring, as the theca of ferns. **1845** LINDLEY *Sch. Bot.* iv. (1858) 25 Flowers regular, with straight anther-valves,..and gyrate foliation. **1861** BENTLEY *Man. Bot.* 211 A circinate or gyrate cyme. **1876** J. S. BRISTOWE *Theory & Pract. Med.* (ed. 2) 324 Sinuous or gyrate bullous bands. **1878** NICHOLSON in *Encycl. Brit.* VI. 373/2 By this 'serial' growth the corallum becomes 'gyrate' or 'meandrine'. **1897** *Allbutt's Syst. Med.* II. 278 The gyrate or ringed form of the patches.

gyrate ('dʒaɪəreɪt, -'reɪt), *v.* [f. L. *gȳrāt-*, ppl. stem of *gȳrāre*: see GYRE *v.*] *intr.* To move in a circle or spiral; to revolve, usually round a fixed point or on an axis; to rotate, whirl.

1830 *Fraser's Mag.* I. 32 Undefined comets that gyrate equally through suns, earths, and satellites. **1847** EMERSON *Repr. Men, Swedenborg* Wks. (Bohn) I. 318 The globule of blood gyrates around its own axis in the human veins, as the planet in the sky. **1858** G. MACDONALD *Phantastes* xvii. 211 With a somerset and a run, [he] threw himself gyrating into the air. **1892** STEVENSON *Across the Plains* 191 Came the dusty night-fliers, to gyrate for one brilliant instant round the flame.

fig. **1885** MISS BRADDON *Wyllard's Weird* II. 124 The rest of Paris was gyrating in the whirlpool of fashionable pleasure.

Hence **gy'rated** *ppl. a.* = GYRATE *a.*; **gy'rating** *vbl. sb.* and *ppl. a.*

1822–34 *Good's Study Med.* (ed. 4) IV. 458 Gyrated dry scall. *Ibid.* 459 The Gyrated Variety [of psoriasis] runs in a migratory course. **1837** CARLYLE *Fr. Rev.* I. III. i, His.. gyratings are at an end. **1860** MAURY *Phys. Geog. Sea* (Low) xix. §795 The gyrating column is never hundreds of miles in diameter. **1871** TYNDALL *Fragm. Sci.* (1879) I. vii. 242 A kind of mystery attaches itself to gyrating water. **1884** *Daily News* 24 Apr. 6 Other articles in the house appearing to perform a gyrating movement.

gyration (dʒaɪə'reɪʃən). Also 8 **giration**. [n. of action f. L. *gȳrāre*: see GYRE *v.* Cf. F. *giration*.]

1. The action or process of gyrating; motion in a circle or spiral; revolution round a fixed centre or axis, turning round, wheeling or whirling; an instance of any of these.

1615 CROOKE *Body of Man* 457 If there had not beene these gyrations in the substance of the braine. **1646** SIR T. BROWNE *Pseud. Ep.* II. iv. 80 The ayre impelled returnes unto its place in a gyration or whirling. **1661** GLANVILL *Van. Dogm.* ix. 81 A French Top, throwne from a cord which was wound about it, will stand as it were fixt..and yet continue in its repeated Gyrations. **1704** NEWTON *Opticks* I. (1721) 123 If a burning Coal be nimbly moved round in a Circle with Gyrations continually repeated. **1768–74** TUCKER *Lt. Nat.* (1834) I. 527 They might then make one giration in a long ellipsis. **1794** ATWOOD in *Phil. Trans.* LXXXIV. 127 *note*, To place the centre of gyration nearly at the same distance from the axis. **1816** KIRBY & SP. *Entomol.* (1843) II. 240 It performs its gyrations alternately from left to right and from right to left. **1834** MRS. SOMERVILLE *Connex. Phys. Sci.* xv. (1849) 140 In the northern hemisphere the gyration [of the wind] is contrary to the movement of the hands of a watch. *Ibid.* 141 Beyond the actual circle of gyration or limits of the storm. **1860** MAURY *Phys. Geog. Sea* (Low) xix. §796 In the gyrations of the storm. **1872** *Daily News* 25 Mar., Snowflakes that danced in eccentric fantastic gyrations. **1882** MINCHIN *Unipl. Kinemat.* 110 M = mass of the whole body and k its radius of gyration about GH. **1897** OUIDA *Massarenes* xi, Women were nevertheless enchanted to be embraced by him in its [the waltz's] giddy gyrations.

b. with reference to immaterial things or *fig.*

1808 J. BARLOW *Columb.* IX. 440 The vast gyration of a thousand years. **1847** DISRAELI *Tancred* II. xiv, His life was a gyration of energetic curiosity. **1852** H. ROGERS *Ecl. Faith* (1853) 35 Such is the appearance of Geo. Fellowes in that rapid gyration to which he has been subjected. **1868** E. EDWARDS *Ralegh* I. ix. 146 His present effort was still more impeded by endless gyrations of irresolution. **1883** S. WADDINGTON *A. H. Clough* 83 The vortex of religious excitement..kept him idly moving in its ceaseless gyrations.

2. *concr.* in *Conch.* One of the whorls of a spiral univalve shell.

Hence **gy'rational** *a.*, characterized by gyration.

1889 in *Century Dict.* (citing R. A. Proctor).

gyrator (dʒaɪə'reɪtə(r)). [as if L. **gȳrātor*, agent-n. f. *gȳrāre* to GYRATE.] **1.** He who or that which gyrates or whirls.

1836 E. HOWARD *R. Reefer* xx, I shall call them the pulsating and the gyrating leg... Whilst you were admiring the undulating grace of the pulsator,..you would find the gyrator had stolen a march upon you. **1895** H. STOPES in *Athenæum* 7 Sept. 325/3 Beautifully made [stone] axes, knives, gyrators. **1908** *Westm. Gaz.* 15 Jan. 3/3 'It's called a diable... He belongs to the best Diabolo Club, and he's never heard it called anything else.' Then he consulted the directions which had come with the box. The first of them began, 'Place the gyrator on the ground.'

2. *Electr.* A passive circuit element which has two pairs of terminals and introduces a phase shift of 180 degrees for one direction of propagation but no phase shift for the reverse direction.

1948 B. D. H. TELLEGEN in *Philips Res. Rep.* III. 87 Another such four-pole [network element], but violating the reciprocity relation, is described by $v_1 = -si_2$, $v_2 = si_1$... We shall denote such a four-pole by the name of ideal gyrator. **1952** *Bell Syst. Techn. Jrnl.* XXXI. 1 The microwave gyrator has been realized by making use of the Faraday rotation in pieces of ferrite placed in the waveguide. *Ibid.* 3 Network synthesis today is based upon the existence of four basic circuit elements: the capacitor, the resistor, the inductor, and the ideal transformer... The introduction of a fifth circuit element, the gyrator, would lead to considerably improved solutions for many network problems. **1957** *Jrnl. Brit. Interplan. Soc.* XVI. 241 The Hall gyrator..is a ferrite device using the Hall effect, which, used at high frequencies, can act as a radar isolator. **1959** H. W. KATZ *Solid State Magnetic & Dielectric Devices* iii. 115 A gyrator preceding a network terminal pair effectively interchanges voltage and current with a scale factor of R ohms. **1971** R. CLAY *Nonlinear Networks & Systems* ii. 55 If a capacitor is connected to a gyrator..the input port appears as an inductor.

gyratory ('dʒaɪərətərɪ), *a.* [as if ad. L. **gȳrātōrius*, f. *gȳrāre* to GYRATE. Cf. F. *giratoire*.] **a.** Moving in a circle or spiral; revolving, whirling.

1816 J. SMITH *Panorama Sci. & Art* II. 52 The mischief produced by the gyratory motion of the air. **1833** HERSCHEL *Astron.* iv. 172 The nutation of the earth's axis is a small and slow gyratory movement. **1858** *Merc. Marine Mag.* V. 197 Several others were more or less implicated in the gyratory mass. **1874** HARTWIG *Aerial W.* viii. 124 Large gyratory columns of water or sand. **1898** *Blackw. Mag.* Oct. 539/2 Solomon studied awhile the gyratory movements of three hawks.

b. Applied to a system of directing road traffic round a roundabout or through a system of one-way streets to avoid the need for one line of traffic to intersect another.

1909 *Westm. Gaz.* 7 Aug. 4/2 The gyratory principle, by which vehicles are directed into circular lines ingeniously devised to avoid intersection. **1926** *Rep. Comm. Police Metropolis, 1925* 16 in *Parl. Papers* (Cmd. 2660) XV. 239 Gyratory systems for the circulation of traffic, after years of discussion, reached the point of practical demonstration this year. **1928** *Observer* 5 Feb. 13/7 Now that every week dedicates a new bunch of streets to the Gyratory System. **1966** *Guardian* 8 Sept. 5/4 A new gyratory road system to ease traffic congestion..is to be built..at Stretford.

gyre (dʒaɪə(r)), *sb. poet.* and *literary*. Also 7 **gire**. [ad. L. *gȳr-us*, ad. Gr. γῦρος ring, circle. Cf. GIRO[1].]

1. A turning round, revolution, whirl; a circular or spiral turn.

1566 DRANT *Horace's Sat.* II. B ij, Fashions..Which..do cum, and goe in circled gyre. **1590** SPENSER *F.Q.* II. v. 8 To ward, Or strike, or hurtle rownd in warlike gyre. **1603** B. JONSON *Satyr*, Pardon, lady, this wild strain,..Elves, apply your gyre again. **1614** BP. HALL *Recoll. Treat.* 494 Other Artizans doe but practise, we still learne; others run still in the same gyre, to wearinesse..our choice is infinite. *c* **1620** T. ROBINSON *M. Magd.* 786 Like to yᵉ top, yᵗ in his gyre doth spin. **1649** BULWER *Pathomyot.* II. i. 71 In all these we may easily maintaine the gyre or circumaction of the Head. **1669** W. SIMPSON *Hydrol. Chym.* 78 Whirling them in oblique gyres. **1814** CARY *Dante, Inf.* XVII. 93 Be thy wheeling gyres Of ample circuit, easy thy descent. **1829** SOUTHEY *Inscrip. Caled. Canal* 2 The glede Wheeling between the mountains in mid air, Eastward or westward as his gyre inclines. **1856** MRS. BROWNING *Aur. Leigh* IV. 1167 Graduating up in a spiral line Of still expanding and ascending gyres. **1920** W. B. YEATS *Michael Robartes* 34 All our scientific, democratic, fact-accumulating, heterogeneous civilization belongs to the outward gyre. **1928** —— *Coll. Poems* (1950) 217 O sages standing in God's holy fire... Come from the holy fire, perne in a gyre. **1929** —— *Let.* (1954) 764, I believe I shall have a poetical re-birth for as I write about my cones and gyres all sorts of images come before me. **1930** R. CAMPBELL *Adamastor* 98 A serpent ..With lifted crest and radiant gyre Revolving into wheels of fire. **1948** C. DAY LEWIS *Poems 1943–47* 64 Earth-souls doomed in their gyres to unwind Some tragic love-tangle. **1962** *Listener* 20 Dec. 1047/2 It is deeply satisfying both as riddle and as poem. The poet evokes an atmosphere of mystery within the frame of the eternal gyre.

2. *concr.* A ring, circle, spiral; also, a vortex.

1590 SPENSER *F.Q.* III. i. 23 She rushing through the thickest preasse Perforce disparted their compacted gyre. **1629** MASSINGER *Picture* II. ii, He..dispersed the armed gire With which I was environed. **1686** GOAD *Celest. Bodies* II. vii. 244 To hurry a great Ship downright in a Dismal Gyre, down into the deep. **1718** BLAIR in *Phil. Trans.* XXX. 893 The Cochlea is a long Cavity consisting of three Gyres or Meanders. **1848** LYTTON *Harold* v. i, The smoke rises in dark gyres to the air. **1881** ROSSETTI *House of Life, Sonn.* xliv, Ah! in your eyes so reached what dumb adieu, What unsunned gyres of waste eternity? **1892** W. E. HENLEY *Song of Sword, Lond. Voluntaries* iv. 10 In genial wave on wave and gyre on gyre.

¶**3.** 'A trance' (Cockeram 1623). *Obs.*⁻⁰

Prob. a mistake. Cf. the following: **1612** DRAYTON *Poly-olb.* v, Streames in whose entrancing gyres Wise nature oft herselfe her workmanship admires.

4. *Comb.*, as ***gyre-circling*** adj.

1881 ROSSETTI *Rose Mary, Beryl-song*, Gyre-circling spirits of fire.

gyre (dʒaɪə(r)), *v. poet.* Also 5, 7 **gire**. [ad. L. *gȳrāre*, f. *gȳrus* (see prec.).]

1. *trans.* To turn or whirl round. *rare.*

c **1420** *Pallad. on Husb.* I. 327 The side in longe vppon the south, let sprede..gire hit from the colde west, if thow conne. **1628** BP. HALL *Rem. Wks.* (1660) 25 With the spightful Philistim, he [the Devil] puts out both the eyes of our apprehension and judgement, that he may gyre us about in the Mill of unprofitable wickednesse. **1885** G. MEREDITH *Diana Crossways* xxii, She was out at a distance on the ebb-sands hurtled, gyred, beaten to all shapes.

†**2.** To revolve round, compass. *Obs.*

c **1420** *Pallad. on Husb.* x. 203 September is with Aprill houris euen, ffor Phebus lijk in either gireth heuen.

3. *intr.* To turn round, revolve, whirl, gyrate.

1593 DRAYTON *Eclog.* II. 71 Which from their proper Orbes not goe, Whether they gyre swift or slow. **1598** YONG *Diana* 10 When to the west the sunne begins to gyre. **1633** P. FLETCHER *Purple Isl.* II. xxxvii, A..groom..Which soon the full-grown kitchin cleanly drains By divers pipes, with hundred turnings giring. *Ibid.* IV. viii, Round about two circling altars gire In blushing red. **1808** J. BARLOW *Columb.* III. 785 Mutual strokes with equal force descend..now gyring prest High at the head, now plunging for the breast. **1814** SOUTHEY *Roderick* XII, The eagle's cry, Who..at her highest flight A speck scarce visible, gyred round and round. **1871** 'L. CARROLL' *Through Looking-Glass* i. 21 'Twas brillig, and the slithy toves Did gyre and gimble in the wabe. **1920** W. B. YEATS *Demon & Beast* in *Coll. Poems* (1950) 210 To watch a white gull take A bit of bread thrown up into the air; Now gyring down and perning there. **1930** E. POUND *XXX Cantos* XXV. 114 Three lion cubs..which born at once began life and motion and to go gyring about their mother. **1951** S. SPENDER *World within World* v. 283 The bomber was gyring and diving.

Hence **'gyring** *vbl. sb.*, revolution, gyration. **'gyring** *ppl. a.*, revolving, whirling, gyrating; also, encircling, encompassing; whence **'gyringly** *adv.*, with revolving motion.

1575 LANEHAM *Let.* (1871) 18 With sundry windings, gyrings, and circumflexions. **1590** PEELE *Polyhymnia* 36 At the shock The hollow gyring vault of heaven resounds. **1594** J. DICKENSON *Arisbas* (1878) 72 One colour teinteth all, Turrets, doores, and gyring wall. **1598** —— *Greene in Conc.* (1878) 150 Wind-tossed waues which with a gyring course Circle the Centers-overpeering maine. **1635** QUARLES *Embl.* IV. ii. (1718) 193 This gyring lab'rinth. **1635** HEYWOOD *Hierarch.* II. 63 They [the Heavens] alter in their gyring more or less. *a* **1640** DAY *Parl. Bees* (1881) 76 The massie world..That on Gyreing [so MS.] spheares is hurld. **1659** TORRIANO, *A-gironda*, giringly, about and about.

gyre-carline ('gaɪə,kɑːlɪn). *Sc.* Also 6 gyr(e)-, gyir-carling, (9 giean carlin). [f. ON. *gýgr* = Norw. dial. *gjure* ogress, witch + CARLINE¹. Cf. ON. *gýgjar-karl* the husband of an ogress.] The mother-witch; a witch, hag.

1535 LYNDESAY *Satyre* 4592 [Folly speaks] My gudame, the Gyre Carling, Leirnde me the Prophesie of Marling. *a* **1605** POLWART *Flyting w. Montgomerie* 661 Leaue boggles, brownies, gyr-carlings and gaists. **1815** SCOTT *Guy M.* iii, The elves and the gyre-carlings. **1822** —— *Pirate* vi, What kind of a country of guisards and gyre-carlines is this!

gyrectomy (dʒaɪə'rɛktəmɪ). *Surg.* [f. GYR(US + -ECTOMY.] Surgical excision or resection of a gyrus of the brain.

1949 J. L. POOL et al. in F. A. Mettler *Selective Partial Ablation of Frontal Cortex* iv. 34 In 3 cases bilateral 'gyrectomy' was carried out; that is, removal of the superior frontal gyri..of the middle frontal gyri..and of the inferior frontal gyri. **1967** HORWITZ & RIZZOLI *Postoperative Complications in Neurosurg. Pract.* iv. 177 Destructive surgery on the cerebral hemispheres in the treatment of intractable pain has been attempted in a variety of ways to which a myriad of names has been applied (lobotomy, leucotomy, gyrectomy, topectomy, etc.).

†**'gyreful,** *a. Obs.* [f. GYRE *sb.* + -FUL.] Full of gyres or turns; circling, whirling.

1566 DRANT *Horace's Sat.* I. i. A vij, Whose carts when they were roulde With gyrefull sway, by coursers swyfte. **1583** STANYHURST *Æneis* (Arb.) 138 Theyre labor hoat they folow: toe the flame fits gyreful awarding.

gyrencephalate (dʒaɪərən'sɛfələt), *a. Zool.* [f. mod.L. *Gyrencephala* (see below), f. GYR-US + ἐγκέφαλος brain (see ENCEPHALA).] Pertaining to or having the characters of the *Gyrencephala*, one of the four main divisions of mammalia in Owen's system, consisting of those in which the cerebrum is convoluted. So **gyren'cephalous** *a.*

1859 OWEN *Classif. Mammalia* 35 These limb-characters can only be rightly applied to the gyrencephalous subclass. **1866** —— *Anat. Vertebr.* II. 272 The Gyrencephalous quadrupeds, as a general rule, have a scrotum. **1875** BLAKE *Zool.* 43 The gyrencephalate sub-class.

gyrer, obs. f. JEERER.

gyrfalcon ('dʒɜː,fɔːlkə n, -,fɔːk(ə)n). Forms: 4–9 jer-, 4, 8– gyr-, (4 gere-), 5–7 gier-, jar(re-, (5 gire-), 4– gerfalcon, etc. (See forms of FALCON.) [a. OF. *gerfaucon*, also *gerfauc* (mod.F. *gerfaut*) = Pr. *girfalc-s*, Sp., Pg. *gerifalte*, It. *girfalco*, *girifalco*, med.L. *gero-*, *giro-*, *gire-*, *gyrofalco*, MHG. *gir-*, *gervalke* (mod.Ger. *gier-*, *geier-*, *gerfalke*), Du. *giervalk*, ON. *geirfálki*.

A compound of the word which appears in Eng. as FALCON; the origin of the first element is disputed, but the prevailing view both among Germanic and Romanic philologists now is that, while the recorded forms in the Teut. langs. are adopted from Fr., the ultimate source is the OHG. *gîr* vulture (MHG. *gîr*, mod.Ger. *geier*), f. the root **gîr* in OHG. *giri*, *gîri* greedy. The suggestion that the med.L. *gyrofalco* is derived from *gȳrus*, *gȳrāre*, and refers to the 'circling' movements of the bird in the air, was made by Gerald de Barri (Giraldus Cambrensis) as early as 1188 (*Top. Hib.* ed. Brewer, I. xiii). A treatise on hunting by the Emperor Frederic II (*d.* 1250) contains a passage (II. iv. 152, ed. 1596) in which the word is said to be either from the Gr. κύριος, lord, or from the Gr. ἱερός sacred. The latter suggestion was prob. based on the current term *falco sacer* denoting a kind of hawk; but according to modern scholars *sacer* in this use (= Fr., Sp., Pg. *sacre* sb.) does not mean 'sacred', but is an adoption of the Arabic *çaqr*. In the 16th c. *hierofalco* was adopted by ornithologists (Aldrovandus, Gesner) as the correct Latin form, probably from the observation that It. *ger-* sometimes represents L. *hier-* (as in *gerarchia* hierarchy); and it is still used as the scientific name of a sub-genus of the genus *Falco*. The view of some recent etymologists, that OF. *gerfaucon* represents a popular L. **hierofalco*, and that the first element of this is from Gr. ἱέραξ hawk, is very improbable.]

In early use, a large falcon, esp. one used to fly at herons; now, any large falcon of the northern regions; esp. the white gyrfalcon of Iceland (*Falco islandus*).

13.. *Guy Warw.* (A.) 823 He schal bring to þe turment þat day..A ger-fauk þat is milke white. **1382** WYCLIF *Job* xxxix. 13 The fether of a strucioun is lic to the fetheris of a ierfakoun and of a goshauk. *c* **1440** *Promp. Parv.* 190/2 Gerfaucun, *herodius*. **1450–70** HOLLAND *Howlat* 319 Geir Falconnis, that gentilly in bewte haboundis. **1526** SKELTON *Magnyf.* 1836 A, syr, thy iarfawcon and thou be hanged togyder. **1580** SIDNEY *Arcadia* (1622) 108 A Ierfaulcon was cast off after her. *a* **1682** SIR T. BROWNE *Tracts* 118 You must not expect to find your gier-falcon there. **1755** SMOLLETT *Quix.* (1803) IV. 87 A saker or jerfalcon darts down upon a heron with a force proportioned to his rise. **1766** PENNANT *Zool.* (1768) I. 134 The..Lanner, Sacre, and the Gyrfalcon are mentioned as natives, in our old game law. **1863** BARING-GOULD *Iceland* 187 A white gerfalcon watches us from yon pile of stones, a bowshot off. **1867** MORRIS *Jason* x. 415 Scarped cliffs here and there, Where screamed the great ger-falcon. **1884** *Girl's Own Paper* 28 June 614/1 The noble gyr or jer falcon of Iceland, which in strength almost rivals the eagle itself. **1910** *Encycl. Brit.* X. 139/1 Next to the typical falcons comes a group known as the 'great northern' falcons... Of these the most remarkable is the gyrfalcon. **1964** *Oxf. Bk. Birds* 46/2 Gyr falcon.

attrib. **1891** C. E. NORTON *Dante's Hell* iv. 20, I saw.. Caesar in armor, with his gerfalcon eyes.

gyrfaunt, variant of GERFAUNT *Obs.*, giraffe.

gyrinid (dʒɪ'rɪnɪd), *sb.* and *a. Ent.* [mod.L., f. *Gyrinidæ*, name of a family of Coleoptera.]

A. *sb.* A member of the Gyrinidæ, a family of aquatic beetles; a whirligig beetle (see WHIRLIGIG *sb.* 4). **B.** *adj.* Of, pertaining to, or designating a beetle of this kind.

1925 *Pap. Michigan Acad. Sci.* V. 430 The first step that one must take in the study of gyrinid affinities is to divest the beetles of their adaptive characters. *Ibid.* 432 Nothing can be surer than that the gyrinids would never have developed in the absence of a surface habitat. **1943** *Brit. Jrnl. Psychol.* Sept. 26 Gyrinid beetles,..maintain a constant general position [in flowing water] by means..of visual perception of the pattern of objects on the adjacent banks. **1955** BORROR & DELONG *Introd. Study Insects* xxii. 339 The gyrinids are oval black beetles that are commonly seen swimming in endless gyrations on the surface of ponds and quiet streams.

gyrle, gyrll, obs. forms of GIRL.

gyrnall, gyrn(e, obs. ff. GIRNEL *Sc.*, GIRN.

gyro ('dʒaɪərəʊ). Colloq. abbreviation of (*a*) GYROSCOPE, (*b*) ***gyro-compass*** (see below).

1910 tr. *Anschütz Gyro Compass* 16 The ordinary mariner's compass merely points to a certain spot known as the magnetic pole, from the direction of which the true North can be deduced. The Gyro, however, avoids this operation by indicating the true North direct. **1914** H. CRABTREE *Spinning Tops & Gyroscopic Motion* (ed. 2) 77 If the position of the ends *N* and *S* of the gyro [gyro-compass] are reversed. **1922** *Encycl. Brit.* XXX. 733/2 In this model [of the gyro compass] three gyros are used in place of the single one of the earlier model. **1964** MRS. L. B. JOHNSON *White House Diary* 24 Mar. (1970) 99 A gyro in a suitcase —that's the machine that keeps the rocket on its proper course. **1966** *Electronics* 17 Oct. 38/3 In a strapdown system ..the gyroscope bearings are connected to the vehicle without gimbals and the gyros roll with the vehicle.

b. *Comb.*, **gyro-bus, -cab**, names given in Science Fiction writing to gyroscopically controlled aircraft; **gyro-car**, (*a*) a mono-rail car or carriage which is balanced by means of gyroscopes driven at high speed in opposite directions; (*b*) a two-wheeled motor-car whose balance and steering are controlled by gyroscopes; **gyro-compass**, a form of gyroscope used as a compass, being continuously driven and specially mounted so that its axis remains parallel to that of the earth; **gyro-horizon** = *artificial horizon*; **gyro-pilot**, a gyro-compass used to steer a vessel or an aircraft without human agency; **gyro-sight**, a gun-sight fitted with a gyroscope; **gyro-stabilizer**, a gyroscopic device for maintaining the equilibrium of a vessel; hence **gyro-stabilized** *a.* (also of a compass).

1936 'J. BEYNON' *Planet Plane* v. 40 Machines of every kind from the dainty flipabout to the massive gyrobus.. started to float in from each quarter. **1956** 'W. TENN' *Time in Advance* (1963) 62 They climbed quickly into one of the many hovering gyrocabs. **1909** *Westm. Gaz.* 8 Nov. 8/3 The gyro-car, as Herr Scherl calls it, is to make a series of runs ..in the Exhibition Hall at the Zoological Gardens. **1909** *Daily Chron.* 11 Nov. 1/6 We waited for the gyro-car to emerge from its shed. **1961** *Ford Bulletin* 14 Apr. 2/5 The Gyron is not the first two-wheeled gyro car. **1970** B. WALLIS in *Daily Tel.* (Colour Suppl.) 16 Oct. 46/2, I am convinced that the car of the future will be a gyroscopically-controlled two-wheeler, with one wheel in the front, the other behind. .. When my gyrocar cornered it would, irrespective of speed, heel over at the correct angle. **1910** tr. *Anschütz Gyro Compass* 10 An accurate means of determining direction by some 'nonmagnetic' appliance is of great importance; this is ..appreciated by many of the large navies, who are installing the Gyro Compass in their submarines. **1911** *Chambers's Jrnl.* 27 May 414/2 The magnetic compass is easily deranged... Its rival is the gyro-compass. **1913** J. H. POYNTING *Earth* 98 That very remarkable invention by the brothers Anschütz, termed the Gyro Compass. **1931** *Times Lit. Suppl.* 22 Jan. 51/3 A speck of dust might cause a gyro compass to 'wander'. **1966** *McGraw-Hill Encycl. Sci. & Technol.* VI. 305/2 Modern gyrocompasses..are now used as the prime navigational instrument on nearly every ship. **1939** *War Illustr.* 29 Dec. 539/2 At ten thousand feet, our gyro-horizon froze. **1942** Gyro horizon [see GYROSCOPE]. **1923** *Westm. Gaz.* 24 Dec., Through the agency of an invention known as the gyro-pilot apparatus, the Cunard liner Laconia, which reached Liverpool yesterday, steered from New York a straight course without human aid. **1924** *Glasgow Herald* 8 Jan. 7 Gyro-Pilot for Cargo Boats. **1936** *Jrnl. R. Aeronaut. Soc.* XL. 555 Air sickness is practically non-existent on..air lines, which use scientific comfort conditioning and which also use gyropilots. **1941** F. H. JOSEPH *Lett. from Brit.* (1942) 55 Boulton-Paul [gun turret] with Gyro-Sight. Improved reflector sight with a rate gyro. **1946** Gyro-stabilised [see GYROMAGNETIC *a.* 2]. **1959** F. D. ADAMS *Aeronaut. Dict.* 87/2 *Gyro-stabilized*, stabilized by a gyro-scope, as in gyro-stabilized compass, gyro-stabilized drift meter. **1963** *New Yorker* 1 June 125 (Advt.), You'll stand at the rail, watch the infinite sea—so smooth to your gyro-stabilized ship. **1921** *Sci. Amer.* 18 June 482/3 The gyro-stablizer damps out the rolling of a vessel. **1946** *Nature* 24 Aug. 250/1 The marine applications fall into three groups, the gyro compass, the gyro pilot and the gyro stabilizer. **1957** *Encycl. Brit.* XI. 51/1 By dealing with each wave increment individually and by exerting a small counteracting force against it at just the right moment, the gyrostabilizer quenches the force of each wave and never allows the vessel to build up a roll averaging more than three or four degrees.

gyro- ('dʒaɪərə), comb. form repr. Gr. γῦρο-ς in sense of 'ring, circle, spiral', as in: **gyroceran** (-'ɒsərən) *a. Conch.* [Gr. κερατ-, κέρας horn], pertaining to the genus *Gyroceras*, typical of the family *Gyroceratidæ* of fossil nautiloid cephalopods having the whorls not contiguous; **gyroceratite** (-'sɛrətaɪt) *Conch.*, a fossil cephalopod of the family *Gyroceratidæ*; hence **gyroceratitic** (-sɛrə'tɪtɪk) *a.*; **'gyrocopter** [after *helicopter*], a kind of helicopter; now *spec.* a small, light, single-seater one (cf. AUTOGIRO); **gyrodactyle** (-'dæktɪl) *Zool.* [Gr. δάκτυλος finger], a trematode worm of the genus *Gyrodactylus*; **'Gyrodyne**, the proprietary name for a type of helicopter which has a horizontal rotor for providing lift and one or more propellers for providing forward thrust; **'gyrofrequency**, the frequency with which a charged particle spirals about the lines of force of a magnetic field through which it is passing; **'gyrograph** (-grɑːf, -æ-) [Gr. -γραφος writing, recording], an instrument for recording revolutions; **'gyroplane** = *gyrocopter*; ‖**,gyropso'riasis** *Med.*, PSORIASIS occurring in circular patches (*Syd. Soc. Lex.* 1886); **gy'ropter** (*disused*) [Gr. πτερόν wing], a rotary-wing aircraft; **'gyrotiller**, a type of cultivator in which the tines rotate about an axis; **'gyrotrope** (-trəʊp) *Electr.* [Gr. -τροπος turning] = COMMUTATOR 1 a (*ibid.*).

1884 *Science* III. Feb. 123/2 The loosely coiled [shell] but with whorls not in contact, *gyroceratitic. **1915** *Aeronautics* 9 June 385/1 The *gyrocopter is a variation of the helicopter operated by a rotary motor. **1934** W. HOLTBY *Pavements at Anderby* (1937) I. 25 The gyrocopter sailed over the rim of the wold and sank silently into the deep meadow. **1962**

Britannica Bk. Yr. 1961 545/2 Among new scientific gadgets there was the gyrocopter, a rotorcraft having both drive to rotors and a normal propeller, and usually a very light single-seater craft. **1965** *Kingston* (Ont.) *Whig Standard* 21 Apr. 6/5 The club members hope to turn their gyrogliders into motorized gyrocopters. **1969** *Courier-Mail* (Brisbane) 1 Apr. 19/2 Gyrocopters are against the law in Australia. Nobody may fly them, even..in the remoteness of his own cattle station. **1864** Cobbold *Entozoa* 44 Those singular ectoparasitic creatures known as the *Gyrodactyles. **1946** *Flight* 14 Nov. 540/1 (*caption*) The Fairey FB-1 research *Gyrodyne model which will be on view at the Paris Show. *Ibid.* 540/2 This is the first of a new class of rotary-winged aircraft known as Gyro-dynes. **1948** *Jrnl. R. Aeronaut. Soc.* LII. 285/1 Delaying the stall by twisting of the blade, or by the use of some alternative configuration, such as the gyrodyne. **1958** Lambermont & Pirie *Helicopters & Autogyros of World* 172 After the end of World War II.. Peter P. Papadakos founded a group of engineers into the Gyrodyne Company of America Inc. for the purpose of perfecting the 'gyro-dyne' concept. **1941** 'R. Stranger' *Dict. Radio & Telev. Terms* 101 *Gyro-frequency. **1962** W. B. Thompson *Introd. Plasma Physics* i. 4 The character of the radiation depends on electron energy; if the energy is low the radiation occurs primarily at the gyrofrequency $\Omega = eB/mc$, where e, m = electron charge, mass, c = velocity of light and B = magnetic field strength. **1817** *Blackw. Mag.* I. 525 A Celestial *Gyrograph..which gives the true bearings, rising, setting, and culminating, of forty of the principal fixed stars, for any hour and minute of the twenty-four hours. **1907** *Nature* 5 Dec. 107/1 The *gyroplane of Messrs. Breguet..revives interest in the attempt to overcome gravity by vertical screw propellers. **1935** *Jrnl. R. Aeronaut. Soc.* XXXIX. 177 Aerodynamic analysis of the gyroplane rotating-wing system. **1969** *Daily Tel.* 10 Mar. 1/8 Mr. Ernest Brooks, 39, the garage owner who designed and built the Mosquito gyroplane, was fatally injured yesterday when it plunged 250 ft. to the ground. *Ibid.*, The tiny £1,000 gyroplane could cruise at 40 mph at 1000 ft and was capable of 80 mph. **1908** *Westm. Gaz.* 14 Aug. 10/2 A new machine, the *Gyropter, or rotary-wing flying machine. **1912** *Yorks. Post* 13 Jan. (leader), Mr. Davidson proposes the building of what he calls a gyropter. **1938** *Encycl. Brit. Bk. of Yr.* 27/2 Combine harvesters, milking machines, *gyrotillers, [etc.]. **1947** *Times* 8 Mar. 4/1 Every available piece of snow-shifting machinery had been pressed into service, including ploughs, tractors, bulldozers, blowers, gyro-tillers, and disc harrows. **1962** J. N. Winburne *Dict. Agric.* 358/2 *Gyrotiller*, a machine used in England to pulverize subsurface soil below depths of ordinary plowing. **1970** G. E. Evans *Where Beards wag All* ix. 106 The gyrotiller—an owd engine that come round and twizzle everything round.

gyrogonite (dʒaɪəˈrɒgənaɪt). *Geol.* [f. gyro- + Gr. γόν-ος seed + -ite.] A petrified seed-vessel of plants of the genus *Chara*, spiral in form, and formerly supposed to be a shell.

1832 De la Beche *Geol. Man.* (ed. 2) 147 Seeds of Charæ, or Gyrogonites, are converted into carbonate of lime, in which the nut is sometimes found within. **1833** Lyell *Princ. Geol.* III. 236 In the limestone I found gyrogonites. **1833** G. A. Mantell *Wonders Geol.* (1838) II. 600 The gyrogonites of the tertiary strata of the Paris basin.

gyroidal (dʒaɪəˈrɔɪdəl), *a.* [f. gyre or gyrus + -oid + -al[1].]

1. *Cryst.* Having a spiral arrangement, as certain planes, etc. in some crystalline forms.

1864 in Webster. **1895** Story-Maskelyne *Crystallogr.* §177 The axes of symmetry..preserve the characteristics of the system, but in the absence of planes of symmetry they do so only by a gyroidal (or alternate) distribution of the poles. The edges consequently are gyroidally grouped in triads *G* round the trigonal axes *o*; and in tetrads *V* round the axes *h*. *Ibid.* §253 The gyroidal position of its faces in respect to the vertical axis.

2. *Optics.* Having the property of turning the plane of polarization to the right or left; rotatory in respect to polarized light.

1864 in Webster.

Hence **gyˈroidally** *adv.*

1895 [see sense 1 above].

gyrolite (ˈdʒaɪərəlaɪt). *Min.* Also guro-. [Named by Anderson 1851; f. Gr. γυρός round + λίθος stone (see -lite).] Hydrous silicate of calcium found in radiated concretions.

1851 *Phil. Mag.* Ser. iv. I. 101 Gurolite. **1851** *Amer. Jrnl. Sci.* Ser. ii. XII. 205 The name gurolite (more correctly gyrolite) alludes to the spherical form of its concretions.

gyromagnetic (ˌdʒaɪərəʊmægˈnɛtɪk), *a.* [See gyro-.] **1.** *Physics.* Of or pertaining to the interdependence of the angular momentum of a spinning charged particle and its resulting magnetic moment; ***gyromagnetic effect*** : any effect arising from this interdependence, esp. the fact that a change in the angular momentum of a freely suspended magnetizable body will produce a change in its magnetic moment, and *vice versa*; ***gyromagnetic ratio***: the ratio of the angular momentum of a spinning charged particle to its magnetic moment; also, the reciprocal of this, expressed either as a true ratio (symbol γ) or as a dimensionless quantity (symbol g').

1922 O. W. Richardson in *Proc. R. Soc.* (1923) A. CII. 538 (*heading*) The magnitude of the gyromagnetic ratio. *Ibid.* 539 We are now practically driven..to the conclusion that the motions of the positively charged parts of the atoms cannot be disregarded in considering these gyromagnetic phenomena. **1922** *Phil. Trans. R. Soc.* A. CCXXIII. 257 (*heading*) On the Richardson gyro-magnetic effect. **1930** S. J. Barnett *Evidence on Elem. Magnet from Res. on Gyromagnetic Phenomena* 12 Rotating a rod about its axis at a speed of *N* revolutions per second magnetizes it exactly as it would be magnetized by applying to it an axial magnetic field with intensity $H = 2\pi sN$, where s is the ratio of the rotary momentum of the elementary magnet to its magnetic moment. This ratio is known as the gyromagnetic ratio, or magneto-mechanical ratio. **1953** C. Kittel *Introd. Solid State Physics* x. 165 Gyromagnetic experiments identify the magnetization in ferromagnetics as arising largely from the electron spin, rather than from the orbital moment. *Ibid.*, The magnetomechanical ratio is defined as the ratio of the magnetic moment to the angular momentum. [*Note*] This quantity..is sometimes called the gyromagnetic ratio, but strictly speaking the gyromagnetic ratio is the reciprocal of the magnetomechanical ratio. **1961** *Encycl. Dict. Physics* III. 551/1 Gyromagnetic phenomena are to be expected in paramagnetic as well as ferromagnetic materials. **1967** *Electronics* 6 Mar. 54/2 The NBS now uses the gyromagnetic ratio of a proton to determine the constancy of its standard voltage.

2. Applied to a type of compass in which a magnetic compass automatically corrects the gradual deviations of a directional gyroscope, which in turn provides the compass reading.

1946 Wells & Glenny in M. Davidson *Gyroscope* iii. ii. 170 A gyro-magnetic compass..should not be confused with a gyro-stabilised magnetic compass. **1952** Hitchins & May *Lodestone to Gyro-Compass* viii. 159 In the gyro-magnetic system a gyroscope is maintained in a nearly fixed direction by intermittent or continuous signals from some sort of magnetic compass. The gyroscope then operates the repeaters. **1957** *Encycl. Brit.* VI. 176/1 In the gyro-magnetic compass..the gyro-direction indicator and magnetic compass are combined in one instrument and the necessity for hand adjustment disappears.

gyromancy (ˈdʒaɪərəmænsɪ). [a. med.L. **gȳromantia*, f. Gr. γῦρο-ς circle, circuit + μαντεία divination. Cf. F. *gyromancie* (Rabelais *giromantie*).] A mode of divination said to have been practised by walking in a circle till the person fell down from dizziness, the inferences being drawn from the place in the circle at which he fell.

1557 North *Gueuara's Diall Pr.* 5 b, All the kyndes of gyromancye, and chiromancye. *a* **1693** *Urquhart's Rabelais* iii. xxv, Have you a mind..to have the truth of the matter yet more fully and amply disclosed unto you..by giromancy, if thou shouldst turn round circles, thou mightest assure thyself from me, that they would fall always on the wrong side. **1855** Smedley *Occult Sci.* 334 Gyromancy was performed by going round continually in a circle, the circumference of which was marked by letters.

gyron (ˈdʒaɪərən). *Her.* Also 6–7 **gyronne**, 7 **geron**. [a. F. *giron*, earlier *geron* (= It. *girone* gyron, *gherone* gore, gusset, Sp. *giron*, *jiron* gusset), ad. OHG. *gêro* triangular piece, gusset: see gore *sb.*[1]] An ordinary of triangular form made by two lines drawn from the edge of the escutcheon to meet in the fesse-point and occupying half of the quarter. Also *attrib.*

Where there is one gyron only, it usually issues from the dexter chief and occupies the second half of the first quarter. (See gyronny.)

1572 Bossewell *Armorie* ii. 77 S. beareth Ermyne, two Gyrons Sable, charged with Cilidon floures proper, a Batune Gules. *Ibid.* 113 b, These particions [*sc.* partition per saltire and per gyron] being the one so lyke the other, for that there is also partie per Gyron, it cannot bee but that there is founde an indifferencie of the use in blazon of the one as of the other. **1610** Guillim *Heraldry* ii. vi. (1660) 71. **1611** Florio, *Gironi*, gerons in armory. **1661** Morgan *Sph. Gentry* ii. vii. 71 The gyron..is a right angled Triangle. **1848** R. Stuart *Glasgow* 99 The *gyron* quarterings of the family of Argyll. **1864** Boutell *Her. Hist. & Pop.* vii. 31 The Gyron..is half of the first quarter of the shield.

gyrondola, obs. variant of girandola.

[**gyronnetty**, *a.* A spurious word in some recent Dicts.; an alteration (after gyron) of *gironnetté*, given as a French word in heraldic dicts. with the explanation 'Finished at the top with points; said of a castle or tower used as a bearing'. This is a blunder for F. *girouetté* 'furnished with a weathercock (*girouette*) of a specified tincture'.]

gyronny (dʒaɪəˈrɒnɪ), *a.* *Her.* Forms: 5 jerownde, 5–6 gerundi(e, 6 geronnie, -ondy, 8 gironne, 7– **gyronny**. [a. F. *gironné* (12th c. *geroné*), f. *giron* gyron: see -y.] Of an escutcheon: Divided into or having gyrons; ***gyronny of eight***, having eight gyrons, i.e. each quarter divided diagonally by lines meeting in the fesse-point.

? *a* **1400** *Morte Arth.* 2891 Thorowe a jerownde schelde he jogges him thorowe. **1486** *Bk. St. Albans, Her.* b iij, Gerundi is called in armys whan the cootarmure is of ix. dyuerse colowris; & a fusitarget with in the cootarmure of whatt colowre that hit be of. *c* **1500** *Sc. Poem Heraldry* 169 in *Q. Eliz. Acad.* 100 Thire be also raschit, as lege or heid, wiche gerondy verry and belly told. **1572** Bossewell *Armorie* ii. 38 b, Geronnie of vj pieces Or and Sable. **1610** Guillim *Heraldry* v. ii. (1611) 240 Hee beareth Gyronny of sixe peeces Sable and Or three Nigroes heads couped Proper. **1713** *Lond. Gaz.* No. 5106/3 A Coat of Arms, being Gironne of Eight Pieces Ermine and Gules. **1864** Boutell *Her. Hist. & Pop.* xiv. §1. 141 Gyronny or and sable.

¶ App. used erron. for gyron.

1696 *Lond. Gaz.* No. 3171/4 The Arms are, a Ship, a Chequer, two Geronies.

†**gyronoˈmonic**, *a.* *Obs. rare*$^{-1}$. [Error for **gyrognomonic*, ad. F. *gyrognomonique*, f. Gr. γῦρο-ς circuit + γνώμων gnomon.] (The passage is merely jargon; the Fr. word, if not a grotesque coinage of Rabelais, may have had some such sense as 'Pertaining to revolution round the dial'.)

a **1693** *Urquhart's Rabelais* iii. xxii, The Mendicant Fryers and Jacobins; who are the two Hemispheres of the Christian World, by whose Gyronomonick Circumbilvaginations.. all the Autonomatick Metagrobolism of the Romish church..is homocentrically poised.

gyrophoric (ˌdʒaɪərəˈfɒrɪk), *a.* *Chem.* [f. mod.L. *Gyrophora*, a genus of lichens (f. Gr. γῦρος circle + -φόρος bearing) + *-ic*.] Only in ***gyrophoric acid*** (see quot.).

1886 *Syd. Soc. Lex.*, *Gyrophoric acid*, an acid obtained from *Gyrophora* or *Umbilicaria pustulata*.

gyroscope (ˈdʒaɪərəskəʊp). *Dynamics.* [ad. F. *gyroscope* (Foucault, 1852): see gyro- and -scope.] **a.** An instrument designed to illustrate the dynamics of rotating bodies, and consisting essentially of a solid rotating wheel mounted in a ring, and having its axis free to turn in any direction. Also used, in various modifications or in conjunction with other equipment, to provide a horizontal or vertical reference direction (as in the artificial horizon and the gyro-compass), to stabilize ships, mono-rail vehicles, etc., and to measure angular velocity and angular acceleration (as in the turn-and-bank indicator and other navigational devices).

The form of this apparatus invented by Foucault is contrived so as to render evident the rotation of the earth, through the tendency of the wheel (being free from the influence of disturbing forces) to maintain its rotation in a fixed plane independently of the earth's motion.

1856 *Amer. Jrnl. Sci. & Arts* Ser. ii. XXI. 119 Foucault placed between the poles of a strong electro-magnet the solid of revolution belonging to the gyroscope. **1857** *Chambers's Jrnl.* 30 May 351/2 To overcome it [*sc.* rolling and pitching]..the professor invented a balanced frame, with free axes for rotation, somewhat on the principle of the gyroscope, which..remains uninfluenced by the.. movements of the ship. **1862** H. Spencer *First Princ.* ii. xxii. §170 (1875) 486 That opposition which the axial momentum of a rotating body makes to any change in the plane of rotation (so beautifully exhibited in the gyroscope). **1862** Sir H. Holland *Ess.* i. 27 The Gyroscope of Foucault ..shews to the eye in a few minutes, by the angular deviation from its plane of rotation, the movement the earth has made in this short space of time. **1871** *Cornh. Mag.* XXIV. 450 It is probable that the principle of the instrument called the gyroscope will be called into action to secure steadiness of motion [for aircraft]. **1879** G. Prescott *Sp. Telephone* 261 [Prof. Dolbear] invented and constructed a gyroscope to run by electro-magnetism. **1891** *Cassell's Fam. Mag.* 187/1 A small gyroscope has also been fitted to the ship's sextants, so as to give an invariable line of sight. **1904** *Daily Chron.* 29 Feb. 4/5 The newest torpedoes, we are told, will have a speed of thirty knots for 3,000 yards, and, thanks to the gyroscope, almost perfect accuracy can be relied upon. **1907** *Standard* 23 Mar., The experiments showed conclusively that gyroscopes could be designed which would exercise a sensible steadying effect upon even the largest passenger steamers on service. **1942** B. A. Shields *Princ. Flight* viii. 297 The gyro horizon, or the artificial horizon as it is often called, also depends on a gyroscope for its operation. **1962** F. I. Ordway et al. *Basic Astronautics* ix. 372 The gyroscope in conjunction with the accelerometer forms the heart of modern space vehicle guidance systems. **1966** Burger & Corbet *Ship Stabilizers* ii. 24 The three types of 'three-frame' gyroscopes discussed are often called 'displacement' gyroscopes because they can measure angular displacement between the framework in which they are mounted and a fixed reference mark—the rotor axle.

b. *Comb.* **gyroscope-compass** = *gyro-compass*; **gyroscope top**, a spinning top on the gyroscope principle, which when spinning may be supported by one end of its horizontal axis.

1909 *Westm. Gaz.* 20 Apr. 9/3 The gyroscope-compass, an invention of Dr. Anschuetz-Kaempfe, of Kiel,..is based upon the familiar principle that a rapidly rotating body tends to keep in the same plane. **1880** *Encycl. Brit.* XI. 352/2 Perhaps the most common form of gyroscope is that which has been largely sold under the name of the gyroscope top. **1921–2** *T. Eaton & Co. Catal.* Fall & Winter 328 The Gyroscope Top..spins at either end or in the middle.

gyroscopic (ˌdʒaɪərəˈskɒpɪk), *a.* [f. as prec.: see -scopic.] Pertaining to or of the nature of the gyroscope; rotatory. Also ***gyroscopic compass*** = *gyro-compass*; ***gyroscopic couple*** (see quot. 1959[2]).

1871 *Cornh. Mag.* XXIV. 451 Since travelling-machines *must* travel swiftly, the gyroscopic portion of the machine may be made to support itself. **1888** *Engineer* LXVI. 364/2 The bearings are of great length and large diameter to stand the gyroscopic action which occurs in a heavy sea on board ship. **1894** *Westm. Gaz.* 30 Oct. 5/1 The second patent is described as 'A new system of Projectiles—styled gyroscopic Projectiles'. **1907** *Standard* 23 Mar., Dr. Schlick's gyroscopic apparatus for steadying ships. **1920** T. W. Chalmers (*title*) The gyroscopic compass. **1928** A. L. Rawlings (*title*) Theory of the gyroscopic compass and its deviations. **1937** *Jrnl. R. Aeronaut. Soc.* XLI. 2 The other dynamic force present in the spin, is the gyroscopic couple, due to the gyroscopic force of the propeller. **1948** A. C. HARDY *Mod. Marine Engin.* III. xvi. 149 The gyroscopic compass operates by the rotation of the earth and the pull of gravity. **1959** N. MAILER *Advts. for Myself* (1961) 183 The inner-directed man—the nineteenth-century businessman would be a prototype—is essentially self-directed, 'gyroscopic', production-minded, set for life from early childhood in pursuit of certain built-in goals. **1959** J. L. NAYLER *Dict. Aeronaut. Engin.* 126 *Gyroscopic couple*, the turning moment which resists any alteration of the inclination of the axis of rotation of a gyroscope. Gyroscopic couples are produced, for instance, by propellers when the plane of rotation is changed, e.g. as in a pull-out, or a spin. **1962** F. I. ORDWAY et al. *Basic Astronautics* v. 204 The probe was fitted with an orientation system that included optical and gyroscopic pickups.

transf. (*jocular*). **1880** P. S. ROBINSON *Noah's Ark* vi. (1882) 156 The giraffe.. would be gratified by a gyroscopic view of the surrounding country.

gyroscopically (dʒaɪərəˈskɒpɪkəlɪ), *adv.* [f. GYROSCOPIC *a.*: see -ICALLY.] By or with a gyroscope; in a gyroscopic manner.

1910 R. M. NEILSON *Aeroplane Patents* II. 64 (*caption*) Herring's gyroscopically-controlled propellers. **1911** *Chambers's Jrnl.* 55/1 The success of the gyroscope in preventing the rolling of ships.. would seem to augur well for the gyroscopically controlled aeroplane. **1970** [see *gyro-car* s.v. GYRO b]. **1971** *Sunday Express* 24 Oct. 11 (Advt.), A low mass pick-up arm gyroscopically pivots in a concentric gimbal mount.

gyrose (ˈdʒaɪərəʊs), *a. Bot.* [ad. mod.L. **gȳrōs-us*, f. GYRUS.] Folded and waved, marked with wavy lines.

1836 LOUDON *Encycl. Plants* Gloss., *Gyrose*, turned round like a crook. **1874** R. BROWN *Man. Bot. Gloss.*, *Gyrose*, marked with wavy lines. **1880** GRAY *Struct. Bot.* 414/1 *Gyrose*, curved backward and forward in turns. **1887** W. PHILLIPS *Brit. Discomycetes* 8 The ribs of the hymenium raised, gyrose, persistent.

gyroso-, (dʒaɪəˈrəʊsəʊ), comb. form of GYROSE, used with the meaning 'gyrose and...'

1887 W. PHILLIPS *Brit. Discomycetes* 8 Pileus inflated, irregularly indulated, gyroso-rugose, brown.

gyrostat (ˈdʒaɪərəstæt). *Dynamics.* [f. GYRO- + Gr. στατ-ός standing, f. στα-, ἱστάναι to stand.] A name given to various forms of gyroscope.

1879 THOMSON & TAIT *Nat. Phil.* I. I. §345 The ordinary gyrostat (a rapidly rotating fly-wheel pivoted as finely as possible within a rigid case, having a convex curvilinear polygonal border, in the plane perpendicular to the axis through the centre of gravity of the whole). **1902** *Encycl. Brit.* XXXII. 578/1 For the purpose of controlling the horizontal direction this boat [*sc.* a submarine] is fitted, in addition to a vertical rudder, with a 'gyrostat', the motion of which instrument is maintained by an electric motor. Previous to making a start the boat must be headed in the direction in which it is intended to move; when the gyrostat, once started, will.. continue to rotate about an axis invariable in direction, and any departure from this will be detected, whether the boat be above the surface or below it. **1922** *Ibid.* XXX. 44/1 Gyrostats are also used in aircraft as azimuth indicators for experimental or test purposes; they may some day be used as part of a gyrostatic compass.

gyrostatic (dʒaɪərəˈstætɪk), *a.* [f. as prec. + -IC.] Pertaining to the gyrostat or gyrostatics; connected with the dynamical theory that a rotating body tends to maintain its plane of rotation.

1879 THOMSON & TAIT *Nat. Phil.* I. I. §345 Let the fly wheels be set each into sufficiently rapid rotation to fulfil the conditions of gyrostatic domination. **1893** SLOANE *Electr. Dict.*, *Gyrostatic action of armatures.* Owing to gyrostatic action a rotating armature resists any change of direction of its axis.

Hence **gyroˈstatically** *adv.*

1879 THOMSON & TAIT *Nat. Phil.* I. I. §345 When all the quantities.. are of the same sign it is easy to find the conditions that must be fulfilled in order that the system may be gyrostatically dominated. **1891** *Athenæum* 19 Dec. 837/2 The Equations of Propagation of Disturbances in Gyrostatically-loaded Media.

gyrostatics (dʒaɪərəˈstætɪks), *sb. pl.* [See prec. and -ICS.] That part of physical science which deals with the rotation of solid bodies.

In recent Dicts.

gyrous (ˈdʒaɪərəs), *a. rare.* [ad. mod.L. **gȳrōsus* GYROSE: see -OUS.] Circular, spiral.

1688 CLAYTON in *Phil. Trans.* XVII. 789 As they pass along with their gyrous or circular Motion, they carry aloft the drie Leaves into the Air. **1800** HURDIS *Fav. Village* 186 The tyrant soaring in the clouds above With gyrous scrutiny the furze-clad hill Closely surveying.

gyrovague (ˈdʒaɪərəveɪg). *Hist. rare.* [a. F. *gyrovague*, ad. med.L. *gȳrovagus*, f. L. *gȳrus* circuit (see GYRE *sb.*) + *-vagus* wandering.] One of those monks who were in the habit of wandering from monastery to monastery.

1801 A. RANKEN *Hist. France* I. I. ii. 224 The Gyrovagues, or Vagabonds, who strolled about from one monastery to another, gratifying too freely their inclinations and appetites.

gyrs(e, gyrss, Obs. Sc. ff. GRASS.

gyrse, gyrsome, vars. GIRSE *Obs.*, GERSUM.

gyrssoppe, variant of GRASSHOP *Obs.*

gyrth(e, gyrtht, vars. GRITH *Obs.* exc. *Hist.*

‖**gyrus** (ˈdʒaɪərəs). *Anat.* Pl. gyri (ˈdʒaɪəraɪ). [L. = circle, circuit, career, a. Gr. γῦρος ring, circle.] A convoluted ridge between grooves or sulci; *esp.* a convolution of the brain. (See also quot. 1846.)

1842 DUNGLISON *Med. Lex.* (ed. 3) 339/2 *Gyrus*, anfractuosity, convolution. **1846** DANA *Zooph.* (1848) 171 Gyri 4 to 5 lines broad. *Ibid.* Gloss., *Gyrus*, a trench together with the sides enclosing it; or, in massive species, the space between the middle of two ridges. **1859** OWEN *Classif. Mammalia* 25 The superficies [of the cerebrum] is folded into more or less numerous gyri or convolutions. **1876** *Trans. Clinical Soc.* IX. 66 The third occipital gyrus. **1887** *Lancet* 17 Sept. 586/2 The region of the angular gyrus .. contains a centre for the raising of the upper eyelid of the opposite eye.

gys, variant of GIS *Obs.*; obs. form of GUISE.

gysar, obs. form of GIZZARD, GUISER.

gysard(e, obs. form of GIZZARD, GUISARD *sb.*[2]

gysarm(e, obs. var. GISARME *Obs.* exc. *Hist.*

gysart, variant of GUISARD *sb.*[2]

gyse, gysen, obs. forms of GUISE *sb.*[2], GIZZEN.

gyser, obs. f. GISARME, GIZZARD, GUISER.

gyserne, obs. variant of GISARME, GIZZERN.

gysour, obs. form of GIZZARD, GUISER.

gyspen, variant of GISPIN *Obs.*

gyss, obs. form of GUISE.

gyssarn, -erne, obs. variants of GISARME.

gyst(e, obs. form of JOIST.

gysyryne, obs. variant of GISARME.

gyte (gaɪt), *sb. Sc.* [? A spelling of *gait*, Sc. form of GET *sb.* in sense 2 b.] A contemptuous word for a child; a brat; a first-year pupil in the Edinburgh High School.

1825-80 JAMIESON, *Gyte, Gyteling*, applied contemptuously, or in ill humour, to a young child. **1894** *Daily News* 28 May 8/5 None of the 'gytes' of his period has told us nearly so much about Mr. Stevenson as Mr. Stevenson has told us.

gyte (gaɪt), *a. Sc.* [Of unknown origin.] Mad, out of one's senses.

1725 RAMSAY *Gentle Sheph.* II. i, The man's gane gyte! **1818** SCOTT *Hrt. Midl.* xxiv, The gudeman's gane clean gyte, I think. **1886** STEVENSON *Kidnapped* xix. 182 Are you gone gyte?

gyte, obs. f. GET *v.*; var. GITE[1] *Obs.*

gyte, gyten, -in, obs. pa. pples. of GET *v.*

gytern(e, obs. variant of GITTERN.

gytlin(g, variant of GETLING.

gytolle, obs. variant of CITOLE.

gyton(e, variant of GETON *Obs.*

gytrash (ˈgaɪtræʃ). *north. dial.* Also guy-. An apparition, spectre, ghost, generally taking the form of an animal.

1847 C. BRONTE *J. Eyre* xii, I remembered certain of Bessie's tales, wherein figured a North-of-England spirit, called a 'Gytrash;' which, in the form of horse, mule, or large dog, haunted solitary ways, and sometimes came upon belated travellers. **1891** ATKINSON *Last Giant Killers* 150 Then another name was called and spelt 'Gytrash'.

Comb. **1847** C. BRONTE *J. Eyre* xii, A Gytrash-like Newfoundland dog.

gytt, obs. form of GET.

gytterne, obs. variant of GITTERN.

gyttja (ˈjɪtʃə). *Geol.* Also gytje. [Sw., = mud, ooze (adopted in its technical sense by H. A. von Post 1862, in *K. Sven. Vetenskaps-Akad. Handl.* 1).] A sediment which is typically black, rich in organic matter, and deposited in productive lakes.

1887 *Encycl. Brit.* XXII. 740/1 In the shallow lakes and enclosed bays of the sea there began to be formed and still is in course of formation a deposit known by the name *gyttja*, characterized by the diatomaceous shells it contains. **1899** *Jrnl. Chem. Soc.* LXXVI. II. 39 At Sandefjord the *gytje* is greasy to the touch, and has the odour of hydrogen sulphide; it is used for mud baths. **1958** F. E. ZEUNER *Dating Past* (ed. 4) iii. 90 There is about one metre of blue lake marl below the polliniferous gyttja. **1970** *Nature* 19 Sept. 1235/1 At a few places, however, there are thin gyttja-like layers a few centimetres thick, which could have formed in pools over permafrost.

gytton, gyttorne, vars. GETON *Obs.*

gyulere, variant of GUILER *Obs.*

Gyv, obs. form of JEW.

gyve (dʒaɪv), *sb. Chiefly pl.* Now *arch.* or *poet.* Forms: *pl.* 3, 6, 7 gives, (5 gyvys), 5-6 guyv(i)es, (7 gieves), 7-8 guives, 4- gyves. *sing.* 6 give, 7 guive, 7- gyve. [ME. *give*, of obscure origin.

The alliteration in ME. poetry shows that the word was originally pronounced with initial (g), and from the spelling *guive* it would appear that this pronunciation continued until the 18th c.; indeed, it is indicated in the pronouncing Dicts. of Sheridan (1780) and Scott (1797). The now prevailing pronunciation with (dʒ) is due to misinterpretation of the graphic form of a word that had become obsolete in oral use. The form points to an OF. **guive* (spelt *give* in *French Chron. Lond.*, 14th c.); Prof. Skeat suggests that this may represent an adoption of some derivative of the Teut. root **wīp-* (OHG. *wīfan* to wind round, LG. *wīp*, a straw-band). But the absence of any record of the word in continental OF. constitutes a serious objection to this conjecture. Can AF. *guive* be an adoption of the synonymous ME. and OE. *widde*, the initial *w* being represented by *gu-*, and the unfamiliar Eng. dental spirant represented by *v* ? If this suggestion be correct, Layamon used both the Eng. and the Fr. form of the word; cf. with quot. *c* 1205 below the following (line 22833) 'Nimeð me þene ilke mon, and doð wiððe an his sweore'.]

A shackle, esp. for the leg; a fetter.

c **1205** LAY. 15538 Giues swiðe grete: heo duden an his foten. *c* **1290** *S. Eng. Leg.* I. 461/145 A-non-riȝht þis holie Man þe Gyues he to-brac. **1306** *Pol. Songs* (Camden) 221 With feteres ant with gyves ichot he wes to-drowe, From the Tour of Londone. **1377** LANGL. *P. Pl.* B. XIV. 51 Shal neuere gyues the greue.. Prisone ne peyne. *c* **1420** *Chron. Vilod.* (Horstm.) 4413 Bot þe gyuys duden þo anon alle to-barst. **1494** FABYAN *Chron.* VI. clxii. 155 The greuous correccyons that he sawe.. as in werynge of irons and guyues. **1505** *Nottingham Rec.* III. 100 Duo paria de guyvies de ferro. **1548** UDALL, etc. *Erasm. Par. Acts* xvi. 60 All the prisoners gyues and other lyke bonds were loosed. **1566** DRANT *Wail. Hierem.* K v b, Pressinge downe, with pondrouse gyves, my feete. **1600** FAIRFAX *Tasso* v. xlii. 83 Hands.. Not to be tide in giues and twisted cords. **1631** J. TAYLOR (Water P.) *Turn Fort. Wheel* (1848) 24 Helpe me.. To fire and powder, Manacles and gives. *a* **1658** CLEVELAND *Wks.* (1687) 253 The benum'd Captive crampt in his cold Gives. **1704** J. PITTS *Acc. Mahometans* viii. 115 The Women of Algier.. wear great Rings, almost like Guives about their Legs. **1774** J. BRYANT *Mythol.* II. 105 We may as well suppose, that a felon would forge his own gyves. **1810** SCOTT *Lady of L.* VI. i, The debtor wakes to thought of gyve and jail. **1828** TENNYSON *Lover's T.* II. 155 Upon his steely gyves. **1829** HOOD *Dream Eugene A.* xxxvi, Eugene Aram walked between With gyves upon his wrist. **1900** *Q. Rev.* Jan. 181 You read of a youth brought up in a country where all the world wore a gyve on the right leg.

b. *transf.* and *fig.*

1587 M. GROVE *Pelops & Hipp.* (1878) 93 Though long I wretch doe weare the giue And carefull clog of heauinesse. **1597** SHAKS. *Lover's Compl.* 242 Playing patient sports in vnconstrain[e]d giues. **1614** BP. HALL *Recoll. Treat.* 251 Not fettred with the gieves of unjust scruples. **1616** B. JONSON *Forest* iv. *To the world*, Such as blow away their liues, And neuer will redeeme a day, Enamor'd of their golden gyues. **1624** FLETCHER *Wife for Month* I. ii, A golden Give, a pleasing wrong. **1700** DRYDEN *Fables, Meleager & Atalanta* 150 Telamon.. happ'd to meet A rising Root, that held his fastned Feet; So down he fell; whom, sprawling on the Ground, His Brother from the Wooden Gyves unbound. **1844** DISRAELI *Coningsby* II. i. 60 The gyves and trammels of office.

gyve (dʒaɪv), *v.* Also 6 give. *Pa. pple.* 3 i-gwived, 4 i-gyved, y-gyvid. [f. GYVE *sb.*] *trans.* To fasten with, or as with, gyves; to fetter, shackle.

c **1290** *Beket* 11 in *S. Eng. Leg.* I. 106 He was sone i-nome, Ase A sclaue forth i-lad and i-don In prisone, And faste was i-gwiued. **1387** TREVISA *Higden* (Rolls) VI. 203 Egwynus byþouȝte hym of þe synnes of his ȝouþe, and gyvede hym self .. and wente so i-gyved to Rome. **1482** *Monk of Evesham* (Arb.) 83 They were gyuyd in fyry feturs and hangyd vp in the myddys of fyre. **1548** UDALL, etc. *Erasm. Par. Mark* vi. 29 Johns head was priuily striken of after he hadde layne a whyle fast gyued in pryson. **1613** HEYWOOD *Silver Age* I. Wks. 1874 III. 86 Gyve his legges in Irons, Till we determine further of his death. **1635** —— *Hierarch.* IV. 268 He the old Dragon gyv'd and bound. **1831** CARLYLE *Sart. Res.* (1858) 79 There was no good Running, so obstructed was the path, so gyved were the feet. **1835** FONBLANQUE *Eng. under 7 Administr.* (1837) III. 199 To fetter their hands, and gyve their legs.

b. *fig.* or with reference to immaterial things.

1377 LANGL. *P. Pl.* B. XX. 191 He.. gyued me in goutes, I may nouȝte go at large. **14..** *Circumcision* in *Tundale's Vis.* (1843) 90 My wittis be so dull with rudenes, And in the cheynes of ignoraunce gyved. **1592** LYLY *Midas* II. ii. 18 Eristus, whose eyes are sticht on Cælia's face, And thoughts gyved to her beautie. **1604** SHAKS. *Oth.* II. i. 171, I will giue thee in thine own Courtship. **1631** HEYWOOD *2nd Pt. Faire Maid of W.* III. Wks. 1874 II. 381 He's gyv'd to me by faith, but else at liberty. **1808** J. BARLOW *Columb.* v. 138 Dependent feelings for a distant throne Gyve the crampt soul that fears to think alone. **1867** CARLYLE *Remin.* II. 147 Hampered and gyved as we were by the genius loci and its difficulties.

gyve, obs. form of GIF *conj.*, GIVE.

gyved (dʒaɪvd), *ppl. a.* [f. GYVE *v.* + -ED[1].] Fastened with gyves; fettered, shackled.

1382 WYCLIF *Gen.* xxxix. 20 [Potiphar] toke Joseph into prysoun, where the gyved men of the kyng weren kept. **1565** COOPER *Thesaurus*, *Compeditus*, fettered, gyued, shackled. **1821** JOANNA BAILLIE *Metr. Leg.*, *Columbus* xlii. 10 These gyved limbs will wear their yoke. **1892** *Pall Mall G.* 29 Sept.

5/2 The practice of arraigning gyved..prisoners in open court..lingered until the time of John Howard.

gyver ('gaɪvə(r)). *slang.* Chiefly *Austral.* and *N.Z.* Also **givo, givor, guiver, guyver.** [Of unknown origin.] Affectation of speech or behaviour, esp. in phr. ***to put on the gyver.*** Also as *adj.*: smart, fashionable.

a **1866** VANCE *Chickaleary Cove* (Farmer & Henley), The stock around my squeeze of a guiver colour see. **1889** BARRÈRE & LELAND *Slang* I. 411/2 *Guiver* (theatrical), flattery, artfulness. **1897** D. MCK. WRIGHT *Station Ballads* (1945) 45 He'd put on 'gyver' enough to last a full-bred actor a week. **1899** W. T. GOODGE *Hits, Skits & Jingles* (1904) 18 And I ain't got the style and the guiver Of them bank clerks and students and sich. **1914** *Bulletin* (Sydney) 14 May, 'E 'ad a bit of guiver wif the secrety. **1916** J. B. COOPER *Coo-oo-ee* x. 142 I'm not takin' any of that sort of 'gyver', you know. **1918** *Chrons. N.Z.E.F.* 5 July 253/1 The 'givor' that kid puts on, you would think he was a captain at least. **1928** J. DEVANNY *Dawn Beloved* xviii. 179 Mrs. Rodda thinks herself too good for anybody else... To hear her and Mrs. Devoy talk! The guyver they put on! **1938** *Observer* 25 Sept. 9/2 Guyver: Make-believe, still used in Anglo-Jewish slang. It is Hebrew for pride, but has now come to mean pretence and is synonymous with..swank. **1948** V. PALMER *Golconda* xxxii. 272 Well, what's all this guyver about the going being tough? **1948** PARTRIDGE *Dict. Forces' Slang 1939–1945* 83 *Givo* or *gyvo*, an adjective which describes any sartorial eccentricity. A 'tiddley-suit' made by a shore-going tailor which has wider bell-bottoms than are permitted by the Service regulations. **1970** D. M. DAVIN *Not Here, Not Now* III. vii. 207, I wouldn't want you to get stuck-up and start putting on the gyver and forgetting your own.

gywe, obs. form of GIVE.

Gywes, Gywene, obs. nom. and gen. pl. of JEW.

gyylde, gyyste, obs. forms of GUILD, JOIST.

gyzard, gyze, obs. ff. GUISARD *sb.*[2], GUISE.

gyzen, obs. form of GIZZEN.

gyzern, gyzzarn, obs. variants of GIZZERN.

H

H (eɪtʃ), the eighth letter of the Roman alphabet, ancient and modern, representing historically the Semitic 𐤇, *Hheth* or *Kheth*, through the Greek **H**, *Heta*, *Eta*, originally the eighth, but, in the later Greek alphabet, after the omission of ϝ (see F), the seventh letter. The Semitic letter represented a laryngal or guttural spirant, or a rough aspirate, and it was with the aspirate value that the letter was originally used in Greek and passed thence into Roman use. (In the later Greek alphabet, H was used as a vowel, to express long *ē*, which had previously not been distinguished from short *e*: see E.) When the Roman alphabet was applied to the Germanic languages, H was used initially for the simple aspirate or breath-sound, which had arisen out of a pre-Germanic or Aryan *k*, through the stages of guttural aspirate (kh), and guttural spirant (x); medially and finally *h* was put for the guttural spirant itself, which, in later times, came to be written *gh* or *ch*: thus, Gothic *hauh*, OHG. *hôh*, OE. *héah*, mod. English *high* (*gh* mute), Scotch *heich*, Ger. *hoch*. In Old English, *h* occurred not only before the vowels, but also before the consonants *l*, *n*, *r*, *w* (representing the pre-Germanic *kl-*, *kn-*, *kr-*, *kw-*, or *q-*), as in *hláf* loaf, *hnecca* neck, *hræfn* raven, *hwá* who; it now stands initially only before vowels. Its power is that of a simple aspiration or breathing, with just sufficient narrowing of the glottis to be audible before a vowel. It is also used to form consonantal digraphs (*sh*, *th*, etc.) with simple sounds; and it is often silent, or merely lengthens a preceding vowel.

The name *aitch*, which is now so remote from any connexion with the sound, goes back through ME. *ache* to OF. *ache* = Sp. *ache*, It. *acca*, pointing to a late L. **accha*, **ahha*, or **aha*, exemplifying the sound; cf. It. *effe*, *elle*, *emme*, etc. (The earlier L. name was *ha*.) The plural occurs as *aitches*, *aches*, *h*s, *h's*.

In late Latin, and in the Romanic languages, the aspirate was no longer pronounced, and consequently often not written; in modern Italian it is entirely omitted, as in *eretico*, *istorico*, *orribile*. In Old French similarly the mute *h* was originally not written, and it was in this form that many Old French words, such as *abit*, *able*, *eir*, *erbe*, *eritage*, *onest*, *onor* or *onur*, *ure* or *oure*, *ympne*, were originally adopted in English. From this stage we derive the still existing forms *able*, *ability*, *arbour* (= *erbere*), *ostler*. But at a later period, imitation of the Latin spelling, by scribes who knew that language, gradually led to the restitution of *h* in the writing of most of these words in French, and thence also in English. In French, the *h*, though thus artificially reinstated in spelling, remained mute; but in England it was gradually, after the usage of the native words, restored in pronunciation, so that at the present day only a very few words, viz. *heir*, *honest*, *honour*, *hour*, with their derivatives, remain with *h* mute; though others, such as *herb*, *humble*, *humour*, were so treated very recently, and are by some people still; and *hostler* (also spelt *ostler*) is so pronounced by the majority. A trace of the former muteness or weakness of *h* in other words is also seen in the still prevalent practice of using *an* before words with initial *h*, not accented on the first syllable, as *heretical*, *historical*, *humane*, *hypotenuse*, and in such archaic forms as 'mine host', and the biblical 'an Hebrew'. In the ME. period, during which *h* was being gradually reinstated in words from Old French, these show great variety of spelling, the same word appearing now with, and now without *h*; this uncertainty reacted upon other words beginning with a vowel, so that these also often received an initial *h* (due probably in some instances, as *habundant*, to a mistaken notion of their etymology). This spelling has been permanently established in the words *hermit* and *hostage*, among others.

In Old English, as in the Teutonic languages generally, initial *h* was strongly and distinctly aspirated. But early in the Middle-English period it was dropped in pronunciation and writing before *l*, *n*, and *r*. The old *hw* was from the 12th c. commonly written *wh*, sometimes *w* only, in Scotch *qwh-*, *quh-*; indicating a variety of pronunciation (see W). Before vowels, in words of Old English or Norse origin, *h* has been regularly retained in the standard spelling and pronunciation: but in many English dialects, especially those of the midl. and southern counties (not in Scotland, Ireland, or in the United States), the aspirate has disappeared as an ordinary etymological element, and is now employed only with other functions, viz. to avoid hiatus (e.g. *the egg*, pronounced *the-h-egg*), and especially in the emphatic or energetic utterance of a syllable with an initial vowel; being then prefixed without distinction to words with or without etymological *h*; thus *horse*, *ass*, usually *òss*, *àss*, emphatically (or after a vowel) *hòss*, *hàss*. In earlier periods, these dialectal habits naturally affected the written language of literature, where their influence was reinforced by the uncertainty that prevailed as to initial *h* in words of Latin-French origin; so that during the Middle-English period, and down to the 17th c., we find numerous instances of the non-etymological absence or (more often) presence of initial *h* in native words also. These characteristics are not confined to English: some modern Dutch and Flemish dialects, especially those of Zealand, Flanders, and North Brabant, have entirely lost *h* as an etymological element, and employ it to avoid hiatus, and to impart emphasis, exactly like the English dialects; while in Old High German, Middle Low German, Middle Dutch, and, above all, Middle Flemish literature, the non-etymological absence and presence of initial *h* is even more marked than in Middle English. In this Dictionary, some of the chief forms found in earlier use with adventitious initial *h* are mentioned in their alphabetical order, with a reference to their proper spelling, especially when this is not seen by simple omission of the *h*; but in other cases it is to be presumed that, when a ME. word in *h* is not entered here, it will be found in the form without *h*.

In recent times, the correct treatment of initial *h* in speech has come to be regarded as a kind of shibboleth of social position; this has resulted in the cultivation of the educated usage in many quarters where it is not native. But even in educated pronunciation, there are cases in which *h* is usually mute, e.g. at the beginning of a syllable after certain consonant groups, as in ex*h*aust, ex*h*ortation, and in such suffixes as *-ham*, *-hope*, in *Chatham*, *Clapham*, *Durham*, *Greenhope*, *Stanhope*, *Tudhope*, *-herd* in *shepherd*, as well as in the pronouns *he*, *his*, *him*, *her*, when unemphatic and as it were enclitically combined with the preceding word, as in 'I met-*h*im on-*h*is horse'. In the corresponding neuter pronoun *it*, originally *hit*, in which the unemphatic use predominates, the *h* was long ago dropped in writing as well as speech. (But in Scotch the emphatic form is still *hit*.)

After a vowel, *h* is regularly silent, and such a vowel being usually long, as in *oh*, *ah*, *bah*, *hurrah*, the addition of *h* (so usual in modern German) is one of the expedients which we have for indicating a long vowel in foreign or dialect words. The silence of *h* in certain positions contributed to the currency of such spellings as the obsolete *preheminence*, *proheme*, *abhominable*.

By the combination of *h* with consonants, numerous digraphs are formed for the expression of simple sounds; the origin of this goes back to the ancient Greek alphabet, which used PH, TH, KH, for the aspirated consonants, which were afterwards provided with single symbols *Φ*, *Θ*, *X*, and sank into simple spirants. In Latin the digraphs were retained, and thence *th*, *ch*, and occasionally *ph*, were taken to represent German spirants or aspirates. In Old English, which had þ, ð, for the sound or sounds represented on the continent by *th*, these digraphs had little currency until after the Norman Conquest, which introduced *th*, *ch*, *gh*, and sometimes *yh*, for certain English sounds, and substituted *wh* for OE. *hw*; the development of a simple sound (ʃ) from the OE. combination *sc*, led, through *sch*, to the digraph *sh*; *ph* and *rh* (pronounced f and r) were adopted from Latin as the representatives of Gr. *φ* and *ῥ*; in more recent times *kh* has been used to express Slavonic and Semitic guttural spirants; *bh*, *dh*, *gh*, *ph*, *th*, *kh*, to represent Sanskrit and Indian aspirates, or other alien sounds; and *zh* (on the analogy, *s* : *z* :: *sh* : *zh*) for the phonetic representation of French *j* in *déjeuner*, symbolized in this Dictionary by (ʒ). (For the history and use of these digraphs, see under their respective initial letters, C, G, etc.)

to drop one's h's (or ***aitches***), to omit initial *h* where it is pronounced in Standard English.

c **1000** Ælfric *Gram.* iii. (Z.) 6, *h* and *k* ȝeendiað on *a* æfter rihte. **1530** Palsgr. 17 The soundynge of this letter H, when he hath his aspiration, and when he hath it nat. *Ibid.*, These words 'honest, honour, habundaunce, habitacion'.. in whiche *h* is written and nat sounded with us. **1562** J. Heywood *Prov. & Epigr.* (1867) 111 Into what place so euer H, may pike him, Where euer thou finde ache, thou shalt not like him. **1573–80** Baret *Alv.*, *H* which corruptly wee name Ach..we in England haue great need of it. **1599** Shaks. *Much Ado* III. iv. 56 *Mar.* For a hauke, a horse, or a husband? *Beat.* For the letter that begins them all, H. **1847** Mrs. Carlyle *Lett.* II. 22 A distinguished magnetiser, who could not sound his h's. **1848** Thackeray *Bk. Snobs* (1881) 220 A drawing-room where the *h* and other points of etiquette are rigorously maintained. **1864** Tennyson *Sea Dreams* 192 Dropping the too rough H in Hell and Heaven. **1886** Ruskin *Præterita* I. 313 They liked, as they did not drop their own *h's*, to talk with people who did not drop theirs. **1888** *Cornh. Mag.* Oct. 365 The letter H is absolutely sacred in the Constitution of the United States. **1892** Boldrewood *Nevermore* I. ii. 41 A very fine young man, but evidently a nobody, inasmuch as he dropped his aitches and so on.

attrib. **1885** *Pall Mall G.* 15 Jan. 4/1 If she can read and write, and is not afflicted with the *h* malady.

b. with reference to the shape of the capital **H.**

1606 Shaks. *Ant. & Cl.* IV. vii. 8, I had a wound heere that was like a T, But now 'tis like an H. **1688** Evelyn *Diary* 18 Aug., The house..a noble uniform pile in the form of a half H.

2. *attrib.* and *Comb.* ***H-block***, one of the H-shaped buildings in the Maze prison in Northern Ireland, the focus of a protest campaign by prisoners claiming 'political' (rather than criminal) status in the late 1970s. ***H-branch***, a branch-pipe joining and proceeding at right angles from two parallel pipes. ***H girder***, ***iron***. ***H hinge***, a type of hinge which when open has the form of an H. ***h-less*** (***aitchless***), adj., without an h or h's; not aspirating the letter h. ***H-piece***, in a force-pump, a piece standing on the wind-bore under the door-piece, by which the water is forced through the door-piece into the standpipe.

1726 in *Maryland Hist. Mag.* (1912) VII. 278 H hinges at 8s per pair. **1836** L. Hebert *Engin. & Mech. Encycl.* I. 674 Another sort, called H..hinges, from their resemblance to those letters, are extensively employed for common purposes. **1875** J. H. Collins *Metal Mining* 147 H-piece. **1888** *Lockwood's Dict. Mech. Engin.*, *H iron*, rolled wrought-iron bar whose section is that of the letter I. Used extensively for building up engineering structures. **1893** *Temple Bar Mag.* July 322 Millionaire cheesemongers who dwell *h*-less in the feudal castles of the poor. **1894** *Times* 1 Mar. 14/5 She..brings 'h'less' Socialists as guests to her husband's house. **1894** Du Maurier *Trilby* II. 135 Hebrew capitalists and aitchless millionaires. **1902** A. C. Harmsworth et al. *Motors* vi. 90 The roof of the house is strengthened at certain points by cross timbers which support two small H girders, and carry iron frames to which are attached pulley blocks. **1960** H. Hayward *Antique Coll.* 142/1 *'H' hinge*, like the cock's head hinge, an early external type of hinge in the form of the letter 'H' extensively used on cupboards of the 16th and 17th cent. [**1976** *Ulster Commentary* Apr. 5/4 New cell units at the Maze Prison... Each unit is in the form of an 'H', each leg of the 'H' containing 25 individual cells with showers, wash-hand basins, toilets, a dining recreation room with TV and games, and a hobbies room.] **1976** *Irish Times* 14 Dec. 5/3 For 11 weeks now sentenced Republican..prisoners in H-block, Long Kesh, have been held in solitary confinement. **1977** *New Statesman* 30 Sept. 439/2 There are five H-blocks completed in the Maze (three more are being built). **1979** [see blanket *sb.* 3]. **1986** *Guardian Weekly* 22 June 5/5 McDonnel, a big boned Belfast man who had joined the blanket and dirty protest in the H Blocks of the Maze, took time off to marry his girlfriend.

II. 3. a. Used like the other letters of the alphabet to denote serial order; applied e.g. to the eighth group or section in classification, the eighth sheet of a book or quire of a MS., etc.

b. Designation of a strong Fraunhofer line at 3969 Å, caused by calcium ions; †orig., (the position occupied by) the H and K lines as a pair. [Named by J. Fraunhofer 1817, in *Ann. d. Physik* LVI. 286.]

1823 tr. Fraunhofer in *Edin. Philos. Jrnl.* IX. 297 The two bands at H are of a very singular nature. **1865** *Phil. Trans.* CLIV. 149 A pair of strong lines..near the extreme refrangible end of the spectrum..may coincide with those of Fraunhofer's H. **1879**, **1967** [see K 3 c].

4. H was a mediæval symbol of 200. H = 200,000. (See Du Cange.)

1727–51 in Chambers *Cycl.*

5. *Music.* The note B natural in the German system of nomenclature (the letter B being used only for B flat).

1880 Stainer & Barrett *Dict. Mus. Terms.* **1880** Gehring in Grove *Dict. Mus.* I. 643/1 H major is a key rarely used..H minor is the key of Schubert's very fine unfinished Symphony.

6. *Math.* In the differential calculus, *h* is used to denote a small increment.

1872 B. Williamson *Diff. Calculus* i. §6 (1873) 4 Let x become $x + h$, where $h = \Delta x$.

7. In *Cryst.*, *h*, *k*, *l* are used for the quantities which determine the position of a plane.

1868 Dana *Min.* Introd. 28. **1895** Story-Maskelyne *Crystallogr.* ii. 19.

8. *Math.*, *Physics.* *H* denotes the Hamiltonian function of classical mechanics or the Hamiltonian operator of quantum mechanics.

1835 W. R. Hamilton in *Phil. Trans. R. Soc.* LXXV. 98 If then we introduce, for abridgement, the following expression H. **1935** Pauling & Wilson *Quantum Mech.* i. 16 Involving a function *H*..called the Hamiltonian function. **1965** W. Hauser *Introd. Princ. Mech.* vi. 194 Whenever the Lagrangian is not explicitly a function of time, the function *H*..referred to as the *Hamiltonian* of the system, is a constant of the motion. *Ibid.* 195 This can be verified by considering the variation of *H*.

9. *Physics.* *h* denotes Planck's constant, the elementary quantum of action (M. Planck 1900, in *Verh. d. Deutsch. Physik. Ges.* II. 245). In more recent usage, the quantum of angular momentum $h/2\pi$ has been represented by $\hbar$.

1901 *Sci. Abstr.* IVa. 230, $\epsilon = h\nu$, where *h* is a constant. **1934** *Physical Rev.* XLVI. 925/2, $\hbar$. **1935** Pauling & Wilson *Quantum Mech.* ii. 25 The constant of proportionality, *h*, is a new constant of nature,..called *Planck's constant* ...$h/2\pi$ [is] a natural unit or quantum of angular momentum. **1955** L. I. Schiff *Quantum Mech.* (ed. 2) i. 7 The product of the uncertainties of the..position and momentum components is at least of the order of magnitude of $\hbar$.

III. Abbreviations. (Those given here with the full stop are frequently used without it.) **H.** = various proper names, as *Henry*, *Helen*; **h.**, (in a ship's log), hail; **H**, (on lead pencils), hard; the various degrees of hardness being denoted by HH, HHH, etc.; **H.**, henry (*Electr.*), heroin; **H** or **h** (*Physics*), horizontal force; **H**, as a direction in a musical score, horns; **H**, designating *horror* films; **h.**, hot, as ***h. and c.***, hot and cold (water);

H or **h.**, hour; **H.**, in the Shipping Register, *Hoy*; **H.** (*Chem.*), Hydrogen; also, hydrogen (bomb); so *H-bomb, -test*, etc.; **H. and D.** (see quots. 1918, 1930); **HB**, (on lead pencils), hard black (denoting a medium hardness); **H.B.C.**, Hudson's Bay Company; **H.B.M.**, His (or Her) Britannic Majesty; **H.C.**, Heralds' College, House of Commons; **H.C.F.** (*Math.*), Highest Common Factor; **H.E.**, His Eminence, His (or Her) Excellency, high explosive; **H.E.I.C.**, Honourable East India Company; **HF**, **H^{F}**, **H$_{F}$**, **Hf**, healthy female(s); **H.F.**, **h.f.**, high frequency; **H.G.**, Horse Guards; **H.H.**, His (or Her) Highness, or His Holiness; **H-Hour**, the hour at which an operation is to begin; cf. D-DAY; **H.I.M.**, His (or Her) Imperial Majesty; **HIV**, human immunodeficiency virus: either of two retroviruses (*HIV-1, HIV-2*) which cause AIDS; also (redundantly) *HIV virus*; cf. *HTLV* below; **H.K.**, Hong Kong (in currency notation); **HM**, **H^{M}**, **H$_{M}$**, **Hm**, healthy male(s); **H.M.**, His (or Her) Majesty; **H.M.C.**, Headmasters' Conference; **H.M.C.**, His (or Her) Majesty's Customs; **H.M.G.**, His (or Her) Majesty's Government; **H.M.I.(S.)**, His (or Her) Majesty's Inspector of Schools; **H.M.S.**, His (or Her) Majesty's Ship or Service; **H.M.S.O.**, His (or Her) Majesty's Stationery Office; **H.N.C.**, Higher National Certificate; **H.O.**, Hostilities Only (see quots.); **H.P.**, half-pay, high pressure, hire purchase, horse-power, hybrid perpetual; **H.P. Sauce**, the proprietary name of a type of spiced brown sauce; **H.Q.**, Headquarters; †**H.q.** or **h.q.**, *hoc quære*, look for this = q.v.; **H.R.H.**, His (or Her) Royal Highness; **H.T.**, **h.t.**, high tension; **HTLV**, human T-cell lymphotropic or lymphocyte virus: any of several retroviruses (*HTLV-1, -2*, etc.) of which one at least (*HTLV-3*, also called *HIV-1*) causes AIDS; cf. *HIV* above; **HUAC**, House [of Representatives] Un-American Activities Committee; **Hz**, hertz (unit of frequency).

1910 N. HAWKINS *Electr. Dict.*, *H. The symbol of induction. The Henry. h. An abbreviation for the henry, the practical unit of induction. **1926** *Clues* Nov. 161/2 **H*, heroin. **1929** *Sat. Even. Post* 13 Apr. 54/3 Heroin is referred to as H. **1933** C. DE LENOIR *Hundredth Man* iv. 61, I opened the packet of H. and took a generous sniff. **1962** K. ORVIS *Damned & Destroyed* v. 42 Suppose I..ask you where to connect for H? **1938** *Ann. Reg. 1937* 339 In June, Lord Tyrell, President of the British Board of Film Censors, introduced a new film classification called '*H' to apply to horror films. Pictures so labelled will not be shown to children under 16, whether accompanied by an adult or not. **1958** *Times* 4 Aug. 10/2 'H' used to, and now 'X' does, among other things, stand for Horror, and the two new films this week..are rich in those qualities [etc.]. **1960** *Spectator* 1 July 20 *The Visit* is old-style *grand guignol* with a few modern H-certificate props. **1901** *Punch* 24 July 64/1 Bathroom (*h. and c.). **1930** *Morning Post* 17 June 20/7, 4 bed-rooms (h. and c. in each). **1937** 'G. ORWELL' *Road to Wigan Pier* xiii. 250 The literary gent in his Tudor cottage with bathroom h. and c. **1950** *Hansard, Commons* 6 Nov. 114, I am not one who criticised the right hon. Gentleman ..for drawing attention to the *H-bomb. **1952** *Manch. Guardian Weekly* 20 Nov. 2/2 The first test model of the H-bomb will be followed shortly by even more violent versions. **1955** *Bull. Atomic Sci.* June 226/2 He asserts that H-war, terrible as it will be, is still better than Communist domination. **1957** *Observer* 8 Sept. 9/3 With bovine stolidity Western man carries on with his H-bomb tests. **1958** 'P. BRYANT' *Two Hours to Doom* 96 Their phoney ending of H-tests. **1959** *Listener* 16 July 88/2 United States H-bombers. **1968** *Times* 29 Oct. 7/3 The first Chinese H-bomb, tested in June last year, probably contained zinc in its construction. **1852** C. H. WEIGALL *Art of Figure Drawing* (Advts.) 14 *H. Moderately hard (used for light sketching). HH. A degree harder (for outlines and fine Drawing). HHH. Very hard (for Architectural Drawing). **1895** *Army & Navy Co-op. Soc. Price List* 563/2 The 'Kohinoor', a high-class drawing Pencil..H, HH, HHH. **1926** R. MACAULAY *Crewe Train* II. xii. 211 She purchased a packet of notepaper and envelopes and a pencil (H.H.) at the post office. **1934** M. V. HUGHES *London Child of Seventies* xiv. 167 'I say, Molly, lend us your Scripture pencil,' Dym would say, for he knew that was an H, and good for his geometry figures. **1948** H. MISSINGHAM *Student's Guide Commerc. Art* II. 57 The degree markings on pencils are:..6H, 4H, 3H—Extra Hard. **1903** A. WATKINS *Photogr.* (ed. 2) 29 A box of one maker's plates marked *H & D 100. **1918** *Photo-Miniature* XV. Mar. (Gloss.), H. & D. (Hurter and Driffield)—used as a prefix to numbers signifying the speed of plates measured by the system devised by these investigators. Fastest plates, H. & D. 400 to 500. **1930** *Sel. Gloss. Motion Pict. Techn.* (*Acad. Motion Pict., Hollywood*), *H and D curve*, the characteristic curve of a photographic emulsion. **1852** C. H. WEIGALL *Art of Figure Drawing* (Advts.) 14 *H.B. Hard and Black (deeper shade than F). **1962** L. DEIGHTON *Ipcress File* xxv. 165, I took his wooden HB pencil. **1732** *Let.* 19 Feb. in *Calendar State Papers, Amer. & West Indies* (1939) 64 That *H.E. and less than five of the Council could not hold Courts of Chancery. **1848** THACKERAY *Van. Fair* li. 453 H.E. Papoosh Pasha, the Turkish Ambassador (attended by Kibob Bey, dragoman of the mission). *Ibid.* lxiii. 571 H.E. Madame de Burst received once a week. **1946** KOESTLER *Thieves in Night* 198 He thought that H.E. went indeed a bit far in demonstrating his dislike of the Hebrew community. **1970** *Catholic Directory* 43 (*heading*) Ireland. The hierarchy at the present time... Armagh. H.E. Cardinal William Conway. **1901** *Daily Chron.* 27 June 3/2 To introduce a very much larger proportion of *H.E. shell. **1915** D. O. BARNETT *Let.* 23 May 153 H.E. is the shell for attacking, because you blow the defenders out of their trenches. **1955** *Bull. Atomic Sci.* Feb. 55/3 The thoroughness of an atomic bombardment's 'area coverage' exceeds that of HE carpet bombing beyond comparison. **1880** *H^{F} [see *HM* below]. **1913** *Year-Bk. Wireless Telegr.* 289 To make the current-distribution over the cross-section more uniform for *H.F. currents. **1923** *Popular Wireless* (Suppl.) 13 Oct. 10 'Plug-in' H.F. Transformers. **1924** *Exper. Wireless* Apr. 397/2 The atmospheric band frequencies which penetrate the H.F. filter. **1942** *Electronic Engin.* XV. 168 A hair-pin filament heated by h.f. current. **1967** *New Scientist* 25 May 455/3 All the frequencies in the HF band that are needed by the many transmitters at the station are produced by processing the 'master' frequency. **1918** in *Amer. Speech* (1944) XIX. 302 'Over the top' is now 'the jump off' and 'zero hour' has changed to '*H hour'. **1927** J. M. SAUNDERS *Wings* (1928) v. 210 The word went out that 'D' day was to be Sept. 12, and that 5 A.M. was to be 'H' hour. **1945** *Hutchinson's Pict. Hist. War 12 Apr.–26 Sept. 1944* 342 No fewer than 13 companies landed on the first tide, at H hour plus 25 minutes to be precise. **1986** *Capital Gay* 11 Apr. 4 An international committee on viral names has been looking into the problem, and was rumoured to have agreed on 'human immune deficiency virus' (HIDV or *HIV). **1986** J.COFFIN et al. in *Nature* 1 May 10 We propose that the AIDS retroviruses be officially designated as the human immunodeficiency viruses, to be known in abbreviated form as HIV. **1986** *Courier-Mail* (Brisbane) 12 Aug. 3/6 He said the antigens of HIV II would have to be incorporated into blood testing to protect supplies. **1987** *Nature* 9 Apr. 610/1 Another is the virus isolated from West Africans with AIDS-like illness and originally called LAV-2 but now renamed HIV-2... These viruses seem to be less closely related to HIV-1 than they are to a virus of healthy African green monkeys. **1987** *Daily Tel.* 17 Apr. 2/6 One of the two blood donors had been found not to be carrying the HIV virus, but the other could not be traced. **1987** *New Scientist* 23 Apr. 20/3 Whereas HIV-2 can infect, at least transiently, primate species that are evolutionarily more distantly related to humans (at least baboons and macaques), HIV-1 infects only humans and chimpanzees. **1952** *Hong Kong Trade Returns* Jan. 1 The unit of value is the Hong Kong dollar, the official rate of exchange being *H.K. $16 = £1 sterling. **1964** *Asia Mag.* 12 July 24/1 According to official figures, on average nearly HK $1 million went into land and building every day in 1963. **1880** *Encycl. Brit.* XIII. 170/2 Table *H^{MF}, comprising all the healthy lives, male and female, included in the observations... Table *H^{M}, comprising the healthy male lives only... Table H^{F}, comprising the healthy female lives. **1898** *Westm. Gaz.* 14 Nov. 8/1 With its premiums and its reversionary bonuses, and its Hm tables and its surrender values. **1905** in *Rep. Headmasters' Conf.* 1905 (1906) 97 The 1903 recommendations of the *H.M.C. favoured solution (*b*) as more in harmony with the existing practice and principles of the Universities. **1966** *Rep. Comm. Inquiry Univ. Oxf.* II. 48 Among men from independent schools, the great majority are from H.M.C. schools. **1938** E. WAUGH *Scoop* II. xii. 137 We don't quite know what he's up to; whatever it is, it doesn't suit *H.M.G.'s book. **1971** *Guardian* 28 July 11/1 Any deal with Ian Smith..would make it impossible for Labour men to support HMG on Europe. **1908** E. M. SNEYD-KYNNERSLEY (*title*) *H.M.I.: Some passages in the life of one of H.M. Inspectors of Schools. **1963** S. MARSHALL *Exper. in Education* ii. 40 The modern H.M.I. sniffs the atmosphere of a school the moment he opens the door. **1905** F. H. COLLINS *Author & Printer* 164/1 **H.M.S.O.*, (His or Her Majesty's) Stationery Office. **1969** *Listener* 20 Feb. 255/3 *Britain: An Official Handbook*, published by HMSO two or three weeks ago at 32s. 6d. **1949** *Educ. in 1948* (Cmd. 7724) 44 (*caption*) *H.N.C. **1967** *Times Rev. Industry* Aug. 70/3 The rising failure rate of the HNC candidates. **1942** PARTRIDGE *Dict. Abbrev.* 48/2 **H.O.*, Hostilities only; applied to a man that has joined for the duration of the war. (Naval.) **1961** B. FERGUSSON *Watery Maze* i. 55 H.O. ('Hostilities Only') ratings—men who had joined the Royal Navy for the duration of the war. **1902** *Encycl. Brit.* XXXII. 151 The *H.-P. valves are worked by means of a simple lever from the L.-P. valve-rods. **1930** *Engineering* 9 May 599/1 Since both the H.P. and L.P. rotors have their own thrust blocks, the two are connected by a Wellmann-Bibby coupling, which permits of free axial expansion. **1945** *Daily Mirror* 6 Sept. 3/2 'Stop *H.P. babies'... Mothers..have to pay for their babies on the hire-purchase system because of the high charges of maternity homes. **1958** *Spectator* 13 June 759/2 They cannot keep up the HP payments. **1959** *New Statesman* 17 Oct. 494/2 The artisan class lives in new houses and pays off the telly and the car on HP. **1869** S. R. HOLE *Bk. about Roses* xi. 174 Marguerite Dombrain, *H.P...an early, reliable, vigorous, bright carmine Rose. **1893** W. ROBINSON *Eng. Flower Garden* (ed. 3) 644/2 Gabriel Luizet, General Jacqueminot and many other H.Ps do not usually bloom after the month of August. **1912** *Trade Marks Jrnl.* 22 May 768 *HP..Sauce and pickles. Edwin Samson Moore, trading as 'The Midland Vinegar Company', 'The Trade Malt Vinegar Company', and as F. G. Garton & Co.,.. Aston Cross,..Warwickshire, vinegar brewer and sauce and pickle manufacturer. **1926–7** *Army & Navy Stores Catal.* 37/1 Sauces..H.P.— -/9. **1940** J. BETJEMAN *Coll. Poems* (1958) 83, I pledge her in non-alcoholic wine And give the H.P. Sauce another shake. **1971** P. WORSTHORNE *Socialist Myth* viii. 171 He [*sc.* Mr. Harold Wilson] manages to retain a little of the working-class-lad-made-good appeal... The H.P.-Sauce style of leadership is a style, so long as it is abnormal. **1909** WEBSTER, *H.Q. **1915** D. O. BARNETT *Let.* 18 Jan. 39 After reporting at Brigade H.Q. we went on to our regiments. **1958** M. SHAARA in 'E. Crispin' *Best SF Three* 23 To heck with the rest. We'll let HQ worry about that. **1931** *Daily Express* 18 Mar. 13/2 Fuller 100 volt *H.T. and G.B. Battery. **1980** B. J. POIESZ et al. in *Proc. Nat. Acad. Sci.* LXXVII. 7415/1 Retrovirus particles with type C morphology were found in two T-cell lymphoblastoid cell lines..and in fresh peripheral blood lymphocytes..from a patient with a cutaneous T-cell lymphoma... The cell lines continuously produce these viruses, which are collectively referred to as *HTLV, strain CR (HTLV$_{CR}$). **1981** *Nature* 19 Nov. 271/2 The antibodies against HTLV are..the first evidence for a specific immune response in humans against a retrovirus. **1982** *Science* 19 Feb. 975/2 HTLV is an acquired, not endogenous, retrovirus. **1984** *N.Y. Times* 22 Apr. 16/3 Federal health officials have scheduled a news conference..to discuss findings made by an AIDS researcher, Dr. Robert Gallo, and his colleagues.. concerning a retrovirus they have reportedly called HTLV-3, for human T-cell lymphotropic virus. **1984** R. C. GALLO et al. in *Science* 4 May 501/1 Here we describe the detection and isolation of HTLV-III from a large number of patients with AIDS and pre-AIDS. **1986** *Sci. Digest* May 24/3 To date, the rarest viral cancer discovered causes T cell leukemia. The culprit virus, HTLV-I, is in the same family as the AIDS virus. **1987** *Oxf. Textbk. Med.* (ed. 2) I. v. 151/2 HTLV-1 is the primary cause of adult T cell leukaemia-lymphoma.., HTLV-2 has yet to be associated with disease though it is probably leukaemogenic. **1966** *Economist* 27 Aug. 817/1 *HUAC, even in its very name, implies an inquisitiveness about individual political beliefs that is unconstitutional. **1968** *Listener* 31 Oct. 566/3 HUAC is trying to investigate how far the Chicago violence was the result of a communist conspiracy. **1958** *Quantities & Units Periodic Phenom.* (ISO Recommendation R 31) 5, 1 *Hz is the frequency of a periodic phenomenon of which the periodic time is 1 s. **1966** *Wireless World* Sept. 50 (Advt.), In order to extend the flat response below 40 Hz the rear of the bass driver is loaded with an acoustic transmission line. **1969** *Sears Catal.* Spring/Summer 8 Frequency response of 35 to 18,000 Hz. Crossover is at 2500 Hz.

h', formerly used for *he* before a vowel or *h*, as *h' is*, *h' had*: see HE.

1663 BUTLER *Hud.* I. I. 409 It was so short, h' had much ado To reach it with his desperate Toe. *Ibid.* 425, I would say eye; for h' had but one. **1704** in *Boccalini's Advert. fr. Parnassus* II. A iv b, The Wrongs H'as felt in Paultry Specimens so long.

† **ha**, *sb.*^{1} *Obs.* Short for HA-HA, a sunk fence.

1766 AMORY *Buncle* (1770) III. 112 There was..a ditch like a ha to keep cattle out. *Ibid.* III. 149, I saw her..walking in the garden, near the ha.

ha (hɑː), *int.* and *sb.*^{2} Also 5–6 **hagh(e**, 7 **haugh**, 8–9 **hah**. [A natural exclamation found in Greek, Latin, most of the mod. Romanic, and all the mod. Teut. langs. The simple *ha!* is not recorded in OE. (which had however the *ha ha!* of laughter), but was used in OF., and is freq. in Eng. from *c* 1300.]

1. An exclamation expressing, according to the intonation, surprise, wonder, joy, suspicion, indignation, etc.

a **1300** *Cursor M.* 4218 Ha! quat þaa bestes war selcuth kene, þat has me refte mi derling dere. *c* **1320** R. BRUNNE *Medit.* 557 Ha, fals Iustyce! where fynst þou þat resun, So for to dampne an ynnocent man? *c* **1460** *Towneley M.* (Surtees) 63 *Pr. Miles.* A, my Lord! *Pharao.* Haghe! **1484** CAXTON *Fables of Æsop* I. ii, Ha knaue, why hast thou troubled and fowled my water? *c* **1489** —— *Sonnes of Aymon* i. 32 Ha, god, what a fayre knyghte is he. **1591** SHAKS. *Two Gent.* II. i. 3 Ha? Let me see: I, giue it me, it's mine. **1596** —— *1 Hen. IV* I. iii. 281 And then the power of Scotland, and of Yorke To ioyne with Mortimer, Ha. **1603** —— *Meas. for M.* II. iv. 42 Ha? fie, these filthy vices. **1611** FLORIO, *Hà* ..an Interiection of chiding, haugh [**1598** hagh?], what? **1626** MASSINGER *Roman Actor* IV. i, Ha! come you resolved To be my executioners? *c* **1709** PRIOR *2nd Hymn Callimachus* 1 Hah! how the laurel, great Apollo's tree, And all the cavern shakes! **1779** SHERIDAN *Critic* I. i, Ha! my dear Sneer, I am vastly glad to see you. **1819** SHELLEY *Cenci* IV. iv. 179 Ha! they will bind us to the rack. **1865** DICKENS *Mut. Fr.* I. vi, 'Good-night, Miss!' said Lizzie Hexam, sorrowfully. 'Hah! Good-night!' returned Miss Abbey with a shake of her head.

b. Sometimes doubled, or preceded or followed by other interjections; as *ha ha!*, *a ha!*, *ah ha!*, † *ha a!* (See also AHA.)

a **1300** *Cursor M.* 4917 Ha ha, traiturs, now wel is sene Queþer þat yee be fule or clene. *Ibid.* 9651 A ha! þat wreche wit-vten freind! *c* **1386** CHAUCER *Nun's Pr. T.* 561 [They] cryden, out harrow and weylaway Ha, ha [*v.r.* a ha] the fox! *c* **1477** CAXTON *Jason* 15 Ha a madame, what is this? **1598** SHAKS. *Merry W.* II. ii. 158 Ah, ha, Mistresse Ford and Mistresse Page, haue I encompass'd you? **1602** —— *Ham.* I. v. 150 Ah ha boy, sayest thou so? **1610** —— *Temp.* v. i. 263 Ha, ha: What things are these?

c. Repeated, *ha ha!*, or oftener, *ha ha ha!* it represents laughter: see HA HA.

2. Used as an interjectional interrogative; esp. after a question; = EH 2. (Chiefly in Shakspere.)

1594 SHAKS. *Rich. III*, I. iii. 234 *Q. M.* Richard. *Rich.* Ha. *Q.M.* I call thee not. **1596** —— *Merch. V.* II. v. 44 What saies that foole of Hagars off-spring? ha. **1604** DEKKER *Honest Wh.* I. xii, Why doe I enter into bonds thus? ha! **1610** SHAKS. *Temp.* II. ii. 61 Doe you put trickes vpon 's with Saluages, and Men of Inde? ha?

3. An inarticulate vocal sound (hɜː or ɜː), expressing hesitation or interruption in speech. Often in collocation with *hum*.

1606 SHAKS. *Tr. & Cr.* III. iii. 284 *Patr.* Ioue blesse great Aiax. *Ther.* Hum. *Patr.* I come from the worthy Achilles. *Ther.* Ha? **1608** —— *Per.* v. i. 84 *Mar.* Hail, sir! my lord, lend ear. *Per.* Hum, ha! **1855** DICKENS *Dorrit* I. xxxi, Laying down such—ha—such unnatural principles. Are you—ha —an Atheist?

B. *sb.*^{2} The interjection taken as a name for itself. Esp. as an expression of hesitation in the combination *hums and ha's*: see HUM, also HAW.

1610 B. JONSON *Alch.* III. ii, You may be any thing, and leave off to make Long-winded exercises; or suck up Your ha, and hum, in a tune. **1622** MABBE tr. *Aleman's Guzman d'Alf* I. 115 Thou wouldst haue..giuen him an Ha, or a Nod. **1764** R. LLOYD *Prol. to Colman's Jealous Wife*, What hands had thunder'd at each *Hah!* and *Oh!* **1820** SHELLEY *Œdipus* I. 228 With a ha! and a hum! I come! I come! **1841** J. T. HEWLETT *Parish Clerk* II. 66 A sort of sound, commendatory, like a *hah!*

ha (hɑː), *v.* Also 9 hah. [f. HA *int.*] *intr.* To utter 'ha!' in hesitation. Chiefly in the combination *to hum (hem) and ha*: see HUM *v.*

1604 DEKKER *Honest Wh.* I. xi, He did not ha: neither hum, hem, nor ha, onely stared me in the face. **1824** SCOTT *Redgauntlet* ch. vii, The former ha'd, eh'd.

ha, *pron.*, ME. form of HE, HEO she, HI they.

ha, ha', worn-down form of HAVE *v.* q.v.

ha' (hɑː). Sc. form of HALL[1].

1780–1836 J. MAYNE *Siller Gun* in Chambers *Pop. Poems Scot.* (1862) 146 The bailies caught the welcome strain, And made the ha' resound again. **1814** SCOTT *Wav.* ix, A gentleman from the south had arrived at the Ha'. **1832–53** D. S. BUCHAN in *Whistle-Binkie* (Scot. Songs) Ser. III. 48 She aye made her hallan to shine like a ha'.

Comb., **ha'-Bible**, the great Bible that lay in the *ha'* or principal apartment; **ha'-folk**, the folk of the hall, kitchen, or common room, the servants; **ha'-house**, the manor-house, the habitation of a landed proprietor.

1786 BURNS *Cotter's Sat. Night* xii, The big ha' Bible, ance his father's pride. **1786** —— *Twa Dogs* 62 An' tho' the gentry first are stechin, Yet ev'n the ha' folk fill their pechan Wi' sauce. **1814** SCOTT *Wav.* x, There were mair fules in the laird's ha' house than Davie Gellatley. **1823** GALT *Entail* I. xix. 158 The big ha' Bible was accordingly removed.. from the shelf where it commonly lay.

haa, obs. form of HAW, azure.

haaf (hɑːf, haf). Also **haave, haff.** [a. ON. *haf* (Sw. *haf*, Da. *hav*) sea, high sea, ocean.]

In Shetland and Orkney: The deep or main sea: now used only in connexion with deep-sea fishing; hence, the part of the deep-sea frequented by fishermen; deep-sea fishing ground or station.

1809 EDMONDSTON *Zetland Isl.* I. 237 The boats set off for the fishing ground, which is called the *haaf*, from 10 o'clock a.m. to 2 o'clock of the afternoon. **1822** SCOTT *Pirate* vi, The careful skipper will sleep still enough in the deep haaf. **1844** W. H. MAXWELL *Sports & Adv. Scotl.* xv, The men employed at the *Haaf*, or the fishing-station most distant from the land. **1888** EDMONDSTON *Home of Naturalist* 168 On returning from a night's fishing at the haaf.

b. *attrib.* and *Comb.* Pertaining to or employed in the haaf or deep-sea fishing, as ***haaf-boat, -boy, -fishing***; **haaf-eel**, a name of the conger-eel; **haaf-fish**, the great seal, *Phoca barbata.*

1793 *Statist. Acc. Scot.* VII. 693 (Jam.) The first master of a boat to the Ha-af, or ling fishing, from Sansting, is now alive. **1806** NEILL *Tour Orkney* 107 (Jam.) Teind has always been exigible on the produce of the haaf fishing. **1808–18** JAMIESON, *Haaf-fish*, the Great Seal, Phoca barbata. **1844** *N. Brit. Rev.* I. 359 A crew of four men and a haave-boy. **1856** ELIZA EDMONSTON *Sk. & T. Shetland Isl.* iv. 43 Engaged in the deep sea or haff fishing. **1866** *Morning Star* 17 Aug. 3/3 The 'haaf' boats from the island of Unst. **1880–4** DAY *Brit. Fishes* II. 251 Haaf-eel, a name given to the common conger in the Moray Firth.

haaf, haak, dial. ff. HALF, HAKE.

haal(e, obs. or dial. forms of HALE *v.*, WHOLE.

haam, dial. form of HAME, HOME.

haanepoot, haanepot, varr. HANEPOOT.

haar (hɑː(r)). *local.* Also **harr, haur.** [a. MDu. *hare* (Du. *haere*) keen cold wind.] A wet mist or fog; esp. applied on the east coast of England and Scotland, from Lincolnshire northwards, to a cold sea-fog.

1662 DUGDALE *Hist. Imbanking* Pref., The air being.. cloudy, gross, and full of rotten harrs. **1671** SKINNER *Etym. Ling. Angl.*, *A Sea Harr*, Lincolniensibus Maritimis Tempestas à mari ingruens. **1777** NIMMO *Hist. Stirlingsh.* 438 In the months of April and May, easterly winds, commonly called *Haars*, usually blow with great violence, especially in the afternoons. **1806** *Gazetteer Scotl.* (ed. 2) 389 The water of the lake [Loch Ness].. never freezes in the severest winter, and, in frosty weather, is covered with a thick haar or mist, which has the appearance of smoke. **1876** *Whitby Gloss.*, *Harr*, mist with small rain. 'A northern harr Brings fine weather from far.' **1889** *N.W. Linc. Gloss.* (ed. 2), *Har*, fog, mist, especially when it is cold. **1892** STEVENSON *Across the Plains* 171 History broods over that part of the world like the easterly haar.

haar, -e, obs. forms of HAIR, HARE.

Haarlem ('hɑːləm). The name of a town in Holland, used *attrib.* in **Haarlem blue**, a variety of blue containing alumina; **Haarlem oil**, 'a proprietary diuretic and stimulant oil' (Dorland 1900).

1885 *Spons' Mech. Own Bk.* 407 Slight differences in the manufacture [of Prussian Blue] cause considerable variation in tint and colour, which leads to the material being known by different names—such as 'Antwerp', 'Berlin', 'Haerlem', 'Chinese' Blue. **1885** *Encycl. Brit.* XVIII. 720/1 Barbados tar, Haarlem oil, Seneca oil, and American oil, all consisting wholly or in large part of crude petroleum, were sold by apothecaries for years before petroleum was obtained by boring. **1906** *Practitioner* Dec. 852 Methyloids.—These are an improved combination of methylene blue, Santal oil, copaiba, Haarlem oil, and cinnamon oil, and are supplied in capsoid form.

haaste, haate, obs. ff. HASTE, HATE, HOT.

hab (hæb), *adv.* (*sb.*) *Obs.* exc. *dial.* [Known in the phrases *hab nab*, *hab or nab*, from *c* 1550. Conjectured to represent some part of the verb HAVE, presumably the pres. subj., OE. *hæbbe*, early southern ME. *habbe*, in conjunction with the corresp. negative form OE. *næbbe*, ME. *nabbe*; the alternative phrase *habbe he* (*ich, we*, etc.), *nabbe he* (*ich, we*, etc.) = 'have he (we, etc.) or have he (etc.) not', accounts fairly for the sense, and answers phonologically; but there is a long gap in the history, between the general disappearance of the *habbe* forms of the verb in ME. and the first examples of *hab nab*.

hab ȝe = have ye, if ye have, occurs in *Sir Ferumbras* c 1380; (*h*)*ab* is still a form of *have* in modern Devonshire and W. Somerset dialect (where also the phrase *hab or nab* is in everyday use), but is exemplified by Elworthy only in (*h*)*ab-m*, for *have'en* = 'have him', where it may be a modern phonetic change, since the dialectal change of *vn* to *bm* is widely spread, in *eb'm* even, *seb'm* seven, and the like.]

1. In the phrases ***hab or nab, hab nab*** (***habs-nabs***), get or lose, hit or miss, succeed or fail; however it may turn out, anyhow; at a venture, at random.

1542 UDALL *Erasm. Apoph.* (1877) 209 Put to the plounge of.. habbe or nhabbe to wynne all, or to lese all. **1580** LYLY *Euphues* (Arb.) 354 Philautus determined, hab, nab, to sende his letters. **1586** J. HOOKER *Girald. Irel.* in *Holinshed* II. 82/2 The citizens.. shot hab or nab at random vp to the roodloft and to the chancell. **1603** FLORIO *Montaigne* II. vi, But hab nab [F. *à toutes adventures*], we can never take too much advantage of it. **1638** FORD *Lady's Trial* II. i, Better stil Habs-nabs good wincke and choose, if one must have her, The other goes without her. **1664** BUTLER *Hud.* II. iii. 990 Cyphers, Astral Characters.. set down Hab-nab, at random. **1707** J. STEVENS tr. *Quevedo's Com. Wks.* (1709) 350 Such.. Sayings are a Discredit to your self.. As for Instance,.. Hab nab, at a venture. **1831** SCOTT *Jrnl.* II. 388 It is all hab-nab at a venture. **1888** ELWORTHY *W. Som. Word-bk.* s.v., 'Then you 'ont take no less?' 'No, I 'ont, not one varden. 'Then I'll ab-m, hab or nab!'

2. quasi-*sb.* In phr. ***at (by) hab or nab*** = prec.; ***by hab or by nab, by habs and nabs***: see quots.

1530 PALSGR. 833 By habbe or by nabbe, *par une voye ou aultre.* c **1540** tr. *Pol. Verg. Eng. Hist.* (Camd. No. 29) 93 While thone sought by happ or nap to subdue thother. a **1612** HARINGTON *Epigr.* IV. (1633) 91 Jack Straw, with his rebellious crew, That set King, Realme and Laws at hab or nab. **1623–4** MIDDLETON & ROWLEY *Span. Gipsy* III. ii, Take heed, for I speak not by habs and by nabs. **1685** *Col. Rec. Pennsylv.* I. 138 Who said you have drawn up an Impeachment against President Moore at hab nab. **1877** *Holderness Gloss.*, *Habs-an-nabs*: Anything done in odd moments or at intervals of leisure, not continuously, is said to be done by *habs-an-nabs.* **1892** M. C. F. MORRIS *Yorksh. Folk-Talk* 41 It is only by stealth as it were, and that 'by habs and nabs', as we say, that a stranger, can learn much of the true folk-talk.

†**hab,** *v. Obs.* [See prec.] In ***hab or nab***, have or not have.

1546 *St. Papers Hen. VIII*, XI. 106 Bernardo sayth the Frenchmen will cum roundely to worke to us at ones, and that we shall habb or nab shortly.

hab, dial. and Black var. of HAVE.

habade, habandoun: see AB- and H.

habanera (hæbə'nɛərə). Also **habanero.** [Sp., short for *danza habanera* Havanan dance, f. *Havana*, capital of Cuba.] A slow Cuban dance and song in 2/4 time. Also *attrib.*

1878 tr. *Bizet's Carmen* 1 'Love the Vagrant', the celebrated Habanera, with English words. **1887** F. C. GOOCH *Face to Face with Mexicans* viii. 289 The *danza* is the most distinctively national of all the dances, and bears a strong resemblance to the *Habanera*, as known in Cuba. **1926** WHITEMAN & MCBRIDE *Jazz* xi. 231 A fox trot was played in a rhythm exactly that of the Habanera or Tango, but much swifter in time. **1958** P. GAMMOND *Decca Bk. Jazz* xv. 176 He uses.. often the minimum outline of a tango or habanera bass.

habara ('hæbərə). Also **habarah, habareh, habra, khabarah.** [Arab. *ḥabara.*] A woman's outdoor silk garment. Also *attrib.*

a **1817** J. L. BURCKHARDT *Trav. Arabia* (1829) I. 339 The women of Mekka and Djidda dress in Indian silk gowns, and very large blue striped trowsers..; over these they wear the wide gown called *habra*, of black silk stuff, used in Egypt and Syria. **1839** E. W. LANE tr. *Thousand & One Nights* (1859) I. 190 It [*sc.* the izár] is now generally made of white calico, but a similar covering of black silk for the married, and of white silk for the unmarried, is now worn by females of the higher and middle classes, and is called a 'habarah'. **1851** *Illustr. Catal. Gt. Exhib.* v. II. 1410 Habara veil, in black silk, for females. **1923** *Sunday at Home* Oct. 51/2 A black Egyptian habareh and veil.

habarion, -ioun, obs. forms of HABERGEON.

habber-: see HABER-.

habberdehoy, var. of HOBBADEHOY.

habble, Sc. form of HOBBLE.

habdabs ('hæbdæbz). *slang.* Also **abdabs.** [Orig. obscure.] Nervous anxiety, the heebie-jeebies, esp. in phr. ***to give*** (a person) ***the screaming habdabs.***

1946 *Penguin New Writing* XXVIII. 177 Come on, kid. This joint gives me the hab-dabs. **1962** *Spectator* 8 June 761/3 *Treasure Island* gives pleasure and excitement to some and the screaming habdabs to others. **1963** *Ibid.* 19 July 72 A desperate tension which the slightest crisis will transform into the screaming abdabs once more. **1966** L. DAVIDSON *Long Way to Shiloh* ii. 28 Uri's whimsy-shrouded secrecy, strenuously maintained throughout the journey, had already brought on a severe attack of the habdabs.

Habdalah (hæv'dɑːlə). Also **Habdala, Havdal(l)ah, Hovdoloh.** [a. Heb. *habhdālāh* separation, division.] A Jewish religious ceremony celebrating the end of the Sabbath; a prayer said at this ceremony.

1733 tr. *B. Picart's Ceremonies & Relig. Customs* I. 62 The Festival concludes with the Ceremony which they call Habdala, as it is observed on the Sabbath. *Ibid.* 65 The Repetition of the Habdala. **1891** M. FRIEDLÄNDER *Jewish Relig.* II. ii. 254 On Sabbath evening, after the close of the Sabbath, we recite the *Habdalah*, in which God is praised for the distinction made between Sabbath and the six week-days. **1892** I. ZANGWILL *Childr. Ghetto* (1893) I. xvi. 151 On Saturday night, immediately after *Havdalah*, Sugarman went to Mr. Belcovitch. *Ibid.* 409 *Havdalah*, ceremony separating conclusion of Sabbath or Festival from the subsequent days of toil. **1941** G. G. SCHOLEM *Major Trends in Jewish Mysticism* ii. 67 An extremely interesting.. magical text, the '*Havdalah* of Rabbi Akiba'. **1957** L. STERN *Midas Touch* III. xx. 150 His other treasures.. a silver spice box and two *Hovdoloh* cups. **1960** *Commentary* June 500/2 To observe the ceremonies of.. the Sabbath meal, the blessing of children, and Havdallah. **1962** B. ABRAHAMS tr. *Life Glückel of Hameln* iv. 102 At the close of Sabbath, while my husband was reciting the *Habdalah.*

‖**habeas.** Short for HABEAS CORPUS, q.v.

1879 SALA in *Daily Tel.* 26 June, The unterrified man moved himself by habeas to the Fleet.

‖**habeas corpora.** *Law.* [L. = thou (shalt) have the bodies.]

1. More fully ***habeas corpora juratorum*** (i.e. of the jury): a process formerly issued out of the Court of Common Pleas, directing the sheriff to compel the attendance of reluctant jurymen.

1476 *Plumpton Corr.* 37, I send you now the habeas corpora and a coppie thereof, and you must desier the sheriffe to serve it. **1535** tr. *Littleton's Nat. Brev.* 223 b (Stanf.) And if thenquest come nat at the day of this wrytte retourned, than shal go an habeas corpora, and after that a distres vnto they come. **1838** CHITTY *Archbold's Pract. Crt. Q.B.* I. I. ii. §8 (ed. 6) 405 If none of the special jurors mentioned in the.. *habeas corpora* appear in court, the cause cannot be tried.

2. More fully ***habeas corpora nuper vicecomitis*** (i.e. of the late sheriff): a process for bringing an ex-sheriff to account to the crown or to his successor.

1838 CHITTY *Archbold's Pract. Crt. Q.B.* I. I. i. §5 (3). (ed. 6) 214 Get your clerk in court to obtain a rule for a habeas corpora to bring in the body of the sheriff.

‖**habeas corpus** ('heɪbiːæs 'kɔːpəs). *Law.* [L. = thou (shalt) have the body (sc. in court).]

A writ issuing out of a court of justice, or awarded by a judge in vacation, requiring the body of a person to be brought before the judge or into the court for the purpose specified in the writ; *spec.* the prerogative writ ***habeas corpus ad subjiciendum***, requiring the body of a person restrained of liberty to be brought before the judge or into court, that the lawfulness of the restraint may be investigated and determined.

[**1231** *Bracton's Note Bk.* (Maitland 1887) 527 Preceptum est uicecomiti quod habeat corpus eius, etc.] **1465** MARG. PASTON in *P. Lett.* No. 503 II. 189 Now ther ys com down an *habeas corpus* for hym. **1585** F. ALFORD in Ellis *Orig. Lett.* Ser. III. IV. 57 An Habeas Corpus since the begynninge of this Queenes time hath bin but 2*s.* 6*d.* in the Common Pleas, and 3*s.* 4*d.* in her Majesties Benche. **1642** *Humb. Desire & Proposit. Lds. & Comm.* 1 Feb. 8 Stopping their *Habeas Corpusses.* **1678** LADY CHAWORTH in *12th Rep. Hist. MSS. Comm.* App. v. 46 Lord Shaftesberie's businesse touching the Habeas Corpus is heard today in the House. **1679** *Act 31 Chas. II*, c. 2 §1 Whensoever any person.. shall bring any Habeas Corpus directed unto any Sheriffe.. Goaler Minister or other Person. **1768** BLACKSTONE *Comm.* (mod. ed.) III. 131 The great and efficacious writ, in all manner of illegal confinement, is that of *habeas corpus ad subjiciendum.* **1827** HALLAM *Const. Hist.* (1876) III. xiii. 9 Bushell.. being committed for non-payment of this fine, sued his writ of habeas corpus from the court of common pleas.

b. Habeas Corpus Act: the name commonly given to the Act 31 Chas. II. c. 2 (1679), whereby the granting and enforcing of this prerogative writ was much facilitated.

1691 C. BLOUNT *Opening of Session* in *Collect. Poems* 20 The *Habeas Corpus* Act, oppos'd, say still The Subjects Rights, is but the Prince's will. **1768** BLACKSTONE *Comm.* (mod. ed.) III. 135 The oppression of an obscure individual gave birth to the famous *habeas corpus* act. **1777** BURKE *Let. to Sheriffs of Bristol* Wks. III. 136 The other [statute] for a partial suspension of the *Habeas Corpus* appears to me of a much deeper malignity. **1857** BUCKLE *Civiliz.* I. vii. 352 By the *Habeas Corpus* Act, the liberty of every Englishman was made as certain as law could make it.

c. *fig.*

1589 *Pappe w. Hatchet* (1844) 38 And with an Habeas corpus to remove them from the Shepheards tarre-boxe to the hangmans budget. **1660** T. GOUGE *Chr. Directions* xviii. (1831) 96 There is not a *habeas corpus* comes to remove thy yoke-fellow, child, or friend, but it is signed by thy heavenly Father. **1775** SHERIDAN *Rivals* III. ii, Here are a great many poor words pressed into the service of this note, that would get their *habeas corpus* from any court in Christendom.

Hence **habeas corpus** *v. trans.* (*nonce-wd.*), to remove or transport as if by a writ of habeas corpus.

1817 KEATS *Wks.* (1889) III. 3 Habeas corpus'd as we are out of all wonder, curiosity, and fear.

habeck, var. HABICK.

‖**habena** (həˈbiːnə). *Anat.* and *Surg.* [L. *habēna* thong, rein, f. *habēre* to hold.]

1. *Anat.* **a.** = FRÆNUM. **b.** = HABENULA.

1839–47 TODD *Cycl. Anat.* III. 677 The pineal gland has no other connexion with the brain than that which these habenæ or peduncles secure for it.

2. *Surg.* 'Formerly applied to a bandage for keeping the lips of wounds together; a uniting bandage' (*Syd. Soc. Lex.* 1886).

1706 PHILLIPS (ed. Kersey). **1753** CHAMBERS *Cycl. Supp.*

habenar (həˈbiːnə(r)), *a.* *Anat.* [f. prec.: see -AR[1].] Of or pertaining to the habena.

‖**habendum** (həˈbɛndəm). *Law.* [L. = 'to be had' or 'to be possessed', gerundive of *habēre* to have.] That part of a deed (beginning in Law Latin with the words *habendum et tenendum*, and in Eng. deeds 'to have and to hold') which defines what estate or interest is thereby granted.

1607 MIDDLETON *Phœnix* II. ii, Now I come to the *Habendum*, to haue and to holde, vse and [etc.]. **1641** *Termes de la Ley* 179 In every deed of Conveyance there be two principall parts, the Premisses, and the Habendum. **1818** CRUISE *Digest* (ed. 2) IV. 30 The description of the things granted need not be repeated in the *habendum*; as it is sufficient that they are described in the premises. **1876** *Wharton's Law Lex.* (ed. 5) s.v. *Deed*, In annuity-deeds and money assignments, the phrase 'To have, hold, receive, and take' is the common form of *habendum*. **1884** ELPHINSTONE *Conveyancing* 100 The clause beginning 'to have and to hold' is the habendum and tenendum combined, and is generally called the habendum.

[**habenry.** Inferred from: '*Habenries*, architectural decorations of some kind, but the exact meaning of the term does not appear to be known. It occurs in Chaucer, some copies reading *barbicans*' (Halliwell). The source is Chaucer's *House of Fame* 1189 (= III. 99), where Skeat, by emendation, reads 'Babewinnes' (see BABOON 1), MSS. and early printed edd. having various misreadings: *MS. Bodl.* Rabewynnes, *MS. Pepys* Babeweuries, edd. 1532 (Thynne), 1598 (Speght) babeuries, 1602 (Speght) habeuries, 1721 (Urry) Barbicans.

1882 OGILVIE, *Habenry*, a barbican; a corner turret. [So *Cent. Dict.*] **1888** *Cassell's Encycl. Dict.*[following Halliwell].]

‖**habenula** (həˈbɛnjʊlə). *Anat.* [L. *habēnula* small thong; hence, small strip of flesh cut out of a wound (Celsus).] 'A small, superficial, grey nucleus of the optic thalamus, situated above and in front of the entrance of the posterior commissure.'

1876 *Quain's Elem. Anat.* (ed. 8) II. 551 A collection of grey matter..called the ganglion of the peduncle of the pineal gland (ganglion of the habenula).

Hence **haˈbenular** *a.*, 'ribbon-like; floating like a thong' (*Syd. Soc. Lex.* 1886).

haˈberance, obs. form of ABEARANCE.

1552 ASCHAM *Germany* 42 Personal pledges..for his good haberance.

haberchoun, obs. Sc. var. HABERGEON.

†**ˈhaberdash**, *sb.* *Obs.* Forms: 5–6 haburdassh, -dashe, haberdash(e. [app. = AF. *hapertas*, of unknown origin, perh. the name of a fabric, which occurs in an Anglo-Fr. customs list of imported peltry, furs, and fabrics, where a parallel and nearly contemporary list has *haberdassherie*. But the English word may, from its date and sense, be a back-formation from HABERDASHER, and *hapertas* may be only a bad AF. spelling of it.

Connexion with mod.Icel. *haprtask* 'haversack' is not possible.]

Petty merchandise, small wares.

1419 *Liber Albus* (Rolls) I. 225 La charge de hapertas, xiid.] **1526** SKELTON *Magnyf.* 1295, I have an hole armory of such haburdashe in store. **1578** T. N. tr. *Conq. W. India* 23 With great store of Haberdash, as bels, necklaces, beades of glasse, collers, points, pinnes, purses, needels, girdels, threed, knives, sissers, pinsers, hammers, hatchets, shirts, Coyfes, headkerchiefs..breeches, coates, clokes, caps, Marriners breeches. **1648** GAGE *West Ind.* 17 To barter with the Spaniards for their small Haberdash, or Iron, Knives, or such things which may help them in their Wars.

fig. **1550–3** *Answ. Papystycall Exhort.* A viij b, Ye vtter soche trashe And pylde haberdashe As laye longe in your mynde.

b. More frequently, ***haberdash ware, wares.***

1477 *Inv. Goods* in Earwaker *Lanc. Wills* (Chetham Soc.) 3 In Dyvers Haburdasshware xs. *c* **1550** *Disc. Common Weal Eng.* (1893) 16 All haberdashe wares, as paper, bothe whyte and browne, glasses [etc.]. **1594** BLUNDEVIL *Exerc.* v. iii. (ed. 7) 533 All sorts of Mercery or Haberdash Ware. **1625** PURCHAS *Pilgrims* II. 1644 One hundred and twentie pieces of Carsies..with divers small Haberdash wares.

†**ˈhaberdash**, *v.* *Obs.* [f. HABERDASHER.] *intr.* To deal in haberdashery or small wares.

1635 QUARLES *Embl.* II. v. (1718) 82 To haberdash In Earth's base wares. **1644** —— *Sheph. Orac.* iv, Leave to haberdash In such small pedling wares.

haberdasher (ˈhæbədæʃə(r)). Forms: 4–6 haberdassher, haburdaissher, -dassher, 4 habirdaschere, -dasshere, 5 habardashar, 6– haberdasher, (7 habber-). [Has the form of a derivative of HABERDASH *sb.* (q.v.), or of the AFr. *hapertas* (quasi **hapertassier*, **haberdassier*); but the actual nature of the relationship between these words is left doubtful by their relative dates, as well as by the undetermined relation in which *haberdash* and *hapertas* stand to each other.]

Formerly, a dealer in a variety of articles now dealt with by other trades, including caps, and probably hats: see quots. In the course of the 16th c. the trade seems to have been split into two, those of: †**a.** A dealer in, or maker of, hats and caps, a hatter (*obs.*); **b.** A dealer in small articles appertaining to dress, as thread, tape, ribbons, etc. Formerly also a drink-seller (as a dealer in 'tape' = spirituous liquor).

1311–12 *Liber Memorandorum* 53 in *Liber Albus* (Rolls) III. 433 Super diversos haberdasshers et capellarios. *c* **1386** CHAUCER *Prol.* 361 An haberdasshere [*v.rr.* habir-, habur-, -daschere, -daissher] and a Carpenter. **1502** ARNOLDE *Chron.* (1811) 108 William Warboys citezen and haburdasher of London. *c* **1515** *Cocke Lorell's B.* (Percy Soc.) 9 Salters, Towelers, and habardashars. *c* **1550** *Disc. Common Weal Eng.* (1893) 64 Haberdashers that sell french or milan cappes, glasses, Daggers, swerdes, gridles and such things. **1561** STOW *Eng. Chron.* (Howe 1615) 869/1 The Milloners, or Haberdashers, in that place, sould mousetrappes, bird cages, shooing hornes, Lanthornes, and Jews trumpes. **1594** NASHE *Unfort. Trav.* 38 Bookes, pictures, beades, crucifixes, why there was a haberdashers shop of them in euerie chamber. [**1720** STRYPE *Stow's Surv.* (1754–5) II. v. x. 278/2 Haberdashers..were also called Milliners, so called from..Milan in Italy, whence the Commodities they dealt in chiefly came; such were Owches, Brooches, Agglets, Spurs, Caps, Glasses, &c.]

a. 1566 *Act 8 Eliz.* c. 11 § 3 For the better and truer making of Cappes and Hattes within this Realme..it shalbe lefull to the Maister and Wardens of the Company of Haberdasshers within the Citie of London..to [etc.]. *c* **1572** GASCOIGNE *Fruites Warre* lxiv, The Haberdasher heapeth wealth by hattes. **1691** WOOD *Ath. Oxon.* III. 699/2 John Fisher a haberdasher of hats and mayor of Northampton. **1711** BUDGELL *Spect.* No. 161 ¶3 He..had won so many Hats, that his Parlour looked like a Haberdasher's Shop. **1711** STEELE *Ibid.* No. 187 ¶7 Mr. Sly, Haberdasher of Hats..has prepared very neat Hats, Rubbers, and Brushes.

b. 1611 COTGR., *Mercerot*, a Pedler, a paltrie Haberdasher. **1617** MINSHEU *Ductor*, An Habberdasher of small wares.. In London also called a Millenier, à Lat. *mille*. i. a thousand, as one hauing a thousand small wares to sell. **1630** MASSINGER *Renegado* II. iii, A great lady dote upon A haberdasher of small wares! **1696** PHILLIPS (ed. 5), *Haberdasher*, one that sells a great many several sorts of Wares, as Riband, Gloves, &c. Also a Seller of Hats. **1708** *Lond. Gaz.* No. 4462/4 William Andrews of London, Haberdasher of small Wares. **1745** *De Foe's Eng. Tradesman* vi. (1841) I. 38 Haberdasher [buys] of the thread merchants. **1755** JOHNSON, *Haberdasher*, one who sells small wares; a pedlar. **1845** J. SAUNDERS *Cab. Pict., Chaucer* 241 Haberdashers were originally a branch of the mercers; and dealt, like them, in small wares. **1821** P. EGAN *Life in London* II. viii. 354 The Haberdasher is busily employed in measuring out tape for his customers. **1828** 'W. T. MONCRIEFF' *Tom & Jerry* III. v. 76 The haberdasher is the whistler, otherwise the spirit-merchant, Jerry—and tape the commodity he deals in. **1893** FARMER & HENLEY *Slang* III. 243/1 *Haberdasher*, (humorously) a publican.

c. *fig.* (cf. *dealer, retailer, vendor*).

1592 NASHE *P. Penilesse* (ed. 2) 21 a, A Haberdasher of Wilde-fowle, or a Merchant venturer of daintie meat. **1597** *1st Pt. Return fr. Parnass.* IV. i. 1235 This haberdasher of lyes. **1664** J. WILSON *Project.* IV. Dram. Wks. (1874) 264 See! your haberdasher of small projects. *a* **1700** B. E. *Dict. Cant. Crew*, *Habberdasher* of Nouns and Pronouns, Schoolmaster or Usher. *a* **1764** LLOYD *New River Head* Poet. Wks. 1774 II. 65 Haberdashers of small jokes. **1827** LYTTON *Pelham* xvi, This 'Haber-dasher of pronouns' was a person of the name of Margot. **1828** *Craven Dial.* s.v., A schoolmaster, alias a haberdasher of nouns and pronouns.

d. *attrib.*

1813 *Examiner* 10 May 296/1 They are altogether haberdasher Statesmen.

Hence **haberdasheress**, a female haberdasher.

1702 T. BROWN *Lett. Dead to Living* Wks. 1760 II. 272, I found..Thalestris the Amazonian, who, as I hinted to you in my last, is become a haberdasheress of small wares.

haberdashery (ˈhæbəˌdæʃərɪ). [f. prec.: see -ERY.]

1. The goods and wares sold by a haberdasher. Also *fig.*

1419 *Liber Albus* III. I. (Rolls) 230 Les Fees de Layn de Spaigne et Haberdasshrie. **1593** NASHE *Christ's T.* (1613) 96 Those are the Syrens, that hang out their shining Silks and Veluets, and dazle Prides eyes with their deceitfull haberdashry. **1690** CHILD *Disc. Trade* (1694) 166 Our own Commodities being some rated very low, as Drapery, Silk Wares, Haberdashery. **1773** G. STEEVENS *Let.* 8 Dec. in *Garrick's Corr.* (1831) I. 588 He might have made many discoveries of consequence to us who deal in the haberdashery of words. **1796** BURKE *Regic. Peace* iii. Wks. VIII. 390 Tape and thread, and all the other small wares of haberdashery and millinery. **1851** MAYHEW *Lond. Labour* I. 373 A highly respectable draper told me that he never could thoroughly understand where hosiery, haberdashery, or drapery, began or ended. **1873** MISS BROUGHTON *Nancy* I. 133, I am involved in a whirlwind of haberdashery, Brussels lace, diamonds. **1923** KIPLING *Independence* 31 He may be festooned with the whole haberdashery of success.

2. The shop or establishment of a haberdasher.

1813 SCOTT *Trierm.* II. Interl. iii, A walking haberdashery, Of feathers, lace, and fur.

3. *attrib.* and *Comb.*, as ***haberdashery-ware***, etc.

1547 *Privy Council Acts* (1890) II. 467 A ship laden with wynes, sylkes, and other haberdasshery wares. **1745** *De Foe's Eng. Tradesman* xlv. (1841) II. 161 Haberdashery-ware from Holland. **1754** RICHARDSON *Grandison* (1781) I. xxxv. 245 A kind of haberdashery shop. **1797–1805** S. & HT. LEE *Canterb. T.* V. 40 In the haberdashery line.

haberdepoies, -poys(e, obs. ff. AVOIRDUPOIS.

1565–73 COOPER *Thesaurus, Amphora*..a pound and a halfe of haberdepoyse weight. **1603** OWEN *Pembrokesh.* (1891) 139 Sold by the haberdepoies pound.

†**haberdine** (ˈhæbədiːn, -dɪn). *Obs.* Forms: 4–6 haburden(ne, 5–7 haberdyne, 6 haberden, -dyn, 6–7 habberdine, haberdin, haberdeen, 7–8 habberdin, -dyn, 6– 9 haberdine, 9 haberdden. [The same word as MDu. *abberdaen* (Du. *abberdaan*), var. of *labberdaen*, supposed by De Vries to be derived from the name of a Basque district, the *tractus Lapurdanus*, F. *le Labourd*, or from *Lapurdum* ancient name of Bayonne; the Basques having been the first to engage in the cod-fishery. The loss of *l-* points to the passing of the word through French: Godef. has *Labordean* 1577; Cotgr. has *abordean, habordean, labordean*; but earlier evidence for the word in Fr. is wanting.] The name of a large sort of cod, used esp. for salting; salt or sun-dried cod.

It was sometimes formerly considered a different species from the common cod and classified as *Asellus Islandicus*.

1300 *Wardr. Acc. Edw. I* (1787) 118 In vendicione diversis per diversa precia 5496 stokf[ish] et Aberden'. [**1370** in Rogers *Agric. & Prices* I. xxiv. 616 In 1370, 140 haburdenne are bought at 1s. each.] **1496** *Naval Accounts Hen. VII* (1896) 166 Ffyssh, cc haberdyne at xxxiij[s] iiij[d] the hundred-lxvj[s] viij[d]. **1530** in Rymer *Foedera* (1710) XIV. 375 Cod and Haberden Eight Hundred. **1538** FITZHERB. *Just. Peas* 156 Fyshers that actually labour to take Lyng Haberdine Lobfyshe. **1573** TUSSER *Husb.* xxiii. (1878) 63 Broome fagot is best to drie haberden on. **1621** BURTON *Anat. Mel.* I. ii. I. i. (1651) 68 Indurate Fish as Ling..Red-herrings.. Haberdine. **1655** MOUFET & BENNET *Health's Improv.* (1746) 230 Our Blood is..corrupted with filthy Fish..salt Herrings, red Herrings, Sprats, Haberdin. **1708** J. CHAMBERLAYNE *St. Gt. Brit.* I. III. ii. (1743) 154 Cod fish, Haberdine, Ling &c. have 124 to the c. [**1867** SMYTH *Sailor's Word-bk.*, *Haberdden*, cod or stock fish dried and cured on board: that cured at Aberdeen was the best.]

b. More fully ***haberdine-fish.***

1573–80 BARET *Alv.* F 578 Habberdine fish, *Asellus salitus*. **1771** PENNANT *Tour Scot.* (1790) 138 Dried cod fish, at that period known by the name of Habberdyn fish.

habergeon (ˈhæbədʒən, həˈbɜːdʒən), **haubergeon** (ˈhɔːbədʒən). Forms: *α.* 3 haubergeun, 4–6 -oun(e, 4–9 -on; also 4–5 hawberjoun, *Sc.* haubrischoun(e, hawbyrschown, haubersion(e, 5 hawburgon, -byrgon, *Sc.* awbyrchowne, 6 haubergyon, haulbergyn, 9 hawbergeon. *β.* ? 3, 4– habergeon; also 3–4 haberion, habiryun, 4–5 haber-, habar-, habir-, habour-, habur-, habyr-, -geon, -gion, -gioun, -gyn(e, -gon, -goun, -gown, -goyne, -jon(e, -joun(e, -jown(e, -jeoun, -jeon, -jun(e, -yon(e, 5 haburioun, 6 habergyn, habarion, habbergion, -jon, -jeoun; *Sc.* haberjone, -choun, -shoune, haberschone, abrichon. (About 100 variants.) [ME. a. F. *haubergeon* (12th c. in Hatz.-Darm.), deriv. (treated as dim.) of OF. *hauberc*, now *haubert*: see HAUBERK and -ON. In Eng. from an early date reduced to *ha-*, though examples of *hau-*, *haw-*, under French influence, contemporary or historical, occur down to the present day. The word has been since the 16th c. only historical, and it was app. after it had become obs. as a living word, that the pronunciation (həˈbɜːdʒən) or (həˈbɜdʒiːɒn), found in Milton, Butler,

Glover, etc., and in some modern dictionaries, arose.]

A sleeveless coat or jacket of mail or scale armour, originally smaller and lighter than a HAUBERK, but sometimes app. the same as that.

[**1285** *Act 13 Edw. I* c. 6 A disz liveree de terre.. haubergeun chapel espe e cutel.] *c* **1340** *Cursor M.* 7521 (Trin.) Helme haburioun [*Gött.* habiryun] on him þei did. **1375** BARBOUR *Bruce* XI. 130 Mony helmys and hawbyrschownys. *c* **1375** *Sc. Leg. Saints, Margaret* 279 Scho wes cled in haubersione Of treutht and of deuocione. **1377** LANGL. *P. Pl.* B. XVIII. 23 In his helme and in his haberioun. **1382** WYCLIF *1 Sam.* xvii. 5 Goliath..was clothid with a maylid hawberioun [**1388** an haburioun hokid]. **1382** —— *Eph.* vi. 14 Þe haberioun of riȝtwysnesse. *c* **1386** CHAUCER *Sir Thopas* 150 Nexte his sherte an Aketoun And ouer that an haubergeoun [*v. rr.* habyrioun, habergoun, haberioun]. **1411** *E.E. Wills* (1882) 19 To Henre my sonne, an aburioun, a ketil Hatte. *c* **1425** WYNTOUN *Cron.* VIII. xxxiii. 22 Throw thre fauld of Awbyrchowne. *c* **1440** *Promp. Parv.* 220/1 Haburyone [*v.r.* haburgyn], or hawberk, *lorica.* *c* **1450** *Mirour Saluacioun* 4129 The haubergeonne whilk his body shuld kepe both vp and doune. **1530** PALSGR. 229/2 Haulbergyn of mayle. **1535** COVERDALE *Rev.* ix. 9 They had habbergions As it were habbergions of yron. **1590** SPENSER *F.Q.* II. vi. 29 Their mightie strokes their haberjeons dismayld. **1600** FAIRFAX *Tasso* I. lxxii. 15 Some dond a curace, some a corslet bright, An hawberke some, and some a haberion. **1611** BIBLE *2 Chron.* xxvi. 14 And Vzziah prepared for them..shields, and speares, and helmets, and habergions. **1663** BUTLER *Hud.* I. iii. 537 The shot let fly.. Lodg'd in Magnano's brass habergeon. **1671** MILTON *Samson* 1119 Then put on all they gorgeous arms, thy helmet And brigandine of brass, thy broad habergeon. **1679** BLOUNT *Anc. Tenures* 23 Their Knights and free-holders to find Corslets and Haubergeons. **1787** GLOVER *Athenaid* VIII. (R.), Above, bright maile, habergeons scal'd in gold. **1864** SIR F. PALGRAVE *Norm. & Eng.* III. 306 The knights are now seen..each covered with his hawbergeon of mail. **1879** BROWNING *Tray* 4 Sir Olaf, the good knight, did don His helm and eke his habergeon.

†**b.** Worn as a rough garment for penance. *Obs.*

c **1386** CHAUCER *Pars. T.* ¶978 Werynge of heyres or of stamyn, or of haubergeons on hire naked flesshe..and swiche manere penances. *Ibid.* ¶980 Of whiche Ihesu crist is moore apayed than of heyres or haubergeouns or hauberkes.

†**c.** Applied to the elytron of a beetle. *Obs.*

a **1637** B. JONSON *Sad Sheph.* II. ii, Scaly beetles, with their habergeons, That make a humming murmur as they fly.

Hence **'habergeoned** (†**hauberiounyd**) *a.*, equipped with a habergeon.

1382 WYCLIF *1 Macc.* iv. 7 Thei sawen the tentis of heithen men stronge, and men hauberiounyd.

†**'haberjet, hauberget.** *Obs.* Also 6 **hauberject**, 8 **haberject**, 9 **halberject**, **-git**. [In med.L. *haubergetum*, a word of obscure origin, app. related to HAUBERK and HABERGEON.] A kind of cloth named in Magna Carta, and in some ancient documents.

[**1216** *Magna Carta 1 Hen. III* §23 Sit..una latitudo pannorum tinctorum & Russettorum & Haubergetorum, scilicet due Ulne infra listas.] **1502** tr. *Great Charter* in Arnolde *Chron.* (1811) 219 And one largenes dyed clothes and of russetis and of hauberiectis, that is to sey two ellis betwyxt the listis. **1706** PHILLIPS (ed. Kersey), *Haberjects, or Haubergets*, a kind of Cloth mention'd in Magna Charta, and other Records. **1865** KINGSLEY *Herew.* II. i. 10 Clothing of..grising or halbergit and lambs' skins. **1861** RILEY *Liber Albus* Gloss. s.v. *Hapertas*, In *Mag. Rot.* 14 *John*, mention is made of 3043 ells *de halbergo albo* 'of white halberject' for the king's use.

†**'habick.** *Obs.* Also **habeck**. [Etymol. unknown.] 'An instrument used in dressing cloth' (Cussans *Handbk. Heraldry* 116).

1660 *Guillim's Heraldry* IV. vii. 288 Sable, a Cheuron Ermine, between two Habicks in chief, and a Tessell in base, proper. This is the bearing of the worshipfull Company of the Cloath-workers. **1864** BOUTELL *Her. Hist. & Pop.* xxi. §11 (ed. 3) 369.

habide, obs. form of ABIDE.

c **1300** *Cursor M.* 22688 Under a fel þai sal habide. *c* **1400** MAUNDEV. (Roxb.) i. 4 It will noȝt habyde þerin.

habil, obs. form of ABLE, HABILE.

habilable ('hæbɪləb(ə)l), *a. rare.* [= mod.F. *habillable*, f. *habiller* to clothe: see -ABLE.] Capable of being clothed.

1831 CARLYLE *Sart. Res.* I. v, The whole habitable and habilable globe.

habilament, variant of HABILIMENT.

habilatory (hə'bɪlətərɪ), *a. rare.* [Arbitrary f. F. *habiller* to dress, or Eng. *habili-ment*, after adjs. etymologically formed in *-atory.*] Having reference to dressing.

1827 LYTTON *Pelham* lxxix. (D.) Accustomed to penetrate the arcana of habilatory art. **1831** CARLYLE *Sart. Res.* I. v, In all his Modes and habilatory endeavours. **1865** —— *Fredk. Gt.* XVIII. vii. VII. 207 Valuable effects, cosmetic a good few of them, habilatory, artistic.

habile ('hæbɪl), *a.* [A variant of ABLE (formerly *hable*, *abil*, etc.), conformed in 16-17th c. to mod.F. *habile* or Lat. *habilis*, and, in modern use, (sense 4) to some extent differentiated: see ABLE *a.*]

†**1.** Fitted, suited; fit, suitable; competent (*to do* something); = ABLE *a.* 2. Chiefly *Sc. Obs.*

c **1425** WYNTOUN *Cron.* IX. xxvi. 78 To that, baith curtas and cunnand He wes, bath habyll and avenand. **1533** BELLENDEN *Livy* IV. 334 Quhilk wes mare habil to have desirit than to have obtenit the tribunate. **1678** MARVELL *Def. Howe* Wks. 1875 IV. 184 Apt and habile for any congenerous action. **1715** *Wodrow Corr.* II. 24 The most habile way to prevent the ruin of this church. **1795** MACKNIGHT *Apostol. Epist.* (1820) I. 624 Many habile and disinterested witnesses.

†**2.** Manageable, handy; = ABLE *a.* 1. *Obs.*

1741 BETTERTON *Eng. Stage* v. 67 The Hands are the most habil members of the Body, and the most easily turned to all sides.

†**3.** Having the capacity or power (*to do* a thing); = ABLE *a.* 4. *Obs.*

1558 KENNEDY *Compend. Tractiue* 71 (Jam.) To be the mair habyl to keip the command of God. **1678** GALE *Crt. Gentiles* III. 32 That God's influxe doth..render the subject habile to act.

4. Having general readiness; handy, ready; skilful, deft, adroit, dexterous.

1485 CAXTON *Chas. Gt.* (1880) 169 Ryol sawe the stroke come, and was habylle, and lepte a syde. **1670** G. H. *Hist. Cardinals* II. III. 189 The most proper and habile person. **1766** MRS. E. GRIFFITH *Lett. Henry & Frances* IV. 38 'Tis like practising Fencing with the left Hand..it renders one more habile, certainly. **1840** T. A. TROLLOPE *Summer in Brittany* II. 223 The most habile writer of monthly fashions. **1886** H. CONWAY *Living or Dead* I. viii. 157 The cards fell quickly from his habile fingers. **1890** *Harper's Mag.* Nov. 894/1 That general training which made educated Americans of earlier generations so habile and adroit.

habiliment (hə'bɪlɪmənt). Forms: α. 5 **abily-**, **abyl(l)y-**, 5-6 **abyle-**, 5-7 **abille-**, **abili-**, 6 **abbili-**, **abilla-**, 7 **abilli-**, **abilia-**, **abliment**. β. Sc. forms (chiefly in senses 1, 3, 4) 6 **abulye-**, **abuilye-**, **abuilie-**, 6-7 **abulȝea-**, **abuilȝie-**, **abulȝa-**, 9 **abuilyiement**. γ. 5 **habyl(l)e-**, **habyly-**, 5-7 **habille-**, 6 **hable-**, 6-7 **habile-**, 6-8 **habilli-**, **habilla-**, 7-9 **habila-**, 6- **habiliment**. See also ABILIMENT, BILIMENT. [a. OF. *habillement*, *abillement*, f. *habiller* to render fit, fit out, f. *habile* fit, suitable: see ABLE. In early use often spelt without initial *h*, esp. in the senses which connected themselves with ABLE, ABILITY; but with the gradual restriction of the word to sense 4 (like mod.F. *habiller*, *habillement*, obviously influenced in sense by F. *habit* clothing), the *h* has been restored. (The Sc. *ly*, *lȝ*, represents Fr. *ll mouillé*.)]

1. (without *pl.*) Outfit, accoutrement, equipment, array, attire, dress. (Now only of personal attire.)

1470-85 MALORY *Arthur* I. xviii, Alle maner of abylement that pretendith to the werre. *c* **1477** CAXTON *Jason* 30 b, Hauyng the forme and habylement of a knight. **1536** BELLENDEN *Cron. Scot.* (1821) I. p. lvi, Thair abulyement was..maid..efter the general gise of the cuntre. **1552** LYNDESAY *Monarche* 4546 Rycht hartfully content Of meit, drynk, and abuilyement. **1590** SPENSER *F.Q.* I. vi. 30 Straunge Lady in so straunge habiliment. **1609** SKENE *Reg. Maj.* 146 The costlie excesse of cleithing, and abulzament of mens bodies. **1753** HANWAY *Trav.* (1762) I. III. l. 229 To keep pace with this romantic extension of habilliment. **1812** S. ROGERS *Columbus* App. 14 In rich habiliment Two Strangers at the Convent-gate. **1842** POE *Murders Rue Morgue* Wks. 1864 I. 202 Numerous changes of habiliment. *fig.* **1894** *Athenæum* 22 Dec. 363/2 The style is the habiliment of the spirit.

†**2.** *pl.* Fittings, apparatus, furniture, gear, outfit, rigging; as of a ship. *Obs.*

1483 CAXTON *Gold. Leg.* 92/1 The cordes and other habyllemens of the shippe bracke.

†**3.** *pl.* Munitions, appliances, implements, or apparatus of war; weapons, warlike stores, etc.

(In this sense the initial *h* was more commonly omitted, doubtless from the recognized connexion with *able, ability*, quasi 'things making *able* for war'.)

1422, etc. [see ABILIMENT]. *a* **1467** GREGORY *Chron.* (Camden) 145 Alle the abyllymentys of werre..as welle pouders, gounnys, and arblastys, schott, or othyr artyleres. **1495** *Act 11 Hen. VII* c. 64 *Preamble*, Shippes with all abilimentis of Werre. **1569** STOCKER tr. *Diod. Sic.* I. iv. 7 To prepare for all such necessarie hablements and engines of warre as were meete. *a* **1642** SIR W. MONSON *Naval Tracts* v. (1704) 489/1 Ammunition, Victuals, or other Abilliments for the War. **1686** *Lond. Gaz.* No. 2120/2 Armour, Munition, Stores..Ordnance, or other Habiliments of War.

†**b.** *esp.* Personal accoutrements for war; armour, warlike apparel; also the trappings of a horse. *Obs.*

c **1489** CAXTON *Sonnes of Aymon* i. 53 Soo beganne eueriche of theym to seke his armes and habylymentes. **1602** MARSTON *Ant. & Mel.* II. Wks. 1856 I. 28 In glistering habilliments of armes. **1611** SPEED *Hist. Gt. Brit.* IX. xvi. §51 He armed himselfe in the dead Knights abillements, with guilt spurres. **1816** SCOTT *Old Mort.* vii, To return his armour and abulyiements at a moment when it was impossible to find a suitable delegate in his stead.

4. *pl.* The apparel, vestments, or garments appropriate to any office or occasion. Applied also, jocularly or grandiloquently, to ordinary clothes. (The chief extant sense.)

(In this sense initial *h* has always prevailed; the connexion with *able, ability*, being less obvious, and that with mod.F. *habit, habillement* more so.)

1491 CAXTON *Vitas Patr.* (W. de W. 1495) III Clothynge and habyllements of the sayd holy fader. **1533** BELLENDEN *Livy* I. (1822) 35 He cled him with riche and riall abulyementis. **1548** HALL *Chron., Hen. VII*, 28 b, Wyth yͤ gartier, coller, mantell, and other habiliamentes apperteyninge to the companyons of the sayde noble ordre. **1589** PUTTENHAM *Eng. Poesie* III. i. (Arb.) 149 They want their courtly habillements. **1591** SHAKS. *Two Gent.* IV. i. 11 My riches, are these poore habiliments. **1642** ROGERS *Naaman* 474 To put on all those abiliments upon him, to kill the fat Calf to welcome him. **1770** MRS. BOSCAWEN in *Mrs. Delany's Life & Corr.* Ser. II. I. 305 We have no winter habiliments. **1848** MRS. JAMESON *Sacr. & Leg. Art* (1850) 218 The Saviour is seen in the habiliments of a gardener. **1867** MISS BRADDON *R. Godwin* II. ii. 30 She saw George Stanmore in his everyday habiliments.

fig. **1614** SIR W. LEIGHTON in Farr *S.P. Jas. I.* 265 All curious quaint abiliments exil'd, In humblest habite now my verse compil'd. *a* **1656** BP. HALL *Rem. Wks.* 98 The earth decks herself in her fresh abiliments of blossomes. **1822** KEBLE *Serm.* i. (1848) 8 Mistaking the circumstances and outward habiliments of things for the things themselves.

†**5.** Anything worn as an ornament; = BILIMENT.

c **1530** LD. BERNERS *Arth. Lyt. Bryt.* (1814) 8 Pyers.. bought for them abylementes and jewelles. **1541** *Act 33 Hen. VIII* c. 5 Any frenche hoode or bonet of veluet, with any habiliment paste or edge of golde perle or stone. **1560** BIBLE (Genev.) *Gen.* xxiv. 22 The man took a golden abillement of half a shekell weight. **1621** AINSWORTH *Annot. Pentat., Gen.* xxiv. 22 Eare-ring: or abillement, jewell, ouch: which was hanged sometime on the eare.

†**6.** *fig.* Mental equipment or qualification; capacity; *pl.* abilities, faculties, powers (of mind). *Obs.*

1585 ABP. SANDYS *Serm.* (1841) 2 How can the Holy Ghost..but require us to bestow all the forces and habiliments we have? **1604** T. WRIGHT *Passions* III. iv. 102 If the impediments of Nature bee but small, And the habiliments otherwise great. **1612** T. TAYLOR *Comm. Titus* i. 9 Wouldest thou haue eloquence added to all these former abilliments? **1633** FORD *Broken Ht.* v. ii, Never lived gentlemen of greater merit, Hope or abiliment to steer a kingdom. *a* **1640** JACKSON *Creed* XI. xlvi. §10 There is a freedom or abiliment to do that which is pleasant and acceptable unto God.

Hence **habili'mental** *a.*, of or relating to attire. **habili'mentary** *a.*, dealing with habiliments.

1837 *New Monthly Mag.* LI. 466 Embodied representatives of antiquity in a moral as well as habilimental point of view. **1845** *Blackw. Mag.* LVII. 731 The result of his habilimentary effort. **1882** HARDY *Two on a Tower* II. vii. 109 Researches among habilimental hulls and husks.

ha'bilimented, *ppl. a.* [f. prec. sb. + -ED².] Equipped, arrayed, apparelled, dressed.

1607 DEKKER *Whore of Babylon* Wks. 1873 II. 257 Habilimented gloriously for warre. **1630** J. TAYLOR (Water P.) *Taylors Frauds* Wks. III. 98 A Chimney-sweeper's wife ..Habilimented like the Diamond Queene. **1630** H. LORD *Persees* Ep. Ded., Habilimented in the ridiculous vesture of his owne Superstitions. **1892** *Chamb. Jrnl.* 1 Oct. 625/1 The staid and decorously habilimented banker.

†**ha'bilitate**, *ppl. a. Obs.* [ad. med.L. *habilitāt-us*, pa. pple. of *habilitā-re*: see next.] Endowed with ability; rendered able; capacitated, qualified.

1622 BACON *Hen. VII*, 12 Not legall, nor habilitate to serue in Parliament.

habilitate (hə'bɪlɪteɪt), *v.* Also ABILITATE. [f. L. *habilitāt-* ppl. stem of *habilitāre* to make fit, enable, f. *habilitās*, aptitude, ABILITY.]

†**1.** *trans.* To endow with ability or capacity; to capacitate, qualify. *Obs.*

1604 T. WRIGHT *Passions* VI. 322 The internall gifts of God..fortifie vs against vice, and habilitate exceedingly to vertue. **1678** MARVELL *Def. Howe* Wks. 1875 IV. 187 A superadded influence, which may habilitate them for action. **1819** SOUTHEY *Hist. Brazil* III. xl. 527 Till a second order from the King should habilitate them so to do.

b. To furnish with means, esp. for the working of a mine. [After Sp. *habilitar.*]

1824 *Ann. Reg.* 212* He then proposed, not to habilitate the mine in the usual way, but to lend money to the miner, that he himself might pay the workmen.

2. *intr.* for *refl.* To qualify oneself for office; *spec.* to qualify as teacher in a German University. [After Ger. *habilitiren.*]

1881 *Contemp. Rev.* June 925 He meant to habilitate as a privat-docent when he returned. **1882-3** SCHAFF *Encycl. Relig. Knowl.* II. 1612 In 1811 he habilitated at Heidelberg with the dissertation, 'De fidei..idea'.

3. *trans.* To clothe, dress, habit. *rare.*

1885 *Longm. Mag.* Dec. 197 Species variously habilitated in artistic patterns. **1888** R. DOWLING *Miracle Gold* II. xxiii. 183 Devils..habilitated in flesh for evil purposes.

Hence **ha'bilitator** [after Sp. *habilitador*], in western U.S. one who habilitates a mine, or furnishes capital for its working under contract with the proprietors.

1889 in *Cent. Dict.*

habilitation (hə,bɪlɪ'teɪʃən). Also ABILITATION. [ad. med.L. *habilitātiōn-em*, n. of action f. *habilitāre*: see HABILITATE *ppl. a.*

Although the obvious connexion with ABILITY led to the dropping of initial *h* in this and the preceding word, in 17th c. the direct Latin derivation finally preserved it.]

The action of enabling or endowing with ability or fitness; capacitation, qualification.

1612 BACON *Ess., Greatness Kingd.* (Arb.) 483 The Things, which we formerly haue spoken of, are but Habilitations towards Armes: And what is Habilitation without Intention and Act? **1713** *Treaty w. Spain* in C. King *Brit. Merch.* (1721) III. 169 All Augmentations of Duties which were introduced in the said Ports.. on occasion of the War, or under the Title of Habilitation, or any other whatsoever, ceasing and being taken away. **1831** *Fraser's Mag.* III. 617 The habilitation of new maritime ports for expediting the intercourse with America. **1861** A. MCCAUL *Ess Proph.* in *Aids to Faith* (1861) 88 He.. had no permanent habilitation to declare the will of God. **1868** M. PATTISON *Academ. Org.* v. 213 I propose that the honour-degrees (M.A., etc.) should of themselves form the habilitation for the office of tutor.

b. The advancing of money on the security of a mine, to enable the owner to work it. (*U.S.*, from Sp. *habilitacion.*)

hability (həˈbɪlɪtɪ). Also 5-6 -te, 6-7 -tie. [An early form of ABILITY, after OF. *habileté*; in this, the *h* was rarely preserved after 1650; but in the 19th c. it has sometimes been restored in sense 2, which goes with *habile* and mod.F. *habileté*.]

†**1.** Early spelling of ABILITY, q.v. *Obs.*

1430-1678 [see ABILITY]. **1723** *State Russia* II. 77 All their Hability consists in crying out with a loud Voice to the Idols.

2. The quality of being habile; deftness; readiness; easy familiarity. [After mod.F. *habileté*.] *rare.*

1840 *Fraser's Mag.* XXII. 64 An hability of conduct which properly constitutes genius in war. **1889** J. M. ROBERTSON *Ess. towards Critical Method* 73 Hability in or familiarity with a given style or form affects our appreciation of it.

habillament, -ement, obs. ff. HABILIMENT.

†**habille,** *v. Obs.* Forms: 5 habyle, -ylle, abele, 5-6 habyll, 5-7 **habille.** [a. F. *habiller, abillier* (13th c. in Hatz.-Darm.), to fit, fit out, put in order, dress, clothe, repr. a late L. type **habiliāre*, f. *habilis* (see HABILE and ABLE); in later use associated with *habit* clothing. Cf. also ABLE *v.* 1, 2, and the Sc. form ABUILYIET.]

1. *trans.* To fit, adapt; = ABLE *v.* 1.

1430-40 LYDG. *Bochas* III. xiii. 86 They ought of reason them self to habyle To haue science of Philosophie.

2. To fit out; to accoutre, array, attire, esp. for war; to apparel, dress; = ABLE *v.* 2.

a **1450** *Knt. de la Tour* (1868) 141 She went into her chaumbre and abeled her self. **1481** CAXTON *Godfrey* i. 19 He dyde do make agayn the chirches, and habylled the holy places. **1489** —— *Faytes of A.* I. vii. 17 Be he habylled rychely in harnoys and mountures. **1491** —— *Vitas Patr.* (W. de W. 1495) I. li. 108 a/2 The holy man Abraham thus habilled and arayed.. lepe up on an horse. *Ibid.* 111 To habylle and put theim in armes. **1652** F. KIRKMAN *Clerio & Lozia* 128 He stayed there so long till Lozia was habilled.

3. To make or pronounce competent, to enable, qualify; = ABLE *v.* 4 b.

1530 PALSGR. 576/2, I habyll, as a man to do a thyng, I make him able, or thynke him suffycient.. I was habylled to handell this mater by better men than you be.

habirgeon, -joun, etc., obs. ff. HABERGEON.

habit (ˈhæbɪt), *sb.* Forms: *α.* 3-5 abit, abyt, 3-6 abite, abyte, (5 abbyte, 6 abbit, -et(te, -ytte, *Sc.* -eit). *β.* 4-7 habite, 5-6 habyte, (5 habet, 6 habitt, habbet, -ett(e, *Sc.* habeit, 6-7 habette), 5- **habit.** [a. OF. *habit, abit* (12th c. in Littré) = Pr. *abit, habit*, It. *abito*; ad. L. *habitus*, noun of action (*u*-stem), from *habēre* to have, *refl.* to be constituted, to be.]

The sense development, as seen in Latin and the modern languages taken together, is thus: *orig.* Holding, having, 'havour'; hence the way in which one holds or has oneself, i.e. the mode or condition in which one is, exists, or exhibits oneself, *a*) externally; hence demeanour, outward appearance, fashion of body, mode of clothing oneself, dress, habitation; *b*) in mind, character, or life; hence, mental constitution, character, disposition, way of acting, comporting oneself, or dealing with things, habitual or customary way (of acting, etc.), personal custom, accustomedness. This development was largely completed in ancient Latin, and had received some extension in OF., before the word became English; in our language, senses were taken, from time to time, from Fr. or L., without reference to their original order of development; hence the chronological order in Eng. is in no way parallel to the original; and the arrangement below is only partly chronological. In mod.F. the word is narrowed down to our branch I, other senses being supplied by *habitude*; thus Eng. 'habit' is co-extensive with the two French words, and its chief sense corresponds not to F. *habit* but to F. *habitude.*

I. Fashion or mode of apparel, dress.

1. a. Bodily apparel or attire; clothing, raiment, dress. *arch.*

a **1225** *Ancr. R.* 12 þe onnesse of o luue & of o wil, þet heo alle habbeð imene wiðinnen hore abit, þet is on. **13..** *E.E. Allit. P.* B. 141 þe abyt þat þou hatz vpon, no halyday hit menskez. **1483** CAXTON *Gold. Leg.* 68/1 Saul thenne changed his habyte and clothyng and dyde on other clothyng. **1592** R. JOHNSON *9 Worthies* F iij, The verie aspect of his outwarde abite. **1607** SHAKS. *Timon* IV. iii. 113 It is her habite onely, that is honest, Her selfe's a Bawd. **1634** SIR T. HERBERT *Trav.* 24 Their habit like to Adams, a few Plaintaine leaves only fixt about their middles. **1651** EVELYN *Diary* 6 Sept., He went about in womens habite. **1725** POPE *Odyss.* IV. 336 In the vile habit of a village slave. **1809** PINKNEY *Trav. France* 111 The chief peculiarity in his habit was a deep lace ruff.

b. with *a* and *pl.* A set or suit of clothes, a dress (of some specified kind). *arch.*

a **1420** HOCCLEVE *De Reg. Princ.* 414 Undir an olde poore habite reignethe ofte Grete vertu. *c* **1440** *Gesta Rom.* lxvi. 305 (Harl. MS.) Weddid.. In a simple Abyt. **1521** *Mem. Ripon* (Surtees) I. 183 To have oon abbit after such fourme. *c* **1665** MRS. HUTCHINSON *Mem. Col. Hutchinson* (1846) 348 The colonel himself had on that day a habit which was pretty rich but grave. *a* **1691** BOYLE *Hist. Air* (1692) 170 Being thinly clothed with one of the digger's habits. **1761-2** HUME *Hist. Eng.* (1806) III. 465 She dressed herself in a rich habit of silk and velvet. **1770** LANGHORNE *Plutarch* (1879) I. 104/1 Women.. were not to go out of town with more than three habits. **1808** *Sk. Charact.* (1813) I. 180 [They] went on horseback, in a uniform habit, all blue and silver.

c. *pl.* Clothes, garments, habiliments. *arch.*

c **1477** CAXTON *Jason* 81 b, Lo here my habytes that be requysite. **1598** YONG *Diana* 257 Your habites denie you to be of any place heereabouts. **1634** MILTON *Comus* 157 Lest the place And my quaint habits breed astonishment. **1734** tr. *Rollin's Anc. Hist.* (1827) V. 170 The latter had put on women's habits over their armour. **1796** MORSE *Amer. Geog.* II. 271 [The bodies of] two princes in the habits they used to wear.

d. Hence in *sing.* A garment; a gown or robe. *arch.*

1714 GAY *Trivia* I. 43 Thy Doily Habit. **1728** T. SHERIDAN *Persius* v. (1739) 66 The Toga was the Habit worn in Peace. **1771** MRS. HARRIS in *Priv. Lett. Ld. Malmesbury* I. 214 Mr. Cambridge borrowed a dress for her, which was pretty and fine, the habit muslin with green and gold sprigs, with a turban and veil. **1852** MRS. JAMESON *Leg. Madonna* (1857) 19 St. Catherine of Siena, her habit spangled with stars.

e. *transf.* and *fig.* Outward form or appearance; guise; 'dress', 'garb'.

1549 COVERDALE, etc. *Erasm. Par. Heb.* 2 Hauing vpon hym the habite of mans body. **1618** WITHER *Motto, Nec Habeo* Wks. (1633) 518, I will ever finde Meanes to maintaine a habit for my Minde Of Truth in graine. **1669** GALE *Crt. Gentiles* I. I. ii. §9 Though Plato thus.. disfigured the habit of his Jewish Traditions. **1824** LONGF. *Autumn* 5 The silvery habit of the clouds. *a* **1839** PRAED *Poems* II. 13 Tory to-day, and Whig to-morrow, All habits and all shapes he wore.

2. *spec.* **a.** The dress or attire characteristic of a particular rank, degree, profession, or function; *esp.* the dress of a religious order; ***the habit***, the monastic order or profession (cf. 'the cowl').

c **1290** *S. Eng. Leg.* I. 20/45 Him-sulf he nam þe Abite þere: and Monek formest bi-cam. *c* **1330** R. BRUNNE *Chron.* (1810) 172 His abite he gan forsake, his ordre lete alle doune. **1362** LANGL. *P. Pl.* A. Prol. 3 In Habite of an Hermite. [**1393** C. In Abit as an Ermite.] *c* **1386** CHAUCER *Monk's T.* 353 In kinges abyt went hir sones tuo. *c* **1430** *Hymns Virg.* (1867) 67 Goo stele an abite, & bicome a frere. **1538** STARKEY *England* I. iv. 127 Frerys whome you wold juge to be borne in the habyte, they are so lytyl and yong. **1642** HOWELL *For. Trav.* (Arb.) 50 So that a Biscayner is capable to be a Cavalier of any of the three habits. **1673** RAY *Journ. Low C.* 17 The several Faculties.. are distinguished by their Habits: Divinity-Students wear constantly Gowns and square Caps. **1709** STRYPE *Ann. Ref.* I. xliii. 471 Puritans, that is, such as refused the habits. **1777** ROBERTSON *Hist. Amer.* (1778) II. v. 129 Magellan, whom the king honoured with the habit of St. Jago. **1827** HALLAM *Const. Hist.* (1876) I. ii. 102 The foreign reformers then in England.. expressed their dissatisfaction in seeing these habits retained. **1894** J. T. FOWLER *Adamnan* Introd. 77 While walking his hands were clasped under his habit.

b. In the Greek Church: ***lesser habit***, the dress of the proficients or monastics of the second degree. ***great*** or ***great angelic habit***, the dress of the monastics of the third degree, termed the perfects.

1772 J. G. KING *Grk. Ch. Russia* 366 [After completing their novitiate] they proceed to take the lesser habit or *σχῆμα*. *Ibid.*, They take.. last of all, the great angelic habit.

3. = RIDING-HABIT: A dress worn by ladies on horseback; a lady's riding-dress.

[**1666** EVELYN *Diary* 13 Sept., The Queene was now in her cavalier riding habit. **1711** STEELE *Spect.* No. 104 ¶3 The Model of this Amazonian Hunting-Habit for Ladies, was, as I take it, first imported from France.] **1798** JANE AUSTEN *Northang. Abb.* (1870) II. vi. 130 Her habit therefore was thrown off with all possible haste. **1824** SCOTT *Redgauntlet* ch. xvii, The elegant compromise betwixt male and female attire, which has now acquired, *par excellence*, the name of a *habit.* **1855** TENNYSON *Maud.* I. xx. i, Whether The habit, hat, and feather, Or the frock and gipsy bonnet Be the neater and completer. **1879** WHYTE-MELVILLE *Riding Recoll.* vii. (ed. 7) 121 The habit and the side-saddle. **1882** MISS BRADDON *Mt. Royal* vii, The St. Aubyn girls were breakfasting in their habits and hats.

II. External deportment, constitution, or appearance; habitation.

†**4.** Bearing, demeanour, deportment, behaviour; posture. *Obs.*

1413 *Pilgr. Sowle* (Caxton 1483) IV. v. 60 Me semyth by semblaunt and by habyte that ye shold be Iustyce. **1489** CAXTON *Faytes of A.* III. i. 168 A stately man of habyte of chere and of maynten. **1586** MARLOWE *1st Pt. Tamburl.* I. ii, Noble and mild this Persian seems to be, If outward habit judge the inward man. **1613** PURCHAS *Pilgrimage* (1614) 154 So of lying or other habit of body. **1642** ROGERS *Naaman* 29 The habit and behaviour of this great Prince. **1687** SEDLEY *Bellam.* III. Wks. 1722 II. 136 What's the meaning of this Habit? I never saw a man so overjoy'd.

5. a. Bodily condition or constitution.

1576 FLEMING *Panopl. Epist.* Epit. A ij b, Of the habite of his body, or corporall proportion.. hee is a faire and well favoured Gentleman. **1626** BACON *Sylva* §354 Cardamon which.. made them grow better, and be of a more active habit. **1711** ADDISON *Spect.* No. 3 ¶3 She would revive.. out of a wasting Distemper, into a Habit of the highest Health and Vigour. **1727-51** CHAMBERS *Cycl.*, *Habit*, in medicine, is what we otherwise call the temperament or constitution of the body; whether obtained by birth, or occasioned by the manner of living. **1782** PRIESTLY *Corrupt. Chr.* I. II. 211 A being.. of a delicate tender habit. **1791** BURKE *App. Whigs* Wks. VI. 136 To bring the patient to a better habit. **1812** AMYOT *Windham* I. 4 A victim to a consumptive habit. **1844** DISRAELI *Coningsby* I. i, Originally .. of a spare habit, but now a little inclined to corpulency.

†**b.** *concr.* The bodily 'system'.

1589 COGAN *Haven Health* (1636) 4 Least.. any of the excrements should hastily be received into the habit of the body. **1652** FRENCH *Yorksh. Spa* x. 91 If it be retained in the habit of the body and veins. **1727-51** CHAMBERS *Cycl.* s.v., A thing is said to *enter the habit*, when it becomes intimately diffused throughout the body, and is conveyed to the remotest stages of circulation. **1733** CHEYNE *Eng. Malady* II. iii. §2 (1734) 138 Water.. would.. dissolve these.. Concretions.. and help to carry them out of the Habit.

†**c.** The outer part, surface, or external appearance of the body.

1652 FRENCH *Yorksh. Spa* xii. 98 The humours being drawn outwardly towards the habit of the body. **1671** GREW *Anat. Plants* III. ii. §3 (1682) 127 Some Parts of Aer, may continually pass into the Body and Blood, by the Habit, or Pores of the Skin. **1725** N. ROBINSON *Th. Physick* 316 The crass, dispirited Serum settles in the Legs, and every where outwardly upon the Habit.

6. *Zool.* and *Bot.* The characteristic mode of growth and general external appearance of an animal or plant. Hence *transf.*; e.g. in *Cryst.* the characteristic mode of formation of a crystal.

1691 RAY *Creation* (1714) 22 The same insect under a different Larva or Habit. **1794** MARTYN *Rousseau's Bot.* xxxii. 492 You know them by their air, or habit, as botanists usually call it. **1826** KIRBY & SP. *Entomol.* IV. 551 When.. you know the name of one species, and find another of the same general habit. **1854** HOOKER *Himal. Jrnls.* II. xxi. 99 Plants.. of a tufted habit. **1870** —— *Stud. Flora* 34 Exotic species with the habit of Nasturtium. **1875** WHITNEY *Life Lang.* v. 90 Languages of other habit than ours. **1895** STORY-MASKELYNE *Crystallogr.* vi. §151 Such differences, then, may generally be held to indicate a mero-symmetrical habit.

†**7.** Habitation, abode. [So in OF.] *Obs. rare.*

1603 FLORIO *Montaigne* I. xxii. (1632) 47 Our greatest vices make their first habit in us, from our infancie.

III. Mental constitution, disposition, custom.

8. The way in which a person is mentally or morally constituted; the sum of the mental and moral qualities; mental constitution, disposition, character.

c **1386** CHAUCER *Knt.'s T.* 520 And shortly turned was al vp so doun Bothe habit and eek disposicioun Of hym. **1579** LYLY *Euphues* (Arb.) 53 If we respect more the outward shape, then the inward habit. **1621** BURTON *Anat. Mel.* I. i. III. xi. (1651) 30 The principal Habits are two in number, Vertue and Vice. **1690** NORRIS *Beatitudes* (1692) 181 It argues a good Habit of Mind. **1719** YOUNG *Revenge* I. i, You .. suit the gloomy habit of my soul. **1895** *Bookman* Oct. 27/1 The lecture plan and the lecturer's habit of mind are visible throughout.

9. a. A settled disposition or tendency to act in a certain way, esp. one acquired by frequent repetition of the same act until it becomes almost or quite involuntary; a settled practice, custom, usage; a customary way or manner of acting. (The most usual current sense. Properly said of living beings; in mod. use occasionally of inanimate things.)

[There is no etymological ground for the distinctive use of 'habit' for an *acquired* tendency; but in philosophical language, such a sense occurs already in Cicero, *Inv.* I, 25, 36, 'habitum appellamus.. item corporis aliquam commoditatem, non natura datam, sed studio et industria partam'. The sense is late in Fr. and Eng.: Cotgr. has '*Habit* .. also an habit; a fashion setled, a vse or custome gotten'.]

1581 PETTIE tr. *Guazzo's Civ. Conv.* I. (1586) 4 b, By long studie and great contemplation.. got an habite and custome to be melancholike. **1591** SHAKS. *Two Gent.* v. iv. 1 How vse doth breed a habit in a man. **1647** COWLEY *Mistress, Soul* ii, That constant they as Habits grow. **1656** tr. *Hobbes' Elem. Philos.* (1839) 348 Habit is motion made more easy and ready by custom. **1662** J. DAVIES tr. *Olearius' Voy. Ambass.* 89 Being thus used from their Childhood, and that habit being as it were converted into a second nature. **1678** CUDWORTH *Intell. Syst.* 158 Habits are said to be an Adventitious and Acquired Nature, and Nature was before defined by the Stoicks to be *ἕξις*, or a *Habit*: so that there seems to be no other Difference between these two, than this, that whereas the One is Acquired by Teaching, Industry and Exercise; the other.. is.. inspired by the Divine Art and Wisdom. **1727** SWIFT *Gulliver* IV. xii, Although it be hard for a man late in life to remove old habits. **1834** MEDWIN *Angler in Wales* I. 18 A dog who once takes to worry sheep never leaves off the habit. **1836-7** SIR W. HAMILTON *Metaph.* (1877) I. x. 178 Both.. are tendencies to action; but.. *disposition* properly denotes a natural tendency, *habit* an acquired tendency. **1837** CARLYLE *Fr. Rev.* I. II. iii, System of Habits, in a word, *fixed ways* of acting and believing. *Mod.* The chimney has a habit of smoking when the fire is first lighted.

b. (Without *a* or *pl.*): Custom, usage, use, wont.

1605 BACON *Adv. Learn.* II. xxii. §8 But allowing his [Aristotle's] conclusion, that virtues and vices consist in habit. **1658** DRYDEN *On the Death of Cromwell* xxxvi, Faction now by habit does obey. **1690** LOCKE *Hum. Und.* II. xxiii. (1695) 156 Which power or ability in Man of doing any thing, when it has been acquired by frequent doing the same thing, is that Idea, we name *Habit.* **1802** PALEY *Nat. Theol.* xxvi. (1819) 449 Habit, the instrument of nature, is a great leveller; the familiarity which it induces, taking off the edge both of our pleasures and of our sufferings. **1876** MOZLEY *Univ. Serm.* vii. 151 It is of the nature of habit to make acts easier and easier.

c. (Usually in *pl.*) Applied to the natural or instinctive practices characteristic of particular kinds of animals, and to natural tendencies of plants.

1774 GOLDSM. *Nat. Hist.* II. IV. i, Many of its [the cat's] habits..are rather the consequences of its formation. **1834** MEDWIN *Angler in Wales* I. 263 A singular exception in the habits of creatures of the feline species. **1852** WOOD *Nat. Hist.* (1862) I. 584 Resembling the hare in general appearance and in many of its habits, the Rabbit is readily distinguished..by its smaller dimensions. **1880** C. & F. DARWIN *Movem. Pl.* 128 Some relation between the habit of cotyledons rising vertically at night or going to sleep, and their sensitiveness..to a touch.

d. ***in the habit*** (†***habits***) ***of doing*** something: having a habit or custom of so doing. So ***to fall*** or ***get into the habit.***

1801 CHARLOTTE SMITH *Solitary Wand.* II. 287 [He] had ..for near two years been in habits of occasional access to him. **1829** K. DIGBY *Broadst. Hon.* I. 66 Some very wise and devout men have been in habits of reading these romances. **1849** MACAULAY *Hist. Eng.* I. 176 He was little in the habit of resisting importunate solicitation. **1879** B. TAYLOR *Stud. Germ. Lit.* 128 The world has fallen into a bad habit of naming everything after something else.

e. *spec.* in *Psychol.* An automatic, 'mechanical' reaction to a specific situation which usually has been acquired by learning and/or repetition.

1859 A. BAIN *Emotions & Will* ix. 519 Some natures are distinguished by plasticity or the power of acquisition, and therefore realize more closely the saying that man is a bundle of habits. **1871** E. B. TYLOR *Primitive Culture* I. i. 1 Custom, and any other capabilities and habits acquired by man as a member of society. **1890** W. JAMES *Princ. Psychol.* I. iv. 104 The moment one tries to define what habit is, one is led to the fundamental properties of matter. The laws of Nature are nothing but the immutable habits which the different sorts of elementary matter follow in their actions and reactions upon each other. **1956** E. R. HILGARD *Theories of Learning* (ed. 2) i. 10 The stimulus-response theorist and the cognitive theorist come up with different answers to the question, What is learned? The answer of the former is 'habits'; the answer of the latter is 'cognitive structures'.

f. The practice of taking addictive drugs (see also quot. 1914). *colloq.* (orig. *U.S.*).

1887 in *Amer. Speech* (1948) XXIII. 246/2 May he continue to wage war against them [*sc.* Chinese opium dens] until the habit has been swept entirely out of existence. **1894** [see OPIUMATE]. **1914** JACKSON & HELLYER *Vocab. Criminal Slang* 41 *Habit*, current amongst dope fiends. Necessity for opiates; a craving; the condition produced by habitual indulgence in drugs... Example: 'I must drop into the hotel donegan (lavatory) and fire (take a hypodermic injection), for I feel my habit coming on.' **1926** J. BLACK *You can't Win* xii. 161 The sufferings they would undergo when there was no more and the 'habit' came on. **1959** *Daily Mail* 17 Oct. 7/3 'Do you have the habit?' He knew she meant 'Do you take drugs?'

†**10.** The condition of being accustomed to something through having constantly to do with it; familiarity. ***on intimate habits***: on intimate terms, familiar. (Cf. HABITUDE 3.) *Obs.*

1586 B. YOUNG tr. *Guazzo's Civ. Conv.* IV. 208 b, Why.. cannot he discourse better of them, who hath had a longer and continuall habit in them? **1600** J. PORY tr. *Leo's Africa* II. 414 By getting an habite of their languages and customes. **1704** HEARNE *Duct. Hist.* (1714) I. 399 Being brought up in this Discipline from Children, they acquir'd a Habit in Science. **1770** BURKE *Pres. Discont.* Wks. 1842 I. 147 The habit of affairs, if, on one hand, it tends to corrupt the mind, furnishes it, on the other, with the means of better information. **1809** SCOTT *Fam. Lett.* 15 Aug. (1894) I. 144 They are on most intimate habits. **1810** *Sporting Mag.* 154 Those who were in the habits of his society. **1859** LEVER *Davenport Dunn* ii. (1872) 20 'One gets a habit of the kind of people', said Lady Lackington.

IV. Literal rendering of L. *habitus* in Logic.

†**11.** *Logic.* The eighth of the categories or predicaments of Aristotle; Having or possession: in Gr. ἔχειν, L. *habitus.* (See CATEGORY 1.) *Obs.*

(Like the other categories, very variously understood and misunderstood by writers on logic.)

1588 FRAUNCE *Lawiers Log.* I. xi. 49 b, The affirmative is called the habite, the negative the privation thereof. **1628** T. SPENCER *Logick* 93 To haue the habit, and to be deprived of the habit are opposed. **1697** tr. *Burgersdicius his Logic* I. ix. 30 Habit is a manner after which clothes, or anything like clothes are put about the body, appended, or in any way adjoined to it. **1837** WHEWELL *Hist. Induct. Sc.* (1857) I. 209 The Categories are the ten heads under which assertions or predications may be arranged;—substance, quantity, relation, quality, time, place, position, habit, action, passion.

V. 12. *Comb.*, as (sense 1, 3) ***habit-bodice, -maker, -man, -shop, -skirt***; (sense 9, esp. 9 e) ***habit-bound*** adj.; ***habit-breaker, -formation; habit-forming*** vbl. sb. and adj., ***-worn*** adj.; †***habit-wise*** adv.; **habit-cloth**, a light broadcloth used for riding-habits and other outer garments; **habit-memory**, one of the two kinds of memory first distinguished by H. Bergson, which consists of motor mechanisms or 'habits' fixed in the organism and which acts in response to an appropriate stimulus, e.g. when repeating a lesson learnt by heart; **habit-neurosis**, a neurosis caused by habit-bound behaviour; **habit pattern**, a pattern of behaviour created by habit; **habit-response**, a response induced by habit; **habit-shirt**, a kind of chemisette with linen collar, worn by women under the outer bodice; **habit spasm** *Med.*, = TIC 1; **habit strength** (see quot. 1958); also called sHR; **habit-training**, the training of an infant or child in regular habits of behaviour, often specifically referring to hygiene, sleeping, and eating.

1892 *Daily News* 2 July 6/7 The becoming *habit-bodice of old, cut away on the hips and fitting like a good glove. **1863** J. G. WHITTIER *Poetical Wks.* (1874) 412/2 But what if, *habit-bound, thy feet Shall lack the will to turn? **1922** W. B. YEATS *Trembling of Veil* 140 Old and habit-bound. **1932** *Brit. Jrnl. Psychol.* July 54 Box 7 [in set of boxes designed for intelligence testing] was introduced as a *habit breaker. **1913** *Lancet* 27 Sept. 964/2 (*title*) A preliminary note on *habit-formation in guinea-pigs. **1936** *Mind* XLV. 290 All habit-formation under the example, instruction, command, influence, of others is propaganda. **1961** *Lancet* 27 Aug. 485/1 Narcotics had not been used for fear of habit-formation. **1899** W. JAMES *Talks to Teachers on Psychol.* p. viii, Maxims relative to *habit-forming. **1913** A. E. LEACH *Food Inspection & Analysis* (ed. 3) xxi. 955 (*heading*) Habit-forming drugs in beverages. **1958** J. CANNAN *And be a Villain* vii. 151, I didn't take any [sleeping pills] last night because if you keep on they might become habit-forming. **1819** *P.O. Lond. Direct.* 84 Tailors and *Habit-Makers. **1769** *Stratford Jubilee* I. i. 12 That valuable creature Mr. Pasquin the *habit-man. **1911** PAUL & PALMER tr. *Bergson's Matter & Memory* ii. 99 (*marginal note of translators*) Automatism has a wide range, and representative memory is often superseded or masked by *habit memory. **1912** *Mind* XXI. 226 M. Bergson, in contrasting these two forms of memory, makes the motor or habit-memory *too* mechanical. **1925** C. FOX *Educ. Psychol.* 140 Take two processes, habit-memory and image-memory respectively. **1907** W. JAMES *Mem. & Stud.* (1911) x. 239 There seems no doubt that we are each and all of us to some extent victims of *habit-neurosis. **1960** G. SANDERS *Mem. Professional Cad* II. iv. 133 Once a man has acquired this *habit pattern it will be intolerable for him to stay home at night. **1964** *Word Study* Feb. 2/2 *Finalize* and *dollar-wise* were deep-seated habit patterns long before Webster's Third displayed them. **1960** B. MALINOWSKI *Sex & Repress. Savage Soc.* 194 The zoologist deals with specific instinctive behaviour, the anthropologist with a culturally fashioned *habit-response. **1834** PLANCHÉ *Brit. Costume* 245 A covering for the neck and throat, similar to what is now called a *habit-shirt. **1751** ELIZA HEYWOOD *Betsy Thoughtless* I. 40 The woman at the *habit-shop in Covent-garden. **1894** *Daily News* 20 June 6/4 The *habit skirt of to-day is surmounted by a riding jacket, generally of a totally different colour. **1888** W. R. GOWERS *Man. Dis. Nervous Syst.* II. v. 586 Children often..present spasmodic movements such as winking, twitching the mouth, jerking the head..which the individuals are unable to control... This condition has been termed 'habit-chorea' ..but..'*habit-spasm' is, I think, a better name. **1940** S. A. K. WILSON *Neurology* II. 1629 In France the word 'tic' has been employed for centuries to denote a habitual, unpleasing gesture; but only within the last 30 years has it been current in English neurology, replacing the incorrect 'habit-spasm' or 'habit-chorea' of prior date. **1948** E. R. HILGARD *Theories of Learning* iv. 83 *Habit strength increases when receptor and effector activities occur in close temporal contiguity. **1951** C. L. HULL *Essentials of Behavior* xiv. 57 We have presented evidence..to indicate the quantitative molar law according to which habit strength (sHR), primary motivation or drive (D), incentive motivation (K)..and the delay in reinforcement (J) respectively operate as functions in the determination of reaction potential. **1958** H. B. & A. C. ENGLISH *Dict. Psychol. Terms* 235/2 *Habit strength or sHr*, (*C. Hull*) an inferred part of the organism that is determined by variation in four empirical determinants: number of reinforcements, amount of reinforcing agents, time between stimulation and response, time between response and reinforcement. **1959** LAMBERT & FILLENBAUM in Saporta & Bastian *Psycholinguistics* (1961) vii. 455/1 An important paper by Pitres..offered a different generalization in order to account for..the effect of aphasia on polyglots. In essence, Pitres' is a habit strength principle which states that the language or languages most used before the aphasic insult will be the first to recover. **1927** A. GESELL in C. W. Kimmins *Mental & Physical Welfare of Child* iii. 40 Wholesome *habit training in infancy lays the foundation of mental health... Feeding, sleeping, bladder control, bowel control—these are not physical matters. They are 'mental'. **1939** E. R. BOYCE *Infant School Activities* 240 Habit-training. The nursery school and class has been closely associated with training in good physical habits and with attention to the health of the child. **1960** I. BENNETT *Del. & Neur. Childr.* v. 181 Difficulties in habit-training may be expected in both delinquent and neurotic children. Both types..are likely to express early difficulties in the form of sleep disturbances, feeding disturbances, or disturbances in bladder or bowel control. **a 1626** BP. ANDREWES *Serm.* xix. (1661) 389 His vigour..holdeth out *habit-wise. **1890** W. JAMES *Princ. Psychol.* I. xvi. 655 These *habit-worn paths of association are a clear rendering of what authors mean by 'predispositions', 'vestiges', 'traces', etc., left in the brain by past experience.

'habit, *ppl. a. Sc. Law.* Also 8 **habite.** [ad. L. *habit-us*, pa. pple. of *habēre* to have, hold.] Held, holden: in the legal phrase **habit and repute**, repr. a med.L. *habitus et reputatus*, in earlier times translated ***halden and repute*** (or ***reputit***), i.e. held and reputed (to be so and so).

[**1503** *Sc. Acts Jas. IV*, c. 23 þe woman..beand repute & haldin as his lachtfull wif. **1551-2** *Eccles. Scot. Statuta* 135 Quæ talium baptizatorum parentes communiter habentur et reputantur. **1681** STAIR *Inst. Law Scot.* IV. xlv. § 4 (1693) 704 In the serving of..terces of relicts, 'commonly holden and repute' is sufficient.] **1753** *Scots Mag.* Sept. 469/1 As habite and repute a common..thief. **1773** ERSKINE *Inst. Law Scot.* I. 86 It is presumed or inferred from cohabitation..joined to their being habite, or held, and reputed, man and wife. **1861** W. BELL *Dict. Law Scotl.* s.v., If the person..be habit and repute a thief—i.e. one who notoriously makes or helps his livelihood by thieving. *Ibid.* s.v., *Execution*, It is sufficient ..that the person..shall have been at the time habit and repute qualified.

b. The phrase ***habit and repute*** is also used quasi-*subst.* for: The fact of being commonly held and reputed (what is indicated by the context).

1754 ERSKINE *Princ. Sc. Law* (1890) 57 If there has been cohabitation and habit and repute for a sufficient time after the parties were free to marry. **1838** W. BELL *Dict. Law Scotl.* s.v., Thus marriage may be constituted by habit and repute..So also habit and repute is an aggravation of a special act of theft. [By a recent Act, *habit and repute* is no longer made matter of charge in the libel.]

habit ('hæbɪt), *v.* [a. F. *habite-r* to have dealings with, possess, cohabit, dwell, inhabit, ad. L. *habit-āre* to have possession of, inhabit, dwell, abide, f. *habit-*, ppl. stem of *habēre*: see prec.]

†**1.** *intr.* To dwell, abide, reside, sojourn. *Obs.*

? *a* **1366** CHAUCER *Rom. Rose* 660 That in her swete song delyten In thilke places as they habyten. **1483** CAXTON *Cato* A viij b, Many men habyten and dwellyn by fayth in the cytees. *a* **1592** GREENE *Alphonsus* I. i, Although he habit on the earth. **1649** EARL MONM. tr. *Senault's Use Passions* (1671) 36 Contraries cannot lodge or habit together.

2. *trans.* To dwell in, inhabit. *arch.*

1598 HAKLUYT *Voy.* I. 435 (R.) Some other towne or place habited, vpon or neer the border of it. **1601** HOLLAND *Pliny* I. 48 The shore of the Æthyopian Ocean, which now is habited. **1847** D. G. MITCHELL *Fresh Glean.* (1851) 250 Hinzelmann who once habited an old castle. **1891** H. S. MERRIMAN *Prisoners & Captives* III. xi. 185 Unless they had habited different parts of the globe.

3. To dress, clothe, attire. (Usually in *pa. pple.*)

1588 SHAKS. *Tit. A.* II. iii. 57 Or is it Dian habited like her? **1656** STANLEY *Hist. Philos.* v. (1701) 174/2 They went proudly habited. **1696** BP. PATRICK *Comm. Exod.* xxix, The High Priest was first habited, and then his Sons. **1737** WHISTON *Josephus Antiq.* XVIII. iii. § 2 He habited a great number of soldiers in their habit. **1866** MRS. H. WOOD *St. Martin's Eve* xxiv, To habit herself as she deemed suitable for her journey. **1889** D. C. MURRAY *Dangerous Catspaw* 55 A group of girls, habited in white flannel.

fig. **1654** TRAPP *Comm. Ezra* viii. 16 Good matter well habited. *a* **1658** FORD, etc. *Witch Edmonton* II. ii, Thy liking is a Glass By which I'll habit my behaviour.

†**4.** To accustom, familiarize, habituate; *pa. pple.* accustomed, practised, used (*to* or *in*). *Obs.*

1615 CHAPMAN *Odyss.* v. (R.), O y'are a shrewd one; and so habited In taking heed. **1627-77** FELTHAM *Resolves* II. iv. 166 A generation of men..That are so habited in falsehood. *a* **1661** FULLER *Worthies* (1840) II. 199 He was so habited to poisons, they became food unto him. **1782** PAINE *Let. Abbé Raynal* (1791) 63 A mind habited to meanness and injustice. **1814** SOUTHEY *Roderick* xx. 11 Habited in crimes.

†**b.** To turn into a habit, render habitual. *Obs.*

1627-77 FELTHAM *Resolves* II. lxiii. 293 When Vices habit themselves into custom and manners. **1660** FULLER *Mixt Contempl.* (1841) 204 Customary sins, habited in us by practice and presumption.

habitability (ˌhæbɪtəˈbɪlɪtɪ). [f. next: see -ITY.] The quality or fact of being habitable.

1714 DERHAM *Astro-Theol.* (1715) p. v, Concerning..the Habitability of the Planets, and a Plurality of Worlds. **1827** *Blackw. Mag.* XXII. 166 There's no kind of furniture like books:—nothing else can afford one an equal air of comfort and habitability. **1880** A. R. WALLACE *Isl. Life* ix. 183 The very habitability of our globe is due to the equalising effects of the waters of the ocean.

habitable ('hæbɪtəb(ə)l), *a.* Also 4 **abitable.** [a. F. *habitable* (14th c. in Littré), ad. L. *habitābilis*, f. *habitāre* to inhabit: see -ABLE.]

1. Suitable for habitation or as a human abode; fit to live in, inhabitable; also *absol.* the habitable globe (cf. Gr. οἰκουμένη).

1388 WYCLIF *Exod.* xvi. 35 Til thei camen in to the lond abitable. **1490** CAXTON *Eneydos* xvi. 62 We haue gyuen her londe habytable. **1555** EDEN *Decades* Contents, The description of the north regions: and howe they are habitable. **1660** HICKERINGILL *Jamaica* (1661) 3 That vulgar division of the World into Zones habitable..and inhabitable. **1667** MILTON *P.L.* VIII. 157 A glimps of Light, conveyd so farr Down to this habitable. **1793** SMEATON *Edystone L.* 195 The habitable part of the building. **1838** DICKENS *Nich. Nick.* xi, A couple of rooms..which some kind of attempt had been made to render habitable.

†**2.** Able or ready to dwell. *Obs. rare.*

1654 tr. *Scudery's Curia Pol.* 68 All the virtues are as habitable, and as content to dwell with the meanest Subject as the mightiest Monarch.

Hence **'habitableness**, the quality of being habitable; fitness for habitation. **'habitably** *adv.*, in a habitable manner.

1653 H. MORE *Conject. Cabbal.* (1713) 13 In respect of its habitableness it is as rightly termed an Earth. *a* **1691** BOYLE *Hist. Air* (1692) 78 To prove not only the habitableness, but healthfulness of that climate and country. **1828** WEBSTER cites FORSYTH for *Habitably.* **1843** MRS. CARLYLE *Lett.* I. 239 The public rooms are in a state of perfect habitableness again.

†**'habitacle.** *Obs.* exc. *Hist.* [a. F. *habitacle* (12th c. in Littré) ad. L. *habitācul-um* dwelling-place, f. *habitāre* to inhabit.]

1. A dwelling-place, habitation.

13.. *Coer de L.* 4149 Thomas..an other stone i-slong To ser Mahouns habitacle. **1382** WYCLIF *Acts* xii. 7 Li3t schoon a3en in the habytacle. **1483** CAXTON *Gold. Leg.* 225/2 Thenne went cristofer to this ryuer & made there his habitacle for hym. **1500-20** DUNBAR *Poems* lxxxv. 14 Haile,

Alphais habitakle! *a* **1691** BOYLE *Hist. Air* (1692) 167 Our bed.. which in this little habitacle was not far from the fire. **1829** SOUTHEY *Epist.* in *Anniversary* 11 Fortune hath set his happy habitacle Among the ancient hills.

fig. and *transf.* **1382** WYCLIF *Eph.* ii. 22 Be ȝe bildid to gidere into the habitacle of God, in the Hooli Gost. *c* **1450** tr. *De Imitatione* III. xxvii. 96 Bringe oute of þe habitacle of myn herte all maner of derkenes. *a* **1555** BRADFORD *Wks.* (Parker Soc.) 356 These our corruptible habitacles, wherein we abide the Lord's leisure. **1684** tr. *Bonet's Merc. Compit.* I. 36 The Bloud-vessels (those genuine Habitacles of noxious Vapours).

2. A canopied niche in the wall of a building. *c* **1384** CHAUCER *H. Fame* III. 104 And eke in each of the pinnacles Weren sundry habitacles. **1875** PARKER *Gloss. Archit., Habitacle*,.. applied also to a niche for a statue. *Ibid.* s.v. *Tabernacle*, Tabernacles were also called Maisons, Habitacles, Hovels, and Housings in ancient contracts.

† **habi'tacule.** *Obs.* [ad. L. *habitāculum* (also found in Eng. use); see prec.] = prec. 1.

c **1374** CHAUCER *Boeth.* II. pr. vii. 44 (Camb. MS.) In the clos of thilke lytul habytacule [*v.r.* habitacle]. **1517** TORKINGTON *Pilgr.* (1884) 20 The habitacule and lordshippe of Kyng Mynos. [**1651** BIGGS *New Disp.* ¶ 112 The topick habitaculum of that contagion.]

† **'habitance.** *Obs.* In 6 -aunce. [a. OF. *habitance*, f. *habiter* to dwell: see -ANCE.] A dwelling-place, habitation.

1590 SPENSER *F.Q.* II. vii. 7 What art thou, man.. That here in desert hast thine habitaunce?

habitancy ('hæbɪtənsɪ). [f. next: see -ANCY.]

1. Residence as an inhabitant; inhabitance.

1792 J. BELKNAP *Hist. New-Hampsh.* III. 268 The qualifications of a representative are two years' habitancy. **1819** W. S. ROSE *Lett.* I. 131 Hospitals.. turning upon some miserable question of habitancy within very confined limits.

2. Inhabitedness, populousness. *rare.*

1837 *Blackw. Mag.* XLI. 735 An escape from the close air and crowded habitancy of the streets.

3. Body or mass of inhabitants collectively.

1832-3 DE QUINCEY *Tradit. Rabbins* Wks. 1860 XIV. 267 Those [persons] do not comprehend the whole habitancy of this well-stocked house. **1862** F. HALL in *Jrnl. Asiat. Soc. Bengal* I Its habitancy may at one time have competed with that of London.

habitant ('hæbɪtənt), *a.* and *sb.* Also 5 aby-, 5-6 -aunt(e. [a. F. *habitant*, ad. L. *habitānt-em*, pr. pple. of *habitāre* to dwell in, inhabit.]

A. *adj.* Inhabiting, indwelling.

1856 R. A. VAUGHAN *Mystics* (1860) II. XII. i. 230 A habitant spirit.

B. *sb.* **1.** One who dwells or resides in a place; a resident, inhabitant, indweller.

1490 CAXTON *Eneydos* Prol. 10 This present boke is necessarye to alle cytezens and habytaunts in townes. *c* **1500** *Melusine* xxx. 221 Thabytants of the Cyte. **1530** PALSGR. 228/2 Habytaunt, a dweller. **1583** STANYHURST *Æneis* III. (Arb.) 74 The habitans in vallye remayned. **1642** HOWELL *For. Trav.* (Arb.) 86 The various habitants of the Earth. *a* **1721** PRIOR *Callimachus* I. 5 To Heaven's great habitants. **1826** DISRAELI *Viv. Grey* IV. vi, The little city of which he was now an habitant.

fig. **1667** MILTON *P.L.* x. 588 Sin, there in power before, Once actual, now in body, and to dwell Habitual habitant. **1818** BYRON *Ch. Har.* IV. cxxi, O Love! no habitant of earth thou art.

‖ **2.** (pronounced (abitɑ̃); pl. often as formerly in F. *habitans*). A native of Canada (also of Louisiana) of French descent; one of the race of original French colonists, chiefly small farmers or yeomen.

1789 *Quebec Gaz.* 5 Feb. 4/1 My Brother Habitants will be .. convinced of the expediency of the regulation. **1791** J. LONG *Voy. & Trav. Indian Interpr.* 167 The Canadians are particularly fond of dancing, from the *seigneur* to the *habitant*. **1836** SIR F. B. HEAD 28 Oct. in *Narrative* vi. (1839) 130 The real interests of the French *habitans* of Lower Canada. **1839** EARL OF DURHAM *Rep. Brit. N. Amer.* 19 Members of the family of some habitant. **1855** W. IRVING *Washington* II. viii. 96 To ascertain the feelings of the *habitans*, or French yeomanry. **1856** OLMSTEAD *Slave States* 682 A hamlet of cottages, occupied by Acadians, or what the planters call *habitans*, poor white, French Creoles. **1881** *Harper's Mag.* Nov. 823 Pirogue as the habitants call it. **1909** *Westm. Gaz.* 10 Apr. 6/2 From school Drummond became a clerk in a telegraph office at Bord-à-Plouffe, a little village on the Rivière des Prairies, where he was in the midst of habitants, lumbermen, and voyageurs. **1966** *Kingston* (Ont.) *Whig-Standard* 27 Aug. 4/3 As the old habitant joke had it, it's okay to t'row out de hank [*sc.* anchor], but suppose there's no rope on the hank?

habitat ('hæbɪtæt). [a. L. *habitat*, 3rd pers. sing. pres. tense of *habitāre*, *lit.* 'it inhabits', in Floras or Faunas, written in Latin, introducing the natural place of growth or occurrence of a species. Hence, taken as the technical term for this.]

1. a. *Nat. Hist.* The locality in which a plant or animal naturally grows or lives; habitation. Sometimes applied to the *geographical area* over which it extends, or the special locality to which it is confined; sometimes restricted to the particular *station* or spot in which a specimen is found; but chiefly used to indicate the kind of locality, as the sea-shore, rocky cliffs, chalk hills, or the like.

[**1762** HUDSON *Flora Anglica* 70 Common Primrose—Habitat in sylvis sepibus et ericetis ubique.] **1796** WITHERING *Brit. Plants* Dict. Terms (ed. 3) 62 *Habitatio*, the natural place of growth of a plant in its wild state. This is now generally expressed by the word Habitat. **1809** *Edin. Rev.* XV. 127 It has also flowered.. after having been transferred from its native *habitat*. **1817** J. BRADBURY *Trav.* 7 A catalogue of some of the more rare plants in the neighbourhood of St. Louis.. together with their habitats. **1840** E. NEWMAN *Brit. Ferns* (1844) 255 The Black Spleenwort.. occurs on rocks as a native habitat. **1857** H. MILLER *Test. Rocks* i. 9 The sea is everywhere now.. the great *habitat* of the Algæ. **1874** J. A. ALLEN in Coues *Birds N.W.* 294 A mixed race has been long known to exist in the region where their habitats adjoin.

b. Hence generally: Dwelling-place; habitation.

1854 LOWELL *Cambridge 30 Yrs. Ago* Pr. Wks. 1890 I. 48 But every thing is not a Thing, and all *things* are good for nothing out of their natural *habitat*. **1869** MISS MULOCK *Woman's Kingd.* III. 54 He reached at last Brook Street, that favourite habitat of physicians. **1871** EARLE *Philol. Eng. Tongue* §372 This word [splotch] has its habitat in Oxfordshire. **1876** GLADSTONE *Homeric Synchr.* 83 Pleas.. for accepting an Asiatic origin and *habitat* for Homer.

2. *Comb.* **habitat form**, the form developed by a race or organism in response to its habitat; **habitat group**, any group of species whose members favour a similar habitat.

1902 F. E. CLEMENTS in *Beiblatt zu den Botanischen Jahrbüchern* LXX. 17 A habitat form is the modified form of a species common to two or more formations produced by a particular formation, i.e. habitat, such as the alpine meadow habitat form of *Campanula rotundifolia*. **1916** B. D. JACKSON *Gloss. Bot. Terms* (ed. 3) 169/1 *Habitat-form*, the impress given to the plant by the habitat. **1898** POUND & CLEMENTS *Phytogeogr. Nebraska* iv. 93 A habitat group is a group of species, which are subject to similar physical conditions, and frequent like habitats. **1959** E. F. LINSSEN *Beetles Brit. Is.* I. 57 This 'bionomic classification', as the method is called, is based on habitat-groups. **1962** *Conservationist* June–July 20/2 Four new life-size dioramas (natural habitat groups) of four types of fish areas in Rochester and Munroe County are featured in permanent exhibitions in the Hall of Natural Science at the Rochester Museum of Arts and Sciences.

habitate ('hæbɪteɪt), *v. rare.* [f. L. *habitāt-*, ppl. stem of *habitāre* to dwell; but by Burton used as a derivative of HABIT *sb.*] **a.** *intr.* To dwell. † **b.** *trans.* To habituate; = HABIT *v.* 4. *Obs.*

1621 BURTON *Anat. Mel.* I. ii. II. vi, They being now habitated to such meditations and solitary places, can indure no company. **1866** J. B. ROSE tr. *Ovid's Fasti* v. 626 Mars habitates in the city of his son. *Ibid.* VI. 936 She doth habitate On Tiber's banks.

habitation (hæbɪ'teɪʃən). Also 4 abitacioun. [a. F. *habi-*, *abitation* (12th c. in Hatz.-Darm.), ad. L. *habitātiōn-em*, f. *habitāre* to dwell, inhabit. '"Habitacion" in whiche *h* is written and nat sounded with us.' Palsgr. 1530, p. 17.]

1. The action of dwelling in or inhabiting as a place of residence; occupancy by inhabitants.

c **1374** CHAUCER *Boeth.* II. pr. vii. 44 (Camb. MS.) A ryht streyt place to the habytasyoun of men. *c* **1386** —— *Monk's T.* 226 He was out cast of mannes compaignye With asses was his habitacioun. *c* **1410** HOCCLEVE *Mother of God* 137 The habitacion Of the holy goost.. Be in myn herte. **1568** GRAFTON (*title*) A Chronicle.. deduced from the Creation of the Worlde, unto the first habitation of thys Islande. **1667** MILTON *P.L.* VII. 622 Every Starr perhaps a World Of destind habitation. **1726** SHELVOCKE *Voy. round World* (1757) 55 Excepting the plantations, and places of habitation. **1897** *Daily Chron.* 1 Feb. 7/4 The premises to be closed.. until they were made fit for human habitation.

2. *concr.* **a.** A place of abode or residence: either the region or country inhabited, or (now more usually) a house, cave, or other particular dwelling-place of man or animal.

1382 WYCLIF *Acts* i. 20 The habitacioun [**1388** abitacioun] of him be maad desert, and be there not that dwellith in it. *c* **1477** CAXTON *Jason* 70 b, Hit pleseth me right well that this noble countre be your habitacion. **1598** BARRET *Theor. Warres* v. ii. 129 Whether the most habitations of the Citie be on high above the alture of the wals. **1662** J. DAVIES tr. *Olearius' Voy. Ambass.* 67 They had no Cities, nor setled Habitations, but liv'd in Woods. **1665** HOOKE *Microgr.* 138 These indeed, seem'd to have been the habitation of some Animal. **1748** F. SMITH *Voy. Disc.* I. 184 The Habitations of the Indians (which we call Cabbins or Tents) are sufficiently wretched. **1859** W. COLLINS *Q. of Hearts* (1875) 44 The nearest habitation to ours was situated about a mile and a half off. **1860** TYNDALL *Glac.* II. iii. 246 To render the planet a comfortable habitation for beings constituted like ourselves.

fig. **1535** COVERDALE *Hab.* iii. 11 The Sonne and Mone remayned still in their habitacion. **1548-77** VICARY *Anat.* iii. (1888) 24 The head of man is the habitation or dwelling place of the reasonable soule. **1597** SHAKS. *2 Hen. IV*, I. iii. 89 An habitation giddy, and vnsure Hath he that buildeth on the vulgar heart.

† **b.** The Jewish tabernacle. *Obs.*

1535 COVERDALE *Num.* vii. 1 Whan Moses had set vp the Habitacion and anoynted it, and sanctifyed it.

3. The name adopted for local branches of the 'Primrose League', a political association established in 1883. (Said to have been suggested by that of 'lodge', used by Masonic societies; cf. also 'tent', 'grove', and the like, similarly used.)

1885 *Primrose League* 13 As a Diploma is issued to every Member, Habitations must be careful to send in the Declarations of every Knight, Dame, or Associate to the Registrar for enrolment. **1892** *Primrose League* in *Albemarle Rev.* Jan. 11 The first Habitation started was for the district of the Strand. *Ibid.* 13 In drawing up the rules it was sought .. to give the affair rather a Masonic character.. Accordingly the local committee was called a Habitation. **1895** *Times* 15 Nov. 6/1 A meeting of the Arthur Balfour Habitation of the Primrose League.

4. A settlement. [After F. *habitation.*]

1555 EDEN *Decades* (Arb.) 45 The interpretacion of certeyne wordes. *Colonie*, an habitacion. [**1809** KENDALL *Trav.* I. ii. 9 In Europe, we speak of settlements, either in a more general sense than colonies, or as included within colonies. The French call them *Habitations*.] **1825** WATERTON *Wand. S. Amer.* I. i. 101 From Simon's to the great fall there are five habitations of the Indians.. These habitations consist of from four to eight huts situated on about an acre of ground.

5. *Comb.* **habitation name**, a place-name in which at least one of the elements denotes an inhabited place; **habitation site** *Archæol.*, a site where there has been a settlement.

1936 *Oxf. Dict. Eng. Place-Names* p. xv, Near habitation-names stand names that originally denoted a pasture-ground or a shelter for the protection of animals, a cowhouse, a cattle-fold, etc. **1962** H. R. LOYN *Anglo-Saxon England* i. 9 There are more British habitation names in the region. **1925** *Antiquaries Jrnl.* Apr. 182 The author has more leisure to examine Meare, a similar habitation-site three miles distant. **1942** *Oxoniensia* VII. 106 The B-beaker and neolithic sherds were drift-sherds from one of the many habitation-sites.. in the neighbourhood. **1962** H. R. LOYN *Anglo-Saxon England* i. 15 This is not to deny the possibility of continuity in habitation sites at places such as London or York. **1971** *World Archaeol.* III. 141 Some of the shelters may have been habitation sites in the past.

habitative ('hæbɪtətɪv), *a.* [f. L. ppl. stem *habitāt-* (see HABITATE) + -IVE.] Of or pertaining to habitation or occupancy by inhabitants.

Now esp. in place-name studies.

1578 [see POSSESSIVE *a.* 2]. **1888** *Archæol. Rev.* Mar. 51 The students of *Toponomastique*, as the French call the modern science of 'habitative nomenclature'. **1929** A. MAWER *Probl. Place-Name Study* iii. 124 By the time that *tun* had become the great habitative suffix there were probably few such groups left. **1961** K. CAMERON *Eng. Place-Names* ii. 27 Place-names.. can be divided into two main types, habitative and topographical. **1967** A. H. SMITH *Place-Names of Westmorland* I. p. xxxviii, The older English settlements are represented by some 30 or more habitative names of parishes and villages.

habita'tivity. *rare.* [ad. F. *habitativité*: cf. prec. and -ITY.] 'The instinct which attaches a person to his own special country or manner of living' *Syd. Soc. Lex.* 1886.

† **'habitator.** *Obs. rare.* [a. L. *habitātor* dweller, agent-n. from *habitāre* to dwell.] A dweller, inhabiter, resident.

1646 SIR T. BROWNE *Pseud. Ep.* VI. x. 325 The longest day in Cancer is longer unto us, then that in Capricorne unto the Southerne habitator.

habited ('hæbɪtɪd), *ppl. a.* [f. HABIT *v.*]

1. Dwelt in, inhabited. *arch.*

1866 *Edin. Rev.* CXXIV. 184 The habited and uninhabitable portions of the globe.

2. Clothed, dressed.

1807 ROBINSON *Archæol. Græca* §10 p. lx, Statues of the Habited Graces. **1865** *Sat. Rev.* 2 Dec. 696/1 How little has been done.. to elevate the habited man above the naked savage!

† **3.** That has become habitual; commonly practised; accustomed. *Obs.*

1605 VERSTEGAN *Dec. Intell.* ii. (1628) 53 This antient and habited vice. **1651** tr. *Life Father Sarpi* (1676) 101 Not superstition, but a constant tenacity, and an habited custom.

† **habition.** *Obs. rare.* In 6 habycyon. [ad. late L. *habitiōn-em*, n. of action f. *habēre* to have.] ? Holding, having; or living, cohabiting.

1502 *Ord. Crysten Men* (W. de W. 1506) IV. xiii. 204 By habycyon carnall in fornycacyon.

habitual (hə'bɪtjuːəl), *a.* (*sb.*) [ad. med.L. *habituāl-is*, f. *habitus* HABIT.]

A. *adj.* † **1.** *Philos.* and *Theol.* Belonging to the 'habit' or inward disposition (see HABIT *sb.* 8); inherent or latent in the mental constitution.

With various shades of meaning, as (*a*) latent in the mind or memory, though not exhibited in action, as in ***habitual knowledge*** or ***cognition*** (in the Scotist philosophy), knowledge latent in the memory, and capable of being called up when occasion presents itself; (*b*) latent or inherent in the character, even when not in active exercise (= DISPOSITIVE), as in ***habitual faith***, ***grace***, ***righteousness***, etc., often opposed to 'actual'; (*c*) potential, virtual, though not practically exercised, as in ***habitual jurisdiction***; (*d*) inherent, native, as opposed to acquired, artificially assumed, or studied; (*e*) subjective, as opposed to 'objective'.

1526 *Pilgr. Perf.* (W. de W. 1531) 160 b, The attencyon that we ought to haue in prayer must be.. not altogyder actuall nor onely habituall. *a* **1535** MORE *Wks.* 732 (R.) The habituall belief is in the childe, verye beliefe, though it be not actuall belieuing and thinking vpon the faith, as the habituall reason is in the childe very reason, though it be not actuall reasoninge and making of sillogismes. *c* **1585** HOOKER *Disc. Justification* §21 The difference of the which operations.. maketh it needfull to put two kindes likewise of sanctifying righteousnesse, *Habituall*, and *Actuall*. *Habituall*, that holynesse, wherewith our soules are inwardly indued, the same instant, when first wee begin to bee the Temples of the holy Ghost. **1615** D. DYKE *Myst. Self-deceiving* 114 There is a double both keeping and breaking of the commandments, habitual and actual. *c* **1656** BRAMHALL *Replic.* iv. 160 With the Romanists themselues I distinguish between habituall and actuall Jurisdiction. **1669** COKAINE *Poems* 74 Her sweet Conditions all the vertues were, Not studied but habitual in her. *a*1716 SOUTH (J.) Art is properly an habitual knowledge of certain rules and maxims. **1837–8** SIR W. HAMILTON *Logic* III. vi. (1860) I. 52 By Objective of Systematic Logic is meant that complement of doctrines of which the Science of Logic is made up; by Subjective or Habitual Logic is meant the speculative knowledge of these doctrines which any individual.. may possess.

2. Of the nature of a habit; fixed by habit; existing as a settled practice or condition; constantly repeated or continued; customary.

1611 COTGR., *Habitual*, habituall; customarie, continuall. **1616** BULLOKAR *Engl. Expos.*, *Habituall*, growne to a habit by long custome. **1635** J. HAYWARD tr. *Biondi's Banish'd Virg.* 128 To deprive women of their naturall feares, though she beleeved them to be rather habituall than naturall. **1681** tr. *Belon's Myst. Physick* Introd., In a Tertian Ague, when it is fix'd and habitual for many days. **1684** R. H. *School Recreat.* 25 Repeat them 'till it becomes habitual to him, to keep his Ground certain, advance.. and observe a due Time. **1790** BURKE *Fr. Rev.* Wks. V. 253 Habitual dissoluteness of manners. **1824** W. IRVING *T. Trav.* I. 108 An Englishman's habitual diffidence and awkwardness of address. **1859** DARWIN *Orig. Spec.* viii. (1873) 205 How unconsciously many habitual actions are performed. **1880** L. STEPHEN *Pope* iv. 92 The thin, drawn features wear the expression of habitual pain.

b. *transf.* Of an agent: That habitually does or is what is denoted by the noun; constantly or customarily occupied in a practice. Of a volcano: Constantly or frequently active or in eruption.

1825 MACAULAY *Ess.*, *Milton* (1854) 5 A habitual drunkard. **1830** LYELL *Princ. Geol.* I. 329 [He] supposed it to have been once a great habitual volcano, like Vesuvius. **1869** *Act 32 & 33 Vict.* c. 99. §1 This Act may be cited as The Habitual Criminals Act, 1869. **1875** HAMERTON *Intell. Life* I. iii. 20 Almost all English people are habitual tea-drinkers.

3. Commonly or constantly used; usual, accustomed.

*a*1654 SELDEN *Table-T.* (Arb.) 100 Proverbs are habitual to a Nation, being transmitted from Father to Son. **1750** SHENSTONE *Rural Elegance* 202 Th' habitual scene of hill and dale. **1820** SCORESBY *Acc. Arctic Reg.* II. 16 The whale-fishers.. who most distinguished themselves by their habitual success in capturing those formidable creatures. **1863** GEO. ELIOT *Romola* II. xxxii, A low stool.. was Romola's habitual seat when they were talking together.

B. *ellipt.* as *sb.* †**1.** A latent or inherent affection of the soul (cf. A. 1 *b*). *Obs. rare.*

1650 O. SEDGWICK *Christ the Life* 22 For the Habituals of Grace.. and.. for the Comfortables of Grace.

2. A habitual criminal, drunkard, etc. *colloq.*

1884 *Gd. Words* 398/2 As a body the 'habituals' are no doubt rightly labelled dangerous. **1895** *Daily News* 13 Apr. 5/1 Four 'habituals' at ten grains a day in every thousand people, would practically account for the whole of the opium lawfully consumed.

Hence **habitu'ality**, the quality or state of being habitual, habitualness; in quot. 1858, the state of being fixed in old habits. **ha'bitualize** *v. trans.*, to render habitual.

1768–74 TUCKER *Lt. Nat.* (1852) II. 517 With the sole expectation of rivetting and habitualizing the three virtues thereby in our hearts. **1801** W. TAYLOR in *Monthly Mag.* XII. 403 Adjectives in *ive*, as *communicative*, *conducive*, *expressive*.. bear to the participles present.. the relation of habituality to actuality. **1858** CARLYLE *Fredk. Gt.* I. III. viii. (1872) 189 With our ponderous Austrian depth of Habituality and indolence of Intellect.

habitually (hə'bɪtjuːəlɪ), *adv.* [-LY².]

†**1.** With respect to habit, disposition, or constitution; inherently, essentially; potentially. (Sometimes opposed to *actually*: cf. prec. 1, and DISPOSITIVELY 1.) *Obs.*

1597 HOOKER *Eccl. Pol.* v. lv. §6 The gifts and virtues which Christ as man hath above men.. make him really and habitually a man more excellent than we are. *a*1639 W. WHATELEY *Prototypes* I. v. (1640) 50 Though Adam were perfect habitually yet not actually, I meane though hee had an ability to attaine perfect knowledge of God and the creatures, yet hee had not yet actually gotten all such knowledge. **1660** BOND *Scut. Reg.* 70 Our Anabaptists, and Puritans.. pretend that the Government originally proceedeth and habitually resideth in the people. **1671** FLAVEL *Fount. Life* vii. 19 If you stand not Habitually ready to leave father [etc.].

2. In the way of habit or settled practice; constantly, usually, customarily.

1682 SIR T. BROWNE *Chr. Mor.* I. xxx, Often repeated acts make us habitually evil. **1790** BURKE *Fr. Rev.* Wks. V. 94 Supreme authority placed in the hands of men not taught habitually to respect themselves. **1883** FROUDE in *Contemp. Rev.* XLIV. 3 A God-fearing man, who prayed habitually at his children's bedside.

ha'bitualness. [f. as prec. + -NESS.] The quality or state of being habitual; customariness.

1668 WILKINS *Real Char.* III. vii. 337 The use of the first Particle, is to denote the Habitualness of any such thing. *a*1729 S. CLARKE *Serm.* cxliv. Wks. 1738 II. 188 The Habitualness of our Obedience. **1860** PUSEY *Min. Proph.* 489 The prophet expresses the habitualness of these visitations by a vivid present.

†**habituary**, *a.* *Obs. rare.* [ad. L. type **habituāri-us*, f. *habitus* HABIT.] = HABITUAL 2.

1627 F. E. *Hist. Edw. II* (1680) 3 How difficult a thing it was to invert the course of Nature.. confirm'd by continuance of practice, and made habituary by custom.

†**habituate** (hə'bɪtjuːət), *ppl. a.* *Obs.* [ad. L. *habituātus*, pa. pple. of *habituāre*: see next.]

1. Made or become habitual; formed into a habit; established by repetition or continuance.

1526 *Pilgr. Perf.* (W. de W. 1531) 94 b, When it is habituate by custome. **1689–90** TEMPLE *Ess. Heroick Virtue* vi. (Jod.), Either native, or habituate. **1720** WELTON *Suffer. Son of God.* I. ii. 33 In an habituate course to pursue its Dictates.

2. Of a person: Grown accustomed (*to* a thing); established in a habit or custom (= HABITUAL 2 b).

1606 BP. ANDREWES *Serm.* II. 203 That we might grow habituate in grace. **1626** BACON *Sylva* §383 Islanders habituate to moist airs. **1679** J. GOODMAN *Penit. Pardoned* II. i. (1713) 143 An old habituate sinner.

habituate (hə'bɪtjuːeɪt), *v.* [f. L. *habituāt-*, ppl. stem of *habituāre* to bring into a condition, f. *habitus* condition, HABIT. Cf. F. *habituer*.]

†**1.** *trans.* To render (anything) habitual, form into a habit. *Obs.*

*a*1613 OVERBURY *Newes from Sea* Wks. (1856) 181 Small faults habituated, are as dangerous as little leakes unfound. **1615** BARGRAVE *Serm.* E iij, No injury.. could habituate in him an Italianate and eternall malice. **1649** BP. HALL *Cases Consc.* iv. (1654) 26 A practice that is now so habituated amongst all nations.

2. To fix (any one) in a habit; to accustom *to*, familiarize *with*. *Pa. pple.* Used, accustomed. Const. *to* (†*in*, †*into*, †*with*), *to do* something.

1530 PALSGR. 577/1 And I may ones habytuate hym in this condiscyon, all is safe. **1628** T. SPENCER *Logick* 61 A man that is habituated with righteousnesse. **1630** BRATHWAIT *Eng. Gentlem.* (1641) 4 To.. habituate him to a more generous forme. *a*1680 CHARNOCK *Attrib. God* (1834) I. 4 He that habituates himself in some sordid lust. **1703** MOXON *Mech. Exerc.* 202 By Use you must habituate your self to let the edge of your Tool bear upon the Work when the Pole.. comes down. **1864** BOWEN *Logic* ix. 308 In minds not habituated to accurate thinking.

absol. **1689** W. ATWOOD *Ld. C.-J. Herbert's Acc. Examined* 58 Mischiefs more remote.. may habituate to Corruption.

†**3.** To settle as an inhabitant (*in* a place). *Obs.* [After F. *habituer*.]

1603 FLORIO *Montaigne* (1634) 548, I shall never be.. so strictly habituated in my country, that I would follow him. **1695** TEMPLE *Introd. Hist. Eng.* Wks. II. 584 (L.) Many.. gentlemen left their families habituated in these countries.

4. To resort to habitually, to frequent. *U.S.*

1872 'OUIDA' *Fitz's Election* (Tauchn.) 185 Lounge in the bay window, habituate the coulisses and employ.. other.. methods for killing time. **1883** *National Baptist* (U.S.) XIX. 769 The places which he habituated and glorified.

habituated, *ppl. a.* [f. prec. vb. + -ED¹.]

†**1.** Made habitual, formed into a habit. *Obs.*

1615 T. ADAMS *Blacke Devill* 55 Any unmortified, habituated, affected sinne. **1653** MANTON *Exp. James* ii. 13 Habituated dispositions, good or bad.

2. Fixed in a habit, accustomed.

1619 JER. DYKE *Counterpoyson* 8 A man may fall into these sinnes, and yet not be an habituated sinner. **1655** R. YOUNGE *Agst. Drunkards* 6 An habituated, infatuated, incorrigible, cauterized Drunkard. **1874** BLACKIE *Self-Cult.* 47 To prevent the stomach from becoming the habituated slave of any kind of food.

habituation (həbɪtjuː'eɪʃən). [ad. med.L. *habituātiōn-em*, n. of action f. *habituāre*: see above. Cf. obs. F. *habituation*.]

1. The action of rendering or becoming habitual; formation of habit. Esp. the formation of such habits as dependence on drugs.

*c*1449 PECOCK *Repr.* III. xix. 415 Habituacioun and custom. **1673** O. WALKER *Educ.* 90 The inclinations and dispositions, which by our own industry and habituations are turned now into natural. **1929** *Jrnl. Pharmacol. & Exper. Therap.* XXXVI. 466 'Habituation' we interpret to mean a condition wherein one becomes accustomed to but not seriously dependent upon a drug. **1960** *Times* 21 Jan. 6/7 The two drugs specifically mentioned in this context are carbromal and bromvaletone. The committee state that cases of habituation arising from the widespread use of these by the public, largely without medical guidance, have been 'numerically very few, but individually serious'. **1962** *Jrnl. Amer. Med. Assoc.* 14 July 93/1 The inherent difficulty in establishing a uniform cut-off point where 'habituation' becomes 'addiction'. **1973** G. G. NAHAS *Marihuana* v. 188 In Egypt 65% of the consumers of hashish declared they were unable to stop although they expressed a wish to discontinue their habituation.

2. The action of habituating or accustoming, or the condition of being habituated (*to* something); esp. in *Psychol.*, the diminishing of response to a frequently repeated stimulus.

1816 KEATINGE *Trav.* (1817) II. 12 Such is the effect of habituation, that.. if passing a river, he hardly puts down his head in effort to drink. **1890** *Spectator* 4 Oct., Power to endure is most usually the result of habituation to work. **1895** *Amer. Jrnl. Psychol.* VII. 82 Gewöhnung, habituation. **1934** H. C. WARREN *Dict. Psychol.* 120/1 *Habituation*, the process of becoming adapted to a given stimulus, situation, or general environment. [A pop. and rather loose term.] **1967** S. ARIETI *Intrapsychic Self* iii. 47 Loss of awareness in the phenomenon of habituation is a parsimonious device used constantly by the nervous system. **1973** S. ROSE *Conscious Brain* ix. 194 The habituation process is.. both a behavioral and a physiological phenomenon.

habitude ('hæbɪtjuːd). Also 5 abitude. [a. F. *habitude* (14th c. in Littré) disposition, habit, ad. L. *habitūdo* condition, plight, habit, appearance, f. *habit-*, ppl. stem of *habēre*.]

1. Manner of being or existing; constitution; inherent or essential character; mental or moral constitution, disposition; usual or characteristic bodily condition, temperament: = HABIT *sb.* 5, 8.

*c*1400 *Lanfranc's Cirurg.* 65 þe leche muste loke þe disposicioun, þe abitude, age, vertu, and complexioun of him þat is woundid. **1540** MORYSINE *Vives' Introd. Wysd.* B iv b, Helthe is a temperat habytude of the bodye. **1579–80** NORTH *Plutarch* (1676) 996 Vertue proceeding from the sincere habitude of the Spirit. **1597** SHAKS. *Lover's Compl.* 114 His real habitude gave life and grace To appertainings and to ornament. **1603** HOLLAND *Plutarch's Mor.* 9 Bodily exercise.. addeth thereto a good habitude and strong constitution. **1677** GALE *Crt. Gentiles* III. 86 Because they had not εὐεξία, a good habitude of soul. **1796** KIRWAN *Elem. Min.* (ed. 2) I. Pref. 7 By a happy comparison of the habitudes of the adjacent fossils. **1870** PROCTOR *Other Worlds* 8 Various as are the physical habitudes which we encounter as we travel over the surface of our globe.

†**2.** Manner of being with relation to something else; relation, respect. *Obs.*

1561 T. NORTON *Calvin's Inst.* IV. 123 He is so conteined in the Sacrament, that he abideth in heauen: and we determyne no other presence but of habitude. **1587** GOLDING *De Mornay* 89 There is a Father, a Sonne, and a habitude of them both, which wee would haue called the Loue, the Union, or the kindnesse of them, that is to wit, the Holy Ghost. **1597** MORLEY *Introd. Mus.* Annot., The habitude (which we call proportion) of one sound to another. **1646** SIR T. BROWNE *Pseud. Ep.* VI. iii. 288 The habitude of this inferiour globe unto the superiour. **1690** LOCKE *Hum. Und.* IV. xi. §14 The same Ideas having immutably the same Habitudes one to another. **1732** BERKELEY *Alciphr.* IV. §21 Proportion.. signifies the habitude or relation of one quantity to another.

†**b.** *in full habitude*: to the full extent, wholly, entirely. *Obs. rare.* (Cf. *in all respects*.)

*a*1661 FULLER *Worthies* (1840) I. 165 Although I believe not the report in full habitude.

†**3.** Familiar relation or acquaintance; familiarity, intimacy; association, intercourse. *Obs.* (Cf. HABIT *sb.* 10.)

1612 DRAYTON *Poly-olb.* xvii. Notes 271 Most kinde habitude then was twixt him and the Pope. **1655** EVELYN *Mem.* (1857) III. 65 The discourse of some with whom I have had some habitudes since my coming home. **1768–74** TUCKER *Lt. Nat.* (1852) II. 314 The entertainment found among their play-fellows, and habitude with the rest of the family. **1796** BURKE *Lett. Noble Ld.* Wks. VIII. 56, I have lived for a great many years in habitudes with those who professed them.

†**b.** *concr.* A person with whom one is familiar; an associate, acquaintance. *Obs. rare.*

1676 ETHEREDGE *Man of Mode* IV. i, La Corneus and Sallyes were the only habitudes we had.

4. A disposition to act in a certain way, arising either from natural constitution, or from frequent repetition of the same act; a customary or usual mode of action: = HABIT *sb.* 9.

1603 FLORIO *Montaigne* II. xi. (1632) 235 A man shall plainly perceive in the minds of these two men.. so perfect an habitude unto vertue, that [etc.]. **1641** MARCOMBES in *Lismore Papers* Ser. II. (1888) IV. 234 Beter for a yong Gentleman not to haue Learned under another then to haue taken an ill habitude. **1683** DRYDEN *Life Plutarch* 21 An habitude of commanding his passions in order to his health. **1736** BUTLER *Anal.* I. v. §2 Many habitudes of life, not given by nature, but which nature directs us to acquire. **1766** *Hist. Europe* in *Ann. Reg.* 14/1 Attachment to those habitudes which they derived from their ancestors. **1805** SYD. SMITH *Mor. Philos.* xvii. (1850) 242 All the great habitudes of every species of animals have repeatedly been proved to be independent of imitation. **1829** LANDOR *Imag. Conv.* Wks. 1846 I. 367/2 The habitude of nearly three months renders this food.. more commodious to my studies and more conducive to my sleep. **1837** *Blackw. Mag.* XLII. 233 The bird, contrary to his habitude, was roosting on a lower perch.

b. (Without *a* or *pl.*) = HABIT *sb.* 9 b.

1599 JAS. I *Βασιλ. Δωρον* (1682) 28 Which.. by long habitude, are thought rather vertue than vice among them. *c*1704 PRIOR *Henry & Emma* 463 Brought by long habitude from bad to worse. **1751** JOHNSON *Rambler* No. 98 ¶11 [They] can be learned only by habitude and conversation. **1826** SOUTHEY in *Q. Rev.* 307 The natural effect of local habitude is to produce local attachment. **1889** *Spectator* 9 Nov. 642/2 In the new land.. the fetters of habitude fall off and the cultivated man will work like the hind.

†**5.** *Chem.* (*pl.*) Ways of acting or 'behaviour' of one substance *with* another; reaction. *Obs.*

1793 HOPE in *Phil. Trans. Edin.* (1798) IV. 10 Habitudes of Strontian mineral with acids. **1818** FARADAY *Exp. Res.* xxxii. (1826) 183 Most authors.. have noticed its habitudes with sulphuric acid. **1832** G. R. PORTER *Porcelain & Gl.* 78 Trial should be made of the habitudes of different colours in combination with their flux.

habitudinal (hæbɪ'tjuːdɪnəl), *a.* [f. L. *habitūdo*, *-inis* HABITUDE + -AL.] Of or pertaining to habit; habitual.

*c*1380 WYCLIF *Sel. Eng. Wks.* (1869) I. 78 But clerkes witen þat þer ben two manere of seyngis, þat ben personel seynge, and habitudinel seynge. **1925** *Glasgow Herald* 12 Apr. 12 Disease.., biologically considered, is of three great kinds—(a) constitutional, (b) occupational or habitudinal, and (c) parasitic and microbic. **1932** J. A. THOMSON *Scientific Riddles* IV. 324 Deeply saturating changes, whether environmental, nutritional, or habitudinal.

‖**habitué** (abitye, hə'bɪtjuːeɪ). [F. *habitué* (fem. *-ée*), pa. pple. of *habituer* to HABITUATE, to bring into a habit.] One who has the habit of going to or frequenting a place; a habitual visitor or resident.

1818 J. W. CROKER *Jrnl.* 7 Dec. in *C. Papers* (1884) I. iv. 122 The habitués of Oatlands give her *étrennes* and receive them in return from her. **1841** LEVER *C. O'Malley* xxvii, A smile in which any habitué of the house would have read our fate. **1849** THACKERAY *Pendennis* xxviii, Old *habitués* of the boxes.

†**ha'bituous,** *a. Obs. rare.* [ad. L. type **habituōsus*, f. *habitus* HABIT.] Belonging to the 'habit' or mental constitution; native.

1633 ROGERS *Treat. Sacram.* I. To Rdr. 12 Whose learned and habituous abilities can farre better performe it.

†**'habiture.** *Obs. rare*⁻¹. [ad. L. type **habitūra*, f. *habit-*: see HABIT.] = HABITUDE.

1599 MARSTON *Sco. Villanie* I. iv, Each Ape.. That can no sooner ken what's vertuous, But will auoid it, and be vitious. Without much doe, or farre fetch't habiture [*rime* cure].

‖**habitus** ('hæbɪtəs). [L.] = HABIT *sb.* 5, 6.

1886 *Syd. Soc. Lex.*, *Habitus*, same as *Habit*, and *Habit of body*. **1886** *Science* 22 Jan. 87/1 The disposition to the disease,—the consumptive habitus.

hable, early form of ABLE: see also HABILE.

hablement, obs. form of HABILIMENT.

hab-nab, hab or nab: see HAB.

haboob (hæ'bu:b). Also **haboub, habub,** etc. [Arab. *habūb* blowing furiously.] A violent and oppressive wind which blows at certain seasons in the Sudan, and which brings with it sand from the desert. Also *transf.*

1897 *Daily News* 2 Oct. 2/1 This was a real haboob—a tornado of sand and small stones. *Ibid.* 4/6 A soldier that had been swept into the river by the merciless haboob. **1928** *Blackw. Mag.* Feb. 259 May is the month of 'haboobs'. **1936** *Jrnl. R. Aeronaut. Soc.* XL. 91 Our captains pay the greatest respect to the 'haboobs' of the Sudan. **1959** R. E. HUSCHKE *Gloss. Meteorol.* 268 *Haboob* (many variant spellings, including *habbub, habub, haboub, hubbob, hubbub*), a strong wind and sandstorm or duststorm in the northern and central Sudan, especially around Khartum, where the average number is about 24 a year. **1973** *Sci. Amer.* Jan. 46/3 The American haboobs are not so frequent as the Sudanese (two or three a year at Phoenix as compared with perhaps 24 a year at Khartoum).

habound, -ance, -ant, etc. obs. ff. ABOUND, ABUNDANCE, etc., very frequent from 14th to 16th c.

habourgioun, -joyn, obs. ff. HABERGEON.

habrik, obs. form of HAUBERK.

habrocome ('hæbrəʊkəʊm). *Zool.* [ad. mod.L. *Habrocoma*, f. Gr. ἁβρός delicate, graceful + κομή hair.] Name of a genus of small South American rodents with large ears like the chinchillas.

‖**habromania** (hæbrəʊ'meɪnɪə). *Path.* [mod.L., f. Gr. ἁβρός graceful, delicate + μανία madness.] A kind of insanity in which the delusions are of a cheerful or gay character.

1854 in MAYNE *Expos. Lex.*

habroneme ('hæbrəʊni:m), *a. Min.* [f. Gr. ἁβρός delicate + νῆμα thread, f. νεῖν to spin.] Having the appearance of fine threads.

1886 in *Syd. Soc. Lex.*

habu ('hɑ:bu:). [Jap.: see quot. 1818.] A venomous pit-viper, *Trimeresurus flavoviridis*, native to the Ryukyu Islands and neighbouring areas.

[**1818** B. HALL *Acc. Voy. Discovery to Great Loo-Choo Island* App., Vocabulary of English and Loo-Choo Words. .. Snake—Háboo.] **1895** *Geogr. Jrnl.* V. 299 The poisonous Trimeresurus.., called *habu* by the natives, is 4 or 5 feet long by 2 inches in diameter, and is an object of universal fear. **1955** *Sci. News Let.* 15 Jan. 36/1 The habu and mamushi, native to certain islands of the Pacific and parts of the Asiatic mainland.

habund, -ant, obs. ff. ABOUND, ABUNDANT.

habur-, habyrgen, -gin, -joun, etc., obs. ff. HABERGEON.

haburden(ne, obs. form of HABERDINE.

haburdepays, obs. form of AVOIRDUPOIS.

habutai ('hɑ:bu:taɪ). Also **-aye, -ae.** [Jap.] A fine soft Japanese silk.

[**1822** F. SHOBERL tr. *Titsingh's Illustr. Japan* 17 Tchouya followed, dressed in two robes of light blue, made of the stuff called *fabita*, with his hands tied behind him.] **1895** *Montgomery Ward Catal.* 12/3 Habutai Silk.. is a very soft, light weight of silk of Japanese make. **1902** *Encycl. Brit.* XXIX. 725/1 Pictures so elaborate and.. accurate as those produced by the *yuzen* process on silk crape or *habutaye.* **1921** *Daily Colonist* (Victoria, B.C.) 7 Apr. 13/6 Black Waists of heavy quality Habutai silk, with tucked fronts and neat collars. **1931** *Stud. Eng. Lit.* (Tokyo) XI. 515 *Habutae*, a kind of silk. This word is regularly used in newspaper advertisements in England. **1950** '*Mercury*' *Dict. Textile Terms* 254/2 A pure dye spotproof silk of the Habutai order, finished with a little lustre.

habyle, habylle, obs. forms of HABILLE *v.*

habyllement, -byly-, obs. ff. HABILIMENT.

hacbus(h, obs. forms of HACKBUSH.

hace, Sc. form of *hoase*, HOARSE *a.*

‖**háček** (‖'hɑ:tʃɛk, 'hæ-). Also **hacek.** [a. Czech, dim. form of *hák* hook.] A name for the diacritic ˇ, which is used in Baltic and Slavonic languages.

When placed above a consonant, it indicates palatalization (as *č* (tʃ), *š* (ʃ)), etc.); when placed above *e*, it indicates the vowel phoneme *jat'.*

1953 W. E. HARKINS *Mod. Czech Gram.* 1 The Latin alphabet has been expanded.. through the use of diacritical marks, called the čárka ˊ, kroužek ˚, and háček ˇ... The single vowel with the háček, ě, is sometimes listed with e. **1959** W. R. & Z. LEE *Teach Yourself Czech* p. xv, All consonant letters marked with a hook (*háček*).. are 'soft'. **1980** R. AUTY in Schenker & Stankiewicz *Slavic Literary Lang.* 169 Hus's lozenge-shaped dot was changed to the 'hook' (*háček*) which lives on as the reversed circumflex of the present-day Czech alphabet. **1984** E. STANKIEWICZ *Grammars & Dict. Slavic Lang.* 3 Hus replaced the medieval system of digraphs with one of diacritics, among which the dot (later replaced by a háček) marked the palatals.

hacendado (ˌæsɛn'dɑ:dəʊ). Also **haciendado.** [Sp.] The owner of an hacienda.

1840 D. TURNBULL *Trav. in West* 98 In the unexpected case of the confiscation of the rural property of a Hacendado, the civil judge of the district.. is directed to proceed to the spot. **1862** MAYNE REID *Tiger Hunter* xix, To the haciendado he hired himself out a part of the year. **1897** *Blackw. Mag.* Nov. 685 The polity of the Mexican haciendado remains unchanged. **1897** *Outing* (U.S.) XXIX. 593/2 The plantation homes of the *haciendados.* **1920** *Glasgow Herald* 22 Sept. 8 The Chilean haciendado. **1934** A. HUXLEY *Beyond Mexique Bay* 284 These lands were once the property of rich *hacendados.* **1962** *Economist* 13 Oct. 157/3 The Constitutionalists [of Mexico] led by Carranza, a *hacendado*, and Villa, a former bandit.

hache (aʃ). Now only as F. [a. F. *hache* (12th c. in Littré) = Sp. *hacha*, It. *accia*:—OHG. **happja*, whence *hęppa*, MHG. *hepe* scythe, bill, sickle.]

†**1.** An axe, hatchet. *Obs.*

[**1283** *De Coupiatoribus providendis* in Rymer *Foedera* (1727) II. 207 Magnam & fortem hachiam, vel securim, ad grossas & parvas arbores succidendas.] **13..** *Coer de L.* 4357 Some caughte a bote and some an hach. *c* **1330** R. BRUNNE *Chron.* (1810) 32 He slouh Colibrant with hache Daneis. *a* **1375** *Joseph Arim.* 503 He hedde an hache vppon heiȝ wiþ a gret halue. **1481** CAXTON *Godfrey* ccx. 307 Holdyng naked swerdes or haches or axis danoys. **1531** ELYOT *Gov.* I. xviii, His sworde or hache of steele.

2. *Prehist. Archæol.* [mod.F. *hache*]: see quot.

1880 DAWKINS *Early Man* 163 The Palaeolithic implements.. consist of the flake, the chopper.. the hâche, or oval pointed implement intended for use without a handle.

hache: see HACHY and HASH.

hache, -ed, hachet: see HATCH, -ED, -ET.

†**hachee.** *Obs.* [a. OF. *hachee, haschiee* pain, anguish, torment.] Pain, pang, torment.

c **1430** *Pilgr. Lyf Manhode* I. liv. (1869) 33 Therfore ye shuldren breke al and brose bi smale gobbettes and parties, in grete syhinges and grete hachees in thinkinge.

hachee, hachey: see HACHY.

‖**hachis** (aʃi). [F.: cf. HACHY.] = HASH.

1751 SMOLLETT *Per. Pic.* (1779) II. xliv. 72 A curious hachis of the lights, liver, and blood of a hare. **1845** DISRAELI *Sybil* (1863) 173 What a hachis you made of it!

hachisch, -ish, var. of HASHISH.

‖**hachure** (aʃyr, hæ'ʃʊə(r)), *sb.* [a. mod.F. *hachure* hatching, f. *hacher*: see HATCH *v.* and -URE.] In *Cartography*, (plur.): The lines used in hill-shading to indicate the more or less steep slope of the surface. Also *attrib.* as in *hachure lines.*

1858 *Merc. Marine Mag.* V. 173 The scale of shade is made to express the degree of slope by the strength of the hachure lines. **1878** HUXLEY *Physiogr.* 12 If the ground is steep, the lines, or hachures, are drawn thick and close together, so that the hilly spots become dark. **1887** J. T. WALKER in *Encycl. Brit.* XXII. 709/2 There are two rival methods of hill-shading—one by horizontal contours, the other by vertical hachures.

ha'chure, *v.* [f. prec. sb.] *trans.* To shade (a map) with hachures to represent the elevations. Hence **ha'chured** *ppl. a.*; **ha'churing** *vbl. sb.*

1864 in WEBSTER. **1885** *Athenæum* 23 May 655/2 The Hill features.. are printed in a separate colour.. making the Map much more picturesque than the usual black hachuring permits. **1894** *Lit. World* 3 Aug. 76 How vividly hachured maps may bring out the important physical features of accidented ground.

†**hachy.** *Obs.* Also 4 **haché,** 7 **hachee, hachey.** [The 14th c. form app. represents an OF. *haché*, from pa. pple. of *hacher* to HASH; the 17th c. *hachee, -ey, -y* may be the same, or may phonetically represent F. *hachis* (1539 in R. Estienne) in same sense. See also HASH.] = HASH.

c **1330** R. BRUNNE *Chron. Wace* (Rolls) 15759 And passed wel þo þat hache; So swete a mete neuer or et he. **1611** COTGR., *Hachis*, a hachey, or hachee; a sliced gallimaufrey, or minced meat. *a* **1648** DIGBY *Closet Open.* (1677) 151 Small cut juycy Hachy of Rabbet, Capon, or Mutton. *Ibid.*, A nourishing Hachy. *a* **1668** SIR W. WALLER *Div. Medit.* (1839) 46 If our forefathers could see our hachees, and olliaes, and hodgpodges.

‖**hacienda** (hæsɪ'ɛndə). [Sp. (a'θyenda) = landed property, estate, domestic work, (OSp. *facienda*, Pg. *fazenda*):—L. *facienda* things to be done, f. *facĕre* to do.] In Spain, and existing or former Sp. colonies: An estate or 'plantation' with a dwelling-house upon it; a farming, stock-raising, mining, or manufacturing establishment in the country; sometimes, a country-house. Also *attrib.*

[**1717** FREZIER *Voy. S. Sea* 135 That they call *La Hazienda de la Marquesa*, or the Marchioness's Estate.] **1760–72** tr. *Juan & Ulloa's Voy.* (ed. 3) II. 116 These extensive tracts of land are divided into Haciendas, or estates belonging to noble families of Lima. **1808** PIKE *Sources Mississ.* III. 256 The Hacienda of Pattos was a square enclosure of about three hundred feet. **1852** TH. ROSS *Humboldt's Trav.* I. xv. 477 A square house (the hacienda or farm) contained nearly eighty negroes. **1860** *Ure's Dict. Arts* (ed. 5) III. 676 Working it on their own account, or, as it is termed, hacienda account. **1881** RAYMOND *Mining Gloss.*, *Hacienda* .. in mining is usually applied to the offices, principal buildings, and works for reducing the ores. **1897** *Blackw. Mag.* Nov. 685/2 The pleasant picture of hacienda life in the land of the Aztecs. **1944** *Harper's Mag.* Aug. 201/2 The Rio Blanco textile works set up in Mexico.. were designed to produce cloth for sale at hacienda stores.

hack (hæk), *sb.*[1] Also 4–5 **hak(e,** 5 **hacc,** 5–7 **hacke.** [In sense 1, known from end of 13th c.; app. cognate with MHG. and Ger. *hacke*, Da. *hakke* pick-axe, mattock, hoe, Du. *hak* hoe, mattock, in Kilian *hacke*; related to HACK *v.*[1] The word is not found in OE., nor in ON. The other senses are prob. of later derivation from the vb.: cf. Da. and Sw. *hak* notch, from *hakken.*]

1. A tool or implement for breaking or chopping up. **a.** Variously applied to agricultural tools of the mattock, hoe, and pick-axe type.

a **1300** *Cursor M.* 1241 He lened him þan a-pon his hak, Wit seth his sun þus-gat he spak. **1483** *Cath. Angl.* 169/2 A Hacc, *bidens, &c. Ibid.* 170/1 An Hak (*A.* hake), *bidens, fossorium, ligo, marra.* **1594** *Vestry Bks.* (Surtees) 36 Payed for sharpinge the church hacke. **1616** SURFL. & MARKH. *Country Farme* 655 Such seeds may be sowne in little furrowes made with a hacke or grubbing axe. **1620** MARKHAM *Farew. Husb.* II. ii. (1668) 4 With these hacks you shall hew and cut to pieces all the earth formerly plowed up furrow by furrow. **1674** RAY *N. C. Words* 34 A *Hack*; a Pick-ax; a Mattock made only with one, and that a broad end. **1797** *Monthly Mag.* III. 34 The custom.. of breaking the ground or clods with a sort of hack. **1855** ROBINSON *Whitby Gloss.*, *Hack*, half a mattock, one without the adze end.

b. A two-pronged tool like a mattock, used for pulling up turnips, dragging dung, etc.; = DRAG 2 e.

1797 *Statist. Acc. Scotl.* XIX. 535 (Jam.) They loosen all the ground completely with a hack, an instrument with a handle of about 4 or 5 feet long, and two iron prongs like a fork, but turned inwards. **1808–25** JAMIESON s.v. *Hack*, *Mudhack*, a pronged mattock, used for dragging dung from carts. **1848** *Jrnl. R. Agric. Soc.* IX. II. 505 They [turnips] are pulled up by a peculiar drag, or 'hack' as it is provincially called [N. Rid. Yorks.].

c. A miner's pick used for breaking stone, esp. in sinking work.

1681 HOUGHTON *Compl. Miner* Gloss (E.D.S), *Hack*, a tool that miners use like a mattock. **1747** HOOSON *Miner's Dict.*, *Hack*, a Tool much used in Mines, where it is soft Work to cut it with. **1851** GREENWELL *Coal-Trade Terms Northumb. & Durh.* 29 *Hack*, a heavy and obtuse-pointed pick, of the length of 18 inches, and weight of 7 lbs., used in sinking or stone work. **1871** MORGAN *Mining Tools* 72 The pick is notably a miner's implement. In different districts it is called either a 'mandrel', 'pike', 'slitter', 'mattock', or 'hack'.

d. A bill for cutting wood: see also quot. 1875.

1875 KNIGHT *Dict. Mech.*, *Hack*, a tool for cutting jags or channels in trees for the purpose of bleeding them. **1881** RAYMOND *Mining Gloss.*, *Hack*, a sharp blade on a long handle used for cutting billets in two.

2. a. A gash or wound made by a cutting blow or by rough or clumsy cutting; a cut, a nick; *spec.* a notch made in a tree to mark a particular spot or to serve as a guide through a wood; a 'blaze' (*U.S.*); a 'chap' in the skin.

c **1575** *Perf. Bk. Kepinge Sparhawkes* (Harting) 34 Take a pece of clene yonge beefe cut.. wᵗ ought hacks or jagges. **1597** LOWE *Chirurg.* (1634) 184 The hackes or rids of the lips, is a solution of continuitie in the tender flesh of the lip. **1606** SHAKS. *Tr. & Cr.* I. ii. 222 Looke you what hacks are on his Helmet. **1808–18** JAMIESON, *Hack*, a chop in the hands or feet. **1887** *Forest & Stream* XXVIII. 179 (Cent.) I went into the woods to cut a hack as a guide in hunting.

b. *Curling.* An indentation made in the ice to steady the foot when hurling the stone.

a **1812** *Acc. Curling* 6 (Jam.) A longitudinal hollow is made to support the foot, close by the tee.. This is called a *hack* or *hatch.* **1892** HEATHCOTE *Skating & Curling* 361 He [the curler] must first fit the tee.. while his right foot rests in the hack or on the heel of the crampit.

c. *Football.* A cut or gash in the skin caused by a kick with the toe of a boot.

1857 HUGHES *Tom Brown* I. vi. (1871) 115 [They] showed the hacks they had received in the good cause. **1880** *Times* 12 Nov. 4/5 Hacks and bruises and hurts more serious are not noticed in the heat of the last few moments.

†**3.** A ridge of earth thrown up by ploughing or hoeing; = COMB 6 c. *Obs.* exc. *dial.*

1744–50 W. ELLIS *Mod. Husb.* III. i. 13 (E.D.S.) That ground which was fallowed in April into broad lands is commonly stirred this month [May] into hacks. *Ibid.* IV. i. 20 (E.D.S.) Plowing the land across in hacks or combs.

4. Hesitation in speech.

1660 H. MORE *Myst. Godl.* VI. xvii. 270 He speaks to this very question.. with so many hacks and hesitations. **1881** F. G. LEE *Reg. Baront.* iv. 46 After many hacks and stammers, he would get through a few sentences of the exordium haltingly.

5. A short dry hard cough.

1885 L. W. CHAMPNEY in *Harper's Mag.* Feb. 370/1 She had a little hack of a cough.

6. An act of hacking; a hacking blow. Also *fig.*, now esp. (*U.S.*) a try, attempt.

1836 D. CROCKETT *Exploits & Adv. Texas* 79 Better take a hack by way of trying your luck at guessing. **1873–4** *Rep. Vermont Board Agric.* II. 238, I have a chance to have several hacks at the weeds before the crop is sown. **1898** M. DELAND *Old Chester Tales* 244, I get more men in a saloon, that's why; and when the show's done I get a hack at 'em. **1969** *New Yorker* 12 Apr. 95/1 We go into the second order of testing,.. which would give us a better hack, a better indication of what we are dealing with.

7. a. = HACKER *sb.* 3. **b.** A spell of hacking on a computer (see HACKING *vbl. sb.* 1 d); an act of gaining unauthorized access to a computer system.

1983 *Your Computer* (Austral.) Sept. 86/3 The first thing I noticed on scanning the list of assembler mnemonics was the complete lack of conditional calls and conditional returns—beloved of 8080 hacks, but which can cause subtle, if not dangerous, coding practices. **1984** *Daily Tel.* 3 Dec. 3/3 It looks possible that a demonstration 'hack' could be arranged by some users to demonstrate that Prestel is vulnerable. **1986** *TeleLink* Sept.–Oct. 56/1 Security in computer communications is an important issue these days, particularly after the much publicized hacks of what were previously thought of as secure systems.

hack, *sb.*[2] Also 6 **hacke**. [In sense 2, another form of the words HATCH and HECK, having the consonant of the latter with the vowel of the former; cf. *hetch*, a variant of *hatch*. The other senses do not run quite parallel with those of *hatch* and *heck*, and it is possible that some of them are of different origin.]

1. *Falconry.* The board on which a hawk's meat is laid. Hence applied to the state of partial liberty in which eyas hawks are kept before being trained, not being allowed to prey for themselves. ***to fly, be at hack***, to be in this state.

1575 TURBERV. *Faulconrie* 175 To convey in the deuise whereon their meate is served called amongst falconers the Hacke. **1828** SIR J. S. SEBRIGHT *Observ. Hawking* 29 Falcons that had flown long at hack, and preyed frequently for themselves before they were taken up. **1852** R. F. BURTON *Falconry in Valley Indus* iv. 43 As soon as they begin to fly strongly they must be taken from hack. **1881** *Macm. Mag.* XLV. 39 The food is put out—one ration for each of the hawks which are 'at hack'.

2. A rack to hold fodder for cattle. ***to live at hack and manger***, i.e. in plenty, 'in clover'. Usually HECK; see also HATCH. ? *Obs.* exc. *dial.*

1674 RAY *N.C. Words* 23 A Hack (*Lincolns.*).. Fæni conditorium, seu præsepe cancellatum signat; a Rack. **1795** in J. Robertson *Agric. Perth* (1799) 543 A small hack full of fine hay. **1818** MISS FERRIER *Marriage* xxvi. (D.), The servants at Lochmarlie must be living at hack and manger. **1825** SCOTT *Jrnl.* 9 Dec., [She] lived with half the gay world at hack and manger.

3. A frame on which bricks are laid to dry before burning; a row of moulded bricks laid out to dry.

1703 T. N. *City & C. Purchaser* 42 The *Hacks* (or Places where they Row them [bricks] up.. to admit the Wind and Air to dry them). **1873** ROBERTSON *Engineer. Notes* 27 He.. wheels them [the bricks] down to the hacks which should be between the moulding shed and kiln. **1896** *Chamb. Jrnl.* XIII. 23/1 The stacking of the bricks in long rows or hacks, about five or six bricks high.

4. = HAKE *sb.*[3] 1.

1808–25 in JAMIESON. **1858** SIMMONDS *Dict. Trade*, *Hack* .. a framework for drying fish.

5. *attrib.* and *Comb.* **hack-barrow**, a barrow on which bricks are conveyed from the moulder's table to the hacks; **hack-bell** (see quot.); **hack-board** = sense 1; **hack-cap**, a cover of straw to protect sun-dried bricks from the rain; **hack-hawk**, a hawk kept 'at hack'; **hack-place** (see quot.); **hack-plank**, one on which bricks are laid to dry.

1891 HARTING *Gloss. Falconry*, **Hack-bells*, large heavy bells put on hawks to hinder them from preying for themselves whilst 'flying at hack'. **1892** *Coursing & Falconry* (Badm. Libr.) 240 As soon as the young hawks have.. returned to feed at evening on the *hack-board. **1882** *Standard* 16 Sept. 8/2 Brickmakers' plant and stock, comprising a large quantity of *hack caps, *hack planks. **1686** BLOME *Gentl. Recreat.* II. 62 **Hack Hawk*, is a Tackler. **1828** SIR J. S. SEBRIGHT *Observ. Hawking* 9 Small leaden bells are sometimes attached to hawk's legs, to prevent them from preying for themselves.. When thus kept, they are termed hack hawks. **1881** *Macm. Mag.* Nov. 39, The '*hack' place.. is an open spot.. where the youngsters will be left at complete liberty for the next few weeks. An open moor or large common serves the purpose admirably.

hack, *sb.*[3] (*a.*) [An abbreviation of HACKNEY, in its various senses, at first in slang use, and mostly familiar or contemptuous. The various senses are connected with those of HACKNEY more closely than with each other. Cf. the following:

a **1700** B. E. *Dict. Cant. Crew*, *Hacks, or Hackneys*, Hirelings. **1721** BAILEY, *Hack*, a common Hackney Horse. **1730–6** —— (folio), *Hack*, a common hackney Horse, Coach, or Strumpet.]

I. 1. A hackney horse; = HACKNEY 1 and 2.

a. A horse let out for hire; *depreciatively*, a sorry or worn out horse; a jade.

1721 BAILEY [see above]. **1739** CIBBER *Apol.* (1756) 26 Beaten Tits, that had just had the Mortification of seeing my Hack of a Pegasus come in before them. **1795** WOLCOTT (P. Pindar) *Lousiad* II. 43 Mount on a Jack-Ass.. astride his braying hack. **1813** H. & J. SMITH *Rej. Addr.* IV. ix, Not spurring Pegasus through Tempè's grove, But pacing Grub-street on a jaded hack. **1829** HOOD *Epping Hunt* xlvii, Butcher's hacks That 'shambled' to and fro. **1840** DICKENS *Barn. Rudge* ii, My horse, young man! He is but a hack hired from a roadside posting house.

b. *spec.* A horse for ordinary riding, as distinguished from cross-country, military, or other special riding; a saddle-horse for the road.

The word implies technically a half-bred horse with more bone and substance than a thorough-bred.

cover-, covert-hack, a horse for riding to the 'meet', or to the covert, where he is exchanged for the hunter. ***park-hack***, a handsome 'well-mannered' horse for riding in the park: so ***town-hack***. ***road-hack***, a horse for riding on the road, travelling, etc.; a roadster.

1798 *Sporting Mag.* XII. 72 Lord Huntley's famous hack. **1841** J. T. HEWLETT *Parish Clerk* I. 228 Six hunters and two cover-hacks. **1856** *Illustr. Lond. News* 12 Apr. 390/3 Sir Charles Knightley.. stuck to his road hack long after his neighbours had taken to post-horses. **1859** *Art of Taming Horses* viii. 132 A cover or country hack must be fast, but need not be so showy in action or handsome as a town hack. **1860** EMERSON *Cond. Life, Power* Wks. (Bohn) II. 340 The hack is a better roadster than the Arab barb. **1861** *Times* 11 July, Every man who.. saunters through Rotton-row from 12 to 2 on a high-priced hack. **1866** MISS BRADDON *Lady's Mile* ii, Society doesn't compel him to ride his park-hack across country. **1872** YOUATT *Horse* iv. (ed. 4) 91 One of those animals rare to be met with, that could do almost anything as a hack, a hunter, or in harness.

2. A vehicle plying for hire; a hackney coach or carriage; = HACKNEY 5. Now only *U.S.*

1704 STEELE *Lying Lover* III. ii, We'll take a Hack—Our Maids shall go with us. **1712** —— *Spect.* No. 510 ¶1, I was the other day driving in a hack thro' Gerard-street. **1752** FIELDING *Amelia* IV. iii, She took a hack and came directly to the prison. **1795** *Boston* (U.S.) *Gaz.* 28 Dec. 3/1 There is but little safety for the ladies and children [in the streets of Boston], but in the hacks. **1823** SCOTT *Fam. Lett.* 11 Feb. (1894) II. 166 To make their way in a noble hack, with four horses. **1872** HOWELLS *Wedd. Journ.* 55 'We must have a carriage', he added.. hailing an empty hack.

†**3.** The driver of a hackney carriage. *Obs.*

1687 MONTAGUE & PRIOR *Hind & Panth. Transv.* 21 [They] slipping through the Palsgrave, bilkt poor Hack. **1713** STEELE *Guardian* No. 14 ¶2 The happy minute.. when our hack had the happiness to take in his expected fare.

4. a. A person whose services may be hired for any kind of work required of him; a common drudge, = HACKNEY 3; *esp.* a literary drudge, who hires himself out to do any and every kind of literary work; hence, a poor writer, a mere scribbler.

a **1700** [see etym. above]. *a* **1774** GOLDSM. *Epit. on E. Purdon*, Here lies poor Ned Purdon.. Who long was a bookseller's hack. **1798** WOLCOTT (P. Pindar) *Tales of Hoy* Wks. 1812 IV. 424 The paper to which he was a hack. **1831** MACAULAY *Ess., Croker's Boswell* (1887) 187 The last survivor of the genuine race of Grub Street hacks. **1865** TROLLOPE *Belton Est.* ii. 22 A hard-working clerical hack. **1895** *Times* 23 Nov. 11/3 The hacks and wire-pullers on his own side in politics.

b. *slang.* A prostitute; a bawd.

1730–6 [see etym. above]. **1864** WEBSTER, *Hack*.. a procuress.

†**5. a.** Anything that is in indiscriminate and everyday use, and is 'hackneyed' or deprived of novelty and interest by such use; a hackneyed sermon, book, quotation, etc: cf. sense 9. *Obs.*

1711 *Vind. Sacheverell* 88 Was not this Sermon of the Doctors a common Hack at Oxford? **1740** DYCHE & PARDON, *Hack*, any thing that is used in common, or upon all occasions, as a horse, cloak, etc. **1775** ASH, *Hack*.. any thing commonly used, any thing used in common. **1790** MAD. D'ARBLAY *Diary & Lett.* (1854) V. 81 *Well* (for that is my hack, as 'however' is my dearest Susanna's) we set off. **1805** G. COLMAN *John Bull* III. i. (Stratm.), You'll find [Fielding's] *Tom Jones*.—Psha! that's such a hack.

b. *slang.* Applied to persons: see quot.

1876 JAS. GRANT *One of the 600* i. 8 The garrison *hacks*, or passé belles, whose names and flirtations are standing jokes.

6. *Naut.* A watch used, in taking observations, to obviate the necessity of moving the standard chronometer. Also ***hack-watch***, ***job watch***.

1851–9 G. B. AIRY in *Man. Sci. Enq.* 3 If a hack-watch is used, the comparison of the hack-watch with the chronometer must be given. **1867** SMYTH *Sailor's Word-bk.*, *Hack watch.* **1881** HAMERSLY *Naval Encycl.*, *Hack.*

II. *attrib.* and *Comb.* (passing into *adj.*).

7. In apposition or *attrib.*, as **a. hack-horse** = sense 1; so ***hack-cob***, ***-poster***. **b.** ***hack-cab***, ***-cabriolet***, ***-carriage***, ***-chaise***, ***-shay*** (see sense 2). **c.** Employed as a hack, at any one's service for literary or other work, for hire, as ***hack attorney***, ***author***, ***moralist***, ***pen***, ***preacher***, ***runner***, ***scribe***, ***writer***; so ***hack-writing***.

a **1734** NORTH *Exam.* III. vii. §52 (1740) 541 And so on to the Hack-Runners and Writers. **1749** FIELDING *Tom Jones* X. ix, Unluckily, a few miles before she entered that town, she met the hack attorney. **1792** WAKEFIELD *Mem.* (T.), Hack preachers employed in the service of defaulters and absentees. **1796** JANE AUSTEN *Pride & Prej.* v, Mrs. Long.. had to come to the ball in a hack chaise. **1814** D'ISRAELI *Quarrels Auth.* (1867) 282 A hack author for the booksellers. **1816** *Sporting Mag.* XLVIII. 239 A fall of 50*l.* per cent... in nag and hack horses. **1826** *Blackw. Mag.* XX. 296/2 You forget the effrontery of the hack-writer in the shame-facedness of the would-be gentleman. **1827** SCOTT *Jrnl.* 27 Apr., The hack-horse patiently trudges to the pole of his chaise. **1834** A. FONBLANQUE *Eng. under 7 Administ.* (1837) III. 163 The journey.. was no more to be accomplished.. with his own horses, so he took hack-posters. **1838** DICKENS *O. Twist* xxvi, He called a hack-cabriolet. **1850** KINGSLEY *Alton Locke* II. ii. 14 My hack-writing was breaking down my moral sense, as it does that of most men. **1851** *London at Table* I. 31, I.. started in a hack cab for the scene of action. **1856** *Illustr. Lond. News* 2 Feb. 126/2 A hack brougham for morning calls. **1868** J. H. BLUNT *Ref. Ch. Eng.* I. 356 Vilifying with their hack pens. **1878** MORLEY *Carlyle* 190 The hack moralist of the pulpit or the press. **1882** E. W. GOSSE *Gray* vii. 142 Three hack-writers.. were copying MSS. for hire. **1933** E. POUND *Let.* 24 Sept. (1971) 247 Teaching damn sight easier way of earning living than hackwriting.

8. *attrib.* Of or belonging to a hack (senses 1, 2), as ***hack-driver***, ***-rider***, ***-stand***. Also HACKMAN.

1812 *Boston Gaz.* 10 Sept., Advt. (Th.), Hack Stand. **1835** in *Southern Lit. Messenger* IV. 197/1 My hack-driver.. assured [me] that there was no other tavern in the city. **1854** M. HARLAND *Alone* xvi, Going to every hack-stand in the city. **1881** *Encycl. Brit.* XII. 196/2 Galloping is a pace not generally indulged in by hack riders. **1889** A. C. GUNTER *That Frenchman* xii, It occurs to her to ask the hack-driver a question. *Ibid.* xiii, Near a hack-stand.. he tells his assistant to jump out.

9. *attrib.* or *adj.* **a.** In common or promiscuous use; hackneyed; trite, commonplace. **b.** Of a hired sort. Also HACK-WORK.

1781 MAD. D'ARBLAY *Diary* June, This, indeed, is now become our hack speech to Mr. Crutchley. **1818** BYRON *Juan* IV. xvii, When the old world grows dull And we are sick of its hack sounds and sights. **1859** KINGSLEY *Misc.* (1860) I. 254 To use a hack quotation. **1862** SHIRLEY *Nugæ Crit.* iii. 156 The hack language on this subject is exceedingly injurious. **1883** *Century Mag.* XXVI. 285, I do more or less work of a hack kind for the magazines.

†**hack**, *sb.*[4] = HACKLE *sb.*[1] 3, cover of a bee-hive.

1658 EVELYN *Fr. Gard.* (1675) 100 Like the cover or hack of a bee-hive.

†**hack**, *sb.*[5] = HACKLE *sb.*[2] 1, a flax-comb.

1658 tr. *Porta's Nat. Magick* IV. xxv. 156 [Flax] kemmed with hackes, till all the membrans be pilled clean.

hack (hæk), *v.*[1] Forms: 3 **acken**, 3–6 **hacke**, **hakke**, (4 *Sc.* **heke**), (6 *pa. pple.* **hact**), 5 **hak(e**, 5– **hack**. [Early ME. *hack-en*, repr. OE. **haccian* (whence *tó-haccian* to hack in pieces):—Common WGer. **hakkôn*: cf. OFris. *to-hakia*, MHG., MLG., MDu., G. *hacken*, mod.Du. *hakken*.]

I. Transitive senses.

1. To cut with heavy blows in an irregular or random fashion; to cut notches or nicks in; to mangle or mutilate by jagged cuts. In earlier use chiefly, To cut or chop *up* or into pieces, to chop *off*. Const. *about*, *away*, *down*, *off*, *up*.

c **1200** *Trin. Coll. Hom.* 139 A maiden bad te kinge his heued, and he hit bad of acken. *a* **1225** *Ancr. R.* 298 Heo hackede of his heaued. **1297** R. GLOUC. (1724) 216 [He] by pece mele hakked yt al to nogte. *c* **1375** *Sc. Leg. Saints*, *Cecile* 205 þu ma heke þaim as þu wil. *c* **1386** CHAUCER *Knt.'s T.* 2007 He.. leet comande anon to hakke and hewe The okes olde. *c* **1440** *Anc. Cookery* in *Househ. Ord.* (1790) 440 Sethe hom, and hak hom smal. **1571** *Mem. Ripon* (Surtees) I. 308 Did cut and hacke away certane pipes of leade. **1596** SHAKS. *1 Hen. IV*, II. iv. 187 My Sword hackt like a Hand-saw. **1653** H. COGAN tr. *Pinto's Trav.* 212 Causing them to be hacked very small. *a* **1716** SOUTH *Serm.* (1737) X. viii. (R.), That man who could stand and see another stripped or hacked in pieces by a thief or a rogue. **1788** BURKE *Sp. agst. W. Hastings* Wks. XIII. 133 The tyrant.. cut and hacked the limbs of British subjects in the most cruel.. manner. **1796** MRS. GLASSE *Cookery* iii. 27 Take the head up, hack it cross and cross with a knife. *a* **1859** MACAULAY *Hist. Eng.* xxiv. (1871) II. 694 Such a partition as is effected by hacking a living man limb from limb. **1886** OVERTON *Evang. Revival 18th Cent.* viii. 152 Buildings.. hacked about to suit the taste of the last century.

2. To make incisions or jags in by other means.

a. Said of frost: To chap or crack the skin. *dial.*

1673 RAY *Journ. Low C.*, *Grison* 417 Our faces were hackt and burnt.. by the Cold. **1808–25** JAMIESON s.v., The hands or feet, when chapped, are said to be *hackit*.

b. *Football.* To kick the shin of (an opponent) intentionally with the toe of the boot. Also in *Rugby Football*. Const. *over*, *up*.

1864 *Blackheathen* 9/1 'Hacking first man up'.. remains at present quite a Rugby rule. **1866** *Daily Tel.* 7 Nov., The practice of 'hacking'.. consists in each side kicking their opponents' shins in so fearful and violent a manner as to disable the players. **1873** H. SPENCER *Stud. Sociol.* viii. 190 Perhaps the 'education of a gentleman' may properly include giving and receiving 'hacking' of the shins at football. **1887** SHEARMAN *Athletics & Football* (Badm. Libr.) 297 The Union Code very properly abolished hacking, tripping, and scragging. **1887** M. SHEARMAN *Athletics & Football* 395 No hacking, or hacking over, or tripping up shall be allowed under any circumstances. **1897** *Encycl. Sport* I. 404/1 *Rugby Football*.. Not only was it legal to hack over the carrier of the ball, but also the first on side, and I have seen as many as four of the van brought to earth by this means. **1963** *Times* 24 Jan. 3/1 It had been agreed [when the laws of Rugby Union were drawn up] that hacking-over and tripping-up should not be permitted.

c. To embarrass, annoy; to disconcert, confuse. Freq. as **hacked** *ppl. a. U.S. slang* or *dial.*

1892 J. C. HARRIS *Uncle Remus & Friends* 349 When you once git 'em hacked dey er hacked fer good; dey des give right up en roll der eyes. **1908** *Dialect Notes* III. 318 We tried to hack the pitcher. **1917** *Ibid.* IV. 413 That joke hacks Steve to this day. **1969** *Rolling Stone* 28 June 19/1 The big word down there is *commercial*... I wouldn't be so hacked off about it if I didn't love country music.

d. To cope with, manage, accomplish; to tolerate, accept; to comprehend; freq. *to hack it. slang* (orig. *U.S.*).

1955 *Antioch Rev.* XV. 379, I can't hack something like stealing. **1968** *Maclean's Mag.* Dec. 29/1, I just couldn't hack teaching any more, it was as simple as that. **1970** *Globe Mag.* (Toronto) 26 Sept. 9/2 You know, they're shooting people at Kent State and we talk about amendments to the Warble Fly Act. I can't hack that; it drives me crazy. **1972** *Sunday Mirror* 16 Apr. 23/3 Now, suddenly and bewilderingly since President Nixon has ordered his legions home, the Arvin is a great little guy who *can* hack it. **1972** *Newsweek* 7 Aug. 18/2, I had proved to the world during my four years in the Senate..that I can hack it.

3. a. To roughen (a grindstone). **b.** To dress (stone) with a hack-hammer.

1862 *Athenæum* 30 Aug. 264 Each grindstone, when new, must itself be rough-ground into shape by the workman; and afterwards, perhaps twice or thrice a day, its worn surface must be fresh roughened for use..processes of 'razing' and 'hacking', as they are called.

4. Applied to various agricultural operations involving cutting or chopping; as, to break up the surface of the ground, to hoe *in* seed, to cut up by the roots, to reap pease, vetches, or the like.

1620 MARKHAM *Farew. Husb.* II. viii. (1668) 4 When you have thus hacked all your ground, and broke in pieces all hard crusts and roughness of the swarth. **1660** SHARROCK *Vegetables* 23 Drawing trenches in the soyle, and then drawing the earth over them with a hoe..and hacking in the seed with the same instrument. **1669** WORLIDGE *Syst. Agric.* (1681) 326 To Hack, that is to cut up Pease or other haw[m]y stuff by the Roots, or to cut nimbly any thing. *a* **1722** LISLE *Observ. Husb.* 36 (E.D.S.) Hacking is breaking the clots abroad after [the lime] is sown. **1807** VANCOUVER *Agric. Devon* (1813) 141 The wheat sown nine or ten pecks to the acre, and hacked in. **1866** ROGERS *Agric. & Prices* I. xxi. 541 It does not seem that the scythe was used for harvest-works, except..for hacking peas. **1888** *Berksh. Gloss.*, *Hack*, to fag or reap vetches, peas, or beans.

5. a. To hoe or plough up (the soil) into ridges: cf. HACK *sb.*[1] 3. **b.** To rake (hay) into rows. *dial.*

1744–50 W. ELLIS *Mod. Husb.* III. viii. 36 (E.D.S.) Combing is also called hacking. **1848** *Jrnl. R. Agric. Soc.* IX. I. 21 [The grass] is 'hacked' into small rows, the hay-makers following each other. **1881** *Leicestersh. Gloss.* s.v. *Hay*, The grass..is next hacked or chopped with a quick action of the rake into windrows.

†**6.** *Mus.* To break (a note). *Obs.*

14.. *Songs & Carols 15th C.* (Percy Soc.) 101 Jankyn crakit notes an hunderid on a knot, And ȝyt he hakkyt hem smallere than wortes to the pot. *c* **1460** *Towneley Myst.* (Surtees) 111 Wille ye here how thay hak, oure syre, lyst, croyne. *Ibid.* 116 Say, what was his song? hard ye not how he crakyd it? Thre brefes to a long. *Ter. Pastor.* Yee, mary, he hakt it. **1496** [see HACKING *vbl. sb.* 2].

†**7.** *fig.* To mangle or 'make a hash of' (words) in utterance. Also *absol. Obs.*

[*a* **1555** LATIMER in Strype *Eccl. Mem.* II. v. 31 [He would] so hawk it [a homily] and chop it that it were as good for them to be without it.] **1598** SHAKS. *Merry W.* III. i. 79 Let them keepe their limbs whole, and hack our English. **1600** HOLLAND *Livy* XXXVIII. xiv. 991 Hacking and hewing his words, as if hee had not been able to speake them out. **1676** [see HACKING *vbl. sb.* 2].

8. To gain unauthorized access to (computer files, etc., or information held in one). *colloq.* (orig. *U.S.*).

1984 *Times* 7 Aug. 16/3 Some of the more popular boards have special sections for hackers. In these may be found a vast amount of information on the systems which are being hacked. **1984** *Daily Tel.* 3 Dec. 3/3 Timefame International ..claimed that its secret identification codes had been 'hacked' early last month, leaving an unauthorised user free to wander through and examine hundreds of screens full of information. **1986** *Ibid.* 16 Apr. 2/6 [He] had told the police he hacked the system 'to publicise British Telecom's negligence'.

II. Intransitive senses.

9. a. To make rough cuts, to deal cutting blows. Const. *at*, †*upon*.

c **1450** *Golagros & Gaw.* 980 He..Hakkit throw the hard weid, to the hede hynt. **1586** J. HOOKER *Girald. Irel.* in *Holinshed* II. 149/1 Two or three hacked vpon him, & gaue him such deadlie wounds that he fell downe and died. **1719** DE FOE *Crusoe* I. ix, I was twenty days hacking and hewing at it. **1888** BURGON *Lives 12 Gd. Men* II. ix. 212 A joint of lamb was being hacked at by the College Dean.

b. Here perh., in a *fig.* or *transf.* sense, belong the following, transl. the Vulgate *molestus esse*, to be troublesome or grievous.

(But Stratmann takes it as a distinct verb.)

a **1300** *E.E. Psalter* xxxiv. [xxxv.] 13 Whils þai to me ware Hackande [Vulg. *molesti essent*]. *Ibid.* liv. 4 [lv. 3] In wrath to me hakand war þai [*molesti erant*].

10. *fig.* †*to hack after*, to aim at, strive for (*obs.*). *to hack at*, to imitate (*dial.*).

1377 LANGL. *P. Pl.* B. XIX. 399 Þat is my kynde, And nouȝte hakke [**1393** to hacke] after holynesse. *a* **1420** HOCCLEVE *De Reg. Princ.* 929 Upon this wofulle thought I hak and hewe. **1828** *Craven Dial.*, *Hack at*, to imitate.

11. Of the teeth: To chatter. *Obs.* exc. *dial.*

c **1320** *Cast. Love* 1640 (Halliw.) Ther shull..here tethe togedur hacke and shake. **1549** COVERDALE, etc. *Erasm. Par. Jas.* 39 Theyr teeth hacked in theyr heade, they were staruen for colde. **1844** S. BAMFORD *Life of Radical* 35, I heard his teeth hacking in his head.

12. a. To hesitate in speech; to stammer. Cf. HACKER *v.* 2. *Obs.* exc. *dial.*

1553 T. WILSON *Rhet.* 62 Hackyng and hemmyng as though our wittes..were a woll gatheryng. **1604** MIDDLETON *Father Hubburd's T.* Wks. (Bullen) VIII. 54 Yours, If you read without spelling or hacking, T. M. **1884** JEFFERIES *Life of Fields* (1891) 155 If any one hacks and haws in speaking, it is called 'hum-dawing'.

†**b.** *trans. to hack out*, to stammer out. *Obs.*

1631 BRATHWAIT *Whimzies* 49 If any..be admitted to his clergy, and by helpe of a..prompter, hacke out his necke-verse. *a* **1682** SIR T. BROWNE *Tracts* 133 Present Parisians can hardly hack out those few lines of the league between Charles and Lewis..yet remaining in old French.

†**13.** To hesitate, to haggle. *Obs.*

1587 CHURCHYARD *Worth. Wales* (1776) 95 They hacke not long about the thing they sell. **1613** PURCHAS *Pilgrimage* VIII. viii. 783 [He] doth according to his wit, without hacking professe Hakluit..his greatest benefactor.

14. To cough with short, dry, oft-repeated cough.

1802 BEDDOES *Hygëia* II. 14 Marianne..has been hacking all the afternoon. Do tell her of some little thing that is good against a cough. **1886** *S. W. Linc. Gloss.* s.v., He has been hacking like that all night.

15. a. To practise hacking (HACKING *vbl. sb.* I d). *colloq.* (orig. *U.S.*).

1982 *Time* 8 Nov. 92/1 In the Hacker's Dictionary, one finds..*gweep* (one who spends unusually long periods of time hacking). **1983** G. L. STEELE *Hacker's Dict.* 13 At MIT, I would sometimes work nights for a month at a time. Now that I am married, I find that I can hack only in spurts. **1986** *New Scientist* 1 May 25/3 Gold and Shifreen argued that they had hacked to draw attention to the risks of poor security on a system carrying financial transactions.

b. To break *into* a computer system by hacking. *colloq.*

1985 *Times* 2 Apr. 18/5 The equipment needed can be used quite legitimately... But it can also be used to hack into other people's computers. **1986** *TeleLink* Sept.–Oct. 25/2 Tom's bank computer was hacked into and his car loan repayments placed in a suspense account, opened specially by the hackers for that purpose.

hack, *v.*[2] [f. HACK *sb.*[2]]

1. *trans.* To place (bricks) in rows upon hacks or drying frames.

1875 KNIGHT *Dict. Mech.* II. 1046 They [bricks] are sundried or *hacked* and temporarily covered with a thatching of straw to protect them. **1884** C. T. DAVIS *Manuf. Bricks, etc.* 126 Each man 'takes in his share', and carefully hacks them in the drying shed. *Ibid.* 221 Pressed bricks are seldom hacked on edge in the sheds, but are laid flatwise.

2. *Falconry.* To keep (young hawks) 'at hack' or in a state of partial liberty.

1883 SALVIN & BRODRICK *Falconry* Gloss. 150 Short-winged Hawks are not hacked; old Falcons are sometimes, when out of health. **1892** *Coursing & Falconry* (Badm. Libr.) 224 If hacking such hawks was not formerly practised.

hack, *v.*[3] [f. HACK *sb.*[3]]

1. *trans.* To make a hack of, to put to indiscriminate or promiscuous use; to make common, vulgar, or stale, by such treatment; to hackney. Also *to hack about, hack to death.*

1745 ELIZA HEYWOOD *Female Spectator* (1748) II. 286 Bred up to the tumbling art..and hacked about at all the petty wells near London. **1762** C. DENIS in *St. James's Mag.* I. 153 If ever tale was hackt about, Grown obsolete, almost worn out, 'Tis that which now I undertake. **1864** *Spectator* No. 1874. 614 We would that so good a name had not been ..hacked about all over the country and in every newspaper, until it goes against the grain to use it. **1882** MISS BRADDON *Mt. Royal* III. i. 3 Her tenderest emotions had been hacked and vulgarized by long experience in flirtation. **1883** *St. James' Gaz.* 14 Dec. 3/2 [An] argument..which is being hacked to death in all the Radical newspapers.

2. To employ as a literary hack, hire for hack-work.

1813 SCOTT *Let. to Lady L. Stuart* 28 Apr. in *Lockhart*, If he takes the opinion of a hacked old author like myself. **1829** —— *Jrnl.* 16 Apr., For being hacked, what is it but another word for being an author?

3. a. *trans.* To employ (a horse) as a hack or road-horse. **b.** *intr.* To ride on horseback at ordinary pace, to ride on the road; distinguished from *cross-country* or *military riding.*

1857 LAWRENCE *Guy Liv.* 64 (Hoppe) He asked her if she would lend him Bella Donna to hack to cover. **1891** *Riding & Polo* (Badm. Libr.) 61 Ponies are good for boys to learn upon.. It is possible to hack them, but they are not hacks in the true sense of the term. **1894** *Field* 9 June p. xli/1 [These] horses have not been trained only hacked and carefully hunted with harriers and foxhounds.

4. *intr.* To ride in a 'hack' or cab. *U.S.*

1879 *Philad. Times* 8 May (Cent. Dict.), Are we more content to depend on street cars and walking, with the accustomed alternative of hacking at six times the money?

¶The sense of *hack* in SHAKS. *Merry W.* II. i. 52, 'These knights will hack', is doubtful. The senses, To be common or vulgar; to turn prostitute; to have to do with prostitutes; and 'to become vile and vulgar' (Johnson and Nares), have been suggested; but the history and chronology of this verb, and of the sb. whence it is derived, appear to make these impossible.

†**hack**, *v.*[4] [Cf. HACK *sb.*[5]] = HACKLE *v.*[3]

1577 B. GOOGE *Heresbach's Husb.* I. (1586) 39 Flax.. combed and hacked upon an iron combe.

hack, obs. form of HAKE, *sb.*[1] and [4].

hack-, stem of HACK *v.*[1] in Comb., in sense 'hacking, chopping'. Hence, †**hack-chip**, a hatchet; **hack-file**, a locksmith's coarse slitting-file (Knight *Dict. Mech.* 1875); **hack-hammer**, an adz-like tool with a short handle, used in dressing stone; **hack-hook** (see quot.); **hack-iron**, (*a*) a miner's pick, = HACK *sb.*[1] I c; (*b*) a chisel for cutting nails (*Cent. Dict.*); **hack-log**, †**hack-stock**, a chopping-block; **hack-saw**, a saw used in metal-cutting.

c **1440** *Promp. Parv.* 220/2 Hachet, or *hakchyp, *securila.* **1831** J. HOLLAND *Manuf. Metal* I. 290 The whole surface of the [mill-]stone chopped with cross lines to make it cut faster, by means of a *hack-hammer. **1875** *Sussex Gloss.*, **Hack-hook*, a curved hook with a long handle, used for cutting peas and tares, or trimming hedges. **1831** J. HOLLAND *Manuf. Metal* I. 195 Striking it upon an upright chisel or *hack-iron. **1831** CARLYLE *Schiller* Misc. Ess. 1872 III. 88 A good enduring *hacklog, whereon to chop logic. **1867** SMYTH *Sailor's Word-bk.*, **Hack saw*, used for cutting off the heads of bolts; made of a scythe fresh serrated. **1411** *Nottingham Rec.* II. 86, j. *hacstok, *jd.* ? *a* **1500** *Chester Pl.* (E.E.T.S.) iii. 69 Here is a good hackstock [*v.r.* hacckinge stocke]; on this yow maye hew and knock. **1660** H. MORE *Myst. Godl.* VIII. i. 363 The very hackstock of Divine vengeance, and the sport and pastime of Misfortune.

hackamore ('hækəmɔə(r)). *U.S.* [? corruption of Sp. *jaquima*, formerly *xaquima*, halter, headstall of a horse (Minsheu).] A halter of horsehair or raw hide having a nose-piece fitted to serve as the head piece of a bridle. Also, a headstall.

1850 W. R. RYAN *Upper & Lower California* I. 152 He overtook me, mounted on a well saddled horse, and leading another by the hackamore. **1889** FARMER *Americanisms*, *Hackamore*, a plaited bridle in use on the plains, made of horse-hair, and used for breaking-in purposes. **1926** D. BRANCH *Cowboy & his Interpreters* 39 But having the 'hackimore' rope fastened to my belt I held to him until help arrived. **1971** A. P. McINNES *Dunlevy* 86 Her only riding equipment was a rawhide hackamore already on the horse's head.

hack-barrow: see HACK *sb.*[2] 5.

hackberry ('hækbɛrɪ). [A phonetic variant of HAGBERRY, q.v.] **1.** A northern name for the Bird-cherry, more commmonly HAGBERRY, q.v.

2. In North America, the fruit of the tree *Celtis occidentalis*, which resembles the bird-cherry in size; also the tree itself, of which there are several varieties, or sub-species.

1796 MORSE *Amer. Geog.* I. 636 Of the natural growth.. we may reckon the..papaw, the hackberry, and the cucumber trees. **1807** PIKE *Sources Mississ.* I. App. (1810) 41 Timber, on both sides, generally hackberry, cottonwood, and ash. **1864** *Chambers' Encycl.* VI. 727 Another American species, *Celtis crassifolia*, often called Hackberry or Hagberry, and Hoop Ash. **1880** *Encycl. Brit.* XI. 360/1 The hackberry tree is of middle size, attaining from 60 to 80 feet in height, and with the aspect of an elm.

hackbolt ('hækbəʊlt). Also **hagbolt**. A local name for the greater Shearwater, *Puffinus major*.

1843 in Yarrell *Hist. Birds* III. 505 *P. Major* is very well known to the Scillonians by whom it is called *Hackbolt*. **1893** NEWTON *Dict. Birds* 11, *Hackbolt*, *hagbolt*, and *hagdown*, names said to be given by the people of Scilly and Man to the larger of the species of Shearwater.

†'**hackbush, 'hagbush.** *Obs.* Also 5 hak(e)buss, 5–6 hacbush, 6 hackbus. [a. rare OF. *haquebusche* (1475), *harquebusche* (1478), a. MFl. *haec-*, *haegbusse*, *hakebus*, *hagebus*, (mod.Du. *haakbus*) = MLG. *hake-*, *hakelbusse*, MHG. *hakenbühse*, (mod.G. *hakenbüchse*); f. *haken*, *hake*, etc. hook + *bühse*, *busse*, *bus* gun, fire-arm; lit. 'hook-gun', so called from the hook originally cast on the gun, by which it was attached to a point of support. In French the usual 16th c. forms were *haquebute* and *(h)arquebuse*, whence HACKBUT and HARQUEBUS.] An early form of fire-arm; = HACKBUT; see etymology, and HARQUEBUS. It was at first a wall-piece, afterwards used in the field with a portable tripod or rest.

1484 in *Harleian MS.* No. 433. lf. 157b, A Warrant to the Constable of the Towre, to delivre to Roger Bikley 8 Serpentynes upon Cartes, 28 Hacbushes with theire frames. **1485** *Naval Accts. Hen. VII* (1896) 50 Hakebusses xij. *Ibid.*

95 Trestelles for hakbusses. **1548** HALL *Chron.* (1809) 787 The Prior of Rome was by a Hackbush slayn.
β. **1539** *Indent.* in *Archæol.* XXII. 69 In the towre at th' end of the whyte wall, 8 double hagbushes. **1547** *Inv.* Ibid. 70 Hagbushes of iron, hagbushes shotte, hagbuttes of croke of iron. **1548** HALL *Chron., Hen. VIII*, 28 With artilerie, as Fawcones, serpentynes, cast hagbushes.

†**hackbushier, hagbushier, hagbusser.** *Obs.* [f. HACKBUSH, HAGBUSH + -IER, -ER.]

1. = HARQUEBUSIER 1.
1524 PACE *Let.* in Strype *Eccl. Mem.* I. App. xi. 21 Skirmishing with four hundred hagbushiers of France. *Ibid.*, Hagbusheirs mynglied among our mentionid light horses.

2. = HARQUEBUS: cf. HARQUEBUSHER 2.
1556 J. HEYWOOD *Spider & F.* lii. 22 Handgoons, hakes, hagbussers, culuerins, slings.

hackbut, hagbut ('hæk-, 'hægbət). *arch.* and *Hist.* Forms: *α.* 6 hacquebute, -buyt, 6–7 hackebutte, 7- haquebut, 7- hackbut (hakebut, hacbutt). *β.* 6–7 hagbutt(e, -bute (6 hagbit, hergbut), 7- hagbut (haguebut). [a. 15–16th c. F. *haquebut, -bute* (*hacque-, aque-, harqbute*), ad. MDu. *hakebus*, or MLG. *hakebusse*: see HACKBUSH. Later in the 16th c., this F. form passed (under influence of It. *archibuso*) through the intermediate *harquebute*, to *harquebuse, arquebuse*, whence the corresponding English forms: see HARQUEBUS.] **1.** An early kind of portable firearm; = HACKBUSH, HARQUEBUS.
α. **1543** TRAHERON *Vigo's Cirurg.* III. II. iii. 116 Woundes made by Hacquebutes. **1583** GOLDING *Calvin on Deut.* cxxvi. 773 Some which had leuer to beare a hackebutte on their shoulder than a distaffe in their hand. **1611** COTGR., *Haquebute*, an Haquebut, or Arquebuse; a Coliuer. **1864** BURTON *Scot. Abr.* I. iv. 167 *note*, The identical hackbut with which Bothwellhaugh shot the Regent Murray.
β. **1541–2** *Act 33 Hen. VIII* c. 6 *Preamb.*, With crossebowes, litil short handgunnes, and little hagbutts. *Ibid.* §2 To seise and take..everie hagbutt and demyhake beinge shorter in lengthe then thre quarters of a Yarde. **1573** *Satir. Poems Reform.* xxxix. 153 Out gais the Hergbut, in the Cannon glydis. **1582–8** *Hist. James VI* (1804) 40 Sorely stressit be shott of hagbute. **1596** DALRYMPLE tr. *Leslie's Hist. Scot.* x. 316 Dischargeng thair hagbitis [L. *bombardis*]. **1808** SCOTT *Marm.* v. iii, A crossbow there a hagbut here.

†**2.** ***hackbut à croc*** (***acroke, of croche, of croke, upon crocke***): see HARQUEBUS 2. *Obs.*
1547 [see HACKBUSH *β*]. **1549** *Compl. Scot.* vi. 41 Mak reddy ȝour cannons..hagbutis of croche, half haggis. **1552** EDW. VI. *Lit. Rem.* (Roxb.) 427 He found in the toune..300 hagbutes of croke. **1563** in Meyrick *Anc. Armour* (1842) III. 37 Hagbutts uppon crocke xiij, whereof xij serviceable. **1580** LD. GREY in Grosart *Spenser's Wks.* I. 472 They had.. muskets and hackbus-acroke.

†**3.** A man armed with a hackbut. *Obs.*
1587 HOLINSHED *Chron. Scot.* an. 1583 (R.) Capteine Lamie..sent with two companies of hackbuts.

4. *Comb.*, as ***hackbut-man***.
1805 SCOTT *Last Minstr.* IV. vi, The German hagbut-men [*v.r.* hackbut-]. **1885** C. W. C. OMAN *Art of War* 93 Under a severe fire from the Spanish hackbutmen.

hackbuteer, -ier (hækbə'tɪə(r)). Also **hag-**. [ad. 16th c. F. *hacquebutier*, f. *hacquebute*: cf. *fusilier, cannonier*.] = next.
c **1610** SIR J. MELVIL *Mem.* (1735) 16 Send to their Help 2000 Hacbutiers. **1805** SCOTT *Last Minstr.* III. xxi, He lighted the match of his bandelier, And wofully scorch'd the hackbuteer. **1873** BURTON *Hist. Scot.* V. liv. 69 Two hundred hagbutiers were sent..to help the master of Forbes.

hackbutter, hagbutter ('hækbətə(r), 'hæg-). *arch.* and *Hist.* Also 6 **haquebuter**, *Sc.* **hagbutar** (**-bitter**). [f. HACKBUT + -ER: see prec.] A soldier armed with a hackbut; a harquebusier.
1544–8 in *Archæol.* XXII. 69 There shall be 150 haquebuters, who shall have good haquebuts. **1548** PATTEN *Exped. Scotl.* in Arb. *Garner* III. 76 Captain of 200 Hackbutters on horseback. **1549** *Compl. Scot.* Epist. 6 He renforsit the toune vitht victualis, hagbutaris, ande munitions. *a* **1627** HAYWARD *Edw. VI* (1630) 24 Of the English one Spanish hackbutter was hurt. **1777** NIMMO *Stirlingsh.* xii. 292 The passage..was lined with an hundred Hagbutters. **1888** *Trans. Glasgow Archæol. Soc.* I. 283 Edinburgh had furnished the hagbutters of his army.

hacked (hækt), *ppl. a.* [f. HACK *v.*[1] + -ED[1].]

1. Chopped; slashed, mangled; having irregular and jagged cuts or wounds; chapped, as by frost.
c **1420** *Pallad. on Husb.* I. 652 Hacked leek or tendir chesis. **1583** STANYHURST *Æneis* I. (Arb.) 22 The weather hackt Troians. **1606** SHAKS. *Ant. & Cl.* IV. viii. 31 Beare our hackt Targets. **1791** COWPER *Iliad* II. 502 His hack'd and riven corslet. **1880** *Antrim & Down Gloss.*, *Hackit hands*, hands chapped from exposure to cold. **1896** *Daily News* 8 Sept. 5/5 The hacked bodies of women and children.

b. *Her.* (See quots.)
1828–40 BERRY *Encycl. Her.*, *Hacked*, as a bend, &c., indented with the indents embowed. **1868** CUSSANS *Her.* (1882) 129 *Hacked*, an indented Charge is thus described, when the notches are curved on both sides, similar to the Teeth of Barnacles.

c. ***hacked quartz***, a variety of quartz presenting incisions, as if produced by hacking it in various directions with a knife or other sharp instrument. (Bristow, *Gloss. Min.* 1861.)

†**2.** ? Spoken with hesitating utterance. *Obs. rare.*
a **1603** T. CARTWRIGHT *Confut. Rhem. N.T.* Pref. (1618) 35 By your cloudy and hacked speaches.

hackee ('hæki:). [Imitative of the animal's cry.] A species of ground squirrel, the Striped or Chipping Squirrel, or Chipmuck, of North America.
1860 in BARTLETT *Dict. Amer.* **1863** WOOD *Illustr. Nat. Hist.* I. 599 The Hackee..is one of the most familiar of North American quadrupeds.

hacker ('hækə(r)), *sb.* [f. HACK *v.*[1] + -ER[1].]

1. One who hacks; one who hoes with a hack.
1620 MARKHAM *Farew. Husb.* II. ii. (1668) 4 One good hacker, being a lusty labourer, will at good ease hack or cut more than half an acre of ground in a day. **1784** *New Spectator* IV. 5/1 Hackers and hewers of reputation.

†**b.** A 'cutter', cut-throat, bully; = HACKSTER.
1581 PETTIE *Guazzo's Civ. Conv.* III. (1586) 135 b, Like these cutters, and hackers, who will take the wall of men, and picke quarrells. **1589** *Pappe w. Hatchet* B b, There is an olde hacker that shall take order for to print them. **1621** BURTON *Anat. Mel.* I. ii. III. xiii. (1651) 118 A common hacker or notorious thief. **1649** BLITHE *Eng. Improv. Impr.* (1653) Ded., How comes City and Country to be filled with Drones and Rogues, our highwaies with hackers, and all places with sloth and wickedness?

†**c.** *fig.* One who mangles words or sense. *Obs.*
a **1603** T. CARTWRIGHT *Confut. Rhem. N.T.* (1618) 606 To make the Author of the Epistle such a hacker and mangler as they themselues be.

2. That which hacks; an implement for hacking, chopping wood, or breaking up earth; a chopper, cleaver; a hoe, mattock.
1481–90 *Howard Househ. Bks.* (Roxb.) 137 Item, for hakkeres ij.*d.* **1688** R. HOLME *Armoury* III. 292/2 The Dutch Cleever, or Chopping Knife, is termed an Hacker, or Hackmes. *a* **1722** LISLE *Husb.* (1752) 214 My labourers came from mowing vetches..not having their hackers with them. **1854** *Jrnl. R. Agric. Soc.* XV. I. 100 Hoeing with a heavy hacker or hoe between the rows. **1879** MISS JACKSON *Shropsh. Word-bk.*, *Hacker*, a short, strong, slightly curved implement of a peculiar kind, for chopping off the branches of fallen trees, etc. **1890** *Gloucestersh. Gloss.*, *Hacker*, a sort of axe for cutting faggots.

b. *U.S.* A tool for making an oblique incision in a tree, as a channel for the passage of sap, gum, or resin.
1875 KNIGHT *Dict. Mech.*

3. a. A person with an enthusiasm for programming or using computers as an end in itself. *colloq.* (orig. *U.S.*).
1976 J. WEIZENBAUM *Computer Power & Human Reason* iv. 118 The compulsive programmer, or hacker as he calls himself, is usually a superb technician. **1977** *Time* 5 Sept. 39/1 Some 500 retail outlets have opened in the past couple of years to sell and service microcomputers—and serve as hangouts for the growing legions of home-computer nuts, or 'hackers' as they call themselves. **1982** *Sci. Amer.* Oct. 110/1 In the jargon of computer science a hacker is someone who spends much of his time writing computer programs. **1983** *Byte* May 298/1 'Hacker' seems to have originated at MIT. The original German/Yiddish expression referred to someone so inept as to make furniture with an axe, but somehow the meaning has been twisted so that it now generally connotes someone obsessed with programming and computers but possessing a fair degree of skill and competence. **1984** *Which Micro?* Dec. 17/3 A hacker might spend more time playing his own version of PacMan than on useful program development. **1986** *A & B Computing* Nov. 16/3 The on-screen help is for the casual user but there's plenty for the hacker who wants to tinker with the software and tailor it for special purposes.

b. A person who uses his skill with computers to try to gain unauthorized access to computer files or networks. *colloq.*
1983 *Daily Tel.* 3 Oct. 3/1 A hacker—computer jargon for an electronic eavesdropper who by-passes computer security systems—yesterday penetrated a confidential British Telecom message system being demonstrated live on BBC-TV. **1985** *U.S.A. Today* 18 Oct. A1/4 A gang of 23 teen-age computer hackers has done 'significant damage' to Chase Manhattan Bank's records. **1986** *TeleLink* Sept.–Oct. 25/2 Just for fun, the hackers decided to drop a few APBs (All Points Bulletins) into the local police computer, with the result that, when out driving in his car, he was repeatedly stopped.

hacker, *v. dial.* [freq. of HACK *v.*[1]]

1. *trans.* 'To hash in cutting, to hack small' (Jam.).
1807 HOGG *Mountain Bard* 18 (Jam.) His throat was a' hackered, an' ghastly was he.

2. *intr.* To hesitate in utterance; to stammer; to 'hum and ha'.
1787 GROSE *Provinc. Gloss.*, *Hacker*, to stutter. S[outh]. **1818** COBBETT *Pol. Reg.* XXXIII. 473 Compared with this, how can one think with patience of the hackering, and stammering [etc.]? **1824** MISS MITFORD *Village* Ser. I. (1863) 115 To stammer and hacker, to bow and curtsey.

3. To haggle.
1833 *Blackw. Mag.* XXXIV. 688 Shall national parsimony..hacker about the remuneration?

hackery ('hækərɪ). *Anglo-Ind.* Also 8 **hackary**, 8–9 **hackree**, 9 **hackaree, hackeray, -ee, -ie, hackrie.** [Origin not clear; perh. a corruption of Hindī *chhakṛā* a two-wheeled bullock-cart.] The common native bullock-cart of India used for the transport of goods; also, in Western India and Sri Lanka, as formerly in Bengal, applied to a lighter carriage (drawn sometimes by horses) for the conveyance of persons.
1698 FRYER *Acc. E. India & P.* 83 We were forced to mount the Indian Hackery, a Two-wheeled Chariot, drawn by swift little Oxen. **1782** W. F. MARTYN *Geog. Mag.* I. 264 The hackrees are in the nature of hackney-coaches; and like them, are let to the public for hire. **1793** W. HODGES *Trav. India* 5 A hackery is a small covered carriage upon two wheels, drawn by bullocks, and used generally for the female part of the family. **1834** CAUNTER *Orient. Ann.* x. 128 Carried in gaudy palankeens, or in hackeries, with gorgeous canopies, drawn by two prancing horses. **1845** STOCQUELER *Brit. India* (1854) 185 For the conveyance of heavy goods, hackries or bullock-carts are available.

hack-file, -hammer: see HACK-.

hackhead, var. of HAKED a pike.

hackia ('hækɪə). = GUAIACUM 2.
1851 *Illustr. Catal. Gt. Exhib.* IV. I. 983/2 Hackia, lignum vitæ, transverse and vertical sections, from River Demerara. **1858** SIMMONDS *Dict. Trade*, *Hackia*, a wood..used for mill cogs and shafts. **1969** S. M. SADEEK *Windswept & Other Stories* 36 The dark East Indian..flicked a piece of paper before him with his hackia stick.

hackie ('hækɪ). *U.S. colloq.* Also **hacky.** [f. HACK *sb.*[3] 2.] A taxi-driver.
1937 *Daily Express* 10 Mar. 6/7 'Hackie' is taxi-driver. **1946** MEZZROW & WOLFE *Really Blues* (1957) viii. 114 Weaving..like an expert hackie in heavy traffic. **1959** 'M. NEVILLE' *Sweet Night for Murder* xiii. 129 And now.. unearth some other blasted hacky that drove me there.

hackin: see next 3.

hacking ('hækɪŋ), *vbl. sb.*[1] [f. HACK *v.*[1] + -ING[1].]

1. a. The action of the verb HACK; chopping, hewing; mutilation, etc. ***hacking off, out***: see quots.
c **1440** *Promp. Parv.* 222/1 Hakkynge, or hewynge, *sectio.* **1621** BURTON *Anat. Mel.* I. ii. III. ii. (1651) 96 Why doth scraping of trenchers offend a third, or hacking of files? **1842–76** GWILT *Archit.* Gloss. s.v., Taking down old plastering from a wall or ceiling is called 'hacking off'. **1881** YOUNG *Every Man his own Mechanic* §1693 The removal of old glass and putty from a sash-frame is termed 'hacking out' in the trade. **1892** E. REEVES *Homeward Bound* 266 There was a lot of horrid hacking and butchery.

b. *Football.* See HACK *v.*[1] 2 b.

c. [After G. *hackung*; cf. F. *hachement.*] Massage with the edge of the hand.
1890 A. KELLGREN *Ling's Syst. Man. Treatm.* 25 Tapotement means hacking or beating. **1893** A. S. ECCLES *Sciatica* 64 Thorough rubbing, kneading, hacking, and passive movements are practised.

d. The use of a computer for the satisfaction it gives; the activity of a hacker (HACKER *sb.* 3). *colloq.* (orig. *U.S.*).
1976 J. WEIZENBAUM *Computer Power & Human Reason* iv. 118 The compulsive programmer spends all the time he can working on one of his big projects. 'Working' is not the word he uses; he calls what he does 'hacking'. **1984** *Times* 7 Aug. 16/2 Hacking, as the practice of gaining illegal or unauthorized access to other people's computers is called. **1984** *Sunday Times* 9 Dec. 15/2 Hacking is totally intellectual—nothing goes boom and there are no sparks. It's your mind against the computer.

†**2.** Breaking of a note; 'mangling' of words or sense: see HACK *v.*[1] 6 and 7. *Obs.*
1496 *Dives & Paup.* (W. de W.) I. lix. 101/1 It were better to say goddes seruyce without note than with note and hackynge of the syllabes and wordes of our prayers. **1676** MARVELL *Mr. Smirke* 6 Having avowed that he had scann'd the Book thorow, this hacking and vain repetition being just like it.

3. *concr.* (Usually **hackin.**) A large kind of sausage or mincemeat pudding which formed, in some districts, part of the 'cheer' on Christmas day.
1674 N. FAIRFAX *Bulk & Selv.* 159 Thus shall we sort out eternity into as many kinds and lengths, as the Darbyshire huswife does her pudding when she makes whitings and blackings, and liverings and hackings. **1674–91** RAY *N.C. Words* 142 A Hackin..*farcimen.* **16..** *Aubrey MS.* (N.), The hackin must be boiled by day break, or else two young men must take the maiden by the arms, and run her round the market place. **1878** *Cumbld. Gloss.*, *Hackin*..a pudding of mincemeat and fruit—used till lately for the family breakfast on Christmas day.

4. *Arch.* (See quot.)
1842–76 GWILT *Archit.* Gloss., *Hacking* in walling, denotes the interruption of a course of stones by the introduction of another on a different level, for want of stones to complete the thickness.

5. *attrib.* and *Comb.* **hacking-block, -stock**, = *hack-log, -stock*; **hacking-knife, -tool**: see quots.
1592 Hacckinge stocke [see *hackstock* s.v. HACK-]. **1823** P. NICHOLSON *Pract. Build.* 422 A Hacking-out Tool is an old broken knife, ground sharp on its edge. **1827** STEUART *Planter's G.* (1828) 46 The lopping and hacking method. **1842–67** GWILT *Archit.* §2226 The hacking knife is for cleaning out the old putty from the rebates where squares are to be stopped in. **1877** *Holderness Gloss.*, *Hackin-block*, a block of wood for chopping meat upon.

'**hacking,** *vbl. sb.*[2] [f. HACK *v.*[3] + -ING[1].] **1.** The action of the vb. (esp. in sense 3).
1879 [see HACK *v.*[3] 4]. **1881** *Encycl. Brit.* XII. 198/2 For hacking purposes a double bridle is almost invariably used.

2. Special Comb. **hacking coat, jacket**, a sports coat suitable for use when riding, often tailored in a tweed with vents at the side or at the back; **hacking length**, the length of a hacking jacket.

1948 'E. CRISPIN' *Buried for Pleasure* vi. 38 He wore jodhpurs, riding-boots, a violent check hacking coat, and a yellow tie. **1954** *New Yorker* 13 Nov. 168/2 A jacket with a center vent and four buttons, or a hacking coat with side vents and slanted flap pockets, is from $125 to $135. **1954** *Irish Digest* Nov. 40 Resplendent in cloth cap, tweed hacking jacket, [etc.].., Huston squires it happily among his beloved Irish. **1959** H. HOBSON *Mission House Murder* ii. 11 My Harris tweed hacking-jacket. **1965** *Punch* 22 Dec. 933/3 Leo McKern's irascible Baron is a splendid comic creation, wrapped in a loud-checked hacking jacket (checks any larger and they wouldn't have fitted on to the material). **1966** *Guardian* 27 July 6/4 Jackets are hacking length.

'hacking, *ppl. a.* [f. HACK *v.*[1] + -ING[2].]

1. That hacks, wounds, or slashes.

1612 W. MARTYN *Youth's Instruct.* 39 These hacking fencers, impudent stage players, beastly drunkards. **1808** SCOTT *Let. to C. K. Sharpe* 30 Dec. in *Lockhart*, Lay hold of ..any other new book you like, and give us a good hacking review of it. **1864** PUSEY *Lect. Daniel* i. 9 That hacking school of criticism, which hewed out the books of Holy Scripture into as many fragments as it willed.

2. ***hacking cough***, a short, dry, frequently repeated cough. Also HECKING, q.v.

[**1642** FULLER *Holy & Prof. St.* II. ii. 55 It was called an Hectick fever; because (saith he) of an hecking cough which ever attendeth that disease.] *a* **1825** FORBY *Voc. E. Anglia, Hacking-cough*, a faint tickling cough. **1835** SIR G. STEPHEN *Search of Horse* vi. 90 The hacking tone of chronic asthma. **1880** MISS BRADDON *Just as I am* xxvii, I have had a hacking cough ever since last September.

Hence **'hackingly** *adv.*

1611 FLORIO, *Alla recisa*, cuttingly, hackingly.

hackle ('hæk(ə)l), *sb.*[1] Forms: 1 **hacele**, 3–4 **hakel(e**, 5 **hakille**, **-yll**, 7 **hackel**, **hacle**, 6– **hackle**. [OE. *hacele* and *hæcele*, wk. fem., 'cloak, mantle, cassock', corresponding, exc. in formative suffix, to OHG *hachul*, MHG. *hachel*, Icel. *hökull* 'priest's cope', Goth. *hakuls* 'cloak', str. masc., also to ON. *hekla* str. f. 'cowled, or hooded frock'.]

†1. A cloak, mantle, outer garment; a chasuble.

c **893** K. ÆLFRED *Oros.* v. x. §3 þa sende him mon ane blace hacelan angean him. *c* **1000** ÆLFRIC *Voc.* in Wr.-Wülcker 153/9 *Clamis*, hacele, *uel* fotsið sciccel. *c* **1200** *Trin. Coll. Hom.* 163 Ðe meshakele of medeme fustane.

2. A covering of any kind, as a bird's plumage, a serpent's skin, etc. *Obs.* exc. *dial.*

13.. *Gaw. & Gr. Knt.* 2081 Vch hille hade a hatte, a myst-hakel huge. *c* **1460** J. RUSSELL *Bk. Nurture* 695 Pecok in hakille ryally. **1658** tr. *Porta's Nat. Mag.* I. 17 The herb Dragon..is full of speckles like a Serpents hackle. **1750** W. ELLIS *Mod. Husb.* III. ii. 116 (E.D.S.) The slug slipped his outer skin, or what we call his hackle in Hertfordshire. **1876** *Whitby Gloss.*, *Hackle*, substance about the person, as flesh, clothing. Property in general. **1892** M. C. F. MORRIS *Yorksh. Folk-Talk* 319 Hackle is the natural covering of any animal, the human skin..'He's got a good hackle ov his back'.

3. **a.** The conical straw roofing of a bee-hive. **b.** The straw covering of the apex of a rick. **c.** The case of a Florence flask.

1609 C. BUTLER *Fem. Mon.* (1634) 26 Swine..rubbing against the hives, and tearing the hackles. **1655** W. MEWE *Let. to Hartlib* in *Ref. Commw. Bees* 49 My Appiary consists of a row of little houses..which I find as cheap at seven yeares end as straw hacles. **1673** RAY *Journ. Low C.* (1738) I. 289 The hackles of old flasks. **1713** WARDER *True Amazons* 44 The Mouse will..shelter himself betwixt the Hackle and the Hive. **1842** AKERMAN *Gloss. Wiltsh. Words, Hackle*, straw covering of the apex of a rick. **1886** TEGETMEIER in *Gd. Words* 810 The old straw hive, which was..to be seen..covered with a straw hackle.

hackle ('hæk(ə)l), *sb.*[2] In 5 **hakell**, 6 **hackel**; see also HECKLE, HATCHEL. [Not recorded in OE.; but the various ME. forms *hechele*, *hetchell* (*c* 1300), *hekele* (*c* 1440), *hakell* (1485), and the later *hatchel*, point to OE. **hacule*, **hęcile*. No corresponding words are recorded in the early stage of any Germanic lang., but MHG. *hachele*, *hechele*, (mod.G. *hechel*), MLG. and MDu. *hekele*, (Du. *hekel*), Da. *hegle*, Sw. *häckla*, all point to OTeut. type **hakilā*, **hakulā*, str. fem. with suffix-ablaut; prob. from the root *hak-* of OHG. **hakjan*, *hęcchen*, *hęcken*, to prick, pierce, stab, and of HOOK, q.v.

It has been suggested that *heckle* came immediately from Du.; but the ME. *hechele*, *hetchell*, testify to an OE. *hęcel*, which would also give *heckle* in the north; so also, the vowel of *hackle*, *hatchel* can be explained only from OE. (Sense 2 is prob. the same word, or from the same root; sense 3 is more doubtful.)]

I. 1. **a.** An instrument set with parallel steel pins for splitting and combing out the fibres of flax or hemp; a flax-comb; = HECKLE, HATCHEL.

1485 *Inv.* in *Ripon Ch. Acts* 368 Unum hakell pro lino. **1599** T. M[OUFET] *Silkwormes* 4 Beetles, hackels, wheeles and frame, Wherwith to bruse, touse, spin and weaue the same. **1797** *Monthly Mag.* III. 301 Mr. Sellars has contrived, by the introduction of steel hackles, in place of wire, to prepare wool, cotton, etc. much more expeditiously, for spinning cordage or lines. **1837** WHITTOCK *Bk. Trades* (1842) 238 Hold the strike of flax in your hand, and break it well upon the coarse hackle.

b. *Hairdressing*. (See quot. 1957.)

1903 A. M. SUTTON *Boardwork* (ed. 2) i. 9 A 'card' or 'hackle', used for disentangling combings, smoothing and mixing hair, is a magnified comb composed of steel spikes or prongs. **1957** V. J. KEHOE *Technique Film & T.V. Make-Up* iii. 34 *Hackle*, a multi-spiked tool which is clamped to a bench and used for combing or carding skeins of hair.

II. 2. Local name of the stickleback.

1655 MOUFET & BENNET *Health's Improv.* (1746) 275 Hackles or Sticklebacks are supposed to come of the Seed of Fishes spilt or miscarrying in the Water. **1661** LOVELL *Hist. Anim. & Min.* 235 Stickle-backs, Hackles; or Harry bannings. **1867** SMYTH *Sailor's Word-bk.*, *Hackle*..a west-country name for the stickleback.

III. 3. **a.** The long shining feathers on the neck of certain birds, as the domestic cock, peacock, pigeon, etc. Also, the feathers on the saddle of a cock. ***a cock of a different hackle***, an opponent of a different character.

a **1450** *Fysshynge w. Angle* (1883) 34 The yelow flye, the body of yelow wull: the wynges of the redde cocke hakyll. **1653** WALTON *Angler* iv. 110 Take the hackel of a Cock or Capons neck..take of the one side of the feather, and then take the hackel, Silk or Crewel, Gold or Silver thred, make these fast at the bent of the hook [etc.]. **1850** D. J. BROWNE *Amer. Poultry Yard* 22 The hackles of the lower part of the back. *Ibid.* 253 In capons..the hackle, the tail feathers, and the spurs grew to a much greater length than in cocks. **1865** KINGSLEY *Herew.* II. iv. 65 Fight it out..with a cock of a very different hackle. **1867** H. B. TEGETMEIER *Pigeons* xi. 117 The hackle, or neck-feathers, should be bright. **1874** *Slang Dict.* 185 *To show hackle*, to be willing to fight. **1884** *Times* 18 Mar. 7 The 42nd [1st Batt. Roy. Highlanders].. received the red hackle as an honourable distinction. **1970** H. E. SMITH *Bantams* i. 9 Feathers towards the stern are correctly called 'saddle hackles'. *Ibid.* iii. 19 The colours of a Red Jungle Fowl..male are neck hackle, golden; saddle hackle, orange.

[¶Quot. 1653 was printed in a mangled and distorted form by Johnson, who founded on it a mistaken explanation, 'Raw silk, any filmy substance unspun'. Although corrected in Todd's Johnson, this bogus sense of *hackle*, with 'flimsy' substituted by Webster for 'filmy', continues to be reproduced in dictionaries.]

b. The hackles of a cock are erected when he is angry; hence ***with the hackles up***, said also of a dog on the point of fighting when the hairs at the top of the neck stand up or of a hound when near the fox and on the point of killing him, also *transf.* of a man when aroused. Hence *hackles* is sometimes put for hair, whiskers, etc.

1881 PHILLIPPS-WOLLEY *Sport in Crimea* 76 As my hackles were now fairly up, I crept and ran as well as I could after my wounded game. **1882** *Pall Mall G.* 31 May 4/2 Not a single hound with his hackles up. **1883** E. PENNELL-ELMHIRST *Cream Leicestersh.* 98 I almost saw the hackles of a good old squire rise as he waved his hat and cheered. **1894** BLACKMORE *Perlycross* 179 He had no moustache to stroke —for only cavalry officers..as yet wore ginger hackles.

4. *Angling*. An artificial fly, dressed wholly or principally with a hackle-feather, or something resembling this; a 'palmer'. Also ***hackle-fly***.

1676 COTTON *Walton's Angler* II. 318 This month also a Plain Hackle or Palmer fly..will kill. **1799** G. SMITH *Laboratory* II. 301 Black-hackle. Body, pale yellow silk, [etc.]. **1867** O. W. HOLMES *Guard. Angel* xxii. (1891) 260 He must go armed with all implements, from the red hackle to the harpoon.

IV. *attrib.* and *Comb.*

5. [from 1] as **hackle bar**, the bar in which the hackle pins are set; **hackle bench** (see quot.); **hackle pin**, **tooth**, one of the teeth of a hackle; **hackle sheet**, a sheet carrying hackles and moving over pulleys.

1875 *Ure's Dict. Arts* II. 431 The object of these guide plates is to support the *hackle bars in passing over the small rollers. *Ibid.* 423 *Hackle bench sometimes revolving so as to present different degrees of hackles at its various angles, sometimes stationary with the gradation of hackles upon its length. *Ibid.* 426 The surfaces being placed so close together that the *hackle pins penetrated the flax from both sides, and hackled at the same time. *Ibid.* 425 Pulleys for carrying the *hackle sheets. *Ibid.* 420 For hand-hackling, the tools used consist of a surface studded..with metal points, called *hackle-teeth.

6. [from III] as ***hackle-feather***, ***-maker***; ***hackle-wise*** adv.; **hackle-fly**: see 4.

1681 CHETHAM *Angler's Vade-m.* x. §3 (1689) 102 An Artifical Palmer-Worm or Fly which is to be made with a Hackle Feather. **1867** F. FRANCIS *Angling* vi. (1880) 244 A capital hot-weather fly dressed hacklewise. **1888** *Daily News* 22 May 2/3 The hackle feathers of the male bird are several feet long.

hackle, *v.*[1] [dim. and freq. of HACK *v.*[1]: cf. MDu. *hakkelen*, having the same relation to *hakken*. Cf. also HAGGLE *v.*]

1. *trans.* To cut roughly, hack, mangle by cutting.

1579–80 NORTH *Plutarch* (1612) 741 Caesar..was hackled and mangled among them, as a wild beast taken of hunters. **1611** CORYAT *Crudities* 274 I have seen a Mountebanke hackle and gash his naked arme with a knife most pittifully to beholde. **1684** *Lond. Gaz.* No. 1959/4 His Hair not shav'd but cut and hackled with a pair of Sheers. **1790** BURKE *Fr. Rev.* Wks. V. 351 The other divisions of the kingdom being hackled and torn to pieces. **1876** T. S. EGAN tr. *Heine's Atta Troll*, etc. 222 'Twill prickle and hackle your faces.

†2. *intr.* To make a hacking. *Obs.*

1589 NASHE *Martins Months Minde* 18 These lustie youthes..hackle at our throate.

Hence **hackled** *ppl. a.*, **'hackling** *vbl. sb.*

1583 BABINGTON *Commandm.* i. (1637) 8 Evill cutting or hackling of the knife. **1842** S. LOVER *Handy Andy* xxv. 214 An old knife whose hackled edge..assisted Andy's own ingenuity in the tearing of his coat.

hackle, *v.*[2] [f. HACKLE *sb.*[1]] *trans.* To cover (a bee-hive) with a hackle or straw roof.

1609 C. BUTLER *Fem. Mon.* (1634) 51 That they be close cloomed..and well hackled down to, or below, the Stool.

hackle, *v.*[3] [f. HACKLE *sb.*[2] 1: cf. HECKLE *v.* in same sense.] **a.** *trans.* To dress (flax or hemp) with the hackle, whereby the fibres are split, straightened, and combed out, so as to be in condition for spinning. Also used of dressing the hair in wigmaking.

1616 [see HACKLING *vbl. sb.*]. **1755** JOHNSON, *Hackle*, to dress flax. **1788** *Trans. Soc. Arts* VI. 164 To be hackled, much in the manner of dressing Flax or Hemp. **1797** MAR. EDGEWORTH *Early Lessons* (1827) I. 217 I am going to hackle the flax..said the woman, and she began to comb the flax with these steel combs. **1866** ROGERS *Agric. & Prices* I. xviii. 426 Small quantities of hemp were grown..and..the produce was hackled and spun by the servants. **1931** G. A. FOAN *Art & Craft of Hairdressing* i. 11/1 When dry the hair is ready for drawing off into roots and points. Taking each section separately the student should lightly hackle the extreme ends. **1966** J. S. COX *Illustr. Dict. Hairdressing* 68/1 *Hackle*, to draw hair through a hackle to disentangle it.

b. *fig.* = HECKLE: see CROSS-HACKLE.

Hence **hackled** *ppl. a.*

1875 *Ure's Dict. Arts* II. 422 Each hackled tress of flax.

hackle, *v.*[4] *Angling*. [f. HACKLE *sb.*[2] III.] *trans.* To dress (a fly) with a hackle-feather.

1867 F. FRANCIS *Angling* xi. (1880) 402 Blue jay hackled over the wing. **1886** PRITT *N. Country Flies* 27 Hackled with a golden feather from a Cock Pheasant's neck.

Hence **hackled** *ppl. a.*, **'hackling** *vbl. sb.*

1867 F. FRANCIS *Angling* xiii. (1880) 475 Where a junction of hackles is to be effected..compare the length of the fibres, so that the hackling may graduate. **1892** *Daily News* 14 Apr. 3/1 In Yorkshire hackled spider flies are the only wear.

hackler ('hæklə(r)). [f. HACKLE *v.*[3]] One who hackles (flax or hemp); a flax-dresser, heckler.

1780 A. YOUNG *Tour Irel.* I. 164 They next send it to a flax-hackler. **1884** *Quiver* Mar. 299/2 Hacklers' disease..is produced by a kind of 'pouce', which being inhaled causes severe tickling in the throat. **1894** *Daily News* 4 July 3/3 All the hacklers die young.

hacklet ('hæklɪt). Also **haglet**. [Origin uncertain.] A small species of sea-gull; the kittiwake.

1855 KINGSLEY *Westw. Ho!* xxxii, From the Gull-rock rose a thousand birds..the choughs cackled, the hacklets wailed. **1856** EMERSON *Eng. Traits, Voy. to Eng.* Wks (Bohn) II. 11 Gulls, haglets, ducks, petrels, swim, dive, and hover around. **1865** GOSSE *Land & Sea* (1874) 74 The kittywake, or hacklet, a very small species of gull.

hackling ('hæklɪŋ), *vbl. sb.*[1] [f. HACKLE *v.*[3] + -ING[1].] The action of the vb. HACKLE[3]; the combing of flax or hemp.

1616 SURFL. & MARKH. *Country Farme* 568 This line after it hath receiued braking and the first hackling, you shall take the strickes, and platting them into a plat of three, make a good bigge roule thereof.

attrib. **1875** *Ure's Dict. Arts* II. 420 In the early period of the linen manufacture, when spinning was done exclusively by hand, no hackling machines were employed. **1839** STONEHOUSE *Axholme* 29. **1849** E. CHAMBERLAIN *Indiana Gazetteer* (ed. 3) 132 A brick building, erected for a hackling house.

hackling[2] and [3]: see after HACKLE *v.*[1] and [4].

hackly ('hæklɪ), *a.* [f. HACKLE *v.*[1] + -Y.] Rough or jagged as though hacked on a small scale; *esp.*, of metals and minerals: Having the surface rough with short sharp points.

1796 KIRWAN *Elem. Min.* (ed. 2) I. 34 The hackly [fracture] presents sharp points, easily perceived in feeling it. **1811** A. T. THOMSON *Lond. Disp.* (1830) 533 It [rhubarb] breaks with a rough hackly fracture. **1846** DANA *Zooph.* (1848) 503 The broad plates..have a very uneven hackly surface. **1849** VARLEY *Rudim. Min.* 16 The native metals.. have a hackly fracture, which may be observed on breaking a piece of thick wire.

hackman ('hækmən). *N.Amer.* [f. HACK *sb.*[3] 2.] The driver of a hack or hackney-carriage; a cabman.

1796 *Boston Directory*, passim. **1806** *Repertory* (Boston) 3 Oct. (Th.), Died, in this town, Mr. Daniel Henry, hackman. **1819** *N.Y. Gaz.* in *Massachusetts Spy* 16 June 3/1 The horses were stopt by the hackmen on the stand. **1850** HAWTHORNE *Amer. Note-Bks.* (1883) 370 We find ourselves in Boston surrounded by eager hackmen. **1879** SALA in *Daily Tel.* 26 Dec., The..hackman..charged us a dollar and a half for what in England would have been an eighteenpenny drive. **1898** H. E. HAMBLEN *Tom Benton's Luck* 56 The line of vociferous hackmen who formed a gauntlet across the exit from the railroad station. **1906** *Daily Colonist* (Victoria, B.C.) 9 Jan. 5/4 A hack case is being heard in the city police court, in which one of the local hackmen is being charged with overcharging.

hackmanite ('hækmənaɪt). *Min.* [ad. Sw. *hackmanit* (L. H. Borgström 1901, in *Geol. Föreningens Stockholm Förh.* XXIII. 563), f. the name of Victor A. *Hackman* (1866–1941), Finnish geologist: see -ITE[1].] A pink or reddish violet variety of sodalite which loses its colour when exposed to daylight but regains it in the dark.

1903 *Jrnl. Chem. Soc.* LXXXIV. II. 304 Hackmanite, a new member of the sodalite group. **1941** *Amer. Mineralogist* XXVI. 441 The induced color change of hackmanite when exposed to ultra-violet light was first observed..on hackmanite from Bancroft, Ontario, which changed from pink to a raspberry shade or deep violet on exposure to ultra-violet light. The induced color faded rapidly and nearly completely on exposure to strong light. **1970** *Physics Bull.* Nov. 487/1 Geologists had found that freshly cleared rocks of a naturally occurring form of sodalite, hackmanite, exhibited a pink colour.

hackmatack ('hækmətæk). Also 8 **hakmantak**, 9 **hacmontac, hackmetack.** [American Indian: see quot. 1792.] The American Larch or Tamarack (*Larix Americana*), found in northern swamps of the United States. Also *attrib.*

1792 J. Belknap *Hist. New-Hampsh.* III. 33 On some mountains we find a shrubbery of hemlock and spruce, whose branches are knit together so as to be impenetrable. The snow lodges on their tops, and a cavity is formed underneath. These are called by the Indians, Hakmantaks. **1821** Dwight *Trav.* I. 36 Hacmontac I take to be an Indian name. **1845** N. P. Rogers in *Whittier's Pr. Wks.* (1889) II. 240 The dark hemlock and hackmatack woods. **1882** *Pall Mall G.* 29 Mar. 11/1 The *Meteor*..is built of oak, hackmatack, and hard pine.

hackney ('hæknɪ), *sb.* (*a.*) Forms: 4 **hakenai, -ne,** 4–5 **hak(e)nei, -ney,** 4–6 **hak(e)nay(e,** 5 **hack-, haknay, (haukenay),** 5–6 **hackenaye, -neye, hakney,** 6 **hackeny, -neie, (hacqne, hacqueneye), haiknay, -ne, -ney,** (*pl.* **hackness, haiknes**), 6–7 **hackneye, -nie,** 6–8 *pl.* **hacknies,** 7 **hacn(e)y,** 7–8 **hackny,** 4– **hackney.** [a. OF. *haquenée* fem. 'an ambling horse or mare, especially for ladies to ride on'; cf. OSp. and Pg. *facanea*, Sp. *hacanea*, It. *acchinea* (Florio), *chinea* 'a hackney or ambling nag': see Diez, Scheler, etc. (In 1373 latinized in England as *hakeneius*: see Du Cange.)

It is now agreed by French and Dutch scholars that MDu. *hackeneie*, *hackeneye*, Du. *hakkenij*, to which some have referred the French word, was merely adopted from the French, thus disposing of conjectures as to the derivation of the word from MDu. *hacken* to hoe. The French *haquenée* and its Romanic equivalents had probably some relationship with OF. *haque*, OSp. and Pg. *faca*, Sp. *haca* 'a nag, a gelding, a hackney' (Minsheu): but, although the word-group has engaged the most eminent etymologists, its ulterior derivation is still unknown.]

I. 1. A horse of middle size and quality, used for ordinary riding, as distinguished from a war-horse, a hunter, or a draught-horse; in early times often an ambling horse; now technically = HACK *sb.*^{3} 1 b.

13.. *Sir Beues* 1255 (MS.A.) Ac nim a liȝter hakenai & lef her þe swerd Morgelai. *c* **1330** R. Brunne *Chron.* (1810) 278 Tille oþer castels about þei sent tueye and tueye In aneus for doute, ilk on on his hakneye. ? *a* **1366** Chaucer *Rom. Rose* 1137 He..loved to have welle hors of prys. He wende to have reproved be Of thefte or moordre, if that he Hadde in his stable ony hakeney. *c* **1386** —— *Can. Yeom. Prol. & T.* 6 His hakeney which þat was al pomely grys. **14..** *Voc.* in Wr.-Wülcker 580/31 *Equillus*, an hakeney. *c* **1440** *Partonope* 3882 A hakeney That ys swyft and ryght well ambling. **1469** *Househ. Ord.* 97 To have viii coursers for his saddle & to them iiii keepers with theyre hakneyes. **1548** Hall *Chron.*, *Hen. VI*, 165 b, The erle of Shrewesbury..because of his age, rode on a litle hakeney. **1577–87** Holinshed *Chron.* II. 20/1 The nag or the hackeneie is verie good for trauelling. **1590** R. Payne *Descr. Irel.* (1841) 7 Carthorsses, mares, and little hackneies are of a very smal price. **1615** G. Sandys *Trav.* 257 The Germans in acknowledgement of their tenure of the Papacie, gaue the Pope yeerly 8. and 40. thousand duckats, together with a white horse. The mony.. at this day is paid, together with the white hackney. **1653** H. Cogan tr. *Pinto's Trav.* 160 Pages, mounted on white Hackneys, having green velvet Saddles. **1678** Butler *Hud.* III. i. 412 Mounted on a Broom, the Nag And Hackney of a Lapland Hag. **1820** Scott *Ivanhoe* ii, He rode..a strong hackney for the road, to save his gallant warhorse. **1831** Praed *Poems* (1865) II. 157 Do you canter down the Row, Upon a very long-tailed hackney? **1843** Youatt *Horse* iv. (ed. 2) 96 The hackney has many of the qualities of the hunter on a small scale. **1890** Boldrewood *Col. Reformer* (1891) 266 The farmer..mounted upon a stout, not over-refined hackney.

†**2.** From an early date mention is found of hackneys hired out; hence the word came often to be taken as, A horse kept for hire. *Obs.* (Cf. also *hackney horse* in 6, HACKNEY-MAN.)

[**1393** Langl. *P. Pl.* C. III. 175 Ac hakeneyes hadde þei none . bote hakeneyes to hyre. **1594** Plat *Jewell-ho.* III. 28 Ride vpon a hired Hackney.] **1614** T. Adams in Spurgeon *Treas. Dav.* Ps. xxvi. 10 It is a wretched thing when justice is made a hackney that may be backed for money. **1626** Meade in Ellis *Orig. Lett.* Ser. I. III. 231 Divers in Town got hacknies, and fled to avoid importunity. **1681** *Lond. Gaz.* No. 1624/4 There was a Brown Nag left by them, supposed to be a London-Hackney. **1715** De Foe *Fam. Instruct.* I. iv. (1841) I. 74 I'll take a hackney, and go to the Mall.

†**b.** *fig.* from 1 and 2, passing into 3. *Obs.*

c **1410** *Sir Cleges* 245 He had non hors..But a staffe was hys hakenay As a man in pouerte. **1600** Dekker *Shoemaker's Holiday* i. (1862) 9 Take him, brave men, Hector of Troy was an hackney to him. **1601** ? Marston *Pasquil & Kath.* I. 31 Trampled on By euery hacknies heeles. **1698** B. F. *Modest Censure* 26 His Criticism is..a hackney to his private Belief and Opinion. **1738** Pope *Epil. Sat.* II. 140 Each spur-gall'd Hackney of the day.

†**3.** One who is used to do mean or servile work for hire; a common drudge, 'fag', 'slave'. Also *fig. Obs.*

1546 J. Heywood *Prov.* (1867) 34 Whan ought was to doo, I was common hackney. **1584** R. Scot *Discov. Witchcr.*, *Disc. Divels* x. (1886) 424 Archangels..are sent onelie about great and secret matters; and angels are common hacknies about euerie trifle. **1668** Pepys *Diary* 11 Feb., Which makes me mad that I should, by my place, become the hackney of this office, in perpetual trouble and vexation. **1669** *Addr. Yng. Gentry Eng.* 8 The idle person is the only common Hackney, and..stands ready to let out himself Post. **1712** J. Wyeth in *Suppl. Ellwood's Autobiog.* (1765) 405 A mercenary Hackney to some of the Clergy. **1784** Cowper *Tiroc.* 620 Such is all the mental food purvey'd By public hacknies in the schooling trade.

†**4.** A woman that hires her person, a prostitute.

1579 Gosson *Sch. Abuse* Apol. (Arb.) 66 Venus..that taught the women in Cyprus to set vp a Stewes too hyre out them selues as hackneies for gaine. **1593** Nashe *Christ's T.* 80 b, When the hackney he hath payde for lyes by him. **1611** Cotgr., *Bringuenaudée*, a common hackney. **1679** Burnet *Hist. Ref.* I. App. 278 [*tr.* N. Sanders] She was so notoriously lewd that she was called an Hackney.

5. A carriage kept for hire; a HACKNEY-COACH.

1664 Pepys *Diary* 18 Apr., Myself being in a hackney and full of people, was ashamed to be seen by the world, many of them knowing me. **1695** Congreve *Love for L.* II. iii, If you won't lend me your Coach, I'll take a Hackney, or a Chair. **1729** Mrs. Pendarves in *Mrs. Delany's Life & Corr.* 141 We were in no bustle of coaches, for no hackneys were allowed to pass. **1825** Hone *Every-day Bk.* I. 1460 He jumped into a Hackney.

II. *attrib.* and *Comb.*

6. a. In apposition, as **hackney horse** = senses 1 and 2; so, ***hackney jade, mare, post-horse, stallion, steed***; also (in analogous sense) ***hackney ass, mule***, and *transf.*, ***hackney-devil***.

1506 Guylforde *Pilgr.* 78 The next daye, Tewysday..we toke our sayd hakney horses and rode to Vyncencia. **1556** Withals *Dict.* (1568) 16 a/1 A hackney horse or horse to be hyred, *equus meritorius*. **1598** Hakluyt *Voy.* I. 400 (R.) There they use to put out their women to hire as we do here hakney horses. **1600** J. Pory tr. *Leo's Africa* I. 25 Their horses of the countrey-breed are..small hackney-jades. *Ibid.* II. 203 Great store of hackney-mules, and asses are kept for travellers to ride upon. **1667** Davenant & Dryden *Tempest* IV. iii. *Syc.* How wilt thou carry me thither? *Steph.* Upon a hackney-devil of thy mother's. **1688** R. Holme *Armoury* II. 150/1 Hackney or Saddle Horses are such as man useth to ride upon for the ease of his Body. **1703** Maundrell *Journ. Jerus.* (1721) 130 Here are Hackney Asses always standing ready equipp'd for hire. **1712** Steele *Spect.* No. 509 ¶8 Mr. Tobias Hobson..was the first in this island who let out hackney horses. **1884** *Hackney Stud Bk.* I. 33 The Modern Hackney Horse may be said to have been the product of the eighteenth century.

b. *attrib.* Of or pertaining to a hackney (horse), as ***hackney hire, pace, saddle, stable, stud***, etc.

1379 *MS. Hostill. Roll, Durh.*, In uno Hakenay-sadyll empt. vjs. viij*d.* **1467** *Mann. & Househ. Exp.* 389 A new hakeney sadylle prise v.s. **1598** B. Jonson *Ev. Man in Hum.* III. v, Out of the old hackney pace, to a fine easie amble. **1659** T. Pecke *Parnassi Puerp.* 56 What for Hackney-hire, was given you. **1754** Foote *Knights* I. Wks. 1799 I. 70 That year the hackney-stable was built. **1809** *British Press* 5 Apr. in *Spirit Pub. Jrnls.* (1810) XIII. 60 [A mare] only of hackney size. **1884** (*title*) Hackney Stud Book.

c. Plying for hire, as HACKNEY-CARRIAGE, -CHAIR, -COACH; also ***hackney-boat, chariot***.

1711 Addison *Spect.* No. 130 ¶4 The..Hackney-boat, which carries Passengers from Leyden to Amsterdam. **1813–14** *Act 54 Geo. III*, c. 147 (*title*), An Act..for authorizing the licensing of a limited Number of Hackney Chariots. **1825** C. M. Westmacott *Eng. Spy* I. 382 Expecting to have met with a hackney rattler, but not one was to be found upon the stand.

†**7. a.** In apposition, or as *adj.* Doing or ready to do work for hire, hireling (also *fig.*); as ***hackney author, clerk, fiddler, gladiator, libeller, preacher, scribbler, sonneteer, tutor, writer***, etc.; also ***hackney pen, tongue***. **b.** *attrib.* or as *adj.* Done by a 'hackney' or for hire, as ***hackney job, writing***. *Obs.*

1589 R. Harvey *Pl. Perc.* (1860) 11 Is it conscience or lucre, that spurgals thy hackney pen? **1660** Wood *Life* (Oxf. Hist. Soc.) I. 361 There were some hackney preachers in the University at this time. **1666** W. Boghurst *Loimographia* 66 Your wild, wanton, hackney fiddlers. **1681** Hickeringill *Vind. Naked Truth* II. 7 A glib Hackney-Tongue he had in his head. **1709** Pope *Ess. Crit.* 419 Some starved hackny sonneteer. *a* **1719** Addison *Lover* No. 39 (Jod.) Booksellers, who set their hackney writers at work for so much a sheet. **1719** Bolingbroke in *Swift's Lett.* (1766) II. 4 What hackney gladiator can you find, By whom the Olympic crown would be declin'd? *a* **1734** North *Exam.* I. i. §7 (1740) 18 The Hackney Libellers of the Faction. *c* **1762** Lloyd *Fam. Ep.* in Chalmers *Eng. Poets* (1810) XV. 118, I must serve some hackney job. *c* **1766** Burke *Tracts Popery Laws* Wks. IX. 336 As hackney Clerks, at the miserable salary of 7*s.* a week.

†**c.** Prostitute. ***hackney-woman***, a bawd. *Obs.*

1616 R. C. *Times' Whistle* vi. 2719 Olde hackny women, they hire out their jades. **1647** R. Stapylton *Juvenal* 36 Hackney-wenches, that ith circus stand. **1678** Butler *Hud.* III. i. 892 No more than every Lover Does from his Hackney-Lady suffer.

†**B.** as *adj.* Worn out, like a hired horse, by indiscriminate or vulgar use; threadbare, trite, commonplace; hackneyed. *Obs.*

1596 Nashe *Saffron Walden* 151 A hackney prouerb in mens mouths euer since K. Lud was a little boy. *a* **1625** Fletcher *Woman pleased* I. i, Law..Her rules and precepts..pamper'd up to cozen him that bought her, When she herself was a hackney, lame, and founder'd. **1714** J. Walker *Suffer. Clergy* 82 The most common and hackney charge in this kind was Tavern haunting and common swearing. **1738** Warburton *Div. Legat.* App. 37 One of his hackney fallacies that run from the end of the book to the other. **1792** W. Boys *Coll. Hist. Sandwich* 293 *note*, The hackney-imputations of drunkeness and swearing.

'hackney, *v.* Now *rare* exc. in *ppl a.* HACKNEYED, q.v. [f. HACKNEY *sb.*]

1. *trans.* To make a hackney of; to use (a horse) as a hack, for general riding purposes; = HACK *v.*^{3} 3 a.

1577 Stanyhurst *Descr. Irel.* in Holinshed *Chron.* (1587) II. 20/1 These horses are best for skirmishes, not for travelling, for their stomachs are such, as they disdaine to be hacknied. **1848** A. B. Evans *Leicestersh. Words, Phrases*, etc. s.v., He'll do very well to drive, but he's not any longer safe to hackney.

fig. **1581** Sidney *Astr. & Stella* cii, Galens adoptiue sonnes, who by a beaten way Their iudgements hackney on, the fault of [*later edd.* on] sicknesse lay.

b. *fig.* To use as a 'hack'.

1837 *Blackw. Mag.* XLI. 277 Hackneyed or spit upon, as the caprice or expediency of the moment prevailed.

†**2.** *trans.* To mount (any one) on a hackney.

1636 Massinger *Gt. Dk. Florence* IV. i, A coach for my money! and that the courtezans know well: Their riding so makes them last three years longer Than such as are hacknied.

†**3.** *intr.* To ride in a hackney-carriage. In quot. ***to hackney it***. *Obs.*

1684 Philo Pater *Observ. Reproved* 6 He..must Trudge on Ten-Toes or Hackney it to Sams Coffee-House.

†**4.** *trans.* To convey in a hackney-carriage.

1784 Cowper *Task* II. 652 To her who..Is hackneyed home unlackeyed.

†**5.** *fig.* To drive hard; to post; to hurry. Also *intr.* (for *refl.*) To run hard, race. *Obs.*

1617 J. Moore *Mappe Mans Mortal.* III. iii. 201 The minutes that hackney at the heeles of time, runne not so fast away. **1631** Quarles *Div. Poems, Samson* (1717) 241 How are thy Angels hackney'd up and down To visit man? **1676** Marvell *Hist. Ess.* Wks. III. 127 Both men and horses and leather being hackneyed, jaded, and worn out upon the errand of some contentious and obstinate bishop. **1781** Cowper *Retirement* 1 Hackneyed in business, wearied at that oar. **1798** W. Hutton *Autobiog.* 41, I had.. paid two shillings for a ticket, been hackneyed through the rooms with violence..and came away completely disappointed.

†**6.** To let *out* for hire. Also *intr.* for *pass. Obs.*

1622 Massinger & Dekker *Virg. Mart.* II. iii, I know women sell themselves daily, and are hacknied out for silver. **1643** G. Wilde *Serm. at St. Maries* 11 Could they have the heart to hackny out this Kingdome. **1679** Prance *True Narr. Pop. Plot* 36 Hackneying forth of Masses for Twelve-pence apiece. *c* **1736** Savage *Poet's Depend. on Statesm.* 26 No will to hackney out polemic strain.

7. To make common by indiscriminate everyday usage; to render too familiar, vulgar, trite, or commonplace. Also with *out*, *about*, *upon*.

1596 Shaks. *1 Hen. IV*, III. ii. 40 So common hackney'd in the eyes of men. **1739** Cibber *Apol.* iv. 78 Plays come to be so hackney'd out, the best Actors will soon feel that the Town has enough of them. **1787** 'G. Gambado' *Acad. Horsemen* (1809) 5, I have had some difficulty in fixing upon a title for my work: A *Vade Mecum* is quite hacknied out. **1817** W. Irving *Life & Lett.* (1864) I. 392, I should not like to have my name hackneyed about among the office-seekers and office-givers at Washington. **1823** T. Jefferson *Writ.* (1830) IV. 376. **1869** Goulburn *Purs. Holiness* viii. 71 Like a popular air..hackneyed upon every street-organ.

†**b.** To undo the freshness or delicacy of. *Obs.*

1785 *Eugenius* II. 28 Young men..who have been hackneyed, from their very infancy, in some of our public seminaries. **1787** T Jefferson *Writ.* (1859) II. 241 Their first and most delicate passions are hackneyed on unworthy objects here. **1792** Mary Wollstonecr. *Rights Wom.* vi. 268 To despise the sensibility that had been excited and hackneyed in the ways of women whose trade was vice. **1808** *Edin. Rev.* XI. 452 Employments which hackney the minds of the other sex.

8. To render habituated, practised, or experienced *in*: often with dyslogistic connotation.

1751 Smollett *Per. Pic.* (1779) IV. xci. 91 Hackneyed as he was in the ways of life. **1801** Mar. Edgeworth *Good French Governess* (1832) 100 Hackneyed in the common language of conversation. **1810** Jane Porter *Scot. Chiefs* lix. 376 Long hackneyed in secret gallantries. **1838** Lytton *Alice* 27 Persons a little hackneyed in the world.

Hence **'hackneying** *vbl. sb.* and *ppl. a.* (in quot. *attrib.*): also **'hackneyer**, one who hackneys.

1801 Southey *Lett.* (1856) I. 181 He begins to discover that hackneying authorship is not the way to be great. **1849** J. Wilson *Christopher under Canvass* in *Blackw. Mag.* LXVI. 254 Every hackneyer of this phrase.

'hackney-'carriage. [f. HACKNEY *sb.* 6 c + CARRIAGE.] Any carriage or vehicle standing or publicly plying for hire.

1796 *Mass. Acts & Laws* (1896) 62 The said Selectmen are hereby authorized to grant licences for such number of Hackney Coaches & Carriages..as they shall judge proper. **1831** *Act 1 & 2 Will. IV* c. 22. §3 Every Hackney Carriage mentioned and described in the Schedule. **1838** Dickens *O. Twist* xlvi, Alighted from a hackney-carriage. **1847** *Act 10 & 11 Vict.* c. 89 §38 Every wheeled Carriage..used in standing or plying for Hire in any Street..and every Carriage standing upon any Street, public or private.. having thereon any numbered Plate required by this..Act ..shall be deemed to be a Hackney Carriage.

'hackney-'chair. Formerly, a sedan chair, subsequently a bath chair or the like, plying publicly for hire. Hence **hackney-chairman**, the bearer, drawer, or keeper of a hackney-chair.

1710 *Act 9 Anne* c. 27 *(title)*, An Act for licensing and regulating Hackney Coaches and Chairs. *Ibid.* c. 23. §8 If any Hackney Coachman or Chairman shall..exact more for his Hire than the several Rates hereby limited. **1776** ADAM SMITH *W.N.* v. ii. (1869) II. 447 The tax upon every hackney coach..and upon every hackney chair. **1840** DICKENS *Barn. Rudge* xvi, Long stands of hackney-chairs and groups of chairmen..obstructed the way.

'hackney-'coach. [f. HACKNEY *sb.* 6c + COACH.] A four-wheeled coach, drawn by two horses, and seated for six persons, kept for hire.

c **1610** [implied in HACKNEY-COACHMAN]. **1635** J. TAYLOR (Water P.) *Old Parr* D iv, They [Coaches] have increased.. to the undoing of the Watermen, by the multitudes of Hackney or hired Coaches: but they never swarmed so thick to pester the streets, as they doe now, till the yeare 1605. **1660** PEPYS *Diary* 7 Nov., Notwithstanding this was the first day of the King's proclamation against hackney coaches coming into the streets to be hired, yet I got one to carry me home. **1777** SHERIDAN *Trip Scarb.* Prol., The streets, some time ago, were paved with stones Which, aided by a hackney-coach, half broke your bones. **1836** DICKENS *Sk. Boz* (1849) 49/2 A regular, ponderous, rickety, London hackney-coach of the old school. **1882** SERJT. BALLANTINE *Exper.* (1890) 16 A machine called a hackney-coach, licensed to carry six people..was the principal mode of locomotion.

attrib. **1623-4** *Althorp MS.* in Simpkinson *Washingtons* p. liii, 6 str. of oates to the hackney coach horses and the hackney horses. **1715** *Lond. Gaz.* No. 5344/3 The Hackney Coach Office in Surry street in the Strand. **1836** DICKENS *Sk. Boz* (1850) 90/1 Rumours were rife on the hackney-coach-stands, that a buss was building, to run from Lisson-grove to the Bank.

'hackney-'coachman. The driver of a hackney-coach.

c **1610** MIDDLETON, etc. *Widow* v. i, My master kisses, as I've heard a hackney-coachman Chear up his mare; chap, chap. **1705** HICKERINGILL *Priest-cr.* II. viii. 77 Chiefly.. Design'd against common Carriers, Waggoners, Hackney Coachmen, and Watermen. **1838** DICKENS *Nich. Nick.* ii, Mr. Bonney bustled up..and knocked a hackney-coachman's knock on the table with a little hammer.

hackneydom ('hæknɪdəm). [f. HACKNEY(ED *ppl. a.* 2 + -DOM. Cf. HACKNEY *v.* 7.] A state of commonplaceness.

1897 G. B. SHAW *Our Theatres in Nineties* (1932) III. 235 The latest attempt to escape from hackneydom and cockneydom is the Chinatown play. **1959** *Times* 30 Nov. 14/3 Again this was a performance that shook the dust of hackneydom from the symphony.

hackneyed ('hæknɪd), *ppl. a.* [f. HACKNEY *v.*]

†**1.** Hired; kept for hire. *Obs.*

1767 G. S. CAREY *Hills of Hybla* 20 On hackney'd steeds, the giddy blockheads fly. *a* **1818** D. STEWART in Jas. Mill *Brit. India* I. II. ix. 385 A village apothecary or a hacknied nurse.

2. Used so frequently and indiscriminately as to have lost its freshness and interest; made trite and commonplace; stale.

1749 HURD *Notes on Horace's Art Poetry* (R.), The tedium arising from hacknied expression. **1785** BOSWELL *Voy. Hebrides* 24 Aug., The old hackneyed objection. **1817** J. SCOTT *Paris Revisit.* (ed. 4) 375 It is the hackneyed complaint that England is without a fine public collection. **1873** SMILES *Huguenots Fr.* I. v. (1881) 82 Along the hackneyed tourist routes. **1887** SYMONDS *Life B. Cellini* (1888) I. Introd. 11 Handling a somewhat hackneyed subject.

3. Habituated by much practice, experienced; sometimes with the ulterior idea of disgust or weariness.

1760 C. JOHNSTON *Chrysal* (1822) III. 146 Hacknied as he was in the ways of wickedness. **1810** SCOTT in *Croker Papers* 10 Oct., Whatever the practised and hackneyed critic may say. **1823** —— *Peveril* xxxix, The hackneyed voluptuary is like the jaded epicure. **1828** D'ISRAELI *Chas. I*, II. vi. 142 Both much too young for hacknied statesmen.

hackney-man ('hæknɪmæn). Forms: see HACKNEY *sb.* [f. HACKNEY *sb.* + MAN.] A man who keeps hackney horses or hackney-carriages for hire; †a servant who attends to a hackney.

1362 LANGL. *P. Pl.* A. v. 161 Hikke þe hakeney mon and hogge þe neldere. **1467** *Mann. & Househ. Exp.* (Roxb.) 398 Paid to the hakneyman in party of payment of the horse that my mastyr hered to ryde to Stoke. **1599** *Soliman & Perseda* I. in Hazl. *Dodsley* V. 281 A hackney-man Should have ten shillings for horsing a gentle-woman. **1601** F. TATE *Househ. Ord. Edw. II* §56 (1876) 43 In the same stable shalbe an hackneyman, who shal keepe the hakene of the house. **1628** EARLE *Microcosm.*, *Carrier* (Arb.) 36 A carryer is his own Hackneyman; for hee lets himselfe out to trauell as well as his horses. **1797** WOLCOTT (P. Pindar) *Out at Last* Wks. 1812 III. 500 The Hackneymen..Shall cry 'My money for my Chaise'. **1845** DISRAELI *Sybil* (1863) 190 The straggling yard of a hackneyman.

†**hackster.** *Obs.* exc. *dial.* Also 7 hacster, haxter. [f. HACK *v.*[1] + -STER.]

1. *lit.* One who hacks, a 'hacker' or 'cutter'; a cut-throat; a swaggering ruffian, swashbuckler.

1581 J. BELL *Haddon's Answ. Osor.* 247 b, If God were such a Royster or hackster that would delight in the slaughter of men. **1610** HOLLAND *Camden's Brit.* I. 11 The hackster, that was hired and sent to kill Marius. **1631** BRATHWAIT *Whimzies, Hospitall-man* 45 To bring an old haxter to the exercise of devotion. **1649** MILTON *Eikon* iii. (1851) 357 Happy times; when Braves and Hacksters..were thought the fittest..to defend his Person. **1658** CLEVELAND *Rustic Rampant* Wks. (1687) 475. **1876** *Whitby Gloss.*, *Hackster*, a murderer; a hewer down of others.

b. A prostitute's 'bully'.

1607 CHAPMAN *Bussy D'Ambois* Plays 1873 II. 58 Thou would'st turne Hackster to any whore.

2. A prostitute. (Cf. HACKNEY *sb.* 4.)

1594 NASHE *Unfort. Trav.* 42 Out whore, strumpet, six penie hackster. **1611** COTGR. s.v. *Danse, Elle sçait assez de la vieille danse*..she hath bin a hackster, a twigger, a good one, in her time.

hackthorn ('hækθɔːn). [ad. Du. *haakedorn*, hook-thorn.] A South African thorny shrub (*Acacia detinens*), also termed 'Wait-a-bit thorn'.

1863 W. C. BALDWIN *Afr. Hunting* 173, I must have had nearly five miles through hack-thorns. **1871** J. MACKENZIE *10 Years north of Orange River* 385 The hack-thorn (*Acacia detinens*) is especially sacred; it would be a great offence to cut down a bough from this tree.

hack-watch: see HACK *sb.*[3] 6.

'hackwood. *local.* The hagberry tree.

1853 G. JOHNSON *Nat. Hist. E. Bord.* I. 58 *Prunus Padus*..The shrub is called Hackwood, and the fruit Hackberry or Hagberry.

hack-work ('hækwɜːk). [HACK *sb.*[3]] Work done by a hack or hired drudge; esp. literary work which a person is hired by a publisher, editor, or other, to do.

1851 SIR F. PALGRAVE *Norm. & Eng.* I. 60 Trade hack-work is of course out of the question. **1875** HAMERTON *Intell. Life* v. ii. (1876) 182 Literary hack-work. **1881** MASSON in *Macm. Mag.* XLV. 159 Such articles of hack-work as might be intrusted conveniently to an unknown young man on the spot.

hacky ('hækɪ), *a.*[1] *colloq.* [f. HACK *v.*[1] + -Y[1].] Of a cough: Characterized by hacking.

Mod. Advt., That rasping hacky cough of yours.

hacky, *a.*[2] *colloq.* [f. HACK *sb.*[3] + -Y[1].] Of the nature of a hack (horse).

1870 *Daily News* 6 June, Britannia [a mare]..she is 'hacky', and in the wrong place here.

hacot, var. HAKED.

†**hacoyte.** *Obs. rare.* [The latter part appears to be OF. *coite*:—L. *culcita* feather-bed, cushion, pillow; but the *ha-* is unexplained, prob. some error.] A cushion or pillow.

1541 COPLAND *Cuydon's Quest. Chirurg.* F iij, The loynes are musculous flesshes lyeng in the sydes of the spondyles of the backe that serue as hacoytes of the synewes [*orig. L.* ut sint illis culcitra].

hacquebute, obs. form of HACKBUT.

hacqueton, hacton, var. of HAQUETON, ACTON.

†**had, hade, hod.** *Obs.* Forms: 1 hád, 2–4 had, 3–4 hade, hod. [OE. *hád* = OS. *hêd*, condition, rank (:—OTeut. **haidu-z*: cf. Goth. *haidus* way, manner, OHG. *heit* m. and fem., person, personality, sex, condition, quality, rank, ON. *heiðr* honour, dignity, Sw. *häder*, Da. *hæder* honour). Being used in comb. with sbs. as in *cild-hád*, *mæȝden-hád*, etc., this word, after its obsolescence as an independent word, remained as a suffix, ME. *-hod*, mod. -HOOD q.v. The sb. after 1200 appears in southern and midl. ME. as *hôd*, in north. as *had*, *hode*; the forms in *a* being much more numerous, it is here treated under *had*, although, if it had lived on, the modern Eng. form would have been *hode* or *hoad*.]

1. Person (in various senses).

c **900** tr. *Bæda's Hist.* IV. xix. [xvii.] (1890) 312 Ænne God on þreom astondnessum oðþo hadum. *c* **1000** *Ags. Gosp.* Matt. xxii. 16 þu ne be-sceawast nanes mannes had. *c* **1000** *Ælfric Gram.* xxii. (Z.) 127 þry hadas synt worda. Se forma had ys þe sprecþ be him sylfum ana. *c* **1175** *Lamb. Hom.* 99 An god..on þreom hadan. *c* **1200** ORMIN 10989 þreo hadess, Faderr and Sune and Haliȝ Gast. *a* **1225** *Ancr. R.* 26 On almihti God, þrile ine þreo hodes.

2. Sex. (Only in OE.)

c **900** tr. *Bæda's Hist.* I. i. (1890) 26 Ælcere yldo and hade. *a* **1000** *Christ* 99 Gewuldrad is se heanra had.

3. Order, rank, degree; holy orders.

c **897** K. ÆLFRED *Gregory's Past.* (Sweet) 3 Æȝðer ȝe godcundra hada ȝe woruldcundra. *c* **900** tr. *Bæda's Hist.* v. xiv. [xiii.] (1890) 436 Wær inn læwdum hade. *c* **1000** ÆLFRIC *Gram.* xi. (Z.) 79 *Gradas*, had oððe stæpe. *c* **1175** *Lamb. Hom.* 101 Bisceopas þes ilcan hades. *c* **1200** ORMIN Ded. 9 Unnderr kanunnkess had and lif. *a* **1225** *Ancr. R.* 318 Munuch, preost, oðer clerk, and of þet hode. *a* **1300** *Cursor M.* 21248 O biscop siþen he tok þe hade. **1340** *Ayenb.* 235 Uor þet hod þet hi habbeþ onderuonge. *c* **1375** *Sc. Leg. Saints, Ninian* 374 Al at to sic had partenyt.

4. State, condition, quality, kind.

Beowulf (Z.) 1297 Hæleþa leofost, on ȝe-siðes had. *a* **1000** *Sal. & Sat.* (Gr.) 408 Leoht hafað hiw and had haliȝes gastes. *c* **1230** *Hali Meid.* 23 Of þeos þre had, meidenhad and widewehad and te þridde wedlached.

had, pa. t. and pple. of HAVE, q.v.

had, mod. form of *hald*, north. f. HOLD *v.*

-had (*-hád*), OE. form of -HOOD *suffix.*

hadada(h ('hɑːdədɑː). Also **hadadaw, haddada, hadeda, hadida.** [Onomatopœic from the bird's raucous call.] A large brown-green ibis, *Hagedashia hagedash.*

1801 J. BARROW *Trav. S. Afr.* I. iv. 264 The Egyptian black *ibis* (*niger*) and another species of *tantalus*, called by the farmers the *haddadas*, were procured at this place. **1846** tr. *Arbousset & Daumas's Narr. Tour Cape G.H.* 190 A large ibis of a brown lustre commonly called by onomatopy *addada*. **1862** J. S. DOBIE *S. Afr. Jrnl.* 10 Oct. (1945) 40 Missed a hadadaw. **1907** *African Monthly* Oct. 445 Flocks of 'ha-di-da' grub silently and unconcernedly in close proximity to the camp. **1952** MACKWORTH-PRAED & GRANT *Birds E. & N.E. Afr.* I. 59 Key to the Adult Storks, Ibises. .. Back bronzy brown, no crest on nape, ridge of bill only red, bare skin confined to front of eye: Hadada *Hagedashia hagedash.* **1953** BANNERMAN *Birds W. & Equat. Afr.* I. 184 West African Hadada. *Hagedashia hagedash brevirostris*... The best guide to the Hadada's identity lies in its loud note —*kah-a-a-a*—uttered frequently, both in flight and on the ground. **1953** R. CAMPBELL *Mamba's Precipice* v. 48 To the forest, on the left bank, flocks of hadadah ibis were flying back to roost. **1957** McLACHLAN & LIVERSIDGE *Roberts's Birds S. Afr.* 39 Hadeda... At a distance it appears dull olive-grey, but metallic reflections on back and wing-coverts may be seen. **1964** C. WILLOCK *Enormous Zoo* vii. 120 Hadada ibises rise with the horrible complaining cry from which they get their title.

Hadassah (hə'dæsə). [Heb., = myrtle, name of the Biblical Esther (Esther 2:7).] An American Zionist women's organization, founded in 1912, which contributes to welfare work in Israel.

1913 H. SZOLD *Let.* 15 July in M. Lowenthal *H. Szold Life & Lett.* (1942) 79 If we can keep up this folder propaganda as the winter's work of Hadassah, we shall be doing admirably. **1952** S. SPENDER *Learning Laughter* vii. 100 In 40 years Hadassah has grown from being a small organization for training a few nurses, into a main channel for transfusing life-blood into a young nation. **1964** D. GREENBURG in *Playboy* Sept. 170/2 Your family..will expect you to be able to relate amusing stories which you have heard..at a meeting of the Hadassah. **1966** H. KEMELMAN *Saturday the Rabbi went Hungry* (1967) i. 8 It fell off and I sewed it on myself. You were at a Hadassah meeting. **1972** *Times* 16 Oct. 6/1 The letter..was addressed to a member of Hadassah, a women's Zionist organisation.

ha day, obs. form of HEY DAY *int.*

†**had-bot, hadbote.** *Obs.* exc. *Hist.* [OE. *hád-bót*, f. *hád* person, degree, order + *bót* recompense, BOOT *sb.*[1]] In *Old English Law*, Compensation for violence or an affront done to a person in holy orders.

a **1000** *Of Eccles. Compens.* in Thorpe *Anc. Laws* (1840) II. 240 And to had-bote, ȝif feorh-lyre wurþe..twa pund to bote. [**1659** in SOMNER *Saxon Dict.* Whence in BLOUNT, COWELL, TOMLINS, WHARTON and mod. Dicts.]

hadda ('hædə), repr. colloq. pronunc. of *had to* or *had a.*

1945 A. KOBER *Parm Me* 34, I hadda do a lotta talking to get her to come here to-night. **1967** 'L. EGAN' *Nameless Ones* xv. 192 Well, she hadda lot of trouble. *Ibid.* 193 She hadda give up an apartment, couldn't afford it. **1969** *Coast to Coast 1967–68* 4 There was that Alsatian they hadda shoot because it wouldn't leave a kid's grave and kept scrabbling at the loose dirt. **1971** 'A. BLAISDELL' *Practice to Deceive* x. 138 'Did you hit her?' 'Naw,..I never hadda chance.'

haddada, hadeda, varr. HADADA(H.

hadden, mod. f. *halden*, north. f. HOLDEN.

hadden, obs. pl. of *had*, pa. t. of HAVE.

hadder, obs. Sc. form of HEATHER.

haddie ('hædɪ). A Sc. dial. variant of *haddo'* = HADDOCK, which, in certain connexions (*caller haddies, Finnan haddies*), has come into somewhat general use.

1816 SCOTT *Antiq.* xxxix, Weel, Monkbarns, they're braw caller haddies. **1832-53** *Whistle-Binkie* (Scot. Songs) Ser. I. 52 The Haggis at first as a haddie was mute. **1844** W. H. MAXWELL *Sports & Adv. Scotl.* xxxiv. (1855) 273 A Finan haddie would have had more charm. **1861** [see FINNAN].

haddo. [? Amer.-Indian.] The humpback salmon (*Oncorhyncus gorbuscha*), a fish closely allied to the salmon, a native of the waters of Kamschatka, Alaska and Oregon.

haddock ('hædək). Forms: 4 haddoc, 4–5 -ok, 5 hadok(e, 5–6 haddoke, 6 hadocke, 6–7 haddocke, 8 hadock, 6– haddock. [Origin uncertain. The suffix *-ock* appears to be diminutive, as in *bullock, dunnock, hillock*, etc.

OF. *hadot*, pl. *hados*, is found in the same sense *c* 1250 (see Godef.), and thus earlier than our first example: it is, however, a very rare word, and, in the opinion of French etymologists, probably from English; its form suggests the Sc. *haddo'*, *haddo's*. The Gaelic *adag* is from Eng.]

1. A fish (*Gadus æglefinus*) allied to the cod, but smaller, abundant in the North Atlantic and the British seas, and much used for food.

1307-8 *Durh. MS. Cell. Roll*, MC Haddoks. **1314** in *Wardr. Acc. 8 Edw. II* 1/12, 2 haddoks 1s. **1327** *Patent Roll 20 Edw. II*, Salt haddoc. *c* **1420** *Liber Cocorum* (1862) 41 Take turbut, haddok, and gode codlyng. *c* **1440** *Promp. Parv.* 220/2 Haddok, fysche, *morius*. **1532** MORE *Confut. Tindale* Wks. 552/1, I knew one that shot at an hart & killed an haddoke. **1615** HEYWOOD *Foure Prentises* I. Wks. 1874 II. 186, I might haue fed the Haddockes. **1681** COLVIL *Whigs*

Supplic. (1751) 48 Shining.. As Haddocks heads do in the dark. **1785** BOSWELL *Voy. Hebrides* 26 Aug., They set down dried haddocks broiled, along with our tea. **1842** MOULE *Her. Fish* in Trench *Mirac.* xxviii. (1862) 387 *note*, A popular idea assigns the dark marks on the shoulders of the haddock to the impression left by St. Peter with his finger and thumb, when he took the tribute-money out of the fish's mouth at Capernaum.

†**b.** Prov. *to bring haddock to paddock*: to spend or lose everything, to come to destitution.

1546 J. HEYWOOD *Prov.* (1867) 82 And thus had he brought haddocke to paddocke. **1577** STANYHURST *Descr. Irel.* in *Holinshed* (1807–8) VI. 23, I had bene like to have brought haddocke to paddocke.

2. Applied, with or without qualification, to other allied fishes, as the Red Cod (*Lotella bacchus*) of New Zealand; ***golden haddock***, the John Dory; ***Jerusalem h.***, the Opah; ***Norway*** or ***Norwegian h.***, the Bergylt or Sea Perch.

1847 CARPENTER *Zool.* §556 The Sebastes, or Norway Haddock, which inhabits the northern seas, and is an important article of food. **1871** HUTTON *Fishes N. Zealand* 115 Red Cod. Also called the Yellow Tail and the Haddock.

3. *Comb.*, as ***haddock-boat***, ***-curing***, ***-smoker***, ***-smoking***; ***haddock-carrying*** adj.; also **haddock-meat** (see quot.); **haddock-tea** (in New England), 'a thin chowder made of haddock' (*Cent. Dict.*).

1769 PENNANT *Zool.* III. 145 The stone-coated worms, which the fishermen call hadock meat. **1883** S. PLIMSOLL in *19th Cent.* XIV. 148 Haddock-carrying vans. **1886** G. R. SIMS in *Daily News* 4 Dec. 5/6 Haddock-smoking can only be carried on in a very few places.

Hence **'haddocker**, a person or vessel employed in fishing for haddock.

haddock, dial. var. of HATTOCK, a shock of corn, a stook.

†**hade** (heɪd), *sb.*[1] *Obs.* exc. *dial.* [Derivation unknown.] A strip of land left unploughed as a boundary line and means of access between two ploughed portions of a field; also, according to some recent writers, a small piece of greensward left at the head or end of arable land upon which the plough turns.

(But the latter sense is perhaps a mistake arising from the identification of *hade* with *head.*)

1523 FITZHERB. *Husb.* §6 The horses may be teddered or tyed vpon leys, balkes, or hades, where as oxen maye not be kept. **1612** DRAYTON *Poly-olb.* xiii. 222 And on the lower Leas, as on the higher Hades, The daintie Clouer growes. **1615** *Map* (C.C.C. Oxon.), The description of certeine arable landes some of them havinge hades of meadow and grasse grounde lieinge in the Southe fielde of Einsham. **1649** BLITHE *Eng. Improv.* 13 Where great Balkes betwixt Lands, Hades, Meares, or Divisions betwixt Land and Land are left. **1848** A. B. EVANS *Leicestersh. Words*, etc., *Hades*.. Headlands, or part of a field not ploughed.

b. *Comb.* **hade-way**, a hade which serves as a way or road between portions of arable land.

1649 BLITHE *Eng. Improv. Impr.* (1652) 80 All your Common Fields were never under Tillage neither, As great part Slades and Hade wayes, and a great part Meadow.

hade (heɪd), *sb.*[2] *Mining* and *Geol.* [Goes with HADE *v.*[2], from which it is app. derived as n. of action.] The inclination of a mineral vein or fault from the vertical; the complement of the *dip*. Also called *underlay* or *underlie*.

1789 MILLS in *Phil. Trans.* LXXX. 94 The principal vein ..has a slight hade to the north-eastward. **1795** *Ibid.* LXXXVI. 40 The yellow argillaceous shistus is again seen with its former hade and range. **1811** PINKERTON *Petral.* II. 578 The hade, slope, or inclination of the vein is chiefly estimated by miners from the lower side. **1851** GREENWELL *Coal-trade Terms Northumb. & Durh.* 29 *Hade*, the slope or inclination of the leader of a slip-dyke. **1851** TAPPING *Derbysh. Lead-mining Terms* (E.D.S.), *Hade*, a slope.. It also signifies a vein that is not perpendicular, but sloping.

b. *Comb.*, as ***hade-slope***.

1874 J. H. COLLINS *Metal Mining* Gloss., *Hade, hadeslope*, the underlie, or inclination of a lode.

†**hade, hode**, *v.*[1] *Obs.* Forms: 1 **hádian**, 2 **hadien**, 2–4 **hodien**. [OE. *hádian*, f. *hád*, HAD holy orders.] *trans.* To ordain.

c **900** tr. *Bæda's Hist.* II. vii[i]. (1890) 118 þæt he biscopas hadian moste. **975** *O.E. Chron.* an. 931 Her mon hadode Byrnstan bisceop to Wintan ceastre. *c* **1200** ORMIN 10881 Hadedd Till bisscopp orr till unnderrpreost. *c* **1275** LAY. 21856 Alle þat hoded were, bissopes and canounes. **1340** *Ayenb.* 235 Of clerkes y-hoded.

Hence **haded** *ppl. a.*; also *absol.*, one in holy orders; **hading** *vbl. sb.*, ordination.

c **1000** *Inst. Polity* in Thorpe *Anc. Laws* (1840) II. 316 Æt hadunge. *a* **1100** *O.E. Chron.* an. 1014 Ealle ʒe hadode ʒe læwede. *c* **1200** *Trin. Coll. Hom.* 31 For ne doð hit none swo ofte se þe hodede. *c* **1200** ORMIN 13255 Att hadedd manness hande. *Ibid.* 15967 Whatt mann sitt iss þatt takeþþ her Forr hadinng aniȝ mede.

hade (heɪd), *v.*[2] *Mining* and *Geol.* [Etymology uncertain; possibly a dialectal form of *head*, retaining the older pronunciation of that word: cf. *tread, trade.*] *intr.* To incline or slope from the vertical, as a shaft, or a vein or fault.

1681 HOUGHTON *Compl. Miner* Gloss. (E.D.S.) s.v., Where any shaft or turn goes descending like the side of a house, or like the descent of a steep hill, it is said to *hade*. **1795** MILLS in *Phil. Trans.* LXXXVI. 40 Which is afterwards seen.. running ENE and WSW, and hading NNW. **1822** G. YOUNG *Geol. Surv. Yorks. Coast* (1828) 177 The dyke, in traversing these hills, hades, or inclines, to the same quarter. **1882** GEIKIE *Text.-bk Geol.* IV. VI. 525 Faults hade in the direction of downthrow, in other words, they slope away from the side which has risen.

Hence **hading** *vbl. sb.* = HADE *sb.*[2]; also *attrib.*

1747 HOOSON *Miner's Dict.* K ij, The side on which the Plim Line will fall is called the Hadeing-side; and according to the Hadeing of this the other flys off, and that we call the Hanging-side. **1875** *Ure's Dict. Arts* II. 778 Hadings signify that some parts of the veins incline.

hade, var. of HAD, *Obs.*

Hadean ('heɪdiːən, heɪ'diːən), *a.* [f. next + -AN.] Of or belonging to Hades.

1839 BAILEY *Festus* xxiv. (1848) 306 Dreams such as gods may dream thy soul possess For ever in the Hadeän Eden-Death. **1878** S. COX *Salv. Mundi* i. (ed. 3) 17 When he stood ..among the spirits in the Hadean prison.

‖**Hades** (heɪdiːz). Also 7–8 **Ades**. [a. Gr. ᾅδης (orig. αἴδης or ἀΐδης) of doubtful origin; in Homer, the name of the god of the lower world, but in later times transferred to his kingdom abode, or house, so that it became a name for the nether world; in LXX and N.T. Greek, used to render Heb. *shĕōl*, the abode of the dead or departed spirits. Introduced into English use *c* 1600, in connexion with theological controversies about the fifth article of the Apostles' Creed.]

1. *Gr. Myth.* **a.** The oldest name of the god of the dead, also called Pluto.

1599 *Broughton's Lett.* xii. 41 By the Poets figments *Hades* was Iupiters brother, both sonnes to Saturne: and so by your own iudges, the penner of the Creede, when he said that Christ descended εἰς ᾅδου, meant that he went into the house of *Hades*. **1667** MILTON *P.L.* II. 964 And by them stood Orcus and Ades, and the dreaded name Of Demogorgon. **1791** COWPER *Iliad* III. 384 The drear abodes Of Ades.

b. *transf.* The kingdom of Hades, the lower world, the abode of departed spirits or shades.

1599 *Broughton's Lett.* xii. 43 Homer presents vnto Vlysses being in Hades, βίαν ἡρακλείαν, the force and strength of Hercules a ghost. **1658** SIR T. BROWNE *Hydriot.* iv. 62 The dead seem all alive in the humane Hades of Homer; yet cannot well speak, prophesie, or know the living, except they drink bloud, wherein is the life of man. **1847** TENNYSON *Princ.* IV. 419 The enthroned Persephone in Hades. **1875** JOWETT *Plato* (ed. 2) I. 417 The old Homeric notion of a gibbering ghost flitting away to Hades.

2. a. After ᾅδης of the Greek New Testament, and hence in the Revised Eng. version: The state or abode of the dead, or of departed spirits after this life; corresp. to the Heb. *Sheol*.

(In the earlier Eng. versions rendered HELL, exc. that in *Acts* ii. 27, 31, Geneva has 'in grave'; hence by some identified with the abode of the devil and his angels.)

1597 H. BROUGHTON *Epistle to Nobilitie* 37 That state to the body is *Sheol*: *Haides* in the Greeke is the very same: and neither of them is euer in Scripture, directlie the state of Eternall Torment. **1599** *Broughton's Lett.* xi. 38 His [Bucer's] conclusion is, that this article *He descended into Hell*, is but an explication of the former *He dyed and was buried*, taking *Hades* for the graue. **1604** BILSON (*title*) The Survey of Christ's Sufferings for Man's redemption; and of his descent to Hades or Hel for our deliverance. **1698** NORRIS *Pract. Disc.* (1707) IV. 150 Of the Place and State whither they are going, the dark invisible *Hades*. *a* **1711** KEN *Hymnarium* Poet. Wks. 1721 II. 127 Shew me the Gulph, that's fixed between The upper Hades, and the sub-terrene. **1881** N. T. (R.V.) *Acts* ii. 31 Neither was he left in Hades, nor did his flesh see corruption.

b. Used trivially as a substitute for *hell* in imprecations, etc.

1912 A. BENNETT *Matador* ii, What the hades are you waiting there for? **1917** [see BLIND *sb.* 11]. **1942** T. BAILEY *Pink Camellia* xxvii. 196 What in Hades is he doing here? **1972** G. BELL *Villains Galore* i. 4 Damn protocol to Hades!

hadida, var. HADADA(H.

Hadith ('hædɪθ). Also **Hadis, Hadithah.** Pl. **Hadithat.** [a. Arab. *ḥadīṯ* a tradition.] The body of traditions relating to Muhammad, which now form a supplement to the Koran, called the Sunna.

a **1817** J. L. BURCKHARDT *Trav. Syria & Holy Land* (1822) 326 An Olema thinks he has attained the pinnacle of knowledge if he can recite all the Koran together with some thousand of Hadeath, or sentences of the Prophet. **1880** *Encycl. Brit.* XI. 367/2 Rejecting the *Hadith*, or traditional sayings of Mahomet. **1883** *Ibid.* XVI. 594/2 The traditions of Mohammed, or *Hadith*, the collective body of which constitutes the *Sunna*, or custom. **1922** *Blackw. Mag.* Mar. 375/2, I treasured this like a *hadis*, an authentic tradition of which I was the custodian. **1924** A. GUILLAUME *Trad. Islam* 15 The hadith literature as we now have it provides us with apostolic precept and example covering the whole duty of man. *Ibid.* 150 Many of the hadith already cited will have shown the good sense, amiability, and liberality of the prophet. **1951** 'N. SHUTE' *Round Bend* v. 137 Legacies are governed by *hadith*, based upon the Koran.

†**had-I-wist, hadiwist.** *Obs.* A phrase (= 'if I had known'), expressing regret for something done in ignorance of circumstances now known; hence, as *sb.* A vain regret, or the heedlessness or loss of opportunity which leads to it.

1390 GOWER *Conf.* I. 105 Upon his fortune and his grace Cometh *had I wist* full ofte a place. *c* **1460** *Urbanitatis* 72 in *Babees Bk.* 15 And kepe þe well from hadde-y-wyste. **1526** *Pilgr. Perf.* (W. de W. 1531) 131 To eschewe.. all slouthfulnes, all negligence, all rashnes.. all had I wyst, all dulnes of perceyuyng our dutyes. **1581** T. HOWELL *Deuises* (1879) 262 Till midst the waues of *had I wist* we floate. **1600** S. NICHOLSON *Acolastus* (1876) 58 Till womens hopes doe end in *Had I wist*. **1613–16** W. BROWNE *Brit. Past.* I. ii. (R.), His late wisht *had I wists*, remorceful bitings. **1876** TRENCH *Synon. N.T.* lxix. 250 What our fathers were wont to call 'hadiwist'.

‖**hadj** (hadʒ, hɑːdʒ). Also 8 **hagge**, 20 **haj, hajj.** [Arab. *ḥajj.*] A pilgrimage to Mecca. Also *transf.*

1704 J. PITTS *Acc. Mahometans* vii. (1736) 218 Be sure to perform the *Al hage*, or *el Hagge*, i.e. the Pilgrimage to Mecca. **1847** DISRAELI *Tancred* IV. v, Who.. could come cringing to El Sham to ask for the contract of the Hadj. **1910** *Encycl. Brit.* XII. 827/1 The word *hajj* is sometimes loosely used of any Mahommedan pilgrimage to a sacred place or shrine, and is also applied to the pilgrimages of Christians of the East to the Holy Sepulchre at Jerusalem. **1930** KIPLING *Limits & Renewals* (1932) 217 He had forbidden music because it was a *haj*.

hadjeen, var. HYGEEN, HAJEEN.

‖**hadji, hajji** ('hadʒi, 'hɑːdʒiː). Also 7 **hagee, haggi, (al)hage, (hatzi), hodge(e, hoggie, -ei, -oi, hogi(e, (hugie),** 7–9 **hadgy,** 8 **hadgee, hagge, hahdgee,** 9 **hodgee, haji.** [Arab. *ḥājī* pilgrim: see HADJ.]

a. The title given to one who has made the greater pilgrimage (on the 8th to 10th day of the 12th month of the Muslim year) to Mecca.

[**1585** T. WASHINGTON tr. *Nicholay's Voy.* III. xxi. 110 Of the Pilgrims of Mecqua by the Turks called Hagislars.] **1612** T. LAVENDER *Trav. 4 Englishm.* 81 They that haue been there [Mecca] but once, are allwaies after called Hogies. **1683** T. SMITH *Acc. Prusa* in *Misc. Cur.* (1708) III, The Haggi, or Pilgrims, that have been at Mecca and Medina, forbear to drink Wine most Religiously. **1753** HANWAY *Trav.* (1762) I. III. xxvi. 111 Myrza Mahommed.. who having made a pilgrimage to Mecca.. was dignified with the title of *hahdgee*. **1881** J. F. KEANE *Six Months Meccah* 144 The day on which I was to acquire the honoured title of Haji. **1892** E. REEVES *Homeward Bound* 205 Hadji is his title, and means that he has been to Mecca.

b. Also given to an Oriental Christian who has visited the Holy Sepulchre at Jerusalem.

1835 WILLIS *Pencillings* II. lvii, A brig, crowded with hajjis to Jerusalem, sailed on the day of my arrival at Smyrna.

hadland ('hædlənd), *sb.*[1] Dial. variant of HEADLAND (sense 1).

1523 FITZHERB. *Surv.* xxi. (1539) 44 The lord hath the hadlandes. **1550** CROWLEY *Epigr. Baylife Arrantes*, His hadland is good ground and beareth all thynge. **1698** WALLIS in *Phil. Trans.* XX. 6 A Quick-set Hedge.. cross the Head of some *Had-Lands* (as they are called). **1854** BAKER *Northamptonsh. Gloss.*, Hadland or Headland.

Hence **hadland** *v. intr.*, to abut or border *upon*.

1649 BLITHE *Eng. Improv. Impr.* (1653) 10 One Furlong butting, or Hadlanding, upon other Furlongs.

†**Hadland**, *sb.*[2] *Obs.* [f. *had*, pa. t. of *have* + *land*: cf. *Lackland.*] A humorous title for one who formerly owned land and has lost it.

1592 GREENE *Upst. Courtier* in *Harl. Misc.* (1810) V. 405 They dub him 'Sir John had Land', before they leave him. **1607** MIDDLETON *Michaelmas Term* v. i, You master prodigal Had-land; away! **1610** J. DAVIES *Commend. Poems, Panegyricke* Wks. (Grosart) 3 *note*, Few Hadlands take pleasure to behold the lands they had.

Hadrianic (heɪdrɪ'ænɪk), *a.* [f. L. *Hadriān(us* + -IC.] Of or pertaining to the Roman emperor Hadrian (A.D. 76–138).

1886 W. P. DICKSON tr. *Mommsen's Provinces of Roman Empire* I. v. 189 In the time of Diocletian we find the district between the two walls evacuated, but the Hadrianic wall occupied still as before. **1897** *Trans. Cumberland & Westmorland Antiquarian & Archæol. Soc.* XIV. 419 Hadrianic inscriptions occur at Chesterholm and Greatchesters. **1911** *Ibid.* New Ser. XI. 390 Vindolana and Magna, although occupied in Hadrianic times as Wall stations, differ from the others in Northumberland. **1921** *Jrnl. Roman Stud.* XI. 51 The idea of a single camp extending from sea to sea is a bold flight of imagination... It became.. a cardinal feature in the 'Hadrianic Theory' of the nineteenth century. **1935** *Burlington Mag.* Feb. 97/1 Hadrianic art was certainly Greek in its nature. **1962** *Guardian* 11 July 5/7 The rampart and ditch of a small Hadrianic fort. **1972** *Daily Tel.* 5 Dec. 12/5 Coins and Antiquities gave £6,800 for a Hadrianic/Early Antonine period Roman marble figure called Paris.

hadrie, obs. Sc. form of HEATHERY.

hadrome ('hædrəʊm). *Bot.* [ad. G. *hadrom* (G. Haberlandt *Physiologische Pflanzenanatomie* (1884) VII. v. 265), f. Gr. ἁδρ-ός thick, bulky + -OME.] The conducting tissue of the xylem, excluding fibres.

1898 H. C. PORTER tr. *Strasburger's Text-bk. Bot.* 102 Other terms often used to designate the vascular bundles are folio-vascular bundles and mestome. The vascular portion is also termed the xylem or hadrome. **1914** M. DRUMMOND tr. *Haberlandt's Physiol. Plant Anat.* vii. 347 The water-conducting vessels and tracheides constitute.. the resistant hadrome portion [of the conducting strand]... The xylem includes the hadrome with its associated wood-fibres... Where.. no wood-fibres are developed, xylem is the exact equivalent of hadrome. **1965** K. ESAU *Plant Anat.* (ed. 2) xii. 272 The parallel term for the xylem is *hadrom*, which refers to the conducting part of the xylem.. excluding the fibers.

Hence **hadro'centric** *a.*, having the hadrome surrounded by the leptome; **'hadromal** [a. G. *hadromal* (F. Czapek 1899, in *Zeitschr. f. physiol. Chem.* XXVII. 163], a hydrolysis product of lignin; *para*-coniferyl aldehyde, $C_6H_2(OH)(OCH_3)CH{:}CHCHO$; **,hadromy'cosis**, a fungal disease of plants in which the xylem is the part most affected.

1899 *Jrnl. Chem. Soc.* LXXVI. I. 560 A substance termed hadromal has been isolated from different woody tissues; it has the properties of a phenol and of an aldehyde. **1900** B. D. JACKSON *Gloss. Bot. Terms* 310/1 *Hadrocentric*, having the hadrome in the centre surrounded by the leptome. **1914** M. DRUMMOND tr. *Haberlandt's Physiol. Plant Anat.* vii. 349 If the hadrome is central and the leptome peripheral, the bundle may be termed *hadrocentric*. **1916** G. H. PETHYBRIDGE in *Sci. Proc. Roy. Dublin Soc.* XV. 87 The fungus mycelium is, at any rate in the early stages of the disease, confined to the wood vessels..and I, therefore, suggest the word 'hadromycosis' for use in this connexion. **1917** *Nature* 22 Feb. 500/2 Plants suffering from the choking of their vessels [by fungi] (hadromycosis). **1928** *Chem. Abstr.* XXII. 399 Czapek's hadromal.., which he considers responsible for the characteristic red color given by wood tissues with phloroglucinol-HCl. **1931** *Hilgardia* V. 197 (*title*) Verticillium hadromycosis. **1952** F. E. BRAUNS *Chem. Lignin* iv. 37 Hadromal occurs in wood as a coniferyl aldehyde cellulose ester. **1971** G. C. AINSWORTH *Ainsworth & Bisby's Dict. Fungi* (ed. 6) 254 Hadromycosis, a disease of plants in which the pathogen is confined to the xylem, *e.g. Verticillium* wilt of potato and tomato.

hadron ('hædrɒn). *Physics.* [f. Gr. ἁδρ-ός thick, bulky + -ON[1]; first used in Russian, with the spelling *adron.*] Any strongly interacting sub-atomic particle. Hence **ha'dronic** *a.*

1962 L. B. OKUN' in *Proc. Internat. Conf. High-Energy Physics* 845/2 In this report I shall call strongly interacting particles hadrons, and the corresponding decays hadronic. **1966** *New Scientist* 26 May 500/1 The particles, so-called baryons and mesons, collectively called hadrons. **1968** *Sci. Jrnl.* Nov. 34/2 Weak decays of hadrons—which are nucleons (neutrons and protons) and their heavy partners. **1969** *Physics Bull.* Jan. 32/1 In high energy hadron collisions, the fraction of the total cross section going into two-body final states decreases rapidly with energy.

hadrosaur ('hædrəusɔː(r)). [ad. mod.L. *Hadrosaurus* (name of the genus), f. Gr. ἁδρό-ς thick, stout + σαῦρος (= σαύρα) lizard.] A genus of gigantic fossil saurian reptiles found in North America.

1877 LE CONTE *Elem. Geol.* III. (1879) 467 The Hadrosaur from New Jersey was twenty-eight feet long.

hadyr, obs. Sc. form of HEATHER.

hae (heː, hɛː, hæː), Sc. form of HAVE.

hæcceity (hɛk'siːɪtɪ, hiːk-). *Scholastic Philos.* Also 7 hæccity. [ad. med.L. *hæcceitāt-em* 'thisness' (Duns Scotus), f. *hæc*, fem. of *hĭc* this.] The quality implied in the use of *this*, as *this man*; 'thisness'; 'hereness and nowness'; that quality or mode of being in virtue of which a thing is or becomes a definite individual; individuality.

1647 R. BARON *Cyprian Acad.* 6 Club-fisted Logick with all her Quiddities..nor Scotus with his hæccities. **1678** CUDWORTH *Intell. Syst.* I. ii. §8. 67 Scholasticks..could not make a Rational Discourse of anything, though never so small, but they must stuff if with their Quiddities, Entities, Essences, Hæcceities, and the like. **1837** WHEWELL *Hist. Induct. Sc.* (1857) I. 244 Duns Scotus..placed the principle of Individuation in 'a certain determining positive entity' which his school called *Hæcceity* or *thisness*. **1890** *Jrnl. Educ.* 1 Nov. 629/1 Of course, if provision is made only for his general humanity and not for what makes him *hic* or *ille*, not for his *hæcceity* as the schoolmen used to say, a man will have cause to complain.

Haeckelian (hɛ'kiːlɪən), *a.* (and *sb.*) [f. the name of E. H. *Haeckel* (1834–1919), German biologist: see -IAN.] Of or pertaining to the opinions of Haeckel; also as *sb.*, a believer in Haeckel's theories. So **Haeckelism** ('hɛkəlɪz(ə)m), **-'ismus**, the opinions and theories of Haeckel.

1894 *Natural Sci.* Mar. 162 We are well content to cease from controversy, to let Calcareous sponges, the Gastrula, and..Haeckelismus take care of themselves. **1897** *Ibid.* Jan. 31 The typical form of the Haeckelian genealogical tree. **1899** E. J. CHAPMAN *Drama of Two Lives* 88 Thus, hæckelism's wondrous gleam Makes clear, to all, how all arose. **1930** G. R. DE BEER *Embryol. & Evol.* xv. 102 There is then no recapitulation in the Haeckelian sense of accelerated repetition of adult stages. **1971** *Nature* 11 June 400/2 The German Monist League..was neither a 'scientific' nor a 'political' body but rather one devoted to Haeckelian naturalism.

hæg, obs. form of HAIK.[2]

hæil, hæle, var. HAIL *a.*, HEAL *sb. Obs.*

hæm, heme (hiːm). [Back-formation from HÆM(OGLOBIN.] **a.** A chelation compound, $C_{34}H_{32}O_4N_4Fe$, of ferrous ion and protoporphyrin, obtained on reduction of hæmatin: the red-coloured non-protein constituent of hæmoglobin.

1925 ANSON & MIRSKY in *Jrnl. Physiol.* LX. 50 Haemoglobin is a conjugated protein consisting of globin and a non-protein part, containing pyrrol nuclei and iron, which we shall call haem. **1939** *Jrnl. Biol. Chem.* CXXXI. 661 Coryell..has applied the Pauling equation..to the oxidation of hemoglobin..and has shown that interaction among the four heme groups will account for the occurrence of an *n* which is not integral. **1956** *Nature* 11 Feb. 275/1 The angular variation of the *g* values enables an accurate determination to be made of the orientation of the hæm and porphyrin planes with respect to the external crystalline axes. *Ibid.* 275/2 Detailed information on the orientation of the hæm planes can be combined with X-ray measurements to calculate the polypeptide chain directions. **1970** R. W. MCGILVERY *Biochem.* ii. 13 The biological function of hemoglobin is therefore derived from both the heme and the peptides... Each of the four peptide chains has its own heme.

b. Any of various compounds of a ferrous or ferric ion and a porphyrin, present in biological pigments.

1948 *Biochem. Jrnl.* XLII. p. xlvii/2 The phase separation of haems has been applied to ox heart muscle. **1962** RIMINGTON & KENNEDY in Florkin & Mason *Comprehensive Biochem.* IV. xii. 563 By far the most important metalloporphyrins..are the iron complexes or hemes. In these nature has exploited the valency change from the ferric to ferrous state and vice versa to establish an electron transport system connecting the intracellular dehydrogenases with atmospheric oxygen. **1966** K. OKUNUKI in Florkin & Stotz *Comprehensive Biochem.* XIV. 233 Four types of haem have so far been known to occur in cytochromes... These are haem *a*, protohaem, haem *c* and so-called haem a_2.

hæma-, hema-, repr. Gr. αἷμα blood; sometimes improperly used as combining form instead of the etymologically regular HÆMATO- or HÆMO-. For such words in *hæma-* see HÆMO-.

These erroneous forms in *hæma-* are nearly all of French origination. Littré has *hémachroïne*, *-dromomètre*, *-dynamique*, *-statique*; to French authors are also due *hémaphéine*, *hematherma*, etc.

In words derived from Gr. αἷμα, the spelling *he-* is favoured in the United States, but is rarely used in Great Britain, except in *hematite*, where it is the prevailing form in industrial and commercial use, and in *hemorrhage* and *hemorrhoid*, in which *hæ-* is however more usual.

hæmachromatosis, hem-, varr. HÆMOCHROMATOSIS.

hæmachrome, -cytometer: see HÆMO-.

hæmad ('hiːmæd), *sb.* [f. Gr. αἷμα blood + -AD, after *monad*, etc.] A blood-corpuscle.

1891 in FOSTER *Encycl. Med. Dict.*

hæmad ('hiːmæd), *adv.* [f. HÆM-AL + -AD in sense 'towards': cf. *dextrad*, *dorsad*.] Towards the hæmal aspect of the body.

1891 FOSTER *Encycl. Med. Dict.*, *Hæmad.* In man, forward; in beasts, downward.

hæmadromograph, etc.: see HÆMO-.

hæmafibrite, hema- (hiːmə'faɪbraɪt). *Min.* [Named 1884, from Gr. αἷμα blood (in reference to its colour) + L. *fibra* fibre + -ITE.] A hydrous arseniate of manganese, of red colour and fibrous structure.

1887 DANA *Manual Min.* (ed. 4) 210.

hæmagglutinate, hem- (,hiːmə'gl(j)uːtɪneɪt), *v.* [f. Gr. αἷμ-α blood + AGGLUTINATE *v.*] *trans.* To cause (red blood cells) to agglutinate. So **,hæma'gglutinating** *ppl. a.*

1921 *Jrnl. Immunol.* VI. 423 In..experiments with normal and 'immune' hemagglutinating sera we have used the slide method. **1922** *Jrnl. Amer. Med. Assoc.* 11 Nov. 1684/1 (*title*) The hemagglutinating fraction of human serums. *Ibid.* 1685/1 The hemagglutinating property is contained in the pseudoglobin fraction. **1936** *Nature* 26 Sept. 554/1 The haemagglutinating substance is present in the cotyledons of the seed of the runner bean. **1956** *Ibid.* 4 Feb. 234/2 Under the conditions of assay, five hæmagglutinating units were regularly inhibited by a minimum of 10–20μ gm. of preparation *IL*-1. **1961** *Lancet* 23 Sept. 718/1 Only 6 strains were found to hæmagglutinate the red cells of more than 5 species.

Also **,hæmaggluti'nation**, the action or process of hæmagglutinating.

1907 *Jrnl. Med. Res.* XVII. 323 Repeated controls have convinced me that the presence and degree of hemagglutination may be detected quite as accurately macroscopically as microscopically. **1919** *Jrnl. Immunol.* IV. 284 The use of hypertonic solutions of sodium chlorid are of no practical value in preventing hemagglutination in complement fixation tests. **1946** *Nature* 27 July 119/1 Vaccinia hæmagglutination is inhibited by appropriate immune sera either of animal or human origin. **1949** *Poultry Sci.* XXVIII. 622 (*title*) A plate hemagglutination-inhibition test for Newcastle disease antibodies in avian and human serums. *Ibid.* 622/1 Virus isolation and neutralization tests are carried out in embryonating chicken eggs; the hemagglutination-inhibition test is done in test tubes. **1969** *New Scientist* 30 Jan. 171/1 The basis of a simple laboratory test—the haemagglutination test—which is widely used in the study of influenza.

hæmagglutinin, hem- (,hiːmə'gl(j)uːtɪnɪn). [f. Gr. αἷμ-α + AGGLUTININ.] A substance that causes agglutination of red blood cells.

1904 *Amer. Jrnl. Med. Sci.* CXXVIII. 669 (*title*) Concerning haemagglutinins of bacterial origin and their relation to hyaline thrombi and liver necroses. *Ibid.* 670 The observations of Hueter..are of interest in connection with our recently acquired knowledge of bacterial haemagglutinins. **1946** *Nature* 27 July 119/1 Work on the hæmagglutinin of vaccinia virus was initiated by an observation by Burnet in October 1941 that a chorioallantoic membrane emulsion agglutinated fowl cells to a low titre. **1969** *New Scientist* 23 Jan. 171/1 The presence of haemagglutinin on the virus surface enables the influenza virus to adhere firmly to the surface of chicken erythrocytes.

hæmagogue, hem- ('hiːm-, 'hɛməgɒg), *a.* and *sb.* [f. Gr. αἷμ-α blood, HÆM(O- + ἀγωγός leading.] **A.** *adj.* Promoting a menstrual or hæmorrhoidal discharge of blood. **B.** *sb.* A medicine which has this quality.

1702 FLOYER *Hist. Cold Bathing* I. ii. (1706) 43 Probably for their Hemagogue Faculty, Hippocrates observes, That Cold Bathing makes bloody Urine worse. **1854** MAYNE *Expos. Lex.*, Hemagogue. **1886** *Syd. Soc. Lex.*, *Hæmagogue.*

hæmal, hemal ('hiːməl), *a. Anat.* [f. Gr. αἷμ-α blood + -AL[1].] Of or belonging to the blood or blood-vascular system; belonging to or situated on or towards that side or region of the body which contains the heart and great blood-vessels: opp. to *neural*; in the case of the Vertebrata and Tunicata, synonymous with *ventral*.

hæmal arch, term used by Owen for the inferior arch of a typical vertebra. ***hæmal cavity***, the cavity formed by a series of hæmal arches (constituted by the ribs, costal cartilages, and breast-bone), and containing the heart, great blood-vessels, and respiratory and digestive organs. ***hæmal spine***, the ventral element of a hæmal arch, represented by a segment of the breast-bone; also (quot. 1868) used by Darwin for a hypapophysis, or process on the hæmal side of the body of a vertebra.

1839–47 *Todd's Cycl. Anat.* III. 1011/2 Near the entry of the hæmal canal. **1848** OWEN *Homol. Vertebrate Skel.* 99 The pleurapophyses defend the hæmal or visceral cavity. **1854** —— *Skel. & Teeth* in *Circ. Sc.* (*c* 1865) II. 48/1 The hæmal arch is formed by a pair of bones called 'pleurapophyses'..by a second pair, called 'hæmapophyses'..and by a bone, sometimes bifid, called the 'hæmal spine'. **1861** J. R. GREENE *Man. Anim. Kingd.*, *Cœlent.* 17 In the Cœlenterata..no distinction between neural and hæmal regions can be noticed. **1868** DARWIN *Anim. & Pl.* I. iv. 122 In a half-wild rabbit..a hæmal spine was moderately well developed on the under side of the twelfth dorsal vertebra. **1878** BELL *Gegenbaur's Comp. Anat.* 217 The close association of the hæmal system and the nerve-tracts. **1891** A. CLARKSON in *Brit. Med. Jrnl.* II. 183 Hæmal Glands.. Certain hitherto undescribed glands which are to be found accompanying the renal artery in some herbivora.

hæmangioma, hem- (,hiːmændʒɪ'əumə). *Path.* Pl. **-ata, -as.** [f. Gr. αἷμ-α blood + ANGIOMA.] (See quot. 1900.)

1890 in BILLINGS *Nat. Med. Dict.* **1900** DORLAND *Med. Dict.* 291/2 *Hemangioma*, angioma containing blood-vessels, but not lymph-vessels; true angioma. **1913** C. P. WHITE *Path. Growth Tumours* vi. 86 Angeiomata..are formed in connection with blood vessels (haemangeioma) or with lymphatic vessels (lymphangeioma). **1961** *Lancet* 22 July 211/2 (*table*) Hæmangiomata. *Ibid.* 26 Aug. 492/2 Patients with coarctation of the abdominal aorta..or large hæmangiomas. **1962** *Ibid.* 6 Jan. 46/1 A capillary hæmangioma of the upper lips, nose, and frontal area seems to be highly pathognomonic of this syndrome. **1970** PASSMORE & ROBSON *Compan. Med. Stud.* II. xxx. 16 It is difficult to draw a dividing line between fibrous xanthomata..and the sclerosing haemangiomata.

Hence **,hæmangioma'tosis**, a condition characterized by the presence of many hæmangiomata.

1912 *Jrnl. Amer. Med. Assoc.* 27 Apr. 1311/1 (*title*) General hemangiomatosis of placenta. **1913** DORLAND *Med. Dict.* (ed. 7) 415/2 Hemangiomatosis, a condition in which multiple hemangiomata are developed. **1970** *Gut* XI. 515 Radiotherapy has been reported..to be of some benefit in..hepatic haemangiomatosis.

hæmanthus, hem- (hiː'mænθəs). *Bot.* [mod.L. (Linnæus *Hortus Cliffortianus* (1737) 127), f. Gr. αἷμ-α blood + ἄνθος flower.] A bulbous plant of the genus so called, belonging to the family Amaryllidaceæ, native to southern and tropical Africa, and bearing umbels of red, pink, or white flowers.

1771 R. WESTON *Universal Botanist* II. 375 Hæmanthus, Blood flower, or African Tulip... Spotted-stalked Guinea Hæmanthus. **1834** *Curtis's Bot. Mag.* LXI. 3373 (*heading*) Hairy, Pink Hæmanthus. **1885** T. BAINES *Greenhouse & Stove Plants* 199/1 Hæmanthus are increased like Amaryllis by offsets which the strong bulbs produce. **1961** *Amateur Gardening* 14 Oct. 29/1 Bulbs of haemanthus can be potted now.

hæmaphæin, -poietic: see HÆMO-.

‖**hæmapophysis** (hiːmə'pɒfɪsɪs). *Anat.* [mod.L.: see HÆMO- and APOPHYSIS. (So called as being situated towards the hæmal aspect of the body.)] Owen's term for that portion of the hæmal arch of a typical vertebra situated between the pleurapophysis and the hæmal spine; represented in the trunk of a vertebrate animal by a costal cartilage.

1849 OWEN *On Limbs* 42 The elements more constantly related to the protection of the vascular or haemal axis..the haemapophyses, [etc.]. **1880** GUNTHER *Fishes* 51 Two haemapophyses which actually coalesce to form on the ventral side the haemal canal for a large trunk of the vascular system.

Hence ˌhæmapoˈphysial *a.*, pertaining to or of the nature of a hæmapophysis.

1839–47 TODD *Cycl. Anat.* III. 965/2 There are developed hæmapophysial arches. **1870** ROLLESTON *Anim. Life* 27.

hæmarthrosis, hem- (hiːmɑːˈθrəʊsɪs). *Path.* Pl. **-oses.** [f. Gr. αἷμ-α + ἄρθρο-ν joint + -OSIS.] Hæmorrhage into a joint.

1883 *Brit. Med. Jrnl.* 22 Sept. 561/2, I diagnosed the case as one of hæmarthrosis. **1891** C. W. M. MOULLIN *Surg.* III. vi. 613 In cases..in which the hæmorrhage is often considerable and the swelling immediate, it may be almost pure blood (hæmarthrosis). **1908** *Practitioner* Apr. 521 Other cases are given..of the association of fatal hæmorrhages from the bowels together with the hæmarthrosis. **1962** *Lancet* 27 Jan. 174/1 Their bleeding is similar to that seen in mild hæmophilia; they have had hæmarthroses, deep intramuscular hæmorrhage, and hæmaturia.

hæmastatic, -tachometer: see HÆMO-.

hæmatal (ˈhiːmətəl), *a.* [f. Gr. αἱματ- blood + -AL¹.] Relating to the blood or blood-vessels.

1886 in *Syd. Soc. Lex.* **1893** in DUNGLISON *Med. Dict.*

hæmataulics (hiːməˈtɔːlɪks). [f. HÆMATO- after *hydraulics*.] The study of the laws of the movement of the blood in the vessels.

1854 MAYNE *Expos. Lex.*, *Hæmataulica*, a term by Magendie for the vascular system; hemataulics.

‖**hæmatemesis** (hiːməˈtɛmɪsɪs). *Path.* [mod.L., f. Gr. αἱματ- blood + ἔμεσις vomiting.] Vomiting of blood.

1800 *Med. Jrnl.* IV. 475 Hæmatemesis. **1806** *Ibid.* xv. 187 This hæmatemesis..being peculiar to the female sex. **1894** *Quain's Dict. Med.* I. 764 Congestion of the portal system is a very frequent cause of hæmatemesis.

hæmatherm, hem- (ˈhiːməθɜːm). *Zool.* [f. mod.L. *Hematherma* sb. pl. (Latreille), erroneously f. Gr. αἷμα blood (see HÆMA-) + θερμ-ός warm.] A warm-blooded animal. So **hæmaˈthermal, hæmaˈthermous** *adjs.*, belonging to the hæmatherms; warm-blooded.

1847 CRAIG, *Hematherms.* **1886** *Syd. Soc. Lex.*, Hæmathermous. **1889** *Cent. Dict.*, *Hemathermal, hæmathermal.*

hæmathorax, erron. form of HÆMOTHORAX.

hæmatic, hematic (hiːˈmætɪk), *a.* and *sb.* [ad. Gr. αἱματικ-ός, f. αἷμα, αἱματ- blood.]

A. *adj.* **a.** Relating or pertaining to blood. **b.** Containing blood, sanguineous. **c.** Acting upon the blood. **d.** Of a blood-red colour (*Syd. Soc. Lex.*).

1854 in MAYNE *Expos. Lex.* **1854–67** C. A. HARRIS *Dict. Med. Terminol.*, *Spanæmic*..a term applied to hæmatic remedies when such remedies impoverish the blood. **1872** PEASLEE *Ovar. Tumours* 42 Boinet divides simple cysts.. into the 'hydatic'..the serous or 'ascitic'; and the 'hematic' (sanguineous) or purulent, but not gelatinous. **1882** *Lancet* I. 316 Hæmatic crises. **1886** *Syd. Soc. Lex.*, *Hæmatic acid*, a substance obtained..when carbonised blood is heated to redness with sodium carbonate and the residue treated with alcohol.

B. *sb.* **1.** A medicine that acts upon the blood.

1854–67 C. A. HARRIS *Dict. Med. Terminol.* s.v., Hæmatics act as restoratives when they enrich the blood, or as spanæmics when they impoverish it. **1881** G. L. CARRICK *Koumiss* 168 It is an excellent hæmatic.

2. hæmatics: That branch of physiology or medicine which treats of the blood.

1854 in MAYNE *Expos. Lex.* **1886** in *Syd. Soc. Lex.*

hæmatid (ˈhiːmətɪd, ˈhɛm-). [f. Gr. αἱματ- blood + -ID.] A red blood-corpuscle.

1888 ROLLESTON & JACKSON *Anim. Life* 335 Blood-corpuscles or haematids. *Ibid.* 353.

‖**hæmatiˈdrosis, hæmathidrosis.** *Path.* [f. HÆMATO- + Gr. ἱδρωσις sweating.] A sweating of blood; effusion of sweat mixed with blood.

1854 in MAYNE *Expos. Lex.* **1876** DUHRING *Dis. Skin* 335 Hæmatidrosis is known also by the names, hæmidrosis, ephidrosis cruenta, and bloody sweats.

hæmatin, hematin (ˈhiːmətɪn, ˈhɛm-). *Chem.* [mod. f. Gr. αἱματ- blood + -IN.]

1. The earlier name of HÆMATOXYLIN.

1819 J. G. CHILDREN *Chem. Anal.* 287 Hematin is the colouring matter of logwood. **1830** LINDLEY *Nat. Syst. Bot.* 92 A peculiar principle, called Hæmatin.

2. A bluish-black amorphous substance with metallic lustre, obtained from red blood-corpuscles, in which it exists as a constituent of hæmoglobin.

1845 G. E. DAY tr. *Simon's Anim. Chem.* I. 5 Protein, and its various modifications—gelatin, bilin, and the products of its metamorphosis—hæmatin, urea, uric acid, &c. **1881** WATTS *Dict. Chem.* VIII. 920 Hæmoglobin is resolved by the action of iodine into hæmatin and globulin.

Hence **hæmaˈtinic** *a.*, of or relating to hæmatin (sense 2); *sb.*, a medicine which increases the amount of hæmatin in the blood. **ˌhæmatiˈnometer**, an instrument for measuring the amount of hæmatin in the blood; so **ˌhæmatinoˈmetric** *a.*, relating to such measurement. ‖**ˌhæmatiˈnuria**: see quot. 1886 (now called *hæmoglobinuria*).

1855 A. B. GARROD *Mat. Med.* (ed. 6) 83 All the preparations of iron appear to act as blood restorers or hæmatinics. **1876** BARTHOLOW *Mat. Med.* (1879) 117 Iron is synergistic as regards haematinic effects. **1885** STIRLING tr. *Landois' Hum. Physiol.* I. 25 In the vessel with parallel sides, or hæmatinometer. **1879** J. R. REYNOLDS *Syst. Med.* V. 468 The existence of hæmatinuria indicates an excessive decomposition of blood corpuscles. **1886** *Syd. Soc. Lex.*, *Hæmatinuria*, the passing of urine containing the colouring matter of the blood without the corpuscles.

†**ˈhæmatine,** *a. Obs.* [ad. Gr. αἱμάτιν-ος of blood, bloody, f. αἱματ- blood: see -INE.] Resembling blood; blood-red.

1658 G. STARKEY *Pyrotechny* xii. 52 The red is the Hematine tincture.

‖**hæˈmatinon, -inum.** [Gr. αἱμάτινον, L. *hæmatinum*, adj. in neuter sing. 'resembling blood, blood-red': see prec.] A red glass found in ancient mosaics and ornamental vases.

1706 PHILLIPS (ed. Kersey), *Hæmatinon*, a kind of red Glass, anciently made into Dishes. **1861** C. W. KING *Ant. Gems* (1866) 74 An entirely red, opaque sort, called Haematinon.

hæmatite, hematite (ˈhɛmətaɪt, ˈhiːm-). *Min.* Formerly also in Lat. form **hæmatites** (hiːməˈtaɪtiːz). Also 6–7 **em-**. The spelling *hem-* is usual in commercial and economic use. [ad. L. *hæmatites*, Gr. αἱματίτης (sc. λίθος) *lit.* blood-like stone, f. αἱματ- blood: see -ITE.] Native sesquioxide of iron (Fe_2O_3), an abundant and widely distributed iron ore, occurring in various forms (crystalline, massive, or granular); in colour, red, reddish-brown, or blackish with a red streak. (Sometimes distinguished as ***red hæmatite***: cf. b.)

α. **1543** TRAHERON *Vigo's Chirurg.* 207 a/2 (Stanf.) Of the stone called ematites. **1601** HOLLAND *Pliny* II. 587 The sanguine load-stone, called Hæmatites. **1750** tr. *Leonardus' Mirr. Stones* 98 Emathitis, or Emathites, is a reddish Stone. **1812** SIR H. DAVY *Chem. Philos.* 384 The purest iron is made from an ore called hæmatites by ignition with charcoal.

β. **1608** TOPSELL *Serpents* (1658) 715 Andreas Balvacensis writeth, that the Bloud-stone called the *Hæmatite*, is made of the Dragons bloud. **1630** J. TAYLOR (Water P.) *Wks.* 33/2 The Onix, Topaz, Iaspar, Hematite. **1688** R. HOLME *Armoury* II. 40/2 The Ematite..is of some called stench blood, for that it stoppeth the..course of flowing. **1849** MURCHISON *Siluria* xix. 463 Chromate of iron, hematite, and magnetic iron-ore. **1863** A. C. RAMSAY *Phys. Geog.* xxxv. (1878) 596 Rich deposits of hæmatite.

b. ***brown hæmatite***: a mineral of a brown or brownish-yellow colour, consisting of hydrated sesquioxide of iron; also called *limonite*.

1805–17 R. JAMESON *Char. Min.* (ed. 3) 230 Reniform brown hematite. **1843** PORTLOCK *Geol.* 113 A layer of earthy brown hematite. **1879** *Cassell's Techn. Educ.* I. 11 Brown iron ore or haematite consists essentially of three equivalents of water united to two of peroxide of iron.

c. *attrib.*

1861 *Lond. Rev.* 16 Feb. 167 We find the Whitehaven district yielding annually upwards of 400,000 tons..of hematite iron ore. **1872** W. S. SYMONDS *Rec. Rocks* x. 392 At Llantrissant in Glamorganshire there are hæmatite iron ores. **1891** *Daily News* 19 Jan. 2/6 A number of the best pig iron makers..particularly hematite producers.

Hence **hæmaˈtitiform, hem-,** *a.*, having the form of hæmatite.

1801 BOURNON in *Phil. Trans.* XCI. 180 Variety 5. Hematitiform.

hæmatitic, hem- (hɛməˈtɪtɪk, hiːm-), *a.* [f. as prec. + -IC.] Pertaining to, consisting of, or resembling hæmatite.

1796 KIRWAN *Elem. Min.* (ed. 2) II. 165 Essential to all hæmatitic ores. **1849** MURCHISON *Siluria* xiii. 321 Spothose and hematitic iron-ores. **1849** DANA *Geol.* ix. (1850) 469 Argillaceous and hematitic iron. **1860** BAIRD, etc. *Birds N. Amer.* 527 It never..has the haematitic tint.

So †**hæmaˈtitical** *a.* = prec. *Obs.*

1805 G. BARRY *Orkney Isl.* (1808) 271 They found hæmatitical iron ore.

hæmato-, hemato- (hiːmətəʊ, hɛmətəʊ), before a vowel **hæmat-, hemat-,** = Gr. αἱματο-, combining form of αἷμα, αἱματ- blood, freely used in Greek, and in many modern scientific terms, chiefly in physiology and medicine. (Several of these have shorter forms in HÆMO-, q.v.)

(The spelling *hæmato-* is more usual in Great Britain; *hemato-* is favoured in U.S.)

hæmaˈtobic, hæmaˈtobious *adjs.* [mod.L. *hæmatobium*, a parasite living in the blood, f. Gr. βίος life], living, as a parasite, in the blood. **ˌhæmatocaˈthartic** *a.* [see CATHARTIC], having the quality of purifying the blood. (Mayne *Expos. Lex.* 1854). **ˈhæmatoˌchrome** [Gr. χρῶμα colour], a red colouring matter developed in some Protozoa at a certain stage of existence. **ˈhæmatoˌcrit** [Gr. κριτ-ής judge], a centrifuge used to estimate the volume occupied by the red blood cells in a sample of blood; the value obtained, expressed as a percentage of the volume of the sample; also earlier **hæmatokrit. ˌhæmatoˈcryal** *a.* [Gr. κρύος cold, frost], belonging to the *Hæmatocrya* or cold-blooded Vertebrata. **ˌhæmatoˈcyanin** = HÆMOCYANIN (Mayne *Expos. Lex.* 1854). **ˈhæmatoˌcyst, ˌhæmatoˈcystis**, a cyst containing blood. **ˈhæmatoˌcyte** [Gr. κύτ-ος cell], a blood-corpuscle; hence **ˌhæmatocyˈtometer**, an instrument for ascertaining the number of blood-corpuscles, = HÆMOCYTOMETER (Dunglison *Lex.*). **ˌhæmatodyˈnamics, -dynaˈmometer** (see HÆMO-). **ˌhæmatoˈgastric** *a.* (see HÆMO-); (Mayne, 1854). †**ˈhæmatoˌgen** [a. G. *hämatogen* (G. Bunge 1885, in *Zeitschr. f. physiol. Chem.* IX. 56)], a yellow powder obtained from egg yolk and supposed to be the precursor of hæmoglobin (*Obs.*). ‖**ˌhæmatoˈgenesis** [see GENESIS], the formation of blood. **ˌhæmatoˈgenic** *a.*, relating to hæmatogenesis; also = next. **hæmaˈtogenous** *a.*, having its origin in the blood. †**hæmaˈtognomist** [Gr. γνώμη means of knowing] (see quot.). **hæmaˈtography** [see -GRAPHY], a description of the blood (Mayne, 1854). **ˌhæmatoˈlytic** *a.* (see HÆMO-). **ˌhæmatomyˈelia** [Gr. μυελ-ός marrow + -IA¹], hæmorrhage into the substance of the spinal cord. **ˌhæmatopaˈthology** (see quot.). **hæmaˈtophagous** *a.* [Gr. -φαγος eating], feeding upon, or living in, blood. ‖**ˌhæmatoˈphilia** = HÆMOPHILIA (*Syd. Soc. Lex.*). ‖**ˌhæmatoˈphobia** = HÆMOPHOBIA (Dunglison, 1857). **ˈhæmatoˌphyte** [Gr. φυτόν plant], a vegetable parasite inhabiting the blood (*Syd. Soc. Lex.* 1886). ‖**ˌhæmatopoiˈesis** [Gr. ποίησις making], the formation of blood. **ˌhæmatopoiˈetic** *a.*, pertaining to hæmatopoiesis (Mayne 1854). **ˌhæmatoˈporphyrin** [a. G. *haematoporphyrin* (F. Hoppe-Seyler *Med.-chem. Untersuch.* (1871) IV. liii. 533): see PORPHYRIN], a dark violet porphyrin compound, $C_{34}H_{38}O_6N_4$, obtained by the action of concentrated acids on hæm or its derivatives. **ˌhæmatoˈsalpinx** [SALPINX 2] (see quot. 1890). **ˈhæmatoˌscope, hæmaˈtoscopy, ˌhæmato-ˈspectroscope** (see quots.). **ˌhæmatoˈstibiite** *Min.* [L. *stibium* antimony], an antimoniate of manganese and iron, the grains of which in thin sections appear blood-red. **ˌhæmatoˈthermal** *a.* [Gr. θερμός warm], warm-blooded = HÆMATHERMAL. **hæmatoˈthorax** (see quot. 1876). ‖**ˌhæmatoˈzoon** (pl. **-ˈzoa**) [Gr. ζῷον animal], an animal parasite inhabiting the blood (Mayne, 1854); hence **ˌhæmatoˈzoan** = prec.; **ˌhæmatoˈzoic** *a.*, of or pertaining to a hæmatozoon.

1888 ROLLESTON & JACKSON *Anim. Life* 844 When the green-coloured organism passes into a resting phase..its colour changes to red, owing to the formation of *haematochrome dissolved in droplets of fat. **1866** *Hæmatocryal [see *hæmatothermal*]. **1854** MAYNE *Expos. Lex.*, **Hæmatocystis*..a hydatid, or cyst containing blood.. a hematocyst. **1890** L. C. WOOLDRIDGE tr. *Bunge's Text-bk. Physiol. & Pathol. Chem.* vi. 102 The iron is more firmly fixed in the nuclein of the yolk of egg than in the albuminates of iron... The nuclein which contained iron..is doubtless the precursor of hæmoglobin, for there is no considerable quantity of any other compound of iron in the yolk. I have therefore proposed that this compound should receive the name *hæmatogen (blood-former). **1934** J. F. MCCLENDON *Man. Biochem.* 112 Bunge..supposed that mammals are born with a store of iron. That led him to look for iron in the eggs of birds, and he found an iron compound which he called hematogen. **1876** tr. *Wagner's Gen. Pathol.* 506 Cysts which arise from blood-vessels, especially veins.. hæmatocystides. *Ibid.* 556 *Hæmatogenic icterus. **1881** *Sci. Amer.* 12 Mar. 161/3 For the dyscrasic or haematogenic origin of Bright's disease. **1866** A. FLINT *Princ. Med.* (1880) 80 Icterus, as thus induced by changes in the blood itself, is called *haematogenous. **1880** J. W. LEGGE *Bile* 229 A hæmatogenous jaundice. **1651** BIGGS *New Disp.* ¶234 These *Hæmatognomists or diviners by the Phœnomena's in the bloud. **1894** *Med. News* 29 Sept. 348/2 (*heading*) A modification of Hedin's *hematokrit. *Ibid.* 350/2 States of comparative health..seem to be of the least importance of all the data necessary for the present status of the hematokrit. **1946** *Nature* 31 Aug. 304/1 These patients had, ..because of the low hæmatocrit, a significantly reduced blood volume. **1958** *Immunology* I. 206 Blood samples were centrifuged in Wintrobe haematocrit tubes. **1966** *Lancet* 24 Dec. 1381/2 Chamberlain and Millard (1963) reduced the hæmatocrit and red-blood-cell volume (R.C.V.) in their patients with polycythæmia by means of oxygen. **1875** R. FOWLER *Med. Vocab.* (ed. 2) 222/1 *Hæmatolytic... 1. Accompanied with the escape of blood from distended capillaries. 2. Applied adj. and subs. to medicines, said to, by long continued use, impoverish the blood. **1886** *Syd. Soc. Lex.*, *Hæmatolytic*, having power to diminish the number of red corpuscles in the blood. **1881** *Brit. Med. Jrnl.* 28 May 852/2 A case of *haematomyelia in a man aged 19. **1940** H. G. WELLS *Babes in Darkling Wood* III. iii. 275 He was equal to hæmatomyelia, a sort of temporary stroke just at the back of the head. **1970** *Archiv. für Toxikol.* XXVI. 56 The apparent sudden onset, the lack of progression,..and the relatively advanced age of manifestation all point to hematomyelia as the cause of the lesion, which in turn follows as a consequence of the increased bleeding tendency associated with benzene poisoning. **1881** HUXLEY in *Nature* No. 615. 347 This modern humoral pathology was essentially blood-pathology (*hæmatopathology). **1854** MAYNE *Expos. Lex.*, *Hæmatophagus*, blood-eating; applied to those insects which seek the blood of animals for their sustenance, as the flea..*hematophagous. **1886** *Syd. Soc. Lex.*, *Hæmatophagous*..also applied to an Hæmatozoon. **1854** MAYNE *Expos. Lex.*, **Hæmatopoiesis*..assimilation of the chyle to blood; blood-making. **1876** tr. *Wagner's Gen. Pathol.* 536 Consecutive changes..which disturb hæmatopoiesis, digestion, respiration, etc. **1885** *Jrnl. Physiol.* VI. 27 The filtrate was reddish and shewed a spectrum which is that of acid *haematoporphyrin. **1902** *Encycl. Brit.* XXXI. 726/2 By mineral acids the iron may be removed, leaving a purplish pigment, Hæmatoporphyrin, which has no power of taking up or giving off oxygen. **1928** J. PRYDE *Recent Adv. Biochem.* (ed. 2) x. 315 It would seem that neither hæmatoporphyrin nor mesoporphyrin is formed in the human body. *Ibid.*, Hæmatoporphyrin has a very powerful light-sensitising action. **1955** *Sci. News Let.* 9 Apr. 240/3 Cancer tissue can be made to glow a bright red under ultraviolet light when a powder called hematoporphyrin is introduced intravenously before surgery. **1955** *Endeavour* XIV. 126/2 Haematoporphyrin.. is accordingly described as 1,3,5,8-tetramethyl-2,4-di-(α-oxyethyl)-porphin-6,7-dipropionic acid. **1884** *Lancet* 2 Feb. 207/2 *Haematosalpinx... Tumours were discovered to the left and right of the uterus. These..proved to be the tubes, full of tar-like blood and firmly adherent. **1890** BILLINGS *Nat. Med. Dict.* 614/1 *Hæmatosalpinx*, collection of blood in the Fallopian tube. **1923** J. M. M. KERR et al. *Combined Text-bk. Obstetr. & Gynæcol.* xli. 612 The fluid.. may extend to the uterine cavity, forming a hæmatometra, and in the most extreme cases it may distend the Fallopian tubes, forming hæmatosalpinges. **1972** C. J. DEWHURST *Integrated Obstetr. & Gynaecol. Postgrad.* i. 12/2 Haematosalpinx is most uncommon except in cases of very long-standing [imperforate membrane], or in association with retention of blood in a fragment of upper vagina. **1886** *Syd. Soc. Lex.*, **Hæmatoscope*, an instrument invented by Hermann to regulate the thickness of the layer of the diluted blood when examined by the spectroscope. **1887** *Jrnl. R. Microsc. Soc.* Ser. II. VII. 470 The determination of the quantity of oxyhæmoglobin by instruments called *hæmatoscopes* or *hæmatospectroscopes*. **1854** MAYNE *Expos. Lex.*, *Hæmatoscopia*, term for an examination of the blood; *hematoscopy. **1887** *Jrnl. R. Microsc. Soc.* Ser. II. VII. 470 *Hæmatoscopy*..a new spectroscopic method of analysing the blood. **1866** OWEN *Anat. Vertebr* I. 7 Vertebrates might be primarily divided..into **Hæmatothermal*, having the four-chambered heart, spongy lungs, hot blood, and *Hæmatocryal*, having less perfect breathing organs, less complex heart, with cold blood. **1852** J. MILLER *Pract. Surg.* xxv. (ed. 2) 315 Blood accumulating within the pleural cavity, may compress the lung, and constitute a dangerous *hæmato-thorax. **1876** tr. *Wagner's Gen. Pathol.* 212 By hæmatothorax is understood hæmorrhage into the pleural cavities.

hæmatoblast (ˈhiːmətəʊˌblɑːst, -ˌblæst). [see HÆMATO- and -BLAST.] **a.** *Phys.* Name given by Hayem to certain yellowish or greenish disks, smaller than the ordinary blood-corpuscles, found in the blood of viviparous Vertebrata; also called *blood-plates*. **b.** *Embryol.* Name given by Wissozky to cells of the mesoderm from which the first blood-corpuscles and blood-vessels originate. (*Syd. Soc. Lex.*)

1876 tr. *Wagner's Gen. Pathol.* 525 The first rudimentary masses of these cells, Heitzmann calls them hæmatoblasts. **1880** *Times* 13 Sept. 4/6 Oxygen..increases the number of red corpuscles and of hæmatoblasts, and the richness of the former in hemoglobin. **1883** *American* VI. 398 The relation of the hæmatoblasts to coagulation.

Hence **hæmatoˈblastic** *a.*

1882 *Lancet* II. 146 The head of the coagulum..contains in the centre a prolongation of the viscid hæmatoblastic material.

hæmatocele, hem- (ˈhiːmətəʊˌsiːl). *Path.* [f. HÆMATO- + Gr. κήλη, tumour, CELE.] A tumour containing extravasated blood.

1730-6 BAILEY (folio), *Hæmatoceˈle*, a Tumour turgid with Blood. **1783** POTT *Chirurg. Wks.* II. 383. **1877** ERICHSEN *Surg.* (1895) II. 1246 By Hæmatocele is meant an accumulation of the blood in connexion with the testicle or spermatic cord. **1878** T. BRYANT *Pract. Surg.* (1879) II. 218 Hæmatocele, usually follows upon some strain or injury.

ˌhæmato-ˈcrystallin. *Chem.* [f. HÆMATO- + CRYSTALLIN.] **a.** The special form of CRYSTALLIN or GLOBULIN found in the blood-corpuscles. **b.** 'A name given to hæmoglobin when it is obtained in a crystalline condition' (*Syd. Soc. Lex.* 1886).

1863-72 WATTS *Dict. Chem.*, *Hæmato-crystallin*, a crystalline substance obtained from blood. It has the composition of the albuminoids, and, if quite pure, would probably be colourless. **1872** J. H. BENNETT *Text-bk. Physiol.* I. 31 According to Hoppe-Seyler and Stokes hæmato-crystallin exists in the blood in two forms. **1878** KINGZETT *Anim. Chem.* 30 There are reasons for regarding hæmatocrystalline as a distinct chemical individual of probably greater complex constitution than fibrin.

ˌhæmato-ˈglobulin. *Chem.* [For *hæmatino-globulin*, f. HÆMATIN + GLOBULIN, as being composed of the two.] The colouring matter of the red corpuscles of the blood; also called **hæmatoˈglobin**: now usually shortened to HÆMOGLOBIN.

1845 G. E. DAY tr. *Simon's Anim. Chem.* I. 43 According to Berzelius, the hæmatoglobulin of human blood contains 100 parts of globulin and 5·8 of hæmatin. **1858** THUDICHUM *Urine* 235 Blood-casts may give up their hæmatoglobuline. **1867** J. MARSHALL *Outlines Physiol.* I. 83 The compound formed by these two substances [i.e. hæmatin or hæmin and globulin] named hæmato-globulin has a great tendency to crystallize even in blood simply set aside.

hæmatoid, hem- (ˈhiːmətɔɪd, ˈhɛm-), *a.* [ad. Gr. αἱματοειδής blood-like: see HÆMATO- and -OID.] **a.** Resembling blood; characterized by the presence of blood. **b.** Consisting of hæmatoidin.

1840 R. LISTON *Elem. Surg.* I. (ed. 2) 176 There are certainly few hæmatoid fungi. **1854** JONES & SIEV. *Pathol. Anat.* (1874) 262 The hæmatoid crystals are occasionally found in apoplectic clots. **1878** T. BRYANT *Pract. Surg.* I. 121 When a soft cancer is filled with blood it is known as a 'hæmatoid variety'.

hæmaˈtoidin, hem-. *Chem.* [f. prec. + -IN.] A yellow or yellowish-red crystalline substance found in extravasated blood; by some supposed to be identical with bilirubin.

1855 tr. *Wedl's Path. Hist.* II. i. 115 *note*, Virchow.. regards them as composed mainly of a new colouring matter, which he called *hæmatoidin*. **1863** *Syd. Soc. Year-bk.* 15 After the chloroform had evaporated, beautiful crystals of hæmatoidine were left. **1885** tr. *Landois' Hum. Physiol.* I. 36 Hæmatoidin crystals have been found in the urine.

hæmatoin (hiːməˈtəʊɪn). *Chem.* [Differentiated from *hæmatin*.] A derivative of hæmoglobin containing no iron.

1876 *Quain's Elem. Anat.* (ed. 8) II. 27 The effects of acids upon hæmatin is to separate the iron and to transform the substance into *hæmatoin* (acid-hæmatin).

hæmatology (hiːməˈtɒlədʒɪ). Also **hem-**. [f. HÆMATO- + -LOGY.] That branch of animal physiology which relates to the blood.

1811 HOOPER *Med. Dict.*, *Hæmatology*..the doctrine of the blood. **1857** in DUNGLISON *Med. Lex.* 440. **1946** *Nature* 21 Sept. 412/1 An International Hematology and *Rh* Conference will be held in Dallas, Texas, on November 15.

Hence **ˌhæmatoˈlogical**, a., relating to hæmatology. (Mayne *Expos. Lex.* 1854.) So also **hæmatoˈlogic** *a.*; **hæmatoˈlogically** *adv.*; **hæmaˈtologist**, one who specializes in hæmatology.

1904 *Lancet* 25 June 1790/2 The next method was demonstrated by Stengel some ten years ago and has since rapidly gained favour amongst hæmatologists, who frequently re-discover it. **1939** *Jrnl. Clin. Invest.* XVIII. 543/2 The serum or plasma iron fluctuations which occur in hematologically equilibrated subjects. **1946** *Nature* 6 July 24/2 We would like to take this opportunity of expressing our thanks to Dr. R. A. Kekwick for advising us on the hæmatological technique. **1947** *Radiology* XLIX. 286/2 The hematologic constituents of the peripheral blood were the most sensitive indicators of radiation effect. **1956** A. H. COMPTON *Atomic Quest* 333 Nuclear chemists,.. metallurgists, hematologists, and meteorologists. **1965** *Math. in Biol. & Med.* (*Med. Res. Council*) III. 90 (*title*) Digital computer as aid to differential diagnosis; use in hematologic diseases.

‖**hæmatoma** (hiːməˈtəʊmə). *Path.* Also in anglicized form **ˈhematome**. [mod.L., f. Gr. type *αἱμάτωμα, n. of product, f. αἱματό-ειν to turn into blood.] 'A bloody tumour or fungus; a swelling containing blood' (*Syd. Soc. Lex.*).

1847-9 TODD *Cycl. Anat.* IV. 125/2 A hæmatoma is then a fibrinous mass..arising from hæmorrhage. **1854** MAYNE *Expos. Lex.* s.v., A hematome. **1876** tr. *Wagner's Gen. Pathol.* 212 Blood-tumors, blood-boils, Hæmatomata. *Ibid.* 218 A hæmorrhage under the surface, especially of cuticular organs, is called hæmatoma or blood-boil.

Hence **hæmaˈtomatous** *a.*, of the nature of or affected with hæmatoma (*Syd. Soc. Lex.* 1886).

1886 *Med. News* XLIX. 536 There were hæmatomatous efflorescences in both dural sacs.

hæmatometer, hem- (hiːməˈtɒmɪtə(r)). [See HÆMATO- and -METER.] **a.** An instrument for measuring the force of the blood = *hæmodynamometer* (see HÆMO-). **b.** An instrument for numbering the blood-corpuscles. So **hæmaˈtometry**, the numeration of the blood-corpuscles.

1854 MAYNE *Expos. Lex.*, *Hematometer*..*Hematometry*.

hæmatose (ˈhiːmətəʊs), *a.* [f. Gr. αἱματ- blood + -OSE.] Full of blood; full-blooded.

1865 *Intell. Observ.* No. 43. 65 The raw meat is supposed to have a reconstituent action, and the alcohol a direct effect on the hæmatose.

hæmatosin, hem- (ˈhɛm-, ˈhiːmətəʊsɪn). *Chem.* [a. F. *hématosine* (Chevreul, 1814), irreg. f. Gr. αἵματος, genitive of αἷμα blood + -IN.] = HÆMATIN 2.

1834 *Good's Study Med.* (ed. 4) I. 550 *note*, Pure oxygen gas will heighten the red colour of hematosine. **1878** A. HAMILTON *Nerv. Dis.* 77 The Cortical substance of the brain was..more or less colored by hæmatosin.

‖**hæmatosis** (hiːməˈtəʊsɪs). [med. or mod.L., a. Gr. αἱμάτωσις (Galen), f. αἱματό-ειν to make into blood.] **a.** The formation of blood, esp. of blood-corpuscles; sanguification. **b.** 'An old term for hæmorrhage.' **c.** The oxygenation of the blood in the lungs (*Syd. Soc. Lex.*).

1696 PHILLIPS (ed. 5), *Hematosis*, Sanguification, or turning into Blood. **1727-51** CHAMBERS *Cycl.*, *Hæmatosis*.. the action whereby the chyle is converted into blood. **1811** HOOPER *Med. Dict.*, *Hæmatosis*, an hæmorrhage or flux of blood. **1866** A. FLINT *Princ. Med.* (1880) 165 The interruption of the function of haematosis in the portion of lung affected. **1879-89** J. M. DUNCAN *Lect. Dis. Women* xvii. (ed. 4), Its return to regularity seems to bring with it a healthy hæmatosis.

hæmatoxylin, hem- (hiːməˈtɒksɪlɪn). *Chem.* [f. mod.Bot. L. *hæmatoxylon*, *-um* logwood (f. HÆMATO- + ξύλον wood) + -IN.] A crystalline substance ($C_{16}H_{14}O_6$) obtained from logwood; colourless when pure, but affording fine red, blue, and purple dyes by the action of alkalis and oxygen; its aqueous solution also affords a fluid used for staining vegetable tissues.

1847 CRAIG, *Hæmatoxyline*..the colouring matter of.. Logwood. **1876** tr. *Wagner's Gen. Pathol.* 317 The calcified parts are not colored by carmine, but are colored blue by hæmatoxylin. **1882** VINES *Sach's Bot.* 947 The net-work readily stains with hæmatoxylin, but the fluid remains colourless.

Hence **hæmatoˈxylic** *a.*, derived from hæmatoxylin.

1892 G. S. WOODHEAD *Pract. Path.* ii. (ed. 3) 81 Hæmatoxylic glycerine is prepared by adding a saturated solution of hæmatoxylin to glycerine saturated with potash alum.

‖**hæmaturia** (hiːməˈtjʊərɪə). *Path.* [f. HÆMATO- + URIA.] The presence of blood in the urine.

1811 in HOOPER *Med. Dict.* **1835-6** TODD *Cycl. Anat.* I. 401/1 An old man subject to hæmaturia. **1886** A. FLINT *Princ. Med.* (1880) 920 Haematuria, or bloody urine, occurs in various diseases. **1894** *Westm. Gaz.* 29 June 3/2 The great plague [at Uganda] is hæmaturia or 'black-water' fever, which..kills 20 per cent. of those attacked.

Hence **hæmaˈturic** *a.*, pertaining to, characterized by, or affected with hæmaturia.

1866 A. FLINT *Princ. Med.* (1880) 923 Haematuric intermittent fever or miasmatic haematuria. **1895** *Daily News* 14 Oct. 6/6 Hæmaturic fever and jiggers appear to be the prevailing curses of Uganda.

hæmautograph (hiːˈmɔːtəgrɑːf, -græf). [f. HÆM(O- + AUTOGRAPH.] The apparatus used in tracing the pulse-curve obtained by opening an artery and allowing the stream of blood to strike against a roll of paper moving in front of it. Hence **hæmautoˈgraphic**, *a.*; **hæmauˈtography**, the operation of recording the pulse-curve in this way.

1885 STIRLING tr. *Landois' Hum. Physiol.* I. 135 Hæmautography. *Ibid.* 136 Hæmautographic curve of the posterior tibial artery of a large dog. **1886** *Syd. Soc. Lex.*, *Hæmautography*. The tracing..closely resembles a sphygmographic tracing, and consists of a primary wave, a dicrotic wave, and slight vibrations in the downward falling line.

hæmerythrin, hem- (ˌhiːmɛˈrɪθrɪn). *Biochem.* [f. Gr. αἷμ-α blood + ERYTHRIN.] A red respiratory pigment in the blood of certain invertebrates.

1903 *Jrnl. Chem. Soc.* LXXXIV. II. 741 Haemerythrin, the pink colouring matter in the blood of *Sipunculus* and a few other worms, is contained in the blood corpuscles. **1950** *Sci. News* XV. 103 A..rare red respiratory pigment is hæmerythrin possessed by certain marine animals. **1963** R. P. DALES *Annelids* iii. 70 Amongst other peculiar features they have enucleate corpuscles containing the respiratory pigment haemerythrin, unique in the Annelida, and found elsewhere only in the sipunculids.

hæmic (ˈhiːmɪk), *a.* [Arbitrary f. Gr. αἷμ-α blood + -IC: the etymological word being HÆMATIC.] Pertaining or relating to the blood; applied *spec.* to a difficulty of breathing caused by a disordered condition of the blood.

1857 DUNGLISON *Med. Lex.* 442 A 'hæmic disease'. **1875** H. C. WOOD *Therap.* (1879) 351 Hæmic respiration is, in other words, greatly interfered with, but not abolished. **1886** *Syd. Soc. Lex.*, *Hæmic asthma*..*Hæmic dyspnœa*.

hæmiglobin, hem- (hiːmɪˈgləʊbɪn, hiːmaɪ-). *Biochem.* [ad. G. *hämiglobin* (Kiese & Kaeske 1942, in *Biochem. Zeitschr.* CCCXII. 122), f. *hämoglobin* haemoglobin, by alteration.] = METHÆMOGLOBIN.

1944 *Chem. Abstr.* XXXVIII. 1537 In expts. dealing with the mechanism of chlorate poisoning, H. and J. [Heubner and Jung] found that hemiglobin (hitherto termed methemoglobin)..served to accelerate its own formation. **1965** *Clin. Chim. Acta* XI. 571 (*heading*) The formation of haemiglobin using nitrites. **1966** *Biol. Abstr.* XLVII. 5186/1 The rate of hemiglobin formation was measured in human blood during drying in air.

hæmin (ˈhiːmɪn). *Chem.* Also **hemin**. [f. Gr. αἷμ-α + -IN, differentiated in form from the regular *hæmatin*.] A deep red crystalline substance obtained from blood, containing hæmatin and hydrochloric acid. Also *attrib.*

1857 in DUNGLISON *Med. Lex.* **1865** WATTS *Dict. Chem.* III. 5 *Hæmin*, a crystallised intensely red substance. **1881** *Ibid.* VIII. 921 It is inferred that hæmin consists, not simply of hæmatin hydrochloride..but of a mixture of that compound with hæmatin and a crystallisable phosphorised substance. **1893** MANN *Forensic Med.* 70 Hæmin crystals are composed of hydrochlorate of hæmatin. **1955** *Sci. News Let.* 29 Oct. 274/1 Hemin, a chemical related to the red color chemical of blood, and protein. **1963** *New Scientist* 25 July

182 Biliverdin is formed by biological degradation of the red blood pigment hemin.

hæmo-, hemo- (hiːməʊ, hɛməʊ), before a vowel **hæm-, hem-** (hiːm, hɛm), repr. Gr. αἱμο-, shortened form of αἱματο- HÆMATO-, combining form of αἷμα blood: cf. Gr. αἱμοπώτης = αἱματοπώτης blood-drinker, αἱμορραγία HÆMORRHAGE. Many words in *hæmo-* occur also in the fuller form HÆMATO-.

Some of these words have been improperly written *hæma-*; a few in which this spelling prevails will be found in their alphabetical places; the rest are entered here under the more etymological form. As regards the spellings *hæ-* and *he-* see note s.v. HÆMA-.

ˌ**hæmochroma'tosis** (erron. **hæma-**) *Path.* [see CHROMATO- and -OSIS] = *bronze diabetes*; '**hæmochrome** (-krəʊm), erron. **hæma-** [Gr. χρῶμα colour], the colouring matter of the blood = HÆMOGLOBIN; hence ˌ**hæmochro'mometer**, 'an apparatus for calculating the amount of hæmoglobin in a liquid by comparison with a standard solution of normal colour' (*Syd. Soc. Lex.*); ˌ**hæmo'chromogen** [CHROMOGEN], a product obtained from hæmoglobin by hydrolysis; '**hæmocœle** (-siːl) [Gr. κοῖλος hollow, κοιλία cavity], the body-cavity of an arthropod or mollusc, analogous to the cœlome of a vertebrate; ˌ**hæmoconcen'tration** (see quot. 1949); ˌ**hæmocy'tometer** (erron. **hæma-**): see quots. and HÆMATO-; ˌ**hæmodi'alysis** *Med.* = DIALYSIS 5 b; hence ˌ**hæmo'dialyser**, an artificial kidney; ˌ**hæmodro'mometer** (also shortened -'drometer), -'dromograph [Gr. δρόμος course: see -METER, -GRAPH], instruments for measuring and registering the velocity of the blood-current; ˌ**hæmody'namic** *a.*, of or belonging to hæmodynamics; ˌ**hæmody'namics** [see DYNAMICS], 'the science of the forces connected with the motion of the blood' (*Syd. Soc. Lex.*); ˌ**hæmodyna'mometer** (erron. **hæma-**), an instrument for measuring the pressure of the blood; **hæmo'gastric** *a.* (erron. **hæma-**) [see GASTRIC], belonging to, or characterized by, effusion of blood into the stomach; ˌ**hæmogenetic** (-dʒɪ'nɛtɪk) *a.* (erron. **hæma-**) [see GENETIC], blood-producing; **hæmo'globulin** *Chem.* = HÆMOGLOBIN; '**hæmogram** [-GRAM], a systematic description of a patient's blood cells. ˌ**hæmo'gregarine** [ad. mod.L. generic name *Hæmogregarina* (B. Danilewsky 1885, in *Archiv für mikroskopische Anatomie* XXIV. 589], a member of a group of coccidian parasites which infest the blood of vertebrates and are transmitted by invertebrates; ˌ**hæmopa'thology**, the pathology of the blood; ˌ**hæmopoi'esis**, var. HÆMATOPOIESIS; **hæmopoi'etic** (see HÆMATO-); ˌ**hæmopoi'etin, -ine** [ad. F. *hémopoïétine* (Carnot & Deflandre 1906, in *Compt. Rend.* CXLIII. 386)], = ERYTHROPOIETIN; '**hæmoscope**, an apparatus for examining the blood; so **hæ'moscopy** (erron. **hæma-**), examination of the blood: see HÆMATO-; ˌ**hæmo'siderin** [a. G. *hämosiderin* (E. Neumann 1888, in *Arch. f. Path. Anat. u. Physiol.* CXI. 27), f. Gr. σίδηρ-ος iron: see -IN[1]], a brownish-yellow granular iron-protein substance used to store iron in the body; ˌ**hæmoside'rosis** [SIDEROSIS], accumulation of hæmosiderin in body tissues; **hæmo'spastic** [Gr. σπαστικός drawing, absorbing], *a.* having the property of drawing blood to a part, as a cupping-glass; *sb.* something having this property (Dunglison, 1857); **hæ'mostasis** [cf. STASIS], stoppage of the flow of blood; '**hæmostat** [cf. -STAT], †(*a*) (see quot. 1900) (*obs.*); (*b*) an instrument for retarding hæmorrhage; **hæmotachometer** (-tə'kɒmɪtə(r)), erron. **hæma-** [Gr. τάχος speed, velocity: see -METER], an instrument for measuring the velocity of the blood-current; so ˌ**hæmota'chometry**, the measurement of this; **hæmo'thorax** (see HÆMATO-); **hæmotrophy** (-'ɒtrəʊfɪ) [Gr. -τροφία nourishment], 'excess of sanguineous nourishment' (Dunglison).

1899 *Brit. Med. Jrnl.* 9 Dec. 1595/1 In the general *haemochromatosis associated with cirrhosis of the liver, the pigment is the haemosiderin and has an ochre yellow colour, which gives to the organs..a most remarkable and characteristic appearance. **1907** *Practitioner* Aug. 214 Haemochromatosis is a rare disease; the pigmentation is often, but not invariably, associated with glycosuria and cirrhosis of the liver. **1932** *Sunday Pictorial* 17 Jan. 6/4 The cause of death was hæmachromatosis, an extremely rare disease of metabolism. **1964** L. MARTIN *Clin. Endocrinol.* (ed. 4) v. 179 In hæmochromatosis the pigmentation is primarily a slaty-grey colour and there is hepatic enlargement with glycosuria. **1885** *Jrnl. Physiol.* VI. 28, I have seen in the lobule of the liver of a pigeon..in one part *haemochromogen, in another biliverdin. **1957** *New Biol.* XXIV. 65 Another possible route for haemoglobin loss is the following. In the gut there is found a compound known as a haemochromogen, which is related to haemoglobin. *Ibid.*, In the laboratory haemochromogen is a breakdown product of haemoglobin. **1882** *Brit. Med. Jrnl.* II. 1005 Two New *Hæmachromometers. **18..** *Jrnl. Microsc. Sc.* XXVIII. 384 (Cent.) The *hæmocœle is divided into five main chambers. **1940** *Acta Med. Scand.* CIII. 548 We shall be able to find hyperglobulinemia without any displacement of the ratio of albumin to globulin in those cases where there is a *hemo-concentration on account of desiccation. **1947** *Radiology* XLIX. 302/2 These dogs also showed a terminal hemoconcentration. **1949** *New Gould Med. Dict.* 453/1 *Hemoconcentration*, an increase in the concentration of blood cells resulting from the loss of plasma or water from the blood stream; anhydremia. **1964** L. MARTIN *Clin. Endocrinol.* (ed. 4) v. 170 Shock is a complex syndrome manifested by hæmoconcentration. **1877** W. R. GOWERS in *Lancet* 798 The *hæmacytometer consists of an apparatus for estimating approximately the number of corpuscles contained in a given volume of blood. **1879** —— *Trans. Clin. Soc.* XII. 67 Ascertaining with the hæmocytometer the corpuscular richness of the blood. **1894** *Quain's Dict. Med.* I. 763 The hæmocytometer may..be employed for ascertaining the globular richness of milk or other liquids. **1959** KUPFER & ROSENAK in *Jrnl. Laboratory & Clin. Med.* Nov. 746 (*title*) A new parallel tube continuous *hemodialyzer. **1963** *Lancet* 12 Jan. 82/2 The dialysing area of the particular hæmodialyser employed is given, together with the urea clearance achieved by its use. **1947** *Q. Cumulative Index Medicus* XLII. 1186/1 Attempted therapy of anuria by intraperitoneal *hemodialysis. **1962** *Lancet* 19 May 1055/1 Hæmodialysis is now commonly applied in acute renal failure. **1968** Hæmodialysis [see DIALYSIS 5 b]. **1888** *Encycl. Brit.* XXIV. 97/2 Chauveau and Lorlet first used their *hæmadromograph in 1860. **1857** DUNGLISON *Med. Lex.* 439 *Hæmadromometer. **1867** J. MARSHALL *Outlines Physiol.* II. 227 The hæmadromometer of Volkmann consists of a bent U-shaped glass tube [etc.]. **1885** T. L. BRUNTON *Text-bk. Pharmacol.* I. xi. (1887) 294 The hæmodrometer shows the rate of circulation in the particular artery experimented on. **1907** *Practitioner* Aug. 217 Although fully recognising the importance of the diastolic pressure, when working at *hæmodynamic problems,..I did not consider it essential. **1961** *Lancet* 12 Aug. 331/1 (*title*) Hæmodynamic effects of guanethidine. **1857** DUNGLISON *Med. Lex.* 439 *Hæmadynamics. **1835–6** TODD *Cycl. Anat.* I. 662/2 The experiments..made with the *hemadynamometer. **1872** *Lancet* I. 675 The mercurial hæmodynamometer gives the pulse-waves. **1858** J. COPLAND *Dict. Med.* III. 138 Hæmagastric or continued yellow fever. **1886** *Syd. Soc. Lex.*, *Hæmogastric*, having blood in the stomach; applied to certain forms of pestilential fever in which blood is vomited. **1859** TODD *Cycl. Anat.* V. 386 The protein compounds..are thus *histogenetic* and **hæmagenetic*. **1876** tr. *Wagner's Gen. Pathol.* 520 Poverty of the blood in *hæmoglobulin and albumen. **1929** R. B. H. GRADWOHL tr. *Schilling's Blood Picture* 17 With the aid of.. simple measures the '*hemogram' is constructed; by its brevity and capacity to express many things it constitutes the basis for the practical usage of the blood picture. **1961** *Lancet* 9 Sept. 568/1 Other studies showed a normal hæmogram and urine analysis. **1908** *Practitioner* Feb. 226 (*heading*) Piroplasmosis, *hæmogregarines and Leishman-Donovan body. **1961** C. H. POPE *Giant Snakes* (1962) 189 No one knows just what hæmogregarines do to their reptile hosts. This technical name for such parasites derives from the fact that they live in red blood cells. **1876** tr. *Wagner's Gen. Pathol.* 517 The chief obstacle to the study of so-called *Hæmopathology. **1900** DORLAND *Med. Dict.* 296/1 *Hemopoiesis. **1948** *Amer. Jrnl. Med. Sci.* CCXV. 411/1 We have noted that a number of chemical substances stimulated hemopoiesis in persons with Addisonian pernicious anemia... One of these, thymine.., is a pyrimidine base. **1964** D. NICHOLS in *Oceanogr. & Marine Biol.* II. 398 Most of the vessels are composed of large, loosely-packed connective tissue cells with scattered regions of haemopoiesis. **1876** tr. *Wagner's Gen. Pathol.* 525 When the lost blood shall have been reproduced by means of food, and by the *hæmopoietic organs. **1947** *Radiology* XLIX. 291/2 These studies indicate a sensitivity of the hemopoietic system of man. **1956** *Nature* 10 Mar. 452/1 Adult mice irradiated with an expectedly lethal dose of X-rays could recover if grafted or injected with hæmopoietic tissue from a normal mouse. **1926** *Chem. Abstr.* XX. 1839 *Hemopoëtin, a substance which appears in the serum of organisms exposed to reduced pressure and has a marked stimulating effect on the bone marrow resulting in increased regenerative capacity of the blood. **1932** WILKINSON & KLEIN in *Lancet* 2 Apr. 721/1 Hæmopoietin may be identified with or allied to Castle's 'intrinsic factor' of normal human gastric juice. *Ibid.* 721/2 This 'enzyme' acting on the proteins in a normal diet may produce a substance which is stored as the active principle in liver until it is required for haemopoietic regeneration... It is proposed temporarily to term this substance in hog's stomach 'haemopoietin'. **1960** *Blood* XVI. 1407 Up to the present the only reproducible sources of hemopoietine are plasma and urine of animals made severely hypoxic. **1970** KRANTZ & JACOBSON *Erythropoietin* i. 4 The plasma factor that increased erythropoiesis had been termed hemopoietine by Carnot and Deflandre; however, as work proceeded, it appeared to be involved exclusively in red cell production .., and erythropoietin became the adopted name. **1896** F. W. MOTT in T. C. Allbutt *Syst. Med.* I. i. 196 When blood corpuscles undergo destruction, as in large extravasations of blood, two substances may be formed—(*a*) **Haemosiderin* and (*b*) *Haematoidin*... Haemosiderin may also be found in the renal epithelium. **1964** S. DUKE-ELDER *Parsons' Dis. Eye* (ed. 14), xvi. 221 A brownish ring, probably due to hæmosiderin, may form in the epithelium encircling the cone (Fleischer's ring). **1972** BALCERZAK & WHEBY in C. E. Mengel et al. *Hematol.* ii. 41 At physiologic levels of tissue iron, slightly more ferretin iron is present than hemosiderin iron. Hemosiderin predominates when excess iron develops. **1909** *Cent. Dict.* Suppl., *Hemosiderosis. **1942** M. M. WINTROBE *Clin. Hematol.* x. 435 Enlargement of the liver with hemosiderosis has been noted in a number of instances [of acute hemolytic anemia]. **1963** H. BURN *Drugs, Med. & Man* (ed. 2) xvi. 159 Among the Bantu in Africa, who use cooking utensils of iron, some of the iron of the pan gets into the food, so that the intake of iron is very high. The absorption of iron continues, and the amount of iron in the liver and other tissues becomes very large. The condition is known as haemosiderosis. **1971** LEAVELL & THORUP *Fund. Clin. Hematol.* (ed. 3) v. 149 Post-transfusional hemosiderosis is an important development in some patients with chronic bone marrow failure or hemolytic anemia who require frequent blood transfusions. Usually the iron is stored in the reticuloendothelial cells. **1843** *Maryland Med. & Surg. Jrnl.* III. 265 (*heading*) On *hæmostasis, and the physical phenomenon of circulation. **1848** DUNGLISON *Med. Lex.* (ed. 7) 411/1 Hæmostasis. **1907** *Practitioner* Aug. 302 Simple serum contains all the coagulating ferments necessary for haemostasis. **1914** *Brit. Med. Jrnl.* 4 July 8/2 (*heading*) Note on haemostasis by application of living tissue. *Ibid.*, I found that a muscle haemostasis would resist as much as 60 to 80 mm. Hg blood pressure. **1962** *Lancet* 27 Jan. 177/1 It is interesting to speculate whether the control could be so low that defective hæmostasis would result despite a normal total prothrombin content. **1900** DORLAND *Med. Dict.* 296/2 **Hemostat*, a proprietary remedy for nose-bleed, containing tannin, quinin sulphate, lard, and benzoic acid: used externally. **1904** F. P. FOSTER *Appleton's Med. Dict.* 1033/2 *Hæmostat*. 1. A hæmostatic forceps or other appliance. **1929** F. A. POTTLE *Stretchers* (1930) 110 The assistant mops it up with a gauze sponge, discovers the point where the blood vessel is severed, and the surgeon clips it with a haemostat, another variety of pincers with handles like manicure scissors. **1969** TROUP & SCHWARTZ in S. I. Schwartz *Princ. Surg.* iii. 106/1 The finger has the advantage of being the least traumatic vascular hemostat. **1867** J. MARSHALL *Outlines Physiol.* II. 228 The *hæmotachometer of Vierordt. **1888** FOSTER *Physiol.* (ed. 5) 222 The Hæmatachometer of Vierordt is constructed on the principle of measuring the velocity of the current by observing the amount of deviation of a pendulum, the free end of which hangs loosely in the stream. **1857** DUNGLISON *Med. Lex.* 440 *Hæmathorax, Hæmatothorax. **1864** T. HOLMES *Syst. Surg.* (1870) II. 589 Hæmo-thorax is hæmorrhage into the cavity of the pleura.

hæmocyanin, hemo- (hiːməʊ'saɪənɪn). *Chem.* Also erron. **hæma-**. [See HÆMO- and CYANIN.] **a.** A blue colouring matter which has been found in human blood. **b.** A substance containing copper, blue when oxidized and colourless when deoxidized, found normally in the blood of some invertebrates.

1845 G. E. DAY tr. *Simon's Anim. Chem.* I. 43 Hæmacyanin, or a blue colouring matter, has been detected by Sanson in healthy blood. **1885** STIRLING tr. *Landois' Hum. Physiol.* I. 12 In cephalopods and some crabs the blood is blue, owing to the presence of a colouring matter (Hæmocyanin) which contains copper.

hæmoglobin, hemo- (hiːməʊ'gləʊbɪn). *Chem.* [Shortened from HÆMATO-GLOBULIN.] The colouring matter of the red corpuscles of the blood, which serves to convey oxygen to the tissues in the circulation; it is a protein which is resolvable into hæm and globin; when oxidized (***oxyhæmoglobin***) it has a bright scarlet colour, and is crystallizable. Formerly called *cruorin*, *hæmatoglobulin*, *hæmoglobulin*, *hæmatoglobin*. Also *attrib.* and *Comb.*

1869 *Syd. Soc. Biennial Retrospect* 3 The specific gravity of hæmoglobin may by calculation be approximately estimated as 1 . 2 to 1 . 3. **1869–72** WATTS *Dict. Chem.* VI. 352 *Hæmoglobin, Hæmatoglobin*, this substance is the only colouring matter of the blood of vertebrate animals. *Ibid.* 353 Hæmoglobin is the only ferruginous constituent of the blood-corpuscles. **1872** HUXLEY *Phys.* iii. 65 Called hæmoglobin from its readily breaking up into globulin and hæmatin. **1876** tr. *Wagner's Gen. Pathol.* 310 Hæmoglobin ..or Hæmatoglobulin..consists of an albumen and a colouring matter hæmatin. **1886** *Syd. Soc. Lex.*, *Hæmoglobin* ..is a colloid, but when combined with oxygen, as oxyhæmoglobin, crystallises according to the rhombic system in plates, or prisms, or tetrahedra..they are bluish red by transmitted light, scarlet by reflected light. **1907** *Yesterday's Shopping* (1969) 510/1 Hæmoglobin Tablets. **1950** *Sci. News* XV. 96 But these lake-dwelling *Daphnia*, if deprived of abundant oxygen in the laboratory, also become pink with newly-formed hæmoglobin in their blood. Thus they have the capacity of hæmoglobin synthesis when stimulated by lack of oxygen, although they do not profit by this gift in nature. *Ibid.* 103 Hæmoglobin is unusual among proteins in having a coloured part of its molecule, a coloured part with characteristic absorption bands in its spectrum which can be measured. **1956** *Nature* 17 Mar. 524/1 There was a drop in the hæmoglobin-level from 81 to 70 per cent when tested by the Sahli method. **1956** *New Biol.* XXI. 55 Sickle-cell haemoglobin is the best known of the abnormal haemoglobins in man, but several other types can be distinguished by electrophoretic and solubility tests. These are known as haemoglobin types C, D, E, G, H, I, J, K, and M. **1957** *Ibid.* XXIV. 61 The mean of the twenty values on the scale gives the 'haemoglobin index' of the population. **1963** R. P. DALES *Annelids* iv. 81 Haemoglobin-containing corpuscles are distributed in the coelomic fluid. **1964** G. H. HAGGIS et al. *Introd. Molecular Biol.* v. 115 In the red blood cell it is the only structure observed between the haemoglobin-laden cytoplasm and the blood plasma. **1968** H. HARRIS *Nucleus & Cytoplasm* vi. 118 The failure of high concentrations of actinomycin D to inhibit decisive events in the differentiation of colonial myxamoebae, of pancreatic cells in the mouse embryo, and of haemoglobin-forming cells in the chick embryo. **1968** *Times* 17 May (*heading*) Structure of haemoglobin solved.

Hence ‖ˌ**hæmoglobi'næmia** (-'niːmɪə) *Path.* [f. prec. and Gr. αἷμα blood, after *anæmia*, etc.], the presence of free hæmoglobin in the fluid part of the blood. ˌ**hæmoglobi'niferous** *a.* [see -FEROUS], containing hæmoglobin. ˌ**hæmoglobi'nometer** [see -METER], an instrument for measuring the quantity of hæmoglobin in blood; whence ˌ**hæmoglobi'nometry**, the measurement of this. ˌ**hæmoglobi'nopathy**, any condition in which the quality of the hæmoglobin in the blood is defective. ‖ ˌ**hæmoglobiˈnuria** (-ˈjʊərɪə) *Path.* [Gr. οὖρον urine], the presence of free hæmoglobin in the urine; whence ˌ**hæmoglobiˈnuric** *a.*, characterized by hæmoglobinuria.

1885 W. ROBERTS *Urin. & Renal Dis.* iv. (ed. 4) 162 *note*, The so-called 'Hæmoglobinæmia' which precedes the change in the urine. **1886** *Syd. Soc. Lex.*, *Hæmoglobinhæmia*, the condition in which hæmoglobin is diffused into the liquor sanguinis, as occurs in some cases of hæmophilia. **1884** *Encycl. Brit.* XVII. 329/2 The blood fluid is often provided with hæmoglobiniferous disks. **1885** STIRLING tr. *Landois' Hum. Physiol.* I. 26 The hæmoglobinometer of Gowers is used for the clinical estimation of hæmoglobin. **1887** *Brit. Med. Jrnl.* 9 July 80 Hæmoglobinometry. **1961** *B.S.I. News* Dec. 27 (*heading*) Sealed glass cells for photometric hæmoglobinometry. **1957** A. W. WOODRUFF et al. in *Brit. Med. Jrnl.* 25 May 1235/1 (*heading*) Terminology of the hereditary haemoglobinopathies with haemoglobin variants. *Ibid.* 1235/2 The term haemoglobinopathy should be used to denote a condition in which the production of normal adult haemoglobin . . is partly or wholly suppressed and it is partly or wholly replaced by one or more haemoglobin variants. **1962** *Lancet* 12 May 1006/2 As the hæmoglobinopathies grow in importance, a monograph taking stock of what we know of thalassæmia is welcome. **1966** *Ibid.* 31 Dec. 1435/1 The situation with respect to diabetes reminds one of attempts to analyse the hæmoglobinopathies before chemical techniques were available for the identification of hæmoglobins to discriminate between possible genotypes. **1866** A. FLINT *Princ. Med.* (1880) 923 A pathological condition of the blood stands in an immediate causative relation to the haemoglobinuria in this affection. **1893** A. DAVIDSON *Hygiene & Dis. Warm Clim.* 181 Bilious hæmoglobinuric fever is met with in Madagascar, Mauritius . . and some parts of Italy.

hæmoid (ˈhiːmɔɪd), *a.* = HÆMATOID *a.* a.
1886 *Syd. Soc. Lex.*, *Hæmoid*, resembling blood.

hæmolymph (ˈhiːməʊlɪmf). *Physiol.* [f. HÆMO- + LYMPH.] The fluid, analogous to blood or lymph, in the body-cavity of some invertebrates.

1885 RAY LANKESTER in *Encycl. Brit.* XIX. 432/1 In Eupolyzoa the cœlom is very capacious; it is occupied by a coagulable hæmolymph in which float cellular corpuscles. **1964** O. KINNE in *Oceanogr. & Marine Biol.* II. 302 Autoradiographs of *Asellus aquaticus* indicate that some 20 to 30‰ of the total body Na is located outside the haemolymph. **1968** H. HARRIS *Nucleus & Cytoplasm* iv. 79 Some authors believe that the proteins of the salivary secretion are not synthesized in the gland, but are simply extracted from haemolymph.

Hence ˌ**hæmolymˈphatic** *a.*, of or pertaining to hæmolymph, or to a circulatory system which is not differentiated into separate blood-vascular and lymphatic systems.

hæmolysis, hem- (hiːˈmɒlɪsɪs). *Med.* [f. HÆMO- + -LYSIS.] The dissolution or lysis of red blood cells with the consequent liberation of their hæmoglobin.

1890 F. TAYLOR *Man. Pract. Med.* 663 The immediate cause of the anæmia is the destruction of red corpuscles in the blood (hæmolysis). **1892** OSLER *Princ. Med.* 725 Increased hæmolysis and dissolution of the hæmoglobin in the blood-serum. **1901** *Jrnl. Chem. Soc.* LXXX. II. 325 Hæmolysis produced by Solanine. **1906** *Practitioner* Nov. 591 The jaundice of the newly born . . is dependent upon changes, probably toxic in character, with excessive hæmolysis. **1947** *Radiology* XLIX. 307/2 Increased red cell hemolysis is indicated by elevated excretion of fecal urobilinogen and urinary bilirubin. **1966** *Lancet* 24 Dec. 1382/1 Pyridium also causes hæmolysis.

Hence **hæˈmolysate**, any preparation obtained from hæmolysed blood; **ˈhæmolyse, -lyze** *v. trans.*, to lyse (red blood cells); also *intr.* (of red blood cells or a preparation of them) to undergo hæmolysis; **ˈhæmolysed, -lyzed, ˈhæmoˌlysing, -ˌlyzing** *ppl. adjs.*; **hæmolysin** (hiːˈmɒlɪsɪn, hiːməʊˈlaɪsɪn) [see LYSIN], any substance which causes hæmolysis; **hæmolytic** (-ˈlɪtɪk) *a.* [Gr. λυτικός loosening, dissolving], destructive of the blood or of the blood-corpuscles; **hæmoˈlytically** *adv.*

1893 *Funk's Stand. Dict.*, Hemolytic. **1897** *Allbutt's Syst. Med.* II. 1044 Pointing to a hæmolytic as well as a simple hæmorrhagic origin for the anæmia. **1900** *Proc. Roy. Soc. Med.* LXVI. 435 Certain blood poisons, viz., the hæmolysines, . . exercise a solvent action only on such red blood corpuscles as are able to unite chemically with them. **1901** *Lancet* 14 Dec. 166/31 Since the discovery of tetanolysin by Ehrlich a series of hæmolysins have been described. **1901** *Trans. Path. Soc. London* LXII. 212 A substance is present in the serum which dissolves or hæmolyses the blood-corpuscles of the rabbit *in vitro*. *Ibid.*, In general every serum that acts hæmolytically on a number of different kinds of erythrocytes possesses a corresponding number of immune bodies and of complements. **1902** *Jrnl. Chem. Soc.* LXXXII. II. 464 Hæmolysin of Bacillus Megatherium. . . In cultures of *B. megatherium* a specific lysin occurs which hæmolyses the corpuscles of guinea-pig, monkey, and man. **1903** *Ibid.* LXXXIV. II. 443 Influence of Cold on the Action of some Hæmolytic Agents. **1908** *Practitioner* Feb. 249 To yield substances which have similar hæmolysing properties to the hæmolytic agent found in tape-worms. **1911** *Jrnl. Amer. Med. Assoc.* 23 Dec. 2059/2 The amboceptor should be used in twice the strength sufficient to hemolyze the corpuscles in from fifteen to twenty minutes. *Ibid.*, The delay in hemolysis with tuberculous serums is striking in contrast to the promptness with which the controls hemolyze. **1916** *Jrnl. Immunol.* I. 37 The hemolyzed cells do not give up an effective hemolysin. **1920** *Nature* 13 May 347/2 The anti-coagulating and hæmolysing action of sodium nucleinate. **1946** *Ibid.* 24 Aug. 269/2 It was found possible to rear first instar bugs to the adult stage by feeding them on defibrinated hæmolysed blood through a mouse skin membrane. **1952** *Q. Jrnl. Exper. Physiol.* XXXVII. 163 The methaemoglobin (MHb) formation which occurs spontaneously in haemolysates of red blood cells occurs much faster when these have been treated so as to remove the posthaemolytic residue. **1957** *Times* 3 Sept. 15/4 Dr. Coombs, whose laboratory test for the diagnosis of haemolytic disease of the new-born infant is in worldwide use. **1962** *Lancet* 8 Dec. 1184/2 The hæmolysate of unfractionated whole-blood cells obtained from the same subject was diluted in the same way. **1967** *Jrnl. Gen. Microbiol.* XLVII. 153 Two haemolysins may be produced by *Escherichia coli*. **1968** *Sci. Jrnl.* Nov. 65/2 The cells are completely disrupted—haemolysed. *Ibid.* 65/3 The cells will haemolyse when subsequently exposed to some mild form of stress. **1972** *Science* 2 June 1030/2 After 72 hours, the tissue culture media were removed and assayed for hemolytically active C4 and C2.

hæmometer (hiːˈmɒmɪtə(r)). [See HÆMO- and -METER.] An instrument for measuring (*a*) the quantity of blood passing through a vessel in a given time; (*b*) the pressure of the blood (= *hæmodynamometer*); or (*c*) the amount of hæmoglobin in the blood (= *hæmoglobinometer*).

1872 RUTHERFORD in *Lancet* I. 675 The *Hæmometer*. I give this name to an instrument invented by Ludwig and Dogiel . . The main object of the instrument is to measure the quantity of blood that flows through a vessel in a given time. **1886** *Syd. Soc. Lex.*, *Hæmometer*, the same as *Hæmodynamometer*. **1887** *Jrnl. R. Microsc. Soc.* Ser. II. VII. 657 Fleischl's Hæmometer . . for the estimation of hæmoglobin in the blood, is based on the colorimetric method.

†**hæmony** (ˈhiːmənɪ). [? f. Gr. αἵμων skilful, or αἱμώνιος blood-red.] Name given by Milton to an imaginary plant having supernatural virtues.

1634 MILTON *Comus* 638 He called it Hæmony, and gave it me . . as of sovran use 'Gainst all enchantments, mildew blast, or damp, Or ghastly Furies' apparition.

hæmophæin (hiːməʊˈfiːɪn). *Chem.* Also hæma-, -phein. [mod. f. HÆMO- + Gr. φαι-ός dusky + -IN. The erroneous spelling *hæma-* follows F. *hémaphéine*.] A brownish substance found in the blood in some cases of jaundice.

1845 G. E. DAY tr. *Simon's Anim. Chem.* I. 40 The ether takes up a certain amount of hæmaphein associated with fat. **1865** WATTS *Dict. Chem.* III. 1 *Hæmaphein*, Bloodbrown.

Hence **hæmoˈphæic** *a.*, characterized by or containing hæmophæin.

1880 J. W. LEGG *Bile* 249 Hæmaphæic jaundice. **1886** *Syd. Soc. Lex.*, Hæmaphæic urine.

‖**hæmophilia** (hiːməʊˈfɪlɪə, hɛməʊ-). *Path.* Rarely anglicized **hæmophily** (hiːˈmɒfɪlɪ). [mod.L., f. HÆMO- + Gr. φιλία affection. Cf. Ger. *hämophilie*, 1828.] A constitutional (usually hereditary) tendency to bleeding, either spontaneously or from very slight injuries; hæmorrhagic diathesis.

1854 JONES & SIEV. *Pathol. Anat.* (1874) 62 Hæmophily appears to be often hereditary. **1864** *Syd. Soc. Year-bk.* 123 Report on Hæmophily. **1872** J. W. LEGG (*title*) A Treatise on Hæmophilia. **1879** KHORY *Princ. Med.* 4 Hæmophilia is . . inherited almost exclusively by males, though capable of transmission through unaffected females.

Hence **hæmophiliac** (-ˈfɪlɪæk) *a.*, affected with hæmophilia; also as *sb.*, a person so affected; **hæmophilic** (-ˈfɪlɪk) *a.*, affected with hæmophilia; also as *sb.*, a hæmophiliac.

1864 *Syd. Soc. Year-bk.* 124 The hæmophilic have for the most part a soft white translucent skin. **1896** *Lancet* 18 Jan. 153/2 An arrest of severe hæmophiliac bleeding from the gums was obtained by an application of calcium phosphate. **1897** *Boston Med. & Surg. Jrnl.* 11 Mar. 227/1 In hemophiliacs, leeching, extraction of the teeth and circumcision are very hazardous operations. **1897** *Lippincott's Med. Dict.* 454/1 *Hæmophilic* . . 2. A person affected with hæmophilia. **1935** WHITBY & BRITTON *Disorders of Blood* xiv. 272 On Mendelian principles a female may be a true hæmophilic if she is the daughter of a hæmophilia-transmitting woman and a hæmophilic male. **1936** *Discovery* Dec. 388/2 A preparation from egg-white, which reduces the clotting time of blood, provides new hope for haemophiliacs. **1938** *New Statesman* 2 July 7/2 Between thirty-five and seventy haemophilics are alive in Greater London to-day. **1946** *Nature* 28 Sept. 447/1 We have been able to study the effect, in some hæmophiliac patients, of a product containing 82 per cent fibrinogen. **1962** *Lancet* 27 Jan. 194/1 A pharmacist who is a hæmophiliac had noted that by taking hesperidin chalcone (a flavonoid) he could ward off haemorrhagic episodes. **1966** DUNLOP & ALSTEAD *Textbk. Med. Treatm.* (ed. 10) 496 In centres with suitable facilities, a supply of this plasma specifically for use in hæmophilics serves a useful purpose. **1967** M. M. WINTROBE *Clin. Hematol.* (ed. 6) xviii. 937/1 Karyotype analysis has been carried out in several of the hemophiliac women and only in 2 instances has the karyotype been abnormal.

‖**hæmophobia** (hiːməʊˈfəʊbɪə). *Path.* [mod.L., f. HÆMO- + -PHOBIA, after *hydrophobia*: see next.] Fear or horror at the sight of blood.
1886 in *Syd. Soc. Lex.*

haemophobous (hiːˈmɒfəbəs), *a. rare.* [f. mod.L. *hæmophobus*, a. Gr. αἱμοφόβος (Galen), f. αἷμα blood + -φοβος fearing.] Afraid of blood, averse to bloodletting.

1684 tr. *Bonet's Merc. Compit.* VI. 188/1 Some hæmophobous Physicians have falsly thought, that drinking cold water was a Remedy that might be subsituted to Bleeding.

hæˈmoptic, hem-, *a.*, bad form of HÆMOPTOIC.
1854 in MAYNE *Expos. Lex.* **1886** in *Syd. Soc. Lex.*

‖**hæmoptoe** (hiːˈmɒptəʊiː). *Path.* [A corrupt or erroneous med.L. form of same derivation as next.] = HÆMOPTYSIS.

1727–51 CHAMBERS *Cycl.*, *Hæmoptysis*, corruptly also called *Hæmoptosis*, and *Hæmoptoe*. **1766** AMORY *Buncle* IV. 283 It makes . . in the lungs, an hæmoptoe. **1772** PERCIVAL in *Phil. Trans.* LXII. 462 The spring is . . celebrated for its efficacy in hæmoptoes. **1777** LIGHTFOOT *Flora Scotica* II. 661 It is also recommended to be taken internally . . for the hæmoptoe. **1794–6** E. DARWIN *Zoon.* (1801) II. 15 That kind of consumption which is hereditary, and commences with slight repeated hæmoptoe. **1876** tr. *Wagner's Gen. Pathol.* 212 Hæmoptysis, or hæmoptoë.

Hence **hæmoptoic** (hiːmɒpˈtəʊɪk) *a.*, affected with, characterized by, or good for, hæmoptoe.

1684 tr. *Bonet's Merc. Compit.* VIII. 267 Nettle . . I think . . is good for hæmoptoïck . . persons. **1862** *Syd. Soc. Year-bk.* 195 Quotidian hæmoptoic fever.

‖**hæmoptysis** (hiːˈmɒptɪsɪs). *Path.* [mod.L. f. HÆMO- + πτύσις spitting, f. πτύ-ειν to spit.] Spitting of blood; expectoration of blood, or of bloody mucus, etc., from the lungs or bronchi.

1646 SIR T. BROWNE *Pseud. Ep.* I. xi. 46 Julian for his hæmoptysis or spitting of bloud, was cured by hony and pine Nuts taken from his Altar. **1799** *Med. Jrnl.* II. 317 Without . . removing pneumonia, or even hæmoptysis. **1849** D. P. THOMSON *Introd. Meteorol.* 20 Very subject to bronchial hæmoptysis.

Hence **hæmoptysic** (hiːməʊˈptɪzɪk, hɛm-), **hæmopˈtysical** *adjs.*, relating to or affected with hæmoptysis.

1834 J. FORBES *Laennec's Dis. Chest* (ed. 4) 173 The hæmoptysical engorgement . . is only a lesser degree of the same affection. **1886** *Syd. Soc. Lex.*, *Hæmoptysic*.

hæmorrhage, hemorrhage (ˈhɛmərɪdʒ). Also 7–8 hæmorrage. [f. as HÆMORRHAGY; for the form of suffix, cf. *-ance* and *-ancy*.] An escape of blood from the blood-vessels; a flux of blood, either external or internal, due to rupture of a vessel; bleeding, esp. when profuse or dangerous.

1671 SALMON *Syn. Med.* III. xxii. 401 Outwardly it stops an Hæmorrhage. **1732** ARBUTHNOT *Rules of Diet* 327 Profuse Hæmorrages from the Nose commonly resolve it. **1873** E. J. WORBOISE *Our New Home* xviii. (1877) 284 Taken very ill with hemorrhage of the lungs. **1880** HUXLEY *Crayfish* 38 It is likely to die rapidly from the ensuing haemorrhage.

fig. **1862** S. LUCAS *Secularia* 210 We might have been mourning to this very hour a fatal political hæmorrhage.

hæmorrhagic, hemo- (hɛməˈrædʒɪk), *a.* [ad. Gr. αἱμορραγικ-ός, f. αἱμορραγία: see HÆMORRHAGY and -IC.] Belonging to, of the nature of, accompanied with, or produced by hæmorrhage.

1804 ABERNETHY *Surg. Obs.* 37 Exciting an hæmorrhagic action in the vessels. **1859** J. TOMES *Dental Surg.* 523 The hæmorrhagic tendency depends upon an abnormal state of the blood. **1881** R. VIRCHOW in *Nature* No. 615. 347 Wepfer, the celebrated discoverer of the hæmorrhagic nature of ordinary apoplexy.

Hence **hæmoˈrrhagically** *adv.*, in a way characterized by hæmorrhage.

1876 tr. *Wagner's Gen. Pathol.* 350 In the blood-vessels of hæmorrhagically inflamed kidneys.

†**hæmoˈrrhagious**, *a. Obs. rare.* [f. L. *hæmorrhagia* + -OUS.] Affected with or of the nature of hæmorrhage.

1753 N. TORRIANO *Gangr. Sore Throat* 39 The Patient's Nose bleeds several Times in the Day, but it is not hæmorrhagious, (i.e. I suppose, he means it is a Dripping, but not a Flux of Blood.)

†ˈ**hæmorrhagy, hemo-**. *Obs.* Forms: 6 emorogie, 7 hemoragie, -rogy, hemeragie, hemorragie, -gy, hæmorragy, hemorrhagie, 7–9 hæmorrhagy, hemo-. Also in Lat. form hæmorrhagia (in 7 hæmor-, hæmorragia). [a. 16th c. F. *emorogie*, *hemorragie*, ad. L. *hæmorrhagia* (Pliny), a. Gr. αἱμορραγία, f. αἱμο- blood- + -ραγια, f. stem ῥαγ- of ῥηγνύναι to break, burst.] = HÆMORRHAGE.

[Some early forms represent med.L. *emorosagia* (Matth. Silvaticus, 1480):

c **1400** *Lanfranc's Cirurg.* 151 If þer folowe emorosogie, þat is to seie, a greet flux of blood. **1562** BULLEYN *Dial. Soarnes & Chir.* 25 b, Amorrosage [*ed.* **1579**, a moresage] or bleding.]

1541 R. COPLAND *Guydon's Quest. Chirurg.*, Yf . . there folowe emorogie or to great flux of blode. **1597** LOWE *Chirurg.* (1634) 290 Hemeragie . . an issuing of the blould in great aboundance. **1612** WOODALL *Surg. Mate* Wks. (1653) 171 They have stayed the Hemoragie or bleeding at the nose. **1621** BURTON *Anat. Mel.* I. ii. v. i, Hæmoragia, or bleeding at nose. **1670** *Phil. Trans.* XXII. 757 This Hæmorragia lasted above a day. **1717** J. KEILL *Anim. Œcon.* (1738) 9 Observations of profuse Hæmorrhagies of the Nose. **1838** J. BELL in *Cooper's Surg. Dict.* 255 In the hemorrhagy of wounds, we cannot always find the artery.

hæmorrhe: see HÆMORRHOID².

hæmorrhoid¹, hemorrhoid (ˈhɛmərɔɪd). Usually in *pl.* Forms (pl.): 4-5 **emeraudes, emeroudis,** 5 **emerowdys,** 6 **em(e)rodes, emor(r)oydes, (-ades), hemerrhoydes,** 6-7 **heme-, hemoroids, -oydes,** 7 **em(e)rods, emroids, hemrods, -roids, hæmrods, hemorroids, hemorrods,** 8 **hæmorroids, hæmorhoids,** 7- **hæm-, hemorrhoids.** (See also EMERODS.) *β.* in Gr.-Lat. form **hæmorrhoides** (-ˈrɔɪdiːz), etc. [a. OF. *emoroyde* (13th c. in Godef. *Suppl.*), in 16th c. *hemorrhoïdes* (Paré), ad. L. *hæmorrhoida* (Pliny), ad. Gr. αἱμορροΐς, accus. sing. αἱμορροΐδα, adj. 'discharging blood', pl. αἱμορροΐδες (sc. φλέβες) veins liable to discharge blood, bleeding piles; deriv. of αἱμόρρο-ος flowing with blood, f. αἱμο- blood- + -ροος flowing. Cf. It. *emmorroide*, Sp. *hemorroide, -ida.*]

1. *pl.* A disease characterized by tumours of the veins about the anus; = PILES, q.v. Rarely *sing.* One of such tumours, a pile.

1398 TREVISA *Barth. De P.R.* VI. xxii. (Tollem. MS.), Slymi water and glewy..heleþ emeroudis [*emeroidas curat*]. *a* **1400**, etc. [see EMERODS]. **1533** ELYOT *Cast. Helthe* (1541) 30 a, The grene leaves [of Rosemary] bruysed doo stoppe the hemorroides. **1541** R. COPLAND *Guydon's Quest. Chirurg.* Qiij, Yf he hath nat had the emorroydes. **1552** HULOET, Hemeroydes or pyles in the fundment. **1578** LYTE *Dodoens* I. v. 11 The roote..healeth the inwarde Hemerrhoydes. **1608** TOPSELL *Serpents* (1658) 739 It is good also against the Hemroids and Piles. **1616** SURFL. & MARKH. *Country Farme* 51 To stay the excessiue flux of the Hemorrhoids. **1634** HARINGTON *Salerne's Regim.* 3 The Hemoroids and Fistula shall graeve him. **1651** BIGGS *New Disp.* ¶288 Ulcers begotten of the hæmorrhoides. **1691** RAY *Creation* I. (R.), To give ease and relief in several pains and diseases, particularly in that of the internal hæmorrhoids. *a* **1707** BP. PATRICK *Autobiog.* (1839) 28 This brought upon me the hoemaroides. **1872** F. G. THOMAS *Dis. Women* (ed. 3) 123 Painful hæmorrhoids. **1877** ROBERTS *Handbk. Med.* (ed. 3) I. 26 The formation of hæmorrhoids as the result of sedentary occupations.

†**2.** *pl.* = Hæmorrhoidal veins. *Obs.* [So in F.]

c **1400** *Lanfranc's Cirurg.* 289 Emoroides ben veines þat endiþ in a mannes ers & ben .v. **1533** ELYOT *Cast Helthe* III. x. (R.), Hemorroides be vaynes in the foundement. **1541** [see HÆMORRHOIDAL 2].

3. *attrib.* or as *adj.* = HÆMORRHOIDAL.

1601 HOLLAND *Pliny* II. 170 They will stanch bloud, [if] it..issue by the hæmorrhoid veins.

Hence **ˌhæmorrhoiˈdectomy**, the surgical removal of hæmorrhoids.

1917 V. C. DAVID in *Surg. Clinics Chicago* I. 543 (*title*) Local anesthesia for hemorrhoidectomy. *Ibid.* 552 Infiltration anesthesia with novocain offers a safe and technically simple method for hemorrhoidectomy. **1949** M. LOWRY *Let.* Oct. (1967) 182 I'm glad you're better now after your operation—the combination of a haemorrhoidectomy with a Catholic institution sounds sadistic. **1967** S. TAYLOR et al. *Short Textbk. Surg.* xxiii. 319 In third degree piles.., haemorrhoidectomy is indicated.

†**hæmorrhoid²**. *Obs.* Also hæmorrhe, and in Lat. form **hæmorrhoïs, -rhus.** [ad. L. *hæmorrhoïs, -ïdem* (Pliny), a kind of poisonous serpent, a. Gr. αἱμορροΐς: etym. as in prec. The forms *hæmorrhe* and *-rhus* go back upon med.L. *hæmorrhous* (Du Cange), Gr. αἱμόρροος.] A serpent whose bite was fabled to cause unstanchable bleeding.

1398 TREVISA *Barth. De P.R.* XVIII. x. (1495) 763 Emorois is a maner adder, and hath that name, for he suckyth the blood of hym that he smyteth. **1601** HOLLAND *Pliny* II. 150 A singular counterpoison..against al serpents, but principally the Hæmorrhoids and the Salamanders. **1608** TOPSELL *Serpents* (1658) 731 Of the Hæmorrhe. This Serpent..is called in Latine, *Hæmorrhous*, to signifie unto us the male, and *Hæmorrhois*, to signifie the female. **1627** MAY *Lucan* IX. (1631) 814 In scaly folds the great Hæmorrhus lyes. **1635** SWAN *Spec. M.* (1670) 440 The wounds of the Hæmorrhois procure unstanchable bleeding. **1774** GOLDSM. *Nat. Hist.* IV. 126 The Hæmorrhois, so called from the hæmorrhages which its bite is said to produce.

hæmorrhoidal, hemo- (hɛməˈrɔɪdəl), *a.* [f. HÆMORRHOID¹ + -AL¹: cf. F. *hémorrhoïdal* (Paré).]

1. *Path.* Of or pertaining to hæmorrhoids.

1651 BIGGS *New Disp.* Summary 228 The hæmorrhoidal blood not putrid. **1827** ABERNETHY *Surg. Wks.* II. 238 Successful in removing hæmorrhoidal excrescences by ligature. **1885** *Lancet* 26 Sept., Hæmorrhoidal Disease.

b. Affected with hæmorrhoids. *rare.*

1646 SIR T. BROWNE *Pseud. Ep.* VII. xviii. 383 The statue of Christ, erected by his hemarroidall patient.

2. *Anat.* Applied to those arteries, veins, and nerves which are distributed to the rectum and adjacent parts. (In quot. 1541 as sb.)

1541 R. COPLAND *Guydon's Quest. Chirurg.*, Fyue braunches of veynes named Emorroides or Emorroidalles. **1671** SALMON *Syn. Med.* III. lxxxiii. 723 If blood abounds bleed the Hæmorrhoidal veins. **1835-6** TODD *Cycl. Anat.* I. 181/1 The hemorrhoidal nerves are directed principally, towards the inferior part of the rectum.

hæmostatic, hemo- (hiːməʊˈstætɪk, hɛm-), *a.* and *sb.* Also erron. **hæma-, hema-.** [mod. f. HÆMO- + Gr. στατικός causing to stand, stopping. In mod.F. *héma-, hémostatique* (Littré).]

A. *adj.* Having the property of stopping hæmorrhage; styptic.

1834 *Lancet* 8 Mar. 889/2, I have resolved upon giving such a view of it [*sc.* torsion of arteries] as will connect it with the other hæmostatic processes now in use in surgery. **1854** MAYNE *Expos. Lex.*, Having the power or property of staunching or stopping a flow of blood, or hemorrhage.. hemostatic. **1864** *Syd. Soc. Year-bk.* 54 On the hæmostatic treatment of Cholera, Hæmorrhage, Exhaustion, etc. **1883** T. HOLMES & HULKE *Syst. Surg.* (ed. 3) I. 351 Hæmostatic remedies become of less and less avail, the longer the blood flows.

B. *sb.* A hæmostatic agent; a styptic.

1706 PHILLIPS (ed. Kersey), *Hæmostatics*, Medicines to stanch Blood. **1883-4** *Med. Ann.* 31/2 The 'puff ball'..a most powerful Hæmostatic.

hæmoˈstatics, hemo-. Also erron. **hyma-, hæma-, hema-.** [See HÆMO- and STATICS.] The hydrostatics of the blood; 'the section of physiology which relates to the laws of the equilibrium of the blood in the vessels' (*Syd. Soc. Lex.*).

1733 S. HALES (*title*) Hymastaticks; or, an Account of some Hydraulick and Hydrostatical Experiements, made on the Blood and Blood-vessels. **1808** YOUNG in *Phil. Trans.* XCIX. 12 Experiments contained in Hales's hæmastatics. **1854** MAYNE *Expos. Lex.*, Hemostatics.

haenapod, var. HANEPOOT.

hæredipety, hæreditary, hæresie, etc.: see HERE-.

haeremai (ˈhaerəmai, anglicized ˈhaɪərɪmaɪ). *N.Z.* Also **haere mai, haire mai, horomai.** [Maori, lit. = come hither.] A Maori term of welcome.

1769 J. BANKS *Jrnl.* 12 Nov. (1962) I. 432 As soon as they [*sc.* the Maoris] came near enough they wav'd and calld *horomai* and set down in the bushes near the beach (a sure mark of their good intentions). **1832** H. WILLIAMS *Jrnl.* in H. Carleton *Life* (1874) I. 112 They were very glad to see us, and gave us the usual welcome, '*haere mai!! haere mai!!*' **1845** E. J. WAKEFIELD *Adv. N.Z.* I. 249 No shouts of *haeremai*, so universal a welcome to the stranger, were to be heard. **1883** F. S. RENWICK *Betrayed* 34 (Morris), Haire mai ho! 'tis the welcome song Rings far on the summer air. **1938** R. D. FINLAYSON *Brown Man's Burden* 9 As the visitors splashed across the ford, that time-honoured cry of welcome broke from every throat. 'Haere mai!' **1943** N. MARSH *Colour Scheme* iii. 55 The Maori people..would like me to greet him with a cordial *haeremai.*

haet, var. HATE *Sc.*, an atom; obs. Sc. f. HOT.

hæved, obs. form of HEAD¹.

haf, obs. pa. t. of HEAVE.

haf(e, haff, obs. forms of HAVE.

hafd(e, hafede, obs. ff. *had*, pa. t. of HAVE.

hafel, bad form of *afell*, pa. t. of AFALLE *v.*¹

a **1175** *Cott. Hom.* 221 þane stede þe se deofel of hafel.

hafeles, hafles, variants of HAVELESS, *Obs.*

‖**haff** (hæf). [Ger., f. (M)LG. *haf* sea, corresp. to ON. *haf*, OE. *hæf* sea.] A shallow freshwater lagoon found at a river mouth, esp. one of those on the Baltic coast.

1859 S. O. BEETON *Dict. Univ. Information* 582/2 *Haff, haf*, an extensive bay or gulf of Pomerania... 2. Of East Prussia... 3. A very extensive bay of the Baltic. **1875** *Encycl. Brit.* III. 294/1 The shore of the Baltic is generally low. Along the southern coast it is for the most part sandy... Where streams come down, there are often fresh-water lakes termed *haffs*, which are separated from the sea by narrow spits called *nehrungs*. **1879** *Ibid.* X. 447/1 The 'haffs' or lagoons on the Baltic. **1933** *Discovery* June 203/1 He writes from experience of fishing in general—on Exmoor, in a Prussian haff, in Cornwall, on Scottish waters, and in Ireland.

haffet (ˈhæfɪt). *Sc.* and *north. dial.* Forms: 6 **halfet, halfhed,** 6-7 **haffat,** 6- **haffet, -it.** [In 16th c. *halfhed, halfet*:—OE. *healfhéafod* the fore part of the head, the sinciput, Ælfric *Gram.* ix. §78.] The side of the head above and in front of the ear; the temple; the cheek.

1513 DOUGLAS *Æneis* IV. xi. 107 Thow thi self thi halfettis als array With haly garland. *Ibid.* IX. xiii. 67 Hys bos helm ..Clynkand abowt hys halfheddis with a dyn. *a* **1605** MONTGOMERIE *Misc. Poems* xxxv. 20 Hir curling loks.. About hir hevinly haffats hings. **1676** W. ROW *Contn. Blair's Autobiog.* xi. (1848) 343 Cuffed on both haffets. **1786** BURNS *Cotter's Sat. Night* 105 His lyart haffets wearing thin an' bare. **1828** SCOTT *F.M. Perth* xix, With the hair hanging down your haffets in that guise. **1870** RAMSAY *Remin.* iii. (ed. 18) 59 Weather-beaten haffets.

attrib. **1794** BURNS *Theniel Menzie's Mary*, Her haffet locks as brown's a berry.

haffle (ˈhæf(ə)l), *v. dial.* [cf. Du. (local) *haffelen* (of a suckling baby) to pull and push at the breast; (of women) to talk a lot, argue.] *intr.* To speak in a hesitant or stammering manner; to prevaricate, shilly-shally. Cf. CAFFLE *v.*

1790 GROSE *Provincial Gloss.* (ed. 2) *Haffle*, to prevaricate. **1825** J. T. BROCKETT *Gloss. N. Country Words* 88 *Haffle*, to waver, to speak unintelligibly. **1869** R. B. PEACOCK *Gloss. Lonsdale* 39/1 *Haffle*, to stammer, to prevaricate, to falter. **1902** in *E.D.D.* s.v., [Nottingham] The doctor, he haffled and caffled, he didn't rightly know what war wrong wi' her himself. **1913** [see CAFFLE *v.*]. **1913** D. H. LAWRENCE *Let.* 3 Mar. (1962) I. 191 The Nottingham people are still haffling and caffling about the children.

hafflin, Sc. var. of HALFING.

hafiz (ˈhɑːfɪz). Also 7 **hafis,** 9 **hafeez.** [Pers., f. Arab. *ḥāfiẓ* watch, guard.] A Muslim who knows the Koran by heart.

1662 J. DAVIES tr. *Olearius' Voy. Ambass.* 314 [The] Turbants..of their Priests, and particularly, of the Hafis, are white. **1819** T. HOPE *Anastasius* (1820) I. x. 192 Who, to obtain the epithet of hafeez, had learnt his whole koran by heart unto the last stop. **1927** *Blackw. Mag.* May 574/2 A hafiz chanted the Koran for the rest of her soul. **1965** *Encycl. Islam* (new ed.) III. 55/2 Ḥāfiẓ..no doubt in youth..earned the right to use the title *ḥāfiẓ* (Ḳur'ān-memorizer), which became his pen-name.

hafnium (ˈhæfnɪəm). *Chem.* [f. *Hafnia* (f. Da. *Havn* harbour (see HAVEN *sb.*), orig. name of Copenhagen (Da. *København*)), mod.L. name of Copenhagen: see -IUM.] A metallic element with a silver lustre usually found associated with zirconium, which it closely resembles chemically, and used in nuclear reactor control rods. Symbol Hf; atomic number 72. Earlier called CELTIUM.

1923 COSTER & HEVESY in *Nature* 20 Jan. 79/2 For the new element we propose the name Hafnium (Hafniae = Copenhagen). **1955** *Sci. Amer.* Oct. 35 In its ores zirconium is invariably accompanied by hafnium, which absorbs neutrons all too readily. **1957** *Bull. Amer. Physical Soc.* II. 269/1 Hafnium's thermionic efficiency in terms of grams evaporated per unit electron emission is slightly greater than that of Th metal. **1967** W. H. KOHL *Handbk. Materials & Techniques for Vacuum Devices* xii. 329/2 The high neutron absorption of hafnium, its excellent corrosion resistance in high-temperature water, and its adequate strength at reactor operation temperatures make this metal suited as a control material.

hafod (ˈhavəd). [W., = summer dwelling.] In Wales = SHIEL.

[**1781** T. PENNANT *Tour in Wales* II. 161 This mountainous tract scarcely yields any corn. Its produce is cattle and sheep, which, during summer, keep very high in the mountains, followed by their owners,..who reside..in *Havodtys*, or summer dairy-houses.] **1952** *Proc. Prehist. Soc.* XVIII. 74 The evidence therefore points to summer pastures, the older pound being used as a corral for cattle, while the lowland farmer set up his hafod within or just outside the wall. **1958** *Rep. R. Comm. Common Land* 274 in *Parl. Papers 1957-8* (Cmnd. 462) X. 1 *Hafod*,..the upland pastures in Wales to which transhumance took place in the summer months. **1963** *Times* 19 Apr. 6/1 Reminiscent of the earliest dwellings in Wales, the 'hafod' or summer home in the mountains, these will be available this season at a peak rental of 12 guineas a week.

haft (hɑːft, -æ-), *sb.*¹ Forms: *α.* 1 **hæft,** 4- **haft,** 5-6 **hafte,** (6 **haughte**). *β.* 4 **hefþe,** 4-6 **hefte,** 4- **heft** (7 **heaft**). [OE. *hæft(e* neut., handle, corresp. to OHG. *hefti* (MHG. *hefte*, G. *heft* neut.), MLG. *hechte* (Du. *hecht, heft*), ON. *hepti*:—(OTeut. **haftjo*m, f. root *haf-* HEAVE, or *hab-* HAVE; app. that by which anything is taken hold of or grasped. (For OE. *æ* for *ę* see Sievers *Ags. Gr.* §89. I. 1.)]

1. a. A handle; esp. that of a cutting or piercing instrument, as a dagger, knife, sickle, etc.

c **1000** ÆLFRIC *Voc.* in Wr.-Wülcker 142/21 *Manubrium*, hæft and helfe. *c* **1000** *Sax. Leechd.* II. 272 ȝegnid þonne.. mid sticcan oþþe mid hæfte. **1382** WYCLIF *Deut.* xix. 5 The axe fleeth the hoond, and the yren, slipt of fro the haft, smytith his freend. **1489** CAXTON *Faytes of A.* II. xxxix. 163 A croked yron well sharp and trenchaunt with a long hafte. **1555** EDEN *Decades* 224 A long dager with a hafte of golde. **1690** *Lond. Gaz.* No. 2525/4, 8 Knives and 8 Forks with Silver Hafts. **1774** GOLDSM. *Nat. Hist.* (1776) VII. 52 The shells of this animal resemble..the haft of a razor. **1866** LAING & HUXLEY *Preh. Rem. Caithn.* 41 One end..was clearly inserted in a socket or haft.

β. **13..** *Seuyn Sag.* (W.) 259 Under heft, and under hond. *c* **1380** *Sir Ferumb.* 791 Tak al-so my swerd..þe hefþe of hym doþ greuaunce to my wounde wyde. **1483** *Cath. Angl.* 179/2 An Hefte, *manubrium, manutentum.* **1551** TURNER *Herbal* I. Hvjb, To make knyffe heftes. *a* **1605** MONTGOMERIE *Misc. Poems* xxxii. 63 Baith heft and blead ar in ȝour hand. *a* **1661** FULLER *Worthies, Suffolk* III. (1662) 73 If the Heaft belonged to Walworth, the Blade, or point thereof at least, may be adjudged to Cavendish. **1878** BROWNING *Poets Croisic* 113 Hilt and heft.

†**b.** Phr. ***loose in the haft*** (*fig.*), unstable, unreliable. ***to have other haft(s) in hand***, to have other business to do, 'other fish to fry'. *Obs.*

c **1325** *Poem Times Edw. II.* 362 in *Pol. Songs* (Camden) 339 Unnethe is nu eny man that can eny craft That he nis a party los in the haft. *c* **1440** *York Myst.* xx. 76 Other haftis in hande haue we. *c* **1460** *Towneley Myst.* (Surtees) 159 For othere haft in hand haue we.

c. *Bot.* Of an iris: the narrow part, or claw, at the base of the petal.

1924 W. R. DYKES *Handbk. Garden Irises* i. 1 An Iris flower consists usually of three outer segments called falls and of three inner segments called standards... The lower part of both the falls and the standards is usually called the haft. **1948** G. ANLEY *Irises* 113 *Haft*, the narrowed portion at the base of a perianth segment.

2. *Comb.*, as *haft-maker*; **haft-pipe** (see quot.).

a **1661** FULLER *Worthies* (1840) III. 395 Bladers, haft-makers, and sheath-makers. **1853** BYRNE *Handbk. for Artisan* 441 Small tools are temporarily fixed by their tangs in a wooden handle to facilitate their presentation to the [grind] stone; the handle is called a haft-pipe.

haft, *sb.*² *Sc.* and *north. dial.* Also heft, ? heff. [Goes app. with HAFT *v.*³]

1. Fixed or established place of abode.

1785 FORBES *Dominie Deposed* 46 (Jam.) I did resolve to change the haft. **1818** SCOTT *Hrt. Midl.* xviii, 'Her bairn,' she said, 'was her bairn, and she came to fetch her out of ill haft and waur guiding'.

2. Settled or accustomed pasture-ground. See also HEFT *sb.*³

c **1800** YOUNG *Ann. Agric.* XXVII. 185 (Cheviots) The haunt which a sheep adopts, in the language of shepherds is called its haft. **1825** JAMIESON, *Heff*, an accustomed pasture ..The attachment of sheep to a particular pasture.

haft, *sb.*³ *midl. dial.* [Origin uncertain: cf. prec.] An island in a pool.

1686 PLOT *Staffordsh.* 232 To see whether the Hafts or Islands in the pooles (upon which they build their neasts) be prepared for them. **1804** BEWICK *Brit. Birds* (1847) II. 210 The owners of some of the fens and marshes in this kingdom ..caused the little islets or *hafts* in those wastes, to be cleared of the reeds and rushes.

haft, *v.*¹ Also 5- heft. [f. HAFT *sb.*¹]

1. *trans.* To fit with, or fix in, a haft or handle.

c **1430** *Pilgr. Lyf Manhode* II. lxxxii. (1869) 105 For to hafte ther-with hire mailettes. **1582** N. LICHEFIELD tr. *Castanheda's Conq. E. Ind.* lxxvi. 155 a, His Dagger and Rapyer..were hafted with pure golde. **1691** WOOD *Ath. Oxon.* II. 528 A bone..with which he said he would haft a knife. **1753** PARSONS in *Phil. Trans.* XLVIII. 380 I used a wire hafted in a glass tube. **1866** *Reader* 22 Sept. 307 Several show in an interesting manner how the stone celts or chisels ..were hafted.

β. *c* **1440** *Promp. Parv.* 235/1 Helvyn or heftyn, *manubrio.* **1483** *Cath. Angl.* 480/1 To Hefte or to make Heftis, *manubriare.* **1871** *Daily Tel.* 1 Nov., By dint of the sharp edge of common sense strongly hefted with broad human and Christian sympathy.

†**2.** To drive *in* up to the haft. *Obs. rare.*

1583 STANYHURST *Æneis*, etc. (Arb.) 143 This mye blade in thy body should bee with speedines hafted.

Hence **'hafting** *vbl. sb.*, fitting with a haft.

c **1440** *Promp. Parv.* 232/1 Heftynge, *manubriacio.* **1538** *MS. Acc. St. John's Hosp., Canterb.*, Payd for haftyng off the ij hand saw. **1607** TOPSELL *Four-f. Beasts* (1658) 487 The bones of Sheep have also their use and employment for the hafting of knifes. **1833** J. HOLLAND *Manuf. Metal* II. 57 The sickle is ready for hafting.

†**haft,** *v.*² *Obs.* [Known only from 16th c., but perh. representing an OE. type **hæftian*, corresp. to OS. *haftôn*, OHG. *haftên* to remain fixed or fast, to stick, Ger. *haften* (to be distinguished from the trans. OE. *hæftan* = OS. *heftian*, Goth. *haftjan*, OHG. *heftan*, Ger. *heften* to make fast, fix, etc.).] *intr.* To use subtilty or deceit, to use shifts or dodges; to haggle, cavil; to avoid coming to the point, hold off, hang back.

1519 HORMAN *Vulg.* (1530) S viij, Haftynge, *dolus malus.* **1557** TUSSER 100 *Points Husb.* lx, Spende none but thyne owne, howsoeuer thou spende: nor haft not to god ward, for that he doth sende. **1600** HOLLAND *Livy* XXVII. xxxix. 967 It was not expedient to lie off and haft any longer. **1603** —— *Plutarch's Mor.* 474 The tyrant, who put them off from day to day, and hafted with them so, as he gave them no audience. **1644** BULWER *Chirol.* 161 One while hafting and wrankling, another while praying and intreating.

Hence †**'hafting** *vbl. sb.*, subtle dealing, dodging, cavilling, trickery; holding off, hesitation, demur. Also *attrib.* in ***hafting point, question***. *Obs.*

1519 HORMAN *Vulg.* (1530) N iv, There is a haftynge poynt, or a false subtylte. **1526** SKELTON *Magnyf.* 707 Craftynge and haftynge contryued is by me; I can dyssemble, I can both laughe and grone. *Ibid.* 1698 To vse suche haftynge and crafty wayes. **1549** COVERDALE, etc. *Erasm. Par. Eph.* Prol., Whan was there more haftyng and craftyng to scrape money to gether. **1565-73** COOPER *Thesaurus*, *Cauilla*..a mocke: a scoffe: an hafting question: a cauill. **1600** HOLLAND *Livy* 377 Why they loitered and made such hafting. **1609** —— *Amm. Marcell.* (N.) He grew enkindled, and without any further hafting or holding off, delivered up all that was demaunded.

haft, *v.*³ *Sc.* and *north. dial.* Also heft. [Goes app. with HAFT *sb.*²: origin uncertain: a connexion suggests itself with G. *heften* to fasten, attach, OS. *heftian* to make fast: but sometimes there seems to be association with HAFT *v.*¹]

1. *trans.* To establish in a situation or place of residence, to locate, fix; *spec.* to accustom (sheep, cattle) to a pasturage.

1728 RAMSAY *Betty & Kate* iv, For sindle times they e'er come back, Wha anes are heftit there. **1823** MACTAGGART *Gall. Encycl.* s.v., Animals are said to be hafted, when they live contented on strange pastures, when they have made a haunt. **1835** MRS. CARLYLE *Lett.* I. 26, I am wonderfully well hefted here; the people are extravagantly kind to me. **1893** HESLOP *Northumb. Gloss.* s.v., To heft, to keep stock upon a certain pasture until accustomed to go there.

b. *intr.* (for *refl.*) To establish itself.

1725 RAMSAY *Gentle Sheph.* I. ii, Ill-nature hefts in sauls that's weak and poor. **1794** S. YOUNG in *Statist. Acc. Scotl.* XII. 86 Such attention..as ought to be paid to stranger, or what is called hefting sheep.

2. *transf.* and *fig.* To set or plant firmly, fix, root, establish, settle.

1755 *Guthrie's Trial* 249 They heft their heart in their own honesty and resolutions, and not in the blessed root Christ Jesus. **1818** SCOTT *Hrt. Midl.* xxxix, The root of the matter was mair deeply hafted in that wild muirland parish than in the Canongate of Edinburgh. **1824** —— *Redgauntlet* let. ix, It may be as well that Alan and you do not meet till he is hefted as it were to his new calling. **1872** DE MORGAN *Budget Paradoxes* 20 It shows how well hafted is the Royal Society's claim.

hafta ('hæftə), repr. colloq. pronunc. of *have to* (see HAVE *v.* 7 c). Chiefly *N. Amer.*

1941 B. SCHULBERG *What makes Sammy Run?* v. 80 That's a honey... I'll hafta remember that one. **1945** A. KOBER *Parm Me* 58, I see... You don't hafta explain. **1952** E. WILSON *Equations of Love* 275 'I don't *haf*ta marry the Aldridge girls,' he said urgently. **1968** N. BENCHLEY *Welcome to Xanadu* vi. 133 You'll hafta carry him.

haftara, haftarot(h): see HAPHTARAH.

hafted ('hɑːftɪd, -æ-), *ppl. a.* [f. HAFT *v.*¹ + -ED¹.] Having or fitted with a haft or handle.

c **1440** *Promp. Parv.* 232/1 Heftyde, *manubriatus.* **1570-6** LAMBARDE *Peramb. Kent* (1826) 366 A shorte blacke hafted knife, like unto an olde halfpeny whitle. **1611** COTGR., *Manché*..hafted, helued. **1767** GOOCH *Treat. Wounds* I. 176 A hafted-needle may prove a very useful instrument. **1888** BELL *Later Age of Stone* 48 Turning up the soil with picks formed of a hafted stone.

hafter ('hɑːftə(r), -æ-), *sb.*¹ [f. HAFT *v.*¹ + -ER¹.] One who makes hafts or handles for tools.

1598 FLORIO, *Manicatore*..a sleeuer, a hafter, a handler. **1831** J. HOLLAND *Manuf. Metal* I. 261 This latter opinion was corroborated by the hafter. **1890** *Daily News* 24 Sept. 2/6 Table-knife hafter.

†**hafter,** *sb.*² *Obs.* [f. HAFT *v.*² + -ER¹.] A caviller, wrangler, haggler, dodger.

1519 HORMAN *Vulg.* 70 b, A flaterynge hafter [*sedulus captator*] is soone espyed of a wyse man. *Ibid.* (1530) N vj, He is a hafter of kynde, *est versutiæ ingenitæ homo.* **1526** SKELTON *Magnyf.* 2485 From crafters and hafters I you forfende. **1573-80** BARET *Alv.* H 11, An hafter: a wrangler: a cauiller, *vitilitigator.* **1611** COTGR., *Tergiversateur*, a flincher,..hafter, dodger, paulterer.

hafue, hafyr, obs. ff. HAVE, HAVER.

hag (hæg), *sb.*¹ Forms: *α.* 3-7 **hegge**, 6-7 **heg.** *β.* 4-7 **hagge**, 6-8 **hagg**, 6- **hag.** [The form *hegge* is found once early in 13th c.; *hagge* once in 14th; otherwise the word is not known till the 16th c. Usually conjectured to be a shortened form of OE. *hægtesse*, *hæhtisse*, *hægtes*, *-tis*, *hegtes* 'fury, witch, hag' = OHG. *hagazissa*, *hagazussa*, *hagzus*, MHG. *hęcse*, Ger. *hexe*, OLG. **hagatussa*, MDu. *haghetisse*, Du. *hecse* (:—OTeut. **hagatusjōn-*).

This derivation suits the sense, but the form-history is not clear, though an OE. **hægge* might perh. be analogous to OE. abbreviated names, such as *Ceadda*, *Ælla*, *Æbbe*, etc. (The ulterior etymology of OTeut. **hagatusjōn-* is itself unknown.) The order of the senses is uncertain; senses 4 and 5 may not belong to this word.]

1. a. An evil spirit, dæmon, or infernal being, in female form: applied in early use to the Furies, Harpies, etc. of Græco-Latin mythology; also to malicious female sprites or 'fairies' of Teutonic mythology. *Obs.* or *arch.*

1552 HULOET, Hegges or nyght furyes, or wytches like unto old women..which do sucke the bloude of children in the nyght, *striges.* **1573** TWYNE *Æneid.* XII. (R), Your filthy foules, and hegges of Limbo low. **1573-80** BARET *Alv.* H 339 A Heg, or fairie, a witch that changeth the fauour of children, *strix.* **1581** J. STUDLEY tr. *Seneca's Hercules Œtæus* 204 b, After ruin made Of goblin hegge, or elfe. **1649** G. DANIEL *Trinarch., Hen. IV*, ccliv, The Grisly Hagge, With knotted Scorpions. **1810** SCOTT *Lady of L.* III. vii, Noontide hag, or goblin grim.

†**b.** Applied to *manes* or shades of the departed, ghosts, hobgoblins, and other terrors of the night.

1538 ELYOT *Dict.*, *Larua*, a spyrite whiche apperethe in the nyght tyme. Some do call it a hegge, some a goblyn. *a* **1557** MRS. M. BASSET tr. *More's Treat. Passion* Wks. 1397/2 Lyke shrycke owles and hegges, lyke backes, howlettes..byrdes of the hellye lake. **1563** B. GOOGE *Egloges* iv. (Arb.) 44 What soeuer thou art..Ghoost, Hagge, a Fende of Hell. **1566** ADLINGTON *Apuleius* 3 Doest thou liue here (O Socrates) as a ghost or hegge to our great shame and ignomie? **1567** DRANT *Horace, Epist.* II. i. (R.), The goddes above are calm'd with verse, with verse the hagges of hell [*carmine manes*]. **1634** MILTON *Comus* 434 Blue meagre hag, or stubborn unlaid ghost.

†**c.** The nightmare. *Obs.*

1632 tr. *Bruel's Praxis Med.* 50 In the Hag or Mare..is no con[v]ulsion, as is in the falling sicknesse. **1696** AUBREY *Misc.* (1721) 147 It is to prevent the Night-Mare (viz.) the Hag from riding their Horses.

†**d.** *fig.* An object of terror, a 'bogey'. *Obs.*

1611 SPEED *Hist. Gt. Brit.* IX. viii. §59 That the Popes Curse was no such deadly and dreadfull Hagge, as in former times they deemed it.

2. A woman supposed to have dealings with Satan and the infernal world; a witch; sometimes, an infernally wicked woman. Now associated with 3.

1587 *Mirr. Mag.*, *Forrex* iii, That hatefull hellish hagge of ugly hue. **1590** SPENSER *F.Q.* I. viii. 46 A loathly, wrinckled hag, ill favoured, old. **1591** SHAKS. *1 Hen. VI*, III. ii. 52 Foule Fiend of France, and Hag of all despight. **1605** —— *Macb.* IV. i. 48 How now you secret, black, and mid-night Hags? **1654** WHITLOCK *Zootomia* 437 The Poets..made the Hag Circes Sister to Æsculapius. **1712** STEELE *Spect.* No. 266 ¶2 One of those Hags of Hell whom we call Bawds. **1728** YOUNG *Love Fame* III. (1757) 101 As hunted hags, who, while the dogs pursue, Renounce their four legs, and start up on two. **1816** SCOTT *Bl. Dwarf* ii, On this moor she used to hold her revels with her sister hags. **1833** HT. MARTINEAU *Cinnamon & P.* iv. 66 The dull roar of the distant sea spoke of hags riding the blast.

3. a. An ugly, repulsive old woman: often with implication of viciousness or maliciousness.

(The place of the first two quots. is doubtful.)

1377 LANGL. *P. Pl.* B. v. 191 With two blered eyghen as a blynde hagge. **1611** SHAKS. *Wint. T.* II. iii. 108 A grosse Hagge: And Lozell, thou art worthy to be hang'd, That wilt not stay her Tongue. *a* **1711** KEN *Urania* Poet. Wks. 1721 IV. 481 The Hagg, who by Cosmeticks smear'd, Fair at first sight appear'd. **1713** STEELE *Englishm.* No. 40. 261 Oppression..makes handsome Women Hags *ante diem.* **1791** COWPER *Odyss.* XVIII. 33 Llike an old hag Collied with chimney-smutch! **1834** LYTTON *Pompeii* III. ix, Perhaps in no country are there seen so many hags as in Italy. **1866** GEO. ELIOT *F. Holt* (1868) 19, 'I am a hag', she said..'an ugly old woman who happens to be his mother'.

b. *fig.* Applied to personifications of evil or of vice. (The place of the first quot. is uncertain.)

a **1225** *Ancr. R.* 216 þe seoue moder sunnen..and of hwuche mesteres þeo ilke men serueð..þet habbeð iwiued o þeos seouen heggen. **1577** tr. *Bullinger's Decades* (1592) 165 Ill fauoured enuie, vgly hagge. **1830** TENNYSON *Poems* 124 Shall the hag Evil die with child of Good?

†**c.** *transf.* Applied opprobriously to a man. (Skelton's use is uncertain.) *Obs.*

a **1529** SKELTON *Dk. Albany* 295 For thou can not but brag, Lyke a Scottyshe hag: Adue nowe, sir Wrig wrag. *a* **1529** —— *Col. Clout* 51 My name ys Colyn Clowte, And [I] purpose to shake owte All my Connyng Bagge, Lyke A clarkely hagge. **1565** GOLDING *Ovid's Met.* IV. (1593) 80 That old hag [Silenus] that with a staffe his staggring limmes doth stay. **1587** —— *De Mornay* xiv. 221 Giue to the oldest Hag that is the same eies that he had when he was yoong. **1676** W. ROW *Contn. Blair's Autobiog.* xii. (1848) 492 Me who am an old hag that must shortly die.

Here perhaps belongs the following:

1553 BALE *Vocacyon* in *Harl. Misc.* (Malh.) I. 357 Than was all the rable of the shippe, hag, tag, and rag called to the reckeninge.

4. † **a.** A kind of light said to appear at night on horses' manes and men's hair. *Obs.* **b.** *dial.* A white mist usually accompanying frost.

1530 PALSGR. 228/2 Hagge, a flame of fyre that shyneth by night, *furolle.* **1656** T. WHITE *Peripat. Inst.* 149 *Flammæ lambentes* (or those we call Haggs) are made of Sweat or some other Vapour issuing out of the Head. **1825** BROCKETT *N.C. Gloss.*, *Hag*,..a white mist, similar to dag. **1855** ROBINSON *Whitby Gloss.*, *Hag*, mist. 'Frost hag', frost haze.

5. A cyclostomous fish (*Myxine glutinosa*) allied to the lamprey, having an eel-like form, and living parasitically upon other fishes. Also HAGFISH.

1823 CRABB *Technol. Dict.*, *Hag*, a particular sort of fish, of an eel-shape..It is of so gelatinous a nature, that when placed in a vessel of sea-water it soon turns it to glue. **1835** KIRBY *Hab. & Inst. Anim.* II. xxi. 373 Those extraordinary animals, the hag and the lamprey. **1881** *Cassell's Nat. Hist.* V. 146 This destruction [of a Haddock] is sometimes accomplished by a single Hag, but as many as twenty have been found in the body of a single fish.

6. *attrib.* and *Comb.*, (chiefly from 2) as ***hag-advocate***, ***-finder***, ***-seed***, ***-witch***; ***hag-born***, ***-steered*** adjs.; ***hag-like*** adv. and adj.; **hag-stone, hag's teeth** (see quots.); **hag-track** = FAIRY-RING.

1718 BP. HUTCHINSON *Witchcraft* Ded. (1720) 17 The odious Names of *Hag-Advocates. **1610** SHAKS. *Temp.* I. ii. 283 The Son, that she did littour heere, A frekelld whelpe, *hag-borne. **1637** B. JONSON *Sad Sheph.* II. ii, That do I promise, or I am no good *hag-finder. **1634** RANDOLPH *Muses' Looking-Glass* I. iii, Her unkemb'd hair, Dress'd up with cobwebs, made her *haglike stare. **1824** J. MORIER *Adv. Hajji Baba* I. xiii. 148 There was also..an old woman of a hag-like and decrepit appearance. **1610** SHAKS. *Temp.* I. ii. 365 *Hag-seed, hence. **1787** GROSE *Provinc. Gloss.* Superstitions 57 A stone with a hole in it, hung at the bed's head, will prevent the night-mare; it is therefore called a *hag-stone. **1867** SMYTH *Sailor's Word-bk.*, **Hag's teeth*, those parts of a matting or pointing interwoven with the rest in an irregular manner, so as to spoil the uniformity. **1858** *Murray's Hand-bk. Kent* Introd. 32 'Fairy rings', sometimes called '*hag-tracks'. *a* **1658** CLEVELAND *Agst. Ale* v, May some old *Hag-witch get astride Thy Bung, as if she meant to ride.

hag, *sb.*² *north. dial.* Also 6-7 **hagg.** [perh. a. ON. *hagi*, Sw. *hage* enclosed field, pasture; cognate with OE. *haga* m., enclosure, place fenced in, MDu. *hāghe* m. and f., hedge, enclosure, thicket of underwood, Du. *haag* f., hedge enclosure, MHG. *hagen*, *hage* m., thicket. Cf. HAW *sb.*¹]

†**1.** (?) A hedge. *Obs.*

c **1470** HENRY *Wallace* XI. 21 Hagis, alais, be laubour that was thar, [were] Fulȝeit and spilt.

2. A wooded enclosure; a coppice or copse.

1589 *Will of Corntwhat* (Somerset Ho.), One close.. adioyning to one hagg of my maisters called Cock crawe..& the lytle hagg. **1600** FAIRFAX *Tasso* VIII. xli. 150 He led me ouer holts and hags. **1788** W. MARSHALL *Yorksh.* Gloss., *Hags*, hanging-woods; or woods in general. **1825** BROCKETT *N.C. Gloss.*, *Hag*,..a wood into which cattle are admitted. **1847-78** HALLIW. s.v., The park at Auckland Castle was formerly called the Hag. **1869** *Lonsdale Gloss.*, *Hag*, an enclosure, a wood. **1878** *Cumbld. Gloss.*, *Hag*, (Central) a woody place intermixed with grass land; (East) a wooded hill.

hag, *sb.*³ *Sc.* and *north. dial.* Also **hagg**. [Of Norse origin: cf. ON. *hǫgg* (:—**haggw*-), cutting blow or stroke, also a hewing-down of trees, *hǫgg-skógr*, 'hag-shaw', wood of felled trees; f. *hǫggva* to hew, HAG *v.*¹ (ON. *ǫ* is regularly repr. by *a* in Eng.: cf. ADDLE *v.*²)]

1. A cutting, hewing, or felling. (See quots.)

1808–18 JAMIESON, *Hag*, one cutting of a certain quantity of wood. **1845** H. FRASER *Statist. Acc. Scotl.* VII. II. 505 At each hagg or felling..these..may produce the sum of £9000. *Ibid.* 520 The value of each hagg or cutting of the woods..amounts to £8260.

2. The stump of a tree left after felling. Also ***hagsnare***.

1615 W. LAWSON *Orch. & Gard.* III. xi. (1668) 33, I see a number of Hags, where, out of one root, you shall see three or four, pretty Oaks, or Ashes straight and tall. **1796** W. MARSHALL *Yorksh.* (ed. 2) Gloss., *Hagsnare*, a stool or stub off which coppice-wood has been cut. **1855** ROBINSON *Whitby Gloss.*, *Hagsnare*.

3. A portion of a wood marked off for cutting; hence, a lot of felled wood, such as is used for fuel.

1796 *Statist. Acc. Scotl.*, *Dunbartonsh.* XVII. 244 (Jam.) They [the oak woods] are of such extent as to admit of their being properly divided into 20 separate hags or parts, one of which may be cut every year. **1803** *Edinb. Evening Courant* 26 Mar. (Jam.) To be exposed for sale by public roup—a hag of wood, consisting of oak, beech, and birch, all in one lot. **1814** SCOTT *Wav.* x, Edward learned from her that the *dark hag*..was simply a portion of oak copse which was to be felled that day. **1825** JAMIESON, *Hag*.. 5. The lesser branches used for fire-wood, after the trees are felled for carpenter-work. **1847–78** [see 4].

4. *Comb.*, as **hag-house**, ? a place for storing firewood; **hag-path**, ? a path through a copse; **hagsnare** (see 2); **hag-staff** (see quot.); **hag-wood**, 'a copse wood fitted for having a regular cutting of trees in it' (Jam.).

1733 *List Chambers in College of Edinb.* in Sir A. Grant *Univ. Edinb.* (1883) II. 192 The Hagg House. Mr. Dawson, Coal-seller. **1816** R. KERR *Agric. Surv. Berwicksh.* 334 (Jam.) Remains of ancient oak forests..which have grown into a kind of copse, or what is termed in Scotland hag woods. **1847–78** HALLIW., *Hag*,..when a set of workmen undertake to fell a wood, they divide it into equal portions by cutting off a rod called a hag-staff, three or four feet from the ground, to mark the divisions, each of which is called a hag. **1887** *N. & Q.* 7th Ser. III. 197 In Warwickshire the rods which mark the boundary of a fall of timber are called *hagg-staffs*. **1889** *Blackw. Mag.* Dec. 826 The poacher..will at evening pass under the wood and down by the 'hag' path.

hag, *sb.*⁴ *Sc.* and *north. dial.* Also **hagg**. [Cf. ON. *hǫgg* (:—**haggw*-), in the sense 'cut-like gap or ravine in a mountain', f. *hǫggva*: see prec., and HAG *v.*¹]

†**1.** A break, gap, or chasm (in a crag or cliff). *Obs.*

a **1300** *Cursor M.* 9886 Þi castel..it es hei sett a-pon þe crag, Grai and hard, wit-vten hag [*Gött.* hagg]. [Cf. **1876** *Whitby Gloss.*, *Hag*, a rock or cliff. 'Built on the face of the hab.' Old local statement.]

2. 'Moss-ground that has formerly been broken up; a pit or break in a moss', i.e. marsh or bog (Jam.). Used in two opposite senses: **a.** A piece of soft bog, esp. in a moor or morass.

1662 DUGDALE *Hist. Imbanking* xlv. 292/2 (trans. *Perambulation of Wigenhale, Norfolk* 13 Hen. IV, 1411) All the warp should be thrown into the Common wayes to fill up haggs and lakes. **1724** RAMSAY *Tea-t. Misc.* (1733) I. 79 The wind's drifting hail and sna' O'er frozen hags, like a' foot ba'. **1787** BURNS *Samson's Elegy* 55 Owre many a weary hag he limpit. **1820** SCOTT *Monast.* xxiii, To assist his companion to cross the black intervals of quaking bog, called in the Scottish dialect *hags*, by which the firmer parts of the morass were intersected. **1864** J. BROWN *Jeems* 15 You slip back, you tumble into a moss-hagg. **1886** STEVENSON *Kidnapped* xiv, I..had to stop..and drink the peaty water out of the hags.

b. One of the turfy or heathery spots of firmer ground which rise out of a peat bog.

1805 SCOTT *Last Minstr.* IV. v, A small and shaggy nag, That through a bog, from hag to hag, Could bound like any Billhope stag. **1861** WHYTE MELVILLE *Tilbury Nogo* 346 The moss or bog being very soft and treacherous, and the little knolls of soft ground—Scotticè, hags—being at that exact distance apart which tempted the ambitious sportsman to a leap, not always a successful one. **1892** H. HUTCHINSON *Fairway Isl.* 241 Beside a large hag of heather.

3. The vertical or overhanging margin of a peat-cutting: the shelving margin of a stream.

1893 HESLOP *Northumbld. Gloss.*, *Hag*, *Peat-hag*, or *Moss-hag*, a projecting mass of peat forming an escarpment on a peat moor, or the points left by edges of water gutters. These hags form miniature ravines on the surface. *Mod. Sc.* (*Roxb.*), There will be trout lying under the hag there.

hag, *sb.*⁵ *dial.* [Cf. HAG *v.*² sense 3 b.]

1887 *S. Cheshire Gloss.*, *Hag*, a task..to work by hag = by task, by the piece, instead of by the day or the week. *Ibid.*, *Hag-master*, the overseer who apportions out the 'hag-work'.

hag, *sb.*⁶: see HAG-BOAT.

hag, *v.*¹ *north. dial.* Also 5–7 **hagge**. [a. ON. *hǫggva* (:—**haggwan*:—OTeut. **hauwan*) to strike or smite with a sharp weapon, to hack, = OE. *héawan*, to HEW: cf. HAG *sb.*³, HAGWORM.]

trans. To cut, hew, chop; = HACK *v.*¹ 1. Also *absol.* or *intr.*

c **1400** *Destr. Troy* 10023 Þai..hurlit þurgh the hard maile, hagget the lere. **1611** COTGR., *Degrader vne forest*, to hagge, or fell it all downe. **1727** WALKER *Peden's Life* in *Biogr. Scot.* 489 (Jam.) They are hashing and hagging them down, and their blood is running down like water. **1811** WILLAN *W. Riding Yorksh. Gloss.*, *Hag*, to cut and shape with an axe. **1836** SIR G. HEAD *Home Tour* 398 Some 'hagged' the coal breaking it in fragments with pickaxes. **1895** CROCKETT *Men of Moss-hags* xxv. 192 Like a man hagging hard wood with a blunt axe.

Hence **hagged** *ppl. a.*; **'hagging** *vbl. sb.*

1825 *Celebrated Trials* V. 362 She drew a pistol, with a new hagged flint from her pocket. **1893** STEVENSON *Catriona* 165 That he should have a hand in hagging and hashing at Christ's Kirk.

hag, *v.*² *Obs.* exc. *dial.* [In sense 1, f. HAG *sb.*¹; senses 2–4 may be of different origin.]

†**1.** *trans.* To torment or terrify as a hag; to trouble as the nightmare. *Obs.*

1598 DRAYTON *Heroic. Ep.* Wks. (1748) 108, I would hag her nightly in her bed, And on her breast lie like a lump of lead. **1662** OGILBY *King's Coronation* 8, I Sorc'ry use, and hag Men in their Beds. **1678** BUTLER *Hud.* III. iii. 20 That makes 'em in the dark see Visions, And hag them-selves with Apparitions. *c* **1700** WATTS *Horæ Lyr.* II. *To Discontented* 40 Haunted and hagg'd where'er she roves.

2. To incite, urge; to 'egg' *on*. Now *dial.*

1587 M. GROVE *Pelops & Hipp.* (1878) 89 Hope doth hag me to encline with pen once for to paynt The staggering staffe whereby I stay. **1881** *Leicestersh. Gloss.*, *Hagg*..to incite; urge; instigate. 'Doon't ye hagg him on.'

3. To fatigue, tire out, 'fag'. Now *dial.*

1674 R. GODFREY *Inj. & Ab. Physick* 184 Nature is not only even jaded, and hag'd, but likewise for the future admonisht. **1742** FIELDING *J. Andrews* IV. xiv, Hagged out with what had happened to her in the day. **1766** *Dodsley's Poets* V. 291 The toilsome employments of mother and wife, Had hag'd the poor woman half out of her life. **1828** *Craven Dial.* s.v., 'I'se fair hagged off my legs.' **1854** BAKER *Northamptonsh. Gloss.*, *Hagg*, to fatigue, to weary.

b. To overwork and underpay, to 'sweat'.

1891 *Labour Commission* Gloss., *Hag principle*, term used to denote the system under which a skilled miner employs an unskilled man, paying him, say, 4*s.* per day, when, possibly, he might have earned 7*s.* or 8*s.* if working for himself. This process is called *hagging*. Crudely put, the *hag principle* is the 'sweating system'.

†**4.** *intr.* To go wearily. *Obs.*

a **1763** BYROM *Poems* (1773) I. 11 We hagg'd along the solitary Road.

hag, hagg, var. of HAKE⁴, fire-arm.

hag-, the stem of HAG *v.*¹ in Comb. (cf. HACK-): **hag-clog, hag-stock**, a block of wood or stump on which firewood is chopped. In quot. 1596, *fig.*

1596 *Seruingman's Comfort* (1868) 116 The chine of Beefe, the hagstocke to these Carpenters, was hewen and squared into diuers parcels. **1828** *Craven Dial.*, *Hag-clog*, a chopping block. **1894** CROCKETT *Raiders* 291 The hag-clog where we cut the branches and wood into billets. *Mod.* (Furness phrase) 'As dull as a hagstock.'

hag-a-bag, obs. var. of HUCKABACK.

hagabusyar, obs. f. HARQUEBUSIER.

†**hagan**. *Obs.* A sort of fishing-net.

1630 *Ducie's Order* in *Descr. Thames* (1758) 78 That no Peter-man do fish with any Hagan or Smelt Net below London Bridge, at any Time of the Year.

Haganah (hɑːgɑːˈnɑː). Also **Hagana**. [ad. Heb. *hᵃgannāh* defence.] A group of Jewish settlers in Palestine who, as an underground defence force, played a leading part in the creation of the state of Israel in 1948.

1923 *Daily Mail* 29 Jan. 6 He knows more about the 'Haganah', the Zionist Self-Defence force, than the authorities in Palestine like. **1949** KOESTLER *Promise & Fulfilment* 96 Specially picked anti-terrorist Haganah squads. **1960** *Guardian* 26 Aug. 5/3 The Hagana was transformed from an underground guerilla force into a regular army. **1973** *Jewish Chron.* 19 Jan. 12/4 The Haganah (Jewish self-defence) movement..ultimately became Israel's army.

hagard, obs. form of HAGGARD.

†**Hagaren**, *a.* *Obs.* Erron. for *hegiran*, of or pertaining to the Hegira.

1614 SELDEN *Titles Hon.* 163 The New Moon of their first Month *Mucharam*..in this Hagaren yeer..was the third day after the true Coniunction or Change.

Hagarene (hægəˈriːn). [ad. L. *Agarēn-us*, f. *Agar*, Hagar.] A reputed descendant of Hagar the concubine of Abraham and mother of Ishmael; an Arab, a Saracen. Also applied in a transferred sense (from Gal. iv. 22–31): see quots.

1535 COVERDALE *Ps.* lxxxii[i]. 6 The tabernacles of the Edomites and Ismaelites, the Moabites and Hagarenes. *a* **1592** H. SMITH *Arrow agst. Atheists* (1637) 46 The Grecians of spite are wont to call the Saracens, Agarens: for that they came not of Sara, but of Agar. *a* **1626** BP. ANDREWES in Spurgeon *Treas. Dav.* Ps. xlvii. 9 The Hagarins, the Turks, and Ishmaelites. **1634** SIR T. HERBERT *Trav.* 152 Mahomet was by birth an Arabian..a Saracen (or rather of discent from Ismael sonne of Hagar, and so a Hagaren). **1854** MILMAN *Lat. Chr.* II. 395 The usual appellation of the Saracens by the Pope is Hagarenes, sons of fornication and wrath. **1856** SPURGEON *Serm.* II. 132 Ye Hagarenes! Ye ceremonialists! Ye hypocrites!

hagas(e, obs. forms of HAGGIS.

hagberry (ˈhægbɛrɪ). Also **hack-, heck-, heg-berry**, and (corruptly) **egg-berry**. [Of Norse origin: Da. *hægge-bær*, Norw. *hegge-bär*, Sw. *hägg-bär* and *hägg*, ON. *heggr*.] A northern name of the bird-cherry, *Prunus Padus*. **b.** Also a less usual synonym of the American HACKBERRY.

1597 GERARDE *Herbal* 1322 Birds Cherrie..in Westmerland..called Hegberrie tree. **1778** LIGHTFOOT *Flora Scot.* 253 Bird-Cherry *Anglis*; Hag-berries *Scotis*. **1794** *Statist. Acc. Perthsh.* IX. 239 (Jam.) On the banks of the Lunan, there is a shrub here called the hack-berry (*prunus padus*) that carries beautiful flowers, which are succeeded by a cluster of fine blackberries. **1818** SCOTT *Let. to Laidlaw* Mar. in *Lockhart*, I shall send..also some Hag-berries. **1825** BROCKETT *N.C. Gloss.*, *Heck-berry*, the bird cherry. **1842** G. TURNBULL in *Proc. Berw. Nat. Club* II. No. 10. 7 By its side the hagberry grew. **1868** ATKINSON *Cleveland Gloss.*, *Hag-berry*, the fruit of the bird cherry... See Egg-berry another form of the word. **1878** BRITTEN & HOLL. *Plant-n.*, Egg-berry, *Prunus Padus* L. Cf. Heckberry. **1879–86** BRITTEN & HOLLAND, give *hackberry*, East. Borders, Cumb., Westm.; add. Roxb., Dumf., Perth; *hag-berry* Scotland generally, Cumb., Westm., N. Lancash., Yorksh.; *heckberry*, Cumb., Yorksh.; *hegberry*, Cumb. **1888** MRS. H. WARD *R. Elsmere* 3 Masses of the white heckberry or bird-cherry.

hag-boat. Rarely **hag**. [Origin unknown: cf. HECK-BOAT.] A kind of vessel formerly used both as a man-of-war, and in the timber and coal trade; latterly 'a clincher-built boat with covered fore-sheets and one mast with a trysail' (Smyth).

a **1700** B. E. *Dict. Cant. Crew*, *Hagboat*, a huge Vessel for Bulk and Length, Built chiefly to fetch great Masts, etc. **1707** *Lond. Gaz.* No. 4329/6 The Mary Hagboat, English-built, Burthen about 350 Tons, 8 Guns. **1711** *Ibid.* No. 4906/2, I met..a French Ship of Thirty-six Guns, a Hag-boat of Twenty-four. **1725** DE FOE *Tour Gt. Brit.* (1748) II. 144 The Ships that bring them [coals], Cats, and Hags, or Hag-boats, Fly-boats, and the like. **1769** FALCONER *Dict. Marine* (1789) Ggb, Hag-boats and pinks approach the figure of cats, the former being a little broader in the stern. **1867** SMYTH *Sailor's Word-bk.*, *Hag-boat*, see Heck-boat. *Heck-boat*, the old term for pinks.

hagbolt: see HACKBOLT.

hagbush, -but(t, obs. ff. HACKBUSH, HACKBUT.

hagden, hagdown. *local.* Also **hagdel, hagdon**. A name of the Greater Shearwater, *Puffinus major*; = HACKBOLT.

1832 W. D. WILLIAMSON *Hist. State Maine* I. 150 The Hagdel [is] of a dark brown colour, about as large as a Murr, though its feathers are longer. **1843** in Yarrell *Hist. Birds* III. 506 Nor could I ascertain that a Greater Shearwater was ever shot..They are commonly known by the name of Hagdowns. **1878** W. A. ANDREWS *Log of Nautilus* 79 Plenty of Mother Carey's chickens, hagdens, and marble-headers. **1885** SWAINSON *Prov. Names Birds* 212 Greater Shearwater ..Hackbolt (Scilly Islands), Hagdown (Dungarvan, Isle of Man.) **1954** FISHER & LOCKLEY *Sea-Birds* i. 26 The Tristan great shearwater also probably reaches its greatest abundance on the North American coast,..where it is known as the 'hagdon'. **1959** BANNERMAN *Birds Brit. Isles* VIII. 141 Wynne-Edwards reminds us that it [*sc.* the sooty shearwater] is known to the fishermen as the hagdown or black hagdon.

hage, haȝe, obsolete forms of AWE.

hagese, -eys, obs. ff. HAGGIS.

'hagfish, hag-fish. [f. HAG *sb.*¹ + FISH *sb.*¹] = HAG *sb.*¹ 5.

1611 COTGR., *Pirot*, the Pirot, or Hag-fish; a kind of long shell-fish. **1884** *Longm. Mag.* Mar. 525 The majority of the fish caught are totally destroyed by hag-fish. **1931** J. R. NORMAN *Hist. Fishes* iii. 41 The related Hagfish (*Myxine*) possesses still more singular habits, and bores right into the fishes it attacks. **1967** *Oceanogr. & Marine Biol.* V. 291 Aqua-lung diving is beginning to provide exact data about the natural habitats of such animals, for example, the hagfish, *Myxine glutinosa*. **1968** *Times* 19 Dec. 4/8 Lampreys, like hagfish, are surviving members of the jawless fishes, the first group of vertebrates to evolve.

‖**Haggadah** (həˈgɑːdə). Also **Hagada(h, Agadah**. [Rabbinical Heb. *haggādāh* (first in Talmud) 'tale', esp. 'edifying tale or story', f. *higgīd* to make clear, declare, tell, Hiphil of **nāgad* to be in front, to be in sight, to be clear or manifest. The Heb. pl. *ha'ggadoth* occurs in Eng. use.]

1. A legend, anecdote, parable, or the like, introduced in the Talmud to illustrate a point of the Law; hence, the legendary element of the Talmud, as distinguished from the *Halachah*.

1856 ETHERIDGE *Jerus. & Tiberias* 182 Hagada is not law, but it serves to illustrate law. **1874** DEUTSCH *Rem.* 17 'Haggadah'..was only a 'saying', a thing without authority, a play of fancy, an allegory, a parable, a tale, that pointed a moral and illustrated a question. **1883** *Encycl. Brit.* XVI. 285/1 This *Haggadah* or *Agadah* varies considerably both in nature and form.

2. The Jewish ritual for the first two nights of the Passover. Also the book containing the text of the service.

1733 tr. *B. Picart's Ceremonies & Relig. Customs* I. 61 Then each of them holding a Glass of Wine in his Hand, says the Hagada. [**1887** JACOBS & WOLF *Catal. Anglo-Jew. Hist. Exhib.* 194 Haggadah Pesach, or Liturgy of the Passover.] **1891** M. FRIEDLANDER *Jewish Relig.* II. iv. 379 The first two evenings of Passover are..called '*seder*-evenings', and the book which contains this Service is generally called *Haggadah*. **1896** W. H. GREENBURG *Haggadah* 6 Upon the first cup one says the benediction... Upon the second cup one recites the Haggada. **1904** *Daily Chron.* 30 Mar. 7/5 Perhaps the whole genius of the celebration of the Passover may be summed up in the words of the Hagadah: 'In every generation each Israelite shall bethink himself as though he had been delivered from Egypt.' **1904** *Jewish Encycl.* VI. 142/2 The opinion of Friedmann..that special books containing the Passover service existed in Talmudic times, is based on a judgment of Raba in favor of a man who claimed a Haggadah..from an estate under the plea that he had lent it to the deceased. **1922** JOYCE *Ulysses* 708 An ancient hagadah book. **1972** *Publishers Weekly* 7 Feb. 16 (Advt.), We have created what we feel is the most unusual Haggadah for Passover 1972... A functional Haggadah with the complete Passover Seder service in both English and Hebrew.

haggaday ('hægədeɪ). *local.* Also 5 **hagin-, haguday,** 9 **hagady.** A kind of door-latch: see quot. 1877.

c **1475** *Voc.* in Wr.-Wülcker 778/20 *Hoc manutentum*, a haginday. **1483** *Cath. Angl.* 169/1 An Haguday, *vectes.* **1610** *Louth* (*Linc.*) *Ch. Acc.* III. 196 (N.W. Linc. Gloss.) To John Flower for hespes..a sneck, a haggaday, a catch and a Ringe for the west gate, ijs. *vjd.* **1847–78** HALLIW., *Haggaday*, a kind of wooden latch for a door. *Yorksh.* **1877** *N.W. Linc. Gloss.*, A *haggaday* is frequently put upon a cottage door, on the inside, without anything projecting outwards by which it may be lifted. A little slit is made in the door, and the latch can only be raised by inserting therein a nail or slip of metal.

Haggadic (hə'gædɪk, -'ɑːdɪk), *a.* Also **Hagadic,** AGADIC. [f. HAGGADAH + -IC.] Of, pertaining to, or of the nature of Haggadah. So **Ha'ggadical** *a.*

1866 *Kitto's Cycl. Bibl. Lit.* III. 167 The Homiletic or Hagadic Exegesis. The design of this branch of the Midrash or exposition is to edify the people of Israel in their most holy faith. **1881** W. R. SMITH *Old Test. in Jew. Ch.* vi. 33 A text encumbered with Haggadic additions. **1882–3** SCHAFF *Encycl. Relig. Knowl.* III. 2298 A feature of this Targum [Job] is its Haggadical character.

Haggadically (hæ'gædɪkəlɪ), *adv.* [f. HAGGADICAL *a.* + -LY².] As in the Haggadah.

1920 OESTERLEY & BOX *Lit. Rabbinical Judaism* 78 The Scriptural lesson..is haggadically developed.

Haggadist (hə'gɑːdɪst). [f. as HAGGADIC *a.* + -IST.] A writer of Haggadoth; one versed in the Haggadah, or Haggadic method.

1882 FARRAR *Early Chr.* I. 516 A Hagadist, or one who dwelt on allegory, legend and historical story more than on the legal precedents of the Halacha. **1891** tr. *Didon's Jesus Christ* I. 200 Jesus did not give the impression of a scribe, a doctor, or a Haggadist..but of a prophet.

Hence **Hagga'distic** *a.*, of, pertaining to, or characteristic of the Haggadists.

1856 ETHERIDGE *Jerus. & Tiberias* 428 The general tone of Jewish preaching in the Middle Ages was not so hagadistic as it had been in the East. **1882** FARRAR *Early Chr.* I. 288 That Hagadistic school of Jewish exegesis.

haggard ('hægəd), *sb.*¹ Also -art. [cf. ON. *heygarðr* stack-yard, f. *hey* hay + *garðr* GARTH.] In Ireland and Isle of Man: A stack-yard.

1586 J. HOOKER *Girald. Irel.* in *Holinshed* II. 44/2 All such cornes as they had in their haggards. *c* **1645** HOWELL *Lett.* II. xxiv, When the Barn was full any one might thresh in the haggard. **1749** MRS. DELANY *Life & Corr.* (1861) II. 511 We saw great quantities of new corn in the haggards as we came along through Staffordshire. **1848** *Act 11 & 12 Vict.* c. 69 §2 The malicious burning of houses, barns, haggards, corn, or other articles or effects. **1894** HALL CAINE *Manxman* 107 She could see the barley stack growing in the haggard.

haggard ('hægəd), *sb.*² [Absolute use of HAGGARD *a.* 1.]

1. A wild (female) hawk caught when in her adult plumage. (With some, in 17–18th c. = peregrine falcon.)

1567 TURBERV. *Epitaphs, etc.* 15 b, Liue like a haggard still therefore, And for no luring care. **1599** SHAKS. *Much Ado* III. i. 36 Her spirits are as coy and wilde, As Haggerds of the rocke. **1607** *Lingua* II. v. in Hazl. *Dodsley* IX. 379 A wondrous flight Of falcons, haggards, hobbies, terselets, Lanards and goshawks. **1766** PENNANT *Zool.* (1768) I. 139 The falcon, the falcon gentle, and the haggard, are made distinct Species, whereas they form only one. **1828** SIR J. S. SEBRIGHT *Observ. Hawking* 32 The older hawks are called haggards: it is these that ornithologists have mistaken for a distinct species, calling it the Peregrine Falcon.

†**b.** *fig.* A wild and intractable person (at first, a female); one not to be captured. *Obs.*

1579 LYLY *Euphues* (Arb.) 74 That if she should yeelde at the first assault, he would thinke hir a light huswife: if she should reiect him scornfully, a very haggard. **1596** SHAKS. *Tam. Shr.* IV. ii. 39, I wil be married to a wealthy Widdow ..which hath as long lou'd me, As I haue lou'd this proud disdainful Haggard. **1680** LD. FALKLAND *Hist. Edw. II*, 67 Their first Act sends Baldock the Lord Chancellour to Newgate, a fit Cage for such a Haggard.

2. *Comb.* *haggard-tercel*; *haggard-like*, *-wise* adv.

1567 TURBERV. *Epitaphs, etc.* 113 b, That Haggard wise doth loue to liue. **1593** NASHE *Christ's T.* (1613) 182 Though Christ..hold out neuer so moouing lures vnto vs, all of them (Haggard-like) wee will turne tayle to. *c* **1620** *Roxb. Ball.* VII. 423 Haggard like, she me abus'd, another taken, and I refus'd. **1727** BRADLEY *Fam. Dict.*, *Hawk*, The Male of a Haggard, the Haggard-Tassel.

†**haggard**, *sb.*³ *Obs.* [? f. HAG *sb.*¹ after such words as *laggard*, *dotard*, etc.] A hag, a witch.

1658 tr. *Porta's Nat. Mag.* VIII. xiv. 232 So children oftentimes effascinate themselves, when their parents attribute it to haggards and witches. **1668** ETHEREDGE *She would if she could* III. i, I protest yonder comes the old haggard. **1715** tr. *C'tess D'Anois' Wks.* 614 She heard the Voice of a Man, and soon after saw an old Haggard.

haggard ('hægəd), *a.* Also 6 **haggarde, haggred,** 6–7 **haggart,** 6–8 **hagard, hagger(e)d.** [Cf. F. *hagard*, 'hagard, wild, strange; froward, contrarie, crosse; vnsociaable, vncompanable, incompatible' (Cotgr.), orig. said of a falcon 'that preyed for her selfe long before she was taken'. According to some, Normand-Picard for *haiard*, deriv. of *haie* 'hedge' ('esprevier hagard est celluy qui est de mue de hayes' Ménagier 14th c. in Littré). But this is very doubtful.]

1. Of a hawk: Caught after having assumed the adult plumage; hence, wild, untamed; said also of an owl (*obs.*).

1567 TURBERV. *Epitaphs, etc.* 15 The haggarde Hauke That stoopeth to no state. **1583** T. WATSON *Cent. Loue* xlvii. (Arb.) 83 In time the Bull is brought to weare the yoake; In time all haggred Haukes will stoope the Lures. **1602** SEGAR *Hon. Mil. & Civ.* IV. xv. 225 Of Falcons some are Gentle and some Haggard. **1604** SHAKS. *Oth.* III. iii. 260. **1637** B. JONSON *Sad Sheph.* III. iii, No Colt is so unbroken! Or Hawk yet half so haggard, or unmann'd! **1682** OTWAY *Venice Preserved* I. i, A haggard Owl, a worthless Kite of Prey. *a* **1734** NORTH *Exam.* II. iv. §117 (1740) 292 As Men catch haggard Hawks, to reclaim, and make them fly at other Quarry. **1814** CARY *Dante* (Chandos) 147 As for the taming of a haggard hawk.

†**2.** *transf.* and *fig.* **a.** Wild, unreclaimed, untrained (often with direct reference to 1). **b.** 'Froward, contrarie, crosse, vnsociable' (Cotgr.).

1580 LYLY *Euphues* (Arb.) 114 Foolish and franticke louers, will deeme my precepts hard, and esteeme my perswasions haggarde. **1583** STANYHURST *Æneis* I. (Arb.) 29 Late a tempest boysterus haggard Oure ships to Libye land with rough extremitye tilted. **1604** R. CAWDREY *Table Alph.* (1613), *Hagard*, wilde, strange, contrary. **1650** B. *Discolliminium* 21 God hath cast most spirits off his hand of common restraint, and let them fly haggard, till they are stark wild. *a* **1683** OLDHAM *Elegies* (1686) 103 At all alike my haggard Love does fly. **1695** BLACKMORE *Pr. Arth.* I. 688 So does the Fiend..rise Through the thick haggair'd Air.

†**3.** In disordered or ragged plumage. *Obs. rare.*

1615 *Val. Welshm.* (1663) D iij a, The Roman Eagle hangs his haggard wings. **1798** COLERIDGE *Picture* 31 The brier and the thorn [shall] Make his plumes haggard.

†**4.** Half-starved; gaunt, lean. *Obs.* (exc. as included in 5).

1630 DAVENANT *Cruel Brother* IV. Dram. Wks. 1872 I. 164 The slave is haggard. At supper..his vain appetite Fed at Nero's rate. *a* **1736** YALDEN *Fox & Flies* (R.), A swarm of half-starved haggard flies, With furie seiz'd the floating prize. **1796** BURKE *Regic. Peace* i. Wks. VIII. 179 The gaunt haggard forms of famine and nakedness.

5. Of a person: Wild-looking; in early use applied esp. to the 'wild' expression of the eyes, afterwards to the injurious effect upon the countenance of privation, want of rest, fatigue, anxiety, terror, or worry.

[**1605** *Tryall Chev.* I. iii. in Bullen *O. Pl.* III. 279 Her looks are haggard and obscure, Which makes me doubtfull sheele not stoope to lure.] **1697** DRYDEN *Virg. Georg.* IV. 370 With hagger'd Eyes they stare, Lean are their Looks, and shagged is their Hair. *a* **1700** —— *Theocritus, Despairing Lover* (R.), Staring his eyes, and haggard was his look. **1757** GRAY *Bard* I. i, Robed in the sable garb of woe, With haggard eyes the Poet stood. **1853** C. BRONTE *Villette* v, Thin, haggard, and hollow-eyed; like a sitter up at night. **1860** TYNDALL *Glac.* I. xi. 77, I had noticed a haggard expression upon the countenance of our guide.

fig. and *transf.* **1735** SOMERVILLE *Chase* III. 465 His haggard Fancy still with Horror views The fell Destroyer. **1827–44** N. P. WILLIS *She was not there* 18 All that tempts the eye and taste, And sets the haggard pulses wild. **1871** SWINBURNE *Songs bef. Sunrise, Bef. Crucifix* 2 At this lank edge of haggard wood. **1876** T. HARDY *Ethelberta* (1890) 72 Till the fire had grown haggard and cavernous. **1883** STEVENSON *Silverado Sq.* 80 From this proposition she recoiled with haggard indignation.

b. Gaunt or scraggy-looking, from the loss of flesh with advancing years. (App. influenced by HAG *sb.*¹, as if 'somewhat hag-like': cf. HAGGED 2.)

1807 CRABBE *Par. Reg.* III. 547 His cheeks were haggard, hollow was his eye. **1840** MISS MITFORD in L'Estrange *Life* (1870) III. vii. 109 To prevent the haggard look which comes upon women who grow thin at fifty. **1858** CARLYLE *Fredk. Gt.* (1865) II. VII. vi. 304 She is getting haggard beyond the power of rouge.

6. *Comb.*, as ***haggard-cheeked, -looking, -wild.***

1794 BURNS *Friend's Amour* viii, Fancy..Reigns, haggard-wild, in sore affright. **1855** BROWNING *Statue & Bust* 162 Hollow-eyed and haggard-cheeked. **1886** W. J. TUCKER *E. Europe* 205 Some dozen haggard-looking crones.

'haggardly, *a.* and *adv.* [f. HAGGARD *sb.*² and *a.* + -LY¹ and ².]

†**A.** *adj.* Like or of the nature of a haggard hawk; wild. *Obs.*

1727 BRADLEY *Fam. Dict.* s.v. *Hawk*, A Hawk..by how much the later you take her, by so much the more Difficulty will she be to be reclaimed and manned, as being more *haggardly* or wilder of Nature.

B. *adv.* In a haggard manner; wildly; gauntly.

1692 DRYDEN *Juvenal's Sat.* vi. 600 How haggardly soe'er she looks at home. **1860** HOLME LEE *Leg. Fairy Land* 39 Her lips paled, her eyes stared haggardly.

'haggardness. [f. as prec. + -NESS.] Haggard quality or condition; wildness as of an unreclaimed hawk; gaunt and worn appearance of face.

1579 LYLY *Euphues* (Arb.) 41 Though the Fawlcon be reclaimed to the fist, she retyreth to hir haggardnesse. **1841** LYTTON *Nt. & Morn.* I. vi, His..haggardness ill became the years of palmy youth. **1876** GEO. ELIOT *Dan. Der.* VII. li, A new haggardness had come in her face.

haggas, obs. form of HAGGIS.

hagged (hægd, 'hægɪd), *a.* Now *dial.* [A late formation from HAG *sb.*¹: prob. influenced by HAGGARD, with which it runs together in sense 2. Perh. in some cases influenced by HAG *v.*²]

1. a. Bewitched. **b.** Witch-like, hag-like. ? *Obs.*

a **1700** B. E. *Dict. Cant. Crew*, *Hagged*, Lean, Witched, Half-Starved. **1706** E. WARD *Hud. Rediv.* I. v. 14 Who grin'd and look'd (the Lord defend her) As hagged as the Witch of Endor. **1765** GRAY *Long Story* 129 The ghostly prudes with hagged face. **1817** SOUTHEY *Let.* 28 May in *Life & Corr.* IV.. 266 [French women] appear to pass at once from youth to hagged old age.

2. Lean, gaunt; haggard; worn-out, fagged.

1694 R. L'ESTRANGE *Fables* 66 A Hagged Carrion of a Wolfe. *a* **1700** [see 1]. **1741** RICHARDSON *Pamela* (1824) I. 62 My red eyes and my hagged looks. **1752** CARTE *Hist. Eng.* III. 312 To see..how hagged and battered she was grown. **1814** SOUTHEY *Roderick* Poet. Wks. 1838 IX. 22 Through the streets he went With haggëd mien. **1860** HUGHES *Tom Brown at Oxf.* xviii, Thou look'st hagged at times, and folk'll see it, and talk about thee.

haggerd, -ered, obs. ff. HAGGARD *a.*

†**haggess, haggiss.** *Obs.* [a. F. *agace*, *agasse* 'a Pie, Piannet, or Magatapie' (Cotgr.), in 13th c. also *agache*, Walloon *aguèse*, med.L. *agasia*, a. OHG. *agazza* pie, also OHG. *agalstra* (MHG. *egelster*, Ger. *elster*: see Kluge). Cf. also HAGGISTER pie, Du. *aakster*, *ekster*, MDu. *aextre*, *extre*, from ODu. and OLG. *agastria*, all from same root as OE *agu* pie.] The magpie.

1599 T. M[OUFET] *Silkwormes* 44 Hardy are Haggesses, but yet giuen to prate. **1655** MOUFET & BENNET *Health's Improv.* (1746) 184 Pyes or Haggisses feed upon Flesh, Eggs, Worms, and Ants.

haggi, obs form of HADJI.

†**hagging.** *Obs. rare.* [f. HAG *sb.*¹ + -ING¹.] The meeting of hags or witches.

1584 R. SCOT *Discov. Witchcr.* Epist. (1886) p. xxi, The witches..their hagging, their riding in the aire. *Ibid.* II. iv. 19 He would spie unto what place his wife went to hagging.

haggis ('hægɪs). Also 5 **hagas(e, hagese, hageys, hagws, (hakkys),** 6 **hagges, -eis, -ise,** 6–8 **haggas, -ass(e, -ess)e,** 7–8 **haggus,** 8 **haggice, -ies,** 9 **-ish, -iss.** [Derivation unknown.

The analogy of most terms of cookery suggests a French source; but no corresp. F. word or form has been found. The conjecture that it represents F. *hachis* 'hash', with assimilation to *hag*, *hack*, to chop, has app. no basis of fact; F. *hachis* is not known so early, and the earlier forms of the Eng. word are more remote from it. Whether the word is connected with *hag* vb., evidence does not show.]

1. a. A dish consisting of the heart, lungs, and liver of a sheep, calf, etc. (or sometimes of the tripe and chitterlings), minced with suet and oatmeal, seasoned with salt, pepper, onions, etc., and boiled like a large sausage in the maw of the animal.

(Now considered specially Scotch, but a popular dish in English cookery down to the beginning of the 18th c. Cf. also quots. 1879–90.)

c **1420** *Liber Cocorum* (1862) 52 For hagese. Þe hert of schepe, þe nere þou take..Hacke alle togeder with gode persole [etc.]. *c* **1430** *Two Cookery-bks.* 39 Hagws of a schepe. Take þe Roppis with þe talowe, & parboyle hem; þan hakke hem smal. *c* **1440** *Promp. Parv.* 220/2 Hagas, puddynge (*S.* hakkys, puddyngys, *H.* hageys). **1508** DUNBAR *Flyting w. Kennedie* 128 The gallowis gaipis eftir thy graceles gruntill, As thow wald for ane haggeis. **1530** PALSGR. 228/2 Haggas a podyng, *caliette de mouton.* **1615** MARKHAM *Eng. Housew.* (1660) 178 This small Oat-meal mixed with blood, and the Liver of either Sheep, Calfe, or Swine, maketh that pudding which is called the Haggas or Haggus, of whose goodnesse it is in vain to boast, because there is hardly to be found a man that doth not affect them. **1675** HOBBES *Odyssey* (1677) 219 Antinous a haggas brought, fill'd up With fat and blood. **1721** BAILEY, *Haggess*, a Sheep's Maw fill'd with minc'd Meat. **1771** SMOLLETT *Humph. Cl.* (1815) 268, I am not yet Scotchman enough to relish their singed sheep's-head and haggice. **1796** MRS. GLASSE *Cookery* v. 85 To make a Scotch Haggass, take the lights, heart, and chitterlings of a calf. **1825** BROCKETT *N.C. Gloss.*, *Haggis*, *Haggish*, a dish..sometimes only of oatmeal, suet and sugar—stuffed into a sheep's maw and boiled. Sold in the Newcastle market. **1836–48** B. D. WALSH *Aristoph., Clouds* I. iv, I neglected to nick a haggis one day I was roasting to dine my relations. **1864** BURTON *Scot. Abr.* I. v. 323 There is something transcendentally Scotch about a haggis. [**1879** MISS JACKSON *Shropsh. Word-bk., Haggis,*.. the smaller entrails of a calf; what the chitterlings are in a pig. **1890** *Gloucester Gloss., Haggus,* calf's chitterlings (Hundred of Berkeley).]

b. *transf.* and *fig.* The paunch.

1836 SIR G. HEAD *Home Tour* 307, I can certainly testify to the inordinate quantity that.. the human haggis will hold.

c. An indolent do-nothing fellow.

1822 CARLYLE in *Early Lett.* (1886) II. 28 The lazy haggises! they must sink when we shall soar.

d. A mixture, hodge-podge; a mess.

1899 *Daily News* 13 Sept. 7/6 They cheerfully go through the curious haggis of social and philanthropic duties served up to them each week. **1928** W. A. J. ARCHBOLD (*title*) Bengal haggis. **1929** H. MARWICK *Orkney Norn* 66/1 He'll just mak a haggis o' the job.

2. *Comb.*, as ***haggis-bag, -maker, -pudding; haggis-fed*** adj.

1483 *Cath. Angl.* 169/1 An Hagas maker, *tucetarius.* **1545** RAYNOLD *Byrth Mankynde* I. xiv. (1634) 51 The bag of an Haggasse pudding. **1787** BURNS *To a Haggis* 37 But mark the rustic, haggis-fed. **1819** *Blackw. Mag.* Sept. 677 More like an empty haggis-bag than any thing else.

haggish ('hægɪʃ), *a.* [f. HAG *sb.*^{1} + -ISH.] Like, resembling, or of the nature of a hag.

1583 STANYHURST *Æneis* I. (Arb.) 27 Mars.. with sweld furor haggish, Lyke bandog grinning. **1601** SHAKS. *All's Well* I. ii. 29 On vs both did haggish Age steale on. **1687** *New Atlantis* I. 329 Guilt leaves an haggish fear that haunts the mind. **1822** *Blackw. Mag.* XI. 11 The beldam's haggish grin. **1886** T. HARDY *Mayor of Casterbr.* i, A haggish creature of about fifty presided.

Hence '**haggishly** *adv.*; '**haggishness**.

1846 WORCESTER, *Haggishley.* **1893** *Dispatch* (Columbus) 2 Mar., [The land] of dazzling beauty and most hideous haggishness in women.

†**haggister.** *Obs.* or *dial.* Also 7 **hagester**, 8 **-ister.** [Cognate with Du. *aakster*, MDu. *aextre*, OLG. *agastria* magpie: see HAGGESS.] A local name of the magpie.

1584 R. SCOTT *Discov. Witchcr.* IV. viii. (1886) 65 The eating of a haggister or pie helpeth one bewitched in that member. **1674** RAY *S. & E.C. Words* 68 *Hagester*, a Magpie. *Kent.* **1802** G. MONTAGU *Ornith. Dict.* (1833), *Hagister*, a name for the Magpie. [**1847–78** in HALLIWELL.]

haggle ('hæg(ə)l), *v.* Also 6–7 **hagle.** [In sense 1, freq. of HAG *v.*^{1} (cf. HACKLE *v.*^{1}); the other senses may possibly have originated from this, though it is not clear that they did. Cf. HIGGLE.]

I. 1. *trans.* To mangle with repeated irregular cuts or cutting blows; to cut clumsily, with uneven jagged edges; to hack, mangle, mutilate.

1599 SHAKS. *Hen. V*, IV. vi. 11 Suffolke first dyed, and Yorke all hagled ouer Comes to him, where in gore he lay.. kisses the gashes That bloodily did yawne vpon his face. **1624** CAPT. SMITH *Virginia* IV. (1629) 145 They not only slew him and his family, but butcher-like hagled their bodies. **1806–7** J. BERESFORD *Miseries Hum. Life* (1826) x. lii, Haggling the nails of your right hand with a pair of blunt scissors held in the left. **1884** ROE *Nat. Ser. Story* vi, That was a good clean cut.. I dislike to see a tree haggled down. *fig.* **1760** LLOYD *The Actor* Wks. I. 14 Your fool.. Who murders what the Poet finely writ, And like a bungler haggles all his wit.

b. *intr.* To make rough or clumsy cuts; to hack.

1768–74 TUCKER *Lt. Nat.* (1852) I. 296 For fear any little motion.. should bend our instrument, and make us haggle or cut awry. **1804** *Man in the Moon* xvii. 131 She haggles at a wing, until it flies off into the plate of one of the astonished guests.

II. 2. *intr.* To cavil, wrangle, dispute as to terms; *esp.* to make difficulties in coming to terms or in settling a bargain; to stickle.

1602 [implied in HAGGLER 2 and 3]. **1611** COTGR., *Barguigner*.. to wrangle, dodge, haggle. **1722** DE FOE *Moll Flanders* (1840) 22 To bid a shilling more, and haggle with them. **1818** SCOTT *Hrt. Midl.* xlii, There were two points on which he haggled. **1853** KINGLSEY *Hypatia* xxi, I recollect well how I used to haggle at that story of the cursing of the fig-tree. **1886** STUBBS *Lect. Med. & Mod. Hist.* xii. 278 The King now haggled about the præmunire.

3. *trans.* To weary or harass with haggling.

1648 CROMWELL *Let.* 20 Aug. in *Carlyle*, We are so harassed and haggled out in this business. *a* **1797** H. WALPOLE *Mem. Geo. II* (1847) II. xi. 359 Moore, and one or two others, were neither awed nor haggled with their inquisitors. **1825** R. P. WARD *Tremaine* II. xxiii. 218 'Old Mr. Barnabus is quoit haggled with it.'

III. 4. *intr.* To advance with difficulty and obstruction: cf. HAGGLER 1. (*Sc.* also *haigle.*)

1583 STANYHURST *Æneis* III. (Arb.) 91 The giaunt, with his hole flock lowbylyke hagling. *Ibid.*, *Conceites* (Arb.) 136 Wheare the great hulck floated, theare now thee cart-wheele is hagling. **1871** CARLYLE in *Mrs. Carlyle's Lett.* II. 36 A Third Edition got done.. Printing haggles forward till October.

Hence **haggled**, '**haggling** *ppl. adjs.*

c **1589** *Theses Martinianæ* 30 Suffer no more of these haggling and profane pamphlets to be published against Martin. **1834** M. SCOTT *Cruise Midge* (1863) 36 The stumps of the haggled brushwood where it had been cleared by the hatchet. **1840** THACKERAY *Paris Sk.-bk.* (1872) 4 The insolence of haggling porters. **1894** CROCKETT *Raiders* (ed. 3) 133 There is a pile of haggled heads by thee.

haggle, *sb.* [f. HAGGLE *v.*] The action of haggling; wrangling or dispute about terms.

1858 R. S. SURTEES *Ask Mamma* xliv. 195 In dealing, a small farmer is never happy without a haggle. **1865** CARLYLE *Fredk. Gt.* XIII. v. V. 55 In the detail of executing, it was liable to haggles. **1865** KINGSLEY *Herew.* xiii, Then the usual haggle began between them.

haggle, dial. var. of HAIL *sb.*^{1} and *v.*^{1}

haggler ('hæglə(r)). [f. HAGGLE *v.* + -ER^{1}.] One who haggles. Cf. also HIGGLER.

†**1.** A clumsy, awkward workman; a bungler. *Obs.* exc. *dial.*

1577 STANYHURST *Descr. Irel.* in Holinshed (1807–8) VI. 5 As neere the pricke as you are, and as verie an hagler as I am, yet the scantling shall be mine. *c* **1589** *Theses Martinianæ* D ij, Alas poore haglers, their fathers are too yoong to outface the least of your sonnes. **1607** DEKKER & WEBSTER *Westw. Hoe* II. ii, Will you, like a haggler's arrow, be down the weather? strike whilst the iron is hot. **1847–78** HALLIW., *Hagler*, a bungler. *Var. dial.*

2. One who haggles or stickles in making a bargain or coming to terms.

1602 DEKKER *Satirom.* Wks. 1873 I. 245 Thy Muse is a hagler, and weares cloathes upon best-be-trust. **1611** COTGR., *Cagueraffe*, a base micher, scuruie hagler, lowsie dodger. **1698** VANBRUGH *Æsop* II. Wks. (Rtldg.) 373/2 Twenty shillings more, twenty shillings less, is not the thing I stand upon. I'se no hagler, gadswookers! **1883** S. C. HALL *Retrospect* II. 502 [He] was anything but a haggler about the prices he paid.

3. An itinerant dealer; a huckster; = CADGER 1, 2. **b.** (See quot. 1851.)

1602 *Act Com. Counc. Lond.* 6 July in *Stow's Survey* V. xxix. (1754) II. 511/1 The open Streets.. ought to be used.. for open Passage.. and not for Hucksters, Pedlars, and Haglers to stand and sit to sell their Wares in. *a* **1661** FULLER *Worthies* I. (1662) 278 Dorsers are Peds or Panniers carried on the backs of Horses, on which Haglers use to ride and carry their Commodities. *a* **1697** AUBREY *Nat. Hist. Surrey* (1719) II. 208 These Rounds of the Haglers.. are not incompatible with a daily Market. *a* **1700** B. E. *Dict. Cant. Crew, A Hagler*, one that Buys of the Country-Folks, and Sells in the Market, and goes from Door to Door. **1851** MAYHEW *Lond. Labour* I. 79 A 'haggler' being.. the middle-man who attends in the fruit and vegetable-markets, and buys of the salesman to sell again to the retail dealer or costermonger.

haggling ('hæglɪŋ), *vbl. sb.* [f. HAGGLE *v.* + -ING^{1}.] The action of the verb HAGGLE. **a.** Wrangling about terms, bargaining with much discussion. **b.** Uneven or clumsy cutting.

a. 1632 SHERWOOD, A haggling, *barguigne.* **1765** COWPER *Wks.* (1835–37) I. 197 Disagreeable haggling and higgling, and twisting and wriggling, to save my money. **1855** MACAULAY *Hist. Eng.* IV. 95 After some haggling he consented to sell.. his pretensions.. for a pension of five hundred pounds a year.

b. 1846 RUSKIN *Mod. Paint.* (1851) I. II. II. iii. §13 Half the chiaroscuro is totally destroyed by the haggling, blackening, and 'making out' of the engravers.

haggly ('hæglɪ), *a.* [f. as prec. + -Y.]

1. Bearing the marks of having been haggled or unevenly and clumsily cut. *dial.*

1825 in JAMIESON. **1887** *S. Cheshire Gloss., Haggly*, hacked uneven.

2. a. Characterized by haggling about terms. **b.** Moving with obstruction and difficulty.

1864 CARLYLE *Fredk. Gt.* IV. 347 A haggly settlement. **1865** *Ibid.* XIII. v. V. 55 It is hoped the Insurrection will go well, and not prove haggly, or hang-fire in the details.

haggred, obs. form of HAGGARD *a.*

haggus, obs. and dial. form of HAGGIS.

haggy, *a.*^{1} [f. HAG *sb.*^{1} + -Y^{1}.] Of or pertaining to a hag.

The sense of quot. 1654 is uncertain: it may belong to HAG *sb.*^{1} 1 or 2.

1654 M. STEVENSON *Occasions Off-spring* 83 Didst thou devise This haggy look, to be thought weather wise? **1964** S. BELLOW *Herzog* (1965) 159 That bitch, Madeleine, whose face looks either beautiful or haggy.

haggy, *a.*^{2} Chiefly *Sc.* [f. HAG *sb.*^{4} + -Y^{1}.] Boggy and full of holes.

1794 *Scots Mag.* Oct. 624/1 The night was neither warm not [*sic*] dry, The road was rough and haggy. **1881** D. THOMSON *Musings among Heather* 62 He thocht he had yet tae cross, A haggy, benty, splashy moss. **1959** D. D. C. P. MOULD *Peter's Boat* vii. 113 This country of bare peat cut with haggy trenches.

hagh)e, haȝe, early ME. forms of HAW *sb.*^{1}

haghel, haȝel, obs. ff. HAIL *sb.*^{1}

†**hagheli, -like**, *adv. Obs.* In 3 (*Orm.*) **haȝhe-.** [a. ON. *hagliga.*] Properly, becomingly.

c **1200** ORMIN 1228 Oxe ganngeþþ haȝheliȝ. *Ibid.* 1231 All haȝhelike & faȝȝre.

†**hagher**, *a. Obs.* Also 3 (*Orm.*) **haȝherr, haher, hawur**, 3–4 **haȝer**, 4 **hauer.** [app. a. ON. *hag-r* handy, skilful; but the retention of the inflexional *-r* of nom. sing. masc. is quite anomalous.] Skilful, clever, dexterous; apt, fit.

c **1200** ORMIN 13471 Forrþi þatt Sannt Anndrew wass Rihht god and haȝherr hunnte. *a* **1225** *Ancr. R.* 52 A ful hawur [*v.r.* haher, haȝer] smið. *a* **1327** *Sat. Consistory Crts.* in *Pol. Songs* (Camd.) 155 Be he never in hyrt so hauer of honde. **13..** *Gaw. & Gr. Knt.* 352 Non haȝer er of wylle.

b. Skilfully wrought.

13.. *Gaw. & Gr. Knt.* 1738 þe haȝer stones Trased aboute hir tressour, be twenty in clusteres.

Hence **haȝ(h)erleȝȝc** [cf. ON. *hagleik-r*], dexterity. **hagherliche, haȝ(h)erlike** *adv.* [cf. ON. *hagliga*], skilfully, aptly, fitly.

c **1200** ORMIN 4906 To rosenn off þin haȝherrleȝȝc. *Ibid.* 6672 Tatt wass haȝherrlike don. **13..** *E.E. Allit. P.* B. 18 He is.. honeste in his hous-hold & hagherlych serued.

'**haghood.** *nonce-wd.* The condition of a hag.

1861 *Macm. Mag.* IV. 324/2 All is over with the toy that he calls woman. Haghood sets in at once.

haginday, obs. form of HAGGADAY.

hagio-, hagi-, combining forms of Gr. ἅγιος holy, saintly; as in '**hagiarchy** [Gr. ἀρχή rule], the rule or order of saints; **hagi-he'roical** *a.*, characterized by saintly heroism; **hagio'mania** [Gr. μανία madness], saintly madness; a mania for sainthood; **hagio-ro'mance**, the romance of a saint's legend; **hagio'typic** *a.*, pertaining to types of saints.

1826 SOUTHEY *Vind. Eccl. Angl.* 323 Personages of the highest order in the *hagiarchy. **1829** —— *Sir T. More* II. 14 Of the most *hagi-heroical austerity. **1797** —— *Journ. Spain* (1808) I. 270 One regular symptom of *hagiomania (if the word may be allowed) is the desire of martyrdom. *a* **1843** —— *Comm.-pl. Bk.* (1849) III. 806 Growing like saint-worship and *hagio-romance. **1886** *Jrnl. Derbysh. Archæol. Soc.* VIII. 84 Such a remarkable *hagiotypic arrangement of saints of the first rank.

hagiocracy (hægɪ'ɒkrəsɪ). [f. Gr. ἅγιος holy + -CRACY.] A government or sovereignty of persons esteemed holy; *spec.* as in quot. 1875.

1846 WORCESTER cites *Eclectic Rev.* **1874** J. E. CARPENTER tr. *Ewald's Hist. Israel* V. 198 The internal weakness.. of the hagiocracy already betrays itself in the one small but significant circumstance of its treatment of the name of God. **1875** *Edin. Rev.* CXLII. 434 *note*, The term 'Hagiocracy'.. is employed by Ewald as the designation of that modified form of the theocratical government which was instituted after the return from the Babylonian Captivity. **1884** FAIRBAIRN in *Contemp. Rev.* Mar. 359 [To make] the Mosaic state the ideal which religious men ought to seek resolutely to realize in a hagiocracy.

‖**Hagiographa** (hægɪ'ɒgrəfə), *sb. pl.* [late L., a. Gr. ἁγιόγραφα, f. ἅγιος holy + γραφή writing, -γραφος writing, written.] The Greek name (lit. 'sacred writings') of the last of the three great divisions of the Hebrew Scriptures (called in Heb. *k'thūbīm* writings) comprising all the books not included under the two divisions of 'the Law' and 'the Prophets'.

These are Psalms, Proverbs, Job; Canticles, Ruth, Lamentations, Ecclesiastes, Esther; Daniel, Ezra, Nehemiah, Chronicles.

1583 FULKE *Defence* (Parker Soc.) 24 These books.. are sometimes called Hagiographa. **1649** ROBERTS *Clavis Bibl.* 501 The Hebrews dividing the whole Scripture into three parts, viz., The Law, the Prophets, and Hagiographa. **1860** *Horne's Introd. Knowl. Script.* (L.), In all there are twenty-two books of the old law; that is, five books of Moses, eight of the prophets, and nine of the Hagiographa. **1884** D. HUNTER tr. *Reuss' Hist. Canon* i. 10 In the time of Josephus the books called the Hagiographa were not yet gathered into a clearly defined collection.

Hence **hagi'ographal** *a.*, of or pertaining to the Hagiographa.

1657 J. COSIN *Canon Script.* 152 (T.) Strabus.. saith that Tobit is to be set among the apocryphal books, and not among the hagiographal. **1732** STACKHOUSE *Hist. Bible* (1767) IV. 284 In the number of hagiographal writers.

hagiographer (hægɪ'ɒgrəfə(r)). [f. med.L. *hagiograph-us*, (f. Gr. ἅγιος holy, saint + -γραφος writing, writer; cf. prec.) + -ER^{1}.]

1. A sacred writer; *spec.* one of the writers of the Hagiographa.

1656 BLOUNT *Glossogr., Hagiographer*, he that writes holy things [citing RALEIGH]. **1703** WHITBY *Paraphr. N.T.* Gen. Pref. 5 They were hagiographers, who are supposed to be left to the use of their own words. **1805** *Edin. Rev.* VII. 95 The Jews.. ranked him [Daniel] only among the number of their hagiographers.

2. A writer of saints' lives; a hagiologist.

1849 SIR J. STEPHEN *Eccl. Biog.* (1850) I. 91 Which chronicle.. has alway been held in much esteem by the hagiographers. **1864** J. H. NEWMAN *Apol.* App. 36 [He] by no means assumes that he is an historian because he is a hagiographer. **1867** FREEMAN *Norm. Conq.* I. v. 390.

hagiographic (hægɪəʊ'græfɪk), *a.* [f. as prec. + -IC, after Gr. -γραφικός: see -GRAPHIC.]

1. Of or pertaining to the Hagiographa.

1888 CAVE *Inspir. O. Test.* viii. 455 There is Hagiographic Inspiration enabling the assimilation of Revelation.

2. Pertaining to the writing of saints' lives.

1819 SOUTHEY in *Q. Rev.* XXI. 378 The Devil began to act a greater part in hagiographic romance. **1893** *Athenæum* 24 June 791/2 A curious compound of genuine historical research and hagiographic adulation.

hagio'graphical, *a.* [f. as prec. + -AL^{1}.] †**a.** Of or pertaining to sacred writings or the sacred Scriptures. *Obs.* **b.** Of or relating to the Hagiographa. **c.** Of or pertaining to biographies of saints.

1585 T. WASHINGTON tr. *Nicholay's Voy.* Ep. Ded. ¶iij, I might adde to these Hagiographicall examples, other..

brought out of prophane Chronologies. **1615** Sir E. Hoby *Curry-combe* ii. 89 The Canon of Hagiographicall Scripture. *a* **1652** J. Smith *Sel. Disc.* vi. 247 That which is Hagiographical, or, as they call it, the dictate of the Holy Spirit. **1864** Pusey *Lect. Daniel* vi. 302 He manifestly intends..hagiographical writers, (as of Solomon he says). **1874** Gilbert in *4th Rep. Hist. MSS. Comm.* 600/1 Preparing some of the hagiographical manuscripts for the press.

hagiographist (hægɪˈɒgrəfɪst). [f. as HAGIOGRAPHER + -IST.] = HAGIOGRAPHER 2.

1817 Southey *Pref. to Malory's Arthur* p. xl, A miraculous conception is the only miracle which the Romish Hagiographists have not bestowed upon their saints.

hagiography (hægɪˈɒgrəfɪ). [f. Gr. ἅγιο-ς holy + -γραφια writing: see -GRAPHY.]

†**1.** = HAGIOGRAPHA. *Obs. rare.*

1812 W. Taylor in *Monthly Rev.* LXVIII. 500 Ecclesiastes..perhaps was not really a part of the Hagiography.

2. The writing of the lives of saints; saints' lives as a branch of literature or legend.

1821 Southey in *Q. Rev.* XXIV. 476 Such tales as these are common in Romish hagiography. **1856** R. A. Vaughan *Mystics* (1860) II. 4 In the hagiography..of the Mohammedan world. **1867** Max Müller *Chips* (1880) III. xiv. 312 A famous name in Cornish hagiography.

hagiolatry (hægɪˈɒlətrɪ). [f. Gr. ἅγιος holy + λατρεία worship.] The worship of saints.

1808 W. Taylor in *Monthly Mag.* XXVI. 207 Reducing the established hagiolatry to that posthumous veneration for the benefactors of the human race, which is the natural religion of every grateful heart. **1855** Milman *Lat. Chr.* (1864) II. IV. vii. 348 The error was in the hagiolatry or adoration of saints, not in the adoration of the image.

Hence **hagiˈolater**, one who worships saints. **hagiˈolatrous** *a.*, given to saint-worship.

1841 G. S. Faber *Provinc. Lett.* (1844) I. 10 That Hagiolatrous Superstition which he deems the Essence of the predicted Apostasy. **1875** Miss Cobbe *False Beasts* 157 As a hagiolater kneels beside the relics of his Saint.

hagiologic (hægɪəʊˈlɒdʒɪk), *a.* [f. HAGIOLOGY (or its Greek elements) + -IC: see -LOGIC.] Of, pertaining to, or connected with hagiology.

1826 Southey *Vind. Eccl. Angl.* 169 Any person versed in hagiologic reading. **1834** J. Raine *Pref. to Reg. Dunelmensis Lib. de Adm. Cuthberti Virt.* (Surtees) p.x, Reginald, one of the most credulous of hagiologic writers.

hagioˈlogical, *a.* [f. as prec. + -AL[1].] = prec.

1872 *Dublin Rev.* Apr. 330 There is a growing tendency..to unfairly depreciate the value of lives of the saints written upon the 'hagiological' method. **1895** *Athenæum* 24 Aug. 255/2 To consist of religious and hagiological anecdota.

hagiˈologist. Also **agio-**. [f. HAGIOLOGY (or its Greek elements) + -IST.] A writer of hagiology; one versed in the legends of saints.

1805 Southey *Madoc* 416 *note*, This miracle is claimed by some Agiologists for St. Baldred. **1837** Sir F. Palgrave *Merch. & Friar* (1844) 204 The Hagiologist assigns an adequate cause. **1871** Tylor *Prim. Cult.* II. 199 The Buddhist theologians and hagiologists.

hagiology (hægɪˈɒlədʒɪ). [f. Gr. ἅγιο-ς holy + -λογια discourse: see -LOGY.] The literature that treats of the lives and legends of saints; also, by extension, of great men or heroes; a work on the lives and legends of the saints.

1807 Southey *Espriella's Lett.* II. 106 There are few finer miracles in hagiology. **1868** Freeman *Norm. Conq.* II. vii. 20 We shall be in danger of mistaking hagiology for history. **1870** Emerson *Soc. & Solit., Clubs* Wks. (Bohn) III. 96 In the hagiology of each nation, the lawgiver was in each case some man of eloquent tongue.

hagioscope (ˈhægɪəʊskəʊp). Also **agioscope**. [f. Gr. ἅγιος sacred, holy + -SCOPE.] A small opening, cut through a chancel arch or wall, to enable worshippers in an aisle or side chapel to obtain a view of the elevation of the host; a squint; also, sometimes applied to a particular kind of window in the chancel of a church.

1839–40 *Hints on Eccl. Antiq.* (Cambr. Camden Soc.) (ed. 2) 18 *Hagioscope.* By this term is intended the aperture made through different parts of the interior walls of a church ..in order that the worshippers in the aisles might be able to see the Elevation of the Host. The technical term in use is 'Squint'..It is hoped..that the new term..may be thought useful. **1844** Paley *Church Restorers* 35 A..chandelier hung from the roof..threw its faint light through a hagioscope upon the founder's tomb by the altar side. **1845** Parker *Gloss. Archit.* (ed. 4) I. 350 (s.v. *Squint*) The name of Hagioscope has lately been applied..but it does not seem desirable to give Greek names to the parts of English buildings. **1848** B. Webb *Continental Eccles.* 192 A late wayside church..with open grated hagioscopes.

Hence **hagioˈscopic** *a.*

1872 *Paroch. Hist. Cornwall* IV. 125 The transept has an hagioscopic communication with the chancel. **1881** *N. & Q.* 6th Ser. IV. 433/2 The sacrist..could command, by a hagioscopic window, the different parts of the mass.

†**hagiosidere.** *Obs. rare.* [ad. Gr. ἁγιοσίδηρον, f. ἅγιος holy + σίδηρος iron.] (See quot.)

1730–6 Bailey (folio), *Hagiosidere*, a Plate of Iron..which the Greeks under the Dominion of the Turks (being prohibited the Use of Bells) strike on, with a Hammer, to call the People to Church.

hagister, var. HAGGISTER, magpie.

hagle, haglet: see HAGGLE, HACKLET.

hagmena, obs. form of HOGMANAY.

hag-ridden (ˈhægrɪd(ə)n), *ppl. a.* Also **hag-rid**. [f. HAG *sb.*[1] + RIDDEN *ppl. a.*]

1. Ridden by a hag; *esp.* afflicted by nightmare.

1684 Otway *Atheist* II. i, He's marry'd, plagu'd, troubled, and Hag-ridden. **1758** Battie *Madness* vii. 49 (Jod.) Thus the glutton..is hag-ridden in his sleep. **1817** Coleridge *Zapolya* i. Prel. 88 Must I hag-ridden pant as in a dream? **1886** T. Hardy *Mayor of Casterbr.* I. xx. 246 When she had not slept she did not quaintly tell the servants next morning that she had been 'hagrid'.

2. Oppressed in mind; harassed.

1702 C. Mather *Magn. Chr.* III. II. xxviii. (1852) 507 He did not allow himself to be hagridden with the enchantments thereof. **1817** Coleridge *Biog. Lit.* 85 So completely hag-ridden by the fear of being influenced by selfish motives. **1891** *Spectator* 4 Apr. 471/1 Our minds are jaded and hag-ridden, as it were, by the physical fatalities of modern science.

hag-ride (ˈhægraɪd), *v.* [f. HAG *sb.*[1] + RIDE *v.*] *trans.* To ride as a hag: see prec.

1661 A. Brome *Songs & Poems* p. xii, When force hag-rid our Land and Seas. *c* **1718** *Lett. fr. Mist's Jrnl.* (1722) I. 164 As for Apparitions and Hag-riding, they are generally the Effects of Imagination and a disturbed animal Faculty. **1817** Scott *Harold* II. xiv, To..hag-ride some poor rustic's sleep. **1893** Stevenson *Catriona* iii. 29 The thought of the dead men hag-rode my spirit.

hag-seed: see HAG *sb.*[1]

hagship (ˈhægʃɪp). [f. HAG *sb.*[1] + -SHIP] The personality of a hag: used as a mock title.

1604 Middleton *Witch* II. ii. (R.), 'Tis the charm her hagship gave me For my duchess' obstinate woman. **1634** Heywood & Brome *Witches Lanc.* IV. H.'s Wks. 1874 IV. 230, I mean to lay the Country for their Hagships. **1785** Mrs. Grant *Lett. fr. Mount.* (1813) II. xix. 96, I fancy their hagships [Macbeth's witches] resided hereabouts.

hag-taper (ˈhægteɪpə(r)). Also 6 **higgis-, hickis-, hig-**; 8 **hagtaber**. [The original form and etymology of the first element are left doubtful by the early instances (*hag-* appears to be late); the second is TAPER *sb.*: cf. Ger. *kerzenkraut* 'taper-wort', MDu. *tortsecruyt* 'torchwort'.] A plant, the Great Mullein (*Verbascum Thapsus*).

1548 Turner *Names of Herbes, Verbascum*, in englishe Mullen higgis taper or Longe wurt. **1562** —— *Herbal* II. 161 The whyte Verbascum is called commonly in English mollen or hickis taper. **1578** Lyte *Dodoens* I. lxxxi. 120 In English..Mulleyn, or rather Wulleyn, Higtape, Torches, and Longworte. **1741** *Compl. Fam.-Piece* I. i. 83 Then put to it a Handful of Hagtaber. **1863** Prior *Plant-n.* s.v., In our modern Floras it is incorrectly spelt *High-taper*. **1876** *Treas. Bot.* 1209/2 The English name, Hig-taper..and Hag-taper.

haguday, obs. form of HAGGADAY.

hague, dial. var. HAW, the fruit.

hagworm (ˈhægwɜːm). *dial.* [a. ON. *hǫggormr*, the adder, f. *hǫgg* (:—*haggw-*) cutting stroke + *ormr* worm. (In different localities *hag* seems to be taken as = copse, hedge, or bog.)] A northern name for the adder or viper; but in some districts applied to the common snake, and in others to the blindworm.

1483 *Cath. Angl.* 169/2 An Hagworme, *jaculus*. **1631** R. H. *Arraignm. Whole Creature* ix. 69 That great hag-worme of a Corroding Conscience. **1787** Grose *Provinc. Gloss.*, *Hag-worms*, snakes of all kinds. *Yorks.* **1828** *Craven Dial.*, *Hag-worm*, a snake, or blind worm, haunting the hag or hedge. **1844** Selby in *Proc. Berw. Nat. Club* II. No. 12. 87 A large specimen of the Slow or Hag-worm, *Anguis fragilis*. **1858** Gen. P. Thompson *Audi Alt.* II. lxvii. 6 A snake (a poor harmless creature, by the way..always excepting the hag-worm). **1891** Atkinson *Moorland Par.* 313, I could account for the presence of the hag worm three or four feet below the surface of the hone.

hagws, obs. form of HAGGIS.

hah, var. of HA *interj.* and *vb.*

ha ha (hɑː ˈhɑː), *int.* and *sb.*[1] Also 7–9 **hah-hah**. [A natural utterance occurring in most languages; cf. Gr. ἁ ἅ, ἇ ἇ, L. *hā hā*, OF. *haha*, *aha*, etc.]

A. *int.* The ordinary representation of laughter.

c **1000** Ælfric *Gram.* xlviii. (Z.) 279 *Ha ha* and *he he* ȝetacniað hlehter on leden and on englisc. *c* **1386** Chaucer *Prioress' Prol* 5 (Harl. MS.) Haha telaws be war for such a iape. **1509** Hawes *Past. Pleas.* XVI. lxviii, Ha, ha! quod he, love doth you so prycke. **1821** Byron *Deformed Transf.* II. iii, *Caes.* (aside and laughing). Ha! ha! here's equity! **1822** Shelley tr. *Goethe's Faust* ii. 31 Ha, ha! your worship thinks you have to deal With men. **18..** W. Jones *Song 'The Monks of Old'* i, For they laugh'd ha! ha! and they quaff'd ha! ha! And lived on the daintiest cheer.

b. *ha ha ha!* and further repetitions express continued laughter.

[*c* **1150** Reginald *Libellus de Vita Godrici* (Surtees) 262 Cum stridore cachinnans, ait, *Hach, Hach, hach.*] **1579** Fulke *Confut. Sanders* 608 Ha ha he, M. Sander hath a pleasaunt witte. **1610** Shaks. *Temp.* II. i. 36 Ha, ha, ha. So: you'r paid. **1691** Ray *Creation* 11, Those accounts..are so excessively absurd and ridiculous, that they need no other confutation than ha, ha, he. **1698** Vanbrugh *Æsop* II. Wks. (Rtldg.) 373/2 Ha! ha! ha! ha! ha! Did ever man behold the like? ha! ha! ha! ha! ha! **1775** Sheridan *Duenna* I. v, Ha! ha! ha! I'll be very particular. **1873** S. T. Smith *My Uncle's Will* 29 By Jove! Ha! ha! ha!—upon my life—ha! ha! ha! ha! *Flor.* What is he laughing at?

B. *sb.* A loud or open laugh.

1806 Surr *Winter in Lond.* (ed. 3) III. 196 Titters from ladies, and ha, ha, ha's from gentlemen. **1837** Carlyle *Fr. Rev.* II. III. v. (1871) 113 Commented on with loud *hahas* and deep grumblings. **1862** *Athenæum* 30 Aug. 280 The *hah-hahs* and guffaws with which certain laughing frogs and jocular toads celebrate their nuptial rites.

Hence **ha ha** (hɑːˈhɑː), *v.*, to utter *ha ha* in laughter; to laugh aloud.

1606 *Sir G. Goosecappe* III. i. in Bullen *O. Pl.* III. 43, I wood have put the third *hah* to it..and *hah, hah, haht* him out of the presence yfaith. **1852** *Fraser's Mag.* XLVI. 456 The hyæna hah! hah's! at the pleasant prospect. **1865** Carlyle *Fredk. Gt.* XVIII. vii, All Regensburg was loud, wailing or haha-ing according to humour.

ha-ha (ˈhɑːhɑː, formerly also hɑːˈhɑː), *sb.*[2] Also **haha, ha! ha!, ha-hah (8 ah, ah)**, 8–9 **haw-haw**. [a. F. *haha* (17th c. in Hatz.-Darm.) 'an obstacle interrupting one's way sharply and disagreeably, a ditch behind an opening in a wall at the bottom of an alley or walk'; according to French etymologists, from *ha!* exclamation of surprise.] A boundary to a garden, pleasure-ground, or park, of such a kind as not to interrupt the view from within, and not to be seen till closely approached; consisting of a trench, the inner side of which is perpendicular and faced with stone, the outer sloping and turfed; a sunk fence.

1712 J. James tr. *Le Blond's Gardening* 28 The End of this Terrass is terminated by..an Ah, Ah, with a dry Ditch at the Foot of it. *Ibid.* 77 Thorough-Views, call'd *Ah, Ah*,..are Openings..to the very Level of the Walks, with a large and deep Ditch at the Foot.., which surprizes..and makes one cry, *Ah! Ah*! from whence it takes its Name. **1724** in Amherst *Gardening* (1895) 234 The walks are terminated by Ha-hah's, over which you see [etc.]. **1749** Lady Luxborough *Lett. to Shenstone* 4 June, The *Ha! Ha*! is digging. **1803** H. Repton *Landscape Gardening* 86 The sunk fence or ha! ha! in some places answers the purpose. **1852** R. S. Surtees *Sponge's Sp. Tour* liii. 300 [The hound] ran a black cart-colt, and made him leap the haw-haw. **1880** *Q. Rev.* Apr. 336 The constant use of Ha-has (or sunk-fences).

b. *transf.* and *fig.*

1773 Mason *Ep. to Sir W. Chambers*, Leap each ha-ha of truth and common sense. **1858** H. Miller *Rambles Geol.* Wks. (1869) 303 These ravines..are *ha-has* of Nature's digging.

c. *attrib.*, as ***ha-ha ditch, fence, wall***.

1769 *De Foe's Tour Gt. Brit.* I. 325 Throwing down the Walls of the Garden, and making, instead of them, Haw-haw Walls. **1774** T. Hutchinson *Diary* 17 Sept., A ha-ha fence at the bottom of the garden. **1849** *Ann. Reg.* 106 The Ha-ha ditch in Kensington Gardens.

haham (ˈhɑːhəm). Also **hakam**; *Yiddish* **chochem** (ˈxɔːxəm), **cacham, chacham, -em.** [ad. Heb. *ḥāḵām* wise, wise man.] One learned in Jewish law; a wise man, savant; *spec.* a Jewish rabbi among Sephardic Jews.

1676 L. Addison *Present State of Jews* (ed. 2) xxvi. 216 In the first rank march the Chachams or Priests. **1733** tr. *B. Picart's Ceremonies & Relig. Customs* I. 46 A Man who hath made the Oral Law his principal Study, he is looked upon by the Generality amongst them as a Doctor, and is therefore called Cacham, or Wise Man. **1892** I. Zangwill *Childr. Ghetto* II. xix. 103 The *Gemorah* says ve muz be vise, *chocham.* **1894** —— *King of Schnorrers* 106 The Haham himself, the Sage or Chief Rabbi of the [Sephardic] congregation. **1901** *Daily Chron.* 23 Nov. 3/2 The vice-presidents include...Mrs. Gaster, wife of the Haham—the spiritual head of the Spanish and Portuguese [Jewish] congregation. **1960** *Jewish Chron.* 8 Apr. 16/1 The Haham or such other person as may for the time being constitute the Ecclesiastical Authority of the Spanish and Portuguese Jews of Great Britain. **1967** D. T. Kauffman *Dict. Relig. Terms* 221/2 *Hakam*, wise one. Chief rabbi in sephardim communities, and among Palestinian Jews in talmudic times. **1968** L. Rosten *Joys of Yiddish* 63 A proud young *chachem* told his grandmother that he was going to become a doctor of philosophy. **1973** *Jewish Chron.* 18 May 8/3 The memorial service was organised by the Haham.

haher, var. of HAGHER *a. Obs.*, skilful.

hahnium (ˈhɑːnɪəm). *Chem.* [f. the name of Otto *Hahn* (1879–1968), German radio-chemist + -IUM.] An artificially produced radioactive element, atomic number 105. Symbol Ha.

1970 A. Ghiorso et al. in *Physical Rev. Let.* XXIV. 1503/1 In honor of the late Otto Hahn we respectfully suggest that this new element be given the name hahnium. **1971** *Nature* 26 Feb. 607/2 The present multi-detector shuttle apparatus is quite a complicated instrument..and its value as a research tool has been proved by the quality of the nuclear spectroscopic data obtained for..hahnium.

hai, obs. form of HAY.

haid, obs. Sc. f. *had*, *hid*.

Haida (ˈhaɪdə), *a.* and *sb.* Also **Haidah, Hydah**. [Native word meaning 'people'.] **A.** *adj.* Of or pertaining to a North American Indian people living on the Queen Charlotte Islands, British Columbia, and on Prince of Wales Island, Alaska. **B.** *sb.* **a.** A member of this people; also in collective sense. **b.** The language of this people.

1841 *Jrnl. R. Geogr. Soc.* XI. 219 The *Haidah* tribes of the Northern Family inhabit Queen Charlotte's Island. *Ibid.*, Since the sea-otter has been destroyed, the Haidahs have become poor. **1862** F. POOLE *Diary* 5 Aug. in *Queen Charlotte Islands* (1871) vi. 73 Two Hydah chiefs and four of their women. *Ibid.* 75 He reciprocated by initiating me into the mysteries of the Hydah tongue. **1869** *Mainland Guardian* (New Westminster, B.C.) 30 Oct. 3/2 We bought a large Hydah canoe for $50, and hired ten siwashes (nine Hydahs and one bog-will Indian), for $10 a month. **1890** J. G. FRAZER *Golden Bough* I. i. 26 When a Haida Indian wishes to obtain a fair wind, he..shoots a raven. **1914** W. H. RIVERS *Kinship & Soc. Organisation* ii. 54 The only people among whom it has been recorded are the Haidahs of Queen Charlotte Island. **1921** E. SAPIR *Lang.* iii. 56 Haida, the Indian language spoken in the Queen Charlotte Islands. **1959** E. TUNIS *Indians* 136/1 In the north the Tlingit and the Haida were related to the Dené. *Ibid.* 136/2 A Haida house. **1969** *Times* 22 Sept. 14/2 A Haida amulet from the Queen Charlotte Islands has a bilaterally symmetrical design.

haidingerite (ˈhaɪdɪŋəraɪt). *Min.* [Named after Von *Haidinger*, an Austrian mineralogist.]

1. A hydrated arsenate of calcium, occurring in minute white crystals.

1827 *Edin. Jrnl. Sc.* VI. 317 I propose to employ the name of Haidingerite to designate the species. **1868** DANA *Min.* (ed. 5) 552. **1875** PLATTNER *Anal. Blowpipe* (ed. Cookesley) 144 Haidingerite, pharmacolite, and picropharmacolite..in the matrass yield much water, especially the latter.

2. Formerly used as a synonym of BERTHIERITE.

1863–72 WATTS *Dict. Chem.* I. 581. **1868** DANA *Min.* 86.

haiduck, variant of HEYDUCK.

haie, obs. form of HAY.

haif, haiff, obs. Sc. forms of HAVE.

haifer, haige, obs. ff. HEIFER, HEDGE.

†**haik**[1], **heyke.** *Obs.* [Cf. EFris. *heike, heik', haike, hoike*: see HUKE.] A kind of cloak or upper garment; app. the same as the HUKE, q.v.

c **1375** *Sc. Leg. Saints, Egipciane* 280 Of þe twa haikis þat he had He tuk þe tane & bakvart kest. *c* **1440** *Promp. Parv.* 232/2 Heyke, garment (*K.* or hewke, *infra*; heyke, cloth; *S.* hayeste garment, or huke), *armelus.* **1488** *Act. Dom. Conc.* 132 (Jam.) Twa govnys, price iij *lb.*, a haik, price x *s.*, a pare of clokis, price x *s.* **1553** *Burgh Rec. Prestwick* (Maitl. Cl.) 51 Ane hayk and ane kyrtyll, price xl *s.* to þe behwf of þe barnis.

‖**haik**[2], **haick** (haik, haɪk). Also 8 **haeg, hayick,** 8–9 **haique, hyke.** [Arab. *hayk*, f. *hāk* to weave.] An oblong piece of cloth which Arabs wrap round the head and body, as an outer garment.

[**1613** PURCHAS *Pilgrimage* (1614) 633 Newes from Barbary..his Turban of course Callico, his Alheik or loose gowne of Lile Grogram.] **1713** S. OCKLEY *Acc. Barbary* 45 Over all this, the best..wear Haegs, or very fine white Blankets, about 6 yards long, and 2 broad. **1797** *Encycl. Brit.* s.v. *Morocco* 27 (Stanf.) The whole wardrobe of a country Moor in easy circumstances consists in a haique for winter, another for summer, [etc.]. **1801** SOUTHEY *Thalaba* IV. 10 *note*, One of these Hykes is usually six yards long and five or six feet broad, serving the Arab for a complete dress in the day. **1825** SCOTT *Talism.* xxvii, Wild forms with their persons covered with haicks. **1891** HALL CAINE *Scapegoat* I. 150 His four Mahommedan wives..were gazing furtively down from behind their haiks.

haik: see HAKE *sb.*[3], [5] and *v.*[1]

haikal (ˈhaɪkəl). [Coptic.] The central chapel of three forming the sanctuary of a Coptic church. Also *attrib.* in **haikal screen**, a screen, often elaborately carved or decorated, which separates the haikal from the body of the church.

1884 A. J. BUTLER *Anc. Coptic Churches* I. i. 28 The screen of the haikal, instead of aligning with that of the side chapels, projects out three or four feet into the choir. **1902** *Encycl. Brit.* XXVII. 238/1 The central division is called the haikal or sanctuary... Haikal screen and choir screen are often sumptuously carved and inlaid. **1935** D. ATTWATER *Catholic Eastern Churches* vi. 139 A church of the Coptic rite has a distinctive arrangement... Within the triple-domed sanctuary (*haikal*) are three altars... On the *haikal*-screen are a few pictures. **1961** O. MEINARDUS *Monks & Monasteries Egyptian Deserts* 302 Part of the haikal screen of the old church can still be seen.

‖**haiku** (ˈhaɪkuː). Also **haikai, hokku.** [Jap.] A form of Japanese verse, developed in the mid-16th century, usually consisting of 17 syllables and originally of jesting character; an English imitation of one.

The *hokku* was originally the opening hemistich of a linked series of *haiku* poems, but is now synonymous with *haiku* and *haikai*. An earlier meaning of *haikai*, an abbreviation of the phr. *haikai no renga* ('jesting linked-verse'), was a succession of *haiku* linked together to form one poem.

1899 W. G. ASTON *Hist. Jap. Lit.* iv. 289 In the sixteenth century a kind of poem known as Haikai, which consists of seventeen syllables only, made its appearance. **1899** *Trans. Asiatic Soc. Japan* XXVII. IV. p. xiv, The *hokku* must be an exceedingly compact bit of word and thought skill to be worth anything—as literature. **1902** *Ibid.* XXX. II. 243 The poets of Japan have produced thousands of these microscopic compositions... Their native name is *Hokku* (also *Haiku* and *Haikai*), which, in default of a better equivalent, I venture to translate by 'Epigram', using that term..as denoting any little piece of verse that expresses a delicate or ingenious thought. **1904** *Westm. Gaz.* 19 Apr. 10/1 The perfect haikai is a Lilliputian lyric of but three unrhymed lines of five, seven, and five syllables respectively—seventeen in all—in which is deftly caught a thought-flash or swift impression... An example..is the following: The west wind whispered And touched the eyelids of Spring: Her eyes, Primroses. **1957** C. BROOKE-ROSE *Lang. Love* 47 Her translations of *haiku* were elegant. **1969** *Radio Times* 15 May 9/1 A sequence of twenty-one sonnets and two haiku on the first American landing in Japan in the mid-nineteenth century.

hail (heɪl), *sb.*[1] Forms: α. 1 **haʒol, -al, -el,** 3 **haȝel, hawel, haul,** 4 **haghil,** 4–5 **hawle, haule.** β. 1 **hæʒl, hæʒel, heʒel,** 3– **hail,** (3 **ail**), 4–6 **hayl(e,** 4–7 **haile,** 5 **hayll(e, hayel.** γ. 7–9 (*dial.*) **haggle.** [Com. Teut.: OE. *haʒol* (*-al, -el*), and *hæʒl* (*hæʒel*):—WGer. **hagal*, **hagl*: cf. OFris. *heyl* (:—*hegl*), MDu. *haghel*, Du. *hagel*, OHG. *hagal*, MHG. and Ger. *hagel*, all masc., ON. *hagl* neut. (Sw., Da. *hagel*):—OTeut. **hag(a)lo-*; perh. cognate with Gr. κɑχλ- in κάχληξ pebble; cf. the notion in *hailstone*. The two OE. types *haʒol* and *hæʒl*, gave the respective ME. types *hawel, hawl*, and *hæil, hayl, hail*, of which the former was southern and came down to the 15th c. Beside these a third type *haggle* directly form Norse, survives in Yorkshire dialect.]

1. Ice or frozen vapour falling in pellets or masses in a shower from the atmosphere. (In spring and summer most frequently occurring in connexion with a thunderstorm.)

α. *a* **1000** *Boeth. Metr.* xxix. 127 Ren æfter þæm, swylce haʒal and snaw. *c* **1000** ÆLFRIC *Hom.* II. 192 Swa micel ðunor and haʒol becom on ðam leodscipe. *c* **1205** LAY. 11975 Haȝel & ræin þer aræs. *Ibid.* 20504 Swa hahȝel [*c* **1275** þe hawel] deð from wolcne. *a* **1300** *Fragm. Pop. Sc.* (Wright) 216 Hi al i-frore ben, Thanne hit is hawel [*v.r.* hawl] pur. *a* **1340** HAMPOLE *Psalter* xvii. 14 Haghil and coles of fire. **1382** WYCLIF *Exod.* ix. 29 Thundres shulen ceese, and hawle [**1388** hail] shal not be. **1422** tr. *Secreta Secret., Priv. Priv.* (E.E.T.S.) 198 God keste ham dovne wyth grete Stonys of hawle..And moche Pepill more were dede by the haule, than by Swerde.

β. *c* **825** *Vesp. Psalter* xvii[i]. 13 Heʒel & colu fyres. *a* **1000** *Phœnix* 60 þær ne hæʒl ne hrim hreosað to foldan. *a* **1000** *Cædmon's Gen.* 808 (Gr.) Cymeþ hæʒles scur. *c* **1250** *Gen. & Ex.* 3046 Ðhunder, and hail, and leuenes fir. *Ibid.* 3183 Oc ðe ail haued so wide spiled, ðat his graue is ðorvnder hiled. **1398** TREVISA *Barth. De. P.R.* VI. xxi. (1495) 210 Water molten of snowe and of hayel is erthly. **1559** W. CUNNINGHAM *Cosmogr. Glasse* 42 Then in this middle region I suppose all Haile, Snow, and suche like is ingendrid. **1638** WILKINS *New World* I. (1684) 130 Thinking (as the Proverb is) that he may use Hail, when he hath no Thunder. **1727–46** THOMSON *Summer* 1144 Down comes a deluge of sonorous hail. **1868** RUSKIN *Pol. Econ. Art* ii. 104 I have seen the hail fall in Italy till the forest branches stood stripped and bare.

γ. [see HAILSTONE.]

2. With *a* and *pl.* A shower or storm of hail; now usually ***hail-storm, hail-shower.***

c **888** K. ÆLFRED *Boeth.* xxxix. §13 Hæʒlas and snawas and se oft ræda ren leccaþ ða eorþan on wintra. *a* **1300** *Cursor M.* 6019 A thonor wit an haile. **1382** WYCLIF *Wisd.* xvi. 16 With newe watris, and hailis, and reynes, they suffreden persecucioun. *c* **1400** *Apol. Loll.* 93 In hailes or tempestis. **1601** SHAKS. *All's Well* V. iii. 33, I am not a day of season, For thou maist see a sunshine, and a haile In me at once. **1788** T. JEFFERSON *Writ.* (1859) II. 458 A very considerable portion of this country has been desolated by a hail.

†**b.** A pellet of hail, a hailstone. *Obs.*

a **1625** FLETCHER *Mad Lover* IV. ii, My head heavy With hails and frosty icicles. **1697** *Phil. Trans.* XIX. 580 Some of the Hail were Eight Inches about.

3. *transf.* and *fig.* A storm, shower, or volley of something falling like hail, esp. of shot.

1590 SHAKS. *Mids. N.* I. i. 244. **1597** —— *Lover's Compl.* 310 That not a heart which in his level came Could 'scape the hail of his all-hurting aim. **1667** MILTON *P.L.* VI. 589 Chaind Thunderbolts and Hail of Iron Globes. **1728** POPE *Dunc.* III. 262 'Mid snows of paper, and fierce hail of pease. **1893** FORBES-MITCHELL *Remin. Gt. Mutiny* 60 A perfect hail of round-shot assailed us.

4. *attrib.* and *Comb.*, as ***hail-shower; hail-like, -stricken*** adjs. Also HAIL-SHOT, -STONE, -STORM.

a **1000** *Andreas* 1259 (Gr.) Veder coledon heardum hæʒelscurum. **1399** LANGL. *Rich. Redeles* I. 26 That neuere had harnesse, ne hayle schouris. **1610** HOLLAND *Camden's Brit.* I. 388 With an haile-like storme of stones Kild him. **1845** DARWIN *Voy. Nat.* vi. (1873) 116 Having finished our dinner of hail-stricken meat.

†**hail**, *sb.*[2] Chiefly *north. Obs.* Forms: 3–4 **hayl,** 3–6 **hail,** 4–5 **haylle,** 4–6 **haile, hayle,** 5 **haille, heylle,** 5–6 **heyle.** [a. ON. *heill* health, prosperity, good luck, cognate with OE. *hǽl*: see HEAL *sb.*]

1. Health, safety, welfare. In northern ME. taking the place of the native Eng. *hele*, HEAL.

a **1400–50** *Alexander* 3272 (Dubl.) When on athyll was so wele in happe and in heyle. *c* **1460** *Towneley Myst.* (Surtees) 73 I am Lord and lech of heyle. *c* **1470** HENRY *Wallace* v. 547 To se his heyle his comfort was the mor. **1549** *Compl. Scot.* vi. 45 The maist part of vs hes gude hail in our body.

b. ***to drink*** (a person's) ***hail***: a modification of the phrase DRINK-HAIL, q.v.

1297 R. GLOUC. (1724) 118 He..custe hire..and glad dronk hire hail.

2. With defining words: ***evil, ill, wroth hail,*** bad luck, misfortune; often used adverbially, with the adj. in dative fem. or some representative thereof: to (one's) hurt, unfortunately, disastrously. Cf. HEAL *sb.*, HALE *sb.*[1] in similar use.

a **1300** *Cursor M.* 6583 Ful iuel hail [*v.r.* ille hayl] brak yee þe dai. *Ibid.* 7320 Ful ilhail [*v.r.* ill a hayle] sal þai it se. *Ibid.* 7335 þis saul haue þai mad þair king..Ful wreþerhail [*v. rr.* wraþer haile, wroþerhele] to þair behoue. *c* **1330** R. BRUNNE *Chron. Wace* (Rolls) 2590 Morgan..wroughte hym self to wroþer haylle. *c* **1386** CHAUCER *Reeve's T.* 169 Ilhayl, by god Aleyn thou is a fonne. *c* **1450** *St. Cuthbert* (Surtees) 5880 þir robbours wand vp þair sayle To þe hey se with euel hayle. *c* **1460** *Towneley Myst.* (Surtees) 61 Wyth yl a haylle! *Ibid.* 89 Ha, ha, goder-haylle!..this is good for the frost. ? *c* **1475** *Sqr. lowe Degre* 299 Alas! it tourned to wroth-hir-heyle. *a* **1529** SKELTON *Elynour Rummyng* 618 God gyve it yll hayle!

hail, *sb.*[3] [A later subst. use of HAIL *int.*, and n. of action f. HAIL *v.*[2]]

1. An exclamation of 'hail!'; a (respectful) greeting or salutation.

1500–20 DUNBAR *Poems* xxxiii. 1 As ȝung Aurora, with cristall haile. *a* **1667** COWLEY *On Virgin* Wks. 1711 III. 53 An Hail to all, let us An Hail return. **1667** MILTON *P.L.* V. 385 The Angel Haile Bestow'd, the holy salutation us'd Long after to blest Marie, second Eve. **1870** *Daily News* 30 Dec., His hail was pleasant, and we bade him 'Good-bye and good luck'.

2. The act of hailing some one; a shout of welcome; a shout or call to attract attention.

1811 WORDSW. *Ep. to Sir G. H. Beaumont* 207 Whence the blithe hail? behold a Peasant stand On high, a kerchief waving in her hand! **1833** HT. MARTINEAU *Vanderput & S.* i. 1 The hail of the pilots or the quay-keepers. **1883** STEVENSON *Treas. Isl.* III. xiv, I could hear hails coming and going between the old buccaneer and his comrades.

b. Phr. ***within hail***: within call, near enough to be hailed; so ***out of hail***, beyond call. Originally nautical phrases.

1697 DAMPIER *Voy.* I. 191 When we came within hale, we found that they were English. **1748** *Anson's Voy.* II. iv. 163 The vessel came within hail of us. **1825** SCOTT *Fam. Lett.* 16 May (1894) II. 267 Your late remove has brought you a good deal more within hail, as the sailors say. **1836** W. IRVING *Astoria* I. 86 Warning them..not to wander away nor be out of hail.

3. *attrib.*, as ***hail-peal***, a peal of salutation or call.

1568 *Hist. Jacob & Esau* I. i. in Hazl. *Dodsley* II. 192 To give my neighbors louts an hail-peal in a morn.

hail, *sb.*[4] *Sc.* [f. HAIL *v.*[3]]

1. *orig.* (At hand-ball, etc.) The act of saluting the dool or goal with the exclamation 'hail!', when it is hit by the ball; hence, the act of hailing or driving the ball to the dool or goal; a 'goal' or victory in one game or round. In phrases, ***to give the hail, to win a hail*** or ***so many hails.***

a **1673** WEDDERBURN *Voc.* 37 (Jam.) *Transmittere metam pila*, to give the hail. *Hic primus est transmissus*, this is the first hail. **1804** TARRAS *Poems* 66 (Jam.) The hails is wun. **1861** J. F. CAMPBELL *Tales W. Highl.* (1892) III. 10 They went to play shinny and Jain won three hales.

2. *transf.* Each of the two goals at hand-ball, football, shinty, and the like.

1843 HARDY in *Proc. Berw. Nat. Club* II. No. 11. 58 The hails, or boundaries of the game, were the..fishing hamlet of Headchesters as one terminus, and the conical height of Hoggeslaw..as the other. **1880** *Boys' Own Book* 130 These posts are the hail or goal.

hail, *sb.*[5], dial. var. of AIL *sb.*[2], the awn of barley.

1880 JEFFERIES *Gt. Estate* 8 The black knots on the delicate barley straw were beginning to be topped with the hail..the hail is the beard of the barley.

†**hail**, *a. Obs.* Forms: 3 **hæil,** 3–4 **heil,** 3–8 **hail,** 3–5 **heyl(e,** 4–7 **haile, hayl(e,** 5 **hayll(e.** [a. ON. *heill* hale, sound, whole = OE. *hál*:—OTeut. **hailo-, hailā-*: see HALE and WHOLE. A ME. equivalent of the northern *hale* and the midl. and southern *hôl, whole*.]

1. Free from injury, infirmity, or disease; sound, unhurt, safe; healthy, robust; = HALE, WHOLE.

c **1205** LAY. 12528 Wunieð her hal and hæil. *c* **1220** *Bestiary* 366 Al heil and sund. *a* **1300** *Cursor M.* 3829–30 He es bath hail and fere, Ya hail and sound, wit-outen were. *c* **1330** *Amis & Amil.* 2232 Y might aschape out of mi wo, Al hayl and hole to be. *c* **1440** *Promp. Parv.* 233/1 Heyl fro sekenesse, *sanus.* **1573** TUSSER *Husb.* xv. (1878) 33 Let timber be haile, least profit doe quaile. **1673** A. WALKER *Leez Lachrymans* 3 The hayl Constitution, the graceful Fashion..of his Youth. **1725** BRADLEY *Fam. Dict.* s.v. *Jaundice*, The Water of a Young Child that's hail.

b. *fig.* Sound, wholesome; pure, uncorrupted.

13.. *K. Alis.* 7036 [He] tok counsaile, That him n'as neither god ne haile. *c* **1460** *Battle of Otterbourne* 92 in *Percy's Reliq.*, He durste not loke on my bred banner, For all Ynglonde so haylle. **1674** N. FAIRFAX *Bulk & Selv.* To Rdr., To shew that a Book..might be understandingly and roundly written, in hail and clear English.

2. In phr. ***hail be thou***, etc. used as a salutation expressing well-wishing or reverence. Hence (in part) HAIL *int.*, q.v.

c **1205** LAY. 14309 Lauerd king, wæs hæil! *Ibid.* 29030 Hail seo þu Gurgmund..hail þine drihtliche men. *a* **1300** *Sat. People Kildare* vi. in *E.E.P.* (1862) 153 Hail be ȝe freris wiþ þe white copis. *c* **1380** WYCLIF *Wks.* (1880) 204 Heil be þou, marie, ful of grace. **1496** *Dives & Paup.* (W. de W.) I. iv. 36/1 Hayle be thou our kynge.

3. Whole, entire. **all hail**: cf. ALL-WHOLE.
a1300 *Cursor M.* 22306 Turn þam till his trouth al hail. a1300 *Floriz & Bl.* 56 'Dame', he sede, 'þis hail is þin, þat win and þat gold eke.'

hail (heɪl), *v.*¹ Forms: α. 1 haȝalian, 3 hauli, 4 haweli. β. 4–7 hayle, 7 haile, 6– hail. γ. 7–9 (*dial.*) haggle. [OE. *haȝalian*:—OTeut. **hag(a)-lôjan*: in ON. *hagla*, MHG. *haglen*, *hagelen*, Ger. *hageln*, Du. *hagelen*, from the sb. The north. dial. *haggle* is from ON. See HAIL *sb.*¹]

1. *intr.* **a.** Impersonally: *it hails* = hail falls.
α. c893 K. ÆLFRED *Oros.* III. v. §1 On sumre tide hit haȝalade stanum ofer ealle Romane. c1290 *S. Eng. Leg.* I. 198/37 Hit bi-gan to þondri and hauli. c1300 *St. Brandan* 32 Hit began to haweli faste.
β. c1425 *Voc.* in Wr.-Wülcker 665/6 *Grandinat*, hayles. 1483 *Cath. Angl.* 169/2 To Hayle, *grandinare*. 1530 PALSGR. 130 *Il grésle*, it hayleth. 1611 BIBLE *Isa.* xxxii. 19 When it shall haile, comming downe on the forest. 1631 WIDDOWES *Nat. Philos.* 19 It hayleth most in Autumne and in the Spring. 1686 GOAD *Celest. Bodies* II. viii. 263 It Hails most in the Wine-Countries. *Mod.* Does it still hail?
γ. 1674 RAY *N.C. Words* 23 It Haggles: It hails. *Var. Dial.* 1855 ROBINSON *Whitby Gloss.* s.v., 'It both haggl'd and snow'd'. 1892 M. C. F. MORRIS *Yorksh. Folk-t.* 319 'It haggled heavy t'last neet'.

b. With subject: (*a*) To pour or send down hail.
c1398 CHAUCER *Fortune* 62 The welkne hath myht to shyne, reyne, or hayle. 1535 COVERDALE *Exod.* ix. 23 The Lorde hayled and rayned vpon the londe of Egipte.
(*b*) To fall as hail.
1859 [see *vbl. sb.* below]. 1879 C. F. HOFFMAN *Monterey* in *Poems of Places, Br. America* 143 Now here, now there, the shot it hailed In deadly drifts of fiery spray.

2. *trans.* To pour down as hail; to throw or send down in a shower with considerable force like hail in a storm.
1570 DEE *Math. Pref.* 35 Such huge Stones..did he with his engynes hayle among them. 1590 SHAKS. *Mids. N.* I. i. 243 He hail'd downe oathes that he was onely mine. 1607 —— *Ant. & Cl.* II. v. 45 Ile set thee in a shower of Gold, and haile Rich Pearles vpon thee. 1847 TENNYSON *Princ.* Prol. 155 Walter hail'd a score of names upon her. 1886 STEVENSON *Dr. Jekyll* III. (ed. 2) 37 Hailing down a storm of blows.

Hence **'hailing** *vbl. sb.* (in first quot. *concr.*).
1538 BALE *Thre Lawes* 1841 Lyghtenynges and haylynges destroyed their corne. 1859 RUSKIN *Two Paths* §12 The hailing of the shot and the shriek of battle.

hail (heɪl), *v.*² Forms: 3–6 haile, hayle, (3 haille, *Orm.* heȝȝlenn), 4–5 heile, 5 heyle, 7–8 hale, 7– hail. [An early deriv. of HAIL *sb.*² and *interj.* which has superseded HAILSE *v.*]

1. *trans.* To salute with 'hail!'; to salute, greet; to receive with expressions of gladness, to welcome.
c1200 ORMIN 2814 He wollde swa Allmahhtiȝ Drihhtin heȝȝlenn. c1205 LAY. 14968 Þus hailede him on þe swicfulle wimman; Lauerd king, wæshail. 1362 LANGL. *P. Pl.* A. IX. 10 Ich heilede hem hendeli. c1440 *Promp. Parv.* 233/1 Heylyn, or gretyn, *saluto*. 1509 HAWES *Past. Pleas.* XX. i, They hayled, Wyth a greate peale of gunnes, at theyr departyng, The marvaylous toure of famous cunnynge. 1725 C. PITT *Vida's Art of Poetry* I. (R.), The ravish'd crowds shall hail their passing lord. 1804 [see HAIL *int.*]. 1849 MACAULAY *Hist. Eng.* I. ii. 183 In Scotland the restoration of the Stuarts had been hailed with delight.

b. With complement (with or without *as*).
1671 MILTON *Samson* 354 Such a Son as all Men hail'd me happy. 1738 GLOVER *Leonidas* I. 396 Extol and hail him as their guardian god. 1807 G. CHALMERS *Caledonia* I. III. vii. 416 The second witch hailed him thane of Cawdor. 1871 R. ELLIS *Catullus* iii. 6 A bird that ever hail'd her Lady mistress.

†**2.** *intr.* To address a salutation *to*; to drink a health to. *Obs. rare.*
c1275 LAY. 18573 For þe king him louede ase his lif, and haylede to his wif.

3. To call or shout to (a ship, a person, etc.) from a distance, in order to attract attention. (Originally and chiefly in nautical use.)
1563 GRESHAM in Burgon *Life* (1839) II. 42 The instant we hadd one hayled another, there rose up soche a great storme. 1624 CAPT. SMITH *Virginia* IV. 128 We anchored.. and in friendly manner sent to hale them. 1692 *Capt. Smith's Seaman's Gram.* I. xvi. 78 *To hail a Ship*..is done after this manner, *Hôa the Ship!* or only *Hôa!* To which they answer *Hâe*. Also to salute another Ship with Trumpets or the like, is called *Hailing*. 1726 G. ROBERTS *Four Years Voy.* 343 Two of them came down to the Sea Side and haled us; I answered, and told them who I was. 1749 FIELDING *Tom Jones* VIII. xii, I heard a voice on a sudden haling me with great familiarity by my Christian name. 1857 LONGF. *Daybreak* 3 It hailed the ships, and cried, 'Sail on'. 1891 *Spectator* 22 Aug., The ignominy of being refused by cabs and omnibuses that he has hailed himself.

4. *intr.* or *absol.* To call out in order to attract attention. (Formerly with *to*; now only *absol.*)
to hail aloft, 'to call to men in the tops and at the mast-head to look out' (Smyth *Sailor's Word-bk.*); *to hail for a trip* (*U.S. colloq.*), 'to state the quantity of the catch during a fishing voyage' (*Cent. Dict.*).
1582 N. LICHEFIELD tr. *Castanheda's Conq. E. Ind.* ii. 7 He ..hasted to the water side, and hailed to our ships. 1633 P. FLETCHER *Purple Isl.* in Farr *S.P. Jas. I* (1848) 190 Unto her sonne she hails. 1798 MILLAR in Nicolas *Disp. Nelson* (1846) VII. p. clv, Captain Berry hailed as we passed. 1888 B. W. RICHARDSON *Son of a Star* I. xiv. 220 A troop of slaves gorgeously dressed, and hailing and shouting as they turned their faces to the rider.

b. *to hail from* (a place): said of a vessel in reference to the port from which she has sailed; hence *transf.* of a person, to come from.
1841 CATLIN *N. Amer. Ind.* (1844) I. i. 2 The country from which he hails. 1873 BLACK *Pr. Thule* xxiv. 397 Ships and sailors hailing from these distant shores. 1888 M. ROBERTSON *Lombard St. Myst.* x, Most of the pupils hailed from France.

hail (heɪl), *v.*³ *Sc.* Also 8 hale. [app. a special use of HAIL *v.*², originating with the phrase *to hail the dool*, i.e. to greet or salute the goal with the exclamation *hail!* when striking it with the ball.] In phrase *to hail the dool*, to reach or strike the goal, to win the goal; *to hail the ball*, to throw or drive the ball to the goal, to win the goal.
a1550 *Christis Kirke Gr.* xxii, Fresch men cam in and hail'd the dulis. 1783 TYTLER *Poet. Rem. Jas. I*, 187 (Jam. s.v. *Dule*) When the [foot]ball touches the goal or mark, the winner calls out, Hail! or it has hail'd the dulis. 1802 SIBBALD *Chron. Scot. Poet.* II. 370 *note* (Jam. s.v. *Dule*) In the game of golf..when the ball reached the mark, the winner, to announce his victory, called, Hail dule! a1809 *Skinner's Misc. Coll. Poet.* 133 (Jam.) The ba'-spell's won, And we the ba' hae hail'd.

hail (heɪl), *int.* Forms: see HAIL *sb.*² and *a.* [An elliptical or interjectional use of HAIL *a.*, the imperative *be*, or some equivalent, as in HAIL *a.* 2, having been originally present: cf. ON. *heill*, and OE. *hál* similarly used.] An exclamation of greeting or salutation; now *poetic* and *rhetorical*, and usually implying respectful or reverential salutation; = L. *ave*, *salve*. **a.** *absol.* with vocative.
c1200 *Vices & Virtues* (1888) 53 'Hail ðu, Marie', he seide. c1275 *Passion our Lord* 191 in *O.E. Misc.* 42 Heyl, he seyde, mayster, to ihesuc þat hi souhte. a1300 *Sat. People Kildare* v. in *E.E.P.* (1862) 153 Hail seint franceis wiþ þi mani foulis. 1382 WYCLIF *Mark* xv. 18 Hail, thou kyng of Iewis. c1440 *Promp. Parv.* 233/1 Heyl, sede for gretynge, *ave, salve*. 1588 SHAKS. *Tit. A.* I. i. 69 Haile Rome: Victorious in thy Mourning Weedes. 1667 MILTON *P.L.* III. 1 Hail holy Light, ofspring of Heav'n first-born. 1738 GLOVER *Leonidas* II. 204 Hail! glorious chief. 1804 J. GRAHAME *Sabbath* 40 Hail, Sabbath! thee I hail, the poor man's day.

b. with *to* [cf. HAIL *sb.*², health, well-being].
1602 SHAKS. *Ham.* I. ii. 160 Haile to your Lordship. 1810 SCOTT *Lady of L.* II. xix, Hail to the chief who in triumph advances! 1820 SHELLEY *To a Skylark* 1 Hail to thee, blithe spirit! 1855 TENNYSON *Maud* III. vi. 42 Hail once more to the banner of battle unroll'd!

hail, Sc. spelling of HALE *a.*; obs. f. HALE *v.*

haile, obs. form of HALE, HEAL.

hailelie, haililie, Sc. spelling of HALELY, *Obs.*

'hailer. [f. HAIL *v.*² + -ER¹.] One who hails, or calls to attract attention.
1880 T. HARDY *Wessex T., Fellow-Townsmen* 130 'Hullo Downe—is that you?' said the driver..The other turned a plump, cheery..face over his shoulder towards the hailer. 1891 *Daily News* 29 Dec. 5/6 Let him hail a 'bus for a penny ride in Fleet-street..the chances are that the hailer will get nothing but a grin.

Haileybury ('heɪlɪbərɪ). The name of a school (Haileybury College) in Hertfordshire, orig. owned by the East India Company, used to designate the system of providing civil servants, or the civil servants themselves, for service in India.
1864 in F. C. Danvers et al. *Mem. Old Haileybury Coll.* (1894) 95, I trust the new men will be found to furnish persons qualified to sustain the character of the Service ..[and] also worthily to fill those high posts of trust..which we now see so happily filled by Haileybury civilians of the old school. 1902 *Encycl. Brit.* XXIX. 451/2 Towards the latter years of the 19th century the last of the old Haileybury civilians, who entered the service as nominees of the East India Company's directors under the system abolished in 1857, were leaving India. 1931 L. S. S. O'MALLEY *Ind. Civil Service* 241 A system of pass examinations, such as the Haileybury entrance examination. 1931 *Times Lit. Suppl.* 18 June 474/3 The modern Civilian is the descendant of the Haileybury students of the early nineteenth century. Whatever the merits or demerits of the Haileybury system, it at least 'led to a tradition of service handed down from generation to generation'.

hail-fellow, *a.* (*adv.*), *sb.* [The familiar greeting or accost 'Hail, fellow!' (now *obs.* or *arch.*), used as a descriptive expression, in various grammatical constructions.
1589 NASHE *Ded. to Greene's Menaphon* (Arb.) 16 Their best lovers would bee much discontented, with the collation of contraries, if I should write over al their heads, Haile fellow well met.]

A. *adj.* On such terms, or using such freedom with another, as to accost him with 'hail, fellow!'; on a most intimate footing; over familiar or unduly intimate.
1580 LYLY *Euphues* (Arb.) 371 Where diddest thou learne that..being suffered to be familiar thou shouldest waxe haile fellowe? 1688 LD. DELAMER *Wks.* (1694) 26 Let not your Servants be over-familiar or haile fellow with you. 1824 SCOTT *Redgauntlet* ch. xv, All's hail-fellow, here. 1886 T. HARDY *Mayor Casterbr.* II. ii. 20 He crossed the room to her..with something of a hail-fellow bearing.

b. So the fuller phrase *hail fellow well met*.
1581 PETTIE *Guazzo's Civ. Conv.* III. (1586) 171 The maister ..being as you say haile fellow well met with his servant. 1586 J. HOOKER *Girald. Irel.* in *Holinshed* II. 105/2 He..placed himselfe..hard at the earle of Ormond his elbow, as though he were haile fellow well met. 1642 ROGERS *Naaman* 463 Gentlemen will be haile fellow well met with Jesters. 1888 RIDER HAGGARD *Col. Quaritch* I. i. 4 He was popular..though not in any hail-fellow-well-met kind of way. 1888 *Graphic* Summer No. 12/3 His hail-good-fellow-well-met shake of the hand.

B. *adv.* On most intimate terms.
1670 EACHARD *Cont. Clergy* 74 The multitude did not go hail fellow well met with Him. 1771 SMOLLETT *Humph. Cl.* I. 26 Apr. Let. i, You see the highest quality and the lowest trades-folk jostling each other, without ceremony, hail-fellow well met. 1847 L. HUNT *Men, Women, & B.* (1876) 91 Palavering rascals, who come, hail-fellow-well-met.

†**C.** *sb. Obs.*
1. An intimate or familiar associate.
1650 R. STAPYLTON *Strada's Low C. Warres* II. 36 It brings men, now hail-fellows with God.
2. The state or footing of intimate friends.
1684 J. GOODMAN *Winter-Evening Confer.* 46 The Master and Servant are at *Hail Fellow*. a1687 COTTON *Poet. Wks.* (1765) 107 This Youth hail Fellow with me made.

hailing ('heɪlɪŋ), *vbl. sb.* [f. HAIL *v.*² + -ING¹.] The action of the verb HAIL²; greeting, salutation; calling out to attract attention.
c1205 LAY. 14442 He com to þan kinge, mid are hailinge. c1380 WYCLIF *Sel. Wks.* III. 351 Heiling..haþ noo vertue among þes freris: for þei saluten ofte fendis. 1548 UDALL *Erasm. Par. Luke* xx. 163 The vanishyng smoke of haillynges and gretinges. 1699 DAMPIER *Voy.* II. i. 157 Ready to fire on us, if we had gone abroad without haling. 1724 R. FALCONER *Voy.* (1769) 13 The other Ship came up to us, and, without hailing, pour'd a Broad-side into the Pyrate.

b. *attrib.*, as *hailing-distance*; **hailing-bough**, one hung up in a house to 'hail' May morning.
1821 CLARE *Vill. Minstr.* I. 11 And dear to him the rural sports of May, When each cot-threshold mounts its hailing bough. 1840 R. H. DANA *Bef. Mast* ii. 4 They passed to leeward of us, and out of hailing distance.

haill, Sc. var. HALE *a.*, or WHOLE.

haill(e, obs. f. HAIL *sb.*² and *v.*², HALE *sb.*⁴

haillely, haillie, etc., Sc. var. HALELY, *Obs.*

Hail Mary, *phr.* and *sb.*
1. The angelic salutation (cf. Luke i. 58) = L. *Ave Maria*.
a1300 *Cursor M.* 10837 'Hail maria', said he, 'ful o grace.' 1340 *Ayenb.* 262 Hayl Marie of þonke uol, lhord by mid þe. 1552 ABP. HAMILTON *Catech.* (1884) 273 Hail Marie ful of grace, our lord is with the.
2. As a devotional recitation = AVE MARY.
c1380 WYCLIF *Sel. Wks.* III. 111 First men seien, Heil, Marie. 1591 *Troub. Raigne K. John* (1611) 50 With fasting and praying, And Haile Marie saying. 1860 FABER *Hymn, Flowers for the Altar* vi, By the picture Lucy loves Hail-Maries will we say. 1881 G. W. CABLE *Mme. Delphine* vi. 32, I am just going to say Hail Marys all the time.

†**hail-mate**, *a. Obs.* = HAIL-FELLOW.
1577 HANMER *Anc. Eccl. Hist.* (1619) 164 He who was haile-mate with the Emperour.

hailscart: see HALESKARTH.

†**hailse**, *v. Obs.* Forms: 4–5 hails, (4 heilse, haylce, haylis), 4–6 hailse, hayls(e (6 helse). [a. ON. *heilsa* to greet, to say hail (*to* a person): cf. HALSE *v.*] *trans.* To greet, salute.
a1300 *Cursor M.* 5046 (Cott.) Þai hailsed him, kneland biforn. c1340 *Ibid.* 7396 (Trin.) Wiþ chere ful swete he heilsed hendely þat prophete. 1377 LANGL. *P. Pl.* B. VII. 160 The mone and the sonne And þe elleuenes sterres, hailsed hym alle. a1400 *Sir Perc.* 404 Do thi hode off, I highte, And haylse hym in hy! 1530 PALSGR. 577/1, I haylse or greete, *je salue*.. Haylse yonder gentylman. 1551 ROBINSON tr. *More's Utop.* I. (1895) 29 When we hadde haylsede thone thother. 1577–87 HOLINSHED *Chron.* III. 1039/1 The Almans or lanceknights..getting neere to the enimies, hailsed them with their harquebut shot. 1585 JAMES I *Ess. Poesie* (Arb.) 73 Fyrie Titan..by his rysing in the Azure skyes, Did dewlie helse all thame on earth do dwell.

Hence †**'hailsing** *vbl. sb.*, greeting, salutation.
a1300 *Cursor M.* 10848 Sco hir vmbi-thoght Quat was þis hailsing he hir broght. c1400 *Melayne* 677 There was none oþer haylsynge Bot stowte wordes and grym. 1596 NASHE *Saffron Walden* N iv b, No wether-cocke..no ewe tree, that he would overslip without haylsing after the same methode.

†**'hail-shot.** *Obs.* [f. HAIL *sb.*¹ + SHOT *sb.*]
1. Small shot which scatters like hail when fired: used in distinction from a ball or bullet.
1485 *Naval Accts. Hen. VII* (1896) 69 Hayle shotte xl. 1555 EDEN *Decades* 114 Owre men were enforced to shute of their byggest pieces of ordinaunce with hayleshotte. 1686 *Lond. Gaz.* No. 2120/8 The discharge of a Pistol loaden with Hail-shot. 1708 MOTTEUX *Rabelais* IV. lxii. (1737) 253 Little Pellets like Hail-shot. 1830 SCOTT *Devorgoil* II. ii, Every hint Is lost on him, as hail-shot on the cormorant.
fig. a1656 HALES *Gold. Rem.* (1688) 193 He shoots his Hail-shot, with his Hail-stones from Heaven. 1680 H. MORE *Apocal. Apoc.* 318 All this hailshot flyes quite over my head.
2. The discharge of such shot. Also *fig.*
1568 GRAFTON *Chron.* II. 1364 There came such thicke Hayleshot of Artillery out of the Towne. 1696 TRYON *Misc.* i. 21 To do them good, I shall venter the Hail-shot of their Tongues.

3. *attrib.*, as ***hail-shot drop.***
1598 MARSTON *Pygmal.* iv. 151 And weepe for anger that the earth was dry..that all the haile-shot drops Could neuer peirce the christiall water tops.

hailstone ('heɪlstəʊn). [f. HAIL *sb.*[1] + STONE *sb.* OE. *hagolstán*, ON. *haglsteinn*, MHG. *hagelstein*, MLG. *hagelstên*, Du. *hagelsteen*, Yorksh. dial. *haggle-steean.*] A pellet of hail.
c **1000** ÆLFRIC *Hom.* I. 52 Orsorh betwux ðam greatum hagolstanum. **13..** *Coer de L.* 2190 The bowmen..shot quarelles and eke stone, As thick as the hail-stone. **1387** TREVISA *Higden* (Rolls) IV. 69 þere fel so grete reyn i-medled wiþ hailstones [*v.r.* hawelstones]. **1563** W. FULKE *Meteors* iv. (1640) 54 b, When the hayle-stones are square, or three-cornerd, the hayle was generated neere the earth. **1646** J. HALL *Poems* I Pamphlets thus like hailstons fly About mine eares. **1774** GOLDSM. *Nat. Hist.* (1776) I. 375 At Hertfordshire, in the year 1697..The hail-stones..being measured, were found to be many of them fourteen inches round. **1860** TYNDALL *Glac.* I. iii. 31 Each hailstone being a frozen cone with a rounded end. **1892** M. C. F. MORRIS *Yorksh. Folk-t.* 319 In the East Riding..hailstones are in some places called 'haggle-steeans'.

'hailstorm, hail-storm. [f. HAIL *sb.*[1] + STORM *sb.*] A violent fall or storm of hail.
1697 *Phil. Trans.* XIX. 577 A Letter..giving Account of a great Hail-storm [in Herts]. **1753** CHAMBERS *Cycl. Supp.* s.v. *Hail*, The mischiefs that violent hail-storms are able to do, is scarce to be conceived. **1813** T. FORSTER *Atmosph. Phænom.* (1815) 252 Hard hailstorms are generally accompanied with thunder and lightning.
fig. **1865** SEELEY *Ecce Homo* v. (ed. 8) 46 Christ bore with undisturbed patience a perpetual hailstorm of calumny.

hailsum, obs. Sc. var. HALESOME.

haily ('heɪlɪ), *a.* [f. HAIL *sb.*[1] + -Y[1].] Consisting of or characterized by hail or hailstorms.
1552 HULOET, Haylye, or full of hayle, *grandinosus.* **1561** DAUS tr. *Bullinger on Apoc.* (1573) 111 Of these is compounded an haylie doctrine, hurtfull doubtles and pestilent. **1611** COTGR., *Gresleux*, haylie. **1703** POPE *Thebais* 495 A rattling tempest..Which the cold north congeals to haily show'rs. **1737** BYROM *Jrnl. & Lit. Rem.* (1856) II. I. 87 A very rainy, snowy, haily, stormy, blustering ride.

haim, var. of HAME; Sc. form of *hame*, HOME.

haimhald, obs. f. HAMALD.

†**hain**, *sb. Obs.* [ME. from Norse. Cf. OSw. *hæghn*, Sw. *hägn* enclosure, hedge, Da. *hegn* hedge, fence. See HAIN *v.*[1]] An enclosure, a park.
c **1205** LAY. 5064 Ne sculde na cniht hærȝien, þær he hauede haines iwald [walled enclosures]. *a* **1440** *Sir Degrev.* 70 Fayere parkes in-wyth haynus, Grett herdus in the playnus [*Thornton MS.* Grete hertes in the haynes, Faire bares in the playnes].

hain (heɪn), *v.*[1] Now *Sc.* and *dial.* Also 5 *Sc.* hane, 6- hayn. [a. ON. *hegna* (Sw. *hägna*, Da. *hegne*) to hedge, fence, protect, preserve, deriv. of OTeut. *hag-* fence, hedge.]
1. *trans.* To enclose or protect with a fence or hedge; *esp.* to preserve (grass) from cattle.
14.. [see HAINED]. **1555** *Sc. Acts Mary* c. 23 It is..ordanit ..that the said wod of Falkland be..keipit and hanit for rysing of young grouth thairof. **1573** in W. H. Turner *Select. Rec. Oxford* 347 Portmeade shalbe hayned and layed freshe from Cattell untyll May daye. **1601** HOLLAND *Pliny* XVIII. xxviii, A ground would be hained in, left lay, and kept for grasse and hey. **1787** WINTER *Syst. Husb.* 328 Ten oxen ..broke into the manured field which had been hayned for mowing. **1794** T. DAVIS *Agric. Wilts* (1813) 258-68 in *Archæol. Rev.* (1888) Mar., Hain up the land, to shut it up for a crop of hay. **1834** *Brit. Husb.* I. xxxi. 486 The uplands are usually 'hayned', or laid up at Candlemas; but richer land is often left open until March.
†**2.** To shut up, confine, restrain. *Obs. rare.*
1636 JAMES *Iter Lanc.* (Chetham) 255 Can mans wise-domme haine The streames of Dee from gliding to yᵉ maine?
3. To spare, save, refrain from consuming or spending. *Sc.*
1508 DUNBAR *Tua mariit Wemen* 386 Quhen he ane hail ȝear wes hanyt. **1572** *Satir. Poems Reform.* xxx. 140 And ȝe wer in yair hands, yai wald not hane ȝow. **1583** *Leg. Bp. St. Androis* 590 *Ibid.* xlv, In Seytoun he remaned, Whair wyne and aill was nothing hayned. **1728** RAMSAY *Fables, Miser & Minos* ii, The Miser..shaw'd the ferryman a knack, Jumpt in, swam o'er, and hain'd his plack. **1825** BROCKETT *N.C. Gloss., Hain*, to save, to preserve. **1826** SCOTT *Diary* 20 Jan. in *Lockhart*, 'Hain your reputation, and tyne your reputation' is a true proverb. **1862** HISLOP *Prov. Scot.* 21 A penny hain'd Is a penny gain'd.
b. *absol.* or *intr.*
1606 WARNER *Alb. Eng.* XVI. ciii. (1612) 406 Yet haine they at their feed. **1737** RAMSAY *Scots Prov.* 72 (Jam.), They that hain at their dinner will hae the mair to their supper.

hain, *v.*[2] *dial.* Also 5-6 heyne, 6 hayn. [app. deriv. form from *hey*, HIGH *v.* to raise, with -EN[5].] *trans.* To raise, heighten, set up.
c **1440** *Promp. Parv.* 230/2 Hawncyn or heynyn (*S.* hawnsyn or yn heyyn), *exalto, elevo, sublevo. Ibid.* 233 (*K.H.*) Heynyn (*P.* heighthyn)..*exalto, elevo.* **1465** MARG. PASTON in *Past. Lett.* No. 499 II. 176, I have spoke with Borges that he shuld heyne the price of the mershe. **1564** *Order* 28 Feb. in Swinden *Gt. Yarmouth* 53 Ordered that the merchants' dinner, or feast..shall be erected and heyned this present year. **1599** NASHE *Lenten Stuffe* 12 Edward the thirde..hayned the price of their priuiledges and not brought them downe one barley Kirnell. **1787** W. MARSHALL *E. Norfolk* (1795) Gloss., *Hain*, to raise, or heighten; as 'to *hain* the rent, the rick, or the ditch'. **1895** RYE *Gloss. E. Anglia, Hain*, to heighten; to rise in price. *Mod. Suffolk.* 'I want my wages hained.'
Hence **haining** *vbl. sb.*
c **1440** *Promp. Parv.* 233/2 Heynynge, *exaltacio, elevacio.*

hainch, Sc. form of HAUNCH.

†**haine.** *Obs.* Also 4-5 hayn(e. [a. F. *haine*, formerly *haïne* (12th c. in Hatz.-Darm.), f. *ha-ïr* to hate; cf. *saisine* from *saisir.*] Hatred.
1387-8 T. USK *Test. Love* Prol., Envye forsothe commendeth nought his reason that he hath in hayn. *c* **1477** CAXTON *Jason* 112 b, Ne of hayne or hate precedent.

haine, var. of HAYNE *Obs.*, a mean wretch.

hained (heɪnd), *ppl. a.* Chiefly *Sc.* [f. HAIN *v.*[1] + -ED[1].] **a.** Fenced, enclosed. **b.** (*Sc.*) Preserved, reserved, spared, saved from consumption.
hained grass, pasture from which grazing cattle have been kept for a time.
14.. *Forest Lawes* c. I. §1 in *Scot. Stat.* I. 323 At þai enter nocht in ony hanyt place of þe woddis with þar bestis. **1579** *Sc. Acts Jas. VI* (1597) §84 Quhatsumever person..pullis or cuttis haned Broome. ? **17..** *Earl Richard, Queen's Brother* vii. in Child *Ballads* IV. cx. (1886) 465/1 You'll have them, and as much haind grass As they all on can gae. **1786** BURNS *Cotter's Sat. Night* xi, The dame brings forth..her weel-hain'd kebbuck. **1786** —— *N.-Y. Salut. to Maggie* 106 I'll flit thy tether To some hain'd rig.

haining ('heɪnɪŋ), *vbl. sb.* Chiefly *Sc.* [f. HAIN *v.*[1] + -ING[1].] Enclosing or preserving; that which encloses or is enclosed; an enclosure.
1535 *Sc. Acts Jas. V*, c. 8 All distroyaris of grenewod be Cutting peling..and siclike of all new hanyngis. *Ibid.* (1597) c. 9 That euerie man..plant woodde and Forrest, and make hedges, and haning for him selfe, extending to three aickers of land. **1571** *Burgh Rec. Peebles* 25 Apr. (Jam. *Supp.*), The Vanelaw to be proclamit waist, seute, and hanyng. **1728** W. STARRAT *Epist.* in *Ramsay's Poems* (1877) II. 276 We'll to the haining drive. *c* **1856** *Denham Tracts* (1895) II. 208 A company of hay-makers, whose work in the adjacent haining had been interrupted by a shower.
b. The preserving of grass from cattle.
1733 P. LINDSAY *Interest Scot.* 37 By this Way we are deprived of the Benefit of Winter-haining. **1829** GLOVER *Hist. Derby* I. 203 The laying or shutting up meadows for hay is, in Derbyshire, called hayning.
c. That which is saved; savings.
1823 GALT *Entail* II. 145 (Jam.) My ain lawful jointure and honest hainings.
d. *attrib.*, as *haining-time.*
1605 *Burgh Rec. Prestwick* 2 Oct. (Jam. *Supp.*), Vnles the samyn guddis be sufficientlie tedderit in hanyng tyme.

hainous, -ly, etc., obs. ff. HEINOUS, -LY, etc.

hainsch, hainsh, Sc. ff. HAUNCH *sb.* and *v.*

hain't, haint, vulgar contr. of *have not.*

haique, obs. form of HAIK[2].

hair (hɛə(r)), *sb.* Forms: α. 1 **hær, hér**, 2-3 **hær**, 2-5 **her**, 4-6 **heer**, 5-6 **heere, here**, (5 **herre**), 6 **hear(e.** β. 4-5 **har, hare**, 4 **hor**, 4-5 **hore**, 5 **haar(e.** γ. 5-6 **heyr(e**, 5-7 **haire, hayre, heir(e**, 6- **hair.** [Com. Teutonic, OE. *hær, hér* = OFris. *hêr*, OS. *hâr* (MDu. *haer*, Du. *haar*), OHG. *hâr*, (Ger. *haar*), ON. *hár* (Sw. *hår*, Da. *haar*):—OTeut. **hǣrom*; not known in Gothic. The α forms are native, from OE., WS. *hær*, Anglian *hér*; the β forms are immed. from ON. *hár*, which gave in ME. *hâr* in northern, and *hôr* in some north midland dialects. The later *heyr, heire, hayre, hair*, is not a normal repr. of ME. *hêr, heer*, the modern Eng. form of which would be (as in 16th c.) *hear* or *here*; it seems to be partly a northern spelling, but mainly due to assimilation to HAIRE.]
I. 1. a. One of the numerous fine and generally cylindrical filaments that grow from the skin or integument of animals, esp. of most mammals, of which they form the characteristic coat; applied also to similar-looking filamentous outgrowths from the body of insects and other invertebrates, although these are generally of different structure.
a **800** *Corpus Gloss.* 1594 *Pilus*, her. *c* **1000** ÆLFRIC *Hom.* I. 236 An hær of eowrum heafde. *a* **1225** *Leg. Kath.* 2288 An her of hare fax. **1382** WYCLIF *Matt.* v. 36 Thou maist not make oon heer whyt, or blak. *c* **1440** *Promp. Parv.* 235/2 Heer (*K., S., P.* here), *capillus.* **1583** HOLLYBAND *Campo di Fior* 335 There will alwayes remaine some heare in the cliffe of the penne.
β. **1340** HAMPOLE *Pr. Consc.* 5007 Na hare sal perishe, ne faile. *c* **1450** *St. Cuthbert* (Surtees) 6961 He had a hare, þe whilk grewe On cuthberts heued. *c* **1460** *Towneley Myst.* (Surtees) 87 Not oone hore. **1483** *Cath. Angl.* 175/2 An Hare, *crinis.*
γ. **1483** *Cath. Angl.* 180/2 An Heire, *pilus. Ibid.* 184/1 A Heyr, *crinis.* **1581** PETTIE *Guazzo's Civ. Conv.* II. (1586) 97 b, A sword..hanging by a haire over his head. **1665** HOOKE *Microgr.* 158 The long hairs of Horses..seem Cylindrical. **1742** FRANCIS *Horace Epist.* II. i. (R.) For hair by hair I pull the horse's tail. **1816** J. WILSON *City of Plague* II. v, And would not hurt a hair upon his head. **1878** HUXLEY *Physiogr.* 70 A hair..is larger when wet than when dry.
b. The plural *hairs* was formerly used = the collective sense 2. [Cf. L. *crines*, Fr. *les cheveux*, Ger. *die haare.*] Now *obs.* or *arch.* as in ***grey hairs***, which is also often taken not collectively.
c **1000** *Ags. Gosp.* Mark i. 6 Iohannes wæs ȝescryd mid oluendes hærum. *c* **1340** *Cursor M.* 8079 (F.) þaire browes ware growen side with heres. **1382** WYCLIF *Luke* vii. 38 And wypide with heeris of hir heed [*R.V.* 1881 the hair of her head]. —— *John* xi. 2 And wipte his feet with hir heeris [*All 16-19th c. versions* with her hair]. *c* **1400** *Destr. Troy* 3989 Gilde hores hade þat gay, godely to se. **1563-87** FOXE *A. & M.* (1596) 42/2 His old age or white heares. **1596** SPENSER *F.Q.* IV. viii. 4 He..would..knocke his head, and rend his rugged heares. **1611** BIBLE *Gen.* xliv. 29 Ye shall bring downe my gray haires with sorrow to the graue. **1715-20** POPE *Iliad* x. 19 He rends his hairs in sacrifice to Jove. **1826** H. N. COLERIDGE *West Indies* 230 Venerable for his white hairs.
c. *fig.* (= 2 b).
1606 G. W[ODCOCKE] tr. *Hist. Ivstine* Ffiv b, A blazing-starre with long haires appeared.
2. *collect.* **a.** The aggregate of hairs growing on the skin of an animal: *spec.* that growing naturally upon the human head; also, hairs collectively or in the mass, as used for manufacturing purposes and the like.
c **1000** *Sax. Leechd.* II. 156 Gif hær to þicce sie. *c* **1200** ORMIN 3208 Hiss claþ wass off ollfenntess hær. *c* **1330** R. BRUNNE *Chron. Wace* (Rolls) 12236 About hure hed hure her to-schaked. *c* **1440** *Promp. Parv.* 235/2 Heer fyrste growynge yn' mannys berde, *lanugo.* **1467** in *Eng. Gilds* (1870) 396 That they wasshe none heare, but benethe the brugge. **1495** *Act 11 Hen. VII*, c. 19 Cussions stuffed with horse here..neetis here, deris here, and gotis here. **1584** [see 8 o].
β. *a* **1300** *Cursor M.* 3662 Esau es rugh wit har. *c* **1300** *Havelok* 235 Handes wringing, and drawing bi hor. *a* **1400-50** *Alexander* 5476 With haare to þaire heelis. *c* **1440** *York Myst.* xxxii. 21 þe hore þat pillis my heed.
γ. *c* **1375** *Sc. Leg. Saints, Egipciane* 225 Hayre scho had, quhyt & streke. **1508** DUNBAR *Tua Mariit Wemen* 21 Kemmet was thair cleir hair. **1561** HOLLYBUSH *Hom. Apoth.* 2 For fallinge of the heyre of the head. **1659** B. HARRIS *Parival's Iron Age* 287 Which makes the hair stand on the heads of such as hear it related. **1774** GOLDSM. *Nat. Hist.* (1776) VIII. 17 Among the hairy caterpillars..the cast skin is covered with hair. **1777** MAD. D'ARBLAY *Early Diary* (1889) II. 169 All our hairs were done to the astonishment of all the company. **1816** BYRON *Prisoner of Chillon* i, My hair is grey, but not with years. **1870** TENNYSON *Holy Grail* 42 She..shore away..all that wealth of hair Which made a silken mat-work for her feet. **1873** MIVART *Elem. Anat.* vii. 238 Our hair and nails are..modifications of the external layer of the skin.
b. *fig.* Applied to the rays or 'tresses' of the sun, the tail of a comet, 'leafy locks' of a tree, etc.
1594 MARLOWE & NASHE *Dido* I. i, Yet shall the aged sun shed forth his hair. **1650** R. STAPYLTON *Strada's Low C. Warres* I. 8 A blazing star..shooting its fiery hair point blank against the Monastery. **1667** MILTON *P.L.* II. 710 Like a Comet..That..from his horrid hair Shakes Pestilence and Warr. **1821** SHELLEY *Prometh. Unb.* I. 168 New fire..Shook its portentous hair beneath Heaven's frown. **1864** SWINBURNE *Atalanta* 1268 The heavy hair of pines.
3. In plants: An outgrowth of the epidermis, consisting of an elongated cell, or a row of cells, usually soft and flexible like the hair of animals. In *Bot.* sometimes extended to other outgrowths of similar origin, as prickles, spore-capsules, etc.: = TRICHOME.
1631 WIDDOWES *Nat. Philos.* 35 The Quince..his fruit hath downie hayre. **1811** MRS. IBBETSON in *Nicholson's Jrnl.* XXX. 1 (*title*), On the Hairs of Plants. **1875** DARWIN *Insectiv. Pl.* 354 The glandular hairs of ordinary plants.. have the power..of absorbing both a solution and the vapour of ammonia. **1875** BENNETT & DYER tr. *Sachs' Bot.* I. iii. 138 Hairs (*Trichomes*) is the term given in the higher plants to those outgrowths which arise only from the epidermis.
4. *transf.* **a.** Applied to various things having the shape, consistency, or appearance of a hair or mass of hair: e.g. threadlike stamens or filaments.
1578 LYTE *Dodoens* VI. i. (655) The yellow heare which groweth in the middle of the Rose is called..in shops and of the Arabian physitions Anthera.
b. In names of plants having foliage fancifully likened to hair: as ***Isis hair, lady's hair***, MAIDENHAIR, ***Venus' hair.***
1551 TURNER *Herbal* I. Biij, It [Adianthum]..may be named in English Venus heyre or ladyes heyre. **1598** FLORIO, *Capelli di venere*, the herbe Maiden-haire, Venus-haire, or our Ladies-haire. **1778** *Eng. Gaz.* (ed. 2) s.v. *Portland*, Among the sea-weeds here is found a sort of shrub, not unlike coral. It is called Isis's Hair.
c. ***African*** or ***vegetable hair***: see quots.
1851 *Offic. Catal. Gt. Exhib.* 1259 'Vegetable hair', made of the leaves of the Algerian dwarf palm-tree..for the use of upholsterers. **1866** *Treas. Bot.* 565 *African Hair*, the fibre of the leaves of the Palmetto, *Chamærops humilis.*
d. Applied to sertularian and other polyps which grow on oyster shells. (*Cent. Dict.*)
e. A spring mechanism which is freed by the HAIR-TRIGGER, q.v.
1864 in WEBSTER.
5. Used as a type of what is of extremely small magnitude, value, or measure; a jot or tittle; an iota; the slightest thing; the least degree. See also *to a hair* in 8 c.
1377 LANGL. *P. Pl.* B. x. 334 Kynghod ne knyȝthod.. Helpeth nouȝt to heueneward one heres ende. *c* **1420** *Anturs of Arth.* xlv, Him lakket no more to be slayne, Butte the brede of hore. **1529** MORE *Comf. agst. Trib.* III. Wks. 1223/1 The prayse had not bene the lesse of one heere. **1536**

LATIMER *2nd Serm. bef. Convocat.* Wks. I. 48 They would not set an hair by the name, but for the thing. **1577** tr. *Bullinger's Decades* (1592) 201 Neither is there one haires difference to choose. **1606** SHAKS. *Tr. & Cr.* III. ii. 191 If I be false, or swerue a haire from truth. *a* **1610** HEALEY *Cebes* (1636) 159 Their estate is not an haire better then the others. **1808–25** JAMIESON, *Hair*, a very small portion or quantity; as *a hair of meal*, a few grains.

†**6.** Taken as the distinctive type of sort or kind; ***of one hair***, of one colour and external quality; hence = sort, kind, nature; stamp, character. *Obs.*

1387 TREVISA *Higden* I. 365 With mylk of a cowe þat is of oon here [*unius coloris*]. **1592** GREENE *Upst. Courtier* in *Harl. Misc.* (Malh.) II. 244 Two notable knaues, both of a haire, and both cosen germaines to the deuill. **1596** SHAKS. *1 Hen. IV*, IV. i. 61 The Qualitie and Heire of our Attempt Brookes no diuision. **1600** TOURNEUR *Transf. Metamorph.* Author to Bk. 6 Expect but flowts, for 'tis the haire of crime. *a* **1625** FLETCHER *Nice Valour* I. i, A lady of my hair cannot want pitying.

7. A cloth, mat, or other fabric of hair used for various purposes in some trades, e.g. in hop-drying, extraction of oils, etc.; a haircloth.

[Historically, the same word as HAIRE, which, in losing the final *e*, has become identical in form with this.]

1485 *Inv.* in *Ripon Ch. Acts* 371 Hayr pro ustrina. **1594** *Fairfax Inv.* in *Archæologia* XLVIII. 130 On Seasterne of leade for barley and a kilne haire. **1848** *Jrnl. R. Agric. Soc.* IX. II. 568 The roof of the building coming on above much nearer the hair than in the modern kilns. *Ibid.* 572 A step-ladder to carry the green hops to lay on the hair. **1884** *Encycl. Brit.* XVII. 742/1 Measured quantities..of [oil-seed] meal are filled into woollen bags..Each bag is further placed within 'hairs', thick mats of horse-hair bound with leather.

II. Phrases and locutions.

8. a. ***against the hair***: contrary to the direction in which an animal's hair naturally lies; contrary to the natural set of a thing; against the grain, inclination, or sentiment. **b.** ***in one's hair***: (*a*) with the hair down; (*b*) bare-headed, without hat or wig; (*c*) being a nuisance or encumbrance, in one's way; usu. with *get* and *have* (orig. *U.S.*); so ***out of one's hair***: out of one's way, not encumbering (see sense 8 q below). **c.** ***to a hair***: to a nicety, with the utmost exactness. **d.** ***hair about the heels***: a mark of under-bred horses; hence *fig.* of persons. †**e.** ***hair and hide, hair and hoof***: every part, entirely, wholly. **f.** ***a hair in one's neck***: a cause of trouble or annoyance. **g.** ***a hair of the dog that bit you, of the same dog*** (or ***wolf***): see DOG *sb.*[1] 17e. **h.** ***a hair to make a tether of***: a slight pretext of which to make a great deal. **i.** ***to comb*** (***a person's***) ***hair*** (*slang*): see COMB *v.* 3. **j.** ***to cut*** (or ***divide***) ***the hair, to split hairs***: to make fine or cavilling distinctions. **k.** ***to keep one's hair on*** (*slang*): to keep cool, not to lose one's head or get excited. **l.** ***to put up, turn up*** (one's) ***hair***: said of a girl when she exchanges her floating hair or ringlets for the dressed hair of womanhood; ***to do*** or ***put up, to let down*** (one's) ***hair*** (i.e. in the toilet); also *fig.*; and of both men and women, ***to let*** (***take***) ***one's*** (***back***) ***hair down***, to throw off reserve, to become confidential. **m.** ***to tear*** (†***rend***) ***one's hair***, i.e. as a symptom of passionate grief. **n.** ***not to turn a hair***: *lit.* of a horse, not to show sweat by the roughening of his hair; *fig.* not to show any sign of being discomposed, ruffled, or affected by exertion. **o.** ***to get*** (a person) ***by the short hairs*** (formerly ***to get*** (a person, etc.) ***where the hair is short***): to have complete control over. **p.** ***to make one's hair curl***: see CURL *v.*[1] 4. **q.** ***out of one's hair***: opp. ***in one's hair*** (sense 8 b (*c*)). **r.** ***to lose one's hair*** (or ***to get one's hair off***): to lose one's temper. **s.** In other expressions: see quots.

a. 1387–8 T. USK *Test. Love* II. iv, Ayenst the heere it tourneth. **1579–80** NORTH *Plutarch* (1676) 388 All went utterly against the hair with him. **1598** SHAKS. *Merry W.* II. iii. 40 If you should fight, you goe against the haire of your professions. **1607** TOPSELL *Four-f. Beasts* (1658) 63 [Cows] in the licking of themselves against the hair. *a* **1627** MIDDLETON *Mayor of Queenborough* III. ii, Books in women's hands are as much against the hair, methinks, as to see men wear stomachers, or night-rails. **1680** HOWE *Bless. Righteous* (1825) 170 Something that crosses them, and goes against the hair. **1827** SCOTT *Chron. Canongate* Introd. iii, He was a wee toustie when you rubbed him again the hair.

b. 1533 CRANMER in Ellis *Orig. Lett.* Ser. I. II. 39 She in her here, my Lord of Suffolke beryng before herr the Crowne. **1606** HOLLAND *Sueton.* 143 Many a time he would shew her to his Souldiours in her haire. **1851** *Oregon Statesman* (Oregon City) 30 Sept. 1/2, I shall depend on your honor..that you won't tell on me, cause if you did, I should have Hetty Gawkins in my hair in no time. **1859** THACKERAY *Virgin.* i, A large grave man in his own hair. **1880** 'MARK TWAIN' *Tramp Abroad* I. xx. 193 What you learn here, you've got to know..or else you'll have one of these..spectacled..old professors in your hair. **1935** S. LEWIS *It can't happen Here* xiii. 123 Maybe there'll be a few Communist cells around here now, when Fascism begins to get into people's hair. **1936** 'J. TEY' *Shilling for Candles* x. 115 She got in my hair until I couldn't bear it another day. **1945** M. LOWRY *Let.* (1967) 49 We had them in our hair all summer. **1951** C. FRY *Sleep of Prisoners* 4 You know what Absalom Said to the tree? 'You're getting in my hair.' **1957** R. WATSON-WATT *Three Steps to Victory* 255 His endurance of a bunch of untidy civilians constantly 'in his hair'.

c. 1606 SHAKS. *Tr. & Cr.* III. i. 157 *Pan.* Youle remember your brothers excuse? *Par.* To a hayre. **1662** J. BARGRAVE *Pope Alex. VII* (1867) 98 Distinguishing between good and bad to a hair. **1765** COWPER *Lett.* 18 Oct., Three or four single men, who suit my temper to a hair. *a* **1834** LAMB *Let. to Coleridge* (L.), I could hit him off to a hair.

d. 1882 H. C. MERIVALE *Faucit of B.* III. II. xxiii. 240 'Hair about the heels', muttered the Count to himself.

e. *c* **1450** *St. Cuthbert* (Surtees) 6860 þai were destroyed, bath hare and hyde. **1705** JEAN IRVINE in *Collect. Dying Test.* (1806) 57 Poor people that would fain have strength to stand by hair and hoof of the truths of God. **1728** P. WALKER *Peden* Pref. (ed. 3) 28 None contending earnestly for Substance and Circumstances, Hair and Hoof of that dear-bought Testimony.

f. *a* **1450** *Ratis Raving* III. 199 Think one the har is in thi nek. **1818** SCOTT *Rob Roy* xxiii, An Bailie Grahame were to get word o' this..it wad be a sair hair in my neck!

h. 1809 SCOTT *Let. to G. Ellis* 3 Nov. in *Lockhart*, Those who wish to undermine it want but, according to our Scotch Proverb, a hair to make a tether of.

j. 1652 SANCROFT *Mod. Policies* in D'Oyly *Life* (1821) II. 241 Machiavel cut the hair when he advised, not absolutely to disavow conscience, but to manage it with such a prudent neglect, as is scarce discernible from a tenderness. **1692** R. L'ESTRANGE *Josephus, Philo's Emb. Caius* x. (1702) 901 To cut a Hair betwixt Satyr and Flattery. **1742** RICHARDSON *Pamela* III. 75 When Persons have a Mind to split Hairs, and to distinguish away the Christian Duties by a Word. **1874** L. STEPHEN *Hours in Library* (1892) I. ix. 316 [He] splits hairs with such surprising versatility.

k. 1883 F. M. CRAWFORD *Dr. Claudius* vi, Keep your hair on, my young friend. **1888** *Pall Mall G.* 4 Aug. 1/2 This is the English way of doing things; they keep their hair on their heads. **1662** [see PUT *v.*[1] 53 a]. **1850** G. H. LEWES in *Leader* 7 Dec. 882/3, I am well aware that a little ranting and 'letting down the back hair' would have 'told' upon the audience with more noisy effect. **1921** W. DE LA MARE *Mem. Midget* iii. 15 On my seventeenth birthday I put up my hair, and was confirmed. **1925** N. COWARD *Vortex* II. 66 Helen and I have just had a grand heart-to-heart talk; we've undone our back hair. **1933** WODEHOUSE *Heavy Weather* vii. 116 You needn't be coy, Beach... No reporters present. We can take our hair down and tell each other our right names. **1951** AUDEN *Nones* (1952) 31 To let their hair down and be frank about The world. **1959** *Listener* 15 Oct. 608/1 Mr. Fredric Warburg has reminded us of this in a volume of autobiography..in which he lets down his hair. **1967** *Guardian* 3 Jan. 2/7 Lively young thing, I recall—but she'll have put her hair up by now. **1967** C. FREMLIN *Prisoner's Base* ix. 67 After you'd gone, Mother—he really let his back hair down. I was right, you know—he *has* been in prison. **1967** B. WOOTTON *In World I never Made* i. 36 Before it became customary for women of all ages to wear their hair short, one of the marks of entering upon adult status was to put one's hair 'up'.

m. 1548 HALL *Chron., Hen. IV*, 14b, This knight.. sobbed, wept, and rent his heare. **1606** SHAKS. *Tr. & Cr.* IV. ii. 113 Teare my bright heire, and scratch my praised cheekes. **1715–20** [see 1 b]. **1802** SOUTHEY *Inchcape Rock* xvi, Sir Ralph the Rover tore his hair And curst himself in his despair. **1855** THACKERAY *Rose & Ring* xix, Tearing her hair, crying and bemoaning herself.

n. 1798 JANE AUSTEN *Northang. Abb.* vii, Hot! he [a horse] had not turned a hair till we came to Walcot church. **1897** BLACKMORE *Dariel* xviii, When I tried her with a lot of little dodges..she never turned a hair—as the sporting people say.

o. 1872 G. P. BURNHAM *Mem. U.S. Secret Service* 207 You've got me where the ha'r is short! What a cursed fool I have been. **1880** 'MARK TWAIN' *Tramp Abroad* I. xx. 184, I had to tackle this miserable language... I've got it where the hair's short, I think. **1888** KIPLING *Wee Willie Winkie* 67 Then they'll rush in, and then we've got 'em by the short hairs! **1928** *Blackw. Mag.* Feb. 150/1 Those Chinhwan really did seem to have got the rest of the world by the short hairs. **1930** SAYERS & EUSTACE *Docts. in Case* I. 25 She's evidently got her husband by the short hairs.

q. 1902 KIPLING in *Sat. Even. Post* 6 Dec. 2/3 Get out o' my back-hair! **1949** 'J. TEY' *Brat Farrar* x. 81 They wouldn't bother to look for him. They would be too relieved to have him out of their hair. **1959** J. MASTERS *Fandango Rock* 173 He wouldn't want to interfere with her big moment, and he'd even managed to keep Peggy out of her hair. **1967** *Boston Sunday Globe* 23 Apr. 18/2 Two vice presidents of the First Pennsylvania Banking and Trust Co., the city's largest and most respected, said the bank paid Karafin and an associate £12,000 a year 'to keep him out of our hair'. **1971** WODEHOUSE *Much Obliged, Jeeves* xvi. 177 He wanted to get Florence out of his hair without actually telling her to look elsewhere for a mate.

r. *c* **1920** D. H. LAWRENCE *Phoenix II* (1968) 120 'Nay—nay,' said Lewis testily. 'Don't get your hair off, Mrs. Goddard.' **1931** T. R. G. LYELL *Slang* 356 *To lose one's hair*, to lose one's temper. 'Last night Jones quite lost his hair and made an awful fool of himself.' **1938** E. BOWEN *Death of Heart* III. ii. 343 *This* is what one gets for being so nicely nonchalant, for saving people's faces, for not losing one's hair.

s. 1579 FULKE *Refut. Rastell* 755 The thinges proued..are but the heire and nayles of the masse, and not the substantiall partes thereof. **1584** FENNER *Def. Ministers* (1587) 13 Hee will..in the next Section tugge it in by the heare. **1586** A. DAY *Eng. Secretary* II. (1625) 80 As when one tells..a lie, to bid him take the haire from his lips.

III. *attrib.* and *Comb.*

9. a. *attrib.* Of, pertaining to, or connected with hair or a hair; made or consisting of hair, or of a texture like hair; as ***hair-bracelet, -broom, -bud, -bulb, -camlet, -cell, -chain, -club*** (CLUB *sb.* 6), ***-combing, -craft, -crape, -crêpe, -fashion, -felt, -fetishism, -fetishist, -fibre, -glove, -goods, -guard, -hat, -list, -merchant, -rope, -scale, -seating, -shaft, -sheath, -substance, -tint, -tip, -work***, etc. Also HAIRBREADTH, -CLOTH, etc.

1673 [R. LEIGH] *Transpr. Reh.* 138 The mode of wearing *hair-bracelets was scarce in use then. **1725** BRADLEY *Fam. Dict.* s.v. *Horse*, Seams, Scabs, and *Hair-brokenness..on the inward Bow of his Knees. **1753** CHAMBERS *Cycl. Supp.* s.v. *Broom*, We say, a birch-broom, a *hair-broom, a rush-broom. **1842** PRICHARD *Nat. Hist. Man* 96 At the origin of each hair two parts are distinguished, the hair-sheath, and the germ or *hair-bud. **1876** DUHRING *Dis. Skin* 34 The root is found..to terminate in a bulb-shaped expansion, termed the *hair-bulb. **1676** *Lond. Gaz.* No. 1107/4 A *Hair-Camblet Coat. **1895** *Montgomery Ward Catal.* 158 *Hair Chains made to order. Send us the hair and we will braid. **1907** N. MUNRO *Daft Days* xxx, The lockets are large and strong, and hair-chains much abound. **1774** MAD. D'ARBLAY *Early Diary* (1889) I. 288 If you are fond of *hair-clubs, you should see the Portuguese ladies' hair! **1940** G. GREENE *Power & Glory* II. iv. 178 There was a hair-slide,.. and a ball of *hair-combings. **1962** *John o' London's* 4 Jan. 14/1 The *haircraft women..used to tour the Swedish countryside..selling their products. **1730** MARTIN in *Phil. Trans.* XXXVI. 454 A Piece of Muslin, or thin *Hair-Crape. **1957** V. J. KEHOE *Technique Film & T.V. Make-Up* xv. 203 **Hair crepe*..may be human hair (Caucasian, Chinese or Indian), yak or a combination of any or all of these types. **1944** KOESTLER in *Horizon* Mar. 162 There are ..certain typical attitudes to life including clothing, *hair-fashion, drink and food. **1951** C. BERG *Unconscious Significance of Hair* vii. 65 The universality of *hair fetishism may be brought into relief by this short instance of its negative aspect: A young woman patient of mine, who had become completely bald,..had an indescribable horror of her predicament being seen or..suspected by anyone. *Ibid.* 61 The *hair fetishist loves the women's hair but frequently has the impulse to despoil or 'castrate' it. **1954** KOESTLER *Invisible Writing* xxiv. 284 The hair-fetishists who loiter in tube-stations with scissors in their pockets. **1858** SIMMONDS *Dict. Trade*, **Hair-gloves*, horsehair gloves used for rubbing the skin in bathing, etc. **1865** DICKENS *Mut. Fr.* II. i, With his decent silver watch..and its decent *hair-guard. **1753** HANWAY *Trav.* (1762) I. v. lxiv. 291 British woollens, such as *hair-list drabs. **1705** *Lond. Gaz.* No. 4098/4 William Taylor..*Hair-Merchant. **1867** EMERSON *Lett. & Soc. Aims* vii. (1875) 179 Bringing it to a *hair-point for the eye and hand of the philosopher. **1577** in Rogers *Agric. & Prices* III. 580 *Hair rope to stake the mill horse. **1863** BATES *Nat. Amazon* v. (1864) 115 At the tip of the moth's body there is a brush of long *hair-scales resembling feathers. **1851** *Offc. Catal. Gt. Exhib.* 535 Specimens of damask and striped *hair-seating, various colours. **1906** *Practitioner* Nov. 692 Complete removal..of the *hair-shaft, together with the root-sheath or papilla. **1924** *Chambers's Jrnl.* 668/2 The process flattens the almost spherical hairshaft and causes it to lean inwards. **1876** DUHRING *Dis. Skin* (1881) 36 The *cortical substance*, termed also **hair-substance*, constitutes the bulk of the hair. **1565** GOLDING *Ovid's Met.* XIV. (1593) 329 The cursed witch had smit Our highest *hairetips with hir wand. **1790** *Columbian Centinel* 13 Oct. 36/4 The Artists' ability in Painting and *Hair-Work may be seen. **1959** *Times* 7 Mar. 9/4 Hairwork jewelry was already popular in the late seventeenth century.

b. *attrib.* For or for the use of the hair; ***hair appointment, -caul, -clasp, -clip, -comb, -conditioner, -cream, -dye, -grip, -lacquer, -lotion, -net, -oil, -ornament, -pad, -preparation, -ribbon, -scissors, -slide*** (SLIDE *sb.* 6), ***-spray, -tonic, -wash***. Also HAIR-BAND, -BRUSH, -PIN, etc.

1938 D. DU MAURIER *Rebecca* xxiv. 402 Mrs. de Winter had a *hair appointment from twelve until one thirty. **1861** C. W. KING *Ant. Gems* (1866) 160 The ear-rings, necklaces, *hair-cauls, or fillets, of the female busts. **1894** A. M. EARLE *Costume Colonial Times* 121 **Hair-clasps.* These ornaments for the hair—clasps to hold up the braided back hair—were advertised for sale in the New York newspapers and in the *Connecticut Courant* of January, 1791, and were worn until a simpler form of hair-dressing appeared about the year 1800. **1957** J. FRAME *Owls do Cry* 55 *Hairclips have been taken from them. **1837** THACKERAY *Ravenswing* i, Two brass *hair-combs set with glass rubies. **1951** *Catal. Exhibits, S. Bank Exhib., Festiv. Brit.* 63/2 *Hair Conditioner. **1926–7** *Army & Navy Stores Catal.* 491/1 *Hair Cream, for fixing the hair. **1843** *Ainsworth's Mag.* III. 554 Invent a new *hair-dye expressly to accommodate his wife. **1933** W. S. MAUGHAM *Sheppey* I. 20, I don't believe there's another man in the business could 'ave sold Mr Bolton a bottle of 'air-dye. **1896** *Woman's Life* III. 462/2 Hair-Bow (Fitted with New Safety *Hair-Grip). **1938** 'J. BELL' *Port of London Murders* vi. 91 The jug..contained..half a bootlace and two rusty hair grips. **1955** *Sci. News Let.* 5 Mar. 150/3 Hair-grips and kirbi-grips are known in America as bobby pins. **1943** *Mod. Beauty Shop* Sept. I. 104 (Advt.), A national publicity campaign is informing women everywhere that *hair lacquer is best applied with an ordinary toothbrush. **1978** ZIZMOR & FOREMAN *Superhair* x. 90 Setting lotions.. contain the same hair lacquers and plasticizers found in aerosol hair sprays. **1906** T. D. LISTER *Chavasse's Advice to Mother* (ed. 16) III. 370 Avoid grease, pomatum, *hair lotions, and all abominations of that kind. **1962** N. MARSH *Hand in Glove* vii. 221 Mr. Period's bedroom smelt of hair lotion. **1810** E. WEETON *Let.* 25 Feb. in *Jrnl. of Governess* (1969) I. 233 A small phial of *hair oil. **1853** MRS. GASKELL *Cranford* xii. 174 The delusive lady was off upon..the merits of cosmetics and hair oils in general. **1870** MISS BRIDGMAN *Ro. Lynne* II. v. 116 There were hair-washes, and hair-oils. **1895** *Montgomery Ward Catal.* 183 Real Tortoise Shell *Hair Ornaments. **1967** H. PORTER in *Coast to Coast 1965–6* 178 They were not discussing the weather or hair-ornaments. **1897** *Sears, Roebuck Catal.* 779/5 *Hair Preparation. **1909** in A. Adburgham *Shops & Shopping* (1964) xiii. 273 A handsome sales-room where are sold.. Hair Preparations,..Hair nets, etc. **1790** J. B. MORETON *W. Ind. Isl.* 98 Two hats..*hair-ribband and hair-dressing. **1688** R. HOLME *Armoury* III. ix. 398 They ought..to be named what kind of cisers they are, whether *Hair cisers.. or Beard cisers. **1895** *Army & Navy Co-op. Soc. Price List* 15 Sept. (Index), *Hair Slides. **1927** *Glasgow Herald* 6 Oct. 11 Her hair-slide was found some distance from the body. **1968** J. IRONSIDE *Fashion Alphabet* 166 A hair slide..is a clip for keeping the hair in place. **1959** *Sears, Roebuck Catal.* Spring & Summer 280/4 Glow *Hair Spray. **1966** *Vogue* Nov. 81 Creamy Skin Perfume..and a hair spray. **1967** W. PINE *Protectors* i. 10 He smelt the scent of her hair-spray. **1895** *Montgomery Ward Catal.* Index, *Hair Tonic. **1897**

Hair tonic [see TONIC *sb.* 1]. **1938** AUDEN & ISHERWOOD *On Frontier* I. i. 28 Surely he's the man who does the hair-tonic advertisements? **1869** D. G. ROSSETTI *Let.* (1965) II. 707 Certainly a *hair-wash would be the unkindest cut of all to bring against the Absalom of modern poetry. **1938** H. NICHOLSON *Let.* 18 May (1966) 342 My hairwash comes from Floris.

c. objective and obj. genitive, as ***hair-buyer, -clasper, -clipper, -curler, -cutter, -dealer, -dryer, -frizzer, -monger, -remover, -seller, -stainer, -straightener, -waver,*** etc.; ***hair-clipping, -colouring, -conditioning, -curling, -cutting, -doing, -drying, -dyeing, -lifting, -nourishing, -picking, -raising, -straightening, -teasing,*** etc., vbl. sbs. and/or ppl. adjs. Also HAIRDRESSER, -SPLITTER, -SPLITTING.

1721 *Lond. Gaz.* No. 5921/4 Mary Penstone..*Hair-buyer. **1859** DARWIN *Orig. Spec.* vi. (1878) 153 Parasite mites..furnished with *hair-claspers. **1895** *Montgomery Ward Catal.* 444/1 The very best *hair clipper in the market. **1930** *Daily Express* 6 Nov. 19/3 A display of the latest type of electrical hair-clippers. **1972** G. DURRELL *Catch me a Colobus* iii. 58 The next thing was carefully to shave the area. .. This was done with an electric hair-clipper. **1886** W. J. TUCKER *E. Europe* 11 Undergoing the process of *hair-clipping. **1959** *Punch* 3 June 752/1 *Hair-colouring (modern usage for hair-dyeing) has become part of a woman's normal routine. **1966** J. S. COX *Illustr. Dict. Hairdressing* 70/2 **Hair-conditioning*, external treatment designed to improve the condition of the hair by means of lotions, creams, massage and the application of steam to the head and hair. **1753** in E. Singleton *Social N.Y. under Georges* (1902) 176 *Hair-curler and peruke-maker from London. **1872** *Rep. Comm. Patents 1870* (U.S.) II. 779/1 Hair-Curler... [A] combination, with a curling-iron tube [etc.]. **1929** *Bookman* May 270/1 A woman's steel hair curlers. **1936** *Discovery* Aug. 250/2 A long ivory rod with a pomegranate finial is probably a hair curler. **1694** *Lond. Gaz.* No. 3036/4 Perriwig-maker and *Hair Cutter. **1889** *Monthly Packet* Christmas 102, I suppose—there—ain't no *hair-cutters up in Heaven? **1832** *Chambers's Edin. Jrnl.* I. 60/2 The announcement *'Hair-cutting rooms' in the window. **1850** DICKENS *Dav. Copp.* vii. 77 My recollections of..canings, rulerings, hair-cuttings, rainy Sundays. **1868** 'HOLME LEE' *B. Godfrey* lii. 295 The hair-cutting parlour behind the shop. **1707** *Lond. Gaz.* No. 4336/8 John Jesson..Grazier and *Hair-dealer. **1875** C. M. YONGE *My Young Alcides* I. vii. 232 In the midst of my *hair-doing..Viola's running in to me. **1895** *Army & Navy Co-op. Soc. Price List* 15 Sept. 180/1 The Princess Patent *Hair Dryer and Burnisher. **1909** *Installation News* III. 7 This Hair-Dryer works..by means of a small..electric fan. **1909** *Westm. Gaz.* 13 Oct. 7/4 One ounce of hair, which she was drawing through the hair-dryer in her hands. **1961** *Times* 26 Apr. 25/4 Domestic appliances such as..hair-driers. **1902** M. BARNES-GRUNDY *Thames Camp* viii. 159 You dive into the sparkling river.., forgetting all about *hair-drying. **1906** *Chambers's Jrnl.* 30 June 495/2 In my lady's room may be found electrically heated curling-irons and an ingenious hair-drying machine. **1872** YEATS *Techn. Hist. Comm.* 96 The art of *hair-dyeing came into vogue. **1762** GOLDSM. *Cit. W.* lxxxviii, Language-masters, music-masters, *hair-frizzers. **1889** 'MARK TWAIN' *Connecticut Yankee* 354, I flung out a *hair-lifting, soul-scorching thirteen-jointed insult. **1840** T. A. TROLLOPE *Summer Brittany* I. 324 The profit thus netted by these *hair-mongers, during a tour through the country. **1647** TRAPP *Comm. Cor.* xi. 14 Homer calleth the Greeks *hair-nourishing men. **1907** *Yesterday's Shopping* (1969) 532/3 *Hair Remover. **1951** M. MCLUHAN *Mech. Bride* 60/2 Hair removers..are backed by long-standing national advertising campaigns. **1713** *Lond. Gaz.* No. 5154/4 William Bell..*Hair-seller. **1725** *Ibid.* No. 6382/11 Charles Parker..*Hair-Stainer. **1898** *Today* 5 Nov. 18/1 'The *Hair Straightener Company manufactures an instrument that will at once remove the curl from the most stubborn hair...' It would be a waste of money..to advertise its wares in a climate like ours, where the moisture of the atmosphere does more *hair straightening than is conducive to feminine happiness. **1966** J. S. COX *Illustr. Dict. Hair-dressing* 74/2 *Hair-straightener*, (1) A preparation to straighten frizzy or over-curly hair. (2) An implement that straightens frizzy hair. **1966** *B.B.C. Handbk.* 25 Could we broadcast something about a new hair straightening cream? **1892** *Queen* 27 Feb. in L. de Vries *Vict. Advts.* (1968) 42/1 Automatic *hair waver and curler..Price 2s. 6d. **1895** *Army & Navy Co-op Soc. Price List.* 15 Sept. 180/2 Hair Wavers (Patent). **1966** J. S. COX *Illustr. Dict. Hairdressing* 75/1 *Hair-waver*, (1) An implement such as waving irons by the use of which hair can be waved. (2) Any apparatus such as a permanent waving machine which heats the hair wound on curlers during the permanent waving process. (3) A person who waves hair.

d. instrumental, as ***hair-bottomed, -hung, -suspended*** adjs. **e.** similative and parasynthetic, as ***hair-coloured, -fissure, -pointed, -stripe, -shaped*** etc. adjs. Also HAIR-STREAK, -STROKE, -WORM.

1818 KEATS *Let.* 5 July (1958) I. 319 *Hair bottomed chairs. **1678** *Lond. Gaz.* No. 1272/4 A *hair-coloured large Suit. **1823** J. BADCOCK *Dom. Amusem.* 138 A *hair fissure is perceptible..in the upper hieroglyphic. **1742** YOUNG *Nt. Th.* II. 300 *Hair-hung, breeze-shaken, o'er the Gulph. **1796** WITHERING *Brit. Plants* (ed. 3) III. 376 Leaves egg-spear-shaped, *hair-pointed. **1832** LINDLEY *Introd. Bot.* 385 Hair-pointed..terminating in a very fine, weak point; as the leaves of many mosses. *Ibid.* 376 *Hair-shaped..the same as filiform, but more delicate, so as to resemble a hair. **1920** *Blackw. Mag.* Aug. 161/2 They would, I understand, be described by tailors as 'fine cachemire with *hair-stripe suitable for gents' morning wear'. **1821** SHELLEY *Prometh. Unb.* I. 398 Like the Sicilian's *hair-suspended sword. **1868** WHITTIER *Among the Hills* I, The hangbird..His *hair-swung cradle straining.

10. Special Combs.: **hair bag**, (*a*) a bag made of hair or of very thin thread; (*b*) a bag in which human hair is kept; (*c*) (see quot. 1966); **hair-ball** (see quot. 1753); **hair-bird**, a popular name of the chipping-bird (*Zonotrichia socialis*) of North America; **hair-bracket** (see quot. 1867); †**hair-bramble**, the dewberry, *Rubus cæsius*; **hair-brown** (see quot.); †**hair-bush**, a bushy head of hair; **hair-button**, a button made with hair; **hair-colour**, (*a*) ? = *hair-brown*; (*b*) the colour of a person's hair; **hair-compasses**, compasses which can be regulated to the utmost nicety; see quot.; **hair-cord**, (*a*) a fabric of which the surface is covered with fine stripes so closely placed as to resemble hairs; (*b*) a cord made of human hair; **hair crack** *Metallurgy* = HAIR-LINE 7; **hair-cut, haircut**, (*a*) an act of cutting the hair by a hairdresser; (*b*) the shape or style in which the hair is cut; (*c*) a customer for a hair-cut; **hair-drawn** *a.*, drawn out as fine as a hair; **hair-eel**, a kind of filiform worm inhabiting stagnant water; **hair-follicle**, the cylindrical depression in the skin from which a hair grows, extending through the corium to the subcutaneous connective tissue; **hair-hygrometer**, a hygrometer depending upon the expansion of hair when exposed to damp; **hair-kiln**, a hop kiln covered with a haircloth on which the hops are spread out to dry; **hair-lead**, a very thin lead used for spacing in printing; **hair-lichen**, an eruption attacking the roots of the hair; **hair-locket**, a locket for holding a lock of hair; **hair-man**, a man who dresses or makes up hair; **hair-mattress**, a mattress stuffed with hair; †**hair-meal**, a hair's breadth, the extent of a hair; **hair-mole (-mold)**, a mole on the skin, having a hair or hairs on it; **hair-moss**, a moss of the genus *Polytrichum*; †**hair-needle** = HAIRPIN; **hair-net** (see NET *sb.*[1] 3); so **hair-netted** *a.*; †**hair-patch**, haircloth; **hair-pencil**, a painter's brush made of camel's hair or the like; **hair-piece**, a length of false hair used to augment the natural hair; **hair-plate**, the plate at the back of a bloomery; **hair-point** *Bot.*, an extension of the nerve at the top of some moss leaves, forming a fine tip; **hair-pyrites**, a synonym of MILLERITE; **hair-raising** *a.*, capable of causing the hair to 'stand on end' through fear or excitement; so **hair-raiser**; **hair-raisingly** *adv.*; **hair-restorer**, a preparation used to promote the growth of hair; **hair-sac** = *hair-follicle*; **hair-salt** [Ger. *haarsalz*,], a name given to alunogen; **hair-seal**, an eared seal of the family *Otariidæ*, sub-family *Tricophocinæ*; **hair-slip**, a place on a green hide where the grain has decayed causing the hair to slip; so **hair-slipped** *a.*, marked with decayed places; †**hair-slitting** *a.*, hair-splitting (*fig.*); **hair-space**, a very thin space used in printing; **hair-spring**, (*a*) the fine hair-like spring in a watch which serves to regulate the movement of the balance-wheel; (*b*) of a trap (perhaps SPRING *sb.*[3] rather than *sb.*[1]); **hair-stone** [Ger. *haarstein*], a synonym of SAGENITE; **hair-style**, a particular way of dressing the hair; hence **hair-styling** *vbl. sb.*; **hair-stylist**; †**hair-tail**, a name given to fishes of the family *Trichiuridæ*, esp. *Trichiurus lepturus*; **hair-tail worm** = *hair-eel*; **hair-tidy**, a tidy [TIDY *sb.* c] for hair-combings; **hair-trim** [TRIM *sb.* 3 d]; **hair-trunk**, a trunk covered with skin retaining the hair; **hair-tuft** (see quots.); †**hair-weed**, a conferva.

1712 MORTIMER *Husb.* II. 2 Haws put in a *Hair-bag, and soaked in Water all Winter..will come up the first Year. **1723** J. NOTT *Cook's & Confectioner's Dict.* §136 To make cider..stamp your Apples, press them in a Hair Bag. **1747** H. GLASSE *Art of Cookery* vi. 65 Strain it through a coarse Hair-bag..then strain it through a Hair-sieve. **1824** J. MORIER *Adv. Hajji Baba* xvii. 188 The different operations of rubbing with the hand, and of the friction with the hair bag. **1911** R. G. ANDERSON in *4th Rep. Wellcome Tropical Res. Lab.* B. 253 By Blood-brotherhood is meant a mutual coalition... The rite..consists in incising the other's forehead..drinking the outflow of blood, smearing an adjacent lock of hair in its residue, and cutting this off to keep..in a neatly woven hair bag as a charm. **1966** J. S. COX *Illustr. Dict. Hairdressing* 69/2 *Hair-bag*,..a bag to hold the queue of a bag-wig. **1712** J. MORTON *Nat. Hist. Northampt.* vii. 451 In the Stomachs of these..the *Hair-Balls are compos'd. **1753** CHAMBERS *Cycl. Supp.*, *Hair-balls*, masses of hair of different shapes and sizes found in the stomachs of cows, oxen, calves, deer, and other animals. **1869** J. BURROUGHS in *Galaxy Mag.* Aug., The social-sparrow, *alias* '*hair-bird', *alias* 'red-headed chipping-bird', is the smallest of the sparrows. **1823** CRABB *Technol. Dict.*, **Hair-bracket*. **1867** SMYTH *Sailor's Word-bk.*, *Hair-bracket*, the moulding at the back of the figure-head. **1578** LYTE *Dodoens* VI. iv. 661 The Bramble is of two sortes..the great and the smal..The lesser berie is called..a *heare Bramble..The fruite is called a Dewberie. **1850** ANSTED *Elem. Course*, **Hair brown*, a colour formed of brown with a little yellow and grey. **1580** HOLLYBAND *Treas. Fr. Tong*, *Chevelure*, the *haire bush. **1583** STANYHURST *Æneis* II. (Arb.) 65 Wee ruffled his hearebush. **1593** *Acc. Bk. W. Wray* in *Antiquary* XXXII. 371, iiij grose of *haire bottonnes. **1785** BOSWELL *Tour Hebrides* i, He wore a full suit of plain brown clothes, with twisted hair-buttons of the same colour. **1615** MARKHAM *Eng. Housew.* (1660) 123 If you will dye your wool of a bright *haire colour. **1657** R. LIGON *Barbadoes* (1673) 36 Pure hair colour dapled with green. *Ibid.* 62 Cockroaches..of a pure hair-colour. **1885** J. BEDDOE *Races of Brit.* xiii. 144 The division of hair-colours..into red, fair, brown, dark, and black. **1906** *Jrnl. Anthropol. Inst.* XXXVI. 325 Such statistics as those..of eye colour, hair colour, as in many anthropological works. **1972** *Woman* 22 Jan. 17 Do you know that British women spend a staggering £10 million a year on changing their hair colour? **1727–51** CHAMBERS *Cycl.* s.v. *Compasses*, *Hair Compasses, so contrived with-in side, as to take an extent to a hair's breadth. **1807** T. YOUNG *Lect. Nat. Philos.* I. x. 101 When great accuracy is required, hair compasses may be employed, having a joint with a spring in one of the legs which is bent a little by means of a fine screw. **1866** in A. Adburgham *Shops & Shopping* (1964) xii. 133, 1 White *hair cord dressing jacket. **1899** T. WATTS-DUNTON *Aylwin* ii. 46 'This is her hair,' he said, taking the hair-cord between his fingers and kissing it. **1920** L. HARMUTH *Dict. Textiles* (ed. 2), *Haircord*, English dress muslin made with thick warp cords. **1923** *Weekly Dispatch* 18 Feb. 12 (Advt.), Useful Shirt in White Haircord Voile. **1951** *Good Housek. Home Encycl.* 34/1 For a..hair cord carpet, herring-bone the raw edges on the underside. **1960** *Textile Terms & Defs.* (ed. 4) 76 *Haircord carpet*, a carpet produced by weaving over unbladed wires. **1896** *Trans. Inst. Naval Archit.* XXXVII. 215 A 10 in. steel shaft..had shown fine *hair cracks on the surface near the propeller. **1925** *Jrnl. Iron & Steel Inst.* CXI. 113 A defect known as *snow-flakes* or *flakes* (America), *hair-cracks* or *hair-lines* (Great Britain), *Flocken* (Germany), and *cassures ligneuses* (France), has received much attention among manufacturers and inspectors of alloy steel forgings. **1959** J. H. THORNLEY *Foundation Design & Pract.* xiii. 103/2 The test for hair cracks consists merely of cleaning the pile and washing or immersing it in a tinted fluid. **1899** *Westm. Gaz.* 5 Dec. 8/1 The trade in Pretoria was kept very busy for about ten days giving the burghers a commando *hair-cut. **1900** *Ibid.* 22 Jan. 2/3 He won mainly on his promise that he would reform the city barber into charging two dollars fifty cents for a hair-cut. **1904** *Daily Chron.* 8 Apr. 4/7 The barbers of Bethlehem, Pa., have raised the price of haircuts from sevenpence to tenpence. **1923** *Glasgow Herald* 10 Feb. 8/8 Commenting upon how few of his customers in recent days had been 'haircuts', he remarked... 'The change of the moon always brings more haircuts out.' **1924** R. MACAULAY *Orphan Island* xviii. §2. 241 They were interrupted by Mr. Albert Edward Smith, who had come for a shave and a hair-cut. **1882–3** SCHAFF *Encycl. Relig. Knowl.* II. 1304 Its lengthy and *hair-drawn dialectics. **1895** BREWER *Dict. Phrase & Fable*, **Hair Eels*, these filiform worms belong to the species *Gordius aquaticus*, found in stagnant pools. **1838** *Penny Cycl.* XII. 9/1 Into each *hair-follicle..there open the ducts of one or two little glands. **1878** NARES *Polar Sea* I. xii. 319 The *hair-hygrometer continues to work in an unsatisfactory manner. **1805** R. W. DICKSON *Pract. Agric.* II. 754 Where *hair kilns are in use..charcoal is had recourse to. **1888** JACOBI *Printer's Vocab.*, **Hair leads*, very thin leads—mostly sixteen to a pica—rarely used nowadays. **1854–67** C. A. HARRIS *Dict. Med. Terminol.*, **Hair Lichen*, an eruption confined to the roots of the hair, followed, after ten days, by desquamation. **1679** *Lond. Gaz.* No. 1379/4 A *Hair Locket, set round with small Table Diamonds. **1689** *Ibid.* No. 2477/4 He took her from a *Hair-man upon the Highway. **1723** *Ibid.* No. 6170/9 James Mathewson.. Hairman. **1836** in *Mass. Hist. Soc. Proc.* (1892) 2nd Ser. VII. 276 Mine an upper berth; a *hair mattress to lie on. **1863** J. NASH *Brit. Pat. 2681*, I..take an ordinary wool, hair, or other mattress, and fasten it..to the top of the spring frame. **1931** *Times* 16 Mar. 2/7 Box-springs, hair mattresses. *c* **1391** CHAUCER *Astrol.* II. §38 Whan the shadwe of the pyn entreth any-thyng with-in the cercle of thi plate an *her-mele. **1680** *Lond. Gaz.* No. 1496/4 A *hair mold on his left Cheek. **1867** J. HOGG *Microsc.* II. i. 311 The undulating *Hair-moss..is found on most shady banks. **1865** M. EYRE *Lady's Walks* xv. 185 Quilts, mittens, *hair-nets, and other articles knitted, of Pyrenean wool. **1873** *Young Englishwoman* Jan. 38/2 Hair nets..may either be worked with coloured silk or, if intended for night wear, with white cotton. **1958** C. FREMLIN *Hours before Dawn* ii. 22 The wisps of untidy grey hair protruding from her hairnet. **1950** J. CANNAN *Murder Included* ii. 21 Elizabeth Hudson,..high-collared, *hair-netted. **1951** E. COXHEAD *One Green Bottle* vi. 164 The hair-netted lady at the next table. *c* **1611** CHAPMAN *Iliad* XIV. Comm., Stuff nothing so substantial, but such gross sowtege or *hair-patch as every goose may eat oats through. **1674** N. COX *Gentl. Recreat.* IV. (1686) 38 Take an Hair-patch, and rub his Body all over. **1763** *Gentl. Mag.* XXXIII. 83/2 Let the spots be gently rubbed with a *hair pencil. **1775** *Phil. Treas.* LXV. 243 It may..be cleansed by wiping it with a soft hair-pencil. **1965** *Listener* 26 Aug. 316/2 Modelling, carving and engraving, prowess with the inked hair-pencil: these complete the specifically aesthetic skills of the Chinese. **1939** *Time* 25 Dec. 2/3 He wears a toupee (*hairpiece or divot in Hollywood) for cinema and most public appearances. **1957** V. J. KEHOE *Technique Film & T.V. Make-Up* vi. 78 Incidentally, a wig covers not only the hair line, but the entire area of the hair on the head, while hairpieces are used to supplement the natural hair growth. **1969** *Times* 20 Mar. 27/1 The man sitting next to you may be wearing a hairpiece. **1881** RAYMOND *Mining Gloss.* s.v. *Bloomary*, The sides are iron plates, the *hair-plate at the back, the cinder-plate at the front, etc. **1818** HOOKER & TAYLOR *Muscologia Brit.* 25 *P[olytrichum] juniperinum*... Except in the want of the *hair-points to the leaves..we can find no essential difference between this and the preceding species [sc. *P[olytrichum] piliferum*]. **1893** H. G. JAMESON *Illustr. Guide Brit. Mosses* 10 The single nerve [of the leaf] may either cease below..or in..the apex, or may run out beyond it so as to be *excurrent*, forming a *mucro*.., *cusp*.., or *hair-point*. **1966** *Oxf. Bk. Flowerless Plants* 74/2 In the form [of *Grimmia apocarpa*] shown here the leaves are tinged reddish-brown and have white 'hair points'. **1805** R. JAMESON *Syst. Min.* II. 263 *Hair- or Capillary-Pyrites. **1897** *Westm. Gaz.* 16 Nov. 3/2 The writer being put on his mettle merely to throw in what an American has felicitously called '*hair-raisers' by the way. **1900** *Daily News* 24 Apr. 7/5 The hair-raising, long, steep descent of Box Hill. **1902** *Daily Chron.* 16 Sept. 3/4 Marvellous yarns of hair-raising perils. **1928** *Daily Express* 17 Aug. 9/1 There were a few hair-raising mishaps, but nobody was hurt. **1957** *Times* 30

Aug. 8/6 A runaway 70-ton Army transporter..careered downhill into the village of Carlton, Notts., to-day at 60 m.p.h. after its brakes had failed... 'It was a hair-raising experience..' said Driver Lee. **1960** *Times* 15 Feb. 15/2 England had left it hair-raisingly late, but it was enough. **1873** *Young Englishwoman* Aug. 414/1 Helena has heard '*hair restorers' so much condemned. **1893** LELAND *Mem.* II. 266 The search for a good hair-restorer..is as vain as the search for happiness. **1866** HUXLEY *Phys.* xii. 292 A *hair*.. is at first wholly enclosed in a kind of bag, the *hair sac.* **1795** SCHMEISSER *Syst. Min.* I. 270 *Hair salt..is of a silvery-white color. **1824** *Pettigrew Papers Shipping & Commercial List* 31 July (D.A.E.), About 500 *hair Seal Skins,..were sold by auction. **1846** R. B. SAGE *Scenes Rocky Mts.* vi. 56 A hair-seal cap and a frock-coat. **1865** BOYD *Swartzen* 106 Greenland hair-seal, South-Sea fur-seal. **1894** LYDEKKER *Roy. Nat. Hist.* II. 107 The fur-seals are, of course, far more valuable commercially than the hair-seals. **1903** L. A. FLEMMING *Pract. Tanning* 265 Grading and Classification of Green Calf-Skins... Second, regular No. 1... Scores are allowed in this grade, but there must be no holes, *hair slips or other bad imperfections. *Ibid.*, Third, good No. 2. This term designates those skins that are slightly hair slipped. **1683** KENNETT tr. *Erasm. on Folly* 139 Our *hair-slitting and irrefragable Doctor. **1843** *Penny Cycl.* XXV. 455/1 The smallest kind, which are called, from their extreme thinness, **hair-spaces.* **1707** MORTIMER *Husb.* xi. 244 With the small Stick (gently put into the hole to stop the knot of the *Hair-spring,..) place it in the Earth in the Moles passage. **1830** KATER & LARDN. *Mech.* xiv. 195 A spiral spring..called a hair spring. **1854** THOREAU *Walden* 37 With consummate skill he has set his trap with a hair springe..and then..got his own leg into it. **1875** KNIGHT *Dict. Mech.* II. 1049 Hair-springs are made of fine steel, which comes upon spools like thread. **1913** *Vanity Fair* (N.Y.) Oct. 91/1 Mme. Fried is prepared to show all of the latest..*Hair Styles. **1944** M. LASKI *Love on Supertax* ix. 84 She longed for some new perfume, a new hair-style. **1963** V. NABOKOV *Gift* ii. 139 He had a remarkable hair style that was also somehow indecent. **1936** *Harper's Bazaar* Mar. 88/4 They specialise particularly in *'Hair Styling', which of course means designing coiffures to fit the individual, as well as carrying them out. **1960** *Guardian* 19 Apr. 2/5 The Princess had led the world's hair-styling fashion. She had been 'an ambassadress' of British hair-styling. **1935** 'MADAME LOUISE' *Mod. Hair Cutting & Styling* 15 A *hair stylist is a hairdresser who has the artistic ability to suggest and create a new hair fashion. **1950** 'P. QUENTIN' *Follower* i. 6 One of her clients at Maurice's, where she worked as a hair-stylist. **1860** GOSSE *Rom. Nat. Hist.* 354 The ribbon-fishes..some of these, as the *hair-tail..are of large size. **1880** GUNTHER *Fishes* 436 The 'Hair-tails' belong to the tropical marine fauna. **1854** MAYNE *Expos. Lex.*, *Hair-Tail Worm*, common name for the *Gordius aquaticus.* **1907** *Yesterday's Shopping* (1969) 1164 Silver-mounted *Hair Tidy. **1918** 'K. MANSFIELD' *Prelude* 11 She..found nothing except a hair-tidy with a heart painted on it. **1935** *Punch* 15 May 592/1 The whole affair of the rejection of Miss Rinse's beaded hair-tidy from our Institute Exhibition has been most unfortunate. **1960** B. SNOOK *Eng. Hist. Embroidery* 116 It suddenly became genteel to embroider..hair tidies, pin-cushions, spectacle and comb cases and what-nots. **1957** S. BECKETT *All that Fall* 30 *Hairtrims and shaves. **1693** *Lond. Gaz.* No. 2832/4 A yellow *Hair Trunk Mail. **1881** POYNTER *Among Hills* I. 311 Her feet planted on her little hair-trunk in front. **1905** E. PHILLPOTTS *Secret Woman* I. ii. 21 The *hair-tufts of his eyebrows had been tawny, but they were now turning. **1923** G. A. GASKELL *Dict. Sacred Lang.* 335/2 Hair tuft between the eyebrows of Buddha: An emblem of spiritual truth within the soul. **1753** CHAMBERS *Cycl. Supp.*, **Hair-weed, conferva*, in botany, the name of a genus of mosses.

hair, *v.* [f. prec. sb.] Hence **hairing** *vbl. sb.*

†**1.** *trans.* (?) To edge with hair or fur. *Sc. Obs.*

1539 *Inv. R. Wardrobe* (1815) 37 (Jam.) Lynit with quhit furring, and harit with martrikis sabill. **1578** *Ibid.* 219 (Jam.) Ane..gowne..pasmentit with silver and a haring of martrikkes.

2. *trans.* To free from hair; to depilate.

1802-14 C. FINLATER *Agric. Surv. Peebles* 81 (Jam.) This practice..was called hairing the butter. **1824** *Mech. Mag.* No. 30. 32 By his method, raw hides, after hairing and baiting, are converted into leather in less than 30 hours. **1888** *Milit. Engineer.* I. II. 55 The hair is removed with a semi-circular knife, called a hairing-knife.

3. *intr.* **a.** 'To produce or grow hair.' (*Cent. Dict.*) **b.** 'To produce hair-like fibres: said of maple-sirup when boiled so low as to string out when dripped from a spoon.' (Funk.)

4. *trans.* To fit hairs to (a violin-bow).

1898 H. R. HAWEIS *Old Violins* 116 Most violinists prefer to pay a small sum and get their bows haired.

hair, obs. form of HARE, HERE *sb.*, HOAR.

hairb, obs. form of HERB.

ˈ**hair-band.** Also 5 -bond(e. A band or fillet to confine the hair.

c **1440** *Promp. Parv.* 236/1 Heere bonde (*P.* herbonde), *vitta.* **1483** *Cath. Angl.* 184/1 An Herebande, *trica, crinale.* **1530** PALSGR. 230/2 Heerbande, *ruban.* **1552** HULOET, Heere bande or heere lace, *discriminale, texta.*

hairbell, -brain, -brained: see HARE-.

hairbreadth (ˈhɛəbrɛdθ).

1. The breadth or diameter of a hair; an infinitesimally small space or distance; a hair's-breadth.

[*c* **1420**: see HAIR *sb.* 5.] **1561** T. NORTON *Calvin's Inst.* III. 259 Let vs not suffer our selues to be led so much as on heare bredth away from this onely foundation. **1611** BIBLE *Judg.* xx. 16 Euery one could sling stones at an haire breadth, and not misse. **1767** FAWKES tr. *Idylls of Theocritus* xiv. 12, I'm within a hair-breadth raving mad. **1815** SCOTT *Guy M.* xlvi, Drawing herself up so as not to lose one hair-breadth of her uncommon height.

2. *attrib.* or as *adj.*: Extremely narrow or close, as ***hairbreadth difference, escape, scape***; hence, ***hairbreadth adventure, risk.***

1604 SHAKS. *Oth.* I. iii. 136 Haire-breadth scapes i' th' imminent deadly breach. **1768-74** TUCKER *Lt. Nat.* (1852) I. 541 The hair-breadth differences of language. **1809** W. IRVING *Knickerb.* VI. ii. (1840) 320 His hair-breadth adventures and heroic exploits. **1871** FREEMAN *Hist. Ess.* Ser. I. i. 9 The hair-breadth scapes of hunted patriots.

ˈ**hair-brede, -breed.** *north. dial.* = prec.

14.. *Camb. MS.* Ff. ii. lf. 38 in *Retrosp. Rev.* Nov. (1853) 103 Oon heere-brede owt of this peyne They have no power to lyfte me. **1562** J. HEYWOOD *Prov. & Epigr.* (1867) 108, I am streight at feedyng within a here breade Where I fed before. **1855** ROBINSON *Whitby Gloss.* s.v., 'She's dying by hair-breeds', by very slow degrees.

hairbrush (ˈhɛəbrʌʃ). **1.** A toilet-brush for smoothing and dressing the hair.

1599 A. M. tr. *Gabelhouer's Bk. Physicke* 259/2 Pinguefye the hayrebrushe in Hartes marrowe, or in stale Bitches milcke, when as you will dresse your hayre. **1851** *Offic. Catal. Gt. Exhib.* 528 Circular hair brushes, capable of revolving either way. **1886** FENN *Master of Ceremonies* i, The nail had been driven in with the back of a hair-brush.

2. Used (chiefly *attrib.*) of a kind of hand-grenade.

1916 J. N. HALL *Kitchener's Mob* ix. 132 Ten or a dozen varieties of bombs were in use... The 'hairbrush', the 'lemon bomb', the 'cricket ball', and the 'policeman's truncheon' were the most important of these, all of them so-called because of their resemblance to the articles for which they were named. **1919** J. MASEFIELD *Battle of Somme* 9 Just before they got us we found some hairbrush bombs. **1923** KIPLING *Irish Guards in Great War* I. 75 The 'stick' hand-grenade of the hair-brush type. **1925** FRASER & GIBBONS *Soldier & Sailor Words* 113 *Hair-brush grenade*, the name for a type of hand-grenade used in the early part of the War, with a handle, the shape of which suggested a lady's hair-brush.

haircloth (ˈhɛəklɒθ). [Cf. HAIRE.]

1. Cloth or fabric made of hair, used for various purposes, as for tents, towels, shirts of penitents and ascetics; also in drying malt, hops, or the like.

1500 *Nottingham Rec.* III. 452 Every peece of hayrcloth. **1582** N. T. (Rhem.) *Matt.* xi. 21 They had done penance in hearecloth and ashes long agoe. **1613** SHERLEY *Trav. Persia* 19 Tents of blacke haire-cloth. **1764** HARMER *Observ.* ii. §17. 75 The same sort of hair-cloth of which our coal-sacks are made. **1850** MRS. JAMESON *Leg. Monast. Ord.* (1863) 220 Chastening herself with haircloth, which she wore under her royal apparel.

attrib. **1632** LITHGOW *Trav.* v. 229 [We] pitched our haire-cloth Tents round about Jacobs Well. **1866** G. MACDONALD *Ann. Q. Neighb.* xxii. (1878) 408, I sat down on a haircloth couch. **1879** *Cassell's Techn. Educ.* IV. 247/1 Milk..poured through a haircloth sieve.

2. An article (as a shirt, towel, etc.) made of this fabric.

1548 UDALL, etc. *Erasm. Par. Matt.* xi. 68 Woulde haue doen penaunce in heerclothes and ashes. **1577** B. GOOGE *Heresbach's Husb.* I. (1586) 10 b, It serveth to convey downe the Malt, after it is watred, unto the hearecloth. **1662** J. DAVIES tr. *Mandelslo's Trav.* 57 The Master of the Bath rubb'd me all over with a hair-cloth. **1753** CHAMBERS *Cycl. Supp.* s.v., Hair-Cloths, in military affairs..are used for covering the powder in waggons, or upon batteries. **1860** PUSEY *Min. Proph.* 176 The ascetic, Jonadab..in his hair-cloth.

hair-do (ˈhɛəduː). Also **hairdo.** [f. HAIR *sb.* + DO *sb.*[1] 2.] **a.** A way or style of dressing the hair (orig. *U.S.*). **b.** A cutting and setting of the hair.

[**1875** J. G. HOLLAND *Sevenoaks* 299 To do the bride's hair and act as the..supervisor of her dress.] **1932** E. FERBER *They brought their Women* (1933) 24 Why don't we wait until I get the new hair-do. **1935** *Mademoiselle* Oct. 42 He shows you how to achieve an evening look with the same hair-do, by drawing up the side curls high above the ears and clipping them with stones. **1941** *Illustrated* 6 Sept. 14/2 (*caption*) Judy tries a new hair-do. **1942** *Chicago Sunday Tribune* 5 July I. 12/2 Spurts of rain inspired feminine picnickers eager to protect holiday hair-dos. **1946** 'S. RUSSELL' *To Bed with Grand Music* iv. 55 Nail-varnish and perfumes and hair-do's. **1959** *Daily Tel.* 31 Dec. 9/7 The 'hair-do' took an hour and a half. **1971** *Petticoat* 17 July 2/2 Why do girls spend pounds on clothes, makeup and hairdos?

ˈ**hairdress.** The mode of dressing the hair; a head-dress.

a **1843** SOUTHEY *Comm.-pl. Bk.* Ser. II. (1849) 336 (heading) Hair-dress of the Madagascarites. **18..** *Amer. Antiquarian* X. 41 (Cent.) The Angakut of Cumberland Sound wear at certain parts the hairdress used by southern tribes.

ˈ**hairdresser.** One whose business is to dress and cut the hair.

1771 SMOLLETT *Humph. Cl.* (1815) 112, I was not above six hours under the hands of the hair-dresser. **1802** MAR. EDGEWORTH *Moral T.* (1816) I. xvi. 131 [He] went to a hairdresser, to have his hair cut and brought into decent order. **1856** B. CORNWALL *Barber's Shop* xvii. (1883) 161 Valets and ladies' maids have usurped the office of the hairdresser.

ˈ**hairdressing.** The action, process, or occupation of cutting and arranging the hair; the business of a hairdresser. Also, a dressing (see DRESSING *vbl. sb.* 4) for the hair.

1771 SMOLLETT *Humph. Cl.* (1815) 184 He..values himself chiefly upon his skill and dexterity in hair-dressing. **1782** JAS. STEWART (*title*) Plocacosmos: or the whole Art of Hair-Dressing. **1872** YEATS *Techn. Hist. Comm.* 299 It is in the Modern Period..that the handicrafts auxiliary to hairdressing have been developed. **1907** *Yesterday's Shopping* (1969) 532/1 Paraffin Hair Stimulant... As a hair dressing it is unrivalled. **1966** J. S. COX *Illustr. Dict. Hairdressing* 71/1 *Hair-dressing*, a liquid preparation of a creamy consistency used to anoint the hair of the head to improve its condition, impart a sheen, facilitate its dressing or hold it in position.

attrib. **1777** JOHNSON *Let. to Boswell* 27 Dec., Mrs. Thrale ran a great black hair-dressing pin into her eye. **1856** W. FERGUSON *Amer. by River & Rail* 67, I..resigned myself into the hands of one of the assistants in 'Phalon's Hair-dressing Saloon'. **1876** J. S. INGRAM *Centenn. Exposition* 701 It contained..ladies' hair-dressing rooms. **1892** *York Co. Hist. Rev.* 60 William Schreiber's Fashionable Shaving and Hair-Dressing Parlors. **1908** *Westm. Gaz.* 29 Feb. 3/2 The hair-dressing sketch shows the Greek silhouette..inspired by Greek ideas. **1909** in A. Adburgham *Shops & Shopping* (1964) xxiii. 273 (*heading*) Ladies Hairdressing Courts. **1966** J. S. COX *Illustr. Dict. Hairdressing* 71/1 *Hair-dressing academy*, in the 18th cent. in Paris these academies were described as follows: 'The academy for teaching the art of female hair-dressing'.

†**haire.** *Obs.* Forms: α. 1 hǽre, hére, 2-3 hære, 3-4 here, 3-6 heare, 4-6 heer(e. β. 3 haiȝre, 3-7 **haire** (4 heiȝre, 4-5 heyre, 4-6 hayr(e, heire, 5 hayr, heyeer, 5-6 hayer, 6 heyer). γ. 4-5 **hare.** [Of this word there were two ME. types, both however going back to WGer. *hâr*jâ* deriv. of *hǎr* hair: the first directly through OE., WS. *hǽre*, Angl. *hére* wk. fem., which regularly became in ME. *hêre, heare, heere*, and, with mutescence of final *e*, *heer*; the second, ME. *haire*, through OF. *haire*, med.L. *haira*:—OFrankish **hârja* (OHG. *hârra*); the form from French survived longest, but is now obs. or merged in HAIR *sb.* (sense 7). The ME. variant *hare* evidently arose from assimilation to the corresponding Norse form of *hair.*] Cloth made of hair, haircloth; *esp.* a hair shirt worn next the skin by ascetics and penitents; extended later to any kind of coarse or harsh fabric, as sackcloth or the like.

α. *c* **825** *Vesp. Psalter* xxxiv. 13 Ic ȝegerede mec mid heran. *c* **1000** *Ags. Gosp.* Matt. xi. 21 Hi dydun dæd-bote on hæran [*c* **1160** *Hatton G.* on hæren] and on axan. *c* **1200** *Trin. Coll. Hom.* 139 Stiue here to shurte. *c* **1205** LAY. 19707 Iscrudde mid heren. *a* **1225** *Ancr. R.* 126 Iudit..ledde swuðe herd lif ..& werede heare. **1340** *Ayenb.* 227 Hy hire ssredde mid þe here. **1387** TREVISA *Higden* (Rolls) V. 109 Marcellus deide y-cloþede in heer. **1430-40** LYDG. *Bochas* IX. ix. (1554) 201 b, Sharpe heares wer also layde asyde. **1529** MORE *Dyaloge* I. Wks. 116/1 [He] fasted, watched, praied & ware heare. **1535** COVERDALE *2 Kings* i. 8 He had a rough heer vpon him.

β. *c* **1250** *Gen. & Ex.* 1977 His cloðes rent, in haiȝre srid. *a* **1300** *Cursor M.* 22510 þe sun..it sal becum..dune and blak sum ani hair [*v.rr.* haire, hayre]. *c* **1350** *Will. Palerne* 4778 Hastili þei hent hem on heiȝresse ful rowe. *c* **1386** CHAUCER *Sec. Nun's Pr. & T.* 133 She..Hadde next hire flessh yclad hire in an haire [*v.rr.* heyre, heire]. *c* **1440** *Promp. Parv.* 221/2 Hayyr, or hayre, *cilicium.* **1530** PALSGR. 228/2 Hayre for parfite men, *hayre.* **1553** in Willis & Clark *Cambridge* (1886) I. 221, iiij yerdes of heire for thalter at viijd the yerde. **1600-1** *Ibid.* II. 482 Helpinge to carrie home ye haires y^t^ were vsed by the Painters ijs. [See also HAIR *sb.* 7.]

γ. **13..** *Cursor M.* 29090 In askes and in hare [? *orig.* haire] and weping and vneses lair [? *orig.* laire]. *c* **1450** *Nom.* in Wr.-Wülcker 725/25 *Hoc cilicium*, a hare.

haire, obs. form of AIR *sb.*[1]

c **1340** *Cursor M.* 19846 (Fairf.) Foure listis lange Vn-to þe haire þer-wiþ hit [a cloth] hange.

haired (hɛəd), *a.* Forms: see HAIR *sb.* [f. HAIR *sb.* + -ED[2].] Having hair; covered with hair or hairs. Often with adj. prefixed, as ***black-haired, golden-haired, long-haired.***

c **1380** WYCLIF *Wks.* (1880) 308 þe sterre herid or beerdid. *c* **1400** *Destr. Troy* 3780 A tulke full faire, Blake horit. *c* **1400** MAUNDEV. (Roxb.) xvii. 78 In Ethiopy er ȝung childer white hared. **1548-77** VICARY *Anat.* v. (1888) 34 He that hath not his Browes heyred is not seemely. **1674** N. COX *Gentl. Recreat.* I. (1677) 106 Crooked-leg'd, and commonly short-hair'd. **1766** PENNANT *Zool.* (1768) I. 30 A good skin well haired is sold for guinea. **1861** HULME tr. *Moquin-Tandon* II. III. v. 149 Others are granulated or haired.

haire mai, var. HAEREMAI.

†ˈ**hairen**, *a. Obs.* exc. *dial.* Forms: 1 hǽren, 4-5 **heren**, 4-6 **heeren**, 6 **haren, hairne**, 6-7 **hearen**, 7- **hairen** (9 *dial.* harren). [OE. *hǽren*, **héren* = OHG. *hârin* (MHG. *hærin*, Ger. *hären*), MDu. *harijn, harin* (Du. *haren*): see HAIR and -EN[4].] Made or consisting of hair; hair-.

971 *Blickl. Hom.* 221 He..hine þa ȝeȝyrede mid hærenum hræȝle. *c* **1000** *Sax. Leechd.* I. 382 Wring ðurh hærenne clað. **1382** WYCLIF *Lev.* xi. 32 Skynnes and heren shertes. **1591** *Widowes Treas.* (1595) F viij b, Strain it through an haren strainer. *a* **1605** MONTGOMERIE *Flyting w. Polwart* 462 An hairne tedder. **1649** JER. TAYLOR *Gt. Exemp.* I. Ad §8. 117 More..afflictive than his hairen shirt was to his body. **1690** W. WALKER *Idiomat. Anglo-Lat.* 385 'Tis bolted through an hairen sack. *a* **1825** FORBY *Voc. E. Anglia* s.v., 'A harren brum', is a hair broom.

†**hairester.** *Obs.* [f. HAIR *sb.* + -STER.] A worker in horsehair.

1415 *Ordo Paginarum* in *York Myst.* Introd. 25 Turnours, Hayresters, Bollers. **1422** *Ibid. note*, Pagina de lez Turnors, Hayresters, et Bollers.

haireve, obs. form of HAIRIF, cleavers.

'hair-grass. [After L. generic name *Aira*, with reference to the slender hair-like branches.] A name for grasses of the Linnæan genus *Aira*.
1759 B. STILLINGFL. *On Grasses* Misc. Tracts (1762) 371 To give such [names] as..approach as near as possible to the Latin names in sound where they could not be interpreted.. Thus I have called the *aira* hair-grass, the *bromus* brome-grass, etc. **1798** *Trans. Soc. Arts* XVI. 123 The grass it now produces (chiefly the aira or hair grass) is so hard and wiry. **1866** *Treas. Bot.* s.v. *Aira*, The tufted Hair-grass..is one of the tallest-growing British grasses.

hairif, hayrif ('hɛərɪf). Forms: 1 **heȝerife**, 4 **hayrive**, 5 **hayryf, heyriff, haryffe (harryf), harofe, harife**, 6 **herif (haylif), haireve**, 7- **hariff**, 8- **hairough**, 9 *dial.* (see quots.). [OE. *heȝerife* wk. fem., app. f. *heȝe* hedge + *rife*, of uncertain meaning. Another OE. name was *heȝeclife*, f. *clifan* to cling, CLEAVE: see *clife*, *clive* under CLEAVERS.] A widely-diffused popular name of Cleavers or Goose-grass, *Galium Aparine*.
c **1000** *Sax. Leechd.* II. 66 Wudu weaxe and heȝerife ȝecnuwa þa togædere. *Ibid.* II. 78 Wyl on wætere æscrinde ..heȝerife, marubian; beþe mid, & þæt lic gnid mid þære heȝerifan. *Ibid.* III. 38 Wyll in buteran þas wyrta elenan moran and heȝerifan. *a* **1387** *Sinon. Barthol.* (Anecd. Oxon.) 37/1 *Rubea minor*, hayrive. **14..** *Nom.* in Wr.-Wülcker 712/20 *Hec uticella*, haryffe. *c* **1440** *Promp. Parv.* 221/1 Hayryf, herbe (*S.* harryyf), *rubea vel rubia minor, et major dicitur* madyr. *c* **1440** *MS. Lincoln* A. i. 17, lf. 283 (Halliw.) Tak wormwod, or harofe, or wodebynde, and stamp it, and wrynge owt the jeuse. *a* **1500** *MS. Sloane* 5, lf. 29 a *Rubia minor*, Hayreff clyuer oþer aron is like to wodruff, and þe sed tuchid will honge in one is cloþis. **1530** PALSGR. 228/2 Haylife an herbe. **1597** GERARDE *Herbal* App., Haireue is Cliuers. **1674-91** RAY *N.C. Words*, *Hariff* and *Catchweed*, goose grasse [*mispr.* goose-grease], *aparine*. **1788** W. MARSHALL *Yorksh.* Gloss., *Hairough*, *galium aperine*, cleavers. **1856** *Farmer's Mag.* Jan. 62 A dressing machine.. for separating cleavers, goose-grass, or hariff from wheat or barley. **1876** *Whitby Gloss.*, *Hairrough* or *Harif*. **1877** *N.W. Linc. Gloss.*, *Hairif*. **1877** *Holderness Gloss.*, *Hairiff*, *Hairup*, *Hairif*. **1879** MISS JACKSON *Shropsh. Word.-bk.*, *Hariffe*. **1881** *Leicestersh. Gloss.*, *Erriff*..*Hayrough* is another and possibly the correct form. **1883** *Hampshire Gloss.*, *Heriff*. **1884** *Cheshire Gloss.*, *Harif*, *herif*. **1890** *Gloucestersh. Gloss.*, *Hairiff*, *harif*, *hariff*, *hariffe*, *hairif*, *haireve*.

hairily ('hɛərɪlɪ), *adv.* [f. HAIRY *a.* + -LY².] With hair or hairiness.
1925 W. DEEPING *Sorrell & Son* xxx, A lone, grim, anthropoid creature, hairily grotesque.

hairiness ('hɛərɪnɪs). [f. HAIRY *a.* + -NESS.] The quality or state of being hairy or covered with hair; hirsuteness.
1398 TREVISA *Barth. De P.R.* v. xv. (1495) 120 By the herynesse therof he defendyth the synewes of the chekes from colde ayre. **1578** BANISTER *Hist. Man* IX. 112 In the Hare such hearynes furthereth her swiftnes. **1665** HOOKE *Microgr.* 146 Cover'd all over with a brown short hairiness. **1828** *Blackw. Mag.* XXIII. 414 Old Father Pan, roaming in all his original hairiness in the forests.

hairing: see HAIR *v.*

'hairish, *a. rare.* [f. HAIR *sb.* + -ISH.] Slightly or partially hairy; †hairy, of hair.
1570 *Gaulfrido and Barnardo le Vayne* (N.), They teare their herish mantels grey. **1578** LYTE *Dodoens* VI. iii. 658 The first kinde of Cistus..hath rounde rough or hearishe stalkes.

†hair-lace. *Obs.* [f. HAIR *sb.* + LACE.] A string or tie for binding the hair; a fillet, headband; also, a fillet in *Archit.*
a **1300** *Land Cokayne* 69 in *E.E.P.* (1862) 158 þe pilers.. wiþ harlas and capitale. *a* **1529** SKELTON *El. Rummyng* 145 Some haue no herelace, Theyr lockes about theyr face. **1580** SIDNEY *Arcadia* III. (1724) II. 485 She took off her hairlace, and would have cut off her fair hair. **1698** FRYER *Acc. E. India & P.* 20 About their Heads they wear an Hairlace.. not to tie their Hair up, which is short enough; but it may be, as our Dames in England, to keep the Wrinkles out of their Foreheads. **1738** SWIFT *Pol. Conversat.* 205 They say, a marry'd Woman has nothing of her own, but her Wedding-Ring and her Hair-Lace.

hairless ('hɛəlɪs), *a.* [f. HAIR *sb.* + -LESS.] Without or destitute of hair; bald; glabrous.
1552 HULOET, Heerles or without heere, or hauing no heere, *depilis*. **1592** SHAKS. *Ven. & Ad.* 487 The..sun.. Whose beams upon his hairless face are fix'd. **1611** COTGR., *Pelé*..pild, hairelesse, bauld. **1836-9** TODD *Cycl. Anat.* II. 523/1 In front this region is concave and hairless. **1883** *19th Cent.* May 759 A toothless, hairless, slow-limbed animal.
Hence **'hairlessness.**
1871 *Athenæum* 27 May 649 This marvellous people (of which hairlessness..is one of the masculine phenomena). **1875** J. HAWTHORNE in *Contemp. Rev.* XXV. 556 His head is hatless..not to mention its hairlessness.

hairlet ('hɛəlɪt). [f. HAIR *sb.* + -LET.] A small or diminutive hair.
1862 *All Year Round* 13 Sept. 8 Mr. Samuelson..adopts the belief that each single hairlet on the fly's foot, serves as a sucking disc. **1881** MIVART *Cat* 287 A rod-like process, provided with long, slender hairlets.

'hair-like, *a.* [f. as prec. + LIKE.] Like or resembling hair; finely drawn out like hair.
1656 BLOUNT *Glossogr.*, *Fibrous*..full of hair-like threads, or strings. **1797** BEWICK *Brit. Birds* (1847) I. 59 *note*, Thinly covered with hair-like feathers. **1892** *Daily News* 7 May 2/8 Seeds..winged or provided with hair-like processes.

'hair-line.
1. A line or rope made of hair.
1731 GRAY in *Phil. Trans.* XXXVII. 33, I took a Piece of a Hair-Line, such as Linnen-Cloaths are dried on. **1870** BLAINE *Encycl. Rur. Sp.* §2946 In..hair lines, each hair in every link should be equally big, round, and even.
2. A very thin or slender line, as the up-stroke of a written letter. *to a hair-line*: to a nicety.
1846 WORCESTER, *Hair-line*..a very slender line. **1870** EMERSON *Soc. & Solit.*, *Work & Days* Wks. (Bohn) III. 64 A carpenter swings his axe to a hair-line on his log. **1884** *Harper's Mag.* Mar. 654/2 The first hair-line of this letter.
3. *Printing.* ***hair-line letter***: A very thin-faced type, generally used for letterings of mounts.
1888 in JACOBI *Printer's Vocab.*
4. = ***hair-cord*** (HAIR *sb.* 10).
1862 *Catal. Internat. Exhibit.*, *Brit.* II. No. 4104, Claret, drab, grey, and fancy hairlines. **1950** '*Mercury' Dict. Textile Terms* 256/1 An imitation hairline fabric, woven from woollen warp and worsted weft.
5. *Typogr.* The thin stroke in a letter form (as distinguished from the stem and the serifs). Also *attrib.*
1896 T. L. DE VINNE in J. Moxon *Mech. Exerc. Printing* 415 No defined width is made for the thin-stroke, which is now called the hair-line. **1932** *Paper & Print* Dec. 326/2 Finely cut serifs, not the hair lines of Bodoni, but cut to a point, are characteristic of some of the latest types. **1970** W. P. JASPERT et al. *Encycl. Type Faces* (ed. 4) p. x, All book types show some variation of thick and thin; in the fifteenth century it was slight, and gradually became more pronounced, until it reached the extreme in the nineteenth century when they became called hair lines. **1972** P. GASKELL *New Introd. Bibliogr.* 29 Didot's first neo-classic type did not show marked contrast, but later developments of the form, by Didot himself and by Bodoni in Italy, resulted by 1800 in faces of great contrast combined with vertical stress and unbracketed, hair-line serifs.
6. The limit-line of the hair on the head.
1922 S. LEWIS *Babbitt* i. 8 A tremendous forehead, arching up two inches beyond the former hair-line. **1936** L. C. DOUGLAS *White Banners* x. 225 The forward curve of the hair-line on the temples. **1959** A. SALKEY *Quality of Violence* viii. 128 The rope round his neck was cutting into the hair-line at the back of his head.
7. *Metallurgy.* In full ***hair-line crack***: see quot. 1949.
1923 J. A. JONES *Woolwich Res. Dept. Rep. no.* 55 51 The occurrence of hair-line cracks at one end of the forgings suggests that trouble might be experienced. **1925** [see *hair crack* s.v. HAIR *sb.* 10]. **1949** R. T. ROLFE *Dict. Metallogr.* (ed. 2) 121 *Hair-line cracks* (or *hair c[racks]*), (1) very fine short cracks occurring in the interior of some steel forgings which have not been allowed to cool sufficiently slowly from the working temperature... (2) The term is also applied to any fine cracks which may occur in metals and alloys. **1962** G. R. BASHFORTH *Manuf. Iron & Steel* IV. ii. 31 When once this [hydrogen-rich] constituent has been formed, its breakdown at low temperatures must result in the formation of hairline cracks, but hairline cracks will not be formed if the breakdown..is brought about at higher temperatures. **1968** *Times* 28 Aug. 21/6 The South of England Electricity Board has had to take its newest..power station..out of commission because of a discovery..of hair-line cracks in welding.
8. In various technical uses: see quots.
1935 *Burlington Mag.* Sept. 109/2 The hair-line sprays with delicate gold leaves. **1955** *Sci. Amer.* May 124/1 Its operation resembles that of a slide rule. You first position the hairline of the slider over the caret between the first four balls. **1960** *Times* 25 Oct. 15/5 He has recovered from a hairline fracture of the wrist. **1961** T. LANDAU *Encycl. Librarianship* (ed. 2) 160/1 *Hair-line rule*, a fine line of varying length used for division of text matter. **1962** *Gloss. Terms Glass Ind.* (*B.S.I.*) §72 *Hair line*, fine cord on the surface of glass. **1967** *Gloss. Paper/Ink Terms for Letterpress Printing* (*B.S.I.*) 12 *Hair lines*, fine filaments of foreign matter which forms barriers preventing the felting of many of the fibres and often leading to web breaks.
9. *fig.* A very thin dividing line. Also *attrib.*
1940 F. SCOTT FITZGERALD *Let.* 21 Sept. (1964) 124, I don't know how this job is going... Things depend on such hairlines here. **1959** *New Statesman* 29 Aug. 235/3 It is this hair-line compromise that Dr Stockwood has now challenged..in his statements, though not in his action, at Carshalton. **1962** *Times* 22 Mar. 3/3 It looked a hairline decision indeed.

hair-lip, erroneous form of HARE-LIP.

'hair-lock. A lock of hair on the head.
c **1000** *Hpt. Gl.* 526 (Bosw.) Hær-loccas, *cincinni*, *crines*. **1583** STANYHURST *Æneis* I. (Arb.) 28 Doune to the wynd tracing trayld hir discheaueled hearlocks. **1820** W. TOOKE tr. *Lucian* I. 493 Shore me of two of my hair-locks.

hairm, hairn, obs. or dial. ff. HARM, HARN.

hairough, local form of HAIRIF.

'hairpin, 'hair-pin. 1. A kind of pin used in dressing and fastening up the hair, fixing a head-dress, etc.
1818 TODD s.v. *Hairneedle*, The modern hairpin kept the hair in certain fanciful shapes. **1838** DICKENS *Nich. Nick.* xix, Kate was dressed to the very last hairpin. **1865** LUBBOCK *Preh. Times* 23 Many of the latter articles found in the Swiss lakes appear..to have been hair-pins.
2. A jocular word for: a person. Also, a thin person. *slang* (orig. *U.S.*).
1879 R. GRANT *Little Tin Gods* 8 That is the kind of a hairpin that he is! **1884** E. W. NYE *Baled Hay* 103 That's the kind of hair pin he is. He never works. **1910** W. M. RAINE *B. O'Connor* 214 Collins ain't that kind of a hairpin. **1959** I. & P. OPIE *Lore & Lang. Schoolch.* ix. 168 The names [for thin people]..are merely descriptive, as..hairpin, [etc.].
3. In full ***hairpin bend, corner***, etc. A sharp bend in a road or course likened to a hairpin in form.
1906 *Daily Chron.* 15 June 6/5 The length and steepness of the rise complicated by a double-hairpin corner. **1906** *Amer. Mag.* LXIII. 176/1 At hairpin turn, perhaps the worst of all, where the course doubles itself, were 500 machines and at least 10,000 people. **1912** *Motor* 23 Apr. Suppl. 2 As we dropped down the gentle 'hairpins' into Voreppe. **1912** G. B. SHAW *Let.* 9 Aug. (1952) 33 A journey of 800 miles includes crawls up endless hairpin zigzags. *Ibid.* 17 Sept. 148 Reversing at impossible hairpin corners. **1914** *Auto-Motor Jrnl.* 410/2 It is not unlike the higher part of Birdlip Hill, starting with a long and steep gradient and ending with a sharp hairpin bend just below the summit. **1923** *Motor Cycle* 13 Sept. 373/1 There is only one acute hair-pin bend, but there are several corners. *Ibid.* 374/1 A rather tricky and loose-surfaced left-hand hairpin was the principal feature of Chinnor Hill. **1957** P. KEMP *Mine were of Trouble* iii. 36 Its sudden ascents and declivities, its blind curves and hairpin bends flanked by unguarded precipices. **1971** D. O'CONNOR *Eye of Eagle* iii. 20, I..was driving up the hairpins that mark the beginning of the Simplon Pass.
4. Other *attrib.* uses.
1887 BURY & HILLIER *Cycling* xiii. 344 In many tangent wheels very fine spokes are used, and their most delicate point is at the bend in the hub, where the double spoke is bent 'hair-pin' fashion. **1895** *Montgomery Ward Catal.* 195 Fancy Chased Hairpin Box. **1906** *Westm. Gaz.* 29 Dec. 15/2 Joined to the ninon with coarse hairpin stitch. **1917** W. OWEN *Let.* 10 Jan. (1967) 426 Celluloid hair-pin box from Boots. **1932** D. C. MINTER *Mod. Needlecraft* 104 (*heading*) Hairpin Work. *Ibid.* 104/1 Hairpin-work D'oyley.

hair-powder. A scented powder made of fine flour or starch, used in the 18th c. for sprinkling the hair or wig in hairdressing; now seldom used except for men-servants.
1663 WOOD *Life* (O.H.S.) I. 475 To my barber for haire powder, 6*d.* **1800** HERSCHEL in *Phil. Trans.* XC. 444, I examined the focus of light, by throwing hair-powder, with a puff, into the air. **1864-5** KNIGHT *Passages Work. Life* I. 220 Hair-powder had altogether gone out.

'hair-ring. A memorial finger-ring set with a small lock of hair.
1696 *Lond. Gaz.* No. 3229/4 An Hair-Ring, set round at the top with Diamonds. **1709** PRIOR *Cupid & Ganymede* 23 Heaps of Hair Rings, and cypher'd Seals.

hair's-breadth, hair's breadth ('hɛəzbrɛdθ). The breadth of a hair; = HAIRBREADTH.
1584 R. SCOT *Discov. Witchcr.* v. v. (1886) 80 Limits.. beyond the which they cannot passe one haires breadth. **1638** BAKER tr. *Balzac's Lett.* (vol. III.) 31 There is not a haires breadth of difference betweene them. **1755** SMOLLETT *Quix.* (1803) I. 101, I am within a hair's breadth of doubting. **1856** DOVE *Logic Chr. Faith* Introd. § 3. 6 Our faith in the fact is not shaken a hair's-breadth.
b. (See quots.)
1706 PHILLIPS, *Hair's-breadth*, a Measure accounted among the Jews the 48th part of an inch. **1832** LINDLEY *Introd. Bot.* 400 A hair's breadth..the twelfth part of a line.
c. *attrib.* or as *adj.*: Extremely narrow or close = HAIRBREADTH 2.
1841 CATLIN *N. Amer. Ind.* (1844) I. x. 72 Our chief conversation was..hairs breadth escapes. **1850** ROBERTSON *Serm.* Ser. II. iv. (1864) 52 To draw some subtle hair'sbreadth distinction. **1868** MILMAN *St. Paul's* 120.

hair-shirt. A shirt made of haircloth, worn by ascetics and penitents. (Cf. HAIRE.)
1737 POPE *Hor. Epist.* I. i. 165 No prelate's lawn, with hair shirt lin'd, Is half so incoherent as my mind. **1869** FREEMAN *Norm. Conq.* III. xii. 213 After her death..a hair-shirt was found on her.
fig. **1884** *Pall Mall G.* 16 Oct. 1/1 If he had chafed less passionately at the hair-shirt of existence.

hair-sieve ('hɛə'sɪv). Forms: see HAIR and SIEVE. A sieve with the bottom made of hair finely woven; usually for straining liquid.
a **1100** *Gerefa* in *Anglia* (1886) IX. 264 Hersyfe, tæmespilan, fanna, etc. *c* **1420** *Liber Cocorum* (1862) 7 Þorowgh a herseve loke þou hit sye. **1530** PALSGR. 230/2 Heer cyve, *sas.* **1769** MRS. RAFFALD *Eng. Housekpr.* (1778) 345 Drain them on a hair sieve. **1894** WILSON *Cycl. Photogr.* 179 *Hair sieve*, a sieve with very fine meshes, used in the washing of gelatino-bromide of silver emulsions.

'hair-splitter. One who 'splits hairs' (HAIR *sb.* 8j); one who makes minute or over-refined distinctions.
1849 CLOUGH *Dipsychus* II. i. 42 A critical hair-splitter! **1853** DE QUINCEY *Autobiog. Sk.* Wks. I. 60 Not the cavilling hair-splitter, but, on the contrary, the single eyed servant of truth. **1857** DARWIN in *Life & Lett.* (1887) II. 105 It is good to have hair-splitters and lumpers. *Note*, Those who make many species are the splitters.

'hair-splitting, *vbl. sb.* The 'splitting of hairs'; the making of over-nice distinctions.
1826 *Blackw. Edin. Mag.* XX. 854/2 A sort of game at hair-splitting. **1857-8** SEARS *Athan.* 15 Metaphysical hair-splitting could hardly show the difference. **1874** H. R. REYNOLDS *John Bapt.* v. i. 306 The hair-splitting of logical Casuistry.

'hair-splitting, *ppl. a.* That 'splits hairs'; that makes over-nice distinctions, over-refining.
1820 T. MITCHELL *Aristoph.* I. p. cxxxv, The hair-splitting niceties of language. **1851** MAYNE REID *Scalp Hunt.* xxxiv, Credit..for their hair-splitting ingenuity. **1856** OLMSTED *Slave States* 121 It takes a more hair-splitting mind, than negroes are generally endowed with, to

think otherwise. **1877** C. GEIKIE *Christ* lvii. (1879) 602 Subjects for dispute to hair-splitting theologians.

hairst, Sc. form of HARVEST.

ˈhair-streak. In full, ***hair-streak butterfly***: A butterfly of the genus *Thecla*; so called from the fine streak-like markings on the wings of some species.

1816 KIRBY & SP. *Entomol.* (1843) II. 19 A small East Indian hair streak Butterfly (*Thecla Isocrates*). **1859** W. S. COLEMAN *Woodlands* (1862) 12 The only butterfly that really feeds on the Oak is the Purple Hair-streak. *Ibid.* 45 The very pretty though not brilliant Brown Hair Streak.

ˈhair-stroke.

1. A very fine line made in writing or drawing; *esp.* a fine up-stroke in penmanship.

1634 PEACHAM *Gentl. Exerc.* 28 The veines..are made with two or three haire stroks with a fine touch of your pen. *Ibid.*, Drawing small haire strokes from the hip to the knee. **1642** FULLER *Holy & Prof. St.* v. x. 393 Those who in matters of opinion varied from the Popes copie the least hair-stroke are condemned for Hereticks. **1781** COWPER *Let.* 23 Apr., You can draw a hair-stroke where another man would make a blot as broad as a sixpence.

2. *Printing.* The fine line at the top or bottom of a letter, a CERIPH. (Knight *Dict. Mech.* 1875.)

hairt, Sc. form of HEART.

ˈhair-trigger. a. A secondary trigger in a firearm, which acts by setting free a spring mechanism called the *hair*, and being delicately adjusted, releases the main trigger by very slight pressure.

1830 E. CAMPBELL *Dict. Mil. Sc.* 249 The hair trigger, when set, lets off the cock by the slightest touch; whereas the common trigger requires a greater degree of force. **1836** T. HOOK *G. Gurney* II. 192 My pistol, which had the hair trigger set, went off. **1851** *Offic. Catal. Gt. Exhib.* 353 Double rifle..with single hair-trigger.

fig. **1876** 'MARK TWAIN' *Tom Sawyer* 226 The inmates were asleep, but it was a sleep that was set on a hair-trigger. **1894** CROCKETT *Lilac Sunbonnet* 23 Her laugh was hung on a hair trigger, to go off at every jest and fancy.

b. *attrib.*: see quots. Also ***hair-trigger flower***, an Australian plant of the genus *Stylidium*, having a very sensitive column of stamens, which move from side to side on the slightest touch. (*Treas. Bot.* 1866.)

1834 M. EDGEWORTH *Tour Connemara* (1950) 4, I had been much amused by my father's account of Dick Martin —'Hairtrigger Dick'. **1886** *Pall Mall G.* 28 May 4/2 What is known in stage parlance as a hair-trigger audience—an audience, that is, of play-goers experienced enough to recognize every delicate bit of acting or skilful contrivance of stage-management. **1892** FITZPATRICK *Secr. Service under Pitt* xxi. 331 His temper was of as hair-trigger a character as the pistols which he carried. **1948** C. DAY LEWIS *Poems 1943–1947* 60 The quick-set ears, the hair-trigger nerves. **1968** *Observer* 1 Sept. 8/7 A hair-trigger laugh.

Hence **ˈhair-triggered** *a.*, having a hair trigger; also **hair-triggerish, -triggery** *adjs.*

1806 *Balance* 7 Jan. (Th.), I know not whether *hair-triggered pistols are in use in Penn. **1824** SCOTT *St. Roman's* xii, There are your hair-triggered rifles, that go off just at the right moment. **1937** L. C. DOUGLAS *Forgive our Trespasses* xv. 304 Intolerant, irascible, pig-headed, hair-triggered. **1945** *Daily Express* 4 June 2/7 The A.A. gunners..had become so hair-triggered that no Allied pilot dare come anywhere near. **1928** GALSWORTHY *Swan Song* II. vi. 162 'I admit,' said Michael, unhappily, 'it's all *hair-triggerish.' **1937** L. C. DOUGLAS *Forgive our Trespasses* ii. 41 He is always so autocratic and *hair-triggery.

hairum-scairum: see HARUM-SCARUM.

hairup, local form of HAIRIF.

hairworm (ˈhɛəwɜːm). An aquatic, nematomorph worm of the order Gordioidea, which, in its larval stages, is a parasite of insects, worms, or fishes.

1658 SIR T. BROWNE *Gard. Cyrus* iv. 65 Gnatworms, Acari, hairworms. **1752** SIR J. HILL *Hist. Anim.* 14 The Hair-Worm, called also the Guinea-Worm..This is the worm that..gets into the flesh of the natives. **1802** BINGLEY *Anim. Biog.* (1813) III. 404 The common hair-worm. The popular name of this worm originated in the notion, that it was produced from the hair of horses and other animals; a notion that is even yet prevalent among the lower classes. **1897** [see *horsehair snake* (HORSEHAIR c)]. **1930** E. C. FAUST *Human Helminthology* xxix. 483 (*heading*) Gordiacea or 'hairworms'. **1951** G. LAPAGE *Parasitic Animals* vi. 175 The larvae of the hairworms may also develop in freshwater worms or fish. **1963** J. B. GOODEY *T. Goodey's Soil & Freshwater Nematodes* (ed. 2) 522 The hairworms or gordiids..occur in freshwater ponds, ditches, streams, lakes, etc.

hairy (ˈhɛərɪ), *a.* and *sb.* Also 4 hari, heeri, 4–5 hery, 4–6 heery, 6 hary, heary, (hearry), heyry, 6–7 hairie, hayrie, -y. [f. HAIR *sb.* + -Y¹.]

A. *adj.* **1. a.** Having much hair; clothed with hair; hirsute.

a **1300** *Cursor M.* 8085 Þair armes hari wit hirpild hid War sette til elbous in þair side. **1388** WYCLIF *Gen.* xxvii. 11 Esau my brother is an heeri man, and Y am smethe. *c* **1400** *Lanfranc's Cirurg.* 106 An hery skyn. **1576** NEWTON *Lemnie's Complex.* (1633) 68 The hotter of complexion therefore that every man is..the hayrier is his body. **1577** B. GOOGE *Heresbach's Husb.* III. (1586) 128 His eares rough and heary. **1774** GOLDSM. *Nat. Hist.* (1776) VIII. 13 Caterpillars..are either smooth, or hairy. **1875** JOWETT *Plato* (ed. 2) III. 60 A bald man and a hairy man are opposed in a single point of view.

b. *transf.*

1609 HOLLAND *Amm. Marcell.* XXV. x. 280 They be called Comets or hairie starres, for that..by the flashing of fire from them, certaine haires seeme to be scattered. **1672–3** MARVELL *Reh. Transp.* I. 48 We call it [a Comet] an Hairy-star. **1697** DRYDEN *Virg. Georg.* II. 559 When Storms have shed From Vines the hairy Honours of their Head.

c. In specific names of animals. **hairy armadillo**, an edentate mammal (*Chaetophractus villosus*) found in Argentina; **hairy frog**, a West African frog (*Trichobatrachus robustus*), the male of which shows filaments of skin on sides and thighs during the breeding season; **hairy woobud** (*oobut*), *Sc.*, a woolly-bear; **hairy woodpecker** *U.S.*, a common woodpecker (*Dendrocopus auduboni* or *D. villosus*) of the eastern parts of North America.

1840 E. BLYTH tr. *Cuvier's Animal Kingdom* 125 The *Pichiy* of Azzara, and an allied species, the *Hairy Armadillo (*Tatou velu*, Az.), resemble the Encoubert. **1892** W. H. HUDSON *Naturalist in La Plata* i. 17 The fourth..is the hairy armadillo, with habits which are in strange contrast to those of its perishing congeners, and which seem to mock many hard-and-fast rules concerning animal life. **1956** G. DURRELL *Drunken Forest* ii. 47 The hairy armadillo is the vulture of the Argentine pampa. **1925** *Jrnl. Morphol. & Physiol.* XL. 342 The occurrence in a frog of long, hair-like processes covering the sides of the body and part of the thighs with a thick growth has excited the curiosity of biologists since the first discovery of this '*hairy frog' nearly twenty-five years ago. **1960** H. W. PARKER tr. *Mertens's World of Amphibians and Reptiles* viii. 138 The male of the large, West African, Hairy Frog..shows hairlike proliferations of the skin 10–15 mm. (0·4–0·6 of an inch) long, at the breeding season; they are completely absent in the female. **1731** M. CATESBY *Nat. Hist. Carolina* I. 19 *Picus medius, quasi villosus.* The *Hairy Woodpecker, weighs two ounces. **1808** A. WILSON *Amer. Ornith.* I. 150 [The] Hairy Woodpecker..is another of our resident birds,..a haunter of orchards, and lover of apple trees, an eager hunter of insects. **1839** J. J. AUDUBON *Ornith. Biogr.* V. 164 The Hairy Woodpecker, *P[icus] villosus*, is a constant resident in our maritime and inland districts. **1880** *Harper's Mag.* Oct. 672/2 *Picus auduboni* is not now recognized as a valid species, but only as a local variety of the hairy woodpecker. **1896** SHARPE *Birds Gt. Brit.* II. 11 On two occasions the Hairy Woodpecker is said to have occurred in the British Islands. **1956** L. W. WING *Nat. Hist. Birds* ii. 26 The Downy and Hairy Woodpeckers of North America bear striking resemblances to each other.

d. ***hairy at*** (***about, in, round***) ***the heel***(***s***) (***fetlocks***): deficient in breeding. So ***hairy-heeled*** adj., and simple **hairy**, in the same sense. *slang.* Cf. HAIR *sb.* 8 d.

1890 R. L. STEVENSON *Mem. & Portr.* 100 That hairy man of business knew his errand well. **1899** A. CONAN DOYLE *Duet* 212, I couldn't stand that chap at any price. A bit too hairy in the fetlocks for my taste. **1905** H. A. VACHELL *Hill* xii, The Rev. Septimus scowled also, because he had always maintained that any Harrovian could accept defeat like a gentleman... 'I always said he was hairy at the heel.' **1906** *Macm. Mag.* Nov. 9, I would join you and cry *Viva Pio Nono!* with the hairiest. **1922** J. BUCHAN *Huntingtower* xi. 213, I can't say I ever liked him... Bit hairy about the heels. **1927** *Blackw. Mag.* Oct. 488/2 He took refuge in..the display..of an honest but slightly hairy heel. **1928** *Observer* 22 Jan. 10/7 (Advt.), There is an Atlantic [locomotive] over there..—a bit hairy about the heel.., but quite sporting on gradients. **1930** A. E. W. MASON *Dean's Elbow* xi, What would those people say..if they knew? Hairy-heeled, eh? **1962** N. MARSH *Hand in Glove* ii. 47, I always say that when people start fussing about family and all that, it's because they're a bit hairy round the heels themselves.

e. Excited, angry, 'out of temper'.

1914 J. JOYCE *Dubliners* 54 She doesn't know my name. I was too hairy to tell her that. **1927** W. E. COLLINSON *Comtemp. Eng.* 116 He got shirty or hairy.

f. ***hairy ape***: a person of a low mental or social type.

[**1922** E. O'NEILL (*title*) The Hairy Ape.] **1931** *Times Lit. Suppl.* 1 Oct. 750/3 The submerged tenth, the hairy apes of society.

g. In various *fig.* and slang senses: difficult (quot. 1848); out-of-date, passé; frightening, hair-raising; crude, clumsy, rough, erratic.

Some examples belong equally under sense 1 b. *transf.*

1848 A. H. CLOUGH *Bothie* ix. 53 He..never once had brushed up his *hairy* Aldrich. **1914** D. O. BARNETT *Let.* 25 Nov. (1915) 13, I..threw a hairy salute! *Ibid.* 2 Dec. 16 It's top-hole fun, with four hairy captains teaching us things. **1934** H. G. WELLS *Exper. Autobiogr.* II. ix. 783 They were not throwing themselves into their parts as the hairy young Italians they were aping would have done. **1946** B. MARSHALL *George Brown's Schooldays* 7 There you go again using great long hairy words. **1950** WENTWORTH & FLEXNER *Dict. Amer. Slang* 239/1 *Hairy*, old, already known, passé; usu. said of a joke or story. **1962** D. SLAYTON in *Into Orbit* 22 If you happen to be pulling a lot of Gs..it might get a little hairy trying to manipulate the controls with all the finesse you'd need. **1966** 'W. COOPER' *Mem. New Man* III. iv. 239 The problem was of the kind that Mike described in his up-to-date slang as 'hairy', meaning complex in surface detail and involving more parameters than anybody would want to cope with simultaneously. In a word, messy. **1966** J. MILES in T. Wisdom *High-Performance Driving* v. 45 You can go just as quickly if you brake and accelerate smoothly. .. If it's hairy its bad. **1966** *Surfer* VII. iv. 48 One of the fastest, hairiest waves I've ever ridden. **1967** *Autocar* 5 Oct. 24/1 This Healey had all the works racing mods which brought the engine power up to 210 b.h.p. and turned what is a hairy and perhaps a slightly clumsy road car into a Ferrari-beating racer. **1968** *Listener* 20 June 816/1 Khe Sanh wasn't too bad. They had good bunkers there, but most places since Tet have been pretty hairy. **1968** *Sun* 12 Nov. 8/5 *Hairy*: a fast driver is a hairy driver. **1968** H. C. RAE *Few Small Bones* I. iv. 39 'Were you ever at one of his parties?'..'Just one... It wasn't my style really. In fact it was pretty hairy... Too many jumped-up gentry.' **1969** J. MORRIS *Fever Grass* xvii. 154 Things may be rough now, baby, but they could get really hairy if you try to cross me. **1971** *New Yorker* 21 Aug. 39 And do you, Elizabeth, take this man, John, to have and to hold, to love and to cherish, until the going gets hairy? **1972** *Times* 14 Oct. 6/2 Lord Snowdon said during a break for an orange juice: 'I was a bit frightened. Some bends are a bit hairy.'

2. a. Consisting of hair or of something resembling hair; hair-like. Now *rare.*

1535 COVERDALE *Song Sol.* vi. 5 Thy hayrie lockes are like a flocke of goates vpon yᵉ mount of Galaad. **1592** SHAKS. *Ven. & Ad.* 625 His brawny sides, with hairy bristles arm'd. **1634** PEACHAM *Gentl. Exerc.* 16 Take a Broome stalke.. chew it betweene your teeth til it..grow heary at the end like a pensill. **1694** *Acc. Sev. Late Voy.* II. (1711) 98 Her Feathers are thready or hairy.

b. Made of hair.

1535 COVERDALE *2 Macc.* x. 26 Gyrded with hayrie cloth aboute their loines. **1561** DAUS tr. *Bullinger on Apoc.* (1573) 94 b, Like an heery sacke which is wouen or made of heeres. **1632** MILTON *Penseroso* 169 The hairy gown and mossy cell. **1712–14** POPE *Rape Lock* II. 25 With hairy springes we the birds betray. **1878** C. STANFORD *Symb. Christ* vii. 177 Clad in hairy raiment such as prophets used to wear.

3. *Bot.* **a.** Covered with short weak thin pubescence.

1597 GERARDE *Herbal* I. xiv. §2. 16 Hairie grasse..is small and little, and rough or hairie like a goate. **1671** GREW *Anat. Plants* I. i. §45 Though the proper leaves are often hairy, yet these are ever smooth. **1776** WITHERING *Brit. Plants* (1796) I. 150 Styles 2, reflected, hairy. **1884** BOWER & SCOTT *De Bary's Phaner.* 70 They preponderate in very hairy plants.

b. In the specific names of plants: see quots.

1597 [see prec.]. **1796** WITHERING *Brit. Plants* (ed. 3) III. 118 Hairy Rest-harrow. **1861** MISS PRATT *Flower. Pl.* VI. 41 Hairy Sedge.

4. *Comb.*, as ***hairy-armed, -arsed, -chested, -clad, -eared, -fibred, -heeled, -legged, -locked, -looking, -nosed*** adjs.; also **hairy-back**, a fish of the family *Trichonotidæ*; **hairy-crown, hairy-head**, species of Merganser.

1530 PALSGR. 315/1 Heary locked that hath syde lockes, *cheuelu.* *c* **1611** SYLVESTER *Du Bartas* II. iv. III. *Schisme* 1039 Fasting hairy-clad. **1797** BEWICK *Brit. Birds* (1847) I. 291 Covered with hairy-looking feathers. **1885** *Encycl. Brit.* XIX. 518/2 The Hairy-nosed Porcupine *H[ystrix] leucura.* **1888** G. TRUMBULL *Names Birds* 69 In..Cabinet of Nat. Hist., Vol. III., 1833, the present species [*Merganser serrator*] is referred to as Hairy-crown. *Ibid.* 74 *Hairy-head*, name in New Jersey of the Hooded Merganser. **1894** FORBES *Monkeys* I. 52 The Hairy-eared mouse-lemur, *Chirogale trichotis.* **1896** LYDEKKER *Roy. Nat. Hist.* V. 392 The remarkable fishes known as hairy-backs..distinguished from the last [*Cepolidæ*] by the jugular position of the pelvic fins, which are in front of the pectorals. **1911** *Encycl. Brit.* XXVIII. 782/1 In the hairy-nosed wombat (*P[hascolomys] latifrons*) of Southern Australia the fur is smooth and silky. **1937** C. W. FERGUSON *Fifty Million Brothers* vii. 96 What is this thing that has..drawn the admiring gaze alike of dictators and hairy-chested novelists? **1944** A. RUSSELL *Bush Ways* xliv. 192, I found there were numberless burrows of the hairy-nosed wombat. **1960** G. SANDERS *Mem. Professional Cad* I. v. 44 Meanwhile the man will applaud in a manner that he feels will demonstrate a fine balance between hairy-chested virility and sensitive intellectuality. **1964** L. MACNEICE *Astrol.* ii. 62 Saturn makes you hairy-chested. **1965** J. S. GUNN *Terminol. Shearing Industry* I. 31 *Hairy-arsed learner*, a man who has probably shorn hundreds of thousands of sheep..but whose skill has been much reduced by age or infirmity. **1967** PARTRIDGE *Dict. Slang* 1164/1 *Hairy-arsed*, no longer young... Mature and hirsute and virile.

B. *sb.* A heavy artillery horse, so called from its hairy fetlocks. *Army slang.*

1899 A. CONAN DOYLE *Duet* 215 The hairies—trooper's chargers, you know. **1924** *Blackw. Mag.* Mar. 365/2 We had the bar placed as high as possible and put the old 'hairies' as hard at the jumps as they could travel. **1930** *Even. Standard* 15 Feb. 15/1 Whipping up the lumbering hairies to a desperate canter. **1959** *Times* 31 Dec. 10/7 No longer should I be dependent on 'hairies' hired from the local cavalry regiment.

hais, Sc. form of *hoase*, HOARSE *a.*

haise, obs. form of *has* (see HAVE *v.*).

haist, etc., obs. Sc. forms of HASTE, etc.

hait, heit (heɪt), *int.* Forms: 4 **hayt, haite, heyt(e, 5 hyte, 6–7 haight, 8– hait.** [Cf. Ger. *hott!*] A word of encouragement or command given to horses to urge them forward; in some dialects, to turn them to one side or the other.

c **1386** CHAUCER *Friar's T.* 245 The Cartere smoot and cryde as he were wood, Hayt [*v. rr.* haite, heyt] Brok, hayt Scot, what spare ye for the stones? *Ibid.* 263 Heyt now quod he. *c* **1460** *Towneley Myst.* (Surtees) 9 Harrer, Morelle, iofurthe, hyte, And let the ploghe stand. *a* **1577** GASCOIGNE *Flowers* Wks. (1587) 101 His thought sayd Haight, his silly speech cryed Ho. **1614** COPLEY *Wits, Fits & Fancies* (N.) Saying to his asse by the way..Haight, beast, and on a God's name. *a* **1825** FORBY *Voc. E. Anglia*, *Hait-wo*, a word of command to horses in a team, meaning, 'go to the left'; for *wo*, in this case, is not stop, but go. **1879** MISS JACKSON *Shropsh. Word-bk.* s.v. *Waggoner's words to horses*, The waggoner, standing to the left of his horses, would address ..the Pin-horse and Shafter alike: 'Haw-woop'..come towards; 'Heit' go from me. The whole team: 'Woo'..stop.

Hence **hait** *v. intr.*, to cry 'hait'.

? *c* **1690** *Bagford Ball.* (Ball. Soc.) 757 And Carters for the sport left Ho and Haiting.

hait, obs. form of HATE, HIGHT, HOT, HOTE.

haith (heθ), *int.* *Sc.* A quasi-oath: a deformation of *faith! i' faith!*

1724 RAMSAY *Gentl. Sheph.* I. ii. sp. 3 Haith, lasses, ye're no blate. **1786** BURNS *Twa Dogs* 149 Haith, lad, ye little ken about it. **1871** C. GIBBON *Lack of Gold* xi, Haith, lass, he'll gar you be sorry some day.

Haitian ('heɪtɪən, 'haɪtɪən, -ʃən), *a.* and *sb.* Also 9 **Haytian.** [f. *Haiti* + -AN.] **A.** *adj.* Of or pertaining to the island of Haiti or Hispaniola in the West Indies, or to the Republic of Haiti situated in the western part of that island. **B.** *sb.* A native or inhabitant of Haiti, or of the Republic of Haiti.

1805 M. RAINSFORD *Hist. Acct. Black Empire of Hayti* 448 Where is that Haytian so vile, Haytian so unworthy of his regeneration, who thinks he has not fulfilled the decrees of the Eternal, by exterminating these blood-thirsty tygers? **1811** *Gentl. Mag.* Sept. 275/1 After the ceremony, their Haytian Majesties..received the sacrament. **1828** J. FRANKLIN *Pres. State Hayti* 6 The partial eulogists of the Haytians go to the length of asserting that they have arrived at a high degree of moral improvement. *Ibid.*, Instances of intelligence have been discovered in the Haytian citizen. **1863** *Chambers's Encyl.* V. 274/1 The inhabitants of the eastern or Spanish portion of Hayti, rising against their Haytian oppressors. **1880** *Encycl. Brit.* XI. 546/1 Haytian Republic. **1964** E. A. NIDA *Towards Sci. Transl.* viii. 181 For Haiti, the Scriptures are published in Haitian Creole, which is essentially a colloquial dialect of French. **1966** G. GREENE *Comedians* I. iii. 75 The walls were hung with pictures by Haitian artists. *Ibid.* 83 The little houses the Haitians constructed for their dead. **1972** *Daily Tel.* (Colour Suppl.) 10 Nov. 23/2 The Haitian government is encouraging the hotel boom with generous concessions.

haiver, haivin, obs. ff. HAVER, HAVEN.

haji, hajji: see HADJI.

hak(e, obs. form of HACK *v.*^{1}

haka ('hɑːkə). *N.Z.* [Maori.] A Maori ceremonial posture dance accompanied by chanting; one danced by members of a sports team, etc.

1832 H. WILLIAMS *Jrnl.* 13 Jan. in H. Carleton *Life H. Williams* (1874) I. 113 They now prepared for their *haka*, or dance. **1845** E. J. WAKEFIELD *Adv. N.Z.* I. 98 A *haka* was now performed by about one hundred and fifty men and women. **1872** A. DOMETT *Ranolf* xv. vi. 19 The *hâka*-dances where she shone supreme. **1907** *Macm. Mag.* Sept. 855 The Maoris are a people with grand manners, and the *haka* is an amusement wherewith they beguile for their guests the long dark evening hours. **1920** *Glasgow Herald* 30 Apr. 9 At the close of the oration the warriors performed the 'Haka' war dance. **1934** *Bulletin* (Sydney) 15 Aug. 11/4 The haka is kept going by Maoriland footballers and hockey players. **1938** R. D. FINLAYSON *Brown Man's Burden* 13 Afterwards there were pois and there were hakas, and there was sure to be a dance. **1957** *N.Z. Listener* 22 Nov. 4/2 One common group ..of Maori words has come right over into New Zealand English—whare, haka and mana (e.g.) have all acquired (when used in English) overtones and extra meanings that were not in the original Maori. They are true New Zealandisms. **1963** *Evening Post* (Wellington) 12 Oct., 'Kamate! Kamate!' the fierce Maori haka rang out today as the 1963–64 All Blacks for Britain had their first haka practice.

hakam, var. HAHAM.

‖**hakama** ('hakama). Also **hakkama.** [Jap.] Loose trousers with many folds in the front, worn in Japan.

1859 A. STEINMETZ *Japan & her People* I. iii. 152 A very peculiar sort of trousers called *hakkama*, which may be called an immensely full-plaited petticoat sewed up between the legs. **1871** A. B. MITFORD *Tales Old Japan* II. 264 The *hakama*, or loose trousers worn by the Samurai. **1893** A. M. BACON *Jap. Interior* vii. 119 The Japanese costume of purple hakama, or kilt-plaited divided skirt, which forms the uniform of the little school-girls. **1963** 'G. BLACK' *Dragon for Christmas* iv. 67 Mr. Kishimura opened the door wearing heavy grey-black silk robes, with the *hakama* over-garment.

hake (heɪk), *sb.*^{1} Also 6 **haake,** 8 **hack.** [Known only from 14th (?) or 15th c.; origin uncertain. Mod. Norw. has *hakefisk*, lit. 'hookfish', applied to fish, as the salmon or trout, with a hooked under-jaw.]

1. A gadoid fish, *Merlucius vulgaris*, resembling the cod. Also extended to the genus *Merlucius*.

[*a* **1310** in Wright *Lyric P.* viii. 31 Alle heo lyven from last of lot, ant are al hende ase hake in chete.] *c* **1430** LYDG. *Min. Poems* (Percy) 201 (Mätz.) Hire skyn is tendyr for to towche, As of an howndfyssh or of an hake. **1555** EDEN *Decades* 273 A fysshe..whiche we caule haddockes or hakes. **1573–80** BARET *Alv.* H i Haake, fish, *Pagrus vel Pagurus.* **1624** CAPT. SMITH *Virginia* VI. 212 Hake you may haue when the Cod failes in Summer. **1769** PENNANT *Zool.* III. 157 The hake is in England esteemed a very coarse fish. **1880** GUNTHER *Fishes* 542 The 'Hake' is found on both sides of the Atlantic ..to a length of four feet. It is caught in great numbers, and preserved as 'Stock-fish'. **1885** J. S. KINGSLEY *Stand. Nat. Hist.* III. 275 The popular name current in England is hake, but in the United States the prefix 'silver' is generally added, to distinguish it from the species of *Phycis*..It is also frequently called whiting, New England whiting, or Old England hake.

b. Applied to other gadoid fish, esp. to species of the genus *Phycis* found on the coast of North America, and to the New England *Lotella rhacinus*.

1871 HUTTON *Fishes N. Zealand* 116 No. 74 (*Lotella rhacinus*)..has been termed the Hake. **1883** *Cassell's Nat. Hist.* V. 274 The greater Fork Beard or Forked Hake..a rare fish in British seas, but ranges round the European coasts and into the Mediterranean. **1885** J. S. KINGSLEY *Stand. Nat. Hist.* III. 273 Three species are common along the eastern American coast, *Phycis chuss, Phycis tenuis*, and *Phycis regius*. The first two are of some economical importance..they are generally known as hakes.

2. *transf.* (See quots.)

1855 ROBINSON *Whitby Gloss.* s.v., 'A greedy hake', a grasping discontented person. **1876** *Mid. Yorksh. Gloss.*, *Hake*..also, a grasping, covetous person.

3. *attrib.* and *Comb.*, as *hake-broil, -fishery, -hook*; **hake's dame,** an English fish, *Phycis blennioides*; also called *forkbeard, forked hake.*

1864 COUCH *Fishes Brit. Isl.* III. 125 Greater Forkbeard. Hake's Dame, Forked Hake, Goat fish. **1865** WHITTIER *Snowbound* 244 The hake-broil on the driftwood coals. **1895** BICKERDYKE *Sea-Fishing* (Badm. Libr.) 390 There are important hake fisheries in Irish waters..and also off Devon and Cornwall. *Ibid.* 152 A large hake hook.

hake, *sb.*^{2} *dial.* [prob. a. ON. *haki* (Sw. *hake*, Da. *hage*) hook; cf. also MDu. *hake*, Du. *haak*, also mod.Ger. *haken* hook. In OE. *haca* occurs only as a gloss of 'pessulus' bolt (*Epinal Gl.* 803).]

1. A hook, esp. a pot-hook.

(The sense in the first quot. is very doubtful.)

1488 *Ld. Treas. Acc. Scot.* I. 100 For cordis and hakkis and ryngis to hyng vp the claythis. **1706** PHILLIPS (ed. Kersey), *Hake*, a Pot-hook. **1795** *Chron.* in *Ann. Reg.* 31 The tea-kettle, and the hake on which it was suspended. **1806** BLOOMFIELD *Wild Flowers, The Horkey* vii, On went the boilers, till the hake Had much ado to bear 'em. *a* **1825** FORBY *Voc. E. Anglia, Hake*, a pothook.

2. The draught iron of a plough; = COPS 3.

1787 W. MARSHALL *E. Norfolk* (1795) Gloss., *Hakes, sb. pl.* the copse or draught-irons of a plow. **1846** *Jrnl. R. Agric. Soc.* VII. I. 34 One end being fastened to the 'hake' of the plough, and the other to the top of the coulter. **1863** MORTON *Cycl. Agric.* II. 720–7 (E.D.S.) *Hake* (*Suff.*), the dentated iron head of a plough.

hake, haik, *sb.*^{3} [Known only from 18th c.; derivation obscure: possibly from the root *hak-* of HATCH and HECK, if not merely a dialectal variation of the latter. It appears to be the prevalent form for sense 1 (which also occurs as HACK *sb.*^{2} 4); in the other senses it seems to be merely a by-form of *hack* and *heck.*]

1. A wooden frame suspended from the roof for drying cheeses; a wooden frame on which fishes are dried; a wooden frame for holding plates. *Sc.*

1768 ROSS *Helenore* 77 A hake was frae the rigging hanging fu' Of quarter kebbocks, tightly made and new. **1880** J. SKELTON *Cruiket Meg* xiii. 145 Plates suspended in a haik above the dresser. **1891** A. MATTHEW *Poems & Songs* 24 Hung like haddocks on a hake. **1895** *Month* Sept. 53 The hake was a triangle of wood studded with nails, and from every nail there hung a haddock.

2. A frame for drying bricks; = HACK *sb.*^{2} 3.

1840 *Jrnl. R. Agric. Soc.* I. III. 352 They [tiles] are placed one upon another on the *hakes* or piles in the sheds till placed in the kiln. **1843** *Ibid.* IV. II. 371 Set them to dry on frames (provincially termed *hakes*), covered with cloth, supported on iron standards.

attrib. **1886** W. A. HARRIS *Techn. Dict. Fire Insur., Hake-houses*, air-drying sheds, for bricks.

3. A rack for cattle to feed at; = HECK.

1863 MORTON *Cycl. Agric.* II. 720–7 (E.D.S.) *Hecks* or *Hakes* (*Lothians*), sparred boxes for holding fodder for sheep. **1891** H. STEPHENS *Bk. Farm* III. 387 Haiks to be fitted over troughs in byres and in cattle-courts.

4. A latticed framework in a mill-race or the like to prevent anything but the water from passing through; = HECK.

1891 *Pall Mall G.* 26 Sept. 2/2 At the 'backwater hakes' adjoining these mills the workmen sometimes break a bar or two, and the salmon coming from the sea get into the dam and are secured in very large numbers.

†**hake,** *sb.*^{4} *Obs.* Also 6 **hack(e, hag(g,** 7 **haque.** [app. an abbreviation of *haquebut, hagbut*, originally in *half-hake* or *demi-hake* = half hackbut, applied to a firearm of shorter length than the *hackbut*. It would appear that for this the simple *hake, haque*, or *hag* was soon substituted.] A short fire-arm used in the 16th c.

c **1538** [see HALF-HAKE]. **1541** [see DEMI-HAKE]. **1548** *Act 2 & 3 Edw. VI*, c. 14 An Acte was made in the [33rd] yere of the late Kinge..for some libertye to shoote in Handegonnes hakes and hacquebuytes. **1556** J. HEYWOOD *Spider & F.* lii. 22 Daggs, handgoons, hakes, hagbussers, culuerins, slings. **1607** COWELL *Interpr., Haque* is a handgunne of about three quarters of a yard long. **1656** in BLOUNT *Glossogr.*

hake, haik (heɪk), *sb.*^{5} *Sc.* and *north. dial.* [f. HAKE *v.*^{1}] (See quots.)

a **1529** SKELTON *Col. Cloute* 252 Howe some synge *Lætabundus* At euery ale stake, With, welcome hake and make. **1825** JAMIESON, *Haik*, a term used to denote a forward, tattling woman. **1828** *Craven Dial.*, *Hakes*, a lounging idle fellow.

hake, haik (heɪk), *v.*^{1} *Sc.* and *dial.* [Origin obscure: cf. Du. *haken* to long, to hanker.]

1. *intr.* 'To go about idly from place to place.'

c **1450** HENRYSON *Mor. Fab.* 73 The caller cryed; How, haike vpon hight, Hald draught, my dowes. **1674–91** RAY *N.C. Words* 34 *To Hake*, to sneak or loiter. **1703** THORESBY *Lett. to Ray* (E.D.S.B. 17) A haking fellow, an idle loiterer. **1811** WILLAN *W. Riding Gloss., Haik, hake*, to lounge, to loiter. **1828** *Craven Dial.*, *Hake*, to go about idly..*about* is generally added. **1855** ROBINSON *Whitby Gloss.*, *To hake*, to lay wait for news; to 'go haking about', prying.

2. *intr.* To go, advance; 'to tramp, trudge or wend one's way: the act implies considerable exertion or endurance' (Jam. *Suppl.*).

c **1450** HENRYSON *Mor. Fab.* 32 The Muske, the little Mouse with all her might, With haste shee haked vnto that hill of hight. *c* **1475** *Rauf Coilȝear* 644 In that hardy in hy, he haiket to that hall For to wit gif Wymondis wynning was thair. *a* **1825** FORBY *Voc. E. Anglia, Hake*, to toil; particularly in walking... 'He has been haking and hattering all day long'.

3. *trans.* To urge; to pester.

1855 ROBINSON *Whitby Gloss.* s.v., 'He hakes my very heart out.' **1892** M. C. MORRIS *Yorksh. Folk-t.* 319 To hake is to follow with inquiries, to annoy, to pester, to hurry on. 'Hake 'em away!' i.e. urge them on almost faster than they are able to go.

hake, *v.*^{2} [f. HAKE *sb.*^{1}] *intr.* To fish for hake. Hence **'haking** *vbl. sb.*

1895 J. BICKERDYKE *Fishing* (Badm. Libr.) xiii. 390 The hakeing season is principally in the autumn and winter.

‖**Hakea** ('heɪkiːə). *Bot.* [mod. Bot. L.: from name of Baron Hake.] A large genus of proteaceous plants, consisting principally of tall shrubs, found in Australia and Tasmania.

1849 C. STURT *Expedit. C. Australia* I. 353 The shrubs for the most part consisted of hakea and mimosae. **1882** *Garden* 10 June 398/1 Banksias and Hakeas are numerous.

haked, hacot ('hækɪd, 'hækət). *dial.* Forms: 1 **hacod, hæced, hæcid,** 7 **hacot,** 8 **hackhead, haget,** 8–9 **haked.** [OE. *hacod, hæced* = OS. *hacud*, OHG. *hahhit, hęhhit* (MHG. *hęchet, hecht*, G. *hecht*), prob. from the root of WGer. **hakjan*, OHG. *hęcken*, to stick, pierce: cf. the other names *pike, ged*, Fr. *brochet.*] A fish, the pike: usually applied to a large sort of pike.

a **700** *Epinal Gloss.* 660 *Mugil*, hæcid. *a* **800** *Erf. Gloss.* Hecid. *a* **800** *Corpus Gloss.* 1342 *Mugil*, hæced. *c* **1000** ÆLFRIC *Colloq.* in Wr.-Wülcker 94 Ælas and hacodas, mynas and æleputan. *c* **1050** *Voc.* Ibid. 443/32 *Mugil*, hacod, oððe heardra. *a* **1667** SKINNER *Etymol. Ling. Angl., Hakot*, occidentalibus adhuc usitatum. **1720** T. COX *Magna Britannia* II. 1053/1 Pikes of a wonderful Bigness, which they call Hakeds. **1759** B. MARTIN *Nat. Hist. Eng.* 107 The neighbouring Meers abound with Fowl and Fish, Eels, Pikes, Hackheads, &c. **1787** BEST *Angling* (ed. 2) 56 In Rumsey mere..are..large Pikes which they call Hagets. **1847** HALLIWELL, *Haked*, a large pike. *Cambr.*

‖**hakeem, hakim** (hə'kiːm). *Oriental.* Forms: 7 **hackeem, hackin,** 7–9 **hakim,** 8–9 **hakem,** 9 **hakeem.** [Arabic *ḥakīm* wise, learned, philosopher, physician, f. *ḥakama* to exercise authority, in deriv. conj. to know, be wise or learned.] A physician or doctor, in Mohammedan countries and in India.

[**1585** T. WASHINGTON tr. *Nicholay's Voy.* III. xii. 93 The common Phisitions which the Turkes call Echim.] **1638** SIR T. HERBERT *Trav.* (ed. 2) 234 The Doctors are nam'd *Hackeems*. **1662** J. DAVIES tr. *Olearius' Voy. Ambass.* v. 220 He brought along with him his *Hakim*, or Physician. **1845** STOCQUELER *Handbk. Brit. India* (1854) 308 Many ignorant *hakeems* who impose..upon the dense population of that locality. **1884** BROWNING *Ferishtah, Family* 51 Why, his reason chimed Right with the Hakim's.

hakeney, hakern, obs. ff. HACKNEY, ACORN.

‖**Hakenkreuz, hakenkreuz** ('hakənkrɔɪts). [Ger.] The Nazi swastika. Also *attrib.*

1931 *Times* 23 Dec. 7/4 A large Nazi Hakenkreuz flag, 'which can be seen for miles', flies from the tallest chimney. **1935** C. ISHERWOOD *Mr. Norris changes Trains* xi. 165 Hitler's negotiations with the Right had broken down; the Hakenkreuz was even flirting mildly with the Hammer and Sickle. **1966** 'M. ALBRAND' *Door fell Shut* xvi. 115 His eyes fell on a large hakenkreuz. To come upon the Nazi insignia so unexpectedly made Bronsky feel slightly sick. **1972** *Oxford Times* 28 July 9 Perhaps he [*sc.* Hitler] hoped the Hakenkreuz would bring bad luck to his enemies.

haker ('heɪkə(r)). [f. HAKE *sb.*^{1} + -ER^1.] A fisherman or a fishing-boat engaged in catching hake.

1880 *Harper's Mag.* Aug. 340/1 The man who fished for hake, and also his boat, was a 'haker'.

'hake's-tooth. [f. HAKE *sb.*^{1} + TOOTH.] The tooth-shell, *Dentalium*.

1731 CAPT. W. WRIGLESWORTH *MS. Log-bk. of the 'Lyell'*, 18 June, The Soundings Red Sand with Hakes teeth. **1881** HAMERSLY *Naval Encycl.*, *Hake's Teeth*, a term for *Dentalium*, a species of shell-fish whose presence in the British Channel serves as a guide to pilots in foggy weather. Also applied to some of the deep soundings in the Channel.

haketon(e, obs. form of HAQUETON, ACTON.

hakille, obs. form of HACKLE.

‖**hakim** ('hɑːkɪm). *Oriental.* Also 7 **haccam, hackame, hackum,** 8 **hackham.** [Arabic *ḥākim* governor, f. *ḥakama* to exercise authority.] A judge, ruler, or governor, in Mohammedan countries and in India; the administrative authority in a district.

1615 BEDWELL *Arab. Trudg.*, The Haccams ofttimes are men of meaner degree. **1713** OCKLEY *Acc. Barbary* 105 Married the next Day by a Priest or Hackham. **1811** *Niebuhr's Trav. Arab.* xxii in Pinkerton *Voy.* X. 37 (Stanf.) I applied to the Hakim or judge of the village. **1866** SIR A. LYALL *Verses in India, Old Pindaree* (1889) 3 Then comes a Settlement Hakim, to teach us to plough and to weed.

hakim, var. of HAKEEM.

†**'haking.** *Obs.* A kind of net, or apparatus with net attached, used for taking sea-fish.

1602 CAREW *Cornwall* 30 a, For the Haking, certain stakes are pitched in the Ose at low water, athwart some Creeke, from shore to shore, to whose feete they fasten a net. *Ibid.*, Of round fish..The generall way of killing these..is by Weares, Hakings, Saynes, Tuckes, and Tramels. *Ibid.*, The tramel..serueth to such vse as the Weare and Haking.

Hakka ('hækə), *sb.* (and *a.*) [Chinese.] A member of a people now dwelling in parts of southern China, especially in the province of Kwangtung or Canton, and in Taiwan, Hong Kong, etc.; also the dialect spoken by this people. Also *attrib.* or as *adj.*

1867 *N. & Q. on China & Japan* I. 66/2 It is a common saying among the Hakkas, that a Punti may study Hakka for many years, and yet not be able to speak it correctly. **1878** H. A. GILES *Gloss. of Reference* 56 *Hakkas*, strangers. A race said to have migrated from the North of China (Kiangsu or Shantung) to the Kuang-tung province at the time of the Yuan dynasty AD 1206–1368. **1879** *Encycl. Brit.* IX. 416/2 Hakkas from the vicinity of Swatow. **1881** J. D. BALL *Easy Sentences Hakka Dial.* p. i, While engaged in my studies in the Hakka dialect I put the sentences in Giles' *Handbook of the Swatow Dialect* into Hakka. **1921** *Outward Bound* July 17/1 He converses freely in Hakka, Cantonese, Mandarin [etc.]. **1926** *Blackw. Mag.* Nov. 628/1 The Hakkas, as wood-cutters and hunters, had already penetrated into the foothills. **1964** *Asia Mag.* 30 Aug. 5/1 (*caption*) Below is a Hakka woman in a work gang in K.L. **1968** 'B. MATHER' *Springers* xviii. 196 The old man at the helm..looked like a Hakka to me. They are fishermen, and nobody's fools. **1971** K. HOPKINS *Hong Kong* 235 Cantonese is very much the predominant language but there are minorities who speak Hakka. **1971** *Nat. Geographic* Oct. 550/1 (*caption*) Curtained hat identifies a Hakka farm-woman. A distinctive group of immigrant Chinese, Hakkas till hillsides in the New Territories.

hal, obs. f. HALE, HALL[1]; pa. t. of HELE *v.*[1]

‖**Halachah, Halakah** (hə'lɑːkə). Also **halacha, -aka.** [Heb. *hălākāh* (pl. *hălākōth*) that which one walks by, f. *hālak* to walk.]

A legal decision regarding a matter or case for which there is no direct enactment in the Mosaic law, deduced by analogy from this law or from the Scriptures, and included as a binding precept in the Mishna.

1856 ETHERIDGE *Jerus. & Tiberias* 182 *Hilkatha*, or *Halaka*, the ultimate conclusion on a matter debated; henceforth constituting a rule of conduct; from *halak*, 'to walk'. **1881** W. R. SMITH *Old Test. in Jew. Ch.* iii. 13 Halacha was legal teaching, systematized legal precept. **1882** FARRAR *Early Chr.* I. 555 He was met by Rabbi Eliezer in the street of Sepphoris, and gave to the Rabbi a Halacha, or legal decision, which pleased him, on Deut. xxiii. 19.

Hence **Ha'lachic** *a.*, of, pertaining to, or relating to the Halachah. **Ha'lachist**, one who deduces laws from the Bible.

1856 ETHERIDGE *Jerus. & Tiberias* 428 An entire systematic discourse..on an halakic thema. **1878** *Academy* 606/1 A great Halakhic teacher in Castille at the time of the expulsion of the Jews from Spain. **1882** FARRAR *Early Chr.* I. 473 The Jewish Halachists, who spend their whole lives in torturing strange inferences out of Levitic regulations.

Halafian (hə'lɑːfɪən), *a. Archæol.* [f. Tell *Halaf* in north-eastern Syria + -IAN.] Denoting the chalcolithic culture which existed in northern Syria and Iraq, characterized by polychrome pottery, evidence of which was first discovered at Tell Halaf.

1937 G. E. WRIGHT *Pottery of Palestine* ii. 30 Painted motifs used by the Palestinian potters are common in the region of the Halâ f pottery... When it comes to the farms, however, the Ghassulian has very little in common with the Halafian. *Ibid.* 31 A type of small bowl with gently rounded sides seems also to be popular in the Halafian culture. **1947** *Iraq* IX. 45 It is evident that there must have been an extensive prehistoric settlement of the T. Halaf period. This Halafian culture has been found throughout the whole of Northern Syria from Ugarit in the west across the Upper Euphrates valley as far as the district of Nineveh on the Tigris. **1950** G. DANIEL *100 Yrs. Archaeol.* vi. 204 The Tell Halaf culture or the Halafian as it was called, could be accurately dated.

halal (hɑː'lɑːl), *v.* Also **hallal.** [f. Arab. *ḥalāl* lawful.] *trans.* To kill (an animal) in the manner prescribed by Muslim law. Hence **halal** *sb.*, lawful food; also *attrib.* and as *adj.*

1855 R. F. BURTON *Personal Narr. Pilgrimage to El-Medinah* I. xiii. 377 To '*halál*' is to kill an animal according to Moslem rites: a word is wanted to express the act, and we cannot do better than to borrow it from the people to whom the practice belongs. **1858** W. JESSE tr. *Ferrier's Hist. Afghans* xxi. 289 They will not eat meat unless it is *halal* (lawful), that is, the animal must have its face turned towards Mecca, and its throat cut in a particular part of the neck. **1877** R. A. STERNDALE *Seonee* 454 *Hālāl.* Slaughtered according to religious law. **1879** F. T. POLLOK *Sport in Brit. Burmah* I. 142 My Mahouts, when they have got down to halal, or cut the throat of a stag, have had a narrow escape. *Ibid.* 179 The mahouts would not eat the stag as it had not been hallaled, so my Madrass servants and the Burmese had it all to themselves. **1883** E. H. AITKEN *Tribes on my Frontier* 167 To allow Peer Khan to make it halal, by cutting its throat in the name of Allah, and dividing the webs of its feet. **1895** *Daily News* 1 June 5/5 The special 'Halál' meal, ordained for the I'd [*i.e.* I'd-uz'zubá Festival] in question, will be provided. **1910** *Scribner's Mag.* Apr. 404/1 Wherever possible the game being hal-lalled in orthodox fashion by the Mahometans. **1952** J. MASTERS *Deceivers* xvii. 193 So the two black goats died, one in the Mohammedan manner, the halal, and one in the Hindu manner, its head struck off at a single blow. **1966** *Guardian* 9 Dec. 8/6 Nuts, spices, curries, meat (avowedly halal at that!). **1970** *Listener* 9 July 44/2 You can get kosher meat next to halal meat.

‖**ha'lalcor.** *East Indies.* Forms: 7 **halalchor, holacueur, holencor, alchore,** 8 **halla-, halichore, hollocore,** 9 **hallalcor.** [Persian (Urdū) *ḥalālkhōr*, f. Arab. *ḥalāl* a thing religiously lawful or indifferent + Pers. *khūr-dan* to eat.] One of the lowest and most despised class in India, Iran, etc., (*lit.*) to whom everything is lawful food.

1662 J. DAVIES tr. *Mandelslo's Trav.* 59 One of those *Holacueurs*, who are wont to march in the head of the Caffilas ..and serve instead of Trumpeters. **1696** OVINGTON *Voy. Surat* 382 (Y.) The Halalchors..are another Sort of Indians at Suratt, the most contemptible. **1698** FRYER *Acc. E. India & P.* 28 As base as the Holencores. **1786** BURNS *Let. to R. Aiken* Oct., Those misguided few..who joined, to use a Gentoo phrase, the 'hallachores' of the human race. **1788** BURKE *Sp. agst. W. Hastings* Wks. XIII. 323 He is wholly driven from all honest society..He becomes an Halichore. **1812** MARIA GRAHAM *Jrnl. Resid. India* 31 (Y.) For the meaner offices we have a Hallalcor or Chandela (one of the most wretched Pariahs).

halas, obs. var. ALAS, *int.*

c **1500** *Melusine* xxxvii. 298 'Halas, Melusyne', sayd Raymondin..'now haue I lost you for euer'. **1610** HOLLAND *Camden's Brit.* (1637) 296 It of Edward King (halas) our Hector, wailes the death.

halatinous (hə'lætɪnəs), *a.* [f. Gr. ἁλάτιν-ος made of salt, f. ἅλς salt: see -OUS.] Saline, salt.

1886 in *Syd. Soc. Lex.*

halation (hə'leɪʃən). [irreg. f. HALO + -ATION.]

a. *Photogr.* The term used to denote the spreading of light beyond its proper boundary in the negative image upon the plate, producing local fog around the high lights, or those portions of the picture which are brighter than the rest of the image (*Cycl. Photogr.*).

1859 G. W. PERRY in *Jrnl. Photogr. Soc. Lond.* 15 Nov., [The phenomenon] to which, until a better one is found, I have applied the term halation. **1881** *Athenæum* No. 2826. 857 Papers read: 'Halation', by Capt. Abney. This was shown not to arise from any turbidity in the glass, but from light being reflected from the back of the plate.

b. A similar effect in television (see quots.).

1937 A. T. WITTS *Television Cycl.* 56 *Halation*, the reflection of image rays by the back of a screen or film. Such reflection produces a blurring of the image as viewed by the observer, or is reproduced on the film. **1940** [see BLOOMING *vbl. sb.*[1] 3]. **1958** *Chambers's Techn. Dict.* Suppl. 983/2 *Halation*, bright annular area around the cathode-ray tube phosphor spot, arising from internal reflection within the glass support.

halawi (hə'lɑːwiː). Also 9 **khalaweh.** [Arab.] A kind of sweetmeat; = HALVA, HULWA.

1836 E. W. LANE *Acct. Manners & Customs Mod. Egyptians* II. 14 The seller of a kind of sweetmeat (*khala'weh*), composed of treacle fried with some other ingredients. **1911** T. E. LAWRENCE *Lett.* (1938) 129 About halawi—I hope you remember the particular sticky sweetmeat of which Thompson & myself used to eat pounds last year. **1913** —— *Home Lett.* (1954) 248 Eat that halawi in my house.

halberd, halbert ('hælbəd, -ət), *sb.* Forms: 5 **haubert,** 6 **hauberd(e, hal-, hawbart, holber, halbearde,** 6–7 **holberd(e,** 7 **hol-, hould-b(e)ard, holbert, harbert, hallbard, halbar,** 6– **halbard, -berd,** 7– **-bert.** [a. OF. *hale-, hallebard* (15th c.), *alabarde* (14th c.) (= Pr., Sp., It. *alabarda*), ad. MHG. *helmbarde*, mod.G. and Du. *hellebarde*, of which the second element is OHG. *barta* (Ger. *barte*), OLG. *barda* (MDu. *baerde*) broad-axe, deriv. of OTeut. **bardo-z* beard. For the first element, two derivations have been suggested; (1) the very rare MHG. *helm, halm* handle, as if 'handled broad-axe', (2) *helm* helmet, with the sense 'axe for smashing helmets'. The latter is, on phonetic and other grounds approved by Kluge, and by Darmesteter. Formerly pronounced (hɔːl-).]

1. A military weapon, especially in use during the 15th and 16th centuries; a kind of combination of spear and battle-axe, consisting of a sharp-edged blade ending in a point, and a spear-head, mounted on a handle five to seven feet long.

1495 *Act 11 Hen. VII*, c. 64 Preamb., Armours Defensives, as..Bowes Billes Hauberts. **1497** *Naval Accts. Hen. VII* (1896) 99 Halberdes of ffaunders making..cxx. Halberdes of London making..x. Halberdes of the forest of Deuon..lx. **1530** PALSGR. 228/2 Halbarde, *halebarde. Ibid.* 229/2 Hauberde, a weapen. *a* **1541** WYATT in *Tottell's Misc.* (*Arb.*) 87 No..Sergeant with mace, with hawbart, sword, nor knife. **1567** TURBERV. *Poems* in Chalmers *Eng. Poets* II. 588/2 For push of pike, for holbers stroke. **1589** *Pasquil's Ret.* 8 To bende euery man the point of his Holberde at her. **1630** WADSWORTH *Pilgr.* viii. 89 Hee..committed mee to the custody of foure souldiers armed with Houldbeards. **1647** CLARENDON *Hist. Reb.* VI. §280 He was slain by a blow with a halbert on the hinder part of his head. **1664** *Flodden F.* vii. 71 Some did in hand their holberds hent. **1720** OZELL *Vertot's Rom. Rep.* I. I. 24 The Offensive [Arms] were the Javelin, the Pike or Halberd, and the Sword. **1855** MACAULAY *Hist. Eng.* III. 375 This wall..the soldiers defended desparately with musket, pike, and halbert.

b. As denoting the rank of a sergeant.

1749 FIELDING *Tom Jones* VII. xi, He..had..so well ingratiated himself with his officers, that he had promoted himself to a halbert. **1796** GROSE *Dict. Vulg. Tongue* s.v., A weapon carried by a serjeant of foot. To get a halbert; to be appointed a serjeant. **1853** STOCQUELER *Milit. Encycl.* s.v., *Old halberd* is a familiar term formerly used in the British army, to signify a person who had..risen to the rank of a commissioned officer.

†**c.** (See quot. 1796.) *Obs.*

1763 *Brit. Mag.* IV. 388 The plaintiff received 300 lashes with a cat-o'-nine-tails at the halberts, under colour of the sentence of a court-martial. **1796** GROSE *Dict. Vulg. Tongue* s.v., To be brought to the halberts; to be flogged *à la militaire*: soldiers of the infantry, when flogged, being commonly tied to three halberts, set up in a triangle, with a fourth fastened across them. **1824** MACAULAY *Gt. Law-suit* Misc. Writ. (1889) 55 My old uncle..would have had some of them up to the halberts.

†**2.** *transf.* A soldier armed with a halberd; a halberdier. *Obs.*

1577–87 HOLINSHED *Chron.* III. 1402/1 Foure thousand men..the great part whereof were shot [= gunners], the other were pikes and halberds. **1603** HOLLAND *Plutarch's Mor.* 1223 Two halberds of Archias guard knocked at the outward gate.

3. (See quot.) ? *Obs.*

1727–51 CHAMBERS *Cycl.*, *Halbert*, among farriers..is a piece of iron, an inch broad, and three or four inches long, soldered to the toe of an horse's shoe, that jets out before; to hinder a lame horse from resting or treading on his toe.

4. *attrib.* and *Comb.*, as ***halberd-bearer, -length, -staff***; **halberd-headed** *a.*, **halberd-shaped** *a. Bot.* (of leaves), shaped like the axe of a halberd; **halberd-shoe** (see sense 3); **halberd-weed**, the West Indian shrub *Neurolæna lobata.*

1775 FLETCHER *Script. Scales* II. §17 Wks. 1795 V. 267 To rank him with an *halbert-bearer. **1866** *Treas. Bot.*, **Halbert-headed*, abruptly enlarged at the base into two diverging lobes, like the head of a halbert. **1571** DIGGES *Pantom.* I. xix. F j b, The distance betwene GE 30 *halberde lenghtes. **1796** WITHERING *Brit. Plants* (ed. 3) III. 587 Leaves egg-shaped..I have not seen any *halberd-shaped. **1880** GRAY *Struct. Bot.* iii. §4. 96 Leaves are Hastate or Halberd-shaped, when the lobes, at the base, point outwards. **1727–51** CHAMBERS *Cycl.* s.v., **Halbert-shoes*.. constrain a lame horse to tread, or rest, on his heel. **1756** P. BROWNE *Jamaica* 315 The *Halbert-weed..generally rises to the height of four or five feet.

Hence **'halberded** *a.*, armed with a halberd.

a **1800** *Loyal Songs* (Mason), The halberted train. **1841** BORROW *Zincali* I. i. §1. 41 The halberded bands of the city.

halberd, *v. rare.* [f. prec. sb.] *trans.* To slash with a halberd.

1874 *Droll Stories fr. Abbeys Touraine* 11 At the risk of having his body halberded by the soldiers.

halberdier (hælbə'dɪə(r)). Also 6 **holbarder, hal-, holberder, halberdear,** 6–8 **halbard(i)er,** 7 **halbertere, -tier, halbeerter, holberteer,** 7–8 **halberdeer, -teer,** 8–9 **halbadier,** 9 **hallebardier.** [a. OF. *hale-, hallebardier* (= Sp. *alabardero*, It. *alabardiere*), f. *halebard* HALBERD: see -IER.] A soldier armed with a halberd; *spec.* a member of certain civic guards carrying a halberd as a badge of office.

1548 HALL *Chron., Edw. IV*, 227 Horsemen, besyde a great number of Lanceknightes and Halberders. **1589** IVE *Instruct.* 73 The Halbardiers maye also fight better in a prease then the Pikemen. **1589** *Pasquil's Ret.* B b, The big bodied Holberders that guarde her Maiestie. **1621** G. SANDYS *Ovid's Met.* v. (1626) 9 Yet Perseus would not venture to inuade The Halbertere Eritheus with his blade. **1649** C. WALKER *Hist. Independ.* II. 87 The King was brought to the Bar by Colonell Hacker with Halberdeers. **1684** *Lond. Gaz.* No. 1956/4 Several Constables, Holberteers and Inhabitants waited their coming. **1760–72** tr. *Juan & Ulloa's Voy.* (ed. 3) II. 49 The company of halbadiers bringing up the rear. **1855** MACAULAY *Hist. Eng.* IV. 4 The royal coach, escorted by an army of halberdiers.

Hence **halber'diered** *a.*, attended by halberdiers.

a **1882** SIR R. CHRISTISON *Autobiog.* (1885) I. ii. 33 The Town Council of the city, robed and halberdiered, walked from the gate to the hall.

'halberdman. = HALBERDIER. Also **'halberdsman.**

1595 DUNCAN *Appendix Etymol.* (E.D.S.), *Satelles*, a halbert man. **1633** SHIRLEY *Bird in Cage* (Fairholt), 'You are one of the guard?' 'A poor halbert-man, sir.' **1638** *Sp. Star Chamber at Censure of Bastwicke*, etc. 30 The

Halbertmen standing round about. **1867** MOTLEY *Netherl.* III. 96 Pikemen as well as halberdsmen carried rapiers.

halbergit, var. HABERJET.

halboie, obs. form of HAUTBOY.

†**halch**, *v. Obs.* exc. *dial.* Forms: 4 **halche(n**, 6–9 **halch**, 9 *dial.* **halsh**. [In senses 1 and 2 app. a dial. variant of HALSE *v.*^{1} and *v.*^{2}; whether sense 3 has risen out of these is not certain.]

†**1. a.** *trans.* To clasp in one's arms, embrace; = HALSE *v.*^{2} 1. *Obs.*

13.. *Gaw. & Gr. Knt.* 939 He hym þonkked þroly, & ayþer halched oþer.

†**b.** *intr.* To hang *upon* in embracing, throw one's arms *upon*. *Obs.* (? *pseudo-archaism.*)

c **1650** *Marr. Gawaine* 65 in Furniv. *Percy Folio* I. 110 To halch vpon him, King Arthur, this lady was full faine.

†**2.** *trans.* To hail, salute, greet; = HALSE *v.*^{1} 3.

1515 *Scot. Field* 52 in *Chetham Misc.* II, When he heard how unkindly his townes they were halched, He piked him to Parice, for thinges that might happen. *c* **1650** *Earle Westmorland* 27 in Furniv. *Percy Folio* I. 301 The Lord Hume halched them right soon, saying, 'banished men, welcome to mee!'

3. a. To fasten, tie, knot. Now *dial.*

13.. *Gaw. & Gr. Knt.* 185 Þat half his armes þer vnder were halched in þe wyse Of a kyngez capados. *Ibid.* 657 Nowe alle þese fyue syþeȝ, forsoþe, were fetled on þis knyȝt, & vchone halched in oþer, þat non ende hade. *Ibid.* 1852 For quat gome so is gorde with þis grene lace, While he hit hade hemely halched aboute. **1828** *Craven Dial.*, *Halsh*, to tie, to fasten, to knot. **1869** *Lonsdale Gloss.*, *Halch.*

b. *Cotton-spinning*, etc. (see quots.). Also **halch-band**.

1892 J. NASMITH *Cotton Spinning* 286 As yarn is always wound off a cop by drawing it upwards,..any such condition of the cop nose results in a number of coils being drawn off simultaneously in an entangled condition. In this case the cop is said to be 'halched', and a good deal of waste is produced when the unwinding takes place. **1901** *N. & Q.* 9th Ser. VIII. 81/1 'Halsh'.—This word is in every-day use in various ways. So far as the cotton trade goes it refers to the band of coloured 'tie yarn' that encircles the 'knot', in addition to the ordinary tie yarn that holds each lea in the knot separately. This is called the 'halsh-band', and when the band is tied the knot is said to be 'halshed'... The 'halsh' is also—in the case of a necktie in the form of a bow, for example—that part in the centre that runs in a vertical or slightly oblique direction, embracing the whole bow... Saddlers also use the word, and possibly it is known in the woollen and worsted industries.

†'**halcydon.** *Obs.* [An incorrect form of *halcyon*, prob. influenced by L. *alcedo* kingfisher.] = HALCYON 1. Hence †**halcy'donian** *a.* [cf. L. *alcedonia* the halcyon days], calm, tranquil.

1611 CORYAT *Crudities* 389 It enioyeth great peace and a very halcedonian time. **1647** A. ROSS *Muse's Interpr.* viii. (1675) 145 The Halcyons or Halcydons were said, I think, to be begot of Lucifer.

halcyon ('hælsɪən, 'hælʃɪən), *sb.* and *a.* Forms: 4 **alceon, alicion,** 6 **alcion, halsion,** 6–7 **halcion,** 7 **alcian,** 6– **alcyon, halcyon.** [a. L. *halcyon*, more properly *alcyon*, a. Gr. ἀλκυών kingfisher.

The spelling ἀλ- *hal-*, is supposed to have arisen out of the fancy that the word was f. ἅλ-ς sea + κύων conceiving, connected with the fable that the halcyon broods upon her nest floating on the calm sea in the 'halcyon days'.]

A. *sb.*

1. A bird of which the ancients fabled that it bred about the time of the winter solstice in a nest floating on the sea, and that it charmed the wind and waves so that the sea was specially calm during the period: usually identified with a species of kingfisher, hence a poetic name of this bird.

1390 GOWER *Conf.* II. 106 (Bodl. MS. 294) Hir briddes ȝit ..Of Alceon þe name bere. **1398** TREVISA *Barth. De P.R.* XIX. lxxix. (1495) 910 In the cliffe of a ponde of Occean, Alicion, a see foule, in wynter maketh her neste and layeth egges in vii dayes and sittyth on brood..seuen dayes. **1545** JOYE *Exp. Dan.* Ep. Ded. (R.), Thei saye, that in the.. coldest tyme of the yere, these halcions (making their nestis in the sea rockis or sandis) wille sitte their egges and hatche forth their chickens. *c* **1592** MARLOWE *Jew of Malta* I. i, How stands the wind? Into what corner peers my halcyon's bill? *a* **1631** DRAYTON *Noah's Flood* (R.), There came the halcyon, whom the sea obeys, When she her nest upon the water lays. *c* **1750** SHENSTONE *Elegies* v. 22 So smiles the surface of the treach'rous main As o'er its waves the peaceful halcyons play. **1819** WIFFEN *Aonian Hours* (1820) 104 The brilliant halcyons..fluttering upon azure wings, appear Loveliest above secluded waters. **1867** *Contemp. Rev.* VI. 252 The alcyon sits her floating nest.

fig. *a* **1649** DRUMM. OF HAWTH. *Poems* Wks. (1711) 39/1 Makes Scotland's name to fly On halcyons wings..Beyond the ocean to Columbus shores. **1880** GOLDW. SMITH in *Atlantic Monthly* No. 268. 200 The halcyons of literature, art, and science were floating on the calm and sunlit sea.

b. In *Zool.* a kingfisher of the Australasian genus *Halcyon*, or of the subfamily *Halcyoninæ*.

1772–84 COOK *Voy.* (1790) V. 1805 We found the halcyon, or great king-fisher, having fine bright colours. **1802** *R. Brooke's Gazetteer* (ed. 12) s.v. *P. William's Sound*, The birds found here were the halcyon, or great kingfisher [etc.].

†**2.** Calm, quietude, halcyon days. *Obs.*

1647 TRAPP *Comm. Matt.* ix. 15 Our halcyons here are but as marriage feasts, for continuance. **1654** —— *Comm. Ps.* ii. 4 By this means the Church had an happy Halcyon. **1748** RICHARDSON *Clarissa* (1811) II. 4 'Tis well one of us does [want courting], else the man would having nothing but halcyon. **1797** MRS. A. M. BENNETT *Beggar Girl* (1813) IV. 144 All, therefore, was halcyon with Mrs. Woudbe.

B. *attrib.* passing into *adj.*

1. Of, or pertaining to, the halcyon or kingfisher. ***halcyon days*** [Gr. ἀλκυονίδες ἡμέραι, L. *alcyonei dies, alcyonides, alcedonia*]: fourteen days of calm weather, anciently believed to occur about the winter solstice when the halcyon was brooding.

[**1540** HYRDE tr. *Vives' Instr. Chr. Wom.* (1592) Pj, Wherefore those daies be called in Latine *Halcionii*, that is as you would say, the Halcion birdes daies. **1545** JOYE *Exp. Dan.* 2a (Stanf.), I remembred the halcyons dayes. **1591** SHAKS. *1 Hen. VI*, I. ii. 131 Expect Saint Martins Summer, Halcyons dayes.] **1601** HOLLAND *Pliny* x. xxxii. (R.), They lay and sit about mid-winter..and the time whiles they are broodie, is called the halcyon daies: for during that season the sea is calm and navigable, especially in the coast of Sicilie. **1605** SHAKS. *Lear* II. ii. 84 Bring oile to fire, snow to the colder moodes..and turne their Halcion beakes With euery gale, and varry of their Masters. [For the allusion see KINGFISHER.] **1839** *Penny Cycl.* XIII. 230/1 The fable of the floating cradle in which during the Halcyon dayes the bird was said to rear its young.

2. Calm, quiet, peaceful, undisturbed. (Usually qualifying *days*.)

1578 *Chr. Prayers* in *Priv. Prayers* (1851) 464 It hath pleased thy grace to give us these Alcyon days, which yet we enjoy. **1631** GOUGE *God's Arrows* v. xvii. 429 Were our daies more halcyon, more quiet and peaceable. **1641** EVELYN *Mem.* (1857) I. 12 Fortifications (a great rarity in that blessed halcyon time in England). **1665** SIR T. HERBERT *Trav.* (1677) 11 When two are seen, they foretel Halcyon weather. **1841** D'ISRAELI *Amen. Lit.* (1867) 250 Peace and policy had diffused a halcyon calmness over the land. **1878** *Masque Poets* 218 The bird of love, in days so truly halcyon, Upon the billows well might build her nest.

†**halcyon**, *v. Obs. rare*$^{-1}$. [f. prec. sb.] *trans.* To calm, tranquillize.

1616 J. LANE *Cont. Sqr.'s T.* 236 Shee, callinge Horbell, Gnartolite, Leyfurco too, thus halcioneth her spite.

†**halcyonian** (hælsɪ'əʊnɪən), *a. Obs.* Also 7 **halci-**. [f. L. *(h)alcyoni-us* of the halcyon + -AN.] Of or pertaining to the Halcyon; calm, quiet, peaceful; = HALCYON B.

1617 DRUMM. OF HAWTH. *Forth Feasting*, What halcyonian days thy reign should give. **1650** A. B. *Mutat. Polemo* 11 Halcionian quiet times at Sea. **1659** HAMMOND *On Ps.* xciv. 15 The halcyonian dayes that the Christians had.

halcyonic, -ite, -oid, var. ALCYONIC, etc.

'**halcyonine**, *a. Ornith.* Of or pertaining to the subfamily of kingfishers (*Halcyoninæ*) of which the genus *Halcyon* is the type.

hald, -en, obs. forms of HOLD, HOLDEN.

haldu ('hældu:). [Hindi.] A tree, *Adina cordifolia*, of the family Rubiaceæ, found in Burma, India, and Thailand; also its yellowish hardwood timber.

[**1881** J. S. GAMBLE *Man. Indian Timbers* 220 ADINA.. *A. cordifolia*..Vern. *Haldu*.] **1920** *Nature* CV. 693/1 *Haldu* (*Adina cordifolia*) is a bright canary-coloured wood notable for the smooth and even regularity of the grain. **1934** *Jrnl. R. Aeronaut. Soc.* XXXVIII. 51 Other timbers used for carving on account of their even structure are Pear (*Pyrus communis*) and the Indian wood known as Haldu (*Adina cordifolia*). **1958** CHOWDHURY & GHOSH *Indian Woods* I. p. xxxvi, In woods like axlewood (*Anogeissus latifolia*), haldu (*Adina cordifolia*) and sandalwood (*Santalum album*), the texture is fine giving a smooth feel.

†**hale**, *sb.*^{1} *Obs.* [A parallel form to HEAL *sb.*, ME. *hele*, and HAIL *sb.*^{2}, conformed in vowel to the adj., OE. *hál*.] Health, well-being, welfare; cure, remedy; = HAIL *sb.*^{2}, HEAL *sb.*

a **1200** *Moral Ode* 202 in *Trin. Coll. Hom.* 226 Ac mihte libbe afre-mo a blisse and an hale. *c* **1200** *Vices & Virtues* (1888) 29 Ne on wele ne on wauȝhe, ne on hale ne on unhale. *c* **1205** LAY. 17755 Þat scal be on þin hale. **1596** SPENSER *Astroph.* 103 All heedlesse of his dearest hale. **1795** BURNS *Poem addressed to Mitchell* v, My hale and weel I'll tak a care o't. [But here perh. only a Sc. dial. form of HEAL *sb.*]

b. ***ill hale***, var. of *ill hail* (HAIL *sb.*^{2} 2), bad luck. In quots. used advb. = Unfortunately, unluckily, disastrously.

a **1300** *Cursor M.* 4905 Ful ilhale [*Fairf.* il haile] did yee þat dede. *c* **1460** *Towneley Myst.* (Surtees) 230 Now illa hale was he borne.

†**hale**, *sb.*^{2} *Obs.* Forms: 1 **healh (heale),** 1–4 **hal,** 4–5 **hale.** [OE. *halh, healh*, infl. *hale, heale*.] A corner, a nook; a secret place.

c **897** K. ÆLFRED *Gregory's Past.* xxxv. 245 Forðæm ælc waȝ bið ȝebieȝed twiefeald on ðæm heale. *c* **1000** *Prose Life St. Guthlac* xx. 82 Hleonian on ðam hale his cyrcan. *a* **1100** *Anglo-Sax. Voc.* in Wr.-Wülcker 326/9 *Angulus*, hyrne, oððe heal. *a* **1250** *Owl & Night.* 2 Ich was in one sumere dale, In one suthe diȝele hale. *c* **1315** SHOREHAM 160 Ac tho hy herde God speke, Wel sone an hal by-gonne threke. *a* **1327** *Pol. Songs* (Camden) 150 We beth honted from hale to hurne. *c* **1450** MYRC 1384 Hast þow do þat synne bale By any wommon þat lay in hale?

†**hale**, *sb.*^{3} *Obs.* Also 5 **halle,** 6 **hail, hall.** [app. a. OF. *hale* (13th c. in Littré), mod.F. *halle* a covered market-place, a. OS. and OHG. *halla*, an area or space covered over. The word is thus in origin a doublet of HALL^{1}, with a different pronunciation and application, due to its French use.] A place roofed over, but usually open at the sides; a pavilion; a tent; a booth, hut, or other temporary structure for shelter.

c **1330** R. BRUNNE *Chron. Wace* (Rolls) 9280 In halles and hales bordes leyd. *c* **1440** *Promp. Parv.* 222/1 Hale or tente, *papilio, scena.* *c* **1440** CAPGRAVE *Life St. Kath.* I. 734 Euery man had plente in hale and in halle. **1480** CAXTON *Chron. Eng.* ccxlii. (1482) 277 The kyng lete make in al hast a long and a large hous of tymbre the which was callid an hale (and couered with tylles ouer) and it was open al about on both sides and at the endes. **1530** PALSGR. 228/2 Hall a long tent in a felde, *tente.* **1572** I. B. *Let.* in Brydges *Cens. Lit.* VII. 240 (N.) Dangerous diseases..to souldiours by reason of lying upon the ground and uncovered, and lykewyse to horses for lacke of hales. **1577–87** HOLINSHED *Chron.* (1807–8) III. 81 Certeine Frenchmen..hearing that the English tents and pavillions were a good waie distant from the armie..spoiled the hails, robbed the tents. **1606** HOLLAND *Sueton* 55 A certaine rate in monie..allowed, For their sumpter-mules, for their tentes and hales.

b. *pl.* (as *sing.*) ? A market-hall [= F. *les halles*].

1541 *Aberd. Reg.* V. 16 (Jam.) The townis consent to mak a halis to mett the wyttal that hapenis to cum to this burgh to sell.

hale (heɪl), *sb.*^{4} Now *rare* or *Obs.* Also 6 *Sc.* **haill.** [f. HALE *v.*^{1}, of which sense 1 may be the imperative, used subst. See also HAUL *sb.*]

1. In ***hoise and hale, hale and how***, exclamations of sailors in hauling something.

1470–85 MALORY *Arthur* VII. xv, Where were many shyppes and maryners noyse with hale and how. **1513** DOUGLAS *Æneis* III. viii. 111 Towart the left, with mony heis and haill, Socht all our flot. **1867** MORRIS *Jason* x. 587 And so drew Argo up, with hale and how, On to the grass. **1890** —— in *Eng. Illustr. Mag.* July 759 Uprose the hale and how of the mariners.

b. The act of haling or hauling.

c **1695** CONGREVE *Taking of Namur* (Seager), Uprooting hills with most tremendous hale.

2. A haul (of fish).

1751 R. PALTOCK *P. Wilkins* xxxiv. (1883) 92/2 It being a large hale, and a shelving bank, I could not lift it.

hale, *sb.*^{5} *Obs.* exc. *dial.* Also 7 **haile.** [app. a. ON. *hali*, Da. *hale* tail: cf. *plough-tail*.]

1. *pl.* The two handles of a plough or wheel-barrow.

1611 COTGR., *Le manche d'une charrue*, a Plough-tayle, or handle; the Plough-hale. **1613** MARKHAM *Eng. Husbandman* I. I. vi. (1635) 36 If your Plough-irons..will not bite on the earth..it is a signe that you hang too heavie on the Plough hales. **1649** BLITHE *Eng. Improv. Impr.* (1653) 190 For the Plough-handles, some call them Stilts, and some Hales, and some Staves. **1725** in BRADLEY *Fam. Dict.* s.v. *Plough.* **1868** ATKINSON *Cleveland Gloss.*, *Hales*, the handles or ends of the plough-stilts: usually in the compound form Plough-hales. **1877** *N.W. Linc. Gloss.*, *Barrow-hale*, the handle of a wheel-barrow.

†**2.** A pot-hook. *Obs.*

1674 RAY *S.& E.C. Words* 68 *A Hale*: (Suff.) i.e. a trammel in the Essex dialect.

†**hale**, *sb.*^{6} *Obs. rare.* = HALO.

c **1440** *Promp. Parv.* 222/1 Hale, or cyrcle a-bowte þe mone, *halo.*

hale (heɪl), *a.* (*adv.*) Forms: α. *Eng.* 1 **hál,** 2–4 **hal,** 3– **hale** (4 **halle, ale, hele,** 8–9 **heal,** *north. dial.* **heale, heeal, heyel, yell**). β. *Sc.* 4 **halle,** 4– **hale,** 5– **hail** (5 **hayle,** 5–6 **haile,** 5– **haill,** 6 **heale, hele,** 6–8 **heal**). [The northern dial. repr. of OE. *hál*, which became in south and midl. dial. *hôl, hool, hole*, WHOLE, but remained in the north *hâl, hale*, in which form it has been taken over in modern times into the literary language in sense 3.

In Scotch from 15th c., long *ā* was spelt *ay, ai*; hence, the later Sc. forms *hayl, hail, haill*, for earlier *hale*, OE. *hál*, must be distinguished from original north Eng. HAIL, in same sense, derived from Norse *heill*. *Heal(e* is a modern Sc. repr. of the closer sound (hi:əl, hɪəl) into which *hale* has now passed, and must be distinguished from Eng. *heal* (hi:l), ME. *hele*.]

A. *adj.* **I. 1.** Free from injury; safe, sound, unhurt. Now only *Sc.* and *north. dial.*

c **1000** *Ags. Gosp.* Matt. x. 22 Se þurh-wunaþ oð ende, se byþ hal. *c* **1200** ORMIN 14818 Godess follc all hal & sund Comm..to lande. *a* **1300** *Cursor M.* 24888 If þou will hale Cum o þis scip to land. **1375** (MS. 1489) BARBOUR *Bruce* III. 92 The King..eschapyt haile and fer. *c* **1400** MAUNDEV. (Roxb.) xvii. 79 It kepez þe lymmes of a man hale. **1513** DOUGLAS *Æneis* (1553) IX. iv. 102 So hele and fere [*ed. Small* hail and feyr] mote sauf me Jupiter. **1567** *Satir. Poems Reform.* iv. 74 It wald mak ony haill hairt sair. **1597** MONTGOMERIE *Cherrie & Slae* 897 Quhyle my heart is heal [*rime* prevail]. **1786** BURNS *Ep. to Major Logan* iii, Hale be your heart, hale be your fiddle. **1802** R. ANDERSON *Cumberld. Ball.* 35 O heale be thy heart! my auld cronie.

2. a. Free from disease, healthy, in good health, well; recovered from disease, healed, 'whole'. Now *Sc.* and *north. dial.*

c **1000** *Sax. Leechd.* I. 74 Þonne bið se man hal on þreora nihte fyrste. *c* **1175** *Lamb. Hom.* 29 Ane wunde..þet ne mei beon longe hwile hal. *a* **1300** *Cursor M.* 13106 Messels er hale, cripels gas right. *c* **1375** (15th c. MS.) *Sc. Leg. Saints* Prol. 125 Of all sekness, and of all bale, In name of Ihesu þai mad haile. *c* **1450** *St. Cuthbert* (Surtees) 3638 [He] had made diuerse hale and fere. **1513** DOUGLAS *Æneis* IV. Prol. 126 Ane hailll mannis estait, In temperat warmnes, nother to cald nor hait. **1579** SPENSER *Sheph. Cal.* July 107 My seely sheepe.. bene hale enough, I trowe. **1597** MONTGOMERIE *Cherrie & Slae* 1474 Our full intent is now To haif ȝe hale. **1792** BURNS *Duncan Gray* iv, Meg grew sick—as he grew heal. **1871** G. MACDONALD *Gospel Women*, in *Wks. Fancy & Imag.* II. 135 Sickness may be more hale than health.

†**b.** *fig.* Free from what is injurious; sound, wholesome. *Obs.*

c **1300** *Cursor M.* 24650 (Edinb.) Þi suet sun sa halle [*v.r.* hale] of hiht. *c* **1320** *Seuyn Sag.* (W.) 693 Hit n'is non hale To leue stepmoderes tale. *c* **1475** *Babees Bk.* 101 Latte ay youre chere be lowly, blythe, and hale. **1563** WINȜET *Four Scoir Thre Quest.* xxxii. Wks. 1888 I. 97 Preist.. that may instruct the peple be hale and syncere doctrine.

3. Free from infirmity; sound in constitution; robust, vigorous. (The current literary sense: now most freq. of old persons.) Often in phr. ***hale and hearty***.

(Not exactly the same as any northern dialect use, and perh. originating in Spenser's use: cf. sense 2, quot. 1579.)

1734 JARVIS *Let. to Swift* 24 Nov. in *S.'s Lett.* (1766) II. 207 Finding my old friend.. so hale at 83–4. **1768–74** TUCKER *Lt. Nat.* (1852) II. 401 The soundest halest constitution may.. catch an infection. **1823** SCOTT *Peveril* i, Then came the strong hale voice of the huntsman soldier with its usual greeting. **1824** DIBDIN *Litr. Comp.* 530 A hale, active, and comprehensive mind. **1860** *Leisure Hour* 174/2 As hale and as hearty.. as ever. **1863** *Good Words* IV. 295/2 He.. was hale and hearty though upwards of a hundred years old. **1865** LIVINGSTONE *Zambesi* xxvi. 541 A hale hearty old age. **1899** *Captain* I. 124/2 Dr. Grace is close on fifty-one, hale and hearty. **1903** T. HARDY *Dynasts* I. I. i. 14 We be the King's men, hale and hearty, Marching to meet one Buona-party. **1928** A. B. CALLOW *Food & Health* 7 In the past many people have been perfectly hale and hearty without having any clear ideas about the science of nutrition.

II. The northern form of WHOLE, in its current senses.

4. Of things material: Whole, entire, unbroken, undivided; undecayed.

c **1200** ORMIN 18512 All hal and unntodæledd. *a* **1225** *Juliana* 31 Sein iuhan.. ase hal com up þrof; as he wes hal meiden. *a* **1300** *Cursor M.* 19313 We find.. þe dors sperd, þe walles hale. *c* **1450** *St. Cuthbert* (Surtees) 6601 Þai fand him all hale liggand. **1533** BELLENDEN *Livy* I. (1822) 96 Ane hede of ane man, with visage hale, but ony corruptioun. **1786** BURNS *Scotch Drink* xxi, Hale breeks.

5. Of things immaterial, time, numbers, etc.: Whole, entire, complete; with no part wanting.

a **1300** *Cursor M.* 419 [Þai] suld be of a numbre hale. *Ibid.* 9262 Fra adam þa ald to crist es tald Sexti hale generacions. **1340** HAMPOLE *Pr. Consc.* 3933 Þe space of alle ane hale yhere. **1508** DUNBAR *Twa Mariit Wemen* 386 Ane hail ȝear. **1513** DOUGLAS *Æneis* (1553) VII. ix. 105 With hale [*ed. Small* haill] routis Ascaneus to reskew. **1802** R. ANDERSON *Cumberld. Ball.* 34 Wad dance for a heale winter neet. **1825** BROCKETT *N.C. Gloss., Hyel, Hale*, whole.

6. a. ***the hale***, the whole, all the; also with possesives, etc.

a **1300** *Cursor M.* 6420 Had godds folk þe hale maistri. **1375** BARBOUR *Bruce* I. 274 The halle condicioun off a threll. *a* **1400–50** *Alexander* 441 Halden heuydman of all þe hale werde. **1558** Q. KENNEDY *Compend. Tractive* in *Wodr. Soc. Misc.* 98 Puttande my heale confidence in God onelie. **1562** WINȜET *Cert. Tractates* iii. Wks. 1888 I. 26 The haill Kirk of God. *a* **1670** SPALDING *Troub. Chas. I* (1829) 6 The laird.., his lady, and haill household. **1816** SCOTT *Antiq.* xv, Him that the hale town kens naething about. **1863** *Tyneside Songs* 25 Aw elways gan The yell hog or nyen.

b. *pl.* The whole of the, all the.

a **1300** *Cursor M.* 2992 And calld his men be for him hale. *c* **1470** HENRY *Wallace* I. 357 Thai lands hayle than was his heretage. **1535** STEWART *Cron. Scot.* (1858) I. 10 Thair victuallis haill were consumit aw. **1557–75** *Diurn. Occurr.* (Bannatyne) 62 The haill lordis past to the tolbuith. **1582–88** *Hist. Jas, VI*, The haill subiects of this realme.

†**7.** All. *Obs.*

a **1300** *Cursor M.* 13303 (Cotton MS.) Tuelue þai war to tell in tale, Quen þat þai war to-gedir hale. *c* **1375** *Sc. Leg. Saints, Thomas* 22 Quhen þu hale ynd has to me Conuertyt.

8. Sole.

c **1375** *Sc. Leg. Saints, Mathias* 137 He hyme mad Hale kepare of al þe thinge. *c* **1470** HENRY *Wallace* I. 140 Protector haile he maid hym of Scotland. **1578–1600** *Scot. Poems 16th C.* II. 153 Thy helpe and haill succour.

9. Possessing full rights as a citizen; not a 'broken man' (BROKEN 9).

1609 SKENE *Reg. Maj.* 80 He is oblissed onely to enter his persone, or bodie, gif he be ane haill man, in the court.

B. *adv.* Wholly, entirely. *Sc.* and *north. dial.*

c **1375** *Sc. Leg. Saints, Egipciane* 102 To þe varld ded vare þai hayle. *c* **1470** HENRY *Wallace* I. 9 Contrar haile thair will. **1508** DUNBAR *Twa Mariit Wemen* 325 Quhen I the cure had all clene and him ourcummyn haill. **1585** JAS. I. *Ess. Poesie* (Arb.) 43 Ane hors, when he is barded haile. **1862** HISLOP *Prov. Scot.* 32 Better ae e'e than hail blind.

hale (heɪl), *v.*[1] Forms: 3- hale; also 4 halie, halye, (halle), 4–6 hayl(e, 5–7 haile, (6 haale), 6–7 (8–9 in sense 4 b) hail. See also HAUL. [a. OF. *haler*, in sense 1 (12th c. in Littré), a. OFrankish *hâlon* = OHG. *halôn, holôn*, modG. *holen*, to fetch, etc., OS. *halôn*, MDu. and Du. *halen*, to fetch, draw, haul, OFris. *halia*, EFris. *halen*, to draw, pull, haul.

Icel. and Sw. *hala*, Da. *hale* (on the ground of which the OFr. word has been erroneously assumed to be from Norse) are late adoptions from LG. (the Icel. perh. from Eng.).]

1. *trans.* To draw or pull. †**a.** Formerly in gen. sense, and in various spec. uses now *obs.* or *arch.*: e.g. to draw *up*, hoist, set (a sail); to take a 'pull' at, toss *off* (liquor); to pull or tear asunder or in pieces; to contract, cause to shrink; to draw back (an arrow) on the string. (= DRAW *v.* in various senses.)

13.. *K. Alis.* 992 They setten mast, and halen saile. **13..** *E. E. Allit. P.* B. 1520 He haled of þe cuppe. *c* **1330** R. BRUNNE *Chron. Wace* (Rolls) 12061 Bowlyne on bouspret to sette and hale. **1398** TREVISA *Barth. De P.R.* v. ii. (1495) 104 The fumositees in the stomak come to the brayne and.. drawe and hale the skynnes of the brayne, and brede ache in the same skynnes. *c* **1440** *Promp. Parv.* 223/1 Halyn, or drawyn, *traho*. **1513** DOUGLAS *Æneis* v. ix. 36 Mynestheus.. Onto the heid has halit wp on hie, Baith arrow and ene etland at the merk. **1549** *Compl. Scot.* vi. 40 Hail al and ane . hail hym vp til vs.. The ankyr vas halit vp abufe the vattir. **1612** DRAYTON *Poly-olb.* xiii. 218 The place that's haled with the crampe. **1621** BURTON *Anat. Mel.* III. ii. II. i. (1651) 450 Thou shalt be haled in pieces with.. some passion or other. **1644** DIGBY *Nat. Bodies* I. xix. (1658) 209 A.. pin of wood, over which they use to hale their lace when they wind it. **1740** NELSON *Wond. Nat. Displayed* III. xxvi. 284 Fastened to a thick Rope, which is haled in by an Engine. **1842** TENNYSON *St. Sim. Styl.* 63 The rope that haled the buckets from the well.

b. To draw or pull along, or from one place to another, esp. with force or violence; to drag, tug. Now superseded in ordinary speech by HAUL.

c **1205** LAY. 16712 Toward Hengest he leop.. and igrap hine bi þan toppe, & hine æfter him halede. **1377** LANGL. *P. Pl.* B. VIII. 95 Dobest.. bereth a bisschopes crosse, Is hoked on þat one ende, to halie men fro helle [**1393** C. XI. 93 And halye with þe hoked ende ille men to goode]. **1483** CAXTON *Gold. Leg.* 363 b/2 She remembryd how Jhesus.. was.. haled forth and mocked. **1570–6** LAMBARDE *Peramb. Kent* (1826) 230 He.. drew and haled the rest out of the doores, by the haire and heeles. **1611** BIBLE *Acts* viii. 3 Saul.. haling men and women, committed them to prison. **1649** JER. TAYLOR *Gt. Exemp.* III. xix. 153 As one hal'd to execution. **1837** CARLYLE *Fr. Rev.* I. v. v, Some score or two.. are indignantly haled to prison. **1873** SMILES *Huguenots Fr.* I. xii. (1881) 244 They were haled before the magistrates, fined and imprisoned.

2. *fig.* To constrain, or draw forcibly *to, into*, or *out of* a course of action, feeling, condition, etc.; to bring *in* violently, drag *in*.

1377–93 [see 1 b]. **1576** FLEMING *Panopl. Epist.* 54 [It] haleth me into a certaine hope of perpetual renowne. **1641** HINDE *J. Bruen* ii. 7 They.. hale and force them by their commands and threats. **1651** HOBBES *Leviath.* IV. xliv. 347 Texts.. haled to their purposes by force of wit. **1697** DAMPIER *Voy.* (1729) I. 493 The Land hales the wind. **1748** RICHARDSON *Clarissa* (1811) III. xxxvi. 216 Inferences, consequences, strained deductions.. haled in to tease me. **1869** FRISWELL *Ess. Eng. Writers* x. 139 Garrick haled on one hand by Tragedy and on the other by Comedy.

†**b.** To harry, molest. *Obs.*

1530 PALSGR. 579/1, I harye, or mysse entreate or hale one. **1641** MILTON *Reform.* II. (1851) 67 To let them still hale us, and worrey us with their band-dogs, and Pursivants. **1847–78** HALLIWELL, *Hale*.. to vex, or trouble; to worry.

3. *absol.* or *intr.* To pull, tug.

1423 JAS. I *Kingis Q.* clxix, Thou art to feble of thy-self.. to clymbe[n] or to hale Withoutin help. **1563–87** FOXE *A. & M.* (1684) III. 276 Hale on apace.. and merrily hoise up your sails. *c* **1580** DRAKE in *The World Encompassed*, etc. (Hakl. Soc. 1854) App. iv. 213, I must have a gentleman to hayle and draw with the mariner, and the maryner with the gentleman. **1612** T. TAYLOR *Comm. Titus* iii. 3 The Minister may hale and pull, but vnlesse the Father draw, none come to the Sonne. **1879** STEVENSON *Trav. Cevennes*, A yoke of.. stolid oxen were patiently haling at the plough.

†**4.** *intr.* To move along as if drawn or pulled; to move with force or impetus, hasten, rush; *spec.* of a ship, to proceed before the wind with sails set, to sail (cf. 1 a). Also *fig. Obs.*

13.. *Gaw. & Gr. Knt.* 136 Þer hales in at þe halle dor an aghlich mayster. *c* **1400** *Destr. Troy* 12286 He.. halit on full hard vnto the hegh Sea. **1667** *Lond. Gaz.* No. 221/1 Several other ships are haleing out of this Harbor. **1727** A. HAMILTON *New Acc. E. Ind.* II. iii. 256 A more convenient Place.. for the Man of War to hale ashore. *Ibid.* 257 That Day that his Ship haled off.

b. To flow, run down in a large stream. *Obs.* exc. *Sc.* and *north. dial.* (In later use written *hail.*)

13.. *E.E. Allit. P.* A. 125 Doun after a strem þat dryȝly halez. *c* **1420** *Pallad. on Husb.* XI. 284 From grapis blake a myghty wyn wole hale. *a* **1529** SKELTON *P. Sparowe* 22, I wept and I wayled, The tearys downe hayled. **1533** BELLENDEN *Livy* I. (1822) 101 The teris begin fast to hale owre hir chekis. *a* **1783** *Willy o' Douglass-dale* xiv. in Child *Ballads* IV ci, An the tears came hailing down. *a* **1835** MOTHERWELL in *Whistle-Binkie* (Sc. Songs) Ser. I. 101 Het tears are hailin' ower your cheek, And hailin' ower your chin. *Mod. Sc.* The sweat was just hailin' off me.

†**c.** *transf.* To project, extend, reach. *Obs.*

13.. *Gaw. & Gr. Knt.* 788 A ful huge heȝt hit [the wall] haled vpon lofte. ? *a* **1400** *Morte Arth.* 2077 The hede [of the spear] haylede owtt behynde ane halfe fote large.

†**hale**, *v.*[2] *Obs.* [Either f. HALE *a.*, or a variant of HEAL *v.* assimilated to HALE *a.*] *trans.* To make hale or whole; to heal.

c **1200** *Vices & Virtues* 71 Ðat þu cunne hes halen. *a* **1300** *Cursor M.* 14157 (Gött.) Þai troud þat he moght þair boþer hale of all his soght. *c* **1330** R. BRUNNE *Chron.* (1810) 7 Fiue woundes That ere not ȝit haled, ne salle be many stoundes. *a* **1340** HAMPOLE *Psalter* xcvii. 2 Þa þat ere halyd [*v.r.* holed] in trouth & luf. **1530** LYNDESAY *Test. Papyngo* 789 In name of Christe thay halit mony hounder, Rasyng the dede, and purgeing the possest.

†**hale**, *int. Obs.* [app. the same as MHG. *hale*, OHG. *halo*, imperative of *halôn, holôn, holen* to fetch, of which emphatic forms *halâ, holâ* were esp. used for hailing a ferry-man: see Hildebrand in *Zeitsch. f. d. Deutschen Unterricht* III. 393.] A cry to call attention.

[See also *E.E. Poems* (1862) 62.]

c **1290** *St. Christopher* 84 in *S. Eng. Leg.* 273 A niȝt in þe oþur half of þe watur, a uoiz þare cam and gradde 'Hale, hale' to seint Cristofre, þat he him þare-ouer ladde.

hale, obs. f. HAIL *v.*[2] and *v.*[3]; var. HELE *v.*[1]

†**hale-bowline.** *Naut. Obs.* [f. HALE *v.*[1]] One fit to hale a bowline; an able seaman.

1627 CAPT. SMITH *Seaman's Gram.* xii. 56 Manned with prest men, being halfe of them scarce hale Boulings. [**1867** SMYTH *Sailor's Word-bk., Haul-bowlings*, the old name for the able-bodied seamen.]

halec, halecize, var. ALEC, ALECIZE.

halecoid ('hælɪkɔɪd), *a.* and *sb.* *Ichth.* [f. mod.L. *Halecoides*, f. *halec, alec*, sauce prepared from small fish, and perh. the fish itself: see -OID.]

A. *adj.* Of or belonging to the herring family. **B.** *sb.* A clupeoid fish.

halecomorphous (ˌhælɪkəʊ'mɔːfəs), *a.* *Ichth.* [f. L. *halec, alec* (see prec.) + Gr. μορφή form + -OUS.] Belonging to the *Halecomorphi*, an order of ganoid fishes, also called *Cycloganoidei*.

†**halecret, hallecret** ('hælkrɪt). *Sc. Obs.* Forms: 6 **halkrig, halkri(c)k**, 9 **halkrike, hal(l)ecret, allecret**. [a. F. *halecret*, in 15–16th c. *allecret, halcret*, of uncertain origin: perh. containing Ger. *hals* neck.] 'A species of corslet, of beaten iron, composed of two pieces for the front and the back' (Littré); according to Meyrick 'a half-suit of light plate armour, worn alike by footmen and horsemen, furnished with long tassels'; used about the middle of the 16th century.

1536 BELLENDEN *Cron. Scot.* v. v. (1821) I. 174 He armyt hym with his halkrig, bow and arowis. **1540** *Sc. Acts Jas. V* (1597) §87 That all vthers.. haue jack of plate, halkrik, or brigitanes. **1801** GROSE *Ant. Arm.* 250 (Jam.) The halecret was a kind of corselet of two pieces, one before and one behind; it was lighter than the cuirass. **1842** MEYRICK *Anc. Armour* II. 206 Officers of infantry in allecrets. *Ibid.* 227 Hallecret.

†**'halely**, *adv. Obs.* Forms: 4 **halic, halik, haali**, *Sc.* **halily**, 4–5 **halli, hally, hali, haly**, 4–6 **halely**, 6 *Sc.* **hailelie, halelie**, 6–7 **hailly**. Northern and esp. Sc. form of WHOLLY, q.v.

a **1300** *Cursor M.* 22931 Sua haali [*Fairf., Gött.* hali] sal þai þan rise þare, þam sal noght want a hefd hare. *Ibid.* 26398 Þan be-houis him screue him halli [*Fairf.* hali] þat will haf halik his merci. **1352** MINOT *Poems* (Hall) iv. 92 For þare þan had þe lely flowre Lorn all halely his honowre. *c* **1400** MAUNDEV. (Roxb.) xxxi. 139 To putte vs all halely in þe mercy of Godd. *a* **1575** *Diurn. Occurr.* (Bannatyne) 302 Haililie left woyd. *a* **1605** MONTGOMERIE *Poems* xxxviii. 18 To vse them hailly as they wold.

halende, var. HEALEND *Obs.*, Saviour.

haleness ('heɪlnɪs). [f. HALE *a.* + -NESS.]

1. Northern dial. form of WHOLENESS, q.v.

a **1340** HAMPOLE *Psalter* ii. 8 The halnes of all creatures.

2. The quality or state of being hale; healthiness, robustness.

1862 SMILES *Engineers* III. 455 Struck by the haleness and comeliness of the English men and women.

haler ('heɪlə(r)). [f. HALE *v.*[1] + -ER[1].] One who hales or hauls. See also HALLIER, HAULER.

1611 COTGR., *Tireur*, a drawer, puller.. haler, lugger. **1755** JOHNSON, *Haler*, he who pulls or hales. **1815** *Pocklington Canal Act* 43 Boatmen, watermen, halers. **1876** MORRIS *Sigurd* I. 17 The halers of the hawsers.

‖**Halesia** (heɪ'liːsɪə). *Bot.* [Named after Stephen Hales, an English botanist, 1677–1761.] A genus of plants (N.O. *Styraceæ*), containing the beautiful Snowdrop or Silver-bell tree of the southern United States, *Halesia tetraptera*, and other species.

1760 J. ELLIS in *Phil. Trans.* Abr. XI. 508 (*title*) Of the Plants Halesia and Gardenia. **1865** PARKMAN *Huguenots* iv. (1875) 58 Here the halesia hangs out its silvery bells.

†**'haleskarth, 'hailscart**, *a. Sc. Obs.* [f. HALE *a.* + *skart, scart*, SCRATCH.] Free from injury: unhurt, unscratched.

1513 DOUGLAS *Æneis* v. v. 72 And brocht his feris hail-scarth to the cost. *a* **1603** in *Moyses' Mem. Jas. VI*, 71 (Jam.) And the brocht the said Will, away hailscart.

halesome ('heɪlsəm), *a.* Forms: 3–4 **halsum**, 4–6 (chiefly *Sc.*) **halesum**, 4–5 (8–9 *Sc.*) **halesome**, 5–6 *Sc.* **hailsum**, 6 **halsome**. [Cf. ON. *heilsamr* salutary.] The northern, and now chiefly Sc. form of WHOLESOME, q.v.

c **1200** ORMIN 10799 Sannt Johaness fullhtninng wass Halsumm and god to fanngenn. *a* **1340** HAMPOLE *Psalter* xxx. 18 Nathynge is halesumere þan to hope in god in all anguys. *c* **1400** MAUNDEV. (Roxb.) xxx. 130 Þe aer es noȝt so gude þare ne so halesome. *c* **1450** *Cov. Myst.* (Shaks. Soc.) 93 Trewly your counselle is ryght good and eylsum. **1597** MONTGOMERIE *Cherrie & Slae* 1381 Nane hailsomer for his behuve. **1813** *Queen's Wake, Kilmeny* iii, Yet you are halesome and fair to see.

Hence **'halesomely** *adv.*, **'halesomeness.**

a **1340** HAMPOLE *Psalter* cxlvii. 7 þai melt halsumly in godis luf. **1483** *Cath. Angl.* 170/2 An Halesomenes, *salubritas.*

halewe(n, obs. form of HALLOW.

†**halewei, -wey.** *Obs.* Forms: 3 **halewei, haliwei(e, halewi, he(a)lewi, halwei, haleweiȝ,** 5 **haliw(h)ey, halyvey.** [ME. *haleweiȝ, heale-, helewi*, pointing to an OE. **hǣlewǣȝ*, **hálwǣȝ*, corresp. to MHG. *heilwâg, -wâc, -awâc, wæge*, ON. *heilvágr*, f. OE. *hǣl*, OHG. *heil*, ON. *heill* health (HAIL *sb.*[2], HEAL *sb.*) + OE. *wǣȝ*, OHG. *wâg*, ON. *vágr* wave, water. Some of the forms show association with *háliȝ* holy. See Grimm *Deutsche Mythol.* II. 551.] A healing water, used both as a drink, and as a lotion for wounds; balm, antidote.

c **1205** LAY. 23071 Heo sculde mid haleweie helen his wunden. *Ibid.* 28617 Heo scal..al me makien mid haleweiȝe drenchen. *c* **1220** *Bestiary* 749 A smel..ðat ouercumeð haliweie wið swetnesse. *a* **1225** *Ancr. R.* 94 Hit is a derne healewi þet no mon ne icnoweð þet naueð hit ismecched. *Ibid.* 282 þu attrest þe mid helewi, & wundest þe mid salue. *a* **1240** *Ureisun* in *Cott. Hom.* 200 Swete iesu mi leof, mi lif, mi leome, min healewi, min huni ter. *Ibid.* 183 Min halwi. *a* **1300** *Land of Cokayne* 84 in *E.E.P.* (1862) 158 þer beþ iiij willis in þe abbei, of triacle and halwei. *c* **1440** *Promp. Parv.* 223/2 Halyvey, or bote a-ȝen sekeness, as treacle or oþer lyke (*K.* haliwey), *antidotum..salutiferum.* ?**14..** *Arundel MS.* 42, f. 93 (Promp. Parv. 223 *note*) *Balsamum*, &c. haliwhey.

half (hɑːf), *sb.* Forms: 1– **half**; also 1 **healf,** (**halb**), 2–3 **alf,** (3 **hælf,** *Orm.* **hallf, elf,** 4 **helf, helue**), 4–5 **halue,** 4–7 **halfe,** (6–7 **haulf(e, hafe**). *Pl.* 4– **halves** (hɑːvz): also 4 **halfis,** 5–7 **-es,** (6 **hawves**), 7–8 **halfs.** [A Com. Teut. sb.: OE. *healf* fem. = OS. *halba* (MDu., MLG. *halve*), OHG. *halba* (MHG. *halbe*), ON. *halfa* (*hálfa*), Goth. *halba* side, half: see HALF *a.* The oldest sense in all the langs. is 'side'.]

I. † **1.** Side; one of the (two) sides (of an object) as a specification of position or direction; the right or left side, the right or left 'hand' (of any one); the direction indicated by the side or hand. *Obs.*

a **700** *Epinal Gloss.* 51 *Altrinsecus*, an ba halbae [*Erf.* halbe, *Corp.* halfe]. **805** *Charter* in *O.E. Texts* (1885) 442 On nænȝe oðre halfe. **862** *Ibid.* 438 An easthalfe. *c* **1000** *Ags. Gosp.* Matt. xx. 21 Sittan, an on þine swiðran healfe, and an on þine wynstran. *c* **1000** *Sax. Leechd.* II. 262 On þa healfe þe þæt sar biþ. *c* **1050** *Voc.* in Wr.-Wülcker 338/8 *Altrinsecus*, on twa healfa. *c* **1200** *Trin. Coll. Hom.* 67 He shodeð þe rihtwise an his rihthalue. *c* **1205** LAY. 14018 A þas hælf þere Humbre. *c* **1340** *Cursor M.* 6263 (Fairf.) þe see on ayþer half ham stode as ij. wallis. **1362** LANGL. *P. Pl.* A. II. 7 'Loke on þe lufthond', quod heo, 'and seo wher [he] stondeþ'..I lokede on þe luft half, as þe ladi me tauhte. **1375** BARBOUR *Bruce* IV. 150 Thai on twa halfis war assalit. *c* **1380** *Sir Ferumb.* 882 þan laid he on þe Sarsyns wykke faste be euery helue. *c* **1400** *Destr. Troy* 1353 Thai soght into the Cite vpon sere haluys. **1495** *Act 11 Hen. VII*, c. 4 §1 On this halfe the fest of Ester. **1532** MORE *Confut. Barnes* VIII. Wks. 805/1 Then thou shalte see me on the backe halfe. [**1600** FAIRFAX *Tasso* IX. lxxiv. 174 The purple morning peeped ore The eastren threshold, to our halfe of land.]

† **2.** *fig.* **a.** One of the opposite sides in a conflict, of the opposite sexes in descent, etc. *Obs.*

a **885** *Will of Alfred* in Earle *Land Charters* 148 Min yldra fæder hæfde ȝecweden his land on ða sperehealfe, næs on ða spinlhealfe. **1297** R. GLOUC. (1724) 217 þe compaynye aþes half muche aneþered was. *Ibid.* 325 He was, in hys moder alf, Seynt Edwardes broþer. *c* **1380** WYCLIF *Sel. Wks.* III. 248 þe Jewis seide þat Crist was not on Goddis halfe. *c* **1400** *Destr. Troy* 13474 His beayell..On his modur halfe. **1563** DOLMAN in *Mirr. Mag., Hastings* lxxviii. 2 On princes halves the myghty god doth fyght.

† **b.** Side, part (as of one of the parties to a transaction). *on* (*in, by*) *the half of*: on the part of, as far as concerns, with respect to. *on this half*: in regard or respect of this, on this account. *Obs.*

1068 *Charter Will. I* in *Eng. Hist. Rev.* Oct. (1896) 741 And þær-to eake on minre healfe ic heom ȝeaf and ȝeuþe ..þæt land. *c* **1230** *Hali Meid.* 7 Nu þenne on oðer half nim þe to þe worlde. **13..** *Coer. de L.* 3302 In myne halff, I graunt the foreward. *c* **1374** CHAUCER *Troylus* IV. 917 (945) It shal not lakke, certeyn, on myn halve. **1480** CAXTON *Chron. Eng.* ccxiii. 199 In that other halfe it was founde by an Enquest..that [etc.]. **1526** SKELTON *Magnyf.* 1032, I am so occupied On this half, & on every syde.

† **c.** Hence *on* (*in*) *the half of*: on the part of, in the name of, as the agent or representative of, for, instead of, on or in behalf of. *Obs.*

c **1200** ORMIN 2830 þatt word..þurrh Gabriæl Wass seȝȝd o Godess hallfe. *a* **1300** *Floriz & Bl.* 144 Ber him þis ring On mine halue to tokning. *c* **1380** *Sir Ferumb.* 99 Send hem boþe on þyn helf. **1480** CAXTON *Chron. Eng.* cxlix. 129 We amonest yow fyrst in the popes half, that [etc.]. **1532** MORE *Confut. Tindale* Wks. 414/1 He would fayne haue his false translacion..sayde and songen a goddes halfe.

† **d.** *on God's half*: in God's name, for God's sake; used to add emphasis to a petition, command, or expression of consent or resignation. *Obs.*

a **1225** *Ancr. R.* 22 Hwo se mei stonden euer on vre Leafdi wurschipe, stonde a godes halue. **1297** R. GLOUC. (1724) 561 He let hom go a Godes half. *c* **1369** CHAUCER *Dethe Blaunche* 370 'A goddys halfe, in goode tyme!' quod I. *c* **1430** *Chev. Assigne* 219 'Go we forthe, fader', quod þe childe, 'vpon goddes halfe!' *a* **1529** SKELTON *El. Rummyng* 501 She yelled lyke a calf, Rise up on God's half.

II. 3. One of two opposite, corresponding, or equal parts into which a thing is or may be divided.

a. Of material objects, in which each half lies on one *side* of the dividing line (thus connected with 1).

c **950** *Lindisf. Gosp.* Mark vi. 23 A half rices mines. **1297** R. GLOUC. (1724) 3 Muche del of Engolond, þe on half al bi Weste. *a* **1300** *Cursor M.* 8715 (Cott.) Wit suerd it [child] sal be delt in tua And aiþer sal haune an half [*Fairf.* half, *Gött.*, *Trin.* a side] in hand. **1535** COVERDALE *2 Sam.* x. 4 Hanun.. shone of the one halue of their beerdes. **1623** SANDERSON *Serm.* I. 89 Making as if he would cut the child into halfs, and give either of them one half. **1666** BOYLE *Orig. Formes & Qual.* 136 In the parting of it into halfes (as when our Hazle Nuts..part in the middle longwise). **1717** FREZIER *Voy. S. Sea* 120 *note*, To unite the two Sides, or Halves of the Float. **1851** CARPENTER *Man. Phys.* 182 A continuation of the sagittal-suture down the middle, dividing it into two equal halves.

b. Of quantities or numbers, in which the half bears the same proportion to the whole as one of the halves of a material object, but all connexion with *side* is lost; a moiety.

c **950** *Lindisf. Gosp.* Luke xix. 8 Heono half godra minra Drihten sello ic ðorfendum [*Ags. Gosp.* Nu. ic sylle ðearfum healfe mine æhta; *Hatton G.* half mine ehte]. **1297** R. GLOUC (1724) 31 [Leir] ȝef hys twei doȝtren half, & half hym self nom. *a* **1300** *Cursor M.* 3999 Ar he þe half o þaa haa slayn. *c* **1489** CAXTON *Sonnes of Aymon* xxi. 464 Yf men had gyven hym the halve of all the worlde. **1563** W. FULKE *Meteors* IV. (1640) 47 They ascend not past the halfe of one mile in height. **1659** B. HARRIS *Parival's Iron Age* 32 Ambition being the one half of the game. **1685** *Gracian's Courtier's Orac.* 157 And in that sense the ingenious Paradox is true: That the half is more than the whole. **1820** SCORESBY *Acc. Arctic Reg.* II. 129 Of this number of whales, considerably above half have been taken by five ships now in the trade. *Ibid.* 223 One-half or three fourths of an inch thick. **1823** —— *Whale Fishery* 5 For sale..at one-half the cost prices.

c. After a cardinal number, as *one...and a half.*

(For the earlier mode of expressing this, see HALF *a.* 2.)

c **1290** *Beket* 14 in *S. Eng. Leg.* I. 107 To ȝeres and an half. **1340** HAMPOLE *Pr. Consc.* 4554 Thre days and an half. **1420** *E.E. Wills* (1882) 46 A bolle pece þat weyyth vij ouunsus & halfe, and halfe a quarter. **1577** B. GOOGE *Heresbach's Husb.* II. (1586) 77 They must be set a foote and a halfe a sunder. **1583** HOLLYBAND *Campo di Fior* 157 An houre and a halfe after we are up. **1673** RAY *Journ. Low C.* 3 We took places in the Passage-Boat for Bruges, and at a League and halfs end came to a Lock. **1700** T. BROWN tr. *Fresny's Amusem. Ser. & Com.* 11 For about three parts and a half of four in the Year. **1817** J. MCLEOD *Voy. Alceste* ii. (1820) 45 One of his attendants..received..about a dozen and a half blows with a flat bamboo.

4. a. More vaguely: One of two divisions more or less approaching equality: esp. with comparatives, as *the larger* or *better half.* †Formerly, sometimes, one of three or more divisions.

a **1300** *Cursor M.* 25046 Four halues o þis werld rond. **1340** *Ayenb.* 16 Ech of þe ilke zeuen [heauedes] him to-delþ ine uele halues. *c* **1400** *Destr. Troy* 13303 The more halfe of my men & my mayn shippis. **1580** etc. Better half [see BETTER *a.* 3 b]. **1614** BP. HALL *Recoll. Treat.* 196 One halfe of the world knowes not how the other lives. **1661** J. CHILDREY *Brit. Baconica* 25 The top of it is hollow like the long half of an Egg. *c* **1730** SWIFT *Direct. Servants* Wks. 1778 X. 331 Swear..it broke into three halves. **1858** A. W. DRAYTON *Sport. S. Africa* 74 The better half of a chicken-pie. **1862** H. SPENCER *First Princ.* II. v. §55 The larger half of the phenomena.

b. *better half*, a wife (or †husband): see BETTER *a.* 3 c. Hence, humorously, *worser half.*

1827 HONE *Every-day Bk.* II. 388 These fair helpmates are as convivial..as their 'worser halves'.

† **5.** One of two partners or co-sharers. *Obs.* Cf. *to go halves*, 7 f.

1520 WHITINTON *Vulg.* (1527) 13 Wheder you wynne or lese, I wyll be your halfe. **1591** FLORIO *2nd Fruites* 25 Master Iohn will you be halfe with me? **1595** SHAKS. *Tam. Shr.* v. ii. 78 *Bap.* Sonne, Ile be your halfe, Bianca comes. *Luc.* Ile haue no halues: Ile beare it all my selfe.

6. Elliptical uses of HALF *a.*, some sb. being omitted. *colloq.*

a. = Half-year. (Sometimes applied to a Term, after the new division of the school-year *c* 1865). **b.** = Half-boot. **c.** = Half-pint, half-gill of spirits. **d.** = Half-back (at Football: cf. HALF- II. i.). Also in Rugby Union, Rugby League, etc. Cf. *fly-half* (FLY *sb.*[2] 8), *scrum-half*. **e.** = Half-mile (race); etc. **f.** *Golf.* A hole or point which is halved. **g.** In Old English prosody = *half-line* (HALF- II. n). **h.** A half-holiday. **i.** Ten shillings, half of £1. *slang.* **j.** A fare or ticket at a reduced (usu. half) rate. Also quasi-*adv.*

1659 WILLSFORD *Scales Comm.* II. 29 Paving tyles..to all these pavements they make halfs, to close the work at the sides and ends.

a. 1820 LEWIS *Lett.* (1870) 3 It..has completely stopped the boats for this half. **1875** A. R. HOPE *My Schoolboy Fr.* 172 This half, all my friends had returned to Whitminster. **1876** *World* V. No. 109. 10 Since the school year has known the triple distribution into terms instead of the *halves* of our boyhood.

b. 1837 DICKENS *Pickw.* x, There's two pair of halves in the commercial.

c. 1888 *Scott. Leader* 27 July 4 To sustain themselves in their public duty by resort to what is technically known as 'a half'. **1891** *Daily News* 15 Apr. 7/1 I heard him call for two halves of ale and a cigar.

d. 1887 SHEARMAN *Athletics & Football* (Badm. Libr.) 306 The best halves were strong thick-set men, rather under than over middle height. **1896** B. F. ROBINSON *Rugby Football* v. 90 The half 'working' the scrummage should rarely try to run him-self. **1897** *Daily Chron.* 16 Feb. 5/6 One change..occurs at half, where Mr. B. plays his first match for London. **1906** GALLAHER & STEAD *Compl. Rugby Footballer* iv. 64 A new line of attack and defence between the halves and the three-quarters. **1951** *Men's Hockey* (Know the Game Series) (1965) 17/2 At long corners..the halves go out behind them. **1960** E. S. & W. J. HIGHAM *High Speed Rugby* vii. 55 Give me a good pair of halves and I will give you a team.

e. 1897 *Whitaker's Alm.* 635/1 The half, after a splendid race, was won by..King.

f. 1881 [see DEAD *a.* 21 b]. **1908** J. BRAID *Advanced Golf* 213 Halves ought rarely to be agreed upon unless the balls are so close to the hole that it is next to impossible for the putts to be missed. **1931** *Daily Tel.* 22 May 18/1 He..secured the necessary 5 for the half and the match. **1959** *Times* 29 May 5/1 Sewell got a brave half at the 18th.

g. 1892 S. A. BROOKE *Hist. Early Eng. Lit.* I. p. x, The Anglo-Saxon line is divided into two halves by a pause. The first half has two 'measures'. **1940** J. R. R. TOLKIEN in J. R. C. Hall tr. *Beowulf* p. xxvii, The Old English line was composed of two opposed word-groups or 'halves'. Each half was an example, or variation, of one of six basic patterns.

h. 1909 P. TRAHERNE *Diary* Nov. (1918) i. 28 By getting up this entertainment on a 'half' when there was nothing else to do I found myself launched into about six rows. **1934** *Neuphilol. Mitt.* XXXV. 130 He will acquire prep-school slang (words such as..*half* 'half holiday').

i. 1931 W. F. BROWN in *Police Jrnl.* IV. 502 They speiled first for stakes of a sprazey,..increasing it..later to a half... This narrative..would in plain English read..They played first for stakes of a sixpence..increasing..later to ten shillings. **1938** G. GREENE *Brighton Rock* I. ii. 30 She's just a buer—he gave her a half.

j. 1935 *Punch* 30 Jan. 137 You two can't go half. You're over age. **1965** *New Statesman* 9 Apr. 567/2 Two adults and three halves, please.

7. Phrases. **a.** † *at halves*, †*to* (*the*) *half*, †*to* (*the*) *halves*: to the extent of a half = HALF *adv.* 1 c; imperfectly, incompletely, by halves (*obs.*). Also, in letting or hiring a house, land, or the like, *to* (*the*) *halves* = so as to have a half-share in the profits (now *U.S.*). **b.** *by halves*: to the extent of a half only; imperfectly, in part; half-heartedly, with half zeal. † **c.** *half in half*: half (to or by half) the total amount; cent per cent (*obs.*). **d.** *in half* or *halves*: into two (more or less) equal parts. **e.** *by half*: by a great deal; much, considerably, far. Esp. in phr. *too clever by half*: trying too hard to be clever. **f.** *to go halves* (cf. 5): to share equally (with a person). **g.** *to cry halves*: to claim a half-share in what is found by another. (See also 2, 3.) **h.** *and a half* (following a sb.): and more; of an exceptional kind. Cf. HEART *sb.* 39 b. *colloq.* **i.** *the half of it*: a significant or more important part of something. Usu. in negative contexts.

a. 1547 SALESBURY *Welsh Dict., Hannery*, to ye halfe. **1577** B. GOOGE *Heresbach's Husb.* (1586) 47 b, He may occupie it by his Bayliffe, or to hawves. **1601** R. JOHNSON *Kingd. & Commw.* (1603) 105 Not at a rent certaine as we do in England, but to halfes, or to the thirds of all graine, fruit and profits, arising of the ground. **1647** W. BROWNE tr. *Gomberville's Polexander* I. 222 I see but at halfes. *Ibid.* 240 To be reveng'd at halfes. *a* **1673** CARYL in Spurgeon *Treas. Dav.* Ps. vi. 8 They do it not to halves, but thoroughly. **1677** HALE *Prim. Orig. Man.* II. vi. 170 In Arphaxad..the great Age of the Ancients was cut to halves. **1682** BUNYAN *Holy War* 115 Nor did I do this to the halves. **1710** PRIDEAUX *Orig. Tithes* ii. 104 It is usual..for the owners to let their Lands to halfs to their Tenants. **1866** LOWELL *Biglow P.* Ser. II. Introd. Poems 1890 II. 188 *To the halves* still survives among us, though apparently obsolete in England. It means either to let or hire a piece of land, receiving half the profit in money or in kind.

b. 1563–87 in FOXE *A. & M.* (K.O.) **1591** SYLVESTER *Du Bartas* I. iv. 6 Faint idle Artizans..Working by halfs. **1641** SYMONDS *Serm. bef. Ho. Comm.* E, Hitherto the work hath been done by the halfes. **1753** HANWAY *Trav.* (1762) II. XIV. i. 343 Nadir, who did nothing by halves, was determined to pull off the mask. **1790** BURKE *Fr. Rev.* Wks. V. 389 A king is not to be deposed by halves. **1863** P. BARRY *Dockyard Econ.* 86 Those charged with the responsibility..should not deal by halves with a question in which all classes have so deep an interest.

c. 1583 STUBBES *Anat. Abus.* II. (1882) 21 Gaining..more than halfe in halfe in euerie thing they buy or sell. **1601** R. JOHNSON *Kingd. & Commw.* (1603) 179 The armie halfe in halfe in number and courage diminished. **1626** BACON *Sylva* §371 By this means they will out-last other Candles of the same stuff, almost half in half. **1655** GURNALL *Chr. in Arm.* I. 57 The price is fallen half in half to what it was. **1762** STERNE *Tr. Shandy* V. iii, My father gained half-in-half, and consequently was as well again off.

d. 1599 H. BUTTES *Dyets drie Dinner* B viij b, First part them in halfes and cut out the Cores. **1706** S. CLARKE *Attrib. God* viii. (R.), When a square cut in halves makes two triangles, those two triangles are still only the two halves of the square. **1821** SHELLEY *Prometh. Unb.* I. 714 Each by lightning riven in half. **1862** *Cornh. Mag.* June 723 The ball ..swift enough to cut the middle stump in half.

e. [*a* **1000** *Boeth. Metr.* xii. 18 Healfe þy swetre.] ?*a* **1400** *Morte Arth.* 2127 Thowe to hye arte by þe halfe, I hete þe in trouthe! **1638** BAKER tr. *Balzac's Lett.* (vol III.) 13 Shee is fayrer by one halfe than shee was before. **1658** COKAINE *Trappolin* I. i, 'Tis better by half than a soldier. **1777** SHERIDAN *Sch. Scand.* IV. iii, Pshaw! he is too moral by half. **1858** WHYTE MELVILLE *Interpreter* xli, Too clever by half. **1889** W. WESTALL *Birch Dene* II. vi. 89 'Nobody can deny as he's clever.' 'Ay, too clever by half.' **1944** L. MACNEICE *Christopher Columbus* 8 Constant ingenuity..often leads to an appearance of being too clever by half. **1961** *Listener* 2

Nov. 717/1 A bad one [*sc.* documentary], whether dull through laziness, or self-conscious or pretentious or too-clever-by-half, can be a real catastrophe.

f. **1678** BUTLER *Hud.* III. iii. 270 For those that save themselves, and fly, Go halves, at least, in th' Victory. **1752** CHESTERF. *Lett.* (1792) III. cclxxxi. 291 If you think I shall win it, you may go my halves if you please. **1835** MARRYAT *Jac. Faithf.* xxxvi, We would go halves, and share it equally. **1851–61** MAYHEW *Lond. Labour* III. 122 (Farmer) He'll then again ask if anybody will go him halves. *a* **1898** *Mod.* I will go halves with you.

g. **1659** CLEVELAND *C. Revived* 1 The devided Damme Runs to the Summons of her hungry Lamb, But when the twin cries Halves, she quits the first. **1730** SAVAGE *Horace to Scæva* 32 (L.) And he, who sees you stoop to th' ground Cries, halves! to everything you've found. **1821** LAMB *Elia* Ser. I. *Imperf. Sympathies*, You cannot cry *halves* to anything that he finds. He does not find but bring.

h. **1636**, etc. [see HEART *sb.* 39 b]. **1832** J. K. PAULDING *Westward Ho!* II. i. 7 Bushfield, too, was here in all his glory, and was not only a whole team, but a team and a half, good measure, as he affirmed. **1837** DICKENS *Pickw.* xlvi. 501, I raythet think the gov'ner vants to have a vord and a half vith you. **1911** T. E. LAWRENCE *Lett.* (1938) 118 Last night was paradise and a half. **1917** *Strand Mag.* LIII. 606/2 Golly! He took a toss and a half! **1959** 'M. M. KAYE' *House of Shade* x. 128 Roaring Rory must have been a hell-raiser and a half in his day.

i. **1932** WODEHOUSE *Hot Water* i. 27 It makes me sick. And that's not the half of it.. She told me I've got to be American Ambassador to France. **1947** 'N. BLAKE' *Minute for Murder* i. 2 'We've not seen the half of it yet,' said the Messenger darkly. 'The half of what?' 'You mark my words, sir. When peace comes, as you might say real peace, there'll be chay-oh in this country.' **1966** M. BREWER *Man against Fear* xi. 117 'You haven't heard the half of it yet.' I went on to tell him about the Carver Street ambush. **1971** M. BABSON *Cover-up Story* x. 109 'How awful,' she said... I nodded, without telling her she didn't know the half of it.

8. *Comb.* **a.** *attrib.*, as *half-share*. **b.** quasi-*adv.*, as *half-partner*, *-sharer*, *-worker*.

1586 T. B. *La Primand. Fr. Acad.* I. (1594) 480 That which.. maketh the will of his halfe-partner to be wholy his own. **1603** DEKKER *Wonderf. Yeare* E iv, Downe she lights this half-sharer, but conueis him into a by-room. **1611** SHAKS. *Cymb.* II. v. 2 Is there no way for Men to be, but Women Must be halfe-workers? **1848** MILL *Pol. Econ.* II. viii. §2 The metayer is at least his landlord's partner, and a half-sharer in their joint gains. **1861** DICKENS *Gt. Expect.* xxv, I presented him with a half-share in my boat.

half (hɑːf), *a.* Forms: 1 healf, hæalf, 1– half; also 5 halve, alfe, halff, 5–7 halfe. [Common Teut.: OE. *healf*, *half* = OFris, OS. (MDu., Du., LG.) *half*, OHG. and Ger. *halb*, ON. *halfr*, (Sw. *half*, Da. *halv*), Goth. *halbs*:—OTeut. **halƀoz*; not known outside Teutonic. The appearance of 'side' as the oldest sense of HALF *sb.* makes the original meaning of the adj. uncertain.]

1. Being one of the two equal parts into which a thing is or may be divided; forming a half or moiety.

a. immediately preceding the sb., and preceded by a defining word (demonstrative or possessive, genitive case, etc.), as *a half length*, *his half share*; *half sheet*. See also *half-sheet* s.v. HALF- II. n.

When the two words constitute a recognized unit or individual, *half* is usually hyphened to the *sb.*, as in *half-crown*: see HALF- II. The limits are necessarily undefined and vague, and the use of the hyphen is a matter of perspicuity in the particular connexion.

835 *Charter* in *O.E. Texts* 447, & him man selle an half swulung an ciollan dene. **859** in Earle *Land Charters* 130 An healf tun que ante pertinebat to wilburgewellan. *c* **1050** *Byrhtferth's Handboc* in *Anglia* VIII. 298 Þrittig daga & tyn tida & healfe tid. *a* **1056** *Charter of Leofwine* in *Cod. Dipl.* IV. 136 Leofwine.. hæfð geboht healfe hide landes. *c* **1175** *Lamb. Hom.* 31 Half oðer þridde lot. *c* **1205** LAY. 18971 Half hundred cnihten. **1393** LANGL. *P. Pl.* C. VII. 267 Ich pynchede on hus half acre. **1535** COVERDALE *Josh.* xii. 6 Vnto the Rubenites, Gaddites and to the halfe trybe of Manasse. **1709** STEELE *Tatler* No. 9 ¶1 The Town has this half Age been tormented with Insects called Easie Writers. **1723** J. NOTT *Cook's & Confect. Dict.* 261c Lay every Cutlet on a half Sheet of Paper. **1828** HUTTON *Course Math.* II. 84 The number of half bricks in the thickness. **1852** E. RUSKIN *Let.* 17 Apr. in M. Lutyens *Effie in Venice* (1965) II. 296, I was very grateful for.. Papa's half sheet about the Ruskins. **1865–6** A. PHILLIPS *Amer. Paper Curr.* II. 148 In five or six weeks the army was on half allowance. **1897** *Bookman* Jan. 122/2 A smudged half sheet of paper.

b. separated from the sb. by demonstrative or defining words, as *half the length*, *half my family*. (Formerly sometimes following the sb.)

The adj. character of *half* appears in OE. and early ME. by its inflexion; in mod. use it is sometimes viewed as a sb. with *of* suppressed, as in 'half (half of, one half of) the men were sick, a quarter or a third of them seriously ill': cf. also quot. 1667.

a **1000** *Judith* 105 (Gr.) Heo healfne forcearf þone sweoran him. *c* **1000** *Sax. Leechd.* II. 78 ȝenim healfe þa sealfe. *c* **1205** LAY. 22441 Halfe þa steden, & halfe þa iweden. *Ibid.* 31814 He brohte ham halue his oxen. *a* **1300** *Cursor M.* 13147 Þof þou ask half mi king-rike. **1377** LANGL. *P. Pl.* B. III. 324 Half a shef of arwes. *a* **1400** CHAUCER *Balade of Compleynt* 2 Compleyne.. might myn herte never My peynes halve. **1486** *Bk. St. Albans* B viij, The space of alfe a quarter of an howre. **1548** HALL *Chron., Edw. IV*, 236 b, Halfe the charges, and halfe the wages of his souldiers. **1667** MILTON *P.L.* v. 559 Scarce the Sun Hath finisht half his journey, and scarce begins His other half in the great Zone of Heav'n. **1724** DE FOE *Mem. Cavalier* (1840) 104 He lost half his men. **1820** SHELLEY *To a Skylark* 101 Teach me half the gladness That thy brain must know. **1823** BYRON *Juan* x. lxiv, The.. wind blew half a gale. **1849** MACAULAY *Hist. Eng.* II. 612 His victory.. had deprived him of half his influence. **1849** [see BATTLE *sb.* 4]. **1864** TROLLOPE *Can you forgive Her?* I. xxxviii. 301 If you are half the woman that I take you to be, you will understand this. **1867** —— *Claverings* I. iii. 38 Though the lord might be only half a man, Julia walked out from the church every inch a countess. **1936** *Discovery* Dec. 397/2 The author has undoubtedly the gift of winning the confidence of his African hosts, which is half the battle. **1944** *Living off Land* i. 15 The correct mental approach to a lesson is often half the battle.

c. esp. with sbs. denoting numbers, quantities, measures of weight, space, time, or money, as *half a dozen, half a bushel, half a pound, half a foot, half an hour, half a crown*. Also *half a bar* (see BAR *sb.*[1] 3 c); *half a bull* [BULL *sb.*[1] 7], half a crown (*slang*).

When these are viewed as independent numbers, amounts, coins, etc., *half* is preceded by *a*, *the*, etc. and hyphened to the sb., as *a half-dozen, the half-bushel, his half-pound, a long half-hour, a bad half-crown*: see HALF- II. *A half-crown* is the former silver coin worth *2s. 6d.*; *half a crown* included the equivalent amount in any coins, e.g. in five sixpences.

1377 LANGL. *P. Pl.* B. v. 31 Hire hed was worth halue a marke. *c* **1386** CHAUCER *Reeve's T.* 324 Thou shalt a Cake of half a busshel fynde. *a* **1450** *Fysshynge w. Angle* (1883) 9 Let it boyle halfe a myle wey and then set hyt down. *c* **1450** *St. Cuthbert* (Surtees) 5058 Noght the space of half a myle, Was done the houre of pryme. *c* **1500** *Melusine* xxxvi. 244 The whiche they recountred a half a myle fro the toun. **1661** J. CHILDREY *Brit. Baconica* 49 At Avering.. there are halfe a dozen, or halfe a score stones little inferiour to the Stonehenge. **1807** CRABBE *Par. Reg.* II. 203 For half an inch the letters stand awry. **1812** J. H. VAUX *Flash Dict.*, *Half a bull*, half a crown. **1859** DICKENS *T. Two Cities* I. ii, Capable of holding about half a Gallon.

d. preceding a relative clause.

(Here it may be a *sb.* with *of* omitted.)

1696 SOUTHERNE *Oroon.* III. i. (Mätz. *Gram.*), If he dares half what he says, he'll be of us. **1733** POPE *Ess. Man* III. 162 Of half that live the butcher and the tomb. **1786** COWPER *Gratitude* 41 All these are not half that I owe.

†**2.** *half*, preceded or followed by an ordinal numeral, was formerly used to express a half-unit less than the corresponding cardinal number; thus OE. *þridda healf*, ME. *thridde half* or *half thrid* = two and a half. *Obs.*

This is an ancient Teutonic mode of reckoning: cf. Ger. *anderthalb* (= OE. *oðer healf*), *dritte halb*, etc. In English it is scarcely found after 1300. The expression is explained in quot. 811 as elliptical: 'two (whole) messuages and a third half-messuage', contracted to *ðridda half haʒa*. Hence the following sb. was originally singular, *ðridde half hýd* = two and a half hide. As in Old Norse, etc., *half* was either declined as an adj. (quot. 891), or stood in the uninflected combining form.

811 *Charter* in *O.E. Texts* 456 Duas possessiunculas et tertiam dimediam, id est in nostra loquela, ðridda half haʒa. **891** *O.E. Chron.*, Se bat wæs ȝeworht of þriddan healfre hyde. *c* **1000** ÆLFRIC *Gen.* viii. 3 Ða wætera.. begunnon to waniȝenne æfter oþer healfhund daȝa. *c* **1200** ORMIN 13777 Þatt sahh & herrde daȝȝwhammliȝ Hallf ferþe ȝer þe Laferrd. *c* **1205** LAY. 32195 Ne wunede þe king þer bute uifte half ȝere. *a* **1300** *Cursor M.* 16599–600 Half feirth of eln was þe length, And oþer half þe brede [of þe rode]. *c* **1300** *Beket* 11 For ful other half ȝer. *c* **1300** *Harrow. Hell* 45 Thritty wynter and thridde half yer Hav y woned in londe her.

3. In reference to space or distance: Half the length (or breadth) of. Now *rare* or *Obs.*

1481 CAXTON *Godfrey* xxvii. 61 They waded in the blood vnto the half legge. **1662** J. DAVIES tr. *Olearius' Voy. Ambass.* 74 Their hair.. hangs down over their shoulders to half their backs. *Ibid.* 302 A Casaque, or Coat, which falls down to half the leg. **1681** *Lond. Gaz.* No. 1628/1 Soon after the Algerine fell astern, and there lay within half Pistol shot. **1692** *Ibid.* No. 2776/4 They saw our Fleet off of Portland, half Channel over. **1727** A. HAMILTON *New Acc. E. Ind.* II. xxxvi. 50 The lower Part of the Frock reaching Half-thigh down.

4. As a measure of degree: Attaining only half-way to completeness or to the actual action, quality, or character in question; falling short of the full or perfect thing; partial, imperfect, incomplete. (Const. as in 1 a.)

In this use now more usually hyphened: see HALF-.

a **1300** *Cursor M.* 27341 He lede penant to half reuing. **1577** tr. *Bullinger's Decades* (1592) 899 Both dawes and halfe fooles may bee made ministers or byshoppes. **1585** T. WASHINGTON tr. *Nicholay's Voy.* IV. v. 116 b, The greater part whereof being halfe christians. **1653** SIR E. NICHOLAS in *N. Papers* (Camden) II. 22 Bargaining, conditional, or half ways beget nothing but factions and divisions. *a* **1765** YOUNG *Wks.* (1767) IV. 81 (Jod.) Half converts to the right. **1816** KEATINGE *Trav.* (1817) I. 198 Contented with half views of things and truths. **1849** MACAULAY *Hist. Eng.* I. 185 A half toleration, known by the name of the Indulgence. **1858** C. HUNT in *Merc. Mar. Mag.* V. 84 Steam should be shut off to half speed. **1862** WHATELY in *Life* (1866) II. 392 A half measure is not a medium between two extremes, but a medium between what is right and what is wrong—between what will effect its purpose and what will not.

half, *v.* Obs. and dial. f. HALVE *v.* (q.v.); also *colloq.* in sense To 'be half', go halves.

1889 *Pall Mall G.* 27 June 5, I asked Sir G. C. if he would 'half'. He consented. I paid for the horse, he repaying me afterwards, and also paying half the training expenses.

half (hɑːf), *adv.* [OE. *half*, *healf*, in composition; in OE. sometimes, and in ME. often, written separate. Both usages are now found, usually with no difference of sense: see HALF- I.]

1. To the extent or amount of half. Hence loosely: In part, partially; to a certain extent, in some degree.

a. qualifying an adjective.

[**971** *Blickl. Hom.* 203 Ða hæþnan leode, þa þe lifdon heora burh healf-cwice.] *c* **1175** *Lamb. Hom.* 81 Half quic ho wes. *c* **1385** CHAUCER *L.G.W.* 1697 *Lucrece*, They were halfe ydel, as hem thoghten. *c* **1425** *Voc.* in Wr.-Wülcker 668/39 *Surdaster, -a, -um*, halfe deffe. **1600** FAIRFAX *Tasso* XIX. civ, Thither she ran with speed, Like one half mad. **1601** HOLLAND *Pliny* I. 96 Halfe wilde beasts. **1657** R. LIGON *Barbadoes* (1673) 64 Fill it half full of water. **1832** AUSTIN *Jurispr.* vi. (1869) 258 Governments which are styled by writers on positive international law *half sovereign states*. **1832** TENNYSON *Lady of Shalott* ii, 'I am half sick of shadows' said The Lady of Shalott. **1878** EDITH THOMPSON *Hist. Eng.* xix. 106 Half wild with rage and grief.

b. qualifying a pa. pple.

c **1380** *Sir Ferumb.* 3569 Er þay wern oȝt helf y-dyȝt, þus barons come oppon hem ryȝt. *c* **1489** CAXTON *Sonnes of Aymon* ix. 228 We ben halfe discomfyted. **1548** HALL *Chron., Edw. IV*, 199 b, The erle had not halfe tolde his tale. **1599** H. BUTTES *Dyets drie Dinner* H vj b, Coleworts.. Halfe sodden, make soluble. **1615** J. STEPHENS *Satyr. Ess.* 8 In her halfe ruin'd cell. *Ibid.* 432, I am halfe perswaded that if hee had but a balladmakers poetry, he would sooner make an Epitaph. **1657** R. LIGON *Barbadoes* (1673) 12 Dinner being near half done. **1711** ADDISON *Spect.* No. 66 ¶5 A Man's Life is half spent before he is taken notice of. **1897** HALL CAINE *Christian* x, Half hidden behind a little forest of palms and ferns.

c. qualifying a pr. pple. or verb.

1423 JAS. I *Kingis Q.* lxxiii, Half sleping and half swoun, in suich a wise. **1500–20** DUNBAR *Poems* lxxxi. 1 This hinder nycht halff sleiping I lay. **1608** BP. HALL *Char. Virtues & V.* 135 Halfe reading every title. **1650** BULWER *Anthropomet.* 162, I half suspect some concurrent affectations. **1674** tr. *Scheffer's Lapland* 12 A bow which a Norwegian can scarce half bend. **1797** MRS. RADCLIFFE *Italian* xxxi, On entering he half turned to look back. **1859** FARRAR *J. Home* 273 He.. half wished he had not come. **1910** W. DE LA MARE *Three Mulla-Mulgars* 63 Half-hiding his face in his jacket. **1918** D. H. LAWRENCE *New Poems* 13 One side shadow, half in sight, Half-hiding the pavement-run.

d. qualifying an adv. or advb. phrase.

a **1310** in Wright *Lyric P.* 40 Nys non so ȝeep, ne half so freo. **1390** GOWER *Conf.* I. 225 There may no mannes privete Ben heled half so well. *c* **1470** HENRY *Wallace* x. 128 Halff in wraith frawart him gan he gang. **1579–80** NORTH *Plutarch* (1612) 740 A man halfe beside himself. **1648** GAGE *West Ind.* 191 The three Spaniards were halfe of the same mind. **1674** S. VINCENT *Yng. Gallant's Acad.* 18 Caudle will not go down half so sweetly as this will. **1706** ADDISON *Rosamond* Wks. 1753 I. 132 The lily was not half so fair, Nor half so sweet the rose. **1724** R. FALCONER *Voy.* (1769) 66, I rowed half round.. the first Day. **1832** Half right, half-left [see HALF- II. d].

2. Used correlatively: *half... half...*.

(Now sometimes hyphened to the following word; but this is unnecessary.)

944 in Earle *Land Charters* 179 Ðonne is þæt land æt snoces cumbe healf þæs cinges healf uncer brentinges. *c* **1000** ÆLFRIC *Voc.* in Wr.-Wülcker 109/16 *Onocentaurus*, healf mann and healf assa. *c* **1205** LAY. 1330 Hit is half mon & half fisc. **1390** GOWER *Conf.* II. 304 He was half man and half beste. **1559** W. CUNNINGHAM *Cosmogr. Glasse* 86 The Sonne.. halfe above the Horizont, and half under. **1581** PETTIE *Guazzo's Civ. Conv.* I. (1586) 23, I ment not that they are halfe good, and halfe evill. **1614** BP. HALL *Recoll. Treat.* 60 An evill man is halfe a beast, and halfe a Divell. **1708** MOTTEUX *Rabelais* IV. lxvii. (1737) 274 With.. one of his Stockins, half on half off, about his Heel. **1810** SCOTT *Lady of L.* I. xxxiv, Half shewing, half concealing all The uncouth trophies of the hall. **1818** M. G. LEWIS *Jrnl. W. Ind.* (1834) 78 A kind of pouting look, half kind, and half reproachful. **1858** ABR. LINCOLN *Sp.* 16 June in *Life* (1890) II. viii. 137, I believe this Government cannot endure permanently half slave and half free.

3. *not half*: a long way from the due amount; to a very slight extent; in mod. *slang* and *colloq.* use = not at all, the reverse of, as 'not half bad' = not at all bad, rather good; 'not half a bad fellow' = a good fellow; 'not half long enough' = not nearly long enough; also (*slang*), extremely, violently, as 'he didn't half swear'.

1583 STOCKER *Hist. Civ. Warres Lowe C.* II. 66 b, Thei were not halfe well prouided to goe awaie vpon the spurre. **1619** DRUMM. OF HAWTH. *Conv. w. B. Jonson* xi. (1842) 11 Sir W. Alexander was not half kinde unto him, and neglected him. **1622** MABBE tr. *Aleman's Guzman d' Alf.* II. I. iii. II. 30 He thought this was hard teaching, he did not halfe like it. **1828** *Craven Dial.* s.v., 'He's nut hauf a bad an', i.e. he is a fair, respectable person. **1851** MELVILLE *Moby Dick* II. xxxi. 215, I don't half like that chap, Stubb. **1859** HUGHES *Scouring W. Horse* vi. 133, I didn't half like the way in which Miss Lucy was running on. **1871** PLANCHÉ *King Christmas*, He never admits a thing is good, but merely 'not half bad'. **1886** J. K. JEROME *Idle Thoughts* Pref., One or two friends to whom I showed these papers in MS. observed that they were not half bad. **1914** H. ASHTON *First from Front* xiv. 99 It wasn't half all right, I tell you. **1919** V. WOOLF *Night & Day* xv. 195, I could live on fifteen shillings a week. .. It wouldn't be half bad. **1920** GALSWORTHY *Foundations* III, in *Plays* (1929) 498 Talk of your sacrifices in the war —they put you on your honour, and you got stout on it. Rations—not 'arf! **1953** L. P. HARTLEY *Go-Between* xiv. 165 And we didn't half enjoy your songs. **1955** E. BOWEN *World of Love* ii. 19 He had no plans: he in fact would not be half sorry if someone said to him he was back for good. **1962** PARKER & ALLERTON *Courage of his Convictions* iii. 143 It doesn't half nark them.

4. Idiomatic uses, in which *half* is now adverbial, though probably originally the adj. or sb.

a. In stating the time of day, ***half past*** (or ***after***) ***one*** or ***one o'clock***, etc. = half an hour past the hour named. (In Scotland, 'half' is often prefixed to the following hour, as in Ger. *halb elf*, etc.)

1750 G. B. DODDINGTON *Diary* (1785) 74 Just at half past twelve she was delivered of a Prince. *a* **1791** GROSE *Olio* (1796) 107 *C.* Pray what's o' clock? *W.* It will be half ten. **1818** JAS. MILL *Brit. India* II. v. v. 494 From half after seven .. they remained exposed to the fire .. till nine o'clock. **1819** BYRON *Juan* I. civ, About the hour Of half-past six. **1853** READE *Chr. Johnstone* 294 Flucker informed her that the nock said 'half eleven'—Scotch for 'half-past-ten'. **1891** *Murray's Mag.* Apr. 445 It was half after eight o'clock one evening.

b. *Naut.* Between the names of two points of the compass, *half* = half a point (i.e. $5\frac{5}{8}°$) from the first towards the second point mentioned.

1726 SHELVOCKE *Voy. round World* (1757) 17 Bearing South East half East, distant six leagues. **1893** EARL DUNMORE *Pamirs* I. 252 We .. altered our course from north to east half-south by the compass.

c. *Naut.* In soundings, *half* before a numeral adds half to it; thus ***half four*** = $4\frac{1}{2}$ fathoms.

1809 TREMENHEERE in *Naval Chron.* XXIII. 191 The ship .. shoaled her water to a half three. **1840** MARRYAT *Poor Jack* xlvii, We shall have *half four* directly, and after that the water will deepen. *c* **1860** H. STUART *Seaman's Catech.* 43 Suppose $4\frac{1}{2}$ fathoms, what soundings would you call? And a half four.

half-, in *comb.* [OE. *half-*, *healf-*, was regularly combined with an adj. or pple., as in *healfewic*, *healfdéad*, *healfhwít*, *healfréad*, *healfsoden*, *healfslǽpiende*; also with a sb., as *healfhéafod* forehead, *healfmann*, *healfpeniȝ*, *healftrendel* hemisphere. In OTeut. *halb-* appears to have been a later substitute for the original *sāmi-*, OE. *sam-*, as in OHG. *sâmiquec*, OS. *sâmquic*, OE. *samcwic* half alive, so *sambærnd* half-burnt, *sambrice* a half-breach; = L. *sēmi-* in *sēmidoctus*, *sēmivīvus*, *sēmicoctus*, *sēmideus*, *sēmihomo*, etc.; Gr. ἡμι- in ἡμιβάρβαρος, ἡμιπλήρης, ἡμιάνθρωπος, ἡμίθεος, etc.; Skr. *sāmi*, in *sāmijīwas* half alive, etc.]

I. 1. With adjectives and pa. pples. Already in OE.: see above. Very common in later use, esp. with pa. pples., to which *half-* may be prefixed whenever the sense suits: e.g. ***half-afraid***, ***-awake***, ***-blind***, ***-crazy***, ***-deaf***, ***-drunk***, ***-full***, ***-human***, ***-learned***, ***-mad***, ***-open***, ***-raw***, ***-ripe***, ***-savage***, ***-true***; ***half-armed***, ***-ashamed***, ***-bent***, ***-buried***, ***-cured***, ***-disposed***, ***-done***, ***-dressed***, ***-eaten***, ***-educated***, ***-finished***, ***-formed***, ***-hidden***, ***-opened***, ***-roasted***, ***-ruined***, etc., etc. With adjs. expressing shape, it implies the form of half the figure, as ***half-cordate***, ***-sagittate***, ***-terete***.

The two elements are often written separately when the adj. is in the predicate (see HALF *adv.* 1); the use of the hyphen mostly implies a feeling of closer unity of notion in the compound attribute, as in *half-blind*, *half-dressed*, *half-raw*, viewed as definite states; but it is often merely for greater syntactical perspicuity, on which ground it is regularly used when the adjective is attributive, thus *I am half dead* (or *half-dead*) *with cold*; a *half-dead dog*.

a. in the predicate.

c **893** K. ÆLFRED *Oros.* III. ix. §4 & funde hiene .. healfcucne. *a* **1000** *Elene* 133 (Gr.) Sume healfcwice flugon on fæsten. *c* **1000** ÆLFRIC *Voc.* in Wr.-Wülcker 163/7 *Subalbus*, healfhwit. *c* **1475** *Nom.* Ibid. 710/3 *Semicecus*, halfblynd. *a* **1626** BACON (J.), The officers of the kings houshold .. must look both ways, else they are but half-sighted. **1704** SWIFT *T. Tub* i. (1709) 29 As if they were half-ashamed to own us. **1712–14** POPE *Rape Lock* IV. 144 Her eyes half-languishing, half-drown'd in tears. **1714** MANDEVILLE *Fab. Bees* (1725) I. 340 A rascal half-drunk. **1725** POPE *Odyss.* III. 144 Leave half-heard the melancholy tale. **1741** RICHARDSON *Pamela* (1824) I. xxi. 271 Being half-vexed, and half-afraid of his raillery. **1826** SCOTT *Jrnl.* (1890) I. 329 Either half-educated or cock-brained by nature. **1844** J. R. LOWELL *Poems* 12 A youth half-smiling. **1845** LINDLEY *Sch. Bot.* v. (1858) 58 Stipules ovate, half-cordate. **1846** 'A LADY' *Jewish Manual* II. v. 216 Dresses made half high are .. unbecoming; they should either be cut close up to the throat or low. **1849** THOREAU *Week on Concord* 399 They are half forgotten ere we have learned the language. **1855** KINGSLEY *Heroes* II. IV. (1868) 123 Stories of it, some false and some half-true. **1858** BAGEHOT *Coll. Works* (1965) II. 55 Half-crazed as she [Meg Merrilies] is described to be. **1863–5** J. THOMSON *Sunday at Hampstead* v, The meat half-done, they tore it and devoured. **1868** DARWIN in *Life & Lett.* (1887) III. 80 Half-sterile, i.e. produce half the full number of offspring. **1880** GRAY *Struct. Bot.* vi. §8. 279 Amphitropous, also termed .. Half-anatropous. **1880** *Contemp. Rev.* Feb. 196. I am more than half-disposed to go along with you in what you say. **1881** 'MARK TWAIN' *Prince & Paup.* 162 He was half-minded to resign. **1893** —— *Man corrupted Hadleyburg* (1900) 269 The station-master .. became pleasant and even half-apologetic. **1904** W. DE LA MARE *Henry Brocken* 76, I glanced at the shock-haired creature, alert, half-human, beside me. **1910** J. MORLEY *Cromwell* (ed. 2) iii. 54 Never more were fish caught there, and the neighbouring town was half ruined. **1923** D. H. LAWRENCE *Birds, Beasts & Flowers* 41 The dim light of full, healthy life That is always half-dark. **1936** *Mind* XLV. 252 What were the views concealed or half-concealed, expressed or half-expressed? **1937** *Brit. Birds* XXX. 240 We have two records of single adults spending one day in the nest when their young were half-fledged. **1961** M. W. BARLEY *Eng. Farmhouse & Cottage* IV. ii. 196 Roofs gabled and half-hipped.

b. as attribute.

1594 HOOKER *Eccl. Pol.* I. viii. §10 Certaine halfewaking men. **1595** SHAKS. *John* III. i. 54 The halfe-blowne Rose. **1625** DONNE *Serm.* lxvi. 667 The Half-present Man, he whose body is here and minde away. **1629** CHAPMAN *Juvenal* Sat. v. 293 That half-eat hare will fall .. to our shares. **1682** N.O. *Boileau's Lutrin* II. 16 And clos'd her speech with an half-dying swoon. **1687** DRYDEN *Hind & P.* III. 409 The clown unread, and half-read gentleman. *a* **1711** KEN *Hymnotheo* Poet. Wks. 1721 III. 333 Half-form'd Words. **1725** POPE *Odyss.* XXII. 196 The half-shut door conceal'd his lurking foes. **1772** HUNTER in *Phil. Trans.* LXII. 453 Half-digested food. **1786** tr. *Beckford's Vathek* (1868) 10 The learned, the half-learned, and those who were neither. **1817** COLERIDGE *Biog. Lit.* 223 In one of his half-earnest, half-joking moods. **1827** SOUTHEY *Hist. Penins. War* II. 679 The half-armed, half-clothed, half-hungered Arragonese. *c* **1827** J. S. MILL in *Adelphi* (1924) I. 689 A half-cultivated taste is always caught by gaudy, affected, and meretricious ornament. **1833** —— *Lett.* (1910) I. 41 It looks like the production of some half-fledged pupil of yours. **1837–9** HALLAM *Hist. Lit.* viii. I. §37 Some half-informed critics. **1838** LYTTON *Alice* 13 Her half-childish, half-womanly grief. **1843** J.S. MILL *Syst. Logic* II. v. ii. 345 It is in those steps of the reasoning which are made in this tacit and half-conscious, or even wholly unconscious manner, that the error oftenest lurks. **1847** MRS. SHERWOOD *Life* xii. 220 A little half-coloured child .. from India. **1851** MELVILLE *Moby Dick* I. xvii. 132 Their half crazy conceits on these subjects. *Ibid.* II. viii. 60 Some sort of a half-hinted influence. **1853/4** J. S. MILL *Draft Autobiogr.* (1961) 116, I had a half formed intention of writing a History of the French Revolution. **1854** THOREAU *Walden* 286 Thus, with half-shut eyes, looking out from the land of dreams. **1858** BAGEHOT *Coll. Works* (1965) II. 72 The undefined, half-expressed .. feelings. **1869** D. G. ROSSETTI *Let.* 27 June (1965) II. 704 A half-crazed charwoman. **1874** J. SULLY *Sensat. & Intuit.* 95 Vague and half-thought out recollections. **1877** WHITMAN *Specimen Days* 104 Some good people may think it a feeble or half-cracked way of spending one's time and thinking. **1895** W. ROBINSON *Eng. Flower Garden* (ed. 4) viii. 118 Shade is not essential, though we think the best effects are attained in half-shady spots. **1897** *Essex Antiquarian* I. 27 When neither stones nor timber were plenty the half-high wall .. was early used, and is still common. **1904** W. H. HUDSON *Green Mansions* xv. 208 Leaving her half-human child to play her malicious pranks in the wood. **1907** *Daily Chron.* 6 Feb. 4/6 Is he really a half-sexed personage? **1908** *Westm. Gaz.* 23 Jan. 2/3 Some trivial gossip in the half-lit hall. *Ibid.* 29 July 3/2 The forces of Free Trade may be confidently reckoned on to squash the half-believed-in promises of Tariff Reform. **1910** W. DE LA MARE *Three Mulla-Mulgars* 120 Her half-blind whitening eyes. **1923** D. H. LAWRENCE *Birds, Beasts & Flowers* 37 Wavering men of old Etruria .. Going with insidious, half-smiling quietness. *Ibid.* 41 The half-secret gleam of a passion-flower hanging from the rock. **1925** T. DREISER *Amer. Trag.* (1926) II. II. xi. 234 He achieved a .. half-apologetic smile. **1927** *Daily Tel.* 15 Nov. 11/7 Most of the ploughing is done with a pair of horses of the half-legged class. **1929** V. WOOLF *Room of one's Own* 127 Those unsaid or half-said words. *a* **1930** D. H. LAWRENCE *Last Poems* (1932) 307 Invisible Between the half-visible hordes. **1931** W. RIPMAN *Eng. Phonetics* 30 Intermediate positions give half-open and half-close vowels. **1932** D. JONES *Outl. Eng. Phonetics* (ed. 3) viii. 38 Half-close vowels are those in which the tongue occupies a position about one-third of the distance from 'close' to 'open'. *Ibid.*, Half-open vowels are those in which the tongue occupies a position about two-thirds of the distance from 'close' to 'open'. **1934** E. LINKLATER *Magnus Merriman* 270 In the country of the blind the half-canned man is king. **1937** *Burlington Mag.* Nov. 234/2 Such half-forgotten artists. **1937** *Mind* XLVI. 83 There is a scale of 'standing-outness' (Abhebung) which reaches from intense experiential clarity to half-conscious habituation. **1941** *Ibid.* L. 10 Some [statements] which would usually be called 'half-joking' or 'not serious', as when the father says, 'The wolves are gaining.' **1949** K. S. WOODS *Rural Crafts Eng.* IV. xiii. 200 The delightfully plump and comfortable curves of old Devon roofs are partly due to the 'hipped' or 'half-hipped' form of the supporting timbers. **1951** W. F. LEOPOLD in Saporta & Bastian *Psycholinguistics* (1961) 355/1 The half-open fricatives were satisfactory as terminal consonants.

c. Hence derivatives, as ***half-dressedness***.

1887 *Daily News* 29 June 5/4 That delicious condition of half-dressedness.

2. With adverbs, as ***half-angrily***, ***-apologetically***, ***-ashamedly***, ***-blindly***, ***-consciously***, ***-divinely***, ***-jokingly***, ***-learnedly***, ***-questioningly***, etc.; ***half-left***, ***-right***, ***-round***, etc. (Cf. HALF *adv.* 1 d.)

c **1700** WATTS *Lyric P.*, *To Mitio* Pt. III. ii. Wks. 1813 IX. 200 Damon is half-divinely blest. **1807** COLERIDGE *Notebk.* (1962) II. 2998, I still half-consciously expect to awake from the night-mair. **1840** CARLYLE *Heroes* v. 296 Struggling half-blindly, as in bitterness of death against that! **1863** MRS. WHITNEY *Faith Gartney's Girlhood* i. 10 Holding the bank-note half-ashamedly in her hand. **1883** *Harper's Mag.* June 141/2 The .. little trot .. lisped, half-coaxingly, half-questioningly. **1913** J. LONDON *Let.* 17 Oct. (1966) 408 He .. is .. half-apologetically explaining that it is the first time. **1923** J. M. MURRY *Pencillings* 271, I was, half-consciously, anxious to be reassured. **1949** M. MEAD *Male & Female* ii. 22 It is often said half-jokingly.

3. With verbs, as ***half-believe***, ***-deify***, ***-fill***, ***-laugh***, ***-make***, ***-murder***, ***-poison***. (Cf. HALF *adv.* 1 c.) Also **half-inch** *v.* (*Rhyming slang*), to 'pinch', to steal; so **half-inching** *vbl. sb.*; **half-lap** [LAP *sb.*[3] 2 b] *v.*, to make a half-lap joint.

1674 WOOD *Life* 2 Feb. (Oxf. Hist. Soc.) II. 281 Men that half-hanged themselves to try how it was. **1727–46** THOMSON *Summer* 1330 Locks, That half-embrac'd her in a humid veil. **1823** J. BADCOCK *Dom. Amusem.* 60 Half-filling a bottle with water. **1825** NICHOLSON *Oper. Mech.* 653 The reason for making the joints half-lapped, or scarfed, [etc.]. **1834** HT. MARTINEAU *Farrers* ii. 25 Two out of the remaining four halfstarted from their chair. **1844** H. STEPHENS *Bk. Farm* II. 296 They are half-lapped in pairs at the centre. **1848** THACKERAY *Van. Fair* xlv, He half-murdered a ferret. **1849** THOREAU *Week on Concord* 192, I half believed that I should get above it. **1850** MARG. FULLER *Woman 19th C.* (1862) 343 Madame Recamier is half reclining on a sofa. **1860** PUSEY *Min. Proph.* 60 The mind which before was .. half-deified. **1878** LOCKYER *Stargazing* 125 We shall not only halve, but half-halve, or quarter the aberration. **1879** FROUDE *Cæsar* xxvii. 477 In Cicero Nature half-made a great man. **1924** J. M. MURRY *Voyage* viii. 152 'I can't help it,' she said, half-laughing at her own confession. **1925** FRASER & GIBBONS *Soldier & Sailor Words* 114 *Half-inch*, to steal. **1948** W. CLEWES *Journey into Spring* ii. 30 We can half-inch those [eggs] from the huts. **1950** T. E. LAWRENCE *Mint* 130 Half-inching is venial, in certain lines of goods. **1952** C. P. BLACKER *Eugenics* 293 The problem family is half-believed to be the product of the capitalistic system. **1972** *Times* 24 Aug. 12/1 If people are going to go around half-inching planets the situation is pretty serious.

4. Special comb.: **half-cut** *a.* (*slang*), half-drunk; **half-equitant** *a.* (*Bot.*) = OBVOLUTE: cf. *demi-equitant*; **half-high** *a.* (see quot.); **half-imperial** *a.*, half imperial-folio size; **half-large** *a.*, (a card) 3 × $2\frac{1}{4}$ inches (Jacobi *Printer's Vocab.*); **half-saved** *a.*, half-witted (*dial.*); **half-shaved** *a.* (*Obs. U.S. slang*), drunk.

1893 FARMER & HENLEY *Slang* III. 250/1 *Half-cut*, half-drunk. **1971** *Radio Times* 18 Nov. 80 Inebriation .. is the sport of all ranks. How many executives can work reasonably effectively unless they are half-cut? **1891** *Daily News* 18 Nov. 3/1 An evening dress to be worn by a very young girl is made '*half-high' .. which means that the bodice is to be cut away to a line mid-way between the neck and bust. **1893** COLLINGWOOD *Life Ruskin* I. 92 Ruskin made sketch after sketch on the *half-imperial board. **1896** *Daily News* 23 Oct. 6/5 He generally completed a half-imperial sketch .. in two hours. **1834** SOUTHEY *Doctor* x. 115 He was what is called *half-saved. Some of his faculties were more than ordinarily acute, but the power of self-conduct was entirely wanting in him. **1871** M. COLLINS *Mrq. & Merch.* I. iii. 100 He was what the villagers called 'half-saved'; not absolutely imbecile. **1818** M. L. WEEMS *Lett.* (1929) III. 225 One night, getting *half shaved, he was easily over-persuaded (a common curse of whiskey) to try his luck at All Fours. *a* **1852** F. M. WHITCHER *Widow Bedott Papers* (1856) xxviii. 354 I've seen that man half shaved on cider afore breakfast in the mornin'.

II. In attributive relation to a sb.

Of these there were already a few instances in OE. (e.g. *healfmann* 'semivir', *healfpeniȝ*, *healftrendel* hemisphere); their number has been enormously increased in later times, especially through the practice of hyphening an adjective and substantive when these have a special or individualized application. These combinations may be distributed among the following classes:

In attributive relation to a sb. **a.** In names of *Coins*, *Weights*, *Measures* of space, quantity, time, etc., as ***half-barrel***, ***-bit***, ***-bottle***, ***-caser*** [CASER[2]], ***-cent***, ***-cooper***, ***-farthing***, ***-firkin***, ***-florin***, ***-foot***, ***-hogshead***, ***-inch***, ***-joe***, ***-litre***, ***-mile***, ***-mutchkin***, ***-peck***, ***-pint*** (also *ellipt.*, a half-pint of beer; see also sense n below), ***-pipe***, ***-pound***, ***-quarter***, ***-quartern***, ***-tierce***. Cf. DEMI- 7. Also HALF-ANGEL, -CROWN, -DOLLAR, -HOUR, -MINUTE, etc. These forms may also be used *attrib.* as in *half-inch board*, *half-mile race*, *half-quartern loaf*, etc.

1494 *Act 11 Hen. VII*, c. 23 Preamb., Every barell, *half barrel and firkyn. *c* **1782** T. JEFFERSON *Autobiog.* Wks. 1859 I. App. 173 The smallest coin .. is the *half-bit, or 1-20 of a dollar. **1877** E. S. DALLAS *Kettner's Bk. of Table* 287 Where are these bottles and *half-bottles of Madeira to be found? **1927** E. HEMINGWAY *Men without Women* (1928) 172 The American lady bought .. a half bottle of Evian water. **1950** T. S. ELIOT *Cocktail Party* I. ii. 51, I found some champagne —Only a half-bottle, to be sure. **1907** H. LAWSON in *Austral. Short Stories* (1951) 70 Felt under his pillow for two half-crowns. 'Here,' he said, 'here's two *half-casers.' *a* **1824** R. PATTERSON cited in WORCESTER 1846 for **Half-cent*. **1889** *Cent. Dict.*, *Half-cent*, a copper coin of the United States .. weighing 94 grains, current from 1793 to 1857. **1836** W. H. MAXWELL *Capt. Blake* II. i, Carrying off diurnally his *half-cooper of port. **1858** SIMMONDS *Dict. Trade*, **Half-farthing*, a British copper coin .. the number .. issued between 1852 and 1854 was 2,621,784. *c* **1440** *Jacob's Well* (E.E.T.S.) 129 þe secunde *half-fote wose in coueytise is raueyne. **1707** *Lond. Gaz.* No. 4337/4, 40 *half Hogsheads, of true neat Bordeaux Brandy. **1820** SCORESBY *Acc. Arctic Reg.* II. 194 Defended by plates of *half-inch iron. **1858** GREENER *Gunnery* 53 An half-inch boiler plate. **1777** J. Q. ADAMS *Wks.* (1854) IX. 470 Guineas, *half joes, and milled dollars in as high estimation as in Pennsylvania. **1921** W. J. LOCKE *Mountebank* i. 7 A thick *half-litre glass of beer. **1967** 'G. CARR' *Lewker in Tirol* iv. 56 He .. ordered a half-litre of wine. **1601** R. JOHNSON *Kingd. & Commw.* (1603) 86 Distant from the towne some *halfe mile. *Mod.* The winner of the half-mile race in the Oxford University Sports. **1816** SCOTT *Antiq.* i, He might have stayed to take a *half-mutchkin extraordinary with his crony the hostler. **1753** *Scots Mag.* June 310/1 Each .. received a *half-peck loaf. **1611** COTGR., *Demi-sextier*, the quarter of a French pinte, and much about our *halfe pinte. **1611** J. DONNE in *Coryat's Crudities* Pref. verse, Can all carouse up thee? No: thou must fit Measures; and fill out for the *half-pinte wit. **1728** E. SMITH *Compleat Housewife* (ed. 2) 151 Pour it into half-pint Basons. **1744** BERKELEY *Let.* 21 Aug. Wks. 1871 IV. 299 Either in half-pint or quarter-pint glasses. **1805** *Med. Jrnl.* XIV. 186 An old half-pint bottle. **1899** R. WHITEING *No. 5 John St.* xi. 107, I .. fell upon roast pork .. and a foaming half-pint. **1937** *Discovery* Sept. 277/1 Fill a half-pint mug. **1966** E. McGirr *Funeral was in Spain* 101 The barman..was morosely polishing half-pint glasses. **1552** Huloet, *Halfe pounde, *selibra*. Halfe pownde wayght, *semissis*. **1535** Coverdale *Neh*. iii. 16 The ruler of the *halfe quarter of Bethzur. **1685** *Lond. Gaz*. No. 2078/4 Lace, three half quarters broad. **1884** F. J. Britten *Watch & Clockm*. 224 Half-quarter repeaters, instead of giving the minutes, strike one additional blow if the half quarter has passed. *Mod. Alm*. 8 Feb., Half-Quarter Day. **1838** Dickens *O. Twist* v, A *half-quartern loaf and a piece of cheese. **1708** Motteux *Rabelais* v. xlv. (1737) 191 A *Half-Tierce, or Hogshead.

b. In *Heraldry* = DEMI- B 1, as ***half-belt***, ***-cheek-bit***, ***-spade***, ***-spear***.

1688 R. Holme *Armoury* III. vii. 44 He beareth Gules, an Horse Bit, Argent. Some do call it..an Half Cheek-Bit. *Ibid*. viii. 5 He beareth Vert, an Half Spade. **1828** Berry *Encycl. Her*. s.v. *Spade*, This..spade is borne in the arms of Swettenham, but they appear as half-spades. **1889** Elvin *Dict. Heraldry*, Half-belt and four buckles.

c. In *Artillery*, *Arms*, denominating a piece of half the size of the full-sized piece, or a shortened size of the latter, as ***half-armour***, ***-cannon***, ***-culverin***, ***-falconet***, ***-head-piece***, ***-lance***. Cf. DEMI- 2–4. Also HALF-PIKE, -SWORD, etc.

1874 Boutell *Arms & Arm*. x. 188 **Half-Armour*, the period of the partial use of armour, extending to the commencement of the 18th century. **1640** Fuller *Joseph's Coat* 1 Cor. xi. 30 (1867) 86 Sometimes He shooteth *half cannon. **1676** *Lond. Gaz*. No. 1116/3 A Battery of 12 Half-Cannon. **1611** Florio, *Mezza testa*, a kind of halfe skull, or *halfe head-peece. **1868** Kirk *Chas. Bold* III. v. i. 332 Armed with a *half-lance.

d. In *Military tactics*, *dress*, etc., as ***half-squadron***, ***-turn***, ***-wheel***; **half-battery**, **-company**, **-distance**, **-file** (see quots.); **half-mounting**, the underclothing and minor articles of apparel belonging to a soldier's outfit in the 18th c. Cf. DEMI- 6. Also HALF-FACE, etc.

1800 *War Office Order* 9 Apr. in Grose *Milit. Antiq*. (1801) II. 186 In lieu of the former articles of cloathing, called half-mounting, two pair of good shoes of the value of five shillings and sixpence each pair. **1832** *Regul. Instr. Cavalry* III. 73 The..troops wheel half right. *Ibid*. 99 The Base Troop wheels more than a half-wheel. *Ibid*. 103 The Troops wheel half-left. **1853** Stocqueler *Milit. Encycl*., *Half-companies* are the same as subdivisions, equal to two stations. *Half-distance* is the regular interval or space between troops drawn up in ranks, or standing in column... *Half-files* is half the given number of any body of men drawn up two deep. **1859** F. A. Griffiths *Artil. Man*. (1862) 11 Right half turn. Front turn. *Ibid*. 30 A battalion in open, or half-distance Column. *Ibid*. 134 Three subdivisions constitute a half-battery.

e. In *Fortification*, as **half-bastion**, **half-caponier** (Sir G. Duckett, *Mil. Dict*.), **half-sap**: see DEMI-BASTION, etc.; **half-merlon**, that solid portion of a parapet which is at the right or left extremity of a battery. Also HALF-CIRCLE, -MOON.

1710 *Lond. Gaz*. No. 4721/1 We shall be obliged to finish it by the half Sap.

f. *Naut*. and *Ship-building*: **half-beam** (see quot. 1850); **half-board**, an evolution by which a sailing vessel is luffed up into the wind with everything shaking, and then, before she has quite lost way, permitted to fall off on the same tack: see BOARD *sb*. 15; **half-breadth** (see quot.); **half-breadth staff**, a rod having marked upon it half the length of each beam in the ship (Knight *Dict. Mech*. 1875); **half-floor**, **-point**, **-port**, **-top**, **half-watch tackle** (see quots.); †**half-wind**, a side-wind. Also HALF-TIMBER.

1836 *Encycl. Metrop*. VI. 415 The *half-beams are all to be of fir. *c* **1850** *Rudim. Navig*. (Weale) 95 *Half-Beams* are short beams introduced to support the deck where there is no framing. **1863** Luce *Seamanship* (ed. 2) 484 In a tideway the *half-board is of great use. **1769** Falconer *Dict. Marine* (1789) D ij b, The breadth of the ship at every top-timber is limited by an horizontal line drawn on the floor-plane, called the *half-breadth of the top-timbers. *c* **1860** H. Stuart *Seaman's Catech*. 66 The '*half-floors'..are pieces of timber placed between the 'cross pieces', to which they are 'coaked' and bolted. **1867** Smyth *Sailor's Word-bk*., **Half-point*, a subdivision of the compass card, equal to 5° 37′ of the circle. *c* **1850** *Rudim. Navig*. (Weale) 122 **Half-ports*, a sort of shutters made of deal, and fitted to the stops of those ports which have no hanging lids. *c* **1860** H. Stuart *Seaman's Catech*. 76 The *half-tops are bolted to the cross trees, and the sleepers are bolted above the trussle trees. **1859** F. A. Griffiths *Artil. Man*. (1862) 317 *A luff tackle, or *half watch tackle*, consists of one double and one single block: the fall is fixed to the single. **1611** Cotgr., *Demivent*, a side-winde, or *halfe-winde.

g. In *Music*, as **half-cadence**, **-close**, an imperfect cadence; **half-demisemiquaver**; **half-rest** (*U.S.*), a minim rest; **half-shift**, **-stop** (see quots.). Cf. DEMI- B. 9. Also HALF-NOTE, -TONE.

1880 Stainer & Barrett *Dict. Mus. T*., **Half-cadence*. If the last chord is the dominant and is preceded by the chord of the tonic, the cadence is called half or imperfect. **1867** Macfarren *Harmony* i. 29 A *half close is when a passage ends upon the chord of the dominant, regardless of what harmony may precede it. **1881** *Academy* 6 Nov. 355 The *half demisemiquaver is still much used. **1880** Stainer & Barrett *Dict. Mus. T*., **Half-shift*, a position of the hand in violin playing. It lies between the open position and the first shift. **1880** C. A. Edwards *Organs* (1881) 146 A stop is a set of pipes that run in order from the one end to the other of the clavier. If this set..discontinues at any portion of the keyboard, it is said to be a *half stop. *Ibid*. Half Stops, properly so called, have practically gone out of fashion.

h. Applied to a stuff which is half of inferior material, as ***half-gauze***, ***-silk***, ***-worsted***, ***-yarn***.

1759 Symmer in *Phil. Trans*. LI. 360 The sort I fixed upon, is what is called *half gauze. **1738** Swift *Pol. Conversat*. 66 Ladies, you are mistaken in the Stuff; 'tis *half Silk. **1796** Morse *Amer. Geog*. II. 217 No fewer than 443 silk-looms, 149 of half-silks. **1594** Blundevil *Exerc*. v. iii. (ed. 7) 533 Worsteds, and *halfe Worsteds.

i. In *Games* and *Sports*, as ***half-marathon***; **half-back** (*Football*), a position immediately behind the 'forwards'; a player in this position; also in other games, e.g. American Football, Rugby Football, Australian Rules; **half-ball** (*Billiards*): see quot. 1850; **half-blast** *Golf*, a shot which is played with half the force of a 'blast' (explosive shot); **half-blue**, the 'colours' (see BLUE *sb*. 9) awarded to a player chosen to represent his university in inter-university contests as second choice to a 'full blue', or to any chosen representative in sports or games not recognized by the Blues Committee as sufficiently important for the award of a 'full blue'; also, a competitor who has gained this award; **half-brassy shot** *Golf*, a brassy shot played with a half swing; **half-captain**, in women's colleges in Oxford, one who has attained a certain degree of proficiency in the management of a boat; so **half-captaincy**; **half-colour**, a badge showing that a stage of proficiency half-way towards getting one's colours has been reached (see COLOUR *sb*.[1] 6 c); **half-court** *Tennis* and *Rackets*, half the court divided by a line (the ***half-court line***) parallel with the side lines; **half-fifteen**, **-forty** *Tennis* (see quot.); **half-forward**, **half-forward flanker** *Austral*. (see quot. 1968); so ***half-forward flank***; **half-hit** (*Cricket*), a faulty hit, the ball falling short of the distance it would have travelled if properly hit; **half-iron shot** *Golf*, an iron shot played with a half swing; **half nelson** *Wrestling*, a hold in which one arm is thrust under the corresponding arm of the opponent and the hand placed on the back of his neck; also *fig*. in phr. ***to get a half-nelson on***, to hold in a crippling position, gain a complete hold over; hence as *v. trans*. with the sense of this phr.; **half-one** *Golf* (see quot.); **half-pin** *Chess*, that position in which a defending man lies between an attacking piece and the defended king and in the line of attack of the attacking piece, but has liberty to move along the line of attack; also, that position in which two defending men lie between the attacking piece and the king so that if either moves the other man becomes pinned; so **half-pinned** *a*.; **half-pinner**, a half-pin problem; **half-shot** *Golf*, a stroke made with a half swing, intended to carry less far than the full shot; **half-stroke** *Golf* = *half-one*; **half swing** *Golf*, a swing of half the usual amount of distance; **half-thirty** *Tennis* (see quot. s.v. *half-fifteen*); **half-topped** *a*. *Golf*, designating a shot in which the ball is partly topped; **half-volley**, (*a*) (*Cricket*, *Football*, etc.), a ball which pitches so that it can be hit or kicked as soon as it rises from the ground; hence also *Cricket*, a ball which pitches just in front of a fieldsman; (*b*) (*Lawn Tennis*), a stroke made when the ball has just left the ground; so ***half-volleyer***; ***half-volleying*** vbl. sb.; also ***half-volley*** vb. Also HALF-BOWL, etc.

1882 *Standard* 20 Nov. 2/8 The *half-backs..effectually checked the threatened danger. **1887** Shearman *Athletics & Football* (Badm. Libr.) 346 A good half-back must be a versatile player. **1887** *Century Mag*. Oct. 892 Behind the quarter-back, and covering the two sides of the field, are the 'half-backs', the cavalry of the team. **1906** Gallaher & Stead *Compl. Rugby Footballer* v. 71 The half back as we know him in New Zealand is the donkey man of the team. **1959** N. Mailer *Advts. for Myself* (1961) 53 He paused, crouched into a halfback's position, waiting for the ball. **1965** *Sun-Herald* (Sydney) 4 July 51 Sydney's half-back flanker Bob Sterling won the President's trophy. **1965** *Advertiser* (Adelaide) 17 July 25 Its half-forward line..was over-run by the powerful South Adelaide half-back line. **1968** Eagleson & McKie *Terminol. Austral. Nat. Football* II. 14 There are three half-backs in each team: left, centre, and right half-back. **1969** *Australian* 24 May 39/2 Ian Bremner, Norm Bussell and Peter Chilton constitute a tight-checking half-back line for Hawthorn. **1850** *Bohn's Hand-bk. Games* 524 A *half ball, or a contact in which the half of one ball is covered by half of the other, produces in each an equal motion, both with regard to direction, strength, and velocity. **1928** *Weekly Dispatch* 24 June 21/6 He played a superb '*half-blast' out of a trap to lay the ball one foot from the cup. **1908** *Westm. Gaz*. 29 July 10/4 The *half-blue for billiards. **1909** *Ibid*. 26 Feb. 12/2 For some time players of lacrosse at Oxford have been urging the Blues Committee to grant them the Half-Blue. **1963** *Times* 5 Feb. 3/3 J. S. Grinalds (Brasenose), an old half-Blue, came back into the defence for the first time this season. **1903** *Westm. Gaz*. 28 Aug. 3/1 The *half-brassy shot approach. **1928** *Daily Express* 7 May 5/2 She may not go on the river unless she is accompanied by a *half-captain or is one herself. Half-captaincies may be had either in rowing, canoeing, or punting. **1929** *Evening News* 18 Nov. 13/5 The player who appears in future bowls international trial matches, but who fails to be selected for the English team, is to receive a '*half-colour'. **1888** *Encycl. Brit*. XXIII. 182/2 A space bounded by the net, the side line, the *half-court line, and the service line. **1895** H. W. W. Wilberforce *Lawn Tennis* 62 The half-court-line dividing the space on each side of the net into two equal parts, called the right and left courts. **1898** *Encycl. Sport* II. 462/2 The half court nearest the dedans is called the 'service side'. *Ibid*., The half-court line..dividing the court lengthways into practically two equal parts. **1961** *Times* 13 Jan. 16/3 Half-court drive down the wall. **1888** *Encycl. Brit*. XXIII. 182/2 *Half-fifteen is one stroke given at the beginning of the second and every subsequent alternate game of a set... Half-thirty is one stroke given at the beginning of the first game, two strokes at the beginning of the second game; and so on, alternately, in all the subsequent games of a set... *Half-forty is two strokes given at the beginning of the first game, three strokes at the beginning of the second game; and so on, alternately, in all the subsequent games of a set. **1963** *Courier-Mail* (Brisbane) 21 Nov. 7/5 A typical commentary from Australian Rules, 'a long drop-kick from the *half-forward flank'. **1968** Eagleson & McKie *Terminology Austral. Nat. Football* II. 14 *Half-forward*, a player occupying a half-forward position, which comes between the centre and full-forward positions. *Ibid*., Half-forwards in the side position are generally referred to as *half-forward flankers*. **1969** *Australian* 24 May 39/2 Bremner will probably be given the task of watching Geelong's mercurial Ken Newland, who will start on a half-forward flank. **1888** *Daily News* 15 Sept. 3/5 Caught at extra mid-off from a *half-hit. **1888** A. G. Steel in Steel & Lyttleton *Cricket* iii. 112 Extra cover-point..may be..placed for half-hits wide on the on—i.e. about half the distance from the batsman that a deep field would stand. **1899** W. Caffyn *Seventy-one not Out* 18 Fielder placed [behind the bowler] for half-hit. **1900** W. A. Bettesworth *Walkers of Southgate* 41 Mr. R. D. Walker, who was fielding in a nondescript sort of place for a half hit, brought off a brilliant catch. **1928** *Daily Tel*. 17 July 17/5 Freeman..had two half-hit fieldsmen. **1895** H. G. Hutchinson *Golf* (ed. 5) iv. 143 The attitude..for the *half-iron stroke. **1905** *Westm. Gaz*. 10 Nov. 4/2 The half-iron shot..cannot be played properly unless turf is taken. **1977** *Washington Post* 7 Mar. D7/2 Dan Rincon of Delaware Track Club led a field of 297 to win the Athletic Shoe Box Classic *half-marathon yesterday. **1985** *Oxford Mail* 2 Mar. 1/5 He had already completed a half marathon at Stratford and was..hoping to go for a full marathon. **1889** W. Armstrong *Wrestling* 230 *Half Nelson, Lancashire. **1896** Ade *Artie* xvii. 154 This thing got the half-Nelson on me before I know it. **1898** *Encycl. Sport* II. 548/2 The half Nelson and heave. **1901** *Black & White Budget* 30 Nov. 315/1 The half-nelson... You grasp your opponent by the right wrist with your left hand, thrust your right hand quickly under his arm at the same time seizing his neck and pressing his head forward. **1903** P. Longhurst *Wrestling* 77 The arm that has the half-nelson hold. **1912** *Daily Chron*. 6 Mar., And Radicals in sunshine bask with Delight to see the clever Asquith Half-Nelson Bonar Law. **1961** *Observer* 26 Nov. 27/1 He gives an exquisite demonstration of the half-nelson generally used to make the unwilling talk. **1966** *New Statesman* 15 July 74/2 He knew..that Sir Alec Douglas-Home had to be..half-nelsoned and regularly thrown out of the ring. **1887** in J. L. Stewart *Golfiana Miscellanea* 299 **Half-one*, a handicap of a stroke deducted every second hole. **1922** Hume & White *Good Companion Two-Mover* 245 The term '*half-pin' arose in 1915, in correspondence between Comins Mansfield and Murray Marble anent No. 122 D, a surprising example, with six half-pins... Greenwood, the composer of this problem, had published a complete half-pinner in 1859. **1926** H. Weenink *Chess Problem* 71 By a Half-pin is understood an arrangement where two Black pieces stand in line in such a way that if either one moves the other becomes pinned by a White piece which has been standing behind both of them waiting to exert its pinning powers. **1928** *Observer* 24 June 25 These three variations are highly complex, the first two illustrating the unpin of the White Q by half-pinned Black Kt's; the third is a half-pin line combined with Black interference. **1891** H. G. Hutchinson *Golf* 26 The principle of the cutting stroke, on the other hand, lies in bringing the head of the iron across that line. It may be applied to a full shot, *half shot, quarter shot or shortest wrist shot. **1893** —— *Golfing* 41 When the distance is less than that for which the three-quarter stroke is used, it is commonly called a half-shot distance. **1896** W. Park *Game of Golf* v. 107 Three-quarter and *half strokes are..much more difficult to play than full shots. **1897** *Encycl. Sport* I. 461 A half-stroke or over, both in singles and foursomes, shall count as one. **1891** H. G. Hutchinson *Golf* 30 Take pains in all *half-swing shots to bring the club-head well and slowly away from the ball before striking. **1896** W. Park *Game of Golf* ii. 39 A club lying on its heel would, in playing through the green, be apt to get away a *half-topped ball. *Ibid*. x. 204 Hazards..should be placed at such distances from the teeing-grounds that, while a well-hit shot will carry them, a topped or half-topped stroke will get in. **1905** *Westm. Gaz*. 23 Aug. 5/1 A lucky half-topped shot. **1953** H. Simmons *Golfers' ABC*, The chip shot not as ought to be, The half-topped seven, scuttled three. **1843** 'A Wykehamist' *Pract. Hints Cricket* 12 All balls pitching between the first line and the crease..are technically termed *half vollies. *Ibid*. 17 A leg half-volley..may be..'dropped into' now and then. **1851** J. Pycroft *Cricket Field* viii. 168 Every one knows the difficulty of making a good half-volley hit off a slow ball. *Ibid*. x. 189 If a bowler has half volleys returned to him, by stretching and stooping after them, he gets out of his swing. **1867** G. H. Selkirk *Guide Cricket Ground* v. 83 The half volley..requires practice to ensure its being picked up properly. **1870** *London Society* Nov. 425/1 The mode of playing a ball so well known at tennis, not quite half-volley. *c* **1880** *A correspondent says*: A half-volley at cricket is a ball bowled up so as to pitch just about the point at which the batsman has a good reach. **1891** W. G. Grace *Cricket* viii. 233 Occasionally you may get a half-volley on the pads. **1897** *Encycl. Sport* I. 621/2 *Half-volley*, a stroke made the moment the ball leaves the ground. **1960** *Times* 21 June 16/1 Taylor half-volleyed a return into the net. **1963** A. Ross *Australia 63* iii. 76 He played at nothing he did not have to, leaving Davidson to flash the odd half-volley through the covers. **1969** *New Yorker* 14 June 45/1 Players call it a half-volley drop shot. Ashe reaches down, lightly touches the rising ball, and sends it on a slow, sharply angled flight toward the net. *Ibid.* 45/3 Ashe, moving up, is again confronted with the need to half-volley. **1912** *Daily News* 11 July 2 A famous *half-volleyer. **1875** 'STONEHENGE' *Brit. Sports* III. I. v. §4. 691 *Half-volleying consists in playing the ball when close to the ground, immediately after it has been dropped.

j. In *Bookbinding*, 'half' signifies that only the back and corners of the binding consist of the material specified; e.g. ***half-calf, half-russia.***

1844 *Catal. Messrs. C. Knight & Co.* 8 Half Morocco or Russia. **1872** O. W. HOLMES *Poet Breakf.-t.* viii. (1885) 192 None of your 'half-calf' economies in that volume! *Mod. Bookseller's Catal.*, Original half sheep.

k. In names of animals, as HALF-APE, HALF-ASS, HALF-SNIPE, etc.

l. Applied to various articles and structures of about half the usual or full size or length, as ***half-bath, -bathroom, -blind, -case, -door, -frame, -furnace, -gaiter, -gown, -hatch, †-head bedstead, -hessian, -hoop*** [cf. HOOP *sb.*[1] 7], ***-hose, -jar, †-kirtle, -sleeve, -stocking, -tester, -tub, -veil, -wicket.*** Cf. DEMI- B. 11. Also HALF-BOOT, etc.

1879 A. VON HARLINGEN in A. H. Buck *Treat. Hygiene & Public Health* I. 373 The *half-bath, in which the bather sits in a tub filled with water to the depth of from ten to twelve inches,.. is adapted to invalids. **1953** R. CHANDLER *Long Good-Bye* xxvii. 171 There was a half-bath off the study. **1959** *News Chron.* 19 June 4/3 A *half-bathroom..has a shower, wash-basin and lavatory, but no bath. **1763** BOSWELL *London Jrnl.* 22 July (1951) 382, I was disturbed by the light..at the earliest dawn, as the windows have only *half-blinds. **1888** JACOBI *Printer's Voc.*, **Half cases*, small cases used for jobbing purposes. **1740** DYCHE & PARDON, *Hasp*, a small iron or brass fastening to a hatch or *half-door. **1844** DICKENS *Mart. Chuz.* iii, The half-door of the bar. **1936** J. TICKELL *See how they Run* ii. 19 The sort of horse's face that looks out over the half-door of a loose-box. **1888** JACOBI *Printer's Voc.*, **Half frames*, small composing frames made to hold one pair of cases only. **1775** F. MARION in *Harper's Mag.* Sept. (1883) 546/1 Black *half-gaiters. **1552** HULOET, *Halfe gowne, *hemitogium.* **1886** WILLIS & CLARK *Cambridge* I. 88 A *half-hatch door. **1598** *Inv. King's Coll.* ibid. III. 325 Item a *halfe head bedsteade of walnuttree. **1837** LYTTON *E. Maltrav.* 76 A pair of *half-hessians completed his costume. **1882** *Times* 31 Jan. 16/6 (Advt.), Single-stone, *half-hoop, and cluster rings. **1892** KIPLING *Lett. of Travel* (1920) 94 His wife..wears half-hoop diamond rings. **1902** *Daily Chron.* 14 June 10/4 The hair.. is surmounted by a half-hoop diadem encrusted with precious stones. **1928** R. HALL *Well of Loneliness* xxi. 198 'I made your mother's engagement ring for him; a large half-hoop of very fine diamonds.' **1960** R. COLLIER *House called Memory* x. 150 Uncle William Henry bought Dora a half hoop of diamonds as an engagement ring. **1851** *Catal. Gt. Exhib.* 588 Lambs-wool and Cashmere hose and *half-hose. **1597** SHAKS. *2 Hen. IV*, v. iv. 24 If you be not swing'd, Ile forsweare *halfe Kirtles. **1689** *Lond. Gaz.* No. 2477/4 A sad coloured Cloth Coat, with..blue *half Sleeves. **1670** NARBOROUGH *Jrnl.* in *Acc. Sev. Late Voy.* I. (1711) 104 Some wear *Half-Stockings. **1803** T. SHERATON *Cabinet Dict.* 44 As to the particular management of beds, and the articles required in mounting them, together with their various classes; these..will most conveniently come under their respective names, as..*Half-tester,..&c. **1859** *Blackw. Mag.* Aug. 229/1 We approached the bed and examined it—a half-tester, such as is commonly found in attics devoted to servants. **1960** H. HAYWARD *Antique Coll.* 279/2 At this period [*sc.* late 17th cent.] a new type of bedstead without footposts was introduced, known as a 'half-tester'. **1726** SHELVOCKE *Voy. round World* (1757) 206 The old stratagem..of turning a light adrift, in a *half tub. **1844** ALB. SMITH *Adv. Mr. Ledbury* (1856) I. viii. 60 The ..*half-wicket that closed the entrance.

m. In various connexions: as ***half-barbarian, -battle, -belief, -believer, -christian, -conformity, -consciousness, -dark, -darkness, -defence, -defender, -dream, -education, -hint, -honesty, -humour, -knowledge, -laugh, -lengthening, -lie, -literate, -look, -mind, -power, -principle, -quotation, -reason, -reasoning, -repentance, -savage, -servant, -service, -sleep, -spacing*** (on a typewriter), ***-view, -whisper.*** (In most of these *half-* has an adverbial force.)

1597 HOOKER *Eccl. Pol.* v. lxii. §9 To speak as half-defenders of the faults. *Ibid.* v. lxxxi. §4 They judge conclusions by demi-premises and half-principles. **1690** LOCKE *Govt.* I. ii. (Rtldg.) 6 It is no injury to call an half-quotation an half-reason. **1736** BUTLER *Anal.* II. viii. 276 Half-views, which shew but Part of an Object. **1768** BOSWELL *Corsica* ii. (ed. 2) 120 A parcel of half-barbarians. **1768–74** TUCKER *Lt. Nat.* (1852) II. 367 A kind of half-reasoning, that suffices to raise difficulties but not pursue them to an issue. **1814** JANE AUSTEN *Mansf. Park* II. vii. 148 A certain half-look attending the..expression of his hope. **1816** —— *Emma* II. xvii. 320 Much that passed between them was in a half-whisper. **1817** J. SCOTT *Paris Revisit.* (ed. 4) 237 A kind of stupefied half-sleep. **1827** HALLAM *Const. Hist.* (1876) II. viii. 57 To admit of no half-conformity in religion. **1836** J. S. MILL in *Westm. Rev.* XXV. 5 See how incapable half-savages are of co-operation. **1838** —— *Ibid.* XXVIII. 454 The sceptics and half-believers of the story. —— *Ibid.* XXXI. 484 Almost all rich veins of original and striking speculation have been opened by systematic half-minds. **1840** CARLYLE *Heroes* iv. 219 Richter says of Luther's words, 'his words are half-battles'. **1860** PUSEY *Min. Proph.* 2 The character of Jehu and his half-belief. *Ibid.* 188 A half-repentance is no repentance. *Ibid.* 199 Another instance of this half-service. **1862** G. BORROW *Wild Wales* II. xxxii. 370 'In truth I am,' said she, with a half laugh. **1865** PUSEY *Truth Eng. Ch.* 3 Unbelievers, or half-believers. **1866** G. MACDONALD *Ann. Q. Neighb.* xxxii, A voice said brokenly in a half-whisper. **1870** LOWELL *Study Wind.* 349 That half-knowledge which is more mischievous in an editor than down-right ignorance. **1881** 'MARK TWAIN' *Prince & Paup.* 208 His senses struggled to a half-consciousness. **1895** KIPLING *Day's Work* (1898) 344 Leading him on to see, more by half-hints than by any direct word, how boys and men are all of a piece. **1898** *Pearson's Mag.* May 539/1 With a half-power steamer which had only one man all told upon her decks. **1900** *Daily News* 18 Aug. 6/1 How she did it she didn't know, she said, in a half-humour manner. **1904** W. DE LA MARE *Henry Brocken* 13 The half-dream [which] weariness brings. **1904** W. B. YEATS *Tables of Law* 9 The formalisms of half-education. **1905** *Westm. Gaz.* 25 Mar. 11/2 The inaccuracies do not matter very much unless they are so gross as to shock the great half-literate. **1926** FOWLER *Mod. Eng. Usage* 399/2 The uneasy half-literates who like to prove that they can spell. **1927** A. CLARKE *Son of Learning* II. 44 In the half-darkness his cowled figure suggests demonic possession. **1928** D. H. LAWRENCE *Lady Chatterley* xvi. 278 She could still see on Connie's face..the half-dream of passion. *a* **1930** —— *Last Poems* (1932) 257 A half-lie causes the immediate contradiction of the half-lie. **1934** BLUNDEN *Choice or Chance* 40 Possessions too,—part fungus and part flower, —Forced on him their half-power. **1934** E. POUND *Eleven New Cantos* xxxix. 45 From star up to the half-dark. **1937** *Mind* XLVI. 101 Postulating a sort of extra, separate half-mind—entelechy—like Driesch. **1938** *Times Lit. Suppl.* 8 Oct. 638/3 The curious delicate half-humour which smiled at his own hypersensitiveness. **1941** T. S. ELIOT *Dry Salvages* ii. 11 The backward half-look Over the shoulder, towards the primitive terror. **1948** —— *Notes Def. Culture* 105 But what is important is to remember that 'half-education' is a modern phenomenon. **1949** KOESTLER *God that Failed* 31 Once or twice she spoke on the telephone to comrades of hers—always in half-words and half-hints. **1953** K. JACKSON *Lang. & Hist. Early Brit.* 342 Half-lengthening of penultimates could not have arisen until after the accent-shift. **1959** E. PULGRAM *Introd. Spectrogr. Speech* viii. 64 The half-power points, whose power is.. proportional to the square of the amplitude. **1961** *Imperial Type Faces* 10 A half-spacing device lends itself to display work. **1962** *Which?* Dec. 359/2 If you leave out a letter, it should be possible, after rubbing out the word, to fit in the extra letter by using half-spacing.

n. In specific combinations: **half-Abo** *Austral.*, a person having one Aboriginal parent (cf. ABO *a.* and *sb.*); **half-adder** [ADDER[1] 3], a unit in an electronic computer (see quot. 1962); **†half-almond stitch**; **half-arm**, half arm's length; **half-arsed, -ass, -assed** *adjs. slang* (orig. *U.S.*), ineffectual, inadequate, mediocre; stupid, inexperienced; **half-barrel** *a.*, semicylindrical (vaulting); **half-belt** (see quot. 1957); **half-bend**, a half fillet for the head; **half-bent**, (*a*) the condition of being half-bent; (*b*) the catch by which the hammer of a gun is placed at half-cock; **†half-bloom**, the round mass of iron taken from the puddling furnace, which was hammered and shingled into a 'bloom'; **half-boarder**, one who has half his board, a day-boarder; **half-box**, a box open at one side; **half-braid** (see quot.); **half-bull**, (*a*) a pontifical letter issued by a new pope before his coronation, so called because the *bulla* is impressed with only one side of the seal, that representing the apostles (Giry); (*b*) [BULL *sb.*[1] 7] *slang*, a half-crown; **half-catch**, (see quots.); **half-cell** *Electr.* (see quot. 1943); **half-centre** (see quot.); **half-chronometer** (see quots.); **half-class**, a class that is half one and half another; **half-column**, a column or pilaster half projecting from a flat surface; **half-commission** *attrib.*, working for or based on half commission; **half-communion**, communion in one kind, as practised in the R.C. Ch.; **†half-compass**, hemisphere: see COMPASS *sb.* 5 b; **half-compression** *attrib.*, designating a device for lessening the compression of the explosive mixture in an internal-combustion engine; **half-course, half-coward** (see quots.); **half-day**, half a working day (cf. DAY *sb.* 8 d); **half-dike**, a sunk fence; **half-dress** (see quot. 1960); **half-duck** = HALF-BIRD; **half-evergreen** *a.*, of a plant that is evergreen in a mild climate; also as *sb.*; **half-flat**, †(*a*) one of the shapes into which a 'bloom' of iron was worked; (*b*) half of a FLAT (*sb.*[2]) or entire storey of a house; **half-foot** (see quot. 1880); **half-frame**, (*a*) *pl.* reading-spectacles consisting of only the lower half of the frames and lenses; also in sing. *attrib.*; (*b*) (*Photogr.*) half the standard 35 mm. picture size; **half-gerund** (see quot. 1924); **half-hatchet**, 'a hatchet with one straight line, all the projection of the bit being on the side towards the hand' (Knight *Dict. Mech.* 1875); **half-header**, a half-brick used to close the work at the end of a course; **half-hose** (see HOSE *sb.* 1 a γ); **half-house**, a shed open at the side; a hovel; **half-hunt** (*Bell-ringing*): see HUNT; **half inferior** *a. Bot.* (see quots.); **half-integer**, any member of the set of numbers obtained by dividing the odd integers by two; hence **half-integral** *a.*; **†half-labour, half-landing**, a landing half-way up a flight of stairs; **half-lap** (see LAP *sb.*[3] 2 b); **half-lattice girder**, one consisting of a single system or row of triangles; **half-lift** [LIFT *sb.*[2] 5 f], a medium-stressed lift in O.E. verse; **half-line** *Pros.* [LINE *sb.*[2] 23 e], half of a line of verse, used esp. of O.E. and related verse; **half-margin** (see quots.); **half-mask**, a mask covering part of the face, such as is worn with a DOMINO; **†half-member**, a semicolon; **half-pass** (see quot. 1948); **half-period**, the HALF-LIFE of a substance; see also quot. 1904; **half-pint** [cf. sense II. a] *fig.*, a small or insignificant person; also *attrib.*; **half-plane** *Math.* (see quot. 1959); **half-plate** *Photogr.* (see PLATE *sb.* 5 c), also *attrib.*; **half-portion**, a half of a portion; *fig.*, a small or insignificant person; **half-press** (see quots.); **half-principal** (*Carpentry*), 'a rafter which does not extend to the crown of the roof' (Knight *Dict. Mech.* 1875); **half-pull** (*Bell-ringing*): see quot.; **half-race** *Bot.* (see quots.); **half-relief** = *demi-relief* (see DEMI- 12); **half-rhyme**, an imperfect or near rhyme; hence **half-rhymed** *ppl. a.*; **half-ripper, half-rip saw**, a finer-toothed ripping saw (see RIPPER 2, RIP-SAW *sb.*); **half-roll** *Aeronaut.*, a manœuvre in which the aircraft turns through 180° about the longitudinal axis; hence **half-roll** *v. intr.*; **half-royal**, a kind of millboard or pasteboard; **half-secret dovetail** (see quot.); **half-shade** (*Painting*), a shade of half the extreme depth; **half-sheet** (*Printing*), the off-cut portion of a duodecimo (Knight, 1875); (see quots.); **half-shoe**, see quot.; also a shoe on one side only of a horse's foot; **half-sibling**, each of two or more individuals having one parent in common; **half-slip**, the lower half of a slip (see SLIP *sb.*[3] 4 c); a petticoat; **half-sole**, that part of the sole of a boot or shoe which extends forward from the shank to the toe; hence **half-sole** *v.*; **half-space** = HALF-PACE 2; **half-speed shaft**, the cam shaft of a four-stroke cycle internal-combustion engine, which rotates at half the speed of the crank shaft; **†half-sphere**, hemisphere; **†half-square** (see quot. 1674); **half-stitch**, a loose open stitch in braid work or pillow-lace making (Caulfeild *Dict. Needlewk.* 259); **half-storey**, an upper storey half the height of which is in the walls and half in the roof; **half-stress** *Pros.*, a secondary stress; **half-stuff** (*Paper-making*), partly prepared pulp; **half-swing plough** (see quot.); **half-term**, a period approximately half-way through a school or other term, often made the occasion of a holiday; freq. *attrib.* as in ***half-term holiday***; **half-text**, a size of handwriting half the size of 'text' or large hand; **half-thickness** *Physics* = HALF-VALUE *thickness*; **half-throw, -travel**, half the full movement of a piston, valve, etc.; **half-tint** (see quot. 1851); **half-title**, the short title of a book often placed in front of the full title; **half-tongue** (*Law*), a jury of which one half were foreigners, formerly allowed to a foreigner tried on a criminal charge; **half-trap**, a semicircular depression in a sewer pipe; **half-turning bolt** (see quot.); **half-uncial**, writing which combines the characters of uncial and cursive; semi-uncial; also *attrib.*; **half-valve** *Mus.* (see quot. 1955); hence **half-valved** *ppl. a.*; **half-valving** *vbl. sb.*; **half-verse** *Pros.*, = *half-line* (above); **half-virgin** = DEMI-VIERGE; **†half-vowel**, a semi-vowel; **†half-vowelish** *a.*, of the nature of a semivowel; **half-water** = HALF-TIDE; **half-watt** *a. Electr.*, applied to a gas-filled incandescent lamp consuming approximately a half-watt per candle-power; **half-wave**, one-half of a complete wave, esp. of electricity or radiation; freq. *attrib.*, utilizing only alternate halves of a sequence of waves, as ***half-wave rectification*** (*Chambers's Techn. Dict.* 1940); half a wave-length long, as ***half-wave antenna, dipole***, etc.; **half-white** = HALF-BREED 2; **half-word, halfword**, a group of consecutive bits, which can be handled as a unit, occupying half a word storage unit of a computer; **half-world**, hemisphere; the demi-monde; also *transf.*

1945 C. MANN in B. James *Austral. Short Stories* (1963) 72 Little black *half-abo. piccaninnies. **1954** *Electronic Engin.* XXVI. 288 Numbers always enter the accumulator loop via the two *half-adders and are therefore automatically added to the previous contents. **1962** *Gloss. Terms Autom. Data Processing* (*B.S.I.*) 60 *Half-adder*, a logic element with two outputs and two inputs to which may be applied signals representing a digit or a number and a single addend or carry digit. **1611** FLORIO, *Mezzo-mandolo*, Seamsters call it the *halfe-almond stitch. **1812** *Sporting Mag.* XXXIX. 18 Each fought at *half-arm for superiority. **1961** A. WEST *Trend is Up* ix. 386 You don't know what it is to worry about what *half-arsed thing your own son is going to pull on you next. **1972** *Observer* 24 Sept. 35/2 The sort of half-arsed dottiness they dish out in West End comedies.

1959 N. Mailer Advts. for Myself (1961) 399 He spent years hobnobbing with gentlemanly shits and *half-ass operators. 1932 Amer. Speech VII. 333 *Half-assed, mediocre; insignificant. 1955 W. Gaddis Recognitions I. v. 183 A half-assed critic..thinks he has to make you unhappy before you'll take him seriously. 1879 Sir G. Scott Lect. Archit. I. 56 The abandonment of the *half-barrel vaulting of the aisles. 1957 M. B. Picken Fasion Dict. 19 *Half b[elt], belt which extends only half-way around body; especially one across back section of garment, as on sports jackets or coats. 1960 Farmer & Stockbreeder 9 Feb. Suppl. 5/1 A..jacket with a half-belt at the back. 1834 Planché Brit. Costume 48 Canute's queen wears..either the diadem or the *half-bend. 1774 Goldsm. Grecian Hist. II. 11 With one leg put forward, and the knee upon the *half-bent. 1881 Greener The Gun 259 A half-bent in the tumbler that prevents the hammer being accidentally pushed down. 1678 Phil. Trans. XII. 934 The Metal runs together into a round Mass or Lump, which they call a *Half-Bloom. 1711 Steele Spect. No. 36 ¶8 They [birds]..may be taken as *Half-Boarders. 1836 E. Howard R. Reefer xiii, The half-boarders whispered their fears to the ushers. 1885 C. T. Davis Manuf. Leather 479 The support is provided with two *half-boxes. 1882 Caulfeild & Saward Dict. Needlework 42 *Half, or Shadow, or Lace Braid, the passement is pricked, as in cloth braid, and twelve pairs of bobbins put on. 1789 *Half bull [see bob sb.[8]]. 1852 Halfbull [see bull sb.[1] 7]. 1906 E. Dyson Fact'ry 'Ands xvi. 216 I've gotter get that 'arf-bull 'r somethin' dangerous may set in. 1890 Daily News 28 Aug. 6/4 What is called the '*half-catch' system—i.e., the owner of the boat (who is usually a fisherman) provides the fishing gear, and receives in return half of the total catch of fish. 1940 Chambers's Techn. Dict. 399/1 *Half-cell. 1943 Gloss. Terms Electr. Engin. (B.S.I.) v. 93 Half cell, of an electrolytic cell: an electrode and that part of the electrolyte with which it is in contact. 1888 Lockwood's Dict. Mech. Engin., *Half-centre, half-centre is sometimes used to denote the position of the crank-pin of an engine when midway between the two dead centres or dead points. 1884 F. J. Britten Watch & Clockm. 115 *Half Chronometer..originally used to denote watches having an escapement compounded of the lever and chronometer, appears now to be applied to fine lever watches which have been adjusted for temperature. 1845 Mrs. S. C. Hall Whiteboy ix. 76 There was nothing..to distinguish L.M. from the *half class—neither gentleman nor farmer. 1726 Leoni Alberti's Archit., Life 4 Four *half Columns of the composite order. 1909 Westm. Gaz. 16 Feb. 7/4 He became a *half-commission man with a firm of stockbrokers. 1927 Sunday Express 13 Mar. 2 A half-commission stockbroker. 1931 Times 16 Mar. 18/1 The Half Commission Practice. 1687 Reflect. Hawk & Panther 27 The *Half-Communion is no older, than the time of Acquinas. 1587 Golding De Mornay vi. 72 The daysun..which inlighteneth not onely the *halfe compasse whereon he shineth, but also euen a part of that which seeth him not. 1901 Motor-Car World II. 317/1 To facilitate starting the engine a *half-compression device is fitted which operates on the exhaust valve through the medium of a second or subsidiary cam attached to the main cam working the exhaust. 1907 Westm. Gaz. 11 Nov. 7/2 The simple half-compression gear. 1883 Gresley Gloss. Coal Mining, *Half-course, half on the level and half on the dip. 1861 Jrnl. R. Agric. Soc. XXII. I. 41 Unless the whole evening's milk is skimmed and added to the whole new morning's milk—in which case the cheese made is '*half-coward'—the produce, whether single or double, is said to be whole-milk cheese. 1791 F. Burney Jrnl. 31 July (1972) I. 2 One precious *half Day I was indulged with my kindest Mr. Lock. 1876 Lady C. Schreiber Jrnl. (1911) I. 477 We found that we could not execute all our little shoppings.., because the Saturday is but a half-day. 1932 Discovery Mar. 71/2 Now the minimum wage [for farm workers] is 30s. per week of five shorter days and a half day. 1973 Daily Tel. 8 Feb. 1/1 The Shadow Cabinet decided to give up a half-day of its Parliamentary time to complete the debate in the Commons. 1805 Forsyth Beauties Scotl. V. 421 Ditches, hedges, and *half-dikes or sunk fences. 1788 E. Sheridan Jrnl. (1960) 138 Great coats made very open before to shew the peticoat—in Undress—*half dress, Night gown and peticoat with fine muslin Aprons—full dress I have not seen. c1810 W. Hickey Mem. (1918) II. xx. 261 A tailor named Knill..advised my having a dark green with gold binding..and for half dress a Bon de Paris with gold frogs. 1815 Belle Assemblée Sept. Pl., Autumnal Walking Dress... The head dress must be either a half-dress cap, or a white satin gipsy, or Wellington hat. 1850 Ladies' Gaz. Fashion Aug. 255/1 Plain mousseline de soie..begins to be a good deal seen in half-dress. 1960 Cunnington & Beard Dict. Eng. Costume 100/2 Half dress, late 18th and 19th c's... The costume worn at day functions and at informal evening ones. 1892 W. J. Gordon Our Country's Birds 10 Local and Popular Names... *Half Duck. 1903 J. A. Hamilton MS. in Red Box 329 Good sport among the half-duck and mussel-duck which abounded at Tudworth. 1934 Webster, *Half-evergreen. 1952 A. G. L. Hellyer Sanders's Encycl. Gardening (ed. 22) 131 Glaucophylla, half-evergreen. 1795 Repert. Arts in J. Holland Manuf. Metal (1831) I. 124 Anconies, bars, *half flats. 1889 Masson in De Quincey's Wks. I. Gen. Pref. 16 A half-flat set of apartments on the second floor of..a house of six such half-flats in all, accessible by a common stair. 1814 J. Sinclair Agric. Scot. App. II. 396 *Half foot, is another method of occupying a farm, equally barbarous in itself, and adverse to improvement. It is not so prevalent in the Highlands, as in some of the Western Isles. 1873 Trans. Highland Soc. 298 Out or led farms like the metayers of France, or the half-foot tenants of the Hebrides. 1880 W. Skene Celtic Scot. III. 370 A kind of tenancy called half-foot, where the possessor of the farm furnished the land and seed corn,..the produce being divided. 1961 Colour Photogr. vi. 249/3 The normal 20-exposure cassette gives 40 *half-frame exposures and the 36-exposure cassette gives 72 so that each colour transparency would cost less than 6d. 1967 A. Flowers in L. Deighton London Dossier 170 Buy one of the half-frame cameras such as the Olympus Pen D2 or the Canon Dial. 1968 J. Hudson Case of Need I. i. 10 'Call me,' Sanderson said, peering over his half frames. 1968 L. Deighton Only when I Larf ii. 17 Strange half-frame spectacles that he peered over abstractedly. 1898 H. Sweet New Eng. Gram. II. 121 The absence of a distinction between common case and genitive in the plural often makes it impossible in the spoken language to distinguish between gerund and *half-gerund, as in to prevent the ladies leaving us, I generally ordered the table to be removed.., where the..alteration of ladies into ladies' would make leaving into a full gerund. Ibid., There seems little doubt that the colloquial half-gerunds in such causal constructions as she caught cold sitting on the damp grass..have arisen through dropping a preposition. 1924 H. E. Palmer Gram. Spoken Eng. 168 In certain constructions the ing form has a function intermediate between that of the present participle and the gerund. Sweet suggests for such cases the term half-gerund. 1737 Bracken Farriery Impr. (1756) I. 342 A Hovel or *half House for them to run into. 1895 R. Kipling in Pall Mall G. 25 Oct. 3/1 When they were tired Kotuko would make what the hunters call a 'half-house'. 1900 B. D. Jackson Gloss. Bot. Terms 118/1 *Half inferior, used of an ovary when the stamens are perigynous. 1940 Chambers's Techn. Dict. 399/1 Half inferior, said of a flower in which the receptacle forms a cup which is adherent to the base of the ovary and partly up its side. 1928 Proc. Physical Soc. XL. 332 The number m can take only certain discrete values (either integers or *half-integers). 1971 P. Hlawiczka Introd. Quantum Electronics xvi. 247 The quantum numbers j_1 and j_2 may be either integers or half integers. 1930 Ruark & Urey Atoms, Molecules & Quanta vii. 187 Many authors use $j + \frac{1}{2}$ instead, when j is *half-integral. 1968 M. S. Livingston Particle Physics ii. 24 Nuclei with an odd number of protons plus electrons, each with half-integral spin, should result in half-integral nuclear angular momenta. 1805 Forsyth Beauties Scotl. II. 443 The rent was frequently paid in kind, or in what was called *half-labour... One-half of the crop went to the landlord. 1910 Daily Chron. 1 Feb. 1/1, I saw the proprietor,..perched on the *half-landing of the stairs. 1965 'T. Hinde' Games of Chance I. i. 16 The black and lemon half-landing bathroom. a1877 Knight Dict. Mech. II. 1049/2 *Half-lattice girder, a form of girder..consisting of horizontal upper and lower bars, and a series of diagonal bars, sloping alternately in opposite directions, and dividing the space between the bars into a series of triangles. 1894 H. Sweet Anglo-Saxon Reader (ed. 7) p. xc, To make up for the want of an accompanying dip, an extra medium-stressed *half-lift is made obligatory. 1967 C. L. Wrenn Study O.E. Lit. 38 Five basic combinations of stress or lift of the voice, half or secondary stress or half-lift, and unstressed syllables. 1864 H. Morley Eng. Writers I. 251 The most important is a heroic poem..extending..to 6357 of the short Anglo-Saxon lines, or *half lines, as they are usually printed. 1900 A. S. Cook Christ of Cynewulf 70 Half-line space. 1910 F. Tupper Riddles of Exeter Bk. 220 The half-line is of the A-type..common in the Riddles. 1927 E. V. Gordon Introd. Old Norse 293 In ON. tradition the unit verse was not the long line, but the half-line, which was called a vísa or line. 1964 English Studies XLV. 38 The patronymic epithet is separated from its antecedent by at least a full half-line. 1965 Ibid. XLVI. 420 In Germanic the basic principle is stress, together with a division into half-lines. 1851 Ord. & Regul. R. Engineers iii. 13 The Paper must be folded in the centre, lengthways, by which it will be divided, equally, into what is technically termed *half-margin. Ibid., All Official Letters for the Inspector-General are..to be written on half margin. 1762 Lowth Introd. Eng. Gram. (1838) 195 The Semicolon, or *Half-member, is a less constructive part, or subdivision, of a sentence or member. 1929 Man. Horsemastership, Equitation & Driving ii. 115 The bending lesson includes..the 'half passage' or '*half pass'... In all lateral movements the forehand must slightly precede the hind quarters. 1948 E. Schmit-Jensen Equestrian Olympic Games App. 95 At the Half Pass the horse moves on two tracks... The outside legs pass and cross in front of the inside legs... The legs on the side to which the horse is moving are the inside legs; those on the opposite side the outside legs. 1904 Goodchild & Tweney Technol. & Sci. Dict. 277/2 The area included in this curve is the first *half period element. Ibid., The effect of the whole wave can be expressed in terms of these half period components. 1905 Nature 13 Apr. 574/1 Different samples gave for the half-period of decay from 52 to 55 seconds. 1942 J. D. Stranathan 'Particles' of Mod. Physics xi. 448 One product of the nuclear disruption was a Ba isotope having a half period of 86 minutes. 1926 Maines & Grant Wise-Crack Dict. 9/1 *Half pint, stunted individual. 1929 W. R. Burnett Little Caesar iv. ii. 117 'Here's the half-pint,' said Killer Pepi, pushing Joe Sansone forward. 1930 G. C. Myers Mod. Parent ix. 165 Here are types of remarks which some parents..will stoop to make: 'What do you think of our half-pint?' 1938 Wodehouse Summer Moonshine xvii. 200 That wonder girl in whose half-pint person were combined all the lovely qualities of woman of which he had so often dreamed. 1943 C. H. Ward-Jackson Piece of Cake 35 Half-pint hero, swaggerer. 1948 'N. Shute' No Highway iii. 82 The little half-pint size, with thick glasses? 1891 *Half-plane [see orthomorphic a. 2]. 1927 H. G. Forder Found. Euclidean Geom. iii. 68 The regions into which a line a separates a plane ω in which it lies are the 'half-planes from a in ω'. 1959 G. & R. C. James Math. Dict. 182/1 Half-plane, the part of a plane which lies on one side of a line in the plane. 1968 P. A. P. Moran Introd. Probability Theory x. 473 In the cases considered the domain is a rectangle, an infinite strip, a half-plane, or infinite quadrant. 1884 F. J. Britten Watch & Clockm. 116 [A] *Half plate..[is] a watch in which the top pivot of the fourth wheel pinion is carried in a cock so as to allow the use of a larger balance. 1888 Jacobi Printer's Voc., Half plate paper, machine made paper of fine and soft texture used for woodcuts. 1877 Design & Work III. 451/1 Half-plate portrait lens. 1892 Photogr. Ann. II. 58 On your slide you require to get all the view on the half-plate negative. 1903 A. Watkins Photogr. (ed. 2) 13 Half-plate is the favourite amateur size. 1907 F. H. Burnett Shuttle xxxviii. 379 Adroit manipulation of 'portions' and '*half portions'..enabled them to add variety to their bill of fare. 1919 Wodehouse Coming of Bill (1920) I. v. 59 He certainly is a kind o' half-portion, ma'am! 1967 —— Company for Henry vii. 130 Even when calling her a squirt and a half-portion he had thought of her as a comely squirt and a half-portion with plenty of sex appeal. 1967 L. Deighton Expensive Place ii. 14 [He] did not like orders for ..charcuterie as a main dish or half-portions of anything. 1883 Percy Smith Gloss. Terms, *Half-press, the work done by one man at a printing-press. 1684 R. H. School Recreat. 90 Ringing at *Half-pulls is now the modern general Practice: that is, when one Change is made at Fore-stroke, another at Back-stroke, etc. 1872 Ellacombe Ch. Bells Devon iii. 36 What the trade would probably consider a 'pull' is, in ringing, termed only a half-pull. 1906 R. H. Lock Variation, Heredity & Evolution v. 141 In the case of a *half-race a small percentage only of seedlings is found to produce plants which show the racial character. Ibid. 145 A half-race might have been defined as a strain in which the character of the complete race is usually latent, and only rarely appears. 1928 B. D. Jackson Gloss. Bot. Terms (ed. 4) 169/2 Half-race, a form intermediate between a species and a variety of it, producing but few seedlings of the racial character, the majority reverting to the specific type. 1830 B. Thorpe tr. Rask's Gram. Anglo-Saxon Tongue 139 Line-Rime is when two syllables, in the same line of verse, have their vowels and the consonants following them alike, which is called perfect rime (consonances), or unlike vowels, and only the following consonants the same, which is called *half rime (assonances). 1860 G. P. Marsh Lect. Eng. Lang. xxv. 553 In Icelandic poetry,..imperfect rhyme is regularly employed, and..is called skothending,..which we may conveniently translate by half-rhyme. Ibid. 560 Although half-rhyme may be said to be peculiar to Icelandic poetry,..yet there are examples of the employment of both full and imperfect line-rhymes in modern English. 1873–4 G. M. Hopkins Note-Bks. (1937) 243 In Icelandic verse an opposite kind of alliteration (skothending) is made use of, namely ending with the same consonant but after a different vowel, as 'bad' 'led', 'find' 'band', 'sin' 'run' (from Marsh, who calls it half-rhyme). 1886 J. M. D. Meiklejohn Eng. Lang. II. 186 The English language is very poor in rhymes, when compared with Italian or German. Accordingly, half-rhymes are admissible..: sun/gone, love/move, allow/bestow, etc. 1936 M. Roberts Faber Bk. Mod. Verse 28 In Owen's war poetry, the half-rhymes almost invariably fall from a vowel of high pitch to one of low pitch. 1960 D. S. R. Welland Wilfred Owen vi. 115 Only in 'Arms and the Boy', 'Wild with All Regrets', and 'Strange Meeting' does he [sc. Wilfred Owen] write in *half-rhymed couplets throughout. 1841 Penny Cycl. XX. 476/2 The ripping-saw, *half-ripper, hand-saw..are saws for the use of one person. 1846, 1875 *Half-rip saw [see rip-saw sb.]. 1926 J. M. Grider War Birds 206, I half rolled on top of him, he *half rolled too. 1934 V. M. Yeates Winged Victory I. iii. 29 The same with the half-roll. Nothing would half-roll like a Camel. A twitch of the stick and flick of the rudder and you were on your back. 1904 Goodchild & Tweney Technol. & Sci. Dict. 277/2 *Half secret dovetail, a dovetail of the form used in a drawer front; it is concealed in a front view, but visible in the side of the drawer when drawn out. 1874 R. Tyrwhitt Sketch. Club 240 Paint the *half-shades in first. 1552 Huloet, *Halfe shoes beynge of suche fashion, that aboue they couer but the toes. 1683–4 J. Moxon Mech. Exerc. Printing (1962) 227 In *Half-sheets, all the Pages belonging to the White Paper and Reteration are Imposed in one Chase, and are plac'd, as you see by the Drafts: of Half-sheet Forms. 1888 C. T. Jacobi Printers' Vocab. 56 Book-work is sometimes printed in 'half-sheet' fashion. When thus printed there are two copies on one sheet. 1914 T. L. De Vinne Mod. Book Composition ix. 336 It is called half-sheet because this larger sheet must be cut in halves before either half can be folded. 1952 E. J. Labarre Dict. Paper (ed. 2) 122/1 Half-sheet, printing a whole sheet of a book so that all the pages of a signature are in one forme. 1964 F. Bowers Bibliogr. & Textual Crit. iv. ii. 109 The work-and-turn method of printing by half-sheet imposition. 1903 Biometrika Nov. 391 The high values, however, found for *half-siblings in the case of the thoroughbreds. 1938 Jrnl. R. Anthrop. Inst. 213 The mother allows the children to invite their half-siblings. 1959 B. Wootton Social Sci. & Social Pathol. iii. 85 Some authors state whether deceased, half- or step-siblings are included, or whether the delinquent himself is counted in the total of family members. 1952 H. Waugh Last seen Wearing (1953) 31 'What about her..under-garments?' '*Half-slip, pants, and bra.' 1957 M. B. Picken Fashion Dict. 313/1 Half slip, any of the various types of slips starting at the waistline. 1795 J. & E. Pettigrew Let. 5 Apr. (MS.) (D.A.E.), I have not got my shoes *halfsoaled yet, as shewmakers are very scarce. 1861 F. W. Robinson No Church ii. I. 71 Two days at Penberriog to rest his ankle and get his boots half-soled. 1823 P. Nicholson Pract. Build. 439 The floor between the two flights is termed a *half-space or resting-place. 1902 A. C. Harmsworth et al. Motors viii. 152 A crank, operated by a connecting rod from the *half-speed shaft on the engine. 1905 Goodchild & Tweney Technol. & Sci. Dict. s.v. Motor Cycles, The half speed shaft, rotating at one half the speed of the crank shaft. 1611 B. Jonson Cataline I. i, Let ..day, At shewing but thy head forth, start away From this *half-sphere. 1662 Pepys Diary 18 Aug., The whole mystery of *off [half] square, wherein the King is abused in the timber which he buys. 1674 Leybourn Compl. Surv. 345 Most Artificers when they meet with Squared Timber, whose breadth and depth are unequal..usually add the breadth and depth together, and take the half for a Mean Square, and so proceed..If the difference be great, the Error is very obnoxious either to Buyer or Seller. 1618 in Willis & Clark Cambridge (1886) I. 206 The *halfe storie to be eight foote and a halfe. 1886 Ibid. II. 737 The dormer-gablets of the half-storey. 1938 A. Campbell Battle of Brunanburh 24 Graz..regarding butu as having a *half-stress on the second syllable. 1961 Rev. Eng. Stud. XII. 345 Long and short syllables must be distinguised in scansion, when they bear either a strong stress or a half-stress. 1766 C. Leadbetter Royal Gauger II. xiv. (ed. 6) 370 In these Mortars the Rags are beaten into what is called *Half-stuff. 1836 Encycl. Metrop. VII. 764 A mill in which the rags are ground to a coarse imperfect pulp, called half stuff. 1912 Chambers's Jrnl. Oct. 671/2 The pulp—at this stage commonly called half-stuff—is fed into beating-engines. 1875 Sussex Gloss., *Half-swing Plough, a plough in which the mould-board is a fixture. 1888 Boy's Own Paper Summer No. 16/2 At *half-term it was Hoskyn's custom to write letters to all the parents with reports of their sons' progress. 1944 L. A. G. Strong All fall Down 55 It's half term, as even you must have realised. 1950 Hodgkinson & Muir in R. M. Scrimgeour North London Collegiate Sch. 1850–1950 v. 101 Miss Drummond spent a half-term morning in her Sussex cottage trying to see whether, if girls spent the whole day at Canons, they could be supplied with adequate teaching there. 1845 Mrs. Carlyle Lett. I. 322 Writing in *half text on ruled paper. 1950 Glasstone Sourcebk. Atomic Energy vii. 170/2 The mass half-thickness, i.e., the actual..*half-thickness multiplied by the density, is almost independent of the material absorbing the gamma rays. 1958 W. K. Mansfield Elem. Nucl. Physics v. 45 To compare the penetrating power of the γ-rays with that of α and β-rays, it is necessary to estimate the half-thickness. **1960** J. N. GREGORY *World of Radio-isotopes* i. 9 The shorter the wavelength of the γ-radiation the greater the half-thickness. **1812** *Examiner* 25 May 328/1 The brilliant lights relieving from a large proportion of *half tints. **1851** *Dict. Archit.*, *Half-tint*,..in a monochrome, it embraces all gradations between positive white and black. **1879** FURNIVALL *New Shaks. Soc. Rep.* 8 The notes on the back of the *half-title of the Part. **1494** *Act 11 Hen. VII*, c. 21 All Attaints..upon any Record, wherein the triall and enquest was by *halfe tongue. *a* **1877** KNIGHT *Dict. Mech.* II. 1050 **Half-turning bolt*, one with a thread occupying one half of its cylindrical surface. **1885** *Encycl. Brit.* XVIII. 153/2 Examples of *half-uncial writing. **1897** H. W. JOHNSTON *Lat. MSS.* 70 Half-Uncials are derived from the uncials and represent the last efforts of the book hand to differentiate itself from the improved business hand of the time... It is also called the Roman Uncial and Pre-Caroline Minuscule. **1912** E. M. THOMPSON *Introd. Gr. & Lat. Palaeogr.* 305 It is the Half-uncial hand which we find employed as far back as the fifth century as a literary hand in the production of formally written MSS. **1926** E. A. LOWE in Crump & Jacob *Legacy of Middle Ages* 209 Before developing a minuscule Irish calligraphers had created a majuscule, the Irish half-uncial as it is styled, of which the Book of Kells, a work of unsurpassed skill and artistry, is the most eminent example. **1946** MEZZROW & WOLFE *Really Blues* i. 12 Yellow's *half-valve inflections and slurs. **1955** L. FEATHER *Encycl. Jazz* vii. 292 *Boy meets Horn*, a showpiece displaying the novel style and tone he popularized using 'half-valve' effect (a squeezed tonal sound obtained by depressing the valve halfway). **1958** S. DANCE in P. Gammond *Decca Bk. Jazz* xxiii. 297 Original creations like *Boy meets horn* with its stifled, half-valved statements. **1956** S. TRAILL *Play that Music* viii. 87 Some players achieve a sort of 'blue note' effect by '*half-valving', which would mean, in our particular example, pressing the middle valve (for a correct E♭) half down. The distortion of tone which this produces is not very attractive, and I would discourage 'half-valving' altogether. **1711** *Half Verse [see HEMISTICH]. **1876** H. SWEET *Anglo-Saxon Reader* p. xcviii, There is often only one alliterative letter in the first half verse. **1907** F. A. BLACKBURN *Exodus & Daniel* p. x, Uncorrected errors are few, though occasional omissions occur, generally of a half-verse. **1938** A. CAMPBELL *Battle of Brunanburh* 16 It will be convenient to group its half-verses in the 'five types' of Sievers. **1946** KOESTLER *Thieves in Night* 165 As obscene and shocking to me as a petting party with a *half-virgin. **1965** N. FREELING *Criminal Conversation* II. xv. 164, I imagined, being full of valuable premedical catch-phrases, that she was 'half-virgin' and therefore despicable. **1577** B. GOOGE *Heresbach's Husb.* I. (1586) 11 Varro devideth his husbandry necessaries into..vowels..*halfe vowels..and mutes. *a* **1637** B. JONSON *Eng. Gram.* iv, L is a letter *half-vowelish. **1883** STEVENSON *Treas. Isl.* IV. xix, The low, sandy spit..is joined at *half-water to Skeleton Island. **1913** *Lighting Jrnl.* I. 207/1 (*heading*) A *half watt lamp!.. The types which it is expected to first develop..operate at an efficiency of half a watt per candlepower. **1915** *Nature* XCVI. 407/1 With electricity generated in modern power-houses, and ordinary metal filament lamps, 750,000 candle-power-hours are generated per ton of coal, compared with 260,000 C.P. per ton of coal when gas and modern gas mantles are used. The extended use of so-called 'half-watt' lamps will soon double this 750,000. **1932** N. ROYDE-SMITH *Incredible Tale* 57 The white glare of the half-watt lamp hanging from the studio roof. **1904** GOODCHILD & TWENEY *Technol. & Sci. Dict.*, **Half wave plate*, a plate of doubly refracting crystal, capable of splitting up a plane polarised ray into two portions, one of which is retarded half a wave length with respect to the other. **1912** *Motor Man.* (ed. 14) ii. 33 When the platinum contacts at the end of the armature touch, one-half of every complete wave flows into the accumulator, and when the contacts separate, the reverse wave of the current is interrupted at the zero or no-voltage line; thus only the half-waves of current flowing in the same direction are used. **1926** R. W. HUTCHINSON *Wireless* viii. 145 If the first half-wave is positive the grid will become positive. *Ibid.*, The next half-wave is negative and this still further lowers the potential of the grid. **1928** *Morning Post* 6 Feb. 3/4 A half wave rectifier. **1943** *Gloss. Terms Telecommunications* (*B.S.I.*) 67 *Half-wave dipole*, a straight aerial symmetrical in regard to its standing-wave current and usually approximately half a wavelength long. **1962** SIMPSON & RICHARDS *Junction Transistors* xii. 276 The same is true of any amplifier, such as the Class AB, whose output is asymmetrical and consists of pulses that are larger than one half-wave. **1962** CORSON & LORRAIN *Introd. Electromagn. Fields* xiii. 446 After having mastered the electric dipole, we shall be able to study the radiation field of the half-wave antenna—the type commonly used for transmitting radio waves. **1866** 'MARK TWAIN' *Lett. fr. Hawaii* (1967) 26 Foreigners and the better class of natives, and '*half whites' in carriages. **1897** —— *Following Equator* 63, I asked after 'Billy' Ragsdale, interpreter to the Parliament in my time—a half-white. **1901** *Daily Colonist* (Victoria, B.C.) 23 Oct. 8/3 In this boat's crew..was Charlie Diamond... He was a Bonin island half-white and is well known to old time sealers. **1959** J. JEENEL *Programming for Digital Computers* ii. 60 One might choose a 12-digit word size for the calculator and have a word represent either one number or a pair of instructions. The single-address instructions would be represented by '*half words'. **1964** Halfword [see BYTE]. **1970** O. DOPPING *Computers & Data Processing* vi. 105 Some machines pack two instructions per cell, and there are different addresses for each half-word, e.g. even addresses for left half-words, odd addresses for right half-words. **1605** SHAKS. *Macb.* II. i. 49 Now o're the one *halfe World Nature seemes dead. **1866** HOWELLS *Venet. Life* xvii. 260 The night's whole half-world. **1881** *Daily Tel.* 3 Feb., The endless intrigues of the 'half-world'. **1870** D. J. KIRWAN *Palace & Hovel* xliii. 613 'Baby Hamilton' is another celebrity of the Half-World. Many stories are told about the recklessness of this girl. **1874** *Porcupine* 21 Feb. 742/1 Those moral magistrates who have so distinctly set their faces against Cremorne and other outdoor haunts of the 'half-world'. **1950** Half-world [see *folk-jazz* s.v. FOLK 6]. **1972** *Times* 6 Apr. 7/5 Away from his chosen half-world, Munby's social life was passed in the first literary and artistic circles of his day.

III. Parasynthetic, as *half-languaged*, *-legged*, *-lived*, *-sensed*, *-sighted* (hence *half-sightedness*), *-sleeved*, *-souled*, *-syllabled*, *-tented*, *-winged*, etc.

1596 R. L[INCHE] *Diella* (1877) 48 Halfe-leg'd Buskins curiously ytide with loopes of burnisht gold. **1615** G. SANDYS *Trav.* 3 The men weare halfe-sleeued gownes. **1651** tr. *Bacon's Life & Death* 7 In the Daylight, they wink and are but half-sighted. **1762** ELLIS in *Phil. Trans.* LII. 662 This genus of insects is placed..under the Hemipteræ or half winged. **1833** BROWNING *Pauline* 167 Like things half-lived, catching and giving life. **1863** HAWTHORNE *Our Old Home* 378 The national half-sightedness. **1865** TYLOR *Early Hist. Man.* iv. 76 Half-languaged men.

‖**halfa** ('hælfə). Also **alfa**, **alpha**, **halfeh**, **hulfa**. [Arab. *ḥalfah*, or *ḥalfā*.] The North African name of species of Esparto grass (*Stipa tenacissima*, *S. arenaria*) used in the manufacture of paper, etc.

1857 SIR W. HOOKER *Rept. Veg. Prod. Algeria, Paris Exhib.* 39 Halfa or Alfa..the Moorish names for certain grasses possessing very strong and tenacious fibres. **1876** W. J. SEATON *Forests & Alpha Algeria* 30 Alpha or hulfa..here covers enormous areas..described by French writers as *mers d'Alpha*. **1877** A. B. EDWARDS *Up Nile* viii. 216 Overgrown..with coarse halfeh grass.

half-a-crown, half-a-dozen, half-an-hour, etc.: see HALF-CROWN, -DOZEN, -HOUR, and HALF *a.* 1 c.

half-and-half, *phrase*.

1. A mixture of two malt liquors, esp. of ale and porter.

1756 *Gentl. Mag.* 299 They had at that house 5 or 6 pints of half and half. *a* **1839** PRAED *Poems* (1864) II. 14 And, o'er a pint of half-and-half, Compose poor Arthur's epitaph. **1880** DISRAELI *Endym.* xx, Our tipple is half-and-half.

2. a. Something that is half one thing and half another, or half this and half that.

c **1814** COLERIDGE *Notes & Lect.* (1874) 264 That finer shade of feeling, the half-and-half. **1840** HOOD *Kilmansegg, Her Precious Leg* xiii. All sterling metal,—not half-and-half. **1890** *Review of Reviews* II. 357/1 It is not all humbug. Agreed, agreed! It is probably a case of half-and-half.

b. A half-breed or half-caste.

1827 J. F. COOPER *Prairie* iii. 58 The half-and-halfs, that one meets in these distant districts, are altogether more barbarous than the real savage. **1922** JOYCE *Ulysses* 315 Pity about her... Or any other woman marries a half and half.

3. *attrib.* or *adj.* That is half one thing and half another; half the thing in question, and half not: often merely an emphatic expression for *half*.

half-and-half jury: a jury chosen half from one class, half from another.

1796 BURNEY *Mem. Metastatio* I. 118 A half-and-half pleasantry, peculiar to our author. **1810** BENTHAM *Packing* (1821) 221 A half and half jury. **1846** J. W. CROKER in *Croker P.* 6 Jan., What is to become of your half-and-half administration? **1870** THORNBURY *Tour Eng.* II. xxiv. 163 Cromwell..hated all half-and-half measures. **1894** *Westm. Gaz.* 23 July 4/3 Trimmers and half-and-half people.

4. as *adv.* In two equal parts; in equal proportions; half...and half not.

1818 MOORE *Mem.* (1853) II. 136, I go half and half with the Longmans. **1827** SCOTT *Diary* 22 July in *Lockhart*, Am I sorry for this truce or not? Half and half. **1837** WHEELWRIGHT tr. *Aristophanes* I. 59 The cup That half-and-half so cunningly was mixed.

5. In a half-intoxicated state.

1715 RAMSAY *Christis Kirke Gr.* II. viii, The manly miller, half and half, Came out to shaw guid will. **1848** DUNCOMBE *Sinks of Lond.* (Fa.), *Half and half*, half seas over, tipsy.

Hence **half-and-'halfed** (-hɑːft), *pa. pple.*; **half-and-'halfer**; **half-and-'halfism**.

1832 *Examiner* 503/2 Toryism is hateful, but he more hated half and half-ism. **1861** *Times* 16 Oct., High bushy hedge-rows—thorn half-and-halfed with ash and other hedge-row trees. **1896** *Daily News* 21 Feb. 6/6 You are not an out-and-out Liberal?..a half and halfer?

†**half-angel.** *Obs.* An English gold coin, worth at different dates, from 3*s.* 9*d.* to 5*s.*; issued from Henry VII to James I.

1503-4 *Act 19 Hen. VII*, c. 5 Thangell and half Angell.. shall go and be currant in payment through all this his Realme. **1542** BOORDE *Introd. Knowl.* i. (1870) 121 The olde noble, the Aungels and the halfe aungels, is fyne golde.

'half-ape. A lemur.

1883 *Cassell's Nat. Hist.* I. 5 The little marmosets..and, linked on to these, the Half Apes or Lemurs.

†**half-ass.** *Obs.* [tr. Gr. ἡμίονος.] A mule.

1587 GOLDING *De Mornay* xxvi. 414 A Halfeasse of Persia shall come and make vs his thralles.

half-baked ('hɑːfbeɪkt), *a.*

1. *lit.* See HALF *adv.* and BAKED; hence, underdone, not thorough, not earnest; raw, crude, ill-digested; half-finished, incomplete, rude.

1621 SANDERSON 12 *Serm.* (1637) 330 Our profest Popelings, and halfe-baked Protestants. *a* **1628** PRESTON *Serm. Bef. His Majestie* (1630) 36 They are either done withoute heate, or but half-baked. **1824** SCOTT *St. Ronan's* xxxi, He must scheme, forsooth, this half-baked Scotch cake!..this lump of oatmeal dough!

2. Deficient in intellect; silly, half-witted. *dial.*

1855 KINGSLEY *Westw. Ho!* iii. (D.), A sort of harmless lunatic, and, as they say in Devon, half-baked. **1893** *Spectator* 24 June 847 Nor could a special variety of intellectual feebleness be better described than by the epithet 'half-baked'.

Hence as *sb.*, a half-baked person. *colloq.* and *dial.*

1866 J. SLEIGH in *Reliquary* VI. 160 *Half-char* or *half-baked*, a foolish fellow. **1892** *Nation* (N.Y.) 4 Aug. 81/2 The half-baked measures by which politicians try so hard to cripple the Australian system. **1923** U. L. SILBERRAD *Lett. J. Armiter* ix. 192, I believe girls were better off really with the old lock-and-key, guard-the-girls sort than with these half-bakeds, who let 'em have their heads.

'half-bap'tize, *v. trans.* To baptize privately or without full rites, as a child in danger of death.

1836 DICKENS *Sk. Boz* ii, He got out of bed..to half-baptize a washerwoman's child in a slop-basin. **1838** —— *O. Twist* ii, The child that was half-baptized, Oliver Twist, is nine years old to-day. **1875** *Sussex Gloss.* s.v., If you please, sir, will you be so good as to half-baptize the baby?

So **half-baptized** *ppl. a.*, baptized privately or without full rites; hence, semi-barbarous, (*dial.*) deficient in intelligence.

1795 SOUTHEY *Joan of Arc* II. Wks. (1853) 16 Irish Kerns, Ruffians half-clothed, half-human, half-baptized. **1875** *Sussex Gloss.* s.v., You must have been half-baptized to water those flowers when the sun was full on them.

'half-beak. A fish of the genus *Hemirhamphus*, having the lower jaw long and ensiform, and the upper short.

1880 GUNTHER *Fishes* 621 The 'Half-beaks' are common between and near the tropics.

'half-,binding. orig. *U.S.* [Cf. HALF-BOUND.] A style of binding of books in which the back and corners are of leather, the sides being of cloth or paper.

1821 M. L. WEEMS *Lett.* III. 325 [Books] in neat half binding, red backs, and corners. **1864** in WEBSTER. **1879** *Cassell's Techn. Educ.* IV. 87. **1881** A. LANG *Library* 67 In half-bindings there is a good deal of room for the exercise of the collector's taste.

'half-bird. (See quot.)

1893 NEWTON *Dict. Birds* 404 *Half-bird*, a common fowler's name for the smaller kinds of Duck, especially the Teal.

†**'half-block**, *sb. Obs. Naut.* A block of which one side is formed by a cheek-piece fastened to an object that forms the other side; = CHEEK-BLOCK.

1794 *Rigging & Seamanship* I. 155 Cheek-blocks, or half-blocks, are made of elm plank.

'half-block, *v.* = BLOCK *v.* 8.

1884 *B'ham Daily Post* 23 Feb. 3/4 Hatters.—Wanted, an Assistant..able to half-block.

'half-blood.

1. The relation between persons having only one parent in common.

1553 *Lett. Patent Edw. VI*, 16 June in *Chron. Q. Jane* etc. (1850) 93 For that the said Lady Mary and Lady Elizabeth be unto us but of the halfe bloud. **1642** FULLER *Holy & Prof. St.* II. xx. 129 What, is a brother by the half bloud no kinne? **1767** BLACKSTONE *Comm.* II. xiv. 227 He is only his brother of the half blood, and for that reason they shall never inherit to each other. **1858** LD. ST. LEONARDS *Handy-bk. Prop. Law* x. 64 The brother of the half-blood, on the part of the father, will inherit next after the sisters of the whole blood on the part of the father and their issue.

attrib. **1882** A. MACFARLANE *Consanguin.* 17 Aunt, half-blood..Brother, half-blood.

2. A person or group of persons related in this way.

1848 WHARTON *Law Lex.*, *Half-blood*, one not born of the same father and mother. **1876** DIGBY *Real Prop.* x. §2 (1). 388 By the change effected by the Inheritance Act, the half-blood, if descended from a common male ancestor, is to take next after any relation in the same degree of the whole blood.

3. One whose descent is only half derived from the blood of a particular race; a half-breed.

1826 H. N. COLERIDGE *West Indies* 147 That rich oriental olive which distinguishes the haughty offspring of the half blood of French or Spaniards.

4. *attrib.* Half-blooded.

1830 in *Wisconsin State Hist. Soc. Coll.* (1892) XII. 185 He is a half Blood St. Regis, with a half Blood Menomonie wife. **1835** C. F. HOFFMAN *Winter in West* I. 215 The driver was also accompanied on the box by a well made young half-blood Chippeway. **1837** H. COLMAN *Rep. Agric. Mass.* (1838) 52, I have slaughtered two half-blood heifers, which have weighed at four years old over 700 lbs. **1873** J. H. BEADLE *Undevel. West* xxi. 406 A handsome half-blood daughter married to a white man. **1943** *Sun* (Baltimore) 4 Dec. 12/6 A further sprinkling of transactions is noted in fine and half-blood wool.

Hence **half-blooded** *a.*, born of different races; *spec.* of superior blood or race by one parent only.

1605 SHAKS. *Lear* v. iii. 80 *Alb.* The let alone lies not in your good will. *Bast.* Nor in thine Lord. *Alb.* Halfe-blooded fellow, yes. **1825** J. NEAL *Bro. Jonathan* III. 375 A half-blooded Indian, of the great Mohawk breed.

'half-boot. [HALF- II. 1.] A boot reaching half-way to the knee, or considerably above the ankle.

1787 COWPER *Let.* 19 Dec., She had half-boots, and laughed at her own figure. **1800** *Sporting Mag.* XV. 49 Half-boots and gilded spurs were a long time used in common visits. **1801** MAR. EDGEWORTH *Belinda* (1833) II. xxiv. 26 Persuaded..to lay aside her half boots, and to equip herself in men's whole boots. **1804** JANE AUSTEN *Watsons* (1879) 340 Nothing sets off a neat ankle more than a half-boot.

1895 *Oracle Encycl.* I. 587/2 The name Caligula..from his wearing the *Caligae*, or half-boots of the common soldiers.

'half-bound, *ppl. a.* Of a book: Having a leather back and corners, with cloth or paper sides: cf. *half-binding.*

1775 SHERIDAN *Rivals* I. ii, They were half-bound volumes, with marble covers! **1863** *Bookseller's Catal.*, Half bound morocco. **1875** *Ure's Dict. Arts* I. 424 If the book is 'half-bound', instead of 'whole-bound', the leather is limited to a strip at the back and a short distance from the back to each side, and to the corners.

†half-bowl. *Obs.* A game played with a hemisphere of wood and fifteen small pins of a conical form.

1477-8 *Act 17 Edw. IV*, c. 3 (1763) Diverses novelx ymagines Jeuez appelles cloish, kayles, half-bowle, handyn & handoute. **1541** *Act 33 Hen. VIII*, c. 9. §11. **1801** STRUTT *Sports & Past.* III. vii. §12. (1810) 241 Half-bowl is practised to this day in Hertfordshire, where it is commonly called rolly-polly.

'half-bred, *a.* (*sb.*) [See BREED *v.*, BRED.]

A. *adj.* **1. a.** Of mixed breed; born of parents of superior and inferior strain; mongrel. Also *fig.*

1701 ROWE *Amb. Step-Moth.* IV. iii. 2022 Half-bred and of the Mungrel Strain of mischief. **1810** *Sporting Mag.* 43 One stallion, and 46 half-bred mares. **1864** *Daily Tel.* 19 July, Lost, a Half-bred Setter and Retriever Dog.

b. Of a sheep. *Austral.* and *N.Z.*

1891 R. WALLACE *Rural Econ. Austral. & N.Z.* xviii. 265 The half-bred sheep, being the various crosses between Merino ewes and long-woolled rams. **1959** BAKER *Drum* II. 116 *Halfbred sheep*, orig. a sheep by a longwool ram from a merino ewe; now loosely applied to the type.

†2. Imperfectly acquainted with the rules of good breeding; under-bred. *Obs.*

a **1732** ATTERBURY *Proverbs* xiv. 6 (Seager) An half-bred man is conceited in his address, and troublesome in his conversation.

B. *sb.* A half-bred horse, pigeon, etc. A half-bred sheep. *Austral.* and *N.Z.*

1848 E. G. WAKEFIELD *Let.* in *N.Z. Jrnl. Agric.* (1950) Feb. 136/3 The want of the more prolific and hardy constitution of the half-bred. **1856** H. H. DIXON *Post & Paddock* x. 171 The best express carriers [pigeons] are half-breds, between an Antwerp and a dragon. **1891** R. WALLACE *Rural Econ. Austral. & N.Z.* xviii. 265 The half-breds, or first crosses, are the most profitable sheep. **1894** G. ARMITAGE *Horse* iv. 47 The half-bred is going..at the top of his pace. **1930** L. G. D. ACLAND *Early Canterbury Runs* i. 7 Corriedales and Half-breds have displaced the Merinos except on the lightest and highest country. **1956** G. BOWEN *Wool Away!* (ed. 2) xii. 134 Half-breds are recognised in New Zealand as a cross between Merinos and one of the English longwool breeds.

half-breed ('hɑːfbriːd). [See BREED *sb.*, and cf. HALF-CASTE.]

†1. A mixed breed or race, sprung from parents of two races. *Obs.*

1775 ROMANS *Hist. Florida* 82 Before the English traders came among them, there were scarcely any half breed, but now they abound among the younger sort. **1858** C. L. FLINT *Milch Cows & Dairy Farming* (1860) ii. 69 Qualities which are, in a measure, artificial..change not only with the breed of one species, but with the different individuals of the same breed, of the same half-breed, and often of the same family.

2. a. One who is sprung from parents or ancestors of different races; orig. and esp., in U.S., applied to the offspring of whites or Negroes and American Indians.

1760 *Newport* (R.I.) *Mercury* 22 Apr. 2/1 On the 18th a Half-Breed, who is a Leader and Head Warrior..came..to Fort Augusta. **1791** W. BARTRAM *Carolina* 440 His mother being a Chactaw slave, and his father a half breed, betwixt a Creek and white man. **1807** PIKE *Sources Mississ.* III. App. (1810) 33 A few civilized Indians and half breeds. **1860** FROUDE *Hist. Eng.* V. 415 The laws which interfered with the marriages of English and Irish, and forbade the inheritance of half-breeds, were relaxed or abolished.

b. *transf.* and *fig.*

1846 *Quincy* (Ill.) *Whig* 27 Jan. 2/4 All the Jacks in the county, consisting of T. H. Owen, John Harper, Backenstos, Bedell, and a few 'half breeds'. **1883** 'MARK TWAIN' *Life on Mississippi* xliv. 402 This reminds me that a remark of a very peculiar nature was made here in my neighbourhood (in the North) a few days ago: 'He hadn't ought to have went.' How is that? Isn't that a good deal of a triumph? One knows the orders combined in this half-breed's architecture without inquiring: one parent Northern, the other Southern. **1952** A. STEVENSON *Speeches* (1953) 179 I'm a half-breed myself. My father was from an old, staunch Democratic family, and he was a Presbyterian. My mother was from an equally old and staunch Republican family and she was a Unitarian.

3. In *U.S. politics*, a name applied in derision to certain Republicans of New York who in 1881 wavered in their party allegiance.

1881 *Daily News* 7 Dec. 4/8 A Cabinet of 'Half-breeds', as the party of Civil Service reform are called. **1888** BRYCE *Amer. Commw.* II. II. xlvi. 203 The 'Stalwart' and 'Half-breed' sections of the Republican party in the same State.. were mere factions..without distinctive principles.

4. *attrib.* (from 1).

a **1762** S. NILES *Wars* in *Mass. Hist. Soc. Coll.* (1861) 4th Ser. V. II. 538 One Molton, a half-breed fellow,..seized the fellow that wounded Mr. Atkins. **1837** HT. MARTINEAU *Soc. Amer.* II. 12 Half-breed boys were paddling about in their little canoes. **1859** THACKERAY *Virgin.* li, A half-breed woman in the fort.

half-brother. [In ME. from *c* 1300; cf. Ger. *halbbruder*, ON. *halfbróðir.*] A brother by one parent only, a brother of the half-blood.

c **1330** R. BRUNNE *Chron.* (1810) 121 Roberd went hir with, Malde's half broþer. *c* **1475** *Nom.* in Wr.-Wülcker 690/13 *Hic germanus*, a halfebrodyre. **1641** *Termes de la Ley* 108 They are termed halfe brothers, or brothers of the halfe bloud. **1715-20** POPE *Iliad* XIV. 265 And seeks the cave of Death's half-brother, Sleep. **1875** JOWETT *Plato* (ed. 2) I. 224 He is my half brother, the son of my mother, but not of my father.

half-butt. *Billiards.* A cue intermediate in length between the ordinary cue and the *long butt*, used to reach a ball beyond the distance for which the ordinary cue is available. (Like the long butt it is made with a piece of heavy wood at the butt-end, to balance the weight of the longer end, which is of light wood.)

1896 *Badminton Libr., Billiards* 97 Half-butts and long-butts, on account of their length, have to be made of pine for lightness' sake..They are cumbrous things, and a disagreeable necessity. *Ibid.* 115 [To be] obliged to use the rest, and, worse still, the half-butt and long-butt, is at any time a drawback.

'half-cap.

†1. A half-courteous salute, shown by a slight movement only of the cap. *Obs.*

1607 SHAKS. *Timon* II. ii. 221 With certaine halfe-caps, and cold mouing nods, They froze me into Silence.

2. A kind of lady's head-dress: see quot.

1893 GEORG. HILL *Hist. Eng. Dress* II. 243 What were called half-caps were worn in the early forties; they were circular head-dresses set well back from the front, and trimmed with bunches of ribbons and flowers at each side, over the ears.

half-caste. Also **half-cast.**

†1. A mixed caste; a race sprung from the union of two castes or races. *Obs.*

1798 WELLESLEY in Owen *Desp.* 15 Several of them are Caffres and people of half-cast.

2. One of a mixed race, a half-breed; *esp.*, in India, one born or descended from a European father and native mother.

1789 MUNRO *Narr. Milit. Oper.* 51 (Y.) Mulattoes, or as they are called in the East Indies, half-casts. **1840** ARNOLD in Stanley *Life & Corr.* (1844) II. ix. 200 To organize and purify Christian Churches of whites and half-castes. **1884** *Century Mag.* XXVII. 919 Much as we admired the Maori race, we were even more struck by the half-castes.

3. *attrib.* (from 1.)

1793 DIROM *Narr. Campaign India* 11 (Y.) Half-cast people of Portuguese and French extraction. **1859** LANG *Wand. India* 284 The daughter of a half-caste merchant. **1869** FREEMAN *Norm. Conq.* III. xiii. 263 No half-caste offspring of Norman or even of..Flemish mothers, but Englishmen of purely English blood.

Hence **half-castism,** a half-caste system.

1896 *Westm. Gaz.* 27 June 8/1 The problem of Half-castism which slavery has been mainly instrumental in bequeathing to South Africa.

half-cheek.

†1. A face in profile, a side-face. *Obs.*

1588 SHAKS. *L.L.L.* v. ii. 620 S. Georges halfe cheeke in a brooch.

2. *Naut.*: see CHEEK 13.

c **1860** H. STUART *Seaman's Catech.* 73 Four half cheeks dowelled and bolted to spindle and side trees.

half-chess. A short chess or plank in a military bridge: see CHESS[2] 4.

1853 SIR H. DOUGLAS *Milit. Bridges* (ed. 3) 68 [They] will bring up two half Chesses and lay them across the Balks.

half-circle.

1. The half of a circle; a semicircle.

1552 HULOET, Halfe circle, *semicirculus.* **1559** W. CUNNINGHAM *Cosmogr. Glasse* 126 Describe in th' intersections in like maner, halfe circles. **1661** J. CHILDREY *Brit. Baconica* 104 A double course of half circles. **1878** NEWCOMB *Pop. Astron.* III. iii. 299 A little more than a half-circle.

2. *attrib.* (See quots.)

1853 STOCQUELER *Milit. Encycl.*, *Half-circle guard*, in fencing, is one of the guards used with the broadsword to parry an inside cut below the wrist. *Ibid.*, *Half-circle parade*, is a parade of the small sword, used against the thrust in low carte.

So **half-'circular** *a.*, semicircular.

a **1847** MRS. SHERWOOD *Life* ii. 19 The half-circular window over the hall-door.

half-cock, *sb.*

†1. Part of a watch: cf. COCK *sb.*[1] 16. *Obs.*

1701 *Lond. Gaz.* No. 3717/4 A Silver Pendulum Minute Watch..with a Bob Ballance, and Glass in the half Cock.

2. Of a fire-arm: The position of the cock or hammer when raised only half-way and held by the catch or half-bent, from which it cannot be moved by pulling the trigger. Hence *to go off (at) half-cock*, to 'go off' prematurely; to speak or act without due forethought or preparation, and consequently to fail in attaining one's object.

1745 [see COCK *sb.*[1] 13 b]. **1752** J. B. MACCOLL in *Scots Mag.* Aug. (1753) 401/2 The..gun was in use, when going to be snapped, to stand at half cock. **1810** *Sporting Mag.* XXXV. 152 It [a gun] went off at half-cock. **1847** *Infantry Man.* (1854) 40 The cock is..to be drawn back to the catch of the half-cock. **1848** LOWELL *Biglow P.* Ser. I. (1880) 38 Now don't go off Half-cock. **1896** *Westm. Gaz.* 6 Jan. 1/3 Poor Doctor Jim! What disasters he brought down upon his country and his company by going off at half-cock!

3. *attrib.*, as **half-cock shot** or **stroke** *Cricket*, a stroke begun as a forward stroke but checked half-way, the ball being allowed to hit the bat.

1888 R. H. LYTTELTON in Steel & Lyttelton *Cricket* ii. 52 He may, after he has got forward and perceived his error, effect a compromise and perform what is sometimes called a 'half-cock stroke'. **1909** *Westm. Gaz.* 17 Apr. 16/2 He may occasionally use a half-cock stroke with the left leg well up to the bat. **1959** *Times* 29 May 4/4 Hallam..made a half-cock shot to be caught and bowled.

So **half-cock** *v. trans.*, to put (a gun) at half-cock.

1833 *Regul. Instr. Cavalry* I. 100 The carbine may be half-cocked. **1847** MARRYAT *Childr. N. Forest* xii, If you choose to half-cock your gun..I will do the same.

half-cocked, *ppl. a.* and *pa. pple.* [See HALF-COCK *v.*] **a.** Of a gun: at half-cock.

1809 [see COCKED *ppl. a.*[2] 2].

b. Partly intoxicated. *dial.* and *slang.*

c **1830** T. WILSON *Pitman's Pay* (1843) 54 Half-cock'd and canty, hyem we gat. **1886** W. H. LONG *I.O.W. Dial.* 120 All on 'em was about half cocked. **1888** [see COCKED *ppl. a.*[2] 2]. **1910** *Dial. Notes* III. VI. 453 *Half-cocked*,..Half drunk.

c. *to go off half-cocked*: to speak or act prematurely. *U.S. colloq.*

1833 *Deb. Congress U.S.* 31 Jan. 1521 The gentleman from Maryland has gone off half cocked. **1877** J. HABBERTON *Jericho Road* xvi. 152 Just like you, always goin' off half-cocked. **1920** S. LEWIS *Main St.* 349 Well—I don't suppose I ought to have gone off half-cocked, and not jollied him along. **1940** E. POUND *Let.* 14 Mar. (1971) 340 No use my going off half-cocked on large subjects whereon I have not yet arrived at conclusion.

d. Incompletely prepared or realized. Also quasi-*advb.*

1946 M. SHULMAN *Zebra Derby* (1947) viii. 45 You know, we're not going into this thing half-cocked. **1953** A. UPFIELD *Murder must Wait* xxi. 186 I've a half-cocked kind of idea.

half-cousin. The child of one's father's or mother's cousin; a second cousin. Sometimes applied to the child of one's own cousin, or to the cousin of one's father or mother.

1871 CARLYLE in *Mrs. Carlyle's Lett.* II. 231 'Sophy', an orphan half-cousin.

half-crown. a. A coin (latterly silver) of Great Britain, of the value of two shillings and sixpence; sometimes used for the equivalent sum, which is regularly expressed by **half-a-crown.** (From 1970 no longer legal tender.)

1542 BOORDE *Introd. Knowl.* i. (1870) 121 The crownes and the halfe crownes..be not so fyne Golde. **1562** TURNER *Herbal* II. 109 b, There is not past an halfe crowne lost. **1692** WAGSTAFFE *Vind. Carol.* xvii. 109 Thirty single Pence with us make a Half-Crown. **1841** E. HAWKINS *Silver Coins Eng.* 142 In 1551 commenced the circulation of crowns, half-crowns, shillings, sixpences, and threepences. **1884** R. L. KENYON *Gold Coins Eng.* 92 Henry VIII..Second Coinage ..Half Crowns Value 2*s.* 6*d.*..Obv. like the reverse of the crowns. Rev. like the obverse of the crowns.

1580 LUPTON *Sivqila* 27 [They] will not sticke to spende halfe a crowne. **1623** *Vox Graculi* in Hone *Every-day Bk.* (1825) I. 54 Half-a-crown's worth of two-penny pasties. **1717** BERKELEY *Tour in Italy* Wks. 1871 IV. 560 A..mark as large as half-a-crown. **1851** MRS. CARLYLE *Lett.* II. 155 Half-a-crown each you may lay out for them.

b. *attrib.*

1620 MIDDLETON *Chaste Maid* I. i, Has no attorney's clerk ..chang'd his half-crown-piece? **1714** MANDEVILLE *Fab. Bees* (1725) I. 347 A man, who keeps an half-crown or twelve-penny ordinary. **1800** HELENA WELLS *C. Neville* I. 165 [To] sit down to half-crown whist with antiquated spinsters.

Hence **half-crowner,** a person who pays a half-crown for a seat at a performance, etc.; a publication costing a half-crown.

1886 H. BAUMANN *Londinismen* 71/2 Half-crowner. **1890** G. B. SHAW *London Music 1888-89* (1938) 288 The half-crowners energetically cried 'Hear, hear'. **1893** FARMER & HENLEY *Slang* III. 250/1 *Half-crowner*, a publication costing 2s. 6d. **1959** *New Statesman* 25 July 106/2 One can watch the half-crowners filing..before the country-house displays of things properly designed and well made.

half-curlew. A local name of the Whimbrel or Jack Curlew, and of the Bar-tailed Godwit, both being smaller than the curlew.

1885 SWAINSON *Prov. Names Birds* 198, 199.

half-dead, *a.* [See HALF *adv.*]

1. In a state in which death seems as likely as recovery; in a state of extreme exhaustion or prostration from sickness or fatigue.

c **1000** *Sax. Leechd.* II. 282 Wiþ þære healf deadan adle. *c* **1175** *Lamb. Hom.* 81 For-whi hit seið alf quic and noht alf ded. **1297** R. GLOUC. (1724) 163 Nys he more þan half ded y lad in a bere. *c* **1400** *Destr. Troy* 6652 Half ded of þe dynt, þer þe duk lay! **1601** R. JOHNSON *Kingd. & Commw.* (1603) 179 Their horses halfe dead through travell. **1864** TENNYSON *Grandmother* ix, And all things look'd half-dead, tho' it was the middle of May.

2. Of a clock: see quots., and DEAD 24 b.

1884 F. J. BRITTEN *Watch & Clockm.* 79 For clocks with shorter than half seconds pendulums the pallets are generally made 'half dead', that is the rests..are formed so as to give a slight recoil to the wheel. *Ibid.* 116 [A] Half Dead Escapement..[is] a clock escapement in which there is a little recoil.

†**half-deal**, *sb.* and *adv. Obs.* [f. HALF *a.* + DEAL *sb.*[1] Cf. HALFENDEAL.]

A. *sb.* 'Half part'; half.

1399 LANGL. *Rich. Redeles* IV. 2 Where was euere ony cristen kynge..þat helde swiche an household be þe halfdelle As Richard. *a* **1400–50** *Alexander* 1368 Hugir by þe halfe dele & hiȝere þan þe toþire. **1548** HALL *Chron., Edw. IV*, 200 Offered hym his eldest daughter..in mariage, with the whole halfedele of his wifes inheritaunce. **1641** PRYNNE *Antip.* 18 Deprived of all Soveraigntie over one halfe-deale of his Kingdome.

B. *adv.* Half.

1399 *Pol. Poems* (Rolls) I. 403 The hie houusinge herborowe ne myghte half-delle the householde. **1513** DOUGLAS *Æneis* VI. ix. 212 All kynd of vicis to comprehend half deill..I mycht nocht rekkin.

'half-deck. [See DECK *sb.*[1]]

1. *lit.* A deck covering half the length of a ship or boat, fore or aft: in this sense still used in some small partly open craft. *spec.* **a.** In old ships of war: A deck extending from the mainmast aftward, situated between the then smaller quarter-deck and the upper or main deck. After the two decks above the main deck were reduced to one, for which the name 'quarter-deck' was retained, 'half-deck' survived only in the expression 'under the half-deck', applied to the part of the main deck from the main mast aftward, formerly covered by the 'half-deck'. †**b.** In colliers: A deck under the main deck, extending forward to near the after-hatch and containing berths, etc., for the crew (*obs.*).

1626 CAPT. SMITH *Accid. Yng. Seamen* 7 As the Captaine doth [make good] the halfe decke; and the quarter Maisters the midships. **1627** —— *Seaman's Gram.* ii. 6 The halfe Decke is from the maine mast to the steareage. **1637** HEYWOOD *Royal Ship* 45 She hath three flush Deckes and a Forecastle, an halfe Decke, a quarter Decke, and a round-house. *a* **1642** SIR W. MONSON *Naval Tracts* III. (1704) 357/1 The other lofty and high charged, with a Half Deck, Fore-Castle, and Copperidge-heads. **1687** *Lond. Gaz.* No. 2291/4 The said Bark is about 50 Tuns, square Stern, without a Head, an half Deck from the main Mast..and a blue painted Stern. **1769** FALCONER *Dict. Marine* (1789), *Half-Deck*, a space under the quarter-deck of a ship of war, contained between the foremost bulk-head of the steerage, and the fore-part of the quarter-deck. In the Colliers of Northumberland the steerage itself is called the half-deck, and is usually the habitation of the ship's crew. **1829** MARRYAT *F. Mildmay* ii, I followed my new friend down the ladder, under the half-deck. **1839** —— *Phant. Ship* xviii, He confined him in irons under the half-deck.

2. A local name in U.S. of the Slipper-limpet, *Crepidula fornicata*, or a related species, which has an under half-shell. (*Century Dict.*)

Hence **'half-decked** *a.*, of a boat, etc.: that is about half covered in or decked; **half-'decker**, a boat which is half-decked.

1872 *Daily News* 3 Aug., The smaller boats, the wherries and the half-deckers, resembled a collection of small white tents. **1882** ELTON *Orig. Eng. Hist.* (1890) 383 Like the half-decked craft which were used by the later Vikings.

half-dime. A silver coin of the United States, value 5 cents, issued from 1792 to 1873 (from 1866 of copper and nickel), popularly called a *nickel*.

1796 T. TWINING *Trav. Amer.* (1894) 170 The silver coins, of dollars, half and quarter ditto, dimes or tenths, and half-dimes.

,half-'dollar. A silver coin of the United States and other countries, equal to 50 cents.

1786 *Jrnls. of Congress* (U.S.) 8 Aug., Resolved..that the silver coins shall be as follows: One coin containing 187 82-100 grains of fine silver, to be called a Half-Dollar. **1792** *U.S. Stat. at L.* 248, 2 Apr. §9 There shall be..struck and coined at the said mint..*Half-dollars*—each to be of half the value of the dollar or unit. **1871** *Worcester's Dict.* App. (Money), Since the act of Congress of June 1853, the half-dollar contains 192 grains of standard silver.

half-dozen, half-a-dozen. The half of a dozen; six (or about six). *Const.*: see DOZEN.

a. **1829** T. L. PEACOCK *Misfort. of Elphin* vi, Some half-dozen..forgers. **1855** THACKERAY *Newcomes* I. 7 Pointing out a half dozen of people in the room. **1865** *Derby Mercury* 15 Feb., I..might have laid hold of some half-dozen at least. *Mod.* Would you like another half-dozen?

b. *c* **1401** *Jack Upland* in *Pol. Poems* (Rolls) II. 69 The cloth of oo man Myȝte hele half a doseyne. **1420–1555** [see DOZEN *sb.* 1]. **1648** GAGE *West Ind.* 12 He offered unto me halfe a dozen of Spanish pistols. *Ibid.* 80 Halfe a dozen Hollanders leapt into the boat after him. **1711** ADDISON *Spect.* No. 1. ¶5 Half a dozen of my select Friends. **1843** BORROW *Bible in Spain* 145 We came suddenly upon half-a-dozen fellows, armed with muskets.

Hence **half-dozenth** *a. colloq.*, sixth.

1840 [see DOZENTH]. **1892** *Eng. Illustr. Mag.* IX. 665 The first or second or half-dozenth attempt.

half-eagle. A gold coin of the United States, of the value of 5 dollars: see EAGLE 5.

1786 in *Amer. Museum* (1789) II. 182/2 There shall be two gold coins; one..equal to five dollars, to be stamped in like manner [to the eagle], and to be called a half-eagle. *a* **1824** R. PATTERSON cited in WORCESTER 1846. **1841** *Congress. Globe* 30 July 269/2 It was an open declaration of war upon the half eagles, the gold currency... This gold, in half eagles, was too good for us. **1852** *Knickerbocker* XL. 323 He was about to contribute a half eagle to the funds. **1868** O. W. HOLMES *Guard. Angel* iii.

half-ebb. The state or time of the tide, when its reflux is half completed.

c **1391** CHAUCER *Astrol.* II. §46 And þere also maist þou wite..wheþer it be..half flode, or quarter flode..half or quarter ebbe. *a* **1490** BOTONER *Itin.* (Nasmith 1778) 153 Et a half flode usque half ebb tunc debet navis transire. **1697** DAMPIER *Voy.* I. 116 It was about half ebb, when one of our men took notice of a Rock. **1862** ANSTED *Channel Isl.* I. i. (ed. 2) 9 The stream flows from half flood to half ebb, and ebbs from half ebb to half flood.

†**halfen**, *v. Obs. rare.* [f. HALF + -EN[5].] *trans.* To make into a half; to sever as a half from the whole.

1677 H. SCOUGAL *Wks.* (1765) 319 Then the halfned soul is left to the doleful resentments of so sad a loss.

†**halfen**, *a. Obs. rare*$^{-1}$. [A pseudo-archaic formation, perh. taken from next.] Half.

1590 SPENSER *F.Q.* III. x. 5 He Malbeccoes halfen eye did wyle; His halfen eye he wiled wondrous well.

'halfendeal, 'halven-, *sb.*, *a.*, and *adv. Obs.* exc. *dial.* In 1 **healfan dǽl**, 3–6 **halfen-, halven-del(e**, 4 **helven-, helvyndel**, 4–5 **halvendell**, 5 **halfon-, -un-, halvundel(e, -dell(e**, 5–6 **halfendell**, 5–7 **halfyndele**, 6–7 **halfendeale**. *β.* 4 **-dole**, 5 **-doole**. *γ.* 4–6 **-dale**. [OE. *þone healfan dǽl*, accus case of *se healfa dǽl*, the half part (see HALF-DEAL, DEAL *sb.*[1], DOLE *sb.*[1]), occurring after verbs of giving and the like, and mechanically retained after the sense of the inflexion was lost.]

A. *sb.* 'Half part'; a half, a moiety.

c **1000** *Apollonius of Tyre* (1834) 12 He..sealde apolloniȝe þone healfen dæl. *c* **1205** LAY. 7093 He hehte..þat he dælde his æhte a twam, And nom þa hæluen dale [*c* **1275** halfendele]. **1297** R. GLOUC. (1724) 5 Ac Schropschire naþ haluendel to þilke bischopriche i wis. *c* **1330** R. BRUNNE *Chron. Wace* (Rolls) 10919 He parted his host in haluendel. *c* **1380** *Sir Ferumb.* 3253 þat haluendol þan diȝte he wiþ-inne forþ to stonde. *c* **1400** *Rom. Rose* 2364 That in oo place thou sette, alle hoole, Thyn herte, withoute halfen doole. *c* **1425** *Craft Nombrynge* 14 þou schalt doubul þat merke þe quych stondes for haluendel on, for too haluedels makes on. **1488–9** *Act 4 Hen. VII*, c. 19 The same halvendele of thissues and profites. **1536** in Strype *Eccl. Mem.* I. xxxv. 274 That the king's highness may have the moyety and halfendale of the dividends. *a* **1656** USSHER *Ann.* vi. (1658) 212 When they had ridd away the halfendeale and dearest part, every man of himself, out of danger. **1888** ELWORTHY *W. Somerset Word-bk.* s.v., I let'n had a full halfen deal, same's off we was to share and share alike.

†**B.** *adj.* Half. *Obs.*

a **1300** *Fragm. Pop. Sc.* (Wright) 22 Evene helven-del than appel heo wolde ȝyve hire liȝt. *c* **1330** *King of Tars* 783 Yit haluendel the child were thyn. *a* **1440** *Sir Degrev.* 812 He passed never out on the playn Halvendel a myle. *c* **1440** *Gesta Rom.* xc. 414 (Add. MS.) The porter..to whome I graunted halfyndele my mede.

†**C.** *adv.* Half, by half. *Obs.*

1387 TREVISA *Higden* I. v. (Rolls) 45 The brede..[is] wel nyh haluendel lasse þan þe lengþe. *c* **1400** *Gamelyn* 272, I have nought yet halvendel sold up my ware. **1590** SPENSER *F.Q.* III. ix. 53 Lampes..halfendeale ybrent.

halfer: see HALVER. [*halfer* is a frequent mispr. for HALSER and HALTER.]

half-face, *sb.*

1. Half of a face; the face as seen in profile; a profile on a coin, etc. Also *attrib.*

1542 BOORDE *Introd. Knowl.* iv. (1870) 137 They haue halfe face crownes. **1561** STOW *Eng. Chron.* (1565) 169 b, A new coyne of siluer; as grotes, halfegrotes, and shyllinges with halfe-faces. **1614** BP. HALL *Recoll. Treat.* 399 Wee sawe a boy there, whose halfe-face was devoured by one of them [wolves]. **1656** J. HARRINGTON *Oceana* (1771) 28 (Jod.) Unless we would draw him with a half face. **1678** BUTLER *Hud.* III. i. 794 Those ravishing and charming Graces, Are all made of two half Faces. **1859** TENNYSON *Elaine* 1255 Then turn'd the tongueless man From the half-face to the full eye.

b. A thin face: cf. HALF-FACED 1, quot. 1595.

2. *Mil.* The action or position of facing half-way to the right or left, i.e. at an angle of 45 degrees.

1833 *Regul. Instr. Cavalry* I. 14 *Right, or Left, Half Face*, each man will make an exact half face, as directed, by drawing back or advancing the right foot one inch, by which the whole will stand individually in echellon. **1847** *Infantry Man.* (1854) 22 Make a half-face to the right.

So **half-face** *v. Mil.*, *intr.*, to make a half-face. Hence **half-facing** *vbl. sb.*

1833 *Regul. Instr. Cavalry* I. 20 The men move on the oblique lines upon which they are..placed..as described in the half-facings. **1853** STOCQUELER *Milit. Encycl.*, To *half-face* is to take half the usual distance between the [front and] right or left face, in order to give an oblique direction to the line.

'half-faced, *a.* [f. prec. sb.]

1. Presenting a half-face or profile. Of a coin: Having a profile stamped upon it; hence, of persons, having a thin, pinched face. So *half-faced groat*, applied contemptuously to a thin-faced man.

1595 SHAKS. *John* I. i, 92–4 Because he hath a half-face, like my father? With halfe that face would he haue all my land, A halfe-fac'd groat, fiue hundred pound a yeere? **1597** —— *2 Hen. IV*, III. ii. 283 This same halfe-fac'd fellow, Shadow, giue me this man: hee presents no marke to the Enemie. **1601** MUNDAY *Downf. R. Earl of Huntington* I iij, You halfe-fac't groat, you thick [? thin] cheekt chittiface. **1634** PEACHMAN *Gentl. Exerc.* 22 The third is onely halfe faced, as you see..Philip and Mary upon a twelve pence.

2. With only half of the face visible.

1593 SHAKS. *2 Hen. VI*, IV. i. 98 Our halfe-fac'd Sunne, striuing to shine. **1607** *Puritan* III. vi. in Steevens *Suppl. Shaks.* (1780) II. 591 (N.) Why cam'st thou in half-fac'd, muffled so? **1814** SCOTT *Ld. of Isles* v. xiii, The half-faced moon shone dim and pale.

3. Imperfect, incomplete, half-and-half.

1592 NASHE *Apol. P. Penilesse* (N.), With other odd ends of your half-faced English. **1596** SHAKS. *1 Hen. IV*, I. iii. 208 Out vpon his halfe-fac'd Fellowship.

1732 NEAL *Hist. Purit.* I. 201 Papists in disguise..Time-servers, and half-faced Protestants. **1824** GODWIN *Hist. Commw.* I. 105 Temporising and half-faced measures.

4. *half-faced camp* (*U.S.*), among frontiersmen: A camp or shelter left open on the south side.

1850 *Americans at Home* I. 95 (Bartlett) Commend me to a hunting-party in a half-faced camp. **1886** *Century Mag.* XXXIII. 379 Sleeping in half-faced camps, where the heavy air of the rank woods was in their lungs all night.

'half-fish. A half-grown salmon: see quot.

1677 JOHNSON in *Ray's Corr.* (1848) 127 A salmon cock, which some call a half-fish, usually about twenty or twenty-two inches, and a whole fish, above that length.

half-flood. The state or time of the flowing tide halfway between low and high water.

c **1391**, *a* **1490** [see HALF-EBB]. **1779** MANN in *Phil. Trans.* LXIX. 622 To shut their gates next the sea a little after half flood. **1867** SMYTH *Sailor's Word-bk.* s.v. *Flood*, When the water begins to rise, it is called a young flood, next it is quarter-flood, half-flood, and top of flood, or high water. **1895** *Pall Mall Mag.* Mar. 378 The river was at half flood.

half-fou' (ha'fu, ha'fʌu). *Sc.* [lit. *half-full.*] A half-bushel.

a **1800** *Sir P. Spens* xi. in Scott *Minstr. Sc. B.*, I brought a half-fou of gude red goud Out o'er the sea wi' me. **1818** SCOTT *Br. Lamm.* vii, There was some half-fous o' aits.

half-galley. A galley of about half the full size.

1687 *Lond. Gaz.* No. 2300/5 Three Gallies, one Half-Gally, and several low Boats. **1794** NELSON 30 July, in Nicolas *Disp.* (1845) I. 463 One whole Galley, two Half Galleys, as reported to me. **1867** SMYTH *Sailor's Word-bk.* s.v. *Galley*, There are also *half-galleys* and *quarter-galleys*, but found..to be of little utility except in fine weather.

half-god. [Cf. OHG. *halbgot* (Ger. *halbgott*).] = DEMIGOD.

c **1374** CHAUCER *Troylus* IV. 1517 (1545) Satiry and fawny..That halue goddes ben of wildernesse. *c* **1385** —— *L.G.W.* Prol. 387 For they ben half goddys in this world here. **1589** PUTTENHAM *Eng. Poesie* I. xvi. (Arb.) 51 Bacchus, Ceres, Perseus, Hercules, Theseus and many other, who..came to be accompted gods and halfe gods or goddesses. **1631** WEEVER *Anc. Fun. Mon.* 39 Those magesticke Heroes, or halfe-gods. **1895** A. NUTT *Voy. of Bran* I. 261 The godlike kin of the heroes, whom the older world called half-gods. **1901** JOYCE *Day of Rabblement* 8 *The Adoration of the Magi*..shows what Mr. Yeats can do when he breaks with the half-gods. **1916** 'Æ' *National Being* ii. 14 The gods departed, the half-gods also. **1951** L. MACNEICE tr. *Goethe's Faust* I. 56 A half-god has dashed it asunder!

†**half-groat.** *Obs.* An English silver coin, of the value of two pence, issued from the time of Edward III till the Commonwealth.

1451 *Sc. Acts Jas. II*, c. 2 At the..half grote [haif coursse] for iiij *d.* **1503–4** *Act 19 Hen. VII*, c. 5 §1 All maner of half grotes or pence of ij[d]. of English coine. **1548** HALL *Chron., Edw. IV*, 192 The coyne..he newly devised..and the silver he called grotes and half grotes. **1841** E. HAWKINS *Silver Coins Eng.* 98 The coins of Edward III were groats, half groats, pennies, halfpennies and farthings.

,half-'guinea. An English gold coin worth 10*s.* 6*d.*, coined from the reign of Charles II to 1813: see GUINEA.

1696 *Act 7 & 8 Will. III*, c. 13 §4 It shall not bee lawfull for any Person..to import Guineas or Halfe-Guineas into this Kingdome. **1727–51** CHAMBERS *Cycl.* s.v. *Coins*, In England, the current species of gold are, the guinea, half-guinea, jacobus, laureat, angel, and rose-noble; the four last of which are now seldom met with.

†**half-hake.** *Obs.* Forms: see HAKE *sb.*[4]: also **half hakk, halfake, -aque, half-hag.** = DEMI-HAKE; a smaller size of hackbut.

c **1538** R. COWLEY in Ellis *Orig. Lett.* Ser. II. II. 100 vj half hakes, a redd pese, a passvolant, ij hackbusshes, and a shipp pese. **1549** *Compl. Scot.* vi. 41 Mak reddy ȝour cannons..hagbutis of croche, half haggis, culuerenis. **1551** *Sc. Acts Mary* (1597) §9 To schutte with the halfe hag, Culuering, or Pistolet. *a* **1562** G. CAVENDISH *Wolsey* (1893) 73 Souches and Burgonyons with gounes and half hakks. **1579** FENTON *Guicciard.* IX. (1599) 369 Fiue hundred footemen with halfaques, and fiftie harquebusiers.

,half-'hardy, *a.* [See HALF- 1 b and HARDY *a.* 4 b.] Of a plant: needing some protection from cold winter weather. Also as *sb.*

1824 LOUDON *Encycl. Gard.* 881 Half-hardy annual border-flowers. **1852** [see HARDEN *v.* 7]. **1862** ANSTED *Channel Isl.* IV. xxi. (ed. 2) 494 List of half-hardy plants. **1904** *Westm. Gaz.* 6 May 10/1 The fuchsias, the heliotrope, the geraniums..are half-hardies. **1960** *Guardian* 25 June 2/6 Most half-hardy plants are..a bit of a nuisance. *Ibid.*, The true alpine enthusiast will turn his nose up at some of these half-hardies. **1972** *Suttons Seeds* (*Catal.*) 18 Dahlias..Can be treated as an annual or as a half-hardy perennial. *Ibid.* 37 The annual phlox. One of the best half-hardy annuals.

'half-headed, *a.* Half-intelligent; deficient in intellect, stupid.

1621–31 LAUD *Sev. Serm.* (1847) 83 Either he is but half-headed to his own principles, or he can be but half-hearted to the 'house of David'. **1660** R. COKE *Power & Subj.* 73 A Company of half-headed lawyers. **1887** *Pall Mall G.* 6 Dec. 9/1 Half-hearted and half-headed advocacy.

'half-hearted, *a.* Not having one's 'whole heart' in a matter; having the heart or affections divided; wanting in courage, earnestness, or zeal.

1611 FLORIO, *Semicorde*, a coward, halfe-hearted. **1621** [see prec.] **1772** FLETCHER *Logica Genev* 108 Some half-hearted Calvinists, who are ashamed of their principles. **1874** MAHAFFY *Soc. Life Greece* v. 154 After a half-hearted search, they go home. **1888** BURGON *Lives 12 Gd. Men* I. iii. 320 [He] found himself surrounded by the perplexed and half-hearted.

†**b.** 'Wanting in true affection, illiberal, ungenerous, unkind.' *Obs.*

1864 in WEBSTER, who cites BEN JONSON.

Hence **half-'heartedly** *adv.*; **-'heartedness.**

1670 CLARENDON *Contempl. Ps.* Tracts (1727) 686 If the heart be divided..there is no blessing for this half-heartedness. **1870** *Pall Mall G.* 27 Sept. 11 Is it that Venice ..sympathizes but faintly and half-heartedly with the master feeling of Italian aspirations? **1881** *Chamb. Jrnl.* No. 918. 495/2 The natural halfheartedness born of years of disappointment. **1888** BURGON *Lives 12 Gd. Men* I. iii. 317 To speak half-heartedly of the Anglican cause.

half-hitch. [See HITCH *sb.*]

1. *Naut.* A hitch formed by passing the end of a rope round its standing part, and then through the bight: the simplest form of hitch.

1769 FALCONER *Dict. Marine* (1789), *Demi-cleff*, a half-hitch on a rope. **1859** F. A. GRIFFITHS *Artil. Man.* (1862) 156 Taking two half hitches round it.

2. A term used by pillow lace makers to denote the loop given to tighten the thread after it has been wound upon the bobbins. (Caulfeild & Saward, *Dict. Needlework*, 1882.)

half-'holiday. Also 7 **half-holyday.**

†**1.** A day which is considered only half a holy day; a saint's day or holy day other than Sunday.

1552 HULOET, Halfe holidaye, *profestus.* **1631** R. BYFIELD *Doctr. Sabb.* 140 The fourth Commandement..concerneth the Sabbath and not halfe holidaies.

2. †**a.** The half of a holy day (used for recreation). **b.** The half (usually the latter half) of a working day, given up to recreation. **c.** A day of which the latter half is taken as a holiday. Also *attrib.*

a **1631** DONNE 80 *Serm.* vii. 75 What a poore halfe-holyday is Methusalems nine hundred yeares to eternity? **1826** in Hone *Every-day Bk.* II. 1195 Half-holiday school-boys. **1845** R. W. HAMILTON *Pop. Educ.* v. (ed. 2) 109 Who does not rejoice in the weekly half-holiday, wherever it is allowed? **1885** *Manch. Exam.* 20 Mar. 8/4 The Saturday half holiday was another ameliorative measure. *Mod.* Wednesday and Saturday are half-holidays.

†**'half-horse**[1]. *Obs.* A centaur. Hence †**half-horsy** *a.*, of the nature of a centaur.

1588 SPENSER *Gnat* 41 Th' halfe-horsy people, Centaures hight. **1591** SYLVESTER *Du Bartas* I. iv. 270 The brave Halfe-horse Phylerian Scout. **1621** G. SANDYS *Ovid's Met.* II. (1626) 38 It pleas'd the Halfe-horse to be so imploy'd.

half horse[2]. *U.S.* [HALF *adv.* 2.] Formerly used in the phr. ***half horse and half alligator*** (see quots.). Usu. *attrib.*

[**1809** 'D. KNICKERBOCKER' *Hist. N.Y.* (1820) IV. ii. 360 The backwood-men of Kentucky are styled half man, half horse, and half alligator, by the settlers on the Mississippi.] **1828** J. HALL *Lett. fr. West* 47 Eight or ten of those 'half-horse and half-alligator' gentry, commonly called Ohio boatmen. **1847** T. B. THORPE *Big Bear of Arkansas* 14 The half horse and half alligator species of men, who are peculiar to 'Old Mississippi'. **1860** *Oregon Argus* 13 Oct. (Th.), These half horse and half alligator sort of politicians are becoming a stench in the nostrils of the American people. **1948** E. N. DICK *Dixie Frontier* 241 More than once a 'half-horse and half-alligator' possessed accurate information on politics and government.

half-hour. The half of an hour; a period of thirty minutes. Also **b. half an hour** (not used with a defining word).

c **1420** *Siege of Rouen* in *Collect. Lond. Cit.* (Camden 1877) 15 With[in] the mount of ij halfe hourys. **1598** B. JONSON *Ev. Man in Hum.* I. v, Faith, some halfe houre to seven. **1777** SHERIDAN *Trip Scarb.* III. ii, She has gone out this half-hour. **1847–8** C. KNIGHT (*title*) Half-hours with the Best Authors. **1892** E. REEVES *Homeward Bound* 96, I have spent one delightful half-hour with him.

b. *a* **1300** *Cursor M.* 24742 It war not half an hore o dai. **1382** WYCLIF *Rev.* viii. 1 Silence is maad in heuen, as half an hour [COVERD. & **1611** aboute the space of halfe an houre]. **1604** *Commons Jrnls.* I. 203/2 He..delivered [the Writ] half an Hour before Eight, at the Fleet. **1663** WOOD *Life* (O.H.S.) I. 479 Till half an houre past six. **1670** NARBOROUGH *Jrnl.* in *Acc. Sev. Late Voy.* I. (1711) 30 In half an hours time. **1745** P. THOMAS *Jrnl. Anson's Voy.* 56 Half an Hour after Eleven we sounded. **1882** H. C. MERIVALE *Faucit of B.* II. I. xvii. 1 A country-town about half-an-hour from London.

Hence **half-'hourly** *a.*, occurring at intervals of half an hour; lasting half an hour. **half-'hourly** *adv.*, at intervals of half an hour, every half-hour.

1807 T. WILLIAMSON *Orient. Sports* II. 197 Pills..given half-hourly. **1827** DE QUINCEY *Murder* Wks. 1862 IV. 71 His ordinary half-hourly beat.

half-im'perial, *sb.*

1. *Hist.* A gold coin of Russia valued originally at 5 and afterwards at 7½ silver roubles.

1839 *Penny Cycl.* XV. 324/1 The half-imperial of 1780, at 15*s.* 4*d.* **1863** KINGLAKE *Crimea* II. 165 Some of the gold Russian coins called 'half-imperials'. **1897** *Daily News* 16 Jan. 3/2 The ukase..orders that imperials and half-imperials shall be minted with the inscriptions '15 roubles' and '7½ roubles' respectively.

2. A size of mill-board (Simmonds *Dict. Trade* 1858).

half-imperial, *a.* See HALF- 4.

†**'halfing**, *adv. Obs.* Also 1 **healfunga**, 4 **halving**, **halfine.** [f. HALF *a.* + -ING.] Half.

c **897** K. ÆLFRED *Gregory's Past.* xxxi. 207 Hit is nyttre ..ðæt hit mon healfunga sprece. *c* **1000** ÆLFRIC *Hom.* I. 126 Na healfunga, ac fulfremedlice. *c* **1375** *Sc. Leg. Saints, Ninian* 869 As he halfine-slepand lay in his bed. **1390** GOWER *Conf.* III. 206 The leon shall..torne away halfing ashamed. *Ibid.* 356 Halving of scorne she said thus.

†**half-island, half-isle.** *Obs.* or *arch.* A peninsula; = DEMI-ISLAND.

1600 HOLLAND *Livy* XXV. xi. 554 Standing as it were in an halfe Island. **1618** BOLTON *Florus* III. vi. 1636 192 Creekes, promontories, straightes, halfe-iles. **1871** R. ELLIS *Catullus* xxxi, Of islands jewel and of half-islands, Fair Sirmio.

half joe. *N. Amer.* [f. HALF- II. a + JOE *sb.*[1]] A Portuguese gold coin, worth 3,200 reis, formerly current in North America. (Cf. *half Johannes*, s.v. JOHANNES.)

[**1772**: see JOE *sb.*[1]] **1775** in *New Hampshire Hist. Soc. Coll.* IX. 88 A Gentleman yesterday gave me a half Jo. **1809** in P. Horry *Life Marion* (1833) 29 He offered..a half joe a-piece for Marion and me to let the recruits go. **1955** E. POUND *Section: Rock-Drill* lxxxix. 53 Doubloons, guineas, half-Joes.

'halflang, *sb.* and *a. Sc.* Also 9 **haaflang.** [f. HALF + *lang*, LONG; but prob. in part altered by popular etymology from HALFLING.]

A. *sb.* = HALFLING *sb.* 1.

1660 in Ure *Hist. Rutherglen* (1793) 65 (Jam.) A man servand, of younger yeires, commonlie a halflang.

b. (See quot.)

1875 *Encycl. Brit.* I. 393/2 A cross betwixt the Cheviot ram and blackfaced ewe..known by the name of *Halflangs.*

B. *adj.* **1.** = HALFLING *a.*

1805 J. NICOL *Poems* II. (Jam.), The haaf-lang chiels assemblin there.

2. Of half length.

1581 *Satir. Poems Reform.* xliv. 188 Braggand Forguson, Vith halflang suord.

half-leg. *U.S.* Half the height of a man's leg. In phr. ***half-leg deep, high.***

1752 J. HEMPSTEAD *Diary* (1901) 599 A great Snow knee deep..last night & this morning half Leg deep & more. **1825** J. NEAL *Bro. Jonathan* I. 112 Natty, makin' his way, through the bushes, half-leg deep. **1832** J. P. KENNEDY *Swallow Barn* II. i. 13 The snow was lying about half-leg deep. **1852** G. N. JONES *Florida Plant. Rec.* (1927) 65, I have a little corn half leg high. **1855** *Ibid.* 133 The spring branch newground [is] knee high, spring branch cut half leg.

'half-length.

1. A portrait of half the full length; one representing the upper half of the person.

1699 C. HOPKINS *Crt. Prosp.* Pref., This Piece was only intended for an Half-Length. **1758** J. KENNEDY *Curios. Wilton-Ho.* 12 Half Length of Philip, Earl of Pembroke. **1762–71** H. WALPOLE *Vertue's Anecd. Paint.* (1786) I. 229 The figures are less than life, and about half lengths. **1812** *Theatrical Inquisitor* I. 21 *Resolved*... That the armorial bearings of the society be a half-length of the American critic, Mr. Snarler. **1911** *Encycl. Brit.* XXII. 128/2 The small half-length of young Martin van Nieumenhoven.

2. *attrib.* or *adj.* Of half the full or entire length.

a **1739** JERVAS in *Pope's Wks.* (1751) VII. 291 (Jod.) Behind some half-length picture.

'half-life. Also **half life. 1.** A life of half the full length; an unsatisfactory way of life. Also *attrib.*, denoting a size of painting half life-size.

1864 *Atlantic Monthly* XIII. 157 (*title*) A half-life and half a life. **1867** D. G. ROSSETTI *Let.* 25 July (1965) II. 624 He would prefer a half-life scale. **1963** *Times Lit. Suppl.* 31 May 393/4 The half-life which men were leading.

2. The time in which the quantity of a substance (or the number of similar objects) in a sample decreases by half, *spec.* (*a*) in *Physics* of a radioactive substance, (*b*) in *Med.* and *Biol.* of a substance accumulated in (an organ of) the body. Also ***half-life period.***

1907 *Jrnl. Chem. Soc.* XCI. II. 1281 Rutherford and others have shown that whilst radium A, B, and C have a life-period of only a few hours, radium D has a half-life-period of forty years. **1954** H. SEMAT *Introd. Atomic & Nucl. Physics* (ed. 3) xi. 363 The value of the half-life of the neutron was calculated from a determination of the density of the neutron beam and the number of neutrons decaying per unit time per unit volume. **1955** *Metabolism* IV. 419 Two patients convalescing from recently active rheumatic fever..had hydrocortisone half-life values which were similar to those seen in the control subjects. **1955** *Sci. Amer.* Aug. 37/1 So the hazard of a given radio-isotope depends basically on a composite quantity called the 'biological half-life'—a measure of the duration of its activity within the body. **1964** *Times* 31 Mar. 11/4 The extension of the half-life concept, familiar in the field of radioactivity, to the break-down of pesticide residues is very welcome. **1971** MURPHY & MUSTARD in J.-M. Paulus *Platelet Kinetics* ii. 26 The slope of the regression curve divided into $-0{\cdot}30103$.. is the estimated platelet half-life. **1971** *Nature* 26 Nov. 233/3 The holes made in leaves by herbivorous insects, the half-life of leaves (four to nine months in most species) and a mass of interesting information about the roots and buttresses of tropical trees. **1972** *Ibid.* 22 Dec. 465/1 Because ^{244}Pu has an 82 m.y. half life, its presence today, 56 half lives after the formation of the Earth, is a most impressive accomplishment.

half-light. A light of half the full intensity; a dim, imperfect light. Also *fig. at, by half lights*: indistinctly, vaguely, dimly.

1625 BACON *Ess., Simulation* (Arb.) 506 What things [are] to be showed at Halfe lights. **1647** TRAPP *Comm. John* i. 5 The former [i.e. light of nature] is but a dim half-light. *a* **1711** KEN *Hymnotheo* Poet. Wks. 1721 III. 199 What by half-Lights to Saints inspir'd was shewn, To you is with all circumstances known. **1875** WHITNEY *Life Lang.* xii. 229 Lines which in a half-light appear definite and fixed.

halfling ('hɑːflɪŋ), *sb.* and *a. Sc.* and *north.* Also 8 **haflin**, 9 **hawflin, halflin.** [f. HALF + -LING.]

A. *sb.* **1.** One not fully grown; a stripling.

1794 *Statist. Acc. Scot., Forfarsh.* XII. 304 (Jam.) Wages of a man servant £10..Of a haflin, £5. **1804** R. ANDERSON *Cumberld. Ball.* 87 She'd little to de, To tek sec a hawflin as he. *Mod. Sc. Advt.*, Baker, Wanted, a stout Halflin, about 3 years at the trade.

2. The half of a silverling or old silver penny.

1820 SCOTT *Ivanhoe* v, 'Not a shekel, not a silver penny, not a halfling'..said the Jew.

B. *adj.* Not fully grown; about the age of 15.

1815 SCOTT *Guy M.* xi, My mother sent me, that was a hafflin callant. **1883** STEVENSON in *Longm. Mag.* II. 381 Religions so old that our language looks a halfling boy alongside. **1895** CROCKETT in *Cornh. Mag.* Dec. 579 She.. ran..more like a halfling lassie than a douce mother of eleven bairns.

'halfling, halflings, *adv.* Now only *Sc.* Forms: *α.* 3 **halflunge**, 5 **-lyng, halvelinge**, 8 **haflen**, 9 **-in.** *β.* 3 (*Orm.*) **hallflinngess**, 6 **halflingis**, 8 **haf(f)lins.** [*a.* f. OE. type ****healflunga***; *β.* with adverbial genitive ending *-es, -s.* Cf. ALLING, -INGS.] To the extent of a half, half; in part, partially.

α. *a* **1225** *Ancr. R.* 354 He nis bute halflunge upo Godes rode. **1423** JAS. I *Kingis Q.* xlix, Thus halflyng louse for haste. *c* **1430** *Pilgr. Lyf Manhode* II. lxxxv. (1869) 106 Haluelinge j foryat Grace dieu.

β. *c* **1200** ORMIN 16575 Off swillke þatt hemm turrndenn swa Hallflinngess to þe Laferrd. **1500–20** DUNBAR *Thistle & Rose* 187 Than vp I lenyt, halflingis in affrey. **1592** *Lyndesay's Wks.* Prol. 3 (Jam.), I stude gazing halflingis in ane trance. **1785** BURNS *Cotter's Sat. Night* vii, While Jenny hafflins is afraid to speak. **1795** MACNEILL *Will & Jean* I. xxi, Haflins seen and haflins hid.

b. quasi-*adj.*

1801 R. GALL *Tint Quey* 175 Wi' Habby Græme the haflins fool. **1824** SCOTT *Redgauntlet* let. xi, My father was then a hafflins callant.

'half-looper. A caterpillar of the *Plusiidæ*: see quot.

1869 *Eng. Mech.* 24 Dec. 345/2 There is a family called the Half-Loopers coming intermediate, with six claspers, of which the..caterpillar of the Gamma moth is an instance.

'half-lop. A fancy name for a rabbit having only one ear pendent.

1868 DARWIN *Variat. Anim. & Pl.* I. 107 When one parent or both are half-lops, that is, have only one ear dependent.

†**halfly**, *adv. Obs.* [-LY[2].] = HALF *adv.*

c **1375** *Sc. Leg. Saints, Ninian* 1418 Til hyme, þat halfly-slepand lay. **1565** J. HALLE *Hist. Expost.* (Percy) 39 Thine arte is halflye wunne. **1622** DRAYTON *Poly-olb.* xxiv. (1748) 358 So holy that him there they halfly deify'd. **1674** N. FAIRFAX *Bulk & Selv.* 167 This is what it is halfly.

'half-man. a. A eunuch. **b.** One who is only half-human, or deficient in humanity.

c **1000** ÆLFRIC *Gram.* viii. (Z.) 27 *Hic..semiuir* healfmann. **1610** HEALEY *St. Aug. Citie of God* XIX. xii. (1620) 720 Calling him halfe-man, for his inhuman barbarism. **1727** SOMERVILLE *Poems* 357 (Jod.) Sha Sefi, among eunuchs bred..Beardless, halfmen. **1932** R. KNOX *Broadcast Minds* vii. 160 We are introduced to a pack of half-men doing a maypole-dance round the Tree. **1941** V. WOOLF *Between Acts* 90 My child's not my child... I'm a half-man. **1954** P. H. JOHNSON *Impossible Marriage* 299 A lot of half-men who don't wash.

c. In Carlyle's use, one of two eminent men whose knowledge and attainments complement those of the other.

1832 CARLYLE in *Fraser's Mag.* VI. 413/2 They were the two half-men of their time: whoso should combine the intrepid Candour, and decisive scientific Clearness of Hume, with the Reverence, the Love, and devout Humility of Johnson, were the whole man of a new time. **1838** MILL in *Westm. Rev.* XXXI. 484 He [*sc.* Bentham] could be a systematic and accurately logical half-man; hunting half-truths to their consequences and practical applications, on a scale both of greatness and of minuteness not previously exemplified. **1953** R. P. ANSCHUTZ *Philos. J. S. Mill* iv. 61 As Carlyle had regarded Hume and Dr. Johnson as the two half-men of their time, so did Mill regard Bentham and Coleridge as 'the great seminal minds' who succeeded them. To Bentham it was given, Mill considered, to discern the truths with which existing doctrines and institutions were at variance; to Coleridge the neglected truths which lay *in* them. Since moreover it was in these terms also that the generality of early Victorians thought about politics, Mill and Carlyle in their turn came to be regarded as the two half-men of that age.

†**half-mark.** *Obs.* The half of a mark; an old English money of account, worth 6*s.* 8*d.*

a **1056** *Charter* in Thorpe *Cod. Dipl.* IV. 136 Mid healf marce goldes. **1393** LANGL. *P. Pl.* C. VI. 134 Hure hefd was worth half mark. **1695** W. LOWNDES *Amendm. Silv. Coin* 64 A Noble which the Law used to call the Hauf Merk. **1891** HUBERT HALL *Antiq. & Cur. Exchequer* 40 The denominations mark and half-mark, so often met with in old accounts, had no existence either in gold or silver currency.

b. *attrib.* Costing half a mark: applied to non-canonical or 'border' marriages. *Sc.*

1663 LAMONT *Diary* 207 (Jam.) Went away..to the borders to be married at the half marke church (as it is commonlie named). **1724–7** RAMSAY *For Sake Somebody* iii, Since ye are content to tye The haff mark bridal band wi' me.

half-marrow. [See MARROW².]

†**1.** A husband or wife; a spouse. *Obs.*

1637 RUTHERFORD *Lett.* (1862) I. 446 A treacherous half-marrow to her husband. **1693** *Sc. Presbyt. Eloq.* (1738) 104 That [she] hath given her sweet Half-Marrow such a Meeting.

2. *Mining.* A partner. (See quots.)

1847–78 HALLIWELL, *Half-marrow*, one of two boys who manage a tram. *North.* **1856** WHELLAN *Hist. Durh.* in *Times* 11 Oct. (1894) 4/6 When two boys of equal size worked together [in 'putting' a load of coal] they were called half-marrows. **1883** GRESLEY *Coal-Mining Gloss.*, *Half-marrow*, a butty or partner.

half-mast. **a.** The half of a mast, half the height of a mast; in the expressions ***at half-mast, half-mast (high)***, at a point at or near the middle of a mast: said esp. of the position of a flag lowered to half the height of the staff as a mark of respect for the dead.

1627 CAPT. SMITH *Seaman's Gram.* ix. 38 Hoise your Sailes half mast high. **1712** W. ROGERS *Voyage* App. 41 Have..your Foretop-sail half-mast, and all your Anchors ready. **1715** *Lond. Gaz.* No. 5333/1 The Flag was hoisted half-Mast high. **1806** A. DUNCAN *Nelson's Fun.* 17 The St. George's jack..was lowered half-mast high. **1891** *Daily News* 8 Oct. 3/1 At Dover the flags on the public buildings and in the harbour are half-mast.

b. *transf.*

1940 L. A. G. STRONG *Sun on Water* 139 With his trousers at half-mast. **1966** *Listener* 10 Feb. 210/1 Its [*sc.* a dog's] tail at half-mast.

Hence **half-mast** *v. trans.*, to hang half-mast high.

1891 *Illustr. Lond. News* 7 Feb. 174/1, I looked for the flag that Helga and I had half-masted. **1892** A. E. LEE *Hist. Columbus* (Ohio) II. 149 Flags were halfmasted, and the..prominent buildings were draped with mourning.

half-measure. [See HALF *a.* 4.] A measure, plan, effort, etc. wanting in the thoroughness or energy required by the circumstances, or necessary for success; procedure characterized by compromise.

1798 BP. WATSON *Let. People Gt. Brit.* (Jod.) Half-measures cannot save us. **1820** *Edin. Rev.* XXXIV. 101 The Academy has taken more than half-measures for improving ..it [art]. **1862** [see HALF *a.* 4]. **1866** KINGSLEY *Herew.* II. i. 4 Who would have advised some sort of compromise, pacifying half-measure. **1881** FREEMAN *Sk. Venice* 380 We feel how vain is the dream of those who think that this or that half-measure has solved it.

half-mile. *attrib.* [f. HALF- II. a.] Extending to, comprising or covering, half a mile. Hence **half-miler**, one who competes in a half-mile race; **half-miling**, the running of such a race.

1799 *Steele Papers* I. 176 The Purse is one hundred and fifty Dollars the first day 3 ½-mile heats. **1901** *Encycl. Sport* I. 48/2 The Amateur Championship meeting has..a Half Mile Race. **1934** T. O. BEACHCROFT *Young Man in Hurry* 49 'All out for the half-mile!'..Why did none of the other half-milers move? **1959** *Times* 18 May 3/3 Down the last back straight Valentin went like a half-miler. **1963** *Times* 27 May 5/6 British half-miling, which has been experiencing something of a renaissance this season, was further strengthened over the weekend.

half-minute. The half of a minute; a space of thirty seconds; also **half a minute**. **b.** *attrib.* and *Comb.*, as ***half-minute gun***; **half-minute glass** (*Naut.*), a sand-glass which determines the time for the running out of the log-line.

1684 T. BURNET *Th. Earth* II. 41 To calculate..an eclipse, to minutes and half-minutes. **1708** N. FROWDE *Life Adv. Voy.* (1773) 140 Half minute Guns were fired the whole Time, and every other Honour shewn to his Memory. **1717** FREZIER *Voy. S. Sea* 7 To answer the Half-minute Glass. **1867** SMYTH *Sailor's Word-bk.* s.v. *Glass*, Half-minute and quarter-minute glasses, used to ascertain the rate of the ship's velocity measured by the log.

half-moon, *sb.*

1. The moon, when only half its disk appears illuminated; more loosely, a crescent.

1530 PALSGR. 230/1 Halfe moone, *croissant de la lune.* **1583** STANYHURST *Æneis* I. (Arb.) 33 With targat, an haulf-moone Lykning. **1631** WIDDOWES *Nat. Philos.* (ed. 2) 13 The Moone..when she is horned, or halfe moone. **1660** HICKERINGILL *Jamaica* (1661) 11 A sharp Iron in form of an half-moon, fastened to a staffe.

2. Applied to various things of the shape of a half-moon or crescent; a figure or outline of this shape; a formation of ships, men, etc., drawn up crescent-wise; the 'Crescent' or Turkish power; on a finger-nail.

1581 STYWARD *Mart. Discipl.* I. 24 The which..is the battaile called the halfe moone. **1596** SHAKS. *1 Hen. IV*, III. i. 100 And cuts me from the best of all my Land, A huge halfe Moone, a monstrous Cantle out. **1608** MIDDLETON *Mad World, my Masters* III. iii, To wear half-moons made of another's hair. **1659** B. HARRIS *Parival's Iron Age* 242 She [Venice] was not able alone, to sustain the weight of the Half-Moon. **1671** MILTON *P.R.* III. 304 See how in warlike muster they appear, In rhombs and wedges, and half-moons, and wings. **1726** AMHERST *Terræ Fil.* xlviii. 256 A half-moon is the Turkish arms. **1883** M. MORRIS *Bk. of Health* 912 The laminæ in the half moon, or lunula, near the root, are not supplied so abundantly with blood-vessels as those beneath the rest of the nail. **1893** H. A. MACPHERSON *Partridges* iv. 173 When he directed the half-moon it was a most beautifully executed manœuvre. **1914** JOYCE *Dubliners* 84 The half-moons of his nails were perfect. **1952** E. GRIERSON *Reptutation for Song* xvii. 144 The nails trimmed short, the half-moons only crescents, almost swallowed by the encroaching skin.

3. *Fortif.* = DEMILUNE 2.

1642 ROGERS *Naaman* 101 Out-workes, halfe-moones and retrenchments to hold the enemy. **1712** E. COOKE *Voy. S. Sea* 149 A Half-Moon, on which six Guns may be planted. **1807** PIKE *Sources Mississ.* (1810) 19 Some were half moons and quite a breastwork.

†**4.** A cuckold; in allusion to his 'horns'. *rare.*

1659 SHIRLEY *Honoria & Mammon* III. i, Bow in homage to your sovereign antlers, Most high and mighty half-moon, prince of beccos.

5. *Mining.* Scaffolding filling up one half the sectional area of a circular *pit-shaft*, on which repairs are done.

1883 GRESLEY *Gloss. Coal-Mining.*

6. *attrib.* and *Comb.* Shaped like a half-moon, as ***half-moon battery, bit, roof, shoe; half-moon-shaped, -like*** adjs.; **half-moon knife**, a double-handed knife used by the dresser of skins for parchment (Knight *Dict. Mech.* 1875); **half-moon spectacles** (or **glasses, specs**), spectacles having lenses shaped like half-moons, used esp. for reading.

1607 TOPSELL *Four-f. Beasts* (1658) 324 Shooe him with half-moon shooes called 'Lunette'. **1772** FORSTER in *Phil. Trans.* LXII. 396 Marks..half-moon shaped. **1794** NELSON 22 Feb. in Nicolas *Disp.* (1845) I. 359 The two guns mounted en barbette, are now making a half-moon battery. **1875** WHYTE MELVILLE *Riding Recoll.* iii. (1879) 58 What I believe is called the half-moon bit, of which the bridoon, having no joint, is shaped so as to take the curve of the animal's mouth. **1952** B. MALAMUD *Natural* 73 Pop, wearing half-moon specs. **1969** 'G.' NORTH *Procrastination of Sergeant Cluff* xiv. 133 The Duty-constable's reading glasses, wire-framed, half-moon, perched on the tip of his nose. **1969** C. BOOKER *Neophiliacs* viii. 207 Lord Home.. looked out over his half-moon spectacles and read the message. **1972** P. TOWNSEND *Zoom!* xi. 190 He put on his half-moon spectacles and glanced over them.

Hence **half-moon** *v. trans.*, to surround like a half-moon; *intr.* to move in a half-moon formation. **half-mooned** *a.*, shaped like a half-moon; semilunate.

1611 CORYAT *Crudities, Praise of Travel*, In his halfe-mooned chair. **1707** FUNNELL *Voy.* (1729) 151 Fins.. stretching to his tail, which is half-moon'd. **1791** MISS SEWARD *Let.* 30 July, A pretty little lawn, half-mooned by the house and shrubberies. **1893** H. A. MACPHERSON *Partridges* iv. 175 Half-mooning should always be done across the drills if possible.

half-'mourner. A name of the Marbled White Butterfly, *Hipparchia Galathea.*

1832 J. RENNIE *Consp. Butterflies & Moths* Index, Half-mourner. **1876** MORRIS *Hist. Brit. Butterflies* 29.

half-'mourning.

1. The second stage or period of mourning, after the expiry of full mourning. **b.** Attire in which the black of full mourning is relieved or replaced by white, or by such colours as grey, lavender, or purple.

1820 MAD. D'ARBLAY *Diary & Lett.* (1854) VII. 273 They had already made up dresses for *half mourning*, of black and white. **1848** THACKERAY *Dinner at Timmins's* iii, She treated herself likewise to a neat, sweet pretty half-mourning. **1856** *Illustr. Lond. News* 29 Mar. 327/2 Half-mourning bareges and muslins.

2. The Marbled White Butterfly; = prec.

half-naked, *a.* As nearly naked as clothed.

1483 *Cath. Angl.* 171/1 Halfe naked. **1552** HULOET, Halfe naked, *seminudus.* **1600** FAIRFAX *Tasso* XX. xvi, This host with whom you must encounter now Are men half-naked. **1713** STEELE *Guardian* No. 52 ¶11 The half-starved and half-naked beggars in your streets. **1828–40** TYTLER *Hist. Scot.* (1864) I. 99 Half-naked..mountaineers.

half-nephew. The son of one's half-brother or half-sister.

1824 [see HALF-NIECE]. **1834** MRS. CARLYLE *Lett.* I. 14 A Frenchman who is her own half-nephew, the son of a sister who was daughter to the same father by a former wife.

†**'halfner.** *Obs. rare*⁻¹. [f. HALF: cf. *partner.*] One who shares to the extent of a half.

1594 CAREW *Tasso* (1881) 85 Of my harmes a halfner ouer right.

halfness ('hɑːfnɪs). [f. HALF *a.* + -NESS.] The condition or quality of being half or incomplete, or of being half one thing and half another; a hesitation between two opinions or courses; half-hearted action; irresoluteness.

1530 PALSGR. 228/2 Halfenesse, *demieté.* **1831** *Fraser's Mag.* III. 131 Such Halfness, such halting between two opinions. **1837** CARLYLE *Fr. Rev.* III. v. vi. (1871) 201 All Girondism, Halfness, Compromise is swept away. *a* **1859** tr. *Goethe's Convers. with Eckerman* in Smiles *Self-Help* i, There is no halfness about them. They are complete men.

half-net, halve-net. *Sc.* [Etymology doubtful: perh. more than one word.] A fishing-net set or held so as to intercept the fish as the tide ebbs. See also quot. 1812.

1538 *Aberd. Reg.* V. 16 (Jam.) An halfnett & half hawnett of the Pott water. **1630** in *Descr. Thames* (1758) 76 All such as have pitched, set or erected any Riff-Hedge, or Half-Net, upon Stakes or otherwise. **1810** CROMEK *Rem. Nithsdale & Galloway Song* 305 (Jam.) He was standing with a halve-net, awaiting the approach of the tide. **1812** SINGER *Agric. Dumfries* 603 *Halve Nets* are a kind of bag-net which catch salmon, gilse, and sea-trout..The persons..entitled to use these and other small nets, are the proprietors within the royalty of Annan.

half-niece. The daughter of one's half-brother or half-sister.

1824 MISS MITFORD *Village* Ser. I. (1863) 223 To pay a.. visit to a half-nephew and niece, or rather a half-niece and her husband.

half-noble. A gold coin issued by Edw. III in 1344 and by succeeding kings to Edward IV.

1480 CAXTON *Chron. Eng.* ccxxv. 231 The halfe noble of the value of thre shyllinges four pens. **1866** CRUMP *Banking* x. 222.

'half-note.

1. *Mus.* †**a.** A half-tone; a semitone. *Obs.*

1597 MORLEY *Introd. Mus.* 3 The ♭ cliefe..is made thus ♭, or thus ♮, the one signifying the halfe note and flatt singing: the other signifying the whole note or sharpe singing. **1684** R.H. *School Recreat.* 120 These are named *Semitones*, or the *Half Notes*, which must be well observed. **1763** J. BROWN *Poetry & Mus.* v. 64 The modern Chromatic Kind is an incidental Ascent or Descent by Half-Notes, with a variable Intervention of whole Notes.

b. A minim.

1847 in CRAIG.

2. The half of a bank-note, cut in two for safety in transmission by post.

1882–93 in BITHELL *Counting-house Dict.*

halfon-, halfundel, var. of HALFENDEAL.

half-pace. [In 1, app. a corruption of earlier *haultpace, haltpace*, HALPACE, q.v. In 2, app. f. HALF + PACE, but prob. an extension of sense 1.]

1. A step, raised floor, or platform, on which something (*e.g.* a throne, dais, etc.) is to be placed or erected. **b.** The platform at the top of steps, on which an altar stands. = FOOT-PACE 2b.

1569 in *Etoniana* (1865) 220, ij half-paces in the hawle for the Bybelers to stand upon. **1593–4** *Bursar's Roll, Peterhouse, Camb.*, Efficienti le halfe pace bibliothecæ. **1622** BACON *Hen. VII*, Mor. & Hist. Wks. (Bohn) 381 The cardinal, standing upon the uppermost step, or half-pace, before the choir. *a* **1734** NORTH *Lives* II. 433 Raised with a half-pace, almost a foot higher than the rest of the room. **1894** *Westm. Gaz.* 10 July 1/2 On the half-pace below the reredos.

2. A broad step or small landing between two half flights in a staircase; = FOOT-PACE 2d.

1611 COTGR., *Aire*, the halfe-pace, or landing place of a half-pace staire. **1677** PLOT *Oxfordsh.* 267 You ascend from one half pace to another, by ascents of 7 steps. **1712** J. JAMES tr. *Le Blond's Gardening* 125 A Half Pace, or Rest of two Paces broad. **1842–76** GWILT *Archit.* Gloss., *Foot pace* or *half pace*, that part of a staircase whereon, after the flight of a few steps, a broad place is arrived at, on which two or three paces may be taken before coming to another step.

Hence **'half-paced** *a.*, having a half-pace.

1603 P. STRINGER *Recept. Q. Eliz. at Oxf.* in Plummer *Eliz. Oxf.* (O.H.S.) 255 An easie half paced stayre, which was of good bredth. **1681** W. ROBERTSON *Phraseol. Gen.* (1693) 1170 The broad step of a halfpaced staire.

†**'half-part.** *Obs.* = HALF *sb.*

1398 TREVISA *Barth. De P.R.* IX. xxv. (1495) 362 The halfe part of mannys lyfe. *a* **1533** LD. BERNERS *Huon* lxxxiv. 264, I wyll gyue hym the halfe parte of my londes. **1595** SHAKS. *John* II. i. 437 He is the halfe part of a blessed man, Left to be finished by such as shee. **1715** LEONI *Palladio's Archit.* (1742) I. 12 If the Column..be divided into 6 half parts.. give 5 halfs of them to the diameter next to the Capitel. **1755** MAGENS *Insurances* II. 100 Within the first Half-Part of the Voyage.

half-pay.

1. Half the usual or full wages or salary; a reduced allowance to an officer in the army or navy when not in actual service, or after retirement at a prescribed time.

1664 PEPYS *Diary* 30 Nov., The Dutch having called in their fleete and paid their men half-pay. **1749** *Refut. Pamph. Navy Bill* 10 Every Officer, whilst he receives the Half-pay, is bound to enter upon Service. **1753** *Scots Mag.* May 261/2 Cashier and Paymaster of the Half-pay. **1823** BYRON *Juan* VIII. ciii, No hero trusteth wholly to half pay. **1844** *Regul. & Ord. Army* 65 Officers upon the Half-Pay who are desirous of being employed upon Full Pay, are to report their wish to the Military Secretary.

2. An officer in receipt of half-pay.

1826 *Ann. Reg.* 170/2 Now, like the other half-pays in London, he must live on plates of beef and goes of gin for the next seven years. **1865** *Pall Mall G.* 21 Aug. 10/2 The half-pays.. have come over in great force.

3. *attrib.*, as ***half-pay officer***, etc.

1715 DK. MARLBOROUGH 30 June in *Lond. Gaz.* No. 5343/1 Filled up with a half Pay Officer. **1727** SOMERVILLE *Poems* 68 (Jod.) Half-pay captains and half-witted beaux. **1889** A. T. PASK *Eyes Thames* 163 Englishmen with small means, of what might be termed the half-pay class.

halfpenny ('heɪpənɪ, *dial.* 'hɑːfpənɪ, 'hɑːpənɪ, 'hapənɪ, 'hapnɪ). Also α. 4–7 **halfe-**, 4–8 **half-, -peny, -ie, -ye**; β. 4 **(alpeny)**, 4–5 **halpeny(e**, 6 **hapeney, happenny**, (*dial.* **hawpny**), 9– **ha'penny, hapenny**. Pl. **halfpennies** ('heɪpənɪz), **halfpence** ('heɪpəns). Also 4 **halpenns**, 5–6 **halpens**. [f. HALF *a.* + PENNY. The pl. *halfpennies* means the individual coins only; *halfpence* is usually collective, or expresses the sum however made up.]

1. a. A coin (formerly of copper, subsequently of bronze) of half the value of a penny; a sum equivalent to two farthings. ***halfpenny farthing*** = three farthings (¾*d.*); ***three halfpence*** or ***a penny halfpenny***, the ordinary expressions for 1½*d.*

The halfpenny was first issued by Edward I, of silver. Under Charles II copper halfpennies were first struck; after 1860 they were of bronze. From Charles I to George III no copper pennies were struck, whence *halfpence* was colloquially used for copper or bronze coins collectively. After the decimalization of the U.K. coinage in 1971, *halfpenny* was often written as two words and pronounced ('hɑːf 'penɪ). It was demonetized on 31 Dec. 1984.

c **1330** R. BRUNNE *Chron.* (1810) 238 Edward did smyte rounde peny, halfpeny, ferthyng. **1382** WYCLIF *Luke* xii. 6 Wher fiue sparrowis ben not seeld for tweyne halpens? **1389** *Eng. Gilds* 98 þe clerke, a peny; þe deen, a alpeny. **1480** CAXTON *Chron. Eng.* cxcviii. 177 Not worth an halfepenye. **1512** *Act 4 Hen. VIII*, c. 19. §14 Those penyes to be taken and have course oonlye for halpens. **1579** *Nottingham Rec.* IV. 193 A quart of ale or bere for a penne and a pynte for a hapeney. **1597** BACON *Ess.* Ep. Ded., They will bee like the late new halfe-pence, which though the Siluer were good, yet the peeces were small. **1654** WHITLOCK *Zootomia* 181 To the Philosopher, three halfpence. **1691** HARTCLIFFE *Virtues* 229 Their As, which is but half-penny-Farthing in our Money, with them weigh'd a Pound. **1699** BENTLEY *Phal.* 440 The Species call'd Nine-pences and Four pence half-penies are gone. **1749** FIELDING *Tom Jones* XIII. viii, There are thousands who would not have contributed a single halfpenny. **1849** LYTTON *Caxtons* 38 He was only unsuccessful in turning my halfpennies into halfcrowns. **1850** W. IRVING *Goldsmith* 79 Adrift upon the town, with but a few half-pence in his pocket. **1969** *Guardian* 30 July 16/1 The halfpenny ceases to be legal tender on Friday [i.e. 1 August]. **1975** *Daily Tel.* 5 May 1/4 Bread prices go up today.., sending the standard loaf up by a halfpenny to 16p.

†**b.** ***halfpenny of gold***: name given to the half-ryal, a piece worth (in reign of Edward IV) 5*s.* *Obs.*

1463 *Bury Wills* (Camden) 15, I beqwethe to the Prior a good purs and a halpenye of gold ther in.

c. ***halfpenny under the hat***, a low game of chance.

1851 THACKERAY *Eng. Hum.* v. (1863) 240 Tom lies on a tomb-stone outside playing at halfpenny-under-the-hat with street blackguards.

d. A halfpenny stamp.

1881 *Stamp-Collector's Ann.* 9 The penny adhesive stamp of the new type.. appeared on the 1st of January, and was followed by the halfpenny and three-halfpence on the 14th October. **1908** *Daily Chron.* 20 Feb. 4/7 Many people.. think it necessary to fortify themselves with penny stamps. Others cram on a couple of half-pennies.

2. Phrases. †***to have one's heart***, or ***hand, on one's halfpenny***, to have a particular object in view (*obs.*). So †***to have one's hand on another halfpenny. more kicks than halfpence***: see KICK *sb.* ***not a halfpenny the worse***; ***a bad halfpenny***. (Cf. PENNY.)

a **1577** GASCOIGNE *Hearbes, etc.* Wks. (1587) 255 But his mystresse having hyr hand on another halfpeny gan thus say unto him. **1589** GREENE *Menaphon* (Arb.) 49 Twere necessarie he tolde us how his heart came thus on his halfepence. **1590** —— *Never too late* Wks. (Rtldg.) Introd. 10 Francesco that was tied by the eies, and had his hart on his halfpeny, could not deny her. **16..** *Notes on Du Bartas*, To Rdr. ii. (N.), But the blinde man, having his hand on another halfe-penny, said, What is that you say, sir? **1603** S. HARSNET *Declar. Egreg. Popish Impostures* 17 Sylueter, Bonifacius, and some other Popes, haue beene errand deuill-coniurers, and yet theyr holinesse not an halfepeny the worse. **1819** J. H. VAUX *Mem.* II. 154 When a man has been upon any errand, or attempting any object which has proved unsuccessful or impracticable, he will say on his return, It's a bad halfpenny; meaning he has returned as he went. **1850** HAWTHORNE *Scarlet Let.* 22 It was not the first time, nor the second, that I had gone away—as it seemed, permanently—but yet returned, like the bad halfpenny. **1895** *Brewer's Dict. Phr. & Fable* (new ed.) 571/2 *I am come back again, like a bad ha'penny.* A facetious way of saying, 'More free than welcome'. As a bad ha'penny is returned to its owner, so have I returned to you, and you cannot get rid of me.

†**3. a.** A small fragment, bit, or piece. *Obs.*

1599 SHAKS. *Much Ado* II. iii. 147 O she tore the letter into a thousand halfpence.

b. A form of ear-mark on cattle and horses. *U.S.*

Cf. *halfpenny slit*, 'an ear-mark given to pigs or sheep' (*E.D.D.*).

1658 *Rec. East Hampton, N.Y.* (1887) I. 151 John Woodroff marked a horse colt with a hapenny under the left eare. **1666** *Early Rec. Portsmouth, R.I.* (1901) 266 A halfpeny from the route [of the ear]. **1667** *Ibid.* 269 A halfpeney out of the r[ight ear]. **1702** *Town Rec. Tops-field, Mass.* (1917) I. 124 A.. horse.. [with] a half penny cut out of the right Ear. **1845** *Early Rec. Portsmouth, R.I.* (1901) 387 The Ear Mark of the Creatures of David Baker is two half pennys before the near or left ear.

4. *attrib.* and *Comb.* **a.** That costs, or involves the outlay of, a halfpenny, as ***halfpenny ballad, dole, loaf, sheet***; of the shape or size of a halfpenny, as ***halfpenny mark***. See also next.

1362 LANGL. *P. Pl.* A. VII. 293 Ne non halfpeny Ale In none wyse drynke. **1419** *E.E. Wills* (1882) 40 Smale Halpeney Loves. *a* **1553** UDALL *Royster D.* III. iii. (Arb.) 45, I will crie halfepenie doale for your worshyp. **1709** *Brit. Apollo* II. No. 70. 3/1, I sent it by the Halfpenny-Post. **1710** *Ibid.* No. 100. 2/2 The Half-Penny Carriage. **1729** E. SMITH *Compleat Housewife* (ed. 3) 86 Slice a half-penny Loaf. **1747** H. GLASSE *Art of Cookery* xv. 140 Your Oven must be as hot as for Halfpenny Bread. **1762** BOSWELL *London Jrnl.* 21 Dec. (1950) 99 A halfpenny roll,.. which I had bought at a baker's. **1865** DICKENS *Mut. Fr.* I. v, A choice collection of halfpenny ballads. **1903** G. B. SHAW *Man & Superman* II. 54 Here comes the New Man, demoralizing himself with a halfpenny paper as usual. **1908** *Chambers's Jrnl.* Jan. 62/1 It ..marks as great advance upon the latter as does the incandescent gas-burner upon the halfpenny dip. **1909** H. G. WELLS *Tono-Bungay* III. iv. 423, I lost three pounds.. at ha'penny nap and euchre. **1914** 'SAKI' *Beasts & Super-Beasts* 116 The office of one of the halfpenny dailies. *a* **1930** D. H. LAWRENCE *Last Poems* (1932) 169 Oh carcase with a board-school mind and a ha'penny newspaper intelligence.

b. Expressing depreciation: To be had for a halfpenny; worth no more than a halfpenny; of contemptible value; trumpery. Also ***three-halfpenny, twopenny-halfpenny***.

1579 TOMSON *Calvin's Serm. Tim.* 481/1 These halfpenie knaues (as they cal them) these syr Iohns that are hired for three halfe pence, or two pence, or two pence halfe pennie. **1673** R. HEAD *Canting Acad.* 93 A *Low-Pad* is a base Sheep-stealing half-penny Rogue. **1721** STRYPE *Eccl. Mem.* II. xv. 370 Patrons.. gave some three half-penny priest a curate's wages. **1726** *Adv. Capt. R. Boyle* 2 Obliged to go on all her halfpenny Errands. **1759** STERNE *Tr. Shandy* I. i, Whether right or wrong, 'tis not a halfpenny matter. **1908** H. L. MENCKEN *Philos. Nietzsche* 284 Reich.. has attained the ha'penny celebrity he seems to crave in much the same manner. **1911** G. B. SHAW *Getting Married* 221 To lie down and let.. every halfpenny journalist walk over us.

halfpennyworth ('heɪpənɪwɜːθ), *sb.* Contracted **ha'p'orth, ha'porth** ('heɪpəθ). Also: α. 1 **healfpeniȝwurþ**, 5 **halpenyworth**, 6 **halpynworth**. β. 5 **halpworthe**, 6 **halporth**, 7 **half-p-worth, halfperth**, 8 **halp'worth, halforth**, 8–9 **ha'p'worth**, (*dial.* **hawporth**). [See WORTH.]

As much as a halfpenny will purchase; hence, a very small quantity.

α. *a* **1035** *Laws of Cnut* xii. (Thorpe) I. 366 Leoht ȝesceot .. healf-peniȝ-wurð wexes æt ælcere hide. **14..** *Voc.* in Wr.-Wülcker 598/26 *Obolatus*, an halfpeny worth. **1479** in *Eng. Gilds* (1870) 425 To serue the pouere people of penyworthes and halfpenyworthes. **1519** *Presentm. of Juries* in *Surtees Misc.* (1888) 32 A halpynworthe off hale for a halpney. **1596** SHAKS. *1 Hen. IV*, II. iv. 591. **1711** ADDISON *Spect.* No. 47 ¶7 To buy a Half-peny worth of Incle at a Shoemaker's. β. *c* **1490** *Promp. Parv.* 224/1 Halpeny worthe.. (*K.* halpworthe), *obolitas, oblata.* **1533** MORE *Debell. Salem* Wks. 132/2, I would wishe none heretike one halporth harme, that had clerely left his heresy. **1692** SOUTHERNE *Wives Excuse* I. i, Three halfperth of farthings. **1719** T. GORDON *Cordial Low Spirits* I. 142 Wearing out three Pens, and exhausting a Halfp'worth of Ink in her Service. **1728** SWIFT *Past. Dial.* Wks. 1755 III. II. 203 A longer ha'p'orth never did I see. **1738** —— *Pol. Conversat.* 169 Bring us a Halfporth of Cheese. **1838** DICKENS *Nich. Nick.* v, A penny loaf and a ha'porth of milk. **1873** BROWNING *Red Cott. Nt.-cap* III. 734 Haste and secure that ha'p'worth, on your life!

b. ***to lose the ship*** (orig. and prop. ***sheep, ewe, hog***) ***for a halfpennyworth of tar***: to lose an object, spoil an enterprize or court failure, by trying to save in a small matter of detail.

Originally referring to the use of tar to protect sore places or wounds on sheep from the destructive attacks of flies. (*Sheep* is dialectally pronounced *ship* over a great part of England.)

1631 CAPT. SMITH *Advt. Planters* 30 Rather.. to lose ten sheepe, than be at the charge of a halfe penny worth of Tarre. **1670** RAY *Proverbs* 103 Ne're lose a hog for a half-penny-worth of tarre [*ed.* **1678** 154 *adds* Some have it, lose not a sheep, &c. Indeed tarr is more used about sheep then swine.]. **1672** J. PHILLIPS *Maronides* VI. 22 And judge you now what fooles those are, Will lose a Hog for a ha'porth of tar. [**1705** J. SPRUEL in J. Smith *Mem. Wool* (1747) II. 66 So as the Proverb is verified, many a Time, we lose the Hog for the Halfpenny.] **1828** *Craven Dial.*, *Haworth*, 'Dunnut loaz t' yow for a hawporth o' tar'. **1869** HAZLITT *Eng. Proverbs* 431 'To spoil the ship for a half-pennyworth of tar.' *Note.* But in Cornwall I heard a version.. more consistent with probability, 'Don't spoil the *sheep* for a ha'porth of tar'. **1891** *Review of Reviews* IV. 576/1 To sink the ship by the refusal of the traditional ha'porth of tar.

†'**halfpennyworth**, *v.* *Obs.* [f. prec. sb.]

1. *intr.* To 'stick at' halfpence; to haggle about minute expenses.

1614 RALEIGH *Hist. World* v. vi. §4. 855 Their halfpenny worthing in matter of Expence when they had adventured their whole Estate in the purchase of a great Empire.

2. *trans.* To deal *out* by halfpennyworths.

1676 MARVELL *Mr. Smirke* 14 He having open'd the whole Pedlers-pack of his malice, which he half-p-worths out.. to his petty Chapmen.

half-pie ('hɑːfpaɪ), *a.* *N.Z. slang.* Also occas. **half-pi.** [perh. ad. Maori *pai* good.] Halfway towards, imperfect, mediocre. Also *absol.* or as *sb.*

c **1926** 'MIXER' *Transport Workers' Song Bk.* 11 There's no half-pie about this kid. **1938** R. FINLAYSON *Brown Man's Burden* 16 She would rather have a Maori who was a real man than a half-pie Pakeha who talked too much. *Ibid.* 78 A few straggling houses and a half-pie store. **1949** H. WADMAN *Life Sentence* I. i. 8 New Zealanders who go home on scholarships and come back half-pi Englishmen. **1952** R. FINLAYSON *Schooner came to Atia* x. 58 Half-pie commie and the gospel-thumpers together! **1955** *Landfall* IX. 274 He hadn't been a real officer, only a half-pie one.

half-pike. Now *Hist.* A small pike, having a shaft of about half the length of the full-sized one. There were two kinds; one, also called a *spontoon*, formerly carried by infantry officers; the other, used in ships for repelling boarders, a *boarding pike*.

1599 MASSINGER, etc. *Old Law* III. ii, Here's a half-pike. **1631** CHETTLE *Hoffman* II. C iij, Ile trie one course with thee at the halfepike, and then goe; come draw thy pike. **1698** FROGER *Voy.* 12 Their ordinary Arms are the Hanger, the Sagay [assagai], which is a very light Half-Pike. **1715** *Lond. Gaz.* No. 5358/2 The Duke of Guise with an Half-Pike in his Hand, being at the Head of the Regiment. **1769** FALCONER *Dict. Marine* (1789), *Demi-pique*, a half-pike, sometimes used to oppose boarders in a sea-fight. **1855** MACAULAY *Hist. Eng.* xiv. III. 422 Camp followers, armed with scythes, halfpikes, and skeans.

b. *Comb.*, as ***half-pike-man***.

1690 J. MACKENZIE *Siege London-Derry* 60/2 That the said Half-Pike-men.. be disarmed.

half-pounder (hɑːf'paʊndə(r)). [f. HALF *a.* + POUND *sb.* + -ER[1].]

1. A gun that fires a shot weighing half a pound. (In quot. *attrib.*) Cf. *four-pounder*, etc.

1800 *Phil. Trans.* XC. 235 We charged a half-pounder swivel with an ounce and an half.. of the mercurial powder.

2. A thing (e.g. a fish) of half a pound weight.

1886 R. C. LESLIE *Sea-painter's Log* x. 202 The great half-pounders are feeding in the broad spreading fords.

half-price.

1. Half the usual or full price; esp. that at which children or poor people are admitted to an entertainment or the like, or that at which people are admitted to a theatre when the performance is half through. Also, the time at which people are so admitted, 'half-time.'

1720 DE FOE *Capt. Singleton* xviii. (1840) 314 It was much better for us to sell all our cargoes here, though we made but half price of them. **1784** COWPER *Task* II. 624 A man o' the town dines late, but soon enough.. To insure a side-box station at half price. **1813** *Examiner* 15 Feb. 108/1 That class ..whom the half-price admits to disturb the order.. of the ..Theatres. **1848** THACKERAY *Bk. Snobs* xlviii, We drank mulled port till half-price. *Mod.* Children under 12, half-price.

2. *attrib.* or quasi-*adj.*

1836 DICKENS *Sk. Boz* ii. (1890) 41 Theatrical converse, arising out of their last half-price visit to the Victoria gallery. **1886** *Cornh. Mag.* July 59 Can this have been the origin of the old English half-price plan?

3. quasi-*adv.* At half-price.

1844 DICKENS *Mart. Chuz.* xxxii, He takes me half-price to the play. **1852** —— *Bleak Ho.* xi, To go half-price to the play.

†**half-rater.** *Obs.* A small racing yacht, so classed from 1891 to 1896; now called an 18-foot boat. (Also *attrib.*)

1894 *Daily News* 10 Sept. 3/4 Conditions.. imposed in order to keep out the ordinary racing half-rater. **1895** *Westm. Gaz.* 30 Jan. 4/1 A half-rater yawl of his design is a novelty.

half-round, *a.* and *sb.*

A. *adj.* Semicircular, in shape or section; semicylindrical; as ***half-bead, bit, channel, chisel, drill, file, gutter, -round, screw***.

half-round spade (*Whaling*), a spade with a blade resembling a carpenter's gouge, used in cutting the blanket piece free from the carcase.

1662 J. DAVIES tr. *Mandelslo's Trav.* 57 Baths.. which were made all halfround. **1671** MILTON *Samson* 1606 A spacious Theatre Half-round on two main Pillars. **1703** MOXON *Mech. Exerc.* 36 With the edge of an half-round File. *Ibid.* 193 Half-round holes or Semi-circles. **1884** F. J. BRITTEN *Watch & Clockm.* 95 For long holes of large diameter nothing beats a half-round drill. **1888** *Lockwood's Dict. Mech. Engin.* (1918) 169 Half-round chisel. **1934** *Burlington Mag.* Nov. 209/2 Chinese details, such as the half-round beads ending in small volutes. **1940** *Chambers's Techn. Dict.* 122/2 *Button-headed screws*, screws having hemispherical heads, slotted for a screwdriver; known also as half-round screws. **1967** *Gloss. Sanitation Terms (B.S.I.)* 13 *Half-round channel*, a channel (def. 2) of semi-circular cross section. *Ibid.* 23 *Half round gutter*, an eaves gutter having a half round cross section.

B. *sb.* **a.** A semicircle; a hemispherical figure.

1718 PRIOR *Knowledge* 638 This fair half-round, this ample azure sky. *a* **1721** —— *Her Right Name* 11 In her forehead's fair half-round. **1811** *Self Instructor* 27 In the midst of the half-round [of the quill]. **1867** *Common Sense Cook Bk.* 38 Half-Round of Beef should be put into cold water.

b. *Arch.* 'A semicircular moulding which may be a bead or torus' (Gwilt *Archit.* 1842–76).

So †**half-rounding** *a.*, forming a semicircle.

1667 MILTON *P.L.* IV. 862 The western point, where those half-rounding guards Just met, and closing stood in squadron joind.

†**half-seal.** *Obs.* The impression of the reverse side or 'foot' of the Great Seal, with which certain documents used to be sealed. (Cf. *half-bull*, under HALF- II n.) Abolished in 1833.

1509–10 *Act 1 Hen. VIII*, c. 16. §4 Lettres patentes.. under the great seale or halfe seale of Englond. **1530** in W. H. Turner *Select. Rec. Oxford* 91 A wrytyng..under the halff seale. **1566** *Act 8 Eliz.* c. 5 Nomynated and appointed by her Maiestie, her heyres or successours, by Commyssion under the Half Seale as it hath ben heretofore used in such Cases. **1641** *Termes de la Ley* 179 Halfe seale is a seale used in Chauncery for the sealing of Commissions unto Delegates upon an appeale in a cause civill or marine. **1832** *Act 2 & 3 Will. IV*, c. 92 §4 Nothing herein..shall..affect..the Right of His Majesty to grant any such Commission under the Great Seal or under the Half Seal as aforesaid, to hear..any Appeal..which may before the said First Day of February [1833] be pending.

half-seas-over. [*Seas* was prob. a genitive case; *half sea's* = half of the sea.]

1. Halfway across the sea.

1551 in Picton *L'pool Munic. Rec.* (1883) I. 107 The commodities..wch ben taken and retorned againe, when they be halfe the seas over. *a* **1618** RALEIGH *Invent. Shipping* 17 That ride it out at Anchor, half Seas over betweene England and Ireland. **1688** *Lond. Gaz.* No. 2396/4 About half Seas over, we discovered the Dutch Fleet. **1831** G. FOWLER *Jrnl. State N. York* 8 It was his intention to have kept below until he thought we were about half seas over, when we surely could not have refused to carry him through.

b. *transf.* and *fig.* Halfway towards a goal or destination, half through with a matter; halfway between one state and another.

1697 VANBRUGH *Relapse* III. ii, That's thinking half-seas over. *a* **1700** DRYDEN (J.), I am half-seas over to death. **1755** *Mem. Capt. P. Drake* I. xiii. 113, I returned them both my sincere Thanks, and thought myself half Seas over. **1823** BYRON *Juan* x. lxi, And hover Upon their airy confine, half-seas-over.

2. Half-drunk. (*humorous.*)

a **1700** B. E. *Dict. Cant. Crew*, *Half Seas over*, almost Drunk. **1714** *Spect.* No. 616. ¶4 Our friend the alderman was half seas over before the bonefire was out. **1880** SPURGEON *J. Ploughm. Pict.* 42 There's nothing too bad for a man to say or do when he is half-seas over.

half-shell. orig. *U.S.* Half an oyster shell. In phr. *on the half-shell*, served in this manner. Also *fig.*

1860 in *Amer. Speech* (1947) XXII. 203/1 Democrats fried,..roasted, or on the half shell. **1861** *Vanity Fair* 30 Mar. 148/1 Hard Shell,..and on the Half Shell Bapt-*ists*,.. and all other *ists*. **1872** E. EGGLESTON *End of World* 155 The eggs..were not roasted on the half-shell. **1880** 'MARK TWAIN' *Tramp Abroad* xlix. 574 Blue points, on the half shell. **1940** A. SIMON *Conc. Encycl. Gastron.* II. 70/1 *Bluepoints* are one of the most popular varieties on the half shell. **1972** E. HARGREAVES *Fair Green Weed* iii. 49 They.. ate..broiled lobster on the half-shell.

†**half-shirt.** *Obs.* A kind of shirt front for men, and chemisette for women, worn in 17th c.

1661 PEPYS *Diary* 13 Oct., This day left off half-shirts, and put on a wastecoate. **1664** *Ibid.* 28 June, This day put on a half-shirt first this summer, it being very hot. **1671** LADY MARY BERTIE in *12th Rep. Hist. MSS. Comm.* App. v. 23 The Dutchesse of Cleveland was very fine in a riche petticoat and halfe shirt, and a short man's coat. **1678** *Lond. Gaz.* No. 1343/4 One Half Shirt, with laced Cravat and Ruffles. *a* **1704** T. BROWN *Table-Talk* in *Collect. Poems* (1705) 128, I hate that Puppy..that goes open breasted; 'tis but a Half-Shirt. **1864** *Chambers' Bk. Days* II. 233/1 Half-shirts were stomachers, richly decorated with embroidery and lace, over which the bodice was laced from side to side.

half-shot, *a. colloq.* (orig. *U.S.*). [f. HALF- 1; cf. SHOOT *v.* 32 d.] Half drunk.

1838 J. C. NEAL *Charcoal Sks.* 13 Moseying is only to be done when a gemman's half shot. **1943** N. MARSH *Colour Scheme* x. 187 'The chap was half-shot,' said Simon. 'They all say he smelt of booze.' **1948** J. M. CAIN *Moth* 64 Stuff for guys in college to gag about when they were half shot with beer.

half-sister. [Not recorded in OE., though *healf-sweostor* was prob. in use: cf. MHG. *halpswester* (G. *halbschwester*), Sw. *halfsyster*, Da. *halvsöster*.]

1. A sister by one parent only.

c **1205** LAY. 8412 He wes his hælue suster sune. **13..** *Gaw. & Gr. Knt.* 2464 Arthurez half suster þe duches doȝter of Tyntagelle. *c* **1400** MAUNDEV. (Roxb.) xxv. 120 Half sisters of þer fader syde wedd þai. **1530** PALSGR. 228/2 Halfe suster, *seur uterine*. **1868** FREEMAN *Norm. Conq.* II. App. 587 The elder Countess Adelaide has been commonly taken to be only a half-sister of William.

fig. **1832** TENNYSON '*Love thou thy land*' 96 Raw Haste, half-sister to Delay. **1872** O. W. HOLMES *Poet Breakf.-t.* v. (1885) 118 The genius for religion..is half-sister to the genius for music.

†2. A lay sister in a convent. *Obs.*

1482 *Marg. Paston's Will* in *Paston Lett.* No. 861 III. 284 Iche hole and half susters at Normans in Norwich.

ˈ**half-snipe.** The jack snipe or lesser snipe, *Scolopax gallinula.* (Cf. *double snipe.*)

1766 PENNANT *Zool.* (1768) II. 360 The French call them *deux pour un*, we the *half snipe*. **1862** C. A. JOHNS *Brit. Birds* 448.

ˌ**half-ˈsovereign.**

1. An English gold coin, nominally worth 50 pence (ten shillings). The sum is also expressed by *half a sovereign.*

Originally (with the sovereign) coined in 1489 (but see quot. 1884); in the 17th c. these coins were superseded by the guinea and half-guinea, for which the sovereign and half-sovereign were again substituted in 1817: see SOVEREIGN.

1503–4 *Act 19 Hen. VII*, c. 5 §1 All maner of Gold of the Coynes of a Sovereyn Halfe Sovereyn [etc.]. **1551** *Proclam. Edw. VI*, in *Wriothesley's Chron.* (1877) II. 59 The half soueraigne of crowne gould of tenne shillinges. **1817** *Proclam.* in *Lond. Gaz.* 11 Oct. 2093/1 To order that certain pieces of gold money should be coined, which should be called 'half sovereigns or ten shilling pieces'. **1884** KENYON *Gold Coins Eng.* 77 This [the ryal] is doubtless the coin mentioned as a half-sovereign in the Statute 19 Henry VII, c. 5..As the reverse is unlike the ryals and the same as that of the sovereigns, it would very likely be popularly called a half-sovereign.

2. The name given by paviors to a 6-in. Purbeck stone pitcher; also to a granite pitching, because it is worth half a sovereign a yard (*Dict. Archit.* 1851).

half-staff. 1. = HALF-MAST.

1708 *Lond. Gaz.* No. 4489/2 The Ships Flags, which were only half-staff high. **1876** BANCROFT *Hist. U.S.* III. xix. 519 Pennants hoisted at half-staff.

†2. Half the length of a staff. *to fight at the half-staff*, to fight at close quarters with staves. *Obs.*

1603 KNOLLES *Hist. Turks* (1621) 517 The Persian horsemen also..bearing staves of good ash..fight with them as occasion servith at the halfe staffe.

half-starved, *a.* Having insufficient food; poorly fed.

1667 MILTON *P.L.* x. 595 Unnam'd, undreaded, and thyself half starv'd. **1713** [see HALF-NAKED]. **1879** GEO. ELIOT *Theo. Such* xv. 266 A half-starved Merry-Andrew.

†**half-strain.** *Obs.* The quality of being half of a good strain or stock and half of an inferior one; half-breed. Also *attrib.*

1673 DRYDEN *Amboyna* v. i, I am but of half-strain courage. **1678** —— *Limberham* III. i, I humbly conceive, you are of the half-strain at least.

Hence †ˈ**half-strained** *a. Obs.*

1682 DRYDEN & LEE *Dk. Guise* IV. iv, Half-strained shop-keepers, got between gentlemen and city wives. **1690** DRYDEN *Don Sebast.* III. i, I'm but a half-strained villain yet.

†ˈ**half-sword.** *Obs.*

1. A small-sized sword. Cf. HALF- II c.

1552 HULOET, Halfe sworde, *semispathium*. **1611** FLORIO, *Mezza arma*, a halfe-sword, any halfe weapon.

2. Half a sword's length. *to be at half-sword*, to be at close quarters with swords.

1589 *Pasquil's Ret.* D b, To meete with his wisedome at the halfe sword. **1596** SHAKS. *1 Hen. IV*, II. iv. 182. *a* **1616** BEAUM. & FL. *Bonduca* v. ii, I was four several times at half-sword with him.

half-thick, *a.* and *sb.*

A. *adj.* Of half the normal thickness: see quots.

1883 *Almondbury & Huddersfield Gloss.*, *Hauf-thick*, when applied to bacon means half-fed, or half-fat, but if to a man, half-witted. **1884** CASSELL, *Half-thick file*, a large coarse file with one rounded and three flat sides. It is used as a rubber-file for coarse work.

†B. *sb.* A kind of cloth. *Obs.*

1693 *Lond. Gaz.* No. 2914/4 Broad-Cloths, Serges half thicks, Duffils, Kerseys. **1745** *De Foe's Eng. Tradesman* xxvi. (1841) I. 258 Kerseys, cottons, half-thicks, duffields.. in Lancashire and Westmorland. **1748** *De Foe's Tour Gt. Brit.* III. 135 Rochdale..very considerable for a Sort of coarse Goods, called *Half-thicks* and *Kersies*.

ˈ**half-tide.**

1. The state of the tide half-way between flood and ebb, when it is half the height of high water.

1669 W. HACKE *Collect. Voy.* III. (1699) 61 A Rock that.. is covered at half Tide. **1862** ANSTED *Channel Isl.* II. ix. (ed. 2) 240 Innumerable pools of water left at halftide.

2. (See quots.)

1633 T. JAMES *Voy.* 62 It flowes halfe tyde, that is, from whence the flood commeth, the water thither returneth, two houres before it be high water. **1762** MORE in *Phil. Trans.* LII. 453 The different tides daily observed between Portsmouth and the Isle of Wight, called there tide and half-tide. **1843** *Penny Cycl.* XXVII. 146/1 When the stream continues to flow up for three hours after it is high-water, it is said to make tide and half-tide; if it continues to flow during one hour and a half, it is said to make tide and quarter-tide, and so on.

3. *attrib.* and *Comb.* Left dry or accessible at half-tide, as *half-tide cavern, rock*; **half-tide basin** or **dock**, one fitted with gates which are closed at half-ebb.

1847 CRAIG, *Half-tide dock*, a basin connecting two or more docks, and communicating with the entrance basin. **1854** H. MILLER *Sch. & Schm.* (1858) 532 Half-tide rocks, very dangerous to the mariner, which lie a full half-mile from the shore. **1862** ANSTED *Channel Isl.* II. ix. (ed. 2) 242 It is not every half-tide cavern that is thus inhabited. **1880** T. STEVENSON in *Encycl. Brit.* XI. 466/1 In order to extend the time during which vessels can enter or leave a wet dock there are two additional works which are often connected with it. These are the entrance-lock and the outer or half-tide basin.

Hence **half-tidal** *a.* = half-tide (*attrib.*).

1885 *Truth* 11 June 920/2 This difficulty might be met by a half-tidal lock and weir.

ˈ**half-ˌtimber,** *sb.* and *a.*

A. *sb. Ship-building.* (See quot.)

1847 in CRAIG. **1849–50** WEALE *Dict. Terms*, *Half-timbers*, in ship-building, those timbers in the cant bodies which are answerable to the lower futtocks in the square body.

B. *adj.* 1. Built half of timber.

1842–76 GWILT *Archit.* Gloss., *Half timber building*, a structure formed of studding, with sills, lintels, struts and braces, sometimes filled in with brickwork and plastered over on both sides. **1874** PARKER *Goth. Archit.* I. i. 10 Half-timber houses..of which the foundations and the ground-floors only are of stone, and the upper part of wood.

2. Made of timber split in half.

1874 J. H. COLLINS *Metal Mining* 42 Timbered with half-timber sets. *Ibid.* 80 In the middle of these half-timber bearers the uprights..are morticed.

Hence **half-timbered** *a.* = B 1.

a **1847** MRS. SHERWOOD *Lady of Manor* IV. xxiv. 80 At the porch of an old half-timbered cottage. **1893** K. L. BATES *Eng. Relig. Drama* 225 The many-gabled, half-timbered edifice of one of Edward VI's Free Grammar Schools.

half-time.

1. a. Half of a (particular) period of time.

1645 PAGITT *Heresiogr.* (1661) 282 Months, weeks, daies, and half-times, and such like Chronology.

b. (See quot.)

1860 O. W. HOLMES *Elsie V.* ii. (1887) 21 It is customary to allow half-time to students engaged in school-keeping, —that is, to count a year, so employed,..as equal to six months of the three years.

c. Half the usual or full time during which work is carried on. (In quot. 1862 as adv.)

1861 *Weekly Times* 13 Oct., Notices of cotton-mills being put upon half-time. **1862** H. SPENCER *First Princ.* II. viii. §72 Factories are worked half-time, or close entirely.

d. (See quot., also 3 below.)

1904 A. B. F. YOUNG *Compl. Motorist* iv. 118 All six valves are interchangeable and mechanically operated by rods worked from a cam shaft which is geared at half-time from the crank-axle.

e. Half the tempo of the performer; an accompaniment at half the tempo of the performer (see quot. 1961).

1938 D. BAKER *Young Man with Horn* iv. 265 They went into half-time together for a short coda. **1961** A. BERKMAN *Singers' Gloss. Show Business* 27 *Half-time*, while the singer continues singing the melody in the normal manner, the rhythmic complement is beat only half as fast as the original count.

f. *Chem.* (See quot.)

1957 *A.S.M.E. Gloss. Terms Nuclear Sci.* (1958) 72/2 *Half-time of exchange*, the time required for half the net realizable exchange of atoms in a chemical exchange reaction to take place.

2. In *Football*, etc., The time at which the first half of the game is completed.

1871 A. G. GUILLEMARD in *Bell's Life* 1 Apr., The call of 'Half-time' found the play exactly in the centre of the ground. **1894** *Times* 23 Feb. 4/2 Before half-time he kicked two goals out of the three registered for Middlesex.

3. *attrib.*, as in *half-time system*, the system by which school-children are enabled to attend school for half the usual time and spend the other half at some remunerative occupation; so *half-time register*, a register of half-time scholars. *half-time survey* of ships: see quot. 1894. **half-time shaft** = *half-speed shaft* (see HALF- II. n).

1861 *Illustr. Lond. News* 13 Apr. 353/3 The extending the half-time system. **1887** *Educational Department Circular* No. 271. 7 Apr., A separate *half-time register* will be kept of all half-time scholars. **1894** H. PASCH *From Keel to Truck* 466 *Half Time Survey*, this applies to wooden and composite vessels, on either of which a special survey is held, when about one half of the time for which they may have been classed, has elapsed. **1904** A. B. F. YOUNG *Compl. Motorist* iii. 49 The projecting part of a cam fixed on the half-time shaft. **1908** *Westm. Gaz.* 15 Oct. 4/2 The lubrication of the engine is carried out by a Dubrulle mechanical lubricator, fitted on the dash-board, and operated by an eccentric on the half-time shaft.

half-timer. One who spends half the usual or full time at anything. *spec.* a. One who works half-time in a factory.

1865 *Daily Tel.* 3 Nov. 5/5 Now a half-timer will get more than he once did for full time. **1883** *Standard* 30 Nov. 2/4 A child entered the mill as a half-timer at ten years old.

b. A half-time scholar: see HALF-TIME 3.

1870 [see FULL-TIMER 1]. **1879** ESCOTT *England* I. 260 The half-timer [at school] is compelled to be regular in attendance. **1890** *Times* 19 Sept. 7/5 Half-timers—that is, children who divide their time between the school and the factory.

half-tone, *sb.*

1. *Mus.* = SEMITONE.

1651 [see TONE *sb.* 4]. **1880** A. J. HIPKINS in Grove *Dict. Mus.* I. 685/1 The mechanism for raising the pitch of the strings [of a harp] one half tone..or two half tones.

2. *Art.* A tone intermediate between the extreme lights and extreme shades; one of the lighter shadows of a photograph, engraving, picture, etc.; esp. in *Printing* and *Photogr.*, a

photo-mechanical illustration printed from a block in which the tones are broken up into small or large dots by the interposition of a glass screen, ruled with fine cross-lines, between the camera and the object; this process. Also *attrib.*

1867 G. W. SIMPSON *Photographs in Pigments* 51 The imperative condition upon which half-tone depends, the exposure of one side of the film to light..seemed to present an insuperable difficulty. **1875** tr. *Vogel's Chem. Light* xv. 251 The pictures were especially wanting in half-tones. **1894** WILSON *Cycl. Photogr.* 179 A picture without half tones is harsh. **1894** *Times* 31 Jan. 3/3 The making of the blocks for the half-tone illustrations. **1911** *Encycl. Brit.* XIV. 325/1 Half-tone blocks..were used in the *Graphic* from 1884. **1937** E. J. LABARRE *Dict. Paper* 155/1 *Halftone paper*, a printing paper suitable for printing half-tone blocks. **1940** *Chambers's Techn. Dict.* 399/2 *Half-tone process*, a process of photographic reproduction in which the varying tones of the original are photographically translated into dots of uniform tone but varying size. **1958** *Times Lit. Suppl.* 17 Jan. 35/2 Such subjects as colour correction by masking, three-colour half-tone printing. **1959** *House & Garden* July 92/4 The publisher has had the sensible idea of backing his colour-plates..with half-tones in black-and-white. **1961** T. LANDAU *Encycl. Librarianship* (ed. 2) 160/2 *Half-tone screens*, transparent plates ruled diagonally with opaque lines at right angles to each other. **1967** KARCH & BUBER *Offset Processes* 541 *Halftone screen*, the ruled, plate glass dot-forming device used to translate continuous tones into halftones.

†**half-tone**, *v. Obs. rare*$^{-0}$. (?) To sing or play in semitones.

1483 *Cath. Angl.* 171/1 To Halfe tone, *semitonare.*

half-track. **1.** [TRACK *sb.*] A vehicle, usu. military, with wheels in front and traction chains in the rear; also *attrib.* Also ***half-tracked*** adj., of such a vehicle.

1927 *Daily Express* 7 Mar. 1/2 Though armoured cars are still tied to roads, the introduction of the half-tracked and the six-wheel carriage will..enable them to move over normal field land. **1935** *Sun* (Baltimore) 9 Feb. 2/3 This force would necessitate acquisition of 285 lightweight tanks ..and 76 half-track cars. **1943-4** *Hutchinson's Pict. Hist. War.* 27 Oct.–11 Apr. 236 Manned by American infantrymen, this half-track vehicle is stolidly ploughing its way through thick mud. **1945** *Times* 24 Mar. 4/1 Infantry with the task-force dropped off the half-tracks in which they travelled and flushed the woods. *Ibid.* 12 May 4/2 There were a few mechanical vehicles, including some of the standard half-tracked troop-carriers. **1955** *Ibid.* 6 June 5/1 Israel forces made use of machine-guns and half-tracked vehicles in an attack on Egyptian positions. **1973** *Jewish Chron.* 19 Jan. 1/1 (*caption*) An Israeli Army half-track vehicle carries civilians across a main square in Jerusalem as the capital lies under the heaviest fall of snow for 21 years.

2. Half the width of a magnetic tape.

1956 G. A. BRIGGS *High Fidelity* xi. 127 A full-width single track tape can always be played on a half-track machine. Half-tracks can, of course, be played with full-width heads only when the adjacent track is unrecorded. **1959** W. S. SHARPS *Dict. Cinematogr.* 101 *Half-track recorder*, a magnetic tape recorder using a recording head covering half the tape width, so that double the playing time is obtained with any given length of tape and speed. **1962** A. NISBETT *Technique Sound Studio* 273 The standard width for the recording of sound programmes is ¼-inch and this may be recorded full, half or quarter track.

half-truth. A proposition or statement which is or conveys only one half or a part of the truth.

1658 MANTON *Exp. Jude* 4 Half-truth hath filled the world with looseness. **1840** MILL *Diss. & Disc.* (1875) I. 398 The noisy conflict of half-truths. **1864** J. H. NEWMAN *Apol.* App. 91 A half-truth is often a falsehood.

b. *attrib.* or *Comb.*

1832 COLERIDGE *Lett.* (1895) 757 Self-designated Tories, and of course half-truthmen.

half-value. A value of a physical property that is half an earlier value; used esp. *attrib.*, as ***half-value period*** = HALF-LIFE 2; ***half-value thickness*** (see quot. 1938).

1903 *Phil. Mag.* V. 578 The activity of the radium emanation decays to half-value in four days. **1908** *Amer. Jrnl. Sci.* XXV. 506 The half-value period of radium is.. about 2000 years. **1910** *Nature* 6 Oct. 431/1 It is proposed that the term 'half-value period' should be used in all cases to represent the term required for a substance to be transformed to half its original value. **1922** *Times Lit. Suppl.* 18 May 318/2 The rate of decay of an element is measured by the 'half-value' period, which may vary from 10^{10} years to 10^{-11} of a second. **1938** R. W. LAWSON tr. *Hevesy & Paneth's Man. Radioactivity* (ed. 2) iii. 37 The intensity of the radiation is reduced to half its value in its passage through a layer of thickness 0·16 mm. Al... Accordingly, the 'half-value thickness' of aluminium for the β-rays from RaE has the value of 0·16 mm. **1955** C. CROXSON in W. C. Newell *Casting of Steel* xii. 531 Some half-value thicknesses for steel are shown in the following table. **1962** F. I. ORDWAY et al. *Basic Astronautics* xii. 500 A useful concept in physical shielding is that of the *half value layer* (HVL) or the thickness of a specific material required to reduce a particular quantity of radiation by half. **1963** W. E. BURCHAM *Nucl. Physics* ii. 30 The interval..during which half the atoms disappear by decay (half-value period or half-life).

half-way, halfway (hɑːfweɪ: see below), *adv.*, *adj.*, *sb.*, and *prep.* [f. HALF *a.* + WAY *sb.*]

A. *adv.* (Stressed *ˈhalfway* when preceding the word it qualifies, *ˌhalfˈway* when following.) At or to half the distance. ***to meet halfway***: see MEET *v.*

c **1386** CHAUCER *Reeve's Prol.* 52 Lo Depeford and it is half wey pryme. **1530** PALSGR. 861/2 Halfe waye, *au milieu du chemyn*, or *a my chemyn.* **1596** SHAKS. *Tam. Shr.* I. i. 62 I-wis it is not halfe way to her heart. **1674** N. FAIRFAX *Bulk & Selv.* Contents, An halfway boundless Bulk. *c* **1696** PRIOR *Love Disarmed* 12 Her bodice half-way she unlac'd. **1717** FREZIER *Voy. S. Sea* 106 A little above half way up a high mountain. **1726** SHELVOCKE *Voy. round World* (1757) 198 Before I had got half way off. **1766** GOLDSM. *Vic. W.* x, About halfway home. **1812** BYRON *Ch. Har.* II. lxix, Combined marauders half-way barr'd egress. **1886** BESANT *Childr. Gibeon* II. vi, The morning service was halfway through. **1926** J. BLACK *You can't Win* (1927) v. 60 She had cleaned up the room till it looked halfway decent. **1938** *Times* 25 May 17/3 He shows how much remains to be done before the standard of life of the West Indian labourer and of the West Indian peasant is raised to a level which can be regarded as halfway tolerable. **1942** *R.A.F. Jrnl.* 16 May 12 There is a drill which must be followed if the voyage is going to be halfway comfortable for everybody. **1960** H. PINTER *Caretaker* III. 77 He's nutty, he's half way gone.

B. *adj.* (Usually stressed *ˈhalfway.*)

1. Midway or equidistant between two points. ***half-way house***, a house (often an inn) situated midway between two towns or stages of a journey, and therefore considered as a convenient halting-place. Also *fig.*

1694 W. BURNABY tr. *Petronius's Satyricon* 21 We could not reach Lycurgus's that Night, and therefore he brought us to a half-way House. **1711** ADDISON *Spect.* No. 511 ⁋3 He was resting with it upon a half-way Bridge. **1793** in *Corr. Ld. Auckland* (1861) II. 515 Yours will be an excellent half-way house, almost as good as the inn at Bromley. **1839** ALISON *Hist. Europe* (1849–50) VII. xlii. §32. 115 The Cape of Good Hope had become a half-way house to their possessions in Bengal. **1856** KANE *Arct. Expl.* I. xvi. 195 My aim was to reach the halfway tent. **1901** S. E. WHITE *Westerners* xix. 164 Copper Creek had begun as a half-way house, and had ended as a camp. **1967** *Canad. Ann. Rev. 1966* 92 There was still need for such things as halfway group homes, preventive delinquency programs [etc.]. **1970** 'T. COE' *Wax Apple* (1973) iii. 24 Halfway houses are places for people returning to society but unable or unwilling to make the plunge all at once. There are halfway houses for ex-drug addicts, former convicts. **1973** *Canadian Antiques Collector* Jan.–Feb. 26/2 The buildings known as half-way houses.. were the inns stationed halfway between the larger centres to accommodate weary travellers.

2. *fig.* That is midway between two states or conditions; half one thing and half another.

169. *Ad Pop. Phaleræ* II. ii. 29 You're then Phanatick, Neuter, Half-way-man, Or mungrel Latitudinarian. **1790** HAN. MORE *Relig. Fash. World* (1791) 231 Some half-way state, something between paganism and christianity. **1855** PRESCOTT *Philip II*, I. II. xi. 261 It fared with this compromise..as with most..half-way measures. **1903** *Daily Chron.* 3 Nov. 4/4 The halfway state between maidenhood and womanhood. **1909** *Ibid.* 31 Dec. 1/5, I am no halfway burglar, and I would kill a man for 2½d. **1962** *Guardian* 19 Nov. 16/1 These buildings are used by the LCC as 'halfway housing' for homeless families.

C. *sb.* **a.** A point or position midway between two extreme points; a halfway place or house.

1634 SIR T. HERBERT *Trav.* 13 Cape of good Hope..being the halfe way into India. *c* **1665** MRS. HUTCHINSON *Mem. Col. Hutchinson* (1848) 46 In the halfway between Owthorpe and Nottingham. **1897** *Daily News* 23 Feb. 3/1 The door opens to a hospitable halfway.

b. The half-way line in a football field.

1960 V. JENKINS *Lions down Under* 202 New Zealand brought the ball back to half-way.

†**D.** *prep.* Half-way up, down, along, etc. *Obs.*

1613 PURCHAS *Pilgrimage* (1614) 488 A cloth..which reacheth halfe way the thigh. **1706** WATTS *Horæ Lyr.* I. *Devotion & Muse* iii, Faint devotion panting lies Half way th' ethereal hill.

ˈhalf-wit. [See WIT *sb.*]

†**1.** One who is only half a wit; a dealer in poor witticisms. *Obs.*

1678 DRYDEN *All for Love* Prol., Half-wits are fleas; so little and so light, We scarce could know they live, but that they bite. **1713** STEELE *Englishman* No. 43. 280 Pen and Ink ..in the Hands of a Half-Wit will do more Mischief than Sword and Dagger. *a* **1720** SHEFFIELD (Dk. Buckhm.) *Wks.* (1753) II. 208 Let the half-wits do it, 'tis their drudgery.

2. One who has not all his wits; a half-witted person. Also *attrib.*

1755 JOHNSON, *Half-wit*, a blockhead or foolish fellow. **1828** in WEBSTER. **1853** A. J. MORRIS *Bible* Introd. 8 Fools and half-wits think themselves justified in calling prophets and apostles to order. **1884** J. H. WYLIE *Hist. Hen. IV*, I. 268 He often acted like a half-wit or a madman. **1938** F. SCOTT FITZGERALD *Let.* Spring (1964) 29 We are setting it aside till we think of a way of half-witting halfwit Hayes and his Legion of Decency. **1960** *Times* 24 Sept. 10/7 Their half-wit uncle.

ˈhalf-ˌwitted, *a.* [f. *half wit* + -ED².]

1706 HEARNE *Collect.* 12 Dec. I. 312 A man of half wit.]

†**1.** Lacking or deficient in (common) sense or reason; simple; senseless. *Obs.*

c **1645** HOWELL *Lett.* (1650) II. 32 To have to doe with perverse, irrationall, half-witted men. **1647** CLARENDON *Hist. Reb.* VI. §102 The half hearted, and half witted people, which made much the major part of both Houses. *a* **1716** BLACKALL *Wks.* (1723) I. 228 As if we should call a Man an idle, vain, empty, shallow-pated, or half-witted Fellow. **1797** GODWIN *Enquirer* I. ii. 8 A self-satisfied, half-witted fellow, is the most ridiculous of all things.

2. Not having all his wits; imbecile; daft.

1712 ARBUTHNOT *John Bull* III. App. ii, A poor, simple.. half-witted, crack-brained fellow. **1732** BERKELEY *Alciphr.* I. §3 A poor half-witted man that means no mischief. **1876** BANCROFT *Hist. U.S.* VI. xxx. 92 A half-witted king, every day growing feebler in mind.

Hence **half-wittedness**.

1832 *Westm. Rev.* XVII. 273 If the attempt to hedge-in gold and silver was unmixed folly, the Mercantile System was the kind of hybrid denominated half-wittedness.

ˈhalf-word. A word or speech which hints or insinuates something, instead of fully asserting it; a hint, suggestion.

c **1369** CHAUCER *Dethe Blaunche* 1022 She wolde not fonde To holde no wight in balaunce By halfe worde ne by countenaunce. **1581** PETTIE *Guazzo's Civ. Conv.* III. (1586) 161 b, He said..he understood by yᵉ halfe word, what the whole ment. **1741** RICHARDSON *Pamela* (1824) I. 118 Only by one rash half-word [he was] exasperated against me. **1856** MRS. BROWNING *Aur. Leigh* VI. 1224 We must scrupulously hint With half-words, delicate reserves.

half-year. The half of a year; six months. As a space of time, expressed by *half a year.* **b.** In Schools, etc. = HALF *sb.* 6 a.

c **907** in Earle *Land Charters* 164 Ymb an oðer healf ȝear. **1154** *O.E. Chron.* an. 1137, xx wintre & half ȝær & viii dæis. *c* **1386** CHAUCER *Reeve's T.* 51 A child þat was of half yeer age. **1473** WARKW. *Chron.* 3 He departed oute of Englonde after halff ȝere. **1596** SHAKS. *1 Hen. IV*, IV. i. 136, I am out of feare Of death, or deaths hand, for this one halfe yeare. **1611** FLORIO, *Mezzannata*, a halfe-yeares rent. **1718** *Freethinker* No. 56. 3 I can open this Half-year with congratulating my Disciples. **1857** HUGHES *Tom Brown* II. i, The Doctor now talking of holiday doings, and then of the prospects of the half-year, what chance there was for the Balliol scholarship [etc.].

half-ˈyearly, *a.* and *adv.*

A. *adj.* Happening every half-year or six months.

1660 WILLSFORD *Scales Comm.* 70 Half yearly or quarterly payments. *Mod.* He pays a half-yearly visit to London.

B. *adv.* Each half-year; twice in a year.

a **1687** PETTY *Pol. Arith.* (1690) 111 The Rents..are paid half yearly. **1884** *Law Rep.* 25 Ch. Div. 717 At liberty to draw out half-yearly the moneys.

halgh(e, halȝ(e, -en, obs. ff. HOLY, HALLOW.

hali, obs. form of HALELY, WHOLLY, HOLY.

halibut (ˈhælɪbʌt, -ət), **holibut** (ˈhɒlɪbʌt). Forms: α. 5–6 **halybutte**, 7 **allebut**, 7–8 **hallibut**, 7– **halibut**. β. 7 **holybut**, 7–8 **hollibut(t**, 8 **hollybut(t**, 7– **holibut**. [app. f. *haly*, HOLY + BUTT *sb.*¹ flat fish: cf. mod.Du. *heilbot* (in Kilian *heylbot*, *eelbot*), LG. *heilbutt*, *heilige butt*, Norse *heilagfiski*, Sw. *helgeflundra*, Da. *helleflynder* i.e. holy flounder: supposed to be so called from being so commonly eaten on holy-days.] A large flat fish (*Hippoglossus vulgaris*), abundant in the northern seas, and much used for food. (Plural *halibuts*, also collectively *halibut.*)

c **1430** *Two Cookery-bks.* 60 Halybutte. Plays fryid. **1570** LEVINS *Manip.* 195/27 Halybutte, fish. **1616** CAPT. SMITH *Descr. New Eng.* 30 Cod, Cuske, Holybut [**1624** *Virginia* VI. 216 Hollibut] Mackerell, Scate. **1620** VENNER *Via Recta* iv. 75 The Hallibut is a big fish, and of great accompt. **1674** RAY *Collect. Words, Sea Fishes* 99 Holibut or Halibut. **1743** *Phil. Trans.* XLII. 612 Sharks, Hollybutts, Red-fish, Trout. **1854** BADHAM *Halieut.* 358 The hippoglossus vulgaris, or holibut..individuals have been captured nearly eight feet in length, four in breadth, and a span thick. **1865** TYLOR *Early Hist. Man.* xi. 302 An Indian canoe was out catching halibut.

b. Applied to other flat fish of the family *Pleuronectidæ*, as the *Greenland halibut* (*Reinhardtius hippoglossoides*), and the *Monterey halibut* or *bastard halibut* of California (*Paralichthys californicus*).

c. *attrib.* and *Comb.*, as ***halibut-killer***; **halibut-broom**, a disgorger for halibut; **halibut-slime**, a kind of sea-anemone, parasitic on halibut.

1883 *Fisheries Exhib. Catal.* 195 Halibut-killer and gobstick for killing the fish and disgorging the hook.

Hence **ˈhalibutter, ˈholibutter**, a vessel engaged in the halibut-fishery.

halic, early ME. form of HALELY, WHOLLY.

halichondroid (hælɪˈkɒndrɔɪd), *a. Zool.* [f. mod.L. *Halichondria*, name of a genus of sponges (f. Gr. ἅλς, ἁλι- sea + χόνδρος cartilage) + -OID.] Related to a group of sponges including *Halichondria palmata*, the largest British sponge.

1887 SOLLAS in *Encycl. Brit.* XXII. 427/2 A very common Halichondroid sponge.

‖**Halicore** (həˈlɪkəriː). *Zool.* [f. Gr. ἅλς, ἁλι- sea + κόρη maiden, lit. 'mermaid'.] Name of the genus of Sirenians, found in the Red Sea and Indian Ocean, to which the Dugong belongs.

1828 J. STARK *Elem. Nat. Hist.* I. 161 Halicore, Cuv... Dugungus, Lacep. **1847** CARPENTER *Zool.* §305 The Dugong or Halicore is a native of the Indian Seas. **1883** *Cassell's Nat. Hist.* II. 269 The Dugong, typical of the genus Halicore, is a living form, ordinarily from ten to twelve feet long.

halidai, obs. form of HOLIDAY, HOLY-DAY.

halide ('heɪlaɪd). *Chem.* [f. HAL(OGEN + -IDE.] A binary compound formed from a halogen and a metal or radical. Also *attrib.*

1876 *Encycl. Brit.* V. 571/2 Acid Halides..may be regarded as the haloid ethers of acid radicles. **1927** N. V. SIDGWICK *Electronic Theory Valency* vi. 88 The halides of the elements show a similar differentiation into volatile non-salts and non-volatile salts. **1938** *Jrnl. R. Aeronaut. Soc.* XLII. 363 An attempt is made to explain the photolysis of silver halides in terms of the concepts of atomic physics. **1948** *Electronic Engin.* XX. 20 If a thin layer of alkali-halide crystals is bombarded with electrons, some electrons are displaced from the halides and secondaries are produced. **1957** *Jrnl. Chem. Soc.* 2071 (*title*) A new preparation of steroid halides.

†**halidom** ('hælɪdəm), **-dome** (dəʊm). *Obs.* or *arch.* Forms: 1 **háliȝdóm**, 2–3 **haliȝdom**, 4 **halydam**, 4–7 **halydom**, **halidam**, 5–6 **holydom(e**, 6 **hollidam(e**, **hollydam**, 6–7 **halli-**, 6–9 **halidome**, 7 **haly-doome**, **holidam(e**, **holydam(e**, 8–9 **halidame**, 3– **halidom**. [OE. *háliȝdóm* = MDu. *heilichdoem* (Du. *heiligdom*), OHG. *heilîgtuom* (Ger. *heiligtum*), ON. *helgidómr* (Da. *helligdom*), f. OTeut. **hailag-*, OE. *háliȝ*, HOLY: see -DOM. The substitution of *-dam*, *-dame*, in the suffix was app. due to popular etymology, the word being taken to denote 'Our Lady'.]

†**1.** Holiness, sanctity. *Obs.*

971 *Blickl. Hom.* 167 Mycel is se haliȝdom & seo weorþunȝ Sancte Iohannes. *c* **1200** ORMIN 2117 Hiss haliȝdom Was godedd himm and ekedd. *a* **1626** BP. ANDREWES *Serm.* xiii. (1661) 488 Then had it His perfect halydome; then it was holy indeed.

2. A holy place, chapel, sanctuary. *arch.*

c **1000** ÆLFRIC *Exod.* xxi. 6 Bringe his hlaford hine to þæs haliȝdomes dura. **1636** JAMES *Iter Lanc.* (Chetham Soc.) 2 They were not onely streets but halydoms. **1820** SCOTT *Monast.* ii, Under the necessity of marching with the men of the Halidome, as it was called, of Saint Mary's. **1839** BAILEY *Festus* v. (1848) 46 The world Is Thy great halidom.

3. A holy thing, a holy relic; anything regarded as sacred. Much used, down to 16th c., in oaths and adjurations.

c **1000** *Laws of Ethelred* III. c. 2 On þam haliȝdome swerian þe him man on hand sylð. *c* **1200** ORMIN 1785 Itt iss Godess arrke, & iss All full off haliȝdomess. *c* **1205** LAY. 15343 Ær he heom hæfden isworen uppen halidom. **1303** R. BRUNNE *Handl. Synne* 5629 Þat dar y swere on þe halydom. **13..** *Gaw. & Gr. Knt.* 2123 As help me God & þe halydam. *a* **1483** *Gild Tailors Exeter* in *Eng. Gilds* 318 As god you helpp and holydom. **1529** MORE *Dyaloge* III. Wks. 237/2 My Lordes all, as helpe me God and halidome maister doctour here sayd vnto me [etc.]. *c* **1561** T. PRESTON *Cambyses* in Hazl. *Dodsley* IV. 244 So help me God and halidom, it is pity of his life. [**1874** STUBBS *Const. Hist.* I. v. 103 *note*, Let the twelve senior thegns..swear on the halidome which shall be put in their hands.]

b. Hence the asseveration: *by my halidom.*

1533 J. HEYWOOD *Johan & Tib* B ij, Nowe so God helpe me, and by my holydome. **1567** *Triall Treas.* in Hazl. *Dodsley* III. 276 Now, by my halidom, it is alone. **1591** SHAKS. *Two Gent.* IV. ii. 136 By my hallidome, I was fast asleepe. **1613** —— *Hen. VIII*, v. i. 117 Now by my Holydame, What manner of man are you? **1765** H. WALPOLE *Otranto* v. (1798) 79 By my halidame, if it should ever be known. **1823** SCOTT *Quentin D.* ii, 'By my halidome, he is ashore.'

halie, obs. form of HALE *v.*, HOLY.

halier, early form of HALYARD.

halieutic (hælɪ'juːtɪk), *a.* and *sb.* [ad. L. *halieuticus*, a. Gr. ἁλιευτικός, f. ἁλιευτής fisher, f. ἁλιεύειν to fish, f. ἅλς the sea.]

A. *adj.* Of or belonging to fishing.

1854 BADHAM *Halieut.* 85 Suggestive of old halieutic associations.

B. *sb. pl.* **halieutics**: The art or practice of fishing; a treatise on fishing.

1646 SIR T. BROWNE *Pseud. Ep.* I. viii. 32 Foure bookes of Cynegeticks or venation, five of Halieuticks or piscation. **1696** J. EDWARDS *Exist. God* I. 192 Other particulars which are mention'd in halieuticks. **1854** BADHAM (*title*) Prose Halieuticks; or Ancient and Modern Fish Tattle.

Hence **hali'eutical** *a.* = HALIEUTIC *a.*; **hali'eutically** *adv.*, in relation to fishing.

1851 *Fraser's Mag.* XLIV. 437 Halieutical. **1883** *Sat. Rev.* 22 Dec. 796 To be halieutically encyclopædic.

Halifax ('hælɪfæks). [The name of a town in the West Riding of Yorkshire.] *go to Halifax*: see GO *v.* 30 b. (Now regarded as a euphemism for *hell.*) Also in phr. *from Hell, Hull, and Halifax, Good Lord, deliver us* (see quot. *a* 1661).

In U.S., sometimes with supposed allusion to Halifax, Nova Scotia.

1630 J. TAYLOR *Works* 115/2 Now if my Whore or Thiefe play well their parts, Give them their due, applaud their good deserts. If ill, to Newgate hisse them, or Bridewell, To any place, Hull, Halifax or Hell. *a* **1661** T. FULLER *Worthies* (1662) Yorks. 189 From Hell, Hull, and Halifax,——deliver us... This is part of the Beggars and Vagrants Letany... Halifax, is formidable unto them for the Law thereof, whereby Theeves taken..in the very Act of stealing of cloath, are instantly beheaded with an Engine, without any further Legal Proceedings. **1669** [see GO *v.* 30 b]. **1807** *Deb. Congress U.S.* (1852) 11 Dec. 1169 Instead of sending it [*sc.* a ship] where he wished it had gone, to Halifax, or to the bottom. **1875**- in *Eng. Dial. Dict.* s.v. **1876** *Congress. Rec.* 4 Aug. 5185/1 'Go to Halifax' was a substitute for a more impious, but not more opprobrious expression. **1882** *Ibid.* 13 July 6015/1 He told them..that he had no further use for them, and they could go home, ashore, or to Halifax. **1920** H. J. JENNINGS *Chestnuts & Small Beer* xiii. 140, I refused to admit that I had made a *faux pas*, and told my critics to go to Halifax.

haliȝ, -en, obs. forms of HOLY, HALLOW.

haligraphy (hə'lɪgrəfɪ). [f. Gr. ἅλς, ἁλι- salt + -γραφια writing.] A treatise or dissertation on the nature and quality of salts.

1854 in MAYNE *Expos. Lex.* **1886** in *Syd. Soc. Lex.*

halik, ME. var. HALELY *Obs.*, wholly.

'hali,keld. *north. dial.* [f. *hali*, HOLY + KELD, a. Norse *kelda* spring, well.] A holy well.

1891 ATKINSON *Moorland Par.* 132 The pins cast into the halikeld.

ha'limetry. [f. Gr. ἅλς, ἁλι- salt + -μετρία measurement.] The measurement of the amount of saline matter in a solution. Hence **hali'metric** *a.*, relating to halimetry. (*Syd. Soc. Lex.* 1886).

halimot(e, var. of HALLMOTE.

halimous ('hælɪməs), *a.* [f. Gr. ἅλιμος of or belonging to the sea (f. ἅλς sea) + -OUS.]

1854 in MAYNE *Expos. Lex.* **1886** *Syd. Soc. Lex.*, *Halimous* ..of, or belonging to, the sea; marine; maritime. Also..of, or belonging to salt; saline; salt.

haling ('heɪlɪŋ), *vbl. sb.* [f. HALE *v.*[1] + -ING[1].] The action of the verb HALE; dragging, hauling.

c **1440** *Promp. Parv.* 223/1 Halynge, or drawynge, *tractus.* **1584** FENNER *Def. Ministers* (1587) 41 By haling and pulling of sentences. **1641** MILTON *Ch. Govt.* II. iii. (1851) 159 The beggarly help of halings and amercements. **1791** R. MYLNE *Rep. Thames & Isis* 27 Cutting down the Trees which annoy the haleing of Boats.

b. *attrib.*, as *haling-path*, *-way.*

1726 *Lond. Gaz.* No. 6447/7 For Towing or Haleing-Paths. **1784** *Mkt. Weighton Drainage Award* 10 A haleing way, or towing path, along the east side of the said canal.

†**'halinitre.** *Obs.* [ad. mod.L. *halinitrum*, f. ἅλς salt + νίτρον nitre.] A name for saltpetre.

1608 TOPSELL *Serpents* (1658) 741 If the fat of a Lizard is mixed with Wheat-meal, Halinitre, and Cumin it maketh Hens very fat. **1672** T. VENN *Compl. Gunner* viii. 10 Artificial Salt-Peter, Sal Nitre, or Halinitre.

'halinous, *a.* [f. Gr. ἅλινος made of or from salt + -OUS.] Containing or consisting of salt; saline. (*Syd. Soc. Lex.* 1886.)

†**hali'ography.** *Obs.* [f. Gr. ἅλς, ἁλι- sea + -γραφια writing.] A description of the sea (Blount *Glossogr.* 1656). So †**hali'ographer**, a describer of the sea (Bailey vol. II. 1727).

‖**haliotis** (hælɪ'əʊtɪs). *Zool.* [f. Gr. ἅλς, ἁλι- sea + οὖς, ὠτ- the ear; so called from their resemblance to the human ear.] A genus of univalve shells, the Ear-shells, the tropical species of which are an important source of mother-of-pearl. One species is found as far north as Guernsey. Also *attrib.*

1752 SIR J. HILL *Hist. Anim.* 118 (Jod.) The great ear shell: the haliotis, with an even edge, and with seven holes. **1845** E. J. WAKEFIELD *Adv. N. Zealand* I. 241 These hooks ..take their name from the *haliotus*[sic]-shell, with pieces of which they are lined. **1883** *Q. Rev.* Jan. 200 Cattle, skins, timber, coal, seaweed, and haliotis, are plentiful enough. **1931** *Oxf. Univ. Gaz.* 17 June 715/2 Toe-bone with carved face and *haliotis* eyes.

Hence **hali'otoid** *a.*, akin to the Ear-shell.

1864 in WEBSTER.

†**halit.** *Obs. rare*⁻¹. [ad. L. *halit-us* breath.] Exhalation, perfume.

1657 TOMLINSON *Renou's Disp.* 377 Their gratious halit.

halite ('hælaɪt). *Min.* [ad. mod.L. *halītes* (Glocker, 1847), f. Gr. ἅλς salt.] Rock salt.

1868 DANA *Min.* 112 *Halite*, common salt. **1879** *Encycl. Brit.* X. 228/2 *Halite* or *Rock-salt* (chloride of sodium) is more widely diffused than was formerly supposed.

halithere ('hælɪθɪə(r)). [ad. mod.L. *Halithērium*, f. Gr. ἅλς, ἁλι- sea + θηρίον beast.] An animal of the genus *Halitherium* of extinct Sirenia.

1880 DAWKINS *Early Man* iv. 80 Halithere, so closely allied to the manatee of Africa and America.

halitosis (hælɪ'təʊsɪs). *Med.* [mod.L., f. L. *halitus* breath + -OSIS.] An abnormally odorous condition of the breath; foul breath.

1874 J. W. HOWE *Breath & Dis.* i. 20 Chronic poisoning from lead, arsenic, or mercury, may also be enumerated as a common cause of halitosis. **1928** *Punch* 17 Oct. 427/1, I shall become a mere mass of degenerate tissues, and flaccid muscles,..with probably a touch of halitosis and lethargy. **1934** S. ROBERTSON *Develop. Mod. Eng.* (1936) XI. 447 Thus *halitosis*, the happy discovery of purveyors of mouth-washes, has found a wider usefulness, and *bad breath* is taboo. **1957** *Times Lit. Suppl.* 12 July 426/4 The dismissed Mulcahy, sadly proud of his porous complexion, bad teeth and occasional morning halitosis.

halituous (hə'lɪtjuːəs), *a.* [f. L. *halitus*: see next.] Of the nature of breath or vapour; vaporous; charged with or characterized by vapour.

1616 J. BULLOKAR *Eng. Expos.*, *Halituous*, vaporous, thin, moist, which may be voided out by the pores. **1684** tr. *Bonet's Merc. Compit.* XVIII. 620 An halituous Poyson is sent from the Antimony. **1757** WALKER in *Phil. Trans.* L. 130 The blueish tincture, which it received from this halituous body. **1886** *Syd. Soc. Lex.*, *Halituous heat*, heat of the body accompanied by a slight moisture on the skin. *H. skin*, a skin covered with slight moisture.

Hence **halitu'osity**, vaporous quality.

1710 T. FULLER *Pharm. Extemp.* 412 Wedelius saith it [the tincture]..concentres the Halituosity..of the Serum.

‖**halitus** ('hælɪtəs). [L. *halitus* breath, f. *halāre* to breathe.] A vapour, exhalation.

1661 EVELYN *Fumifugium* Misc. Writ. I. (1805) 227 The same dangerous halitus of char-cole. **1675** —— *Terra* (1729) 14 Evaporating the malignant Halitus's and impurities of the imprisoned Air. **1758** W. BORLASE *Nat. Hist. Cornwall* 25 The faintings which seize the workmen, are owing..to.. the heat..not to a sulphureous or mineral halitus. **1875** T. HAYDEN *Dis. Heart* 9 If the pericardium be laid open..its serous surface will be found moistened..by a fine halitus.

haliwei, -wey, var. of HALEWEI, *Obs.*

Haliwerfolk ('hælɪwə,fəʊk). *Obs.* exc. *Hist.* Forms: 1–2 **haliwere(s)folc**, 2 **-werefolk**, 3–4 **-warfolc**, **-folk**, 4–5, 9 (*Hist.*) **-werfolk**, **-folc**, 5 **-waresfolc**, **-ueresfolch**, 8 **-wor-folk**, 9 **halywerfolc.** Also, corruptly, 4 **(h)aliwarcfolk**, 7– **haly-**, **holy-**, **-wark-**, **-work-**, **-folk.** [OE. **haliȝweresfolc*, people of the holy man or saint (cf. Bæda IV. xxvii. þone halȝan wer... Cuþbyrht).] The folk of the holy man or saint (Cuthbert); those who held their lands by the service of defending the body, relics, and territory of St. Cuthbert; also the county of Durham wherein they dwelt.

Called in Life of St. Cuthbert, *c* 1450 (Surtees) 4608 'Cuthbert folk', 7517 'þe saint pople'.

1099–1126 *Charter* in *Finchale* (Surtees) 20 Rannulfus.. ominibus hominibus suis, Francis et Anglis, de Haliweresfolc, salutem. ?**12..** *Charter* in *Newminister Cartulary* (Surtees) 133 Unam bovatam terræ in Cunsdine, quæ est in Haliwerefolc. *c* **1303** *Reg. Pal. Dunelm.* (Rolls) III. 39 Antiquiores totius Haliwarfolk' et Northumbriæ. **1430** *Feodarium Prioratus Dunelm.* (Surtees) (*passim*), Haliwerfolc, Haliwaresfolc, Halieuresfolch. **1816** SURTEES *Hist. Durham* I. xxxiii, The tenants of St. Cuthbert, who pleaded their privilege of Halywerfolc. **1892** BOYLE *County of Durham* 74 The tenants..on several occasions claimed that they were Haliwerfolk, the folk or men of the holy man (*wer*).

¶ In some 14th c. documents (after *wer* was obsolete), misunderstood and corrupted as *halywark-folk*, i.e. people who had the *holy work* of defending the body etc. of St. Cuthbert.

1311 *Reg. Pal. Dunelm.* (Rolls) I. 8 A senioribus de Aliwarkfolk' et Northumbriæ. **1316** *Rot. Parl* 9 *Edw. II*, No. 8 *Ibid.* IV. 137 In libertate episcopi Dunolmensis de Haliwarcfolks. **1610** HOLLAND *Camden's Brit.* I. 736 They pleaded..that they were Haliwerke folkes, and held their lands to defend the Corps of Saint Cuthbert. **1627** SPEED *England* (1666) P b, Whose charge..was to keep and defend the corps of S. Cuthbert their great adored Saint, and therefore they termed themselves, The holy work folks. **1846** *Brockett's N.C. Gloss.* (ed. 3) 207 The *Halywercfolk* or holy work people.

halk, obs. Sc. form of HAWK.

†**halke.** *Obs.* [Only in ME.: perh. a dim. of OE. **halh*, *healh*, corner: see HALE *sb.*[2]] A corner, recess, hiding-place.

a **1300** *K. Horn* 1119 He lokede in eche halke Ne seȝ he nowhar walke Aþulf his felawe. **1340** *Ayenb.* 210 Bide þine uader of heuene ine halke. *c* **1385** CHAUCER *L.G.W.* 1780 *Lucretia*, In he comyth in to a priue halk. *c* **1491** *Chast. Goddes Chyld.* 93 O thou edder..tornynge hyder and thyder by a thousande holettes and halkes. [**1598** SPEGHT *Chaucer's Wks.* Rdr. to Chaucer (R.), Where hast thou dwelt good Geffrey al this while?.. In haulks, and herne, God wot, and in exile.]

halket ('hælkɪt). The large grey seal, *Halichœrus gryphus.* (*Cent. Dict.*)

halkri(c)k, -krig, -krike, var. HALECRET.

hall[1] (hɔːl). Forms: 1– **hall**, 1 **heall**, **heal**, 3–7 **halle**, (4 **alle**), 4–7 **hal**, **haule**, 5 (**hale**, **awle**), 5–6 **hawl(l)e**, 6 **haull**, *Sc.* 5 **hawe**, 8– **HA'**. [Com. Teut.: OE. *heall* str. f. = OS., OHG. *halla* (MLG., MDu., MHG. *halle*, Du. *hal*), ON. *hǫll*, *hall-* (Sw. *hall*, Da. *hal*):—OTeut. **hallâ-*:—**halnâ-*, deriv. of ablaut series *hel-*, *hal-*, *hul-* to cover, conceal.]

†**1.** A large place covered by a roof; in early times applied to any spacious roofed place, without or with subordinate chambers attached; a temple, palace, court, royal residence. *Obs.* in gen. sense.

Beowulf (Z.) 89 He doȝora ȝe-hwam dream ȝehyrde hludne in healle. *a* **1175** *Cott. Hom.* 231 Þat se hlaford into þar halle come. *c* **1205** LAY. 28033 Þa postes..þa heolden up þa halle. **1297** R. GLOUC. (1724) 540 He wende & lai withoute toun, atte kinges halle. **1340** HAMPOLE *Pr. Consc.* 8098 Loverd! better es a day lastand In þi halles þan a thowsand. *c* **1400** MAUNDEV. (Roxb.) v. 15 þ ai make pittes in þe erthe all aboute þe hall. **1447** BOKENHAM *Seyntys* (Roxb.) 32 The virgyne, wych stant.. In the hey weye, venus halle by. **1500–20** DUNBAR *Poems* lxxxv. 75 Trywmphale hall, hie tour royall Of Godis celsitud. **1606** HOLLAND *Sueton.* 211 Being once Emperour did set up also in his Haule (or Court yard) the Lineall processe and race of his house.

fig. **971** *Blickl. Hom.* xiv. 163 Seo heall þæs Halȝan Gastes. **1450–1530** *Myrr. our Ladye* 148 Whiche hathe dwelled in the halle of the maydens wombe. *c* **1460** *Towneley Myst.* 33 Doufe, byrd fulle blist, fayre myght the befalle!.. Fulle welle I it wist thou wold com to thi halle. **1868** TENNYSON *Lucretius* 136 Stairs That climb into the windy halls of heaven.

2. a. The large public room in a mansion, palace, etc., used for receptions, banquets, etc., which till nearly 1600 greatly surpassed in size and importance the private rooms or 'bowers' (see BOWER *sb.*[1] 2); a large or stately room in a house. ***in hall***, was often rhetorically contrasted with ***in the field***. ***servants' hall***: the common room in a mansion or large house in which the servants dine.

c **1200**, etc. [see BOWER *sb.*[1] 2]. *a* **1225** *Leg. Kath.* 1470 In halle & i bure. *c* **1325** *Poem Times Edw. II* 252 in *Pol. Songs* (Camden) 334 And nu ben theih liouns in halle, and hares in the feld. **14..** *Nom.* in Wr.-Wülcker 723/7 *Hoc atrium*, a hawlle. *c* **1450** *Bk. Curtasye* 388 in *Babees Bk.* 311 In halle make fyre at yche a mele. **1500–20** DUNBAR *Poems* lxvi. 23 The honourable vse is all ago, In hall and bour, in burgh and plane. **1530** PALSGR. 228/2 Halle in a house, *salle.* *a* **1533** LD. BERNERS *Huon* cxi. 383 The ryche chambers that were on the syde of the hall. **1586** A. DAY *Eng. Secretary* II. (1625) 78 When by a part we understand the whole, as to say.. a *hall* for a house. **1662** J. DAVIES tr. *Olearius' Voy. Ambass.* 16 The Hall for Audience is on the right hand of the Court. **1717** FREZIER *Voy. S. Sea* 261 The first Room is a large Hall, about 19 Foot Broad, and between 30 and 40 in Length. **1727–51** CHAMBERS *Cycl.* s.v., The hall.. in the houses of ministers of state, public magistrates, &c., is that wherein they dispatch business and give audience. **1834** *W. Ind. Sketch Bk.* I. 152 One [compartment] occupying nearly half the area, which was designated 'the hall', and appropriated to the ordinary daily purposes of drawing and dining-room. **1840** DICKENS *Barn. Rudge* xvi, To quarrel in the servants' hall while waiting for their masters and mistresses. **1874** PARKER *Goth. Archit.* I. iii. 89 Part of the great Norman hall remains, now converted into the servants' hall.

b. *transf.* The company assembled in a hall.

1412–20 LYDG. *Chron. Troy* I. v, At her comynge gladdeth all the halle.

3. The residence of a territorial proprietor, a baronial or squire's 'hall'.

(In early use, not separable from 1.)

c **1000** *Ags. Gosp.* Matt. ix. 23 Se hælend com in-to þas ealdres halle. *c* **1400** *Destr. Troy* 8683 Within houses & hallis hard was þere chere. **14..** *Metr. Voc.* in Wr.-Wülcker 625/19 *Quactum*, halle, howse. **1596** SHAKS. *Tam. Shr.* II. i. 189 But Kate, the prettiest Kate in Christendome, Kate of Kate-hall. **1807** CRABBE *Par. Reg.* III. 235 In town she dwelt;—forsaken stood the Hall. **1832** MACAULAY *Armada* 60 The warlike errand.. roused in many an ancient hall the gallant squires of Kent. **1864** TENNYSON *Aylmer's Field* 36 Aylmer followed Aylmer at the Hall, And Averill Averill at the Rectory Thrice over; so that Rectory and Hall, Bound in an immemorial intimacy, Were open to each other.

4. A term applied, esp. in the English universities, to a building or buildings set apart for the residence or instruction of students, and, by transference, to the body of students occupying it. **a.** Originally applied at Oxford and Cambridge to all residences of students, including the Colleges when these came to be founded. Now only *Hist.*, *arch.*, or *poetic* for 'academic buildings'.

At Cambridge this use survived till modern times, when some of the smaller colleges, though corporations, were still called *halls*; the older designation survives, for distinction's sake, in the name of Trinity Hall.

[**1379** *Patent Roll Rich. II*, I. 32 (New Coll. Oxon.) Custos et scholares collegii, domus, sive aulæ prædicti.] *c* **1386** CHAUCER *Reeve's T.* 83 Poure clerkes two That dwelten in this halle of which I seye. **1474** in Wood *City of Oxford* (O.H.S.) I. 126 Tenementum magistri et scholarium Collegii vulgariter nuncupati University Halle. ? **15..** *Ibid.* I. 580 Gardinum quod pertinet ad Collegium de Queen Hall. **1847** TENNYSON *Princess* Prol. 140 Pretty were the sight If our old halls could change their sex, and flaunt With prudes for proctors, dowagers for deans, And sweet girl-graduates in their golden hair. **1886** tr. *Statutes of Trinity Hall* in Willis & Clark *Cambridge* Introd. 17 The house [*domus*] which the aforesaid college shall inhabit, shall be named the Hall [*aula*] of the Holy Trinity of Norwich.

b. After the institution of the colleges, applied specifically to those buildings and societies which, unlike the colleges, were governed by a head only (and not by head and fellows), and whose property was held in trust for them, they not being bodies corporate. (Cf. COLLEGE 4.)

The 'Halls' were originally very numerous, but in Queen Elizabeth's time only eight remained in Oxford, and they are now almost extinct.

1535–6 *Act 27 Hen. VIII*, c. 42 §1 Provostshippes, Maister-shippes, Halles, Hostelles. **1568** GRAFTON *Chron.* II. 950 In Oxford.. he founded also Magdaleyn Hall. **1611** FLORIO, *Allóggio*.. also a skollers house, as the halls in Oxford, that haue no lands, but all liue of themselues. **1683** WOOD *Life* 18 May (O.H.S.) III. 47 A Master of every College and Hall to have procuratoriall power during the duke of York's being at Oxon. **1784** COWPER *Task* II. 699 In colleges and halls, in ancient days, When learning, virtue, piety and truth Were precious. **1877** *Statutes of Univ. Oxf. Commissioners* (1882) 215 A Statute for the Union of Balliol College and New Inn Hall. **1896** *Kelly's Oxford Directory* 91 The halls are governed by the *Statuta Aulularia*, a code of regulations originally formed by the University, and since amended by Convocation. *Ibid.* 92 The four Dyke Scholarships formerly belonging to this hall [St. Mary] have now been suppressed.

c. In recent times applied to buildings in University towns, established, whether by the Universities or not, for the use of students in the higher learning, sometimes enjoying the privileges of the University and sometimes not: e.g. at Oxford, private halls for the residence of undergraduate members of the University, under the charge of a member of Convocation; theological halls (e.g. Wycliffe Hall), halls for women students (e.g. Somerville Hall, Lady Margaret Hall).

For the last two classes the name 'college' has also been assumed: see COLLEGE 4 e.

Divinity Hall, the name applied to the theological department of the Scottish Universities, and to the theological colleges of the Nonconformist churches.

1879 *Minutes of Committee of Assoc. for Education of Women* 21 June, The Scholarship to be called the Mary Somerville Scholarship tenable at Somerville Hall for 3 years. **1879** *Times* 23 June, Other exhibitions and scholarships have been and will be awarded by the Lady Margaret and Somerville Halls. **1882** *Addenda to Statutes (Oxford)* 879 §1 Of the granting of Licenses to open private Halls. *Ibid.* §6 Of the Conditions upon which a Private Hall may become a Public Hall of the University. **1896** *Kelly's Oxford Directory* 94 To open a suitable building as a private hall for the reception and tuition of matriculated students who shall be admissable to degrees.. the proprietor of such hall is to bear the title of 'Licensed Master'.

d. In American colleges: A room or building appropriated to the meetings of a literary or other society; also the society itself.

1888 J. A. PORTER in *Cent. Mag.* Sep. 751 The twin literary societies, or 'halls', generally secret, and always intense in mutual rivalry, which have been institutions at every leading college in the land. *Ibid.*, Oliver Ellsworth, afterward Chief-Justice.. founded Clio Hall at Princeton, and a few years later, in 1769, Whig Hall arose at the same college.

5. a. In English colleges, etc.: The large room in which the members and students dine in common.

1577 in Willis & Clark *Cambridge* (1886) III. 371 The Comedie played publiklie in the hawlle at Christmas. **1683** WOOD *Life* 19 May, They went into the hall [of Queen's Coll. Oxford], and viewed the pictures of King Charles I and his queen. **1853** C. BEDE *Verdant Green* vi, That he might make his first appearance in Hall with proper éclat. **1877** BLACKMORE *Cripps* xix. (1895) 111 Will you dine in hall with me? *Mod.* Concert in Balliol Hall.

b. *transf.* The dinner in a college hall.

1859 HUGHES *Tom Brown at Oxf.* i, You ought to dine in hall perhaps four days a week. Hall is at five o'clock. *a* **1890** R. F. BURTON in *Life* (1893) I. 74 The time for 'Hall', that is to say for college dinner, was five p.m.

6. A house or building belonging to a guild or fraternity of merchants or tradesmen.

At these places the business of the respective guilds was transacted; and in some instances they served as the market-houses for the sale of the goods of the associated members; as *Apothecaries' Hall, Haberdashers' Hall, Merchant Tailors' Hall, Saddlers' Hall*, etc. etc. in London. See also *cloth-hall* (CLOTH 19), COMMON HALL, GUILD-HALL, etc.

c **1302** [see COMMON HALL 1]. *c* **1386** CHAUCER *Prol.* 370 To sitten in a yeldehalle on a deys. **1548** HALL *Chron. Hen. VI*, 170 The Mayre.. ordeyned, that all Wardeins of misteries, should assemble their felowship in their particular hawles. **1632** MASSINGER & FIELD *Fatal Dowry* v. i, And therefore use a conscience (tho' it be Forbidden in our Hall towards other men). **1654** WHITLOCK *Zootomia* 233 Examine the truth of it at Stationers Hall. **1708** *New View Lond.* 593 An Alphabetical Account of Companies and their Halls. **1869** ARUNDELL *London & Liv. Comp.* 187 The custom of possessing magnificent halls had not.. become general.

7. a. A large room or building for the transaction of public business, the holding of courts of justice, or any public assemblies, meetings, or entertainments. (See also MUSIC-HALL, TOWN-HALL, etc.)

1297 R. GLOUC. (1724) 390 The tour he made of Londone, Wyllam þys proute kyng, And muche halle of Londone, þat so muche was þoru all thyng. **1382** WYCLIF *Matt.* xxvii. 27 Thanne kniȝtis of the president takynge Jhesu in the mote halle. **1568** GRAFTON *Chron.* II. 237 The king and the Erle went hand in hand to the great Hall of the Towne. **1732** LEDIARD *Sethos* II. IX. 334 They desir'd the ambassadors to go out of the hall. **1802** M. CUTLER in *Life, etc.* (1888) II. 79 The House [Congress].. adjourned.. for the purpose of giving opportunity to workmen to fix some ventilators, which were greatly wanted in the Hall. **1826** H. N. COLERIDGE *West Indies* 193 The Court House.. contains a hall on the ground floor for the Assembly.

†**b.** ***the Hall***, Westminster Hall, formerly the seat of the High Court of Justice in England; hence, the administration of justice. *Obs.*

1548 HALL *Chron., Hen. VI*, 185 b, To Westmynster, and there set in the hawle, with the scepter royall in his hand. **1613** SHAKS. *Hen. VIII*, II. i. 2 Whether away so fast?.. Eu'n to the Hall, to heare what shall become Of the great Duke of Buckingham. **1738** POPE *Epil. Sat.* II. 218 To Virtue's work provoke the tardy Hall.

†**c.** A formal assembly held by the sovereign, or by the mayor or principal municipal officer of a town; usually in phr. ***to keep hall, call a hall.*** *Obs.* (see also COMMON HALL.)

1551–2 EDW. VI *Jrnl.* 7 Jan. in *Lit. Rem.* (Roxb.) II. 388, I went to Detford to dine there, and brake up the halle. **1568** GRAFTON *Chron.* (1809) II. 526 [Christmas] kept at Greenewiche with open hous-hold, and franke resorte to the Court (which is called keping of the Hall). *c* **1665** MRS. HUTCHINSON *Mem. Col. Hutchinson* (1848) 162 Whereupon a hall was called, and the danger of the place declared to the whole town. **1684** *Lond. Gaz.* No. 1956/4 The next day the Mayor called a Hall, and.. swore all the Aldermen.

d. Also in *pl.* (occas. in *sing.*), abbrev. of *music-hall*.

1862 A. J. MUNBY *Diary* 29 Mar. in D. Hudson *Munby* (1972) 119 Socially speaking, the audience were a good deal higher than those I have seen in similar Halls at Islington & elsewhere. **1867** DICKENS *Lett.* 16 Dec. (1880) II. 318, I have to go to the hall to try an enlarged background. **1895** CHEVALIER & DALY *A. Chevalier* 115 He was one of the few actors of any prominence who had migrated to the halls. **1898** J. D. BRAYSHAW *Slum Silhouettes* 29 He've tried every small 'all in town, even the pubs wot gits up 'smokers'. **1905** MORTON & NEWTON (*title*) Sixty years' stage service, being a record of the life of Charles Morton, 'the Father of the Halls'. **1923** N. COWARD *Coll. Sk. & Lyrics* (1931) 75 Doing a turn of me own on the halls—very trying work—and so cosmopolitan. **1934** T. S. ELIOT *Rock* i. 25 Robey's on the 'alls; but this gentleman.. used to hentertain the toffs. **1942** E. BLOM *Mus. in Eng.* x. 168 The 'halls' were the last places where anybody would have thought of going for the sake of music. **1967** *Listener* 8 June 760/2 The vital and self-confident art of the halls.. a London Sound to set beside the Liverpool sort.

8. The entrance-room or vestibule of a house; hence, the lobby or entrance passage.

(The entrance-room was formerly often one of the principal sitting-rooms, of which many examples still remain in old country houses.)

1663 GERBIER *Counsel* 10 The Hall of a private-house, serving for the most part but for a Passage. **1706–7** FARQUHAR *Beaux' Strat.* I. i, The Company.. has stood in the Hall this Hour, and no Body to shew them to their Chambers. **1790** J. B. MORETON *W. Ind. Isl.* 24 Do not keep loitering about the hall or piazza. **1848** THACKERAY *Dinner at Timmins's* iii, Fitz tumbled over the basket.. which stood in the hall. **1897** M. HAMILTON *McLeod of Camerons* 259 They were still standing in the hall of the hotel.

†**9.** A space in a garden or grove enclosed by trees or hedges. *Obs.*

1712 J. JAMES tr. *Le Blond's Gard.* 19 Groves.. Close-Walks, Galleries, and Halls of Verdure. *Ibid.* 49 You should always.. make something Noble in the Middle of a Wood, as a Hall of Horse-Chesnuts, a Water-work.. or the like.

†**10.** = HALLING. *Obs.*

1845 PARKER *Gloss. Archit.* (ed. 4) I. 197 They [the walls] were also sometimes hung with tapestry or carpeting, and a set of hangings of this kind was occasionally called a *Hall* or *Hallyng*.

11. In allusive phrases: ***bachelor's hall***, an establishment presided over by an unmarried man, or a man in the absence of his wife. †***cutpurse hall***, †***ruffian's hall***, a place where cutpurses or ruffians congregate, or exercise their pursuits. ***liberty hall***, a place where one may do as one likes.

1615 TOMKIS *Albumazar* III. vii, 'Tis the cunningst nimmer Of the whole Company of Cut-purse-Hall. **1632** MASSINGER *City Madam* I. ii, My gate ruffian's hall! What insolence is this? **1773** GOLDSM. *Stoops to Conq.* II. (Globe) 652/1 This is Liberty-hall, gentlemen. You may do just as you please. **1840** DICKENS *Old C. Shop* i, I'll have my Bachelor's Hall at the counting-house. **1844** —— *Mart. Chuz.* xi, 'Bachelor's Hall, you know, cousin', said Mr. Jonas. **1885** C. F. HOLDER *Marvels Anim. Life* 226 Captain Sol, who was a widower, and kept bachelor's hall, so to speak.

†**12.** ***a hall! a hall!*** a cry or exclamation to clear the way or make sufficient room in a crowd, esp. for a dance; also to call people together to a ceremony or entertainment, or to summon servants.

1592 SHAKS. *Rom. & Jul.* I. v. 28 A Hall Hall, giue roome, and foote it Girles. **1599** CHAPMAN *Hum. dayes Myrth* Plays 1873 I. 103 A hall, a hall, the pageant of the Butterie. **1623** MIDDLETON *Entertainment at Lord Mayor's* Wks. (Bullen) VII. 373 A hall! a hall! below, stand clear. **1689** S. SEWALL *Diary* 19 Mar. (1878) I. 249 When the people cry'd, a Hall, a Hall, the Aldermen came up two by two, the Mace carried before them. **1808** SCOTT *Marm.* v. xvii, Lords to the dance,—a hall! a hall!

13. *attrib.* and *Comb.*, as ***hall-bible***, ***-board***, ***-book***, ***-ceiling***, ***-chair***, ***-chimney***, ***-cleaner***, ***-clock***, ***-feast***, ***-floor***, ***-hearth***, ***-keeper***, ***-lamp***, ***-man***, ***-pillar***, ***-porter***, etc.; ***hall-like*** adj.; also **hall-bedroom** *U.S.*, a small bedroom partitioned off at one end of a hall; **hall-bed roomer** *U.S.*, one who sleeps in this; **hall-boy**, a page-boy in a large house; a call-boy in the hall of a hotel or the like; **hall day** = COURTDAY 1; **hall-disputation**, **hall-exercise**, a disputation in a college hall; **hall-full**, as many as a hall will hold; †**hall-reader**, one who read the Bible or other book in the college hall; **hall-room** *U.S.*, a room at the end of and of the width of a hall; also *v. intr.*, to live in such a room; †**hall-spoon**, a spoon made of hall-marked silver; **hall stand**, a piece of furniture used to receive umbrellas, hats, coats, and brushes usually situated near the front door in the hall of the house; **hall-table**, (*a*) a large, solid table belonging to the hall in a mansion; (*b*) a small table situated in the hall near the front door; **hall-tree** *U.S.*, a hall stand or hat rack. Also HALL-HOUSE, -MARK, etc.

1738 *New Hampsh. Probate Rec.* II. 280 Samuel Brewster shall have.. ye *Hall Bed Room. **1886** H. JAMES *Bostonians*

II. xxi. 44 One of his rooms was directly above the street-door of the house; such a dormitory, when it is so exiguous, is called in the nomenclature of New York a 'hall bedroom'. **1922** A. BENNETT *Lilian* I. vi. 57 In New York it would have been termed a hall-bedroom. **1934** L. MUMFORD in W. Frank et al. *Amer. & Alfred Stieglitz* ii. 35 Lonely young men and women from the country..faced their first year in the city from hall bedrooms on the top-floor rear of unamiable boarding-houses. **1899** J. L. WILLIAMS *Stolen Story* 230 Like many an other lonely *hall-bed roomer. **1884** *N.Y. Herald* 27 Oct. 2/2 Janitors and *hall boys in attendance. **1885** C. M. YONGE *Nuttie's Father* II. xiii. 158 The hall boy, an alert young fellow, had already dashed down the steps. **1892** —— *That Stick* I. ii. 23 He had been hall boy to a duke, footman to a viscountess, valet to an earl. **1912** L. J. VANCE *Destroying Angel* xx, The hall-boys said you were busy on the telephone. **1672** *Acc. Christ's Coll.* in Willis & Clark *Cambridge* (1886) III. 368 The *Hall-Bible is bound in 1672. **1786, 1823** Ha' bible [see HA']. **1864** DICKENS *Mut. Fr.* I. ii. 5 The Veneering establishment, from the *hall-chairs..to the grand pianoforte. **1939** A. CLARKE *Sister Eucharia* i. 7 The stage is seen to be quite bare except for two high hall chairs. **1746** M. HUGHES *Jrnl. Late Rebellion* Back of Title, Entered in the *Hall-Book of the Company of Stationers. **1807** WORDSW. *White Doe* IV. 23 The hall-clock..points at nine. **1585** HIGINS tr. *Junius' Nomenclator* 371 *Dies fastus*..An *hall day: a court day: a day of pleading, as in terme time at Westminster hall, &c. **1700** LUTTRELL *Brief Rel.* (1857) IV. 642 A private verdict was given, and will be affirmed the next hall day in court. **1460** *Lybeaus Disc.* 1765 Amydde the *halle flore. **1883** BLACK *Shandon Bells* xxviii, A *hall-full of men smoking pipes. **1705** HEARNE *Collect.* 12 Nov., A *Hall Keeper for Blackwell Hall. **1834** *W. Ind. Sketch Bk.* I. 153 A common *hall lamp was suspended from one of the centre beams. **1883** D. COOK *On Stage* I. ix. 204 There is no situation in the world where a man can better study his kind than the *hall-porter's chair of a London theatre. **1934** *Punch* 5 Aug. 164/2 The hall-porter moved wearily across the floor to take my luggage. **1919** T. K. HOLMES *Man fr. Tall Timber* i. 3 'Shucks! why didn't you say H. Harvey Stafford?' interrupted the *hall-man. **1886** WILLIS & CLARK *Cambridge* III. 369 The desk which was used by the *Hall-Reader. **1859** *Ladies' Repository* XIX. 466/2 The little *hall-room is just large enough for the boys to sleep in. **1886** S. W. MITCHELL *R. Blake* (1895) v. 39 Miss Darnell had for her own use a like space on the third floor, leaving to Miss Wynne a bed-chamber..known as a hall-room. **1906** 'O. HENRY' *Four Million* (1916) xiv. 139 The restaurant was next door to the old red brick in which she hall-roomed. *Ibid.* 140 Schulenberg was to send three meals per diem to Sarah's hall-room. **1688** *Lond. Gaz.* No. 2339/4, 15 Spoons, 4 being *Hall Spoons gilt. **1882** *Times* 31 Jan. 16/6 (Advt.), A very fine carved oak bookcase, two cabinets, a ditto *hall stand and table. **1897** R. KRON *Little Londoner* (1917) 28 Not far from the door, there are an umbrella-stand, a hat-rack, with several pegs on it, and a large looking-glass; if the three are combined, such a piece of furniture is called a hall-stand. **1911** *Daily Colonist* (Victoria, B.C.) 4 Apr. 19/1 (Advt.), Oak Hall Stand, Brussels Rugs. **1943** K. TENNANT *Ride on Stranger* iii. 23 By applying her eye to one of the coloured panes in the front door, she could make out the dim bulk of a hall-stand. **1952** J. GLOAG *Short Dict. Furnit.* 282 Hall stands were often made wholly of cast iron. **1682** MRS. BEHN *City Heiress* 52 Being drunk, and falling asleep under the *Hall-table. **1808** SCOTT *Marm.* VI. Introd. 52 The huge hall-table's oaken face, Scrubb'd till it shone. **1869** L. M. ALCOTT *Little Women* II. xxiii. 327 He..never..expressed ..surprise at seeing the Professor's hat on the Marches' hall-table. **1902** H. JAMES *Wings of Dove* II. iv. 82, I shan't leave mine [*sc.* my letters] on the hall-table. *a* **1941** V. WOOLF *Haunted House* (1943) 44 She touched the letters on the hall table. **1891** *Harper's Mag.* June 79/1 One could distinguish..the *hall tree, whereon Rhodes's hat swung in its place. **1900** E. E. PEAKE *Darlingtons* ix. 79 She..walked back to the sitting-room, stopping to touch up her hair before the glass in the hall-tree. **1954** J. STEINBECK *Sweet Thursday* xviii. 108 He busted two windows and run off with the deer-antler hall-tree.

Hall^{2}. *Physics.* The name of Edwin H. *Hall* (1855–1938), American physicist, used attrib. to designate an effect discovered by him and various quantities associated therewith (see quot. 1958).

1902 Hall effect [see *electric potential* s.v. ELECTRIC *a.* 2 b]. **1922** GLAZEBROOK *Dict. Appl. Physics* II. 468/2 The effect of a magnetic field upon the electrical conductivity of metals, first discovered by Lord Kelvin in 1856 and known as the Hall effect, is very marked in the case of bismuth wire or plates. **1940** *Chambers's Techn. Dict.* 400/1 *Hall effect*, a change in the distribution of current in a strip of metal, due to a magnetic field. **1958** *Van Nostrand's Sci. Encycl.* (ed. 3) 784/1 In 1879 Hall..discovered that if a strip of gold-leaf, carrying an electric current longitudinally was placed in a magnetic field with the plane of the strip perpendicular to the direction of the field, points directly opposite each other on the edges of the strip acquired a difference of electric potential... The transverse electric potential gradient per unit magnetic field intensity per unit current density is called the 'Hall coefficient' for the metal in question... The Hall angle is the ratio of E_y..to the field E_x... The Hall mobility is the mobility of the electrons or holes in a semiconductor as measured by the Hall effect. **1965** PHILLIPS & WILLIAMS *Inorg. Chem.* I. vi. 195 Other methods which measure the mobility of the electrons, e.g. measurement of the Hall effect, also permit a distinction to be made between the two mechanisms of electron migration.

hall, obs. form of HAUL.

hallabaloo: earlier form of HULLABALOO.

hallachore, hallalcor: see HALALCOR.

†**hallage** ('hɔːlɪdʒ). *Obs.* Also 7 halledge. [a. F. *hallage* (13th c. in Hatz.-Darm.), f. *halle* market-hall + -AGE.] A fee or toll paid for goods sold in a mercantile hall or market; see quot. 1607.

1607 COWELL *Interpr.*, *Hallage* is a fee due for cloths brought for sale to Blackwell hal in London. **1648** in Picton *L'pool Munic. Rec.* (1883) I. 181 Paid for townes customes and hallage iij^{li}. **1664** *Ibid.* 298 Goods distreyned for anie towns custome of Halledge. **1678** *Act of Common-Council, London* B j a, All sorts of Broad..Cloths..brought unto, pitched, and harboured in Blackwell-Hall..there to remain till..the Duties of Hallage herein after-mentioned also [be] paid. **1720** STRYPE *Stow's Surv.* II. v. 181/1.

hallal, var. HALAL *v.*

hallali ('hæləlɪ). [Echoic.] A bugle call. Also *fig.*

1885 G. MEREDITH *Diana of Crossways* II. ii. 55 He knew enough to blow his huntsman's horn... His hallali rang high. **1898** —— *Reading of Life* 77 Right loud the bugle's hallali elate Rang forth. **1920** *Q. Rev.* July 13 The hallali was sounded in a famous letter to Lord Grey de Wilton, the candidate for Bath, in which Disraeli accused the Ministers of having for five years harassed every trade. **1923** W. J. LOCKE *Moordius & Co.* x. 140 On the stroke of four the orchestra of French hunting horns blew the *hallali*.

†**halla'lloo,** *sb.* ? *Obs.* [Extended form of HALLOO. Cf. also *halla-*, HULLABALOO.] Shouting, loud and excited vociferation.

1730 FIELDING *Tom Thumb* I. v, Would I had heard..The hallalloo of fire in every street! **1749** —— *Tom Jones* IV. viii, So roared forth the Somersetshire mob an hallaloo.

hallan ('hælən). *Sc.* and *north. dial.* Also 6–8 halland, 8 hallon, 8–9 hallen. [perh. derivative or dim. of HALL^{1}.] A partition wall in a cottage; particularly, that between the door and the fireplace, which shelters the room from the draught of the door; also the inside porch formed by this partition.

1490–91 *MS. Hostill. Roll, Durh.*, Pro dalbura murorum, gabellorum, hallandorum, per xiv dies. **1500–20**, etc. [see HALLAN-SHAKER]. **1728** RAMSAY *Fables, Monk & Miller's Wife* 249 Hab got a kent, stood by the hallan. *a* **1774** FERGUSSON *Farmer's Ingle*, When he out o'er the halland flings his een. **1829** HOGG in *Blackw. Mag.* XXVI. 48 The family being at prayers when she went..she stood still behind the hallan.

b. *Comb.*, as ***hallan-end, -pin, -post, -side.***

1725 RAMSAY *Gent. Sheph.* III. ii, A foundling that was laid Down at your hallon-side ae morn in May. **1825** BROCKETT *N.C. Gloss.*, *Hallen-pin*, a pin fixed upon the hallen for the purpose of hanging up coats, hats, etc. **1894** CROCKETT *Raiders* 55 John and Rab were hid at the back of the hallan-end.

'hallan-,shaker. *Sc.* A beggar who stands shaking the hallan; a vagabond, sturdy beggar.

1500–20 DUNBAR *Poems* xiv. 57 Sic knavis and crakkaris.. Sic halland schekkaris. *a* **1605** POLWART *Flyting w. Montgomerie* 758 Land lowper, light skowper..Halland shaker, draught raiker. **1785** *Jrnl. fr. Lond.* 4 (Jam.) Staakin about like a hallen-shaker. **1816** SCOTT *Antiq.* iv, I and a wheen hallenshakers like mysell.

hallbard, obs. form of HALBERD.

hall-door. a. The door of a hall or mansion. **b.** The door leading into the hall or entrance-room of a house; the front door.

c **1205** LAY. 30153 Wið uten his halle dure. *c* **1410** *Sir Cleges* 287 The vsscher at the hall dore was Wyth a staffe stondynge. **1568** GRAFTON *Chron.* II. 73 Fyndyng the Hall dore of the Palace of Caunterbury shut against them, they went to an inwarde backe dore. **1791** MRS. RADCLIFFE *Rom. Forest* vi, Several times she went to the hall-door in order to look into the forest. **1808** SCOTT *Marm.* v. xii. (*Lochinvar* vii), They reached the hall door and the charger stood near. **1848** C. BRONTË *J. Eyre* xi, The hall-door, which was half of glass, stood open.

halle, obs. form of HALE *sb.*^{3}, *a.* and *v.*

Hallé ('hæleɪ). Applied *attrib.* to an orchestra, concerts, and other musical events which owe their inception to Charles *Hallé* (orig. Carl Halle) (1819–1895). Also used *absol.*

1852 MRS. GASKELL *Let.* 7 Dec. (1966) 217 We have 3 Hallé tickets for Thursday. *c* **1860** —— *Lett.* (1966) 614 Beautiful Hallé last night. **1936** R. C. K. ENSOR *England 1870–1914* x. 327 Outside the metropolis..the chief purveyor of orchestral concerts [was] the Hallé orchestra. **1954** *Grove's Dict. Music* (ed. 5) V. 542/2 In 1895 the Hallé concerts had become a national institution. *Ibid.* 544/1 Philip Godlee, the former Chairman of the Hallé. *Ibid.*, The Hallé Choir had also had its vicissitudes. *Ibid.*, Concerts outside the Hallé series. **1957** *Times Lit. Suppl.* 1 Nov. 652/3 There is something wrong with a system of public finance that rewards hard work and the enterprise to secure solvency with a cut in the next year's subvention, as was the Hallé's experience. **1968** *Guardian* 29 Mar. 10/6 Our North Midlands scout, driving hard to attend a Hallé concert in Hanley, had to pause at a garage for repairs... 'I'm going to the Hallé in Hanley.'

hallecret: see HALECRET.

‖**hälleflinta** (hɛlə'flɪntə). *Min.* [Sw. = hornstone, f. *häll* flat rock + *flinta* hornstone, flint.] A name given to a very fine-grained variety of gneiss, generally free from mica, and resembling felsite.

1878 LAWRENCE tr. *Cotta's Rocks Class.* 213 Felsite has also received the names of petrosilex, and in Scandinavia hälle-flinta. **1879** RUTLEY *Study Rocks* xii. 214 Those varieties termed hälleflinte and hornstone having a peculiar flinty aspect. **1880** *Academy* 20 Nov. 370 The Chinese Rocks are allied to hälleflinta.

Hence **hälleflintoid** *a.*, of or like hälleflinta.

1888 BLAKE in *Q. Jrnl. Geol. Soc.* XLIV. 280 Some more hälleflintoid rock (well shown in a quarry by the roadside).

‖**Hallel** (hæ'leːl, 'hælɛl). [Heb. *hallēl*, inf. and imper. 'praise, celebrate', a vb. in the Piel conjugation, with which Ps. cxiii begins.] A hymn of praise, consisting of Psalms cxiii to cxviii inclusive, sung at the four great Jewish feasts. Also *attrib.*

Great Hallel, a hymn of praise consisting of Psalm cxxxvi, and, according to some, of part of Psalm cxxxv, sung on occasions of great joy.

1702 ECHARD *Eccl. Hist.* (1710) 190 After this they proceeded to sing the hymn, or rather to finish the *Hallel*, which in all consisted of six Eucharistical psalms, beginning at the 113th and concluding with the 118th. **1876** C. M. DAVIES *Unorth. Lond.* 209 That Last Supper..with its simple Hallel-Hymn. **1877** C. GEIKIE *Christ* lv. (1879) 662 At the Feast of Tabernacles, the great Hallel was daily sung in their processions.

hallelujah, -iah (hælɪ'luːjə), *int.* and *sb.*^{1} Also 6 **halleluya, 6–7 halleluia(h, 7 halaluiah.** [a. Heb. *hallĕlū-yāh* 'praise (ye) Jah (= Jehovah)'; the verb is the imper. plural of *hallēl*: see prec.]

1. a. The exclamation 'Praise (ye) the Lord (Jah, or Jehovah)', which occurs in many psalms and anthems; hence, a song of praise to God; = ALLELUIA *int.* and *sb.*^{1}

1535 COVERDALE *Ps.* cv[i]. (*heading*) Halleluya. *Ibid.* 48 Let all people saye: Amen, Amen. Halleluya. **1557** N. T. (Genev.) *Rev.* xix. 1, I heard the voyce of muche people in heauen saying, Halleluiah. **1625** SANDERSON *Serm.* I. 115 The abridgement is short, which some have made of the whole book of Psalms but into two words, *hosannah*, and *hallelujah*. **1667** MILTON *P.L.* VII. 634 And the Empyrean rung With Halleluiahs. **1738** WESLEY *Hymn*, '*Lift up your Heads*' iv, Their Hallelujahs loud and sweet With our Hosannas join. **1818** SCOTT *Hrt. Midl.* ii, That the psalms they now heard must be exchanged in the space of two brief days for eternal hallelujahs or eternal lamentations.

b. = Hallelujah-chorus.

1880 GROVE *Dict. Mus.* I. 646 He [Handel] has written other Hallelujahs or Allelujahs.

c. *attrib.* and *Comb.*, as **hallelujah-band, -victory** (see quots.); **hallelujah-chorus,** a musical composition based on the word 'hallelujah'; **hallelujah-lass,** a popular name for a female member of the Salvation Army.

a **1763** BYROM *Ep. Gentl. Temple* (R.) Tune the hallelujah song anew. **1872** O. SHIPLEY *Gloss. Eccl. Terms*, *Hallelujah Band*, a sect of Protestant dissenters. **1880** GROVE *Dict. Mus.* I. 646 The Hallelujah Chorus in the Messiah is known to everyone. **1886** F. HUME *Myst. Hansom Cab* (1887) xvi. 109 It appears that she had been in the Army as a hallelujah lass. **1889** REDDELL *Fact, Fancy & Fable* 247 *Hallelujah Victory*, That gained by newly converted Bretons, led by Germanus, Bishop of Auxerre, in 429. They went into battle shouting 'Hallelujah!' **1967** W. S. SMITH *London Heretics* III. v. 238 In 1879..more than 2,000 fellow citizens packed into Livingston Hall nightly to listen to the 'Hallelujah Lasses'.

2. A semi-Christian religion practised among the Carib-speaking peoples of Guyana.

1946 F. W. KENSWIL *Childr. Silence* vi. 13 Aboriginal Indians are a very religious set of people... Those of the hinterland of this colony [British Guiana] have their own religion which they call 'Hallilieujah'. This Hallilieujah is said to have been conceived, in the dim past, by an Indian whose name was Bi-chi-wung. **1955** *Times* 22 June 11/7 The most primitive religion which they still practise is a debased version of Christianity called Hallelujah... It..seems to date from some time in the nineteenth century.

halle'lujah, *sb.*^{2} [Taken as the same word as prec.: but of uncertain origin.] = ALLELUIA *sb.*^{2}, the wood-sorrel. Prior *Plant-n.* 1863.

1920 *Sunday at Home* June 569/2 Oxalis, the wood-sorrel, was known as hallelujah,..from its blossoming between Easter and Whitsuntide, when psalms were sung ending in the word hallelujah. **1923** *Times Lit. Suppl.* 3 May 293/3 How happy is the country polyonymosity that hails it also as sheep-sorrel,..hallelujah,..and God Almighty's bread-and-cheese?

hallelujatic, -iatic (,hælɪluː'jætɪk), *a.* Of or pertaining to the Hallelujah; = ALLELUIATIC.

a **1818** *Christian Antiq.* II. 119 (T.) Called halleluiatick psalms. **1888** D. R. THOMAS *Hist. St. Asaph* 7 This engagement, which has been handed down as 'The Halleluiatic Victory'.

†**halle'lujous, -'uious,** *a. Obs.* = prec.

1645 QUARLES *Sol. Recant.* v. 46 Thus when thy awfull presence shall draw near These Hallalujous Courts.

haller, obs. form of HELLER^{1}, a coin.

hallew, obs. form of HALLOO *v.*

halleyr, obs. form of HALYARD.

hallful ('hɔːlfʊl). [f. HALL *sb.*^{1} + -FUL 2.] As many or as much as will fill a hall.

1905 *Daily Chron.* 17 Feb. 3/6 The entertainment of a whole hallful of poor children. **1909** *Westm. Gaz.* 26 Sept. 6/3 What a hallful it was that received him with ringing, rousing, rollicking cheers!

hall-house. *Obs.* exc. *local.*

†**1.** A house or edifice that is a hall. *Obs.*

1467 *Ord. Worcester* xli. in *Eng. Gilds* 393 Citezen or straunger that hyreth eny chambour in that seide halle house [the Guild-hall].

2. The principal living-room in a farm-house. **1564** *Durham Depos.* (Surtees) 80 The testament was maid in his haull house, upon a holloday. **1575–6** *Ibid.* 268 The said Thomas was soore sike, lyinge in his hall house. **1599** *Acc.-Bk.* in *Antiquary* XXXII. 242 In the hawle house.

3. The farm-house, as distinguished from the cottages on the farm. **1603** OWEN *Pembrokesh.* (1891) 191 And then was the old tenant at Mydsomer to remove out of the hall house.

4. (Sc. *ha' house*) A manor-house; = HALL[1] 3. **1702** *Lond. Gaz.* No. 3826/4 At Latimers in Bucks..is a fair large Hall-house fit for a Person of Quality. **1712** ADDISON *Spect.* No. 517 ¶2 Captain Sentry, my master's nephew, has taken possession of the hall-house, and the whole estate. **1814** SCOTT *Wav.* x, Saying 'there were mair fules in the laird's ha' house than Davie Gellatley'.

halli, var. HALELY *Obs.*, wholly.

halliard: see HALYARD.

halliballoo: HULLABALOO.

hallibut, hallidome: see HALI-.

†**hallier**[1]. *Obs.* Also 4 **halyer**. [f. HALE *v.*[1], perh. after an OF. *halier, hallier*: cf. *sawyer*.]

1. One who hales or hauls; a hauler. **1479** *Off. Mayor Bristol* in *Eng. Gilds* 425 Ne soffir not the halyers to hale it all awey. **1644** PRYNNE & WALKER *Fiennes' Trial* 44 Cannons..might with ease have been easily drawne off, being downe the hill, and many Halliers horses ready at hand for that service.

2. Earlier form of HALYARD, q.v.

3. A kind of net for catching birds. **1727** BRADLEY *Fam. Dict.* s.v. *Call*, Then place your Net, call'd a Hallier, quite round..each Part about twenty Foot distant from the Cage.

†**hallier**[2]. *Obs.* [f. HALL *sb.*[1] 4: cf. med.L. *aulārius* in same sense.] A student in a hall at Oxford University. **1587** HARRISON *England* II. ii. (1877) I. 87 The students also that remaine in them [Oxford hostels or halls] are called hostelers or halliers.

†**'halling**[1]. *Obs.* Also 5 **hawlyng(e**, 5–6 **hallyng**. [f. HALL *sb.*[1] + -ING: cf. *bedding, flooring*.] Tapestry or painted cloth for the walls of a hall. **1418** *E.E. Wills* (1882) 35 Alle the hustilmentis of Beddyng, hallyng, pottys & pannes. **1427** *Mem. Ripon* (Surtees) I. 329 Unum pannum pinctum vocatum hawlyng. **1483** *Cath. Angl.* 179/1 An Hawlynge, *auleum*. **1522** *Bury Wills* (Camden) 115 A hallyng of steynyd clothe w[t] rynnyng vynys and leves w[t] bestes and birdes. **1566** *Eng. Church Furniture* (Peacock) 94 Item one vale which our vicare haith and he haith made a halling therof.

halling ('hælɪŋ), *sb.*[2] [Norw., from *Hallingdal*, a valley in southern Norway.] A Norwegian country-dance in triple rhythm; also, the music for such a dance. **1866** PLESNER & RUGELEY-POWERS tr. *Björnson's Arne* ii. 13 Nils played; and the two gentlemen each gave a dollar for him, and then asked for the *halling*. **1924** *Glasgow Herald* 31 May 4 We have no space here to describe the wonderful Halling dance. **1947** A. EINSTEIN *Mus. Romantic Era* xvii. 320 Many of these dances show evidence of great age and uninterrupted tradition—the leaping dance (*springar*) in $\frac{3}{4}$ meter and the *halling* in duple meter.

'hallion, hallyon. *Sc.* and *north. dial.* Also **hullion**. [Origin uncertain. Cf. F. *haillon* rag.] A term of contempt: A low or scurvy fellow; an idle, worthless fellow. **1786** BURNS *Addr. Beelzebub* 37 They..tirl the hallions to the birses. **1789** D. DAVIDSON *Seasons* 26 (Jam.) Some rustic hallion. **1808–18** JAMIESON, *Hullion*. **1817** SCOTT *Rob Roy* iv, This is a decentish hallion. **1825** BROCKETT *N.C. Gloss.*, *Hallion*, a term of reproach. **1895** CROCKETT *Men of Moss-hags* xxx. 223, I can manage the hullions fine.

hallite ('hælaɪt). *Min.* [Named from Halle in Germany.] A synonym of Aluminite or Websterite. **1837** DANA *Min.* **1872** WATTS *Dict. Chem.* III. 6.

halliyard, rare obs. form of HALYARD.

'hall-mark, *sb.* [f. HALL *sb.*[1] 6, f. the name of the London assay office at Goldsmith's Hall.]

a. The official mark or stamp used by statutory Hall-marking Authorities in marking the standard of gold and silver articles assayed by them, without which articles of these metals may not legally be sold.

The present U.K. assay offices are in Birmingham, London, Sheffield, and Edinburgh.

1721 *Lond. Gaz.* No. 5974/3 That the same [silver wares] have the Hall-Mark thereon. **1852** A. RYLAND *Assay Gold & S.* 4 Every one has observed that all plate bears certain marks;—these are generally five in number and are called the *Hall-marks*, or assay marks. **1884** BRITTEN *Watch & Clockm.* 150 Birmingham.—Hall mark, an anchor in a square frame for gold, and an anchor in a pointed shield for silver. **1887** *Academy* 1 Jan. 15/3 The hall-mark was a Lombardic capital T, the mark for the year 1496–7.

b. *fig.* A distinctive mark or token of genuineness, good breeding, or excellence. **1864** *Daily Tel.* 1 Sept., A guardsman, bearing on him the 'Hall mark' of Alma. **1887** *Pall Mall G.* 21 Mar. 3/1 The stamping with a hall-mark (called a degree) is not the only, or perhaps even the chief, function of a university. **1894** WOLSELEY *Marlborough* I. 140 The hall-mark of real military genius.

'hall-mark, *v.* [f. prec. sb., after MARK *v.*] *trans.* To stamp with a hall-mark. Also *fig.* **1773** *Rep. Comm. Assay Offices* 25 He bought the Knives and Forks..and believed at that Time they had been Hall marked,..and refused selling them when he found they were not Hall marked. **1852** A. RYLAND *Assay Gold & S.* 135 Express instructions..to have the plate Hall-marked. **1892** G. S. LAYARD *C. Keene* ii. 36 It certainly never occurred to them that Nature had hall-marked him 'genius'.

Hence **'hallmarked** *ppl. a.*, **-marking** *vbl. sb.* **1879** *Blackw. Mag.* Aug. 202 Its hall-marking is no guarantee for quality. **1884** BRITTEN *Watch & Clockm.* 116 The hall marking of all watch cases of gold or silver made in Great Britain..is compulsory. **1888** *Athenæum* 22 Dec. 852/1 On the plea that the articles were not hall-marked. *Mod.* (*fig.*) Not hall-marked on every link.

hallmote, halmote ('hɔːlməʊt). Forms: 2–5 **halimot**, 4 (7–8 *Hist.*) **halymote**, *Hist.* 6 **haylemot**, 6–9 **halimote**, **heal-gemot**, 7–9 **halmot**, 8 **hallimote**, 8–9 **hal(l)mote**, 9 **hallmoot**. [Early ME. *hal-imot, -ymote*, repr. an OE. * *heall-ȝemót*, f. *heall* HALL[1] + *ȝemót* meeting, assembly.]

1. The court of the lord of a manor, held in the hall; a court-baron. **1101** *Laws Hen. I*, c. 9 §4 in Thorpe *Anc. Laws* I. 517 Et omnis causa terminetur vel hundreto, vel comitatu, vel halimoto socam habencium, vel dominorum curiis. *Ibid.* c. 20 §1. 528 In causis omnibus et hallemotis pertinentibus. *c***1205** LAY. 31997 Hu Aðelstan her com..hu he sette halimot, & hu he sette hundred. **1591** LAMBARDE *Archeion* (1635) 15 The Court Baron, anciently called Heal-gemot, and corruptly Haylemot, that is..the Court of the Hall, Mannor, or chiefe place. **1607** COWELL *Interpr.*, *Halymote* is a court Baron..the etymologie is the meeting of the tenents of one hall or maner. **1846** *Brockett's N.C. Gloss.* (ed. 3) I. 206 *Halmot-court*..The name is still kept up in Durham county, in the bishop's manors. **1892** GARNIER *Hist. Eng. Landed Int.* 63 Private courts, such as those of the King's Thane and Halmote.

*fig. a***1327** *Pol. Songs* (Camden) 154 Upo lofte The devel may sitte softe, And holden his halymotes ofte.

2. The court of an incorporated trade-guild or 'company'. *a***1633** COKE *Inst.* IV. (1669) l. §9 The Court of Hall-mote. This is..as much as to say the Hall Court, *i. Conventus Civium in Aulam publicam*, every Company of London having an Hall wherein they keep their Courts, and this Court anciently called *Hall-mote* or *Folk mote*. **1708** J. CHAMBERLAYNE *St. Gt. Brit.* I. III. x. (1743) 209 The court of Halmote, or Assembly of every Guild or Fraternity. **1892** HAZLITT *Livery Comp. Lond.* 104 In 30 Edward I the Bakers were allowed to hold four hall-moots yearly, to determine all offences committed in their business.

¶ It has been erroneously analysed as 'holy or ecclesiastical court'. **1655** FULLER *Ch. Hist.* VI. ii. §22 All these appeared at the Hali-mote or Holy Court of the Cellarer. **1670** BLOUNT *Law Dict.*, *Halimote*..also a Holy or Ecclesiastical Court. **1797** *Jacob's Law Dict.* s.v. *Halymote, Called the holymote or holy-court, Curia Sanctimotus*, for regulating the bakers of the city.

hallo, halloa (hə'ləʊ), *int.* and *sb.* [A later form of HOLLO (*hollow, holloa*), q.v. Cf. Ger. *hallo, halloh*, also OHG. *halâ, holâ*, emphatic imper. of *halôn, holôn* to fetch, used esp. in hailing a ferryman. Also written *hullo(a, hillo(a, hello*, from obscurity of the first syllable.] A shout or exclamation to call attention, or expressing some degree of surprise (e.g. on meeting some one unexpectedly). Cf. HALLOO. Freq. used as a greeting, etc., on a telephone. Also, repeated, as a locution indicating surprise. Cf. HELLO *int.* b, HULLO *int.* **A.** as *interj.* **1840** DICKENS *Barn. Rudge* x, 'Halloa there! Hugh!' roared John. **1864** H. SPENCER *Illustr. Univ. Progr.* 217 Any phrase with which one may be heard to accost the other—as 'Hallo, are you here?' **1942** A. CHRISTIE *Body in Library* ii. 24 Hallo, 'allo, 'allo, what's this? **1972** *Police Rev.* 10 Nov. 1473/2 You could have a walking, talking plastic Policeman ..saying 'Allo, allo, allo.'

B. as *sb.* *a***1898** *Mod.* I gave a loud halloa. Loud halloas were now heard in all directions. **1932** *N. & Q.* 6 Aug. 105/2 The telephonic 'hallo'.

hallo, halloa (hə'ləʊ), *v.* [f. prec.] *intr.* To shout or exclaim 'hallo!' **1781** MAD. D'ARBLAY *Diary* May, They were all halloaing at this oddity. **1863** KINGSLEY *Water Bab.* 6 The groom saw him, and halloed to him to know where Mr. Grimes..lived. **1884** *Pall Mall G.* 7 Nov. 2/2 There must be no halloaing before we are out of the wood.

hallock, var. HOLLOCK, *Obs.*, a Spanish wine.

Hall of Fame. orig. and chiefly *U.S.* **1.** A place where famous persons are commemorated, as the Hall of Fame for Great Americans in New York City or the National Baseball Hall of Fame and Museum at Cooperstown, New York State. *U.S.* **1901** *Land of Sunshine* Jan. 61 The Columbia College 'Hall of Fame' includes various more or less useful Americans and excludes Edgar Allan Poe. **1913** W. P. EATON *Barn Doors & Byways* 122 Only a year or two ago a red fox was seen in New York City,..on the wooded hillside sloping toward the Harlem River at University Heights near the Hall of Fame. **1957** *Encycl. Brit.* III. 166E/2 On June 12, 1939, the National Baseball Hall of Fame and Museum was dedicated at Cooperstown, N.Y. *Ibid.* XI. 106B/2 The Hall of Fame for Great Americans is a semicircular granite colonnade on the campus of New York university... It was established in 1900..and was dedicated in 1901. **1975** *New Yorker* 17 Nov. 150/3 Concluding his acceptance speech at Cooperstown, when he was taken into the Baseball Hall of Fame: 'And I want to thank the tremendous fans'.

2. *transf.* and *fig.* **1903** H. HAPGOOD *Autobiogr. Thief* xii. 265 Whenever I square it and go to work I am nailed, because my mug is in the Hall of Fame. **1927** *My Oklahoma* June 14/1 In the Hall of Fame of the aboriginals there is no name like that of Sequoyah. **1941** J. S. HUXLEY *Uniqueness of Man* xii. 252 Who really is who?.. *Who's Who* should provide the answer ..In what proportion are the different professions and occupations represented in the Annual Hall of Fame? **1950** *Sport* 22–28 Sept. 18/2 Jack left his father's butcher's shop in his native Belfast to carve a niche in the football hall of fame. **1977** *Time* 16 May 57/3 The moment passes, but not before it is inducted into the Hall of Fame of the mind. **1986** *ZX Computing Monthly* Oct. 34/4 A range of options including joysticks and starting levels is provided and a full high score 'hall of fame' is included.

Hence **Hall of Famer**, one elected or belonging to a Hall of Fame (esp. in *Baseball*). **1948** *Age-Herald* (Birmingham, Ala.) 24 Mar. 15/6 'It looks as if I'll be here for awhile,' the baseball hall of famer explained. **1976** *Billings* (Montana) *Gaz.* 16 June 3C/8 Gaylord Perry moved past Hall of Famers Bob Feller and Warren Spahn into sixth place on the all-time strikeout list Tuesday night.

halloo (hə'luː), *int.* and *sb.* [Goes with HALLOO *v.*; it may be a varied form of HOLLO *int.* and *sb.*, suited to a prolonged cry intended to be heard at a distance.] An exclamation to incite dogs to the chase, to call attention at a distance, to express surprise, etc. **A.** as *interj.* [**1605** SHAKS. *Lear* III. iv. 79 Pillicock sat on Pillicock hill, alow; alow, loo, loo.] *a***1700** DRYDEN (J.), Some popular chief..but cries halloo, And, in a trice, the bellowing herd come out. **1728** SWIFT *Mullinix & Timothy* Wks. 1755 III. II. 213 Will none of the Tory dogs pursue, When through the streets I cry *halloo*? **1796** SCOTT *Wild Huntsman* i, The Wildgrave winds his bugle-horn, To horse, to horse! halloo! halloo! **1875** JOWETT *Plato* (ed. 2) III. 311 Halloo! I said, I begin to perceive a track.

B. as *sb.* (See also VIEW-HALLOO.) **1707** FRIEND *Peterborow's Cond. Sp.* 211 Be sure..you answer with an English Halloo. **1810** SCOTT *Lady of L.* II. XXXVII, The minstrel heard the far halloo. **1859** *Art of Taming Horses, &c.* xii. 201 When hounds do not come up to the huntsman's halloo till moved by the whipper-in, they are said to dwell. **1885** W. A. B. HAMILTON *Mr. Montenello* II. 47 A piercing view-halloo announces the much-desired event.

halloo (hə'luː), *v.* Also 7 **hallew**. [Either f. HALLOO *int.* and *sb.*, or a variant of earlier HALLOW *v.*[2], with shifted stress as in OF. *ha'loer, il ha'loe*.]

1. a. *intr.* To shout 'halloo' to dogs in order to urge them on. **b.** *trans.* To urge on or incite with shouts.

It is doubtful whether the first two quotations belong here or to HALLOW *v.*[2]

1568 *Hist. Jacob & Esau* I. ii. in Hazl. *Dodsley* II. 195 Then maketh he [Esau] with his horn such toohing and blowing, And with his wide throat such shouting and hallooing. **1606** J. CARPENTER *Solomon's Solace* xli. 162 Admonitions whereby he halleweth men away from those vanities. **1717** PRIOR *Alma* II. 312 Old John halloos his hounds again. **1826** SCOTT *Jrnl.* 17 Feb., Many who have hallooed me on at public meetings, [etc.]. **1836** H. ROGERS *J. Howe* viii. (1863) 214 Bishops, who hallooed on the inferior clergy..in this cruel and ignoble sport.

2. *intr.* To shout in order to attract attention; to holla. **1722** DE FOE *Plague* 105, I halloo and call to them till I make them hear. **1791** MRS. RADCLIFFE *Rom. Forest* i, His conductor then hallooed. **1805** WORDSW. *Waggoner* III. 124 Hallooing from an open throat, Like travellers shouting for a boat. **1807** PIKE *Sources Mississ.* (1810) 25 We were.. hallooed after to go into every lodge to eat. **1814** JANE AUSTEN *Mansfield Park* (1870) III. vii. 333 Hallooing out at sudden starts.

b. Proverb. ***not to halloo until one is out of the wood***, not to shout till one is safe from robbers in the forest; esp. *fig.* not to exult till all danger or difficulty is past. **1801** W. HUNTINGTON *Bank of Faith* 85 But, alas! I hallooed before I was out of the wood. **1876** FAIRBAIRN in *Contemp. Rev.* June 137 He halloos, not only before he is out of the wood, but before he is well into it.

3. *trans.* To shout (something) aloud. **1602** MARSTON *Ant. & Mel.* III. Wks. 1856 I. 31 He might fall thus, upon the breast of earth, And in her eare halloo his misery. **1814** JANE AUSTEN *Mansf. Park* (1870) III. viii. 341 The servants hallo'd out their excuses from the kitchen. **1851** D. JERROLD *St. Giles* xiii. 134 He hallooed into the gaping ears of the landlady the terrible intelligence.

Hence **ha'llooing** *vbl. sb.* and *ppl. a.* **1568** [see sense 1]. **1748** F. SMITH *Voy. Disc.* I. 24 We heard a Hallooing from Shorewards. **1808** J. BARLOW *Columb.* VI. 540 And with hallooing blast Shake the vast wilderness.

halloo-baloo, -bo-loo: see HULLABALOO.

hallow ('hæləʊ), *sb.*[1] Usually in pl. **hallows**. Forms: 1 **hálga**, *fem.* **hálȝe**, 2–4 **halȝe**, **-ȝie**, **haleȝe**, **haliȝ**, etc.; also 3–4 **halwe**, **halewe**, 4 **halu**,

4-6 halow(e, etc. Plural: α. 1 **hálᵹan, 2-4 halȝen, 2 halechen, 3 haleȝ(h)en,** *Orm.* **hallȝhenn, alhen;** also 3-5 **halwen, halewen** (3 **haluwen,** 4 **hawen),** 5 **halowen.** β. 3 **halhe,** 3-4 **halwe.** γ. 4 **halȝhes, -is, haliȝhis, halyȝhs,** 4-5 **haloȝh(e)s;** also 3-5 **halwes,** 4 **(alwes), hal(e)wis, halouys, hawlouys, halus,** 4-5 **halowis, -ous(e, -owse,** 4-6 **halow(e)s,** 5 **halewes, -oes, (aleues),** 6- **hallows,** (6-7 **-es).** [OE. *hálᵹa*, definite form of *háliᵹ* adj. holy (*se hálᵹa, seo hálᵹe*, the holy (man, woman), *þa hálᵹan* the holy ones), used at length as an ordinary weak sb. (Cf. Ger. *der heilige, die heiligen*, L. *sanctus*, It. *santo*, F. *saint*.) The *-en* plural was retained in the south during the ME. period, while *halwes* appeared in midl. and north before 1300. In the radical form *háliᵹ*, the *á* became regularly *ō*, and the *iᵹ* became *-y*; but in *hálᵹa* the consonant group caused shortening of the *á* to *a*, and the *ᵹ* before a back-vowel produced *w*, between which and the *l* was developed *o*, as in *arrow*, *widow*, etc. Cf. HALLOW *v.*¹]

1. A holy personage, a SAINT. (Little used after 1500, and now preserved only in ALL-HALLOWS and its combinations, q.v.)

a **885** *Will of Alfred* in Earle *Land Ch.* 148 On godes naman and on his haliᵹra. *c* **1000** ÆLFRIC *Hom.* II. 142 Cuðberhtus se halᵹa siððan ᵹefremode mihtiᵹlice wundra on ðam mynstre wuniᵹende. *c* **1000** —— *Saints' Lives* (E.E.T.S.) II. 52 Swa swa seo haliᵹe [St. Mary] ær foresæde. **1154** *O.E. Chron.* an. 1137 §5 Hi sæden openlice ðæt crist slep & his halechen. *c* **1200** *Trin. Coll. Hom.* 5 Ure louerd wile cume and alle his haleȝen mid him. *c* **1200** ORMIN 6009 Bitwenenn Godess hallȝhenn. *a* **1225** *Juliana* 76 As hit deh alhen [*MS. B.* halhe] to donne. **1230** *Hali Meid.* 19 Dream ..þat nane halwes ne mahen. *a* **1240** *Lofsong* in *Cott. Hom.* 217 Imennesse of haluwen. *c* **1290** *S. Eng. Leg.* I. 53/227 Heiȝ halewe in heouene is. **1297** R. GLOUC. (1724) 82 Grete halwe.. As Seynt Cristyne & Seynt Fey. *Ibid.* 233 Mony ys the holy halwe, that her y bured ys. *Ibid.* 255 Ye relykes of halewen yfounde were. *a* **1300** *Cursor M.* 10402 Of halus hei in heuen blis. *Ibid.* 29549 (Cott. Galba) It takes him fro þe cumpany of halows. *c* **1300** *Ibid.* 22592 (Edin.) Es na halȝie [*v. rr.* halu, halwe] vndir þe heuin. **13..** *Sir Beues* 1218 (MS. A.) Deliure a þef fro þe galwe, He þe hateþafter be alle halwe! [*v. rr.* alle halowse, al halowes]. *c* **1325** *Prose Psalter* li[i]. 9 In þe syȝt of þyn halwen. *c* **1330** R. BRUNNE *Chron.* (1810) 182, I vowe to Saynt Michael, & tille halwes þat are. **1340** HAMPOLE *Psalter* v. 15 Ymange aungels & haloghs. **1340** —— *Pr. Consc.* 5119 Alle his halghes sal with him come. *c* **1350** *Will. Palerne* 371 To crist & to hal alwes. *c* **1380** WYCLIF *Wks.* (1880) 48 Acursed of god of fraunseis and of alle hawen. *c* **1386** CHAUCER *Prol.* 14 To ferne halwes [*v.r.* halowes] kowthe in sondry londes. **1387** TREVISA *Higden* (Rolls) I. A chirche of al halwen..oure Lady is after Crist cheef halwe of al mankynde. *c* **1400** MAUNDEV. (Roxb.) xiii. 60 Him þai honoure and wirschepes before all oþer halowes. *c* **1430** *Pilgr. Lyf Manhode* II. cxlvii. (1869) 133 Ayenst god and alle hise halwen. *c* **1440** *Sir Gowther* 380 Yet may she sum good halowe seche. *c* **1489** CAXTON *Sonnes of Aymon* iii. 99, I swere you vpon all halowes. *Ibid.* xix. 418, I swere to you, sire, by all halowen. **1553** BECON *Reliques of Rome* (1563) 238 Martyrs, Confessours, and virgines, and the halowes of God. **1647** *Pol. Ballads* (1860) I. 67 Watson, thee I long to see By God, and by the Hallowes. [**1876** FREEMAN *Norm. Conq.* V. 284 Men said openly that Christ slept and His hallows. (See quot. 1154.)]

2. In *pl.* applied to the shrines or relics of saints; the gods of the heathen or their shrines.

In the phrase *to seek hallows*, to visit the shrines or relics of saints; orig. as in sense 1, the saints themselves being thought of as present at their shrines. Cf. quot. *c* 1440 in 1.

c **1200** *Vices & Virtues* (1888) 3 Ðo menn ðe halleð gode behaten god te donne, oðer halȝe to sechen. *c* **1385** CHAUCER *L.G.W.* 1310 *Dido*, Sche sekith halwis & doth sacryfise. *c* **1400** *Destr. Troy* 650 Swiftly to sweire vpon swete haloghes. *Ibid.* 10948 With Sacrifice solemne [þai] soghten þere halowes. *c* **1489** CAXTON *Sonnes of Aymon* xxvi. 552, I wylle..that ye bere wyth you the halowes for to make theym swere thervpon. **1523** SKELTON *Garl. Laurel* 1636 Right is over the fallows Gone to seke hallows. **1561** *Schole-ho. Wom.* 309 in Hazl. *E.P.P.* IV. 117 On pilgremage then must they go, To Wilsdon, Barking, or to some hallowes.

b. *holy of hallows*: see HOLY.

3. hallow- in *Comb.* (chiefly in *Sc.*) is used for ALL-HALLOW- = All Saints'-, in HALLOW-DAY, HALLOW-E'EN, HALLOWMAS, HALLOW-TIDE; also **hallow-fair**, a fair or market held at Hallowmas; **hallow-fire**, a bonfire kindled on All-hallow-e'en, an ancient Celtic observance.

1795 MACPHERSON *Wyntoun's Cron.* Gloss., Halow-fair is held on the day of all saints. **1799** *Statist. Acc. Scotl.* XXI. 145 (Jam.) But now the hallow fire, when kindled, is attended by children only.

hallow (ˈhæləʊ), *sb.*² Forms: 5 **halow,** 6- **hallow,** 7-9 **hallo, halloo.** [f. HALLOW *v.*² Often identified in spelling with HALLOO, although pronounced with stress on first syllable.] A loud shout or cry, to incite dogs in the chase, to help combined effort, or to attract attention.

c **1440** *Promp. Parv.* 223/2 Halow, schypmannys crye, *celeuma.* **1583** STANYHURST *Æneis* II. (Arb.) 45 With shouting clamorus hallow. **1603** DRAYTON *Bar Wars* II. (R.), With noise of hounds and halloos as distraught. **1634** MILTON *Comus* 481 List! list! I hear Some far-off hallo break the silent air. **1783** COWPER *Epit. Hare* 4 Whose foot ne'er tainted morning dew, Nor ear heard huntsmen's hallo. **1837** W. IRVING *Capt. Bonneville* III. 226 Gallopping, with whoop and halloo, into the camp.

†**hallow,** *sb.*³ *Obs.* [prob. the same word as HALLOW *sb.*², transferred to the material encouragement given to the hounds.] The parts of the hare given to hounds as a reward or encouragement after a successful chase.

c **1420** *Venery de Twety* in *Rel. Ant.* I. 153 Whan the hare is take, and your houndes have ronne wele to hym ye shul blowe aftirward, and ye shul yef to your houndes the halow, and that is the syde, the shuldres, the nekke, and the hed, and the loyne shal to kechonne. **1486** *Bk. St. Albans* E iij b, Wich rewarde when oon the erth it is dalt With all goode hunteris the halow it is calt. **1576** TURBERV. *Venerie* 174 Which the Frenchman calleth the reward, and sometimes the quarey, but our old Tristram calleth it the hallow. **1688** R. HOLME *Armoury* II. 188/1 Hallow..a reward given to Hounds, of beast that are not beasts of Venery.

hallow (ˈhæləʊ), *v.*¹ Forms: 1 **hálᵹian,** 2-3 **haleȝe(n,** 2-4 **-iȝe(n,** 2-5 **-we(n,** 3 **(alȝen),** *Orm.* **hallȝhenn,** 3-4 **halȝe(n,** **-ie(n,** 3-5 **halewe(n,** 3-7 **halow(e,** (4 **halu, -ugh,** 5 **helewe, hawlowe),** 6- **hallow.** [OE. *hálᵹian, -ode*, = OS. *hêlagôn* (M.Du. *hēligen, heiligen*), OHG. *heilagôn* (Ger. (*heiligen*), ON. *helga* (Sw. *helga*, Da. *hellige*), Com. Teut. deriv. of *hailag-* HOLY. For the ME. shortening of the *á* to *a*, see HALLOW *sb.*¹]

1. *trans.* To make holy; to sanctify, purify.

c **1000** *Ags. Gosp.* John xvii. 19 Ic halᵹiᵹe me sylfne þæt hiᵹ syn eac ᵹehalᵹode. *c* **1000** ÆFRIC *Exod.* xix. 10 Ȝehalᵹa hiᵹ todæᵹ. *c* **1200** ORMIN 10803 He wollde uss hallȝhenn. *a* **1225** *Ancr. R.* 396 Jesu Cristes blod þet haleweð boð þeos oðre. *a* **1340** HAMPOLE *Psalter* xvii. 28 Traist in him þat he will halighe þe. **1340** *Ayenb.* 237 Miȝtoul uor to halȝy ham þet hit onderuongeþ. **1382** WYCLIF *John* xi. 55 Many of the cuntree stiȝeden vp to Jerusalem the day bifore pask, for to halowe them selue. *Ibid.* xvii. 17 Halwe thou hem in treuthe. *c* **1532** DEWES *Introd. Fr.* in Palsgr. 954 To halowe, *sainctifier.* **1638** BAKER tr. Balzac's Lett. (vol. III). 25 Those women whose teares Antiquitie hath hallowed. **1837** R. NICOLL *Poems* (1843) 1 Chief of the Household Gods Which hallow Scotland's lowly cottage-homes! **1892** WESTCOTT *Gospel of Life* 299 Christianity..meets and hallows our broadest views of nature and life.

2. To consecrate, set apart (a person or thing) as sacred to God; to dedicate to some sacred or religious use or office; to bless a thing so that it may be under the particular protection of a deity, or possess divine virtue. *arch.*

971 *Blickl. Hom.* 205 Gif hit sie mannes ᵹemet þæt he circean halᵹian sceole. *a* **1175** *Cott. Hom.* 223 On þan seofeðan deȝ he ȝeendode his wurc..and þane deȝ halȝode. *c* **1205** LAY. 17496 þe king..hæt halȝien þe stude, þe hæhte Stanhenge. **1297** R. GLOUC. (1724) 358 The pope asoyled & blessed Wyllam & al hys..And halewede hys baner. *a* **1300** *Cursor M.* 8867 Quen þat þe temple halughd was. **1398** TREVISA *Barth. De P.R.* XVI. lxxxvi. (1495) 582 Saphire stone was syngulerly halowed to Appolin. **1494** FABYAN *Chron.* I. cxxxii. (R.), For to dedicate and halowe the monastery of Seynt Denys in moost solempne wyse. **1547** BOORDE *Introd. Knowl.* i. (1870) 121 The Kynges of Englande doth halowe euery yere Crampe rynges. **1579** SPENSER *Sheph. Cal.* Feb. 210 Often crost with the priestes crewe, And often halowed with holy water dewe. **1648** GAGE *West. Ind.* 152 Candlemas day..Bring their Candles to be blessed and hallowed. **1868** FREEMAN *Norm. Conq.* II. vii. 112 Leo..entered France..to hallow the newly built church of his monastery.

†**b.** To consecrate (a person) to an office, as bishop, king, etc. *Obs.*

c **900** tr. *Bæda's Hist.* I. xvi. [xxvii.] (1890) 62 Se halᵹa wer Agustinus..wæs ᵹehalᵹod ercebiscop Ongolþeode. *c* **1000** *O.E. Chron.* an. 979 On þys ᵹeare wæs Æþelred to cininge ᵹehalᵹod. **1154** *Ibid.* an. 1135 And halechede him to kinge on midewintre dæi. *c* **1325** *Metr. Hom.* 79 Thir nonnes when that thai halowid ware, Thai toke thaire leue hame to fare. [**1871** FREEMAN *Norm. Conq.* IV. xviii. 179 And there..the Lady Matilda was hallowed to Queen by Archbishop Eldred. **1872** E. W. ROBERTSON *Hist. Ess.* 207 In the reign of Offa..Ecgfrith was 'hallowed to king'.]

†**c.** To consecrate (the eucharistic elements). *Obs.*

c **1200** ORMIN 1727 Þær he Cristess flæsh and blod Hanndleþþ, hallȝheþþ, and offreþþ.

3. To honour as holy, to regard and treat with reverence or awe (esp. God or his name).

a **1000** *Hymns* v. 2 (Gr.) Sy þinum weorcum halᵹad noma niððа bearnum! *c* **1000** *Ags. Gosp.* Matt. vi. 9 Fader ure þu þe ert on heofene, sye þin name ᵹehalᵹed. *a* **1300** *Cursor M.* 25104 Halud be þi nam to neuen. **1382** WYCLIF *Deut.* xxxii. 51 Ȝe halwide not me amonge the sones of Yrael. *a* **1440** *Sir Degrev.* 91 They hade halowed hys name Wyth gret nobullé. *c* **1600** SHAKS. *Sonn.* cviii, Euen as when first I hallowed thy faire name. **1611** BIBLE *Matt.* vi. 9 Our father which art in heauen, hallowed be thy Name. **1645** USSHER *Body Div.* (1647) 358 To hallow the name of God, is to separate it from all profane and unholy abuse, to a holy and reverend use.

4. *trans.* To keep (a day, festival, etc.) holy; to observe solemnly.

971 *Blickl. Hom.* 37 Halᵹiaþ eower fæsten. *c* **1175** *Lamb. Hom.* 45 To haliȝen and to wurðien þenne dei þe is icleped sunne dei. *c* **1380** WYCLIF *Sel. Wks.* III. 85 Have mynde to halwe þin holiday. **1389** *Eng. Gilds* (1870) 17 Euery brother & sister..shullen halwen euermore ye day of seint George. *a* **1533** LD. BERNERS *Gold. Bk. M. Aurel.* (1546) D vij b, Halowyng the feasste of themperours natiuitie. **1552** ABP. HAMILTON *Catech.* (1884) 66 Remember that thow hallow the Sabboth day. **1796** COLERIDGE *Left Place of Retirement* 10 Hallowing his Sabbath-day by quietness.

†**b.** *absol.* To keep holy day. *Obs.*

c **1200** *Trin. Coll. Hom.* 155 Hure riht time þenne men fasten shal oðer halȝen. **1303** R. BRUNNE *Handl. Synne* 929 Haleweþ wyþ us at þe noun In þe wurschyp of oure lady. **1496** *Dives & Paup.* (W. de W.) I. xviii. 51/1 Tyme to halowe and tyme to labour.

hallow (ˈhæləʊ), *v.*² Forms: 4-7 **halow,** 6-8 **hallow,** 7-9 **hallo, halloo.** See also HOLLOW. [ME. *halow-en*, corresp. to and prob. a. OF. *hallo-er* to pursue crying or shouting.]

1. *trans.* **a.** To chase or pursue with shouts. **b.** To urge on or incite with shouts. **c.** To call or summon *in*, *back*, etc. with shouting.

c **1340** *Cursor M.* (Trin.) 15833 þei..foule halowed him.. as he had ben an hounde. *c* **1369** CHAUCER *Dethe Blaunche* 379 þe hert found is I-halowed and rechased fast long tyme. **1399** LANGL. *Rich. Redeles* III. 228 He was halowid and y-huntid, and y-hote trusse. **1530** PALSGR. 577/2, I halowe houndes with a krye. **1587** FLEMING *Contn. Holinshed* III. 1003/1 To hallow home cardinall Poole their countriman. **1674** N. COX *Gentl. Recreat.* I. (1677) 99 Hallow in your Hounds untill they have all undertaken it. **1696** S. SEWALL *Diary* 13 Jan. (1878) I. 419, I went to Sheaf and he hallowed over Jno. Russell again. *a* **1713** ELLWOOD *Autobiog.* (1765) 265 Clapping their Hands and hallowing them on to this evil Work. **1812** *Sporting Mag.* XXXIX. 184 They [fox hounds] were then halloed back.

2. *intr.* To shout, in order to urge on dogs to the chase, assist combined effort, or attract attention.

c **1420** *Anturs of Arth.* v, The hunteres they haulen [= halwen], by hurstes and by hoes. *c* **1440** *Promp. Parv.* 224/1 Halowyn, or cryyn as schypmen (*P.* halowen with cry), *celeumo.* **1525** LD. BERNERS *Froiss.* II. lxi. [lxiv.] 209 They.. halowed after them as thoughe they had ben wolues. **1567** W. WREN in Hakluyt *Voy.* (1589) 149 When they hallowed we hallowed also. **1612** DRAYTON *Polyolb.* xiii. 216 The shepherd him pursues, and to his dog doth halow. **1634** MILTON *Comus* 226, I cannot halloo to my brothers. **1815** W. H. IRELAND *Scribbleomania* 2 Though loudly the Bards all against me may halloo, I rank with the time a true chip of Apollo.

3. *trans.* To shout (something) aloud.

? *a* **1400** *Morte Arth.* 3319 What harmes he has hente he halowes fulle sone. **1601** SHAKS. *Twel. N.* I. v. 291 Halloo your name to the reuerberate hilles. **1676** DRYDEN *Aurengz.* v. i. 2226 In your Ear Will hallow, Rebel, Tyrant, Murtherer. **1812** H. & J. SMITH *Rej. Addr.* ix. (1873) 82 And never halloo 'Heads below!'

Hence **ˈhallowing** *vbl. sb.* and *ppl. a.*

13.. *Gaw. & Gr. Knt.* 1602 There watȝ blawyng of prys in mony breme horne, Heȝe halowing on hiȝe. **1483** *Cath. Angl.* 172/1 An Halowynge of hundis, *boema.* **1569** J. SANFORD tr. *Agrippa's Van. Artes* Pref., The hallowinge Hunter, will set his houndes and hawkes upon me. **1597** SHAKS. *2 Hen. IV*, I. ii. 213 Hallowing and singing of Anthemes. **1755** B. MARTIN *Mag. Arts & Sc.* 156 Making great Noises by hallowing, hooting, etc.

†**ˈhallow,** *int. Obs.* [app. a variant of *hollo* interj., influenced by HALLOW *v.*², *sb.*²] An exclamation to arouse to action, or to excite attention.

1674 BUTLER *Geneva Ballad* 63 Heark! How he opens with full Cry! Hallow my Hearts, beware of Rome.

hallow, obs. or dial. form of HOLLOW *a.*

ˈHallow-day. *dial.* [In 1, short for ALL-HALLOW-DAY, q.v.; in 2, from HALLOW *sb.*¹]

1. All Saints' day, the first of November.

1596 DALRYMPLE tr. *Leslie's Hist. Scot.* IX. 200 Jn Edʳ vpon a [= a'] Halow day, rais sik a wind and wethir. **1711** *C.M. Lett. to Curat* 10 In any time of K. Edward the 6th's Reign, preceeding Hallow-day 1552. **1854** H. MILLER *Sch. & Schm.* (1858) 292 We had completed all our work ere Hallowday.

2. A saint's day; a holy day, a holiday.

a **1825** FORBY *Voc. E. Anglia, Hallowday*, a holiday. *a* **1829** *Clerk's Twa Sons o Owsenford* xvi. in Child *Ballads* III. lxxii. (1885) 175/2 Till the hallow days o Yule.

hallowed (ˈhæləʊd, ˈhæləʊɪd), *ppl. a.* [f. HALLOW *v.*¹ + -ED¹.] Sanctified, blessed, consecrated, dedicated.

c **900** tr. *Bæda's Hist.* IV. xxxii. [xxxi.] (1890) 380 Ðone ᵹehalᵹodan lichoman Cuðberhtes. *a* **1300** *Cursor M.* 29256 Wit ani halud [*v.r.* halowde] thing. *a* **1340** HAMPOLE *Psalter* xix. 2 A halighid kyrke. **1512** *Act 4 Hen. VIII*, c. 2 §1 In eny Churche Chapell or halowed place. **1655** FULLER *Ch. Hist.* v. iv. §28 That the Hallowed oyl is no better than the Bishop of Rome his grease or butter. **1804** J. GRAHAME *Sabbath* 1 How still the morning of the hallowed day! **1859** S. LONGFELLOW *Hymn* i, Again, as evening shadow falls, We gather in these hallowed walls.

Hence **ˈhallowedly** *adv.*; **ˈhallowedness.**

1828 SCOTT *F.M. Perth* xxvii, In all the hallowedness of resignation. **1834** H. O'BRIEN *Round Towers Irel.* 364 As hallowedly expressive as they were ever before. **1866** ALGER *Solit. Nat.* II. 49 Lest their hallowedness be profaned.

Hallow-e'en. *Sc.* [Shortened from *All-Hallow-Even*: see ALL-HALLOW 4.] The eve of All Hallows' or All Saints'; the last night of October. Also *attrib.*

In the Old Celtic calendar the year began on 1st November, so that the last evening of October was 'old-year's night', the night of all the witches, which the Church transformed into the Eve of All Saints.

1556-1698 [see *All Hallow Eve*, ALL-HALLOW 4]. **17..** *Young Tamlane* in *Border Ministr.* (1869) 478 This night is Hallowe'en, Janet, The morn is Hallowday. **1773** FERGUSSON *Eclogue* 18 Nae langer bygane than sin Halloween. **1785** BURNS *Halloween* ii, To burn their nits, an' pou their stocks, An' haud their Halloween. **1808-18** JAMIESON, *To haud Halloween*, to observe the childish or superstitious rites appropriated to this evening. **1864** *Chambers' Bk. Days* II. 519/1 The evening of the 31st of October, known as All Hallows' Eve or Halloween. It is the night set apart for a universal walking abroad of spirits. **1883** J. HAWTHORNE in *Harper's Mag.* Nov. 930/2

Halloween is the carnival-time of disembodied spirits. **1884** Q. VICTORIA *More Leaves* 69 We saw the commencement of the keeping of Halloween.

attrib. **1795** *Statist. Acc. Scotl.* XV. 517 Formerly the *Hallow Even Fire*, a relic of Druidism, was kindled in Buchan.

'hallower. [f. HALLOW *v.*[1] + -ER[1].] One who or that which hallows, sanctifies, or consecrates; a sanctifier, consecrator.

1382 WYCLIF *Ezek.* xxxvii. 28, I the Lord, halewer of Yrael. *c* **1440** *Promp. Parv.* 224/2 Halware of holydayes, *celebrator.* **1548** CRANMER *Catech.* 140 The holy gost, is yᵉ commen sanctifier or halower. **1607** *Schol. Disc. agst. Antichr.* II. vi. 62 The..grande hallower and consecrator of al holy things.

'hallowing, *vbl. sb.*[1] [f. as prec. + -ING[1].] The action of the verb HALLOW; consecration, dedication, sanctification.

c **900** tr. *Bæda's Hist.* I. xvi. [xxvii.] (1890) 72 Æt biscopes halȝunge. *a* **1300** *Cursor M.* 10215 Þe haluing Of temple. **1398** TREVISA *Barth. De P.R.* IX. xxxi. (1495) 368 Thenne men goon wyth processyon to the fonte halowinge. **1482** *Churchw. Acc. Yatton* (Som. Rec. Soc.) 113 Costs for hawluyng of the Cherche erde. **1668** WILKINS *Real Char.* 397 Consecrating or Hallowing. **1875** MANNING *Mission H. Ghost* v. 127 The hallowing of the name of God is that He may be known, and worshipped..and honoured by all His creatures.

'hallowing, *ppl. a.*[1] [f. as prec. + -ING[2].] That hallows; sanctifying.

c **1175** *Lamb. Hom.* 103 Twa sarinesse beoð, an is þeos uuele oðer is halwende. *a* **1225** *St. Marher.* 18 Wið þe halwunde fur of þe hali gast. **1738** WESLEY *Psalms* v, On Thee, O God of Purity, I wait for hallowing Grace. **1885** *Athenæum* 14 Feb. 226/1 The civilizing and hallowing influence of Christianity.

hallowing, *vbl. sb.*[2] and *ppl. a.*[2]: see after HALLOW *v.*[2]

Hallowmas ('hæləumæs). Forms: See HALLOW *sb.*; also 4 **hallomese, halumes,** 6 **hollomass,** 7 **hallamas.** [Shortened from *All-Hallow-mass*: see ALL-HALLOW 5.] The feast of All Hallows or All Saints. Also *attrib.*, as ***Hallowmas-day, -eve.***

1389 in *Eng. Gilds* (1870) 60 Ye soneday be-forn halwemesse day. *Ibid.* 69 Ye souneday next after halumesday. *c* **1450** *Merlin* 97 At halowmasse Antor made hys sone knyght, and at yoole he come to logres. **1590** GREENWOOD *Collect. Sclaund. Art.* Fivb, Your solempne and double feasts of your hollomass, Christmass, Candlemass. **1593** SHAKS. *Rich. II*, v. i. 80 She came adorned hither like sweet May; Sent back like Hallowmas, or short'st of day. **1688** R. HOLME *Armoury* III. 268/2 Sow Wheat before Hallowmas Eve. **1786** BURNS *Twa Dogs* 123 As bleakfac'd Hallowmass returns. *a* **1832** SCOTT *St. Swithin's Chair*, On Hallow-Mass Eve the Night-Hag will ride. **1876** GRANT *Burgh Sch. Scotl.* II. xiv. 469 The old quarterly terms for paying the school fees were Lammas, Hallowmas, Candlemas, and Beltane.

† **'Hallow-tide.** *Obs.* Forms: 5 **halow-,** 6 **halon-, halun-, hallon-,** 7 **hallen-, hallow-tide.** [Shortened from *All-Hallow-tide*, †*all hallowentyde*: see ALL-HALLOW 6.] The season of All Saints; the first week of November.

c **1450** *Merlin* 100 Antor hadde made his eldeste sone knyght at the halowtide be-fore yoole. *c* **1530** LD. BERNERS *Arth. Lyt. Bryt.* (1814) 444 The which shal be now at this Halontyde. **1573** TUSSER *Husb.* xxi. (1878) 55 At Hallontide, slaughter time entereth in. **1606** W. KELLETT in *Lismore Papers* Ser. II. (1887) I. 95 Against michelmas or hallentide. **1609** *Nottingham Rec.* IV. 292 On Saint Mathew daye, and so till Hallowtyd.

halloysite (hə'lɔɪzaɪt). *Min.* [Named 1826, after d'Halloy, a Belgian geologist; see -ITE.] A clay-like earthy mineral, a hydrated aluminium silicate, resulting from the decomposition of felspar.

1827 *Edin. Jrnl. Sc.* VI. 183 Halloysite, a new mineral species. **1837** THOMSON in *Proc. Berw. Nat. Club* I. No. 5. 157 Adheres to the tongue like Halloysite. **1849** DANA *Geol.* iii. (1850) 208 The Halloysite group of minerals.

Hallstatt ('halʃtat). The name of a village in Upper Austria, the site of an ancient necropolis, where rich archæological finds have been made, used *attrib.* to denote a phase of the early Iron Age, and the type of civilization of that period. So **Hall'stattian** *a.*

1866 J. LUBBOCK *Addr. Primæval Antiquities Archæol. Inst.* 17 The significance of the absence of silver in the Hallstadt find is greatly increased when we see that in the true Iron age..silver was used. **1869** —— *Pre-Historic Times* (ed. 2) i. 24 M. Ramsauer..director of the salt mines at Hallstadt, near Salzburg, in Austria, has discovered an extensive cemetery belonging to this transitional period. *Ibid.* 25 Another interesting point in the Hallstadt bronze, as in that of the true Bronze Age, is the absence of silver, lead, and zinc. **1893** *Funk's Stand. Dict.* I. 812/3 Hallstattian. **1900** tr. *Deniker's Races of Man* 315 The so-called 'Hallstattian' period lasted in Central Europe, France, and Northern Italy from the tenth or ninth to the sixth century B.C. The Hallstattian civilisation flourished chiefly in Carinthia, Southern Germany, Switzerland, Bohemia, Silesia, Bosnia, the south-east of France, and Southern Italy. **1905** *Brit. Mus. Guide Antiq. Early Iron Age* 36 The drum-shaped brooch..is also not uncommon in the Hallstatt period. *Ibid.* 39 The Hallstatt stage of culture is well represented at Glasinatz. **1931** *Times Lit. Suppl.* 1 Oct. 753/3 Scanty traces of Hallstatt immigrants. **1958** *Ibid.* 19 Sept. 526/2 The general reader..will meet..the well-known cultures of Hallstatt and La Tène.

hallucal ('hæl(j)u:kəl), *a. Anat.* [f. HALLUX (*halluc-*) + -AL[1].] = next.

1889 *Century Dict.* mentions 'hallucal muscles'.

hallucar ('hæl(j)u:kə(r)), *a. Anat.* [f. as prec. + -AR.] Of or belonging to the hallux or great toe.

1856-8 W. CLARK *Van der Hoeven's Zool.* II. 620 Posterior feet with clawless hallucar wart, or pollex none.

hallucinant (hæ'l(j)u:sɪnənt), *sb.* and *a.* [f. HALLUCIN(ATE *v.* + -ANT[1].] **A.** *sb.* **a.** Someone who experiences hallucinations. **b.** A drug that induces hallucinations. **B.** *adj.* Producing or experiencing hallucinations.

1895 tr. *Nordau's Degeneration* I. iii. 32 The women devotees..did not merely believe that the hallucinant maiden had herself seen the vision, but all of them saw the Holy Virgin with their own eyes. **1910** A. W. VERRALL *Bacchants of Euripides* 72 In a hallucinant working by suggestion..such effects are perfectly natural. **1932** A. HUXLEY *Brave New World* iii. 63 Euphoric, narcotic, pleasantly hallucinant. **1964** *Punch* 30 Dec. 1013/2 Someone who knew her potions, her febrifuges and hallucinants.

hallucinate (hæ'l(j)u:sɪneɪt), *v.* [f. pa. ppl. stem of L. (*h*)*allūcinārī* (more correctly *ālūcinārī*), to wander in mind, talk idly, prate. Cf. F. *halluciner.*]

† **1.** *trans.* To deceive. *Obs. rare*[−0].

1604 R. CAWDREY *Table Alph., Hallucinate*, to deceiue, or blind. **1623** COCKERAM, *Hallucinate*, to deceiue.

2. *intr.* To be deceived, suffer illusion, entertain false notions, blunder, mistake. Also, to have a hallucination or hallucinations. Now chiefly *U.S.*

1652 GAULE *Magastrom.* 88 If prognosticators have so often hallucinated..about naturall effects. **1666** G. HARVEY *Morb. Angl.* ix. 75 Physicians do extreamly hallucinate in the discern of their causes. **1751** WARBURTON *On Pope* III. 287 (Jod.) It is no wonder that the verbal criticks should a little hallucinate in this matter. **1840** CARLYLE *Heroes* v. (1858) 329 The man who cannot think and see; but only hallucinate, and missee the nature of the thing. **1847** WEBSTER, Hallucinate. **1930** C. SPEARMAN *Creative Mind* x. 135 A man hallucinated that the clothes of the girls 'flew off them'. **1958** E. DUNDY *Dud Avocado* III. vi. 270 My first thought was that I had gone stark raving mad..and that I was now hallucinating in a looney bin. **1964** 'A. CROSS' *In last Analysis* iii. 31 Had such an idea crossed her mind, Kate would have decided that..she was 'hallucinating'. **1973** *Publishers Weekly* 19 Mar. 61/3 He describes her and is told, bluntly, that he is hallucinating.

3. *trans.* To affect with hallucination; to produce false impressions or perceptions in the mind of.

1822-34 *Good's Study Med.* (ed. 4) III. 117 Pascal himself was..so hallucinated with hypochondrism as to believe that he was always on the verge of an abyss. **1877** WRAXALL tr. *Hugo's 'Misérables'* I. iv, The scaffold..has something about it that hallucinates.

Hence **hal'lucinated, ha'llucinating** *ppl. adjs.*

a **1763** BYROM *Ep. to Friend* (R.), Some poor hallucinating scribe's mistake. **1886** GURNEY *Phantasms of Living* I. 461 The hallucinated person..imagined [etc.]. **1892** A. B. BRUCE *Apologetics* Introd. 27 It may be mistaken hallucinated conviction. **1903** E. WHARTON *Sanctuary* II. iv. 137 That hallucinating distinctness which belongs to the midnight vision. **1966** *New Statesman* 18 Feb. 233/2 Jennifer Dawson writes about the surface pain of living—with hallucinating effect.

hallucination (hæl(j)u:sɪ'neɪʃən). [ad. late L. *ālūcinātiōn-em* (*all-, hall-*), n. of action f. *ālūcinārī*: see HALLUCINATE *v.* Cf. F. *hallucination* (Dict. Acad. 1835).]

1. The mental condition of being deceived or mistaken, or of entertaining unfounded notions; with *a* and *pl.*, an idea or belief to which nothing real corresponds; an illusion.

a **1652** J. SMITH *Sel. Disc.* iv. 70 Notions..arising from the deceptions and hallucinations of sense. **1660** H. MORE *Myst. Godl.* v. xvi. 198 The Exposition is a mere hallucination. **1856** R. A. VAUGHAN *Mystics* (1860) I. 33 Reason..is not swept away by the hallucinations of sentiment.

2. *Path.* and *Psychol.* The apparent perception (usually by sight or hearing) of an external object when no such object is actually present. (Distinguished from *illusion* in the strict sense, as not necessarily involving a false belief.)

1646 SIR T. BROWNE *Pseud. Ep.* III. xviii. 153 If vision be abolished it is called *cæcitas*, or blindnesse, if depraved and receive its objects erroneously, Hallucination. **1859** HULME tr. *De Boismont's Hallucinations* Introd. 7 The most celebrated men have been liable to hallucinations, without their conduct offering any signs of mental alienation. **1886** GURNEY *Phantasms of Living* I. 459 The definition of a sensory hallucination would thus be a percept which lacks, but which can only by distinct reflection be recognised as lacking, the objective basis which it suggests.

hallucinative (hæ'l(j)u:sɪnətɪv), *a.* [f. *hallūcināt-*, pa. ppl. stem of L. *hallūcinārī* (see HALLUCINATE) + -IVE.] Productive of hallucination.

1873 J. FORSTER *Dickens* IX. i, The vividness of Dickens' imagination..[he] finds..to be simply hallucinative.

ha'llucinator. *rare.* [late L., agent-n. f. *hallūcinārī.*] One who hallucinates.

1860 WORCESTER cites *North Brit. Rev.*

hallucinatory (hæ'l(j)u:sɪnətərɪ), *a.* [f. *hallūcināt-*, pa. ppl. stem of L. *hallūcinārī* to HALLUCINATE + -ORY.] Characterized by, pertaining to, or of the nature of hallucination. Hence **halluci'natorily** *adv.*

1830 *Fraser's Mag.* I. 748 The indolent and hallucinatory oisivity of Campbell. **1843** CARLYLE *Past & Pr.* III. x, Hallucinatory visions rise. **1917** C. R. PAYNE tr. *Pfister's Psychoanalytic Method* xvii. 467 Then every time, out of hate and expiation, he changed hallucinatorily the feared one into the death's head. **1959** G. D. PAINTER *Marcel Proust* I. 178 They were irresistibly comic, and at the same time hallucinatorily accurate.

‖ **hallucinė** (hæ'l(j)u:sɪne). *rare.* [Fr.] A person who regularly suffers from hallucinations.

1886 *Buck's Hand-bk. Med. Sci.* III. 481/1 Nowadays the hallucinés hear voices through the telephone, and feel electric shocks. **1898** *Daily News* 20 Sept. 4/5 Genius goes somehow with what we call hysteria, most persons of genius being epileptic, or 'hallucinés'. **1909** W. JAMES *Let.* 19 Sept. in R. B. Perry *Thought & Char. W. James* (1935) II. lviii. 123, I strongly suspect Freud, with his dream-theory, of being a regular *halluciné.*

hallucinogen (hæ'l(j)u:sɪnədʒɛn). [f. HALLUCIN(ATION + -O + -GEN.] A drug which causes hallucinations (see HALLUCINATION 2).

1954 A. HOFFER et al. in *Jrnl. Mental Sci.* C. 30 When the literature is examined to catalogue these hallucinatory substances, which for convenience we have called the hallucinogens, one is struck by their small number. **1954** A. HUXLEY *Doors of Perception* 6 Lysergic acid, an extremely potent hallucinogen derived from ergot. **1955** *Jrnl. Mental Sci.* CI. 318 There are so few hallucinogens known that we must study intensively the types of sub-groups and molecules which cause hallucinations. **1958** *New Scientist* 28 Aug. 715/3 More recently..several hallucinogens have been observed which produce, in addition to other symptoms of schizophrenia, auditory hallucinations. **1969** *Times* 24 Jan. 6/6 The fly agaric fungus yields one of the most potent and anciently used hallucinogens, inducing a slight trembling followed by illusions.

So **ha,llucino'genic** *a.*, being or containing such a drug; causing hallucinations.

1952 *Jrnl. Mental Sci.* XCVIII. 311 There are many other hallucinogenic drugs, but none has either such striking properties or such a simple chemical constitution as mescaline. **1958** *Sci. News* XLVII. 36 Other lines of research..include the search for substances that antagonize the hallucinogenic drugs. **1959** *Times Lit. Suppl.* 27 Feb. 113/4 We believe our evidence points to a role for the hallucinogenic mushroom in the origins of the religious idea in primitive society. **1960** *Times* 31 Dec. 9/7 A liana of which the boiled juice has hallucinogenic effects. **1965** *Listener* 23 Sept. 465/1 It is a powerful mind-changer of the hallucinogenic variety. **1968** *Times* 13 Nov. 16/1 Many well known hallucinogenic drugs, such as LSD and mescaline, cause mice to exhibit the curious behaviour pattern of head twitching.

hallucinosis (hæ,l(j)u:sɪ'nəʊsɪs). *Psychiatry.* [f. HALLUCIN(ATION + -OSIS.] A disorder of the nervous system associated particularly with alcoholism, marked by persistent hallucinations, commonly auditory, with little if any impairment of consciousness.

1905 S. PATON *Psychiatry* xi. 300 Acute alcoholic hallucinosis. **1908** *Practitioner* Jan. 9 The acute hallucinosis and paranoidal forms of alcoholic insanity. **1912** OSLER & McCRAE *Princ. & Pract. Med.* (ed. 8) III. i. 399 Alcoholism. .. There is a condition termed *acute hallucinosis*, in which auditory hallucinations are marked..and the mental disturbances are fixed. Ideas of persecution are common. There are intermediate forms between this and the ordinary delirium tremens. **1914** *Amer. Jrnl. Insanity* LXX. II. 369 (*title*) Study of hallucinosis. **1962** HENDERSON & GILLESPIE *Text-bk. Psychiatry* xii. 291 Accompanied by..clear and orderly thinking, willing and acting; there is no real or genuine hallucinosis. **1964** LANDIS & METTLER *Varieties Psychopathol. Experience* xiv. 312 The horror, torture, and pain experienced during delirium tremens or alcoholic hallucinosis have been described many times.

‖ **hallux** ('hæləks). *Anat.* Pl. **halluces** ('hæl(j)usi:z). [mod.L., corrupted from *allex* (*allic-*) the great toe (Isidore *Gloss.*), found once in Plautus in phr. *allex viri* a 'thumb of a man', a thumbling.] The innermost of the digits (normally five in number) of the hind foot of an air-breathing vertebrate; the great toe; in birds (when present) usually either the inner or the hind toe. (Corresponding to the *pollex* or thumb of the fore limb.)

1831 R. KNOX *Cloquet's Anat.* 161 The Toes..are distinguished..by their numerical names..The first is also called the Great Toe, (*hallux*). **1839** W. JARDINE *Brit. Birds* II. 53 All [Insessores] have the hallux, or hind toe. **1872** NICHOLSON *Palæont.* 388 In the Emeu, Cassowary,..the hallux is..absent. **1875** tr. *Schmidt's Desc. & Darw.* 280 Prehensile hind feet with their opposable hallux.

hallway. orig. *U.S.* An entrance-hall or passage leading to various rooms in a house or building.

1877 J. HABBERTON *Jericho Road* 173 It passed through the narrow hallway which separated the cell from the jailor's apartments. **1882** *Harper's Mag.* Feb. 347 Entering the Senate hallway. **1883** ROE *Ibid.* Dec. 45/1 The hallway..is wide, and extends to a small piazza in the rear. **1920** B. CRONIN *Timber Wolves* ii. 41 He stood hesitating at the entrance to the musty hallway. **1953** L. KUPER *Living in Towns* ii. 13 The front doors..give direct access to hallway and staircase. **1959** *Shropsh. Mag.* Mar. 9/2 He has a beautiful wooden chest in his hallway. **1971** *Real Estate Rev.* Fall 104/2 A woman who had been attacked in the common hallway of her apartment house.

hally, obs. form of HALELY (*wholly*), HOLY.

hallybaloo: see HULLABALOO.

hallyer, obs. form of HALYARD.

hallyly, obs. form of HALELY, HOLILY.

halm: see HAULM.

‖**halma** (ˈhælmə). [a. Gr. ἅλμα leap, f. ἅλλεσθαι to leap.] A game played on a checkerboard of 256 squares, by two persons with 19 men each, or four persons with 13 each, each player's men being placed in a corner of the board and moved towards the opposite corner, the characteristic move consisting of a leap over any man in an adjacent square into a vacant square beyond, or of a series of such leaps. Named also *hoppity*.

1890 *Daily News* 31 Jan. 5/2 She had better stay in the drawing-room and play *halma* with her sisters. **1891** *Ibid.* 30 Sept. 5/1 Halma is offered as a cheap and safe substitute for chess, but Halma, like football, is being ruined by professionalism.

halmeshouse, obs. form of ALMS-HOUSE.

1530 PALSGR. 228/2 Halmeshouse, *aumoniere*.

halmot, obs. or arch. form of HALLMOTE.

halo (ˈheɪləʊ), *sb.* Also 6 **halon**, 7–8 in L. form **halos**. Pl. **haloes, halos** (also 9 **halones**). [= F. *halo*, It. *alone*, Sp. *halon*, ad. L. *halōs*, a. Gr. ἅλως threshing floor, disk of the sun, moon, or a shield. The Romanic forms imply a L. type **halo, -ōnem*, which is also used in mod.L.]

1. a. A circle of light, either white or prismatically coloured, seen round a luminous body and caused by the refraction of light through vapour; *spec.* that seen round the sun or moon, commonly of 22 or 46 degrees radius, with the red extremity of the spectrum inside the circle.

The definite size of halos and the arrangement of their prismatic colours distinguish them from *coronæ*, which are phenomena of diffraction, varying in size and having the red outside: see CORONA 1, quot. 1849. But the two words are often treated as synonymous.

1563 W. FULKE *Meteors* iii. (1640) 34 The Circle caled Halon is a garland of divers colours that is seen about the Sunne, the Moone, or any other Starre. *Ibid.* 36 Halon is seen about Candles, in smoky places, as are baths and kitchins. **1603** HOLLAND *Plutarch's Mor.* 1202 Rainbowes, haloes or garlands about the Sunne, Moone, etc. **1635** SWAN *Spec. M.* v. §2. (1643) 128 This appearance is commonly called Halo; and the matter..of it is a cloud. **1762** FALCONER *Shipwr.* I. 190 A mighty halo round the lucid sphere, Cross'd and divided, did on high appear. **1813** T. FORSTER *Atmosph. Phænom.* (1815) 100 A double halo is not a very common occurrence..simple halones are generally about 45° in diameter.. Triple halones are extremely rare occurrences. **1860** *Cornh. Mag.* II. 568 The halos..In summer..announce rain; in winter, thaw.

b. Applied to other circular luminous appearances; hence, by extension, to other things in the form of a circle or ring.

1813 SHELLEY *Q. Mab* i. 102 That [light] which, bursting from the Fairy's form, Spread a purpureal halo round the scene. **1844** A. WELBY *Poems* (1867) 33 The sunlight round thy mossy cell A golden halo weaves. *a* **1881** ROSSETTI *House of Life* ii, When Death's nuptial change Leaves us for light the halo of his hair.

c. A coloured circle, such as those around the nipples, and those which surround vesicles or pustules; = AREOLA 3.

1706 PHILLIPS (ed. Kersey), *Halo*, or *Halos*..also a reddish Spot or Circle of Flesh which encompasses each Nipple in the Breasts of Women. **1807–26** S. COOPER *First Lines Surg.* (ed. 5) 352 An ulcer of the cornea..its margin is surrounded by a slight halo of lymph. **1822–34** *Good's Study Med.* (ed. 4) IV. 479 Eruption of minute, acuminated vesicles..occasionally surrounded by a blushing halo.

d. *pl.* The rings of lighter and darker colour, usually concentric, in the yolk of an egg, the result of its deposition in successive layers.

1886 in *Syd. Soc. Lex.*

e. A style in women's hats (worn at the back of the head with the brim thus framing the face). Also *attrib.* and *Comb.*, as ***halo-brim(med), hat, style***, etc.

1899 *Daily News* 22 Apr. 8/4 Some of the new models [*sc.* hats] are intended to be put on in the halo style. **1903** *Daily Chron.* 24 Oct. 8/4 The hat makes a halo in front. **1934** *Times* 22 June 17/4 A brown halo hat. **1935** *Times* 17 June 11/3 Felt halos are made with a velvet cap in front, and cost 3½ guineas. *Ibid.* 2 Oct. 17/4 A pale blue halo-brimmed hat. **1952** E. GRIERSON *Reputation for Song* xxvii. 244 Laura..wore a little black halo-hat to frame her pallid face.

f. A more or less circular bright or dark area formed in various photographic processes (see quots.).

1941 *Amer. Speech* XVI. 316/2 *Halo*, the effect obtained in portraiture when a strong back-light is used. **1961** G. MILLERSON *Technique Telev. Production* iii. 49 *Haloes* (throw-off). A black aureole surrounding an over-bright high-contrast area, and obliterating the nearby picture. **1967** KARCH & BUBER *Offset Processes* 541 *Halo*, a luminous circle or aura around the halftone dot.

2. The circle or disk of light with which the head is surrounded in representations of Christ and the Saints; a nimbus.

1646 SIR T. BROWNE *Pseud. Ep.* v. viii. 247 Our Saviour, and the Virgin Mary..are commonly drawne with scintillations, or radiant Halo's about their head. **1866** MAX MÜLLER *Chips* (1880) III. vii. 186 Few saints, if any, did deserve their halo better than St. Louis.

3. *fig.* The ideal glory with which a person or thing is invested when viewed under the influence of feeling or sentiment.

1813 BYRON *Giaour* iii, Expression's last receding ray, A gilded halo hovering round decay! **1824** W. IRVING *T. Trav.* I. 207 Encircled by a halo of literary glory. **1857** BUCKLE *Civiliz.* I. xii. 690 That halo which time had thrown round the oldest monarchy in Europe. **1867** FREEMAN *Norm. Conq.* I. v. 390 Hagiographers have of course surrounded him with a halo of sanctity and miracle.

4. *attrib.* and *Comb.*, as ***halo-zone***; ***halo-bright, -girt, -like*** adjs. **halo blight, spot**, either of two bacterial diseases caused by species of *Pseudomonas*, *P. coronafaciens* affecting oats, and *P. phaseolicola* affecting beans of the genus *Phaseolus*; characterized by brown spots surrounded by yellowish-green rings on leaves; **halo effect** *Psychol.*, the favourable bias in interviews, intelligence tests, and the like generated by an atmosphere of approbation; also *transf.*

1920 C. ELLIOTT in *Jrnl. Agric. Res.* XIX. 139 This 'halo-blight' is a disease which occurs to at least some extent each year throughout the oat-growing sections of the central and eastern States. **1930** W. H. BURKHOLDER in *Mem. Cornell Univ. Agric. Exper. Station* No. 127 37 The most striking symptom [of *Phytomonas medicaginis phaseolicola*] arises from a local infection, and is the spot to which Miss Hedges has applied the term *halo blight*. **1954** A. G. L. HELLYER *Encycl. Garden Work & Terms* 115 *Halo blight*, a disease of beans also sometimes known as halo spot. **1955** *Sci. Amer.* June 83 Bacterial blight of beans..embraces a group of diseases: common blight, fuscous blight and halo blight, each caused by a different bacterium. **1971** M. NOBLE in J. H. Western *Dis. Crop Plants* iii. 33 In New South Wales an inspection scheme for bean (*Phaseolus*) seed has been in operation..for control of halo blight. **1971** J. COLHOUN in *Ibid.* x. 211 Halo blight of oats..is not regarded as constituting an economic problem in the British Isles. [**1926** E. H. MAGSON in *Brit. Jrnl. Psychol. Mon. Suppl.* 9 89 It must be pointed out that it is quite unnecessary to employ a new technical term such as 'halo' or 'aura' to cover these cases.] **1938** *Brit. Jrnl. Psychol.* Jan. 285 Such general impressions, often called 'halo effects', have already been noted to affect the diagnosis of personal qualities. **1940** R. S. WOODWORTH *Psychol.* (ed. 12) v. 143 Another error [in rating intelligence tests] is known as the 'halo effect'. If an individual creates a favourable impression by his excellence in one trait, you are apt to rate him near the top in every trait. **1967** *Guardian* 20 Dec. 1/6 Mrs. Castle..agreed that the new Act had a 'halo' effect in that it made drivers more careful. **1833** BROWNING *Pauline* 320 Halo-girt with fancies of my own. **1845** HIRST *Poems* 132 A glory dances Halo-like around her. **1928** *Jrnl. Agric. Res.* 1 Mar. 428 Halo spot is known to occur in Georgia, Florida, and Connecticut. **1871** B. TAYLOR *Faust* (1875) II. I. ii. 10 The highest virtue like a halo-zone Circles the emperor's head.

ˈ**halo**, *v.* [f. prec. sb.] *trans.* To surround, encompass, or invest with a halo. *lit.* and *fig.* Also with *round*. Hence ˈ**haloing** *vbl. sb.* and *ppl. a.*

1801 SOUTHEY *Thalaba* IX. xxvii, The fire That haloed round his saintly brow. **1832** J. WILSON in *Blackw. Mag.* XXXI. 176 The burning light with which Minerva haloed his head. **188.** R. G. H[ILL] *Voices in Solit.* 14 The Spring ..with a haloing rainbow crowns her head. **1887** T. HARDY *Woodlanders* I. xiii. 244 The two lamps of a carriage, haloed by the fog. **1967** *Gloss. Paper/Ink Terms for Letterpress Printing* (*B.S.I.*) 9 *Haloing*, the appearance of vehicle from the ink round half-tone dots or characters.

halo- (hæləʊ), combining form of Gr. ἅλς, ἁλός sea, salt, as in ˈ**halobiont** *Ecol.*, an organism that lives in a saline habitat; hence ˌ**halobiˈontic** *a.*; ˌ**halobiˈotic** *a. Ecol.*, living in the sea; ˌ**haloˈchromism** *Chem.* [ad. G. *halochromie* (Baeyer & Villiger in *Ber. d. Deut. Chem. Ges.* (1902) XXXV. 1190)], the property possessed by certain colourless or faintly coloured compounds of becoming brilliantly coloured in the presence of acids or of certain other compounds; **haloˈlimnic** *a. Biol.*, living in fresh water but having an affinity with marine forms; **haloˈmorphic** *a. Soil Sci.*, (of a soil) containing, or developed under the influence of, large quantities of salts other than calcium carbonate; ˈ**halophyte** *Ecol.* [ad. mod.L. *halophyta* (J. F. Schouw *Grundtræk til en almindelig Plantegeographie* (1822) 138)], a plant which is adapted to grow in saline conditions; so **haloˈphytic** *a.*, growing, or adapted to grow, in saline conditions; **haloˈplankton**, marine plankton; ˈ**halosere** *Ecol.* (see quot. 1930[1]); ˈ**halowax** [HALO(GEN + WAX *sb.*[1]] (see quots.).

1928 K. E. CARPENTER *Life Inland Waters* ix. 228 Other *halobionts are: all known species of *Ephydra* (Diptera).. and several species of *Ochthebius, Philydrus*, and *Paracymus* (Coleoptera). **1937** ALLEE & SCHMIDT *Hesse's Ecol. Animal Geogr.* xix. 370 'Halobionts' are limited to water of rather high salt content, and are more or less salt-tolerant stenohaline forms. **1928** K. E. CARPENTER *Life Inland Waters* ix. 228 Above this concentration, species rapidly diminish in numbers, and above 10 per cent. are only found the true *'halobiontic' forms, which rarely, or never, occur in waters other than saline. **1909** WEBSTER, Halobiotic. **1927** R. S. LULL *Org. Evol.* (rev. ed.) v. 70 *Halobiotic or Marine Realm. **1902** *Rep. Brit. Assoc.* 119 Reference may be made to some recent work of v. Baeyer and Villiger on dibenzylidene acetone and triphenyl methane. They refer to the constitution of colourless substances which form highly coloured salts, and term the phenomenon **halochromism*. **1944** *Hackh's Chem. Dict.* (ed. 3) 395/1 *Halochromism*, the formation of colored salts from colorless organic bases by the addition of acids. **1952** K. VENKATARAMAN *Chem. Synthetic Dyes* I. viii. 326 In the phenomenon of halochromism, the neutral organic compounds, which become brilliantly colored on the addition of hydrogen ion, are colored to about the same depth and intensity by the addition of neutral substances such as boron trichloride or stannic chloride instead of hydrogen ion. **1898** J. E. S. MOORE in *Proc. R. Soc.* LXII. 453 They probably belong to the same quasi-marine, or what I shall in future call the *Halolimnic group. **1903** —— *Tanganyika Probl.* vii. 141 The animals forming the invertebrate section of this peculiar group have an obviously marine aspect, and on that account I have spoken of them elsewhere as forming a halolimnic series in Lake Tanganyika—that is to say, they form a group of animals which, although living in a fresh-water lake, have at the same time the characters of animals that are typical of the sea. **1904** *Westm. Gaz.* 26 May 5/2 The shells of the halolimnic gasteropods. **1922** *Nature* 5 Jan. 28/1 The halolimnic forms..exhibit a marine-like appearance. **1938** *U.S. Dept. Agric. Yearbk.* 1169 **Halomorphic soils*, a suborder of intrazonal soils, the properties of which are determined by the presence of neutral or alkali salts, or both. **1968** R. W. FAIRBRIDGE *Encycl. Geomorphol.* 273/1 Other desert soils are intra-zonal ..and either contain appreciable amounts of calcium carbonate (the pedocal soils) or have relatively high concentrations of other soluble salts (the halomorphic soils). **1886** WEBSTER Add., *Halophyte. **1894** F. W. OLIVER et al. tr. *Kerner's Nat. Hist. Plants* I. 74 Plants which only flourish abundantly on soils rich in alkaline salts are called halophytes. The same name has also been applied to plants which only thrive in sea-water. **1903** W. R. FISHER tr. *Schimper's Plant-Geogr.* 90 Halophytes can thrive on ordinary soil..without any addition of common salt. **1909** GROOM & BALFOUR tr. *Warming's Oecol. Plants* liv. 219 A halophyte..is one form of xerophyte. **1966** *New Scientist* 2 June 575/1 Because of the removal of water by transpiration or in the harvested crop, the concentration of salts in the system will rise so that even halophytes will suffer. **1895** G. HENSLOW *Orig. Plant Struct.* 83 *Halophytic plants, and others yielding ethereal oils. **1950** *Engineering* 26 Mar. 610/3 While..salt..is being washed out of the soil..the vegetation will still be halophytic. **1909** GROOM & BALFOUR tr. *Warming's Oecol. Plants* xxxviii. 160 The plankton of salt water may be subdivided into neritic and oceanic *halo-plankton. **1927** R. S. LULL *Org. Evol.* (rev. ed.) iii. 43 Marine or halo-plankton. **1929** WEAVER & CLEMENTS *Plant Ecol.* iv. 74 Hydroseres in saline areas are distinguished as (salt) *haloseres. **1930** *Jrnl. Ecol.* XVIII. 201 *Halosere*, the sere commencing in saline water or upon saline soil. *Ibid.* 229 (*heading*) Communities developing within the halosere. **1964** K. A. KERSHAW *Quantitative & Dynamic Ecol.* iii. 39 Clements similarly termed the stages of salt marsh succession a halosere. **1922** *Halowax* (*Condensite Co. of America*) 3 *Halowax for impregnating paper round electrical condensers. *Ibid.* 4 Halowax is a trade name for chloro-naphthalene substitution products, i.e., products in which chlorine atoms are substituted for those of hydrogen in the naphthalene. **1928** *Daily Express* 10 Jan. 3/7 The.. Anti-Knock Compound..is a liquid consisting of tetra-ethyl lead, ethylene dibromide, halowax oil and red aniline dye. **1947** J. C. RICH *Materials & Methods of Sculpture* vi. 157 *Halowax* is a synthetic wax with a high melting point. It is a strong and hard material and imparts a milky opaqueness to a cool wax formula. **1963** R. F. WEBB *Motorist's Dict.* 121 *Halowax*, a type of oil, blended with a tetra-ethyl lead compound used to lubricate the working parts of some mechanical superchargers.

haloed (ˈheɪləʊd), *ppl. a.* [f. HALO + -ED.] Surrounded or invested with a halo.

1791 E. DARWIN *Bot. Gard.* I. 105 Ray'd from his lucid breast and halo'd brow. **1894** MRS. H. WARD *Marcella* I. 107 A wide sky holding a haloed moon.

halogen (ˈhæləʊdʒɛn). *Chem.* [mod. f. Gr. ἅλς, ἁλο- salt + -GEN; cf. F. *halogène*] An element or substance which forms a salt by direct union with a metal. The halogens are chlorine, fluorine, bromine, iodine, and the compound cyanogen. In mod. use, any of the elements of group 7 of the periodic table, viz. fluorine, chlorine, bromine, iodine, and astatine.

1842 *Proc. Amer. Phil. Soc.* II. 219 The epithet halogen is applied to bodies whose binary compounds with metals are deemed salts. **1867** C. L. BLOXAM *Chem.* 10 A salt-radical or halogen is a substance which forms an acid when combined with hydrogen. Examples.—Chlorine, which forms hydrochloric acid (HCl); Cyanogen (C_2N), which forms hydrocyanic acid (HC_2N). **1872** WATTS *Dict. Chem.* III. 6 *Halogen*, the electro-negative radicle of an haloid-salt. **1880** *Nature* XXI. 290 Displacement between oxygen and the halogen elements united with metals. **1884** T. S. HUMPIDGE tr. *Kolbe's Short Text-bk. Inorg. Chem.* 96 The halogens or salt-producers. The four elements chlorine, bromine, iodine, and fluorine are grouped together under this name. **1959** *Nomencl. Inorg. Chem.* (I.U.P.A.C.) 6 The use of the collective names: halogens (F, Cl, Br, I, and At),..may be continued.

Hence **haˈlogenated** *a.*, combined with a halogen. **halogeˈnation**, the introduction of an atom of a halogen into a molecule of a compound by addition or substitution. **haˈlogenous** *a.*, of the nature of a halogen.

1846 SMART Suppl. s.v., The simple halogenous bodies or halogens at present known, are chlorine, fluorine, iodine and bromine. **1882** *Nature* XXV. 353 The action of halogenated..radicals on the potassic compound of pyrol. **1911** *Chem. Abstr.* V. 1436 (*heading*) Halogenation of benzene monohalides... The expts...were carried out at 55–75° without a diluent. **1965** PHILLIPS & WILLIAMS *Inorg. Chem.* II. xii. 463 Some of the interhalogens provide convenient solvents for halogenation reactions, particularly in view of their partial ionization.

halography (hæ'lɒgrəfɪ). [mod. f. Gr. ἅλς, ἁλο- salt + -GRAPHY; cf. F. *halographie.*] The or a description of salts.
1854 in MAYNE *Expos. Lex.*

haloid ('hælɔɪd, 'hæləʊɪd), *a.* and *sb. Chem.* [f. Gr. ἅλς salt + -OID.]
A. *adj.* Having a composition like that of common salt (sodium chloride, NaCl); applied to all salts formed by the simple union of a halogen with a metal, as potassium iodide, KI. Now *rare.*
1841 *Penny Cycl.* XX. 369/2 Common salt is the principal of a class composed of a metal and such bodies as chlorine, iodine, bromine, and fluorine, and the radicals of the hydracids, and which are included by Berzelius in his class of *haloid-salts*..because in constitution they are analogous to sea-salt. **1863–74** WATTS *Dict. Chem.* III. 6 The term haloïd is still occasionally applied to the chlorides, bromides, iodides, fluorides, and cyanides. **1873** *Fownes' Chem.* (ed. 11) 537 Haloid Ethers are Compounds of hydrocarbons with halogens. **1875** *Ure's Dict. Arts* II. 782 Modern ideas on the constitution of salts have greatly tended to weaken the old distinction between haloïd salts and oxysalts.
B. *sb.* A salt of this nature. Superseded by *halide.*
1846 in WORCESTER. **1854–67** C. A. HARRIS *Dict. Med. Terminol.* s.v. *Halogens*, Salts thus formed are termed haloids. **1881** S. THOMPSON in *Design & Work* 24 Dec. 454 Chief amongst those substances are chlorine and the haloids.

halok, halock ('heɪlək). *Sc.* [Origin unknown.] A light thoughtless girl or young woman. Hence **halokit** *a.*, giddy, thoughtless, foolish, crazy.
1508 DUNBAR *Tua Mariit Wemen* 465 Hutit be the halok lase a hunder ȝeir of eild! **1675** *Rutherford's Rel. Lett.* Postscr. 270 A well-meaning kind of harmless, though half hallocked Persons. **1724** RAMSAY Tea-t. Misc. (1733) I. 90 Shangymou'd, halucket Meg.

halology (hæ'lɒlədʒɪ). [mod. f. Gr. ἁλο- salt + -LOGY; cf. F. *halologie.*] That branch of chemistry which treats of salts.
1854 in MAYNE *Expos. Lex.*

'halomancy. [mod. f. Gr. ἁλο- salt + μαντεία divination, -MANCY; cf. F. *halomancie.*] Divination by means of salt.
1864 WEBSTER, *Alomancy.*

halometer (hæ'lɒmɪtə(r)). [f. as prec. + -METER.] An instrument for measuring the external form, angles, and planes of the crystals of salts.
1854 in MAYNE *Expos. Lex.*

halonate ('heɪləʊnət), *a. Bot.* [f. mod.L. *halōn-*, HALO *sb.* + -ATE[2].] Surrounded by an outer ring.
1911 CROMBIE & SMITH *Brit. Lichens* II. 359 Halonate.. surrounded by an outer circle. **1921** A. L. SMITH *Handbk. Brit. Lichens* 102 Spores ellipsoid or oblong..usually with a hyaline mucilaginous epispore (halonate). **1959** U. K. DUNCAN *Guide to Study of Lichens* 64 Th. Fries..cited the halonate character of the spores [of *Rhizocarpon*] as the distinguishing factor.

halophile ('hæləʊfaɪl), *sb.* and *a. Med.* [a. F. *halophile*, f. Gr. ἁλο- salt + φίλος loving.]
A. *sb.* **1.** A name given by Berzelius to the extractives of the urine.
1844–53 G. BIRD *Urin. Deposits* iii. (ed. 4) 103 Berzelius has..described such a yellow colouring matter under the name of halophyle. **1886** in *Syd. Soc. Lex.*
2. *Ecol.* An organism which grows in or can tolerate saline conditions.
1928 K. E. CARPENTER *Life Inland Waters* ix. 229 These 'halophiles' are true freshwater species endowed with powers of resistance. **1965** B. E. FREEMAN tr. *Vandel's Biospeleol.* xiii. 196 The Pogoninae are for the most part halophiles. **1966** T. D. BROCK *Princ. Microbial Ecol.* iii. 47 Halophiles are in ionic equilibrium with their environment.
B. *adj. Ecol.* Growing in or tolerating saline conditions.
1909 *Cent. Dict.* Suppl., Halophile. **1961** *Times Rev. Industry* June 82/1 A gradual increase of the halophile (or, better, salt-resisting) plants..at the fringe of the oasis and the great desert beyond.

halophilic (,hæləʊ'fɪlɪk), *a. Ecol.* [f. HALOPHIL(OUS *a.* + -IC.] Growing in or tolerating saline conditions, halophilous.
1919 *Jrnl. Bacteriol.* IV. 177 (*title*) A preliminary report upon some halophilic bacteria. **1964** *Oceanogr. & Marine Biol.* II. 161 Few studies have been made of the role of detritus as a food for halophilic Crustacea. **1971** M. ALEXANDER *Microbial Ecol.* viii. 181 Some populations are obligately halophilic.

halophilous (hæ'lɒfɪləs), *a.* [f. as HALOPHILE *sb.* and *adj.*: see -OUS.] 'Salt-loving'; growing in salt marshes.
1888 F. A. LEES *Flora W. Yorksh.* 81 Certain Halophilous (salt-loving) plants.

halosaurian (,hæləʊ'sɔːrɪən). *Palæont.* [f. mod.L. *Halosaurus*, f. Gr. ἁλο- sea + σαῦρος lizard: see -IAN.] A marine saurian, as the extinct ichthyosaur or plesiosaur.
1884 tr. *Claus' Zool.* 177 The Halosaurians, with their best known genera Ichthyosaurus and Pleiosaurus, are entirely peculiar to the secondary period.

halosaurus (,hæləʊ'sɔːrəs). [mod.L. (see quot. 1863); see HALOSAURIAN.] A deep-water marine fish of the genus so called, characterized by an elongated body and long tapering tail. Hence **'halosaur**, a member of the family Halosauridæ, which includes both fossil and living fishes; **,halo'sauroid** *a.*, of, pertaining to, or resembling a fish of this kind; also as *sb.*
[**1863** J. Y. JOHNSON in *Proc. Zool. Soc.* 406 *Halosaurus*, gen. nov. Body elongated, clothed with cycloid scales;..tail compressed and tapering to a point.] **1893** *Funk's Stand. Dict.*, Halosauroid, a. & n. **1897** *Proc. Zool. Soc.* 268 On *Echidnocephalus*, a Halosauroid Fish from the Upper Cretaceous Formation of Westphalia... Thanks to..new specimens of *Halosaurus* obtained by the 'Challenger' Expedition, it is now possible to demonstrate that..the strange Halosauroid type was already completely developed before the end of the Cretaceous period. **1904** G. A. BOULENGER in *Cambr. Nat. Hist.* VII. xxii. 622 The conformation of the pectoral arch has much in common with that of the Halosaurs. *Ibid.* 624 In *Halosaurus* the scales of the lateral line..are scarcely enlarged. **1957** R. CAMPBELL *Portugal* iv. 68 In the depth of Setúbal they were visited by many weird monsters,..notably, the *halosaurus* with a long undulating tail. **1963** *New Scientist* 10 Jan. 80 The deeper-living benthic fishes, those that live at depths beyond 2,000 metres, are..halosaurs (Halosauridae). **1971** *Nature* 2 Apr. 279/1 They include the halosaurs, which are known to develop from leptocephalus larvae, and the spiny eels or notacanths.

halotechny ('hæləʊteknɪ). [ad. F. *halotechnie* (Dict. Acad. 1762), f. Gr. ἁλο- salt + τεχνή art.] That branch of chemistry which deals with salts. So **halo'technic** *a.*, relating to halotechny.
1800 *Monthly Mag.* IX. I. 588 [A school to study] the formation of salts, and the extraction of acids and alkalies.. which he calls the *halotechnic* school. **1854** MAYNE *Expos. Lex.*, *Halotechnia*..old term for that branch which treats of salts: halotechny.

halothane ('hæləθeɪn). [f. HALO(GEN + E)THANE.] A volatile liquid, $CF_3CHBrCl$, with a characteristic odour, used as a general anæsthetic.
1957 *Lancet* 8 June 1196/1 Dr Foster has done a great service by his letter of June 1, if only by drawing attention to errors in the use of 'Fluothane' (halothane). *Ibid.* 7 Sept. 493 To date, cardiac arrest has been reported in five patients anæsthetised with halothane. **1961** *Brit. Med. Dict.* 653/1 *Halothane*, B.P. Commission approved name for 2-bromo-2-chloro-1:1:1-trifluoroethane, a volatile, non-explosive anaesthetic, more powerful than ether. **1971** *Nature* 1 Oct. 353/1 Cats anaesthetized with 50% nitrous oxide in oxygen and 1% halothane.

halotrichine (hæ'lɒtrɪkaɪn). *Min.* [f. Gr. ἁλο- salt + θρίξ, τριχ- hair: see -INE.] A variety of halotrichite from the Solfatara, near Naples.
1863–72 WATTS *Dict. Chem.* III. 6. **1868** DANA *Min.* (ed. 5) 655.

halotrichite (hæ'lɒtrɪkaɪt). *Min.* [Named by Glocker, 1839, f. as prec. + -ITE.] Iron alum, occurring in yellowish-white, fibrous masses.
1849 NICOL *Min.* 323. **1868** DANA *Min.* (ed. 5) 654 *Halotrichite*, Silky fibrous. Yellowish-white. Taste inky-astringent. **1875** PLATTNER *Blowpipe* 208 Halotrichite fuses in the matrass in its water of crystallization.

†**halover.** *Obs.* [f. HALE (or HAUL) *v.* + OVER *adv.*] A portage.
1699 S. DAMPIER *Voy.* II. II. 120 The Halover is a small Neck of Land, parting the Sea from a large Lagune. It is so call'd by the Privateers, because they use to drag their Canoas in and out there.

halow, obs. f. HALLOO *v.*, HALLOW *sb.* and *v.*

Halowe Thursdaye, obs. f. HOLY THURSDAY.

haloxylin, -ine (hæ'lɒksɪlɪn). [f. Gr. ἁλο- salt + ξύλον wood + -IN.] An explosive; see quot.
1883 H. S. DRINKER *Explosive Compounds* 60. **1895** *Dict. Explosives* 17 Haloxyline, An explosive (patented 1866) in which a powdered cellulose substance and a rapid explosive are added to charcoal and saltpetre.

halp, obs. pa. t. of HELP.

†**halpace, haltpace.** *Obs.* Forms: α. 6 hault-, halt-pase. β. 6 halpace, hal(l)pas. [a. 16th c. f. *hault pas, haut pas*, lit. 'high step'; see also HALF-PACE, HAUT-PAS.] = HAUT-PAS; HALF-PACE 1.
α. **1540–1** ELYOT *Image Gov.* 60 a (Stanf.) A haulte pase.. at the ende of the Theatre, where the emperour shoulde sytte in his maiestie. **1587** FLEMING *Contn. Holinshed* III. 1382/2 The edge of the haltpase, or mounting floore.
β. **1507** *Will of J. Saunders* (Somerset Ho.), An halpace of Tymbre werk..for the Organs theron to stonde. **1519** *Churchw. Acc. St. Giles Reading* 7 For halpasis to the Awters xvjd. **1548** HALL *Chron.* (1809) 606 On the aultare was a deske or halpace. **1577–87** HOLINSHED *Chron.* III. 857/1 On the altar an halpas..and on the same halpas stood twelue images.

halpens, -peny, obs. ff. *halfpence*, HALFPENNY.

†**halper**, *v. Obs.* [a. Ger. *holpern* (1540 in Kluge) to stumble, vacillate: see Grimm.] To stumble, go unsteadily, go backward and forward.
1596 NASHE *Saffron Walden* L iv, If..he is not well acquainted with the place, he goes filthely halpering, and asking cap in hand from one shop to another, where's such a house and such a signe? **1599** —— *Lenten Stuffe* 54 Hee might have tooke him at his proffer, which since he refused, and now halperd with him, as he eate up the first, so would he eate up the second.

halpworth, halpynworth, obs. ff. HALFPENNYWORTH.

halse, hals, *sb.* Now *Sc.* and *north. dial.* hause, hawse (hɔːs). Forms: 1 hals, heals, 3 *Orm.* halls, 4–7 hals(e, (4 halce, 6 halsz, halss, hawes, heylis, 7 hose), 7–9 hause, hass(e, 8–9 hawse. [Com. Teut.: OE. *hals, heals* = OFris., OS., OHG., ON. *hals*:—OTeut. *holso-z:—pre-Teut. *kolsos: cf. L. *collum*, earlier *collus*, from *colsus.]
1. The neck.
a **1000** *Cædmon's Gen.* 385 Mid þy me god hafað ȝehæfted be þam healse. *c* **1200** ORMIN 4777 Side, & halls, & hæfedd. *c* **1330** R. BRUNNE *Chron.* (1810) 279 Þe Scottis be alle schent, & hanged bi þe hals. **1377** LANGL. *P. Pl.* B. Prol. 170 To..Knitten on a colere..And hangen it vp-on þe cattes hals. *c* **1422** HOCCLEVE *Jereslaus' Wife* 712 Hire þat from the roope kepte his hals. **1575** J. STILL *Gamm. Gurton* v. ii. in Hazl. *Dodsley* III. 240 Many a truer man than he has hanged up by the halse. *a* **1605** MONTGOMERIE *Poems* xxxv. 45 Hir halse more vhyt Nor I can wryt. **1616** BULLOKAR *Eng. Expos.*, *Halse* [*Obs.*], a necke. **1825** BROCKETT *N.C. Gloss.*, *Hause*, the neck. A very old word. **1893** *Northumbld. Gloss.*, *Hass, Hause*, the neck, the throat.
2. The throat, gullet.
c **1440** *Promp. Parv.* 224/1 Hals, or halce, throte, *guttur.* *c* **1440** *Bone Flor.* 1474 Hyt stekyth in my hals, I may not gete hyt downe. **1572** *Satir. Poems Reform.* xxxviii. 34 With baitis in our hals. **1697** W. CLELAND *Exped. Highland-host* 448 Poems 22 He got of Beer a full bowl Glass, which got bad passage at his Hasse. **1819** J. HODGSON in J. Raine *Mem.* (1857) I. 241 His words stuck in his hause. **1855** ROBINSON *Whitby Gloss.*, *Hause*, the throat.
†**3.** *transf.* A narrow neck of land or channel of water. *Obs.*
[Cf. The 'Hawse Inn' at South Queensferry.]
c **1470** HENRY *Wallace* VII. 808 Throuch out the moss delyuerly thai ȝeid; Syne tuk the hals, quharoff thai had most dreid. **1513** DOUGLAS *Æneis* I. iv. 8 Ane havin place with ane lang hals or entre. **1536** BELLENDEN *Cron. Scot.* (1821) I. p. xxvii, Nidisdail..beginnis with ane narow and strait hals.
4. A narrower and lower part of a line of hills, joining two heights; a *col*: in the form HAUSE, q.v.
†**5.** Phr. ***to hold in hals***, to flatter, beguile, delude with false professions. *Obs.*
c **1560** A. SCOTT *Poems* (S.T.S.) xxiii. 23 Hir fenȝeit wordis..held me in the hals. **1583** *Satir. Poems Reform.* xlv. 783 With mony flattering taill and fals He held that bischop in the hals. **1616** HART *Pref. to Barbour's Bruce* (1620) 14 (Jam.) Edward had..long time holden them in the hals, upon vain hope of the kindgdome.
6. *attrib.* and *Comb.* Of or pertaining to the neck, as ***halse-bone*** (***bane***), ***-riband***; †**hals-man**, executioner, headsman; **hawslock, hasslock**, the wool on the neck of a sheep.
1794 *Ritson's Scott. Songs* I. 50 (Jam.) There's gowd in your garters, Marion; And silk on your white *hauss-bane. **1818** CARLYLE *Early Lett.* (Norton) I. 148 Tell him..to write instanter if he wish his head to continue above his hass-bone. **1725** RAMSAY *Gent. Sheph.* I. i, A tartan plaid spun o' good *hawslock woo. **1820** *Blackw. Mag.* VI. 664 Card them through each other like black wool and white hawslock. *a* **1659** CLEVELAND *Scots Apostacy* II. 14 Do Execution like the *Hals-man's Sword.
Hence †**halsed** *a.*, having a neck, -necked. *Obs.*
1536 BELLENDEN *Cron. Scot.* (1821) I. p. xxxiv, Ane lang mand, narrow halsit, and wyid mouthit.

†**halse**, *v.*[1] *Obs.* Forms: 1 **halsian, healsian**, 2 **hælsien**, 2–3 **halsi(en**, 3–6 **halse**. [OE. *halsian, healsian*, ? from earlier *hálsian = OHG. *heilisôn* to augur, expiate, ON. *heilsa* to hail, greet (with good wishes):—OTeut. *hailosôjan, f. *hailos weal, well-being, prosperity: see HEAL *sb.*]
1. *intr.* To augur, divine, soothsay; to declare in the name of something divine or holy. (Only OE.)
c **1050** *Gloss.* in Wr.-Wülcker 354/13 *Ariolandi*, on wigbede to halsienne.
2. *trans.* To call upon in the name of something divine or holy; to exorcize, adjure, conjure; to implore, entreat, beseech.
c **825** *Vesp. Psalter* xxxvi[i]. 7 Underðioded bio ðu dryhtne & halsa hine. *c* **870** *Halsuncge* in *O.E. Texts* 176 Ic eow [ðe] halsiȝe on fæder naman..þæt ȝe to þys husle ne gangen. *c* **897** K. ÆLFRED *Gregory's Past.* xxxii. (E.E.T.S.) 213 Ic eow healsiȝe broður for ðæm tocyme Dryhtnes Hælendan Kristes. *c* **1000** *Ags. Gosp.* Matt. xxvi. 63 Ic halsiȝe þe [*Lindisf.* ic halsa ðec, *Rushw.* ic halsio þe, *Hatt.* ic hælsiȝe þe] ðurh þone lyfiendan god, þæt ðu secȝe us ȝyf þu sy crist godes sunu. *a* **1225** *Ancr. R.* 114 Þurh þeo ilke neiles ich

halse ou ancren, nout ou, auh do oðre, uor hit nis no neod. *Ibid.* 348 Ich halsie ou..þet ʒe wiðholden ou from vlesliche lustes. *a* **1225** *St. Marher.* 17 Ich halsi þe o godes nome. *c* **1386** [see HALSEN *v.* 1]. **14..** *Pol. Rel. & L. Poems* (1866) 85 He was so agast of þat grysyly gose..He halsed hit þorow goddes myȝte. **1553** BECON *Reliques of Rome* (1563) 244* The whiche wicked spirite is halsed or coniured or caste out of hym.

3. To hail, salute, greet. [= HAILSE *v.*, of which it may be a by-form.]

1375 BARBOUR *Bruce* VII. 116 Thai met the Kyng and halsit him thar. *c* **1375** *Sc. Leg. Saints, Johannes* 618 He met a pilgrime in the gat, þat haliste hyme, and sad þusgat. **1498** *Caxton's Chron. Eng.* VI. The holy ymages of sayntes bowed downe to hym whan the body of hym was broughte in to the chyrche..& honourably hym halsyd. **1583** STOCKER *Hist. Civ. Warres Lowe C.* II. 12 Thei so brauely halsed him with Harquebouze shotte. **1596** DALRYMPLE tr. *Leslie's Hist. Scot.* x. 354 Sa tha all salute and halse her.

halse, *v.*[2] *Obs.* exc. *Sc.* (hɑːs, hɔːs). Forms: 4–5 **hals,** 5–6, 9 **halse,** 5, 8 **hawse,** 6 **haulse,** 6–7 **hause,** 9 **hass.** [Either an independent deriv. of *hals,* HALSE neck = OHG. *halsan, -en, -on,* MHG. *halsen* to throw one's arms about the neck of, embrace; or a sense developed upon HALSE *v.*[1], through association with HALSE *sb.* In many passages it is difficult to distinguish it from HALSE *v.*[1], sense 3, since either 'salute' or 'embrace' makes sense.]

1. *trans.* To embrace.

a **1300** *Cursor M.* 4357 Sco can hals him son wit þis And bedd him mothes for to kys. *c* **1400** *Lanfranc's Cirurg.* 174 As whanne he halsiþ a womman wiþ hise hondis. *c* **1440** *Gesta Rom.* lxix. 320 (Harl. MS.) He ran for gladnesse, and halsid hire, and kist hire. *c* **1440** *Promp. Parv.* 224/1 Halsyn, *amplector.* **1530** PALSGR. 577/1, I halse one, I take hym aboute the necke, *je accolle.* **1596** SPENSER *F.Q.* IV. iii. 49 Each other kissed glad, And lovely haulst..And plighted hands. **1674–91** RAY *N.C. Words* (E.D.S.), *Hose, Hause,* to hug, or carry in the arms, to embrace. **1733** *Cock-laird-Orph. Caled.* (Chambers 1829), He hawsed, he kiss'd her, And ca'ed her his sweet. **1819** SCOTT *Noble Moringer* i, He halsed and kiss'd his dearest dame.

absol. c **1430** *Syr Gener.* (Roxb.) 9614 There thei halsed and thei kist.

†**b.** *transf.* and *fig. Obs.*

a **1340** HAMPOLE *Psalter* iv. 3 Ʒe hals & kys & sekis wiþ traiuaile, vanyte and leghe. *a* **1547** SURREY *Praise mean Estate* in *Tottell's Misc.* (Arb.) 27 Who so gladly halseth the golden meane, Voyde of dangers..hath his home. **1636** RUTHERFORD *Lett.* (1862) I. 179 To come nigh Christ and hause Him and embrace Him.

†**2.** To encompass by going round. [= L. *complecti.*] *Obs. rare.*

a **1340** HAMPOLE *Psalter* lxvii. 11 Vmgifis syon & halsis it.

halse, s.w. dial. form of HAZEL *sb.*

halse, halser, -ier, obs. ff. HAWSE, HAWSER.

halsen, *a. s.w. dial.* Also **-on.** [f. *halse,* HAZEL + -EN.] Of hazel.

1586 J. HOOKER [of Exeter] *Girald. Irel.* in Holinshed II. 178/1 He caused a number of flakes and hurdels to be made of halson, allers, and withie rods. **1888** ELWORTHY *W. Somerset Word.-bk.* s.v., A hazel-rod is..a 'halsen stick'.

halsen, *v. Obs.* exc. *dial.* In 3 **halsni,** 4 **helsny,** 6 **halson,** 6–7 **halsen.** [Extended form of HALSE *v.*[1], as if from an OE. **háls-,* **hǽlsnian.*]

†**1.** *trans.* To call upon in the name of something holy, to adjure; = HALSE *v.*[1] 2. *Obs.*

c **1290** *S. Eng. Leg.* I. 479/587 Ich halsni þe a-godes name þat þou wende to Marcilie. **1340** *Ayenb.* 253 Ich you helsny þet ye..loki uram wilninges. *c* **1386** CHAUCER *Prioress' T.* 193 O deere child I halsen [so *Heng.*; *v.rr.* halse, hailse, hailese] thee In vertu of the hooly Trinitee, Tel me what is thy cause for to synge.

2. To augur, foreshow by auspices, prognosticate; in mod. s.w. dial., to augur ill, predict evil *of.*

1586 J. HOOKER *Girald. Irel.* in Holinshed II. 181/1 Some speciall points of his late seruice..which doo halson and giue a hope that he will *Addere colophonem,* and bring that land to a full and perfect gouernment and regiment. **1888** ELWORTHY *W. Somerset Word-bk.* s.v., 'Her'll halseny all the day long 'bout every body.'

Hence **'halsening** *vbl. sb.,* augury, prognostication; **halsening** *ppl. a.,* auguring, boding.

1586 J. HOOKER *Girald. Irel.* in Holinshed II. 52/2 He tooke ship in Milford hauen, but for hast he left to doo his deuotion and oblation at saint Dauids, which was but an euill halsoning. **1587** FLEMING *Contn. Holinshed* III. 305/2 Which his halsening in the end came partlie to effect. **1602** CAREW *Cornwall* 1 b, This ill-halsening hornie name [Cornwall] hath..opened a gap to the scoffes of many. *Ibid.* 133 b, But this halsening, the present flourishing estate of that Kingdome, utterly convinceth of falsehood. **1746** *Exmoor Scolding* (E.D.S.) 56 Thee wut..Oll vor whistering and pistering, and hoaling and halzening, of cuffing a Tale.

†**halsfang, healsfang.** *O.E. Law* Also 1 **halsehang, halfehang,** 7–9 **healfang.** [OE., f. *hals, heals,* neck, HALSE *sb.* + *fang* seizure, catching, booty.] A word used in the OE. or Anglo-Saxon Laws, meaning app. originally some punishment and afterwards the fine in commutation thereof. The legal antiquaries since *c* 1600 have taken it to mean the pillory; but this is strongly combated by Schmid, *Gesetze der Angelsächsen* s.v.

a **1000** *Laws of Wihtræd* c. 12 (Schmid) ʒif ceorl buton wifes wisdome deoflum ʒelde, he sie ealra his æhta scyldiʒ and heals-fange. *a* **1000** *Laws of Edmund* II. c. 7 Of þam dæʒe on XXI niht gilde man heals-fang. *a* **1135** *Laws Hen.* I. c. 14 §3 Mediocris thaini, equus cum apparatu suo, et arma ejus, et suum halsfange in Westsexa; in Myrcenis duae librae. *Ibid.* c. 76 §1 Et debet halsfang primo reddi, sicut weræ modus erit. **1607** COWELL *Interpr.* s.v. *Pillorie,* This was among the Saxons called *Healsfang* of (*Heals*) a necke and (*Fang*) to take. **1609** SKENE *Reg. Maj.* 121 The Baxter sall be put vpon the Pillorie (or 'halsfang') and the Browster upon the Cockstule. **1848** WHARTON *Law Lex., Healfang* or *Halsfang,* the pillory; also a pecuniary mulct, to commute for standing in the pillory.

†**halsier.** *Obs. rare*[−0]. [Origin uncertain: perh. to be connected with *halser,* HAWSER.] See quots. and HALSTER.

1583 J. HIGINS tr. *Junius' Nomenclator* (N.), *Helciarius,*.. an halsier, or he which haleth and draweth a ship or barge alongst the river by a rope: also he that draweth up burthens and packes into a ship. **1548** FLORIO, *Alzaniere,* a halsier or he that haleth a ship or barge by a rope: a halse or halsier in a ship. **1658** [see HALSTER].

†**halsing,** *vbl. sb.*[1] *Obs.* [f. HALSE *v.*[1] + -ING[1].]

1. Exorcizing, exorcism.

870 Halsuncge [see HALSE *v.*[1] 2]. *a* **1039** *Laws of Cnut* I. c. 4 (Schmid) Micel is seo halsung and mære is seo halʒung þe deofla afyrsað. **1387** TREVISA *Higden* (Rolls) III. 11 He [Solomon] fonde up halsynge coniuresouns forto slake wiþ siknesse.

2. Supplication, entreaty.

c **825** *Vesp. Psalter* cxlii[i]. 1 Dryhten..onfoh halsunge mine. **971** *Blickl. Hom.* 87 Mid wependre halsunga hine bædon. *a* **1225** *Ancr. R.* 330 Mid þus onwille halsunge, weopeð & gret efter sume helpe.

3. Greeting, salutation.

1375 BARBOUR *Bruce* VII. 117 The Kyng thame thar halsing ʒuld. *c* **1440** *York Myst.* xii. 149 *Ang.* Hayle! Marie! full of grace..*Maria.* What maner of halsyng is þis?

halsing, *vbl. sb.*[2] [f. HALSE *v.*[2] + -ING[1].] Embracing, embrace.

1387 TREVISA *Higden* (Rolls) VII. 139 Her housbonde halsynges. **1393** LANGL. *P. Pl.* C. VII 187 Handlynge and halsynge and al-so þorw cussynge Excitynge oure aiþer oþer til oure olde synne. **1598** R. BERNARD tr. *Terence, Heautont.* v. i, I will say nothing of hausing and kissing. **1613** MARKHAM *Eng. Husbandman* I. I. ii. (1635) 7 Affable without haussing or kissing.

halsome, -sum, obs. forms of HALESOME.

halss, halsz, obs. forms of HALSE *sb.*

halst, obs. 2 sing. pres. of HOLD *v.*

†**halster.** *Obs. rare*[−0]. = HALSIER.

First found in Kersey's ed. of Phillips as a variant of the latter's *halsier,* and hence in various Dicts.; of the statement of Halliwell and Smyth, that it is a west-country term, no confirmation has been found.

[*a* **1658** PHILLIPS, *Halsier,* a term in Navigation, he that draws the Halser or Cable wherewith boats are towed along some Channel.] **1706** —— (ed. Kersey), *Halsier,* or *Halster.* **1721** BAILEY, *Halsier, halster.* **1731–1800** —— *Halser, halster.* **1775** ASH, *Halster.* **1847–78** HALLIWELL, *Halster*..*West.* **1867** SMYTH *Sailor's Word-bk., Halster,* a west-country term for a man who draws a barge along by a rope.

†**'halswort.** *Obs.* [f. HALSE *sb.* + WORT.] *lit.* Throatwort: a name app. given in OE. times to different plants, either having throat-like flowers, or supposed to cure maladies of the throat. Cockayne includes under it *Campanula Trachelium,* Throatwort; *Bupleurum,* Hare's-ear, *Scilla autumnalis,* Autumnal Squill; and *Symphytum album,* White Comfrey; others apply it to Orpine.

c **1000** *Sax. Leechd.* I. 158 þysse wyrte wyrttruman ðe man halswyrt nemneð. *c* **1000** *Ælfric's Voc.* in Wr.-Wülcker 134/22 *Auris leporis,* halswyrt. *a* **1387** *Sinon. Barthol.* (Anecd. Oxon.) 23 *Halsewort,* i. crassula major. *c* **1450** *Voc.* in Wr.-Wülcker 599/27 *Orpina,* orpine *vel* halsewort.

halt (hɔːlt), *sb.*[1] Also (6–7 **alto,** 7 **alt),** 8 **hault.** [Orig. in phrase *to make halt* = Ger. *halt machen,* f. *halt* 'hold', holding, stoppage, stand. The German military phrase was before 1600 taken into the Romanic langs., as Sp. *alto hacer,* It. *far alto,* F. *faire halte* or *alte,* whence the Eng. forms *to make alto, make alt,* and finally *make halt.* From the military vocabulary the word passed into hunting, travelling, and general use.] **a.** A temporary stoppage on a march or journey.

1591–1598 [see ALTO *sb.*[1]]. **1622** F. MARKHAM *Bk. War* v. iii. §4. 171 To make stands (which some call *Altoes* or *Hallts*)..whereby the souldier may be refresht when he is weary with travell. **1623** [see ALT[1]]. *a* **1625** EARL SOMERSET in *Cabala* I. (1654) 1, I understand of some halt you made, and the Cause of it. **1660** F. BROOKE tr. *Le Blanc's Trav.* 10 Part of the Caravane made an halt. **1662** J. DAVIES tr. *Olearius' Voy. Ambass.* 63 Without any halt by the way. **1667** MILTON *P.L.* VI. 532 To descrie the distant foe..In motion or in alt. *Ibid.* XI. 210 And on a Hill made alt. **1709** *Lond. Gaz.* No. 4583/4 The Duke of Marlborough commanded an Hault. **1856** KANE *Arct. Expl.* II. xv. 154 Seeing them come to a halt above the island. **1868** *Regul. & Ord. Army* §1144 On arrival at the destination, the Halt is to be sounded. **1880** T. HARDY *Trumpet Major* xxviii, Leaving them at halt, he proceeded rapidly onward. *Mod.* Here let us make a halt.

attrib. **1869** E. A PARKES *Pract. Hygiene* (ed. 3) 396 On the halt day the men should wash..their clothes.

b. A small railway station without the ordinary accommodation or staff, at which only local trains normally stop.

1910 *Offic. Guide L.N.W.R.* (ed. 15) 410 Rail motor car halts at Wendlebury, Charlton, and Oddington. **1914** *Railway Mag.* Aug. 152/2 The provision of the 'halts' on the new line has been much appreciated locally. **1921** *Dict. Occup. Terms* (1927) §706 *Halt attendant;* a porter who attends at roadside halt, where there is no proper station staff. **1973** *Country Life* 7 June 1612/4 A halt or unstaffed stopping place where trains called only if required.

Hence **'haltless** *a.,* without a halt.

1856 KANE *Arct. Expl.* I. xxix. 379 An unbroken ice-walk of..twenty haltless hours.

halt, *sb.*[2] [f. HALT *v.*[1] and *a.*]

1. A halting or limping, a limp. *arch.*

1599 SHAKS. *Pass. Pilgr.* 308 A cripple soon can find a halt. [Cf. HALT *v.*[1] 1, *c* 1374]. **1775** JOHNSON, *Halt,* the act of limping; the manner of limping. **1789** BRAND *Hist. Newcastle* I. 310 *note,* He had a halt in walking, occasioned by a lameness in one of his legs.

2. The disease foot-rot in sheep. *Obs.* or *local.*

1750 W. ELLIS *Mod. Husb.* IV. i. 124 (E.D.S.) About Buckingham town they call [foot-rot] the halt. **1757** DYER *Fleece* (1807) 56 Long rains in miry winter cause the halt.

halt (hɔːlt), *a. arch.* and *literary.* Forms: 1 **healt,** 1– **halt;** 3 *Orm.* **hallte,** 5 **halte,** 5–7 **hault.** [A Com. Teut. adj.: OE. *halt, healt* = OFris., OS. *halt* (MDu. *halt, hout,* OHG., MHG. *halz,* ON. *haltr* (Sw., Da. *halt*), Goth. *halt-s:*—OTeut. **halt-oz.*] Lame; crippled; limping.

[*a* **700** *Epinal Gloss.* 589 *Lurdus,* laempihalt; *Erf.* lemphihalt.] *c* **893** K. ÆLFRED *Oros.* III. i. (1883) 96 Ænne wisne mon, þeh he healt wære, se wæs haten Ageselaus. *c* **1200** ORMIN 15499 Þe blinde ʒaff he wel to sen, & hallte wel to ganngenn. *a* **1225** *St. Marher.* 20 Nan misbilimet bern, nowðer halt ne houeret. *c* **1330** *Cursor M.* 20885 (Fairf.) Halt men he gaf þe fote. *c* **1440** *Promp. Parv.* 224/1 Halte, or crokyd, *claudus.* **1526–34** TINDALE *John* v. 3 Halt and wyddered, waytynge for the movynge off the wather. **1612–16** W. BROWNE *Brit. Past.* I. ii. (R.), To waite upon the gout, to walke when pleases Old January hault. **1784** COWPER *Task* I. 471 Halt, and weary of the path they tread. **1859** TENNYSON *Guinevere* 42 If a man were halt or hunch'd.

fig. **1691** WOOD *Ath. Oxon.* II. 214 Many..made very imperfect and halt returns. **1866** *Lond. Rev.* 3 Mar. 246/1 The case proceeds in a halt, cumbersome style.

b. *Comb.,* as *halt-footed* adj.

1422 tr. *Secreta Secret., Priv. Priv.* (E.E.T.S.) 176, I ne ham not maymet in handis ne in armes, thegh y be halte-footed. **1877–8** MORLEY *Crit. Misc.* (1888) I. 205 Hollow and halt-footed transactions.

halt (hɔːlt), *v.*[1] Forms: 1 **healtian, haltian,** 5–6 **halte,** 6–7 **hault(e,** 4– **halt.** [OE. *haltian, healtian* = OS. *haltôn* (MDu. *halten, houten*), OHG. *halzên* (MHG. *halzen*), f. HALT *a.*]

1. *intr.* To be lame, walk lame, limp. *arch.*

c **825** *Vesp. Psalter* xvii. 46 Bearn fremðe aldadon & haltadon. *c* **897** K. ÆLFRED *Gregory's Past.* xi. 65 Stæppað rythe, ne healtiʒeað leng, ac beoð hale. *a* **1300** *Cursor M.* 3942 All his liue þan halted he. *c* **1374** CHAUCER *Troylus* IV. 1429 (1457) It is ful hard to halten vn-espied By-fore a crepul for he kan þe craft. **1382** WYCLIF *Gen.* xxxii. 31 He forsothe haltide with the too foote. *c* **1489** CAXTON *Sonnes of Aymon* vii. 175 But bayarde wente haltynge. **1530** PALSGR. 582/1, I haulte, I go nat upright of one of my legges or of bothe. **1607** SHAKS. *Timon* IV. I. 24 Thou cold Sciatica, Cripple our Senators, that their limbes may halt As lamely as their Manners. **1611** BIBLE *Ps.* xxxviii. 17, I am ready to halt. **1684** BUNYAN *Pilgr.* II. (1862) 317, I am not inclined to halt before I am lame. **1780** COWPER *Progr. Err.* 560 Halting on crutches of unequal size. **1868** HELPS *Realmah* iii. (1876) 29 He halted slightly in his walk.

†**2.** To cease haltingly or hesitatingly *from* (a way or course); to fall away. *Obs.*

c **900** tr. *Bæda's Hist.* v. xx[ii]. (1890) 472 Hi..fram rihtum stiʒum healtiað. *a* **1340** HAMPOLE *Psalter* xvii. 49 Þai haltid fra þaire stretis. **1613** PURCHAS *Pilgrimage* (1614) 277 Whom the Jesuites..report to halt from his former Mahumetisme, and to incline to Gentilisme.

3. To walk unsteadily or hesitatingly; to waver, vacillate, oscillate; to remain in doubt.

Esp. in the scriptural phrase 'to halt between two opinions'; now often associated with HALT *v.*[2]

1382 WYCLIF *1 Kings* xviii. 21 How long halt ʒe into two parties? [**1611** How long halt ye between two opinions?] **1613** PURCHAS *Pilgrimage* (1614) 343 Their religion halteth betwixt divers religions of the Turkes, Persians, and Christians. **1631** GOUGE *God's Arrows* II. ii. 134 Such as halted, in some things doing that which was good, in other things that which was evill. **1875** FREEMAN *Norm. Conq.* (ed. 2) III. xii. 150 No longer halting between his loyalty and his plighted oath. **1881** J. GRANT *Cameronians* I. iii. 37 The conversation halted irregularly between music and literature.

4. *fig.* To proceed 'lamely', imperfectly, or faultily; to be at fault; to be defective in logic, analogy, measure, rime, etc., as a syllogism, metaphor, or verse; not to go 'on all fours'.

1436 *Pol. Poems* (Rolls) II. 159 Allas! oure reule halteth, hit is benome. **1548** GEST *Pr. Masse* 108 Doo they not know that eche comparison halteth and in some matters discordeth? **1576** FLEMING *Panopl. Epist.* 388 That usuall verse, althoughe it hault in one syllable. **1581** MULCASTER *Positions* iv. (1877) 22 How so euer men hault in doing of their duetie. **1602** SHAKS. *Ham.* II. ii. 339 The Lady shall say her minde freely; or the blanke Verse shall halt for't. **1678** R. BARCLAY *Apol. Quakers* v. §24. 175 All Comparisons halt in some part. *a* **1771** GRAY *Corr.* (1843) 228 Where the verse seems to halt, it is very probably occasioned by the transcriber's neglect.

†5. To fail in soundness or straightforwardness of conduct; to use shifts, play false. *Obs.*

1412–20 LYDG. *Chron. Troy* I. v, Yet in the truth somewhile doth he halte. **1585** Q. ELIZ. in *Four C. Eng. Lett.* 29, I cannot halt with you so muche as to denye that I have seen suche evident shewes of your contrarious dealings. **1600** HOLLAND *Livy* XXXII. xxx. 828 Some doubt and suspition they had, that their allies haulted, and were not sound of al four.

halt (hɔːlt), *v.*² Also 7 alt. [f. HALT *sb.*¹; cf. F. *halter* (17th c.), Ger. *halten* to hold, to stop.]

1. a. *intr.* To make a halt; to make a temporary stoppage in a march or journey. (At first a military term only, but sometimes in later use a mere synonym of 'stop'.)

1656 BLOUNT *Glossogr.*, *Halt*, or to make an halt..to stop, stay, or make a stand or pause. **1662** J. DAVIES tr. *Olearius' Voy. Ambass.* 15 Halting and advancing according to the orders. **1672** T. VENT *Milit. Discipl.* viii. 20 *note*, The word *Alt* doth signify to make a stand, and is derived from the Dutch word *Halt*, which is as we say *hold*. **1686** *Abridgem. Eng. Milit. Discipl.* 117 As soon as the Body is marched as far as is intended, they are to be commanded to Halt. **1748** *Anson's Voy.* II. xii. 265 They halted on our first approach, and never advanced afterwards. **1853** C. BRONTË *Villette* xxi, We took a walk into the country and halted for refreshment at a farm. **1854** WOOD *Anim. Life* (1855) 398, I would defy the best trained cavalry horse to have halted more instantaneously.

b. *Mil.* In the imperative, a word of command. Also formerly used as a command in traffic regulations and on road signs. So ***halt notice***, ***sign***. Also *transf.*

1796 *Instr. & Reg. Cavalry* (1813) 69 The officer of the second division gives the word *Wheel!*..and then *Halt! Dress!* when the wheel is completed. **1932** E. WALLACE *When Gangs came to London* xx. 175 He caught Terry's eye and abruptly changed the subject. When they were outside: 'What was that halt sign?' demanded Jiggs. **1935** *Highway Code* 21 (*caption*) Halt sign. **1958** A. WILSON *Middle Age of Mrs. Eliot* II. 153 David, recognizing the Grimm quotation as a halt sign, laughed too. **1965** D. M. DEVINE *His Own Appointed Day* I. ii. 17 Left, here. Then turn right at the halt sign. **1967** M. SUMMERTON *Memory of Darkness* ii. 21 He had driven through a halt sign, and collided with an on-coming tanker. **1969** *Times* 15 July 7/3 What are the advantages of the Give Way signs? Why cannot the Ministry go back to the old safer Halt notices?

2. *trans.* To cause to halt; to bring to a stand; to stop.

1805 LAKE in Owen *Wellesley's Desp.* 533 The flight of Holkar..induced me to halt the army. **1827** STEUART *Planter's G.* (1828) 275 When the machine has got within forty or fifty yards of the place, it is proper to halt the horses.

Hence **halted** *ppl. a.*, brought to a stand.

1796 *Instr. & Reg. Cavalry* (1813) 15 Wheels of divisions of the squadron or line, are made on a halted, or on a moveable pivot. **1847** *Infantry Man.* (1854) 62 Wheeling round the halted file.

halt, obs. 3 sing. pres. of HOLD *v.*

halt, obs. form of HAUGHT *a.*

haltand, -ane, var. HAUTAIN *a. Obs.*

halte, obs. var. of HOLT, copse.

halter (ˈhɔːltə(r)), *sb.*¹ Forms: 1 **hælfter**, 3–5 **haltre**, (4 **haltyr**, 6 **aulter**), 6–7 **haulter**, 3– **halter**. β. 2 **helfter**. 5 *north.* **heltir**, **-yr(e**, 5–6 **helter(e**. [OE. *hælftre* = OHG. *halftra* (Ger. *halfter*), MDu. *halfter*, *halter*, OLG. *heliftra*, MLG. *helchter*, *halter*:—WGer. **halftra-*, **haliftra-*, f. root **halƀ-*, whence OHG. *halb*, MLG. and MDu. *helve*, OE. *helfe*: see HELVE. The primary sense was 'that by which anything is held': cf. L. *capistrum* halter. The *f* between *l* and *t* was lost in ME. as in MDu. and MHG.]

1. a. A rope, cord, or strap with a noose or head-stall, by which horses or cattle are led or fastened up.

a **1000** *Gloss.* in Wr.-Wülcker 199/14 *Capistrum*, hælfter, *uel* cælfster. *a* **1100** *Ibid.* 332/18 *Capistrum*, hælfstre. *c* **1175** *Lamb. Hom.* 53 þet is þes deofles helfter. *a* **1250** *Owl & Night.* 1028 Hom ne mai halter ne bridel Bringe. **1390** GOWER *Conf.* II. 48 And trusse her halters forth with me. **14..** *Nom.* in Wr.-Wülcker 727/44 *Hoc capistrum*, a heltyr. *c* **1450** *St. Cuthbert* (Surtees) 5361 þe hors heltirs to breke he ran. **1497** *Naval Acc. Hen. VII* (1896) 119 Horsharnes without halters. **1546** J. HEYWOOD *Prov.* (1867) 44 It wolde haue made a hors breake his halter sure. **1760–72** tr. *Juan & Uloa's Voy.* (ed. 3) II. 240 The nooses, or halters, are thongs of a cow's hide. **1835** LYTTON *Rienzi* v. v, The horse runs from one hand, the halter remains in the other.

b. A strap attached to the top of a backless bodice and looped round the neck; also, a bodice with such a strap or cut so as to give a similar effect. Hence *attrib.* and *Comb.*, as ***halter neck(line)***, ***top***.

1935 *Mademoiselle* Aug. 1/2 (*caption*) Trunks with halter top. **1936** *New Yorker* 18 Jan. 50/2 When a dress terminates in a halter neck, they have an ingratiating habit of putting a little bolero jacket over it. **1939** M. B. PICKEN *Lang. Fashion* 102/3 Halter neckline..introduced about 1933. Used in sports and evening clothes. **1948** N. MAILER *Naked & Dead* (1949) II. vii. 229 In the brothel the girls wear halters and trim panties with a tropical print. **1953** BERG *Dict. New Words* 91/1 *Halter*, a woman's bodice, held in place by straps around the neck and across the back, so as to leave the arms and the back free. **1958** J. D. MACDONALD *Executioners* (1959) iv. 59 Nancy wore very short red shorts..and a yellow linen halter. **1959** *Vogue Pattern Book* June/July 23 A full, floating skirt and bare back halter top for a sun dress. **1971** *Vogue* Dec. 64/1 Black silk jersey halter-neck dress ..£70.

2. a. A rope with a noose for hanging malefactors.

c **1460** *Towneley Myst.* (Surtees) 313 Ye shalle clym on helle crokkys With a halpeny heltere. **1481** CAXTON *Reynard* (Arb.) 32 Hadde we an halter which were mete for his necke and strong ynough we shold sone make an ende. **1548** HALL *Chron., Hen. VIII*, 63 One after another in their shertes, and every one a halter about his neck. **1596** SHAKS. *Merch V*, IV. i. 379 *Por.* What mercy can you render him Anthonio? *Gra.* A halter gratis, nothing else for Gods sake. **1722** SEWELL *Hist. Quakers* (1795) I. IV. 295 Break not our ecclesiastical laws, for then ye are sure to stretch by a halter. **1852** MISS YONGE *Cameos* I. xxvii. 220 The archers and men-at-arms were hung in halters to every tree in the forest.

fig. **1583** GOLDING *Calvin on Deut.* xviii. 105 A Childe.. if his father let him haue his Swindge lyke a Goose: hee putteth the halter about his Neck by cockering of him too much. **1642** FULLER *Holy & Prof. St.* I. vi. 15 The same counsels observed are chains to grace, which neglected prove halters to strange undutifull children. **1860** KINGSLEY *Misc.* I. 84 Raleigh..finding that James was betraying him, and sending him out with a halter round his neck.

b. Used typically for death by hanging; 'the gallows'.

1533 FRITH *Another bk. agst. Rastell* 337 Which doth rather purchase them a halter than the remission of sins. **1679** BURNET *Hist. Ref.* an. 1554 (R.), Ready to offer up their lives to the halter, or the fire, as God should appoint. **1790** PENNANT *London* (R.), Edward..resigned to them the monopoly of the ax and halter. **1864** TENNYSON *Aylmer's Field* 520 Scared with threats of jail and halter.

3. *attrib.* and *Comb.*, as ***halter-chain***, ***-maker***, ***-place***, ***-seller***, ***-strap***, ***-string***; ***halter-proof*** adj.; **halter-break** *v. U.S.*, to accustom (a horse, etc.) to a halter; to break by means of a halter; **halter-cast** *ppl. a.* (see quots.); **halter hitch** (see quot. 1944); †**halter-man**, a hangman. Also HALTER-SACK, -SICK.

1837 *N.Y. Mirror* 28 Oct. 140/3 The moose has been frequently tamed, and unlike the common deer, can be *halter-broken as easily as a horse. **1860** J. G. HOLLAND *Miss Gilbert's Career* xix. 350 You want to halter-break 'em when they're little and get 'em kind o' wonted to the feel of the harness. **1868** *Rep. Iowa Agric. Soc. 1867* 117 My colts are halter-broken as soon as foaled. **1883** W. H. BISHOP in *Harper's Mag.* Oct. 725/2 They are halter-broke, and turned loose again. **1704** WORLIDGE *Dict. Rust.*, **Halter Cast* happens thus: when a Horse endeavours to scrub the itching part of his Body near the Head or Neck, one of his hinder Feet entangles in the Halter..by the violent strugling of the Horse to disingage himself, receives sometimes very dangerous hurts in the hollow of his Pastern. **1813** *Sporting Mag.* XLII. 58 Danger of being halter cast, which has proved fatal to so many horses. **1831** J. HOLLAND *Manuf. Metal* I. 183 *Halter-chains..used with bridles. **1944** C. W. ASHLEY *Bk. Knots* ii. 44 *Halter hitch.* Horses are hitched with this knot the world over. The end is stuck loosely through the loop, which is not tightened. The knot is easily slipped after removing the end from the loop. **1947** *Times Lit. Suppl.* 15 Nov. 594/4 When he was seven he was given a pony on condition that he mastered a halter hitch. **1596** NASHE (*title*) Haue with you to Saffron-walden, or, Gabriell Harueys Hunt is vp. Containing a full Answere to the eldest sonne of the *Halter-maker. **1638** *Conceited Lett.* (N.), *Halter-men and ballet-makers were not better set aworke this many a day. **1630** J. TAYLOR (Water P.) *Trav.* Wks. III. 80/1 The priuiledges of this graund *Haulter-master are many. **1704** *Lond. Gaz.* No. 4082/4 A bay Nag..with..a Dent cross his Nose in the *Halter-place. *a* **1679** EARL OF ORRERY *Guzman* 111, By your Charms you may make your self *Halter-proof. *c* **1515** *Cocke Lorell's B.* (Percy) 5 Hary *halter seler at tyborn. **1753** CHAMBERS *Cycl. Supp.*, **Halter-Strap* or *String*, a cord, or long strap of leather, made fast to the head-stall, and to the manger, to tye the horse.

halter (ˈhɔːltə(r)), *sb.*² [f. HALT *v.*¹ + -ER¹.]

1. One who halts or limps, as a cripple.

c **1440** *Promp. Parv.* 224/1 Haltare, *claudicator*. **1552** in HULOET. **1749** LAVINGTON *Enthus. Methodists & Papists* (1820) 205 Calling him one-eyed, halter, baldpate.

2. One who wavers; a waverer.

c **1611** SYLVESTER *Du Bartas* II. iv. IV. *Decay* 315 Double Halters between God and Gold. **1684** RENWICK *Serm.* vii. (1776) 92 O halters! take heed and be admonished.

ˈhalter, *v.* Also 6 haltren; β. 5 heltryn. [f. HALTER *sb.*¹]

1. *trans.* To put a halter upon (a horse or the like); to fasten *up* with a halter.

c **1440** *Promp. Parv.* 235/1 Heltryn beestys, *capistro*. **1530** PALSGR. 577/2, I halter, I tye in a halter, *Iencheuestre*. **1617** MARKHAM *Caval.* I. 75 When the colt is haltered. **1881** FENN *Off to Wilds* xxix. (1888) 203 The horses were haltered up to the wheels.

fig. **1647** TRAPP *Comm. Matt.* xxii. 12 He was muzzled or haltered up, that is, he held his peace, as though he had had a bridle or a halter in his mouth. **1650** R. STAPYLTON *Strada's Low C. Warres* II. 35 Should they now halter themselves, called by a woman's voice?

†**b.** *to halter apes in hell*: see APE *sb.* 6. *Obs.*

1584 PEELE *Arraignm. Paris* IV. ii, All that be Dian's maids are vow'd to halter apes in hell.

2. *fig.* To put a restraint or check upon; to bridle; to fetter; to hamper.

1577 B. GOOGE *Heresbach's Husb.* III. (1586) 130 A faire feelde, that the Steeres may..not be feard, or haltred, with trees, or bushes. **1679** *Hist. Jetzer* 22 They thought they had made him their own, and halter'd up his Conscience.

3. To catch or entrap with a noose or lasso.

1573–80 BARET *Alv.* H 54 To halter, or intangle, *laqueum injicere alicui*. **1597–8** BP. HALL *Sat.* (1753) 70 Or halter finches through a privy doore. *a* **1625** BEAUM. & FL. *Wit without M.* IV. ii, What pretty gins thou hast to halter woodcocks! *a* **1732** ATTERBURY (T.), Catching moles and haltering frogs. **1760–72** tr. *Juan & Ulloa's Voy.* (ed. 3) I. 416 They are very dextrous in haltering a bull at full speed ..The noose is made of cow hide.

4. To put a halter about the neck of (a person); to hang (a person) with a halter.

1616 HAYWARD *Sanct. Troub. Soul* I. xii. (1620) 248 A cord, to halter me in hell. **1649** G. DANIEL *Trinarch., Rich. II*, civ, The Great ones..hanged are, The Rest were halter'd, Pardon'd; and 'twas faire. **1765** *Meretriciad* 49 Silent and sad as any Rogue cou'd be, That halter'd rode, to dreaded Tyburn tree. **1894** *Voice* (N.Y.) 13 Sept., The Chicago bombthrowers who were haltered for practising their principles.

fig. **1633** T. ADAMS *Exp. 2 Peter* iii. 3 Lusts..to serve him like Absalom, and halter him at the next bough. **1639** FULLER *Holy War* v. vii. (1647) 239 Suffered to have rope enough, till they had haltered themselves in a Præmunire.

Hence **ˈhaltering** *vbl. sb.*

1591 PERCIVALL *Sp. Dict.*, *Cabestrage*, haltering. **1598** FLORIO, *Capestratura prima*, the first haltering of a coult.

haltered (ˈhɔːltəd), *ppl. a.* [f. HALTER *sb.*¹ or *v.*] Having a halter on; fastened with or as with a halter; *fig.* fettered, hampered.

1520 *Treat. Galaunt* in Furniv. *Ballads fr. MSS.* I. 452 They go haltered in them as horse in the stable. **1606** SHAKS. *Ant. & Cl.* III. xiii. 130 A halter'd necke, which do's the Hangman thanke, For being yare about him. **1811** BYRON *Hints from Hor.* 281 A halter'd heroine Johnson sought to slay—We saved Irene, but half damn'd the play.

†**ˈhalterer.** *Obs. rare*⁻⁰. In 5 helterere. [f. HALTER *sb.*¹ + -ER¹.] A halter-maker.

c **1425** *Voc.* in Wr.-Wülcker 651/35 *Hic capistrius*, helterere.

‖**halteres** (hælˈtɪəriːz), *sb. pl.* Also **alteres**. [Gr. ἁλτῆρες (in sense 1), f. ἅλλεσθαι to leap.]

1. Weights, similar to dumb-bells, held in the hands to give an impetus in leaping.

1533 ELYOT *Cast. Helthe* xxxiii. (1541) 47 The plummets, called of Galen Alteres, whiche are nowe moch vsed with gret men..are verrye good to be vsed fastynge, a lytel before breakefast or dyner. **1857** BIRCH *Anc. Pottery* (1858) I. 414 The halteres or leaping dumb-bells, are seen hung up. **1896** *Daily News* 6 Apr. 5/7 An ordinary long jump..made with the help of halteres or leaping dumb-bells.

2. *Entom.* The pair of knobbed filaments, also called *balancers* and *poisers*, which in dipterous insects take the place of a pair of posterior wings.

1823 in CRABB *Technol. Dict.* **1834** MCMURTRIE *Cuvier's Anim. Kingd.* 449 The halteres are entirely exposed. **1874** LUBBOCK *Orig. & Met. Ins.* i. 23 The hinder pair being represented by minute club-shaped organs called 'halteres'.

halteridium (hæltəˈrɪdɪəm). *Zool.* Pl. **-ia**. [mod.L. (A Labbé 1894, in *Archives de Zoologie expérimentale et générale*, 3e série, II. 129), f. Gr. ἁλτήρ weight used in leaping.] A name for the gametocytes of the protozoan genus *Hæmoproteus*, which is parasitic in birds, used when the gametocytes were erroneously considered to be a separate genus.

1901 G. M. STERNBERG in *Pop. Sci. Monthly* LVIII. 367 The mosquito..could not transmit the malarial parasite of man or another similar parasite of birds (halteridium). **1901** *Practitioner* Mar. 278 One of the malaria-like organisms of birds, namely, halteridium. **1962** J. D. SMYTH *Introd. Animal Parasitol.* ix. 107 These gametocytes [of *Hæmoproteus columbæ*] are shaped like a curved sausage and encircle the nucleus in a halter-fashion, and are sometimes referred to as *Halteridia*, as they were at one time called by the generic name of *Halteridium*.

†**halter-sack.** *Obs.* [f. HALTER *sb.*¹ + SACK.] A 'gallows-bird': a term of obloquy.

1598 FLORIO, *Capestro*, a rope, a halter, a headstall. Also a wag, a halter-sack, or gallowes-clapper. **1611** *Ibid.*, *Capestrello*..a haltersacke, a waghalter. **1611** BEAUM. & FL. *King & no K.* II. ii, Away, you halter-sack, you. *a* **1616** —— *Triumph of Hon.* i, Thy beginning was knapsack, and thy ending will be halter-sack.

halter-sick, *sb.* and *a.* [prob. originating in an error for prec.] **A.** *sb.* = HALTER-SACK.

1617 MINSHEU DUCTOR, An Halter-sicke, or one that the gallowes groanes for, a knauish boy.

B. *adj.* (Cf. *death-sick*.)

1820 W. TOOKE tr. *Lucian* I. 511 You..villainous, infamous halter-sick miscreant.

haltie, obs. form of HAUGHTY *a.*

halting (ˈhɔːltɪŋ), *vbl. sb.*¹ [f. HALT *v*¹ + -ING¹.] The action of limping or walking lamely.

c **1440** *Promp. Parv.* 224/2 Haltynge, *claudicacio*. **1581** PETTIE *Guazzo's Civ. Conv.* III. (1586) 147 b, And when he shall walke upright by himselfe, he may boldlie take uppe others for haultinge. **1672** SIR T. BROWNE *Lett. Friend* xiii. (1881) 136 Whether lameness and halting do still encrease among the inhabitants.

b. *transf.* and *fig.* (See HALT *v*¹. 4, 5.)

c **1430** *Pilgr. Lyf Manhode* III. xxx. (1869) 152 Ther is noon haltinge so foul as lyinge. **1589** R. HARVEY *Pl. Perc.* 7, I would the woorst were curbd with a checkthong, as bigge as a towpenny halter, for halting with a Queene so good and gratious. **1627** SANDERSON *Serm.* I. 269 Without hollowness, halting, and hypocrisie. *a* **1680** GLANVILL *Serm.* v. (R.),

They lay in wait for our haltings. **1851** HELPS *Comp. Solit.* vi, A wonderful halting in their logic.

'halting, *vbl. sb.*[2] [f. HALT *v.*[2]] The action of making a halt; stopping; chiefly *attrib.* At or on which a halt is made, as ***halting ground, morning, point.*** (See also HALTING-PLACE.)

1759 ROBERTSON *Hist. Scot.* I. v. 347 After halting three hours, she set out for Hamilton. *c* **1813** MRS. SHERWOOD *Stories Ch. Catech.* xxiv. 249 *Halting Morning*, the morning when there is no parade. **1856** KANE *Arct. Expl.* II. x. 110 When they reached any of the halting-huts. **1869** E. A. PARKES *Pract. Hygiene* (ed. 3) 62 When halting ground is reached, it may be necessary to filter the water.

'halting, *ppl. a.* [f. HALT *v.*[1]]

1. That halts; limping, lame.

1382 WYCLIF *Micah* iv. 6, I schal gedere the haltinge. **1483** *Cath. Angl.* 172/2 Haltande, *claudicans.* **1564–78** BULLEYN *Dial. agst. Pest.* (1888) 81 Better is an haltyng man whiche kepeth the right waie than the swift runner..that wandereth a straie. **1849** M. ARNOLD *Sonn. to Friend* 6 That halting slave, who in Nicopolis Taught Arrian.

2. *fig.* Maimed; defective, imperfect, faulty.

1533 FRITH *Another Bk. agst. Rastell* (1829) 228 That halting verse shall run merrily..upon his right feet. **1611** BIBLE *Transl. Pref.* 7 If anything be halting, or superfluous, or not so agreeable to the originall, the same may bee corrected. **1877** L. MORRIS *Epic Hades* III. 248 How to reach with halting words That infinite perfection.

3. Hesitating, wavering, shifting.

1585 ABP. SANDYS *Serm.* (1841) 273 Their halting hearts ..their friendly words and malicious deeds. **1875** STUBBS *Const. Hist.* II. xvii. 601 The weak and halting policy of Edward II. **1878** B. TAYLOR *Deukalion* II. ii. 60 An easy way Between two worlds to suit the halting crowd.

Hence **'haltingly** *adv.*, in a halting manner; limpingly, lamely (*lit.* and *fig.*). **'haltingness**, defectiveness, imperfection, faultiness.

1580 HOLLYBAND *Treas. Fr. Tong*, *Boistement*, haltingly. *a* **1603** T. CARTWRIGHT *Confut. Rhem. N.T.* (1618) 341 Him that walketh in the way, although it be haltingly. **1881** CHR. ROSSETTI *Pageant*, etc. 169 This Life is full..Of haltingness and baffled shortcoming.

'halting-place. [f. HALTING *vbl. sb.*[2]] Place of halting; temporary stopping place.

1797 BEWICK *Brit. Birds* (1847) I. p. xxiv. *note*, In their long migratory flight..to their halting places. **1837** DICKENS *Pickw.* ii, [They] had resolved to make Rochester their first halting-place.

halt-pace, var. of HALPACE, *Obs.*

†**haltstring.** *Obs. rare.* = STRINGHALT.

1673 *Lond. Gaz.* No. 823/4 A dark brown Mare..having the haltstring in both the hinder leggs when she is cold.

haltyn, var. HAUTAIN *a.*, *Obs.*

halud, obs. pa. pple. of HALLOW *v.*

haluka: see CHALUKAH.

halurgist ('hælədʒɪst). [f. Gr. ἅλ-ς salt + -ουργος working + -IST.] A worker in salt.

1756 C. LUCAS *Ess. Waters* II. 82 It is by the halurgists, or workers in salt, called scum.

halurgy ('hælədʒɪ). [f. as prec. + -ουργία a working: cf. *metallurgy*.] Salt-working.

1853 TH. ROSS *Humboldt's Trav.* III. xxxi. 255 A long residence in the salt-producing districts of Europe, and the labours of practical halurgy. **1854** in MAYNE *Expos. Lex.*

halus, haluuen, haluwen: see HALLOW *sb.*[1]

halutzim (hɑː'luːtsɪm), *sb. pl.* Also **chalutzim, haluzim.** [Heb. *ḥălûṣ.*] Jewish pioneers entering Palestine in order to build up their future national home.

1921 *Daily Mail* 11 Apr. 6/5 The 'Haluzim' are the Jewish pioneers who are flocking into Palestine to help in building up the Jewish National Home. **1923** *Daily Mail* 18 July 7 Tel Aviv..is the headquarters of the Rutenberg Company and also of a number of co-operative building societies run by young Jewish halutzim pioneers. **1923** W. P. LIVINGSTONE *Galilee Doctor* 261 The halutzim, or 'pioneers'. **1971** D. MEIRING *Wall of Glass* ix. 71 A few other Second Aliyah men from Russia, calling themselves Chalutzim, pioneers.

halva ('hælvə, ‖hal'vaː, x-). Also **halvah, halvas, halwa.** [ad. Turk. *helva*, mod. Gr. *halvas*, Arab. *ḥalwā* HULWA.] A sweetmeat made of sesame flour and honey.

1846 I. F. ROMER *Pilgrimage* II. ii. 33 The vender of sweetmeats with a tempting array of *halva* and 'lumps of delight' set out upon a wooden tray borne upon his head. **1908** *Daily Chron.* 12 June 4/7 A Greek merchant in the East-end, who..would sell you..black olives, rose leaf jam, and halvas. *a* **1916** 'SAKI' *Toys of Peace* (1919) 134 A tin of the best Smyrna halva. **1917** KIPLING *Eyes of Asia* (1918) 80, I eat..halwa and puri (native dishes). **1945** A. KOBER *Parm Me* 5 'Halvah', a Turkish confection. **1953** H. MILLER *Plexus* (1963) x. 352, I see Halvah and Baklava too. **1962** *Listener* 24 May 931/2 *Halva cake.* Many of the Greek cakes and pastries are beyond the scope of the home cook, but here is a simple one. **1964** W. MARKFIELD *To Early Grave* (1965) ii. 34 He brought a bagful of Hershey bars and Charms and sour balls and chocolate-covered halvah. **1973** *Sunday Express* 23 Sept. 7/1 From the first time he tasted halva as a child Gholamali Rastegar was obsessed by the traditional Arabic sweetmeat made from honey.

'halvans, *sb. pl.* [Deriv. of *half, halve*: cf. '*halvans* half-produce of labour, given instead of wages' (*West Cornwall Gl.*).]

1849–50 WEALE *Dict. Terms, Halvans*, in Cornish, the refuse ore. **1874** J. H. COLLINS *Metal Mining* Gloss., *Halvans*, the refuse heap of mines, which still contain a small portion of ore, the residue of the dressing processes.

Hence **'halvaner** (see quots.).

1858 SIMMONDS *Dict. Trade, Halvanner*, a miner who dresses and washes the impurities from crude ores. **1880** *W. Cornwall Gloss., Halvaner*, one who receives the half produce of his labour.

halve (hɑːv), *v.* Forms: 4–6 **halfe**, 5–8 **half**, 4– **halve.** [ME. *halfen, halven* f. HALF *sb.*]

1. *trans.* To divide into two halves or equal parts; to share equally; to deal *out*, take, or complete the half of; to reduce to half.

a **1300** *E.E. Psalter* liv. 24 Man-slaer and swykel his dayes halfe sal. *a* **1420** HOCCLEVE *De Reg. Princ.* 1246 What I have, I wole it with you halve. **1483** *Cath. Angl.* 170/2 To Halfe, *mediare, dimidiare.* *a* **1568** ASCHAM *Scholem.* (Arb.) 39 Not trobled, mangled, and halfed, but sounde, whole, full, and hable to do their office. **1641** W. BRAY *Sermon* 23 The Church of Rome..halfes out to them an imperfect Sacrament. **1647** H. MORE *Song of Soul* II. App. lxxxi, Not lightened entire, But halfed like the Moon. **1703** T. N. *City & C. Purchaser* 54 The setting off..being halfed. **1789** COLERIDGE *Philedon* Poems I. 5 The fervid Sun had more than halved the day. **1869** E. A. PARKES *Pract. Hygiene* (ed. 3) 5 These quantities might..in most cases be halved. *fig.* **1638** WOTTON *Lett., Rem.* (L.), Our Nicholas, for I account him at least halfed between us, tells me that [etc.]. **1878** BROWNING *La Saisiaz* 59 Power that sinks and pettiness that soars, all halved and nothing whole.

†**b.** To attain or amount to the half of. *Obs.*

1382 WYCLIF *Ps.* liv. 24 [lv. 23] Men of blodis and trecherous shul not haluen ther daȝes. **1398** TREVISA *Barth. De P.R.* XVIII. xv. 775 There is a manere wylde oxe that..in eyther of hys hornes may halfe the mesure that hyghte Boz.

2. *Carpentry.* To fit (timbers) together by HALVING, q.v. Also *intr.* for *pass.*

1804 *Trans. Soc. Arts* XXII. 43 An upright bar, with the horizontal bars halved into it. **1851** J. S. MACAULAY *Field Fortif.* 159 The ends notched out so as to halve into each other.

3. In *Golf*, ***to halve a hole*** (***with*** another), to reach it in the same number of strokes. Also, ***to halve a round, a match.***

1857 *Chambers' Inform.* II. 693/1 When players are very equally matched, neither party has, at the close of a day's play, gained an advantage; every round has been halved, hence the match itself is halved, and remains to be played another day. **1894** *Daily News* 23 Apr. 2/5 They ultimately halved the match. **1894** *Times* 28 Apr. 13/3 Both players reached the green in 3, and the hole was halved in 5.

†**4.** *intr.* To render half service or obedience.

1566 ASCHAM *Divæ Elizab.* Wks. (1761) 183 Saul, first halfing with God, (as when God gave Amalec into his hand) then halting in religion. **1613–80** [see HALVING *vbl. sb.*[1] 1 b].

Hence **halved** (hɑːvd), **halving**, *ppl. adjs.*

1619 W. SCLATER *Exp. 1 Thess.* (1630) 439 A mangled and halfed Decree of God. **1641** 'SMECTYMNUUS' *Vind. Answ.* vi. 84 This you call a faithlesse and a halved citation. **1815** J. GILCHRIST *Labyrinth Demol.* 41 Suited only to halfing and crooked thinkers. **1894** *Westm. Gaz.* 24 Apr. 7/2 After a halved match.

halve, obs. form of HALF *sb.*

halvelings ('hɑːvlɪŋz), *adv.* [Cf. HALFLING.] In half, in two halves.

1846 J. BAXTER *Libr. Pract. Agric.* (ed. 4) I. 397 The horizontal poles are cleft halvelings, and nailed or tied to the uprights.

halvendeal: see HALFENDEAL.

halve-net: see HALF-NET.

halver[1] ('hɑːvə(r)). Also 7 **halfer.** [f. HALVE *v.* + -ER[1].]

1. *Obs.* One who halves; one who has a half share in anything; a partner.

1625 BP. MOUNTAGU *App. Cæsar* II. v. 141 If your selves and such Halfers in opinion, *omnium horarum homines.* **1633** *Terrier Tieths Swinton* in *N. & Q.* 6th Ser. (1885) XI. 366 The inhabitants of Swinton as likewise the lands are partly Wholers and partly Halfers to the Churches or Parsonages of Wath and Mexborough. **1637** RUTHERFORD *Lett.* 8 Sep. (1675) 85 Enough to me..that Christ will have Joy and Sorrow Halfers of the Life of the Saints. *a* **1787** J. BROWN (Haddington) *Sel. Rem.* (1807) 305 Christ is more than halver with me in this cleanly cross.

2. *dial.* and *U.S.* A half-share; esp. in *halvers!* as an exclamation claiming half of something found. Cf. HALF *sb.* 7 g. Esp. in phr. ***do by halvers, go halvers*** (***with***).

1517 *Aberdeen Burgh Recds.* 24 July (Spalding Cl.) Scho had ane young swyne in hawfaris betuix hir and Ellene Crippill. **1816** SCOTT *Antiq.* xxiii, The beggar exclaimed, like a Scotch school-boy when he finds anything, 'Nae halvers and quarters—hale o' mine ain, and nane of my neighbour's. **1825** BROCKETT *N.C. Gloss.* s.v., If the finder be quick he exclaims 'no halfers—findee keepee, losee seekee'. **1865** 'MARK TWAIN' *Celebr. Jumping Frog* (1867) 36 No man can say he ever see him do anything by halvers. **1873** J. H. BEADLE *Undevel. West.* iv. 93 'I'll go halvers with him,' shouts the conservative-looking chap. **1887** *S. Cheshire Gloss., Hafers*..the ordinary word which is used to claim half of any treasure-trove. **1932** W. FAULKNER *Light in August* xviii. 394 Byron Bunch, that weeded another man's laidby crop, without any halvers.

¶ Pegge in *Anonym.* IV. xlii. (*a* 1796) proposes *halfer* as the proper form for *havier* 'a castrated fallow deer'; whence in Todd and later Dicts.

halver[2]. One who fishes with a halve-net or half-net.

1812 SINGER *Agric. Dumfries* 603 The halvers, or persons who claim and practise this kind of fishing.

halving ('hɑːvɪŋ), *vbl. sb.*[1] [f. HALVE *v.*]

1. The action of the vb. HALVE; division into two equal parts; sharing equally.

c **1430** *Art Nombryng* (E.E.T.S.) 6 The halfyng of euery nombre. **1613** PURCHAS *Pilgrimage* (1614) 41 The often halfing of ages.

†**b.** The rendering of half service, divided obedience. *Obs.*

1613 BP. HALL *Recoll. Treat.* (1614) 700 Against halving, hee will bee served with all the heart. **1642** BP. REYNOLDS *Israel's Petit.* 16 To reprove and humble us, for our Hypocrisie and halvings with God. *a* **1680** BROOKS in Spurgeon *Treas. Dav.* Ps. cxix. 145 God neither loves halting nor halving; he will be served truly and totally.

2. *Carpentry.* A method of fitting two pieces of timber together by cutting out half the thickness of each, so as to let them into each other.

1842–76 GWILT *Archit.* Gloss., *Halving*, a method of joining timbers by letting them into each other. It is preferable to mortising. **1881** YOUNG *Every Man his own Mechanic* §437 *Halving* is the simplest mode of performing the operation to which the term 'scarfing' is applied.

halving, *vbl. sb.*[2] [f. *halve*, HALF(-NET) + -ING[1].] Fishing with a half-net.

1791 *Statist. Acc. Scotl., Dumfriessh.* II. 16 (Jam.) A second mode of fishing, called haaving or hauling. **1812** SINGER *Agric. Dumpfries* 604 In halving, all animosities are forgot.

halvundele, var. of HALFENDEAL.

halwa, var. HALVA.

halwe, halwy, obs. forms of HALLOW.

halwei, var. of HALEWEI, *Obs.*

haly, var. of HALELY *adv.*

halyard, halliard, haulyard ('hæljəd, hɔːl-). *Naut.* Forms: α. 4–5 **halier**, 5–6 **hallyer**, (5 **halyher, halleyr, hayllyer**, 6 **hellier**, 7 **harriar**). β. 7–9 **hallyard**, 7– **halliard, halyard**, (7 **halli-yard, hallyeard**), 8– **haulyard.** [orig. *halier, hallyer*, the same as HALLIER, f. HALE *v.*: in 17th c. perverted by association with *yard*]

1. A rope or tackle used for raising or lowering a sail, yard, spar, or flag.

1373 *Indenture* in Riley *Lond. Mem.* (1868) 370, 2 haliers, 2 yerderopes..2 shettes. **1495–7** *Naval Acc. Hen. VII*, (1896) 106 Ropes cald Hawsers, Cranerope, Gynne ropes, Haliers, Cartropes. *Ibid.* 197 Hallyers for the foresale. **1592** WYRLEY *Armorie* 144 Not any helliers end, Hawser, boolina, but soone he will amend. **1611** COTGR., *Guinderesse*..the mizen halliards; the rope whereby the mizen sayle is hoysed vp. **1612** DEKKER *If it be not good* Wks. 1873 III. 293 Let goe your Harriars, let goe, amaine louere amaine. **1627** CAPT. SMITH *Seaman's Gram.* v. 21 The Halyards belong to all masts, for by them we hoise the yards to their height. **1751** SMOLLETT *Per. Pic.* (1779) I. ii. 16 From the sprit-sail-yard to the mizen top-sail haulyards. **1762** FALCONER *Shipwr.* II. 13 The bow-lines and the hall-yards quickly gone. **1835** MARRYAT *Jac. Faithf.* viii, Clap on, both of you, and get another pull at those haulyards. **1867** SMYTH *Sailor's Word-bk., Halliards, Halyards, Haulyards.* **1879** TENNYSON *Defence of Lucknow* i, Banner of England..Shot through the staff or the halyard.

b. With defining word prefixed: as ***crow-foot halyards***, lines through a block on the lower stay, and bent to the crow-foot on the awning (Hamersly *Naval Encycl.*); ***peak-halyards***, those used on gaffs and hooked to the peak; ***signal-halyards***, light lines extending from the deck to the trucks or gaff-ends, used for hoisting signal-flags; ***throat-halyards***, those that are used on gaffs, hooked to the jaws, etc.

1770 WINN in *Phil. Trans.* LX. 191 The pendant halliards, which pass over a sheave in the truck, on the top-gallant-mast-head. **1833** MARRYAT *P. Simple* xxviii, A tail-block and the studding-sail haulyards. **1836** —— *Midsh. Easy* xvii, Made it fast to the peak halyards and hoisted it up.

2. *attrib.*, as ***halyard block***; **halyard-rack**, a wooden framework in which the running part of any halyard is kept coiled, so as to be always clear for running.

1833 MARRYAT *P. Simple* xii, I'll come to an anchor on the topsail halyard rack. *c* **1860** H. STUART *Seaman's Catech.* 75 The mizen cap has a bolt on the after part for the peak halyard block.

halyer, var. HALLIER.

halymote, halyvey, obs. ff. HALLMOTE, HALEWEI.

ham (hæm), *sb.*[1] (*a.*) Forms: 1 **ham(m, hom(m**, 3–4 **homme**, 3–7 **hamme**, 5 **hame**, 5– **ham.** [OE. *ham(m, hom(m*, str. f. = OHG. *hamma*, MHG. *hamme*, Ger. dial. *hamm*, angle of the knee, Du. *hamme* (Kilian) *ham* 'ham'; cf. also, with single *m*, OHG. *hama*, MHG. *hame*, Flem. *hame*, ON.

hǫm: app. f. an OTeut. **ham-*, **hamm-* to be crooked.]

A. *sb.* **I. 1. a.** That part of the leg at the back of the knee; the hollow or bend of the knee.

c **1000** ÆLFRIC *Gloss.* in Wr.-Wülcker 160/13 *Poples*, hamm. *c* **1000** *Sax. Leechd.* II. 68 Moneᵹum men ᵹescrincað his fet to his homme. *Ibid.* ᵹebeþe þa hamma mid þam stan baðe. *a* **1225** *Ancr. R.* 122 Mid hommen iuolden, þet is, cneolinde. *c* **1290** *S. Eng. Leg.* I. 360/42 þe senewes in his hamme schronken. **13..** *E.E. Allit. P.* B. 1541 His cnes cachchez to close and cluchches his hommes. *c* **1400** *Lanfranc's Cirurg.* 295 Loke in his hamme, vnder his knee. **1530** PALSGR. 228/2 Hamme of the legge, *jarret*. **1581** MARBECK *Bk. of Notes* 921 We must not suppose that he doth sit with bended hammes. **1679** *Confinement* 31 With supple ham, and pliant knee. **1801** STRUTT *Sports & Past.* III. v. 210 He hangs by his hams upon a pole. **1831** BREWSTER *Nat. Magic* x. (1833) 254 He broke it to pieces by the tendons of his hams.

b. By extension: The back of the thigh; the thigh and buttock collectively. Usually in *pl.*

1552 HULOET, Hamme, *femur*. **1573-80** BARET *Alv.* H 57 The vtter part of the thigh, the hamme, *fœmur*. **1676** HOBBES *Iliad* (1677) 190 He cannot, without trembling, quiet sit; But dances on his hams, and changes hue. **1796** MORSE *Amer. Geog.* II. 562 They sit on their hams, with their legs and arms disposed in the manner of monkeys. **1875** F. HALL in *Lippincott's Mag.* XVI. 753/1 Squatting on their hams at respectful distance.

c. In quadrupeds: The back of the hough; the hough.

1607 TOPSELL *Four-f. Beasts* (1658) 317 A kinde of Scab breeding in the ham, which is the bent of the bough. **1678** *Trans. Crt. Spain* II. 156 To cut the hammes of the Mules of the Coach. **1735** SOMERVILLE *Chase* I. 250 His [a hound's] round Cat Foot, Strait Hams, and wide-spread Thighs.. confess his Speed.

2. The thigh of a slaughtered animal, used for food; *spec.* that of a hog salted and dried in smoke or otherwise; also, the meat so prepared.

1637-50 ROW *Hist. Kirk* (Wodrow) 324 Mr. Henrie Blyth had such antipathie aganis an ham, that no sooner did he heare a ham spoken of but he swarfed. **1711** STEELE *Spect.* No. 14 ¶8 A Jew eat me up half a Ham of Bacon. **1712** PRIOR *Extempore Invitation* 4 If they can dine On bacon-ham, and mutton-chine. **1734** W. SNELGRAVE *Guinea & Slave Trade* 210 Several Westphalia Hams, and a large Sow. **1775** ROMANS *Hist. Florida* 331, I purchased some bear, bacon and venison hams of them. **1833** MARRYAT *P. Simple* xxv, A smoked mutton ham. **1854** THACKERAY *Rose & Ring* xiv, She took out.. some slices of ham.

3. *attrib.* and *Comb.*, as ***ham-curing***, ***-pie***, ***-sandwich***, ***-smoker***; **ham-beetle**, one of several American beetles whose larvæ are destructive to hams, esp. *Corynetes* (*Necrobia*) *rufipes*, the red-legged ham-beetle; **hamfatter** *U.S. slang*, an ineffective actor or performer; (also ***hamfat***) a mediocre jazz musician; so ***hamfat man***, etc.; **ham-fisted** *a.*, having large or clumsy hands, heavy-handed, awkward; bungling; hence **ham-fistedly** *adv.*, **ham-fistedness**; **ham-footed** *a.*, clumsy, awkward, stupid; **ham-handed** *a.*, = *ham-fisted*; hence **ham-handedly** *adv.*, **ham-handedness**; **ham loaf** orig. *U.S.*, a shaped mass of chopped cooked ham intended to be cut into slices; **ham-tail**, ? a (horse's) tail of a rounded shape like a ham.

1848 DICKENS *Dombey* vi, The old-established Ham-and-Beef Shop. **1907** *Daily Chron.* 23 Oct. 4/4 Spinning, or bread-baking, or *ham-curing. **1880** G. A. SALA *America Revisited* (1882) I. iv. 66 Every American who does not wish to be thought 'small potatoes' or a *'ham-fatter' or a 'corner loafer'. **1889** *Cent. Dict.*, *Hamfatter*,.. a term of contempt for an actor of a low grade, as a negro minstrel. Said to be derived from an old-style negro song called 'The Ham-fat Man'. **1932** 'SPINDRIFT' *Yankee Slang* 20 *Hamfatter*, loudly-dressed and loudly-decorated dude. **1938** *N.Y. Amsterdam News* 12 Mar. 17 The Harlem Hamfats grind out the tune. **1946** MEZZROW & WOLFE *Really Blues* 58 A lot of beat up old hamfats.. sang and played. **1959** S. B. CHARTERS *Country Blues* 86 The singing of these little 'hamfat' bands never reached the artistic intensity of men like Blind Lemon. **1966** *New Yorker* 11 June 160/2 Most of the musicians playing in these clubs are old men... They're hamfat musicians. In the old days, the rough musicians kept pieces of ham fat in their pockets to grease the slides of their trombones. **1928** *Daily Mail* 7 May 6/4 *Ham Fisted.—Applied to pilots who are heavy on controls, or generally clumsy. **1928** *Sunday Express* 24 June 8/3 Two thousand lumber-jacks were in town, ham-fisted great fellows with hair on their chests and pine needles growing out of their ears. **1938** C. S. FORESTER *Ship of Line* 51 God damn and blast all you hamfisted yokels. **1942** H. ALLEN in Forbes & Allen *Ten Fighter Boys* 15 A dog-fight with a Hun very rarely entails a considered aerobatic movement as an evasive action. In fact, the more ham-fisted the movement, the better its effect. **1960** *Times* 20 Oct. 8/1 The play's basic idea implies a less ham-fisted humour than the authors can supply. **1964** *Punch* 2 Sept. 355/1 Some *ham-fistedly insensitive moments. **1963** *Times* 16 Feb. 9/3 The campaign cannot be written off because of the *hamfistedness of its beginnings. **1960** E. S. & W. J. HIGHAM *High Speed Rugby* 26 One *'ham-footed' forward.. makes a present of the ball to the other side. **1961** *Sunday Express* 7 May 14 Is he so thick-soled, ham-footed? **1918** W. A. BISHOP *Winged Warfare* 30 First the instructor would tell me I was *'ham-handed'—that I gripped the controls too tightly with every muscle tense. **1918** *Punch* 3 Apr. 222/2 *Second P[ilot]*... I was getting ham-handed and mutton-fisted, flapping the old things every day. **1930** C. DIXON *Parachuting* 93 The pilot with sensitive hands is a better pilot than one with non-sensitive hands. The latter are bluntly called 'ham-handed'. **1934** E. LINKLATER *Magnus Merriman* 98 Are you trying to insult me, or is that your ham-handed idea of a compliment? **1946** *Times* 3 Dec. 8/3 There should be no ham-handed bulk purchasing of stuff which was not really wanted. **1958** *New Statesman* 12 Apr. 458/3 Much of the recipient's pleasure is taken away by the very ham-handed invitation. **1964** *Economist* 11 Apr. 168/1 The FMC has gone a bit *hamhandedly about its job. **1928** O. STEWART *Aerobatics* 50 One of the main objectives in finesse is the development of good 'hands'... *Ham-handedness is not often a gift of unkind fate; it is not necessarily incurable. **1963** *Economist* 8 June 1046/1 The Kennedy Administration has contributed its own moments of hamhandedness. **1902** *Encycl. Brit.* XXVI. 558/2 Hamburger steak with onions, veal loaf, *ham loaf. **1907** *Daily Chron.* 23 Sept. 7/5 Veal loaf, ham loaf, beef loaf. **1733** POPE *Hor. Sat.* II. i. 46 None deny.. Darty his *Ham-pie. *c* **1847** J. S. COYNE in M. R. Booth *Eng. Plays of 19th Cent.* (1973) IV. 186 We used to go together to Greenwich, with a paper of *ham sandwiches in my basket. **1866** 'MARK TWAIN' *Lett. fr. Hawaii* (1967) 68 The Sandwich Islanders always squat on their hams, and who knows but they may be the old original 'ham sandwiches'? **1872** 'L. CARROLL' *Through Looking-Glass* vii, I fed him with—with—with Ham-sandwiches and Hay. **1880** RUSKIN *Fathers have told Us* I. i, If he has bought his ham-sandwich, and is ready for the 'En voiture, messieurs'. **1972** B. EVERITT *Cold Front* xv. 145 The boy.. sat between us, polishing off a gigantic ham sandwich. **1829** T. HOOK *Bank to Barnes* 164 *Ham-smoker, and pork-butcher. **1705** *Lond. Gaz.* No. 4183/4 A.. Gelding.. with a *Ham Tail. **1611** COTGR., *Veine iartiere*, the garter veine, or *hamme veine.

4. Phr. **ham and beef** *Rhyming slang*, the chief warder in a prison; **ham and eggs**, a dish consisting of fried ham and eggs.

1941 J. PHELAN *Murder by Numbers* iv. 46 There's the ham-and-beef and tickety-boo making rounds. **1962** *John o' London's* 25 Jan. 82/2 A chief warder or prison officer is known in rhyming slang as a *ham and beef*. **1837** W. H. WILLS *Jrnl.* in *S. Hist. Assoc. Pub.* VI. 473 They gave me fryed ham and eggs and biscuit, bread & Coffee. **1838** DICKENS *Let.* 1 Feb. (1965) I. 366 We have had for breakfast, .. ham and eggs. **1967** C. DRUMMOND *Death at Furlong Post* iii. 31 'Get me ham and eggs,' he said.

II. 5. a. [App. short for *hamfatter*.] An inexpert performer; (also ***ham actor***, ***actress***) an ineffective or over-emphatic actor, one who rants or overacts. *slang* (orig. *U.S.*).

1882 *Illustr. Sport. & Dram. News* 23 Dec. 355/2 'Banjo Hams' are held up to scorn. *Ibid.*, One writer proudly describes himself as 'no ham, but a classical banjo player'. **1903** S. A. CLAPIN *New Dict. Amer.* 220 *Ham*, in theatrical parlance, a tenth-rate actor or variety performer. **1911** *Hampton's Mag.* Aug. 178/1 It was the voice of what is known as a 'ham', because Shakespeare once wrote a play. A 'ham' actor. **1926** H. C. WITWER *Roughly Speaking* 223 Ham actors get a extra split week at a picture house if their fearful monologs put the ladies on the broiler. **1928** *Daily Express* 20 June 9/4 Sophie Tucker will, in all probability, appear in a revue next autumn... 'You have never seen me in revue,' Sophie reminded me, 'I am a ham actor too, you know.' **1933** 'HAY' & 'ARMSTRONG' *Orders are Orders* II. 51 'We'd better have Harvey.. to double for him.'.. '*That* old ham actor?' **1936** WODEHOUSE *Laughing Gas* xviii. 200 Just one of these ham actors that's jealous of a fellow's screen genius. **1941** E. WILSON *Wound & Bow* i. 61 Dickens had a strain of the ham in him, and, in the desperation of his later life, he gave in to the old ham and let him rip. **1947** N. MARSH *Final Curtain* xii. 179 A squalid little ham actress. **1957** V. J. KEHOE *Technique Film & T.V. Make-Up* i. 15 The expression 'ham' actor originated from those performers who rubbed ham rind on their faces as a base for their colored powders when they could not afford the more expensive and less odoriferous oils. **1958** *Times* 16 Apr. 3/2 'He thought I was an old ham,' says Miss Seyler indulgently.

b. An inexpert or over-theatrical performance; ham acting. *slang*.

1942 R. CHANDLER *High Window* (1943) xxx. 195 Don't feed me the ham. I've been in pictures. I'm a connoisseur of ham. **1959** *Times Lit. Suppl.* 20 Feb. 95/3 Charles Dickens.. saw Lemaître in his late period and was swept off his feet, but what he says might apply equally well to ham acting. In fact, it sounds suspiciously like ham. **1959** *Listener* 28 May 954/2 The mummer who thinks that all acting before his time was 'ham'.

6. An amateur telegraphist; now esp. an amateur radio operator. *slang* (orig. *U.S.*).

1919 C. H. DARLING *Jargon Bk.* 17 *Ham*, a student telegraph operator. **1922** *Glasgow Herald* 18 Aug. 6 Any person who passes a test prescribed by the Government can obtain a licence to 'send' radio messages in the United States, and in popular parlance one who has qualified and taken this 'Radio Operator Amateur—First Grade' certificate is dubbed a 'ham'. **1928** *Collier's* 22 Sept. 26 The amateur radio 'hams' have the ends of the earth for neighbors. **1929** *Amer. Speech* IV. 288 At either end of a wire an unskillful operator is a 'lid', 'ham', 'bum' or 'plug'. **1936** *Daily Herald* 19 Sept. 7/5 (Advt.), Do you ever hear the 'hams'? It appears that ' hams' is American for amateur radio transmitters... Of course, the 'hams' use the short wavelengths. **1955** *Sci. News Let.* 19 Mar. 188/2 Now it will be easier for a blind person to qualify for a license as a radio 'ham'. **1957** *Oxford Mail* 9 Nov. 4/5 The Russians invited radio 'hams' throughout the world to send details to Radio Magazine, Moscow, of reception from their satellites. **1967** *New Scientist* 11 May 322/3 The army of radio 'hams', who reach out over fantastic distances with their single sideband transmitters and receivers, are about to be reinforced. **1973** D. LEES *Rape of Quiet Town* vi. 90 He'd heard the radio ham speaking into a microphone.

III. 7. [Partly from *ham-fisted*, *-handed* adjs.] An incompetent boxer or fighter. *U.S. slang*.

1888 *Missouri Repub.* 27 Mar. (Farmer), He is a good fighter but will allow the veriest ham to whip him. **1929** *Sat. Even. Post* 14 Dec. 144/3 They want me to slug with this big ham.

B. *attrib.* or as *adj.* **1.** Characteristic of or relating to a ham actor or an inexpert performer; self-consciously theatrical. *slang*.

1935 H. WILLIAMS *4 Yrs. Old Vic* xi. 186 Young players to-day are scared of being what they call 'ham', which I suppose is an abbreviation of what used to be termed 'ham-bone'. **1938** *Evening Standard* 26 July 7/2 We hear a great deal about 'ham' acting nowadays. As far as I can judge, 'ham' acting is the habit of rolling sonorous speeches round the tongue and delivering them with extravagant relish to the gallery. **1944** AUDEN *Sea & Mirror* in *For Time Being* iii. 56 The schmalz tenor never quite able at his big moments to get right up nor the ham bass right down. **1958** B. NICHOLS *Sweet & Twenties* xvii. 231 His conception of aristocracy was strangely out of date, and more than a little 'ham'. **1958** *Observer* 4 May 15/7 It is one of the most extraordinary exhibitions of ham acting I've ever seen.

2. [Partly from *ham-fisted*, *-handed* adjs.] Clumsy, ineffective, incompetent. *slang*.

1941 M. ALLINGHAM *Traitor's Purse* xii. 133 Campion's thin hands remained expressionless and Lugg's great ham-fists did not stir. **1942** FORBES & ALLEN *Ten Fighter Boys* p. xv, What he obviously intended to do on overshooting me was to flick over and spin down, but being a little ham, he overdid the manœuvre and came the right way up. *Ibid.* 84, I didn't stay to argue, but went bowling down in the hammest manner possible. **1949** 'J. TEY' *Brat Farrar* xiv. 124 He was.. reluctant to submit that tender mouth to the ham hands of a Westerner. **1963** *Times Lit. Suppl.* 1 Feb. 71/1 Nothing he hated more than 'ham' writing and 'prefabricated' characters.

ham, *sb.*[2] *local.* [OE. *ham(m*, *hom(m*, str. m. = OFris. *ham*, *hem*, *him*, NFris. *hamm*, EFris. *ham*, *hamm* a pasture or meadow enclosed with a ditch, LGer. *hamm* piece of enclosed land (on the Rhine, 'meadow'); WFlem. *ham* meadow, in Kilian *hamme*, *ham* 'pratum pascuum'; a word confined on the continent to the Frisian and Lower Saxon area, where its specific application varies as in England.] A plot of pasture ground; in some places esp. meadow-land; in others *spec.* an enclosed plot, a close. Found in OE., and still in local use in the south; in some places surviving only as the name of a particular piece of ground.

901-9 *Charter of Eadweard* in *Cod. Dipl.* V. 166 Ðanon on ᵹerihte to Scealdæmeres hamme. ? *c* **1000** *Ibid.* V. 383 Ða hammas ða ðer mid rihte toᵹebyriaþ. **1617** MINSHEU *Ductor*, A *Hamme* or a little plot of ground growing by the riuers or Thames side, commonly crooked, and beset with many willow trees or osiers. *c* **1630** RISDON *Surv. Devon* (1810) 6 Between the North and the South Hams (for that is the ancient name) there lieth a chain of hills. **1702** *Lond. Gaz.* No. 3838/4 The said Fair will be kept.. upon a Place.. called the Ham. **1796** W. MARSHALL *West Engl.* I. 33 The forests [would] be converted, by degrees, into common pastures, or hams. **1880** WILLIAMS *Rights of Common* 91 Within these two meadows were several hams or home closes of meadow. **1881** BLACKMORE *Christowell* iv, The sheep-wash corner in the lower ham.

ham, *sb.*[3] The OE. *hám* HOME, which, in composition, has been shortened to *ham*, as in *Hampstead*, *Hampton* (:—*Hámtún*), *Oakham*, *Lewisham*, etc., and, in this form, is sometimes used by historical writers in the sense 'town, village, or manor' of the Old English period.

1864 I. TAYLOR *Words & Places* (1882) 82 In the Anglo-Saxon charters we frequently find this suffix (ham) united with the names of families, never with those of individuals. **1872** E. W. ROBERTSON *Hist. Ess.* 118 A separate homestead apart from the ham of the vill. **1874** GREEN *Short Hist.* 3 The home or 'ham' of the Billings would be Billingham.

†**ham**, *v.*[1] *Obs. rare.* [f. HAM *sb.*[1]] = HAMSTRING *v.*

1618 *Crt. & Times Jas. I* (1849) II. 114 The bailiffs assaulted him in his coach, hammed his horses, and threatened no less unto himself.

ham (hæm), *v.*[2] *slang.* [f. HAM *sb.*[1]] To act in a 'hammy' manner, to over-act. Freq. const. *up*. Hence '**hammed-up** *ppl. a.*; '**hamming** *vbl. sb.* and *ppl. a.*

1933 STANLEY & MAXFIELD *Voice* 268 Hamming. **1937** *Printers' Ink Monthly* Apr. 54 *Ham it*, overacts [*sic*] for emphasis—bluster. **1944** L. A. G. STRONG *Director* xxii. 166 What with toning my voice down to that kid's mewing, and then trying to balance that hamming bloody idiot. **1946** *Daily Tel.* 18 Nov. 6/6 Thomas Mitchell, after a deal of recent hamming, is a convincing detective. **1955** A. HUXLEY *Genius & Goddess* 16 The performance was on the corny side; but it was a sympathetic part and, though she dearly loved to ham it up, Beulah was not merely a treasure. **1955** T. STERLING *Evil of Day* ix. 110 'Any actor would give twenty years of his life to play the part.'.. 'I thought if I told you what it was you'd ham it.' **1957** *Listener* 12 Sept. 402/3 Nor does he purvey anything of Wales as it is—rather the hammed-up version of Wales that the stupider sort of Englishman prefers. **1957** *Observer* 10 Nov. 19/2 The temptation of second-feature hamming. **1958** M. DICKENS *Man Overboard* ii. 27 She had hammed her scene with the seducer at the final run through. **1960** S. H. COURTIER *Gently dust Corpse* iii. 38 Hamming it now, thought Birch, and it's time they were brought to their senses. **1965** *Listener* 18 Nov. 795/1 Marie Bell.. hams it up in a smugly self-conscious cameo portrayal. **1973** E. PAGE *Fortnight by Sea* xii. 132 A hammed-up impression of a military man.

ham, obs. var. *am* (see BE *v.*); obs. f. HOME.

hamac, **hamaca**, etc., obs. ff. HAMMOCK.

hamacratic (hæmə'krætɪk), *a.* [f. Gr. ἅμα together + κράτος rule + -IC.] Pertaining to government based on mutual action.

1838 F. LIEBER *Political Ethics* II. cxxviii. I. 414 More of a hamacratic character.

hamada(h), varr. HAMMADA.

Hamadan ('hɑːmədɑːn). The name of a town in north-west Iran, used *attrib.* or *ellipt.* to denote a kind of carpet or rug (see quot. 1960).

1901 J. K. MUMFORD *Oriental Rugs* xi. 199 There is little difficulty in distinguishing the Hamadan carpet from all other weavings. **1932** P. SELVER tr. *Čapek's Tales from Two Pockets* 184 By Jove, if it isn't a Hamadan... and sometimes there are some fine Karavams and Kelims to be picked up. **1960** H. HAYWARD *Antique Coll.* 138/1 Hamadan is the marketing centre for Kurdish rugs and they are often known by this name. Heavy, long pile of great durability, rather coarse in stitch but well coloured, designs often embellished with animal figures. Hamadan rugs are frequently described as 'Persian'.

hamadryad (hæmə'draɪæd). Pl. **-ads**: also in Lat. form **hamadryades** (-ədiːz). [ad. L. *Hamādryas*, a. Gr. Ἁμαδρυάς, chiefly in pl. *Hamādryad-es*, Ἁμαδρυάδ-ες wood-nymphs, f. ἅμα together with + δρῦς tree]

1. *Gr.* and *Lat. Mythol.* A wood-nymph fabled to live and die with the tree which she inhabited.

c **1386** CHAUCER *Knt.'s T.* 2070 In whiche they woneden in reste and pees Nymphus, ffawnes, and Amadrides [*v. rr.* amadries, Amadryes]. **1390** GOWER *Conf.* II. 336 With suche, as Amadriades Were cleped wodemaidens tho. **1590** SPENSER *F.Q.* I. vi. 18 The wooddy nymphes, faire Hamadryades,..And all the troupe of light-foot Naiades. **1664** EVELYN *Sylva* Concl. §13 (R.) The fittest sacrifice for the royal oaks, and their hamadryads. **1769** JOHNSON *Lett. to Mrs. Thrale* 14 Aug., Nothing has deterred these audacious aldermen from violating the hamadryads of George Lane. **1873** LOWELL *Among my Bks.* Ser. II. 166, I am not sure that the tree was a gainer when the hamadryad flitted and left it nothing but ship-timber.

transf. **1791** W. BARTRAM *Carolina* 357 An innocent frolic with this gay assembly of hamadryades [Indian girls].

2. *Zool.* **a.** A large, very venomous, hooded serpent of India (*Naja hamadryas*, or *Hamadryas* (*Ophiophagus*) *elaps*), allied to the cobra.

1863 WOOD *Illustr. Nat. Hist.* III. 140 The Serpent-eating Hamadryas.. feeds almost wholly on reptiles. **1894** *Daily News* 4 June 7/5 When the Zoological Gardens were first opened, a hamadryad, imported with a selection of cobras, ate up fifty pounds' worth of the latter before its nature was discovered.

b. A large baboon of Abyssinia (*Cynocephalus hamadryas*).

1894 *Daily News* 6 Dec. 5/3 Four hamadryads are now the sight of the day at the Jardin d'Acclimatation in Paris..M. Milne-Edwards gives the hamadryad a high character for intellect.

hama'dryas. [See HAMADRYAD 2 b.] ***hamadryas baboon*** = HAMADRYAD 2 b.

1932 S. ZUCKERMAN *Soc. Life Monkeys & Apes* xii. 200 The barks of the Chacma are almost indistinguishable from those of the Hamadryas baboon. **1967** *Listener* 6 Apr. 459/3 The gelada baboon and the hamadryas baboon.

hamal: see HAMMAL.

hamald, hamelt, hamel ('hem(ə)ld, -(ə)lt, -(ə)l), *a.* (*sb.*) *Sc.* Forms: 5 **hameholde**, 6 **hamald, hammald, hamhald,** 6–7 **haim(e)hald, haymhald(e,** 8–9 **hamelt, -eil, -el, -il,** 9 **hamilt.** [A deriv. of *hame* HOME, app. akin to ON. *heimoll, heimull, heimill* homely, domestic, household-.]

Belonging to home, domestic; home-grown, home-made; homely, vernacular; unpolished.

? *a* **1400** *Morte Arth.* 1843 Hethynge es hame holde, vse it who so wille. **1513** DOUGLAS *Æneis* I. ii. 27 Cariand to Italy Thair vincust hammald goddis. **1597** SKENE *De Verb. Sign.* s.v. *Haimhaldarf*, Hamhald lint, or haimhald hemp, is that quhilk growis at haime. **1722** RAMSAY *Three Bonnets* IV, Thus I ha'e sung in hamelt rhyme. *a* **1774** FERGUSSON *Poems* (1789) II. 24 (Jam.) To chaunt their hameil lays. **1805** J. NICOL *Poems* I. 93 (Jam.) To send some hamelt, rustic lays. **1809** *J. Skinner's Misc. Poet.* 179 Critic, or bard, or hamil kine, Or high degree. **1832–53** *Whistle-Binkie* (Scot. Songs) Ser. III. 5 Auld hamilt cheer.

†**B.** *sb.* In phr. ***borgh of haimhald*** (*Old Sc. Law*), a pledge exacted from a seller of an article that it is home produce. *Obs.*

c **1400** *Burrow Lawes* c. 128. §1 Na man sall buy any thing within burgh, without the seller finde him sufficient borgh of haymhalde. *c* **1575** BALFOUR *Practicks* (1754) 210 Except the sellar find him ane sufficient pledge thairanent, and borgh of hamehald. **1609** SKENE *Reg. Maj.* 15.

Hence †**hamald, haimhald** *v.* (*Old Sc. Law*), to prove (something withholden or claimed by another) to be one's own property. *Obs.*

c **1575** BALFOUR *Practicks* (1754) 523 The persewar sall hame-hald, and with him away have, the said beist or cattel. **1609** SKENE tr. *Quon. Attach.* c. 10 §6 The challenger sall haymhalde [*debet haymaldare*] that thing, as his awin.

hamamelis (hæmə'miːlɪs). [mod.L. (J. F. Gronovius in Linnæus *Genera Plantarum* (ed. 2, 1742), a. Gr ἀμαμηλίς medlar.] A shrub or small tree of the genus so called, which is native to North America and Eastern Asia, belongs to the family Hamamelidaceæ, and includes several species bearing yellow flowers late in winter before the leaves appear; a witch-hazel. Also, the extract made from the leaves and bark of *Hamamelis virginiana.* So **hama'melin**, the dried extract.

1743 J. BARTRAM *Observ. Trav. Pensilvania to Canada* 19 July (1751) 35 Now we came to most excellent level ground ..full of tall timber..and shrubs, as opulus, green maple, hornbeam, hamamelis. **1760** J. LEE *Introd. Bot.* 332 Witch Hazel, *Hamamelis.* **1890** BILLINGS *Med. Dict.*, *Hamamelin*, name given to a dry powdered extract of hamamelis. **1898** *Rev. Brit. Pharm.* 10 Fresh hamamelis-leaves are macerated in a little more than double their volume of water and alcohol. **1900** M. THORN in W. D. DRURY *Bk. Gardening* xi. 386 The Hamamelis here mentioned may be propagated by grafting in February or early March. **1910** *Practitioner* July 128 Dry skins..must be cleaned with cold cream,..Any teleangiectasis must be treated with very hot water, to which is added hamamelis. **1911** J. U. LLOYD in *Bull. Lloyd Libr.* XVIII. 47 The preparation known as distilled hamamelis, or distilled extract of hamamelis, introduced by Pond about the middle of the nineteenth century. **1941** R. C. WREN *Potter's Cycl. Bot. Drugs* (ed. 5) 376 The concentration 'Hamamelin' is used for piles mostly in form of suppositories. **1949** *National Formulary* (B.M.A.) 79 Suppositories, each containing 3 gr of dry extract of hamamelis, to be dispensed. **1969** *Jrnl. Roy. Hort. Soc.* XCIV. 85 Hamamelis should be planted, if possible, not too far from the house.

Haman ('heɪmən). **1.** The name of the chief minister of Ahasuerus who was hanged on the gallows prepared for Mordecai, as related in the Book of Esther, used allusively (phr. ***to hang as high as Haman***). So **Ha'manic** *a.*

1644 R. BROWNE *Ld. Digbies Designe to betray Abingdon* 7 When their blinded Party shall..see him in his colours, they will at last pity..a Prince that makes use of such a wicked head..: And..may know who is that Haman which blasts Mordecai's petition. **1647** *Mercurius Melanchol.* No. 3. 13 What is honour, but another Haman? This day a companion with a King, on the morrow hanging on the gallowes. **1650** J. TRAPP *Comm. O.T.* Isa. lxi. 2 All Hamans be hanged up at that feast-royal, at the last day especially. **1816** SCOTT *Old Mort.* xxvii, The whig Captain Balfour..swore..that if the garrison was not gi'en ower the morn by daybreak, he would hing up the young lord, poor thing, as high as Haman. **1842** BARHAM *Ingol. Leg.* 2nd Ser. 57 I'll hang you, like Haman! **1881** H. ADLER in *19th Cent.* Dec. 813 Prof. Goldwin Smith renews his onslaughts upon Jews and Judaism with an acerbity and virulence which I may be permitted to term Hamanic.

2. Haman's ears, formerly **Haman's fritters**, fritters or cakes eaten by the Jews at the festival of Purim.

1846 'A LADY' *Jewish Man.* vii. 123 Haman's Fritters. **1949** *Housewife* May 50/1 The pudding that we ate..on Purim was appropriately called Hamaan's Ears—lovely crisp flaps of thin pastry sprinkled with sugar and cinnamon. **1961** *Times* 23 Dec. 9/1 'Haman's ears': a cake eaten by Jewish people at the festival of Purim, to commemorate the downfall of Haman, their persecutor.

hamarchy ('hæmɑːkɪ). [f. Gr. ἅμα together + -αρχία rule.] (See quot.)

1838 F. LIEBER *Political Ethics* II. cxxviii. I. 411 Hamarchy..is that polity which has an organism..in which a thousand distinct parts have their independent action, yet are by the general organism united into one..living system.

hamart, Sc. form of HOMEWARD.

hamartia (hə'mɑːtɪə). [a. Gr. ἁμαρτία fault, failure, guilt.] The fault or error which entails the destruction of the tragic hero (with particular reference to Aristotle's *Poetics*).

[**1789** T. TWINING *Aristotle's Treat. Poetry* 308 Dacier confounds himself and his readers in his note about *Thyestes.* He mistakes Aristotle's sense of ἁμαρτια.] **1895** S. H. BUTCHER *Aristotle's Theory Poetry & Fine Art* viii. 300 But with him [*sc.* Macbeth] the ἁμαρτία, the primal defect, is the taint of ambition. **1927** F. L. LUCAS *Tragedy* iv. 102 If we seek the *hamartia* in more modern tragedy like Ibsen's, it becomes clearer than ever that an intellectual mistake is all that the term need mean. **1956** H. HOUSE *Aristotle's Poetics* vi. 94 All serious modern Aristotelian scholarship agrees.. that 'hamartia' means an error which is derived from 'ignorance of some material fact or circumstance'. **1968** D. W. LUCAS in *Aristotle's Poetics* 302 The essence of *hamartia* is ignorance combined with the absence of wicked intent.

hamartiology (həmɑːtɪ'ɒlədʒɪ). *Theol.* [mod. f. Gr. ἁμαρτία sin + -LOGY.] The doctrine of sin; that part of theology which treats of sin.

1875 LIGHTFOOT *Comm. Col.* (ed. 2) 119 The hamartiology of the Old Testament has its counterpart in the soteriology of the New. **1879** FARRAR *St. Paul* II. 195 Righteousness and sin, soteriology and hamartiology, are the fundamental thoughts in St. Paul's theological system.

Hence **hamarti'ologist**.

1890 *Microcosm* (N.Y.) Mar., Scientific and scriptural hamartiologists.

hamartoma (hæmɑː'təʊmə). *Path.* [mod.L., ad. G. *hamartom* (E. Albrecht 1904, in *Verh. d. deutsch. path. Ges.* VII. 153), f. Gr. ἁμαρτ-άνω to go wrong: see -OMA.] A tumour-like mass resulting from the faulty growth or development of normal cells or tissue.

1904 *Index. Med.* II. 142/2 (*index*) Hamartoma. **1909** J. G. ADAMI *Princ. Path.* I. III. xxiii. 749 We must be governed here by our conception of the meaning of the word *angioma.* .. If we restrict it to mean a tumor, due to the independent growth of vessels, they [*sc.* other tumors having vessels as their main constituent] must be cast out of this class. To provide a class for them Albrecht has suggested the term *Hamartoma.* **1950** G. P. WRIGHT *Introd. Path.* xxvii. 479 Striking examples of the vascular hamartomas may be seen in the simple, cavernous, or more complicated plexiform, overgrowths of blood vessels that form congenital nævi, birth-marks,..or vascular warts. **1970** S. D. KOBERNICK tr. *Masson's Human Tumors* I. ii. 77 In one category, heterotopia consists of tissues which belong to the region where they are encountered, but have escaped the organization of this region and are found in excess: these are Hamartomas.

hamate ('heɪmət), *a.* [ad. L. *hāmāt-us* furnished with or shaped like a hook, f. *hām-us* hook: see -ATE[2].] Furnished with hooks, or having the shape of a hook; hooked. (Chiefly in *Nat. Hist.*)

1744 BERKELEY *Siris* §227 To explain cohesion by hamate atoms is accounted *ignotum per ignotius.* **1854** WOODWARD *Mollusca* (1856) 108 Teeth single, hamate.

hamated ('heɪmeɪtɪd), *a.* [f. as prec.] = prec.

1697 *Phil. Trans.* XIX. 685 Small hamated or crooked Prickles. **1704** SWIFT *Mech. Operat. Spirit* Misc. (1711) 294 Nothing less than a violent Heat can disentangle these Creatures from their hamated Station of Life.

Hamathite ('heɪməθaɪt). [f. *Hamath*, the biblical name for Hama in western Syria + -ITE[1].] An inhabitant of the ancient Syrian city of Hamath; also, a script found in the Taurus mountains, now called 'Hittite'. Also *attrib.*

1611 BIBLE *Gen.* x. 18 The Aruadite, the Zemarite, and the Hamathite. **1880** *Encycl. Brit.* XII. 26/1 Professor Sayce's view that the Hittites were the authors of the Hamathite hieroglyphics. **1926** D. G. HOGARTH *Kings of Hittites* 2 Hamathite territory is..the nearest to Galilee in which any sure evidence of occupation by Hittite civilization ..has yet appeared. **1952** O. R. GURNEY *Hittites* 3 The same script had been noticed by E. J. Davis on the great rock-carving over a stream at Irriz in the Taurus mountains. Davis had then called the script 'Hamathite'.

† **'hambargh.** *Obs.* or *dial.* Forms: 5 **hamberwe, -burwe,** 8–9 **howmbark.** [f. HAME[2] + OE. *-beorȝ, -berȝ* = *ȝebeorȝ* protection: cf. *héafod-beorȝ* helmet, *healsbeorȝ* hauberk, gorget. The elements are the same as in the synonymous BARGHAM, (*berhom, brecham, barkum*).] The collar of a draught horse; a bargham or brecham.

13.. *Gloss W. de Biblesw.* MS. Arundel 220 lf. 302 (Way *Promp. Parv.* 33) Les cous de chiuaus portunt esteles (*gloss* hames, *MS. Phill.* hamberwes). Coleres de quyr (*gloss* beruhames). **14..** *Voc.* in Wr.-Wülcker 580/23 *Epyphium*, an hamborwe. *Ibid.* 599/12 *Epifium*, an hamburwe. *c* **1746** J. COLLIER (Tim Bobbin) *Lanc. Dial.* Wks. (1862) 52 His wig ..on lee like o howmbark on his shilders.

Hence †**'hambargh** *v. trans.*, to put a collar on.

14.. *Voc.* in Wr.-Wülcker 580/24 *Epyphio*, to hamburwe.

hamber, hambir, obs. ff. HAMMER.

hamber, obs. form of AMBER *sb.*[2]

1481 CAXTON *Reynard* (Arb.) 14 Vij hamber barelis ful.

hambergite ('hæmbəgaɪt). *Min.* [ad. G. *hambergit* (W. C. Brögger 1890, in *Zeitschr. f. Kryst. und Min.* XVI (Specieller Th.). 65), f. the name of A. *Hamberg* (1863–1933), Sw. mineralogist, who discovered it: see -ITE[1].] A basic borate of beryllium, $Be_2(OH)BO_3$, occurring in colourless orthorhombic crystals that have strong double refraction.

1890 *Jrnl. Chem. Soc.* LVIII. II. 1078 Hambergite, discovered by A. Hamberg in 1889, and named after him by the author, crystallises in the rhombic system. **1962** R. WEBSTER *Gems* I. xvi. 265 Hambergite..was originally found in southern Norway in material of non-gem quality, but a discovery has now been made of large colourless crystals in central Madagascar.

hamber-line ('hæmbəlaɪn). *Naut.* Also **hambro-line.** [corr. of *Hamburgh.*] (See quot. 1867.)

1793 J. MACDONELL *Diary* in C. M. Gates *Five Fur Traders* (1933) 75 The canoe line..consists of fine Hambro lines loosely twisted upon one another. **1853** SIR H. DOUGLAS *Milit. Bridges* (ed. 3) 109, 2 skeins of hamber line, to lash the planks to the outside cables. **1867** SMYTH *Sailor's Word-bk.*, *Hamber*, or *Hambro'-line*, small line used for seizings, lashings, etc. **1961** F. H. BURGESS *Dict. Sailing* 108 *Hambro, Hambroline*, a small line, made of three strands of hemp, hard laid, sometimes tarred, and used for lacings, seizings, etc.

hamble, *v. Obs.* exc. *dial.* Forms: 1 **hamelian,** (3 *pa. pple.* **heomelede**), 4 **hameled, hamled,** 7–9 **hamble, hamel,** 9 **hammel.** [OE. *hamelian* to mutilate = OHG. *hamalôn*, MHG. *hameln*, ON. *hamla* to maim, mutilate; from an adj. appearing on OHG. as *hamal* maimed, mutilated, whence mod.G. *hammel* a castrated sheep.]

1. *trans.* To mutilate, maim; to cut short, dock; *spec.* to cut off the balls of the feet of (dogs) so as to render them unfit for hunting.

(Erroneously taken in 17th and 18th c. as = *hamstring.*)

a **1050** *O.E. Chron.* an. 1036 Sume hi man blende, sume man hamelode. *c* **1204** LAY. 11206 He heomelede þa reuen, nalde he mænne bi-lefuen. *c* **1374** CHAUCER *Troylus* II. 915 (964) Algate a fot is hameled of þy sorwe. *c* **1394** *P. Pl. Crede* 300 Hosen in harde weder y-hamled by þe ancle. **1607**

COWELL *Interpr.*, *Hameling* of dogges, or hambling, is all one with the expeditating of dogges. **1616** BULLOKAR *Engl. Expos.*, *Hameled*, cut off, abated (*obs.*). [**1727–51** CHAMBERS *Cycl.*, *Hameling*, or *Ham-stringing*, the act of cutting the great tendon, vulgarly called the *ham-string*.]

2. *intr.* To walk lame. *dial.*

1828 *Craven Dial.*, *Hamel*, to walk lame. **1863** MRS. TOOGOOD *Yorksh. Dial.*, *Hamlin*, walking lame.

Hence †**hamble-shanked** *a.*, maimed or lame in the leg.

1661 K. W. *Conf. Charact.*, *Informer* (1860) 47 A club-footed, hambleshanckt..hircocerous.

hamblet, obs. form of HAMLET.

hambo ('hambʊ). [f. *Hambo*, name of a parish in Hälsingland, Sweden.] A Swedish folk dance in ¾ time.

1925 *Blackw. Mag.* Jan. 79/1 We had been dancing in the Nylocks barn—dancing polskas and hambos. *Ibid.* Feb. 196/2 We only play old Swedish tunes..only old peasant polskas, hambos, and waltzes.

'ham-bone. 1. The bone in a ham of hog meat; also, such a bone with the meat attached. Also (in *pl.*) *transf.*

1855 W. G. SIMMS *Forayers* 340 He had..brought with him the ham-bone and bread which he had so hastily appropriated. **1866** 'MARK TWAIN' in *Harper's Mag.* Dec. 111/1 We have only left a lower end of a ham-bone, with some of the outer rind and skin on. **1908** J. LONDON *Let.* 22 Dec. (1966) 275, I have to get down on my ham-bones and beg forgiveness. **1972** P. DICKINSON *Lizard in Cup* vi. 97 He found a bone in a trash-can—a bit of ham-bone.

2. An inferior or amateur actor, esp. one who speaks in a spurious Negro accent; a mediocre musician. *U.S. slang.*

1893 P. H. EMERSON *Signor Lippo* v. 11 Hambones! I told you so. I could vardy that when I heard them joggering. **1905** W. MELVILLE *No Wedding Bells for Her* II. iii, You are green, Ham bones means them as pays to act, which they can't do, and so saves the manager engaging deserving actors. **1942** BERREY & VAN DEN BARK *Amer. Thes. Slang.* §583/18 *Hambone*, an unconvincing blackface dialectician. **1960** B. KEATON *Wonderful World of Slapstick* (1967) 13 Because I was also a born hambone, I ignored any bumps.. I may have got at first on hearing audiences gasp.

3. A sextant. *Naval slang.*

1938 F. A. WORSLEY *First Voy. in Square-Rigged Ship* viii. 144 What altitude have you got on that hambone, Stringer? **1962** GRANVILLE *Dict. Sailor's Slang* 58/1 *Ham-bone*, sextant which is of much the same shape.

hambro, hambro-line, vars. HAMBER-LINE.

Hamburg, -burgh ('hæmbɜːg, -bərə). [*Hamburg*, a city of North Germany.]

1. (Also ***Hamburg grape***) Name of a black variety of the grape, of German origin, which is specially adapted to hothouse cultivation.

1838 *Penny Cycl.* X. 500/2 Grapes..The following are suitable for a vinery:—Black Frontignan, Black Prince, Black Hamburg. **1892** BARRON *Vines & Vine Cult.* (ed. 3) 139 The Black Hamburgh Grape is stated to have been imported from Hamburgh in the early part of the last century by Mr. John Warner..Hence it became known as Warner's Black Hamburgh, i.e. Mr. Warner's Black Grape from Hamburgh..The best known [of its German names, are] Trollinger, and Frankenthaler, which, of late years, has been much adopted in this country by some as synonymous with Black Hamburgh, by others as representing a larger and coarser variety.

2. Name of a small variety of the domestic fowl.

1857 *Chambers' Inform. People* I. 647/2 True-bred Hamburgs never shew any inclination to sit..The Hamburgs are very timid, shy fowls, and easily distressed. **1885** TEGETMEIER in *Encycl. Brit.* XIX. 645/1 The Hamburghs, erroneously so called from a name given them in the classification adopted at the early Birmingham shows, are chiefly breeds of English origin.

3. ***Hamburg steak***: see STEAK 2 c.

Hamburger. Also -burgher, †-bourger. [G. *Hamburger* a native or inhabitant of Hamburg in Germany.] **1.** A native or inhabitant of Hamburg. Also *attrib.* or as *adj.*

1616 G. CAREW *Let.* Jan. (1860) 81 The Kinge of Denmarke..purposeth to build a stronge fort vppon the River of Elbe, requiringe the Hambourgers to permitt 3,000 of his men to passe throughe there towne. **1653** W. GEE *Let.* 16 June in M. M. Verney *Memoirs* (1894) III. ii. 56 They had been fired upon by an English ship, and had pursued 'a Hamburger'. **1737** *London Mag.* Feb. 81/2 (*heading*) Of the City of Hamburgh, with several Observations on the Hamburghers, and other Germans. **1798** D. WORDSWORTH *Jrnl. Visit to Hamburgh* (1941) I. ii. 21 Hamburgher girls with white caps. **1856** GEO. ELIOT in *Westm. Rev.* IX. 14 The fair Hamburghers acted in the spirit of Johnson's advice to Hannah More. **1932** L. GOLDING *Magnolia St.* II. iv. 314 The stolid young Hamburgers who went out rowing on Sundays on the Alster. **1966** *Guardian* 5 Nov. 7/3 He had the welfare of the sleeping Hamburghers in mind.

2. (Now freq. with lower-case initial.) In full ***Hamburger steak*** = ***Hamburg steak*** (see STEAK 2 c); also, a kind of sausage. Now, chopped beef, spiced and flavoured, formed into a cake and fried, often served between two halves of a toasted bun. So ***hamburger bar***, etc. orig. *U.S.*

1889 *Walla Walla* (Wash.) *Union* 5 Jan. 2/4 You are asked if you will have 'porkchopbeefsteakhamandegg hamburgersteakorliverandbacon'. **1901** ADE *40 Mod. Fables* 285 After the kid had been carried out of the Ring looking like a Hamburger Steak. **1902** *Encycl. Brit.* XXVI. 558/2 Hamburger steak with onions. **1908** 'YESLAH' *Tenderfoot S. Calif.* xiv. 118 Out of date eggs, last year's hamburger and over ripe limburger. **1912** I. COBB *Back Home* 147 A vendor ..sold to the same customers..odorous hamburger and flat slabs..of striped ice-cream. **1920** *Chambers's Jrnl.* 348/2 Hamburger steaks and German pot roasts. **1929** E. HEMINGWAY *Farewell to Arms* II. xv. 106 They had the look of not too freshly ground hamburger steak. **1931** B. STARKE *Touch & Go* iv. 58 A truck driver transporting two huge draft horses took us to Bryan, where he grandly 'set 'em up' to hamburgers and coffee. **1943** *R.A.F. Jrnl.* Aug. 10 She held a pair of..gloves in one hand and a hamburger sandwich in the other. **1950** *Manch. Guardian Weekly* 6 Apr. 3 After much pleasantry over the hamburgers and hot dogs. **1957** *London Mag.* Dec. 19 There is a pier with all the usual sideshows, hot dog, hamburger and ice-cream stands. **1960** *Times* 30 Jan. 11/7 The mounting number of hamburger bars suggests that it is here to stay.

Hamburg parsley: see PARSLEY 1, 2.

†**hame**[1]. *Obs.* Forms: 1 ham, (in comb.) -hama, -homa (5 haum), 4–6 hame. [OE. *-hama* = OS., OHG. *-hamo* in comb. 'covering, garment', MHG. *-hame, -ham*; also ON. *hams*, (Da. *ham*) snake's slough, cf. *hames* in quot. 13...] A covering, *esp.* a natural covering, integument; skin, membrane, slough (of a serpent).

Beowulf (Z.) 1570 Bil eal ðurh-wod fægne flæsc-homan. *c* **1000** *Voc.* in Wr.-Wülcker 276/23 *Camisa*, ham. **13..** *K. Alis.* (Laud MS. 385) Neptenabus..takeþ hym hames of dragon. *Ibid.* 391 Offe he cast his dragons hame. *c* **1440** *Promp. Parv.* 224/2 Hame, thyn skynne of an eye, or oþer lyke, *membranula*. *c* **1440** CAPGRAVE *Life St. Kath.* III. 1132 All þis ilk tyme þer was a hame Of blyndenes be-for þis ermytes yȝe. **1544** PHAER *Regim. Lyfe* (1553) C vj a, An Adders hame sodden in wine. **1546** —— *Bk. Childr.* x. 5 The hame or skynne of an adder or a snake, that she casteth.

hame[2] (heɪm). Also 6 haame, haume, 8 *dial.* hawm, 9 heam, *dial.* haam, *Sc.* haim. [Not known before 1300. Corresponds to MDu. *hame, haem*, MHG. dial. *hame*, Du. *haam*, LG. Westph. *ham*: perh. from an OTeut. root **ham-* to hold against, hinder.] **a.** Each of two curved pieces of wood or metal placed over, fastened to, or forming, the collar of a draught horse.

1303 R. BRUNNE *Handl. Synne* 11496 3yt wyl þey neuer shryue here shame, So are þey bounde yn þe fendes hame. **13..** [see HAMBARGH]. **1483** *Cath. Angl.* 172/2 A Hame of a horse. **1501** DOUGLAS *Pal. Hon.* I. 425 Euyr hamis conuenient for sic note, And raw silk brechamis ouir thair halsis hingis. **1577** B. GOOGE *Heresbach's Husb.* I. (1586) 11 b, Collers, Bridle reynes, Headstalles..Haames. **1611** COTGR., *Attelles*, the haumes of a draught horses collar; the two flat sticks that incompasse it. **1616** SURFL. & MARKH. *Country Farme* 538 Horses with open collars, and large hames. **1794** W. FELTON *Carriages* (1801) II. 146 The Heams are the two irons made to fix round the neck collar. **1883** J. P. GROVES *From Cadet to Captain* xxii. 223 Harnessing..Nellie's ponies..he managed to get the hames upside down, with the kidney-links on the top of the collars.

b. *attrib.* and *Comb.*, as ***hame-loop, -maker, -rein, -strap, -terret, -tug***.

1794 W. FELTON *Carriages* (1801) II. 139 The Heam-Tugs..are riveted to the heam-loops. **1826** *Sporting Mag.* XVIII. 393 A pole-chain may be unhooked, or a hame strap get loose. **1902** *Daily Chron.* 9 July 3/6 Why a tight hame rein should be used on so many builders' and other carts is ..a puzzle. **1908** *N. & Q.* 10th Ser. X. 106 At the foot of a hill leading from Blackrock, near Brighton, to Rottingdean is a board with the inscription: 'Please slacken hame-rein on going uphill.'

hame, obs. and Sc. f. HOME; obs. f. HAM, HAULM; var. HEM *Obs.*, them.

hameil: see HAMALD.

†**hamel**[1]. *Obs.* exc. *dial.* Also hamell, -il. [a. OF. *hamel* (13th c. in Littré). mod.F. *hameau*, (med.L. *hamellum*), dim. of **ham* (Picard *ham, hem*), a. WGer. *haim* village, dwelling, HOME.] = HAMLET.

c **1514** *Exam. Cokeye More* in *Chetham Misc.* (1856) II. 7 How feere the town or hamell of Aynsworth extends. **1523** FITZHERB. *Surv.* xv. (1539) 33 No townschyppe nor hamell. **1708** *Termes de la Ley* 390 *Hamlet, Hamel*, or *Hampsel* are diminutives of *Ham*, which signifies an Habitation. *c* **1746** J. COLLIER (Tim Bobbin) *Lanc. Dial.* Wks. (1862) p. xxxvii, They look'nt on im as th' Hammil-Scoance. **1885** *Cheshire Gloss.*, *Hamil Sconce*, the light of the village or hamlet.

hamel[2] ('hɑːməl, ‖'haməl). *S. Afr.* [Afrikaans = Du. *hamel*, G. *hammel* castrated ram; cf. HAMBLE *v.*] A wether.

1835 A. SMITH *Diary* 22 Apr. (1939) I. 376 If relatives rich, sometimes kill ten oxen and ten hamels. **1871** H. H. DUGMORE *Remin. Albany Settler* 14 A dozen of startled hamels, just separated from a large flock, would be likely to try a driver's legs, and lungs too, in crossing it. **1895** W. C. SCULLY *Kafir Stories* 28 Would your father have let me die rather than take a hamel from the flock of a rich, lazy boer, who never counts his sheep? **1896** R. WALLACE *Farm. Ind. Cape Col.* xvii. 346 Ram lambs are..'sorted' to make wethers or hamels. **1950** *Cape Times* 14 Dec. 13/6 At an auction sale..hamels fetched £6 11s.—the highest price for hamels in this district.

hamel, variant of HAMALD, HAMBLE.

hamelet, hamelt: see HAMLET, HAMALD.

†**hamel-tree.** *Obs.* or *dial.* (See quot.)

1740 [W. ELLIS in] *Lond. Mag.* 386 That cross Piece of Wood, to which the Wheel-horses in a Coach are fasten'd, which I call a *Hamel-tree*.

hamely, Sc. form of HOMELY.

hamer, hamester, obs. ff. HAMMER, -STER.

‖**hamerkop** ('hɑːməkɒp, 'hamərkɔp). *S. Afr.* Also semi-anglicized **hammerkop** ('hæ-). [Afrikaans, f. *hamer* hammer + *kop* head.] = HAMMER-HEAD 4.

1834 A. SMITH *Diary* 7 Dec. (1939) I. 163 A Basutu said the hammerkop gives rain. **1887** *Encycl. Brit.* XXII. 578/1 It [sc. *Scopus umbretta*]..is the 'Hammerkop' (Hammerhead) of the Cape colonists. **1890** [see HAMMERHEAD 4]. **1895** *Funk's Stand. Dict.*, Hamerkop. **1946** *Cape Argus* 7 Dec. 2 Hamerkops are remarkable fowl... The hamerkop's nest is a huge affair, generally in a tree. **1952** *Cape Times Week-end Mag.* 8 Nov. 6 A solitary hamerkop flies homeward every evening. **1964** C. WILLOCK *Enormous Zoo* vii. 120 Hammerkops, the queer brown bird with the blunt head that gives it its name, pick over scraps in the rotting papyrus stems. **1966** E. PALMER *Plains of Camdeboo* xi. 195 We never saw the hamerkop in numbers. **1971** *Country Life* 28 Oct. 1127/2 Hammercops, curious bulky brown birds with crests and thick bills, flew about in pairs.

hamesucken, †**-soken** ('heɪmsʌk(ə)n). *Old Eng.* and *Sc. Law.* Forms: 1 hámsócn, 3 hamsokne, 4 hamsokene, homsokne; *Hist.* 7–9 hamsoken, homesoken; *Sc.* 7 haimsuckin, -suken, 8 -sucken, 7– hamesucken. [OE., f. *hám* home, dwelling + *sócn* fem., seeking, visiting, attack, assault, ON. *sókn* attack.]

1. The crime of assaulting a person in his own house or dwelling-place. Now only in Scotch Law.

a **1000** *Laws of Edmund* II. c. 3 Be mund-brice and be ham-socnum. *c* **1030** *Laws of Cnut* II. c. 62 (63) Gif hwa ham-socne ȝewyrce ȝebete þæt mid fif pundan. *c* **1250** BRACTON *De. Leg. Angl.* III. II. xxiii. (Rolls) II. 464 Ham-sokne, quæ dicitur invasio domus contra pacem domini regis. **1387** TREVISA *Higden* (Rolls) II. 95 Hamsokene oþer Ham-fare, a rese i-made in hous. *c* **1575** BALFOUR *Practicks* (1754) 541 Na man may challenge ane uther of hamesucken, bot for assailȝeing him at his awin proper house and dwelling-place. **1753** *Stewart's Trial* 123 In the crime of hamesucken, he and his accomplices might be all equally principals. **1773** ERSKINE *Inst. Law Scotl.* 719 Haimesucken..is the crime of beating or assaulting a person within his own house. **1827** SCOTT *Jrnl.* I. 367 Half a dozen Selkirk processes, among others one which savours of Hamesucken.

2. A franchise of holding pleas of this offence and receiving the penalties imposed on the offender; also the penalty or mulct itself. (By English legal antiquaries variously misunderstood and erroneously explained.)

1020 *Charter of Cnut* in Earle *Land Charters* (1888) 233 þæt he beo his saca and socne wyrðe and grið bryces, and ham socne and forstealles and infangenes þeofes. *c* **1250** *Gloss. Law Terms* in *Rel. Ant.* I. 33 *Hamsokne*, quite de entrer en autri ostel á force. *c* **1290** FLETA I. xlvii. §18 (1647) 63 Hamsokne [signat] quietantiam misericordiæ intrusionis in alienam domum vi & injuste. **1579** RASTELL *Expos. diff. Words* 132 *Home soken* (or *hame soken*), that is, to bee quite of amerciaments for entring into houses violently and without licence, and contrary to the peace of the king. And that you holde plea of such trespasse done in your Court, and in your lande. **1717** *Blount's Law Dict.* (ed. 3), *Homesoken, Hamsoken*..the Privilege or Freedom which every Man hath in his House; and he who invades that Freedom is properly said *facere Homesoken*. This I take to be what we now call *Burglary*. *Ibid.*, It is also taken for an Impunity to those who commit this crime. **1769** BLACKSTONE *Comm.* IV. xvi. 223 Burglary, or nocturnal housebreaking..which by an antient law was called hame-secken, as it is in Scotland to this day. **1861** RILEY *Liber Albus* Gloss. 326 *Hampsokne*, literally House-protection, i.e. the protection from assault afforded by a man's house.

‖**hametz** ('hɑːmɛts, x-). Also **chametz, chometz**, etc. [Heb. *ḥāmēṣ*.] Leaven, or food that has been mixed with leaven, prohibited during the Passover.

1891 M. FRIEDLÄNDER *Jewish Relig.* 377 The head of the family..examines his residence thoroughly, and keeps the *chametz*, which he has found, in a safe place till the next morning. *Ibid.* 378 All the *chamets* that is left after the first meal on the 14th of *Nisan* must be removed. **1892** I. ZANGWILL *Childr. Ghetto* II. xxiv. 124 'Where is the Rabbi?' 'Up in the bedrooms gathering the *Chomutz*..hunting with a candle for stray crumbs.' **1960** *Jewish Chron.* 8 Apr. 35/1 The Rev. S. Black..told the boys and girls of Pesach and its meaning. Of the search for chametz (leavened bread). **1960** *Commentary* June 499/2 Removing bread (but not other *hametz*) from the house on Passover. **1973** *Jewish Chron.* 9 Feb. 12/5 He is convinced that no one eats *hametz* during Passover.

†**'hamfare.** *Old Law. Obs.* [OE. type **hámfaru*, f. *hám*, home, dwelling + *faru* going, passage, expedition.] = HAMESUCKEN 1.

a **1135** *Laws Hen. I*, c. 80 §11 Hamsocna est, vel hamfare, si quis premeditate ad domum eat..et ibi eum invadat, si die vel nocte hoc faciat. **1387** [see HAMESUCKEN]. **1610** HOLLAND *Camden's Brit.* I. 223. **1670** BLOUNT *Law Dict.*, *Hamfare*. **1717** *Ibid.* (ed. 3) *s.v.*, I rather think that *Hamfare*..is a Breach of the Peace in a House.

hamhald, obs. form of HAMALD.

Ham Hill stone, Ham stone. A Somerset stone, representative of the lower part of the Upper Lias, quarried in the Ham Hill quarry near Yeovil and used widely for building purposes in the area.

1889 H. B. WOODWARD in *Proc. Bath Nat. Hist. & Antiquarian Club* VI. 182 The celebrated building-stone of Ham Hill, near Yeovil.. is not without geological interest... The Ham Hill stone is mainly composed of sand and comminuted shells. **1918** *Q. Jrnl. Geol. Soc.* LXXIV. 169 At Ham Hill.. the portion of *moorei* date is exposed in the big quarry on the hill and the main mass of it is a 'freestone'—the celebrated Ham-Hill Building-Stone. In the big quarry the sequence is as follows: 1. Sand.. 2. 'Riddings'.. 3. Ham-Hill Stone. **1936** G. POLLETT *Song for Sixpence* ix. 76 This grey Ham stone is most satisfying to the eye. **1961** *Countryman* LVIII. III. 439 Sophisticated strangers are not yet trying to buy the lovely old Ham-stone farmhouses.

Hamidian (hæˈmɪdɪən), *a.* [f. the name of Abdul *Hamid* II + -IAN.] Pertaining to or resembling the rule of Abdul Hamid, Sultan of Turkey from 1876 to 1909. Hence **Haˈmidianism**.

1908 *Westm. Gaz.* 1 Aug. 2/3 Thirty years of wandering in the Hamidian wilderness. **1908** *Daily Chron.* 24 Oct. 4/4 The Hamidian rule. *Ibid.* 18 Dec. 4/4 A reversion to Hamidianism. **1930** *Times Lit. Suppl.* 4 Dec. 1047/3 His spy-system appears to have been Hamidian in its extent and efficiency.

Hamidieh (hæˈmɪdɪeɪ). [f. the name of Abdul *Hamid* II + *-ieh* adj. suffix.] A body of Kurdish cavalry formed by the Turks in 1891.

1898 H. A. G. PERCY *Diary Asiatic Turkey* 83 Zekki,.. the reputed founder of the Hamidieh System. **1901** *Westm. Gaz.* 27 Aug. 2/2 The Hamidie Cavalry.. defy the Porte by ignoring its commands. **1902** *Encycl. Brit.* XXV. 665/2 A tribal militia force (Hamidieh), consisting of 48 regiments, is formed somewhat on the lines of Cossacks.

hamiform (ˈheɪmɪfɔːm), *a.* [f. L. *hāmus* hook: see -FORM.] Hook-shaped.

a **1849** MAUNDER cited in WORC. (1860).

hamil, hamilt: see HAMALD.

hamillet, obs. form of HAMLET.

Hamiltonian (hæmɪlˈtəʊnɪən), *a.* (*sb.*) [f. the surname *Hamilton* + -IAN.]

A. *adj.* **a.** Pertaining to James Hamilton (1769–1831), or to his system of teaching languages. **b.** Pertaining to the Scottish philosopher and logician, Sir William Hamilton (1788–1856). **c.** Pertaining to or invented by the Irish mathematician, Sir William Rowan Hamilton (1805–65), as ***Hamiltonian equation, function, operator***. **d.** Pertaining to or holding the doctrines of the American statesman, Alexander Hamilton, a leader of the Federalist party (1757–1804). **B.** *sb.* A follower of any of the above.

1826 SYD. SMITH *Wks.* (1869) 531 We would have Hamiltonian keys to all these books. **1858** S. A. ALLIBONE *Dict. Eng. Lit.* I. 755 *Hamilton, James*, 'author of the Hamiltonian system', excited much attention in the learned world by his publications.. of interlinear English translations of books in various languages. **1864** BOWEN *Logic* viii. 228 (heading) The Hamiltonian Doctrine of Syllogisms. *Ibid.* 252 Under the Hamiltonian doctrine of eight fundamental Judgments, we have five hundred and twelve conceivable Moods. **1879** H. ADAMS *Gallatin* 174 (Cent.) Laying entirely aside the general proposition that the Hamiltonian Federalists considered a national debt as in itself a desirable institution.

Hamiltonism (ˈhæmɪltənɪz(ə)m). [f. as prec. + -ISM.] The doctrine or philosophy of Sir William Hamilton (see prec. b).

1867 MILL *Exam. Hamilton* iii. (ed. 3) 37 This is Kantism, but it is not Hamiltonism.

hamirostrate (heɪmɪˈrɒstrət), *a.* [f. L. *hāmus* hook + *rostr-um* beak: see -ATE².] Having a hooked beak.

In mod. Dicts.

Hamite (ˈhæmaɪt), *sb.*¹ and *a.* Also 7–9 **Chamite**, 9 **Khamite**. [f. *Ham* (formerly spelt *Cham*, Heb. *hām* Gr. χάμ, L. *Cham*), name of the second son of Noah (Gen. vi. 10) + -ITE.]

A. *sb.* †**1.** A follower of Ham: used as a term of obloquy. (Cf. Gen. ix. 22–25.) *Obs. rare.*

1645 PAGITT *Heresiogr.* (1647) 59 Terming.. us.. Balamites, Chamites, Cainites.

2. A descendant of Ham; a person belonging to one of the nations or tribes supposed to be descended from Ham (cf. Gen. ix. 18, 19), viz. the Egyptians and other African races.

1854 C. C. J. BUNSEN *Chr. & Mankind* IV. (*title*) The Asiatic origin of the Khamites or Egyptians. **1860** R. S. POOLE in *Dict. Bible* I. 742 Egypt may have been the first settlement of the Hamites whence colonies went forth.

B. *adj.* = Hamitic (see below).

1842 PRICHARD *Nat. Hist. Man* 144 The Phoenicians or Canaanites, both being Chamite, and not Shemite, nations. **1871** P. SMITH *Anc. Hist. East* 6 The Hamite Race.. is located in Africa and South Arabia.

Hence **Hamitic** (hæˈmɪtɪk) *a.*, belonging to the Hamites; esp. applied to a group of African languages, comprising the ancient Egyptian, and the Berber, Galla, and allied extant languages; **ˌHamiticiˈzation**, the action of becoming Hamitic; **Haˈmiticized** *a.*, having become Hamitic; **Hamitism** (ˈhæmɪtɪz(ə)m), the fact of being a Hamite; **ˈHamitoid** *a.*, resembling the Hamitic type.

1844 G. S. FABER *Eight Diss.* (1845) II. 273 Of Hammitic Origin. **1854** C. C. J. BUNSEN *Chr. & Mankind* III. 183 Chamitism, or ante-Historical Semitism. *Ibid.*, The Chamitic deposit in Egypt. **1860** FARRAR *Orig. Lang.* 215 The Egyptian language belongs then to a Chamitic family. **1861** J. G. SHEPPARD *Fall Rome* iii. 116 Considering Hamitism as nothing more than a special form of Semitism, and altogether unconnected with the Turanian family. **1877** DAWSON *Orig. World* xii. 260 The Semitic and Hamitic mythologies are derived from the primeval cherubic worship of Eden. **1880** A. H. SAYCE *Introd. Sci. of Lang.* II. vii. 181 A number of dialects.. are classed together as Ethiopian or Khamitic. **1884** *Nature* 17 Apr. 581/1 These peoples should apparently be regarded rather as Negroes affected by Hamitic than as Hamites affected by Negro elements. In other words, they are Negroid rather than Hamitoid. **1911** H. H. JOHNSTON *Opening up of Africa* iii. 91 The earlier and more elaborate of these works were inspired by Semites and executed by Hamiticized negroes. **1923** G. W. MURRAY *Eng.-Nubian Dict.* Introd., In the case of Nubian, the process of Hamiticization has gone so far that it has borrowed Hamitic personal-endings for its verb, Hamitic case-endings for its noun, and possesses a vocabulary largely Hamitic. **1936** *Discovery* June 171/1 The first great group of hamiticised Negroes, the Nilotes, constitute a well-defined physical type.

hamite (ˈheɪmaɪt), *sb.*² [ad. mod.L. generic name *Hamites*, f. *hām-us* hook: see -ITE.] A fossil cephalopod having a shell of a hooked shape.

1832 DE LA BECHE *Geol. Man.* (ed. 2) 265 The hard black limestone (containing an abundance of Scaphites, Hamites, Turrilites, and other fossils). **1847** ANSTED *Anc. World* x. 244 A hooked shell.. called a Hamite.

Haˈmito-Seˈmitic, *a.* Designating the language family including Hamitic and Semitic languages. Also as *sb.* Also **Haˈmitic-Seˈmitic** *a.* and *sb.*

1909 *Cent. Dict.* Suppl., *Hamito-Semitic*, relating to the peoples speaking Hamitic and Semitic languages which are considered members of one linguistic stock. **1936** *Science & Society* I. 25 He records similarities.. between pronouns in Hamitic-Semitic. **1939** L. H. GRAY *Foundations of Lang.* 357 Second in importance only to the Indo-European linguistic family comes the Hamito-Semitic group. **1964** R. H. ROBINS *Gen. Ling.* viii. 307 The Hamito-semitic family, represented by classical Arabic and the Arabic languages and dialects of the Middle East and North African coast.

†**ˈhamkin.** *Obs.* [? f. HAM *sb.*¹] (See quot.)

1616 BULLOKAR *Engl. Expos.*, *Hamkin*, a pudding made vpon the bones of a shoulder of mutton, all the flesh being first taken off. [So in COCKERAM, BLOUNT].

hamlet¹ (ˈhæmlɪt). Also 4 **hamelat, hamillet**, 4–6 **hamelett(e**, 4–7 **hamelet**, 6 **hamlette**, 7 **hamblet**. [a. OF. *hamelet*, in AFr. also *hamelete, hamlette*, (med.L. *hameletum, -letta*), secondary dim. of *hamel*: see HAMEL.] A group of houses or small village in the country; *esp.* a village without a church, included in the parish belonging to another village or a town. (In some of the United States, the official designation of an incorporated place smaller than a village.)

c **1330** R. BRUNNE *Chron.* (1810) 310 þe fote men ilk a flok, A pouere hamlete toke, þe castelle Karelauerok. *Ibid.* 340 He died at a hamelette, men calle it Burgh bisandes. **1483** *Cath. Angl.* 172/2 A Hamelett, *villula*. **1546** in *Eng. Gilds* (1870) 222 Wᵗ vij lyttle hamlettes therto belonging. **1604** *View of Fraunce* C b, One hundred thirtie two thousand of Parish Churches, Hamlets, and Villages of all sorts. **1675** OGILBY *Brit.* Introd. 3 The Hamlets of the Tower made up 2 Regiments. **1750** GRAY *Elegy* iv, The rude forefathers of the hamlet sleep. **1820** SCOTT *Monast.* i, A small village or hamlet, where.. some thirty or forty families dwelt together. **1888** BRYCE *Amer. Commw.* II. II. xlviii. 247 Ohio.. divides her municipal corporations into (*a*) cities.. (*b*) villages.. and (*c*) hamlets, incorporated places with less than 200 inhabitants.

attrib. **1641** *Commons Jrnls.* II. 262 For the Hamlet Men, it was Harvest-time. **1879** JEFFERIES *Wild Life in S. Co.* 123 The thatcher, the most important perhaps of the hamlet craftsmen.

b. *transf.* The people of a hamlet. (*poetic.*)

1726–46 THOMSON *Winter* 422 Hamlets sleeping in the dead of night. **1850** TENNYSON *In Mem.* x, Where the kneeling hamlet drains The chalice of the grapes of God.

Hence **ˈhamleted** *a.*, located in a hamlet. **hamleˈteer**, an inhabitant of a hamlet. **ˈhamletize** *v. U.S.*, to incorporate as a hamlet; hence **hamletiˈzation**.

1627–77 FELTHAM *Resolves* II. xlix. 256 Hamletted in some untravelled village of the duller Country. **1825** T. CROMWELL *Hist. Colchester* 102 Overcoming a feeble opposition from the Tower Hambleteers. **1876** T. HARDY *Ethelberta* (1890) 283 Going back to give the rudiments of education to remote hamleteers. **1893** *Dispatch* (Columbus) 9 Feb., The controversy concerning the hamletizing of Bullitt Park. *Ibid.*, Annexation, not hamletization, should occur.

Hamlet² (ˈhæmlɪt). The name of the prince of Denmark who is the hero of Shakespeare's play of this name, in allusive phr. ***Hamlet without the Prince*** (***of Denmark***): a performance without the chief actor or a proceeding without the central figure.

[**1775** *Morning Post* 21 Sept., *Lee Lewes* diverts them with the manner of their performing Hamlet in a company that he belonged to, when the hero who was to play the principal character had absconded with an inn-keeper's daughter; and that when he came forward to give out the play, he added, 'the part of Hamlet to be left out, for that night.'] **1818** BYRON *Let.* 26 Aug. (1830) II. 445 My autobiographical essay would resemble the tragedy of Hamlet.., recited 'with the part of Hamlet left out by particular desire'. **1820** LADY GRANVILLE *Let.* 22 Aug. (1894) I. 161, I am not used to be news-monger and perhaps I leave out Hamlet. **1825** SCOTT *Talisman* (1883) 5 The title of a 'Tale of the Crusaders' would resemble the playbill, which is said to have announced the tragedy of Hamlet, the character of the Prince of Denmark being left out. **1859** G. MEREDITH *Ordeal R. Feverel* I. vii. 109 'What have you been doing at home, Cousin Rady?' 'Playing Hamlet, in the absence of the Prince of Denmark.' **1902** *Daily Chron.* 22 Apr. 3/1 Of what avail is it to promise 'entirely new scenery' for 'Die Meistersinger', if the part of Hans Sachs is to be practically eliminated from the performance? And yet this 'Hamlet-without-the-Prince' method is consistently pursued season after season at Covent Garden. **1910** *Times Weekly* 17 June 452 The army without Kitchener is like Hamlet without the Prince of Denmark. **1918** L. STRACHEY *Emin. Victorians* 86 The Catholic Church without the absolute dominion of the Pope might resemble the play of Hamlet without the Prince of Denmark. **1967** J. PRESCOT *Case Counterfeit* viii. 96 Without Drax one can't do a thing. Hamlet without the Prince of Denmark, I guess. **1972** *Publishers Weekly* 3 Apr. 22/3 The article.. in the March 6th *PW* was an attempt to stage Hamlet without the Dane.

Hence **ˈHamletish** *a.*; **ˈHamletism**, an attitude resembling that of Hamlet; **ˈHamletize** *v. rare*, to soliloquize or meditate after the manner of Hamlet.

1844 HEBBE & MACKAY tr. *Sealsfield's Life in New World* 267 Halloo! Mr. Howard! Hamletizing? **1852** H. MELVILLE *Pierre* VII. vi. 191 In this plaintive fable we find embodied the Hamletism of the antique world. **1854** 'G. GREENWOOD' *Haps & Mishaps in Europe* iii. 53 Herr Devrient is a handsome, Hamlet-ish man, with a melancholy refinement of voice. **1905** *Daily Chron.* 11 Apr. 4/7 Let us forget Hamletism and all its ills. **1920** D. H. LAWRENCE *Women in Love* xiv. 205 One shouldn't talk when one is tired and wretched.—One Hamletises, and it seems a lie. **1923** —— *Stud. Classic Amer. Lit.* ix. 180 So Dana sits and Hamletizes by the Pacific—chief actor in the play of his own existence. **1936** *Times Lit. Suppl.* 5 Sept. 711/2 Adams's madness is, indeed, a trifle Hamletish. **1945** W. FOWLIE in *Mod. Reading* XII. 210 He is the one contemporary writer who has driven out from his nature all traces of hamletism, and yet he writes constantly about Hamlet. **1952** A. R. D. FAIRBURN *Strange Rendezvous* 25 He has played the gravedigger to many a Hamletish posture of my soul.

hamloun, in *Gaw. and Gr. Knt.*, error for *hauiloun*, HAVELON *v.*

hamly, -nes, obs. north. ff. HOMELY, -INESS.

hamlynge, obs. form of AMBLING.

c **1440** *Eng. Conq. Irel.* (E.E.T.S.) 89 Vnneth he wolde ryde any hamlynge hors but mych trottynge hors.

hammack, hammacoe, etc.: see HAMMOCK.

hammada (hæˈmɑːdə). *Geol.* Also **hamada(h)**. [f. Arab *ḥammāda*.] A flat rocky area of desert blown free of sand by the wind, typical of the Sahara.

1853 J. RICHARDSON *Narr. Mission Cent. Afr.* II. iv. 60 Aghadez is situated on a hamadah, or lofty plateau of sandstone and granite formation. **1857** H. BARTH *Trav. N. & Cent. Afr.* I. v. 133 Overweg and I had no time to lose in preparing for our journey over the hammáda, or plateau. **1886** *Encycl. Brit.* XXI. 149/2 Nearly all the rest of the Sahara consists.. of undulating surfaces of rock (distinguished as *hammada*),.. and regions of sandy dunes. **1934** W. FITZGERALD *Africa* I. ii. 60 Rocky wastes with the bare exposure of fissured rocks as dominant features of the scene, form the 'hamada' type of the Sahara. **1966** *McGraw-Hill Encycl. Sci. & Technol.* IV. 76/2 Ordinarily, a hammada is a bare rock surface composed of relatively flat-lying consolidated sedimentary rocks from which overlying softer sediments have been stripped, principally by wind erosion.

‖**hammal, hummaul** (haˈmaːl). Also 8–9 **hamaul**, 9 **hamal, khamal**. [Arab. *hammāl* porter, f. *hamala* to carry.] A Turkish or Oriental porter; in Western India, a palanquin-bearer.

1766 GROSE *Voy. E. Ind.* (1772) I. 120 (Y. s.v. *Hummaul*) The Hamauls or porters, who make a livelihood of carrying goods to and from the warehouses. **1839** MISS PARDOE *Beauties of Bosph.* 38 (Stanf.) Here the khamals deposit the heavy bale. **1845** STOCQUELER *Handbk. Brit. India* (1854) 93 The palankeen-bearers (called hammals at Bombay). **1878** H. M. STANLEY *Dark Cont.* I. i. 37 Hamals, bearing clove and cinnamon bags. **1962** J. FLEMING *When I grow Rich* iii. 44 Heavily disguised as *hamals*, or human mules. **1967** J. RATHBONE *Diamonds Bid* xii. 105 Grey-clad hamals, porters who will carry anything anywhere.

hammald, obs. form of HAMALD.

‖**hammam, hummaum** (haˈmaːm). Also 7– **hamam**; and see HUMMUM. [Arab. *ḥammām* bath.] An Oriental bathing establishment, a Turkish bath.

1625 PURCHAS *Pilgrims* II. ix. 1419 (Stanf.), I went to the Hammam. **1704** J. PITTS *Acc. Mohammetans* 47 They have many Hammams or Wash-houses to bath themselves in. **1820** T. S. HUGHES *Trav. Sicily* I. vi. 174 (Stanf.) We proceeded to the public hummaum, or Turkish bath. **1832** GELL *Pompeiana* I. vi. 87 The first chamber of an oriental *hamam*. **1844** *Mem. Babylonian P'cess* II. 33 There.. she is free from the jealous espionage of her lord, which stops at the hammam's threshhold.

hammed (hæmd), *a.* [f. HAM *sb.*[1] + -ED[2].] Having hams; usually in comb., as CAT-HAMMED, ***fickle-hammed***.

1711 *Lond. Gaz.* No. 4808/4 Stolen or stray'd..a bay Gelding..fickle hamm'd.

hammel, variant of HAMBLE, HEMEL.

hammer ('hæmə(r)), *sb.* Forms: 1 hamor, 1–3 homer, 1–5 hamer, 4 hamyr, 4–5 hamur, 5 hamere, hamour(e, -owre, 6 *Sc.* hemmir, 6– hammer, *β.* 5 hambir, -yr, 5–7 hamber. [Common Teutonic: OE. *hamor, -er, hǫmer* = OS. *hamur* (MDu., Du. *hamer*), OHG. *hamar* (Ger. *hammer*), ON. *hamarr*. The Norse sense 'crag', and possible relationship to Slav. *kamy*, Russ. *kamenʹ* stone, have suggested that the word originally meant 'stone weapon'.]

1. a. An instrument having a hard solid head, usually of metal, set transversely to the handle, used for beating, breaking, driving nails, etc. Hence, a machine in which a heavy block of metal is used for the same purpose (see STEAM-HAMMER, TILT-HAMMER, TRIP-HAMMER).

knight of the hammer, a blacksmith or hammerman. ***throwing the hammer***, an athletic contest, consisting in throwing a heavy hammer as far as possible.

a **1000** *Juliana* 237 Carcernes duru..homra ȝeweorc. *c* **1000** *Ags. Voc.* in Wr.-Wülcker 272/36 *Malleus*, hamer. *c* **1050** *Ibid.* 182/23 *Porticulus*, hamor. *a* **1225** *Ancr. R.* 284 Wultu þet God nabbe no fur in his smiððe—ne belies—ne homeres? *c* **1369** CHAUCER *Dethe Blaunche* 1164 As hys brothres hamers ronge Vpon hys Anuelet vp and doon. **1413** *Pilgr. Sowle* (Caxton 1483) IV. xxx. 78 Withouten strook of hamour. *c* **1440** *Promp. Parv.* 225/1 Hamur (*v. rr.* hambyr, hamowre), *malleus*. **1528** in Rye *Cromer* (1889) 55 Withe too grett yerne hambers. **1555** EDEN *Decades* 161 Such maces and hammers as are vsed in the warres. **1606** SHAKS. *Ant. & Cl.* V. ii. 210 Mechanicke Slaues With greazie Aprons, Rules, and Hammers. **1717** DE FOE *Mem. Ch. Scotl.* II. 38 He that has a Nail to drive, will not want a Hammer. **1851** D. WILSON *Preh. Ann.* (1863) I. II. ii. 359 The perforated oblong stone for a hammer. **1851** RICHARDSON *Geol.* 473 [Those] known by the name of Sedgwick's, and by that of De la Beche's geological hammer. *Ibid.* 474 Mineralogical hammers of various forms. **1859** *Autobiog. Beggar boy* 4 The marriage was celebrated in a common lodging house in Gretna Green. I believe the ceremony was performed by a knight of the hammer.

b. *fig.* A person or agency that smites, beats down, or crushes, as with blows of a hammer. Cf. L. *malleus*, O.F. *martel*.

[**1308** *Inscr. on tomb of Edw. I*, in *Westm. Abbey*, Edvardus Primus: Scotorum Malleus: Hic est: MCCCVIII: Pactum serva.] **1382** WYCLIF *Jer.* I. 23 Hou to-broke and to-brosid is the hamer of al erthe? **1387** TREVISA *Higden* (Rolls) VI. 43 Saladinus..þe strong hamer of Cristen men. **1614** SYLVESTER *Bethulia's Rescue* IV. 30 Let my victorious hand Be scourge and hammer of this Heathen Band. **1655** FULLER *Ch. Hist.* III. xiv. §14 As *malleus Scotorum*, the hammer or mauler of the Scots, is written on the tomb of King Edward the First in Westminster; *incus Scotorum*, the anvil of the Scots might as properly be written on the monument (had he any) of Edward the Second. **1674** HICKMAN *Quinquart. Hist.* Epist. (ed. 2) A iv b, St. Austin (the hammer of Pelagianism). **1679** J. GOODMAN *Penit. Pardoned* II. i. (1713) 154 Broken by the hammer of affliction. **1873** EDITH THOMPSON *Hist. Eng.* xxviii. ¶5 Thomas Cromwell..has been called 'the Hammer of the Monks'.

2. In various specific senses or uses:

a. A lever with a hard head arranged so as to strike a bell, as in a clock.

1546 *Ludlow Churchw. Acc.* (Camden) 26 Item, for shotynge on hammer and a sprynge. **1601** CORNWALLYES *Ess.* xi, A Clocke, whose hammer was stricken by an Image like a Man. **1864** SKEAT *Uhland's Poems* 319 Within the gray church-tower The hammer strikes the midnight hour. **1872** ELLACOMBE *Ch. Bells Devon* i. 22 At Exeter..each bell has a sort of clock hammer striking on the outside.

†**b.** The knocker of a door. *Obs.*

1585 HIGINS tr. *Junius Nomencl.* 214/2 *Cornix*..the ring or iron hammer wherewith we knocke at the doore. **1591** PERCIVALL *Sp. Dict.*, *Aldáua de puerta*, the ring or hamer of a doore. **1625–6** PURCHAS *Pilgrims* II. 1661 They neuer knock at the Gate (for there is no Ring or Hammer). **1627** *Lisander & Cal.* VI. 104 They heard againe great knocking at the gate by the hammer thereof.

c. *Fire-arms.* (*a*) In a flint-lock, a piece of steel covering the flash-pan and struck by the flint; (*b*) in a percussion-lock, a spring lever which strikes the percussion-cap on the nipple; (*c*) applied to analogous contrivances by which the charge is exploded in various modern kinds of guns.

1590 SIR J. SMYTH *Disc. Weapons* II. 47 To strike just upon the wheeles being fire-lockes, or upon the hammers or steeles, if they be Snap-hances. **1745** DESAGULIERS tr. *Gravesande's Nat. Philos.* I. 108 To drive the Cock, which carries the Flint against the Hammer. **1833** *Regul. Instr. Cavalry* I. 30 The flint strikes the hammer. **1851** *Offic. Catal. Gt. Exhib.* 1203 Percussion-gun, with an improved under-box and a safety hammer.

d. A small bone of the ear; the malleus.

1615 CROOKE *Body of Man* 531 With three Bones, the smallest of the whole body..the first is called the *Hammer*, the second the *Anuile*, the third the *Stirrop*. **1718** J. CHAMBERLAYNE *Relig. Philos.* (1730) I. xiii. §5 The Auditory Bones are four in Number, the Hammer, the Anvil, the Stirrup, and between the Anvil and Stirrup there lies a small Bone. **1879** CALDERWOOD *Mind & Br.* 71 The first bone has a rounded head, a narrow neck..its shape has led to its name hammer.

e. A small hammer or mallet used by auctioneers to indicate by a rap the sale of an article. Hence in phrases, as ***to bring*** (***send, put up***) ***to the hammer***, to sell by auction; to ***go*** or ***come to*** or ***under the hammer***, to be sold by auction.

(A similar hammer is used by a chairman to call a meeting to order.)

1717 FRIOR *Alma* III. 571 When my dear volumes touch the hammer. **1784** COWPER *Task* VI. 291 Oft as the price-deciding hammer falls. **1828** MARLY *Life Planter Jamaica* 181 These girls were brought to the hammer to pay their father's debts, being held to be part of his moveable property. **1842** TENNYSON *Audley Crt.* 59 His books..Came to the hammer here in March. **1856** READE *Never too late* x, He threatened to foreclose, and sell the house under the hammer. **1857** RUSKIN *Pol. Econ. Art* ii. (1868) 128 If you like it, keep it; if not, send it to the hammer.

f. (*a*) A small wooden mallet with a padded end or head, held in the hand, with which the strings of a dulcimer or similar instrument are struck. (*b*) A part of the action of a pianoforte, consisting of a slender wooden shank and a padded wooden head, which strikes the strings when the corresponding key is pressed down.

1774 *Specif. J. Merlin's Patent* No. 1081 A set of Hammers of the nature of those used in the kind of Harpsichords called Piano Forte. **1783** *Specif. J. Broadwood's Patent* No. 1379 The hammers which strike the strings. **1840** *Penny Cycl.* XVIII. 140/1 The action of the square piano-forte, on its first introduction, consisted of a key, a lifter, a hammer, and a damper. **1879** STAINER *Music of Bible* 52 The leap from a dulcimer to a pianoforte would have been immediate, if the first instruments with keyboards had hammers wherewith to strike the strings. **1880** HIPKINS in Grove *Dict. Mus.* I. 468/2 The dulcimer, laid upon a table or frame, is struck with hammers.

†**3.** A small iron-forge. *Obs.*

1674 RAY *Collect. Words, Of Iron Work* 127 In every forge or hammer there are two fires at the least.

†**4.** A disease in cattle. *Obs.*

[Cf. Cotgr. *Marteau*, 'also, the Stithie (a beasts disease)'.] **1616** SURFL. & MARKH. *Country Farme* 94 The Stithie happening to the Oxe, being otherwise called a Mallet or Hammer, is knowne when the beast hath his haire standing vpright all ouer his bodie. **1688** R. HOLME *Armoury* II. 172.

5. A match at throwing the hammer. (See note to sense 1.)

1897 *Whitaker's Alm.* 635/1 J. Flanagan..won the Hammer with 131 ft. 11 in.

6. Phrases. ***hammer and tongs*** (colloq.): with might and main (like a blacksmith showering his blows on the iron taken with the tongs from the forge-fire). ***hammer and pincers***: a phrase descriptive of the noise made by a horse striking the hind-foot against the fore-foot: cf. CLICK, FORGING. ***hammer and sickle***: an emblem consisting of a crossed hammer and sickle, used as a symbol of the industrial worker and the peasant, e.g. on the national flag of the U.S.S.R.; hence used allusively of Soviet-type Communism. ***Thor's hammer, h. of Thor***: (*a*) the hammer carried by the god Thor in Norse mythology; (*b*) a figure somewhat like a cross (= FYLFOT); (*c*) a prehistoric ornament resembling a hammer. ***up to the hammer*** (colloq. or slang): up to the standard, first-rate, excellent.

1708 *Brit. Apollo* No. 56. 3/2 I'm now coming at you, with Hammer and Tongs. **1799** *Sporting Mag.* XIV. 187 To go hammer and pincers, is to over-reach and strike the hinder toe upon the fore-heel. **1801** *Ibid.* XVII. 119 For Hammer and Pinchers, or over-reaching. **1833** MARRYAT *P. Simple* xxxv, Our ships were soon hard at it, hammer and tongs. **1865** KINGSLEY *Herew.* iv, By Thor's hammer boys, see if I do not return some day. **1882** MABEL PEACOCK in *Academy* 7 Oct. 259 You shall mark your food with the hammer of Thor, and think you are signing a holy sign. **1884** W. C. RUSSELL *Jack's Courtship* in *Longm. Mag.* III. 241 What cooking there was in it was up to the hammer. **1887** FRITH *Autobiog.* I. xxi. 277 He turns to me, and we went at it hammer and tongs. **1921** *Times* 20 Sept. 4/6 The subjects of the..designs [of Bolshevist postage stamps] are symbolical of Labour..the 20 roubles a shield charged with the device of a hammer and sickle crossed. **1933** H. G. WELLS *Shape of Things to Come* III. §11. 330 There was still no discord with Russia; there the blazon of the wings was put up side by side with the old hammer and sickle. **1935** E. WEEKLEY *Something about Words* 27 A new ideal in literature and poetry, a kind of 'hammer and sickle' conception of artistic composition. **1937** H. G. WELLS *Brynhild* v. 65 It might be possible to indicate whether the flavouring [of a book] were sexual, intellectual, left, right, or detective, by some variation in the general design, an obelisk, for example, the hammer and sickle, the swastika or what-not. **1958** *Listener* 5 June 928/2 An Algiers broadcast said the choice was 'between the Hammer and Sickle and the Cross of Lorraine'.

7. Combinations. **a.** attrib., as ***hammer-bar, -beat, -bolt, -boy, -clang, -drudge, -mark, -rod, -shed, -spring, -stroke***, etc.; (sense 2 f *b*) as ***hammer-butt, -felt, -fork, -rail, -shank***; **b.** objective, similative, and instrumental, as ***hammer-beater, -catcher, -wielder***; ***hammer-like, -proof, -shaped, -strong*** adjs. **c.** Special combs.: **hammer-action**, (*a*) action of or as of a hammer; (*b*) those parts of a piano which compose and control the hammers; **hammer-axe**, a tool consisting of a hammer and axe combined (Craig, 1847); **hammer-block**, the steel face of a steam-hammer; **hammer-blow**, a blow or stroke of a hammer; also in the steam-engine (see quot.); **hammer-cap**, a cap covering the cock of a gun; **hammer-cramp**, a form of cramp or spasm to which hammermen are liable; **hammer-dress** *v. trans.*, to dress (stone) by strokes of a hammer; **hammer drill**, a percussion drill; **hammer-fish**, the hammer-headed shark; **hammer-flaw, -flush**, the flakes of heated iron struck off by a hammer; **hammer-gun**, a gun fired by means of a hammer (see 2 c); **hammer-hard** *a.*, made hard by hammering; **hammer-harden** *v. trans.*, to harden (metals) by hammering; **hammer-lock** *Wrestling*, a position in which a wrestler is held with one arm bent behind his back; also *fig.*; so **hammer-lock** *v. trans.*; **hammer-mill**, a water-mill driving a hammer in a small forge; **hammer-oyster** = *hammer-shell*; **hammer-palsy**, paralysis of the arm caused by use of the hammer; **hammer-pick**, a tool with a head formed as a hammer on one side and a pick on the other; **hammer-pike**, 'a long-shafted weapon, like the *war-hammer*..carried by the subalterns in charge of the flag under the First [French] Empire' (Farrow, *Milit. Encycl.* 1885); **hammer-pond**, a pond in which water for driving a *hammer-mill* is stored; **hammer-price** *Stock Exchange*, the price realized for shares (of a defaulter) closed at the hammer; **hammer-rifle**, a rifle fired by means of a hammer; **hammer-scale**, the coating of oxide which forms on red-hot iron and can be separated by hammering (also called *forge-scale*); **hammer-sedge**, *Carex hirta*; **hammer-shark**, the hammer-headed shark; **hammer-shell**, the hammer-shaped shell of a bivalve mollusc of the genus *Malleus*; also the animal itself (also called *hammer-oyster*); **hammer-slag, -slough** = *hammer-scale*; **hammer-stone**, a prehistoric stone implement resembling, or used as, a hammer; **hammer-thrower** (see sense 1, note); **hammer-throwing** (see sense 1, note); **hammer-toe** (see quot.); **hammer-tongs**, tongs having projecting pins for holding hammer-heads or other articles with holes punched in them; **hammerwise** *adv.*, in the manner of a hammer; **hammer-work**, (*a*) work performed with a hammer; (*b*) something constructed or shaped with the hammer; **hammer-wrought** *a.*, worked into shape with the hammer, as iron, brass, etc. Also HAMMER-BEAM, etc.

1885 *Encycl. Brit.* XIX. 71/2 An altered German harpsichord, the *hammer action of which..may have been taken from Schroeter's diagram. *Ibid.* 72/1 In Frederici's upright grand action..the movement is practically identical with the hammer action of a German clock. **1906** *Westm. Gaz.* 22 Mar. 7/2 The explosion, which was probably caused by the hammer action of the water. **1927** PEAKE & FLEURE *Priests & Kings* 165 Perforated hammer-axes..are said to have been found [at Tripolye]. **1847** EMERSON *Poems* (1857) 54 The joiner's *hammer-beat. **1382** WYCLIF *Job* xli. 15 His herte..shal be streyned as the stithie of an *hamer betere. **1861** W. FAIRBAIRN *Iron* 121 The *hammer-block is guided in its vertical descent by two planed guides or projections. **18..** *Jrnl. Franklin Inst.* CXXIII. 42 (Cent.) The so-called *hammer-blow in locomotives is the irregularity of the pressure exerted between the wheel and rail, which arises from the vertically-unbalanced action of the counter-weights placed in the wheel to neutralize the horizontal action of the piston and other moving parts. **1881** *Instr. Census Clerks* (1885) 42 Forge and *Hammer Boy. **1909** *Westm. Gaz.* 19 Aug. 9/4 There has been a considerable shortage of hammer boys in most of the mining districts. **1840** *Penny Cycl.* XVIII. 141/2 Block passed through the *hammer butt. **1896** HIPKINS *Pianoforte* Gloss., *Hammer-Butt*, the centred butt of the hammer-shank in the so-called English action, shaped with the notch against which the sticker of the hopper works. **1823** CRABB *Technol. Dict.*, **Hammer-cap*. **1883** R. MACDONNELL in *Brit. Med. Jrnl.* 12 May 912 (*title*) *Hammer-cramp. **1837** HT. MARTINEAU *Soc. Amer.* II. 191 There are four viaducts of *hammer-dressed sandstone. **1854** H. MILLER *Sch. & Schm.* (1858) 272 He hammer-dressed his stones with fewer strokes than other workmen. **1939** J. D. S. PENDLEBURY *Archaeol. Crete* iii. 98 The stones are invariably hammer-dressed, the saw not yet being used for masonry. **1940** *Chambers's Techn. Dict.* 401/1 *Hammer-dressed*, a term applied to stone surfaces left with a rough finish produced by the hammer. **1908** R. PEELE *Compressed Air Plant for Mines* xx. 249 Numerous small air *hammer drills..have come into favor in the past few years... The hammer drill strikes a light blow. **1922** *Encycl. Brit.* XXXI. 958/1 Machine drills underwent important changes during 1910–20, especially in the development of the 'hammer' drills... In the hammer drill, the bit is held stationary..and is struck a rapid succession of blows by the reciprocating piston-like hammer. **1592** G. HARVEY *Pierce's Super.* 183 The grossest *hammer-drudge in a country. **1890** *Daily News* 12 Nov. 5/5 A local tuner had ingeniously brightened the tone of a piano by anointing the *hammer-felts with a mixture of whiting and glue. **1835** BOOTH *Analyt. Dict.* (Worc.), **Hammer-Fish*, a rapacious fish; the balance-fish. **1729** SHELVOCKE *Artillery* IV. 182 Take of the Filings of Iron or of *Hammerflaw. **1644** RUSHW. *Hist. Coll.* III. II. 742 The Line strongly guarded with *Hammer-guns and Murtherers. **1886** *Daily News* 16 Sept. 7/2 He used a breech-loading double-barrelled hammer gun, with two triggers within a guard. 1703 MOXON *Mech. Exerc.* 31 *Hammer-hard, is when you harden Iron, or Steel, with much hammering on it. 1694 *Ibid.* 92 The Iron-Saws are only *Hammer-hardned. 1846 GREENER *Sc. Gunnery* 105 We recommend hammer-hardening in all mixtures containing iron. 1752 SIR J. HILL *Hist. Anim.* 301 (Jod.) The squalus with a very broad transverse *hammer-like head. 1897 *Pearson's Mag.* III. 638 Hammer lock and Nelson on the ground. 1905 *Daily Chron.* 21 Feb. 7/4 The very thought of being *'hammer-locked' should be enough to deter the most confirmed 'disorderly'. 1906 E. DYSON *Fact'ry 'Ands* vi. 72 Jest you take a 'ammerlock holt iv yerself, 'n' 'ave some dam consideration fer others. 1907 G. B. SHAW *Let.* 23 Sept. (1956) 107 Short of giving Phyllis a leading part, and thus giving you the hammer lock on him, I dont know what to do. 1944 *Infantry Jrnl.* (U.S.) June 25 He got his Jap in a hammerlock. 1965 *Economist* 4 Dec. 1072/2 These are fuzzy far-off dreams, considering the right wing's hammerlock on the Republican party today. 1610 HOLLAND *Camden's Brit., Sussex* 306 Pooles and waters..of sufficient power to driue *hammer milles, which beating upon the iron, resound all ouer the places adjoyning. 1884 *Contemp. Rev.* Aug. 326 To form ponds for driving the hammer-mills. 1756 T. AMORY *J. Buncle* (1770) I. xiii. 55 Of all the curious shells..the *hammer oyster was what I wondered at most. 1854 WOODWARD *Mollusca* (1856) 261 The 'hammer-oyster' is remarkable for its form, which becomes extremely elongated with age; both ears are long, and the umbones central. 1869 W. FRANK-SMITH in *Lancet* 27 Mar. 427 (*title*) Hephæstic Hemiplegia (*Hammer Palsy). 1887 HISSEY *Holiday on Road* 366 *Hammer-ponds. 1895 C. R. B. BARRETT *Surrey* vii. 168 Parallel to the road.. I see a long series of hammer ponds. 1900 *Westm. Gaz.* 4 June 7/1 He can have the stock closed at the *hammer price. 1901 *Ibid.* 13 May 9/1 The actual dealings in the shares being between £6 and £8 per share and the hammer price £2. 1840 *Penny Cycl.* XVIII. 141/2 (Piano-forte) *Hammer rail. 1907 *Yesterday's Shopping* (1969) 634 *Hammer rifles. 1920 G. BURRARD *Notes on Sporting Rifles* 15 Hammerless ejectors are better than non-ejectors and hammer rifles. 1884 F. J. BRITTEN *Watch & Clockm.* 118 *Hammer Rods.. in a Turret Clock..connect the movement with the hammers. 1866 *Treas. Bot.*, *Hammersedge, *Carex hirta*. 1896 HIPKINS *Pianoforte* 29 Cedar has been much used for *hammer-shanks on account of its elasticity. 1877 BRYANT *Poems, Sella* 146 Hideous *hammer-sharks, Chasing their prey. 1890 W. J. GORDON *Foundry* 13 The blast-furnaces that stand near the *hammer-shed. 1711 *Phil. Trans.* XXVII. 349 A sort of Rock or Tree-Oyster, call'd by some a **Hammer-Shell* from its Shape. 1736 *Specif. Kingsmill Eyre's Patent* No. 553 There is then added..a certain small quantity of..*hammer slough. 1823 CRABB *Technol. Dict.* s.v. *Hammer*, **Hammer-spring*, the spring on which the hammer of the gun-lock works. 1847 *Infantry Man.* (1854) 107 The little finger touches the hammer-spring. 1872 J. EVANS *Anc. Stone Implem.* 29 The *hammer-stones used in the manufacture of flint hatchets. 1891 D. WILSON *Right Hand* 41 Similar hammer-stones occur in Danish peat-mosses. 1580 in Farr *S.P. Eliz.* (1845) II. 310 The steele obeyeth the *hammer-stroke. 1899 *Daily News* 18 July 7/2 The *hammer-throwers were out in the morning. 1968 *Listener* 11 July 49/2 There have been a number of marriages..between hammer-throwers and female discus-throwers. 1873 MISS BRADDON *L. Davoren* Prol. ii, Geoffrey Hossack practises *hammer-throwing with an iron crowbar. 1886 *Syd. Soc. Lex.*, **Hammer-toe*..a distortion of the second toe..so that it is bent upwards at an angle, the two terminal phalanges being flexed. 1894 *Daily News* 4 May 6/4 That resemblance to a section of a square arch which is known..as 'hammer toe'. 1888 *Pall Mall G.* 6 July 11/1 A second will..thump down his fist, *hammerwise, to nail his arguments. 1398 TREVISA *Barth. de P.R.* XVI. iv. (Tollem. MS.), No þinge streccheþ more with *hamoure-werke þan golde. 1846 ELLIS *Elgin Marb.* I. 107 Made several statues of this hammer-work.

hammer, *sb.*² Prob. = Ger. *ammer*, the yellow bunting or YELLOW-HAMMER, q.v.

1606 CHAPMAN *Mons. D'Olive* IV. (D.), S'light I ever took thee to be a hammer of the right feather.

hammer, *v.* [f. HAMMER *sb.*¹]

I. *trans.* **1.** *lit.* **a.** To strike, beat, or drive with or as with a hammer.

*c*1430 *Pilgr. Lyf Manhode* IV. xviii. (1869) 184 Whan I haue..beten him and hamered him. *c*1532 DEWES *Introd. Fr.* in *Palsgr.* 950 To hamer, *marteler*. 1642 J. GOODWIN (*title*) Anti-Cavalierism..for the suppressing of that butcherly brood of Cavaliering incendiaries, who are now hammering England. 1864 SKEAT *Uhland's Poems* 334 He hammered the anvil hard into the ground! 1890 BAKER *Wild Beasts* II. 167 They commenced hammering the good dogs with their heavy bamboos. 1907 F. H. BURNETT *Shuttle* xxxviii. 379 Jem Belter, who 'hammered' a typewriter. 1959 M. SHADBOLT *New Zealanders* 26 The Potoki boys hammered the piano and banged the drums.

b. To fasten with or as with a hammer, e.g. by nailing; to drive *up*, *down*, etc., with a hammer.

*c*1450 *Mirour Saluacioun* 152 Crist as he was ruthfully hamerd upon the croce. 1742 YOUNG *Nt. Th.* I. 247 There beings..Are hammer'd to the galling oar for life. 1847 TENNYSON *Princ.* v. 358 All that long morn the lists were hammer'd up. 1873 J. RICHARDS *Wood-working Factories* 35 If the hooks are hammered down too hard.

c. To beat out, as metal, with a hammer; to shape with blows of a hammer.

1522 [see HAMMERED]. 1605 CAMDEN *Rem.* 200 The Lord hath dilated me by hammering me vpon the anvild. *a*1712 W. KING *Ovid's Art of Love* 16 Is it not hammer'd all from Vigo's plate? 1851 D. WILSON *Preh. Ann.* (1863) I. II. i. 331 Armillæ of pure gold, hammered into rounded bars. 1875 JOWETT *Plato, Cratylus* (ed. 2) II. 232 This is hammered into shape. 1878 SMILES *Robt. Dick* xiii. 94 Has been literally hammered out by the force of the waves.

2. *fig.* **a.** (from 1 c.) To devise, design, contrive, or work out laboriously; to put into shape with much intellectual effort. Often with *out*. (Frequent in 17th c. 'Used commonly in contempt' J.)

1583 STANYHURST *Æneis* IV (Arb.) 96 What broyle Tyrus angrye doth hammer. *Ibid.* 108 Hym shee left daunted with feare, woords duitiful hamring For to reply. 1589 GREENE *Menaphon* (Arb.) 82 He hammered in his head many meanes to stay the faire Samela. 1628 CHAS. I in Rushw. *Hist. Coll.* (1659) I. 631 The profession of both Houses in the time of hammering this Petition. 1681 NEVILE *Plato Rediv.* 125 The Peers are Co-ordinate with the Commons in presenting and hammering of Laws. 1751 *Affect. Narr. Wager* 139 He endeavoured to hammer out some excuses for him. 1819 BYRON *Juan.* I. clxii, At first he tried to hammer an excuse. 1887 SAINTSBURY *Hist. Elizab. Lit.* viii. (1890) 314 Songs like these are not to be hammered out by the most diligent ingenuity.

†**b.** To discuss, debate. *Obs.*

1594 CAREW *Huarte's Exam. Wits* (1616) 117 A question, much hammered betweene Plato and Aristotle.

c. To drive by dint of reiterated argument or persuasion (as an idea, etc. into a person's head).

1646 J. HALL *Horæ Vac.* 63 Others it must either be forced and hammered into. 1844 COL. HAWKER *Diary* (1893) II. 241 Hammering into his head the designs I wished for. 1850 KINGSLEY *Alt. Locke* Pref. (1879) 97 That priggishness and forwardness..are soon hammered out of any Cambridge man. 1866 W. COLLINS *Armadale* III. xiv, Hammering common sense into his head.

d. *Stock Exchange slang.* (*a*) To declare (a person) a defaulter (see quot. 1887). (*b*) To beat down the price of (a stock, etc.); to depress (a market).

1865 *Harper's Mag.* XXX. 619 The chronic bears were amusing themselves by 'hammering' i.e. pressing down the price of Hudsons. 1883 *Pall Mall G.* 17 Oct. 5/2 Having omitted to settle within that time [the three days' grace] he was promptly 'hammered'. 1887 *Financ. Critic* 19 Mar., The head Stock Exchange waiter strikes three strokes with a mallet on the side of a rostrum in the Stock Exchange before making formal declaration of default of a member. Thus, to be 'hammered', is to be pronounced a defaulter. 1890 *Daily News* 28 Jan. 6/4 Bears were induced to hammer the market on bad shipments reported from Glasgow.

e. To inflict heavy defeat(s) on, in war, games, etc.; to strike forcefully; to beat up. *colloq.*

1948 PARTRIDGE *Dict. Forces' Slang 1939–45* 90 *Hammer*, to shell severely. To inflict a heavy defeat on. 1959 *Times* 28 May 4/6 Smith hammered Slade for two fours and a six. 1973 *Times* 5 Jan. 17/5 Challenging the well-entrenched leaders in the United Kingdom car rental industry seems to hold no fears for Crook. He is hoping to hammer them on both quality and price. 1973 *Courier & Advertiser* (Dundee) 14 Feb. 5/3 He was severely injured about the face and his dentures were broken. He had no doubt that he had been 'hammered'.

II. *intr.* **3. a.** *lit.* To deal blows with or as with a hammer; to strike a succession of heavy blows; to thump.

13.. *Gaw. & Gr. Knt.* 2311 þaȝ he homered heterly, hurt hym no more. 1413 *Pilgr. Sowle* (Caxton 1483) IV. xxx. 78 To bete or hameren vppon his hede by yeuynge of counceylle contrary to his plesaunce. 1586 J. HOOKER *Girald. Irel.* in *Holinshed* II. 32 We haue no leasure to serue the Muses, but to be hammering with weapons. 1886 STOKES *Celtic Ch.* (1888) 349 He found an English tourist hammering away with a geologist's hammer. 1891 E. PEACOCK *N. Brendon* I. 186 The lawyer..hammered on the door with his heavy whipstock.

b. Of a pipe: to make a knocking noise, as when a flow of liquid is suddenly stopped by turning a tap. (Cf. WATER-HAMMER 2.)

1889 P. HASLUCK *Model Engin. Handybk.* 108 The pump, owing to its not being filled properly at each stroke, will hammer very much.

4. *fig.* †**a.** To devise plans laboriously, 'cudgel one's brains', debate or deliberate earnestly (*upon*, *on*, *at*, *of*); with *upon*, sometimes, To reiterate, persist in, insist upon. *Obs.*

1591 SHAKS. *Two Gent.* I. iii. 18 That Whereon, this month I haue bin hamering. 1598 GRENEWEY *Tacitus' Ann.* XV. viii. 232 He came againe to Rome, hammering greatly with himselfe of going to the prouinces of the East. 1647 TRAPP *Comm. Matt.* v. 18 This the heathens had.. hammered at. 1777 J. Q. ADAMS *Fam. Lett.* (1876) 293 We have been several days hammering upon money.

†**b.** Of an idea: To present itself persistently to one's mind as matter of debate; to be in agitation.

1588 SHAKS. *Tit. A.* II. iii. 39 Blood, and reuenge, are Hammering in my head. 1593 G. FLETCHER *Rich. III*, xviii. Poems (Grosart) 151 So still a crowne did hammer in my head. 1667 DRYDEN *Sir Martin Mar-all* I. i. (R.), A thousand things are hammering in his head; 'tis a fruitful noddle, though I say it.

c. To work hard, toil; to make persistent and laborious attempts. Const. *at*.

1755 JOHNSON, *Hammer*, to work; to be busy: in contempt. 1826 SCOTT *Jrnl.* 7 May, Hammered on at the Review till my backbone ached. 1874 L. STEPHEN *Hours in Libr.* (1892) II. ii. 41 He liked..to hammer away at his poems in a study where chaos reigned supreme. 1887 T. A. TROLLOPE *What I remember* I. ix. 215 The examiner had been hammering away at the man next before me for an inordinate time. 1892 A. S. WILKINS in *Bookman* Oct. 26/2 Hammering away at a point which he wished to enforce.

5. To make reiterated laborious efforts to speak, to stammer. Now only *dial.*

1619 R. WESTE *Bk. Demeanor* 109 in *Babees Bk.* 294 If in thy tale thou hammering stand, or coughing twixt thy words. 1685 WOOD *Life* 21 Feb. (O.H.S.) III. 132 He hammered so long for a Latin word for an 'address'. *c*1817 HOGG *Tales & Sk.* III. 351 Was he hammering over the name. 1855 ROBINSON *Whitby Gloss.*, *To Hammer*, to speak confusedly, to stammer.

hammerable ('hæmərəb(ə)l), *a. rare.* [f. prec. vb. + -ABLE.] Capable of being hammered, or beaten out with a hammer; malleable.

1611 COTGR., *Malleable*, mallable, tractable, hammerable. 1623 LISLE *Ælfric on O. & N. Test.* Pref. 4 That cleere and hammerable glasse of old.

'hammer-beam. *Arch.* A short beam projecting from the wall at the foot of a principal rafter in a roof, in place of a tie-beam.

1823 in P. NICHOLSON *Pract. Build.* Gloss. 1843 *Ecclesiologist* II. 57 The wallpieces, spandrils and hammer-beams are plain. 1876 GWILT *Encycl. Archit.* Gloss., *Hammer Beam*, a beam acting as a tie at the feet of a pair of principal rafters, but not extending so as to connect the opposite sides. 1879 *Cassell's Techn. Educ.* VII. 38/1 Rows of hammer-beams, terminating in beautifully-carved figures of angels.

attrib. 1831 *Sat. Rev.* 3 Sept. 292 The hammer-beam roof ..once more shows its ancient pitch.

hammer-cloth. [Derivation unknown.

The conjecture in quot. 1854 is obviously untenable: the coachman's 'box' is not known before 1600. De Quincey, *Autobiog. Germ. Stud.*, 1836, (Wks. 1889 II. 83) has a conjecture that *hammer-cloth* is 'a corruption from *hamper-cloth*.' Prof. Skeat has compared Du. *hemel* 'heaven, canopy, tester', citing from Hexham *den Hemel van de koetse* 'the Seeling of a Coach.' But these suggestions are not corroborated by the evidence. See also HAMMOCK-CLOTH, with which this is either connected or confused.]

A cloth covering the driver's seat or 'box' in a state or family coach. (In quot. 1465 applied to a material.)

1465 *Mann. & Househ. Exp.* 315 My mastyr bout of Baron of Hadlegthe xlj. elles of hamerclothe. 155. in *Archæol.* XVI. 91 (D.) Hamer clothes, with our arms and badges of our colours, and all other things apperteininge unto the same wagon. 1736 WEST *Let.* in *Gray's Poems* (1775) 10, I never knew before that the golden fangs on hammercloths were so old a fashion. 1794 W. FELTON *Carriages* (1801) I. 153 Hammer Cloths are among the principal ornaments of a Carriage. 1854 KNIGHT *Once upon a Time* II. 18 The [coach] man carried a hammer, pincers, nails, ropes, and other appliances in case of need; and the *hammer-cloth* was devised to conceal these..remedies for broken wheels and shivered panels.

Hence **hammer-clothed** (-klɒθt, -ɔː-) *a.*, provided with a hammer-cloth.

1862 SALA *Accepted Addr.* 182 The great..heavy hammer-clothed, double-seated family Carriage.

hammered ('hæməd), *ppl. a.* [f. HAMMER *v.* + -ED¹.] Beaten out or shaped with a hammer.

1522 *Bury Wills* (Camden) 116 A ewer of pewter hamerd. 1593 SHAKS. *Lucr.* 951 To spoile Antiquities of hammerd steele. 1671 MILTON *Samson* 132 The hammered cuirass. *a*1700 DRYDEN *Disc. Epick Poetry* (R.), I had certainly been reduced to pay the publick in hammered money, for want of milled. 1816 KEATINGE *Trav.* (1817) II. 136 The quays.. faced with hammered stone. 1863 P. BARRY *Dockyard Econ.* Pref. 11 If rolled armour-plates were to be pronounced superior to hammered plates.

b. Of grapes: Having innumerable marks as if they had been hammered into shape, a result of good cultivation.

1882 *Garden* 21 Jan. 50/3 The berries of the Vines with their roots outside were hammered, while those on the inside ones were not.

hammerer ('hæmərə(r)). [f. as prec. + -ER¹.]

1. One who hammers or wields a hammer; often, one who plies the geologist's hammer, a geologist. Also, as a specific occupation.

1611 COTGR., *Marteleur*, a hammerer; one that worketh with a hammer. 1631 R. H. *Arraignm. Whole Creature* xii. §5. 146 All the late Hammerers of Papists. 1861 WILSON & GEIKIE *Mem. E. Forbes* xii. 378 The geologists..half-a-dozen stalwart hammerers. 1890 *Nature* 4 Sept., A source of regret to the whole brotherhood of hammerers. 1909 *Westm. Gaz.* 8 Feb. 3/1 The man was a 'hammerer'—i.e., a driver of rivets into boilers, &c. 1921 *Dict. Occup. Terms* (1927) §278 *Hammerer*,..flattens saw blades,..by..striking any curved part with hammer.

2. 'The three-wattled bell-bird of Costa Rica, *Chasmorhynchus tricarunculatus*' (Cent. Dict.).

'hammer-head.

1. The head or striking part of a hammer.

1562 J. HEYWOOD *Prov. & Epigr.* (1867) 144 The hammer hed..werth [= weareth] quite out. 1896 HIPKINS *Pianoforte* 30 The flattened shape of the hammer-head favours a musical quality of tone in soft playing that distinguishes many good pianos when the hammers are nearly worn out.

2. A head, likened to a hammer; a blockhead. (Cf. *beetle-head.*) *Obs.*

1532 MORE *Confut. Tindale* Wks. 645/1 Is not ther an hamer hed more meete to make horshoune in hel, then to constre yᵉ scripture in earth. 1581 J. BELL *Haddon's Answ. Osor.* 4 b, Your owne foolish lying wordes properly forged in that hammerhead of yours. 1628 GAULE *Pract. The.* (1629) 216 The Hammer-heads sate lately vpon like consultation. 1947 R. TAYLOR *Bar Nothing Ranch* (1949) xvi. 151 The meanest old hammerheads under her tutelage became as cooing doves.

3. a. A hammer-headed shark; so called from the great lateral expansions of the head. **b.** An American fish, *Hypentelium nigricans*, having a head of hammer-like shape.

1861 COUCH *Brit. Fishes* I. 71 The Hammer Head is a rare wanderer to our seas. 1880 GUNTHER *Fishes*, The 'Hammerheads' or Hammerheaded Sharks belong to the most formidable fishes of the ocean.

4. An African bird, the shadow-bird or umber-bird (*Scopus umbretta*); from the shape of the head with its occipital crest and long stout bill.

1890 *Sat. Rev.* 1 Feb. 139/2 The umbre is known in South Africa as the hammerkop or hammer-head. **1895** *Pop. Sci. Monthly* 773 That singular bird known as the hammer-head.

5. ***hammer-head crane*** = *hammer-headed crane*.

1910 *Encycl. Brit.* VII. 371/1 The Titan is portable and the hammer-head crane fixed. **1938** *Jane's Fighting Ships* 37 Fitting out berth equipped with giant 25 ton Hammerhead Crane.

'hammer-,headed, *a.* [f. prec. + -ED².]

1. a. Having a head shaped like that of a hammer.

1567 GOLDING *Ovid's Met.* VII. 74 Their hammer headed Joawles Are ioyned to their shoulders iust. **1752** SIR J. HILL *Hist. Anim.* 301 (Jod.) The balance fish and the hammerheaded shark. **1865** DICKENS *Mut. Fr.* I. ix, A long hammer-headed old horse.

b. ***hammer-headed crane*** (see quot. 1910).

1908 A. TOLHAUSEN tr. *Böttcher's Cranes* IX. 492 (*title*) Hammer-headed crane of 150 tons, constructed by the Duisburger Maschinenbau-A.-G. **1910** *Encycl. Brit.* VII. 370/2 The so-called 'hammer-headed' crane consists of a steel braced tower, on which revolves a large horizontal double cantilever; the forward part of this cantilever or jib carries the lifting crab, and the jib is extended backwards in order to form a support for the machinery and counter-balance.

2. *fig.* Dull in intellect; stupid; beetle-headed.

1552 HULOET, Hammer headed knave, *Tuditanus.* **1600** NASHE *Summer's Last Will* Epil. in Hazl. *Dodsley* VIII. 92 Hammer-headed..clowns. **1855** DICKENS *Dorrit* (Househ. Ed.) 402/2 You hammer-headed woman.

hammering ('hæmərɪŋ), *vbl. sb.* [-ING¹.]

1. The action of striking, knocking, or beating out with a hammer; the dealing of hard reiterated blows as with a hammer. Also *fig.*

1563 W. FULKE *Meteors* v. (1640) 67 Copper is most like to Silver in the waight, and in the hammering. **1612–15** BP. HALL *Contempl., O.T.* XX. xxi, After a thousand hammerings of the menaces of Gods law. **1768–74** TUCKER *Lt. Nat.* (1852) II. 676, I have found the first working too laborious to leave me strength for a second hammering. **1811** *Sporting Mag.* XXXVII. 18 He stood the hammering of his antagonist..with uncommon firmness. **1883** W. E. NORRIS *No New Thing* III. xxxv. 224 I'll give you such a hammering that you won't do it again for a year.

attrib. **1824** W. IRVING *T. Trav.* II. 41 My door became a hammering place for every bailiff in the county. **1875** BUCKLAND *Log-bk.* 32 A beaver using his tail as a hammering instrument.

2. *fig.* †**a.** Devising, contriving, or constructing.

1589 *Pappe w. Hatchet* (1844) 34 Newe alterations were in hammering. **1626** *Crt. & Times Chas. I* (1848) I. 150 There is a hammering..a brave design to set forth the next spring.

b. *Stock Exchange slang.* (See HAMMER *v.* 2 d.)

1893 *Times* 19 Dec. 11/3 'Bears' assisted the decline by 'hammering'.

c. Of grapes: see HAMMERED b.

1882 *Garden* 21 Jan. 50/3 The views of those who have maintained that the hammering was due to culture more than anything else.

3. Hesitation in speech, stammering.

1731 *Wodrow Corr.* (1843) III. 489, I never..saw so much hammering and indecency in delivery. **1828** *Craven Dial., Hammering*, stammering.

hammering *ppl. a.* That hammers.

1639 S. DU VERGER tr. *Camus' Admir. Events* 129 That puts a thousand hammering suspitions into thy head. **1895** *Athenæum* 24 Aug. 257/1 It is the hammering alliteration which he especially adopts.

hammerkop: see HAMERKOP.

hammerless ('hæməlɪs), *a.* [f. HAMMER *sb.*¹ + -LESS.] Without a hammer: *esp.* of a gun.

1875 'STONEHENGE' *Brit. Sports* I. I. ii. §4. 44 The hammerless gun. **1886** *Badm. Libr., Shooting* (1895) 34 In matter of safety the hammerless has the advantage of the hammer gun.

hammerman ('hæməmæn). A man who works with a hammer. *spec.* **a.** A smith or worker in metal. **b.** A blacksmith's unskilled assistant or 'striker'. **c.** A man who manipulates a steam-hammer. **d.** *Coal-mining*: see quot. 1829.

1483 *Charter Town Council Edinb.* 2 May, The Hammermen Craft, bayth blacksmyths, goldsmiths, lorymeris, saidlaris. **1535** COVERDALE *Isa.* xli. 7 The Smyth comforted the moulder, and the Ironsmyth the hammerman. **1619** *Canterbury Marriage Licences* (MS.) Anthony Pullen of Hawkhurst, hamorman. **1697** EVELYN *Numism.* vii. 226 Not only the Hammer men, but the very Court of Moneyers itself. **1769** *De Foe's Tour Gt. Brit.* IV. 103 The fourteen incorporated Trades are: Surgeons, Goldsmiths..Farriers, Hammermen, Wrights, Masons [etc.]. **1817** *Sporting Mag.* L. 17 After the manner of a hammer-man at a forge. **1818** SCOTT *Hrt. Midl.* xxix, The hammermen of Edinburgh are to my mind afore the world for making stancheons, ring-bolts, fetter-bolts, bars, and locks. **1829** GLOVER *Hist. Derby* I. 58 When the holers have finished their operations, a new set of men, called hammer-men, or drivers, enter the works. These fall, or force down, large masses of coal, by means of long and sharp iron wedges. **1880** *Harper's Mag.* Dec. 59 The hammer-man, in a swinging seat, times the turning of his rod of steel to the quick stroke of the hammer.

'hammersmith. A smith who works with a hammer; a hammerman.

1382 WYCLIF *Gen.* iv. 22 Tubalcaym, that was an hamer smyth. **1683** PETTUS *Fleta Min.* I. (1686) 318 When such proof is found by the Magnet..then the Hammer-smiths..use further to prove..it. **1756** NUGENT *Gr. Tour* II. 201 Ziegenhals..remarkable for its great number of hammersmiths, and a manufacture of glass. **1887** *Standard* 8 Apr. 2/4 The men are blacksmiths and hammersmiths.

'hammer-tail. **a.** 'In a striking clock, a continuation of the hammer stalk that is lifted by the pins in the pin wheel' (Britten *Watch & Clockm.* 1884). **b.** In a pianoforte: see quot. 1896.

1805 *Trans. Soc. Arts* XXIII. 355 Fixed with the hammer-tail to the hammer-bar by means of a pin. **1884** F. J. BRITTEN *Watch & Clockm.* 252 For lifting the hammer tails of small clocks, pins in the wheel..do very well. **1896** HIPKINS *Pianoforte* Gloss., *Hammer-tail*, a prolongation of the hammer-head shaped so as to be caught in its descent by the check.

†**hammerwort.** *Obs.* The Wall-pellitory.

c **1000** *Sax. Leechd.* I. 374 Genim..hamor wyrte blosman. *a* **1100** *Ags. Voc.* in Wr.-Wülcker 300/22 *Perdicalis*, homorwyrt. **1597** GERARDE *Herbal* App., Hammerwort is Pellitorie of the wall.

hammily: see HAMMY *a.*

‖**hammochrysos** (hæməʊ'kraɪsɒs). *Min.* [L. (Pliny), a. Gr. ἀμμόχρυσος, f. ἄμμος sand + χρυσός gold.] A sparkling stone mentioned by the ancients; perhaps yellow micaceous schist, or the sand from it.

1706 in PHILLIPS (ed. Kersey). **1750** tr. *Leonardus' Mirr. Stones* 110. **1868** DANA *Min.* 302. **1876** T. HARDY *Ethelberta* (1890) 321 Nearly everything was glass in the frontage of this fairy mart, and its contents glittered like the hammochrysos stone.

hammock¹ ('hæmək). Forms: α. 6–9 **hamaca**, 7 **-acca, -acco, -ackoe, hammacho,** 8 **hamacoe,** 8–9 **hammacoe.** β. 7 **hamack(e, hammac(k, -aque, amack, hamock, hammok,** 8 **hammoc,** 8–9 **hamac,** 7– **hammock.** [a. Sp. *hamaca* of Carib origin; cf. F. *hamac* (1555 in Hatz.-Darm.).]

1. A hanging bed, consisting of a large piece of canvas, netting, etc. suspended by cords at both ends; used esp. by sailors on board ship, also in hot climates or seasons on land.

α. **1555** EDEN *Decades* 200 Theyr hangynge beddes whiche they caule *Hamacas*. **1596** RALEIGH *Discov. Gviana* 55 They lay each of them in a cotten Hamaca, which we call brasill beds. **1613** R. HARCOURT *Voy. Guiana* in *Harl. Misc.* (Malh.) III. 191 Hamaccas, which are Indian beds, most necessary in those parts. **1638** SIR T. HERBERT *Trav.* (ed. 2) 7 Saylers, who..get forthwith into their beds (or hamackoes) [**1677** or hamacks]. **1761** *London Mag.* XXX. 220 Orders were..given for sewing him up in a hamacoe, in order to bury him. **1794** *Rigging & Seamanship* I. 170 To keep the hammacoes in the stantions. **1847** PRESCOTT *Peru* (1850) II. 101 Carried on the shoulders of the natives in the *hamacas*, or sedans, of the country.

β. **1626** CAPT. SMITH *Accid. Yng. Seamen* 11 A Hamacke, the lockers, the round-house. **1657** R. LIGON *Barbadoes* (1673) 45 Lye down and rest them in their Hamocks. **1675** *Mistaken Husband* v. i. in *Dryden's Wks.* (1884) VIII. 626 It cannot be so convenient as a Hammaque. **1698** FROGER *Voy.* 134 There is nothing but Famine that can draw them out of their Amacks. **1723** J. ATKINS *Voy. Guinea* (1735) 112 Travelling is in Hammocks..slung cross a Pole and bore up at each end by a Negro. **1804** NELSON 26 Apr. in Nicolas *Disp.* (1845) V. 514 Seamen's beds and hammocks are very much wanted. **1840** R. H. DANA *Bef. Mast* xxviii. 93, I went aboard, and turned into my hammock.

2. *transf.* Applied to the suspended nest of the hangbird or American oriole; and to the suspended case made by the caterpillars of certain moths.

1856 BRYANT *Poems, Strange Lady* vii, And there the hang-bird's brood within its little hammock swings. **1859** DARWIN *Orig. Spec.* vii. 208 A caterpillar which had completed its hammock up to, say, the sixth stage of construction. **1874** CARPENTER *Ment. Phys.* I. ii. §60 (1879) 61 There is a Caterpillar that makes a very complicated hammock.

†**3.** = HAMMOCK-CLOTH 1. *Obs. rare*⁻¹.

1690 *Lond. Gaz.* No. 2612/4 Lost..a Coach-Horses Hammock of Crimson and Musk Colour Caffaw fringed with the same colours.

4. *Comb.*, as ***hammock-bearer***; ***hammock-cradled*** adj.; **hammock-batten**, one of the battens or strips of wood nailed to the ship's beams, from which the hammocks are slung; **hammock chair**, a folding reclining-chair with canvas support for the body, suitable for use in a sitting-room or garden; a deck-chair; **hammock-clew, -clue**, the series of small cords (**hammock-lines**) by which a hammock is suspended at each end; **hammock-man**, one of two or more men employed in carrying a hammock slung on poles; **hammock-moth** (see quot.); **hammock-nettings**, *orig.* rope nettings in which the hammocks when rolled up were stowed away on board ship, these being lashed or hung to the **hammock-rails** above the bulwarks; hence, the long troughs afterwards constructed for this purpose on the top of the bulwarks of the spar-deck in a man-of-war; **hammock-rack** = *hammock-batten*; **hammock-shroud**, a hammock used as a shroud in which to bury a corpse at sea.

1867 SMYTH *Sailor's Word-bk.*, **Hammock Battens* or *Racks*, cleats or battens nailed to the sides of a vessel's beams, from which to suspend the seamen's hammocks. **1819** *Edin. Rev.* XXXII. 389 Carried by *hammock-bearers at a foot pace. **1881** *Graphic* 18 June in L. de Vries *Vict. Advts.* (1968) 127/1 The *Yankee hammock chair..costs but 17s. 6d. complete. **1885** *Army & Navy Co-op. Soc. Price List* II. 1478 Portable Hammock Chairs. **1971** *Country Life* 1 Apr. (Suppl.) 44/2 (Advt.), Early 19th century hammock chair in mahogany upholstered in deep-buttoned Havana brown leather. **1794** *Rigging & Seamanship* I. 62 *Hammock-lines are made from groundtows. **1734** W. SNELGRAVE *Guinea & Slave Trade* 25, I had six *Hammock-men, who relieved one another by turns. [**1777** SUCKLING in Laughton *Lett. & Disp. Nelson* 9 The Commanding Officer should always be particular in having the hammocks well stowed in the nettings.] **1899** *Cambr. Nat. Hist.* VI. 379 The *Hammock-moth, *Perophora sanguinolenta*, of the centre of South America, the larva of which constructs its own portable habitations out of its own excrement. **1833** M. SCOTT *Tom Cringle* (1862) 349 Heavy bulwarks four feet high, surmounted by *hammock-nettings. **1833** MARRYAT *P. Simple* xv, The captain..stood upon the weather *hammock-rails, holding by the main-rigging. **1850** TENNYSON *In Mem.* vi, His heavy-shotted *hammock-shroud Drops in his vast and wandering grave.

hammock²: see HUMMOCK.

hammock-cloth. [The relation of sense 1 to HAMMOCK¹ is not apparent.]

†**1.** A cloth for the back of a horse. *Obs.*

1685 *Lond. Gaz.* No. 2060/4 A Hammock Cloth for a Coach Horse, of a Dark-hair-color'd Cloth Imbroider'd with Red and White. **1687** *Ibid.* 2270/4, 2 Hammock Cloaths of green Flowred Velvet on a white Ground, both fringed with Scarlet and White.

2. = HAMMER-CLOTH. (? By confusion.)

1830 MISS E. EDEN *Let.* in Mrs. Swinton *Lady de Ros* (1893) 41, I thought a hammock-cloth would be better under those circumstances than a dicky.

3. *Naut.* A cloth used for covering the hammocks to protect them from wet when stowed in the nettings on the top of the bulwarks.

1804 NELSON 28 July in Nicolas *Disp.* (1846) VI. 120 The want of these hammock-cloths will be severely felt, and there is none on board to cover the men's bedding. **1842** J. F. COOPER *Jack o' Lantern* I. 148 The hammocks were not stowed, and the hammock-cloths had that empty and undressed look so common to a man-of-war in the night.

Hammond organ ('hæmənd 'ɔːgən). *Mus.* [See quot. 1960.] The proprietary name of an electric organ produced by the Hammond Organ Company, in which sounds are produced by generating and combining electric currents of suitable frequencies; applied also to similar instruments; also *ellipt.* as *Hammond*.

1935 *Electronics* VIII. 156 (*caption*) The Hammond electric organ. **1936** *Proc. Inst. Radio Engin.* XXIV. 1446 The amount of agreement and departure from this tempered scale of frequencies found in the Hammond organ have been listed in his [*sc.* Hammond's U.S.] patent No. 1,956,350. **1957** *Gramophone* Apr. 426/3, I confess that the Hammond organ is an instrument which I find hard to accept in the field of popular music. **1960** GAMMOND & CLAYTON *Guide Pop. Mus.* 100 *Hammond organ*, an electrical instrument invented by Laurens Hammond in 1929. The Hammond Instrument Company of Chicago was formed in this year and began marketing the instrument in 1935... In 1938 the Aeolian-Hammond Player-Organ was produced, an entirely mechanical instrument. **1970** *Melody Maker* 3 Oct. 15/1 Having squeezed every possible sound from his Hammonds, the Moog was the natural progression.

hammy ('hæmɪ), *a.* [f. HAM *sb.*¹ + -Y.]

1. Characterized by the presence of ham. Also, resembling ham.

1861 WYNTER *Soc. Bees* 103 The eating-house connoisseur..ordered a slice of beef cut with a hammy knife. **1877** E. S. DALLAS *Kettner's Bk. of Table* 413 It was a grand hit this—the introduction of the hammy taste.

2. Of, pertaining to, or characteristic of a ham actor or ham acting. *slang.*

1929 T. WOLFE *Look Homeward, Angel* (1930) xxvii. 367 With fat hammy sonority he welcomed them. **1933** STANLEY & MAXFIELD *Voice* II. iii. 80 In particular, the prolongation of the vowel sounds associated with the consonants m, n and l is cheap and 'hammy'. **1946** *Penguin New Writing* XXVIII. 182 Toni..put on a hammy deep-in-thought act. **1965** G. MCINNES *Road to Gundagai* vi. 106 His part..was..hammy enough, but Carson managed to ham it up a good deal further. **1973** 'D. JORDAN' *Nile Green* xxxv. 171 Condon raised an eyebrow in a hammy attempt to be supercilious.

Hence (sense 2) **'hammily** *adv.*

1942 *Time* 27 Apr. 61 The talented author..has told one of the most hackneyed of all sentimental yarns, and told it hammily. **1958** *Spectator* 7 Feb. 175/2 Rather hammily acted but extremely well sung. **1961** *John o'London's* 14 Sept. 307/1 The plot is hackneyed to the point of imbecility, the slapstick hammily archaic.

hamose (heɪ'məʊs), *a.* [ad. L. type **hāmōsus*, f. *hāmus* hook.] Having hooks, hooked.

1709 *Brit. Apollo* II. No. 19.2/1 Compos'd of less Hamose and Twining Particles. **1886** in *Syd. Soc. Lex.*

hamour(e, obs. form of HAMMER.

hamous ('heɪməs), *a.* ? *Obs.* [f. L. *hām-us* hook + -OUS.] = HAMOSE.

1665 HOOKE *Microgr.* 6 Hamous, or hooked particles. 1758 BORLASE *Nat. Hist. Cornwall* 256 A hamous crooked little fang.

hamper ('hæmpə(r)), *sb.*[1] Also 4-5 -ere, 6 -ier, 7 -ire: see also HANAPER. [A phonetic reduction of HANAPER, by elision of middle vowel, and assimilation of *np* to *mp*, as in *ampersand*.]

1. A large basket or wickerwork receptacle, with a cover, generally used as a packing-case. In earlier times a case or casket generally; but from 1500 usually of wickerwork.

1392 *Acct.* in *Exped. Earl Derby* (Camden) 196 Pro emendacione vnius serure de j hampere. *c* 1425 *Voc.* in Wr.-Wülcker 659/10 *Hic cophinus*, hampere. 1490 [see HANAPER 1]. 1494 FABYAN *Chron.* VII. 607 The mayer and aldermen yode vnto the kynge, and presented hym with an hamper of golde, and therin a thousande pounde of fayre nobles. 1528 *Test. Ebor.* (Surtees) V. 254 A hamper of wikers wth writinges in yt, *jd.* 1530 PALSGR. 203/1 Casket or hamper, *escrayn.* 1552 HULOET, Hamper for women to put in spindels or bottomes of threade. 1598 BARRET *Theor. Warres* V. ii. 131 Baskets, hampiers, and small hand-panniers. 1603 HOLLAND *Plutarch's Mor.* 345 His mother had hidden him within a little corne flasket or twiggen hamper. 1610 *Althorp MS.* p. vi. in Simpkinson *Washingtons*, 3 hampers for the plate covered with sayle skinnes, and all of them with lockes and keyes. 1661 PEPYS *Diary* 27 Sept., We found a hampire of millons sent to me also. 1666 *Ibid.* 21 Sept., A hamper of bottles of wine. 1790 WOLCOTT (P. Pindar) *Adv. to Future Laureate* Wks. 1812 II 333 Like Porters sweating underneath a hamper. 1837 DICKENS *Pickw.* iv, Undo the hamper, Joe. *Mod.* Christmas hampers have taxed the resources of the Parcel Office.

b. Of definite size or measure (*U.S.*): in New York, an oyster-basket holding two bushels; in Virginia, a measure of small fish holding about a bushel. (*Cent. Dict.*)

†**2.** = HANAPER 3. *Obs.*

1503-4 *Act 19 Hen. VII*, c. 29 *Preamble*, Fine and fee to your Highnesse in your hamper..to be payde. *a* 1577 SIR T. SMITH *Commw. Eng.* (1609) 58 The Clarke of the Hamper is hee that doth receiue the fines due for euery Writ sealed in this Court. 1647 HAWARD *Crown Rev.* 1 Livery out of the Hamper 28. 08. 4. 1714 J. FORTESCUE-ALAND *Pref. to Fortescue's Abs. & Lim. Mon.* 39 An Annuity of 180 Marks out of the Hamper.

3. *Comb.*, an ***hamper-maker***. Also **hamperful**.

1411 *Close Roll 12 Hen IV*, (dorso), Petrus Sandhurst, hamper-maker. 1812 COL. HAWKER *Diary* (1893) I. 55, I could kill a hamperful of partridges in the neighbourhood.

'**hamper**, *sb.*[2] [f. HAMPER *v.*[1]]

†**1.** Something that hampers, or prevents freedom of movement; a shackle. *Obs.*

1613-16 W. BROWNE *Brit. Past.* I. v, His shackles, shack-lockes, hampers, gives, and chaines His linked bolts. *a* 1624 BP. M. SMITH *Serm.* (1632) 34 If they wil needs entangle themselves with those hampers that are made against practisers against the state, who can helpe them?

2. *Naut.* Things which form a necessary part of the equipment of a vessel, but are in the way at certain times. (See esp. TOP-HAMPER.)

1835 MARRYAT *Jac. Faithf.* xxxix, The boat.. immediately filled, and turned over with us, and it was with difficulty that we could escape from the weighty hamper that was poured out of her. 1873 DIXON *Two Queens* I. IV. ii. 182 Their vessels..with heavy hamper and a flowing sail.

hamper ('hæmpə(r)), *v.*[1] [Occurs first *c* 1350, in northern writers; actual origin uncertain; possibly from a radical *ham-* (? *hamm-*), found in Icel. *hęmja*, pa. t. *hamdi* to restrain, hold back from roving, Ger. *hemmen*, MHG. *hęmmen*, MG. *hamen* to restrain, clog, hamper: see Kluge. The ending is that of a freq. or dim.; but the phonology is obscure.]

1. *trans.* To obstruct the free movement of (man or beast), by fastening something on, or by material obstacles or entanglements; to fasten, bind, fetter, shackle, clog; to entangle, catch (*in* something).

c 1350 *Will. Palerne* 1115 Hampres him so harde, to sum cost þat he drawe. 1480 CAXTON *Chron. Eng.* ccxxiii. 220 We be now y lodged bytwene our enemyes and yf they mowe vs hampre ther is no bote but deth. *c* 1537 *Thersites* in Hazl. *Dodsley* I. 395, I will hamper some of the knaves in a bridle. 1600 J. PORY tr. *Leo's Africa* II. 418 They passe the nights in prisons..hampered and yoaked together like brute beasts. 1642 MILTON *Apol. Smect.* (1851) 267 Not contented to be caught in every other gin, but he must be such a novice, as to be still hamper'd in his owne hempe. 1725 DE FOE *Voy. round World* (1840) 339 He caused them to be hampered with ropes, and tied together. 1749 F. SMITH *Voy. Disc.* II. 231 At five we engaged with Ice..and were hampered in it until eleven. 1873 DAVIES *Mount. & Mere* ii. 11 The Carp were hampered in the rushes.

†**b.** To restrain by confinement.

c 1440 *Bone Flor.* 1175 Syr Emere..hamperde hym in hys holde. *c* 1470 HENRY *Wallace* VII. 446 Mad folk with fyr hampryt in mony hauld. 1583 STANYHURST *Æneis* I. (Arb.) 19 Where blusterus huzing Of wynds in Prison thee great king Æolus hampreth.

c. To derange (a lock or other mechanism) so as to impede its working.

1804 MISS S. LEE *Life of a Lover* VI. 264 (L.), I hampered the lock of the library door, so that I might be secure of interrupting those who should intrude themselves. 1860 W. COLLINS *Wom. White* III. x. 405 He has hampered the lock.

2. *fig.* and *gen.* To impede or obstruct in action; †**a.** to restrain, fetter (*obs.*); **b.** to entangle, encumber, or embarrass, with obstacles or difficulties. (Now the common use.)

c 1350 *Will. Palerne* 441 þat barne, For wham myn hert is so hampered. *Ibid.* 668 So loue now me hampris. ? *a* 1366 CHAUCER *Rom. Rose* 1493 That proude hertid Narcisus.. Myght on a day ben hampred so For love. *c* 1485 *Digby Myst.* (1882) III. 722, I am hampord with hate! 1548 UDALL *Erasm. Par. Luke* xxiv. (R.), To snibbe and hamper the hardenesse of herte that reigned in the people. 1612 *Proc. Virginia* 24 in *Capt. Smith's Wks.* (Arb.) 106 He so hampered their insolencies that they brought the 2 prisoners. 1654 TRAPP *Comm. Ps.* xxxiv. 13 The Tongue is an unruly member, and can hardly be hampered. 1775 SHERIDAN *Duenna* I. iv, If I could hamper him with this girl. 1812 WELLINGTON *Let. to Earl of Liverpool* 27 Mar. in Gurw. *Desp.* IX. 14, I believe no officer at the head of an army was ever so hampered. 1846 RUSKIN *Mod. Paint.* (1848) I. I. II. iii. §5. 41, I do not mean to hamper myself with any fine-spun theory. 1878 BOSW. SMITH *Carthage* 296 The duty of protecting her had often seriously hampered his movements. 1891 FREEMAN *Sk. fr. French Trav.* 117 The builder was hampered by the existence of aisles.

3. To tie up together, pack up; to put together into one bundle or parcel. (Cf. also HAMPER *v.*[3] 2.)

13.. *E.E. Allit. P.* B. 1284 þe golde of þe gazafylace.. Wyth alle þe vrnmentes of þat hous, he hamppred togeder. 1890 BOLDREWOOD *Col. Reformer* (1891) 198 The unconsidered trifles counted, priced, or hampered up together.

†**4.** *fig.* (with *up*) To fasten up, make fast. *Obs.*

c 1590 GREENE *Fr. Bacon* vi. 136 To avoid ensuing jars Ile hamper vp the match, Ile..wed you here.

Hence '**hampering** *vbl. sb.* and *ppl. a.*; also '**hamperer**, one who or that which hampers.

1812 L. HUNT in *Examiner* 21 Sept. 595/1 Fresh hamperings..with a new ally. *a* 1837 in Lockhart *Scott* xli. (1839) V. 352 *note*, Tis a sad hamperer of genius. 1861 WILSON & GEIKIE *Mem. E. Forbes* ii. 40 No hampering pecuniary restrictions were laid upon him in his early days.

'**hamper**, *v.*[2] *Obs.* exc. *dial.* [Derivation obscure.] To strike, beat. (*trans.* and *intr.*)

a 1529 SKELTON *Ware the Hauke* 325 Masyd, wytles, merry smyth, Hampar with your hammer, upon thy styth. *c* 1590 GREENE *Fr. Bacon* vii. 118 Out with your blades And hamper these jades. 1828 *Craven Dial.*, *Hamper*, to beat. 1847-78 HALLIWELL, *Hamper*, to beat. *North.*

'**hamper**, *v.*[3] [f. HAMPER *sb.*[1]: cf. the following passage in which there is a word-play on the sb.:

1603 DEKKER *Grissil* (Shaks. Soc.) 6 I'll hamper somebody if I die, because I am a basket-maker.]

1. *trans.* To load with hampers; to present with a hamper (*humorous*).

1725 BAILEY *Erasm. Colloq.* (1877) 325 (D.) One ass will carry at least three thousand such books, and I am persuaded you would be able to carry as many yourself, if you were well hampered. 1838 BRENTON *Life E. St. Vincent* II. ix. 155 It was a common expression with the receiving clerks in the dock yards, to say that 'they had not been hampered', as a reason for refusing to receive inferior articles into store..The 'hampering' meant a bribe in the shape of a hamper of wine [etc]. 1894 *Westm. Gaz.* 13 Dec. 3/3 There is something particularly charming in being 'hampered' at Christmas-time.

2. To pack in a hamper. (Cf. also HAMPER *v.*[1] 3.)

1775 ASH, *Hamper*..to put up in a hamper. 1846 in WORCESTER.

hampered ('hæmpəd), *ppl. a.* [f. HAMPER *v.*[1] + -ED[1].] Fettered, entangled, impeded, encumbered, embarrassed: see the verb.

1633 G. HERBERT *Temple, Home* xi, As an entangled, hamper'd thing. 1635 QUARLES *Embl.* III. xv. (1718) 186 These fleshly fetters, that so fast involve My hamper'd soul. 1890 BOLDREWOOD *Col. Reformer* (1891) 108 A toiling owner of a small station, a hampered purchaser of a larger one.

Hence '**hamperedly** *adv.*; '**hamperedness**.

1831 CARLYLE *Let.* in Froude *Life in Lond.* (1882) II. viii. 211 The worst thing about our establishment is its hamperedness. 1837 —— *Mirabeau* in *Misc. Ess.* (1888) V. 254 Count de Mirabeau 'rides in the garden of forty paces' with quick turns, hamperedly.

†'**hamperman**. *Obs.* **a.** An official in charge of the hamper or hanaper. **b.** A bearer of a hamper.

1526 *Househ. Ord.* 171 The said gentleman-usher, sewer, hampermen, groomes, pages, and yeomen ushers..to have the reversion of the said service. 1631 BRATHWAIT *Whimzies, Pedler* 140 Something he would gladly leave the young hamperman, his hopefull heire.

hampier, -ire, obs. ff. HAMPER *sb.*[1]

Hampshire ('hæmpʃə(r)). **a.** The name of a county in the south of England, used (chiefly *attrib.*) to designate a breed of sheep; also ***Hampshire Down***; also designating a breed of pig.

a 1661 T. FULLER *Worthies* (1662) Hants. 2 Hantshire Hoggs, are allowed by all for the best Bacon. 1813 C. VANCOUVER *Gen. View Agric. Hampshire* 371 The.. common Hampshire ewe will cost from 25*s.* to 40*s.* each. 1825 LOUDON *Encycl. Agric.* 1123/2 The heath sheep, old Hampshire, or Wilts breeds. 1875 *Encycl. Brit.* I. 392/2 These sheep are now usually classed as Sussex Downs and Hampshire Downs, the former being the most refined type of the class.., and the latter..having a heavier fleece, stronger bone, and somewhat coarser and larger frame. *Ibid.* 400/2 The Berkshire and Hampshire hog seems originally to have been from the same stock, but by some early cross acquired the thicker carcase, prick-ears, shorter limbs, and earlier maturity of growth, by which they are characterised. 1886 C. SCOTT *Sheep-farming* 12 The Hampshire Down, though a larger sheep than the Southdown, does not mature so early. 1957 *Encycl. Brit.* XVII. 920/1 The Hampshire breed [of pig] originated in England and was later introduced into the United States... Hampshires possess good growing and fattening qualities. 1962 J. N. WINBURNE *Dict. Agric.* 361/1 *Hampshire swine*, an American, lard-type breed of black, white-belted swine. 1971 *Farmers Weekly* 19 Mar. 77/4 It was a risky step to take from the viewpoint of ..Hampshire Down enthusiasts.

b. ***Hampshire hog***: a colloq. or derogatory term for a native of Hampshire; also, a dish of boiled bacon and vegetables.

[1622 DRAYTON *Polyolbion* II. xxiii. 70 As Hamshire long for her, hath had the tearme of Hogs.] *c* 1720 *Vade Mecum for Malt-Worms* I. 50 Now to the Sign of Fish let's jog, There to find out a Hampshire Hog. 1861 C. M. YONGE *Stokesley Secret* i. 9 'You could not be more right if you were a Hampshire hog,' said Sam. 1937 J. RAYNER *Shell Guide to Hampshire* 26/1 Hampshire Hog. You boil 4 to 5 lb. of bacon ..in an iron saucepan, keep the extracted bacon hot on the hob, and put..cabbages.. into the water... You can put potatoes in as well. *Ibid.* 30 There are three sorts of Hampshire hog, and they have given the county the subsidiary name of *Hoglandia*. One, the inhabitant of the county. Two, the less domestic animal from whose frequency the inhabitant gets his name... And three, the dish. 1944 in A. Wykes *Royal Hampshire Regiment* (1968) v. 104, I reckon us little lot of Hampshire Hogs have done well for his nibs Adolf in this invasion. 1963 C. MACKENZIE *My Life & Times* II. 169 She was a Dorset woman, and both she and her husband had a profound contempt for what they called the Hampshire hogs with whom they were condemned to live.

c. *pl.* The Royal Hampshire Regiment.

1904 *Westm. Gaz.* 14 June 8/2 The Hampshires, who mustered ten officers and 484 men. 1968 A. WYKES *Royal Hampshire Regiment* v. 107 The Hampshires, with..the Dorsets and Devons, were the three battalions of infantry forming one of the spearheads that was to land on the Arromanches beach.

Hampstead Heath ('hæmpstɛd hiːθ). The name of a district in north London, (*a*) used in *Rhyming Slang* to designate the teeth; also *Hampsteads*; (*b*) ***Hampstead Heath sailor*** (see quot. 1889).

1887 *Referee* 6 Nov. 7/3 She'd a Grecian 'I suppose', And of 'Hampstead Heath' two rows In her 'sunny south' that glistened Like two pretty strings of pearls. 1889 BARRÈRE & LELAND *Dict. Slang* I. 444/2 *Hampstead Heath sailor*.., a term of ridicule—no sailor at all. 1932 *Daily Express* 25 Jan. 6/6 (*heading*) 'Hampsteads' and 'Yobs'. A common expression for the feet is 'plates o' meat' and for the teeth 'Hampstead Heath'... These become simply 'plates' for feet and 'Hampsteads' for teeth. 1962 R. COOK *Crust on its Uppers* (1964) ii. 23 The rot had set in something horrible with her hampsteads and scotches.

hamseen, var. KHAMSIN.

hamshackle ('hæmʃæk(ə)l), *v.* [app. of Sc. or northern dial. origin; possibly f. radical *ham-*, as in HAMPER *v.*[1] + SHACKLE *v.*; but the first element also occurs as *hab-*, *hap-*, *hob-*, *hop-*.] *trans.* To shackle (a horse or cow) by a rope or strap connecting the head with one of the forelegs; hence *fig.* to fetter, curb, restrain.

1802 J. SIBBALD *Chron. Scot. Poetry* Gloss. (Jam.) *Hamschakel*, to fasten the head of a horse or cow to one of its fore legs, to prevent its wandering too far in an open wild. 1825 BROCKETT *N.C. Gloss.*, *Hamshackle*, to fasten the head of an animal to one of its forelegs. Vicious cows and oxen are often so tied, especially when driven to slaughter. 1847 in CRAIG. 1864 in WEBSTER.

hamsoken, -sokne, obs. ff. HAMESUCKEN.

hamster ('hæmstə(r)). Also 6 **hamester**, 9 **hampster**. [a. Ger. *hamster*; so in MHG.; OHG. had *hamastro* masc., OS. *hamstra* fem., corn-weevil.]

A species of rodent (*Cricetus frumentarius*) allied to the mouse and rat, found in parts of Europe and Asia; it is of a stout form, about 10 inches long, and has cheek-pouches in which it carries the grain with which it stores its burrows; it hibernates during the winter. Also applied to other pouched rodents allied to or resembling this.

1607 TOPSELL *Four-f. Beasts* (1658) 413 The skins of Hamsters are very durable. 1744 GOLDSM. *Nat. Hist.* (1862) I. VI. i. 454 The Cricetus, or German rat, which Mr. Buffon calls the hamster. 1849 *Sk. Nat. Hist.*, *Mammalia* IV. 69 Fortunately for England the hamster is not indigenous within the precincts of the island. 1886 *Edin. Rev.* Apr. 350 Dormice and hamsters are found in the stony region South of Judea.

b. Also ***hamster-mouse***, ***-rat***.

1607 TOPSELL *Four-f. Beasts* (1658) 411 *heading*, Of the Hamester-mouse. 1829 E. JESSE *Jrnl. Nat.* 151 The hairs of the hamster mouse..have a central perforation, apparently uninterrupted throughout their whole length. 1853 KINGSLEY *Hypatia* xviii, You purblind old hamster-rat.

c. The fur of the hamster.

1895 *Spectator* 23 Nov. 722/1 Lining-furs, such as squirrel, hampster, musk-rat.

hamstring ('hæmstrɪŋ), *sb.* [f. HAM *sb.*[1] + STRING *sb.*]

a. In human anatomy, one of the tendons (four inner and one outer) which form the sides of the ham or space at the back of the knee; they are the tendons of the semimembranosus, semitendinosus, gracilis, sartorius, and biceps muscles of the thigh. **b.** In quadrupeds, the great tendon at the back of the 'knee' or hough in the hind leg; it is the *tendo Achillis*, corresponding to that of the heel in man.

1565 GOLDING *Ovid's Met.* II. (1593) 53 Hir hamstrings and her knees were stiffe. **1600** HOLLAND *Livy* 462 (R.) Wounding their backes, and cutting their hamstrings. **1688** R. HOLME *Armoury* III. 293/1 A Leg of Veal or Mutton hung by the Ham String on a Hook. **1804** ABERNETHY *Surg. Obs.* 260, I also drew the integuments gently towards the inner ham-string.

hamstring ('hæmstrɪŋ), *v.* Pa. t. and pple. -stringed (-strɪŋd), -strung (-strʌŋ). [f. prec. sb.]

1. *trans.* To cut the hamstrings of, so as to lame or disable; also to cut the muscle or tendons of the small of the whale.

1675 PRIDEAUX *Lett.* (Camden) 33 If they should know this to, they would hamstring me. **1831** YOUATT *Horse* i. (1847) 4 The Israelites were commanded to hough or ham-string the horses that were taken in war. **1865** *Reader* 17 June 676 Poor Cyrill Lucar was ham-stringed by order of the Sultan in 1638.

2. *transf.* and *fig.* To disable as if by hamstringing; to cripple, destroy the activity or efficiency of.

1641 MILTON *Reform.* II. (1851) 47 So have they hamstrung the valour of the Subject by seeking to effeminate us all at home. *a* **1678** MARVELL *Poems, Damon the Mower*, Ham-stringed frogs can dance no more. **1719** T. GORDON *Cordial Low Spirits* I. 129 A Reason sufficient, why Oaths ought not to Hamstring the Ambassadors. **1858** CARLYLE *Fredk. Gt.* III. ii. (1865) I. 144 Thought all hamstrung, shrivelled by inveterate rheumatism.

hamular ('hæmjulə(r)), *a.* [f. L. *hāmul-us* small hook + -AR.] Of the form of a small hook; hooked; applied *spec.* in *Anat.* to processes of certain bones.

1839–47 TODD *Cycl. Anat.* III. 271/2 The Pterygoid processes.. present in each of these species distinct hamular processes. **1854** OWEN *Skel.* in *Circ. Sc.* I. 249 A hamular process is sent off from the head of the tibia and fibula.

hamulate ('hæmjuːlət), *a.* [f. as prec. + -ATE.] **a.** *Bot.* Having a small hook at the tip (*Syd. Soc. Lex.* 1886); also = HAMULOSE, a. **b.** *Anat.* = HAMULAR.

hamule ('hæmjuːl). [ad. L. *hāmulus* small hook, dim. of *hāmus* hook.] = HAMULUS.

1847 CRAIG, *Hamule*, in Anatomy, any little crookedlike process.

hamulose (hæmjuː'ləʊs), *a. Bot.* [f. L. *hāmul-us* small hook + -OSE.] **a.** Covered with little hooked hairs or bristles. **b.** Having a small hook, hamulate.

1860 in WORCESTER (citing GRAY). **1866** in *Treas. Bot.* **1886** in *Syd. Soc. Lex.*

hamulous ('hæmjuːləs), *a. Bot.* [f. as prec. + -OUS.] = prec.

1684 tr. *Bonet's Merc. Compit.* VIII. 279 Take the hamulous Pericarpium of the Teazle.

‖**hamulus** ('hæmjuːləs). Pl. **hamuli** (-aɪ). [L. *hāmulus*, dim. of *hāmus* a hook.]

a. *Anat.*, *Zool.*, and *Bot.* A small hook or hook-like process, as in certain bones, in feathers, etc.; in *Bot.* a hooked bristle. **b.** *Obstetric Surg.* A hook-shaped instrument for extracting the fœtus.

1727–51 in CHAMBERS *Cycl.* **1855** HOLDEN *Hum. Osteol.* (*1878*) *101* The external or orbital surface has a vertical ridge upon it which terminates below in a small lancet-like process or tongue, termed hamulus. **1886** *Syd. Soc. Lex.*, *Hamulus* .. The hook-like portion of the pterygoid process of the sphenoid bone. Also, a term for the unciform bone.

hamur, hamyr, obs. ff. HAMMER.

[**hamylone**, in *Rel. Ant.* I. 154, error for *hauylone*, HAVELON *sb.*]

hamyne = *amen*, AIM *v.*

1530 in PALSGR. 577/2.

Han (hæn). Designating a Chinese dynasty (206 B.C.–220 A.D.) marked by the introduction of Buddhism, the extension of Chinese rule over Mongolia, the revival of letters, and increase of wealth and culture.

1736 R. BROOKES tr. *Du Halde's Gen. Hist. China* I. 346 (*heading*) The Fifth Dynasty, called *Han*, which had twenty-five Emperors in the Space of 426 Years. **1837** *Penny Cycl.* VII. 81/1 About the year 201 B.C., the race of Tsin was succeeded by that of Hân, which filled one of the most celebrated periods of Chinese history. **1876** *Encycl. Brit.* V. 644/1 Lew Pang was then proclaimed emperor (206 B.C.) under the title of Kaou-te, and the new line was styled the Han dynasty. **1930** *Times Lit. Suppl.* 2 Oct. 774/3 The majority seem to reflect the Han style... Two famous homonymous generals who flourished under the Han dynasty. **1935** A. TOYNBEE *Study of Hist.* (ed. 2) II. 373 The Han Empire and the Kushan Empire marched with one another in Central Asia for at least a century. **1971** *Ashmolean Mus. Rep. of Visitors 1970* 51 Imperial seals of the 17th and 18th centuries as well as some early Han types.

han = *haven*, obs. inf. and pres. t. pl. of HAVE *v.*

Han, obs. form of KHAN.

han', Sc. form of HAND *sb.* and *v.*

Hanafite ('hænəfaɪt). Also Hanef-, -ifite. [f. Arab. *ḥanafī* (f. *Ḥanīfah* personal name) + -ITE.] A member of one of the four sects or schools of the Sunnites or orthodox Muslims, following the rite of Abu Hanīfah of Kufah (*c* 700–770). Also *attrib.* or *adj.*

[**1738** J. PITTS *Relig. & Mann. Mahometans* 57 The Hamifees.. put their Hands on their Belly. **1841** LANE *Arab. Nts.* I. 17 This class consists of four sects, Hanafees, Sháfe'ees, Málikees, and Hambelees.] **1880** *Libr. Univ. Knowl.* VII. 292 Hanifah.. founder of the Hanifites, the oldest of the sects of Mohammedans considered orthodox. **1887** *Encycl. Brit.* XXII. 661/1 The Hanafite rite is official in the Turkish empire.

‖**hanami** (hanami). [Jap.] (See quots.).

1891 A. M. BACON *Jap. Girls & Women* x. 295 The *hanami*, or picnic to famous places to view certain flowers as they bloom in their season. **1902** L. HEARN *Kottō* x. 97 All of us.. should make up a party, and enjoy our *hanami* together. **1965** W. SWAAN *Jap. Lantern* iv. 47 This collection is suitable for such festive occasions as *hanami* (flower- and more particularly cherry-blossom-viewing).

†**hanap** ('hænəp). *Obs.* exc. *Hist.* [a. OF. *hanap* (= Prov. *enap*), drinking-vessel, cup, ciborium:—O Frankish **hnapp-* = OHG. *hnapf*, *napf* = OE. *hnæp*, *hnæpp*, Du. *nap*, cup, bowl, basin.] A drinking-vessel, a wine-cup or goblet. Now applied, as an antiquarian term, to mediæval goblets of ornate character.

1494 FABYAN *Chron.* VII. 540 Kyng Rycharde gaue vnto the Frenshe Kyng an hanap or basyn of golde, wᵗ an ewir to the same. **1530** PALSGR. 54 *Hanap* is olde romant, though I fynde it used in Froissart. **1823** SCOTT *Quentin D.* iv, He had indeed four siluer hanaps of his own. **1853** SOYER *Pantroph.* 365 Charles the Bald gave to the Abbey of St. Denis a hanap, said to have belonged to Solomon. **1879** C. DICKENS *Dict. Lond.* (1884) 25/1 A.. collection of mazers and hanaps and cups. **1894** *Times* 19 July 4/4 A silver-gilt bulb hanap and cover, on three feet formed as draped male figures on diamond-shaped plinths.. German, end of the 15th century.

hanaper ('hænəpə(r)). *Obs.* exc. *Hist.* Also 5 **hanypere, hanapre**, 7 **haniper, hanper**. [a. OF. *hanapier* case to hold a hanap: see prec. and HAMPER *sb.*[1]]

†**1.** A case for a hanap or hanaps; a plate-basket; a repository for treasure or money. Cf. HAMPER *sb.* 1. (In quot. 1570–6 perh. transferred from 3.)

[**1380** *Thorne's Chron.* (Du C.), Hi 4 bacini in uno Hanaperio. Item undecim ciphi argentei.. cum suis hanaperiis.] *c* **1440** *Promp. Parv.* 226/1 Hanypere [*c* **1490** *MS. K.* hamper], *canistrum, cartallus.* **1570–6** LAMBARDE *Peramb. Kent* (1826) 285 The yeerely maintenance thereof [the Chapel at Hakington] was to be drawn from the same Hanaper [St. Thomas's offerings at Canterbury] and to be bestowed on certain Secular Chanons.

2. A round wicker case or small basket in which documents were kept: see quots. and references.

[**1292** *Indenture* 30 Dec. in *Stat. Scotl.* I. 117 (*red*) Item vij Haneparios quos magister Thomas de Karnoto olim Cancellarius Scocie misit.. In quorum uno haneperio ixˣˣ & xvij littere, etc. **1323–4** *Bp. Stapleton's Kalendar* 17 Edw. II. lf. 59 In hanaperio de Virgis, ad hoc signum.. Carte et scripta de feoffamentis & donacionibus Regis Anglie [242 Documents]. **1768** BLACKSTONE *Comm.* III. 49. **1796** J. ANSTEY *Pleader's Guide* (1803) 45 The Writ Original.. Which erst in mouldy hamper slept By Lawyers Hanaper yclept. **1836** PALGRAVE *Antient Kal. & Inv.* (Rec. Comm.) I. Introd. 28 Upon a recent inspection of a bag of deeds.. I found that it contained the hanaper so described.. and within the hanaper were all the several deeds with their seals in the highest state of preservation. **1838** *Blackw. Mag.* XLIII. 658 Surprised that you should rake up such rubbish as this from the old hanapers of empiricism. **1891** HUBERT HALL tr. *Memorand. Scacc. 42 Ed. III* in *Antiq. & Curios. of Exch.* ii. 53. **1891** SCARGILL-BIRD *Guide Documents in P.R.O.* Introd. 13.

3. The department of the Chancery, into which fees were paid for the sealing and enrolment of charters and other documents. Abolished by Statute 2 & 3 Wm. IV, c. 11 (1832).

So called, according to some, because documents that had passed the Great Seal were here kept *in hanaperio*, in a hanaper (sense 2), until the fees thereon were paid; others have taken the name as orig. applied (in sense 1) to the *fiscus* in which the money thus accruing was itself kept: so Du Cange, s.v. *Hanaperium*.

***Clerk, Controller, Warden of the Hanaper*:** see quots.

[**1314** in *Red Bk. Exch.* (Rolls) 920 Qe le Clerk del Hanaper de notre Grant Seal rende son acounte a notre Escheqier. **1326** *Ibid.* 932 Les acountes.. des issues du seal de la Chauncellerie par le clerk gardeyn del Hanaper. **1350** *Close Roll 24 Edw. III* in Rymer *Foedera* (1825) III. I. 196 Rex dilecto clerico suo.. custodi hanaperii cancellariæ nostræ. **1433** *Rolls of Parlt.* IV. 433 Status Reventionum.. Regni.. De Exitibus Hanaperii.. M·viᶜ·Lxviijli. iijs. iiijd.] **1455** *Rolls of Parlt.* V. 317/1 That this.. Acte.. be not prejudiciall.. to the clarke of oure Hanaper. *a* **1483** *Liber Niger* in *Househ. Ord.* (1790) 29 Twyce in every yere the clerke of the hanapre should calle a newe householde rolle oute of the King's countynghouse. **1534** *Act 26 Hen VIII*, c. 3 §2 And that the said clarke of the Hanaper shall make a true and juste accompte thereof [sc. of the moneys received for first-fruits, etc.], as he is bounde to do of the money receyved of the profites of the Kings greate seale. **1536** *Statutes Irel. 28 Hen. VIII* (Bolton, 1621, 108) The writings obligatorie or money taken for the same shall rest, remaine, and abide in the hands of the underthesaurer, or in the Hanaper of the kings Chauncerie in Ireland. **1607** DAVIES *Lett. Earl Salisb.* i. (1787) 233 The commission was drawn and sealed in the haniper. **1607** COWELL *Interpr.*, Haneper of the Chauncerie, anno 10 R. 2. cap. prim., seemeth to signifie as *fiscus* originally doth in Latine. —— *Ibid.*, Clerk of the hamper or hanaper.. is an officer in Chawncerie .. otherwise called warden of the hamper.. whose function is to receiue al the mony due to the kings maiestie, for the seales of charters, patents, commissions, and writs, as also feese due to the officers for enrolling and examining the same. *Ibid.*, Controller of the hamper.. which is an officer in the Chauncerie attending on the Lord Chaunceler or Keeper daily in the terme time... His office is to take all things sealed from the clerke of the hanaper.. and to enter the same into a speciall booke. **1720** STRYPE *Stow's Surv.* (1754) I. II. ii. 354/1 They recieve it [their rent of five marks] very duly, either out of the Exchequer, or Hanaper even until this present. **1768** BLACKSTONE *Comm.* III. 49. **1842** *Act 5 & 6 Vict.* c. 103 §1 The following Offices of the High Court of Chancery, namely, the Offices of Clerks of the Enrolments.. Comptrollers of the Hanaper.. are hereby abolished. **1845** LD. CAMPBELL *Chancellors* (1857) I. Introd. 6 The place where the Chancellor carried on his business.. was divided between the 'Hanniper' or hamper, in which writs were stored up; and the 'Petty Bag'.

hanapoot, var. HANEPOOT.

‖**hanashika** (hanaʃika). [Jap.] A professional story-teller.

1891 A. M. BACON *Jap. Girls & Women* x. 294 Public halls, where professional story-tellers, the *hanashika*, night after night, relate long stories to crowded audiences. **1936** K. NOHARA *True Face of Japan* v. 120 A *hanashika*, or story teller, is telling innocent stories.

†**'hanaster, 'hanster.** *Obs.* Also 4 **hauncer**, ? 5 **handster, -ester.** [The earliest form cited by Brian Twyne from Oxford City documents is *hauncer*; *hanster* occurs in 14–15th c.; *handester* is mentioned by Twyne as also found by him; the usual form after 1500 was *hanaster*, latinized *hanasterius*. The earlier forms *hauncer*, *hanster*, favour the view that the word was a derivative of *hansa* or *hanse*: cf. esp. *hansing* s.v. HANSE.] The name given (in the city of Oxford) to persons paying the entrance-fee of the guild-merchant (see HANSE 2), and admitted as Freeman of the City.

1321–2 *Oxf. City Doc.*, in *Twyne's MSS.* XXIII. 241 [in *Rot. Comp. Camerariorum* de anno xvº Regis Edw. II.] Item, summa recᵗ des Hauncers hoc anno vij li. xi s. **1393** *Ibid.* [In *Rot. Comp. Camerar.* de an. 17º Ric. II.] Item recept, de admissis in gilda hoc anno 17 li. 2s. **1399** *Ibid.* [In alio rentali sive computo de 23º Ric. II.] Item recept. de Hansters hoc anno 7 li. 2s. 6d. **1410** [in *Rot. Comp.* de xiº Henr. IV] Comput. de Hansteris hoc anno 14 li xis. 6d. **1519** *Title of List* in Turner *Select. Rec. Oxford* 23 Hanasterii ibidem tempore Johannis Traves maioris, Walteri Gover et Johannis Kyng Camerariorum, Anno regni regis Henrici Octavi undecimo. *c* **1608** BRYAN TWYNE *MSS. Collecta* XXIII. 241 (*Note* to quot. 1399) *Hansters*, sive ut alibi legitur ibidem *Handesters*.. Conjicio autem hoc vocabulo denotari illos quos frequentius illic vocari observavimus *Intrantes* sive *Admissos* eo anno *in gildæ Aulam.* [margin] *Hansters* et *Hanasters*, et sunt apprentitii ad libertatem civitatis vocati, et ita dicuntur Oxoniæ hodierno die, vocabulo ab Hanse deriuato. **1887** C. W. BOASE *Oxford* 44 In the sixteenth century they [the chamberlains] were still joined with the mayor in admitting the new hanasters or members of the trading corporation. **1890** GROSS *Gild Merchant* II. 194 Oxford.. Those admitted to the Gild or freedom seem to have borne the name 'hanasters'. Among the town muniments there is a book containing lists of the latter.

'Hanbalite. Also Ham-. [f. Arab. *ḥanbalī* (f. pers. name *Hanbal*) + -ITE.] A member of the strictest of the four sects of orthodox Muslims, following the rite of Ahmad Ibn Hanbal (A.D. 780–855). Also *attrib.* or *adj.*

[**1841** (*Hambelee*) see HANAFITE. **1865** W. G. PALGRAVE *C. & E. Arabia*, Those of the Hanbalee sect.] **1886** BLOUNT *Dict. Sects* 283/1 Four sects, named after their founders, Hanifites, Malekites, Shafeites, and Hanbalites, who differ in some unimportant points of ritual and Koranic interpretation. **1887** *Encycl. Brit.* XXII. 661/1 The *Hanbalites*, whose system is the strictest, have practically disappeared in the *Málikites*.

hance (hɑːns, -æ-), *sb.* Also 6 **hawnce, hawnse, haunse**, 7 **haanse**, 6–9 **hanse, haunce.** [perh. a. AF. **haunce* = OF. *hauce*, *haulce*, later *hausse* rise, elevation, raised part, f. *hausser* see HANCE *v.*]

†**1.** The lintel of a door or window. *Obs.*

1534 MORE *On the Passion* Wks. 1295/2 He commaunded .. they shoulde bysprincle the postes and the hawnce of their doores with the bloud of the lambe. *Ibid.* 1297/2 Marke ourselfe.. in the hawnce of oure foreheade, wyth the letter of *Tau.* **1552** HULOET, Haunce of a dore or other lyke, *limen .. supercilium.* **1585** HIGINS tr. *Junius' Nomenclator* 213/2 *supercilium*.. the hanse of a doore. **1611** COTGR., *Claveau* .. the Haunse, or Lintell of a doore. **1618** [see 5].

2. *Naut.* **a.** A curved rise from a lower to a higher part, as of the fife-rails or bulwarks from the waist to the quarter-deck. Also erroneously *hanch* or *haunch*. **b.** = HAUNCH.

(Viewed from the 'higher part', the ' rise' was a fall or descent; hence, the explanation in Harris and later Dicts.)

1637 HEYWOOD *Royal Ship* 41 Upon the Hances of the waste are foure Figures. **1664** E. BUSHNELL *Compl. Shipwright* 11 Then set off the Tumbling Home, at the Height of the two first Haanses. **1710** J. HARRIS *Lex. Techn.*, *Hances* (in a Ship) are Falls or Descents of the Fife-Rails, which are placed on Banisters on the poop, Quarter-Deck, &c., down to the Gangway. *c* **1850** *Rudim. Navig.* (Weale) 123 *Hance* or *hanch.* A sudden fall or break, as from the drifts forward and aft to the waist. Also those breaks in the rudder, &c., at the parts where it suddenly becomes narrower. **1867** SMYTH *Sailor's Word-bk.*, *Hances*, spandrels; the falls or descents of fife-rails.

3. *Arch.* The arc of smaller radius at the springing of an elliptical or many-centred arch. Now usually viewed as the 'haunch' of the arch, and often so spelt: cf. HAUNCH.

1703 MOXON *Mech. Exerc.* 33 A part of the Ellipsis..which is called the *Hanse*; The other part..is called the *Scheam.* **1725** W. HALFPENNY *Sound Building* 9 If the Arch is required to be quicker or flatter on the Hanse. **1828** J. M. SPEARMAN *Brit. Gunner* (ed. 2) 269 The exterior surface is formed by two planes touching the curvé on the hances, and meeting in a ridge over the vertex of the arch.

b. (See quot.)

1842–76 GWILT *Archit.* Gloss., *Hance*, the small arch which often joins a straight lintel to a jamb. Hence the term *Hance arch.*

†**4.** *transf.* A curved or rounded part of a body. Cf. HAUNCH. *Obs. rare.*

1778 *Phil. Trans.* LXVIII. I. 69 The last shot..struck..against a former shot..with the hance of its end so as to flatten it in that part.

5. *Comb.*, as **hance-head** = 1.

1618 in Willis & Clark *Cambridge* (1886) I. 207 The Jawmes and munions to be of white stone with hance heads also of white stone. **1886** *Ibid.* 112 The arches, or hanse-heads, were cut out of the window-heads, which are now square at the top.

Hence **hanced** *a.*, provided with a hance.

1886 WILLIS & CLARK *Cambridge* III. 555 Rectangular windows divided by monials into two or three lights, each light being 'hansed' or arch-headed.

†**hance**, *v.* *Obs.* Forms: 4–6 **haunce**, 4–7 **hauns(e**, 5 **hawnce**, 6 **haunsh**, 6–7 **hance**. [app. a. AF. **hauncer* for OF. *haucer*, *haulcer* (F. *hausser*) to raise. Cf. ENHANCE.] *trans.* To raise, lift, elevate, exalt; = ENHANCE 1. 2.

1303 R. BRUNNE *Handl. Synne* 12436 Alle þese kalle men 'cyrcumstaunces' þat vn to þe grete dede men haunces. **1382** WYCLIF *Ps.* xxxvi[i]. 35 The vnpitouse aboue hauncid. *c* **1440** *Jacob's Well* (E.E.T.S.) 121 To ben haunsyd in hyȝe estate. *c* **1440** *Promp. Parv.* 230/2 Hawncyn, or heynyn ..*exalto, elevo, sublevo.* ? *a* **1500** *Chester Pl.* (E.E.T.S.) v. 424 He haunshed our kinde on high. *Ibid.* vi. 98 Meeke also he haunsed has. *c* **1500** *Melusine* xlix. 326 Or euer the geaunt myght have haunced his Clubbe. **1513** MORE in Grafton *Chron.* (1568) II. 791 Every thing was haunsed above the measure. **1583** STANYHURST *Æneis* IV. (Arb.) 110 Yt toe the skytyp is haunced.

b. (?) To excite with liquor, 'elevate'.

1630 J. TAYLOR (Water P.) *Trav.* Wks. III. 78/1 At the Table..every man did his best endeauour to hauns mee for my welcome. [Cf. NARES s.v. *Hanced.*]

Hence † **'hancing** *vbl. sb.*, raising, elevation.

1382 WYCLIF *Jer.* xlix. 16 Thin owne hauncyng desceyuede thee. **1589** *Pappe w. Hatchet* (1844) 36 The hogshead was euen come to the hauncing, and nothing could be drawn from him but dregs.

hancel, obs. form of HANDSEL.

†**hancenhede.** *Obs.* In 4 **haun-.** [app. a deriv. of HANCE *v.*; as if f. a ppl. adj. **hauncen* + *-hede*, -HEAD.] The condition of being 'lifted up'; pride, haughtiness.

1303 R. BRUNNE *Handl. Synne* 5164 þe fyrst ys ouer moche drede, þe touþer ys proude hauncenhede.

hanch (hɑːnʃ, -æ-), *v.* Now chiefly *Sc.* Also 6 **hantch**, 7 **haunsh**, 9 **hansh.** [a. obs. F. *hancher* 'to gnashe or snatch at with the teeth' Cotgr.] *trans.* and *intr.* To snatch, snap at, or bite with violent or noisy action of the jaws; said of large dogs, wild beasts, cannibals, or greedy men.

a **1400–50** *Alexander* 774* þar liggez lymmes of laddes, leggez and harmes..Som hanchyd of þe heued, som þe handez etyn. **1535** COVERDALE *Ps.* vii. 2 Lest he hanch vp my soule like a lyon. —— *Isa.* v. 29 They shal roare, and hanch vp the praye. *a* **1662** R. BAILLIE *Lett.* (1841) I. 252 A number greidilie hanshit at the argument..bot came not near the matter. **1808–25** JAMIESON, *Hansh.* **1834** M. SCOTT *Cruise Midge* (1863) 38 Several men had been terribly torn by the Blood-hounds who..stood gasping and barking and hanching at us, at the entrance of the opening.

Hence **hanch**, *sb. Sc.*, a voracious snap.

1808–18 in JAMIESON. **1880** *Antrim & Down Gloss.* s.v., 'The dog made a hanch at me.'

hanch, hanck, obs. ff. HAUNCH, HANK.

hanckleth, obs. Sc. form of ANKLE *sb.*

c **1538** LYNDESAY *Syde Taillis* 123 Syder nor may thair hancklethis hyde. **1596** DALRYMPLE tr. *Leslie's Hist. Scot.* I. 94 Thair cotes war syd evin to the hanckleth.

hancockite ('hænkɒkaɪt). *Min.* [f. the name of E. P. *Hancock* (*c* 1834–1916), American artist and amateur mineralogist, who discovered it: see -ITE[1].] A variety of epidote rich in strontium and lead.

1899 PENFIELD & WARREN in *Amer. Jrnl. Sci.* CLVIII. 339 (*heading*) Hancockite. *Ibid.* 343 A considerable quantity of hancockite was taken from the mine at one time, and it is the most abundant of the new species described in this paper. It is named after Mr. E. P. Hancock of Burlington, N.J. **1900** *Jrnl. Chem. Soc.* LXXVIII. II. 88 Hancockite. This occurs as brownish-red, cellular masses of minute, lath-shaped crystals, which are mono-clinic. **1968** I. KOSTOV *Mineral.* 309 Hancockite contains Pb and Sr.

hand (hænd), *sb.* Forms: *α.* 1–5 **hond**, 4 **hoond(e**, 4–6 **honde.** *β.* 1– **hand**, 4 **haunde**, 4–7 **hande.** *Plural. α.* 1 **honda**, 2–4 **honde**, 4 **hond**; 1 **handa**, 2–4 **hande.** *β.* 2–5 **honden**, (2 -**an**, 5 -**on**). *γ.* 4 **heind**, 4–5 **hend**, **hende.** *δ.* 3–6 **hondes.** 4–5 -**is**, 5 -**us**, -**s**; 4–7 **handes**, 5 -**us**, 5–6 -**is**, -**ys**, 4– **hands.** [Com. Teut.: OE. *hand*, *hǫnd*, fem. *u*-stem, pl. *-a*, = OFris. *hand*, *hond* (pl. *honda*), OS. *hand* (pl. *hendi*), OHG. *hant* (pl. *henti*), ON. *hǫnd* (genit. *handar*, pl. *hendr*), Goth. *handus* (pl. *handjus*). Regarded by some as belonging to Goth. *-hinþan*, pa. pple. *-hunþans* to seize; but this is doubtful. The original OE. pl. *handa*, ME. *hande*, was (like other plurals in *-e*), superseded in ME. by *handen*, and this eventually by *handes*, *hands.* Northern Eng. had in 14–15th c. an umlaut-plural *hend* from Norse.]

A. Illustration of the plural forms.

α. *c* **1000** *Ags. Gosp.* John xx. 20 He æt-ywde him his handa [*Lindisf.* ða hónd, *Rushw.* hond], and his sidan. *c* **1160** HATTON *Gosp.* Matt. iv. 6 On heora hande. *c* **1175** *Lamb. Hom.* 149 His fet and his honde. *c* **1200** ORMIN 14673 Abraham..band itt fét & hande. *a* **1300** *K. Horn* 112 Wringinde here honde. *c* **1330** *Amis & Amil.* 156 Therto thai held vp her hond. *c* **1380** *Sir Ferumb.* 2658 He hew of heuedes, armes, and haunde.

β. *c* **1160** *Hatton Gosp.* John xx. 20 He ateowede heom hys handen. *c* **1175** *Lamb. Hom.* 23 His fet and his hondan. *Ibid.* 91 Heo setten heore honden [101 here hondan] ofer ilefde men. *c* **1290** *S. Eng. Leg.* I. 10/304 Oþur heore hondene oþur baþeden al. *c* **1400** A. DAVY *Dreams* 95 He vnneiled his honden two. *c* **1420** *Chron. Vilod.* 1224 My hondon and my fete.

γ. *a* **1300** *Cursor M.* 3566 His hend [*v.rr.* hende, handes, hondes] vnquemli for to quak. *Ibid.* 17142 (Gött.) Take vte mi herte bituix þi heind [*Cott.* hend]. **1340** HAMPOLE *Pr. Consc.* 3214 Bunden by hend and fete. *c* **1400** MAUNDEV. (Roxb.) ii. 5 þe pece..to þe whilk his hend ware nailed. *c* **1460** *Towneley Myst.* (Surtees) 7 God has maide man with his hend. *c* **1475** *Babees Bk.* 200 Somme holde the clothe, somme poure vpon his hende.

δ. *c* **1205** LAY. 10187 Heo letten heom draȝen vt oðer bi hondes oðer bi fot. *a* **1300** *Cursor M.* 3678 Sco..couerd þar-wit his hands [*v. rr.* handis, handes, hondes] als. **1382** WYCLIF *2 Sam.* xvii. 2 The hoondis feblid. *c* **1400** *Apol. Loll.* 28 þe handus leyd vpon. *c* **1430** *Stans Puer* 22 in *Babees Bk.* 29 þin hondis waische also. **1535** COVERDALE *Ps.* lxxxvii[i]. 9, I..stretch out my hondes vnto the.

B. Signification.

General arrangement. I. The simple word. *The member, its use, its position, 1–6. ** As representing the person, 7–10. *** As put for its capacity or performance, 11–17. **** Something like a hand, 18–22. ***** That which is held in the hand, 23–24. II. Phrases. * With governing preposition, 25–36. ** With verb and preposition, 37–42. *** With governing verb, 43–47. **** With qualifying adjective, 48–52. ***** With an adverb, 53–55. ****** With another noun, 56–61. ******* Proverbial phrases and locutions, 62. III. Attributive uses and Combinations, 63–65.

I. The simple word. * *The member, its action, its position, its symbolic use.*

1. The terminal part of the arm beyond the wrist, consisting of the palm and five digits, forming the organ of prehension characteristic of man. The name is also given to the similar members forming the terminations of all four limbs in the quadrumanous animals or monkeys.

c **825** *Vesp. Psalter* cxxvi[i]. 4 Strelas in honda mæhtȝes. *Ibid.* cxxviii[i]. 7 Ne ȝefylleð hond his se ripeð. *c* **1000** *Ags. Voc.* in Wr.-Wülcker 264/32 *Manus*, hand. *c* **1250** *Gen. & Ex.* 3336 Moyses hield up his hond. *c* **1386** CHAUCER *Prol.* 107 In his hand [*v.rr.* hond, honde] he baar a myghty bowe. *c* **1460** *Towneley Myst.* (Surtees) 125, I bryng rekyls..Here in myn hende. **1548** HALL *Chron.*, *Edw. IV*, 234 Then eche Prince layed his right hand on yᵉ Missal, and his left hand on the holy Crosse, and toke there a solempne othe. **1601** R. JOHNSON *Kingd. & Commw.* (1603) 108 As long as their hands were able to holde a penne. **1700** T. BROWN tr. *Fresny's Amusem. Ser. & Com.* 67 Here walk'd a French Fop with both his Hands in his Pockets. **1817** COLERIDGE *Sibyl. Leaves* (1862) 215 And when the Vicar joined their hands, Her limbs did creep and freeze. **1828** STARK *Elem. Nat. Hist.* I. 31 This opposition of a fifth member to the other four constitutes what is properly called the *hand.* **1842** TENNYSON *Break, Break, Break* iii, O for the touch of a vanish'd hand. **1863** HUXLEY *Man's Place Nat.* ii. 90 The Gorilla's hand is clumsier, heavier, and has a thumb somewhat shorter in proportion than that of a man; but no one has ever doubted its being a true hand.

b. The terminal part of the fore-limb in quadrupeds, esp. when prehensile; the fore-foot. Also more widely applied to the terminal part of any limb of an animal when prehensile. In *Anat.* and *Zool.*, the terminal part of the 'arm' or fore-limb in all vertebrates above fishes; also applied to the prehensile claw or chela in crustaceans, and formerly to the tarsus of the anterior leg in insects.

1382 WYCLIF *Prov.* xxx. 28 A lisard with hondis cleueth. **1535** COVERDALE *Ibid.*, The spyder laboureth with hir handes. **1607** TOPSELL *Four-f. Beasts* (1658) 341 [A hyæna] coming to a Man asleep in a Sheep-cot, by laying her left hand or fore-foot to his mouth, made or cast him into a deed-sleep. **1639** T. BRUGIS tr. *Camus' Mor. Relat.* 159 The Lizard..raceth out with her tayle, the markes which with her hands she printed in the sand. **1727–51** CHAMBERS *Cycl.*, *Hand*, in falconry, is used for the foot of the hawk..*Hand*, in the manage..sometimes..stands for the fore-feet of an horse. **1852** DANA *Crust.* I. 428 Hands subtuberculate.

†**c.** *transf.* The whole arm. *Obs.*

1615 CROOKE *Body of Man* 728 The vpper ioyntes are called by the common name of the *Hand*, for the Ancients accounted the whole member from the shoulder to the fingers ends to bee all the Hand. **1661** LOVELL *Hist. Anim. & Min.* 302 The limbs are divided into the hands and feet, and the hand into the shoulder, cubit, and extremity. **1727–51** CHAMBERS *Cycl.* s.v., The hand, among anatomists, extends from the shoulder to the fingers ends: this is called also the *greater hand.*

†**d.** The trunk of an elephant. *Obs.*

1607 TOPSELL *Four-f. Beasts* (1658) 162 They reverence the Sun rising, holding up their trunck or hand to heaven. [**1843** MACAULAY *Lays, Prophecy of Capys* xxiv, The beast who hath between his eyes The serpent for a hand.] **1859** TENNYSON *Vivien* 576 The brutes of mountain back..with their serpent hands. [Cf. Skr. *hasti* the 'handed'.]

e. *fig.*

1592 T. TIMME *10 Eng. Lepers* B b, Moses and Aaron are but Gods hands, Gods lieutenants here in earth. **1653** A. WILSON *Jas. I*, Pref. 5, I..look to be Anatomized myself by the Hand of Opinion. **1724** R. FALCONER *Voy.* (1769) 3 Safe from the griping Hands of the Law. **1877** BROCKETT *Cross & Cr.* 32 To crumble beneath the hand of time.

f. *pl.* In Association Football, the illegal handling of the ball.

1894 BRANSCOMBE & 'ROSS' *Morocco Bound* II. 28 The statute demands A free kick for hands! **1897** [see HANDLING *vbl. sb.* 1 c]. **1967** *Assoc. Football* (Know the Game Series) 28 (*caption*) Area covered by 'Hands'.

2. In reference to the use of the hand for grasping, holding, or retaining; hence used to denote possession, custody, charge, authority, power, disposal: usually in phr. *in* (*into*, *to*, etc.) *the hands of*, *in other hands*, etc.

c **825** *Vesp. Psalter* xxx[i]. 16 [15] Genere me of hondum feonda minra. *c* **1000** *Ags. Ps.* (Th.) cxviii[i]. 109 Is sawl min symble on ðinum holdum handum. *c* **1290** *Beket* 357 in *S. Eng. Leg.* I. 116 þe bischopriches fullen boþe In-to þe kingus hond. *a* **1300** *Cursor M.* 22265 þar sal he bath yield up of hand, His corun and his king wand. *c* **1400** *Lanfranc's Cirurg.* 140 Manye men dieden in hise handis bi þis wey. *c* **1400** MAUNDEV. (Roxb.) vi. 18 Many oþer landes he haldes in his hand. *a* **1530** PACE *Let. to Wolsey* in Ellis *Orig. Lett.* Ser. III. lxxxi. 199 In Pacquett off Lettres..comyn to my handis thys mornynge. **1548** HALL *Chron.*, *Hen. VI*, 106 The Frenchemen..thinkyng the victory to be in their handes. **1606** DEKKER *Sev. Sinnes* 35 They..take the lawe into their owne handes, and doe what they list. **1611** BIBLE *Gen.* xvi. 6 Behold, thy maid is in thy hand. **1709** STEELE *Tatler* No. 53 ¶11 The Citadel will be in the Hands of the Allies before the last Day of this Month. **1849** MACAULAY *Hist. Eng.* I. 593 The land..round his pleasure grounds was in his own hands. **1889** DOYLE *M. Clarke* iii. 25 Not once in a month did a common newsletter fall into our hands.

b. In Roman Law (tr. L. *manus*): the power of the husband over his wife.

1875 POSTE *Gaius* I. §111 Possession invested the husband with right of Hand after a whole year of unbroken co-habitation. *Ibid.* Comm. (ed. 2) 97 According to Cicero, the wife was only called materfamilias when subject to Hand. **1875** MAINE *Hist. Inst.* xi 313 [In early Roman Law] the wife was said to come under the hand of her husband.

3. In reference to action performed with the hand, and hence (*fig.*) to action generally; thus, often = agency, instrumentality: esp. in phr. *by the hand(s of*, *by* (a person's) *hand.*

c **825** *Vesp. Psalter* cviii[i]. 27 Ðæt witen ðætte hond ðin ðeos is. *c* **1000** *Ags. Ps.* (Th.) lxxvi. 17 [lxxvii. 20] Folc þin ðu feredest..þurh Moyses mihtiȝe handa. *c* **1175** *Lamb. Hom.* 91 þa warhte god feole tacne..þurh þere apostlan hondan. *c* **1440** *Jacob's Well* (E.E.T.S.) 235 Makyth clene ȝoure handys, þat is, ȝoure werkys. **1535** COVERDALE *Judg.* vi. 36 Yf thou wilt delyuer Israel thorow my hande. **1586** T. B. *La Primaud. Fr. Acad.* I. 4 If everie one did not put to his helping hand for the correction and reformation of them. **1639** DU VERGER tr. *Camus' Admir. Events* 58 To suffer by the hands of the hangman. **1662** STILLINGFL. *Orig. Sacr.* III. i. §8 If some..attribute such things to Gods immediate hand. **1712** W. ROGERS *Voy.* 305, I sent it by the Hand of an Enemy. **1772** PRIESTLEY *Inst. Relig.* (1782) I. 226 Many..eminent Stoics died by their own hands. **1847** DE QUINCEY *Sp. Mil. Nun* Wks. III. 11 She could turn her hand to anything.

b. Part or share in the doing of something: esp. in phrase, *to have a hand in.*

1597 SHAKS. *2 Hen. IV*, v. ii. 140 In which you (Father) shall haue formost hand. **1625** BACON *Ess.*, *Empire* (Arb.) 303 His Queen had the principall hand in the Deposing and Murther of her Husband. **1776** GOLDSM. *Vic. W.* i, We had two romantic names in the family; but I solemnly protest I had no hand in it. **1837** C. M. GOODRIDGE *Voy. S. Seas* (1843) 122, I am at a loss myself to discover what hand the moon could have had in it.

4. In reference to the position of the hands, one on each side of the body: Side (right or left); hence more generally, side, direction, quarter. Also *fig.* (See also 10 and 32 h, i, j.)

c **1000** ÆLFRIC *Gen.* xlviii. 13 Sette Ephraim on his swiþran hand þæt wæs on Israheles wynstran hand. *c* **1205** LAY. 14734 Heo iseȝen an heore riht hond, a swiþe fæier æit-lond. *c* **1320** *Sir Tristr.* 357 Chese on aiþer hand Wheþer þe leuer war Sink or stille stand. **1513** MORE in Grafton *Chron.* (1568) II. 795 At the last he came out..with a Bishop on every hand of him. **1535** STEWART *Cron. Scot.* II. 93 All Gallowa and Walis of Annand, And all the dalis on the efter hand. **1548** HALL *Chron.*, *Hen. VIII*, 73 On the other hande or syde of the gate, was set a pillar. **1583** HOLLYBAND *Campo di Fior* 91 When you are there, turne on the right hand, and then on the left hand. **1627** J. Doughty *Divine Myst.* (1628) 12 Schoolmen do alwaies incline to the worse hand. **1711** Addison *Spect.* No. 3 ¶5 The Floor, on her right Hand, and on her left, was covered with vast Sums of Gold. **1884** *Manch. Exam.* 8 Sept. 8/6 The mountains on either hand become loftier and steeper.

b. *fig.* In various phrases with present participles, expressing a way, direction, or tendency as opposed to its contrary; as ***on*** (***upon, in, of***) ***the mending hand***, i.e. in the way to mend or recover, getting better; so also with *advancing, growing, thriving, declining, gaining, losing, suffering, giving, receiving*, etc. *arch.* and *dial.*

1598 Grenewey *Tacitus' Ann.* I. ii. 3 Giuing out that Augustus was on the mending hand. **1651** N. Bacon *Disc. Govt. Eng.* II. xviii. (1739) 95 What the Chancery was in times past, hath been already shewed; still it is in the growing and gaining hand. **1701** J. Law *Counc. Trade* (1751) 187 When the nation shall once be brought as much upon the thriving or growing, as now it is upon the declining hand. **1789** Wesley *Wks.* (1872) XII. 439 Mr. Wrigley..is now also on the mending hand. **1828** *Craven Dial.* s.v., 'To be on the mending hand', to be in a state of convalescence. **1858** Carlyle *Fredk. Gt.* VI. iv. (1865) II. 166 Freidrich Wilhelm's ill-humour..has long been upon the growing hand.

†**c.** In phr. ***at a bad hand, at the worst hand***, = positions, case. *Obs.*

c **1489** Caxton *Sonnes of Aymon* xiv. 352 He saw well that his folke was at the worste hande. **1621** Bp. Mountagu *Diatribæ* III. 421 Paulus..at worst hand hath related it in good and true Latine. **1640** Fuller *Joseph's Coat* iv. (1867) 144 Is the world at this bad hand..that one must be far from trusting their nearest friends?

5. As used in various ways in making a promise or oath; *spec.* as the symbol of troth-plight in marriage; pledge of marriage; bestowal in marriage. Also as a symbol of acceptance of an invitation to dance.

c **1320** *Sir Tristr.* 50 Þer to þai bed her hond To heiȝe and holden priis. *c* **1330** *Amis & Amil.* 156 Therto thai held vp her hond. **13..** *Coer de L.* 604 On the book they layde her hand, To that forewarde for to stand. **1390** Gower *Conf.* I. 95 Have here min honde, I shal the wedde. *a* **1440** *Sir Eglam.* 245 '3ys', seyde the erle, 'here myn honde!' Hys trowthe to hym he strake. **1586** W. Massie *Marriage Serm.*, Many a one for land takes a foole by the hand. **1605** Shaks. *Lear* IV. v. 31 More convenient is he for my hand Than for your Ladies. **1775** Sheridan *Duenna* III. vii, In obedience to your commands, I gave him my hand within this hour. **1813** Jane Austen *Pride & Prej.* I. xviii. 208 When the dancing recommenced..and Darcy approached to claim her hand. *a* **1817** —— *Northanger Abbey* (1818) II. i. 15 After aspiring to my hand, there was nobody else in the room he could bear to think of. **1828** Scott *F.M. Perth* xxix, Catharine's hand is promised—promised to a man whom you may hate. **1871** L. Stephen *Playgr. Eur.* ii. (1894) 47 Marriage is honoured, and the heart always follows the hand.

†**6.** Hence, In oaths and asseverations. (See also right hand.) *Obs.*

a **1300** *Cursor M.* 3313 'Say me now', he said, 'be þi hand, Has þou any fader liuand?' **1596** Shaks. *Tam. Shr.* I. i. 194 Master, for my hand, Both our inuentions meet and iumpe in one. **1599** —— *Much Ado* IV. i. 327 *Bene.* Tarry good Beatrice, by this hand I loue thee. *Beat.* Vse it for my loue some other way then swearing by it. **1601** —— *All's Well* III. vi. 76 By the hand of a souldier I will undertake it. **1636** Davenant *Platonic Lovers* Wks. (1673) 386 A comely old fellow, by this hand.

** *As representing the person.*

7. In reference to the person who does something with his hands; hence often denoting the person in relation to his action.

1590 Spenser *F.Q.* I. xi. 5 The Nourse of time and everlasting fame, That warlike handes ennoblest with immortall name. **1598** Barret *Theor. Warres* III. ii. 77 The quadrate of ground..wherein many hands are brought at one time to fight. **1615** J. Stephens *Satyr. Ess.* 242 Except some charitable hand reclaimes him. **1724** A. Collins *Gr. Chr. Relig.* 177 The Pentateuch..was translated..by different hands. **1893** E. M. Thompson *Gk. & Lat. Palæogr.* xi. 150 Additions..by the hand that retouched the writing.

b. *spec.* In reference to an artist, musician, writer, actor, etc. as the performer of some work; hence sometimes used to denote the person himself.

1644 Evelyn *Mem.* (1857) I. 70 Painted in miniature by rare hands. **1665** Boyle *Occas. Refl.* Pref. (1845) 9 These Papers..[as well] as those of the same hand that have preceded them. **1696** tr. *Du Mont's Voy. Levant* 86 Paintings, by the most celebrated Hands. **1738** *Daily Post* 12 July, A Band of Musick, consisting of the best hands from the Opera, and both the Theatres. **1790** Paley *Horæ Paul.* i. 7 Everything about them indicates that they come from the same hand. **1965** *Listener* 3 June 835/3 A major document of the post-Symbolist movement in Spain, with English versions by eleven hands, the 'hands' including W. S. Merwin,..and James Wright.

8. A person employed by another in any manual work; a workman or workwoman.

1655 Mrq. Worcester *Cent. Inv.* §14 Many hands applicable to the same force, some standing, others sitting. **1657** R. Ligon *Barbadoes* (1673) 42 Those hands..that must be employed in their building. **1721** Berkeley *Prev. Ruin Gt. Brit.* Wks. III. 200 Manufactures, which..would employ many hands. **1771** Franklin *Autobiog.* Wks. 1840 I. 29 My son has lately lost his principal hand by death. **1778** *Eng. Gaz.* (ed. 2) s.v. *Kettering*, Near 2000 hands are said to be employed here in the manufactory of shalloons, tammies and serges. **1856** Olmsted *Slave States* 433 The children beginning as 'quarter-hands', advancing to 'half-hands', and then to 'three-quarter hands'; and, finally, to 'full hands'. **1886** Froude *Oceana* i. 7 The 'hands' and the 'hands'' wives and children.

b. *spec.* Each of the sailors belonging to a ship's crew. ***all hands***: the whole crew.

1669 Sturmy *Mariner's Mag.* I. 18 Come aft all hands. **1712** W. Rogers *Voy.* 312 In the Morning we put 35 good Hands aboard her. **1726** G. Roberts *Four Years Voy.* 13, I shipped Hands and began to get things ready as fast as I could. **1820** Scoresby *Acc. Arctic Reg.* I. 515 All hands on board perished. **1834** Medwin *Angler in Wales* II. 144 Another hand would not have been amiss. *Ibid.*, She has just hands enough to weigh anchor.

c. Hence (colloq.) ***all hands***: all the members of a party, esp. when collectively engaged in work.

1703 Farquhar *Inconstant* IV. i, Come, gentlemen, all hands to work. **1726** G. Roberts *Four Years Voy.* 263 Then all Hands went to fishing. **1860** Dickens *Uncomm. Trav.* v, If all hands had been got together, they would not have more than half filled the room.

9. *colloq.* Used (with defining adj.) of a person in reference to his ability or skill in doing something. (See also old *hand*.) Usually with *at*.

1792 Cowper *Let.* 30 Mar. He..might be one of our first hands in poetry. **1797** G. Washington *Let.* Writ. 1892 XIII. 422 A rare hand at all obsolete claims that depend much on a good memory. **1830** J. H. Newman *Lett.* (1891) I. 227, I am a bad hand at criticising men. **1833** Ht. Martineau *Loom & Lugger* II. iii. 45 He was always but a poor hand at writing a letter. **1858** A. W. Drayson *Sporting S. Africa* 48 'Do you sketch?' 'Well, I'm no hand at that'. **1870** E. Peacock *Ralf Skirl.* II. 280 He was a good hand at singlestick.

b. *colloq.* or *slang.* Used (with defining adj.) of a person in reference to his action or character.

1798 I. Milner in *Life* ix. (1842) 162 His moral character was exceedingly bad..he is still a loose hand. **1860** Russell *Diary India* II. 146 (Hoppe) Little S., the Major's partner..is well known as a cool hand.

†**10.** Used of or in reference to a person as the source from which something is obtained (cf. 4):

a. as the source of information, etc. (usually with defining adj. indicating the degree of trustworthiness.) *Obs.*

1614 J. Chamberlain in *Crt. & Times Jas. I.* (1848) I. 334, I have heard it, through several ways, from good hands. **1662** J. Davies tr. *Olearius' Voy. Ambass.* 164 He had it from a very good hand, that the King of Poland had sent an Ambassador. **1717** Lady M. W. Montagu *Let. to C'tess Mar* 30 Jan., An account..which I have been very solicitous to get from the best hands. **1811** J. W. Croker in *C. Papers* June (1884), I hear from a good hand that the King is doing much better.

†**b.** as the supplier of goods: in phrases denoting rate or price (with qualifying adj.), as ***at the best hand***, most profitably or cheaply; so ***at the better hand, at the dear hand***. *Obs.*

1552 Huloet, Bye dearer, or at the last hande. **1582** N. Lichefield tr. *Castanheda's Conq. E. Ind.* xxxiii. 82b, To the end our Merchaunts..might..buye theyr Spices at the better hande. **1599** Hakluyt *Voy.* II. II. 3 For the procuring of which..commodities at the best and first hand. **1696** J. F. *Merchants' Ware-ho.* 11 The whole sute is generally sold at the best hand for three Pound ten. **1712** Steele *Spect.* No. 288 ¶3 Buying and importing..Linens, and Pictures, at the best hand. **1767** Cowper *Let. to Hill* 14 May Wks. 1837 XV. 16, I might..serve your Honour with cauliflowers and broccoli at the best hand.

c. With ordinal numerals, indicating a series of so many persons through whom something passes. See also first hand, second hand.

1439 *Rolls of Parlt.* V. 32/1 Your Lieges selle the Merchandises..in the said Contres, and at the first hand bye ayeinward Merchandises of the same Contres. **1551** Edw. VI *Lit. Rem.* (Roxb.) II. 504 We should by all thinges at the first hand of straungers. **1589** *Hay any Work* 44, I had it [the tale] at the second hand. **1624** Bedell *Lett.* xi. 141 You haue it but at the third, or fourth hand, perhaps the thirtieth or fortieth. **1713** Ockley *Acc. Barbary* Pref. (1718) 11 The Uncertainty which attends the writing Things at second Hand. **1888** Bryce *Amer. Commw.* I. xxv. 273 Very few of the members..had been in England so as to know her constitution..at first hand.

*** *As put for its capacity or performance.*

11. Capacity of doing something with the hand, and hence of doing generally; skill, ability, knack.

1398 Trevisa *Barth. De P.R.* v. xxviii. (1495) 137 We sayen thyse haue a good hond, that is to vnderstonde, a good crafte of wrytynge other of payntynge. **1539** Latimer *Serm. & Rem.* (1845) 416 You be indeed *scius artifex*, and hath a good hand to renew old bottles. **1586** Day *Eng. Secretary* II. (1625) 130 The perfection of his hand in the variety and neat delivery of his letters in writing. **1699** Bentley *Phal.* 297, I cannot but take notice of his unlucky Hand, whenever he meddles with Authors. **1708** Motteux *Rabelais* v. xx, I have no hand at making of Speeches. **1791** Mrs. Radcliffe *Rom. Forest* ii, I had always a hand at carpentry. **1881** E. D. Brickwood in *Encycl. Brit.* XII. 197/1 The 'hand for crust' which is denied to many cooks and cannot be learned.

12. *Horsemanship.* In various expressions referring to the management of the reins and bit with the hand; often = skill in handling the reins.

1375 Barbour *Bruce* II. 120 For thar na horss is in this land Sa wycht, na ȝeit sa weill at hand. **1581** Pettie *Guazzo's Civ. Conv.* III. (1586) 157b, The father..ought in this doubt, to carrie a heavie hand, rather than a light, on the bridle. **1686** N. Cox *Gentl. Recreat.* IV. (ed. 3) 54 In a short time he will..be at such command upon the hand, that he will strike at what rate you please. **1725–51** Chambers *Cycl.* s.v., A horseman is said to have *no hand*, when he only makes use of the bridle unseasonably. **1807** Sir R. Wilson *Jrnl.* 22 June in *Life* (1862) II. viii. 279 She not only sits gracefully but has a master's hand. **1875** Whyte Melville *Riding Recoll.* v. (1879) 73 Strong of seat, and firm of hand. **1881** E. D. Brickwood in *Encycl. Brit.* XII. 197/1 Much depends on the rider having good hands... A rider with good hands never depends upon his reins for retaining his seat. *Ibid.* 199/1 A jockey must therefore..have a hand for all sorts of horses, and in the case of two and three year olds a very good hand it must be.

b. See quot.

1727–51 Chambers *Cycl.* s.v., *Hand* is also used for a division of the horse into two parts, with respect to the rider's hand. The *fore-hand* includes the head, neck, and fore-quarters. The *hind-hand* is all the rest of the horse.

13. The performance of an artist, etc; execution, handiwork; style of execution; 'touch'. †Also *concr.* The product of artistic skill; handiwork.

1667 Milton *P.L.* IX. 438 Among thick-wov'n Arborets and Flours Imborderd on each Bank, the hand of Eve. **1671** —— *P.R.* IV. 57 Carved work, the hand of famed artificers In cedar, marble, ivory or gold. **1762–71** H. Walpole *Vertue's Anecd. Paint.* (1786) III. 77 By what I have seen of his hand, particularly his own head at Houghton, he was an admirable master. **1883** *Athenæum* 30 June 834/2 An exhaustive acumen in discriminating styles and 'hands' [in prints].

b. Touch, stroke (in phr. *last hand*, etc.).

1648 Gage *West Ind.* Ep. Ded. A iij b, The last hand of the Painter. **1707** Luttrell *Brief Rel.* (1857) VI. 132 An opportunity of putting the last hand to the happy union of the 2 kingdoms. **1755** T. Amory *Mem.* (1769) II. 154 An itinerary I am giving the last hand to. **1760–72** tr. *Juan & Ulloa's Voy.* (ed. 3) II. 291 Willing to put the finishing hand to our principal work. **1865** M. Arnold *Ess. Crit.* ix. 376 The compiler did not put his last hand to the work.

14. A turn or innings in certain games, as cricket, racquets, billiards. (See also 23 c.)

17.. *Laws of Cricket* in Grace *Cricket* (1891) 15 To allow 2 minutes for each man to come in when one is out, and 10 minutes between Each Hand to mark yᵉ Ball, that it may not be changed. **1819** Hazlitt in *Every-day Bk.* (1825) 868 The four best racket-players of that day..Davies could give any one of these two hands a time, that is half the game. **1884** *Lillywhite's Cricket Ann.* 45 Fine all-round fielding enabled them to get Marylebone out for 80 in their second hands. **1894** *Times* 6 Mar. 7/2 (Racquets) Mr. Dawkins opened, and in the sixth hand he went from 5–3 to 14–3. **1897** *Daily Chron.* 16 Feb. 5/6 (Billiards) Peall had four or five hands to score 16, but the champion could only muster a 40 and a 50.

b. A member of a cricket eleven.

1731 in H. T. Waghorn *Cricket Scores* (1899) 4 The Duke's hands came in first. **1874** *Baily's Monthly Mag.* Dec. 155 Seven of the eleven..were new hands.

†**c.** A score in cricket. *Obs.*

1833 J. Nyren *Young Cricketer's Tutor* 104 He would often get long hands. **1836** *New Sporting Mag.* Oct. 361 [Which number] added to the byes they stole, and the wide balls bowled, sufficed to make a hands of eighty-six runs. **1875** *Baily's Monthly Mag.* Sept. 273 Let me see him make a good hand against good bowling.

15. A round of applause. Esp. in present-day use in phr. ***to give*** (or ***get***, etc.) ***a big*** (or ***good***) ***hand***: to give, etc., a large round of applause (orig. *U.S.*).

1590 Shaks. *Mids. N.* V. i. 444 Giue me your hands, if we be friends, And Robin shall restore amends. **1838** Dickens *Nickleby* xxix. 284 He has gone on night after night, never getting a hand and you getting a couple of rounds at least. **1849** *Theatrical Programme* 18 June 30 Buskin's part goes without a hand—Lamp carries off all the honours. **1883** G. B. Shaw *How to become Mus. Critic* (1960) 48 The dance-tunes, played by an indifferent band, went almost without a hand. **1886** *Lantern* (New Orleans) 6 Oct. 4/3 Their act always pulls a big hand. **1896** *Punch* 10 Oct. 180/2 Aeschylus ..wrote tragedies in blank verse, but they are not now played at any London theatre. He would not get a 'hand' nowadays. **1922** C. Sandburg *Slabs of Sunburnt West* 39 It's a good act—we got a good hand. **1924** H. A. Vachell *Quinney's Adv.* 179 The second curtain fell without 'a hand'. **1927** Prince of Wales in *Even. News* 7 Oct. 6/5 They both do a great deal of hard work for the British Legion. It may be I am more the fellow who travels about and gets the hands. **1932** A. J. Worrall *Eng. Idioms* 40 He always gets a good hand when he appears in a London theatre. **1948** *Prairie Club Bull.* June 14 Three lusty cheers and a big hand for Charles, Our Star Square Dance Host! **1959** *Listener* 28 May 958/3 A deed which earned what our Quiz compères insist on calling 'a big hand'.

16. The action of the hand in writing and its product; handwriting; style of writing; *esp.* as belonging to a particular person, country, period, profession, etc. (See also court-hand, short-hand, etc.).

1390 Gower *Conf.* III. 305 To make an ende And write ayein her owne honde. **1513** More in Grafton *Chron.* (1568) II. 782 Written in Parchement in a fayre set hande. **1530** Palsgr. 433/1 He goeth to the writyng scole, but his hande appayreth every daye. **1542** Udall *Erasm. Apopth.* II. (1877) 251 Written in greate letters of texte hande. **1576** Fleming *Panopl. Epist.* 276 He wrote a running hand. **1660** Willsford *Scales Comm.* To Rdr. A ij, Mr. Nathanael Sharp, who writeth all the usuall hands writ in this Nation. **1705** Hearne *Collect.* 31 Aug., A French woman writ the Proverbs..in variety of Hands. **1709** Steele & Addison *Tatler* No. 110 ¶4 A Letter which he acknowledged to be his own Hand was read. **1840** Lytton *Money* I. iii, But he will recognize my hand. **1893** E. M. Thompson *Gk. & Lat. Palæogr.* xix. 301 We find it convenient to treat the cursive or charter-hand as a separate branch of mediæval English writing apart from the literary or book-hand.

b. ***hand of writ, write*** (*Sc.*) = prec. sense; also *transf.* said of the person.

1816 Scott *Antiq.* xv, 'Div ye think naebody can read hand o' writ but yoursell?' **1870** Ramsay Remin. v. (ed. 18) 118, I am not a good *hand of write.* **1890** Stevenson *Vailima Lett.* (1895) 14, I request a specimen of your hand of write.

17. The name of a person written with his own hand as an attestation of a document; signature. *Obs.* or *arch.*, exc. in phrases in which *hand* is now understood more literally. So also *under the hand of*, 35 d. ***note of hand***: see NOTE.

1534 *Act 26 Hen. VIII*, c. 3 §4 Euery writinge.. subscribed with the hande and name of the clerke of the hanaper. **1548** HALL *Chron., Hen. VIII*, 29 Notwithstandynge his othe..and his awne hand and seale. **1607** DEKKER *Hist. Sir T. Wyatt* Wks. 1873 III. 84 Will you not subscribe your hand with other of the Lords? **1611** SHAKS. *Wint. T.* IV. iv. 288 *Dor.* Is it true too, thinke you. *Autol.* Fiue Iustices hands at it, and witnesses more then my packe will hold. **1640** S. D'EWES in *Lett. Lit. Men* (Camden) 167 A petition..from the Cittie of London accompanied with fifteene thousand hands. **1666** PEPYS *Diary* 25 Sept. (1879) IV. 92 By Coach to Lord Brouncker's, and got his hand to it. **1726** SHELVOCKE *Voy. round World* (1757) 41 In witness whereof, we have hereunto set our hands and seals. *Mod.* (Form of testing clause) As witness the hands of the said A. B. and C. D.

**** *Something like or of the size of a hand.*

18. An image or figure of a hand.

*c*825 *Vesp. Psalter* cxiii. [cxv.] 7 Honda habbað and ne grapiað. **1535** COVERDALE *Ibid.*, Their ymages..haue handes and handle not. **1644** BULWER *Chirol.* 165 The custome of the Romans..to erect a statue of Mercurie with the Fore-Finger pointing out the maine road, in imitation whereof..we have in such places notes of direction; such is the Hand of St. Albans. **1688** R. HOLME *Armoury* II. xvii. 399/1 He beareth Vert, a Hand proper, holding of a Pen. **1717** FREZIER *Voy. S. Sea* 242 The Ladies wear..a little Jeat Hand..called *Higa*, the Fingers closed, but the Thumb standing out. **1858** O. W. HOLMES *Aut. Breakf.-t.* ix, A great wooden hand,—a glove-maker's sign.

b. A conventional figure of a hand with the forefinger extended (☛), used in writing or printing to draw attention to something.

1612 BRINSLEY *Pos. Parts* (1669) p. iv, A Hand pointing at some places which are of most necessary use.

c. A device shaped like a hand.

1830 M. EDGEWORTH *Let.* 6 Dec. (1971) 439 Mr. Turner ..had shewn me the bank of England and the famous machine-*hand* which weighs the guineas without assistance from mortal touch. **1873** *Young Englishwoman* Jan. 52/1 Will any one..tell her how to clean white..gloves. She possesses wooden hands for stretching them on. **1926–7** *Army & Navy Stores Catal.* 1008/2 Dairy utensils... Scotch hands [for shaping butter].

19. The pointer or index which indicates the divisions of a dial, esp. that of a clock or watch. (See HOUR-, MINUTE-, SECONDS-HAND.)

1575 LANEHAM *Let.* (1871) 55 The handz of both the tablz stood firm and fast, allweyz poynting too iust too a clok. **1592** SHAKS. *Rom. & Jul.* II. iv. 119. **1661** *Humane Industry* 100 Now this animated needle shews with the Lilly-hand.. the North. **1720** *Lond. Gaz.* No. 5863/4 A striking Gold Watch with an Alarm, Hour-Hand and Minute-Hand. **1781** COWPER *Retirement* 681 An idler is a watch that wants both hands, As useless if it goes as when it stands. **1846** LONGF. *Old Clock on Stairs* ii, Half-way up the stair it stands, And points and beckons with its hands.

20. A lineal measure, formerly taken as equal to three inches, but now to four; a palm, a HAND-BREADTH. Now used only in giving the height of horses and the like.

1561 EDEN *Arte Nauig.* I. xviii. 19 Foure graines of barlye make a fynger: foure fingers a hande: foure handes a foote. **1661** LOVELL *Hist. Anim. & Min.* 102 Prickles..of two or three hands length. **1664** BUTLER *Hud.* II. i. 694 A Roan Gelding twelve Hands high. **1810** *Sporting Mag.* XXXVI. 196 A galloway under fourteen hands. **1857** G. LAWRENCE *Guy Liv.* (Tauchn.) 67 (Hoppe) A chestnut standing full sixteen hands.

21. As a measure of various commodities (the single articles or parts being sometimes compared to fingers). **a.** A bundle of tobacco-leaves tied together. **b.** A certain quantity of water-cress. **c.** Five oranges or herrings. **d.** A palmate root of ginger. **e.** One of the clusters, each containing from 8 to 20 fruits, into which a bunch of bananas or plantains naturally divides.

1726 G. ROBERTS *Four Years Voy.* 102 In another Locker, I found four or five Hands of Tobacco. **1756** P. BROWNE *Civil & Nat. Hist. Jamaica* II. ii. 119, I have sometimes seen a hand of ginger weigh near half a pound... The larger spreading roots are called Hands in Jamaica. **1851** MAYHEW *Lond. Labour* I. 92 (Hoppe) A single hand being 5 oranges. *Ibid.* 150 We buy the water-cresses by the 'hand'. One hand will make about five halfpenny bundles. **1861** *Ibid.* III. 163 Five herrings make a hand. **1879** J. R. JACKSON in *Encycl. Brit.* X. 603/2 Uncoated ginger..the 'races' or 'hands' [are] from 3 to 4 inches long. **1886** *U.S. Consular Rep.* No. 65. 216 (Cent). The fruit [banana]..consists of a stock on which are from four to twelve clusters called hands. **1888** PATON & DITTINAR in *Encycl. Brit.* XXIII. 425/1 The leaves..[of tobacco] are made up into 'hands', or small bundles of from six to twelve leaves. **1894** in *Pop. Sci. Monthly* XLIV. 497 A hand [banana] may contain from a dozen to twenty fruits or 'fingers'.

22. *Cookery.* A shoulder of pork. (Formerly applied to part of a shoulder of mutton.)

1673 S. C. *Rules of Civility* x. 102 A Shoulder of Mutton is to be cut like a semicircle betwixt the flap and the hand. *a* **1825** FORBY *Voc. E. Anglia*, *Hand (of Pork)*, the shoulder joint of a hog, cut without the blade-bone. **1863** MRS. GASKELL *Sylvia's L.* I. 62 Flitches of bacon and 'hands' (i.e. shoulders of cured pork..) abounded.

***** *That which is held in the hand.*

23. In games of cards: The cards dealt to each player; the handful of cards held by each at the beginning of the game. Also, the cards held at any stage of such a game as Poker.

1630 *R. Johnson's Kingd. & Commw.* 41 He that winnes the game, gets not onely the maine Stake, but all the Bets by follow the fortune of his hand. **1694** CONGREVE *Double Dealer* II. i. Plays (1887) 122 Then I find it's like cards: if either of us have a good hand, it is an accident of fortune. **1726** SWIFT *Th. Various Subj.* Wks. 1778 XI. 358, I must complain the cards are ill shuffled, till I have a good hand. **1881** *Knowledge* No. 4. 83/2 In whist each player is to consider his partner's hand as well as his own. **1889** R. GUERNDALE *Poker Bk.* 25 To fill your hand, to improve it by the draw. **1913** 'A. B. LOUGHER' *Poker* 13 The next process is that of drawing to fill the hands.

b. The person holding the cards. ***elder*** or ***eldest hand***, the person who plays first; so ***younger hand***, ***second***, ***third hand***, etc.

1589, etc. [see ELDER *a.* 4, ELDEST 5]. **1663** DRYDEN *Wild Gallant* IV. i, Zounds, the rogue has a quint-major, and three aces younger hand. **1746** HOYLE *Whist* (ed. 6) 22 You are an elder Hand. **1828** T. AIRD in *Blackw. Mag.* Dec. 713/1 A fag partner at whist when a better fourth hand is wanting.

c. A single round in a game, in which all the cards dealt at one time are played.

1622 MABBE tr. *Aleman's Guzman d'Alf.* II. 123 When I had wonne two or three hands, I tooke pleasure now and then to lose a little. **1771** SMOLLETT *Humph. Cl.* (1815) 66 They take a hand at whist, or descant upon the General Advertiser. **1837** DICKENS *Pickw.* vi, The odd trick at the conclusion of a hand. **1876** *World* V. No. 113. 17 We have a room where we can take a hand at whist.

d. *fig.*

In many phrases, as *to* PLAY *into the hands of another*, *to* FORCE *the hand of*, *to* SHOW *one's hand*, etc., for which see the verbs. ***to declare one's hand*** (fig.): to reveal one's circumstances or aims. (Cf. DECLARE *v.* 11.)

1600 HOLLAND *Livy* XXV. xxxiv. 575 They..expected certainely to haue another hand as good as this. *a* **1626** BACON (J.), There was never a hand drawn, that did double the rest of the habitable world, before this. **1777** SHERIDAN *Sch. Scand.* IV. iii, I have a difficult hand to play in this affair. **1882** B. HARTE *Flip* ii, Until you saw my hand. **1887** RIDER HAGGARD *Jess* xiii, You don't show me your hand like this for nothing. **1922** D. H. LAWRENCE *England, my England* 271 Upstairs Fanny evaded all the thrusts made by his mother, and did not declare her hand.

†**24.** A handle. *Obs.*

1523 FITZHERB. *Husb.* §23 Holde downe the hynder hand of his sith, that he do not endent the grasse. **1549** *Ludlow Churchw. Acc.* (Camden) 40 For makynge a hand to our lady belrope. **1715** DESAGULIERS *Fires Impr.* 142 The little Hand to turn the Cylinder or Shutter. **1764** V. GREEN *Surv. Worcester* 232 The business called handling..i.e. putting the hand to cups.

b. The part of a gun grasped by the hand.

1881 GREENER *Gun* 433 The circumference of the hand may be obtained by passing a string round it immediately behind the trigger-guard... The usual hand is about 5-in. in circumference for 12-bores.

II. Phrases.

* *With governing preposition.*

(See also AFOREHAND, AFTERHAND, *asidehand* (s.v. ASIDE IV), BEFOREHAND, BEHINDHAND, *between-* (Sc. *atween-*) *hands* (BETWEEN *prep.* 3 b); NEARHAND, NIGH-HAND, OFF-HAND, UNDER-HAND.)

25. at hand.

a. Within easy reach; near; close by. (Sometimes preceded by *close*, *hard*, *near*, *nigh*, *ready*.)

a **1300** *Cursor M.* 15710 He es cummand negh at hand þe tresun has puruaid. *Ibid.* 17922 (Gött.) He cums at hand to slak ȝur site. *a* **1400–50** *Alexander* 81 Artaxenses is at hand, & has ane ost reryd. **1535** COVERDALE *Ps.* cxviii[i]. 151 Be thou nye at honde also (o Lorde). **1548** HALL *Chron., Hen. V*, 46 b, Their enemies wer ever at hande. **1667** MILTON *P.L.* II. 674 Satan was now at hand. **1750** JOHNSON *Rambler* No. 19 ¶15 Forced to produce not what was best but what happened to be at hand. **1840** DICKENS *Barn. Rudge* x, Have you a messenger at hand?

b. Near in time closely approaching. (Sometimes qualified as prec.) Also † *at hands*.

c **1200** ORMIN 16147 Himm þinnkeþþ þatt hiss herrte shall Tobrestenn neh att hanndess. *a* **1300** *Cursor M.* 14206 If he mai slepe, hele es at hand. *c* **1400** *Destr. Troy* 396 And she at hond for to haue husband for age. **1526–34** TINDALE *2 Thess.* ii. 2 As though the daye of Christ were at honde. **1662** J. DAVIES tr. *Olearius' Voy. Ambass.* 34 The end of both his Voyage and life were neer at hand. **1724** DE FOE *Mem. Cavalier* (1840) 39 The diet at Frankfort is at hand. **1820** KEATS *St. Agnes* viii. The hallowed hour was near at hand. **1868** J. H. BLUNT *Ref. Ch. Eng.* I. 433 Further great changes were at hand.

†**c.** At the immediate moment; at the start. *Obs.*

1601 SHAKS. *Jul. C.* IV. ii. 23 Hollow men, like Horses hot at hand, Make gallant shew..But when they should endure the bloody Spurre..Sinke in the Triall. **1640** FULLER *Joseph's Coat* iii. (1867) 133 Some men's affection spends itself with its violence, hot at hand, cold at length. **1650** —— *Pisgah* II. xiv. 297 Rebellion, though running so at hand, is quickly tyred..Loyalty is best at a long course. **1705** STANHOPE *Paraphr.* II. 223 Many..though hot at hand, yet quickly abate of their Speed.

†**d.** = By hand: see 26 a. *Obs.*

1595 SHAKS. *John* v. ii. 75 A Lion fostered vp at hand.

†**e.** At the wrist. *Obs.*

[*c* **1386** CHAUCER *Prol.* 193 (Harl. 7334), I saugh his sleues purfiled atte hond [*Six texts* at the hond] Wiþ grys.] **1697** *Lond. Gaz.* No. 3256/4 The Coat buttoned close at Hand.

†**f.** At close quarters in conflict; fighting hand to hand (*with*). Also *at hands*. *Obs.* (Cf. *to come to hands*, 37 b.)

1565–73 COOPER *Thesaurus* s.v. *Cominus*, *Pugnare cominus cum hoste*, to fight at hand, or hand to hand with hys enimy. *a* **1608** SIR F. VERE *Comm.* 97 When they were come up and at hands with the enemy.

†**g.** ***at (on, upon) any hand***: on any account, in any case. So ***at no hand***: on no account, by no means. *Obs.*

c **1430** *Syr Tryam.* 995 He never sir James slowe at none honde. **1553** T. WILSON *Rhet.* (1580) 200 The feined Fables ..would not bee forgotten at any hande. **1568** GRAFTON *Chron.* II. 27 The Welshmen would at no hand geve him any oportunitie to fight with them. **1620** VENNER *Via Recta* Introd. 11 It is at no hand to be allowed. **1646** BUCK *Rich. III*, I. 35 His secret drift was, to apt and prepare the Duke to a Rebellion at any hand. **1690** NORRIS *Beatitudes* (1694) I. 128 This the Gravity of Zeno's School will, at no hand, permit.

†**h.** ***at every hand***: on all hands. *Obs.*

1690 W. WALKER *Idiomat. Anglo-Lat.* 48 It is believed at every hand.

†**i.** ***at*** (a person's) ***hand***: near him, close by him, in attendance upon him, at his disposal, subject to him, (also ***at the hand***, ***at hand unto***). ***at one's own hand***: at one's own disposal, one's own master. *Obs.* or *dial.*

1382 WYCLIF *1 Chron.* xviii. 17 Forsothe the sonys of Dauid [were] first at the kyngis hond. *c* **1430** *Syr Gener.* 2066 Al the gretest of that lond Because of mede were at his hond. **1508** DUNBAR *Tua mariit Wemen* 12, I hard..Ane hie speiche, at my hand. **1613** PURCHAS *Pilgrimage* (1614) 136 The Gibeonites..were at hand unto the Levites in the meanest offices about the..Temple. **1619** *Canterbury Marriage Licences* (MS.), Lidia Webb..nowe at her owne hand, her parents being all dead. **1700** *Pennsylv. Archives* I. 130 The proprietors did not set up a government at their own hands but were authorized.

j. ***at the hand(s of***: from the hands of; from. (Expressing the immediate source, after such verbs as *receive*, *take*, *find*, *seek*, *require*, etc. See AT *prep.* 11.)

a **1035** *Laws of Cnut* I. c. 22 To onfonne..æt bisceopes handa. *c* **1200** ORMIN 9261 To wurrþenn fullhtnedd att hiss hannd. **1535** COVERDALE *Job* ii. 10 Seing we haue receaued prosperite at the honde of God. **1548–9** (Mar.) *Bk. Com. Prayer, Visitation of Sick*, You may fynde mercy at our heauenly fathers hande. **1662** J. DAVIES tr. *Olearius' Voy. Ambass.* 288 The King would take it very ill at their hands. **1749** FIELDING *Tom Jones* v. iii, The many little favours, received..at his hands. **1768–1884** [see AT *prep.* 11 b]. **1893** F. W. MAITLAND in Traill *Social Eng.* ii. 165 He had just received the Christian faith at the hands of Roman missionaries.

26. by hand.

a. With the hand or hands; by manual action or labour, as opposed to machinery, or to natural processes.

1549 COVERDALE, etc. *Erasm. Par. 2 Tim.* 21 The ghospell, whiche I delyuered vnto thee..delyuer likewise by handes vnto others. **1562** T. TIMME *Ten Eng. Lepers* G ij, They bring up by hand crammed and franked foules and beastes. **1653** WALTON *Angler* xi. 204 Many will fish for the Gudgion by hand. **1662** J. DAVIES tr. *Olearius' Voy. Ambass.* 163 A very great bank, so even, that it seems to have been done by hand. **1709** STEELE *Tatler* No. 89 ¶6, I was bred by Hand. **1846** J. BAXTER *Libr. Pract. Agric.* (ed. 4) I. 278 Implements employed in the preparation of flax by hand. **1861** DICKENS *Gt. Expect.* ii, She had brought me up 'by hand'. **1881** *Truth* 19 May 686/2 Embroidery done by hand.

b. By, past, aside (as in *to put by hand*); usually *pred.* or *adj.* laid aside, done with, disposed of; past, finished, over. *Sc.*

1637 RUTHERFORD *Lett.* (1830) 199 Many ells and inches of the short thread of your life are by-hand since I saw you. *Ibid.* I. xi. (1664) 32 The greatest part but play with Christianity, they put it by hand easily. **1782** SIR J. SINCLAIR *Observ. Scot. Dial.* 53 (Jam.) A good thing by-hand: a good thing over.

c. ***by the hand***: expeditiously, readily, straightway. (Cf. *from hand* 28 a.)

1658 GURNALL *Chr. in Arm.* verse 14. ix. §1. (1669) 38/2 That they should grow rich by the hand.

27. for one's own hand. For one's own interest or benefit, on one's own account.

1828 SCOTT *F.M. Perth* xxxiv, 'I fought for my own hand', said the Smith. **1869** TENNYSON *Coming of Arthur* 218 Each But sought to rule for his own self and hand. **1879** FROUDE *Cæsar* ix. 92 Lesbos was occupied by adventurers, who were fighting for their own hand.

28. from hand.

†**a.** 'Out of hand', at once, immediately. [Cf. Ger. *von der hand.*] *Sc. Obs.*

1535 STEWART *Cron. Scot.* II. 607 The Danis..Wand saill to top, and saillit syne fra hand. **1535** LYNDESAY *Satyre* 440 Gude sirs, I sall be reddie, evin fra hand. ? *a* **1550** *Freiris of Berwik* 378 in *Dunbar's Poems* (1893) 297 The caponis als ȝe sall ws bring fra hand. **1558** in *Miscell. of Wodr. Soc.* (1844) 265 Fra hand, eftir that the mater wes schawin to me, I persauit.

†**b.** Out of reach, away, off. *Obs.*

1608 D. T. *Ess. Pol. & Mor.* 15 b, And the reason heereof is not farre from hand.

29. in hand.

a. *lit.* (Held or carried.)

1390 GOWER *Conf.* II. 338 With a bow in honde. **1508** DUNBAR *Gold. Targe* 110 Cupide the king, wyth bow in hand. **1632** J. HAYWARD tr. *Biondi's Eromena* 61 With sword in hand. **1784** COWPER *Task* IV. 239 With brush in hand and pallet spread. **1887** *Pall Mall G.* 23 Feb. 3 Suppose that it went cap in hand to every Government in Europe. *Mod.* There sat a reporter pencil in hand to take down his words.

†**b.** ***in hand***, ***in one's hand***: (led) by the hand, or by a string, or the like. *Obs.*

c **1385** CHAUCER *L.G.W.* Prol. 213 And from a fer com.. The god of love and in his hande a quene. **1423** JAS. I *Kingis Q.* 79 Ech in his stage, and his make in his hand. **1513**

DOUGLAS *Æneis* II. vii. [vi.] 47 Panthus..in his hand also Harling him eftir his litle nevo, Cummis. **1641** *Termes de la Ley* 126 s.v. *Dogge-draw*, A Hound that hee leadeth in his hand. **1684** R. H. *School Recreat.* 21 Trot him about in your Hand a good while: Then offer to Mount. **1782** C. A. BURNEY in *Mad. D'Arblay's Early Diary* (1889) II. 305, I charged him to bring his sister in his hand. **1796** MRS. E. PARSONS *Myster. Warn.* II. 237 Bringing your friend in your hand.

†**c.** ***in hand***: in the company or presence of a person, or in attendance on him. ***to come in hand***: to present oneself, appear. ***to hold in hand***: to attend on. *Obs.*

a **1300** *Cursor M.* 22239 (Edinb.) Firste sale be descenciune, are antecriste sal cum in hande. *Ibid.* 2432 (Cott.) þe king..commaunded..Men suld him mensk and hald in hand. *Ibid.* 3916 Ilkan wit oþer went in hand.

d. In actual or personal possession, at one's disposal; †in early use, Under one's authority, subject to one; in one's charge; in custody. (Also ***in hands***.)

c **1200** ORMIN 17990 þe Faderr..hafeþþ ȝifenn himm inn hannd To weldenn alle þingess. *a* **1300** *Cursor M.* 15813 Petre was in hand nummen for forfait he had don. *c* **1400** MAUNDEV. (Roxb.) iv. 12 Cristen men ware wont for to hafe þat citee in hand. *c* **1530** A bird in hand [see BIRD *sb.* 6]. **1551** T. WILSON *Logike* (1580) 86 Promised to give hym a greate somme of money..and gave hym..halfe in hande. **1623** BINGHAM *Xenophon* 22 The Milesian..being in hand to the Kings people, escaped away naked to the Grecians. **1627** J. CARTER *Exp. Serm. Mount* 38 It lyeth us in hand, seriously to consider what our practice is. **1633** T. STAFFORD *Pac. Hib.* I. vii. (1810) 98 Then Desmond O Conner layed hold upon James Fits Thomas, and said, My Lord you are in hand. **1690** LOCKE *Hum. Und.* II. xxi. (1695) 146 Apt to judge a little in Hand better than a great deal to come. **1751** *Affect. Narr. Wager* 43 With a little yet in Hand, we were almost starving. **1844** M. HENNELL *Soc. Syst.* 50 To make.. purchases..according to convenience and cash in hand. **1884** CURTIS PRICE in *Law Times Rep.* LI. 157/2 His scrupulous desire to keep the mansion-house in hand. *Mod.* You may keep the offer in hand till the 20th.

†**e.** In expectation or suspense (with *hold*, *keep*). *Obs.*

c **1369** CHAUCER *Dethe Blaunche* 1019 Hyr lust to holde no wyght in honde. *c* **1374** —— *Troylus* II. 426 (477) But that I nyl not holden hym yn honde. **1653** H. COGAN tr. *Pinto's Trav.* xxxviii. 152 Not to hold him longer in hand. **1824** SCOTT *St. Ronan's* xviii, The rogue-lawyers, after taking fees, and keeping me in hand for years.

f. In process; being carried on or actually dealt with in any way. (See also *take in hand* 42.)

c **1386** CHAUCER *Reeve's T.* 115 It shal be doon, quod Symkyn..What wol ye doon whil that it is in hande? *c* **1460** *Towneley Myst.* (Surtees) 147 Som what is in hand, what ever it meyn. **1513** MORE in Grafton *Chron.* (1568) II. 757 No warre in hande, nor none towarde. **1586** A. DAY *Eng. Secretary* I. (1625) 22 The matters or newes in hand amongst us. **1692** LD. MOLESWORTH *Acc. Sweden* 109 Though it be something forreign to the Matter in hand. **1719** DE FOE *Crusoe* II. vii, Having much business in hand. **1888** BURGON *Lives 12 Gd. Men* II. xi. 332 He..gave his whole attention to whatever he had in hand. **1895** *Manch. Guard.* 19 Oct. 4/8 The work..is now well in hand.

g. ***in hand with***: occupied or engaged with, dealing with; in conference with, endeavouring to persuade (also ***in hands with***). *Obs.* or *dial.* †***in hand to do*** something: occupied in doing it. *Obs.* (See also *to go in hand with*, 39.)

1470–85 MALORY *Arthur* x. lxii, I shal neuer be at ease in my herte tyl I be in handes with them. **1509** BARCLAY *Shyp of Folys* (1874) II. 25 Another with Grece and Cesyll is in honde. **1515** SUFFOLK in *State Papers Hen. VIII* (*For. & Dom.*) II. I. 26 The Queen was in hand with me the first day I [came], and said she must be short with me. **1539** BIBLE (Great) *Ps.* lvi. 2 Myne enemyes are daylye in hande to swalow me vp. **1604** JAS. I *Counterbl.* (Arb.) 111 Is it not a great vanitie, that a man cannot heartily welcome his friend now, but straight they must bee in hand with Tobacco? **1633** BP. HALL *Hard Texts* 598 Zerubbabel, who is now in hand to build the Temple. **1635** LAUD *Wks.* (1860) VII. 116 For the statutes, I am in hand with them. [**1825–80** JAMIESON s.v., He's in hands wi' Jean.]

h. ***in hand***: under control, subject to discipline. (Originally a term of horsemanship, cf. b.)

1832 *Prop. Regul. Instr. Cavalry* III. 64 They will have their horses in hand..with their heads well up. **1856** *Athenæum* 6 Dec. 1491 An Irishman..who has been kept well in hand at a tight University in his calf-days. **1874** L. STEPHEN *Hours in Library* (1892) I. iv. 151 If he had strong passions..he kept them well in hand.

i. Preceded by a numeral denoting a number of draught horses, etc. driven by one person. See FOUR-IN-HAND.

1890 *Pall Mall G.* 20 June 2/1 An eight-in-hand team.

†**j.** ***in any hand***: in any case, at any rate: = 25 g. *Obs.*

1601 SHAKS. *All's Well* III. vi. 45 Let him fetch off his drumme in any hand. **1622** MABBE tr. *Aleman's Guzman d'Alf.* II. 150, I would not in any hand..he should slip his necke out of the collar.

k. *Billiards.* Of the cue-ball: having been retrieved by hand, after being pocketed, and having been placed on any selected spot within the D preliminary to the next stroke.

1860 'R. CRAWLEY' *Handy Bk. Games* xiii. 106 Your ball being in hand, you must play for the hazard that shall bring the object-ball back to the opposite cushion. **1904** S. A. MUSSABINI *Mannock's Billiards* v. 228 The cue-ball is 'in hand' with the red ball, presenting a straightaway winning hazard into the right middle pocket.

l. *N.Z.* (See quots.)

1930 L. G. D. ACLAND *Early Canterbury Runs* i. 5 Until wire fences were introduced about 1862, all sheep on the plains were kept more or less in hand. The practice was for a shepherd to go round the boundary once or twice a day. **1933** —— in *Press* (Christchurch) 28 Oct. 15/7 Sheep are in hand when you have them in a mob near you.

30. of..hands. a. ***of one's hands*** (rarely ***hand***): in respect of one's actions, of action, of valour in fight: usually with ***valiant***, ***proper***, etc. ***a man of his hands***: a man of valour, skill, or practical ability. *arch.*

a **1300** *Cursor M.* 7 O brut þat bern bald of hand. **13..** *Coer de L.* 2092 Three gentil barouns of England, Wise of speech, doughty of hand. **1375** BARBOUR *Bruce* IX. 481 This Schir Eduard..Wes of his handis a nobill knycht. **1470–85** MALORY *Arthur* II. xvii, Ye are..the man of moost prowesse of your handes lyuyng. **1513** DOUGLAS *Æneis* IX. iii. 130 Mony thousand douchty men of handis. *c* **1530** H. RHODES *Bk. Nurture* 73 in *Babees Bk.* 84 A man of his handes with hastynesse Should at no tyme be fylde. **1598** SHAKS. *Merry W.* I. iv. 27 He is as tall a man of his hands, as any is between this and his head. *a* **1635** NAUNTON *Fragm. Reg.* (Arb.) 47 He loved sword and buckler men, and such as our Fathers were wont to call men of their hands. **1886** SIR F. POLLOCK *Oxford Lect.* iv. 108 Learning to be a man of your hands with another weapon or two besides.

†**b.** ***of all hands***: on all hands (see 32 h), on all sides, on the part of every one; also (quot. 1588) in any case. *Obs.*

1548 HALL *Chron.*, *Hen. VII*, 6 b, Callyng him of al handes kynge. **1588** SHAKS. *L.L.L.* IV. iii. 219 Of all hands must we be forsworne. **1621–31** LAUD *Serm.* (1847) 45 Then there is 'joy', 'great joy', of all hands. **1715** M. DAVIES *Athen. Brit.* I. 260 Both are own'd of all hands to be spurious.

31. off hand.

a. See OFF-HAND. **b.** ***off one's hand(s)***: out of one's charge or control. ***to take off one's hands***: to relieve one of the charge or responsibility of.

1636 RUTHERFORD *Lett.* I. ccx. (1675) 394 The scattered Flock once committed to me, and now taken off my Hand by himself. **1676** WYCHERLEY *Pl. Dealer* v. ii, He has seemed to make his wench rich, only that I might take her off his hands. **1698** FRYER *Acc. E. India & P.* 81 Good Masters, who had taken off of his hands more Flesh in that time..than he had sold in some Years before. **1765** FOOTE *Commissary* I. Wks. 1799 II. 9 A friend of the lady's will take the child off her hands. **1889** *The County* xxii, I have taken him off your hands.

32. on hand, upon hand.

a. In one's possession; in one's charge or keeping: said of things, or of work or business which one has to do. ***to have on hand***: to have with one; to be charged with, have the care or responsibility of; to have in order to deal with or dispose of; to be about or engaged on.

c **1025** *Interl. v. Rule St. Benet* (Logeman) 75 Swa hwylce þinc on handum mid hælicum ofoste si becumen. *c* **1205** LAY. 248 Al þat lond þat Eneas heore fader hefde on hond. **1390** GOWER *Conf.* I. 94 Thou hast on honde such a game. **1470–85** MALORY *Arthur* I. xvii, These xj kynges haue more on hand than they are ware of. **1548** UDALL, etc. *Erasm. Par. John* 91 b, It onely lyeth you vpon hande to fyght manfully. **1815** E. S. BARRETT *Heroine* I. 59 We have other matters on hands. **1818** JAS. MILL *Brit. India* II. IV. v. 470 If he possessed in India any money on loan or merchandize on hand. **1853** LYTTON *My Novel* I. ix, The abode..which had so evidently hung long on hand. *Mod.* We have at present a large stock of tweeds on hand.

†**b.** Said of evil, harm, etc. affecting a person. ***to have on hand***: to have to bear or suffer. *Obs.*

c **1200** *Moral Ode* 192 þet ure eldre misduden, we habbeþ uuele on honde. *c* **1350** *Leg. Rood* (1871) 62 Fader, what harm es þe on hand. **1390** GOWER *Conf.* II. 12 For ever he hath drede upon honde.

†**c.** In or into one's presence; present; at hand. ***to bring on hand***: to bring in, introduce. ***to nigh on hand***: to draw nigh, approach. *Obs.*

a **1300** *Cursor M.* 4937 Sargantz send i son on hand þat in þair gare mi god þai fand. *Ibid.* 10680 To bring a custom neu on hand. *c* **1400** *Destr. Troy* 11362 Noy..neghis on hond. *Ibid.* 12265 Onone come the nyght & neghit vppon hond. *a* **1400–50** *Alexander* 4791 A new note neghis on hand.

†**d.** ***on (an) hand***: favourably, prosperously.

c **1200** *Trin. Coll. Hom.* 177 Here tuder swiðe wexeð and wel þieð and goð wel on hond. *c* **1205** LAY. 22313 Wind heom stod an honde. *a* **1250** *Owl & Night.* 1649 Me þuncþ þat þu me gest an honde.

e. At hand; in attendance (*U.S.*).

1856 OLMSTED *Slave States* 372 The slaves they had employed never would be *on hand*, when the hour for relieving came. **1887** J. HAWTHORNE *Trag. Myst.* x, Jonson proposed to be on hand again before breakfast. **1891** *Chicago Inter Ocean* 16 Feb., I heard that he was about to make a sale, and I was on hand.

†**f.** On in time, as time goes on. *Obs.*

c **1205** LAY. 7165 þeos children weoxen an hond þat heo mihten halden lond. *Ibid.* 12711 Ah þene nome hit losede an hond. *a* **1225** *Ancr. R.* 326 þe wunde þet euer wurseð an hond. *c* **1320** *Sir Tristr.* 933 On hand Mani man wepen sare For ransoun to yrland.

g. ***on, upon, one's hands*** (rarely ***hand***): resting upon one as a charge, burden, or responsibility, or as a thing to be dealt with or attended to; opp. to ***off one's hands***.

1528 ROY *Rede me* (Arb.) 134, I haue wife and children vpon my hande. **1568** GRAFTON *Chron.* II. 1167 Kerseis, and Collons, lay on their handes. **1639** T. BRUGIS tr. *Camus' Mor. Relat.* 214 Seeing three men upon his hands, what could he doe? **1700** T. BROWN tr. *Fresny's Amusem. Ser. & Com.* 48 Persons..that have a great deal of Idle Time lying upon their Hands. **1790** BURNS *Tam O'Shanter* 78 That night, a child might understand, The Deil had business on his hand. **1799** HAN. MORE *Fem. Educ.* (ed. 4) I. 110 Were we thrown a little more on our own hands. **1889** J. S. WINTER *Mrs. Bob* (1891) 158, I have this house on my hands till next October.

h. ***on all hands***, ***on every hand***: on all sides, in all directions, to or from all quarters.

1601 R. JOHNSON *Kingd. & Commw.* (1603) 105 They are oppressed on all hands. **1604** SHAKS. *Oth.* II. i. 86 The grace of Heauen, Before, behinde thee, and on euery hand Enwheele thee round. **1700** DRYDEN *Pref. Fables* (Globe) 506 It is agreed on all hands that he writes even below Ogilby. **1775** SHERIDAN *Duenna* I. iv, I have heard it on all hands. **1856** R. A. VAUGHAN *Mystics* (1860) II. VIII. vii. 66 The shameful servility of some, the immoral life of others, the bigotry of almost all, repelled him on every hand. **1893** *Law Times* XCV. 227/2 It is admitted on all hands.

i. ***on (the) one hand***, ***on the other hand***, are used (besides the physical sense 4) to indicate two contrasted sides of a subject, circumstances, considerations, points of view, etc.

1638 BAKER tr. *Balzac's Lett.* (vol. III.) 55 My mother.. being sicke on one hand, and my selfe on the other. **1705** BOSMAN *Guinea* 434 We are obliged to depart without our Money: But on the other hand, the next time we come hither, we are sure to be honestly paid. **1711** ADDISON *Spect.* No. 101 ¶2 If men of eminence are exposed to censure on the one hand, they are as much liable to flattery on the other. **1741** WATTS *Improv. Mind* I. v. §5 But there is a danger of mistake in our judgment of books, on the other hand also. **1871** SMILES *Charact.* i. (1876) 10 Either being elevated on the one hand, or degraded on the other. *Mod.* This is the larger; on the other hand, its flavour is not quite so fine.

†**j.** So formerly ***on either hand***, ***on some hands***, ***on this hand***. *Obs.*

1655 BP. HALL *Rem. Wks.* (1660) 205 Here we live with men, yea beasts, yea, if (on some hands) I should say with incarnate Devils, I should not [etc.]. **1662** STILLINGFL. *Orig. Sacr.* II. vii. §2 It is no question on either hand whether God may require these things or no. **1769** BURKE *Corr.* (1844) I. 188 On this hand I would not choose a very shy and cold behaviour.

k. ***on any hand***: see 25 g.

33. out of hand.

a. At once, immediately, straight off; without premeditation, suddenly; extempore.

13.. *Gaw. & Gr. Knt.* 2285 Dele to me my destine, and do hit out of honde. *c* **1485** *Digby Myst.* (1882) I. 214 Redde him of his lyff out of hand a-non. **1578** LYTE *Dodoens* III. lxxxviii. 427 Aconit is..very hurtful to mans nature, and killeth out of hande. **1692** R. L'ESTRANGE *Josephus, Antiq.* XV. xi. (1733) 413 Salome and her Faction were Tooth and Nail for dispatching her out of Hand. **1794** GODWIN *Cal. Williams* 82 Bid him finish the business out of hand. **1883** F. M. CRAWFORD *Dr. Claudius* vii. 114 She will marry you out of hand after a three months' engagement.

b. The opposite of *in hand* (in various senses: see 29): No longer in process; done with; not led by the hand; from or as a result of some treatment (quot. 1823); out of or beyond control.

1597 SHAKS. *2 Hen. IV*, III. i. 107 Were these inward Warres once out of hand, Wee would (deare Lords) vnto the Holy-Land. **1807** COLERIDGE *Lett.* (1895) 513 Do what you have to do at once, and put it out of hand. **1823** J. BADCOCK *Dom. Amusem.* 153 Though repeated with muriatic acid also, it comes out of hand in a most enviable state of whiteness. **1883** W. E. NORRIS *No New Thing* III. xxxv. 223 Your temper seems to have got rather out of hand.

c. ***to eat*** (or ***feed***) ***out of one's hand*** (see EAT *v.* 3 d).

1958 HAYWARD & HARARI tr. *Pasternak's Dr. Zhivago* I. vii. 212 'Well, have they had their tails twisted yet? Are they keeping quiet now?' 'The shopkeepers, you mean?.. Feed out of your hand!'

34. to hand.

a. Within reach, accessible, at hand; †near, close by, close up, to close combat (*obs.*); into one's possession or presence. (See also *to come to hand*, 37 a.)

a **1300** *Cursor M.* 11235 Sli[k] clathes als sco had to hand. *Ibid.* 14142 His sisters serued him to hand. *c* **1400** *Rom. Rose* 4198 It were foly to prece to honde. *c* **1440** CAPGRAVE *Life St. Kath.* v. 992 Ffor be his massageris sente he me to hande Al my sustenauns. **1590** SPENSER *F.Q.* I. xi. 8 By this, the dreadful Beast drew nigh to hand. *Ibid.* II. vi. 19 Him needed not long call; shee soone to hond Her ferry brought. **1750** FRANKLIN *Let.* Wks. 1887 II. 166, I sent this essay.. and have since heard nothing of it, which makes me doubt of its getting to hand. **1845–6** TRENCH *Huls. Lect.* Ser. I. iv. 69 Evidences ready to hand.

b. ***to hand***, ***to one's hand***: into subjection, under control.

1607 TOPSELL *Four-f. Beasts* (1658) 241 Alexander..at last wan the horse to hand. *c* **1630** RISDON *Surv. Devon* §266 (1810) 275 He..brought the hawk to hand. **1720** DE FOE *Capt. Singleton* iv. (1840) 63 Some of these they had brought so to their hand, that they taught them to go and come.

c. ***to (unto) one's hand(s***: ready for one, without exertion on one's own part.

1581 W. CHARKE in *Confer.* IV. (1584) Ff ij b, I English it to your hande, because you deale not with the Greeke. **1606** SHAKS. *Ant. & Cl.* IV. xiv. 29 What thou would'st do Is done vnto thy hand. **1661** BRAMHALL *Just Vind.* iii. 53 The Court of Rome had done that to their hands. **1701** W. WOTTON *Hist. Rome, Commodus* i. 188 The Work is done to your Hands already by your Father. **1855** BROWNING *A Light Woman* xiv, Robert Browning, you writer of plays, Here's a subject made to your hand!

35. under hand.

†**a.** In subjection, under control or rule; under one's charge or care. *Obs.*

a **1300** *Cursor M.* 6442 (Cott.) þis ilk folk..þat moyses had vnder hand. *c* **1340** *Ibid.* 4261 (Trin.) Ioseph..haþ his godes vndir honde.

b. Secretly, stealthily: see UNDERHAND.

1611 TOURNEUR *Ath. Trag.* III. iii. Wks. 1878 I. 92 He does it under hand. **1705** BOSMAN *Guinea* (1707) 49 Selling this Liquor by their Emissaries under-hand.

c. ***under one's hand(s***: under one's action, charge, care, or treatment.

1535 COVERDALE *Exod.* xxi. 20 He that smyteth his seruaunt..that he dye vnder his handes. **1659** D. PELL *Impr. Sea* 72 As a Physician doth to see many patients dying under his hands. **1700** S. L. tr. *Fryke's Voy. E. Ind.* 16 We had a Man, who had lost a Limb..under our Hands to cure.

d. ***under the hand of***: with the signature of. (Cf. 17.)

1633 T. STAFFORD *Pac. Hib.* I. vii. (1810) 98 Letters which were intercepted and brought to mee (under the Presidents hand). **1700** S. L. tr. *Fryke's Voy. E. Ind.* 70 An especial Order under my hand. **1726** *Adv. Capt. R. Boyle* 309 The Lady.. gave it my Wife, without any thing under my Hand. **1891** *Law Times* XCII. 125/1 The rule which makes it necessary to stamp with a sixpenny stamp an agreement under hand only.

unto one's **hand**: see 34 c. **upon hand**: see 25 g, 32 g.

36. with..hands.

†**a.** ***with one's hands, with (seventh, twelfth,*** etc.) ***hand***: by oath, by the testimony of (seven, twelve, etc.) witnesses. (See Du Cange s.v. *Juramentum.*) *Obs.*

1484 *Surtees Misc.* (1888) 43 He welbe at all tymes redy to prove and make good eythre upon a book or els with his handes. **1609** *Leges Marchiarum* in *Stat. Scotl.* I. 84*/2 He sall purge him þerof at þe merchis..with þe sevynt hand. **1658** CLEVELAND *Rustic Rampant* Wks. (1687) 472 The Abbot with his twelfth Hand..should swear.

b. ***with both hands*** (fig.): with all one's might; †fully, freely (quot. 1624). (See also *to play with both hands*, 40.)

[**1340** HAMPOLE *Pr. Consc.* 1258 þe world..Agayn us fightes with twa handes.] **1611** BIBLE *Micah* vii. 3 That they may doe euill with both hands earnestly. **1624** BEDELL *Lett.* viii. 118 All this is yeelded with both hands. **1871** L. CARROLL *Through the Looking-Glass* ix. 188 You couldn't deny that, if you tried with both hands.

** *With verb and preposition.* (See also *bear in hand* (BEAR *v.* 3 e), *bring on h.* (32 c above), *come in h.* (29 c), *have in h.*, *on h.* (29 f. 32 a, b), *hold in h.* (29 c, e), *take off one's hands* (31 b).)

37. come to hand.

a. To come to one, or within one's reach, to arrive, to turn up: to be received or obtained.

a **1300** *Cursor M.* 19893 þan com þaa thre men him to hand. *c* **1400** *Sowdone Bab.* 2401 Thai slowen down þat came to honde. **1513** MORE in Grafton *Chron.* (1568) II. 782 To put on such harnesse as came next to their handes. **1603** KNOLLES *Hist. Turks* (1658) 72 The common people..eat whatsoever comes to hand. **1807** T. JEFFERSON *Writ.* (1830) IV. 101 The enclosed letter..came to hand yesterday. **1875** JOWETT *Plato* (ed. 2) III. 358 Seizing any weapon that comes to hand.

b. ***come to (one's) hands***: to come to close quarters, engage hand to hand. (Cf. 25 f.)

1551 ROBINSON tr. *More's Utop.* II. (1895) 257 The battell come to their handes. **1623** BINGHAM *Xenophon* 74 Who came to hands, before the whole Armie ioyned. **1882** STEVENSON *New Arab. Nts.* (1884) 237, I want to come to my hands with them, and be done.

†**38. fall in hand(s.** *Obs.* (Cf. 29 f, g.)

†**a.** To fall to blows; to come to words *with*. (Also *fall on hand.*) *Obs.*

1448 *Paston Lett.* No. 60 I. 74 When they met to gyder, they fell in handes togyder, and [Sir Robert] smot hym.. with hys sord. *Ibid.* No. 711 III. 72, I felle on hande with hym for Matelaske Kerre. **1529** MORE *Comf. agst. Trib.* III. Wks. 1224/1 She fel in hand with hym and all to rated him. **1605** CAMDEN *Rem.* (1637) 275 His wife fell in hand with him, and asked him; What will you do, list you not to put forth your selfe as others doe?

†**b.** ***fall in hands with***, or *to do* something: to set about, take in hand. *Obs.*

1529 MORE *Dyaloge* 30 b/1 Or he fall in hand wyth the tone or the tother. **1577–87** HOLINSHED *Chron.* (1807–8) II. 83 King Stephan..fell in hand to besiege the residue of those places which the rebels kept. **1611** BIBLE *Transl. Pref.* 10 Neither..were we the first that fell in hand with translating the Scripture into English. **1641** BEST *Farm. Bks.* (Surtees) 141 Neaver to fall in hands with mole catchinge till St. Marke day bee past.

†**39. go in hand, on hand.** *Obs.* (Cf. 29 f, g.)

†**a.** ***go in hand with***, or *to do* something: to engage or deal with, be about; to proceed with.

1534 MORE *On the Passion* Wks. 1323/2 Our Sauiour foorthwyth went in hande with the instytutynge of..the blessed Sacramente. **1587** HARRISON *England* II. i. (1877) I. 38, I will..go in hand with the limits..of our seuerall sees. **1639** SANDERSON *Serm.* II. 124 [That] he should..go in hand with it himself, with all convenient care and speed.

†**b.** To come to be dealt with or treated. *Obs.*

1553 GRIMALDE *Cicero's Offices* (*c* **1600**) 159 b, When Atreus part should goe in hand [*cum tractaretur Atreus*].

†**40. play on** (or **with**) **both hands.** To practise double dealing, act with duplicity. *Obs.*

1549 *Compl. Scot.* xi. 89 The kyng of ingland playit vitht baytht the handis. **1613** PURCHAS *Pilgrimage* (1614) 358 He slew..King of the Hunnes, for playing on both hands.

†**41. stand** (one) **in** (or **on**) **hand.** To concern; to be incumbent on; to be the duty or business of. (Cf. 32 g.)

c **1555** *Fisher's Life* lf. 118 It standeth vs in hand..to prostrate ourselves before him. **1583** GOLDING *Calvin on Deut.* Pref. Ep. 3 It standeth us on hand to strengthen ourselves in the infallible certaintie of the holy Christian Religion. **1654** H. L'ESTRANGE *Chas. I* (1655) 89 It stood him in hand to stand upon his guard. **1786** I. PERKINS *Poem* in H.R. Stiles *Bundling* (1869) 99 Sence it doth stand each one in hand To happyfy his life.

42. take in hand, †on hand. To take the charge or responsibility of; to set oneself to carry out or deal with; to undertake; sometimes *spec.* to undertake the discipline, care, or cure (of a person).

a. with *simple obj.*

a **1300** *Cursor M.* 25928 þis hali wark j tak on hand. **1375** BARBOUR *Bruce* I. 268 Wedding is the hardest band That ony man may tak on hand. **1390** GOWER *Conf.* I. 34 Where dedly werre is taken on honde. **1535** COVERDALE *Ps.* c[i]. 4, I wil take no wicked thinge in honde. **1581** PETTIE *Guazzo's Civ. Conv.* I. (1586) 22 To morrow..we wil take againe our matter in hand. **1608–11** BP. HALL *Medit. & Vows* II. §12 Before I take any man in hand, I will knowe whether hee be a thorne or a nettle. **1749** FIELDING *Tom Jones* VII. iii, Very obedient to me she was when a little child, before you took her in hand. **1885** G. ALLEN *Babylon* xi, I've taken you in hand. *Mod.* It is a difficult task that you have taken in hand.

b. with *inf.* (*arch.* or *dial.*)

1307 *Elegy Edw. I*, v, That oure kynge hede take on honde, Al Engelond to ȝeme ant wysse. *c* **1380** *Sir Ferumb.* 143 To take an hond aȝen hym to take þe fyȝte. **1526** TINDALE *Luke* i. 1 For as moche as many have taken in hond to compyle a treates off thoo thynges. **1676** HOBBES *Iliad* I. 268 T'appease Achilles I will take in hand. *Mod.* (*north. dial.*) He took in hand to inform the others.

*** *With verb governing* hand. (For other phrases, as BEAR *a hand*, FORCE (*a person's*) *hand*, HOLD (*one's*) *hand*, JOIN *hands*, KISS *the hand*, LAY *hands on*, LEND *a hand*, SET *hand* (*to*, *on*), SHAKE *hands*, STRIKE *hands*, TRY *one's hand*, WASH *one's hands of*, etc., see the verbs. *to have a hand in*: see 3 b above. *to show one's hand*: see 23 d.)

43. change hands. To substitute the left hand for the right and the converse; to pass from one hand to another, from one person's hand or possession to another's (cf. 2).

1670, 1732 [see CHANGE *v.* 2]. **1826** H. N. COLERIDGE *West Indies* 100 The property in the soil must change hands. **1849** MACAULAY *Hist. Eng.* II. 160 The whole soil would soon change hands.

44. give (one's) **hand.**

a. To present or hold out the hand to be grasped, in token of salutation, bargaining, etc.

1596 SHAKS. *Tam. Shr.* II. i. 320 Giue me your hands, God send you ioy, Petruchio, 'tis a match. **1601** —— *Jul. C.* v. v. 49 Giue me your hand first. Fare you wel my Lord. **1876** T. HARDY *Ethelberta* (1890) 114 She gave him a hand so cool and still that Christopher..was literally ashamed to let her see and feel his own.

†**b.** *fig.* ***to give hands***: to consent, agree (*to*); to pledge oneself. *Obs.*

1594 CAREW *Huarte's Exam. Wits* (1616) 24 So they all gaue hands to this opinion, saue onely Aristotle. **1708** OCKLEY *Saracens* (1848) 432 So they gave him their hands to be subject to him.

c. ***to give a hand***: to help a person. Also, ***to lend a hand*** (see LEND *v.*[2] 2 e).

1860 in A. F. Ridgway *Voices from Auckland* 71 His young wife..will readily give him a hand at the crosscut for a few hours. **1880** *Daily Tel.* 26 Nov., A policeman gave him a hand up. **1949** J. ROUTH in *Granta* Christmas ed., 'Here, let me give you fellows a hand,' I suggested.

45. make a hand. a. To make one's profit; to make a success *of*, to succeed or speed with. Freq. with qualifying adj., as *fair*, *fine* (often ironical), *good*, etc.

1538 LONDON in *Lett. Suppress. Monast.* (Camden) 234 They mak ther handes by leesys, salys of wodde, and of ther plate. **1583** GOLDING *Calvin on Deut.* iii. 15/1 All is one with them, so as they may make their hand. **1613** SHAKS. *Hen. VIII*, v. iv. 74 Y' haue made a fine hand fellowes? **1669** W. HACKE *Collect. Orig. Voy.* iii. (1699) 69 We should have made a better hand of them. **1702** C. MATHER *Magn. Chr.* VII. App. (1852) 596 Through the disadvantages of their feet by the snow they could make no hand on it. **1727** SWIFT *Gulliver* II. iii, The farmer..concluding I must soon die, resolved to make as good a hand of me as he could. **1808** WINDHAM *Let.* 21 Oct. in *Sp. Parl.* (1812) I. 98, I do not find that I make much hand (I should rather perhaps say much *foot*) in walking. **1890** BOLDREWOOD *Col. Reformer* (1891) 90, I don't suppose you'd have made much hand of them by yourself.

b. ***to make a hand of (with)***: to make away with, make an end of, 'do for'. *Obs.* or *dial.*

1577–87 HOLINSHED *Chron.* (1807–8) III. 142 They falling to the spoile made a hand, and therewith departed. **1583** STUBBES *Anat. Abus.* II. (1882) 55 To giue them such medicines..as will soone make a hand of them. **1601** HOLLAND *Pliny* IX. lx, It makes a hand with it, and digesteth it presently. **1678** BUNYAN *Pilgr. Progr.* 93 He [Moses] had doubtless made a hand of me, but that one came by, and bid him forbear. **1864** CARLYLE *Fredk. Gt.* XV. v. (1871) VI. 8 Hungarian Majesty..attacks Seckondorf furiously..in mid-winter; and makes a terrible hand of him. **1887** *Chesh. Gloss.* s.v., I mun know about th' markets afore I sell: I dunna want to be made a hand on.

46. put (one's) **hand. a.** ***to put one's hand***: to exert oneself, use one's energies; now always with *to*: to set about, undertake (a piece of work).

1388 WYCLIF *Luke* ix. 62 No man that puttith his hoond to the plouȝ, and biholdynge bacward, is able to the rewme of God. **1439** in *Fenland N. & Q.* (1905) July 222 And yat ..ye wole at yis tyme..putte youre handes and ese us by wey of lone of ye somme of C marc. *c* **1450** *St. Cuthbert* (Surtees) 6056 þat to þi seruyce puttys þair hands. **1535** COVERDALE *Deut.* xii. 18 All y[t] thou puttest thine hande vnto. **1631** J. PRESTON *Treat. Effect. Faith* 45 If God himselfe put not his hand to the worke no man is able to believe. **1633** J. HALL *Hard Texts* Zech. xi. 9, I will not put my hand to redresse it. **1879** M. J. GUEST *Lect. Hist. Eng.* ix. 80 Whatever he put his hand to, he did it 'with all his might'.

b. ***to put*** (one's) ***hand(s) on,*** (†***in***, †***unto***): to lay hands on (see LAY *v.*[1] 21 c); †to do violence to (*Sc. Obs.*); to get hold of, seize (also *fig.*).

1535 COVERDALE *Exod.* xxii. 8 ([He] shal sweare) that he hath not put his hande vnto his neghbours good. **1837** C. M. GOODRIDGE *Voy. S. Seas* (1843) 44 [We] got into her with such articles as we could immediately put our hands on. **1842** J. H. NEWMAN *Par. Serm.* VI. viii. 111 Perhaps..we can put our hand, as it were, on a time in our childhood [when, etc.]. **1972** L. HENDERSON *Cage until Tame* vii. 57 Right now he couldn't put his hands on a hundred quid.

47. take the hand of. To take hold of the hand which is given or offered; to join hands.

1565 *Child Marriages* (E.E.T.S.) 68 The said Roger and Ellin..toke handes together. **1610** SHAKS. *Temp.* I. ii. 376 Come vnto these yellow sands, And then take hands. **1771** MRS. E. GRIFFITH *Lady Barton* II. 274 A pair..as firmly united as any that ever took hands, from the first wedding in Eden, down to this present day. *Mod.* Take my hand; I will lead you safely.

**** *With adjective qualifying* hand.

(For other phrases, as BLOODY *hand*, EVEN *hand*, FREE *hand*. HELPING *hand*, HIGH *hand*, LOOSE *hand*, OLD *hand*, RED *hand*, SINGLE *hand*, STRONG *hand*, UPPER *hand*, etc., see the adjectives. See also LEFT HAND, OVERHAND, RIGHT HAND, SECOND HAND, etc.).

48. better hand. †**a.** Superiority, the 'upper hand'; precedence.

1523 [see BETTER *a.* 5]. **1555** W. WATREMAN *Fardle Facions* II. xi. 243 The name of the Turkes hath gotten the bettre hande, and the other [Saracens] is out of remembraunce. **1568** GRAFTON *Chron.* II. 341 If they might have the better hande of us. **1632** MASSINGER & FIELD *Fatal Dowry* II. i, To let strong nature have the better hand. **1641** J. TRAPPE *Theologia Theol.* 2 That the Gospel should have the better hand of the Law.

b. See 10 b, 45 a.

49. clean hands. *fig.* Freedom from wrong-doing, innocence or uprightness of life: see CLEAN *a.* 3 g.

1382 WYCLIF *Job* xvii. 9 The riȝtwis shal holden his weie, and with clene hondis adde strengthe. **1539** BIBLE (Great) *Ps.* xxiv. 4 He that hath cleane handes and a pure hert. **1667** PEPYS *Diary* 19 May, My Lord Treasurer..is said to die with the cleanest hands that ever any Lord Treasurer did. **1896** MORLEY in *Liberal Mag.* Dec. 495 You would go..into the councils of Europe with clean hands.

50. first hand. a. ***at (the) first hand***: see 10 c above, and FIRST HAND. †**b.** ***at first hand***: at first. *Obs.*

1600 HOLLAND *Livy* XXV. xxxvii. 577 At first hand they wist not what to doe.

†**51. good hand.** ***to get*** or ***have a good hand against***: to get or have a decided advantage over. *Obs.* (See also *make a good hand of*, 45 a.)

1600 HOLLAND *Livy* VII. vii. 253 The other armie..got a good hand against their enemies. **1652–62** HEYLIN *Cosmogr.* III. (1673) 160/1 A prince who since he came to age, hath had a good hand against the Turks.

†**52. higher hand.** Superiority in contest, mastery. *Obs.*

a **1225** *Leg. Kath.* 758 ȝef ha mahen on me þe herre hond habben. **13..** *Coer de L.* 5239 And who that haves the heyer hand Have the cyte and al her land. *c* **1386** CHAUCER *Prol.* 399 If þat he faughte and hadde the hyer honde. *c* **1450** *Merlin* 124 That he myghte haue the hier honde.

***** *With an adverb.*

53. hand in, out. ***to have one's hand in***: to be actively engaged, to be in habitual practice, to be at it; to be in practice. ***his hand is out***: he is out of practice, not in working order.

c **1460** *Towneley Myst.* (Surtees) 220 Yit efte, whils thi hande is in, Pulle ther at with som kyn gyn. **1586** A. DAY *Eng. Secretary* I. (1625) 44 There was no rake-hell..but his hand was in with him, and that he was a copesmate for him. **1588** SHAKS. *L.L.L.* IV. i. 137 And if my hand be out, then belike your hand is in. **1667** BARROW in Rigaud *Corr. Sci. Men* (1841) II. 54 Now my hand is in, I will add briefly these theorems. **1749** CHESTERF. *Lett.* (1792) II. cxcviii. 246 Write a line or two of it every day to keep your hand in. **1828** *Craven Dial.* s.v., *To have the hand in*, to be accustomed to business. **1848** *Mem. Tod of Balerno* 17 There are particular seasons when..his hand is out, when he is unable to wield the pen, when imagination flags. **1875** M. PATTISON *Casaubon* 354 Mere exercises to keep his hand in.

54. hands off! *colloq.* Keep off! let (the person or thing) alone! a peremptory order to cease or desist from touching or interference. Also *attrib.*

1563 BECON *Display. Pop. Masse* Wks. III. 42 Take thys bread, sayth..Christ..Hande of, saye ye papistes. Gape and we will put it in your mouthes. *c* **1592** MARLOWE *Massacre Paris* II. iv, Hands off, good fellow; I will be his bail. **1637** B. JONSON *Sad Sheph.* I. ii, Hand off, rude ranger! —Sirrah, get you in. **1883** STEVENSON *Treas. Isl.* III. xiv, 'Hands off!' cried Silver leaping back a yard. **1902** *Daily Chron.* 23 Jan. 7/1 A protest must be made against the hands-off policy. **1908** *Times Lit. Suppl.* 3 Sept. 283/3 The hopelessly *doctrinaire* character of the 'hands-off' individualism.

b. *Aeronaut.* Used as *adj.* and *adv.* in connection with an automatically controlled aircraft.

1932 *Flight* 20 May 443/1 By means of the adjustable tail plane the machine can be trimmed to fly 'hands off'. **1935** *Jrnl. R. Aeronaut. Soc.* XXXIX. 1041 Control of this airplane when operating on one engine was carefully studied with the result that it can be flown 'hands off'. **1959** *Times* 18 Sept. 7/3 Some 4,000 'hands off' landings have been made. **1966** *Electronics* 3 Oct. 134 On the last orbit, it guided Gemini II into a hands-off reentry and landing virtually down the stacks of the recovery ships. **1968** *New Scientist* 1 Feb. 251/1 Several companies have developed artificial stabilization systems which enable the helicopter to be flown 'hands-off'.

55. hands up! An order or direction to people to hold up their hands to signify assent, etc.; also, a robber's, policeman's, etc., order to preclude resistance. Also in *Curling* (see quot. 1897).

1873 J. MILLER *Life amongst Modocs* 193 Hands up, gentlemen! **1887** J. HAWTHORNE *Trag. Myst.* xviii, Hands up—every soul of you! **1897** *Encycl. Sport* I. 264/1 *Hands up*, the command of the Skip.. to stop sweeping. *a* **1898** *Mod.* (at school). Hands up, those who have the right answer! **1910** *Encycl. Brit.* VII. 646/1 Curling has a language which contains many curious terms... *Hands up*! stop sweeping.

****** *With another noun.*

(See also HAND AND GLOVE, HAND OF GLORY, HAND OVER HEAD, HAND TO MOUTH, etc.)

56. hand..fist. a. ***hand over fist*** (colloq.) = HAND OVER HAND. Also, esp., *fig.* of the making of money.

1825 W. N. GLASCOCK *Naval Sketch-Bk.* (1826) I. 26 The French.. weathered our wake, coming up with us, 'hand over fist', in three divisions. **1833** S. SMITH *Life Major J. Downing* (1834) 116 They.. clawed the money off of his table, hand over fist. **1861** M. B. CHESNUT *Diary* 8 Aug. (1949) 107 Fitzhugh Lee and Roony are being promoted hand over fist. **1880** W. C. RUSSELL *Sailor's Sweetheart* II. iii. 173 A heavy squall was coming up hand over fist along with the wind. **1884** in *L'pool Daily Post* 9 Jan. (1885) 6/2 [It] enables.. lighter and better rigged whalers to get away from them, as the phrase goes, 'hand over fist'. **1888** 'R. BOLDREWOOD' *Robbery under Arms* xxvii, We.. made money hand over fist. **1901** *Daily Chron.* 27 Dec. 3/3 To use a phrase common to the Anglo-Saxon, they have been making money hand-over-fist. **1929** J. B. PRIESTLEY *Good Companions* II. vii. 445 She lost money hand-over-fist for weeks and weeks—and not a murmur—and now she is beginning to get a little back again. **1963** *Times* 12 June 13/4 It pays hand over fist always to take the secondary roads that run along the 'wrong' sides of rivers in preference to the main roads that run along their 'right' sides.

b. ***hand to fist*** (colloq.) = HAND TO HAND.

1652-3 WOOD *Life* 4 Mar., Going to the ale-house.. they set hand to fist, and drunk very desperatly. **1705** HICKERINGILL *Priest-cr.* I. (1721) 59 Killing a Lyon and a Bear, Hand to Fist. **1760** FOOTE *Minor* I. Wks. 1799 I. 245 He and Jenny Cummins drank three flasks, hand to fist, last night. **1811** SCOTT *Fam. Lett.* Sept (1894) I. vii. 229 The Edinburgh reviewers have been down on my poor *Don Roderick*, hand to fist.

57. hand and foot (also in earlier use ***f. and h.***, ***feet and hs.***, ***hs. and f.***) are often found in collocation; usually (now always) in adverbial construction; esp. in phr. ***to bind hand and foot*** (in mod. use sometimes *fig.*). ***to wait upon*** or †***serve (to) hand and foot***: to wait upon or serve assiduously. (See also FOOT *sb.* 26 b.)

c **950** *Lindisf. Gosp.* John xi. 44 ȝebundeno foet & hond. *c* **1000** *Ags. Gosp.* Ibid., þe dead wæs ȝebunden handan & fotan. *c* **1200** *Vices & Virt.* (1888) 17 And binden me, baðe handen and fiet. *a* **1300** *Cursor M.* 14355 Bath fete and hand þar was he bunden. *c* **1330** *Assump. Virg.* (B.M. MS.) 70 Sche.. seruede hem to hande & fote. *c* **1420** *Sir Amadace* (Camd.) lviii, To serue him wele to fote and honde. **1639** S. DU VERGER tr. *Camus' Admir. Events* 56 He is forth-with bound hand and foot. **1893** *Law Times* XCIV. 502/2 The Divisional Court held themselves bound hand and foot by the authorities. *a* **1898** *Mod.* They expect to be waited on hand and foot. **1955** L. P. HARTLEY *Perfect Woman* x. 96 He has everything he wants and servants who wait on him hand and foot.

58. hand...hand. (See also HAND IN HAND, HAND OVER HAND, HAND TO HAND.)

† **a.** ***hand by hand, hand for hand***: = HAND TO HAND, at close quarters; side by side. ***hand of hand, hand with hand, to hand and hand, with hand to hand***: = HAND TO HAND. *Obs.*

c **1205** LAY. 174 Hond wið honde, fuhten þa heȝe men. **13..** *Coer de L.* 4364 Hand be hand to geve bekyr. *c* **1400** *Sowdone Bab.* 394 That thai myght fight with hem anoon, Honde of honde. **1430-40** LYDG. *Bochas* IV. ix. (1554) 107 The King and he walking hand by hand. **1490** CAXTON *Eneydos* liv. 150 To fyghte wyth hym hande for hande. **1535** STEWART *Cron. Scot.* I. 371 Tha kingis.. raid togidder to the toun, Hand for hand. **1548** HALL *Chron., Hen. V*, 56 b, To get upon the walles and with hand to hand to graple with his enemy. **1553** BRENDE *Q. Curtius* III. 33 Being enforced to joyne hand for hand, they valiantly used the sworde.

b. ***from hand to hand***: from one person to another; through a series or succession of hands. (Cf. 10.)

1561 T. NORTON *Calvin's Inst.* I. 18 Their writings came to posteritie.. from hand to hand. **1660** F. BROOKE tr. *Le Blanc's Trav.* 10 The word was given from hand to hand through the company. **1882** BESANT *Revolt of Man* ix. 217 This tract had been circulated from hand to hand.

c. ***hand under hand***: bringing each hand successively below the other, as in climbing down a rope, etc.: the opposite of HAND OVER HAND.

1804 *Naval Chron.* XI. 92 [He] let himself down, hand under hand, by a rope.

59. hand and thigh. *Old Irish Law.* (See quot.)

1873 W. K. SULLIVAN *Introd. to O'Curry's Anc. Irish* I. 172 Ultimately, however, daughters appear to have become entitled to inherit all if there were no sons. The land thus given to a daughter was called 'an inheritance of hand and thigh'. *Ibid.*, An explanation of why the estate 'of hand and thigh' was one-third the estate of a *Fiath*.

60. hand's turn. *colloq.* A stroke of work.

1828 *Craven Dial.* s.v., She winna do a hands-turn. **1881** *Queen* LXX. 522/3 She.. has to be waited on by the maids rather than doing a hand's turn for herself or you.

61. hands-across-the-sea, used *attrib.* of an act, etc., performed by one country as a gesture of friendship to an overseas country.

1899 *Westm. Gaz.* 1 Feb. 1/4 Mr. Tree has a new drama in his mind—an old-time hands-across-the-sea subject. **1955** *Sci. News Let.* 5 Feb. 88/3 The Missouri Commission is interested in the experiments, not only as a 'hands-across-the-sea gesture'.. but because the Missouri bunny might also be susceptible to the dread disease, and advance knowledge would permit more effective preventive action. **1957** *Times Lit. Suppl.* 25 Oct. 635/2 What is this but empty rhetoric of the 'hands-across-the-sea' brand? **1971** C. FICK *Danziger Transcript* (1973) 88 It was supposed to be a hands-across-the-sea sort of thing.

******* *Proverbial phrases and locutions.*

62. a. In comparisons, as ***as bare, flat, as one's hand***. **b.** ***like hand and glove***, etc.: see also HAND AND GLOVE. † **c.** ***to have long hands***: see quots. **d.** ***to have one's hands full***: to have enough to do or as much as one can do, to be fully occupied. **e.** ***many hands make light work***. **f.** ***in the turn(ing) of a hand***: in a moment, instantly (cf. *in the twinkling of an eye*). **g.** In other expressions: see quots. (***to have a hand in the pie***: see PIE. ***to play into a person's hands***: see PLAY.) **h.** ***hands down***: with ease, with little or no effort; unconditionally, submissively; orig. in the racing phr. ***to win hands down***, referring to the jockey dropping his hands, and so relaxing his hold on the reins, when victory appears certain.

a. *c* **1420** *Siege Rouen* in *Collect. Lond. Cit.* (Camden) 4 Buschys and brerys and boughys they brende And made hyt as bare as my honde. **1876** BROWNING *Nat. Magic* i, The room was as bare as your hand. **1883** *Harper's Mag.* Dec. 147/1 That coast.. is flat as your hand, as we say.

b. **1798** G. WASHINGTON *Lett.* Writ. 1893 XIV. 129 He.. has been as familiar with all.. as the hand is with the glove.

c. **1583** HOLLYBAND *Campo di Fior* 17 What if I should call thee theefe? What if I should say that thou hast long handes? **1828** SCOTT *F.M. Perth* vi, His father is a powerful man—hath long hands—reaches as far as he can.

d. **1470-85** MALORY *Arthur* XX. xxii, Ye shalle haue bothe your handes ful of me. **1625** MASSINGER *New Way* V. i, You shall have your hands full Upon the least incitement. **1724** DE FOE *Mem. Cavalier* (1840) 65 Horn.. had his hands full with the main battle. **1874** STUBBS *Const. Hist.* (1875) I. xii. 479 The king had his hands full in Poictou.

e. **14..** *Sir Beues* 3012 (MS. M.) Thoughe Ascaparde be neuer so starke, Many handes make lyght warke! **1539** TAVERNER *Erasm. Prov.* (1552) 36 Many handes make a lyghte burthen. **1663** F. HAWKINS *Youth's Behav.* 90 Many hands make light work.

f. *a* **1300** *Cursor M.* 23223 Quils þou moght turn þi hand abute, It suld worth rose witvten dute. **1599** H. BUTTES *Dyets drie Dinner* F v, In the turne of an hand: in the twinckling of an eye. *a* **1632** T. TAYLOR *God's Judgem.* I. II. xxxvi. 289 In the turning of an hand they were all in flames.

g. **1561** DAUS tr. *Bullinger on Apoc.* (1573) 133 b, Thou must hold vp thy hand to thine eares for me: that is to say, thou shall confirme me this by an oath. **1617** MORYSON *Itin.* III. I. ii. 17 He that writes often, shall often receiue letters for answere: for one hand washeth another.

h. **1867** 'PIPS' *Lyrics & Lays* 155 There were good horses in those days, as he can well recall, But Barker upon Elepoo, hands down, shot by them all. **1882** *Moonshine* 3 June 265 (*caption*) Won!! 'Hands Down'. **1913** MRS. H. WARD *Mating of Lydia* II. xii, That I should surrender, hands down, to a lot of trumpery complaints and grievances. **1920** W. B. MONEY *Humours of Parish* 126, I started off in the race in full nigger costume, and won hands down. **1958** *Times* 14 Aug. 9/7 Double this speed, however, and the submarine wins hands down.

III. Attributive uses and Combinations.

63. *attrib.* **a.** Of or belonging to the hand, as ***hand-clasp, -gesture, -gout, -grasp, -guard, -kiss, -movement, -reach, -rest, -skill, -touch, -turn, -wave***, etc. **b.** Worn on the hand, as ***hand-fetter, -ring, -ruffle, -shackle***.

1887 JEFFERIES *Amaryllis at the Fair* 85 Books.. bound in the best style of *hand-art. **1583** STANYHURST *Æneis* IV. (Arb.) 105 Fayth plighted in *handclaspe. **1897** HALL CAINE *Christian* xi, Their hands met in a long hand-clasp. **1930** R. PAGET *Babel* ii. 56 The large number of ideas which cannot be symbolized directly by *hand-gesture. **1962** *Listener* 1 Mar. 382/2 The energy and urgency of hand gesture, visible in his recent drawings, has extended itself on the larger scale of these paintings. **1616-61** HOLYDAY *Persius* 325 When the knotty *hand-gout has once broke Their joynts. **1893** *Daily News* 11 Jan. 2/1 Losing their foothold and *handgrasp on the ladder ways. **1874** BOUTELL *Arms & Arm.* viii. 128 At the handle the shaft [of the lance] passed through a small circular shield, or *hand-guard (called a vamplate). **1861** C. READE *Cloister & Hearth* ii. 32 A sweet little coaxing *hand-kiss. **1958** F. HARRIS *My Life & Loves* V. i. 28 She sent me back with an imperious hand-kiss. **1637** *Bp.'s Transcr. of Register S. Geo. Martyr* (Canterbury), [Signed] William Welton by W his *hand mark. **1924** R. M. OGDEN tr. *Koffka's Growth of Mind* v. 254 During the *hand-movements, the gaze is directed fixedly upon the object. **1795** SOUTHEY *Joan of Arc* IX. 258 At his side Within *hand-reach his sword. **1904** GOODCHILD & TWENEY *Technol. & Sci. Dict.* 279/1 **Hand rest*, the T-shaped support for supporting hand-turning tools in working at a lathe when a slide rest is not used. **1922** JOYCE *Ulysses* 225 Two carfuls of tourists passed slowly, their women sitting fore, gripping frankly the handrests. **1845** JAMES *A. Neil* ii, His collar and *hand-ruffles were of lace. **1549** HOOPER *10 Commandm.* xi. Wks. (Parker Soc.) 405 A manacle or *hand-shackle to keep them from doing of ill. **1883-4** J. G. BUTLER in *Bible-Work* II. 131 Daily labor, *hand-toil or brain-toil. **1859** *Bentley's Q. Rev.* July 544 When it comes to shifts and *hand-turns.. we are utterly at a stand.

c. That is or may be held or carried in the hand, portable; as ***hand-anvil, -baggage, -camera*** (so ***hand-camerist***); ***-candle, -candlestick, -lamp, -lantern, -lexicon, -litter, -mirror, -luggage, -microphone, -mike, -net, -props, -screen, -specimen, -spectroscope, -tray***, etc.

1889 *Pall Mall G.* 21 Sept. 6/1 The two travellers.. stowed their *hand-baggage away in their compartment. **1902** *Daily Chron.* 27 Feb. 3/3 The Boer delegates have only brought with them hand-baggage. **1889** *Photogr. News* 15 Nov. 755/1 For the *hand camera there is, I believe, a great and wide field of usefulness. **1890** *Anthony's Photogr. Bull* III. 1 Both to the stay-at-home and the tourist the hand camera has become a necessity. **1910** *Chambers's Jrnl.* Sept. 588/1 Hand-cameras are made in a thousand patterns. **1892** *Photogr. Ann.* II. 52 It is this ungentlemanly abuse of the hand camera which brings the whole class of *hand camerists into disrepute. **1897** C. M. HEPWORTH *Animated Photogr.* xiii. 96 Subjects which are suitably lighted and otherwise 'possible' for the hand camerist may be safely attempted with a cinematographic camera. **1682** *Lond. Gaz.* No. 1706/8 One large Candlestick and Socket, one *hand Candlestick, Snuff-pan, and Snuffers. **1892** A. HEALES *Archit. Ch. Denmark* 31 A king is holding up a similar *hand-cross. **1862** *Illustr. Lond. News* 11 Jan. 51/1 With a *hand-eye-glass disposed across the nose. **1895** STORY-MASKELYNE *Crystallogr.* viii. §1. 388 The contact- or *hand-goniometer. **1831** CARLYLE *Sart. Res.* I. x, Thou.. wilt walk through thy world by the sunshine of what thou callest Truth, or even by the *hand-lamp of what I call Attorney-Logic. **1836** *Mechanics' Mag.* XXV. 317 The fact is that no *unguarded* light should ever be permitted in any stable, warehouse, cellar, or bed chamber; cheap, convenient, and even elegant hand lamps and lanterns suited to these uses, are met with in abundance. **1869** DUNKIN *Midn. Sky* 8 He has furnished himself with a *hand-lamp. **1940** *Chambers's Techn. Dict.* 401/2 *Hand-lamp*, a portable electric-light fitting suitable for carrying in the hand. Also called *inspection-lamp, portable-lamp*. **1965** 'LAUCHMONEN' *Old Thorn's Harvest* x. 134 They all sit down near to their handlamps. **1862** MARSH *Eng. Lang.* iii. 49 In a *hand-lexicon of any modern tongue. **1888** LD. MACNAGHTEN in *Law Rep. Ho. Lords* xiii. 55 Passengers take the lighter articles of luggage—or *'hand-luggage' as it is called,—in the carriage with them. **1908** *Daily Chron.* 8 Jan. 4/4 Glancing furtively at that terrible piece of hand-luggage, a New York Sunday newspaper. **1924** W. J. LOCKE *Coming of Amos* iv, Maxime possessed himself of her hand-luggage. **1970** *New Yorker* 16 May 41/3 'Any hand luggage?' says the clerk, peering over the top of the counter. **1968** *Radio Times* 20 June 58/1 For long I have been puzzled about the use of *hand microphones. **1968** *Punch* 3 Jan. 29/1 He does know precisely what he's about when he clutches a *handmike and sings. **1888** *Harper's Mag.* Dec. 162/1 An ivory backed *hand-mirror. **1726** SHELVOCKE *Voy. round World* (1757) 16 A little *hand nest of drawers. **1856** KANE *Arct. Expl.* II. xxiv. 243 Birds.. caught in their little *hand-nets. **1933** P. GODFREY *Back-Stage* iii. 34 'Props' is an abbreviation of 'stage properties', and therefore *'hand-props' are things handled by the actors, such as fans, snuff-boxes, etc. **1891** D'O. CARTE in *Pall Mall G.* 5 Dec. 1/3 There were some 3000 *hand-properties employed in 'Ivanhoe', and 10 scenes. **1826** MISS MITFORD *Village* Ser. II. (1863) 342 Painted shells and roses.. on card-racks and *hand-screens. **1815** W. PHILLIPS *Outl. Min. & Geol.* (1818) 198 By the examination of *hand specimens. **1871** tr. *Schellen's Spectr. Anal.* lxix. 418 The *hand-spectroscope of Huggins. **1481-90** *Howard Househ. Bks.* (Roxb.) 228 A payre of *hand-trayes. **1535** COVERDALE *Num.* xxxv. 18 Yf he smyte him with an *handweapon of wodd.

d. Managed or worked with the hand (sometimes *spec.* with one hand); driven or operated by manual power, as distinguished from that of an animal or a machine; as ***hand-bat, -bellows, -besom, -brake, -brush, -card*** (in cotton-spinning), ***-carriage, -comb, -drill, -drum, -feed, -flail, -harpoon, -hook, -lathe, -lever, -machine, -mangle***, †***-mell*** (= mallet), ***-mortar, -piercer, -pump, -punch*** (hence as *vb.*), ***puppet, -quern, -rake, -rope, -sail, sewing-machine, -shears, -shell, -sled, -sledge, -sleigh, -tool, -wagon, -wheel***, etc. **e.** Made or done by hand, as ***hand-embroidery***.

1781 SMEATHMAN in *Phil. Trans.* LXXI. 181 *note*, Beaten level.. with their feet and a kind of *hand-bat or beetle. **1665** HOOKE *Microgr.* 23 Blowing now and then the Coles with *hand-Bellows. **1894** *Westm. Gaz.* 4 Sept. 4/2 To stop the train at the proper place by the application of the ordinary *hand-brake only. **1913** *Autocar Handbk.* (ed. 5) xiv. 216 In some Coventry Daimler cars the *hand brake can be caused either to withdraw the clutch or not when it is applied. **1959** *Times* 15 Dec. 13/5 Consternation clutches at the heart while the driver clutches the handbrake. **1968** *Sun* 12 Nov. 8/5 *Handbrake turn*, the technique involving using the handbrake instead of reverse gear, for negotiating 'impossible' hairpins. **1747** H. GLASSE *Art of Cookery* xvii. 150 Let them be scrubed clean with a *Hand-Brush and Sand, and Fuller's Earth. **1904** J. VAIZEY *More about Pixie* (1910) i. 7 She went down on her knees, and swept up the dust with a small hand-brush. **1879** *Cassell's Techn. Educ.*

IV. 273/1 Carding..was performed by a pair of *hand-cards upon the knee. **1745** Ellis *Mod. Husb.* VI. ii. 14 This Farmer..carried his Wheat-sheaves into his Barn on a Sunday, by *Hand-carriage. **1859** Dickens in *All Year Round* (1860) 11 Aug. 422/2 A hand-carriage, drawn by a man... I saw within it an old man. **1882** *Encycl. Dict.* I. 685/2 The slivers are made by *hand-combs. **1710** *Lond. Gaz.* No. 4712/4 Several Persons..did attempt to murther ..Mr. Stone..wounding him with a *Hand-Crow. **1770–4** A. Hunter *Georg. Ess.* (1803) I. 431 The seed must be drilled by a *hand-drill. **1864** J. A. Grant *Walk across Africa* viii. 144 A band of *hand-drums is near the sultan's hut, giving lighter dance-music for the amusement of the boys and girls. **1879** Stainer *Music of Bible* 149 It was a tambour, timbrel, or *hand-drum. **1958** E. Borneman in P. Gammond *Decca Bk. Jazz* xxi. 275 A male leader and a small group..who accompanied themselves on..hand drums,..and gong-gong. **1940** *Chambers's Techn. Dict.* 401/1 **Hand feed*, the hand operation of the feed mechanism of a machine tool, as distinct from an automatic feed. **1962** *Gloss. Autom. Data Proc.* (*B.S.I.*) 91 *Hand-feed punch*, a key punch into which punched cards have to be fed manually one at a time. **1820** Scoresby *Acc. Arctic Reg.* II. 233 The *hand-harpoon is placed upon the nick or rest with its stock. **1765** Croker *Dict. Arts & Sc.*, **Hand-Hook*, an instrument used by smiths to twist square iron. **1873** *Young Englishwoman* Mar. 131/1 A most useful..*hand-machine ..at the low price of 39s. **1927** T. Woodhouse *Artificial Silk* 81 Practically coincident with the hand knitting of jumpers and the like came the hand-machine knitting. **1882** Pebody *Eng. Journalism.* xv. 107 He used to..make use of his mother's *hand-mangle to work off impressions of type. **1600** *Vestry Bks.* (Surtees) 133 For a *handmell, and crosspin of iron, to mend or make bald-rigs for our bells. **1704** *Lond. Gaz.* No. 4059/3, 2 Hawitzers, and 100 *Hand-Mortars. **1667** Primatt *City & C. Build.* 26 Whether they draw Water with Buckets, or *Hand-Pumps, or Chain-Pumps. **1962** *Gloss. Autom. Data Proc.* (*B.S.I.*) 91 **Hand punch*, a key punch into which punched cards have to be fed manually one at a time. *Ibid.* 96 *Hand punch*, a tape punch operated directly by hand. **1967** A. Battersby *Network Analysis* (ed. 2) xv. 264 Their decisions are hand-punched on to special cards. **1950** *Dryad Handicraft Catal.* 74 *Hand puppets and string puppets. **1957** *Encycl. Brit.* XIV. 906/1 Hand puppets can be of wood, plaster,..or stuffed cloth. *c* **1000** Ælfric *Judg.* xvi. 21 Heton hine grindan æt hira *hand-cwyrne. **1878** Lecky *Eng. in 18th C.* II. v. 26 The only mills for grinding corn were hand-querns, turned by a woman's hand. **1523** Fitzherb. *Husb.* §28 A man or woman folowythe the mower with a *hande-rake halfe a yarde longe, with . vii. or . viii. tethe. **1495–7** *Naval Acc. Hen. VII*, (1896) 267 *Hande ropes—xviij; takes for the mayne sayle —ij. *a* **1698** Temple (J.), The seamen will neither stand to their *handsails, nor suffer the pilot to steer. **1881** Du Chaillu *Land Midn. Sun* II. 256 The women were up and busy sharpening the *hand-scythes. *a* **1877** Knight *Dict. Mech.* II. 1058/1 **Hand sewing-machine*, a form of sewing-machine in which the parts are pivoted jaws, operated in the manner of scissors. **1876** Fox Bourne *Locke* II. xi. 193 The coin being cut with *hand-shears, and stamped with hand-hammers. **1767** H. Brooke *Fool of Qual.* (1792) IV. 53 (Stanf. s.v. *Granada*) They tossed their granadoes or *hand-shells among us. **1746** *Coll. New H. Hist. Soc.* IX. 141 [I] went to mill with a *hand sled. **1780** in *Coll. Mass. Hist. Soc.* (1905) 7th Ser. V. 6 [They] hall their wood on hand sleds. **1843** *Knickerbocker* XXII. 294 The serjeant's hand-sled, piled with wood. **1877** *Rep. Vermont Board Agric.* IV. 92 Provided with a handsled, the boy would first roll on to it the back log. **1848** R. M. Ballantyne *Hudson's Bay* (1890) 83 The *hand-sledge is a thin flat slip or plank of wood... Indians invariably use it when visiting their traps, for the purpose of dragging home the animals or game they may have caught. **1856** Kane *Arct. Expl.* II. xxv. 249 They have given us hand-sledges for our baggage. **1829** G. Head *Forest Scenes* 203 [The trees] had been..removed by means of small *hand sleighs purposely prepared for them. **1836** C. P. Traill *Backwoods of Canada* 110 We were overtaken on our return by S—with a handsleigh, which is a sort of wheelbarrow, [etc.]. **1841** G. Powers *Hist. Sk. Coos* 70 A rude hand sleigh. **1936** D. McCowan *Anim. Canad. Rockies* xii. 103 An experienced trapper..delivered it on a hand sleigh. **1931** *Engineering* 9 Jan. 62/3 The roll adjusting gear is operated by a single *handwheel, through an arrangement of steel bevel and spur gears. **1940** *Chambers's Techn. Dict.* 402/1 *Hand wheel*, a grooved pulley provided with a cranked handle and mounted on a universal form of vice, used for driving a lathe or other tool by hand. **1948** *Brit. Jrnl. Psychol.* Mar. 149 The pointer..moved steadily away from the line, and required a compensatory movement of the handwheel at a rate of 1 r.p.m. to keep it on the line. **1879** *Cassell's Techn. Educ.* IV. 255/2 The ores are generally brought to surface by means of a common hand-whim.

64. a. *objective* and *obj. genitive*, as ***hand-binder***, ***-clapping***, ***-holding*** (hence as a back-formation ***hand-hold*** vb.), ***-kissing***, ***-spoiler***, ***-warmer***, ***-washing***; ***hand-wringing*** adj.

1585 Higins tr. *Junius' Nomenclator* 196/2 *Manicæ*.. manicls, or *handbinders. **1838** Carlyle *Misc.* (1857) IV. 144 If rumour and *hand-clapping could be credited. **1888** D. C. Murray *Weaker Vessel* i, A dropping fire of hand-clapping. **1948** B. G. M. Sundkler *Bantu Prophets S. Afr.* vi. 189 After the hymn..sung with gusto and more handclapping, the testimonies begin. **1959** I. & P. Opie *Lore & Lang. Schoolch.* vi. 94 Bangor children find that an innocent hand-clapping game goes neatly to the words. **1963** *Movie* Apr. 12/1 Newsreel photographers were often forced to *hand-hold their cameras. **1908** *Daily Chron.* 13 Mar. 4/6 *Hand-holding ensures a rapid means of communication between the hand and the heart or brain. **1960** C. Day Lewis *Buried Day* v. 94 Hand-holdings and childish kisses. **1868** Yates *Rock Ahead* iii. v, The ladies exchanged sweet *handkissings. **1836** E. Howard *R. Reefer* xxvi, I brought up to her the penitent *hand-presser. **15..** *Aberd. Reg.* V. 15 (Jam.) Maisterfull and violent *handputting in his dekin. **1884** *Pall Mall G.* Extra 24 July 14/2 *Hand-warmers fitted with charcoal pans. **1879** Farrar *St. Paul* (1883) 43 The Talmud..devotes one whole treatise to *hand-washings. **1964** M. Hynes *Med. Bacteriol.* (ed. 8) ii. 22 Nevertheless the main sterilizing action of hand-washing is the mechanical removal of epithelial scales and surface bacteria. **1603** Dekker *Wonderfull Yeare* C, You desolate *hand-wringing widowes.

b. *instrumental* = With the hand, by hand; *esp.* as distinguished from what is done by machinery; as ***hand-coloured*** ppl. adj., ***-colouring***, ***-comber***, ***-combing***, ***-done***, ***-drawn*** ppl. adjs., ***-dressing***, ***-eating***, ***-feed*** vb., ***-feeding***, ***-fed***, ***-fired*** ppl. adj. (so ***hand-firing***), ***-fisher***, ***-flung***, ***-held***, ***-hewn*** (ppl.) adjs., ***-hidden*** ppl. adjs., ***-kill*** vb., ***-knit*** adj. (also as *sb.*), ***-knitted*** ppl. adj., ***-knitting***, †***-laboured***, ***-milker***, ***-milking***, ***-moulded*** ppl. adjs., ***-operated***, ***-rear*** vb., ***reared*** ppl. adj., ***-rub*** vb., ***-rubbed***, ***-set*** ppl. adjs., ***-sew*** vb. (so ***hand-sewing***, ***-sewn***), ***-spun***, ***-thrown***, ***-tooled*** ppl. adjs., ***-tufted*** pa. pple. and ppl. adj., ***-turned***, ppl. adjs., ***-washing*** (see also 64 a), ***-weaver***, ***-weaving***, ***-woven*** ppl. adj., ***-wrought*** ppl. adj., etc.

1796 W. Marshall *West. Eng.* I. 142 (E.D.S.) With a Beating-axe..large chips, shavings or sods are struck off.. This operation is termed *hand-beating. **1869** *Eng. Mech.* 31 Dec. 377/2 The prints..were.. finished by *hand-colouring. **1894** H. Speight *Nidderdale* 304 This was in the days of *hand-combing and hand-weaving. **1907** N. Munro *Daft Days* xvii. 151 Another *hand-done bill upon the counter. **1908** *Westm. Gaz.* 28 Dec. 5/2 Insets of hand-done crochet form one of the newest designs. **1907** *Yesterday's Shopping* (1969) 737/1 *Hand-drawn linen. **1937** *Evening News* 15 Mar. 3/6 (Advt.), Hand-drawn top collar. **1957** Manvell & Huntley *Technique Film Music* iii. 167 Attempts at creating hand-drawn sound-tracks have been in progress since the coming of the sound film. *Ibid.*, He built up a sound-track of hand-drawn musical effects, mixing them occasionally with normal orchestral instruments to give variety. **1857** Livingstone *Trav.* xi. 206, I often presented my friends with iron spoons, and it was curious to observe how the habit of *hand-eating prevailed. **1805** Forsyth *Beauties Scotl.* I. 421 The snow..render[s] it necessary to *hand-feed their flocks of sheep. **1960** *Farmer & Stockbreeder* 29 Mar. 65/1 To the busy shepherd, *hand-feeding may not seem worth while. **1968** *Gloss. Terms Offset Lithogr. Printing* (*B.S.I.*) 24 *Hand feeding*, the manual placing of single sheets of paper or other material to the machine lays. **1846** J. Baxter *Libr. Pract. Agric.* (ed. 4) I. 191 Cattle, when *hand-fed. **1880** *Libr. Univ. Knowl.* (N.Y.) XI. 404 The joints should be carefully *hand-filled with fine screened sand. **1963** *Times* 23 May 7/3 Existing *hand-fired plant still in fair condition. **1908** *Chambers's Jrnl.* Aug. 624/1 Owing to the fact that unscreened British coal is extensively employed in Hamburg *hand-firing is more generally adopted. **1961** *Listener* 12 Oct. 583/2 'Hand-firing', or the fact that the fuel has to be brought to the boiler, is the drawback of all solid-fuel boilers. **1855** 'P. Paxton' *Captain Priest* 147 In the deeper places of such streams must the *handfisher seek his prey. **1913** Kipling *Songs from Books* 113 But Tubal fashioned the *hand-flung spears. **1923** Glazebrook *Dict. Appl. Physics* IV. 393/2 The *hand-held camera implies 'exposures' of brief duration. **1969** *Daily Tel.* (Colour Suppl.) 10 Jan. 18 (*caption*) The photograph was taken by astronaut Anders with hand-held Hasselblad. **1969** *Jane's Freight Containers 1968–69* 584/1 All four motors are controlled from a single hand-held push-button control unit. **1938** M. K. Rawlings *Yearling* xiv. 143 The thick *hand-hewn slabs of the shingled roof. **1969** *Computers & Humanities* III. 240 The work of Hagelman and Barnes is born into competition with one of the last of the hand-hewn concordances. **1859** Tennyson *Vivien* 895 Face *Hand-hidden, as for utmost grief. *c* **1575** *Chalm. Air* c. 25 in Balfour *Practicks* (1754) 585 Gif ony Fleshour.. slayis or *hand-killis ony beif or flesh with his awin handis. **1920** F. Scott Fitzgerald *This Side of Paradise* (1921) i. ii. 63 The *hand-knit, sleeveless jerseys were stylish. **1958** Handknit [see bawneen]. **1959** *Manch. Guardian* 29 July 5/1 Woollens fall into two classes, the cashmere jerseys, sweaters, and cardigans..and the Scottish handknits. **1967** *Harper's Bazaar* Sept. 49 The neck, High-polo-ed, hand-knit. **1881** *Sylvia's Home Jrnl.* in A. Adburgham *Shops & Shopping* (1964) xvii. 189 The largest stock in the kingdom of *hand-knitted socks and stockings. **1952** M. Laski *Village* viii. 135 A skirt and a hand-knitted jumper. **1902** *Daily Chron.* 20 Dec. 5/2 Another ancient industry is at its last gasp—viz., the *hand-knitting of Kilmarnock bonnets. **1961** J. G. Davis *Dict. Dairying* (ed. 2) 740 The War of 1914–18, because of the acute shortage of *hand milkers, gave an unexpected impetus to the adoption of machine milking. **1915** J. London *Let.* 26 Jan. (1966) 446 Get Timms' experience with *hand-milking labor conditions. **1960** *Farmer & Stockbreeder* 8 Mar. 55/2 In the past when hand-milking was the rule. **1854** H. Miller *Sch. & Schm.* xiii. (1858) 287 This same *hand-moulded pottery of the bronze period. **1936** *Discovery* Nov. 350/1 The Electrotor meter has a *hand-operated pump movement. **1893** G. D. Leslie *Lett. to Marco* xix. 128 The futility of attempting to *hand-rear them. **1894** *Daily News* 2 Oct. 6/6 Both with natural and *hand-reared birds. **1859** F. A. Griffiths *Artil. Man.* (1862) 224 *Hand-rub and bandage legs. **1862** Beveridge *Hist. India* III. vii. iii. 101 Two attendants whose duty it was to hand-rub (*shampoo*) their master. **1908** *Daily Chron.* 23 Oct. 9/4 All *hand-set [type] becomes unnecessary. **1938** *Times Lit. Suppl.* 26 Mar. 204/3 Hand-set in most attractive type. **1895** *Montgomery Ward Catal.* 318/3 Hame Strap, *hand sewed. **1919** Barrie *Alice Sit-by-the-Fire* I. 21 You *hand-sew them and stretch them over a tin cylinder. **1946** *Nature* 14 Dec. 868/1 The speed of expert *hand-sewing, thirty stitches per minute, is slow and laborious compared with that of machine work. **1961** T. Landau *Encycl. Librarianship* (ed. 2) 161/1 *Hand sewing*, usually sewing through the fold by hand on the sewing frame, to suspended cords or tapes arranged across the back of a book. **1887** *Col. & Indian Exhib., Rep. Col. Sect.* 401 A handsome pair of men's *hand-sewn Wellingtons. **1911** *Rep. on Labour & Social Conditions in Germany* III. vi–vii. 101, I could have my boots soled and heeled with this quality of leather, and hand-sewn for 3s. 5d. **1959** *Times* 7 Mar. 9/2 A pigskin-covered whip, tightly stretched and handsewn, makes a pleasing and serviceable article. **1647** Trapp *Comm. Matt.* v. 11 There are tongue-smiters, as well as *hand-smiters. **1892** *Eastern Morning News* (Hull) 16 Feb. 2/8 *Hand-split laths. **1895** *Daily News* 15 June 5/3 A piece of *hand-spun and hand-woven cloth. **1884** Roe *Nat. Ser. Story* v, A profitable crop..can only be grown by careful *hand-thinning. **1909** *Westm. Gaz.* 22 Oct. 4/2 The barbed spear used..is a *hand-thrown weapon. **1933** *Archit. Rev.* LXXIV. 38/1 (*caption*) These are hand-thrown pieces on the wheel. **1895** 'Mark Twain' in *North Amer. Rev.* July 2 An illustrated, gilt-edged, tree-calf, *hand-tooled, seven-dollar Friendship's Offering. **1931** *Times Lit. Suppl.* 25 June p. vii/2 The Swiss hand-tooled bindings are disappointing. **1906** *Daily Chron.* 5 June 4/5 Killybegs carpets, which are *hand-tufted by the peasants. **1922** Joyce *Ulysses* 697 Handtufted Axminster Carpet. **1962** *BSI News* Feb. 17/1 Methods for the determination of colour fastness of textiles to a number of agencies, for example, soda boiling, *handwashing, [etc.]. **1827** G. Higgins *Celtic Druids* 263 *note*, I wish to God our poor *hand-weavers could as easily migrate to Sydney. **1843** *Penny Cycl.* XXVII. 177/2 In *hand-weaving, the weaver suspends his operations from time to time in order to apply dressing to his warp. **1772** A. Young in R. Dossie *Mem. Agric.* (1782) III. 27 [I] *hand-weeded it, Aug. 22nd. **1807** *Ann. Reg.* 861 The plants are twice hand-weeded. *c* **1000** *Ags. Gosp.* Mark xiv. 58 Ic towurpe þis *hand-worhte tempel. **1881** *Truth* 19 May 686/1 The train..was covered with hand-wrought embroidery. **1880** L. Higgin *Handbk. Embroidery* 62 Neutral-tinted *hand-woven linen. **1925** A. Huxley *Let.* 2 Nov. (1969) 258 We bought..twelve yards of hand woven material.

c. *locative*, etc. In or as to the hands; as ***hand-bound***, ***-gyved***, ***-lopped***, ***-shackled***, ***-tied*** ppl. adjs.

?*c* **1600** *Distracted Emp.* i. i. in Bullen *O. Pl.* III. 176 Better *hand-bounde wrastell with the Sea. **1837** Carlyle *Fr. Rev.* III. i. i. (1872) 4 A poor Legislative..had let itself be *hand-gyved.

d. *similative*, etc., as ***hand-footed***, ***-high***, ***-like***, ***-shaped*** adjs.

1890 O. Crawfurd *Round the Calendar* 147 The wall running by the garden paths, *hand-high. **1802** Bingley *Anim. Biog.* (1813) I. 63 The *hand-like conformation of their fore-feet. **1796** Withering *Brit. Plants* (ed. 3) IV. 102 Branches widening, *hand-shaped.

65. Special Combs. †**hand-adventure**, a single-handed contest; **hand-alphabet**, an alphabet of signs made by the hands, a 'deaf-and-dumb' alphabet; **hand-bag**, (*a*) a light travelling-bag, (*b*) a lady's bag for accessories; **hand-balancer**, an acrobat; **hand-bible** *slang* = holy stone *sb.*; **hand block** (see block *sb.* 7), a block used in printing textiles by hand; also *attrib.*; hence **hand-blocked** *a.* (cf. *block-printed* adj.); **hand-blown** *ppl. a.*, of glass blown by a craftsman; **hand-board** *U.S.*, a board in front of a preacher or speaker; **hand-buckler**, a small shield held in the left hand to parry an adversary's sword-thrusts; **hand-cannon**, an early portable fire-arm of the cannon type; **hand-car** (*U.S.*), a light car propelled by cranks or levers worked by hand, used in the inspection and repairing of a railway line; **hand-chair**, a Bath chair; hence **handchairman**, one who draws a Bath chair; **hand-darg** (*Sc.*), a day's work of manual labour; **hand-drop** (see quot.); †**hand-evil**, gout in the hands; **hand-fight**, a fight at close quarters, or hand to hand; **hand-fish**, a pediculate fish, having the pectoral fin articulated; **hand-fives**, the usual game of fives as distinguished from bat-fives (see fives[2] 1); **hand-flower**, the flower of the *hand-plant* (q.v.) or **hand-flower-tree**; †**hand-friend**, (?) a friend at hand, or who will 'stand by' one in case of need; **hand-gear**, the starting-gear of an engine; **hand-hole**, a hole giving passage for little more than the hand; **hand-in** (*Tennis*), the person who is serving the ball; †**hand in and hand out**, the name of a game with a ball in 15th c.; **hand-jam** *v.* (*Mountaineering*), to wedge a hand in a crack as a handhold; hence as *sb.*; also **hand-jamming** *vbl. sb.*; **hand-jive** (see quot. 1961); hence **hand-jiving** *vbl. sb.*; **hand-laid** *ppl. a.* (cf. *laid paper*); **hand-language**, the art of conversing by signs made with the hands; †**hand-laying** (*hond leggynge*), imposition of hands, ordination; **hand-lead** (*Naut.*), a small lead used in taking soundings less than 20 fathoms; **hand-letter** *v.* (see quots.); hence ***hand-lettered*** ppl. adj., ***hand-lettering*** vbl. sb.; **hand-light** (*Gardening*), a bell-glass (= handglass 2); †**hand-loose** *a.*, free from restraint; †**hand-maker**, one who makes gain fraudulently (cf. 45 a); so †**hand-making**; **hand-mast** (see quots.); also *attrib.* as ***hand-mast piece***, ***spar***; †**hand-muff**, a boxing glove; **hand-mule** (see quot. 1892); also *attrib.* as ***hand-mule spinner***; **hand orchis**, a name for *Orchis maculata*, from the finger-like lobes of the tubers; **hand-out** (*Tennis*), the person to whom the ball is served; **hand-pick** *v. trans.*, to pick by hand; also *fig.*; so **hand-picked** *ppl. a.*; **hand-piece, handpiece**, (*a*) the part of a dental drill that is held in the hand; (*b*) the part of a sheep-shearing machine that is held in the shearer's hand; **hand-pin** (*Gunnery*), see quot.; **hand-plant**, a Mexican tree (*Cheirostemon *platanoides*, N.O. *Sterculiaceæ*), having large flowers with bright red stamens, which are united at the base and then spread in five finger-like bundles; **hand-plate,** (*a*) = *finger-plate*; (*b*) a small plate to pass over the surface of work to be tested; † **hand-point**, a children's game, the same as *span-counter*; **hand-pollinate** *v. trans.*, to pollinate by hand; so ***hand-pollination***; **hand-post**, a guide-post at the parting of roads, a FINGER-POST *sb.*; **hand-print**, the mark left by the impression of a hand; also (quot. 1886), a representation of a hand; **hand-promise**, a solemn form of betrothal among the Irish peasantry; **hand-quill**, one of the large pinion feathers of a bird; † **hand-reaching** [cf. Ger. *handreichung*], used by Coverdale for ministration or contribution; **hand-reading**, palmistry; so ***hand-reader***; **hand-screw** (see quot. 1850); also *attrib.* as ***hand-screw-maker***; † **hand-shaft** (see quot.); **hand signal**, a manual indication by the driver of a motor vehicle, pedal cycle, etc., of his intention to stop, turn, etc.; † **hand-sleeve**, a sleeve reaching to the wrist; **hand-spring**, a summersault in which the body is supported by the hands while the feet are in the air; **hand-stand**, an act in gymnastics in which the body is supported by the hands while the feet are in the air; also *attrib.*; † **hand-stripe** = HAND-STROKE; † **hand-stuff**, app. some sort of refuse; **hand-swipe**, a shadoof worked by hand for raising water; † **hand-table**, a writing tablet; **hand-taut** *a.* = *hand-tight*; **hand-tennis**, tennis in which the ball is struck with the hand, not with a racket; **hand-tight** *a.*, as tight as it can be drawn or fixed by the hand; † **hand-timber**, small wood; **hand-towel**, a small towel for wiping the hands after washing; **hand traverse** *Mountaineering* (see quots. 1897, 1957); **hand-tree** = *hand-plant*; **hand-wave** *v.*, to smooth the surface of (a measure of corn) with the hand, instead of using a strike; † **hand-whip**, a riding-whip; † **hand-wolf**, a wolf brought up by hand.

1649 H. WATSON *Valentine & Orson* xiii. 59 All this *hand-adventure now knitting up in this manner. **1680** DALGARNO *Didascolocophus* viii. 73, I have at last fixt upon a Finger or *Hand-alphabet according to my mind. **1837** *Penny Cycl.* VIII. 283/1 We shall give his hand-alphabet. **1862** *Englishwoman's Domestic Mag.* July 143 Portable umbrellas.. may easily be carried in the *hand-bag. **1867** A. D. WHITNEY *L. Goldthwaite* ii. 32 Their hand-bags were hung up. **1880** MISS BRADDON *Just as I am* xlv, She had her waterproof.. and a hand-bag. **1896** G. B. SHAW *Let.* 9 Nov. (1965) 700, I want to buy a handbag for the journey. **1899** O. WILDE *Importance of being Earnest* I. 37 'Where did the charitable gentleman who had a first-class ticket for this seaside resort find you?..' 'In a handbag.'..' A handbag?' **1913** *Vanity Fair* Dec. 79/2 The latest novelty in hand bags. **1923** *Weekly Dispatch* 13 May 14 Crocodile Calf handbag. **1937** *Discovery* Dec. 374/2 Ladies' shoes and hand-bags. **1968** *New Society* 22 Aug. 266/1 Non-U handbag/U bag (the thing carried by women). **1927** *Daily Tel.* 30 Aug. 12/6 Masu, the Japanese *hand-balancer and juggler. [*a* **1865** SMYTH *Sailor's Word-Bk.* (1867) 98 *Bible*,.. a squared piece of freestone to grind the deck with sand in cleaning it; a small holystone, so called from seamen using them kneeling.] **1908** O. ONIONS *Pedlar's Pack* 109 That was Ben, and i' the Dolphin, where all they knew o' Bibles was the *hand-bibles they holystoned the decks wi'. **1839** URE *Dict. Arts* I. 215 The *hand blocks are made of sycamore or pear-tree wood, or of deal faced with these woods. **1936** *Archit. Rev.* LXXIX. 291/1 Any artist of decorative faculties can create patterns for printed cretonnes or linens,.. provided he is sufficiently familiar with the advantages and drawbacks of roller-printing, screen-printing and handblock-printing. **1928** *Daily Express* 9 Jan. 5/2 The new.. *hand-blocked linens are a boon. **1931** *Ibid.* 21 Sept. 5/2 Pure silks, whose hand-blocked patterns have all been designed by famous.. British artists. **1928** *Ibid.* 28 May 7/2 An exhibition of *hand-blown and enamelled glass. **1958** *Archit. Rev.* CXXIV. 256 These fittings are made of thick handblown glass in white or dark grey-green with inner shades masking the bulbs. **1734** *Col. Rec. Georgia* III. 130 Part of the Twenty one Pieces of Mahogany, Ash, Sycamore, Ilex and Red Bay Timber the Growth of Georgia used in the Experiments for making *Hand Boards &c. **1845** A. WILEY in *Indiana Mag. Hist.* (1927) XXIII. 165 Behold the.. awkward man arise and place his chair before him for his pulpit and hand-board. **1857** P. CARTWRIGHT *Autobiogr.* xx. 203 They drove a stake down, and nailed a board to it,.. and this was my hand board. **1847–73** HALLIWELL, **Hand-cannon*, a musket. **1874** BOUTELL *Arms & Arm.* Notes 293 The hand-cannon soon gave place to the hand-gun. **1850** LYELL *2nd Visit U.S.* II. 14, I left the *hand-car and entered a railway-train, which carried me in one hour into the town. **1894** *Westm. Gaz.* 3 Sept. 5/1 A relief train carrying hand-cars eventually rescued them from their perilous position. **1622** MABBE tr. *Aleman's Guzman d' Alf.* I. 37 It seemed to mee a *Silla de manos*, or easie *hand-Chair. **1857** DUNGLISON *Med. Lex.* 447 **Hand-drop, Wrist-drop.* A popular term for the paralysis of the hand, induced by the action of lead. **1562** TURNER *Baths* 6 b, It is good.. for the *handeuell and fote euell. **1586** J. HOOKER *Girald. Irel.* in Holinshed II. 168/1 Where-vpon they fell at *hand-fight. **1849** GROTE *Greece* II. lx. (1862) V. 286 A strenuous hand-fight then commenced. **1847** CARPENTER *Zool.* §564 The *Cheironectes*, or *Hand-fish, bears a strong resemblance to the common Angler in its structure and habits; but its fins are still more capable of motion, enabling it to walk along the ground almost in the manner of quadrupeds. **1905** *Westm. Gaz.* 17 Mar. 4/1 Our game of *hand-fives is perhaps the closest approach we have to the central type of the games. **1822** C. WELLS *Stories after Nature* (1891) 17 There is one thing greater than revenge, and *hand-friend to our cause —it is mercy. **1842** G. FRANCIS *Dict. Arts*, etc. **Hand-gear.* **1846** WORCESTER, *Hand-Gear*, an arrangement of levers and other contrivances for opening and shutting the valves of a steam-engine. *a* **1877** KNIGHT *Dict. Mech.* II. 1055/1 **Hand-hole*, a small hole at or near the bottom of a boiler, for the insertion of the hand in cleaning, etc. It is closed by a hand-hole plate. **1967** *Gloss. Sanitation Terms* (*B.S.I.*) 24 *Handhole*, a small opening with an access cover to provide for the inspection, repair or cleaning of the inside of a vessel or pipe. **1875** 'STONEHENGE' *Brit. Sports* III. I. v. §4. 690 If the *hand-in makes one, the game is called vantage. **1477** *Act 17 Edw. IV*, c. 3 Diversez novelx ymaginez Jeuez appelez Cloishe Kaylez half Kewle *Hondyn & Hondoute & Quekeborde. **1540** *Order Hen. VIII* in Rymer *Fœdera* (1710) XIV. 707 Keper aswell of the Playes of Hande oute and al Keyles. **1948** H. C. PARKER *Climbs on Gritstone* I. 37 The crack facing the Pinnacle is climbed, with the use of an awkward *hand jam, to the second chockstone. **1937** *Mountaineering Jrnl.* V. 138/1 A crack in the right-hand corner of the rectangular grass platform was climbed with the aid of small holds and *hand jamming. **1957** CLARK & PYATT *Mountaineering in Brit.* xvi. 237 A new method of hand-jamming, enabling a hold to be obtained in a cleft with far more flexibility and far less pain than the previously accepted method. **1958** M. PUGH *Wilderness of Monkeys* 33 There was no room for dancing but here and there couples were *hand-jiving and one girl expressed ecstasy by pulling her hair down into her eyes. **1958** *Radio Times* 14 Feb. 5/1 The world of skiffle, rock 'n' roll, jazz, and the hand-jive. **1961** PARTRIDGE *Dict. Slang* Suppl. 1125 *Hand-jive*, system of rhythmic hand-movements in time to music where floor is too crowded to allow people present to jive (dance), esp. as in coffee bars. **1958** *Punch* 12 Feb. 288/3 *Hand-jiving only employs the dancer from the waist up and affords a great saving on Espresso space, the calf muscles and shoe-leather. **1899** *Hand-laid [see DECKLE 2]. **1680** DALGARNO *Didascolocophus* viii. 73 Neither.. is it so proper a medium of interpretation between persons present face to face, as a *Hand-language. **1387** TREVISA *Higden* (Rolls) V. 243 Unwis *hond leggynge is chalenged of þe [Pope Leo]. **1745** P. THOMAS *Jrnl. Anson's Voy.* 314 Sometimes we should have seven Fathom on one Side of the Ship, and no Ground with the *Hand Lead on the other. **1828** J. M. SPEARMAN *Brit. Gunner* (ed. 2) 384 The hand-lead-line, which is generally 20 fathoms in length, is marked at every 2 or 3 fathoms. **1889** *Century Dict.*, **Hand-letter*, an impress on a book-cover by movable types from a hand-stamp. **1960** G. A. GLAISTER *Gloss. Bk.* 171/1 *Hand-letters*, brass letters, mounted in wooden handles, which are used by the finisher for lettering the title, etc., on the cover of a hand-bound book. **1907** N. MUNRO *Daft Days* xvii. 150 A large *hand-lettered bill was in each window. **1969** 'I. DRUMMOND' *Man with Tiny Head* xv. 171 A hand-lettered sign. **1967** KARCH & BUBER *Offset Processes* iv. 117 A few Filmotype lettering styles unlike the usual type faces appear to be special *handlettering. **1824** M. R. MITFORD *Our Village* 13 A melon bed!—fie! What a grand pompous name was that for three melon plants under a *hand-light! **1860** DELAMER *Kitch Gard.* (1861) 78 A *handlight or bell-glass. **1882** *Garden* 4 Feb. 72/1 Cuttings.. root readily under a small handlight. **1596** DALRYMPLE tr. *Leslie's Hist. Scot.* v. 304 The peple lyke a cumpanie of Wylde beistes, *hand louse. **1549** LATIMER *3rd Serm. bef. Edw. VI* (Arb.) 97 A *hande maker in hys office, to make his sonne a great man. **1549** COVERDALE, etc. *Erasm. Par. Jude* 23 *Handmaking of gaynes, which thinge dooeth moste principally defile the doctrine of Christe. **1830** MARRYAT *King's Own* III. i. 11 We can carry away a top-mast, and make a new one out of the *hand-mast, at sea. **1875** LASLETT *Timber* 232 Hand-mast.. is a technical term applied.. to a round spar, holding at the least 24, and not exceeding 72, inches in circumference. **1867** SMYTH *Sailor's Word-bk.*, **Hand mast-spar*, a round mast; those from Riga are.. over 70 feet long by 20 inches diameter. **1814** *Sporting Mag.* 93 In the on-set the combatants wore *hand-muffs. **1834** HT. MARTINEAU *Moral* II. 59 *Hand-mules are worked in pairs. **1892** *Labour Commission* Gloss., *Hand-mules*, spinning-machinery, driven by steam power and manual labour combined, used in producing yarn. **1875** 'STONEHENGE' *Brit. Sports* III. I. v. §4. 690 if the player who fails to return the ball is the server or hand-in, he becomes *hand-out. **1831** *Sutherland Farm Rep.* 72 in *Brit. Husb.* (1840) III, A few boys and girls *hand-pick the whole. **1881** *Chicago Times* 4 June, Good to choice mediums [*sc.* beans] were quotable at $2.25 & 2.40 per bu. for hand-picked. **1898** *Advance* (Chicago) 3 Mar. 282/1 [Loyola] face to face with individuals, hand-picking souls from the fire. **1907** *Westm. Gaz.* 12 Sept. 5/1 The most expensive of the ordinary coals—'large hand-picked coal'. **1918** *Times* 23 Jan. 6/3 True, there has been a widespread feeling that the Irish Convention was handpicked. **1925** J. GREGORY *Bab of Backwoods* xii. 157 An able-bodied trio, hand-picked by William Badger. **1928** *Daily Express* 11 July 1/2 A handpicked 'National' Assembly for Parliament. **1949** I. DEUTSCHER *Stalin* 353 Its members, though they had all been hand-picked by Stalin.. differed on means and methods. **1959** *Manch. Guardian* 1 July 4/5 The director.. hand-picks his best students for design jobs in the potteries. **1889** C. A. HARRIS *Princ. & Pract. Dentistry* (ed. 12) 526 Its use will also keep the *hand-piece in good condition. **1914** J. B. PARFITT in N. G. Bennett *Sci. & Pract. Dental Surg.* 326 Hand-pieces.. are often liable to get very much soiled. **1949** F. SARGESON *I saw in my Dream* 115 The whirring of the hand-pieces. **1950** *N.Z. Jrnl. Agric.* May 463/3 Thorough scrubbing of the shearing board with disinfectant and the cleansing of handpieces are also worthwhile practices. **1960** *Farmer & Stockbreeder* 23 Feb. 67/2 Entrants for the final at the Royal Show.. will be judged using their own handpieces. **1963** J. OSBORNE *Dental Mechanics* (ed. 5) x. 212 For these purposes.. small rotary stones in a handpiece are advisable. **1900** H. LAWSON *Over Sliprails* 49 Scraping old splashes of paint off the brass and *hand-plate. **1881** GREENER *Gun* 262 Another pin will then be seen in the rear end of the trigger-plate, remove this pin (occasionally this '*hand-pin' is placed in the reverse way). **1830** LINDLEY *Nat. Syst. Bot.* 36 The *Hand plant of Mexico. **1659** TORRIANO, *Al-palmo*, the play our children call, At span-counter, or at *Hand-point. **1918** *Nature* 15 Aug. 470/2 To *hand-pollinate the flowers of a soft-shelled tree with pollen from a tree of similar character. **1954** A. G. L. HELLYER *Encycl. Garden Work* 130/2 As a result of the *hand-pollination, seed may be formed. **1886** R. TUCK *Handbk. Biblical Difficulties* II. 324 This *hand-print is made in order to avert the 'evil eye'. **1894** 'MARK TWAIN' IN *Cent. Mag.* Feb. 553 The hand-print of one twin is the same as the hand-print of the fellow-twin. **1966** *New Scientist* 3 Mar. 539/2 The use of handprints has spread from the charge room to the clinic. Three paediatricians.. have reported.. that newborn babies with congenital defects frequently have abnormal palm and fingerprints. **1791** J. HAMPSON *Mem. Wesley* III. 101 A clergy-man is like a *hand-post; if he shew the way, it is not necessary he should walk in it himself. **1830–3** CARLETON *Traits & St., Going to Maynooth* (Cent.), Few would rely on the word or oath of any man who had been known to break a *hand-promise. **1535** COVERDALE *Acts* vi. 1 Their wyddowes were not loked vpon in the daylie *handreachinge. **1902** *Daily Chron.* 28 Nov. 6/3 S.S.,.. *'hand reader',.. appeared.. to answer a charge of pretending to tell fortunes by palmistry. **1867** A. R. CRAIG *Bk. of Hand* 31 In obedience to the stern dictates of the *hand-reading art. **1960** C. STORR *Marianne & Mark* ii. 29 She asked if I wanted the cards or the crystal or a hand reading. **1765** CROKER *Dict. Arts & Sc.*, **Hand-Screw*, an instrument more usually called a jack. **1819** *P.O. Lond. Direct.* 63 Smith and Hand-screw-maker. *c* **1850** *Rudim. Navig.* (Weale) 123 *Hand-screws* or *jacks*. This engine is used to cant beams or other weighty timbers: it consists of a box of elm containing cogged iron wheels of increasing powers. The outer one, which moves the rest, is put in motion by a winch. **1598** FLORIO *Sommessa*, the length of a span or hand-breadth, a *hand shaft so called of our drapers. **1922** *Collier's* 7 Jan. 8/1, I am asked by Collier's to suggest a simple, universal, and almost automatic system of *hand signals for the automobile driver. **1934** *Amer. Speech* IX. 114/2 On the way to business [by car],.. those who drive have to make allowances for.. hand signals. **1960** E. H. CLEMENTS *Honey for Marshal* v. 94 He made the hand-signal impatiently.. as the lorry still seemed shackled by its own indecision. **1965** PRIESTLEY & WISDOM *Good Driving* vi. 47 The Highway Code.. lists the three hand signals. **1585** HIGINS tr. *Junius' Nomenclator* 172/1 *Manica*.. the *handsleeue: the sleeue of a garment. **1686** *Lond. Gaz.* No. 2192/4 A Purple Wastcoat, with narrow Gold Lace on the Hand sleeves. **1875** W. CARLETON *Farm Legends* (1885) 88 He al'ays could.. Make somersets on the mow, *Hand-springs, cart-wheels, an' such. **1895** *Nation* (N.Y.) 19 Dec. 437/3 Children.. throwing handsprings and standing on their heads. **1899** H. BUTTERWORTH *How To* iv. 15 (*heading*) *Hand stand. **1909** W. SKARSTROM *Gymnastic Kinesiology* 74 But in raising the legs and inverting the body to the 'Hand stand' there is at first a considerable bend at the hips and more flexion in the elbows than occurs in 'Free Front Rest'. **1946** 'J. TEY' *Miss Pym Disposes* vi. 111 When she goes out from thees [*sic*] plaace [*sic*] it will not matter any longer that she can do a handstand better than anyone else. **1951** *Swimming* (E.S.S.A.) v. 87 Before attempting handstand dives, you must be able to maintain a steady hand balance.. grip the end of the board with the hands,.. you can then throw up or press up into the armstand position. **1959** *Times* 17 Feb. 3/2 The little girl with upraised arms about to perform a handstand. **1555** W. WATREMAN *Fardle Facions* II. vi. 152 To fighte it oute at *hand stripes. **1690** *Lond. Gaz.* No. 2597/4 If any Brown Paper-maker will Buy either Rags, Ropes or *Hand-stuff of said Company, they may be supplied at the Companies Warehouse. **1799** *Naval Chron.* II. 314 Dealers in.. what is called hand stuff and old stores. **1862** RAWLINSON *Anc. Mon.* I. 271 The use of the *Hand swipe.. is mentioned by Herodotus and even represented upon the sculptures. *c* **1440** *Promp. Parv.* 225/2 *Hand tablys.. *pugillaris*. *c* **1860** H. STUART *Seaman's Catech.* 33 Heave *hand taut. **1825** HONE *Everyday Bk.* 865 **Hand-tennis* still continues to be played.. it is now called fives. **1794** *Rigging & Seamanship* I. 167 **Hand-tight*. A moderate degree of tension on a rope, as to make it straight. **1881** YOUNG *Every Man his own Mechanic* §443. 194 This tongue should fit the groove somewhat tightly indeed in the manner called by joiners 'hand tight' meaning so tight that it cannot readily be pulled out with the hand. **1664** *Husbandm. Practice* (N.), Fell *hand-timber from the full to the change. **1598** FLORIO *Worlde of Wordes* 355/1 *Sciugatóio*, a *hand-towell, a wiper, a rubbing cloth. **1778** in P. Ziegler *King William IV* (1971) ii. 26, 2 Dozen of Hand Towels. **1972** M. KENYON *Shooting of Dan McGrew* iv. 32 In the.. men's room he was drying his face on a hand-towel. **1897** O. G. JONES *Rock-Climbing* xvii. 268 We each in turn ventured on the **hand-traverse* from above... It is so named because the climber hangs by his hands,.. and traverses across the face by sheer strength of his arms. **1935** D. PILLEY *Climbing Days* i. 17 Above this the 'hand traverse' faced us. A crack.. offers sloping and not very good holds to the hands.. the slab gives a little friction to the knees, but not very much. **1957** COLLOMB *Dict. Mountaineering* 84 *Hand traverse*, a horizontal movement across a broad flake of rock, the body being supported entirely on the hands which grip the edge of the flake. **1837** *Penny Cycl.* VII. 28/1 Called the '*hand-tree', in consequence of its stamens being so arranged as to present an appearance somewhat similar to that of a human hand. **1641** BEST *Farm. Bks.* (Surtees) 104 The millers will say that they had as leave haue corne stricken, as soe *handwaved, and left hollowe in the midst. **1791** *Statist. Acc. Scotl.* II. 533 (Jam.) Measured by hand-waving, i.e. they are stroked by the hand about four inches above the top of the firlot. **1683** *Lond. Gaz.* No. 1835/4 One short *Hand-Whip, with a Silver twist about the Handle. *a* **1611** BEAUM. & FL. *Maid's Trag.* IV. i, Though I am tame.. I may leap, Like a *hand-wolf, into my natural wildness, And do an outrage.

† **hand**, *sb.*[2], var ANDE *Obs.*, breath.

1340 HAMPOLE *Pr. Consc.* 775 His nese oft droppes, his hand stynkes.

hand (hænd), *v.* [f. HAND *sb.*[1]]

1. *trans.* To touch or grasp with the hand, lay hands on, lay hold of; to work or manage with the hand, manipulate, handle; also *fig.* to deal with, treat of. *Obs.* exc. in technical use: see quots.

1610 SHAKS. *Temp.* I. i. 25 If you can command these Elements to silence.. wee will not hand a rope more. **1611** —— *Wint. T.* II. iii. 63 Let him that makes but trifles of his eyes First hand me. *Ibid.* IV. iv. 359 When I was yong, And handed loue, as you do. *a* **1721** PRIOR *Lady's Looking-glass* 29, I hand my oar. **1786** J. WEDGWOOD in *Phil. Trans.* LXXVI. 397 What we call handing or slapping the clay, an operation by which its different parts are intermixed. **1879** *Cassell's Techn. Educ.* IV. 414/1 Brought up..to full perfection by 'handing', i.e. brisk rubbing with the palm of the hand.

2. *Naut.* To take in, furl (a sail).

1634 SIR T. HERBERT *Trav.* 5 The Sailers..handing in their sailes, and standing on the Deckes..in their wet clothes. *a* **1642** SIR W. MONSON *Naval Tracts* III. (1704) 364/1 With Ten Sailors to hand the Sails. **1720** DE FOE *Capt. Singleton* xiv. (1840) 239 We were glad to hand all our sails. **1790** BEATSON *Nav. & Mil. Mem.* I. 192 The mizen top-sail was handed to prevent the mast and rigging from falling about their ears. **1881** *Daily Tel.* 28 Jan., 'They must be handing the maintopsail', I thought.

3. To lead or conduct by the hand; to assist with the hand in mounting a step, alighting, etc.

a **1631** DONNE (J.), Angels did hand her up, who next God dwell. **1638** SIR T. HERBERT *Trav.* (ed. 2) 120 The Sultan and Shawbander handed him out of his Bardge. **1697** DAMPIER *Voy.* I. 15 Our tallest men stood in the deepest place, and handed the sick, weak, and short men. **1764** FOOTE *Mayor of G.* I. Wks. 1799 I. 169 Enter Mrs. Sneak, handed by the Major. **1821** CLARE *Vill. Minstr.* I. 34 He hands her o'er the stile. **1862** TROLLOPE *Orley F.* xiii, He handed her into the carriage.

4. a. To deliver or pass with the hand or hands. (Also with adverbs, as *about, in, over.*) *spec.* To deliver or serve (food) at a meal. Also with passive force: to be served, to be delivered. Also with *round.*

1650 SIR T. BROWNE *Pseud. Ep.* v. vi. (1658) 298 Judas.. was so near, that our Saviour could hand the sop unto him. **1692** *Royal Proclam.* 13 Sept. in *Lond. Gaz.* No. 2802/1 Persons who..shall..hand or bring any such Libel to the Press. **1711** ADDISON *Spect.* No. 58 ¶3 There were several Satyrs and Panegyricks handed about. **1726** G. ROBERTS *Four Years Voy.* 329, I would hand the Hat and his Arms to him. **1802** C. WILMOT *Let.* 3 Jan. (1920) 27 Cakes,.. Lemonade, &c., continually handing about the Room. **1803** M. WILMOT *Let.* 13 May in *Russ. Jrnls.* (1934) I. 13 Soup was handed round. **1816** *Sporting Mag.* XLVIII. 173 You may as well hand me over the money. **1837** DICKENS *Pickw.* iv, Come, hand in the eatables. **1844** 'J. SLICK' *High Life N.Y.* II. 250 The niggers..dodged about, fillin plates and a handin em round. **1851** *London at Table* II. 44 Don't omit to hand the vegetables and sauces. **1891** E. PEACOCK *N. Brendon* I. 201 Hilary handed the paper to Sir Sampson. **1901** F. H. BURNETT *Making of Marchioness* I. iv. 134 'I ought to go and help hand cake,' she said. **1945** M. ALLINGHAM *Coroner's Pidgin* i. 11 I'm going to 'and round at the reception. **1964** S. H. NOWELL-SMITH *Edwardian England* iv. 183 At smart tables, dishes were now handed by the servants—service *à la russe*, as it was called.

b. *transf.* and *fig.* To deliver, pass, transfer, transmit. Now only with adverbs, as ***to hand down***, i.e. to a later generation or age; ***to hand on***, i.e. to the next in a series or succession; ***to hand over***, i.e. to another's possession, keeping, etc.

1642 SIR T. BROWNE *Relig. Med.* I. §49 In a vacuity.. there wants a body or Medium to hand and transport the visible rays of the object unto the sense. **1659** D. PELL *Impr. Sea* 401, I would hand this word unto the Merchants of our Land also. **1692** E. WALKER *Epictetus' Mor., In praise of Epictetus*, Every word..Your hearers have receiv'd as from an Oracle, And handed down to us. **1698** FRYER *Acc. E. India & P.* 176 A Story handed by Tradition. **1865** KINGSLEY *Herew.* ix, The father handed on the work. **1875** JOWETT *Plato* (ed. 2) V. 5 His function of chief speaker is handed over to the Pythagorean philosopher.

c. To give, convey: often with implication of palming-off or imposing. *U.S.*

1901 MERWIN & WEBSTER *Calumet 'K'* ii. 21, I told him he ought to give it to somebody else, and he handed me a lot of stuff about my experience. **1908** 'O. HENRY' *Options* (1916) 30 I've had it handed to me in the neck, too. **1925** F. LONSDALE *Spring Cleaning* 11 You ought to have heard the stuff they have handed over to her about you! **1926** J. BLACK *You can't Win* vi. 75 You'll..maybe get grabbed off a train and handed thirty days at Colorado Springs. **1970** *Morning Star* 17 Feb., The American Civil Liberties Union has condemned sentences for contempt handed down by Judge Julius Hoffman.

d. *to hand it to*: to acknowledge the superiority of; to congratulate; freq. in phr. ***you have*** (***got***) ***to hand it to*** (someone). orig. *U.S.*

c **1906** J. F. KELLY *Man with Grip* 14 You must hand it to the Jap. **1923** H. L. FOSTER *Beachcomber in Orient* xiv. 377, I do not like John [Chinaman]... But, to use the vernacular, you have to hand it to him. **1923** *Harper's Mag.* Apr. 558 You've got to hand it to that kid... He's stood everything and never squealed a yelp. Some young tough, believe me! **1926** G. D. H. & M. COLE *Blatchington Tangle* xli. 279 'I must hand it to you, sir,' the pseudo-American acknowledged. **1926** E. WALLACE *Ringer* I. 11 The Ringer's clever. I hand it to him. **1927** 'A. BERKELEY' *Mr. Priestley's Problem* ii. 30 'Guy, I hand it to you,' Laura was shrieking. **1965** *Listener* 30 Sept. 498/1 You've got to hand it to the Jerries, they know how to make cars. **1973** D. JORDAN *Nile Green* xxi. 85, I had to hand it to him: he hadn't missed a trick.

5. To join the hands of. *rare.*

1643–1881 [see HANDED 3].

†**6.** *intr.* To go hand in hand, concur. *Obs.*

1624 MASSINGER *Renegado* IV. i, Let but my power and means hand with my will.

hand and glove, (also with - -), *pred.* or *adj. phr.* Also (later) **hand in glove**. In constant close relations, on very intimate terms.

1680 R. MANSEL *Narr. Popish Plot* 103 Mrs. Cellier, to whom Mr. Willoughby was such a Croney, that they were hand and glove. **1780** COWPER *Table T.* 173 As if the world and they were hand and glove. **1867** TROLLOPE *Chron. Barset* I. xxiv. 206 He's not hand-and-glove with Lord Derby.

β. **1799–1800** BURDON *Pursuits Lit.* I. 47 (L.) Our author is here hand in glove with Providence. **1881** BESANT & RICE *Chapl. of Fleet* I. iv, The Doctor is..hand-in-glove with the bishop. **1889** *County* xxii, Priestman and the new Lady Sandilands are already hand in glove.

'hand-axe, -ax. a. An axe to be wielded by one hand; anciently a battle-axe.

1297 R. GLOUC. (1724) 26 He ne dradde noȝt þo that handaxe, as it was y sene. *c* **1300** *Havelok* 2553 Hand-ax,.. gisarm, or spere. **1375** BARBOUR *Bruce* XII. 57 The hand ax schaft ruschit in twa. **1498** *St. Giles' Charters* (1859) Pref. 41 Ane hand-ax or sword. **1886** J. H. KENNEDY in A. E. Lee *Hist. Columbus* (1892) II. 372 The other..with only a handax and jackplane made a drum cylinder.

b. A prehistoric stone implement, *esp.* a bifacially worked cutting tool typical of certain Lower and Middle Palæolithic industries. (Cf. COUP DE POING.)

1878 *Brooklyn Monthly* May 143/2 Another pattern have the groove extending partly round; other are wholly without a groove, and are of a pattern sometimes called hand axes. **1914** J. GEIKIE *Antiquity of Man in Europe* ii. 44 The *coup de poing* or hand-axe still occurs, but is rare, and would seem to have gone out of use in early Mousterian times. **1955** J. S. WEINER *Piltdown Forgery* xiii. 185 At Olorgesailie in Kenya Leakey found some good examples of these spherical stone balls with the Hand-axe culture. **1959** J. D. CLARK *Prehist. S. Afr.* ii. 41 *Handaxe*, a heavy all-purpose tool, often pear-shaped and some 8–9 inches in length. Believed to have been used in the hand without hafting. **1972** *Times Lit. Suppl.* 31 Mar. 371/2 The chopper and biface core tools generally known as hand-axes.

hand-ball.

1. A ball for throwing with the hand.

a **1400–50** *Alexander* 1771 Se quat I send to þe, son, þi-selfe with to laike, A hatt & and a hand-balle, & a hernepanne. **1483** *Cath. Angl.* 173/1 An Hand balle, *pila manualis*. **1846** GREENER *Sc. Gunnery* 296 Throw a hand-ball against any moveable body, and it will displace that body.

2. A game played with such a ball in a space between two distant goals.

(An annual hand-ball contest (usually on a holiday in spring) is an ancient institution in towns, villages, and parishes in the south of Scotland: see BALL *sb.*[1] 4 b.)

1581 MULCASTER *Positions* xxvii. (1887) 105 The litle handball is counted to be a swift exercise. **1777** BRAND *Pop. Antiq.* (1870) I. 98 It was customary in some churches for the Bishops and Archbishops themselves to play with the inferior clergy at hand-ball..even on Easter-day itself. **1801** STRUTT *Sports & Past.* II. iii. 84 The game of handball was indiscriminately played by both sexes. **1897** *Harper's Mag.* XCIV. 256/1 In a large open space reserved for the boys to play handball.

3. A hollow ball of india-rubber punctured so as to emit a spray of fluid when pressed in the hand.

1888 *Med. News* LII. 639 Whether the spray be given with a handball spray apparatus or with a small steam vaporizer. **1896** T. C. ALLBUTT *Syst. Med.* I. 305 The hand-ball sprays are used at ordinary temperatures.

4. A game resembling fives.

1886 G. H. BENEDICT *Spaldings Hand Bk. Sporting Rules* 45 A game of hand ball shall consist of twenty-one aces, to be played with a ball about two inches in diameter. **1910** *Encycl. Brit.* X. 450/2 Handball, of ancient popularity in Ireland and much played in the United States, is practically identical with fives. **1957** *Ibid.* IX. 339/1 Certain forms of the games [of fives] in the United States, in Ireland and in some parts of the north of England are known as handball. *Ibid.* XI. 141/1 There is evidence that handball originated in Ireland about a thousand years ago. *Ibid.* 142/1 The game of Irish handball..was played on a hard clay floor, with one wall of stone,..against which the ball was struck. **1961** J. S. SALAK *Dict. Amer. Sports* 215 *Handball*, a wall game in which a black rubber ball is struck with the hand against a wall, or walls, the ball being struck alternately by opposing players. **1968** *Globe & Mail* (Toronto) 17 Feb. 48/1 (Advt.), Regulation-size squash and handball courts.

†**hand-band.** *Obs.* [Cf. ON. *handaband* a joining or shaking of hands.] Covenant made by joining hands; covenanted condition, union, or possession.

a **1300** *Cursor M.* 3915 Wit wijf and child, and al hand-band, Ilkan wit oþer went in hand. *Ibid.* 13428 O wijf for-sok he hand-band. *c* **1460** *Towneley Myst.* (Surtees) 43 God gif the to thyn handband The dew of heven and frute of land.

hand-barrow. [BARROW *sb.*[3] 1 a.] A flat, rectangular frame of transverse bars, having shafts or 'trams' before and behind, by which it is carried.

14.. *Voc.* in Wr.-Wülcker 572/2 *Ce[no]vectorium manuale*, an handberwe. **1511** *Demaundes Joyous* in *Promp. Parv.* 225/1 *note*, What thinge shall be hardest to hym to knowe? *R.* A hande-barowe, for of that he shall not knowe whiche ende shall goo before. **1587** FLEMING *Contn. Holinshed* III. 1548/1 Caried from the gaole to the place of iudgement, some vpon handbarrowes. **1669** WORLIDGE *Syst. Agric.* (1681) 322 Barrow, is of two sorts; either a Hand-barrow, or a Wheel-barrow. **1854** H. MILLER *Sch. & Schm.* xxii. (1860) 234/1 We could see..a dead body borne forth by two persons on a hand-barrow.

†**b.** A similar flat barrow having a wheel. *Obs.*

1521 *MS. Acc. St. John's Hosp., Canterb.*, For a hand barow whele vjd. **1555** EDEN *Decades* 333 Hand barrowes bothe with wheeles and without wheeles.

c. *Comb.* **handbarrow beggar**, a mendicant cripple carried from door to door on a stretcher, as formerly customary in Scotland.

'hand,basket. [BASKET *sb.*] A basket to be carried in the hand.

1495–7 *Naval Acc. Hen. VII* (1896) 197 Hand baskettes for brede—ij; Maundes to bere in ffleshe—ij. **1583** HOLLYBAND *Campo di Fior* 97 Buye a salate, and radishes, and cheries. Take the hand-basket. **1671** CROWNE *Juliana* III. Dram. Wks. 1873 I. 69, I can see when I see, surely; I don't carry my eyes in a hand-basket. **1768–74** TUCKER *Lt. Nat.* (1852) I. 281 He prepares the materials at home, and brings them all together in a hand-basket.

attrib. **1560** BECON *New Catech.* Wks. 1844 II. 339 That their wives be no dish-clouts, nor no hand-basket-sloys, nor no drudges, nor yet slavish people, but fellow-heirs with them of everlasting life.

'handbell. A small bell rung by being swung in the hand, as distinguished from one rung by a bell-pull, bell-rope, etc.

a **1000** *Charter of Leofric* in *Cod. Dipl.* IV. 275 Nu ða synd .xiii. upphangene and .xii. handbella. **1570** LEVINS *Manip.* 57/20 A Handbell, *tintinnabulum.* **1688** R. HOLME *Armoury* III. 461/2 A Saint Bell, or Hand Bell..is held in a mans hand, and soe rung. **1859** W. COLLINS *After Dark* (Tauchn.) 307 (Hoppe) He took up the hand-bell to ring for lights. **1894** J. T. FOWLER *Adamnan* Introd. 43 The abbot or bishop called the brethren together by the sound of a hand-bell.

b. That carried by a town-crier or bellman.

c **1500** *Maid Emlyn* in *Anc. Poet. Tracts* (Percy) 18 The handbell ofte dyd she tolle, Full great sorowe makynge. **1681** W. ROBERTSON *Phraseol. Gen.* (1693) 1066 It passes about like an hand-bell. **1837** CARLYLE *Fr. Rev.* I. v. v, Criers rushing with hand-bells: 'Oyez, oyez, All men to their Districts to be enrolled!' **1880** A. MCKAY *Hist. Kilmarnock* (ed. 4) 130 A hand-bell was rung through the streets when a person departed this life.

c. *spec.* A bell specially constructed with a leathern handle, and the clapper made and attached in a particular way, for *handbell-ringing.*

d. *attrib.* and *Comb.*, as ***handbell-shaped*** adj.; also **handbell-ringer**, one who performs musically on handbells; **handbell-ringing**, a musical performance executed by a company of ringers with handbells tuned to different notes.

1889 HURST *Horsham* Gloss., *Handbellringer*, at Christmas handbell ringers go round to different towns or villages with their bells.

hand'bill[1]. [BILL *sb.*[1] 4.] A light bill or pruning knife.

1523 FITZHERB. *Husb.* §127 Take a sharpe hatchet or a handbyll and cut the settes. **1702** EVELYN in *Pepys' Diary* VI. 254 With his handbill and pruning knife.

'handbill[2]. [BILL *sb.*[3]] A printed notice or advertisement on a single page, intended to be delivered or circulated by hand. Sometimes applied to a small bill to be posted on walls, etc.

1753 *World* No. I. 3 Who make their appearance either in hand-bills, or in weekly or daily papers. **1793** *Regal Rambler* 26 Lucifer drew up a most inflammatory hand-bill. **1837** HOWITT *Rur. Life* II. v. (1862) 152 A large hand-bill in the post-office window offering a reward of 100*l.* for the apprehension of a delinquent. **1864** KNIGHT *Passages Work. Life* I. v. 218 [He] had the indiscretion to circulate a hand-bill from house to house.

'hand-blow, 'handy blow. [f. HAND *sb.* + BLOW *sb.*[1] The form with *handy-* found *a* 1600, as also in *handy-cuff, -grip, -stroke*, etc., appears to be due to the co-existence of *handwork* and *handiwork* from 14th c.] A blow with the hand; a cuff. Usually in *pl.* ***to come to hand(y)-blows***, to come to blows at close quarters; so ***to fall to, be at hand*** (or ***handy-***)***blows***.

α. **1577–87** HOLINSHED *Chron.* III. 1138/1 The enimie boldlie approcheth, the pike is offered, to handblowes it commeth. **1587** FLEMING *Contn. Holinshed* III. 1997/2 At length through shot..scalding water and handblowes they were repelled. **1643** [ANGIER] *Lanc. Vall. Achor* 26 The Enemy came on desperately, even to hand-blows.

β. **1587** HARMER tr. *Beza's Serm.* 162 (T.) By whose means the matter came to handie-blows. **1632** LITHGOW *Trav.* III. 114 Belaboured him soundly with handy blowes. **1639** R. WARD *Animadv. War* XIV. I. ccl, An instrument called a Flaile, used..when the Enemy is at handy blowes. **1783** AINSWORTH *Lat. Dict.* (Morell) I. s.v. *Blow*, To come to handy blows, *Cominus pugnare.* **1870** MORRIS *Earthly Par.* I. I. 316 Nought of handy blows I know.

'hand-bolt, *sb.* ? *Obs.* [BOLT *sb.*[1] 6.] A handcuff. Also *fig.*

1816 *Trial Berkeley Poachers*, The hand-bolt hurt us. **1831** *Examiner* 467/1 [He] pronounces the nomination boroughs conservative—the hand-bolts of the Commons.

Hence **'hand-bolt** *v. trans.*, to handcuff.

1816 *Trial Berkeley Poachers* 44 Colonel Berkeley, and several more came up to us, and hand-bolted us. **1831** *Lincoln Herald* 22 July 2/3 'Constable, do your duty—handbolt them.'

handbook ('hændbʊk). [Found in OE. in form *handbóc, -bók*, as a rendering of L. *manualis* and Gr.-L. *enchiridion.* But the current word was introduced after Ger. *handbuch* in 19th c.]

A small book or treatise, such as may conveniently be held in the hand; a manual.

†**a.** in OE. The MANUAL of ecclesiastical offices and ritual. *Obs.*

a **900** *Canons of Ælfred* 21 in Thorpe *Laws* II. 350/15 Ða halȝan bec, saltere and pistolboc, sangboc and handboc. *c* **1050** *Byrhtferth's Handboc* in *Anglia* VIII. 321 Enchiridion þæt ys manualis on lyden & handboc on englisc. *a* **1100** *Voc.* in Wr.-Wülcker 327/26 *Manualis*, handlin oððe handboc. *c* **1367** *Eulogium Hist.* (1863) III. v. lxxxii. 9 Librum in sinu quod ipse vocabat manuale, quod Anglice vocabat handbok. **1563-87** FOXE *A. & M.* (1596) 130/1 A booke of his owne making in his owne toong, which in the English speach he [K. Alfred] called a handbooke, in Greeke called it Enchiridion, in Latin a manuell.

b. A compendious book or treatise for guidance in any art, occupation, or study; *spec.* a book containing concise information for the tourist.

1814 (*title*) A Handbook for modelling wax flowers. **1833** NICOLAS *Chronol. Hist.* Pref. 19 What the Germans would term, and which, if our language admitted of the expression, would have been the fittest title for it, 'The Hand-book of History'. **1836** (*title*) A Hand-Book for Travellers on the Continent [Murray's]. **1838** H. ROGERS *Introd. Lect. Eng. Gram. & Comp.* 70 Such tasteless innovations as 'Morning-land' (*Morgen-land*) for the East, and 'hand-book' (*hand-buch*) for 'manual'. **1843** *Fraser's Mag.* XXVII. 649 The compiler of this *Handbook* [Murray's Handbook to N. Italy] (we are obliged to use his coined word by way of distinction) does not give the prices. **1863** *Reader* 21 Feb. 190 If by handbook he intends anything of a guide, he has failed in his object.

c. A betting-book; ***handbook man***, a bookmaker. Also ***hand-booking***, bookmaking. *U.S.*

1894 *Voice* 20 Sept., In every saloon which boasts a ticker are to be found men who will register a bet to any amount. These 'handbook' men are all [etc.]. **1903** *N.Y. Evening Post* 14 Sept., A case where an officer arrested a handbook man. **1904** *N.Y. Times* 13 June 1 The handbooking possibilities on the Derby. **1946** *Chicago Daily News* 26 June 14/2 The mob was..operating hand-books with full knowledge of your police department.

†**'hand-borow.** *Obs.* [See BORROW *sb.*] *lit.* 'hand-pledge' or security; according to Spelman, Cowell, and their copiers, a name for one (or each) of the nine sureties associated with the HEADBOROW in a frank-pledge.

(It does not appear where the 16th c. antiquaries got the word, no trace of which has been found in OE. or ME.)

1626 SPELMAN *Gloss.*, *Handborowe*, in Decuriis seu Friborgis vnus e nouenis est, decimo, quem Headboruw vocant, suppositus. **1672** MANLEY *Cowell's Interpr.*, *Hand-borow*, A Surety, a manual Pledge, that is, an inferior Undertaker; for *Head-borow* is a superior or Chief Instrument, *Spelm.* **1848** WHARTON *Law Lex.* s.v. *Head-borough*, The head boroughs were the chief of the ten pledges, the other nine being denominated *hand-borows*, or inferior pledges.

'handbow. [BOW *sb.*[1]] An ordinary bow in which the string is drawn and released by hand, as distinguished from a CROSS-BOW.

1535 COVERDALE *1 Macc.* vi. 51 He made all maner ordinaunce: handbowes, fyrie dartes, rackettes. **1549** *Compl. Scot.* vi. 42 Mak reddy ȝour corsbollis, hand bollis, fyir speyris. **1600** J. PORY tr. *Leo's Africa* II. 160 Neither had they any other weapons but hand-bowes (for crosse-bowes were not then used).

'handbreadth. Also 6 handbreth, -breath, 8- hand's breadth, handsbreadth. A Unit of lineal measure in many countries and periods, founded on the width of the adult human hand, a PALM; formerly estimated as one-fourth of a foot, but now as four inches.

1535 COVERDALE *1 Kings* vii. 26 The thicknesse was an handbreth. **1559** W. CUNNINGHAM *Cosmogr. Glasse* 56 A Hande breadth. Conteyninge in it 4 Fingers. A Fote. Conteyninge in it 4 Hande breadth. **1653** H. COGAN tr. *Pinto's Trav.* lxvi. 267 Within nine hand-bredths of the Water. **1843** MACAULAY *Lays Anc. Rome, Horatius* xlv, The good sword stood a hand-breadth out Behind the Tuscan's head. **1875** WHYTE MELVILLE *Riding Recollect.* iv. (1879) 65 A handsbreadth behind the girths.

'handbrede. *Obs.* exc. *north. dial.* Also 4 handibre(e)de, *erron.* 6 hand-brode, 8 -broad, 8-9 *dial.* -breed. [BREDE *sb.*[2]] = prec.

c **1000** ÆLFRIC *Gloss.* in Wr.-Wülcker 158/11 *Palmus*, span *uel* handbred. **1388** WYCLIF *Ezek.* xl. 43 The brenkis of tho boordis ben of oon handibreede [**1382** of oo palme]. ?*a* **1400** *Morte Arth.* 2229 Hurttes his herne-pane an haunde-brede large. *c* **1420** *Pallad. on Husb.* III. 361 Vp to goon Ouer the hed too hondbrede is his kynde. **1551** TURNER *Herbal* I. Q v b, Twoo handbredes from that place. **1577** B. GOOGE *Heresbach's Husb.* II. (1586) 55 A handbrode in height. **1726** *Nat. Hist. Irel.* 89 The thickness of two handbroads or there-abouts. **1792** BURNS *Willie's Wife* iii, Ae limpin leg a hand-breed shorter. **1828** *Craven Dial.*, *Hand-breed.* **1893** *Northumbld. Gloss.*, *Handbraed.*

hand-'broad, *a.* Of the width of a hand.

1612-15 BP. HALL *Contempl.*, *O.T.* XVIII. viii, A hand-broad cloud. *a* **1711** KEN *Hymns Evang.* Poet. Wks. 1721 I. 10 The hand-broad Cloud shall the expanse bedew. **1865** KINGSLEY *Herew.* iii, Ill-lighted by a hand-broad window.

'hand-,canter. [CANTER *sb.*[3]] A gentle, easy canter. Cf. HAND-GALLOP.

1836 GEN. P. THOMPSON *Exerc.* (1842) IV. 73 The Whigs ..have probably made up their minds to carry their Bill through in a hand canter. **1893** EARL DUNMORE *Pamirs* I. 284 We had seven miles to ride to the city, which we did at a hand canter.

'hand-cart. A small cart pushed or drawn with the hands.

1810 *Hull Improv. Act* 56 Any..dray, hand-cart, wheel-barrow. **1884** F. M. CRAWFORD *Rom. Singer* I. 44 A man who was selling cabbage in the street stopped his hand-cart.

'handclap. [CLAP *sb.*[1]] **a.** A clap of the hands; the brief space of time which this takes, an instant.

1822 HOGG *Perils of Man* III. 205 (Jam.) It is God speed, or spulyie wi' thee in three handclaps. **1864** BURTON *Caerngorm Mountains* 77 In a hand-clap, in it swept.. dashing everything before it. **1962** A. NISBETT *Technique Sound Studio* ii. 33 You can use a hand-clap to give a rough guide to the reverberation.

b. Applause.

1907 *Daily Chron.* 1 Oct. 4/5 The curtain goes up..to some feeble handclaps from invited guests. **1908** *Westm. Gaz.* 13 Mar. 7/3 The chairman of the company.., with the directors, entered the room, a hand-clap greeting them.

c. ***slow handclap***: slow applause expressing disapproval. Also (with hyphen) as vb. Hence ***slow hand-clapping*** vbl. sb.

1953 *Britannica Bk. of Year* 638/2 The freedom of usage seen in the formation of compounds also allows frequent changes in function, so that verbs, for example, may be formed from nouns. Examples are: to slow-handclap. **1955** MILLER & WHITINGTON *Cricket Typhoon* 215 Indeed, they jeered and slow-handclapped Cowdrey. **1958** F. C. AVIS *Boxing Ref. Dict.* 103 *Slow handclap*, ironic applause expressed by means of a very slow clapping of the hands. **1959** *News Chron.* 13 July 4/6 Some cynical dons..were giving the slow hand-clap to the end of the procession. **1961** *Guardian* 3 Apr. 1/7 All the slow hand-clapping and hysterical cheering. **1966** *Listener* 20 Jan. 88/2 This destructive criticism was nothing compared with the..slow-handclaps and final booing.

†**'handcloth.** *Obs.* [See CLOTH *sb.* 1.] A towel, a napkin; a duster.

c **1000** ÆLFRIC *Hom.* I. 426 Ic ȝeseo Godes engel standende ætforan þe mid hand-claþe, and wipaþ þine swatiȝan limu. *c* **1200** *Trin. Coll. Hom.* 163 Hire handcloðes and hire bord cloðes ben makede wite. *c* **1475** *Voc.* in Wr.-Wülcker 773/10 *Hoc manitergium*, a hand-clothe. [**1839** H. ROGERS *Ess.* II. iii. 143 We cannot now speak, as did our Saxon ancestors..of hand-clath (hand-cloth) for towel.]

'handclout. *dial.* [See CLOUT *sb.*[1] 4.] = prec.

1788 W. MARSHALL *Yorksh.* Gloss., *Handclout*..a towel.

'handcraft. Manual skill, power, or work; = HANDICRAFT 1. Hence **handcraft** *v. trans.*; **handcrafted** *ppl. a.*

a **975** *Edgar's Canons* § 11 in Thorpe *Laws* II. 246 (Bosw.) We læraþ þæt preosta ȝehwilc to-eacan lare leorniȝe handcræft ȝeorne. *c* **1000** ÆLFRIC *Hom.* I. 392 Mid his handcræfte he teolede his and his ȝeferena forþ-dæda. *c* **1100** *Rule St. Benedict* lvii. (Durh. Chapt. MS. B. iv. 24) To be ceapienne æniȝ þing heora handcræftes. *c* **1205** LAY. 4899 þurh his hænde craftes [*c* **1275** þorh his hendi craftes]. *c* **1400** *Lanfranc's Cirurg.* 18 So þat it be don with hand craft [*MS. B.* hande crafte]. **1483** *Cath. Angl.* 173/1 An Hand crafte, *mechania*. **1533** MORE *Answ. Poysoned Bk.* Wks. 1062/1 Menne of handcraft. **1555** W. WATREMAN *Fardle Facions* Pref. 8 Diuers inuencions of handekraftes and sciences. **1599** MARSTON *Sco. Villanie* 166 Euery broking hand-crafts artizan.

1849-53 ROCK *Ch. of Fathers* III. x. 358 Our Anglo-Saxon goldsmiths' hand-craft. **1933** *Catholic News* (Johannesburg) Mar. 15 (Advt.), Hand-craft tailored suits. **1965** *Punch* 3 Nov. 645/3 The stone, being hand-crafted and set, remained in place for more than a month before it was washed away in a rain-storm. **1967** *Listener* 5 Jan 21/2 The bowls appear hand-crafted instead of factory-manufactured. **1968** C. LEADER *Angry Darkness* iv. 39 The tiny shops were filled.. with old silver and hand-crafted copper and brass. **1968** J. ARNOLD *Shell Book of Country Crafts* 59 Machine- and mass-production, together, have had a tremendous impact ..on hand-crafts. **1971** *Daily Colonist* (Victoria, B.C.) 24 Oct. 4/2 All the fuel injection parts had to be handcrafted.

†**'handcraftman.** *Obs.* Also β **handcrafty man.** [f. prec.; in β implying a derivative adj. *handcrafty*.] = HANDICRAFTSMAN.

1463-4 *Rolls of Parlt.* V. 506/2 Artificers, handcrafty men and women..have been gretely empoveryshed. **1483** *Act 1 Rich. III*, c. 9 § 1 Beyng an Artificer or handcrafty man. **1520** *Caxton's Chron. Eng.* VII. 159/1 The same evenynge the handcrafty men of the towne arose. *a* **1529** SKELTON *Vox Populi* 194, I meane the handecrafteman. **1564-78** BULLEYN *Dial. agst. Pest.* (1888) 6 Ause I haue many of my sirename here..yea, honast handcraftie men.

'handcraftsman. [lit. *handcraft's man.*] = prec. Hence **handcraftsmanship.**

1530-1 *Act 22 Hen. VIII*, c. 13 Preamb., Supposyng that Straungers usyng bakyng, bruyng, surgerye or wrytyng, shulde be hand craftesmen..suche handcraftesmen as were entended by any the sayde Estatutes.

1923 *Daily Mail* 22 Jan. 6 (Advt.), A specialised handcraftmanship places these brushes as a blessing [etc.]. **1933** *Archit. Rev.* LXXIII. 253/1 The subject of handcraftsmanship and mass production has been touched upon. **1954** B. GRIFFITHS *Golden String* ix. 137 If a society is to be really human, there will always be a need for the hand-craftsman. **1961** *John o' London's* 7 Sept. 275/2, I think no one today, save a few incurable rustic-romantics and starry-eyed handcraftsmen, will imagine that a solution is to be found.

handcuff ('hændkʌf), *sb.* Also *dial.* **handycuff.** [f. HAND *sb.* + CUFF *sb.*[1] 3 in same sense (of which a single instance is known of 1663).

The first examples of the sb. imply that it arose in the north. For connexion with OE. *handcops*, there is no historical evidence.]

A manacle, or shackle for the hand, consisting of a divided metal ring which is locked round the wrist. Handcuffs are used in pairs, connected by a short chain or jointed bar, so as to fasten the hands of a prisoner together or secure him to the hand of the officer who has him in custody.

1775 ASH, *Handcuff*, an iron instrument to confine the hand. **1808-18** JAMIESON, *Handcuffs*, manacles. **1814** SCOTT *Wav.* xxvii, 'A rash promise..is not a steel handcuff: it may be shaken off.' **1818** TODD, *Handcuff*, a manacle, a fetter for the wrist. [No quot.] **1828** *Craven Dial.*, *Handy-cuffs*, handcuffs. **1865** DICKENS *Mut. Fr.* I. xii, The Inspector put a pair of handcuffs in his pocket.

'handcuff, *v.* [f. HAND *sb.* + CUFF *v.*[2], in same sense.] *trans.* To put handcuffs on; to manacle, shackle the hands of.

1720 DE FOE *Capt. Singleton* v. (1840) 79 Tied two and two by the wrist, as we handcuff prisoners. **1754** W. HAY *Ess. Deformity* 26 (T.) If he cannot carry an ox, like Milo, he will not, like Milo, be handcuffed in the oak, by attempting to rend it. **1837** HT. MARTINEAU *Soc. Amer.* III. 313 To handcuff and fetter your fellow-man.

Hence **handcuffed** ('hændkʌft), *ppl. a.*, **'handcuffing** *vbl. sb.*

1784 COWPER *Tiroc.* 819 Bedlam's closeted and handcuffed charge. **1859** JEPHSON *Brittany* iii. 35, I should like to have the handcuffing of you.

handed ('hændɪd), *a.* [f. HAND + -ED.]

1. Having hands; esp. of some specified kind.

1552 HULOET, Handed longe, or longe handes hauynge. **1613** PURCHAS *Pilgrimage* (1614) 816 It hath the body of a Fox, handed and footed like a Monkie. **1674** N. FAIRFAX *Bulk & Selv.* To Rdr., We and others of the Handed Philosophers. **1791** E. DARWIN *Bot. Gard.* II. iii. 1781 Nor handed moles, nor beaked worms return.

b. Very frequently in parasynthetic compounds, as ***empty-***, ***hard-***, ***open-***, ***two-***, ***four-handed.***

1526 SKELTON *Magnyf.* 2257 Ye both well handyd. **1611** BIBLE *Lev.* xxi. 19 A man that is broken footed, or broken handed. **1632** LITHGOW *Trav.* III. 88 [They] doe not use to come empty handed. **1894** LD. WOLSELEY *Marlborough* II. xlix. 40 A peculiarly indulgent or open-handed master.

2. = PALMATE.

1854 MAYNE *Expos. Lex.*, *Handed Fucus*..common name for the *Fucus palmatus*.

3. Joined hand in hand.

1643 MILTON *Divorce* Pref. (1851) 15 If any two be but once handed in the Church. **1667** —— *P.L.* IV. 739 Into thir inmost bower Handed they went. **1881** D. C. MURRAY *Joseph's Coat* III. xxxiv. 234 They sat handed, looking at each other now and then, but quite wordless.

handedness ('hændɪdnɪs). [f. HANDED *a.* + -NESS.] The tendency to, or the preference for, the use of either the right or the left hand. Also *transf.*

1921 *Trans. Utah Acad. Sci.* II. 59 (*title*) The problem of handedness. *Ibid.* 62 It is argued by some that a child's handedness is a result of imitating its parents. **1936** F. A. E. CREW in *Jrnl. Genetics* XXXIII. 67 It seemed to me necessary to examine each rat..for evidence of this right-hand and left-hand turning habit,... [68] In any examination of handedness the experimentation must not be complicated by the presence of an alternating light. **1937** *N. & Q.* 10 July 32/1 The First Series of an exhaustive scientific work on the subject of 'Handedness'. **1961** *Lancet* 12 Aug. 363/1 The left hemisphere is usually dominant for speech regardless of the handedness of the individual. **1962** *Listener* 10 May 814/3 Proteins..contain amino acids (all of one particular handedness) joined together. **1973** *Sci. Amer.* May 27/3 Background data, including..length of postpartum separation from siblings and handedness of the mother.

Handelian (hæn'diːlɪən), *a.* and *sb.* [f. the name of Georg Friedrich *Handel*, originally *Händel* (1685–1759), German musician + -IAN.]

A. *adj.* Of, pertaining to, or characteristic of Handel, or his style of composition. **B.** *sb.* One who favours or imitates the style of Handel.

1770 *Priv. Lett. 1st Ld. Malmesbury* (1870) I. 205 Tenducci is amazingly improved; in his part the old Handelian songs were left out. **1788** F. BURNEY *Diary* (1842) IV. IV. 231 The concert was very Handelian. **1808** S. WESLEY *Lett.* (1875) 9 This would nettle the Handelians devilishly. **1825** LAMB *Lett.* (1888) II. 132 My sister's cold is as obstinate as an old Handelian, whom a modern amateur is trying to convert to Mozart-ism. **1865** J. HULLAH *Transition Per. Music* 244 It 'bears so genuine a Handelian impress'. **1885** *Athenæum* 28 Feb. 288/1 Revivals of Handelian oratorio. **1911** LADY GUTHRIE in R. L. Orr *Ld. Guthrie* (1923) 258 Those dusky simple souls interpreting the glorious Handelian strains. **1966** K. AMIS *Anti-Death League* 349 The series of florid, rather Handelian amens swung to its close.

hander[1] ('hændə(r)). [f. HAND *v.* + -ER[1].] One who hands, delivers, or passes. Also with adverbs, *down*, *in*, *out*, etc. *spec.* = HANDLER 2.

1678 *Lond. Gaz.* No. 1288/4 The Hander of it to the Press. **1680** DRYDEN *Religio Laici* 361 Grant they were The handers down. **1746** *Acct. of Cock-fight* in *42nd Ann. Rep. Deputy Keeper P. R.* 166 In such manner as is usual for handers to account to ten. **1794** *Sporting Mag.* III. 169

Called 'handers' or 'setters to'. **1824** Miss Mitford *Village* Ser. I. (1863) 123 An excellent hander of muffins and cake. **1850** L. Hunt *Autobiog.* xix. 303 The hander down of his likeness to posterity.

'hander². [f. hand *sb.* + -er¹ 1.]

1. A blow on the hand.

1868 J. Greenwood *Purgat. Peter the Cruel* v. 149 (Farmer) You've got to take your handers. **1887** *Times* (weekly ed.) 1 July 7/4 The matron gave her six 'handers' with a cane.

2. *-hander* in comb., **a.** as back-hander, a back-handed blow; **b.** as *left-hander*, a left-handed man.

1882 *Daily Tel.* 12 June, The next comer, Scotton, the left hander..played out time.

handewark, -werk, *sbs.*: see handiwork.

† **'handfast**, *sb. Obs.* [app. f. hand *sb.* + fast *a.*: an unusual formation for a sb. Senses 3, 4, go with handfast *v.*]

I. 1. Firm hold or grip with the hands.

1545 Raynold *Byrth Mankynde* ii. v. (1634) 118 That part of the which she hath handfast. **1582** N. Lichefield tr. *Castanheda's Conq. E. Ind.* xxxiii. 81 a, He could not escape, forsomuch as our men caught handefast of him. **1622** R. Hawkins *Voy. S. Sea* (1847) 105 Such were the blowes he gave them with his pinnions, as both left their hand-fast, being beaten blacke and blewe.

fig. **1577** Bull *Luther's Comm. Ps. Grad.* (1615) 30 By faith to lay sure handfast on Gods eternal mercy and Grace. **1645** Pagitt *Heresiogr.* (1662) 55 You seem to have good handfast of your opinion. *a* **1656** Hales *Gold. Rem.* (1688) 61 If we search it, we shall find some Hand-fast, some Circumstance that will make it easie to be born.

b. *in handfast*, in hold, held fast.

1611 Shaks. *Wint. T.* iv. iii. 795 If that Shepheard be not in hand-fast, let him flye.

2. A handle by which anything is grasped: e.g. of a flail. *local.*

1893 Baring-Gould *Cheap Jack Z.* I. 180 Zita took both flails..there was a deep bruise in the 'handfast' of one. *Ibid.* The leather thongs that attached the flapper to the handfast were twisted.

II. 3. The joining of hands in making a bargain.

1626 Middleton *Anything for Qt. Life* v. ii, A firm covenant, signed and sealed by oath and handfast.

4. A contract or covenant; *spec.* a betrothal or marriage contract.

1611 Shaks. *Cymb.* i. v. 78 The Remembrancer of her, to hold The hand-fast to her Lord. *a* **1616** Beaum. & Fl. *Wit at Sev. Weapons* v. i, Here in Heaven's eye, and all Love's sacred powers..I knit this holy hand fast, and with this hand, The heart that owes this hand, ever binding..Both heart and hand in love, faith, loyalty. **1872** E. W. Robertson *Hist. Ess.* 175 In its original acceptation the word *handfast* simply meant a contract of any sort, though it seems to have been gradually applied almost exclusively to a marriage contract. **1884** J. Payne *Tales fr. Arabic* I. 119 Then they assembled together..and made a covenant and handfast of fealty with him.

5. *Comb.*, as *handfast-maker*.

1610 Holland *Camden's Brit.* i. 388 (D.) Britona, handfast-maker shee, All clad in Laurell green.

'handfast, *a.* [In senses 1, 2, orig. pa. pple. of handfast *v.*]

† **1.** Contracted by the joining of hands; espoused.

Also 'Betrothed by joining of hands in order to cohabitation, before the celebration of marriage' (Jamieson).

c **1200**, etc. [see handfast *v.* 1]. **1470–85** Malory *Arthur* x. xxxvii, Anone he made them hand fast and wedded them. **1484** in *Ripon Ch. Acts* (Surtees) 162 *note*, 'I take the Margaret to my handfest wif.' **1532** More *Confut. Tindale* Wks. 728/1 Vpon the day when they should haue been made handefaste and ensured together. *c* **1565** Lindesay (Pitscottie) *Chron. Scot.* 26 (Jam.) This Isobel was but hand-fast with him, and deceased before the marriage. **1610** Holland *Camden's Brit.* i. 384 Tame and Isis meeting in one streame become hand-fast (as it were) and joyned in Wedlocke.

fig. **1546** Bale *Eng. Votaries* i. 63 b (T.) A vyrgine made handfast to Christ.

† **2.** Bound; having the hands fast; manacled.

c **1400** *Gamelyn* 437 þou shalt stond up by the post as þou were hond fast. **1611** Cotgr., *Emmanoté*, manacled, handfast. **1632** Lithgow *Trav.* x. 463 At last being loosed from these Pinnacles of paine, I was hand-fast set on the floore.

3. Having a firm grip of the hand; tight-fisted, close-fisted. *lit.* and *fig.*

1603 Knolles *Hist. Turks* (1638) 227 Being also much more handfast than were his honourable predecessors. **1606** Breton *Praise Vert. Ladies* Wks. (Grosart) 57 (D.) Some will say women are covetous: are not men as handfast? **1845** Carlyle *Cromwell* (1871) I. 15 Ludlow, a common handfast, honest, dull and indeed partly wooden man. **1887** *Kentish Gloss.* s.v., 'Old George is middlin' handfast today' (said of a good catch at cricket).

handfast ('hændfɑːst, -æ-), *v. Obs.* exc. *Hist.* Also 3–6 **-fest**(e. Pa. pple. **-ed**; in earlier use **hand-fast**. [In sense 1, early ME. a. ON. *hand-festa* to strike a bargain by joining hands, to pledge, betroth, f. *hand-* hand- + *festa* to fasten, make fast, settle, pledge, bind in wedlock, betroth. The other senses appear to be independent formations from *hand* and *fast*: cf. handfast *sb.* 1.]

I. 1. *trans.* To make a contract of marriage between (parties) by joining of hands; to betroth (two persons, or one person *to* another).

c **1200** Ormin 2389, Ȝho wass hanndfesst an god mann þatt Josæp wass ȝehatenn. *c* **1375** *Sc. Leg. Saints, Cecile* 16 Scho..Ves handfast vith a ȝungmane, þat in maryag vald hire haf tan. **1474** Caxton *Chesse* ii. i. Bij b, A right fayr mayde..which was assured & handfast vnto a noble yong gentilman of cartage. **1483** *Cath. Angl.* 173/1 To Handefeste, *fedare, subarrare*. **1541** Coverdale *Chr. State of Matrim.* (1543) 43 b (Brand), Every man lykewyse must esteme the parson to whom he is handfasted none otherwyse than for his owne spouse, though as yet it be not done in the Church ner in the Streate. **1565–73** *Durham Depos.* (Surtees) 242 Lancelott Eyttes, the said Janett grandfather, dyd handfast them. **1624** Heywood *Gunaik.* vii. 337 The Auspices of Auguries were Southsayers and such as used to handfast or contract marriages. **1808–25** Jamieson, *To handfast*, to betrothe by joining hands, in order to cohabitation, before the celebration of marriage. **1849** Jas. Grant *Kirkaldy of Gr.* ix. 90 Margaret, daughter of Lord Crichton, to whom he had been betrothed or hand-fasted.

fig. **1555** L. Saunders in Coverdale *Lett. Mart.* (1564) 191 He hath..handfasted vs hys chosen children vnto hys deare sonne our Christ. **1631** *Celestina* vii. 81 If you will but hand-fast your affections each to other. **1680** G. Hickes *Spirit of Popery* 7 Mr. Andrew Cant..called unto them to come, and be hand-fasted unto Christ by Subscribing the Contract.

† **b.** Said of the man: To engage in a marriage contract. Also *refl. Obs.*

14.. *Eger & Grime* 1274 in Furniv. *Percy Folio* I. 394 Gryme handfasted that faire Ladye. **1577–87** Holinshed *Scot. Chron.* (1805) II. 125 Which earl by letters of procuracie..affied and handfasted the foresaid ladie Margaret in all solemne wise. **1611** Cotgr., *Accorder vne fille*, to handfast, affiance, betroath himselfe vnto a maiden. **1666** Sancroft *Lex Ignea* 40 We list not to hand-fast ourselves to God Almighty.

c. *intr.* (for *refl.*)

1850 *N. & Q.* 1st Ser. II. 151/2 John Mac-Vic Ewen..had handfasted (as it was called) with a daughter of Mac Ian of Ardnamurchan.

† **d.** *fig.* To engage with an earnest; to give earnest of. *Obs.*

1630 Lord *Banians* Introd., Handfesting the Reader with as good hopes, as may bee expected from a subject of this nature.

II. † **2.** To grasp, seize with the hand; to take fast hold of. Also *fig. Obs.*

c **1530** H. Rhodes *Bk. Nurture* 96 in *Babees Bk.* (1868) 84 Learne thou to handfast honesty. **1562** Bulleyn *Dial. Soarnes & Chir.* 25 b, A newe labour and care will handfaste you. **1602** Warner *Alb. Eng.* x. lix. (1612) 262 Euen this grand-Captaine of the Hosts..Hand-fasting now the Altar clames that priuiledge in vaine. **1652–62** Heylin *Cosmogr.* ii. (1682) 156 One of the Children hand-fasted the spear.

† **3.** To make fast the hands of, to manacle. *Obs.*

1586 J. Hooker *Girald. Irel.* in *Holinshed* II. 134/2 He was taken prisoner, and handfasted, and so kept for a space. **1611** Cotgr., *Emmanoter*, to manacle; to handfast, or tie the hands together.

'handfasted, *ppl. a. Obs.* exc. *Hist.* [f. handfast *v.*]

1. Contracted or engaged by joining of hands; betrothed. Also *fig.* in spiritual sense.

1535 Coverdale *Deut.* xxii. 27 The handfested damsell. **1555** L. Saunders in Coverdale *Lett. Mart.* (1564) 212 We be handfasted vnto hym as the spiritual spouse of so heauenly an husband. **1637** Rutherford *Lett.* (1862) I. 339, I am glad that ye are still handfasted with Christ.

b. (See quots. and handfasting b.)

1820 Scott *Monast.* xxv, She is not my wife, but she is handfasted with me, and that makes her as honest a woman. *Ibid.*, When we are handfasted, as we term it, we are man and wife for a year and a day,—that space gone by, each may choose another mate, or at their pleasure, may call the priest to marry them for life—and this we call handfasting.

† **2.** With hands firmly grasped, hand in hand.

1592 R. D. *Hypnerotomachia* 12 b, Dauncing in a ring, with theyr armes spred abrode, and hanfasted, man with man and woman with woman.

† **'hand,fastening**. *Obs.* = handfasting.

[*c* **1000** Ælfric *Voc.* in Wr.-Wülcker 115/7 *Mandatum*, handfæstnung.] *c* **1545** Coverdale *Ord. Ch. Denmark* Wks. (Parker Soc.) I. 480 Even at their hand-fastening, (when the knot of holy wedlock is fast knit) there are present the father and mother of the parties.

† **'handfaster**. *Obs.* [f. as next + -er¹.] One that 'handfasts', or makes a contract between parties; the maker of a nuptial contract or union.

1598 Grenewey *Tacitus' Ann.* xi. ix. 151 That shee should heare the words of the Auspices, or hand-fasters. **1649** Bulwer *Pathomyot.* Pref. 17 Any Physiological Handfaster that can marry them stronger together, might doe it if he pleas'd.

'handfasting, *vbl. sb. Obs.* exc. *Hist.* [f. handfast *v.* + -ing¹. Cf. Sw. *handfästning* solemn engagement.] Betrothal.

1530 Palsgr. 183 *Vnes fiansayles*, an assuryng or handfastynge of folkes to be maryed. **1561** Daus tr. *Bullinger on Apoc.* (1573) 256 In matrimonie there is a contract or makyng sure, there is a coupling or handfasting of eyther partie, and finally mariage. *a* **1603** T. Cartwright *Confut. Rhem. N.T.* (1618) 167 After they had in their handfasting, solemnly professed before God..they would live [etc.]. **1691** Nicholson *Gloss. Northanhymb.* 142 Hand-festing. *Contractus Matrimonialis.* **1880** T. A. Spalding *Eliz. Demonol.* 5 The betrothal, or handfasting.

b. Formerly treated as an uncanonical, private, or even probationary form of marriage. See Brand *Pop. Antiq.* (1870) II. 46, Jamieson s.v.

1541 Coverdale *Chr. State of Matrim.* (1543) 43 b (Brand) In some places..at the Handefasting ther is made a greate feaste and superfluous Bancket, and even the same night are the two handfasted personnes brought and layed together, yea, certan wekes afore they go to the Chyrch. **1774** Pennant *Tour Scotl. in 1772* i. (1790) 91 Among the various customs now obsolete, the most curious was that of hand-fisting, in use about a century past. **1805** Forsyth *Beauties Scotl.* II. 284 This was called *hand-fasting*, or hand in fist. **1884** *Spectator* 16 Feb. 224/2 A rude morality even attached to the probationary marriage, made by the joining of hands or 'hand-fasting'. **1888** *Durham Parish Bks.* App. (Surtees) 371 In vol. XXI of the Surtees Soc. publications.. interesting instances will be found of such *handfasting* (as it was called) in private houses or elsewhere, being proved and recognised in court.

† **'handfastly**, *adv. Obs.* [-ly².] By solemn engagement made by joining hands; firmly.

1577–87 Holinshed *Scot. Chron.* (1805) II. 237 The which if the Scots would most holilie and handfastlie promise.

† **'handfastness**. *Obs.* [-ness.] The condition of being fast bound; firm attachment.

1545 Raynold *Byrth Mankynde* ii. vii. (1564) 83 b, Great motions..wherby many times the handfastnesse of the Cotilidons is broken.

handfist, -ing, erron. ff. handfast, -ing.

handful ('hændfʊl), *sb.* [OE. *handfull* str. fem., plur. *handfulla*, f. *hand* + *full* adj.: cf. ON. *handfyllr*, Ger. *handvoll*.

Though composed, like *mouthful*, of sb. and adj., the compound was in OE. and ME. a true sb., inflected as a whole; hence its plural is properly *handfuls*, not *handsful*.]

1. a. A quantity that fills the hand; as much or many as the hand can grasp or contain.

a **700** *Epinal Gloss.* 645 *Manticum*: handful beouuas [*Corpus Gl.* beowes]. *c* **1000** *Lamb. Ps.* cxxv[i]. 6 (Bosw.) Berende handfulla heora. *c* **1000** Ælfric *Lev.* ii. 2 Nime hira ane handfulle smideman. *a* **1225** *Ancr. R.* 254 An honful ȝerden. **1382** Wyclif *Gen.* xxxvii. 7, I wenede vs to bynden hondfullis in the feelde..and ȝoure hondfullis stondynge al aboute to loute myn hondful. **1378–8** T. Usk *Test. Love* Prol. 112 And glene my handfuls of the shedinge after their handes. *c* **1489** Caxton *Sonnes of Aymon* iii. 107 Ye ben not worth an hanfull of strawe. **1555** Eden *Decades* 242 The negros or blacke Moores..gaue golde by hole handfuls. **1590** Shaks. *Mids. N.* iv. i. 41, I had rather haue a handfull or two of dried pease. **1613** Purchas *Pilgrimage* (1614) 794 Others ful of Gold in powder, each containing two handfuls. **1791** Cowper *Iliad* xviii. 690 In frequent handfuls, there, they bound the sheaves. **1875** Jowett *Plato* (ed. 2) I. 53 To throw in salt by handfuls.

b. Through later analysis into sb. + adj., the plural has been improperly made *handsful*.

1480 Caxton *Chron. Eng.* clxi. 144 The noble burgeys.. cast oute at hir wyndowes gold and siluer hondes ful. **1563** Hyll *Art Garden.* (1593) 108 Take three or four handes full of the Straw-berrie leaues. **1664** Pepys *Diary* (1879) III. 1 Of yᵉ flowers of Sᵗ. John's Wort two Handsfull, of yᵉ Leaves of Plantan, of Alehoofe, of each three handfulls. **1683** *Pennsylv. Archives* I. 64, 20 handsfuls of Wampum. **1770** Langhorne *Plutarch* (1879) II. 727/2 Throwing incense into the fire by handsful. **1863** Bates *Nat. Amazon* ix. (1864) 254 Throwing handsfull of sand and sticks at it.

2. A small company or number; a small quantity or amount. (Usually *depreciative*.)

1525 Ld. Berners *Froiss.* cccxcix. (R.), Ye se yonder your enemyes, they be but a handefull of men. **1536** *Rem. Sedition* 2 a, The ignorant souldiours were here thus taught, a handful of witte to be moch more worth than a horslode of strengthe. **1588** Shaks. *L.L.L.* iv. i. 149 His Page atother side, that handfull of wit. **1633** Earl Manch. *Al Mondo* (1636) 148 The longest liver hath but a handfull of dayes. **1748** *Anson's Voy.* iii. x. 414 Conquered about an age since by an handful of Tartars. **1828** Planché *Desc. Danube* 62 Passing a handful of villages. **1838** Dickens *Nich. Nick.* xxiii, Mrs. Crummles herself has played to mere handfuls. **1876** Freeman *Norm. Conq.* V. xxv. 550 They kept their own tongue, borrowing only a handful of words from the British tongue.

† **3. a.** A lineal measure of four inches; = hand *sb.* 20. *Obs.*

c **1450** Lonelich *Grail* l. 620 Thorwh the scholdere it [the knife] Cam thore A large handful and wel More. **1547** Boorde *Introd. Knowl.* xxiv. (1870) 185 A cap of sylke..of .iii. handfoll longe. **1600** Hakluyt *Voy.* (1810) III. 134 A tree..foureteene handfuls about. **1707** Sloane *Jamaica* I. Pref., Raised some few handfuls high. **1731–37** J. Tull *Horse-hoeing Husb.* (1822) 194 A handful high.

† **b.** *spec.* used in measuring the height of horses.

1535 *Act 27 Hen. VIII*, c. 6 §2 Two mares..of the altitude or height of .xiii. handefulles at the least. **1541–2** *Act 33 Hen. VIII*, c. 5 §1 Every horse..to be..in heyght xiiij handfulles, reconynge and accounting to every handfull foure ynches. **1607** Topsell *Four-f. Beasts* (1658) 256 In height it was about twenty two handfuls and three fingers. **1676** *Ibid.* No. 1080/4 A bay Gelding 14 handful high.

4. *fig.* As much as one can manage; an affair or person with which one has one's hands full.

1755 Johnson, *Handful*..4. As much as can be done. **1887** Miss Braddon *Like & Unlike* i, I can assure you he was a handful even for me. **1891** *Spectator* 17 Jan., The troublesome boy..the boy that is generally described by his attendants as a 'handful'.

5. *slang.* A five years' prison sentence.

1930 J. Lait *Big House* i. 6 A five-year sentence is a 'handful'. **1953** M. Gilbert *Fear to Tread* ix. 118 He's had a two-stretch... He'll collect a handful next time. **1966** *New*

Society 31 Mar. 22/2 Going up for a handful (receiving a sentence of five years' imprisonment).

Hence 'handful *v.*, to deal *out* by handfuls.

1625 Bp. Hall *Serm.* Wks. (1837) V. 215 Not sparingly handfulled out to us, but dealt to us by the whole load.

'hand-'gallop. An easy gallop, in which the horse is kept well in hand to prevent excess of speed.

1675 *Mistaken Husb.* IV. vi. in *Dryden's Wks.* (1884) VIII. 626 If it rides but a Trot or a hand gallop. **1771** Smollett *Humph. Cl.* I. 29 May, I have.. seen a waggon pass.. at the hand-gallop. **1859** Lang *Wand. India* 11 She.. goes off at a canter, which soon becomes a hand gallop.

fig. **1697** Dryden *Virg. Georg.* Ded., He is always.. upon the hand-gallop. **1709** *Brit. Apollo* II. No. 16. 3/2 Sometimes an Hand-Gallop She goes in her Strains.

hand-glass.

1. A magnifying-glass held in the hand to help the eyesight.

1822–34 *Good's Study Med.* (ed. 4) III. 153 Thirty-two either wore spectacles or used hand-glasses. **1837** Marryat *Dog-fiend* xxviii, He.. pulled a pair of hand-glasses out of his pocket.. and.. commenced reading.

2. *Hort.* A portable glass shade used for protecting or forcing a plant.

1788 G. White *Selborne* lxv. 304 The hail broke.. all my garden-lights and hand-glasses. **1824** Loudon *Encycl. Gardening* (ed. 2) 287 The wrought-iron hand-glass is composed of solid iron sash-bars, and may therefore be formed of any shape or height. **1828** in Webster. **1838** *Penny Cycl.* XII. 40/1 A hand-glass.. keeps the temperature in which the plant breathes higher than the external air. **1851** Glenny *Handbk. Fl. Gard.* 25 The perennials may be raised from cuttings, under a common hand-glass.

3. A small mirror with a handle.

1882 Besant *Revolt of Man* iv. (1883) 94 She took up a hand-glass, and intently examined her own face.

4. *Naut.* A half-minute or quarter-minute sand-glass used for measuring the time in running out the log-line.

1875 in Knight *Dict. Mech.*

hand-grenade ('hændgrɪˌneɪd). Also 7–9 -grenado, 7–8 -granado.

1. An explosive missile, smaller than a bombshell, thrown by hand.

a **1661** Fuller *Worthies* II. (1662) 61 If they lye board and board they throw hand-Granadoes with stinck-pots into the ship which make so noisom a smell that, [etc.]. **1684** J. Peter *Siege Vienna* 43 A Hundred fresh Men armed with Hand-Granadoes. **1719** De Foe *Crusoe* II. ix, The boatswain.. called for a hand-grenado, and threw it among them. **1809–10** Coleridge *Friend* (1865) 83 The result and relict of this author-like hand-grenado. **1859** F. A. Griffiths *Artil. Man.* 91 A Land service Hand grenade weighs 1 lb. 13 oz., and may be thrown from 40 to 60 feet.

2. A glass bottle containing a chemical, to be broken in order to extinguish fire.

1895 *Army & Navy Coöp. Soc. Price List* Sept. 286 Fire Extinguishers (Imperial Hand Grenade).. The Harden Star Hand Grenades.

Hence **hand-gre'nading** *vbl. sb.*, the throwing of hand-grenades.

1882 *Standard* 25 Aug. 3/7 [They] remained on the camp side of the river, escalading, hand grenading, and double lock bridge building. **1884** *Milit. Engin.* I. II. 102 The squad will then be put through the hand grenading drill in slow time. *Ibid.* 105 The stores being arranged in the same order as for hand-grenading.

handgrip. Also -gripe, handy-, handigrip(e. [OE. *handgripe*, f. *grīpan* to gripe, grip. In 16th c. varied with *handy-gripe, handy gripe*, after *handiwork*: cf. also handy *a.*]

1. Grasp, seize with the hand. ***to come to handgrips***, to come to close combat. So ***to be at*** or ***in handgrips***.

α. *Beowulf* (Z.) 965 For hand-gripe minum. *a* **1300** *Cursor M.* 4002 Sal i slip And fal noght in his hand grip. **1571** Golding *Calvin on Ps.* lxii. 2 He commeth to handgripes ageine. **1589** Puttenham *Eng. Poesie* III. xix. (Arb) 228 A iollie man.. Good at hand grippes, better to fight a farre. *a* **1618** Sylvester *Panaretus* 1258 Hee, that both Globes in his own hand-gripe holds. **1831** Carlyle *Sart. Res.* II. iv, Now at actual handgrips with Destiny herself. **1858–** *Fredk. Gt.* IV. ii. (1865) I. 281 The Bridge of Cassano; where Eugene and Vendôme came to handgrips.

β. **1542** Udall *Erasm. Apoph.* II. 185 b, Fyghtyng in warre ought to bee within handye grypes. **1601** Holland *Pliny* II. 567 *margin*, Two wrestlers.. at handy-gripes. **1755** *Mem. Capt. P. Drake* II. v. 188 Unless we left our Swords, and promised not to go to handy Grips. **1895** *Newcastle Daily Jrnl.* 2 Feb., At other places, where they have come into handi-grips with the invaders.

2. Grip or firm pressure of the hand in greeting.

1884 E. Yates *Recoll.* (Tauchn.) II. iii. 115 With his warmest hand-grip. **1885** *New Bk. Sports* 99 The laird exchanges a hearty hand-grip with him.

3. The handle by which a grip is taken.

1887 *N. Y. Semi-weekly Tribune* 16 Aug. (Cent.), The handle or handgrip [of a sword].

†handgriping. *Obs.* Also handi-. [f. hand + griping *vbl. sb.*] + prec. 1, 2.

1577 Hanmer *Anc. Eccl. Hist.* (1619) 284 When they ioyned together, and came to handigriping. **1700** Congreve *Way of World* IV. xii, The heart-heavings and the handgripings.

†'handgrith. *O.E. Law.* [See grith.] Peace, protection, or security given by the king's hand.

a **1000** *Laws of Edw. & Guthrum* i þæt ciric-grið binnan wagum and cyninges hand-grið efne unwemme. **1717** in *Blount's Law Dict.* (ed. 3).

'handgun. **a.** A name for any fire-arm carried and fired in the hand (with or without a rest), as opposed to a great gun or cannon. Apparently *Obs.* (in actual use) before 1700; the term has been revived in the 20th c. (orig. in the U.S.).

1446 in *Archæologia* XXII. 63 Bought ii handgunnes deere. *c* **1449** Marg. Paston in *Paston Lett.* No. 67 I. 83 Wykets.. to schote owte atte, bothe with bowys and with hand gunnys. **1473** Warkw. *Chron.* (Camden) 13 Kynge Edwarde.. hede withe hym.. three hundred of Flemynges with hande-gonnes. **1541** *Act 33 Hen. VIII*, c. 6 Preamb., Crossebowes, little short Handguns, and little Hagbuts. **1580** Hollyband *Treas. Fr. Tong, Arquebuse*, a handgunne. **1697** Dampier *Voy.* I. 117 They having not above 3 or 4 Hand-guns, the rest of them being arm'd with Lances. **1874** Boutell *Arms & Arm.* 293 Hand-guns.. in our own country.. seem to have been used as early as 1375. **1957** *Amer. Speech* XXXII. 191 The word handgun is very old... Since the 1930s its use as a generic term in place of pistol [etc.]... Recent use has made familiar, at least in writing, such derivatives as.. handgun work,.. applied to shooting the handgun at paper targets. **1961** Webster, *Handgun*, a firearm held and fired with one hand. **1968** *Economist* 22 June 43/3 California's Department of Justice estimates that there are 3·5 million concealable hand-guns (pistols and revolvers) within the state.

b. *Comb.*, as ***handgun-maker, handgun-shot.***

1599 Hakluyt *Voy.* II. I. 79 The handgunshot was innumerable and incredible. **1647** Haward *Crown Rev.* 26 Handgun-maker: Fee. —— 24. 6. 8.

Hence **†handgunner; handgunning** *vbl. sb.*

1530 Palsgr. 229/1 Han[d]gonner, *coulevrinier*. **1957** *Amer. Speech* XXXII. 190 It is inevitable.. that colloquialisms of the handgunner overlap with those of the rifleman. *Ibid.* 191 Handgunning offers a great diversity of matches (slow, timed, and rapid fire).

†hand-habend, *a.* (*sb.*) *O.E. Law.* Also 3 -habbynde, 4 -habbing, 6 *Sc.* -havand, [Early ME. form of OE. **hand-hæbbend* 'hand-having', for which the phrase actually found is *æt hæbbendre handa* 'at or with a having hand'. The form *habend* was subseq. more or less modernized.] Of a thief: Having (the thing stolen) in hand. Also applied as *sb.* to the offence, and to the franchise of holding plea thereof.

[*a* **725** *Laws of Wihtræd* c. 26 (Schmid), Gif man frigne man æt hæbbendre handa gefo. *a* **940** *Laws of Æthelst.* IV. c. 6 Quicunque sit [fur] sit handhabenda, sit non handhabenda, si pro certo sciatur. *Ibid.* v. Proem §2 Se þe æt hæbbendre handa gefangen sy. *c* **1125** *Laws of Hen. I*, c. 59 §20 Forisbannitum, aut furem handhabendum.] *c* **1250** Bracton III. II. xxxii. §2 Ubi latro deprehensus est.. hondhabende & bacberende. **1292** Britton I. xxx. §6 Acun .. robbeour seisi de soen larcyn handhabbynde et bacberinde. *a* **1300** *Floriz & Bl.* 668 Felons inome hond habbing. **13..** *Seuyn Sag.* (W.) 691 Who is founde hond-habbing, Hit nis non nede of witnessing. *c* **1575** Balfour *Practicks* (1754) 39 Thieves.. apprehendit in manifest thift, sic as handhavand and back-beirand. **1609** Skene tr. *Quoniam Attach.* c. 39 §1 Gif he is taken.. in handhauang theift, or roborie. **1828** Scott *F.M. Perth* iv, Our outfang and infang, our hand-habend, our back-bearand, and our blood-suits.

'hand-ˌhammer. A hammer that is used in one hand; the smith's working hammer, as distinguished from the two-handed *sledge-hammer*, etc.

c **1050** *Gloss.* in Wr.-Wülcker 448/2 *Malleolus*, hand-hamur. **1606** Birnie *Kirk-Buriall* (1833) 36 Lucrifaction, like Jacobs, whose wealth was the winning of his owne hand-hammers. **1703** Moxon *Mech. Exerc.* 3 The Hand-hammer, which is.. of such weight, that it may be weilded.. with one hand at the Anvil. **1876** Fox Bourne *Locke* II. xi. 193 Silver.. coins being cut with hand-shears, and stamped with hand-hammers.

'hand-hoe, *sb.* A hoe managed by the hands, as distinguished from a horse-hoe, etc.

1744–50 W. Ellis *Mod. Husb.* IV. i. 7 A Man, with the common Hand-hough, may directly follow, and pull up the loose Mould to the Stalks. **1853** *Catal. Roy. Agric. Soc. Show Gloucester* 111 A Hand Hoe for Corn and Turnips.

hand-hoe, *v. trans.* To hoe by hand. Hence **'hand-hoeing** *vbl. sb.*, **'hand-hoer.**

1733 J. Tull *Horse-hoeing Husb.* x. 45 'Tis seldom that these Rolled Turneps can be Hand-Ho'd at the Critical time. **1744–50** W. Ellis *Mod. Husb.* IV. i. 15 This Machine .. will.. fit the remaining Turneps for Hand-houghing. **1797** A. Young *Agric. Suffolk* 52 Many.. make it a rule to hand-hoe their broad-cast crops. **1846** McCulloch *Acc. Brit. Empire* (1854) I. 89 They are.. planted in drills, hand-hoed, and horse-hoed. **1895** *Economic Rev.* Oct. 455 [This] necessitated a greater width of idle soil between each wheat-plant than that required by the Italian hand-hoer.

handhold ('hændhəʊld). [See hold *sb.*]

1. Hold for the hand, grip with the hands; that by which one can hold on in climbing. Also *fig.*

1643 Tuckney *Balme of G.* 17 Let the desperatenesse of the cure prove an handhold for our faith in prayer to fasten on. **1655** Gurnall *Chr. in Arm.* I. 164 Be very careful of giving thine enemy hand-hold. *a* **1688** Bunyan in Spurgeon *Treas. Dav.* Ps. lxix. 2, I had.. left myself neither foot-hold, nor hand-hold, amongst all the stays and props in the precious word of life. **1892** *Badm. Libr., Mountaineer.* vii. 225 Whenever there is any handhold obtainable. **1893** C. Wilson *Mountaineer.* vii. 121 If really good handholds are plentiful, the rocks are easy. *Ibid.*, Various anomalous kinds of handhold are met with upon more difficult rocks; for instance, finger-tip holds, side-holds, and holds facing downwards.

2. That portion of any implement that is grasped by the hand, e.g. the part of a fishing-rod immediately above the reel.

1833 J. Holland *Manuf. Metal* II. 43 A strong spring forming the head or hand-hold.

handiblow, var. of handblow, q.v.

handicap ('hændɪkæp), *sb.* [A word of obscure history. Two examples of the sb., and one of the verb, are known in 17th c.; its connexion with horse-racing appears in the 18th; its transferred general use, esp. in the verb, since 1850. It appears to have originated in the phrase 'hand i' cap', or 'hand in the cap', with reference to the drawing mentioned in sense 1.]

1. The name of a kind of sport having an element of chance in it, in which one person challenged some article belonging to another, for which he offered something of his own in exchange. (Also *fig.*)

On the challenge being entertained, an umpire was chosen to decree the difference of value between the two articles, and all three parties deposited forfeit-money in a cap or hat. The umpire then pronounced his award as to the 'boot' or odds to be given with the inferior article, on hearing which the two other parties drew out full or empty hands to denote their acceptance or non-acceptance of the match in terms of the award. If the two were found to agree in holding the match either 'on' or 'off', the whole of the money deposited was taken by the umpire; but if not, by the party who was willing that the match should stand. (See *Notes & Queries* 23 June, 1855).

This sport is described under the name of *Newe Faire*, in *Piers Plowman* A. v. 171, B. v. 328, C. VII. 377, where 'Clement þe cobelere caste of his cloke', for which 'Hikke þe hakeneyman' wagered his hood, and 'Robyn þe ropere' was named for 'a noumpere', to ordain how much 'who-so haueth the hood shuld haue amendes of the cloke'. For reference to a similar sport in Scandinavia and Germany (where called *Freimarkt*), see *Germania* XIX. (1847) 1, *Engl. Stud.* V. 150. A recent example occurs in R. S. Surtees 'Mr. Sponge's Sporting Tour' ch. xlv, in which the challenge is between a gold watch and a horse. In later times the result became the subject of further betting on the part of the bystanders: see *The Sportsman* 17 April 1897, 5/5.

? *a* **1653** G. Daniel *Idyl* ii. 120 Ev'n those who now command, The inexorable Roman, were but what One step had given: Handy-Capps in Fate. **1660** Pepys *Diary* 18 Sept., Here some of us fell to handicap, a sport that I never knew before, which was very good. **1832** *Mem. Sir J. Campbell* I. xi. 300 Buying horses by what is called handy-cap; a kind of lottery, which everybody knows. **1852** R. S. Surtees *Sponge's Sp. Tour* xlv.

2. *Horse-racing.* (orig. *attrib.*) †**a.** ***handicap match***: a match between two horses, the arrangement of which was made in accordance with the sport of handicap in 1, the umpire here decreeing the extra weight to be carried by the superior horse, and the parties drawing as in 1 to declare whether the match should be 'on' or 'off', with the same chances as to the forfeit-money. *Obs.*

(Such matches are recorded as early as 1680, but the term 'handicap' does not appear.)

1754 *Pond's Racing Calendar* p. xxxii, Rules concerning Racing in general, with a Description of a Post and Handy-Cap Match.. A Handy-Cap Match, if for *A. B.* and *C.* to put an equal Sum into a Hat, *C*, which is the HandyCapper, makes a Match for *A.* and *B.* which when perused by them, they put their Hands into their Pockets and draw them out closed, then they open them together, and if both have Money in their Hands, the Match is confirm'd; if neither have Money, it is no Match: In both Cases the Hand-Capper draws all the Money out of the Hat; but if one has Money in his Hand, and the other none, then it is no Match; and he that has the Money in his Hand is intitled to the Deposit in the Hat. If a Match is made without the Weight being mentioned, each Horse must carry ten Stone. [So in 'Rules of Racing' in *Racing Calendar* 1826, and Blaine *Encycl. Rural Sports* ed. 1832.]

b. ***handicap race*** (shortened ***handicap***): a horse-race in which an umpire (the handicapper) decrees what weights have to be carried by the various horses entered, according to his judgement of their merits, in order to equalize their chances. So ***handicap plate, sweepstakes***, etc.

1786 Pick *Sportsman & Breeder's Vade Mecum* I. 103 (Newmarket) Handicap Plate of 83 gs. for all ages. Two Middle Miles. Won by Mr. Fox's Balloon.. 13 others started. **1789–90** Weatherby *Racing Calendar* 194 (Curragh, June Meeting) Handicap plate of 50 gs. from the Red Post home. Mr. Hamilton's King David, by High-flyer, 6 yrs. old, 8 st. 12 lb.; Mr B. Daly's Little Moll, 5 yrs. old, 6 st. 12 lb. [and 2 other horses]. **1793–4** *Ibid.* 288 (Races to come: Bath.) The day after the Races, a Handicap Sweepstakes of 5 gs. each, for horses, etc, of all ages, two miles. The horses to be named to the Clerk of the Course by eight o'clock the evening before running, and the Stakes to be then paid. **1806** *Sporting Mag.* XXVIII. 184 Six horses entered for a Handicap-plate of £50. **1812** *Ibid.* XXXIX. 99 Four or five of the greatest Handicaps, to be run for at Newmarket next Spring. **1856** H. H. Dixon *Post & Paddock* iv. 75 The luckiest of handicaps was the Chester Cup of 1853, when 131 out of 216 horses accepted. *Ibid.* vii. 114 In these more degenerate days of light-weights and handicaps. 1858 *Jockey Club Rules* 17 in Blaine *Encycl. Rur. Sports* (1870) 373/1 If a horse shall fraudulently run.. The owner shall.. return any sum.. won in plates, matches, or sweepstakes (whether handicap or not), which the said horse may have won. *Ibid.* 39. 374/1 In all handicaps with twenty subscribers, when the highest weight accepting is under 8 st. 12 lb., it is to be raised to that weight.. but in all minor handicaps and in two-year-old handicaps.. the highest weight.. is to be raised to 8 st. 7 lb. 1862 *Times* 2 Jan., The most prolific source of mischief, perhaps, on the Turf, is the increase and magnitude of the handicaps. There is no beast so miserable, but that he may possibly succeed in a handicap. 187. *Rules of Racing* in J. Rice *Hist. Brit. Turf* (1879) II. 367 A 'handicap' is a race in which the weights which the horses are to carry are to be adjusted after the time limited for entering or naming, according to the handicapper's judgment of the merits of the horses, for the purpose of equalizing their chances of winning.. A free handicap is one in which no liability for stake or forfeit is incurred until acceptance, and no entry need be made.

3. Any race or competition in which the chances of the competitors are sought to be equalized by giving an advantage to the less efficient or imposing a disadvantage upon the more efficient.

Besides the method of weighting, as in 2, this may be done in various ways, according to the nature of the game, as by requiring the superior competitor to accomplish a greater distance (*i.e.* giving a start to the inferior), to do it in a shorter time, to play with fewer men or pieces, etc.

1875 J. D. Heath *Croquet Player* 87 There is a variety called Time Handicaps, in which, if the game be not concluded at the expiration of a given time, the player who is ahead wins. 1895 *Badminton Libr., Billards* 439 No two men should play in the same handicap when one can give the other much more than a third of the game.

4. The extra weight or other condition imposed on a superior in favour of an inferior competitor in any athletic or other match; hence, any encumbrance or disability that weighs upon effort and makes success more difficult.

1883 E. Pennell-Elmhirst *Cream Leicestersh.* 153 Two minutes at such a time is.. a heavy handicap on the efforts of hounds. 1890 *Pall Mall G.* 25 June 1/3 The president.. will not be called upon for an address, as this is felt to be a severe tax upon the person and a handicap on the post. *Ibid.*, His broken wing is a heavy handicap to him, and his chances against fox and stoat are now reduced to a minimum. 1894 H. H. Gibbs *Colloquy on Currency* 231 If other nations are injured by the absence of that advantage, what is to prevent them from altering their laws, throwing off the handicap, and riding with equal weights?

5. (See quot.)

1868 Brewer *Phr. & Fable, Handicap*, a game at cards not unlike Loo, but with this difference—the winner of one trick has to put in a double stake, the winner of two tricks a triple stake, and so on. Thus: if six persons are playing, and the general stake is 1s., and A gains three tricks, he gains 6s., and has to 'hand i' the cap' or pool, 3s. for the next deal. Suppose A gains two tricks and B one, then A gains 4s. and B 2s., and A has to stake 3s. and B 2s. for the next deal. [No confirmation has been found.]

6. *attrib.*, as ***handicap match, plate, prize, race.***

1754, etc. Handicap-match, -plate [see 2]. 1856 H. H. Dixon *Post & Paddock* x. 175 At York about 10,000 [cards] are sold on the Handicap day. 1897 *Whitaker's Alm.* 633/2 The A.A.A. rules fixed a limit of ten guineas for handicap prizes [in foot races]. *Ibid.* 649/2 The *Hester*.. was more successful in handicap matches, winning 5 firsts and 4 seconds.

'handicap, *v.* [f. prec. sb., or of same origin.]

†**1.** *trans.* To draw or gain as in a game of chance. *Obs. rare.*

1649 G. Daniel *Trinarch., Hen. V.* xcviii, The Treasurer .. for a price Mercates his Maister to extend his purse: And handy-capps some Crownes: may the boot rise To the boot worthy.

2. *intr.* To engage or take part in a handicap match (see handicap *sb.* 2).

1839 *Blackw. Mag.* XLV. 353, I need not explain.. the art and mystery to give and take the long odds knowingly, to make a 'book', to 'handicap', and to 'hedge'. 1856 Lever *Martins of Cro' M.* 36 He had mingled in turf experiences.. and betted and handicapped with men of fortune.

3. a. *trans.* To equalize the parties to a handicap, by decreeing the 'odds' to be given.

1852 R. S. Surtees *Sponge's Sp. Tour* xliv, 'Who shall handicap us? Captain Guano, Mr. Lumpleg, or who?' .. 'Name me arbitrator', muttered Jack.

b. *fig.* To equalize the chances of competing or contrasted things.

1865 *Daily Tel.* 17 Oct. 5/3 You can't handicap Paris and London as to vice.. Paris can still give two stone of iniquity.

4. *trans.* To weight race-horses in proportion to their known or assumed powers, in order to equalize their chances.

1856 H. H. Dixon *Post & Paddock* xii. 198 The present system of handicapping we believe to be vicious in the extreme; and our impression of a true English handicap is, that no horse should carry more than 9st. 9lbs., or less than 5st. 5lbs. 18.. *View Eng. Racer & Saddle Horse* in *Youatt's Horse* iv. (1872) 74 Four horses were handicapped by Dr. Bellyse at Newcastle-under-Lyne. 1881 E. D. Brickwood in *Encycl. Brit.* XII. 202/2 When well-known winners entered for a race, other competitors withdrew, and sport was spoiled. A remedy was devised in handicapping, that is, apportioning a table of weights to the competitors.. in proportion to their known or assumed demerits.

5. *trans.* To weight, hamper, or otherwise 'penalize' a superior competitor in any match or contest, so as to reduce his chances in favour of inferior competitors. More generally, To place any one at a disadvantage by the imposition of any embarrassment, impediment, or disability; to weight unduly.

1864 *Reader* 9 July 57 He is handicapped with the weight of his own reputation. 1865 *Sat. Rev.* 4 Feb. 132/2 A man of real mathematical ability must be very heavily handicapped to allow competitors of inferior talent to meet him with any chance of success. 1868 *Pall Mall G.* 23 July 3 Not only are our crack shots, our best billiard players, our fleetest runners, and our grandest racehorses handicapped to let the worthless have a chance for the prizes, but even statesmen, clergymen, and soldiers are managed similarly. 1868 Rogers *Pol. Econ.* xxii. (1876) 298 If the law handicaps one kind of labour and so hinders its employment. 1880 *Standard* 15 Dec., The British farmer is so severly handicapped that he cannot possibly compete with the American farmer. 1884 *Lillywhite's Cricket Annual* 1 They were handicapped in their out-play by the absence of their best bowler. 1885 *Times* (weekly ed.) 6 Nov. 7/3 A high expenditure and heavy taxation handicaps a country. 1887 Jessopp *Arcady* i. 6 The inevitable something which handicaps any one who comes as a stranger into the parish. 1894 H. H. Gibbs *Colloquy on Currency* 231, I thought.. our system.. much to our advantage, and that other nations not enjoying it were handicapped in the race.

Hence **'handicapping** *vbl. sb.* and *ppl. a.*; **'handicapped** *ppl. a.*, of persons, esp. children, physically or mentally defective. Also *absol.* as *sb.*

1856 H. H. Dixon *Post & Paddock* ii. 46 Dr. Bellyse, whose love of handicapping and cock-fighting was so [great]. 1889 W. T. Linskill *Golf* iii. (1895) 15 Another form of odds is 'so many holes up'. This is handicapping by holes and not by strokes. 1915 L. D. Wald *House on Henry St.* 117 (*caption*) The Handicapped Child. 1919 *School & Society* 29 Aug. 256/2 There are, of course, other types of mentally handicapped children who should be sharply differentiated. 1942 *Q. Jrnl. Speech* Feb. 81/1 The child who is still babbling, lisping, stuttering.. at thirty-six months of age is just as handicapped.. as the child with a misshapen back. 1958 *Times Lit. Suppl.* 21 Nov. p. xiii/2 The approach is strictly a practical one and even extends to the needs of handicapped children. 1958 P. Townsend in N. Mackenzie et al. *Conviction* 118 The handicapped.. still are treated too often as second-class citizens. 1959 *Housewife* June 33 Chronically sick or handicapped people.

handicapper ('hændɪkæpə(r)). [f. prec. vb.]

a. One who handicaps; *spec.* the public official who decrees what weights the different horses are to carry in a handicap.

1754 [see handicap *sb.* 2a]. 1856 H. H. Dixon *Post & Paddock* xii. 199 Handicappers do well in a large handicap if they get two-fifths of the horses to accept, and a third of the acceptances to the post. 1861 Whyte Melville *Good for Nothing* II. xlii. 202 You are bad handicappers, ladies! 1862 *Times* 2 Jan., An honest handicapper is in the hands of the public runners of horses and utterly at their mercy, and the runners of horses are as completely at the mercy of the dishonest handicapper. 1875 J. D. Heath *Croquet Player* 91 Referee (and handicapper, when necessary) should be appointed, to superintend the various games, and to settle disputes.

b. A horse running in a handicap race.

1895 *Starting Price* 23 Mar. 1/3 *Barbary*.—A second-rate handicapper, but bad-tempered and disappointing. 1955 *Times* 25 Aug. 2/6 That fine handicapper Durante put up a splendid performance under 9 st. 7 lb. in coming away in the last two furlongs to beat Naval Patrol by five lengths.

handicraft ('hændɪkrɑːft, -æ-). Also 6–8 **handycraft**; and as 2 words or with hyphen. [A development of earlier handcraft, after the original pair *handwork, handiwork*.]

1. Manual skill: skilled work with the hands.

*c*1275 [see handcraft]. 1477 Norton *Ord. Alch.* iv. in Ashm. (1652) 49 In this Warke finde ye nothing shall, But handie-crafte called Arte Mechanicall. *c*1570 *Pride & Lowl.* (1841) 22 Coonning in handy craft and facultie. 1658 J. Robinson *Eudoxa* i. 16 All kind of Handicraft, or Art. 1682 Grew *Anat. Plants* Ep. Ded., A Piece of Natures Handicraft. 1857 Ruskin *Pol. Econ. Art* 61 You ask of him nothing but a little quick handicraft. 1863 Bates *Nat. Amazon* I. 79 He prefers handicraft to field labour.

2. A manual art, trade, or occupation.

1548 Cranmer *Catech.* 46b, They also teache vs diverse waies of marchaundise, many handycraftes. *a*1661 Fuller *Worthies, Cheshire* 181 He [Speed] was first bred to a handicraft, and as I take it to a Taylor. 1703 Moxon *Mech. Exerc.* Pref. 6 Smithing is.. as curious a Handy-Craft, as any is. 1845 S. Austin *Ranke's Hist. Ref.* II. 27 Students left the university and went home to learn a handicraft. 1872 Yeats *Growth Comm.* 286 Improvements were introduced into agriculture and the handicrafts.

†**3.** A handicraftsman, artizan, workman. *Obs.*

1586 T. B. *La Primaud. Fr. Acad.* i. 698 Made by Masons, Carpenters, Geometricians, Sawyers, Ioiners, and other handy-crafts. 1650–66 Wharton *Poems* Wks. (1683) 398 Repining Tradesmen, and Poor Handicrafts. 1708 J. Chamberlayne *St. Gt. Brit.* i. ii. xii. (1743) 99 He hath also the Oversight of.. Handicrafts and Artisans.. in the King's Service. 1745 *De Foe's Eng. Tradesman* Intro., Those who make the goods they sell, though they keep shops, are called Handicrafts. 1821 Scott *Kenilw.* xxv, [Beshrew thy heart for the word], replied the handicraft.

4. *attrib.*, passing into *adj.* = 'manual, practical'.

1662 J. Chandler *Van Helmont's Oriat.* 59 We see by handicraft-demonstration, that the Air in deep Wells and Cellers is stable in the same point of heat. 1663 F. Hawkins *Youth's Behaviour* 79 Handy-craft-trades, which require the labour of the hand. 1692 tr. *Sallust* 67 Sollicite Handicraft Tradesmen and Slaves. 1816 Keatinge *Trav.* (1817) II. 139 The ingenuity of the handicraft people here is very striking. 1845 J. Saunders *Cab. Pict. Eng. Life, Chaucer* 202 The inhabitants.. who lived by the cultivation of trade, commerce, and the arts hardicraft and mental.

'handi,craftship. *rare.* [-ship.] Exercise of handicraft, workmanship.

1835 *Blackw. Mag.* XXXVII. 927 Did he furnish the materials for the handicraftship of others?

'handi'craftsman. Formerly also as 2 words, or with 1 or 2 hyphens; also *β.* **handicraftman.** [lit. *handicraft's man*, man of handicraft: cf. craftsman.] A man who exercises a handicraft; one employed in a manual occupation.

1551 Robinson tr. *More's Utop.* ii. iv. (1895) 148 A handicraftes man doth so earnestly bestowe hys vacaunte and spare houres in learninge. 1586 T. B. *La Primand. Fr. Acad.* i. 698 Bakers, Cookes, Vintners, and other handy-crafts-men. 1603 Holland *Plutarch's Mor.* 450 All other artisans and handi-craftsmen. 1758 J. Blake *Plan Mar. Syst.* 23 All the handy-crafts-men.. particularly carpenter's mates, caulkers. 1849 Ruskin *Sev. Lamps* v. §24. 160 From the mass of available handicraftsmen the power is gone.

β. 1580 Hollyband *Treas. Fr. Tong, Gens de mestier*, handiecraft men. 1590 Shaks. *Mids. N.* iv. ii. 10 The best wit of any handycraft man in Athens. 1660 R. Coke *Justice Vind.* 24 Mechanical handicraft-men, and husbandmen. 1788 Priestley *Lect. Hist.* v. li 394 No security for handicraftmen and traders. 1854 Hawthorne *Eng. Note-Bks.* (1879) II. 346 Be he.. scholar, handicraftman, or what not.

Hence **'handi'craftsmanship.**

1882 *Pall Mall G.* 13 Nov. 4 The man who best united literary handicraftsmanship with the highest scientific and technical mastery of his subject.

'handicrafts,woman. [after handicrafts-man.] A woman who exercises a handicraft.

1846 Worcester cites *Gent. Mag.* 1857 Miss Mulock *Th. ab. Wom.* iv. (1858) 69 The class which I have distinguished as handicraftswomen. 1865 F. Hall *Daśá-rúpa* Pref. 18 A female devotee, or a handicraftswoman.

handicuff. Also handy-. [f. hand *sb.* or handy *a.* + cuff *sb.*[2]: app. after *fisticuff.*] *pl.* Blows with the hands; fighting hand to hand. Also *fig.*

1701 *Dial. betw. Marphorio & Pasquin* 12 By the Posture you are in, I suppose you are for handy-Cuffs. 1726 Shelvocke *Voy. round World* (1757) 271 [They] must have gone to handy cuffs with the enemy. 1761 Sterne *Tr. Shandy* III. xxi, His rhetoric and conduct were at perpetual handy-cuffs. 1816 C. James *Milit. Dict.* (ed. 4) 383/2 *Jeux de main*, manual play, or what are vulgarly called handicuffs.

handicuff, dial. var. of handcuff.

handie-talkie ('hændɪˌtɔːkɪ). Also **Handie-Talkie, handy-talky.** [After walkie-talkie.] Name of a light form of walkie-talkie two-way radio set, easily carried in the hand.

1942 *Nat. Geogr. Mag.* Nov. 680 Churchill.. is holding a 'handie-talkie' radio used for conversation between ground points and planes in the air. 1943 *Time* 27 Sept. 83/2 (Advt.), He'll talk his way out.. with his two-way 'handy-talkie'... The 'handy-talkie' is only one of many radio communication devices of our armed forces. 1960 *Times* 8 Mar. 15/3 The equipment is known as a Handie-Talkie and has been produced to replace the heavier walkie-talkie sets used during the last war. 1969 S. Greenlee *Spook who sat by Door* xiii. 113 Cops spoke busily into their car radios and handy-talkies.

handigrip, variant of handgrip.

handil(l, obs. forms of handle.

'handily, *adv.* [f. handy *a.* + -ly[2].] In a handy manner or way; expertly; †manually.

1611 Florio, *Manoalmente*, manually, handily. 1719 De Foe *Crusoe* i. iv, Not being able to guide it so handily. 1832 Ht. Martineau *Life in Wilds* vi. 78 She used.. the threads of flax more handily than they.

†**'handiment.** *Obs.* Handling, management.

1660 Fisher *Rustick's Alarm* Wks. (1679) 194 In thy heedless handiment of this more General Subject.

handiness ('hændɪnɪs). [f. handy *a.* + -ness.]

1. The quality of being handy or expert.

1647 Trapp *Comm.* 1 *Pet.* i. 12 Girding implies, 1. Readinesse, 2. Nimblenesse, handinesse, handsomenesse. 1755 in Johnson. 1829 Carlyle *Misc.* (1857) II. 60 If he have any handiness in the business. 1867 Smiles *Huguenots Eng.* ii. (1880) 22 He could.. do any sort of work requiring handiness and dexterity.

2. The quality of being easily or conveniently handled; manageableness, convenience.

1877 W. H. White *Naval Archit.* (1882) 461 Handiness is held to be an essential quality in most classes of war ships. 1879 *Cassell's Techn. Educ.* ix. 166 The all-important qualities of stability when travelling, and handiness in turning.

handing ('hændɪŋ), *vbl. sb.* [f. hand *v.*]

1. The action of the verb hand, in various senses.

1651 Hobbes *Leviath*, i. ii. 8 Like handing of things from one to another. 1758 J. Blake *Plan Mar. Syst.* 7 In knotting and splicing, in handing and reefing of sails.

†**2.** A handle. *Obs. rare.*

1703 Moxon *Mech. Exerc.* 51 The Wood work belonging to the Jack, is a Barrel, a Spit-wheel and a Handing of the Winch.

3. *attrib.* **handing-post** (*local*), finger-post.

1880 Jefferies *Hodge & M.* I. 24 On the handing-post at the lonely cross-roads. 1882 Nares *Seamanship* (ed. 6) 96 It [powder] is passed.. from one handing-room to the other, and then on deck.

hand in glove: see HAND AND GLOVE.

hand in hand (also with - -), *adv. phr.* (*a.*, *sb.*). [See HAND *sb.* 58.]

1. *adv. phr.* With hands mutually clasped; each holding the other's (or another's) hand.

c **1500** *Three Kings' Sons* (E.E.T.S.) 33 Than wente they two hand yn hand vndir the clothe of estate. **1667** MILTON *P.L.* XII. 648 They hand in hand, with wandring steps and slow, Through Eden took thir solitarie way. **1762–71** H. WALPOLE *Vertue's Anecd. Paint.* (1786) III. 117 The portraits of dwarfs hand in hand by Sir Peter Lely. **1870** THORNBURY *Tour Eng.* I. xii. 236 They dance hand-in-hand through [the] streets.

b. *fig.* In conjunction, side by side, concurrently; *to go hand in hand with*, to keep step with.

1576 FLEMING *Panopl. Epist.* 341 The same..as it were running hand in hande with his wonderfull knowledge. **1641** BROME *Jovial Crew* I. i. Wks. 1873 III. 358 Thy charity there goes hand in hand with mine. **1788** FRANKLIN *Autobiog.* Wks. 1840 I. 177 The debates went on daily hand in hand with the Indian business. **1874** GREEN *Short Hist.* i. §3. 31 The industrial progress of the Mercian Kingdom went hand in hand with its military advance.

2. *attrib.* or adj. Going hand in hand or side by side; well-matched.

1611 SHAKS. *Cymb.* I. iv. 75 As faire, and as good: a kind of hand in hand comparison. **1817** L. HUNT *To T. L. H.* iv. Poet. Wks. (1860) 258 Ah, first-born of thy mother..My bird when prison-bound, My hand in hand companion.

b. The name given to a Fire Insurance Office in London, founded in 1696; implying the mutual sharing of risks.

1781 COWPER *Friendship* 106 Like hand in hand insurance plates. **1798** W. TAYLOR in *Monthly Rev.* XXVII. 493 It may be defined a *hand-in-hand* assurance office for securing mercantile credit.

3. *sb.* **a.** A representation of two hands mutually clasped. **b.** Mutual clasping of hands. **c.** A company of persons hand in hand.

1710 STEELE *Tatler* No. 245 ¶2 A broad thick Gold Ring with a Hand in Hand graved upon it. **1842** TENNYSON *Vis. Sin* 162 Loving tears, And the warmth of hand in hand. **1880** G. MEREDITH *Trag. Com.* (1881) 252 The whole Alpine hand-in-hand of radiant heaven-climbers.

handiron, obs. form of ANDIRON.

c **1475** *Voc.* in Wr.-Wülcker 770/2 *Hee andena*, a handyryn. **1731** FIELDING *Grub St. Op.* I. xi, The very handirons..have not more brass in them than thy forehead.

handistroke, by-form of HANDSTROKE.

handiwork ('hændɪwɜːk). Forms: 1 **handȝeweorc**, 2–4 **handi-**, **hondiwerc**, **-werk(e**; 6 **handye-**, **-ie-**, 6- **handy work**, 7- **handiwork**. [OE. *hand-ȝeweorc*, f. *hand* + *ȝeweorc* work (a collective form). OE. had also *handweorc* HANDWORK containing the simple *weorc* work. As *ȝeweorc*, *iwork* did not survive in ME., *handiwerc*, was naturally analysed as a compound of the simple *werc*, with *handi*, often written separately, and treated as an adj.: see HANDY. See also, under HANDWORK, the ME. northern form *hande-werk*.]

1. Work of the hands; a thing or collection of things made by the hands of any one.

c **1000** ÆLFRIC *Deut.* iv. 28 And ȝe þeowiaþ fremdum Godum, manna hand ȝeweorc. c **1175** *Lamb. Hom.* 129 And sette hine ouer his hondiwerc. a **1225** *St. Marher.* 10 Help me þin hondi werc. c **1340** *Cursor M.* 1589 (Trin.) His owne hondiwerke so soone Wolde god not hit were for-done. **1535** COVERDALE *Ps.* xviii[i]. 1 The very heauens declare the glory off God, and the very firmament sheweth his handye worke. **1635** QUARLES *Embl.* III. x, I am thy handy-worke, thy creature, Lord. a **1680** BUTLER *Rem.* (1759) I. 126 The Pagans heretofore Did their own Handy-works adore. **1795** WOLCOTT (P. Pindar) *Pindariana* Wks. 1812 IV. 230 To see the handiworks of God In sun and moon and starry sky. a **1839** PRAED *Poems* (1864) II. 112 To see the sempstress' handiwork.

2. Work done by the hands or by direct personal operation or agency. Sometimes, the work of man's hands as opposed to nature.

c **1000** *Ags. Ps.* (Th.) ix. 15 On his hand ȝeweorce byð ȝefangen se synfulla. **1540** COVERDALE *Fruitf. Less.* iii. Wks. (Parker Soc.) I. 350 They..undertake to get their own living with their handy-work. **1551** T. WILSON *Logike* (1580) 44 b, An Image whiche is an artificial thyng, is made by the handie worke of man. **1658** BROMHALL *Treat. Specters* v. 327 The cave..seemed as if it had been made by handywork. **1674** N. FAIRFAX *Bulk & Selv.* 67 The shapes of nature being of another kind of make than those of handy-works. **1820** HAZLITT *Lect. Dram. Lit.* 2 What they performed was chiefly nature's handy-work.

b. Work (of any kind); doing, performance.

1838 DICKENS *O. Twist* xxix, That was your handiwork, Giles, I understand. **1874** GREEN *Short Hist.* viii. §5. 510 The Liturgy and Canons had been Laud's own handiwork.

3. Manual employment: working with the hands, as opposed to *head-work*; practical work. [Cf. HANDY.]

1565 J. HALLE *Hist. Expost.* (Percy) 41 Chirurgery is *Operatio manualis*, that is handye worke. Wherefore..call it the handye worke of medicine. **1603** KNOLLES *Hist. Turks* (1621) 1326 The Estates..have raised handiworks as well as traffike and navigation to the highest point of perfection. **1669** WOODHEAD *St. Teresa* II. vii. 55 She accounted Handy-work a great means of advancing, and perfecting her Religions. **1703** MOXON *Mech. Exerc.* Pref. 2 To what purpose would Geometry serve, were it not to contrive Rules for Handy-Works? **1866** J. BROWN *Horæ Subs.* Ser. I. Pref. *note*, We wish we saw more time, and more handiwork, more mind spent upon anatomy and surgery.

‖**handjar, hanjar** ('hændʒə(r)). Also 7 **handiarre, haniar**; see also KHANJAR. [Pers. (Arab.) *khanjar* dagger.] A Persian or Turkish dagger or sword-knife.

1603 KNOLLES *Hist. Turks* (1621) 1313 He stabbed her with his handiarre. **1625–6** PURCHAS *Pilgrims* II. IX. 1588 (Stanf.) They always weare a Haniar (that is, a Dagger) set with rich stones. **1696** PHILLIPS (ed. 5), *Hanjar*, a certain kind of Dagger worn by the Bashaws Wives. **1873** DIXON *Two Queens* I. v. i. 234 He hung a Moorish hanjar on his thigh. **1887** *Pall Mall G.* 5 Oct. 1/2 A Montenegrin noble..greatly encumbered in his play by the revolvers and handjar in his belt.

handkerchief ('hæŋkətʃɪf, -iːf), *sb.* Forms: α. 6 **handekerchefe, -carcheff, handcercheue, -kerchef**, 6–7 **-kerchiefe**, 7 **-kercheefe, -chife, -chiffe, hankerchief**, 7- **handkerchief**. β. 6–7, 9 (*dial.* and *vulgar*) **handkercher, hankercher**, 9 *dial.* **hancutcher**. [f. HAND *sb.* + KERCHIEF, q.v. also for the form *handkercher*. The latter was common in literary use in 16–17th c., and remained the current spoken form for some time after *handkerchief* was commonly written (cf. quot. 1866); it is still a common dialect and vulgar form.]

a. A small square of linen, silk, or other fabric (which may be embroidered, fringed, etc.), carried in the hand or pocket (***pocket-handkerchief***) for wiping the face, eyes, or nose, or used as a kerchief to cover the head, or worn about the neck (***neck handkerchief*** or ***neckerchief***). Phr. ***to drop the handkerchief***: ***to throw*** (or ***fling***) ***the handkerchief***.

to drop or throw the handkerchief, i.e. in young people's games, in which he or she to whom it is thrown runs after and tries to catch the other; hence, allusively, to signify that one may be run after, to invite courtship.

1530 PALSGR. 229/1 Handekerchefe, *mouchover*. **1557** N.T. (Genev.) *Acts* xix. 12 From his body, were broght vnto the sycke, napkyns or handkerchefs. **1563** MAN *Musculus' Commonpl.* 274 a, The shadow of Peter, the handcercheue of Paull. **1604** SHAKS. *Oth.* III. iii. 434 Haue you not sometimes seene a Handkerchiefe Spotted with Strawberries, in your wiues hand? **1684** BUNYAN *Pilgr.* II. 76 He also wiped mine Eyes with his Hankerchief. **1722** *Lond. Gaz.* No. 6056/1 The Santo Sudario (or Holy Handkerchief)..is to be exposed. **1749** H. WALPOLE *Let.* 20 July (1903) II. 396 Till all the juries of matrons have finished their inquest, one shall not care to make one's choice—I was going to say—*throw one's handkerchief*, but at present that term would be a little equivocal. **1764** —— *Let.* 5 June (1904) VI. 78 Lord Tavistock has flung his handkerchief to Lady Elizabeth Keppel. **1768–74** TUCKER *Lt. Nat.* (1852) II. 477 When, on looking through the window, we see the women pulling their handkerchiefs over their heads, we take this for a sign that it is beginning to rain. **1786** E. SHERIDAN *Jrnl.* 21–23 Jan. (1960) 79 The hankerchiefs are not so much puff'd out and there is now a very pretty sort of hankerchief much worn open at the neck and exactly made and trim'd like a Boy's shirt. **1825** R. WARD *Tremaine* II. xxxix. 338, I imagine he must do something more than merely throw his handkerchief. **1825** H. WILSON *Mem.* II. 11 The system at White's Club..is..never to black ball any man, who ties a good knot in his handkerchief. **1859** GEO. ELIOT *A. Bede* 29, I think his blue linen handkerchief was very wet with tears. **1870** *Brewer's Dict. Phr. & Fable* 384/1 '*The committee was at a loss to know whom to throw the handkerchief to*' (The *Times*)..the allusion is to the game called in Norfolk 'Stir up the dumplings', and by girls 'Kiss in the ring'. **1897** *Outing* (U.S.) Apr. 71/2, I was hoping that they would have an English May-pole dance, but instead they played 'drop the handkerchief', which Philip said, though not so ancient, was more fun. **1932** *Times Lit. Suppl.* 16 July 506/3 If he hesitate today whether he shall throw the handkerchief to Germany or Russia, does not such an embarrassment prove his power?

β. c **1532** DEWES *Introd. Fr.* in *Palsgr.* 907 The hande kercher..*mouchoir*. **1583** HOLLYBAND *Campo di Fior* 31 Put this hande-kircher at thy girdle, to make cleane thy nose. **1583** in *North. N. & Q.* I. 77 Gloves, hand-carchaes, gyrdylles. **1601** SHAKS. *All's Well* v. iii. 322 Mine eyes smell Onions, I shall weepe anon: Good Tom Drumme lend me a handkercher. **1666** PEPYS *Diary* (1879) IV. 46, I took occasion to fall out with her [my wife] for buying a laced handkercher without my leave. **1828** *Craven Dial.*, *Hancutcher*, handkerchief. **1837** THACKERAY *Yellowpl.* (1887) 29 A blue bird's-eye handkercher. [**1866** LOWELL *Biglow P.* Introd. Poems 1890 II. 166 Voltaire tells his countrymen that *handkerchief* was pronounced *hankercher*..This enormity the Yankee still persists in.]

b. *attrib.* and *Comb.*, as ***handkerchief blouse, -box, -case, -cloth, dress, -hat, -loom, -monger, -pin, pocket, sachet, table, -turban***, etc.; **handkerchief-head** (see quot. 1942).

In several of the collocations applied to parts of costume made up of squares resembling or suggesting handkerchiefs.

1711 SWIFT *Jrnl. to Stella* 4 May, I have been a mighty handkerchiefmonger. **1790** E. WYNNE *Diary* 17 Jan. (1935) I. ii. 30 Betzy bought..a handkerchief pin. **1880** L. HIGGIN *Handbk. Embroidery* 106 (Advt.), Handkerchief sachets, from £3. 3s. **1885** J. J. MANLEY *Brit. Almanac Comp.* 25 There was also a remarkable handkerchief-loom exhibited. **1890** LD. LUGARD *Diary* 27 Mar. (1959) I. iv. 161, I..presented the women with a return present viz. a dhoti of 'handkerchief cloth'. **1893** 'MARK TWAIN' in *Cent. Mag.* Dec. 238/2 She took off her handkerchief-turban. **1895** *Montgomery Ward Catal.* Index, Handkerchief Boxes and Cases. **1896** E. TURNER *Little Larrikin* x. 106 She had conceived the idea of making Ruffy a present of a handkerchief-sachet. **1899** *Daily News* 1 July 4/3 The revival of the handkerchief dress. **1900** *Westm. Gaz.* 9 Aug. 3/2 The handkerchief blouse. **1903** *Daily Chron.* 18 July 8/4 The sleeves are handkerchief ones. **1922** JOYCE *Ulysses* 99 His inner handkerchief pocket. **1932** D. C. MINTER *Mod. Needlecraft* 246/1 *Handkerchief case*..oblong folded to form pocket and flap. **1942** *Amer. Mercury* LV. 95 *Handkerchief-head*, sycophant type of Negro; also an Uncle Tom. **1950** A. LOMAX *Mr. Jelly Roll* (1952) v. 231 This corny old handkerchief-head would assert that Count Basie did not know piano. **1956** S. LONGSTREET *Real Jazz* 147 A 'handkerchief-head' is an old-fashioned Negro who doesn't know his rights. **1960** *Encounter* XIV. II. 39 The Negro officer isn't a 'handkerchief head', an Uncle Tom. **1960** H. HAYWARD *Antique Coll.* 138/2 *Handkerchief table*, an American term for a single-leaf table with leaf and top triangular in shape. Closed, the table fits in a corner, opened it is a small square. **1963** *Sunday Express* 3 Nov. 19/1 A group of handkerchief hats in pastel glove leather. **1971** P. D. JAMES *Shroud for Nightingale* v. 170 An embroidered handkerchief sachet with a dozen handkerchiefs carefully folded.

Hence '**handkerchiefful**; † '**handkerchiefly** *a.*, such as calls for the use of a handkerchief.

1753 C. CIBBER in *Richardson's Corr.* (1804) II. 177 Having as handkerchiefly a feeling of it as Mr. Sylvester himself. **1876** *Daily News* 27 Oct. 5/3 An orderly produced a handkerchiefful of bread and cheese.

'**handkerchief**, *v. rare.* [f. prec. sb.] **a.** *intr.* To use a handkerchief. **b.** *trans.* To cover or wipe with a handkerchief.

1754 RICHARDSON *Grandison* (1811) II. xvi. 179 The servants entering with the dinner, we hemmed, handkerchiefed, twinkled, took up our knives and forks. **1778** MAD. D'ARBLAY *Diary* Sept., I began now a vehement nose-blowing, for the benefit of handkerchiefing my face.

handky, var. HANKY[1].

'**hand-labour**. Labour or work of the hands, manual labour; †'art' as opposed to nature; now, usually, manual as opposed to machine work.

1549 COVERDALE, etc. *Erasm. Par. Thess.* 3 We wrought with our handelabour. **1610** HOLLAND *Camden's Brit.* I. 548 Strong..as well by naturall situation as hand-labour. **1640** SANDERSON *Serm.* II. 176 St. Paul..at Corinth..maintained himself a long while together with his own hand-labour. **1832** *Veg. Subst. Food* xvii. 385 The hoeing of a cane-field..was [formerly] always effected by hand labour.

Hence '**hand-,labourer**, a worker with his hands.

1598 FLORIO, *Manifattore*..a hand-labourer. **1878** *N. Amer. Rev.* CXXVII. 265 The mere hand-laborer is thrown out of employment.

handlangwhile: see HANDWHILE.

handle ('hænd(ə)l), *sb.*[1] Forms: 1 **handle**, 3 **hondel**, 4–6 **handel(l**, 5 **handele, handyl(l(e, andyll**, 5–6 **handil(l**, 5- **handle**. [OE. *handle*, deriv. of HAND.]

1. a. That part of a thing which is made to be grasped by the hand in using or moving it.

a **800** *Corpus Gloss.* 1904 *Stiba*, handle. c **1000** ÆLFRIC *Gloss.* in Wr.-Wülcker 104/11 *Stiba*, sulhhandla. a **1225** *Juliana* 59 Forte turnen þat hweol wið hondlen. **1398** TREVISA *Barth. De P.R.* XIX. cxxviii. (1495) 933 An handell by the whyche he is heue hyther and thyther. c **1400** MAUNDEV. (1839) xxiii. 249 To smyte an hors with the handill of a whippe. **1470–85** MALORY *Arthur* I. iii, He handled the swerd by the handels. **1577** B. GOOGE *Heresbach's Husb.* II. (1586) 109 b, The handles, or steeles of Husbandmennes tooles. **1605** SHAKS. *Macb.* II. i. 34 Is this a Dagger, which I see before me, The Handle toward my Hand? **1798** FERRIAR *Illustr. Sterne* vi. 177 Do you not consider what a handle a long beard affords to the enemy? **1860** TYNDALL *Glac.* I. xviii. 127 The handle of my hatchet.

b. Phr. (orig. *U.S. colloq.*) ***to fly off*** (or ***off at***) ***the handle*** (*fig.* from an axe): to be carried away by excitement; to lose self-control; now usually, to lose one's temper. Also, in same sense, ***to go*** (or ***be***) ***off the handle***. ***to go off the handle***: to die.

1843–4 HALIBURTON *Attaché* (Farmer), He flies right off the handle for nothing. **1872** O. W. HOLMES *Poet Breakf.-t.* x. (1885) 258 My old gentleman means to be Mayor..before he goes off the handle. **1888** KIPLING *Phantom Rickshaw* 2 Pansay went off the handle,..all that nonsense about ghosts developed. **1898** —— *Day's Work* 78 How are we to do our work if you fly off the handle that way? **1908** C. E. MULFORD *Orphan* xxii. 271 He reckoned you would..get good and mad, fly off the handle, and raise h—l generally. **1915** A. CONAN DOYLE *Valley of Fear* I. v. 82 A kind of wave of jealousy would pass over him and he would be off the handle and saying the wildest things in a moment. **1932** KIPLING *Limits & Renewals* 157 Jimmy went off the handle at once; and Nicol kept patting him on the back. **1958** *Times* 3 Nov. 11/7 Montgomery flew off the handle and told the Minister of Defence..that he must find out whether Bevin still stood by what he said. **1964** L. NKOSI *Rhythm of Violence* 64 Calm down, for God's sake! Everybody's flying off the handle. What's the matter with everybody?

c. ***to the handle, up to the handle***: thoroughly, completely, up to the hilt. *U.S. colloq.*

1833 *Louisville Publ. Adv.* 9 May, He is determined to carry the contest 'to the handle'. **1835** A. B. LONGSTREET *Georgia Scenes* 234 We'll all go in for you here up to the handle. **1843** T. C. HALIBURTON *Attaché* 1st Ser. I. viii. 119 Give me your figgery-four, Squire, I'll go in up to the handle for you. **1855** *Knickerbocker* XLV. 435 (Th., s.v. *Up*), He was enjoying his trip 'up to the handle'. **1860** *Ibid.* LV. 415 He had for the last few years used a boy and dog as fencing material; he found it 'a good institution'; they did the thing up to the handle. **1877** J. HABBERTON *Jericho Road* xi. 101 If he isn't playin' possum right up to the handle, then he is a fool.

d. ***to give, use, the long handle*** (Cricket): to hit freely and continuously.

1888 STEEL & LYTTLETON *Cricket* ii. 77 Hold the bat nearer the top and give her the long handle. **1903** WARNER in H. G. Hutchinson *Cricket* 71 As a rule the hitting or 'long-handle game', as it has been called, pays best under these circumstances [*sc.* on a sticky wicket]. **1928** *Daily Express* 20 Dec. 3/2 Ryder set about the bowlers unmercifully, using the long handle.

2. *transf.* **a.** Something resembling a handle; in *Bot.* = MANUBRIUM. ***handle of the face***: used jocularly for the nose.

1639 T. DE GRAY *Compl. Horsem.* 39 The crocks and handles of the scull. **1673** S. C. *Rules of Civility* 102 A Leg of Mutton is cut above the handle, by thrusting the Knife as deep into it as one may. **1708** MOTTEUX *Rabelais* v. v, Carbuncles.. which undermine the Handles of their Faces. **1887** *Modern Society* 27 Aug. 864 (Farmer) A restless.. old lady, with an immense handle to her face.

b. A small basket with a handle, in which soft fruit is packed for the market.

1900 *Daily Express* 30 June 5/5 French red currants reached 1s. 3d. a basket or 'handle'.

c. A measure of beer, approx. 1 pint. *N.Z.*

1938 R. D. FINLAYSON *Brown Man's Burden* 40 'A handle of beer,' Mr. Puttle was saying easily to the barman. **1943** J. A. W. BENNETT in *Amer. Speech* XVIII. 89 [In New Zealand] beer is dispensed in *handles* (in Australia, *pots*) or *half-handles*. **1947** 'A. P. GASKELL' *Big Game* 57 'He gets one handle every day,' said George [barman]. **1956** *N.Z. Listener* 8 June in J. Reid *Kiwi Laughs* (1961) 204 They still drink beer out of handles, sixpence a pop.

3. *fig.* **a.** That by which something is or may be taken hold of; one of two or more ways in which a thing may be taken or apprehended (in phr. ***to have two handles, to take a thing by the best handle***, etc.); a fact or circumstance that may be 'laid hold of' or taken advantage of for some purpose; an occasion, opportunity, excuse, pretext.

a **1535** MORE *Wks.* 330 (R.) He would gladly catch holde of some small handell to kepe hys money fast. **1633** G. HERBERT *Temple, Confession* iv, Fiction Doth give a hold and handle to affliction. **1679** tr. *Burgersdicius his Logic* II. xiii. 56 A dilemma is.. as it were a syllogism with two handles and catching one both ways. *a* **1716** SOUTH *Serm.* (1716) IV. 196 Hope and Fear are the two great Handles, by which the Will of Man is to be taken Hold of. **1732** LEDIARD *Sethos* II. VIII. 224, I would not give this handle to calumny. **1770** LANGHORNE *Plutarch* (1879) II. 1061/1 He took care to give her no handle against him. **1876** GLADSTONE *Homeric Synchr.* 168 Where tradition afforded any sort of handle for the purpose.

b. In colloq. phr. *to get a handle on*, to gain control over (a situation, etc.); to acquire the means of understanding or of forming an opinion about. orig. *U.S.*

1972 *New Yorker* 14 Oct. 131/2 Scribner.. said to me, 'I don't think people have any idea of how tough it is for anyone in this job to get a handle on anything.' **1977** *Verbatim* Sept. 8/1 It is such a common saying but I can't seem to get a handle on how it started. **1977** *Listener* 20 Oct. 498/1 In the 1930s, it was fairly easy to get a handle on the politics of the screenwriting community. **1982** S. BELLOW *Dean's December* xiii. 246 You're reading books, talking to academics, trying to get the right handle on things. **1984** *Miami Herald* 27 Mar. 26/4 I'm still trying to get a handle on our offense.

4. a. ***a handle to one's name*** (colloq.): a title of rank, honour, or courtesy attached to the name.

1833 MARRYAT *P. Simple* iv, 'Mister Coxswain! thanky, Sir, for giving me a handle to my name.' *Ibid.* lxiv, 'Captain O'Brien', said the general. 'Sir Terence O'Brien, if you please, general. His Majesty has given me a handle to my name'. **1855** THACKERAY *Newcomes* xxiii, She.. entertained us with stories.. mentioning no persons but those who 'had handles to their names', as the phrase is. **1886** *Illustr. Lond. News* 23 Jan. 94/3 Very distinguished young women, with handles to their names.

b. A person's name; a nickname. *slang* (orig. *U.S.*).

1870 J. C. DUVAL *Adv. Big-Foot Wallace* xxxviii. 236, I would rather be called 'Big-Foot Wallace' than 'Lying Wallace'... Such handles to my name would not be agreeable. **1927** *Dialect Notes* V. 449 Whut's yer handle? **1935** *Amer. Speech* X. 18/2 *Monicker*, a genuine name, as distinguished from an alias. Modern *handle*. **1964** D. VARADAY *Gara-Yaka* xx. 180 One was Toothless Annie... She had come by her 'handle' when a hysterical grass-eater had kicked her teeth in. **1969** C. F. BURKE *God is Beautiful, Man* (1970) 82 One night Jesus met a guy named Nicodemus. How's that for a handle?

5. *attrib.* and *Comb.* Of, belonging to, or next to, the handle, as ***handle-end, -hand***; forming the handle, as ***handle-piece, -stick***; having a handle, as ***handle-cup, -dish, -net***; †**handle-band** (see quots.); **handle-bar**, a transverse bar, usually curved, with a handle at each end, connected with the driving- or steering-wheel of a cycle, by which the vehicle is guided by hand; *pl.* the right- and left-hand parts of which this is composed; also *attrib.*, *spec.* of a (usually large) moustache of handle-bar shape.

1532 in Rogers *Agric. & Prices* III. 568/2 Greenwich. Welsh mats.. Frail mats.. *Handleband. 99 lb. @/4. [**1882** *Ibid.* IV. 578 The edges of these mats appear to have been bound with a material called handleband, which.. is probably coarse hempen tape.] **1887** *Graphic* 3 Dec. 619 These machines.. are fitted with adjustable handles and seat rod. Well finished in black enamel, with plated hubs, *handle bars, &c. **1894** *Million* V. 377/1 Pick up your dress with your right hand, take hold of the handle bar with your left. **1898** *Science Siftings* XV. 170/1 Handle-bars in which the drop is greater than four inches below the seat are.. dangerous. **1908** *Westm. Gaz.* 15 Apr. 10/2 A contributor to the *Motor Cycle* advises motor-cyclists to carry handle-bar mirrors on their machines. **1908** *Daily Chron.* 21 Nov. 9/4 One cannot effect this unobserved change when other than handle-bar control is fitted. **1909** *Captain* Aug. 448/2 Home-made Handlebar-grips. **1923** H. L. WILSON *Oh, Doctor!* xxiv. 333 [He] threw a confident leg across the saddle and worshipfully grasped the spreading handle bars. **1933** G. P. JACKSON *White Spirituals* 65 An elderly man with handle-bar moustache. **1941** *Penguin New Writing* VIII. 17 One man was huge and swarthy, with a handlebar moustache. **1953** M. DICKENS *No More Meadows* vii. 295 Chap with the handlebar moustache. Real Pilot-Officer Prune type. **1968** *Which?* Aug. 231/2 Turn the handlebars—the steering should not be too tight or too loose. *Ibid.* 232/1 If the brake levers are too far from the handlebar grips, a child with small hands might find it difficult to work them. **1972** J. ROSSITER *Rope for General Dietz* ii. 23 We both had the enormous handlebar moustaches *de rigueur* in the RAF at that time. **1669** WORLIDGE *Syst. Agric.* (1681) 260 Your Lines.. of good, fine and strong *handle-bound Pack-thread. **1717** FREZIER *Voy. S. Sea* 65 A Wooden Instrument.. consisting of a *Handle-Cup at one End, and a long Beak. **1897** MARY KINGSLEY *W. Africa* 325 The patterns he puts at the *handle-end of his swords. **1703** MOXON *Mech. Exerc.* 17 You must dip your *Handlehand, and mount your end-hand a little. **1834** MEDWIN *Angler in W.* I. 45 Ash for the bottom or *handle-piece.

Hence **handleless** *a.*, without a handle.

1873 TRISTRAM *Moab* ii. 22 Three handleless, saucerless blue china cups. **1887** A. STORY *Fifine* I. 62 A young moon hanging like a handleless sickle in the sky.

handle ('hænd(ə)l), *sb.*[2] [f. HANDLE *v.*[1] 1.] The feel of or sensation produced by goods, especially textiles, when handled.

1884 W. S. B. McLAREN *Spinning* 19 It is not merely the coarseness or fineness of the fibre which guides him, but also the softness and kind 'handle', as it is called. **1898** *Daily News* 7 Mar. 2/1 For softness and beautiful handle they have no equal. **1927** T. WOODHOUSE *Artificial Silk* 2 The handle of many artificial silk articles of commerce compares favourably with that of most of the corresponding textures in the other branches of the textile industry. **1961** *Times* 26 Oct. p. iv, A new type of paper.. which had all the qualities —good surface and opacity, good colour and crispness of 'handle'. **1962** *Which?* Aug. 240/2 The blanket.. felted considerably and had a harsh 'handle'. **1968** J. IRONSIDE *Fashion Alphabet* 210 The filaments are 'crimped' to resemble wool, giving a warm, soft 'handle'. **1970** *Nature* 17 Oct. 212/1 The 'handle' and 'feel' of fabrics.

handle ('hænd(ə)l), *v.*[1] Forms: 1 **handlian, hondlian,** 2–4 **handlen,** 3 **hondlien,** 3–4 **hondlen,** 4–5 **hondel,** 4–6 **handell, -il(l, -yll(e,** 4–7 **handel,** 5 **hondle,** 6 *Sc.* **hanel,** 4– **handle.** [OE. *handlian* = OLG. *handlôn*, OHG. *hantalôn* to take or feel with the hands (MHG. and Ger. *handeln*), ON. *họndla* to lay hold of; deriv. of HAND *sb.*]

I. To manipulate, manage.

1. a. *trans.* To subject to the action of the hand or hands: in earlier use, *esp.*, to touch or feel with the hands, to pass the hand over, stroke with the hand; later, to take hold of, turn over, etc., in the hand, to employ the hands on or about.

to handle a horse, to get him accustomed to the hand. *to handle a dog*, etc., to hold and set him on in a fight or contest.

c **1000** ÆLFRIC *Gen.* xxvii. 12 Gif min fæder me handlaþ and me ȝecnæwð. *c* **1000** *Sax. Leechd.* III. 204 Ylpes ban handlian. *c* **1200** ORMIN 18913 Þatt menn himm mihhtenn cnawenn & handlenn himm. *a* **1225** *Ancr. R.* 178 He ne mei iðolien þet me hondle his sor. *c* **1380** WYCLIF *Wks.* (1880) 49 A weeg of siluer.. þei wolen handil faste. *c* **1400** *Gamelyn* 82 [He] bi gan with his hand to hondel his berd. **1530** PALSGR. 578/1 She can handell a chylde dayntely. **1631** WEEVER *Anc. Fun. Mon.* 301 This merry deuill.. would haue handled him with rough Mittins, as the prouerbe is. *a* **1698** TEMPLE (J.), The hardness of the winter forces the breeders there to house and handle their colts six months every year. **1717** FREZIER *Voy. S. Sea* 118 I have handled and felt it. **1825** HONE *Every-day Bk.* I. 992 The dogs to be handled by Mr. Edwards [at a baiting]. **1888** BURGON *Lives 12 Gd. Men* I. i. 41 It is impossible to handle these volumes without the deepest interest. **1890** BOLDREWOOD *Col. Reformer* 93 I'll do nothing but handle him [a horse] to-day.

absol. *c* **1275** *Passion of our Lord* 607 in *O.E. Misc.* 54 Hondleþ nv and iseoþ. þat gost naueþ none bon Ne vleys. **1535** COVERDALE *Ps.* cxiii. 15 [cxv. 7] They haue handes and handle not. **1748** HARTLEY *Observ. Man* I. iii. 386 A Brute is supposed to speak.. or to handle.

b. *intr.* (for *refl.*) To have a (specified) feel, behaviour, action, etc. when handled.

1727 BRADLEY *Fam. Dict.* s.v. *Hop-garden*, If they handle moist or clammy when you squeeze them they are fit to bag. **1847** *Jrnl. R. Agric. Soc.* VIII. I. 77 The wheat.. soon handles cold and damp. **1881** GREENER *Gun* 250 If the balance is not the same, they will handle as if of different bends. **1946** *Mod. Lang. Notes* LXI. 443 The use, in advertising, of the 'potential intransitive', in such examples as 'this car *operates, handles* smoothly'. **1958** *Times* 23 Sept. 14/2 Sceptre, handling excellently, rounded the mark to the sound of loud hootings. **1962** *Which? Car Suppl.* Oct. 142/1 It [*sc.* the car] handled very securely. **1972** *Country Life* 23 Mar. 703/3 The machine handles well, and I discovered no snags.

2. a. *trans.* To ply or wield (something, e.g. a tool or weapon) with the hand; to manipulate.

c **1205** LAY. 1338 He hihte hondlien kablen. *c* **1300** *Havelok* 347 Þe beste knicht þat euere micte.. handlen spere. *c* **1385** CHAUCER *L.G.W.* 2594 *Hypermnestra*, That ypermystra dar nat handele a knyf. **1535** COVERDALE *1 Chron.* ix. [viii.] 40 The children of Vlam were valeaunt men, and coulde handell bowes. **1576** FLEMING *Panopl. Epist.* 437 That I may see.. how well you handle your penne. **1611** BIBLE *Gen.* iv. 21 Iubal.. was the father of all such as handle the harpe and organ. **1631** GOUGE *God's Arrows* v. xi. 421 More fit.. to handle a mattocke then to hold a musket. **1741–3** WESLEY *Jrnl.* (1749) 61 As soon as they could handle a knife and fork, they were set to our table. **1872** *Even. Standard* 10 Aug. (Farmer), Her Royal Highness .. appears to handle the ribbons in a very skilful manner.

b. *Mil.* (See quots.)

1684 R. H. *School Recreat.* 46 *Handle your Charger*, Gripe fast your Bandilier or Charger, hold it even with the Muzzle. *Ibid.* 48 *Handle your Musket*.. step forward, and lay your Right-hand on the Muzzle. **1844** *Regul. & Ord. Army* 265 To all other Officers they [sentinels] are to carry or handle their Arms. **1853** STOCQUELER *Milit. Encycl.*, *Handle Arms!* .. by which the soldier is directed to bring his right hand briskly up to the muzzle of his firelock, with his fingers bent inwards.

c. *Tanning.* (See quot., and HANDLER 3.)

1839 URE *Dict. Arts* 764 They [*sc.* the hides].. are successively transferred into other pits with stronger ooze; all the while being daily *handled*, that is, moved up and down in the infusion. **1875** *Ure's Dict. Arts* III. 83 s.v. *Leather*, The hides.. are *handled*, at first several times a day; that is, they are drawn out of the pits, or moved up and down in the liquor.

d. *Cricket.* (See quots.)

1788 in H. T. Waghorn *Dawn of Cricket* (1906) 98 Their opponents were superior to them in handling [*sc.* fielding] the ball. **1797** in G. B. Buckley *Fresh Light on 18th Cent. Cricket* (1935) 184 Handling b. in play. **1841** *Manchester Chron.* 24 July, John Ogden.. handled the ball well [i.e. as bowler].

3. a. To manage, conduct, direct, control: (*a*) a thing, animal, or person; †(*b*) a matter, course of action, etc. (sometimes = carry out, perform, transact).

1523 FITZHERB. *Husb.* §68 Yet at manye tymes they [mares] maye drawe well, if they be well handled. **1548** HALL *Chron.*, *Rich. III.* 11 b, While these thynges were thus handeled and ordered in Englande. **1582** N. LICHEFIELD tr. *Castanheda's Conq. E. Ind.* lxi. 125 b, The skirmish was valiantly handled. **1598** BARRET *Theor. Warres* IV. i. 93 Most of his actions are to be handled in the face and view of the enemie. **1669** STURMY *Mariner's Mag.* I. 17 Thus you see the Ship handled in fair weather and foul. **1679–1714** BURNET *Hist. Ref.* an. 1529 (R.) [To] see with what moderation as well as justice the matter was handled. **1874** WHYTE MELVILLE *Uncle J.* (Tauchn.) II. ii. 3 A smarter officer never handled a regiment. **1891** *Law Times* XC. 463/2 Adepts in marshalling facts and handling witnesses.

†**b.** *refl.* To conduct oneself, behave. *Obs.*

1540 HYRDE tr. *Vives' Instr. Chr. Wom.* (1592) A vij, So you have handled your selfe in all the order and course of your life. **1548** UDALL *Erasm. Par.* Pref. 18. **1869** E. PEACOCK *Two Deaths* in *Once a Week* 27 Mar. 230 And one with cruel, bitter words, Handleth herself right scornfully.

4. To use, do something with; to make due use of.

[*c* **1394** *P. Pl. Crede* 108 We hondlen no money, but menelich faren.] **1647** WARD *Simp. Cobler* 3 The devill desiers no better sport then to see light heads handle their heels. **1796** GROSE *Dict. Vulg. Tongue* s.v., To know how to handle one's fists; to be skilful in the art of boxing. **1842** TENNYSON *Walking to Mail* 16 He lost the sense that handles daily life. **1860** RUSKIN in A. Ritchie *Rec. Tennyson, etc.* 29 Sept. (1892) 137 It struck me.. that you depended too much on blending and too little on handling colour.

II. To deal with, treat.

5. a. To deal with, operate upon, do something to; to treat.

1542 BOORDE *Dyetary* xi. (1870) 260 It wyll make good drynke or euyl; euery thinge as it is handled. **1630** *R. Johnson's Kingd. & Commw.* 53 With the French, lesse [meat], but well handled. **1665** HOOKE *Microgr.* Pref. D ij, So vast is the variety of Objects.. so many different wayes there are of handling them. *a* **1774** PEARCE *Serm.* III. xv. (R.), [He] fears to expose a good cause by his method of handling it. **1828** SCOTT *F.M. Perth* vii, You would be as much afraid of handling this matter, as if it were glowing iron. **1879** *Athenæum* 8 Nov. 603/3 The most difficult of all musical forms to handle successfully.

b. To deal with, treat, 'serve', 'use' (in a specified way); to act in some specified way towards.

a **1225** *Juliana* 46 Me seli meiden hu derstu nu hondlin me ant halden me swa hardeliche. *a* **1300** *Cursor M.* 19206 Quen þai to þeir breþer þare Had tald hu þai handeld war. *c* **1400** *Gamelyn* 10 Deth was comyn him to & handlid him ful sore. **1535** COVERDALE *Prov.* xxiv. 29, I wil handle him, even as he hath dealte with me. **1555** EDEN *Decades* 33 The miserable Ilande men whom they handeled moste cruelly. **1638** BAKER tr. *Balzac's Lett.* (vol. III) 163 Lucan; whom Scaliger hath handled so hardly. **1705** BOSMAN *Guinea* 26 Men whose good Name and Reputation I shall always handle very tenderly. **1861** TULLOCH *Eng. Purit.* iv. 417 He was handled twenty times worse than he had been before. **1894** R. BRIDGES *Feast of Bacchus* I. 405 Handle him kindly.

†**c.** *intr.* To 'deal', act (in a specified way).

1535 COVERDALE *Ps.* cxviii[i]. 78 Let the proude be confounded, which handle so falsly agaynst me. **1581** MARBECK *Bk. of Notes* 616 They handle together with good faith.

6. a. To deal with or treat in speech or writing; to treat of, discuss; † formerly sometimes = to confer about, discuss in a deliberative asssembly.

c **1050** *Byrhtferth's Handboc* in *Anglia* (1885) VIII. 304/24 Þa þing þe we nu handledon. **1303** R. BRUNNE *Handl. Synne* 94 For þys skyle hyt may be seyde 'Handlyng synne'. **1480** CAXTON *Descr. Brit.* 30 The cause was handled and ytreated bitwene the forsaid primates. **1551** T. WILSON *Logike* (1580) 41 The Preacher handeled his matter learnedly. **1621** ELSING *Debates Ho. Lords* (Camden) 126 To discusse the matter of oathe.. which is appoynted to be handled that daye. **1641** WILKINS *Math. Magick* I. ii. (1648) 12 Astronomy handles the quantity of heavenly motions. **1725** WATTS *Logic* IV. ii. §6 The very same theme may be handled .. in several different methods. **1868** NETTLESHIP *Ess.*

Browning Introd. I, I could not within reasonable limits handle both criticism and interpretation.

†**b.** *intr.* or *absol.* To treat, discourse, confer.

1596 DALRYMPLE tr. *Leslie's Hist. Scot.* x. 378 Tha hanelit anent the Mariage of the Quene. **1658** A. FOX *Wurtz' Surg.* II. xxvi. 177 In the Chapter which handleth of exiccated Members. **1673** WOOD *Life* 12 Oct., They finding that I had handled upon that point, Peers altered it.

7. To treat artistically; to portray or represent (in a particular style).

1553 EDEN *Treat. Newe Ind.* (Arb.) 17 A deuyll made of copper, and that so workemanly handeled that he semeth like flaming fire. **1603** DRAYTON *Bar. Wars* VI. xliii, The story of his fortunes past In lively pictures neatly handled was. **1850** LEITCH *Müller's Anc. Art* §204. 193 The countenance is always handled in a less spirited manner. **1860** KINGSLEY *Misc.* II. 77 Our painting is only good when it handles landscapes and animals.

8. To have in hand or pass through one's hands in the way of business; to trade or deal in; to buy and sell. *U.S.*

1888 C. D. WARNER in *Harper's Mag.* Apr. 776/1 It does not pay to 'handle' books, or to keep the run of new publications. **1889** *Pall Mall G.* 13 Feb. 3/1 Large jobbing houses who handle all the new and standard publications in considerable numbers to supply small dealers. **1897** *Glasgow Her.* 12 Feb. 7/2 Export houses which handle steel rails.

Hence **handlable, -eable** (ˈhændləb(ə)l), †**ˈhandlesome** (*obs.*), *adjs.*, capable of being handled.

1611 COTGR., *Maniable*, tractable, wieldable, handleable. **1674** N. FAIRFAX *Bulk & Selv.* 47 All feelers numb, nothing handlesom. **1893** *Field* 25 Feb. 297/1 She [a boat] must be handleable by one man in all ways and weathers.

handle, *v.*^{2} [f. HANDLE *sb.*^{1}] *trans.* To furnish with a handle; to affix the handle to.

1600 T. MASHAM in *Hakluyt's Voy.* III. 695 Wee were informed, that their bowes were handled with golde. **1701** C. WOLLEY *Jrnl. in N. York* (1860) 52 With a flint, handled the Indian way. **1888** BELL *Later Age of Stone* 36 You may now ask how these implements were handled.

handleability (ˌhænd(ə)ləˈbɪlɪtɪ). [f. HANDLEABLE *a.*: see -ITY.] Ease of handling.

1947 N. BALCHIN *Aircraft Builders* v. 31 The problem was one of combining performance with 'handleability' and toughness of condition. **1949** *Jrnl. R. Aeronaut. Soc.* LIII. 962/1 The general 'handleability' of an aero-plane must not be lost sight of in a welter of requirements which might lead to excessive stability. **1970** *Amat. Photographer* 22 Apr. 55/2 An indefinable quality of a camera is its 'handleability'.

handled (ˈhænd(ə)ld), *a.* [f. HANDLE *sb.*^{1} and *v.*^{2} + -ED.] Furnished with or having a handle: *esp.* with defining word, as ***long-handled, ivory-handled***. Used in *Heraldry* when the handle of a tool or weapon is figured of a different tincture from the blade, as 'a sickle or, handled gules'.

1785 COWPER *Let.* 24 Dec., It..is hinged, handled, and mounted with silver. **1836** T. HOOK *G. Gurney* I. 6 Smart-handled knives. **1888** BELL *Later Age of Stone* 19 The modern aborigines of Australia use daggers formed of handled flakes. **1889** *Pall Mall G.* 31 July 5/2 As for the 'handled' names..Mr. Knowles produces four Duchesses [etc.].

handled, var. of ANLETH (ON. *andlit*), *Obs.*, countenance.

c **1250** in *Pol. Rel. & L. Poems* 214 Bleye was his fair handled [*v.r.* neb].

handler (ˈhændlə(r)). [f. HANDLE *v.* + -ER^{1}.]

1. a. One who handles (in *lit.* and *fig.* senses: see HANDLE *v.*^{1}). In *Football*, One who plays 'Rugby'.

1398 TREVISA *Barth. De P.R.* VIII. xiii. (1495) 320 Chaungers handlers of syluer. **1540** COVERDALE *Confut. Standish* Wks. (Parker Soc.) II. 429 An unreverent handler of God's word. **1607** TOPSELL *Four-f. Beasts* (1658) 177 A cunning Archer or handler of a Gun. **1663** BLAIR *Autobiog.* ii. (1848) 25 Outgivings to traders and handlers in this Kingdom. **1889** *Pall Mall G.* 16 Mar. 3/1 The rough play which has prevailed this winter, both among the dribblers and the handlers.

b. Something that has a specified feel when handled: cf. HANDLE *v.*^{1} 1 b.

1848 *Jrnl. R. Agric. Soc.* IX. II. 444 They..are often bad handlers, and slow feeders.

2. *spec.* **a.** One who holds and sets on a dog or a game-cock in a fight or contest; one who shows the points of dogs at a trial, etc.

1825 HONE *Every-day Bk.* I. 996 The..dogs darted at the ..lion, amid the horrid din of the cries of their handlers. **1828** MARLY *Life Planter Jamaica* (ed. 2) 320 In the temporary cock-pit..The handlers made their appearance. **1897** *Field* 6 Feb. 168/1 Each hound has a handler. They work the dogs in front of the judges. **1931** *Our Dogs* 23 Oct. 296 Handlers and Breakers. Gun dogs wanted for training or boarding. **1959** *Times* 18 Sept. 7/5 Of the nine handlers who took part in the opening event—the hired shepherds' championship—only two failed to complete the course.

b. A police officer who is in charge of a trained dog.

1959 B. J. FARMER *Murder Next Year* xxi. 134, I know Sergeant Cristobel... He's handler for a trained Alsatian. **1962** *Times* 29 Dec. 6/7 Minivans..containing two highly trained police dogs with their handlers. **1971** B. CALLISON *Plague of Sailors* 10 They're not dogs, they're bloody werewolves. What d'you handlers do for leave, spend it in the bloody jungle?

c. *Boxing.* (See quot. 1961.)

1950 J. DEMPSEY *Championship Fighting* 9 His handlers threw in the towel. **1960** *Times* 1 Sept. 4/4 It took several seconds of rough first aid by his handlers before he was able to regain his seat. **1961** J. S. SALAK *Dict. Amer. Sports* 216 *Handlers*, the chief second and assistant seconds of a boxer during a contest. **1973** *Sunday Express* (Trinidad & Tobago) 8 Apr. 29/2 (*caption*) One of his handlers..is near tears after Ali lost a 12 round non-title bout.

3. *Tanning.* A pit containing a weak tannin infusion, in which the hides are 'handled': see HANDLE *v.*^{1} 2 c.

1777 MACBRIDE in *Phil. Trans.* LXVIII. 115 The leather is ready for the ooze, and at first is thrown into smaller holes, which are termed handlers. **1879** *Cassell's Techn. Educ.* v. 311 The pits containing the weakest solutions are called 'handlers'.

4. [f. HANDLE *v.*^{2}] A workman who fastens the handles to vessels, tools, etc.; a hafter.

1598 FLORIO, *Manicatore*..a sleeuer, a hafter, a handler. **1881** *Porcelain Works, Worcester* 21 The turner..having completed the form of the cup it is passed to the Handler.

handles, var. ANDLESS, *Sc. Obs.*, breathless.

handless (ˈhændlɪs), *a.* [f. HAND *sb.*^{1} + -LESS.]

1. Without hands; deprived of hands.

1483 *Cath. Angl.* 173/2 Handles, *mancus, mancatus*. **1588** SHAKS. *Tit. A.* III. i. 67 What accursed hand Hath made thee handlesse in thy Fathers sight? **1607** DAY *Trav. Eng. Bro.* (1881) 87 For which thou shalt go handless to thy graue. **1867** SWINBURNE in *Fortn. Rev.* Oct. 428 There is no such thing as a dumb poet or a handless painter.

2. *fig.* Not doing, or not able to do, anything with the hands; incapable or incompetent with the hands, or in action. *Obs.* exc. *dial.*

1413 *Pilgr. Sowle* (Caxton 1483) IV. xxxii. 81 Wherfor is he nought handeles, for he hath full power to helpen and comforten all. *c* **1586** C'TESS PEMBROKE *Ps.* LXXVI. ii, The mighty handlesse grew as men that slumbered. *a* **1658** J. DURHAM *Expos. Rev.* vii. (1680) 34 Believers have not a handlesse Mediator. **1854** *Phemie Millar* 28 You are truly a poor handless thing. **1897** BARRIE *Margaret Ogilvy* 128 He is most terribly handless.

ˈhand-line.

1. A line to be worked or drawn by hand; *esp.* a fishing line worked without a rod.

1674 N. COX *Gentl. Recreat.* III. (1677) 20 Fasten your Hand-lines or drawing Cords, which must be at the least a dozen, a fathom long. **1766** PENNANT *Zool.* (1776) I. 343 (Jod.) The same rapidity of tide prevents their using hand-lines. **1895** *Oracle Encycl.* II. 105 The fishery is carried on by hand-lines..the bait being cuttlefishes, shell-fishes, etc.

2. *Naut.* 'A line bent to the hand-lead, measured at certain intervals with what are called *marks* and *deeps* from 2 and 3 fathoms to 20' (*Sailor's Word-bk.*).

1897 MARY KINGSLEY *W. Africa* 415 We want a hand-line for soundings.

Hence **ˈhand-liner**, one who uses a hand-line for fishing. **ˈhand-lining** *vbl. sb.*, fishing with a hand-line. **hand-line** *v.*, to fish with a hand-line; to pull in a fishing-line by hand.

1887 MARQ. LORNE in *Fortn. Rev.* Mar. 464 A fleet engaged wholly in handlining and trawling. **1935** A. J. CRONIN *Stars look Down* II. xix. 437 Old Macer..had to make the best of it by hand-lining off shore for whiting. **1969** *Islander* (Victoria, B.C.) 7 Sept. 6/1 Peter began commercial fishing, handlining for cod. **1972** *Shooting Times & Country Mag.* 24 June 15/3, I was at one stage handlining in like fury to keep in touch and then suddenly as the fish passed us, was slipping line out to the running fish.

handling (ˈhændlɪŋ), *vbl. sb.* [f. HANDLE *v.*^{1} and ^{2} + -ING^{1}.] **I.** The action of the vb. HANDLE.

1. a. The action of touching, feeling, or grasping with the hand; management with the hand, wielding, manipulation; laying hands on; treatment in which the hands are effectively (or roughly) used.

c **1000** ÆLFRIC *Hom.* II. 182 Æt ðam cristenan menn ..ðone ðe se eadiᵹa Benedictus na handlunge..fram his bendum alysde. *a* **1225** *Ancr. R.* 60 Mid sweorde of deadliche hondlunge. **1398** TREVISA *Barth. De P.R.* III. xxiii. (1495) 71 In a stronge man and fleshly the pulse is gropyd and knowe wyth stronge and harde handlyng. **1512** in Willis & Clark *Cambridge* (1886) I. 608 Made and set vpp after the best handlyng and fourme of good workmanship. **1669** PEPYS *Diary* 19 May, To perform what was commanded, in the handling of their arms. **1795** *Gentl. Mag.* July 581/2 Irony, like Satire, is one of those edged tools which require careful handling. **1861** HUGHES *Tom Brown at Oxf.* ix. (1889) 76 There might be some reason in the rough handling he had got.

b. Quality perceived by feeling with the hand.

1881 J. P. SHELDON *Dairy Farming* 8/1 Fat soon accumulates..and forms the 'quality' or 'handling' which indicates the extent to which she [a cow] may be considered fit for the butcher.

c. In games, the illegal touching of the ball.

1882 in Charles-Edwards & Richardson *They saw it Happen* (1958) 300 For a breach of rule, which forbids handling, a free kick was awarded against the Etonians. **1897** *Encycl. Sport* I. 429/1 *Handling*, or *Hands*, touching the ball with any part of the arm when in play. Only the goal-keeper can do so without a penalty. 'Hands' is given against the offender.

d. [HANDLE *v.*^{1} 1 b] The way in which a motor vehicle handles.

1962 *Which? Car Suppl.* Oct. 143/1 Its handling was very secure, but the car was badly affected by side winds. **1967** *Autocar* 28 Dec. 5/3 In general the handling of the car was satisfactory.

2. *fig.* Dealing with a thing or person; treatment; management.

1530 PALSGR. 229/1 Handelyng, entreating, *traictement*. **1538** STARKEY *England* I. i. 21 Apply your selfe to the handelyng of the materys of the commyn wele. **1632** LITHGOW *Trav.* II. 66 The Venetians, Ragusans, and Marseillians haue great handling with them. **1776** JOHNSON 28 Mar. in *Boswell*, A woman of fortune being used to the handling of money, spends it judiciously. **1886** J. R. REES *Pleas. Book-Worm* ii. 37 De Quincey, with his marvellous handling of English prose.

3. Artistic manipulation: cf. HANDLE *v.*^{1} 7.

1771 SIR J. REYNOLDS *Disc.* iv. (1876) 360 What the painters call handling; that is, a lightness of pencil that implies great practice, and gives the appearance of being done with ease. **1840** THACKERAY *Crit. Rev.* Wks. 1886 XXIII. 147 A miniature..remarkable for its brilliancy of colour and charming freedom of handling. **1859** GULLICK & TIMBS *Paint.* 231 Handling is that part of the mechanical 'execution' or manipulation of a picture which exhibits the pencilling or play of the brush.

4. [f. HANDLE *v.*^{2}] The action or process of putting on the handles of vessels, etc.

1764 V. GREEN *Surv. Worcester* 232 Part of the business called handling and spouting, i.e. putting the hand to cups.

5. *attrib.*

1866 GEO. ELIOT *F. Holt* II. xxix. 211 If they were not touched in the right handling-place. **1882** JAMES PATON in *Encycl. Brit.* XIV. 384/2 After colouring, the hides pass on to the handlers or handling pits. **1895** *Daily News* 27 Nov. 5/3 Under Rugby Union rules..a determined affort is being made to revive the interest in the handling game [Rugby Union Football]. **1927** *Observer* 27 Mar. 28 In spite of the progress Rugby has made, the Association game at the Schools..has fully held its own with the handling code. **1949** *Archit. Rev.* CV. 218 The east bay includes..the polymer handling bay. **1954** *Economist* 11 Sept. 8/2 The central terminal area, which will hold the permanent control tower and the passenger handling buildings, is now being completed. **1955** *Times* 6 July 4/4 A long handling rush by Britain looked dangerous and from a loose scrum in the opposing twenty-five their backs gained possession for O'Reilly to cut in and score. **1962** *Which?* Dec. 367/1 Labour costs were covered, but there was a 'handling charge' of 2s. 6d. **1969** *Times* 13 Jan. 11/2 The increase in the handling margins would be nearer to 100 than 10 per cent.

II. †**6.** A handle. *Obs.*

c **1450** LONELICH *Grail* xxviii. 275 Thus the lettres of the handelyng spak. **1460** CAPGRAVE *Chron.* 117 The swerd..in the handelyng thereof was closed on of thoo IIII nayles that were in Cristis handis and feet. *c* **1500** *Melusine* xix. 65 They were as grete as the handlyng of a fan.

†**ˈhandlings,** *adv. Obs.* [In OE. *handlinga* adv.; in ME. with adverbial gen.: see -LING, -LINGS.] Hand-to-hand, at close quarters.

c **1000** ÆLFRIC *Hom.* I. 386 þæt he handlinga æniᵹne man acwealde. *a* **1300** *Cursor M.* 3933 Sammen handlinges wristeld þai.

hand-list, *sb.* [Cf. *hand-book*] A list of books, etc. in a form handy for reference.

1855 HALLIWELL (*title*) A brief hand-list of books.. illustrative of..Shakespeare. **1893** *Edin. Even. Disp.* 22 Apr. 2/3 To provide a hand-list for this library.

Hence **handlist** *v. trans.*, to enter (books, etc.) in such a list.

1888 NICHOLSON *Bodleian Library in* 1882–7 445 The Librarian also commenced..handlisting the considerable accumulations of inscribed fragments of papyrus. **1897** —— *Oxf. Univ. Gaz.* 18 May 509/1 [He] handlisted the entire collection of Mr. Hallam's MSS., consisting of 144 vols.

†**ˈhandlock.** *Obs.* [See LOCK *sb.*] A shackle for the hands; a manacle, a handcuff.

1532 *St. Papers Hen. VIII*, II. 158 The malefactour wished that he had the King in the ende of a hand lokk, and the Deputie in the other ende. **1600** HAKLUYT *Voy.* (1810) III. 313 Who should also have kept me companie in a handlocke with the rest. **1633** T. STAFFORD *Pac. Hib.* I. ii. (1810) 35 The White Knight, and his sonne in law..Whom in hand-lockes he carried away with him.

ˈhandlock, *v.* [f. prec. sb.; cf. also LOCK *v.*] *trans.* To handcuff. Also *transf.* Chiefly in *pa. pple.*

1586 J. HOOKER *Girald. Irel.* in *Holinshed* II. 21/2 The king..commanded him to be handlocked and fettered, with an other prisoner. **1826** SCOTT *Woodst.* xxxvi, Still holding his..friend's arm enclosed and hand-locked in his. **1829** H. MURRAY *N. Amer.* I. iv. 197 The son was still kept handlocked.

ˈhand-loom. a. A weaver's loom worked by hand as distinguished from a power-loom.

1833 SIR D. BARRY *Factory Comm. Rep.* App. A. 3. 42 Thinks her daughter's health rather better than when at the handloom. **1843** *Penny Cycl.* XXVII. 182/2 If [the weaver] clings to the hand-loom, his condition will become worse from day to day.

b. *ellipt.* in *pl.* for *handloom linens*.

1890 *Daily News* 10 Mar. 2/7 Flax and Linens.—Belfast.. In brown power loom linens the demand continues very languid..Handlooms are unchanged.

c. *attrib.* and *Comb.*

1833 SIR D. BARRY *Factory Comm. Rep.* App. A. 3. 43 *note*, The power-loom dressers have been all hand-loom weavers. **1837** *Penny Cycl.* VIII. 99/2 Hand-loom weaving is altogether a domestic manufacture. **1893** *Daily News* 27 Apr. 7/3 Drills and handloom goods dull.

Hence **ˈhand-loomed** *a.*

1928 *Daily Express* 13 July 3/6 Hand-loomed leathers.. are a vogue in exclusive handbags. **1966** A. ADBURGHAM *View of Fashion* 135 Hand-loomed skirts.

† **'handly**, *a. Obs.* [f. HAND *sb.* + -LY¹.] Used by the hands; manual; mechanical.

c **1400** *Lanfranc's Cirurg.* 129 To remeue a boon wiþ handely [*MS. B*, handly] instrumentis. *Ibid.* 40 Remeuynge of þe boon wiþ handliche instrumentis.

'hand-made, *a.* **a.** Made by hand. Formerly distinguished from the work of nature (= artificial), now usually from that of machinery.

1613 PURCHAS *Pilgrimage* (1614) 511 A hand-made strait of Sea water. **1840** *Penny Cycl.* XVII. 209/2 Hand-made paper is now commonly marked with the name of the maker, and the date of the year when it was made. **1879** LUBBOCK *Sci. Lect.* v. 156 Hand-made pottery is abundant. **1959** HALAS & MANVELL *Technique Film Animation* vi. 69 The animated film is essentially a hand-made art. **1968** *Times* 31 Aug. 19/4 Some biographical facts (including the..item of her using the blue hand-made paper fabricated for Colette).

b. *fig.*

1936 *Punch* 7 Oct. 418/2 (*heading*) The hand-made short story. **1937** B. H. L. HART *Europe in Arms* iv. 49 The fortified region..is garrisoned by units of varying composition which are 'hand-made' to suit the sector allotted to them. **1958** *Listener* 9 Oct. 549/2 By the very terms of his [*sc.* de Gaulle's] own newly adopted hand-made constitution, the President must not be anything but an arbitrator.

handmaid ('hændmeɪd), *sb.* [f. HAND *sb.* + MAID. Cf. OE. *handþeᵹn* personal attendant or servant, also the ME. phrase 'to serve any one to hand', HAND *sb.* 34 a, 56.]

1. A female personal attendant or servant: **a.** in literal sense. *arch.*

1382 WYCLIF *Ps.* cxxii[i]. 2 As the eᵹen of the hondmaide in the hondis of hir ladi. **1398** TREVISA *Barth. De. P.R.* I. (1495) 7, I am the handmayde of the lorde. **1548** HALL *Chron., Hen. V*, 61 b, The goddesse of warre called Bellona ..hath these .iij. handmaides ever of necessitie attendyng on her, bloud, fyre, and famine. **1613** SHAKS. *Hen. VIII*, II. iii. 72 Vouchsafe to speake my thankes, and my obedience, As from a blushing Handmaid, to his Highnesse. **1806** SURR *Winter in Lond.* (ed. 3) I. 122 With Dinah, her sturdy handmaid, as her attendant. **1856** MRS. BROWNING *Aur. Leigh* II. 412 To be the handmaid of a lawful spouse.

b. *fig.* (in common use).

1592 DAVIES *Immort. Soul* v. vi, As God's Handmaid, Nature, doth create Bodies. **1779** WESLEY *Collect. Hymns* Pref. 5 Poetry..keeps its place as the handmaid of Piety. **1875** STUBBS *Const. Hist.* III. xxi. 533 Heraldry became a handmaid of chivalry.

†**c.** A vessel employed to attend upon a larger one; a tender. *Obs.*

1599 HAKLUYT *Voy.* II. II. 121 Vnto which 4 ships [under Sir Francis Drake] two of her pinasses were appointed as hand-maids.

2. A moth (also ***handmaid moth***), *Datana ministra*, of the family *Bombycidæ*.

1869 NEWMAN *Brit. Moths* 473 The Handmaid (*Naclia Ancilla*).

3. *attrib.* and *Comb.* Also ***handmaid-like*** adj.

1629 MILTON *Christ's Nat.* 242 Her sleeping Lord with handmaid lamp attending. **1725** POPE *Odyss.* XXII. 459 Full fifty of the handmaid train. **1814** MRS. J. WEST *Al. de Lacy* I. 61 With handmaid-like humility of judgment. **1855** TENNYSON *Enid* 400 [He] let his eye..rest On Enid at her lowly handmaid-work.

Hence † **'handmaid** *v. nonce-wd. Obs.*

1655 FULLER *Hist. Camb.* Ep., Natural Philosophy, which should hand-maid it to Divinity.

'hand,maiden. [f. HAND *sb.* + MAIDEN: see prec.] = HANDMAID. **a.** *lit.* (*archaic*).

a **1300** *E.E. Psalter* cxxii. 2 Als eghen of hand-maiden klene, In hende of hir levedy bene. **1382** WYCLIF *Gen.* xxi. 10 Throw out this handmayden and the sone of hir. **1483** *Cath. Angl.* 173/2 An Handemayden, *abra, ancilla.* **1611** BIBLE *Luke* i. 48 He hath regarded the lowe estate of his handmaiden. **1826** MISS MITFORD *Village* Ser. II. (1863) 353 Who filled an equivocal post in the household, half handmaiden and half companion. **1849** MACAULAY *Hist. Eng.* I. 330 During several generations..the relation between divines and handmaidens was a theme for endless jest.

b. *fig.*

1581 MULCASTER *Positions* xli. (1887) 243 To haue the handmaiden sciences to attend vpon their mistres profession. **1875** JOWETT *Plato* (ed. 2) IV. 28 Health and temperance..are the handmaidens of virtue.

So **handman** *dial.*, manservant, serving-man.

1754 J. SHEBBEARE *Matrimony* (1766) I. 245 She..went to Bed to the Handman.

'hand-me-down, *sb.* and *a. dial.* and *colloq.* [f. the verbal phr. *to hand down* (see HAND *v.* 4 b).] **A.** *sb.* That which is handed down, as an heirloom, a second-hand garment, etc.; also, a ready-made garment. **B.** *adj.* Having been handed down or passed on; = REACH-ME-DOWN *a.* So ***hand-me-down shop***, etc. Also *fig.*

1874 HOTTEN *Dict. Slang* 187 *Hand-me-downs*, second-hand clothes. **1882** G. W. PECK *Peck's Sunshine* 213 A hand bill for a Chicago hand-me-down clothing store. **1888** *New York World* 5 Mar. (Farmer), A twelve-dollar suit of hand-me-downs. **1889** *Sporting Times* 29 June (Farmer), Trousers..which all over proclaim themselves entitled to the epithet of hand-me-down. **1896** ADE *Artie* xviii. 70 They'll be workin' for some Reub that come into town wearin' hand-me-downs. **1897** *Congress. Rec.* 25 Mar. 274/1 These cheap-johns, ready-made, 'hand-me-down' statesmen. **1904** *Boston Herald* 15 Oct. 2 He wears a cheap suit of 'hand-me-down' clothing. **1909** *Daily Chron.* 2 July 7/4 He got it from a lady admirer..and he wanted me to 'ave it as a hand-me-down. **1914** JOYCE *Dubliners* 150 His little old father kept the hand-me-down shop in Mary's Lane. **1925** S. LEWIS *Martin Arrowsmith* viii. §2 A dirty old office, with hand-me-down chairs and a lot of second-hand magazines. **1935** A. J. CRONIN *Stars look Down* II. xiii. 375 A little hand-me-down factory. **1954** M. MEAD *Growing up in New Guinea* 188 Their myths are dull hand-me-downs. **1960** *Economist* 31 Dec. 1382/1 Many large corporations are still flying converted bombers and hand-me-down transports, but these are being supplemented by the newer, smaller light models. **1966** *New Yorker* 5 Nov. 197 To dramatize this hand-me-down truth.

'hand-mill. A grinding mill consisting of one millstone turned upon another by hand, a quern. Now, also, applied to a simple machine for grinding coffee, or the like, worked by hand-power.

1563-87 FOXE *A. & M.* (1596) 75/2 Quirinus the bishop of Scescanius having a handmill tied about his necke, was throwne headlong from the bridge into the flood. **1573-80** BARET *Alv.* H 92 An Handmill: a querne. **1792** A. YOUNG *Trav. France* 536 Feudal tyranny in Bretagne, armed with the judicial power, has not blushed even in these times at breaking hand-mills. **1875** W. MCILWRAITH *Guide Wigtownshire* 43 A quern-stone, or upper half of an ancient hand-mill.

'hand-mould.

1. A small mould managed with the hand; e.g. one used in casting hand-made type.

1399 LANGL. *Rich. Redeles* II. 155 He mellid so þe matall with þe hand-molde, That [þey] lost [of þeir] lemes þe leuest þat þey had. **1875** in KNIGHT *Dict. Mech.*

†**2.** An apparatus for holding the hands in correct position in pianoforte-playing. *Obs.*

1819 COL. HAWKER *Diary* (1893) I. 179, I..presented my pianoforte hand-moulds to Messrs... Pleyel, which they approved and accepted for their manufactory.

hand-off (hænd'ɒf, -ɔː-), *v. Rugby Football.* [f. HAND *v.* + OFF *adv.*] *intr.* To push off an opponent with the hand. Also *trans.* Hence **'hand-off** *sb.*, the action of pushing off an opponent.

1897 *Encycl. Sport* I. 429 *Handing-off*, pushing off an opponent who endeavours to impede a player running with the ball. **1920** *Times* 8 Nov. 6/2 The wings ran well and were not afraid to 'hand-off'. **1922** *Daily Mail* 8 Dec. 12 A dangerous scoring wing with a powerful hand-off and an elusive swerve. **1923** W. J. A. DAVIES *Rugby Football* 135 Coates..ran with his head half turned to the right..which gave one the impression that he was waiting and was anxious to hand-off some one. **1928** *Observer* 19 Feb. 27/1 [He] has a fine kick, with a strong hand-off. **1959** *Times* 21 Sept. 3/5 Gray, who used his hand-off effectively.

hand of glory. [A transl. of F. *main de gloire*, a deformation, by 'popular etymology', of OF. *mandegloire, mandeglore, mandegore* (Godefroy), orig. *mandragore* mandrake.]

Originally applied, in French, to a charm formed of the root of a mandrake; afterwards, in consequence of the deformation of the word, applied to a charm made of the hand of an executed criminal: see quot. 1816 and context.

1707 *Curios. in Husb. & Gard.* 284 Mountebanks..make of it [mandrake] what we call a Hand of Glory..They..make believe, that by using some little Ceremonies, the Silver they lay near it, will increase to double the Sum every Morning. **1787** GROSE *Provinc. Gloss.* Superstitions 73-5. **1816** SCOTT *Antiq.* xvii, 'De hand of glory..is hand cut off from a dead man, as has been hanged for murther, and dried very nice in de shmoke of juniper wood' [etc.]. **1840** BARHAM *Ingol. Leg.* (*title*) The Hand of Glory.

hand-organ. A portable barrel-organ played by means of a crank turned with the hand.

1796 MORSE *Amer. Geog.* II. 334 Hand-organs, and other musical inventions. **1892** G. S. LAYARD *C. Keene* i. 8 A hand-organ turned with might and main by the busy sister.

hand-organist, one who plays a hand-organ.

1896 HOWELLS *Impr. & Exp., Tribul. Cheerf. Giver* iv. 162 Ought one to give money to a hand-organist?

hand-out. [f. HAND *v.* + OUT *adv.*; see also HAND *sb.* 65.]

1. a. That which is handed out; *spec.* (*a*) food or alms given to a beggar at the door; (*b*) a gift of money. orig. *U.S.*

1882 SWEET & KNOX *Texas Siftings* 195 If I can't get a 'hand-out' for it I can at least expatiate on its merits. **1887** M. ROBERTS *Western Avernus* 71 'Bummers' is American for beggars, and a 'hand out' is a portion of food handed out to a bummer or a tramp at the door when he is not asked inside. **1896** *Dialect Notes* I. 418 *Hand-out*, clothes such as a tramp asks for. **1896** ADE *Artie* vi. 50, I see barrel-house boys goin' around for hand outs that was more on the level than you was. **1903** *Daily Chron.* 4 Apr. 5/2 The weekly hand-out for the butcher. **1904** 'O. HENRY' *Trimmed Lamp* (1916) 32 Pretty soon I was in the free-bed line and doing oral fiction for hand-outs among the food bazaars. **1925** W. CATHER *Professor's House* 195 He soon drank up all his wages. When Rapp picked him up there he was living on hand-outs. **1931** C. MASSIE *Confessions of Vagabond* vii. 74 Tramps will often travel a hundred miles to one particular spot where they are sure to get a 'hand-out'. **1946** WODEHOUSE *Joy in Morning* vi. 45, I can well imagine a man of conservative views recoiling from one which might come asking for handouts for the rest of its life. **1959** *Daily Tel.* 27 July 12/6 The report in yesterday's newspapers that Mr. Nixon, on an early morning visit to a Moscow market, had tried to give a 100-rouble note as a 'hand-out' to a worker. **1968** *Globe & Mail* (Toronto) 3 Feb. B4/3 Poor countries realize part of the burden lies on them... They're no longer just looking for handouts.

b. *attrib.*; *spec.* providing light refreshments in a handy form.

1910 *Salt Lake Tribune* 27 Nov. 32/7 On the first floor 'hand-out' luncheons were being served. **1928** F. N. HART *Bellamy Trial* viii. 277, I would take a good walk, get a bite to eat at one of the hand-out places in the vicinity of the station. **1960** *Farmer & Stockbreeder* 22 Mar. 79/3 The future of our industry is going to rely much more on capital grants than on hand-out grants.

2. Matter handed out to or by the newspaper press; more generally, matter handed out from any source to convey information, guidance, etc.

1927 *Amer. Speech* II. 242/1 To get pictures and 'hand-outs', that is, prepared statements given to the press by officials or other prominent persons. **1929** *Literary Digest* 12 Oct. 7/1 Mr. Shearer told..how he gave the newspaper men at Geneva 'hand-outs' to help them in preparing their despatches. **1929** *Sat. Even. Post* 7 Dec. 213/2 We have public-relations experts who do their stuff by means of propaganda in the press and hand-outs to the newspaper boys and girls. **1942** *Punch* 8 July 8/2 An N.C.O. distributes hand-outs in which we are warned that the information given on this course is going to be the most secret. **1942** *Gen* 15 Sept. 24/2 White feather hand-outs..to men and women not in uniform have now reached epidemic proportions. **1945** *Ann. Reg. 1944* 251 The Spanish official 'hand-out'.. was a masterpiece of nebulous verbiage. **1951** *Manch. Guardian Weekly* 23 Nov. 2 Fakes a handout to several of his team. **1958** *Punch* 8 Jan. 84/2 B.O.A.C. hadn't given me a free briefcase full of handouts for nothing. **1959** 'H. HOWARD' *Deadline* viii. 66 A little loose-leaf notebook issued as a free handout by Hopalong Cassidy Enterprises. **1965** *Spectator* 22 Jan. 92/2 The handout is a (necessary) curse of modern political life. It shackles the speaker and bores his audience, but it delights the reporter. **1972** 'G. BLACK' *Bitter Tea* (1973) iv. 63 Not a handout likely to satisfy a newspaper reporter, Inspector.

hand over hand, *adv. phr.* (*a.*) Chiefly *Naut.*)

a. With each hand brought successively over the other, as in climbing up or down a rope, or rapidly hauling at it.

1736 COOKE in *Phil. Trans.* XL. 380 A lusty young Man attempted to go down (hand over hand, as the Workmen call it) by means of a single Rope. **1769** FALCONER *Dict. Marine* (1789), *Main avant*, the order to pull on a rope hand-over-hand. **1857** HUGHES *Tom Brown* II. iv, Up went Martin, hand over hand.

b. *fig.* With continuous advances; said of a vessel, etc. approaching or giving chase to another.

1830 MARRYAT *King's Own* xiii, The frigate was within a mile of the lugger, and coming up with him hand over hand. **1890** BESANT *Armorel of Lyonesse* I. 38 The second boat.. came up hand over hand, rapidly overtaking the first boat.

c. *attrib.* or *adj.* (with hyphens). **hand-over-hand stroke**, a style of swimming in which each arm is alternately brought out of the water from behind and with a circular sweep returned to the water in front. Also as *adv. phr.*

1856 'STONEHENGE' *Brit. Sports* 516/2 The Hand-over-Hand style is a very rapid mode of swimming. **1859** M. THOMSON *Cawnpore* 86 (Hoppe) With mere hand-over-hand labour it was wearisome work. **1872** H. GURR *Art of Swimming* 25 To Swim Hand-over-hand. **1884** *Leisure Hour* June 343/1 A final hand-over-hand climb. **1904** R. THOMAS *Swimming* 139 The hand-over-hand is the most ancient stroke, at all events that is recorded.

Hence **,hand-over-'hander.**

1924 R. CLEMENTS *Gipsy of Horn* vi. 104 Sending the royal yards aloft to a rattling hand-over-hander.

hand over head, *adv. phr.* (*a.*, *sb.*) Now *rare* or *Obs.*

1. *adv. phr.* Precipitately, hastily, rashly, recklessly, without deliberation; †indiscriminately.

c **1440** *Bone Flor.* 475 Than they faght hand ovyr hedd. **1549** LATIMER *7th Serm. bef. Edw. VI* (Arb.) 185 So adict as to take hand ouer hed whatsoeuer they say. **1600** HOLLAND *Livy* XXII. iii. 433 He would..do all in hast, hand over head, without discretion. **1650-3** tr. *Hales' Dissert. de pace* in *Phenix* (1708) II. 369 The ruder sort..shall hand-over-head follow the Authority of others. **1775** MAD. D'ARBLAY *Let. to Crisp* 8 May in *Early Diary*, I don't urge you, hand over head, to have this man at all events. **1839** JAMES *Louis XIV*, III. 240 A lavish guardian, who..spent the estate hand-over-head.

2. *attrib.* or *adj.* (with --). **a.** Precipitate, rash, reckless; †indiscriminate.

a **1693** URQUHART *Rabelais* III. xxiii. 193 In a hand-over-head Confusion. *a* **1825** FORBY *Voy. E. Anglia, Hand-over-head*, thoughtlessly extravagant. **1866** LE FANU *All in Dark* II. xix. 156 They never think what they are doing, girls are so hand-over-head.

b. *Cricket.* Designating a style of bowling (see OVERHAND *a.* 2).

1899 A. LANG in *Daily News* 22 July 4/2 The modern hand-over-head style.

†**3.** Phr. ***to play at hand over head***, to act precipitately or rashly; in quot. app. with allusion to climbing (cf. HAND OVER HAND). *Obs.*

1589 R. HARVEY *Pl. Perc.* 2 Neuer will I..play at hand ouer head so high, but where I may feele sure footing.

'hand-paper.

1. A make of paper having the figure of a hand in the water-mark.

1855 R. HERRING *Paper & P. Making* 79 An open hand with a star at the top, which was in use as early as 1530, probably gave the name to what is still called hand paper.

1868 Brewer *Dict. Phr. & Fab., Hand paper*..so called from its water-mark..☞.

2. Hand-made paper.

handpike: see HANDSPIKE.

'hand-play. *arch.* Interchange of blows in a hand-to-hand encounter: an OE. phrase, revived by some modern writers.

a **1000** *Cædmon's Exod.* 327 Heard handpleȝa. *a* **1050** *O.E. Chron.* an. 1004 (1865) 138 *note*, þæt hi næfre wyrsan handpleȝan on Angel cynne ne ȝemitton. [**1867** Freeman *Norm. Conq.* I. v. 350 They never met in all England with worse handplay.] **1884** *Pall Mall G.* 2 May (Cassell), Memories of Scandinavian glee in the hard hand-play of battle.

'hand-press. A press worked by hand; *esp.* a printing-press so worked, as distinguished from one worked by steam or other power. Hence **hand-pressman.**

1679 Duddell in R. Mansel *Narr. Popish Plot* (1680) 54 Mr. Willoughby did once ask him, if he could make a Hand-Press, in order to Printing. **1840** Lardner *Geom.* 191 With hand-presses..two hundred and fifty copies were obtained per hour from the same types, which required the work and superintendence of two men. **1967** E. Chambers *Photolitho-Offset* i. 3 The operation of printing consists, first, in damping the stone—with a wet sponge in hand-press printing or with a wet roller in power-press work.

'hand-rail. A rail or railing supported on balusters or uprights, as a guard or support to the hand at the edge of a platform, stairs, etc.

1793 Smeaton *Edystone L.* §54 The hand-rail of the balcony. **1865** Mrs. Whitney *Gayworthys* ix. (1879) 92 The shattered gig, thrown on its side, crashed up against the handrail of the bridge. **1892** J. C. Blomfield *Hist. Heyford* 46 A wooden staircase with a single handrail.

So **'hand,railing**, (*a*) the making of handrails; (*b*) = HANDRAIL.

1823 P. Nicholson *Pract. Build.* 204 The whole of the art of hand-railing depends on finding the section of a cylinder. *a* **1833** J. T. Smith *Bk. for a Rainy Day* (1845) 65 It was only enclosed by a low and very old hand-railing. **1888** *Pall Mall G.* 3 Oct. 2/1 Classes for..wood carving, etching, hand railing and chasing and repoussé work.

handraulic (hæn'drɔːlɪk), *a.* [f. HAND *sb.* + HYD)RAULIC *a.*] Of something done by hand rather than by machine. Hence **han'draulically** *adv.*

1948 Partridge *Dict. Forces' Slang* 90 *Handraulic power*, ..with a pun on hydraulic. *Ibid.* 103 *Johnny Armstrong*, the elementary motive power known in the Navy as 'handraulic', used for 'pully-haully' work. **1962** *Times* 4 Aug. 8/6 The ease with which even a battleship could be set in motion 'handraulically' was once vividly demonstrated. *Ibid.* 8/7 'Rolling ship' is more than just a spectacular display of 'handraulic' power. It is a good way of getting refloated. **1963** *Flight International* LXXXIII. 291/3 There are two general approaches to automation of the complex organisation of a traffic control centre: either a complete system is designed and tested more or less in isolation and transferred as an entity from the experimental stage into the working, or the existing 'handraulic' system is improved step-by-step until a clearer picture of an ultimate requirement emerges.

† **'hand-ruff.** *Obs.* [See RUFF.]

1. A ruff worn on the hand or wrist.

1591 Percivall *Sp. Dict., Polaymas*, hose without feete, hand rufs.

2. A game at cards.

1611 Cotgr., *Ronfle*, hand-Ruffe, at Cards..To play at hand-Ruffe.

hand running, *adv. phr. dial.* or *colloq.* Straight on; in continuous succession. Cf. *end-running*.

1828 *Craven Dial.* s.v., 'He did it seven times hand-running.' **1860** in Bartlett *Dict. Amer.* **1877** *N.W. Linc. Gloss.* s.v., 'There was six deaths from th' fever hand-running.' **1885** Howells *Silas Lapham* (1891) II. 70 Irene's been up two nights hand running.

† **handsal**, *v. Obs. rare.* In 3 hondsal. [a. ON. *handsala* to make over by stipulation, f. *handsal* bargain, f. *hand* hand + *selja* to hand over, make over.] *trans.* To hand over.

a **1225** *Juliana* (Royal MS.) 6 Ant ȝettede him his dohter, & wes sone ihondsald al hire unwilles.

'hand-sale. [f. HAND *sb.* + SALE.] See quots. (In some uses a corruption or conjectural explanation of AUNCEL.)

1607–1691 [see AUNCEL]. **1767** Blackstone *Comm.* II. 448 (Seager) Anciently among all the northern nations shaking of hands was held necessary to bind the bargain: a custom which we still retain in many verbal contracts: a sale thus made was called handsale (*venditio per mutuam manuum complexionem*). **1888** Elworthy *W. Somerset Word-bk., Handsale weight*, any article purchased by poising it in the hand so as to judge of the weight without actual weighing, is called *handsale weight*.

'hand-saw. A saw managed by one hand.

1411 *Nottingham Rec.* II. 86, j hondsawe. **1497** *Naval Acc. Hen. VII* (1896) 324 Also for an handesaw price vj^{d}. **1573–80** Baret *Alv.* H 78 A hand sawe..*vne scietie, ou petite scie.* **1596** Shaks. *1 Hen. IV*, II. iv, 187 My Buckler cut through and through, my Sword hackt like a Hand-saw. **1664** Cotton *Scarron.* Pref. (D.), 'Tis all the world to a handsaw but these barbarous Rascals would be so ill-manner'd as to laugh at us as confidently as we do at them. **1798** Greville in *Phil. Trans.* LXXXVIII. 413 A stone-cutter was sawing rock crystal with a hand-saw. **1867** Smyth *Sailor's Word-bk., Hand-saw*, the smallest of the saws used by shipwrights, and used by one hand.

b. In the following, *handsaw* is generally explained as a corruption of *heronshaw* or *hernsew*, dial. *harnsa*, heron. (Other conjectures taking *hawk* in a different sense from the bird have also been made.) No other instances of the phrase, (except as quotations from Shakspere), have been found.

1602 Shaks. *Ham.* II. ii. 367, I am but mad North, North-West: when the Winde is Southerly, I know a Hawke from a Handsaw.

handsbreadth: see HANDBREADTH.

handsel, hansel ('hændsəl, 'hænsəl), *sb.* Forms: 3 **handselne, (handsselle),** 4 **hancel,** 5 **hanselle,** 5–7 **hansell,** 6 **hansselle,** 6–7 **handsell,** 6– **hansel, handsel.** [The form corresponds to OE. *handselen* glossed 'mancipatio' (giving into the hands of another), or to ON. *handsal*, 'giving of the hand, promise or bargain confirmed by joining or shaking hands', also, in same sense, *handseld*; cf. OSw. *handsal*, Sw. *handsöl* money, etc. handed over to any one, gratuity, 'tip'. But though there are some quotations (sense 2 b) which may have the simple sense of 'gift', the general notions of 'omen, gift to bring good luck, luck-penny, auspicious inauguration or first use', which run through the English uses of the word, are not accounted for by the sense of these OE. and ON. words. Cf. however Da. *handsel* 'handsel, earnest-money', also Ger. *handgeld*, *handgift*, *handkauf*, and esp. F. *étrenne*, OF. *estreine*, the senses of which are exactly parallel to our 2, 3, 4.

c **1050** *Voc.* in Wr.-Wülcker 449/29 *Mancipatio*, handselen.]

† **1.** Lucky prognostic, omen, presage, augury; token or omen of good luck. *Obs.*

c **1200** *Vices & Virtues* 29 Sum oðer dwel hie drieð, and seggeð þat he nafde naht gode han(d)sselle ðe him þat sealde. *c* **1200** *Trin. Coll. Hom.* 11 Warienge and handselne and time and hwate and fele swilche deueles craftes. **1303** R. Brunne *Handl. Synne* 369 Of hancel y can no skylle also, Hyt ys nouȝt to beleve þarto..For many hauyn glade hancel at þe morw And to hem or euyn comþ mochyl sorw. *c* **1475** *Partenay* 4885 Where the Erle shold haue ill hansell anon. **1500** *Ortus Vocab.*, Strena est bona sors, *Anglice* hansell. **1573** Twyne *Æneid* x. Ee ij, Æneas first the rusticke sort sets on For happy hansils sake [*omen pugnæ*]. **1579–80** North *Plutarch* To Rdr. (1676) Av b, Among the cries of good handsell [Amyot, *cris d'heureux presage*] and the wishes of good luck..one was; Happier be thou than Augustus. **1681** Glanvill *Sadducismus* II. (1726) 305 He had it [a pewter dish] from Alice Duke for good Handsel for his Daughter, who had lately lain in.

2. A gift or present (expressive of good wishes) at the beginning of a new year, or on entering upon any new condition, situation, or circumstances, the donning of new clothes, etc.; originally, deemed to be auspicious, or to ensure good luck for the new year, etc. [= L. *strena*, F. *étrenne.*]

13.. *Gaw. & Gr. Knt.* 66 Syþen riche forth runnen to reche honde-selle, Ȝeȝed ȝeres ȝiftes on hiȝ, ȝelde hem bi hond. *Ibid.* 491 This hanselle hatz Arthur of auenturus on fyrst, In ȝonge ȝer. **1375** Barbour *Bruce* v. 120 Sic hansell to the folk gaf he Richt in the first begynnyng, Newly at his ariwyng. **1500–20** Dunbar *New Year's Gift to King* iii, God giue the guid prosperitie..In hansell of this guid new ȝeir. *c* **1530** in *Pol. Rel. & L. Poems* 38 Iuellis pricious cane y non fynde..To sende you..þis newe yeres morowe, Wher-for lucke and good hansselle My herte y sende you. *c* **1532** Dewes *Introd. Fr.* in *Palsgr.* 945 To geve the first hansel, *estrinér.* **1650** Fuller *Pisgah* II. ix. 189 The Syrian Kings civilly tendered their service, to give it as good handsell to so good a work. **1723** De Foe *Col. Jack* (1840) 22 As it was the first time..he took *1l.* 5*s.* from my part, and told me I should give him that for handsel. **1784** Burns '*There was a lad*' ii, 'Twas then a blast o' Janwar' win' Blew hansel in on Robin. **1831** Carlyle *Sart. Res.* I. ix, Neighbour after neighbour gave thee as handsel, silver or copper coins. **1856** Ld. Cockburn *Mem.* ii. (1874) 95 About the New Year..every child had got its handsel, and every farthing of every handsel was spent there. **1883** *Longm. Mag.* Apr. 656 It was the immemorial custom for servants to receive handsel or first gifts of the year on this day.

† **b.** Gift, present, given on any occasion; reward.

1390 Gower *Conf.* II. 373 If I might ought of love take, Such hansel have I nought forsake. **1399** Langl. *Rich. Redeles* IV. 91 Some..were be-hote hansell if þey helpe wold To be seruyd sekirly of þe same siluere. **1513** Douglas *Æneis* IX. x. 104 Sik bodword heir the twys takyn Troianis Sendis for hansell to Rutilianis.

† **c.** *ironically.* A 'dressing' given or received.

1470–85 Malory *Arthur* VIII. xvi, Anon with lytel myght he was leyd to the erthe, And as I trowe sayd sir Sagramore ye shal haue the same handsel that he hadde. **1583** Rich *Phylotus & Emelia* (1835) 29 That your daughter should bestowe suche hansell on her housband as she hath alreadie bestowed vpon me.

3. A first instalment of payment; earnest money; the first money taken by a trader in the morning, a luck-penny; anything given or taken as an omen, earnest, or pledge of what is to follow.

[*a* **1400** *Sir Beues* 3109 (MS. A.) Her þow hauest liþer haunsel, A worse þe be-tide schel.] **1569** Golding *Heminges Post.* Ded. 4 Accept this Booke as a first hansell. **1571** Campion *Hist. Irel.* i. (1633) 60 Take this..but for hansell, the gaine is to come. **1597** Hooker *Eccl. Pol.* v. lvi §11 The apostles terme it sometime..the pledge of our heauenly inheritance, sometime the hansell or earnest of that which is to come. **1614** B. Jonson *Barth. Fair* II. ii, Bring him a sixe penny bottle of Ale; they say, a fooles handsell is lucky. **1630** Massinger *Renegado* I. iii, Nothing, sir—but pray Your worship to give me hansell. **1787** Grose *Prov. Gloss.* Superstitions 64 It is a common practice among the lower class of hucksters, pedlars, or dealers..on receiving the price of the first goods sold that day, which they call hansel, to spit on the money, as they term it, for good luck. **1809** R. Langford *Introd. Trade* 132 *Hansel*, a small sum on account, confirming the agreement. **1851** Mayhew *Lond. Labour* I. 369 'Who'll give me a handsel—who'll give me a handsel?'

4. The first use, experience, trial, proof, or specimen of anything; first taste, foretaste, first fruits: often with the notion of its being auspicious of what is to follow.

1573 Twyne *Æneid* XI. Gg iij, Here now remaine the spoiles, and hansell, of the hautie kinge [*de rege superbo Primitiæ*] Mezentius loe here lies. **1589** Greene *Menaphon* (Arb.) 71 Had not Samela passed by..he should like inough haue had first handsell of our new Shepheards sheepehooke. **1601** Holland *Pliny* II. 504 But this Perillus was the first himselfe that gaue the hansell to the engine of his own inuention. **1639** Horn & Rob. *Gate Lang. Unl.* lxi. §655 That a novice, or young beginner, which sets up a trade, may give a taste, hansell or tryall of his skill to the Masters of the Company. **1730** Fielding *Rape upon Rape* III. iii, I have not seen one Prisoner brought in for a Rape this Fortnight, except your Honour. I hope your handsel will be lucky. **1837** Lockhart *Scott* Oct. an. 1818 Such was the handsel, for Scott protested against its being considered as the house heating of the new Abbotsford. **1868** Atkinson *Cleveland Gloss., Handsel, hansel*..the first use of anything, from a shop to a new implement, of whatever kind.

5. *attrib.* and *Comb.* **handsel Monday**, the first Monday of the year (usually according to Old Style), on which New Year's handsel is given. (*Sc.*)

1585 Higins tr. *Junius' Nomenclator* 80 The first bridall banket after the wedding daye: the good handzell feast. **1788** Burns '*I'll kiss thee yet*' ii, Young Kings upon their hansel throne, Are no sae blest as I am, O! **1793** *Statist. Acc. Scotl.* V. 66 Besides the stated fees, the master [of the parochial school] receives some small gratuity, generally 2*d.* or 3*d.* from each scholar on handsel Monday. **1795** *Ibid.* XV. 201 *note*, On the evening of Handsel Monday, as it is called.. some of his neighbours came to make merry with him. **1815** Scott *Guy M.* xxxii, Grizy has..maybe a bit compliment at Hansel Monanday. **1825** Brockett *N.C. Gloss., Hansel-Monday*, the first Monday in the New Year, when it is customary to make children and servants a present.

handsel, *v.* [f. HANDSEL *sb.*]

1. *trans.* To give handsel to (a person); to present with, give, or offer, something auspicious at the commencement of the year or day, the beginning of an enterprise, etc.; to inaugurate the new year to (any one) with gifts, or the day to (a dealer) by being his first customer; to present with earnest-money or a luck-penny in auspication of an engagement or bargain.

c **1430** *Pilgr. Lyf. Manhode* II. cxviii. (1869) 119 It [a horn] hath be maad euere sithe j was born. And of him I was hanselled [*de li je fu estrenée*]. **1483** *Cath. Angl.* 174/1 To Hanselle, *strenare, arrare.* **1530** Palsgr. 578/2, I hansell one, I gyve him money in a mornyng for suche wares as he selleth, *je estrene.* **1583** Stocker *Hist. Civ. Warres Lowe C.* I. 153 Being in this sort hanseled with a newyeeres gift. **1611** Cotgr., *Estrener*, to handsell, or bestow a New-yeares gift on. *c* **1645** Howell *Lett.* (1650) II. Jan. 1641 *The Vote*, Then let me something bring May hansell the New-Year to Charles my King. *Mod. Sc.* When I was at school, the custom of handselling the master on Handsel Monday still flourished in Scotland.

2. To inaugurate with some ceremony or observance of an auspicious nature; to auspicate.

1600–62 I. T. *Grim the Collier* II. in Hazl. *Dodsley* VIII. 426 Let's in, and handsel our new mansion-house With a carousing round of Spanish wine. **1636** Fitz-Geffray *Holy Transport.* (1881) 189 Who com'st from heauen to blisse the earth, To handsel with thy bloud thy blessed birth. **1645** Rutherford *Tryal & Tri. of Faith* (1845) 207 That they may handsel the new throne with acts of mercy. **1661** Morgan *Sph. Gentry* III. ix. 101 Romulus having hanselled it with his brother's blood made it an asylum for all commers. **1677** W. Hubbard *Narrative* II. (1865) 44 Capt. Samuel Holioke handseled his Office with the Slaughter of four or five of the Enemy. **1746** Mrs. Delany *Let. to Mrs. Dewes* in *Life & Corr.* 437 Having ordered Mr. Langhorne to send in a little wine to your cellar at Welsbourne, by way of hanselling a new place. **1881** Besant & Rice *10 Years' Tenant*, etc. *Sweet Nelly* I. 200 I wanted to present her with something to hansel friendship.

b. *fig.* (*ironical*).

1583 Stocker *Hist. Civ. Warres Lowe C.* II. 52 He was by and by handsled with a Pistoll. **1611** Speed *Hist. Gt. Brit.* IX. xxiv. 274 The Gallies were assayled by Sir John Winkefield, who with his small ships so hanselled their sides, as they were forced to creepe by the Shore. **1632** Brome *Court Beggar* II. i. Wks. 1873 I. 200 Take heede I begin not now, and handsell your Ladies house..and your gentle-woman's presence here with a fist about your eares. **1699** Farquhar *Constant Couple* III. v, I'll hansel his woman's clothes for him!

3. To inaugurate the use of; to use for the first time; to be the first to test, try, prove, taste.

1605 Chapman, etc. *Eastward Ho* II. i, My lady..is so ravished with desire to hansel her new coach. **1612** T. Taylor *Comm. Titus* i. 8 Haman shall hansell his owne gallowes. **1746** *Tom Thumb's Trav. Eng. & Wales* 104 The Earl of Morton, who erected the Scotch Maiden, was himself the first who hansell'd it. **1841** Brewster *Mart. Sc.*

III. iii. (1856) 202 However, we hanselled your cup. **1873** F. HALL *Mod. Eng.* ii. 35 No expression was ever yet used which some one had not to handsel. **1892** DOBSON *18th C. Vignettes* 34 Joseph Warton had handselled them [Spence's unpublished 'Anecdotes'] for his 'Essay on Pope.'

Hence '**handselling** *vbl. sb.*

1885 BLACK *White Heather* iii, A more substantial hand-selling of good luck.

hand-seller, handseller. [f. HAND *sb.* + SELL *v.*: app. not from *handsel.*] **a.** An itinerant auctioneer, who sells by 'Dutch auction'; a 'cheap Jack'. **b.** A street-dealer who carries his stock-in trade in a basket, tray, or the like.

1851 MAYHEW *Lond. Labour* I. 328 In the provinces, and in Scotland, there may be 100 'cheap Johns', or, as they term themselves, 'Han-sellers'. *Ibid.* 354 The sellers of tins, who carry them under their arms, or in any way.. apart from the use of a vehicle, are known as *hand-sellers*. The word *hand-seller* is construed by the street-traders as meaning literally *hand seller*, that is to say, a *seller* of things held or carried in the *hand*. **1865** *Daily Tel.* 21 Dec. 5/2 A glib 'hand-seller'.. mounted on his rostrum, dilates upon the contents of the volumes which he has to sell. **1879** *Era* 6 Dec., Wanted, One First-class Handseller and Planksman. Apply to Mr. T. H., Auction Vans, Chipping-Norton.

So **hand-selling**.

1851 MAYHEW *Lond. Labour* I. 329 Sometimes its a better game than 'han-selling'. **1879** T. DIXON in W. B. Scott *Autobiog. Notes* II. 267–8 There is a plan of dealing in books called hand-selling, which is selling by a kind of auction. The upset price.. is gradually reduced, till somebody takes it.

† '**handsenyie.** *Obs.* Also **and-**. Sc. form of ENSIGN *sb.*, in various senses.

1572 *Hist. Jas. VI* (1825) 139 Capten James Bruce.. Johne Robesoun, in Braydwodside, his andsenyé. *a* **1575** *Diurn. Occurr.* (Bannatyne) 330 Handsenyie of Scotland.. wes set on the castell heid of Edinburgh. **1591** R. BRUCE *Eleven Serm.* P viij a (Jam.), He gaue them handseinyeis of his visible presence, as was the tabernacle, the ark. *a* **1605** MONTGOMERIE *Poems* lix. 8 Funerall mark and handsenȝie.

† '**handservant.** *Obs.* [Cf. *handmaid.*] A servant attending upon one; an attendant.

1578 *Chr. Prayers* in *Priv. Prayers* (1851) 443 The devil, and his handservant the world.

handset ('hændsɛt). Also **hand-set.** [HAND *sb.* + SET *sb.*[2]] A telephone transmitter and receiver combined in a single instrument.

[**1914** SMITH & CAMPBELL *Automatic Teleph.* vi. 131 The telephone instrument follows the general form which is so popular on the Continent, making large use of the combined transmitter and receiver, sometimes known as the hand microphone set.] **1930** *Electr. Commun.* VIII. 265/2 The tendency towards more comfortable and convenient apparatus has been evidenced.. finally by the development of handsets, or as they are sometimes called, 'micro-telephones'. **1955** 'N. SHUTE' *Requiem for Wren* 283 They repeated it and booked the call, and I put down the handset. **1962** A. NISBETT *Technique Sound Studio* 176 For telephones a standard hand-set can be similarly adapted, so that the bell may be worked by a press-button. **1972** C. DRUMMOND *Death at Bar* v. 127 There was a call box... He had to wait ten minutes while a young citizen.. quacked into the handset.

'**handshake,** *sb.* **a.** A shake of the hand: cf. HAND-SHAKING.

1873 TRISTRAM *Moab* xviii. 344, I gave him a hearty hand-shake. **1878** BROWNING *Poets Croisic* 130 Let me return your handshake!

b. A gift of money.

1960, etc. [see *golden handshake*]. **1968** *Times* 3 July 26/6 (*headline*) Dockers told of handshake. *Ibid.*, An offer of bigger 'golden handshakes'. **1971** *Financial Mail* (Johannesburg) 26 Feb. 649/2 (Advt.), However you invest with the United, you get a handsome handshake.

handshake ('hændʃeɪk), *v.* [Back-formation from HAND-SHAKING.] *intr.* To shake hands. So '**hand,shaker**.

1898 H. JAMES *Two Magics* 8 We handshook and 'candlestuck', as somebody said, and went to bed. **1905** *Westm. Gaz.* 2 Nov. 12/1 As the line moves forward each hand-shaker is steadily pushed along. **1928** *Daily Express* 28 Aug. 8/3 Hearty handshakers. **1940** *Amer. Speech* XV. 211/2 Those who try to get promotions by pull with officers are called handshakers or suction kids. **1964** G. B. SCHALLER *Year of Gorilla* x. 240 The Belgians are the most confirmed handshakers I have ever met.

'**hand-'shaking.** Shaking of hands in greeting or leave-taking.

1805 WORDSW. *Waggoner* III. 45 What tears of rapture, what vow-making, Profound entreaties, and hand-shaking! **1859** GEO. ELIOT *A. Bede* 50 That pleasant confusion of laughing interjections, and hand-shakings, and 'How are you's'. **1883** BLACK *Shandon Bells* xxx, There was much hand-shaking on the steps of the Abercorn Club. **1964** ROSE & ZIMAN *Camford Observed* vii. 129 *Handshaking*: at Oxford the Master of a College interviews every undergraduate at the end of each term and hears a report on his progress by his Tutor. **1965** *Listener* 16 Sept. 425/2 A hand-shaking tour of the Soviet Union.

† '**handsmooth,** *a.* and *adv.* *Obs.* exc. *dial.*

A. *adj.* Level or flat as if smoothed with the hand; smooth to the hand.

1530 PALSGR. 452/2, I beate downe to the grounde, or I beate down hande smothe, *je arrase*. This castell was beate downe hande smothe with ordonaunce. **1558** MORWYNG *Ben Gorion* (1567) 6 Iudas.. spedely set upon them, beat them downe handsmoth. **1590** T. WATSON *Death Sir F. Walsingham* 233 Poems (Arb.) 165 O heards and tender flocks, o handsmooth plains. *a* **1603** T. CARTWRIGHT *Confut. Rhem. N.T.* (1618) 595 This Epistle.. beateth it down as hand-smooth as it doth the sacrifices.

b. *fig.* Flat, plat, unqualified.

1612 W. SCLATER *Minister's Portion* Ep. Ded., Having no such evidence.. to carry away so handsmooth a conclusion.

B. *adv.* Flatly; downright; without check, interruption, or qualification.

1600 ABP. ABBOT *Exp. Jonah* 500 He fretteth and chafeth hand-smooth with the Lord. **1610** HEALEY *St. Aug. Citie of God* 768 This they avouch, hand-smooth. **1631** *Celestina* XI. 130 Shee.. will seaze hand-smooth on a whole drove of us at once. **1659** H. MORE *Immort. Soul* II. xvii. (1662) 137 All things goe on hand-smooth for it, without any check or stop. **1682** MRS. BEHN *City Heiress* III. i, Let 'em accuse me if they please, I come off hand-smooth with *Ignoramus*. *a* **1825** FORBY *Voc. E. Anglia*, *Hand-smooth*, uninterruptedly, without obstacle; also entirely.. 'He ate it up handsmooth'.

handsome (hæn(d)səm), *a.* (*adv.*) Forms: 5 **hondsom**, 5–6 **handsum**, 5–8 **handsom**, 6 **handesom(e**, **hansum**, 6–7 **hansom(e**, 6– **handsome.** [Known only from 15th c., f. HAND *sb.* + -SOME: cf. *toothsome*. Cf. early mod. (16th c.) Ger. *handsam*, Ger. dial. and EFris. *handsam*, early mod. Du. *handsaem*, Du. *handzaam*, all in sense 1.]

A. *adj.* † **1. a.** Easy to handle or manipulate, or to wield, deal with, or use in any way. *Obs.*

c **1435** *Torr. Portugal* 1301 Sir Torrent gaderid good cobled stonys, Good and handsom ffor the nonys. *c* **1440** *Promp. Parv.* 225/2 Handsum, or esy to hond werke ..(*Pynson* hansum), *manualis*. *c* **1450** LONELICH *Grail* xiv. 695 Lyghtere and more hondsom it was Thanne his owen [ax]. **1551** ROBINSON tr. *More's Utop.* II. (1895) 262 Both easy to be caried, and handsome to be moued. **1598** GRENEWEY *Tacitus' Ann.* II. iv. 37 Neither were the barbarous huge targets, and long pikes so handsome, among trees and low shrubs, as darts and swords.

† **b.** Handy, ready at hand, convenient, suitable. *Obs.* or *dial.*

1530 TINDALE *Prol. Lev.* in *Doct. Treat.* (1848) 428 Beware of allegories; for there is not a more handsome or apt thing to beguile withal than an allegory. **1545** RAYNOLD *Byrth Mankynde* (1564) 93 b, Whiche of these partes shall seeme moste commodious and handsome to take it out by. **1577** B. GOOGE *Heresbach's Husb.* IV. (1586) 183 b, Carry all your Coames into some handsome place, where you meane to make your Honie. **1577** *St. Aug. Manual* Pref., A short and handsome abridgement of the chosen sayinges of the holy fathers. **1600** HOLLAND *Livy* XXV. xxix. 571 Whatsoeuer came next to their hands, and lay handsome for them, they rifled. **1678** CUDWORTH *Intell. Syst.* 505 *Δίκαιον* quasi *διᾳιὸν*; the Letter Cappa, being only taken in for the more handsom pronunciation. **1807** PIKE *Sources Mississ.* (1810) 7 On the west shore, there is a very handsome situation for a garrison. **1851** CARLYLE *Sterling* III. iii. (1872) 184 A handsome shelter for the next two years.

2. a. Of action, speech, etc.: Appropriate, apt, dexterous, clever, happy: in reference to language, sometimes implying gracefulness of style (cf. 3, 6). ? *Obs.* exc. *U.S.*

1563–87 FOXE *A. & M.* (1596) 9/2 He wrote a sharpe and an handsome letter to Celestinus. **1642** ROGERS *Naaman* 239 An handsome sudden evasion. **1652–62** HEYLIN *Cosmogr.* I. (1682) 121 They fell upon this handsom project. **1690** LUTTRELL *Brief Rel.* (1857) II. 106 Mr. Recorder in a handsome speech congratulated the King on his happy successe in Ireland. **1712** STEELE *Spect.* No. 455 ¶2 Close Reasoning, and handsome Argumentation. **1749** FIELDING *Tom Jones* XV. xi, He determined to quit her, if he could but find a handsome pretence. **1837** HT. MARTINEAU *Soc. Amer.* III. 83 They use the word 'handsome' much more extensively than we do: saying that Webster made a handsome speech in the Senate.

b. Of an agent: Apt, skilled, clever. *Obs.* exc. in *U.S.*, or as associated with other senses.

1547 SALESBURY *Welsh Dict.*, *Hylaw*, handsome. **1561** T. NORTON *Calvin's Inst.* IV. xx. (1634) 735 O handsome expositors! **1570** LEVINS *Manip.* 162/11 Handsome, *scitus*. **1574** HELLOWES *Gueuara's Fam. Ep.* (1577) 83 You would haue bene more handsome to colour Cordouan skinnes, then to haue written processe. *a* **1631** DRAYTON *Moon-Calf* (R.), If some handsome players would it take, It (sure) a pretty interlude would make. **18..** *Presbyterian* (*Americanisms*), A writer is styled 'a very handsome author', meaning a good and clever one, and quite irrespective of his appearance, which may be the reverse of comely. **1883** *Standard* 22 Feb. 3/7 The bitch was a most handsome winner when she killed.

† **3.** Proper, fitting, seemly, becoming, decent.

1597 HOOKER *Eccl. Pol.* V. xxix. §3 Came to Church in hansome holiday apparell. **1610** BARROUGH *Meth. Physick* V. xvi. (1639) 304 Let all things be clean and handsome about him. **1624** FLETCHER *Rule a Wife* III. i, Go get you handsom. **1654** in *Whitlock's Zootomia* To Author A iv b, Wit, Learning, and Variety of matter, put into a handsom Dresse.

4. a. Of fair size or amount; 'decent', fair, considerable, moderately large. Now *unusual*.

1577 B. GOOGE *Heresbach's Husb.* II. (1586) 66 b, So groweth it to a handsome height, meete to shadowe hearbes. *a* **1649** WINTHROP *New Eng.* (1825) I. 7 The wind at E. and by N. a handsome gale with fair weather. **1670** NARBOROUGH *Jrnl.* in *Acc. Sev. Late Voy.* I. (1711) 31 Cut the Bodies in good handsome pieces. **1725** BRADLEY *Fam. Dict.* s.v. *Age*, Two handsome Glasses of this Water may be drank every Morning fasting. *c* **1730** BURT *Lett. N. Scotl.* (1818) I. 164 They export pretty handsome quantities of pickled salmon. **1812** BRACKENRIDGE *Jrnl.* in *Views Louisiana* (1814) 231 It continues a handsome width. **1851** CARLYLE *Sterling* I. iii. (1872) 14 The soil, everywhere of handsome depth.

b. Of a sum of money, a fortune, a gift, etc.: Considerable. Now (by association with 5) in stronger sense: Ample, generous, liberal, munificent.

1577 B. GOOGE *Heresbach's Husb.* I. (1586) 10 b, I graunt I coulde make a good handsome gayne of them. **1660** F. BROOKE tr. *Le Blanc's Trav.* 270 Having.. given him a handsome piece of money to unlock his secret. **1788** PRIESTLEY *Lect. Hist.* V. liii. 410 To get handsome fortunes by small profits, and large dealings. **1811** *Sporting Mag.* XXXVIII. 210 By a *handsome* price he meant a good price. **1835** MARRYAT *Jac. Faithf.* xxxix, She has been told that he has left you something handsome. **1855** THACKERAY *Rose & Ring* vii, King Valeroso also sent Sir Tomaso.. a handsome order for money. **1881** *Daily Tel.* 28 Jan., His pay.. very much handsomer than his brother Jack gets.

c. Humorously, of a reproof or punishment: Ample, strong, severe, 'fine'.

1726 *Adv. Capt. R. Boyle* 131 And reproach'd me in a handsome Manner. **1796** GROSE *Dict. Vulg. Tongue*, *Handsome Reward*, This, in advertisements, means a horse-whipping. **1824** SCOTT *St. Ronan's* xi, Finding the cowboy, with a shirt about him.. and treating him to a handsome drubbing.

5. a. Of conduct, etc.: Fitting, seemly, becoming; courteous, gracious, polite. Now in stronger sense, denoting a quality that evokes moral admiration (cf. sense 6): Generous, magnanimous.

1621 FLETCHER *Pilgrim* IV. ii, Was it fair play? did it appear to you handsome? **1673** S. C. *Rules of Civility* 56 Because it is not so handsom to sit full in his face, it will be esteemed good Breeding, if he place himself *en profile* or something side ways. **1693–4** GIBSON in *Lett. Lit. Men* (Camden) 219 'Twill be handsome for me first to apply myself to the Provost, for fear it should otherwise be not well taken. **1782** OPIE in J. J. Rogers *Opie & Wks.* (1878) 24, I was introduced to Sir Josh. who said many handsome things of me both to my face and behind my back. **1830** J. H. MONK *Bentley* 115 Through this handsome conduct of the dean the dispute was amicably settled. **1863** MRS. C. CLARKE *Shaks. Char.* vi. 142 In the sequel, however, Ford does make a handsome atonement.

b. *spec.* Of military exploits: Soldierly, gallant, brave, admirable. *Obs.* or *arch.*

1665 MANLEY *Grotius' Low C. Warres* 293 Now was a very handsom Sally made out of Coevorden. **1726** SHELVOCKE *Voy. round World* (1757) 454 [The] second lieutenant, who made a handsom resistance. **1812** WELLINGTON *Disp.* 4 Aug. in *Examiner* 31 Aug. 552/2, I enclose.. [a] report of a very handsome affair with the enemy's cavalry.

6. a. Having a fine form or figure (usually in conjunction with full size or stateliness); 'beautiful with dignity' (J.) 'fine'. (The prevailing current sense.)

1590 SPENSER *F.Q.* II. iv. 3 A handsom stripling. **1601** R. JOHNSON *Kingd. & Commw.* (1603) 69 The streetes.. more neate and handsome then those of Italy. **1604** SHAKS. *Oth.* IV. iii. 37 This Lodouico is a proper man.. A very handsome man. **1622** WITHER *Mistr. Philar.* Wks. (1633) 710 Who could dote on thing so common As meer outward handsome Woman? **1662** J. DAVIES tr. *Olearius' Voy. Ambass.* 17 Young Lords, very handsome, both as to Face and Body. **1717** LADY M. W. MONTAGU *Let. to C'tess Mar* 10 Mar., She appeared to me handsomer than before. **1783** COWPER *Lett.* 10 Nov., I can look at.. a handsome tree, every day of my life with new pleasure. **1841** JAMES *Brigand* ii, He was one of the handsomest and most splendid Cavaliers of his day. **1849** —— *Woodman* ii, A large and handsome room, lined entirely with beautiful carved oak. **1846** J. BAXTER *Libr. Pract. Agric.* (ed. 4) I. 281 New and vigorous shoots, producing much better and handsomer plants. **1855** THACKERAY *Rose & Ring* xvii, She is very pretty, but not so *extraordinarily* handsome.

b. Used, sometimes ironically, to address, or as a designation of, a handsome person. *colloq.* (orig. *U.S.*).

1921 J. DOS PASSOS *Three Soldiers* (1922) VI. ii. 334 'Teach him how to salute,' the officer had said and Hand-some had stepped up to him and hit him. **1940** S. LEWIS *Bethel Merriday* i. 13 'Hya, Toots. Hya, handsome,' said her brother. **1945** E. WAUGH *Brideshead Revisited* I. v. 104 Be a sport, handsome: no one's seen anything but you. **1963** 'H. CALVIN' *It's Different Abroad* ii. 7 Laurent turned to him and sneered. 'Okay, handsome,' he said.

B. *adv.* = HANDSOMELY (in various senses). Now only in vulgar use, exc. in proverb ***handsome is as*** (also ***that***) ***handsome does***.

? *a* **1400** *Morte Arth.* 2128 Thowe arte to hye by þe halfe, I hete þe in trouthe! Thowe salle be handsomere hye, with þe helpe of my Lorde! **1591** *Troub. Raigne K. John* (1611) 53 This geere doth cotton hansome, That couetousnesse so cunningly must pay the lechers ransome. **1597** SHAKS. *2 Hen. IV*, II. iv. 303 Proue that euer I dresse my selfe handsome, till thy returne. **1766** GOLDSM. *Vic. W.* i, She would answer, 'they are as Heaven made them—handsome enough, if they be good enough; for handsome is that handsome does'. **1796** GROSE *Dict. Vulg. Tongue* s.v., Handsome is that handsome does; a proverb frequently cited by ugly women. **1840** DICKENS *Barn. Rudge* i, Do you suppose Highwaymen don't dress handsomer than that? **1847** F. A. DURIVAGE in W. T. Porter *Quarter Race in Kentucky* 48 She aint no Wenus, Sir,.. but handsome is as handsome does. **1950** A. CHRISTIE *Murder is Announced* xiii. 139 'Such a handsome young man.'.. 'Handsome is as handsome does... Much too fond of poking fun at people.' **1963** *Times* 5 June 4/3 But handsome is as handsome does, and his job was done when he was caught off the last ball, when Kent still had a wicket to spare. **1970** G. GREER *Female Eunuch* 56 Men were slipping into relative anonymity and 'handsome is as handsome does'.

† '**handsome,** *v.* *Obs.* [f. prec. adj.] *trans.* To make handsome (in various senses); to fit, adapt; to make seemly or becoming, bring to a proper condition (also with *up*); to beautify, adorn.

1555 W. WATERMAN *Fardle Facions* App. 324 Let the ploughe be handesomed for them also, acording to their sortes. **1593** DONNE *Sat.* i, Him.. all repute For his device, in handsoming a suit [of clothes].. to have the best conceit. **1600** SURFLET *Countrie Farme* I. x. 48 He shall ouerlooke his warren to stoare it a new, and to handsome vp the earths. **1657** R. LIGON *Barbadoes* (1673) 42 Some of the Planters that meant to handsom their houses, were minded to send for gilt leather, and hang their rooms with that.

handsomeish ('hænsəmɪʃ), *a. nonce-wd.* [f. as prec. + -ISH.] Somewhat handsome.

1754 RICHARDSON *Grandison* (1811) VI. 339 He is a fine, jolly, hearty, handsomeish man.

handsomely ('hænsəmlɪ), *adv.* [f. as prec. + -LY[2].] In a handsome manner.

†**1.** Conveniently, handily, readily. *Obs.*

1547-64 BAULDWIN *Mor. Philos.* (ed. Palfr.) 77 Heauy things shall little grieve him that can handsomely bear them. **1577** B. GOOGE *Heresbach's Husb.* IV. (1586) 173 If you can handsomely convey them, it is best to bring from the Sea, little Rockes with the Weedes and all uppon them. **1653** GODDARD *Let.* 28 July in *Mert. Reg.* II. 396, I finde that I cannot handsomely or indeed without great preiudice.. come to Oxford. **1669** SHADWELL *Royal Shepherdess* IV. Wks. 1720 I. 280 If thou canst handsomely, do it, and be back early in the morning.

†**2.** Fitly, appropriately, aptly. *Obs.*

1553 T. WILSON *Rhet.* (1580) 6 Though he can handsomely sette them together. **1561** T. NORTON *Calvin's Inst.* III. 202 How much more fitly and more handesomely might these thinges be applied by way of allegorie. **1635-56** COWLEY *Davideis* IV. *note* 13 The 20 years of the Arks abiding at Curiath-jearim will be handsomely made up. **1693** SALMON *Bates' Dispens.* II. (1713) 606 Heterogenous Bodies, which can never handsomly mix together. **1711** ADDISON *Spect.* No. 13 ¶4 He says very handsomly.. that he does not act for gain.

†**3.** Skillfully, dexterously, cleverly. *Obs,*

1551 ROBINSON tr. *More's Utop.* I. (1895) 100 To handle the matter wyttelye and handesomelye for the purpose. **1624** T. SCOTT *2nd Pt. Vox Pop.* 57, I have known some under the cullour of selling Tobacco have carried Letters handsomly, privily in the balls or roules. **1648** GAGE *West Ind.* 26 The cards were handsomely shuffled. **1655** FULLER *Ch. Hist.* I. i. §7 The Iesuite handsomely answers, That Peter was then probably from home.

b. Carefully; without haste, gently, gradually. Now only *Naut.* (Cf. CANNILY.)

1550 COVERDALE *Spir. Perle* xxii. (1588) 212 He hath a sure eie to the stern to rule that as handsomly and cunningly as he can. **1570** DEE *Math. Pref.* 31 Poure in water, handsomly. **1658** ROWLAND *Moufet's Theat. Ins.* 915 Lay it handsomely and as closely on as the sick can endure it. **1769** FALCONER *Dict. Marine* (1789), *Lower handsomely!* and *lower cheerly!* are opposed to each other, the former being the order to lower gradually, and the latter to lower expeditiously. **1832** MARRYAT *N. Forster* v, Ease off the main sheet, handsomely my lad—not too much. **1867** SMYTH *Sailor's Word-bk., Handsomely,* signifies steadily or leisurely; as 'lower away handsomely' when required to be done gradually and carefully. The term 'handsomely' repeated, implies 'have a care; not so fast; tenderly'.

4. With becoming or elegant action; in good style, neatly, elegantly. Now *rare.*

1582 MUNDAY *Eng. Rom. Life* in *Harl. Misc.* (Malh.) II. 179 After they are risen, they fold vp theyr sheetes handsomelie. **1684** BUNYAN *Pilgr.* II. 161 The girl was to be commended, for she answered the Musick hansomely. *a* **1754** FIELDING *Journey* I. xxv, Instruct a child in the science of coming handsomely into a room. **1809** M. CUTLER in *Life Jrnls. & Corr.* (1888) II. 341 Dr. Griffin preached a good sermon, handsomely delivered. **1870** *Daily News* 16 Apr., In the end, Kirkup threw his man handsomely.

b. Ironically, in reference to reproof or punishment: Severely, 'finely', 'in fine style'.

1553 T. WILSON *Rhet.* 2 Phavorinus the Philosophier did hit a yong man over the thumbes very handsomely. **1628** SHIRLEY *Witty Fair One* I. iii, You take pains to whip me so handsomely. **1716** LADY M. W. MONTAGU *Let. to C'tess Mar* 3 Aug., We were all Sunday night tossed very handsomely. **1838** DICKENS *Nich. Nick.* xxvii, The Frenchman who cleaned you out so handsomely last night.

5. In accordance with what is becoming in conduct; courteously, graciously; decently; now in stronger sense, Generously, magnanimously.

1548 UDALL *Erasm. Par. Luke* vi. 74 That it maie please God handsomly and fauourably to send the good aide of his spirite. **1660** F. BROOKE tr. *Le Blanc's Trav.* 21 He maintained them handsomely, and near his person. **1708** N. FROWDE *Life Adv. Voy.* (1773) 120 If I could handsomely have refrained going to the House. **1827** J. W. CROKER in *Diary* 18 Feb., The Duke spoke handsomely of Canning in all their personal intercourse. **1884** *Manch. Exam.* 11 June 4/7 It is admitted..that in giving this pledge the Government have acted handsomely.

b. Liberally, generously, amply; usually in reference to a payment or gift.

1735 P. T. in *Pope's Lett.* I. Suppl. 20 If you'll pay the Paper and Print, and allow me handsomely for the Copy. **1778** JOHNSON in Mad. D'Arblay *Diary* 26 Sept., 'He must come down very handsomely with a settlement.' **1861** M. PATTISON *Ess.* (1889) I. 41 Edward..granted new privileges to the Hanse association, for which they were always ready to pay handsomely.

6. So as to have a fine or pleasing aspect; admirably, beautifully.

1610 SHAKS. *Temp.* v. i. 293 Goe Sirha, to my Cell..trim it handsomely. **1657** R. LIGON *Barbadoes* (1673) 14, 10 Soldiers..as proper men as I have seen, and as handsomely cloathed. **1766** GOLDSM. *Vic. W.* xxxi, He now therefore entered, handsomely drest in his regimentals. **1812** BRACKENRIDGE *Views Louisiana* (1814) 130 A vast plain.. handsomely diversified with prairie and woodland.

handsomeness ('hænsəmnɪs). [f. as prec. + -NESS.] The quality of being handsome.

†**1.** Convenience, handiness; fitness. *Obs.*

1530 PALSGR. 229/1 Hansomnesse, *aduenanteté.* **1552** HULOET, Boke whyche for hansomenes may be caried in iourney. **1626** BACON *Sylva* §14 For hansomeness sake..it were good you hang the upper Glass upon a Nail.

†**2.** Skill, dexterity, ability, cleverness; propriety, becomingness, decency. *Obs.*

1555 W. WATREMAN *Fardle Facions* II. vi. 151 Teachinge them to ride, to shote..with great diligence, and handsomenes. **1611** COTGR., *Habileté*..readinesse, handsomenesse, dexteritie. **1656** JEANES *Fuln. Christ* 66 There may be decency or handsomnesse in the first usage of a thing.

3. Graciousness, courtesy (*obs.*); magnanimity, liberality.

a **1616** BEAUM. & FL. *Wit without M.* I. i, He will not look with any handsomeness Upon a woman. *Mod.* We must admit the handsomeness of the reward.

4. Seemliness or pleasantness of aspect, or (*obs.*) of style; elegance, neatness; beauty, comeliness; in mod. use, beauty of a somewhat stately kind.

1598 HAKLUYT *Voy.* I. 248 (R.) Townes and villages also, but built out of order, and with no hansomeness. *a* **1616** BEAUM. & FL. *Wit without M.* I. i, A goodly woman; And to her handsomeness she bears her state, Reserved and great. **1687** SETTLE *Refl. Dryden* 75 Hansomeness in a man I have heard of..but never of Beauty before. **1827** HARE *Guesses* Ser. I. (1873) 32 Handsomeness is the more animal excellence, beauty the more imaginative. **1892** E. REEVES *Homeward Bound* 195 Admiration of the picturesque handsomeness of the men.

hands-on, *a.*[1] [f. *hands,* pl. of HAND *sb.* + ON *prep.* and *adv.*; cf. *hands off!* s.v. HAND *sb.* 54.]

1. a. Involving direct participation in an activity (esp. the use of computers or a computer keyboard), in order to gain practical experience of it; of experience, training, etc.: practical, rather than theoretical or second-hand.

1969 *Times* 27 Oct. 19/4 Elsewhere there are perhaps half a dozen IBM 1130s—the Sloan school has one in the basement—used for 'hands-on' calculations by students. **1971** *Computers & Humanities* VI. 35 At least eighteen seem, from their course descriptions, to offer 'hands-on' experience with computers. **1978** *Nature* 3 Aug. 413/3 The presence of scientists will also allow 'hands-on' experiments to be tried out, in contrast to previous life-science experiments in space which were fully automated. **1979** *Personal Computer World* Nov. 113/3 (Advt.), Intensive weekend courses in BASIC including hands-on mini computer operation. **1983** *Your Computer* (Austral.) Aug. 7/1 There will also be a series of 'hands-on' workshops for conference delegates who want first-hand experience with a small computer system. **1983** *New Scientist* 17 Nov. 486 (*caption*) Hands-on science: learn about pumps by playing with water. **1987** *Courier-Mail* (Brisbane) 18 Feb. 8/6 (Advt.), Hands-on marketing workshops. A series of two day practical marketing workshops will be held in Brisbane.

b. Of a person: having practical experience; experienced or prepared to become involved in the practical aspects of an activity (esp. a job).

1977 *Chicago Tribune* 2 Oct. XII. 36/7 (Advt.), Immediate placement for versatile 'hands-on' individuals with current state-of-art, solid state, TTL, CMOS components and microprocessors. **1978** *Detroit Free Press* 16 Apr. F3/5 (Advt.), Must be a hands on person with some mechanical ability. **1984** *Austral. Financial Rev.* 9 Nov. 4/5 (Advt.), Successful candidates will need to be self-motivated, 'hands-on' people who enjoy being involved in building a new enterprise. **1986** *New Yorker* 3 Feb. 100/2 Though he has been celebrated for being a hands-on mayor, he explained that he delegated many things to his commissioners.

c. Performed or experienced at first hand.

1978 *Fortune* 31 Dec. 48 Through hands-on management and attention to the bottom line, the chief executive who got his job by accident has transformed the company. **1983** *Observer* 17 Apr. 19/3 By..going for a policy of direct hands-on control, Green is adamant that he can quadruple Tilling's present return on sales. **1985** *Globe & Mail* (Toronto) 10 Oct. B20/3 (Advt.), The successful candidate will have a solid record of achievement in 'hands-on' management established over several years experience. **1986** *Wanganui Chron.* 19 Feb. 10/8 (Advt.), This is a hands-on position and involves stock and quality control, in charge of small staff and counter sales.

2. Of an exhibit: that can be handled. Of a museum, display, etc.: containing exhibits of this kind.

1975 *Hands-on Museums* (U.S. Educational Facilities Laboratories) 4 Hands-on museums..provide school students with educational experience typically not possible within the school house. **1983** *New Scientist* 17 Nov. 485/2 The first of..several dedicated 'hands-on' science centres in Britain. **1984** *Tropical Times* 21 Mar. 7/2 Admission includes hands-on Science Gallery exhibits.

handspike ('hændspaɪk), *sb.* Also 7 -spiek, -speck, 7-8 -speek, 9 -spec. [ad. early mod. Du. *handspaecke,* mod. Du. *handspaak,* in same sense (f. *spaak,* MDu. *spake* pole, rod). In Eng. app. assimilated to SPIKE (or in quot. 1615 to *pike*).]

1. A wooden bar, used as a lever or crow, chiefly on ship-board and in artillery-service. It is rounded at the one end by which it is held and square at the other, and usually shod with iron.

1615 E. S. *Britain's Buss* in Arb. *Garner* III. 627 Two or three handpikes, of ash. **1626** CAPT. SMITH *Accid. Yng. Seamen* 31 A gunners quadrant, a hand spike, a crow of iron, to mount a peece. **1648-78** HEXHAM *Dutch Dict., Handtspeecke,* Bar, or Hand-Spiek. **1691** T. H[ALE] *Acc. New Invent.* 119 Nautical Staticks, and Mechanicks, relating to Pullies and Crows, Handspecks. **1696** PHILLIPS (ed. 5), A *Handspeek,* a Wooden Leaver, used in stead of a Crow of Iron to traverse the Ordnance [**1706** (ed. Kersey), or to heave in a Windlass to weigh up the Anchor]. **1748** F. SMITH *Voy. Disc.* I. 53 The Ice..was cleared from the Head of the Ship with Handspikes. **1836** MARRYAT *Midsh. Easy* xiv, Jack knocked him down with a handspike. *c* **1850** *Rudim. Navig.* (Weale) 123 *Handspec.* **1860-75** *Ure's Dict. Arts* (ed. 7) II. 782 *Handspike,* a strong wooden bar, used as a lever to move the windlass and capstan in heaving the anchor.

2. Incorrectly for Sc. *handspake,* HANDSPOKE.

3. *attrib.* and *Comb.*, as ***handspike-end, -man***; **handspike-ring** (*Artill.*), the thimble on the trail transom of a gun, for the handspike by which it is manœuvred.

1859 F. A. GRIFFITHS *Artil. Man.* (1862) 208 The assistant handspikemen will attend the compressors. **1883** STEVENSON *Treas. Isl.* IV. xx, Pretty handy with a handspike-end.

'handspike, *v.* [f. prec. sb.] *trans.* To move or strike with a handspike.

1776 in *Harper's Mag.* Sept. (1883) 547/2 In the act of hand-spiking up the Canon into the embrasure. **1837** MARRYAT *Dog-fiend* vi, He never would have handspiked *me.*

'handspoke. In Sc. -spake, -spaik, -spike. [See SPOKE.] A spoke or bar of wood carried in the hand; *spec.* one of those used in carrying the coffin at a funeral in Scotland.

1727 WALKER *Remark. Pass.* 140 (Jam.) Friends would not suffer them to put their hands to a handspaik, tho' they offered. **1816** SCOTT *Antiq.* xxxi, The coffin, covered with a pall, and supported upon handspikes by the nearest relatives. **1850** *Loudon's Encycl. Gard.* 515 The carrying lever, or handspoke is used in pairs for carrying tubs of plants or other bodies..Two of them united to a platform of boards form the common hand-barrow.

'hand-staff.

1. A staff-like handle; *spec.* that part of a flail by which it is held.

14.. *Voc.* in Wr.-Wülcker 594/47 *Manutercium,* an hand-staf. *Item*..an handele. *c* **1440** *Promp. Parv.* 165/2 Fleyl staffe or honde staffe. **1688** R. HOLME *Armoury* III. 333/1 The Caplings [of a flail]..are the strong double Leathers made fast to the top of the Hand-staff. **1827** H. NEELE *Rom. Hist.* (1831) I. 77 Every English lance was red to the hand-staff with blood. **1831** J. HOLLAND *Manuf. Metal* I. 161 By means of the reciprocating motion of a lever to which [in bellows] the racket or handstaff is attached.

†**2.** A popular name of some asterism; according to Jamieson, 'supposed to be Orion's sword'. *Obs.*

1513 DOUGLAS *Æneis* VIII. Prol. 154 The son, the sevin sternis, and the Charll wane, The elwand, the elementis, and Arthuris hufe, The horne and the hand staff. *a* **1605** MONTGOMERIE *Flyting w. Polwart* 419 Be the.. Charlewaine, Be the hornes, the handstaff, and the king's ell.

†**3.** A staff carried as a weapon. *Obs.*

The word is a literal rendering of the Hebrew.

1611 BIBLE *Ezek.* xxxix. 9 They..shall..burne the weapons..the bowes and the arrowes, and the handstaues [*marg.* iauelins, **1382** WYCLIF stafs of hond] and the speares.

†**'handstone.** *Obs.* A stone that can be lifted or thrown with the hand.

1598 GRENEWEY *Tacitus' Ann.* IV. xi. 107 The barbarians ..now threw hand-stones against the rampire. *a* **1725** A. SIMSON *Descr. Galloway* (1823) 27 (Jam.) A cairn, or great heap of small handstones, with five or six high stones erected.

handstroke ('hændstrəʊk). Also **handi-, handystroke.** [f. HAND *sb.* + STROKE. For the variant *handistroke, handy stroke,* cf. HAND-BLOW and HANDY *a.*]

†**1.** A stroke or blow with the hand. ***to come to handstrokes*** (***handy strokes***), to come to blows or hand-to-hand fighting. So ***to be at handstrokes,*** etc.

α. **1523** LD. BERNERS *Froiss.* I. xx. 30 They shulde soone assemble to gether to fyght at hande strokes. **1548** HALL *Chron., Hen. VI,* 90 After thei came to hande strokes: greate was the fight. **1625-6** PURCHAS *Pilgrims* II. 1486 Immediately we came to handstrokes. *c* **1840** MANNING *Let. to Archdeacon Hare* in Purcell *Life* (ed. 4) I. 163 Till I can come, as Hobbes says, to handstrokes with you.

β. **1548** HALL *Chron., Hen. V,* 50 When thei came to handystrokes. **1589** *Disc. Voy. Spaine & Port.* (1881) 104 Having beaten an Enemie at handie strokes. **1602** *Hist. Eng.* in *Harl. Misc.* (Malh.) II. 455 To..bring the matter to handy strokes. **1692** R. L'ESTRANGE *Josephus, Wars* III. xix. (1733) 687 Provoking them to handy Strokes.

2. *attrib.* (See quot.)

1880 C. A. W. TROYTE in Grove *Dict. Mus.* I. 219/2 [The bell] would in swinging past that point raise the rope; this gives the ringer a second pull..and this is called the 'handstroke' pull.

hands-up ('hændzʌp), *v.* [f. the order *hands up!* (see HAND *sb.* 55).] *intr.* To put up the hands in token of surrender. Also *trans.*, to cause to surrender. So **'hands-up** *sb.*, the action of putting up the hands (in quot. *attrib.*); **'hands-,upper,** one who surrenders. Also **'hand-up** *sb.*, one who throws up his hands.

1901 *Comtemp. Rev.* Mar. 327 A small patrol..went..to the farm of a 'hands upper', *i.e.*, one who had surrendered his arms. **1901** *Daily Chron.* 12 Nov. 5/4 They regard themselves as quite the aristocrats of the camp, and much superior to the 'hands-uppers', as they have delighted in calling the children of less obstinate patriots. **1901** 'LINESMAN' *Words by Eyewitness* 239 The refugee camps within the British lines, wherein dwell the hundreds of Dutchmen who have surrendered, or 'hands-upped'. **1902** *Westm. Gaz.* 20 Mar. 7/1 Trooper Long..was grabbed by the throat by a 'hands-up' prisoner, who threw down his rifle. **1902** *Appleton's Ann. Cycl.* 629/2 The Boers who had accepted British sovereignty at various times since the fall of Bloemfontein and Pretoria, contemptuously called 'handups' by the others. **1915** *Observer* 4 Apr. 7/2 We have now a case of 'hands-upping', the first in this war, by a whole unit of Germans. **1923** *Daily Mail* 9 Mar. 10 The Germans after 'hands-upping' Rumania proceeded literally to turn out their pockets. **1928** *Observer* 17 June 7 Those faint-hearted ones who are 'hand-uppers' in regard to aviation. **1929** J. BUCHAN *Courts of Morning* III. 307 They hands-upped like lambs. We've gotten a nice little bag——fourteen hundred and seventy-three combatant soldiers.

†**hand-tame**, *a. Obs.* Tame and submissive to handling; mild, gentle. Hence **hand-tameness**, submissiveness, gentleness, mansuetude; also **handtamed** *ppl. a.*, reduced to submission.

*a***1300** *E.E. Psalter* xxxiii[i]. 3 (Mätz.) Here handtame [*mansueti*] and faine withal. *Ibid.* xliv. [xlv.] 5 For sothnes, and handtamenes, And rightwisenes, þat in þe es. *c***1325** *Poem Times Edw. II*, 398 in *Pol. Songs* (Camden) 341 To waxen al hand-tame that rathere weren so proude. *a***1400-50** *Alexander* 504 As scho were hand-tame. *c***1460** *Towneley Myst.* (Surtees) 98 We ar mayde hand tamyd, Withe these gentlery men.

hand to hand, *adv. phr.* (*a.*) Also †**hand unto hand** (*obs. rare*). With close approach of hands; at close quarters; man to man. (Chiefly in reference to fighting.)

*c***1400** *Destr. Troy* 10351 Neuer hond vnto hond harmyt he nother. *a***1533** LD. BERNERS *Huon* xliii. 144 To fyght with me hand to hande. **1589** R. HARVEY *Pl. Perc.* 9 My selfe drinking hand to hand with the founder of them. **1640** LD. KYNALMEAKY in *Lismore Papers* Ser. II. (1888) IV. 147 The King went imediately with him, and there talk'd hand to hand some three houres. **1847** GROTE *Greece* (1862) III. xl. 434 A close combat hand to hand was indispensable.

b. *attrib.* or *adj.* (with --).

1836 LYTTON *Athens* (1837) I. 478 The hand-to-hand valour of the Greeks. **1879** FROUDE *Cæsar* xiv. 209 In these hand-to-hand engagements there were no wounded.

hand to mouth, *phr.* (*a.*, *sb.*)

1. *from hand to mouth*: by consuming food as soon as it is obtained; with attention to immediate wants only; without provision for the future; improvidently, thriftlessly.

1509 BARCLAY *Shyp of Folys* (1874) II. 45 Theyr vayne myndes to farther thynges is dull Saue on that which from hande to mouth is brought. **1571** GOLDING *Calvin on Ps.* lxviii. 11 Hungery folkes that are fed from hand too mouth. **1660** HICKERINGILL *Jamaica* (1661) 56 No supply, But just from hand to mouth, no Granary. **1790** COWPER *Let. to Newton* 5 Feb., I subsist as the poor are vulgarly said to do, from hand to mouth. **1887** JESSOPP *Arcady* Introd. 14 We in the country are one and all living from hand to mouth.

2. *attrib.* or *adj.* (with --). Involving immediate consumption (or, *transf.*, disposal of goods) as soon as obtained; aiming at the satisfaction of present needs only; improvident.

1748 RICHARDSON *Clarissa* (1811) III. 181 Contented with hand-to-mouth conveniencies. **1860** W. G. CLARK *Vac. Tour* 10 The hand-to-mouth purblind policy of your Government. **1892** W. PIKE *Barren Ground N. Canada* 71 Very agreeable after the hand-to-mouth existence we had been leading.

3. *sb.* Lack of provision for the future.

1864 TENNYSON *En. Ard.* 116 Low miserable lives of hand-to-mouth.

hand-vice. A vice that may be held in one hand. Sometimes applied to a small movable vice that can be fixed to a bench.

1611 COTGR., *Oberon*..the hand-vice, or toole, wherewith a Locksmith holds a key as he files it. **1669** STURMY *Mariner's Mag.* II. 53 You should have a Hand-Vice, so made as to screw into the edge of a Board for your use. **1703** MOXON *Mech. Exerc.* 5 The Office of the Hand-Vice, is to hold small work in, that may require often turning about. **1822** IMISON *Sc. & Art* II. 426 Fix a hand-vice to some part of it where no work is intended to be.

hand-waled, *ppl. a. Sc.* Also 7 -weal'd, 8-9 -wailed. [See WALE *v.*] Chosen or selected by hand; individually or carefully selected, picked.

1671 *True Nonconf.* 293 Communicating with hand-weal'd companions. **1719** RAMSAY *Ep. to Hamilton* 2 Sept. 74 Sic wordy, wanton, hand-wail'd ware. **1727** WALKER *Remark. Pass.* 58 (Jam.) To apprehend and bring to condign punishment our hand-wail'd murderers. **1818** SCOTT *Hrt. Midl.* x, The hand-waled murderers, whose hands are hard as horn to wi' haudin the slaughter-weapons. [By Scott app. thought to refer to wales on the hands.]

So **hand-waling (-wailling)**, *vbl. sb.*

1709 ? W. GUTHRIE *Serm.* 15 (Jam.) Tho' ye be a singular waill'd companie..and the best that by hand wailling can be waill'd out of Clydesdale.

handwarp: see HANDYWARP.

†'**handwhile.** *Obs.* Also *β.* **handlanglewhile**, *mod. Sc.* **hanla'while.** [OE. *hand-hwīl*: see HAND and WHILE *sb.*] A moment, an instant, a span (of time).

*c***1000** ÆLFRIC *Hom.* I. 294 Ða tid ōðōe ða hand-hwile þe min Fæder ʒesette þurh his mihte. *c***1200** ORMIN 12166 þatt deofell let te Laferrd seon..inn an hanndwhile..þe kinedomess alle. *a***1225** *Ancr. R.* 146 Hure þet is agon in one handhwule! **1377** LANGL. *P. Pl.* B. XIX. 267 þise foure.. harwed in an handwhile al holy scripture. *c***1400** *Destr. Troy* 11030 Halpe hym to horse in a hond qwhile. **1556** J. HEYWOOD *Spider & F.* xxx. 23 Conscience euery handwhile thou doste cry. **1646** F. HAWKINS *Youth's Behav.* (1663) 27 Contradict not at every hand-while, that which others say.

β. *c***1460** *Towneley Myst.* (Surtees) 109, I may not syt at my note, A hand lang while. **1802** J. SIBBALD *Chron. Scot. Poetry* Gloss. (Jam.), *Handwhile*, vulg. *Hanla-while*, a short time. *Mod. Sc.* He canna sit still a hanla' while.

'**hand-woman.** *Obs.* or *dial.*

†**1.** A female attendant; a handmaid. *Obs.*

*a***1300** *Cursor M.* 2593 Sar..had hir wit a hand womman, þat agar hight. *Ibid.* 10906, I am mi lauerd hand-wimman.

2. (*dial.*)

1847-78 HALLIWELL, *Hand-woman*, a midwife. *Devon.*

handwork ('hændwɜːk). Forms: 1 -weorc, 3-5 -werk, 6- work; also *β.* 3-5 **hande-**, (**honde-**) **-werk, wark.** [OE. *hand-weorc*, found beside the more frequent *hand ʒeweorc* HANDIWORK. In ME. the northern dialect had *hande-werk*, as if f. an inflected form of *hand*; perh. after ON. *handa-verk*. When the *e* became mute in 14th c., this also sank into *hand-werk*.]

†**1.** A thing or quantity of things wrought or made by the hands; = HANDIWORK 1. *Obs.*

*a***1000** *Riddles* xxi. 7 Sinc hondweorc smiþa. *a***1300** *E.E. Psalter* cxxxvii[i]. 8 þi hend-werke ne forsake for-þi. *c***1325** *Metr. Hom.* 71 This Makary Come unto the cyte..To sell thar hys handwerke. *a***1420** HOCCLEVE *De Reg. Princ.* 3340 His handwerk and his creature. **1594** KYD *Cornelia* in Dodsley *O. Pl.* (1780) II. 253 Thou heaven's hand-work Fair Illium. **1895** MORRIS *Beowulf* 16 The best of all war-shrouds, The hand-work of Weland.

β. *c***1200** ORMIN 5054 Mann iss Godess handewerrc. *a***1300** *Cursor M.* 1155 (Cott.) Mi handewark als egges me. *c***1340** *Ibid.* 20222 (Fairf.) Kepe þi hande werk fra shame. *c***1470** HENRY *Wallace* II. 186 Quhi will thow giff thi handewark for nocht?

2. Work done with the hands; working with the hands; manual operation or labour; now esp. as distinguished from work done by or with machinery.

?*a***1000** *Eccles. Inst.* 3 in Thorpe *Laws* II. 404 (Bosw.) þurh ðæt handweorc. *c***1400** *Rom. Rose* 6683 Of his hond-werk wolde he gete Clothes to wryne hym. **1552** LATIMER *Serm. & Rem.* (1845) 41 They think they get their livings with their own handwork. **1570** DEE *Math. Pref.* 39 The Architect..directeth the Mechanicien, to handworke. **1601** HOLLAND *Pliny* II. 531 One brasen image he had of Mentors hand-worke. **1856** EMERSON *Eng. Traits, Wealth* Wks. (Bohn) II. 74 The incessant repetition of the same hand-work dwarfs the man. **1874** MICKLETHWAITE *Mod. Par. Churches* 261 We hear a great deal about 'handwork'; everything must be handwork. **1897** *The Chiswick Press* 4 The reputation for Handwork which they have acquired.

'**hand-worked** (-wɜːkt), *ppl. a.* Worked, made or done by hand, and not by mechanism.

1818 TODD, *Handworked*, made with hands; formed by workmanship. **1861** W. F. COLLIER *Hist. Eng. Lit.* 440 The substitution of the steam printing-machine for the hand-worked printing-press. **1887** *Pall Mall G.* 19 Aug. 8/2 Hand-worked bilge pumps. **1891** *Ibid.* 1 June 7/2 A specimen of a hand-worked gun now in use in the navy.

'**hand-ˌworker.** One who works with his hands: opposed variously to one who works with his head, one who employs the hands of others, or one who works with a machine.

1844 COBDEN in *League* 10 Aug., Be he..merchant, manufacturer or handworker. **1862** T. MORRALL *Needle-making* 20 The hand-workers' prices were much reduced by the machines. **1896** L. ECHENSTEIN *Woman under Monasticism* 238 The productions of the old hand-worker.

'**hand-working.** Working with the hands; manual labour or operation. Also *attrib.*

In first two quots. a literal transl. of Gr. χειρουργία surgery.

*c***1400** *Lanfranc's Cirurg.* 7 (MS. B.), For þe ende and þe prophyte of surgerye ys of hand wyrchynge..whyche techiþ vs to worche with handes in a Mannes body. **1548-77** VICARY *Anat.* i. (1888) 13 Ipocras sayth, that Surgerie is hande working in mans body. **1580** SIDNEY *Ps.* XIX. i, The firmament..Shewes His hand-working wonders.

†'**handworm.** *Obs.* An acarid, the itch-insect (*Sarcoptes scabiei*) which burrows in the hands.

*a***800** *Corpus Gloss.* 320 *Briensis*, honduyrm. *c***1000** *Voc.* in Wright 288/4 *Urcius*, hand-wyrm. **14..** *Metr. Voc.* in Wr.-Wülcker 625/6 *Curio*, hondworme. **1530** PALSGR. 229/1 Handeworme, *ciron.* **1630** J. TAYLOR *Wks.* (N.), All the world is..to the heavens, as a hand-worme or nit may be compared to the world. **1677** HALE *Prim. Orig. Man.* III. v. 274 That Animal that well near escapes his sight by reason of its smalness, as the *Acarus*, the *Cyro* or Hand-worm. *a***1693** URQUHART *Rabelais* III. xxi. 181 Fleas, Punies, Handworms.

'**hand-wrist.** *Obs.* exc. *dial.* [OE. *hand-wrist, -wyrst*, f. HAND + WRIST, *wyrst*, OFris. *wriust* wrist, and instep, Ger. *rist* instep.]

1. The wrist or joint of the hand. Now *dial.*

*a***1000** *Ags. Gloss* in Wr.-Wülcker 216/24 *Cuba, i. ulna*, elnboga, *uel* hondwyrst. *c***1050** *Ibid.* 356/20 *Articulus*, handwyrst. *c***1325** *Gloss W. de Biblesw.* in Wright *Voc.* 147 *Le cou de la meyn*, the hand wriste. **1560** FRAMPTON in Strype *Ann. Ref.* I. xx. 244 The blood sprang out at my hand-wrists, where I was tied. **1650** CROMWELL *Let.* 4 Sept. in *Carlyle*, Colonel Whalley only cut in the handwrist. **1809** PARKINS *Culpepper's Eng. Physic. Enl.* 212 Bruised and applied to the soles of the feet and hand-wrists. [In Somersetsh., Wiltsh., and Glouces. Dialects.]

†**2.** A cuff. *Obs. rare.*

1707 J. STEVENS tr. *Quevedo's Com. Wks.* (1709) 229 Ruffles and Hand-wrists, to appear in sight, and represent Shirt-Sleeves.

†'**handwrit.** *Obs.* [f. HAND *sb.* + WRIT: cf. OE. *handʒewrit*, and HANDWRITING; also Sc. *hand of writ*: see HAND 16 b.] Handwriting; autograph; signature.

*c***1200** ORMIN 13566 þurrh Moysæsess hande writt. **1536** BELLENDEN *Cron. Scot.* (1821) II. 390 He demandit thaim gif thay kend thair handwrittis and selis. **1560** in Tytler *Hist. Scot.* (1864) III. 397 An assured promise under their hand-writs. **1616** W. HAIG in J. Russell *Haigs* vii. (1881) 160 Which he pretends was of my handwrit. **1693** *Sc. Presbyt. Eloq.* (1738) 116 Deny your own Hand-Write if you dare?

handwrite ('hændraɪt), *sb. Sc., Ir.*, and *U.S.* [f. HAND *sb.* + WRITE *sb.*[1] 5. Cf. HANDWRIT and *hand of writ, write* (HAND *sb.* 16 b).] Handwriting.

1483- in *Dict. Older Scot. Tongue.* **1617** in W. K. Tweedie *Sel. Biogr.* (1847) I. 95, I receaved a letter..whilk albeit it wanted a subscription, yet by the handwrite..I knew to be yours. **1638** S. RUTHERFORD *Lett.* (1664) 14 His hand write, & his seal. **1688** in R. Wodrow *Hist. Suff. Ch. Scot.* (1722) II. 633 You..adhered to your preaching Book, and declared the same to be your own Hand-write. **1836** B. TUCKER *Partisan Leader* (1861) 16 (Th.), He has got a paper in the captain's hand-write to show him the way. **1856** W. G. SIMMS *Eutaw* 429 (Th.), Thar's his name in handwrite!.. Hyar's a boy that reads this hand-write. **1880** W. H. PATTERSON *Gloss. Antrim* 49 Whose hand write is that? **1907** N. MUNRO *Daft Days* xv, She knew she could never sustain the standard of hand-write, spelling, and information Bud had established in her first epistle. **1923** *Dialect Notes* V. 209, I know his hand write.

'**handwrite**, *v. rare.* [prob. a back-formation from *hand-written*, written by hand, like *hand-made*, etc.: see HAND *sb.* 64 b.] *trans.* To write with the hand, or with one's own hand.

1849-53 ROCK *Ch. of Fathers* III. ix. 223 A fine psalter.. hand-written. **1871** *Athenæum* 13 May 584 To prove that Francis hand-wrote the Junian letters is not to demonstrate that he composed them. **1878** BROWNING *Poets Croisic* xcv, I myself Hand-write what's legible yet picturesque.

handwriting ('hændraɪtɪŋ). [Cf. L. *manuscriptum*, Gr. χειρόγραφον.]

1. Writing with the hand; manuscript as distinguished from print, etc.; the writing of a particular hand or person, or that pertaining to a particular time or nation.

1500-20 DUNBAR *Poems* lix. 16 Versis off his awin hand vryting. **1639** T. BRUGIS tr. *Camus' Mor. Relat.* 199 A young man that could artificially counterfeit all manner of hand writing. **1783** BURKE *Rep. Comm. India* Wks. XI. 215 A paper in his own handwriting. **1891** SCOTT & DAVEY *Historical Documents* 46 The study of handwritings. **1893** E. M. THOMPSON *Hand-bk. Gk. & Lat. Palæogr.* Pref. 7 As he grows up the child developes a handwriting of his own, diverging more and more from the models.

2. That which is written by hand; manuscript; a piece of written matter; a written document or note. *Obs.* or *arch.*

1534 TINDALE *Col.* ii. 14 He..hath put out the hand-writinge that was agaynst vs. **1535** COVERDALE *Job* i. 17 He gaue him the sayde weight of syluer vnder an hand-writinge. **1576** FLEMING *Panopl. Epist.* 155 When hand writing and Epistles passe too and fro in absence and distance. **1631** *Star Chamb. Cases* (Camden) 66 To forge 4 parchment leaves of an olde handwriting. **1791** MRS. RADCLIFFE *Rom. Forest* viii, Adeline took it up, and opening it perceived a hand-writing.

fig. **1831** BREWSTER *Nat. Magic* ii. (1833) 10 The optic nerve is the channel by which the mind peruses the hand-writing of Nature on the retina. **1928** R. FRY in *S.P.E. Tract* XXXI. 331 *Ecriture*. Has a special sense in regard to painting, and refers to the rhythm of the handling of paint. *Handwriting* has hardly acquired this use, but perhaps might be adequate. **1959** *Sunday Times* 10 May 19/5 Certain designers possess an accuracy of taste and a precision of expression which produce an identifiable handwriting... Dior's was a great handwriting. **1959** *Observer* 20 Sept. 18/4 A style policy which is recognisably the 'handwriting of the store'. **1960** *Observer* 28 Feb. 5/3 Leonardo's left-handedness, his preoccupation with things observed.. contribute to what Sir Kenneth [*sc.* Clark] calls his 'handwriting'. **1961** R. SETH *Anat. Spying* vi. 97 The individual's use of the morse-key is as distinctive as his handwriting—in fact, it is referred to as 'handwriting'.

3. *attrib.*, as **handwriting expert**, one who makes a study of handwriting in order to determine the authorship of disputed documents, to detect forgeries, etc.

1894 *Strand Mag.* VIII. 293/1 The methods employed by handwriting experts. **1897** *Westm. Gaz.* 2 Dec. 5/1 M. Bertillon, the famous handwriting expert, one of the witnesses at the Dreyfus trial. **1898** *Ibid.* 17 Jan 7/2 The testimony of hand-writing 'experts'. **1967** G. B. MAIR *Girl from Peking* iv. 52 Our handwriting experts say that they *could* have been written by the same person.

handy, *sb. north. dial.* [f. HAND *sb.*]

1. See quot. 1825.

1681 *Inv.* in *Biggar & Ho. of Fleming* (1862) 62 Item to Andrew Murray ane Say a handy and a seck rindle. **1818** *Edin. Mag.* Dec. 503 (Jam.), I flang the hannie frae me. **1825** BROCKETT *N.C. Gloss.*, *Handy*, a small wooden vessel with an upright handle. **1847-78** HALLIWELL, *Handy*, a piggin.

2. A hand-bier.

1909 *Daily Chron.* 8 June 2/5 Hearses, Handys, Biers, &c. **1922** *Daily Mail* 4 Nov. 10 The charges for licences on motor-hearses and handys.

handy ('hændɪ), *a.* [In sense 1, app. developed from the first element in HANDIWORK (q.v.), which was often written separately as *handi, handie, handy*, being app. taken as an adj. = 'manual', and so extended to other words, as *labour*, *occupation*, *operation*, *art*, and the like. In the later senses (after 1600), it appears to be a normal derivative of HAND *sb.* + -Y. (Not directly connected with *hendy*.)]

†**1. a.** Of, or done by, the hand: manual. *Obs.*

[*a* **1310** in Wright *Lyric P.* xix. 60 Thin hondy werk nult thou lete. **1477** NORTON *Ord. Alch.* in Ashm. (1652) 49 But handie crafte called Arte Mechanicall. **1581** MARBECK *Bk. of Notes* 1077 A Temple of mans handy worke.] **1535** COVERDALE *Haggai* i. 11 Vpon men and vpon catell, yee and vpon all handy laboure. **1541** R. COPLAND *Guydon's Quest. Chirurg.* A iij, Thynges belongynge to handy operacyon. **1551** ROBINSON tr. *More's Utop.* II. (1895) 148 He is taken frome hys handy occupation. **1576** NEWTON *Lemnie's Complex.* (1633) 17 Tinkers, Carters, Tipplers, handy Artificers. **1585** T. WASHINGTON tr. *Nicholay's Voy.* IV. xxvii. 146 He was punished by death as a private person, but not by handye execution. **1612** WOODALL *Surg. Mate* Pref. Wks. (1653) 5 *Chirurgia*, or the Handy part of healing. **1631** WEEVER *Anc. Fun. Mon.* 150 Whose exercise was.. handy labour, digging and filling vp againe their graues. **1713** S. SEWALL *Diary* 15 Sept. (1879) II. 398 Took the Churches Handy vote; Church sat in the Gallery.

†**b.** Wielded by the hand; hand to hand.

1586 WARNER *Alb. Eng.* II. vii. (1612) 29 Then fettle they to handy Armes.

2. a. Ready to hand; near at hand; conveniently accessible or ready for use.

1650 FULLER *Pisgah* I. 400 It was placed very handy, and convenient for such as went up to sacrifice. **1775** ROMANS *Hist. Florida* App. 54, I..found mahogany growing so handy that I took in about 4000 feet of it in a very few days. **1852** MRS. STOWE *Uncle Tom's C.* xx, Knocked down with the shovel or tongs, which ever came handiest. **1894** R. BRIDGES *Feast of Bacchus* II. 760, I happen to have it handy.

b. Phr. ***handy by***, ***to***: conveniently situated for. *dial.* and *U.S.* So ***handy for*** (general colloq.).

1825 J. JENNINGS *Observ. Dial. W. Eng.* 133 I've hir'd 'twar handy ta tha zea. **1893** 'O. THANET' *Stories of Western Town* 136 It is customary in the Lossing Building to say, 'We are so handy to the cars.' **1934** H. G. WELLS *Exper. Autobiogr.* II. viii. 602 A miscellany of people came and went there and to lodgings handy-by the smaller house at Dymchurch. **1968** *Globe & Mail* (Toronto) 17 Feb. 45 (Advt.), Not one street to cross to get to public school. Handy to shopping plaza. Beautiful view over park.

3. a. Convenient to handle or hold in the hand; easy to be manipulated, managed, or directed.

1694 MOXON *Mech. Exerc.* 195 Use has made the Mawl more handy for them. **1776** J. Q. ADAMS *Wks.* (1854) IX. 382 The galleys first built..were too large to be handy. **1880** *Times* 25 Dec. 7/4 The ship sails well..Steers well under all circumstances, and is very handy. **1897** A. LANG in *Bookman* Jan. 115/2 The volume is delightfully handy, and the type excellent.

b. ***handy dog*** (see quots.). *N.Z.*

1933 L. G. D. ACLAND in *Press* (Christchurch) 25 Nov. 15/7 Some dogs will both head and huntaway and are called handy dogs. **1968** *N.Z. News* 28 Aug. 16/1 A pack usually has several 'huntaways', a 'heading' dog and a 'handy' dog. .. The handy dog is generally versatile at all jobs.

4. Ready or clever with the hands; dexterous; able to turn the hand to anything.

1662 J. DAVIES tr. *Olearius' Voy. Ambass.* 89 They are very handy, and easily imitate any thing they see done. **1790** J. B. MORETON *W. Indies* 43 Two smart handy boys or girls. **1824** MISS MITFORD *Village* Ser. I. (1863) 112 A man..of that peculiar universality of genius which forms, what is called in country phrase, a handy fellow. **1847** DE QUINCEY *Sp. Mil. Nun* v. (1853) 9 She was a handy girl. She could turn her hand to anything. **1874** L. STEPHEN *Hours in Library* (1892) I. ix. 300 That strange ingenuity which makes an American the handiest of all human beings.

5. handy- in *comb.* **a.** (from sense 1, or having the same origin): **handy-blow**: see HAND-BLOW; **handy-craft**: see HANDICRAFT; †**handy-fight**, a hand-to-hand fight; †**handy-frame**, what is framed by the hands, handiwork; **handy-grip**(e: see HANDGRIP; **handystroke**: see HANDSTROKE; †**handythrift**, what a man earns with his hands; **handy-work**: see HANDIWORK; †**handywright** [repr. OE. **handȝewyrhta*], a worker with his hands, a mechanic. **b.** (from senses 2-4): **handy-billy** (see quot.); **handybook** (*nonce wd.*) = HANDBOOK; **handy-man**, (*a*) a man of general utility, a man useful for all sorts of odd jobs; (*b*) a sailor; **handy-sized** *a.*, of a convenient or suitable size.

1858 SIMMONDS *Dict. Trade*, *Handy-Billy. **1867** SMYTH *Sailor's Word-bk.*, *Handy-billy*, a small jigger purchase, used particularly in tops or the holds, for assisting in hoisting when weak-handed. A watch-tackle. **1933** J. MASEFIELD *Bird of Dawning* 56 We handed up the handy billy, they made it fast to the davit-head. **1867** BUCHAN (*title*) *Handy Book of Meteorology. **1888** *Athenæum* 20 Oct. 522 (Cent.) Handbooks, or handybooks, may be designed or used in two different ways. **1601** B. JONSON *Poetaster* v. i, Castor his horse, Pollux loves *handy-fights. **1597** MIDDLETON *Wisd. Sol. Paraphr.* xvi. 4 Say, is your god like this, whom you ador'd, Or is this god like to your *handy-frame? **1872** *Times* 27 Aug. (Farmer), The result is he cannot be called a *handy-man. **1887** *N. & Q.* 7th Ser. III. 514 Often heard among labourers, handy-men, and artizans. *a* **1898** *Mod. Advertisem.* Handy-man wanted, used to horses and cows and make himself generally useful. **1899** H. BEGBIE *Handy Man* iii, And the babe sleeps sound in her cot o' nights, and the trader may plot and plan, For under the stars on the rolling deep stands the vigilant Handy Man. **1900** *People* 1 Apr. (Ware), The handy man. High praise for the naval brigade. **1927** *Scots. Observer* 19 Mar. 15/3 The need for a *handy-sized and attractive edition of the Gospels. **1961** *Times* 7 Feb. 17/5 Few owners are building handy-sized tankers these days. *a* **1592** GREENE *Orpharion* Wks. (Grosart) XII. 86 He should gette it with his *handy-thrift. **1674** N. FAIRFAX *Bulk & Selv.* 193 Isaac Habrechtus that cunning *Handywright who made the Clock at Strasburgh.

'handy-'dandy, *sb.* or *adv. phrase.* Also **handy-bandy**, **-pandy**, **-spandy**. [A riming jingle on *hand*, or its childish diminutive *handy*.]

A. *sb.* **1. a.** A children's game in which a small object is shaken between the hands by one of the players, and, the hands being suddenly closed, the other player is required to guess in which hand the object remains.

The transferred use in sense 3 implies that the child's play was known before that date.

1585 HIGINS tr. *Junius' Nomenclator* 297/2 s.v. *Arteres*, The play called handie dandie. **1598** FLORIO, *Bazzichiare*, to shake between two hands, to play handy-dandy. **1601** DEACON & WALKER *Answ. Darel* 73 A little yong child playing at handie dandie happely..to make choise of that hand, wherein the pin or the point is placed. **1622** MABBE tr. *Aleman's Guzman d' Alf.* I. II. ii. 112, I learned to play at Cock-All, at Handy-Pandy, and at Nine-holes [*à la taba, al palmo y al hoyuelo*]. *a* **1764** LLOYD *Cobbler of Cripple-gate* 103. **1801** STRUTT *Sports & Past.* IV. iv. 349. **1847-78** HALLIWELL s.v., He whirls his hands round each other, crying, 'Handy-spandy, Jack-a-dandy, which good hand will you have?' **1887** *S. Cheshire Gloss.*, *Handy-Bandy*, the name of a game. A person conceals an object in one of his two closed hands, and invites his companion to tell which hand contains the object in the following words: Handy-Bandy, sugar-candy, Which hand wun yo have?

b. ***to play handy-dandy***. Often *fig.*

1579 TOMSON *Calvin's Serm. Tim.* 319/2 Yet these mates will come hither and play handidandy. *c* **1585** R. BROWNE *Answ. Cartwright* 2 Master Cartwright would playe at handie dandie with vs, and yet not giue vs that hand which we doe choose. **1683** WILLIAMS *Answ. Hunt's Postscr.* 20 All the Arts and Acts of Parliament afterwards, which..played handy-dandy with the Crown. **1862** CARLYLE *Fredk. Gt.* VIII. v. (1865) III. 46 You cannot play handy-dandy with a King's Crown, your Majesty! say his new Ministers.

c. The words used, as in the game, in offering a choice, or when it is indifferent which of two things is chosen; = 'Choose which you please'.

1598 CHAPMAN *Bl. Begg.* Plays 1873 I. 16 Why loe heere we are both, I am in this hand, and hee is in that, handy dandy, prickly prandy, which hand will you haue. **1605** SHAKS. *Lear* IV. vi. 157 Change places, and handy-dandy, which is the Iustice, which is the theefe? **1687** SETTLE *Refl. Dryden* 51 The expression is so excellent in either sense that *Handy Dandy*, 'tis no matter which you choose. **1965** *New Statesman* 3 Dec. 879/3 Change places, handy-dandy and the tone..could almost be Peter Simple on Dr. Castrumba. **1966** *Ibid.* 15 Apr. 539/3 Handy-dandy, which is the Underground Man and which is the complacent bourgeois?

†**2.** Transposition, shifting, as from hand to hand.

1615 SIR E. HOBY *Curry-combe* iii. 110 But is not heere olde handy pandy, when sentences shall be tossed from one place to another, without the Authors aduise?

†**3.** Something held or offered in the closed hand; a covert bribe or present. *Obs.*

1362 LANGL. *P. Pl.* A. IV. 61 Wro[n]g þenne vppon Wisdom wepte to helpe Him for his handidandi Rediliche he payede [**1377** B. IV. 75 Thanne wowed wronge wisdome ful ȝerne, To make his pees with his pens handi-dandi payed. **1393** C. v. 68 On men of lawe wrong lokede and largelich hem profrede, And for to haue of here help handy-dandy payede.]

B. *Adverbially.* With change of places; alternately, in rapid alternation.

a **1529** SKELTON *Sp. Parrot* 176 Donatus be dryven out of schole, Prisians hed broken, now handy dandy And *inter didascolos*, is reckoned for a fole. **1679** R. L'ESTRANGE *Answ. to Appeal fr. Country to City* 20 These people..can set Governors and Subjects handy-dandy to Box one another like Punchinello's Puppets, when they please.

handy-pandy, -spandy: see prec.

handyron, -yn, obs. forms of ANDIRON.

†**'handywarp.** *Obs.* Also **handwarp**. [f. HANDY *a.* 1 + WARP *sb.*] A kind of cloth made in the 16th c., of which app. the warp was prepared in some particular way.

1552 *Act 5 & 6 Edw. VI*, c. 6 §1 All and everie colored Clothe or Clothes..of lyke sortes commonlye called Handy-warpes. *Ibid.*, All Whites..made in the saide Shires or elswhere as Coxsall Whites Glaynesfordes and other beinge Handwarpes. **1565** GOLDING *Ovid's Met.* VI. (1593) 127 Or on the rocke doth spinne the hand-warpe woofe Or else imbroidereth. **1606-7** *Act 4 Jas. I*, c. 2 §1 Every White Cloth ..of like makinge commonlye called Handywarpes.

hane, Sc. var. of HAIN *v.*; obs. form of KHAN.

‖**haneg, hannege, hanega**, obs. forms of FANEGA, a Spanish measure of capacity.

1588 PARKE tr. *Mendoza's Hist. China* iii. 7 You shall haue a haneg [of rice] for a ryall of plate. **1600** HAKLUYT *Voy.* III. 461 Halfe a hannege of maiz. **1717** FREZIER *Voy. S. Sea* 117 Corn..6000 Hanegas..the Hanega weighing 150 Pounds.

[**hanelon, -oune**, erron. ff. HAVELON *sb.* and *v.*]

hanepoot ('hɑːnəˌpɔːt, -ˌpʊət). *S. Afr.* Also **haanepoot**, **haanepot**, **haenapod**, **hanapoot**, and (corruptly) **honeypot**. [Afrikaans, f. Du. *haan* cock + *poot* foot.] **1.** The grape-variety Muscat of Alexandria, a table grape often also used for making wine and for raisins.

c **1798** LADY A. BARNARD in A. W. C. Lindsay *Lives of Lindsays* (1849) III. 403 The Honipot grape.., a fleshy white grape, which is of the Muscatel nature and excellent. **1801** J. BARROW *Trav. S. Afr.* I. 65 A large white Persian grape, called here the haenapod. **1855** W. R. KING *Campaigning in Kaffirland* (ed. 2) 190 The most deliciously flavoured grapes, one sort, called the 'honeypot',..of immense size. **1878** T. J. LUCAS *Camp Life* 36 A fine fleshy well-favoured variety called hanne poot. **1887** *Colonial & Indian Exhib., Rep. Col. Sect.* 136 Raisins are made from the Haanepot grape. **1896** R. WALLACE *Farm. Ind. Cape Col.* x. 202 Of grapes the Haanepoot..and the Barbarossa are considered the best for the British market. **1927** *Daily Express* 8 Apr. 5 The Cape grapes..either the gros Colmars or the white Hanapoots. **1945** *Cape Times* 30 Mar. 4/7 The hanepoots are golden-brown and sweet. **1946** *Ibid.* 11 Feb. 6/5 In 1938-39 it was easy to buy good hanepoots at six or eight lb. for a shilling. **1971** *Rand Daily Mail* 28 July 15 The Spanish variety was thought to be the forebear of the Hanepoot grapes of today.

2. A sweet white wine made from hanepoot grapes.

1804 R. PERCIVAL *Acct. Cape of Good Hope* xi. 188 The Hanepod made from a large white grape is very rich, but scarce and dear. **1952** C. L. LEIPOLDT *300 Yrs. Cape Wine* xv. 203 A more common Hanepoot wine is a golden coloured, fairly sweet wine, of which several kinds are on the market. **1966** C. DE BOSDARI *Wines of Cape* (ed. 3) vi. 66 There are also the Muscadels,..from Hanepoot..to Frontignac.

hang (hæŋ), *v.* Pa. t. and pple. **hung** (hʌŋ), **hanged** (hæŋd). Forms: see below. [The history of this word involves that of two OE. and one ON. verb; viz. (1) the OE. str. *hón* (:—*hâhan*), *heng* (? *héng*), *hangen*, (*hǫngen*), trans.; (2) the OE. weak *hangian*, *hangode*, *-od*, (also *hǫng-*), intr. = OFris. *hangia*, OS. *hangôn* (for OHG. *hangên*); (3) the ON. causal vb. *hęngjan* trans. = OHG. *hęngan*, MHG., MDu. *hengen*. OE. *hón* = OS. and OHG. *hâhan*, MHG. *hâhen*, *hân*, MLG. *hân*, MDu. *haen*, represented the OTeut. reduplicating vb., with consonant-exchange (*grammatischer wechsel*), *hâhan* (from earlier **haŋhan*), *hehâh* (pl. *hehaŋgun*), *haŋgan-*, in Gothic, *hâhan*, *haihâh*, *haihâhun*, *hâhan-* (levelled under the present tense form). In WGer. and Norse, the pa. t. had the type *heŋg*: OS. *heng*, OHG. *hiang*, MHG. *hienc*, Ger. *hing*, ON. *hekk*, pl. *hengu*; OE. *heng* (? *héng*), ME. *heng*, *hieng*, *heyng*, *hing*. The pa. pple. *hangen* also varied in OE. and ME. with *hǫngen* (as in *lang*, *long*, etc.). Already in ON. the present stem *hâh-* had been ousted by the weak form *hanga*, and in the Middle period a similar change took place in all the WGer. langs.: MHG. *hâhen*, *hangen*, MDu. *hâen*, *hangen*, ME. *hôn*, *hangen* (*hongen*). This identified the old trans. vb. with the intr. *hangian*, *hongian*, so that both had now for the pres. t. *hang* (*hong*); in consequence of which the strong pa. t. and pa. pple. *heng* (*hing*), *hangen* (*hongen*), and the weak forms, *hangede* (*hongede*), *-ed*, became also generally confounded in sense, and (with some exceptions) used indiscriminately. Meanwhile the ON. causal verb *hęngja* came into northern Eng. as *heng(e*, also (with Eng. change of (-ɛŋ) to (-ɪŋ), *hing*; at first app. with weak inflexion and trans. sense, *hengde*, *henged*, *hingde*, *hinged*; but soon, by assimilation to the 3rd ablaut-class of str. verbs, with a pa. t. *hang*, varying in north. midl. with *hong*, both trans. and intr. At this period (13-15th c.), therefore, while the south had pres. t. *hang*, *hong*, and pa. *heng*, *hing*, the north had conversely pres. *heng*, *hing*, pa. *hang*, *hong*. Finally the northern inflexion *hing*, *hang*, was completed by the pa. pple. *hung*, which in the 16th c. penetrated into general Eng.; where arose a new pa. t. *hung* (like *sing*, *sung*, *sung*), in presence of which the earlier *heng*, *hing*, and *hong* became obs. The weak inflexion *hanged* however continued in use (being the only one used in Bible versions from Coverdale to 1611, though Tindale had also *houng*); but was gradually superseded by *hung* in the general sense, trans. and intr., leaving *hanged* only in the special trans. sense (3) 'put to death by hanging', owing prob. to the retention of this archaic form by judges in pronouncing capital sentences. The distinction is found already in Shakspere, and is established in the objurgatory expressions 'You be hanged!' 'I'll be hanged if I do', and the like. Nevertheless southern speakers and writers still often say 'the man was hung' instead of 'hanged'. In the northern dialects, on the other hand, the distinction runs all through the verb, the special sense 'put to death by hanging' being expressed by *hang*, *hang'd*, *hang'd*, while the general verb is *hing*, *hang*, *hung*; the present tense *hing* extends into England as far south as Northamptonshire: see A. 1 ϵ, quot. 1821. In those dialects, therefore, *hing* and *hang* are distinct verbs, differing both in sense and inflexion; but in Standard English, there being only the single form *hang* for the present tense, it is necessary to treat all the forms together. (*Hang* is parallel in inflexion to FANG *v.*)

The distinction of trans. and intr. has always tended to break down. The strong verb was orig. trans. in WGer. and in OE., *hangian* being the intr.; but in ON., *hanga, hekk, hangenn* was intr., and the causal *hengja* trans.; *hengen* is only trans in Ormin, but Cursor M. and Hampole have *heng, hing*, both trans. and intr., like the contemporary southern *hang, hong*. Cf. also mod. Ger., in which the true intr. *hangen* is archaic, and ordinarily superseded by the trans. *hängen*, though the pa. tenses *hing* intr. and *hängte* trans. remain distinct in use.]

A. Inflexional Forms.

1. Present tense stem.

α. 1–3 **hó-** (inf. **hón**, imper. **hóh**, 3rd sing. ind. **hóþ**, pl. ind. and imper. **hóð**). (Only *trans.*)

c **1000** *Ags. Gosp.* Matt. xxiii. 34 ȝe hiȝ ofsleað and hoð and swingað on eowrum ȝesomnungum. —— John xix. 6 Hoh hyne, hoh hyne.. Nime ȝe hine and hoð. *c* **1160** *Hatton Gosp.* ibid., Hoh hine, hoȝ hine. *c* **1205** LAY. 10009 þat be king heom sculde don oðer slan oðer hon. *a* **1250** *Owl & Night.* 1123 Me þe hoþ in one rodde.

β. 1 (*intr.*) **hang(i)-**, 3– (also *trans.*) **hang-**.

c **1000** ÆLFRIC *Gram.* xxvi. (Z.) 157 *Pendeo*, ic hangiȝe. *c* **1000** ÆLFRIC *Hom.* I. 596 Swa haliȝ wer hangian ne sceolde. *a* **1300** *Cursor M.* 5015 (Cott.) Elles wil þai.. Your eldest sun or hefd or hang [*Fairf.* hange, *Trin.* honge]. **1382** WYCLIF *Matt.* xxii. 40 In these two maundementis hangith al þe lawe and prophetis. *c* **1440** *Promp. Parv.* 225/2 Hangyn, by the selfe, *pendeo*. Hangyn a thynge on a walle, or other lyke, *pendo, suspendo*. **1653** WALTON *Angler* ii. 62 Come, hang him upon that Willow twig. *Mod.* Hang it in front of the fire, and let it hang all night.

γ. (*a*) 3–4 (*intr.*) **hong(i)-**; 3–5 (also *trans.*) **hong-** (**hongue, honge**); (*b*) 3 **heongi-** *intr.*, **heong-** *trans.*

(*a*) *c* **950** *Lindisf. Gosp.* Matt. xxii. 40 In ðisum tuæm bibodum all ae stondes *vel* honges [*Rushw.* ealle ae hongað]. *c* **1205** LAY. 510 Alle heo sculden hongien [*c* **1275** hongie] on heȝe treowen. *c* **1275** *Ibid.* 5715 þat an hii solle hongy. **1297** R. GLOUC. (1724) 448 He suor, honge he ssolde Anon. *c* **1300** *St. Brandan* 555 The cloth that so heȝe hongeth there. **1340** *Ayenb.* 31 Hit behoueþ yelde oþer hongy.

c **1290** *S. Eng. Leg.* I. 10/312 Ore louerd þaron to hongue. **1297** R. GLOUC. (1724) 561 Ich mai honge vp min ax. *c* **1340** *Cursor M.* 11890 (Fairf.) Traytours, he saide.. I sale honge ȝou [*Cott., Gött.* hing]. **1362** LANGL. *P. Pl.* A. IV. 20 Hong on him an heui Bridel. *c* **1380** WYCLIF *Wks.* (1880) 316 Knottis.. hongynge bifore. *c* **1420** *Pallad. on Husb.* IV. 375 Let picche her pedifeet, & honge hem hie. **14..** *Eger & Grime* 122 in Furniv. *Percy Folio* I. 358 Faire on his brest he cold it honge.

(*b*) *c* **1205** LAY. 26474 Alle heo sculleð heongien [*c* **1275** hongi] heȝe uppen treouwe. *Ibid.* 12281 Heo gunnen heongen [*c* **1275** honge] cniues.

δ. *north.* and *n. midl.* 2–6 **heng.** *trans.* and *intr.*

[*c* **1200** ORMIN *henngenn: see 2ε]. *c* **1330** R. BRUNNE *Chron. Wace* (Rolls) 16182 Dide henge his lymes on a bow. **13..** *Gaw. & Gr. Knt.* 182 A much berd as a busk ouer his brest henges. **1426** AUDELAY *Poems* 1 Hye on galouys fore to heng. *c* **1449** PECOCK *Repr.* II. x. 199 Make Crist plesid with hem which henge in him. **1538** STARKEY *England* I. iv. 118 Many mennys materys heng in sute.

ε. *north.* and *n. midl.* 3– **hing-** (4–6 **hyng-**) *trans.* and *intr.*

a **1300** *Cursor M.* 4946 If yee giue dome, þan sal þai hing [So all MSS.]. *Ibid.* 16020 To hefd him or to hing. *c* **1330** R. BRUNNE *Chron.* (1810) 172 Galwes do ȝe reise & hyng þis cheitefe. *c* **1400** MAUNDEV. (Roxb.) ii. 5 Hingand apon þat crosse. **1423** JAS. I. *Kingis Q.* lxxxix, Thaire hudis oure thaire eyne thay hyng. *c* **1440** *York Myst.* xxxvi. 77 3a, late hym hyng! **1483** *Cath. Angl.* 186/1 To Hynge, *pendere*. **1570** LEVINS *Manip.* 135/36 *Hing*, to hang. **1601** WEEVER *Mirr. Mart.* B vj b, Whose bloudy flaggs like fierie streamers hing. **1637** RUTHERFORD *Lett.* (1862) I. 265 To hing your vessels.. upon the Nail. **1821** CLARE *Vill. Minstr.* I. 46 Nodding bulrush down its drowk head hings. *Ibid.* II. 168 The lane-path where the dog-rose hings. **1826** J. WILSON *Noct. Ambr.* Wks. 1855 I. 356 Hing 't on my thoomb. *Mod. Sc.* Hing it up, and let it hing for a day.

2. Past Tense.

α. 1 **heng** (? **héng**), pl. **hengon**; 2–6 **heng**, pl. **henge(n**; 4 **heeng, -e(n**, 4–6 **henge**, 6 **heyng.** Orig. *trans.*; also 4–6 *intr.*

c **1000** ÆLFRIC *Gen.* xli. 13 Hine man heng. *c* **1000** *Ags. Gosp.* Luke xxiii. 33 þar hiȝ hine hengon [*c* **1160** *Hatton Gosp.* hengen]. **1154** *O.E. Chron.* an. 1137 §7 [Hi] him on rode hengen. *a* **1300** *Cursor M.* 8498 (Gött.) He.. henge [*Cott., Fairf.* hang(e, *Trin.* heng] þer-on, his folk to bie. *c* **1340** *Ibid.* 18561 (Trin.) þei him henge [*C.* hang, *F., G.* hanged]. **13..** *Coer de L.* 5712 Hys crouper heeng al full off belles. *a* **1350** *Childh. Jesus* 641 (Mätz.) His picher on þe sonnebeme he hieng. **1382** WYCLIF *Ps.* cxxxvi[i] . 2 Wee heengen [**1388** hangiden] vp oure instrumens. *c* **1400** MAUNDEV. (1839) viii. 93 The Tree of Eldre, that Judas henge him self upon. **1413** *Pilgr. Sowle* (Caxton 1483) I. xv. 10 For me thou henge vpon the crosse. *c* **1450** *Merlin* 53 His legges and his reynes hengen above the water. **1485** CAXTON *Chas. Gt.* 13 Agabondus.. after henge his wyf. **1526** *Pilgr. Perf.* (W. de W. 1531) 242 b, The thefe that heng vpon the crosse by our lorde. **1596** *King & Barker* 8 in Hazl. *E.P.P.* I. 4 Blake kow heydys sat he apon, The hornys heyng besyde.

β. 4–5 **hing(e, hyng, hynge.** *trans.* and *intr.*

c **1340** *Cursor M.* 17035 (Laud) While he hyng on that tre [*Cott., Gött.* hang, *Trin.* hong]. **1412–20** LYDG. *Chron. Troy* III. xxii. (MS. Digby 230, lf. 106 b/2), Vpon his arme he hinge [*MS. Digby* 232, lf. 82 b/1, heng] his hors rene. *c* **1450** *Cov. Myst.* (Shaks. Soc.) 379 He hynge hymself upon a tre. **1460** CAPGRAVE *Chron.* (Rolls) 214 Anon the Kyng.. hing [*mispr.* hung] the Januensis, and mad a new Capteyn. **1494** FABYAN *Chron.* I. ccxlii, Thys mater hynge in argument.. by the space of xv dayes. **1532** *Gower's Conf.* VIII. (ed. Berthelet) (R. Supp.), A pair of bedes blacke as sable She toke and hynge my necke about.

γ. 1 **hangode**, 2–4 **hangede** (4 **-ude**), 4– **hanged.** Orig. *intr.*; from 3- also *trans.* (the only form of pa. t. in 16th c. Bible versions, exc. occas. Tindale). Now only *trans.*, in sense 3.

c **1000** ÆLFRIC *Hom.* II. 240 Ðaða Crist hangode on rode for ure alysednysse. *c* **1200** *Vices & Virtues* 51 Ðe hali rode ðe Crist on hangede. *c* **1205** LAY. 29559 Heo.. nomen tailes of rehȝen, and hangede on his cape. *c* **1340** *Cursor M.* 19344 (Fairf.) þe quilk ȝe hanged [*Cott., Gött.* hang] with fals assise. *a* **1350** *Childh. Jesus* 23 (Mätz.) Iesus hangude is picher on þe sonne beme. **1382** WYCLIF *Matt.* xxvii. 5 Goyinge awey he hangide [*v.r.* heeng, **1388** hongide] hym with a grane. **1539** BIBLE (Great) *Matt.* xxvii. 5 And went and hanged hym selfe. *Mod.* [see B. 3.]

δ. 3–4 **hongede (-ide)**, 4 **honged.** Orig. *intr.*

c **1205** LAY. 13109 þe hod hongede adun. *a* **1225** *Ancr. R.* 106 þe munt of Caluarie, þer ure Louerd hongede. *c* **1340** *Cursor M.* 11898 (Trin.) þerynne þei honged him bi þe fete. **1382** WYCLIF *Gen.* xl. 22 The tother he hongide [**1388** hangide] in a gibete. ——*Josh.* ii. 21 She hongide [*v.r.* heeng, **1388** hangide] a litil reed coord in hir wyndowe.

ε. *north.* and *n. midl.* 3 **hengde**, pl. **-en**, 4 **henged.** Orig. *trans.*; in 4 also *intr.*

c **1200** ORMIN 9952 And henngdenn himm o rode. *Ibid.* 13773 þatt Judisskenn laþe follc, þatt henngde Crist o rode. **13..** *Gaw. & Gr. Knt.* 732 þe colde borne.. henged heȝe ouer his hede in hard ysse-ikkles. **1340** HAMPOLE *Pr. Consc.* 5260 Als he henged on þe rode tre. **1382** WYCLIF *Gen.* xxiv. 47 So I hengide [**1388** hangide, *v.r.* hynge] eer ryngis to honoure the face of hir.

ζ. *north. dial.* 3–4 **hinged**, 4 **hynged (-id, -ud).** *trans.* and *intr.*

a **1300** *Cursor M.* 8080 (Cott.) Lang and side þair brues wern, And hinged all a-bout þair hern. *Ibid.* 16676 (Cott. & Gött.) A theif on aiþer side þai hinged [*Fairf.* hong, *Tr.* heng]. *a* **1340** HAMPOLE *Psalter* xxi. 1 When he hyngid on þe crosse. **1340** —— *Pr. Consc.* 5334 þe man.. þe whilk yhe hynged on þe rode. *c* **1410** *Hampole's Psalter* cviii. 7 (Laud MS.) His dayes was few þat hyngid him selfe.

η. *north. dial.* 3– **hang.** *trans.* and *intr.*

a **1300** *Cursor M.* 4468 (Cott.) Apon ilk bogh.. hang winberis inogh [*Fairf.* hange, *Gött.* hing, *Trin.* henge]. *Ibid.* 18415 (Cott.) þe Iuus me hang bi-side iesu [*Gött.* hanged, *Laud* hanggyd, *Trin.* honged]. *c* **1400** MAUNDEV. (Roxb.) ii. 5 þat pece.. on whilk his body hang. **1578** *Ps.* li in *Scot. Poems 16th C.* II. 116 The thief that hang on thy right hand. *Mod. Sc.* He hang his bonnet on the peg. A man that hang aboot the place.

θ. *n. midl.* 3–7 **hong**, 3–5 pl. **-e(n**, 5–6 **honge**, 6 **houng, hoong.** *trans.* and *intr.* (But the 16–17th c. instances may perh. mean *hung*.)

c **1275** LAY. 29559 Hii.. nemen rohȝe tayl.. and honge[n on h]is cope. *a* **1310** in Wright *Lyric P.* xxv. 68 For love thou hong on rode tre. *c* **1340** *Cursor M.* 16717 (Trin.) þo þeues þat bi him honge. *Ibid.* 20336 (B.M. Add. MS.) Mi sone þei hongen on a tre. *c* **1386** CHAUCER *Knt.'s T.* 1564 The rynges on the temple dore that honge [*Camb.* henge]. **1513** MORE in Grafton *Chron.* (1568) II. 781 Nothing ware that the axe hong so nere his awne heade. **1526–34** TINDALE *Matt.* xxvii. 5 He.. went and hounge hym sylfe [*later vv.* hanged]. —— *Acts* x. 39 Whom they slew and honge [*later vv.* hanged] on tree. **1577–87** HOLINSHED *Chron.* (1807–8) II. 219 Then he hoong altogither on his sleeve. *Ibid.* III. 163 At this answer the duke hoong the groine. **1602** *2nd Pt. Return fr. Parnass.* I. ii. 222 Hearers hong vpon his melting tong [*rime* he song].

ι. 6– **hung.** *trans.* and *intr.* The current form.

1577 E. HOGAN in Hakluyt *Voy.* (1589) 157 Some of them.. hung down their heads like dogs. **1597** DANIEL *Civ. Wars* VII. (R.), That which hung by more than by one nail. **1636** G. SANDYS *Paraphr. Ps.* (Cassell) [Thou] hung'st the solid earth in fleeting air. **1662** J. DAVIES tr. *Olearius' Voy. Ambass.* 49 They.. hung about his neck some Pipes. *Mod.* I hung the pictures where they hung before.

3. Past Participle.

α. 1–5 **hangen** (5 **-yn**). β. 3–5 ***hange**, 5 **hang.**

a **1000** *Elene* 852 (Gr.) On hwylcum ðara beama bearn wealdendes.. hangen wære. *c* **1250** *Gen. & Ex.* 4074 Ðe bidde ic hangen ðat he ben. **1482** *Monk of Evesham* (Arb.) 38 Some were hangyn on galows.

14.. *Sir Beues* 4051 (MS. M.) With skyll he shall be hang and drawe. *c* **1460** *Towneley Myst.* (Surtees) 226 Lo so hy thay have hym hang.

γ. 3–4 **hongen.** δ. 3–4 **yhonge**, 4–5 **honge.**

c **1330** R. BRUNNE *Chron.* (1810) 172 Better.. þan to be hongen in þi frendis sight.

1297 R. GLOUC. (1724) 174 Hys sseld.. was þanne yhonge wast Aboute ys ssoldren. *a* **1400–50** *Alexander* 779 (Ashm.) Has a helme on his hede, and honge on his swyre A schene schondirhand schild.

ε. 4– **hanged.** (Now only in sense 3.)

c **1330** R. BRUNNE *Chron.* (1810) 50 Edrik was hanged on þe toure. **1377** LANGL. *P. Pl.* B. Prol. 176 þo þe belle was ybouȝt, and on þe beiȝe hanged. **1413** *Pilgr. Sowle* (Caxton 1483) III. iii. 51 Hye bemes and long on which were many hanged. **1535** COVERDALE *Hos.* ii. 8 Which she hath hanged vpon Baal. **1610** SHAKS. *Temp.* I. i. 35 If he be not borne to be hang'd. **1626** BACON *Sylva* §319 The Apple hanged in the Smoak. **1703** MAUNDRELL *Journ. Jerus.* (1732) 143 There were also hang'd in the Wall two small Bells. **1703** MOXON *Mech. Exerc.* 202 When no weight is hanged to it. *Mod.* They were hanged, drawn, and quartered.

ζ. 4–5 **honged, -ud, -id.**

c **1388** *Tract in Wyclif's Sel. Wks.* III. 472 He wolde raþer be hongud. **1426** AUDELAY *Poems* 3 Thevys al day hongud thay be. **1483** CAXTON *Gold. Leg.* 152 a/1 Theron he was honged tyl hys Armes were out of Joynte.

η. *north.* and *n. midl.* 3–6 **henged** (5–6 **-yd**).

c **1200** ORMIN 1018 þatt waȝherifft wass hennged tær. *c* **1300** *Havelok* 2480 To þe galwes drawen.. And þore ben henged wit two feteres. **1538** STARKEY *England* I. iv. 119 Hengyd wythout mercy or pyte.

θ. 4–5 **hinged, hynget**, 5 *Sc.* **hingit.**

c **1400** MAUNDEV. (Roxb.) ii. 5 þe crosse on whilk Dismas þe gude theefe was hynged. *a* **1400–50** *Alexander* 779 (Dubl.) And hynget vmby þar shwyre A shemerand sheld. *c* **1450** *Golagros & Gaw.* 438, I war wourthy to be Hingit heigh on ane tre.

ι. *north.* 6 **hingen (-in, -yn).** *rare.*

1513 DOUGLAS *Æneis* V. vi. 49 Ane arrow cais.. Hingin [*ed.* **1553** hingyn] by a braid tische of gold.

κ. 6– **hung.** The current form.

1592 SHAKS. *Ven. & Ad.* 103 Over my altars hath he hung his lance. **1594** —— *Rich. III*, I. i. 6 Our bruised armes hung vp for Monuments. **1697** DRYDEN *Virg. Georg.* I. 214 Baits were hung on Hooks. *Mod.* [see B. 1.]

B. Signification.

I. Transitive senses.

1. a. To place (a thing) so that it is supported from above, and takes, below the point of support, the position due to the action of gravity or any external force; to fasten, hook on, or attach to an object above; to suspend.

c **1000** *Sax. Leechd.* I. 362 Wið fefore nim blæces hundes deades þone swyþran foten sceancan, hoh on earm. **1297** R. GLOUC. (1724) 174 Hys sseld.. was þanne yhonge wast Aboute ys ssoldren. **1398** TREVISA *Barth. De P.R.* XIX. cxii. (1495) 918 Ostryches egges ben hangyd in chyrches for lyghtnesse for they ben so grete and selden seen. **1526** TINDALE *Matt.* xviii. 6 Yt were better for hym that a millstone were hanged aboute his necke. **1595** SHAKS. *John* III. i. 199 And hang a Calues-skin on his recreant limbs. **1647** WARD *Simp. Cobler* 8 He.. will for a need hang Gods Bible at the Devills girdle. **1666** PEPYS *Diary* 23 Aug., All the afternoon.. hanging things, that is my maps and pictures and draughts. **1769** BLACKSTONE *Comm.* IV. 202 It was frequently usual for the court to direct the murderer, after execution, to be hung upon a gibbet in chains. **1818** SHELLEY *Rev. Islam* III. xxv. 4 Hung them on high by the entangled hair. **1865** DICKENS *Mut. Fr.* (Tauchn.) III. 68 (Hoppe) I'll have a bell hung from this room to yours. *a* **1898** *Mod.* The artists whose pictures have not been hung in this year's Academy Exhibition. **1896** R. FRY *Lett.* (1972) I. 168 Tonk's *Broadstairs* is a terrible thing to hang: it is so spotty and brilliant that it knocks the other things to pieces. **1967** *Listener* 2 Mar. 296/2 More rewarding, and better hung,.. is the loan exhibition of graphics.

fig. **1340** *Ayenb.* 40 þe ualse demeres, þet ham zelue hongeþ more of one half þanne of anoþre. **1597** HOOKER *Eccl. Pol.* v. viii. §2 Why we should hang our iudgement vpon the Churches sleeue. **1671** MILTON *Samson* 59 God.. hung it [my strength] in my hair. **1873** HOLLAND *A. Bonnic.* xii. 203 He had hung the sweetest and highest hopes of his life upon me.

b. To suspend or tie up (bacon, beef, etc.) in the air to mature, to dry for preservation, or (game, venison) to become 'high'.

1599 H. BUTTES *Dyets drie Dinner* I vj b, Fallow Deere.. fat, very well chased, hang'd untill it be tender. **1697** DAMPIER *Voy.* I. 43 The meat they string up, and hang it a drying. **1796** MRS. GLASSE *Cookery* iii. 20 If your venison be very sweet, only dry it with a cloth, and hang it where the air comes. **1863** *Morn. Star* 1 Jan. 5 Potter.. said game is not fit to eat until it has been hung.

†**c.** To hook (a fish). *Obs.*

1674 N. COX *Gentl. Recreat.* IV. (1677) 46 The Pike.. being hung, he hath drawn the Duck clear under water. *a* **1683** OLDHAM *Passion of Byblis* Wks. (1686) 134, I should have first with art disguis'd the hook.. And found him hung at least before I strook. **1787** BEST *Angling* (ed. 2) 168 *Hang a fish*, hook him.

d. To suspend floating without attachment in the air, or in space.

1382 WYCLIF *Job* xxvi. 7 He.. hangeth vp the erthe vp on nouȝt. **1591** SYLVESTER *Du Bartas* I. iii. 971 Heavie things, hang'd in the Aire must fall. **1646** J. GREGORY *Notes & Obs.* (1650) 56 Over this Tohu or Nothing it was that he stretched the north or firmament and then hanged the Earth upon the same Nothing.

2. *spec.* To attach or suspend in such a way as to allow of free movement about or on the point of attachment; e.g. to hang a door (on its hinges), a coach (on springs), the tongue, the under jaw, etc. Also, to attach in a well-balanced or poised position, as to hang a scythe (on its 'snead').

1535 COVERDALE *Neh.* vi. 1 Had I not hanged the dores vpon the gates. **1697** DRYDEN *Virg. Georg.* III. 597 If a swarthy Tongue Is underneath his humid Palate hung. **1724** *Lond. Gaz.* No. 6318/2 A.. Spring.. to be used in hanging of Coaches. **1738** SWIFT *Pol. Convers.* 4, I warrant, this Rogue's Tongue is well hung. **1852** LANMAN *Daniel Webster* 20 (Cent.) He complained to his father that his scythe was not hung right. Various attempts were made to hang it better, but with no success. **1867** SMYTH *Sailor's Word-bk.*, *Hanging the rudder*, so as to allow the pintles to fall into their corresponding braces. **1881** YOUNG *Every Man his own Mechanic* §836 To shew its construction and the mode adopted in 'hanging' it [a door].

3. To fasten up or suspend on a cross or gibbet, as a mode of capital punishment; † **a.** formerly, *spec.* to crucify; **b.** now, *spec.* to put to death by suspension by the neck.

In this sense, *hanged* is now the specific form of the pa. tense and pa. pple.; though *hung* is used by some, esp. in the south of England.

c **1000** ÆLFRIC *Hom.* II. 308 Het se wælhreowa hine hon on heardre hengene. **1154** *O.E. Chron.* an. 1137 §7 [Hi] him on rode hengen for ure Drihtines luue. *a* **1225** *St. Marher.* 5 Hongeð hire on heh. *a* **1225** *Juliana* 28 þe reue.. het hire hon up ant hongin biþe toppe. **1297** R. GLOUC. (1724) 509 The king.. hangede men gultles. *c* **1320** *Sir Tristr.* 1797 Sche swore bi godes rode þai schuld ben hong and drain. *c* **1330** R. BRUNNE *Chron.* (1810) 247 As a þefe slawen, on galwes hanged hie. **13..** *Coer de L.* 3692 The devyl hange you be a corde! *c* **1400** *Destr. Troy* 7573 To be hangit in hast, or his hede tyne. **1465** *Paston Lett.* No. 99 I. 135, I was arestyd.. and was thretenyd to have ben hongyd, drawen, and quarteryd. **1548** HALL *Chron., Hen. VIII*, 16 Caused hym to be hanged, in the Palaice of Westminster, where he hong twoo daies. **1667** PEPYS *Diary* 4 Apr., He had hanged him at the yard's arm, without staying for a Court-martiall. **1711** E. WARD *Vulgus Brit.* III. 33 And like a Trew Blew Moderator Would Hang him first, and Try him a'ter.

1721–2 R. Wodrow *Suffer. Ch. Scotl.* (1838) I. i. iv. §4. 357/1 That he should be hanged at the cross of Edinburgh ..and after he was hanged dead, that his head be severed from his body. *c* **1801** C. K. Sharpe in *Mem.* (1888) I. 25 Paul slew his sire, was hanged, and hung in chains. **1817** Shelley *Address* Pr. Wks. 1888 I. 372 These men were..at last brought to the scaffold and hung. **1828** Scott *F.M. Perth* xxx, I hope they hanged the villain high enough? **1838** Dickens *O. Twist* lii, To be hanged by the neck, till he was dead—that was the end. **1896** *Globe* 18 Nov. 1/4 No one would have hung a dog upon the evidence. **18..** *Times* 11 Sept., Alleging the dictum of a Judge: 'Beef, Sir, is hung, men are hanged'.

c. *refl.* To commit suicide by hanging.

a **1300** *Cursor M.* 16504 A rape..fast he fest abute his hals, þer-wit him-self he hang. **1388** Wyclif *Matt.* xxvii. 5 He passide forth, and ȝede, and hongide hym silf with a snare. *c* **1460** *Towneley Myst.* (Surtees) 142 Let thame go hang thame. **1585** T. Washington tr. *Nicholay's Voy.* ii. 42 He constrayned them of dispaire and anger to hang themselves. **1590** Shaks. *Mids. N.* v. i. 366 If hee that writ it had..hung [*Qq.* hanged] himselfe in Thisbies garter. **1657** R. Ligon *Barbadoes* (1673) 51 Such an one that hang'd himself. **1855** Ld. Lonsdale in *Croker Papers* (1884) III. xxix. 323 You may regard it as only giving them rope to hang themselves! **1884** *Chamb. Jrnl.* 10 May 293/1 Zeno hanged himself at the ripe old age of ninety-eight.

d. Used as an imprecation, or as a strong expression of anger, vexation, or impatience. Also, ***I'll be hanged if...***, ***I'll see*** (***you***, etc.) ***hanged first***, as emphatic forms of angry refusal or denial.

13.. *Coer de L.* 4414 Hangyd be he that this toun yelde, To Crystene men, whyl he may leve! *c* **1392** Chaucer *Compl. Venus* 33 Jelousie be hanged be a cable! **1589** *Pappe w. Hatchet* 4 And so fare well, and be hangd! **1596** Shaks. *Tam. Shr.* ii. i. 301 Ile see thee hang'd on sonday first. **1598** —— *Merry W.* iii. iii. 196 Hang him, dishonest rascal! **1607** —— *Timon* iv. iii. 87 Hang thee, Monster! *Ibid.* v. i. 134 Speake and be hang'd. **1602** *2nd Pt. Return fr. Parnass.* iii. iii. 1296 Hang me if he hath any more mathematikes then wil serue to count the clocke. **1675** Hobbes *Odyssey* (1677) 208 But, hang him!..labour for his living he will not. **1703** Steele *Tend. Husb.* iii. ii, No, hang it! **1711** Addison *Spect.* No. 57 ¶7 I'll be hanged if you and your silent Friend there are not against the Doctor. **1712** Arbuthnot *John Bull* iii. ix, Part with my country-seat..I'll see him hanged first. **1738** Swift *Pol. Convers.* 82 She's immensely rich.—Hang her! they say, her Father was a Baker. **1779** Mrs. Thrale in *Mad. D'Arblay's Diary* 20 Oct., I would have sent to you, but hang it, thought I, if I only name her [etc]. **1836** Marryat *Midsh. Easy* xiii, But hang me if I hadn't the best of the argument. **1851** Mrs. Carlyle *Lett.* II. 143 I'll be hanged if I ever give you anything another time. **1852** R. S. Surtees *Sponge's Sp. Tour* xix, 'Hang the rain!' exclaimed Jawleyford. **1862** Thackeray *Round. Papers, De finibus* 276 'Be hanged to you, can't you leave me alone now?' **1889** J. K. Jerome *Three Men in a Boat* 246 'Well, hang it all, I've done more than old J., anyhow.' **1894** R. Bridges *Feast of Bacchus* v. 1541 'You and your Persian customs be hanged, Sir.'

4. a. To let droop or bend downward; to cause to lean or slope over.

1593 Shaks. *2 Hen. VI*, ii. iii. 45 Thus droupes this loftie Pyne, and hangs his sprayes. **1596** —— *1 Hen. IV*, iii. ii. 81 But rather drowz'd, and hung their eye-lids downe. **1697** Dampier *Voy.* I. 490 The Clouds began to hang their heads to the Eastward, and at last moved gently that way. **1827** Clare *Sheph. Cal.* 34 Where the snow-drop hings Its silver bell.

b. ***to hang the head*** (***down***): i.e. as a sign of shame, despondency, contrition, or sheepishness. So ***to hang the lip***, etc.

c **1205** Lay. 15688 Þa heng heo hire hæfued & heolde touward bræsten. *c* **1375** Chaucer *Troylus* iii. 1030 (1079) And þerwithal he heng a-doun his hed. *c* **1380** Wyclif *Serm.* Sel. Wks. I. 69 Crist comfortiþ his children..þerfore shulden þei rere þer heedis..and nouȝt hong þere heedis doun. **1548** Hall *Chron., Rich. III*, 54 Although he was there wᵗ all a litle vexed, beganne somewhat to hang yᵉ hedde [**1568** Grafton Began somwhat to hang the lip]. **1760** C. Johnston *Chrysal* (1822) II. 56 He hung down his head, and..withdrew quite abashed. **1786** Burns *Tam Samson's Elegy* iii, The Brethren o' the mystic level May hing their head on woefu' bevel. **1790** Mrs. Lennox *Euphemia* xxxv. III. 2 Miss Bellenden hangs her fair head at this intelligence. **1797** Mary Robinson *Walsingham* III. 173 The landlord hung his brow, abashed and selfreproved. **1887** Besant *The World went* vi. 48 He began to hang his head again, and to be despondent.

c. ***to hang the groin, a leg, an arse*** (vulgar): to hesitate or hold back; to be reluctant or tardy; to hang back.

1577–87 Holinshed *Chron.* (1807–8) III. 163 At this answer, the duke hoong the groine. **1596** Harington *Metam. Ajax* (1814) 61 Some of our rude countrymen english this hanging an arse. **1599** Marston *Sco. Villanie, Ad Rithmum* 194. **1633, 1663** [see arse 1 b]. **1828** *Craven Dial.* s.v. *Hing*, 'To hing an a—', to loiter. **1883** Stevenson *Treas. Isl.* i. v, You have your hands on thousands, you fools, and you hang a leg!

5. To furnish or decorate *with* things suspended about or around; *esp.* to deck or ornament (a place) with tapestry or hangings.

1451 [see hanged 3]. **1484** Caxton *Fables of Poge* (1889) 1 He saw the bedde rychely couerd & the walles wel hanged. **1523** Ld. Berners *Froiss.* I. xxxiv. 48 The hall of the towne was apparelled and hanged, as though it had ben the kynges chamber. **1568** Grafton *Chron.* II. 183 Conveyed her through the Citie, which then was richely hanged. **1634** Sir T. Herbert *Trav.* 38 Their eares hung with five, six, or eight Rings. **1697** Dryden *Virg. Past.* vi. 124 Till unperceiv'd the Heav'ns with Stars were hung. **1722** *Lond. Gaz.* No. 6084/2 The first Room was hung with Bayes. **1809** R. Langford *Introd. Trade* 121 How many yards of paper.. will hang a room?

6. a. ***to hang fire***: (of a fire-arm) to be slow in communicating the fire through the vent to the charge; hence *fig.* to hesitate or be slow in acting.

(It is doubtful if this is really transitive: it is perhaps connected with 17.)

1781 Thompson in *Phil. Trans.* LXXI. 278 In consequence of which the piece is slower in going off, or, as sportsmen term it, is apt to hang fire. **1801** Scott *Let. to G. Ellis* 7 Dec. in *Lockhart*, Leyden's Indian journey..seems to hang fire. **1815** *Sporting Mag.* XLVI. 120 He..was sure the jury would not hang fire in giving him a verdict. **1853** Kane *Grinnell Exp.* xxii. (1856) 174 It is a flint-lock concern, and half the time hangs fire. **1892** *Literary World* 27 May 509/2 A book produced anonymously hung fire for six weeks.

b. *fig.* To reduce to, or hold in, a state of indecision or inaction; *esp.* in phr. ***to hang a jury***, to prevent (as a juryman) a jury from reaching a verdict (cf. 17 c). *U.S.*

1778 G. Washington *Let.* 15 June in *Writings* (1834) V. 405, I am hung in suspense. **1848** E. Bryant *California* xxvi. 291 The jury, after the case was referred to them, were what is called 'hung'; they could not agree. **1868** *Harper's Mag.* Mar. 542/2 The jury..returned with a verdict in favor of the *plaintiff*! On remonstrating with the Mexican why he did not 'hang' the jury, the lawyer asked him, 'Why did you bring in a verdict against yourself?' **1967** *Guardian* 3 Apr. 2/7 The lone juror who finally hangs the jury will not emerge,..unless at the start his view has some support.

7. a. To catch or fasten in something.

18.. *Georgia Scenes* 17 (Cent.) Jake hung his toe in a crack of the floor, and nearly fell. **1882** Nares *Seamanship* (ed. 6) 183 If the crosstrees hang the mast..heave the mast up.

b. To tie or hitch up (a horse). (Cf. 28 e.) Chiefly *U.S.*

1835 *Southern Lit. Messenger* I. 581 Having arrived at Blank, we *hung* our horses, as Virginians always do after riding them. **1843** 'R. Carlton' *New Purchase* xxvi, While *hanging* Dick to a gate post. **1900** H. Lawson *On Track* 30 He got down, wondering what was up, and hung his horse to the last post but one. **1916** J. B. Cooper *Coo-oo-ee!* xii. 164 You made the remark that 'you'd tie up your horse'—an Australian 'hangs' his horse to a fence.

II. Intransitive senses.

8. a. The proper verb expressing the position or posture of a thing unsupported beneath, and kept from falling by being attached above; usually implying motion or mobility of the unattached parts: To remain fastened or suspended from above; to depend, dangle, swing loose.

c **1000** Ælfric *Hom.* I. 466 His loccas hangodon to ðam anccleowum. *c* **1205** Lay. 13109 Þe hod hongede adun. *a* **1300** *Cursor M.* 3067 On þat tre hinges frut ful gode. **1398** Trevisa *Barth. De P.R.* xiii. xxiv. (1495) 456 A drope hangynge fallynge or stondynge. *c* **1440** *York Myst.* xlviii. 21 He ete the appill I badde schulde hyng. **1548** Hall *Chron., Hen. VIII*, 3 Her heire hangyng downe to her backe, of a very great length. **1585** T. Washington tr. *Nicholay's Voy.* iv. iii. 115 b, They hadde theyr Woodknife or skaine hanging at their girdle. **1597** R. Johnson *Seven Champions* i. i. (1867) 7 Another apartment, where hung the richest armour in the world. **1662** J. Davies tr. *Olearius' Voy. Ambass.* 305 Sheep..with the Ears hanging down. **1674** tr. *Scheffer's Lapland* 93 They have alwaies some [water] hanging over the fire in a kettle. **1774** Goldsm. *Nat. Hist.* (1776) IV. 246 It often also hangs by the tail, which is long and muscular. **1842** Tennyson *Morte d'Arthur* 219 Curls.. clotted into points and hanging loose. **1861** M. Pattison *Ess.* (1889) I. 45 Among the portraits which hung above were two allegorical pieces.

b. In various proverbs and phrases.

1548 Hall *Chron., Hen. VI*, 168 b, By whose misgovernaunce..his aucthoritie [might] hang in a very small thred. **1581** Pettie *Guazzo's Civ. Conv.* ii. (1586) 97 b, With a sword still hanging by a haire over his head. **1707** Watts *Hymn, 'Thee we adore, Eternal Name'* v, Great God! on what a slender Thread Hang everlasting Things! **1818** Scott *Rob Roy* xxvi, Na, na! let every herring hing by its ain head, and every sheep by its ain shank. **1838** De Quincey *Wks.* (1863) XV. 43 *note*, During the currency of the three Sundays on which the banns were proclaimed by the clergyman from the reading-desk, the young couple elect were said jocosely to be 'hanging in the bell-ropes', alluding perhaps to the joyous peal contingent on the final completion of the marriage.

c. Of flesh for food: To be suspended or fastened up in the air to dry, mature, or become 'high': cf. 1 b.

1861 Mrs. Beeton *Househ. Managem.* (1880) 528 A hare ..is better to hang without being paunched.

d. (By transposition of subject and adjuncts): To be furnished or adorned with things suspended or attached.

13.. *Coer de L.* 5712 Hys crouper heeng al full off belles. **1737** Bracken *Farriery Impr.* (1757) II. 95 He is apt..to hang all over with a kind of dewy Sweat. **1872** Black *Adv. Phaeton* xiii. 181 Bands of sand..hanging with every variety of wild flower.

9. To be supported or suspended at the side, as on a hinge or pivot, so as to be free to turn or swing horizontally.

a **1300** *Cursor M.* 18104 He..brast þe brasen yates sa strang, And stelen croc þat þai wit hang [*Gött.* lock þat þar-on hang]. **1869** W. C. Hazlitt *Eng. Prov. & Proverbial Phrases* 7 A creaking door hangs long on its hinges.

10. *spec.* **a.** Of a person: To be suspended *on* or *upon* a cross, gibbet, gallows, etc.; to suffer death in this way; esp. as a form of punishment. Also as an imprecation: cf. 3 c. Now usu. in phr. ***to go hang***: to go and be hanged; to 'go to the devil'; to be dismissed or rejected; freq. ***let*** (***it***, etc.) ***go hang***.

c **1000** Ælfric *Hom.* II. 256 Þes halȝa Hælend hangað her unscyldiȝ. *a* **1225** *Ancr. R.* 106 He [our Lord] ase he hongede, muhte habben hore breð..amidden his neose. *a* **1300** *Cursor M.* 12218 Worthi he war on gebet hang. **1340** *Ayenb.* 218 Þanne hit behoueþ þet hi yelde: oþer þet hi hongi. Vor ase me zayþ: 'oþer yelde: oþer hongi'. *c* **1489** Caxton *Sonnes of Aymon* xxii. 481 He shall see me hange shamfully. **1596** Shaks. *1 Hen. IV*, ii. i. 74 If I hang, Ile make a fat payre of Gallowes. **1606** —— *Ant. & Cl.* ii. vii. 59 Go hang sir, hang: tell me of that? Away. **1610** —— *Temp.* ii. ii. 53 [She] Would cry to a Sailor, goe hang. **1712–14** Pope *Rape Lock* iii. 22 Wretches hang that jurymen may dine. **1879** Browning *Ned Bratts* 24 Betting which knave would 'scape, which hang. **1881** C. Gibbon *Dead Heart* v, 'The Count..may go hang for me.' **1921** R. Hichens *Spirit of Time* xii. 203 Hold on to the best in yourself and let all the rest go hang. **1937** J. Betjeman *Coll. Poems* (1958) 41 Other cars all go hang My little bus is enough for us. **1960** M. Sharp *Something Light* xix. 174 Louisa instantly resolved to let the room go hang. **1973** *Physics Bull.* June 345/3 It would even be proper for SRC to decide to support (say) only 20 post-graduate schools of chemistry and to let the rest go hang.

b. To be in desperate difficulties. *slang.*

1874 Hotten *Slang Dict.* 187 *Hanging*, in difficulties. A man who is in great straits, and who is, therefore, prepared to do anything desperate to retrieve his fortunes, is said, among sporting men, to be 'a man hanging', i.e. a man to whom any change must be for the better. **1889** Barrère & Leland *Dict. Slang* I. 446/2 *To hang* (popular and sporting), to be in a desperate state.

11. a. To have the top bending or projecting beyond the lower part; to bend forward or downward; to lean over; also, to incline steeply (see hanging *ppl. a.* 2).

Beowulf (Z.) 1362 Se mere..ofer þæm hongiaþ hrinde bearwas. *c* **1400** *Lanfranc's Cirurg.* 82 Ordeyne þe lyme so þat þe mouþ of þe wounde hange dounward. **1546** Langley *Pol. Verg. De Invent.* iii. x. 77 a, Dædalus..first inuented the plomline, whereby the Euenes of the Squares bee tried whether they batter or hang ouer. **1568** Tilney *Disc. Mariage* D vij, The top of a highe rocke, which hung over the sea. **1598** Greneway *Tacitus' Ann.* xii. viii. 165 The high hils which hanged ouer them. **1641** F. Hawkins *Youth's Behav.* (1663) 19 Go not with thy head too high, nor too low, nor hanging to the right, or left. **1818** Shelley *Rev. Islam* i. xxiii, The mountains hang and frown Over the starry deep. **1851** Greenwell *Coal-trade Terms Northumb. & Durh.* 29 *Hang*, to incline or dip. **1871** Freeman *Norm. Conq.* IV. xviii. 191 The later castle, whose picturesque turrets and battlements hang so proudly over the river at its feet.

b. To lean or watch *over* (with care and anxiety, as a sick or dying person).

1792 S. Rogers *Pleas. Mem.* i. 45 O'er infant innocence to hang and weep. **1855** Tennyson *Maud* i. xix. iv, When only Maud and the brother Hung over her dying bed.

c. *Iron-founding.* = scaffold *v.* 5.

1878 *Jrnl. Iron & Steel Inst.* XII. 202 When a furnace 'hangs' on one side, a more common occurrence with small old furnaces than with large modern ones, a system prevailed in some works of putting half a pig of lead in above the part that was fast. **1908** R. Forsythe *Blast Furnace* 242 When the stock becomes wedged so tightly that it can no longer descend, the furnace is said to 'hang'.

d. Of a horse: to veer towards one side.

1951 E. Rickman *Come racing with Me* ii. 16 Sarda II 'hanging' towards Native Heath..who won by a short head. **1958** J. Hislop *From Start to Finish* xi. 128 Courses such as Epsom and Lewes, where the ground slopes towards the rails and horses tend to hang that way. **1965** *Observer* (Colour Suppl.) 30 May 34 If he starts to hang before he tires a jockey can generally straighten him up.

12. a. To remain suspended without visible support; to rest, float (in the air, etc.).

c **1200** Ormin 7339 Þe sterrne comm rihht till þatt hus.. And..heng þæroferr stille. *c* **1305** *St. Christopher* 210 in *E.E.P.* (1862) 65 In þ'eir hi [arewes] honge aboue him. **1563** W. Fulke *Meteors* iv. (1640) 46 b, A Cloud is a vapor cold and moyst, drawne..by the heate of the Sunne, into the middle region..where, by cold it is so knit together that it hangeth. **1658** Willsford *Secrets Nat.* 111 If the Stars.. seem to hang as if they were ready for to fall, it argues [etc.]. **1712** Addison *Spect.* No. 420 ¶3 To see so many Worlds hanging one above another. **1850** Tennyson *In Mem.* cvii. 10 Yon hard crescent, as she hangs Above the wood. **1883** Stevenson *Treas. Isl.* iii. xiv, The few birds..still hung in alarm above the heads of the intruders.

b. *fig.* Of an evil or doubt: To hover *over* one, ready or liable to fall; to impend, be imminent; esp. in phrase, ***to hang over*** (***one's***) ***head***.

1548 Hall *Chron., Edw. IV*, 219 The greate calamities and adversities, whiche then did hang over her hed, and were likely..to fall. **1552** *Bk. Com. Prayer* Communion, How sore punishmente hangeth ouer your headès. **1651** Hobbes *Leviath.* ii. xxv. 133 The punishment hanging over us for our sins. **1664** *Flodden F.* iv. 34 Now since at hand such danger hings. **1783** *Polite Trav.* 76 Embittered as they were by..the popular odium which hung over them. **1865–6** H. Phillips *Amer. Paper Curr.* II. 72 Uncertainty hung over the movements of the British troops in New York.

13. a. To rest *on*, *upon* (†*of*, etc.) for support or authority; to depend *upon*; to be dependent *on*.

c **1000** Ælfric *Hom.* II. 314 Hi ealle [ȝesette] hangiað on ðisum twam wordum. *c* **1200** *Moral Ode* 312 in *Trin. Coll. Hom.* 229 Al hit hangeð and halt bi þese twam worde. **1382** Wyclif *Gen.* xliv. 30 The lijf of hym hongith [**1388** hangith] of the lijf of this. **1413** *Pilgr. Sowle* (Caxton 1483) iii. iv. 52, I had made..one of yow Chaunceler and another tresorer in whiche offyces specially hanged alle the gouernaunce. **1471** Ripley *Comp. Alch.* iv. xiv. in Ashm. (1652) 147 And in two thynges all our entent doth hing. **1538** Starkey *England* i. i. 14 The vnyuersal and true law of nature..no thyng hangyng of the opynyon and folysch fansy of man. **1660** R. Coke *Power & Subj.* 202 The proces hanging upon such writs. **1718** Prior *Pleasure* 299 Does life or death Hang on the wrath or mercy of my breath? **1824** L. Murray *Eng. Gram.* (ed. 5) I. 444 A sentence composed of several members linked together, and hanging upon one another. **1852** TENNYSON *Ode on Wellington* 240 One, upon whose hand and heart and brain Once the..fate of Europe hung.

b. To remain or rely in faith or expectation; to count or depend confidently *on*, *upon* (†*of*). ?*Obs.*

1393 LANGL. *P. Pl.* C. xv. 214 And hope hongeþ ay þer-on to haue þat treuthe deserueþ. *c* **1400** *Destr. Troy* 8089 At hir wordes, I-wis, the worthy was glad; Hengit in hope, held hym full gayne. **1549** COVERDALE, etc. *Erasm. Par. Heb.* 18 But what thing was it that made him more dearly beloued of God then his brother Cayn: Forsoth faith, wherby he wholy hanged of him. **1625** *Gonsalvio's Sp. Inquis.* Pref. D ij b, Matters which hee vnderstandeth not, whereby he must needs hang altogether of other mens opinions. **1817** MAD. D'ARBLAY *Wanderer* V. 123 Determined..to hang..solely upon herself.

c. To remain in consideration or attention.

c **1340** HAMPOLE *Prose Tr.* 37 Hafe in mynde his manhede sumtyme..bot leue of sone and hyng noghte to lange þareappone. *c* **1491** *Chast. Goddes Chyld.* 92 A man shall put suche myswenyng away from hym, ne dwelle not ne henge not longe therupon. **1557** N. T. (Genev.) *Luke* xix. 48 All the people hanged vpon him when they heard him. **1638** BAKER tr. *Balzac's Lett.* (vol. III.) 215 You have auditors.. they run after your words, and hang at your mouth. **1766** FORDYCE *Serm. Yng. Wom.* (1767) II. viii. 18 Attention will hang upon her words. **1864** TENNYSON *En. Ard.* 873 Enoch hung a moment on her words.

14. To attach oneself for support; to cling, hold fast, adhere. **a.** with arms, claws, mouth, etc.

c **1330** *Assump. Virg.* (B.M. MS.) 653 The Iewe þat henge apon þe bere [l. 615 To þe bere he cleued fast]. **1393** LANGL. *P. Pl.* C. IV. 227 Thou hast hanged on myn hals elleuen tymes. *c* **1465** *Eng. Chron.* (Camden 1856) 47 Yonge childrynne lay ded in the stretis, hangyng on the ded modris pappis. **1583** STUBBES *Anat. Abus.* II. (1882) 43 Halt, blind, lame..hanging vpon his sleue..crauing of releefe. **1596** SHAKS. *Tam. Shr.* II. i. 310 Shee hung about my necke, and kisse on kisse Shee vi'd so fast. **1622** SPARROW *Bk. Com. Prayer* (1661) 376 Notorious sinners..begging the prayers ..hanging upon the knees of all that entered into the Church. **1711** ADDISON *Spect.* No. 31 ¶2 The dogs..would hang upon their Prey by their Teeth. **1885** *Manch. Exam.* 5 June 8/4 Two young maids..hang with laughing glee on his arms.

b. Of things: To stick, adhere, cleave.

1639 S. DU VERGER tr. *Camus' Admir. Events* 130 Whose foote hanging in one of his stirrups, and the Mule setting himselfe to run..drag'd. **1662** J. DAVIES tr. *Olearius' Voy. Ambass.* 305 The fat hangs to them in great gobbets. **1688** J. SMITH *Baroscope* 37 The Mercury will never play free therein, but hang to the Sides. **1860** TYNDALL *Glac.* I. vii. 51 Secondary glaciers..hanging on the steep slopes.

c. To stick close, so as not to leave or let go.

1508 DUNBAR *Flyting w. Kennedie* 226 With..all the toun tykis hingand at thy heilis. **1697** BENTLEY *Phal.* etc. *Ep. Euripides* (1836) II. 213 Give me an advocate that will stick close, and hang upon a cause. **1735** SOMERVILLE *Chase* II. 227 The patient Pack Hang on the Scent unweary'd. **1838** THIRLWALL *Greece* xl. V. 119 Alexander..hung upon their rear, obstructed their march.

d. Of the wind: To remain persistently in a certain point of the compass.

1671 R. BOHUN *Wind* 142 The Easterly are..very often the most freezing winds, especially if they hang somewhat towards the North. **1697** DAMPIER *Voy.* I. 82 The Winds hung in the western quarter betwixt the N.W. and the West, so that we could not get much to the Westward. **1748** *Anson's Voy.* III. vi. 351 The winds hanging in the northern board. **1781** NELSON 5 Mar. in Nicolas *Disp.* I. 40, I am sorry the wind hangs so much Western board, as it must hinder the sailing of the Grand Fleet. **1865** GOSSE *Land & Sea* (1874) 6 On one occasion the wind had hung long from the westward.

e. To attach oneself as a dependant or parasite; to be a hanger-on.

1535 COVERDALE *Prov.* xix. 6 The multitude hangeth vpon greate men. **1613** SHAKS. *Hen. VIII*, III. ii. 367 Oh how wretched Is that poore man, that hangs on Princes fauours? **1691** WOOD *Ath. Oxon.* I. 584 His son Edm. lived by hanging on Gentlemen, and by his shifts. **1766** GOLDSM. *Vic. W.* iii, Crowds of dependants..hung upon him for a time. **1832** *Examiner* 268/1 They..continued to hang on the parish.

15. a. To cling or adhere as an encumbrance or drag; to be a burdensome or depressing weight.

c **1450** *Golagros & Gaw.* 1176 As tuiching this thing That now hingis on my hart. **1592** SHAKS. *Rom. & Jul.* V. i. 71 Contempt and beggery hangs vpon thy backe. **1653** WALTON *Angler* ii. 50, I begin to be weary; yester dayes hunting hangs stil upon me. **1700** BP. PATRICK *Comm. Deut.* xxviii. 68 Though some, as I said before, were sold at a very vile rate, next to nothing; yet others hung upon the sellers hands. **1760** C. JOHNSTON *Chrysal* (1822) III. 6 Something hangs upon your spirits. **1821** SHELLEY *Prometh. Unb.* I. 436 Most heavy remorse hangs at my heart.

b. esp. of time.

1711 ADDISON *Spect.* No. 93 ¶2 Several Hours of the Day hang upon our Hands. **1768–74** TUCKER *Lt. Nat.* (1852) II. 316 So much time hanging heavy upon our hands for want of employment. **1770** GRAY in *Corr. w. N. Nicholls* (1843) 104 To pass my solitary evenings, which hung much lighter on my hands before I knew him. **1892** W. PIKE *Barren Ground N. Canada* 137 With these attractions and a fair supply of books, time did not hang at all heavily.

16. *fig.* To be attached as an adjunct or connected circumstance.

1596 SHAKS. *Tam. Shr.* IV. i. 60. **1598** —— *Merry W.* I. iv. 159 Wel, thereby hangs a tale. **1688** KENNET in *Magd. Coll. & Jas. II* (O.H.S.) 258 Thereby hangs a tale. **1847** L. HUNT *Men, Women, & B.* II. iv. 52 Thereby hangs an anecdote that shall be noticed presently.

17. a. To be or remain in dubious suspense; to be doubtful or undecided. Also *to hang in the wind.*

1382 WYCLIF *Deut.* xxviii. 66 Thi lijf shal be as hongynge before thee. **1430–40** LYDG. *Bochas* I. xiv. (1554) 27 b, Althea..Gan sore muse and henge in a balaunce. *c* **1500** *Melusine* xxxi. 228 Wherfore the cyte henge in balaunce to be delyuered & gyuen ouer to the Sarasyns. **1551** T. WILSON *Logike* (1580) 77 b, The Counsaill have long debated..and as yet the matter hangeth in suspence. **1555** J. PROCTOR *Hist. Wyat's Rebell.* in Arb. *Garner* VIII. 70 Such..as hung in the wind, as neuters. **1679** T. SIDEN *Hist. Sevarites* 95 We began to hang between fear and pleasure. **1732** POPE *Ess. Man* II. 7 He hangs between; in doubt to act, or rest. **1862** MRS. CARLYLE *Lett.* III. 144 He has been hanging betwixt life and death. **1881** *Daily Tel.* 28 Jan., I..hung in the wind a moment before asking leave to step down. **1881** JOWETT *Thucyd.* I. 65 A battle was fought which hung equally in the balance.

†**b.** To remain unsettled or unfinished; to be held in process or in abeyance: often with a notion of delay. See also HANGING *ppl. a.* 3. *Obs.*

1494 *Sc. Acts Jas. IV* (1597) §57 The summoundes that ar now dependand and hingand betuixt ony parties. **1538** STARKEY *England* I. iv. 118, I see many mennys materys heng in sute ii, iij, or iiij yere. **1666** PEPYS *Diary* 27 Oct., While the business of money hangs in the hedge. **1728** W. SMITH *Ann. Univ. College* 321 The Cause would never have hung upon the Hedges so long as it did.

c. Of a jury: to fail to agree. (Cf. 6 b and HUNG *ppl. a.* 3.) *U.S.*

1859 BARTLETT *Dict. Amer.*, *To hang*, to stick fast, come to a stand still; as, the jury hung, and 'the man got a new trial'. **1929** *Randolph Enterprise* (W. Va.) 24 Oct. 5/1 The jury hung up on the case and were discharged.

18. Of a note in music: To be prolonged.

1597 MORLEY *Introd. Mus.* 81 He woulde saie it hangeth too much in the close. **1779** BURNEY *Infant Music.* in *Phil. Trans.* LXIX. 198 A particular note hung, or, to speak the language of organ builders, ciphered, by which the tone was continued without the pressure of the finger.

19. a. To remain with motion suspended.

1667 MILTON *P.L.* VI. 189 A noble stroke he lifted high, Which hung not. **1847** TENNYSON *Princ.* VII. 64 Ida came behind Seen but of Psyche: on her foot she hung A moment, and she heard.

b. To slacken motion perceptibly; *spec.* in *Cricket* (see quots.) and *Baseball*. Occas. *trans.*

1838 *Bell's Life* 8 July 4/4 The dead state of the ground, which prevented the balls from working, and caused them to hang considerably. **1897** K. S. RANJITSINHJI *Jubilee Bk. Cricket* 77 The ball is made to hug the ground when it pitches, and to rise slowly afterwards, or 'hang', as it is called by cricketers... With some bowlers it either 'hangs' or more often comes fast off the pitch owing to something in their regular action. **1897** *Encycl. Sport* I. 246/1 A ball 'hangs' which rises unexpectedly slowly from the pitch. **1906** JEPHSON in H. G. Hutchinson *Cricket* 103 He ran up and delivered the ball, to all appearances, exactly similarly each time; but one found now that the ball was hanging in the air, now that it was on to one surprisingly soon. **1928** *Funk's Stand. Dict.* I. 1112/1 *Hang* (Sport), to slacken speed perceptibly and unexpectedly: said of a ball in flight in various games, and of a boat between strokes, in rowing. **1967** *Boston Globe* 5 Apr. 51/6 'It was a bad pitch,' Bennett admitted. 'I was trying to pitch low and instead I hung a high curve ball for him to hit.'

c. *to hang to* (see quot.).

1888 *Lockwood's Dict. Mech. Engin.* 172 *Hang to*, a term having several applications. A file hangs to its work when it cuts without slip. A saw hangs to, when it feels as though being drawn into the timber. A pattern hangs to the sand when it delivers with difficulty.

20. To remain as unwilling to depart or move on; to loiter, linger, as with expectation or interest: often with the implication of parasitical attachment. Cf. *hang on*, 26. Also, esp. *U.S.*, ***to hang around*** (a person, place, etc.). So ***hang-arounder.***

1830 *Corrector* (Sag Harbor, N.Y.) 26 June 1/3 What a number of young gentlemen you have in this city—hanging round the corners—standing in hotel doors. **1842** TENNYSON *Godiva* 2, I hung with grooms and porters on the bridge, To watch the three tall spires. **1847** J. S. ROBB *Streaks of Squatter Life* 133 Every time I come up from Lusiane, I found Jess hangin' round that gal. **1854** KINGSLEY *Hypatia* ix, Groups of monks, priests..and citizens..were hanging about the courtyard. **1856** KANE *Arct. Expl.* II. iv. 49 This same deer has been hanging round the lake. **1861** DICKENS *Gt. Expect.* xxxviii, Drummle so hung about her..that I resolved to speak to her concerning him. **1883** F. M. PEARD *Contrad.* xxxiv, Stephen..hung by her side while she gathered the flowers. **1885** 'C. E. CRADDOCK' *Prophet Gt. Smoky Mts.* 8, I hev seen that critter, that thar preacher, a-hangin' round you-uns house a powerful deal lately. **1892** *Law Times* XCIII. 490/1 The witnesses had to be kept hanging about. **1897** S. T. CLOVER *Paul Travers' Adv.* 51, I guess I can fix you out if you hang around here, but keep shady. **1915** N. L. MCCLUNG *In Times like These* vi. 72 Although the polls are only open every three or four years, if women .once get into the way of going to them, they will hang around there all the rest of the time. **1938** O. NASH *I'm Stranger Here Myself* 234 The hang-arounders' cheerful chirrups. **1939** I. BAIRD *Waste Heritage* xi. 136 He hung around the window then he stopped in the doorway and tried the door in case there was anyone inside the store could say whether Eddy had been hanging around. **1950** A. LOMAX *Mr. Jelly Roll* 57 Buddy Bolden, the most powerful trumpet player I've ever heard..and the absolute favourite of all the hangarounders in the Garden District. **1970** G. F. NEWMAN *Sir, You Bastard* viii. 244 He didn't hang around afterwards. **1973** *Melody Maker* 25 Aug. 27 In a front room in Shepherds Bush, however, plots are being hatched—and hang about, because I'm not going to bore you with yet another..yarn.

†**21.** To hanker *after* or *for*. *Obs.*

c **1672** WOOD *Life* (O.H.S.) I. 475 His mind still hung after antiquities and musick. **1684** SOUTHERNE *Disappointment* II. i, Alphonso..whom my heart hangs after for its peace.

III. In combination with adverbs.

22. hang back. *intr.* To resist advance by one's weight or inertia; *fig.* to show unwillingness to advance or come forward; to be backward.

1581 PETTIE *Guazzo's Civ. Conv.* II. (1586) 110 So if hee hang backe, hee shall bee halled forward with honour. **1673** DRYDEN *Marr. à la Mode* II. i, Pr'ythee do not hang back so. **1709** ADDISON *Tatler* No. 81 ¶4 Another, that hung back at the Entrance, and would have excused himself. **1819** J. W. CROKER in *C. Papers* 4 May, Peel and Plunkett were hanging back, each unwilling to speak first. **1872** BLACK *Adv. Phaeton* x. 140 The horses hanging back from the pole [of the phaeton] in this fashion.

23. hang behind. *intr.* To lag behind and retard progress.

1674 N. COX *Gentl. Recreat.* I. (1677) 16 When Hounds hang behinde, and beat too much upon the scent or place, we say, They Plod.

24. hang in. *intr.* To persist in spite of adversity (as of a boxer app. facing defeat); to hold out or endure; also, to wait around. Freq. *imp.* and with *there*. *colloq.* (chiefly *U.S.*).

1969 *New Yorker* 14 June 44/3 He tries a careful, hang-in-there, soft crosscourt top-spin dink. **1971** E. E. LANDY *Underground Dict.* 98 Hang in (there). **1971** *Atlantic Monthly* May 6/1 [President Nixon] has a long history of coming from behind..and of confronting adversities, and it would be in his nature to hang in there and fight. **1972** *Dict. Contemp. & Colloq. Usage* (Eng.-Lang. Inst. Amer.) 15/1 *Hang in* there, buddy, you'll soon feel better. To make sense; to fit in or carry through, as a conclusion that is appropriate for what went before. **1974** *New York* 18 Mar. 39 Rose Mary Woods is hanging in, but her friends say it has been difficult. **1979** J. HELLER *Good as Gold* 347 Hang in there, if you can, until his eyes turn glassy and he starts to yawn. **1982** *Observer* 26 Sept. 25/7 Mrs Mao had him down and almost out, but he hung in. **1984** J. ARCHER *First among Equals* xii. 134 'No, no,' said Simon. 'I'll hang in there now that I've waited this long.'

25. hang off. a. *intr.* To cease to cling; to leave hold.

1590 SHAKS. *Mids. N.* III. ii. 260 Hang off thou cat, thou bur; vile thing let loose.

b. To show hesitation in coming to close quarters or to an agreement; to hang back, demur.

1641 TRAPP *Theologia Theol.* 238 Moses..hung off a great while from going to Pharaoh with a message of dismission. **1669** PEPYS *Diary* 3 Jan., I, out of my natural backwardness, did hang off, which vexed her. **1686** GOAD *Celest. Bodies* I. xii. 44 We hang off, and seem loth to come upon the Stage. **1894** *Daily News* 18 Sept. 2/7 Buyers hanging off to an unusual extent.

26. hang on. a. *intr.* To remain clinging, to continue to adhere: usually implying expectation, or unwillingness to sever one's connexion.

1860 MRS. CARLYLE *Lett.* III. 61 Charlotte..is still hanging on at her mother's..with nothing to do. **1861** DUTTON COOK *P. Foster's D.* II. 56 What does he do now? Oh, he hangs on at the Nonpareil. **1884** CHURCH *Bacon* iii. 61 The shrewd and supple lawyers who hung on to the Tudor and Stuart Courts. **1893** FARMER *Slang*, *To hang on by one's eyelashes*..to persist at any cost, and in the teeth of any discouragement. **1899** G. B. SHAW *Let.* 20 Apr. (1931) 260 She is always hanging on by her eyebrows, whereas the German is comfortably seated in a solid, permanent, broadbottomed engagement. **1931** *Times Lit. Suppl.* 12 Mar. 193/1 Lacking roots in the soil of any particular country, Whistler had always to 'hang on by his eyebrows'. **1935** *Yachting* Dec. 82/3 *Hanging on by the eyelids*, the seaman's vivid description of his situation during a very heavy gale. **1958** *Listener* 21 Aug. 259/2 Each aircraft hangs on to the tail of the one directly in front.

b. *to hang it on*: to delay or protract a matter; cf. *to hang it out*, 27 d. (*slang.*)

1812 J. H. VAUX *Flash Dict.*, *Hang it on*, purposely to delay or protract the performance of any task or service you have undertaken, by dallying and making as slow a progress as possible. **1823** EGAN *Grose's Dict. Vulg. Tongue.*

c. To wait. Freq. in *imp.*, be patient, be reasonable!

1939 J. B. PRIESTLEY *Let People Sing* x. 262 I'd better hang on and have a word with her. **1941** BAKER *Dict. Austral. Slang* 34 *Hang on!*, be reasonable! Not so fast. **1971** *Woman's Own* 27 Mar. 26/1 Hang on a minute... I'm coming with you.

d. Used in 'hold the line'. conversation in the sense of 'hold the line'.

1936 R. LEHMANN *Weather in Streets* I. iv. 70 Hang on a moment... Mummy wants to speak to you. **1960** *Daily Tel.* 15 Aug. 17/5 Switchboard operators have been trained not to keep any caller 'hanging on'. **1969** S. HYLAND *Top Bloody Secret* i. 37 'Shall I tell him you're coming?' 'Yes please. Tell him to hang on'.

e. *to hang on to* (something): to retain.

1871 TROLLOPE *Eustace Diamonds* (1873) I. xvi. 220 It was manifest enough that she meant 'to hang on to them' [*sc.* the diamonds]. **1936** 'M. INNES' *Death at President's Lodging* ix. 166 He had in his possession certain valuable documents... Umpleby simply hung on to them. **1971** 'D. HALLIDAY' *Dolly & Doctor Bird* ii. 16 The hotel wouldn't let her hang on to her room.

f. *to hang one on*: to deal (someone) a blow.

1908 K. MCGAFFEY *Sorrows of Show-Girl* 200 Hauling off wifey hangs one on Alla's map. **1960** B. CRUMP *Good Keen Man* 44 I'd thought for a moment he was going to hang one on me. The idea..had got his goat all right. **1966** *Punch* 19 Jan. 69/1 There are moments when most of us have felt the keenest desire to hang one on the boss's chin and walk out.

g. Used in various technical senses (see quots.).

1963 *Amer. Speech* XXXVIII. 118 *Hang on*, to maintain a proper position for the receiver while it is coupled to the tanker's air refueling boom. 'Dingbat 27, can you hang on if I start a slow turn to the left?' **1967** *Gloss. Mining Terms (B.S.I.)* x. 7 *Clip on* or *hang on*, to attach a tub or tubs to a haulage rope by a clip or shackle.

27. hang out. a. *intr.* To protrude with downward direction.

c **1400** *Lanfranc's Cirurg.* 59 Wiþ open mouþ..his tunge hangiþ out. **1590** SHAKS. *Mids. N.* IV. ii. 42 Let not him that playes the Lion, paire his nailes, for they shall hang out for the Lions clawes. **1674** N. COX *Gentl. Recreat.* I. (1677) 120 The canine Teeth..hang out very long.

b. *trans.* To suspend (a sign, colours, or the like) from a window, on a projecting pole, a rope, etc.; to display as a sign or signal. Also, *to hang out to dry*: to suspend (wet washing) on a clothes-line in the open so that it can dry. Hence *transf.* in *Cricket*: *hang one's bat out to dry* (see quots.).

to hang out one's shingle (*U.S. colloq.*) to put up one's sign-board or door-plate, to establish oneself in business.

1564 in *Vicary's Anat.* (1888) App. iii. 166 Takynge care, that they..doe neyther hange or beate oute..eny maner of beddynge or apparrell. **1600** J. PORY tr. *Leo's Africa* II. 129 While women are bathing themselves, they hang out a rope at the first entrance of the house, which is a signe. **1654** WHITLOCK *Zootomia* 79, I will..be the Physitian, and hang out an Urinall. **1712** ADDISON *Spect.* No. 265 ¶6 The Whig and Tory Ladies begin already to hang out different Colours. **1884** BESANT *Childr. Gibeon* 2 When she was hanging out the clothes. **1893** *N.E.D.* s.v. *Clothes* sb. pl., *Clothes-line, rope*, a cord or wire on which to hang out washed clothes to dry. *a* **1898** *Mod.* Flags and banners were hung out in honour of the royal visit. **1895** C. B. FRY in *Badminton Mag.* Aug. 132 He [*sc.* the young player on hard wickets] gets into the habit of moving his right leg, leaving his bat hanging out to dry, and playing crooked. **1925** *Country Life* 25 July 142/1 In playing forward..never 'hang your bat out to dry' by not advancing your left foot to the pitch of the ball; if you do, you have neither power nor control.

c. *intr.* To reside, lodge, live (*colloq.* or *slang*). Also, of a job: to be available, to be found.

1811 *Lex. Balatronicum* s.v., *The traps scavey where we hang out*, the officers know where we live. **1837** DICKENS *Pickw.* xxx, I say, old boy, where do you hang out? **1876** GEO. ELIOT *Dan. Der.* xxxvii. (D.), I've found two rooms at Chelsea..and I shall soon be ready to hang out there. *c* **1926** 'MIXER' *Transport Workers' Song Book* 69 When there is a job hanging out. **1931** T. LYELL *Slang* 364, I hear you've got a job in Foster's factory. Where does it actually hang out? **1931** D. RUNYON *Guys & Dolls* (1932) ii. 35 He cannot have a whole lot of sense, or he will not be hanging out with Handsome Jack. **1935** *Forres, Elgin & Nairn Gaz.* 6 Nov. 4/5 (*heading*) Later American word-imports... Phrases are very numerous:—Where do you hang out? **1936** WODEHOUSE *Laughing Gas* ii. 23 The head of the family has always hung out at the castle.

d. (*Australian colloq.*) *to hang it out* = 'to hang it on', 26 b. Also without *it*: to endure, hold out. Chiefly *Austral.* and *N.Z.*

1890 BOLDREWOOD *Col. Reformer* (1891) 236 As long as they have their grub and their wages they'll hang it out, one again the other. *Ibid.* 341 The rest of the time you'll have to hang it out the best way you can. **1939** J. DELL *Nobody ordered Wolves* ii. 14 B. and P. offered her twelve thousand ..but I told her to hang out and sure enough Bill sold her to M.B.G. for fourteen thousand flat. **1941** BAKER *Dict Austral. Slang* 34 *Hang out*, to endure: to delay (a matter). **1944** J. FULLARTON *Troop Target* xi. 87 I've been pretty crook for the last hour. But I wanted to hang out till we saw a house. **1946** K. TENNANT *Lost Haven* ix. 132 The old punt had broken down at last. He had been hoping against hope that it would hang out until the war ended, but the luck was against him.

e. Slang phr. *to let it all hang out*: to be uninhibited or relaxed; to be candidly truthful. orig. *U.S.*

1970 C. MAJOR *Dict. Afro-Amer. Slang* 76 *Let it all hang out*, to be uninhibited, free. **1972** *National Observer* (N.Y.) 27 May 17/3 Give it expression, they say, 'Let it all hang out.' If it 'all hangs out', it is bound to do some good. **1972** *Village Voice* (N.Y.) 1 June 51/1 No names, of course, will be used; he doesn't expect everyone will be as willing as he is to let it all hang out.

28. hang together. a. *intr.* To adhere together loosely or without rigid attachment.

c **1400** *Lanfranc's Cirurg.* 48 Ouþer a boon is not kutt al atwo but sum of his substaunce is don awey..or ellis he hangiþ togidere. **1673** RAY *Journ. Low C.* (1738) I. 421 Bastons of wood hacked and cleft (but so as the pieces hang together).

b. To be coherent or consistent; to constitute a coherent or consistent whole.

1553 T. WILSON *Rhet.* (1580) 107 The rather their tale maie hang together. **1594** SHAKS. *Rich. III*, III. vi. 4 Here is the Indictment..And marke how well the sequell hangs together. **1699** BENTLEY *Phal.* 47 How can these two stories hang together? **1885** *Manch. Exam.* 22 Sept. 5/1 There are many things in the Berlin Treaty which do not hang well together.

c. To hold together; to be associated, united, or mutually dependent; *spec.* (of a person) to keep body and soul together, to continue to exist.

1551 T. WILSON *Logike* (1580) 25 b, Therefore it hangeth together as Germaines lippes, as we use to saie. **1598** SHAKS. *Merry W.* III. ii. 13 As idle as she may hang together for want of company. **1644** MILTON *Jdgm. Bucer* Wks. 1738 I. 284 Many Marriages hang as ill together now, as ever they did. **1697** COLLIER *Immor. Stage* iv. §3 (1730) 140 Let us now see how Sir Tunbelly hangs together. **1760** C. JOHNSTON *Chrysal* (1822) III. 24 We have always been remarkable for hanging well together. **1894** *Westm. Gaz.* 14 June 3/1 Someone having said to him, 'You know, Franklin, we must all hang together in this matter', he instantaneously replied, 'Yes, or we shall assuredly all hang separately!'

29. hang up. a. *trans.* To fasten a thing on high so that it is supported only from above; to suspend on a hook, peg, or the like. Also *absol.* = to hang up the receiver of a telephone at the end of a conversation; *to hang up on*: to break off telephonic communication with.

a **1300** *Cursor M.* 12072 And be þe har he vp him hang þat all moght se him spek him to. **13..** *Gaw. & Gr. Knt.* 477 Now sir, heng vp þyn ax. *c* **1440** *Anc. Cookery* in *Househ. Ord.* (1790) 447 Honge hit up in a clothe a lytel while. **1686** N. COX *Gentl. Recreat.* IV. (ed. 3) 28 A Range of Presses made with Peggs in them to hang up Saddles [etc.]. **1726** *N. Riding Rec.* VIII. 174 All Mayors..are hereby ordered to hing or cause to be hung up this order in some public place. *a* **1898** *Mod.* Let me hang up your overcoat. **1911** A. B. SMITH *Mod. Amer. Teleph.* xxvi. 759 When the subscribers are through talking, they hang up their receivers. **1928** E. WALLACE *Double* viii, 'Oh, Mr. Staines!.. What a dull life yours must be!' And then she hung up on him, and left him feeling like a spanked child. **1928** F. N. HART *Bellamy Trial* iii. 101 He'd hung up, I guess. Anyway he didn't answer. **1952** A. BARON *With Hope, Farewell* 103 He managed to say, 'Thank you,' and was about to hang up. **1960** *Daily Tel.* 15 Aug. 17/5 Several directors and secretaries of firms told me that they hung up within a minute if they could not get through. **1968** 'P. BARRINGTON' *Accessory to Murder* vii. 125 Mrs. Lindley heard the click of the receiver and became indignant. He'd almost hung up on her.

b. Phrases. *to hang up* (*one's sword, gun*, etc.): to put aside in disuse; to give up using. *to hang up one's hat*: see quots.; *to hang up one's boots*, to give up playing a game; *to hang up the spoon*, to die; *to hang up a record*, to set up a record.

[**1297** R. GLOUC. (1724) 561 Ich mai honge vp min ax, febliche ic abbe agonne. **1595** *Maroccus Ext.* p. v, And therewith mee thinkes I see him hang the hat upon the pin againe. **1659** B. HARRIS *Parival's Iron Age* 46 Before we sheath our sword, and hang it upon the nail.] **1826** H. N. COLERIDGE *West Indies* 249 And having fought through the Peninsula hung up his sword *non sine gloria*. **1847** MARRYAT *Childr. N. Forest* v, A little more practice, and I will..hang my gun up over the chimney. **1855** TROLLOPE *Warden* xix, Eight hundred a year, and as nice a house as any gentleman could wish to hang up his hat in. **1888** ELWORTHY *W. Somerset Word-bk.* s.v., When a man marries and goes home to the wife's house to live, he is said to 'hang up his hat'. **1925** O. JESPERSEN *Mankind, Nation & Individ.* ix. 166 There are countless variants [for 'to die']..take an earth bath, hang up the spoon, snuff the candle, snuff it. **1930** *Publishers' Weekly* 15 Mar. 1508/2 A record sale was hung up..on Tuesday... Four hundred and ten copies of the book were sold in one hour. **1938** D. RUNYON *Take it Easy* xv. 283 Professor D. says he has no doubt that under the old rule Nicely-Nicely will hang up a record that will endure through the ages. **1942** BERREY & VAN DEN BARK *Amer. Thes. Slang* 44 *Reside*, hang up one's hat. *Ibid.* 132 *Die*, hang up one's hat. *Ibid.* 242 *Hang up one's hat*,..to be perfectly at ease, make oneself at home. **1949** F. SARGESON *I saw in my Dream* II. xiii. 113 Some said that..he'd have had more self-respect if he'd told the girl to go and hang her hat up somewhere else. **1963** *Times* 23 Jan. 3/4 Johnson, Miller, and Johnston hung up their boots soon afterwards and two years later Benaud began to build the side.

†**c.** To hang on a gibbet (= sense 3); hence as an imprecation (= 3 c). *Obs.*

1588 SHAKS. *L.L.L.* IV. iii. 54 The shape of Loues Tiburne, that hangs vp simplicitie. **1592** —— *Rom. & Jul.* III. iii. 57 Hang vp Philosophie: Vnlesse Philosophie can make a Iuliet, Displant a Towne. **1771** GOLDSM. *Hist. Eng.* IV. 10 Feversham, immediately after the victory, hanged up above twenty prisoners. **1774** —— *Grecian Hist.* II. 59 If Philip takes the city, he will hang up Aster.

d. To put 'on the shelf' or into abeyance; to keep back, delay, detain for an indefinite time. Also *to hang it up*, to chalk it up, to give credit. *slang.*

1623 F. RYVES *Let.* 8 Oct. in *Abp. Ussher's Lett.* (1686) 301 After a while, that Negotiation was hung up upon the Nail, in expectance of the Princes return. **1803** G. ROSE *Diaries* (1860) II. 33 He might hang the matter up..as long as he pleased. **1841** *Swell's Night Guide* Gloss., *Hang it Up*, to go on Credit. **1844** W. H. MAXWELL *Sports & Adv. Scotl.* xiii. (1855) 118 The Roost of Sumburgh will..'hang up' a vessel among its..currents..for days together. **1874** 'MARK TWAIN' & WARNER *Gilded Age* I. xiii. 172 The Colonel muttered something to the barkeeper about 'hanging it up'. **1884** *Pall Mall G.* 20 Oct. 1/1 Carried by a larger majority than that which hung up the Franchise Bill in July. **1890** *Spectator* 12 July 37/2 The proposal..to hang up Bills which might be proceeded with in another session of the same Parliament without beginning *de novo*. **1942** S. H. ADAMS *Tambay Gold* xiv. 191 They hung me up for the parking fee.

e. To fasten or tie up (a horse). *Austral. colloq.*

1858 W. KELLY *Life in Victoria* (1860) 49 In Melbourne there are posts sunk in the ground almost opposite every door... Fastening your horse to one of these posts is called 'hanging him up'. **1890** BOLDREWOOD *Col. Reformer* xvi. 185 The gentleman in advance hung up his horse and walked into the house. **1895** *Pall Mall Mag.* Sept. 104 He hung up his horse to that post. **1966** 'J. HACKSTON' *Father clears Out* 118 On the Saturday many good hacks were hung up at the hotel.

f. *intr.* To be suspended on a wall, etc. Also, to suspend movement or action; to stop or stay.

1667 PEPYS *Diary* 22 July, In my Lord's room..where all the Judges' pictures hung up. **1845** *Greenfield Fish. Rec., Chowan, N.C.* 6 May in N. E. Eliason *Tarheel Talk* (1956) 276 Made 2 hauls & hung up [for the fishing season]. **1854** *Congress. Globe* App. 108 (Th.), In reading the President's message,..he got befogged, and, in the language of the Kentucky boatman, 'hung up for the night.' **1874** E. EGGLESTON *Circuit Rider* xvi, You mou't get a place 'bout a mile furder on whar you could hang up for the night. **1895** *Dialect Notes* I. 372 A mower, when rain was coming on: 'I reckon we'll have to hang up for all day.'

g. *Cab-drivers' slang.* (See quots.)

1930 'A. ARMSTRONG' *Taxi* xii. 164 'Hanging it up' is loitering past a theatre to snatch a fare away from the recognized rank. **1939** H. HODGE *Cab, Sir?* I. v. 50 Policemen in these outer districts are more easy-going than in the West End. So I chance 'hanging it up' as we call it, near the door, keeping my engine running in case the policeman looks too nasty.

hang (hæŋ), *sb.* [f. prec. vb.]

1. a. The action of hanging, drooping, or bending down; also, a downward inclination, slope, or bend; a declivity.

1807 VANCOUVER *Agric. Devon* (1813) 50 Yarcombe is favorably situated on the south-east hang of a hill. *c* **1850** *Rudim. Navig.* (Weale) 140 *Ram-line.* A..line..used for the purpose of forming the sheer or hang of the decks. **1850** L. HUNT *Autobiog.* i. (1860) 25 Never shall I forget her face.. with that weary hang of the head on one side.

b. A slackening or suspension of motion. Also in *Cricket* (see HANG *v.* 19 b).

1866 *Morning Star*, The objectionable hang at the termination of the stroke [of an eight-oar] had almost entirely disappeared. **1867** F. FRANCIS *Angling* v. (1880) 182 A trout usually rests where the hang and eddy of the stream will give him the best chance. **1888** R. H. LYTTELTON in Steel & Lyttelton *Cricket* ii. 48 Any break, hang, or rise that the bowler or the ground may impart to the ball must almost inevitably produce a bad stroke. **1897** K. S. RANJITSINHJI *Jubilee Bk. Cricket* 78 The ideal bowler..should do his best to acquire a command of off-break and leg-break, 'top' and 'hang'. **1901** [see BUMP *sb.*[1] 1 c].

2. The mode in which a thing hangs or is poised; *spec.* of a painting or work of art.

a **1797** MRS. M. GODWIN *Posth. Wks.* (1798) IV. 121 Death could not alter the rigid hang of her limbs. **1864** WEBSTER s.v., The hang of a scythe or of a discourse. **1878** JEFFERIES *Gamekeeper at H.* 6 So accustomed is he to its balance and 'hang' in the hand that he never thinks of aiming. **1885** MISS BRADDON *Wyllard's Weird* III. 22 She believed that for the hang of a skirt..she could hold her own with any house in London. **1959** *Listener* 5 Mar. 422/3 The Secretary of the Society, with no previous experience of the compromise necessary in rooms so unsuited to the display of very modern painting, has achieved a remarkably successful hang. **1964** *Guardian* 21 Apr. 9/1 At the great Tate Gallery exhibitions..the brilliance of the hang has invariably been cancelled out by the failure of..the lighting engineers.

3. *to get the hang of*: to become familiar with the proper wielding or use of a tool; *fig.* to get to understand, manage, master, deal with as an adept; to acquire the knack of. (orig. *U.S. colloq.*)

1845 N. S. PRIME *Hist. Long Island* 82 (Bartlett) After they have..acquired the hang of the tools for themselves. **1847** DARLEY *Drama in Pokerville* 67 (Farmer) The theatre was cleared in an instant..all running to get the hang of the scrape. *a* **1860** T. PARKER in J. Weiss *Life* (1864) II. 434, I ..think I have got the hang of the people and their institutions. **1860** O. W. HOLMES *Elsie V.* xxii. (1892) 245 Your folks have never got the hang of human nature. **1881** *Spectator* 12 Feb. 223 They..have not yet got the hang of good biography. **1883** CRANE *Smithy & Forge* 21 The hammer is one of those tools that the workman gets used to, or 'gets the hang of'. **1890** *Daily Chron.* 4 Apr. 7/2 He gets what some call 'the hang' of the place. **1895** R. KIPLING in *Century Mag.* Dec. 271/1 I'm getting the hang of the geography of that place. **1918** *War Illustr.* 13 July 372/3 On the second day I had a 'flip' round the aerodrome to get the 'hang' of the country. **1931** H. G. WELLS *Work, Wealth, & Happiness of Mankind* (1932) 1 Never before has there been this need and desire to 'get the hang' of the world as one whole. **1957** *Listener* 17 Oct. 606/1 Children..in their desire to get the hang of their surroundings.

4. *concr.* (*dial.*) Something that hangs or is suspended; a hanging mass or clump; a crop of fruit; a hang-net.

a **1825** FORBY *Voc. E. Anglia*, *Hang*, a crop of fruit. 'A good tidy hang of apples'. **1857** KINGSLEY *Two Y. Ago* xxv, It might be..one of the 'hangs' with which the club-water was studded, torn up and stranded. **1873** *Act 36 & 37 Vict.* c. 71 Sched. iii, License Duties for each..Weir, hang, baulk, garth, goryd, box, crib, or cruive..£12. 0. 0.

5. *not..a hang*: an angry or impatient equivalent of 'not a bit', 'not in the least': usually with *care*. Cf. HANG *v.* 3 d, DAMN *sb.* 2.

1861 H. KINGSLEY *Ravenshoe* xliii. (Farmer), She looks as well as you by candlelight, but she can't ride a hang. **1876** 'OUIDA' *Winter City* vi. 125 She don't care a hang what anybody says of her.

6. (*a*) *hang of a*: an Australian and N.Z. intensive phrase, variously spelt (*hangava, hanguva*, etc., and in altered forms, e.g. *hangashun*), used informally, sometimes with adverbial force, of something big, bad, vexatious, etc., of its kind. Also *like hang*, like hell. Cf. HELLISHING, HELLISHUN.

1941 BAKER *N.Z. Slang* vi. 51 Expressions..in constant use by our youngsters..hangava, hangashun. **1943** J. A. W. BENNETT in *Amer. Speech* XVIII 90 The intensives hanguva, hangershun. **1945** F. SARGESON *When Wind Blows* ii. 14 They got down in a hang of a hurry. *Ibid.* iii. 16 All this was because Charlie was hang of a funny to be with. **1949** *Landfall* III. 145 Gosh, Dad's hangava crabby with you! **1950** B. SUTTON-SMITH *Our Street* ii. 33 It's a hang of a wet day. **1960** N. HILLIARD *Maori Girl* 64 It hurts like hang.

hang-, the verb-stem used in comb. in various constructions; as **hang-back**, one who hangs back or hesitates; **hang-bench** (dial. *hing-bench*), in *Lead-mining*, a piece of timber forming part of a stow, which is pinned to the sole-tree by wooden pins; **hang-choice**, a choice between two evils; **hang-fair** (see quot.); **hang-five, -ten** *Surfing* = *hanging five, ten* (HANGING *ppl. a.* 6); so *to hang five, ten*; **hang-gallows**, *a.* destined or fit for the gallows; *sb.* a gallows-bird; **hang-glider**, (*a*) a suspension glider, controlled and stabilized by deliberate movements of the operator's body, which is suspended upright in the framework of the machine; (*b*) one who operates a hang-glider; hence [as a back-formation] **hang-glide** *v. intr.*; **hang-gliding** *vbl. sb.*; **hang-head** *a.*, that hangs its head; †**hang-lipped** *a.*, having hanging or drooping lips; †**hang-lock**, a hanging lock, a padlock; **hang-nest**, a bird that constructs a pensile nest, a HANGBIRD; **hang-net**, a kind of net which is set vertically; †**hang-on**, a hanger-on, a mean dependant; **hang-out** (*slang*): see quots.; †**hang-rope**, †**hang-string**, †**hang-up** = *hang-gallows*; **hang-up** *slang*, drawback, fault; difficulty, fixation, 'thing'; also *attrib.*

1866 *Public Opinion* 31 Dec. 720 'You mean Emancipation!' exclaim the *hang-backs. **1653** MANLOVE *Lead-mines* 268 (E.D.S.) Stowes, Crosses, Holes, *Hange-benches. **1747** HOOSON *Miner's Dict.* P iij b, The Sole-trees and Hang-benches are fastned together with Pins of Wood. **1851** TAPPING *Gloss. Derbysh. Lead-mining Terms* (E.D.S.), *Hange-benches* or *Hing-benches*. **1816** SCOTT *Antiq.* xxx, I hope Saint Patrick sung better than Blattergowl's precentor, or it would be *hang-choice between the poet and psalmist. **1811** SOUTHEY in *Q. Rev.* VI. 283 Regarding an execution as a holiday, which..they call *hang-fair. **1962** D. MUIRHEAD *Surfing in Hawaii* viii. 80 (*caption*) Film-maker Walt Phillips *hangs five at Halewia, Hawaii. **1969** *Observer* 3 Aug. 35/1 He may 'nose ride', balancing on the very front of the board to achieve a 'hang five' or 'hang ten', with five or ten toes over the tip of the board. **1785** GROSE *Dict. Vulg. Tongue*, **Hang gallows look*, a thieving or villainous appearance. **1790** *By-stander* 233 A hang gallows rascal without money. *Ibid.* 298, I was sent to Coventry, as an incorrigible hang gallows. **1828** *Craven Dial.*, *Hang-gallows*, a villain; a proper subject or pendant for the gallows. **1986** *Washington Post* 28 Feb. D5/1 You can polish up your banjo-playing at an Appalachian crafts workshop in West Virginia. Or learn to *hang-glide on the beach at Nags Head in North Carolina. **1930** V. W. PAGÉ *Henley's ABC of Gliding & Sailflying* (1931) 202 On '*hang' gliders the lateral and longitudinal stability and the angle of attack are controlled by shifting the weight of the pilot. **1969** K. MUNSON *Pioneer Aircraft 1903–14* 125/2 The unpowered D.1 was launched from a 4-wheel trolley chassis for its first take-off in 1907 with Colonel Capper aboard. However, when it was damaged in a crash-landing further tests were abandoned in favour of the D.3 'hang-glider'. **1972** *Daily Tel.* 7 June 13/8 Considerable interest is being revived in hang gliders and at least four groups are now working on prototype flying wings... They rely on the pilot's leg-work to become airborne and span and performance is limited by the power of the human shoulder. **1973** *Sunday News* (N.Y.) *News Mag.* 16 Sept. 28/1 'It is the most beautiful, the quietest, the cleanest sport,' says one hang glider. **1973** *Daily Colonist* (Victoria, B.C.) 21 Aug. 16/3 She was flying a Black Hawk hang glider made of black plastic sheeting stretched on aircraft tubing and cable. It has a 38-foot wingspan and a 15-foot keel. **1978** *Guardian* 10 Apr. 2/4 Britain's 60 top hang-gliders spent the weekend 1,000ft. above the Sussex Downs. **1986** *Washington Post* 21 May Health 14/1 Type T personalities include not only hang gliders, mountain-climbers and round-the-world balloonists, but also artists, scientists and entrepreneurs. **1971** *Soaring* June 3/1 The photograph is of Taras Kiceniuk, Jr. '*'ang glidin'' in our group-owned Rogallo hang glider at Soledad Pass, California. **1972** *Daily Tel.* (Colour Suppl.) 13 Oct. 10/3 In America the sport of 'hang gliding'..is becoming extremely popular. **1973** *Daily Colonist* (Victoria, B.C.) 6 July 15/1 Hang gliding is the closest you can get to flying free. **1871** G. MACDONALD *Wild Flowers* in *Wks. Fancy & Imag.* III. 27 *Hang-head Bluebell. **1574** *Durham Depos.* (Surtees) 313 She..did heare the said Janet Wilkinson call the said Katheryne '*hange lipped witche'. **1411** *Nottingham Rec.* II. 86, j. *henglok, ijd. **1587** *Vestry Bks.* (Surtees) 26 Item given for a key to a hinge locke, jd. **1713** DERHAM *Phys. Theol.* IV. xiii. 233 *note*, The Icterus minor, and the Jupujuba, or whatever other Name the American *Hang-nests may be called by. **1868** WOOD *Homes without H.* xiii. 241 The Baltimore Oriole goes by many names..such as Hang Nest and Hanging Bird, from the beautiful pensile nest which it makes. **1812** *Agric. Surv. Dumfr.* 605 (Jam.) *Hang-nets are larger in the mesh than any other nets, and are stretched upright between stakes of about ten feet long, placed at regular distances of about eight feet. **1873** *Act 36 & 37 Vict.* c. 71 §39 No byelaw made under the authority of this section shall limit the length of a hang net. **1589** *Hay any Work* (1844) 45 Ungodly bishopps, with their *hangones and parasites. *Ibid.* 69 What is that you Bb. and your hangones will not saye by Walde-graue. **1852** BRISTED *5 Years in Eng. University* (Farmer), The fourth of July I celebrated by a *hang-out. **1893** FARMER *Slang*, *Hang out*, a residence; a lodging; and (American university) a feast; an entertainment. **1895** *Harper's Mag.* Apr. 712/1 He [the tramp]..calls his clubhouse a hang-out. **1895** *Century Mag.* Oct. 943/1 In the afternoon some thirteen boys appeared at the 'hang-out'. **1896** *Atlantic Monthly* Jan. 67/2 His wanderings ended..oftener in some distracting vagabond's 'hang-out' in a neighboring city. *a*1911 D. G. PHILLIPS *Susan Lenox* (1917) II. x. 248 She avoided the tough places, the hang-outs of the gangs. **1951** R. CAMPBELL *Light on Dark Horses* 244 But I had still another hang-out. That was the Harlequin Restaurant. **1957** *New Yorker* 5 Oct. 66/3 The most energetic dancer of her day, gyrating nightly at the Stork Club and other hangouts of the quality. **1960** *Guardian* 9 Nov. 8/6 Basement hangouts which have a vogue and then disappear. **1968** *Globe & Mail Mag.* (Toronto) 13 Jan. 7/3 It is 3 a.m. in a steam bath known as an after-midnight homosexual hangout. **1570** LEVINS *Manip.* 170/6 *Handgrope, *furcifer*. **1675** COTTON *Scoffer Scoft* 40 A pretty Child thou art..little *Hang-string. **1963** *Pix* 28 Sept. 62/2 **Hang ten*, ten toes over the nose of the board. **1967** *New Yorker* 25 Feb. 18/1 *The endless Summer*—A hang-ten documentary about surfing in various parts of the world. **1562–3** *Jack Juggler* in Hazl. *Dodsley* II. 151 You have cause now to thank this same *hang-up. **1959** *Daily Colonist* (Victoria, B.C.) 16 Apr. 2/6 Man—Omnibus salutation extended to men, women, domestic animals—saves cool cat hangup of remembering names. **1967** A. DIMENT *Dolly Dolly Spy* ii. 27 Hash..is non-narcotic but whether..it leads you on to the hang up drugs I don't know. **1967** *Melody Maker* 27 May 10/6 All these hang-ups are eliminated by the truth—this is a great record. *Ibid.* 29 July 10/5 There are all sorts of hang-up noises going on in the background. **1967** *Ottawa Jrnl.* 31 May 39/2 Your husband's hang-up dates back to childhood and you must treat it as an illness, which it is most assuredly. **1967** *Crescendo* Dec. 27/4 He was always very kind and patient with me, as he was..with all people. A great degree of sensitivity to people's hang-ups, you know—he'd never put you on a spot. **1968** *Melody Maker* 22 June 2 The group didn't want the hang up of worrying about recording specific singles. **1968** *Observer* 22 Dec. 21/1 People have this hang-up about art. A woman will worry for days about spending money on a painting: is it a good investment, can she trust her own judgment? The same woman will spend £150 on a dress..without giving it a thought. **1973** *Black World* Apr. 17/1 Depressing piece about pushers, junkies, whores and their hang-ups.

hangable ('hæŋəb(ə)l), *a. rare.* [See -ABLE.]

1. Capable of being or liable to be hanged.

1595–6 in Tytler *Hist. Scot.* (1864) IV. 238 [James VI..was resolved no more to use great men or chancellors in his affairs, but such as he could correct, and were] 'hangable'. **1719** OZELL tr. *Mission's Mem.* 122 All those People calling themselves Bohemians or Egyptians, are hangable as Felons at the Age of 14 Years.

2. Of an offence: Punishable by hanging.

1815 MISS MITFORD in L'Estrange *Life* (1870) I. 323 It does not..appear that he ever committed any hangable or transportable offence.

3. That may lead to hanging.

1836 T. HOOK *G. Gurney* (1850) III. iii. 351, I felt none of that hangable, drownable desperation about her.

So **hanga'bility**, capacity of being hanged.

1829 LAMB *Lett.* xvii. To Procter 157 The theoretical hangibility (or capacity of being hanged, if the judge pleases) of every infant born with a neck on.

hangar (See below). [Fr.; ulterior origin uncertain: see Du Cange, Diez, Littré.]

‖**a.** (hɑ̃gar). A covered space, shed, or shelter, *esp.* for carriages.

1852 THACKERAY *Esmond* III. xiii, Mademoiselle, may we take your coach to town? I saw it in the *hangar*. **1861** tr. *Du Chaillu's Equat. Afr.* xv. 253 The people gathered..under the immense *hangar* or covered space. **1886** SHELDON tr. *Flaubert's Salammbo* vii, The rumbling chariot..halted under a wide hangar.

b. ('hæŋə(r)). A shed for the accommodation of aircraft or spacecraft.

1902 *Daily Chron.* 31 Oct. 5/3 Mr. Santos Dumont..will construct a hangar in the Bois de Boulogne. **1935** H. G. WELLS *Things to Come* ix. 48 Inside an aeroplane hangar. **1962** A. SHEPARD in *Into Orbit* 97, I tried to avoid moving into Hangar S—our quarters at the Cape—for as long as I could. **1962** V. GRISSOM *Ibid.* 119 On 1 July the capsule was taken from the hangar to the launching pad to be mated to the Redstone.

hangarage ('hæŋərɪdʒ). [Blend of *hangar* and *garage*.] Accommodation for aircraft in a hangar.

1932 *Flight* 10 Nov. 1044/1 When I thought I was almost beaten, I suddenly won, and hangarage was granted. **1961** R. HIGHAM *Brit. Rigid Airship* vii. 121 This caused a tremendous demand for hangarage and other means of storing gear under cover. **1970** M. KELLY *Spinifex* iii. 54 Hangarage for twenty planes. Full servicing workshops.

hangashun, hangava, etc.: see HANG *sb.* 6.

hangbird ('hæŋbɜːd). [f. HANG *v.* + BIRD *sb.*] A bird that builds a hanging nest; *esp.* an American oriole of the family *Icteridæ*.

1789 J. MORSE *Amer. Geogr.* 59 Upwards of one hundred and thirty American Birds have been enumerated ..[including the] Hangbird, Heron, Little white Heron. **1794** S. WILLIAMS *Hist. Vermont* 118 Hangbird, *Oriolus icterus*. **1824** Z. THOMPSON *Gazetteer Vermont* 18 The singing birds are the robin, thrush,..springbird, goldfinch and hangbird. **1831** J. Q. ADAMS *Mem.* (1867) VIII. 426 The oriole of Baltimore is the fiery hang-bird. **1856** BRYANT *Poems, Gladness of Nature* ii, There are notes of joy from the hang-bird and wren. **1868** WHITTIER *Among Hills* 1, The hang-bird overhead, His hair-swung cradle straining.

†**'hang-by.** *Obs.* exc. *dial.* (hing-by). [f. HANG- vb.-stem + BY *adv.* and *prep.*]

1. A contemptuous term for a dependant or hanger-on.

1579 GOSSON *Sch. Abuse* (Arb.) 40, I meane those hange-byes whome they succour with stipend. **1599** B. JONSON *Cynthia's Rev.* v. iii, Enter none but the Ladies, and their Hangbies. **1655** FULLER *Hist. Camb.* 9 To condemn the whole University for a hand-full of Hang-byes, such as never were matriculated members therein. **1855** ROBINSON *Whitby Gloss.*, A *Hing-by*, an adherent, a dependent, a flatterer.

2. An appendage, an adjunct.

*c*1585 R. BROWNE *Answ. Cartwright* 35 Why then will he haue the Lordes discipline..to be but an accident or hangby to the Church? **1620** THOMAS *Lat. Dict.*, *Appendix*..a pent-house..a processe, a hangby, a labell. **1661** K. W. *Conf. Charac.*, *Old Hording Hagg* (1860) 89 Her hands are the clumsie hangbyes of her body.

3. *attrib.*

1641 R. BROOKE *Eng. Episc.* I. i. 3 Creatures, and hang-by Dependants.

'hang-dog, *sb.* and *a.* [f. HANG *v.* + DOG *sb.*[1]: cf. *cut-throat*.]

A. *sb.* A despicable or degraded fellow fit only to hang a dog, or to be hanged like a dog.

1687 CONGREVE *Old Bach.* III. vi, There's the hangdog his man. **1772** NUGENT tr. *Hist. Friar Gerund* I. 476 The Hang-dogs who murdered Christ. **1840** THACKERAY *Catherine* ix, Paws off..You young hang-dog.

b. *attrib.* in *apposition*.

1828 SCOTT *F.M. Perth* xxii, How can thy traffic with the hang-dog executioner be of avail to serve me? **1862** SALA *Ship Chandler* ii. 21 That hang-dog buccaneer, who had Captain Kidd for a grandfather.

B. *adj.* Of, befitting, or characteristic of a hang-dog; low, degraded; having a base or sneaking appearance.

1677 OTWAY *Cheats of Scapin* III, i, A squinting, meager, hang-dog countenance. **1826** SCOTT *Jrnl.* 7 Jan., I can't have the hang-dog look which the unfortunate Theseus has. **1873** MISS BROUGHTON *Nancy* III. 191 With an extremely hang-dog air. **1893** *Westm. Gaz.* 15 Feb. 3/2 They sat silent and hang-dog throughout.

hang-down ('hæŋdaʊn), *sb.* and *a.* [f. phrase *to hang down* (see HANG *v.* 8).] **A.** *sb.* That which hangs down, *spec.* in certain technical uses. **B.** *adj.* That hangs down.

1888 *Lockwood's Dict. Mech. Engin.* 172 *Hang down*, or *hanger*, a bearing suspended from a roof or beam for the journal of a shaft. **1904** GOODCHILD & TWENEY *Technol. & Sci. Dict.* 279/2 *Hang down* (Eng.), a frame for suspending a bearing from a roof or beam.—(Foundry), the sling which supports heavy weights in the foundry; the upper ends of the rods of the sling are attached to the travelling crane. **1906** KIPLING *Actions & Reactions* (1909) 212 As Guiseppe [*sic*] unshipped the working mechanism of the organ (it developed a hang-down leg) from its wheels. **1967** *Punch* 31 May 804/2 Vintage varieties of [cider] apples (with names such as Dabinett, Woodbine, Slack-Ma-Girdle, Hangdown, Sheep's Nose) can be used for no other purpose.

hange, var. of HENGE[1], 'pluck' of a sheep, etc.

hanged (hæŋd), *ppl. a.* [f. HANG *v.* + -ED[1].]

1. Suspended, etc.; see the verb. (Now *Obs.* in the general sense; the form in use being HUNG.)

2. Put to death by hanging by the neck.

1470–85 MALORY *Arthur* VII. xvi, The syghte of these hanged knyghtes. **1508** DUNBAR *Flyting w. Kennedie* 187 Reistit and crynit as hangitman on hill. **1599** MINSHEU *Dial. Sp. & Eng.* 68 A rope of a hanged man. **1876** *Mr. Gray & Neighb.* I. 205 England was 'merrie'..for the hangers, though scarcely quite so 'merrie' and pleasant, perhaps, for the hanged.

b. As an expletive (also *advb.*): 'Confounded', 'cursed'.

1887 *Poor Nellie* (1888) 102 A hanged uncomfortable position for a fellow to be in. *Ibid.* 105 A confounded bad dinner and hanged bad wine.

†**3.** Furnished or decorated with hangings. *Obs.* or *arch.*; usually HUNG.

1451 in Willis & Clark *Cambridge* (1886) III. 351 An hanged bed. **1562** J. HEYWOOD *Prov. & Epigr.* (1867) 179 Walles, Som seeld, som hangd. **1626** BACON *Sylva* §144 Musick is better in Chambers Wainscotted than Hanged. **1876** BREWER *Eng. Studies* iii. (1881) 117 The king's chamber and the rooms adjoining were matted and hanged.

hangee (hæŋ'iː). *nonce-wd.* [f. HANG *v.* + -EE.] A person who is hanged.

1831 GEN. P. THOMPSON *Exerc.* (1842) I. 424 Now let us, the *hangees* that are to be, sift and examine this position. **1886** *Pall Mall G.* 27 Apr. 3 Why should the hangee be subjected to the hands of a bungler?

hanger[1] ('hæŋə(r)). [OE. *hangra*, pl. *-an*, deriv. of HANG *v.* Now identified in form and feeling with the next. See Napier & Stevenson, *Crawford Charters* in *Anecd. Oxon.* 134.] A wood on the side of a steep hill or bank: cf. HANGING *ppl. a.* 2 b.

*c*938 *Charter* in *Cod. Dipl.* III. 409 Ealle þa hangran betweonan ðam weȝe and ðam ðe to Stanleaȝe liȝþ. *c*987 *Ibid.* III. 229 Of ðam hangran suþ to þære stræt. **1789** G. WHITE *Selborne* lxxxvii, A considerable part of the great woody hanger at Hawkley was torn from its place and fell down, leaving a high freestone cliff naked and bare. **1822** in Cobbett *Rur. Rides* (1885) I. 179 These hangers are woods on the sides of very steep hills. **1851** COBDEN in Morley *Life* (1882) II. iii. 91 The nightingale and cuckoo are already heard in the hanger. **1883** G. ALLEN *Col. Clout's Cal.* xxxv. 202 It [wild service-tree] grows sparingly in hangers and copses.

hanger[2] ('hæŋə(r)). Also 5–6 *Sc.* **hingar(e, -er**, 6 **hengar**. [f. HANG *v.* + -ER[1].] One who or that which hangs.

1. a. One who suspends a thing from above; often in *comb.* as *bell-hanger*, *paper-hanger*, etc. (q.v. under the first element). *spec.* One of those who select and hang the pictures for an exhibition (e.g. that of the Royal Academy).

1791–1851 Bell-hanger [see BELL *sb.*[1] 12]. **1865** *Pall Mall G.* 7 Apr., The hangers of the year are Messrs E. M. Ward, Millais, and E. W. Cooke. It is not unusual for the hangers to limit their own contributions. **1894** *Westm. Gaz.* 16 Mar. 1/2 So soon as a man is elected to full membership he becomes a hanger for the next exhibition..Hangers are almost as anxious to be excused as High Sheriffs.

b. One who puts a person to death by hanging, or causes him to be hanged.

c **1430** *Pilgr. Lyf Manhode* II. xcv. (1869) 110 Afterward j wole be drawere and hangere of thee. **1680** AUBREY *Lives Eminent Men* (1813) II. 351 A very severe hanger of highwaymen. **1876** [see HANGED 2].

†**c.** One who hesitates or wavers: see HANG *v.* 17. *Obs.*

1536 STARKEY *Let.* 30 July in *England* (1871) p. xxxix, You schal fynd me..to be no sterter, wauerar nor hengar in the wynd.

2. Something that hangs down or is suspended.

†**a.** A piece of tapestry hanging. †**b.** A hat-band with a part hanging loose behind. †**c.** A pendant; also *attrib.*, as ***hanger-pearl***. †**d.** A bell-rope. **e.** A pendant catkin. **f.** A local name for the sea-weed tangle.

a **1483** *Liber Niger* in *Househ. Ord.* 78 The chief yeoman of this office hathe in charge..cuppes of silver & leather, tankardes, & earthe asshen cuppes..hangers & all that other stuffe of this office. **1488** *Inv.* in Tytler *Hist. Scot.* (1864) II. 391 Item a collar of gold maid with elephantis and a grete hingar at it. **1513** DOUGLAS *Æneis* x. iii. 35 Or in the crownell pycht, or rych hynger, Quhilk dois the nek array. **1516** in *Inv. R. Wardrobe* (1815) 25 (Jam.) Item, ane black hatt with ane hingar contenand ane greit ruby balac. Item, v hattis of silk without hingaris. *c* **1565** LINDESAY (Pitscottie) *Chron. Scot.* (1728) 159 And also commanded her to take what hingers or tapestry-work..she pleased. **1578** in *Inv. R. Wardrobe* (1815) 266 (Jam.) A small carcan with hingar perll and small graynis anamalit with blak. **1767** H. BROOKE *Fool of Qual.* (1859) II. 225 (D.) On pulling the hanger of a bell, the great door opened. **1869** BLACKMORE *Lorna D.* xvii, The hangers of the hazel, too, having shed their dust to make the nuts.

g. (See quot. 1905.)

1905 CALKINS & HOLDEN *Art Mod. Advertising* 352 Hangers are printed or lithographed cards of various shapes and sizes, to be hung up in a store. **1927** in *John Edwards Mem. Foundation Q.* (1969) V. IV. 144 In-closed find a folder... Also we have a large hanger and dealers order blank.

3. Something that overhangs; in *Mining*, The rock over the lode or vein; the 'roof'.

1631 JORDEN *Nat. Bathes* xiv. (1669) 136 Most metals breeding between a Hanger and a Lieger..are seldome above a foot thick. **1811** PINKERTON *Petral.* II. 585 The rock on both sides, or, in the miners' language, the *roof* and the *sole*, the *hanger* and the *leger*, is altered and decomposed.

4. a. A contrivance by which anything is hung; a rope, chain, or hook used to suspend something; a support for a journal-box, etc., of a shafting. Also *attrib.*

1864 WEBSTER s.v. *Pulley*. **1873** J. RICHARDS *Wood-working Factories* 27 Having the hanger-plates ready,..mount the shaft in the hangers and invert them. *Ibid.* 65 The rods and fingers or studs are now generally furnished with hangers for the smaller shafts. **1882** NARES *Seamanship* (ed. 6) 134 Pass the gaskets and clew hangers. **1896** *Daily News* 10 Jan. 2/7 The spring hanger of the tender broke.

†**b.** A loop or strap on a sword-belt from which the sword was hung; often richly ornamented.

1598 B. JONSON *Ev. Man in Hum.* I. iv, This other day, I happened to enter into some discourse of a hanger, which..both for fashion and workmanship, was most peremptory beautiful and gentlemanlike. **1599** MINSHEU, *Talabarte*, sword hangers. *Tiros de espada*, sword hangers. **1601** HOLLAND *Pliny* II. 483 Their sword-girdles, hangers, and bawdricks, gingle again with thin plates of siluer. **1602** SHAKS. *Ham.* v. ii. 157. **1648** *Bury Wills* (Camden) 217, I give vnto my nephew..my guilt wrought sword and the girdle and hangers to it. **1676** HOBBES *Iliad* (1677) 289 The boys with silver hangers were adorn'd And golden swords.

c. A loop by which anything is hung, as the loop at the back of the neck in a coat, etc.; the loop of a hunting-whip or crop.

1684 *Lond. Gaz.* No. 1935/4 He had a Whip with a red Handle and a Buff hanger at the end of it.

d. A chain or iron rod to which a pot or kettle is hung by means of a pot-hook in the old-fashioned kitchen fireplace. Hence *transf.* A nursery name for the stroke with a double curve (*ι*), one of the elementary forms in learning to write; usually in the phrase ***pot-hooks and hangers***.

1599 MINSHEU, *Llares*, or *Ollares*, pot hangers. **1608** *Withals' Dict.* 186 To hang as the pots doe uppon their hangers. **1738** SWIFT *Pol. Convers.* Introd. 82 His Skill in making Pot-hooks and Hangers with a Pencil. **1809** W. IRVING *Knickerb.* (1849) 127 But little skilled in the mystery of combining pot-hooks and hangers. **1896** *Longm. Mag.* Nov. 64 The old iron 'hangers' for pots are common.

e. A coat- or dress-hanger.

1873 *Young Englishwoman* Feb. 91/1 The two different kinds of hangers..will be found very advantageous for hanging up heavy articles of dress, as winter cloaks, etc. **1908** *Daily Chron.* 26 Feb. 8/5 Every coat and every skirt should have a hanger to itself. **1934** L. A. G. STRONG *Corporal Tune* II. iv. 151 It does clothes no good to stay all folded up. The sooner they're out and on hangers the better. **1955** M. ALLINGHAM *Beckoning Lady* iii. 38 She was carrying a newly pressed dress on a hanger. **1970** *New Yorker* 28 Feb. 34/3 There are no hangers for suits which have always had hangers.

5. hanger-on. a. A follower or dependant (*familiarly* and often *disparagingly*).

1549 *Lansdowne MSS.* 238 lf. 292 The multytude of Reteynours and hangers on. **1603** SIR R. CECIL in Ellis *Orig. Lett.* Ser. II. III. 206 Among some hangers-on upon the Court. **1727** SWIFT *Wonder of Wonders* Wks. 1755 II. II. 54 He is a perpetual hanger-on: yet no-body knows how to be without him. **1864** BURTON *Scot Abr.* I. iii. 142 Scotland was for the first time treated as a needy and troublesome hanger-on of France.

†**b.** An appendage, an adjunct. *Obs.*

1552 LATIMER *Serm. Lord's Prayer* vi. (1845) 419 But here is one addition, one hanger on: 'As we forgive them that trespass against us'. **1674** N. FAIRFAX *Bulk & Selv.* To Rdr., All the words about body and hangers on to body.

c. *Coal-mining.* The same as *onsetter*, a workman who puts the corves or tubs into the 'cage' or 'chair' at the bottom of the pit-shaft. Formerly these were hung on to the end of the rope or chain.

1858 SIMMONDS *Dict. Trade*, *Hanger-on*, a miner employed at the bottom of the shaft in fixing the skip or bucket to the chain. **1893** *Daily News* 5 July 5/7 Three young fellows who were employed as hangers on at the pit bottom.

6. *Comb.* **hanger-back**, one who hangs back (see HANG *v.* 22); **hanger-board** (see quot. 1893).

1923 *Q. Register* May 583 He never..played the calculating hanger-back. **1962** *Times* 10 Aug. 9/4 Young novelists..must realize..that, however many people will unwisely refrain from reading their daring first novels, their own mothers, and even their own grandmothers, will not be among the hangers-back. **18..** *Electr. Rev.* (U.S.) XII. 8 (Cent. Dict.), Electrical connection between the conducting-wires and lamps must be made through a suitable hanger-board. **1893** T. O'C. SLOANE *Stand. Electr. Dict.*, *Hanger board*, a board containing two terminals, a suspending hook, and a switch, so that an arc lamp can be introduced into a circuit thereby, or can be removed as desired.

hanger[3] ('hæŋə(r)). Also 6 **hangre**, 7 **hangar**; β. 6 **hynger**, **henger**, 7 **hinger**. [app. the same as HANGER[2], from HANG *v.*; though possibly not of Eng. formation: cf. early mod.Du. *hangher*, '*slootdeghen* [rapier], pugio de zona pendens'.

The suggestion has been offered that this is the same word as the Pers. Arab. *khanjar*: see HANDJAR. But, although 'hanger' has sometimes been employed to translate the latter (prob. with a notion of etymological identity) neither history nor phonology appears to support the conjecture.]

A kind of short sword, originally hung from the belt.

1481–90 *Howard Househ. Bks.* (Roxb.) 285 My lord paied for a hanger for hymselff viij. *s.* iiij. *d.* **1483** *Act 1 Rich. III*, c. 12 §2 No Merchaunt Straungier..[shall] bring into this Realme..Knyves, Hangers, Taillourshires, Scisors, Andyrons. *c* **1500** in *Ripon Ch. Acts* (Surtees) 303 Cum gladiis vocatis hyngers vel baselardys. **1530** PALSGR. 229/1 Hangre a weapen, *bracquemart*. **1558** *Nottingham Rec.* IV. 408, I give and bequeath to James Hartley my henger and my dagger. **1589** R. HARVEY *Pl. Perc.* (1860) 33 The sight of a Hanger rusted in the sheath hanging by ones side. **1619** *Naworth Househ Bks.* (Surtees) 105 A silke belt for my Lord's hinger. **1682** N. O. *Boileau's Lutrin* II. 182 Yet, on my word the Knave had wit in's Anger, And wisely took along his rusty Hanger. **1698** FROGER *Voy.* 12 Their ordinary Arms are the Hanger, the Sagay, which is a very light Half-Pike, and the Bow. **1719** DE FOE *Crusoe* I. xv, I made him a belt with a frog hanging to it, such as in England we wear hangers in; and in the frog, instead of a hanger, I gave him a hatchet. **1831** SCOTT *Cast. Dang.* i, A small crooked sword, like what we now call a hanger.

hang-fire ('hæŋfaɪə(r)). [f. phrase *to hang fire* (see HANG *v.* 6).] A delay in the explosion of the charge of a gun or of a blasting charge. Also *transf.*

1892 W. W. GREENER *Breech-Loader* 170 Nothing is more tantalising to the sportsman than miss-fires; hang-fires, too, are a great nuisance. **1899** *Kynoch Jrnl.* Oct.–Nov. 6/2 Hang fires, soft shots, high pressures, and other defects. **1936** L. B. LYON *Bright Feather Fading* 40 Dove's hang-fire height A long way falls. **1955** *Times* 16 May 12/5 There is..no hang-fire in a story which..lacks the long dramatic suspense of the year before.

hangi ('hæŋɪ). *N.Z.* [Maori.] A Maori earth-oven in which food is placed on heated stones.

1861 *Richmond-Atkinson Papers* I. 697 They had made a 'hangi' just before the front windows. **1882** W. D. HAY *Brighter Britain* II. iii. 153 Fish and meat were frequently roasted on the clear side of the fire..but the great national culinary institution was the earth-oven, the kopa or hangi. **1905** W. SATCHELL *Toll of Bush* xxx. 343 At least the recipients of the hangi should partake of his hospitality. **1905** W. BAUCKE *Where White Man Treads* 16 For in their season he [*sc.* the Maori] could supplement his dry fare..with the tender bulbous shoots of the tii (cabbage tree), at heart white and delicate, baked in a haangi. **1959** *Weekly News* (Auckland) 30 Dec. 42 Recently, 3404 guests sat down in relays to the wedding breakfast, cooked Maori style, in a hangi—a stone-lined pit—and served in woven flax. **1963** B. PEARSON *Coal Flat* xxii. 372 Yesterday..we had the *hangi* ready.

hangie ('hæŋɪ). *Sc.* [f. HANG *v.*]

1. A term of reproach: ? hangman or gallows-bird; a worthless fellow.

1787 BURNS *Addr. to Deil* ii, Hear me, auld Hangie, for a wee, An' let poor damned bodies be.

2. A drift-net.

1889 *Scott. Leader* 11 Mar. 5 The use of the hangie or drift-net on the waters of the Tay.

hanging ('hæŋɪŋ), *vbl. sb.* [f. HANG *v.* + -ING[1].] The action of the verb HANG.

1. The action of suspending or fact of being suspended; suspension.

c **1400** *Lanfranc's Cirurg.* 24 Bi him [ligament] þe membris ..schulden ben y-teied, þe whiche þat neden hangynge. **1596** SHAKS. *1 Hen. IV*, II. iv. 446 A foolish hanging of thy nether Lippe. **1667** *Lond. Gaz.* No. 136/4 The New Invention of Major Thorny Franke, for the hanging of Coppers. **1703** MOXON *Mech. Exerc.* 153 The Hanging of Doors, Windows, etc. **1711** ADDISON *Spect.* No. 81 ¶2 Like the hanging out of false Colours.

2. The action of putting to death on the gallows, etc., or the fact of being so put to death.

a **1300** *Cursor M.* 22860 Thoru þair aun gilt Wit hefding, draght, or hanging spilt. **1460** CAPGRAVE *Chron.* (Rolls) 190 Where Thomas was juged to drawying, hanging, and hedyng. **1562** J. HEYWOOD *Prov. & Epigr.* (1867) 129 Weddyng and hangyng are desteny. **1601** SHAKS. *Twel. N.* I. v. 20 Many a good hanging preuents a bad marriage. **1738** SWIFT *Pol. Convers.* 78 'Twas her Fate; they say, Marriage and Hanging go by Destiny. **1855** MACAULAY *Hist. Eng.* xxi. IV. 677 That, of all sights, that in which the English most delighted was a hanging.

3. A downward slope or curve; esp. in *Shipbuilding* (see quots.)

1684 R. H. *School Recreat.* 83 The chusing out your Ground, and preventing the Windings, Hangings, and many turning Advantages of the same, whether..open wide Places..or in close Bowling-Alleys. **1711** W. SUTHERLAND *Shipbuild. Assist.* 160 Hanging; the opposite to Snying, when the middle of the Plank appears lower than the Ends, but circular. *c* **1850** *Rudim. Navig.* (Weale) 123 *Hanging*, declining in the middle part from a horizontal right line, as the hanging of the decks, hanging of the sheer, etc.

4. *fig.* †**a.** Dependence. *Obs.*

c **1430** *Pilgr. Lyf Manhode* I. xxxiii. (1869) 21 For þat oon hath his comyng out, and his hanginge, of þat ooþer.

b. The condition of being in suspense or left over for an indefinite time; also ***hanging-up***.

1638 BAKER tr. *Balzac's Lett.* (vol. II.) 86 If..pretenders avoid a sudden falling, it is by enduring a tedious hanging, receiving perpetuall affronts. **1890** *Pall Mall G.* 20 June 7/1 This measure authorized the 'hanging up' of bills by either House provided..that the consent of the Crown were obtained. **1892** *Ibid.* 27 Jan. 2/2 A hanging-up resolution is never satisfactory.

5. *concr.* **a.** Something that hangs or is suspended; something attached, an appendage; also *fig.* (Usually in *pl.* Also ***hangings-on.***)

1549 LATIMER *2nd Serm. bef. Edw. VI* (Arb.) 55 As it foloweth in the texte wyth the appurtenaunces and hangynges on. **1552** —— *Serm. in Lincoln* i. 63 These be sequels or hangings on, wherewith the chiefe dish is poudred. **1611** SHAKS. *Cymb.* III. iii. 63 In one night A Storme..Shooke downe my mellow hangings: nay my Leaues. **1633** P. FLETCHER *Purple Isl.* III. vii, Many a cragge dependeth; Like to the hangings of some rockie masse.

b. *Iron-founding.* = SCAFFOLDING *vbl. sb.* 2 a.

1878 *Jrnl. Iron & Steel Inst.* XII. 202 The modern system of putting the material round the in-wall and allowing it to roll to the centre, has diminished the heat at the in-wall of the furnace and greatly reduced the hanging and scaffolding. **1948** G. R. BASHFORTH *Manuf. Iron & Steel* I. x. 165 Hanging, which is sometimes referred to as wedging, is similar to scaffolding, but is due to carbon deposition.

6. *spec.* **a.** A piece of drapery with which a bedstead, the walls of a room, etc., are hung; a curtain or the like; also the material for this.

1431 in Rogers *Agric. & Prices* III. 550/3 Hanging to hall with a border of Cowchye work 11*s.* **1530** PALSGR. 129/1 Hangyng for a bedde, *accoustrement de lict*. **1663** COWLEY *Verses & Ess.*, *Country Mouse*, Behind a Hanging in a spacious room. **1758** JOHNSON *Idler* No. 13 ¶10 A hanging that is to represent Cranmer in the flames. **1836** B. CORNEY *Bayeux Tapestry* 3 A piece of hanging which belongs to the cathedral church of Bayeux.

b. *pl.* The pieces, folds, or masses of tapestry or other stuff, with which a room or bed is hung; also extended to wall-paper (*paper-hangings*).

1485–6 *Naval Acc. Hen. VII* (1896) 46 Hangings of Say to hang aboute the Ship, oon of vj peces. **1566** *Eng. Ch. Furniture* (1866) 71 Quishions for his house and hanginges for his bedd. **1593** DONNE *Sat.* iv. (R.), Though his face be as ill As theirs, which in old hangings whip Christ. **1673** DRYDEN *Marr. à la Mode* IV. iv, No more than a picture in the hangings. **1716** *Lond. Gaz.* No. 5434/3 Paper painted, or stained for Hangings. **1877** M. M. GRANT *Sun-Maid* i, He pushed back the hangings as he continued speaking.

7. A steep slope or declivity of a hill. Now *local*.

c **1400** MAUNDEV. (Roxb.) ix. 34 þai er in þe hingand [*en le declin*] of þe hill. **1489** CAXTON *Faytes of A.* II. xii. 113 Went vpon the hangynge of a montayne for to byholde. **1578** LYTE *Dodoens* I. xcviii. 140 Ladies Mantell groweth..in the hanging of hilles. **1622** BACON *Hen. VII* Mor. & Hist. Wks. (Bohn) 332 Upon the brow or hanging of a hill. **1888** G. VENABLES *Garianonum Greetings* ii. 3, 'The Hanging', which forms part of the Garden and Grounds of the Rectory here. **1888** *Berksh. Gloss.* s.v., E'll vind moor partridges on the hangin' yander'n anywher.

8. *attrib.* and *Comb.*, as (sense 2) ***hanging day***, ***matter***, ***time***; (sense 6) ***hanging-cloth***, ***-paper***; **hanging clamp** (see quot.); **hanging committee**, the committee who decide the hanging of pictures in an Exhibition (e.g. that of the Royal Academy); **hanging-head**, **-post**, **-stile**, the post or upright which bears the hinges of a door or gate; †**hanging-holder**, an attendant; **hanging-needle**, a seine-needle, used in attaching a fishing-net to the cork-line and foot-line; **hanging-press**, a press in which clothes are hung.

c **1850** *Rudim. Navig.* (Weale) 123 **Hanging clamp*, a semicircular iron with a foot at each end, to receive nails, by which it is fixed to any part of the ship to hang stages to, etc. *c* **1500** *Melusine* xxvi. 206 Cyteseyns had hanged theire houses withoutforth toward the stretes, with theire best and rychest *hangyng clothes. **1817** *Sporting Mag.* L. 33 A painter having some interest with one of the *Hanging Committee. **1866** *Reader* 12 May 476 The hanging committee could not possibly have found artists to occupy them so worthily. **1795** tr. *Moritz's Travels* 60 Last Tuesday was (what is here called) *hanging day... I only heard tolling at a distance the death-bell of the sacrifice to justice. **1806** *Balance* (Hudson, N.Y.) 11 Nov. 355 (Th.), Next Friday [the newspaper] promises to make its debut. Friday —that's hanging day—but no matter. **1857** D. G. Rossetti *Let.* June (1965) I. 325 *Friday* is the hanging day. **1888** Elworthy *W. Somerset Word-bk.*, **Hanging-head*, same as Hanch; the upright part of a gate, to which the hinges are attached. **1624** Fletcher *Wife for a month* I. ii, You scurvy usher..thou poor base *hanging-holder. **1755** Johnson s.v., A *hanging matter. **1861** Sala *Dutch Pict.*, *Ship-Chandler* (L.), It's a hanging matter to touch a penny's worth of them. **1752** Lady Luxborough *Let. to Shenstone* 19 July, My *hanging-paper is arrived, and the cracks of the ceiling have been filled. **1792** *Trans. Soc. Arts* X. 30 The limb of a Chestnut..was put down as a *hanging post for a gate, and carried the gate..fifty-two years. **1743** Wesley *Wks.* (1872) XIII. 174 They broke..the *hanging-press. **1845** Mrs. S. C. Hall *Whiteboy* xi. 93 What in Ireland is called a hanging press, in which ladies suspend their dresses. **1823** P. Nicholson *Pract. Build.* 225 **Hanging Stile*, the stile of a door or shutter to which the hinge is fastened; also, a narrow stile fixed to the jamb on which a door or shutter is frequently hung.

hanging ('hæŋɪŋ), *ppl. a.* (*prep.*) [f. as prec. + -ING².] That hangs.

1. a. Supported above, and not below; suspended, pendulous; projecting downwards; drooping.

1483 *Cath. Angl.* 186/2 Hyngynge, *pendulus, suspendens.* **1577** B. Googe *Heresbach's Husb.* II. (1586) 115 b, The eares ..if they bee great and hanging, are signes of a Jade. **1591** Percivall *Sp. Dict.*, *Himacas*, hanging beds. **1610** Holland *Camden's Brit.* I. 690 The land there is hollow and hanging. **1626** Capt. Smith *Accid. Yng. Seamen* 11 A hanging cabben, a Hamacke. **1726** Leoni *Alberti's Archit.* I. 31/1 Huge pieces of hanging Stone. **1882** Shorthouse *J. Inglesant* II. 228 It faded more and more into the hanging darkness.

b. *hanging sleeve*, a loose open sleeve hanging down from the arm; formerly worn by children and young persons. Hence **hanging-sleeved** *adj.*

1659 Gauden *Tears Ch.* 580 The Popes..being then in their bibs and hanging-sleeves. **1683** *Apol. Prot. France* iv. 46 Children..in their Nurse's arms, or not out of their Hanging-sleeves. **1742** Richardson *Pamela* IV. 301 When I was a Girl, or when I was in Hanging-sleeves. **1748** —— *Clarissa* Wks. 1883 VIII. 406 The hanging-sleeved, go-carted property of hired slaves. **1826** Scott *Woodstock* v. **1841** Lane *Arab. Nts.* I. 71 In which case they kiss the end of the hanging-sleeve.

2. a. Leaning over, overhanging; steep, declivitous.

a **1350** *Guy Warw.* (A.) 5270 þan com þer bi an hongend hille..Guyoun. **1480** Caxton *Chron. Eng.* ccxxiii. 222 They ..met the baillol and his companye at an hongyng bought of the more in a streit passage. **1513** Douglas *Æneis* III. iv. 40 Vndir a hingand hewch. **1598** Florio, *Silo*..he that hath a skowling looke..or hanging eie-browes. **1626** Bacon *Sylva* §600 To bring Water, from some Hanging Grounds, where there are Springs. **1787** Winter *Syst. Husb.* 99 The branches, or smaller drains..are cut a-cross the ground with a hanging level. **1847** James *J. Marston Hall* vii, The dark man with the heavy hanging brow.

b. Of a wood, garden, walk, etc.: Situated on a steep slope, top of a wall, etc. so as to hang over or appear to do so.

Hanging Gardens (of Babylon), a transl. of L. *pensiles horti* (Quintus Curtius), κρεμαστοὶ κῆποι (Plutarch, etc.).

c **1170** *Newminster Cartul.* (Surtees) 75 Le Hangande scauhe. **1487** *Ibid.* 263 Hanhand bray. **1705** Addison *Italy* 315 We call hanging Gardens, such as are planted on the Top of the House. **1712** —— *Spect.* No. 415 ¶3 The Walls of Babylon, its hanging Gardens. **1753** Hanway *Trav.* (1762) II. I. ix. 48 They abound in lofty trees, and different kinds of hanging walks. **1791** Mad. D'Arblay *Diary* 7 Aug., Hills..mostly covered with hanging woods. **1815** J. Fernie *Hist. Dunfermline* 16 On the sides or slopes of the mound, and at the back of the houses are hanging gardens. **1871** L. Stephen *Playgr. Eur.* i. (1894) 5 Its lovely grouping of rock and hanging meadow. **1931** H. Crane *Let.* 21 Sept. (1965) 381 Dense tropical foliage and veritable hanging gardens. **1971** R. Russell tr. *Ahmad's Shore & Wave* i. 13 He had conjured up a picture of the hanging gardens of Malabar Hill in Bombay, overlooking the sea.

†**3. a.** Remaining in suspense or abeyance; pending.

c **1460** in Arnolde *Chron.* (1811) 192 The lebel or artycles of the cause ayenst hym before you in the courte of cristiante moued and hanging. **1590** Spenser *F.Q.* I. ii. 16 Both stand sencelesse..Forgetfull of the hanging victory.

†**b.** Pending, during; orig. with a sb. in absolute construction; when placed before the sb., liable to be treated as a prep.; cf. DURING, and Fr. *pendant*; *this hanging* (= Fr. *cependant*), pending this, meanwhile. *Obs.*

a **1420** Hoccleve *De Reg. Princ.* 2654, I rede also how that, hangyng a stryfe Bitwene Kyng Porrus and a lord clept Fabrice. *c* **1489** Caxton *Sonnes of Aymon* i. 50 This hangynge, the duke..came afore the kynge. **1491** —— *Vitas Patr.* (W. de W. 1495) I. xciii. 127 b/1 Hangynge this tyme was a philosophre in the sayd cyte. *c* **1500** *3 Kings Sons* 91 This tyme hangyng, ye may leue garrisons in this Reaume. **1568** Grafton *Chron.* II. 151 This matter thus hangyng, the king [etc.]. **1621** Elsing *Debates Ho. Lords* (Camden) 52 The patent was gyven up, hanging the suyte. **1628** Coke *On Litt.* 13 a, Hanging the process, the defendant conveyeth the land.

4. Having a downward cast of countenance; gloomy-looking. (Often with play on HANG *v.* 3.)

1603 Shaks. *Meas. for M.* IV. ii. 34 A good fauor you haue, but that you haue a hanging look. **1607** Middleton *Michaelmas Term* IV. iii, Like a hanging morn, a little waterish awhile. **1766** T. Amory *J. Buncle* (1825) III. 79 He had the most hanging look I have ever seen. **1855** Browning *Fra Lippo* 308 Have you noticed, now, Your cullion's hanging face?

5. In transitive sense: That causes (persons) to be hanged; addicted to hanging. Chiefly *hanging judge*. Also *transf.*

1848 Thackeray *Van. Fair* xlii, Celebrated as a hanging judge. **1929** J. B. Priestley *Good Companions* II. iv. 339 Your Bruddersfordian is a hanging judge of anything that costs money. **1937** 'G. Orwell' *Road to Wigan Pier* ix. 178 The worst criminal..is morally superior to a hanging judge. **1963** *Times* 9 Mar. 9/6 He became an advocate of reform and a hanging judge of the powers that be in politics, commerce and agriculture. **1972** M. Gee *In my Father's Den* 121 Price ..is a combination public relations man and hanging judge.

6. In various specific collocations or combinations, as **hanging ball** (*Golf*), a ball lying on a downward slope; **hanging barrel**: see quot.; † **hanging basin**, a basin with a hole in the bottom suspended so that the water might run from it into another vessel below; **hanging bird** = HANGBIRD; **hanging bits**, small plates of iron fixed to the upright iron bar of a stocking-frame and having projecting studs which come into contact with the caster-backs; **hanging-block** (see quot. *a* 1884); **hanging-bowl** *Archæol.*, name given to certain Celtic or Saxon bowls that were suspended from the roof; **hanging bridge**, a suspension-bridge; see also quot. *a* 1877; **hanging buttress**, 'a buttress supported upon a corbel, and not standing solid on the foundation' (Webster 1864); **hanging-coal, -side, -wall** (*Mining*), that which hangs or leans over the working; **hanging-compass** (see quot. *a* 1865); † **hanging-dog** *a.* = HANG-DOG; **hanging drop** *Biol.*, a drop of liquid suspended from a cover glass fitting on to a special transparent cell or microscope slide, by means of which living microorganisms or cells in the drop may be examined microscopically; usu. *attrib.*; **hanging five, ten** *Surfing*, used, freq. *attrib.*, with reference to the placing of all the toes of one foot (or of both feet) over the front edge of a surfboard; **hanging gale**: see GALE; **hanging glacier** (see quot. 1940); **hanging glider** = *hang-glider* (see HANG-); **hanging guard**, a guard in fencing, esp. sabre-play: see quots.; also known as 'high seconde'; **hanging inden(ta)tion**, (*a*) *Printing* (see INDENTATION 3 and INDENTION 2); (*b*) *Librarianship* (see quot. 1941); † **hanging jack**, a roasting jack hung before a fire; **hanging knee** (see quot.); † **hanging laver** = *hanging basin*; **hanging lie** *Golf*, the position of a ball when it rests on ground sloping downwards in the direction of play; † **hanging lock**, a padlock; **hanging-moss**, a lichen or moss that hangs in long fringes from the limbs of trees; **hanging paragraph** = *hanging indent(at)ion*; **hanging pawn** *Chess*, one of two advanced pawns which are side by side with no pawns on the adjacent files that can support them; **hanging press**, a sliding book-press or case in a library which hangs, supported above, in front of a fixed press, so that it can be drawn out to permit access to the shelves behind; also called a *sliding press*; **hanging shelf**, a suspended shelf; **hanging side** (see *hanging-coal*); **hanging steps** (see quot. 1904); **hanging ten**, see *hanging five* above; **hanging valley**, a valley which is abruptly cut across by the steep side of a larger valley or a sea-cliff; **hanging valve**, a hinged valve which falls open by the action of gravity; † **hanging-waggon**, a coach hung on springs; **hanging wall** see *hanging-coal*; **hanging wardrobe**, (*a*) a wardrobe designed to accommodate clothes hanging at full length; (*b*) a row of hooks on which clothes may be hung.

1857 *Chambers' Inform.* II. 695/2 *Hanging balls..are caused by a little rise of the ground close behind the ball, from whatever cause. **1884** F. J. Britten *Watch & Clockm.* 120 [A] *Hanging Barrel..[is] a going barrel whose arbor is supported only at the upper end. **1558** *Bury Wills* (Camden) 150 Syxe *hanginge basons of latton, iij wasshinge basons of latton. **1759** B. Stillingfl. *Econ. Nat.* in *Misc. Tracts* (1762) 92 The *hanging bird..fixes it[s nest] upon the bough of some tree hanging over the water. **1868** Wood *Homes without H.* xiii. 241 The Baltimore Oriole goes by many names..such as Hanging Bird, from the beautiful pensile nest which it makes. **1829** Glover *Hist. Derby* I. 242 In 1714..Hardy added the caster-back and *hanging-bits [to the stocking-frame]. *a* **1865** Smyth *Sailor's Word-bk.* (1867) 366 **Hanging-blocks*..are sometimes fitted with a long and short leg, and lash over the eyes of the topmast rigging; when under, they are made fast to a strap. *a* **1884** Knight *Dict. Mech.* Suppl. 436/2 *Hanging block*, a block through which the top-sail tye is rove, then through the tye-block on the yard, and the standing part made fast to the mast head. **1940** *Burlington Mag.* Dec. 180/2 The two bronze *hanging-bowls (believed to be lamps) with enamelled escutcheons and mounts. **1956** I. S. Maxwell in D. L. Linton *Sheffield* 122 The presence of three hanging-bowls from this same area may perhaps indicate that Celtic art survived for a long time in this remote district. **1962** H. R. Loyn *Anglo-Saxon England* i. 14 In the case of.. hanging-bowls, some of the richest work culturally of the whole settlement period may be attributed to Celtic craftsmen. **1815** *Niles' Weekly Register* IX. 92/1 The main post-road..crosses the Brandywine on a *hanging bridge. *a* **1877** Knight *Dict. Mech.* II. 1060/2 *Hanging-bridge.* 1. A hollow, vertical partition depending from the bottom of a boiler and serving to deflect the flame... 2. *a.* A suspension bridge. *b.* A truss-frame bridge. **1881** Raymond *Mining Gloss.*, **Hanging-coal*, a portion of the coal-seam which, by the removal of another portion, has had its natural support removed, as in holing. *a* **1865** Smyth *Sailor's Word-bk.* (1867) 366 **Hanging-compass*, a compass so constructed as to hang with its face down-wards. **1667** J. Lacy *Sauny the Scot* v. Dram. Wks. (1875) 386 Looks he not like a disbanded officer with that *hanging-dog look there? **1885** *Jrnl. R. Microsc. Soc.* V. 117 The '*hanging drop'..has some great..disadvantages. **1892** *Phil. Trans. R. Soc.* B. CLXXXIII. 130 Cultures in hanging drops, made in sterilised cells under the microscope. *Ibid.* 136, I..prepared a hanging drop culture of this. **1908** *Practitioner* Aug. 264 By observation of hanging-drop preparations from growth in glucose broth. **1970** Passmore & Robson *Compan. Med. Stud.* II. xviii. 13/1 The presence of flagella is usually inferred by observing..motility in hanging drop preparations of fluid cultures. **1963** *Sunday Mail Mag.* (Brisbane) 5 May 12/5 **Hanging five*, five toes over the nose of the board for maximum speed. **1965** P. L. Dixon *Compl. Bk. Surfing* vi. 78 Riding forward is a term used here to cover all sorts of nose-riding styles like hanging five and ten toes over. **1894** J. W. Gregory in *Q. Jrnl. Geol. Soc.* L. 515 The 'corrie' or '*hanging glaciers'. **1902** *Encycl. Brit.* XXXI. 23/1 Hanging glaciers (*i.e.*, glaciers perched on steep slopes) often discharge themselves over steep rock-faces, the snout breaking off at intervals. **1940** C. M. Rice *Dict. Geol. Terms* 168/1 *Hanging glacier*, a glacier of small size on so steep a slope that the ice breaks off and falls from its lower end. **1932** J. Manchot tr. *Kronfeld's On Gliding & Soaring* 254 '*Hanging Glider' is the literal translation of the German 'Hängegleiter'. **1956** *Flight* LXIX. 270/1 This also was a 'hanging' glider. **1707** *Hope's New Meth. Fencing* 12 Of the advantage that the *Hanging-Guard hath over all, or most of the other Guards. **1889** A. Hutton *Cold Steel* 8 The Hanging Guard..is formed by dropping the point to a level with the opponent's right hip, raising the hand as high as the head, the edge to be uppermost—and looking at the opponent under the shell of the sword. **1893** *Westm. Gaz.* 3 July 3/1 The old hanging guard has been discarded, and in its place a position of 'engage,'..has been adopted. **1927** *Amer. Speech* II. 239/2 The *hanging indention is built just the opposite of a paragraph. **1941** *A.L.A. Catalog Rules* (ed. 2) p. xxv, *Hanging indention*, a form of indention in which the first line begins at author indention and succeeding lines at title indention. **1961** T. Landau *Encycl. Librarianship* (ed. 2) 161/1 Hanging indentation. **1660** Pepys *Diary* 4 Feb., They were buying of a *hanging-jack to roast birds on. *c* **1850** *Rudim. Navig.* (Weale) 123 **Hanging knee*, those knees against the sides whose arms hang vertically or perpendicularly. **1462** *Test. Ebor.* II. (Surtees) 256 A *hangyng laver with the halling, a cesterne. **1483** *Act. 1 Rich. III*, c. 12 §2 No Merchant Stranger..shall bring into this Realme..hanging candlesticks..hanging lauers. **1493** *Bury Wills* (Camden) 82 My best hangyng lauour stondyng in my parlour. **1909** P. A. Vaile *Mod. Golf* pl. 96 The stance and address for a *hanging lie. **1424** in Rogers *Agric. & Prices* III. 549/1, 6 *hanging locks 1/6. **1495–7** *Naval Acc. Hen. VII* (1896) 261 Hangyng lokes to the Storehouse dore. **1497** in *Ld. High Treas. Acc. Scot.* 2 Nov., Tua hingand lokkis to the thesaure kist. **1959** L. M. Harrod *Librarians' Gloss.* (ed. 2) 140 *Hanging..paragraph. **1964** T. L. Kinsey *Audio-Typing & Electric Typewriters* vii. 66 New paragraph to be typed as a hanging paragraph. **1927** *Brit. Chess Mag.* XLVII. 269/2 The fact that Black has completed his development so early with no other disadvantage than being saddled with the '*hanging Pawns' goes to show that the nightmare..is ended. **1943** R. Fine *Ideas Chess Openings* iv. 131 The hanging Pawns need not be feared by White because of his excellent development. **1726** Swift *Gulliver* I. II. ii. 179 The Cradle was put into a small Drawer..and the Drawer placed upon a *Hanging-shelf for fear of the Rats. **1825** J. Neal *Bro. Jonathan* I. 188 A hanging shelf.. loaded with cheeses; ropes of onions; dried apples, [etc.]. **1881** S. P. McLean *Cape Cod Folks* ii. 31 In one dark recess I came into forcible contact with a hanging-shelf of pies. **1962** *Williamsburg Reproductions Catal.* 12 An approved reproduction of a hanging shelf of English design, about 1760. **1881** Raymond *Mining Gloss.*, **Hanging-side*, or *Hanging-wall*, or *Hanger*, the wall or side over the vein. **1876** *Notes Building Construction* II. 108 *Hanging steps are fixed at one end only. **1904** Goodchild & Tweney *Technol. & Sci. Dict.* 279/2 *Hanging steps*, stone steps having one end built into a wall. **1962** *Austral. Women's Weekly* Suppl. 24 Oct. 3/2 **Hanging ten*, a trick method of riding with toes tucked over the front of the surfboard. **1963** *Observer* 13 Oct. 15/4 The critical 'hanging ten' stance, in which the surfer speeds across the wave with his 10 toes actually hanging over the nose of the 10-ft. surfboard. **1900** W. M. Davis in *Proc. Boston Soc. Nat. Hist.* XXIX. 288 In the spring of 1899, I sent a brief note..to..Mr. G. K. Gilbert of Washington, telling him that all the lateral valleys seemed to be 'hung up' above the floors of the trunk valleys. His reply was long in coming..and he suggested that such laterals should be called '*hanging valleys'—a term I have since then adopted. He fully agreed that hanging valleys presented unanswerable testimony for strong glacial erosion. **1932** Auden *Orators* I. 22 Arguments from the other side of the lake on the formation of hanging valleys. **1938** *Sat. Rev. Lit.* 1 Jan. 17/3 We go..to hear a well-informed ranger explain how a glacier makes a U-shaped valley, leaving hanging valleys to dump waterfalls over the edge. **1952** H. W. Tilman *Nepal Himalaya* II. xii. 149 In a sort of hanging valley, where the slope eased off.. we began searching for a camp site. **1963** D. W. & E. E. HUMPHRIES tr. *Termier's Erosion & Sedimentation* v. 126 It may have tributaries, but these are often 'hanging valleys' with waterfalls. **1968** R. W. FAIRBRIDGE *Encycl. Geomorphol.* 522 Interesting examples of hanging valleys may also be seen entering fjords, notably in Norway and New Zealand. Hanging valleys also occur sometimes along non-glaciated coasts where the rate of cliff retreat is higher than the adjustment potential of the smaller streams, e.g., in the chalk cliffs in the south of England. They are also to be seen along youthful fault scarps. **1585** HIGINS tr. *Junius' Nomencl.* 266/2 *Pilentum*.. an *hanging waggon: a stately waggon for ladies and gentlewomen: a coch. **1777** HOOLE *Comenius' Vis. World* (ed. 12) 109 Great persons are carried .. in a hanging-waggon, which is called a coach. **1778** W. PRYCE *Mineralogia Cornubiensis* II. i. 79 When the Miners dig down.., then the roof, i.e. the upper, the *hanging wall, or incumbent wall of the Lode or Fissure, is.. over their heads. **1875** *Ure's Dict. Arts* (ed. 7) II. 782 **Hanging-wall*.. the rock which hangs over the lode. **1883** *Standard* 20 Jan. 1/5 The hanging wall is composed of granite. **1901** *Daily Colonist* (Victoria, B.C.) 31 Oct. 6/3 The quartz in the hanging wall here assayed £39.60 and that on the footwall £4.80. **1970** W. SMITH *Gold Mine* iv. 9 Rod pondered the unfortunate choice of mining terminology that had named the roof of an excavation 'the hanging wall'. **1896** *Heal & Son Catal.* 169 The 'Eversfield' Suite.. consisting of 2 ft. 9 in. *Hanging Wardrobe, [etc.]. **1907** *Yesterday's Shopping* (1969) 278/2 Hanging Wardrobe, in oak, teak and mahogany —6 hooks. **1972** *Country Life* 25 May (Suppl.) 37/1 Full length, Hanging Wardrobe in the Chippendale style. It is 4 feet 3 inches wide, 7 feet 2 inches high and 21 inches deep.

Hence †'**hangingly** *adv.*, in a hanging manner.

1548–67 THOMAS *Ital. Gram.*, *In pendente*, hangeyngly, or in doubte.

hangle, var. of HENGLE *Obs.*

hangman ('hæŋmən). [f. HANG *v.* + MAN.]

1. A man whose office it is to hang condemned persons; also more generally, an executioner, a torturer, racker. ***common hangman***, the public executioner.

1393 LANGL. *P. Pl.* C. VII. 368 þe hangeman of tyborne. **1483** *Vulgaria abs Terentio* 10 b, See how froward a face 300n hangeman makes. **1526** TINDALE *Mark* vi. 27 The kynge sent the hangman and commaunded his heed to be brought in. **1622** MABBE tr. *Aleman's Guzman d'Alf.* II. 328 Since the Hang-man dealt so roughly with him.. racking as much from him as there needed no farther confession. **1647** CLARENDON *Hist. Reb.* II. §51 A Paper.. avowed to contain the matter of the Treaty, was burned by the Common Hang-man. **1785** GROSE *Dict. Vulg. Tongue*, *Hangman's wages*, thirteen pence halfpenny, which according to vulgar tradition was thus allotted, one shilling for the execution, and three halfpence for the rope. **1849** MACAULAY *Hist. Eng.* ii. I. 175 The Commons began by resolving.. that the Covenant should be burned by the hangman in Palace Yard.

b. *transf.* A term of reprobation; also used playfully. Also *fig.*

1553 T. WILSON *Rhet.* (1580) 123 Amplification.. to call a naughtie fellowe theef, or hangman, when he is not knowne to bee any suche. **1599** SHAKS. *Much Ado* III. ii. 11 He hath twice or thrice cut Cupids bow-string, and the little hang-man dare not shoot at him. **1645** MILTON *Colast.* Wks. (1851) 373 You suffer'd this nameles hangman to cast into public such a despightfull contumely.

2. *attrib.* and *Comb.*

1825 CAMPBELL *To Memory Spanish Patriots* v, Manglers of the martyr's earthly frame! Your hangmen fingers cannot touch his fame. **1859** GEN. P. THOMPSON *Audi Alt.* II. lxxxvii. 56 Put to two deaths at once by the hands of a hangman-judge. **1865** DICKENS *Mut. Fr.* I. xii, 'It strikes me rather as a hang-man air.'

Hence **hangman-like** *a.* and *adv.*; '**hangmanship**, the office or function of hangman.

1684 OTWAY *Atheist* v. (1735) 107 Six or seven arm'd rogues with hangmanlike faces. **1824** LANDOR *Imag. Conv.* Ser. I. Wks. 1846 I. 23, I abominate and detest hangmanship. **1881** SWINBURNE *Mary Stuart* IV. i. 137 [They] rage not hangmanlike upon the prey. **1883** *Birmingham Weekly Post* 22 Sept. 4/7 To decide upon the claims of 1,200 candidates for the hangmanship of England.

'**hangment.** *Obs.* exc. *dial.* [f. HANG *v.* + -MENT: perh. after *judgement.*]

1. Hanging.

c **1440** *Promp. Parv.* 225/2 Hangement [*v.r.* hongment], *suspendium, suspencio.* *c* **1440** *Gesta Rom.* xxxvi. 146 (Harl. MS.) This is to seye, My soule hathe choson hongment. *c* **1449** PECOCK *Repr.* III. viii. 324 Power into hangement and into deeth. **1888** ELWORTHY *W. Somerset Word-bk.*, *Hangment*.. also hanging, execution.

2. (See quots.)

1825 BROCKETT *N.C. Gloss.*, s.v., To play the hangment, is to be much enraged, to play the very deuce. **1828** *Craven Dial.*, *Hangment*.. an expression of surprise, as, 'what the hangment!' **1887** *Pall Mall G.* 19 Oct. 6/1 'What the dickens have you to do with it?.. who the hangment are you?'

'**hang-nail.** [f. HANG *v.* + NAIL; but historically an accommodated form of *angnail*; cf. AGNAIL 3.] A small piece of epidermis partially detached, but hanging by one end, near to a nail.

1678 R. L'ESTRANGE *Seneca's Mor.* xxiii. (1705) 482 The Ripping of a Hang-nail is sufficient to Dispatch us. *a* **1825** FORBY *Voc. E. Anglia*, *Hang-nail*, a minute portion of the cuticle, rising and slivered off about the roots of the finger-nails. **1842** FR. A. KEMBLE *Rec. Later Life* (1882) II. 219 Will you.. be so good as to remember what a hang-nail is like?

hang-over, hangover ('hæŋ,əʊvə(r)). orig. *U.S.* [HANG *v.* 17.] **1.** A thing or person remaining or left over; a remainder or survival, an after-effect. (Later quots. influenced by sense 2.)

1894 *Outing* (U.S.) XXIV. 67/2 Then there are a few 'hang-overs' who have tried before, and two or three green candidates. **1920** C. SANDBURG *Smoke & Steel* 153 A hangover of summer song. **1922** H. CRANE *Let.* 23 June (1965) 77 Since I have been writing ads a certain amount of hangover work to be done evenings. **1930** L. DENNY *Amer. conquers Brit.* 9 That easily inspired hatred of Germany remained as a hang-over in America long after it had been thrown over by the British. **1939** C. DAY LEWIS *Child of Misfortune* 136 At the beginning of his second University year, he was still suffering a little from the hang-over of public-school education. **1941** *Ann. Reg. 1940* 232 Owing to shortage of labour.. as much as any hang-over from the Civil War, the.. harvests were all unsatisfactory. **1958** *Economist* 20 Dec. 1054/2 There has been a slight move away from the previous invariable association of every increase in unemployment with a mental picture of lean and hungry men, in hangover from the grim thirties. **1959** *Times Rev. Industry* Dec. 54/3 Only just recovered from the ghastly hangover of that [buying] spree. **1963** *Times Lit. Suppl.* 8 Feb. 87/2 The bitter taste of the humanitarian hangover. **1973** *Daily Tel.* 19 Feb. 6/4 The oversized dormitories.. are hang-overs from the old lunatic asylums.

2. The unpleasant after-effects of (esp. alcoholic) dissipation.

1904 'G. WURDZ' *Foolish Dict.*, *Brain*,.. usually occupied by the Intellect Bros.,—Thoughts and Ideas—as an Intelligence Office, but sometimes sub-let to Jag, Hang-Over & Co. **1912** W. IRWIN *Red Button* 93 This was the first time in his life that Tommy North had ever admitted a 'hangover'. **1935** D. L. SAYERS *Gaudy Night* viii. 161 'How's Miss Cattermole?' 'Bad hang-over. As you might expect.' **1942** *New Statesman* 11 July 26/1 But the use of myths has a similar effect to the use of alcohol: an inevitable hang-over follows the original elation. **1957** *Listener* 18 July 105/2 Its [*sc.* coffee's] ability to quicken the spirits, and, above all, to remove the vestiges of those severe hang-overs which afflicted our hard-drinking fore-fathers. **1959** N. MAILER *Advts. for Myself* (1961) 220 It was the only good writing I ever did directly from a drug, even if I paid for it with a hangover beyond measure. **1962** K. ORVIS *Damned & Destroyed* ix. 59 Her eyes were walled in panic, flaming with hangover pain.

3. *Electr.* (See quots.)

1940 *Chambers's Techn. Dict.* 402/1 *Hang-over*, the delay in restoration of speech-operated switches, as in the *Vodas*, to ensure the non-clipping of weak final consonants of words. **1943** *Gloss. Terms Telecommun.* (*B.S.I.*) 12 *Hangover time*, of an echo-suppressor, the interval of time that elapses between the instant when the operating signal ceases to be applied at the input terminals of the echo-suppressor and the instant when the suppression loss is reduced to 6 db. **1961** G. A. BRIGGS *A to Z in Audio* 95 A perfect loudspeaker would cease to vibrate immediately any applied signal is cut off. Failure to do so is mainly due to resonance, and the unwanted output is sometimes referred to by the unpleasant word hangover. Its effect is to colour the reproduction and spoil the transient response. The worst offender is often the cabinet. **1967** W. E. PANNETT *Dict. Radio & Telev.* 125 *Hangover*, lack of 'attack' and extended decay in sound reproduction. It is most apparent with transients and is usually due to a resonance or insufficient damping in the system.

Hence '**hang-,overish** *a.*, somewhat affected by a hang-over.

1936 'P. QUENTIN' *Puzzle for Fools* viii. 62, I felt a bit hang-overish, but that was nothing new.

†'**hangrell.** *Sc. Obs.* [f. HANG *v.* (Cf. MDu. *hangereel* a term of reproach, a gallows-bird.)] A gallows; see also quot. 1802.

a **1605** POLWART *Flyting w. Montgomerie* 772 Gleyd gangrell, auld mangrell! to the hangrell, and sa pyne. **1802** SIBBALD *Chron. Scot. Poetry* Gloss. (Jam.), *Hangarell*, *hangrell*, an implement of the stable, upon which bridles, halters, etc. are hung.

Hang Seng (hæŋ sɛŋ). The name of a bank in Hong Kong, used *attrib.*, as ***Hang Seng index***, to designate an index of the (average) movement in the price of selected securities on the Hong Kong stock exchange.

1969 *South China Morning Post* (Hong Kong) 22 Nov. (Business News Suppl.) p.i/4 The Hang Seng Bank.. has developed an index to give investors and other people interested in the Hong Kong Stock Exchange a general guide to share price movements... The Hang Seng Index, as it will be called, is expected to prove as useful as the Dow Jones.. and other indices are on other world markets. **1971** *Investors Chron.* 12 Mar. 806/2 Early in 1968 the Hang Sheng [*sic*] index stood at 60. **1976** *Economist* 6 Mar. 93/1 The Hang Seng index.. has now pulled sharply ahead. **1985** *Daily Tel.* 18 Feb. 21 The Hang Seng index.. jumped more than 50 points through the barrier on Friday.

†'**hangster.** *Obs. rare.* [ME. *hangestre*, fem. of *hangere*, HANGER: see -STER.] = HANG-WOMAN.

c **1430** *Pilgr. Lyf Manhode* III. xviii. (1869) 144 Now, quod j, art thow an hangestere? Ye, certeyn, quod she.

hangul[1] ('hʌŋgʊl). Also hungal. [Kashmiri *hāngul.*] A deer, *Cervus cashmiriensis*, related to and perhaps a race of the red deer.

1858 A. L. ADAMS in *Proc. Zool. Soc.* XXVI. 529 *Cervus cashmeriensis*.. *Barra Singa* and *Hanglu* of the Cashmerees. **1869** A. A. A. KINLOCH *Large Game Shooting* 44 Cashmeerie hangul. **1898** R. LYDEKKER *Deer of all Lands* 83 The Hangul —*Cervus cashmirianus.* **1922** *Blackw. Mag.* Mar. 334/1 The hungal or Kashmir stag, found on the western side of Chamba. **1955** I. T. SANDERSON *Living Mammals of World* 251/1 The real Red Deer... include.. the Hangul of Kashmir. **1973** *Times* 20 Feb. (India Suppl.) p. xi/3 The lordly Hangul, the most magnificent of deer, also dwell here.

‖**hangul**[2] ('hangul). Also hankul. [Korean, f. *Han* Korea + *kul* script, alphabet.] The Korean national phonetic alphabet (formerly called ONMUN).

1951 C. OSGOOD *Koreans & their Culture* xvi. 323 Books were printed in the native alphabet, ŏnmun (or hangŭl), with the innovation of having the characters run horizontally from left to right instead of vertically. **1953** D. PORTWAY *Korea* vii. 122 Sino-Korean words can be transcribed into hangul. **1966** S. McCUNE *Korea* xiii. 182 One of the benefits of the Korean phonetic writing system, *hangul*.. has been that it could be quickly learned by those who speak Korean. **1972** P. M. BARTZ *S. Korea* iv. 39/1 In its modern form, *Hangul* consists of 24 phonetic symbols and is considered one of the most ingenious writing systems ever devised. **1972** *Computers & Humanities* VI. 264 The entries are transcriptions of the Korean syllabary (hangul) used to annotate those Chinese characters.

†**hangum-tuum.** *humorous.* [Perh. a parody on *judicium tuum*, or *et ideo habeat judicium suum*, 'and therefore let him have his judgement'; a phrase found in court rolls, referring to hanging.]

c **1650** *Dialogue on Oxford Parl.* in *Harl. Misc.* (1808–12) II. 127 (D.), *Tom.* They shall not come and rob him by a strong hand. *Will.* They durst hardly do that; for then it had come to hangum-tuum.

†'**hangwite.** *Old Law.* A penalty and offence mentioned in Domesday Book, and in *Leges Willelmi*: see quots.

1086 *Domesday* I. 262 b, Hangeuuitham faciens in ciuitate [de Cestre] x. sol. dabat. Propositus autem regis uel comitis hanc forisfacturam faciens xx. solid. emendabat. *a* **1195** *Charter Rich. I.* in *Wetherhal Register* (1897) 30 Quiete.. de Ferdwita et hengwita.. et de blodwita. *a* **1200** *Laws of Will. I*, I. c. 4 Si quis latronem sive furem, sine clamore et insecutione ejus, cui dampnum factum est, ceperit, et captum ultra duxerit, dabit x. solid. de henwite [*Fr. text* hengwite], et ad primam divisam faciet de eo justitiam. Quod si eum ultra primam divisam sine justitiarii licentia duxerit, erit in forisfacto xl. sol. *c* **1250** *Gloss. Law Terms* in *Rel. Ant.* I. 33 *Hangwite*.. Quite de larum pendu sanz sergant. **1579** RASTELL *Expos. diff. Words*, *Hangwit*, that is to be quite of a theefe or felone hanged without iudgement, or escaped out of your custody. **1641** *Termes de la Ley* 179.

hang-woman. *nonce-wd.* A woman who performs the function of a hangman.

1883 *Philad. Press* 30 Aug. 4, In Ireland, a sheriff once, not being able to find a hangman, hired a hangwoman. **1884** *Pall Mall G.* 4 Jan. 11/1 Some amusing tales about sextons and hangmen (and of one hang-woman).

hangworthy ('hæŋwɜːðɪ), *a. rare.* [f. HANG *v.* + WORTHY: cf. *blameworthy*, *trustworthy*, etc., in which, however, the first element is a sb.] Worthy to be hanged.

1580 SIDNEY *Arcadia* (1622) 426 To lay their hang-worthy neckes vpon the constancie of his promised pardon. *c* **1670** *Expost. Let. Men Buckhm.* 2/2 Most Hang-worthy Gentlemen! **1888** *Scott. Leader* 22 June 4 A provisional list of the half-a-dozen most hangworthy of my confreres.

‖**Hanif, Haneef** (ha'niːf). [Arab. *ḥanīf*, app. the same as Heb. *ḥanēf* impious.

It has been conjectured by Sprenger and others that in Mohammed's early days there was a sect of reformed Jews, who professed to follow the religion of Abraham, to whom enemies gave the epithet *ḥanēf*, 'impious', and that Mohammed, being misled as to the meaning of the word, adopted it in a good sense.]

A name or epithet applied in the Koran to Abraham; hence, also, to one sincere or orthodox in the faith of Islam. By historical writers, applied to a sect of religious reformers, with many of whose tenets Mohammed identified himself, as professing to restore the religion of Abraham.

Hence **Hanifism, Hanifite** (**Hanee-, Hany-**) *sb.* and *a.*

1734 SALE tr. *Koran* vi. 79, I [Abraham] have turned my face to him who originated the heaven and the earth, as a hanif, and I am not of the idolaters. **1877** J. E. CARPENTER tr. *Tiele's Hist. Relig.* 94 To constitute Hanyfism into a religion, a fixed doctrine, an organised worship, and a divine sanction were needed. These were provided by Mohammed. **1877** DODS *Mohammed, Buddha & Christ* ii. 85 He aimed [at first] at nothing else than to restore the religion of Abraham, the Hanyfite creed. **1883** *Encycl. Brit.* XVI. 546/2 There were individuals who were not content with a negation, and sought a better religion.. They were called Hanifs, probably meaning 'penitents', men who strive to free themselves from sin. They did not constitute a regular sect, and had in fact no fixed and organized views.

‖**haniwa** ('haniwa). [Jap.] A clay image or cylinder of a type anciently placed outside Japanese sepulchres.

1931 G. B. SANSOM *Japan* I. i. 7 Outside the mounds, but evidently associated with them, are found clay figures (known as *haniwa*). **1960** B. LEACH *Potter in Japan* vi. 136 Haniwa figures from A.D. 600. **1970** *Oxf. Compan. Art* 607/1 'Tomb figures' or *haniwa*, clay cylinders some of which were decorated with human or other figures. **1972** *Mainichi Daily News* (Japan) 7 Nov. 5/5 Shards of cylindrical Haniwa had been found at the site.

hanjee, var. KHANJEE.

hank (hæŋk), *sb.* Also 6 hanc, 6–7 hanke, 7–9 hanck(e. [Found in 14th c.; app. from Norse: cf. ON. *hǫnk* fem. (:—**hanku*), genit. *hankar* hank, coil, skein, clasp; also *hanki* m., the hasp or clasp of a chest; Sw. *hank* m., string, tie-band, rowel;

Da. *hank* handle (as of a basket), ear of a pot. (The connexion of senses 6 and 7 with the others is not certain.)]

1. A circular coil or loop of anything flexible.

1483 *Cath. Angl.* 173/2 An Hank. **1513** DOUGLAS *Æneis* II. v. [iv.] 34 As he [Laocoon] etlis thair hankis to have rent, And with his handis thame away have draw. **1674** N. COX *Gentl. Recreat.* IV. (1677) 40 Tie them fast with the two ends of the Silk, that they may hang in so many Hanks. **1688** R. HOLME *Armoury* III. iii. 107 An Hank is a slipping made up into a knot. **1859** R. F. BURTON *Centr. Afr.* in *Jrnl. Geog. Soc.* XXIX. 196 The hair..is usually twisted into many little ringlets or hanks. **1877** W. THOMSON *Voy. Challenger* I. ii. 119 The stems..were coiled in great hanks round the trawl-beam.

2. A skein or coil of thread, yarn, etc.; a definite length of yarn or thread in a coil.

A hank of cotton yarn contains 840 yds.; of worsted yarn 560 yds. *to make a ravelled hank*, to entangle a skein hence *fig.* 'to put anything into confusion' (Brockett).

1560 ROLLAND *Crt. Venus* II. 694 Ane Reill..To reill thair hankis..of reid gold wyir. **1633** *Naworth Househ. Bks.* (Surtees) 328 For sixe hanckes and 3 cutts of yarne. **1776–7** *Act 17 Geo. III*, c. 11 §11 Every several hank of such worsted yarn shall..contain seven raps or leas. **1834** MEDWIN *Angler in Wales* I. 41 Knotting my hanks of gut. **1835** URE *Philos. Manuf.* 102 In cotton yarns, the rule of numbering is very simple, being the number of hanks, each eight hundred and forty yards long, requisite to form one pound in weight. Thus No. 40, written 40's., denotes yarns of which forty hanks weigh one pound. **1880** *Harper's Mag.* Sept. 534/2 The ceilings [were] hung with hanks of blue yarn. **1888** *Century Mag.* XXXVI. 768/2 These little silken 'hanks' were sometimes..prettily colored. **1957** *Vogue Knitting Bk.* L. 70/2 (Advt.), 3, 4 & 2-ply Super Botany Wool. oz. hanks 1/5. **1966** *Which?* Feb. 53/2 Most yarns are sold in balls nowadays; we tested only nine still sold in the hank.

fig. *a* **1745** SWIFT *To Dr. Sheridan* 31 Thy words together ty'd in small hanks, Close as the Macedonian phalanx. **1896** *Home Missionary* (N.Y.) July 136 The tangled hank has yet many knots and hitches.

3. a. A loop of string, wire, or the like, used to fasten things together, or to hang a thing up by; *spec.* in rural use, A bight of rope or a withy used as the fastening of a gate or hurdle.

1388–9 *Abingdon Acc.* (Camden) 57, j hank pro cemetar'. **1617** MARKHAM *Caval.* VI. 9 If his Rider start him sodainly, or hold his hankes too straite. **1641** BEST *Farm. Bks.* (Surtees) 16 Yow are to make your hankes 3 quarters of a yarde in length, and to putte to everie barre yow sende to fielde a hanke. **1788** W. MARSHALL *Yorksh.* Gloss., *Hank*, a with, or rope, for fastening a gate. **1855** ROBINSON *Whitby Gloss.*, *Hank*, a rope-loop for fastening a gate.

b. *Naut.* A hoop or ring of rope, wood, or iron, fixed upon the stays, to seize the luff of the fore-and-aft sails, and to confine the staysails thereto, at different distances (Smyth *Sailor's Word-bk.*).

1711 W. SUTHERLAND *Shipbuilder's Assist.* 134 Fore-sheet, Main-sheet, Hanks, Swifter. **1769** FALCONER *Dict. Marine* (1789), *Anneaux d'étai*, the hanks of a stay-sail. **1794** *Rigging & Seamanship* I. 88 *Reef-hanks*, short pieces of log-line, or other small line, sewed at certain distances on the reefs of boom-sails. **1840** R. H. DANA *Bef. Mast* xxxv. 132 A rattling of hanks announce that the flying-jib has come in. **1883** *Harper's Mag.* Aug. 450/1 Then comes a foresail, which is fitted with hanks to the fore-stay.

c. *hank for hank*: see quots.

1760 C. JOHNSTON *Chrysal* (1822) II. 238 Able to go, hank for hank with any thing that swims the sea. **1794** *Rigging & Seamanship* II. 251* *Hank-for-hank*, when two ships tack and make a progress to windward together. **1867** SMYTH *Sailor's Word-bk.*, *Hank for hank.*

4. *fig.* **a.** A restraining or curbing hold; a power of check or restraint: esp. in *to have a hank on* or *over any one*. Now *rare* or *dial.*

1613 T. POTTS *Disc. Witches* (Chetham) P iv a, The said witches..had then in hanck a child of Michael Hartleys. **1706** FARQUHAR *Recruit. Officer* II. ii, 'Twill give me such a hank upon her pride. **1721** STRYPE *Eccl. Mem.* II. xxi. 172 So that their landlords might have them [the tenants] upon the hank. **1771** SMOLLETT *Humph. Cl.* (1815) 251 Humphry had this double hank upon her inclinations. **1825** BROCKETT *N.C. Gloss.* s.v., To keep a good hank upon your horse, is to have a good hold of the reins. **1851** DE QUINCEY *Ld. Carlisle on Pope* Wks. 1862 XII. 45 He had defied all the powers of Chancery to get a hank over him.

b. Connexion, entanglement; *no hanks with*, no relations with, nothing to do with. *dial.*

1888 ELWORTHY *W. Somerset Word-bk.*, *Hanks*, connection or dealings with—used only with a negative construction..I have heard people warned..'not to have no hanks' with a certain horse, or with an undesirable bargain. **1893** *Wiltsh. Gloss.* s.v., 'I won't ha' no hank wi' un', will have nothing at all to do with him.

c. *Wrestling.* In the Cumberland and Westmorland style, a throw made by putting the left leg between the legs of an opponent, catching his left leg, and leaning or pulling backwards. Also *back-hank*.

1870 W. ARMSTRONG *Wrestliana* 44 Robinson lifted him up like a cat lifting a mouse, when, Plaskett immediately put in the hank. **1888** *Encycl. Brit.* XXIV. 690/2 Each man tries to throw his adversary by using the 'buttock',..the 'crossbuttock',..or the 'back-hank'. **1898** *Encycl. Sport* II. 547/2 The hank, when manipulated by an expert wrestler, becomes one of the hardest and most dangerous falls of all.

5. The handle of a jug or pot. *dial.*

c **1530** in Gutch *Coll. Cur.* II. 318 The mending of twoo Pottle Pottis..the gilding and mending the hancs lyddes and saudering them in sartaigne places. **1847–78** HALLIWELL, *Hank*, a handle. *Somerset.*

6. A baiting of an animal.

1785 GROSE *Dict. Vulg. Tongue* s.v., *A Smithfield hank*, an ox rendered furious by over driving and barbarous treatment. **1812** J. H. VAUX *Flash Dict.*, *Hank*, a bull-bait, or bullock-hunt. **1813** *Sporting Mag.* XLII. 24 To appear at a mill, a hanck, or a dog-fight. **1881** *Diprose's Annual* 64/2 The needful preparations for these Tiger Hanks. *Ibid.* 66/2 Thus ended my first, though..not my last tiger hank.

7. A propensity; an evil habit. *dial.*

1721 BAILEY, *Hank*, a Habit, Custom or Propensity of Mind. **1825** BROCKETT *N.C. Gloss.*, *Hank*, a habit. **1828** *Craven Dial.* s.v., 'Shoe's gitten a sad hank o' runnin out ot neets.' **1878** *Cumbld. Gloss.*, *Hank*, an evil habit.

hank (hæŋk), *v.* Also 4 **hanc, haunk,** 4–7 **hanke,** 7 **hanck.** [Known from 13th c.; prob. from Norse: cf. ON. *hanka* to coil, refl. *hankask* to coil oneself up, f. *hǫnk*, *hank-* sb.: see prec. (The connexion of senses 5 and 6 is uncertain.)]

1. a. *trans.* To fasten by a loop or noose; to entangle; to catch by any loop-like part. Now *dial.*

[*c* **1205** LAY. 25872 Beoð þine feðer-heomen Ihannked mid golde.] *a* **1300** *Cursor M.* 16044 Ful herd þai did [him] hanc, And bonden broght him forth as thef. *c* **1450** HENRYSON *Mor. Fab.* 50 The Lyon fled and..Fell in the net and hankit fute and head. **1513** DOUGLAS *Æneis* VII. iii. 10 At the schoyr wndir a gresy bank, Thair nauy can thai ankir fast and hank. **1617** MARKHAM *Caval.* VI. 44 He shall hold [the reynes] fast betweene his fore-finger and his thumbe, and then hanke them about his hand twice. **1858** R. S. SURTEES *Ask Mamma* liii. 242 Others hank their horses on to the crook at the door. **1894** CROCKETT *Lilac Sunbonnet* 39 There he hung, hanket by the waistband o' his breeks.

fig. **1357** *Lay Folks Catech.* 456 Dedli synnes..gastely sla ilk mannes saule, That er hanked [*Lamb. MS.* bound] in al or in any of tham. **1744** E. ERSKINE *Serm.* Wks. (1871) III. 201 The heart of the bride being thus hanked or catched with the glory of the Bridegroom.

b. *Wrestling.* To throw (an opponent) by means of the hank (see HANK *sb.* 4 c).

1881 *Sportsman's Year-Bk.* 314 The next fall resulted in favour of Pooley, who hanked his adversary. **1894** *Carlisle Patriot* 13 July 7/4 (Cumbld. Gloss. 1899), J— was hanked, S— trying the inside click.

†**2.** To hang. *Obs.* (Perh. a scribal error.)

c **1465** *Eng. Chron.* (Camden 1856) 10 The kyng pardoneth the thy drawyng and hankyng, but thyn hed shalle be smyte of.

3. *intr.* To hang or remain fastened; to 'catch.' (In quot. 1547 prob. a misprint.)

1547 HOOPER *Declar. Christ* viii. (Zurich) Hij, The same bodye that hankyd upon the crose. *a* **1616** BEAUM. & FL. *Scornf. Lady* v. iv, You should have hankt o' th' bridle, Sir, i' faith. *Mod. Sc.* Take care that your line does not hank on the bushes.

4. *trans.* To make up (thread) in hanks.

1818 TODD, *Hank*, to form into hanks. Used in the north of England. **1825** in BROCKETT *N.C. Gloss.*

5. To bait: cf. HANKER *sb.*[1] *slang.*

1823 [see HANKER *sb.*[1]] **1893** in FARMER *Slang.*

†**6.** *intr.* = HANKER *v.* 1, 2. *Obs.*

1589 C. OCLAND in *Lett. Lit. Men* (Camden) 71 Where I hanked after plentie I have runne upon scarcetie. **1716** *Cuckoo* in *Jacobite Songs* (1871) 23 He'll fley away the wild birds that hank about the throne.

Hence **hanking** *vbl. sb.*

1641 BEST *Farm. Bks.* (Surtees) 16 The 8th thinge belonge to barres is fold-hankes or hankinges, as they call them, which is as thicke againe as plough-string, beinge a loose kinde of two plettes. **1820** J. CLELAND *Rise & Progr. Glasgow* 45 The hanking of handspun yarn.

† **'hanker,** *sb.*[1] *Obs.* [f. HANK *sb.* 6 or *v.* 5 + -ER[1].] One who takes part in bull-baiting.

1811 *Lexicon Balatronicum*, *Bull Hankers*, persons who over-drive bulls, or frequent bull baits. **1823** EGAN *Grose's Dict. Vulg. Tongue*, *Bull Hankers*, men who delight in the sport of bull-hanking; that is, bull-baiting, or bullock-hunting. **1825** HONE *Every-day Bk.* I. 1171 [Smithfield] drovers, and bullock-hankers.

'hanker, *sb.*[2] [f. HANKER *v.*] A longing after something; a secret yearning.

1827 BEDDOES *Let.* Oct. in *Poems* p. lxxvii, Nothing but the desperate hanker for distinction..ever set me upon rhyming. **1881** T. HARDY *Laodicean* III. ix, She has not shown a genuine hanker for anybody yet.

hanker ('hæŋkə(r)), *v.* [Not known before 1600; history obscure. Mod.Du. has *hunkeren* (Plantijn, 1673, *hungkeren*), dial. *hankeren*, in same sense. Generally thought to be frequentative and intensive deriv. of HANG *v.*, but cf. HANK *v.* 6.]

1. *intr.* To 'hang about', to linger or loiter *about* with longing or expectation. Now *dial.*

1601 F. GODWIN *Bps. of Eng.* 539 [He] hauing hankered a long time about the Chauncery. **1641** MILTON *Reform.* II. (1851) 66 But let us not..stand hankering and politizing, when God..points us out the way to our peace. *a* **1652** BROME *Eng. Moor* I. i. Wks. 1873 II. 3, I was hankring at an ordinary, In quest of a new Master. **1713** WARDER *True Amazons* 53 If you find any [hornet] hankering about your Bees. **1858** HUGHES *Scouring of W. Horse* viii. 198, I used to hanker round the kitchen, or still-room, or wherever she might happen to be.

2. To have a longing or craving. Const. *after*; less usually with *for*, or *infin.*

In Johnson's time 'Scarcely used but in familiar language'; now common in literature.

1642 ROGERS *Naaman* 111 The soules misery is..that she is alway hankering and catching at every shadow and vanity. **1652** NEEDHAM tr. *Selden's Mare Cl.* 248 The Saxons inhabiting the shore over against us, hanker'd after it. **1768–74** TUCKER *Lt. Nat.* (1852) II. 15 The mind..always hankering after what she has not. **1835** THIRLWALL *Greece* I. viii. 325 The tendency of human nature to hanker after all that is forbidden. **1850** KINGSLEY *Alt. Locke* x, To be told what you've been hankering to know so long. **1856** MRS. BROWNING *Aur. Leigh* IX. 514 That Romney dared to hanker for your love.

Hence **'hankerer,** one who hankers; **'hankering** *ppl. a.*; whence **'hankeringly** *adv.*, in a hankering manner.

1845 LD. CAMPBELL *Chancellors* cxxiv. (1857) VI. 84 The bishops..had among them hankerers after the exiled family. **1859** KINGSLEY *Misc.* (1860) I. 286 Hankerers after fame and power. **1864** WEBSTER, *Hankeringly.*

hankering ('hæŋkərɪŋ), *vbl. sb.* [f. prec. + -ING[1].] A mental craving or longing.

1662 J. BARGRAVE *Pope Alex. VII* (1867) 79 He had an ambitious hankering after a cap. **1678** BUTLER *Hud.* III. ii. 239 And felt such Bowel-Hankerings, To see an Empire all of Kings. **1712** STEELE *Spect.* No. 431 ¶3, I then took a strange Hankering to Coals; I fell to scranching 'em. **1771** FRANKLIN *Autobiog.* Wks. 1840 I. 16, I still had a hankering for the sea. **1893** A. JESSOPP *Stud. Recluse* vii. 217 The hankering for what we call sympathy is the virtue—or the vice—of advanced civilisation.

hankle ('hæŋk(ə)l), *v. dial.* Also 7–8 **hanckle.** [f. HANK *v.* + dim. and freq. ending -LE.] *trans.* † **a.** To fasten lightly. *Obs.* **b.** To twist or entangle; also *fig.*

1621 SANDERSON *12 Serm.* (1637) 356 An unruly Coult.. fettered and side-hanckled for leaping. **1781** J. HUTTON *Tour to Caves* Gloss., *Hanckle*, to entangle. **1825** BROCKETT *N.C. Gloss.*, *Hankle*, to twist, to entangle thread, silk, or worsted. **1855** ROBINSON *Whitby Gloss.*, *Hankled* or *Handkled*, joined hand-in-hand in a pursuit. 'They hankled him on', enticed him to unite.

hanksite ('hæŋksaɪt). *Min.* [Named in 1885 after H. G. Hanks, mineralogist, California: see -ITE.] Sulphate and carbonate of sodium, found in hexagonal prisms of white or yellowish colour.

1885 *Amer. Jrnl. Sc.* Ser. III. XXX. 133 Hanksite, a new anhydrous sulphato-carbonate of sodium.

hankul, var. HANGUL[2].

hanky[1] ('hæŋkɪ). Also **handky, hankie.** Nursery and colloquial name for HANDKERCHIEF.

1895 J. DAVIDSON *Earl Lavender* iv. 73 They..sighed, and looked up, and the schoolmaster's wife used her handky. **1902** *Westm. Gaz.* 17 Dec. 8/2 Lovely ladies' hankies in dainty lawn. **1924** E. MARSH tr. *La Fontaine's Fables* 52 Every occurrence was referred to her; Whether one lost a hanky or a lover. **1939** [see ACCESSORIZE *v.*]. **1953** [see *fly-whisk* s.v. FLY *sb.*[1] 11]. **1967** N. FREELING *Strike Out* 133 Janine was snuffling in a silly little hanky.

hanky[2]. = HANKY-PANKY. *rare.*

1924 GALSWORTHY *White Monkey* II. iv, On our floor, with Michael outside the door, one would know there couldn't be any hanky.

hankyl, obs. form of ANKLE *sb.*

c **1475** in Wr.-Wülcker 751/4 *Hec cavilla*, a hankyl.

hanky-panky ('hæŋkɪ'pæŋkɪ). *slang.* [An arbitrary formation, prob. related to *hocus pocus*, *hoky-poky*.] Jugglery, legerdemain; trickery, double dealing, underhand dealing.

1841 *Punch* I. 88 (Farmer) Only a little hanky-panky. **1847** ALB. SMITH *Chr. Tadpole* xlvii. (1879) 409 Necromancy, my dear Sir—the hanky-panky of the ancients. **1864** E. YATES *Broken to Harness* xxxviii, If there was any hanky-panky, any mystery I mean. **1881** *Athenæum* 27 Aug. 265/1 Madame Blavatsky's hanky-panky with teacups and cigarettes. **1887** BLACK *Sabina Zembra* 461 He won't play hanky-panky with me.

attrib. **1865** B. BRIERLEY *Irkdale* I. 292 Any sort o' hanky-panky work. **1882** *Mrs. Raven's Tempt.* III. 41 Some hanky-panky trick of hers.

hanlawhile: see HANDWHILE.

hann, var. of KHAN, caravanserai.

'hannayite. *Min.* [Named 1878 after J. B. Hannay of Manchester: see -ITE.] Hydrous phosphate of magnesium and ammonium found in slender yellowish crystals in the guano of Skipton Caves.

1879 *Min. Mag.* III. 108 Hannayite..found at the Skipton caves, Victoria.

Hannibal ('hænɪbəl). The name of the famous Carthaginian general, who fought against Rome in the third century B.C. Hence, *allusively*, a great general. (Also, in Shakes., humorously confounded with CANNIBAL.) † *Hannibal eye*, a blind eye.

1585 T. WASHINGTON tr. *Nicholay's Navig.* Ded. ¶iii b, Were it not that I feare the censure of some politike Hanniball. **1603** SHAKS. *Meas. for M.* II. i. 187 Proue this, thou wicked Hanniball. *a* **1652** R. BROME *New Acad.* III. ii. in *Wks.* (1873) II. 58, I passe For a brisk youth, but for my Hannibal eye here.

Hence **Hannibalian** (hænɪ'beɪlɪən), **Hannibalic** (-'bælɪk) *adjs.*, of, pertaining to, or characteristic of Hannibal.

1678 J. D. (*title*) The History of Appian..In Two Parts. The First consisting of the Punick..and Hannibalick Wars. **1862** W. P. DICKSON tr. *Mommsen's Hist. Rome* II. III. vi. 189 Thus ended the second Punic, or as the Romans more correctly called it, the Hannibalic, war. **1880** *Encycl. Brit.*

XI. 444/2 In the year 202 B.C. the Second Punic, or, more properly, the Hannibalian War was at an end. **1886** H. F. LESTER *Under two Fig Trees* 135 And baby had registered a Hannibalic vow. **1934** A. TOYNBEE *Study Hist.* II. v. 162 The advance of the Roman frontier..was a direct.. consequence of the Hannibalic War itself.

Hanover (ˈhænəʊvə(r), orig. stressed as in Ger. haˈnoːvər). [Ger. *Hannover.*] **1.** The name of a North German town, the capital of a region of the same name, formerly an Electorate of the Empire, later a province of Prussia; in 1714 the Elector of Hanover became king of England. ***go to Hanover*** = begone, be off (cf. *go to Hexham, Bath, Jericho*); so ***to send to, wish at Hanover.*** Hence, **Hanoverian** (hænəʊˈvɪərɪən) *a.*, of or pertaining to Hanover or the House of Hanover; *sb.* an inhabitant of Hanover; also, an adherent of the House of Hanover. †**Hanoverianize,** †**Hanoverize** *vbs., trans.* to make Hanoverian; *intr.* to become Hanoverian.

17.. SWIFT *Wks.* (1768) VII. 264 And now God save this noble realm, And God save eke Hanover; And God save those who hold the helm, When as the King goes over. **1744** *Lond. Mag.* 649 Our Hanovranised Ministers here. **1775** ASH, *Hanoverian*, belonging to Hanover..A native of Hanover. *a* **1797** H. WALPOLE *Mem. Geo. II*, III. 179 Sir John Philipps reproached Pitt with Hanoverizing. **1827** MACAULAY *Hallam's Const. Hist.* Ess. (1887) 78 Like William and the princes of the Hanoverian line. **1869** ROGERS *Hist. Gleanings* I. 37 It became manifest that the law of the Hanoverian succession would be respected.

2. Phr. ***what the Hanover***, an expression of irritation or impatience. *dial.* or *colloq.*

1902 *Eng. Dial. Dict.* III. 56/2 What the Hanover do I care about it? **1914** D. H. LAWRENCE *Prussian Officer* 223 'What the Hanover's got you?' asked Whiston. 'Nothing. Can't I get up?' **1915** —— *Rainbow* i. 27 He went home..wondering What the Hanover!

hanper: see HANAPER.

‖**Hans** (hans). A familiar abbreviated form in German and Dutch of *Johannes*, John; hence, a German or Dutchman.

1569 HARDING in *Jewel's Sedit. Bul* (1570) 5 Accused by Hicke, Hob, and Haunce, and judged by Jacke and Gill. **1667** LD. ORRERY *State Lett.* (1743) II. 202 We shall give Monsieur, or Hans, or both, good entertainment. **1855** MACAULAY *Hist. Eng.* IV. 485 For Hans, after filling the pockets of his huge trunk hose with our money..would, as soon as a press gang appeared, lay claim to the privileges of an alien.

†**b.** ***Hans-in-kelder*** (Dutch, lit. Jack-in-cellar): an unborn child; cf. Ger. *Hänschen im keller*.

1635 BROME *Sparagus Garden* III. iv. Wks. 1873 III. 159 Come here's a health to the Hans in Kelder, and the mother of the boy, if it prove so. **1648** NEEDHAM *Mercurius Pragmaticus* No. I. Aiij b (Stanf.), The Birthday of that precious new government; which is yet but a Hans-en-kelder. **1656** in BLOUNT *Glossogr.* **1663** DRYDEN *Wild Gallant* v. ii, It seems you are desirous I should father this hans en kelder here. **1785** in GROSE *Dict. Vulg. Tongue.*

hans, obs. form of HANSE.

Hansard[1] (ˈhænsəd). *Hist.* [f. HANSE + -ARD. (As a surname, Hansard occurs early in 13th c., but its identity is doubtful.)] A member of one of the establishments of the German Hanse.

1449 *Rolls Parlt.* V. 144/2 Hanser. **1453** *Ibid.* V. 230/2 Another Subsidie..of every Venecian, Esterlynge.. Lumbard, Hanszard, Prucier, and also other Straungers Merchauntz. *Ibid.*, Hansard. **1832** MCCULLOCH *Comm. Dict.* (1852) 655 The merchants of the Hanse towns, or Hansards, as they were then commonly termed, were established in London at a very early period. *Ibid.* 656 The Hansards were every now and then accused of acting with bad faith. **1890** CUNNINGHAM *Growth Eng. Comm. Early & Mid. Ages* §121 At the beginning of the fifteenth century the Hansards found that their monopoly of the Baltic trade was threatened.

Hansard[2] (ˈhænsəd, -ɑːd). The official report of the proceedings and debates of the Houses of Parliament; colloq. so called as having been compiled for a long period by Messrs. Hansard. Also *transf.*

1876 L. STEPHEN *Hours in Library* II. 154 Hansard was not, and newspapers were in their infancy. **1880** *Gentl. Mag.* CCXLVI. 79 The Queensland legislature..has its own official daily Hansard.

Hansardize (ˈhænsədaɪz), *v.* [f. prec. + -IZE.] *trans.* To confront (a member of Parliament) with his former utterances as recorded in 'Hansard'; to prove (a person) to have formerly expressed a different view or opinion. Also *absol.*

1869 HUXLEY in *Sci. Opinion* 5 May 506/2 I do not wish to *Hansardize* Sir William Thomson by laying much stress on the fact that, only fifteen years ago, he entertained a totally different view of the origin of the sun's heat. **1869** LD. GRANVILLE *Sp. in Ho. Lords* 15 June, I will venture now —to use a word, an admirable word invented by the noble lord opposite—to Hansardise. **1894** *Athenæum* 15 Dec. 822/2 M. Ollivier goes out of his way to attack Thiers by 'Hansardizing' him, as the Prime Minister Lord Derby used to say.

Hence ˌ**Hansardiˈzation**, the action of 'Hansardizing'.

1883 HUXLEY in *Jrnl. Educ.* 1 Mar. 97/2 That process so hateful to members of Parliament, which may be denoted by the term 'Hansardization'.

Hanse (hæns, ‖ˈhanzə). *Hist.* Also 2–7 **hans,** 6–7 **haunce, haunse.** [a. OF. *hanse*, and med.L. *hansa*, a. OHG. (and Goth.) *hansa* (= OE. *hós*) military troop, band, company, MHG. *hanse* fellowship, association, merchants' guild.

The early examples of this word relating to England occur in Latin charters and other documents, and in the L. form *hansa*, the precise sense of which, e.g. in the phrase 'gilda mercatoria et (*or* cum) hansa', is often difficult to determine. See the discussion of the word in Gross, *The Gild Merchant* I. Appendix C. The following two main senses may be distinguished, but the order of their appearance in Eng. is not clear.]

1. A company or guild of merchants in former times; an association of merchants trading with foreign parts; the merchant guild of a town; also, the privileges and monopolies possessed by it; sometimes, app., the guild-hall or 'hanse-house'.

The ***Old Hanse*** was the Fellowship of the London Merchants which had a monopoly of the foreign trade of London since Norman times; the ***New Hanse*** was the company of Merchant Adventurers first incorporated in 1497, which received charters from Henry VII in 1505 and Elizabeth in 1566.

1199 *Charter of K. John to Dunwich* in Brady *Boroughs* (1790) App. 10 Concessimus etiam eis hansam, et Gildam Mercatoriam, sicut habere consueverint. **1297** in *Lib. Cust.* (Rolls) I. 71 Quod non sunt del Hauns de Amyas, Corbie, et Nele, nec aliquid habent in societate cum hominibus eorundem partium, nec cum creditoribus ejusdem Hanciæ. **1552–3** in *Hist. MSS. Comm. Rep. Cecil Papers* I. 132 [Petition to Lord Chancellor, from the] New Haunce [of the Merchant Adventurers, for redress of their grievances against those of the] Old Haunce. **1587** FLEMING *Contn. Holinshed* III. 275/1 A deed, in which king John granted to the citizens of Yorke a guildhall, hanse, and other liberties. **1594** PLAT *Jewell-ho.* III. 89 Offering to exchange their freedome, both of the olde Haunce and of the newe, for this multiplying Art [of alchemy]. *c* **1600** *Brit. Mus. Add. MS.* 18913, lf. 23 (Gross I. 195 *note*) Euerie persone admitted into the Freedome of the Fellowshippe of Merchant Adventurers of the Realm of England shall pay at suche his admission yf he come in one the old hanse, as yt ys termed, 6*s.* 8*d.* sterlinge, And yf he come in one the new hanse, tenn markes sterlinge. **1623** tr. *Favine's Theat. Hon.* II. iv. 79 Made among one part of them a Hanse, that is to say, a League and Societie. **1872** COSMO INNES *Lect. Scott. Legal Antiq.* III. 114 All the burghs beyond the Munth had a confederacy called by the name of Hanse. [But it is disputed whether this was the meaning or effect of the *liberum ansum* conferred by K. William the Lion, 1165–1214, upon all his burgesses north of the Munth: see Gross I. 197.] **1890** GROSS *Gild Merch.* I. 198 *note*, This Hanse of London flourished in the thirteenth and fourteenth centuries.. Bruges and Ypres were at the head of this league, which originally consisted of seventeen towns of Flanders, and North France.

b. *spec.* The name of a famous political and commercial league of Germanic towns, which had also a house in London. *pl.* The Hanse towns or their citizens.

1305 in *Lib. Cust.* I. 112 Quod Alemanni de Hansa, mercatores Alemanniæ, sint quieti de ij solidis, ingrediendo et exeundo..ad Portam de Bisshopesgate. **1485** in *Mat. illust. Reign Hen. VII* (Rolls) I. 115 The merchants of the Hanze in Almayne, having a house in the city of London, commonly called Guyldhall Theutonicorum. **1503–4** *Act 19 Hen. VII*, c. 23 'For þe Stillyard', To the prejudice hurt or charge of the seid merchauntes of the Hanse. **1598** HAKLUYT *Voy.* I. 155 [They] passed through the chiefe cities of the Hanse and treated in such sorte with the Burgomasters of them that [etc.]. *a* **1618** RALEIGH *Invent. Shipping* 24 The rest, the Popes, then the Hanses, and lastly the Turks have in effect ruined. **1890** GROSS *Gild Merch.* I. 196 In charters conferred by English kings upon the Teutonic Hanse, gild and hanse are used synonymously.

2. The entrance-fee of a mediæval trading guild; also, a toll or impost levied upon merchants or traders not of the guild.

[This was a very early sense of *hansa*: see Du Cange.]

1200 *Charter of K. John to Ipswich* (Gross II. 121) Ad ponendum se in Gilda et ad hansam suam eidem Gilde dandam. **1279** *Andover Gild Rolls* (Gross II. 292) Quod non tenetur aliquid super Gildam quam tenet, pro qua interrogatus fuit soluere suum hans. **13..** *K. Alis.* 1571 (MS. Laud) He gaf þe bisshopp to gode hans, Riche Baizes besauntz & pans. *Ibid.* 2935 Sendith ows, to gode hans, On hundreþ þousande besauntz From ȝer to ȝerne molke ȝee faile. **1659** *Brit. Mus. Add. MS.* 18913, lf. 19 (Gross I. 195 *note*) For all Hanses, Fines and Broakes att Admissions, and all Broakes condemned in Court for any kind of Transgressions against the orders of the Fellowshipp. **1890** GROSS *Gild Merch.* I. App. C. 194 The term 'hanse' was most commonly used to denote a mercantile tribute or exaction, either as a fee payable upon entering the gild merchant, or as a toll imposed upon non-gildsmen before they were allowed to trade in the town.

3. *attrib.* and *Comb.*, as **hanse-house**, the house in which the members of a hanse met, a guild-hall; sometimes = sense 1; †**hanse-penny**, a payment levied by a hanse; also ***hanse-gild***, etc. **b. Hanse city, Hanse town**, one of the towns of the German Hanse or Hanseatic League; so ***Hanse association, league, merchant***, etc.

a **1135** *Charter of Thurstan to Beverley* in Rymer *Fœdera* (1816) I. 10 Volo ut burgenses mei de Beverlaco habeant suam hanshus. **1337** *Andover Gild Rolls* (Gross II. 333) Et solutum est eadem die de Hanspanes..iis. xid. **1585** in Poulson *Beverlac* I. 330 The rent, revenewes, yssues, profittyes, and comoidytyes perteyninge to the hanse house and comynaltie of the same towne. **1876** FREEMAN *Norm. Conq.* V. xxiv. 472 The men of York had their Hanse-house; the men of Beverley should have their Hanse house too. **b. 1571** *Act 13 Eliz.* c. 14 Merchant strangers..from the lxxii. hanse Townes. **1598** HAKLUYT *Voy.* I. 155 The common society of the Hans marchants. **1601** R. JOHNSON *Kingd. & Commw.* (1603) 76 Not subject to the duke, but a free and hanstown. **1630** *R. Johnson's Kingd. & Commw.* 268 Of Hanse cities there were 72, mutually bound by ancient leagues to enjoy common privileges and freedomes. **1753** HANWAY *Trav.* (1762) II. I. iii. 14 Hamburg is well known to be a hanse town. **1787** A. ANDERSON *Hist. Comm.* I. 502 The naval superiority of the Hans-League at this time [1474]. **1861** M. PATTISON *Ess.* (1889) I. 41 Edward.. granted new privileges to the Hanse association.

Hence **hansing** *vbl. sb.*, as in ***hansing-silver***, money paid for admittance into a hanse.

1304 in *Collect. Buriensia* Add. MS. 17391 (Gross *Gild Merch.* II. 32) ij solidos et unum denarium, quam quidem solutionem vocant inter se hansing-silver.

hanse, obs. form of HANCE.

Hanseatic (hænsɪˈætɪk), *a.* Also 7 **anse-, ansiatike, hansiatick, -tique.** [ad. med.L. *hanseāticus*, f. MHG. *hanse*: see HANSE.] Of or pertaining to the German Hanse.

1614 SELDEN *Titles Hon.* Pref. Ciij, The Hansiatique Societie, beginning about CIƆ.CC. of Christ some while before Frederique the second. **1662** J. DAVIES tr. *Olearius' Voy. Ambass.* 27 'Tis numbred among the Hanseatick Towns. **1665** MANLEY *Grotius' Low C. Warres* 265 Deventer, formerly a free City of the Anseatike League. **1796** MORSE *Amer. Geog.* II. 275 The Hanseatic association, commonly called the Hanse towns. **1861** M. PATTISON *Ess.* (1889) I. 44 The free towns of Lübeck, Bremen, and Hamburg as heirs of the corporate estate of the Hanseatic League, became possessed of the Steelyard.

b. as *sb.* A member of the Hanse.

1787 A. ANDERSON *Hist. Comm.* I. 502 Any city of the Hanseatics.

hansel: see HANDSEL.

†**hanselin.** *Obs. rare.* In 4–5 **hanselyn(e, hanslyne, hanse lyne, haunseleyn** (also **anslet**). [a. OF. *hainselin, hamselin.*] A kind of jacket or 'slop', worn by men in the 14th c.

c **1386** CHAUCER *Pars. T.* ¶348 The horrible disordinat scantnesse of clothyng, as been thise kutted sloppes or haynselyns [*v.rr.* hanselyns, haunseleynys, hanse lynes, hanslynes, anslets].

Hansen (ˈhænsən). *Med.* The name of G. H. A. Hansen (1841–1912), Norwegian physician, used *attrib.* and in the possessive to designate *Mycobacterium leprae*, the causative agent of leprosy, which he discovered, and occas. leprosy itself, as ***Hansen('s) bacillus, Hansen's disease.***

1903 *Jrnl. Path. & Bacteriol.* VIII. 260 These bacilli had some resemblance in form to Hansen's bacilli. **1914** *Jrnl. R. Microsc. Soc.* 569 (*heading*) Behaviour of the Hansen bacillus in vitro. **1938** DORLAND *Med. Dict.* (ed. 18) 430/1 *Hansen's disease*, leprosy. **1947** *Amer. Jrnl. Public Health* Mar. 313 (*title*) Education in Hansen's disease. **1955** *Sci. News Let.* 21 May 322/3 Changes in the proteins in the blood of patients with Hansen's disease (leprosy) were reported. **1970** A. W. WOODRUFF *Alimentary & Haematol. Aspects Trop. Dis.* i. 3 Hansen's bacilli will readily be found in the second [disease].

†**hanse-pot.** *Obs.* Also **haunce-, haunch-.** An ornamental pot or vase of some kind.

1561 *Gifts to Queen* in Nichols *Progr. Q. Eliz.* I. 111 A haunce-pott of allabaster garnished with silver. **1575** *Inv. Abp. Parker's Goods* in *Archæologia* XXX. 25, ij hance potts withe Angells wings chased on the bellies, withe covers annexed, weyinge xliij oz. **1590** *Inv. Sir T. Ramsey, ibid.* XL. 336 vj hanse potts parcell gilt poiz lxxxv oz.

†**hanskin.** *Obs.* [ad. Ger. *Hänschen*, dim. of HANS.] (Cf. HANS, and Eng. use of *Jack.*)

1631 BRATHWAIT *Whimzies, Sayler* 89 Stares cannot bee more faithfull in their society, than these hanskins in their fraternity.

hansom(e, -sum, obs. ff. HANDSOME.

hansom cab (ˈhænsəm). Also short **hansom.** [f. *Hansom*, surname of an architect who in 1834 patented a vehicle with some of the essential features of this cab.] A low-hung two-wheeled cabriolet holding two persons inside, the driver being mounted on a dickey or elevated seat behind, and the reins going over the roof.

1852 COL. HAWKER *Diary* (1893) II. 343 A flying hansom cab, which cut along almost at railway speed. **1882** SERJT. BALLANTINE *Exper.* ii. 20, I have lived to see an archbishop in a hansom cab! **1884** MCCARTHY *Eng. under Gladstone* xiii. 250 Joseph Aloysius Hansom, who invented the Hansom cab, died this year [1882].

β. **1847** *Punch* XIII. 193 The Hansoms were rattling. **1870** DISRAELI *Lothair* xxvi. (D.), He hailed a cruising hansom ..''Tis the gondola of London', said Lothair, as he sprang in. **1893** *19th Cent.* Mar. 470 The hansom as we know it bears little resemblance to the cumbrous vehicle designed by the inventor.

b. *attrib.* as ***hansom cab-driver, -cabman.*** *β.* ***hansom-driver; hansom-borne*** adj.

1849 THACKERAY *Pendennis* II. xxxvi. 346 The cabman, although a Hansom cabman, said thank you for the gratuity which was put into his hand. *a* **1860** ALB. SMITH *Med. Student* (1861) 17 Dashing up to the door as Hansom cab-drivers are wont to do.

Hence **'hansom** (*it*) *v.*, (cf. CAB *v.*, COACH *v.*), to travel or go in a hansom. **hanso'meer** (*nonce-wd.*), the driver of a hansom.

1890 BARING-GOULD *Arminell* xli, To think that I..a raging Democrat, should be hansoming it to and fro between my Ladies and Honourables. **1893** F. F. MOORE *Gray Eye or So* III. 50 Driving as fast as the hansomeer thought consistent with public safety. **1894** MISS BROUGHTON *Beginner* xi, One slippery January morning as she hansoms it along.

hant, ha'nt. Obs. and local U.S. form of HAUNT *sb.*

han't, ha'n't, vulgar contr. of *have not*.

hant, pa. t. of HENT, *Obs.*

hantle ('hɑ:nt(ə)l, -æ-). *Sc.* and *north. dial.* [Not known before *c* 1700; origin obscure.

It has been conjectured to be identical with Da. and Sw. *antal*, 'number, quantity, multitude', which suits the sense, but presents historical and phonetic difficulties, esp. as to the initial *h* in Sc.; it has also been viewed as composed of *hand* + *tale* number, which suits the form, and as a corruption of *hankle*, or of *handful*: the last is unlikely, seeing that *handful, handfu'* itself exists in all the dialects.]

A (considerable) number or quantity; a good many, a good deal.

1692 *Sc. Presbyt. Eloq.* (1738) 149 Here's a great Hantle of Bonny-braw well-fac'd young Lasses. **1814** SCOTT *Wav.* xxix, He has a hantle siller. **1816** —— *Antiq.* xvi, A hantle letters he has written. **1823** J. WILSON *Marg. Lyndesay* xxxiii, They make the avenue look a hantle tosher. **1896** MASSON in *Edinb. Even. News* 14 Nov. 4/2 Scotland had been a hantle the better for having had him. [In Glossaries of Cumberland, Mid Yorkshire, Whitby, etc.; in Lancashire and Cheshire Gl. *Hantle, hontle* 'a handful'.]

‖**hantu** ('hæntu:). [Malay.] An evil spirit, a ghost.

1821 J. LEYDEN tr. *Malay Annals* vi. 54 He saw a hantu, or spectre. **1839** T. J. NEWBOLD *Straits of Malacca* II. xii. 191 The Hantu Ribut is the storm fiend that howls in the blast. **1900** W. W. SKEAT *Malay Magic* iv. 101 *Hantu* and *sheitan* are generic terms for evil spirits, the former being the Malay term. *Ibid.* 103 The Hantu Kubor (Grave Demons) are the spirits of the dead, who are believed to prey upon the living. **1927** H. M. TOMLINSON *Gallions Reach* xxx. 239 They tell me this land is full of hantus, things that ought not to be about; souls now stowed safely away in Gehenna. **1959** *Listener* 8 Oct. 579/3 The spirits, or *hantus*, as they were called in Maly, were not always of human beings. **1962** *Times* 30 June 10/6 There was the *hantu* that brings the lightning.

Hanukkah, var. CHANUKAH.

hanum: see KHANUM.

Hanuman (hʌnʊ'mɑ:n). Also **hoonoomaun, huniman**, etc. [Hind., Hindi *hanumān* (Skr. *hanumant*, f. *hanumat* large-jawed).] **1.** *Hindu Mythology.* Proper name of a monkey-chief; a semi-divine monkey-like creature, to whom extraordinary powers were attributed in legend.

1814 SOUTHEY in J. W. Robberds *Mem. W. Taylor* (1843) II. 427 For the last ten years..Buonaparte..was the God Hanuman—the monkeys, whom he commanded, did the mischief. **1883** *Trans. Asiatic Soc. Japan* XI. 270 For greater safety Râmachandra..stationed Hanuman, the monkey-god..to guard the palace. **1886** YULE & BURNELL *Hobson-Jobson* s.v. *Lungoor*, The monkey-god Hunimān. **1936** E. G. BOULENGER *Apes & Monkeys* ix. 215 The uncanny revenge taken by priests..upon an Englishman, who..insulted the image of Hanuman in a wayside temple. **1965** P. C. JAY in I. DeVore *Primate Behavior* vii. 197 One kind of monkey, the langur, has also had an important part in the traditions and epics of India and is often referred to in its role as the monkey deity Hanuman.

2. (with small initial) An Indian monkey, *Presbytis entellus*, venerated by Hindus.

1843 E. BLYTH in *Jrnl. Asiatic Soc. Bengal* XII. 174 The Hoonumans are strictly protected. *Ibid.*, I know of one locality where the whole numerous community of Bengal Hoonumans appears to consist of males only. **1867** T. HUTTON in *Proc. Zool. Soc.* 944 The particular species of Monkey to which the name of Hoonoomaun now more especially and properly applies is known to naturalists as the *Semnopithecus entellus*. **1891** J. L. KIPLING *Beast & Man in India* iii. 65 Of late years the tradesmen who form the bulk of the members of our municipalities have felt that there are too many Hanumāns abroad. **1897** *Q. Rev.* Oct. 395 No visitor to Hindostan..can have failed to see the sacred Monkey or Hanuman. **1936** E. G. BOULENGER *Apes & Monkeys* ix. 215 The sacred langur, or hanuman..ranges over India from the Deccan northward to the south bank of the Ganges. In its *rôle* of a sacred animal, dedicated to the god Hanuman, it is unique.

Hanunóo ('hɑ:nənəʊ). [Native name.] A member of a people inhabiting southern Mindoro in the Philippines; also, the language of this people.

1949 *Amer. Anthropologist* LI. 269 The Hanunóo raise their own cotton and indigo, and weave and dye skirts, blankets, and other fabrics with considerable skill. *Ibid.*, While visiting in dingy Hanunóo huts, large piles of bamboo poles, four to six feet long, were found. *Ibid.* 271 The ambáhan 'literary' language is either an archaic form of Hanunóo, or a rarer type known as *binúkid*. **1963** J. LYONS *Structural Semantics* iii. 38 Hanunóo color categories.

hanylon, in *Bk. St. Albans*, error for HAVELON *v.*

hanypere, obs. form of HANAPER.

haole ('haʊlɪ, 'haəli). *Hawaiian.* [Native word.] One who is not a native Hawaiian; a white man. Also *attrib.* or as *adj.*

[**1825** W. ELLIS *Jrnl. Tour Hawaii* vii. 151 We had escaped, only because we were *haore*, (foreigners.) No Hawaiian..would have done so with impunity.] **1843** J. J. JARVES *Scenes Sandwich Islands* iii. 104 One brings vegetables, another fish..in short, any thing and every thing which they suppose the *haole*, (foreigner,) to want. **1866** 'MARK TWAIN' *Lett. fr. Hawaii* (1967) 161 But the thing was tabu..to foreigners—haoles. *Ibid.* 202 To the natives all whites are haoles—how-ries—that is, strangers, or more properly, foreigners. **1905** *Daily Chron.* 24 June 3/1 Stevenson 'fell in love' with the Polynesians,..and was consequently unjust to the *haoles*, or white people. *c* **1938** L. MUMFORD *Report on Honolulu* in *City Development* (1946) 75 A lasting link between their ancient ways and the less primitive life lived by the various haole groups that have followed. **1954** *Ellery Queen's Myst. Mag.* Oct. 8/2 The *haole*—white—characters are fiction. The Hawaiians..are authentic. **1970** *Language* XLVI. 981 Ever-increasing pressure for the use of English from 'haoles' (main-land whites) and others.

haoma ('haʊmə). [Zend.] = HOM.

1890 *Ann. Rep. Smithsonian Inst.* 91 On the position of the Haoma in the Avesta of the Parsees. **1953** *Trans. Philol. Soc.* 22 Old Ind. *durósa-*, Avestan *dūraoša-*, the epithet of soma and haoma.

haori ('ha:ori). [Jap.] A short loose coat worn in Japan.

1877 *Trans. Asiatic Soc. Japan* V. I. 8 A *haōri*,—the upper mantle worn by the military class. **1880** F. V. DICKINS tr. *Chiushingura* (new ed.) iii. 16 Badge or device on the sleeves and back of the *haori* or mantle. **1896** L. HEARN *Kokoro* vi. 94 Haori, a sort of upper dress, worn by men as well as women. **1897** J. LA FARGE *Artist's Lett. from Japan* 274 Women under their umbrellas wore the graceful short overcoat they call *haori*, and tottered over the wet ground on high wooden pattens. **1907** *Daily Chron.* 15 May 3/5 The little ornament on his haori (the gown) was the family crest. **1922** J. STREET *Mysterious Japan* ii. 19 One or two of them wore the graceful and dignified *hakama* and *haori*—the silk skirt and coat of formal native dress. **1970** J. KIRKUP *Japan behind Fan* 125 There are even some small garments, jackets called *haori*, made from decorated paper. **1972** *National Geographic* CXLI. 692/2 In a quiet way several of the men were equally impressive in somber-hued kimonos complete with *haori*, the elegant outer jacket of dark silk.

hap (hæp), *sb.*[1] *arch.* Also (3 heppe), 3–7 **happe**, 4–6 **hape, happ.** [Early ME. a. ON. *happ* neut., chance, hap, good luck. The same root is found in OE. *ȝehæp* adj., fit, *hæplíc* equal.]

1. Chance or fortune (good or bad) that falls to any one; luck, lot.

c **1205** LAY. 3857 His hap [*c* **1275** heppe] wes þa wurse. *Ibid.* 4894 Brennes wes swiðe hende, his hap wes þe betere. **1297** R. GLOUC. (1724) 447 Gode cas & hap ynou..com to þe kyng. *c* **1330** R. BRUNNE *Chron.* (1810) 59 He had bien in his courte, whan his happe was more hard. *c* **1400** *Destr. Troy* 4671 Þai comyn to the cost..And þere hyt into hauyn as hom happe felle. *a* **1533** LD. BERNERS *Huon* clxi. 618 Alas what hap and desteny haue I. **1630** *R. Johnson's Kingd. & Commw.* 56 If you have the good hap to come into their houses. **1667** MILTON *P.L.* IX. 421 He sought them both, but wish'd his hap might find Eve separate. **1770** WARING in *Phil. Trans.* LXI. 379 It has not been my hap to meet with it elsewhere. **1810** SCOTT *Lady of L.* II. iii, Remember then thy hap erewhile A stranger in the lonely isle. **1884** BESANT *Childr. Gibeon* II. iv, Sickness and suffering, birth and death, good hap and evil hap.

2. (with *pl.*) An event or occurrence which befalls one; a chance, accident, happening; often, an unfortunate event, mishap, mischance.

c **1205** LAY. 18215 He wes his hire-mærke in æuer ælche happe. **1390** GOWER *Conf.* I. 43 A wonder hap which me befelle. **1483** CAXTON *Gold. Leg.* 273 b/1 That I be no more constreyned to haue soo many cursidnesses or ylle happes. **1591** *Troub. Raigne K. John* (1611) 38 No redress to salue our awkward haps. **1711** STEELE *Spect.* No. 154 ¶3, I entertained the Company..with the many Haps and Disasters. **1849** GEO. ELIOT in *Life* (1885) I. 201, I have nothing to tell you; for all the 'haps' of my life are so indifferent.

†**3.** Good fortune, good luck; success, prosperity. *Obs.*

a **1225** *Leg. Kath.* 187 Bisohte him help, and hap And wisdom. *a* **1300** *Cursor M.* 5564 Drightin þam sent bath happ and sele. **1377** LANGL. *P. Pl.* B. xx. 383 Now kynde me auenge, And sende me happe and hele. *c* **1440** *Gesta Rom.* lxxi. 388 (Add. MS.) He had hape in all thing that he bought. **1557** *Tottell's Misc.* (Arb.) 255 My hap is turned to vnhappinesse. **1681** W. ROBERTSON *Phraseol. Gen.* (1693) 471 Some have the hap; some stick in the gap. **1813** SCOTT *Trierm.* III. Introd. iii, Be it hap, or be it harm.

4. Absence of design or intent in relation to a particular event; fortuity; chance or fortune, considered as the cause or determiner of events. (Occasionally personified.)

1340 *Ayenb.* 24 Huanne þe lheuedi of hap heþ hire hueȝel y-went to þe man. *c* **1374** CHAUCER *Boeth.* v. pr. i. 117 (Camb. MS.) Hap is an vnwar bytydynge of causes assembled in thingis þat ben don for som other thinge. *c* **1385** CHAUCER *L.G.W.* 1773 *Lucrece*, Hap helpeth hardy man alday. *c* **1420** *Pallad. on Husb.* III. 710 Hit is bot happe of plaunte a tre to gete. **1534** MORE *On the Passion* Wks. 1311/1 Thynges accompted to fall vnder chaunce and hap. **1645** USSHER *Body Div.* (1647) 50 Nothing semeth to passe by meer hap or chance. **1888** *Quiver* May 504/2 By curious hap..[she] was actually located at 'The Beeches'. *Mod.* As hap would have it, I went there also.

†**b.** In phr.: *by* (*through, in, on*) *hap*: haply, by chance, casually; perchance, perhaps. Also, in same sense. *on* (*upon, in*) *haps. Obs.*

1388 WYCLIF *Josh.* xiv. 12 If in hap the Lord is with me, and Y mai do hem awai, as he bihiȝte to me. *c* **1400** *Lanfranc's Cirurg.* 66 (MS. B.) Þenne by hap sum grete drope of blod may be congelyde togedre. *a* **1400–50** *Alexander* 4936 Þou sall here apon happis..Þat neuire hathill vndire heuen herd bot þi-selfe. **1533** MORE *Confut. Barnes* VIII. Wks. 775/1 Yf it fortuned them to fal vppon it by happe. **1625** HART *Anat. Ur.* II. xi. 122 One may through hap..hit the naile on the head. **1642** FULLER *Holy & Prof. St.* III. xii. 181 They must needs hit the mark sometimes, though not by aim, by hap.

†**c.** *in hap*: in case. *Obs.*

c **1340** *Cursor M.* 6801 (Trin.) In happe he hap on bac nor bed Cloþ to hule him but þat wed. **1388** WYCLIF *Dan.* iv. 24 In hap God schal forȝyue thi trespassis.

hap, *sb.*[2] *north. dial.* [f. HAP *v.*[2]] A covering of any kind.

1724 RAMSAY *Tea-t. Misc.*, *Hap me with thy petticoat*, Grant me for a hap that charming petticoat. **1787** BURNS *Brigs of Ayr* 25 When the stacks get on their winter hap. **1846** *Brockett's N.C. Gloss.* (ed. 3) I. 209 *Hap* is a cover of any kind of stuff, but generally applied to one of coarse material. **1868** ATKINSON *Cleveland Gloss.*, *Haps*, over-clothes; rugs, shawls, great coats, etc.

hap (hæp), *v.*[1] *arch.* Also 4–7 **happe**, 5 **hape.** [ME. *happe(n*, f. HAP *sb.*[1]: cf. ODan. *happe* to chance.]

1. *intr.* To come about by 'hap' or chance; to happen, come to pass, occur, chance. **a.** with the event expressed either by a sb. or pron. preceding the verb as subject, or by a clause or infinitive following it, the verb being then generally preceded by *it*. Formerly with auxiliary *be* instead of *have*.

1340–70 *Alisaunder* 521 A Lioun..may lightlych driue Of hertes an holle herde as happes ilome. *c* **1374** CHAUCER *Troylus* v. 796 Happe how happe may, Al sholde I deye, I wole here herte seche. **1377** LANGL. *P. Pl.* B. vi. 47 Wel may happe in heuene, þat he worth worthier sette. **1398** TREVISA *Barth. De P.R.* v. ii. (1495) 103 Suche euyll shape..happyth selde in wymmen. *c* **1400** *Destr. Troy* 7553 As hit happit of þes hynd, herkyn a while! *c* **1489** CAXTON *Sonnes of Aymon* iii. 86 Theyr fayne aventure that was happed to theym that daye. **1509** FISHER *Fun. Serm. C'tess Richmond* Wks. (1876) 306 The perylles..whiche dayly..myght haue happed vnto her. **1523** LD. BERNERS *Froiss.* I. lxxvi. 97 It happed so well for hym, that it rayned all night. **1554–9** in *Songs & Ball.* (1860) 2 For nowe is hapt that I fearedde least. **1596** SHAKS. *Tam. Shr.* IV. iv. 107 Then wherefore should I doubt: Hap what hap may, Ile roundly goe about her. *a* **1677** BARROW *Serm.* Wks. 1716 I. 22 What can hap to him worthy to be deemed evil? **1808** SCOTT *Marm.* III. xiv, Thus oft it haps, that..A feather daunts the brave. **1880** TENNYSON *Battle Brunanburh* xv, Never had huger Slaughter of heroes.. Hapt in this isle.

†**b.** with an indirect object (dative). (Const. as in a.) *Obs.*

c **1380** *Sir Ferumb.* 1634 To schewe to þe þorw my sawe, how þat ous is hapid. *c* **1385** CHAUCER *L.G.W.* 634 *Cleopatra*, In the se it happede hem to mete. *c* **1430** *Syr Gener.* (Roxb.) 5577 If any thing hap him amys. **1509** HAWES *Past. Pleas.* XVI. xxx, It may me happe a remedy to fynde.

2. To have the hap, fortune, or luck (*to do* something, or with clause).

(With the indirect obj. of 1 b changed into the subject, thus '*him* (it) happed to come', '*he* happed to come'.)

1393 LANGL. *P. Pl.* C. XII. 114 Yf þou happe..þat þow hitte on clergie. *c* **1400** *Lanfranc's Cirurg.* 100 (MS. B.) Ofte tymes alle þese causes happe to come togedres. **1566** T. STAPLETON *Ret. Untr. Jewel* IV. 55 If the Skie fal, we may happe to catche Larkes. **1612** DRAYTON *Poly-olb.* i. 9 He of the race of Troy a remnant hapt to find. **1714** GAY *Sheph. Week, Thursday* 8 A maiden fine bedight he hapt to love. **1814** SCOTT *Ld. of Isles* III. xiii, Where'er I happ'd to roam.

3. To come or go by chance; to light or chance *on* or *upon*. Cf. HAPPEN *v.* 4.

1390 GOWER *Conf.* II. 205 If ye happe therupon Ye shal be riche men for ever. **1548** W. PATTEN *Exp. Scotl.* in Arb. *Garner* III. 92 Whose Grace..had happed upon a fellow like a man. **1590** RECORDE, etc. *Gr. Artes* (1646) 154, I have a generall rule for the fraction that may hap in this worke. **1603** DRAYTON *Bar. Wars* v. xl, But he is hap'd into his earthly hell. **1718** BP. HUTCHINSON *Witchcraft* xv. (1720) 168 He chanced to hap upon a Boy. **1762** FOOTE *Orators* II. Wks. 1799 I. 217 Was it yourself that was happing about here but now? **1863** A. B. GROSART *Small Sins* Pref. Note (ed. 2) 14 [This book] I have not been fortunate enough to hap upon.

†**4.** To have luck (of some kind), to speed, or fare (well or ill). *Obs.*

c **1350** *Will. Palerne* 3340 Ȝe wite þei do wrong, þe worse schul þei happe. **1377** LANGL. *P. Pl.* B. III. 284 Riȝte as agag hadde, happe shul somme. *a* **1400** *Octouian* 1437 Thorgh Godes grace well he hapte. **1601** ? MARSTON *Pasquil & Kath.* III. 391 Your ship (the Hope-well) hath hapt ill, returning from Barbarie.

†**5.** ? To take one's luck. *Obs. rare.*

1575 R. B. *Appius & Virginia* in Hazl. *Dodsley* IV. 151 Therefore hap and be happy, hap that hap may.

Hence **happing** *ppl. a.*

1593 Q. ELIZ. tr. *Boethius* (E.E.T.S.) 17 Thinkes thou that this world is wheeled by rash and happing chaunce? *Ibid.* 103 It coms not of nought, for it hath his own proper occasion, of which the happing and unlookt for luck, seems to haue wrought this hap.

hap, *v.*[2] Now only *Sc.* and *dial.* Also 4–7 **happe**, 6 **hop.** [Derivation unknown. Its distribution from East Anglia and Lancashire to Scotland seems to point to Norse origin.]

1. *trans.* To cover up or over.

13.. *E.E. Allit. P.* B. 626 þre mettez of mele menge & ma kakez, Vnder askez ful hote happe hem byliue. *c* **1400** *Destr. Troy* 12627 Fund a bag full bret.. Happit at þe hede of his hegh bed. **1501** DOUGLAS *Pal. Hon.* Prol. 38 The dasy and the maryguld vnlappit Quhilks all the nicht lay with their leuis happit. **1560** ROLLAND *Crt. Venus* I. 399 With hir awin hand scho happis me. **1570** LEVINS *Manip.* 27/18 *Happe*, to cover. **1813** HOGG *Queen's Wake, Kilmeny* vi, Her bosom happed wi' flowerets gay. **1891** L. KEITH *Halletts* II. ix. 189 How softly they [leaves] fell and happed the graves!

†**b.** *transf.* and *fig. Obs.*

c **1400** *Destr. Troy* 9198 What wildnes, or worship, waknet my hert For to hap her in hert, þat hates my-seluyn? *c* **1420** *Pallad. on Husb.* III. 214 This sk[e]p vnto the tree thow bynde & happe. **1576** GASCOIGNE *Philomene* (Arb.) 102 Stonie walles Which fast (in hold) hir hapt.

2. To cover for warmth, as with extra clothing or bed-clothes; to wrap; to 'tuck *up*' (in bed).

a **1300** *Cursor M.* 6802 (Gött.) He has nouþer on bac nor bedd, Clath to hap him. *c* **1330** R. BRUNNE *Chron. Wace* (Rolls) 9017 He gaf hym drynke poysoun, And happed hym warme, and bad hym slepe. *c* **1440** *York Myst.* xviii. 195, I pray þe Marie happe hym warme. **1465** J. PASTON in *Paston Lett.* No. 528 II. 235 Worsted for dobletts, to happe me thys cold wynter. **1551** ROBINSON tr. *More's Utop.* II. (1895) 151 If he had them he should not be the better hapt or couered from colde. **1591** NASHE *Prognost.* 21 [He] shall hop a harlot in his clothes all the yere after. **1647** H. MORE *Song of Soul* I. I. xxiv, A lucid purple mantle in the West Doth close the day, and hap the Sun at rest. **1674** RAY *N.C. Words* 23 *To Happe*: to cover for warmth. **1724** RAMSAY *Tea-t. Misc.* (*title*) Hap me with thy Petticoat. *a* **1825** in FORBY *Voc. E. Anglia*. **1863** MRS. TOOGOOD *Yorksh. Dial.*, Hap up the children well in bed, it's varry cold. **1865** KINGSLEY *Herew.* xxiv, His chaplain hapt him up in bed. **1893** STEVENSON *Catriona* 277, I took my cloak to her and sought to hap her in the same.

†**3.** To put or lay as a covering (*on*). *Obs.*

13.. *Gaw. & Gr. Knt.* 655 His clannes & his cortaysye croked were neuer, And pite, þat passez alle poyntez, þyse pure fyue Were harder happed on þat haþel þen on any oþer.

Hence **happed** *ppl. a.*; also **hap-warm**, a warm wrap or cloak (*dial.*).

1641 BEST *Farm. Bks.* (Surtees) 17 Well happed sheepe are the best for an hard faugh. *a* **1774** FERGUSSON *Hallow-Fair* 4 Whan fock.. Their winter hap-warms wear.

†**hap**, *v.*[3] *Obs.* Also 6–7 happe. [a. F. *happer* to seize suddenly, a. Du. *happen* to snatch, seize.] *trans.* To seize.

1574 tr. *Littleton's Tenures* 80 b, The feoffour entrethe and happethe the possession of the deede poll. **1611** COTGR., *Happer*, to hap, or catch; to snatch or graspe at. **1613** SIR H. FINCH *Law* (1636) 30 The Lord that first can happe the Wardship of his heire, shall haue it.

hap, *v.*[4] *Sc.* Also 9 haup. *trans.* and *intr.* To turn to the right: used in the management of horses in the yoke, and esp. as a call to a horse so to turn; opposed to *wynd*, turn to the left. Hence *fig.* ***neither to hap nor to wynd***, to take neither one course nor the other.

a **1745** MESTON *Poems* (1767) 16 (Jam.) But he could make them turn or veer, And hap or wynd them by the ear. **1794** SCOTT *Let. to Miss Rutherford* 5 Sept. in *Lockhart*, In carters' phrase [she] would neither hap nor wynd till she got rid of him. **1816** R. KERR *Agric. Surv. Berwicksh.* 503 (Jam.) Formerly, in speaking to their horses, carters employed *hap* and *wynd* in ordering them to either side, now mostly *high-wo* and *jee*.

hap, Sc. form of HOP; obs. form of HEAP.

hapalote ('hæpələʊt). [ad. mod. Zool. L. *hapalōtis*, f. Gr. ἁπαλός soft + οὖς, ὠτ-, ear.] An Australian genus of rodents of the mouse family, having large tapering soft ears, and enlarged hind legs somewhat like those of the jerboa.

[**1887** H. H. HOWORTH *Mammoth & Flood* 370 Six or more species of hapalotes and mus have been found in the Wellington valley caves.]

‖**hapax legomenon** ('hæpæks lɪ'gɒmənɒn). Pl. **hapax legomena**. Also simply **hapax**. [Gr. ἅπαξ λεγόμενον (thing) once said.] A word or form of which only one instance is recorded in a literature or an author.

[**1654** J. TRAPP *Minor Prophets* 605 'Tis ἅπαξ λεγόμενον read only here: and hence this variety of interpretations. **1801** W. MAGEE *Atonement & Sacrifice* 336 [The book of Job's] very great antiquity, and uncommon sublimity of elevation, which has occasioned a greater number of ἁπαξ λεγομενα, and expressions difficult to be understood.] **1882** FARRAR *Early Chr.* I. xi. 236 The number of the *hapax legomena* is remarkable, and some of them are full of picturesqueness. **1931** *English Studies* XIII. 124 An article that should certainly find a place in a miscellany in honour of the brave defender of Wulfila as a translator: Collitz on two hapax legomena in Wulfila's translation. **1956** J. WHATMOUGH *Poetic, Scientific & other Forms of Discourse* ii. 37 The *hapax legomenon*, although statistically it hardly differs from a word of very low occurrence.. is nevertheless anomalous, just like the scazon in Greek comedy. **1957** C. BROOKE-ROSE *Langs. Love* iv. 34 She saw herself go through the minutiæ of scansion, dialect forms, emendation, haplography, *hapax legomena* and *anacolutha* in Beowulf. **1962** *Amer. Speech* XXXVII. 54 He.. rejects a Middle English *hapax* as a genuine idiom unless he can trace it back to an Old Norse.. word.

hape, obs. form of APE.

c **1475** *Voc.* in Wr.-Wülcker 759/24 *Hec simia*, a hape.

ha'pence, var. *halfpence* s.v. HALFPENNY.

hapeney, obs. form of HALFPENNY.

ha'penny, hapenny, varr. HALFPENNY.

†**hap-harlot.** *Obs.* Also 6 hopharlot, hap-harlat, 7 *erron.* hap-hartlet, 8 happarlet, hapherlet. [f. HAP *v.*[2] + HARLOT varlet, knave: cf. *wrap-rascal*.] A coarse coverlet.

1552 HULOET, Happe harlot, couerlet so called, *matta, teges*. **1573–80** BARET *Alv.* H 122 A *Hapharlat*, a course couering made of diuers shreds. **1577** HARRISON *England* II. xii. (1877) I. 240 Our fathers.. haue lien full oft vpon straw pallets, on rough mats couered onelie with a sheet vnder couerlets made of dagswain or hopharlots. **1656** BLOUNT *Glossogr.*, *Haphartlet*. **1706** PHILLIPS (ed. Kersey), *Hapherlet* or *Happarlet*. *a* **1825** FORBY *Voc. E. Anglia*, *Hap-harlot*, a coarse coverlit.

haphazard ('hæp,hæzəd), *sb.*, *a.* and *adv.* [f. HAP *sb.*[1] + HAZARD: lit. 'hazard of chance'.]

A. *sb.* **a.** Mere chance or accident; fortuity. Chiefly in phr. ***at, by*** (†***in***) ***haphazard***, by mere chance, without design; at random, casually.

1575 R. B. *Appius & Virginia* in Hazl. *Dodsley* IV. 106 [One of the dramatis personæ] Haphazard. **1576** FLEMING *Panopl. Epist.* 227 It is hap hazard, if you escape undamnified. *Ibid.* 237 Happe hasarde it is, if you be not prest out for a souldier. **1577** HANMER *Anc. Eccl. Hist.* (1619) 339 The interchangeable course of these calamities, commeth not to passe by hap hazard. **1642** ROGERS *Naaman* 21 One that goes not to worke at a meere hap-hazard. **1726** LEONI *Designs* Pref. 1/1 Ornaments thrown together at hap-hazard. **1862** BEVERIDGE *Hist. India* II. v. viii. 479 Everything was left to a kind of hap-hazard. **1889** *Spectator* 23 Nov., The.. hereditary principle, with all its necessary haphazard.

†**b.** A matter of chance. *Obs.*

1594 CAREW *Huarte's Exam. Wits* (1616) 268 If the generation take not effect at the first comming, it is a great hap hazard, but that at the second a female shalbe begotten. *a* **1680** CHARNOCK *Attrib. God* (1834) I. 557 How many events.. seem to persons ignorant of these counsels to be a hap-hazard.

B. *adj.* Characterized by haphazard; dependent upon chance or accident; random.

1671 MAYNWARING *Anc. & Mod. Phys.* 101 This is not a time to practice with hap hazard medicines. **1805** SOUTHEY *Lett.* (1856) I. 346 But his praise and his censure are alike haphazard and worthless. **1872** BLACK *Adv. Phaeton* xxvii. 365 Some haphazard remark. **1875** J. C. COX *Ch. Derbysh.* I. 208 Fragments of coloured glass.. inserted in a haphazard fashion.

C. *adv.* In a haphazard manner; at haphazard; at random; casually.

1857 DICKENS *Lett.* (1880) II. 30 We came here haphazard, but could not have done better. **1873** H. SPENCER *Stud. Sociol.* xv. 383 Knowledge of human nature gained hap-hazard. **1883** F. HARRISON *Choice Bks.* (1886) 395 This new social system did not come hap-hazard.

Hence †**hap'hazarder** (*obs. nonce-wd.*), ? one who ventures at haphazard. **hap'hazarding**, haphazard action. **hap'hazardly** *adv.*, in a haphazard manner, at haphazard. **hap'hazardness**, haphazard quality or character; also **hap'hazardry**.

1573 G. HARVEY *Letter-bk.* (Camden) 142 Who but happ hazarder in Madame fortunes lapp? *a* **1819** J. WATT in *Athenæum* 6 Sept. (1890) 311/2 [He fell upon most of his best things by a kind of chance, or, as James Watt put it, by] 'random haphazarding'. **1887** *Athenæum* 14 Sept. 336 [*Κυβεία*] in Ephes. iv. 14.. is translated *sleight*: the proper rendering seems to be recklessness, haphazardness. **1874** BURNAND *My time* xxv. 232 This haphazarding sort of profession. **1887** *Chamb. Jrnl.* 26 Nov. 754 Seating them quite haphazardly. **1932** V. WOOLF *Common Reader* 2nd Ser. 63 But with all this haphazardry, the *Letters*.. provide their own continuity. **1949** *Scrutiny* Sept. 196 *Antony and Cleopatra* has none of the haphazardries of *Pericles*. **1959** *Times Lit. Suppl.* 7 Aug. 459/1 A tape-recorder.. that can reproduce in all their haphazardry the jumbled rhythms of modern conversation.

‖**haphtarah** (haf'tɑːra). Also **haftara, haphtara, hapht(h)orah**. Pl. **-rot(h)**. [Heb. *haphṭārāh*, pl. *haphṭārōth*, lit. conclusion, f. *pāṭar* to bring to an end.] The lesson from one of the Prophets, which is associated with each lesson from the Law (called *parashah*), and is read after it in the Jewish synagogue on the sabbath.

1723 MATHER *Vind. Bible* 362 Which custom of reading these Haphthorahs as an addition to the law paraschas, still continues. **1891** M. FRIEDLÄNDER *Jewish Relig.* II. 347 The lesson from the Prophets is called *haphtarah*, 'conclusion'. **1907** I. ZANGWILL *Ghetto Comedies* 141 You shall read the *Haphtorah* (prophetic section) next *Shabbos*. **1932** C. ROTH *Hist. Marranos* xiii. 326 A translation of the Bible.. contained a list of the *Haftarot* (Prophetical lessons). **1973** *Jewish Chron.* 2 Feb. 23/4 During the reading I sat with anticipation awaiting his rendering of the haftara.

hapless ('hæplɪs), *a.* Also 6–7 -les, -lesse. [f. HAP *sb.*[1] + -LESS.] Destitute of 'hap' or good fortune; unfortunate, unlucky, luckless.

1568 GRAFTON *Chron.* II. 2 Desyryng to ende their haplesse lyfe. *a* **1592** GREENE *Alphonsus* v. Wks. (Rtldg.) 243/2 O hapless hap! o dire and cruel fate! **1635** J. HAYWARD tr. *Biondi's Banish'd Virg.* 181 The object of an hopelesse and haplesse love. **1667** MILTON *P.L.* IX. 404 O much deceav'd, much failing, hapless Eve! *a* **1720** SHEFFIELD (Dk. Buckhm.) *Wks.* (1753) I. 5, I.. wish my hapless life a shorter date. **1867** SMILES *Huguenots Eng.* x. (1880) 170 Nor did distinction in learning protect the hapless Protestants.

'haplessly, *adv.* [f. prec. + -LY[2].] In a hapless manner; unfortunately, lucklessly; unhappily.

a **1631** DRAYTON *Wks.* IV. 1560 (Jod.) If ought it ail'd, or haplessly it cry'd. **1865** KINGSLEY *Herew.* ix, He haplessly for himself thought he had a grievance. **1887** SWINBURNE *Locrine* III. i. 41 This came By chance—mishap—most haplessly for thee.

'haplessness. *rare.* [f. as prec. + -NESS.] Hapless condition.

In recent Dicts.

haplite ('hæplaɪt). *Min.* [f. Gr. ἁπλοῦς (see next) + -ITE.] (See quot.)

1879 RUTLEY *Stud. Rocks* xii. 211 Aplite or haplite.. also termed semi-granite or granitell, is a rock.. consisting of a crystalline-granular admixture of felspar and quartz.

haplo-, combining form of Gr. ἁπλό-ος, contr. ἁπλοῦς single, simple, as in **haplocardiac** (hæpləʊ'kɑːdɪæk), *a.* [Gr. καρδία heart], having a heart of simple structure; belonging to the *Haplocardia* or *Brachiopoda*. ‖**Ha'plocerus** [Gr. κέρας horn], generic name of the Rocky Mountain sheep; hence **ha'plocerine** *a.* **haplocyemate** (-saɪ'iːmət), *a.* [Gr. κύημα embryo], developed directly from a more or less elongated gastrula (*Cent. Dict.* cites J. A. Ryder). **haplomorphic, -ous** (-'mɔːfɪk, -əs), *adjs.* [Gr. μορφή shape], of simple form; belonging to the *Haplomorpha*, a division of medusans and also, in some classifications, of gastropods. **haplopetalous** (-'pɛtələs) *a.*, monopetalous; also, having a single row of petals (*Syd. Soc. Lex.* 1886). **'haplophase** *Biol.*, the phase in the life-cycle of an organism when the nuclei are haploid. **'haplopore** *Zool.*, an isolated pore on the surface of the theca of certain cystoids (order Diploporita) in which the pores usu. occur in pairs; also, a thecal canal that ends in one of these pores. **haplostemonous** (-'stiːmənəs), *a.* *Bot.* [Gr. στήμων stamen], having a single circle or row of stamens. **haplotomy** (hæ'plɒtəmɪ) [Gr. ἁπλοτομία], a simple cutting or incision (Mayne *Expos. Lex.* 1854).

1925 E. B. WILSON *Cell* (ed. 3) 1132 *Haplophase*, that phase of the life-history, particularly in the antithetic alternation of generations in plants, in which the nuclei are haploid. **1957** FISCHER & HOLTON *Biol. & Control Smut Fungi* vii. 245 The point at which the haploid nuclei are reunited in conjugate association determines the duration of the haplophase. **1899** *Rep. Brit. Assoc. 1898* 917 The simple or irregular haplopores become connected in pairs (diplopores). **1962** D. NICHOLS *Echinoderms* xi. 138 The diploporite *Aristocystites*.. is flask-shaped, with a theca composed of many irregularly arranged plates pierced by haplopores and diplopores. **1880** GRAY *Struct. Bot.* vi. §2. 177 *note*, The andrœcium or the blossom is said to be Isostemonous or Haplostemonous when the stamens are of one series equal in number to that of the ground-plan of the blossom.

b. *Genetics.* Used as a prefix to designate the presence of only one of a pair of homologous chromosomes.

1924 T. H. MORGAN in E. V. Cowdray *Gen. Cytol.* xi. 720 The offspring are of two kinds, one kind normal with two chromosome IV's, the other kind with only one IV. These haplo-IV flies also give an interesting result if crossed out to a stock that carries a recessive factor in chromosome IV. **1932** SINNOTT & DUNN *Princ. Genet.* (ed. 2) ix. 185 One whole IV chromosome is missing from the 'Diminished' flies; they have only one of the pair of small chromosomes and are thus known as haplo-IV individuals.

haplodont ('hæpləʊdɒnt), *a.* and *sb.* [f. HAPLO- + Gr. ὀδούς, ὀδοντ- tooth.]

A. *adj.* **1.** Having the crowns of the molar teeth simple or single, and not divided into ridges, etc.

2. Belonging to the *Haplodontidæ*, a family of North American rodents, called sewellels.

B. *sb.* One of the *Haplodontidæ*.

haplography (hæ'plɒgrəfɪ). [f. HAPLO- + -GRAPHY.] Single writing; the unintentional writing of a letter or word, or series of letters or words, once, when it should be written twice. (The opposite of DITTOGRAPHY.)

1888 GOW *Comp. Classics* 55 *Haplography* or *Lipography*.. is a special and very common case of omission. **1896** W. M. LINDSAY *Introd. Latin Textual Emend.* iii, The commonest kind of omission is that known as Haplography.. In Virgil *G.* IV. 311, for example, *Miscentur, tenuemque magis, magis aera carpunt*. Some MSS. offer *tenuemque magis aera*, omitting the second *magis*.

haplohedral (hæpləʊ'hiːdrəl), *a.* *Cryst.* [f. HAPLO- + Gr. ἕδρα seat, base + -AL[1].] Applied to a system or form in which each normal bears only one face.

1878 GURNEY *Crystallogr.* 54. **1895** STORY-MASKELYNE *Crystallogr.* v. 105 Where for each of its origin-planes the system or form belonging to it has only one plane extant parallel to the origin-plane, the system or form will be termed haplohedral.

haploid ('hæplɔɪd), *a.* (and *sb.*). *Biol.* [a. G. *haploid* (E. Strasburger 1905, in *Jahrb. f. wissensch. Bot.* XLII. 62), f. Gr. ἁπλό-ος single:

see -PLOID.] Having a single set of unpaired chromosomes, as in a gamete or germ-cell; made up of cells the nuclei of which contain such a set of chromosomes. (Distinguished from DIPLOID, etc.) Also as *sb.*, a haploid individual. Hence **'haploidy**, the state or condition of being haploid.

1908 W. H. LANG tr. *Strasburger's Text-Bk. Bot.* (ed. 3) I. i. 165 The organism with the single number of chromosomes may be termed the haploid, or haploid generation, that with the double number the diploid, or diploid generation. **1914** G. N. CALKINS *Biol.* ix. 209 The chromatin of the nucleus collects in a thick fibrous mass on one side of the nucleus (synapsis stage) and from it emerge one-half as many chromosomes as are formed at ordinary vegetative divisions (in modern terminology this is called the haploid number). **1922** *Amer. Naturalist* LVI. 57 There is one striking difference between haploidy for X and haploidy for an autosome. **1925** *Nature* 10 Oct. 537/2 (*heading*) Haploidy in the male sawfly. **1926** T. H. MORGAN *Theory Gene* x. 139 A cell with one set of chromosomes is said to be haploid, and an individual made up of such cells is..called.., by extension, a haploid. **1946** *Nature* 17 Aug. 239/2 Since the basic haploid number of *Artemia salina* is known to be 21, the present race must be considered as decaploid with a slight augmentation of the number of 105 tetrads. **1957** C. P. SWANSON *Cytol. & Cytogenetics* vi. 159 In plants, where haploidy has been more commonly observed as an abnormality than in animals, the haploid individuals can generally be characterized as being smaller than their diploid progenitors. **1968** J. A. SERRA *Mod. Genetics* III. xx. 150 The course of meiosis is expected to be different in haploids derived from diploids than it is in haploids derived from polyploids.

haplology (hæ'plɒlədʒɪ). [f. HAPLO- + -LOGY.] The utterance of one letter, syllable, or word instead of two. Cf. HAPLOGRAPHY.

1895 M. BLOOMFIELD in *Amer. Jrnl. Philol.* XVI. 411 The philosopher who coined *symbolatry* after *idolatry* (the latter εἰδωλολατρεία changed by haplology.)

haplont ('hæplɒnt). *Biol.* [a. G. *haplont*, f. HAPLO- + Gr. ὤν, ὀντ- being: see ONTO-.] A sexual organism that is haploid at all stages of its life other than the zygote, which is diploid; an organism at a stage, or during the stages, in its life cycle at which it is haploid. So **ha'plontic** *a.*, characteristic of, or having the characteristics of, a haplont.

1920 *Bot. Abstr.* V. 214 (*heading*) Biology and morphology of the male haplonts of some Oenotheras. **1925** E. B. WILSON *Cell* (ed. 3) vi. 492 The spores..receive the haploid number of chromosomes and develop without fertilization into a haploid, gamete-producing 'sexual' generation, known as the haplont (in plants the gametophyte) which intervenes between meiosis and the gamete-formation. **1929** *Hereditas* XIII. 311, I propose the terms haplontic and diplontic sterility. **1938** *Bot. Rev.* IV. 135 It is more probable that the above-described diplohaplontic Ulvaceae and Cladophoraceae arose from a haplontic ancestor than from a primitive ancestral type with alternating unicellular haploid and diploid phases. **1951** M. O. P. IYENGAR in G. M. Smith *Man. Phycol.* iii. 59 *Protosiphon* is another member of the Siphonales which is a haplont and not a diplont like the majority of the Siphonales. **1964** PRIESTLEY & SCOTT *Introd. Bot.* (ed. 4) xxxiii. 499 If this is confirmed the nuclei in the Vaucheria thallus would be haploid and the life-cycle haplontic with the zygote (and zygospore) the only cell representing the diploid stage.

haply ('hæplɪ), *adv.* Now *arch.* or *poet.* Also 4 hapliche, 5–7 happely. [f. HAP *sb.*[1] + -LY[2]. The form *happely* connects this with HAPPILY.] 'By hap'; by chance or accident; perhaps, perchance; mayhap, maybe.

1362 LANGL. *P. Pl.* A. VI. 104 Þe dore I-closet..to [kepe] þe þer-oute; Hapliche, an Hundred ȝer er þou eft entre. **1483** CAXTON *Gold. Leg.* 76 b/1 Or I was unworthy to them or happely they were unworthy to me. **1526** TINDALE *Acts* v. 39 Lest haply ye be founde to stryve agaynst god. **1604** SHAKS. *Oth.* IV. ii. 44 If happely you my Father do suspect. **1650** R. STAPYLTON *Strada's Low C. Warres* II. 33 Some of them may be negligent..and some happely ignorant. **1667** MILTON *P.L.* IV. 378 My dwelling haply may not please.. your sense. **1703** ROWE *Fair Penit.* I. i. 147 Hap'ly I stole unheeded to her Chamber. **1750** GRAY *Elegy* 97 Haply some hoary-headed swain may say [etc.]. *a* **1862** BUCKLE *Civiliz.* III. v. 481 This age, haply, may not witness the emancipation.

ha'p'orth: see HALFPENNYWORTH.

happ, happe, obs. ff. HAP.

happen ('hæp(ə)n), *v.* Forms: 4–5 happene(n, hapnen, 4 hapene, -in, -yne, 4–6 happine, -yn(e, 5 happin, -on, 4–8 hapne, (*infl.* hapneth, hapned, etc.), 5– happen. [ME. f. HAP *sb.*[1] + -EN[5] 2, or extended form of HAP *v.*]

1. *intr.* To come to pass (*orig.* by 'hap' or chance); to take place; to occur, betide, befall. The most general verb to express the simple occurrence of an event, often with little or no implication of chance or absence of design. **a.** with the event expressed by a simple subject. (Formerly sometimes with *be* as auxiliary.) Said ominously of an accident or some serious thing (*spec.* death) happening to a person, with vague subject, *anything, something*.

c **1375** *Sc. Leg. Saints, Magdalena* 392 Þu mycht sone peryste be Be storme þat hapnis in þe se. **1526** TINDALE *Mark* x. 32 What thinges shulde happen vnto him. **1528** LYNDESAY *Dreme* 56 The mater hapnit thus. **1540–1** ELYOT *Image Gov.* (1549) 153 He shewed there all that was hapned. **1651** HOBBES *Leviath.* II. xxx. 175 The greatest evill that can happen in this life. **1709** STEELE *Tatler* No. 5 ¶8 There happened between these Two Men a Dispute about a Matter of Love. **1795** H. NELSON *Let.* 10 Mar. (1945) II. 18 A glorious death is to be envied; and if anything happens to me, recollect that death is a debt we must all pay. **1811** PRINCESS CHARLOTTE *Let.* 11 Oct. (1949) 9, I am going again on Monday at 1, unless anything should happen between this time & that. **1829** *Blackw. Mag.* June 719/1 In the event of 'any thing happening to his father', as the modern phrase for the termination of man's mortal career runs. **1862** *Cornhill Mag.* (1863) VIII. 574 Doctor says I shall not last long, so I don't think I shall be removed before anything happens. **1875** JOWETT *Plato* (ed. 2) I. 131 He would like to know what will happen to him. **1884** G. C. DAVIES *Peter Penniless* x, It isn't a night for any man to be left out in if anything has happened to him. **1885** RIDER HAGGARD *K. Solomon's Mines* ii, I will..arrange that in the event of anything happening to us or to you, that your son shall be suitably provided for. **1965** N. DUNN *Talking to Women* 40 Lots of people they plan and they put this away for when they get old and that type of thing and then anything happens and who has it, their kids, don't they?

b. *impersonally*, with or without *it*. The event may be expressed by a *subord. clause* or *infin. phr.* following the vb.

c **1375** *Sc. Leg. Saints, Petrus* 464 Sa happinnyt þan in þat stede þar wes dede lyand a ȝong man. *Ibid., Bertholemeus* 73 Gyf it hapyne sa þat he Wil thole hyme of ȝou fundyn be. *c* **1400** MAUNDEV. (Roxb.) xxv. 118 If it hapne þat any man ..dye by þe way. *c* **1475** *Rauf Coilȝear* 382 That I haue hecht I sall hald, happin as it may. **1577** B. GOOGE *Heresbach's Husb.* I. (1586) 13 b, If there happened to be any thing broken. **1582** N. LICHEFIELD tr. *Castanheda's Conq. E. Ind.* ii. 6 b, It happened not so. **1660** BLOUNT *Boscobel* I. (1680) 47 Some of their party..might quarter at the house (as had often hapned). **1700** T. BROWN tr. *Fresny's Amusem. Ser. & Com.* 127 It happening to Rain. **1796** JANE AUSTEN *Pride & Prej.* vii. (1833) 24 As it happens, they are all of them very clever.

†**c.** with an indirect object (dative): To befall. Constr. as in a or b. *Obs.* or *dial.*

13.. *E.E. Allit. P.* B. 27 Þe haþel clene of his hert hapenez ful fayre. *c* **1375** *Sc. Leg. Saints, Johannes* 147 It hapnyt syne þir ȝunge men twa Vith Johne, þare master, for to ga. *c* **1400** *Destr. Troy* 8831 Now fryndes, in faith, vs is faire happont. *c* **1450** *Mirour Saluacioun* 3178 If hym hapne to haf enemys. **1523** *Act 14 & 15 Hen. VIII*, c. 4 §3 If..it shall happen any such person or persons to retourne into the realme. **1596** SPENSER *State Irel.* (Globe) 612/1 Yf it should happen the Captayne suddaynly to dye, or to be slayne in battell. **1654** H. L'ESTRANGE *Chas. I* (1656) 52. **1801** E. HELME *St. Margaret's Cave* III. 272 Lest any vexatious accident should happen him by the way. **1815** E. S. BARRETT *Heroine* II. 123 No harm shall happen you.

†**d.** With *out.* (Cf. *to fall out.*) *Obs.*

a **1643** LD. FALKLAND in *View some Exceptions*, etc. (1646) 124 The case he puts is morally impossible to happen out. **1684** tr. *Eutropius* VII. 106 It happened out that these two Consuls..were slain. **1701** SWIFT *Mrs. Harris' Petition* Wks. 1755 III. II. 60 Here's an ugly accident has happen'd out.

†**2.** With *to, unto*: To fall to the lot of; to fall into the hands of; to come in the way of. *Obs.*

1574 WHITGIFT *Def. Aunsw.* I. Wks. 1851 I. 154 If temporal dominion or possession happen to the minister of the gospel. **1581** SAVILE *Agric.* (1622) 186 His Pretorship also he passed ouer in the same sort, with the like silence: for none of the iudiciall places happened vnto him. *a* **1626** BACON *Max. & Uses Com. Law* (1636) 37 All such duties, rents, reliefes, wardships, coppyholds or the like, that had hapned unto him. **1686** W. DE BRITAINE *Hum. Prud.* x. 53 So little a part of it, as that which will happen to my share. *a* **1764** R. LLOYD *Fam. Lett. Rhimes* Wks. 1774 II. 85 More compassion..Than always happens to the share Of the more cruel human fair.

3. a. To have the hap or fortune (*to do* something).

(With the indirect obj. of 1 c changed into the grammatical subject; cf. HAP *v.*[1] 2.)

13.. *Cursor M.* 3602 (Gött.) Þu may hapin to sla sum dere. **1390** GOWER *Conf.* I. 239 Supplaunt with his slie caste Full ofte happeneth for to mowe Thing which another man hath sowe. **1577** B. GOOGE *Heresbach's Husb.* IV. (1586) 160 b, If they happen to eate Lupines, they will straight swell under the eyes. **1613** PURCHAS *Pilgrimage* (1614) 740 One of their Ships..happened to strike on a great Whale with her full stemme. **1792** *Gentl. Mag.* 17/2 The conversation happened to turn on the lottery. **1838** DICKENS *Nich. Nick.* iii, I happen to know that she is. **1871** MORLEY *Voltaire* (1886) 8 The impression that the hearer..happens to have formed.

b. Used with varying degrees of intensity to support or imply an assertion, const. *inf.* Also used impersonally, in which case it is sometimes followed by a subordinate clause.

1933 F. BALDWIN *Innocent Bystander* (1935) v. 95 She happens to be my only sister's child and I have an interest in her. **1937** S. LEWIS in *Colophon* Feb. 220 *Main Street*, which is always put down as my first book, happens to have been my seventh. **1956** N. COWARD *South Sea Bubble* II. i, *Ch.* You have got it in for her, haven't you? *C.* Certainly not. I just don't happen to like the way she goes on. **1957** B. & C. EVANS *Dict. Contemp. Amer. Usage* 217/1 We happen to like her. *Ibid.*, It happens we like her. **1973** 'M. INNES' *Appleby's Answer* vii. 74 You don't happen to have any cigarettes?

4. a. To chance to be or to come; to come or go casually; to make one's appearance; to 'turn up', occur. *Obs.* or *dial.* exc. as in b.

a **1400–50** *Alexander* 2364 Alexander with his armee.. Has happend ȝit ai hedire to þe herre of his faes. *c* **1470** HENRY *Wallace* v. 351 Scho..tald his eyme, that he was hapnyt thar. **1513** DOUGLAS *Æneis* II. viii. 30 He felt himself hapnit amyd his fone. **1657** W. COLES *Adam in Eden* cl, The knots or kernels that happen in any part of the body. **1755** *Mem. Capt. P. Drake* I. v. 37 Two other Officers..coming up to us, asked how we happened abroad so late? **1776** G. SEMPLE *Building in Water* 85, I once happened in Company with a very ingenious Gentleman. **1800** WEEMS *Washington* i. (1877) 5 Some young Americans happening at Toulon. **1818** SCOTT *Hrt. Midl.* xxxiii, It's the only book thou canst not happen wrong in.

b. with *on, upon* (occas. *of*): To come upon by chance or casually, to chance to find or meet with.

1533 MORE *Apology* 5 [They] can not yet happen on them, but after longe sekynge. **1535** COVERDALE *Esther* vi. 1 They happened on the place where it was wrytten [etc.]. **1548** HALL *Chron., Edw. IV*, 190 The capitain..happened by chaunce of a fishar man. **1605** CAMDEN *Rem.* (1637) 312 If sometime you happen of an uncouth word. **1701** LUTTRELL *Brief Rel.* (1857) V. 71 The Harwich..happ'ned upon a quick sand. **1776** G. SEMPLE *Building in Water* 33 When we were driving our Piles, we often happened on some of the large Stones. **1883** W. H. BISHOP in *Harper's Mag.* Oct. 715/2 'Pockets' of precious metals happened upon by miners. **1888** RIDER HAGGARD *Col. Quaritch* xii, I had just happened of him up a tree when you began to halloa.

c. with *into*. *Obs.* exc. *U.S.*

1569 J. SANFORD tr. *Agrippa's Van. Artes* 143 a, If at any time a riche man happen into his handes, [etc.]. **1643** *Myst. Iniq.* 36 They happened into the company of a..Priest. **1707** FUNNELL *Voy.* (1729) 193 If they do chance to come amongst them and happen into their hands. **1889** *Boston* (Mass.) *Jrnl.* 29 Oct. 2/3 Happening into a book auction sale in Boston.

d. *happen in*: To go or come in casually; *esp.* to 'drop' in (at a house); also ***happen along, around, back, by, over.*** *U.S.* ***happen in with***, to fall in with, to meet casually. *Sc.* and *Eng. dial.*

1749 in G. O. Seilhamer *Hist. Amer. Theatre* (1888) I. 29 Joseph Morris and I happened in at Peacock Bigger's and drank tea there. **1838** J. F. COOPER *Homeward Bound* viii. 112, I only happened in..to make a first call. **1845** C. M. KIRKLAND *Western Clearings* 116 He could hardly have 'happened in' at a more fortunate juncture. **1872** E. EGGLESTON *Hoosier Schoolmaster* xxxiii, Miss Nancy just happened over at Mrs. Thomson's humble home. **1873** MRS. WHITNEY *Other Girls* xxxiii (1876) 422 A friend or two happening in now and then to see them. **1882** A. PERCY *Twice Outlawed* 101 Under-sheriff Knight, of Pepin county, happened along that way. **1883** W. BLAIKIE in *Harper's Mag.* Nov. 905/1 Just happen in with them at meal-time. **1893** MCCARTHY *Red Diamonds* I. 34 Say, stranger, have you any objection if I happen in here along of you? **1893** R. D. WIGGIN *Polly Oliver's Problem* (1894) ii. 20 A swarm of horrid insects might happen along and devour the plants. **1901** W. CHURCHILL *Crisis* III. ii. 366, I happened around at Colonel Carvel's this afternoon. **1930** R. FROST *Coll. Poems* 67, I go nowhere on purpose: I happen by. **1931** D. RUNYON *Guys & Dolls* (1932) 261 There we are away over by the East River in the early morning, with no other taxis in sight, and a cop liable to happen along any minute. **1953** H. MILLER *Plexus* (1963) viii. 228 We were literally without a cent when he happened along. **1970** G. F. NEWMAN *Sir, You Bastard* viii. 246 She had decided she would just happen back. **1970** *New Yorker* 26 Sept. 35/3 She held the paper in place with her left arm..and to any of the girls who happened in before she fell asleep she explained that she was taking forty winks.

5. *trans.* (by ellipsis from 4 b.) To meet with casually, to incur. *dial.*

1868 ATKINSON *Cleveland Gloss.*, *Happen*, often used actively, in the sense of, To meet with, to incur. **1884** *Pall Mall G.* 16 Oct. 2/2 Men-of-war are constantly..happening mischances of one kind or another.

6. *intr.* To be successful; esp. in ***it's all happening***, there is much activity or success. *slang.*

1949 A. SHAW *Vocab. Tin-Pan Alley* in *Music Libr. Assoc. Notes* Dec. 44/1 A song happens..when the preparatory work results in a successful bid for popularity. **1962** *Down Beat* 8 Nov. 38 It sounded like they were all striving to create ..but it didn't really happen. **1966** *Crescendo* Mar. 2/3 'It's all happening' was one of the more tiresome items in the pseudo-hip phrase books of the recent past. It seldom meant much while it was in fashion, but there has now arisen a situation which it describes exactly. For it really *is* all happening for Stan Tracey this year. **1967** *Ibid.* Feb. 19/1 It's all been happening at the Village Vanguard lately. *Ibid.* Dec. 27/4 We could either go back to New York with a flop show, or try to stay over and make a band happen. **1971** *Melody Maker* 9 Oct. 18/5 The guitar solo didn't happen.

†**'happen,** *a. Obs.* Also 4 -yne. [Deriv. of HAP *sb.*[1] or *v.*[1]: suffix uncertain.] Fortunate, happy, blessed.

13.. *E.E. Allit. P.* C. 13–15 Þay arn happen þat han in hert pouertė..þay ar happen also þat haunte mekenesse. **13..** *Gaw. & Gr. Knt.* 56 Þe hapnest vnder heuen. *c* **1375** *Sc. Leg. Saints, Placidas* 31 Happyne man is he þat, befor he þire taknis se, Penance to do here wil begyne.

Hence †**'happenly** *adv.*, fortunately, happily.

c **1375** *Sc. Leg. Saints, Marcus* 25 Þare he sa hapinly wrocht þane þat mony sawle to criste he wane.

happen, *adv. north. dial.* [app. HAPPEN *v.* in pres. subjunctive: cf. *mayhap* (in north. dial. *mappen*).] Mayhap, perhaps, maybe, perchance.

1790 MRS. WHEELER *Westmld. Dial.* 59 Weest happen git an Organ then. **1828** *Craven Dial.*, *Happen*, used as an adverb, probably, perhaps. **1848** C. BRONTË *J. Eyre*, She'll happen do better. **1865** T. BRIERLY in Harland *Lanc. Lyr.* 246 Happen the ice may let in.

†**happenable,** *a. Obs. rare.* [-ABLE.] Capable of happening; that may possibly happen.

a **1659** OSBORN *Queries* Misc. (1673) 583 Through a confluence of all events happenable to Man.

happenchance: see HAPPENSTANCE.

happening ('hæp(ə)nɪŋ), *vbl. sb.* [-ING[1].]

1. The action of the vb. HAPPEN; occurrence.

1551 T. WILSON *Logike* (1580) 13 By accidentall happenyng. **1601** CORNWALLYES *Disc. Seneca* (1631) 8 The every daies hapning of such things. **1885** *Law Times Rep.* LII. 684/1 Waiting for the happening of any future event.

2. (with *pl.*) An event, occurrence; a chance.

1581 J. BELL *Haddon's Answ. Osor.* 169 No place is left to the happenynges of fortune. **1628** GAULE *Pract. The.* (1629) 107 The many and strange alterings and happenings to Men. **1748** HARTLEY *Observ. Man* I. iii. 338 The Happenings must bear nearly the same Ratio to the Failures. **1895** H. P. ROBINSON *Men born equal* 101 The happenings of the next day or the next month. **1896** S. R. CROCKETT *Grey Man* xxviii, I could not find it in my heart to tell him of the happening. **1896** *Black & White* 27 June 824/2 Before the final coorious happening, there was a fire in a croft of auld Applebird's. **1899** *Daily News* 5 Apr. 2/4 Such a happening would almost certainly have had much more serious results had it been a horsed carriage. **1907** *Westm. Gaz.* 30 Dec. 2/2 The Denshawi incident is not viewed by all exactly alike, but it was decidedly a regrettable happening. **1921** E. E. CUMMINGS *Let.* 22 Apr. (1969) 75 The feria is..a double happening. There were the grounds..and there were the torros.

3. a. An improvised or spontaneous theatrical or pseudo-theatrical entertainment. Also in extended use, any spontaneous or 'vital' display. orig. *U.S.*

1959 *Nation* (N.Y.) 24 Oct. 260/2 The first exhibition is not of painting but is an 'event' consisting of eighteen 'happenings' by Allan Kaprow. **1962** *Listener* 5 Apr. 604/1 It was with their series of 'happenings' that these artists first reached the public. Happenings, usually staged in downtown lofts, were performances, improvised round basic ideas that left a good deal to chance and action on the night. Actors and décor mingled intimately with the audience. **1963** *Guardian* 13 Mar. 8/7 The latest form of 'way out' entertainment in Washington, DC, is a Happening ..a goofy party. **1963** *Observer* 15 Sept. 27/6 The last day.. gave us our notorious nude, who was towed across the musicians' gallery as part of a rehearsed 'Happening'. **1966** *Ibid.* 17 Apr. 11/4 Here are the long-term..effects of having the television cameras in the House... Politics comes to be regarded as a series of dramatic scenes. A Budget or a Bill is seen..as a happening. **1969** *Listener* 13 Mar. 339/2 The Japanese city is not a design that has been done badly: it's the negation of design, an urban happening with its own special vitality. **1970** *Daily Tel.* 29 Dec. 10 Tomorrow the 1,600 delegates will see a 'happening' called 'Thank God We're Normal' performed by 70 boys and girls from.. comprehensive schools in London.

b. *Art.* (See quot. 1962.)

1962 *Listener* 5 Apr. 604/2 The room-sized collages called happenings or situations are works of art that actually simulate the environment. *Ibid.* 605/1 In his happenings, he [*sc.* Dine] used cheap materials and found objects, lifted from the city's waste. **1965** *Times Lit. Suppl.* 25 Nov. 1044/2 Happenings may be seen as the logical extension of the collage principle.

happening, *ppl. a.* [f. HAPPEN *v.* + -ING².]

1. That happens; occurring; chancing.

1530 PALSGR. 229/1 Happenyng, *aduenant.* **1551** T. WILSON *Logike* (1580) 42 b, An Ague maie be the happenyng cause. **1593** Q. ELIZ. tr. *Boethius* (E.E.T.S.) 91 Of the succession of Chaunce, of hapning Luckes.

2. Casual, chance, occasional. *Sc.*

a **1605** POLWART *Flyting w. Montgomerie* 560 Hapning haires blawin withersuns aback. *Mod. Sc.* I have been there at a happening time. You may still find a happening apple on the tree.

happenny, obs. and dial. f. HALFPENNY.

happen-so ('hæp(ə)nsəʊ). Chiefly *U.S.* [f. HAPPEN *v.* + SO *adv.*] A chance event.

1904 *Westm. Gaz.* 13 Sept. 1/3 Politics..may or may not be mixed up in it. It is just a happen-so if they are. **1938** M. K. RAWLINGS *Yearling* xxiv. 310 Gittin' that buck was pure happen-so. **1962** M. & G. GORDON *Journey with Stranger* (1963) ix. 62 That Japanese girl—didn't have anything to do with us... It was just a happen so.

happenstance ('hæp(ə)nstəns). Chiefly *U.S.* [Amalgam of HAPPEN(ING + CIRCUM)STANCE *sb.*] A chance event; a coincidence. Occas. in altered form **happenchance**. Also *attrib.*

1897 *Outing* (U.S.) XXX. 557/1, I guess it was just a 'happenstance'. **1911** *Dialects Notes* III. 544 *Happenchance, happenstance,* happening, circumstance. Used facetiously. Blend-formations. **1937** *John o' London's* 12 Mar. 986/3 The buyer of *Human Psychology*..will be given the opportunity to defile his vocabulary with such terms as 'happenstance'. **1941** *Sat. Even. Post* 22 Mar. 24/3 Even if by happen-chance a hailstorm didn't come along and ruin the crop, there was always something to fight. **1946** M. C. SELF *Horseman's Encycl.* 306 The introduction of polo to England was pure happen-chance. **1960** *Listener* 7 Jan. 17/2 They shrewdly refused to attribute this to happenstance. **1963** D. B. HUGHES *Expendable Man* (1964) v. 149 The abortionist hadn't killed her, he would have no need of the happenstance tool. **1965** *Observer* (Colour Suppl.) 13 Apr. 27/2 Balloon races have a fixed beginning, all right, but their finishing line is a matter of happenstance. **1966** OGILVY & ANDERSON *Excurs. Number Theory* x. 117 Again the last fraction, which we wish to discard, is ½ (it need not have been—that was just happenstance). **1969** *Sci. Jrnl.* May 9/3 Berry could say little, beyond suggesting that the use of several sleeping pills by both Schweickart and Frank Borman, who suffered a vomiting attack on the *Apollo 8* flight, was probably a 'happenstance'. **1973** *Tablet* 17 Feb. 155/2 'Falsifiability' is duly, recorded—not long after fall-out', with which some might think positivism has a more than happenchance..connection.

†**happer,** *v.*¹ *Obs. rare.*⁻¹ [Cf. MDu. *haperen* to hesitate, stutter (Kilian), Ger. *hapern* to stick, stop: see Grimm.] *intr.* ? To stutter.

1519 HORMAN *Vulg.* 75 A foule anger: in the whyche the mouthe foometh: the nostrellys droppethe: and the tonge happarthe.

†**happer,** *v.*² *Obs.* or *dial.* [In quot. 1587, app. freq. of *hap*, HOP *v.*; in the s.w. dial. use perh. a different word.] *intr.* (See quots.)

1587 HARMER tr. *Beza's Serm.* xix. 242 A new swarme of locusts..to happer and swarme throughout the worlde [*pour formillier parmi le monde*]. **1847–78** HALLIWELL, *Happer*, to crackle; to patter. *West.* **1888** ELWORTHY *W. Somerset Word-bk., Happery,* v.i. and adj., snap or crackle.

happer, Sc. form of HOPPER *sb.*

happi-coat ('hæpɪkəʊt). Also **happy-**, (ellipt.) **happi.** [Jap. *happi* a kind of coat.] A Japanese loose outer coat of various materials; a similar fashion garment.

1880 *Trans. Asiatic Soc. Japan* VIII. 344 Young men often wore a red *Happi* with large sleeves. **1890** B. H. CHAMBERLAIN *Things Japanese* 94 But *jinrikisha*-men wear the *happi.* **1931** E. V. GATENBY in *Studies Eng. Lit.* (Tokyo) XI. Oct. 515 *Happi-coat,* often misspelt 'happy' coat. **1933** 'R. CROMPTON' *William—the Rebel* vi. 121 'Go and put on my happi coat, William,' she said. **1948** M. ALLINGHAM *More Work for Undertaker* (1949) vi. 70 She wore a gay little happi-coat. **1970** J. KIRKUP *Japan behind Fan* 127 Here there was a crowd of men in *happi* coats. **1971** *Daily Tel.* 1 Nov. 11/1 They want to trot around in tuxedo trouser outfits, Japanese happi coats, or pedal-pusher pants. **1971** *Catal. Exhib. C. Beaton's Fashion* (V. & A. Mus.) 54/1 A beige suede 'happi coat'..worn with tapering suede trousers.

happify ('hæpɪfaɪ), *v.* [f. HAPPY *a.* + -FY.] *trans.* To make happy. (Now *U.S.*)

1612 SYLVESTER *Trag. Hen. Gt.* 642 This Prince..One short Mis-hap for ever Happifies. **1656** S. H. *Gold. Law* 88 It will surely conduce to prolong your days, besides happyfying them. **1786** I. PERKINS *Poems* in H. R. Stiles *Bundling* (1869) 99 To happyfy his life. **1837–40** HALIBURTON *Clockm.* (1862) 79 If that don't happify your heart, then my name's not Sam Slick. **1875** M. B. EDDY *Science & Health* vi. 315 To happify existence by constant intercourse with those adapted to elevate it is the true motive for marriage. **1892** *Spectator* 9 Apr. 497/1 Finding infants whom she could wash and dress and happify among the alleys and courts of the East-End. **1905** *Daily Chron.* 13 July 4/4 Her jargon about 'happifying existence' jars upon one after the Scriptural phrase, 'making glad the hearts of men'. **1945** L. SHELLY *Jive Talk Dict.* 12/2 *Happify,* to make happy. **1955** *Watchtower* 15 Mar. 182/2 Keeping these happifying thoughts in mind, we are determined to maintain our integrity faithfully.

Hence '**happified** *ppl. a.*

a **1853** ROBERTSON *Lect.* ii. (1858) 63 Purged of the idea of ..happified selfishness. **1865** E. BURRITT *Walk to Land's End* 461 This happified convention.

happiless, *a. rare.* [erron. f. HAPPY *a.* + -LESS.] Void of happiness.

1618 FIELD *Amends for Ladies* IV. i. in Hazl. *Dodsley* XI. 144 Because man does not so, Shall we conclude his making happiless? **1870** *Daily News* 3 Nov., The hopeless, happiless condition of this poor girl.

happily ('hæpɪlɪ), *adv.* Also 4–7 **happely.** [f. HAPPY *a.* + -LY².] In a happy manner.

1. By chance; perchance; = HAPLY. *arch.*

1377 LANGL. *P. Pl.* B. v. 624 þe dore closed..to kepe þee with-outen Happily an hundreth wyntre. *a* **1400** *Gloss.* in *Rel. Ant.* I. 8/2 *Fortassis,* happylyche. *c* **1400** *Apol. Loll.* 109 þat appily I be not greuid to denay God. **1570–6** LAMBARDE *Peramb. Kent* (1826) 493 Such as happily will demaund, what reason this custome..hath. **1601** SHAKS. *Twel. N.* IV. ii. 57. **1613** PURCHAS *Pilgrimage* (1614) 91 Happily..they intended Neptune, or I know not what Devill. **1693** SIR T. P. BLOUNT *Nat. Hist.* 432 Happily there may not be so considerable Alterations in the gravity of the Atmosphere far off at Land. **1890** I. TAYLOR *Orig. Aryans* 18 The Iranian traditions may take us back for three, or happily, for four thousand years.

2. With or by good fortune; fortunately, luckily, successfully. (Now often in weakened sense, expressing that it is well that things are so.)

c **1350** *Will. Palerne* 2495 No gom miȝt hem finde, so happiliche þei hem hidde. *c* **1470** HENRY *Wallace* v. 986 Schir Jhone the Grayme to thaim come happely. **1568** GRAFTON *Chron.* II. 266 It chaunced so happely the same time for the Englishmen that [etc.]. **1613** SHAKS. *Hen. VIII,* v. ii. 0, I am glad I came this way so happily. **1756–7** tr. *Keysler's Trav.* (1760) II. 421 How happily several members of the Arcadian academy have succeeded. **1871** MORLEY *Voltaire* (1886) 110 The case happily stands alone in his biography.

3. With successful or satisfactory adaptation to circumstances; aptly, fitly, appropriately; felicitously.

1577 B. GOOGE *Heresbach's Husb.* IV. (1586) 168 She happely resteth with him, whom in her lifetime she so earnestly served. **1596** SHAKS. *Merch. V.* II. ii. 191 Thou art to wilde, to rude, and bold of voyce, Parts that become thee happily enough. **1634** W. TIRWHYT tr. *Balzac's Lett.* (vol. I.) 341 After those haue bin rightly conceiued, they are as happily to bee expressed. **1662** STILLINGFL. *Orig. Sacr.* I. i. §20 Some (I will not say how happily) have conjectured, that [etc.]. **1774** J. BRYANT *Mythol.* I. p. xiii, Their chronology ..coincides very happily with the accounts given by Moses. **1849** MACAULAY *Hist. Eng.* I. 412 Minds..happily constituted for the cultivation of science purely experimental. **1874** GEO. ELIOT in *Life* (1885) III. 235 A capital example of your happily-planned publication.

4. With mental pleasure or content. *happily ever after*: see HAPPY *a.* 7 b.

In early instances difficult to distinguish from 2 and 3.

1513 MORE in Grafton *Chron.* (1568) II. 788 To marry himself wherin he should never happily love. **1591** SHAKS. *Two Gent.* I. iii. 57 He writes How happily he liues, how wellbelou'd. **1682** NORRIS *Hierocles* 134 Which they once happily enjoy'd. **1711** STEELE *Spect.* No. 254 ⁋3 A very loving Couple most happily paired. **1871** R. ELLIS *Catullus* lxi. 19 So with Mallius happily Happy Julia weddeth. **1875** JOWETT *Plato* (ed. 2) V. 397 Those who would live happily should..do no wrong to one another.

happiness ('hæpɪnɪs). [f. as prec. + -NESS.] The quality or condition of being happy.

1. Good fortune or luck in life or in a particular affair; success, prosperity.

1530 PALSGR. 229/1 Happynesse, *prosperité.* **1591** SHAKS. *Two Gent.* I. i. 14 Wish me partaker in thy happinesse, When thou do'st meet good hap. **1614** RALEIGH *Hist. World* II. v. i. §1. 263 This also..was a part of her happinesse; that she was neuer ouer-laied with too great warres at once. *a* **1704** T. BROWN *Sat. of Antients* Wks. 1730 I. 24 Whether..we follow them by the only force of natural happiness, or instinct. **1705** BOSMAN *Guinea* 277 It is a very great Happiness, and particular Providence of God, that the Sea and Rivers here seem..to contest. *Mod.* When in Switzerland I had the happiness to meet a friend whom I had not seen for many years.

b. in *pl.*

1601 R. JOHNSON *Kingd. & Commw.* (1603) 36 Nature hath..heaped into this teritorie..all those delightful happinesses. **1678** OTWAY *Friendship in F.* 18 Ten thousand happinesses wait on you. **1739** CIBBER *Apol.* (1756) I. 69 It was therefore one of our greatest happinesses. **1885** SPURGEON *Treas. Dav.* Ps. cxxviii. 2 Heaped up happinesses in the plural belong to that man who fears the Lord.

2. The state of pleasurable content of mind, which results from success or the attainment of what is considered good.

1591 SPENSER *Ruines of Time* 357 Like beast [that] hath no hope of happinesse or blis. **1611** SHAKS. *Cymb.* V. v. 26 To sowre your happinesse, I must report The Queene is dead. **1667** MILTON *P.L.* VIII. 621 Let it suffice thee that thou know'st Us happie, and without Love no happiness. **1725** WATTS *Logic* II. v. §3 Happiness consists in the attainment of the highest and most lasting natural good. **1734** POPE *Ess. Man* IV. 1 Oh Happiness! our being's end and aim! Good, Pleasure, Ease, Content! whate'er thy name. **1851** H. SPENCER *Soc. Stat.* Introd. 5 Happiness signifies a gratified state of all the faculties. **1868** BAIN *Ment. & Mor. Sc.* III. i. §8 Each one's happiness may be defined as the surplus gained when the total of pain is subtracted from the total of pleasure.

b. *greatest happiness of the greatest number,* as a principle of moral and political action: first enunciated by Hutcheson 1725, thence taken into Italian 'la massima felicità nel maggior numero' by Beccaria *Dei Delitti e delle Pene* (Monaco, 1764) 4 (English translation 1766); thence in Priestly 1768, and Bentham 1776; at the instance of Gen. P. Thompson, 1829, shortened to 'greatest happiness principle', 'rule of greatest happiness'.

1725 HUTCHESON *Ideas Beauty & Virtue* iii. § 8. 164 That Action is *best* which accomplishes [**1726** procures] the *greatest Happiness* for the *greatest Numbers*; and that worst, which in like manner occasions Misery. **1768** PRIESTLEY *Ess. on Govt.* **1776** BENTHAM *Fragm. on Govt.* Wks. 1843 X. 142. **1829** GEN. P. THOMPSON *Exerc.* (1842) I. 130 The latest improvement, therefore, of the philosopher [Bentham]..is to dismiss the superfluous 'greatest number', and declare that the just object of politics and morals, is simply 'the greatest happiness'..And the accessary proposition is, that the greatest aggregate of happiness must always include the happiness of the greatest number. *Ibid.* 240 The rule of the greatest happiness evidently includes the motive. **1834** *Ibid.* III. 118 But these [ascetics] too, were pursuers of the Greatest-Happiness Principle..after a sort. **1894** B. KIDD *Soc. Evolut.* x. (1895) 290 'The greatest happiness of the greatest number—long a prominent doctrine in English politics.

3. Successful or felicitous aptitude, fitness, suitability, or appropriateness; felicity.

1599 SHAKS. *Much Ado* II. iii. 191, *Clau.* He is a very proper man. *Princ.* He hath indeed a good outward happines. **1602** —— *Ham.* II. ii. 213 How pregnant (sometimes) his Replies are? A happinesse That often Madnesse hits on. **1635** N. R. *Camden's Hist. Eliz.* III. 361 The charge of the whole fleet she committed to Charles Howard of Effingham..of whose happinesse she had a very good persuasion. *a* **1668** DENHAM in *Guardian* No. 164 ⁋3 There being certain graces and happinesses peculiar to every language. **1779–81** JOHNSON *L.P., Cowley* Wks. II. 23 He..reduces it from strength of thought to happiness of language. **1826** DISRAELI *Viv. Grey* IV. i, Possessing no vigour of language, and gifted with no happiness of expression.

happing, *vbl. sb.*¹ [f. HAP *v.*¹ + -ING¹.] The action of the verb HAP¹; in quot., Fortune.

? *a* **1400** *Morte Arth.* 3958 Here es the hope of my hele, my happynge of armes!

'**happing,** *vbl. sb.*² [f. HAP *v.*² + -ING¹.] **a.** The action of the verb HAP²; covering up. **b.** *concr.* A covering; a coverlet, quilt, rug.

a **1340** HAMPOLE *Psalter* Canticles 510 þou reft him all þe happynge þat he had of þi chosen men. *c* **1440** *Promp. Parv.* 227/1 Happynge, or hyllynge. **1503** in Nicolas *Test. Vetust.* (1826) I. 450 Stuffe of bedding..a quilt happing..a square happing, white and black..a chike happing. **1629** GAULE *Holy Madn.* 134 How fraile a Carkasse..is shrouded under so gorgeous Happings. **1893** *Illustr. Lond. News* Christm. No. 23/2 Her head smothered in the bed-happings.

†**happious**, *a. Obs. rare*⁻¹. [f. HAP *sb.*¹, or HAPPY *a.*, after words of Fr. origin in -OUS.] Fortuitous; 'chancy'.

1387-8 T. USK *Test. Love* I. x, This worlde..governed, not with unstedfast or happyous thing, but with rules of reson.

happy ('hæpɪ), *a.* [f. HAP *sb.*¹ + -Y.]

†**1.** Coming or happening by chance; fortuitous; chance. *Obs. rare.*

1513 DOUGLAS *Æneis* v. Prol. 3 The wery hunter to fynd his happy pray. **1677** HALE *Prim. Orig. Man.* III. ii. 258 Any happy concourse of Atoms.

2. a. Having good 'hap' or fortune; lucky, fortunate; favoured by lot, position, or other external circumstance.

1375 BARBOUR *Bruce* I. 121 Wys men sayis he is happy That be othir will him chasty. *c***1400** *Destr. Troy* 11217 He is happy, þat a harme hastely amendes. *c***1440** *Promp. Parv.* 226/2 Happy, *fortunatus*. *c***1470** HENRY *Wallace* I. 376 Happy he was, tuk fysche haboundanle. **1546** J. HEYWOOD *Prov.* (1867) 7 Happy man happy dole. *c***1572** GASCOIGNE *Fruites Warre* lxxvi. Wks. 1869 I. 166 He..Weenes yet at last to make a happie hande By bloudie warre. **1719** DE FOE *Crusoe* I. xi, I was so happy as not to be thereabouts at that time. **1741** MIDDLETON *Cicero* I. VI. 495 The happy set of liberty, plenty, and letters. **1895** L. J. SMITH in *Law Times Rep.* LXXIII. 692/1 A testator in the happy position of having..realty both in Lancashire and in America.

†**b.** Blessed, beatified. *Obs.* ***of happy memory***, a phrase conventionally applied to the deceased.

1526 TINDALE *Jas.* i. 25 He shalbe happi in his dede. *c***1550** CHEKE *Matt.* v. 3 Happi be yᵉ beggars in sprijt. **1604** E. G. *D'Acosta's Hist. Indies* I. iv. 15 As the happy Chrysostome hath learnedly spoken. **1611** BIBLE *John* xiii. 17 If yee know these things, happy are ye if ye doe them. **1693** *Humours Town* 69 To the Assigns of Tom. Saffold, of happy Memory. **1700** T. BROWN tr. *Fresny's Amusem. Ser. & Com.* 84 Prettier than Dony of Happy Memory.

c. ***happy land***, a prosperous, favourable, etc., land; *spec.*, heaven.

1787 S. STENNETT in J. Rippon *Selection of Hymns* 584, I stand, And cast a wishful Eye, To Canaan's fair and happy Land. **1806** T. G. FESSENDEN *Democracy Unveiled* (ed. 3) I. 85 Such principles, alas, will flood Columbia's 'happy land' with blood. **1845** C. H. BATEMAN *Children's Hymn-Bk.* 36 There is a happy land Far far away. **1893** M. DANVERS *Grantham Myst.* xiii, The old 'un will soon join the young 'un in the happy land. **1902** *Daily Chron.* 6 Feb. 5/2 During the great..strike..a rhyme went round beginning 'There is a happy land, far, far way [*sic*], Where no blacklegs ever go'. **1943** M. KANTOR (*title*) Happy land. **1959** I. & P. OPIE *Lore & Lang. Schoolch.* xvii. 365 There is a happy land by the 'Red School' Where Miss Macdonald stands, preaching like a fool.

3. Characterized by or involving good fortune; fortunate, lucky; prosperous; favourable, propitious. (Now used only in certain collocations, in which there is association with senses 4 or 5.) Also in certain familiar or conventional special collocations: ***happy day***, wedding day; ***happy days!***, a drinking toast; similarly, esp. in aviation circles, ***happy landings!***; ***happy ending***, an ending in a novel, play, etc., in which the characters acquire spouses, money, do not die, etc.; ***happy event***, the birth of a baby; ***happy pair***, an engaged or newly wedded couple; ***happy release***, (esp.) death; ***many happy returns***: see RETURN *sb.* 2b.

1340 HAMPOLE *Pr. Consc.* 1334 Continuel happy commyng Of worldly gudes, es a takenyng Of þe dampnacion þat sal be. **1434** MISYN *Mending of Life* xii. 130 A Ioyfull hap & happy ioy. *a***1533** LD. BERNERS *Huon* xlvii. 157 It was happy for them that the wether was so fayre. **1576** FLEMING *Panopl. Epist.* 378 What king in his adventures hath had more happie successe? **1634** SIR T. HERBERT *Trav.* 2 In lesse then one houre..we enjoyed a happie blast. **1697** DRYDEN *Alexander's Feast* I The Lovely Thais by his side, Sate like a blooming Eastern Bride..Happy, happy, happy Pair! **1702** C. SEDLEY (*title*) The happy pair: or, a poem on matrimony. **1734** W. SNELGRAVE *Guinea* 277 It proved very happy for me. **1739-40** S. RICHARDSON *Pamela* (1740) II. 151 May I hope, my Pamela, said he, that next Thursday shall certainly be the happy Day? **1789** G. PARKER *Life's Painter* xiv. 115 (*title*) The happy pair. **1789** LADY NEWDIGATE *Let.* 2 June in A. E. Newdigate-Newdegate *Cheverels* (1898) vi. 84 Many happy returns of yᵉ day to us my Dʳ Love. **1821** [see RETURN *sb.* 2b]. **1838** DICKENS *Nickleby* (1839) xiv. 124 Many happy returns of the day, my dear. **1839** MURCHISON *Silur. Syst.* I. xxxvi. 489 When one of those happy accidents occurs. [**1848** MRS. GASKELL *Mary Barton* I. xi. 205 So anticipating a happy ending to the course of her love, however distant it might be, she fell asleep.] **1850** THACKERAY *Pendennis* II. xxxvii. 357 The ardent Foker pressed onwards the happy day. **1850** DICKENS in *Househ. Words* 19 Oct. 74/1 His wife unfortunately took to drinking..before happy release in every point of view. **1861** —— *Gt. Expect.* xi, 'This is my birthday, Pip'. I was going to wish her many happy returns. **1864** —— in *All Year Round* 1 Dec. 7/2 Then I shouldn't have the agonies of trying to understand him which was a happy release. **1884** H. JAMES in *Longman's Mag.* Sept. 506 Another would say that it depends for a 'happy ending' on a distribution at the last of prizes, pensions, husbands, wives, babies, millions, appended paragraphs and cheerful remarks. **1913** G. B. SHAW *Quintessence of Ibsenism* (rev. ed.) 192 The substitution of a sentimental happy ending for the famous last scene. **1929** E. BOWEN *Joining Charles* 122 She was such a good soul—it seemed quite a happy release. **1934** *Evening News* 25 July 4/5 Ronnie swallowed half the whisky... 'Happy landings, Phyllis..dear!'.. The powder left his fingers, missed the glass. **1934** R. S. LAMBERT *For Filmgoers Only* 68 'Happy endings' are in much greater evidence on the screen than, for instance, in the play. **1934** E. WHARTON *Backward Glance* vii. 147 The American public always wants..a tragedy with a happy ending. **1935** G. GREENE *Basement Room* 106 'Your health, my dear. You look younger than ever.' 'Happy days,' Amy said. **1938** —— *Brighton Rock* v. v. 213 'When's the happy day?' Cubitt said and they all smiled. **1940** PARTRIDGE *Dict. Clichés* 100 *Happy event, a* or *the*, the birth of a child; esp. the first in a family: mostly lower-middle class: from ca. 1880. **1946** T. RATTIGAN *Winslow Boy* I. 29 Happy pair, I think, is the phrase that is eluding you. **1951** J. B. PRIESTLEY *Festival at Farbridge* II. i. 199 'Happy days!' cried Mobbs. 'Cheers!' said the Major gloomily. **1953** P. FRANKAU *Winged Horse* III. ii. 199 The glass lifted. 'Happy Landings,' Carey said. **1957** N. FRYE *Anat. Criticism* 104 Most students of literature prefer to keep in the middle distance..run-of-the-mill Elizabethan sonnets and love lyrics,..nineteenth-century happy-ending novels. **1960** *Times* 9 Jan. 7/7 The further analysis of 'happy events' that occurred in 1959..reveals 7,070 births. **1966** T. WALSH *Face of Enemy* (1968) 62 Another drink was handed to him... 'Happy days, old boy.' **1969** *Times* 20 Mar. 16/2 Aunt Juju, in her harping upon 'happy events'..knows more about life and death than Hedda.

4. a. Having a feeling of great pleasure or content of mind, arising from satisfaction with one's circumstances or condition; also in weakened sense: Glad, pleased.

1525 LD. BERNERS *Froiss.* II. clxxxvii. [clxxxiv.] 572 Therfore it is an olde prouerbe: he is nat poore yᵗ is happy. **1562** J. HEYWOOD *Prov. & Epigr.* (1867) 145 Better be happy then wise. **1635** SHIRLEY *Coronat.* v, Heaven created him, To make her happy. *a***1699** LADY HALKETT *Autobiog.* (1875) 5 Resolved to leave England since he could not be Hapy in itt. *a***1732** GAY *Songs & Ball, New Song on New Similes* (1784) II. 117 Full as an egg was I with glee, And happy as a king. **1773** in *Wilkes' Corr.* (1805) IV. 161, I am happy at your liking Eastbourn so well. **1785** PALEY *Mor. Philos.* I. vi. (1830) 15 In strictness, any condition may be denominated happy, in which the amount or aggregate of pleasure exceeds that of pain. **1847** MARRYAT *Childr. N. Forest* xi, We will do all we can to make you happy. **1891** O. W. HOLMES *Lett.* Oct., I am glad to hear that you are well and busy, which is, I think, the same as being happy.

b. Freq. with neg., as ***not*** (***at all***), ***not entirely***, ***not quite happy about*** (or ***with***), usually indicating substantial dissatisfaction. Cf. NOT *adv.* 10b.

1947 *People* 22 June 7/5 The receiving club were not at all happy about this. **1967** N. FREELING *Strike Out* 21, I dropped a monstrous clanger, letting anybody see I wasn't happy, but..I'm still not happy. **1971** *Guardian* 2 Dec. 11/2 She says, with some delicacy, that the studio, Paramount, was 'not happy with it' and failed to promote it.

c. ***happy family***: (*a*) a conventional description of a harmonious family; also *fig.*; (*b*) (see FAMILY *sb.* 2b); (*c*) *Austral.*, a popular name of the grey-crowned babbler (*Struthidea cinerea*); also called ***happy jack***.

1868 F. HARRISON *Let.* 11 Nov. in *Geo. Eliot's Lett.* (1955) IV. 484, I know of no worse instance of the monkey-like criticism of the day, than the way in which the hedge-sparrows of the reviews (forgive this 'happy family' of metaphors) chirrup out their blame or praise. **1901** [see APOSTLE III]. **1927** T. E. LAWRENCE *Lett.* (1938) 539 The happy family is the squadron or flight, and the misery of discipline..is resident in depots and work-shops. **1932** *Week-end Rev.* 30 July 139/2 You just treat 'em like one big, happy family. **1939** *Times Lit. Suppl.* 14 Jan. 27/1 In spite of the title she has given to her book, Miss Stevenson's heroine comes from anything but a happy family. **1945** BAKER *Austral. Lang.* xii. 211 The Grey-crowned Babbler is known..as the..happy family, happy jack. **1946** VISCT. MONTGOMERY *El Alamein* Fore-word, The Eighth Army was a very happy family. **1958** N. W. CAYLEY *What Bird is That?* (ed. 2) 69 Also called Grey Jumper, Happy Family. **1963** *Austral. Encycl.* I. 385/1 Babblers..commonly known as catbirds (or caties), chatterers, happy families, and apostle-birds.

d. ***happy families***: a game played with a pack of special cards, each card depicting on its face a member of a tradesman's family of four; it is the aim of each player to make as many complete families as he can.

1881 *Cassell's Bk. In-Door Amusem.* 142 The well-known game of Happy Families is nothing but a variation of Spade the Gardener. **1918** 'C. DANE' *First Blade* xxv, An early passion for Happy Families. **1954** E. HYAMS *Stories & Cream* 50 'Play cards, pal?'.. The other man said, in a rather nasty way, 'Ah, 'appy families, I suppose?' **1955** J. LEHMANN *Whispering Gallery* IV. 225 We were like a pack of cards for Happy Families.

5. a. Successful in performing what the circumstances require; apt, dexterous; felicitous.

happy dispatch: see DISPATCH, HARA-KIRI. ***happy warrior***, applied conventionally to an excellent soldier; also *fig.*

*c***1340** *Cursor M.* 3505 (Fairf.) He was happy to gammys sere Of beste of wode of fowels of riuer. ?*a***1400** *Morte Arth.* 3878 Hardyeste of hande, happyeste in armes. *a***1533** LD. BERNERS *Gold. Bk. M. Aurel.* (1546) G viij, He was apt and happie in armes. **1591** SHAKS. *Two Gent.* IV. i. 34 Haue you the Tongues? *Val.* My youthfull trauaile, therein made me happy. **1715** BENTLEY *Serm.* x. 338 Our English Translators have not been very happy in their Version of this Passage. **1738** SWIFT *Pol. Convers.* Introd. 3 One Gentleman is happy at a Reply; another excels in a Rejoinder. **1806** [see WARRIOR II. 2]. **1884** G. SHAW-LEFEVRE in *19th Cent.* Jan. 37 The artist..has been most happy in depicting the parents reposing in death. **1915** D. O. BARNETT *Let.* 1 July 200 The 'happy warrior' who did the deed is in my platoon, one Finlay, and his hair is red. **1924** F. D. ROOSEVELT in *N.Y. Times* 27 June 4/3 He [*sc.* Alfred E. Smith] is the 'Happy Warrior' of the political battle-field. **1959** *Listener* 12 Nov. 843/3 Ernest Jones was a happy warrior.

b. Of actions, etc.: Characterized by fitness for the circumstance or occasion; appropriate, fitting, felicitous.

*c***1340** *Cursor M.* 4677 (Fairf.) þorou his awen happy [*v. rr.* scel-wis, witti] rede He filled wiþ wine baþ quyte and rede. **1591** SHAKS. *1 Hen. VI*, III. ii. 18 Saint Dennis blesse this happy Stratageme. **1596** —— *1 Hen. IV*, v. iv. 162 If a lye may do thee grace Ile gil'd it with the happiest tearmes I haue. **1662** STILLINGFL. *Orig. Sacr.* I. i. §8 The happy use the Primitive learned Christians made of all those passages. **1779** SHERIDAN *Critic* II. i, A most happy thought. **1779** COWPER *Lett.* 21 Sept., The situation is happy, the gardens elegantly disposed. **1793** BEDDOES *Math. Evid.* 82 His definition appears to me far from happy. **1862** MILL *Utilit.* 84 This happy thought was considered to get rid of the whole difficulty. **1879** MCCARTHY *Own Times* II. xxix. 391 No comparison could be more misleading or less happy. *Mod.* No happier reply could have been given.

c. ***happy medium*** = *golden mean* (GOLDEN *a.* 5c).

1778 *English Mag.* Feb. 59/2 All extremes are ridiculous: the happy medium is to be aimed at. **1782** J. PRIESTLEY *Hist. Corrupt. Chr.* I. II. viii. 272 Other persons..were able..to hit the happy medium between the popish doctrine of merit ..and that of the total insignificance of good works. **1901** ADE *Forty Modern Fables* 51 Moral: only one in a thousand ever strikes the happy medium. **1920** *Ladies' Home Jrnl.* Oct. 163/2 There is a happy medium. **1947** K. TENNANT *Lost Haven* (1968) x. 164 Ain't there no bloody happy medium?

d. Exhibiting harmony or co-operation, esp. ***happy ship***, a ship on which the crew work together harmoniously; also *transf.* of the conduct of any organization.

1905 *Westm. Gaz.* 9 Dec. 16/1 There never was a 'happier ship', and from captain to cabin-boy all worked cordially together. **1916** 'TAFFRAIL' *Pincher Martin* iii. 43 The *Belligerent* was notoriously a happy ship. **1929** T. E. LAWRENCE *Home Lett.* (1954) 375 The camp is comfortable, & the airmen say it is a happy place. **1950** W. J. M. MACKENZIE in G. F. M. Campion *Brit. Govt. since 1918* 83 A branch or a department may be a theoretical monstrosity and yet be a 'happy ship'; and traditionally a 'happy ship' is the only efficient ship. **1955** *Times* 10 May 5/6 A visit to our Combined Training team recently gave the pleasant impression of a thoroughly 'happy ship' and, without undue confidence, that it will take a very good team indeed to beat them. **1958** P. KEMP *No Colours or Crest* iii. 26 *Fidelity* was not a happy ship. **1958** *Observer* 31 Aug. 19/3 The team was an undeniably happy one with immense spirit.

e. Of drugs: in certain colloquial phrases with the sense 'intended to produce or induce happiness', e.g. ***happy dust***, cocaine; ***happy pill***, a tranquillizer.

1922 E. MURPHY *Black Candle* I. vii. 67 The boxes were found to contain cocaine, or 'happy-dust'. **1929** H. MILES tr. *Morand's Black Magic* I. i. 12 Cocaine (or 'happy-dust', as Congo said). **1937** E. ST. V. MILLAY *Conversation at Midnight* IV. 114 Your head's So full of dope, so full of happy-dust..you're just a drug Addict. **1956** A. HUXLEY *Let.* 14 Mar. (1969) 791 The present mass consumption of 'Happy Pills', (Miltown-Equanil). **1964** E. DUNDY *Old Man & Me* xviii. 176 Those heart-shaped 'happy-pills' of soft musty mauve, pale blue, or apple-green, with that faint incision down their middles. **1966** I. ASIMOV *Fantastic Voyage* i. 11 You've got that tranquillizer gleam in your eye, doctor. I don't need any happy pills.

6. *colloq. humorous.* Slightly drunk; 'elevated'.

1770 *Gentl. Mag.* XL. 559 To express the Condition of an Honest Fellow..under the effects of good fellowship, it is said that he is..Happy. **1833** MARRYAT *P. Simple* xxx, An opportunity of making himself a 'little happy'.

b. ***happy hour*** (orig. *U.S.*), a period of time (usu. in the early evening) during which drinks are served in a bar, etc., at reduced prices, or when free hors-d'œuvres are available.

1961 *Providence Jrnl.* 4 July 24/2 All went home happy except the Newport police..and those deprived of their happy hour at the cocktail bar. **1967** *Atlantic Monthly* July 58/2 There have been other near tragedies which are, in retrospect, awfully good happy-hour bar stories. **1979** *Tucson Mag.* Feb. 101/2 Free hors d'oeuvres during happy hour (4-8). **1985** *Times* 12 Aug. 8 Most restaurants and bars have been forced to forget about 'happy hour' where drinks are cheaper.

7. *Comb.* as ***happy-hearted***, ***-making***, ***-natured***, ***-seeming***, ***-tempered***.

1597 DANIEL *Civ. Wars* Poems (1717) 208 Yet happy-hapless Day, blest ill-lost Breath, Both for our better Fortune, and your own! *c***1630** MILTON *Time* 18 Him, to whose happy-making sight..When once our heavenly-guided soul shall climb. **1858-61** J. BROWN *Horæ Subs.* (1863) 163 A singularly happy, and happy-making man. *Ibid.*, *Miss Stirling Graham* (1882) 173 She retained to the last her happy-heartedness. **1864** E. H. W. *Sonn. & Poems, Longest & Shortest*, 'O summer day! so soon away!' The happyhearted sigh and say. **1921** D. H. LAWRENCE *Sea & Sardinia* 56 Old wood..happy-seeming as iron never can be. **1924** M. A. LOWNDES *Terriford Myst.* iii. 35 Yet she looked so happy-natured. **1946** E. SITWELL *Fanfare for Elizabeth* xv. 155 Katherine Parr, a happy-natured, placid woman. **1952** S. SPENDER *Learning Laughter* 103, I never noticed such a happy-seeming family.

b. Used in certain comparative or hyperbolical phrases, e.g. (***as***) ***happy as the day*** (***is long***); ***as happy as Larry*** (see LARRY *sb.*³). Also, with reference to the happy endings of fairy tales, novels, etc., ***happy*** (also ***happily***) ***ever after***(***wards***).

1786 COWPER *Let.* 9 Feb. (1904) II. 462 We will be as happy as the day is long. **1823** C. LAMB *Let.* 6 Jan. (1935) II. 361 May your granaries be full..and you as idle and as happy as the day is long! **1853** C. M. YONGE *Heir of Redclyffe* II. xii. 187 Guy..and Amy..were in a course of living very happy ever after. **1858** LYTTON *What will he Do?* IV. VIII. iii.

61 And then they would live happy ever afterward as in fairy tales. **1864** Geo. Eliot *Let.* 23 Nov. (1956) IV. 168 He is as happy as the day is long—and very good—one of those creatures to whom goodness comes naturally. **1873** L. Troubridge *Life amongst Troubridges* (1966) viii. 67 The hero and heroine.. marry comfortably off in the end and live happily ever after. **1905** *Westm. Gaz.* 1 July 7/1 This, of course, is the so-called 'happy-ever-after' ending: in most cases the comedies of this type are.. artificial. **1925** R. Hall *Saturday Life* xi. 122 Eight weeks ago she had seemed as happy as the day. **1938** *Times Lit. Suppl.* 15 Jan. 43/3 Thus a story which.. ends on a happily-ever-after note. **1960** *Observer* 8 Feb. 14/7 There's a nasty rumour in some studios that the next fad will be 'happy ever after' endings. **1963** *Harper's Bazaar* May 11 The happy-ever-after heroine is you!

† **happy**, *v. Obs.* [f. prec. adj.] *trans.* To render happy.

c **1600** Shaks. *Sonn.* vi, That use is not forbidden usery Which happies those that pay the willing lone. **1600–26** *Breton's Pasquil's Message* iii, While onely Trueth.. Happieth the Heart, and makes the Soule divine. **1632** Heywood *2nd Pt. Iron Age* v. Wks. 1874 III. 419 We are happied euer.

-happy. Used freely during and since the 1939–45 war as the second element in many combinations: **a.** In a dazed, nervous, or light-headed state as a result of excessive strain, e.g. by exposure to bombs (*bomb-happy*), anti-aircraft fire (*flak-happy*), the desert (*sand-happy*), etc. **b.** Acting in an irresponsible, obsessive, or precipitate manner, e.g. *gadget-happy* (= obsessed with the acquisition of gadgets), *trigger-happy* (= liable to shoot at anything at any time). Cf. also *slap-happy*.

† **happy-be-lucky**, *adv. Obs.* = next.

1633 T. James *Voy.* 40 We must goe forward: happy be luckie. **1708** Motteux *Rabelais* v. x, Happy be lucky, 'tis all a case.

'happy-go-'lucky, *adv.*, *a.* (and *sb.*)

A. *adv.* Just as it may happen; as luck will have it; haphazard.

1672 Wycherley *Love in Wood* I. i, You have your twenty guineas in your pocket for helping me into my service; and, if I get into Mrs. Martha's quarters, you have a hundred more—if into the widow's, fifty:—happy go lucky! **1699** Sir T. Morgan *Progr. France* in Arb. *Garner* IV. 641 The Redcoats cried, 'Shall we fall on in order, or happy-go-lucky'. **1705** Hickeringill *Priest-er* iv. (1721) 238 Hittee Missee, happy go lucky, as the blind Man kill'd the Crow. **1802** *Sporting Mag.* XX. 272 Messrs. Hubbards resisted [the action] on the plea of having sold him 'happy go lucky' (meaning the purchaser was to take him with all faults, for better for worse.)

B. *adj.* Of persons or their actions: Taking things as they happen to come; easy-going.

1856 Reade *Never too late* xv, The first thing was to make Carter think and talk, which he did in the happy-go-lucky way of his class. **1863** Kingsley *Water Bab.* vi. 241 There were never such comfortable, easy-going, happy-go-lucky people. **1880** 'T. McGrath' *Pict. fr. Irel.* 7 Forced habits of industry not natural to the happy-go-lucky Celt.

C. *sb.* **a.** A happy-go-lucky person. **b.** Happy-go-lucky quality or character.

1851 H. Melville *Whale* xxvii. 128 A happy-go-lucky; neither craven nor valiant. **1893** S. Pope in *Times*, There had been a good deal of 'happy-go-lucky' in the manner in which the election was conducted.

Hence **happy-go-luckiness**; **happy-go-luckyism** *nonce-wd.*

1893 Yonge & Coleridge *Strolling Players* xxii. 187 Her Irish happy-go-luckiness. **1928** *S.P.E. Tract* xxix. 269 The fertility and happy-go-luckiness of Elizabethan English. **1952** G. Raverat *Period Piece* iii. 49 The casual happy-go-luckiness.. which was one of her most attractive qualities. **1889** Ld. Desart *Little Chatelaine* II. xxiv. 136 The atmosphere of happy-go-luckyism she had come into.

haprune, obs. form of apron.

14.. *Voc.* in Wr.-Wülcker 770/7 *Hec limas*, a haprune.

† **haps**, *adv. Obs.* Also 6 happes [f. hap *sb.*[1], with adverbial *-s*: cf. perhaps.] 'By hap', haply perhaps, perchance.

1589 Nashe *Anat. Absurd.* ciij b, Who so snatcheth up follies too greedilie may happes prove a wittome whiles he fisheth for finer witte. **1595** —— *P. Pennilesse* (ed. 2) Ep. to Printer A ij, I might haps (halfe a yeare hence) write the returne of the Knight of the Post from Hell. **1622** Callis *Stat. Sewers* (1647) 94 It may haps be objected on the other part, That [etc.].

haps(e, happys, obs. forms of hasp.

hapten ('hæptən). *Immunol.* Also **-ene**. [ad. G. *hapten* (K. Landsteiner 1921, in *Biochem. Zeitschr.* CXIX. 303), f. Gr. ἅπτειν to fasten.] A substance, usu. of low molecular weight, which cannot by itself elicit an antibody, but which can do so when combined with another substance, usu. a protein, the antibody thus produced being capable of reacting either with the free or the combined hapten.

1921 *Chem. Abstr.* XV. 3317 (*heading*) Heterogeneous antigens and haptenes. **1926** *Proc. Soc. Exper. Biol. & Med.* XXIII. 343 Active fractions of the specific part of the heterogenetic antigen, haptene, were obtained by fractional precipitation with alcohol. **1928** *Jrnl. Immunol.* XV. 595 Specifically reacting non-antigenic substances—so-called haptens—play a great part in the constitution of the antigens of animal cells and bacteria. **1931** C. H. Browning in *Syst. Bacteriol.* (*Med. Res. Council*) VI. 206 These non-protein substances when isolated do not by themselves cause antibody production *in vivo*; therefore Landsteiner has classed them as 'haptens' in contrast to true antigens. **1969** *New Scientist* 12 June 575/1 Low molecular weight chemicals (haptens) which are themselves non-antigenic but become antigenic when conjugated to 'carrier' proteins.

Hence **hap'tenic** *a.*

1932 *Dorland's Med. Dict.* (ed. 16) 616/2 *Haptenic*, pertaining to or caused by haptens. **1966** *Lancet* 24 Dec. 1419/1 The capacity to manifest contact allergy to a haptenic substance is impaired in persons with leprosy.

hapteron ('hæptərɒn). Pl. **haptera**. [mod.L., badly f. Gr. ἅπτειν to fasten.] An organ of attachment by which certain aquatic plants or algæ fasten themselves to rocks.

1895 M. C. Potter tr. *Warming's Handbk. Syst. Bot.* I. 10 Hairs and organs of attachment (rhizoids and haptera), which biologically serve as roots, are developed. **1909** Groom & Balfour tr. *Warming's Oecol. Plants* lxii. 241 Lithophytes require *haptera* by which they can attach themselves to rock, unless the thallus itself adheres closely to this. **1967** C. D. Sculthorpe *Biol. Aquat. Vasc. Plants* v. 111 It creeps over the rocks to which it adheres by hairs or by exogenous projections known as haptera, which secrete a cement from their discoid tips.

haptic ('hæptɪk), *a.* (and *sb.*) [ad. Gr. ἁπτικ-ός able to come into contact with, f. ἅπτειν to fasten.] **a.** Of, pertaining to, or relating to the sense of touch or tactile sensations. **b.** Having a greater dependence on sensations of touch than on sight, esp. as a means of psychological orientation. Also *absol.*, a haptic person.

1890 in Billings *Med. Dict.* **1904** *Amer. Jrnl. Relig. Psychol.* May 33 The scourging, thorns, spear and other tactile or haptic sensations come next. **1939** *Mind* XLVIII. 360 There is the notion of pure 'touch', and there are 'kinæsthetic experiences', and we can have the one without the other; but when we speak of 'the world of touch', or 'tactile æsthetics', we are referring to the data provided by an intimate combination of them both and for this sense Prof. Révész uses the adjective 'haptic'. *Ibid.* 364 How does Prof. Révész find out whether the blind have tactile æsthetic experiences? Does he treat haptics seriously in their own right? **1954** *Archit. Rev.* CXVI. 400/3 Some of his ugly, tumescent pots are brutally haptic, and if it were not for the paintings on them, might be the work of primitive men, moulding bulbous petitions for fruitful wives. **1964** *Listener* 30 July 156/2 Sight becomes such a preponderant source of information as the child grows, that even those who are basically haptic types come to have a secondary dependence on visual imagery. **1966** *Publ. Amer. Dial. Soc.* 1964 xlii. 41 A complete record of the segmental, paralinguistic, kinesic, and haptic systems, none of which is within the grasp of the linguist today. **1971** *Which?* Oct. 304/1 Scleral (sometimes called haptic) lenses, about the size of a 5p piece, cover the whole front of the eye.

So **'haptical** *a.*, **'haptically** *adv.*; **'haptics** *Psychol.* and *Linguistics* [ad. G. *haptik* (M. Dessoir 1892, in *Arch. f. Physiol.* 242)], the study of touch and tactile sensations, esp. as a means of communication.

1895 E. B. Titchener in *Amer. Jrnl. Psychol.* VIII. 82 (*heading*) A psychological vocabulary.. *haptik*, haptics. **1899** *Amer. Jrnl. Psychol.* XI. 25 Haptical images, beside being vague and ill-defined, offer peculiar difficulties. **1904** G. S. Hall *Adolescence* II. ix. 5 Haptics is thus a paleopsychic field *par excellence*, and the exploration of this most extended of all senses involves a study of the entire dermal area. **1964** *Listener* 30 July 156/2 Those who are.. essentially haptically minded—in other words, who primarily orientate themselves by means of touch, and their own bodily feelings and muscular sensations. **1966** *Publ. Amer. Dial. Soc.* 1964 xlii. 48 Haptics is that sub-system of nonlanguage communication which conveys meaning through physical contact. **1972** W. M. Austin in A. L. Davis *Culture, Class, & Lang. Variety* viii. 147 The highly social animals.. greet each other haptically by briefly holding each other's muzzles in their mouths.

haptine ('hæptɪn, -i:n). *Immunol.* [a. G. *haptine* (Ehrlich & Morgenroth 1900, in *Berlin. klin. Wochenschr.* 30 July 683/2), f. Gr. ἅπτειν to fasten: see -ine[5].] In Ehrlich's theory of immunization, a receptor detached from the parent-cell, circulating freely in the bloodstream, and acting as a protection against infection by combining with the foreign substance which would produce it. Cf. haptophore *a.* (and *sb.*)

1900 E. F. Bashford tr. P. Ehrlich in *Proc. R. Soc.* LXVI. 448 The sifting of the material obtained by observation is rendered more difficult by the occurrence under normal conditions of a great number of quite unlooked for bodies furnished with haptophore groups and arising from diverse organs, and which we may designate collectively as haptines. **1902** *Brit. Med. Jrnl.* 12 Apr. 918/1 Every normally functionating cell throws off large numbers of side chains, either as isolated complexes, or in connection with complement. These side chains are spoken of as haptines (Ehrlich). **1932** Hewlett & McIntosh *Man. Bacteriol.* (ed. 9) v. 168 Ehrlich termed the diverse free receptors which occur in the body fluids in various circumstances 'haptines'.

haptoglobin (hæptəʊ'gləʊbɪn). *Biochem.* [ad. F. *haptoglobine* (Polonovski & Jayle 1940, in *Compt. Rend.* CCXI. 518), f. Gr. ἅπτειν to fasten + hæm)oglobin.] Any of several proteins of the a_2-globulin group that occur in blood serum and are able to combine with free hæmoglobin to form fairly stable complexes.

1941 in *Index Medicus* XXIX. 190/2. **1956** *Nature* 29 Sept. 695/1 Since differences in the haptoglobins of individuals determine their inherited serum groups, we suggest that the system comprising these groups be known as the 'haptoglobin system'. **1961** *Lancet* 23 Sept. 722/1 Normal sera contain three types of haptoglobins, which are now known to occur in three genetically controlled combinations. **1966** E. S. West et al. *Textbk. Biochem.* (ed. 4) xv. 573 Only the haptoglobins of types 1-1 and 2-2 have been shown to be homogeneous compounds... Type 2-1 haptoglobin has been found to be heterogeneous by ultracentrifugation.

haptophore ('hæptəʊfɔə(r)), *a.* (and *sb.*) *Immunol.* Also **-phor**. [a. G. *haptophor* (P. Ehrlich 1898, in *Deutsch. med. Wochenschr.* 22 Sept. 599/2), f. Gr. ἅπτειν to fasten + -o + -phore.] Applied, in Ehrlich's theory of immunization, to that group of atoms in the molecule of a toxin or other substance which enables it to combine with the corresponding receptors of a cell. Also *absol.* So **hapto'phoric**, **hap'tophorous** *adjs.*

1899 tr. P. Ehrlich in *Trans. Jenner Inst. Prevent. Med.* (2nd Ser.) 11, I have already.. touched upon the question whether.. the toxin molecule contains two independent groups, of which the one (the toxophore) conditions the toxicity, and the other (the haptophore) the combining property. *Ibid.* 12 With the help of the haptophore groups, the toxin molecule becomes 'anchored' to the cell. **1902** Vaughan & Novy *Cellular Toxins* (ed. 4) 182 Both the toxophil groups of the cell, and the cytophil groups of the toxin may be designated as haptophorous bodies. **1902** *Brit. Med. Jrnl.* 29 Mar. 785 The atom arrangement, or group in the toxin, which corresponds to the receptor, he [*sc.* Ehrlich] calls the 'haptophoric group'. **1904** *Ibid.* 10 Sept. 574 Although the toxophoric group may be similar, the haptophor is dissimilar. **1938** W. Bulloch *Hist. Bacteriol.* xi. 275 Of the two, the haptophore is the more stable. Ehrlich considered that the toxophoric atom group can deteriorate to a non-toxic state although the haptophoric group may at the same time remain unchanged. **1960** *New Biol.* XXXI. 104 It was very hard to conceive that 'haptophores' could pre-exist.

haptotropism (ˌhæptəʊ'trəʊpɪz(ə)m, -'trɒpɪz(ə)m, hæp'tɒtrəpɪz(ə)m). *Bot.* [ad. G. *haptotropismus* (L. Errera 1884, in *Bot. Zeitung* 5 Sept. 564), f. Gr. ἅπτειν to fasten: see tropism.] The phenomenon whereby plant organs, as the tendrils of climbing plants, exhibit tropic movements in response to the stimulus of touch. Hence **hapto'tropic** *a.*

1892 L. Errera in *Ann. Bot.* VI. 373 Thus, the geotropic, heliotropic, hydrotropic, haptotropic curvatures arise, which are familiar to vegetable physiologists. **1900** B. D. Jackson *Gloss. Bot. Terms* 118/2 *Haptotropism*, curvature induced in climbing plants by the stimulus of a rough surface. **1924** M. Skene *Biol. Flowering Plants* iv. 298 The response to contact stimulus is termed haptotropism. **1934** Webster, Haptotropic. **1953** Fritsch & Salisbury *Plant Form & Funct.* (rev. ed.) xxix. 263 Certain tropic growth-curvatures result from direct contact with a foreign body and are described as haptotropic. **1965** Bell & Coombe tr. *Strasburger's Textbk. Bot.* (new ed.) 375 Many plants.. are sensitive to touch... This phenomenon is termed haptotropism (thigmotropism).

hapu ('hɑ:pu:). *N.Z.* Also (erron.) **harpu**. [Maori.] A clan, sub-tribe, or small community.

1843 E. Dieffenbach *Trav. N.Z.* II. iii. ix. 361/2 Hapu —tribe, family. **1857** C. F. Hursthouse *New Zealand* I. 162 The 70,000 semi-civilized natives now in New Zealand are divided into some dozen chief tribes, and into numerous sub-tribes and 'Harpu'. **1873** *Jrnls. Ho. Reps. N.Z.* III. App. G. vii. 87 (Morris), Were not all your hapu present when the money was paid? **1891** *Rep. Australas. Assoc. Adv. Sci.* III. G. 378 (Morris), Tribes or nations, each of which was divided into hapus, and the hapus into families. **1921** H. Guthrie-Smith *Tutira* viii. 52 In sympathy with this *hapu* or sub-tribe and its old-world ways. **1949** P. Buck *Coming of Maori* (1950) iii. i. 333 To denote the groupings in English, the *iwi* has been termed tribe and the *hapu* a sub-tribe. **1960** N. Hilliard in C. K. Stead *N.Z. Short Stories* (1966) 241 He's East Coast, he don't know the *hapus* up our way.

hapuku, hapuka ('hɑ:pu:ku:, -kə). *N.Z.* Also formerly **whapuku**, etc. [Maori *hapuku*.] A large marine food fish, *Polyprion oxygeneios*; = cod *sb.*[3] 2 b and grouper 2.

1838 J. S. Polack *New Zealand* I. ix. 322 Some deep banks lie off the east coast, on which the *kanai*, or mullet, *wapuka*, or cod-fish, and.. salmon abound. **1844** W. Wakefield in *N.Z. Co. Rep.* XXXVI. 31 Aug. 137 The habouka is taken in great quantities near the fishing town. *c* **1845** in C. F. Hursthouse *New Zealand* (1857) I. 217 We've .. lowing herds on every side, Hapuka in every tide. **1855** R. Taylor *Te Ika a Maui* 411 *Hapuku*, or *whapuku* commonly called the cod, but a much richer fish in flavor. **1859** A. S. Thomson *Story N.Z.* I. 30 The Hapuku is the largest New Zealand salt-water fish. **1944** *Mod. Jun. Dict.* (Whitcombe & Tombs) (ed. 7) 193 *Hapuka, hapuku*, the Maori name for a large edible fish, also called 'groper'. Often mispronounced 'ha-pu'-ka'. **1960** Doogue & Moreland *N.Z. Sea Angler' Guide* 209 Groper or *Hapuku*... Other names: *Polyprion oxygeneios*; whapuku (Maori)... The word 'hapuka' is a corruption of hapuku. **1966** *Encycl. N.Z.* I. 907/1 Hapuku or groper (*Polyprion oxygeneios*).. is a large, heavy, deep-sea fish closely related to the bass.

ha'p'worth, contracted f. HALFPENNYWORTH.

haque, -but, var. HAKE *sb.*[4], HACKBUT.

haqueton ('hæktən). *Obs.* exc. *Hist.* Forms: 5 **hacton**, 5–9 **haqueton**, 6 **hocton**, **hugtoun**, 6–7 **haketon(e**, **ho(c)queton**, 9 **hauqueton**, **hawketon**, 6– **hacqueton**; see also ACTON. [A later modification of ME. *aketoun*, ACTON (q.v.), after OF. *hocqueton*, *hocton*, F. *hoqueton*.]

A stuffed jacket or jerkin worn under the mail; a jacket of leather or the like plated with mail: = ACTON.

a **1400** *Octavian* 878 When he on Florent hacton caste. *c* **1477** CAXTON *Jason* 16 He percid hit and the hauberk and the haqueton. **1523** LD. BERNERS *Froiss.* I. ccccxix. 734 Hocquetons and gantlettes of steele. **1560** ROLLAND *Crt. Venus* I. 91 His Hugtoun was of Crammesie veluet. **1599** THYNNE *Animadv.* (1875) 31 'Haketon' is a slevelesse Iackett of plate for the warre, couered withe anye other stuffe. *a* **1693** URQUHART *Rabelais* III. vii. 65, I am.. weary of wearing.. Hoquetons. **1820** SCOTT *Ivanhoe* xxviii, To see the gore trickle down his rich embroidered hacqueton. **1830** JAMES *Darnley* xxxi, He was dressed in a hacqueton, or close jacket of buff leather.

har, obs. form of HAIR, HER (*her*, *their*), HIGHER, HOAR; var. of HAAR, HARRE.

haracana, harancane, early ff. HURRICANE.

harach, var. of HARATCH.

† **'harageous**, *a. Obs.* Also 5 **haraious**, **-iows**, **hareious**, **harageus**. [perh. repr. an OF. **arageux*, related to *aragier* to become furious, *aragié* furious, *aragement*, *aragerie*, *aragison*, rage, fury.] Stern, cruel, violent.

? *a* **1400** *Morte Arth.* 1645 They hye to þe holte, thes harageous knyghttez. *Ibid.* 1834 The hethene harageous kynge appone the hethe lyggez. *c* **1440** *Promp. Parv.* 227/1 Haraiows, or sterne.. *austerus*, *rigidus*. **14..** *Medulla*, *MS. Cant.* in *Promp. Parv.* 227 *note*, *Immanis*, haraious, grete, cruelle or dredefulle.

Hence † **harageously** *adv. Obs.*, cruelly.

c **1440** *Jacob's Well* (E.E.T.S.) 76 Whan þou hast dysdeyn of symple folk.. & hareiously takyst on wyth hem.

‖ **harai goshi** ('harai 'goʃi). [Jap., f. *harai*, *harau* to sweep + *goshi*, *koshi* loin, waist.] A throw in Judo.

1941 M. FELDENKRAIS *Judo* vi. 114 Japanese experts are generally smaller than their foreign opponents, and still they find no difficulty in throwing them by *Haraï-Goshi*, for example. **1954** E. DOMINY *Teach yourself Judo* 190 Harai Goshi,.. Sweeping Loin Throw. **1957** TAKAGAKI & SHARP *Techniques of Judo* II. iii. 31 Techniques such as *harai-goshi*. **1965** *New Statesman* 14 May 760/2 My son.. has applied the old Harai Goshi, a very effective throw in judo.

‖ **hara-kiri** (ˌhɑːrə'kiːriː). Also corruptly **hari-kari**, **hurry-curry**. [Japanese (colloquial and vulgar), f. *hara* belly + *kiri* cut. (The more elegant expression is said to be *seppuku*.)] Suicide by disembowelment, as formerly practised by the samurai of Japan, when in circumstances of disgrace, or under sentence of death. Also called (by Englishmen) *happy dispatch*: see DISPATCH *sb.* 4. Also *transf.*

1856 *Harper's Mag.* Mar. 460 (*title*) Hari-kari of Japan. **1859** *Times* 18 Aug. 10 These officers no longer perform hari-kari, or in other words disembowel themselves, rather than survive the disgrace of admitting foreigners. **1862** HOLMES *Hunt after Captain* in *Old Vol. of Life* (1891) 58 He will very commonly consent to the thing asked, were it to commit hari-kari. **1871** A. B. MITFORD *Old Japan* II. 195 The ceremony of hara-kiri was added afterwards in the case of persons belonging to the military class being condemned to death. **1888** *Scott. Leader* 17 Mar. 4 The Liberal Unionist party.. will hesitate long before committing 'hari-kari' in that fashion. **1888** J. L. ATKINSON in *Boston* (Mass.) *Jrnl.* 7 June, Hara-kiri, the Japanese method of self-destruction in the baronial days, was practiced only by the Samurai, who were the two-sworded retainers of the barons or Daimiyos.. Hari-kiri is rarely if ever heard of as being done in Japan nowadays.

hara(l)d, harat, obs. forms of HERALD.

haram, var. of HAREM.

harambee (hə'ræmbiː). [Swahili.] Pulling or working together; co-operation; the slogan of the Kanu government of Kenya at the time of independence. Also *attrib.*

1963 *Times* 13 Aug. 6/4 The farmers.. joined him in the shout of 'Harambee'—the rallying call to the people of Kenya. *Ibid.* 12 Dec. (Kenya Suppl.) p. ii/7 They ran an effective Kanu government on the theme of *harambee* (working together) and at the pre-independence talks.. they broadly won.. all their main objectives. **1969** *Reporter* (Nairobi) 16 May 40/1 The farmers of Nyanza Province.. are giving an example to the rest of the country in launching *harambee* self-help schemes. **1971** *E. Afr. Standard* (Nairobi) 13 Apr. 2/4 The self-help work carried out by the people on a harambee basis was intended to make them join hands together in the development of a strong nation. *Ibid.*, Harambee groups should offer cooperation to one another in giving donations to fund-raising meetings.

harangue (hə'ræŋ), *sb.* Forms: 5 **arang**, 7 **har(r)ange**, **harang**, 8 **harrangue**, 7– **harangue**. [In Scottish writers from *c* 1450: in Eng. after 1600: a. OF. *arenge* (14–15th c.), *harangue* (16th c.), ad. med.L. *harenga* in same sense, It. *aringa*, Pr., Sp. *arenga*; 68 cf. It. *aringo* place of declamation, arena, etc. Referred by Diez to OHG. *hring*, MHG. *ring*, ring, circle of auditors, spectators, etc., arena.] A speech addressed to an assembly; a loud or vehement address, a tirade; formerly, sometimes, a formal or pompous speech.

a **1450** *Ratis Raving* I. 243 To tell the al how mycht befall, To lang arang men wald it call. **1595** DUNCAN *App. Etymol.* (E.D.S.), *Oratio*, a praier, a harang, speeche. **1605** BACON *Adv. Learn.* I. vii. §2. 32 Sweetely touched with eloquence and perswasion of Bookes, of Sermones, of haranges. *c* **1610** SIR J. MELVIL *Mem.* (1735) 313 All who heard his grave Harangue. **1611** COTGR., *Sermon*.. an Harang, or Oration, made vnto the people. **1660** *Trial Regic.* 86 He made a long harrange about that horrid Act. **1711** STEELE *Spect.* No. 32 ¶2 Mr. President began an Harangue upon your Introduction to my Epistle. **1791** COWPER *Odyss.* II. 112 Telemachus, intemp'rate in harangue. **1834** MACAULAY *Pitt* Ess. (1854) 298 He uttered his spirit-stirring harangues. **1838** THIRLWALL *Greece* III. 219 He called an assembly.. and made a harangue in vindication of his past conduct.

b. *Comb.*, as **harangue-maker**, one who makes a harangue; *spec.* the speaker or chairman in the old Scottish parliament.

1560 in Tytler *Hist. Scot.* (1864) III. 127 Harangue-maker. **1759** ROBERTSON *Hist. Scot.* II. App. 141 His lieutenant for this time, is chosen speaker of the parliament, or harangue-maker as these men call it.

harangue, *v.* Also 8 **harrangue**. [a. F. *haranguer* (15–16th c. in Hatz.-Darm.), 'to make an Oration; to preach or speak long vnto', Cotgr.]

1. *intr.* To make an address or speech to an assembly; to deliver a harangue; to declaim.

1660 EVELYN *Mem.* 4 July, I heard Sir Samuel Tuke harangue to the House of Lords. **1709** STEELE & SWIFT *Tatler* No. 67 ¶19 Such as harangue in Pulpits. **1766** GOLDSM. *Vic. W.* xi, My wife.. undertook to harangue for the family. **1809–10** COLERIDGE *Friend* (1837) II. 14 There is no subject, which men in general like better to harangue on than politics. **1855** MACAULAY *Hist. Eng.* IV. 437 Haranguing against each other, moving votes of censure.

2. *trans.* To address in a harangue; to make a formal public speech to.

1682 WOOD *Life* 31 May, Thence to the Physick Garden where Dr. (Robert) Morison harangued him [the Moorish ambassador]. **1781** GIBBON *Decl. & F.* II. xliii. 591 He often harangued the troops. **1802** MAR. EDGEWORTH *Moral T.* (1816) I. xv. 119 Heard the voice of T.R.. haranguing the mob. *a* **1862** BUCKLE *Misc. Wks.* (1872) I. 553 In the sixteenth century ambassadors were obliged to harangue princes in Latin.

b. To urge *out of* or *into* by haranguing.

a **1678** MARVELL *Wks.* II. 307 (R.) The author.. indeavoured to harangue up the nation into fury against tender consciences. **1737** BRACKEN *Farriery Impr.* (1757) II. 128 The Doctor.. harangues them out of the little Sense they have.

Hence **ha'ranguing** *vbl. sb.* and *ppl. a.*

1708 R. O. in *Hearne's Collect.* 2 Jan. (O.H.S.) II. 91 Ye Haranguing Tribe yt fills ye dignitys in ye Church. **1741** MIDDLETON *Cicero* I. vi. 435 His talent at haranguing. **1850** MAURICE *Mor. & Met. Philos.* (ed. 2) I. 158 The haranguing style to which Plato was in general so averse.

haranguer (hə'ræŋə(r)). [f. prec. vb. + -ER[1].] One who harangues or addresses an assembly; a noisy declaimer.

a **1668** DAVENANT *To the Noble Widow* Wks. (1673) 306 More Brains than would serve the head of a Giant Or all the Haranguers of Paris and London. **1681** DRYDEN *Abs. & Achit.* 509 With them join'd all th' haranguers of the throng, That thought to get preferment by the tongue. **1741** MIDDLETON *Cicero* I. v. 397 Those haranguers of the mob. **1858** HOGG *Like Shelley* I. 430 To look the petulant little haranguer in the face.

haras ('hærəs, ‖ arɑ). Now treated as Fr. Forms: 4 **harace**, 4, 9 **harras**, 5 **hareys**, **harrasse**, **(haryage)**, 6 **harres**, **harreise**, **harrage**, 7 **harace**, **harase**, 4– **haras**. [a. OF. *haraz* (12th c.), later *haras* 'horses and mares kept only for breed' (Cotgr.), in med.L. *haracium*, of uncertain origin; Diez suggests relationship to Arabic *faras* horse.] An enclosure or establishment in which horses and mares are kept for breeding; hence, †a stud, breed, or race of horses (*obs.*).

[**1292** BRITTON III. vii. §5 As vaches et a genices et as harascz des jumentz et des poleyns en boys.] *a* **1300** *Land Cokayngne* 35 in *E.E.P.* (1862) 157 Nother harace, nother stode. **13..** *Guy Warw.* (A.) 5710 As wicked coltes out of haras. *c* **1420** *Pallad. on Husb.* IV. 840 This craft in gentyl haras is to charge. *c* **1425** WYNTOUN *Cron.* VIII. xxii. 55 (Jam.) Ane haryage.. he had gud, That had swlyk twelf in til his stud. *c* **1450** *Cov. Myst.* (1841) 147 3ondyr is an hous of haras that stant be the wey. **1540–1** ELYOT *Image Gov.* (1549) 127 Who setteth by a ragged, a restie or ill fauoured colte, because that the harreise, wherof that kinde is comen .. wanne the price of rennyng at the game of Olympus? **1594** CAREW *Huarte's Exam. Wits* (1616) 306 A mare of a good harrage. **1602** —— *Cornwall* 24 a, Nature denying a great harace. **1792** A. YOUNG *Trav. France* 54 Supporting a wretched haras (stud). **1887** *Times* 24 Dec. 10/1 The foreign haras which were established.. in various countries on the Continent created a most serious drain upon our resources in this country. *Ibid.* 10/2 The establishment of a Government haras, or breeding station.

harass ('hærəs), *v.* Also 7 **harraze**, **har(r)asse**, 7–8 **harrass**. [a. F. *harasser* (1562 in Godef.) 'to tire or toyle out, to spend or weaken, wearie or weare out by ouertoyling; also, to vex, disquiet, importune, harrie, hurrie, turmoile, torment' (Cotgr.); perh. a derivative form of OF. *harer* to set a dog on.]

† **1.** *trans.* To wear *out*, tire *out*, or exhaust with fatigue, care, trouble, etc. *Obs.* or *dial.*

a **1626** BACON (J.), These troops came to the army but the day before, harassed with a long and wearisome march. **1656** BLOUNT *Glossogr.*, *Harasse*.. to tire or toyl out, to spend or weaken, weary, or wear out. **1697** DRYDEN *Virg. Georg.* III. 214 When athirst, restrain 'em from the Flood; Their Bodies harrass, sink 'em when they run. **1713** ADDISON *Cato* v. i, Nature oppress'd, and harrass'd out with care, Sinks down to rest. **1720** W. GIBSON *Diet. Horses* x. (1731) 159 After they [horses] have been harass'd, and gone through their assigned Tasks.. they should be rid gently out of the Manage. **1760–72** tr. *Juan & Ulloa's Voy.* (ed. 3) I. 37 They are so harrassed with labour, and their wages so small.

† **2.** To harry, lay waste, devastate, plunder. *Obs.*

a **1618** RALEIGH *Mahomet* (1637) 65 Burnt and harrazed the Countrie. **1665** MANLEY *Grotius's Low C. Warres* 261 While they harassed the Fields. **1684** *Scanderberg Rediv.* vi. 137 Parties which Harrassed and Plundred and Burnt all the Country. **1710** PRIDEAUX *Orig. Tithes* iv. 198 The Danish War.. very cruelly harassed this Land.

3. To trouble or vex by repeated attacks.

1622 BACON *Hen. VII*, 63 (R.) To harrasse and wearie the English, they did vpon all aduantages set vpon them with their light-horse. **1727** SWIFT *Let. Eng. Tongue* Wks. 1755 II. I. 183 The Britains.. daily harrassed by cruel inroads from the Picts. **1783** *Polite Trav.* 77 The new settlers had.. no enemy to harrass them. **1838** THIRLWALL *Greece* III. 343 The Argives continued.. to harass the Epidaurians with repeated incursions. **1865** PARKMAN *Huguenots* i. (1875) 8 The Indians unceasingly harassed their march.

4. To trouble, worry, distress with annoying labour, care, perplexity, importunity, misfortune, etc.

1656 BLOUNT *Glossogr.*, *Harasse*.. also to vex, disquiet, etc. **1695** WOODWARD *Nat. Hist. Earth* III. i. (1723) 158 Alarmed and harrassed by Earthquakes. **1738** JOHNSON *London* 166 The griefs that harass the distress'd. **1855** MILMAN *Lat. Chr.* (1864) III. VI. iii. 415 A mind harassed by the perplexing state of affairs. **1855** TENNYSON *Maud* I. xix. 22 Vext with lawyers and harass'd with debt.

transf. **1737** WHISTON *Josephus*, *Antiq.* I. i. §4 When it [the ground] should be harassed by their labour, it should bring forth some of its fruits.

5. *techn.* To scrape or rub.

1875 *Ure's Dict. Arts* III. 93 To soften the skins after dyeing, they are harassed by a knife, the point of which is curved upwards.

Hence **'harassed** *ppl. a.* (whence **'harassedly** *adv.*); **'harassing** *ppl. a.* (whence **'harassingly** *adv.*). Also **'harassable** *a.*, capable of being harassed. **'harasser**, one who or that which harasses. **'harassery** (*nonce-wd.*), harassing action.

1882 J. HAWTHORNE *Fort. Fool* I. xiv, She.. knew where his *harassable points were and how to irritate them. **1693** CHAS. DRYDEN tr. *Juvenal*, *Sat.* VII. (1697) 178 Whether he should.. into Quarters put his *harrass'd Men. **1726** SHELVOCKE *Voy. round World* (1757) 217 Not.. a seat whereon to rest our harrassed limbs. **1884** L. J. JENNINGS in *Croker papers* I. xii. 359 His successor.. passed a harassed life. **1891** *Harper's Weekly* 19 Sept. 710/2 On the edge of life, fighting anxiously, *harassedly, for a foothold. **1707** *Lond. Gaz.* No. 4322/1 Fire and Sword, the too too fatal *Harassers of these bordering Places. **1805** G. ELLIS *Spec. E.E. Rom.* I. 23 (R.) Unnumbered harassers Of the Fleet and Scots. **1834** J. W. CROKER in *C. Papers* 10 Dec. (1884), Well may you talk of 'harassing cares'. The first that I dread for you are the personal *harasseries of individual pretenders. **1833** HT. MARTINEAU *Berkeley the Banker* I. vii. 137 You must have had.. an extremely *harassing day, Sir. **1868** FREEMAN *Norm. Conq.* II. ix. 389 The harassing attacks of the nimble Welsh. **1822** W. TAYLOR in *Monthly Rev.* XCIX. 290 The roads became *harassingly bad. **1886** *Sat. Rev.* 20 Mar. 417 Schumann literature.. has become almost harassingly voluminous.

'harass, *sb.* [f. prec. vb.] Harassment.

1667 WATERHOUSE *Fire Lond.* 66 This late harrass of us by a more than Gottish and Vandallique fire. **1748** RICHARDSON *Clarissa* (1811) IV. xliii. 286 The harasses and doubts under which I have laboured. **1814** BYRON *Lara* II. xi, The daily harass, and the fight delay'd. **1875** M. PATTISON *Casaubon* 31 He struggles, all through a life of harass, to have his time for himself.

'harassing, *vbl. sb.* [f. HARASS *v.* + -ING[1].]

a. The action of the verb.

1689 DILLINGHAM *Myst. Iniq. Anatomised* 35 The harassing, spoiling, and imprisonment of the Nonconformists. **1842** MANNING *Serm.* (1848) I. 238 To be set free from the harassing of indwelling evils.

b. *attrib.*, as **harassing agent**, a gas intended for use in harassing or incapacitating an enemy, a rioting crowd, etc., without being lethal; also ***harassing gas***.

1968 R. CLARKE *We All fall Down* iii. 40 No weapons of any kind are manufactured at Porton, although the harassing agent known as CS was developed there in the early 1950s. **1972** W. F. BIDDLE *Weapons Technology & Arms Control* xix. 286 The object of a harassing agent is to make it impossible for opposing troops either to stay in an area or to carry out their military duties. Harassing agents are not necessarily intended to be lethal. **1969** *New Scientist* 30 Jan. 219/2 The other major class of agents in use are the harassing gases CS, CN and DM. They are supposedly non-lethal.

harassment ('hærəsmənt). [f. HARASS *v.* + -MENT.] The action of harassing, or the fact of being harassed; vexation, worry.

1753 HANWAY *Trav.* (1762) I. III. xxix. 126 The perpetual harassments which the Tartars usually give a regular army. **1806** *Edin. Rev.* IX. 146 The harassment of these applications. **1893** BEATRICE HARRADEN *Ships Night* (1894) 6 A face..pathetic because of its undisguised harassment.

‖**ha'ratch.** Also **harach, haratsh.** The same as CARATCH, the poll-tax levied by the Turks on their Christian subjects.

1745 R. POCOCKE *Trav.* in Pinkerton *Voy.* (1811) X. 729 (Stanf.) The galleys go out every summer round the islands to collect the harach or Christian poll tax. **1813** BYRON *Br. Abydos* II. xx. *note*, 'Rayahs',—all who pay the capitation tax, called the 'Haratch'. **1884** W. CARR *Montenegro* 27 *note*, To escape the haratch and the tribute of children.

harateen: see HARRATEEN.

harauld, obs. form of HERALD.

harbagar, -be(n)ger, obs. ff. HARBINGER.

harbar, -ber, obs. forms of HARBOUR *sb.* and *v.*

harbarie, var. of HARBOURY, *Obs.*

harbary, var. of HERBARY.

harbegeon, incorrect form of HABERGEON.

†**'harbergage, 'herbergage.** *Obs.* Forms: 4-5 herber-, herbur-, herby-, (4 harbi-), 5 herbergh-, herbe-, herba-, harbergage, (harbergach), 5-6 herbi-, 6 erbigage, (herbadge). [a. ONF. *herbergage* (*herbeg(h-*, *herbag-*, *heberg-*, *harbegage*), = Central OF. *herberjage* (*herbaj-*, *heberge-*, *harberj-*), f. *herberge, herberger*, in ONF. *herberghe, -gue, herberghier, -beguier*: see HARBINGER.]

1. Lodging, entertainment.

c **1386** CHAUCER *Cook's Prol.* 5 This Millere hadde a sharpe conclusion Vpon his argument of herbergage [*v. rr.* harbigage, herburgage]. *c* **1400** MAUNDEV. (1839) viii. 97 This is the same Julyan, that men clepe to for gode Herberghgage [*Roxb.* xi. 48 gude herbery]. *a* **1420** HOCCLEVE *De Reg. Princ.* 1264 Withe rich hoost he toke his herbegage. **1430-40** LYDG. *Bochas* VI. xi. (1554) 155 b, Such ..Should of custome haue their harbergage In that citie. **1439** W. BYNGHAM in Willis & Clark *Cambridge* (1886) I. Introd. 56 For the free herbigage of poure scolers of gramer. *c* **1445** *Ibid.* 54 He hyrd hym loginge for his scolers and for harbergach of his stor and hustilmentes for his howseholde. **1502** *Privy Purse Exp. Eliz of York* (1830) 74 Making herbigage there by the space of iiij dayes.

2. Place of lodging or entertainment; inn.

13.. *Minor Poems fr. Vernon MS.* 626/8 His Innes & his orchardus..Halles, & herbergages, heiȝ vppon heiht. ? *a* **1400** *Morte Arth.* 2475 Hyes to the harbergage thare the kynge houys. *Ibid.* 3014 At the herbergage. *c* **1475** *Partenay* 1017 Euery man went to hys erbigage.

†**harberger,** earlier form of HARBINGER.

†**harbergery, herbergery.** *Obs.* Forms: 4 herbergery(e, -i(e, herbagery, -ie, herbergrye. -borgerie, (harbergary), 4-5 herbe-, harburgery. [a. OF. *herbergerie* (*herbegerie, hebergerie, habergerie*, etc.), f. *herbergere* HARBINGER, *herbergier* to lodge; see HARBINGE *v.* and -ERY 1 b.]

1. Lodging, entertainment.

1303 R. BRUNNE *Handl. Synne* 10106 þarfore makeþ he none herbergerye. *c* **1330** —— *Chron.* (1810) 203 At þe dangu þat nyght he tok his herbegerie. *c* **1340** *Cursor M.* 14709 (Fairf.) His herbagery sal be in helle. **1382** WYCLIF *Gen.* xxiv. 32 He ladde hym into the hows of herbergrye [**1388** the ynne]. **1387** TREVISA *Higden* v. ix. (Rolls) V. 403 Oon to þe bisshop and his meyne to fynde harburgy [*v. rr.* herbergrye, herbergerye].

2. Place of lodging or entertainment; inn.

a **1300** *Cursor M.* 8286 Make þam a riche herbergeri [*v. rr.* herbageri, herbergery, wonyng]. **1382** WYCLIF *Luke* xxii. 11 Where is the herborgerie [**1388** chaumbre] where I schal ete pask with my disciplis? **1390** GOWER *Conf.* III. 99 The splen is to malencoly Assigned for herbergery. *c* **1440** *Bone Flor.* 1760 At thys burges hows he toke hur downe, There was hur harburgerie.

harbergh, -berow(e, etc., obs. ff. HARBOUR.

harberie, -ry: see HARBOURY, -BRY, *sb.* and *v.*

harbert, obs. form of HALBERD.

harbesher, -biger, obs. ff. HARBINGER.

'harbin. A local name of the COAL-FISH (*Merlangus carbonarius*), at a certain age.

1806 NEILL *Tour Orkney, etc.* 209 (Jam.) The appearance of the coal-fish varies much with its age: hence a new series of provincial names. In Orkney it is 1. a sillock; 2. a cooth; 3. a harbin; 4. a cudden; and 5. a sethe. **1836** YARRELL *Brit. Fishes* (1841) II. 251. **1861** COUCH *Brit. Fishes* III. 84.

harbinge ('hɑːbɪndʒ), *v.* Forms *α.* 5-7 **herberge,** 5 **herbige.** *β.* 6, 9 **harbinge,** 7 **herbinge.** [ME. *herberge, herbige*, a. OF. *herbergier, herbigier* (3rd sing. pr. *herberge, -bige*): see next, and cf. HARBOUR *v.*]

†**1. a.** *trans.* To lodge. **b.** *intr.* (for *refl.*, as in OFr.) To take up one's quarters. *Obs.*

c **1475** *Partenay* 1313 And ther ooste myght see ful fast herbiging. **1515** *Caxton's Chron. Eng.* IV. 35 b/1 A wyse man ..that was herberged a nyght in his house. **1561** STOW *Eng. Chron., Universities* x. (R. Supp.), Fro the reuerence and eminence of the personages therein harbinged. **1596** NASHE *Saffron Walden* 91 One Master Bradburies, where the late deceased Countesse of Darbie was then harbinged. **1601** F. TATE *Househ. Ord. Edw. II*, §56 (1876) 42 They shal..make the liveree of hay for horses herberged out of the court. *a* **1603** T. CARTWRIGHT *Confut. Rhem. N. T.* (1618) 30 The creature and the Creator, which if they were well herbinged should not haue lien so neere together.

2. [*nonce-use* from *harbinger.*] *trans.* To be a harbinger of, to announce beforehand.

1868 WHITMAN *Sel. Poems, Starting fr. Paumanok* 17 The future of the States I harbinge. **1897** *Mem. F. O. Morris* 83 Harbinging the return.

harbinger ('hɑːbɪndʒə(r)), *sb.* Forms: *α.* 2-7 herberger(e, 4 herborgere, 4-7 herbergeour, 5 herberjoure, -owre, 5-7 herberjour, -barjour, 6 her-, harburger, 6- 7 harberger, -geour. *β.* 5-6 herbeger(e, harbyger, herbejeour, 6 herbe-, herbigeour, harbiger, -bagar, -besher. *γ.* 5 herbengar, 5-8 herbenger, 6 herbynger, 6-7 herbinger, harbenger, 6- harbinger, (6 arbinger). [Early ME. *herbergere* and *herbergeour*, a. OF. *herbergere* (*-begiere, habergiere*), in obl. case *herbergeor* (*-geur, -geour, -jur, heb-, hab-*) one who provides shelter or lodgings (= med.L. *heribergātor, herebergiātor*), agent-n. from vb. *herbergier* (*-bargier, -begier, -bager, -bigier, har-*) to provide lodgings for (= med.L. *heribergāre*), f. OF. *herberge* = med.L. *heri-, hereberga* lodging, quarters (for an army, etc.), a. OHG. and OLG. *heriberga* lit. 'shelter for an army', f. *hari, heri*, host, army + *-berga* (= OE. *-berȝ, -beorȝ*) protection, shelter, f. *bergan* to protect. Already in OHG. this word had been extended from the original military sense, to mean 'place of entertainment, lodging': see HARBOUR. The form *herbegere*, occurring in OF. and ME., was in the latter changed to *herbenger*, whence, with *har-* for *her-* (as also sometimes in OF.), the current *harbinger*: cf. *passenger, messenger, wharfinger*. See also HARBOURER.]

†**1.** One who provides lodging; an entertainer, a host; a HARBOURER. ***common herberger***, a common lodging-house keeper. *Obs.*

α. *c* **1175** *Lamb. Hom.* 143 þe herbe[r]gers, þe þolemode, þe elmesfulle..sculen beon icleoped on þe fader riht halue. **1340** *Ayenb.* 39 Robberes and kueade herbergeres [*MS.* herberȝeres] þet berobbeþ þe pilgrimes an þe marchons. **1382** WYCLIF *Rom.* xvi. 23 Gayus, my herborgere [**1388** oost] greetith ȝou wel. *c* **1440** *Promp. Parv.* 235/2 Herberiowre, *hospiciarius*. **1502** ARNOLDE *Chron.* (1811) 26 Comon herburgers in the same cite and in the subbarbes.. as well as oder comon harburgers free and of the same fraunches.

β. *c* **1400** *Rom. Rose* 5000 Gronyng and Grucchyng, hir herbeiours..tellen hir, erliche and late, That Deth stondith armed at hir gate. *Ibid.* 7585 With sory happe to youre bihove, Am I to day youre herbegere! Go, herber yow elleswhere than heere.

2. One sent on before to purvey lodgings for an army, a royal train, etc.; a purveyor of lodgings; in *pl.*, an advance company of an army sent to prepare a camping-ground; a pioneer who prepares the way. *Hist.* and *arch.* †***Knight Harbinger***: an officer in the Royal Household (the office was abolished in 1846).

α. *c* **1386** CHAUCER *Man of Law's T.* 899 The fame anon thurgh out the toun is born..By herbergeours [*v.r.* -jours], that wenten hym biforn. ? *a* **1400** *Morte Arth.* 2448 Thane come þe herbariours, harageous knyghtez. **1530** PALSGR. 228/2 Harberger, *fourrier du roy*. *a* **1562** G. CAVENDISH *Wolsey* (1893) 64 His harbergers passyng byfore to provyde lodgyngs for his trayne.

β. **1460** *Paston Lett.* No. 357 I. 525 The Harbyger of my Lord of Marche. **1470-85** MALORY *Arthur* VII. xxviii, Thenne ther cam the herbegeours from kynge Arthur for to herborowe hym and his kynges. **1514** BARCLAY *Cyt. & Uplondyshm.* (Percy Soc.) p. liii, Men must win the Marshall or els herbegere With price or with prayer. **1548** HALL *Chron., Hen. VIII* (an. 5) (1809) 555 The English cariers that came with the Harbeshers to take ground..tooke certayne wagons with beere and vitaill. **1552** HULOET, Harbiger, to appoint lodginges for the traine of princes, *epistathmi*. **1555** ABP. PARKER *Ps.* cv, To them as herbeger Lo Joseph sold to servitude.

γ. **1471** *Arriv. Edw. IV* (Camden) 27 Theyr herbengars were come afore them as ferre as Sudberrye. **1524** *State Papers Hen. VIII*, II. 115 He shalle not sett his men too coyne uppon the Kinges subjectes..but by bille made by the arbinger. **1525** LD. BERNERS *Froiss.* II. cxxviii. [cxxiv.] 364 They had sent before their herbyngers to take vp their lodgynges. **1623** tr. *Favine's Theat. Hon.* II. xii. 185 Where the Herbinger had before marked the lodgings for Otho. **1635** N. R. *Camden's Hist. Eliz.* IV. 567 The chief Magistrate ..as an Harbinger appoynting out their billet. **1708** J. CHAMBERLAYNE *St. Gt. Brit.* I. II. xii. (1743) 105 They have a gentleman harbinger to provide lodging for them. **1743** *List King's Officers above Stairs* ibid. II. 190 William Cowper, Esq.; Knight-Harbinger. **1877** MISS YONGE *Cameos* IV. ii. 25 Harbingers were sent before, to prepare quarters for all this train.

3. One that goes before and announces the approach of some one; a forerunner. Mostly in *transf.* and *fig.* senses, and in literary language.

β. *a* **1550** *Hye way Spyttel Hous* 834 in Hazl. *E.P.P.* IV. 60 These to our place have dayly herbegers.

γ. *c* **1572** GASCOIGNE *Fruites Warre* (R.), Hope is harbenger of all mishappe. **1630** MILTON *May Morning*, Now the bright morning star, day's harbinger, Comes dancing from the east, and leads with her the flowery May. *a* **1638** MEDE *Wks.* III. (1672) 702 His Harbinger John had now finished his Message. **1765** H. WALPOLE *Otranto* iii, First came two harbingers with wands. Next a herald. **1768** BEATTIE *Minstr.* I. xxxvi, Proud harbinger of day..Fell chanticleer! **1820** W. IRVING *Sketch Bk.* II. 359 The boding cry of the tree-toad, that harbinger of storm. **1874** H. AINSWORTH *Merry Eng.* I. iv, A harbinger, apparelled in the royal livery, had been sent on to announce the approach of the Princess. **1875** STUBBS *Const. Hist.* II. xiv. 72 The prophet and harbinger of better days coming.

†**4.** = HARBOURER 2. *Obs. rare.*

1741 *Compl. Fam. Piece* II. i. 289 In Harbouring the Hart, the Huntsman or Harbinger must..put his Hound before him, and beat the Outside of the Springs or Thickets.

5. harbinger of spring. A small umbelliferous herb of North America, *Erigenia bulbosa*, which flowers in March in the Central States. In its tuberous root, twice ternate leaves, and small white flowers, it resembles the Earth-nut of Great Britain.

1868 ASA GRAY *Man. Bot. Northern U.S.* (ed. 5).

Hence **'harbingership,** the office or position of a harbinger. **'harbingery** (*nonce-wd.*), the act or function of a harbinger (in sense 3).

1613 PURCHAS *Pilgrimage* (1614) 242 Thou shalt go one houre before; and presently caused his head to be smitten off. An unhappie Harbengership in regard of his Art. **1887** SAINTSBURY *Hist. Elizab. Lit.* ii. 46 They do not come in with the somewhat ostentatious usherment and harbingery, which for instance laid the even more splendid bursts of Jeremy Taylor open to the sharp sarcasm of South.

'harbinger, *v.* [f. prec. sb. (in sense 3).] *trans.* To act as a harbinger to; to announce, presage.

1646 G. DANIEL *Poems* Wks. 1878 I. 24 To Harbinger his learned name. **1662** COKAINE *Ovid* I. i, Before..I for this untimely courtesy Make thee to harbinger my soul in death! **1794** COLERIDGE *Relig. Musings* Poems I. 88 More bright than all the angel blaze That harbinger'd thy birth. **1814** SOUTHEY *Roderick* XVIII. 299 The star that harbingers a glorious day. **1875** EMERSON *Lett. & Soc. Aims* v. 131 Heralded and harbingered by smiles and greetings.

harbor, var. spelling of HARBOUR.

harborie: see HARBOURY.

†**harborough, -borow,** etc. ME. forms of HARBOUR *sb.* and *v.*

†**'harborous,** *a.* *Obs.* Also 6 herber-, herbo(u)r-, harber-, harbour-, etc. [f. HARBOUR *sb.*[1], after words in -OUS from French, e.g. *humorous.*]

1. Affording harbour or shelter; given to hospitality.

1526 TINDALE *1 Tim.* iii. 2 A bishoppe must be..honestly aparelled, harberous, apt to teache. —— *1 Pet.* iv. 9 Be ye herbrous and that without grudginge. **1550** BALE *Apol.* 38 An other sorte promyseth their howse to be herbourouse to the howsehold of fayth. *a* **1613** OVERBURY *Observ. France* Wks. (1856) 237 Their nature, which is easie and harborous to strangers. **1632** VICARS *Virg. Æneid* 72 In this kinde harb'rous town.

2. Furnished with harbours or havens for ships.

[**1589** FLEMING *Virg. Georg.* III. 49 That water at the first Was harborous to brode wide ships, now harborous to wains.] **1612** DRAYTON *Poly-olb.* i. 5 Her haven angled so about her harbrous sound. **1641** HEYLIN *Help to Hist.* (1671) 266 A Countrey harborous on either side with commodious Havens. **1702** C. MATHER *Magn. Chr.* III. II. vii. (1852) 397 This is a well known sea, called Euxine, or harborous.

harbory: see HARBOURY.

harbour, harbor ('hɑːbə(r)), *sb.*[1] Forms: *α.* 2 hereberȝe, 3 herburȝe, -byrȝe, 3 herberȝe, 4 herboru, herbergh, -berw, -beruh, 4-5 herberwe, -berewe, -borewe, -borwe, -boruhe, -borouȝ, -borw, -burhe, -burgh(e, 4-6 herberow(e, -borow(e, 5 herbarwe, -barow, -barou, -bourgh, 5-6 herboroghe, -borough(e, 6 herberough, -bourough, -burrouh. *β.* 4 herbore, -bure, 4-5 -ber(e, 5-6 -bour(e. *γ.* 5 harburrow, 5-6 harbarow(e, -brough(e, 5-7 harborow(e, 6 harberowe, -bourgh, -borrow, -bourough, 6-7 harborough(e. *δ.* 5 harbar, 6-7 harboure, 6- harbor, harbour, (7 harber). [Early ME. *hereberȝ(e, herberȝ(e*, corresp. to an OE. **herebeorȝ*, f. *here* army, host = *-beorȝ, -e* protection, shelter, not recorded, but found in the cognate langs., OHG. *hęre-, hęre-, herberga* (MHG. and mod.G. *herberge*), OLG. *hęriberga* (MDu. *herberghe*, Du. *herberg*) all fem., ON. *herbergi* neuter (Sw. *herberge*). The ME. word has been assumed to be from Norse; but the phonology points rather to an OE. type (original, or perh. after the Norse). The subsequent history shows two lines of phonetic change, viz. the change of *her-* to *har-*, usual with *er-* before a consonant (as in *bark, barrow, hart, marsh*, and the pronunciation of *clerk, sergeant, Berkshire, Hertford*, etc.); and the weakening of the second element to *-ber*, *-bor*, *-bour*; the current *harbour* exhibits both of these changes. The late ME. form remains in place names, e.g. *Market Harborough*.

Harbour is now the standard spelling of both the noun and the verb in the U.K., while *harbor* prevails in the United States.]

1. Shelter, lodging, entertainment: sojourn, abode.

α. *c* **1150** *Homily* (Kluge *Leseb.* 72) Na synderlice onoðren herbyrȝe. *c* **1175** *Lamb. Hom.* 69 þe node habbeð ȝiuen heom red, Mid hereberȝe and mid fode. *c* **1250** *Gen. & Ex.* 1392 If ȝhe miȝte taken Herberȝe for hire frendes sake[n]. **1382** Wyclif *Wisd.* xviii. 4 Withoute hurting of good herberewe [**1388** herbore]. *c* **1386** Chaucer *Pars. T.* ¶957 Neede of cloþing and herberwe [*v. rr.* herborugh, harborowe, herboruhe]. *c* **1440** *York Myst.* xiv. 6 Graunt vs gode herborow þis nyght. **1470–85** Malory *Arthur* x. ix, They.. praid the lord of the castel of herburgh. **1530–1** *Act 22 Hen. VIII*, c. 12 If any personne.. geue any herborowe moneye or lodgeynge to any beggers. **1553** Brende *Q. Curtius* D ij, That Alexander shoulde fynde no herborow [*v.r.* herberowe] there. **1573** G. Harvey *Letter-bk.* (Camden) 166 Frendly voutsave him herburrouh.

β. **1340** Hampole *Pr. Consc.* 6153 Of herber grete nede I had, Yhe herbed me with hert glad. **1388** Wyclif *Ecclus.* xxix. 31 To seke herbore [*v.r.* herberow] fro hous in to hous. *c* **1400** *Ywaine & Gaw.* 2940 Whi wil thou her thi herber tane? **1538** Bale *Brefe Com.* in *Harl. Misc.* (Malh.) I. 207 Helpe alwayes the poore, with herbour, foode, and aparell. **1552** *Ord. St. Bartholomew's* E j b in *Vicary's Anat.* (1888) App. xvi. 310 For the herboure and succour of the dere members of Christes body. **1575** Laneham *Let.* (1871) 9 To take herbour.

γ. *c* **1410** Love *Bonavent. Mirr.* vi. (1510) C iv, She.. asked harborowe in dyvers places. *c* **1435** *Torr. Portugal* 260 What crystyn man axithe harburrow here? **1549** Coverdale, etc. *Erasm. Par. Rom.* 34 Lette them have harbroughe. **1571** Campion *Hist. Irel.* i. (1633) 62 Those cursed exactions of diet and harborow. **1598** in Picton *L'pool Munic. Rec.* (1883) I. 115 Whoesoever.. shall lodge or gyve harborough to any rouges. [Cf. Market Harborough.]

δ. **1548** Udall, etc. *Erasm. Par. Matt.* xxv. 115 Whan I was a straunger and nedy of harboure. **1592** *Nobody & Someb.* in Simpson *Sch. Shaks.* (1878) II. 289 Nobody takes them in, provides them harbor. **1663** Dryden *Wild Gallant* III. i, All I desire of you is but harbour for a minute. **1684** Bunyan *Pilgr.* II. 148 Our great Want.. was Harbor and good Company. **1691** Ray *Creation* II. (1704) 253 They serve for the Harbour.. of various Animals. **1791** Cowper *Odyss.* II. 397 Give harbour in thy breast on no acount To after-grudge or enmity. **1814** Scott *Ld. of Isles* I. xxvi, To harbour safe, and friendly cheer, That gives us rightful claim.

2. a. A place of shelter or sojourn; lodgings, quarters, resting-place; place of entertainment, inn; place of refuge, asylum. *Obs.* exc. *dial.*

cold harbour, a place of shelter from the weather for wayfarers, constructed by the wayside. Hence, a frequent name of a locality, and in comb. *Cold Harbour Lane.*

α. *c* **1300** *Havelok* 742 þore were Of here herboru herborwed þere. **1377** Langl. *P. Pl.* B. x. 406 Holicherche, þat he[r]berwe is and goddes hous to saue. *c* **1386** Chaucer *Prol.* 765, I saugh nat this year so myrie a compaignye Atones in this herberwe [*v. rr.* herborowe, harborowe, herberw, herburhe] as is now. *c* **1450** *Merlin* 539 Thei fonde nether house ne herberowe. **1530** Palsgr. 230/2 Herboroghe, *logis*. *a* **1637** B. Jonson *Discoveries* Wks. (Rtldg.) 743/1 To have his arms set up in his last herborough.

β. **1340** Hampole *Pr. Consc.* 448 With-in his awen moder body, Whar his herber with-in was dight. *c* **1449** Pecock *Repr.* 523 Dyuerse Ostries or Herbouris for to logge the more multitude.

γ. ? *c* **1475** *Sqr. lowe Degre* 179 Yf ye may no harbroughe se, Than must ye lodge under a tre. **1530** Palsgr. 169 *Herberge*, an harborowe. **1579** Twyne *Phisicke agst. Fort.* I. v. 6 a, Thy harborow or Inne, or rather thy pryson. **1600** Holland *Livy* XXVI. xli. 616 That the legions from out of their winter harboroughs, should there meete together.

δ. **1483** *Cath. Angl.* 174/2 An Harbar, *hospicium*. **1570** Levins *Manip.* 222/36 Harboure, *hospitium*. **1590** Spenser *F.Q.* I. I. 7 Fair harbour that them seems: so in they entred are. **1642** Rogers *Naaman* 462 They will capitulate for their honour to go out of their harbour, with their pikes traild.. and in array. **1711** Addison *Spect.* No. 110 ¶2 Ivy and Elder-Bushes, the Harbours of several solitary Birds. **1868** Atkinson *Cleveland Gloss.*, *Harbour*, shelter, lodging.

†**b.** The 'house', mansion, or position of the sun or a planet in the zodiac. *Obs.*

c **1386** Chaucer *Frankl. T.* 307 To ech of hem his tyme and his seson As thyr herberwe [*v. rr.* herborwe, harborowe, hebour] chaungeth lowe or heighe.

c. The covert or place of retreat of wild animals.

1576 Fleming tr. *Caius' Eng. Dogs* in Arb. *Garner* III. 234 Terriers.. driue them out of their hollow harbours. **1615** J. Stephens *Satyr. Ess.* 310 Hee dreames of.. a Bucke lodged, or a Hart in harbor. **1622** T. Scott *Belg. Pismire* 74 They resort to those places as to their harboroughs or couerts. **1741** *Compl. Fam. Piece* II. i. 289 When you intend to find out the Harbour or Layer of a Hart. **1884** Jefferies *Red Deer* vi. 103 The stag.. When he has settled himself down he is said to be 'in harbour'.

d. *fig.*

1548 Udall, etc. *Erasm. Par. Mark* iv. 35 Fynde any quietnesse, or sure harborowe. **1591** R. W. *Tancred & Gismunda* v. ii. in Hazl. *Dodsley* VII. 85 Ah, pleasant harborough of my heart's thought! **1674** Brevint *Saul at Endor* 268 These saving Harbers. **1805** Wordsw. *Prelude* I. 11 In what vale Shall be my harbour?

3. a. A place of shelter for ships; *spec.* where they may lie close to and sheltered by the shore or by works extended from it; a haven, a port.

α. [*c* **1205** Lay. 28878 Sexisce men.. seileden to londe, And herberȝe token.. Bi-ȝeonde þere Humbre.] *c* **1386** Chaucer *Prol.* 403 To rekene wel his tydes His stremes.. His herberwe and his moone, his lodemenage. **1555** W. Watreman *Fardle Facions* Pref. 11 Thei.. digged out herborowes, where their shippes might ride saulfe fro the storme.

β. **1582** N. Lichefield tr. *Castanheda* I j b, The Ports, Herbours, and Riuers, where he tooke in fresh water.

γ. *a* **1547** Surrey *Æneid* IV. 53 Also the Sirtes, unfriendly harbroughe. **1555** Eden *Decades* 350 A byght or bay as thowgh it were a harbarowe. **1578** Bourne *Invent.* 11 They must cheyne their Hauen or harborrow. **1600** Hakluyt *Voy.* (1810) III. 121 They put into the foresayde Harborough. **1614** Raleigh *Hist. World* II. (1634) 302 A Harborow of great capacitie, being in former times but an open bay.

δ. **1582** N. Lichefield tr. *Castanheda's Conq. E. Ind.* lxii. 126 b, Their harbour or hauen is verie good. **1603** Knolles *Hist. Turks* (1638) 119 They were not able to put into the Harbor. **1697** Dryden *Virg. Georg.* IV. 609 A Station safe for Ships, when Tempests roar, A silent Harbour, and a cover'd Shoar. **1802** *Med. Jrnl.* VIII. 23 Some of the men of war, then in the harbour. *a* **1839** Praed *Poems* (1864) II. 178 Like a wreck that is drifting to harbour, I come to thee, Lady, at last.

b. An airship shed or hangar.

1909 *Chambers's Jrnl.* Oct. 659/2 Work in connection with the other Zeppelin air-ships is so far advanced that as soon as the halls, or harbours, as they are called, are ready it will only be necessary to put the parts together. **1912** C. B. Hayward *Pract. Aeronaut.* 36 To the only two airship sheds or 'harbors' exceeding 400 feet in length.. no less than nine had been added [in France].

c. (See quot. 1948.)

1935 *Jrnl. R. United Service Inst.* Nov. 747 The aeroplane cannot hit a moving tank with a bomb, but when the tanks harbour, the aircraft will make every effort to locate and bomb them... The bombing of tanks in harbour will cause immediate dispersion. **1948** Partridge *Forces' Slang* 91 *Harbour*, halting place for the night for guns and tanks. Also a verb.

4. *Glass-making.* A large shallow trough-like box with handles or wheels used for holding the mixed ingredients or 'batch' and conveying them to the pot for fusion.

1891 *Sale Catal. Glass Wks. Stourbridge*, Seven mixing harbours. **1897** *Correspondent*, Each harbour of separate mixture is placed around the furnace before each pot for the purpose of filling.

5. *attrib.* and *Comb.* (in sense 3), as ***harbour-admiral***, ***-bar***, ***-buoy***, ***-duty***, ***-light***, ***-room***, ***-town***, etc.; **harbour-due**, a charge for the use of a harbour (usually in *pl.*); **harbour-gasket**, **-log**, **-watch** (see quots.); **harbour-master**, an officer who has charge of a harbour, and of the mooring of ships, etc. therein; hence ***harbour-mastership***; **harbour seal** *N. Amer.*, the common seal, *Phoca vitulina*, found along the shores of northern oceans; **harbour-side**; **harbour stow**, furling in a body (cf. furling *vbl. sb.* 1); so **harbour-stowed** *a.*; **harbourward** *adv.*, towards the harbour.

1829 Marryat *F. Mildmay* iv. The *Gladiator*, the flagship of the *harbour-admiral. **1798** Coleridge *Anc. Mar.* VI. xv, We drifted o'er the *Harbour-bar. **1864** Tennyson *Sailor Boy* 2 He rose at dawn and, fired with hope, Shot o'er the seething harbour-bar. **1842** —— *Audley Court* 85 The bay was oily calm; the *harbour-buoy.. With one green sparkle ever and anon Dipt by itself. **1718** *Bridlington Pier Act*, All such tools, *harbour-dues, or other dues. **1863** Fawcett *Pol. Econ.* x. vii. (1876) 614 A harbour due is.. paid for the accommodation obtained by shipping. **1867** Smyth *Sailor's Word-bk.*, **Harbour-gaskets*, broad, but short and well-blacked gaskets.. for showing off a well-furled sail in port. **1858** *Merc. Marine Mag.* V. 371 A *Harbour-Light will be established. **1867** Smyth *Sailor's Word-bk.*, **Harbour-log*, that part of the log-book which.. relates only to transactions while the ship is in port. **1769** Falconer *Dict. Marine* (1789), *Maître de ports*, an *harbour-master, or officer appointed to take care of a port. **1884** G. Allen *Philistia* I. 37 The honourable sinecure of a *harbour-mastership. **1847** Grote *Greece* II. xliv. (1862) IV. 9 To provide *harbour-room at once safe and adequate. **1766** J. Banks *Diary* Oct. in A. M. Lysaght *Joseph Banks in Newfoundland & Labrador* (1971) II. 145 They [*sc.* the fishermen] divide them [*sc.* the seals] into five sorts which they call Square Phipper Hooded Seal Heart or houke Bedlamer and *harbour seal, which last stays in the Countrey all the year. **1832** J. McGregor *British America* I. iii. 107 The harbour seal (phoca vitulina).. does not seem to be migratory. **1958** A. W. Cameron *Canad. Mammals* 55 Apart from the grey seal, the harbour seal is the only member of the tribe that ordinarily spends the summer in southern Canada. **1964** E. P. Walker et al. *Mammals of World* II. 1302 (*caption*) Hair or harbor seals (*Phoca vitulina*). **1947** Crowther & Whiddington *Science at War* 180 Larger explosive charges can be used, and their effects registered by electrical recording on the *harbour-side. **1962** *Daily Tel.* 11 Aug. 14/5 It was then decided to take Coweslip, still low in the water, to the nearby harbourside home of Mr. B. A. L. **1969** *Jane's Freight Containers 1968–69* 56/2 D & F Harborside Terminal. **1886** R. Brown *Spunyarn & Spindrift* xxv. 311 Every rope in its place and hauled taut, every sail neatly furled in a *harbour-stow. **1924** R. Clements *Gipsy of Horn* v. 98 A 'harbour stow' we gave them, rolling the canvas into a neat skin as though it were covered with a jacket and passing the gaskets at regular intervals like seizings. **1924** J. Masefield *Sard Harker* 24 She was in lovely order; yards squared, harbour-stowed. *c* **1611** Chapman *Iliad* II. (R.), Halos *harbor-towne, that Neptune beats upon. **1867** Smyth *Sailor's Word-bk.*, **Harbour-watch*, a division or subdivision of the watch kept on night-duty, when the ship rides at single anchor.

† **harbour**, *sb.*[2] *Obs.* [A frequent spelling of arbour *sb.*[1] from 16th c., intermediate between the earlier *herber*, *erber*, and the present form.]

a. A grass-plot, a green = arbour 1. **b.** A bower or retreat covered with climbing shrubs and plants.

a. **1505** *Will of M. Huntyngdon* (Somerset Ho.), My body to be buried in our lady Harbar of the Cathedrall Church of Hereford. [**1573** *Richmond. Wills* (Surtees) 234 My bodye to be buried within yᵉ arbour on the north side off the churche of Richmonde.] **1804–20** *Hereford Cath., Sexton's Bk. of Fees*, For Ground in the Cathedral Lady Harbour, or Cloister, 4s. 6d.

b. **1563** [see arbour 5.] **1593** G. Fletcher *Licia, etc.* xxvi. (Grosart) 107 Where loving Wood-bine, doth the Harbour binde. **1613** R. Cawdrey *Table Alph.* (ed. 3), *Ombrage*, shade, harbor, or bower to rest vnder. **1762** *Gentl. Mag.* 222 A gravel walk.. with a covered harbour at each end of it. *a* **1790** Warton *Poet. Wks.* (1802) II. 194 An avenue so cool and dim Shall to an harbour, at the end, In spite of gout, entice a friend.

Hence ˈ**harboured** *ppl. a.*, = arboured.

1615 G. Sandys *Trav.* 136 We rid in shallow cradles, two on a Camell: harboured aboue, and couered with linnen.

harbour *sb.*[3], var. of arbor *sb.*[1]

1797 *Monthly Mag.* III. 222 Effected by a jagged wheel, fixed on the barrel harbour.

harbour, harbor (ˈhɑːbə(r)), *v.* Forms: *α.* 2 **hereburеȝen**, **herborȝen**, 3 **herber(e)ȝen**, **hereborwen**, 3–5 **herberwen**, **herborwen**, 4 **herberghen**, **herborghen**, **herbarwen**, **herbweren**, 4–5 **herberghwen**, **herberewen**, 4–6 **herberowe(n**, 5 **hereboroghe**, **herburghe**, **herberrowe**, 5–6 **herborowe**, 6 **herberoughe**, **herbrough**. *β.* 3–7 **herber(e(n**, 4–5 **herbor**, 5 **herbar**, 6 **herbowr(e**, *γ.* 4–6 **harborough**, 5 **-bergh**, **-berough**, **-burrow**, **-bourrow**, 5–6 **-borowe**, 6 **-barow**, **-brough**. *δ.* 5 **harbur**, 5–6 **harber**, 6 **harbar**, 6– **harbor**, **harbour**. See also *herbery*, harbry *v.* [f. harbour *sb.*, in its various phonetic forms:—OE. type **herebeorȝian*, corresp. to ON. *herbergja*, *-byrgja*, to lodge, harbour; OHG. *heribergôn*, MHG., MDu., Ger., Du. *herbergen* intr. and trans. Cf. also *herberge*, early form of harbinge *v.*, from OF. *herberger* (which was ultimately the same word).]

I. *trans.* †**1. a.** To provide a lodging or lodging-place for; to shelter from the weather or the night; to lodge, entertain. *Obs.*

α. *c* **1150** *Homily* (Kluge *Leseb.* 73) Swa swa leofne gyst heo hire husede and innlice herebyreȝode. *c* **1175** *Lamb. Hom.* 23 þu.. fedest wreche men and hereburеȝest and scrudest. *c* **1290** *S. Eng. Leg.* I. 260/146 To hereborewi Miseise men. *c* **1380** Wyclif *Sel. Wks.* III. 201 Cloþe.. and herberwe hem. *Ibid.* 317 þere he schal be hereberowid. *c* **1440** *Promp. Parv.* 236/1 Herberwyn [*v.rr.* herbergwyn, herborowen] or receyvyn to hereboroghe. **1530–1** *Act 22 Hen. VIII*, c. 12 To lodge and herberough any persone.. of charitee or almes. **1540** Taverner *Postils, Exhort. bef. Communion*, We have not hymselfe now.. to herbrough him. **1557** *Jest Mylner Abingt.* 157 in Hazl. *E.P.P.* III. 106 Herberowe us to night.

β. *a* **1300** *Cursor M.* 15494 To spek o iesu þar he was herberd in þat tun. **1382** Wyclif *Acts* x. 32 Symound, that is named Petre; this is herborid in the hous of Symound coriour. *c* **1400** *Isumbras* 524 Bot mete ne drynke couthe he gete none, Ne house to herbere hyme inne. *a* **1510** Douglas *King Hart* II. 264 Ȝe sall nocht herbere me and Eis at anes. **1609** Skene *Reg. Maj., Stat. Robt. I.* 20 Na man be herbered or lodged in the houses or granges.

γ. *c* **1435** *Torr. Portugal* 262, I wold harburrow the full fayne. *c* **1450** *Mirour Saluacioun* 1252 To harbergh the nedy wagring. **1530** Palsgr. 579/1, I intende to harborowe folkes no more. **1565** Golding *Ovid's Met.* II. (1593) 29 Tethis who doth harbrough me within her surges wide. **1587** *Sivqila* in *Polimanteia* (1881) Introd. 18 To al them that harborough such a guest.

δ. *c* **1440** *Bone Flor.* 1971 He harberde hym far therfro All behynde men.. Hys sekenes was so felle. **1557** *Ord. Hospitalls* E ij, Those [children] that are harboured in the Howse. **1601** Shaks. *Twel. N.* II. iii. 102 She harbors you as her kinsman.

fig. **1630** Prynne *Anti-Armin.* 1 Which would willingly harbour themselues, vnder the roofe.. of the Church of England. **1671** Milton *Samson* 458 The anguish of my soul, that suffers not Mine eye to harbour sleep.

b. *absol.* To show hospitality.

1534 Tindale *Rom.* xii. 13 Diligently to harboure [**1535** Coverd. Be glad to harbarow. **1539** (Great Bible), Be readie to harboure.]

†**2.** To quarter (soldiers or retainers); to assign lodgings to, to billet; *refl.* to take up quarters, encamp. Also *absol.* *Obs.*

c **1330** R. Brunne *Chron.* (1810) 149 Nouþer cite ne burgh myght þei in herberd be. *c* **1350** *Will. Palerne* 1626 Alle þe genge of grece was gayli resseyued & herbarwed hastely. *c* **1450** *Bk. Curtasye* 427 in *Babees Bk.* 312 The marshalle shalle herber alle men in fere. **1480** Caxton *Chron. Eng.* cii. 83 They comen.. in grete companyes and lodged and herburghed hem in the countrey al aboute where they wold. *a* **1483** *Liber Niger* in *Househ. Ord.* 32 Within the kinges gates no man shall harborow or assigne but this chamberlayn or usher. **1523** Ld. Berners *Froiss.* I. cclvi. 381 They.. layde siege about Monsac, and harbored themselfe, as though they wolde nat go thence in a moneth. **1648** Gage *West Ind.* 90 [We] were.. harboured in a green plot of ground resembling a meadow.

3. a. To give shelter to, to shelter. Formerly often in a good sense: to keep in safety or security, to protect; now mostly dyslogistic, as to conceal or give covert to noxious animals or vermin; to give secret or clandestine entertainment to noxious persons or offenders against the laws.

α. ? *a* **1366** Chaucer *Rom. Rose* 491 The gardin was not daungerous To herberwe briddes many oon. **1393** Langl. *P. Pl.* C. xxii. 320 Ordeyne þe an hous, peers, to herberghen in thi cornes. *c* **1430** *Pilgr. Lyf Manhode* i. cxxv. (1869) 66 This scauberk is cleped humilitee..in whiche thow shuldest thi swerd herberwe. **1484** Caxton *Fables of Æsop* i. xx, The swalowe..herberowed her in the plowgh mans hows.

β. **1420** *Surtees Misc.* (1888) 17 Yt lette noght William Selby to herber hys tymber apon the same walle. **1502** Arnolde *Chron.* 83 Yf any freman..suffer ony wares or marchaundises..to be kepte or herbowryd in his house.

γ. **1579** J. Stubbes *Gaping Gulf*, To harborough the persecuted Christians in your owne kingdome.

δ. *c* **1460** *How Marchande dyd Wyfe betray* 148 in Hazl. *E.P.P.* I. 201 Y swere..Y wylle neuyr harbur the kyngys felone. **1472** *Presentm. Juries* in *Surtees Misc.* (1888) 25 Oone panyermaker..harbers suspect persones in his hous. **1576** Fleming *Panopl. Epist.* 180 Ignoraunt what lewdnes lurketh, and what heynousnesse is harboured in the deedes they go about. **1633** T. Stafford *Pac. Hib.* i. xviii. (1810) 193 Traitours, which harboured themselves in the bogs and woods. **1659** D. Pell *Impr. Sea* 106 *note*, I would have Captains to say that our ships shal harbour no such Sailors. **1700** S. L. tr. *Fryke's Voy. E. Ind.* 44 These Woods harbour vast numbers of Monkeys. **1711** Addison *Spect.* No. 131 ¶5 He wishes Sir Roger does not harbour a Jesuit in his House. **1759** tr. *Duhamel's Husb.* i. vi. (1762) 12 Dung harbours insects. **1849** Macaulay *Hist. Eng.* I. 641 After the conviction of the rebels whom she had harboured. **1851** *Illustr. Catal. Gt. Exhib.* 780 Cocoa-nut fibre..does not harbour vermin. *Mod. Newsp.* A tobacconist was fined £100 for harboring smuggled tobacco.

fig. **1650** Hubbert *Pill Formality* 15 It is a dangerous thing to harbor a Traytor within your brest. **1820** Scott *Ivanhoe* xxiv, What religion can it be that harbours such a villain? **1842** H. Rogers *Ess.* I. i. 33 Harbouring every vagrant story that may ask shelter in his pages.

†**b.** Of a place, etc.: To afford accommodation or room for; to contain, hold. *Obs.*

1362 Langl. *P. Pl.* A. ii. 40 Bote þer nas halle ne hous þat miht herborwe þe peple. **1398** Trevisa *Barth. De P.R.* v. iii. (1495) 106 The mydle moder beclyppyth the brayne and herboryth and holdeth togyders the veynes of the brayne. *c* **1440** *York Myst.* xv. 125 It [a horn spoon] will herbar fourty pese. **1587** Golding *De Mornay* ix. 115 That there is but one God, and that The Ayre, The Heauen, the Sea, the Earth, and Hell..were harbered in his breast from all Eternitie. **1667** Boyle *Orig. Formes & Qual.*, The specifick actions of a Body that harbours subordinate Forms. **1680** —— *Produc. Chem. Princ.* v. 240 The Aeriall particles, that are wont to be harboured in the Pores of that liquor.

4. *fig.* To entertain within the breast; to cherish privately; to indulge. Now usually in reference to evil thoughts or designs.

1393 Langl. *P. Pl.* C. viii. 258 In þyn hole herte to herberghwen alle treuthe. **1576** Fleming *Panopl. Epist.* 337 O heart appointed even from thy creation to harbour kindenesse. **1583** Stanyhurst *Æneis* i. (Arb.) 17 Such festred rancoure doo Sayncts celestial harbour? **1601** F. Godwin *Bps. of Eng.* 353 The citizens..harboring their old grudge. **1602** Rowlands *Tis Merrie when Gossips meete* 20, I know that beauteous wenches are enclinde, To harbour hansome men within their minde. **1766** Fordyce *Serm. Yng. Wom.* (1767) I. iii. 109 They will be tempted to harbour suspicions. **1781** Cowper *Convers.* 561 Hearts..that harbour at this hour That love of Christ and all its quickening power. **1849** Macaulay *Hist. Eng.* II. 70 He believed them to harbour the worst designs. **1850** W. Irving *Goldsmith* i. 28 It was impossible for him to harbour resentment.

5. To shelter (a ship) in a haven or harbour.

1555 Eden *Decades* 2 Naturall hauens, of capacitie to harborowe greate nauies of shippes. **1600** J. Pory tr. *Leo's Africa* ii. 232 A faire haven, where the ships of Alger are safely harboured. **1633** P. Fletcher *Purple Isl.* xii. lii, Harbour my fleshly bark safe in thy wounded side. **1693** *Lond. Gaz.* No. 2849/4 Directions..how to Harbour a Ship in the same with Safety. **1887** Bowen *Virg. Æneid* iv. 375, I..Harboured his vessels, saved from death his mariner band.

6. To trace (a stag) to his 'harbour' or lair. Also *transf.*

1531 Elyot *Gov.* i. xviii, A few nombre of houndes, onely to harborowe, or rouse, the game. **1576** Turberv. *Venerie* 239 We herbor and unherbor a Harte, we lodge and rowse a Bucke. **1637** B. Jonson *Sad Sheph.* i. ii, Here's Little John hath harbord you a Deere. **1741** [see harbinger 4]. **1886** Wood in *Gd. Words* 690 A..tigress had been tracked..and at last 'harboured', as Stag-hunters say, in a small thicket. **1892** H. Hutchinson *Fairway Isl.* 6, I can harbour a stag against any man on Exmoor.

II. *intr.* **7.** To shelter oneself, lodge, take shelter; to encamp; later, often with some notion of lurking or concealment. *arch.* or *Obs.*

c **1200** *Trin. Coll. Hom.* 87 ȝif he mai þer-inne herberȝen. **1303** R. Brunne *Handl. Synne* 10290 Lete hym herber yn hys hous. *c* **1374** Chaucer *Boeth.* ii. pr. vi. 53 Wont to sleen hys gestes þat herburghden in hys hous. *c* **1380** *Sir Ferumb.* 5251 Thar herborghede þe king & ys barouns, Wyþ-oute tentes oþer pauyllouns. *c* **1400** *Rowland & O.* 745 Vnder a Mountayne þey herberde þan Besyde a reuer. *c* **1450** *Merlin* 125 Ye sholde not fynde an house in to herberowe. **1593** Shaks. *3 Hen. VI*, iv. vii. 79 Now for this Night, lets harbor here in Yorke. **1686** Plot *Staffordsh.* 448 Others say that the Robbers themselves harbour'd here. *c* **1750** Shenstone *Econ.* i. 52 Beneath one common roof Thou ne'er shalt harbour. **1805** Wordsw. *Waggoner* i. 59 Where the Dove and Olive-Bough Once hung, a Poet harbours now. **1807** Pike *Sources Mississ.* ii. (1810) 200, I was suspicious that possibly some party of Indians might be harboring round.

fig. *c* **1489** Caxton *Blanchardyn* liv. 207 Neither sleepe nor quiet could harber in her head. **1569** J. Sanford tr. *Agrippa's Van. Artes* 105 b, But nowe this plague..doth not onely herberoughe emonge temporall men. **1590** Marlowe *Edw. II*, v. Wks. (Rtldg.) 214/1 Think not a thought so villanous Can harbour in a man of noble birth. **1655** tr. *De Parc's Francion* I. 33 [To] suffer such a thought to harbour in our minds. **1760** Law *Spir. Prayer* ii. 161 No vice can harbor in you. **1796** *Hist. Ned Evans* I. 266 If envy could have harboured in such a breast as Sophia's.

8. Of an animal: To have its retreat or resort; *spec.* said of a stag.

1599 H. Buttes *Dyets drie Dinner* M viij, It is a Seafish..It harboureth some time about the shore. **1610** Guillim *Heraldry* iii. xiv. (1660) 166 You shall say that a Hart Harboureth. **1613** Purchas *Pilgrimage* (1614) 862 Penguin..cannot flie,..feeds on fish and grasse, and harbors in berries. **1650** Fuller *Pisgah* iii. ix. 338 Here the bellowing Harts are said to harbour..the belling Roes to bed. **1772–84** Cook *Voy.* (1790) V. 1680 The place where the turtle were known to harbour. **1869** Phillips *Vesuv.* iii. 46 In the woody parts wild boars frequently harboured.

9. a. Of a ship (or its crew): To take shelter or come to anchor in a haven or harbour. Also *fig.*

1583 Stanyhurst *Æneis* iii. (Arb.) 72 Wee saulflye dyd harbor in hauen. **1611** Shaks. *Cymb.* iv. ii. 206 To show what coast thy sluggish crare Might easiliest harbour in. *a* **1642** Sir W. Monson *Naval Tracts* iii. (1704) 331/2 He might have Harbour'd in Falmouth. **1718** Sewall *Diary* 12 May (1882) III. 184 Wind was Contrary that was forc't to harbour at Marblehead. **1842** Browning *Waring* ii. ii. 2 We were sailing by Triest Where a day or two we harboured.

b. Of tanks, military forces, etc.: to shelter; to halt for the night. Cf. senses 7 and 9 a.

1935, **1948** [see harbour *sb.*[1] 3 c]. **1956** W. Slim *Defeat into Victory* 498 That night our leading troops harboured two hundred and forty miles from Rangoon.

Hence **'harboured, 'harbouring** *ppl. adjs.*

1388 Wyclif *Wisd.* v. 15 An herborid man of a dai, that passith forth. **1743** J. Davidson *Æneid* viii. 267 Calling his vanquished Sons into his Azure Bosom and harbouring streams. **1833** Wordsw. *Warning* 44 Harboured ships, whose pride is on the sea. **1835** I. Taylor *Spir. Despot.* viii. 361 A harboured grudge and exasperation.

harbourage, -orage ('hɑːbərɪdʒ). Also 6 **herberage.** [f. harbour *sb.*[1] + -age: cf. the earlier ME. *herbergage*, harbergage, from French.]

1. Shelter, lodging; = harbour 1.

1570 *Henry's Wallace* xi. 1236 *note*, Now in hewin he has his herberage [**1470** heretage]. **1595** Shaks. *John* ii. i. 234 Your King..Craues harbourage within your Citie walles. **1634** Heywood *Maidenh. well Lost* ii. Wks. 1874 IV. 124 You shall not want nor foode, nor harborage. **1816** Scott *Old Mort.* viii. Did you give him harbourage in this very house? **1859** Tennyson *Enid* 281 Where can I get me harbourage for the night?

transf. and *fig.* **1829** I. Taylor *Enthus.* x. 297 Both infidelity and heresy have, till of late, found harbourage in the supposed or pretended corruption or uncertainty of the canon. **1876** F. E. Trollope *Charming Fellow* II. xi. 174 An idea to which..he would give no harbourage.

2. A place of shelter; a lodging; = harbour 2.

1651 N. Bacon *Disc. Govt. Eng.* ii. xxvi. (1739) 113 Happy England, if the same prove good Harbourage for a fainting Nation! **1820** Scott *Ivanhoe* xxviii, The worst of these harbourages..would unquestionably be more fitting for your residence than the abode of a despised Jew. **1883** *Graphic* 19 May 498 The island has been a harbourage of conspiracy and sedition.

3. Shelter for ships, shelter in a haven: cf. harbour 3.

[*a* **1680** Butler *Rem.* (1759) I. 412 That Enemy..winddriven on the British Coast, would find safe Harbourage in Milford.] **1850** Blackie *Æschylus* I. 38 Harsh harbourage, hard hammocks, and scant sleep. **1861** Smiles *Engineers* II. 204 He..took soundings all round the proposed harbourage. **1884** W. C. Smith *Kildrostan* 33 The new stonepier That was to make safe harbourage for the boats.

harbourer, -orer ('hɑːbərə(r)). [f. harbour *v.* + -er[1]. This took up sense 1 of *herberger*, harbinger, after that word came to be used chiefly in senses 2, 3.]

1. One who harbours, shelters, or entertains; an entertainer, a host. Also *fig.* Now more usually dyslogistic.

1548 Udall *Erasm. Par. Luke* viii. (R.) Of an harbourer of deuils, was he sodainly made a disciple, and scholar of Jesus. **1577** B. Googe *Heresbach's Husb.* i. (1586) 45 Eyther..harberours of Antes..or else breeders of..weedes. **1624** T. Scott *2nd Pt. Vox Populi* 28 Abettors, maintainors, concealors of their plots or haberours of their persons. **1652** J. Audley *Eng. Commw.* 29 It became the Commons to be harborers of the people. **1710** Strype *Life Abp. Grindal* an. 1582 (R.) A great nurse of pious men, and harbourer of exiles for religion. **1847** De Quincey *Sp. Mil. Nun* Wks. III. 19 Not to the Don as harbourer of his daughter. **1892** *Daily News* 25 Jan. 5/3 Unpolished granite..is a sad harbourer of soot and dust.

2. *Stag-hunting.* One whose office it is to trace a deer to its covert.

1651 Davenant *Gondibert* ii. xxix, Old Forrest Spys, the Harborers With hast approach. **1674** N. Cox *Gentl. Recreat.* (1677) 72 The Harbourer having taught his Hound to draw mute always round the outside of the Covert. **1884** Jefferies *Red Deer* vi. 104 The work of the 'harbourer' is to find where a runnable stag is in 'harbour' on the morning of the meet.

Hence **'harbouress, -oresse,** a hostess.

1624 Heywood *Gunaik.* ix. 428 Mary..was a devout harboresse,..that gladly entertained the disciples of Christ.

'harbouring, *vbl. sb.* [f. harbour *v.* + -ing[1].] The action of the verb harbour, in various senses.

a **1300** *Cursor M.* 14709 His herbering sal last in hell. **1382** Wyclif *Rom.* xii. 13 Kepinge, hospitalite, that is, herboringe of pore men. *c* **1489** Caxton *Sonnes of Aymon* i. 28 Lorde god, that wythin the holy wombe..toke thy herbowrynge. **1576** Turberv. *Venerie* 141 There is not so muche skill to be used in lodgyng of a Bucke as in harboring of a harte. **1600** J. Pory tr. *Leo's Africa* ii. 376 Places for the..docking, and harbouring of his warlike gallies. **1631** *Star Chamb. Cases* (Camden) 56 Here was an harbouring of a popish priest.

b. *attrib.*, as ***harbouring house, place.***

1535 Stewart *Cron. Scot.* (1858) I. 10 Tha saw evin at thair hand Ane herbering place. **1585** Fleetwood in Ellis *Orig. Lett.* Ser. i. II. 302 Harboringe Howses for Maisterles Men, and for such as lyve by theifte. **1605** Waymouth in *Harper's Mag.* Apr. (1883) 708/2 The most..secure harboring river that the world affordeth.

harbourless ('hɑːbəlɪs), *a.* For early forms see harbour *sb.*[1] [f. harbour *sb.*[1] + -less.]

1. Destitute of shelter, houseless, homeless.

c **1200** Ormin 6166 Himm þatt iss herrberrȝhelæs þe birrþ herberrȝhe findenn. *c* **1380** Wyclif *Wks.* (1880) 129 Þo men þat not herberwid suche pore herberweles. **1382** —— *Matt.* xxv. 35, I was herberlesse [**1526** Tindale herbrouelesse (**1534**) herbourlesse; **1535** Coverd. harbourlesse] and ȝee..herberden me. **1470–85** Malory *Arthur* vii. xxxii, For kyng Arthurs sake he shall not be herberoules. **1526** *Pilgr. Perf.* (W. de W. 1531) 153 b, Harbourynge the harboroughles. **1609** Bible (Douay) *Isa.* lviii. 7 The needie, and herberles bring in into thy house. *a* **1677** Manton *Exp. Lord's Pr. Matt.* vi. 11 We should soon be shiftless, harbourless, begging from door to door. **1829** J. Donovan *Catech. Counc. Trent* i. iv. §11 He is born in poverty; he is born as a harbourless stranger.

†**2.** Of a place: That affords no shelter. *Obs.*

1565 Golding *Ovid's Met.* i. (1593) 7, I entred by and by The harbroughlesse and cruell house. **1589** Warner *Alb. Eng.* ii. Prose Addit. (1612) 334 The harbourlesse Desart.

3. Without harbours or havens for ships.

1600 Holland *Livy* 352 (R.) The haven-lesse and harbourlesse coasts of Italie. **1795** Anna Seward *Lett.* (1811) IV. 107 A vast ocean, howling and harbourless. **1857** Ruskin *Pol. Econ. Art* i. (1868) 16 The sea roars against your harbourless cliffs—you have to build the breakwater.

†**'harboursome,** *a. Obs.* [f. harbour *sb.*[1] + -some.] Given to hospitality, hospitable.

1584 Lodge *Alarum* 79 Harden not your hearts..releeve the poore, be harboursome.

†**'harboury, 'harb(e)ry,** *sb. north. dial.* and *Sc. Obs.* Forms: 4 **herberi,** 4–6 **-ery(e, herbry(e,** 5 **herbre,** 5–6 **harbery,** 5–7 **-erie,** 6 **harbry, -rie, harbarie, -ory, -orie,** 6–7 **harbourie,** 7–9 **harboury.** [In 13th c. northern Eng. *herberi*, parallel to ME. *herberȝe, herberwe*; perh. immediately a. ON. *herbergi* (see harbour *sb.*[1]); but possibly with a suffix *-y* or *-ry*.]

1. Shelter, lodging, harbourage; = harbour *sb.*[1] 1. In quot. 1375, military encampment.

a **1300** *Cursor M.* 14135 To þis castel was iesus cald Til herberi [*Fairf.* herborwe] als i forwit tald. **1375** Barbour *Bruce* xvii. 298 Till gret lordis, ilkane syndri, Ordanit ane felde for thar herbry. *a* **1400** *Relig. Pieces fr. Thornton MS.* 28 Ne clathes to þe nakede ne herbery to þe herberles. *c* **1470** Henry *Wallace* vii. 472 Sewyn scor with him that nycht tuk herbry thar. *c* **1475** *Rauf Coilȝear* 41 He na harberie had for his behufe. **1552** Abp. Hamilton *Catech.* (1884) 244 He giffis the meit, drink, and claith and harbory. **1552** Lyndesay *Monarche* 5942 Oftymes ȝe gaue me Herberye. **1570** Levins *Manip.* 107 These..in *rye* are formed of substantives as of armour, armorie..of harbour harbourie, *hospitium*. **1609** Skene *Reg. Maj., Stat. David II*, 44 All they quha sellis bread and aill, sall receaue passengers in herberie within their houses. **1619** Sir J. Sempill *Sacrilege Handl.* 50 For harboury, No certaine dwelling place. **1862** Hislop *Prov. Scot.* 96 He that's ill o' his harboury is gude at the way-kenning.

2. A place of shelter, a lodging-place; = harbour 2.

c **1325** *Metr. Hom.* 63 Thar was na herberie To Josep and his spouse Marie. **1375** Barbour *Bruce* ii. 280 Sa till thar herbery wend sall thai. *c* **1475** *Rauf Coilȝear* 675 Thair was ane hailsum harbery. **1513** Douglas *Æneis* xi. x. 95 It is a stelling place and sovir harbry, Quhar ost in staill or enbuschment may ly. **1549** *Compl. Scot.* xv. 135 Hareyt furtht of house and herberye. **1570** Levins *Manip.* 104/29 Harborie, *hospitium*. **1583** *Leg. Bp. St. Androis* Pref. 94 in *Satir. Poems Reform.* xlv, Leaving the heavinlie harbrie whair he satt.

3. Shelter for ships; a harbour.

15.. *Ship Laws* in *Balfour's Practicks* (1754) 625 Quhair ony great presse of shippis lyis in ane harberie. **1576** in W. McIlwraith *Guide Wigtownshire* (1875) 90 All the ports, creeks, harbories, and landing-places. **1617** *Ibid.*, The burgh and harbourie of Stranraer. *c* **1640** *Sc. Acts Chas. I* (1814) V. 95 The said burgh of Pittenweyme..hes ane guid and saiff harberie.

4. *Comb.*, as ***harboury-place.***

1513 Douglas *Æneis* iii. i. 31 Ane ancyant and ane tender herbry place To Troianis. **1562** Winȝet *Cert. Tractates* i. Wks. 1888 I. 4 We..exhort the latter marinaris..to..direct it to sum mair sure harbery place.

harbrough(e, obs. ff. harbour *sb.* and *v.*

†**'harbry, 'herbery,** *v. north. dial.* and *Sc. Obs.* Forms: 4 **herbery, herbory,** 4–6 **herbri, herbry,** 6–7 **harbry, harberie.** [In 14th c. *herbery, herbry*, a northern doublet of harbour *v.*, perh. immediately a. ON. *herbergja*: cf. harboury *sb.*]

1. *trans.* To shelter, lodge: = harbour *v.* 1.

1375 Barbour *Bruce* ii. 300 And bad thaim herbery thaim that nycht. *c* **1375** *Sc. Leg. Saints, Magdalena* 218 Nane wald herbry þam in house. **14..** *Burgh Laws* c. 85 (Skene 90) Na man..aw to harbery ony strangear in his house langar þan a nycht. **1500–20** Dunbar *Poems* lxvi. 29 Nor veseit the seik, nor..Harbreit the wolsome. ? *a* **1550** *Freiris of Berwik*

239 in *Dunbar's Poems* (1893) 293, I will herbry no gaistis heir perfay. **1609** SKENE *Reg. Maj.* 129 Na man sovld harbrie strangers.

2. To anchor (a ship) in a haven or harbour.

1513 DOUGLAS *Æneis* I. vi. 159 Thi schippis and fallowschip.. Other ar herbryit in the havin. **1562** A. SCOTT *Poems* (S.T.S.) i. 205 Þat Lord may harbary so thy bairge.

3. *intr.* To take shelter, to lodge; to come into a haven, to land.

c **1475** *Rauf Coilȝear* 710 Quhen he harbreit with me. **1513** DOUGLAS *Æneis* I. viii. 81 We ar defendit to herbry on the sand.

Hence †ˈ**harbrying, herbreyng** *vbl. sb.*

1375 BARBOUR *Bruce* IX. 703 Strange men had tane herbreyng In the place.

harburrow, obs. form of HARBOUR *sb.* and *v.*

harcabuz, obs. form of HARQUEBUS.

harcarrah: see HIRCARRA.

harcelet, var. HASLET.

harcken, obs. form of HEARKEN *v.*

hard (hɑːd), *a.* (*sb.*) Forms: 1 heard, 2–4 herd, (3 ard, *Orm.* harrd), 3–7 harde, (6 heard, herde), 4– hard. [A Common Teut. adj.: OE. *heard* = OFris. *herd*, OS. *hard* (MDu. *hart(d)*, MLG. *hard, harde*, Du., LG. *hard*), OHG. *hart, harti, herti* (MHG. *hart, herte*, Ger. *hart*), ON. *harðr* (Sw. *hård*, Da. *haard*), Goth. *hardus*:—OTeut. **hardús*, corresp. to pre-Teut. **kartús* = Gr. κρατύς strong, powerful. Like other adjs. in *-us*, *hardus* became in WGer. partly a *jo*-stem *hardja-*, whence OHG. *harti, herti*; but there is no trace of this in OS. and OE.]

A. *adj.* **I.** Passively hard: resisting force, pressure, or effort of some kind.

1. a. A primary adjective expressing consistency of matter: That does not yield to blows or pressure; not easily penetrated or separated into particles; firm and resisting to the touch; solid, compact in substance and texture. The opposite of *soft*.

Beowulf (Z.) 2509 Billes ecʒ, hond and heard sweord. **971** *Blickl. Hom* 221 Mid hærenum hræʒle swiþe heardum & unwinsumum. *c* **1000** *Sax. Leechd.* II. 182 Wiþ heardum swile þæs maʒan. *c* **1175** *Lamb. Hom.* 129 Weter of þan herda flinte. *a* **1300** *Cursor M.* 6390 (Gött.) Of þe hard stan. *c* **1375** *Sc. Leg. Saints, Machor* 707 Ȝoure hartis ar herd as flynt. *c* **1400** MAUNDEV. (Roxb.) xvii. 79 Þai er so hard þat þare may na metell pulisch þam. *c* **1440** *Promp. Parv.* 227/1 Harde yn towchynge, or felynge.. *durus.* **1594** T. B. *La Primaud. Fr. Acad.* II. 148 The substance thereof is thicke, and harder then any other skinne, and therefore it is called the harde mother. **1607** E. TOPSELL *Hist. Foure-footed Beastes* 188 Prescribing him a diet; which is to drink water, and to eat hard Egs. **1638** SIR T. HERBERT *Trav.* (ed. 2) 240 Sallads, acharrs, and hard egs. **1657** R. LIGON *Barbadoes* (1673) 72 Leaves.. extreamly stiff and hard. **1674** tr. *Scheffer's Lapland* 12 The hair of both Sexes is generally black and hard. **1690** LOCKE *Hum. Und.* II. v. (1695) 54 That being generally call'd hard by us, which will put us to Pain, sooner than change Figure by the pressure of any part of our Bodies; and that, on the contrary, soft, which changes the Situation of its parts upon an easie and unpainful touch. **1764** REID *Inquiry* v. §2 Wks. I. 120/1 When the parts of a body adhere so firmly that it cannot easily be made to change its figure, we call it hard. **1860** TYNDALL *Glac.* I. ii. 10 If it did not yield in the slightest degree it would be perfectly hard. **1860** PUSEY *Min. Proph.* 541 Harder than adamant. **1962** L. DEIGHTON *Ipcress File* xxi. 143, I was loaded with anchovy,.. hard egg and salmon.

†**b.** Undigested (in the stomach). *Obs.*

1687 R. L'ESTRANGE *Answ. Diss.* 31 Neither is it.. Only the bespoken Thanks, at last, that lyes so Hard in our Author's Stomach. **1696** TRYON *Misc.* iii. 88 Suppers lie hard in the Stomach.

c. *hard fist*, an ungloved fist. Also *attrib.*

1887 *Daily News* 27 Jan. 5/5 Time was when the opening night was a velvet-glove contest. The hard-fist battle was postponed.

d. *hard iron, hard lead*: see quots.

1881 MAXWELL *Electr. & Magn.* II. 44 Iron which retains its magnetic properties when removed from the magnetic field is called Hard iron. **1881** RAYMOND *Mining Gloss., Hard lead*, lead containing certain impurities, principally antimony.

e. Of a lawn tennis court: made of asphalt or other hard material, as distinguished from a grass court.

1889 H. W. W. WILBERFORCE *Lawn Tennis* v. 19 Most people on a dry ground or a 'hard' court use brown leather or buck-skin shoes with thick, smooth, red rubber soles. **1909** *Westm. Gaz.* 30 Mar. 12/3 It is possible to place too much significance on hard-court results, grass conditions in England being so materially different. **1959** *Daily Tel.* 1 June 1/4 The French hard-court championships. **1973** G. MITCHELL *Murder of Busy Lizzie* i. 10 A sunken garden, a hard tennis court, miniature golf.

f. Of silk: retaining its natural gum. Also applied to a worker in hard silk.

a **1877** KNIGHT *Dict. Mech.* 2180/2. **1878** A. BARLOW *Hist. Weaving* 395 Before the gum has been boiled off the silk it is said to be hard silk. **1921** *Dict. Occup. Terms* (1927) §399 *Hard hand* (silk); general term for any worker engaged in treating silk while still hard, *i.e.*, before it is degummed.

g. Of porcelain: made of hard paste; *hard paste*: see PASTE *sb.* 3 b, PORCELAIN 1 note.

1814 REES *Cycl.* XXVIII. Dd 4/2 Porcelain made of the best proportions of these two substances.. is called hard porcelain. **1832** G. R. PORTER *Treat. Porcelain & Glass* iii. 43 This paste is not so cohesive or viscous as that which forms hard porcelain. **1848** H. R. FORSTER *Stowe Catal.* 6 The celebrated Porcelain of Dresden, or more properly, Meissen,.. is the most choice.. of German fabrication. The material is termed 'hard paste'. **1869** LADY C. SCHREIBER *Jrnl.* (1911) I. 44 A bird on a raised sort of foot, *possibly* hard paste English. **1879** Hard-paste [see PASTE *sb.* 3 b]. **1881** *Harper's Mag.* Feb. 368/1 There are now hard or true porcelain manufactories in New York. **1885** *Encycl. Brit.* XIX. 642/1 Bristol porcelain is of interest as being the first hard natural porcelain made in England. **1909** *Chambers's Jrnl.* Nov. 751/1 China manufactured in the eighteenth century was of two kinds—namely, 'hard' paste or true porcelain, and 'soft' paste or artificial china. **1968** *Canad. Antiques Collector* Aug. 27/1 Hard-Paste porcelain is unaffected by the file where it is 'free from the glaze'. **1968** J. ARNOLD *Shell Bk. Country Crafts* 234 Hard porcelain, already glazed, is fired at 1300°–1400°C., causing complete fusion.

h. In many specific collocations, e.g. ***hard brass, cheese, coke, cure, glaze, lights, mixture, pavior, pitch, solder, solderer, soldering, stock.*** Also ***hard coal*** = ANTHRACITE; ***hard rubber*** = EBONITE, VULCANITE 2; ***hard soap***, see SOAP *sb.* 2.

1873 E. SPON *Workshop Rec.* 1st Ser. 10 Hard Brass, for Casting.—25 parts copper, 2 zinc, 4.5 tin. **1888** *Lockwood's Dict. Mech. Engin., Hard Brass.*—(1) Brass which has not been annealed after drawing or rolling... (2) Hammered brass, and brass which contains a large proportion of tin. **1902** *Encycl. Brit.* XXVII. 355/1 A perfect Leicester is perhaps the most attractive of all the so-called 'hard' cheese. **1957** 'K. CURRAGH' *Lady into Cook* 68 Cheese Soufflé... 4 tablespoons grated cheese (Parmesan or any hard cheese). **1846** *N.Y. Morning Express* 2 Oct. 4/2 Hard Coal is a little higher owing to the increased traffic and freight. **1960** *Gloss. Coal Terms (B.S.I.)* 8 *Hard coal*, all coal of higher rank than lignite. In the U.S.A. the term is restricted to anthracite. **1979** *Sci. Amer.* Jan. 28/3 Hard coal (anthracite and the various grades of bituminous coal) and soft coal (brown coal and lignite). **1888** *Lockwood's Dict. Mech. Engin., Hard coke*, oven coke. **1907** Hard cure [see CURE *sb.*[1] 11]. **1909** *Westm. Gaz.* 9 Nov. 12/1 Fine Hard Cure Para Rubber. **1962** J. T. MARSH *Self-Smoothing Fabrics* vi. 80 Another feature of the treatment with triazones is the necessity for a 'hard cure', e.g. for 2 to 3 min. at 150°C or 1 to 2 min. at 165°C. **1814** REES *Cycl.* XXVIII. Ee 2/2 The hard and less fusible glaze of the hard porcelain, which is mostly feldspar. **1839** URE *Dict. Arts* II. 1016 The hard glaze of pipeclay ware. **1930** *Sel. Gloss. Motion Pict. Techn.* (*Acad. Motion Pict., Hollywood*), *Hard lights.* (1) Arc lights. (2) Illumination from arcs, in general. Refers to the sharp shadows cast. **1909** *Practitioner* Feb. 266 The mixture of the cocculus with beer .. was kept by brewers' druggists, and sold to brewers under the name of 'multum' or 'hard mixture'. **1904** GOODCHILD & TWENEY *Technol. & Sci. Dict.* 280/1 *Hard paviors*.., malm bricks, over-burnt and slightly blemished in colour, used for paving, coping, etc. **1879** *Encycl. Brit.* X. 100/1 If the heat is forced, and the distillation [sc. of coal-tar] continued, a large amount of 'heavy' or 'dead oils' is obtained, and the mass left in the still is 'hard pitch'. **1860** Hard rubber [see VULCANITE 2]. **1846** *Pat. Jrnl.* 1 Aug. 174/2 Hard solder. Melt together two pounds of copper and one pound of tin. **1873** E. SPON *Workshop Rec.* 1st Ser. 364, 2 parts of good silver and 1 of ordinary brass pins, well melted, is a good, useful jewellers' hard solder. *a* **1877** KNIGHT *Dict. Mech.* II. 1061/2 *Hard solder*, the solder used for uniting the more infusible metals. Spelter solder and silver solder are the two principal varieties. **1879** *Spon's Encycl. Industr. Arts* I. 324 Alloys employed for joining metals together are termed 'solders' and they are commonly divided into two classes: hard and soft solders. **1902** *Young Engineer* I. 104 The art of soldering may be divided into two distinct classes —soft soldering,.. and hard soldering, in which the solders are composed of gold, silver, copper, zinc, or brass. **1921** *Dict. Occup. Terms* (1927) §262 *Brazer, brazier; hard solderer*; joins together parts of steel, iron, brass or copper articles by brazing or hard soldering. **1836** *Penny Cycl.* V. 409/1 The bricks are now separated for sale; the hard sound stocks are the best, and are worth from 1*l.* 10*s.* to 2*l.* a thousand. **1879** *Notes Building Constr.* III. 105 Hard Stocks are overburnt bricks, sound, but considerably blemished both in form and colour. **1904** GOODCHILD & TWENEY *Technol. & Sci. Dict.* 69/2 Those [bricks] which are less overburnt are termed 'hard stock', and are useful for many building purposes.

2. Of money: In specie as opposed to paper currency. See also quot. 1882.

1706 FARQUHAR *Recruiting Officer* IV. iii, Your mother has a hundred pound in hard money, lying.. in the hands of a mercer. **1779** A. ADAMS in *J. Q. Adams' Fam. Lett.* (1876) 365 Corn is sold at four dollars, hard money, per bushel. **1825** BENTHAM *Ration. Rew.* 154 Husbandmen, like other labourers, are paid in hard money by the week. **1830** GALT *Lawrie T.* v. viii. (1849) 230 We were to get hard cash to meet a run. **1878** *N. Amer. Rev.* CXXVI. 157 The nomination of Governor Tilden, upon a hard-money resumption platform. **1882** BITHELL *Counting-ho. Dict., Hard cash*, a term used to distinguish metallic money, from ..paper money... Often popularly used to denote bank notes, and other documents of undoubted value, in contradistinction to mere book debts, or commercial rights.

3. Said of the pulse when the blood-tension is high, so that the artery feels firm and not easy to be compressed.

1727–52 CHAMBERS *Cycl.* s.v. *Pulse*, A hard Pulse signifies 1. That the membrane of the artery is drier than ordinary.. 3. That the arteries are full [etc.]. **1803** *Med. Jrnl.* IX. 508 A full if not a hard pulse. **1846** J. BAXTER *Libr. Pract. Agric.* (ed. 4) I. 440 The pulse.. is hard and full—not weak and oppressed.

4. a. Not easy to wear out or cause to give way; capable of great physical endurance and exertion; formerly, *esp.*, hardy and bold in fight. Now chiefly in sense approaching 1.

Beowulf (Z.) 342 Wlanc wedera leod word æfter spræc heard under helme. *c* **1200** ORMIN 1596 And ȝiff þin heorrte iss harrd and starrc, And stedefasst o Criste. *c* **1205** LAY. 18958 Brutael þat is a cniht swiðe herd. *c* **1380** *Sir Ferumb.* 808 Fir[umbras] was hard, & suffrede wel. *c* **1400** MAUNDEV. (1839) xxi. 253 Þei ben full harde folk and moche peyne and wo mow suffren. **1577** B. GOOGE *Heresbach's Husb.* I. (1586) 13 b, A hard fellowe, brought up from his childehood to labour. **1607** TOPSELL *Four-f. Beasts* (1658) 119 Yet is the black Hound harder and better able to endure cold, then the other which is white. **1697** DRYDEN *Virg. Georg.* I. 95 Men, a hard laborious Kind. **1857** G. LAWRENCE *Guy Liv.* 65 (Hoppe) [The horses] are both in hard condition, so it [a race] can come off in ten days. **1885** *Times* 11 Feb. 8/1 The men.. look as hard as nails and fit for anything.

†**b.** Firm, steadfast, unyielding. *lit.* and *fig.* *Obs.*

1340 HAMPOLE *Pr. Consc.* 662 A man es a tre, þat standes noght harde, Of whilk þe crop es turned donward. *a* **1661** FULLER *Worthies* (1840) III. 174 His name in Saxon soundeth a pearl, to which he answered in the preciousness of his disposition, clear and hard.

†**c.** Inured, hardened, obdurate. *Obs.*

1606 SHAKS. *Ant. & Cl.* III. xiii. 111 When we in our viciousnesse grow hard. **1607** —— *Timon* IV. iii. 269 Thy Nature, did commence in sufferance, Time Hath made thee hard in't.

5. a. Difficult to do or accomplish; not easy; full of obstacles; laborious, fatiguing, troublesome.

a **1340** HAMPOLE *Psalter* vi. 4 Ful hard it is to be turnyd enterly til þe bryghthed and þe pees of godis lyght. *c* **1440** *Promp. Parv.* 227/1 Harde yn knowynge, or warkynge, *difficilis.* **1559** W. CUNNINGHAM *Cosmogr. Glasse* 97 It is as harde, and laborus, to get the Longitude. **1611** BIBLE *Transl. Pref.* 2 So hard a thing it is to please all. **1653** WALTON *Angler* ii. 60, I see now it is a harder matter to catch a Trout then a Chub. **1711** STEELE *Spect.* No. 36 ¶8 How hard a thing it is for those to keep Silence who have the Use of Speech. **1876** MOZLEY *Univ. Serm.* iv. 90 Often.. what we must do as simply right.. is just the hardest thing to do.

b. Of the object of an action. Const. *inf.*, or *of, in*, with sb. expressing the action.

c **1200** ORMIN 6326 And tatt iss swiþe strang and harrd To forþenn her onn eorþe. *a* **1300** *Cursor M.* 16992 (Gött). His pine was hardir [*Cott.* herder] for to drei. *a* **1420** HOCCLEVE *De Reg. Princ.* 825 But paiement is harde to gete now adayes. **1513** MORE in Grafton *Chron.* (1568) II. 767 Hard it is to be wrested out. **1577** B. GOOGE *Heresbach's Husb.* III. (1586) 143 Other remedies more harde to bee com by. **1599** H. BUTTES *Dyets drie Dinner* E b, Chestnuts.. are hard of digestion. **1653** WALTON *Angler* viii. 168 He is a very subtle fish and hard to be caught. **1768** STERNE *Sent. Journ.* (1778) II. 112 (*Case of Consc.*), I was hard to please. **1833** HT. MARTINEAU *Tale of Tyne* iii. 64 It is a hard thing to manage. **1873** BURTON *Hist. Scot.* V. lxii. 382 She was hard to be entreated in this affair.

c. Of the subject of an action: Not easily able or capable; having difficulty in doing something. Const. *inf.*, or *of* with sb. denoting action or faculty. *Obs.* exc. in ***hard of hearing***.

c **1300** *Cursor M.* 9326 Men sua herd of vnder-stand. *a* **1400** *Serm. agst. Miracle-plays* in *Rel. Ant.* II. 50 Yvil and hard of bileve. *a* **1533** LD. BERNERS *Huon* cxxvi. 464 We ar hard of byleue that this shall be. **1564** *Child Marriages, etc.* (E.E.T.S.) 134 The testatrixe was hard of hearinge. **1579–80** NORTH *Plutarch* (1612) 179 Of slow capacitie, and hard to learn and conceive. **1726–7** SWIFT *Gulliver* III. x, He.. found the natives.. very hard to believe that the fact was possible. **1858** DICKENS *Lett.* (1880) II. 55, I have been very hard to sleep too, and last night I was all but sleepless. **1861** —— *Gt. Expect.* xxxvii, I am hard of hearing. **1871** B. TAYLOR *Faust* (1875) II. II. iii. 148 Wise words in hard ears are but lifeless lore. **1950** *Lancet* 11 Nov. 532/2 Practical courses.. on audiometry and hearing-aids, hard-of-hearing children, [etc.]. **1968** *Brit. Med. Bull.* XXIV. 256/2 There may be a real problem in distinguishing the hard of hearing from those with organic intellectual impairment or autism.

d. (*to do something*) ***the hard way***: (to do it) by one's own unaided efforts, through bitter experience, or by the most difficult method.

1931 D. RUNYON *Guys & Dolls* (1932) xiii. 276 'Charley,' he says, 'do you make it the hard way?' **1938** *Collier's* 2 Apr. 16 (*title*) The hard way. **1945** N. L. MCCLUNG *Stream runs Fast* ix. 80 You learned everything the hard way. **1951** 'N. SHUTE' *Round Bend* 1, I came into aviation the hard way. **1954** M. CROFT *Spare Rod* I. ii. 12 I'm starting you off the hard way. **1958** *Observer* 26 Jan. 15/8 Making a movie the hard way spiritually and intellectually is the thing that really matters. **1958** *Listener* 28 Aug. 292/1 Unqualified men who come up what used to be called 'the hard way'. **1959** *Times Lit. Suppl.* 4 Dec. 701/4 The Japanese failed to recognize it in the 1930s, and learnt it the hard way. **1971** D. LEES *Rainbow Conspiracy* ix. 135 In the end I nearly found the reservoir the hard way.

6. a. Difficult to penetrate with the understanding; not easy to understand or explain.

[**1382** WYCLIF *2 Pet.* iii. 16 Epistlis.. in whiche ben summe harde thinges in vndirstondinge.] *c* **1450** tr. *De Imitatione* III. xlviii. 118 Knouleche of many harde questiouns. **1535** COVERDALE *Ps.* lxxii[i]. 16 Then thought I to vnderstonde this, but it was to harde for me. **1663** F. HAWKINS *Youth's Behav.* 73 Dictionary.. a Lexicon, a Book wherein hard words and names are mentioned and unfolded. **1720** SWIFT *Lett. Yng. Clergym.* Wks. 1841 II. 201 Obscure terms, which by the women are called hard words. **1888** BURGON *Lives 12 Gd. Men* II. xii. 364 To ask hard questions.

b. ***hard word***, used *dial.* in various senses, e.g. pass-word, abuse, scandal, marriage proposal, refusal. Phr. ***to put the hard word on*** (someone) *Austral.* and *N.Z. slang*, to ask for a favour or a loan, esp. to ask a woman for her favours.

1831 S. LOVER *Legends & Stories of Ireland* 1st Ser. p. xxiii, *Hard word*, hint. **1843** W. CARLETON *Traits & Stories Irish Peasantry* I. 78 So I gives Jack the hard word [*sc.* pass-word]. **1891** B. STOKER *Snake's Pass* xvi, He would send the hard word round the country about me and my leman. **1899**

Somerville & 'Ross' *Exper. Irish R.M.* vi. 123, I had said what is called in Ireland 'the hard word' [*sc.* marriage proposal]. 1905 *Eng. Dial. Dict.* III. 63/1 Ah assed him for a shillin', an' he gev mi t'hard-word.

1919 W. H. Downing *Digger Dial.* 28 *Hard word*, an outrageous demand. (Put the hard word on.) 1927 J. Devanny *Old Savage* 144 He thinks she is putting the 'hard word' on him. 1943 *Coast to Coast 1942* 215 A tradesman notorious for putting the hard word on his typists. 1947 I. Douglas *Opportunity in Australia* 89 *Put the hard word on*, to cadge for a loan or favour. 1959 Baker *Drum* iv. 38 Establishing a suitable vantage point to 'put the hard word on' her. 1960 D. Lockwood *Fair Dinkum* ii. 11 He didn't put the hard word on me once, and my credit is still good. 1969 *N.Z. News* 28 May 1/1 (*headline*) Pilots put hard word on airline. 1970 *N.Z. Listener* 21 Dec. 8/3 'Don't you think hitching's a little dangerous for females?' 'Well, some sheilas I know have had the hard word put on them.'

7. Difficult to deal with, manage, control, or resist. † ***too hard for***, too much for, more than (one) can manage. ***hard case***, a difficult case to treat or deal with; a person that cannot be reclaimed, a hardened criminal, a 'bad lot'. orig. *U.S.* In Australia and New Zealand, an amusing or eccentric but adventurous person, a 'character'; also called ***hard doer*** (see doer 5), ***hard shot, hard thing***. See also sense 11 below.

1588 Shaks. *L.L.L.* ii. i. 258 *Boy.* What then, do you see? *Lad.* 2. I, our way to be gone. *Boy.* You are too hard for me. 1605 Verstegan *Dec. Intell.* ii. (1628) 31 The Hollander was too hard for the Frenchman, and threw him downe. 1726 Shelvocke *Voy. round World* (1757) 330 If we found the enemy too hard for us. 1750 Chesterf. *Lett.* (1792) III. ccxl. 101 A man who is master of his matter will with inferior parts be too hard..for a man of better parts who knows his subject but superficially. 1836 W. T. Porter *Quarter Race Kentucky* (1854) 38 A 'hard case' called Emanuel Allen. 1842 *Life in West* 323 A canoe full of 'hard cases' (vagabonds) had passed up the river. 1848 Ruxton *Life in Far West* 71 (Farmer) La Bonte had lost all traces of civilised humanity, and might justly claim to be considered as hard a case as any of the mountaineers then present. *a* 1891 Stevenson (Dixon), He was a fellow-clerk of mine, and a hard case. 1920 *Punch* 7 Apr. 266/1 The hard-case mates a-bawlin'. 1928 *Sunday Express* 8 Jan. 4 With memories that go back to the days of 'cracker-hash', 'lobscouse', and hard-case, blue-nose, Nova Scotia mates. 1928 *Sunday Dispatch* 29 July 2 Half a dozen particularly hard-case units of the Flying Squad. *a* 1936 Kipling *Something of Myself* (1937) ii. 22 It [*sc.* a school]..had been made up..by drafts from Haileybury..and, I think, a percentage of 'hard cases' from other schools.

1896 H. Lawson *In Days when World was Wide* (1900) 197 Cause of half the fun that's started—'Hard-case' Dan—Isn't like a broken-hearted, Ruined man. 1896 —— *While Billy Boils* in *Wks.* (1948) 54 Steelman was a hard case... There was no shaking off Steelman. 1900 —— *Over Sliprails* in *Ibid.* 273 After dinner a humorous old hard case mysteriously took us aside. 1918 *Chrons. N.Z.E.F.* 7 June 204 Without a smoke he was a hard thing. 1938 'R. Hyde' *Nor Years Condemn* ix. 184 Fred's a hard shot. 1940 F. Sargeson *Man & Wife* (1944) 64 He was the hardest case bloke you ever came across. 1943 —— in *Penguin New Writing* XVII. 66 He looked a bit of a hard-shot. 1950 'A. P. Gaskell' in *Landfall* IV. 18 Cliff was a hard case.

b. Of facts: incapable of being denied or explained away, 'stubborn'.

1887 *Graphic* 29 Jan. 123/1 Hard Facts. 1906 *Daily Chron.* 11 Apr. 3/4 A few more hard-fact letters and less of this soft imagining might have made the body of the book as interesting as the appendix. 1929 Chesterton *Poet & Lunatic* iv, Thank God for hard stones; thank God for hard facts. 1956 A. H. Compton *Atomic Quest* 311 The hard fact is that war, like business, reduces to a question of gain versus cost. 1973 *Daily Tel.* 8 May 7/2 We have been unable to substantiate the allegations. We have few hard facts to go on but are continuing our investigations.

c. Of news or information: factual, real, objective, reliable, substantiated.

1938 E. Waugh *Scoop* ii. i. 117 There isn't any hard news. 1948 *Newsweek* 16 Aug. 51/1 The bulk of the broadcast time is given over to so-called 'hard news'—that is, straight newscasts of what is going on in the world and in the United States. 1956 A. J. Ayer *Probl. of Knowl.* iii. 92 Those who have sought to erect an edifice of knowledge on the basis of what Bertrand Russell..has called 'hard data', have commonly agreed that such data were yielded by sense-perception. 1958 *Listener* 16 Aug. 239/2 This would yield some interesting and some relatively 'hard' evidence. 1958 *Economist* 13 Sept. 815/2 Two hard items for the agenda. 1959 Duke of Bedford *Silver-Plated Spoon* ix. 185 Newspapers do not encourage telephone calls to the other side of the world unless they are in possession of pretty hard information. 1963 *Ann. Reg. 1962* 520 Upon receiving the first preliminary hard information of this nature..I directed that our surveillance be stepped up.

8. a. Of a nature or character not easily impressed or moved; obdurate; unfeeling, callous; hard-hearted.

Beowulf (Z.) 166 Atol angengea..heardra hynða. 971 *Blickl. Hom.* 57 Manige men beoð heardre heortan. *c* 1250 *Gen. & Ex.* 3061 Ðis weder is softe, And ðis king hard, And brekeð him eft ðat forward. *c* 1386 Chaucer *Man of Law's T.* 759 Why wil thyn harde fader han thee split? *c* 1440 *Promp. Parv.* 227/2 Harde demare, or domys mann wytheowte mercy. 1568 Grafton *Chron.* II. 282 There was not so heard a hart, if they had seene them but would have had pittie upon them. 1697 Dryden *Virg. Georg.* iv. 466 So wretched is thy Son, so hard a Mother thou. 1822 Lamb *Elia* Ser. ii. *Detached Th. on Bks.*, With his hard eyes, casting envious looks at them all the while. 1864 Tennyson *Grandmother* 17 You think I am hard and cold.

†**b.** ***to die hard***: to die obdurate or impenitent. *Obs.* See also hard *adv.* 3, die *v.*[1] 3.

1709 *Tatler* No. 63 ¶5 Most Writers..seem to place a peculiar Vanity in dying hard. 1712 Swift *Let. Dr. King* 8 Dec. (T.), He died hard, as their term of art is here, to express the woeful state of men, who discover no religion at their death. 1730–46 Thomson *Autumn* 490 Who saw the villain..dying hard, Without complaint. 1796 Grose *Dict. Vulgar T.* s.v. *Dye hard* or *game*, To dye hard, is to shew no signs of fear or contrition at the gallows.

9. Not easily moved to part with money; stingy, niggardly, 'close'. Cf. hard-fisted.

1362 Langl. *P. Pl.* A. i. 165. 1393 *Ibid.* C. ii. 188 Aren none hardur ne hongryour þan men of holy churche, Auerouse & euil-willed whanne thei ben auaunsed. 1530 Palsgr. 314/2 Harde, as one that is a nygarde, *chiche.* 1568 Grafton *Chron.* II. 49 He was free and liberall to straungers, and heard and holdyng from his familiers and servaunts. 1849 Macaulay *Hist. Eng.* II. 282 Many wondered that a man..could be so hard and niggardly in all pecuniary dealings.

10. Not easily moved by sentiment; of a practical, shrewdly intelligent character. See also hardhead.

1747 *Col. Rec. Pennsylv.* V. 147 The French have hard heads. 1824 R. B. Peake *Americans Abroad* i. i. (Farmer), We Americans have got hard heads. 1853 Lytton *My Novel* ii. iv, My books don't tell me that it is a good heart that gets on in the world: it is a hard head.

II. Actively hard: pressing severely; severe.

11. a. Difficult to bear or endure; not easy to suffer, put up with, or consent to; pressing severely; severe, rigorous, oppressive, cruel. ***hard case***: applied to a sailing-ship on which conditions are rough; ***hard lines***: see line *sb.*[2] 6; ***hard luck***: see luck *sb.* 1; also *attrib.*; ***hard-lying money***: corruption of ***hard line money*** (see line *sb.*[2] 6); hence ***hard lyer***; (joc.) ***hard-liar***.

971 *Blickl. Hom.* 49 þæt he þonne..onfo þæs heardestan þeowdomes. *Ibid.* 95 þonne biþ þam eft heard dom ȝeteod. *c* 1175 *Lamb. Hom.* 49 þurh þreo herde weies. *c* 1200 Ormin 1442 Harrd and hefiȝ þine inoh. 1297 R. Glouc. (1724) 213 In such ard cas as hym vel. 1340 Hampole *Pr. Consc.* 4539 And do þam to hard dede at þe last. *c* 1477 Caxton *Jason* 77 b, [He] had grete sorow in his corage whan he was aduertised of these harde tydinges. 1576 Fleming *Panopl. Epist.* 39 It was his hard lucke and curssed chaunce. 1600 J. Pory tr. *Leo's Africa* ii. 102 Fearing hard measure, if they should be carried unto the king. 1751 Jortin *Serm.* (1771) II. ii. 29 We think our position particularly hard. 1825 Hone *Every-day Bk.* I. 218 It is a little hard, indeed, that I should have these fine compliments and severe reproaches at the same time. 1893 Selous *Trav. S.E. Africa* 109 The life these people lead is a hard one. 1920 *Blackw. Mag.* Mar. 322/2 The mate of a Yankee hard-case. 1924 R. Clements *Gipsy of Horn* vi. 111 He signed away as Third Mate on a hard-case Yankee barque. 1900 Ade *More Fables in Slang* (1902) 18 Her Hard-luck story. 1906 B. von Hutten *What became of Pam* ii. viii, Learning..something of..his hard-luck story. 1919 H. L. Wilson *Ma Pettengill* iv. 109 She said it [*sc.* the letter] would tell a new hard-luck tale for non-payment of a note. *Ibid.* 134 It was another hard-luck letter. 1959 P. H. Johnson *Humbler Creation* v. 32 The hard-luck stories of all parsons whose luck would never get any better. 1916 'Taffrail' *Pincher Martin* iv. 56 'They ain't so bad,' he murmured. 'You gits a tanner a day, 'ard lyers in 'em.' 1920 —— *H.M.S. Anonymous* xv. 291 What d'you think the government pay us one and six hard lyers for? Twenty seven extra bloomin' pounds per annum. 1916 —— *Pincher Martin* iv. 56 Men serving in destroyers receive sixpence a day extra pay. It is known as 'hard-lying money'. 1925 Fraser & Gibbons *Soldier & Sailor Words, Hard-lying money*, the extra allowance granted to officers and men for service in destroyers and torpedo boats, and as compensation for wear and tear of uniform and clothing, etc. Extended in the War to the crews of motor launches and other auxiliary small craft. (Abolished in 1923.) 1927 *Daily Express* 10 Oct. 3 Sometimes, in recompense for discomforts endured, the crews of drifters draw what is termed 'hard-lying money' (those who receive this are naturally known as 'hard liars').

b. Of time.

1390 Gower *Conf.* I. 312 It hath ben sene and felt full ofte, The harde time after the softe. *c* 1477 Caxton *Jason* 45 b, The time must be taken as hit cometh, is hit hard or softe. 1705 Hickeringill *Priest-cr.* ii. viii. 73 Money is Money, a very necessary Commodity in Hard times. 1812 Shelley *Address* Prose Wks. 1888 I. 228 There are always bad men who take advantage of hard times. 1861 Hughes *Tom Brown at Oxf.* viii, They had a hard time of it too, for my father had to go on half-pay. 1890 Lecky *Eng. in 18th C.* VII. 14, 1793 was eminently a 'hard year', and great numbers of labourers were out of employment.

c. Of the weather, etc.: Severe, rigorous, violent. In ***hard winter*** there is often present a notion of the frozen state of the ground, etc.

1552 Huloet, Harde winter or verye colde, *sæuissima Hyems.* 1568 Grafton *Chron.* II. 37 A blasyng starre, whereupon folowed an hard Wynter. 1679–88 *Secr. Serv. Money Chas. & Jas.* (Camden) 81 He said Majesties bounty and charity..in respect of the extreme hard weather. 1686 *Lond. Gaz.* No. 2199/4 With a hard gale or Wind at S.S.W. *a* 1691 Boyle *Hist. Air* (1692) 115 Very hard frost. Thames frozen. Carts went over. 1697 Dampier *Voy.* I. 16 We had extraordinary hard Rain. 1700 S. L. tr. *Fryke's Voy. E. Ind.* 299 A very hard Storm fell upon us in the way. 1755 Magens *Insurances* II. 98 Any Thing that falls over board [or] is spoiled or damaged by hard Weather. 1769 Falconer *Dict. Marine* (1789) Ss iv b, It is called a storm or hard gale. 1814 *Sporting Mag.* LXIV. 62 To catch..wood-pigeons in hard weather. 1884 *Nonconf. & Indep.* 16 Oct. 1006/1 We shall have a 'hard' winter. 1890 Boldrewood *Col. Reformer* (1891) 160 A grizzled, hard-weather-looking old sea-dog.

12. a. Of persons: Harsh or severe in dealing with any one. Const. (†*to*), *on, upon.*

c 1000 *Ags. Gosp.* Matt. xxv. 24 Hlaford ic wat þæt ðu eart heard mann, þu ripst þær ðu ne seowe. *a* 1123 *O.E. Chron.* an. 1043 Heo wæs þan cynge hire suna swiðe heard. *a* 1300 *Cursor M.* 28743 Sin crist is buxum to vnbind, Qui sal man preist ouer hard find. *c* 1450 tr. *De Imitatione*, i. xiii. 14 Be not harde to him þat is tempted, ȝeue him comfort. 1613 Purchas *Pilgrimage* (1614) 84 Heavie and hard neighbours to the Church in Judea. 1682 *Lond. Gaz.* No. 1737/2 The French..are very hard upon the Tenants to make them pay their Rents, with all their Arrears. 1738 Swift *Pol. Convers.* 19 Colonel, why so hard upon poor Miss? 1862 Trollope *Orley F.* xiv, Felix began to perceive that he had been too hard upon her.

b. Of things, actions, etc.: Characterized by harshness or severity; unfeeling, cruel, harsh, rough.

a 1000 *Crist* 1443 Ic þæt sar for ðe..ȝeþolade hosp and heard cwide. 1393 Langl. *P. Pl.* C. i. 122 God shal take veniaunce..Wel harder and grettere..þan euere he dude on ophni. 1435 Misyn *Fire of Love* i. xii. 26 þai fed me comonly or on hard maner. 1552 Huloet, Hard fare, *aridus uictus.* 1593 Shaks. *2 Hen. VI*, iv. ix. 45 He is fierce, and cannot brooke hard language. 1663 Butler *Hud.* i. i. 3 When hard words, jealousies, and fears Set folks together by the ears. 1784 Cowper *Task* i. 123 Hard fare! but such as boyish appetite Disdains not. 1864 Burton *Scot Abr.* I. iii. 109 All was rough, hard, and ungenial. 1887 R. Garnett *Carlyle* viii. 135 She almost invariably took a hard view of persons and things.

c. Strict, without abatement or concession.

1612 Earl of Dorset *Lett.* in *Crt. & Times Jas. I*, 210 He will have but a hard bargain of it. 1647 Ward *Simp. Cobler* 30 They never complain of me for giving them hard measure, or under-weight. 1870 R. B. Brough *Marston Lynch* xvii. 163 A man who had possessed the power to drive a hard bargain. 1968 *Times* 26 Aug. 7/2 The House of Commons today must take a hard look at British defence policy.

d. *Pol.* Designating a strict or hard-line faction at the wing of a political party or of the political spectrum, esp. as ***hard left, right***. Cf. hardshell *sb.* 3, loony *a.* 2; contr. with soft *a.* 11 c.

1975 *New Left Rev.* Nov.–Dec. 69 For the foreseeable future, then, the hard right has the initiative in Turkey. 1976 *National Observer* (U.S.) 17 Apr. 5/5 It is a fact that the hard-left liberals don't like him. 1977 [see soft *a.* 11 c]. 1985 *Mail on Sunday* 3 Mar. 10/5 Intelligence chiefs believe the explosion..was the work of the new hard-Left of the outlawed Irish National Liberation Army. 1986 *Tribune* 12 Sept. 7/5 On some recent nec votes she has been in a hard Right minority of just two with Ken Cure.

III. In various transferred senses.

13. Having the aspect, sound, etc., of what is physically hard (sense 1); harsh or unpleasant to the eye or ear, or to the æsthetic faculty.

1513 [implied in hard-favoured]. 1599 Shaks. *Much Ado* v. ii. 38, I can finde out no rime..for scorne, [but] horne, a hard rime. 1622 Middleton & Rowley *Changeling* ii. ii, When we're us'd to a hard face, 'tis not so unpleasing. 1682 Grew *Anat. Plants* Pref., Some of the Plates..are a little hard and stiff. *a* 1700 Dryden (J.), His diction is hard, his figures too bold, and his tropes..insufferably strained. *a* 1744 Pope *Answ. to Mrs. Howe* 6 A Virgin hard of Feature. 1754 Eeles in *Phil. Trans.* XLIX. 142 And form what the sailors call a hard dry sky. 1830 Capt. T. Hamilton *C. Thornton* (1845) 47 A stiff and raw-boned looking matron, hard in feature. 1854 Hawthorne *Eng. Note-Bks.* (1879) II. 170 A generally hard outline of country. 1872 Tennyson *Lynette* 1083 Then that other blew A hard and deadly note upon the horn. 1876 Humphreys *Coin Coll. Man.* xxv. 363 The hard and peculiar style of the period. 1882 Besant *Revolt of Man* iii. (1883) 72 It was a hard face even when she smiled. 1894 *Brit. Jrnl. Photog.* XLI. 51 Very dense, or as we should call it now, *hard*, negatives.

14. a. Applied to water holding in solution mineral, especially calcareous, salts, which decompose soap and render the water unfit for washing purposes.

1660 F. Brooke tr. *Le Blanc's Trav.* 18 The water was sharp and hard, but nothing brackish. 1756 C. Lucas *Ess. Waters* I. 83 Hard waters are the best for builders and plasterers. 1805 W. Saunders *Min. Waters* 305 A very hard water, curdling soap, and possessing a large portion of selenite and earthy carbonats. 1849 Claridge *Cold Water-cure* (1869) 85 Hard water makes the skin rough, but soft water, on the contrary, renders it smooth.

b. Of liquor: Harsh or sharp to the taste; acid; sour from being stale. Now *dial.* or *slang.*

1581 Pettie tr. *Guazzo's Civ. Conv.* ii. (1586) 73 Neither hard wine is pleasant to the tast, neither haughtie behaviour acceptable in companie. 1592 Greene *Disc. Coosnage* iii. 20 Hee tastes the other pinte of wine..it dranke somewhat harde. *a* 1700 B. E. *Dict. Cant. Crew, Hard Drink*, that is very Stale, or beginning to Sower. 1833 *Drakard's Stamford News* 1 Oct., To prevent beer from getting acetous, or what is called hard.

c. Intoxicating, spirituous, 'strong'. *colloq.* orig. *U.S.*

1789 F. Asbury *Jrnl.* (1821) II. 304 [A] drink made of one quart of hard cider, [etc.]. 1810 M. L. Weems *Lett.* (1929) III. 13 What could possibly have kept me from hard drink? 1840 *Congress. Globe* 13 Feb. 197/3 He had heard..the same arguments preached nine hundred and ninety-nine times over a barrel of hard cider. 1848 *Ibid.* 27 Apr. 688/2 They had charged him [*sc.* President Harrison] with drinking hard cider. 1857 *Spirit of Times* 3 Jan. 281/1 It was not infrequent, as late as the hard-cider campaign of 1840,.. that [etc.]. 1861 H. W. Harper *Lett. from N.Z.* (1914) iv. 67 Order up some hard stuff to give them something to drink. 1879 *Boston Trav.* 20 Sept. (Cent.), Before the court..for selling hard liquor, when he had only a licence for selling ale. 1884 J. Purves in *Gd. Words* May 330/2 Two or three kegs of the 'hard stuff'. 1888 *Pall Mall G.* 17 Sept. 7/2 The consumption of 'hard liquors'.. has steadily decreased. 1946 F. Sargeson *That Summer* 35 They all started on hard stuff and went on to beer later. 1964 C. Willock *Enormous Zoo* ix. 169 With a hard drink in the hand the day lengthens and softens. 1965 O. A. Mendelsohn *Dict. Drink* 90 *Cider*,.. .. If fermented and therefore alcoholic, the term hard cider is frequently used.

d. Of oil (see soft *a.* 23 d).

e. Of drugs: dangerous and habit-forming, addictive, e.g. heroin and cocaine.

1955 *Amer. Speech* XXX. 87 *Hard stuff*, opium. 1965 'MALCOLM X' *Autobiogr.* vii. 110 As the pros did, I too would key myself to pull these jobs by my first use of hard dope. I began with .. sniffing cocaine. 1967 *Listener* 10 Aug. 169/2 Nothing on earth would persuade me to try LSD or the hard drugs. 1967 *Times* 7 Oct. 5/3 The Court said that anyone supplying a child with a hard drug was doing a terrible deed which called for grave punishment... The Court refused an application .. for leave to appeal against .. conviction .. of supplying a dangerous drug (six tablets of heroin). 1969 J. GARDNER *Compl. State of Death* ix. 167 You start on pot and straight off you're mixing with people who've graduated to the hard stuff.

f. Of nuclear sites and structures (see quot. 1960). Also applied to nuclear missiles.

1958 R. D. BOWERS in *Air Univ. Q. Rev.* X. 91 It would be useful to know how the cost of a hard base compares to that of a soft base if they have equal measures of merit (cost per surviving missile). 1960 *Amer. Speech* XXXV. 302 The adjective *hard* is now used in certain parts of the Air Force .. to refer to the resistance to atomic explosions of airfields, missile launching pads, command posts, and other structures, their resistance coming from underground location or toughness of structure or both. 1962 *Listener* 29 Mar. 547/2 The American development of missiles such as Minuteman which can be fired from strongly protected pits in the ground—the so-called hard missile sites—as well as the Polaris submarines. 1965 H. KAHN *On Escalation* vii. 136 Let the reader assume .. that both the Soviet Union and the United States have 10,000 hard and dispersed missiles on each side.

15. *Comm.* Of prices: High and unyielding; stiff. Said also of the market, etc.

1838 D. WEBSTER *Private Corr.* (1856) II. 37 Money is very hard, all along the coast, from here [i.e. Washington, D.C.] North. 1882 *Pall Mall G.* 1 July 5/2 Yesterday's Money Market was extremely hard. 1892 *Daily News* 11 Feb. 2/5 In American cotton .. prices are reported harder.

16. *Phonetics.* Popularly applied to certain consonants: **a.** to the letters *c*, *g*, when they have their original 'back' or guttural sounds (k, g), as distinguished from the palatal and sibilant sounds (tʃ, ts, s, dʒ, etc.) into which they have passed in various languages; **b.** to the breath consonants (k, t, p, and sometimes x, ʃ, s, θ, f) as opposed to the corresponding voiced consonants (g, d, b; ɣ, ʒ, z, ð, v).

[*c* 1620 A. HUME *Brit. Tongue* vii. (1870) 17 Quhen the hammer and the stiddie are ane, the difference is in the hardnes and softnes of the tuich; as may be seen in ca and ga, ta and da.] 1775 J. WALKER *Dict.* Introd. 13 Shewing that the preceding *c* and *g* in these words are soft, which might possibly be mistaken, and pronounced hard, if written *changable, peacable*. 1828 WEBSTER *Dict.* Introd. 36 When *a* is preceded by the gutturals hard *g* or *c*. 1846 WORCESTER *Dict.* Introd. 15 *G* before *e*, *i*, and *y*, is sometimes hard and sometimes soft. *Ibid.* 19 *Th* .. has two sounds; one, hard, sharp, or aspirate, as in *thin* .. the other flat, soft, or vocal, as in .. *then, breathe*. 1877 PAPILLON *Man. Comp. Philol.* iii. (ed. 2) 32 Consonants .. *a. Tenues* .. also called 'sharp', 'hard', 'surd'.

17. *Physics.* **a.** Of radiation: having great penetrating power.

1902 *Encycl. Brit.* XXVIII. 52/2 If the exhaustion of the bulb is carried further, so that there is a considerable increase in the potential difference between the cathode and anode and therefore in the velocity of the cathode rays, the Röntgen rays have much greater penetrating power and are often called 'hard rays'. 1938 R. W. LAWSON tr. *Hevesy & Paneth's Man. Radioactivity* (ed. 2) iv. 49 The wave-length of the 'hard' γ-radiation is so small that even crystals are of no avail here as diffraction gratings. 1940 *Nature* 8 June 903/2 (*title*) Absorption of hard cosmic rays and mesotron decay. 1943 *Electronic Engin.* XVI. 54 Short wave, or hard, radiation penetrates more deeply into the tissues. 1955 *Gloss. Terms Radiology* (*B.S.I.*) 12 *Hard radiation*, a term used to describe qualitatively the more penetrating types of X-rays, beta rays and gamma rays.

b. Of a vacuum: complete or almost complete. Of a vacuum tube or thermionic valve: containing a high vacuum.

1899 W. CROOKES in *Rep. Brit. Assoc. Adv. Sci. 1898* 23 Röntgen suggests a convenient phraseology; he calls a low vacuum tube, which does not emit the highly penetrating rays, a 'soft' tube, and a tube in which the exhaustion has been pushed to an extreme degree, in which the highly penetrating rays predominate, a 'hard' tube. 1919 R. STANLEY *Textbk. Wireless Telegr.* (ed. 2) II. 22 With a hard vacuum none of these varying effects are present... The hard valve, made by Langmuir, was called by him a Pliotron. 1923 E. W. MARCHANT *Radio Telegr.* v. 61 *Hard Valves.*—The only way in which this can be achieved is by exhausting the air so completely from the bulb that there is nothing but a pure electron discharge. 1931 DUNCAN & DREW *Radio Telegr. & Telephony* (ed. 2) 214 The degree of vacuum in the tube would change and some tubes became *soft* (having less vacuum) while others became *hard* (having a higher vacuum, with little or no gas present). 1940 *Chambers's Techn. Dict.* 403/1 *Hard tube*, a high-vacuum discharge tube. 1943 *Gloss. Terms Telecomm.* (*B.S.I.*) 28 *Hard vacuum tube*, a vacuum tube evacuated to such a degree that its electrical characteristics are essentially unaffected by ionisation of included gas. 1953 *Electronic Engin.* XXV. 241 A blocking oscillator was first used as a hard-valve time-base in 1923. 1962 F. I. ORDWAY et al. *Basic Astronautics* xi. 449 The hard-vacuum condition of space.

IV. Intense, strenuous, violent.

†**18.** Intense in force or degree; strong, deep, profound. *Obs.*

971 *Blickl. Hom.* 59 On þone heardestan stenc. *c* 1489 CAXTON *Sonnes of Aymon* xiv. 323 Thei fell in to so harde a slepe that thei forgate richard. 1535 COVERDALE *Gen.* ii. 21 The Lorde God caused an herde slepe to fall vpon man. 1807 PIKE *Sources Mississ.* (1810) 30 Passed some large islands and remarkably hard ripples.

19. a. Carried on or performed with great exertion, energy, or persistence; unremitting; (of study) close; involving great labour or effort; vehement, vigorous, violent. Qualifying a noun of action, and akin to HARD *adv.*

Beowulf (Z.) 577 No ic on niht ȝefræȝn .. heardran feohtan. *a* 1300 *Cursor M.* 5527 Wit herd werckes þai held þam in. *c* 1450 *Merlin* 446 Full harde and felon was the bateile ther. 1548 HALL *Chron., Hen. VI*, 87b, A sore conflict and an hard encountre. 1596 SHAKS. *1 Hen. IV*, IV. iii. 23 Their courage with hard labour tame and dull. 1600 HOLLAND *Livy* L. Argt. 1239 Hard hold [*magno certamine*] there was about him. 1629 MASSINGER *Picture* II. ii, A day's hard riding. 1714 MANDEVILLE *Fab. Bees* (1733) II. 417 Many .. kill themselves with hard drinking. 1727 SWIFT *Gulliver* III. iv. 200, I had obtained by hard study a good degree of knowledge. 1760–72 tr. *Juan & Ulloa's Voy.* (ed. 3) I. 29 Reduced to have recourse to mean and hard labour for subsistence. 1821 CLARE *Vill. Ministr.* II. 55 My hard day's work is done. 1855 MACAULAY *Hist. Eng.* IV. 445 The fight must be long and hard. 1884 HON. I. BLIGH in *Lilywhite's Cricket Ann.* 3 A fine specimen of hard hitting.

b. ***hard labour***: labour imposed upon certain classes of criminals during their term of imprisonment; see quot. 1865. ***hard swearing***, swearing (as a witness) persistently and tenaciously to one effect regardless of perjury; hence often a euphemism for 'perjury'.

1853 *Act 16 & 17 Vict.* c. 99 §6 Every Person .. ordered to be kept in Penal Servitude .. may during such term be kept to Hard Labour. 1865 *Act 28 & 29 Vict.* c. 126 §19 Hard Labour for the Purposes of this Act shall be of Two Classes, consisting, 1st, of Work at the Tread Wheel, Shot Drill, Crank, Capstan, Stone-breaking, or .. other like Description of hard bodily labour. 1887 *Spectator* 20 Aug. 1114 There is not, we fancy, much false-swearing; but there is probably a considerable amount of hard-swearing. 1892 T. SECCOMBE in *Dict. Nat. Biog.* XXIX. 37/1 The hard swearing of Oates and Bedloe .. overcame any scruples on the part of the jury. 1896 *Westm. Gaz.* 29 July 5/1 The term 'hard' now has no particular meaning except as applied to the kind of labour called 'first-class hard labour'. 1905 *Daily Chron.* 10 July 5/2 Hard-labour convicts. *Ibid.* 6 Nov. 5/6 Hard-labour prisoners. 1908 *Ibid.* 7 Jan. 4/6.

20. Acting or carrying on one's work with great energy, exertion, or persistence; unremitting, persistent. Qualifying an agent-noun: cf. prec. sense.

1663 *Flagellum, or O. Cromwell* (ed. 2) 5 A hard Student for a week or two. 1747 tr. *Le Blanc's Lett. Eng. & Fr. Nations* I. 327 The Goths .. are said to have been hard-drinkers. 1813 LD. ELDON *Sp. in Parl.* 18 May in *Examiner* 24 May 326/1 For him .. and others who were hard labourers. 1859 KINGSLEY *Misc.* (1860) I. 151 The hardest rider for many a mile round. 1895 J. W. BUDD in *Law Times* XCIX. 543/1 Every hard worker .. requires sufficient and regular holidays.

V. Phrases and Combinations.

21. † ***to the hard*** .. (with various sbs.): to the very... Also, ***at (the) hard*** .. (*obs.*). † ***at hard edge***, at close conflict, in actual contact (*obs.*). [This app. began with things that were actually *hard*, and was thence extended to others. (See exhaustive article by Dr. Fitzedward Hall, in (N.Y.) *Nation* 24 May 1894.] ***hard at it*** (cf. 19); ***hard cases make bad law*** (see quot. 1903); ***to play hard to get*** (cf. PLAY *v.* 34), to pretend to remain aloof, to act or behave as if unapproachable or uninterested; also ***hard-to-get*** attrib. phr., aloof, unapproachable.

c 1400 MAUNDEV. (1839) xxviii. 283 Wee weren cast doun and beten down .. to the hard erthe be wyndes, and thondres. 1470–85 MALORY *Arthur* I. xiv, Their hors knees brast to the hard bone. *c* 1489 CAXTON *Sonnes of Aymon* xii. 305 He clove his hede to the harde teeth. 1526 TINDALE *John* ii. 7 Filled them up to the harde brym. 1528 MORE *Dyaloge* II. Wks. 187/1, I am in this matter euen at the harde wall, & se not how to go further. *a* 1553 UDALL *Royster D.* I. i. (Arb.) 12 Vp is he to the harde eares in loue. 1581 J. BELL *Haddon's Answ. Osor.* 457 To mainteyne a lye in any matter whatsoever, even to the hardhedg, as they say. 1591 HARINGTON *Orl. Fur.* XXXIII. lxxii. (1634) 273 They might a thousand times at hard-edge meet And neither blade thereby a gap would get. 1635 N. R. tr. *Camden's Hist. Eliz.* II. 213 That he might follow the report of his comming at the hard heeles. 1726 SHELVOCKE *Voy. round World* (1757) 203, I kept all the canvas .. at hard bats-end. 1754 RICHARDSON *Grandison* (1812) I. 120, I will never meet at hard-edge with her.

1749 FIELDING *Tom Jones* III. VII. v. 32 Pray who hath been the Occasion of putting her into those violent Passions? Nay, who hath actually put her into them? Was not you and she hard at it before I came into the Room? 1811 JANE AUSTEN *Let.* 30 Apr. (1932) 278 By this time I suppose she is hard at it, governing away—poor creature! 1923 J. S. HUXLEY *Ess. Biologist* iii. 119 The two are hard at it, shaking their heads. 1964 C. WILLOCK *Enormous Zoo* i. 13 The circular saws were soon hard at it.

1854 G. HAYES in W. S. Holdsworth *Hist. Eng. Law* (1926) IX. App. 423 Sur. B. [*i.e.* Baron Surrebutter] A hard case. But hard cases make bad law. 1903 V. S. LEAN *Collectanea* III. 479 Hard cases make bad law. i.e. lead to legislation for exceptions. 1909 *Spectator* 22 May 809/1 'Hard cases make bad law', and also bad policy. 1945 A. KOBER *Parm Me* 32 'I played "hard to get". Y' know,' he amplified, 'like I couldn't be bothered.' 1951 WODEHOUSE *Old Reliable* xi. 132 Why are you pulling this hard-to-get stuff on Joe? 1951 AUDEN *Nones* (1952) 18 But that Miss Number in the corner Playing hard to get. 1959 P. CAPON *Amongst those Missing* 194 To be blunt, you sort of strike me as playing hard to get. 1959 J. FLEMING *Miss Bones* xv. 168 Is she playing hard-to-get? he thought angrily. 1961 *Times* 26 Oct. 18/1 Miss Nancie Jackson's Millamant is a statuesque blonde, playing hard-to-get while keeping our sympathy. 1962 *Guardian* 8 Feb. 7/4 The wish to create a hard-to-get atmosphere for the coming negotiations.

22. *Comb.* Parasynthetic compounds, as ***hard-billed***, having a hard bill; so ***hard-backed***, ***-based***, ***-boned***, ***-burdened***, ***-coated***, ***-conditioned***, ***-edged***, ***-eyed***, ***-faced***, ***-fated***, ***-feathered***, ***-fortuned***, ***-glazed***, ***-haired***, ***-leaved***, ***-lipped***, ***-mailed***, ***-minded***, ***-nailed***, ***-named***, ***-natured***, ***-skinned***, ***-spirited***, ***-textured***, ***-timbered***, ***-toiled***, ***-visaged***, ***-walled***, etc.; **hard-grained**, having a hard grain; *fig.* of a close or unsympathetic character; †**hard-necked**, †**hard-nolled**, obstinate, stiff-necked; †**hard-witted**, dull at learning. Also HARD-FAVOURED, -FEATURED, etc.

1853 MRS. GASKELL *Cranford* xvi. 312 Mr. Peter said he was tired of sitting upright against the *hard-backed uneasy chairs. 1959 Hardbacked [see HARDBACK 2]. 1959 *Listener* 31 Dec. 1140/1 Within a few years it [*sc.* the American Strategic Air Command] will have at its disposal enough '*hard-based' missiles—that is, either housed in protected subterranean sites or mounted on mobile carriers—to make it impossible for any surprise attack to succeed at all. 1774 GOLDSM. *Nat. Hist.* (1790) V. 339 (Jod.) *Hard-billed singing-birds. 1797 BEWICK *Brit. Birds* (1847) I. p. v, The hard-billed birds .. which live chiefly on seeds. 1636 EARL STRAFFORDE *Lett. & Disp.* (1739) II. 20 An austere *hard-conditioned Man. 1954 J. R. R. TOLKIEN *Two Towers* 22 Long slopes they climbed, dark, *hard-edged against the sky. 1964 *English Studies* XLV. 28 Nor are registers hard-edged pigeon-holes. 1841–4 EMERSON *Ess., Experience* Wks. (Bohn) I. 173 Moaning women, and *hard-eyed husbands. 1871 J. G. WHITTIER *Marguerite* in *Wks.* (1898), By her bed the *hard-faced mistress sat. 1958 B. NICHOLS *Sweet & Twenties* 145 Harding was a hardfaced provincial politician. 1591 PERCIVALL *Sp. Dict., Encañonarse las aves*, to be *hard feathered. 1928 *Daily Express* 6 Oct. 11/7 A *hard-glazed lacquer work upon tin-plate. 1847 TENNYSON *Princ.* Prol. 178 *Hard-grained Muses of the cube and square. 1852 DICKENS *Bleak Ho.* xxii, A hard-grained man, close, dry, and silent. 1926 J. MASEFIELD *Odtaa* xiii. 223 Hi crackled through some *hard-leaved scrub. 1849 ROSSETTI *Let.* 27 Sept. (1965) I. 60 Hunt reads Dumas, *hard-lipped. 1961 *John o' London's* 6 July 57/2 One of his virtuoso essays in hard-lipped sensitivity. 1879 G. M. HOPKINS *Sermons* (1959) 18 Christ has .. made us deaf here, .. with his hands *hardnailed out and appealingly stretched on the cross. 1910 W. DE LA MARE *Three Mulla-Mulgars* xvii. 232 Long, hairy, hard-nailed toes. 1683 KENNETT tr. *Erasm. on Folly* (1709) 53 All those *hard-named fellows cannot make So great a figure as a single quack. 1889 F. M. PEARD *Paul's Sister* II. 192 A handsome, imperious, *hard-natured woman. 1535 COVERDALE *Baruch* ii. 30 It is an *hardnecked people. 1586 J. HOOKER *Girald. Irel.* in *Holinshed.* II. 134/2 That effrenated and hardnecked people. 1388 WYCLIF *Ecclus.* xvi. 11 If oon hadde be *hard nollid, wondur if he hadde be giltles. 1552 HULOET, *Hard skynned, *duricorius*. 1664 H. MORE *Myst. Iniq., Apol.* 541, I dare appeal even to the *hardestspirited person to judge of it. 1937 E. SITWELL *I live under Black Sun* 141 A sour *hard-textured unripe plum. 1593 SHAKS. *3 Hen. VI*, II. i. 55 Hewes downe and fells the *hardest-tymber'd Oake. 1721 *Lond. Gaz.* No. 6009/3 George Parsons .. *hard visag'd, with a narrow Cloth Drab coloured Coat on. *a* 1568 ASCHAM *Scholem.* (Arb.) 31 When they meete with a *hard witted scholer, they rather breake him, than bowe him.

23. a. In names of trees and plants: **hard-corn**, a general name for wheat and rye; **hard fescue** (see FESCUE *sb.* 4); **hard-grass**, a name given locally to various coarse dry grasses, e.g. *Dactylis glomerata*, *Lepturus incurvatus*, species of *Sclerochloa*, *Rottbœllia*, etc.; †**hard-hay**, *Hypericum quadrangulum*; †**hard-how**, a name of the Marigold, *Calendula officinalis*; **hard-rush**, *Juncus effusus*; **hard-tinder fungus**, *Boletus igniarius*; **hard wheat**, any wheat having a hard grain rich in gluten; also *attrib.* Also HARDBEAM, -HACK, -HEAD. **b.** In other connexions, chiefly technical: **hard bargain**, a thing or person not worth its cost; see also 12 c; **hard bop** (see BOP *sb.*[2]); **hard-bread**, a kind of hard-baked cake or biscuit; **hard cheddar**, **cheese** *colloq.*, hard luck (see also sense 1 h above); **hard chine** [CHINE *sb.*[3] 2] (see quot. 1961); so **hard-chined** *a.*; **hard copy** (see quots.); **hard core**, (*a*) (see CORE *sb.*[1] 7 d); (*b*) an irreducible nucleus or residuum; also a stubborn or reactionary minority; something blatant or intractable; freq. *attrib.*; **hard cover** orig. *U.S.*, (of a book) a stiff binding case, chiefly (with hyphen) *attrib.*; also **hard-covered** *a.* = *hard-bound* (HARD *adv.* 8 d); **hard currency**, (*a*) in specie as opposed to paper currency, metallic currency (*obs.*); (*b*) (see quot. 1949); **hard-dirt**, (see quot.); **hard disc** *Computing*, a disc (DISC *sb.* 2 g) that is rigid and has a large storage capacity, as distinct from the smaller-capacity floppy disc; **hard dot** *Printing* (see quot. 1968); **hard-edge**, a style of painting (see quot. 1962[1]); also freq. *attrib.*; **hard facing** *Metallurgy*, the application to the surface of a metal of a protective hard material resistant to wear, corrosion, etc.; hence **hard-faced** *a.*; **hard finish**, **-ing**, in *Plastering*, the third and last coat, consisting of fine stuff laid on to the depth of about an eighth of an inch; **hard fish**, (see quot.); **hard glass**, a borosilicate glass (cf. PYREX); **hard hat**, (*a*) a hat made of hard or stiffened felt; a bowler hat; (*b*) a tin helmet; (*c*) a person who wears a tin helmet, *spec.* a construction worker; (*d*) a person who is reactionary or conservative; also *attrib.*; **hard-hitter (hat)** *Austral.* and *N.Z. colloq.*, = BOWLER[3]; **hard-holing** (see quot.); **hard landing** *Astronaut.*, an uncontrolled landing in which the vehicle is destroyed; so **hard lander**; **hard-line** *attrib.*, adhering to a hard or firm policy without abatement or concession (cf. sense 12c); so **hard-liner**; **hard-nosed** *a.*, (*a*) (see quot. 1889); (*b*) *U.S. slang*, obstinate, stubborn; **hard pad**, a form of distemper in dogs and sometimes other animals; **hard pear**: see HARDPEER; **hard-rock**, (*a*) *attrib.* or as *adj.* (*N. Amer.*), 'experienced in underground work in hard massive formations;—said of a miner' (Webster 1934); (*b*) (*N. Amer. slang*) as noun phr., a hard, craggy person; also *attrib.*; (*c*) a type of strident music; **hard sell** orig. *U.S.*, aggressive salesmanship or advertising; also *attrib.*; **hard-sell** *v.*; **hard-selling**; **hard-sold** *ppl. a.*; **hard shoulder** (see quot. 1955); **hard-standing** (occas. **hard-stand**) (see quots. 1951, 1956); **hard top**, (*a*) a rigid or fixed roof of a motor-car (as opposed to one of soft material); also a car so fitted; (*b*) (see quot. 1957); **hard tube** (see sense 17b); **hard twist**, a hard-spun yarn, a yarn with more than the usual amount of twist; **hard valve** (see sense 17b); **hard waste** (see quot.); **hardway** = HARD B. 4.

1867 SMYTH *Sailor's Word-bk.*, *Hard bargain , a useless fellow; a skulker. **1893** J. A. BARRY *S. Brown's Bunyip, etc.* 48 Let a couple of the hard-bargains sling their hammocks in the after-hold. **14..** *Nom.* in Wr.-Wülcker 739/37 *Hoc colifium*, *hardbred. **1781** HEATH in R. Putnam *Mem.* (1903) 187 The major is gone to the commissary to obtain some hard bread if possible. **1835** in J. B. Thoburn *Stand. Hist. Oklahoma* (1916) vi. 74 The ration of bread shall be one pound of wheat flour, Indian meal, or hard bread. **1857** W. CHANDLESS *Visit Salt Lake* ii. 11 What we call rolls, in America are ycleped biscuits, and biscuits in their turn hard bread. **1866** PRIME in *Harvard Mem. Biog.*, *G. W. Batchelder* II. 10 He has divided his last cake of hard-bread, and compelled me to take it. **1905** G. E. COLE *Early Oregon* i. 12 Having no salt junk or hard bread left. **1931** 'N. BELL' *Life & Andrew Otway* 464 'He knew all about cutting throats. Seen a bit in his time.' '*Hard cheddar. I reckon a bullet'd be my mark if I wanted to pass in my checks.' *Ibid.* 465 No, I don't see how you can blame the bleedin' government. Hard cheddar on you but—. **1876**, etc. *Hard cheese [see CHEESE *sb.*[1] 2 d]. **1913** C. MACKENZIE *Sinister St.* I. II. i. 149, I thought it hard cheese on her. **1973** J. I. M. STEWART *Mungo's Dream* xxii. 270 It was hard cheese on him coming up against another top-class specimen. **1912** *Motor Boat Man.* (ed. 5) v. 44 'Miranda IV'..has a single step... The *hard chine or angular bilge is not an essential feature. **1951** *Engineering* 8 June 680/2 In general, the appraisal of the respective merits and demerits of round-bilge, hard-chine and stepped hulls is fair and temperate. **1961** F. H. BURGESS *Dict. Sailing* 110 *Hard chine*, a feature of a boat in which the topsides and bottom meet at an angle instead of curving to a round bilge. **1967** *Jane's Surface Skimmer Systems 1967–68* 86/2 A small sports hydrofoil, the ST-1 has a typical hard-chine type hull of wooden construction. **1966** *Amer. Speech* Oct. 235 *Lightning*, a wood-planked, *hard-chined boat made for racing. **1964** *Gloss. Automated Typesetting* (C.I.S.) 17 **Hard copy*, a printed (typewritten) record or copy of machine output. **1964** T. W. MCRAE *Impact of Computers on Accounting* vi. 165 An intermediate device, the computer, is necessary to translate the 'magnetic' records into a 'hard copy' format suitable for audit. **1936** *Nature* 12 Sept. 441/2 Possibly 200,000 would be practically unemployable on any ordinary basis—the '*hard core' as it is called. **1940** *Economist* 3 Feb. 193/2 One of the more encouraging developments of the last few months is a substantial loosening of what has hitherto been regarded as the 'hard core' of unemployment. **1951** J. CORNISH *Provincials* 24 The party was acknowledged even by the hard-core cynics to be a credit to the Dunseith brothers. **1955** *Treatm. Brit. P.O.W.'s in Korea* (H.M.S.O.) 25 This camp..was the home of the hard core of Other Rank reactionaries—men who had distinguished themselves by their heroic resistance to all Chinese brutality. **1956** *Ann. Reg. 1955* 300 A hard core of Karens in both zones maintained resistance. **1958** *Daily Mail* 15 Aug. 2/1 More than 100 hardcore EOKA terrorists have been netted in the anti-terrorist operation. **1958** *Listener* 11 Dec. 982/1 In seven 'hard core' States, no Negro child attends a white school. **1959** F. VAN P. BRYAN in Ernst & Schwartz *Censorship* (1964) xix. 130 A work of literature..stands on quite a different footing from hard core pornography. **1961** R. KEE *Refugee World* iii. 26 Weiss, the Frankfurt jeweller..was a 'hard-core' case in 1950. **1968** *Times* 2 Sept. 2/7 Heathrow airport..could, perhaps, be called the hard core of Britain's noise problem. **1973** *Times Lit. Suppl.* 20 Apr. 451/5 The leading modern writer of hard-core science fiction. **1608** in *N. & Q.* 8th Ser. XI. 201/2 The *hard corne fielde to be made before the feast of St. Mathewe. **1646** *Yorksh. Roy. Compos. Papers* I. 94, 350 stooks hardecorn, 49 stooks barley. **1949** in *Amer. Speech* (1952) XXVII. 148 *Hard-cover reprints. *Ibid.*, Hard-cover reprint house. **1951** *Sat. Rev. Lit.* 12 May 31/1 Much of the reading involves books whose quality does not justify any particular consideration just because the pages are bound inside a hard cover. **1951** *Publishers' Weekly* 12 May 1949 Each issue will be a hard-cover book. **1957** *Economist* 5 Oct. 45/1 Critics of mass market publishing suspect that it spreads mediocrity, even to the hardcover business. **1960** *News Chron.* 10 Jan. 3/7 The Heinemann group..published..an expurgated version of 'Lady Chatterley'..in hard cover in this country. *Ibid.* 3/8, I would immediately bring out a hard-cover edition. **1968** *Times* 14 Sept. 21/4 The whole inquiry relates exclusively to hard-cover sales. **1952** *Amer. Speech* XXVII. 147 (*heading*) Books: hard-bound, hard-cased, *hard-covered, limp-covered. **1851** J. H. GREEN *Twelve Days in Tombs* 33 The politicians were fiercely discussing the '*hard' and 'soft' currency question. **1940** *Economist* 6 Apr. 609/1 The phenomenon of a 'free' rate diverging from the 'official' rate occurs only in respect of those so-called 'hard' currencies for which official rates are fixed by the Bank of England (notably American dollars). **1948** *Hansard Commons* 29 Jan. 1247 As a hard-currency market, the United States is of great importance. **1948** *Ibid.* 9 Mar. 1003 Does the Chancellor of the Exchequer think it right to spend over £60 million a year in hard currency? **1949** *Times* 10 Sept., *Hard currency*, a term without precise meaning. In general, when used in relation to this country, it means the currency of any country with which this country has an adverse balance of payments in current transactions which has to be settled in gold or dollars... Hard currency is..a relative rather than an absolute term, reflecting as it does the relation between one currency and another. **1950** *Engineering* 10 Feb. 144/1 Vehicles for export to hard-currency countries. **1957** *Times* 2 Sept. 27/2 Canadians last week enjoyed the mixed blessing of having the world's hardest currency. **1969** *Listener* 20 Feb. 229/3 Arthritis would have helped me break into the hardest of hard-currency resort areas. **1851** MAYHEW *Lond. Labour* (1861) II. 281 '*Hard-dirt', or 'hard-core', consisting of the refuse bricks, chimney-pots..broken bottles..oyster-shells, &c., which form part of the contents of the dustman's cart. **1978** *Practical Computing* July–Aug. 31/3 Also on display is a *hard-disc system which uses Pertec 10Mbyte discs. **1982** *Times* 26 Oct. 15/7 Hard disks are made to a far higher degree of precision, using an aluminium platter that is extremely finely ground and polished before the magnetic oxide coating is applied. **1983** *Pop. Computing* Sept. 168 The standard Winchester hard disk is permanently attached to its recording unit. **1961** DUGAN & PINE in *Penrose Ann.* LV. 135 (*title*) The *hard-dot positive in gravure. *Ibid.*, The need for a 'hard-dot' in the positive plates. **1968** *Gloss. Terms Offset Lithogr. Printing* (*B.S.I.*) 15 *Hard dot*, a half-tone dot with a high edge density. **1961** *Times* 6 June 16/5 The '*hard-edge' abstractions of recent years. **1962** *Guardian* 18 Jan. 7/7 During the last three years..a new branch-line in British painting has opened up and been loosely labelled the 'hard-edge school'... The paintings tend to be precisely geometric, crisp..and totally withdrawn from any personal emotive content. *Ibid.* 12 July 6/4 Hard-edge is socially useful..but it is neither art nor painting. **1962** *Listener* 21 June 1080/2 Kelly is a 'hard-edge' abstractionist. He balances simple areas of sharply defined flat colour one against the other. **1965** *New Statesman* 30 Apr. 693/2 The exhibition effects an uneasy marriage between, on the one hand, hard-edge abstraction and stain painting, fields in which the Americans easily excel, and, on the other, optical art. **1960** *Jrnl. Iron & Steel Inst.* CXCIV. 269/3 *Hard-faced rolls had a useful service life five times as long as the usual steel rolls. **1930** *Ibid.* CXXII. 542 Welded-on overlays or '*hard facings' have been applied to drill bits and other tools to combat abrasion. **1931** *Ibid.* CXXIV. 634 The author cites a number of applications of hard facing and indicates the economy of the process. **1730** W. WARREN *Collect.* in Willis & Clark *Cambridge* (1886) I. 231 The side-walls..of yᵉ Chapel done with *Hard finishing (as 'tis call'd) and Stucco-work. **1808–18** JAMIESON, **Hard fish*, cod, ling, &c., salted and dried. **1904** S. P. MULLIKEN *Method Identification Pure Org. Compounds* I. 10 Prepare an ignition-tube 8–10 cm. in length from a piece of *hard-glass combustion tubing. **1937** *Discovery* Nov. 360/2 Pyrex and other hard glasses. **1965** PHILLIPS & WILLIAMS *Inorg. Chem.* I. xiv. 545 Hard glass or pyrex is made from mixed boron (30 per cent) and silicon oxides. **1806** J. GALPINE *Brit. Bot.* §44. 10 *Rotbollia incurvata*, sea *hard-grass. **1961** R. W. BUTCHER *Brit. Flora* II. 978 *Parapholis* (*Lepturus*) *incurva*. The curved hard-grass is a small, tufted annual with many erect, curved stems 1–6 in. high. *Ibid.* 979 *Parapholis strigosa*. The sea hard-grass is a small, tufted annual with many slender, solitary, erect or bent stems 6–18 in. high. **1935** A. J. POLLOCK *Underworld Speaks* 51/1 **Hard hat*, a derby. **1945** BAKER *Austral. Lang.* 181 The Australian equivalents of what the Englishman calls a bowler and the American a derby. Here are our contributions: boxer,..hard hat, [etc.]. **1953** *Collective Bargaining Agreement Giant Yellowknife Gold Mines* 3 Protective devices..shall be provided by the Company, but this shall not include personal necessities such as hard hats, hard toed boots and gloves. **1956** H. M. NEWELL *Dam* xvii. 84 Workmen were cocooned in clothing till he couldn't recognize them... Beneath their hard-hats, stocking caps or scarves or kerchiefs tied under their chins. **1963** A. LUBBOCK *Austral. Roundabout* 21, I was given a white tin hat, as it is a regulation that these safety helmets must be worn in the 'hard hat' areas of the mines. **1970** *Sunday Tel.* 14 June 12/7 All the dangerous implications of 'hard-hat' demonstrations by flag-waving workers who see the anti-war movement as a betrayal. **1970** *Sunday Mail* (Brisbane) 14 June 21/2 A 'Hard Hat' is a construction worker, but his helmet symbolises all those beefy blue-collar workers who have suddenly become the knuckleduster on the strong right arm of President Nixon's silent majority. **1972** D. E. WESTLAKE *Cops & Robbers* (1973) v. 63 It was one of those huge office buildings being constructed there, and the hardhats kept steady working away at it. **1597** GERARDE *Herbal* II. cli. §4. 434 S. Peters woort, Square or great S. Iohns grasse: and of some *Hardhay. **1895** J. ROBERTS *Diary* 7/2, I had long ere this put on my own clothes..of the 'masher' type—white shirt, *hard-hitter, tight trousers, etc. **1907** H. LAWSON *Romance of Swag* (1948) 478 Jim sat in his shirt-sleeves, with his flat-brimmed, wire-bound, 'hard-hitter' hat on. **1924** H. T. GIBSON *That Gibbie Galoot* i. 1, I didn't mind so much when my former mates sat on my hard-hitter hat. **1932** N. SCANLAN *Pencarrow* xxiv. 242 Then hats. Of course they must have hard hitters..black bowler hats—hard hitters as they were usually called in the colony. **1891** *Labour Commission Gloss.*, **Hard Holing*, hard strata underneath the coal which has to be holed or curved. **1597** GERARDE *Herbal* App., *Hardhow is Marygolds. **1962** F. I. ORDWAY et al. *Basic Astronautics* v. 176 (*caption*) Exterior view of Ranger lunar *hard lander. **1958** *Times* 28 Mar. 10/3 The first [*sc.* landing on the moon] would be a simple shot, ending either in a '*hard' (uncontrolled) landing or a circling of the moon. **1967** *Technology Week* 23 Jan. 61/1 (Advt.), Grumman is engaged in major application research to develop vehicles for soft and hard landings on Mars. **1962** *Times Lit. Suppl.* 21 Dec. 992/5 The '*hard-line' periodical *Literatura i zhizn*, which has up to now dealt exclusively with the literature of the Russian Federation, will close down. **1964** *Economist* 18 Jan. 206/1 CIA's..reputation as a 'hard-line' agency. **1965** *New Statesman* 7 May 710/3 Among those whose toughness stiffened the rebels' will to resist were..the 50 or 60 'hard line' communists. **1970** *Guardian* 28 Oct. 4/6 He has not concealed his hardline views, but has avoided coming into direct public confrontation with the party leadership. **1963** *Sat. Rev.* 25 May 22/2 The fact that war has now become an instrument of mutual suicide..has made no dent in the thinking of *hardliners. **1966** *Observer* 17 Apr. 2/8 Vice-President Humphrey—widely regarded as a hard-liner on Asia. **1969** *Guardian* 5 Mar. 8/1 Hardliners of the Right and the Left will say..that there is no middle way in Latin-American politics. **1889** *Cent. Dict.*, **Hard-nosed*, in hunting, having little or no sense of smell: said of dogs. **1927** *Hollis St. Theatre Prog.* (Boston) 19 Sept. Gloss., *Hard nosed*, stubborn. **1949** *Penguin New Writing* XXXVIII. 49 And *there* there is a lock, too, with the saint who welched three times in charge of the keys, who can be trusted not to be too hard-nosed. **1965** *Economist* 3 Apr. 27/2 Washington has got pretty 'hard-nosed' about criticism of its Congo policy. **1971** *New Society* 7 Jan. 26/1 A whole host of prophetic ravers and hard-nosed technocrats. **1973** *Times* 8 Feb. 23/2 Dolly's hard-nosed business approach to publishers probably did not have universal support. **1948** MACINTYRE et al. in *Vet. Rec.* 28 Feb. 103/1 We now recognise a condition which we have tentatively called '*hard pad disease'. **1950** A. C. SMITH *Dogs since 1900* 35 The disease should be more properly termed canine encephalitis... It became known as 'hard-pad' because a curious symptom..is a hardening of the pads. **1958** *New Yorker* 22 Feb. 31/3 Even the fact that foxes are now carrying a disease called hardpad is insufficient reason for shooting a fox. **1923** 'B. M. BOWER' *Parowan Bonanza* iv. 56 Tommy's an old, *hard-rock man. **1926** *Amer. Speech* II. 87/1 The old hardrock miners (now nearly extinct) were either single jackers or double jackers. **1949** *Chicago Daily News* 9 Apr. 1/6 A machinist drilling with a crew of hardrock miners 75 feet below the surface. **1950** W. R. BIRD *This is Nova Scotia* 19 One night..he ran up against a hardrock from Spencer's Island, and when the fracas ended he had been completely thrashed. **1962** K. ORVIS *Damned & Destroyed* xvi. 119 A hard-rock by the name of Welch. **1965** *Globe & Mail* (Toronto) 6 Jan. 24/9 Page [is] a hard-rock defensive back. **1967** *Boston Sunday Herald* 26 Mar. I. 11/2 ' Sing-Out' shook Saunders Theater with its mesmeric hard-rock beat. **1969** *Rolling Stone* 28 June 38/2 Drummer, hard-rock, blues, heavy, wants dependable group with horns. **1952** *Business Week* 9 Aug. 40 A few months ago everyone had keyed himself up to the '*hard sell'. **1957** 'E. MCBAIN' *Con Man* (1960) iii. 31 It's the hard sell and the soft sell, anywhere you go. **1958** D. DELMAN (*title*) The hard sell. **1959** *Times Lit. Suppl.* 13 Nov. 662/3 One does not see any examples..of what is called 'hard-sell' advertising. **1961** *Economist* 14 Jan. 114/2 The need for the 'hard sell' is evident. **1963** *Guardian* 16 Nov. 14/7 It is difficult to hard-sell the honest song the way they do the contemporary counterfeit. **1963** *New Scientist* 19 Sept. 613/1 The reader cannot miss the hard-sell line of advertising copy. **1966** *Ibid.* 21 July 125/1 Whatever one may think of the 'hard-sell' methods employed by big American corporations, they obviously work. **1960** *Economist* 8 Oct. 158/2 The current slump in sales has also prompted many firms to return to the '*hard-selling' practices of earlier recessions. *Ibid.* 172/1 The fuel-economy services offered by the coal and oil industries to sell their products may not prove serious competition for an independent organisation like Nifes, which may end up refereeing between them for hard-sold firms. **1955** *Times* 6 July 10/1 The motorways are to be constructed to modern standards, with *hard shoulders of 9 ft. (land hardened and laid down for vehicles to get safely off the running lanes). **1959** *Ibid.* 4 Nov. 9/7 The hard shoulder, used by vehicles for emergency stops, has collapsed at one point under the weight of a heavy lorry. **1973** *Scotsman* 12 Jan. 11/4 Twenty-six of the accidents were on the inside lane or hard shoulder. **1944** *R.A.F. Jrnl.* Aug. 259 Our lorries, drawn up on the *hardstanding ground, beside lines of gliders. **1951** *Gloss. Aeronaut. Terms* (*B.S.I.*) III. 22 *Hard standing*, a prepared hard surface for parking aircraft or heavy vehicles. **1956** W. A. HEFLIN *U.S.A.F. Dict.* 245/1 *Hardstand*, any paved, compacted, or otherwise specially-prepared surface or area set up either for parking an airplane or ground vehicle, or for storing supplies and equipment. *Ibid.* 245/2 *Hardstanding*, the facility provided by hardstands. **1957** *Times* 1 Mar. 9/6 These are certainly the aircraft which one sees on the hardstanding. **1960** *Guardian* 19 May 1/6 The rural council intends to provide hard-standing for caravans. **1968** *Bucks Examiner* 2 Aug. 2/7 Hardstanding for the parking of one coach or coaches. **1859** W. S. COLEMAN *Woodlands* (1862) 74 Gigantic specimens of the *Hardtinder fungus (*Boletus igniarius*). **1949** FRAZEE & BEDELL *Automotive Fundamentals* 82 The convertible sedan features the same entrance and seating arrangements as are found in the regular *hard-top sedan. **1951** *Amer. Automobile* Mar. 78/3 Plymouth has adopted entirely new designations... The coming hardtop will be called Belvidere. **1952** *Autocar* 12 Dec. 1663/1 The hardtop style of roof is now used on all bodies, whether they have two or four doors. **1956** *Sat. Rev.* 7 Apr. 40/2 The number of enclosed theatres now colloquially known as 'hard tops' declines. **1957** *Amer. Speech* XXXII. 239 The conventional movie house under a roof is now referred to as a hardtop. **1959** 'S. RANSOME' *I'll die for You* iv. 43 Two Burt Fishers ..driving two identical Chevy hard-tops. **1967** *Guardian* 3 Oct. 5/3 The price of the hard top has gone up to £1,255. **1897** *Sears, Roebuck Catal.* 186/1 This suit is made from genuine Michigan *hard twist cassimere. **1921** T. WOODHOUSE *Yarn Counts* vii. 87 There are..exceptional degrees of twist, some..of which might exceed the value of the so-called hard twist. **1963** A. J. HALL *Textile Sci.* iii. 114 In a similar manner much the same considerations apply in a multi-ply yarn if the two or more single yarns present are only slightly or highly twisted (often referred to as soft and hard twist) together. **1921** *Dict. Occup. Terms* (1927) §362 *Breaker*, **hard waste*; *hard waste tenter* ; feeds and operates machine which opens out hard cotton waste (waste from ring frames and from reeling and winding machines, cop bottoms and other thready waste) in preparation for re-spinning, or for use in manufacture of gun cotton. **1865** *Cornh. Mag.* Apr. 467 The owner was walking on the beach, or *hardway, at the mouth of the river whither the Ellen was bound. **1812** in H. Davy *Elem. Agric. Chem.* (1813) 133 *Hard wheat always sells at a higher price in the market than soft wheat. *Ibid.*, The flour of hard wheat is in general superior to that made from soft. **1843** *Penny Cycl.* XXVII. 301/2 There are three principal varieties... These are the hard wheats, the soft wheats, and the Polish wheats. **1856** J. C. Morton *Cycl. Agric.* II. 1005 *T[riticum] vulgare durum*, hard African wheat. **1908** *Westm. Gaz.* 1 July 6/3 The hard-wheat lands of Canada. **1971** *Times* 23 Jan. 21/4 Britain should take commodities like oil, wine, hard wheat.

B. *sb.* (elliptical use of the adj.).

1. a. [The adj. used absolutely.] That which is hard, something hard; hardship.

a **1250** *Owl & Night* 459 Ne recche ich noȝt of winteres reve; Wan ich i-s[e]o that cumeth that harde, Ich fare hom to min erde. *c* **1350** *Will. Palerne* 472 But ȝif myn hauteyn hert þe harde a-sente. **1795** A. Shirrefs *Sale Catal.* 3 (E.D.D.), A plain North-country bard, Who fain would cripple through the hard. **1808** Jamieson *Dict. Scot. Lang.*, *Hard*, difficulty, hardship. *To come through the hard*, to encounter difficulties, to experience adverse fortune. **1858** G. Roy *Generalship* vi. 101 The bits o' bairns run a great risk o' coming through the hard. **1902** *Westm. Gaz.* 10 July 10/1 He had 'come through the hards' himself. **1904** *Daily Chron.* 27 May 3/4 She is a lady who.. has given her life to nursing, and has gone through its hards.

b. Phrases. † ***of* (*by, with*) *hard***, with difficulty. † ***on, with hard***, with violence, fiercely. † ***at the hardest***, at the utmost. ***let the hardest come to the hardest, when hard comes to hard***: if, or when, the worst comes to the worst. ***in the hard***, in hard cash, 'down'.

1297 R. Glouc. (1724) 17 Corineus ther with harde smot. **13..** *Guy Warw.* (A.) 1726 Y com fram Lombardy Of hard y-schaped for þe maistrie. *c* **1380** Wyclif *Serm.* Sel. Wks. II. 100 Þes synneris bi hard ben turnid to God. **1382** —— *Eccl.* i. 15 Peruerted men of hard ben amendid. *a* **1400–50** *Alexander* 3004 He with hard schapid. *a* **1450** *Knt. de la Tour* (1868) 81 Atte the hardest, for a while, thou wilt not goo ferre. *c* **1470** Henry *Wallace* v. 845 He.. Hewyt on hard with dyntis sad and sar. **1670** Eachard *Cont. Clergy* 114 Let the hardest come to the hardest; if they can get by heart, *Quid est fides?* **1727** P. Walker in *Biog. Presbyt.* (1827) I. 266 When Hard came to Hard, of Boots, Thumbikins, and Fire-matchs. **1830** Galt *Lawrie T.* II. i. (1849) 43 Four hundred and thirty-three dollars.. counted out to me in the hard. **1864** Carlyle *Fredk. Gt.* IV. 598 Now that hard had come to hard.

c. In various technical applications.

1855 *First Rep. Adulteration of Food* 2 in *Parl. Papers* *1854–5* VIII. 221 Bread is adulterated with mashed potatoes, alum, 'hards', and sometimes.. with sulphate of copper. **1921** *Dict. Occup. Terms* (1927) §238 *Sider, hard* (needles); burnishes sides of sewing machine needles in the hard, *i.e.*, after hardening on revolving bob with oil and emery. **1937** *Archit. Rev.* LXXXI. 269/2 Scrap lead may contain other metals, such as the tin in solder, resulting in what is known as 'hards'. **1956** F. S. Atkinson in D. L. Linton *Sheffield* 268 The 'hards' of the Barnsley seam and, to a lesser extent, of the Parkgate or Deep Hard, make an excellent locomotive coal. **1960** *Gloss. Coal Terms* (*B.S.I.*) 12 *Hards*, a commercial term for the larger sizes of dull hard coal, in contrast to 'brights'.

d. Also ***hard-on*** sb. (and as adj.). An erection of the penis. *slang.*

1893 Farmer & Henley *Slang* III. 269/1 *Hard-bit* (or *bit of hard*). 1. The *penis* in erection. *Ibid.* 270/1 *Hard-on* adj. phr., prick-proud. **1922** Joyce *Ulysses* 527 What, boys? That give you a hardon? **1937** Partridge *Dict. Slang* 375/2 *Have a hard up*, to have a priapism. **1966** N. Behn *Kremlin Let.* I. iv. 56 When he wasn't plundering I suppose he was raping. He was more like a dog with a hard-on than a man with a mission. **1967** A. Wilson *No Laughing Matter* III. 377 He pulled up her red woollen dress.. but still no hard. **1971** B. W. Aldiss *Soldier Erect* 44 The bromide damped down desire—you really had to work to get a hard on, whereas before it always flipped up naturally. **1971** B. Thornberry tr. Hansen & Jensen's *Little Red School-Bk.* (ed. 2) 95 When boys get sexually excited, their prick goes stiff. This is called having an erection or 'getting a hard on'. **1972** *Screw* 12 June 10/2 Billy and I talked down our hardons and.. went downstairs to load the truck.

†**2.** The hard part, the shell. *Obs.*

c **1420** *Pallad. on Husb.* VIII. 135 Of squyllis whyte, al raw, taak of the hardis.

†**3.** Hard or firm ground. *Obs.*

1576 in W. H. Turner *Select. Rec. Oxford* (1880) 385 That hurst or bancke is of hard, and some gravell. **1629** *Drayner Conf.* (1647) A iij b, The Inhabitants upon the Hards, and the Bankes within the Fennes.

4. A firm beach or foreshore; also, a sloping stone roadway or jetty at the water's edge for convenience in landing and putting out. (Hence, at Portsmouth, a street which adjoins the landing; also called the 'Common Hard'.)

1838 Dickens *Nich. Nick.* xxiii, [At Portsmouth] the Common Hard, a dingy street leading down to the dockyard. **1866** *Daily Tel.* 11 Jan. 4/4 The loves of the 'Hard' are proverbially of brief duration. **1886** R. C. Leslie *Sea-painter's Log* iv. 64 Well-known sheltered beaches, or 'common hards', as they were called. These hards still remain in old seaports. **1893** *Northumbld. Gloss.*, *Hard*, a firm foreshore, used for beaching vessels. **1896** Charpentier *Guide to Southsea & Portsmouth* 76 The Hard is not a beautiful place now-a-days. **1897** Max Pemberton in *Windsor Mag.* Jan. 268/1, I have started from the hard of the boathouse with fingers.. benumbed.

5. *U.S. Political slang.* **a.** = hardshell *sb.* 3. **b.** One of the supporters of Senator Benton of Missouri about 1850, so called from their advocacy of 'hard money'.

1847 Robb *Squatter Life* 91 (Farmer) Hards, softs, whigs and Tylerites were represented. **1888** Bryce *Amer. Commw.* II. II. xlvi. 203 The Hunkers and Barnburners who divided the Deomcratic party forty years ago, and subsequently passed into the 'Hards' and the 'Softs', began in genuine differences of opinion about canal management and other State questions.

6. A slang abbreviation of *hard labour*.

1890 *Globe* 26 Feb. 1/4 Seven days' incarceration, with or without hard. **1896** *Daily News* 19 Dec. 6/5 They don't hang them nowadays, but give them six months' hard.

7. ***hard and sharp***, (?) a kind of bit. ? *Obs.*

1787 'G. Gambado' *Acad. Horsemen* (1809) 36 *note*, Were a Pig to be driven in a hard and sharp, or a Weymouth.

8. Tobacco in a cake.

1865 T. Archer *Pauper, Thief & Convict* v. 83 Peaceable companions.. smoking pipefuls of 'hard' which they cut from a flat cake with their clasp-knives. **1898** G. Bartram *White-headed Boy* iv. 102 Packages of shag tobacco, lumps of sweetened 'hard'. *Ibid.* 105 Lind me a hand.. with this lump o' harrd. **1898** *Daily News* 24 Feb. 3/1 Mr. Atkins.. pulled at his pipe until he floated off into dreamland on a whiff of 'hard'.

hard, *adv.* Forms: see the adj. [OE. *hearde* = OS. *hardo*, OHG. *harto* (MHG. *harte*), f. hard *a.*] In a hard manner.

1. a. With effort, energy, or violence; strenuously, earnestly, vigorously; violently, fiercely. In early use, sometimes = intensely, exceedingly, extremely.

c **1000** Ælfric *Hom.* II. 256 Him hearde ðyrste. *a* **1200** *Moral Ode* 157 Þer we muȝen bon eþe offerd and herde [*v.r.* harde] us adreden. *c* **1290** *S. Eng. Leg.* I. 28/81 Huy tormenteden him harde and stronge. *c* **1330** R. Brunne *Chron.* (1810) 33 Yit þe kyng Anlaf so hard gan he chace. *c* **1340** *Cursor M.* 20736 (Trin.) Þidurwarde þei hyȝed hem harde. *c* **1400** *Destr. Troy* 8215 Ector.. macchit hym so harde. *c* **1440** *Gesta Rom.* ii. 5 (Harl. MS.) Grete labour þat he hadde on the day afore made him to slepe hard. **1535** Coverdale *2 Chron.* xviii. 33 A certayne man bended his bowe harde. *c* **1586** C'tess Pembroke *Ps.* LIV, Strangers.. Who hunt me hard. **1634** Peacham *Gentl. Exerc.* 68 Presse it downe hard. **1697** Dampier *Voy.* I. 338 He strikes the Gong as hard as he can. **1722** De Foe *Col. Jack* (1840) 128 We worked hard, lodged hard, and fared hard. **1776** Foote *Capuchin* I. Wks. 1799 II. 388 His majesty looked at me very hard. **1860** Hughes *Tom Brown at Oxf.* xi, Pulling 'hard all' from Sandford to Iffley, and then again from Iffley over the regular course. **1867** Trollope *Chron. Barset* II. xlvi. 16 He ..bid the cabman drive hard.

b. Of the weather, wind, snow, rain, frost, etc.

13.. *Sir Beues* 4580 (MS. A.) Þe wind blew hardde wiþ gret rage. **1628** Digby *Voy. Medit.* 51 It blew hard all night. **1697** Dampier *Voy.* I. 13 It rained very hard. **1798** Nelson 28 Dec. in Nicolas *Disp.* III. 212 The next day it blew harder than I ever experienced since I have been at sea. **1864** Mrs. Carlyle *Lett.* III. 237 If it.. snows as hard there as here. *Mod.* Last night it froze hard.

c. Very, extremely. *U.S. colloq.*

1850 N. Kingsley *Diary* (1914) 97 Mr. Hopkins is hard sick. *a* **1910** 'O. Henry' *Trimmed Lamp* (1916) 16 He isn't a millionaire so hard that you could notice it, anyhow.

2. a. So as to bring or involve oppression, pain, trouble, difficulty, or hardship; severely; cruelly, harshly. See also hard-set 1.

c **1205** Lay. 8814 Ich wes.. hærde [*c* **1275** herde] biðrungen. *a* **1300** *Cursor M.* 3470 Als womman þat ful hard was stad. *a* **1340** Hampole *Psalter* vii. 12 Þe harder will he punysch. **1393** Langl. *P. Pl.* C. I. 28 Al.. lyueden ful harde, In hope to haue a gode ende. *c* **1460** *Towneley Myst.* (Surtees) 59 Fulle hard halden ar we here. **1579–80** North *Plutarch* 124 (R.) The poor geese were so hard handled. **1699** Dampier *Voy.* II. II. 38 Having fared very hard already. **1712** Addison *Spect.* No. 271 ¶4, I shall be very hard put to it to bring my self off handsomly. **1771** *Junius Lett.* l. 260, I will not bear hard upon your.. friend. **1885** *Daily News* 20 Feb. 5/6 Hard put to it to veil their feelings.

†**b.** With an uneasy pace. *Obs.*

1583 Hollyband *Campo di Fior* 283 He troteth hard, He will breake all my bones. **1600** Shaks. *A.Y.L.* III. ii. 331 He [Time] trots hard with a yong maid, between the contract of her marriage, and the day it is solemnizd. **1681** *Lond. Gaz.* No. 1649/8 Dark Brown Gelding.. Trots very hard. **1688** R. Holme *Armoury* II. vii. 150 A trotting horse, when he sets hard, and goes of an uneasy pace. **1824** Scott *St. Ronan's* vii, I am heated, and my pony trotted hard.

c. ***to go hard with*** (a person): to fare ill with him, to prove to his serious hurt or disadvantage; with *but*, introducing a statement of what will happen unless prevented by overpowering difficulties. See also go *v.*

1530 Palsgr. 550/1 It shall go harde but I wyll fynde one mater or other to breake hym of his purpose. **1591** Shaks. *Two Gent.* I. i. 86 It shall goe hard but ile proue it by another. **1596** —— *Tam. Shr.* IV. iv. 109 It shall goe hard if Cambio goe without her. **1596** —— *Merch. V.* III. ii. 292 It will goe hard with poore Anthonio. **1705** Hickeringill *Priest-cr.* IV. 231 Not a Farthing abated.. which goes hard in Hard-times. **1809** W. Irving *Knickerb.* (1861) 87 It shall go hard but I will make it afford them entertainment. **1855** Prescott *Philip II*, I. iii. 51 It might have gone hard with the envoy, had the mistake not been discovered.

3. With difficulty, hardly; scarcely. ***to die hard***: see die *v.*[1] 3.

1382 Wyclif *Luke* xviii. 24 How hard thei that han richessis schulen entre in to the rewme of God. **1536** Latimer *Serm. bef. Convoc.* Wks. I. 41 Now hard and scant ye may find any corner.. where many of his children be not. **1604** Shaks. *Oth.* I. ii. 10 With the little godlinesse I haue I did full hard forbeare him. **1626** Bacon *Sylva* §830 Solid bodies foreshow rain, as boxes and pegs of wood when they draw and wind hard. **1810** Scott *Lady of L.* III. xi, And hard his labouring breath he drew. **1811–68** [see die *v.*[1] 3]. **1888** Bryce *Amer. Commw.* III. lxxxiii. 100 Now, though it dies hard, its monopoly of office is departing.

4. Firmly, securely; tightly; fast. Now *rare.*

a **1225** *Juliana* 59 And bunden hire þerto hearde and heteueste. *c* **1400** *Gamelyn* 346 Gamelyn was i-take and ful hard i-bounde. *c* **1440** *Promp. Parv.* 227/2 Harde sett (*P.* or obstynat) yn wyckydnesse.. *obstinatus*. **1500–20** Dunbar *Poems* xxxii. 48 All the hollis wes stoppit hard. **1596** Spenser *F.Q.* v. iv. 22 With both his hands behinde him pinnoed hard. **1602** Shaks. *Ham.* II. i. 87 He tooke me by the wrist, and held me hard. **1703** Moxon *Mech. Exerc.* 206 A Pin.. to fit hard and stiff into the round Hole. **1833** L. Ritchie *Wand. by Loire* 241 Bound hard and fast.

5. a. So as to be hard; to hardness. (Often qualifying a pa. pple. See also 8 d.)

1340 Hampole *Pr. Consc.* 6455 Þus may men se by an egge hard dight, How heven and erthe and helle standes right. *c* **1465** *Eng. Chron., Hen. VI* (Camden 1856) 55 The Thamise and othir grete rivers were so hard frosen that hors and cariage myȝte passe ovir. **1563** W. Fulke *Meteors* (1640) 10 Being very neere compact, and as it were hard tempered together. **1632** J. Lee *Short Survey* 12 Lapland, where all rivers.. and lakes are hard frozen. **1766** Lane in *Phil. Trans.* LVII. 456 A piece of common tobacco-pipe hard-baked. **1854** Ronalds & Richardson *Chem. Technol.* (ed. 2) I. 124 The coke should be hard burnt.

b. On a hard surface, floor, etc.

1577 B. Googe *Heresbach's Husb.* IV. (1586) 161 The harder they lie, the sooner they fatte. **1607** Topsell *Four-f. Beasts* (1658) 237 That so he may lie soft and stand hard. **1886** Stevenson *Kidnapped* xviii. 173 'Ye maun lie bare and hard, and brook many an empty belly.'

6. a. In close proximity, of time or place; close. ***hard upon*** (***on***), close before or after so as to press upon. Now chiefly in ***to run*** (a person) ***hard***. See also hard by.

c **1410** Love *Bonavent. Mirr.* xxviii. (Sherard MS.), Answerde harde ageyn reprouynge hem. **1506** Guylforde *Pilgr.* (Camden) 62 [We] laye amost harde abrode the grete vggly rokkes. **1526** Tindale *Acts* xviii. 7 Whose house ioyned harde to the sinagoge. **1535** Coverdale *Job* xvii. 1, I am hard at deathes dore. —— *Ps.* xxi[i]. 11 Trouble is harde at honde. **1582** N. Lichefield tr. *Castanheda's Conq. E. Ind.* xii. 29 b, The King.. came in a great boate hard to our Fleete. **1598** Barckley *Felic. Man* (1631) 519 The shee-wolfe.. whose covetousnesse is followed hard at the heeles with envy. **1771** Foote *Maid of B.* III. Wks. 1799 II. 230 You are hard upon sixty. **1813** Scott *Trierm.* II. Interl. i, While conjuring wand Of English oak is hard at hand. **1864** D. G. Mitchell *Sev. Stor.* 285 It was now hard upon three o'clock. **1865** Thackeray in *Daily News* (1896) 27 Jan. 4/7 Who will one of these days run you hard for the Presidentship. **1897** F. Hall in *N. & Q.* 17 Apr. 310/1 Incongruity which trenches hard on nonsense.

b. *Naut.* Expressing the carrying of an action to its extreme limits, as in ***hard-a-lee, -a-port, -a-starboard, -a-weather***: see the second elements. (Hence **hard-a-ported, hard-a-starboarded** *pa. pples.*, put hard a-port, a-starboard. Also **hard-a-weather** *adj.*, able to stand the utmost rigours of the weather.)

1549 *Compl. Scot.* vi. 40 Hail doune the steir burde lufe harde a burde. **1679** Sturmy *Mariner's Mag.* (1684) 15 The helm is hard aweather. **1707** *Lond. Gaz.* No. 4380/2 We clap'd our Helm hard a Starboard. **1800** Weems *Washington* xi. (1877) 151 Washington then seized the helm, with a gallant hard-a-lee. **1848** *Blackw. Mag.* LXIII. 87 [He] wore a remarkably hard-a-weather pilot-coat. **1883** *Law Times Rep.* XLIX. 332/2 The Margaret.. had her.. helm hard-a-starboarded. **1892** *Ibid.* LXVII. 251/1 The pilot ordered the helm of the Merchant Prince to be ported, and shortly afterwards to be hard-a-ported.

†**7.** Parsimoniously. *Obs. rare.*

1711 Steele *Spect.* No. 155 ¶3 The Rogues buy as hard as the plainest and modestest Customers they have.

8. In Comb., qualifying ppl. adjs., to which *hard* is always united by a hyphen when they are used attributively, and generally also when they are used predicatively unless the order is reversed; thus, 'A hard-boiled egg', 'Do you prefer it hard-boiled?' 'Will you have it boiled hard?'. The advb. is used thus in nearly all its senses, and the number of combinations is unlimited. Examples:

a. With effort, strenuously, violently, etc., as ***hard-biting, -bit, -contested, -drinking, -driven, -driving, -fought, -hitting, -hurled, -ridden, -riding, -running, -sought, -swearing, -trotting, -worked, -working***, etc.; **b.** With hardship, severely, etc., as ***hard-besetting, -bested, -bred, -faring, -judging, -kept, -lived, -living, -looking, -pressed, -pressing, -tried, -used***, etc.; **hard-hit**, severely stricken by misfortune, grief, or disaster; deeply in love; **hard-pushed**, in difficulties; **hard run** *U.S.*, in difficulties or want, esp. with regard to money; **hard-wearing**, able to stand a considerable amount of wear. **c.** With difficulty, as ***hard-acquired, -bought, -earned, -gained, -got, -learnt, -won, -wrung***, etc. **d.** So as to be hard, tight, etc., as ***hard-baked, -beaten, -braced, -cured, -dried, -pressed***, etc. **hard-bound** orig. *U.S.*, (of books) bound in boards; **hard-cased** *U.S.* = *hard-bound*. **e. hard-bound**, slow in action; costive, constipated; **hard-drawn**, drawn when cold, as wire; †**hard-holding**, close-fisted, niggardly; †**hard-laced**, strait-laced, strict and precise; **hard-spun**, tightly twisted in spinning.

1858 W. ELLIS *Vis. Madagascar* viii. 206 *Hard-baked reddish earth. **1592** SHAKS. *Ven. & Ad.* 985 O *hard-believing love, how strange it seems Not to believe, and yet too credulous! **1634** MILTON *Comus* 857 In *hard-besetting need. **1886** KIPLING *Dep. Ditt.* (ed. 2) 108 What a *hard-bit gang were we. **1741** RICHARDSON *Pamela* (1824) I. 157 The *hard-bought victory. **1946** *Publishers' Weekly* 5 Oct. 1971/1 Several publishers of *hard-bound reprints offer new series or expanded ones. **1952** *Amer. Speech* XXVII. 148 The ubiquitous 'paper-back'..is undoubtedly the cause of a reversal in bookbinding nomenclature. Whereas the board-bound used to be the normal and expected kind of book it is now necessary to use the qualifying adjectives *hard-bound, hard-cased*, or *hard-covered* when one refers to any book not in paper covers. **1959** *Times Lit. Suppl.* 6 Nov. p. xxxviii/4 It is estimated that more than 233,000,000 copies were sold in 1957, as against 32,000,000 hard-bound adult trade books. **1735** POPE *Ep. Arbuthnot* 182 The Bard ..strains, from hard-bound brains, eight lines a year. **1632** BROME *Northern Lasse* I. i. Wks. 1873 I. 1 Some *Hard-bred Citizen. **1951** *Publishers' Weekly* 2 June 2357 Using the conventional method, eight to ten hours is a fair estimate of the time required to build in each batch of *hard-cased books. It takes that long for paste to set and hinges to be formed. **1780** NAIRNE in *Phil. Trans.* LXX. 334 A piece of *hard-drawn iron wire. **1875** HOWELLS *Foregone Concl.* viii. 119 *Hard-drinking, hard-riding, hard-swearing, foxhunting English parsons. **1902** 'MARK TWAIN' in *North Amer. Rev.* Dec. 762 The poor and the *hard-driven. **1949** R. K. MERTON *Social Theory* (1951) 17 A small, hard-driven group of professors. **1951** M. MCLUHAN *Mech. Bride* 157/1 The cowboy is as non-erotic as the *hard-driving executive. **1770** BURKE *Pres. Discont.* (T.), To take their *hard-earned bread from the lowest offices. **1847–9** HELPS *Friends in C.* Ser. I. (1854) I. 28 The hard-earned gains of civil society. **1864** BURTON *Scot Abr.* I. ii. 91 The *hard-fighting clans near the Border. *a* **1666** FANSHAW *On Ld. Strafford's Trial* (T.), [The] *hard-fought field. **1839** THIRLWALL *Greece* VI. 175 Defeated in a hard-fought battle. **1860** 'OLD SHEKARRY' *Hunting Grounds of Old World* i. 19, I feel sure he is *hard hit. *Ibid.* 20 A bright crimson pool..showed that he was hard hit. **1884** G. C. DAVIES *Peter Penniless* xix. 145 Hard Hit. **1891** M. E. BRADDON *Gerard* xxix, You've been hard hit. **1909** H. G. WELLS *Ann Veronica* ix, She saw her aunt in tears, her father white-faced and hard hit. **1839** *Q. Rev.* LXIII. 25 Our *hard-hitting Irish labourers. **1889** *Spectator* 12 Oct., He was swift, adroit, hard-hitting. **1955** *Times* 16 July 5/3 His plea was for an immediately available joint military force of hard-hitting character. **1962** *Christian Cent.* 26 Sept. 1164/1 Hard-hitting new book and films to help you combat communism. **1876** G. M. HOPKINS *Poems* (1918) 22 A released shower, let flash to the shine, not a lightning of fire *hard-hurled. **1580** SIDNEY *Arcadia* (1622) 206 Like a *hard-kept warde new come to his lands. **1581** J. BELL *Haddon's Answ. Osor.* 194 So sparyng a niggard, and *hardelaced. **1878** J. P. HOPPS *Princ. Relig.* iv. 17 All life's hard-earned virtues and *hard-learnt lessons. **1921** GALSWORTHY *To Let* II. i, A look of life *hard-lived. **1884** 'MARK TWAIN' *Huck. Finn* 89 A couple of mighty *hard-looking strangers. **1915** A. CONAN DOYLE *Valley of Fear* v. 79 They were a mighty hard-looking crowd. **1825** MILL *Speech* in *Autobiogr.* (1924) 282 The Lion, finding himself *hard-pressed, called together the aristocracy of the forest. **1891** Hard-pressed [see PRESSED *ppl. a.*[1]]. **1961** *New Scientist* 16 Mar. 664/3 Hard-pressed managers and engineers can hope to read only a tiny fraction of it. **1938** *New Statesman* 20 Aug. 282/1 Mr. Lennox Robinson..said that..it was not fair to press the lecturer. But the S.J...was a *hard-pressing man. **1950** D. GASCOYNE *Vagrant* 43 And the heart's slowly dulled By the hard-pressing years. **1807** J. BARLOW *Columb.* VII. 259 To aid her *hard-pusht powers. **1834** [ASA GREENE] *Perils of Pearl St.* 123 (Bartlett), We began to be hard pushed. Our credit, however was still fair. **1852** R. S. SURTEES *Sponge's Sp. Tour* iv. 17 A *hard-riding ..sort of sportsman. **1822** J. FOWLER *Jrnl.* 22 June (1898) 163 We have left them all behind, and will be *hard run for meat. **1834** *Deb. Congress U.S.* 10 Mar. 848 Men, I say, who, to use the mercantile phrase, are 'hard run' to make ends meet, and only wanting an honorable excuse to fail. **1845** *N.Y. Tribune* 1 Nov. (Bartlett), We knew the Tammany party were hard run; but we did not know it was reduced to the necessity of stealing the principles of Nativism. **1865** ROSSETTI *Let.* 27 July (1965) II. 562 I'm dreffle hard run for tin till the end of next week when I shall have some. **1939** C. MORLEY *Kitty Foyle* 324 Everybody there looked so hard-run it cheered me up. **1952** C. DAY LEWIS tr. *Virgil's Aeneid* v. 98 The *hard-running waves off Malea. **1963** *Times* 29 May 3/5 Hard-running fairways and small, sometimes tricky greens. **1909** J. JUSSERAND *Lit. Hist. Eng. People* III. 162 His [*sc.* Shakespeare's] most wonderful inventions were not *hard-sought finds. **1906** GOODCHILD & TWENEY *Technol. & Sci. Dict.* 864/2 s.v. *Yarn*, The yarn is defined as soft spun, medium spun, *hard spun, according to the amount of twist it has received. **1906** *Daily Chron.* 1 Oct. 3/2 Its purpose of helping the *hard-tried bookseller. **1664** PEPYS *Diary* (1879) III. 27 A *hard-trotting sorrell horse. **1906** GOODCHILD & TWENEY *Technol. & Sci. Dict.* 833/1 s.v. *Warp*, The term applied to the series of spun threads, usually stronger and *harder twisted than the weft. **1962** J. T. MARSH *Self-Smoothing Fabrics* xi. 168 Cotton voiles with their hard-twisted yarns may be impregnated on a mangle whose bowls have been wrapped with a fine cloth. **1950** *Mind* LIX. 407 Difficulties which can in one sense of a *hard-used word be called 'philosophical'. **1909** *Daily Chron.* 11 June 7/5 Everything possible to be done is achieved in the endeavour to make it *hard-wearing. **1928** *Observer* 1 Apr. 13 [This] Lingerie is amazingly hard-wearing. *a* **1845** HOOD *The Mary* 58 *Hardwon wages, on the perilous sea. **1894** 'MARK TWAIN' in *Century Mag.* Jan. 330/1 He was coarsely fed and *hard worked. *a* **1930** D. H. LAWRENCE *Phoenix* (1936) 74 The busy, hard-worked-looking woman. **1774** GOLDSM. *Nat. Hist* (1790) II. 224 (Jod.) The *hardworking wives of the peasants. **1856** KANE *Arct. Expl.* I. xxviii. 371 Five nights' camping out in the snow, with hard-working days between. **1605** SYLVESTER *Du Bartas* II. iii. IV. *Captaines* 786 A rude Clown, whose *hard-wrought hands, before Nothing but spades, coulters, and bils had bore.

†**hard**, *v. Obs.* [OE. *heardian* = OS. *hardôn* (MDu., MLG., Du., LG. *harden*), OHG. *hartên* and *hartôn* (MHG. *harten*), orig. intrans., f. *hard-* adj. HARD; but already in late OE. used also for the cognate trans. vb. *hiẹrdan, hyrdan* = OFris. *hęrda*, OS. *gi-hęrdian*, OHG. *hartian, hęrtan*, ON. *hęrða*, Goth. *ga-hardjan* to make hard.]

1. *intr.* To be or become hard. *lit.* and *fig.*

c **1000** *Sax. Leechd.* I. 76 Seoð þonne þa wyrte oð þæt heo heardiȝe. *a* **1225** *Ancr. R.* 220 Ure Louerd spareð a uormest þe ȝunge & þe feble..Auh so sone so he isihð ham hearden, he let arisen & awakenen weorre. **1382** WYCLIF *Ps.* lxxxix. 6 Inwardli harde he and waxe drie. **1398** TREVISA *Barth. De P.R.* XIX. lxi. (1495) 898 Wexe meltyth..in hete and hardyth in colde. *c* **1440** *Promp. Parv.* 227/1 Hardyn, or growyn harde, *dureo, induresco.*

2. *trans.* To make hard, harden. **a.** *lit.*

c **1000** *Sax. Leechd.* II. 188 þæt wyrmð and heardaþ þone maȝan. **1398** TREVISA *Barth. De P.R.* VII. xiv. (1495) 233 Medycynes that drye and harde. *c* **1420** *Pallad. on Husb.* I. 436. When that is drie..harde hit wel. *c* **1440** *Promp. Parv.* 227/1 Hardyn, or make harde, *induro.* **1491** CAXTON *Vitas Patr.* (W. de W. 1495) I. xxxiii. 28 a/1 A salte humour, the whyche by the hete of the sonne..was harded as yce.

b. *fig.* To deprive of feeling or emotion; to render callous, obstinate, or obdurate.

c **1205** LAY. 5871 And auer alc god mon harde [*c* **1275** hardi] hine sulue. *c* **1380** WYCLIF *Sel. Wks.* III. 324 Heretikis hardid in here Errour. **1382** —— *Exod.* xiv. 8 The Lord hardide the herte of Pharao. *c* **1440** CAPGRAVE *Life St. Kath.* IV. 1098 Soo ar ȝe harded with obstinacye. *a* **1618** SYLVESTER *Job Triumph.* I. 723 He sees their harts y[t] hard them In Guiles and Wiles.

Hence **harded** *ppl. a.*; **harding** *vbl. sb.* and *ppl. a.*

c **1386** CHAUCER *Sqr.'s T.* 237 Hardyng of metal. **1398** TREVISA *Barth. De P.R.* VII. lxx. (1495) 291 Hardyng medycyne rennyth the matere. **1412–20** LYDG. *Chron. Troy* III. xxvii, His herded herte of stele. **1620** SHELTON *Quix.* IV. xxvi. 205 Bodies of harded Cork trees.

hard(e, obs. pa. t. of HEAR; obs. f. HOARD.

hard and fast, *a.*

1. *Naut.* (See quot. 1867.)

1867 SMYTH *Sailor's Word-bk.*, *Hard and fast.* Said of a ship on shore. **1895** LD. C. E. PAGET *Autobiog.* iv. (1896) 80 Finding the ship hard and fast, he had nothing for it but to remain quietly on board.

2. Rigidly laid down and adhered to.

1867 J. W. HENLEY *Sp. in Ho. Com.* 11 Apr., Whether the franchise is to be limited by a hard and fast line. —— 28 May, The House has deliberately, after long consideration, determined to have no 'hard and fast line'. **1867** W. H. GREGORY *Sp. in Ho. Com.* 28 May, What were the whole of the fancy franchises but 'a hard and fast line'? It was very easy to affix a nickname. **1875** JOWETT *Plato* (ed. 2) I. 412 Who are the wicked, and who are the good, whom we venture to divide by a hard and fast line? **1881** J. EVANS *Anc. Bronze Implem.* i. 1 It is impossible to fix any hard and fast limits for the close of the Stone Period. **1890** BP. STUBBS *Primary Charge* 45 We are none of us in a condition to lay down a hard and fast rule about inspiration.

hard-and-'fastness. The condition of being hard and fast; hard and fast character.

1903 *Daily Chron.* 5 Mar. 3/3 The 'hard-and-fastness' of experience. **1904** *Westm. Gaz.* 18 June 13/2 By denying the hard-and-fastness and asserting the strictly provisional character of the forms or categories.

Hardanger ('hɑːdæŋə(r)). The name of a district in west Norway used *attrib.* or *absol.* in names of things connected with Hardanger, as *Hardanger cloth, embroidery, fiddle, violin.*

1883 J. M. FLEMING *Old Violins & their Makers* v. 177 In the Exhibition of 1862, a specimen of their class of work —a Hardanger violin—was exhibited. **1900** GROVE *Dict. Mus.* (ed. 2) IV. 663/1 The Halling...is accompanied on the Hardanger fiddle.., a violin strung with four stopped and four sympathetic strings. **1908** *Sears, Roebuck Catal.* 527/5 Hardinger [*sic*] Canvas. **1928** *Funk's Stand. Dict.*, *Hardanger*, ornamental needlework in the pattern of diamonds or squares, made at Hardanger. **1930** tr. *T. de Dillmont's Encycl. Needlework* 580 This border is a specimen of the Norwegian openwork known under the name of 'Hardanger' embroidery. **1957** M. B. PICKEN *Fashion Dict.* 159/1 *Hardanger cloth*, soft cotton cloth of excellent quality. *Ibid.*, *Hardanger embroidery*, heavy, symmetrical, Norwegian needlework done in elaborate diamond or square pattern. **1972** P. A. WHITNEY *Listen for Whisperer* vii. 120 What you heard was one of our Hardanger fiddles.

hardback ('hɑːdbæk). **1. a.** Name in West Indies of a coleopterous insect.

1750 G. HUGHES *Barbadoes* 82 The Hardback. This fly is about half an inch long..Its membranaceous wings are defended with sheaths or shell-wings. **1958** J. CAREW *Wild Coast* ii. 22 Hector..watched a hardback beetle crawling up the wall...'Boy, if you kill all the hardbacks that come in here you will make a mess of my clean floor.' **1959** P. CAPON *Amongst those Missing* 66 The insects..whirred and buzzed ..and the noise made by the hardbacks..kept Harry's nerves on the stretch.

b. Name of a river fish of Central America.

1883 J. G. WOOD in *Sunday Mag.* Nov. 676/2 Many of these rivers are inhabited by a fish (*Callichthys*) popularly called the Hassar or Hardback.

2. A book bound in stiff boards; cf. PAPERBACK(ED). Also *attrib.* So **hard-backed** *a.* (see also HARD *a.* 22).

1954 *New Republic* 26 Apr. 18 (*heading*) New novels: hardbacks or paperbacks. **1957** *Harper's Mag.* Sept. 94/3 Is it not possible that he may come away reading nothing but paperback books, that he will have become attuned to never spending $4.50 on a hardback? **1958** *Economist* 8 Nov. Suppl. 1/1 The retailer's margin on paperbacks is just as profitable as on hardbacks... A hardback order may well be topped up with a couple of 'quality paperbacks'. **1959** *Times* 24 Nov. 6/4 Most 'respectable' American publishers respect the British publisher's hardbacked and paperbacked book rights. **1960** *Times* 3 Feb. 17/4 The big paperback publishers are not hardback publishers but specialists in what is virtually a new genre. **1970** G. GREER *Female Eunuch* 170 Love affairs whether in cheap 'romance' comic-papers or in hard-back novels.

hard-bake ('hɑːdbeɪk). [f. HARD *a.* + BAKE *v.* and *sb.*] A sweetmeat made of boiled sugar or treacle with blanched almonds; 'almond toffee'.

1825 HONE *Every-day Bk.* I. 51 Show-glasses, containing ..hard-bake, brandy-balls, and bull's-eyes. **1848** THACKERAY *Van. Fair* lvi, A taste..for hardbake and raspberry tarts.

attrib. **1849** THACKERAY *Pendennis* II. v, Brandy-ball and hardbake vendors.

hardball ('hɑːdbɔːl). *N. Amer.* [f. HARD *a.* + BALL *sb.*[1]; cf. SOFTBALL 2 a.] **1.** = BASE-BALL.

a **1883** G. W. BAGBY *Sel. Misc. Writings* (1885) II. 19 He must now learn to cut jackets, play hard-ball, choose partners for cat and chermany, be kept in. **1939** in WEBSTER Add. **1941** *Sun* (Baltimore) 24 Apr. 15/2 He played softball in junior high, and hardball for an American Legion team. **1974** *Plain Dealer* (Cleveland, Ohio) 19 Oct. 5-D/1 We both knew Eric Miller from our days at St. Ed. He had expressed an interest in athletics and we knew that he backed a AAA hardball team.

2. *fig.* Tough, uncompromising dealings or activity (esp. in political contexts); chiefly in phr. *to play hardball. slang.*

1973 P. J. BUCHANAN in *Black Panther* 6 Oct. 17/3 There are things that are certainly utterly outrageous... Then, there is dirty tricks, then there is political hardball, then there is pranks. **1977** *Washington Post* 6 Sept. B5/5 Washingtonians usually know better. They know that people play political hardball here. **1978** *Globe & Mail* (Toronto) 21 Feb. 7/1 The House could be a dangerous place... No more days of gentle badinage between Tory Bill and his friend Stephen. From now on it's going to be hardball. **1983** *Fortune* 18 Apr. 118/2 If anyone wants to play hardball, Cub can operate in the 5% to 6% range and still be profitable, because its costs are so lean. **1985** *New Yorker* 15 Apr. 100/2 Word was leaked from the White House in mid-March that members of the President's party who did not support his programs should not expect reëlection help. Such 'hardball' is not new, but it is not Reagan's style.

Hence **'hard-baller**, one who 'plays hardball' or engages in aggressive, uncompromising activity; **'hardball** *v. trans.*, to (attempt to) persuade or coerce in this way.

1976 *Time* 27 Dec. 52/1 Grodin plays the honcho as a hard-baller of the sort that used to hang around the Nixon White House. **1983** *Washington Post* 13 Oct. DC1 The manager has picked Frederick Dorsey, a deputy D.C. corporation counsel with a background in civil rights, to face hardballers C & P Telephone Co. in a series of high-stakes hearings next month. **1984** *Observer* 15 July 7/5 She rebelled occasionally, hard-balling O'Neill into attaching to a Bill an Amendment that would help her District, by threatening to kill a million dollar pork-barrel destined for his.

hardbeam ('hɑːdbiːm). ? *Obs.* [f. HARD *a.* + BEAM tree.] The HORNBEAM, *Carpinus Betulus.*

c **1000** *Sax. Leechd.* I. 398 Ælces treowcynnes..butan heardan beaman. **1545** ASCHAM *Toxoph.* (Arb.) 123 Steles be made of diuerse woodes as brasell,..hardbeame [etc.]. **1597** GERARDE *Herbal* 1296 It is also called..in English Hornbeame, Hardbeame, Yoke Elme, and in some places Witch hasell. **1801** STRUTT *Sports & Past.* II. i. 54 [Arrows] made of oak, hardbeam, or birch.

hard-bitten, *a.* [f. HARD *adv.* + BITTEN *pa. pple.* (here used actively: cf. *ill-spoken*).] Given to hard biting; tough in fight.

1784 SIR M. HUNTER *Jrnl.* (1894) 65 So hard-bitten an animal that all the torture you can use will not make him leave his hold. **1815** SCOTT *Guy M.* liii, They will be hard-bitten terriers will worry Dandie. **1857** HUGHES *Tom Brown* II. viii, Such hard-bitten, wiry, whiskered fellows.

hardboard. [BOARD *sb.* 3.] A stiff type of board made from wood-pulp fibre. Also *attrib.*

1929 C. J. WEST *Bibliogr. Pulp & Paper Making 1900–1928* 157 (*heading*) Preparation of hard boards. **1934** *House Building 1934–1936* xxvii. 264 (Advt.), Insulite is an ideal material for the lining of walls and ceilings... Insulite products include Hardboard and Boards for Roof Insulation. **1939** *Chem. Abstr.* 2675 A process of making dense hardboard sheet products, which consists in subjecting fibrous wood or woody lignocellulose material.. to a heat treatment. **1959** *Times* 18 May 10/4 Composite hardboard..is displacing traditional panelled construction in many buildings. **1959** *Housewife* June 32 Many of the huts are divided..by hardboard partitions.

hard-boil, *v.* [Back-formation f. next.] *trans.* To boil (an egg) until hard-boiled. Also *transf.*

1895 'MARK TWAIN' in *Harper's* Nov. 886 No more time to decide it than it takes to hard-boil an egg. *a* **1930** D. H. LAWRENCE *Etruscan Places* (1932) 16 He [*sc.* a shepherd] is the faun escaping again out of the city precincts... You cannot hard-boil him. **1963** *Listener* 10 Jan. 103/3 Hard-boil the eggs. **1973** *Nature* 23 Mar. 258/2 Considerably less than 12 h is required, either at 91° or 86° C, to hard-boil an egg.

hard-boiled, *a.* [f. *to boil hard*, where *hard* is a predicative adj. Cf. HARD *adv.* 8.]

1. Of an egg: boiled till the white and yolk are solid.

1723 J. NOTT *Cook's & Confect. Dict.* No. 21, Mince..the Yolks of hard boil'd Eggs. **1747** H. GLASSE *Cookery* (1784) 71 Chop two or three hard-boiled eggs fine. **1833** MARRYAT *P. Simple* xxv, We found hard-boiled eggs, bread, and a smoked mutton ham. **1846** A. Soyer *Gastron. Regen.* 445 Prepare a border of hard-boiled eggs. **1968** C. Roden *Bk. Middle Eastern Food* 99 (*heading*) Fried hard-boiled eggs.

2. Of articles of clothing: stiff, hard. *U.S.*

1903 A. Adams *Log of Cowboy* ix. 58 That fellow in front of the drug store over there with the hard boiled hat on. **1919** S. Lewis *Free Air* 86 To Claire, traveling men were merely commercial persons in hard-boiled suits.

3. Hardened, callous; hard-headed, shrewd. orig. *U.S.* Hence, of measures, practical.

1886 'Mark Twain' *Speeches* (1923) 137 Hard-boiled, hide-bound grammar. **1915** in *Amer. Speech* (1937) 260 Hard boiled egg who wouldn't bid 90 on 100 aces. **1919** in F. A. Pottle *Stretchers* (1930) 354 We are too hard-boiled to make much of a demonstration. *Ibid.* 358 Two hardboiled Irish sergeants are terrorizing the barrack. **1926** *Publishers' Weekly* 10 July 120/1 Stone..being hard-boiled, waited a few days to notice any appreciable increase in sales. **1926** *Ladies' Home Jrnl.* 26 Aug., The hard-boiled cynic has a shell it [*sc.* satire] can never penetrate. **1928** *Weekly Dispatch* 3 June 10/3 From its obscure beginning down in the 'tough' section of New York, up through the 'hard-boiled' wards of the great city, into municipal politics and thence into the Governor's chair. **1929** A. Conan Doyle *Maracot Deep* vi. 153 The hard-boiled Scanlan actually fell down in a faint. **1931** Buck & Anthony *Bring 'Em Back Alive* 163 It is all a hard-boiled proposition of not treading on the other fellow's feet for fear he may rise up and poke his big toe in your eye. **1932** E. Wilson *Devil take Hindmost* viii. 80 That man of iron..a drastic-minded and hard-boiled Dane. *Ibid.* 82 There is a Detroit type which..has some of the energy and hard-boiled bluffness of the Chicagoans. **1934** *Archit. Rev.* LXXV. 116/2 Yet those old houses are safe and kind and probably better employed in modifying some hard-boiled business man's mentality. **1942** *Mind* LI. 274 It certainly is difficult to remain a stoic or a cynic, to be 'hard-boiled', for a long time. **1959** *Encounter* Sept. 62/2 The disregard of truth in favour of hard-boiled scientific ideals. **1968** *Times* 27 Sept. 2/3 Mr. Heath's hard-boiled image is beginning to crack.

Hence **hard-'boiledly** *adv.*; **hard-'boiledness**.

1933 H. J. Massingham *London Scene* iv. 76 No other quarter of London is so consciously, hard-boiledly, shamelessly middle-class [*sc.* as Kensington]. **1934** Webster, Hard-boiledness. **1936** *Times Lit. Suppl.* 28 Mar. 255/2 Pareto apprehended the essential 'hardboiledness' of politics by personal and bitter experience. **1939** A. Huxley *After many a Summer* i. vii. 86 He dreaded for her the influence of so much cynicism and hardboiledness.

'hard-burned, -burnt, *a.* [hard *adv.* 8 d.] Made hard by intensified firing.

1851 C. Cist *Cincinnati* 214 Walls of hard-burnt brick. **1869** *Rep. Comm. Agric. U.S. 1868* 360 Hard-burned terra cotta pipes. **1893** Kate Sanborn *Truthf. Wom. S. California* 45 Half-cylindrical plates of hard-burnt clay.

hard by, *prep.* and *adv.* Somewhat *arch.* [hard *adv.* 6 + by *prep.* and *adv.*]

A. *prep.* Close by; in close proximity to; close to, very near to. (Now only of place.)

1526 Tindale *Acts* xxvii. 7 We saled harde by the costes off Candy. **1659** D. Pell *Impr. Sea* 575 *note.* Your ships were hard by drowning. **1682** Milton *Hist. Mosc.* v. Wks. 1738 II. 143 They saw many Whales very monstrous hard by their Ships. **1849** Macaulay *Hist. Eng.* I. v. 628 Hard by the remains of Monmouth were laid the remains of Jeffreys.

B. *adv.* In close local proximity; close by, very near; †also *transf.* close at hand in time.

1535 Coverdale *Obad.* 15 The daye off the Lorde is harde by vpon all Heithen. **1590** Greene *Mourn. Garm.* (1616) 43, I will place thee in a Farme house of mine hard by adioining. **1717** Berkeley *Tour in Italy* 19 Jan. Wks. 1871 IV. 527 Hard by we saw the remains of the circus of Sallustius. **1800** Wordsw. *Pet Lamb* 58 Our cottage is hard by. **1886** Ruskin *Præterita* I. ix. 300 The lily of the valley wild in the copses hard by.

hardel(l, obs. forms of hurdle.

hardely, obs. form of hardily, hardly.

harden ('hɑːd(ə)n), *v.* [f. hard *a.* + -en[5]: cf. ON. *harðna*, which is, however, only intr. *Harden* has taken the place of OE. *heardian*, ME. *hard-en*, to hard.]

I. *trans.* **1. a.** To render or make hard; to indurate.

c **1200** Ormin 1487 Tu..grindesst itt [corn], and cnedesst itt, And harrdnesst itt wiþþ hæte. *Ibid.* 1567 Þu bakesst Godess laf And harrdnesst itt þurrh hæte. **1513** Douglas *Æneis* vi. xii. 55 The spot of filth hardynit [*concretam labem*] in the spreit. **1555** Eden *Decades* 97 Pykes and dartes hardened at the endes with fyere. **1632** J. Lee *Short Surv.* 12 Fishes dryed and hardened with the frost. **1710** J. Clarke *Rohault's Nat. Phil.* (1729) I. 159 The Heat must be but moderate, to harden Bodies. **1793** [see 7]. **1860** Tyndall *Glac.* i. xi. 73 The snow was hardened by the night's frost.

transf. and *fig.* **1733** Pope *Ess. Man* iii. 193 Thy Reason.. shall..Entangle Justice in her net of Law, And right, too rigid, harden into wrong. **1856** H. Rogers *Ess.* II. viii. 373 The strong metaphorical language of Christ became hardened into the doctrine of Transubstantiation. **1874** Green *Short Hist.* iv. §3. 177 The rise of a lawyer class was everywhere hardening customary into written rights. **1880** Earle *Philol. E.T.* §405 Many of these [adjectives] are hardened into substantives, as *commandant, inhabitant.*

b. *spec.* of metals.

1797 *Encycl. Brit.* VIII. 310/1 There are several ways of hardening iron and steel, as by hammering them, quenching them in cold water, &c. *a* **1877** Knight *Dict. Mech.* II. 1060/2 Iron is surface hardened by heating to a bright red, sprinkling with prussiate of potash, allowing to cool to a dull red, and cooling with water. **1957** *Encycl. Brit.* VI. 906/2 After the blades are forged or cut out they are hardened by heating in a suitable furnace to the correct temperature and then quenched.

†**2.** To render bold or stout in action; to embolden, confirm; to incite to action. *Obs.*

c **1200** Ormin 1574 Itt hardneþþ all þe gode manness heorrte, To þolenn..All þatt tatt iss unnselþe. **13..** *K. Alis.* 1200 He..hardneth al his men. **1375** Barbour *Bruce* xii. 500 The horss with spuris hardnyt thai. *c* **1470** [see hardened *ppl. a.* 2]. **1658** Cleveland *Rustick Rampant* Wks. (1687) 502 Greyndcob's Stubbornness hardens on the Clowns.

3. To make difficult of impression or emotion; to make callous or unfeeling.

a **1300** *Cursor M.* 5908 Þe hert o pharaon..es mar Hardend for mi sau þan ar. **1382** Wyclif *Ps.* xciv. [xcv.] 8 Wileth not hardne ȝoure hertis. **1611** Bible *John* xii. 40 He hath blinded their eyes, and hardened their heart. **1712** Steele *Spect.* No. 456 ⁋ 1 Men hardened beyond the Sense of Shame or Pity. **1735** Berkeley *Querist* §390 The disbelief of a future state hardeneth rogues against the fear of death. **1825** Lytton *Falkland* 54, I hardened my heart against his voice.

4. To make persistent or obdurate in a course of action or state of mind.

c **1400** *Destr. Troy* 9966 His hert was so hardonet all in hote loue. **1615** J. Stephens *Satyr. Ess.* 272 Sacke and strong liquours hardens him in his custome. **1681** Dryden *Abs. & Achit.* 145 Harden'd in Impenitence. **1826** Scott *Woodst.* vi. He hardened himself..to the act. **1885** *Manch. Exam.* 6 May 4/7 It would..confirm and harden her in a policy of settled hostility to this country.

†**5.** To maintain stiffly, affirm. *Obs.*

c **1200** Ormin 18219 Teȝȝ wolldenn bliþeliȝ Harrdnenn, ȝiff þatt teȝȝ mihhtenn, þatt teȝȝre Bapptisstess fulluhht Wass bettre. *a* **1300** *Cursor M.* 12239 He hardens [*Fairf.* arguis; *Trin.* argueþ of] suilkin thing þat i ne wat end ne beginning.

6. To make firm and tight.

1523 Fitzherb. *Husb.* §126 For with the wyndynge of the edderynges: thou dost lose thy stakes & therfore they must nedes be dryuen newe and hardened agayne. **1769** Falconer *Dict. Marine* (1789), *Retenue*, fastened, or hardened home in its place. *Ibid.* G b, The forelock..is thrust through a narrow hole..where it is hardened home by a hammer. **1882** Nares *Seamanship* (ed. 6) 205 Studding-sail tacks..will..want hardening out.

7. a. To render hardy, robust, or capable of endurance. Chiefly of the physical constitution. ***to harden off***: to inure (plants) to cold by gradually reducing the temperature of a hot-bed or forcing-house or by increasing the time of exposure to wind and sunlight.

1577 B. Googe *Heresbach's Husb.* i. (1586) 6 b, Being hardened with labour in peace, they might the better be able to abyde the travayle of warres. **1601** R. Johnson *Kingd. & Commw.* (1603) 4 The sharpenes of the place which doth harden them. **1793** Beddoes *Calculus* 162 It is not true.. that cold hardens children as it hardens steel. **1852** *Beck's Florist* Aug. 174 The principal secret of preserving half-hardy plants over the winter with indifferent accommodation, lies in their being rooted early and gradually hardened afterwards. **1873** *Young Englishwoman* May 238/1 Everything which has been kept in the house during the winter for summer planting, or raised in a frame ..should be gradually hardened to endure the changes of life in the open air.... This 'hardening off', as the gardeners term it [etc.]. **1875** Ruskin *Hortus Inclusus* (1887) 34 [They] never put me through any trials to harden me, or give me decision of character. **1905** *Terms Forestry & Logging* 13 *Harden off*, to prepare seedlings in the seedbed for transplanting by gradually exposing them to wind and sunlight. **1909** *Daily Chron.* 5 June 9/5 This cool treatment or 'hardening off' process. **1912** *Chambers's Jrnl.* Dec. 848/1 Plants raised in this frame require no hardening off. **1933** *Jrnl. R. Hort. Soc.* LVIII. 117 Such young plants are generally well hardened-off, and receive but little check when transferred to their new quarters. **1970** C. Lloyd *Well-Tempered Garden* ii. 54 When they [*sc.* the cuttings] have rooted, they can be..returned to a close atmosphere but then gradually hardened off by the admission of more air.

b. To render (a nuclear missile or base) hard (see hard *a.* 14 f).

1958 R. D. Bowers in *Air Univ. Q. Rev.* X. 90 Another possibility..might be to harden our sites. *Ibid.* 92 Repeating the analyses and assigning various values to the parameters should provide a good feeling for the payoff in hardening missile sites. **1960** *Times* 11 Feb. 11/6 Though land-based missiles can be 'hardened' by burying them and surrounding them with concrete they are still vulnerable to ..nuclear attack. **1972** *Sci. Amer.* June 15/3 Attempts to 'harden' such fixed missile-launchers (that is, to increase their resistance to the effects of nuclear explosions) are in the long run doomed to futility.

8. *Phonetics.* To make a sound 'hard'. Cf. hard *a.* 16.

1871 *Public Sch. Lat. Gram.* §12. 8 Poets sometimes.. harden v- vocalis into v- consonans: as, *gen-va* for *ge-nu-a.*

II. *intr.* **9.** To become hard.

c **1420** *Liber Cocorum* (1862) 37 In playand water þou kast hit schalle, To harden. **1596** Dalrymple tr. *Leslie's Hist. Scot.* I. 47 A mater that wirkis out of the stanes, and hardnes throuch the calde nature of the Sey. **1796** Morse *Amer. Geog.* II. 114 As they are of a petrifying quality, they harden ..into various forms. **1833** Lardner *Manuf. Metal* II. 314 Pure iron may..be superficially converted into steel, so as to harden, temper, and receive a fine polish. **1847** Tennyson *Princ.* iii. 254 That we might..watch The sandy footprint harden into stone.

fig. **1863** Geo. Eliot *Romola* iii. xiv, That cold dislike.. was hardening within him. **1891** *Eng. Illustr. Mag.* Oct. 65 The weather was hardening into what promised to be half a gale. **1891** *Law Times* XCII. 99/2 This natural sequence hardened first into custom and then into law.

10. To become hard in feeling, emotion, constitution, etc.

1667 Milton *P.L.* i. 572 Now his heart Distends with pride, and hardning in his strength Glories. **1780** Cowper *Progr. Err.* 590 There hardening by degrees, till double steeled, Take leave of nature's God, and God revealed. **1865** Kingsley *Herew.* ii. 64 He hardened into a valiant man. **1873** Miss Thackeray *Old Kensington* xii. 105 Though he might have softened to Lady S., he now hardened to himself. **1884** Pae *Eustace* 62 He said they would soon harden to the work.

11. *Comm.* Of prices: To become higher, to rise; to stiffen. Cf. hard *a.* 15.

1674–91 Ray *N.C. Words* 24. s.v., The Market Hardens, i.e. Things grow dear. **1828** *Craven Dial., Harden*, to advance in price; 't' corn rayther hardens'. **1882** *Daily Tel.* 4 May, Prices are hardening on the Continent.

Hence **'hardening** *vbl. sb.* and *ppl. a.*

1630 *R. Johnson's Kingd. & Commw.* 234 By hardning and custome. **1725** Pope *Odyss.* ix. 292 Half the white stream to hard'ning cheese he prest. **1823** J. Badcock *Dom. Amusem.* 138 The plate..has received an injury in the hardening. **1885** J. J. Manley in *Brit. Alm. Comp.* 18 The butter is placed in a Danish cooler or hardening box. **1877** *Encycl. Brit.* VI. 734/1 The hardening is accomplished by heating the blade to a cherry-red heat and suddenly quenching it in cold water. **1902** *Daily Chron.* 18 Jan. 5/4 The hardening of new-arrived drafts [of troops] is most noticeable. **1902** A. Bennett *Anna of Five Towns* viii. 176 The 'hardening-on' kiln, a minor oven where for twelve hours the oil is burnt out of the colour in decorated ware. **1908** *Westm. Gaz.* 15 Apr. 1/3 The inexorable and hardening passage of twenty years. *Ibid.* 21 Aug. 5/4 There has been a great hardening on the part of the merchants, who were formerly placing the stones [*sc.* diamonds] on the market for anything they could fetch. **1930** *Economist* 5 Apr. 758/2 The hardening of bill rates, which put a further reduction of the Bank Rate out of court for the time being. **1936** *Forestry* X. 124 By exposure to suitable, but not damagingly low, temperatures plants are rendered more resistant to frost; this is the process known as hardening, and takes place naturally during the autumn. **1940** *Economist* 6 Jan. 12/2 These difficulties have already had as their effect a general hardening of prices. **1959** *Chambers's Encycl.* X. 686/2 Most fixing solutions also contain a tanning or hardening agent which unites with the gelatin of the emulsion layer, increases its melting-point and reduces its swelling in water. **1970** *New Yorker* 17 Oct. 171/1 These maneuvers have all added up to what one astute observer of the talks has described as 'a hardening of the arteries'.

harden, herden, hurden ('hɑːd(ə)n), 'hɜːd(ə)n), *sb.* and *a. local.* Forms: α. 5–7 hardin, -yn, 5–9 harden, 6–9 harding. β. 5–9 herden, 6–9 hurden. [Belongs to hards *sb.*; it is prob. a derivative in *-en* rather than the OE. *heordan*, ME. *herden* sb. pl., and may have been orig. adj., although the sb. use appears earlier in our quots. *Harden* appears to be northern and eastern; *herden, hurden* midl. and western; some northern dialects have the form harn, q.v.]

A. *sb.* A coarse fabric made from the hards of flax or hemp.

c **1430** *Durham MS. Cell. Roll*, Pro viij uln. panni vocati Herdyng, ij s. **1462** J. Paston in *P. Lett.* No. 449 II. 101 Nat withstandyng, ther herden at Wyggenalle shall be don this day. **1495** *Nottingham Rec.* III. 38 Duo parea linthiaminum de harden. **1570** *Bury Wills* (Camden) 156 One payer of sheets of hurden. **1615** Markham *Eng. Housew.* ii. v. (1668) 134 That which comes from the flaxe being a little towed again in a pair of Wooll Cards, will make a course harding. **1708** T. Ward *Eng. Ref.* ii. (1716) 235 (D.) A shirt he had made of coarse harden, A collar-band not worth a farthing. **1881** D. C. Murray *Joseph's Coat* II. xxiv. 257 The tumbled herden which did duty for linen.

b. *attrib.* and *Comb.*

1601 Holland *Pliny* xix. i, After the stalkes of the Flax be wel dried, they are to be beaten and punned..with an hurden mallet or tow-beetle. *a* **1652** Brome *City Wit* iv. ii. Wks. 1873 I. 348 You hurden smock'd sweaty slutters.

B. *adj.* Made of harden.

1522 *Test. Ebor.* (Surtees) V. 147 A hardyn apperon. **1542** *Richmond. Wills* (Surtees) 31 Item vij score of lyn garne, and iiij score of hardyng garne vij[s]. viij[d]. **1545** Ascham *Toxoph.* (Arb.) 118 An herden or wullen cloth waxed. **1641** Best *Farm. Bks.* (Surtees) 67 A course hempe or harden cloath. *a* **1652** Brome *New Acad.* iii. i. Wks. 1873 II. 47 The hurden smock with lockram upper-bodies. *a* **1763** Shenstone *Ess., On Dress* (1765) 124 The country-fellow..appears genteel ..when he is hedging in his hurden frock. **1824** Mrs. Sherwood *Waste Not* ii. 2 They wore a linsey petticoat and herden apron. **1887** D. C. Murray *Old Blazer's Hero* (1889) 87 With a corner of her herden apron.

†**b.** Clothed in harden. *Obs.*

1658 Cleveland *Rustick Rampant* Wks. (1687) 453 The.. Ring-leaders of the hurden rustick Raggamuffins.

,hardena'bility. *Metallurgy.* [f. harden *v.*: see -ity.] The extent to which a metal may be hardened (see also quot. 1954).

1932 *Jrnl. Iron & Steel Inst.* CXXVI. 609 (*heading*) Factors affecting the inherent hardenability of steel. **1950** J. H. Bateman *Materials of Construction* 411 The surface hardness and the distance from the surface of the hardening effect are measures of the hardenability of steel. **1951** *Engineering* 14 Dec. 764/2 He said that in some circumstances an alloy content was necessary in order to achieve the necessary hardenability of the steel. **1954** *Gloss. Terms Iron & Steel (B.S.I.)* i. 16 *Hardenability*, the property which determines the depth and distribution of hardness after quenching under specified conditions. *Ibid., Hardenability test*, a test to assess hardenability. A common example is the Jominy test.

hardened ('hɑːd(ə)nd), *ppl. a.* [f. harden *v.* + -ed[1].]

1. Rendered hard, indurated.

1590 Spenser *F.Q.* i. xi. 24 Upon his crest the hardned yron fell. **1676** Dryden *Aurengz.* i. i. 365 The laborious Hind Whose harden'd Hands did long in Tillage toil. **1730**

[see QUENCHING *vbl. sb.* 1]. **1874** BOUTELL *Arms & Arm.* ii. 38 Bronze or hardened brass.

2. Rendered unfeeling or callous; hard-hearted; obdurately settled or determined in a course.

c **1375** *St. Leg. Saints, Mathias* 455 Sum sa hardnyt ware þat þai Vald trew til hyme be na way. *c* **1470** HENRY *Wallace* x. 283 Thai hardnyt hors fast on the gret ost raid. **1576** FLEMING *Panopl. Epist.* 65 Some are..so hardened..that they care not for their countrie. *a* **1605** MONTGOMERIE *Devot. Poems* iv. 59 Stoup, hardint hairt, befor the Lord. **1722** DE FOE *Plague* (1754) 42 The very Buryers of the Dead, who were the hardnedest Creatures in Town. **1740** WESLEY *Wks.* (1872) I. 285, I was desired to pray with an old hardened sinner. **1850** SCORESBY *Whaleman's Advent.* (1859) ix. 124 The most hardened grumbler.

3. Rendered hard (see HARD *a.* 14 f).

1960 *Aeroplane* XCIX. 588/2 In the case of Atlas, this hurried development has resulted in four different types of operational launch site—unprotected, semi-protected, semi-hardened and hardened—and immense cost has been a feature of the programme. **1962** *Listener* 5 Apr. 605/2 A relatively small number of 'hardened', invulnerable, I.C.B.M.s.

Hence **'hardenedness.**

1571 GOLDING *Calvin on Ps.* xxxii. 3 The hardenednesse of our flesh. **1790** G. WALKER *Serm.* II. xxix. 309 A kind of brutality and hardendness.

hardener ('hɑːd(ə)nə(r)). [f. HARDEN *v.* + -ER[1].]

1. One who hardens; *spec.* one whose work is to harden metals; one who case-hardens guns, etc.

1611 COTGR., *Affermisseur*..a stiffener, hardner. **1755** in JOHNSON. **1845** *P. Parley's Ann.* VI. 181 Misfortune is not a hardener of the heart. **1881** *Academy* 8 Jan. 30 A grand zoologist, not a mere hardener and slicer of microscopic stuff. **1886** *Pall Mall G.* 15 May 14/1 When the grinding is completed the blades are returned to the hardeners to be reset.

2. That which hardens. **a.** *Photogr.* Any chemical used in the making of gelatine negatives to prevent the melting or frilling of the film in warm weather.

1909 *Cent. Dict.* Suppl., Hardener [Photogr.]. **1930** *Sel. Gloss. Motion Techn.* (*Acad. Motion Pict., Hollywood*), *Hardener*, solution used to harden photographic emulsion. **1948** A. L. M. SOWERBY *Dict. Photogr.* (ed. 17) 362 A hardener containing 1½ per cent. of potash alum, used at this *p*H value, may be expected to raise the melting point of the gelatine.

b. In various technical applications (see quots.).

1903 *Westm. Gaz.* 30 Nov. 2/1 The hardening temperature for the steel called 'high carbon' is difficult to define; for the personal equation comes into play, and with different hardeners the variation in hardening temperature often reduces the quality of the steel. **1945** R. T. ROLFE *Dict. Metallogr.* 101 *Hardeners*, alloys prepared for the purpose of adding small quantities of additional elements to molten metals. **1951** *Gloss. Terms Plastics* (*B.S.I.*) 17 *Hardener*, a material used to promote the setting of certain types of synthetic resin. **1959** *Gloss. Packaging Terms* (*B.S.I.*) 13 *Hardener*, a chemical used to promote the setting of adhesive. **1966** A. W. LEWIS *Gloss. Woodworking Terms* 43 *Hardener*, liquid used to speed up the setting of resin glue. **1967** E. CHAMBERS *Photolitho-Offset* ix. 130 Potassium alum is recommended as a *hardener* in preference to chrome alum which, although more potent, loses its hardening power after short use and forms a sludge.

harder ('hɑːdə(r)). *S. Afr.* Also 8 harter, 20 haarder. [a. Afrikaans *harder*, Du., LG. *harder*, OE. *heardhara*, *heardra*.] Any of various species of the grey mullet family (Mugilidæ), of which *Liza ramada* and *M. cephalus* are well known.

1731 G. MEDLEY tr. *Kolben's Pres. State Cape Good-Hope* II. 193 There is..about the Cape a Sort of Herrings the Cape-Europeans call Harters. **1838** D. MOODIE tr. *Record* 13 We..caught and salted 400 large steenbrass, and about 2,000 harders. **1892** SIMMONDS *Dict. Trade* (new ed.), *Harder*, a kind of mullet about twelve inches long, caught near the coasts of the Cape colony. **1947** K. H. BARNARD *Pict. Guide S. Afr. Fishes* 81 The family of Grey Mullets, called in South Africa Harders or Springers (*Mugilildae*) is economically very important. **1962** *Cape Argus* (Mag. Sect.) 11 Aug. 1/7 Bunches of harder, maasbanker and pilchards and many other kinds of fish. **1971** *Daily Dispatch* (East London, Cape Province) 8 Mar., There were hundreds of haarders (mullet) in the bay itself.

Harderian (hɑː'dɪərɪən), *a. Anat.* [f. the name of J. J. Harder (Swiss anatomist 1656–1711) + -IAN.] ***Harderian gland***: the lubricating gland of the nictitating membrane or 'third eyelid', in the inner angle of the eye of birds and some mammals.

1835–6 TODD *Cycl. Anat.* I. 307/1. **1859** *Ibid.* V. 543/1 Ruminants are provided with an Harderian gland.

†**hardfast**, *a. Obs.*$^{-0}$ Dense. Hence **hardfastness** *nonce-wd.*, density.

1674 N. FAIRFAX *Bulk & Selv.* 147 For the sake of its hardfastness or closeness.

'hard-favoured, *a. arch.* [See HARD *a.* 13 and FAVOUR *sb.* 9.] Having a hard or unpleasing 'favour', appearance, or look; ill-favoured, ugly.

1513 MORE in Grafton *Chron.* (1568) II. 758 Richard the thirde sonne..was..hard favoured of visage. *a* **1592** GREENE & LODGE *Looking Glasse* Wks. (Rtldg.) 141/1 As hard-favoured a devil as ever I saw. **1768** BOSWELL *Corsica* iii. (ed. 2) 226 The Corsicans are in general of small stature, and rather hard-favoured. **1852** DICKENS *Bleak Ho.* xix, Humouring the joke with a hard-favoured smile.

Hence **hard'favouredness.**

1585 T. WASHINGTON tr. *Nicholay's Voy.* II. viii. 42 Because of his hardfavourednesse and deformity. *a* **1665** J. GOODWIN *Filled w. the Spirit* (1867) 56 The fat [kine] had need..to have been..twenty times seven times fatter than they were, to have wrought a cure upon the leanness and hardfavouredness of the other.

'hard-featured, *a.* [See HARD *a.* 13.] Having hard, harsh, or unpleasing features.

1748 SMOLLETT *Rod. Rand.* xlix. (1804) 338 A tall raw-boned man with a hard-featured countenance. **1836–7** DICKENS *Sk. Boz* (1850) 94/1 The old hard-featured man..is a county Member. **1874** MOTLEY *Barneveld* II. xxiii. 424 A hard-featured but commanding and not uncomely woman.

Hence **hard'featuredness.**

1856 RUSKIN *Mod. Paint.* IV. v. xix. §22 That absence of perception of the Beautiful, which introduced a general hardfeaturedness of figure into all German and Flemish early art.

hard fern. A general name for ferns of the genus *Lomaria*, as the Northern Hard Fern, *Lomaria* (*Blechnum*) *Spicant*, of Europe.

1828 SIR J. SMITH *Eng. Flora* IV. 316 *Blechnum boreale*, Northern Hard-fern. **1830** HOOKER *Brit. Flora* 449. **1862** ANSTED *Channel Isl.* II. viii. (ed. 2) 182 The *blechnum*, or hard fern, is plentiful in both islands.

'hard-fisted, *a.* [Cf. HARD *a.* 9.] Stingy, niggardly.

a **1656** BP. HALL *Balm of Gilead* (T.), None are so gripple and hard-fisted as the childless. **1890** *Daily News* 9 Sept. 4/7 Women..this soft-handed but hard-fisted sex.

Hence **hard'fistedness.**

1869 MARQ. SALISBURY *Sp. in Ho. Lords* 22 July, A spirit of hard-fistedness which even Shylock would have envied.

'hardhack. *U.S.* [f. HARD *a.* + (?) HACK *v.*] A low shrub, *Spiræa tomentosa*, common in New England, having dense terminal panicles of rose-coloured or white flowers.

1832 W. D. WILLIAMSON *Hist. State Maine* I. 116 The Hardhack, a barren bush, usually chooses poor cold ground for its residence and growth. **1851** S. JUDD *Margaret* II. i. (Ward) 198 A bunch of the white hardhack, a cream-like flower, innerly blushing. **1866** LOWELL *Biglow P.* Introd. Poems 1890 II. 203 Our narrow New England lanes..where no better flowers were to be gathered than goldenrod and hardhack. **1880** *Harper's Mag.* Dec. 85 Them mulleins an' hardhacks in the buryin'-ground. **1968** E. R. BUCKLER *Ox Bells & Fireflies* vi. 95 The hardhacks, with roots like the roots of wisdom teeth, to be kept back from the edges of the cleared land.

hardhake: see HARDHAW.

'hard-handed, *a.*

1. Having hard hands, from manual labour.

1590 SHAKS. *Mids. N.* v. i. 72 Hard handed men, that worke in Athens heere, Which neuer labour'd in their mindes till now. **1883** S. C. HALL *Retrospect* I. 271 The hard-handed men of the working classes.

†**2.** Niggardly, penurious, close-fisted. *Obs.*

1593–5 NORDEN *Spec. Brit., M'sex* II. (1598) 16 More or lesse, as the passengers were bountifull or hard-handed.

3. Ruling with a firm or cruel hand; severe.

1641 MILTON *Reform.* II. (1851) 36 The easie, or hard-handed Monarchy's. **1784** COWPER *Task* III. 827 The cruel gripe That lean hard-handed poverty inflicts.

Hence **hard'handedness.**

1885 A. MACLAREN *Week Day Addr.* 126 The insolence and hardhandedness of Roman rule.

†**'hardhaw.** *Obs.* [Cf. HARDHEAD[1] 6.] Knapweed. Also **hardhake.**

c **1450** *Alphita* (Anecd. Oxon.) 83 *Iacea nigra*..Bulwed uel hardhaw. **14..** *MS. Trin. Coll. Camb.* R. 14, 32 *Jacea nigra*, Hardhake.

'hardhead[1], hard-head.

1. a. A hard-headed person; one not easily moved; one dull of intellect.

1519 HORMAN *Vulg.* 63 Some men counte them nygardis and hardheedis that wyll haue a rekenynge of exspensis. **1576** FLEMING *Panopl. Epist.* 36 A flintie fellowe and a hard head. **1650** BULWER *Anthropomet.* 22 Hard-head and Block-head, terms of reproach with us. **1848** DURIVAGE *Stray Subj.* 110 (Farmer) Most of the passengers had disappeared for the night, and only a knot of hard-heads were left upon deck. **1967** P. JONES *Fifth Defector* xiii. 190 I'd advise you to keep your mouth shut and let the hardheads handle it at embassy level.

b. A person not easily affected by alcohol.

1860 E. COWELL *Diary* 19 Mar. (1934) 41 Mr. Van Orden a very pleasant, but, to Sam, very dangerous companion being a great drinker, and one of the 'Hard Heads' whom drink does not seem to hurt.

†**2.** A contest of butting with the head. Also *hard-heads. Obs.*

1681 DRYDEN *Spanish Friar* v. ii. I have been at hard-head with your butting citizens. **1687** —— *Hind & P.* II. 443 Both play at hard-head till they break their brains. **1831** SCOTT *Jrnl.* 16 Oct., He has been at hard-heads with the rogues, and come off with advantage.

3. The name of several fishes: **a.** The sea scorpion or father-lasher, *Cottus scorpius*. **b.** The grey gurnard, *Trigla gurnardus*. **c.** The menhaden (*New England*).

1803 SIBBALD *Hist. Fife & Kinross* 128 (Jam.) *Scorpius major nostras*; our fishers call it Hardhead. **1810** NEILL *List of Fishes* 14 (Jam.) *Trigla Gurnardus*. Crooner or Crointer. It is known by a variety of other names, as Captain Hardhead [etc.]. **1837** HAWTHORNE *Twice-told T.* (1851) II. vi. 91 The very air was fishy, being perfumed with dead sculpins, hardheads, and dogfish. **1867** SMYTH *Sailor's Word-bk.*, *Hard-head*..on our coasts the father-lasher or sea-scorpion, *Cottus scorpius*.

4. The Californian grey whale, *Rhachianectes glaucus*: so called from its habit of butting boats.

1860 *Merc. Marine Mag.* VII. 213 They have a variety of names among whalemen, as 'Hard-head', 'Devil-fish'.

5. The ruddy duck, *Erismatura rubida*, more fully called *hard-headed dipper* (Atlantic Coast, U.S.) (*Cent. Dict.*)

6. The plant Knapweed. Also ***hard-heads.***

1794 MARTYN *Rousseau's Bot.* xxvi. 401 Common or Black Knap-weed..which the country people in some places call Hard-heads. **1828** *Craven Dial.*, *Hard-heads*, Knapweed. **1861** MISS PRATT *Flower. Pl.* III. 250 Hard-head.

7. A variety of sponge.

1883 *Fisheries Exhib. Catal.* (ed. 4) 160 The principal varieties..are known as sheep-wool, white reef, abaco velvet, dark reef, boat, hardhead, grass, yellow and glove.

8. A residual alloy of tin, iron, and arsenic, produced in the refining of tin.

1881 in RAYMOND *Mining Gloss.*

'hardhead[2]. *Obs.* exc. *Hist.* Also hardit. [? A corruption of F. *hardit*, *hardi* (in Cotgr. *ardit*, *ardy*) HARDY; said to be from *hardi*, surname of Philip III of France, under whom the coin was first issued.] A Scottish copper coin of Mary and James VI, of the value of about three halfpence English money. App. the same as the LION.

1563 in Pitcairn *Crim. Trials Scotl.* I. 440 Convict of contirfeeting of the prenting irnes..of ane Lyone callit þe Hardheid. *a* **1572** KNOX *Hist. Ref.* Wks. 1846 I. 365 (MS. G) Daylie thair was suche numbers of Lions (alias called Hard-heids) prented, that the basenes thairof maid all thingis exceiding dear. **1644** D. HUME *Hist. Douglas* 334 (Jam.) A certain brasse or copper coyne (called Hardheads). **1893** *Antiquary* Mar. 105 Coins found in St. Queran's well 1869..James VI hardheads or bodles.

'hard-headed, *a.* **1.** *lit.* Having a hard head.

†**2.** Not easily turned, as a horse; *fig.* obstinate, stubborn. *Obs.*

1583 GOLDING *Calvin on Deut.* x. 57 We bee hardheaded and thinke that all that euer is sayde is but a mockerie. **1607** TOPSELL *Four-f. Beasts* (1658) 240 It must be regarded that the Horse in leading be not drawn after you, for so will he be made hard headed, unwilling to follow. **1642** CHAS. I *Answ. to Earles of Bristol & Dorset* 7 By which we may rectifie this hard-headed distraction.

3. Not easily influenced by sophistry or sentiment; matter-of-fact, logical, practical. Cf. HARD *a.* 10.

1779 MAD. D'ARBLAY *Diary* Oct., Mrs. Dickens is..a sensible, hard-headed woman. **1883** *Pall Mall G.* 14 Dec. 1/1 Standing..at Bradford before five thousand hard-headed Yorkshiremen. **1888** BRYCE *Amer. Commw.* II. lxxiv. 609 A shrewd, cool, hard-headed man of business.

Hence **hard'headedly** *adv.*; **hard'headedness.**

1848 H. ROGERS *Ess.* I. vi. 317 A proof of his indomitable hard-headedness. **1886** *Pall Mall G.* 16 June 5/2 To deal with an irresponsible romancer thus hardheadedly may seem like breaking a butterfly on a wheel.

'hard-heart, *a. arch.* = HARD-HEARTED.

1475 *Bk. Noblesse* 66 It wolde make an harde hert man to falle the teris of his yen. **1616** J. LANE *Cont. Sqr.'s T.* (Chaucer Soc.) 120 *note* 5 Are they not hard-hart butchers remedies? **1895** MRS. K. T. HINKSON *Miracle Plays* v. 74 O hard-heart little town!

†**hard heart**, *v. Obs.* [f. next.] *trans.* To make hard of heart, to render hard-hearted.

1581 J. BELL *Haddon's Answ. Osor.* 27 After the Duke had hard harted himselfe, and waxed insolently obstinate. *Ibid.* 246 Even so Pharao..was..hard harted by God.

'hard-hearted, *a.* [f. *hard heart* + -ED[2].] Having a hard heart; incapable of being moved to pity or tenderness; unfeeling; unmerciful.

c **1205** LAY. 11990 Nes næuere na mon iboren..þæt hæleð weore swa stærc Ne swa hærd iheorted. **1340** HAMPOLE *Pr. Consc.* 7505 Here es no man lyland Swa hard-herted. *c* **1374** CHAUCER *Boeth.* II. metr. vi. 43 (Camb. MS.) He was so hard hertyd, þat he myhte ben domes man or Iuge of hyr dede beaute. *c* **1430** *Hymns Virg.* (1867) 126 Y cowde not wepe, y was so hard hertyd. **1600** J. PORY tr. *Leo's Africa* II. 51 Such a..horrible conflicte, that..would have affrighted any man, were he never so hard harted. **1613** PURCHAS *Pilgrimage* (1614) 736 Neither can the hard-hearted Rockes breake these yeelding Vessels. **1708** PRIOR *Turtle & Sparrow* 287 She soon grew sullen; I hard-hearted. **1855** MACAULAY *Hist. Eng.* xiv. III. 400 That he might die the same hardhearted, wicked Jeffreys that he had lived.

Hence **hard'heartedly** *adv.*; **hard'heartedness.**

1583 GOLDING *Calvin on Deut.* i. 3 Because of their hard-hartednesse and stubbornesse. *Ibid.* clxxxiv. 1142 Let vs deale not so hardheartedlie. **1682** SIR T. BROWNE *Chr. Mor.* 67 The dens..where malice, hardheartedness, and oppression love to dwell. **1810** BENTHAM *Packing* (1821) 186 These are the sort of persons whom so hardheartedly..we see him thus devising plans for getting rid of. **1837** SYD. SMITH *Wks.* (1867) II. 270 A hardheartedness produced by the long enjoyment of wealth and power.

†**hardhede.** *Obs. rare*$^{-1}$. [f. HARD *a.* + *-hede*, -HEAD.] Hardness.

c **1440** *Jacob's Well* (E.E.T.S.) 236 In hyȝe hylles of pryde arn iiij. wyckednessys, þat arn, dryehed, hardhed, bareynhed, & a foul fall doun.

†**hardhewe.** *Obs.* Also 6 hardewes. [app. f. HARD *a.*: second element uncertain.] The wild Chicory, *Cichorium Intybus.*

a **1500** *Sloane MS.* 5. 6/2 *Cicoria*..Ang[lice] hardhewe. **1548** TURNER *Names of Herbes* (1881) 44 *Intybus sylvestris*.. in englishe Succory or hardewes.

†**'hard-hewer.** *Obs.* A stonemason.

1447-8 in Willis & Clark *Cambridge* (1886) I. 400, xxiiij masons of kent called hard hewers. *c* **1515** *Cocke Lorell's B.* (Percy Soc.) 9 Tylers, brycke leyers, harde hewers. **1548** *Act 2 & 3 Edw. VI*, c. 15 §3 No person..shall..lett or disturbe any..joyner, hardhewer, sawyer, tyler, pavyer, glasyer [etc.]. **1602-3** *Canterbury Marriage Licences* (MS.), Will's Jacobe de ffolkston hardhewer. **1637** *Articles for building Wye bridge* cited in Pegge *Kenticisms.*

Hardian: see HARDYAN *a.* and *sb.*

hardie, var. HARDY.

‖**hardiesse** (ardi'ɛs). [a. F. *hardiesse* (12-13th c. in Hatz.-Darm.), f. *hardi* HARDY. Adopted from OFr. in 14-15th c.; and anew as an alien loan-word in 18th c.] Hardihood, boldness.

1340 *Ayenb.* 83 Ine prouesse byeþ þri þinges to-deld, hardyesse strengþe an stedeuestnesse. **1390** GOWER *Conf.* I. 147 Cowardy It torneth into hardiesse. **1475** *Bk. Noblesse* 29 In lessing youre courage ne abating your hardiesse. **1761** H. WALPOLE *Lett.* (1857) III. 411 (Stanf.) The frank *hardiesse* of the answer saved him. **1832** *Edin. Rev.* LVI. 48 Fantastic or startling *hardiesses* of expression.

†**hardifly**, *adv. Obs. rare.* [? repr. OF. *hardivement*, f. *hardif* hardy.] A by-form of HARDILY.

c **1500** *Melusine* xxxi. 231 They of poytou receyued them moch hardyfly, and wete it wel that there was grete losse of peple of bothe partyes.

hardihead ('hɑːdɪhɛd). *arch.* [f. HARDY *a.* + -HEAD.] = next.

1579 SPENSER *Sheph. Cal.* Ded. 12 Craue pardon for my hardyhedde. **1590** —— *F.Q.* I. iv. 38 Enflam'd with fury and fiers hardyhed. *a* **1764** LLOYD *Progr. Envy* Poet. Wks. 1774 I. 139 Fly, reckless mortals, fly, in vain is hardy-head. **1889** F. W. BOURDILLON in *Athenæum* 5 Oct. 454/1 True maiden art thou in thy dread; True maiden in thy hardi-head.

hardihood ('hɑːdɪhʊd). [f. HARDY *a.* + -HOOD.] The quality or condition of being hardy.

1. Boldness, hardiness; audacity.

1634 MILTON *Comus* 650 With dauntless hardihood, And brandish'd blade, rush on him. **1849** MACAULAY *Hist. Eng.* vii, More than one day..was retrieved by the hardi-hood with which he rallied his broken battalions. **1860** MAURY *Phys. Geog. Sea* ii. §82 That the winds do make currents in the sea no one will have the hardihood to deny.

2. Robustness (of body or constitution). *rare.*

1794 S. WILLIAMS *Vermont* 165 Amidst the rudeness and hardihood of the savage state. **1807** G. CHALMERS *Caledonia* I. II. vi. 304 The vigour of his mind was properly supported by the hardyhood of his body. **1861** DELAMER *Fl. Gard.* 148 Their hardihood is not to be depended on, and they can only be trusted as conservatory plants here.

hardily ('hɑːdɪlɪ), *adv.* [f. HARDY *a.* + -LY².] In a hardy manner.

1. Boldly; courageously, with hardihood.

a **1225** *Leg. Kath.* 676 Hald hardiliche [*v.r.* herdeliche] on þæt tu hauest bigunnen. *a* **1300** *Cursor M.* 12953 Herdili [*Gött.* hardli] he yode him nerr. **13..** *Guy Warw.* (A.) 2966 Now..fiȝt þai agin ardiliche. *c* **1430** *Pilgr. Lyf Manhode* II. xxvi. (1869) 85 Go, quod she, hardiliche, with oute dredinge rude entendement. **1596** DALRYMPLE tr. *Leslie's Hist. Scot.* VIII. 72 Nochtheles he sparet nocht to speik hardilier. **1600** HOLLAND *Livy* 461 (R.) At the first the Gaules and Spanyards..mainteined the conflict right hardily. **1799** BP. HORSLEY *Speech* July (R.), Confidently and hardily I make the assertion, and I challenge confutation. **1860** PUSEY *Min. Proph.* 313 They could foretell hardily, because they could not yet be convicted of untruth.

†**2.** Robustly; not tenderly. *Obs. rare.*

1674 N. COX *Gentl. Recreat.* IV. (1686) 41 Horses that run abroad all Winter, which however hardily bred, and kept [etc.]. **1748** RICHARDSON *Clarissa* (1811) III. iii. 29 She loves to use herself hardily. **1793** BEDDOES *Catarrh* 167 Among those hardily brought up.

†**3.** *Parenthetically.* = It may be boldly said; freely, certainly, assuredly, by all means. In later use changed through *hardely* to *hardly. Obs.*

c **1300** *Cursor M.* 23767 (Edin.) Hardilik [*v.r.* hardeli] es he cuard, þat nankin part mai pol of hard. *c* **1386** CHAUCER *Merch. T.* 68 Alle othere manere giftes, hardily [*so 4 MSS.*; 2 hardely]..alle been giftes of Fortune. *c* **1400** *Destr. Troy* 1934 þou hardly no hede of þi hele toke..When þou entrid our Ile. *c* **1440** CAPGRAVE *Life St. Kath.* IV. 1348 There lyue noon better at this day, hardyly. *a* **1529** SKELTON *P. Sparowe* 270 No, no, syr, hardely. *a* **1553** UDALL *Royster D.* I. ii. (Arb.) 19 Yea now hardly lette me alone. **1553** T. WILSON *Rhet.* (1580) 4 Bee he Preacher, Lawier, yea, or Cooke either hardely. **1600** HOLLAND *Livy* XXIV. viii, Elect him Consull hardly, and good leave have you.

‖**hardim** ('hɑːdɪm). In 5 hardan. [Arab. *ḥarḏawn*, lizard, land crocodile.] An agamoid lizard, *Stellio vulgaris*, of the Levant.

1398 TREVISA *Barth. De P.R.* XVIII. xxi. (1495) 780 Al his [chameleon's] body is rough and sharpe as the body of an Hardan. **1860** WOOD *Illustr. Nat. Hist.* (1863) III. 88 *Hardim*, the Arab name for the Stellio. **1884-5** *Standard Nat. Hist.* III. 414 (Cent.) The hardims are of an olive green color shaded with black, and below a pale yellow.

hardiment ('hɑːdɪmənt). *arch.* [a. OF. *hardiment* (in Godef.), f. *hardi* HARDY: see -MENT.] Boldness, courage, daring, hardihood.

c **1374** CHAUCER *Troylus* IV. 505 (533) Artow in Troye and hast noon hardiment To take a womman which þat loueth þe? *c* **1430** *Pilgr. Lyf Manhode* IV. xxiv. (1869) 189, I wot neuere how þou hast take hardement to turne ayen to me. **1500-20** DUNBAR *Poems* xxvii. 20 He tynt all hardyment, Ffor feir he chaingit hew. **1600** FAIRFAX *Tasso* VI. xxxiv. 100 Our foes fierce courage, strength and hardiment. **1791** COWPER *Iliad* VII. 203 This brunt of hostile hardiment severe. **1803** WORDSW. '*Vanguard of Liberty*', Vanguard of Liberty, ye men of Kent..Now is the time to prove your hardiment! **1813** SCOTT *Rokeby* I. vii, The full carouze, that lent His brow a fiercer hardiment.

†**b.** A deed of daring, a bold exploit. *Obs.*

1375 BARBOUR *Bruce* XII. 509 Mony ane hardyment douchtely Wes thair eschewit [= achieved]. **1596** SHAKS. *1 Hen. IV*, I. iii. 101 He did confound the best part of an houre In changing hardiment with great Glendower. **1601** WEEVER *Mirr. Mart.* C vj, Tis often seen, ill-pleasing accidents Proceed from rage and hare-braind hardiments. **1611** SHAKS. *Cymb.* v. iv. 75 Like hardiment Posthumus hath To Cymbeline perform'd.

hardiness ('hɑːdɪnɪs). [f. HARDY *a.* + -NESS.] The quality or condition of being hardy.

1. Boldness, daring; audacity; hardihood. Now somewhat *rare.*

1297 R. GLOUC. (1724) 64 He..the emperour with stod, And dredde of hys hardynesse. **1393** LANGL. *P. Pl.* C. XXI. 80 No boye hadde hardynesse hym to touche in deyinge. *c* **1450** *Merlin* 231 A yonge knyght of grete hardynesse. **1561** EDEN *Arte Navig.* Pref. ℭℭj, Accoumpting desperatnesse for boldenesse, rashnesse for hardinesse. **1647** CLARENDON *Hist. Reb.* VI. §261 There being none that had the hardiness yet to declare..for the King. **1814** SOUTHEY in *Q. Rev.* XII. 76 [Du Bartas] coining words when he did not find them ready minted for his use, introducing new compounds, good or bad, with equal hardiness. **1866** R. CHAMBERS *Ess.* Ser. I. 27 To execute a purpose so lofty..would have..required great hardiness of heart.

2. Capability of endurance, physical or mental. Now chiefly, Physical robustness.

1642 MILTON *Apol. Smect.* Wks. (1847) 80/1 Preserving the Body's health and hardiness. **1781** GIBBON *Decl. & F.* II. xl. 490 Luxury enervated the hardiness of their minds and bodies. **1789** BENTHAM *Princ. Legisl.* vi. §9 The external indications of hardiness are the firmness of the muscular fibres and the callosity of the skin. **1834** *Penny Cycl.* II. 189/1 [The apple] from its hardiness and great abundance, is one of the most important productions of cold climates. **1879** *Cassell's Techn. Educ.* IV. 39/1 The extreme hardiness of the race.

¶ Catachr. for *hardness.* (Often an error of copyists and editors.)

1559 TAVERNER *Gard. Wysed.* I. 3 a, The office of a capitayne is agaynst rebelles to use hardynesse, and agaynst his liege subiectes, gentylnesse. **1596** SPENSER *State Irel.* (Globe) 640/1 Great endurours of cold, hunger, and all hardiness.

†**harding.** *Obs. rare*⁻¹. A slowly developing plant: cf. HASTING. In quot. *transf.*

1581 MULCASTER *Positions* iv. (1887) 19 Ripenes in children is not tyed to one time, no more then all corne is ripe for one reaping..Some be hastinges and will on, some be hardinges, and drawe backe.

hardish ('hɑːdɪʃ), *a.* [f. HARD *a.* + -ISH.] Somewhat hard (in various senses).

1580 HOLLYBAND *Treas. Fr. Tong*, *Duret*, hardish. *a* **1592** GREENE *Alphonsus* IV. Wks. (Rtldg.) 240/2 For my pillow.. The hardish hillocks have suffic'd my turn. **1676** TEMPLE *Let. to King* Wks. 1731 II. 423 With Terms something hardish. **1747** *Gentl. Mag.* 55 In 8 days it grew hardish, and in 14 quite dry. **1864** BURTON *Scot Abr.* I. iv. 160 It will require a hardish course of reading.

†**hardiship.** *Obs. rare*⁻¹. [f. HARDY *a.* + -SHIP.] Hardy behaviour, courage.

a **1240** *Wohunge* in *Cott. Hom.* 271 Moni man þurh his strengðe and hardischipe ek makes him lued and ȝerned.

hardishrew ('hɑːdɪʃruː). Now *local.* Also 7 hardyshrew, hardshrew, 9 (*dial.*) hardistraw, hardistrow. [app. f. HARDY *a.* + SHREW.] A name variously applied to the field-mouse, harvest-mouse, and shrew-mouse.

1601 HOLLAND *Pliny* I. 234 In Italy the hardy shrews are venomous in their biting. **1656** W. D. tr. *Comenius' Gate Lat. Unl.* ¶193 The Rat, Hardshrew, and whole herd of mice, enemies to corn. **1686** PLOT *Staffordsh.* 222 A Hardishrew or Nursrow (as they here call them,) i.e. a field-mouse. **1847-78** HALLIWELL, *Hardishrew*, a field-mouse. *Staff.* Also called the *hardistraw.* **1882** *W. Worcestersh. Gloss.*, *Hardishrew*, The field-mouse; also *Hardistraw.* **1884** *Upton Gloss.*, *Hardistrow*, a shrew-mouse.

†**hardiss, hardysse**, *v. Obs. rare.* [f. *hardiss-*, extended stem of OF. *hardir*, f. *hardi* HARDY.] *trans.* To make hardy, embolden.

1297 R. GLOUC. (1724) 204 So muche..he truste To hym sulue & to hardyssy ys men. *Ibid.* 426 Vor so wel he vaȝt, & hys men hardyssede echon.

†**'hardlaik.** *Obs.* [a. ON. *harðleikr* hardness, harshness.] Hardship, harshness, severity.

c **1400** *Destr. Troy* 3476 With hardlayke & harme, þat happyn shall after. *Ibid.* 8124 The shall happon in helle hardlaikes mo.

hardly ('hɑːdlɪ), *adv.* Forms: see HARD *a.* [f. HARD *a.* + -LY².] In a hard manner.

†**1.** With energy, force, or strenuous exertion; vigorously, forcibly, violently. *Obs.*

c **1205** LAY. 7480 Hardliche [*c* **1275** hardeliche] heo heowen. *Ibid.* 16700 Samuel þæt sweord an-hof And hærdeliche adun sloh. *c* **1305** *St. Christopher* 82 in *E.E.P.* (1862) 62 He..step hardeliche & faste. *c* **1460** *Towneley Myst.* (Surtees) 247 Lay on him hardely, And make hym go his gate. ? *a* **1550** *Freiris of Berwik* 552 in *Dunbar's Poems* (1893) 303 Stryk, stryk herdely, for now is tyme to the. **1607** TOPSELL *Serpents* (1658) 625 The Lamprey caught fast hold on his hand, biting hardly. **1713** STEELE *Guardian* No. 58 ¶6 I..drink stale beer the more hardly, because, unless I will, nobody else does. **1818** MRS. SHELLEY *Frankenst.* iv. (1865) 68 My pulse beat so quickly and hardly, that I felt the palpitation of every artery.

†**2.** Boldly, daringly, hardily. *Obs.*

a **1225** *Ancr. R.* 268 Heo..þet, wið swuche goste, herdeliche ne uihteð. *a* **1300** *Cursor M.* 12953 (Gött.) Hardli [*Fairf.* baldeli] he ȝode him nere. *c* **1400** *Rowland & O.* 446 Feghte one, dere Sone, hardely. *c* **1489** CAXTON *Sonnes of Aymon* viii. 194 Lete vs goo to it hardly For we durste well assaylle the devylle when ye be wyth vs. **1566** PAINTER *Pal. Pleas.* I. 99 b, Speake hardly thy minde. **1622** BP. ANDREWES *Serm.* (ed. 18) 258 Keep on your hats, sit even as you do hardly.

†**3.** Firmly. *Obs.*

a **1225** *Ancr. R.* 268 Herdeliche ileueð þet al þe deofles strencðe melteð þuruh þe grace of þe holi sacrament. *c* **1440** CAPGRAVE *Life St. Kath.* v. 264 Leue this doctryne hardyly as ȝoure crede! **1583** STANYHURST *Æneis, Conceites* (Arb.) 138 In brest of the godesse, Gorgon was coketed hardlye.

4. With hard pressure; with severity or rigour; severely, rigorously, harshly.

1523 LD. BERNERS *Froiss.* I. cxxx. 158 He is hardely matched, wherfore he hathe nede of your ayde. **1568** GRAFTON *Chron.* II. 190 Two Bishops and an Abbot..were hardly and streightly kept in strong prison so long as the king lyved. **1573** G. HARVEY *Letter-bk.* (Camden) 3, I besout [him]..that he wuld not deale so hardly bi me. **1603** KNOLLES *Hist. Turks* (1621) 51 The unconstant people.. now began to speak hardly of him. *a* **1656** BP. HALL *Rem. Wks.* (1660) 32 Being shipped at Deep, the Sea used us hardly. **1766** GOLDSM. *Vic. W.* xxxi, How is it, Sir, that this poor man..is used thus hardly? **1853** A. J. MORRIS *Business* I. 10 Conscience is hardly bestead by the demands of life. **1886** *Law T.* 20 Feb. 283/2 The rule worked hardly.

5. With trouble or hardship; uneasily, painfully.

1535 COVERDALE *Ps.* xxi[i]. 29 They that lye in the dust, and lyue so hardly. **1548** HALL *Chron.*, *Hen. VII*, 41 Cornysh-men..gate theyr lyvyng hardly by minynge and diggyng tinne and metall. **1630** *R. Johnson's Kingd. & Commw.* 118 The Husbandmen live hardly. **1705** BOSMAN *Guinea* 108 The Money we get here is indeed hardly enough acquired. **1712** SEWALL *Diary* 17 June (1879) II. 352 Mr. White condescending to ride before, sitting hardly. **1840** MACAULAY *Ess.*, *Clive* (1887) 555 What is made is slowly, hardly, and honestly earned.

6. Not easily, with difficulty. *Obs.* exc. as contained in 7.

1535 COVERDALE *Wisd.* ix. 16 Very hardly can we discerne the thinges that are vpon earth. **1582** N. T. (Rhem.) *Luke* xviii. 24 How hardly [TIND., CRANM., *Geneva*, with what difficulty] shal they that haue money enter into the kingdom of God? **1597** HOOKER *Eccl. Pol.* v. ii. §2 We are hardliest able to bring such proofe..as may satisfie gainesayers. **1598** GRENEWEY *Tacitus' Ann.* IV. xvi. 116 Vnto whom accesse was hardliest obtained. **1650** FULLER *Pisgah* 270 Bitumen.. quickly kindled, hardly quenched. **1708** BURNET *Lett.* (ed. 3) 123 When it has rain'd ever so little..the Carts go deep, and are hardly drawn. **1766** FORDYCE *Serm. Yng. Wom.* (1767) II. xiv. 271 Easily provoked and hardly pacified. **1822** KEBLE *Serm.* i. (1848) 17 The rock, to which Solomon hardly won his way after many hard conflicts.

7. Barely, only just; almost not; not quite; scarcely. (In early use only gradually distinguished from 6. Formerly sometimes (as still in vulgar use) with superfluous negative.)

1553 EDEN *Treat. Newe Ind.* (Arb.) 7 It hardelye agreeth with the pinciples of Philosophie and common experience. **1601** HOLLAND *Pliny* I. 310 Being so little. (as hardly the finenesse thereof cannot be seen). **1601** R. JOHNSON *Kingd. & Commw.* (1603) 89 All which will hardly amount to fower score pounds. **1674** N. COX *Gentl. Recreat.* III. (1677) 59 Either of these will not suffer him to keep hardly flesh upon his back. **1698** FRYER *Acc. E. India & P.* 142 When Day broke I could hardly believe my Eyes. **1710** STEELE *Tatler* No. 193 ¶1, I had hardly entered the Room, when I was accosted by Mr. Thomas Dogget. **1783** HAILES *Antiq. Chr. Ch.* i. 2 We can hardly place it earlier. **1840** DE QUINCEY *Style* Wks. XI. 262 With a life of leisure, but with hardly any books. **1860-1** FLO. NIGHTINGALE *Nursing* 46, I need hardly say, that [etc.]. **1874** GREEN *Short Hist.* ii. §7. 100 A year had hardly passed. [*Mod.* (*vulgar*) I couldn't hardly tell what he meant.]

8. In close proximity, closely; = HARD *adv.* 6.

1584 in *Spenser's Wks.* (Grosart) I. 483 Being hardlie followed by certaine kearnes. **1603** KNOLLES *Hist. Turks* (1621) 35 They were so hardly pursued. **1880** *Daily News* 12 Nov. 2/1 They are hardly run by some of the English Potteries.

†**9.** *Parenthetically.* Certainly, assuredly, by all means: see HARDILY 3. *Obs.*

10. *Comb.* (with *ppl. adjs.*), as ***hardly-acquired, -earned, -labouring, -rendered, -removed, -used.***

1625 K. LONG tr. *Barclay's Argenis* III. xii. 190 Tokens of his hardly-removed sicknesse. **1858** MRS. OLIPHANT *Laird of Norlaw* II. 31 Many a hardly-labouring soul, full of generous plans and motives, has seen a stranger enter into its labours. **1866** TROLLOPE *Belton Est.* II. vi. 158 The hardly-used groom had returned from his futile afternoon's inquiry. **1882** OUIDA *Maremma* I. 34 With her hardly-earned gains. **1890** W. STEBBING *Peterborough* ix. 176 The honour and loyalty of the hardly-used veteran. **1937** *Discovery* Aug. 240/2 The hardly-won natural gem. **1952** C. P. BLACKER *Eugenics* 282 Each hardly-won improvement in human conditions.

hard-meat. ? *Obs.* Corn and hay used as fodder, as opposed to grass.

1481-4 E. PASTON in *P. Lett.* No. 859 III. 280, I had my horsse with hym at lyvery.. I payed for hard mete ever to hym. **1523** FITZHERB. *Husb.* §66 A cowe shall gyue more mylke with a lyttell grasse and strawe.. thanne she shall doo with hey and strawe.. for the harde meate dryeth vp the mylke. **1641** BEST *Farm. Bks.* (Surtees) 73 If there fall a good thicke snowe and frosts with it.. it will make them fall to theire hard-meate most sharpely and keenely. **1737** BRACKEN *Farriery Impr.* (1757) II. 85 To suffer Horses to lie at Hard-meat.. for Weeks.

†**b.** *fig.* ***at (to) hard meat***: in close confinement; under strict restraint. *Obs.*

1594 NASHE *Unfort. Trav.* 16 Dreame.. that I am close at hard meate at Windsore or at Hampton Court. **1642** BAKER tr. *Malvezzi's Disc. Tacitus* 459 They meant to hold Augustus (as the saying is) to hard meat, and make him grant what they demanded. **1725** SWIFT *Let. to Pope* Wks. 1761 VIII. 46, I hear nothing of our friend Gay, but I find the court keeps him at hard meat.

hard metal. 1. Any of various alloys valued for their hardness.

1729, 1845 [see METAL *sb.* 5]. **1911** *Encycl. Brit.* XXI. 339/1 Hard metal (96 parts of tin, 8 of antimony and 2 of copper), a mixture very closely resembling.. 'Britannia metal'.

2. (See quot. 1967.)

1936 *Jrnl. Iron & Steel Inst.* CXXXIV. 66A The author discusses the application of hard metal alloys and of diamond substitutes (such as tungsten carbide) to the hard-facing of tools. **1960** *Ibid.* CXCIV. 532/1 The final section is devoted to a consideration of materials used for cutting tools, namely unalloyed tool steels, alloyed tool steels,.. hard metals, i.e. sintered tungsten carbide and the like. **1967** A. K. OSBORNE *Encycl. Iron & Steel Industry* (ed. 2) 195/1 *Hard metals*, powdered carbides of tungsten, tantalum, or titanium, cemented into solid masses by mixing with powdered cobalt or nickel, then cold pressing and sintering. Used for cutting tools, wire drawing dies, and parts subjected to heavy wear and abrasion.

hard-mouthed, ('hɑːdmaʊðd, -maʊθt), *a.*

1. Having a hard mouth: said of a horse not easily controlled by the bit or rein.

1617 MARKHAM *Caval.* II. 106 When they haue either hard mouthed horses, or runne away Iades. **1682** *Lond. Gaz.* No. 1708/4 A Spring Snaffle, that Commandeth with the greatest ease.. all hard-mouthed Run-away Horses. **1854** WOOD *Anecd. Anim. Life* (1855) 398 Little hard-mouthed animals.. perfectly independent of bit and bridle.

2. *fig.* Self-willed, obstinate.

1686 D'URFEY *Commw. Women* I. i. 5 They are so hard mouth'd, there's no dealing with 'em. **1704** SWIFT *Mech. Operat. Spirit* Misc. (1711) 299 Wonderfully headstrong, and hard-mouth'd. **1722** DE FOE *Moll Flanders* (1840) 311 Two wenches, a couple of hard-mouthed Jades. **1800** A. CARLYLE *Autobiog.* (1860) 432 Robertson's soothing manner prevented his being hard-mouthed with him.

hardness ('hɑːdnɪs). Forms: see HARD *a.* [f. HARD *a.* + -NESS.] **a.** The quality or condition of being hard; difficulty of penetration, solution, apprehension, performance, endurance; inflexibility, rigidity, stiffness, harshness; rigour, severity, cruelty; obduracy, obstinacy; hardiness, etc.: see HARD *a.*

a **700** *Epinal Gloss.* 871 *Rigore*, heardnissæ. *c* **1000** *Ags. Gosp.* Matt. xix. 8 For eower heorte heardnysse. *c* **1000** *Sax. Leechd.* I. 296 Wiþ ðæs maʒan heardnysse. *c* **1025** *Rule St. Benet* (Logeman) 96 Beon ʒebodenne ealra heardnessa and stiðnissa. *c* **1175** *Lamb. Hom.* 47 He mihte noht iþolie þe herdnesse of þe rapes. *a* **1300** *Cursor M.* 19325 (Gött.) Þai durst no hardnes þaim do. **1390** GOWER *Conf.* II. 71 Hys lady.. With hardnesse his herte fyreth. *c* **1440** *Jacob's Well* (E.E.T.S.) 195 Hardnes of clothyng on bak & in bed. *c* **1440** *Promp. Parv.* 227/2 Hardenes of knowy(n)ge, or dede doynge.. *difficultas.* *a* **1529** SKELTON *Now synge we, etc.* 75 Jesu.. That for man suffred great hardnes. **1552** *Bk. Com. Prayer, Litany*, From hardnesse of hearte.. Good lord, deliuer us. **1573-80** BARET *Alv.* N 108 Hardnesse is sparing of expenses, niggardship. **1577** B. GOOGE *Heresbach's Husb.* I. (1586) 14 The tediousnesse and hardnesse thereof driveth them away. *Ibid.* IV. 160 b, Powre in Plaister, or some liquid thing, that may come to a hardnesse in the shell. **1579** E. K. *Gloss. Spenser's Sheph. Cal.* Mar. 23 By reason of Winters hardnesse. **1596** SPENSER *F.Q.* IV. viii. 27 Enur'd to hardnesse and to homely fare. **1598** BARCKLEY *Felic. Man* (1631) 440 Wealth maketh a woman proud, beauty suspected, and hardnesse of favour lothsome. **1604** SHAKS. *Oth.* III. iv. 34 Oh hardnes to dissemble! **1691** RAY *Creation* (1714) 164, I have armed thee with courage and Hardness to attempt the Seas. **1697** DRYDEN *Virg. Georg.* IV. 155 Honeycombs of Golden Juice.. T' allay the Strength and Hardness of the Wine. **1704** *Collect. Voy. & Trav.* (Churchill) III. 53/2 Because of the Hardness of the Weather. *a* **1745** SWIFT (J.), The tenants poor, the hardness of the times. **1822-34** *Good's Study Med.* (ed. 4) III. 191 When hardness of hearing depends upon a deficiency of cerumen. **1836** *Penny Cycl.* VI. 142/1 Carbonate of lime.. to this in part the hardness of water is owing. **1862** MRS. H. WOOD *Mrs. Hallib.* II. xxvi. (1888) 290 A stony hardness settled on the young lady's face. **1883** *Manch. Exam.* 3 Dec. 4/1 The tendency of the rates was firm, owing to the hardness of the short loan market. **1895** STORY-MASKELYNE *Crystallogr.* i. 8 The hardness of crystals in different directions has been estimated by means of an instrument termed a sclerometer.

b. With *a* and *pl.* An instance of this quality; a hardship.

1340 *Ayenb.* 236 Hit be-houeþ þet uless beate and wesse be dissiplines and be hardnesses. *c* **1374** CHAUCER *Boeth.* IV. pr. v. 102 (Camb. MS.) So as god.. yeueth.. to goode folk hardnesses and to shrewes he grauntyth hym hir wyl. **1658** JER. TAYLOR *Let. to Evelyn* in *Evelyn's Mem.* (1857) III. 102 One of the hardnesses will be that you must over-come even this just and reasonable grief. *a* **1700** DRYDEN (J.), Sculptors are obliged to.. make many ample folds, which are insufferable hardnesses. **1790** *By-stander* 43 The crudest hardnesses.. are to be rubbed off.

c. *spec.* The degree of resistance of a mineral to abrasion or scratching.

1784 R. KIRWAN *Elem. Mineral.* I. App. 171 (*heading*) Table of the comparative hardness of different Species of Stones, extracted chiefly from the Memoirs of Stockholm, for 1768. Mr. Quist, the author of this Memoir determined the hardness of most of the following stones. **1904** GOODCHILD & TWENEY *Technol. & Sci. Dict.* 279/2 *Hardness*, the hardness of a mineral is determined by noting which of the standard minerals the specimen may be scratched by, and which of the ten it will scratch.

d. Of radiation (cf. HARD *a.* 17 a).

1926 R. W. LAWSON tr. *Hevesy & Paneth's Man. Radioactivity* IV. i. 45 The shorter the wave-length of the γ-rays, the greater is their penetrating power through matter, or the greater their 'hardness'.

†'**hardock.** *Obs.* Also **hor-dock, hardoke.** [app. f. OE. *hār*, ME. *hôr*, HOAR + DOCK.] Some coarse weedy plant: probably burdock.

The burdock has hoary foliage. (Some have however suggested that the word is a misprint for *burdock* itself; and various other conjectures have been offered.)

1605 SHAKS. *Lear* IV. iv. 4 (Fol. 1) Crown'd.. with Hardokes [*Qq.* hor-docks, *Fol. 2* hardocks], Hemlocke, Nettles, Cuckoo flowres, Darnell, and all the idle weedes that grow.

hardometer (hɑː'dɒmɪtə(r)). [f. HARD *a.* + -O + -METER.] An instrument for measuring the hardness of metals.

1934 H. O'NEILL *Hardness of Metals* iii. 90 The 'Firth Hardometer'.. is an excellent bench instrument. **1940** *Jrnl. R. Aeronaut. Soc.* XLIV. 845 The following chapter carries on the hardness tests with details of the Rothwell test, the Firth hardometer, the Firth-Brown variable load hardometer and notched bar impact testing. **1946** *Firth Brown Gloss. Metall. Terms* 26 *Firth hardometer*,... For testing harder materials a pyramid diamond indenter is recommended and can be supplied with the [Brinell] machine in addition to the hardened steel ball. **1958** *Oxf. Univ. Gaz.* 10 Mar. 772/1 Mr. Allen also completed the examination of about 40 Bronze Age implements of copper and bronze by hardometer.

hard-on: see HARD *sb.* 1 d.

'**hard-pan.** orig. *U.S.* [See PAN.]

1. A firm subsoil of clayey, sandy, or gravelly detritus; also, hard unbroken ground.

1817 T. DWIGHT *Trav. New Eng.* (1821) I. 374 What is here called hard pan, a very stiff loam, so closely combined, as wholly to prevent the water from passing through it. **1828** WEBSTER, *Pan*, among farmers, the hard stratum of earth that lies below the soil; called the *hard pan.* **1829** H. MURRAY *N. Amer.* II. III. i. 273 The farmer comes to what Mr. Spafford calls hard-pan, a stiff impenetrable surface on which no vegetable substance will grow. **1883** *Century Mag.* Nov. 113 The New [World] is for the most part yet raw, undigested hard-pan. **1886** MARQ. LORNE in *Gd. Words* 166 Large quantities of loose rock and hardpan. **1963** D. W. & E. E. HUMPHRIES tr. *Termier's Erosion & Sedimentation* 406 *Hardpan*, an English agricultural term (used mainly in the U.S.A., Africa and Australia) for a horizon in podsolic and lateritic soils hardened by precipitation and cementation. **1968** *New Scientist* 10 Oct. 79/3 The number of rice paddies under cultivation in some Far Eastern countries could be doubled using an asphalt 'hardpan'.

2. *fig.* Lowest level or foundation; bottom; 'bed-rock'.

1852 W. B. PIKE in *N. Hawthorne & Wife* (1885) I. 444 Almost all the novel-writers I have read, although truthful to nature, go through only some of the strata; but you are the only one who breaks through the hard-pan. **1860** HOLMES *Elsie V.* viii, Mr. Silas Peckham had gone a little deeper than he meant, and come upon the 'hard-pan', as the well-diggers call it, of the Colonel's character. **1872** B. TALBOT in *Amer. Ann. Deaf* July 135 Down in the very hard-pan of ignorance.. must the workman prepare a bed for this foundation. **1883** H. A. BEERS in *Century Mag.* June 285/2 But it [a book] didn't appear to get down to hard-pan or to take a firm grip on life.

3. *attrib.* and *Comb.*

1870 J. K. MEDBERY *Men & Myst. Wall St.* 212 Hard pan is soon reached, and both old world and new are full of hard-pan capitalists. **1889** K. MUNROE *Golden Days* xi. 122 To tell the honest hard-pan truth. **1907** R. W. SERVICE *Songs of Sourdough* (1908) 77 When a man gits on his uppers in a hard-pan sort of town. **1928** *Bull. Amer. Soil Survey Assoc.* IX. 33 Immaturely developed soils may have a hardpan-like horizon.

hardpeer ('hɑːtpɪə(r)). *S. Afr.* Also **hardepeer,** and anglicized **hard pear.** [Afrikaans; f. Du. *hard* hard + *peer* pear.] A small tree of the Cape, *Olinia cymosa*, having hard wood; also applied to other trees (see quot. 1913).

1801 J. BARROW *Trav. S. Afr.* I. 340 Hard peer... Uses.. Sometimes in waggons. **1851** *Catal. Gt. Exhib.* IV. 1. 951 Pear (hard). **1874** LINDLEY & MOORE *Treas. Bot.* Suppl. s.v. *Olinia*, The plant grows in rocky thickets and woods at the Cape, where it is known as Hardpeer. **1880** Hard Pear [see PEAR *sb.* 3]. **1887** C. A. MOLONEY *Sk. Forestry W. Afr.* 354 Hardpeer of the Cape.. Shrub 4 to 10 feet high. **1913** PETTMAN *Africanderisms, Hard Pear.* (1) In Natal this name is given to *Pleurostylia capensis.* (2) In the Cape Colony it is applied to *Strychnos Henningsii.* **1961** PALMER & PITMAN *Trees S. Afr.* lii. 297 *Strychnos Henningsii. Hard pear,* hardepeer... This tree should not be confused with the 'hard pear' of the Knysna forests, which is *Olinia cymosa*, and which belongs to a different family.

hards, hurds (hɑːdz, hɜːdz), *sb. pl.* Now *local.* Forms: α. 1 heordan, 2-3 heorden, 4-5 herdes, -is, 4-7 hurdes, 5-6 heerdis, hyrdes, -ys, -is, 6-7 hirds, 6- hurds. β. 4-6 hardes, -is, -ys, 5- hards. [OE. *heordan* fem. pl.: cf. early mod.Du. *herde, heerde* 'fibra lini' Kilian (not in Hexham). Corresp. to OLG., OFris. *hêde*, NFris. *hêde, heed*, MLG., MDu., Da. *hede*, LG. *hede, heden, heen*:—OTeut. type **hizdôn-*; cf. Goth. *mizdô*, OS. *mêd(a*, OE. *meord.* The form *hards* is north. and n. midl., *herds* or *hurds* s. midl. and west. These are in form plural, but are sometimes construed as sing. Cf. HARDEN *sb.* and *a.*] The coarser parts of flax or hemp separated in hackling.

α. *c* **725** *Corpus Gloss.* 1908 *Stuppa*, heordan. *c* **1050** *Gloss.* in Wr.-Wülcker 451/27 *Naptarum*, heordena. *a* **1225** *Ancr. R.* 418 Nexst fleshe ne schal mon werien no linene cloð, bute ȝif hit beo of herde and of greate heorden. *c* **1350** *Leg. Rood* (1871) 81 Hir clathes.. bigan to brin Als herdes þat had bene right dry. ? *a* **1366** CHAUCER *Rom. Rose* 1233 A sukkenye, That not of hempe ne heerdis was. **1398** TREVISA *Barth. De P.R.* VIII. xliii. (Tollem. MS.), Yf suche a stone is set aforne þe sonne, hurdes set þerto beþ tende and set on fyre. *c* **1400** *Lanfranc's Cirurg.* 35 A plumacio.. maad of herdis [*B.* hurdes] or of towe. *c* **1440** *Promp. Parv.* 241/1 Hyrdys, or herdys of flax, or hempe, *stuppa.* **1530** PALSGR. 183 *Vnes estovpes*, a locke of towe or hurdes. **1555** EDEN *Decades* 193 It [coco-nut] is inuolued and couered with many webbes much lyke vnto those hyrdes of towe whiche they vse in Andalusia. **1737** BRACKEN *Farriery Impr.* (1756) I. 292 Wounds.. dress'd with Hurds. **1837** WHITTOCK, etc. *Bk. Trades* (1842) 238 Hold the strike of flax stiff in your hand, and break it well upon the coarse hackle, saving the hurds to make harder cloth of.

β. **1375** BARBOUR *Bruce* XVII. 612 Pik and ter als haf thai tane, And lynt and hardiss with brynstane. **14..** *Nom.* in Wr.-Wülcker 696/9 *Hec stupa*, a hardes. **1526** *Pilgr. Perf.* (W. de W. 1531) 48 Chyppes, hey, & hardes, whiche be maters apt to burne. **1656** W. COLES *Art of Simpling* 64 A Cokar tree, whose hairy stuff or hards which is next the outer bark doth make cordage and tackle for ships. **1795** M. MADAN *Persius* 145 *note*, The coarse part of flax, tow, hards, oakum to calk ships with. **1818** SCOTT *Fam. Lett.* 16 Jan. (1894) II. 8 These Regalia.. were smuggled out by a clergyman's wife under quantity of hards of lint. *a* **1825** FORBY *Voc. E. Anglia, Hards*, coarse flax.

hard scrabble (hɑːd 'skræb(ə)l). *U.S. colloq.* [cf. SCRABBLE *v.* 4.] **1.** 'A place thought of as the acme of barrenness where a livelihood may be obtained only with great difficulty. Also attrib. Often as a proper name.' (*Dict. Americanisms.*)

1804 LEWIS & CLARK *Orig. Jrnls.* (1905) VII. 38 Got on our way at hard Scrable Perarie. **1904** *Pittsburgh Gaz.* 7 July 4 In the early days of my ministry.. I was sent to take charge of a little hard-scrabble circuit. **1949** *Sat. Even. Post* 30 Apr. 22/3 She was the daughter of a hard-scrabble rancher. **1972** *Science* 26 May 891/1 The reservoir would back up along the creek and inundate 125 small, hardscrabble farms that lay along 24 miles of the stream's flood-plain.

2. 'A vigorous effort made under great stress.' (*Dict. Americanisms.*)

1812 *Salem Gaz.* 29 May 2/3 Presidential Hard Scrabble! **1851** H. MELVILLE *Moby Dick* II. xxx. 205 While taking that hard-scrabble scramble upon the dead whale's back. **1854** S. HALE *Lett.* (1919) 7 By a well-organised hard-scrabble, Luc. and I get the breakfast things washed by nine o'clock. **1972** *Sat. Rev.* 26 Feb. 31/3 [Ulster] Catholics.. enjoy the benefits of.. an economy that may be hardscrabble but is still substantially more prosperous than the South's.

hard-set, *a.* [f. SET *pa. pple.*]

1. In a hard or difficult position; beset by difficulty or trouble.

1387 TREVISA *Higden* (Rolls) IV. 55 Þere Hanibal was harde sette [*infestatus*] foure dayes wiþ Galles. *c* **1475** *Rauf Coilȝear* 449, I sall hald that I haue hecht, bot I be hard set. **1737** BRACKEN *Farriery Impr.* (1756) I. 254 The poor Creature is very hard set to drive his Water from him. **1890** BOLDREWOOD *Col. Reformer* (1891) 221, I have sent for some books.. Until they arrive, I shall be rather hard-set.

2. Set so as to be hard or firm.

1813 SIR R. WILSON *Diary* II. 448 More like Egypt's alluvium during the inundation than hard-set soil. **1890** *Nature* 16 Oct. 602/1 Beds of rigid lava and hard-set ash.

b. Of eggs: That have been subject to incubation.

1879 JEFFERIES *Wild Life in S. Co.* 339 Some say it is the hardset eggs he [the snake] prefers.

c. Of the features, etc.: Rigidly set.

1855 TENNYSON *Maud* I. iv. iv, I.. smile a hard-set smile, like a stoic.

3. Determined, obstinate.

1818 SCOTT *Hrt. Midl.* xiii, It's a hard-set willyard beast this o' mine.

'**hardshell, 'hard-shell,** *a.* and *sb.*

A. *adj.* **1.** *U.S.* Having a hard shell: applied to some crustaceans and molluscs, as crabs, clams, etc. Also applied to the fruit of a nut-tree.

1798 *Spectator* (N.Y.) 7 Nov. 2/5 Hardshell almond trees. **1818** *Amer. Monthly Mag.* II. 296 The hard shell clam.. is cooked by roasting. **1855** *Knickerbocker* XLVI. 222 'Hard-shell' clam-catchers. **1942** M. K. RAWLINGS *Cross Creek* xvii. 226 We have four turtles, the gopher;.. the hard-shell cooter; the soft-shell; and the alligator cooter.

2. *fig.* Rigid and uncompromising in religious orthodoxy.

Hardshell Baptists (U.S.), a strict sect of Baptists, of extreme Calvinistic views.

1838 W. Y. ALLEN *Diary* 17 July in *S.W. Hist. Q.* (1914) XVII. 54 Was introduced to Daddy Spraggins, a Hardshell

Baptist preacher. **1846** J. J. HOOPER *Adv. Simon Suggs* i. 13 He lived with his father, and an old 'hard shell' Baptist preacher. **1857** ELLIOTT *Sp. in Ho. Representatives* (Bartlett), A regular member of the Hardshell Baptist Church. **1864** *Spectator* No. 1875. 643 'Hardshell Churchmen' is the title of an article in this number, and the epithet is applied to Lord Robert Cecil's party. **1890** *Spectator* 8 Feb., The tough and hard shell type to which Judaism owes such strength and permanence as it has ever possessed. **1893** *Daily Tel.* 15 May 5/5 Like the American Hardshell Baptists they hold that there is nothing like religion.

B. *sb.* **1.** A creature with a hard shell; a hard-shelled crab or clam. Also *fig.*, a stubborn or unemotional person. (*U.S.*)

1858 *South. Cultivator* XVI. 187/2 We have, however, one or two specimens in our eye of the genus, *hard shell*, who still do as their *daddies* did. **1916** H. L. WILSON *Somewhere in Red Gap* iv. 135 A grouchy old hardshell with white hair and whiskers whirling about his head. **1919** T. K. HOLMES *Man fr. Tall Timber* xiii. 156 I've ridden up here from Tall Timber Junction to get acquainted with you hardshells.

2. = Hardshell Baptist: see A. 2. (*U.S.*)

1845 *Knickerbocker* XXVI. 285 A 'Hard-Shell' recently turned a 'Soft-Shell' out of church. **1848** JONES *Sketches Trav.* 30 (Farmer) The old hard-shell laid about him like death. **1855** *Putnam's Monthly* V. 190 The claim of 'Hard-Shells', touching their familiarity with the Bible. **1872** E. EGGLESTON *Hoosier Schoolmaster* xii, Of course the Hardshells are prodigiously illiterate. **1908** *Dialect Notes* III. 319 *Hardshell*, a Primitive Baptist.

3. *U.S. Politics.* A member of the more conservative of the two factions into which the Democratic party in New York state was divided in 1852 and following years.

1853 *N.Y. Tribune* 2 Apr. (Bartlett), The difference between a Hardshell and a Softshell is this: one favors the Execution of the Fugitive Slave Law and goes for distribution of the offices among the Nationals, while the other is a loud stickler for Union and Harmony. **1864** SALA in *Daily Tel.* 18 Nov., After Democrats and Republicans, Hunkers and Hardshells, Miscegenators and Copperheads, have been replaced by honester and abler politicians.

hardshelled, *a.* **1.** Having a hard shell; = HARDSHELL *a.* 1.

1611 COTGR. s.v. *Reffe*, An hard-sheld nut. **1782** J. H. ST. J. DE CRÈVECŒUR *Lett. Amer. Farmer* iv. 135 The shores.. abound with the soft-shelled, the hard-shelled, and the great sea clams. **1796** B. HAWKINS *Lett.* (1916) 17 A grove of dwarf hard shelled hickory trees. **1839** C. F. BRIGGS *Adv. H. Franco* II. i. 2 Close by, was a negro opening hard-shelled clams. **1865** *Trans. Ill. Agric. Soc.* V. 408 Beetles, or, as they are sometimes called, 'hard-shelled bugs' . **1942** M. K. RAWLINGS *Cross Creek Cookery* xvii. 191 Why does a hard-shelled cooter lay a soft-shelled egg, and a soft-shelled cooter lay a hard-shelled egg?

2. *fig.* = HARDSHELL *a.* 2. Also, hardened, callous.

1842 J. S. BUCKINGHAM *Slave States Amer.* I. 197 The Baptists [in Macon, Georgia] are of the order called here 'Hardshelled Baptists'. **1872** W. MATHEWS *Getting on in World* xi. 153 There is no man so 'hard-shelled' that his soul cannot be reached by kindness. **1904** *N.Y. Herald* 23 Oct. 16 There are a good many hard shelled Bryan men who intend to vote for Roosevelt. **1909** R. A. WASON *Happy Hawkins* 108 It was a hard-shelled book. **1941** J. STUART *Men of Mountains* 331 If you could see all of us Republicans, Democrats, Methodists, Forty-Gallon Baptists, Hard shelled Baptists,.. shaking hands and asking the other how he is after the long night o' sleep. **1965** *Times Lit. Suppl.* 25 Nov. 1046/1 Various forms of hard-shelled Establishment versus dissent.

hardship ('hɑːdʃɪp). [f. HARD *a.* + -SHIP.]

†**1.** The quality of being hard to bear; hardness; rigour; severity; painful difficulty. *Obs.*

a **1225** *Ancr. R.* 364 Herdschipe of liue. **1676** LADY CHAWORTH in *12th Rep. Hist. MSS. Comm.* App. v. 35 Lady Latimer was delivered with much hardship on Wednesday, the child dead.

2. A condition which presses unusually hard upon one who has to endure it; hardness of fate or circumstance; severe toil or suffering; extreme want or privation.

c **1400** *Destr. Troy* 2686 What vnhappe & hardship hapnes the to! **1671** MILTON *P.R.* I. 341 Men to much misery and hardship born. **1697** DRYDEN *Virg. Georg.* II. 667 Inur'd to Hardship, and to homely Fare. **1775** BURKE *Sp. Conc. Amer.* Wks. III. 110 The Durham act.. confines the hardship of want of representation to the case of subsidies. **1847** GROTE *Hist. Greece* II. xlvii. (1862) IV. 179 He had his share of the benefit as well as of the hardship. **1889** RUSKIN *Præterita* III. i. 18 Resolute choice of a life of hardship.

b. With *a* and *pl.* An instance of this.

a **1225** *Ancr. R.* 6 Swuche oðre heardschipes þet moni flechs mai þolien. **1654** WHITLOCK *Zootomia* 33 The unwelcome hardships of Winter. **1722** DE FOE *Relig. Courtsh.* I. i. (1840) 26 A hardship that never was put upon any one before. **1832** HT. MARTINEAU *Demerara* ii. 14 The hardships inflicted on himself and his brother partners.

†**c.** An infliction of severity or suffering; a piece of harsh treatment. *Obs.*

17.. SWIFT (J.), To recover the effects of their hardships upon us. **1780** BURKE *Corr.* (1844) II. 369, I do not know that I have ever offered.. a hardship, or even an affront, to the religious prejudices of any person whatsoever.

hardshrew, obs. form of HARDISHREW.

hard stone, 'hardstone. a. Any type of hard stone. **b.** A precious or semi-precious stone.

The earliest examples are instances of the informal union of *hard* adj. and *stone*.

1568 GRAFTON *Chron.* II. 434 He buylded of hard stone, the bewtifull Librarie in the gray Friers in London, now called Christes Hospitall. **1613** [see STONE *sb.* 2]. **1733** W. TOWNESEND *Let.* 28 Aug. in *Archit. Rev.* (1945) XCVIII. 105/3 Eight feet below the top of ye hardstone plinth. **1905** *Daily Chron.* 11 July 5/7 The hard-stone works. **1921** *Dict. Occup. Terms* (1927) §572 *Banker hand, hewer* or *mason*; *hard-stone banker mason*; cuts, and if necessary saws, blocks of stone at 'banker'. **1931** *Times* 16 Mar. 22/4 Chinese hard-stone carvings. **1935** *Burlington Mag.* June 299/1 (*title*) An exhibition of hardstone carvings. **1936** *Ibid.* Aug. 91/2 A few jades and hard-stones. **1958** *Times* 2 Dec. 12/5 Chinese porcelain and hardstones realized £9,585 at Christie's yesterday.

hard-tack. [f. HARD *a.* + TACK *sb.* in fig. application: cf. *hard fare.*] Ship-biscuit; hence, ordinary sea fare in general. Also, hard bread or biscuits generally. Also *fig.* and *attrib.*

1836 *Knickerbocker* VIII. 203 When I was the size of that monkey there, who knows how to do nothing but gnaw hard tack. **1841** LEVER *C. O'Malley* lxxxviii. (Farmer), No more hard-tack.. no salt butter, but a genuine land breakfast. **1853** KANE *Grinnell Exp.* xxxvi. (1856) 326 Another set of fellows adhered pertinaciously to their salt junk and hard tack. **1869** *Mayne Reid's Mag.* June 513. **1888** *Century Mag.* XXXVI. 614/1 A little rabbit that kept.. nibbling at our bread and hard-tack. **1899** T. HALL *Tales* 108 A meal of raw bacon, hard-tack and cold water. **1909** *Daily Chron.* 8 July 9/2 Of all the hard-tack breads.. I have found.. the small ringed bread of Siberia the most substantial. **1931** *Economist* 5 Dec. 105/1 It has paved the way.. for the real hard-tack committee work on the thousand practical problems of the constitution builder. **1955** W. FOSTER-HARRIS *Look of Old West* ii. 56 Hardtack.. was hard, unleavened bread, baked in cakes.. about 3 inches square, decorated with what looked like nail punctures. **1960** *Economist* 15 Oct. 219/1 Some of those who raised left-wing political rather than hard-tack organisational questions being shouted down by genuine party workers.

hardtail ('hɑːdteɪl). *U.S.* [f. HARD *a.* + TAIL *sb.*[1]] **a.** A marine fish, *Caranx crysos*, found in the western parts of the Atlantic Ocean.

1884 G. B. GOODE *Fisheries U.S.* I. 324 The Jurel—Caranx Pisquetus. This fish, known about Pensacola as the 'Jurel', 'Cojinua', and 'Hard-tail'. **1902** JORDAN & EVERMANN *Amer. Food & Game Fishes* 306 The runner, hard tail, or jurel, reaches a foot or more in length.. and is a food-fish of considerable importance. **1968** *OECD Multiling. Dict. Fish* 139 *Caranx crysos*... Also called runner, hardtail, crevalle.

b. *slang.* A mule.

1917 A. G. EMPEY *Over Top* 294 *Hard tails*, mules. **1931** 'D. STIFF' *Milk & Honey Route* 207 *Hard tails*, mules usually old ones. So named because they show little response to the skinner's whip. Young mules are shave-tails. **1966** *Publ. Amer. Dial. Soc.* XLVI. 26, I was driving an old pair of hard tails.

hard 'up, *advb.* and *adj. phr.* (*sb.*)

1. *adv. Naut.* Said of the tiller when it is put as far as possible to windward, so as to turn the ship's head away from the wind. (Usually as a command.)

1612 DEKKER *If it be not good* Wks. 1873 III. 293 Whoes at Helme? beare vp hard: and hard vp. **1840** R. H. DANA *Bef. Mast* xxxi. 117 'Ice on the lee bow!' 'Hard up the helm!' **1875** BEDFORD *Sailor's Pock. Bk.* x. (ed. 2) 354 Hard up the helm, *la barre au vent.*

2. *adj.* Hard put to it; in difficulties; in want, *esp.* of money; in destitution. ***hard up for***, sorely at a loss for. *colloq.* (of slang origin).

1821 HAGGART *Life* 104 (Farmer) There I met in with two Edinburgh snibs, who were hard up. **1840** DE QUINCEY *Style* IV. Wks. 1860 XI. 322 As hard up for water as the Mecca caravan. **1852** DICKENS *Bleak Ho.* xi, He was in want of copying work to do, and was.. hard up! **1886** J. K. JEROME *Idle Thoughts* 2 You don't feel nearly so hard up with elevenpence in your pocket as you do with a shilling. **1889** BESANT *All in a Garden Fair* II. ii, Every man in England who was hard up or had a hard-up friend.

3. *sb.* (See quots.)

1851 MAYHEW *Lond. Labour* I. 3/2 The cigar-end finders, or 'hard-ups', as they are called. **1905** *Daily Chron.* 17 May 6/7 In tramp phrase they [*sc.* cigar and cigarette ends] are known as 'hard-ups', and are smoked along the road. **1933** 'G. ORWELL' *Down & Out* xxxii. 236 Hard-up—tobacco made from cigarette ends. **1959** *Listener* 5 Mar. 406/1 We roll a couple of 'hard-ups' to smoke. Hard-ups are made of tobacco we collect from cigarette ends.

Hence **hard-'upness, hard-'up(p)ishness.** *slang* and *colloq.*

1859 D. G. ROSSETTI *Let.* 23 June (1965) I. 353 As for hardupishness.. I have been literally penniless for two days. **1870** SALA *Dickens* 45 The occasional 'harduppishness' of a young man striving to attain a position. **1876** HINDLEY *Adv. Cheap Jack* (Farmer), There were frequent.. collapses from death or hard-upness. **1882** *Times* 13 Mar. 11 Enough to account for the general 'hard-uppishness', as it has been called. **1888** MCCARTHY & PRAED *Ladies' Gallery* II. i. 8 My old familiar condition of hard-up-ness.

hardware ('hɑːdwɛə(r)). [See WARE.]

1. a. Small ware or goods of metal; ironmongery.

c **1515** [implied in HARDWAREMAN]. **1723** *Lond. Gaz.* No. 6146/10 John Lowe.. Haberdasher of Hard-Ware. **1774** PENNANT *Tour Scotl. in 1772.* 10 Locks, hinges, cast-iron and other branches of hardware. **1844** H. H. WILSON *Brit. India* I. 535 Pedlars.. with a pack of scissors or other hardware at their backs.

b. Weapons.

1865 L. N. BEAUDRY *Hist. Rec. 5th N.Y. Cavalry* (1868) 38 Capt. Hammond.. charged upon the rebels.., crying as he flew forward, 'give them your hardware, boys!' **1885** *Daily News* 12 Nov. 5/4 The chances are that the authorities.. may have had an eye on such kind of 'hardware' [*sc.* torpedoes]. **1914** JACKSON & HELLYER *Vocab. Criminal Slang* 42 *Hardware*,.. weapons; knives; razors; tools and paraphernalia used by safe-crackers [etc.]. **1929** *Amer. Speech* V. 59 His [*sc.* a Nebraska cowboy's] fire arms are frequently called his 'hardware'. **1955** *Bull. Atomic Sci.* Apr. 168/2 How much does our superiority in hardware contribute to our over-all security? **1966** *New Yorker* 29 Oct. 236 Oh, put your hands up, dear. He's got the hardware. **1967** *Observer* 11 June 11/2 The wholesale destruction this week of expensive hard-ware has brought home to some Arabs the folly of an extravagant armament policy.

c. The physical components of a system or device as opposed to the procedures required for its operation; opp. *software*.

1947 D. R. HARTREE *Calculating Machines* 14 The ENIAC... I shall give a brief account of it, since it will make the later discussion more realistic if you have an idea of some 'hardware' and how it is used, and this is the equipment with which I am best acquainted. **1953** A. D. & K. H. V. BOOTH *Automatic Digital Calculators* xv. 169 The engineering difficulties encountered in this type of machine are great, and a considerable increase in the size and complexity of the 'hardware' seems inevitable. **1960** [see ALGORITHMIC *a.*]. **1960** *Times* 21 Mar. 13/6 Academician Sedov.. knows the hazards of 'hardware' projected into space. **1960** *Times* (Computer Suppl.) 4 Oct. p. iii/7 Both punched card and computer 'hardware' will continue to develop very rapidly. **1962** J. GLENN in *Into Orbit* 6 The engineers and technicians had to start from scratch to develop the capsule and some of the other pieces of hardware which we are using. **1963** *Engineering* 23 Aug. 246/1 Hardware means the apparatus or machinery of computing, both the main instrument and its peripheral or ancillary equipment. **1964** *Daily Tel.* 14 Feb. 29/8 Engineers are leaving because.. they cannot rely on.. early development being continued to the 'hard-ware' stage. **1965** *New Scientist* 4 Nov. 331/1 All necessary hardware [for computers] exists today and is in production, but getting a comprehensive system off the ground requires the creation of a great deal of software. **1968** *Lebende Sprachen* XIII. 3/1 The practical requirements for the manned lunar landing program are being translated into hardware, experiments and programs. **1968** *Brit. Med. Bull.* XXIV. 198/2 Elaborate hardware is not a substitute for a thoroughgoing analysis of the whole area of medical vocabularies, procedures, information and systems for the care of patients. **1969** *Computers & Humanities* III. 139 Hardware refers to the physical apparatus while software describes the program languages that permit efficient use of the hardware.

d. Various slang and colloquial senses.

1839 *Spirit of Times* 1 June 153/3 He prepared to swallow his fifth invoice of 'hardware' [*sc.* whisky]. **1945** L. SHELLY *Jive Talk Dict.* 12/2 *Hardware*, flashy jewelry. **1951** I. SHAW *Troubled Air* vii. 105 When the rating goes up, I buy my hardware [*sc.* jewellery] at Cartier's. **1963** *Amer. Speech* XXXVIII. 206 *Hardware*, slang for a medal or trophy won in a skiing competition. **1968** *Times* 9 Sept. 6/7 Prince William has some useful leisure hard-ware—like a private aircraft.

2. *attrib.* and *Comb.*, as ***hardware dealer, factory, merchant, trade***; **hardware paper**, a make of durable wrapping-paper; **hardware store** orig. *U.S.*, an ironmongery shop.

1724 SWIFT *Drapier's Lett.* Wks. 1755 V. II. 14 Mr. Wood.. a hard-ware-dealer, procured a patent.. to coin 108,000*l.* in copper. **1789** *Boston Directory*, Whitwell,.. hardware store. **1848** MILL *Pol. Econ.* I. iv. §1. (1876) 35 Suppose.. that the capitalist is a hardware manufacturer. **1862** TROLLOPE *Orley F.* vi. 36 A.. man in the hardware line. **1886** *Harper's Mag.* June 48/1 Wrapping the stem [of the peach-tree].. with strong hardware or sheathing paper. **1964** M. GALLANT in R. Weaver *Canad. Short Stories* 2nd Ser. (1968) 60 Across the Alps was the name of a hard-ware store and its address on the other side of Montreal. **1972** *P.O. Telephone Directory, London Yellow Pages Classified* (North) 152/1 Barker's Hardware Stores Ltd, 43 High St.

'hardwareman. Also 6 harder man. [f. prec.] A manufacturer of or dealer in hardware.

c **1515** *Cocke Lorell's B.* (Percy Soc.) 10 Harde waremen, mole sekers, and ratte takers. **1548** HALL *Chron., Hen. VIII*, 65 Then the French harder men opened their wares, and made the Taylers hal lyke to the paunde of a marte. **1577** HARRISON *England* III. ix. (1877) II. 64 Grindstones for hardware men. **1858** GREENE *Gunnery* 181 The persuasive eloquence of the itinerant hardwareman.

hard-wired (hɑːd'waɪəd), *a.* [f. HARD *a.* or *adv.* + WIRED *ppl. a.*] **1.** *Computing.* Employing or containing permanently connected circuits designed to perform a specific, unchangeable, function; (of a function) achieved by such circuits; built *into* a device in this way.

1969 *Mechanised Accounting* Nov. 54/2 Central to the entire System 21 structure is the microprocessor and its various hard-wired microprograms. **1973** *Sci. Amer.* May 11 (Advt.), It computes in totally algebraic logic and is equipped with immediate-response hardwired functions. **1974** *Physics Bull.* Dec. 568/1 (Advt.), This instrument—our ND 100—is the most powerful hardwired analyzer ever made available commercially. **1981** *Sci. Amer.* Apr. 71A/2 It is a rule of thumb in computer science that an operation can be executed fastest when it is hardwired into the computer rather than programmed as part of a program. **1985** *Personal Computer World* Feb. 177/1 Handshaking is hardwired through CTS or DTR, or can be carried out in software if required.

2. *transf.*, esp. with reference to the brain and its function.

1971 *New Scientist* 16 Sept. 615/2 These cells are hard-wired and ready for action as soon as the kitten opens its eyes. **1975** *Sci. Amer.* June 87/3 The product of 'hard-wired', or fixed, visual pathways originating at the retina and terminating in the cortex. **1977** C. SAGAN *Dragons of Eden* ii. 29 The brain is completely hard-wired: specific cognitive functions are localized in particular places in the brain.

Hence [as a back-formation] **hard-'wire** *v. trans.*, to provide with, or make as, a permanent electric connection.

1983 *Austral. Microcomputer Mag.* Nov. 28/2 Data security may be achieved by hardwiring the fixed disk unit into a special power outlet that can be locked in the off position. **1985** *Computer Equipment* Sept. 39/1 This now enables them to hard-wire links from the 56M central file server to all the required terminals in the factory.

'hardwood, *sb.*

1. a. The wood or timber of deciduous trees, as distinguished from that of pines and firs; in some localities *spec.* that of oak and ash. Mostly *attrib.*, as in ***hardwood tree, forest***, etc. Chiefly *Sc.* and *U.S.*

1568 *Kirton-in-Lindsey Chruchw. Acc.* in *N.-W. Lincoln. Gloss.*, William Chapman, iij lode of hardwodde. **1813** Geo. Robertson *Agric. Surv. Kincard.* 343 (Jam.) Deciduous trees, or what is here called hard wood; in distinction from the evergreens or firs, whose timber is comparatively softer. *a* **1817** T. Dwight *Trav. New Eng.* (1821) II. 165 Hard-wood land; or land, producing oak and other kinds of wood, which are called hard, in opposition to pine, and other soft kinds. **1828** *Craven Dial.*, *Hardwood-trees*, Deciduous trees, in contradistinction to evergreens and the fir tribe. **1840** *Knickerbocker* XXVIII. 337 Most unexceptional 'hardwood' land. **1864** Lowell *Fireside Trav.* 146 The rounded..outline of hard-wood trees. **1869** *Trans. Ill. Agric. Soc.* VII. 578 Some elevated ridges..called technically, hard wood ridges..escaped wholly, or in part the effects of the fire. **1880** *Libr. Univ. Knowl.* (N.Y.) X. 149 Forests of hardwood diversified by groves of sugar maple. **1897** Mary Kingsley *W. Africa* 641 Do not start a plantation on soil that is not growing hard-wood forest. *a* **1898** *Mod.* Will you have it of deal or hardwood? **1903** S. E. White *Forest* viii. 89 The trunks of the hard-wood forest. **1911** *Daily Colonist* (Victoria, B.C.) 15 Apr. 18/1 We mail on request an illustrated catalogue of plain and fancy hardwood floors with prices attached. **1968** E. R. Buckler *Ox Bells & Fireflies* xxi. 297, I stand on top of the hardwood hill.

b. *ellipt.* A hardwood tree.

1905 J. Nisbet *Forester* I. III. iv. 419 Pit-planting is the usual method of growing Oak and all other kinds of hardwoods. **1908** *Westm. Gaz.* 15 Aug. 15/3 The tender colours of the hardwoods bursting towards summer glory. **1972** *Country Life* 16 Mar. 653/3 The number of trees by species ..together with some idea of their quality (in the case of hardwoods, veneer, good or..low-grade mining and fencing timber).

2. a. In Australia, applied to many kinds of timber resembling teak, *esp.* to *Backhousia Bancroftii*, used in building and fencing. **b.** A West Indian shrub, *Ixora ferrea*.

1888 Candish *Whispering Voices* 108 Sitting on a block of hardwood..Is the grayhaired forest feller. **1890** Boldrewood *Miner's Right* iii. 24 A hammer-like piece of hardwood above a plate of tin. **1891** *Pall Mall G.* 19 Jan. 2/1 Hardwood can be found in any quantity from the Dutch boundary to the Louisiade group.

'hard-wooded, *a.* **a.** Having hard wood. **b.** Of hardwood as opposed to pine or fir; deciduous.

1858 Glenny *Gard. Every-day Bk.* 111/1 Hard-wooded plants want most attention. **1897** Mary Kingsley *W. Africa* 91 This will become a forest of soft-wooded plants and palms; and finally of hard-wooded trees.

hardy ('hɑːdɪ), *a.* Also 3–4 **herdi, -y,** (4 **ardi**). [a. F. *hardi*, nom. sing. *hardiz* (11th c. in Hatz.-Darm.) = Pr. *ardit*, It. *ardito*, pa. pple. of OF. *hardir*, Pr. *ardir*, It. *ardire* to harden, make hard, bold, etc., a. WGer. **hardjan*, Goth. *hardjan*, OHG. *hartjan* to make hard, f. *hard* HARD *a.*]

1. Bold, courageous, daring. **a.** Of persons, their manner, etc.

a **1225** *Leg. Kath.* 1745 Porphire and Auguste wurðen..se swiðe wilcweme, and se hardi. *c* **1275** Lay. 4181 Six hundred cniþtes of alle þe kenneste and of þan hardieste. *a* **1300** *Cursor M.* 15503 We er herdi [*v.rr.* hardi, hardy] men i-nou agains iudas vr fa. **13..** *Guy Warw.* (A.) 1136 Gode kniȝt and ardi in fiȝt. *c* **1380** Wyclif *Serm.* Sel. Wks. I. 343 Petre was..hardi in axing. *c* **1420** *Avow. Arth.* xvii, The hed of that hardy, He sette on a stake. **1568** Grafton *Chron.* III. 94 A good Knight and hardie of his handes. **1587** Fleming *Contn. Holinshed* III. 1343/1 Philip duke of Burgognie, surnamed the hardie. **1625–6** Purchas *Pilgrims* II. 1043 No man is so hardy as to ride on horse-back by a church. **1765** H. Walpole *Otranto* i. (1798) 25 Art thou so hardy, as to dare my vengeance? **1827** Hallam *Const. Hist.* (1876) I. iv. 185 In this treatise such a hardy spirit of innovation was displayed..that [etc.]. **1885** *Manch. Exam.* 13 June 5/2 No one..would be hardy enough to take up the reins after he had thrown them down.

b. Of actions, qualities, etc.

a **1225** *Ancr. R.* 248 Herdi bileaue bringeð þene deouel a vlihte. *c* **1340** *Cursor M.* 7659 (Fairf.) þis batal was hardy I-nogh. **1585** T. Washington tr. *Nicholay's Voy.* I. 20 *note*, A hardie enterprise of certaine knights. **1685** Evelyn *Mem.* (1857) II. 253 He..has served the Court interest on all the hardiest occasions. **1783** Johnson *Let. to J. Fowke* 19 Apr., Silenced by a hardy denial of facts. **1884** E. Reclus in *Contemp. Rev.* May 633 A hardy stroke on the Stock Exchange.

2. *opprobriously.* Presumptuously bold, audacious; rashly bold, showing temerity. Cf. FOOLHARDY.

a **1225** *Ancr. R.* 56 þu, a wrecche sunful mon, ert so swuðe herdi to kesten kang eien upon ȝunge wummen. *a* **1340** Hampole *Psalter* ix. 42 þat na man be hardy him to heghe abouen þe stabilnes of haly men. *c* **1450** *Merlin* 37 Thei sholde not be so hardy be-fore me to make yow no lesynge. **1483** *Cath. Angl.* 175/1 Hardy..*temerarius, qui sine consilio agit.* *c* **1489** Caxton *Sonnes of Aymon* xxii. 474 Yf Reynawd were soo hardy to doo ony harme vnto richarde of normandy, I sholde hange hym wyth myn owen handes. **1699** Bentley *Phal.* 503 What shall we say now to such a hardy Writer, as this is? **1890** *Sat. Rev.* 1 Feb. 150/1 A warning to others not henceforward to be so hardy.

†3. Strong, enduring, tough. *Obs.*

c **1381** Chaucer *Parl. Foules* 176 The byldere ok & ek the hardy [*v.r.* harde] assh.

4. a. Capable of enduring fatigue, hardship, rigour of the weather, etc.; physically robust, vigorous.

1548 Hall *Chron.*, *Hen. VI*, 150 A tall and a hardye personage. **1600** J. Pory tr. *Leo's Africa* II. 32 How strong and hardie I was, and how I could endure the cold and tempestuous season. **1667** Milton *P.L.* IV. 920 [Art] Thou then they Less hardie to endure? **1774** Goldsm. *Nat. Hist.* (1776) V. 183 When once grown up, turkies are very hardy birds. **1783** *Polite Trav.* 105 Northward of the bay, even the hardy pine is seen no longer. **1853** J. H. Newman *Hist. Sk.* (1873) II. I. ii. 93 The hardy mountaineers of the Caucasus.

b. *Hort.* Able to grow in the open air throughout the year. ***half hardy***, able to do this except in winter, when shelter is required. ***hardy annual***, an annual plant that may be sown in the open ground, or that ripens its seed and sows itself year after year. Also *fig.*, a subject that comes up year after year in Parliament, or in the newspapers. ***hardy perennial***, a herbaceous plant with a perennial rootstock; also *fig.*

1664 Evelyn *Kalendarium Hortense* in *Sylva* 59 Auriculas ..need not be hous'd; it is a hardy Plant. **1783** T. Blaikie *Diary of Scotch Gardener* (1931) 187 A little way from St Germains..ther is a Curious Gentelman one Mr. Trochereau who has a curious collection of hardy exotick plants. **1813** [see BORECOLE]. **1831** *Athenæum* 5 Nov. 718 This, truly, is 'a hardy Annual'! **1852** Half-hardy [see HARDEN *v.* 7]. **1852** R. Buist *Amer. Flower-Garden Directory* (ed. 5) 29 Hardy Annuals..are possessed of much beauty of hue. **1870** Lowell *Study Wind.*, *Chaucer* (1886) 216 It may well be doubted whether Roman literature, always a half-hardy exotic, could ripen the seeds of living reproduction. **1871** S. Hibberd *Amateur's Flower Gard.* 188 Many of the hardy annuals are weedy and short-lived. **1892** *Pall Mall G.* 16 Aug. 4/2 (Farmer) Readers..are once more filling the columns of that journal with 'Is Marriage a Failure?' The hardy annual is called 'English Wives' this time. **1900** J. M. Abbott in W. D. Drury *Bk. Gardening* viii. 260 Hardy herbaceous perennials are a very popular set of plants. **1916** 'Taffrail' *Pincher Martin* xiv. 248 The subjects most often brought under discussion, however—the hardy perennials, so to speak—were: [etc.]. **1944** A. Huxley *Let.* 9 Apr. (1969) 502, I am very glad to hear the good news of *The Art of Seeing*. The book has all the appearance of a hardy perennial. **1967** C. O. Skinner *Madame Sarah* vii. 132 Thousands of playgoers travelled thousands of miles to sob over Marguerite Gauthier's departure from life..in that hardy perennial whose actual title is *La Dame aux Camélias*. **1967** C. Lloyd *Hardy Perennials* i. 9 The hardy perennial possesses every virtue that you could require of a plant, except for a permanently visible structure.

c. Of actions, qualities, etc.

1601 Chester *Love's Mart.*, *K. Arthur* liii, The Saxons men of hardie strength. **1674** tr. *Scheffer's Lapland* 124 The Laplanders lead a miserable and hardy kind of life. **1845** Ford *Hand-bk. Spain* I. 53 The horses of Navarre..are still esteemed for their hardy strength.

5. *Comb.*, as ***hardy-limbed***, ***-mannered***, ***-witted***, etc.

1598 Sylvester *Du Bartas* II. ii. II. *Babylon* 650 Ronsard ..hardy-witted, handleth happily All sorts of subject, stile, and Poesie. **1825** Moore *Mem.* (1853) IV. 339 The sexton, a shrewd, hardy-mannered fellow.

'hardy, *sb.* Also **hardie.** [prob. f. HARD, or HARDY *a.*] The vertical bar or blade of hard iron with a sharp edge, on which nailmakers cut or strike off the shaped nail from the iron rod; also, a movable piece, called also 'fuller', fitting into a socket in an anvil, used for similar purposes by blacksmiths.

1870 *Gd. Words* Apr. 247 My bore and hardy must be done, Or I cannot make good nails. **1875** Knight *Dict. Mech.*, *Hardy*..A chisel or fuller having a square shank for insertion into a square hole in an anvil called a *hardy-hole*. **1894** *Amer. Ann. Deaf* June 150 [Blacksmith's tools] a poker, a rake, a shovel, a sprinkler, a hardy. **1957** R. Lister *Decorative Wrought Iron-Work* ii. 13 The square hole through the heel is called a *hardie hole*. *Ibid.* 228 *Hardie*, a small chisel, used in the anvil. **1964** [see *hot set* s.v. HOT *a.* 12 c]. **1965** A. F. Shirley *Metalwork Techniques* vi. 84 Metal ..should be heated where it is to be cut and this part placed on the hardie and hammered to form a vee cut.

†'hardy, *v. Obs.* [f. HARDY *a.*]

1. *trans.* To make hardy or bold; to encourage.

a **1225** *Leg. Kath.* 2163 Hardi min heorte. **1297** R. Glouc. (1724) 218 Lucye, to hardy ys men, prykede her and þer. *c* **1350** *Will. Palerne* 1156 Forto hardien þe hertes of here heiȝh burnes. *c* **1430** *Pilgr. Lyf Manhode* I. lxxi. (1869) 41 Al gates j hardied me and went wel nyh to hire.

2. *intr.* To become bold. *nonce-use.*

1823 Lamb *Elia* Ser. II. *Old Margate Hoy*, Still hardying more and more in his triumphs over our simplicity.

Hardyan, Hardian ('hɑːdɪən), *a.* and *sb.* [f. the name of Thomas *Hardy* (1840–1928), novelist and poet + -IAN.] Characteristic of the works of T. Hardy. Also *sb.*, an admirer or follower of Hardy. Similarly **Hardy'esque** *a.*

1910 R. Brooke *Let.* Jan. (1968) 216 That abysmal darkness..inspired me with thousands of Hardyesque short poems about people whose affairs went dismally wrong. **1927** H. Crane *Let.* 29 May (1965) 300 A footnote of Hardian doom. **1929** *Sat. Rev.* 24 Aug. 221/2 But in the dialogue of the rustics it shows a delicious Hardyesque sense of humour. **1931** *Times Lit. Suppl.* 28 May 423/1 Confirmed and receptive Hardians..will know how many..approach it with preconceptions of various degrees of falseness. **1941** Blunden *Thomas Hardy* 271 It can be admitted by almost any Hardyan that the poor passages in his work are an offering to the wanton or the unsympathetic critic. **1944** —— *Cricket Country* 142 An unspoken Hardyan complaint. **1960** C. Day Lewis *Buried Day* vi. 111 The rich Dorset accents and the Hardy-esque names.

†'hardy'dardy. *Obs.* [A reduplicated extension of HARDY: cf. *handy-dandy*.] **a.** Rash or foolish daring. **b.** A daring fellow, dare-devil.

a **1529** Skelton *Sp. Parrot* 450 So myche hardy dardy and so lytell manlynes. **1593** R. Harvey *Philad.* 80 A very hardydardy in deede as euer liued.

hardyshrew, obs. form of HARDISHREW.

hare (hɛə(r)), *sb.* Forms: 1–2 **hara**, 2– **hare**, (4–5 **haar(e, hayre,** 5 **are,** 6–7 *Sc.* **hair(e).** [A Com. Teut. sb.: OE. *hara*, = OFris. *hase* (WFris. *haeze*, MDu. *haese*, *hāze*, Du. *haas*), OHG. *haso* (MHG., MLG., mod. Ger. *hase*), ON. *here*, *heri* (Sw., Da. *hare*):—OTeut. **hason-*, **hazon-*, cognate with OPruss. *sasins* (for *szasins*) hare. Cf. also Skr. *çaça* (? for *çasa*) hare. Relationship to the OE. adj. *hasu*, *heasu* 'grey, ash-coloured' is doubtful. The OE. and Norse words show rhotacism, the latter with resulting umlaut.]

1. a. A rodent quadruped of the genus *Lepus*, having long ears and hind legs, a short tail, and a divided upper lip.

The common hare of Great Britain and Europe (*L. timidus*), is a timid, watchful, and very swift animal. 'Its eyes are so situated, that the animal can see nearly all around it' (Carpenter); hence, prob., the popular saying that it sleeps with its eyes open (Topsell): cf. *hare-eyed*, *hare's eye*, *hare-sleep*, in 6. A less common species or subspecies is the Alpine or varying hare (*L. variabilis*). In North America there are several species or subspecies, of which *L. Americanus* comes closest to the common European hare.

a **700** *Epinal Gloss.* 608 *Lepus, leporis*, hara [*Erf. Gloss.* hæra]. **1154** *O.E. Chron.* an. 1086 (Earle) 222 He sætte be þam haren þæt hi mosten freo faran. *a* **1250** *Owl & Night.* 383 Ich mai iseon so wel so on hare. *c* **1330** R. Brunne *Chron.* (1810) 210 About þei gan him chace, and hunted him als hayre. **1382** Wyclif *Lev.* xi. 6 An haar [**1388** hare] forsothe [is vnclene], for and he chewith kude. **1436** *Pol. Poems* (Rolls) II. 186 Skynnes of otere, squerel, and Irysh are. **1486** *Bk. St. Albans* F vj, A Trippe of haaris. **1597** Montgomerie *Cherrie & Slae* 15, I saw the hurcheoun and the hair, Quha fed amangis the flowris fair. **1678** Marvell *Growth Popery* 23 As much out of order, as if..an Hare had crossed his way. **1684** R. H. *School Recreat.* 8 The Hare the first Year a Leveret, 2 a Hare, 3 a great Hare. **1820** Keats *Eve of St. Agnes* i, The hare limp'd trembling through the frozen grass. **1847** Carpenter *Zool.* §236 The Alpine or varying Hare (so named from its usual residence, and from the changes of colour which it undergoes), inhabits the northern parts of Scotland, the mountainous parts of Ireland, and has been occasionally seen in the mountains of Cumberland. **1884** *St. James' Gaz.* 7 Aug. 4/2 The white hare has risen in value during the last two seasons.

b. The male or buck hare is sometimes called *Jack hare*. During March (the breeding season) hares are wilder than at other times; hence the proverbial saying ***as mad as a March hare***.

1529 More *Supp. Soulys* Wks. 299/2 As mad not as a march hare, but as a madde dogge. *a* **1631** Drayton *Nymphidia*, Oberon..grew as mad as any hare, When he had sought each place with care, And found his queen was missing. **1741** *Compl. Fam.-Piece* II. i. 300 The Males are usually call'd *Jack Hares*. **1783** Cowper *Epit. on Hare* 8 Old Tiny..Who, nursed with tender care,..Was still a wild Jack hare. **1812** H. & J. Smith *Rej. Addr.* IV. viii, For what is Hamlet, but a hare in March? **1865** L. Carroll *Alice's Adv. Wonderland* vi. (1886) 90 'In that direction..lives a Hatter: and in that direction..lives a March Hare..they're both mad.'

2. Phrases and Proverbs. ***to hold*** (or ***run***) ***with the hare and run*** (or ***hunt***) ***with the hounds***; ***to run with hare and hounds***: to try to keep in with both sides; to play a double part. ***first catch your hare*** (i.e. as the first step to cooking him): a direction jestingly ascribed to Mrs. Glasse's Cookery Book, but of much more recent origin.

† ***to hunt for*** or ***catch a hare with a tabor***; † ***to take hares with foxes***, † ***to seek a hare in a hen's nest***, also ***to set the tortoise to catch the hare***: to seek to do something almost impossible. † ***to kiss the hare's foot***: to be late. † ***to have two hares afoot*** or ***to run after two hares***: to undertake too many things. ***to get the hare's foot to lick***: to obtain very little. ***to make a hare of***: to make ridiculous. † ***to set the hare's head (foot, hare-pie) against the goose-giblet***: to let one thing serve as a set-off to another. ***here*** or ***there the hare went*** or ***goes away***: here or there the matter ended. Also, expressions referring to Æsop's Fable of the Race between the Hare and the Tortoise.

1399 Langl. *Rich. Redeles* I. 58 Men myȝtten as well haue huntyd an hare with a tabre As aske ony mendis ffor þat þei mysdede. *c* **1440** *Jacob's Well* (E.E.T.S.) 263 þou hast a crokyd tunge heldyng wyth hownd and wyth hare. **1539** Taverner *Erasm. Prov.* (1552) 36 As I say in our Englyshe prouerbe: Set the hares head against the gose gyblet. [See also **1546** J. Heywood *Prov.* (1867) 52; **1607** Dekker *Westw. Hoe* V. iv, Dram. Wks. 1873, and *note*.] **1546** J. Heywood *Prov.* (1867) 17 And yet shall we catche a hare with a taber, As soone as catche ought of them. **1562** *Ibid.* 137 Holde with the hare and run with the hounde, run thare As wight as the hounde, and as wyse as the hare. **1577** Stanyhurst *Descr. Irel.* in *Holinshed* (1807–8) VI. 52 But in deed it is hard to take hares with foxes. **1595** Shaks. *John* II. i. 137 You are the Hare of whom the Prouerb goes Whose valour plucks dead

Lyons by the beard. **1599** Porter *Angry Wom. Abingd.* (Percy Soc.) 103 Hee is gone to seek a hayre in a hennes nest .. which is as sildome seene as a blacke swan. **1600** Holland *Livy* xxxv. xlv. 914 And here went the hare away. **1613–16** W. Browne *Brit. Past.* II. ii, We had need Make haste away, unlesse we meane to speed With those that kisse the Hares foot. **1633** Rowley *Match Midn.* v. in Hazl. *Dodsley* XIII. 88 As I have been bawd to the flesh, you have been bawd to your money; so set the hare-pie against the goose-giblets. **1658–9** Burton *Diary* 9 Mar. (1828) IV. 108 Keep to your debate. You have two hares a-foot. You will lose both. *a* **1683** Sidney *Disc. Govt.* II. xxiii. (1704) 151 An ill Hare is said to make a good Dog. **1690** *Turn-Coat of Times* iv. in *Roxb. Ball.* (1883) IV. 515, I can hold with the Hare, and run with The Hound: Which no body can deny. **1798** Malthus *Popul.* (1817) III. 113 It would appear to be setting the tortoise to catch the hare. **1818** Scott *Let. to Croker* 5 Feb. in *Lockhart*, The poor clergyman [got] nothing whatever, or, as we say, the hare's foot to lick. **1830** W. Carleton *Traits & Stories* II. 111 What a hare Mat mad iv 'im; .. and did not lave him a leg to stand upon. **1855** Thackeray *Rose & Ring* xiv, 'A soldier, Prince, must needs obey his orders: mine are .. to seize wherever I should light upon him—' 'First catch your hare! ..' exclaimed his Royal Highness. **1858** *Times* 25 Aug. 6/2 Bitter experience has taught us not to cook our hare before we have caught it. **1896** *Daily News* 20 July 8/2 The familiar words, 'First catch your hare', were never to be found in Mrs. Glasse's famous volume. What she really said was, 'Take your hare when it is cased'. **1938** J. Cary *Castle Corner* x. 562 That fella thought he'd made a hare of me, but I knew one trick better.

3. *fig.* Applied to a person, in various allusive senses.

c **1325** *Poem Times Edw. II*, 252 in *Pol. Poems* (Camden) 334 Nu ben theih liouns in halle, and hares in the feld. **1650** R. Stapylton *Strada's Low C. Warres* VI. 7 At the very first charge .. this hare in a Helmet fled out of the Field. **1729** Swift *Libel on Dr. Delany, etc.* 53 Thus Gay, the hare with many friends, Twice seven long years the Court attends. **1864** Tennyson *Aylmer's F.* 490 The .. distant blaze of those dull banquets made The nightly wirer of their innocent hare Falter before he took it.

b. He who lays the 'scent' (usually paper torn into fragments) which the 'hounds' follow in the sport ***hare and hounds*** (also called 'paper-chase'; see *paper chase* s.v. paper *sb.* 12): used *lit.* and *fig.*

a **1845** Hood *To Mr. Malthus* i, You're quite enough to play at hare and hounds. **1857** Hughes *Tom Brown* I. vii, Please, sir, we've been out Big-side Hare-and-Hounds, and lost our way. **1883** W. H. Rideing in *Harper's Mag.* July 178/2 A flushed little 'hare' bounds past us, distributing the paper 'scent' in his course, and followed a quarter of an hour afterward by the panting and baffled 'hounds'. **1920** T. S. Eliot *Sacred Wood* 11 Coleridge is apt to take leave of the data of criticism, and arouse the suspicion that he has been diverted into a metaphysical hare-and-hounds. **1938** Partridge *World of Words* ix. 261 Well worth the hare-and-hound chase through the dictionary. **1963** *Daily Tel.* 5 Feb. 20/6 Throughout his speech he was constantly heckled and interrupted, but the scene cannot be described as 'Hare and hounds'.

4. One of the southern constellations, *Lepus*.

1551 Recorde *Cast. Knowl.* (1556) 268 Vnder the feete of Orion, is there a constellation of 12 starres, named the Hare. *a* **1701** Creech *Manilius* v. ix. 61 The Hare appears, whose active Rays supply A nimble force. **1839** *Penny Cycl.* XIII. 444/2 *Lepus* (the Hare), one of the old constellations, said by Hyginus to be in the act of running from Orion's dog.

5. = sea-hare, a molluscous animal, *Aplysia depilans*.

1591 Sylvester *Du Bartas* I. v. 89 Foot-less, and finnless (as the baneful Hare, And heat-full Oyster). **1601** Holland *Pliny* II. 71 It represseth the poison of the venomous fish called the sea-Hare. **1847** Carpenter *Zool.* §917 The *Aplysia*, commonly termed Sea-Hare .. from the peculiar form of the superior pair of tentacula, which are flattened and hollowed like the ears of a quadruped.

6. *attrib.* and *Comb.* **a.** attrib., as ***hare-back, -catcher, -chase, -drive, -flesh, -hunter, -park, -pie, -skin, -sleep, -soup***. **b.** objective or obj. gen., as ***hare-hunting, -shooting*** sbs. and adjs. **c.** similative, as ***hare-like, -mad*** adjs. **d. hare-coursing**: see coursing *vbl. sb.*[1] 2; **hare-eyed**, *a.*, having eyes that look all round, or that are never closed: see sense 1, note; **hare-hearted** *a.*, timid; †**hare-hound**, a dog for hunting hares; **hare-kangaroo**, a small kangaroo of the genus *Lagorchestes*, so called from its resemblance to a hare in size and colour; **hare-pocket**, a pocket in a shooting-coat, made of a size to hold a hare; **hare's eye** = lagophthalmia: see quot.; **hare's fur** *Ceramics*, a brown or black glaze streaked with silvery white or yellow used on some Chinese pottery; †**hare-shaw** = hare-lip; **hare-sighted** *a.*, short-sighted; †**hare-sleep**, a very light sleep; †**hare's-tooth** (see quot.). Also hare-brain, -foot, etc.

1583 Stubbes *Anat. Abus.* II. (1882) 36 Some leather .. wil straight-way become browne as a *hare backe. **1752** Sir J. Hill *Hist. Anim.* 356 (Jod.) The vulture leporarius, or *hare-catcher. **1840** D. P. Blaine *Encycl. Rural Sports* v. i. 562 The credit of the organisation of the sport of *hare coursing .. [is] without all doubt the undisputed property of the English. **1972** *Times* 5 Feb. 1/2 The House of Commons ended its Friday sitting in uproar and confusion when the Hare Coursing (Abolition) Bill was talked out. **1884** Speedy *Sport* xiii. 216 A large bag of ptarmigan is not usually obtained in connection with a *hare-drive. **1611** Tarlton *Jests* (1844) 12 To which he said little, but, with a squint eye, as custome had made him *hare eyed, hee looked for a jest to make them merry. **1612** Chapman *Death Pr. Henry* D, Frantick Distemper & Hare-eyd vnrest. **1614** Rowlands *Fooles Bolt* 33 Two right *Hare-harted coward Fooles. **1679** T. Blount *Anc. Tenures* 42 With .. two *Harehounds, or Greyhounds. *a* **1744** Pope *Let. M. & T. Blount* (T.), I .. then ride out a hunting .. How can a .. *hare-hunter hope for a minute's memory? **1735** Somerville *Chase* II. Argt., Description of the *Hare-hunting in all its Parts. **1864** Sir S. Northcote *Lect. & Ess.* iii. (1887) 89 A hare-hunting farmer. *a* **1592** H. Smith *Wks.* (1867) II. 483 The *hare-like coward runs his ways. **1620** Middleton *Chaste Maid* III. ii, Here's a day of toil well pass'd over, Able to make a citizen *hare-mad. **1674** N. Cox *Gentl. Recreat.* (1667) 100 The largest *Hare-Parks that ever I heard of, and the best furnished .. are in Ireland. **1633** *Hare-pie [see 2]. **1664–5** Pepys *Diary* 23 Jan., Dined upon a hare pye. **1870** Ouida *Held in Bondage* 21 Audit and hare-pie had not much temptation for us that morning. **1925** G. Burrard *Big Game Hunting* 281 Two '*hare' or 'poacher' pockets will be found most useful on occasions. **1950** *Q. Jrnl. Forestry* XLIV. 60 The map should be made .. to fit into the forester's hare pocket. **1727–51** Chambers *Cycl.* s.v. *Eye*, **Hare's Eye, Oculus Leporinus* .. a disease arising from a contraction of the upper eye-lid .. so that the patient is obliged to sleepe with the eye half-open. **1899** S. W. Bushell *Oriental Ceramic Art* xxvii. 724 The most highly appreciated ware at the tea-testing parties .. was the dark-colored pottery of the province of Fuchien .. the tea-bowls of which were known to Chinese virtuosos as '*hare's-fur bowls'. **1934** *Burlington Mag.* May 214/1 *Temmoku* tea bowls with the 'hare's fur' glaze.... They have a blackish stone-ware body, and a thick, lustrous black glaze streaked with hair lines of brown and silver. **1959** G. Savage *Antique Coll. Handbk.* 52 The black glazed wares of Honan are of great interest, and tea-bowls with a variegated dark brown glaze, known as 'hare's fur', came from Chien-an in Fukien Province. **1597** Lowe *Chirurg.* (1634) 185 The *Hare-shaw is a defectuositie of nature which happeneth .. in the Lip, Eare or Nose .. sometimes found cloven or they come in the world. **1627–77** Feltham *Resolves* I. xxv. 45 'Tis indiscretion that is *Hare-sighted. **1719** De Foe *Crusoe* I. xiv, A cap, which I had made of a *hare-skin. **1832** Carlyle *Remin.* I. 36 Hare-skins would accumulate into the purchase money of a coat. *a* **1700** B. E. *Dict. Cant. Crew*, **Hare-sleep*, with Eies a'most open. **1804** Scott *Let. to Ellis* 21 Aug. in *Lockhart*, *Hare soup may be forthcoming in due season. **1607** Topsell *Four-f. Beasts* (1658) 208 Whatsoever Beast be born in your flock, having that mark upon them, which is commonly called *Hares-tooth, never suffer them to suck their dam.

7. In names of plants: as †**hare's-ballocks**, popular name for species of Orchis; **hare's-bane**, *Aconitum Lagoctonum*; **hare's-beard**, the Great Mullein; †**hare-bottle**, Knapweed; **hare's colewort, house, lettuce, palace, thistle** (also ***hare-thistle***), names for the Sow-thistle, *Sonchusoleraceus*; **hare's-eye**, the Red Campion, *Lychnis diurna*; **hare's-meat**, Wood-sorrel; **hare-nut** (*dial.*), the Earth- or Pig-nut; **hare-parsley**, Wild Chervil, *Anthriscus sylvestris*; **hare's-tail (grass)**, a species of grass, *Lagurus ovatus*; **hare's-tail rush**, Single-headed Cotton-grass, *Eriophorum vaginatum*. Also hare-bell, etc.

1562 Turner *Herbal* II. 128 b, Whyt Satyrion .. or in other more vnmanerly speche, *hares ballockes. **1597** Gerarde *Herbal* II. cclvi. §2. 630 Mullein is called .. of some *Hares bearde. **1620** Markham *Farew. Husb.* II. viii. (1668) 40 The weeds which are most incident there-unto, are Twitch .. besides Thistles, *Harebottles. **1597** Gerarde *Herbal* II. xxxi. §8. 232 Sowthistle is called .. of some *Brassica leporina*, or *Hares Colewort. *Ibid.* App., *Hares eie is *Lychnis syluestris*. **1607** Topsell *Four-f. Beasts* (1656) 209 An herb called *Lactuca Leporina* .. that is, Hares-lettice, *Hares-house, Hares palace. [*c* **1000** *Sax. Leechd.* I. 226 Se hara .. mid þysse wyrte hyne sylfne ȝelacnað, for þy heo ys lactuca leporina ȝenemned.] **1597** Gerarde *Herbal* II. xxxi. §2. 229 The stalk of *hares lettuce or smooth Sowthistle, is oftentimes a cubite high. **1703** Thoresby *Let. to Ray* (E.D.S.), **Hare-nut*, [an] earthnut. *c* **1516** *Grete Herball* cccli. T v/2 *Palacium leporis*, *hares palays, is an herbe lyke Spurge, but it hath longer and ryper leues .. It is called hares palays. For yf the hare come vnder it, he is sure that no beest can touche hym. **1874** *Young Fancier's Guide* 4 July (Britten & H.), There is a plant known as *hare parsley, of which rabbits are extremely fond. **1879** Britten & Holland *Plant-n.*, *Hare Parsley*, in Aubrey's Wilts .. This [*Anthriscus sylvestris*] is no doubt the plant intended. **1806** J. Galpine *Brit. Bot.* §41. 10 *Lagurus ovatus*, *hare's-tail-grass. **1597** Gerarde *Herbal* 232 Apuleius calleth it [Sowthistle] *Lactuca Leporina*, or *Hares Thistle.

†**hare**, *v.*[1] *Obs.* Also 7–8 **hair**. [Origin not clear: in sense 1 app. allied to harry *v.*; sense 2 may have some association with hare *sb.*]

1. *trans.* To harry; to worry; to harass.

1523 Ld. Berners *Froiss.* I. ccxv. 271 The other parte of the same company .. sayd, howe they wolde se the pope and cardynalles .. or els to hare and to pyll the countre. [*Ibid.* 272 So thus they haryed the pope, the cardynals, and the marchauntes about Auygnon.] **1548** Hall *Chron.*, *Edw. IV* (1809) 330 The Princes of Burgoyne had not been so plucked hared & spoyled of her faire townes & Castles as she was. **1674** N. Cox *Gentl. Recreat.* (1677) 110 Let the Hounds kill the Fox themselves, and worry and hare him as much as they please.

2. To frighten, to scare.

1659 B. Harris *Parival's Iron Age* 153 Who .. so staggered and hared him, that he could not make one word of answer. **1687** R. L'Estrange *Answ. Diss.* 47 To Hair Them out of their Wits with Croking. **1692** Locke *Educ.* §67 To hare and rate them thus at every turn, is not to teach them. **1721** Strype *Eccl. Mem.* III. xiii. 122 Being but simple before, he was now haired out of his wits indeed. **1732** Gay *Distress'd Wife* II. Wks. (1772) 285 Your ladyship hares one so. **1750** Chesterf. *Lett.* (1792) III. ccxli. 106 Little minds are in a hurry .. they run, they hare, they puzzle, confound, and perplex themselves.

Hence **hared**, **'haring** *ppl. adjs.*

a **1618** Sylvester *Job Triumph.* I. 128 While Hee yet spake, there came Another in, Hared and hot. *a* **1700** B. E. *Dict. Cant. Crew*, *Hared*, Hurried. **1755** T. Amory *J. Buncle* (1825) I. 23 The multitude are thereby .. rendered a hairing, staring, wrathful rabble.

hare, *v.*[2] [f. hare *sb.*] *intr.* †**a.** To double like a hare. **b.** To run or move with great speed. Also with *it*.

1893 Farmer & Henley *Slang*, *To hare it*, to retrace one's steps; to double back. **1908** D. Coke *House Prefect* xi. 141 He had heard .. the order, 'Hare'! Now 'Hare'! is Seftonian for 'Run—and run jolly quick'! *a* **1914** J. E. Raphael *Mod. Rugby Football* (1918) 262 Receiving the ball well inside his own half-way, Palmer commenced to 'hare' for the touch-line. **1917** P. Gibbs *Battles of Somme* 173 There were other trenches ahead, and the men 'hared' off to these. **1923** Wodehouse *Inimitable Jeeves* xiv. 178, I .. hared it rapidly to the spot. **1957** *Listener* 19 Dec. 1046/1 The producer .. can't go haring about collecting the items. **1958** *Woman* 11 Jan. 47/1, I hared up to London, left my book with the publishers and went to my flat. **1963** *Times* 13 June 5/1 Boulter took over by the backstraight and went haring away past 660 yards in 1 min. 21.1 sec.

hare, obs. f. haar, hair, haire, hoar.

hare, obs. form of *are* (see be), ere.

hare, obs. form of air *adv.*, before.

c **1375** *Sc. Leg. Saints, Laurentius* 763 Rycht as þe feynd sad hyme hare.

harebell, hare-bell ('hɛəbɛl). Also 7–8 **hare's-bell**, 9 **hairbell**. [f. hare *sb.* + bell: perh. as growing in places frequented by hares.]

1. The wild hyacinth, *Scillanutans*: = blue-bell 2.

1387–8 *Compotus of Mary C'tess of Derby* 2 P' armilaus domine et capucio broid' cum harebells. **14..** *Nom.* in Wr.-Wülcker 713/9 *Hec bursa pastoris*, harebelle. **1597** Gerarde *Herbal* 99 The blew Harebels or English Jacint is very common throughout all England. **1611** Shaks. *Cymb.* IV. ii. 222 The azur'd Hare-bell, like thy Veines. **1613–16** W Browne *Brit. Past.* II. iii, The Hare-bell .. for her stainless azure blue, Claims to be worn of none but those are true. **1620** Parkinson *Paradisi* II. xi. 122 Our English Iacinth or Hares-bels is so common euery where, that it scarce needeth any description. **1786** tr. *Beckford's Vathek* (1868) 13 The ground was strewed with violets, hare-bells, and pansies. **1802** *Trans. Soc. Arts* XX. 203 The root of the *Hyacinthus non scriptus*, the plant commonly called Blue-Bells, or Hare-Bells. **1879** Britten & Holland *Plant-n.*

2. The Round-leaved Bell-flower, *Campanula rotundifolia*: = blue-bell 1.

(This application appears to have arisen in Scotland, where the Campanula is much more abundant than the wild hyacinth. Sometimes, with reference to the slender stalk, altered to *hairbell*, which Lindley tried to establish in this sense, leaving *harebell* to its original use in sense 1. Originally, in English use, 'Blue-Bell' was *Campanula*, 'Hare-bell' was *Scilla*, 'Hair-bell' non-existent.)

1765 Mickle *Sir Martyn* I. (R.), On Desmond's mouldering turrets slowly shake The trembling rie-grass, and the hare-bell blue. **1790** Burns *Elegy Henderson* v, Mourn little harebells, o'er the lee. **1810** Scott *Lady of L.* I. xviii, E'en the slight hare-bell raised its head, Elastic from her airy tread. **1810** Southey *Kehama* VII. vii, Gently as the dews of night that gem And do not bend the hare-bell's slenderest stem. **1866** *Treas. Bot.* 208/2 *Campanula rotundifolia*, Hare-bell, or .. Hair-bell, the Blue-bell of Scotland. *a* **1882** Whittier *To* —— 5 Poet. Wks. 162 Banks inclined, With trembling harebells hung.

3. *attrib.*, as ***harebell blue***.

1909 *Daily Chron.* 15 June 7/5 The dress linens .. have been prepared in many exquisite shades of leaf-green, pale primrose, hare-bell blue. **1925** T. Dreiser *Amer. Trag.* III. xvi. 647 His harebell eyes showing only cold .. practical logic. **1940** C. Day Lewis *Poems in Wartime* 8 This hare-bell height of calm. *Ibid.* 9 The climb To a tremulous, hare-bell crest. **1969** R. Godden *In this House of Brede* (1970) i. 39 Dame Veronica of the wistful hare-bell blue eyes.

'hare-brain. Also hair-. [f. hare *sb.* + brain. The spelling *hair-brain*, suggesting another origin for the compound, is later, though occasional before 1600.]

†**1.** One who has a brain like a hare's, or no more brain than a hare; a giddy or reckless person. *Obs.*

1550 Bale *Apol.* 29 Thys rashe kynde of vowyng .. he may wele bequethe to his madmen, hys harebraynes. *a* **1553** Udall *Royster D.* I. iv. (Arb.) 27 Ah foolish harebraine, This is not she. **1621** Burton *Anat. Mel.* I. ii. III. ix. (1651) 105 What a company of hare-brains have done in their rage. *a* **1670** Hacket *Abp. Williams* II. 137 (D.) The hare-brains among us are engaged with them.

Comb. **1542** Udall *Erasm. Apoph.* 237 Vndiscretely or harebrainlike, he would nedes .. bee reputed .. for an Academique.

2. *attrib.* or *adj.* = hare-brained.

1566 T. Stapleton *Ret. Untr. Jewel* IV. 109 The most outragious and harebrayne stomaches of the Donatistes. **1586** A. Day *Eng. Secretary* I. (1625) 79 For love is measured .. not by a haire-braine furie, but by a discreete and moderate ascention. **1588** Fraunce *Lawiers Log.* Ded. ¶¶ij b, Newfangled, youngheaded, harebrayne boyes. **1660** J. Sharp in *Lauderd. Papers* (Camden) I. 57 Were the game .. to be reacted, ther would be few of those hairbrain men .. now found. **1882** Stevenson *New Arab. Nts.* (1884) 6 They also handed on to me a hare-brain humour. **1886** *American* XII. 309 Hairbrain schemes of economic policy.

Hence †**'harebrainness.** *Obs.*

1598 R. Haydocke tr. *Lomazzo's Tr.* II. 72 Hare-brainnesse hath ridiculous, furious, and phantasticall motions.

'hare-brained, *a.* Also hair-. [parasynth. f. *hare brain* + -ed[2]. For the form *hair-*, see prec.]

Having or showing no more 'brains' or sense than a hare; heedless, reckless; rash, wild, mad. Of persons, their actions, etc.

1548 HALL *Chron., Hen. V*, 216 b, My desire is that none of you be so unadvised or harebrained as to be the occasion that [etc.]. **1581** PETTIE *Guazzo's Civ. Conv.* III. (1586) 148 If his sonne be haughtie, or haire brained, he termeth him courageous. **1615** J. STEPHENS *Satyr. Ess.* 100 Whilst they, out of a hare-brained lunacie desire battaile. **1643** PRYNNE *Sov. Power Parl.* I. (ed. 2) 42 The hair-brain'd advise of his young Cavalieres. **1738** SWIFT *Polite Convers.* 144 Perhaps it will make me hare-brain'd. **1818** HAZLITT *Eng. Poets* vii. (1870) 172 The excesses of mad, hairbrained, roaring mirth. **1862** MRS. H. WOOD *Mrs. Hallib.* III. xxii, Keeping hare-brained follies at arm's-length.

Hence **'hare-brainedly** *adv.*; **'hare-brainedness**.

a **1577** GASCOIGNE *Fruite of Fetters* (R.), Fansie.. farewell, whose badge.. in my hat full harebrayndly, thy flowers did I weare. **1656** BLOUNT *Glossogr.*, *Cerebrosity*, brainsickness, hairbrainedness. **1659** D. PELL *Impr. Sea* Ep. Ded. C ij, Profane, and giddy hairbrainedness.

'hare-bur. [cf. HARDOCK.] Burdock.

1866 *Treas. Bot.*, Hareburr, *Arctium Lappa.* [**1879** BRITTEN & HOLLAND *Plant-n.*, *Hareburr*.. perhaps a misprint for Hurrburr.]

†**'hare-cop.** *Obs.* [? f. HARE *sb.* + COP head.] ? = HARE-BRAIN *sb.*

1567 *Damon & Pithias* in Hazl. *Dodsley* IV. 75 A merry harecop 'tis, and a pleasant companion.

'hare-finder. A man whose business is to find or espy a hare in form.

1599 SHAKS. *Much Ado* I. i. 186 Or doe you play the flowting iacke, to tell vs Cupid is a good Hare-finder? **1611** MARKHAM *Countr. Content* I. vii. (1668) 43 The Hare-finder should give the Hare three sohows before he put her from her Lear. **1676** SHADWELL *Virtuoso* III. Wks. 1720 I. 364 *Clarinda.* You stare about like a Hare-finder; what's the matter? *Longvil.* Faith, madam, I expected to have met your Sister here. **1824** MISS MITFORD *Village* Ser. I. (1863) 185 Rat-catcher, hare-finder, and broom-maker.

harefoot, hare-foot.

1. Also *hare's foot.* The foot of a hare, or a foot resembling a hare's; *spec.* a long narrow foot found in some dogs.

1748 RICHARDSON *Clarissa* (1811) II. 118 (D.) Better a hare-foot than none at all; that is, than not to be able to walk. **1901** *Encycl. Sport* I. 329/2 *Harefoot*, a long, narrow foot, carried far forward. **1945** C. L. B. HUBBARD *Observer's Bk. Dogs* 161 American standards permit hare-feet. **1952** R. LEIGHTON *Compl. Bk. Dog* (ed. 6) v. 80 Faults: [in Boxer].. hare's feet.

†**2.** A nickname for a swift-footed person.? *Obs.*

c **1410** *Chron. Eng.* 899 in Ritson *Metr. Rom.* (1802) II, Harald, Godwyne sone He was cleped Harefot, for he was urnare god. **14..** *Bromton Chron.* in Twysden *Hist. Angl. Script. decem* (1652) 932 Propter levitatem pedum & cursus Haraldus Harefot communiter extitit appellatus. *a* **1491** ROUS *Hist. Reg. Angl.* 105 Haroldus Harfote quasi levis in cursu ut lepus aliquis.

†**3.** A plant; = HARE'S-FOOT I. ? *Obs.*

c **1265** *Voc. Plant.-n.* in Wr.-Wülcker 555/6 *Auencia*, hare-fot. *a* **1387** *Sinon. Barthol.* 24 Harefote, *avancia.* **1570** LEVINS *Manip.* 178/29 Harefoote, herb, *lagopus.*

†**4.** Name given to the ptarmigan and other species of *Lagopus*, from the densely feathered feet. ? *Obs.*

[**1706** PHILLIPS, *Haresfoot*.. also a kind of Bird.] **1755** JOHNSON, *Harefoot.* 1. A bird. *Ainsworth.*

5. Used adverbially: swiftly. *poet.*

1939 T. S. ELIOT *Family Reunion* I. ii. 60 What of the terrified spirit Compelled.. To rise toward the violent sun .. Harefoot over the moon?

Hare Krishna ('hɑːreɪ 'krɪʃnə). [f. Hindi *hare* O God! + *Kṛishṇa* name of an incarnation of the god Vishnu.] The title of a chant or mantra based on a name of the Hindu deity Vishnu; used esp. as an incantation by members of a religious cult in the U.S. and elsewhere; hence *attrib.* or *absol.* to designate this cult or its members.

1968 *New Yorker* 17 Aug. 36 Newspaper pictures of the poet [*sc.* Ginsberg] chanting '*Hare Krishna*' at one of Leary's sellout psychedelic celebrations. **1970** *Time* 3 Aug. 31 He [*sc.* David Hoyt] became a member of the Hare Krishna cult and custodian of the Radha Krishna temple. **1971** *Times* 5 July 3/6 The founder of the Hare Krishna Movement, his Divine Grace A. C. Bhaktivedanta, did not make his expected appearance. **1971** E. LARSEN *Strange Sects & Cults* viii. 164 Small groups of smiling English youngsters.. could be seen slowly dance-marching in file through London's West End.. to the accompaniment of some tinkling Oriental instruments, chanting 'Hare Krishna' and offering passers-by literature on their 'Krishna Consciousness Movement'. **1972** G. V. HIGGINS *Friends of Eddie Coyle* xi. 68 Near the first subway kiosk the Hare Krishnas sang and danced, wearing saffron robes and tattered gray sweaters.

hareld ('hærəld). Also **herald, harold.** [ad. mod.L. *Harelda* (Stephens 1824), arbitrary alteration of earlier *Havelda*, from Icel. name *havelle.*] A species of sea-duck, *Harelda glacialis.*

1841 SELBY in *Proc. Berw. Nat. Club* I. No. 9. 261 *Harelda glacialis*, Long-tailed Hareld. **1863** KINGSLEY *Water Bab.* vii. (1889) 258 Harlequins and eiders, harolds and garganeys.

hare-lip ('hɛə'lɪp). Also 8 **hair-.** [f. HARE *sb.* + LIP.]

1. Fissure of the upper lip, caused by the arrest of development in the upper lip or jaw; so called from the resemblance to the cleft lip of a hare.

1567 HARMAN *Caveat* 82 Wylliam Coper with the Harelyp. **1590** SHAKS. *Mids. N.* v. i. 418 Neuer mole, harelip, nor scarre. **1634** T. JOHNSON *Parey's Chirurg.* I. ii. (1678) 2 The Chirurgeon.. cicatriceth cloven lips, commonly called Hare-lips. **1785** R. CUMBERLAND in *Observer* No. 98 ¶11 [He] had a remarkable hair-lip, which exposed to view a broken row of discoloured teeth. **1855** HOLDEN *Hum. Osteol.* (1878) 98 In cases of double hare-lip, where the fissure is not confined to skin, the pre-maxillary bones on each side fail to unite with the rest of the upper jaw.

2. ***hare-lip sucker***, a fish, *Quassilabia lacera*, of the Ohio river and its tributaries, remarkable for the conformation of the mouth.

Hence **hare-lipped** (-lɪpt) *a.*, having the upper lip cleft like the hare.

1607 TOPSELL *Four-f. Beasts* (1658) 208 If the childe prove not Hare-lipt. **1775** ADAIR *Amer. Ind.* 277, I spoke.. to a hair-lipped warrior among them. **1854** BADHAM *Halieut.* 114 The hideous, hare-lipped uranoscopus.. the singular position of whose eyes attracted early the attention of naturalists.

harelot, obs. form of HARLOT.

harem, haram ('hɛərəm). Also 7 **haramm,** 8 **harram** (hɑː'ræm); 9 **hareem, harīm** (hɑː'riːm). [a. Arab. *ḥaram*, and *ḥarīm* lit. (that which is) prohibited or unlawful, that which a man defends and fights for, as his family, a sacred place, sanctuary, enclosure; the women's part of the house; wives, women; from *ḥarama* to prohibit, forbid, make unlawful. The two Arabic words are practically synonymous, *esp.* in countries where Arabic is not the vernacular. From the first come the earlier Eng. *haram* and *harem*; from the second the later *harim, hareem*; see also sense 3.]

1. a. The part of a Muslim dwelling-house appropriated to the women, constructed so as to secure the utmost seclusion and privacy; called also *seraglio*, and in Persia and India *zenana.*

1634 SIR T. HERBERT *Trav.* 62 He has three hundred women in his Seraglio (called here Haram). *Ibid.* 148 The other women belonging to Seraglioes or Haramms, live discontented. **1698** FRYER *Acc. E. India & P.* 132 The Governor sent for me to visit his Lady in the Haram. **1718** LADY M. W. MONTAGU *Let. to C'tess Mar* 10 Mar., I have been in a harem, where the winter apartment was wainscoted with inlaid work of mother-of-pearl. **1753** HANWAY *Trav.* (1762) I. III. xxxiv. 157 The harram is magnificent, consisting of a square within its own wall of brick. **1864** ENGEL *Mus. Anc. Nat.* 220 This drum is especially used in the hareems. **1872** BAKER *Nile Tribut.* xx. 349 Brought by the Abyssinian traders to be sold for the Turkish harems.

b. *transf.* and *fig.*

1823 SCOTT *Peveril* xlix, [She] stood with her arms folded on her breast, with an humble air, as different from that which she wore in the harem of the Duke of Buckingham as that of a Magdalene from a Judith. **1870** EMERSON *Soc. & Solit., Books* Wks. (Bohn) III. 86 A man's library is a sort of harem. **1872** O. W. HOLMES *Poet Breakf.-t.* viii. 248, I must have my literary harem, my *parc aux cerfs*, where my favorites await my moments of leisure and pleasure.

2. a. The occupants of a harem collectively; the female members of a Muslim family; *esp.* the wives and concubines collectively of a Turk, Persian, or Indian Muslim.

1781 COWPER *Anti-Thelypthora* 108 Seraglios sing and harems dance for joy. **1821** BYRON *Sardan.* I. i, Were it less toil.. To head an army than to rule a harem? **1855** BURTON *Pilgr. Meccah* xv. (1893) I. 295 The kitchen.. being as usual occupied by the 'Harim'. **1879** E. K. BATES *Egyptian Bonds* I. iii. 37 The Viceroy's harem were disporting themselves on the sand.

b. *transf.* and *fig.* Applied *spec.* to the family units of various animals.

1784 COWPER *Task* IV. 447 Where chanticleer amidst his haram sleeps In unsuspecting pomp. **1855** THACKERAY *Newcomes* II. xxxvi. 324 Could our hearts let in such a harem of dear friendships. **1860** MOTLEY *Netherl.* (1868) I. ii. 47 In the harem entertained for him in the Louvre many pitfalls entrapped him. **1898** D. S. JORDAN *Fur Seals* I. 57 The average size of a harem.. is about thirty females to a single bull. **1932** S. ZUCKERMAN *Soc. Life Monkeys & Apes* xi. 178 Sokolowsky's account of sexual life in a chimpanzee harem is by far the best that has hitherto appeared. **1948** A. L. RAND *Mammals E. Rockies* 26 In the autumn.. the bull elk come down from the mountains to gather their harems. **1955** L. DARLING *Seals & Walruses* 24 There are an average of forty cows in a fur seal's harem. **1964** G. DURRELL *Menagerie Manor* i. 32 The peacock.. leading his vacant-eyed harem towards their roosting place.

3. A Muslim sacred place or area; one which is prohibited to any but the Faithful. More usually in form *harām*, Arabic *ḥarām*, forbidden, sacred place.

1855 BURTON *Pilgr. Meccah* xv. (1893) I. 294 We all set out in a body to the Harim.. a duty which must not be delayed by the pious. **1883** A. THOMSON *Holy Land* vi. 106 On the summit of Mount Moriah.. there spreads the noble enclosure of the Haram.

4. Comb., as ***harem-court, -wall***; ***harem-bred*** adj.; **harem dress**, a dress with a harem hem; **harem hem**, a hem which draws in the material which then billows over it; **harem skirt**, a loose trouser-like skirt as worn in a harem, or an imitation of one; hence ***harem-skirted*** adj.

1829 *Bengalee* 226 Humble puppet, Haram slave. **1853** KINGSLEY *Hypatia* xviii, Wulf came rapidly down stairs, through the hall into the harem-court. **1883** A. THOMSON *Holy Land* viii. 138 To sink shafts as near as possible to the prohibited distance, and then to approach the Haram walls by tunnelling underneath. **1890** C. W. C. OMAN *Hist. Greece* 187 A mere harem-bred despot. **1911** *Sphere* 11 Mar. 219 The opinions of London and Paris over the harem skirt seem to be as divided as is the costume itself. **1927** *Delineator* June 21 *Chéruit* was the first to make taffeta frocks in great puffs with harem hems. **1952** *California Stylist* May, The harem dress.. mushrooming fullness on a delicate stem. **1957** *Punch* 14 Aug. 191/1 His cocktail and evening dresses are harem skirted, and there was a bright yellow harem trouser-dress. **1958** J. LAVER *Edwardian Promenade* vii. 163 Two symbolic kinds of skirt: the harem skirt and the hobbleskirt. **1958** *Vogue* Mid-Sept. Extra Issue 77/4 Electric blue chiffon softly wrapping a tiny waist and gently curving into a harem hem. **1966** *Sunday Times* (Colour Suppl.) 27 Feb. 32/4 Paul Poiret's harem dress.. was inspired by Bakst's designs.

haremlik ('hɛərəm-, hə'riːmlɪk). [Turk., f. HAREM + *-lik* place.] = HAREM I.

1920 *Blackw. Mag.* Nov. 661/2 High above their bench and entered from the Haremlik, is an iron grille or cage, in which the Padishah could overhear unseen his Ministers' deliberations. **1936** N. M. PENZER *Harēm* i. 16 Relations with European powers soon gave rise to the coining of a word that would embrace not only the *harēmlik* and the *serāmlik* but the entire Royal buildings as a whole.... The word *seraglio* was chosen. **1941** *Archit. Rev.* XC. 101/2 The houses were divided vertically into two parts—the *Haremlik* or women's quarters, and the *Selamlik* for the men.

ha'rengiform, *a.* [f. mod. Zool. L. *harengus* herring + -FORM.] Having the form of a herring.

1828 in WEBSTER; and in later Dicts.

†**'hare-pipe.** *Obs.* [f. HARE *sb.* + PIPE.] A trap for catching hares.

1389 *Act 13 Rich. II*, Stat. I. c. 13 §1 Nene use furettes haies rees hare pipes ne cordes. *c* **1485** *E.E. Misc.* (Warton Club) 45, I have an hare-pype in my purce, Hit schal be set al for thi sake. **1576** TURBERV. *Venerie* 200 As you may take a hare with Harepypes or such like gynnes. **1603** *Act 1 Jas. I*, c. 27 §1 Everie person.. which.. shall.. take, or destroy any Hares with any Harepipes, Cordes, or with any such Instrumentes. **1615** W. LAWSON *Country Housew. Gard.* (1626) 45 You must have.. an Hare-pipe for an Hare. **1821** *Sporting Mag.* IX. 11 Hare-pipes, gins, snares.

hare's-ear ('hɛəzɪə(r)). [From the shape of the leaves.] The name given to species of *Bupleurum* (N.O. *Umbelliferæ*), and *Erysimum* (N.O. *Cruciferæ*), having auricled leaves. ***bastard hare's-ear***, a name for *Phyllis Nobla* (N.O. *Cinchonaceæ*), a shrub found in the Canary Isles.

1597 GERARDE *Herbal* II. clxxix. 485 Which hath caused me to call it Hares eares, hauing in the middle of the leafe some hollownesse resembling the same. **1861** MISS PRATT *Flower. Pl.* I. 131 *Erysimum orientale* (Hare's-ear Treacle Mustard). **1866** *Treas. Bot.*, *Bupleurum*, Hare's-ear, Thorow-wax.

'hare's-foot.

1. A species of clover (*Trifolium arvense*), with soft hair about the flowers. Also called ***hare's-foot trefoil.*** (See also HAREFOOT.)

1562 TURNER *Herbal* II. 26 a, Lagopus maye be called in Englishe Haris foot or rough clauer. **1713** J. PETIVER in *Phil. Trans.* XXVIII. 62 Its blush Flowers stand in a round flusey Head, like our Haresfoot. **1861** MISS PRATT *Flower. Pl.* II. 109 *Trifolium arvense* (Hare's-foot Trefoil).

2. The Corkwood tree (*Ochroma Lagopus*) of the West Indies and Central America; so called from the dehiscent ripe fruit with the cotton of the seeds protruding from it. *Treas. Bot.* 1866.

3. a. A hare's foot used in applying rouge, etc., to the face.

c **1800** [see *burnt cork* s.v. BURNT *ppl. a.* 7]. **1827** L. T. REDE *Road to Stage* 38 Burn a cork to powder, wet it with beer (which will fix the colouring matter), and apply it with a hare's-foot, or a cloth. **1835** DICKENS *Sk. Boz* (1836) II. 206 The young lady with the liberal display of legs, who is kindly painting his face with a hare's foot. **1859** E. WINSTANLEY *Shifting Scenes Theatr. Life* xxi. 200 There are pots of rouge, hare's feet, powder-boxes. **1877** 'HARESFOOT & ROUGE' *How to 'Make-up'* 13 Then with a hare's foot apply a colouring of Rouge to the cheeks. **1939–40** *Army & Navy Stores Catal.* 1097/1 Theatrical make-up... Hares' feet.

b. See HAREFOOT I.

4. *attrib.* **hare's-foot fern**, a name of *Davallia canariensis*; also extended to other species, as (in Australia) *D. pyxidata.* **hare's-foot sedge**, *Carex lagopina.* **hare's-foot trefoil**: see I.

1861 MISS PRATT *Flower. Pl.* VI. 27 Hare's-foot Sedge.. a very rare plant. **1866** *Treas. Bot.*, *Davallia*, a.. genus of polypodiaceous ferns.. They have scaly creeping rhizomes, which feature has given rise to the name of Hare's Foot Fern, applied to *D. canariensis.* **1882** *Garden* 29 Apr. 301/3 *Davallia Fijiensis Plumosa* [is] a very elegant Hare's-foot Fern.

harestane, -strang(e, Sc. ff. HOARSTONE, STRONG.

'hare-'warren. A warren or breeding-place for hares.

1647 in Rushw. *Hist. Coll.* IV. II. 878 Another Rendezvous of the Army was upon the Hare-warren near

Kingston. **1668** SEDLEY *Mulberry Gard.* IV. i, Like a pack of hounds in a hare warren. **1774** FOOTE *Cozeners* II. Wks. 1799 II. 161 He puts me in mind of a pack of hounds in a hare-warren; by eternally shifting the game, the pursuit never ends. **1829** *Sporting Mag.* XXIII. 392 A county..which..has degenerated..into a mere hare-warren and pheasant-mew.

harewe, obs. form of ARROW.

harewood ('hɛəwʊd). Also **hairwood, airwood** (8 **aire-**); and simply 7 **ayer, ayre.** [ad. dial. G. *aehre, ehre*, or its apparent source Friulian, etc. *ayar, ayer, aire*:—Rom. **acre* = L. *acer* maple.] Stained sycamore wood, used by cabinet-makers.

1664 EVELYN *Sylva* I. x. 28 The Timber [of Maple] is far superiour to Beech for all uses of the Turner... Also for the lightness (under the name Ayer) imploy'd often by those who make Musical-instruments. **1676** T. MACE *Musick's Mon.* 49 Next, what Wood is Best for the Ribbs. The Air-wood is absolutely the Best. *Ibid.* 64 A Lute made of Ayre. **1723** *Evening Post* 30 May, He has ..some fine Aire-wood for furnishing the Insides [of harpsichords]. **1843** HOLTZAPFFEL *Turning* etc. I. 107 A variety of sycamore, which is called harewood, is richer in figure and sometimes striped. **1873** E. SPON *Workshop Rec.* 1st Ser. 414/1 Have the veneers ready, which must be air-wood. *Ibid.* 423/2 Hair-wood. **1899** *Daily News* 22 June 8/7 A cabinet..of inlaid satin, hare, and other woods. **1901** *Westm. Gaz.* 9 May 1/3 On satin and harewood banded with rosewood. **1947** J. C. RICH *Materials & Methods of Sculpture* x. 296 English sycamore, or Harewood, is actually a variety of maple. It is a light-colored, fine-grained, figured wood and is generally available in the form of thin planks. **1968** *Times* 26 Nov. 13/6 A pair of George III satinwood and harewood commodes. **1973** *Country Life* 7 June 1587/1 A pembroke table in the silvery green of harewood.

‖**harfang** ('hɑːfæŋ). Also **harphang.** [a. F. *harfang* (1760 in Hatz.-Darm.), a. Sw. *harfång* the snowy owl, f. *har(e* hare + *fånga* to catch.] The Great Snowy Owl.

1774 GOLDSM. *Nat. Hist.* (1862) II. II. vii. 55 The Harfang, or Great Hudson's Bay Owl of Edwards..the largest of all the nocturnal tribe. **1847** CARPENTER *Zool.* §382 The Harfang or Great Snowy Owl..is found in very high northern latitudes, of both the Old and New World. **1884** *N.Y. Herald* 27 Oct. 5/2 It was I who killed the harphang.

harga-, harge-, harguebush(e, etc., obs. ff. HARQUEBUS, etc.

Hargrave ('hɑːgreɪv). The surname of Lawrence *Hargrave* (1850–1915), an Australian pioneer in Aeronautics, used *attrib.* to designate a cellular box-kite invented by him in 1894.

1900 R. S. BAKER *Boy's Bk. Inventions* vi. 210 Those [tailless kites] of the Hargrave model giving the impression of a number of big pasteboard boxes with the bottoms knocked out. **1908** W. H. STORY tr. *Hildebrandt's Airships* x. 117 (*caption*) Hargrave kite. *Ibid.* x. 121 Four Hargrave kites were used. **1945** BAKER *Austral. Lang.* x. 200 Hargrave box kite.

†**hargulater.** *Obs.* Also **-atier, hargo-, hargeletier, argolatear.** Variant forms of ARGOLETIER: see quot. 1598.

1581 STYWARD *Mart. Discipl.* II. 123 Sending alwaies before 100 Hargulaters on Horsebacke. **1591** GARRARD *Art Warre* 197 The Argolateares are to gallop the field and scale the side of a squadron. **1598** BARRET *Theor. Warres* Gloss. 251 *Hargulatier*..is the souldier seruing on horsebacke, vnarmed, vsing a Calliuer with a snap hance. **1625** MARKHAM *Souldiers Accid.* 26 Whosoeuer is a good Musquetier cannot chuse but be a good Hargeletier.

harhalde, obs. form of HERALD.

hariant, obs. form of HAURIENT.

haricot ('hærɪkəʊ, -kɒt), *sb.* Also 7 **aricot,** 8 **arico, harricot,** 8–9 **harico, harrico.** [a. F. *haricot* (16th c. in Littré), in 14th c. *hericoq de mouton* (Hatz.-Darm.), *hericot* (Littré), in sense 1; in sense 2 Hatz.-Darm. cite *fevre de haricot* of 1642. Origin uncertain: see Littré.]

1. A ragout (originally of mutton, now sometimes of other meat). Also *attrib.*

[**1611** COTGR., *Haricot*, mutton sod with little turneps, some wine, and tosts of bred crumbled among.] **1706** PHILLIPS (ed. Kersey), *Haricot*, a particular way of dressing Mutton-cutlets, or several sorts of Fowl and Fish in a Ragoo with Turneps; also a kind of French beans. **1769** MRS. RAFFALD *Eng. Housekpr.* (1778) 102 Harico of a Neck of Mutton. **1816** CATHERINE HUTTON in *W. Hutton's Autobiog.* Concl. 90 Harico of mutton and gooseberry pudding. **1870** *Daily News* 16 Nov., Irish stew or haricot mutton.

2. A leguminous plant of the genus *Phaseolus*, especially *P. vulgaris*, the common Kidney-bean or French-bean: also ***haricot bean.*** Applied both to the plant and the beans or seeds. Also ***haricot blanc, pod, vert.*** See BEAN *sb.* 3.

1653 H. COGAN tr. *Pinto's Trav.* xxvi. 99 A little meal, aricot beans, onions..wherewith we made the best shift we could. **1706** PHILLIPS (ed. Kersey), *Arico*, the French-Bean, or Kidney-Bean [see also 1]. **1792** A. YOUNG *Trav. France* 353 Another course is to sow rye; after that millet; and with this *harricots*, or kidney-beans. **1815** M. BIRKBECK *Journ. thro' France* 16 Women were every where hoeing French beans (*Haricos*). **1845** E. ACTON *Mod. Cookery* xv. 328 The haricot blanc is the seed of a particular kind of French bean. **1861** DELAMER *Kitch. Gard.* 90 On the Continent..the ripe seeds, or haricots proper, are largely cultivated for winter use. **1869** E. A. PARKES *Pract. Hygiene* (ed. 3) 175 Haricot beans frequently form part of the vegetables. **1877** E. S. DALLAS *Kettner's Bk. Table* 242 (*heading*) Haricot pods, what the French call haricots verts; called also French beans. **1907** *Yesterday's Shopping* (1969) 45/1 Vegetables, preserved, in Tins..Haricots Verts, extra fins—tin, 0/7½. **1941** A. SIMON *Conc. Encycl. Gastron.* III. 46/2 In the U.S.A...there is a variety of canned String Beans..marketed under the name of *Haricots verts.* **1966** *Harrod's Food News* Sept. 2/1 Haricot Verts—8 oz. 3/3. **1967** *Listener* 20 Apr. 533/3 Chefs who bite the *haricots verts* or spit on the icing sugar. **1970** *Sat. Rev.* 3 Oct. 44/3 *Cassoulet*..usually includes goose..sausages, and *haricots blancs* or white beans.

Hence **haricot, harico** *v. trans.*, to make into a haricot (sense 1).

1769 MRS. RAFFALD *Eng. Housekpr.* (1778) 141 To harico a Neck of Mutton. **1805** *Sporting Mag.* XXV. 226 Veal cutlets, haricoed mutton.

haridan, harier: see HARRIDAN, HARRIER.

harif, -iff, -of, dial. forms of HAIRIF.

Harijan ('hærɪdʒən). [a. Skr. *harijana*) person who has received the grace of the god Vishnu, f. *Hari* Vishnu + *jana* person.] The name given by Gandhi to the Untouchables in India. Also as *adj.*

1931 M. K. GANDHI *Bleeding Wound* (1932) ix. 40 Only the other day a friend suggested to me that the word Harijana (man of God) be substituted for the word 'antyaja' (the 'lastborn') that is being used for 'untouchables'... I am delighted to adopt that word. **1932** *Ibid.* App. 186, I would like to assure my Harijan friends, as I would like henceforth to name them, that..I am wedded to the whole..agreement. **1958** G. MIKES *East is East* 162 But the untouchables—the *harijans*—are still not regarded as human beings. **1960** *Times* 23 May 13/7 Many more Harijan children are now attending the village schools. **1966** *New Statesman* 11 Feb. 190/1 Already the leader of the untouchables..has won a seat in the cabinet..in recognition of the 70-odd Harijan votes cast against Desai. **1969** *Times* 13 Oct. (India Suppl.) p. vi/2 In Porbander, in spite of Gandhi's dream and work to eradicate untouchability and the Government's enlightened policy during the past 22 years, Harijans must still draw water from separate taps. **1973** *Times* 20 Aug. 12/1 Harijans, or 'Children of God', the name coined by Mahatma Gandhi—and now generally used—for the Untouchables.

hari-kari, erron. form of HARA-KIRI.

†'**hariolate,** *v. Obs.* Cf. also ARIOLATE, etc. [f. L. *hariolāt-*, ppl. stem of *hariolārī* to divine, foretell, f. *hariolus* soothsayer.] *intr.* To soothsay; also, in 17th c., to practise ventriloquism. Hence †'**hariolating,** †**hario'lation;** also †'**hariole** *v.* (*nonce-wd.*), to divine, guess; †'**hariolize,** to soothsay.

1592 WARNER *Alb. Eng.* VII. xxxv. (1612) 168 The lad was loftie, for himself he hariolized well, At full he could his lessons, and a formale lie would tell. **1656** BLOUNT *Glossogr.*, *Hariolation*, a fore-telling or South-saying. **1656** T. ADY *Candle in Dark* 80 The imposture of Hariolating or speaking in the belly. **1660** tr. *Amyraldus' Treat. conc. Relig.* III. ii. 333 What is the guess of hariolation of two or three to the constant opinions of a whole multitude? **1677** J. WEBSTER *Witchcr.* vi. 121 The Genii hariolating forth of the belly. **1833** C. WORDSWORTH in *Ann. Early Life* (1891) I. 130, I think I may venture to hariole [*rime* carriole].

hariot, obs. form of HERIOT.

†**harish** ('hɛərɪʃ), *a. Obs.* [f. HARE *sb.* + -ISH.] Of the nature of a hare; mad, foolish.

1552 HULOET, Harishe, or of a hare. **1579** TOMSON *Calvin's Serm. Tim.* 693/1 Our harish and madde zeale. **1581** J. BELL *Haddon's Answ. Osor.* 420 b, More then harishe maddnes.

hark (hɑːk), *v.* Forms: 2 **herkien,** 3 **harkien,** (3–4 **herc**), 3–5 **herken,** 4–6 **herk(e,** 6–8 **harke, heark,** 6– **hark.** [Early ME. *herkien*:—OE. type **heorcian* corresp. to OFris. *herkia, harkia* (WFris. *herckjen, harckjen*, NFris. *harke*); in ablaut relation with MDu. *horken, horcken* (Kilian) mod. Flem. dial. *heurken, horken*, MHG. and mod. Ger. *horchen*; from an ablaut series *herk-, hark-, hork-*. OHG. *hôrechen*, MHG. *hôrchen*, perh. owe their long *ô* to the influence of *hôren* to hear. The change of OE. *eo*, ME. *e*, to *a* is regular: cf. OE. *beorc* bark, *deorc* dark: the Sc. form is still *herk* as in *derk, berk*, etc.]

1. *trans.* To give ear or listen to; to hearken to, hear with active attention.

c **1175** *Lamb. Hom.* 31 Bluðeliche he wule herkien þet þe preost him leið on. *c* **1200** *Vices & Virt.* (1888) 19 Harkið hwat se haligast seið. *c* **1325** *Lai le Freine* 147 Sone after she gan herk Cokkes crowe, and houndes berk. *c* **1385** CHAUCER *L.G.W.* 1276 *Dido*, Now herkith how he schal his lady serue. *c* **1489** CAXTON *Sonnes of Aymon* ix. 246 Herke what we wyll telle you. **1513** DOUGLAS *Æneis* XII. x. 30 Now harkis quhat I purpos do this tyde. **1526** SKELTON *Magnyf.* 401 What, I say, herke a worde. **1598** YONG *Diana* 282 Harke but one worde that I shall say vnto thee. *c* **1680** BEVERIDGE *Serm.* (1729) I. 506 Hark what he himself here saith. **1830** TENNYSON *To J.M.K.*, Hating to hark The humming of the drowsy pulpit-drone.

2. *intr.* To give ear, hearken, listen. **a.** with *to.*

a **1300** *Cursor M.* 14030 (Gött.) Herk to me a stund. **1513** DOUGLAS *Æneis* IX. Prol. 6 Quha tharto harkis fallis in fragilite. **1579–80** NORTH *Plutarch* Amiot to Rdrs. (R.), A certain singular pleasure in hearking to such as be returned from some long voyage. **1580** SIDNEY *Ps.* XVII. i, Just Lord, to my suit hark. **1646** CRASHAW *Temperance* in *Steps to Temple* (1670) 207 Hark hither, Reader, wilt thou see Nature her own Physitian be? **1785** BURNS *Vision* I. 25 Had I to guid advice but harkit. **1855** LYNCH *Rivulet* LXIX. v, We hark with holy fear To the lingering sounds sublime. **1887** G. M. FENN *Dick o' the Fens* vii, Hark at him!..young squire ar'n't going to eat any more bacon, 'cause it's cruel to kill the pigs. **1894** CROCKETT *Raiders* 178 Hark to the rattle of the guns. **1895** 'G. MORTIMER' *Like Stars that Fall* xiii, 'You're so spry, I can't trust you for a grass widow.' 'Hark at him!' laughed Mrs. Larpenti.

b. *absol.* Chiefly in *imperative.*

a **1300** *Cursor M.* 21378 Herc, and i sal tel yow. *c* **1440** *Promp. Parv.* 237/1 Herkyn, and take heede, and ley to þe ere..*asculto.* **1513** DOUGLAS *Æneis* II. Prol. 15 Harkis, ladyis, ȝour bewtie was the caus. **1591** SHAKS. *1 Hen. VI*, I. v. 27 Hearke Countreymen, eyther renew the fight Or teare the Lyons out of Englands Coat. **1610** —— *Temp.* IV. i. 262 Harke, they rore. *c* **1709** PRIOR *2nd Hymn Callimachus* 4 Hark! he knocks. **1821** BYRON *Heaven & Earth* iii. 727 Hark, hark! Deep sounds..Are howling from the mountain's bosom. **1821** CLARE *Vill. Minstr.* II. 86, I knew her well And her whole history, if ye'll hark, can tell.

c. In the imperative the nom. *ye* is often added (also written *hark'ee, harkee*); less commonly *hark you*, and by confusion *hark thee* (cf. *fare thee* well).

1588 SHAKS. *Tit. A.* II. i. 99 Why harke yee, harke yee, and are you such fooles, To square for this? **1591** —— *Two Gent.* III. i. 127 Harke thee: I will goe to her alone. **1605** B. JONSON *Volpone* v. i, But, heark you: Remember, what your ladyship off'red me. **1708** MOTTEUX *Rabelais* IV. lxiv. (1737) 261 Harkee me, dear Rogue! **1709** STEELE *Tatler* No. 38 ¶9 Hark'ee, No Names. **1711** BUDGELL *Spect.* No. 150 ¶9 Hark you, Sirrah, I'll pay off your extravagant Bills once more. **1751** E. MOORE *Gil Blas* Prol (R.), But hearkee, poet!—won't you though? says I. **1836–48** B. D. WALSH *Aristoph., Knights* II. iii, Harkee, Quick haul up your ponderous dolphins. **1838** LYTTON *Alice* 69 Hark ye! one word more with me, sir, and you quit my service to-morrow.

†**3.** *trans.* To get to hear of, find out by inquiry and listening; = HEARKEN *v.* 8. *Obs.*

1561 T. HOBY tr. *Castiglione's Courtyer* (1577) N vij b, Those that go alwaies harking out the loues of others, & disclose them so point by point.

4. *intr.* Used in hunting, etc., as a call of attention and incitement, esp. in conjunction with an adverb directing what action is to be performed: hence denoting the action: see below. Cf. also HARK *sb.*

1610 SHAKS. *Temp.* IV. i. 258 *Pro.* [setting on dogs] Fury, Fury: there Tyrant, there: harke, harke. Goe, charge my Goblins that they grinde their ioynts.

a. ***hark away, forward, in, off***: to proceed or go away, forward, in, draw off.

1737–1801 [see HARK *sb.*]. **1816** 'QUIZ' *Grand Master* VIII. 228 Hark! forward, sportsmen—'tis the same. **1824** MACTAGGART *Gallovid. Encycl.* s.v. *Haurk*, When the hunter hears by them [terriers] the situation they are in, he bawls down to *haurk to him, haurk to him, ye wee blasties.* **1826** *Sporting Mag.* XVII. 270 The word was given 'Yoi—hark in, hark'. **1844** DISRAELI *Coningsby* I. v, I think the hounds are too hot to hark off now. **1846** R. E. EGERTON-WARBURTON *Hunting Songs* v. (1883) 15 Away! Hark, away! ..Ne'er slacken your pace.

b. ***hark back.*** Of hounds: To return along the course taken, when the scent has been lost, till it is found again; hence *fig.* to retrace one's course or steps; to return, revert; to return to some earlier point in a narrative, discussion, or argument.

1829 *Sporting Mag.* XXIV. 175, I must 'hark back', as we say in the chace. **1868** HOLME LEE *B. Godfrey* xli. 225 Basil must needs hark back on the subject of the papers. **1877** CRUTTWELL *Hist. Rom. Lit.* 223 The mind of Lucretius harks back to the glorious period of creative enthusiasm. **1882** STEVENSON *Stud. Men & Bks., J. Knox* 349 He has to hark back again to find the scent of his argument. **1895** F. HALL *Two Trifles* 31 To hark back to *scientist*..I am ready to pit it against your *agnostic.*

c. *trans.* ***hark on, forward***: to urge on with encouraging cries. ***hark back***: to recall.

1813 HOGG *Queen's Wake* 178 Scho herkit on her revining [i.e. ravening] crew. **1834** SIR H. TAYLOR *Artevelde* I. i. 9 (D.) There is but one that harks me back. **1852** THACKERAY *Esmond* II. ix, Yelling and harking his bloody war-dogs on. **1865** DASENT *Jest & Earnest* (1873) I. 209 He..harked forward his packs of hounds with a cheer.

d. ***hark after***: to go after, to follow.

1899 B. TARKINGTON *Gentleman fr. Indiana* vii. 109 Men were running around a corner of the court-house, and the women and children were harking after.

5. *intr.* To speak in one's ear; to whisper or mutter. *Sc.* and *north. dial.*

1583 *Leg. Bp. St. Androis* 168 in *Satir. Poems Reform.* xlv, Auld Captane Kirkburne to him harkit. **1697** W. CLELAND *Poems* 99 (Jam.) Then some began to hark and rown. **1785** R. FORBES *Dominie Deposed* 38 (Jam.) Then whispering low to me she harked. **1851** *Cumbld. Gloss.*, *Hark*, to whisper and to listen.

Hence '**harking** *vbl. sb.* and *ppl. a.*; also '**harker** *Sc.*, a listener.

1530 PALSGR. 229/1 Harkyng, *escout, audience.* **1583** STANYHURST *Æneis* II. (Arb.) 47 Thee les he furth pratled, thee more wee longed in harcking. *a* **1700** B. E. *Dict. Cant Crew, Harking* [**1785** GROSE, *Hark-ye-ing*], whispering on one side to borrow Money. **1825** JAMIESON s.v., Harkers never hear a gude word of themselves. **1885** LADY GREVILLE *Creatures of Clay* I. xvii, The sense that I was bound to another woman would prevent any vain harkings back.

hark, *sb.* [f. HARK *v.*] **a.** An act of harking. **b.** A whisper, a privy communication. *Sc.* **c.** A shout starting or urging on the hounds in the chase; also ***hark away***. **d.** ***hark back***: a retracing of steps, a backward move.

1737 M. GREEN *Spleen* 83 Exulting at the hark-away. **1786** *Lounger* No. 87. 300, I have not forgotten.. the encouraging Hark forward to a cautious hound. **1743** GARRICK *Lethe* I. Wks. 1798 I. 20 All hie to the midnight hark-away. **1798** *Sporting Mag.* XII. 5 The chace an oblique 'hark back' of two miles. **1801** BLOOMFIELD *Rural T.* (1802) 114 Ye peaceful Streams that wind along Repeat the Hark-away. **1810** SCOTT *Lady of L.* I. iii, With hark and whoop and wild halloo No rest Benvoirlich's echoes knew. **1820** HOGG *Wint. Even. T.* II. 207 (Jam.) Take heart till I tell you the hark of my mind. **1859** MASSON *Brit. Novelists* ii. 152 The attempt .. is interesting as a hark-back to mediævalism.

harka ('hɑːkə). [a. Moroccan Arab. *ḥarka* military expedition, classical Arab. *ḥaraka* movement.] A body of Moroccan irregular troops.

1903 *Daily Chron.* 18 Sept. 4/6 The regions in the Sahara affected by the recent incursions of the Moorish harkas. **1909** *Ibid.* 26 July 1/5 The harka.. consisted of about 15,000 Kabyles. **1925** *Blackw. Mag.* Nov. 624/1 [He] led out a harka to fight in the national cause.

harkaboise, etc., obs. forms of HARQUEBUS.

harkee = *hark ye*: see HARK *v.* 2 c.

harken, *v.*, etc.: see HEARKEN, etc.

harl, harle, *sb.*[1] Also 9 *dial.* hurle: see also HERL. [app. = MLG. *herle, harle, harrel, harl*, LG. *harl*, EFris. *harrel* fibre of flax or hemp.]

1. A filament or fibre (of flax or hemp).

[**13..** see HERL 1.] **1649** BLITHE *Eng. Improv. Impr.* (1653) 262 The watering of it [flax] opens, and breakes the harle the best. **1677** YARRANTON *Eng. Improv.* 54 Beating and often dressing will cause the Harle to open. **1743** MAXWELL *Sel. Trans. Soc. Impr. Agric. Scot.* 331 (Jam.) Broken pieces of straw, hanging in a great measure loose upon the harle or flax. **1882** JAGO *Cornw. Gloss., Hurle*, a filament.

2. A barb or fibre of a feather: cf. HERL.

[*a* **1450**, etc. see HERL 2.] **1877** BLACKMORE *Cripps* ii, The ribs and harl of feathers. **1884** *St. James' Gaz.* 21 June 6/2 The body is made entirely of peacock's harl. **1884** BLACKMORE *Tommy Upm.* I. 254, I began to chew the harl [of a quill pen].

harl, *sb.*[2] *dial.* [f. HARL *v.*[2]]

1. A tangle; a knot; a confusion; *fig.* mental confusion.

a **1697** AUBREY *Nat. Hist. Wilts* 51. **1825** BRITTON *Beauties Wilts* (E.D.S.), *Harl*, something knotted, or entangled. **1889** *N.W. Linc. Gloss.* s.v., Jimmy H... is e' such 'n a harl as niver was. **1888** *Berksh. Gloss.* s.v., If 'e dwoant mind thee 'ooll get that string in a harl.

2. A leash of hounds. *local.*

1827 *Sporting Mag.* XXI. 26 In the [county] I live in, they call a couple and a half, or three hounds, a 'harl' of hounds. **1847–78** HALLIWELL, *Harle*..(2). Three hounds. *Oxon.* This corresponds to a leash of greyhounds.

harl, *sb.*[3] *Sc.* [f. HARL *v.*[1]]

1. The act of harling or dragging.

1808–18 in JAMIESON.

2. That which is harled or scraped together.

1808–25 JAMIESON s.v., 'He got a harle of silver.'

3. A small quantity, a scraping (of anything). Also *fig.*

1821 *Blackw. Mag.* Jan. 400 (Jam.) Ony haurl o' health I had was aye about meal-times. **1893** STEVENSON *Catriona* 101 And see if I cannae get a little harle of justice out of the military man.

4. An implement for 'harling' or raking mud or soft manure; a wide hoe-like scraper for scraping the soft mud off roads.

1825 in JAMIESON.

5. A composition of lime and gravel or sand; roughcast.

1869 R. L. STEVENSON *Let.* 18 June in *Scribner's Mag.* (1899) XXV. 42/1 The houses, white with harl. **1898** J. J. BURGESS *Tang* ii. 23 The gable was white, for the 'harl' had been picked off in the spring. **1940** 'M. INNES' *Secret Vanguard* ix. 92 The walls of the sort of rough-cast which in Scotland is called harl.

harl, *v.*[1] *Sc.* and *north.* Also 3–9 harle, 6 harrell, 6 *Sc.* haurl. [Origin unknown.

Although there are instances of confusion (perh. only scribal) of *harl* and *hurl*, the two verbs appear to be distinct; in mod. Sc. they are distinct in use.]

1. *trans.* To drag: usually with the notion of friction or scraping of the ground.

c **1290** *S. Eng. Leg.* I. 391/4 Alle þat comen bifore him: luþere Men to-drowe And harleden heom out of þe londe. *Ibid.* 226/245 þe wynd hem harlede vp & doun: in peryls meni on. **1297** R. GLOUC. (1724) 487 King Richard this noble kniȝt Acres nom so, & harlede so the Sarazins, in eche side aboute. *a* **1300** *Cursor M.* 29533 (Cott. Galba) Cursing es þe fendes lyne þat harles a man to hell pine. *c* **1375** *Sc. Leg. Saints, Barnabas* 442 In ane rape for-owte chesone þai harlyt hyme one to presone. *c* **1400** *Destr. Troy* 2968 A ship ..Halyt into havyn, harlit with ropes. **1500–20** DUNBAR *Poems* lxxii. 52 Thai harlit him furth with raip and corde. **1535** COVERDALE *1 Esdras* iv. 48 Y^t they shulde harle cedre trees from Libanus vnto Ierusalem. **1573** J. DAVIDSON *Commend. Uprichtnes* xxx, Harling thame beforr Princes and Kings. *a* **1813** A. WILSON *Rab & Ringan* Poet. Wks. 147 Frae house to house they harled him to dinner. **1816** SCOTT *Old Mort.* viii, They should never harle the precious young lad awa' to captivity.

†**b.** To drag in a vehicle. *Sc. Obs.* (Cf. HURL.)

1557–75 *Diurn. Occurr.* (Bannatyne) 69 Harling of thame throw the toun in ane cart. *a* **1575** *Ibid.* 341 The Magistrates causit harrell him in ane cairt throw the toun.

c. To scrape roads with a 'harl'. *South Scotl.*

2. *intr.* (for *refl.*) To drag or trail oneself, to go with dragging feet.

1500–20 DUNBAR *Poems* xxxix. 29 And lairdis in silk harlis to the eill. **1710** in *Collect. Dying Testimonies* (1806) 166, I had heard the curates and harled after the bulk of the.. ministers. **1888** BLACK *In Far Lochaber* vii, To go away harling here and harling there out o'er the country.

b. *intr.* To come as if dragged off.

1785 BURNS *Halloween* xxiii, 'Till skin in blypes came haurlin.

3. *trans.* To rough-cast with lime mingled with small gravel.

c **1730** [see HARLING below]. **1805** FORSYTH *Beauties Scotl.* IV. 455 The habitations.. are generally built of stone and clay, and pointed or harled with lime. **1885** *Blackw. Mag.* Apr. 441/1 It was whitewashed or 'harled' as they say in the North.

4. *intr.* To troll for fish: see below.

Hence **harled** *ppl. a.*, **harling** *vbl. sb.*

c **1730** BURT *Lett. N. Scotl.* (1754) I. 65 On the outside they.. face the work all over with mortar thrown against it with a trowel, which they call harling. **1867** F. FRANCIS *Angling* x. (1880) 385 The fishing.. is mostly from a boat, and the style is called 'harling'. **1884** Q. VICTORIA *More Leaves* 348 The inn is merely a small, one-storied, 'harled' house. **1891** *Daily News* 9 Feb. 6/3 You are rowed about the vast expanse of water in a stout boat, with a large phantom minnow, blue or brown, let out, by fifty yards of line, behind the boat.. This is the process of 'harling'.

harl, *v.*[2] *dial.* [Etymol. uncertain.

Prob., from the sense, a different word from prec.]

1. *trans.* To entangle, twist, or knot together; to ravel or confuse.

13.. *Gaw. & Gr. Knt.* 744 þe hasel & þe haȝ-þorne were harled al samen. *a* **1722** LISLE *Husb.* (1752) 171 [Barley] harled or fallen down. **1876** *Whitby Gloss., Harl'd*, or *hurl'd*, warped or crooked. **1881** *Isle of Wight Gloss., Harl*, to entangle; to get thread into knots.

b. *intr.* (for *refl.*) To become entangled, twisted, or confused.

1609 C. BUTLER *Fem. Mon.* C v b, Twisting them [a bundle of reeds or straws] fast together in your hand, let the band harle or double in the very top of the Head. *a* **1722** LISLE *Husb.* (1752) 212 If corn harles or lodges, a scythe cannot carry a cradle.

2. *trans.* (See quots.)

1787 GROSE *Provinc. Gloss., Harle*, to harle a rabbit; to cut and insinuate one hind leg of a rabbit into the other, for the purpose of carrying it on a stick. **1877** *N.W. Linc. Gloss.* **1878** JEFFERIES *Gamekeeper at H.* 35 An adept at everything, from 'harling' a rabbit upwards.

harlakeene, -ken(e, -kin, obs. ff. HARLEQUIN.

harlas, var. of HAIR-LACE *Obs.*, fillet.

harlat, -ry, obs. forms of HARLOT, -RY.

harleian (hɑː'liːən, 'hɑːlɪən), *a.* [ad. mod.L. *Harleiānus*, f. surname Harley.] Of or belonging to Robert Harley Earl of Oxford (1661–1724), and his son Edward Harley; esp. in reference to the library of books and MSS. collected by them, of which the MSS. were purchased in 1753 by the British nation and deposited in the British Museum.

1744–6 (*title*) The Harleian Miscellany: a Collection of.. Pamphlets and Tracts.. selected from the Library of Edward Harley, second Earl of Oxford. **1754** (*title*) Act of 26 Geo. II, for the purchase of the Museum or Collection of Sir Hans Sloane, and of the Harleian Collection of MSS. **1808** A Catalogue of the Harleian MSS. in the British Museum. **1895** ZAEHNSDORF *Sh. Hist. Bookbinding* 12 The Harleian style took its name from Harley, Earl of Oxford. It was red morocco with a broad tooled border and centre panels.

Harlem ('hɑːləm). The name of a predominantly Black area in Manhattan, New York, used *subst.*, *attrib.* or in *Comb.* to designate a strongly swinging jazz style. Also as quasi-*adj.*

1934 C. LAMBERT *Music Ho!* III. vii. 201 By jazz, of course, I mean the whole movement roughly designated as such, and not merely that section of it known as Afro-American, or more familiarly as 'Harlem'. *Ibid.* viii. 224 American jazz is either too Hollywood or too Harlem—it rarely suggests the dusty panorama of American life. **1946** R. BLESH *Shining Trumpets* xiii. 315 Harlem piano was, more than any other style, akin to the player piano, no doubt because many Harlem pianists made early player rolls. **1947** R. DE TOLEDANO *Frontiers of Jazz* p. ix, Harlem Jazz is.. much more commercial, there's less going on, and therefore it's easier to understand. **1958** C. FOX in P. Gammond *Decca Bk. Jazz* vii. 87 A percussive, striding style of playing.. still called.. 'Harlem Piano'. **1959** M. T. WILLIAMS *Art of Jazz* (1960) iii. 17 The Harlem style of James P. Johnson and Fats Waller.

Harlemese (hɑːlə'miːz). [f. prec. + -ESE.]

A regional type of speech used by the inhabitants of Harlem. Also *attrib.* or as *adj.*

1928 *Opportunity* VI. xi. 346/2 Dr. Fisher writes with equal authority and zest of.. his Harlemese version of a sermon on the battle of Jericho, the technique of piano moving, [etc.] **1932** *Ibid.* X. x. 320/2 The escapades of these two roustabouts and the 'Harlemese' which they use so glibly. **1942** *Amer. Mercury* July 84 She offers a sketch of Harlem life couched in Harlemese. **1963** A. BONTEMPS *Amer. Negro Poetry* p. xvi, Hughes's art can be likened to that of Jelly Roll Morton and the other creators of jazz. His sources are street music. His language is Harlemese. **1972** *Listener* 27 Jan. 125/3 [They] assume we know Brooklynese ..and Harlemese, and Bronxese. **1973** *Black World* Mar. 81 His [*sc.* Langston Hughes'] language has been appropriately called Harlemese: vibrant, rhythmic, direct, and racy.

Harlemite ('hɑːləmaɪt). [f. HARLEM + -ITE[1].]

A person born in or residing in the Harlem area in the city of New York.

1890 *Harlem Local Reporter* 1 Mar. 2/5 The average Harlemite is in a continuous swim of development and prosperity. **1896** *N.Y. Dramatic News* 4 July 6/3 With music nightly the place will be of great benefit to Harlemites. **1897** *Outing* (U.S.) XXX. 488/1 As a contrast to the scope and aim of the Harlemites,.. the Riverside Wheelmen, of New York, may be quoted. **1926** A. NILES in W. C. Handy *Blues* 22 His satire on the prissy and citified Harlemite. **1950** A. LOMAX *Mr. Jelly Roll* II. 78 The passionate enthusiasm of a Harlemite for baseball. **1958** C. FOX in P. Gammond *Decca Bk. Jazz* vii. 86 The 'twenties found many Harlemites.. throwing parlour-socials (or rent parties). **1971** *Black Scholar* June 18/1 The Harlemites appearing in the simple stories are.. 'like the knights and courtiers in *Le Morte d' Arthur*'.

harlequin ('hɑːlɪkwɪn, -kɪn), *sb.* Forms: 6 harlicken, 7 harlaken(e, -keen(e, -kin, arlequin, 7– harlequin. [a. Fr. *harlequin* (1585 in Hatz.-Darm.), *arlequin*, ad. It. *arlecchino*.

The Italian word is possibly the same as OFr. *Hellequin, Herlequin, Herlekin, Hierlekin, Hielekin, Helquin, Hennequin*, a devil celebrated in mediæval legend, esp. in *la maisnie Helequin, Harlequini familia* (Miège), a company or troop of demon horsemen riding by night. Of this the ultimate origin is possibly Teutonic. See Diez, Mahn *Etymol. Untersuch.*, Godefroy, Skeat.]

I. 1. a. A character in Italian comedy, subsequently in French light comedy; in English pantomime a mute character supposed to be invisible to the clown and pantaloon; he has many attributes of the clown (his rival in the affections of Columbine) with the addition of mischievous intrigue; he usually wears particoloured bespangled tights and a visor, and carries a light 'bat' of lath as a magic wand.

(In reference to quot. 1590, it may be noticed that the *arlecchino* is said, in Italian Dictionaries, to have originally represented the simple and facetious Bergamese man-servant. Cf. the stage Irishman.)

1590 NASHE *Almond for Parrat* Ded., Taking Bergamo in my waye homeward.. It was my happe.. to light in felowship with that famous Francattip' Harlicken, who.. asked me many particulars of the order and maner of our playes. **1606** DAY *Ile of Guls* II. iii, Like a Harlakene in an Italian comedy. **1607** DAY, etc. *Trav. Eng. Bro.* (1881) 56 Here's an Italian Harlaken come to offer a play to your Lordship. **1612** HEYWOOD *Apol. Actors* II. 43 To omit all the Doctors, Zawnyes, Pantaloones, Harlakeenes, in which the French, but especially the Italians, have beene excellent. **1676** DRYDEN *Epil. Etheredge's Man of Mode*, Those nauseous Harlequins in Farce may pass. **1704** ADDISON *Italy* (1766) 68 Harlequin's part is made up of blunders and absurdities. **1727** FIELDING *Love in Sev. Masques* II. i, A man of sense acts a lover just as a Dutchman would a harlequin. **1756** FOOTE *Eng. fr. Paris* I. Wks. 1799 I. 107 A bundle of contradictions, a piece of patch-work, a mere harlequin's coat. **1757** SMEATON in *Phil. Trans.* L. 204 As if an harlequin had leaped thro' the window. **1759** JOHNSON *Gen. Concl. Brumoy's Grk. Theat.* (R.), They represented.. a complete tragedy or comedy in the same manner as dumb harlequin is exhibited on our theatres. **1778** J. Q. ADAMS *Diary* 28 Apr. Wks. 1851 III. 146 In the evening we went to the Italian comedy, where I saw a harlequin for the first time. **1817** BYRON *Beppo* iii, Harlequins and clowns, with feats gymnastical. **1858** HAWTHORNE *Fr. & It. Jrnls.* I. 81 The papal guard in their.. party-colored dress.. looking not a little like harlequins.

b. *transf.* A buffoon in general; a fantastic fellow.

1878 CARLYLE in Ld. R. Gower *My Remin.* xxvii. (1883) II. 175 [He called Beaconsfield] 'that melancholy harlequin'.

2. A small breed of spotted dogs. So G. *harlekin* (Grimm).

1774 GOLDSM. *Nat. Hist.* III. viii. 286 The mongrel kind ..the Dutch mastiff, the harlequin,.. and the Dane.

3. More fully ***harlequin duck***. A northern species of duck, *Histrionicus minutus*, with fantastically variegated plumage.

1772 FORSTER in *Phil. Trans.* LXII. 419 *Anas. A. Histrionica*.. Harlequin Duck. **1863** KINGSLEY *Water Bab.* vii. 269 Swans and brantgeese, harlequins and eiders. **1876** SMILES *Sc. Natur.* xiii, The Harlequin.. and the Eider duck visit the loch occasionally in winter. **1884** *Harper's Mag.* Apr. 706/2 Harlequin-ducks of the gayest plumage.

4. The Oriental or noble opal. Also *attrib.*

1873 C. ROBINSON *N.S. Wales* 62 Opals.. Amongst the polished stones are some of the harlequin class.

II. 5. *attrib.* or as *adj.* Having the characteristics of a harlequin or of his dress; burlesque, ludicrous; particoloured.

harlequin china, service, set, a name given to a set of cups, etc., of different colours and patterns.

1779 WILKES *Corr.* (1805) V. 223 A formal declaration of war by harlequin heralds. **1806–7** J. BERESFORD *Miseries Hum. Life* (1826) VI. i, A china Shakspeare and Milton in Harlequin jackets. **1859** HELPS *Friends in C.* Ser. II. I. Addr. to Rdr. 10 At this Harlequin period of the world what is written one week may seem obsolete the next. **1871** MRS. WHITNEY *Real Folks* xiii. (Cent.), She had six lovely little harlequin cups on a side-shelf in her china-closet.. rose, and brown, and gray, and vermilion, and green, and blue.

6. *Comb.*, as *harlequin-leap, -preacher; harlequin-looking* adj. Also **harlequin bat**, an

Indian species, *Scotophilus ornatus*, of pale tawny-brown, variegated with white spots; **harlequin beetle**, a South American longicorn beetle, *Acrocinus longimanus*, with particoloured elytra; **harlequin brant**, the American white-fronted goose, *Anser albifrons gambeii*, also called *pied* or *speckled brant*; **harlequin bug** *Austral.*, either of two bugs with brightly-coloured markings, *Dindymus versicolor* or *Tectocoris diophthalmus*; **harlequin cabbage-bug**, an American hemipterous insect, *Murgantia histrionica*, having brilliant markings; †**harlequin deer**, ? a particoloured fallow deer; **harlequin duck**: see 3; **harlequin (eye)glasses, spectacles**, spectacles with the frame tilted upwards at the corners (named from their resemblance to a harlequin's mask); **harlequin fish**, (*a*) *Rasbora heteromorpha*, a small cypriniform fish found in Thailand, Malaya, and Sumatra; (*b*) *Othos dentex*, the scarlet rock cod, a perciform fish found along the coasts of south and west Australia; **harlequin-flower**, a name of the South African genus *Sparaxis*, N.O. *Iridaceæ*, with great variety of colouring; **harlequin fly**, a fly of the genus *Chironomus*; **harlequin garrot**, the golden-eye duck or pied wigeon, a species of *Clangula*; **harlequin (Great) Dane**, a Great Dane having a black and white coat; **harlequin moth**, the magpie moth, *Abraxas grossulariata*; **harlequin opal** = HARLEQUIN *sb.* 4; **harlequin pigeon**, an Australian Bronze-wing pigeon; **harlequin ring** (see quot.); **harlequin rose**, a variety of rose with striped petals; **harlequin smiler**, *Merogymnus eximius*, a small Australian perciform fish; **harlequin snake**, the coral-snake and other species of *Elaps*, so called from their variegated colouring of orange and black.

1865 WOOD *Homes without H.* viii. (1868) 176 The magnificent insect which is known to entomologists as the *Harlequin Beetle..belongs to the wood-burrowers. **1882** *Stanford's Compend. Geogr., Central Amer.* 128 The most deadly enemy of the gum-elastic tree is..the well-known 'harlequin beetle'. **1945** K. C. MCKEOWN *Austral. Insects* xv. 81 The commonest and best known species [of Pyrrhocoridæ] is the striking red and black insect popularly known as the *Harlequin Bug (*Dindymus versicolor* Sch.), found throughout Australia, and attacking apples and other fruits. **1970** T. E. WOODWARD et al. in *Insects of Australia* (C.S.I.R.O.) xxvi. 450/1 *Tectocoris diophthalmus* (Thunb.), the 'harlequin bug' of Queensland, attacks the bolls of cotton, and is common on other malvaceous plants. **1872** C. V. RILEY in *4th Ann. Rep. Missouri Entomol.* 35 *Harlequin cabbage bug. **1778** *Eng. Gazetteer* s.v. *Ickworth*, A park well stocked with the fine *harlequin-deer. **1945** 'L. LEWIS' *Birthday Murder* (1951) i. 7 Her *harlequin eyeglasses became crooked on her pointed face. **1961** WODEHOUSE *Service with Smile* ix. 130 She was regarding him austerely through her harlequin glasses. **1956** M. WEST *Gallows on Sand* x. 115 A school of *harlequin fish flirted away from my descent, their tube-like bodies flashing blue and gold, their ugly faces smiling like a circus clown's. **1959** *Times* 3 Mar. 7/1 The 'guinea pigs' in these experiments are inch-long harlequin fish..from south-east Asia. **1900** MIALL & HAMMOND (*title*) The structure and life history of the *harlequin fly (*Chironomus*). **1956** *Nature* 17 Mar. 534/1 The family Chironomidae has scarcely been studied at all in New Zealand... Known colloquially as the 'Harlequin fly', they are, it seems, almost ubiquitous. **1863** BARING-GOULD *Iceland* 162 A magnificent *harlequin garrot floated unmoved within a stones throw. **1800** *Harlequin Dane [see DANE 2]. **1909** *Daily Chron.* 28 July 7/1 A black and white or harlequin Great Dane. **1948** 'SIGMA' in B. Vesey-Fitzgerald *Bk. Dog* II. 420 When smart men drove a well-appointed turnout, a Dalmatian or harlequin Great Dane was necessary to complete the picture. **1813** *Examiner* 1 Feb. 69/2 A *harlequin-leap through a window. **1835** WILLIS *Pencillings* I. xv. 111 The *harlequin-looking Swiss guard. **1887** *Col. & Indian Exhib., Rep. Col. Sect.* 70 Some specimens are of a rare kind, known as '*Harlequin' opals. **1847** LEICHHARDT *Jrnl.* vii. 227 We saw two flocks of the *harlequin pigeon (*Peristera histrionica*). **1760** JORTIN *Erasm.* II. 195 Stories of a *Harlequin-Preacher, who used to surprise his audience with his monkey-tricks. **1877** W. JONES *Finger-ring* 414 *Harlequin-rings..were so called because they were set round with variously-coloured stones. **1876** T. HARDY *Ethelberta* (1890) 194 They were striped, red and white, and appeared to be leaves of the *Harlequin rose. **1955** A. ROSS *Australia 55* ix. 118 Sharks..whose presence causes..coral trout and *Harlequin Smilers suddenly to evaporate. **1964** T. C. MARSHALL *Fishes of Great Barrier Reef* 326 Harlequin Smiler *Merogymnus eximius*. **1885** C. F. HOLDER *Marvels Anim. Life* 131 The coloring of the *harlequin [snake]..is exceedingly rich. **1940** *Optometric Weekly* 19 Dec. 1262 The *Harlequin spectacle frame is protected by patents. **1962** J. BRAINE *Life at Top* xii. 154 Her harlequin spectacles didn't make her expression any less severe.

Hence **harlequina, -ess**, a female harlequin. **harlequi'nesque, harle'quinic** *adjs.*, having the style of a harlequin. **harle'quinically** *adv.*, after the manner of a harlequinade. **'harlequinism**, the performance of a harlequin; action characteristic of a harlequin. **'harlequinize** *v.*, to convert into a harlequin; to dress or do up in fantastical colouring.

1867 *Harlequina [see HARLEQUINADE a.] **1882** STEVENSON *New Arab. Nts.* II. xii. 222 His blouse was stained with oil colours in a *harlequinesque disorder. **1785** in *Cornh. Mag.* (1883) June 718 Humorous and characteristic masks; among the best of which we reckon..a whimsical *harlequiness. **1804** *Miniature* No. 4. 14 (*title*) Ode to the Rainbow, in the genuine Fantastical, Unmeaning, *Harlequinic Style of Sentimental Sonneteers. **1824** W. TAYLOR in *Monthly Rev.* CIII. 47 The Tale..is..so *harlequinically metamorphosing. **1808** *Edin. Rev.* XII. 203 The philosophical *harlequinism of that valiant knight. *a* **1852** WEBSTER *Wks.* (1877) I. 345 In popular governments, men must not..be disgusted by occasional exhibitions of political harlequinism. **1876** MISS BROUGHTON *Joan* II. viii. III. 225 The small dining-room..is travestied indeed and *harlequinized like the rest of the house.

harlequin, *v.* [f. prec. sb.] **a.** *trans.* To conjure *away*, like harlequin in a pantomime. *rare.* **b.** *intr.* To play the harlequin. *rare.* **c.** *trans.* To colour, decorate with contrasting colours. So **'harlequined** *ppl. a.*

1737 M. GREEN *Spleen* (1807) 148 And Kitten, if the humour hit Has harlequin'd away the fit. **1828** WEBSTER, *Harlequin*, to play the droll; to make sport by playing ludicrous tricks.

1941 'R. WEST' *Black Lamb* II. 304 A slope of long grass harlequined with flowers. **1959** *Housewife* June 5 The two colours daringly harlequinned. **1963** *Harper's Bazaar* July 44 Shetland jumper—white, harlequinned in different greys. **1965** D. FRANCIS *For Kicks* iv. 49 She wore a black and white harlequined ski-ing jacket.

harlequinade (hɑːlɪk(w)ɪ'neɪd), *sb.* [a. F. *arlequinade* (1769 in Hatz.-Darm.), f. *h)arlequin*: see -ADE.] A kind of pantomime; that part of a pantomime in which the harlequin and clown play the principal parts.

1780 T. DAVIES *Mem. Garrick* I. x. 129 He formed a kind of harlequinade, very different from that which is seen at the Opéra Comique in Paris, where harlequin and all the characters speak. **1823** *Sismondi's Lit. Eur.* (1846) I. xv. 439 A specimen of these old harlequinades. **1827** W. S. in Hone *Every-day Bk.* II. 502 In 1717, the first harlequinade..was performed at the theatre in Lincoln's Inn Fields. **1867** *Morn. Star* 27 Dec., The harlequinade subsequent to the transformation scene was cleverly supported by Mr. —— (harlequin), Mdlle. —— (columbine), Mr. —— (pantaloon), Miss —— (harlequina), and Mr. —— (clown).

b. *transf.* Buffoonery; fantastic procedure.

1828 MACAULAY *Ess., Hallam* (1887) 93 No unity of plan, no decent propriety of character and costume, could be found in the wild and monstrous harlequinade [reign of Chas. II]. *a* **1849** POE *Longfellow, Willis, etc.* Wks. 1864 III. 334 Every trick of thought and every harlequinade of phrase.

c. A piece of fantastic particoloured work.

1874 MICKLETHWAITE *Mod. Par. Churches* 72 An elaborate harlequinade of stripes and diamonds on a raw blue or red ground, called illumination.

Hence **harlequi'nadish** *a.*, *nonce-wd.*, of the nature of a harlequinade.

1859 SALA *Tw. round Clock* (1861) 417 All is jarring, discordant, tawdry and harlequinadish.

harlequi'nade, *v.* [f. prec. sb.: cf. *to masquerade*.] *intr.* To play the harlequin; to act fantastically. Hence **harlequi'nading** *vbl. sb.* and *ppl. a.*

1788 'A. PASQUIN' *Childr. Thespis, Tom Blanchard*, Broad Humour the province of wit is Invading, And his efforts are weaken'd by harlequinading. **1823** *New Monthly Mag.* VII. 515 The three pirates who..harlequinade it in the air on the banks. **1880** VERN. LEE *Stud. Italy* iii. 175 The stream of masks harlequinading along. **1894** *Cornh. Mag.* Feb. 160 As fantastic as the harlequinading tits.

†**'harlequinery.** [a. F. *arlequinerie*, f. *h)arlequin*: see -ERY.] Pantomime, harlequinade.

1741 RICHARDSON *Pamela* (1811) IV. 89 The French taste is comedy and harlequinery; the Italian, music and opera. **1794** MRS. PIOZZI *Synon.* I. 167 Feats of harlequinery.

Harley ('hɑːlɪ). *Harley Street*: name of a street in London associated with eminent physicians and surgeons; hence used allusively for the specialists of the medical profession.

1830 *New Monthly Mag.* II. 220 Harley-street was..in an uproar at these monstrous stipulations. **1905** G. B. SHAW *Shaw on Shakes.* (1962) 1 A regular company..holding itself as exclusively above the casual barnstormer as a Harley Street consultant holds himself above a man with a sarsaparilla stall. **1958** B. NICHOLS *Sweet & Twenties* xi. 138 The sort of people who always contribute to symposiums—a bishop, a general..an 'eminent Harley Street surgeon'. **1961** L. MUMFORD *City in History* iv. 105 'Harley Street', 'Madison Avenue', 'State Street', are shorthand expressions not just for occupations, but for a whole way of life that they embody. **1972** M. GILBERT *Body of Girl* xvii. 156 Two Harley Street surgeons discussing a difficult case.

harlicken, obs. form of HARLEQUIN.

†**'harlock.** *Obs.* Some flower not identified.

It cannot be the same as *hardock*; and *charlock*, proposed by some, does not flower in May, and is not likely to have been used for decoration.

a **1631** DRAYTON *Dowsabel*, This Maiden..Went forth when May was in the prime, To get sweet setywall, The honey-suckle, the harlock, The lily, and the lady-smock, To deck her summer hall.

harlot ('hɑːlət), *sb.* Forms: 3– harlot; 3–4 herlot, (3 *pl.* har-, herloz), 4 harelot, harlatte, 4–6 harlote, -lotte, 5–6 -lat, 6 harllott. [As a word of masculine gender found early in 13th c., as feminine in 15th c.; a. OF. *herlot, harlot, arlot* masc., lad, young fellow, base fellow, knave, vagabond = Pr. *arlot* vagabond, beggar, It. *arlotto* 'a lack-latin or hedge-priest' (Florio), 'glutton, greedy gut, great eater' (Baretti); cf. med.L. *arlotus, erlotus* glutton (Mahn); OSp. *arlote, alrote* lazy, sluggardly, loafing; OPg. *alrotar* to go about begging, Pg. to mock. Of this widely-diffused Romanic word, the ulterior history and origin are uncertain: see suggestions in Diez, Mahn *Etymolog. Untersuch.* No. 155, and Skeat.

The random 'conjecture' of Lambarde, 1570–6, retailed by many later writers, that *harlot* in sense 5 c was derived from the name of Arlette or Herleva, mother of William the Conqueror, could have been offered only after the earlier senses and uses of the word were forgotten.]

†**1.** A vagabond, beggar, rogue, rascal, villain, low fellow, knave. In later use (16–17th c.), sometimes a man of loose life, a fornicator; also, often, a mere term of opprobrium or insult. *Obs.*

a **1225** *Ancr. R.* 356 And beggen ase on harlot, ȝif hit neod is, his liueneð. *c* **1330** R. BRUNNE *Chron.* (1810) 317 A foule herlote him slowe [*un ribaud li tuayt*]. **1377** LANGL. *P. Pl.* B. XVII. 108 He was vnhardy, þat harlot and hudde hym *in inferno*. *c* **1386** CHAUCER *Reeve's T.* 348 Ye false harlot, quod the Millere, hast? *c* **1460** *Towneley Myst.* (Surtees) 248 Outt, harro! what harlot is he That says his kyngdom shalbe cryde? **1508** KENNEDIE *Flyting w. Dunbar* 359 Herefore, fals harlot, hursone, hald thy tong. **1549** LATIMER *3rd Serm. bef. Edw. VI* (Arb.) 86 Was not thys a sedyciouse harlot? **1561–77** *Durham Depos.* (Surtees) 107 That I called him openly 'beggerly harlot and cutthrote'. *c* **1620** Z. BOYD *Zion's Flowers* (1855) 103 A man a harlot, and a wife a whoore. **1659** D. PELL *Impr. Sea* 37 What should you do with such Harlots in your Service? which calls for holiness, and better principled men.

†**2.** An itinerant jester, buffoon, or juggler; one who tells or does something to raise a laugh. *Obs.*

a **1340** HAMPOLE *Psalter* xxxix. 6 Hoppynge & daunnceynge of tumblers and herlotis, and oþer spectakils. **1362** LANGL. *P. Pl.* A. VII. 48 Hold not þou with harlotes, here not heore tales. *c* **1380** WYCLIF *Sel. Wks.* III. 352 Mynstrel and joȝelour, tumbler and harlot, wole not take of þe puple bifore þat þei han shewid þer craft. **14..** *Nom.* in Wr.-Wülcker 694 *note*, *Hic scurra*..harlot. **14..** *Medulla*, *MS. Cant.* (Promp. Parv.), *Gerro*, a tryfelour, or a harlott. **1483** *Cath. Angl.* 175/2 An Harlott, *balatro* (A. *histrio*) ..*ioculator, -trix.*

†**3.** Applied to a male servant or attendant; a menial: cf. KNAVE, in similar use. *Obs.*

13.. *E.E. Allit. P.* B. 39 þen þe harlot with haste helded to þe table. *c* **1386** CHAUCER *Sompn. T.* 46 A sturdy harlot wente ay hem bihynde, That was hir hostes man, and bar a sak. *c* **1450** *Merlin* 9 When hir suster com..she brought with her a grete hepe of harlotys. **1536** BELLENDEN *Cron. Scot.* (1821) I. 55 He repudiat his nobil quene..and gart his vicious harlotis deforce hir.

†**4.** = 'Fellow'; playfully 'good fellow'. *Obs.*

c **1386** CHAUCER *Prol.* 647 He [Somonour] was a gentil harlot and a kynde A bettre felawe sholde men noght fynde. *a* **1634** CHAPMAN *Revenge Hon.* Wks. 1873 III. 325 That is an harlot. Prithee be musical and let us taste The sweetness of thy voice.

5. Applied to a woman. **a.** As a general term of execration. (Cf. 1.) *rare.*

c **1485** *Digby Myst.* (1882) I. 326 What, ye harlottes, I haue aspied certeyn That ye be traytours to my lord the kyng. **1823** CARLYLE *Early Lett.* (Norton) II. 236, I bullyrag the sluttish harlots of the place.

†**b.** A female juggler, dancing-girl, ballet-dancer, or actress. (Cf. 2.) *Obs.*

1483 *Cath. Angl.* 175/2 An Harlott..*ioculatrix, pantomima..histrix.*

c. *spec.* An unchaste woman; a prostitute; a strumpet.

(Very frequent in 16th c. Bible versions, where Wyclif had *hoore*, whore; prob. as a less offensive word.)

1432–50 tr. *Higden* (Rolls) I. 249 The harlottes at Rome were callede *nonariæ*. **1513** MORE in Grafton *Chron.* (1568) II. 784 King Edwarde woulde say that he had three concubines..the thirde the holyest harlot in the realme. **1526** TINDALE *Luke* xv. 30 Thy sonne..which hath devoured thy goodes with harlootes [WYCL. hooris; *Rhem.* whoores]. **1535** COVERDALE *Job* xxxi. 9 O then let my wife be another mans harlot. **1570–6** LAMBARDE *Peramb. Kent* (1826) 200 Robert, the Duke of Normandie, had issue by a Concubine (whose name..was Harlothe, and after whom, as I coniecture, such incontinent women have ever since beene called Harlots). **1573–80** BARET *Alv.* H 170 An harlot, a whore, a strumpet, *meretrix.* [The only sense mentioned.] **1667** MILTON *P.L.* IV. 766 Not in the bought smile Of Harlots, loveless, joyless, unindeard. **1718** PRIOR *Pleasure* 905 To each new harlot I new altars dress. **1826** SCOTT *Woodst.* iii, A tyrant and a harlot were fitting patron and patroness for such vanities. **1859** TENNYSON *Vivien* 819 Tho' harlots paint their talk as well as face, With colours of the heart that are not theirs.

fig. **1560** BIBLE (Genev.) *Isa.* i. 21 How is the faithful citie become an harlot! [WYCL. **1382** a strumpet; **1388** an hoore.] **17..** PHILIPS *Wit & Wisdom* (R.), Wit is a harlot beauteous to the eye. **1827** POLLOK *Course T.* v, The Church a harlot then, When first she wedded civil power. **1860** PUSEY *Min. Proph.* 298 The wealth..shall go to another harlot, Nineveh.

†**6.** Applied to unchaste persons of both sexes. *Sc.*

1563 WINȜET *Four Scoir Thre Quest.* liii. Wks. 1888 I. 109 Gif the harlotis, for quhais causs matrimonie is violatit or adnullit, may mary wthiris. *Ibid.* 110 The twa harlotis to be ȝokit vp in a prætendit band of matrimonie.

b. Hence, *play the harlot.* (Chiefly of women.)

1535 COVERDALE *Ezek.* xvi. 28 Thou hast played the whore also with the Assirians..Yee thou hast played the harlot. **1541** *Lond. Chron. Hen. VIII* in *Camd. Misc.* IV. 16 Hanggid and quartarid..for playing the harlottes with queen Kataryn that then was. **1596** DALRYMPLE tr. *Leslie's Hist. Scot.* IX. 226 Nobil men..with quhom she was accuiset to play the harlat. **1611** BIBLE *Hos.* iii. 3 Thou shalt not play the harlot. **1885** BIBLE (R.V.) App., [American Revisers' renderings] Substitute..'play the harlot' for 'go a whoring' and 'commit whoredom'.

†**7.** Applied to the pointed boots worn in the 14th c. *Obs.*

13.. *Eulog. Hist.* (Rolls) III. 231 Habent etiam caligas.. quas cum corrigiis ligant ad suos 'paltokkos' quæ vocantur 'harlottes' [*v.r.* harlotes], et sic unus 'harlot' servit alteri.

8. *attrib.* passing into *adj.*: That is a harlot; of or pertaining to a harlot.

a **1300** *Cursor M.* 27932 Harlot sagh, speche o disur, rimes vnright, gest of Iogolur. **13..** *K. Alis.* 3336 Thow him clepedst an harlot gome: Now thow seist he is the beste knyght. *c* **1380** *Sir Ferumb.* 1234 'Wat! harlot gadelyng.. mote þou be heȝe an-honge!' *c* **1470** HENRY *Wallace* I. 219 Rouch rewlyngis apon thi harlot fete. **1570** BUCHANAN *Ane Admonit.* Wks. (1892) 24 Godles papistes, harlat protestantis. **1590** SHAKS. *Com. Err.* II. ii. 138 And teare the stain'd skin of my Harlot brow. **1667** MILTON *P.L.* IX. 1060 The Harlot-lap Of Philistean Dalilah. **1742** POPE *Dunc.* IV. 45 A Harlot form, soft gliding by. *a* **1774** W. HARTE *Vis. Death* (R.), Colours laid on with a true harlot grace; They only show themselves, and hide the face. **1879** FARRAR *St. Paul* xviii. I. 331 The harlot city which had made the nations drunk with the..wine of her fornications.

9. *Comb.* **harlot-house**, a brothel or stews.

1659 D. PELL *Impr. Sea* Ep. Ded. C viij, The Mercenary Harlot houses that bee in the Italian..and Spanish Cities.

'harlot, *v.* [f. prec. sb.] *intr.* To play the harlot. Hence **harloting** *vbl. sb.* and *ppl. a.*

1641 MILTON *Animadv.* i. Wks. (1847) 58/2 They that spend their youth in loitering, bezzling, and harlotting. **1675** WYCHERLEY *Country Wife* v. iv, O! thou harloting harlotry! hast thou done't then? **1697** C. LESLIE *Snake in Grass* (ed. 2) 35 By their own Argument, all the Quakers are Harlotted from the Church of Christ. **1864** *Daily Tel.* 9 Feb., How about the courtesans harlotting in your streets?

†**'harlotize,** *v. Obs. trans.* To make a harlot of; to characterize as a harlot; to call harlot.

1589 WARNER *Alb. Eng.* VI. xxx. (1612) 150 Is it to harlotize, thinkst thou, a Goddesse, wrong too small?

harlotry ('hɑːlətrɪ), *sb.* (*a.*) [f. HARLOT *sb.* + -RY.]

†**1.** Buffoonery, jesting; ribaldry, scurrility, scurrilous talk; obscene talk or behaviour. *Obs.*

c **1325** *Song Merci* 132 in *E.E.P.* (1862) 122 Now harlotrie for murþe is holde, And vertues turnen in-to vice. *c* **1340** *Cursor M.* 27623 (Fairf.) Of pride be-comis..manikin vnnaite oþer þing, Als sange of harlotery & lesing. **1377** LANGL. *P. Pl.* B. v. 413, I haue leuere here an harlotrie or a somer game of souteres, Or lesynges to laughe at. **1382** WYCLIF *Eph.* v. 4 Either filthe, or foly speche, or harlotrie [**1388** harlatrye; **1526–34** TINDALE gestinge; **1582** *Rhem.* scurrilitie], that perteyneth not to thing. *c* **1440** *Jacob's Well* (E.E.T.S.) 134 Þe v. inche is harlotrie, makyng iapys a-forn folk, in pleying at þe spore, at þe bene, at þe cat. **1483** *Cath. Angl.* 176/1 To do Harlottry, *scurrari.* **1578** *Gude & Godlie Ballatis* Title-p., Diueris vtheris Ballattis changeit out of prophane Sangis in godlie sangis, for auoyding of sin and harlatrie. **1809** SCOTT *Fam. Lett.* 10 Sept., To reprint..the only original Caxton..with all the superstition and harlotrie which the castrator..chose to omit.

†**2.** Filth, trash. *Obs.*

1467 *Ordin. Worcester* in *Eng. Gilds* 374 Item that no man caste donge or harlotry at the slipp, ner vpon the key. *Ibid.* 398 That non persone cast eny donge of eny manere harlotre in the Slippe goynge to Severne.

3. Profligacy or vice in sexual relations, unchastity; the conduct of a harlot; dealing with harlots; the practice or trade of prostitution.

1377 LANGL. *P. Pl.* B. XIII. 353 Lechoures..of her harlotrye and horedome in her elde tellen. *c* **1386** CHAUCER *Merch. T.* 1018 Thanne shal he knowen al hire harlotrye. *c* **1400** *Destr. Troy* 5024 In hordam & harlatry vnhyndly to lye. **1530** PALSGR. 229/1 Harlottrye, *paillardyse.* **1570** LEVINS *Manip.* 104/30 Harlotrie, *meretricium.* **1645** RUTHERFORD *Tryal & Tri. Faith* (1845) 37 This..causeth Joseph see nothing in harlotry, but pure, unmixed guiltiness against God. **1858** FROUDE *Hist. Eng.* IV. xviii. 65 Happy contrast to the court, with its intrigues and harlotries.

4. *concr.* A harlot; a term of opprobrium for a woman. (In 1821 *collective.*)

1584 PEELE *Arraignm. Paris* IV. iii, A harlotry, I warrant her. **1596** SHAKS. *1 Hen. IV*, III. i. 198 A peeuish selfe-will'd Harlotry. **1663** DRYDEN *Wild Gallant* III. ii, You are a company of proud harlotries: I'll teach you to take place of tradesmen's wives. **1754** RICHARDSON *Grandison* (1781) III. iv. 26, I expect you will produce the little harlotry. **1821** BYRON *Sardan.* II. i. 126 He loved his queen—And thrice a thousand harlotry besides. *c* **1836** LANDOR *Imag. Conv.* Wks. II. 91/2, I have no patience with the bold harlotry.

5. *fig.* Meretriciousness, illegitimate attractiveness.

1768 G. MASON *Eng. Gard.* I. (R.), The simple farm eclips'd the garden's pride, Ev'n as the virgin blush of innocence, The harlotry of art. **1794** MATHIAS *Purs. Lit.* (1798) 57 They will then perceive..the harlotry of the ornaments. **1824** *Blackw. Mag.* XVI. 425 To throw off..the harlotry of the imagination.

†**B.** *attrib.* or as *adj.* Base, scurvy, filthy, worthless, trashy. *Obs.*

1579–80 NORTH *Plutarch* (1676) 305 A young Harlotry filth. **1598** GRENEWEY *Tacitus' Descr. Germ.* I. 259 Cattle plentie, but for the most part harletry runts. ?*c* **1600** *Distracted Emp.* II. i. in Bullen *O. Pl.* III. 193 Thys vertue is The scurvyest, harlottryest, undoeing thynge That ever mixte with rysing courtyers thoughts. *a* **1607** J. RAYNOLDS *Proph. Haggai* iv. (1649) 57 No building was to be found.. unles it be three or four harlotrey houses. **1663** DRYDEN *Wild Gallant* III. ii, I squorn your harlotry tricks, that I do.

harm (hɑːm), *sb.* Forms: 1–3 **hearm**, 2–5 **herm**, 3 (**harem**), **hærm**, (**ærme**), (3–5 **arme**), 3–7 **herme**, **harme**, (4 **harim**, **arm**, 5 **harome**), 6 *Sc.* **hairm(e**, 3– **harm**. [Com. Teutonic: OE. *hearm*, corresp. to OFris. *herm*, OS. *harm*, OHG. *harm*, *haram* (mod.G. *harm*), ON. *harmr* grief, sorrow, rarely harm, hurt (Sw. *harm*, Da. *harme*):—OTeut. **harmo-z*: perh. cogn. w. Skr. *śrama* labour, toil.]

1. a. Evil (physical or otherwise) as done to or suffered by some person or thing; hurt, injury, damage, mischief. Often in the set phrase 'to do more harm than good'.

Beowulf (Z.) 1893 No he mid hearme of hliðes nosan, gæs[tas] grette. *a* **1123** *O.E. Chron.* an. 1101 His men mycel to hearme æfre ȝedydon. **1297** R. GLOUC. (1724) 277 To gret harm to al þys lond, the gode kyng he slou. *c* **1340** *Cursor M.* 4898 (Fairf.) Do ham na arme in na way. *c* **1380** *Sir Ferumb.* 2578 Þay mowe noȝt her y-wys hem-selue fram herme saue. *c* **1384** CHAUCER *H. Fame* II. 537 Thou shalt have no harme truely. *c* **1400** MAUNDEV. (1839) iv. 23 Sche doth non harm to no man, but ȝif men don hire harm. **1442** *Searchers' Verdicts* in *Surtees Misc.* (1888) 18 Ye same place has taken mikel herm for defaut of a gutter. *c* **1530** H. RHODES *Bk. Nurture* 28 in *Babees Bk.* 72 Vnto your Elders gentle be, agaynst them say no harme. *a* **1586** *Satir. Poems Reform.* xxxv. 59 Ȝe knaw quhat hairme he hes susteind. **1632** LITHGOW *Trav.* II. 62 What harme was done by us amongst the Infidels, we were not assured. **1657** R. LIGON *Barbadoes* (1673) 62 Caterpillars..do very great harm. **1705** HICKERINGILL *Priest-cr.* I. (1721) 21 Harm watch, Harm catch. **1791** MRS. RADCLIFFE *Rom. Forest* x, I meant no harm. **1809** *Q. Rev.* May 305 The story should be suppressed altogether, as one which will do more harm than good. **1849** MACAULAY *Hist. Eng.* II. 44 Aware that the divulging of the truth might do harm. **1857** DICKENS *Dorrit* II. xxix. 723, I should have done you more harm than good, at first. **1875** JOWETT *Plato* (ed. 2) V. 331 Rains doing harm instead of good. **1914** G. B. SHAW *Misalliance* p. xxix, These rare cases actually do more harm than good.

b. With *a* and *pl.* An evil done or sustained; an injury, a loss.

a **1000** *Cædmon's Gen.* 756 Ealle synt uncre hearmas ȝe-wrecene. *c* **1200** *Vices & Virtues* (1888) 59 Ǣr ðu muȝe þoliȝen alle harmes and scames and bismeres. *c* **1380** WYCLIF *Sel. Wks.* III. 349 Oþer bodili harmes. *c* **1461** *Paston Lett.* No. 428 II. 73 Of ij harmys the leste is to be take. **1583** BABINGTON *Commandm.* viii. (1637) 73 Wise is hee, whom other mens harmes can cause to take heede. **1728** MORGAN *Algiers* II. iv. 263 The inconceivable Harms he did to Christendom. **1863** LONGF. *Wayside Inn, Birds of Killingworth* xix, They..from your harvests keep a hundred harms.

c. ***out of harm's way***: Out of the way of doing or of sustaining injury.

a **1661** FULLER *Worthies* (1840) I. xviii. 61 Some great persons..have been made sheriffs, to keep them out of harm's way. **1697** DAMPIER *Voy.* I. 207 He took care to keep himself out of harms way. **1711** STEELE *Spect.* No. 136 ¶4 People send Children..to School to keep them out of Harm's way. **1890** H. M. STANLEY *Darkest Africa* I. xiv. 333 They had..migrated in time out of harm's way.

†**2.** Grief, sorrow, pain, trouble, distress, affliction. Also with *a* and *pl.* ***to make harms*** (quot. 1375): to make lamentation. *Obs.*

a **1000** *Cædmon's Gen.* 751 Eac is hearm gode, mod-sorȝ ȝemacod. *a* **1300** *Cursor M.* 24089 Þis harm mi hert it held sa hard. *c* **1375** *Sc. Leg. Saints, Johannes* 68 Mony ane Of hir kine..Folowit hyr, makand harmys. *c* **1386** CHAUCER *Sqr.'s T.* 578, I wende verraily That he had felt as muche harm as I Whan þat I herde hym speke and saugh his hewe. **1570** *Satir. Poems Reform.* xxi. 197 Sic hauie harme sall happin to ȝour hart. **1627** F. E. *Hist. Edw. II* (1680) 47 He lays aside his Arms, for harms to feed his humour.

†**3.** Pity, a pity. (Cf. F. *dommage.*) *Obs.*

c **1430** *Syr Gener.* (Roxb.) 4230 It was harme it wanted oght. **1535** STEWART *Cron. Scot.* III. 44 Sobbit full soir that harme wes for to heir.

4. *attrib.* and *Comb.*, as ***harm-doer***, ***-doing***, ***-taking***; ***harm-averting***, ***-eschewing*** adjs.

c **1220** *Bestiary* 389 Husebondes hire haten for hire harm dedes. **1386** in Rymer *Fœdera* (1709) VII. 526/2 Þair sall not be at þa Rydings no Harme doynges. **1477** EARL RIVERS (Caxton) *Dictes* 81 Them..yᵗ ben harmedoers and loueth falshode and desepcion. **1571** GOLDING *Calvin on Ps.* xxxiv. 11 To live quietly..without any harmetaking. **1641** MILTON *Ch. Govt.* I. v, I judge they may pass without harm-doing to our Cause. **1889** R. B. ANDERSON tr. *Rydberg's Teut. Mythol.* 102 Harm-averting songs.

harm, *v.* Forms: 1 **hearmian**, 2–3 **haremen**, **hearmen**, **hærmen**, 2–5 **herme**, 3–4 **hermien**, 3–7 **harme**, 4 **harmi**, **-y**, 6 **arme**, 4– **harm**. [OE. *hearmian*, f. *hearm* HARM *sb.*: cf. OHG. *harmjan*, *harmen*, *hermen* to calumniate, injure.]

To do harm (to); to injure (physically or otherwise); to hurt, damage. Orig. *intr.* To be hurtful, with dative (like L. *nocēre*), which was sometimes in ME. expressed by *to*, but generally became a simple object, making the verb *trans.*

c **1000** ÆLFRIC *Hom.* I. 140 Gif ðu hine forȝitst, hit hearmað þe sylfum and na Gode. *c* **1000** in *Leg. Rood* 105 Þeah þe hit hearmiȝe sumum. *c* **1175** *Lamb. Hom.* 107 To hermen alle monnen. *a* **1225** *Ancr. R.* 64 Þe wise mon askeð ..hweðer ei þing hermeð more wummon þene hire eien. **1340** *Ayenb.* 23 To oþren ha wyle harmy..to miszigge to ham þet he wyle harmi. **1393** LANGL. *P. Pl.* C. III. 248 And holy churche þorw hem worth harmed for euere. **1548** HALL *Chron., Hen. VI*, 175 Protractyng of tyme onely hurted and harmed the Kyng. **1653** WALTON *Angler* vii. 153 Harme him as little as you may possibly, that he may live the longer. **1659** D. PELL *Impr. Sea* 77 *note*, An High Elme..in the midst of a Garden..harms all round about it. **1784** COWPER *Task* VI. 578 He that hunts Or harms them there, is guilty of a wrong. **1875** JOWETT *Plato* (ed. 2) I. 291 When a man has no sense he is harmed by courage.

b. *absol.* To do harm or injury.

1362 LANGL. *P. Pl.* A. III. 136 And hongeþ him for hate þat harmede neuere. **1546** J. HEYWOOD *Prov.* (1867) 23 She can no more harme than can a she ape. **1633** P. FLETCHER *Ps.* cxxvii. (R.), As arrows..Where they are meant, will surely harm, And if they hit, wound deep and dread.

Hence **harmed**, **'harming** *ppl. adjs.*

c **1440** *Promp. Parv.* 228/1 Harmyd, *dampnificatus.* **1563** HYLL *Art Garden.* (1593) 149 They temper the harming force of the colde of it.

harm, -e, obs. forms of ARM *sb.*[1]

a **1400–50** *Alexander* 3237 He..clepys hym in harmez.

‖**harmala** ('hɑːmələ), **harmel** ('hɑːmɛl). [Late L., = Gr. ἅρμαλα, from Semitic; cf. Arab. *ḥarmil* wild rue, whence the form *harmel*; cf. F. *harmale* (1694 in Hatz.-Darm.).]

Wild rue, *Peganum Harmala*, a plant native to Southern Europe and Asia Minor. Also *attrib.*, as **harmala red**, a red colouring matter obtained from the seeds of the plant. Hence **harmaline** ('hɑːməlaɪn), *Chem.*, a white crystalline alkaloid ($C_{13}H_{14}N_2O$) obtained from the seeds of wild rue. **harmalol** ('hɑːməlɒl), another alkaloid ($C_{12}H_{12}N_2O$), from the same source.

c **1000** *Sax. Leechd.* II. 140 Sealf..armelu..wyl on buteran to sealfe. **1753** CHAMBERS *Cycl. Supp.*, *Harmala, Harmel*, or wild rue. **1847** CRAIG, *Harmaline.* **1865** WATTS *Dict. Chem.* III. 7 The seeds contain about 4 per cent. of alkaloids of which one-third consists of harmine and two-thirds of harmaline. *Harmala red*, the seeds of harmala contain also a red colouring matter. **1889** *Watts' Dict. Chem.*, *Harmalol.*

†**'harman.** *Thieves' Cant. Obs.* [Origin of first syllable uncertain, ? from *hardman*; *-man(s* as in *crackmans*, *darkmans*, etc.]

1. pl. ***harmans***, the stocks.

1567 HARMAN *Caveat* (1869) 84 *The harmans*, the stockes. *Ibid.* 86 So may we happen on the Harmanes.., So we maye chaunce to set in the stockes. **1609** DEKKER *Lanthorne & Candle-lt.* C iij b, To put our stamps in the Harmans.

2. Short for *harman beck*: A constable.

1725 *New Cant. Dict.*, *Harman*, a Constable. *a* **1791** GROSE *Olio* (1796) 231 When I leave Nan in the vile Harman's hands. **1829** LYTTON *Disowned* 8 The worst have an awe of the harman's claw.

Hence †**'harman-beck** [*beck*, BEAK *sb.*[3]], a constable; the parish-constable or beadle.

1567 HARMAN *Caveat* (1869) 84 *The harman beck*, the Counstable. **1609** DEKKER *Lanthorne & Candle-lt.* C iij b, The Ruffin cly the nab of the Harman beck. **1641** BROME *Joviall Crew* II. Wks. 1873 III. 388 Let's..bowse in defiance o' th' Harman-Beck. **1822** SCOTT *Nigel* xxxv, I am not the lad to betray any one to the harman-beck.

harmatian (hɑː'meɪʃən), *a.* [irreg. f. Gr. ἅρματ-chariot + -IAN.] (See quots.)

1774 BURNEY *Hist. Mus.* (1789) I. 386 Plutarch enumerates the changes which he made in the Harmatian, or chariot air. **1861** J. S. ADAMS *5000 Mus. Terms*, *Harmatian* or *chariot air*, a spirited martial air employed to animate the horses that drew the chariot during battle.

‖**harmattan** (hɑː'mætən, in 18th c. 'hɑːmətæn). Also 7 **harmetan**, **hermitan**, 8 **-atan**, (**air-mattan**). [From *haramata*, the name in the Fanti or Tshî lang. of W. Africa.

According to Norris in Phil. Trans. LXXI. 52 (1780) 'a corruption of *Aherramantah*, compounded of *Aherraman* to blow and *tah* tallow, grease, with which the natives rub their skin to prevent their growing dry and rough'; but acc. to Christaller, Dict. Asante & Fante Lang. (Basel 1881), a borrowed foreign word, viz. 'Sp. *harmatan*, an Arabic word'. (But no such Arabic word has been found.)]

A dry parching land-wind, which blows during December, January, and February, on the coast of Upper Guinea in Africa; it obscures the air with a red dust-fog.

1671 R. BOHUN *Wind* 195 Of the Harmetans in Guiny. **1688** J. HILLIER *Lett. fr. Cape Corse* in *Misc. Cur.* (1708) III. 365 We had a dry North and North-Easterly Wind, call'd an Hermitan, and it overcame the Sea-Brize. **1723** J. ATKINS *Voy. Guinea* (1735) 149 Air-mattans, or Harmatans, are impetuous Gales of Wind from the Eastern Quarter about Midsummer and Christmas. **1725** J. REYNOLDS *View Death* (1735) 30 And Harmatans revenge the richness of their oar. **1845** DARWIN *Voy. Nat.* i. 5 During those months when the harmattan is known to raise clouds of dust high into the atmosphere. **1906** F. B. ARCHER *Gambia Colony* i. 27 This excessive dryness is undoubtedly due to the severe 'harmattan' experienced in the locality. **1963** W. SOYINKA *Lion & Jewel* 22 The dew-moistened leaves on a Harmattan morning.

attrib. **1671** R. BOHUN *Wind* 196 The Harmetan Winds, so called by the Natives, come..in December about Christmas. **1803** T. WINTERBOTTOM *Sierra Leone* I. ii. 2 *note*, Known by the name of the harmattan wind. **1828** CARLYLE *Misc.* (1872) I. 187 The Harmattan breath of doubt.

harmel: see HARMALA.

harmer ('hɑːmə(r)). [f. HARM *v.* + -ER[1].] One who or that which harms; an injurer.

1583 BABINGTON *Commandm.* viii. (1637) 69 Harmers of the commodities which they inioy. 1838 J. STRUTHERS *Poetic Tales* 14 Fell Boreas, cruel harmer.

†**harme'say, harmi'say.** *Sc. Obs.* Also 6 harmissa. [Origin uncertain: it perh. contains the word *harm*.] A cry of grief or distress; = 'alas'.

a 1487 *How Good Wife taught her Dau.* 102 Than 'had I wittyn!' will thai say, With mony 'allas' and harmesay. 1535 STEWART *Cron. Scot.* II. 84 'Bot now', he said, 'allace, and harmissa! For all that welth is went full far awa'. 1552 LYNDESAY *Monarche* 5973 Than sall thay say, With mony hydous harmesay, Allace! gude Lorde. 1603 *Philotus* clv, Allace, and harmisay..quhat sall I say?

harmful ('hɑːmfʊl), *a.* [f. HARM *sb.* + -FUL.] Fraught with harm or injury; injurious, hurtful.

a 1340 HAMPOLE *Psalter* lxi. 10 It is a harmefull winninge to win cattell and tine rightowsnes. 1388 WYCLIF *Prov.* i. 22 Hou long foolis schulen coueyte tho thingis that ben harmful to hem silf. *c* 1460 FORTESCUE *Abs. & Lim. Mon.* xiv, How harmefull it wolde be to the kynge, and to his reaume, yff his commons were pouere. 1549 UDALL, etc. *Erasm. Par. Heb.* iv. (R.), An harmfull person. 1562 J. HEYWOOD *Prov. & Epigr.* (1867) 95 Better is..A harmelesse lie, than a harmefull true tale. 1625 K. LONG tr. *Barclay's Argenis* v. v. 344 Fame is ever quicker..to bring us harmefull news, then such as we desire. 1697 DRYDEN *Virg. Georg.* I. 115 And sleepy Poppies harmful Harvests yield. 1814 CARY *Dante, Par.* IV. 65 That other doubt Which moves thee, is less harmful. 1885 *Manch. Exam.* 15 May 4/7 To establish and endow a particular form of religion by the State is harmful to religion generally.

harmfully ('hɑːmfʊlɪ), *adv.* [f. prec. + -LY².] In a harmful manner; injuriously, mischievously.

c 1374 CHAUCER *Boeth.* II. pr. i. 21 (Camb. MS.) Cast a-way hir þat pleyyth so harmfully. 1534 MORE *On the Passion* Wks. 1274/2 To see theyr fayned friend..so harmefully disceiue them. 1633 BP. HALL *Hard Texts* 353 Men that were harmfully troublesome. 1891 *Leeds Mercury* 25 May 5/3 The thought..operated harmfully upon his mind.

'**harmfulness.** [f. as prec. + -NESS.] The quality of being harmful; injuriousness.

1580 SIDNEY *Arcadia* v. Wks. 465 This Daiphantus.. disguised himself like a woman; which being the more simple and hurtless sex might easier hide his subtile harmfulness. 1696 TRYON *Misc.* i. 12 Whether it be in Vertue, or in Harmfulness. 1850 KINGSLEY *Alt. Locke* i, Deeds and words, of the harmfulness of which I had no notion.

harmine ('hɑːmaɪn). *Chem.* [f. HARMA(LA + -INE.] An alkaloid ($C_{13}H_{12}N_2O$) contained in the seeds of HARMALA, or obtained by oxidation of harmaline. (Discovered in 1847.) Hence **har'minic acid**, an acid ($C_{10}H_8N_2O_4$) obtained by oxidation of harmine.

1864 WEBSTER, *Harmine.* 1865 WATTS *Dict. Chem.* III. 10 *Harmine*..is a weaker base than harmaline. 1889 *Ibid.*, *Harminic acid.*

'**harming,** *vbl. sb.* [f. HARM *v.* + -ING¹.] The action of the verb HARM; harm, injury, hurt. In quot. *a* 1300 = sorrow, grief.

a 1300 *Cursor M.* 9385 A! lauerd, gret herming was þar. *c* 1470 HENRY *Wallace* I. 110 Erle Patrik..harmyng did ws mast. 1623 DRUMM. OF HAWTH. *Cypress Grove* Wks. (1711) 117 The harming of the one is the weakning of the working of the other. 1719 D'URFEY *Pills* I. 189 Dreadful harming.

harmissa, var. of HARMESAY *Obs.*

harmless ('hɑːmlɪs), *a.* [f. HARM *sb.* + -LESS.] **1.** Free from harm or injury; unhurt, uninjured, unharmed. Now *rare*.

c 1290 *S. Eng. Leg.* I. 72/39 Harmles he feol and hol man i-novȝ. *c* 1385 CHAUCER *L.G.W.* 2664 *Hypermnestra*, To passen harmlesse of that place, She graunted hym. 1480 CAXTON *Chron. Eng.* ccxiv. 201 The scottes escaped harmelees. 1587 *Mirr. Mag.*, *Sabrina* xvi, Drowne mee, and let my mother harmlesse goe. 1685 COTTON tr. *Montaigne* I. 482 Some..undertook by this means..to save harmless the religion of others. 1848 THACKERAY *Van. Fair* xii, Pecking up her food quite harmless and successful.

2. Free from loss, free from liability to punishment, or to pay for loss or damage; *esp.* in *to save harmless*.

1418 *E.E. Wills* (1882) 33 That þᵉ same Ionet saue and kepe harmeles myn heirs..a-ȝens Iohn Roe. 1481 CAXTON *Reynard* (Arb.) 46 Yf ye saue me harmles in the spirituel court. 1592 WEST *1st Pt. Symbol.* §103E, That he the same R.S...shall acquite, discharge, and from time to time for euer saue harmelesse the said H.M. and J. his wife. 1651 J. MARIUS *Bills of Exchange* 23 Giving Bond to save harmelesse. 1755 MAGENS *Insurances* I. 112 It was agreed to keep the king harmless. 1818 CRUISE *Digest* (ed. 2) IV. 472 A person.. covenanted..that he would save the lessee harmless from any claiming by, from, or under him.

3. Free from guilt; innocent. *arch.*

1297 R. GLOUC. (1724) 509 Harmles me him nom, & mid hors to drou, & suþþe anhunge him. 13.. *E.E. Allit. P.* A. 675 Þe ryȝt-wys man schal se hys face, Þe harmlez haþel schal com hym tylle. 1529 MORE *Dyaloge* IV. Wks. 279/1 To the helpe and defence of his good and harmelesse neyghbour, against yᵉ malice and crueltie of yᵉ wrong doer. 1594 *1st Pt. Contention* vi. 24 In Pomphret Castle harmelesse Richard was shamefully murthered. 1627-77 FELTHAM *Resolves* I. xxix. 50 How happy..those things live, that follow harmless Nature? 1863 MRS. C. CLARKE *Shaks. Char.* v. 134 Up to the very last scene, she bears him harmless of all suspicion.

4. Doing or causing no harm; not injurious or hurtful; inoffensive, innocuous.

1533 MORE *Answ. Poysoned Bk.* Wks. 1047/1 They loue better hunger and thurste, then the harmelesse lacke of them bothe. 1593 SHAKS. *2 Hen. VI*, III. i. 71 The sucking Lambe, or harmelesse Doue. 1653 WALTON *Angler* i. 16 The most honest, ingenious, harmless Art of Angling. 1718 MOTTEUX *Quix.* (1733) II. 279 The harmlessest Fellow in the World. 1809-10 COLERIDGE *Friend* (1865) 29 One of the most harmless of human vanities. 1894 J. T. FOWLER *Adamnan* Introd. 32 The harmless snake.

5. *Comb.*, as ***harmless-looking***.

1890 MARIE CORELLI *Wormwood* III. 248 Liquid.. harmless-looking as spring-water.

'**harmlessly,** *adv.* [f. prec. + -LY².] In a harmless manner; without causing or receiving injury.

1561 T. NORTON *Calvin's Inst.* IV. xx. (1634) 740 They might behave themselves harmlesly and quietly together. 1653 WALTON *Angler* i. 32 He had spent that day..both harmlesly and in a Recreation that became a Church-man. 1796 MORSE *Amer. Geog.* II. 301 Their balls passed harmlessly over the heads of the Russians. 1880 McCARTHY *Own Times* IV. 83 The sudden tumult was harmlessly over.

'**harmlessness.** [f. as prec. + -NESS.] The state or quality of being harmless; inoffensiveness.

1596 THOMAS *Lat. Dict.* (1606), *Innocentia*, innocencie, integritie, harmelessenesse. 1646 P. BULKELEY *Gospel Covt.* v. 382 Justnesse in dealing without holinesse, is but heathenish harmlessnesse. 1758 WARBURTON *Div. Legat.* Pref. Wks. 1811 IV. 55 Its harmlessness or malignity is the only matter of inquiry. 1879 *Cassell's Techn. Educ.* IX. 151/1 The absolute harmlessness of the safety matches.

†'**harmoge.** *Obs.* [L. *harmogē* = Gr. ἁρμογή joining, fitting, arrangement, f. ἁρμόζειν to fit.] A harmony of colours or sounds.

1601 HOLLAND *Pliny* II. 528 As for the apt coherence of one colour with another, the ioint as it were between, and the passage from one to another, they named it Harmoge. 1662 EVELYN *Chalcogr.* v. 128 The alteration could no more certainly be defin'd, then [by] the Semitons or Harmoge in Musick.

harmole, harmehole, obs. ff. ARMHOLE.

c 1425 *Voc.* in Wr.-Wülcker 637/17 *Hec acella*, harmole. *c* 1475 *Pict. Voc.* Ibid. 748/21 *Hoc bachium*, a harmehole.

‖**harmonia** (hɑː'məʊnɪə). *Anat.* [L. *harmonia*, a. Gr. ἁρμονία joining, joint, agreement, harmony, etc.; in Galen, 'the union of two bones by mere apposition'. See also HARMONY.] A kind of suture in which the two bones are apposed to each other by plane or nearly plane surfaces.

1657 *Physical Dict.*, *Harmonia*, is the juncture of a bone by a line. 1842 E. WILSON *Anat. Vade M.* (ed. 2) 41 The Harmonia suture is the simple apposition of contiguous surfaces. 1881 MIVART *Cat* 121 The adjoined even edges form what is termed an harmonia or false suture.

†**harmoniac** (hɑː'məʊnɪæk), *a.* *nonce-wd.* [f. Gr. ἁρμονία HARMONY + -AC.] Relating to harmony, or to the cultivation of music; = HARMONIC *a.* 1. Also *absol.*

1771 MRS. J. HARRIS in *Priv. Lett. Ld. Malmesbury* I. 212 They talk of nothing but the charms of the Harmoniac meeting. *Ibid.* 216 The Harmoniac met last night..The Harmoniac is over.

†**harmo'niacal,** *a.* *Obs.* [f. as prec. + -AL¹.] Full of harmony, harmonious; harmonical.

1536 *Primer Hen. VIII*, Jesus, the honor Angelicall, To them so sweet armoniacall. 1620-55 I. JONES *Stone-Heng* (1725) 23 There's no one Structure..wherein more clearly shines those harmoniacal Proportions. *a* 1660 HAMMOND *19 Serm.* v. Wks. 1684 IV. 592 To tune him to that sweet harmoniacal Gospel temper. 1693 J. BEAUMONT *On Burnet's Th. Earth* I. 71 Another mind, to whom other harmoniacal Laws may be more pleasing.

harmonial (hɑː'məʊnɪəl), *a.* *rare.* [f. L. *harmonia*, a. Gr. ἁρμονία HARMONY + -AL¹.]

Pertaining to or characterized by harmony or agreement; harmonious. (In quot. 1622, Relating to collation of parallel passages: see HARMONY 6.)

1569 SANFORD tr. *Agrippa's Van. Artes* 30b, A certaine Harmoniall daunsinge of the heauenly Bodies. 1622 CALLIS *Stat. Sewers* (1647) 121 Seeing the Statute Law can receive no due construction, but by the rules of the Common Law, I have..made a harmonial composition of them both. 1691 TRYON *Wisd. Dictates* 111 All Vegitative Foods..are far more agreeable and harmonial than Flesh or Fish. 1884 *Nonconf. & Indep.* 17 Jan. 55/3 The peeping moon contributes to the harmonial rivalry of colour.

†**har'monian.** *Obs.* *rare*⁻¹. [f. L. *harmonia* HARMONY + -AN, after *musician*.] One versed in harmony or music; a musician.

1603 HOLLAND *Plutarch's Mor.* 1257 Lasus the harmonian ..brought a great change into Musicke.

harmonic (hɑː'mɒnɪk), *a.* and *sb.* [ad. L. *harmonic-us*, a. Gr. ἁρμονικός skilled in music, musical, in neut. pl. ἁρμονικά as sb., theory of music, music, f. ἁρμονία HARMONY: see -IC. Cf. F. *harmonique* (14th c. in Hatz.-Darm.).]

A. *adj.* **1. a.** Relating to music, musical; in reference to ancient music, Relating to melody as distinguished from rhythm. *Obs.* exc. in specific uses.

harmonic hand: a figure of the left hand, having the finger-joints marked with the syllables denoting the notes of Guido Aretino's scale. ***harmonic telegraph***: see quot. 1884; also, ***harmonic telegraphy***.

1570 LEVINS *Manip.* 121/33 Harmonicke, *harmonicus.* 1603 HOLLAND *Plutarch's Mor.* 1259 The Harmonique skill conteineth the knowledge of intervals, compositions, sounds, notes and mutations. 1694 W. HOLDER *Harmony* (1731) Introd., Of the Nature of Sound in General; and then, more particularly, of Harmonick Sounds. 1782 BURNEY *Hist. Mus.* II. 90 No proof can be found in the writings of Guido that the Harmonic Hand was of his construction. 1852 DICKENS *Bleak Ho.* xi, At the Sol's Arms, where the Harmonic Meetings take place. 1878 *Telegraphic Jrnl.* VI. CXXXIII. 348/1 Gray's harmonic telegraph can now be seen in operation at the Paris Exhibition. 1880 W. H. HUSK in Grove *Dict. Mus.* I. 82 An association for..printing the best music..called the Royal Harmonic Institution. *Ibid.* 691 Harington..born in 1727 ..founded the Harmonic Society of Bath. 1884 KNIGHT *Dict. Mech.* Supp., *Harmonic telegraph*, a telephone, which sends messages by audible musical tones. 1902 *Westm. Gaz.* 8 Jan. 6/2 The extensive adoption of..harmonic telegraphy. 1925 *Telegr. & Teleph. Jrnl.* XI. CXXII. 152/2 Mr. Cromwell Varley, who seems to have been the first to get hold of the fundamental idea of harmonic telegraphy, of sending into the telegraph line a number of different frequencies of signalling current at the same time and sorting them out at other stations.

b. Addicted to music; musical. *nonce-use.*

1796 BURNEY *Mem. Metastasio* II. 200 Heroes of the harmonic family. *Ibid.* II. 377 Take care of your health, for the honour of the harmonic family.

2. a. Sounding together with pleasing effect; harmonious, in harmony, concordant.

harmonic triad, an old name for the common chord.

1667 MILTON *P.L.* IV. 687 With Heav'nly touch of instrumental sounds In full harmonic number joind. 1728 POPE *Dunc.* II. 254 Ass intones to Ass, Harmonic twang! of leather, horn and brass. *c* 1800 K. WHITE *Music* vi, Softest flutes or reeds harmonic join'd. 1845 *Encycl. Metrop.* V. 774 *Harmonic triad*..another name for the common chord. 1872 HUXLEY *Phys.* viii. 212 A tuning-fork may be set vibrating, if its own particular note or one harmonic with it, be sounded in its neighbourhood.

b. Melodious, tuneful, sweet-sounding. *rare.*

1815 W. H. IRELAND *Scribbleomania* 36 Harmonic and vigorous poesy.

3. *Mus.* Relating to harmony (as distinct from melody and rhythm); belonging to the combination of musical notes in chords.

1661 BLOUNT *Glossogr.* (ed. 2), *Harmonick*..that pertains to harmony, which is the accord of divers sounds or notes. 1784 SIR W. JONES *Mus. Modes Hindus* Wks. 1799 I. 413 Natural philosophy..limits the number of mixed, or harmonick, sounds to a certain series. 1869 OUSELEY *Counterp.* i. 1 When we look at a piece of harmonized music from the harmonic point of view, we confine our attention to the chords of which it is composed. 1879 *Sat. Rev.* 6 Dec. 699 Chromatic notes are used..for two..purposes—a harmonic purpose in modulation to new keys, and a melodic purpose in ornamentation.

4. a. *Acoustics* and *Mus.* Applied to the tones produced by the vibration of a sonorous body in aliquot parts of its length (see B. 2); relating to such tones.

harmonic scale: the scale formed by the series of harmonics of a fundamental note. ***harmonic minor mode*** or ***scale***: see quot. 1884. ***harmonic series*** = ***harmonic scale***. ***harmonic stop***: an organ-stop in which each of the pipes is pierced with a small hole in the middle of its length, so as to give the note corresponding to half the length; e.g. the ***harmonic flute***.

1831 BREWSTER *Nat. Magic* viii. (1833) 182 The acute sounds given out by each of the vibrating portions are called harmonic sounds. 1867 TYNDALL *Sound* iii. 123 The sounds of the Eolian harp are produced by the division of suitably stretched strings into a greater or less number of harmonic parts by a current of air passing over them. 1880 E. J. PAYNE in Grove *Dict. Mus.* I. 665 Any brass instrument, such as the hunting horn or military bugle..yields the familiar harmonic scale. 1880 E. J. HOPKINS *Ibid.* 666 Harmonic stops have in recent years come into great favour. 1881 C. A. EDWARDS *Organs* 157 [The] Harmonic-flute..is an open flue stop..of extreme beauty, the tone being full and fluty. 1884 MAITLAND in Grove *Dict. Mus.* IV. 666/2 Harmonic minor is the name applied to that version of the minor scale which contains the minor sixth together with the major seventh, and in which no alteration is made in ascending and descending. 1889 E. PROUT *Harmony* (ed. 10) vii. §171 This form is known as the Harmonic Minor Scale, the other two being called Melodic Minor Scales. 1910 *Encycl. Brit.* XIII. 1/1 The unisonous quality of octaves is easily explained when we examine the 'harmonic series' of upper partials.

†**b.** *Optics.* Applied to 'accidental' or subjective complementary colours, formerly supposed to be analogous to harmonic sounds. *Obs.*

1831 BREWSTER *Optics* xxxvi. 309 As in acoustics, where every fundamental sound is..accompanied with its harmonic sound, so..the sensation of one [colour] is accompanied by a weaker sensation of its accidental or harmonic colour. 1858 G. BARNARD *Landscape Paint.* 29 The term harmonic has been applied to accidental colours because the primitive and its accidental colour harmonise with each other in painting.

5. *Math.* **a.** Applied to the relation of quantities whose reciprocals are in arithmetical progression (e.g. $1, \frac{1}{2}, \frac{1}{3}, \frac{1}{4}, \ldots$); or to points, lines, functions, etc., involving such a relation; = HARMONICAL 7.

(This application, which originated with the ancient Pythagoreans, is generally held to have arisen from the fact that a string or other sonorous body, divided into segments whose lengths are $\frac{1}{2}$, $\frac{1}{3}$, $\frac{1}{4}$, etc. of the total length, gives a definite series of musical notes whose relations are of fundamental importance in harmony; see A. 4, B. 2.)

harmonic average = *harmonic mean*. ***h. conjugates***, each of the two pairs of points AB, CD, in relation to the other pair, in a straight line ACBD divided harmonically at C and B. ***h. division***, division of a line at four points A, C, B, D, such that the lengths AC, AB, AD, are in harmonic proportion; also analogous division of an angle or other magnitude. ***h. pencil***, a system of four straight lines in a plane meeting at one point, such as to divide harmonically every straight line that cuts them. ***h. progression***, the relation of a series of quantities whose reciprocals are in arithmetical progression, or such a series itself. ***h. proportion***, the relation of three quantities in harmonic progression; the second is said to be a ***harmonic mean*** between the first and third. ***h. range*** or ***row***, a series of four points in a straight line, forming two pairs of harmonic conjugates. ***h. ratio*** = *harmonic proportion*. ***h. series*** = *harmonic progression*; esp. the series $1 + \frac{1}{2} + \frac{1}{3} + \frac{1}{4} + \ldots$

1706 W. Jones *Syn. Palmar. Matheseos* 79 Whence, if the 2 first Terms of an Harmonic Proportion be given, the 3d. is readily found. **1862** Mulcahy *Mod. Geom.* 7 Four right lines drawn from the same point and cutting a right line harmonically (called a harmonic pencil) will also cut harmonically any other right line meeting them. **1866** Brande & Cox *Dict. Sci., Lit., & Art* II. 96/1 *Harmonic Progression or Series*, a series of numbers such that any three consecutive terms are in harmonic proportion. **1881** Casey *Sequel to Euclid* 88 If *C* and *D* be harmonic conjugates to *A* and *B*, *AB* is called a harmonic mean between *AC* and *AD*. **1885** Leudesdorf *Cremona's Proj. Geom.* 41 If..the harmonic range..be projected upon any other straight line, its projection..will also be a harmonic range. **1895** Story-Maskelyne *Crystallogr.* §63. 75 Harmonic division of a zone. *Ibid.*, The harmonic division of an angle. **1942** G. James *Math. Dict.* 199/1 *Harmonic ratio.* If the cross ratio of four points (or four lines) is equal to -1, it is called a harmonic ratio and the last two points are said to divide the first two harmonically. **1949** G. & R. C. James *Math. Dict.* 23/2 The harmonic average is the reciprocal of the arithmetic average of reciprocals of the observations. **1964** Crowder & McCuskey *Topics in Higher Analysis* iv. 193 Since $\sqrt{(n+1)}/n > 1/n$ for all $n > 0$, and

$$\sum_{n=1}^{\infty} 1/n$$

is the harmonic series that diverges,

$$\sum_{n=1}^{\infty} \sqrt{(n+1)}/n$$

also diverges.

b. harmonic motion, a periodic motion, which in its simplest form (***simple harmonic motion***) is like that of a point in a vibrating string, and is identical with the resolved part, parallel to a diameter, of uniform motion in a circle.

harmonic function, a function consisting of a series of terms, each of which expresses a harmonic motion; in a wider sense, any function that satisfies a differential equation of a class of which that expressing a simple harmonic motion is the first example. ***harmonic analysis***, the calculus of harmonic functions, an important part of modern mathematical analysis. ***harmonic curve***, a curve in which the ordinates are a simple harmonic function of the abscissæ; a curve of sines. ***harmonic analyser***, an integrating machine invented by Lord Kelvin for producing mechanically the harmonic constituents of meteorological, tidal, and other curves. ***harmonic current***, an alternating current the variations of which, graphically represented, follow a harmonic curve.

1867 Thomson & Tait *Nat. Phil.* I. i. §53 Simple harmonic motion..Such motions [are] approximately those of the simplest vibrations of sounding bodies..whence their name. *Ibid.* §56 The velocity of a point executing a simple harmonic motion is a simple harmonic function of the time. *Ibid.* §75 A complex harmonic function, with a constant term added, is the proper expression..for any..periodic function. *Ibid.* I. i. App. B, The..method..commonly referred to by English writers as that of 'Laplace's Coefficients'..is here called spherical harmonic analysis..A spherical harmonic function is defined as a homogeneous function, *V*, of *x*, *y*, *z*, which satisfies the equation $\frac{d^2V}{dx^2} + \frac{d^2V}{dy^2} + \frac{d^2V}{dz^2} = 0$. **1882** Minchin *Unipl. Kinemat.* 7 If a point ..moves..round in a circle with constant velocity, the foot ..of the perpendicular from the point on any diameter of the circle moves backwards and forwards..with a motion which is called a simple harmonic motion. **1908** *R. Soc. Catal. Sci. Papers 1800–1900* I. *Pure Math.* 402/1 (*title*) Harmonic analyser. **1910** *Hawkins's Electr. Dict.* 193/1 Harmonic current.

c. *Electr.* Of or relating to harmonics (harmonic *sb.* 2b), as ***harmonic distortion***, non-linear distortion of a wave-form in which harmonics of the original frequencies are introduced into it; ***harmonic generator***, a device that generates and combines harmonics of one or more sinusoidal oscillations to produce a complex wave-form; ***harmonic interference***, interference caused by the reception of harmonics of a transmitted signal of some other frequency; ***harmonic selective signalling*** (see quot.).

1929 K. Henney *Princ. Radio* xvii. 450 We determined the percentage of harmonic distortion that occurred in an amplifier when it worked over a curved characteristic. **1930** *Terms & Def. Telegr. & Teleph.* (*B.S.I.*) 21 *Harmonic selective signalling*, signalling a number of stations on one circuit by means of alternating or pulsating currents of different frequencies, each individual station being tuned to one frequency only. A calling station can call any selected station independently of the others by employing the frequency particular to the selected station. **1930** *Proc. Inst. Radio Engin.* XVIII. 31 If a receiver with poorly designed selective circuits is subjected to relatively high local field intensities one of the radio-frequency tubes may be overloaded and may then function as a modulator or harmonic generator. *Ibid.*, Complaints of harmonic interference are, at times, received by the operators of broadcast stations which can be traced directly to deficiencies in the design of the receivers employed. **1931** *Trans. Amer. Inst. Electr. Engin.* L. 811/1 The vacuum-tube harmonic generators of present practise are fundamentally amplifiers operated under conditions of input voltage and grid bias. **1962** A. Nisbett *Technique Sound Studio* 249 Harmonic distortion is most easily caused by flattening of peaks in the waveform. *Ibid.*, 1% harmonic distortion is not usually noticeable.

6. Relating to or marked by harmony, agreement, or concord (in general sense); harmonizing in aspect or artistic effect; harmonious in feeling, etc.

1756 T. Amory *J. Buncle* (1770) I. i. 33, I came to a little harmonic building, that had every charm and proportion architecture could give it. **1784** J. Potter *Virtuous Villagers* I. 110 Souls..united by harmonic union. **1796** H. Hunter tr. *St. Pierre's Stud. Nat.* (1799) II. 3 The most harmonic of all contrasts. **1893** J. Pulsford *Loyalty to Christ* II. 435 He is Harmonic Man, He is God manifested.

7. *Anat.* Belonging to or of the nature of a harmonia, q.v.

1826 Kirby & Sp. *Entomol.* (1828) III. xxxiv. 402 *note*, A harmonic suture is when the margins of two flat bones simply touch each other without any intermediate substance.

B. *sb.*

1. *pl.* A theory or system of musical sounds or intervals; that part of acoustics which relates to music. (Rarely in *sing.*) *Obs.* exc. in reference to ancient systems.

1709–29 V. Mandey *Syst. Math., Arith.* 48 That the Lovers of Musick may have the Proportions in view..we thought it convenient in this place to expose the Harmonicks of the Ingenious John Kepler. **1760** Stiles in *Phil. Trans.* LI. 698 Harmonic was divided into these seven parts; 1. of sounds, 2. of intervals, 3. of genera, 4. of systems, 5. of tones, 6. of mutations, 7. of melopœia. **1837** Whewell *Hist. Induct. Sc.* (1857) I. 50 The truths of Harmonics..were cultivated with much care.

2. a. (Short for *harmonic tone*.) One of the secondary or subordinate tones produced by vibration of the aliquot parts of a sonorous body (as a string, reed, column of air in a pipe, etc.); usually accompanying the primary or fundamental tone produced by the vibration of the body as a whole. Also called *overtones* or *upper partials* (as being of higher pitch than the fundamental tone).

Harmonics are sometimes produced independently, as in the violin and other stringed instruments by varying the point of contact of the bow, or by lightly pressing the string with the finger at special points, and in certain wind instruments by varying the force or direction of the breath. ***natural harmonics***: the series of harmonics naturally produced by the vibration of a string, etc., in halves, thirds, quarters, and so on; also, on instruments of the violin class, harmonics obtained from an open string, those from a stopped string being called ***artificial harmonics***. ***grave harmonic***: a name sometimes given to a low tone resulting from the combination of two tones = *differential tone*.

1777 Sir W. Jones *Ess. Arts* Poems, etc. 196 These accessory sounds, which are caused by the aliquots of a sonorous body vibrating at once, are called harmonicks, and the whole system of modern Harmony depends upon them. **1831** H. Melvill in *Preacher* II. 281 The harmonics of some Italian musician. **1880** E. J. Payne in Grove *Dict. Mus.* I. 664 The harmonics..determine..as has been lately proved by Helmholtz, the quality of musical tones. *Ibid.* 665 Natural harmonics..are an important resource in harp music..Brass instruments are richest in the practical employment of harmonics. **1884** Haweis *My Musical Life* i. 26–7 Playing all sort of melodies in flute-like harmonics.

b. *Electr.* In an alternating circuit, a component current whose frequency is a multiple of the fundamental; also, a corresponding electro-magnetic oscillation.

1894 *Amer. Jrnl. Sci.* CXLVIII. 379 The presence of upper harmonics in an alternating current wave. *Ibid.* 383 For every harmonic of the inducing current we shall have a harmonic electromotive force of the same frequency in the resonant circuit. **1919** R. Stanley *Text-bk. Wireless Telegr.* (ed. 2) II. 164 When the fundamental oscillations in a circuit are accompanied by other subsidiary oscillations the latter are called harmonics. **1955** *Sci. Amer.* June 43/3 They act like radio transmitters, emitting radio waves at the critical frequency and at harmonics of this frequency.

3. *Math.* = *harmonic function* (A. 5b), in the wider sense. ***spherical harmonic***, a harmonic function having a relation to Spherical Geometry akin to that which functions expressing harmonic motion have to Plane Geometry. Such are ***spherical solid harmonics***, ***spherical surface harmonics***, ***sectorial***, ***tesseral***, and ***zonal harmonics***, etc.

1867 Thomson & Tait *Nat. Philos.* I. i. App. B, General expressions for complete spherical harmonics of all orders. **1873** Maxwell *Electr. & Magn.* I. 163 When the poles are given, the value of the harmonic for a given point on the sphere is a perfectly definite numerical quantity. **1885** Watson & Burbury *Math. Th. Electr. & Magn.* I. 67 To express the potential at any point *P* of any distribution of matter in a series of spherical solid harmonics. *Ibid.* 68 It is evident that the density of this distribution on the sphere must by symmetrical about *OC*, and must therefore be expressible in a series of zonal harmonics with *OC* as axis.

harmonica (hɑːˈmɒnɪkə). Also 8 **armonica**. [fem. of L. *harmonicus* harmonic, used subst.]

1. Name of several different musical instruments.

a. An instrument invented by Dr. B. Franklin, consisting of a row of hemispherical glasses fitted on an axis turned by a treadle and dipping into a trough of water, played by the application of the finger; an improvement of the earlier 'musical glasses'. Also applied to other forms in which the tones are produced in various ways from graduated glass bowls or tubes. **b.** An instrument consisting of a row of glass plates mounted on a resonance-box and struck with hammers. **c.** A kind of mouth-organ; also applied to other wind-instruments with reeds. (See also harmonicon.)

1762 Franklin *Lett.* Wks. 1887 III. 204 In honor of your musical language, I have borrowed from it the name of this instrument, calling it the Armonica. **1778** *Phil. Surv. S. Irel.* 453 The invention of the musical glasses, now improved into the *harmonica*. **1831** Carlyle *Misc.* (1857) II. 207 His genius is not an Æolian harp, but a scientific harmonica. **1863** Tyndall *Heat* viii. §301 The flame would sing..as in the well known case of the hydrogen harmonica. **1880** Grove *Dict. Mus.* I. 663 The name Harmonica is now used for a toy-instrument of plates of glass hung on two tapes and struck with hammers. **1880** A. J. Hipkins *Ibid.* 667 In England keyboard harmonicas with bellows were known by the name of Seraphine. **1895** *Montgomery Ward Catal.* 241/1 Concert harmonica, 10 double holes, 40 reeds, brass reed plates, celluloid covers, absolutely perfect in tone. **1938** S. G. Hedges *Hohner Harmonica Band Bk.* iii. 15 Harmonicas are made in several keys, the principal being G and C. **1966** L. M. Fox *Instruments Pop. Mus.* xiii. 84 Some harmonicas have a slider stop which can switch into play a second row of reeds tuned a semitone higher. **1973** *Advocate-News* (Barbados) 24 Feb. 3/6 (Advt.), Attention all musicians.. Just arrived:—..Harmonica Holders.

2. Name given to different organ-stops.

1840 *Specif. Organ, Town Hall, Birmingham* in Grove *Dict. Mus.* II. 601 On Solo Manual..Harmonica, 4 ft. **1852** Seidel *Organ* 98 Harmonica..is a register of a most refined, delicate tone. **1880** Stainer & Barrett *Dict. Mus. T.*, *Harmonica*..A name sometimes given to a mixture stop on foreign organs.

harmonical (hɑːˈmɒnɪkəl), *a.* Also 6 **armonical**. [f. as harmonic + -al[1].]

1. Marked by harmony or agreement; harmonious, concordant: = harmonic *a.* 6. (In later use mostly *fig.* from 4.) Now *rare*.

1531 Elyot *Gov.* I. xx, Sterres and planettes, and their motions harmonicall. **1586** T. B. *La Primaud. Fr. Acad.* I. (1589) 415 To distribute liberally and according to harmonicall proportion their gifts, graces, and good turnes. **1676** Cudworth *Serm. 1 Cor.* xv. 57 (ed. 3) 81 The soul of man was harmonical as God at first made it, till sin, disordering the strings and faculties, put it out of tune. **1691–1701** Norris *Ideal World* II. xii (1704) 465 The harmonical consent of these two Divine writers. **1851** Ruskin *Stones Ven.* I. xx. §18 The arrangement of shadows ..in certain harmonical successions.

2. Relating to or obtained by collation of parallel passages in different books: see harmony 6.

1612 T. Taylor *Comm. Titus* i. 11 Partly by the expresse texts of Scripture: partly by harmonical, parallel, and sutable places. **1697** C. Leslie *Snake in Grass* (ed. 2) 354 One Harmonical Gospel made out of the four Gospels.

†**3.** Belonging or relating to music, musical: = harmonic *a.* 1. *Obs.*

1603 Holland *Plutarch's Mor.* 581 (R.) To judge of song and harmonical measures. **1626** Bacon *Sylva* §105 After euery three whole Notes Nature requireth, for all Harmonicall vse, one Halfe-Note to be interposed. **1796** Hutton *Math. Dict.*, *Harmonical Interval*, the difference between two sounds, in respect of acute and grave. **1837** Whewell *Hist. Induct. Sc.* (1857) I. 255 What new harmonical truth was illustrated in the Gregorian chant?

†**b.** In ancient Greek music: = enharmonic 1.

1603 Holland *Plutarch's Mor.* 486 (R.) Among sundry kinds of music, that which is called chromatical..enlargeth ..the heart, whereas the harmonical contracteth and draweth it in.

†**4.** Of sounds, etc., esp. of musical notes: Harmonious, concordant, consonant; sweet-sounding, tuneful: = harmonic *a.* 2. *Obs.*

15.. *Proverbis* in *Antiq. Rep.* (1809) IV. 409 In the Speris of the planettis makynge sownde armonical. **1596** Fitz-Geffray *Sir F. Drake* (1881) 24 Fetch Orpheus harpe with strings harmonicall. **1626** Bacon *Sylva* §873 Harmonicall Sounds, and Discordant Sounds are both Actiue and Positiue. **1727–51** Chambers *Cycl.* s.v., Harmonical intervals..are the same with concords. **1774** Mitford *Harmony of Lang.* 186 The Italian has harmonical graces which the English cannot reach.

†**b.** *transf.* Of verse: Rhythmical, melodious, sweet-sounding. *Obs.*

1589 Puttenham *Eng. Poesie* II. (Arb.) 144 This ditty of th' Erle of Surries, passing sweete and harmonicall. **1652** Ashmole *Theat. Chem. Brit.* Proleg. 12 Unlesse their Verses ..were form'd with an Harmonicall Cadence.

5. Relating to harmony, or the combination of notes in music: = harmonic *a.* 3. ? *Obs.*

1727–51 Chambers *Cycl.* s.v., In its more proper and limited sense, harmonical composition.. may be defined, the art of..concerting several single parts together, in such manner as to make one agreeable whole. **1795** Mason *Ch. Mus.* i. 10 Not only the effect of musical sounds in melodious succession, but of these too in harmonical combination.

†**6.** = harmonic *a.* 4. *Obs.*

1727–51 Chambers *Cycl.* s.v., Harmonical sounds are produced by the parts of chords, etc. which vibrate a certain number of times while the whole chord vibrates once.

7. *Math.* = HARMONIC *a.* 5. †*harmonical numbers*: numbers in harmonic progression (*obs.*).

1569 J. SANFORD tr. *Agrippa's Van. Artes* 25b, Of Harmonical Numbers, and Geometrical. **1597** MORLEY *Introd. Mus.* Annotat., Harmonical proportion is..when the greatest of three termes is so to the least as the difference of the greatest and middle termes is to the difference of the middle and least. **1727-51** CHAMBERS *Cycl.* s.v., Harmonical series is a series of many numbers in continual harmonical proportion. **1881** CASEY *Sequel to Euclid* 89 The reciprocals of lines in arithmetical progression are in harmonical progression. **1882** C. SMITH *Conic Sect.* (1885) 53 *PQ:FS::PR-PQ:PS-PR*, so that *PQ PR PS* are in harmonical proportion.

†**b.** as *sb.* (*pl.*) Straight lines forming a harmonic pencil; quantities in harmonical progression. *Obs.*

a **1746** MACLAURIN *Algebra* (1779) 456 Any right line which meets four harmonicals is cut by the same harmonically. **1796** HUTTON *Math. Dict.* s.v., The reciprocals of Harmonicals are arithmeticals.

†**8.** *Anat.* = HARMONIC *a.* 7. *Obs.*

1578 BANISTER *Hist. Man* I. 5 A simple line, and Harmonicall meting, haue the Bones of the nose.

harmonically (hɑːˈmɒnɪkəlɪ), *adv.* [f. prec. + -LY².]

†**1.** In the way of harmony or agreement; agreeingly, harmoniously. (Sometimes *fig.* from 2.) *Obs.*

1604 T. WRIGHT *Passions* v. § 3. 175 A flexible..voice, accommodated in manner correspondent to the matter.. conueyeth the passion most aptly..and almost harmonically. **1613** F. ROBARTS *Rev. Gosp.* 65 What point soeuer the fathers do harmonically and with consent of all, agreeingly maintain. **1681** FLAVEL *Meth. Grace* xiii. 265 One and the same spirit harmonically works in all believers through the world.

†**2.** With harmony or concord of sounds; concordantly, tunefully, harmoniously. *Obs.*

1589 PUTTENHAM *Eng. Poesie* II. i. (Arb.) 79 Poesie is a skill to speake and write harmonically. **1691** NORRIS *Pract. Disc.* 109 A Lute..though never so Harmonically Set and Tuned, yields no Musick till its Strings be artfully touched. **1751** JOHNSON *Rambler* No. 88 ⁋3 The sounds of the consonants are less harmonically conjoined.

3. *Mus.* In relation to harmony.

1775 STEELE in *Phil. Trans.* LXV. 74 These two specimens of melody..are harmonically the same, though rhythmically different. **1880** C. H. H. PARRY in Grove *Dict. Mus.* I. 676 Otherwise they [the chords] would have no notes in common and the connection between them harmonically would not be ostensible.

4. *Math.* In a harmonic relation or proportion.

1597 MORLEY *Introd. Mus.* Annot. (∴) ij, If you diuide the same [diapason] harmonically. **1603** HOLLAND *Plutarch's Mor.* 1255 Plato..intending to declare harmonically the harmony of the foure elements of the soule..in each interval hath put downe two medieties of the soule, and that acording to musical proportion. **1676** *Phil. Trans.* XI. 745 One only line cut in three parts, which Line he calls cut harmonically. **1706** W. JONES *Syn. Palmar. Matheseos* 79 When 3 Terms are so disposed..they are said to be Harmonically Proportional. **1882** C. SMITH *Conic Sect.* (1885) 53 If *PQRS* be a harmonic range, then *Q* and *S* are said to be harmonically conjugate with respect to *P* and *R*.

†**har'monicalness.** *Obs.* 'Harmonical' quality; tunefulness, harmoniousness.

1691-8 NORRIS *Pract. Disc.* (1711) III. 209 That connexion that is between such Motions upon it [the lute] and the Harmonicalness of its sound.

harmonichord (hɑːˈmɒnɪkɔːd). [ad. F. *harmonicorde*, f. *harmonium* + *corde* CHORD.] A keyboard instrument invented by Kaufmann in 1810, in which the tone (resembling that of a violin) was produced by the friction of a revolving cylinder, charged with rosin, against the strings.

1835 *Suppl. to Mus. Library* II. July 71 The harmonichord was not quite in tune. **1880** in GROVE *Dict. Mus.*

†**harmonician** (hɑːməʊˈnɪʃən). *Obs.* [f. HARMONIC + -IAN: cf. *musician*.] One versed in harmony or musical theory.

1760 STILES in *Phil. Trans.* LI. 699 The modes admitted by the Aristoxenians were thirteen..to which two more were added by later harmonicians. **1776** SIR J. HAWKINS *Hist. Mus.* I. III. vii. 334 Ptolemy and the rest of the Greek harmonicians.

harmonicon (hɑːˈmɒnɪkən). [a. Gr. ἁρμονικόν, neut. sing. of ἁρμονικός HARMONIC.] A name given to various musical instruments.

a. = HARMONICA I a. **b.** = HARMONICA I b; also applied to instruments similarly constructed. **c.** A mouth-organ consisting of a row of free reeds arranged in a case so as to give different notes by expiration and inspiration. **d.** A kind of barrel-organ with a number of stops imitating various orchestral instruments; also called *orchestrion*. **e.** *chemical harmonicon*, an apparatus in which musical tones are produced by flames of hydrogen or other gas burning in glass tubes.

1825 *Specif. F. H. Smith's Patent* (U.S.) 7 Apr., Musical glasses, called the Grand harmonicon. **1842** *Mechanic's Mag.* XXXVII. 70 The pressure of the performer's finger.. is the great charm of such instruments as the harmonicon [etc.]. **1864** ENGEL *Mus. Anc. Nat.* 11 Instruments consisting of a series of pieces of sonorous wood..made to vibrate by being beaten with a stick or hammer, like our harmonicon. **1875** LOEWY & FOSTER tr. *Weinhold's Introd. Exp. Phys.* 374 As in the glass-harmonicon which consists of strips of glass affixed to cords at the nodal points. *Ibid.* 379 The apparatus..has been termed the chemical harmonicon. **1880** STAINER & BARRETT *Dict. Mus. T.*, *Harmonicon*, a toy instrument which consists of free reeds inclosed in a box in such a way that inspiration produces one set of sounds, respiration another. **1885** *Daily News* 17 Aug. 6/1 (Stanf.) A very great curiosity is the rock harmonicon, or musical stones..'reduced to music' by Crosthwaite, of Keswick.

harmonious (hɑːˈməʊnɪəs), *a.* Also 6 **armonious**, *Sc.* **ermonius**. [ad. F. *harmonieux* (14th c.), f. *harmonie* HARMONY: see -OUS.]

1. Marked by harmony, agreement, or concord; agreeing, accordant, concordant, congruous; having the parts or elements in accord so as to form a consistent or agreeable whole.

1638 T. WHITAKER *Blood of Grape* 6 If contraries shall bee adhibited to a harmonious temper, 'tis the cause of discord. **1643** MILTON *Divorce* II. xiii, The..statutes of God..are most constant and most harmonious each to other. **1753** HOGARTH *Anal. Beauty* viii. 40 A..harmonious order of architecture in all its parts. **1804** J. GRAHAME *Sabbath* 816 Th' ethereal curve of seven harmonious dyes. **1820** W. IRVING *Sketch Bk.* I. 40 The very difference in their characters produced an harmonious combination.

b. Marked by agreement of feeling or sentiment; free from discord or dissent; consentient, unanimous.

1724 *Wodrow Corr.* (1843) III. 116, I..am glad Mr. Paisley's call will be harmonious. **1849** MACAULAY *Hist. Eng.* II. 213 No constitutional question had ever been decided..with more harmonious consent. **1870** E. PEACOCK *Ralf Skirl.* I. 160 A long and not quite harmonious interview with his wife.

2. Characterized by harmony of sounds; sounding together with agreeable effect; in harmony, concordant; tuneful, sweet-sounding; full of harmony.

1549 *Compl. Scot.* vi. 64 His ermonius sang. **1570** DEE *Math. Pref.* 22 As, for Astronomie, the eyes; So for Harmonious Motion, the eares were made. *c* **1586** C'TESS PEMBROKE *Ps.* XLVII. iii, Hark, how did ring Harmonious aire with trumpetts sound. **1633** G. HERBERT *Temple, Aaron* i, Harmonious bells. **1784** COWPER *Task* I. 767 Your songs confound Our more harmonious notes. **1836-7** DICKENS *Sk. Boz, Miss Evans & Eagle* 140 They formed an harmonious quartett. **1853** C. BRONTE *Villette* xli, His voice..mixed harmonious with the silver whisper..[of] light breeze, fountain, and foliage.

b. *transf.* Of persons: Singing, playing, or speaking tunefully or agreeably.

1530 PALSGR. Introd. 15 The frenchemen..covet..to be armonious in theyr speking. **1592** GREENE *Groat's W. Wit* (1617) 11 The sight and hearing of this harmonious beauty. **1738** GLOVER *Leonidas* I. 400 Harmonious youths..In loftysounding strains his praise record. **1880** GROVE *Dict. Mus.* I. 655/1 The popular air known as 'The Harmonious Blacksmith'.

harmoniously (hɑːˈməʊnɪəslɪ), *adv.* [f. prec. + -LY².] In a harmonious manner.

1. In the way of agreement or congruity; in harmony; so as to form a consistent whole.

1632 PORTER *Old Mus. Airs* in *Brit. Bibl.* (1812) II. 319 Who hath a human soule and musicke hates, Hates his owne soule that's made harmoniously. **1695** LD. PRESTON *Boeth.* III. 151 The Sovereign Good which ruleth all things powerfully, and disposeth them softly and harmoniously. **1819** MONTGOMERY *Hymn 'The glorious universe around'* ii, All His works with all His ways Harmoniously unite.

b. With harmony of feeling or sentiment.

1671 J. WEBSTER *Metallogr.* xii. 178 They..did harmoniously agree. **1770** BURKE *Pres. Discont.* (R.), It was their wish to see publick and private virtues not dissonant and jarring..but harmoniously combined. **1883** FROUDE *Short Stud.* IV. I. xii. 159 They were now able to work harmoniously together.

2. With harmony of sounds; tunefully.

1611 COTGR., *Melodieusement*, melodiously, harmoniously, musically, tunably. **1635** SHIRLEY *Coronat.* v. (R.), A king's name Doth sound harmoniously to men at distance. *a* **1720** SHEFFIELD (Dk. Buckhm.) *Wks.* (1753) I. 269 Poetry, harmoniously divine.

har'moniousness. [f. as prec. + -NESS.] Harmonious condition or quality.

1679 KING in G. Hickes *Spirit of Popery* (1680) 37 Harmoniousness and Oneness in the things of God. **1696** TOWERSON *Serm. Ch. Mus.* 27 The Organ..both by the Lowdness, and the Harmoniousness thereof doth..carry the Voices of Men along with it.

harmoniphon, -phone (hɑːˈmɒnɪfən, -fəʊn). [mod. f. Gr. ἁρμονία HARMONY + -φωνος -sounding. Cf. F. *harmoniphon* (Littré).]

A musical instrument consisting of a tube like that of a clarinet, inclosing a set of free reeds governed by a keyboard like that of a harmonium. Also applied to a musical box with a combination of reeds and pipes.

1839 *Mus. World* Oct. 410 The Harmoniphon..lately invented by M. Paris of Dijon..resembles..the concertina ..but it is played by keys like those of a pianoforte. **1880** *Libr. Univ. Knowl.* X. 335 When they [musical boxes] have a combination of reeds and pipes, they are known as flutes, celestial voices, and harmoniphones. **1884** *Encycl. Brit.* XVII. 106/2 Barrel organs, mechanical flutes, celestial voices, harmoniphones.

harmonist (ˈhɑːmənɪst). [f. HARMONIZE *v.*: see -IST; cf. F. *harmoniste* (18th c. in Hatz.-Darm.).]

1. One skilled in musical harmony. **a.** A player, singer, or composer of 'harmonies' or tuneful sounds; a musician. Also *fig.* A poet (cf. *singer*).

1742 YOUNG *Nt. Th.* III. 81 Sweet Harmonist! and beautiful as sweet! **1791** HUDDESFORD *Salmag.* 83 Ballads I have heard rehears'd By harmonists itinerant. *a* **1800** COWPER *Lines to Dr. Darwin* 3 Sweet harmonist of Flora's court! **1828** WORDSW. *Power of Sound* xii, The Ocean is a mighty harmonist.

b. A composer skilled in harmony (as distinguished from melody, etc.); one versed in the theory of harmony, a writer on harmony.

a **1790** ADAM SMITH *Imit. Arts* II. Ess. (1795) 174 A musician may be a very skilful harmonist, and yet be defective in..melody..and expression. **1873** LOWELL *Among my Bks.* Ser. II. 284 Milton was a harmonist rather than a melodist. **1880** E. GURNEY *Power of Sound* 271 Modern harmonists are unwilling to acknowledge that the minor triad is less consonant than the major.

c. One of a school of ancient Greek musical theorists who founded the rules of music on the subjective effects of tones, not on their mathematical relations, as the *canonists* did.

1570 DEE *Math. Pref.* 22 The Controuersie betwene the auncient Harmonistes, and Canonistes.

2. One who collates and harmonizes parallel narratives, or the like; one who makes a harmony, *esp.* of the Gospels: see HARMONY 6.

1713 NELSON *Life Bp. Bull* (1714) 140 He chargeth the Harmonist with confounding the Terms of Scripture. **1871** FREEMAN *Hist. Ess.* (1872) 17 The..careful translator and harmonist of the English Chronicles. **1896** W. F. ADENEY *How to read the Bible* 108 The temptation of the harmonist is to smooth away all differences between the accounts he has set himself to bring into line.

3. One who reduces something to harmony, agreement, or concord; a harmonizer.

1809-10 COLERIDGE *Friend* (1865) 78 The intelligence which..controls..occurrences, is..represented..under the name..of the supreme harmonist. **1840** LYTTON *Pilgr. Rhine* xix, The swayers and harmonists of souls. **1876** FAIRBAIRN in *Contemp. Rev.* June 140 The harmonists of science and religion he rated as little better than knaves.

b. *pre-established harmonist*, one who accepts the doctrine of pre-established harmony: see HARMONY I. (*nonce-use.*)

1838 *Blackw. Mag.* XLIV. 234 The occasionalists and pre-established harmonists.

4. (with capital *H.*) One of a communistic religious body in the United States, founded by Geo. Rapp of Würtemberg in 1803; they settled in Pennsylvania, and founded a town called Harmony (whence their name), and another called Economy.

1824 BYRON *Juan* XV. xxxv, When Rapp the Harmonist embargo'd marriage. **1875** *N. Amer. Rev.* CXX. 227 The followers of Rapp at Economy (the Harmonists).

harmonistic (hɑːməˈnɪstɪk), *a.* and *sb.* [f. prec. + -IC.]

A. *adj.* Belonging to the work of a harmonist (sense 2); relating to the collation and harmonizing of parallel passages.

1860 ELLICOTT *Life Our Lord* i. 19 *note*, Modern writers on harmonistic study. **1881** WESTCOTT & HORT *Grk. N.T.* II. 124 Its most dangerous work is 'harmonistic' corruption, that is, the partial or total obliteration of differences in passages otherwise more or less resembling each other.

B. *sb.* (Also in *pl.*) Harmonistic studies; the branch of Biblical criticism which seeks to harmonize the Gospels or other parts of the Scripture narrative.

1875 J. B. MᶜCLELLAN *N. Test.* 372 The present entirely independent contribution to Harmonistics. **1886** A. B. BRUCE *Mirac. Elem. in Gosp.* iv. 137 The old Harmonistic.. reduced the divergent narratives into conformity..on the principal that [etc.].

Hence **harmo'nistically** *adv.*, in the manner of a harmonist; in relation to a 'harmony' of writings.

1885 J. S. BLACK tr. *Wellhausen's Proleg. Hist. Israel* v. i. 154 The precept being thus harmonistically doubled.

harmonium (hɑːˈməʊnɪəm). [a. F. *harmonium* (invented by Debain, *c* 1840), deriv. of Gr.-L. *harmonia* or Gr. ἁρμόνιος harmonious: cf. *melodium*.]

A keyboard instrument, the tones of which are produced by free metal 'reeds', tongues, or 'vibrators', actuated by a current of air from bellows, usually worked by treadles; a kind of reed-organ.

Strictly distinguished from the *American organ* by the fact that the air is driven outwards through the reed-pipes, whereas in the latter it is sucked inwards; but the name is sometimes extended to include the American organ.

1847 *Illustr. Lond. News* 7 Aug. 95/2 Pianos, melodiums, harmoniums, eolinas, &c. too dear at any price. **1879** STAINER *Music of Bible* 27 What could the musical historian of a thousand years hence gather of the construction of a harmonium [etc.], from the derivation of their respective names? **1880** MISS BRADDON *Just as I am* xxxiv, The schoolmistress began her voluntary on the harmonium.

Hence **har'moniumist**, one who plays a harmonium.

1886 *Standard* 18 Mar. 8/6 A Clergyman's daughter wishes for an engagement as Harmoniumist.

harmonization (ˌhɑːmənaɪˈzeɪʃən). [f. next + -ATION.] The action or process of harmonizing.

1. a. Reduction to harmony or agreement; reconciliation.

1837 G. S. FABER *Justification* xlix, The required harmonisation of the apparently opposite declarations. **1879** H. SPENCER *Data of Ethics* viii. §54. 147 That harmonization of constitution with conditions forming the limit of evolution.

b. Agreement in colour.

1897 R. KEARTON *Nature & Camera* 252 Their wonderful harmonisation with the sand upon which they lay stretched. **1925** R. W. G. HINGSTON in E. F. Norton *Fight for Everest, 1924* 262 We are attracted by their example of harmonization, the pale grey colour of their fur blending well with the upland soil.

2. *Mus.* The adding of harmony to a melody.

1880 E. GURNEY *Power of Sound* 248 The harmonisation of melodies.

harmonize (ˈhɑːmənaɪz), *v.* Also 5 **armonyse.** [a. F. *harmoniser* (15–16th c. in Hatz.-Darm.), f. *harmonie* HARMONY: see -IZE.]

†**1.** *intr.* To sing or play in harmony. *Obs. rare.*

1483 CAXTON *Gold. Leg.* 255 b/2 The Thrones Songen, the domynacyons maden melodye, The pryncypates armonysed.

2. a. *intr.* To be in harmony (*with*); to accord, agree (in sense, sentiment, feeling, artistic effect, etc.).

1629 LIGHTFOOT *Erubhim* 153 R. Tancuman shewes how the making of the Tabernacle harmonizeth with the making of the world. **1839** JAMES *Louis XIV*, III. 24 It harmonizes well with his general character. **1850** M. COSH *Div. Govt.* II. i. (1874) 129 Green..harmonises with red. *Mod.* The colours do not harmonize.

b. *Mus.* To be in harmony, form a concord.

1855 BAIN *Senses & Int.* II. ii. §10 The sounds that harmonise are..related to one another numerically in the number of their vibrations.

3. *trans.* To bring into harmony, agreement, or accord; to make harmonious.

a. To make harmonious or concordant in sound; to attune. (In quot. 1791, to fill with harmony or music.)

1700 DRYDEN *Cymon & Iph.* 34 Love first invented verse, and form'd the rhime, The motion measur'd, harmoniz'd the chime. **1791** W. BARTRAM *Carolina* 286 Most of these beautiful creatures who annually people and harmonize our forests and groves..are birds of passage. **1864** TENNYSON *Sea Dreams* 247 A music harmonizing our wild cries.

b. To reduce to internal harmony; to render tranquil or peaceful; to make agreeable in artistic effect. Also *absol.*

1727–46 THOMSON *Summer* 467 Every passion aptly harmoniz'd. **1749** JOHNSON *Irene* III. i, When social laws first harmonized the world. **1798** ANNA SEWARD *Lett.* (1811) V. 136 Those habits of style which..harmonize and inspirit. **1812** BYRON *Ch. Har.* II. xlviii, Bluest skies that harmonize the whole. **1850** ROBERTSON *Serm.* Ser. III. iv. (1872) 59 It is the graces of the Spirit which harmonize the man, and make him one.

c. To bring into agreement (two or more things, or one thing *with* another); to reconcile.

1767 A. YOUNG *Farmer's Lett. People* 22 The wise policy ..is to harmonize agriculture and manufactures. **1845** MAURICE *Mor. & Met. Philos.* in *Encycl. Metrop.* II. 588/1 An attempt to harmonize the doctrines of the schools. **1871** L. STEPHEN *Playgr. Eur.* iv. III. 259 A man must have harmonised himself with the scenery.

d. To form a harmonious combination *with*.

1852 *Art-Jrnl.* Apr. 117/3 If it is necessary that the colours of the different articles of dress should..harmonise with each other. **1862** *Englishwoman's Domestic Mag.* May 60/1 Flowers, and shells, and coloured fabrics that harmonise admirably with themselves and with the tropical scenery among which she lives. **1925** R. W. G. HINGSTON in E. F. Norton *Fight for Everest, 1924* 265 Then unexpectedly the bird alights, the crimson colour vanishes, the white spots disappear, and the bird again harmonizes with the hill. **1949** *Oxf. Jun. Encycl.* II. 72/1 Colour is used in one of the following ways: to break up the outline of the body, or to make it harmonize completely with the background, or to provide obliterative shading.

4. *Mus.* To add notes, usually of lower pitch, to the notes of (a melody) so as to form chords; to add harmony to. Also *absol.*

1790 (*title*) Songs Composed by Mrs. Hodges. Harmonised and Published by Mr. Hullmandel. **1875** OUSELEY *Harmony* iv. 57 Take these three notes as a melody to be harmonized. **1875** —— *Mus. Form* ii. 4 Any man may learn how to harmonise correctly.

Hence **ˈharmonized** *ppl. a.*; **ˈharmonizing** *vbl. sb.* and *ppl. a.*

1643 LIGHTFOOT *Glean. Ex.* (1648) 23 The serious Harmonizing of the foure Evangelists together..will make this..cleare. **1789** W. GILPIN *Wye* (ed. 2) 61 Fogs.. spreading over the landscape a beautiful, grey harmonizing tint. **1871** FREEMAN *Hist. Ess.* Ser. I. iv. 86 A harmonized narrative of the martyrdom. **1872** *Daily Tel.* 11 Jan., The harmonising of labour and capital.

harmonizer (ˈhɑːmənaɪzə(r)). [f. prec. + -ER[1].] One who harmonizes (see the verb).

1678 CUDWORTH *Intell. Syst.* 215 Plutarch [supposed].. that all the substance of..the world did exist from eternity, unmade; so that God was only the orderer, or the methodizer and harmonizer, thereof. **1861** J. S. ADAMS *5000 Mus. Terms, Harmonizer*..is generally applied to those musicians who add passages to the productions of others, fill up scanty pieces, or garnish popular airs. **1865** DICKENS *Mut. Fr.* III. vi, You, Sir, harmonizer with myself in opinions.

b. *spec.* = HARMONIST 2.

1713 NELSON *Life Bp. Bull* (1714) 103 Our Judicious Harmonizer. **1762** W. CLEAVER *Char. David* 5 Disdain for commentators and harmonizers. **1871** LIGHTFOOT *Revis. N.T.* iv. 159 Some harmonizer devised the statement.

harmon mute (ˈhɑːmən mjuːt). [perh. f. HARMONICA.] A type of mute for a trumpet or trombone, also called *wa-wa mute*. Hence **harmon-muted** *a.*

1955 L. FEATHER *Encycl. Jazz* ii. 64 The sounds produced by both trumpet and trombone were changed by..a variety of mutes, including the straight, cup and Harmon mutes and the rubber plunger. **1966** *Crescendo* Dec. 29/2 A slow, moody piece, with flute and Harmon-muted trumpet. **1967** *Ibid.* Feb. 26/2 Pull out the tube on your harmon mute.

harmonogram (hɑːˈmɒnəgræm). [f. as HARMONOGRAPH: see -GRAM.] A figure or curve drawn by a harmonograph.

1902 *Pearson's Mag.* Apr. 445/1 Not only can an infinity of varying harmonograms be produced with one ratio of pendulum length, but the ratio can be altered. **1962** R. QUIRK *Use of English* (*dust jacket*), The Harmonogram illustrated on this jacket is Crown Copyright, Science Museum, London.

harmonograph (hɑːˈmɒnəgrɑːf, -æ-). [f. as next + -GRAPH.] An instrument for tracing curves representing sonorous vibrations.

1879 *Jrnl. Sci.* N.S. I. 508 Mr. W. J. Wilson exhibited a new harmonograph and figures drawn by it. **1880** *Athenæum* 20 Nov. 679/1 Mr. Bosanquet..gave the mathematical theory of the curves drawn by the harmonograph.

harmonometer (hɑːməˈnɒmɪtə(r)). [ad. F. *harmonomètre*, irreg. f. *harmonie* HARMONY + *mètre* (see -METER).] An instrument for measuring the harmonic relations of musical notes.

1823 CRABB *Technol. Dict.*, *Harmonometre.* **1828** WEBSTER, *Harmonometer.* **1861** J. S. ADAMS *5000 Mus. Terms, Harmonometre*, a string drawn between two points, over bridges so arranged as to be lengthened or shortened at pleasure, and used for measuring the harmonic relations.

harmony (ˈhɑːmənɪ). Forms: 4–6 **armonie, -ny(e,** (5 **armeny, ermony),** 6 **harmonye,** 6–7 **harmonie,** 6– **harmony.** [a. F. *harmonie* (12th c. in Hatz.-Darm.), = Pr., Sp., It. *armonia*, ad. L. *harmonia*, a. Gr. ἁρμονία joining, joint, agreement, concord of sounds, music, f. stem ἁρμο- of ἁρμός joint, ἁρμόζειν to fit together, arrange.]

1. Combination or adaptation of parts, elements, or related things, so as to form a consistent and orderly whole; agreement, accord, congruity.

pre-established harmony, in the philosophy of Leibnitz, a harmony between mind and matter, e.g. between the body and soul, established before their creation, whereby their actions correspond though no communication exists between them.

c **1532** DEWES *Introd. Fr.* in *Palsgr.* 1058 Others have sayd that it [the operation of God] is a maner of armonie. **1597** HOOKER *Eccl. Pol.* V. xxxviii. §1 The soule it selfe by nature is, or hath in it, harmonie. **1605** BACON *Adv. Learn.* I. iv. §6 (1873) 32 The harmony of a science, supporting each part the other, is..the true and brief confutation..of all the smaller sort of objections. **1745** *De Foe's Eng. Tradesman* ii. (1841) I. 18 Here is a harmony of business, and everything exact. **1814** SOUTHEY *Roderick* XXI. 382 To heavenliest harmony Reduce the seeming chaos. **1847** LEWES *Hist. Philos.* (1867) II. 273 His [Leibnitz's] favourite hypothesis of a Pre-established Harmony (borrowed from Spinoza). **1860** TYNDALL *Glac.* II. xxiv. 353 Where other forces mingle with that of crystallization, this harmony of action is destroyed.

b. Phr. ***in harmony***: in agreement or accordance, consistent, congruous. So *out of harmony*.

1816 KEATINGE *Trav.* (1817) I. 42 He may always be sure of finding nature in harmony with herself. **1849** MACAULAY *Hist. Eng.* II. 149 This mode of attack..was in perfect harmony with every part of his infamous life. **1853** MAURICE *Proph. & Kings* i. 11 The *vox populi* was the *vox Dei* even when the two voices seemed most utterly out of harmony.

2. Agreement of feeling or sentiment; peaceableness, concord. (Sometimes as *fig.* from 4.)

1588 GREENE *Pandosto* (1843) 25 Coveting no other companion but sorrowe, nor no other harmonie but repentance. **1667** MILTON *P.L.* VIII. 605 Harmonie to behold in wedded pair More grateful then harmonious sound to the eare. **1780** COWPER *Progr. Err.* 140 Love, joy, and peace make harmony more meet. **1844** H. H. WILSON *Brit. India* III. 408 The harmony which had thus been re-established with the Court of Baroda.

b. *Harmony Society*: see HARMONIST 4.

1874 J. H. BLUNT *Dict. Sects, Harmony Society*, a community formed in 1805 by..George Rapp, on the principle of having all things common.

3. Combination of parts or details in accord with each other, so as to produce an æsthetically pleasing effect; agreeable aspect arising from apt arrangement of parts.

1650 BULWER *Anthropomet.* 86 To make up the perfect harmony of a Face. **1780** HARRIS *Philol. Enq.* Wks. (1841) 419 How pleasing the harmony between hills and woods, between rivers and lawns? **1879** *Cassell's Techn. Educ.* III. 192 Harmony results from an agreeable contrast.

4. The combination of musical notes, either simultaneous or successive, so as to produce a pleasing effect; melody; music, tuneful sound. (The earliest sense in English; in mod. use more or less associated with sense 5.)

harmony of the spheres: see SPHERE.

c **1384** CHAUCER *H. Fame* III. 306 Songes ful of Armonye. **1413** *Pilgr. Sowle* (Caxton 1483) v. viii. 99 The trees folowed him [Orpheus] and the stremes stoden to heren his armony. **1531** ELYOT *Gov.* I. xx, Dauid..playinge swetelye on a harpe, with his pleasant and perfect harmonie reduced his [Saul's] minde in to his pristinate estate. **1610** SHAKS. *Temp.* III. iii. 18 What harmony is this? my good friends, harke. **1667** MILTON *P.L.* VII. 560 Ten thousand Harpes that tun'd Angelic harmonies. **1756–7** tr. *Keysler's Trav.* (1760) III. 276 Inraptured with the harmony of a choir of angels. **1828** WORDSW. *Power of Sound* xiv, Harmony, blest queen of smiles and tears, With her smooth tones and discords just.

b. *gen.* Pleasing combination or arrangement of sounds, as in poetry or in speaking; sweet or melodious sound.

a **1529** SKELTON *Replyc.* 337 For all his armony In metricall muses. **1632** J. HAYWARD tr. *Biondi's Eromena* 14 Somewhat solaced in hearing the sweete harmony of her name. **1780** COWPER *Table T.* 701 Harmony, strength, words exquisitely sought. **1864** TENNYSON *Milton.* O mighty-mouthed inventor of harmonies. **1876** tr. *Blaserna's Sound* iii. 46 The poets speak often, and not without reason, of the harmony of the waves.

5. *Mus.* The combination of (simultaneous) notes so as to form chords; that part of musical art or science which deals with the formation and relations of chords; the structure of a piece of music in relation to the chords of which it consists.

Distinguished from *melody*, which is the succession of notes forming an air or tune; and, in strict modern use, from *counterpoint*, which is the combination of melodies; but also used of any music in parts, and sometimes in early use synonymous with *counterpoint*.

1526 *Pilgr. Perf.* (W. de W. 1531) 291 They excede or passe all ioyes as moche as armony passeth melody. **1616** BULLOKAR *Eng. Expos.*, *Harmonie*, delightfull musicke of many notes. **1727–51** CHAMBERS *Cycl.* s.v. *Harmonical*, The art of harmony has long been known under the name of counterpoint. **1782** BURNEY *Hist. Mus.* II. 451 Figurative harmony, consisting of three or four different melodies moving together in consonance. **1867** MACFARREN *Harmony* i. 19 Singing in harmony of three parts. **1875** OUSELEY *Mus. Form* i. 2 A knowledge of Harmony and Counterpoint. **1879** MACFARREN *Counterp.* i. (1881) 2 Harmony is the simultaneous sounding of several notes, and includes concords and discords.

6. A collation of passages on the same subject from different writings, arranged so as to exhibit their agreement and account for their discrepancies; now chiefly used of a work showing the correspondences between the four Gospels and the chronological succession of the events recorded in them.

1588 *Marprel. Epist.* (Arb.) 8 The Harmonie of the Confessions of all those Churches..Which Harmonie was translated and printed by..Thomas Thomas. **1607** A. WILLET (*title*) An Harmonie vpon the First Booke of Samvel ..diuers readings compared, [etc.]. **1727–51** CHAMBERS *Cycl.*, *Evangelical harmony*, a title of diverse books, composed to show the uniformity and agreement of the accounts given by the four Evangelists. **1732** HARLEY (*title*) An Essay for composing a Harmony between the Psalms and other parts of Scripture. **1756** J. MACKNIGHT (*title*) Harmony of the four Gospels. **1896** W. F. ADENEY *How to read the Bible* 108 A 'harmony' of the Gospels is an attempt to arrange the several contributions of the four evangelists, so that they shall all fall into their right places in a common story.

7. *Anat.* = HARMONIA.

1615 CROOKE *Body of Man* 443 It..is distinguished from the wedge bone by the bastard seame called a Harmony, which is accounted for the ninth Suture. **1668** CULPEPPER & COLE *Barthol. Anat.* Man. IV. v. 340 There are..in the Skul, also many harmonies, where the bones are joyned together. **1841–71** T. R. JONES *Anim. Kingd.* (ed. 4) 312 A species of 'harmony', as it is technically termed by anatomists—two plates of the skeleton being accurately and immoveably fitted to each other, but without being decidedly fastened together by serrated edges.

harmost (ˈhɑːmɒst). Also 8 **harmoste.** [ad. Gr. ἁρμοστής, f. ἁρμόζειν to fit, settle, regulate.] One of the governors sent out by the Lacedæmonians during their supremacy (after the Peloponnesian war) to control the subject cities and islands.

1775 in ASH. **1797** HOLCROFT *Stolberg's Trav.* (ed. 2) IV. xci. 65 After the battle of Leuctra..the Spartans sent no more Harmostes. **1852** GROTE *Greece* IX. 261 The few details which we possess respecting these harmosts..are all for the most part discreditable. **1873** SYMONDS *Grk. Poets* Ser. I. i. (1877) 27 Her generals and harmosts made use of their authority for the indulgence of their private vices.

harmosty (ˈhɑːməstɪ). [f. prec. + -Y, as if after a Gr. *ἁρμόστεια.] The office of a harmost.

1852 GROTE *Greece* II. lxxiii. IX. 345 Lucrative posts, harmosties and others, all monopolised by the Peers.

†**ˈharmosyn.** *Obs. rare.* [ad. Gr. ἁρμόσυνος (Hesych.) = ἁρμοστής.] = HARMOST. Hence **harmoˈsynian** (*rare*), in same sense.

1594 *Mirr. Policy* (1599) 162 In the Spartane Commonweale they had certain set Officers named Harmosyns, who had in charge to punish the insolencie of women. **1788**

Chambers' Cycl. s.v., Harmosynians were magistrates among the Spartans.

harmotome ('hɑːmətəʊm). *Min.* Also *erron.* **harmotone.** [a. F. *harmotome* (Haüy), f. Gr. ἁρμός joint + -τομος cutting; app. in reference to the fact that the octahedron divides parallel to the plane that passes through the terminal edges.]

A hydrous silicate of aluminium and barium, commonly occurring in cruciform twin crystals of various colours. Also called *cross-stone*.

1804 R. Jameson *Syst. Min.* I. 222 Cross-stone.. Harmotome. Haüy. **1851** Richardson *Geol.* ii. (1855) 25 An especial value was assigned to the mineral *harmotome*, or cross-stone, on account of the sacred emblem of which it was supposed to be the type. **1881** *Cassell's Pop. Educ.* VI. 333 *Harmotome*..being frequently found in twin crystals or macles, so regular as to form in section a Maltese cross.

harn (hɑːn), *sb.*[1] *Obs.* exc. *Sc.* Usually in pl. **harns,** *Sc.* **hairns** (hernz). Forms: 2 **hærnes,** 3–4 **hernes,** 4–5 **harnys,** 4–7 **harnes,** 5 **herns, (hernys, harneys,** 6 **harnis),** 6– **harns,** 8– *Sc.* **hairns.** [Late OE. or early ME. *hærnes*, ME. *hernes*; app. from Norse: cf. ON. *hjarne*, *-ni* wk. masc. (:—**hernon-*, **herznon-*) brain (Sw. *hierna* fem., Da. *hierne*); also OHG. *hirni* (MHG. *herne*, Ger. *hirn*) neut., MLG. *herne*, *harne*, MDu. *herne* fem. and neut., *hersene*, *harsene* fem. (Du., in pl. only, *hersenen*, *hersens*, *har-*), all going back to an orig. neuter **hirzni*, **hirsni*, which subseq. passed into fem. in MDu. The OTeut. **herzn-*, **hersn-*, was co-radicate with Skr. *çîrshn-* head, and Gr. κρανίον skull, perh. also with L. *cerebrum* brain.] Brain; brains.

a **1154** *O.E. Chron.* an. 1137 Me dide cnotted strenges abuton here hæued and uurythen to ðæt it gæde to þe hærnes. *c* **1300** *Havelok* 1808 Was non of hem that his hernes Ne lay ther ute ageyn the sternes. **1303** R. Brunne *Handl. Synne* 5032 Þe harnes lay vpp on þe stone. **1375** Barbour *Bruce* xii. 56 He the hed till harnys claf. *c* **1440** *Promp. Parv.* 237/2 Hernys, or brayne (*S.* harneys), *cerebrum*. **1501** Douglas *Pal. Hon.* iii. lxxxix, My harnis trimblit besily. **1570** Levins *Manip.* 32/39 Harne, *cerebrum*. **1672** *Depos. Cast. York* (Surtees) 187 She did take the ax and knocked her husbands harnes out. **1693** *Scot. Presbyt. Eloq.* (1738) 138 And make the Hairns of these Malignants a Hodge podge. **1828** *Craven Dial.*, *Harns*, brains. **1834** M. Scott *Cruise Midge* (1863) 65 My harns are strangely confused. **1894** Crockett *Raiders* (ed. 3) 375 In ten minutes, that wife's a weedow, an' gatherin' up her man's harns in a napkin.

harn, *a.* and *sb.*[2] Also 6–7 **harne.** [A contracted form of harden *a.* and *sb.*]

A. *adj.* = harden *a.*

1571 *Satir. Poems Reform.* xxix. 17 On sonday his garmont wes of ane harne sek. **1855** Robinson *Whitby Gloss.* s.v., A wide setten harn apron. **1862** Hislop *Prov. Scotl.* 22 As coarse as Nancie's harn sark,—three threads out of the pound.

B. *sb.*[2] = harden *sb.*

1622–3 *Inv.* in *Best's Farm. Bks.* (Surtees) 162 *note*, Six pound and a half of harden harne, and three of femble harne, 4s. **1651** *Carlisle Crt. Leet Rolls* in Ferguson & Nanson *Munic. Rec. Carlisle* (1887) 292 For buying lincloth harne and yarne before the markett bell ring. **1790** Burns *Tam o' Shanter* 171 Her cutty sark, o' Paisley harn. **1793** *Statist. Acc. Scotl.*, *Perthsh.* VI. 236 (Jam.) Weavers who.. manufacture..what they call Harn, and coarse packing cloth. **1806** Forsyth *Beauties Scotl.* IV. 42 Coarse fabrics, provincially called *tweels*, *harns*, and *straikens*.

harness ('hɑːnɪs), *sb.* Forms: 3–5 **harnais,** 4 **hernis,** 4–5 **harnays, hernays, -eys, oys, -es,** 4–6 **harnes,** 4–7 **her-, harneis(e, -eys(e,** 5 **har-, hernas, harnysse, harnoys,** 5–7 **harnesse,** 4– **harness** (6 **-ys, -iss, -ass,** 6–7 **-ish,** 7 **-ois, -ace).** See also irnes(s. [ME., a. OF. *harneis*, *-ois* (*her-*), mod.F. *harnais* (Picard *harnas*), whence also Pr., Sp. *arnes*, Pg. *arnez*, It. *arnese*, med.L. (*h*)*arnesium*, *har-*, *hernasium*, *harnascha*, *harnasch* (neuter). Ulterior origin uncertain: the OF. derived vb. *harnesquier*, *-eschier*, shows that *harneis* represented an earlier **harnesc*, L. type **harniscum*. From the Fr. came also MHG. *harnesch*, *-nasch*, *-nas* (12th c.), Ger. *harnisch* masc.; MDu. *harnas*(*ch*), Du. *harnas* neut.; Icel. *harneskja* fem.

Often assumed to be of Celtic origin, on the strength of mod. Breton *harnez*, *hernez*, (1) old iron, (2) harness, cuirass (Le Gonidec), compared with mod. Welsh *haiarn* iron (OW. *hearn*, OIr. *iarn*:—Proto-Celtic **isarno-*). But Thurneysen, *Keltoromanisches* 36, points out fatal difficulties, phonetic and chronological. Breton *harnez* (in this sense) is prob. from French.

In the obscurity that surrounds the origin of the word, the primary sense and the order of sense-development remain uncertain. Several specific uses appear in Engl. about the same time; and the arrangement here followed is provisional. It seems probable that a general sense of 'equipment, furniture, outfit, gear, tackle', is the original.]

1. Tackle, gear, furniture, armament; the equipment or mounting of any thing; e.g. of a ship, a fishing-rod, the metal-work of a girdle, etc. (*obs.*). Still used of the mechanism by which a large bell is suspended and rung.

[**1294** *Rolls of Parlt.* I. 128/2 Harnesia ad navem illam spectantia. **1333–4** *Durham MS. Cell. Roll*, In.. emendacione hernes del fyschors'. **1423** *Act 2 Hen. VI*, c. 17 Null Orfeour ne Juellour nautre homme qe oepere harneis dargent.] *a* **1450** *Fysshynge w. Angle* (1883) 6 Ye muste furst lurne to mak ȝowr harnes þat ys to sey your rod your lynys ..& your hokes. **1483–4** *Act 1 Rich. III*, c. 12 No..maner Gurdels nor eny Harnes wrought for Gurdels. **1530** Palsgr. 229 Harnesse for a gyrdelle, *ferreure*. **1632** J. Hayward tr. *Biondi's Eromena* 11 A bastard Galley of three and thirty banks..and adorning her with double harnesse, tackling and furniture.

2. a. The defensive or body armour of a man-at-arms or foot-soldier; all the defensive equipment of an armed horseman, for both man and horse; military equipment or accoutrement. *Hist.* or *arch.*

c **1330** R. Brunne *Chron.* (1810) 309 Norreis & Surreis.. With hors & herneis at Carlele mad samnyng. *a* **1450** *Golagros & Gaw.* 566 All the harnes thai hade, Baith birny and breist-plade. **1470–85** Malory *Arthur* ix. xl, Youre harneis & horses haue ben fayre and clene kepte. **1489** Caxton *Faytes of A.* i. i. 2 To make harnoys of yron and steel. **1535** Coverdale *1 Kings* xx. 11 Let not him yᵗ putteth on yᵉ harnes make his boast like him yᵗ hath put it of. **1581** Savile *Tacitus' Hist.* i. lxxix. (1591) 44 A kind of harnish.. composed of iron plates or stiffe bend-lether. **1605** Shaks. *Macb.* v. v. 52 Ring the Alarum Bell, blow Winde, come wracke, At least wee'l dye with Harnesse on our backe. **1606** Holland *Sueton.* Annot. 5 Enoplia was a kinde of Moriske daunce after a warlike manner in harnois. **1611** Bible *1 Kings* xxii. 34 A certain man drew a bow at a venture, and smote the king of Israel betweene the ioynts of the harnesse. *a* **1680** Butler *Rem.* (1759) I. 219 Old Knights-errant in their Harness fought. **1852** Longf. *Warden Cinque Ports* xi, A single warrior, In sombre harness mailed.

fig. **1503** Hawes *Examp. Virt.* xi. (Arb.) 46 Good hope thy legge harneys shall be. **1558** Bp. Watson *Sev. Sacram.* i. 2 Christe..hath armed vs with a seuen fold harnes, that is to say, with the seuen giftes of the holy gost. **1607** Rowlands *Famous Hist.* 54 What scales of Harness arm that crooked nose And teeth? **1835** Lytton *Rienzi* iii. iii, Men who win power, easily put on its harness, dignity. **1857** Lawrence *Guy Liv.* iv. 35 To watch him in his training, and spy out the joints in his harness. [Cf. **1611** above].

b. Phrase, *to harness*: cf. *to arms*.

1475 *Bk. Noblesse* 69 Alle the comyns..[stode]sodanly to harneys and rebelled ayenst the duc of Exetyr. **1548** Hall *Chron.*, *Hen. VII*, 42 b, Cryes were made, every man to harneys.

c. With *a*: A suit of mail: see quot. 1559.

c **1489** Caxton *Sonnes of Aymon* i. 44 Many fayr harneyses shynyng. **1548** *Act 2 & 3 Edw. VI*, c. 2 Preamb., Souldiors well furnished with good Horses and Harnesses. **1559** *Lanc. Wills* I. 153 My soune..shall have one harnys that ys to saye a plate coote or jacke a sallett a payre of speutes and a halbert. **1720** Strype *Stow's Surv.* (1754) II. v. xxxi. 566/2 Such able men as had white Harnesses. **1828** Scott *F.M. Perth* iii, Had the laird not wanted a harness.

†**d.** *transf. pl.* Men in harness; men-at-arms.

? *a* **1400** *Arthur* 314 Than hadde he out of Normandye.. Fowre skore þowsand harneys.

e. (See quot. 1940.) Also called ***ignition harness***.

1938 R. Keen *Wireless Direction Finding* (ed. 3) xiii. 523 To reduce the capacity of the screening of the cables, and to avoid the bulk and inconvenience of large numbers of separately screened leads, the whole wiring system of an engine may be built into a unit known as 'screening harness'. Fig. 405 shows such a harness..for a Bristol 'Pegasus' radial engine. **1940** *Chambers's Techn. Dict.* 404/1 *Harness*, the entire system of screened ignition leads enclosed within their screening tubes to prevent electro-magnetic radiation from affecting the radio-receiving equipment. **1956** W. A. Heflin *U.S.A.F. Dict.* 262/2 *Ignition harness*, a system or assembly of wires, together with any shielding or conduits inclosing them, for conducting electric current from the distributor to the spark plugs of an aircraft engine.

†**3.** The baggage or portable equipment of an army, a party of travellers, etc. *Obs.*

a **1300** *Cursor M.* 11642 Bath ass and ox at wit þam war, And bestes þat þair harnais [*v. rr.* hernays, harneis] bar. *c* **1330** R. Brunne *Chron.* (1810) 236 Þis burgeis..Þe may & hir herneis did led vnto þe kyng. *c* **1380** *Sir Ferumb.* 1748 Oure harneys comeþ her be-hynde wiþ to hundred men araid. *c* **1400** *Rom. Rose* 7477 Whan the pilgrymes commen were..Hir harneis nigh hem was algate.

4. a. The trappings or accoutrements of a horse: formerly including those used in riding, but now confined to the gear or tackle of a draught horse or other animal. 'The traces of draught horses, particularly of carriages of pleasure or state: of other carriages we say *geer*' (J.). ***double harness***, harness for two draught horses working side by side; ***single harness***, harness for a draught horse working alone; ***in harness***, side by side, together. Often *fig.*

1303 R. Brunne *Handl. Synne* 4599 To wynne hors and harnyse. *c* **1350** *Will. Palerne* 4281 No seg vnder heuene.. araiȝed more beter..Of hors & of harneys & alle oþer gere. *c* **1380** *Sir Ferumb.* 3664 Þe sadel..With gold was fret and pretious ston, and þe harneys was of golde. *c* **1440** *Promp. Parv.* 228/1 Harneys for hors, *falere*. **1463** *Bury Wills* (Camden) 34 My beste hors with sadil and brydil, with alle the beste harneys for oon hors longyng therto. **1530** Palsgr. 229/2 Harnesse for the plough horse, *harnoys de cherue*. **1600** Holland *Livy* xxxix. xxxi. 1043 C. Calpurnius.. highly praised the horsemen, and rewarded them with rich harnish and trappings. **1636** Davenant *Witts* Wks. (1673) 215 Another Coach it drives from the Strand! Then have at the Harnace. **1688** R. Holme *Armoury* iii. 336/1 Horses are fastned by their Harnish..to draw the Coach. **1743** *Boston Post-Boy* 28 Nov. 4/1 *Advt.*, A fine open chariot, with the harnesses for two horses. **1824** R. Stuart *Hist. Steam Engine* 22 It then bears itself quietly under the harness, (like good horses). **1834** Medwin *Angler in Wales* II. 39 Wild horses..which had never before been in harness. **1838** *Lexington Observer & Rep.* 2 June, We soon hitch'd traces to trot in double harness. **1846** R. Ford *Gatherings from Spain* viii. 88 Those who have a friend with whom they feel they can venture to go in double harness, had better do so. **1862** *Catal. Internat. Exhib.*, *Brit.* II. No. 4732 Double and single harness, pads, collars, round reins, pole pieces. **1873** 'Mark Twain' & Warner *Gilded Age* 373 He and I are sworn brothers on that measure; we work in harness. **1901** 'M. Gray' *Four-Leaved Clover* i, And it's about time you went in double harness. I go better in single. To confess the solid truth, I was born an old maid. **1907** G. B. Shaw *John Bull's Other Island* i. 20 In the main it is by living with you and working in double harness with you that I have learnt to live in a real world and not in an imaginary one. **1937** D. L. Sayers *Busman's Honeymoon* vii. 152 It was her own feelings that didn't seem to be quite pulling in double harness with her intelligence. **1967** *Listener* 2 Feb. 177/3 Prokofiev enthusiasts will be delighted to see that Milstein has now recorded the two violin concertos in harnesss.

b. *fig.* Working equipments; the conditions, routine, and obligations of regular work. ***in harness***, in the routine of daily work; ***to die in harness***, i.e. in the midst of work.

1841 Thackeray *Gt. Hoggarty Diamond* ii, In early times, before we were well in harness. **1841** Emerson *Lect.*, *Man the Reformer* Wks. (Bohn) II. 237 He must..take on him the harness of routine and obsequiousness. **1868** Holme Lee *B. Godfrey* xvii. 101 Queer pair to run i' harness. **1871** L. Stephen *Playgr. Eur.* xii. (1894) 279 After a holiday, the day on which we resume harness joins on to the day on which we dropped it. **1875** Hamerton *Intell. Life* x. vii. 371 The finest intellects have never lived in harness. **1875** [see die *v.* 3]. **1883** S. C. Hall *Retrospect* I. 193 Palmerston..died, as he had lived, in harness, working to the last. **1889** Baring-Gould *Pennycomequicks* II. xviii. 26 If you insist on going into harness at once, in two years I shall be attending your funeral.

c. From their resemblance to the harness of a horse (see sense 4 a above): straps so arranged that they can be fitted for the protection of travellers in an aeroplane or car. Also used of straps fitted (*a*) on a dog, instead of a collar; (*b*) on a parachute; (*c*) in a perambulator; (*d*) round a child and held by an adult as a safety lead or leash. Also called *safety harness*.

1895 *Montgomery Ward Catal.* 484/2 Pug dog harness, black or russet leather. **1897** H. Dalziel *Brit. Dogs* (ed. 2) III. 43 A kind of dog-harness to mitigate the evils of.. choking by the collar. **1935** C. G. Burge *Compl. Bk. Aviation* 538/1 Safety belts and safety harness have been specially designed for use in aircraft... Harness must hold the wearer firmly in his seat against upward accelerations. **1939** *Sewing Machine & Pram Gaz.*, *Buyers' Guide* Apr. 30 (*caption*) This firm have a very wide selection of reins and safety belts... A typical model of Safety harness is illustrated. **1945** C. H. Ward-Jackson *Piece of Cake* (ed. 2) 38 *Harness*, strap holding one to one's seat in an aircraft. **1951** *Gloss. Aeronaut. Terms* (*B.S.I.*) iii. 13 *Harness*, an assembly of straps or cords worn by a parachutist or employed to suspend an inanimate load to which the parachute is attached. **1962** *Times* 23 Jan. 5/6 Every approved harness [in a motor-car] has a quick-release catch. **1962** *Which?* Jan. 8/1 The buckles of the three harnesses that survived the test crash intact were easy to release. **1963** *B.S.I. News* May 34 Safety harness for babies... The types dealt with will be suitable for attachment to perambulators, push chairs and high chairs. Provision will also be made for use of reins with the harness, when the child is able to walk. **1971** J. Philips *Escape a Killer* (1972) i. ii. 24 She unbuckled the dog's harness. **1972** P. Cleife *Slick & Dead* xviii. 233 Tripping the quick-release of my harness, I leapt from my seat.

5. †**a.** Household and personal equipment; furniture; apparel. *Obs.*

1340 *Ayenb.* 24 Þe diȝtinge of his house wyþ eyse of loste, and oþre manere harneys. *c* **1350** *Will. Palerne* 1582 William ..wel him a-tyred Gayli in cloþes of gold & oþer gode harneis. *c* **1440** *Promp. Parv.* 228/1 Harneys, or hustylment (*K.* instrumentys longynge to howsolde), *utensile*. *c* **1440** *Gesta Rom.* xl. 159 (Harl. MS.) She dude of hir harnes, and come, and laye downe by him. **1511** *Yatton Churchw. Acc.* (Somerset Rec. Soc.) 131 Of Iohn Gurnan for yᵉ Church harnes. **1602** Fulbecke *Pandectes* 47 They had about their harneys certaine yron buttons.

b. Uniform, clothes. ***harness bull, cop***, a policeman in uniform. *U.S. slang* (chiefly *criminals'*).

1891 'Mark Twain' *What is Man?* (1917) 225 At the Metropolitan in New York they sit in a glare, and wear their showiest harness. **1899** B. W. Green *Word-bk. Virginia Folk-Speech* 178 *Harness*,..clothing, dress garments. **1903** A. H. Lewis *Boss* 262 [The] Captain sends along a couple of his harness bulls from Mulberry Street. **1914** Jackson & Hellyer *Vocab. Criminal Slang* 42 *Harness*, general currency. A uniform... A 'harness bull' is the commonest form of the term's use. **1926** J. Black *You can't Win* iv. 31 The 'harness cop' who had been at the front door went back to his beat. *Ibid.* xii. 165 We're bang up against the city prison when a big, flat-footed, harness bull steps out an' yaffles us. **1930** E. H. Lavine *Third Degree* ii. 12 'Wise detectives', who dread going back into 'harness', or uniform, ..sail along the lines of least resistance. **1931** 'D. Stiff' *Milk & Honey Route* iv. 45 Any harness bull can tell you where the municipal lodging house..is to be found. **1972** J. Godey *Three Worlds* (1973) iii. 32 The cops. From the chief on down to the harness bulls.

6. The apparatus in a loom by which the sets of warp-threads are shifted alternately to form the shed; the mounting.

1572 in W. H. Turner *Select. Rec. Oxford* 341 That every weaver have in his house or shop from the summe of 16 bores to the summe of 700 harneyses and slayes, 3 beares betweene every harnys. **1826** in *Patents for Invent.* (1861) 88 (*Weaving*) These healds or harness, when complete, are formed by what I shall term double perfect loops. **1831** G. R. Porter *Silk Manuf.* 216 Heddles, which are commonly called the harness of the loom. **1836** Ure *Cotton Manuf.* (1861) II. 224 The harness of the draw-loom is not confined by leaves but every cord carries a mail or loop for the warp. **1888** EGGLESTON in *Century Mag.* XXXVI. 529/2 When Barbara had tied a broken string in the 'harness' of the loom, she resumed her seat on the bench.

†**7.** Privy members. Also, ***privy harness.*** *Obs.*

1382 WYCLIF *Gen.* ix. 22 The privey herneis of his father. *c* **1386** CHAUCER *Wife's Prol.* 136 Euery wight..That hath swich harneys as I of tolde. **1387** TREVISA *Higden* (Rolls) III. 453 þere [in Nysa] men heleþ her prive herneys wiþ þynne leves. **15..** *Frere & Boye* in Ritson *Anc. Pop. P.* (1791) 45 Unnethes on hym he had one cloute..His harneys for to hyde.

†**8.** Ware, gear; *fig.* affairs, matters. *Obs.*

c **1386** CHAUCER *Pars. T.* ¶900 Why þat a man synneþ as by which temptaciou n or by excitynge of oþer folke..and alle such maner harneys. *c* **1440** *York Myst.* xv. 102 Loo! here slyke harnays as I haue, A baren broche by a belle of tynne At youre bosom to be.

9. *attrib.* and *Comb.*, as (in sense 4) ***harness-boss, -horse, -maker, -polisher, -room, -tie, -work***; (in sense 6) ***harness-board*** (see quot.), ***-cord, -twine***; ***harness-bearing*** adj.; also **harness-clamp** (see quot.); **harness (horse) racing**, a race between horses harnessed to vehicles; also **harness race** (Webster, 1909); †**harness-man** = HARNESS-BEARER, an armour-bearer; **harness-plate**, electroplated metal work used in harness; hence **harness-plater** (see quot.); **harness-tub** = HARNESS-CASK; **harness-weaver** (see quot.).

1590 SPENSER *F.Q.* II. xi. 43 Jove's *harnesse-bearing bird. **1875** KNIGHT *Dict. Mech.*, **Harness-board*, the compass-board of a loom, having holes through which pass the neck twines. **1852** DICKENS *Bleak Ho.* lxvi, The polishing..of stirrup-irons, bits, curb-chains, *harness-bosses. **1875** KNIGHT *Dict. Mech.*, **Harness-clamp* (Saddlery), a kind of vice used to hold leather while being stitched. **1836** URE *Cotton Manuf.* (1861) II. 224 The *harness cords of a draw-loom. **1861** WALSH & LUPTON *Horse* xv. 272 Hacks and *Harness-horses demand nearly as much time and care to prepare them for their work. **1889** DK. BEAUFORT *Driving* (Badm. Libr.) 74 A harness horse in regular work ought to be fed four times a day. **1853** C. MORFIT *Tanning, etc.* 152 '*Harness' leather is blackened in the grain. **1611** COTGR., *Armorier*, an armorer, or *Harnesse-maker. **1889** DK. BEAUFORT *Driving* (Badm. Libr.) 94 It is adviseable..for the harness-maker to see the horse he is required to fit with a collar. **1530** PALSGR. 229/2 *Harnesman, *armigere.* **1858** SIMMONDS *Dict. Trade*, **Harness-plater*, a workman who electro-plates the metal work for harness. **1901** *World Almanac* 266 *Harness racing. **1909** *Ibid.* 213 Harness horse racing. **1947** *Newsweek* 8 Sept. 71/1 Harness racing is doing very well in keeping up with the flashy bankrolls of the times. **1968** *Globe & Mail* (Toronto) 3 Feb. 36/2 About the only sure thing in harness racing is that Russ Miller..will come up with something special each year. *Ibid.* 17 Feb. 44 (Advt.), Nine harness races today. **1971** *Guardian* 9 June 6/5 Trotting or harness racing, which has become a major sporting attraction in Australia and the United States, is making a comeback in its place of origin, the Yorkshire dales and fells. **1889** DK. BEAUFORT *Driving* (Badm. Libr.) 89 The *harness-room should be provided with a fireplace or some kind of stove. **1858** SIMMONDS *Dict. Trade*, **Harness Weavers*, operatives employed in Paisley in weaving the more complicated patterns of shawls. *Mod.* Horses for quiet *Harness-work.

Hence **'harnessry** *rare*, harness collectively; **'harnessy** *a. colloq.*, smacking of harness.

1824 WIFFEN *Tasso* VII. lxxxii, With chariots, harnessries, and helms. **1892** *Field* 14 May 729/1 She [a mare] seemed a bit heavy about the neck, and 'harnessy'.

'harness, *v.* Forms: *α.* 4 harneyschen, 4–6 -esch(en, 6 harnisch. *β.* 4–5 harneyse(n, -eise(n, -ayse(n, -esse(n, -as(se(n, hernays, 5–6 harnys(e, -es, 5–7 -ass, 6 -esse, 7 -ise, 6– harness. [In form *harnesche*, a. OF. *harneschier* (12th c. in Hatz.-Darm.), Picard *harnesquier*, later *harnaskier*, *harnascher*, *harnacher* (Rom. type **harnescāre*, cf. Pr. *arnescar*), f. *harnesc-*, OF. *harneis* HARNESS. The *β.* forms are formed from, or conformed to, the sb.]

†**1.** To furnish, equip, accoutre; esp. to mount, or ornament with fittings of some precious material.

c **1380** *Sir Ferumb.* 3665 Brydel and paytrel and al þe gere Wiþ fyn gold y-harneysed were. *c* **1386** CHAUCER *Prol.* 114 A gay daggere, Harneised wel and sharpe as point of spere. *c* **1400** MAUNDEV. (Roxb.) XIX. 86 Brade gyrdils of silke, wele hernayst with gold and preciouse stanes. **1418** *E.E. Wills* (1882) 34 My Baselard harneysed with siluer. **1470–85** MALORY *Arthur* VIII. xxxiv, A fayre horse harnest with gold. **1534** *Eng. Ch. Furniture* (1866) 193, ij verges paynted made for the chamberlaynes harneseid at bothe endes with syluer. **1877** *Jrnl. Archæol. Inst.* XXXIV. 300 [Wooden drinking-cups] hooped and mounted or 'harnessed' in silver.

2. a. To equip in 'harness' or armour; to arm, to accoutre. *arch.*

13.. *Gaw. & Gr. Knt.* 592 So harnayst as he watz he herknez his masse. **1375** BARBOUR *Bruce* IX. 710 [Thai] schot furth, fra thai harnast war. *c* **1380** *Sir Ferumb.* 2929 Harneyscheaþ 3ow with-oute lette. *c* **1440** *York Myst.* xxviii. 195 Both armed and harneysed 3e be. *c* **1537** *Thersites* in Hazl. *Dodsley* I. 395 When I am harnessed well. **1682** BUNYAN *Holy War* 46 Harness yourselves for the war. **1868** FREEMAN *Norm. Conq.* II. ix. 324 Their decks were thick with warriors harnessed for the battle.

fig. **1531** TINDALE *Exp. 1 John* (1537) 79 They..harnesse themselues with the meditacyon of those thinges which Christ suffered. **1547** BOORDE *Introd. Knowl.* xiii. (1870) 156 Now am I harnest, and redy, Doche for to speke. **1556** J. OLDE tr. *Gualter's Antichrist* 36 The Leoparde..hade foure winges, and was harnessed wyth as many hornes.

†**b.** To equip (a place) defensively; to fortify.

1611 BIBLE *Macc.* iv. 7 They saw the campe of the heathen, that is was strong, and well harnessed.

3. To put harness on (a horse or other beast of burden or draught); now confined to draught animals, *esp.* carriage-horses, and the like. Also *fig.*, now chiefly to utilize (a river, waterfall, natural forces, atomic energy) for motive power.

13.. *K. Alis.* 4708 He dude quyk harnesche hors, And sette theron heore cors. **1483** *Cath. Angl.* 176/1 To Harnes, *epiphiare, falerare.* **1530** PALSGR. 579/2 Be your horses harnessed yet? it is tyme to go to ploughe. **1535** COVERDALE *Jer.* xlvi. 4 Yee harnesse youre horses, & set youre selues vpon them. **1684** *Scanderbeg Rediv.* iv. 54 Followed by above 200 of the Lords..all splendidly Array'd, and their Horses extraordinarily Harnessed. **1715–20** POPE *Iliad* XXIV. 990 The Trojan train Their mules and oxen harness to the wain. **1890** MISS BROUGHTON *Alas!* III. 285, I should like to buy a little cart to harness him to.

absol. **1864** CARLYLE *Hist. Fredk. Gt.* XVII. iv. IV. 548 Mitchell was harnessing for Potsdam.

fig. **1698** FRYER *Acc. E. India & P.* 115 Others that are harness'd with the Apron-strings of Trade. **1775** SHERIDAN *Rivals* I. i, I wish they were once harnessed together in matrimony. **1856** DOVE *Logic Chr. Faith* I. ii. 72 Philosophy ..must..harness herself and work. **1894** *Westm. Gaz.* 5 Dec. 3/1 We may any day have news flashed to us by cable that Niagara is harnessed, and its stupendous power brought into ordinary commercial uses. **1927** A. CHRISTIE *Big Four* xvii. 258, I believe that she has, to a certain extent, succeeded in liberating atomic energy and harnessing it to her purpose. **1935** *Discovery* Feb. 41/1 The business of harnessing cosmic rays, of forcing them to do the work of electricity, is proceeding apace. **1955** *Times* 19 May 3/6 This monster is, of course, the huge underwater vessel Nautilus ..propelled by 'the dynamic force of the universe', which somehow he has succeeded in harnessing. **1965** *Listener* 3 June 823/1 This seems..to make sense: harnessing individual and group enthusiasm to enrich the region.

†**4.** To dress, clothe, apparel, array. *Obs.* or *arch.*

c **1400** *Rom. Rose* 2647 Ryse on morwe up erly, Out of thy bedde, and harneyse thee. **1467** *Eng. Gilds* (1870) 408 Alle the hole crafte, shallen wayte vppon the seid Baillies..in ther best arraye harnesid. **1562** J. HEYWOOD *Prov. & Epigr.* (1867) 90 A goose is harnest in hir white fethers. **1647** TRAPP *Comm. Matt.* vi. 7 With two [wings] they covered or harnessed their feet. **1848** KINGSLEY *Saint's Trag.* IV. i, I am harnessed light as any foot-page.

Hence **'harnessing** *vbl. sb.*; also *concr.* trappings, accoutrement. **'harnesser**, one who harnesses.

1596 DALRYMPLE tr. *Leslie's Hist. Scot.* VIII. 129 Certane horssis..harnest wᵗ braue harnessings. **1611** COTGR., *Harnacheur*, a harnesser of a horse. **1796** MORSE *Amer. Geog.* II. 35 The deer, whose harnessing is very simple. **1837** DICKENS *Pickw.* ix, The whole process of harnessing had to be gone through afresh.

† **'harness-bearer.** *Obs.* An armour-bearer.

1563 W. FULKE *Meteors* (1640) 31 *note*, The Eagle, Jupiters harnesse-bearer. **1581** MARBECK *Bk. of Notes* 338 The Philistines..were ouercome of Jonathas and his harnesse-bearer. **1611** SPEED *Hist. Gt. Brit.* v. vi. §12. 34 His seruant and harnesse-bearer.

'harness-cask. *Naut.* A cask or tub with a rimmed cover used on board ship (and in Australia) for keeping the salt meats for present consumption. Also *harness-tub* (see HARNESS *sb.* 9).

1818 *Aberd. Jrnl.* 2 Dec. (Jam.), Some thieves..breaking open a harness cask on deck, stole about one cwt. of beef. **1840** R. H. DANA *Bef. Mast* xxx. 109 Before any of the beef is put into the harness-cask. **1867** SMYTH *Sailor's Word-bk.*, *Harness-cask*, a large conical tub for containing the salt provisions intended for present consumption. **1889** BOLDREWOOD *Robbery under Arms* (1890) 12 Father..began to look at the harness-cask, which stood in a little back skillion.

harnessed ('hɑːnɪst), *ppl. a.* [f. HARNESS *v.*]

†**1.** Furnished, equipped; mounted with silver or other metal. *Obs.*

1426 *E.E. Wills* (1882) 76 A swerd harnesed, a wodeknyf harnesed. **1478** *Churchw. Acc. Croscombe* (Somerset Rec. Soc.) 20 A harneyste gyrdell. **1538** *Bury Wills* (Camden) 136 One harnest gyrdyll callyd a dymysent blacke sylke.

†**2.** Armed, in armour. *Obs.*

c **1460** *Launfal* 377 Ten well yharneysyth men. **1530** PALSGR. 231/1 Hernyst man, *homme darmes.* **1595** SHAKS. *John* v. ii. 132 This harness'd Maske, and vnaduised Reuell. **1658** BROMHALL *Treat. Specters* II. 163 The Ægyptians, until that time, had never seen an harnessed Souldier. **1679** CROWNE *Ambit. Statesm.* I. 5 Nature..Doe's alwaies leave some tender place unguarded, About unmatchable vast harnest animals.

3. Yoked, in harness.

1483 *Cath. Angl.* 176/2 Harnessed, *faleratus.* **1596** SHAKS. *1 Hen. IV*, III. i. 221 The houre before the Heauenly Harneis'd Teeme Begins his Golden Progresse in the East. **1725** POPE *Odyss.* xv. 56 Join the harnessed coursers to the car. **1887** BOWEN *Virg. Æneid* III. 113 Hence are the harnessed lions that trail their sovereign's throne.

4. harnessed antelope, a West African antelope, *Tragelaphus scriptus*, whose markings present the appearance of a set of small harness. Also called *bushbuck*.

c **1789** *Encycl. Brit.* IV. 149/1 The scipta or harnessed antelope..has straight horns nine inches long, pointing backwards. **1893** LYDEKKER *Horns & Hoofs* 250 The typical harnessed antelopes are small and elegant animals. **1899** H. A. BRYDEN *Great & Small Game of Africa* 453 (*heading*) The bushbucks. Genus Tragelaphus. The harnessed antelopes, or bushbucks,..may be arranged as follows:— A... 1. The Bongo (*T. euryceros*). 2. The Nyala (*T. angasi*)... 3. West African Bushbuck (*T. gratus*). 4. Situtunga (*T. Spekei*)... 5. Lesser Bushbuck (*T. scriptus*). The last is represented by several local races. **1960** *Times* (Nigeria Suppl.) 29 Sept. p. xxi/4 The bushbuck, also called harnessed antelope from the pattern of white stripes on its coat, remains widespread.

† **'harnessment.** *Obs.* = HARNESS *sb.* 2.

1610 HOLLAND *Camden's Brit.* I. 174 To euery Knight he allowed..100 shillings for his harnessements.

harnish, -ois, etc., obs. ff. HARNESS.

harn-pan. *Sc.* and *north. dial.* Also 6 *erron.* **hardyn-.** [HARN *sb.*¹] The skull, the brain-pan.

a **1300** *Cursor M.* 7277 His hernpan [*Gött.* harn panne] he brak wit chance. **1340** HAMPOLE *Pr. Consc.* 5298 þe thornes hym prikked til þe harnpane. *c* **1440** *Promp. Parv.* 237/1 Herne panne of þe hed, *craneum.* **1549** *Compl. Scot.* xvii. 154, I am leukand gyf i can fynd my fathers hardyn pan amang thir dede mennis banis. **1613** T. POTTS *Disc. Witches* (1845) K b, He is naild sore by the heart and hand, And holy harne Panne. **1821** *Joseph the Book-Man* 18 He'd swear the harnpans he'd knock in, Of fools who would persist in jokin'. **1828** *Craven Dial.*, *Harn-Pan*, the skull.

b. (Sense obscure.)

a **1400–50** *Alexander* 1713 A ball..þe barne with to play A herne-pann es of a berne of brende gold [*cancram auream*] yeuen. *Ibid.* 1895 þe herne-pan, þe hand-ball þe hatt made of twiggis.

harns *sb. pl.*, brains: see HARN.

harnser, dial. form of HERONSEW.

haro: see HARROW *v.*², HARROW *int.*

haroer, obs. form of HARRIER¹, HARROWER.

harold, var. of HARELD (duck).

harold(e, -rood, -rotte, obs. ff. HERALD.

haron, harow(e, obs. ff. HERON, ARROW.

1426 *Surtees Misc.* (1888) 4 Certayn peces in shappe and fourme of harowes. *c* **1475** *Pict. Voc.* in Wr.-Wülcker 812/37 *Hec sagitta*, a harow.

haroses, haroset(h, varr. CHAROSET(H.

harow(e, obs. ff. HARROW *sb.*, *v.* and *int.*

harp (hɑːp), *sb.*¹ Forms: 1 hearpe, (hærpe), (2 herpe, 3 hearpe), 3–7 harpe, 4– harp. [Com. Teut.: OE. *hearpe* = OLG. **harpa*, MDu. *harpe* (Du. *harp*), OHG. *harpha, harfa*, (Ger. *harfe*), ON., Sw. *harpa*, Da. *harpe*:—OTeut. **harpôn-*. Thence late L. *harpa* and derived Romanic words.]

1. a. A stringed musical instrument, which, in its usual form, consists of a framework of wood fitted with a series of strings of definite lengths which are played with the fingers, (or, in some earlier types, with a plectrum). Also *spec.* one used by Anglo-Saxon minstrels.

The modern harp is roughly triangular in form and furnished with pedals for raising the tone of the strings by a semitone, in double-action harps by two semitones.

c **825** *Vesp. Psalter* xxxii[i]. 2 In hearpan ten strenga singað him. *c* **1000** ÆLFRIC *Gen.* xxxi. 27 Mid timpanum and mid hearpum. *c* **1175** *Lamb. Hom.* 97 He [David] on 3eo3oþe herpan lufede. *c* **1290** *S. Eng. Leg.* I. 23/127 þe harpe he heng vp bi þe wouh. **1382** WYCLIF *Gen.* iv. 21 Tubal..was the fadre of syngerys in harp and orgon. **1535** COVERDALE *Ps.* xcvi[i]. 5 Prayse the Lorde vpon the harpe, synge to the harpe with a psalme of thanksgeuynge. **1667** MILTON *P.L.* VII. 258 They..touch't thir Golden Harps. **1767** PERCY *Ess. Anc. Eng. Minstrels* 9 In the early times it was not unusual for a Minstrel to have a servant to carry his harp. **1791** COWPER *Odyss.* VIII. 301 Our pleasures are the feast, the harp, the dance. **1807** ROBINSON *Archæol. Græca* II. xvii. 174 The harp originally consisted of four strings, to which Terpander added other three. **1807** S. TURNER *Hist. Anglo-Saxons* (ed. 2) II. 407 Of the harp, Bede mentions, that in all festive companies it was handed round, that every one might sing in turn. **1889** RUSKIN *Præterita.* III. 166 The harp is the true ancient instrument of Scotland, as well as of Ireland. **1898** S. A. BROOKE *Eng. Lit. fr. Beginnings to Norman Conq.* iv. 82 We should place ourselves..in the hall..when the benches are filled..and hear the Shaper strike the harp to sing this heroic lay. **1903** L. F. ANDERSON *Anglo-Saxon Scop* 36 The harp was the instrument most used by the scop. **1942** J. C. POPE *Rhythm of Beowulf* 91 If the harp were keeping time, the voice might omit the first accent of a verse.. without causing the slightest confusion. **1957** *Rev. Eng. Stud.* VIII. 7 The clear song of the bard is accompanied by the music of the harp.

fig. **1704** POPE *Windsor For.* 280 Where Cowley strung His living harp. **1781** COWPER *Retirement* 325 Man is a harp whose chords elude the sight, Each yielding harmony, disposed aright. **1784** —— *Task* VI. 747 Sweet is the harp of prophecy. **1842** TENNYSON *Locksley Hall* 33 Love took up the harp of Life, and smote on all the chords with might.

b. ***double harp***: one having two sets or rows of strings differently tuned. ***triple harp***: one with three such sets. ***Æolian harp***: see ÆOLIAN 2.

1552 HULOET, Double harpe, called a roote, *barbitos.* **1880** STAINER & BARRETT *Dict. Mus. T.*, *Double harp.*

c. A representation of a harp.

1785 GROSE *Dict. Vulg. Tongue* s.v., Harp is also the Irish expression for woman, or tail, used in tossing up in Ireland, from Hibernia being represented with a harp, on the reverse of the copper coins of that country. **1843** *Q. Rev.* Sept. 586 A small volume under the title of the 'Spirit of the Nation', with a vignette emblem of the harp without the Crown. **1873** BOUTELL *Her. Anc. & Mod.* 158 *Harp*..headed with the upper part of a winged angel—originally called a Welsh harp. It is the national device of Ireland, and it is borne in the Irish quarter of the Royal arms.

d. Also **mouth harp** = MOUTH-ORGAN, harmonica. *colloq.* (orig. *U.S.*).

1887 *Scribner's Mag.* Oct. 481/1 She displayed a flimsy red silk handkerchief and a child's harp. **1903** ADE *In Babel* 40 I'd walked from Loueyville over to Terry Hut with a nigger that played the mouth harp. **1963** *Amer. Speech* XXXVIII. 246 *Harp* or *mouth harp* 'harmonica'. **1965** *Melody Maker* 10 July 12/6 For the best blues sound you have to..play the harp in a transposed manner.

e. An Irishman. *U.S. slang.*

1904 'No. 1500' *Life in Sing Sing* xiii. 249/1 *Harp*, an Irishman. **1926** T. BEER *Mauve Decade* iv. 162, I sewed up his head for a young Italamerican who had been trying to impress the haughty Harps on his street. **1936** J. DOS PASSOS *Big Money* 75 The foreman was a big loudmouthed harp.

†**2.** Phr. ***to agree** (etc.) **like harp and harrow***: not to agree at all (the things being utterly different, though their names alliterate). *Obs.*

1563 BECON *Displ. Pop. Masse* (1637) 299 The Lords Supper and your peevish, popish private masse doe agree together..as the common proverbe is, like harpe and harrow, or like the hare and the hound. **1624** GATAKER *Transubst.* 203 These things hang together like harp and harrow, as they say. **1700** T. BROWN tr. *Fresny's Amusem. Ser. & Com.* 34 [Bethlehem] Bedlam..whether the Name and Thing be not as disagreeable as Harp and Harrow?

3. The northern constellation Lyra.

1551 RECORDE *Cast. Knowl.* (1556) 264 An other constellation, whiche is called the Harpe. **1697** CREECH *Manilius* v. II. 67 Next shines the Harp. **1839** *Penny Cycl.* XIV. 225/2 Lyra (the Harp), one of the old constellations, representing the lyre of Mercury..or of Orpheus.

†**4.** The name given to two Irish coins bearing the figure of a harp. **a.** = *harp-groat*: see 8. **b.** Short for *harp-shilling*: see 8 and HARPER¹ 2. *Obs.*

1542 RECORDE *Gr. Artes* (1575) 198 There is an other Grote called a Harpe, which goeth for 3*d.* **1561** *Proclam.* in *15th Rep. Hist. MSS. Comm.* App. III. 122 The said pece called the Reade Harpe shalbe taken and receyved onely for and at two pence currant of this realme. **1606** J. ROWLEY in *Lismore Papers* Ser. II. (1887) I. 90, I..desired you to be pleased to make me over 100ˡⁱ in harpes.

5. Applied to various mechanical contrivances: **a.** A screen or sieve used in sifting and cleansing grain from weed-seeds, etc. *Sc.* **b.** An oblong frame filled up with parallel wires and used as a screen for sifting sand, coal, etc. *Sc.* **c.** *Cotton Manuf.* 'A concave grating in a scutching-machine through which the refuse falls as the cotton is driven forward by the revolving beater' (Knight *Dict. Mech.* 1875).

1768 *Specif. Patent* No. 896 A wire harpe which sifts out all the gross sand, dust, small wheat, etc. **1788** *Patent* No. 1645 Harp for separating the straw from the corn. **1830** *Mechanic's Mag.* XIV. 162 The year following [1795] he introduced..what he denominated *plain harps*, to receive the straw as it fell from the shaker and give it also a shaking motion. **1897** *Alloa Jrnl.* 24 July 3 He was threatening [him] for not giving him his harp (a riddle for coals).

6. Also ***harp-shell***: A mollusc of the genus *Harpa* of family *Buccinidæ*, and its shell.

1751 SIR J. HILL *Hist. Anim.* 150 Harp Shell. **1837** *Penny Cycl.* IX. 455/2 The genus [Harpa]..is more especially abundant at the Mauritius and the neighbouring islands, whence the finest of the more common species and the many-ribbed harps are procured. *Ibid.*, The most precious ..is the Many-ribbed Harp (*Harpa imperialis*). **1863** WOOD *Nat. Hist.* III. 373 The general colours are tolerably similar throughout the Harps, but each species always preserves its peculiar individuality. *Ibid.* 377 The Harp-shells are only found in the hottest seas.

7. Also ***harp-seal***: The Greenland seal: so called from the harp-shaped dark marking on the back.

1784 PENNANT *Arctic Zool.* 165 The Newfoundland Seal-hunters call it the *Harp, or Heart* Seal, and name the marks on the sides the saddle. **1847** CARPENTER *Zool.* §202 The *Greenland*, or *Harp Seal*, is remarkable for the changes of colour which it undergoes. **1854** *Chamb. Jrnl.* I. 76 Four varieties..the young *harp* and young *hood*, the old *harp* and the *bedlamer*, or old *hood*. **1885** *Boston* (Mass.) *Jrnl.* 25 Apr. 2/3 Steamer Ranger..returned to St. John's with 35,600 prime young harps.

8. *attrib.* and *Comb.*, as ***harp-form, -maker, -note, -player, -solo, -twanging, -woman; harp-fingering, -like, -shaped*** adjs.; ***harp-wise*** adv.; **harp-file**, a wire hook for filing papers, attached to a harp-shaped piece of iron (Funk); **harp-fish**, a fish of the genus *Lyra*, the Piper; †**harp-groat**, an Irish coin having the figure of a harp on the reverse; **harp-lute** (see quot.); **harp-master, -mistress**, a teacher of harp-playing; **harp-seal**: see sense 7; **harp-shell**: see sense 6; †**harp-shilling**, an Irish coin having the figure of a harp on the reverse: see HARPER¹ 2; †**harp-star**, Vega, the chief star in Lyra. Also HARP-STRING.

1661 LOVELL *Hist. Anim. & Min.* 233 *Harp fish hath a hard and dry flesh, yet sweet enough if eaten boiled with vinegar. **1753** CHAMBERS *Cycl. Supp.* s.v. *Lyra*, The lyra cornuta or horned harp fish..a fish of an octangular form, covered all over with long scales. **1543** in O'Curry *Mann. Anc. Irish* (1873) III. 274 An hundred pounds sterling in *harp grotes. **1861** J. S. ADAMS *5000 Mus. Terms*, **Harp-Lute*, an instrument having twelve strings and resembling the guitar. *c* **1515** *Cocke Lorell's B.* (Percy) 10 *Harpe makers, leches, and upholsters. **1819** *Hermit in Lond.* II. 185 That gentleman is my daughter's *harp-master. **1852** MISS MITFORD *Recollect* II. 101 The dismissal of the poor little *harp-mistress. **1813** SCOTT *Trierm.* I. v, Had a *harp-note sounded here, It had caught my watchful ear. **1591** *Fearf. Effects 2 Comets* (Halliw.), *Harpe shillings shall not passe for twelvepence. *a* **1592** GREENE *Jas. IV*, III. ii. (Rtldg.) 204/2 What shall I be, then? faith, a plain harp-shilling. **1601** HOLLAND *Pliny* XVIII. xxvi. I. 590 The Dolphin star riseth in the morning, and the morrow after, the *Harp-star Fidicula. **1626** BACON *Sylva* §223 You may try it without any sound board along, but only *Harp-wise, at one end of the strings.

†**harp** *sb.*² In 7 **harpe**. = HARPY 4. *Obs.*

1671 H. M. tr. *Colloquies Erasmus* 514 The Ducks and Seaguls, the Harpe and the Buzzard..The Harpe and the Kite against the Buzzard.

harp, *v.* [OE. *hearpian*, f. HARP *sb.*¹ Cf. MDu., Du. *harpen*, MHG. *harpfen*, Ger. *harfen*.]

1. *intr.* To play on a harp.

c **888** K. ÆLFRED *Boeth.* xxxv. §6 He mihte hearpian þæt þe wudu wagode. *c* **1205** LAY. 20311 He cuðen harpien wel an his child-haden. **1377** LANGL. *P. Pl.* B. XVIII. 405 Many hundreth of angeles harpeden and songen. **1525** *Tale of Basyn* 82 in Hazl. *E.P.P.* III. 47 He harpys and gytryns and syngs well ther-too. **1629** MILTON *Nativity* 115 The helmed cherubim, And sworded seraphim..Harping in loud and solemn quire. **1879** BUTCHER & LANG *Odyss.* 208 Among them harped the divine minstrel Demodocus.

2. *fig.* ***to harp upon, on** (†**of**), **a, one, the same** (etc.) **string***: to repeat a statement or dwell on a subject to a wearisome or tedious length.

1513 MORE in Grafton *Chron.* (1568) II. 773 The Cardinall made a countenaunce to the Lord Haward that he should harpe no more upon that string. *c* **1526** FRITH *Disput. Purgat.* (1829) 117 See how he harpeth all of one string. **1625** *Gonsalvio's Sp. Inquis.* 13 They are sure still harping on their old string. **1685** *Refl. Baxter* 25 He harps much upon that jarring String. **1837** CARLYLE *Fr. Rev.* II. v. vi. (1872) 198 Harping mainly on the religious string.

3. Hence, ***to harp on, upon,** (†**of, about**)*: to dwell wearisomely upon in speech or writing.

1562 *Apol. Priv. Masse* (1850) 19 The great matter you harp on. **1602** SHAKS. *Ham.* II. ii. 189 Still harping on my daughter. **1634** SIR T. HERBERT *Trav.* 103 This word revenge he still harpt upon. **1712** STEELE *Spect.* No. 504 ⁋2 Ever harping upon things they ought not to allude to. **1837** DISRAELI *Venetia* II. x, Still harping of her father.

b. ***harp on*** (intr.): to continue harping.

1856 MISS YONGE *Daisy Chain* II. xii, 'It would be a comfort', harped on Mr. Rivers, dwelling on the subject.

†**4.** *trans.* To play (notes, etc.) upon a harp. *Obs.*

a **1300** *Cursor M.* 7430 (Gött.) Harpand a sang bifor þe king. *c* **1320** *Sir Tristr.* 572 He..harpeþ notes swete. **1483** CAXTON *Gold. Leg.* 172 b/1 An harpe on whiche..he wold harpe anthemes. **1526** TINDALE *1 Cor.* xiv. 7 Howe shall it be knowen what is pyped or harped? **1777** WARTON *Ode* x. Poems 67 A tale..Never yet in rime enroll'd, Nor sung, nor harp'd in hall and bower.

b. To render in verse, to 'sing'.

1808 J. BARLOW *Columb.* VIII. 322 What avails To harp for you these known familiar tales?

†**5.** *trans.* To play upon, twang (a string, etc.).

1628 GAULE *Pract. The.* (1629) 44 The Promise made, the Prophets harpe the string.

b. *fig.* (*intr.*). To 'play' (*upon*). *rare.*

1830 GEN. P. THOMPSON *Exerc.* (1842) I. 228 They fear the orators who harp upon the bad passions of the people.

6. *intr.* To make a sound like that of the harp.

1657 S. PURCHAS *Pol. Flying-Ins.* 59 Yet shall you hear them if you listen in an evening harping like Mise (as if Mise were gnawing on every side). **1823** BYRON *Island* II. xviii, No dying night-breeze, harping o'er the hill.

7. *trans.* To give voice to, to guess.

1605 SHAKS. *Macb.* IV. i. 74 Thou hast harp'd my feare aright. **1818** SCOTT *Br. Lamm.* iv, The old dame had..harped aright the fear of the Lord Keeper. **1821** BYRON *Sardan* II. i. 420 Thou hast harp'd the truth indeed!

†**b.** *intr.* ***to harp at***: To guess at. *Obs.*

1611 COTGR. s.v. *Taston, Parler à taston*, to speake by ghesse or coniecture, onely to harpe at the matter. **1670** MILTON *Hist. Eng.* IV. Wks. (1851) 178 Rugged names of places unknown, better harp'd at in Camden, and other Chorographers.

8. *trans.* To bring *out of, into*, a place or state by playing on the harp.

a **1529** SKELTON *Replyc.* 341 At his resurrection he harped out of hell Olde patriarkes and prophetes in heuen with him to dwell. *a* **1800** *Glenkindie* in Jamieson *Pop. Ballads* (1806) I. 91 He'd harpit a fish out o' saut water, Or water out o' a stane. *a* **1828** *Water o' Wearie's Well* in Buchan *Anc. Ballads*, He's harped them all asleep. **1871** TENNYSON *Last Tourn.* 328 He could harp his wife up out of Hell.

harpacticid (hɑːˈpæktɪsɪd). *Zool.* [f. Gr. ἁρπακτικ-ός rapacious + -ID³.] One of the family Harpacticidæ, tiny copepod crustacea. Also as *adj.*

1909 G. SMITH in *Cambr. Nat. Hist.* IV. iii. 62 *Euterpe acutifrons*..exhibits the structure of a typical Harpacticid. **1932** *Discovery* Sept. 287/2 The Cyclopids and Harpacticids are, of course, represented in ponds and streams on the surface. **1957** *New Biol.* XXIV. 70 Yet other free-living copepods belong to the group called harpacticids. **1961** J. GREEN *Biol. Crustacea* iii. 45 Some crustaceans (e.g. harpacticid copepods) do not have a heart.

harpacticoid (hɑːˈpæktɪkɔɪd). *Zool.* [f. as prec. + -OID.] One of the order Harpacticoida, very small worm-like copepod crustacea. Also as *adj.*

1946 *Nature* 28 Dec. 935/1 Its [sc. *Bathynella*'s] habitat..is analogous to that of the interstitial harpacticoid copepods. **1952** J. CLEGG *Freshwater Life Brit. Isles* xii. 176 There are about forty-six species of Harpacticoids in Britain. **1956** *Nature* 11 Feb. 289/2 The sample contained..one harpacticoid copepod and numerous nematodes. **1961** J. GREEN *Biol. Crustacea* v. 72 There may be one sac, as in many calamoids and harpacticoids, or two sacs as in most cyclopoids. **1970** *Nature* 24 Oct. 323/2 These fish use their gill rakers to strain off the minute animals such as harpacticoid copepods.

†**harpagon.** *Obs.* [ad. L. *harpago, -ōnem*, f. Gr. ἁρπάγη grappling-hook.] A grappling-hook.

1553 BRENDE *Q. Curtius* F v, Certaine instrumentes where-with they myght pul downe the workes that their enemies made, called Harpagons. [**1600** HOLLAND *Livy* 746 (R.) Yron hookes at the end (which the souldiers call *harpagones*) for to take hold upon the Roman ships.]

†**harped**, *a.* *Obs.* [f. HARP *sb.*¹ + -ED².] Having a harp; bearing the figure of a harp, as ***harped groat*** = *harp-groat*: see HARP *sb.* 8.

1547 BOORDE *Introd. Knowl.* iii. (1870) 133 In Irlond they haue Irysh grotes, & harped grotes, & Irysh pens.

harper¹ (ˈhɑːpə(r)). Forms: 1 harperi, hearpere, herpere, herperi, 3 harpare, 4–5 -or, -our, 5 -owre, -ure, herper, 6 harpar, 4- harper. [OE. *hearpere* = MHG. *harpfære*, ON. *harpari*:—OTeut. type **harparjo-z*, f. *harpôn-* HARP *sb.*¹: see -ER¹. ME. had also the AFr. form *harpour* = F. *harpeur*, OF. *harpeor*, late L. *harpātōr-em*.]

1. a. One who harps or plays upon a harp.

a **800** *Leiden Gloss.* 147 in Sweet *O.E. Texts* 115 *Fidicen*, harperi. *c* **888** K. ÆLFRED *Boeth.* xxx. §6 Ðæs hearperes wif. **1297** R. GLOUC. (1724) 272 Menestral he was gode ynou, & harpare in eche poynte. **13..** *E.E. Allit. P.* A. 880 As harporez harpen in her harpe, þat nwe songe þay songen ful cler. **1413** *Pilgr. Sowle* (Caxton 1483) v. viii. 99 The poete Orpheus was so swete an harpoure that the trees folowed him. **1483** *Cath. Angl.* 176/2 An Harper, *citharedo.* **1580** *Nottingham Rec.* IV. 194 Gevyn to the blynde harpar xij*d.* **1662** T. CROSSMAN *Hymn, 'Jerusalem on high'*, The Harpers ..Harping on harps of gold. **1767** PERCY *Ess. Anc. Eng. Minstrels* 7 Much greater honours seem to have been heaped upon the northern scalds..than appear to have been paid to the minstrels and harpers of the Anglo-Saxons. **1846** GROTE *Greece* I. vii. (1862) II. 189 The Lesbian harper Terpander. **1883** VIGFUSSON & POWELL *Corpus Poeticum Boreale* p. lv, In England an innovation appears, the harper who sits at the king's feet. **1912** W. M. DIXON *Eng. Epic & Heroic Poetry* 61 The braggart, the coward, the bard or harper, cunning with the glee-wood..all are there.

b. Phr. ***have at** (**among**) **you, harpers***: see quot. 1785.

1542 J. HEYWOOD *Prov.* (1867) 65 Haue among you blynd harpers (sayde I) The mo the merier. *a* **1625** FLETCHER *Mad Lover* I. ii, He has a battalia now in's brains. He draws out; now Have at ye, Harpers! **1641** M. PARKER (*title*) The Poet's Blind Man's Bough; or have among you, my Blind Harpers. **1785** GROSE *Dict. Vulg. Tongue* s.v. *Harp*, Have among you, my blind harpers; an expression used in throwing or shooting at random among a crowd.

†**2.** Applied to various Irish coins current in the 16th and 17th c., bearing the figure of a harp; *esp.* the *harp shillings*, worth 9*d.* of English money. *Obs.* exc. *Hist.*

1598 E. GILPIN *Skial.* (1878) 40 Art thou yet to learne A harper from a shilling to discerne? **1607** HEYWOOD *Fayre Mayde* Wks. 1874 II. 26 Your shilling prov'd but a harper. **1726–31** TINDAL *Rapin's Hist. Eng.* XVII. (1743) II. 157 Elizabeth coined also Irish Money, namely, shillings called Harpers. **1839** W. J. THOMS *Anecd. & Trad.* 54.

3. The harp-seal (*Cent. Dict.*).

harper² (also *harpier*), app. error for HARPY.

1586 MARLOWE *1st Pt. Tamburl.* II. vii, Now doth ghastly Death With greedy talents gripe my bleeding heart, And like a harpy [so 8vo; *Qo.* harper] tires upon my life. **1605** SHAKS. *Macb.* IV. i. 3 Harpier cries, 'tis time, 'tis time.

harpineer: see HARPOONEER.

harping (ˈhɑːpɪŋ), *vbl. sb.* [f. HARP *v.* + -ING¹.] The action of the vb. HARP; playing upon the harp; the sound of the playing of a harp.

c **888** K. ÆLFRED *Boeth.* xxxv. §6 He hi hæfþ ȝeearnod mid his hearpunga. *c* **1205** LAY. 24193 Þer wes harepinge and song. **13..** *K. Alis.* 1043 Pipyng, and eke taboryng, Sytolyng, and ek harpyng. *c* **1425** *Thomas of Erceld.* 315 [Thomas] saide 'harpynge kepe I none, ffor tonge es chefe of mynstralsye'. **1671** MILTON *Samson* Introd., A chorus of heavenly harpings and song between. **1802** HEBER *Palestine* 26 Mysterious harpings swell the midnight gale.

b. *fig.* (See HARP *v.* 2, 3.)

1546 J. HEYWOOD *Prov.* (1867) 79 He..did fall, From harping on that stringe, to faire flattring speeche. **1768–74** TUCKER *Lt. Nat.* (1852) II. 236 Continual harpings upon the same string. **1820** W. IRVING *Sketch Bk.* (1859) 149 He made infinite merriment by harpings upon old themes. **1888** BURGON *Lives 12 Gd. Men* II. ix. 171 The Examiner.. persisted in harping on his own one idea.

c. Verses, poetry, 'song'.

1819 BYRON *Proph. Dante* I. 144 And yet my harpings will unfold a tale. **1857** H. REED *Lect. Brit. Poets* ix. 323 The evil spirit..charmed to rest by the harpings of his muse.

d. *Comb.*, as †***harping glee***, harp music.

a **1300** *Cursor M.* 7251 Sampson..was sle on harpingleu [*Gött.* harping glew, *Trin.* harp glew].

'harping, *ppl. a.* [f. as prec. + -ING².] That harps or plays on a harp. Also *transf.*

1641 MILTON *Ch. Govt.* II. Introd., A sevenfold Chorus of Hallelujah's and harping Symphonies. **1865** KINGSLEY *Herew.* xix, He was a dancing, harping fellow.

†**harping-iron** (ˈhɑːpɪŋˈaɪən). *Obs.* [Related to F. *harper* to grapple, grasp, clasp, etc. (Cotgr.), also *harpin* a boat-hook.] A barbed spear or

javelin used for spearing whales and large fish; a harpoon. (In quot. 1734, a grappling-iron.)

1596 NASHE *Saffron Walden* 37, I haue prouided harping yrons to catch this great Whale. **1613** PURCHAS *Pilgrimage* (1614) 839 A Crocodile or some other monster..which thrust out a tongue like a harping iron. *c* **1645** HOWELL *Lett.* (1650) III. 21 With his harping Iron he can draw ashore the great Leviathan. **1665** G. HAVERS *P. della Valle's Trav. E. India* 328 We..strike them with a broad instrument, full of barbs, called an Harping-iron. **1701** C. WOLLEY *Jrnl. in N. York* (1860) 38 The tow..is a line fastend to the Harping-iron about 50 fathoms long. **1734** tr. *Rollin's Anc. Hist.* IV. VIII. xiv. 90 Nicias had provided harping irons to grapple them. **1814** W. BROWN *Hist. Propag. Chr.* II. 455 They..insert it [poison] in the point of their arrow or harping iron.

harpings ('hɑːpɪŋz), *sb. pl. Naut.* Also 7 **harping**, 8–9 **harpins, harpens.** [? f. HARP *sb.*]

1. a. The fore-parts of the wales which encompass the bow of a ship and are fastened to the stem, being thicker than the after-parts in order to sustain the shock of plunging into the sea. **b.** Pieces of oak, forming an extension of the ribbands, for holding the cant-frames of a vessel in place until the outside planking is worked.

1658 PHILLIPS, *Harpings*, the breadth of a ship at the bow. **1664** E. BUSHNELL *Compl. Shipwright* 14 The Sweep of the Harping. **1711** W. SUTHERLAND *Shipbuild. Assist.* 53 The Channel-wales, which are crooked, call'd Harpings. **1869** SIR E. J. REED *Shipbuild.* xx. 432 Before any frames are hoisted staging is erected at the topsides, and the sheer or gunwale harpins are suspended from it. **1879** *Cassell's Techn. Educ.* IV. 190/1 The timbers are secured by means of a longitudinal 'harpin' or 'ribband' wrought along under the floors and secured to them.

2. ***cat-harpings***: the ropes or (now more generally) iron cramps that serve to brace in the shrouds of the lower-masts behind their respective yards, so as to tighten the shrouds and also give more room to draw the yards in when the ship is close-hauled. Also ***cat-harping legs***.

1626 CAPT. SMITH *Accid. Yng. Seamen* 15. **1627** —— *Seaman's Gram.* v. 21 Cat harpings are small ropes runne in little blockes from one side of the ship to the other, neere the vpper decke to keepe the shrouds tight for the more safety of the mast from rowling. *a* **1700** B. E. *Dict. Cant. Crew, Catharpin Fashion*, when People in Company Drink cross, and not..according to the Sun's motion. **1779** COOPER in *Phil. Trans.* LXIX. 161 We saw one of our best seamen hanging by his feet in the main catharpins struck dead. **1833** MARRYAT *P. Simple* vii, The midshipman told me these were called the cat-harpings, because they were so difficult to climb, that a cat would expostulate if ordered to go out by them.

† **'harping-spear.** *Obs.* = HARPING-IRON.

1657–83 J. EVELYN *Hist. Religion* (1850) I. 82 Even him [Leviathan], with his harping spear, he boldly encounters. **1738** tr. *G. de Lucca's Mem.* 248 These Harping-Spears are pointed..extreamly sharp, with Beards to hinder them from coming out.

harpist ('hɑːpɪst). [f. HARP *sb.*[1] + -IST.] A (professional) harper.

1613–16 W. BROWNE *Brit. Past.* II. v, That Oeagrian harpist, for whose lay, Tigers with hunger pinde and left their pray. **1856** CAPERN *Poems* (ed. 2) 141 'Twas a little fairy harpist Playing on the subtle air. **1890** *Guardian* 24 Sept. 1472/2 Mr. John Thomas, harpist to the Queen. **1898** S. A. BROOKE *Eng. Lit. fr. Beginnings to Norman Conq.* ii. 41 As far as we can go back with certainty we find the Teutonic ..harpists and singers. **1948** K. MALONE in A. C. Baugh *Lit. Hist. England* I. 46 Whether Scilling was Widsith's harpist or a fellow scop..we cannot tell.

'harpless, *a. rare.* Without a harp.

1859 *Emin. Men & Pop. Bks.* 177 The performer was soon left harpless.

harponier: see HARPOONEER.

harpoon (hɑː'puːn), *sb.* Also 7–8 **harpon.** [ad. F. *harpon* 'a crampiron wherewith Masons fasten stones together' (Cotgr., 1611) = Sp. *arpon*, Pg. *arpão*, deriv. of F. *harpe* dog's claw, cramp, cramp-iron, clamp (1485 in Hatz.-Darm.), ad. L. *harpē* (*harpa*) = Gr. ἅρπη sickle, scimitar. Cf. the earlier HARPING-IRON.]

†**1.** A barbed dart or spear. *Obs.*

1625 PURCHAS *Pilgrims* I. III. 118 (Stanf.) Their weapons halfe-Pikes, headed with Iron as a Harpon. **1697** DAMPIER *Voy.* (1729) I. 7 Throwing the Lance, Fisgig, Harpoon, or any manner of Dart. *Ibid.* 10 The women..prevent them from doing any injury to each other by hiding their Lances, Harpoons, Bows and Arrows.

2. a. A barbed spear-like missile, to the handle or shank of which a long line of rope is attached; it is used for capturing whales and large fish, being either hurled by the hand or fired from a gun.

1694 *Acc. Sev. Late Voy.* II. (1711) 8 Saw a Whale, and flung into him three Harpoons. **1704** *Naval Chron.* XII. 32 Taking whales by the Gun-harpoon. **1778** *Phil. Trans.* LXVIII. 395 A very large shark was struck with the harpon. **1846** GREENER *Sc. Gunnery* 318 The gun projected the harpoon into the crown of the [whale's] head, burying it two feet deep. **1874** MARKHAM *Whaling Cruise* 26 The manner in which the harpoons are fitted is first with about twelve fathoms for a gun harpoon, and three for a hand harpoon, of the best white untarred hemp rope [etc.].

b. *Med.* A trocar-like surgical instrument for removing small pieces of living tissue of examination.

1876 J. S. BRISTOWE *Theory & Pract. Med.* (1878) 719 The extraction by means of a suitable instrument (harpoon) of fragments of striped muscular tissue. **1897** *Allbutt's Syst. Med.* II. 1057 The harpoon designed..for this purpose produces an unsurgical wound.

3. *attrib.* and *Comb.*, as ***harpoon-arrow, -barb, -head, -maker, -shaft***; **harpoon-fork**, a kind of hay-fork worked by tackle in loading or unloading hay; **harpoon-gun**, a gun for firing a harpoon; **harpoon-rocket**, a bomb-lance for killing whales; **harpoon-shuttle**, a long shuttle or needle used for sewing mats for hydraulic dikes and jetties.

1874 BOUTELL *Arms & Arm.* vi. 92 Two curved pieces of iron, or blades (probably like small *harpoon barbs). **1820** SCORESBY *Acc. Arctic Reg.* II. 226 The *harpoon-gun was invented in 1731. **1874** MARKHAM *Whaling Cruise* 27 The harpoon gun is fixed on a swivel in the bows of the boat. **1835** SIR J. ROSS. *Narr. 2nd Voy.* xviii. 280 He brought back a hook and a *harpoon head. **1858** SIMMONDS *Dict. Trade*, **Harpoon-maker*. **1856** KANE *Arct. Expl.* II. xiii. 135 A capstan-bar..invaluable for its adaptation to *harpoon-shafts. **1847** EMERSON *Repr. Men, Goethe* Wks. (Bohn) I. 389 He stripped him [the Devil]..of horns, cloven foot, *harpoon tail.

har'poon, *v.* [f. prec. sb.: cf. F. *harponner* (1634 in Hatz.-Darm.).] *trans.* To strike or spear with a harpoon.

1774 PENNANT *Tour Scotl. in 1772*, 168 A basking shark that had been harpooned. **1780** COXE *Russ. Disc.* 56 Sea animals which they harpoon with their bone lances. **1867** PEARSON *Hist. Eng.* I. 2 They harpooned the whale.

b. *transf.* and *fig.*

1806–7 J. BERESFORD *Miseries Hum. Life.* (1826) IX. xxxix, Trying often to harpoon a floating pat of butter. **1872** O. W. HOLMES *Poet Breakf.-t.* iii. (1885) 67 The Master harpooned a breakfast-roll.

harpooneer (hɑːpuː'nɪə(r)). Now *rare.* Also 7 **harpoonier**, 7–8 **harponier**, 7–9 **harpin-**, 8 **harponeer.** [f. HARPOON *sb.* + -EER[1], -IER. (The form and date suggest a. Fr. **harponnier*.)] = next.

1613 PURCHAS *Pilgrimage* (1614) 742 A Shallop, in which the Harponier stands ready, with both his hands to dart his Harping iron. **1667** R. NORWOOD in *Phil. Trans.* II. 567 When the Harpineer..sees his opportunity, he strikes his Harping-Iron into the Whale. **1695** BLACKMORE *Pr. Arth.* x. 174 So when Battavian Harpooniers assail, With their sharp Launces, some prodigious Whale. **1752** BOND in *Phil. Trans.* XLVII. 430 The harpooneer, as they call him, sits rowing in the head of the boat, and observes certain silent signals, which the boat-steerer gives him, to inform him, that he is near enough to strike the whale. **1874** MARKHAM *Whaling Cruise* 14 The harpooneer is in charge of the boat and pulls the stroke-oar.

harpooner (hɑː'puːnə(r)). [f. HARPOON *v.* + -ER[1]. Cf. F. *harponneur* (17th c.).] One who hurls or fires a harpoon.

1726 SHELVOCKE *Voy. round World* (1757) 420 They seldom can want a supply of this [fish], the men being expert harpooners. **1829** MARRYAT *F. Mildmay* xiii, The harpooner poised his weapon. **1878** MARKHAM *Gt. Frozen Sea* vii. 86 Selecting the largest of the three as his victim, our harpooner carefully laid his gun.

'harpress. *rare.* [f. HARPER + -ESS. Cf. OF. *harperesse* (15th c.)] A female harper.

1814 SCOTT *Wav.* xxii, An aspen which overhung the seat of the fair harpress.

† **'harpsical.** *Obs.* (Also **harpsecol, harpsicol,** vulg. **haspicols**). A corrupt form of HARPSICHORD, prob. after *virginal*.

1616 CHAPMAN *Homer's Hymne to Apollo* 29 Then strait did fall To studie of the harp and harpsicall All th' Immortals. **1668** H. MORE *Div. Dial.* v. xxxviii. 447 Some well-strung Harpsicall or Theorbo. **1704** *Collect. Voy.* (Churchill) III. 38/2 Their Quils..serve for Harpsicals. **1706** PHILLIPS (ed. Kersey), *Harpsecord* or *Harpsecol*. **1752** FOOTE *Taste* I. Wks. 1799 I. 12 Playing upon the haspicols. **1773** GOLDSM. *Stoops to Conq.* IV. i, Her pretty long fingers, that she twists this way and that, over the haspicholls.

harpsichord ('hɑːpsɪkɔːd). Also 7 **arpsicord, harpsicord,** 8 **harpsecord.** [ad. obs. F. *harpechorde* (Cotgr.) = It. *arpicordo* (Radino 1592, Florio 1598), mod.L. *harpichordium* (*a* 1558 in Scaliger *Poetics* VIII), f. L. *harpa* harp + *chorda*, It. *corda* string. The intrusive *s*, due apparently to some mistake, appears in the earliest English instances.]

A keyboard instrument of music (resembling in appearance the grand piano), in which the strings were plucked and set in vibration by quill or leather points set in jacks connected by levers with the keys. (In use esp. from 16th to 18th c.)

double harpsichord, one having an extra string to each key, sounding an octave higher than the others, and a second keyboard to control the extra strings.

1611 COTGR., *Harpechorde*, an Arpsicord or Harpsicord; a Dulcimer. **1664** EVELYN *Diary* 5 Oct., There was brought a new-invented instrument of music, being a harpsichord with gut-strings, sounding like a concert of viols with an organ. **1694** *Phil. Trans.* XVIII. 72 In Organs and Harpsicords, where the Notes are fixt, the proper Ascent and Descent cannot be made but only beginning from some Keys. **1766** PENNANT *Zool.* (1812) I. 280 The quills of ravens sell for twelve shillings the hundred, being of great use in tuning the lower notes of a harpsichord. **1775** SHERIDAN *Duenna* II. iii, Black and white alternately, just like the keys of a harpsichord. **1848** DICKENS *Dombey* xxix, She went up stairs to set forth the bird waltz on the harpsichord. **1896** HIPKINS *Hist. Pianoforte* 75 The harpsichord is a double, triple—in some instances, quadruple—spinet, the sounds being excited by a jack and quill plectrum, the same as in the spinet or virginal.

b. *attrib.* and *Comb.*, as ***harpsichord-lesson, -maker, -making, -master, -player, -wire***, etc.

1772 BRYDONE in *Phil. Trans.* LXIII. 167, I cut a quantity of harpsichord-wire into short pieces. **1773** BARRINGTON *Ibid.* 266 The harpsichord-tuners find it more difficult to tune these extreme parts. **1789** BURNEY *Hist. Mus.* IV. 307 Sandoni, a harpsichord-master and composer of some eminence. *Ibid.* 540 An exquisite harpsichord-player. **1876** STAINER & BARRETT *Dict. Mus. T., Harpsichord graces*, certain turns and ornaments employed in playing upon the harpsichord, introduced for the most part as compensation for the lack of sustaining power in the instrument. **1896** HIPKINS *Hist. Pianoforte* 79 The palm for excellence in harpsichord-making is due to the famous Ruckers family.

Hence **'harpsi,chordist**, a harpsichord-player.

1878 L. WINGFIELD *Lady Grizel* II. xi. 283 The Duke's foreign valet was a neat harpsichordist.

† **harpsicon**, corruption of prec.

1633 A. H. *Partheneia Sacra* 144 (T.) Let them run divisions on the harpsicon or virginals. **1660–1** PEPYS *Diary* 26 Feb., There saw the new Harpsicon made for Mrs. The. **1683** PETTUS *Fleta Min.* II. 12 The strings of the Harpsicon.

'harp-string. One of the strings of a harp.

c **1000** *Apollonius of Tyre* (Th.) 17 He þa hearpe-strengas mid cræfte astirian ongan. *c* **1384** CHAUCER *H. Fame* II. 269 Whan men harpe strynges smyte Whether hyt be moche or lyte Loo with the stroke the ayre to-breketh. *c* **1430** LYDG. *Hors, Shepe & G.* 68 in *Pol. Rel. & L. Poems* 17 Of the shepe is cast A-way no thynge..For hapre stryngis his Ropys seruythe Ichoone. **1814** SCOTT *Ld. of Isles* I. iii, He spoke, and on the harp-strings died The strains. **1833** N. ARNOTT *Physics* (ed. 5) II. 230 A harp-string, while vibrating as it sounds, appears like a flat transparent riband.

‖ **harpuisbos** (harpø'yːsbɔs). Also 9 **harpuisbosje** (-bɔsi) and (semi-anglicized) **harpuis, arpuse,** or **rapuis bush.** [Afrikaans, f. *harpuis* resin + *bos* bush.] An evergreen shrub belonging to the genus *Euryops*, esp. the resin-bush, *E. multifidus*.

[**1793** tr. *C. P. Thunberg's Trav. Europe, Afr., & Asia* I. 211 A species of *Coccus*, called *Harpuys*, that was found on the branches of trees, was said to prove mortal to sheep.] **1811** W. J. BURCHELL *Trav. S. Afr.* (1822) I. xii. 259 The inhabitants of this district, when in want of resin, use as a substitute, a gum which exudes from different species of shrubs; which they therefore call *Harpuis bosch* (Resin bush). **1815** A. PLUMPTRE tr. *Lichtenstein's Trav.* II. 176 A shrub, which grows from two feet to three feet and a half high, called by the colonists *harpuisbosjes*, the rosin tree. **1846** H. H. METHUEN *Life in Wilderness* 112 We again were in danger of being burnt; a sea of flame raging on one side of the road, and consuming the resinous *arpuse* bushes with a roaring noise, audible a long way off. [**1912** *East London Dispatch* 22 Aug. 5 (Pettman), Mr. Moffatt (Tarka) brought up the question of the noxious *rapuis* which had hitherto baffled their efforts.] **1926** O. SCHREINER *From Man to Man* xi. 353 They burnt harpuis bushes on the lands at home. **1952** *Cape Argus* (Mag. Section) 1 Nov. 1/7 The yellow of the harpuisbos.

harpy ('hɑːpɪ). [ad. L. *harpȳ-ia*, usually in pl. *harpȳiæ* = Gr. ἅρπυιαι 'snatchers' (cf. ἁρπάζειν to snatch away, seize), in Homer used to personify whirlwinds or hurricanes, in Hesiod said to be sisters of Aello and Iris, in later mythology represented as hideous winged monsters. Perh. immediately a. F. *harpie* (14th c. in Hatz.-Darm.).]

1. *Gr.* and *Lat. Myth.* A fabulous monster, rapacious and filthy, having a woman's face and body and a bird's wings and claws, and supposed to act as a minister of divine vengeance.

1540 PALSGRAVE tr. *Acolastus* N iv b, Such were the harpies, as Virgil discribith them. **1610** SHAKS. *Temp.* III. iii. 83 Brauely the figure of this Harpie has thou Perform'd (my Ariell); a grace it had, deuouring. **1671** MILTON *P.R.* II. 462 Both table and provision vanished quite With sound of harpies' wings, and talons heard. **1736** BUTLER *Anal.* I. iii. Wks. 1874 I. 51 His vices..like so many harpies, craving for their accustomed gratification. **1868** TENNYSON *Lucretius* 159 Strangers at my hearth Not welcome, harpies miring every dish. **1873** SYMONDS *Grk. Poets* viii. 263 The Harpies were wind-tossed films of frothy cloud; the Sirens daughters of foam and mist.

b. A conventional representation or figure of a harpy, as in Heraldry.

1572 BOSSEWELL *Armorie* II. 111 b, An Harpie Vert, Wynged de Or. **1610** GUILLIM *Heraldry* III. xxvi. (1611) 183 The Harpey..should be giuen to such persons as haue committed manslaughter. **1823** CRABB *Technol. Dict.* s.v., The field is, *or*, a harpy displayed, crined, crowned, and armed, *or*. **1873** BOUTELL *Her. Anc. & Mod.* 158 *Harpy*, a fabulous heraldic creature, represented as a vulture with a woman's head and neck.

2. *transf.* and *fig.* A rapacious, plundering, or grasping person; one that preys upon others.

1589 WARNER *Alb. Eng.* v. xxviii. (R.), Plucke downe those grating harpies that Seduce our king amis. **1643** *Myst. Iniq.* 45 The insolent carriage of Prince Rupert, and his Harpyes. **1775** JOHNSON *Tax. no Tyr.* 5 The harpies of taxation. **1859** THACKERAY *Virgin.* xviii, Was it my mother-in-law, the grasping, odious, abandoned, brazen harpy? **1884** *St. James' Gaz.* 4 Apr. 4/2 Mr. Commissioner Kerr has begun a crusade against legal 'harpies'.

3. The HARPY-EAGLE.

1838 *Penny Cycl.* X. 175/2 The harpy is stated to be a solitary bird, frequenting the thickest forests, where it feeds upon the sloths. **1856** KNIGHT *Cycl. Nat. Hist.* II. 698 The Harpies, or Fishing Eagles, with short wings.

4. The moor-buzzard, *Circus æruginosus.*

1838 *Penny Cycl.* X. 183/1 *Circus æruginosus*..is the..Moor-Buzzard, Marsh-Harrier, Duck-Hawk, Harpy, and White-headed Harpy. **1862** *Chambers's Encycl.* V. 252.

5. The HARPY-BAT, q.v.

6. *attrib.* and *Comb.*, as ***harpy advocate, breed, fury, grin, lawyer, pettifogger, race, raven***; ***harpy-footed, harpy-like*** adjs.; **harpy-monument**, a monument found at Xanthus in Lycia, on which are figures resembling harpies.

1621 BURTON *Anat. Mel.* Democr. to Rdr. 32 They..undo one another to enrich an Harpy advocate. *Ibid.* II. i. IV. i. 209 That he be not over-careless or covetous, Harpy-like to make a prey of his patient. **1667** MILTON *P.L.* II. 596 Thither by harpy-footed Furies hail'd. **1749** SMOLLETT *Regicide* II. vii, Why let in A train of harpy sorrows to my breast? **1767** WESLEY *Jrnl.* 11 Aug., The harpy-lawyers are..disappointed. **1853-78** W. SMITH *Class. Dict.* 298 In the famous Harpy monument recently brought from Lycia to this country, the Harpies are represented in the act of carrying off the daughters of Pandareus. **1866** TROLLOPE *Claverings* xxiv, Woman,—altogether of the harpy breed!

Hence **harpyian** (erron. **harpeian, harpyan**) *a.*, belonging to or characteristic of a harpy.

1644 VICARS *Jehovah-Jireh* 46 For fear of their Harpeian paws. *c* **1728** E. PRIOR *Lament.* in Willis & Clark *Cambridge* (1886) II. 676 Those harpyan claws.

'harpy-'bat. A name given to two or more species of bat found in the East Indies.

1883 *Cassell's Nat. Hist.* I. 276 The Harpy Bat (*Harpyia cephalotes*)..the Molucca Bat of Pennant and Shaw, inhabits the islands of Celebes and Amboyna. *Ibid.* 308 The Harpy Bat (*Harpiocephalus harpia*) is about two inches and a half long, with a tail nearly two inches in length..observed in India, at Darjeling, and the Khasia hills.

'harpy-'eagle. A large and powerful bird of prey (*Thrasyaëtus harpyia*, or *Harpyia destructor*) larger than the golden eagle, with crested head and fan-shaped tail, a native of South America.

1830 T. ATTWOOD *Let. to Wife* 21 June in C. M. Wakefield *Life* x. (1885) 143, I went on Saturday to see the harpy eagle, and a most grand and beautiful creature he is. **1883** *Cassell's Nat. Hist.* III. 276 Although from its size and courage..generally called the *Harpy Eagle*, it is evident from its structure that it is a Buzzard.

harquebus, arquebus ('hɑːkwɪbəs, 'ɑːk-), *sb.* Also †harquebut, †harquebush. Forms: *α.* 6 harquebutt(e, -but. *β.* 6 arkbussh, 6-7 harga-, hargu-, harguebush(e, harquebush. *γ.* 6-7 harga-, hargu-, hargue-, -buse, buze, hargwebusse, harkaboize, harquebuz(e, -busse, 7 hargebuse, harguebus(s)e, 7-8 harquebuse, 7- -buss, 6- harquebus. *δ.* 6 arcubos(e, 7 -buse, arquebwze, 7-9 arquebuss, 8-9 -bus, -buse. [a. 16th c. F. (*h*)*arquebuse* (*-bute*, etc.). The MHG. *hake*(*n*)*bühse*, MLG. *hakebusse* (see HACKBUSH), was transformed in It., by popular etymology, into *arcobugio, -buso* (*arco* bow + *bugio, buso* 'hollow, hole', in reference to the hollow barrel, and to its taking the place of the bow or arbalest), also later *archibugio, -buso* (cf. Sp. *arcabuz*); under the influence of the It., the earlier French name *haquebute* (see HACKBUT) was changed through the intermediate *harquebute, harquebuse*, to *arquebuse*. These French forms were in turn adopted in English, where also the influence of the earlier *hackbush, hagbush*, gave rise to the mixed forms *harquebush, hargubush, harguebusse*, etc.]

1. The early type of portable gun, varying in size from a small cannon to a musket, which on account of its weight was, when used in the field, supported upon a tripod, trestle, or other 'carriage', and afterwards upon a forked 'rest'. The name in German and Flemish meant literally 'hook-gun', from the hook cast along with the piece, by which it was fastened to the 'carriage'; but the name became generic for portable fire-arms generally in the 16th century, so that the type with the hook was subsequently distinguished as *arquebuse à croc*: see 2.

According to Wendelin Boeheim, *Handbuch der Waffenkunde* (Leipzig 1890) 447, 455, the hook of the original *hakenbühse* was intended to hold on to a wall or other fixed object, partly to support the weight of the barrel and partly to diminish the recoil. Maximilian I (early 16th cent.) introduced the portable tripod which could be put together in the field. The forked rest came in about 1520, with the Spanish musket.

α. **1574** *Lanc. Lieutenancy* I. (Chetham Soc.) 42 Sir Thomas Hesketh Knight to furnishe..Harquebuttes ij.

β. **1532** ELYOT *Let. to Dk. Norkolk* 14 Mar. in *Gov.* (1883) Life 80 Arkbusshes and crossebowes, I thowght theim innumerable. *a* **1557** *Assault of Cupid* in *Tottell's Misc.* (Arb.) 173 The hargabushe..dims the ayre with misty smokes. **1625** MARKHAM *Souldiers Accid.* 5 If you haue Harquebushes (which are now out of vse with vs). **1688** R. HOLME *Armoury* II. 153/1 Wounds..either with Arrows, or with the Harquebush, or Gun-shot.

γ. **1555** EDEN *Decades* 4 Crossebowes, bylles, hargabuses. **1562** J. SHUTE tr. *Cambine's Turk. Wars* Ep. Ded. **j b, Yf he vse the harquebuze he is..shotte to deathe with harquebuzes. **1575** CHURCHYARD *Chippes* (1817) 85 As you see..crowes flie out of a wood, when a harkaboize is shotte of. **1590** SIR J. SMYTH *Disc. Weapons* Cj b, Caliuers..being of a greater length and heighth of bullet, and more ranforced than Harquebuzes. **1622** F. MARKHAM *Bk. War* I. ix. 33 Harquebusses I cannot allow in this place, because they are grown out of vse, and can by no means make their encounter good where the Musquet is opposed against them. **1634** T. JOHNSON *Parey's Chirurg.* XI. (1678) 270 Harquebuse, a word..borrowed from the Italians, be reason of the touch-hole by which you give fire to the Piece. *a* **1674** MILTON *Hist. Mosc.* iv. (1851) 494 A Peal of 170 Brass Ordnance..and 20000 Harquebuzes twice over. **1753** HANWAY *Trav.* (1762) II. VI. ii. 153 A kind of harquebuses, which carry a handful of musket balls. **1805** SCOTT *Last Minstr.* IV. xxix, Level each harquebuss on row; Draw, merry archers, draw the bow. *a* **1864** HAWTHORNE *S. Felton* (1879) 23 The heavy harquebus.

δ. *c* **1540** PEPWELL in Ellis *Orig. Lett.* Ser. II. II. 64 They do ocupy her now..with Arcubozys, wiche gyvythe doble the stroke of a hand gon. **1603** KNOLLES *Hist. Turks* (1621) 982 In battell they use the arcubuse and scimitar. **1605** CAMDEN *Rem.* (1657) 208 Chambers, slinges, arquebwze. **1813** BYRON *Giaour* 521, Each armed, as best becomes a man, With arquebuss and ataghan. **1829** W. IRVING *Chron. Conq. Granada* II. lxx. 178 A chance medley combat ensued, with lances, arquebuses, cross-bows, and cimeters.

†**2. harquebus à croc** (corruptly *of crock*): 'An arquebuss supported on a rest by a hook of iron fastened to the barrel. From the size of its calibre it was used to fire through loop-holes' (Meyrick *Anc. Armour* 1824). *Obs.*

(As this was exactly the original *hakenbühse*, the addition *à croc*, 'with hook', was doubtless made after the etymological meaning of *haquebute* or *arquebuse* was forgotten, and the name extended to fire-arms which had no *haken* or *croc*. Littré identifies the *croc* with the *fourchette* or *rest*, but one of his quotations has 'chacun une harquebuse à croc sans fourchette' and another explains the use of the *croc*: 'harquebuses à croc, que l'on ne peut bien tirer si elles ne sont liées et accrochées sur du bois', tied and *hooked* upon wood.)

[**1547**, etc. see HACKBUSH, -BUT]. **1572** *Inv.* in Whitaker *Hist. Craven* (1812) 334, 11 harquebusses of crocke. **1611** COTGR., *Arquebuse à croc*, an harguebuse a-crocke (somewhat bigger than a musket). **1625** J. GLANVILLE *Voy. Cadiz* 27 Oct. (Camden) 75 By the faire carrieng of their peices Itt was manifest that some of them were Harquebush of Crocke. **1627** CAPT. SMITH *Seaman's Gram.* xiv. 69 For Curriours, Hargabusacrocks [**1653-92** Harquebusses]..Bastard-muskets, Coliuers. **1653** H. COGAN tr. *Pinto's Trav.* lxix. 280 All the Elephants carried wooden castles on their backs, from whence they shot with Musquets..and a great number of Harquebuses a crock, each of them ten or twelve spans long. **1678** tr. *Gaya's Arms of War* 87 The Arquebuss a Crock is made of Iron, in form of a great Musket. It may be fired three hundred times a day..The Bullet of it weighs three ounces. *a* **1693** LUDLOW *Mem.* (1771) 31 A great wall-gun called a Harquebuz de Croq being fired from the top of the castle.

3. *collectively.* Soldiers armed with harquebuses.

1594 PEELE *Alcazar* IV. Eij, Garded about With full fiue hundred hargubuze on foote. **1602** MARSTON *Ant. & Mel.* I. iii, Maine squares of pikes, millions of harguebush. **1638** FORD *Lady's Trial* IV. ii, Yongster Brogen-foh, with four-score hargubush.

4. *attrib.* and *Comb.*, as ***harquebus shot, -man.***

1574 G. BAKER *Oleum Magistr.* title-p., The which Oyl cureth..Wounds, Contusion, Hargubush Shot [etc.]. **1598** BARRET *Theor. Warres* 134, 600 quintals of hargubuze powder. **1600** DYMMOK *Ireland* (1843) 34 Towards the northeast not more than halfe an hargubuz shott. **1687** *Knolles' Hist. Turks* (1787) 829/1 Grasold, General of the Italians, there slain with a Harquebuse Shot.

†**harquebus**, *v.* To shoot as a harquebus.

a **1693** URQUHART *Rabelais* III. xxvi. 217 Harcabuzzing.

harquebusade, arq- (ˌhɑːkwɪbə'seɪd, ˌɑːk-). Also -ada, -ado. [a. F. (*h*)*arquebusade*: see prec. and -ADE, -ADA, -ADO.]

†**1.** A shot from a harquebus. *Obs.*

1590 SIR R. WILLIAMS *Disc. Warre* 26 The soldiers..discharged a salue of hargubusaides on the poore people. **1591** GARRARD *Art Warre* 213 (Stanf.) Hauing shot sixe or 7 Hargabuzades a peece. **1633** *Batt. Lutzen* in *Harl. Misc.* (Malh.) IV. 190 He..was beaten down with a storm of harquebusado's. **1721** BAILEY, *Arquebusade*, a Shot of an Arquebuse.

2. A continuous discharge of harquebus-shots. Cf. *cannonade, fusillade.*

1562 J. SHUTE tr. *Cambine's Turk. Wars* 36b, Their aunswere was, with the faire Cannonade, harquebuzade and such lyke. **1849** JAS. GRANT *Kirkaldy of G.* xiv. 133 They opened a brisk harquebusade on the assailants.

3. (in full ***harquebusade-water***): A lotion regarded as a specific for gunshot and other wounds.

1747 CHESTERF. *Lett.* (1792) I. cxxiii. 330 Thank you for the Arquebusade water which you sent her. **1758** MRS. DELANY *Life & Corr.* (1861) III. 503 Poor John cut a terrible gash in..his hand. I washed it well with arquebuzade. **1758** J. S. *Le Dran's Observ. Surg.* (1771) Aa iij b, Add more or less Arquebusade Water. **1839** LADY LYTTON *Cheveley* I. xi. 242 Let me get you something—a little salvolatile, or some arquebusade.

†**harquebusery.** *Obs.* [a. F. (*h*)*arquebuserie* (1551 in Godef.), f. *harquebuse*: see HARQUEBUS and -ERY.] Harquebuses collectively; the employment of harquebuses in warfare, harquebus-fire.

1589 IVE *Fortif.* 36 To assure himselfe from the artillerie and harquebuserie of the towne. *Ibid.* 37. **1590** SIR J. SMYTH *Disc. Weapons* 27 Men of warre, that do neither understand the true effects of Mosquetterie, Harquebuzerie, nor Archerie. *Ibid.* 47.

†**'harquebusher, -butter.** *Obs.* Also 6 **harkebuzer, harquebusar.** [f. HARQUEBUS (in its various forms) + -ER[1].]

1. = HARQUEBUSIER.

1567 SIR N. THROGMORTON in Robertson *Hist. Scot.* (1759) II. App. 41 These lords haue for the guard of their town 450 Harqubushers. **1577-87** HOLINSHED *Chron.* III. 962/1 Manfullie assailed by the harquebutters. **1587** FLEMING *Contn. Holinshed* III. 1980/1 Two hundred harquebutters on horsebacke. **1601** R. JOHNSON *Kingd. & Commw.* (1603) 224 With..two thousand harquebushers. **1641** BAKER *Chron.* (1679) 290/2 Assailed by the Harquebusars.

2. A harquebus. Cf. HACKBUSHIER 2.

1573-80 BARET *Alv.* G 635 A gunne called an arquebusher, *sclopus.*

harquebusier, arquebusier (ˌhɑː-, ˌɑːkwɪbə'sɪə(r)). Forms: *α.* 6 **hargu-, harquebutier.** *β.* 7 **hargubisheer.** *γ.* 6- **harquebusier,** (6 **harke-, hargabusier, hargubuzier,** 9 **harquebussier**). *δ.* 7 **arcabuzier,** 7- **arquebusier.** [a. 16th c. F. *arcabusier* (1533), (*h*)*arquebusier -butier*, f. (*h*)*arquebus*, HARQUEBUS. See also the earlier equivalents HACKBUSHIER, HACKBUTTER, -BUTEER.] A soldier armed with a harquebus.

1548 *Acts Privy Counc.* (1890) II. 202 For the wages of cc harquebutiers. **1553-4** *Q. Jane & Q. Mary* (Camden) 45, vij hagabusyars of Wyats company. **1555** EDEN *Decades* 288 A band of hargabusiers on horsbacke. **1568** DK. NORFOLK in Campbell *Love-lett. Mary Q. Scots* (1824) 17 Two hundred harkebusiers being in the court. **1578** T. N. tr. *Conq. W. India* 39 His Hargabushiers and Crossebowmen. **1579** DIGGES *Stratiot.* 82 The Harquebuzier with a light Brigandine. **1611** COTGR., *Haquebutier*, an Arquebusier, or small shot. **1633** T. STAFFORD *Pac. Hib.* II. xxi. (1810) 418 And gaue occasion of skirmish..with some hundred hargubisheers. **1656** BLOUNT *Glossogr.*, *Arcabuzier.* **1670** COTTON *Espernon* I. III. 108 Three hundred Harquebusiers on Horse-back. **1800** *Hist. Europe* in *Ann. Reg.* 175/2 Sixteen arquebuziers to each regiment. **1825** SOUTHEY in *Q. Rev.* XXXII. 387 Bayard..would give no quarter to harquebussiers. **1858** MOTLEY *Dutch Rep.* ii. 272 Arquebusiers, spearsmen and halberdmen.

harquebut, obs. form of HARQUEBUS.

†**harr,** *v. Obs.* or *dial.* Also 9 haur. [Of echoic origin: cf. ARR *v.*[2], HURR *v.*] *intr.* To snarl as a dog; to make a rough guttural trill. Hence **harring** *vbl. sb.* (in Montg. *harrand*).

1387 TREVISA *Higden* (Rolls) II. 159 Som vseþ..harrynge, and garrynge grisbayting. *a* **1605** MONTGOMERIE *Misc. Poems* iii. 61 ȝe think my harrand something har. **1656** T. ADY *Candle in Dark* 77 A witch or false prophet as had that devilish imposture of harring in their throats to deceive the people, called of some Ventriloquism. *Ibid.*, They spoke with a counterfeit voyce of harring in the throat. *c* **1746** J. COLLIER (Tim Bobbin) *View Lanc. Dial.* Gloss., *Harr*, to snarl like an angry dog. **1825** JAMIESON, *Haur*, to speak with what is called a burr in the throat. *Lanarks.*

harr, var. HAAR, sea-fog.

†**harrage,** *v. Obs.* A form used by Fuller, app. as = HARRY or HARASS (cf. *ravage*).

1655 FULLER *Ch. Hist.* VIII. ii. §16 That this [Diocese] of Lincolne, harraged out before, should now lie fallow. **1655** —— *Hist. Camb.* Pref. §1 Of late the Danes..had harraged all this Countrey. *a* **1661** —— *Worthies* (1840) II. 131 Living in a harraged land.

harrage, -ras(e, -asse, obs. ff. HARAS, a stud.

harrald(e, harrat, obs. ff. HERALD *sb.*

harrass, obs. form of HARASS *v.*

†**'harrateen.** *Obs.* Also harateen. A kind of linen fabric formerly used for curtains, bed-furniture, and the like. Also *attrib.*

1711 DK. NEWCASTLE *Let. to Dk. Montagu* 26 Sept. (*Sotheby's Catal.* 15 May 1897) Six field Bedsteads wth Crimson harateen furnitures. **1748-9** *General Advertiser* No. 4440 Ready-Made Furnitures..either of Harrateen, Cheney, Flower'd Cotton, Checks. **1756** H. WALPOLE *Corr.* (1820) II. 4 (D.) A wretched hovel..half its nakedness barely shaded with harateen stretched till it cracks. **1762** SMOLLETT *Sir L. Greaves* xvi. (D.), Thick harateen curtains were close drawn round the bed. **1825** ESTHER HEWLETT *Cottage Comforts* v. §67. 36 If you have curtains..the best..are linen check harrateen.

Comb. **1770** *Sketchley & Adams' B'ham Direct.*, Haywood, John, 15 Cherry Street, Harrateen maker.

†**harrawnte,** ? *ppl. a. Obs.* [perh. = OF. *harant*, pr. pple. of *harer* to incite dogs, etc. by shouts, orig. to shout, a. OHG. *haren* to cry, shout. See Skeat *Trans. Phil. Soc.* 1891-3, 362.] ? Shouting.

? *a* **1400** *Morte Arth.* 2449 Thane come the herbariours, harageous knyghtez, The hale batelles on hye harrawnte ther-aftyre.

†**harre, har.** *Obs.* exc. *dial.* Forms: 1 heorr, hior, 3-5 herre, 4-7 harre, 5-6, 9 *dial.* har. [OE. *heorr* (*hior*) fem. and m., and *heorra* m.; the

former corresp. to MDu. *herre, harre*, Du. *har, harre*, fem., the latter to ON. *hjarre, -ri* m.:—OTeut. types **herrâ-* and **herron-*.]

1. The hinge of a door or gate; in modern dialect use, the heel of a gate which bears the hinges: cf. HARROW *sb.*[2]

Beowulf (Z.) 999 Heorras to-hlidene. *c***725** *Corpus Gloss.* 423 *Cardo*, heor. *c***1000** *Lamb. Ps.* cxlvii. 2 [13] (Bosw.) He ʒestrangode heorran geata ðinra. *c***1200** *Trin. Coll. Hom.* 113 Ure helende brac þo þe irene herre and alto shiurede þe ȝiaten. *c***1386** CHAUCER *Prol.* 550 Ther nas no dore þat he ne wolde heue of harre. **1398** TREVISA *Barth. De P.R.* VIII. vi. (1495) 304 As the sharp corner of a dore meueth in the herre. **1483** CATH. ANGL. 176/2 An Harre of a dore, *cardo.* **1513** DOUGLAS *Æneis* II. ix. [viii.] 72 Furth of har the stapillis hes he bet. **1611** COTGR., *Chardonnereau*, the harre of a dore; the peece, band, or plate, that runnes along on the hindge-side of some dores. **1893** HESLOP *Northumb. Gloss.*, *Har*, the upright pieces of a gate known as the back har and the fore har.

fig. *c***888** K. ÆLFRED *Boeth.* xxxiv. §7 Seo hior ðe eall god on hwearfaþ. *c***1380** WYCLIF *Wks.* (1880) 472 Cardenals ben an herre to þe fendis hous.

2. *fig.* A cardinal point; an important matter.

*c***1000** *Sax. Leechd.* III. 84 Æfter þam feowor heorren heofenes and eorðan. **1388** WYCLIF *Prov.* viii. 26 Erthe, and floodis, and the heris of the world. *c***1440** *York Myst.* xxxi. 143, I hope we gete some harre hastely at hande.

3. *out of harre*: out of joint, out of order.

*a***1327** *Pol. Songs* (Camden) 318 Wer never dogges there Hurled out of herre. **1390** GOWER *Conf.* II. 139 Wherof this world stant out of herre. *c***1440** CAPGRAVE *Life St. Kath.* II. 891 More out of herre, þan is a foole þat can not se be-fore. *c***1460** *Towneley Myst.* (Surtees) 195 Alle is out of har, and that shalle he yrk. **1526** SKELTON *Magnyf.* 921 All is out of harre.

harreise, harres, obs. ff. HARAS, a stud.

harriage, harrage, var. AVERAGE *sb.*[1]

*a***1712** FOUNTAINHALL in M. P. Brown *Suppl. Decis.* (1826) IV. 358 (Jam.) The services..of harriage and carriage. **1795** *Statist. Acc. Scot., Perths.* XV. 605 Harrage.

Harrian, var. HURRIAN *sb.* and *a.*

harriar, obs. var. of HALYARD.

harrico(t, obs. forms of HARICOT.

harridan (ˈhærɪdən). Also 8 **harradan**, 8–9 **haridan**. [Generally supposed to be an alteration of F. *haridelle* an old jade of a horse (16th c. in Hatz.-Darm.); also, a gaunt ill-favoured woman (Littré); but connecting forms are not known.] A haggard old woman; a vixen; 'a decayed strumpet' (J.): usually a term of vituperation.

*a***1700** B. E. *Dict. Cant. Crew, Harridan*, one that is half Whore, half Bawd. **1706** FARQUHAR *Recruit. Officer* v. vi, D'ye hear, d'ye hear, you plaguy harridan, how those bullets whistle! **1727** POPE *Macer* 24 And in four months a batter'd harridan. *a***1745** SWIFT *Misc. Poems* (1807) 57 The nymphs with whom you first began, Are each become a harridan. **1860** EMERSON *Cond. Life, Consid.* Wks. (Bohn) II. 426 This identical hussy was a tutelar spirit in one house, and a haridan in the other. **1865** *Public Opinion* 31 Dec. 714/1 The harpy and harridan of the establishment was punished.

attrib. **1820** MOORE *Mem.* (1853) III. 102 The old harridan landlady.

fig. **1864** BURTON *Scot. Abr.* II. 299, I heartily consign that old harridan Etiquette, with all her trumpery, to [etc.]

Hence †**harriˈdanical** *a.* *nonce-wd.* *Obs.*

1725 MRS. PENDARVES in *Mrs. Delany's Life & Corr.* (1861) I. 118 Her old harridanical mother-in-law has stripped her house in town of all its furniture.

harrier[1] (ˈhærɪə(r)). [f. HARRY *v.* (which see for the phonology) + -ER[1]. See also HARROWER[2].]

1. One who harries, ravages, or lays waste.

1596 DALRYMPLE tr. *Leslie's Hist. Scot.* I. 121 Reiuers, Raikers, Herrieris of the ground. **1600** HOLLAND *Livy* III. lxviii. 135 Robbers and harriers of our fields. **1868** LOWELL *Pictures fr. Appledore* II. 54 She hides her mountains and her see From the harriers of scenery.

†**2.** (See quots.) *Obs.*

1591 PERCIVALL *Sp. Dict.*, *Harre*, the voice of a harrier or driuer of beasts, *Eia.* **1598** FLORIO, *Vatigaro*, a harrier, a drouer, a driuer of cattell.

3. (Also †*harrower*.) A name for falcons of the genus *Circus*, and their allies: cf. HEN-HARRIER, MARSH-HARRIER.

1556 WITHALS *Dict.* (1568) 4a/2 A haroer, *rubetarius.* **1565–73** COOPER *Thesaurus, Rubetarius*, a kinde of haukes called an henne harroer. **1611** COTGR., *Bondrée*, a kind of short winged Eagle..some call her a Harrower. **1691** RAY *Collect. Words* Pref. (E.D.S.) 3 Called a *hen-harrier* from chasing, preying upon, and destroying of poultry. **1833** R. MUDIE *Brit. Birds* (1841) I. 99 The harriers are..very indefatigable in their hunting, and highly destructive of the feathered tribes, and also of rabbits.

4. *Comb.* (from sense 3): **harrier eagle**, *Circaetus gallicus*; **harrier-hawk**, a hawk of the American genus *Micrastur*.

1883 *Cassell's Nat. Hist.* III. 270 They retain the facial ruff of the Harriers, and hence the name of Harrier-Hawk. *Ibid.* 284 The Common Harrier Eagle (*Circaetus gallicus*).. found all over Southern and Central Europe.

harrier[2] (ˈhærɪə(r)). Also 6 **haryer**, 7–8 **harier**. [app. f. HARE *sb.* + -IER; but perh. orig. the same word as HARRIER[1], associated with and referred to *hare*: cf. 2nd quot. 1576.]

1. A kind of hound, resembling the fox-hound, but smaller, used for hunting the hare.

1408 *Privy Seal* (20 Aug.) 9 Hen. IV. (No. 5874) La garde de nos chiens appellez hayrers. **1413** *Rot. Pat.* 1 Hen. V. pt. 3, memb. 19, 12 June, Custodiam canum nostrorum vocatorum 'hayreres'. **1446** *Issues of Excheq.* (ed. Devon), [Hounds called] heireres. **1542** UDALL *Erasm. Apoph.* 127 b, There bee harryers or buckehoundes. **1576** TURBERV. *Venerie* 165 A hounde whiche is a perfect good haryer. **1576** FLEMING tr. *Caius' Dogs* in Arb. *Garner* III. 233 That kind of dog whom Nature hath endued with the virtue of smelling, and draweth into his nostrils the air of the scent of the beast pursued and followed..we call *Leverarius*, Harriers. **1679** BLOUNT *Anc. Tenures* 39 A Kenel of little Hounds called *Harriers.* **1723** *Lond. Gaz.* No. 6194/6 A Pack of Harriers. **1846** J. BAXTER *Libr. Pract. Agric.* (ed. 4) I. 217 Harriers in general are much slower in the pursuit than fox-hounds.

b. In *pl.* A pack of such hounds; including the persons, huntsmen and others, following the chase.

1877 BLACK *Green Past.* xx, The harriers had met at Willowby Clump. **1882** MISS BRADDON *Mt. Royal* x, The harriers met at Trevena.

2. A member of a 'hare-and-hounds' team.

1891 *Daily News* 16 Dec. 5/6 The first prize for the best costumed 'harrier' was awarded to Mr. E. J. Bagot. **1893** *Birkenhead News* 9 Dec. 7/3 A little diversion was caused through one of the Rock Ferry Harriers falling into a ditch in attempting to leap over it.

Harriet Lane (ˌhærɪət ˈleɪn). *slang* (chiefly *Naut.*). [f. the name of a famous murder victim; cf. FANNY ADAMS.] Preserved meat, esp. Australian tinned meat.

1896 in FARMER & HENLEY *Slang* IV. 153/2. **1909** B. LUBBOCK *Deep Sea Warriors* ix. 117 I'd rayther eat this here than the Harriet Lane we get served out for our Sunday dinner. **1909** J. R. WARE *Passing Eng.* 150/2 *Harriet Lane*, Australian canned meat—because it had the appearance of chopped up meat; and Harriet Lane was choppped up by one Wainwright. **1916** 'TAFFRAIL' *Carry on!* 28 'Fanny Adams' and 'Harriet Lane' were the names once given to the preserved meat issued to seamen. **1932** J. W. HARRIS *Days of Endeavour* viii. 134 A meal of pantiles and cold 'Harriet Lane' is provided. **1938** W. E. DEXTER *Rope-Yarns* 30 On Sunday we were allowed 1 lb. of preserved meat, known as 'Harriet Lane', from the name of a woman who had disappeared.

harring: see HARR *v.*

†**ˈHarrington.** *Obs.* exc. *Hist.* A brass farthing token, coined by John, Lord Harrington, under a patent granted him by James I in 1613.

['Now [1613] my lord Harrington obtained a Patent from the King for the making of Brasse Farthings, a thing that brought with it some contempt though lawfull.' Spark *1st 14 Years Jas. I* (1651) I. xxix. 56.]

1616 B. JONSON *Devil an Ass* II. i. 83, I will not bate a *Harrington* o' the summe. **1632** —— *Magn. Lady* IV. iii. *a***1639** WOTTON *Let.* 12 Aug. in *Rel. Wott.* (1672) 558, I have lost four or five friends, and not gotten the value of one Harrington.

ˈharringtonite. *Min.* [f. proper name *Harrington* + -ITE.] A variety of Mesolite.

1834 *Edinb. New Philos. Mag.* XVII. 186 (Dana). **1843** PORTLOCK *Geol.* 218 Harringtonite forms veins or layers in the..greenstone of Portrush. **1868** DANA *Min.* §381 The variety named Harringtonite by Thomson.

Harris (ˈhærɪs). The name of the southern section of the island of Lewis with Harris in the Outer Hebrides, used (chiefly *attrib.*) to designate the hand-woven tweed produced by the inhabitants of this region. Also *ellipt.* (*Harris* is a proprietary term in relation to tweed manufactured in the island of Lewis with Harris.)

1892–3 *T. Eaton & Co. Catal.* Fall & Winter 11/2 The finest Harris tweed with detachable cape. **1894** *Strand Mag.* VIII. 661/2 My tailor tells me that Harris tweed cannot wear out. **1898** *Daily News* 5 July 2/4 The delightful 'Harris', 'Shetland', and 'Sutherland' tweeds that were being shown. **1924** GALSWORTHY *White Monkey* II. ii. 131 Very elegant in smoke-grey Harris tweeds. **1939** 'N. BLAKE' *Smiler with Knife* ii. 33 Her trim, green Harris-tweed suit. **1949** H. WADMAN *Life Sentence* 5 We have no tailors who know how to handle Harris. **1971** *Stornoway Gaz.* 21 Aug. 6/7 (Advt.), Gent's Harris heavy knit crew necks.

ˈharrisbuck. [Named after Sir W. C. Harris, by whom it was discovered in 1837: see *Proc. Zool. Soc.* 1838 p. 2.] The Sable Antelope of South Africa, *Hippotragus niger*.

1863 W. C. BALDWIN *Afr. Hunting* 187, I saw this morning three beautiful harrisbucks. **1876** MISS FREWER tr. *J. Verne's 3 Englishm. & 3 Russians* ix. 71 They brought down a couple of harrisbucks. **1894** LYDEKKER *Royal Nat. Hist.* II. 287.

harrish, obs. form of HARSH.

harrisite (ˈhærɪsaɪt). *Min.* [f. proper name *Harris* + -ITE.] A variety of copper-glance, with cubic cleavage.

1865 WATTS *Dict. Chem.* III. 14 *Harrisite*, a variety of cuprous sulphide, Cu^2S, occurring in the Canton mine, Georgia. **1868** DANA *Min.* §61 *Harrisite*..is chalcocite with the cleavage of galena.

†**harro**, *v.* *Obs. rare.* (See quots.)

1575 LANEHAM *Let.* (1871) 13 The swift fleeting of the Deer afore..the hoounds harroing after, az they had bin a number of skiphs too the spoyle of a karuell. **1825** JAMIESON, To Harro, Hirro, v.n. and a., to huzza, to halloo.

harroer, obs. f. HARRIER[1], HARROWER.

Harrogate (ˈhærəʊgeɪt). Name of a borough in the West Riding of Yorkshire (now in N. Yorkshire) used *attrib.* to designate (*a*) a medicinal water originating in Harrogate, (*b*) the proprietary name of a kind of toffee.

1771 SMOLLETT *Humph. Cl.* I. 229 Harrigate-water, so celebrated for its efficacy in the scurvy..is supplied from a copious spring. **1867** BLOXAM *Chem.* 45 The Harrowgate water is eminently sulphureous. *Ibid.* 654/1 (*index*) Harrogate water. **1890** in A. DAVIS *Package & Print* (1967) 64 (Advt.), Farrah's Original Harrogate Toffee. **1910** *Trade Marks Jrnl.* 28 Dec. 2069 Farrah's Harrogate Toffee... John Farrah, Limited..Harrogate; Toffee Manufacturers. **1931** W. HOLTBY *Poor Caroline* vii. 278 Eleanor came.. bringing..the caramels and Harrogate toffee that Caroline loved. **1938** *Harrogate Spa Med. Jrnl.* Apr. 17 All the Harrogate waters are chemically unstable in contact with oxygen, indicating a measure of activity not common to most mineral springs. **1967** H. JOHNSON in C. Ray *Compleat Imbiber* IX. 141 Harrogate water is bottled to this day. **1967** E. S. TURNER *Taking Cure* iii. 40 Knaresborough..was to become eclipsed in reputation by the near-by 'stinking' wells, the source of 'Harrogate water'.

†**ˈharrohen.** *Obs. rare*[−1]. [f. HARROW *v.*[2] + HEN; cf. HARRIER[1] 3.] The Hen-harrier.

1575 TURBERV. *Faulc.* 55 The harrohen or capped kyte.

harrold, harrotte, obs. ff. HERALD.

Harrovian (hæˈrəʊvɪən), *a.* and *sb.* [f. mod.L. *Harrōvi-a* Harrow + -AN.]

A. *adj.* Of or pertaining to Harrow school. **B.** *sb.* One educated at Harrow.

1864 R. CHAMBERS *Bk. of Days* II. 177 The Harrow Shootings were abolished in 1771... The Harrovians deeply regretted the ending of their old amusement. **1885** *Athenæum* 28 Mar. 402/1 Many eyes besides those of Harrovians must recently have turned with interest..to the great school upon the hill.

harrow (ˈhærəʊ), *sb.*[1] Forms: 4 **haru, harou, harewe**, 4–5 **harwe**, 5–6 **harow(e**, 7 **harrowe**, 5– **harrow**. [ME. *harwe*, answering to an OE. **hearwe* or **hearȝe*: app. related to MLG. (MDu.) *harke*, Du. *hark* rake, also ON. *herfi, hervi* (Sw. *harf, härf*, Da. *harv*) harrow; but the form-relations are obscure, and the ulterior origin uncertain.]

1. A heavy frame of timber (or iron) set with iron teeth or tines, which is dragged over ploughed land to break clods, pulverize and stir the soil, root up weeds, or cover in the seed. Sometimes made in two halves, and then locally called *the harrows*.

*a***1300** *Cursor M.* 12388 For plogh and haru [*v.rr.* harwe, harou] cuth he dight. *a***1350** *Childh. Jesus* 1365 (Mätz.) Ouȝht..þat scholde to harewe oþur to plouȝ, He couþe it wurchen. **1377** LANGL. *P. Pl.* B. XIX. 268 þise foure.. harwed in an handwhile al holy scripture, Wyth two harwes þat þei hadde..Id est, vetus testamentum & nouum. [**1393** C. XXII. 272 eythes.] *a***1400–50** *Alexander* 1063 A harrow foreheld ouer with tyndez. *c***1440** *Promp. Parv.* 228/2 Harowe [*v.r.* harwe], *erpica.* **1573** TUSSER *Husb.* xvii. (1878) 37 A barlie rake toothed, with yron and steele, like paier of harrowes. **1577** B. GOOGE *Heresbach's Husb.* I. (1586) 23 b, The Harrowe, is an instrument crosse lettused, to breake the Cloddes withall, and to cover the seedes. **1816** J. SMITH *Panorama Sc. & Art* II. 626 The harrow is employed after the plough..to produce a more complete pulverization of the soil. **1897** *N. & Q.* 8th Ser. XI. 432/2 She was an adept at the management of cart and harrows.

fig. **1824–46** LANDOR *Imag. Conv.* Wks. II. 382 Under the harrow of affliction.

b. With various defining words, as *Berwickshire harrow*, † *back harrow*; **revolving harrow**, a harrow of which the teeth are fixed on radiating arms, so as to revolve horizontally. Also *brake* (or *break*) *harrow* (BRAKE *sb.*[3] 4), BUSH HARROW, *chain-harrow* (CHAIN *sb.* 19), etc.

1616 SURFL. & MARKH. *Country Farme* 541 Breake the clods..and then with your back-harrowes runne ouer them againe. **1805** FORSYTH *Beauties Scotl.* (1808) V. 420 Break-harrows and rollers are almost as yet confined to a few proprietors. **1826** LOUDON *Encycl. Agric.* (1831) 414 The Berwickshire harrow is the most perfect implement of the kind in general use.

c. Phrases and locutions.

*c***1380** WYCLIF *Serm.* Sel. Wks. II. 280 Cristene men may seye, as þe poete seiþ in prouerbe—þe frogge seide to þe harwe, cursid be so many lordis. **1523** FITZHERB. *Husb.* §15 It is an olde sayinge, The oxe is neuer wo, tyll he to the harowe goo. **1802–12** BENTHAM *Rationale of Evidence* (1827) I. 385 *note*, Kept like toads under a harrow. **1806–7** J. BERESFORD *Miseries Hum. Life* (1826) XII. vii, Placed, and held, under the harrow. **1818** SCOTT *Rob Roy* xxvii, 'Ower mony maisters, as the paddock said to the harrow, when every tooth gae her a tig.' **1825** JAMIESON s.v., *To rin awa' with the harrows*, applied to those who do not reason fairly; especially, when they go on..disregarding any thing that has already been said in reply. **1827** SCOTT *Jrnl.* (1890) II. 94 If I die in the harrows, as is very likely, I shall die with honour. **1889** *Spectator* 12 Oct., The Armenians and Cretans are already under the harrow.

2. *transf.* A similar contrivance used for other purposes: see quots., and cf. HEARSE.

1548 HALL *Chron., Hen. V*, 48 b, They have imagined caltrappes, harowes and other new trickes to defende the force of the horsmen. **1611** BIBLE *1 Chron.* xx. 3 Hee brought out the people..and cut them with sawes, and with harrowes of yron, and with axes. **1660** JER. TAYLOR *Duct.*

Dubit II. ii. (R.), That David made the people of the Ammonites to pass under saws and harrows of iron is not safely imitable by Christian souldiers.

†**b.** A kind of sledge: also *harrow-sled*. *Obs.*

15.. *Tourn. Tottenham* 203 in Hazl. *Ritson's Songs* (1877) 81 Sum broght gret harows Ther husbandes for to hom fech. **1552** HULOET, Harrowe sled, *traha*.

c. In *Fortification*: see quot.

1788 *Chambers's Cycl.*, *Harrow*, in Fortification, is a Gate made of timber, whose dimensions are commonly six by four inches, and six inches distant from each other, well fastened to three or four cross bars, and secured with iron.

d. In *Gold-mining*: see quots.

1869 R. B. SMYTH *Goldf. Victoria* Gloss. 613 Harrows are fixed to the pole of a puddling machine, and being dragged round, divide and mix the auriferous clays with water. **1888** F. HUME *Mad. Midas* I. v, The wash dirt being put into these, there was an iron ring held up by chains, having blunt spikes to it, which was called a *harrow*.

3. A diagonal arrangement of soldiers; also of migratory fowl in the air.

1876 HOLLAND *Sevenoaks* xii. 158 The wild geese flying over..had called to Jim..and he had looked up at the huge harrow scraping the sky. **1891** *Cornh. Mag.* Dec. 643 (*temp. Edw. III*) Let your men form a harrow on either side of the ridge. *Ibid.* 647 The four-deep harrow formation which gave strength to their array, and yet permitted every man to draw his arrow freely without harm to those in front.

4. [From the verb.] The act of harrowing.

1871 R. ELLIS *Catullus* lxiv. 13 Scarcely the wave foamed white to the reckless harrow of oarsmen.

5. *attrib.* and *Comb.*, as *harrow-beam*, *-maker*, *-man*, *-pin*, *-tooth*; *harrow-shaped* adj.; **harrow-bull** [see BULL *sb.*[5]], one of the pieces of wood which form the frame of the harrow; **harrow-cultivator**, a modification of the harrow supported on wheels; **harrow-spindle**, one of the 'slots' or crosspieces which are mortised through the 'bulls'; **harrow-tine** (†**-tind**) = *harrow-tooth*.

1523 FITZHERB. *Husb.* § 15 An oxe-harowe, the whiche is made of sixe smal peces of timbre, called *harowe-bulles.. in euery bull are syxe sharpe peces of yren, called harowe tyndes. **1616** SURFL. & MARKH. *Country Farme* 662 Harrow-buls, Harrow-teeth. **1483** *Cath. Angl.* 176/2 An Harow or a *harow maker, *erpicarius*. **1826** LOUDON *Encycl. Agric.* (1831) 528 The *harrow-man's attention..should be constantly directed to [etc.]. **1530** PALSGR. 229/2 *Harowe pynne, *cheuille de herse*. **1860** PUSEY *Min. Proph.* 67 *Harrow-shaped planks, set with sharp stones. **1641** BEST *Farm. Bks.* (Surtees), The smallest sort of them for *harrowe-spindles. **1483** *Cath. Angl.* 176/2 An *Harow toothe, *paxillus*. **1828** SCOTT *F.M. Perth* ii, Plough-graith and harrow-teeth!

harrow, *sb.*[2] *dial.* = HARRE, hinge.

1528 *MS. Acc. St. John's Hosp. Canterb.*, Paid for..ye harrow of a gate. **1863** BARNES *Dorset Dial.*, *Harrow of a gate*, the backer upright timber of a gate by which it is hung to its post.

Harrow, *sb.*[3] *Cricket.* The name of a public school at Harrow in Middlesex, used *attrib.* to designate: a bat of less than full size (also *ellipt.*); 'a stroke by which the ball is driven in the direction of mid-off' (Lewis); also, an ineffectual attempt at such a stroke; 'the position of the fieldsman placed for the Harrow drive' (Lewis).

1851 J. PYCROFT *Cricket Field* ix. 171 'I beg your pardon, sir,' he..said.., 'but ain't you Harrow?'—'Then we shan't want a man down there,'..; 'stand for the "Harrow drive", between point and middle wicket.' **1877** C. BOX *Eng. Game Cricket* 451 *Harrow drive.* Some persons define this phrase to mean a fluke in the slips, after an ineffectual attempt to play forward. **1887** J. LILLYWHITE *Cricketers' Ann.* (Advt.), 7 Youth's Cane-handled Bats. Harrow size. **1922** D. J. KNIGHT *First Steps to Batting* i. 13 For a boy of 14 or 15 who has chosen a Harrow 2 lbs. 2½ oz. should be satisfactory. **1958** *Times* 22 May 15/4 It was pure pantomime with Chinese cuts and Harrow drives flying off Lobb's bat. **1970** *Times* 6 Mar. 16/8 His one escape was from a 'Harrow' drive, off McKenzie, which narrowly missed his leg stump.

harrow ('hærəʊ), *v.*[1] Forms: see HARROW *sb.*[1] [f. HARROW *sb.*[1]: cf. mod.G. *harken* to rake, Sw. *harfva*, Da. *harve* to harrow.]

1. *trans.* To draw a harrow over; to break up, crush, or pulverize with a harrow. So *harrow over*. *harrow in*, to cover in (seed, etc.) by harrowing.

a **1300** *Cursor M.* 21303 Þe toiþer he saus efter þe sede, Þe thrid it harus efter wit spede. **1377** [see HARROW *sb.*[1] 1]. *c* **1440** *Promp. Parv.* 228/2 Harwyn, *erpico*. **1530** PALSGR. 579/2 He that soweth his seedes must harowe the grounde by and by, for els the byrdes wyll eate it awaye. **1611** BIBLE *Job* xxxix. 10 Canst thou binde the Vnicorne with his band in the furrow? or will he harrow the valleyes after thee? **1759** tr. *Duhamel's Husb.* I. ix. (1762) 52 Harrow over your ground, with a heavy wide-tooth'd harrow. **1772** T. SIMPSON *Vermin-Killer* 13 When the farmer sows his seed, before he harrows it in. **1834** Low *Agric.* (1847) 412 In a fortnight or more after planting, the whole field is to be harrowed.

fig. **1650** W. BROUGH *Sacr. Princ.* (1659) 482 To plow up thy heart, and harrow thy whole man. **1654** TRAPP *Comm. Ps.* xv. 4 It is evill to sow reports and slanders but worse to harrow them in.

b. *absolutely.*

1393 LANGL. *P. Pl.* C. VI. 19 Heggen oþer harwen oþer swyn oþer gees dryue. **1565–73** *Durham Depos.* (Surtees) 104 Harrawinge and sawinge upon a Sondaye. **1882** OUIDA *Maremma* I. 3 They will..plough, and harrow, and sow.

c. *intr.* (for *passive*). Of land: To suffer harrowing; to turn out under the harrow.

1841 *Jrnl. R. Agric. Soc.* II. II. 183 It [soil] never failed.. to harrow down as mellow as possible.

†**d.** *back-harrow*, *bull-harrow*: see quots. *Obs.*

1552 HULOET, Harrow corne when it is in grase, called back harrowe, *pectino*, *sarrio*. **1780** A. YOUNG *Tour Irel.* II. 208 Bull harrow it, that is with harrows without teeth.

†**2.** *transf.* To cut through as a harrow; to 'plough' (the sea, etc.). *Obs.*

1583 STANYHURST *Æneis* I. (Arb.) 33 His launce staffe thee dust top turuye doth harrow. *Ibid.* III. 76 The sea by our mariners with the oars cleene canted is harrowd.

3. To tear, lacerate, wound (physically).

1633 T. ADAMS *Exp. 2 Peter* i. 16 The thorns harrowing his sacred head. **1735** SOMERVILLE *Chase* II. 119 Th' impatient Rider..With galling Spurs harrows his mangled Sides. **1786** tr. *Beckford's Vathek* (1834) 67 Harrowing his cheeks with a few scratches.

†**b.** To tear *up*. *Obs.*

1604 A. SCOLOKER *Diaphantus* (1880) 36 Ile haue reuenge, or harrow vp my will.

4. To lacerate or wound the feelings of; to vex, pain, or distress greatly. (Rarely with *up*.)

1602 SHAKS *Ham.* I. i. 44 It harrowes me with fear and wonder. *Ibid.* I. v. 16, I could a Tale vnfold, whose lightest word Would harrow vp thy soule. *c* **1630** SANDERSON *Serm.* II. 305 Our thoughts are so pulled and harrowed this way and that way. **1634** MILTON *Comus* 565 Amaz'd I stood, harrow'd with grief and fear. **1735** SOMERVILLE *Chase* IV. 485 Th' ambitious Wretch, whose discontented Soul Is harrow'd Day and Night. **1816** KEATINGE *Trav.* (1817) I. 152 Dreadful stories, whereby the minds of good people.. are harrowed up. **1865** MERIVALE *Rom. Emp.* VIII. lxviii. 337 His gentle nature was harrowed by the misery around him.

†**b.** To vex, disturb. *Obs.*

1609 HOLLAND *Amm. Marcell.* XXI. x. 177 He [Julian] harrowed the memoriall [*memoriam vexavit*] of Constantine, as one that had beene a deviser of innovation.

†**5.** To castrate. *Obs.*

1753 *Stewart's Trial* 139 He wants to harrow him [a horse] this spring. *Ibid.* 179 At the harrowing.

Hence '**harrowed** *ppl. a.*, '**harrowing** *vbl. sb.*

1523 FITZHERB. *Husb.* §12 As moche plowynge and harow-ynge. **1552** HULOET, Harrowed after the maner of backe harrowynge, *pectitus*. **1785** G. WASHINGTON *Writ.* (1891) XII. 225 After three ploughings and three harrowings, sowed millet. **1788** FALCONBRIDGE *Afr. Slave Tr.* 41 The harrowed parts of the back of the unoffending seaman. **1847** DISRAELI *Tancred* II. xvi, 'I cannot leave her', thought the harrowed Tancred. **1888** *Athenæum* 11 Aug. 189/3 The inevitable harrowing of the reader's feelings.

harrow ('hærəʊ), *v.*[2] Forms: 1 **herȝian**, 3 **herehen, herhen**, 3–4 **herȝen**, 4 **herwen, herewe, harwe, harrewe, haru, horu**, 4–5 **harewe**, 4–6 **harow(e, haro**, 6 **herow**, 6– **harrow**. [A by-form of HARRY *v.*, OE. *herȝian*, of which the pa. t. and pa. pple. *herȝode*, *herȝod*, and vbl. sb. *herȝung* regularly became in ME. *herwede*, *herwed*, *herwyng*, whence, by change of *-er* before cons. to *-ar*, and levelling, came ME. *harwe*, *harowe*, *harrow*.]

trans. To harry, rob, spoil. **a.** Used especially in the phrase *to harrow hell*, said of Christ.

c **1000** [see HARROWING below]. *a* **1225** *St. Marher*, 10 Þu herehedest helle. *a* **1300** *Cursor M.* 26026 Of hell it harus þe hard prisun. **13..** *Sir Beues* (MS. A.) 4469 Be him, þat herwede helle. *c* **1386** CHAUCER *Miller's T.* 326 By hym that harwed [*v.rr.* hariede, haried, harowed] helle. *c* **1500** *How Plowman lerned Pater-Noster* 39 in Hazl. *E.P.P.* I. 211, I byleve in Jhesu Cryste, Whiche suffred dethe and harowed hell. **1589** *Hay any Work* 39 Let him tell what our Sauiour Christ should do, if he did not harrow Hell. **1624** BP. MOUNTAGU *Gagg* 218 This was before Christ harrowed Hell. **1625** USSHER *Answ. Jesuit* 374 Christ spoiled, or (as they were wont to speake) harrowed Hell. **1850** NEALE *Med. Hymns* (1867) 168 Christ hath harrowed hell.

b. In the general sense of HARRY *v.*

1606 J. CLAPMAN *Hist. Gt. Brit.* I. III. xvi. 142 These Picts ..did oft-times harrow the borders. **1643** PRYNNE *Sov. Power Parl.* I. (ed. 2) 112 The County of Glocester, (which they have pitifully harrowed and spoiled). **1782** SIR W. JONES *Speech Reform. Parl.* Wks. 1799 VI. 719 They racked and harrowed the people. **1814** SCOTT *Ld. of Isles* V. xv, Long harrow'd by oppressor's hand.

Hence '**harrowed** *ppl. a.*; '**harrowing** (OE. *herȝung*) *vbl. sb.*, spoiling (of hell), also in general sense, plundering, sacking (of a country).

c **1000** ÆLFRIC *Hom.* I. 228 Hell oncneow Crist, ðaða heo forlet hyre hæftlingas ut, þurh ðæs Hælendes herȝunge. *a* **1450** *Chester Pl.* xvii. (Harl. MS. 2013) See that you doe well, In pagente sett out the harrowinge of helle. **1586** WARNER *Alb. Eng.* I. vi, And then in harrowed Hell (Pyrithous buried) he nor she, nor Theseus longer dwell. **1599** SANDYS *Europæ Spec.* (1632) 184 The harrowing and desolating of the Countrey. **1654** COKAINE *Dianea* III. 234 He came to the harrowing of our Island. **1859** WEDGWOOD *Dict. Eng. Etymol.* s.v. *Harry*, The harrowing of hell was the triumphant expedition of Christ after his crucifixion, when he brought away the souls of the righteous who had..been held captive in hell since the beginning of the world.

†**harrow, haro** ('hærəʊ), *int. Obs.* Forms: 4 **harou, -ow, -awe**, 4–6 **harowe, harrowe**, 4–7 **harrow** (5 **a rowe**), 5–7 **harro**, 6 **harrok, haroll**, 5– **haro**. [a. OF. *haro*, *harou*, *hareu*, *harol*, *harau*, *hero*, of obscure origin. The popular notion, found already in 14th c., that the expression was *ha Rou!*, a call upon Rou, Raoul, or Rollo, duke of Normandy, is not consistent with the OF. forms of the word.]

1. A cry of distress or alarm; a call for succour. *to cry harrow* (on any one): to denounce (a person's) doings. *Obs.* since *c* 1600. (Modern instances are either after ME., or from mod.F.)

13.. *Seuyn Sag.* (W.) 480 Sche..gradde 'Harow!' with gret rage. **1340** *Ayenb.* 31 Hauanne þe man..nele arere þet heued to gode be zorȝe ne grede harou be ssrifte. *c* **1386** CHAUCER *Miller's T.* 100 Lat be Nicholas Or I wol crie, out, harrow, and allas. —— *Reeve's T.* 152 Iohn..gan to crie harrow and weylaway Oure hors is lorn. **1413** *Pilgr. Sowle* (Caxton) I. vii. (1859) 6 Lete us cryen a rowe and oute upon them all! *c* **1460** *Towneley Myst.* (Surtees) 307 Oute, haro, out, out! harkyn to this horne. **1481** CAXTON *Reynard* (Arb.) 66, I crye out harowe on them that so falsely haue belyed me. **1513** DOUGLAS *Æneis* XII. x. 126 Thai rent thar hair, with harrow, and allaik. **1525** LD. BERNERS *Froiss.* II. clxxxviii. [clxxxiv.] 574 Out, harowe, what myschife is this. **1530** PALSGR. 501/2 My mother was afrayde there had ben theves in her house, and she kryed out haroll alarome. **1590** SPENSER *F.Q.* II. viii. 46 Harrow and well away! After so wicked deede why liv'st thou lenger day? *a* **1643** W. CARTWRIGHT *Ordinary* III. i. in Hazl. *Dodsley* XII. 253 Harrow, alas! I swelt here as I go. [**1863** SALA *Capt. Dangerous* II. iv. 133 You may cry Haro upon me for a Cynic. **1894** F. S. ELLIS *Reynard* 208 Harowe! I cry on that vile crew.]

‖**2.** In Law of Normandy and Channel Isles, in form *haro!*: see quots.

1682 WARBURTON *Hist. Guernsey* §43 (1822) 100 *Clameur de Haro*, is thus practised. When any man finds another entering upon his possessions..crying out three times *haro*, he in the king's name discharges any workmen..from proceeding or any person from employing them or others.. afterwards he commences his action in the court. If he neglect so to do, then the person against whom the *haro* was cried, may..bring his action against him who cried *haro*. **1862** ANSTED *Channel Isl.* IV. xxiii. (ed. 2) 539 Encroachments on property are sometimes met by a very peculiar exclamatory appeal, called 'Ha! Ro!' repeated thrice. It is considered to be the remains of an old appeal to Rollo, Duke of Normandy, and is followed by action.

3. as *sb.* The calling of *harrow!*; outcry.

c **1440** *York Myst.* xxxi. 84 Þanne gete we some harrowe full hastely at hande. **1535** STEWART *Cron. Scot.* (1858) I. 124 Thair wes no thing bot harrok, how and cry.

harrower[1] ('hærəʊə(r)). [f. HARROW *v.*[1]]

1. One who harrows land.

c **1440** *Nom.* in Wr.-Wülcker 687/16 *Hic harpicator*, a haroer. **1552–72** HULOET, Harrower, when it is backe harrowed, or weeder, *sarritor*. **1641** BEST *Farm. Bks.* (Surtees) 140 Harrowers have usually 3*d.*, or 3*d.* two quarters a day. **1688** R. HOLME *Armoury* III. 243/2 Good Plowman, Sower, Harrower, and Carter.

†**2.** [f. HARROW *sb.*[1]] A harrow-maker. *Obs.*

1483 *Cath. Angl.* 176/2 An Harow or a harow-maker (*A.* a Harower), *ericarius*.

3. One who harrows (the soul, feelings).

1814 MRS. J. WEST *Alicia de Lacy* IV. 283 Harrowers of the soul and slow consumers of the body. **1889** WHITBY *Awaken. Mary Fenwick* III. ii. 58 A glorifier of maudlin sentimentality, a harrower of feelings.

'**harrower**[2]. *Obs.* or *arch.* Also 5 **harwere**, 6 **harroer**. [f. HARROW *v.*[2]]

1. A spoiler: a by-form of HARRIER[1]. *harrower of hell*, an appellation of Christ.

c **1450** *Cov. Myst.* (Shaks. Soc.) 160 We xulle telle..How harwere of helle Was born this nyght.

2. A bird of prey; = HARRIER[1] 3, q.v.

harrowing, *vbl. sb.*: see HARROW *v.*[1] and [2].

harrowing ('hærəʊɪŋ), *ppl. a.* [f. HARROW *v.*[1]] That harrows or lacerates the feelings; acutely distressing or painful.

1810 SCOTT *Lady of L.* IV. vi, My soul with harrowing anguish torn. **1884** COLERIDGE in *Law Rep.* 14 Q. Bench Div. 279 Other details yet more harrowing..were presented to the jury.

Hence '**harrowingly** *adv.*, '**harrowingness**.

1799 W. TAYLOR in *Monthly Rev.* XXVIII. 179 Scarcely any single figure so divinely yet harrowingly expressive. **1843** *Fraser's Mag.* XXVII. 19 The prayer for annihilation is more harrowingly terrific. **1883** *Academy* 29 Dec. 426 The ..tragic and sordid harrowingness [of life].

harrumph (hæ'rʌmf). Chiefly *U.S.* Also **harrump**. [Imitative.] A guttural sound made by clearing the throat. Also *fig.* So as *vb.*, to make this sound; to speak in a rasping or guttural voice; to make a comment implying disapproval.

1936 'J. TEY' *Shilling for Candles* iv. 34 'Howdyudo. Harrumph!' He cleared his throat. **1941** *Time* 16 June 29/2 This touching appeal evoked a harrumph from the New York *Times*. **1942** *N.Y. Herald Tribune Books* 11 Jan. 13 He seems to be a figure of fun, with his..fairly continuous harrumphing. **1943** *Time* 11 Oct. 86 The State Department harrumphed and other U.S. oil companies stood on their legal, unenforceable rights. **1957** *Ibid.* 2 Sept. 23/2 Harrumphed one official: 'The best way of putting it would be to say at this point we are tolerant of Dr. Nkrumah's actions.' **1965** G. MCINNES *Road to Gundagai* ii. 33 The Captain harrumphed. **1967** *New Yorker* 25 Feb. 99 My goodness, Henry, you're much too young to be going *har-rumph*, *har-rumph* all the time! **1970** *Times Lit. Suppl.* 29 Jan. 113 Across the room he'd go, singing and harrumphing.

†**harry**, *sb.*[1] *Obs.* [f. HARRY *v.*] The act of harrying; devastation, molestation, vexation.

c **1330** R. BRUNNE *Chron.* (1810) 157 Ne þorgh non oþer harie to do him reise his schelde.

Harry ('hærɪ), *sb.*² Also 4-7 **Herry.** [ME. *Herry*, from *Henry* by assimilation of *nr* to *rr*; *er* subseq. becoming *ar*, as in HARRY *v.*] A familiar equivalent of the Christian name Henry (whence also the feminine name *Harriet*, originally = Henriette); used also in transferred applications, and as part of many appellatives.

I. 1. The proper name.

c **1386** CHAUCER *Cook's Prol.* 34 And ther-fore Herry Bailly by thy feith Be thou naf[t] wrooth. **1519** *Interlude 4 Elem.* in Hazl. *Dodsley* I. 30 The most wise prince the seventh Herry. **1648** MILTON *Sonnet to Lawes*, Harry, whose tuneful and well-measured song [etc.].

2. As a generic name for: **a.** A country fellow (? *obs.*). **b.** A young Englishman of a low-class type: cf. 'ARRY.

1796 GROSE *Dict. Vulg. Tongue, Harry*, a country fellow. **1828** *Craven Dial., Harry*, a country man, a rude boor. **1874** *All Year Round* XII. 617 We have all been introduced to Harry at home..We do not style him 'Arry, as some offensively and in the worst taste do.

c. ***flash Harry***: an ostentatious, loudly-dressed, and usually ill-mannered man; cf. FLASH *a.*³ Also *attrib.*

1960 J. RAE *Custard Boys* II. xiii. 158 'They're just a lot of smart Alecs.' 'Flash Harrys,' suggested Peter. **1960** *Times* 31 Oct. 16/4 He registers emotional upset by a slightly raised eyebrow, and then briskly readjusts his flash-Harry tie. **1962** *Times* 22 May 15/4 Her flash-Harry boy-friend.

3. pl. ***Harrys*** or ***King Harrys***: playing cards of the second quality.

1842 *Bradshaw's Jrnl.* 16 Apr. (in *Philol. Soc. Trans.* 1867, 63) The best cards are called Moguls, the others Harrys and Highlanders. **1866** in *Stationer & Fancy Trades Register* 1 Sept. (Ibid.). The different qualities of cards are distinguished as Moguls, Harrys, Highlanders, and Merry Andrews. **1867** FRY *Playing-Card terms* (Ibid. 64) Harrys, so called from the device on the wrappers.

II. With qualification, *Old*, *Lord*, *blind*.

4. **Old Harry**: A familiar name for the Devil: see also OLD and NICK. ***to play Old Harry with***: to play the devil or the mischief with; to work mischief upon; to ruin.

1777 BRAND *Pop. Antiq.* (1870) III. 54 In the north of England Old Harry is also one of the popular names of the devil. **1796** in GROSE *Dict. Vulg. Tongue.* **1824** SCOTT *Redgauntlet* ch. viii, There is none but Ould Harry, as I know of, that can match ye. **1837** MARRYAT *Dog-fiend* xlvii, They've played Old Harry with the rigging. **1842** BARHAM *Ingol. Leg., Merch. Venice* Moral, Pitch Greek to old Harry, and stick to Conundrums! **1880** MRS. LYNN LINTON *Rebel of Family* II. ix, These evening damps and chills play Old Harry with one's bronchial tubes.

5. (See quots.)

a **1700** B. E. *Dict. Cant. Crew, Old Harry*, a Composition used by Vintners, when they bedevil their Wines. **1796** GROSE *Dict. Vulg. Tongue, Old harry*, a composition used by vintners to adulterate their wines.

6. ***by the Lord Harry***: a form of swearing; of doubtful origin.

1687 CONGREVE *Old Bach* II. i, By the Lord Harry he says true. **1708** MOTTEUX *Rabelais* IV. xx. (1737) 87 Sound, Friend, in the Lord Harry's Name. **1821** BYRON *Epigr. Braziers' Addr. Caroline*, By the Lord Harry! They'll find.. much more. **1890** BESANT *Demoniac* xv, Then, by the Lord Harry..if the Devil wins this time, you shall be the prize show of the mad-house!

7. **blind Harry**: see BLIND *a.* 16.

8. ***to box Harry***: see BOX *v.*² 3 b.

III. Combinations.

9. **a.** In apposition: **harry-banning**, a local name of the three-spined stickleback. **harry-bird**, the Greater Shearwater (*Puffinus major*). **Harry Denchman**, **Harry Dutchman**, local names of the hooded or Danish crow. †**harry-lion**, 'a horse-godmother' (Halliwell). **harry-long-legs**, the cranefly or daddy-long-legs. †**harry-ruffian**, a swaggerer.

1661 LOVELL *Hist. Anim. & Min.* 235 Stickle-backs, Hackles: or *Harry bannings, are naught and unwholesome. **1778** *Eng. Gazetteer* s.v. *Pembrokeshire*, The puffin and the *harry-bird breed in holes, and commonly in those of the rabbits. **18..** W. G. WATERS *Words not in Forby* in *Norf. Arch.* VIII. 167 **Harry Denchman*, the Danish crow. **1885** SWAINSON *Prov. Names Birds* 86 Hooded crow (*Corvus cornix*)..*Harry Dutchmen. **1607** *Christmas Prince* (1816) 33 Good-wife Spiggot..her selfe staulked in the middest like a great *Harry-Lion (as it pleased the audience to terme it). **1676** COTTON *Angler* II. 338 We have also this month a *Harry-long-legs. **1781** MAD. D'ARBLAY *Diary* 14 Sept., A Harry Longlegs..after much trial to catch, eluded me. **1851** S. JUDD *Margaret* II. i. (1871) 160 She has caught a harry-long-legs and holds it by one of its shanks. **1609-10** CORBET *Elegie on Ravis* Poems (1807) 5 When I past Paules, and travell'd in that walke Where all oure Brittaine-sinners sweare and talk; Ould *Harry-ruffians, bankerupts, southsayers.

b. In arbitrary appositive uses of which a few have emerged as set expressions, e.g. **Harry Flakers** *Naut. slang*, exhausted; **Harry Flatters** *Naut. slang*, (of the sea) calm; **Harry Freeman's** (also **Harry Frees**) chiefly *Naut. slang*, a gift; also as *adj.*, free; **Harry James** *slang*, nose.

1925 FRASER & GIBBONS *Soldier & Sailor Words* 115 *It's Harry Freeman's*, a gift. Something gratis. (Navy.) **1929** F. C. BOWEN *Sea Slang* 64 *Harry Frees*, the name given in the Grand Fleet to the very welcome fruit and vegetables sent up as gifts by the public. **1935** 'L. LUARD' *Conquering Seas* xii. 139, I don't expect to supply cigarettes Harry Freemans. **1941** C. GRAVES *Life Line* 154 Fortunately, the sea has dropped and it is Harry Flatters. Harry Flatters means flat calm, and Harry is used as a predicate for almost any expression. **1946** *Lancet* 2 Feb. 177/1 Get in there, and strip off Harry Nuders. **1950** T. E. LAWRENCE *Mint* 32 Sort of thing the civvies in London pay fifty quid for, we get harry-freeman's. **1958** F. NORMAN *Bang to Rights* 36 Plenty of dust floating about in the air, which gets..up your Harry James. **1962** *John o' London's* 14 June 571/2 'Harry Flakers' to mean worn out after a party or heavy work. *Ibid.*, 'Harry Flatters' for a flat calm sea. **1962** P. PURSER *Peregrination 22* xxii. 99 It's okay for our kind of thing but it would be Harry Grimmers for ordinary civilians. **1966** F. SHAW et al. *Lern Yerself Scouse* 58, *I wuz lookin fer some Arry Freeman's*, I was looking for something for nothing. *a* **1966** M. ALLINGHAM *Cargo of Eagles* (1968) viii. 103 Get me a Harry pinkers—a large one. **1969** *Guardian* 14 Mar. 10/5 It's derisory, old boy, they'll turn it down harry nem-conners. *Ibid.*, Harry shambles, old boy... In the old Imperial Aircraft days..the engineer would bring the old kite down harry plonkers on the grass.

10. *attrib.* **Harry groat**, a groat coined by Henry VIII; the ***old Harry groat***, is that which bears the king's head with a long face and long hair. **Harry noble**, a gold coin of Henry VI. **Harry racket**, a name of Blindman's buff. **Harry sovereign**, a sovereign of Henry VII or Henry VIII.

1633 MARMION *Antiquary* II. in Hazl. *Dodsley* XIII. 456 A piece of antiquity; sir, 'tis English coin; and if you will needs know, 'tis an old *Harry groat. **1681** HICKERINGILL *Vind. Naked Truth* II. 26 In Henry the Eighths time, (when a Harry-groat was the chiefest Silver-Coyne). **1456** *Sc. Acts. Jas. II*, c. 7 Mone of vþer cuntreis..sik as the *henry Ingliss noble. **1488** *Ld. High Treas. Acc. Scot.* I. 80 Item, in Hari nobilis and salutis fourti and ane. **1497** *Ibid.* 345 Item, to Hannis, gunnar..a quartar of ane Harj nobill. **1611** COTGR., *Capifou*, a play..not much vnlike our *Harry-racket, or Hidman-blind. *Ibid.*, *Cline-mucette*, the game called Hodman-blind; Harrie-racket; or, are you all hid. **1615** J. STEPHENS *Satyr. Ess.* 371 She hath old *harry soveraignes.. to give away on her death bed.

harry ('hærɪ), *v.* Forms: 1 **herȝian**, 2-4 **herȝian**, 3 **hereȝen**, **hærȝien**, **herien**, 3-4 **herȝen**, 4 **herijen**, **harre**, **hare**, **hari**, 4-7 **hery(e**, 5 **heryȝen**, 4-6 **hary(e**, 6-9 *Sc.* **herry**, 7 **harrie**, 6- **harry**. See also HARROW *v.*² [OE. *hęrȝian*, *hęrian*, = OLG. *herron*, MLG., MDu. *heren*, *hergen* (*heregen*, *herien*), OHG. *harjôn*, *herjôn*, *herron*, MHG. *heren*, *herjen*, *herigen*, *hergen*, ON. *herja*, Da. *hærge*:—OTeut. type **harjôjan*, f. **harjo-* host, army, HERE *sb.* It is notable that in this word the OE. *ȝ* from *j*, though originally palatal (cf. pple. *heriende* in Ælfred's *Orosius*), passed over into the guttural spirant, giving *w* in ME. This prob. took place first before the back vowels, in pa. t. *herȝode*, pa. pple. *herȝod*, vbl. sb. *herȝung*, whence, by extension, the ME. present, *herwhe*, *herwe*, *harwe*, HARROW *v.*², beside the normal *herȝe*, *heryhe*, *herry*, *harry*. In ME. the native word may have run together with OF. *harier*, *herier*, *herrier*, in same sense.]

1. *intr.* To make predatory raids or incursions; to commit ravages.

c **893** K. ÆLFRED *Oros.* I. i. §19 Þa Cwenas herȝiað hwilum on ða Norðmen. *Ibid.* ii. §1 He wæs heriende & feohtende fiftiȝ wintra. *a* **1000** *O.E. Chron.* an. 794 (Earle) 59 Þa hæðenan on Norðhymbrum herȝodon. **1154** *Ibid.* an. 1014 (Earle) 151 Hi..sceoldan..ealle ætȝædere faran and herȝian. *c* **1205** LAY. 14000 Þurh þi lond heo ærneð, and hærȝieð, and berneð. *c* **1565** LINDESAY (Pitscottie) *Chron. Scot.* (1728) 6 They passed through the country and herried and slew wherever they came. **1610** HOLLAND *Camden's Brit.* I. 86 Harrie and make havock of all. *a* **1616** BEAUM. & FL. *Bonduca* II. iii, Harrying for victuals. **1837** CARLYLE *Fr. Rev.* III. I. i, The Prussians were harrying and ravaging about Metz. **1867** FREEMAN *Norm. Conq.* (ed. 3) I. v. 312 The Danes spread themselves over the country, harrying.

2. *trans.* To overrun (a place or territory) with an army; to ravage by war or invasion; to lay waste, sack, pillage, spoil.

c **1205** LAY. 1640 He..herȝede þat lond. **1375** BARBOUR *Bruce* XIX. 280 The scottis men all cokdaill Fra end till end thai heryit haill. *c* **1460** *Batt. Otterbourne* 14 in *Percy's Rel.*, And boldely brente Northomberlonde, And haryed many a towyn. **1547** J. HARRISON *Exhort. Scottes* 209 How the countrey hath been ouer runne, spoyled and heried. **1581** SAVILE *Tacitus' Hist.* III. xlix. (1591) 143 Italie he harried as a conquered countrey. *a* **1649** DRUMM. OF HAWTH. *Hist. Jas. II*, Wks. (1711) 31 The earl of Huntly burnt and herried all the lands of the earl of Murray. **1670** MILTON *Hist. Eng.* II. Wks. (1847) 500/1 The Saxons with perpetual landings and invasions harried the South coast of Britain. **1855** MACAULAY *Hist. Eng.* IV. 73 One band..harried the county of Wicklow. **1874** GREEN *Short Hist.* i. §1. 6 Pirate-boats were harrying the western coast of the island.

†**b.** *spec.* To despoil *hell*; as said of Jesus Christ after his death; = HARROW *v.*² a. *Obs.*

c **1200** *Trin. Coll. Hom* 23 For to þe time cam þat he hereȝede helle. *a* **1240** *Lofsong* in *Cott. Hom.* 205 [He] þuruh his holi passiun werþ þene deouel adun and heriede helle. *a* **1300** *Cursor M.* 1446 Til þat our lauerd haird [*v.r.* heried] hell. *c* **1450** *Mirour Saluacioun* 3032 This helle entered Jhesu..And of alle savles there inne he heryde it.

c. To rob (birds' nests). The current word in mod.Sc.

1637-50 Row *Hist. Kirk* (1842) p. xxxii, I was informed, that some parichoneris..did herit craw nestes. **1816** SCOTT *Antiq.* vii, Mony a kittywake's and lungies's nest hae I harried up amang thae very black rocks. **1894** CROCKETT *Raiders* 75, I had come over to harry gleds' nests.

3. To harass (persons) by hostile attacks, forced exactions, or rapacity; to despoil.

a **1300** *Cursor M.* 29340 Þaa þat pouer men ouer-lais, and herijs [*v.r.* robbes] þam. **13..** *E.E. Allit. P.* B. 1179 He herȝed vp al Israel. **1500-20** DUNBAR *Poems* xiii. 34 Sum is put owt of his possessioun; Sum herreit, and on creddens dynis. **1635** RUTHERFORD *Lett.* (1862) I. 148 It is His honour His servants should not be herried and undone in His service. **1786** BURNS *Addr. Beelzebub* 37 While they're only poind't and herriet. **1816** SCOTT *Old Mort.* viii, Harried and undone!—body and gudes!

b. To drive forth stripped of house or goods. *Sc.*

1549 *Compl. Scot.* xv. 135 Sic vane hope..hes gart mony of vs be hareyt furtht of house and herberye. **1552** ABP. HAMILTON *Catech.* (1884) 49 Quhasa..hurtis ony uther man and hareis him out of house and harbarie. **1603** JAS. I. *Sp. Hampton Crt. Confer.* in Fuller *Ch. Hist.* x. i, I will make them conform themselves; or else I will harry them out of the land, or else do worse. **1755** JOHNSON s.v., In Scotland it signifies to rob, plunder, or oppress..as—'he harried me out of house and home'; that is, he robbed me of my goods and turned me out of doors.

4. To worry, goad, torment, harass; to maltreat, ill-use, persecute; to worry mentally.

a **1400-50** *Alexander* 4484 And othire harlotry ȝe hant þat heris þe goste. **1530** PALSGR. 579/1 Why do you harye the poore felowe on this facyon? **1609** HOLLAND *Amm. Marcell.* 214 He was haunted and harried with the horrible apparitions and spectres of Furies. **1653** H. COGAN tr. *Pinto's Trav.* iv. 8 Being wearied with harrying those poor bodies in such fashion, they cast them all battered to pieces into the Sea. **1764** JOHNSON *Let. to Dr. Taylor* 22 May, That your mind should be harried it is no wonder. **1859** TENNYSON *Guinevere* 358 Thou their tool, set on to plague ..and harry me.

†5. To ravish, violate. *Obs.*

1591 HARINGTON *Orl. Fur.* XII. vi, Thus in his sight to have his mistresse hary'd. **1607** TOURNEUR *Rev. Trag.* I. iv. Wks. 1878 II. 36 He harried her among a throng of Panders.

6. To plunder, carry off in a marauding raid (cattle, etc.). Now *Sc.*

1579 FENTON *Guicciard.* III. (1599) 115 The cattell being harried by the one and the other. **1600** HOLLAND *Livy* X. ii. 352 They..harrie and drive away prises both of men and cattell. **1808** SCOTT *Marm.* I. xix, Harried the wives of Greenlaw's goods. **1830** GALT *Lawrie T.* VI. viii. (1849) 288 Herrying the webs and yarn of the country wives.

7. To drag. *Obs.* or *dial.*

13.. *E.E. Allit. P.* C. 178 Sembled þay were, Herȝed out of vche hyrne. **1340** HAMPOLE *Pr. Consc.* 4305 (Harl. MS. 6923. lf. 62), And deuylles salle harre hym up evene In the ayre. *c* **1386** CHAUCER *Pars. T.* ¶97. *c* **1430** *Life St. Kath.* xxiv. (1884) 53 Than anoon þe holy mayde was haryed forth to turment. *c* **1440** *Promp. Parv.* 227/2 Haryyn, or drawyn, *trahicio.* **1494** FABYAN *Chron.* VII. 429 Then the corps.. were haryed to Thamys syde, where..there in the rubbusshe & sande..they buryed or conueyed these .iii. bodyes. **1530** PALSGR. 579/2 He haryeth hym aboute as if he were a traytour. **1604** T. WRIGHT *Passions* II. iii. §4.73 Like wild horses drawing a coach..herrying and herling their Maister at their pleasure. **1613** R. CAWDREY *Table Alph.* (ed. 3), *Harrie*, pull violently. **1624** HEYWOOD *Gunaik.* I. 17 Harrieng the virgin thence. **1845** EMILY BRONTE *Wuthering Heights* xxxiv. 280 'Th' divil's harried off his soul', he cried.

†**harry**, *int. Obs.* Also 5 **harrer**, 6-7 **aree.** A call to a horse; = HAIT.

c **1440** *Promp. Parv.* 221/2 Hayht, harry. *c* **1460** *Towneley Myst.* (Surtees) 9 Harrer, Morelle, iofurthe, hyte, And let the ploghe stand. **1599** MINSHEU *Sp. Dict., Harre* (Sp.), a voice of carters to their horses, saying, aree, gee, haight, etc.

†**harry-carry.** *Obs.* (See quots., and cf. HURRY-CURRY).

1493-4 *Ordinance* in *Yarmouth Bk. Entries* (*Norf. Archæol.* (1855) IV. 262) Now of late divers of the same inhabitants have devised carts, called Harry Carries, and the owners of the same being called Harry Carmen, set..boys and girls to go with the said carts..Every harry carry man, keeping a harry carry to get money by the same, shall keep to go with the same one hable man. **1870** THORNBURY *Tour Eng.* II. xix. 37 These narrow rows [at Yarmouth] created a necessity for a special low, long narrow vehicle, first introduced in Henry the Seventh's time, and hence popularly known as 'Harry-carries'.

harrying ('hærɪɪŋ), *vbl. sb.* Forms: see the vb. [OE. *herȝung*, f. *herȝian* to HARRY: see -ING¹.] Warlike incursion; devastation, laying waste; ravaging, plundering, raiding.

c **900** tr. *Bæda's Hist.* I. ix. [xi.] (1890) 42 Seo herȝung wæs þurh Alaricum Gotena cyning ȝeworden. *c* **1000** *O.E. Chron.* an. 994 (Earle) 132 *note*, Hi..worhton þæt mæste yfel..on bærnette and hereȝunge and on man slyhtum. *a* **1250** *Prov. Ælfred* 90 in *O.E. Misc.* 108 To werie þat lond wiþ hunger and wiþ herivnge. **1557-75** *Diurn. Occurr.* (Bannatyne) 194 The hereing of Bothuile Mure. **1871** FREEMAN *Hist. Ess.* Ser. I. viii. 216 The coasts of Britain.. desolated by their harryings.

'**harry-net.** *Obs.* or *dial.* The same as HARRY-WATER *net*: see below.

1805 *Leslie of Powis* 79 (Jam.) He does not know what a harry-net is. **1867** SMYTH *Sailor's Word-bk., Harry-net*, a net with such small meshes, and so formed, as to take even the young and small fish.

†**Harry-Soph.** *Obs.* [Shortened from *Henry-Sophister*, latinized *Sophista Henriciānus*, as given by Fuller: see quot. 1661. (By an academic joke referred to Gr. ἐρίσοφος very wise.)] A class of students in the University of Cambridge: see quots.

a **1661** FULLER *Worthies* (1662) 151 *An Henry-Sophister.* So are they called, who after four years standing in the University, stay themselves from commencing Bachelors of Arts, to render them..more capable of preferment. Several reasons are assigned of their name..The truth is this, in the reign of King Henry the eighth, after the destruction of Monasteries, learning was at a loss, and the University.. stood at a gaze what would become of her. Hereupon many Students staid themselves, two, three, some four years, as who would see, how their degrees, (before they took them) should be rewarded and maintained. **1795** *Gentl. Mag.* 20 (Farmer) A Harry, or errant Soph.. is one who, having kept all the terms, by statute required previous to his law-act, is *hoc ipso facto* entitled to wear the same garment, and, thenceforth, ranks as batchelor, by courtesy. **1852** *Cambridge Univ. Cal.* 38 A student who has declared for Law or Physic, may put on a full-sleeved gown, when those of the same year, who go out at the regular time, have taken their degree of Bachelor of Arts. He is then styled a Harry-Soph (ἐρισοφος).

Harry Tate ('hærɪ 'teɪt). [Stage-name of R. M. Hutchison (1872–1940), music-hall comedian.] Used *attrib.* or in the possessive to designate anything incompetent or disorderly. Also (by *Rhyming slang*), a state, usually of nervous excitement or irritability.

1925 FRASER & GIBBONS *Soldier & Sailor Words* 115 *Harry Tate's Cavalry*, a nickname occasionally applied in jest to Yeomanry. *Ibid.*, *Harry Tate's Navy*, a nickname occasionally used in jest for the Royal Naval Volunteer Reserve. **1929** F. C. BOWEN *Sea Slang* 64 *Harry Tate's Navy*, before the war a term of derision applied to the Royal Naval Volunteer Reserve generally, but dropped completely since they showed their value. During the War it was generally applied to the Auxiliary patrol, particularly the Motor Boat Reserve. **1932** 'P. P.' *Rhyming Slang* ii. 21 *Harry Tate*, state. **1935** *Brit. Jrnl. Psychol.* Jan. 359 Native courts have been established [in Uganda]... Their methods have been described as 'Harry Tate' procedure; but they are generally successful in arriving at the facts.

† **'harry-water**, *a.* and *sb.* Also 6 herriewater. [f. HARRY *v.* + WATER.]

1. *adj.* That harries or despoils the water. As *sb.*, short for *harry-water net*, a kind of net with meshes so small as to catch very small fish.

1579 *Sc. Acts Jas. VI*, c. 89 That destroyes the Smoltes and frye of Salmound.. be Polkes, Creilles, Trammel-nets, and Herrie-waters.

2. *transf.* and *fig.* Cf. *drag-net*.

1552 LYNDESAY *Monarche* 4761 Their herywater they spred in all countries. **1620** A. SYMSON *Christ's Test. Unf.* E viij (Jam.), [The doctrine of Purgatory] is ane herrie-water-net, and hath ouer-spread the whole waters. **1629** Z. BOYD *Last Battell* 488 (Jam.) Alexander had fished the whole world with his herrie-water-net.

harse, -er, obs. ff. HARSH, HAWSE, HAWSER.

harsegaye, var. of ARCHEGAY, *Obs.*

1876 in VOYLE *Milit. Dict.*

† **'harsell**, *v. Obs. rare.* [a. F. *harceler*, in 15th c. *harceller*, for *herceler*, f. OF. *herser* to harrow.] *trans.* To aggravate, exacerbate.

1603 FLORIO *Montaigne* III. xiii. (1632) 614 He.. in stead of appeasing, doth harsell and wring them.

harsh (hɑːʃ), *a.* Forms: 3–6 **harsk**, 4 **arsk**, 5 **harske, hars**, 6 **harse, harshe, har(r)ysh(e**, 6–7 **harrish**, 6– **harsh**. [ME. *harsk*, a northern word, found from *c* 1300, agrees in form (but hardly in sense) with OSw. *harsk*, Sw. *härsk*, Da. *harsk* rank, rancid, rusty (as bacon), not recorded in ONorse; also in form and sense with MLG. and mod.G. *harsch* harsh, rough. As a general Eng. word, *harsh* (*harrish*) is not found before 16th c. There is a northern by-form HASK.

Ulterior etymology obscure: conjectured to be a deriv. in *-sk*, *-sh*, of *hard* (quasi *hardsk*), or of the root *har-* in *harm*.]

1. Disagreeably hard and rough to the touch; coarse in texture; rugged.

a **1300** *Cursor M.* 21343 Leon dantand harsk and herd. *c* **1375** *Sc. Leg. Saints, Baptista* 278 Ine to arsk hare he wes clede. ? *a* **1400** *Morte Arth.* 1084 Harske as a hundefisch.. So was þe hyde of þat hulke hally al over! **1513** DOUGLAS *Æneis* IV. x. 9 Amang buskis harsk. **1600** J. PORY tr. *Leo's Africa* I. 36 A kinde of harsh haire like goates. **1606** N. BAXTER *Sidney's Ourania* D ij, Our spokes beene blunt rude harrish uncooth. **1626** BACON *Sylva* §516 The Pith and the Kernel.. are both of a harsh substance. **1737** BRACKEN *Farriery Impr.* (1756) I. 322 An old Horse's Mouth being naturally harsh and thin of Flesh upon the Roof. **1876** PAGE *Adv. Text-Bk. Geol.* iv. 85 Volcanic ash and dust feel harsh to the finger.

2. Repugnant or unpleasant to other bodily senses. **a.** Unpleasantly rough to the taste; astringent.

c **1440** *Promp. Parv.* 228/2 Harske, or haske, as sundry frutys (*P.* hars, or harske). **1533** ELYOT *Cast. Helthe* II. vii. (1541) 20 b, [Grapes] which are in taste bytter or harryshe. **1551** T. WILSON *Logike* Ded. (1580) A ij b, This fruite.. maie perhaps in the first tastying, seeme somewhat rough and harshe in the mouthe. **1626** BACON *Sylva* §40 Such Astriction is found in Things of an Harrish Tast. **1637** MILTON *Lycidas* 3, I come to pluck your berries harsh and crude. **1809** PINKNEY *Trav. France* 139 The water.. is so harsh that it cannot be drunk. **1831** J. DAVIS *Manual Mat. Med.* 258 Black Oxide of Mercury.. is.. of a harsh taste.

b. Disagreeably rough to the ear; jarring, discordant.

1530 [implied in HARSHNESS]. **1568** GRAFTON *Chron.* II. 49 He was harrish of voyce, but yet eloquent. **1597** HOOKER *Eccl. Pol.* V. xxvii. §2 Certain harsh and vnpleasant discords. ? **1630** MILTON *At a Solemn Music* 20 And with harsh din Broke the fair musick. **1670** NARBOROUGH *Jrnl.* in *Acc. Sev. Late Voy.* I. (1711) 65 The Men have a harsh Language, and speak ratling in the Throat. **1870** E. PEACOCK *Ralf Skirl.* II. 217 Loud and harsh as the scream of the peacock. **1892** W. MINTO in *Bookman* Nov. 56/2 They are the only harsh notes in a volume of delightful verse.

c. Of rough aspect; unpleasing or inharmonious to the eye; forbidding.

1774 GOLDSM. *Nat. Hist.* (1776) IV. 200 His face tanned, and all his lineaments.. harsh and blackened by the sun. **1837** W. IRVING *Capt. Bonneville* III. 141 The red glare of the fires upon these wild groups and harsh faces. **1841** W. SPALDING *Italy & It. Isl.* I. 177 The energy and harsh proportions, sometimes reaching the height of caricature.. in the bronze and terra-cotta figures. **1894** WILSON *Cycl. Photogr.* 179 A picture without half tones is harsh.

d. Disagreeable or forbidding in general physical effect; attended with discomfort; rough, rude.

1613 PURCHAS *Pilgrimage* (1614) 422 The Kirgessen.. Iteseliti, harsh names of harsher people in those most harsh and horrid desarts. **1681** DRYDEN *Abs. & Achit.* To Rdr., The physician.. prescribes harsh remedies to an inveterate disease. **1841** JAMES *Brigand* ii, The harsh and boisterous state of the weather. **1856** KANE *Arct. Expl.* II. xxi. 211 A cache of meat deposited.. in this harsh wilderness.

3. Repugnant or roughly offensive to the feelings; severe, rigorous, cruel, rude, rough, unfeeling. **a.** Of actions, systems, etc.

1579–80 NORTH *Plutarch* 503 (R.) His speech was not harsh nor churlish, but verie mild and pleasant, as appeareth by the letters he wrote. **1588** SHAKS. *L.L.L.* V. ii. 289 It can neuer be, They will digest this harsh indignitie. **1659** W. CHAMBERLAYNE *Pharonnida* I. iii. (1850) 55 Whatever crime's the cause Of this harsh sentence. **1709** LADY M. W. MONTAGU *Let. to Miss A. Wortley* 21 Aug., Repent of your harsh censure. **1849** MACAULAY *Hist. Eng.* II. 90 Under the harsh administration of Laud.

b. Of persons.

1580 SIDNEY *Arcadia* 431 (N.) The verie shining force of excellent vertue, though in a very harrish subject. **1596** SHAKS. *Merch. V.* IV. i. 123 Not on thy soale: but on thy soule harsh Jew Thou mak'st thy knife keene. **1790** BURKE *Fr. Rev.* Wks. V. 328 As conquerors, they have imitated the policy of the harshest of that harsh race. **1875** JOWETT *Plato* (ed. 2) III. 109 He is a harsh master to his servants.

4. Repugnant to the understanding or taste; grating upon the mind or æsthetic faculty; strained, forced; lacking smoothness, unpleasing, ungraceful.

1594 WILLOBIE *Avisa* (1880) 12 Easie to be vnderstood, without harrish absurdity. **1624** CAPT. SMITH *Virginia* Pref. 1 Though the beginning may seeme harsh.. a pleasanter Discourse ensues. **1710** BERKELEY *Princ. Hum. Knowl.* §38 It sounds very harsh to say we eat and drink ideas. **1841** MYERS *Cath. Th.* 130 No harsh transitions Nature knows. **1897** GRENFELL & HUNT *Λόγια Ἰησοῦ* iii. 10 An accusative after *νηστεύειν*, 'fast to the world' is very harsh.

5. *Comb.* **a.** Parasynthetic, as ***harsh-featured***, ***-mannered***, ***-syllabled***, ***-tongued***, ***-voiced*** adjs. **b.** Adverbial, as ***harsh-blustering***, ***-echoing***, ***-grating***, ***-resounding***, ***-sounding*** adjs. **c.** † **harsh-weed**, a name for Knapweed, *Centaurea Scabiosa* (Sir J. Hill *Herb. Brit.* 1760).

1735 SOMERVILLE *Chase* IV. 155 Thy threat'ning voice, *Harsh-echoing from the hills. **1863** I. WILLIAMS *Baptistery* Pref. (1874) 14 Uncouth shapes, *Harsh-featur'd.. rude of limb. *a* **1743** SAVAGE *Wks.* (1775) II. 75 (Jod.) Bars *harsh-grating. **1593** SHAKS. *Rich. II*, I. iii. 135 With *harsh resounding Trumpets dreadfull bray. **1595** —— *John* IV. ii. 150 In rude *harsh sounding rimes. **1870** BRYANT *Iliad* I. I. 30 *Harsh-tongued! thou ever dost suspect me. **1850** LYNCH *Theo. Trin.* v. 73 Wisdom is not *harsh-voiced.

harsh, *v. rare.* [f. prec. adj.]

† **1.** *intr.* To give a harsh sound; to creak. *Obs.*

1583 STANYHURST *Æneis* I. (Arb.) 32 Gates with the metal dooe creake in shrilbated harshing. *Ibid.* II. 63 At leingth with rounsefal, from stock vntruncked, yt harssheth.

2. *trans.* To rub or clash roughly against.

1889 H. A. C. DUNN *Fencing* vii. 98 The defender parries tierce with a crisp tap, taking care not to harsh his blade.

harshen ('hɑːʃ(ə)n), *v. rare.* [f. HARSH *a.* + -EN[5].] *trans.* To render harsh.

1824 *Mirror* III. 123/1 Sounds of harmony, harshened into discord. **1850** KINGSLEY *Alt. Locke* xxxii, A soured and harshened spirit. **1880** BERTHA THOMAS *Violin-Player* II. x. 248 In a strange harshened accent.

'harshish, *a. nonce-wd.* [f. as prec. + -ISH.] Somewhat harsh.

1841 BROWNING *Pippa Passes* ii, How to Jonah sounded harshish, Get thee up and go to Tarshish.

harshly ('hɑːʃlɪ), *adv.* [f. as prec. + -LY[2].] In a harsh or disagreeably rough manner; roughly, rudely, discordantly, unpleasantly, severely, unfeelingly, etc.: see the adj.

c **1375** *Sc. Leg. Saints, Margaret* 437 þe maydine.. hynt hyme harskly be þe hare. **1590** SHAKS. *Com. Err.* IV. iv. 7 'Twill sound harshly in her eares. **1599** THYNNE *Animadv.* (1875) 32 Althoughe yt sholde be improperlye or harsely applied. **1667** MILTON *P.L.* XI. 537 Like ripe Fruit.. Gatherd, not harshly pluckt. **1784** COWPER *Task* VI. 503 Truths Not harshly thundered forth, or rudely pressed. **1849** MACAULAY *Hist. Eng.* II. 214 A harsh code harshly enforced.

harshness ('hɑːʃnɪs). [f. as prec. + -NESS.] The quality of being harsh; unpleasant roughness, discordance, severity, rigour, etc.: see the adj.

c **1375** *Sc. Leg. Saints, Agnes* 122 With harsknes he can hir assalȝe. **1500–20** DUNBAR *Poems* xxii. 19 For harsknes of hir carlich throt. **1530** PALSGR. Introd. 15 To avoyde all maner harshenesse.. whan many consonantes come betwene the vowelles. **1562** TURNER *Herbal* II. 86 Hartis tung.. hath a byndyng taste with an harrishnes. **1695** ADDISON tr. *Virg. Georg.* IV. Wks. 1721 I. 21 Luscious sweets, that.. Correct the harshness of the racy juice. *a* **1782** BLAIR *Lect.* xviii. 18 Harshness arises from unusual words; from forced inversions.. and too much neglect of smoothness and ease. **1847** TENNYSON *Princ.* II. 289 My needful seeming harshness, pardon.

† **'harshy**, *a. Obs. rare.* [f. as prec. + -Y.] Of harsh quality or character.

1583 STANYHURST *Æneis* III. (Arb.) 77 Theartoo skriches harshye reioyning. **1607** *Barley-Breake* (1877) 28 The harshie rockes are all to totters rent.

harsk(e, obs. forms of HARSH.

harslet: see HASLET.

harst, a Sc. form of HARVEST.

† **'harstrang, 'horestrong.** *Obs. Herb.* [Introd. 1562 from Du. *harstrang*, = Ger. *harnstrenge* strangury, f. *harn* urine + *strenge* tightness, rigidity.] Hog's Fennel, *Peucedanum officinale*.

1562 TURNER *Herbal* II. 83 b, Peucedanum is named.. in Duch Har strang, and because we haue no other name for it .. it may be called in Englishe also Har strang. *Ibid.* 84 Harstrang.. will make hys hede ache and be dusy that gathereth it. **1578** LYTE *Dodoens* II. cviii. 298 It is called.. in Englishe also *Peucedanum*, Horestrong, or Hore-strange. **1601** HOLLAND *Pliny* II. 430 If the head be annointed with Castoreum incorporat with oile of roses and Harstrang. **1879** PRIOR *Plant-n.*, *Harstrong*, or *Horestrong*.

hart (hɑːt). Forms: 1 **heorut, heorot**, 1–4 **heort**, 3–6 **hert**, 4–6 **herte**, 5–6 **harte**, 5– **hart**. [ME. *hert*, OE. *heort*, *heorot* = OLG. *hirot* (MDu., Du. *hert*, LG. *hart*), OHG. *hiruz*, *hirz* (MHG. *hirz*, Ger. *hirsch*, from earlier *hirsz*), ON. *hjǫrtr* (Sw., Da. *hiort*):—OTeut. **herut-*, perh.:—**herwut-*, **herwot-*, with dental formative *-t*, appended to a stem cognate with L. *ceruo-s*; perh. related to Gr. *κερατ-* horn, as if = 'the horned'.]

1. The male of the deer, esp. of the red deer; a stag; *spec.* a male deer after its fifth year.

c **825** *Vesp. Psalter* xli[i], 2[1] Swe swe heorut ȝewillað to waellum wetra. *c* **888** K. ÆLFRED *Boeth.* xxxv. §6 Nan heort ne onscunode nænne leon. *c* **1205** LAY. 26762 Swa hund þene heort driueð. **1297** R. GLOUC. (1724) 376 Wo so.. slou hert oþer hynde. *c* **1385** CHAUCER *L.G.W.* 1121 (*Dido*) Ne hound for hert or wilde bor or der. **1398** TREVISA *Barth. De P.R.* v. xxv. (1495) 134 As it faryth in horses, camelles, and hartes. **1526** *Pilgr. Perf.* (W. de W. 1531) 226 As the hart renneth to the water. **1602** *2nd Pt. Return fr. Parnass.* II. v. 889 Your Hart is.. the fourth yeare a Stagge, the fift yeare a great Stag, the sixt yeare a Hart. **1611** BIBLE *Ps.* xlii. 1 As the Hart panteth after the water brookes. **1741** *Compl. Fam. Piece* II. i. 289 To find out the Harbour or Layer of a Hart. **1814** SCOTT *Ld. of Isles* IV. ii, See him dart O'er stock and stone like hunted hart.

† **b.** ***hart of grease***, a fat hart. ***hart of ten***, a hart with ten branches on his horns. ***hart royal***, a hart that has been chased by a royal personage.

c **1380** *Sir Ferumb.* 1750 Gyrfacouns y-muwed & white stedes, & hertes of gresse y wene. *a* **1440** *Sir Degrev.* 249 Hys proud hertes of grese Bereth no chartur of pes. *c* **1550** *Adam Bell* in Furniv. *Percy Folio* (1868) III. 421 Eche of them slew a hart of greece The best they could there see. **1598** MANWOOD *Lawes Forest* 24 b, If the King or Queene doe hunt or chase him, and he escape away aliue, then.. he is called a Hart Royall. *Ibid.* iv. §6. 28 When a Hart is past his sixt yeere, he is generally to be called a Hart of Tenn. **1637** B. JONSON *Sad Sheph.* I. ii, A great, large deer! *Rob.* What head? *John.* Forked: a hart of ten. **1674** N. COX *Gentl. Recreat.* (1677) 6 If hunted by the King, a *Hart Royal*. **1822** SCOTT *Nigel* xxvii, There is a pleasure in looking at a hart of grease.

2. *Comb.*, as ***hart-like*** adj., ***hart-skin***; **hart-berry**, a local name of the Bilberry; † **hart-bramble**, Buckthorn; † **hart-evil** (see quot.); † **hart-fly**, an insect. ? the stag-beetle; † **hart-horse**, tr. Gr. *ἱππέλαφος*, 'lit. the horse-deer, perhaps the rusa, *Cervus Aristotelis*' (Liddell & Scott); † **hart-hound**, a stag-hound; † **hart-root, hart's-root** (see quots.); **hart's-balls** = *hart's truffles*; **hart's black** (see quot.); † **hart's-crest**, the imaginary horns on the forehead of a cuckold; † **hart's-eye**, a plant: see quot.; † **hart's-head** (see quot.); † **hart's-trefoil**, Melilot = HARTCLOVER; **hart's-truffle**, a kind of underground fungus (*Elaphomyces*); † **hart-thorn** [tr. L. *spina cervina*], Buckthorn, *Rhamnus catharticus*; † **hart-wolf**, a fabulous animal, a hybrid between a deer and a wolf.

c **1000** *Sax. Leechd.* II. 332 Cnua þonne *heorot brembel leaf. **1727** BAILEY vol. II, **Hart Evil* (with Farriers), the Stag-evil, a Rheum or Defluxion, that falls upon the Jaws and other Parts.. of a Horse, which hinders him from eating. **1610** GUILLIM *Heraldry* III. xviii. (1611) 152 As the *Hart-fly Beetle, Ladi-cow, [etc.] **1550** J. COKE *Eng. & Fr. Heralds* vii. (1877) 59 Greyhoundes, *harthoundes, buckehoundes, and begles. **1598** SYLVESTER *Du Bartas* II. i. IV. *Handicrafts* 402 With *Hert-like legs. **1611** COTGR., *Libanot*, Hearbe Frankincense.. *Hart-root. **1677** LITTLETON *Lat. Dict.*, *Harts-root, *libanotis* [= rosemary]. **1823** CRABB *Technol. Dict.*, *Hart-Root*, the *Athamanta* of Linnæus. **1866** *Treas. Bot.*, *Hart'sballs, *Elaphomyces*. **1851** *Dict. Archit.*, **Hart's Black*, that substance remaining.. after the spirits, volatile salt and oil, have been extracted from hartshorn.. when.. levigated it answers the purpose of painters nearly as well as ivory black. **1600** J. LANE *Tel-troths Message* 44 The married men might.. shunne the

*Harts crest to their hearts content, With cornucopia, Cornewall, and the horne. **1607** TOPSELL *Four-f. Beasts* 126 Elaphoscum: (that is, as some call it *Harts eye, others Hart-thorne, or grace of God, others wild Ditany). **1686** PLOT *Staffordsh.* 26 [Clouds] in the form of the letter V, jagg'd on each side..called by the water-men the *Harts-head. **1483** *Cath. Angl.* 177/1 An *Hartskyn..*nembris.* **1624** HARINGTON *Sch. Salerne* in *Babees Bk.* 255 In the Summer-time I chiefly commend garments of Harts-skinnes, and Calues-skins. **1640** PARKINSON *Theat. Bot.* Table, *Harts Trefoile is Mellilot. **1866** *Treas. Bot.* 389 *Deer balls*, a synonym of *Hart's Truffles..*Elaphomyces.* **1607** *Hart-thorne [see *hart's-eye*]. **1611** FLORIO, *Spina ceruina*, the wilde Harthorne. **1577** EDEN & WILLES *Hist. Trav.* 295 *Harte Woolfes..engendred eyther of a Woolfe and a Hynde, or a Hart and a bitch Woolfe. **1660** F. BROOKE tr. *Le Blanc's Trav.* 166 They have..Hart-Wolves brought up to hunt their own kinde.

hart, obs. f. HEART; obs. var. *art* (see BE).

hartal (ˈhɑːtæl, ‖ˈhʌrtɑːl). *India.* [Hind. *hartāl* for *haṭṭāl* lit. 'locking of shops' (Skr. *haṭṭa* shop, *tālaka* lock, bolt).] Organized shutting of shops and cessation of business, to serve, usually, as a protest against government legislation or a political situation, or as an act of mourning.

1920 *Blackw. Mag.* Apr. 441/1 What I had seen there of the crowds at the Hartal..had made me nervous. **1921** *Q. Rev.* July 54 He proclaimed a universal 'hartal', or cessation from business, as a protest against the Rowlatt legislation. **1922** *Ibid.* Oct. 417 Gandhi was preparing a *Hartal* at Bombay. **1931** *Daily Tel.* 6 Jan. 9/5 The Moslems enforced a complete 'hartal' (day of mourning or strike). **1955** *Times* 18 Aug. 8/5 A hartal to be observed throughout India on Friday was called here to-day by the Goa liberation committee in memory of the Indians killed by Portuguese fire on Monday. **1958** J. V. BONDURANT *Conquest of Violence* iii. 36 Non-cooperation may include strike, walk-out, *hartal*, and resignation of offices and titles. *Ibid.* iv. 119 The *hartal* is usually of short duration—a day or two. Shops close and work ceases. *Hartal* is also employed at times of national mourning. **1962** A. CARTER *Direct Action* 8 At the beginning of the Rowlatt Act Satyagraha Gandhi called on his followers for a 'hartal'—a day of abstention from work and of fasting and prayer.

hart-clover, hart's clover. [f. HART: see quot. 1664.] A name for Melilot.

*c***1000** *Sax. Leechd.* I. 120 Ðeos wyrt þe man..heort-clæfre nemneð. *c***1425** *Voc.* in Wr.-Wülcker 644/36-7 *Hoc trifolium*, hartclauer. *Hic sicassis, idem.* **1644** R. TURNER *Botanalogia* 199 In English Melilot, Kings Claver, and Harts Claver, because Deer delight to feed upon it. **1674-91** RAY *N.C. Words* 35 Hart-claver, Melilot. **1879** PRIOR *Plant-n., Hart's Clover.*

harte, obs. f. ART *sb.*; also of HEART, q.v.

*c***1375** *Sc. Leg. Saints, Nycholas* 56 His fadir..Gert informe hyme..In liberale hartis. *Ibid., Eugenia* 52 Scho had leyryte..Of þe sewine sciens al þe harte.

‖**hartebeest, hartbeest** (ˈhɑːtəbiːst, ˈhɑːtbiːst). Also in Afrikaans form **hartebees.** [S. Afr. Du., f. Du. *hert* hart + *beest* beast.]

a. A kind of antelope (*Alcephalus caama*) common in South Africa.

1786 SPARRMAN *Voy Cape G.H.* II. xiv. 199 The hartbeest ..is the most common of all the larger gazels. **1824** BURCHELL *Trav.* II. 99 One of our party fell in with the fresh remains of a *kaama* or *hartebeest.* **1834** PRINGLE *Afr. Sk.* 11 Where the gnu, the gazelle and the hartèbeest graze. **1884** J. COLBORNE *Hicks Pasha* 198, I saw a magnificent herd of hartebeeste quietly grazing. **1959** *Cape Times* 27 Jan. 2/6 Rare kinds of buck, such as eland and red hartebees. **1961** L. VAN DER POST *Heart of Hunter* III. xiv. 178 Once, the story says, Mantis appeared to the children of the early race as a dead Hartebees.

b. *attrib.*, as **hartebeest house, hut,** 'a frail structure of "wattle and daub", so called, apparently, because a similar primitive structure was often erected by the earlier hunters' (Pettman); also **hartebeeste house.**

[**1815** A. PLUMPTRE tr. *Lichtenstein's Trav.* II. 95 Not far from this wretched cabin stood a somewhat more spacious, but very ruinous straw hut, of the sort which is here called *hartebeesthuisje.*] **1818** B. H. LATROBE *Jrnl.* 256 A hartebeest-house, being a roof, put upon a wall about two feet in height. **1863** W. C. BALDWIN *Afr. Hunting* i. 16 What is called a hartebeest house, of very tall reeds, stuck close together in a kind of trench dug for them in bundles, and meeting over head. **1873** F. BOYLE *To Cape for Diamonds* 242 A colony of Hottentot women had seized possession of our 'hartebeest's hut'. **1898** W. C. SCULLY *Vendetta of Desert* iv. 23 Uncle Diederick lived in a structure known in South Africa as a 'hartebeeste house'.

harth(e, obs. form of HEARTH.

hartheled, obs. var. of *hardled*, HURDLED.

harth-pace, erron. f. HALF-PACE: cf. HATHPACE.

1667 PRIMATT *City & C. Build.* II. (1680) 70 You may make these Stairs..Harth-pace-stairs, and so have one or two landing-places.

hartichoke, -chough, etc., obs. ff. ARTICHOKE.

1688 R. HOLME *Armoury* II. 76/2 The Artechoke (or vulgarly an Hartichough).

hartin (ˈhɑːtɪn). *Min.* [Named from *Oberhart* in Styria: see -IN.] A fossil resin ($C_{10}H_{17}O$) found in the lignite of Oberhart.

1863-82 WATTS *Dict. Chem.* III. 14.

hartite (ˈhɑːtaɪt). *Min.* [f. as prec. + -ITE.] A fossil resin found with hartin.

1863-82 WATTS *Dict. Chem.* III. 14.

hartleberry, obs. form of HURTLEBERRY.

Hartleian (hɑːˈtliːən, ˈhɑːtlɪən), *a.* and *sb.*

A. *adj.* Of or pertaining to the doctrines of David Hartley (1705-57), regarded as the founder of the English associationist school of psychologists. **B.** *sb.* One of the Hartleian school.

1803 *Edin. Rev.* I. 476 The unnecessary complication of the Hartleyan theory. **1817** COLERIDGE *Biog. Lit.* (1882) 57 This *Caput mortuum* of the Hartleian process has been rejected by his followers. **1859** J. MARTINEAU *Ess., etc.* (1891) III. 564 The thorough-faced Hartleyian walks through these startling paradoxes.

hart-royal. a. See HART 1 b. **b.** See quot.

1755 JOHNSON, *Hart-royal*, a plant; a species of buck-thorn plantain. [App. an error in J.: cf. HARTSHORN 3.]

hartshorn (ˈhɑːtshɔːn). [f. *hart's* (possessive of HART) + HORN.]

1. The horn or antler of a hart; the substance obtained by rasping, slicing, or calcining the horns of harts, formerly the chief source of ammonia.

*c***1000** *Sax. Leechd.* I. 234 Wiþ heafod sare, heortes hornes axan fif peneᵹa ᵹewæᵹe drinc. *c***1420** *Pallad. on Husb.* I. 937 Brent hertis horn. **1578** LYTE *Dodoens* IV. lxxx. 544 Putting thereto Hartes horne burnt and washed. **1646** SIR T. BROWNE *Pseud. Ep.* 335 So of the suffitus of a torch, doe Painters make a velvet blacke..so of burnt Harts horn a sable. **1655** MRQ. WORCESTER *Cent. Inv.* §83 A Rasping-Mill for Harts-horn. **1718** QUINCY *Compl. Disp.* 8 The Spirit of Animals, as what is procur'd from Hartshorn. **1732** ARBUTHNOT *Rules of Diet* 264 Calcin'd Hartshorn. **1796** MRS. GLASSE *Cookery* xxi. 334 The shavings of hartshorn.

2. ***spirit of hartshorn***, also simply ***hartshorn***: the aqueous solution of ammonia (whether obtained from harts' horns or otherwise). ***salt of hartshorn***: carbonate of ammonia; smelling salts.

1685 BOYLE *Salub. Air* 109 A colourless Liquor, namely Spirit of Hartshorn or of Sal-armoniac. *a***1698** TEMPLE *Gout* (R.), The Count..gave me a receipt of the salt of hartshorn, by which a famous Italian physician..had performed mighty cures. **1709** STEELE *Tatler* No. 23 ¶2 Down she fell..Hartshorn! Betty, Susan, Alice, throw Water in her Face. **1807** T. THOMSON *Chem.* (ed. 3) II. 6 Ammonia..was known by the name of *volatile alkali*; it was also called *hartshorn*, because..obtained by distilling the horn of the hart. **1875** H. C. WOOD *Therap.* (1879) 557 In the use of hartshorn..it is necessary to exercise care, lest injury should be done to the delicate mucous membrane.

†**3.** Applied to two plants having leaves branched like a stag's horn: **a.** Buck's-horn Plantain, *Plantago Coronopus* (also **hartshorn plantain**); **b.** Swine's Cress, *Senebiera Coronopus. Obs.*

1578 LYTE *Dodoens* I. lxiv. 93 The first Crowfoote or Hartshorne..bringeth forth vpon each side of the leafe three or foure shorte startes or branches, almost like to the branches of a Hartes horne. *Ibid.* 95 We may also call it Hartes horne Plantayne, Buckehorne Plantayne. **1656** CULPEPPER *Eng. Phys. Enl., Bucks-horn*, it is also called Harts-horn..the Vertues are held to be the same of Bucks-horn plantane. **1674** N. COX *Gentl. Recreat.* (1677) 142 Juice of an Herb called Harts-horn. **1866** *Treas. Bot.*, Hart'shorn, *Plantago Coronopus.*

4. *attrib.* and *Comb.*, as ***hartshorn drops, -rasper, shavings, tea***; †**hartshorn beetle**, the stag-beetle; **hartshorn jelly**, a nutritive jelly made formerly from the shavings of harts' horns, now from those of calves' bones; **hartshorn plantain** (see 3).

1658 ROWLAND *Moufet's Theat. Ins.* 1005 The πλατύκερως, or *Harts horn Beetle is called *Lucanus* by Nigidius. **1706-7** FARQUHAR *Beaux Strat.* IV. i, Here, here, let's see the *Hartshorn-drops. **1813** J. THOMSON *Lect. Inflam.* 641 Hartshorn drops, and such-like stimulating fluids. **1769** MRS. RAFFALD *Eng. Housekpr.* (1778) 210 To make *Hartshorn Jelly. **1883-4** *Cassell's Dict. Cookery* 308 *Hartshorn Jelly*—Boil half a pound of hartshorn shavings in four pints of water for three hours. **1725** *Lond. Gaz.* No. 6382/11 Richard Sill..*Harthorn-Rasper. **1747** WESLEY *Prim. Physic* (1762) 48 Two ounces of *Hartshorn shavings. *a***1762** LADY M. W. MONTAGU *Song to Lady Irwin* i. Lett., etc. 1887 II. 511 'Tis too soon for *hartshorn tea.

ˈ**hart's-tongue.** [A transl. of med.L. *lingua cervi*; so named from the shape of the long entire fronds: so Ger. *hirschzunge*, Da. *hertstong*, Fr. *langue de cerf*, etc.] The common name of the fern *Scolopendrium vulgare*; also extended to other species of the genus; rarely applied to some other polypodiaceous ferns, as *Olfersia cervina* and *Polypodium Singaporianum.* So **hart's-tongue fern.**

*c***1325** *Gloss. W. de Biblesw.* in Wright *Voc.* 162 *Cerflange*, hertis-tounge. ?*c***1350** *O.E. Med. Gloss.* in *Archæol.* XXX. 409 Hertistonge, *lyngua cervi.* *c***1440** *Promp. Parv.* 238/1 Hertys tongue, herbe, *scolopendria, lingua cervi.* *a***1450** *Alphita* (Anecd. Oxon.) 103 *Lingua ceruina..gall.* cerflange, *ang.* herttonge. **1562** TURNER *Herbal* II. 86 b, Hartis tunge.. hath nether stalk sede nor floure. **1589** COGAN *Haven Health* (1636) 179 Fumitory, Harts-tong..and such like cooling herbes. **1854** S. THOMSON *Wild Fl.* III. (ed. 4) 285 The hart's-tongue fern grows in bunches of long plain leaves. **1882** *Good Cheer* 37 Glossy fronds of hartstongue were uncurling among the wet stones.

hartwort (ˈhɑːtwɜːt). [A 16th c. spelling of HEARTWORT, q.v.]

1. Applied by early herbalists to their genus *Seseli*, including various umbelliferous plants now placed elsewhere.

Seseli æthiopicum is now *Laserpitium latifolium*, Herb Frankincense.

1562 TURNER *Herbal* II. 135 a, Seseli Ethiopicum groweth in diuerse partes of hyghe Germanye..som call it hartzwurt ..wherefore we maye call it Hartwurt, wyth the Duche men, vntyll we fynde a better name for it. **1611** COTGR., *Siler*, the hearbe Seseli, Hartwort. **1668** WILKINS *Real Char.* II. iv. §4. 90 Umbelliferous Herbs of Finer Leaves.. Hart-wort. **1693** SALMON *Bates' Dispens.* (1713) 23/2 Hart-wort, or Bastard Lovage. **1714** *French Bk. of Rates* 89 Hart-wort per 100 weight, 01 00. **1715** PETIVER in *Phil. Trans.* XXIX. 239 Shrub Hartwort, Ray 476, c. 5 [=*Bupleurum fruticosum*]. **1886** *Syd. Soc. Lex., Hartwort*, the *Laserpitium siler*, and the *Tordylium maximum.* H. French, H. of Marseilles, *Seseli tortuosum.*

2. A book-name for *Tordylium maximum*, one of the plants formerly included in the genus *Seseli.*

1787 WITHERING *Brit. Plants* (ed. 2) I. 269 **1824** J. E. SMITH *Eng. Flora* I. 103. **1846** SOWERBY *Eng. Bot.* (ed. 3), Great-Hart-Wort, *Tordylium Maximum.* **1866** *Treas. Bot.*, Hartwort, *Tordylium.*

harumfrodite (hɛəˈrʌmfrədaɪt). *Jocular slang.* Also **harumphrodite, herumfrodite.** [After *hermaphrodite.*] = HERMAPHRODITE *sb.* and *a.* So **haˌrumphroˈditic** *a.*, characteristic of an hermaphrodite.

1896 [see GIDDY *a.* 3 b]. **1924** *Blackw. Mag.* Aug. 235/1 Take the young Jot from the plough and turn him to Pope's 'Rape of the Lock' or Shelley's 'Adonais', and you will make a comfortless harumphroditic amphibian of him. **1953** *Essays & Studies* VI. 103 A Welsh writer writes in Welsh.. and those others who make articulate some two-thirds of the nation are, according to taste, 'lost to the English' or base harumphrodites.

harum-scarum (ˈhɛərəmˈskɛərəm), *adv.*, *a.*, and *sb. colloq.* Also 7-9 **harum-starum,** 8 **hare'um scare'um, hairum-scairum,** 8-9 **harem-scarem.** [A riming combination, app. f. HARE *v.*[2] + SCARE *v.*, sometimes taken as = *hare 'em, scare 'em.*]

A. *adv.* Recklessly, heedlessly, wildly. ? *Obs.*

1674-91 RAY *S. & E.C. Words* 101 To *Hare*, to affright or make wild; to go *harum starum.* **1740** *Round about our Coal Fire* i. (Farmer), While Tom run harum scarum to draw a jug of ale. **1785** GROSE *Dict. Vulg. Tongue* s.v., Running harum scarum, said of any one running or walking carelessly ..and in a hurry, after they know not what. **1803** JANE PORTER *Thaddeus* xii. (1831) 114, I should not like a son of mine to run harum-scarum through my property.

B. *adj.* Reckless, careless, heedless in action; wild rash. (Of persons and their actions.)

1751 SMOLLETT *Per. Pic.* (1779) I. viii. 71 Such a hare'um scare'um blood of a bitch. **1780** MAD. D'ARBLAY *Diary* May, He seemed a mighty rattling harem-scarem gentleman. **1801** MAR. EDGEWORTH *Belinda* iii. (D.), What I call harum-scarum manners. **1832** LYTTON *Eugene A.* II. vii, A dissolute, harum-scarum fellow..always in debt. **1861** LD. R. MONTAGU *Mirror in America* 66 A mere harum-scarum scramble after the whim of the hour is not government.

C. *sb.* **a.** A reckless, unregulated person. **b.** Reckless action or behaviour.

1784 *Unfortunate Sensibility* I. 39 More mischief..than such a hare'em scare'em as I could accomplish in twenty years. **1868** HOLME LEE *B. Godfrey* xxvi. 133 His reminiscences of Basil as a handsome harum-scarum. **1886** E. L. BYNNER *A. Surriage* i. 11 Had a tidal wave swept over the rocks and played at harum-scarum? **1896** J. MORLEY in *Daily News* 18 June 3/3 Instead of humdrum you..have got harum scarum.

Hence **harum-ˈscarumness**, recklessness.

1863 HAWTHORNE *Our Old Home* (1883) I. 345 Accustomed to a life-long luxury of dirt and harum-scarumness. **1883** L. WINGFIELD *A. Rowe* I. ii. 35 A reckless Hibernian harum-scarumness in pecuniary matters.

‖**haruspex** (həˈrʌspɛks). Pl. **haruspices** (-ɪsiːz). Also 6-9 **aruspex,** 7 anglicized as **(h)aruspick, -pect.** [L. *(h)aruspex*, f. a root appearing in Skr. *hirâ* entrails + L. *-spic-* beholding, inspecting.] One of a class of ancient Roman soothsayers, of Etruscan origin, who performed divination by inspection of the entrails of victims, and in other ways.

1584 R. SCOT *Disc. Witchcr.* IX. iii. (1886) 138 Another sort of witching priests called *Aruspices*, prophesied victorie to Alexander, bicause an eagle lighted on his head. *c* **1605** ROWLEY *Birth Merl.* IV. i. 331 Not an Aruspex with his whistling spells. **1652** GAULE *Magastrom.* 313 Alexander.. called his aruspicks to inspect the entrayls. **1741** MIDDLETON *Cicero* I. VI. 454 These terrors alarmed the City, and the Senate consulted the Haruspices. **1879** FROUDE *Cæsar* xxvi. 458 'Am I to be frightened', he said, in answer to some report of the haruspices, 'because a sheep is without a heart?'

haruspical (həˈrʌspɪkəl), *a.* Also **ar-.** [ad. L. *(h)aruspicāl-is*, f. *haruspex, -icem*: see prec.] Belonging to, or having the function of, a haruspex. So †**haˈruspicate (ar-)** *a.* [L. type **haruspicārī, haruspicāt-*], in same sense.

1652 GAULE *Magastrom.* 26 Their oracles, augurs, and all the aruspicate presagers. *Ibid.* 307 The haruspicall diviners.

Ibid. 327 A great aruspicall diviner would needs forewarn Cæsar.

haruspication (hərʌspɪ'keɪʃən). [n. of action f. L. type *haruspicārī* to act as HARUSPEX: see above and -ATION.] Divination by inspection of the entrails of animals.

1871 TYLOR *Prim Cult.* I. 111 Haruspication belongs.. especially to the Malays and Polynesians. *Ibid.* 112 Haruspication has died out more completely than almost any magical rite.

haruspice, anglicized form of HARUSPEX: cf. F. *aruspice*.

1828 in WEBSTER, who cites *Encyc. Adam*.

†**ha'ruspicine, arus-**. *Obs.* [ad. L. *haruspicīn-a*, fem. of *haruspicīn-us* belonging to a haruspex, used as sb. (sc. *ars*).] = HARUSPICY. So †**haruspi'cinal (ar-)** *a.*, relating to haruspicy; †**haru'spicinate (ar-)** *v. intr.*, to practise haruspicy; †**haru'spiciny (ar-)** = HARUSPICY.

1581 SAVILE *Tacitus' Hist.* II. iii. (1591) 54 The skill and arte of Haruspicine. **1652** GAULE *Magastrom.* 189 Augurizing, auspicating, and aruspicinating. *Ibid.* 294 Tages..taught the Hetrurians the aruspicinall discipline. *a* **1693** URQUHART *Rabelais* III. xxv. 210 Will you have a trial of your Fortune by the Art of Aruspiciny?

haruspicy (hə'rʌspɪsɪ). Also 6–9 **ar-**. [ad. L. *haruspicium*, f. *haruspic-em*: see HARUSPEX.] The practice or function of a haruspex; divination by inspection of the entrails of victims.

1569 J. SANFORD tr. *Agrippa's Van. Artes* 51 b, Of Aruspicie, which is a kinde of soothsaying. **1759** B. STILLINGFL. tr. *Cal. Flora* Pref. in *Misc. Tracts* (1762) 236 This institution of augury seems to have been much more antient than that of aruspicy. **1895** *Folk-Lore* Mar. 63 The old Roman haruspicy exists among the Hawaiians.

Harveian ('hɑːviːən), *a.* [f. the name of William *Harvey* (1578–1657), English physician, who discovered how the blood circulated + -AN.] Pertaining or relating to, expounded by, or commemorating Harvey.

1755 T. LEMAN *Some Mem. Life & Writings Late Dr. Richard Mead* 27 In 1723, Dr. Mead was appointed to speak the anniversary Harveian oration, before the members of the college of physicians. **1837** *London Med. Gaz.* 8 July 565/1 The College of Physicians continues to show their classic taste in the Harveian Oration. **1839** J. TURNER *Reg. Exper. Living Animals* 34 As a sceptic of the Hunterian and Harveian doctrines, I here take my stand. **1880** *Encycl. Brit.* XI. 505/1 Caspar Hoffmann,..admitting the truth of the lesser circulation in the full Harveian sense. *Ibid.* 506/2 The Harveian Orations. **1903** *Lancet* 6 June 1608/1 The Harveian Lectures of the Harveian Society of London. **1928** *Daily Tel.* 15 May 14/3 MSS., books, pictures, and other objects of Harveian interest. **1972** *Times Lit. Suppl.* 7 Apr. 403/3 (Advt.), Qualified cataloguer (temporary) urgently required... Applications..to: Harveian Librarian, Royal College of Physicians of London.

harvest ('hɑːvɪst), *sb.* Forms: 1–2 **hærfest, herfest,** (1 **hærfæst**), 3–6 **hervest,** 4–5 **hervist, -vyst, -wist,** 5 **harveste,** (**-weste, -waste, -wyste, her(r)ust, eruyst**); 3– **harvest,** (*Sc.* 8–9 **hairst,** 9 **ha'arst, harst, herst**). [OE. *hærfest, hęrfest* = OFris. *herfst* (mod.Fris. dial. *harvst, hearst, herst*), MDu. and Du. *herfst*, MLG. *hervest, hervst*, (LG. *harvst, harfst*), OHG. *herbist* (MHG. *herbest*, Ger. *herbst*), all masc.; ON. (with loss of *r* and contraction) *haust* neut. (orig. masc., Sw., Da. *höst* m.):—OTeut. **harƀisto-z, -usto-z*, perh. from a root **harƀ-* = L. *carpĕre* to pluck, crop, cf. Gr. καρπός fruit.]

1. The third of the four seasons of the year, the autumn. *Obs.* exc. *dial.*, or passing into sense 2.

902 *Charter Bp. Denewulf* in *Cod. Dipl.* V. 151 To hærfestes emnihte sie simne aȝyfed. *c* **1050** *Byrhtferth's Handboc* in *Anglia* (1885) VIII. 299 þa feower timan.. lengten, sumor, hærfest, & winter. *a* **1100** *Voc.* in Wr.-Wülcker 317/7 *Autumnus*, herfest. *a* **1225** *Ancr. R.* 412 þe holi rode dei, þe latere, þet is ine heruest. *c* **1290** *S. Eng. Leg.* I. 12/393 Aftur heruest he comez i-lome. **1387** TREVISA *Higden* (Rolls) VI. 107 þe evenes of þe day and þe nyȝt is ones in þe Lente and efte in hervest. **1422** tr. *Secreta Secret., Priv. Priv.* lxvi. (E.E.T.S.) 243 Al the olde Phylosofers the yere dyuysedyn in fowre Parties, wyche ben callid Veere, Somer, Herrust, and Wyntyr. *Ibid* 245 Of Herust. **1551** RECORDE *Cast. Knowl.* (1556) 32 The 14 day of September ..with it beginneth Haruest, which is the third quarter of the year. **1646** SIR T. BROWNE *Pseud. Ep.* VI. iii. 287 Countries, whose constitutions admit not such tempestivity of harvest. **1774** M. MACKENZIE *Maritime Surv.* 78 Toward the End of Harvest, when the Days are turning short.

2. The season for reaping and gathering in the ripened grain.

(Not distinctly marked from prec. sense before 14th c.)

a **1100** *Gerefa* in *Anglia* (1886) IX. 261 On hærfeste ripan. *c* **1300** *St. Brandan* 692 Thapplen were ripe y-nouȝ riȝt as hit harvest were. **13..** *E.E. Allit. P.* B. 523 Sesounez schal yow neuer sese of sede ne of heruest. **1382** WYCLIF *Gen.* xxx. 14 And Ruben goon out in tyme of wheet heruest into the feeld. **1390** GOWER *Conf.* II. 202 The man, whiche hath his londe tilled, Awaiteth nought more redely The hervest. *c* **1420** *Pallad. on Husb.* IV. 252 Reserue in heruest hem that seed shal brynge. **14..** in *Archæol.* LIV. I. 164/106 July for eruyst. **1483** *Cath. Angl.* 177/1 Harvest, *autumpnus, messis.* **1483** *Presentm. Juries* in *Surtees Misc.* (1888) 28 And cutes corn in harwyste. **1535** COVERDALE *2 Sam.* xxi. 9 Whan yᵉ barly haruest begynneth. **1611** BIBLE *Prov.* x. 5 He that sleepeth in haruest, is a sonne that causeth shame. **1667** MILTON *P.L.* XI. 899 Seed time and Harvest, Heat and hoary Frost Shall hold thir course. **178.** BURNS *Song* Robin shure in hairst, I shure wi' him. **1856** STANLEY *Sinai & Pal.* v. (1858) 242 The harvest of Palestine is in April or May.

b. *transf.* The season for the gathering of other annual products.

1697 DRYDEN *Virg. Georg.* IV. 337 Two Honey Harvests fall in ev'ry Year.

c. *transf.* and *fig.* (From 2 and 3.)

1535 COVERDALE Jer. li. 33 The doughter of Babilon hath bene in hir tyme like as a threszshinge floore, but shortly shal hir haruest come [**1382** WYCLIF, ȝit a litil, and come shal the tyme of his reping]. **1599** SHAKS. *Much Ado* I. iii. 27 It is needful that you frame the season for your owne haruest. **1613** PURCHAS *Pilgrimage* (1614) 674 The Lent..so weakening their bodies, that the Moores make that their Harvest of Abissine captives. **1648** GAGE *West Ind.* 93 Fellow-labourers in that harvest of souls. **1841** LONGF. *God's-acre* iii, The great harvest, when the archangel's blast Shall winnow, like a fan, the chaff and grain.

3. The reaping and gathering in of the ripened grain; the gathering in of other products.

1526 TINDALE *John* iv. 35 Loke on the regions: For they are whyte allredy vnto harvest [1388 WYCLIF, ben..to repe]. *c* **1532** DEWES *Introd. Fr.* in *Palsgr.* 950 To go to hervest, *moissoner.* **1606** SHAKS. *Ant. & Cl.* II. vii. 26 The Seeds-man Vpon the slime and Ooze scatters his graine, And shortly comes to Haruest. **1667** MILTON *P.L.* IV. 981 A field Of Ceres ripe for harvest. **1797** WASHINGTON in *Sir J. Sinclair's Corr.* (1831) II. 27, I..shall read it..so soon as I have passed through my harvest, which is now nearly finished. **1880** MRS. WHITNEY *Odd or Even* xii. 98 When the great hay harvest was not actually amaking.

b. Proverbs and phrases. ***to make a long harvest for*** or ***about a little corn.*** ***lord of the harvest***, (*a*) the proprietor or farmer to whom the crops belong, hence applied to God (Matt. ix. 8); (*b*) the head reaper, harvest-lord. ***lady of the harvest***, (*a*) the woman chosen to receive honour at the harvest-home; cf. HARVEST QUEEN; (*b*) the female 'mate' of the head reaper, harvest-lady.

1534 TINDALE *Matt.* ix. 38 Wherfore praye the Lorde of the harvest [**1526** harvest lorde] to sende forthe laborers into hys harvest. **1546** J. HEYWOOD *Prov.* (1867) 38 Surely..ye haue in this time thus worne, Made a long haruest for a little corne. **1600** DEKKER *Shoemaker's Holiday* ii. (1862) 12, I am sure you make that garland for me against I shall be lady of the harvest. **1710** *Tusser Redivivus* in *Hone's Every-day Bk.* (1827) II. 1158 He that is the lord of harvest is generally some stayed sober-working man. **1826** *Ibid.* 1167 The lord of the harvest accompanied by his lady (the person is so called who goes second in the reap)..enters the parlour where the guests are seated, and solicits a largess from each of them.

4. The ripened grain or fruit; the corn-crop.

1526 TINDALE *Matt.* ix. 37 The hervest is greate [WYCLIF, there is myche ripe corne] but the laborers ar feawe. **1573-80** BARET *Alv.* H 206 Haruest was so plentifull, that barnes would not hold it. **1697** DRYDEN *Virg. Georg.* III. 311 The waving Harvest bends beneath his [Boreas'] Blast. **1791** COWPER *Iliad* XVIII. 689 Along the furrow here, the harvest fell. **1870** YEATS *Nat. Hist. Comm.* 80 Those who sow and reap her bountiful harvests are often without bread.

b. The season's yield of any natural product.

1607 TOPSELL *Four-f. Beasts* (1658) 421 This ought to be no marvail, that there should be so great a harvest and store of these Mice. **1697** DRYDEN *Virg. Georg.* II. 753 The Vine her liquid Harvest yields. **1880** C. R. MARKHAM *Peruv. Bark* xii. 409 The harvest of bark, in 1879..amounted to 106,000 lbs. **1881** *Times* 29 July 4/1 The climatic conditions on which the grouse harvest depends.

5. *fig.* The product or 'fruit' of any action or effort: a supply produced or appearing, a 'crop'.

1576 FLEMING *Panopl. Epist.* 225 They shal gather such gleaning as agree with your harvest, namely the same vertue wherwith you are indued. **1594** SHAKS. *Rich. III*, v. ii. 15 To reape the Haruest of perpetuall peace. **1693** DRYDEN *Juvenal* (J.), Let us the harvest of our labours eat. **1771** *Junius Lett.* xliv. 235, I am not now sanguine enough to expect a more plentiful harvest of parliamentary virtue in one year than another. **1833** LYELL *Elem. Geol.* xix. (1874) 336 A rich 'harvest' of fossil ferns has been obtained from them.

6. *attrib.* and *Comb.* **a.** Of or pertaining to the autumn or harvest.

1382 WYCLIF *Jude* 12 Heruest trees with outen fruyt. *c* **1449** PECOCK *Repr.* III. xvi. 383 Thoruȝ al an haruest cesoun. *a* **1529** SKELTON *E. Rummyng* 278 Another..wyth her doth brynge Her haruest gyrdle, her weddynge rynge. **1577** B. GOOGE *Heresbach's Husb.* I. (1586) 24 We here doo call *Fruges*, all sortes of harvest grayne. **1602** CAREW *Cornwall* (1811) 120 The ordinary covenants of most conventionary tenants are, to..do harvest journies, grind at the mill [etc.]. *a* **1621** J. VICARS in *Sylvester's Wks.* (1880) I. 10/2 All thy full-ear'd Harvest-Swathes. **1688** R. HOLME *Armoury* III. viii. 336 An Harvest Bottle of Leather. **1697** DRYDEN *Virg. Georg.* II. 286 No toiling Teams from Harvest-labour come So late at Night. **1730-46** THOMSON *Autumn* 1128 The harvest-treasures all Now gather'd in. **1797** *Statist. Acc. Scotl.* XIX. 384 The former tenant..kept a piper..and gave him his harvest-fee. **1801** ELIZ. SCOT *Alonzo & Cora* 50 'Twas on a cheerful harvest-morn. **1842-4** H. STEPHENS *Bk. of Farm* (1891) III. 88 Harvest Forks..used in the loading of corn require to have long shafts. **1873** SYMONDS *Grk. Poets* iii. 91 The voice of the harvest-bird brings Theognis sorrow. **1884** MISS SURTEES *Harvest Home* 16 For that harvest-day the fields are white.

b. Of or pertaining to the harvest-home.

1602 CAREW *Cornwall* 68 (Brand) The harvest dinners are held by every wealthy man. **1606** *Choice, Chance, etc.* (1881) 28 Another [would] swell with pride, as if she were Mistris of the Haruest cart. **1809** SCOTT *Poacher* 115 The harvest-feast grew blither when he came. **1821** CLARE *Vill. Minstr.* I. 27 All the feats that crown the harvest supper night. **1827** HONE *Table Bk.* II. 333 Harvest-Catch in Norfolk. **1884** MISS SURTEES *Harvest Home* 17 Compel them to come in to the Master's Harvest-home, to the great Harvest Supper.

c. objective, as ***harvest-bearing*** adj. **d.** adverbial, as ***harvest-trudging*** adj.

1845 MRS. NORTON *Child of Isl.* (1846) 184 When harvest-trudging clowns went singing by. **1871** BRYANT *Odyss.* v. 557 The harvest-bearing earth.

7. Special comb.: **harvest-apple**, a small apple ripening in August; **harvest-bell**, (*a*) a bell rung in harvest time; (*b*) a flower, the Autumn bell, *Gentiana Pneumonanthe*; **harvest-cock**, a salmon of a certain age; **harvest doll**: see quot., also cf. HARVEST QUEEN; †**harvest ears**: see quot.; **harvest festival, thanksgiving**, a thanksgiving service for the ingathering of the harvest, at which the church is usually decorated with grain, fruit, etc.; **harvest-fever**, an autumnal fever; **harvest-fish**, the butter- or dollar-fish of North America, a species of *Stromateus*; **harvest-fly**, a name in U.S. for species of *Cicada*, which appear during harvest time; **harvest-folk**, the people engaged in harvesting; **harvest-goose** = *harvest-home goose*; **harvest-hand, -hind, -swain**, a reaper in the harvest-field; **harvest-herring, -mackerel**, one caught during harvest; **harvest-hog**, 'a young sheep, that is smeared at the end of harvest, when it ceases to be a lamb' (Jam.); **harvest-lady** and **harvest-lord**, the couple of reapers who lead the others in the harvest-field; see also 3 b; **harvest-louse, -mite** = HARVEST-BUG, **harvest-play**, 'the vacation of a school during harvest' (Jam.); **harvest-rig** *Sc.*, (*a*) a ridge, rig, or 'land' of a harvest-field, between two furrows; the harvest-field so divided; (*b*) the couple, man and woman, who reap together during the harvest, cutting a 'rig' conjointly; **harvest-saver**, a machine for economically drying hay, etc. when cut in wet weather; **harvest-spider**, a long-legged spider, *Phalangium*, common in harvest-fields; **harvest-tick**, (*a*) = HARVEST-BUG; (*b*) any small spider of the family *Leptidæ*; **harvest-trow** (*dial.*) = HARVEST MOUSE; **harvest-wench, -woman**, a female reaper; **harvest-work**, the work of reaping and gathering in the harvest (so ***harvest-worker***).

1597 GERARDE *Herbal* II. ciii. §4. 355 Calathian Violet..is called..of some *Haruestbels. **1860** *N. & Q.* 2nd Ser. X. 356 To ring what is called the 'Harvest Bell'..to warn the labourers in the harvest fields when to begin and cease their labour. **1861** *Act* 24 & 25 *Vict.* c. 109 §4 All migratory fish of the genus salmon, whether known by the names ..*harvest cock, sea trout, white trout..or by any other local name. **1777** BRAND *Pop. Antiq.* (1849) II. 20 Not half a century ago, they used everywhere to dress up something ..at the end of harvest which was called a *Harvest Doll. **1608** *Withals' Dict.* 46 Thine eares be on pilgrimage..as they say commonly, thou hast on thy *haruest eares. *Vestræ peregrinantur aures.* **1882** J. PARKER *Apost. Life* I. 43 Pentecost was a *harvest festival. **1891** C. CREIGHTON *Epidem. Brit.* 409 Autumnal or *harvest-fever, was a pestilential fever. **1885** KINGSLEY *Stand. Nat. Hist.* III. 191 The species known in Massachusetts and New York as the butter-fish, in New Jersey as the *harvest fish. **1753** CHAMBERS *Cycl. Supp.*, **Harvest-fly, Cicada*..the name of a large fly, remarkable for the noise which it makes in the summer-months, and particularly about the time of harvest. **1870** RILEY *Rep. Nox. Ins.* 131 Reminding one of the mode of escape of our Harvest-flies (*Cicadæ*). **1573** TUSSER *Husb.* lvii. (1878) 132 In haruest-time, *haruest folke, Seruants and all should make, altogether, good cheere in the hall. **1577** B. GOOGE *Heresbach's Husb.* II. (1586) 63 The mowers and Harvest folkes..carrie great peeces of them to the Field with them. *c* **1400** *Rel. Ant.* II. 113 A yong wyf and an *arvyst-gos, Moche gagil with bothe. **1891** T. HARDY *Tess.* I. 178 *Harvest-hands being greatly in demand just then. **1547** BOORDE *Introd. Knowl.* ix. (1870) 149 We haue *harvest heryng, & good hawkes. **1697** DRYDEN *Virg. Past.* II. 10 *Harvest Hinds, o'erspent with Toil and Heats. **1549** *Compl. Scot.* vi. 66 Gylmyrs and dilmondis, and mony *herueist hog. *a* **1825** FORBY *Voc. E. Anglia*, **Harvest-lady*, the second reaper in the row..but does not seem to have been ever so regularly greeted by the title, except on the day of harvest-home. **1573** TUSSER *Husb.* xlvi. (1878) 129 Grant *haruest lord more by a penie or twoo, to call on his fellowes the better to doo. *a* **1825** FORBY *Voc. E. Anglia*, *Harvest-lord*, the principal reaper, who goes first, and whose motions regulate those of his followers. **1775** ASH, **Harvestlouse*, an exceeding small insect very troublesome in harvest time. **1874** RILEY *Rep. Nox. Ins.*, 'Jiggers' or *Harvest Mites, *Leptus irritans. L. Americanus.* **1877** A. MURRAY *Econ. Entomol.* 117 *Trombidiidæ* (Harvest mites). **1884** *Health Exhib. Catal.* 148/1 Models of *Harvest Savers, already adopted on twenty of the chief estates in the country. **1852** WOOD *Nat. Hist.* (1863) III. 677 Sometimes the *Harvest-spider is seen scrambling over the grass with wonderful speed. **1883** J. CURTIS *Farm Ins.* 200 The harvest-bug..is closely allied..to our tick..described by Dr. Geer under the name of *Acarus Phalangii* from its infesting the harvest-spider *Phalangium Opilio.* **1648** HERRICK *Hesper.*, *Hock-cart* 13 The *harvest swaines, and wenches bound For joy, to see the hock-cart crown'd. **1886** *Syd. Soc. Lex.*, **Harvest ticks*, the species of the Genus *Leptus.* **1880** JEFFERIES *Gr. Ferne F.* I. 90 Looking at a nest of *harvest-trows, as the tiny mice are called that breed in the grass. **1758** JOHNSON *Idler* No. 71 ¶14 He saw some reapers and *harvest-women at dinner. **1562** *Act 5 Eliz.* c.

4 §16 Persons..accustomed to goe into other Shires for *Harvest worck.

harvest ('hɑːvɪst), *v.* [f. prec. sb.]

1. a. *trans.* To reap and gather in (the corn, or, by extension, other ripe crop).

c **1400** MAUNDEV. (1839) xxx. 300 Men hervesten the Corn twyes a ȝeer. **1719** [see HARVESTING *vbl. sb.*] **1776–90** PENNANT *Tour Scotl.* (T.), I have seen a stock of reeds harvested and stacked, worth two or three hundred pounds. **1858** GLENNY *Gard. Every-day Bk.* 222/1 The general crop [of onions] must be pulled, if not already harvested. *Mod.* The tenants had to harvest the lord's grain for him.

b. *intr.* To gather in the corn-crop.

1891 *Daily News* 28 Apr. 2/5 Texas and Southern Kansas can harvest in June and July.

c. *trans.* To kill or remove (wild animals belonging to a local population) so as to provide food (or other useful product) or sport, or to reduce the population.

1947 *Biol. Abstr.* XXI. 1602/2 14 tagged fish were recaptured later by anglers, suggesting that only a small % of the sauger crop is being harvested. **1948** *Jrnl. Wildlife Managem.* XII. 78/1 In 13 years of harvesting the surplus, 546 deer have been taken. **1960** *Biol. Abstr.* XXXV. 2529/1 *Aeromonas* caused heavy mortality of golden shiners..when these fish were harvested and moved to holding tanks. **1961** *Listener* 7 Sept. 348/2 Now 500 to 1,000 hippo are being harvested annually for food. **1970** *Daily Tel.* 30 Oct. 4/8 The tablets were made from the livers of seals harvested in Alaska in 1964. **1973** *Times* 10 Oct. 6/8 Shellfish in Italian waters can be harvested again after a month-long ban brought about by cholera.

d. To remove (cells) from a culture made *in vitro* or *in vivo*; to remove (cells, tissues, organs, or embryos) from an animal for experimental purposes.

1946 *Nature* 9 Nov. 677/2 Table 2 shows the general metabolic activities of normal cells compared with those of cells harvested from a culture grown for 90 min. in the presence of 10 units [of] penicillin per ml. medium. **1957** *Jrnl. Cellular & Compar. Physiol.* XLIX. 369 Various numbers of HeLa cells were added to duplicate Warburg flasks and oxygen consumption was measured for 68·5 hours. The results..indicated that..the rate of oxygen consumption was related linearly to number both of cells inoculated and cells harvested. **1960** *Biol. Abstr.* XXXV. 460/2 (*heading*) Effects of 2,4-dinitrophenol on endogenous respiration of yeast harvested during the first budding cycle. **1971** *Nature* 17 Dec. 385/3 The lymphoid organs are always harvested 24 h after the injection of labelled cells. **1972** *Ibid.* 24 Mar. 169/1 Macrophages were harvested from the peritoneal cavity 10 days after the second immunization. **1972** *Science* 5 May 519/1 Pregnant animals were killed 3 days later and the embryos were harvested.

2. *transf.* To gather and lay up in store; to 'reap', to husband.

1888 *Pall Mall G.* 26 Jan. 10/1 He..has watched Chicago's growth for fifty years, and harvested a fortune of about £40,000 from that city's prosperity. **1889** M. E. CARTER *Mrs. Severn* III. III. xii. 258 The whole of her money was spent. That was soon, for she did not try to harvest it.

Hence **'harvested** *ppl. a.*

1632 SHERWOOD, Haruested, *mestivé.* **1766** PENNANT *Zool.* (1768) I. 8 Artificial shelter, and harvested provision. **1887** RUSKIN *Præterita* II. xi. 404 The pendant gold of the harvested maize.

harvest-bug. A minute mite or acarid troublesome during harvest; also called *harvester, harvest-louse, -mite, -tick* (see HARVEST *sb.* 7). That common in England is a larval form of *Tetranychus* (*Leptus*) *autumnalis*; those in the U.S. are species of *Tetranychus* and *Trombidium*.

1768–74 TUCKER *Lt. Nat.* (1852) I. 371 The flea and the gnat regale on his blood; the harvest-bug burrows in his flesh. **1771** G. WHITE *Selborne* xxxiv. 89 This animal (which we call an harvest-bug) is very minute..of a bright scarlet colour. **1861** HULME tr. *Moquin-Tandon* II. VI. vi. 305 The wound of the Harvest bug occasions an acute burning and insupportable itching.

harvester ('hɑːvɪstə(r)). [f. HARVEST *v.*]

1. A reaper.

1589 PEELE *Eglogue Gratulatorie* Wks. (Rtldg.) 562/2. **1595** —— *Old Wives T.* ibid. 452/1 Soft, who have we here? our amorous harvesters [*Qo.* haruest starres]. **1621** QUARLES *Div. Poems, Esther* (1638) 91 The Harvester with bubling brow Reaping the interest of his painefull plough. **1809** PINKNEY *Trav. France* 243 The French ladies..are fond of habiting themselves as harvesters. **1886** *Syd. Soc. Lex.*, *Harvesters' disease*, Duclaux's term for a disorder to which persons working out of doors in the hot summer of 1859 were subject.

2. Applied to various insects: **a.** = *harvesting ant*. **b.** 'A harvest-man, daddy-long-legs' (Funk). **c.** A harvest-bug.

1882 ROMANES *Anim. Intell.* 97 The following points of interest in the habits of the European harvesters [ants].

3. A reaping machine; *esp.* one which also binds up the sheaves. Also, a machine for gathering in any particular crop, as a ***cane harvester***. **harvester cutter**, one of the section knives of a harvester; **harvester-thresher**, a machine for both harvesting and threshing. Cf. *combine harvester*.

1848 *U.S. Pat.* 21 Nov., Harvester. **1851** C. CIST *Sk. Cincinnati* 161 Harvesters and mowing-machines. **1858** SIMMONDS *Dict. Trade, Harvester*, an American machine for cutting clover and timothy seed, &c. **1875** KNIGHT *Dict. Mech.*, *Harvester-cutter grinder*, a machine adapted to the grinding of the section knives of harvesters, which are riveted to the knife-bar. **1882** *Advance* (Chicago) 17 Aug. 524 With the extensive Harvester Works ..and other manufactories building. **1884** *Pall Mall G.* 5 Dec. 2/2 The price of sheaf-binding harvesters. **1893** *Jrnl. R. Agric. Soc.* Dec. 702 Trials of Self-binding Harvesters. **1911** *Daily Colonist* (Victoria, B.C.) 5 Apr. 1/3 Large shipments of harvester machinery are arriving from overseas points. **1929** NEWMAN & BLACKABY (*title*) Report of the trials of the combined harvester-thresher in Wiltshire, 1928. **1950** *Engineering* 17 Nov. 391/3 Attempts to solve the potato-harvester problem. **1971** *Farmers Weekly* 19 Mar. 83/3 One man with the buckrake comfortably kept pace with a double-chop harvester.

harvest-field. A field in which the corn is being reaped or gathered in; a corn-field in harvest. Also *transf.* and *fig.*

1730–46 THOMSON *Autumn* 286 Thus to pick The very refuse of those harvest-fields. **1850** SCORESBY *Whaleman's Advent.* vi. (1859) 79 The great harvest-field of American whalers. **1855** TENNYSON *Brook* 227 My brother James is in the harvest-field. **1870** BRYANT *Iliad* I. II. 41 Like the harvest-field, when west winds stoop suddenly from above.

harvest home, harvest-home.

1. The fact, occasion, or time of bringing home the last of the harvest; the close of the harvesting.

1596 SHAKS. *1 Hen. IV*, I. iii. 35 His Chin new reapt, Shew'd like a stubble Land at Haruest-home. **1693** DRYDEN *Persius* IV. 64 At harvest-home, and on the shearing-day. **1757** R. BENTLEY tr. *Hentzner's Trav. Eng.* 79 (Brand) We happened to meet some country people celebrating their Harvest Home; their last load of corn they crown with flowers. *a* **1826** L. HUNT *Months* in *Hone's Every-day Bk.* I. 1059 Harvest-home is still the greatest rural holiday in England. **1844–61** H. ALFORD *Hymn*, Come, ye thankful people, come, Raise the song of Harvest-Home.

fig. **1598** SHAKS. *Merry W.* II. ii. 287, I will vse her as the key of the Cuckoldly-rogues Coffer, and ther's my harvest-home. **1606** *Sir G. Goosecappe* v. i. in Bullen *O. Pl.* III. 85, I have cride haruest home of thus much judgment In my greene sowing time. **1818** SHELLEY *Lines Euganean Hills* 230 Sheaves of whom are ripe to come To destruction's harvest home.

b. A shout or song of rejoicing on that occasion.

1648 HERRICK *Hesper.*, *Hock-cart* 6 Crown'd with the eares of corne, now come, And, to the pipe, sing harvest home. **1691** DRYDEN *K. Arthur* v. i, Come, my boys, come; And merrily roar our harvest home. **1814** SCOTT *Ld. of Isles* I. Introd., The last blithe shout hath died upon our ear, And harvest-home hath hush'd the clanging wain.

2. The festival or merry-making to celebrate the successful homing of the corn, called in Scotland 'the kirn'. (Now rarely held.)

1573 [see 3]. **1648** HERRICK *Hesper.*, *Country Life*, Thy wakes..Thy sheering-feast, which never faile; Thy harvest-home; thy wassaile bowle. **1798** BLOOMFIELD *Farmer's Boy*, *Summer* 290 The long-accustomed feast of Harvest-home. **1864** *Chambers' Bk. of Days* ii. 376/2 In England, the festival of ingathering passes generally under the endeared name of harvest-home. **1891** *Daily News* 21 Sept. 3/2, I have nowhere found any survival of the old-fashioned 'harvest home'. 'No; it is quite gone. The Union killed that.'

3. *Comb.*, as ***harvest-home call, song***; **harvest-home goose**, one killed and eaten at the harvest-home feast; also called ***harvest-goose***.

1537 TUSSER *Husb.* xc. (1878) 181 For all this good feasting, yet art thou not loose, Till ploughman thou giuest his haruest home goose. **1813–43** *Brand's Pop. Antiq.* (1849) II. 19 The Suffolk peasantry use..the following Harvest-home song: Here's a health to the barley-mow! *Ibid.* 29 This 'Harvest-home' Call is the one generally made use of in the county of Devon.

harvesting ('hɑːvɪstɪŋ), *vbl. sb.* [f. HARVEST *v.* + -ING[1].] **a.** The reaping and housing of grain, etc.; also *transf.*, the gathering up of resources.

1719 DE FOE *Crusoe* I. viii, The end of all my harvesting. **1841–4** EMERSON *Ess.*, *Prudence* Wks. (Bohn) I. 95 In the harvesting of fruits in the cellar. **1860** MOTLEY *Netherl.* (1868) I. xiv. 78 In more remote regions..the thrifty soldier thought that there might be..good harvesting for his sword.

b. *attrib.*

1836 *U.S. Pat.* 28 June, Harvesting machine. **1875** KNIGHT *Dict. Mech.*, *Harvesting-machine.* **1881** *Times* 18 May 11/4 Employment on English harvesting work. **1892** *Ibid.* 20 Jan. 10/5 The Hon. Walter Abbott Wood, the inventor, and founder of the manufactory, of the harvesting machines..died..on the 15th inst...aged 76.

'harvesting, *ppl. a.* [f. as prec. + -ING[2].] That reaps or gathers in and stores up grain, etc. ***harvesting ant***, a kind of ant which gathers and stores up the seeds of grasses; ***harvesting mouse*** = HARVEST MOUSE.

1873 MOGGRIDGE *Ants & Spiders* I. 52 These harvesting ants will be found all round the shores of the Mediterranean. **1882** ROMANES *Anim. Intell.* 102 The harvesting or agricultural ants of Texas. *Ibid.* 365 Of the harvesting mouse Gilbert White says:—One of their nests I procured this autumn.

'harvestless, *a.* [-LESS.] Devoid of harvests or crops; sterile, unproductive.

1868 MENKEN *Infelicia* 81 Break up the harvestless ridges where we starved. **1875** TENNYSON *Q. Mary* v. i, Harvest-less autumn, horrible agues, plague.

'harvestman.

1. A labourer in the harvest-field; a reaper; *esp.* one who leaves home to obtain harvest work.

1552 HULOET, Haruest man, *messor.* **1611** BIBLE *Isa.* xvii. 5 And it shall bee as when the haruest-man gathereth the corne. **1774** JOHNSON *Diary* 4 Sept. in *Boswell*, I saw the harvest-men very decently dressed. **1894** *Times* 14 Aug. 15/1 It can hardly be said that the weather of last week was on the side of the harvestman.

2. A name given to certain insects which abound in the fields in harvest-time; *esp.* a long-legged spider of the family *Phalangidæ*.

1830 *Withering's Brit. Plants* II. 85 *note*, Among the almost infinite variety of insects which haunt Grasses..is the *Gryllus viridissimus*..in Devonshire called the Harvest-man from the season of its appearance. **1847** CARPENTER *Zool.* §765 The *Phalangidæ*, or Harvest-men, have two thread-like palpi, terminated by a small hook. **1872** RILEY *Rep. Nox. Ins.* 17 These animals are popularly called 'Grand-Daddy-Long-Legs' in this country, but are also known as 'Harvest men' and 'Grandfather-Gray-Beards'.

harvest month. The month during which the harvest is gathered in; originally (like Ger. *herbstmonat*, Icel. *haustmánuðr*) a name of September; but in Robert of Gloucester of August.

c **1000** ÆLFRIC *Gram.* ix. (Z.) 43 September, hærfestmonoð. **1297** R. GLOUC. (1724) 61þe nexte moneþ afturward, þat heruest moneþ ys, He let clepe aftur hym August y wys. **1826** in *Hone's Every-day Bk.* (1827) II. 1155 Had my journey taken place during the present harvest month.

harvest moon. The moon which is full within a fortnight of the autumnal equinox (22 or 23 Sept.), and which rises for several nights nearly at the same hour, at points successively further north on the eastern horizon.

1706 WATTS *Horæ Lyr.*, *Vict. Poles over Osman* 5 Wks. 1813 IX. 275/1 Seventy harvest-moons Fill'd his wide gran'ries with autumnal joy. **1747** FERGUSON in *Phil. Trans.* XLIV. 538 All the Phænomena of the Harvest-Moon become very plain by this additional Part. **1803** LEYDEN *Scenes Infancy* I. 267 The waning harvest-moon shone cold and bright. **1832** LYTTON *Eugene A.* I. xii, The broad harvest-moon was in the heavens, and filled the air as with a softer and holier day. **1868** LOCKYER *Elem. Astron.* iv. §30.

harvest mouse. A very small species of mouse (*Mus messorius*, or *Micromys minutus*), which builds its nest in the stalks of growing grain; it is the smallest of British quadrupeds, being just over 2 inches in length.

1812 *Pennant's Zool.* I. 149 *heading*, Harvest Mouse. **1839** *Penny Cycl.* XV. 505/1 The Harvest Mouse. White, of Selborne, who suggests the name of *Mus minimus*, appears to be the first who drew the attention of naturalists to this the smallest of British quadrupeds. **1849** *Sk. Nat. Hist.*, *Mammalia* IV. 67 The harvest mouse is insectivorous as well as granivorous.

harvest queen. A name given **a.** to Ceres, the goddess of agriculture and crops; **b.** to a young woman chosen from the reapers (or an image or doll dressed up, cf. *harvest-doll*), to whom was given a post of honour at the harvest-home.

1579 SPENSER *Sheph. Cal.* Aug. 36 Well mought it beseme any haruest Queene. **1597–8** BP. HALL *Sat.* v. ii, He stole the daughter of the Harvest-Queen. **1667** MILTON *P.L.* IX. 842 Adam..had wove Of choicest Flours a Garland to adorne Her Treses, and her rural labours crown, As Reapers oft are wont thir Harvest Queen. **1778** HUTCHINSON *View Northumbld.* II. Anc. Customs 17 In some places I have seen an image apparelled in great finery, crowned with flowers.. This they call the *Harvest Queen*, and represents the Roman Ceres. **1827** HONE *Every-day Bk.* II. 1161.

c. = *harvest-lady*: see HARVEST 7. *local.*

a **1825** FORBY *Voc. E. Anglia* s.v. *Harvest Lady*, The Dictt. call this personage the Harvest-Queen; Dr. D. E. Clark says that, on inquiry in Cambridgeshire, he understood that to be the denomination. He would not have received such information in Norfolk. **1847–78** HALLIWELL s.v. *Harvest-lady*, The second reaper is also called the harvest-queen.

harvestry. The act or work of harvesting; also, that which is harvested (Ogilvie, *Suppl.*, citing Swinburne).

harvest-tide. = next.

c **1200** ORMIN 11254 O sumerr, and onn herrfesstid, O winnterr, and o lenntenn. *a* **1300** *Cursor M.* 4060 He-self was on þe feld biside To geder corn in herueistide. **1513** DOUGLAS *Æneis* VI. v. 31 As in the first frost eftir hervist tyde. **1874** GREEN *Short Hist.* v. §5. 250 In the long interval between harvest-tide and harvest-tide, work and food were alike scarce in the mediæval homestead.

harvest time. The time of harvest; the season of autumn (*obs.*).

1362 LANGL. *P. Pl.* A. VII. 107 He schulde ben huyred þer-aftur whom haruest tyme come. **1470–85** MALORY *Arthur* XX. xi. 815 It befel vpon a daye in heruest tyme. **1611** BIBLE *2 Sam.* xxiii. 13 [They] came to Dauid in the haruest time. **1842** TENNYSON *Dora* 53 At last a fever seized On William, and in harvest time he died.

b. *fig.* The time for reaping reward or gathering in results.

1782 MAD. D'ARBLAY *Let. to Crisp* Aug., This is the harvest time of your life. **1876** BANCROFT *Hist. U.S.* III. xiv. 214 But Gage..whiled away his harvest-time of honor.

Harvey ('hɑːvɪ), *sb.* **1.** [Reputed to be named after Gabriel Harvey, d. 1630.] A kind of cooking- and cider-apple; different varieties are named ***golden Harvey, Siberian Harvey***, etc.

1640 PARKINSON *Theat. Bot.* in R. Hogg *Fruit Man.* (1875) 67 Harvey apple, a faire, greate, goodly apple; and very well relished. **1741** *Compl. Fam. Piece* I. v. 262 Your Apples must be Pippins, Pearmains, or Harveys. *Ibid.* II. iii.

352 Harvey Apple, Aromatick Pippin. **1834** *Penny Cycl.* II. 189/2 The best varieties [for cider] are..the Siberian Harvey..and above all, the golden Harvey, or brandy apple.

2. The name of Peter *Harvey* (see quot. 1959), English publican, in ***Harvey's Sauce*** (now a proprietary trade-mark). Also ***Harvey Sauce*** and *ellipt.*

1817 [see KETCHUP]. **1856** DICKENS in *Household Words* XIII. 555/2 The grocer's hot pickles, Harvey's Sauce, Doctor Kitchener's Zest. **1870** —— *E. Drood* xi. 80 A condiment of a profounder flavor than Harvey. **1876** *Trade Marks Jrnl.* 28 June 198 Harvey's Sauce for Fish, Game, Steaks etc. Prepared from the Original Receipt, only at E. Lazenby's Fish Sauce Warehouse. *Ibid.* 199 Harvey's Sauce —Caution: The admirers of this celebrated Sauce are.. requested to observe that each bottle bears the well-known Label signed 'Elizabeth Lazenby'. **1905** E. WHARTON *House of Mirth* I. xiv. 243 A bottle of Harvey sauce on the sideboard. **1959** *Tradition (E. Lazenby & Co.)* Jan. 2/1 The history of Elizabeth Lazenby can really be dated from 1760. In that year, a Mr. Peter Harvey, owner of an inn called the 'Black Dog' in Bedfont, Middlesex, invented a thin sauce known as 'Harvey's Sauce'. So good was it that many of his customers endeavoured to obtain the recipe, and one of them, a certain London grocer named M. Lazenby, offered to buy it, but Peter Harvey refused to part with his secret. Mr. Lazenby..married Harvey's sister, Elizabeth. As a wedding present, Peter Harvey gave Elizabeth..the recipe for his famous sauce. **1967** A. DAVIS *Package & Print* 44 It is likely that by the end of the eighteenth century Burgess's essence of anchovies..and Lazenby's Harvey's sauce were on the market in labelled bottles not noticeably different from those in which they were to enter the twentieth.

'Harvey, *v.* [After the surname of the inventor.]

a. To harden (steel) by a process invented by H. A. Harvey of New Jersey, (patented in England 1888, No. 401); = HARVEYIZE. **b.** To fit or supply (a ship) with armour-plates so treated. Hence **'Harveyed** *ppl. a.*

1894 *Daily News* 21 June 2/6 The Harveyed Steel Plate has now been adopted. **1894** *Times* 12 July 8/4 The 'Harveyed' plates in the tests did not show any marked superiority over the St. Chamond plate. **1894** *Westm. Gaz.* 18 Oct. 6/1 The royalties on plates ordered to be 'Harveyed', though not yet completed. **1896** *Daily News* 21 Aug. 5/8 The vessel..is Harveyed to the water line.

Also **'Harveyize** *v.*, **-ized** *ppl. a.*

1891 *Pall Mall G.* 2 Nov. 6/3 The trial of two nickel steel plates Harveyised. **1892** *Ibid.* 2 Nov. 6/3 A patent known as high-carbon nickel Harveyized armour for the protection of men-of-war. **1894** *Times* 6 June 7/4 'Harveyized' steel plates will stop the heaviest cannon shot.

Harvey Wallbanger: see WALLBANGER.

harwe, ME. form of HARROW *sb.* and *v.*

hary, -er, obs. forms of HARRY, HARRIER.

harytage, obs. form of HERITAGE.

harzburgite ('hɑːtsbɜːgaɪt). *Petrogr.* [ad. G. *harzburgit* (H. Rosenbusch *Mikrosk. Physiogr. d. Min. u. Gesteine* (ed. 2, 1887) II. i. 270), f. *Harzburg*, name of a town in Saxony: see -ITE[1].] A rock of the peridotite group consisting basically of orthopyroxene and olivine.

1890 *Mineral. Mag.* IX. 41 The typical norite has 49·23 *per cent.* of silica,..the well-known 'schillerfels' or bastite-serpentine-rock (Harzburgite of Rosenbusch) 42·36. **1922** *Mineral. Abstr.* I. 396 The rocks of Mansjö Mtn. (61½°N., 15½°E.), Sweden, include crystalline lime-stone and gneiss with intruded amphibolites and later harzburgite and eulysite. **1924** *Trans. Geol. Soc. S. Afr.* XXVI. 14 The recognisable harzburgites exhibit fairly considerable differences in composition and grain. **1965** G. J. WILLIAMS *Econ. Geol. N.Z.* x. 149/1 Hutton (1942) identified chromite grains in dunite-serpentinite and harzburgite-serpentinite in a tributary of Gentle Annie Creek in western Otago. **1970** *Nature* 28 Mar. 1227/2 Most of the volcanics were basic, but during the upper Cretaceous ultrabasics (harzburgite, lherzolite, dunite and anorthosite) were intruded.

has, 3rd sing. pres. Ind. of HAVE *v.*

has, obs. var. of AS, ASS *sb.*; ME. f. HOARSE *a.*

a **1300** *Cursor M.* 1073 A ded has. *c* **1375** *Sc. Leg. Saints, Nycholas* 301 Has he bad, sa haf þai done. **14..** *Voc.* in Wr.-Wülcker 700/33 *Hic onager*, a wyld has.

hasagai var. of HASSAGAI, ASSAGAI *sb.*

hasar, rare obs. f. HAWSER.

†**hasard, -art,** *a.* (*sb.*) *Sc. Obs.* [app. a deriv. of OE. *hasu, haswe*, or ON. *hǫss*, accus. *hǫsvan* (:—*hasu-*) 'grey, ash-coloured'. See -ARD.]

A. *adj.* Grey-haired, hoary. **B.** *sb.* A grey-haired man.

1513 DOUGLAS *Æneis* IV. Prol. 164 Thow ald hasart lychour, fy for schame. *Ibid.* VI. v. 17 This ald hasard careis our fludis hoit Spretis and figuris in his irn hewit boit. *Ibid.* VII. viii. 100 Ouersett with hasart hayr and faynt dotage.

hasard, obs. form of HAZARD.

has-been ('hæzbiːn), *sb.* (*a.*) [perf. tense of BE *v.*] **1. a.** One that *has been* but is no longer: a person or thing whose career or efficiency belongs to the past, or whose best days are over. Also **hasbeen.**

1606 BIRNIE *Kirk-Buriall* (1833) 34 Being now but umwhile, and as an hes-beene. **1786** BURNS *Inventory* 8 My han' afore's a gude auld has-been. **1827** HONE *Every-day Bk.* II. 820 John Jones may be described as 'one of the *has beens.*' **1853** B. F. TAYLOR *Jan. & June* (1871) 206 Dilapidated 'has-beens', and despised 'used-to-be's'. **1879** G. F. JACKSON *Shropsh. Word-bk.* 180 'Er's a good owd 'as bin. **1904** *Philadelphia Even. Tel.* 9 Nov. 5 Parker and his party are among the has beens. **1905** B. TARKINGTON *In Arena* 3 I'll potter along trying to look knowing and secretive, like the rest of the has-beens. **1914** G. ATHERTON *Perch of Devil* I. 70 The obsolete notions that made most of our relations a sort of premature has-beens. **1929** *Psyche* Apr. 27 The age when physicians are divided into Has-beens and Neverwozzers. **1972** J. WAMBAUGH *Blue Knight* (1973) vii. 104 When I retire I'm just a has-been.

b. *attrib.* or *adj.*

1819 *Hermit in London* II. 133 A has-been battered beau.

2. *pl.* Old times. *U.S.*

1904 W. H. SMITH *Promoters* v. 91, I met old Bishop Slosher..and just for has-beens I took him to lunch with me.

hase, obs. form of AS *adv.*

c **1420** *Anturs of Arth.* xix, Pride with his purtenans, hase prophetes haue told.

hase, obs. form of HOARSE, HAZE.

hasel, -ell, obs. forms of HAZEL.

hasenpfeffer ('hɑːzən(p)fɛfə(r), 'hɑːs-). [G.] A highly seasoned rabbit stew.

1892 *Sun's Guide to New York* 16 Pork and beans, *hassenpfeffer*, and corned beef and cabbage are equally palatable over there. **1909** L. MEIER *Art of German Cooking* vii. 142/2 (*heading*) Hasenpfeffer. **1967** P. McGERR *Murder is Absurd* x. 127 There's a restaurant in Baltimore that has a real knack with Hasenpfeffer.

hasert, obs. form of HAZARD.

hash (hæʃ), *v.* Also 7 **hache.** [a. F. *hache-r*, f. *hache* hatchet: see HACHE.]

1. *trans.* To cut (meat) into small pieces for cooking; to make into a hash.

1657 R. LIGON *Barbadoes* (1673) 34, I gave them some tastes of my Cookery, in hashing, and fricasing this flesh. **1725** BRADLEY *Fam. Dict.* s.v. *Mushroom*, You must hash a Piece of Veal or Fowl. **1727** W. MATHER *Yng. Man's Comp.* 28 Hash, to mince Meat. **1853** SOYER *Pantroph.* 136 Meat hashed small and well peppered.

2. *fig.* Also ***hash over, up.***

1742 POPE *Dunc.* IV. 231 Be sure I give them Fragments, not a Meal; What Gellius or Stobæus hash'd before, Or chew'd by blind old Scholiasts o'er and o'er. **1794** MATHIAS *Purs. Lit.* (1798) 385 His own stale scraps..Hash'd up and season'd with an old man's spleen. **1880** *Academy* 25 Sept. 219 Pleased at seeing his waifs and strays of thought thus hashed up. **1920** F. S. FITZGERALD *This Side of Paradise* (1921) iv. 129 The things..they had hashed and rehashed for many a frugal conversational meal. **1931** LOEB & SCHENKER *Please stand By* I. iv. 45 But drop up anyway, I have something I want to hash over with you. **1950** *New Yorker* 16 Dec. 26/1 Asked him in to hash over a point or two. **1958** *Times Lit. Suppl.* 5 Sept. 493/3 It is the classic film formula, the sort of thing that dead-beat script-writers hash up for B. pictures.

3. To cut up, to slash or hack about; to mangle. Also *fig.* Now *Sc.* and *dial.* Also *intr.*

1663 BUTLER *Hud.* I. iii. 838 He..rain'd a storm Of blows so terrible and thick, As if he meant to hash her quick. **1727** WALKER *Peden's Life* in *Biogr. Scot.* 489 (Jam.) They are hagging and hashing them down, and their blood is running down like water. **1829** SCOTT *Jrnl.* 10 Feb., Hashed and smashed as my time is, who can make anything of it? **1893** STEVENSON *Catriona* 165 A hand in hagging and hashing at Christ's Kirk.

Hence **hashed** (hæʃt) *ppl. a.*, **'hashing** *vbl. sb.*; **'hasher**, one who hashes or makes a hash; also *U.S. slang*, a waiter or waitress in a restaurant; **'hashery** *U.S. slang*, a hash-house, a cheap eating-house.

17.. *Battle Sheriff Muir* 1715 in Child *Ballads* (1864) VII. 159 There was such hashing, and broad swords a-clashing. **1768–74** TUCKER *Lt. Nat.* (1852) II. 648 The cuttings, the roastings, and hashings they undergo. *a* **1845** HOOD *Clubs* iii, The Cook's a hasher—nothing more. **1870** *Alaska Times* (Sitka) 8 Jan. 1/3 Having lately opened a hashery, I send you this my rules and regulations. **1901** *Munsey's Mag.* XXIV. 568/2 The salary was ten times what she was getting at the hashery. **1916** A. B. DUNN in *Editor* 11 Mar. 297/2 Hasher, meaning waitress. **1957** J. KEROUAC *On Road* (1958) 172 Her honest labors in the hashery. **1960** *Listener* 18 Aug. 250/2 When it came to making an impression on the 'hashers' in the railroad 'beaneries', the boomers really let themselves go... The 'hashers' were girls chosen for their looks. **1961** *Amer. Speech* XXXVI. 271 Somewhere on your run you will spend some time at a truck stop..while the hasher serves your diesel.

hash (hæʃ), *sb.*[1] Also 7 **hache.** [f. HASH *v.*, taking the place of the earlier *haché, hachee, hachey*, HACHY, and HACHIS, from French.]

1. Something cut up into small pieces; *spec.* a dish consisting of meat which has been previously cooked, cut small, and warmed up with gravy and sauce or other flavouring.

1662–3 PEPYS *Diary* 13 Jan., I had..at first course, a hash of rabbits, a lamb. **1678** R. L'ESTRANGE *Seneca's Mor.* (1702) 510 They are only Hache, made up of the Fragments that remain'd. **1709** ADDISON *Tatler* No. 148 ¶9, I..passed my Eye over several Hashes, which I do not know the Names of. **1796** MRS. GLASSE *Cookery* v. 47 Lay..thin sippets round the dish, and pour in your hash. **1863** ELIZA ACTON *Mod. Cookery* 205 If the meat in a hash or mince be allowed to boil, it will immediately become hard.

2. *transf.* and *fig.* Old matter 'served up' or presented in a fresh form; now often coloured by or associated with 3.

1672–3 MARVELL *Reh. Transp.* II. 368 To serve up to the Reader continually the cold Hashes of plain repetition. **1759** GOLDSM. *Pol. Learn.* x, Old pieces are revived..the public are again obliged to ruminate over those hashes of absurdity. **1860** DARWIN in *Life & Lett.* (1887) II. 319 Chiefly a well-done hash of my own words.

3. a. A mixture of mangled and incongruous fragments; a medley; a spoiled mixture; a mess, jumble. Often in phr. ***to make a hash of***, to mangle and spoil in attempting to deal with.

1735 POPE *Donne Sat.* iv. 52 The Hash of tongues A Pedant makes. **1747** H. WALPOLE *Lett. H. Mann* 23 Feb. (1833) II. 274 (Farmer) About as like it, as my Lady Pomfret's hash of plural persons and singular verbs or infinitive moods was to Italian. **1833** J. H. NEWMAN *Lett.* (1891) I. 459 Froude writes up to me we have made a hash of it. **1847** LD. HOUGHTON in *Life* (1891) I. ix. 402 Lord Grey has made somewhat of a hash of New Zealand and its constitution. **1868** FREEMAN *Norm Conq.* II. App. 595 They there-fore make a strange hash of the story.

b. Phr. ***to settle*** (a person's) ***hash***: to reduce to order; to silence, subdue; to make an end of, 'do for'. *slang* or *colloq.*

1803 I. CRUIKSHANK *Olympic Games* 16 June (*caption*), I think the first round will settle his hash. **1807** *Massachusetts Spy* 14 Oct. 4/1 This settles all the hash. **1809** T. G. FESSENDEN *Pills Poetical* 114 We therefore mean to make a dash, To settle fighting Europe's hash. **1822** [see SETTLE *v.* 21 b]. *a* **1825** *Song* in BROCKETT s.v., The hash of the Yankees he'll settle. **1849** E. E. NAPIER *Excurs. S. Africa* II. 389 My finger was in an instant on the trigger, and another second would have settled his hash. **1864** BROWNING *Youth & Art* xiv, You've to settle yet Gibson's hash. **1930** R. H. MOTTRAM *Europa's Beast* xii. 292 He's settled my hash, right enough. **1933** C. ST. J. SPRIGG *Fatality in Fleet St.* x. 124 What are you going to do? Settle his hash and drop him overboard?

4. A term of obloquy, applied to a person who 'makes a hash' of his words, etc. *Sc.*

1655 in Brockett *N.C. Gloss.* (1846) I. 211 [In 1655, Henry Hedley was fined 3*s.* 4*d.* for calling William Johnson, one of the stewards of the Company of Bricklayers and Plasterers] 'a slavering hash'. **1722–30** RAMSAY *Fables* i, *Twa Books*, I canna thole the clash, Of this impertinent auld hash. **1785** BURNS *Ep. Lapraik* xii, A set o' dull, conceited hashes. **1816** SCOTT *Old Mort.* xxviii, 'What was I wanting to say..to his honour himsell..ye muckle hash?'

5. A trade name for waste paper of the lowest quality.

1893 *Westm. Gaz.* 4 July 5/3 'Hash', the paper of lowest marketable value, can be collected and sorted without loss.

6. *attrib.*, as *hash-dish, -meat*; **hash browns** chiefly *U.S.*, = *hashed brown potatoes* s.v. HASHED *ppl.a.* b; more fully, **hash-brown(ed) potatoes; hash-house** chiefly *U.S. colloq.*, a cheap eating-house, boarding house, etc.; also *attrib.*; **hash-joint** *U.S. slang* = *hash-house*; **hash-mark** *U.S. slang*, a military service stripe; **hash sign** [cf. *hash-mark*: prob. ult. f. HATCH *v.*[2], altered by popular etymology], the symbol #, esp. used before a numeral (as in N. Amer.) to indicate a following number; the 'number sign'; **hash-slinger** *U.S. slang*, a waiter or waitress; **hash-up** *slang*, a hastily cooked meal; also *fig.*, something concocted afresh from existing material; a reworking.

1917 I. C. B. ALLEN *Mrs. Allen's Cook Bk.* 400 *Hash Browned Potatoes. **1948** H. L. MENCKEN *Amer. Lang.* Suppl. II. 388 Of late there has been a strong tendency..to omit the *-ed* ending... Examples: *mash* potatoes, *hash-brown* potatoes, [etc.]. **1969** *Drive-In & Carry-Out* July 16 (Advt.), Choose either regular or crinkle cut french fries.. and shoestring as well as hash browns. **1973** M. DAVIS *Potato Bk.* 20/1 Fry..uncovered. Turn with a spatula to brown both sides. These are known variously as 'cottage fries', 'home fries' or 'hash browned' potatoes. **1975** J. LEHRER *We were Dreamers* vii. 109 I had..a whopping serving of Mrs. King's hash browns. **1979** *United States 1980/81* (Penguin Travel Guides) 336 Hash-brown potatoes and salads are specialties. **1986** R. BRANDON *Left, Right & Centre* xxi. 119 Taggart ordered eggs, bacon and hash browns. **1869** *Territorial Enterprise* (Virginia, Nev.) 21 Sept. 3/1 The Mayor proposes to double the tax on all '*hash houses'. **1875** *Scribner's Monthly* July 277/1 In the slang vernacular, an eating place is a 'hash house'. **1883** *Daily Tel.* 10 Jan. 5/4 (Farmer), Fifteen-cent restaurants, commonly called hash-houses. **1895** W. C. GORE in *Inlander* Dec. 116 *Hash-house*, boarding house. **1897** *Outing* (U.S.) XXX. 362/1 It has its swell hotels..and its 'hash-houses'. **1900** H. LAWSON *On Track* in *Prose Wks.* (1948) 223 Fourpenny hash-houses (good beds, 6d.). **1903** A. H. LEWIS *Boss* xx. 273 His is this deadfall on Barclay Street, with that hash-house keeper to give him th' dough for his checks. **1936** I. L. IDRIESS *Cattle King* xviii. 170 Sid Kidman found every hotel, every boarding-house, every hash-house, every room crowded. **1966** 'P. QUENTIN' *Puzzle for Fiends* (1947) xxiv. 171 You'll have to take that job in a hashhouse after all. **1960** N. HILLIARD *Maori Girl* 221, I see the hotels and the hash-houses. **1895** W. C. GORE in *Inlander* Dec. 116 **Hash-joint*, boarding-house. **1930** J. DOS PASSOS *42nd Parallel* 101 Passing the same Chink hashjoint for the third time. **1909** *Man-o' Warsman* Dec. 24/1 First Sergeant John J. Maloney earned another *hash-mark. **1935** G. & S. LORIMER *Heart Specialist* vi. 168 Slim and Shorty each had two gold stripes on their left sleeve that Slim called hash marks because they were service stripes and stood for the number of years of free food they'd had on Uncle Sam, he said. **1706** MRS. CENTLIVRE *Love at a Venture* v. Wks. (1723) 312 Your Father..swears..he'll slice me into *Hash-meat. **1984** *Which Micro?* Dec. 12/2 Neither user-defined characters, nor the '*hash' sign could be reproduced. **1986** *Guardian* 20

Feb. 15 Would I please therefore oblige her by using the musical notation provided (I gather that it is called a hash sign). **1868** *Gold Hill News* (Nevada) 6 May, The nice young man of Washoe may or may not be some kind of a clerk, a *hash-slinger, or a check-guerrilla. **1895** W. C. GORE in *Inlander* Dec. 116 *Hash-slinger*, table waiter. **1946** *Amer. Speech* XXI. 86 The cooks and 'hashslingers' of former years went off to war or to the shipyards. **1895** A. W. PINERO *Second Mrs. Tanqueray* II. 71 Dreams are only a *hash-up of one's day-thoughts. **1902** *N.Z. Illustr. Mag.* VI. 452 While sharing their 'hash-up', he had [determined] to pitch camp on the [gum] field. **1914** *Auto-motor Jrnl.* 816/2 The so-called 'motoring notes' in the daily press are a thinly disguised hash-up of the best stuff in the motor press proper. **1970** *Times* 28 Feb. p. iv, A style perilously close to certain Colour Supplement hash-ups and clearly aligned for Over-ground consumption.

hash, *sb.*[2] Colloq. abbrev. of HASHISH.

1959 N. MAILER *Advts. for Myself* (1961) 245 Drawing upon hash, lush, Harlem, Spanish wife, Marxist culture [etc.]. **1967** *Listener* 31 Aug. 262/2 If people use dangerous machinery.. while they are high on hash, the consequences may be..brash. **1968** A. DIMENT *Gt. Spy Race* viii. 143 What do you and Riordan do for a living—I thought he was just another part-time hash pusher? **1972** P. DICKINSON *Lizard in Cup* x. 157 'It's morphine she's been on?' said Pibble. But Tony shook her head. 'Just grass. Hash.'

hashed ('hæʃt), *ppl. a.*[1] [f. HASH *v.* + -ED[1].]

a. Of food (esp. meat): cut into small pieces for cooking; made into a hash.

1653 H. COGAN tr. *Pinto's Trav.* xix. 66 A great Skillet full of Rice with hached Lard. **1865** TROLLOPE *Belton Est.* xxv. 298 The breast of a hashed fowl.

b. ***hashed brown potatoes*** chiefly *U.S.*, a dish made of cooked potatoes, chopped (often pressed together to form a cake) and then fried until brown. Cf. *hash browns* s.v. HASH *sb.*[1] 6.

1900 J. D. REES *Compl. Cook Bk.* 118 (*heading*) Hashed brown potatoes. **1946** *Good Housekeeping* Mar. 92/1 Hashed brown potatoes, with their golden-brown, crusty outside.. are a number one favorite with men. **1959** *House Beautiful* Jan. 102/4 The shredded and diced potatoes, sometimes called hashed brown or shredded potato patties, are excellent.

Hashimite ('hæʃɪmaɪt), *a.* and *sb.* Also **Hashemite.** [f. the name of *Hāšim*, great-grandfather of Muhammad + -ITE[1].]

A. *adj.* Of, pertaining to, or characteristic of the Hashimites. **B.** *sb.* A member of an Arabian princely family claiming descent from Hashim.

1697 H. PRIDEAUX *True Nature of Imposture in Life Mahomet* 5 From him [*sc.* Hashem] the Kindred of Mahomet are called Hashemites. **1757** S. OCKLEY *Hist. Saracens* (ed. 3) I. 6 Hashem the great grandfather of Mahomet, whose descendants were from him called Hashemites. **1883** *Encycl. Brit.* XV. 672/1 Native princes claiming descent from the Prophet—the Háshimite emírs of Mecca..—attained to great authority and aimed at independence. **1949** KOESTLER *Promise & Fulfilment* xvi. 177 Transjordan was and is as interested in a solution on these lines as the Jews, in view of the age-old rivalry between the Hashimite and Saudite dynasties. **1958** *Spectator* 7 Feb. 159/2 The Hashemites of Transjordan or Iraq. **1973** *Times* 22 Sept. 5/1 Despite a spiritual attachment to the guerrillas and a distaste for Hashemite rule, Jordan's Palestinian majority view any guerrilla return with far less enthusiasm than Arabs elsewhere.

Hashimoto (hæʃɪ'məʊtəʊ). *Med.* The name of H. *Hashimoto* (1881–1934), Japanese surgeon, used in the possessive to designate struma lymphomatosa, a disease (described by him in 1912), usu. of women and probably of autoimmune origin, in which the thyroid is enlarged, usu. symmetrically, and infiltrated by lymphoid tissue, as ***Hashimoto's disease, goitre, struma (lymphomatosa), thyroiditis.***

1935 *Arch. Surg.* XXXI. 424 No cervical adenitis is present in association with Hashimoto's struma. **1936** STEDMAN *Med. Dict.* (ed. 13) 475/2 *Hashimoto's disease*, struma lymphomatosa. **1937** J. H. MEANS *Thyroid & its Dis.* xix. 503 The histology of Hashimoto's goiter is that of extensive lymphoid infiltration. **1956** *Jrnl. Clin. Endocrinol.* XVI. 1570 (*title*) An unusual iodinated protein of the serum in Hashimoto's thyroiditis. **1962** *Times* 30 Nov. 19/4 Hashimoto's disease, in which there is a gradual destruction of the thyroid gland. **1968** *Brit. Med. Bull.* XXIV. 224/2 Shown are the observed frequencies of occurrence of signs, symptoms and results of laboratory tests in three diseases: Hashimoto's disease, simple goitre and thyroid cancer. **1972** BASTENIE & ERMANS *Thyroiditis & Thyroid Function* v. 110 The formal criteria of Hashimoto's goitre, namely a recently developed symmetrical and homogeneous goitre, the presence of very high thyroid antibody titres, and the diffuse lesions characteristic of the disease. *Ibid.* 118 The progress of untreated Hashimoto's thyroiditis is variable.

‖**hashish, hasheesh** ('hæʃɪʃ, ha'ʃi:ʃ). Also (6 **assis**), 9 **haschisch, -ish, hachisch, -ish, hachshish.** [Arab. *ḥashīsh* dry herb, hay, the dry leaves of hemp powdered, the intoxicant thence prepared.]

The top leaves and tender parts of the Indian hemp (which in warm countries develop intoxicating properties) dried for smoking or chewing, in Arabia, Eqypt, Turkey, etc. Cf. BHANG, an Indian preparation of the same plant.

1598 W. PHILLIPS *Linschoten* I. (1885) II. 116 Bangue..is made in three sorts..The first by the Ægyptians is called Assis, which is the poulder of Hemp, or of Hemp leaves. **1613** PURCHAS *Pilgrimage* VI. viii. 502 A compound called Lhasis, one ounce whereof being eaten, causeth laughing, dalliance and makes one as it were drunken. **1811** tr. *Niebuhr's Trav. Arab.* cxx. in Pinkerton *Voy.* X. 153 (Stanf.) As they have no strong drink, they, for this purpose, smoke Haschisch, which is the dried leaves of a sort of hemp. **1855** H. SPENCER *Princ. Psychol.* (1872) I. I. vi. 103 It is a well known result of hashish to give an excessive vividness to the sensations. **1856** EMERSON *Eng. Traits, Character* Wks. (Bohn) II. 59 They chew hasheesh; cut themselves with poisoned creases. **1892** *Pall Mall G.* 29 Feb. 3/3 Victims to the excessive use of hasheesh.

fig. **1859** SALA *Tw. round Clock* (1861) 113 If you put a single grain of philosophic hachisch into that pacific calumet of his. **1884** H. D. TRAILL in *Contemp. Rev.* Apr. 575 Entranced by the haschish of Mr. Frederic Harrison's eloquence.

b. *attrib.*, as ***hashish-house, -insanity, -smoker.***

1883 H. H. KANE in *Harper's Mag.* Nov. 944/1 (*title*) A hashish-house in New York. *Ibid.*, A large community of hashish smokers. **1884** *St. James Gaz.* 22 Mar. 5/1 Intoxicating effects which recommend the drug to hashish-eaters in India. **1897** ALLBUTT *Syst. Med.* II. 901, I doubt very much if hasheesh insanity can be at present diagnosed by its clinical character alone.

hashmagandy (ˌhæʃmə'gændɪ). *Austral.* and *N.Z. slang.* Also **hash-me-gandy, hash magandy.** [f. HASH *sb.* 1.] A type of stew.

1919 W. H. DOWNING *Digger Dial.* 28 *Hashmagandy*, an insipid and monotonous army dish. **1941** BAKER *N.Z. Slang* vi. 54 Terms bequeathed to us by shearers and tramps and farmers..that appear to have originated this century..*hash-me-gandy*, station stew. **1945** —— *Austral. Lang.* 81 For stews our only original contributions appear to be *hash-me-gandy* and *mulliga stew.* **1951** L. G. D. ACLAND *Early Canterbury Runs* 381 *Hash-me-gandy*, station stew.

hashy ('hæʃɪ), *a.* [f. HASH *sb.*[1]] Of the nature of a 'hash', or mixture of mangled fragments.

1891 *Athenæum* 3 Oct. 452/1 A tale..duplicated in that famous collection, showing the hashy manner in which it was put together.

Hasid, -ic, -im, -ism: see CHASID, CHASSID.

†**hask, haske,** *sb. Obs.* [cf. HASSOCK 3.] (See quot. 1579.)

1579 SPENSER *Sheph. Cal.* Nov. 16 Phoebus..hath.. taken vp his ynne in Fishes haske [*gloss.*, a haske is a wicker pad, wherein they vse to cary fish]. **1598** FLORIO, *Cauagna*, ..a fishers basket, or haske. **1611** DAVISON *Poems* 38 (N.) The joyfull sunne, whom cloudy winter's spight Had shut from us in watry fishes haske.

hask (hɑ:sk, -æ-), *a.* Now *dial.* [app. a by-form of *harsk*, northern form of HARSH.] Rough and hard to the touch or taste, *esp.* from the absence of moisture; coarse and dry. Also used as *adv.*

c **1440** *Pallad. on Husb.* VII. 124 Al hugely and haske [L. *rauce*]. *c* **1440** *Promp. Parv.* 228/2 Harske or haske, as sundry frutys, *stipticus, poriticus.* **1747** HOOSON *Miner's Dict.* M ij b, Curled and adorned after the same manner by Spar, but hask and dry, and of no pleasant Colour at all. **1825** BROCKETT *N.C. Gloss.*, *Hask*, coarse, harsh, rough, parched..A hask wind is keen and parching..Coarse worsted is hask to the feeling. **1828** *Craven Dial.* s.v., 'Hask grass', rough, coarse grass. **1855** ROBINSON *Whitby Gloss.*, *Hask*, deficient in moisture. ' Hask bread', oft said to be as 'hask as chopped hay'. **1885** F. H. BOWMAN *Struct. Wool* Gloss. 354 *Hask*, dry and hard or unpliable.

b. *fig.* Harsh in sound, tone, or manner. *Sc.*

1594 A. HUME *Hymns*, etc. Ep. to Rdr., Rude Scottish and hask verses. **1643** R. BAILLIE *Lett. & Jrnls.* (1841) II. 63 The petition of the Londoners got so hask and insnareing an answer.

c. Dry, husky: as a cough.

a **1722** LISLE *Husb.* 343 They have in Wilts a disease on their cows, which they call a hask or husky cough.

hask, obs. form of ASK.

a **1300** *Cursor M.* 26465, I hask þe þen if it be nede.

†'**haskard.** *Obs.* Also **-erd.** [Of uncertain derivation; the suffix as in *bast-ard*, etc.: its locality is opposed to its being a derivative of the northern HASK *a.*] A man of low degree, a base or vulgar fellow. Also *attrib.*

1491 CAXTON *Vitas Patr.* (W. de W. 1495) I. cxl. 152 b/1 As..he came out of the hous of a comyn woman He mette wyth a lewde haskarde, whyche for to doo the sayd synne of lechery went to the hous. **1519** HORMAN *Vulg.* 31 Declaryng a very folysshe and an haskard felowe vnder the person of Thersyte. **1523** SKELTON *Garl. Laurel* 606 They be haskardis & rebawdis. **1569** NEWTON *Cicero's Olde Age* 14 Priuate persons and haskerds of low degree. **1574** WITHALS *Dict.* 60/2 A haskarde, or of lowe degree, *proletarius.*

Hence †'**haskardly** *a.*, vulgar, low, base. †'**haskardy**, baseness; haskards collectively.

1576 NEWTON *Lemnie's Complex.* (1633) 208 Some haskerdly peizaunts, and rascall persons. **1575** LANEHAM *Let.* (1871) 4 Ouerthroun at last by Berthreds Hascardy. **1577–87** HOLINSHED *Chron.* (1807–8) III. 81 Treason and haskardie in thus leaving their camp at the very point of fight.

haskinize ('hæskɪnaɪz), *v.* [f. the name of S. E. *Haskin*, the inventor of the process + -IZE.] *trans.* To submit (green timber) to a process by which it becomes hard and durable through the application of heat of over 212°F. under a pressure of 200 pounds to the square inch. So ˌ**haskini'zation.**

1897 S. E. HASKIN (*title*) Haskinizing—Vulcanizing—for the preservation of wood from decay. **1908** W. R. FISHER tr. *Gayer's Forest Utiliz.* (ed. 2) 509 The process is termed Haskinisation or Vulcanisation, and has given good results on the Manhattan Railway, New York.

†**haskness.** *Obs.* [f. HASK *a.*] Hoarseness, huskiness.

1519 HORMAN *Vulg.* 28 He hath a great haskenes [*graui asthmate implicatur*]. **1540** EARL OF BATH in Ellis *Orig. Lett.* Ser. II. II. 158, I am..sore aggreved with the agew myxte with a cough & haskenes. **16..** in J. Thompson *Ann. Influenza* (1863) 9 A dry cough; pain of the breast, haskness and roughness of the throat.

†**haskwort.** *Obs.* [Badly formed in imitation of Ger. *halskraut*, f. *hals* neck + *kraut* plant (perh. with some suggestion of HASK *a.*): cf. HALSWORT.] Name given by Lyte to two species of Bell-flower, *Campanula Trachelium* and *C. glomerata.*

1578 LYTE *Dodoens* II. xx. 170 This Throtewurte or Haskewurte..is..of three sortes, that is to say, the great and the small, and the creeping kinde. *Ibid.* 172 The Plante may be very wel called Haskewurte, or Throtewurte..in high Douch Halszkraut: in base Almaigne Halscruyt. **1863** in PRIOR *Plant-n.* (1879) 105.

†'**hasky,** *a. Obs.* or *dial.* [f. HASK *a.* + -Y.] Dry and stony, as soil; gravelly.

1649 BLITHE *Eng. Improv. Impr.* (1652) 157 Dry, haskey, sandy, hungry Land. *Ibid.* 187 St. Foyn is a French Grass much sowed there, upon their barren, dry, hasky Lands. **1840** *Jrnl. R. Agric. Soc.* I. IV. 403 Clover seldom succeeds on sandy loam, or thin hasky land.

hasle, obs. form of HAZEL.

haslet ('heɪslɪt), **harslet** ('hɑ:slɪt). Forms: α. 4–5 **hastelet,** 4–7 **hastlet,** 5 **hasselet,** 6 **haselet,** 6–7 **haslett, -e,** 7– **haslet.** β. 6– **harslet,** (7 **harselet,** (**harsnet**), 8 **harcelet**). [a. OF. *hastelet* (mod.F. *hâtelettes*) roasted meat, dim. of *haste* a spit, a piece of roasted meat (cf. obs. F. *hastilles* 'th' inwards of a beast', Cotgr.):—L. *hasta* spear. The spelling *harslet* appears to arise from the long *ā*.] A piece of meat to be roasted, *esp.* part of the entrails of a hog; pig's fry; also, the 'pluck' or 'gather' (heart, liver, etc.) of other animals, as the sheep, calf, etc.

13.. *Gaw. & Gr. Knt.* 1612 He britnez out þe brawen in bryȝt brode scheldez & hatz out þe hastlettez. ? *c* **1390** *Form of Cury* (1780) 83 Hastlets of Fruyt. Take Fygs iquarterid, Raysons hool, [etc.]. *a* **1440** *Sir Degrev.* 1399 Hastelettus in galantyne. *c* **1450** *Two Cookery-bks.* 106 Take a Turbut, and kut of þe vynnes in maner of a hastelette, and broche him on a rounde broche, and roste him. **1530** PALSGR. 229/2 Haselet of a hogge, *haste menve.* **1653** H. COGAN tr. *Pinto's Trav.* xxx. 121 Concerning hogs..some..sell nothing but the chitterlings, the sweet-breads, the blood, and the haslets. **1796** MRS. GLASSE *Cookery* ii. 7 In a hog..the haslet which is the liver and crow, kidney and skirts. **1812** COMBE *Picturesque* XXVI. 106 A rich Haslet at the fire, Will give you all you can desire. **1872** FRERE *Aristoph.*, *Frogs* II. 242 Keep quiet—and watch for a chance of a piece of the haslets.

β. **1585** HIGINS tr. *Junius' Nomenclator* 87 A haggise: some call it a chitterling: some a hogs harslet. **1664** PEPYS *Diary* 10 Mar., A good hog's harslet, a piece of meat I love. **1739** 'R. BULL' tr. *Dedekindus' Grobianus* 235 A roasted Harslet on the Table stood. **1866** FELTON *Anc. & Mod. Gr.* I. v. 365 Poultry and meat..calf's pluck, pig's harslet and chine.. finished the course.

attrib. **1677** CHARLETON *Exercit. de diff. et nomin. Anim.* (ed. 2) 13 Apexabones, Harslet-Puddings.

Hasmonean (hæzməʊ'ni:ən), *sb.* and *a.* Also **Ash-, -æan, Asmonean, -æan.** [f. mod.L. *Asmōnæus*, f. Ἀσαμωναῖος (Josephus) = *ḥašmōnây*, name of the reputed grandfather of Mattathias.] **A.** *sb.* A member of a Jewish dynasty or family to which the Maccabees belonged. **B.** *adj.* Of or pertaining to this dynasty.

1620 LODGE tr. *Josephus* XIV. xxviii. 381 Thus ended the estate of the Asmoneans, after 120. and sixe yeeres. *Ibid. marg.*, The end of the Asmonean family. **1832** H. COTTON *Five Bks. Maccabees* 50 Ashmonæan princes. **1834** *Penny Cycl.* II. 485 Asmonæans. **1880** *Encycl. Brit.* XIII. 421/2 A certain priest Mattathias, of the family of the Hasmonæans. **1898** *Expositor* Apr. 273 The Hasmonean priestly dynasty. **1926** E. F. SCOTT *1st Age Christianity* i. 16 In virtue of his priestly descent the Asmonaean king could also hold the office of high-priest. **1956** A. TOYNBEE *Historian's Approach to Religion* x. 134 A short-lived Hasmonaean successor-state. **1973** *Sci. Amer.* Jan. 80/2 We would know nothing of the political fortunes of the Hasmonean dynasty, which followed the Maccabean revolt.

hasp (hɑ:sp, -æ-), *sb.* Forms: α. 1 **hæpse,** 3–7 **haspe,** (6 **happys, hosp**), 4– **-hasp** (7– *dial.* **hapse**). β. (*north.*) 2–7 **hespe,** 5– **hesp.** [OE. *hæpse* (:—**hæspe*) wk. fem. 'fastening, clasp, hasp'; cf. OHG. *haspa* fem., a reelful of yarn, MHG. *haspe, hespe* reel, hinge, hinge-hook, Ger. *haspe* hasp, clamp, hinge, hook, *dial.* reel, *häspe* ham of the leg; MLG. *hespe, haspe* hinge, MDu. *haspe* hasp or fastening of a door, reel, skein of yarn, *hespe* hinge, joint, ham, ON. *hespa* wk. fem. 'wisp or skein of wool, hasp, fastening'. The sense-history of the group is obscure, and it may be doubted whether the 'hasp' of a door, and a 'hasp' of yarn, though in form identified in all the langs., were originally the same word. (But cf. HANK.)]

I. 1. A contrivance for fastening a door or lid: now chiefly applied to a hinged clasp of metal which passes over a staple and is secured by a pin or padlock; also (in a trunk or box), a hinged plate of metal with a projecting piece of the nature of a staple which fits into a hole and is secured by the lock.

c **1000** ÆLFRIC *Saints' Lives* II. 328 Sum sloh mid slecge swiðe pa hæpsan. *c* **1150** *Voc.* in Wr.-Wülcker 546/42 *Sera*, hespe. **13..** *Coer de L.* 4083 Undernethe is an hasp, Schet with a stapyl and a clasp. *c* **1386** CHAUCER *Miller's T.* 284 To the chambre dore he gan hym dresse.. And by the haspe [*Lansdowne* hespe] he haaf it of atones. *a* **1420** HOCCLEVE *De Reg. Princ.* 1104 Up is broke lok, haspe, barre, and pynne. *c* **1470** HENRY *Wallace* VII. 416 Stapill and hesp. **1515** *Pilton Churchw. Acc.* (Som. Rec. Soc.) 70 For mendyng off a happys.. ij[d]. **1560** *Ludlow Churchw. Acc.* (Camden) 96 A stapulle and a haspe for the.. chest. **1572** *Nottingham Rec.* IV. 145 Stapyles, hespes, and brages. **1631** *MS. Acc. St. John's Hosp., Canterb.*, For charnells and haspes for the two chests in our hall. **1674** RAY *S. & E.C. Words* 80 In Sussex for hasp, clasp, wasp, they pronounce hapse, clapse, wapse. **1680** *Lond. Gaz.* No. 1537/4 One Sugar-Box.. with a Hasp to fasten it on one side. **1852** MRS. STOWE *Uncle Tom's C.* xv, 'This trunk has got to be shut and locked'.. The hasp snapped sharply in its hole. **1886** HALL CAINE *Son of Hagar* II. i, The pony was tied to the hasp of the gate.

b. Applied to other simple contrivances for fastening a door, casement window, etc.; also, a latch for a sash window.

1772 *Phil. Trans.* LXII. 138, I fastened the other end with a small hasp to one of the jambs. **1855** TENNYSON *Maud* I. xiv. ii, If a hand.. were laid On the hasp of the window. **1855** ROBINSON *Whitby Gloss.*, *Hesp*, the door-fastener or button which turns on a pivot in the centre. **1876** GWILT *Archit.* Gloss., *Hasp*, the fastening to a common casement. **1885** *Law Times* 315/2 He must not break a pane to undo the hasp of the window. **1886** FENN *Master of Ceremonies* vi, The spring of the window hasp.

c. 'A semi-circular clamp turning in an eye-bolt in the stem-head of a sloop or boat, and fastened by a forelock in order to secure the bowsprit down to the bows' (Smyth *Sailor's Word-bk.*).

d. *O. Eng. and Sc. Law.* ***by hasp and staple***: see quots.

[*c* **1250** BRACTON V. IV. XV. 14 (Rolls) VI. 138 Seysina facta ..vel per nuntium, per fustim, vel per baculum, vel per haspam. **1292** BRITTON II. ix. §6 Deliverer al purchaceour la seisine par le haspe ou par le anel del uihs, ou par encousture de la porte.] **1569** in Balfour *Practicks* (1754) 175 Or he sould be saisit be hesp and stapill, as the commoun use is within burgh. **1861** W. BELL *Dict. Law Scotl.*, *Hasp and Staple* is the form of entering an heir in a burgage subject.. The claimant alleges his title, and proves it by witnesses; on which the bailie declares him to be heir, and makes him take hold of the hasp and staple of the door as a symbol of possession, and then enter the house and bolt himself in. [Entry by hasp and staple is now obsolete under Conveyancing and Land Transfer (Scotland) Act, 1874 (37 & 38 Vict. c. 94 §25).]

2. A clasp or catch for fastening two parts of a garment, the covers of a book, etc.

a **1300** *Body & Soul* in *Map's Poems* (Camden) 338 A denkles cope for to bere al brennynde on him was kest, With hote haspes i-mad to spere. *c* **1400** *Destr. Troy* 5254 The haspes of his helme heturly brast. *a* **1698** EVELYN *Voy. Marry-land* (R.), A curious hasp The manteau 'bout her neck to clasp. **1715** *Pancirollus' Rerum Mem.* I. IV. ii. 155 Shoes.. either lac'd close.. or else clasp'd with Taches or Hasps. **1829** HOOD *Eug. Aram* vi, He strain'd the dusky covers close, And fix'd the brasen hasp.

3. (?) A handle of a trunk or case.

a **1774** GOLDSM. *To Sir J. Reynolds* (R.), Four [men] got under each trunk, the rest surrounded, and held the hasps. **1868** W. COLLINS *Moonst.* (1889) 118 An old japaned tin case, with a cover to it, and a hasp to hang it up by.

II. 4. A hank or skein of yarn, thread or silk; a definite quantity of yarn, the fourth part of a spindle.

a **1400** *Octouian* 1442 The brydel was made of chaynys, Of grete haspys wer the reynys. *c* **1400** *Destr. Troy* 3899 Here huet on his hede as haspis of silke. *c* **1440** *Promp. Parv.* 238/1 Hespe of threde, *mataxa, haspum, filipulus.* **1792** *Statist. Acc. Scotl., Fifesh.* VI. 43 (Jam.) About 30 years ago.. a hesp or slip, which is the fourth part of a spindle, was thought a sufficient day's work for a woman.

†5. A reel for winding yarn, thread, or silk. *Obs.* [Only in Dicts. Perh. an error of Skinner.]

1671 SKINNER *Etymol. Ling. Ang.*, *Hasp*, alabrum seu Instrumentum Textorium in quod filum fusi evolvitur. **1730-6** BAILEY (folio), An *Hasp*, a Reel to wind Yarn on. **1828** WEBSTER *Hasp*, a spindle to wind thread or silk on (*local*).

III. 6. 'An instrument for cutting the surface of grass-land; a scarifier' (Webster 1864).

7. *attrib.*, as ***hasp-lock.***

1881 YOUNG *Every Man his own Mechanic* §865 The hasp-lock used for trunks and portmanteaus.

hasp, *v.* Also 1 hæpsian, 4-7 haspe; 9 *dial.* hesp. [OE. *hæpsian*, f. *hæpse* HASP *sb.*]

1. *trans.* To fasten with, or as with, a hasp.

c **1000** ÆLFRIC *Gram.* xxxvii. (Z.) 220 Ic scytte sum loc oððe hæpsige. **13..** *E.E. Allit. P.* B. 419 With-outen.. Hurrok, oþer hande-helme hasped on roþer. *a* **1375** *Joseph Arim.* 205 A dore.. haspet ful faste. *c* **1400** *Destr. Troy* 8593 Ector.. haspit on his helme, & his horse toke. *c* **1440** *Gesta Rom.* lxxxvii. 408 (Harl. MS.) Be not a-ferde.. for I shall haspe the dore, and pynne it with a pynne. **1570** LEVINS *Manip.* 35/37 To Haspe, *obserare.* **1611** COTGR., *Aggraffer*.. to buckle, or haspe. **1727** BRADLEY *Fam. Dict.* s.v. *Bee hive*, A small light Wooden Shutter, to hasp in cold Weather on the Outside. **1854** H. MILLER *Sch. & Schm.* (1858) 15 The companion-head was hasped down. **1869** *Lonsdale Gloss.*, *Hesp*, to hasp or fasten the latch of a door. **1882** *Mrs. Raven's Tempt.* II. 181 She went to the window and hasped it.

†b. *fig.* To fasten *together*, unite firmly.

1362 LANGL. *P. Pl.* A. I. 171 So harde heo beoþ with Auarice I-haspet to-gedere [**1393** —— C. II. 193 So harde hath aueryce hasped hem to-gederes].

†2. To clasp, embrace. *Obs.*

13.. *Gaw. & Gr. Knt.* 1388 He happpez his fayre hals his armez wyth-inne, & kysses hym. *c* **1400** *Destr. Troy* 367 Hailsyng of hed bare, haspyng in armys. **1607** TOURNEUR *Rev. Trag.* III. v. Wks. 1878 II. 91 If hee tooke mee haspt within his bed.

†3. To gird with mail or tight-fitting clothes; to buckle.

13.. *E.E. Allit. P.* C. 381 He askez heterly a hayre & hasped hym vmbe. **13..** *Gaw. & Gr. Knt.* 281 If I were hasped in armes on a heȝe stede. *Ibid.* 831 Alle hasped in his heȝ wede.

†4. To confine or fasten (in a tight place); to lock *up*. *Obs.*

1680 ELIZ. CELLIER in Howell *St. Trials* (1816) VII. 1187 He told me.. that he had been squeezed and hasped into a thing like a trough, in a dungeon under ground. **1699** GARTH *Dispens.* v. (1700) 65 Haspt in a tombril.. With one fat slave before, and none behind. **1711** STEELE *Spect.* No. 132 ¶2 Being hasped up with thee in this publick Vehicle. *Ibid.* No. 155 ¶2, I keep a Coffee-house.. I am unavoidably hasped in my Bar.

Hence **'hasping** *vbl. sb.*

1611 COTGR., *Aggraffement*, a hooking, clasping.. a hasping.

†haspede. *Obs. rare.* [deriv. of HASP.] A clasp, a hook.

13.. *E.E. Allit. P.* C. 189 By þe haspede he hentes hym þenne, & broȝt hym vp by þe brest.

haspicholls, -cols, corruptions of HARPSICAL, HARPSICHORD.

hass, dial. var. of HALSE; obs. form of ASS *sb.*

hassagai, -ay, var. ASSAGAI *sb.*

1731 MEDLEY *Kolben's Cape G. Hope* I. 65 Dexterity in throwing the Hassagaye. **1813** *Edin. Rev.* XXI. 69 The same Caffre.. with his hasagai attacks the horny elephant. **1885** *Cassell's Techn. Educ.* IV. 160 The hassagay-tree (*Curtisia faginea*) one of the largest timber-trees in Africa.

hassar ('hæsə(r)). [? native S. American name.] One of the genus *Callichthys* of siluroid fishes, found in the rivers of tropical America, and remarkable for building a regular nest and being able to travel considerable distances over land.

1865 W. HOUGHTON in *Intell. Observ.* No. 40. 262 These hassars, as they are called. **1883** WOOD in *Sunday Mag.* Nov. 676 Many of these rivers.. are inhabited by a fish.. popularly called the Hassar, or Hardback. *Ibid.* 676/2 The Hassar is as good a walker as the Climbing Perch.

hassard, obs. form of HAZARD.

hassassin, an etymological var. of ASSASSIN.

1826 LINGARD *Hist. Eng.* (ed. 4) II. 403 *note*, The Sheik or old man of the mountain, the chief of the Hassassins.

hassel(l, hasser, obs. ff. HAZEL, HAWSER.

Hassid, -ic, -im, -ism: see CHASID, CHASSID.

hassle ('hæs(ə)l). *colloq.* (chiefly *N. Amer.*). Also hassel. [Eng. and U.S. dial.: see *E.D.D.* and Wentworth *Amer. Dial. Dict.*] A quarrel, argument, fuss; a difficulty, problem; trouble. Also as *vb.*, to quarrel, argue; to worry, harass.

1945 *Down Beat* 15 Feb. 1/5 Building bands is getting to be a habit with Freddie Slack. He broke up his last few after booking hassels. **1946** *Sat. Even. Post* 31 Aug. 72/2 'Hassle' is a gorgeously descriptive word which lately has won wide usage in show business. **1950** B. SHULBERG *Disenchanted* (1951) ix. 102 She's actually a society girl.. who's had a hassel with her family and wants to prove she can get by on her own. **1957** J. KEROUAC *On Road* (1958) 50 We'll both understand purely and without any hassle that we are simply stopping talking. **1959** F. W. HOUSEHOLDER in Saporta & Bastian *Psycholinguistics* (1961) 18/1 The chief metaphysical bones hassled over in recent years concern such points as 'biuniqueness'. **1967** *Boston Sunday Globe* 23 Apr. 25/1 Now the zoning hassle has switched across the city to.. where the Greek Orthodox Church is petitioning for a rezoning to allow a developer to erect.. a $1.8 million office building complex. **1969** *Rolling Stone* 17 May 11/2 All other [*sc.* dancing clubs] had collapsed or been hassled to death. **1971** *Frendz* 21 May 16/1 The Edgar Broughton Band toured Germany earlier this year and were involved in some heavy hassles with the promoters of the various gigs.

hasslock: see HALSE *sb.* 6.

hassock ('hæsək), *sb.* [OE. *hassuc*, of uncertain etymology. Some have conjectured derivation from Welsh *hesg* sedges. It is doubtful whether sense 4 is the same word.]

I. 1. A firm tuft or clump of matted vegetation; *esp.* of coarse grass or sedge, such as occurs in boggy ground; a 'tussock', Sometimes applied to an insulated clump of bushes or low trees.

986 *Charter of Æthelred* in Kemble *Cod. Dipl.* No. 655 III. 223 Of ðam weȝe on ðone hassuc upp an hrofan hricge. [**1147** *Found. Charter Sawtrey Abbey* in Dugdale *Mon. Angl.* (1682) I. 853 Pastores.. nostri super exteriores hassocos versus Walton inter pratum & mariscum debent stare.] *c* **1430** *Pilgr. Lyf Manhode* III. vi. (1869) 139 And thanne the olde made me gon vp on a gret hassock. *c* **1440** *Promp. Parv.* 228/2 Hassok, *ulphus.* **1597** GERARDE *Herbal* II. xxi. §5. 209 Leaues, spread vpon the grounde in manner of a turffe or hassocke. **1662** DUGDALE *Hist. Imbanking* Pref., The stink of smoaky hassocks. **1769** *De Foe's Tour Gt. Brit.* III. 332 Moss.. lay above the Ground, in little Heaps.. called Hassocks, which were full of Holes, like an Honeycomb. **1805** R. W. DICKSON *Pract. Agric.* (1807) I. 444 Great tufts of rushes &c. called hassocks. **1807** VANCOUVER *Agric. Devon* (1813) 286 With much difficulty I could step from one hassock to another, in laying out the drains. **1814** MISS MITFORD In L'Estrange *Life* (1870) I. 270 The down is entirely spotted with small islets (the country people call them hassocks) of low trees and luxuriant underwood. **1843** WHITTIER *Pr Wks.* (1889) I. 321, I was stumbling over the rough hassocks, and sinking knee-deep in the black mire. **1871** J. R. NICHOLS *Fireside Sc.* 111 After digging out the hassocks and burning them.

b. *transf.* A 'shock' of hair.

1785 *Jrnl. fr. Lond. to Portsmouth* in *Poems in Buchan Dial.* 7 (Jam.) Wi' a great hassick o'hair hingin.. about her haffats. **1818** SCOTT *Rob Roy* xxxiv, His tatty pow, that ne'er had a better covering than his ain shaggy hassock of hair! [*a* **1825** FORBY *Voc. E. Anglia*, *Hassock-head*, a shock head; a bushy and entangled growth of coarse hair.]

2. A thick firm cushion or bass, often stuffed with rushes or straw, used to rest the feet on, and *esp.* in places of worship to kneel upon.

According to Forby s.v. '*hassocks* in bogs were formerly taken up.. shaped, trimmed, and dressed.. to make kneeling much easier than on the pavement of the church.' Hassocks of turf or peat, formerly used in the church, are still (1897) preserved at Lower Gravenhurst in Bedfordshire.

1516 in Rogers *Agric. & Prices* III. 564/3, 20 hassocks for pews. **1625** FLETCHER & SHIRLEY *Nt. Walker* v. i, Buy a mat for your bed, buy a mat! A hassock for your feet. **1667** *Vestry Bks.* (Surtees) 202 For a hassock and a matt for our Minister, 6d. **1711** ADDISON *Spect.* No. 112 ¶2 To make them kneel.. he gave every one of them a Hassock and a Common-prayer Book. **1784** COWPER *Task* I. 748 Knees and hassocks are well-nigh divorc'd. **1881** BESANT & RICE *Chapl. of Fl.* I. viii, A stately pew with red serge seats and hassocks. **1887** MISS BRADDON *Like & Unlike* iii, They made her comfortable upon the sofa, with a hassock for her feet.

†3. A rush basket: cf. HASK *sb. Obs.*

1573-80 BARET *Alv.* H 209 A hassocke, a baskette made of twigges or rushes, *scripiculum.*

II. 4. The soft calcareous sandstone which separates the beds of ragstone in Kent.

1706 PHILLIPS (ed. Kersey), *Hassock*, soft Sand-stone. **1765** *Univ. Mag.* XXXVII. 58/2 Mortar.. made.. of chalk, sand, or hassock. **1851** *Dict. Archit.* s.v., The sandstone that separates the beds of the Kentish rag is known by the name of hassock and hassock stone, the latter.. when the sand is agglutinated enough to allow its being raised in block. **1879** RUTLEY *Stud. Rocks* xiv. 281 The calcareous sandstones in the Hythe beds in Kent are locally termed hassock.

III. 5. *Comb.*, as ***hassock-grass, -plough;*** **hassock-filler**, a device for stuffing hassocks; **hassock-knife**, an implement for chopping off hassocks.

1699 *Post Boy* 24-6 Jan. in *N. & Q.* 7th Ser. XI. 168 They were all arm'd, some with Guns, some with.. Hassock-knives. **1797** A. YOUNG *Agric. Suffolk* 161 The plough made on purpose, and called a hassock plough, cut laterally much beyond the line of its draught. **1863** KINGSLEY *Water Bab.* i. 34 The hassock-grass and sedges tumbled him over. **1875** KNIGHT *Dict. Mech.*, *Hassock-filler*, a device consisting of a curb and a charging cylinder, whereby the stuffing is packed into the cover.

Hence **'hassock** *v. trans.*, to furnish with hassocks (sense 2).

1842 BARHAM *Ingol. Leg.*, *Sir Rupert*, He.. resolves to.. new-cushion and hassock the family pew.

hassocky ('hæsəkɪ), *a.* [f. HASSOCK + -Y.]

1. Abounding in hassocks or clumps.

1645 G. BOATE *Nat. Hist. Irel.* (1726) 62 Hassocky bogs. **1649** BLITHE *Eng. Improv. Impr.* ix. (1633) 61 Your hassocky morish rough Land. **1863** BARING-GOULD *Iceland* xix. 336 A horse cannot keep up with it over the broken hassocky ground.

2. Of the nature of or consisting of calcareous hassock.

1710 *Brit. Apollo* III. No. 70. 2/1 A Rockey or Hassucky sort of Ground. **1881** WHITEHEAD *Hops* 17 The loams.. and hassocky detritus of the Hythe beds. **1894** B. FOWLER in *Proc. Geol. Assoc.* XIII. 362 Towards Bramshott the beds became very hassocky.

hast, 2nd pers. sing. pres. ind. of HAVE.

hast, obs. form of HASTE.

†hastal, *a. Obs. rare.* [ad. L. type **hastāl-is*, f. *hasta* spear.] Spear shaped.

1671 GREW *Anat. Plants* I. vii. §3 (1682) 45 It [the cover of the seed] is.. Hastal, in *Lactuca.*

‖**hasta la vista** ('asta la 'vista). [Sp.] Goodbye, au revoir (used chiefly in Spanish contexts).

1935 C. MORLEY (*title*) Hasta la vista, or, A postcard from Peru. **1940** A. HUXLEY *Let.* 5 Jan. (1969) 449 Well, bless you both. Give our loves to the love-worthy. Hasta la vista. **1967** C. ARMSTRONG *Gift Shop* ix. 76 Dorinda had bade him a gay *hasta la vista* in Copenhagen and gone off. **1967** K. GILES *Death in Diamonds* ix. 168 'Come and stay with us...' 'I hope to. Hasta la vista.'

[**hastard,** prob. a scribal error for HASKARD.

a **1529** SKELTON *Earl Northumberland* iv. 24 (MS. Reg. 18 D II. lf. 165) Vilane hastardis in þer furious tene.. Confeterd togeder of commonn concente Falsly to slo þer moste singlar goode lorde.]

† **'hastary.** *Obs. rare.* [ad. L. *hastāri-us* belonging to the spear, subst., a spearman; f. *hasta* spear. Cf. F. *hastaire.*] A spearman.

1589 IVE *Instruct. Warres* 104 Before the first rankes of the Hastaries.

hastate ('hæsteɪt), *a.* [ad. L. *hastātus*, f. *hasta* spear: see -ATE² 2.]

1. Formed like a spear or spear-head; spear-shaped.

1854 WOODWARD *Mollusca* (1856) 117 Lingual teeth.. elongate, subulate, or hastate. **1856-8** W. CLARK *Van der Hoeven's Zool.* I. 667 *Astacus*..Lamellar appendage, dentiform or hastate. **1874** COUES *Birds N. W.* 665 Crescentic or hastate spots. **1885** CASTLE *Sch. Fencing* 44 The hastate weapons: pike, partisan..and poleaxe.

b. *Bot.* Of leaves: Narrowly triangular nearly to the base, where two lateral lobes project at right angles to the midrib.

1788 J. LEE *Introd. Bot.* III. v. (ed. 4) 191 *Hastate*, Javelin-shaped; when they are triangular, the Base and Sides hollowed, and the Angles spreading. **1794** MARTYN *Rousseau's Bot.* xxvii. 427 Hastate leaves that are quite entire. **1870** HOOKER *Stud. Flora* 313 *Rumex acetosella*; diœcious, lower leaves hastate. **1880** GRAY *Struct. Bot.* iii. §4.96 Leaves..Hastate or Halberd-shaped.

2. *Comb.*, as *hastate-auricled, -leaved.*

1864 *Sowerby's Bot.* I. 187 Hastate-leaved Scurvy-grass. **1883** BENTLEY *Bot.* 159 When the lobes of such a leaf are separated from the blade..it is auriculate or hastate-auricled.

† **'hastated,** *a.* [f. as prec. + -ED.] = prec.

1748-52 SIR J. HILL *Hist. Plants* 597 (Jod.) The hastated-leaved arum with a clavated spadix. **1753** CHAMBERS *Cycl. Supp.* s.v. *Leaf.* **1791** W. BARTRAM *Carolina* 478 Towards the tops..they became trifid, hastated, and lastly lanceolate.

'hastately, *adv.* [-LY².] In a hastate fashion; chiefly in comb. with adjs., denoting a combination of the hastate with another shape, as *hastately-cordate, -lanceolate, -sagittate, -two-eared*, etc.

1831 DON *Gardener's Dict.* Gloss., Hastately-sagittate.

ha'stato-, combining form of L. *hastātus* HASTATE, used like *hastately.*

1829 LOUDON *Encycl. Plants* Gloss., *Hastato-lanceolate*, between halbert-shaped and lanceolate. **1850** HOOKER & ARNOTT *Brit. Flora* 462 *Arum maculatum*..leaves all radical, hastato-sagittate.

haste (heɪst), *sb.* Forms: 3- **haste**; also 3-8 **hast**, 4-5 **haast(e**, 4-6 *Sc.* (and Coverd.) **haist**, 5 **hayste**. [a. OF. *haste* (12th c. in Hatz.-Darm.), mod.F. *hâte*:—WGer. **haisti-*, in OE. *hǽst, hést* fem., violence, fury = Goth. *haifsts* fem., strife, contest; cf. OE. *hǽste* adj. violent, vehement, impetuous = OFris. *hâst, hǽst*, OHG. *heisti, heist.* The French word was taken back into Middle Dutch, and thence into other Teut. langs.: cf. MDu. *haeste, haest*, Du. *haast*, MLG. and LG. *hast*, Ger. *hast* haste.]

I. 1. Urgency or impetuosity of movement resulting in or tending to swiftness or rapidity; quickness, speed, expedition (properly of voluntary action). Opposed to leisurely motion or action. (Most freq. in phrases: see 4 a, 5.)

a **1300** *Cursor M.* 5198 To bidd hast now es nan sa frek. *c* **1386** CHAUCER *Miller's T.* 359 This asketh haste. **1526** *Pilgr. Perf.* (W. de W. 1531) 48, I shall do more in a daye than my brother in twayne, for all his haste. **1582** N. LICHEFIELD tr. *Castanheda's Conq. E. Ind.* vii. 17 a, They fled, and made away with great hast. **1697** DAMPIER *Voy.* I. 13 The old man would have stayed us here..but our business required more haste. **1796** GOLDSM. *Ess.* xv. Wks. (Globe) 328/1 In situations where the action seems to require haste. **1888** A. K. GREEN *Behind Closed Doors* iv, To make him understand the necessity of haste.

2. Such quickness of action as excludes due consideration or reflection; hurry, precipitancy, want of deliberation, rashness. (See also 4 b, 6.)

a **1300** *E.E. Psalter* lxxvii[i]. 33 Þair daies waned in unnaitnesse, And þair yheres with haste ware lesse. *c* **1374** CHAUCER *Troylus* v. 1605 Greuous to me god-wot is youre vnreste, Your haste. *a* **1533** LD. BERNERS *Huon* xcix. 320 An yll haste is not good. *c* **1645** HOWELL *Lett.* (1650) II. 29 Hast and choler are enemies to all great actions. **1781** COWPER *Retirement* 725 Friends, not adopted with a school-boy's haste. **1832** TENNYSON *'Love thou thy land'* 96 Raw Haste, half-sister to Delay.

3. The condition of being obliged to act quickly on account of having little time; eagerness to get something done quickly; hurry. (See also 4 c, d.)

c **1385** CHAUCER *L.G.W.* 794 *Thisbe* (MS. Gg. 4.27), This tisbe hath..so gret haste Piramus to se. **1470-85** MALORY *Arthur* I. x, After the hast of the letters, they gaf hem this ansuer that [etc.]. **1548** HALL *Chron., Hen. VI*, 93 b, These joly gallantes left behynde theim for hast, all their tentes. **1581** SAVILE *Agric.* (1598) 198 Many halfe dead..were left for haste of winning the fielde. **1710** STEELE *Tatler* No. 200 ¶4 The urgent Hast of another Correspondent. **1828** SCOTT *F.M. Perth* xxxiv, She advanced, breathless with haste. **1872** J. F. CLARKE *Self-Culture* 58 (Cent.) The haste to get rich.

II. Phrases.

4. *in haste.* **a.** (in sense 1.) With energetic speed; quickly, expeditiously (also, †*an, on haste* (obs.): see AN *prep.*). So *in all haste* (arch.), as quickly as possible, with all speed.

a **1300** *Cursor M.* 13402 Þai fild a cupp þan son in hast. *a* **1300** *K. Horn* 615 He sloȝ þer on haste On hundred bi þe laste. *c* **1380** *Sir Ferumb.* 3608 Richard prykede forþ an haste, Ase harde as he may þraste. *a* **1400-50** *Alexander* 2817, I sall hele [= recover] all in hast. **1567** *Satir. Poems Reform.* v. 50 Reuenge in haist the cruell act. **1667** MILTON *P.L.* x. 456 Forth rush'd in haste the great consulting Peers. *a* **1791** WESLEY *Wks.* (1830) XII. 287 Though I am always in haste I am never in a hurry. **1859** TENNYSON *Enid* 1391 'Not dead!' she answer'd in all haste. **1868** LYNCH *Rivulet* CXVII. i, Arise, sad heart, arise in haste.

b. (in sense 2.) With excited quickness; without deliberation, hurriedly, hastily, in a hurry.

1513 MORE in Grafton *Chron.* (1568) II. 782 Scribled forth in hast at aduenture. **1535** COVERDALE *Ps.* cxv. 11, I sayde in my haist: All men are lyers. **1677** LAUDERDALE in *L. Papers* (Camden) III. lvii. 89 So as they may not trouble us any more in hast. **1689** BURNET *Tracts* I. 1 Who has seen so little, and as it were in hast. **1710-11** SWIFT *Let. to Mrs. Johnson* 16 Jan., I dined to-day with Dr. Cockburn, but will not do so again in haste, he has generally such a parcel of Scots with him.

c. (in sense 3.) With quickness of action due to being pressed for time; with speed, speedily.

1513 MORE in Grafton *Chron.* (1568) II. 759 One Mistlebrooke..came in great haste to the hous of one Pottier. **1584** POWEL *Lloyd's Cambria* 221 The king leuied an armie in Hast. **1699** GARTH *Dispens.* v. 60 In hast a Council's call'd. **1727** SWIFT *Gulliver* III. i. 181 Four or five men running in great haste up the stairs. **1845** S. AUSTIN *Ranke's Hist. Ref.* III. 607 Prepared at any moment to send such as might be demanded in haste.

d. (in sense 3.) As predicate, often with *infin.*: Eager to get something done quickly; in a hurry.

1591 SHAKS. *Two Gent.* I. iii. 89 Your Father calls for you, He is in hast, therefore I pray you go. **1700** RAY in *Lett. Lit. Men* (Camden) 205, I am in no hast for them, but can well wait your leisure. **1759** ROBERTSON *Hist. Scot.* I. III. 196 Mary was in no haste to return into Scotland. **1782** COWPER *Gilpin* 198 So turning to his horse, he said, 'I am in haste to dine'. **1812** J. WILSON *Isle of Palms* III. 935 No sooner come than in haste to go.

5. a. *to make haste*: To put forth energy producing speed; to move or act with quickness; to use expedition, to hasten. (Often with *inf.*)

1535 COVERDALE *Ps.* xxxix. [xl.] 13 Make haist (o Lorde) to helpe me. **1582** N. LICHEFIELD tr. *Castanheda's Conq. E. Ind.* vii. 19 b, Making hast to the shore, and atteining the same, they ran away. **1662** J. DAVIES tr. *Olearius' Voy. Ambass.* 13 One while to march on very slowly, another, to make more haste. **1749** FIELDING *Tom Jones* VI. x, It was necessary for him to make haste home. **1837** DICKENS *Pickw.* vii, Make haste down, and come out. **1847** JAMES *J. Marston Hall* ix, I made as much haste as I could to get away.

b. *to make haste slowly*, after L. *festina lente* (Suet. *Aug.* 25).

1744 B. FRANKLIN *Poor Richard* (1890) Apr. 146 Make haste slowly. **1831** *Deb. Congress U.S.* 4 Feb. 98 Thus far the committee have 'made haste slowly'. **1938** M. TEAGLE *Murders in Silk* iii. 22 Easy, son. Let's make haste slowly. Does Conner know where the knife came from?

c. *Cricket.* Of a ball: to come up from the pitch with increased speed.

1888 A. G. STEEL in Steel and Lyttelton *Cricket* iii. 123 Every now and then one of their balls will, in cricket slang, 'make haste from the pitch'. **1904** P. F. WARNER *How we recovered Ashes* ix. 177 The ball made haste off the pitch, kept a little low, and clean beat Duff. **1920** —— *Cricket Reminisc.* ii. 19 Australia, where the bowler who makes haste off the pitch is the most useful type.

6. In proverbs and phrases: chiefly in sense 2.

c **1375** BARBOUR *Troy-bk.* II. 1682 Of fule haist cummis no speid. **1546** J. HEYWOOD *Prov.* (1867) 5 Hast maketh waste. *Ibid.*, The more haste the lesse speede. **1556** ROBINSON tr. *More's Utop.* (ed. 2) To Rdr. (Arb.) 19 With more hast then good spede I broughte it to an ende. **1621** QUARLES *Argalus & P.* (1678) 29 Acts done in haste, by leisure are repented. **1869** FREEMAN *Norm. Conq.* III. xiv. 323 The more haste was emphatically not the better speed. **1869** HAZLITT *Eng. Prov.* 153 Haste trips up its own heels. **1883** HT. P. SPOFFORD in *Harper's Mag.* Mar. 573/1 She married him in all haste—to repent in all leisure. **1897** E. PHILLPOTTS *Lying Prophets* 346 [Cornish phrase] More haste, more let. *Mod.* More haste, less (or worse) speed.

III. 7. *Comb.*

1552 HULOET, Haste maker, *accelerator.* **1576** FLEMING *Panopl. Epist.* 262 Festination or hast making. **1851** HELPS *Comp. Solit.* xi. (1874) 199 There is no occasion for being excessively emulous, or haste bitten.

haste (heɪst) *v.* Forms: see prec. [a. OF. *haster* (11th c. in Hatz.-Darm.), mod.F. *hâter*, f. *haste, hâte*, HASTE *sb.* Cf. Du. *haasten*, Ger. *hasten*, Da. *haste*, Sw. *hasta*, all from Fr.] Now chiefly literary, the ordinary word being *hasten.*

1. *trans.* To cause to move more quickly; to urge, drive, or press on; to quicken, accelerate, hurry.

a **1300** *Cursor M.* 26737 Hast noght þi scrift on þiskin wis. *c* **1330** R. BRUNNE *Chron.* (1810) 42 Fals Edrike þat þam þider hasted. **1398** TREVISA *Barth. De P.R.* IV. iii. (1495) 83 Dryenesse hastyth aege. *c* **1489** CAXTON *Sonnes of Aymon* xxvi. 562 The children of reynawde hasted somoche the ii. sones of foulques..that thei..were..wery. *a* **1533** LD. BERNERS *Huon* lix. 206 They were so hastyd and pursewyd. **1607** SHAKS. *Cor.* V. i. 74 Let's hence, And with our faire intreaties hast them on. **1786** BURNS *Auld Farmer's N.-Y. Salut. Mare* xiv, Thou..just thy step a wee thing hastit.

2. *refl.* = 3. *arch.*

a **1300** *Cursor M.* 5018 Yee most yow hast on your fare. *c* **1380** WYCLIF *Wks.* (1880) 469 þey shulden..haaste hem to make aseeþ. *c* **1475** *Rauf Coilȝear* 550, I will not haist me ane fute faster on the way. **1535** COVERDALE *Ps.* cxl. [cxli.] 1 Lorde, I call vpon the: haist the vnto me. **1667** MILTON *P.L.* XI. 104 Hast thee, and from the Paradise of God..drive out the sinful Pair. **1869** LOWELL *Foot-Path* iv, I look and long, then haste me home.

3. *intr.* To make haste; to come or go quickly; to act with haste or expedition; to be quick, hurry; (of time or events) to come on or approach rapidly. (Often with *to* and *inf.*)

a **1300** *Cursor M.* 2837 'Haste', he said, 'þan þeder yaar'. *c* **1375** *Sc. Leg. Saints, Johannes* 112 þe seknes na remed Ma haf, bot hastis to þe dede. **1388** WYCLIF *Ps.* lxix. [lxx.] 1 Lord, hast thou to helpe me. **1581** MULCASTER *Positions* xli. (1887) 234 If the reward were good, he would hast to gaine more. **1614** RALEIGH *Hist. World* V. iii. (1736) I. 689 He hasted away towards Utica. **1667** MILTON *P.L.* IV. 867 O friends, I hear the tread of nimble feet Hasting this way. **1712** POPE *Messiah* 23 See Nature hastes her earliest wreaths to bring. **1849** C. BRONTË *Shirley* xxiv, The hour is hasting but too fast. **1871** R. ELLIS *Catullus* viii. 4 Still ever hasting where she led.

hasteful ('heɪstfʊl), *a. rare.* [f. HASTE *sb.* + -FUL.] Full of haste; hurrying, hurried. Hence **'hastefully** *adv.*, in haste, expeditiously.

1610 HOLLAND *Camden's Brit.* I. 388 With hastfull hot desire. **1873** J. DUNS *Mem. Sir J. Y. Simpson* xv. 519 In the excitement of hasteful travel. **1890** SARAH J. DUNCAN *Soc. Depart.* 308 We got hastefully back, three-quarters of an hour before she sailed. **1895** *Daily Tel.* 25 Mar. 7/4 This hasteful, bustling and forgetful age.

† **hasteler, hastler.** *Obs.* [app. a. AF. **hasteler*, f. **hastele* (whence secondary dim. *hastelet*: see HASLET), dim. of *haste*, mod.F. *hâte* spit, broach:—L. *hasta* spear; cf. the 12th c. L. equivalent *hastalārius* (? *hastellārius*), also *hastelāria* the place where broaches were kept (Du Cange). In this sense, Godefroy has only OF. *hasteeur, hasteur*:—med.L. *hastātōr-em* (Du Cange).]

An officer of the kitchen, who superintended or attended to the roasting of meat; also, a turn-spit.

[? *c* **1175** *Constit. Domus Regis* in *Liber Niger Scacc.* (Hearne) I. 348 De Magna Coquina..Hastalarius.] *c* **1420** *Liber Cocorum* (1862) 1 Þis hasteler, pasteler, and potagere. *c* **1440** *Promp. Parv.* 229/1 Hastlere, þat rostythe mete ..*assator, assarius.* **1563-87** FOXE *A. & M.* (1684) III. 715 Saying that Nicholas Cadman was Noyes Hastler, that is, such a one as maketh and hasteth the fire.

hasteless ('heɪstlɪs), *a.* [f. HASTE *sb.* + -LESS.] Without haste. Hence **'hastelessness**, complete absence of haste or hurry.

1873 W. CORY *Let. & Jrnls.* (1897) 313 Men who are as the stars, unconscious, hasteless, stedfast. **1883** JEFFERIES in *Longm. Mag.* June 192 Hastelessness is the only word one can make up to describe it.

hastelet, obs. form of HASLET.

† **'hasteling.** *Obs. rare.* In 7 **hastling.** [f. HASTE + -LING.] A hasty person.

1629 GAULE *Holy Madn.* 203 Haue after the Hastling; nay haue at him with an encounter as resolute, as speedy.

† **'hastely, hastly,** *adv. Obs.* Forms: 3-4 **hastelich(e, -lyche,** 4 **-lik** (superl. **-lokest**), 4-5 **-li,** 4-6 **-ly, -lie,** 5-6 *Sc.* (and Coverd.) **haistely,** 5-7 *Sc.* **-lie,** 6 *Sc.* **hestely;** also 4-6 **hastly,** 6 *Sc.* **haistlie.** [f. HASTE *sb.* + -LY²; perhaps, in its origin, a variant of *hastily*, the *e* at length becoming mute.]

1. = HASTILY 1.

c **1290** *S. Eng. Leg.* I. 3/71 He liet him cristni hasteliche. *a* **1300** *Cursor M.* 15224 Sua hasteli als he might. **1377** LANGL. *P. Pl.* B. XIX. 466 The lawe wil I take it, þere I may hastlokest it haue. **1380** *Lay Folks Catech.* (Lamb. MS.) 1373 Accidy þat is slownesse Whan a man schuld do a good dede hastly. *a* **1400-50** *Alexander* 3784 As hastely as he it herd, his ostis he flittis. *c* **1475** *Rauf Coilȝear* 113 Twa cant knaifis of his awin haistelie he bad. *c* **1489** CAXTON *Sonnes of Aymon* xx. 451 He called hastly the duke naymes. **1500-20** DUNBAR *Poems* xxii. 59 Gif I mend nocht hestely. **1535** COVERDALE *Ps.* liv. [lv.] 15 Let death come hastely vpon them. **1596** DALRYMPLE tr. *Leslie's Hist. Scot.* x. 268 Haistlie ..to the west cuntrie to the Quene he past. **1609** SKENE *Reg. Maj.* 102 Als haistelie as he may.

2. = HASTILY 2.

1552 HULOET, Hastely or rashelye, *præcipitanter.*

hasten ('heɪs(ə)n), *v.* [Extended form of HASTE *v.*, after the numerous verbs in -EN⁵.]

1. a. *trans.* To cause to make haste; to urge on; to accelerate, expedite, hurry: = HASTE *v.* 1.

1565-73 COOPER *Thesaurus* s.v. *Festino, Mortem in se festinauit*, he hastned his owne death. **1579** SPENSER *Sheph. Cal.* May 152 Sorrowe ne neede be hastened on. **1600** E. BLOUNT tr. *Conestaggio* 28 Sebastian..hastened his departure, impatient of the least delaies. **1659** B. HARRIS *Parival's Iron Age* 210 These preparations hastened the king to Nottingham. **1707** *Curios. in Husb. & Gard.* 181 Nitre mixt with Water..is excellent to hasten the Vines. **1719** DE FOE *Crusoe* I. xx, We had three leagues to go, and our guide hastened us. **1816** J. SMITH *Panorama Sc. & Art* II. 141 A jet of water is admitted to hasten the condensation. **1854** TOMLINSON *Arago's Astron.* 121 The ultimate effect..was discovered in hastening, not in deferring, the time of the appearance of the comet!

† **b.** To dispatch or send in haste. *Obs.*

1611 BIBLE *1 Kings* xxii. 9 Hasten hither Micaiah the sonne of Imlah. **1652** SIR E. NICHOLAS in *N. Papers*

(Camden) 309, I pray be still pressing the K. of France to hasten his effectual letters. **1674** *Essex Papers* (Camden) I. 178 Your Exce will now have hastened over to me 34 foot Companys. **1748** RICHARDSON *Clarissa* (1811) VIII. 40 If there be anything in Brand's letter that will divert me, hasten it to me.

2. *intr.* To make haste; to come, go, or act quickly; to be quick; to hurry: = HASTE *v.* 3. (Often with *to* and *inf.*) ***to hasten slowly***: cf. HASTE *sb.* 5 b.

1568 GRAFTON *Chron.* II. 399 King Richard.. hastened not a little to set all things.. in order. *c* **1600** SHAKS. *Sonn.* lx, So do our minutes hasten to their end. **1611** BIBLE *Gen.* xviii. 6 Abraham hastened into the tent, vnto Sarah. **1659** B. HARRIS *Parival's Iron Age* 142 Nor did he hasten to beat them out of his country. **1719** DE FOE *Crusoe* (L.), I hastened to the spot whence the noise came. **1874** GREEN *Short Hist.* viii. §7. 534 Scotland.. hastened to sign the Covenant. **1907** *Spectator* 12 Jan. 43 'Hasten slowly' is a very good motto in Imperial politics. **1958** *Oxford Mail* 14 Aug. 1/3 The Government is still hastening slowly on re-expansion.

Hence **'hastened** *ppl. a.*; **'hastening** *vbl. sb.* and *ppl. a.*

1631 MILTON *Epit. Marchioness Winchester* 46 Presaging tears, Which the sad morn had let fall On her hastening funeral. **1648** GAGE *West Ind.* 95 For the speedier hastening of our second breakfast. **1671** MILTON *Samson* 958 Thy hasten'd widowhood. **1770** GOLDSM. *Des. Vill.* 51 Ill fares the land, to hastening ills a prey, Where wealth accumulates and men decay.

hastener ('heɪs(ə)nə(r)). [f. prec. + -ER1.]

1. One who or that which hastens. Also *Services' slang* (see quot. 1946).

1587 TURBERV. *Trag. T.* (1837) 156 He and.. his Queene .. that hastners of King Albyons bane had beene. **1686** A. SNAPE *Anat. Horse* IV. xvi. 177 The Muscles.. called *Acceleratores* or Hastners. **1751** JOHNSON *Rambler* No. 169 ¶7 Pride and indigence, the two great hasteners of modern poems. **1943** C. H. WARD-JACKSON *Piece of Cake* 35 *Hastener*, a letter asking for a reply to a previous letter. **1946** J. IRVING *Royal Navalese* 92 *Hastener*, a letter or a 'Minute' asking for a reply to some previous correspondence. **1955** *Times* 12 May 11/4 Those who were once temporary soldiers may recall how they used to send 'hasteners' for the stores they wanted.

2. A stand or screen for concentrating the heat of the fire on a roasting joint of meat; a haster. *dial.*

1847–78 HALLIWELL, *Hastner*, same as *Haster*. **1858** in SIMMONDS *Dict. Trade*. **1888** [see HASTER].

† **'hasteness.** *Obs.* [Cf. HASTELY.] By-form of HASTINESS.

1413 *Pilgr. Sowle* (Caxton 1483) IV. ii. 59 Withouten fowle rebukynge or hastenesse of vengeaunce. *c* **1450** R. *Gloucester's Chron.* (1724) 482/1 *note* (MS. Coll. Arms) His eyen.. as sperkelyng fuyre, as lightnyng with hastenesse.

haster ('heɪstə(r)). *dial.* [f. HASTE *v.* + -ER; but cf. OF. *hasteur* turnspit, s.v. HASTELER, and see HASTERY.] = HASTENER 2.

1829 HUNTER *Hallamsh. Gloss.* 48 (Hall.) *Haster*, a tin meat-screen, to reflect the heat while the operation of roasting is going on. **1839** A. BYWATER *Sheffield Dial.* (1877) 34 Shoo tumbled backards, and nockt haster uppat beef. **1888** *Sheffield Gloss.*, *Hastener* or *Haster*.

† **'hastery.** *Obs.* [f. OF. *haster* to roast (see *hasté* in Godef.), f. *haste* spit + -ERY.] The process or art of roasting meat; roast meats collectively.

c **1420** *Liber Cocorum* (1862) 5, I wylle schawe, Tho poyntes of cure.. Of Potage, hastery and bakun mete. *Ibid.* 38 Here endys oure hastere þat I of spake. **1511** *Earl Northumbld.'s Househ. Bk.* in *Antiq. Repert.* (1809) IV. 244 A Yoman Cooke.. Who doith hourely attend in the Kitching at the Haistry for roisting of Meat.

hastif, -ly, -ness: see HASTIVE, -LY, -NESS.

hastifoliate (hæstɪ'fəʊlɪət), *a. Bot.* [f. L. *hasta* spear + *foli-um* leaf: see -ATE2.] Having spear-shaped leaves. Also **hasti'folious** *a.*

1886 *Syd. Soc. Lex.*, *Hastifoliate*. **1889** *Cent. Dict.*, *Hastifolious*.

hastiform ('hæstɪfɔːm), *a.* [ad. L. type **hastiformis*, mod.F. *hastiforme*, f. L. *hasta* spear: see -FORM.] Spear-shaped.

1886 in *Syd. Soc. Lex.*

† **'hastihede.** *Obs. rare*−1. [f. HASTY + *-hede*, -HEAD.] Hastiness, haste.

1390 GOWER *Conf.* II. 245 Eche of hem in hastihede Shall other slee.

hastile ('hæstaɪl), *a. Bot.* [ad. L. type **hastīlis*, f. *hasta* spear: see -ILE. Cf. L. *hastīle* spear-shaft.] = HASTATE.

1864 WEBSTER cites GRAY.

hastilude ('hæstɪl(j)uːd). *Obs.* exc. *Hist.* [ad. med.L. *hastilūdus*, *hastilūdium*, f. L. *hasta* spear + *lūdus* play.] Spear-play; a name for a kind of tilt or tournament.

1586 FERNE *Blaz. Gentrie* 366 In any Tilt, Iust, Hastilude or Turney. *c* **1640** J. SMYTH *Lives Berkeleys* (1883) I. 148 To concurre with swords, fight at barriers, excercise hastyludes. **1845** *Gentl. Mag.* II. 239 That tangible memorial of round table hastiludes still preserved in the building. **1879** DIXON *Windsor* I. xviii. 187 One sport, called hastiludes, was no less dangerous than war itself.

hastily ('heɪstɪlɪ), *adv.* Forms: 4–5 **hastilich(e, -li(e, -le,** (*superl.* **-lokest**), 4–6 **hastyly,** 6 *Sc.* **haistily, -yly:** 4– **hastily.** [f. HASTY *a.* + -LY2. Cf. also HASTIVELY, HASTELY.] In haste.

1. Quickly, speedily, expeditiously; †soon, without delay, shortly, suddenly (*obs.*); rapidly, swiftly. Now usually with implication of being pressed for time: Hurriedly.

a **1300** *Cursor M.* 17288 + 153 To petre & his deciples hastile tell ȝee, þat he is risen. *c* **1385** CHAUCER *L.G.W.* 1989 *Ariadne*, To come & speke with us hastily. *c* **1400** MAUNDEV. (1839) xv. 162 The mone envyrouneth the Erthe more hastyly than ony other Planete. **1549** *Compl. Scot.* vi. 58 Ane sterne.. callit ane comeit, quhen it is sene, ther occurris haistyly eftir it sum grit myscheif. **1590** SPENSER *F.Q.* I. ii. 6 Up he rose, and clad him hastily. **1664** EVELYN *Kal. Hort.* (1729) 219 Over-hastily blooming Trees. **1766** GOLDSM. *Vic. W.* xxx, He took the letter, and hastily read it over. **1874** GREEN *Short Hist.* iii. §2. 123 The Northern nobles marched hastily to join their comrades.

2. With undue haste excluding consideration or forethought; precipitately, rashly, inconsiderately.

1586 A. DAY *Eng. Secretary* I. (1625) 129 Young men.. by the.. want.. of aged experience, are hastily led thereunto. **1712** ADDISON *Spect.* No. 279 ¶1 That the Reader may not judge too hastily of this Piece of Criticism. **1858** FROUDE *Hist. Eng.* xviii. IV. 9 She had married hastily, and as hastily grown weary of her choice.

3. With quickness of temper; in sudden anger.

1573 TUSSER *Husb.* ix. (1878) 17 To hate reuengement hastilie. **1755** JOHNSON, *Hastily*.. 3. Passionately; with vehemence.

hastiness ('heɪstɪnɪs). [f. as prec. + -NESS.] The quality or condition of being hasty.

†**1.** Quickness, swiftness, rapidity; suddenness.

c **1330** R. BRUNNE *Chron.* (1810) 256 þi manace.. in hastynes suorn. *c* **1440** *Promp. Parv.* 229/1 Hastynesse, *idem quod* Haaste. **1450–1530** *Myrr. our Ladye* 2 The shortnes.. of thys lyfe, the hastynes of dethe. **1591** SPARRY tr. *Catton's Geomancie* 24 All hastinesse and swiftnesse is appointed vnto ♂ and ☿.

2. Undue quickness; precipitancy; hurriedness.

c **1386** CHAUCER *Melib.* ¶167 (Harl.) ȝe moste also dryue out of ȝour herte hastynes [4 *MSS.* hastifnesse].. For.. þe comune prouerbe is þis; þat he þat soone demeth soone repentith. **1477** EARL RIVERS (Caxton) *Dictes* 88 Hastinesse of speche maketh men to erre. **1561** T. NORTON *Calvin's Inst.* I. 28 That people with a certaine hote hastinesse, brake out oftentimes to seke them idols. **1641** BAKER *Apol. Laymen* 189 Oh the wonderfull dammage that is incurred by hastinesse and precipitancy. **1751–73** JORTIN *Eccl. Hist.* (R.), Epiphanius was made up of hastiness and credulity. **1888** *Academy* 21 Jan. 49/1 Hastiness of execution.

3. Quickness of temper; tendency to sudden anger or irritation, passion.

1297 R. GLOUC. (1724) 474 He acorsede alle thulke men.. That of an false preste ne abbe eke him nouȝt. That word he sede ofte in hastinesse. *c* **1430** *Life St. Kath.* (Gibbs MS.) 77 He waxed nyȝe wood by hedy hastynesse. **1526** *Pilgr. Perf.* (W. de W. 1531) 110 Hastynesse or irefulnesse. **1596** DALRYMPLE tr. *Leslie's Hist. Scot.* I. 105 Thair ouir haistines, and ouer bent to reuenge. **1749** FIELDING *Tom Jones* Wks. 1775 III. 73 You have a little too much hastiness in your temper. **1830** D'ISRAELI *Chas. I*, III. v. 73 Laud.. had the bluntness and hastiness of a monastic character.

†**b.** A fanciful name for a 'company' of cooks.

c **1491** CAXTON *Bk. Curtesye* (ed. 2) finis, A Hastynes of cookes.

hasting ('heɪstɪŋ), *vbl. sb.* [f. HASTE *v.* + -ING1.] The action of the verb HASTE; making haste, speeding; expedition, acceleration.

a **1350** *Childh. Jesu* 1590 (Mätz.) þo Josep was comen in hastingue. **1398** TREVISA *Barth. De P.R.* VII. iv. (1495) 224 The cause of hastynge of Manasses deth. ? *a* **1400** *Arthur* 377 Bedwer wyþ alle hastynge Tolde Arthour alle þis þynge. **1568** *Knt. of Curtesy* 25 He praieth you in all hastynge To come in his court for to dwell.

hasting, *ppl. a.* and *sb.* [f. as prec. + -ING2.]

A. *ppl. a.*

1. That hastes, speeding: see the verb.

1632 MILTON *Sonn.* ii, My hasting days fly on with full career. **1870** EMERSON *Misc. Papers, Plutarch* Wks. (Bohn) III. 343 To keep up with the hasting history.

†**2.** That ripens early: applied to varieties of fruit or vegetables. *Obs.*

1578 LYTE *Dodoens* I. xxxv. 52 The huskes be.. like a great hasting or garden pease. **1611** COTGR., *Hastiveau*.. a hasting apple, or peare. **1719** LONDON & WISE *Compl. Gard.* 243 How to raise hasting Strawberries. **1753** CHAMBERS *Cycl. Supp.*, *Hasting Pear*,.. It ripens in July.

B. *sb.* [ellipt. use of the adj.]

†**1.** An early-ripening fruit or vegetable; *spec.* a kind of early pea. *Obs.* (or now only *local*).

1573 TUSSER *Husb.* xviii. (1878) 45 Sowe hastings now, if land it alow. **1585** HIGINS tr. *Junius' Nomenclator* 101/2 *Ficus præcox. Figue hastive.* A rathe fig ripened before the time: an hasting. **1664** BUTLER *Hud.* II. *Ep. to Sidrophel* 22 To cry Green-Hastings. **1727** POPE, etc. *Art of Sinking* 115 Common cryers.. persuade people to buy their oysters, green hastings, or new ballads. **1878** *Science Gossip* Aug. 190 A day or two since I heard the cry 'Green Hastings!'.. fifty years ago, it was the usual cry for green peas.

†**2.** Applied to persons who hasten or make haste (with allusion to prec. sense). Only in *pl.*

1546 J. HEYWOOD *Prov.* (1867) 35 Toward your woorkyng ye make such tastingis, As approue you to be none of the hastingis. **1581** [see HARDING]. *a* **1661** FULLER *Worthies, Sussex* (1811) II. 385 Now men commonly say they are none of the Hastings, who, being slow and slack, go about business with no agility. *a* **1700** B. E. *Dict. Cant. Crew*, *You are none of the Hastings*, of him that loses an Opportunity.. for want of Dispatch.

hastish ('heɪstɪʃ), *a. dial.* [f. HASTE *sb.* or *v.* + -ISH.] = HASTY *a.* 4.

1749 FIELDING *Tom Jones* XVI. iii, [An ignorant woman says] A very hastish kind of gentleman.

† **'hastity.** *Obs. rare.* In 4 **hastite.** [Worn down from OF. *hastiveté*, f. *hastif* hasty: see next. Cf. *jollity*, F. *joliveté*.] Hastiness, haste.

c **1340** *Cursor M.* 2909 (Trin.) þen coom a doom in hastite To hem þat longe had spared be.

† **'hastive, 'hastif,** *a. Obs.* Also 3–5 **-yf(e, -ife, -yve.** [a. OF. *hastif, -ive*, mod.F. *hâtif, -ive*, speedy, hurried, impetuous, f. *haste*, mod. *hâte* HASTE *sb.* + -IVE. See also HASTY, which is in origin a doublet of this word.]

1. Speedy, swift: = HASTY *a.* 1.

1382 WYCLIF *Jer.* xxxvi. 29 Hastif shal come the kinge of Babiloyne, and waste this lond. **1390** GOWER *Conf.* II. 56 And make many hastif rodes. *a* **1420** HOCCLEVE *De Reg. Princ.* 2092 Dethe was to hastyfe, To renne on the.

b. Of fruit, etc.: Maturing early; early, forward: = HASTY *a.* 1 d.

1727–51 CHAMBERS *Cycl.*, *Hastive*, a French term, sometimes used in English for early, forward.. The hastive fruits are strawberries and cherries. We have also hastive peas, etc.

2. Precipitate, rash: = HASTY *a.* 3.

1297 R. GLOUC. (1724) 458 Folc hastyf hii beþ ek ynou, & also wyþout rede. **1340** *Ayenb.* 184 Of hastif red hit uorþingþ efterward. *c* **1374** CHAUCER *Troylus* IV. 1540 (1568) (MS. Gg. 4. 27) Hastyf man wanted neuere care. *c* **1430** *Syr Gener.* (Roxb.) 4984 Treulie thou were a litle to hastife.

3. Quick-tempered, passionate (= HASTY *a.* 4); in a passion, angry.

1297 R. GLOUC. (1724) 414 Renable nas he noȝt of tonge, ac of speche hastyf. *c* **1330** R. BRUNNE *Chron.* (1810) 177 Richard was hastif, & ansuerd þat stund, Certes þou lies cheitiff, & as a stinkand hund. *c* **1410** *Chron. Eng.* 667 in Ritson *Met. Rom* II. 298 The king was hastif ant starte up, Ant hente the thef by the top. **1489** CAXTON *Faytes of A.* I. vii. 17 That he be not testyf, hastyf, hoot ne angry.

† **'hastively, hastifly,** *adv. Obs.* [f. prec. + -LY2.] Hastily, quickly, speedily.

a **1327** *Pol. Songs* (Camden) 190 Facccheþ me the traytours y-bounde.. hastifliche ant blyve. *a* **1350** *Childh. Jesu* 1631 (Mätz.) He answerede him ful hastifli.

† **'hastiveness, hastifnesse.** *Obs.* [f. prec. + -NESS.] Hastiness, rashness, passionateness.

c **1330** R. BRUNNE *Chron.* (1810) 129 If any man mad pleynt of clerk for hastiuenesse. *c* **1386** CHAUCER *Melib.* ¶167 Ye moste also dryue out of youre herte hastifnesse. **1390** GOWER *Conf.* III. 99 Fool hastifnesse.

† **hasti'vess.** *Obs.* In 4 **hastiwes.** [a. AF. *hastivesse*, f. *hastif*, *hâtif* HASTIVE.] = prec.

[**1292** BRITTON IV. ix. §8 Acuns.. mentent par fole hastivesce.] *c* **1325** *Metr. Hom.* 159 Quen we hald our hert fra wreth, And hastiwes.

† **ha'stivity.** *Obs.* In 5 **hastyvyte:** see also HASTITY. [a. OF. *hastiveté*, mod.F. *hâtiveté*, f. *hastif* HASTIVE: see -ITY.] = prec.

c **1450** in *Pol. Poems* (Rolls) II. 242 Vengeaunce and wrathe in an hastyvyté.

hastler, hastlet, obs. ff. HASTELER, HASLET.

hastly: see HASTELY.

hasty ('heɪstɪ), *a.* (*sb.*, *adv.*) [a. OF. *hasti* for *hastif* (pl. *hastis*), mod.F. *hâtif, -ive*, f. *haste*, *hâte* HASTE *sb.*: see HASTIVE, and cf. JOLLY, TARDY. The termination was doubtless from the first identified with native *-i*, *-y* from OE. *-iȝ*; and it is noticeable that the other Teutonic langs. have formed corresponding adjs. of that type: Du. *haastig*, Ger., Da., Sw. *hastig*.] Marked by haste; acting, moving, performed, etc. with haste.

1. Speedy, quick, expeditious; swift, rapid (in action or movement); sudden. *arch.* exc. as in b.

c **1340** *Cursor M.* 5324 (Trin.) þe kynge lete write lettres .. wiþ hasty fare. **1340** HAMPOLE *Pr. Consc.* 1548 Gret hasty myscheves.. þat tyll þe world er nere command. **1465** *Paston Lett.* No. 508 II. 200 Lete me have word in as hasty tyme as ye may. *c* **1511** *1st Eng. Bk. Amer.* (Arb.) Introd. 28/1 This people hathe a swyfte hasty speche. **1551** TURNER *Herbal* I. Bij a, Thys wolfbayne of all poysones is the most hastye poison. **1648** MILTON *Tenure Kings* (1650) 59 We wish hasty ruin to all Tyrants. **1697** DRYDEN *Virg. Georg.* I. 174 When impetuous Rain Swells hasty Brooks. **1722** DE FOE *Plague* (1756) 198 A very smart and hasty Rain. **1770–4** A. HUNTER *Georg. Ess.* (1803) I. 24 The dung of pigeons is a rich and hasty manure. **1810** SCOTT *Lady of L.* I. xviii, The sportive toil.. Served too in hastier swell to show Short glimpses of a breast of snow.

b. Speedy or quick on account of having little time; hurried.

1590 SIR J. SMYTH *Disc. Weapons* 5 b, A hastie retraite. **1746** BERKELEY *Let. to Prior* 20 May, Wks. 1871 IV. 317. I have written these hasty lines in no small hurry. **1750** GRAY *Elegy* xxv, Brushing with hasty steps the dews away. **1834** MEDWIN *Angler in Wales* II. 113 Aberdovey, of which I made a hasty common-ink sketch. **1844** WILSON *Brit. India* III. 9 [He] had scarcely.. time to cast a hasty glance at the novel circumstances around him. **1874** L. STEPHEN *Hours in Library* (1892) II. i. 20 Rasselas..is ill calculated for the hasty readers of to-day.

c. Requiring haste or speed; made in haste. *spec.* in *Cookery*: see also HASTY PUDDING.

c **1386** CHAUCER *Miller's T.* 359 (Harl. MS.) This axeþ hast, and of an hasty [5 *MSS.* hastif] þing Men may nought preche or make taryyng. **1577** B. GOOGE *Heresbach's Husb.* IV. (1586) 184 Sommer Hony, or hasty hony, made in thirty daies after the tenth of June. **1657** *North's Plutarch* Add. Lives (1676) 90 He [Columbus] built a hasty Fort with wood and earth. **1742** P. FRANCIS *Horace, Ep.* I. xvi. 91 To purchase hasty wealth. **1883** *Cassell's Dict. Cookery, Hasty Puff.*

†**d.** That ripens or comes to maturity early in the season; early, forward [L. *præcox*]: = HASTING *ppl. a.* 2. *Obs.*

c **1440** *Promp. Parv.* 228/2 Hastybere, corne..*trimensis.* **1523** FITZHERB. *Husb.* §12 Hasty pees..be sowen before Christmasse. **1611** BIBLE *Isa.* xxviii. 4 As the hastie fruite before the summer. **1626** BACON *Sylva* Introd. to §422 How to make the Trees..more Hastie and Sudden, than they vse to be. **1693** EVELYN *De la Quint. Compl. Gard.* I. 131 Hasty, or Forward-Cherries.

†**2.** Eager to get something done quickly; in a hurry. In early use sometimes nearly = Ready, willing: cf. *quick.*) Usually with *inf. Obs.*

c **1375** *Sc. Leg. Saints, Effame* 70 His hasty lykine til fulfil. *a* **1450** *Knt. de la Tour* (1868) 62 No wise woman aught to be hasty to take upon the new noualitees of array. **1483** CAXTON *Gold. Leg.* 376 a/2 She was hasty for to obeye and constaunte to suffre. *a* **1533** LD. BERNERS *Huon* lxvi. 227 How is it that ye be so hasty to departe? **1592** *Nobody & Someb.* in Simpson *Sch. Shaks.* (1878) I. 344 The Queene is not so hasty of your death. **1597** SHAKS. *2 Hen. IV*, IV. v. 61 Is hee so hastie, that hee doth suppose My sleepe, my death? **1754** FOOTE *Knights* II. Wks 1799 I. 85 'Tis partly to prevent bad consequences, that I am..so hasty to match him.

3. Characterized by undue quickness of action; precipitate, rash, inconsiderate.

c **1430** LYDG. *Min. Poems* 223, I have harde..That haste mene sholde wante no woo. *c* **1440** *Promp. Parv.* 228/2 Hasty..*preceps.* **1568** GRAFTON *Chron.* II. 44 Hastie and furious of heart, and unware of perilles. **1651** HOBBES *Leviath.* III. xxxvii. 237 Aptitude..to give too hasty beleefe to pretended Miracles. **1762** GOLDSM. *Cit. W.* ii, I..will not be hasty in my decisions. **1802** *Med. Jrnl.* VIII. 505 He has been led into many hasty assertions. **1875** JOWETT *Plato* V. 146 Do not be hasty in forming a conclusion.

4. Of persons or their dispositions: Quickly excited to anger, quick-tempered, passionate, irritable. Of words or actions: Uttered or done in sudden anger or irritation.

1526 *Pilgr. Perf.* (W. de W. 1531) 93 b, Testinesse or impacyency, is a frayle & hasty disposycyon, or rather accustomed & vsed vyce of angre. **1530** PALSGR. 315/1 Hastye, disposed to be angry. *a* **1533** LD. BERNERS *Huon* xliii. 143 Be not dyspleasyd yf I spake eny hasty worde. **1535** COVERDALE *Prov.* xiv. 29 Wrath and haistie displeasure. **1611** BIBLE *Ibid.*, Hee that is hasty of spirit, exalteth folly. **1781** GIBBON *Decl. & F.* III. 45 The natural disposition of Theodosius was hasty and choleric. **1878** SEELEY *Stein* II. 129 Do you suppose I do not know myself to be hasty and irritable?

B. as *sb.* The murrain which attacks cattle. *Sc.*

1812 *Agric. Survey Scotl., Caithness* 200 (Jam.) Called the murrain (provincially *hasty*), because the animal dies soon after it is seized with it. **1815** *Ibid., Sutherland* 101 The disease called murrain or *heasty*, prevailed among the black cattle of this county.

†**C.** as *adv.* Hastily; quickly, rapidly, soon.

c **1450** LYDG. *Secrees* 847 Discrecyon..That hasty wyl medle on nouthir syde. **1549** *Compl. Scot.* vi. 54 Mercurius ..quhilk makkis reuolutione nyne dais mair haistiar nor dois Venus..is ay sene befor the soune rysing, and haisty eftir that the soune is cum to the vest orizon.

D. *Comb.*, as ***hasty footed, -minded, -witted.***

1590 SHAKS. *Mids. N.* III. ii. 200 Wee haue chid the hasty footed time, For parting vs. **1596** —— *Tam. Shr.* v. ii. 40 An hastie witted bodie. **1736-1816** *Ainsworth's Lat. Dict.*, Hasty-minded, *fervens animi.*

†**hasty**, *v. Obs.* exc. *Sc.* [f. prec.] = HASTE *v.*

a **1340** HAMPOLE *Psalter* lxxvii. 37 þaire dayes fayld in vanyte and þaire ȝeris wiþ hastiynge [*cum festinacione*]. *c* **1400** tr. *Secreta Secret., Gov. Lordsh.* (E.E.T.S.) 105 He peyned him to hasty þe Mule. **1533** BELLENDEN *Livy* I. (1822) 2 Thay will haisty thameself to here thir novelties and recent dedis. *Mod. Sc.* He told them to hastie.

†'**hastyfully**, *adv. Obs.* Corrupt form of HASTIVELY under the influence of HASTY.

c **1500** *Melusine* xxxi. 231 He..putte hym emong the sarasyns more hastyfully than thunder falleth fro heuen.

hasty pudding. A pudding made of flour stirred in boiling milk or water to the consistency of a thick batter; in some parts applied to a similar preparation of oatmeal (usually called 'porridge'); in U.S. made with Indian meal and water.

1599 H. BUTTES *Dyets drie Dinner* F ij, I can thinke of no fitter name than an hasty pudding. For I protest in so great haste I composed it, that [etc.]. **1600** J. PORY tr. *Leo's Africa* II. 45 They cast barlie-meale into boiling water..stirring the same..Then setting this pap or hastie-pudding upon the table. **1633** HEYWOOD *Eng. Trav.* II. Wks. 1874 IV. 28 Like a hastie Pudding, longer in eating, then it was in making. **1741** *Compl. Fam.-Piece* I. ii. 160 Take a large Pint of Milk, put to it 4 Spoonfuls of Flour.. and boil it into a smooth Hasty-Pudding. **1769** *De Foe's Tour Gt. Brit.* III. 243 The common Breakfasting here-abouts is Hasty-pudden, made of Oatmeal and Water boiled to a Paste. **1820** W. IRVING *Sketch Bk., Leg. Sleepy Hollow* (1865) 438 Great fields of Indian corn..holding out the promise of cakes and hasty pudding. **1879** B. F. TAYLOR *Summer-Savory* i. 7 Their green knapsacks are growing plump with rations of samp, hasty-pudding, and Indian bread. **1881** *Harper's Mag.* Jan. 227/1 Cod-fish balls for breakfast on Sunday morning,.. and fried hasty-pudding. **1948** *Newsweek* 5 Jan. 66/1 Cook in an iron pot; turn out on a dish and the result: hasty pudding.

†'**haswed**, *a. Obs.* [f. OE. *hasu, haswe* grey, tawny + -ED.] Marked with grey or brown.

c **1250** *Gen. & Ex.* 1723 Sep or got, haswed, arled, or grei, Ben don fro iacob fer a-wei.